# GENERAL INFORMATION

SEE VOLUME 1

How to Use the Engine Performance Section
Engine Performance Safety Precautions
Diagnostic Routine Outline
1980-91 Maintenance Reminder Lights
Using Mitchell's Wiring Diagrams
Trouble Shooting
Engine Overhaul Procedures
General Cooling System Servicing
Gear Tooth Contact Patterns
Drive Axle Noise Diagnosis
Anti-Lock Brake Safety Precautions
Hydraulic Brake Bleeding
Wheel Alignment Theory & Operation
Commonly Used Abbreviations
English-Metric Conversion Chart

# PORSCHE

# SAAB

# SUBARU

# SUZUKI

# TOYOTA

# VOLKSWAGEN

# VOLVO

# LATEST CHANGES & CORRECTIONS

*NOTE: For Eagle Summit information, see Chrysler/Mitsubishi Contents page.*

| See Acura through Hyundai Volume 1 | See Infiniti through Nissan Volume 2 |
|---|---|
| *ACURA* | *INFINITI* |
| *AUDI* | *ISUZU* |
| *BMW* | *JAGUAR* |
| *CHRYSLER/MITSUBISHI* | *LEXUS* |
| *DAIHATSU* | *MAZDA* |
| *FORD MOTOR CO.* | *MERCEDES-BENZ* |
| *GENERAL MOTORS* | *NISSAN* |
| *GEO* | |
| *HONDA* | |
| *HYUNDAI* | |

**PORSCHE**
**Through**
**VOLVO**
*VOLUME 3*

# 1991 MITCHELL® IMPORTED CARS LIGHT TRUCKS & VANS SERVICE & REPAIR

**The Leader in Professional Estimating and Repair Information.**

Mitchell International

ACKNOWLEDGMENT

Mitchell International thanks the domestic and import automobile and light truck manufacturers, distributors, and dealers for their generous cooperation and assistance which make this manual possible.

---



Published By

MITCHELL INTERNATIONAL
9889 Willow Creek Road
P.O. Box 26260
San Diego, California 92196-0260

ISBN0-8470-0615-8



Customer Service Numbers:

Subscription/Billing Information:
1-800-648-8010 or 619-578-6550

Technical Information:
1-800-854-7030 or 619-578-6550

Or Write: P.O. Box 26260, San Diego, CA 92196-0260

# PORSCHE

# 1990-91 PORSCHE CONTENTS

## GENERAL INFORMATION [1]

### ALL MODELS



[1] – For all GENERAL INFORMATION, see front of Volume 1.

## ENGINE PERFORMANCE

### INTRODUCTION



### EMISSION APPLICATIONS



## ENGINE PERFORMANCE (Cont.)

### SERVICE & ADJUSTMENT SPECIFICATIONS



### ON-VEHICLE ADJUSTMENTS



### THEORY & OPERATION

# 1990-91 PORSCHE CONTENTS (Cont.)

## ENGINE PERFORMANCE (Cont.)



## ELECTRICAL



## WIRING DIAGRAMS



## SAFETY EQUIPMENT

# 1990-91 PORSCHE CONTENTS (Cont.)

## ENGINES

### 3.6L 6-CYLINDER



## CLUTCHES

### AWD & RWD



## DRIVE AXLES

### AWD FRONT AXLE SHAFTS



### RWD AXLE SHAFTS



## BRAKES

### DISC



## WHEEL ALIGNMENT

### SPECIFICATIONS & PROCEDURES



## SUSPENSION

### FRONT



### REAR

# 1990-91 PORSCHE CONTENTS (Cont.)

## STEERING

### STEERING COLUMNS



### POWER RACK & PINION



## TRANSMISSION SERVICING

### AUTOMATIC TRANSMISSION



### MANUAL TRANSMISSION SERVICING



### TRANSMISSION REMOVAL & INSTALLATION

# 1990-91 ENGINE PERFORMANCE
# Porsche Introduction

## 1990-91 MODEL COVERAGE

| MODEL | BODY CODE | ENGINE | ENGINE ID | FUEL SYSTEM | IGNITION SYSTEM |
|---|---|---|---|---|---|
| 911 Carrera 2/4 | A [1] | 3.6L (M64/01) [2] | B | PFI (DME) [3] | Magnetic [4] |
| 911 Carrera 2/4 | B [5] | 3.6L (M64/01) [2] | B | PFI (DME) [3] | Magnetic [4] |
| 911 Carrera 2/4 | C [6] | 3.6L (M64/01) [2] | A | PFI (DME) [3] | Magnetic [4] |

[1] - 2-Door Coupe.
[2] - M64/02 with Tiptronic 4-speed automatic transmission.
[3] - Digital Motor Electronics (DME) engine management system.
[4] - Ignition system is an integral part of DME engine management system.
[5] - Targa (Body Code "E" in 1990).
[6] - Cabriolet (Body Code "E" in 1990).

## VIN DEFINITION

**WPOAB296*MS410001**

① ② ③ ④ ⑤ ⑥ ⑦ ⑧ ⑨ ⑩ ⑪ ⑫ ⑬ ⑭ ⑮ ⑯ ⑰

① Indicates Nation of Origin.
②③ Indicates Make.
④ Indicates Series.
**⑤ Indicates Engine.**
⑥ Indicates Restraint System.
⑦⑧ Indicates Vehicle Type (along with 12th digit).
⑨ Indicates Check Digit
**⑩ Indicates Model Year.**
⑪ Indicates Assembly Plant.
⑫ Indicates Vehicle Type (along with 7th and 8th digits).
⑬⑭⑮⑯⑰ Indicates Serial Number.

91H16490

## ENGINE CODE LOCATION

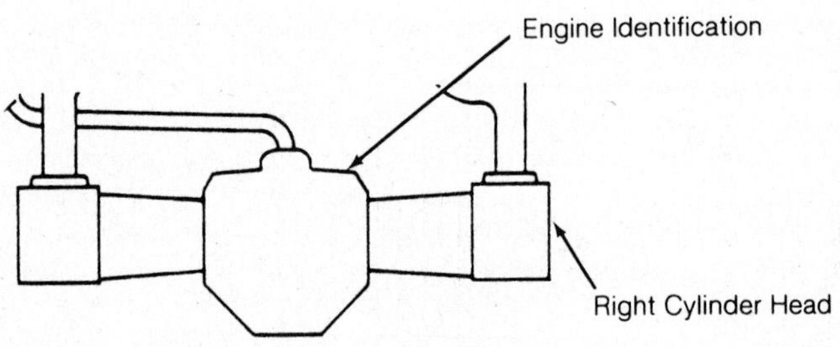


Courtesy of Porsche of North America, Inc.

*MODEL YEAR VIN CODE APPLICATION*

| VIN Code | Model Year |
|---|---|
| K | 1989 |
| L | 1990 |
| M | 1991 |

# Emission Applications

*1990-91 PORSCHE EMISSION*

| Model, Engine & Fuel System | Emission Control Systems & Devices | Remarks |
|---|---|---|
| 911 Carrera 2/4 3.6L (PFI) | PCV, EVAP, TWC, FPR, SPK, $O_2$, CEC, CE [1] | [1] - 1991 California only. |

**CE** - CHECK ENGINE Light
**CEC** - Computerized Engine Controls
**EVAP** - Fuel Evaporative System
**FPR** - Fill Pipe Restrictor
**PCV** - Positive Crankcase Ventilation
**PFI** - Port Fuel Injection
**$O_2$** - Oxygen Sensor
**SPK** - Spark Control System
**TWC** - Three-Way Catalyst

# 1990-91 ENGINE PERFORMANCE
# Service & Adjustment Specifications

## 911 Carrera 2/4

## INTRODUCTION

Use this article to quickly find specifications related to servicing and on-vehicle adjustments. This is a quick-reference article for when you are familiar with adjustment procedure and only need a specification.

## CAPACITIES

*BATTERY SPECIFICATIONS*

| Application | Amp Hr. Rating |
|---|---|
| 911 Carrera 2/4 | 72 |

*FLUID CAPACITIES*

| Application | Quantity |
|---|---|
| Crankcase (Including Filter) | |
| Oil Change Capacity | [1] 9.5 qts. (9.0L) |
| Total Oil Capacity | [1] 12.2 qts. (11.5L) |
| Automatic Transaxle (Dexron-II) | [2] 9.5 qts. (9.0L) |
| Manual Transaxle (SAE 75 W 90) | |
| 911 Carrera 2 | 3.8 qts. (3.6L) |
| 911 Carrera 4 | |
| Front Axle | 1.27 qts. (1.2L) |
| Rear Axle | 4.02 qts. (3.8L) |

1 – Check oil level with vehicle on level ground. Ensure engine is running at idle and normal operating temperature.
2 – Differential oil capacity is 1.9 pts. (0.9L) with Tiptronic automatic transaxle. Use SAE 75 W 90 oil.

## QUICK-SERVICE

### SERVICE INTERVALS & SPECIFICATIONS

*REPLACEMENT INTERVALS*

| Component | Miles |
|---|---|
| Air Filter | 30,000 |
| Fuel Filter | 30,000 |
| Oil & Oil Filter | 15,000 |
| Spark Plugs | 30,000 |
| "V" Belt & Polyrib Belt | 30,000 |

*BELT ADJUSTMENT*

| Application | [1] Deflection In. (mm) |
|---|---|
| "V" Belt | 13/64-25/64 (5-10) |

1 – With light pressure applied to center of belt.

## MECHANICAL CHECKS

### ENGINE COMPRESSION

Check engine compression with engine at normal operating temperature and specified cranking speed, all spark plugs removed (on dual plugs, remove exhaust side only), and throttle wide open.

*COMPRESSION SPECIFICATIONS*

| Application | Specification |
|---|---|
| Compression Ratio | 11.3:1 |
| Compression Pressure | |
| Normal | 142-184 psi (10-13 kg/cm²) |
| Minimum | 107 psi (7.5 kg/cm²) |
| Maximum Variation | |
| Between Cylinders | 22 psi (1.5 kg/cm²) |

### VALVE CLEARANCE

Adjust valve clearance with engine cold. See VALVE CLEARANCE SPECIFICATIONS table. Adjust valves in firing sequence: 1-6-2-4-3-5. Marks for TDC of each cylinder are located 120 degrees apart on crankshaft pulley.

*VALVE CLEARANCE SPECIFICATIONS*

| Application | In. (mm) |
|---|---|
| Intake & Exhaust (Cold) | .004 (.10) |

## IGNITION SYSTEM

### IGNITION COIL

*IGNITION COIL RESISTANCE – Ohms @ 68°F (20°C)*

| Application | Primary | Secondary |
|---|---|---|
| 911 Carrera 2/4 | .4-.6 | 5000-7200 |

### FIRING ORDER & TIMING MARKS

***NOTE:*** ***For location of ignition timing mark, see ON-VEHICLE ADJUSTMENTS article.***

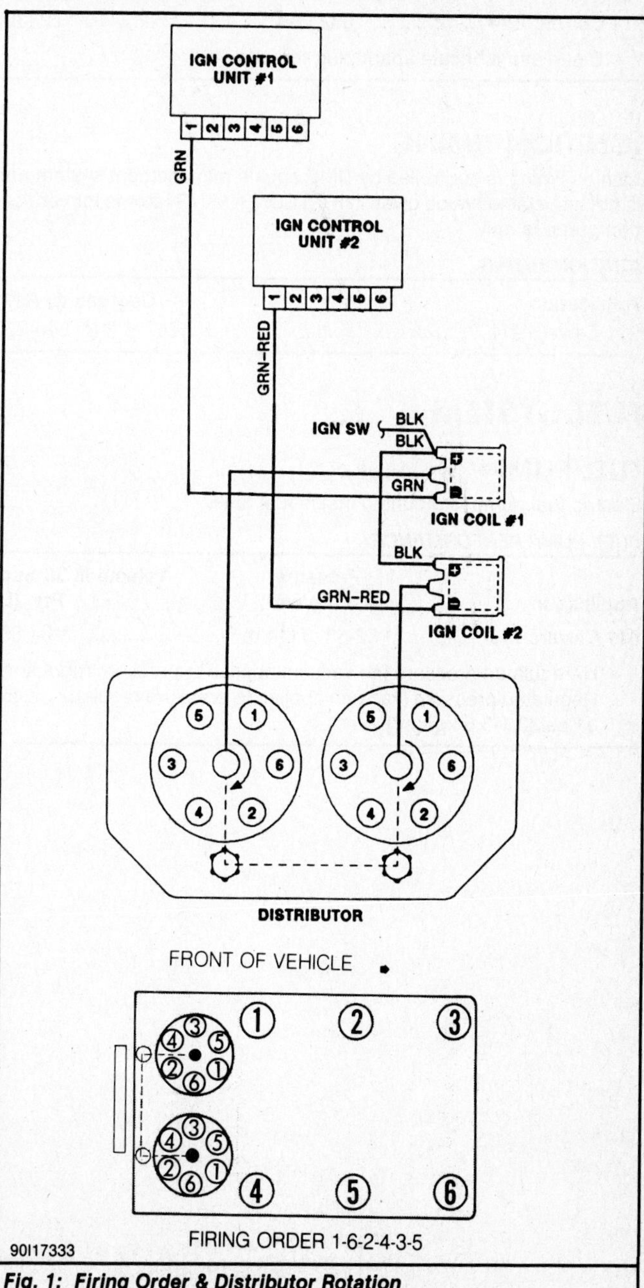


*Fig. 1: Firing Order & Distributor Rotation (Double Ignition System)*

# 1990-91 ENGINE PERFORMANCE
# Service & Adjustment Specifications (Cont.)

## HIGH TENSION WIRE RESISTANCE

*HIGH TENSION WIRE RESISTANCE* [1]

| Application | Ohms |
|---|---|
| Plug Connectors | 3000 |
| Distributor Cap Connector | 1000 |

[1] – Cap and plug connector only.

## SPARK PLUGS

*SPARK PLUG TYPE*

| Application | Bosch No. |
|---|---|
| 911 Carrera 2/4 | FR 5 DTC |

*SPARK PLUG SPECIFICATIONS*

| Application | Gap In. (mm) | Torque Ft. Lbs. (N.m) |
|---|---|---|
| 911 Carrera 2/4 | .032 (.8) | [1] 22 (30) |

[1] – Clean and lubricate spark plug threads.

## IGNITION TIMING

Ignition timing is controlled by DME engine management system and is not adjustable. Value given in IGNITION TIMING table is for verification purpose only.

*IGNITION TIMING*

| Application | Degrees @ RPM |
|---|---|
| 911 Carrera 2/4 | TDC ± 3 @ 840-920 |

## FUEL SYSTEM

### FUEL PUMP

Electric fuel pump is mounted inside fuel tank.

*FUEL PUMP PERFORMANCE*

| Application | Pressure psi (kg/cm²) | Volume in 30 Sec. Pts. (L) |
|---|---|---|
| 911 Carrera 2/4 | [1] 52-58 (3.6-4.0) | 1.8 (.85) |

[1] – Unregulated pressure (no vacuum applied to pressure regulator). Regulated pressure (vacuum applied to pressure regulator) is 45-51 psi (3.1-3.5 kg/cm²).

## INJECTOR RESISTANCE

*INJECTOR RESISTANCE*

| Application | Ohms |
|---|---|
| 911 Carrera 2/4 | 16 |

## IDLE SPEED & MIXTURE

*IDLE SPEED & CO LEVEL*

| Application | Idle RPM | CO Level |
|---|---|---|
| 911 Carrera 2/4 | 840-920 | [1] .4-1.2 % |

[1] – With oxygen sensor connected. Measurement is taken in front of catalytic converter.

## FAST IDLE SPEED

Fast idle speed is controlled by DME engine management system and is not adjustable.

## THROTTLE SWITCHES

**Idle Speed Switch** – See THROTTLE SWITCHES RESISTANCE table. For additional information, see ON-VEHICLE ADJUSTMENTS article.

**Full Throttle Switch** – See THROTTEL SWITCHES RESISTANCE table. For additional information, see ON-VEHICLE ADJUSTMENTS article.

**Throttle Valve Potentiometer** – See ON-VEHICLE ADJUSTMENTS article for adjustment information.

*THROTTLE SWITCHES RESISTANCE*

| Application | Ohms |
|---|---|
| **Idle Speed Switch** [1] | |
| Throttle Valve Closed | Less Than 10 |
| Throttle Valve Open [2] | Infinite Resistance |
| **Full Throttle Switch** [3] | |
| Throttle Valve Closed | Infinite Resistance |
| Throttle Valve Open [4] | Less Than 10 |

[1] – Resistance is measured between terminals No. 1 and No. 2.
[2] – Throttle valve angle must be greater than one degree.
[3] – Resistance is measured between terminals No. 2 and No. 3.
[4] – Throttle valve must be at least 2/3 open.

## 911 Carrera 2/4

## ENGINE MECHANICAL

Before performing any on-vehicle adjustments to fuel or ignition systems, ensure engine mechanical condition is okay.

## VALVE CLEARANCE

Adjust valve clearance with engine cold. See VALVE CLEARANCE SPECIFICATIONS table. Adjust valves in firing sequence: 1-6-2-4-3-5. Marks for TDC of each cylinder are located 120 degrees apart on crankshaft pulley.

***VALVE CLEARANCE SPECIFICATIONS***

| Application | In. (mm) |
|---|---|
| Intake & Exhaust (Cold) | .004 (.10) |

## IGNITION TIMING

Ignition timing is controlled by DME engine management system and is not adjustable. Value given in IGNITION TIMING table is for verification purpose only.

***IGNITION TIMING***

| Application | Degrees @ RPM |
|---|---|
| 911 Carrera 2/4 | TDC ± 3 @ 840-920 |

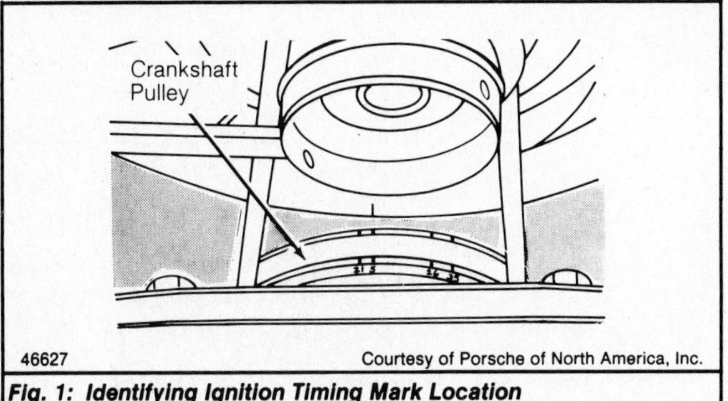


46627 Courtesy of Porsche of North America, Inc.

***Fig. 1: Identifying Ignition Timing Mark Location***

## IDLE SPEED & MIXTURE

### COLD (FAST) IDLE

Fast idle speed is controlled by DME engine management system and is not adjustable.

### IDLE MIXTURE

***NOTE: Mixture adjustment is NOT part of normal tune-up procedure and should NOT be performed unless fuel injection components and/or control units are replaced, or vehicle fails emission testing.***

**1)** Connect exhaust gas test line to test point in front of catalytic converter. By-pass idle stabilization system. Connect CO tester and tachometer. When engine is at operating temperature, turn regulating screw or by-pass screw on throttle until proper base idle speed is obtained.

**2)** Pull off rubber cap and disconnect plug for oxygen sensor at left side of engine compartment. If CO level is not correct, adjust mixture screw. Screw is located on airflow meter.

**3)** Always adjust mixture from lean to rich using Adjusting Wrench (P 377). Reconnect plug for oxygen sensor. Coat threads of test connection with molybdenum paste and install.

***IDLE SPEED & CO LEVEL***

| Application | Idle RPM | CO Level |
|---|---|---|
| 911 Carrera 2/4 | 840-920 | [1] .4-1.2 |

[1] – With oxygen sensor connected. Measurement is taken in front of catalytic converter.

## IDLE SPEED

Only base idle speed can be adjusted. The Digital Motor Electronic (DME) engine management system processes idle speed switch position, engine temperature and engine speed, then signals idle speed positioner to change idle speed as necessary. If idle speed control fails, control diaphragm is moved to a given clearance against the stop, allowing minimum operation.

## THROTTLE SWITCHES

### IDLE SPEED SWITCH

**911 Carrera 2/4 (M/T) – 1)** Disconnect throttle position sensor. Using an ohmmeter, check continuity between idle switch terminals No. 1 and No. 2. *See Fig. 2.* With throttle valve closed, ohmmeter reading should be less than 10 ohms.

**2)** Open throttle valve beyond one-degree angle. With throttle valve open, ohmmeter reading should be infinity. If ohmmeter readings are not as specified, adjust idle switch.

**3)** To adjust switch, use a 0.036" (0.9 mm) feeler gauge to adjust clearance between idle speed switch housing and drag lever when throttle valve is closed. *See Fig. 3.*

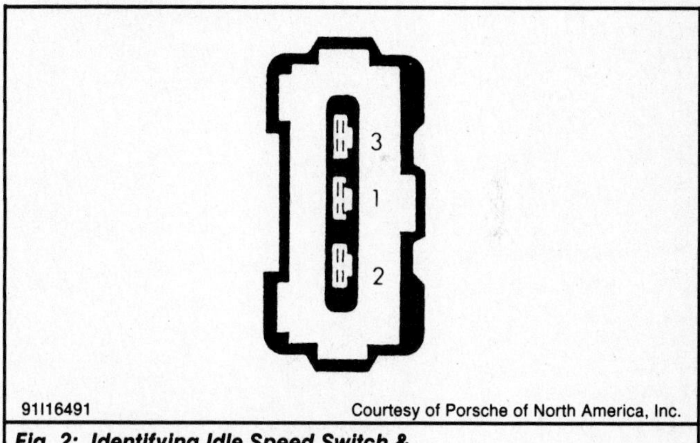


91I16491 Courtesy of Porsche of North America, Inc.

***Fig. 2: Identifying Idle Speed Switch & Full Throttle Switch Terminals***

### FULL THROTTLE SWITCH

**911 Carrera 2/4 (M/T) – 1)** Disconnect throttle position sensor. Using an ohmmeter, check continuity between full throttle position switch terminals No. 2 and No. 3. *See Fig. 2.* With throttle valve closed, ohmmeter reading should be infinity.

**2)** Open throttle valve at least 2/3 of the way. With throttle valve open, resistance should be less than 10 ohms. If ohmmeter readings are not as specified, adjust full throttle switch.

**3)** The full throttle switch must be adjusted so the switch contacts will close at throttle angle of about 70 degrees. *See Fig. 3.*

# 1990-91 ENGINE PERFORMANCE
## On-Vehicle Adjustments (Cont.)

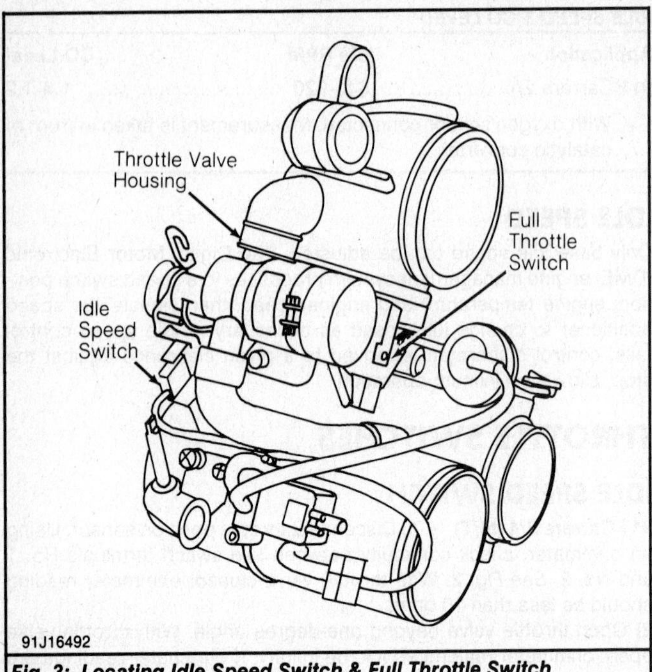


**Fig. 3: Locating Idle Speed Switch & Full Throttle Switch**

***THROTTLE SWITCHES RESISTANCE***

| Application | Resistance |
|---|---|
| Idle Speed Switch [1] | |
| Throttle Valve Closed | Less Than 10 Ohms |
| Throttle Valve Open [2] | Infinite Resistance |
| Full Throttle Switch [3] | |
| Throttle Valve Closed | Infinite Resistance |
| Throttle Valve Open [4] | Less Than 10 Ohms |

[1] – Resistance is measured between terminals No. 1 and No. 2.
[2] – Throttle valve angle must be greater than one (1) degree.
[3] – Resistance is measured between terminals No. 2 and No. 3.
[4] – Throttle valve must be at least 2/3 open.

## THROTTLE VALVE POTENTIOMETER

**911 Carrera 2/4 (A/T)** – Automatic transmission (Tiptronic) vehicles have a throttle valve potentiometer instead of a full throttle switch on throttle valve housing. The potentiometer is used exclusively for transmission control. In addition to the potentiometer, a full throttle switch for DME control unit, and an adjustment switch for throttle valve potentiometer are also located on throttle valve housing. Adjust throttle valve potentiometer so that a click is heard when the small diameter throttle valve plate begins to open.

***NOTE: DO NOT confuse the throttle valve potentiometer adjustment click with the click produced by idle speed switch contacts.***

## 911 Carrera 2/4

# INTRODUCTION

This article covers basic description and operation of engine performance-related systems and components. Read this article before diagnosing vehicles or systems with which you are not completely familiar.

# AIR INDUCTION SYSTEM

## RESONANCE FLAPS

Intake system is divided by 2 resonance flaps. This allows the natural occurrence of intake air oscillations to draw more air into the engine.

Resonance flaps are activated by Digital Motor Electronics (DME) control unit via a resonance flap solenoid, which opens resonance flaps with the help of a diaphragm valve when engine speed is greater than 5500 RPM. Solenoid is connected with a vacuum supply tank.

Solenoid and diaphragm valve will close when engine speed drops to less than 5400 RPM. To avoid seizure of resonance flaps (from deposits in intake), solenoid is activated briefly each time ignition is turned on. This causes resonance flaps to move from closed to open position, and back to closed.

***NOTE: On 1991 models, the aluminum intake runners have been changed to plastic. To reduce noise, a muffler has also been fitted between the idle speed stabilizer and the intake system.***

## THROTTLE VALVE ASSEMBLY

To improve engine pickup and transition behavior during slow acceleration, movement of throttle valve assembly has been modified so that smaller diameter throttle valve plate moves in the open direction first. Large diameter throttle valve plate is also opened via a drag arm, after first throttle valve is opened approximately 5 degrees. In addition, idle speed switch must open before small throttle valve plate moves.

***NOTE: On 1991 models, a single-flap throttle valve assembly is used in conjunction with the new plastic intake runners. Because of these changes, the control and venting lines, the air box, and the hoses for the venturi tube are also modified.***

# COMPUTERIZED ENGINE CONTROLS

All models are equipped with Digital Motor Electronics (DME) engine management system. *See Fig. 1*. The DME system uses various sensors to monitor intake air volume, engine speed, crankshaft position, intake air temperature and throttle position. Signals from these sensors, along with the start and oxygen sensor signals, are sent to the DME control unit. The control unit uses the input from these sensors to determine the correct fuel amount and ignition timing.

## DME CONTROL UNIT

A 55-pin DME control unit monitors and controls all engine management functions. *See Fig. 2*. The DME control unit is located under driver's seat. The DME control unit has the ability to store fault codes related to fuel injection and ignition system. Detected faults remain stored for at least 50 engine starts.

On 1990 models, the DME control unit harness connector includes 2-pin and 3-pin harness connector leads that must be bridged to battery positive (B+) or ground, depending on the state (California) and whether vehicle is equipped with a manual or automatic (Tiptronic) transmission. The process of bridging these leads is known as control unit coding.

All 1991 models are equipped with a modified DME control unit (Part No. 964 618 124 00). Control unit coding distinctions are only made between manual and automatic transmissions. The state (California) coding feature has been deleted. The modified control unit also has the ability to activate CHECK ENGINE light.

***NOTE: Components are grouped into 2 categories. The first category covers INPUT DEVICES, which control or produce voltage signals monitored by the control unit. The second category covers OUTPUT SIGNALS, which are components controlled by the control unit.***

## INPUT DEVICES

Vehicles are equipped with different combinations of input devices. Not all devices are used on all models. To determine input device usage on a specific model, see WIRING DIAGRAMS article in ENGINE PERFORMANCE. The available input signals include the following:

**Airflow Sensor** – Sensor is located in the air stream of airflow meter and supplies air volume information to DME control unit. The control unit uses this and other information to regulate fuel injection rate.

Airflow meter incorporates an airflow measuring plate. Airflow plate is connected to a potentiometer and opens when engine draws in air. Potentiometer informs control unit of the engine load by transmitting an electrical signal determined by the position of measuring flap. Potentiometer also signals control unit when fuel enrichment is necessary to prevent loss of engine power during sudden acceleration or deceleration.

**Detonation (Knock) Sensors** – Engine is fitted with 2 knock sensor brackets, each with a knock sensor attached. These brackets unite No. 1 and 3 cylinders, and No. 4 and 6 cylinders. If engine knock is detected, ignition timing for pertinent cylinder is retarded 3 degrees. If engine knock continues, ignition will continue to be retarded in 3-degree decrements (up to 9 degrees maximum). When engine knock stops, ignition timing is returned in small steps to its optimal value.

**Engine Speed/Reference Mark Sensor** – Speed sensor is mounted on an adjustable bracket with reference mark. Sensor measures engine speed by monitoring teeth on flywheel signal ring gear. Sensor sends 2 voltage pulses to the DME control unit as each tooth passes.

Reference mark sensor is located on crankcase flange. Sensor detects crankshaft position in relation to TDC and sends signal to control unit. Sensor is triggered by reference mark sender ring gear on flywheel.

**Engine Temperature Sensor** – Sensor is located in cylinder head, near No. 3 cylinder. Sensor supplies information on engine temperature to control air/fuel ratio (as engine temperature varies during cold start) and spark timing.

**Hall Effect Sensor** – Hall Effect sensor is installed in the double-ignition distributor. Hall Effect sensor identifies ignition timing of No. 1 cylinder and appropriately assigns signals of both knock sensors to firing order.

**Idle Speed Switch** – Switch is used to sense closed throttle position and is mounted on throttle housing, opposite full throttle switch. Idle speed switch signals DME control unit when to control idle stabilization and coasting fuel cutoff.

**Intake Air Temperature Sensor** – Sensor is located in air stream of airflow meter and supplies incoming air temperature information to control unit. The DME control unit uses this, along with other information, to regulate fuel injection rate.

**Full Throttle Switch** – The full throttle switch is mounted on throttle housing. Full throttle switch signals DME control unit of optimum power demands.

***NOTE: On 1991 models, the oxygen sensor has been modified to work in conjunction with the new DME control unit. The new oxygen sensor may ONLY be used with the new DME control unit. The oxygen sensors CANNOT be identified by physical appearance. The part number must be used to properly distinguish the NEW sensor (Part No. 258 003 024) from the OLD sensor (Part No. 258 003 084).***

**Oxygen Sensor** – Oxygen sensor is mounted in engine exhaust stream, in front of catalytic converter. Sensor supplies a low voltage signal (less than 0.5 volt) when fuel mixture is lean (high oxygen), and a higher voltage (up to one volt) when fuel mixture is rich (low oxygen). This rich-to-lean fluctuating signal is used by the DME control unit in calculations of air/fuel mixture (fuel injector) control.

# 1990-91 ENGINE PERFORMANCE
## Theory & Operation (Cont.)

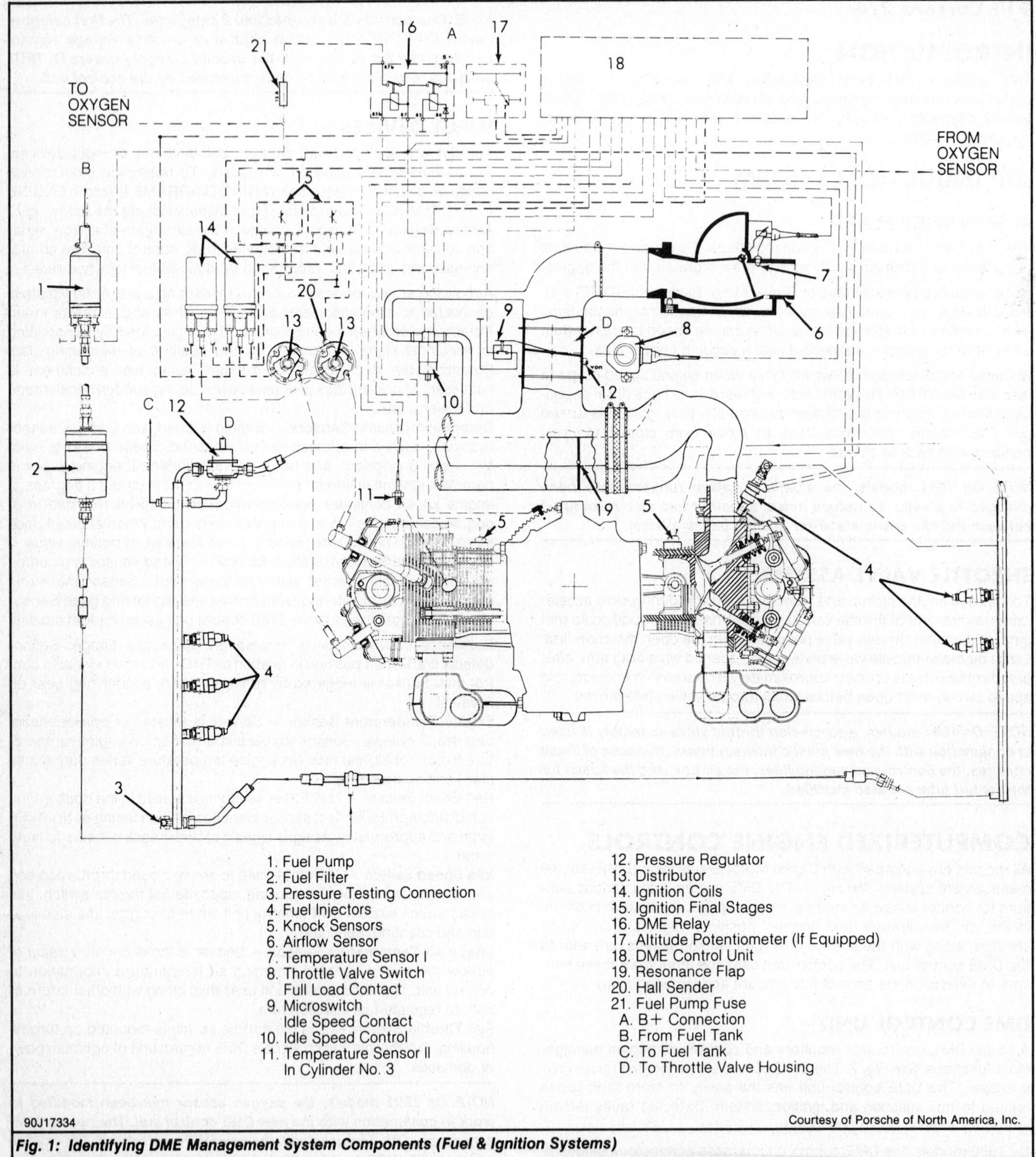


***Fig. 1: Identifying DME Management System Components (Fuel & Ignition Systems)***

The oxygen sensor has 3 wires: 2 for heater element (power and ground), and a single wire for oxygen sensor signal. The oxygen sensor heating element allows sensor to reach operating temperature faster. Heating element is energized through the fuel pump/DME relay when ignition is turned on. Connector from sensor to wiring harness are located near flywheel engine speed/reference mark sensor connector.

## OUTPUT SIGNALS

***NOTE: Vehicles are equipped with different combinations of computer-controlled components. Not all components listed below are used on every vehicle. For theory and operation on each output component, refer to indicated system after components.***

# 1990-91 ENGINE PERFORMANCE
# Theory & Operation (Cont.)

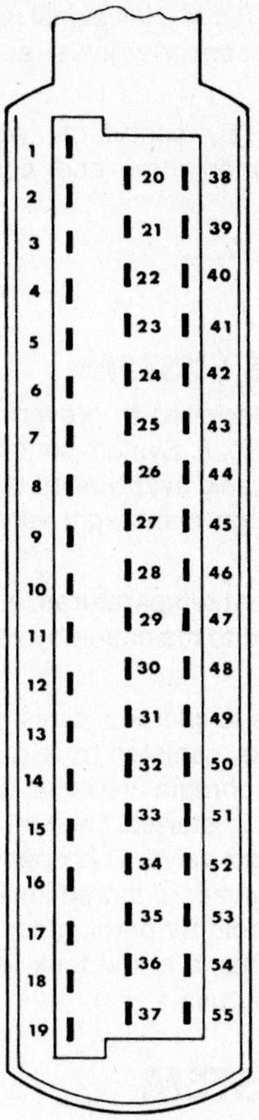

1. Ignition Signal (Output Stage)
2. Ground (Output Stage Shield)
3. DME Relay Ground (Fuel Pump)
4. Idle Speed Control
5. Fuel Tank Venting Solenoid
6. Engine RPM (To Tachometer)
7. Airflow Sensor Signal
8. Hall Effect Sensor Signal
9. Not Used
10. Oxygen Sensor (Ground Shield)
11. Knock Sensor No. 1
12. Airflow Sensor (Power Supply)
13. Diagnostic Connector (L)
14. Ground
15. Fuel Injector No. 3
16. Fuel Injector No. 6
17. Fuel Injector No. 1
18. Battery Voltage (Keep Alive Memory)
19. Ground
20. Not Used
21. Diagnostic Connector (Engine Knock Yes/No)
22. CHECK ENGINE Light Control
23. Resonance Flap Solenoid
24. Ground
25. Not Used
26. Ground (Airflow Meter)
27. Not Used
28. Oxygen Sensor Signal
29. Knock Sensor No. 2
30. Shield/Ground (Ground Shield For Hall Effect Sensor & Knock Sensors. Knock Sensor Ground.)
31. Hall Effect Sensor (+)
32. Fuel Consumption Gauge
33. Fuel Injector No. 5
34. Fuel Injector No. 4
35. Fuel Injector No. 2
36. Not Used
37. Ignition Voltage (From DME Relay)
38. Not Used
39. DME Coding
40. A/C Compressor
41. A/C Switch
42. Not Used
43. Not Used
44. Intake Air Temperature Sensor
45. Engine (Coolant) Temperature Sensor
46. Altitude Potentiometer (If Equipped)
47. Engine Speed/Reference Mark Sensor (+)
48. Engine Speed/Reference Mark Sensor (Ground Shield)
49. Not Used
50. A/C-Heating System Regulation
51. Not Used
52. Idle Speed Switch
53. Full Throttle Switch
54. DME Coding Connector
55. Diagnostic Connector (K)

91A16493

Courtesy of Porsche of North America, Inc.

***Fig. 2: Identifying DME Control Unit Input/Output Signals***

**A/C Compressor Control** – See A/C COMPRESSOR CONTROLS under MISCELLANEOUS CONTROLS.

**CHECK ENGINE Light** – See CHECK ENGINE LIGHT under SELF-DIAGNOSTIC SYSTEM.

**DME (Fuel Pump) Relay** — See FUEL DELIVERY under FUEL SYSTEM.

**Double Ignition** – See IGNITION TIMING CONTROL SYSTEM under IGNITION SYSTEM.

**Fuel Injectors** – See FUEL CONTROL under FUEL SYSTEM.

**Fuel Tank Vent Solenoid** — See EVAPORATIVE EMISSIONS SYSTEM under EMISSION SYSTEMS.

**Idle Speed Control** – See IDLE SPEED CONTROL under FUEL SYSTEM.

**Resonance Flap Solenoid** — See RESONANCE FLAPS under AIR INDUCTION SYSTEM.

## FUEL SYSTEM

### FUEL DELIVERY

**Fuel Pressure Regulator** – Pressure regulator is located at end of injection collection line. *See Fig. 1.* Pressure regulator maintains constant fuel pressure to fuel injectors.

**Fuel Pump & Fuel Pump Relay** – Electric fuel pump is located in fuel tank and maintains a constant fuel supply to injection system. *See Fig. 3.* Power for fuel pump is supplied by the DME relay. Fuel pump portion of DME relay is energized by the DME control unit.

1. Fuel Tank
2. Expansion Tank
3. Fuel Pump
4. Fuel Filter
5. Charcoal Canister
6. Flushing Air Pipe
7. To Engine
8. Fuel Return

90A17335

Courtesy of Porsche of North America, Inc.

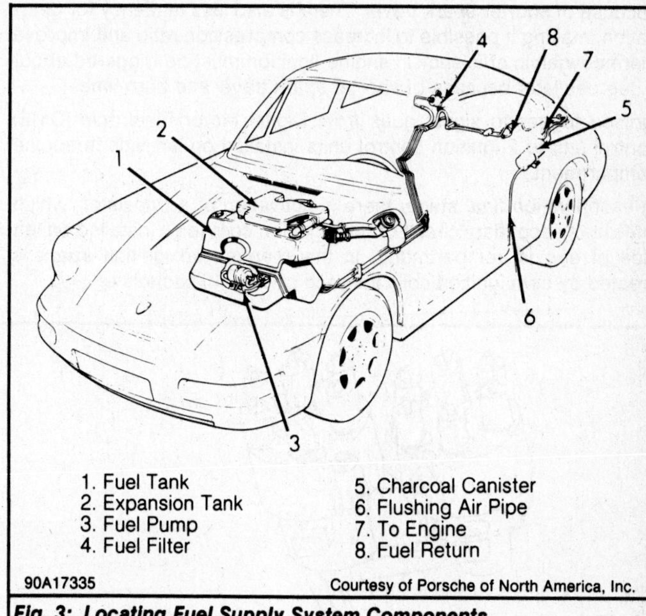

***Fig. 3: Locating Fuel Supply System Components***

# 1990-91 ENGINE PERFORMANCE
# Theory & Operation (Cont.)

## FUEL CONTROL

The DME control unit meters the amount of fuel distributed to each cylinder by sequential control of fuel injectors. The amount of fuel reaching each cylinder is controlled separately, once for each working (compression) stroke, according to firing order. Injection timing can be changed depending on engine temperature, engine speed and load, or other engine operating conditions.

**Fuel Injectors** – A fuel rail links fuel pressure regulator with fuel injectors. Each cylinder is provided with a solenoid-operated injector, which sprays fuel toward backside of each inlet valve. The DME control determines the length of time each injector is open. The injector's on time determines amount of fuel delivered.

## IDLE SPEED CONTROL

All models use an air regulating valve (idle speed positioner) to provide auxiliary air valve operation and idle speed stabilization. Air regulating valve is located near throttle body and is controlled by DME control unit. When necessary, air regulating valve will adjust air by-pass opening to maintain both cold and warm engine idle speeds.

**Air Regulating Valve** – Valve controls air by-pass opening around throttle. When necessary, control unit operates air regulating valve to stabilize idle speed.

## IGNITION SYSTEM

### IGNITION TIMING CONTROL SYSTEM

The engine speed/reference mark sensor sends a signal to DME control unit. The control unit uses this signal to fire coils for secondary ignition. Based on information received from data sensors, spark control allows DME control unit to determine the exact instant that ignition is required.

**Detonation Retard Operation** – See DETONATION (KNOCK) SENSORS under INPUT DEVICES.

**Double-Ignition System** – Two spark plugs per cylinder ignite air/fuel mixture. With this system, burn time of air/fuel mixture is shorter because of shorter spark travel. There is also less tendency for detonation, making it possible to increase compression ratio and improve thermodynamic efficiency in engine. Ignition must be triggered about 6 degrees later because of shorter spark travel and burn time.

Ignition triggering signal goes from Digital Motor Electronic (DME) control unit to 2 ignition control units installed on left side in engine compartment.

In each ignition final stage, there is activation of a transistor, which interrupts secondary circuit of both ignition coils (also installed on left side of engine compartment). In this manner, an ignition spark is created by both ignition coils for each cylinder in sequence.

A Hall Effect sensor, installed in the double-ignition distributor, identifies cylinder No. 1 (ignition TDC). *See Fig. 4*. Hall signal is required by DME for assignment of both knock sensor signals, as well as for sequential fuel injection control.

Each distributor rotor is controlled by centrifugal weights. This ensures alignment between distributor rotor and corresponding ignition contact in distributor cover.

## EMISSION SYSTEMS

### EVAPORATIVE EMISSIONS SYSTEM

Fuel evaporation control system is designed to prevent fuel vapors from escaping into atmosphere. *See Fig. 5*. System consists of a non-vented fuel tank filler cap, expansion tank, evaporation tank, charcoal canister, fuel tank vent solenoid, purge diaphragm valve, restrictor and connecting lines and hoses.

Expanded fuel, caused by high ambient temperatures, is collected in expansion tank. Liquid fuel is returned to main tank by venting action as fuel is used from main tank.

Fuel vapor passes through a vent line to charcoal canister where it is stored. A second vent line connects canister to a purge control diaphragm valve. Purge control diaphragm valve is closed when engine is not running. When engine is started, manifold vacuum is applied to top fitting of purge diaphragm valve. This opens an internal passage in diaphragm valve, allowing vapors stored in charcoal canister to be drawn into the intake manifold for burning during the combustion process. Purge line also contains a fuel tank vent solenoid which is controlled by the DME control unit.

## SELF-DIAGNOSTIC SYSTEM

The DME control unit has the ability to store fault codes related to fuel injection and ignition system. Detected faults remain stored for at least 50 engine starts. If positive battery cable or DME control unit connector is disconnected, the fault code memory and system adaptation will be cleared. For additional information, see SELF-DIAGNOSTICS article.

### CHECK ENGINE LIGHT

All 1991 models are equipped with a CHECK ENGINE light, which comes on if a component related to fuel injection and ignition system fails. The CHECK ENGINE light is installed in oil temperature/pressure gauge cluster. For additional information, see SELF-DIAGNOSTICS article.

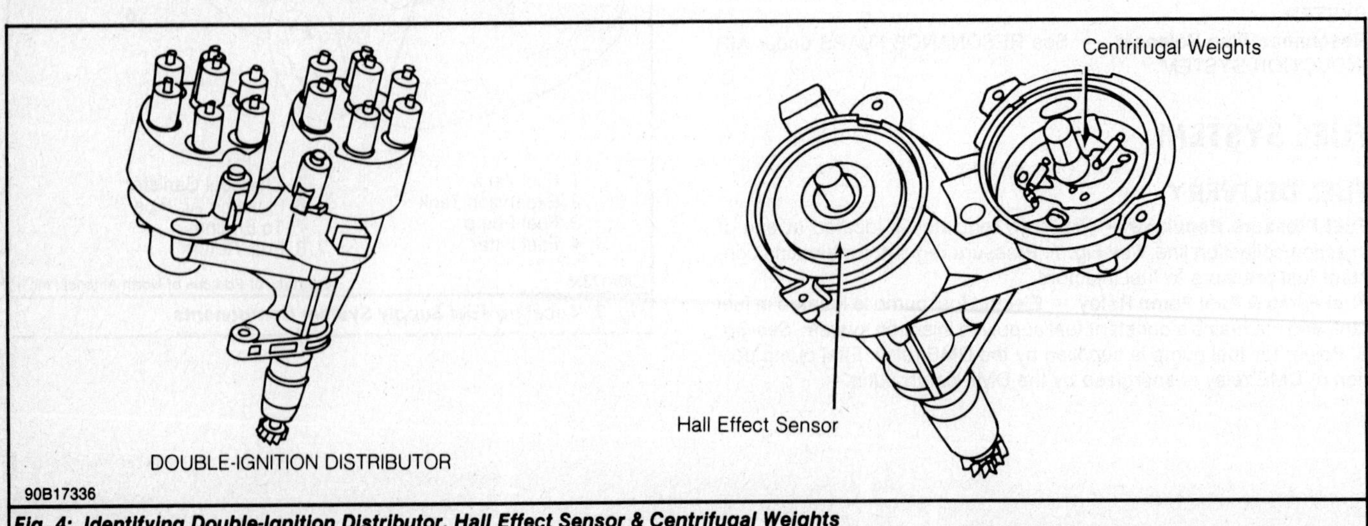


*Fig. 4: Identifying Double-Ignition Distributor, Hall Effect Sensor & Centrifugal Weights*

# 1990-91 ENGINE PERFORMANCE
# Theory & Operation (Cont.)

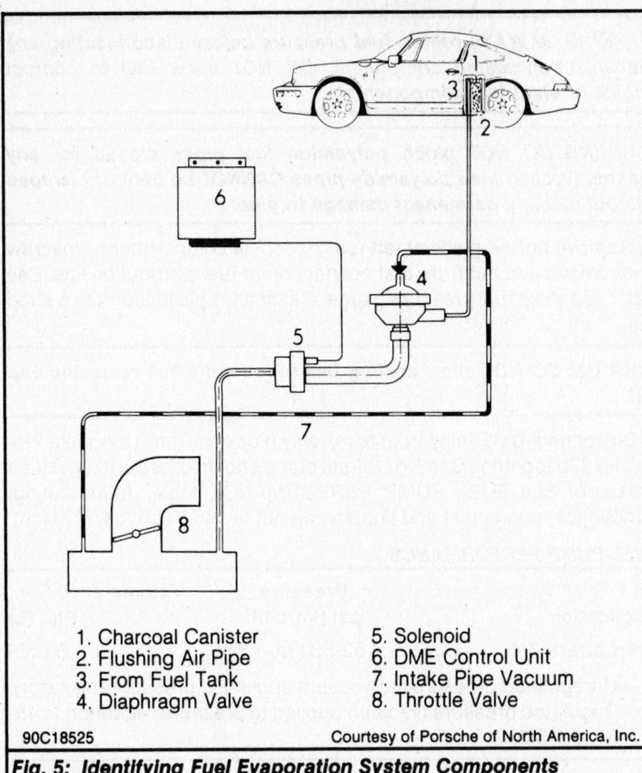


**Fig. 5: Identifying Fuel Evaporation System Components**

## MISCELLANEOUS CONTROLS

***NOTE: Although not considered true engine performance-related systems, some controlled devices may affect driveability if they malfunction.***

## A/C COMPRESSOR CONTROLS

Specific information is not available from manufacturer. The DME control unit, however, receives input and sends output signals over terminals No. 40 (A/C compressor), 41 (A/C switch) and 50 (A/C-heating system regulation).

# 1990-91 ENGINE PERFORMANCE
# Basic Diagnostic Procedures

## 911 Carrera 2/4

## INTRODUCTION

The following diagnostic steps will help prevent overlooking a simple problem. This is also where to begin diagnosis for a no-start condition.

The first step in diagnosing any driveability problem is verifying the customer's complaint with a test drive under conditions problem reportedly occurred.

Before entering self-diagnostics, perform a careful and complete visual inspection. Most engine control problems result from mechanical breakdowns, poor electrical connections or damaged/misrouted vacuum hoses. Before condemning the computerized system, perform each test listed in this article.

***NOTE: Perform all voltage tests with a Digital Volt-Ohmmeter (DVOM) with a minimum 10-megohm input impedance, unless stated otherwise in test procedure.***

## PRELIMINARY INSPECTION & ADJUSTMENTS

### VISUAL INSPECTION

Visually inspect all electrical wiring, looking for chafed, stretched, cut or pinched wiring. Ensure electrical connectors fit tightly and are not corroded. Ensure vacuum hoses are properly routed and not pinched or cut. See VACUUM DIAGRAMS article to verify routing and connections (if necessary). Inspect air induction system for possible vacuum leaks.

### MECHANICAL INSPECTION

**Compression** – Check engine mechanical condition with a compression gauge, vacuum gauge or an engine analyzer. See engine analyzer manual for specific instructions. Always disconnect the engine speed/reference sensor for compression tests. If this is not done, dangerous high voltages and insulation damage to the following may result: ignition coil, high-voltage distributor, and ignition leads.

***WARNING: DO NOT use ignition switch during compression tests on fuel-injected vehicles. Use a remote starter to crank engine. Fuel injectors are triggered by ignition switch during cranking mode and can create a fire hazard or contaminate engine's oiling system.***

*ENGINE COMPRESSION*

| Application | psi (kg/cm²) |
|---|---|
| Normal Compression Pressure | 142-184 (10-13) |
| Minimum Compression Pressure | 107 (7.5) |
| Maximum Variation Between Cylinders | 22 (1.5) |

**Exhaust System Backpressure** – Exhaust system can be checked with a vacuum or pressure gauge. Remove $O_2$ sensor or air injection check valve (if equipped). Connect a 1-10 psi pressure gauge and operate engine at 2500 RPM. If exhaust system backpressure is greater than 1 3/4 - 2 psi, exhaust system or catalytic converter is plugged.

If a vacuum gauge is used, connect vacuum gauge hose to intake manifold vacuum port and start engine. Observe vacuum gauge. Open throttle part way and hold steady. If vacuum gauge reading slowly drops after stabilizing, check exhaust system for restriction.

## FUEL SYSTEM

### FUEL PRESSURE

Begin basic diagnosis of fuel system by determining fuel system pressure.

***WARNING: ALWAYS relieve fuel pressure before disconnecting any fuel injection-related component. DO NOT allow fuel to contact engine or electrical components.***

***WARNING: DO NOT pinch polyamide fuel pipes closed for any reason. Rubber-lined polyamide pipes CANNOT be bent or clamped without causing permanent damage to pipe.***

**1)** Remove hot-air guide at left rear of engine compartment. Unscrew and remove cap nut from test connection of fuel distribution line. *See Fig. 1*. Connect fuel pressure gauge. Catch any spilled fuel with a shop rag.

***CAUTION: DO NOT allow sealing ball to fall out when removing cap nut.***

**2)** Disconnect DME relay from fuse/relay block and jump terminals No. 30 and 87b together. *See Fig. 1*. Fuel pump should operate at specified pressure. See FUEL PUMP PERFORMANCE table. After testing, remove test equipment and tighten cap nut to 108 INCH lbs. (12 N.m).

*FUEL PUMP PERFORMANCE*

| Application | Pressure psi (kg/cm²) | Volume in 30 Sec. Pts. (L) |
|---|---|---|
| 911 Carrera 2/4 | [1] 52-58 (3.6-4.0) | 1.8 (.85) |

[1] – Unregulated pressure (no vacuum applied to pressure regulator). Regulated pressure (vacuum applied to pressure regulator) is 45-51 (3.1-3.5).

***NOTE: Digital Motor Electronic (DME) relay terminal numbers are marked on the relay socket.***

### FUEL PUMP VOLUME TEST

**1)** Remove hot-air blower at left rear of engine compartment. Disconnect fuel return line from fuel distributor. Catch any spilled fuel with a shop rag.

**2)** Connect a test hose from fuel distributor to measuring receptacle. Disconnect DME relay from fuse/relay block. Jump terminals No. 30 and 87b together. *See Fig. 1*. Fuel pump should operate. Allow fuel pump to operate for 30 seconds. Volume delivered into receptacle should be at least 1.8 pts. (.85 L).

## IGNITION CHECKS

**Spark** – Check for spark at coil wire and at each spark plug wire using a high output spark tester. Check spark plug wire resistance, on suspected wire(s), from cap to plug connector. Resistance should NOT be greater than 4000 ohms.

**Ignition Coil Primary Resistance** – **1)** Ensure ignition switch is off. Disconnect wires from primary terminals of ignition coils to isolate them from system.

**2)** Set ohmmeter at x1 scale. Connect ohmmeter leads to both primary terminals. Reading should be .4-.6 ohm. If reading is not as specified, replace ignition coil.

**Ignition Secondary Resistance** – **1)** Ensure ignition switch is off. Remove wire from coil tower. Set ohmmeter at x1000 scale. Connect ohmmeter leads to ignition coil positive terminal and coil tower.

**2)** Reading should be 5000-7200 ohms. If reading is not as specified, replace ignition coil.

**Distributor Cap & Spark Plug Leads** – Resistance of distributor cap suppression resistors should be 1000 ohms (each). Resistance of spark plug lead suppression resistors should be 3000 ohms (each).

# 1990-91 ENGINE PERFORMANCE
## Basic Diagnostic Procedures (Cont.)

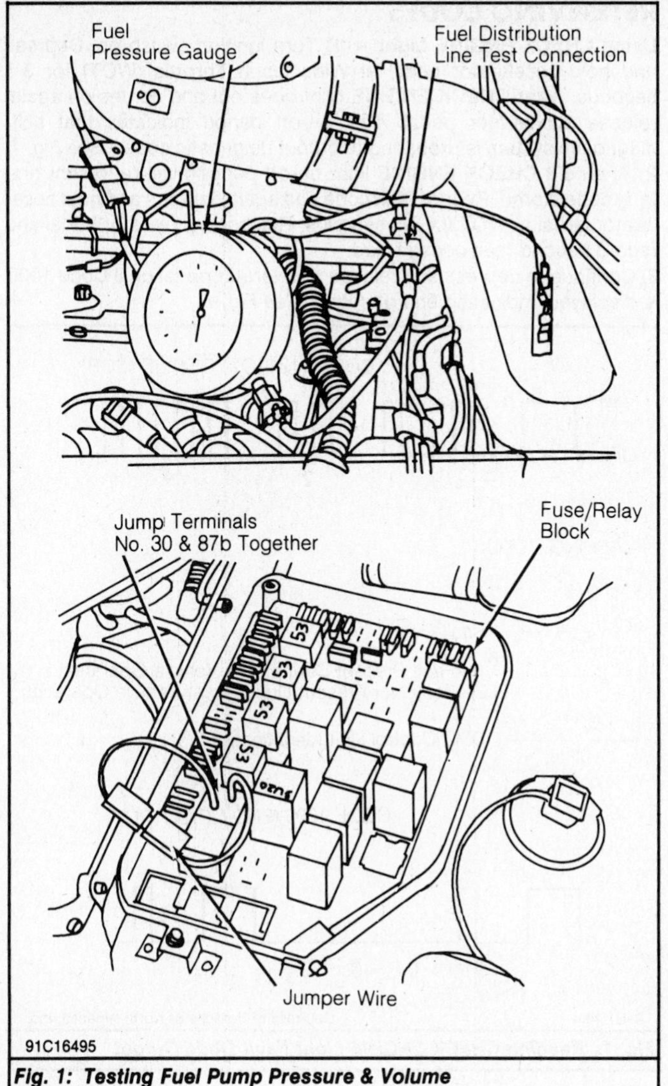


***Fig. 1: Testing Fuel Pump Pressure & Volume***

## IDLE SPEED & IGNITION TIMING

Ensure idle speed and ignition timing are set to specification. Idle speed and ignition timing are controlled by DME engine management system and are not adjustable. Values given in IGNITION TIMING SPECIFICATIONS and IDLE SPEED SPECIFICATIONS tables are for verification purpose only.

***IGNITION TIMING SPECIFICATIONS***

| Application | Degrees @ RPM |
|---|---|
| 911 Carrera 2/4 | TDC ± 3 @ 840-920 |

***IDLE SPEED SPECIFICATIONS***

| Application | Idle RPM |
|---|---|
| 911 Carrera 2/4 | 840-920 |

## SUMMARY

If no faults were found while performing BASIC DIAGNOSTIC PROCEDURES, proceed to SELF-DIAGNOSTICS article.

# 1990-91 ENGINE PERFORMANCE
# Self-Diagnostics

## 911 Carrera 2/4

## INTRODUCTION

If no faults were found while performing BASIC DIAGNOSTIC PROCEDURES, proceed with self-diagnostics. Also see SYSTEM & COMPONENT TESTING article.

***NOTE: Only limited information on the self-diagnostic system is available from manufacturer.***

## SELF-DIAGNOSTIC SYSTEM

The Digital Motor Electronics (DME) control unit has the ability to store fault codes related to fuel injection and ignition systems. Detected faults are stored for at least 50 engine starts. If positive battery cable or DME control unit connector is disconnected, fault code memory and system adaptation will be cleared.

**Hard Failures –** Hard failures cause CHECK ENGINE light to illuminate and remain on until problem is repaired. If light comes on and remains on (light may flash) during vehicle operation, cause of malfunction must be determined using diagnostic (code) charts. If a sensor fails, the control unit will use a substitute value in its calculations to continue engine operation. In this condition, commonly known as limp-in mode, vehicle runs but driveability will not be optimum.

**Intermittent Failures –** Intermittent failures may cause CHECK ENGINE light to flicker or illuminate. Light goes out after intermittent fault goes away. However, the corresponding trouble code will be stored in ECU memory. If fault does not reoccur within a certain time frame, related code will be erased from ECU memory. Intermittent failures

may be caused by sensor, connector or wiring related problems. See INTERMITTENTS in TROUBLE SHOOTING – NO CODES article.

## CHECK ENGINE LIGHT

All 1991 models are equipped with a CHECK ENGINE light. Light comes on if component related to fuel injection and/or ignition system fails. The CHECK ENGINE light is installed in oil temperature/pressure gauge cluster. Light comes on as a self-test when ignition switch is in ON position.

After engine starts, throttle valve closes, and CHECK ENGINE light goes out to indicate that no codes are present. If CHECK ENGINE light remains on, a fault is present (hard failure) in DME engine management system. If CHECK ENGINE light comes on (flickers) while driving, a fault in DME engine management system has been identified (intermittent failure).

If idle speed switch is open during starting, the CHECK ENGINE light will come on. As soon as the idle speed switch closes while driving, the CHECK ENGINE light goes out after a 4-second delay.

If full throttle switch is faulty (shorted to ground), the CHECK ENGINE light will remain on constantly. Some fault codes CANNOT be displayed using the CHECK ENGINE light. In such cases, retrieve fault code(s) through diagnostic connector, and repair condition(s) causing CHECK ENGINE light to come on. See USING DIAGNOSTIC CONNECTOR under RETRIEVING CODES.

## RETRIEVING CODES

**Using CHECK ENGINE Light – 1)** Turn ignition switch on. Depress and hold accelerator pedal at Wide Open Throttle (WOT) for 3-5 seconds. After CHECK ENGINE light goes out and comes on again, release accelerator pedal. This on-off period indicates that self-diagnostic system is preparing to output diagnostic codes. *See Fig. 1*.

**2)** The next CHECK ENGINE light on-off periods will represent first fault code stored. Record fault code and again depress and hold accelerator pedal at WOT for 3-5 seconds. Release accelerator pedal and record second fault code stored.

**3)** Continue to depress and release accelerator pedal until Code 1000 is displayed, indicating end of output. *See Fig. 1*.

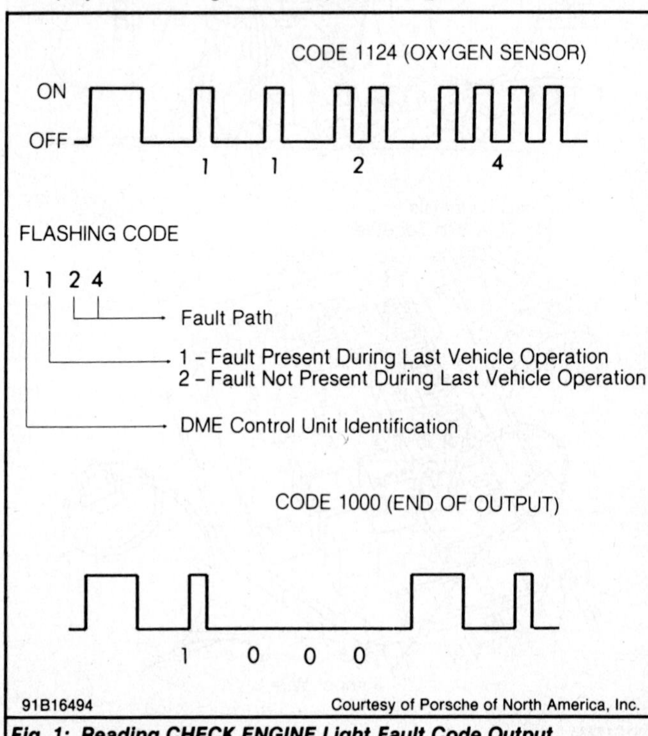


***Fig. 1: Reading CHECK ENGINE Light Fault Code Output***

**Using Diagnostic Connector – 1)** Ensure transmission is in Park or Neutral, and ignition is off. Diagnostic connector is located underneath a cover, in front passenger's footwell. Connect Porsche System Tester (9288), or Porsche Flashing Code Tester (9268) with Adapter Lead (9268/2) to diagnostic connector.

**2)** If system tester is used, turn tester on and follow instructions displayed. In addition to reading fault memory, it is possible to activate a number of components with this tester.

**3)** If flashing code tester and adapter lead is used, the 4-digit fault code(s) will be flashed by the tester. If the number 1 is displayed in the second digit of the code, then fault was present during the last vehicle operation. If the number 2 is displayed in the second digit, then fault was not present when vehicle was last operated. See FAULT CODE IDENTIFICATION table.

# 1990-91 ENGINE PERFORMANCE
# Self-Diagnostics (Cont.)

### FAULT CODE IDENTIFICATION

| Code [1] | System Affected | Probable Cause |
|---|---|---|
| 1000 [2] | | End Of Output |
| 1111 | DME Power Supply | Power Supply Less Than 10 Volts Or Greater Than 16 Volts |
| 1112 [2] | Idle Speed Switch | Short In Ground Circuit |
| 1113 | Full Throttle Switch | Short In Ground Circuit |
| 1114 [2] | Engine Temperature Sensor | Open Circuit |
| 1121 [2] | Airflow Sensor | [3] Signal Not Plausible |
| 1123 [2] | Oxygen Sensor | Air/Fuel Mixture Too Rich Or Too Lean |
| 1124 [2] | Oxygen Sensor | Open/Shorted Circuit Or Faulty Sensor |
| 1125 | Intake Air Temp. Sensor | Open/Short Circuit |
| 1131 | Knock Sensor No. 1 | [3] Signal Not Plausible |
| 1132 | Knock Sensor No. 2 | [3] Signal Not Plausible |
| 1133 | Knock Regulation | Knock Computer Faulty |
| 1134 | Hall Effect Sensor | Open/Short Circuit |
| 1141 [2] | DME Control Unit | DME Control Unit Faulty |
| 1151 [2] | Fuel Injector No. 1 | Open/Short Circuit |
| 1152 [2] | Fuel Injector No. 2 | Open/Short Circuit |
| 1153 [2] | Fuel Injector No. 3 | Open/Short Circuit |
| 1154 [2] | Fuel Injector No. 4 | Open/Short Circuit |
| 1155 [2] | Fuel Injector No. 5 | Open/Short Circuit |
| 1156 [2] | Fuel Injector No. 6 | Open/Short Circuit |
| 1500 [2] | System Okay | No Faults Stored In Memory |

[1] – Except for Code 1000 and Code 1500, the second digit of all other codes can also be a 2, indicating that fault did not exist during last operation of vehicle.
[2] – On 1991 models, these codes can also be displayed by CHECK ENGINE light. Other flashing codes are also possible but DO NOT represent a warning regarding CHECK ENGINE light.
[3] – Signal of a monitored component is not conforming with memory contents of DME control unit. The control unit recognizes that there is a faulty signal, but cannot always recognize the cause of the faulty signal.

## READING INPUT & OUTPUT SIGNALS

***NOTE:** Some input and output signals can be checked with both testers. See INPUT SIGNALS CODE IDENTIFICATION and OUTPUT SIGNALS CODE IDENTIFICATION tables.*

### INPUT SIGNALS CODE IDENTIFICATION

| Code | Input Signals | [1] Action |
|---|---|---|
| 1000 | End Of Output | |
| 1332 | 10 – Idle Speed Switch | Operate Accelerator Pedal Lightly |
| 1333 | 11 – Full Throttle Switch | Operate Accelerator Pedal To Wide Open Throttle |
| 1334 | [2] 12 – A/C Activation | Switch On Air Conditioning |
| 1335 | [3] 13 – A/C Activation | Switch Off Air Conditioning |

[1] – After action is taken, LED should go out and 0000 should be displayed on tester after about 3 seconds.
[2] – Input occurs at terminal No. 41 of DME control unit.
[3] – Input occurs at terminal No. 40 of DME control unit.

### OUTPUT SIGNALS CODE IDENTIFICATION

| Code [1] | Output Signals |
|---|---|
| 1311 | 1 – Fuel Injector No. 1 |
| 1312 | 2 – Fuel Injector No. 2 |
| 1313 | 3 – Fuel Injector No. 3 |
| 1314 | 4 – Fuel Injector No. 4 |
| 1315 | 5 – Fuel Injector No. 5 |
| 1316 | 6 – Fuel Injector No. 6 |
| 1321 | 7 – Idle Speed Control |
| 1322 | 8 – Fuel Tank Vent Solenoid |
| 1323 | 9 – Resonance Flaps |

[1] – Activation of component may cause difficult engine starting afterward.

## CLEARING CODES

**Using CHECK ENGINE Light –** Ensure fault causing CHECK ENGINE light to come on has been repaired, then depress and hold accelerator pedal at WOT for more than 12 seconds. The CHECK ENGINE light goes out briefly after 3, 7 and 10-second intervals to indicate that fault code memory has been cleared.

**Disconnecting DME Control Unit Connector –** To clear codes stored in memory, momentarily disconnect the electrical connector from DME control unit. The fault code memory and system adaptation will be cleared.

***NOTE:** Fault code memory may also be cleared using Porsche system tester or Porsche flashing code tester.*

## DME CONTROL UNIT LOCATION

The DME control unit is located under the driver's seat.

## SUMMARY

If no hard fault codes (or only pass codes) are present, driveability symptoms exist or intermittent codes exist, proceed to BASIC DIAGNOSTIC PROCEDURES article or SYSTEM & COMPONENT TESTING article.

# 1990-91 ENGINE PERFORMANCE
# System & Component Testing

### 911 Carrera 2/4

## INTRODUCTION

Before testing separate components or systems, perform procedures in BASIC DIAGNOSTIC PROCEDURES article. Since many computer-controlled and monitored components set a trouble code if they malfunction, also perform procedures in SELF-DIAGNOSTICS article.

***NOTE: Testing individual components does not isolate shorts or opens. Perform all voltage tests with a Digital Volt-Ohmmeter (DVOM) with a minimum 10-megohm input impedance, unless stated otherwise in test procedure. Use ohmmeter to isolate wiring harness shorts or opens.***

## TESTING PRECAUTIONS

**1)** ALWAYS turn ignition switch off, or disconnect battery for resistance tests. ALWAYS disconnect the engine speed/reference sensor for compression tests. If this is not done, dangerous high voltages and insulation damage to the following components may result: ignition coil, high-voltage distributor and ignition leads.
**2)** NEVER connect a capacitor to ignition coil terminals. NEVER connect ignition coil terminal No. 1 to ground. The ignition coil and DME control unit could be damaged.
**3)** NEVER connect battery leads or test light to ignition coil terminal No. 1. The DME control unit will be damaged. NEVER disconnect ignition lead from ignition coil secondary terminal during engine operation.
**4)** Voltage flashover from ignition coil secondary terminal to ignition coil primary coil terminals (No. 1 and 15) must be avoided. The DME control unit could be damaged.
**5)** When testing, the secondary circuit of the ignition system MUST be suppressed at all times with 4000-ohm resistance (1000-ohm distributor cap suppression resistor; 3000-ohm spark plug lead suppression resistors).
**6)** ALWAYS turn ignition switch off or disconnect battery BEFORE disconnecting ignition or DME control unit connectors. Electrostatic discharge may damage DME control unit.
**7)** NEVER disconnect battery while engine is running. Reversed battery polarity could damage ignition or DME control unit. DO NOT exceed a charging voltage of 16 volts (including when using a battery charger).

***NOTE: Complete system and component testing information is not available from manufacturer. Only components with informations available are covered in this article.***

## COMPUTERIZED ENGINE CONTROLS

### DME CONTROL UNIT

**CHECK ENGINE Light Control Circuit (1991 Models) – 1)** Disconnect DME control unit connector. *See Fig. 2*. Check the CHECK ENGINE light control circuit by grounding DME control unit wiring harness connector terminal No. 22 and turning ignition on.
**2)** If CHECK ENGINE light fails to come on, check bulb and wiring harness (circuit) between DME control and instrument cluster. See WIRING DIAGRAMS article in ENGINE PERFORMANCE.

***NOTE: If CHECK ENGINE light control circuit is faulty, a fault code may be stored in memory. See SELF-DIAGNOSTICS article.***

**Diagnostic Circuit – 1)** Locate 19-pin diagnostic connector underneath cover in front passenger's footwell. Use DVOM to check wiring harness (circuit) continuity between pin No. 7 (Orange/Blue wire) of 19-pin diagnostic connector and DME control unit terminal No. 13. *See Fig. 2*.
**2)** Use DVOM to check wiring harness (circuit) continuity between pin No. 8 (Orange/White wire) of 19-pin diagnostic connector and DME control unit terminal No. 55. If circuit continuity does not exist, check wiring harness for open circuits or circuits shorted to ground. If circuit continuity is okay, go to next step.
**3)** Use DVOM to check voltage at pin No. 7 (Orange/Blue wire) of 19-pin diagnostic connector. Repeat voltage check at pin No. 8 (Orange/White wire) of 19-pin diagnostic connector. Voltage readings must be greater than 8 volts with ignition on. If voltage is not as specified, check wiring harness for open/short circuits. See WIRING DIAGRAMS article in ENGINE PERFORMANCE.

**Ground Circuits – 1)** Use DVOM to check continuity to ground on Digital Motor Electronics (DME) control unit ground circuits at terminals No. 14, 19, 24 and 30. *See Fig. 2*. See WIRING DIAGRAMS article in ENGINE PERFORMANCE. Ensure ohmmeter reading is zero ohm.
**2)** If reading is not zero ohm, repair open ground circuit. Check DME ground wires on cylinder No. 1 intake pipe and fuel filter mount. Check ground strap between body and transmission/engine. Ensure all electrical connections are securely attached and free of corrosion.

**Power Circuits – 1)** Disconnect DME control unit connector. Connect DVOM between terminal No. 24 (ground) and terminal No. 18 (battery voltage; keep-alive memory). *See Fig. 2*. DVOM should indicate battery voltage. If battery voltage is not present, check Red wire back to fuse block and battery, or Brown ground wire. See WIRING DIAGRAMS article in ENGINE PERFORMANCE.
**2)** Connect DVOM between terminal No. 24 (ground) and terminal No. 37 (ignition signal from DME relay). *See Fig. 2*. Turn ignition on. DVOM should indicate battery voltage. If battery voltage is not present, check Gray/Brown wire back to DME relay, or Brown ground wire. See WIRING DIAGRAMS article in ENGINE PERFORMANCE.

***NOTE: On vehicles equipped with anti-theft system, check power supply from ignition lock to terminal No. 86 of DME relay via the anti-theft system control unit. See WIRING DIAGRAMS article in ENGINE PERFORMANCE.***

## ENGINE SENSORS & SWITCHES

**Airflow Sensor – 1)** Connect DVOM between ground and terminal No. 3 of airflow sensor wiring harness connector. *See Fig. 1*. Turn ignition on to check voltage supply to sensor. If reading is 4.7-5.3 volts, go to next step. If voltage is not 4.7-5.3 volts, check Blue/Green wire back to DME control unit.
**2)** Disconnect air filter hose. Using jumper wires, connect terminal No. 3 of airflow sensor wiring harness connector with terminal No. 3 of sensor, and terminal No. 4 of wiring harness connector with terminal No. 4 of sensor.
**3)** Connect DVOM between ground and airflow sensor terminal No. 2. Turn ignition on to check voltage drop across sensor. With airflow sensor plate closed, reading should be 250-260 millivolts.
**4)** Using a screwdriver handle, press airflow sensor plate to full throttle position. Reading should gradually increase to about 4.6 volts. If voltage values are incorrect, replace airflow sensor.

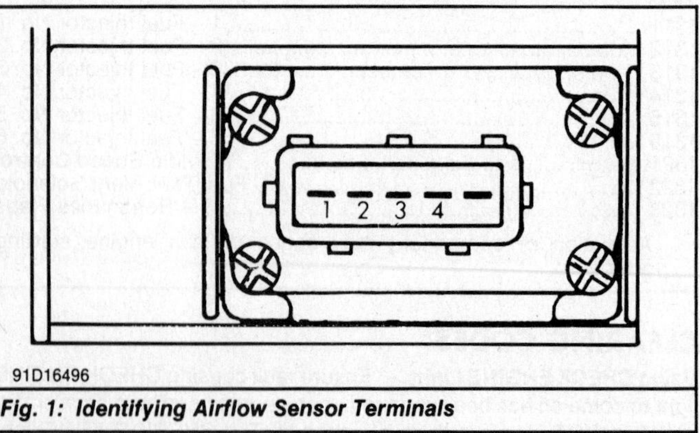


*Fig. 1: Identifying Airflow Sensor Terminals*

**DME Relay – 1)** Disconnect DME control unit connector. Connect a jumper wire between terminal No. 3 (DME relay ground) and terminal No. 24 (ground). *See Fig. 2*.

# 1990-91 ENGINE PERFORMANCE
# System & Component Testing (Cont.)

**2)** Turn ignition on and ensure fuel pump runs. If fuel pump does not run, check fuses, DME relay, Black/White wire to DME relay, Green/Black wire to fuel pump, or fuel pump. See WIRING DIAGRAMS article in ENGINE PERFORMANCE.

**Engine (Coolant) Temperature Sensor** – Disconnect DME control unit connector. Connect DVOM between terminal No. 30 (ground) and terminal No. 45 (engine temperature sensor). *See Fig. 2.* See ENGINE (COOLANT) TEMPERATURE SENSOR RESISTANCE table. If readings are incorrect, check resistances directly on sensor.

***ENGINE (COOLANT) TEMPERATURE SENSOR RESISTANCE***

| Temperature °F (°C) | Ohms |
|---|---|
| 32 (0) | 4400-6800 |
| 59-86 (15-30) | 1400-3600 |
| 104 (40) | 1000-1300 |
| 176 (80) | 250-390 |
| 212 (100) | 160-210 |

**Full Throttle Switch** – **1)** Disconnect DME control unit connector. Connect DVOM between terminal No. 24 (ground) and terminal No. 53 (full throttle switch). *See Fig. 2.* With throttle valve closed, ohmmeter reading should be infinity.

**2)** Open throttle valve at least 2/3 of the way. With throttle valve open, resistance reading should be less than 10 ohms. If ohmmeter readings are incorrect, measure resistance directly at full throttle switch and adjust if necessary. See ON-VEHICLE ADJUSTMENTS article.

**Idle Speed Switch** – **1)** Disconnect DME control unit connector. Connect DVOM between terminal No. 24 (ground) and terminal No. 52 (idle speed switch). *See Fig. 2.* With throttle valve closed, ohmmeter reading should be less than 10 ohms.

**2)** Open throttle valve beyond 1-degree opening angle. With throttle valve open, ohmmeter reading should be infinity. If ohmmeter readings are incorrect, measure resistance directly at idle speed switch and adjust if necessary. See ON-VEHICLE ADJUSTMENTS article.

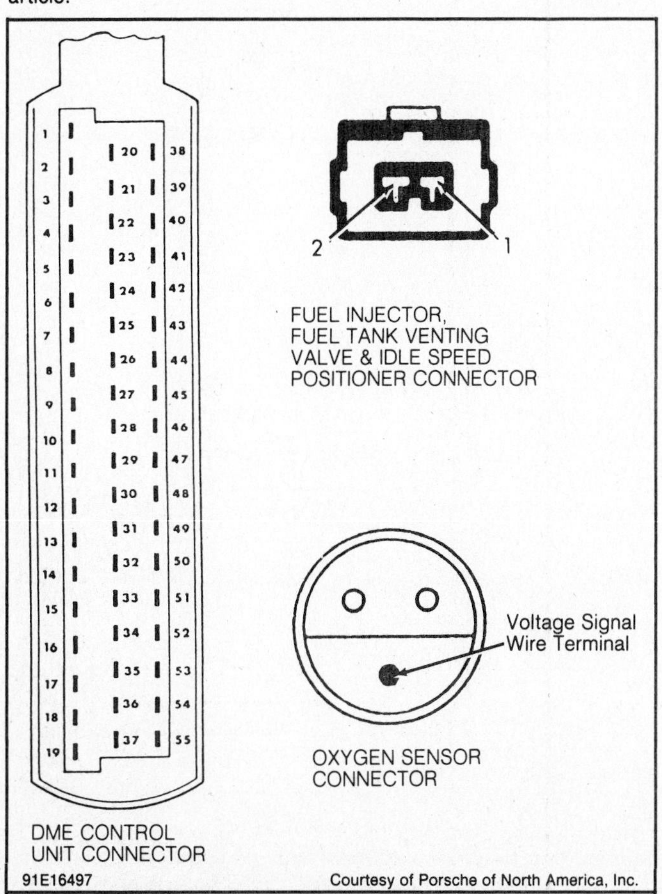


***Fig. 2: Identifying DME Control Unit, Fuel Injector & Oxygen Sensor Connectors***

**Intake Air Temperature Sensor** – **1)** Disconnect DME control unit connector. Connect DVOM between terminal No. 26 (airflow meter ground) and terminal No. 44 (intake air temperature sensor). *See Fig. 2.* See INTAKE AIR TEMPERATURE SENSOR RESISTANCE table.

**2)** If readings are incorrect, check resistances directly on sensor by connecting ohmmeter between terminals No. 1 and 4 at intake air temperature (airflow) sensor. *See Fig. 1.*

***INTAKE AIR TEMPERATURE SENSOR RESISTANCE***

| Temperature °F (°C) | Ohms |
|---|---|
| 32 (0) | 4400-6800 |
| 59-86 (15-30) | 1400-3600 |
| 104 (40) | 1000-1300 |

**Knock Sensors** – Check knock sensors and brackets for proper installation. Check sensor connectors for loose, corroded or damaged terminals. Check knock sensor circuits/wiring harness. See WIRING DIAGRAMS article in ENGINE PERFORMANCE. If necessary, replace knock sensors.

***NOTE: Specifications and other testing information are not available from manufacturer. If a knock sensor is faulty, ignition timing will be retarded 6 degrees on crankshaft.***

**Oxygen Sensor** – **1)** Disconnect oxygen sensor connector. Start and warm engine to normal operating temperature. Connect DVOM between ground and oxygen sensor voltage signal wire. *See Fig. 2.*

**2)** Note voltage on DVOM. Accelerate engine to enrich mixture, and note voltage reading on DVOM. DVOM must indicate a change in voltage signal. Reading will vary between 150-900 millivolts depending on air/fuel mixture.

## FUEL SYSTEM

### FUEL DELIVERY

***NOTE: For fuel system pressure testing, see BASIC DIAGNOSTIC PROCEDURES article.***

### FUEL CONTROL

**Fuel Injectors** – **1)** Disconnect fuel injector connector. Connect DVOM between ground and terminal No. 2 of fuel injector connector. *See Fig. 2.* Turn ignition on and check voltage supply to fuel injector. If battery voltage is not indicated, check Red/White wire back to fuse/relay block. See WIRING DIAGRAMS article in ENGINE PERFORMANCE.

**2)** If battery voltage is present, use DVOM to measure resistance across injector terminals. If resistance is not approximately 16 ohms, replace injector. Repeat test for each injector.

## IDLE CONTROL SYSTEM

***NOTE: Idle speed is not adjustable. For adjustment of idle switch and full throttle switch, see ON-VEHICLE ADJUSTMENTS article.***

**Idle Speed Positioner** – Disconnect idle speed positioner connector. Connect DVOM between ground and terminal No. 2 of idle speed positioner wiring harness connector. Turn ignition on and check supply voltage to positioner. Reading should be battery voltage. If battery voltage is not indicated, check Red/White wire back to fuse/relay block. See WIRING DIAGRAMS article in ENGINE PERFORMANCE.

## IGNITION SYSTEM

***NOTE: For ignition system checks, see BASIC DIAGNOSTIC PROCEDURES article.***

# 1990-91 ENGINE PERFORMANCE
# System & Component Testing (Cont.)

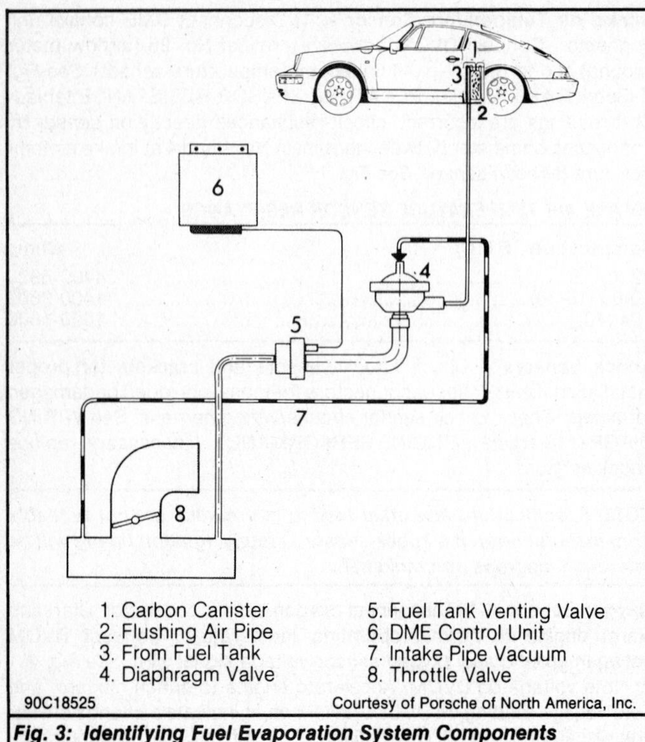


*Fig. 3: Identifying Fuel Evaporation System Components*

## EMISSION SYSTEMS & SUB-SYSTEMS

### FUEL EVAPORATION

**Fuel Tank Venting Valve** – Disconnect fuel tank venting valve connector. Connect DVOM between ground and terminal No. 1 of fuel tank venting valve wiring harness. *See Fig. 2.* Turn ignition on and check voltage supply to valve. Reading should be battery voltage. If battery voltage is not indicated, check Red/White wire back to fuse/ relay block. See WIRING DIAGRAMS article in ENGINE PERFORMANCE.

**Purge Diaphragm Valve** – Remove diaphragm valve from vehicle. Blow air through side fitting on valve. Little or no air should pass through valve. Apply vacuum to top fitting of diaphragm valve with a hand-held vacuum pump. Vacuum should hold, and air blown in, through side fitting, should now pass freely out bottom fitting of diaphragm valve.

## 911 Carrera 2/4

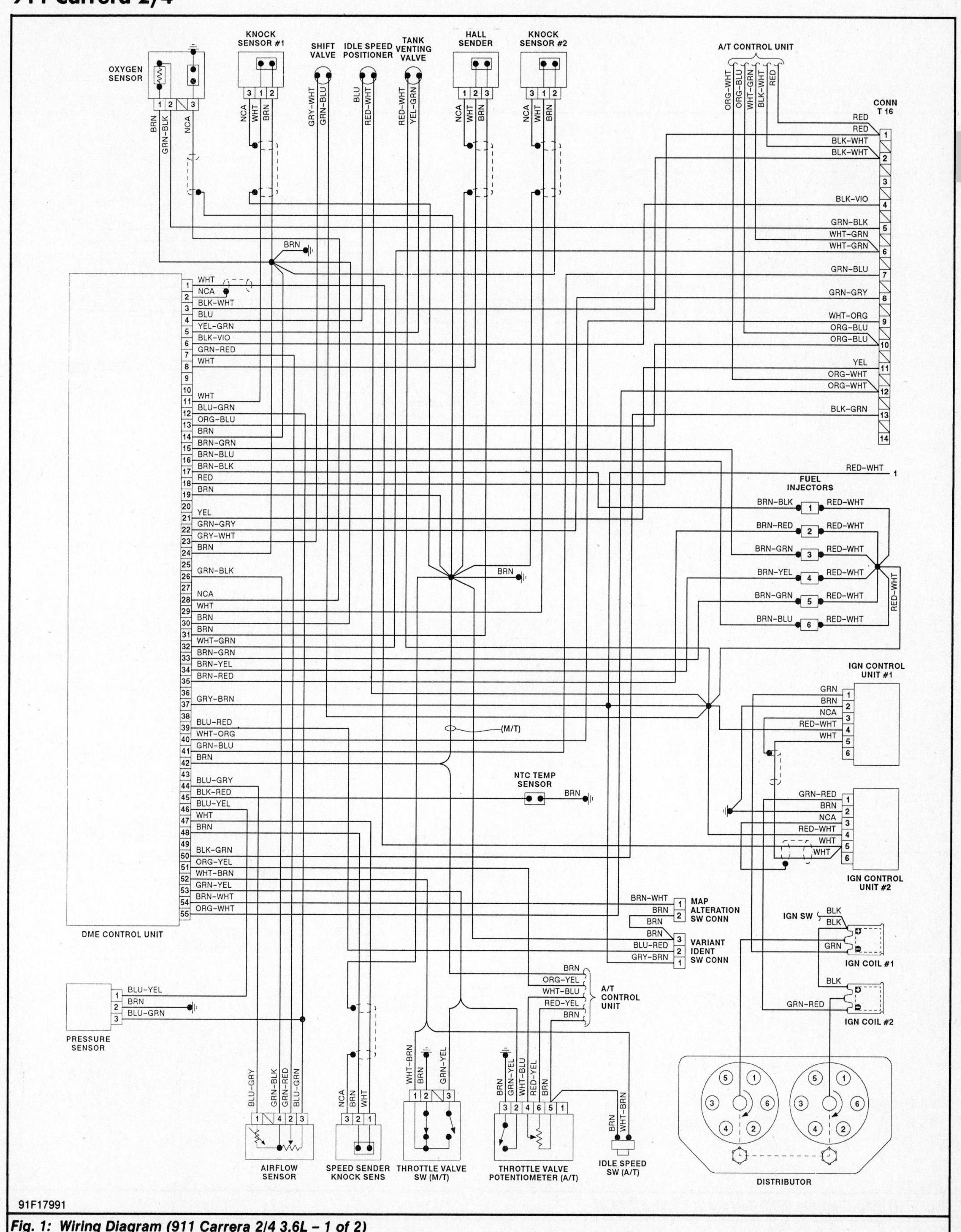


*Fig. 1: Wiring Diagram (911 Carrera 2/4 3.6L – 1 of 2)*

# 1990-91 ENGINE PERFORMANCE
## Wiring Diagrams (Cont.)

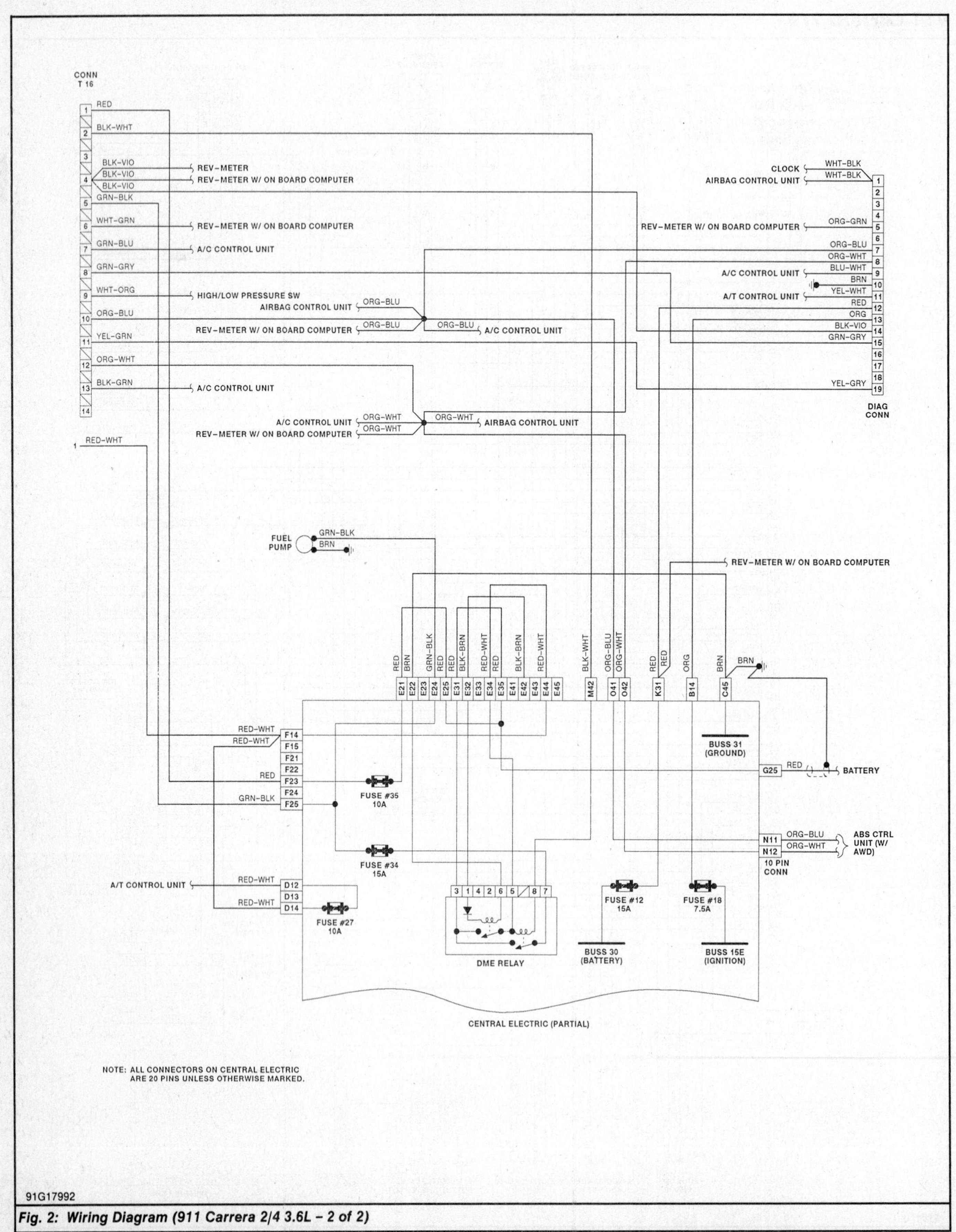


*Fig. 2: Wiring Diagram (911 Carrera 2/4 3.6L - 2 of 2)*

# 1990-91 ELECTRICAL
# Starters

### 911 Carrera 2/4

## DESCRIPTION

Starter is a brush-type, series-wound electric motor with an overrunning clutch. Field frame is enclosed by commutator end frame and drive bushing and carries pole shoes and field coils. A spline armature shaft drive end carries drive assembly.

## TROUBLE SHOOTING

***NOTE: See TROUBLE SHOOTING article in GENERAL INFORMATION.***

## ON-VEHICLE TESTING

### CIRCUIT TEST

**1)** Ensure battery is fully charged and electrical connections are clean and tight. With ignition switch in crank position, measure voltage at spade terminal of starter solenoid. If reading is at least 8 volts, go to step **3)**.
**2)** If reading is not as specified, measure voltage at ignition switch. If reading is at least 8 volts, check wiring between ignition switch and starter solenoid. If reading is not as specified, replace ignition switch.
**3)** Measure voltage at field terminal of starter solenoid. If reading is at least 8 volts, repair or replace starter. If reading is not as specified, replace starter solenoid.

## REMOVAL & INSTALLATION

**Removal (Carrera 2) - 1)** Starter is located on right side of transmission. Disconnect and shield negative battery cable. Raise and support vehicle. Remove undercover. Remove axle shafts from differential. Remove hot air tubes. Remove gearshift cable fork head at neutral safety switch actuating lever.
**2)** Remove bracket securing gearshift cable to transmission and set cable aside. Disconnect electrical connector from neutral safety switch. Remove stabilizer bar from vehicle. Place a transmission jack under transmission. Remove 6 bolts securing transmission rear support to vehicle body. Lower transmission slightly.
**3)** Remove upper starter nut from starter. Remove protective cap (if equipped) and electrical wires from starter. Remove lower starter bolt and ground strap. Remove starter. Inspect teeth of transmission flex plate for damage. Repair as needed.
**Installation -** Ensure sufficient space exists between starter electrical wires. Install protective cap (if equipped) over electrical connections at starter. To complete installation, reverse removal procedure. Check starter and gear selector operation. Tighten nuts and bolts to specification. See TORQUE SPECIFICATIONS table.
**Removal (Carrera 4) - 1)** Starter is located on right side of transmission. Disconnect and shield negative battery cable. Raise and support vehicle. Remove undercover. Remove undercover support. Remove axle shafts from differential. Remove hot air tubes.
**2)** Remove clutch slave cylinder from transmission, and set slave cylinder aside. DO NOT disconnect slave cylinder hose from slave cylinder. Remove upper starter bolt from starter. Remove protective cap (if equipped) and electrical wires from starter. Remove lower starter nut and ground strap. Remove starter. Inspect teeth of transmission flywheel for damage. Repair as needed.
**Installation -** Ensure sufficient space exists between starter electrical wires. Install protective cap (if equipped) over electrical connections at starter. To complete installation, reverse removal procedure. Check starter and clutch operation. Tighten nuts and bolts to specification. See TORQUE SPECIFICATIONS table.

## OVERHAUL

Information is not available from manufacturer.

## STARTER SPECIFICATIONS

Information is not available from manufacturer.

## TORQUE SPECIFICATIONS

***TORQUE SPECIFICATIONS***

| Application | Ft. Lbs. (N.m) |
|---|---|
| Axle Shaft-To-Transmission Bolt | |
| 8-mm | 31 (42) |
| 10-mm | 59 (80) |
| Stabilizer Bar-To-Body Bolt | 17 (23) |
| Stabilizer Bar-To-Stabilizer Link Nut | 34 (46) |
| Transmission Support-To-Body Bolt | 34 (46) |

# 1990-91 SAFETY EQUIPMENT
# Air Bag Restraint System

## 911 Carrera 2/4

***WARNING:** To avoid injury from accidental air bag deployment, read and carefully follow SERVICE PRECAUTIONS and all WARNINGS.*

***NOTE:** For information on air bag DIAGNOSIS & TESTING or DISPOSAL PROCEDURES, see MITCHELL'S AIR BAG SERVICE & REPAIR MANUAL, DOMESTIC & IMPORTED MODELS.*

## DESCRIPTION & OPERATION

Air bag system consists of an air bag with gas generator, ignition unit, control unit and impact sensors. During a frontal collision, impact sensors send a signal through control unit to air bag. In the ignition process, a solid propellant inside gas generator ignites in a fraction of a second. A driver-side air bag is located on steering wheel center pad and a passenger-side air bag is located above glove compartment.

## SERVICING

Manufacturer recommends air bag system inspection 4, 8 and 10 years from date of manufacture. After 10 years, system inspection is recommended every 2 years.

## SYSTEM OPERATION CHECK

Turn ignition switch to ON position. AIR BAG light on instrument panel should come on for approximately 5 seconds and then go off. If AIR BAG light fails to come on, remains on longer than 5 seconds or comes on during driving, air bag system service is necessary.

## SERVICE PRECAUTIONS

Observe these precautions when working with air bag systems.

- Disable air bag system before servicing any air bag or steering column component. See DISABLING & ACTIVATING AIR BAG SYSTEM.
- Wait about 10 minutes after disabling air bag system before servicing. Air bag system voltage is maintained for about 10 minutes after system is disabled. Failure to wait 10 minutes before servicing system may cause accidental air bag deployment and possible personal injury.
- Because of critical operating requirements of system, DO NOT service any air bag component. Repair is made by replacement only.
- DO NOT allow grease, oil, cleaning solutions or similar substances to contact air bag units.
- DO NOT subject air bag units to temperatures warmer than 195°F (90°C).
- Replace air bag units, impact sensors and control units which have fallen from a height of 1.5 feet or more.
- DO NOT install additional trim, labels or stickers on steering wheel or in area of passenger-side air bag.
- DO NOT repair or modify air bag system wiring.
- Air bag system must be disabled before electric welding can be performed on vehicle.
- DO NOT route wires from other electrical equipment in vicinity of air bag wire harness.

## DISABLING & ACTIVATING AIR BAG SYSTEM

***WARNING:** Wait about 10 minutes after disabling air bag system before servicing. Air bag system voltage is maintained for about 10 minutes after system is disabled. Servicing system before 10 minutes may cause accidental air bag deployment and possible personal injury.*

To disable air bag system, turn ignition off. Disconnect and shield negative battery cable. To activate air bag system, reconnect negative battery cable. Perform a system operation check to ensure system is functioning properly. See SYSTEM OPERATION CHECK.

## REMOVAL & INSTALLATION

***WARNING:** Follow air bag service precautions to prevent accidental air bag deployment and personal injury. See SERVICE PRECAUTIONS.*

***NOTE:** After component replacement, check system to ensure proper operation. See SYSTEM OPERATION CHECK.*

### DRIVER-SIDE AIR BAG UNIT

**Removal – 1)** Follow air bag service precautions. See SERVICE PRECAUTIONS. Disable air bag system. See DISABLING & ACTIVATING AIR BAG SYSTEM.

**2)** Driver-side air bag unit is located on steering wheel. Unscrew 2 air bag unit Torx screws from rear of steering wheel. Disconnect air bag electrical connector, and remove air bag unit. *See Fig. 1.*

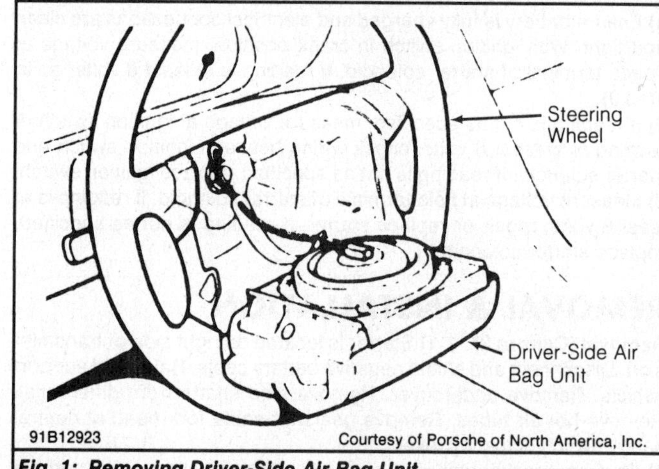


***Fig. 1: Removing Driver-Side Air Bag Unit***

**Installation –** To install, reverse removal procedure. Install new Torx screws, and tighten to specification. See TORQUE SPECIFICATIONS table at end of article. Activate air bag system. See DISABLING & ACTIVATING AIR BAG SYSTEM. Check AIR BAG light to ensure system is functioning properly. See SYSTEM OPERATION CHECK.

### CONTACT UNIT

**Removal – 1)** Follow air bag service precautions. See SERVICE PRECAUTIONS. Disable air bag system. See DISABLING & ACTIVATING AIR BAG SYSTEM.

**2)** Contact unit is attached to combination switch, located under steering wheel trim panel. *See Fig. 2.* Ensure front wheels face straight ahead. Remove driver-side air bag unit. See DRIVER-SIDE AIR BAG UNIT under REMOVAL & INSTALLATION.

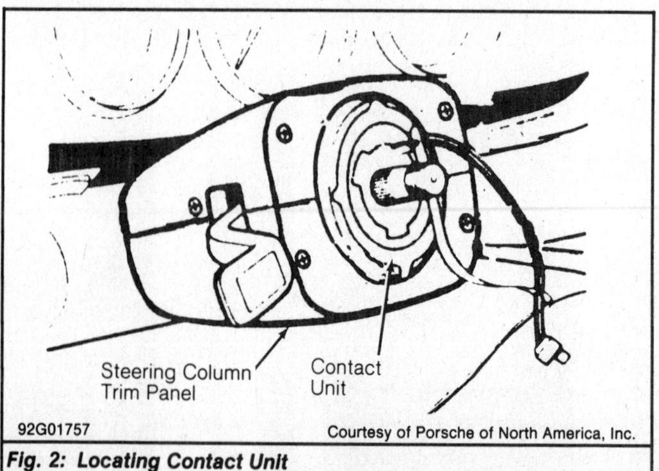


***Fig. 2: Locating Contact Unit***

# 1990-91 SAFETY EQUIPMENT
# Air Bag Restraint System (Cont.)

**3)** Remove steering wheel. See STEERING WHEEL under REMOVAL & INSTALLATION. Remove steering column trim panel. Remove contact unit screws from combination switch. Disconnect contact unit electrical connector, and remove contact unit. *See Fig. 3.*

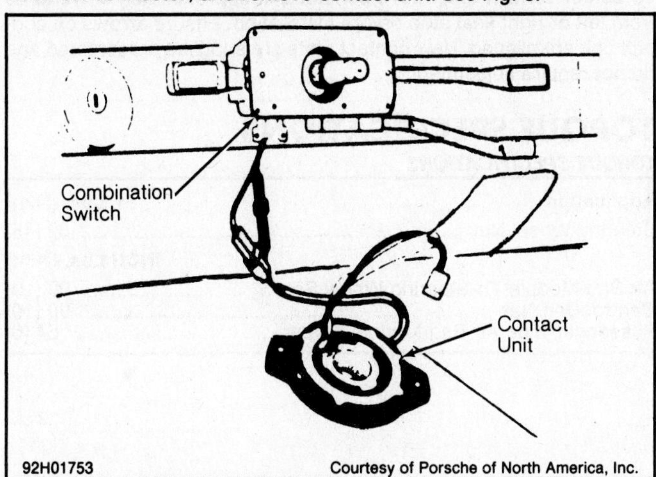


***Fig. 3: Removing Contact Unit***

**Installation - 1)** Ensure front wheels face straight ahead. To center contact unit, move unit approximately 4 1/2 turns from left or right final stop before installation. Ensure arrows on contact unit are aligned. New contact units are supplied precentered.
**2)** To install remaining components, reverse removal procedure. Activate air bag system. See DISABLING & ACTIVATING AIR BAG SYSTEM. Check AIR BAG light to ensure system is functioning properly. See SYSTEM OPERATION CHECK.

## IMPACT SENSORS

**Removal - 1)** Follow air bag service precautions. See SERVICE PRECAUTIONS. Disable air bag system. See DISABLING & ACTIVATING AIR BAG SYSTEM.
**2)** Impact sensors are located in left and right sides of luggage compartment, in front of spring strut domes. Disconnect impact sensor connector. Remove shear nuts using Special Tool (9259). Remove impact sensor.
**Installation - 1)** To install, reverse removal procedure. Ensure impact sensor is well-grounded. Install new shear nuts. Hex head of shear nut rounds off when correct torque is obtained.
**2)** Reactivate air bag system. See DISABLING & ACTIVATING AIR BAG SYSTEM. Check AIR BAG light to ensure system is functioning properly. See SYSTEM OPERATION CHECK.

## PASSENGER-SIDE AIR BAG UNIT

**Removal - 1)** Follow air bag service precautions. See SERVICE PRECAUTIONS. Disable air bag system. See DISABLING & ACTIVATING AIR BAG SYSTEM.
**2)** Passenger-side air bag unit is located on right side of instrument panel. Remove glove box. Disconnect air bag unit electrical connectors. Remove radio and radio mounting frame. Remove heater/air conditioner controls and mounting frame.
**3)** Remove ashtray and knee guard. Remove 3 screws and bottom air bag flap. Remove 4 screws from top air bag flap. Press flap forward and then downward (flap is attached by a brace). Remove 5 air bag mounting screws. *See Fig. 4*. Move air bag unit downward, and remove.
**Installation -** To install, reverse removal procedure. Install new air bag attaching screws, and tighten to specification. See TORQUE SPECIFICATIONS table at end of article. Activate air bag system. See DISABLING & ACTIVATING AIR BAG SYSTEM. Check AIR BAG light to ensure system is functioning properly. See SYSTEM OPERATION CHECK.

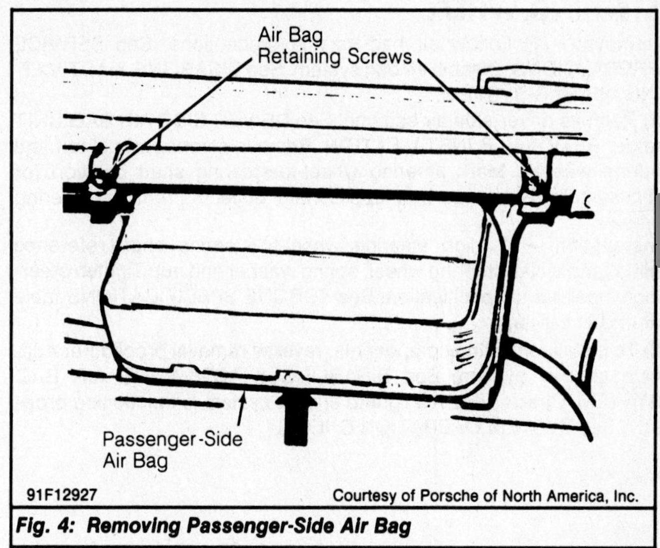


***Fig. 4: Removing Passenger-Side Air Bag***

## AIR BAG CONTROL UNIT

**Removal - 1)** Follow air bag service precautions. See SERVICE PRECAUTIONS. Disable air bag system. See DISABLING & ACTIVATING AIR BAG SYSTEM.
**2)** Air bag control unit is located on a cross panel, behind center console. Remove center console and glove box. Remove fuse block. Disconnect electrical connectors from control unit. *See Fig. 5.*

***NOTE: 6-pin connector is attached with a red tab lock, which is destroyed when removed. Connector must be attached with a green tab after installation.***

**3)** Guide all wire harnesses for impact sensors back into passenger compartment. Loosen straps along wire harness. Remove shear-off nuts using Special Tool (9259). Remove control unit retaining nuts. Remove air bag control unit along with water protection cap.

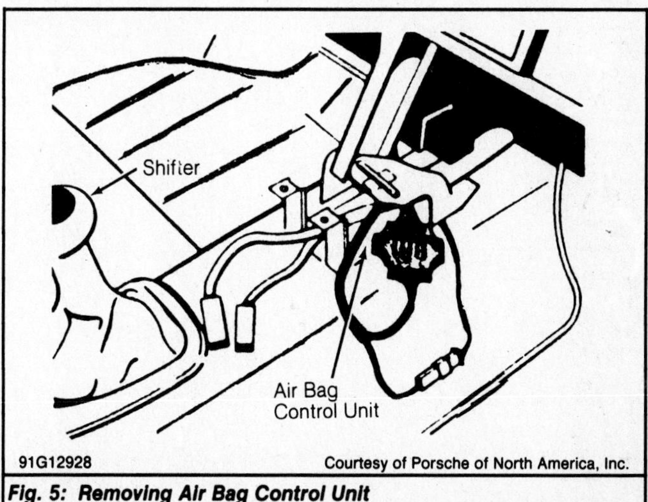


***Fig. 5: Removing Air Bag Control Unit***

**Installation - 1)** To install, reverse removal procedure. Install shear-off nuts diagonally. Hex head of shear nut rounds off when correct torque is obtained. Tighten control unit nuts to specification. See TORQUE SPECIFICATIONS table at end of article.
**2)** Activate air bag system. See DISABLING & ACTIVATING AIR BAG SYSTEM. Check AIR BAG light to ensure system is functioning properly. See SYSTEM OPERATION CHECK.

# 1990-91 SAFETY EQUIPMENT
# Air Bag Restraint System (Cont.)

## STEERING WHEEL

**Removal - 1)** Follow air bag service precautions. See SERVICE PRECAUTIONS. Disable air bag system. See DISABLING & ACTIVATING AIR BAG SYSTEM.

**2)** Remove driver-side air bag unit. See DRIVER-SIDE AIR BAG UNIT under REMOVAL & INSTALLATION. Remove steering wheel nut and spring washer. Mark steering wheel-to-steering shaft position for reassembly reference. Use appropriate puller to remove steering wheel.

**Installation - 1)** Align steering wheel-to-steering shaft reference mark, and install steering wheel, spring washer and nut. Tighten steering wheel nut to specification. See TORQUE SPECIFICATIONS table at end of article.

**2)** To install remaining components, reverse removal procedure. Activate air bag system. See DISABLING & ACTIVATING AIR BAG SYSTEM. Check AIR BAG light to ensure system is functioning properly. See SYSTEM OPERATION CHECK.

## ADJUSTMENTS

### CONTACT UNIT

To center contact unit, move contact unit approximately 4 1/2 turns from left or right final stop before installation. Ensure arrows on contact unit are aligned. New contact units are supplied precentered and do not require adjustment.

## TORQUE SPECIFICATIONS

***TORQUE SPECIFICATIONS***

| Application | Ft. Lbs. (N.m) |
|---|---|
| Steering Wheel Nut | 32 (45) |
| | **INCH Lbs. (N.m)** |
| Air Bag Module-To-Steering Wheel Screw | 90 (10) |
| Control Unit Nut | 90 (10) |
| Passenger-Side Air Bag Module Screw | 54 (6) |

# 1990-91 SAFETY EQUIPMENT
# Steering Column Switches

## 911 Carrera 2/4

***WARNING: Vehicles are equipped with Supplemental Restraint System (SRS). Use extreme caution when working on steering column components. Air bag could deploy. Before any repairs are performed, disconnect and shield negative battery cable. Wait about 10 minutes to allow system to electrically discharge before attempting any repairs.***

## TESTING

Testing information is not available from manufacturer.

## REMOVAL & INSTALLATION

### STEERING WHEEL & HORN PAD

***WARNING: Vehicles are equipped with Supplemental Restraint System (SRS). Before working on steering column components, disconnect and shield negative battery cable. Wait about 10 minutes to allow system to electrically discharge before attempting any repairs.***

**Removal - 1)** Place wheels in straight-ahead position. Disconnect and shield negative battery cable. Remove Torx screws securing air bag module to steering wheel.

**2)** Disconnect air bag electrical connector, and remove air bag module from steering wheel. *See Fig. 1*. Set air bag module aside with padded side facing up. Remove steering wheel nut and spring washer. Mark position of steering wheel to steering shaft for installation reference. Use appropriate puller to remove steering wheel.

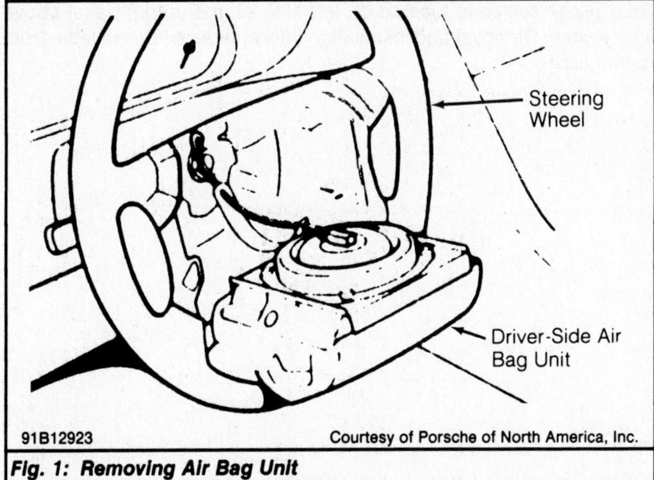


***Fig. 1: Removing Air Bag Unit***

**Installation - 1)** Align steering wheel to steering shaft. Ensure electrical wires are not pinched during installation of steering wheel. Install spring washer and nut.

**2)** Tighten nut to specification. See TORQUE SPECIFICATIONS table at end of article. To complete installation, reverse removal procedure. Install new Torx screws. Check horn operation.

### COMBINATION SWITCH

***NOTE: Combination switch includes cruise control, headlight/turn signal and wiper/washer switches.***

**Removal - 1)** Ensure front wheels are in straight-ahead position. Disconnect and shield negative battery cable. Remove steering wheel. See STEERING WHEEL & HORN PAD under REMOVAL & INSTALLATION. Remove steering column trim panel. Disconnect contact unit electrical connectors.

**2)** Remove screws securing contact unit to combination switch, and remove contact unit. *See Fig. 2*. Disconnect combination switch electrical connectors, and remove combination switch from steering column.

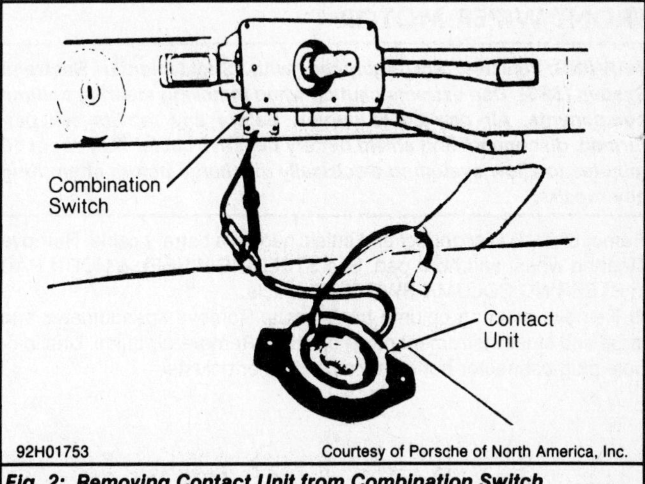


***Fig. 2: Removing Contact Unit from Combination Switch***

**Installation -** To install, reverse removal procedure. To center contact unit, move unit approximately 4 1/2 turns from left or right final stop before installation. Ensure arrows on contact unit are aligned. Tighten steering wheel nut to specification. See TORQUE SPECIFICATIONS table.

## TORQUE SPECIFICATIONS

***TORQUE SPECIFICATIONS***

| Application | Ft. Lbs. (N.m) |
|---|---|
| Steering Wheel Nut | 33 (45) |
| | **INCH Lbs. (N.m)** |
| Air Bag Module-To-Steering Wheel Screw | 90 (10) |

# 1990-91 SAFETY EQUIPMENT
# Wiper/Washer Systems

### 911 Carrera 2/4

## DESCRIPTION

Vehicles are equipped with a 3-speed wiper motor with an intermittent cycle. A rear wiper and headlight washer system are optional. Headlight washer operates only when headlights are on.

## TESTING

Testing information is not available from manufacturer.

## REMOVAL & INSTALLATION

***NOTE: Vehicles are equipped with Supplemental Restraint System (SRS). See AIR BAG RESTRAINT SYSTEM article in SAFETY EQUIPMENT for service precautions and disabling and activating air bag system.***

### FRONT WIPER MOTOR

***WARNING: Vehicles are equipped with Supplemental Restraint System (SRS). Use extreme caution when removing steering column components. Air bag could deploy. Before any repairs are performed, disconnect and shield battery negative cable. Wait about 10 minutes to allow system to electrically discharge before attempting any repairs.***

**Removal - 1)** Disconnect and shield negative battery cable. Remove steering wheel and horn pad. See STEERING WHEEL & HORN PAD in STEERING COLUMN SWITCHES article.

**2)** Remove steering column trim panels. Remove speedometer and large and small instrument panel clusters. Remove air guide. Unclip 6-pole plug connector behind small instrument cluster.

**3)** Remove 4 screws securing heating and air conditioning cover, and remove cover. Open luggage compartment lid and support lid. Remove left side spring from luggage compartment lid. Remove wiper motor linkage nut.

**4)** Remove 3 screws securing wiper motor to support bracket. Remove ground cable bolt, and disconnect ground cable. Disconnect wiper motor electrical connector. Remove wiper motor through cutout for speedometer.

**Installation -** Install motor on bracket and connect wiring. Crank arm and wiper link on wiper motor should form a straight line when installed. To complete installation, reverse removal procedure. Tighten steering wheel nut to 33 ft. lbs. (45 N.m). Check wiper motor operation.

### FRONT WIPER SWITCH

For removal and installation of front wiper switch, see COMBINATION SWITCH in STEERING COLUMN SWITCHES article.

### FRONT WASHER MOTOR

Front washer motor is mounted in washer reservoir. Reservoir is located in left front fender under door flap. Removal and installation information is not available from manufacturer.

### REAR WIPER MOTOR

Rear wiper motor is located in engine compartment. Removal and installation information is not available from manufacturer.

### REAR WIPER SWITCH

Rear wiper switch is located on left side of instrument panel above light switch. Removal and installation information is not available from manufacturer.

# 1990-91 ENGINES
# 3.6L 6-Cylinder



## 911 Carrera 2/4

***NOTE: For repair procedures not covered in this article, see ENGINE OVERHAUL PROCEDURES article in GENERAL INFORMATION.***

## ENGINE IDENTIFICATION

Engine may be identified by using Vehicle Identification Number (VIN) stamped on a metal pad, located near lower left corner of windshield. The fifth character identifies the engine model.

***ENGINE IDENTIFICATION CODES***

| Application | Engine Type | Engine ID |
|---|---|---|
| 911 Carrera 2/4 | | |
| Manual Transmission | M64/01 | [1] |
| Tiptronic Transmission | M64/02 | [1] |

[1] - "A" or "B" identifies engine as 3.6L.

## ADJUSTMENTS

### BLOWER BELT

**1)** Adjust blower drive belt by adding or removing spacer washers between impeller housing and pulley half.
**2)** Adjust initial "V" belt tension so belt can be pressed in .394-.591" (10-15 mm) by hand pressure at midpoint between pulleys. Remove one spacer washer from between pulley half and housing, and install it in front of pulley section. Check for final belt deflection of .2" (5 mm).

***NOTE: If "V" belt is stretched so only one spacer washer remains between pulley half and impeller housing, replace belt. Belt must not contact bottom of "V" in pulley.***

**3)** Install outer belt pulley half. Insert spacer washers not used for adjustment between outer pulley half and clamping cap.
**4)** Tighten pulley mounting nut to 32-65 ft. lbs. (45-90 N.m). Ensure pulley halves run true; otherwise, belt wear may be greatly increased. Maximum radial pulley runout is .006" (.15 mm) and maximum lateral runout is .008" (.20 mm). Run vehicle 30-60 miles. Check and readjust belt as necessary.

### VALVE CLEARANCE ADJUSTMENT

***CAUTION: Adjust valves with engine cold.***

**1)** Raise and support vehicle. Remove rear wheels. Remove hot air blower (electric fan) to access oxygen sensor connector. Disconnect oxygen sensor connector. Remove 4 10-mm screws for engine paneling on side of engine. Push oxygen sensor rubber grommet downward through engine paneling on left side of engine.
**2)** Remove engine cover from underside of engine. Remove complete exhaust system, except for heat exchanger. Remove side panels from engine. Disconnect spark plug cables from spark plugs. Remove valve covers.
**3)** Rotating crankshaft clockwise, set piston No. 1 to TDC of compression stroke. TDC mark on pulley must align with crankcase seam or locating mark on blower housing. Check valve clearance on cylinder No. 1, and adjust as necessary. Valve clearance is .004" (.10 mm) for intake and exhaust valves.
**4)** Check valves in cylinder firing order. Firing order is 1-6-2-4-3-5. *See Fig. 1*. Rotate engine clockwise (120 degrees) until next mark aligns with crankcase seam or locating mark on blower housing. Adjust valves for cylinder No. 6. Continue rotating crankshaft clockwise until all valves have been checked and adjusted (as necessary).
**5)** Use new valve cover seals. Use new self-locking nuts on valve covers. Tighten valve cover bolts to specification. See TORQUE SPECIFICATIONS table at end of article.

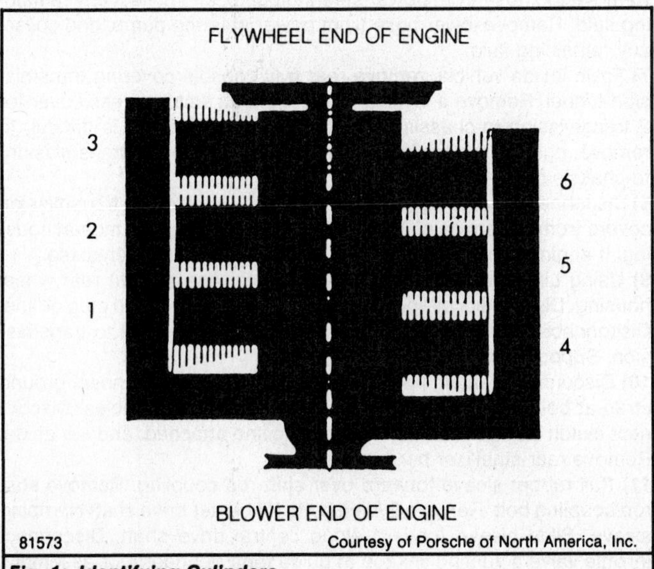

***Fig. 1: Identifying Cylinders***

### VALVE TIMING ADJUSTMENT

***CAUTION: Use extreme care when turning crankshaft or camshafts to avoid valve-to-piston contact. DO NOT turn crankshaft or camshafts if any resistance is felt. Severe engine damage may result.***

**1)** Rotating crankshaft clockwise, set piston No. 1 to TDC of compression stroke. TDC mark on pulley must align with crankcase seam or locating mark on blower housing. Position both camshafts with punch marks up. *See Fig. 2*.
**2)** If camshaft(s) do not have punch marks, position camshafts so key groove points up. Position Auxiliary Chain Tensioner (9401) against timing chain. Tighten bolt on auxiliary chain tensioner until recess on plunger is just visible.
**3)** An alignment hole on camshaft sprocket should align with camshaft. Insert dowel pin. If alignment holes are not aligned (camshaft has moved), rotate crankshaft until No. 1 piston is at TDC of compression stroke again. Ensure camshafts are positioned properly. Repeat steps **2)** and **3)**.

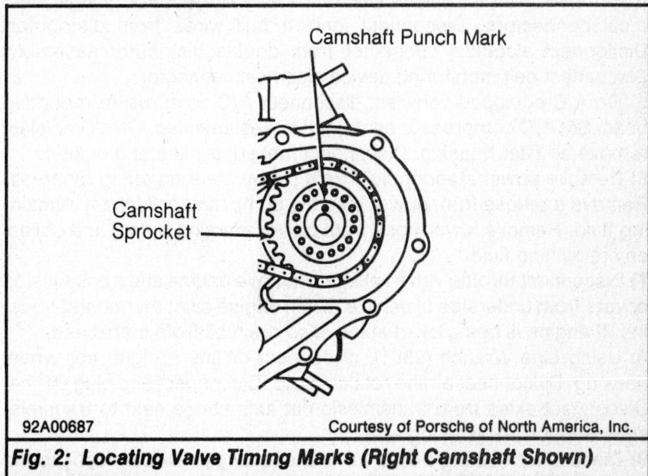

***Fig. 2: Locating Valve Timing Marks (Right Camshaft Shown)***

## REMOVAL & INSTALLATION

***CAUTION: DO NOT start engine with ground strap between transmission and chassis disconnected or Digital Motor Electronics (DME) control unit will be destroyed.***

### FUEL PRESSURE RELEASE

Turn ignition off. Access fuse panel in luggage compartment. Remove fuel pump/oxygen sensor fuse. Start engine. Allow engine to run until it stalls. Crank engine to ensure residual fuel pressure is released.

# 1990-91 ENGINES
# 3.6L 6-Cylinder (Cont.)

## COOLING AIR BLOWER

***CAUTION: When air ducts and baffle plates are reinstalled, openings and gaps must not exist or engine damage may result.***

**Removal – 1)** Blower may be removed (complete or with alternator only) with engine in vehicle. Air deflector plates between cylinders can only be detached with engine out of vehicle and camshaft housing(s) removed.

**2)** Detach screws holding upper air channel. Hold alternator pulley, loosen pulley mounting nut and remove belt. Remove nuts from blower housing mount strap, and loosen strap.

**3)** Remove blower housing and alternator off locating peg and toward rear. Mark wiring connectors on alternator for reassembly reference. Detach wiring from alternator. Remove blower housing with alternator assembly.

**Installation –** Position blower housing and alternator on crankcase locating peg. Reconnect alternator wiring. To complete installation, reverse removal procedure.

## ENGINE

***NOTE: Engine and transmission is removed as an assembly from underneath vehicle.***

**Removal & Installation (Carrera 2) – 1)** Release fuel pressure. See FUEL PRESSURE RELEASE under REMOVAL & INSTALLATION. Disconnect negative battery cable. Raise and support vehicle. Position supports for vehicle so transmission supports can be removed later. Remove rear wheels.

**2)** Disconnect 6 electrical connections at intake manifold assembly. Remove cable clip from airflow sensor. Remove hot air blower (electric fan) from engine.

**3)** On left side of engine compartment, disconnect carbon canister hose, brake booster vacuum hose, reference mark sensor electrical connector, knock sensor electrical connector, temperature sensor electrical connector, cruise control electrical connector, oxygen sensor connector and fuel return line. If fuel tank is full, connect an extra piece of fuel line to vehicle fuel return line. Pinch off extra fuel line connected to vehicle fuel return line to prevent fuel from leaking.

**4)** Remove cover for engine electrics board. Disconnect multiple electrical connectors. Disconnect ignition coil wires from distributor. Disconnect electrical connector from double distributor assembly. Disconnect belt monitoring device electrical connector.

**5)** On A/C-equipped vehicles, disconnect A/C compressor mounting bolts. Set A/C compressor aside with hoses attached. On all vehicles, remove air filter housing. Disconnect fuel supply line at fuel filter.

**6)** Remove power steering fluid from power steering pump reservoir. Remove top hose from power steering pump, and collect any remaining fluid. Remove lower hose from power steering pump, and collect any remaining fluid.

**7)** Disconnect throttle valve linkage. Remove engine and transmission covers from underside of vehicle. Drain engine oil at thermostat housing. If engine is being overhauled, also drain oil from crankcase.

**8)** Using Line Wrench (9501), disconnect oil line at right rear wheel housing. Disconnect oil line retaining clip. Disconnect and plug oil line. Disconnect axles from transmission at axle flange next to transmission. Support axles using wire.

**9)** Disconnect heating hoses at heat exchanger. Disconnect ground strap at bottom starter mounting. Disconnect starter cables. Disconnect throttle valve actuating linkage at underfloor assembly guide tube. Disconnect transmission selector lever cable at transmission.

**10)** Disconnect transmission selector lever cable holder at transmission. Disconnect electrical connector located next to transmission selector cable holder. Remove rear stabilizer bar from vehicle. Disconnect 2 remaining oil line connections at right rear wheel housing. Plug remaining oil line connections at right rear wheel housing.

**11)** Remove engine guard bracket. Reinstall bolts for engine guard bracket as bolts are a contact surface for engine mounting plate used in engine removal. Connect Engine Mounting Plate Adapter (9111/1), Support Plate (9111/2) and Engine Mounting Plate (9111/3) to a jack. Position jack under engine. Attach mounting plates and adapter to engine. Slightly preload jack.

**12)** Remove transmission transverse crossmember bolts. Remove engine mounting bolts. Lower engine/transmission assembly approximately 4". Disconnect electrical connector at airflow meter. Disconnect electrical connector at transmission. Ensure all vacuum, oil, fuel and electrical lines leading from engine are disconnected. Slowly lower engine/transmission assembly from vehicle.

**13)** To separate engine from transmission, remove starter from transmission. Hang Torque Converter Holder (9325) behind starter ring gear. Attach brace for torque converter holder to starter mounting bolt holes. Torque converter holder will prevent torque converter from falling out during separation.

***CAUTION: Ensure Torque Converter Holder (9325) is positioned properly. If holder is not positioned properly, torque converter may fall out when transmission is separated from engine.***

**14)** Connect Transmission Holder (9324) to transmission mounting bores on sides of transmission case. Attach an overhead support to transmission holder. Slightly preload overhead support. Remove engine-to-transmission bolts. Separate transmission from engine. To install, reverse removal procedure.

**Removal (Carrera 4) – 1)** Release fuel pressure. See FUEL PRESSURE RELEASE under REMOVAL & INSTALLATION. Disconnect negative battery cable. Raise and support vehicle. Position supports for vehicle so transmission supports can be removed later. Remove rear wheels.

**2)** Disconnect differential lock control/pump assembly electrical connector located in luggage compartment. Disconnect 5 electrical connections at intake manifold assembly. Remove cable clip from airflow sensor. Remove hot air blower (electric fan) from engine.

**3)** On left side of engine compartment, disconnect carbon canister hose, brake booster vacuum hose, reference mark sensor electrical connector, knock sensor electrical connector, temperature sensor electrical connector, cruise control electrical connector, oxygen sensor connector and fuel return line. If fuel tank is full, connect an extra piece of fuel line to vehicle fuel return line. Pinch off extra fuel line connected to vehicle fuel return line to prevent fuel from leaking.

**4)** Remove cover for engine electrics board. Disconnect multiple electrical connectors. Disconnect ignition coil wires from distributor. Disconnect electrical connector from double distributor assembly. Disconnect belt monitoring device electrical connector.

**5)** On A/C-equipped vehicles, disconnect A/C compressor mounting bolts. Set A/C compressor aside with hoses attached. On all vehicles, remove air filter housing. Disconnect fuel supply line at fuel filter.

**6)** Remove power steering fluid from power steering pump reservoir. Remove top hose from power steering pump, and collect any remaining fluid. Remove lower hose from power steering pump, and collect any remaining fluid.

**7)** From inside vehicle, remove rear tray console covering transmission tunnel. Remove a layer of PVC. Remove small access cover for 2 transmission-to-chassis bolts. If small access cover is difficult to remove, push cover out from under vehicle. Remove 2 transmission-to-chassis bolts.

**8)** Disconnect throttle valve linkage. Remove engine and transmission covers from underside of vehicle. Drain engine oil at thermostat housing. If engine is being overhauled, also drain oil from crankcase.

**9)** Using Line Wrench (9501), disconnect oil line at right rear wheel housing. Disconnect oil line retaining clip. Disconnect and plug oil line. Disconnect axles from transmission at axle flange next to transmission. Support axles using wire.

**10)** Disconnect heating hoses at heat exchanger. Disconnect ground strap at bottom starter mounting. Disconnect starter cables. Disconnect clutch slave cylinder with hydraulic line attached, and set aside. Remove rear stabilizer bar from vehicle.

**11)** Pull rubber sleeve forward over shift rod coupling. Remove shift rod coupling bolt. Remove 2 Allen bolts for center drive shaft clamping sleeve. Slide sleeve forward along central drive shaft. Disconnect throttle valve actuating linkage at guide tube of underfloor assembly.

# 1990-91 ENGINES
# 3.6L 6-Cylinder (Cont.)

**12)** Place a self-made support across center drive shaft assembly to keep center drive shaft from falling during engine removal. Remove wheel-to-wheel slave cylinder mounting bolts. Remove Allen bolt for interaxle differential lock slave cylinder. Without disconnecting hydraulic lines, hang both slave cylinders aside.
**13)** Disconnect remaining oil line connections at right rear wheel housing. Plug remaining oil line connections at right rear wheel housing. Remove engine guard bracket. Reinstall bolts for engine guard bracket as bolts are a contact surface for engine mounting plate used in engine removal.
**14)** Connect Engine Mounting Plate Adapter (9111/1), Support Plate (9111/2) and Engine Mounting Plate (9111/3) to a jack. Position jack under engine. Attach mounting plates and adapter to engine. Slightly preload jack.
**15)** Remove transmission transverse crossmember bolts. Remove engine mounting bolts. Slowly lower engine/transmission assembly until center drive shaft contacts self-made support. Disconnect electrical connector at airflow meter. Ensure all vacuum, oil, fuel and electrical lines leading from engine are disconnected. Pull engine/transmission assembly slightly to rear of vehicle. Slowly lower engine/transmission assembly from vehicle.
**16)** To separate engine from transmission, disconnect electrical connectors from starter and back-up light switch. Remove clutch release shaft bolt. Remove clutch release shaft from transmission.
**17)** Attach an overhead support to transmission. Slightly preload overhead support. Remove 4 engine-to-transmission bolts. Separate transmission from engine. Using Wrench (P119), remove upper mounting nut on starter.
**Installation (Carrera 4) – 1)** Lubricate all sliding surfaces of clutch release mechanism and gear teeth of drive shaft with long-term grease. Position release fork in release bearing. Using adhesive tape, fix position of release fork. Mount transmission to engine.
**2)** Ensure seals are positioned properly on clutch release shaft. *See Fig. 3.* Guide clutch release shaft with sealing rings into release fork. Remove adhesive tape through assembly hole. Pack needle bearing cap with long-term grease. Install needle bearing cap and bracket onto clutch release shaft. Tighten bracket into place using bolt.

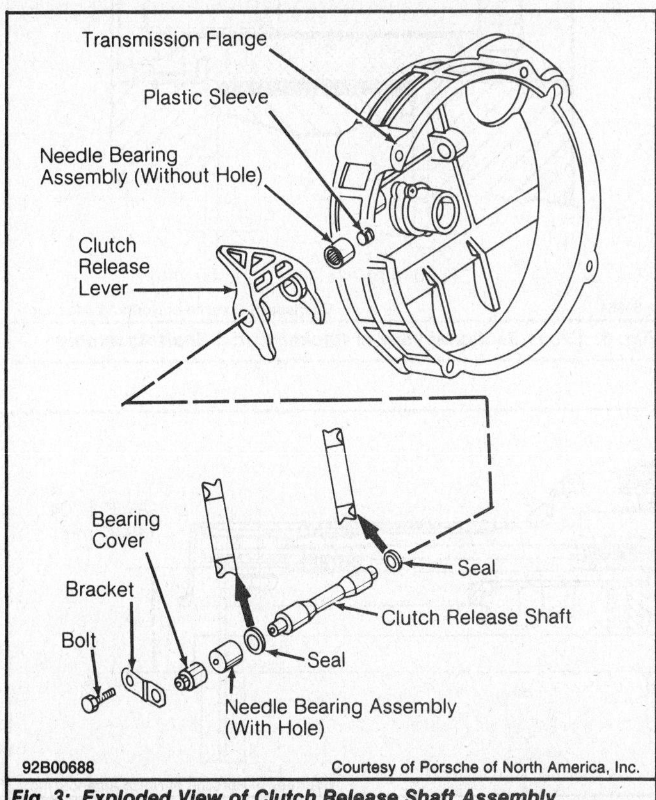


*Fig. 3: Exploded View of Clutch Release Shaft Assembly*

**3)** During engine installation, ensure heat exchanger hoses are not pinched. Slide heat exchanger hoses onto heat exchangers just before engine/transmission assembly is in position. Ensure inner rubber seal on heat exchanger is seated correctly. To complete installation, reverse removal procedure.

## INTAKE MANIFOLD

**Removal & Installation – 1)** Release fuel pressure. See FUEL PRESSURE RELEASE under REMOVAL & INSTALLATION. Disconnect negative battery cable. Remove hot air blower (electric fan) and ducts from engine.
**2)** On A/C-equipped vehicles, disconnect A/C compressor mounting bolts. Set A/C compressor aside with hoses attached. On all vehicles, remove air filter housing. Remove alternator/blower belt.
**3)** Remove alternator/blower assembly from engine. See COOLING AIR BLOWER under REMOVAL & INSTALLATION. Disconnect fuel inlet and return lines. If fuel tank is full, connect an extra piece of fuel line to vehicle fuel return line. Pinch off extra fuel line connected to vehicle fuel return line to prevent fuel from leaking.
**4)** Disconnect electrical connector from double distributor assembly. Label and remove all spark plug wires from double distributor assembly. Remove double distributor assembly from engine.
**5)** Ensure all vacuum, fuel and electrical lines are disconnected from intake manifold assembly. Remove intake manifold mounting bolts. Remove intake manifold assembly from engine. To install, reverse removal procedure.

## EXHAUST MANIFOLD

**Removal & Installation – 1)** Disconnect heating hoses at heat exchanger. Raise and support vehicle. Remove engine and transmission covers from underside of vehicle. Disconnect hot air distributor pipe from exhaust manifolds.
**2)** On right exhaust manifold, remove exhaust manifold-to-exhaust cross pipe flange bolts. On left exhaust manifold, remove exhaust manifold-to-catalytic converter flange bolts. Remove oxygen sensor (if necessary). On both exhaust manifolds, remove mounting bolts.
**3)** Remove exhaust manifold from engine. When removing left exhaust manifold, exhaust cross pipe is removed with left manifold as an assembly. To install, reverse removal procedure.

## CYLINDER HEAD

***NOTE: If camshaft housing is removed, any single cylinder head may be removed. If camshaft housing is left attached to cylinder heads, heads and camshaft housing may be removed as an assembly.***

**Removal & Installation – 1)** Remove engine from vehicle. See ENGINE under REMOVAL & INSTALLATION. Remove intake manifold. See INTAKE MANIFOLD under REMOVAL & INSTALLATION. Remove exhaust manifold(s) as necessary. See EXHAUST MANIFOLD under REMOVAL & INSTALLATION.
**2)** Remove rocker arm covers and gaskets. Rotating engine with crankshaft, position camshaft as necessary and remove rocker arms for bank of cylinder heads being serviced. See ROCKER ARM under REMOVAL & INSTALLATION.
**3)** Rotate crankshaft until No. 1 piston is at TDC of compression stroke. Disconnect timing chain tensioner oil supply lines between crankcase and timing chain housing covers. Remove covers, and discard gaskets. Remove chain tensioner(s). Remove timing chain. See TIMING CHAIN under REMOVAL & INSTALLATION.

***CAUTION: DO NOT rotate crankshaft or camshafts with timing chains removed. Engine damage may occur.***

**4)** Remove camshaft(s). See CAMSHAFT under REMOVAL & INSTALLATION. If a single cylinder head is being removed, remove cylinder head bolts for individual cylinder head being serviced.
**5)** If all cylinder heads from one side of engine are being removed together, remove timing chain housing mounting nuts from crankcase.

# 1990-91 ENGINES
# 3.6L 6-Cylinder (Cont.)

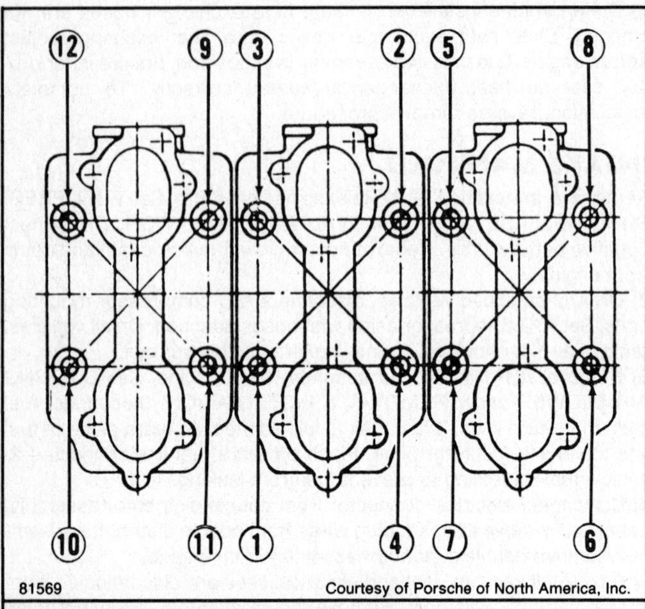


*Fig. 4: Cylinder Head Tightening Sequence*

Remove cylinder head nuts. Remove cylinder heads and timing chain housing as an assembly. To install, reverse removal procedure. Use new gaskets when reassembling engine. Tighten cylinder head bolts in sequence. *See Fig. 4*.

## CRANKSHAFT OIL SEALS

**Removal & Installation (Blower End Main Bearing)** – Remove belt pulley. Pry out seal. Coat new seal with oil, and press in place.

**Removal & Installation (Flywheel End Main Bearing)** – Remove flywheel. Remove oil seal. Coat new seal outer edges with sealing compound. Press seal into crankcase until seal is flush with face of crankcase.

## TIMING CHAIN

**Removal** – **1)** Remove muffler and rear cooling shroud. Disconnect timing chain tensioner oil supply lines between crankcase and timing chain housing covers. Remove timing chain covers. Discard gaskets.

***NOTE: Note timing chain tensioner position when removing. Ensure oil feed hole is positioned properly when installing.***

**2)** Rotate crankshaft to bring No. 1 piston to TDC of compression stroke. Remove timing chain tensioners from timing chain housing. Using Camshaft Holding Wrench (9191), hold camshaft sprocket from rotating. Remove camshaft sprocket center bolt.

**3)** Using Dowel Pin Remover (P-212), remove dowel pin aligning camshaft sprocket onto camshaft flange. Remove timing chain tensioner blade and chain guides. Remove camshaft sprocket.

**4)** Remove master link clip, and separate chain. Remove endless type timing chain by grinding 2 rivet ends from any link. Remove link and chain.

***NOTE: Timing chain installed from factory is an endless type. Replace factory chain with a master link type.***

**Installation** – **1)** Ensure camshaft sprockets are parallel and aligned. *See Fig. 5*. Parallel alignment of sprockets must not exceed .010" (.25 mm). Seat intermediate shaft and camshafts against thrust collars (push toward flywheel) before measuring alignment.

**2)** Camshaft sprocket alignment may be adjusted using .02" (.5 mm) shim spacers between camshaft sprocket flange and sealing flange (if necessary). Normally, 3 shims are located under left camshaft sprocket (1-3 cylinders) and no shims under right camshaft sprocket.

**3)** When installing master link type chain, ensure closed end of master link clip faces direction of travel. Install timing chain tensioner blade and chain guides. Adjust valve timing. See VALVE TIMING ADJUSTMENT under ADJUSTMENTS.

**4)** Using Camshaft Holding Wrench (9191), hold camshaft sprocket from rotating. Install camshaft sprocket center bolt. Use new gaskets during installation. When installing chain tensioners, ensure oil feed hole points up on left tensioner. Ensure oil feed hole points down on right tensioner. To complete installation, reverse removal procedure.

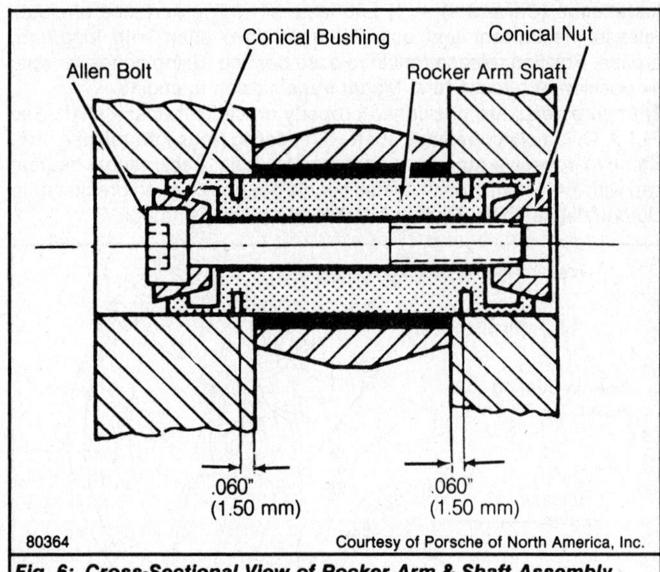


*Fig. 6: Cross-Sectional View of Rocker Arm & Shaft Assembly*

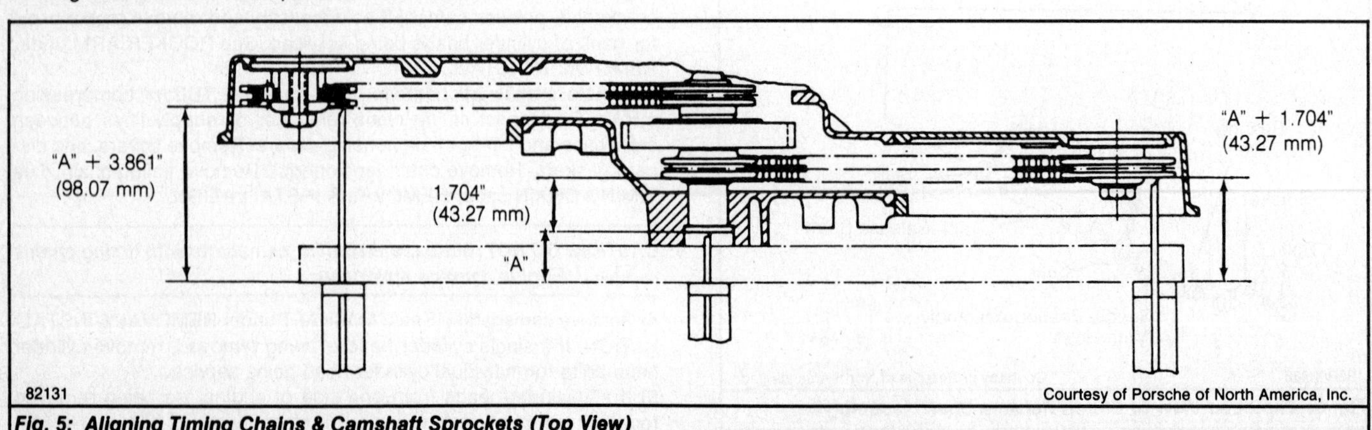


*Fig. 5: Aligning Timing Chains & Camshaft Sprockets (Top View)*

Housing
Bearings
Sprocket
Left
Camshaft
Right
Camshaft
82132
Courtesy of Porsche of North America, Inc.

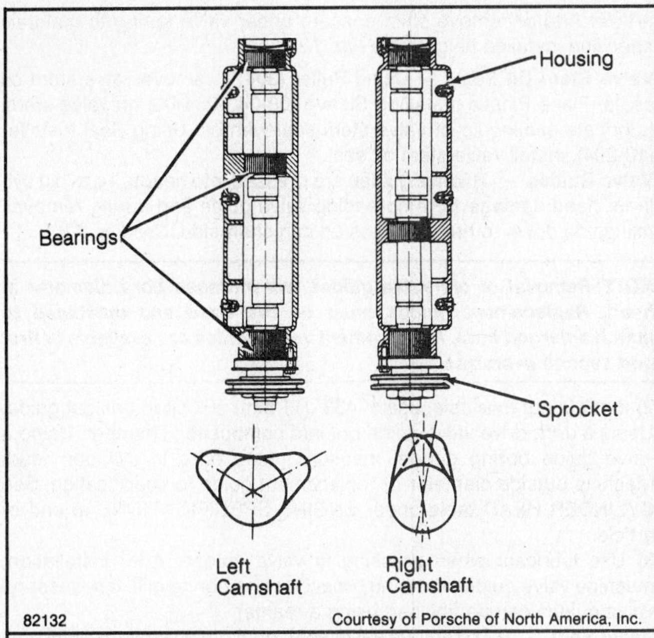

*Fig. 7: Positioning Camshafts in Camshaft Housings*

Right
Left
82130
Courtesy of Porsche of North America, Inc.

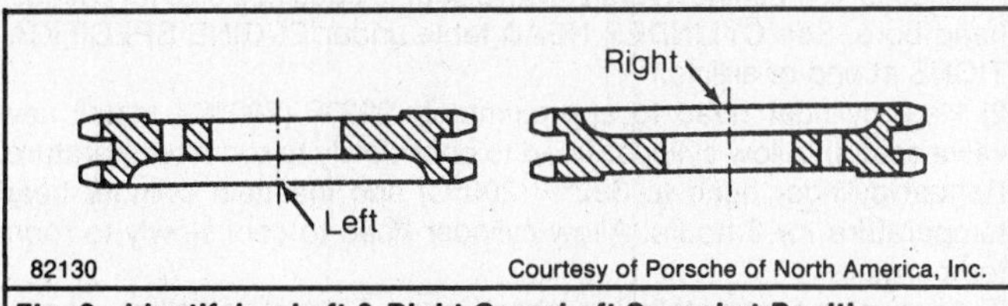

*Fig. 8: Identifying Left & Right Camshaft Sprocket Positions*

## ROCKER ARM

***NOTE: Rocker arm and shaft assembly cannot be removed until cam lobe pressure is relieved.***

**Removal & Installation – 1)** Remove rocker arm covers and gaskets. Rotate crankshaft and camshafts to relieve cam lobe pressure on rocker arm being removed. If necessary, loosen nut on valve adjusting screw and back off adjusting screw.

**2)** Using a 6-mm Allen wrench, loosen rocker arm shaft bolt. Remove Allen-head bolt, conical bushing and conical nut. *See Fig. 6*. Slide rocker shaft out of cylinder head, and remove rocker arm.

**3)** Check rocker arm, shaft bore and shaft for wear, and replace as necessary. Install rocker arm shaft with Allen-head bolt facing either No. 2 or 5 cylinder. Center shaft properly in housing, and tighten Allen-head bolt. *See Fig. 6*.

## CAMSHAFT

**Removal – 1)** Remove engine from vehicle. See ENGINE under REMOVAL & INSTALLATION. Remove rocker arm covers and rocker arms. See ROCKER ARM under REMOVAL & INSTALLATION. Remove timing chain. See TIMING CHAIN under REMOVAL & INSTALLATION.

***NOTE: Note timing chain tensioner position when removing. Ensure oil feed hole is positioned properly when installing.***

**2)** Remove timing chain covers, and discard gaskets. Rotate crankshaft to bring No. 1 piston to TDC of compression stroke. Remove timing chain tensioners from timing chain housing. Using Camshaft Holding Wrench (9191), hold camshaft sprocket from rotating. Remove camshaft sprocket center bolt.

**3)** Using Dowel Pin Remover (P-212), remove dowel pin aligning camshaft sprocket onto camshaft flange. Remove camshaft sprocket. Remove camshaft flange. Remove camshaft sealing flange. Remove camshaft.

1
2
3
4
5
6
7
8
9
10
11
12
13
1. Valve Spring Keepers
2. Valve Spring Retainer Cap
3. Inner Valve Spring
4. Outer Valve Spring
5. Valve Seals
6. Valve Spring Seats
7. Valve Spring Spacer
8. Valve Guide
9. Exhaust Valve
10. Valve Seat
11. Intake Valve
12. Head Nut
13. Helicoil
92C00690
Courtesy of Porsche of North America, Inc.

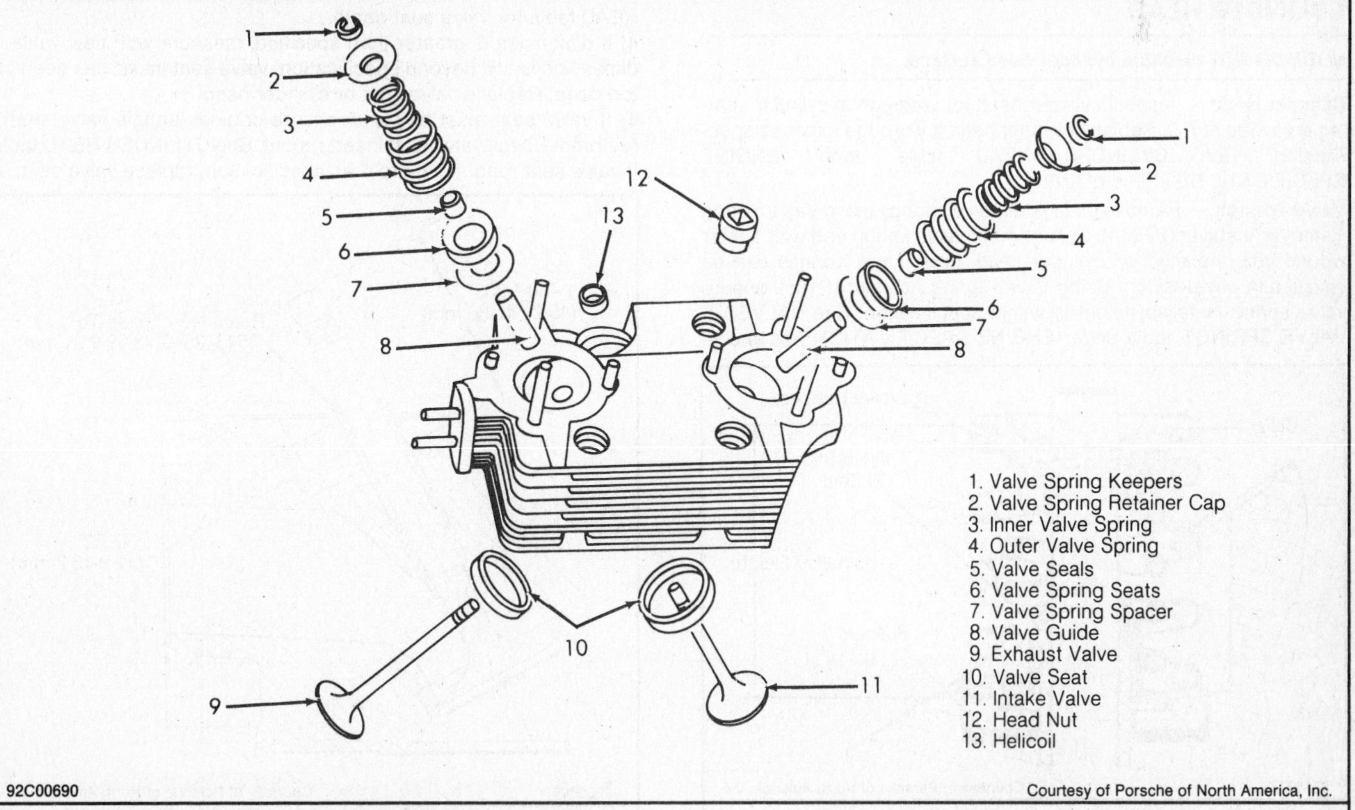

*Fig. 9: Exploded View of Cylinder Head Assembly*

# 1990-91 ENGINES
# 3.6L 6-Cylinder (Cont.)

**4)** Check oil injection tubes in camshaft housing for damage. If replacement is needed, drill a 3/8" deep hole in end plug using a 1/2" drill bit. Cut 6-mm threads using bottoming tap, and pull out end plug with 6-mm screw and spacer. DO NOT damage sealing surface during plug removal.

**5)** Before removing injection tube, note oil hole locations in tube for installation reference. Separate oil hole bores must face up (toward valve covers). Double bores face cam bearing surface. Loosen centering screws, and slide out injection tube.

**Installation - 1)** Lubricate oil injection tube bore. Slide in new tube. Apply sealant to new end plug. Install plug about .012" (.30 mm) deeper than sealing surface. Expand plug before installation if it does not fit tightly in bore.

**2)** Install and position camshafts in housings. *See Fig. 7*. Install sealing flange with new gasket and "O" ring, and tighten mounting bolts. Install thrust washer, shim spacer and Woodruff key. Install camshaft sprocket flange. When installing chain tensioners, ensure oil feed hole points up on left tensioner. Ensure oil feed hole points down on right tensioner.

**3)** Install timing chain and camshaft sprockets with sprockets in proper locations. *See Figs. 5 and 8*. Check timing chain alignment. See TIMING CHAIN under REMOVAL & INSTALLATION. Install chain guides and camshaft sprockets. Install chain tensioners.

**4)** Install rocker arm shaft assemblies. To complete installation, reverse removal procedure. Adjust valve timing as necessary.

### INTERMEDIATE SHAFT

**Removal & Installation -** Crankcase housing must be split to access intermediate shaft. See CRANKCASE HOUSING under OVERHAUL. Remove intermediate shaft from right crankcase half. Remove sprocket circlips. Remove sprockets from shaft. To install, reverse removal procedure. Ensure intermediate shaft bearings are positioned properly.

## OVERHAUL

### CYLINDER HEAD

***NOTE: DO NOT machine cylinder head surface.***

**Cylinder Head -** Inspect cylinder head for warpage at cylinder seating area. *See Fig. 9*. Replace cylinder head if warpage exceeds specification. See CYLINDER HEAD table under ENGINE SPECIFICATIONS at end of article.

**Valve Springs -** Remove and install valve springs using Valve Spring Remover/Installer (P200a). Ensure outer valve spring end with tighter wound coil is placed on cylinder head. Inner valve springs can be installed in any position. Using Valve Spring Adjuster (P10c), ensure valve spring installed height is within specification. See VALVES & VALVE SPRINGS table under ENGINE SPECIFICATIONS at end of article. Add or remove shim spacers under valve spring to maintain specified installed height. *See Fig. 10*.

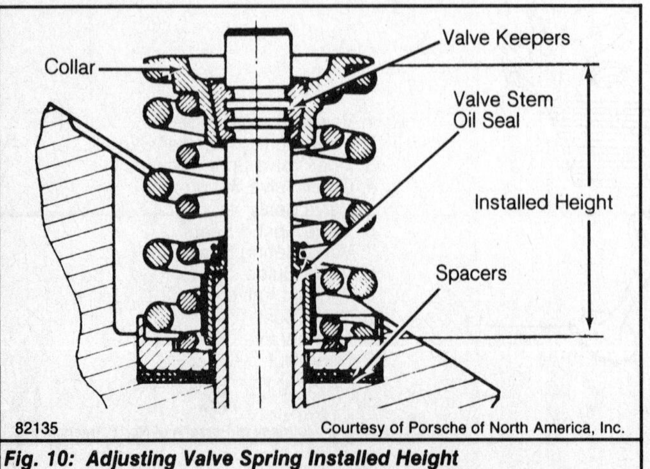


***Fig. 10: Adjusting Valve Spring Installed Height***

**Valve Stem Oil Seals -** Using Puller (3047), remove valve stem oil seals. Place Plastic Installing Sleeve (00-043-084-00) on valve stem. Lubricate sealing lip of valve stem seal with oil. Using Seal Installer (10-204), install valve stem oil seal.

**Valve Guides - 1)** Valve guides are pressed into heads. To avoid cylinder head damage from spreading valve guide end during removal, mill guide down to head surface on camshaft side. *See Fig. 11*.

***NOTE: Removal of old valve guides will increase bore diameter in head. Replacement guides must be oversized and machined to match enlarged bore. Replacement valve guides are available in first and second oversizes.***

**2)** If mill is not available, use a .433" (11 mm) drill bit to drill out guide. Using a drift, drive valve guide out into combustion chamber. Using a valve guide boring gauge, measure guide bore in cylinder head. Machine outside diameter of replacement guide to specification. See CYLINDER HEAD table under ENGINE SPECIFICATIONS at end of article.

**3)** Use lubricant when pressing in valve guides. After installation, machine valve guide I.D. using broach or fine boring mill. If necessary, valve guides can be finished using a reamer.

**Valve Seat - 1)** To remove valve seat, grind away seat material until loose in cylinder head. Drive seat out. Measure I.D. of valve seat bore. If necessary, machine oversize valve seat to specified size for cylinder head bore. See CYLINDER HEAD table under ENGINE SPECIFICATIONS at end of article.

**2)** Heat cylinder head to approximately 392°F (200°C). Install new valve seat(s). Allow cylinder head to cool slowly to room temperature. Reheat cylinder head to 392°F (200°C) and maintain cylinder head temperature for 2 hours. Allow cylinder head to cool slowly to room temperature.

**3)** After valve seat installation, check insert depth by installing respective valve in guide and measuring distance from tip of valve stem to bottom of shim cavity (without shims). *See Fig. 11*. See CYLINDER HEAD table for valve seat depth.

**4)** If dimension is greater than specified, measure with new valve. If dimension is still beyond specification, valve seat insert has been cut too deep. Replace valve seat or cylinder head.

**5)** If valve seat must be recut, ensure original 3-angle valve seat is restored. Check valve seat insert runout. See CYLINDER HEAD table. If valve seat runout is more than specification, replace valve seat.

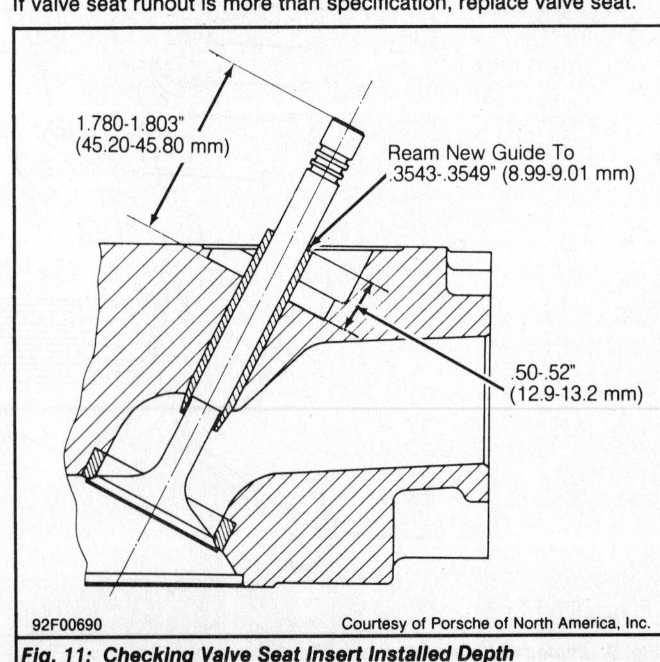


***Fig. 11: Checking Valve Seat Insert Installed Depth***

# 1990-91 ENGINES
# 3.6L 6-Cylinder (Cont.)

**Valves – 1)** Clean valves. Grind or replace valve(s) and/or inserts as necessary. Check valve stem-to-valve guide clearance. See CYLINDER HEAD table under ENGINE SPECIFICATIONS at end of article. Replace valve or valve guide as necessary.
**2)** Ensure valve length is within specification. See VALVES & VALVE SPRINGS table under ENGINE SPECIFICATIONS at end of article. If valve length is not within specification, replace valve(s).
**Valve Seat Correction Angles –** Information is not available from manufacturer.

## VALVE TRAIN

**Rocker Arm Shaft Assembly –** With rocker arm shaft assembly disassembled, check rocker arm shaft bore inside diameter. Check outside diameter of rocker arm shaft. Check rocker arm bore and width. Check rocker arm housing width. See ROCKER ARM ASSEMBLY table under ENGINE SPECIFICATIONS at end of article.

## CRANKCASE HOUSING

**Removal & Disassembly – 1)** With camshaft housings, cylinder heads, cylinders, timing chain covers, tensioners and sprockets removed, detach chain guides. Remove crankcase breather cover, oil pressure sensor, thermostat and flywheel.
**2)** Remove accessory drive belt assembly. Detach and remove intermediate shaft axial adjustment cover. Detach breather outlet nozzle.
**3)** Remove all 8-mm nuts connecting crankcase halves. Remove 2 cap nuts (under oil cooler flange) from No. 1 main bearing studs. Remove all through bolts. Loosen No. 7 main bearing stud nut (through left timing chain housing opening.)
**4)** Lift left crankcase half from right crankcase half. Lift out crankshaft. Unfasten lock tabs on oil pump mounting nuts. Remove nuts and oil pump together with connecting shaft, intermediate shaft and timing chains.
**Inspection – 1)** Examine crankcase halves for cracks and damage. Inspect sealing surfaces for flatness and cleanliness. Repair or replace crankcase and related components as necessary.
**2)** Clean off gasket material using solvent and/or sharp-edged scraper. Clean out oilways using round wire brush, and flush out entire system of oil passages with solvent and compressed air.
**3)** Ensure annular pressure relief groove cut around No. 7 main bearing through bolt (on left crankcase half sealing surface) is free of dirt and/or sealing compound.
**4)** Measure main bearing bores. See CRANKSHAFT MAIN BEARINGS under OVERHAUL. Replace any broken cylinder head studs. If necessary, retap threads in crankcase, apply Loctite 270 and install a new cylinder head stud.
**Reassembly & Installation – 1)** Attach right crankcase half to work stand. Fit crankcase with matching crankshaft and intermediate shaft gears for center-to-center and backlash measurements before crankcase reassembly. See INTERMEDIATE SHAFT under OVERHAUL.
**2)** After gear matching procedure, place intermediate shaft together with connecting shaft and oil pump (without timing chains) into crankcase. Turn shaft by hand. Ensure intermediate shaft, connecting shaft and oil pump rotate without binding.
**3)** If binding, reset each shaft's splines in relation to each other. Remove intermediate shaft, connecting shaft and oil pump from crankcase without disassembling.
**4)** If removed, install oil screens (at connecting webs below bearing supports), and fasten by bending sheet metal tabs over. Determine proper main bearing insert sizes. See CRANKSHAFT MAIN BEARINGS under OVERHAUL.
**5)** Install No. 2-7 main bearing inserts into both crankcase halves. Ensure grooves machined in bearing supports of crankcase halves and bearing insert guide tabs align and oil passages in inserts and crankcase coincide.
**6)** Place No. 1 (blower end) main (thrust) bearing inserts in position in both crankcase halves. Place new oil seal ring into groove of oil pump suction passages, in right crankcase half. Ensure seal ring is properly seated.
**7)** Install assembled oil pump, connecting shaft and intermediate shaft (with timing chains) in crankcase half. Install oil pump mounting nuts with new sheet metal lock tabs, and bend tabs over lock nuts after tightening.
**8)** Install new "O" ring and oil seal in No. 8 bearing insert. Mark position of centering hole on insert flank, and slide insert onto crankshaft journal. Using Connecting Rod Props (P-221), stand up cylinder No. 1 and 2 connecting rods.
**9)** Apply oil and molybdenum disulfide grease to all bearing journals. Install crankshaft assembly in right crankcase half with No. 8 bearing insert centering bore aligned with dowel pin in crankcase.

***CAUTION: DO NOT allow dowel pin to fit into oil passage provided in bearing insert or oil will not reach bearing and severe engine damage will result.***

**10)** Coat main bearing oil seal O.D. with sealant, and ensure seal fits flush with outer crankcase exterior. Install Timing Chain Props (P-222) and remaining connecting rod props. Ensure new seal rings are installed in oil passage connecting left and right crankcases and between oil pump and left crankcase half.
**11)** Apply thin coat of sealant to both crankcase mating surfaces. Ensure no sealant reaches bearing insert seats or surfaces. Carefully inspect final component locations. Attach left crankcase half to right crankcase half.
**12)** Lubricate crankcase through bolts (long bolts) and bolt seals with oil. Place insulator on bolts near bolt heads. Slide seals over bolt ends using Seal Installer (P-9511). Slide "O" ring near bolt head. DO NOT slide "O" ring completely to bolt head. Slide "O" ring on bolt shank to where bolt shank starts to enlarge near bolt head.

***CAUTION: DO NOT turn crankcase through bolts (long bolts) after installation into crankcase as "O" rings may become damaged. Tighten crankcase nuts.***

**13)** Install and tighten crankcase 8-mm bolts (short bolts) until crankcase halves come in contact with each other. Insert crankcase through bolts (long bolts) into crankcase assembly. Place insulator on bolts near bolt threads. Using Seal Installer (P-9511), slide seals over bolt ends. Install nut onto crankcase bolt (long bolt). Tighten nuts to specification in sequence. *See Fig. 12*. See TORQUE SPECIFICATIONS table at end of article.
**14)** Install a temporary protective sleeve over end of connecting rod assemblies until pistons are installed. Install flywheel. Ensure crankshaft turns freely in crankshaft housing and timing chains remain clear. Complete remaining engine assembly as necessary.

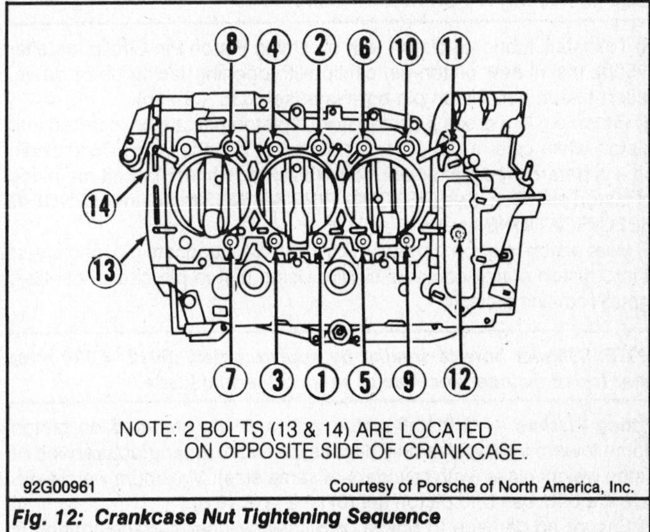


***Fig. 12: Crankcase Nut Tightening Sequence***

# 1990-91 ENGINES
# 3.6L 6-Cylinder (Cont.)

## PISTON & CYLINDER ASSEMBLY

***NOTE: Cylinder bore is smaller by approximately .0012" (.030 mm) near top of cylinder because of varying thermal loads.***

**Piston & Cylinder Assembly – 1)** With camshaft housing and cylinder head(s) removed, mark piston and cylinder for reassembly reference. Remove cooling air shrouds as necessary. Remove cylinder(s).

**2)** Remove piston pin circlips. DO NOT allow circlips to drop into crankcase. Heat piston to approximately 176°F (80°C). Remove pin, and mark piston pin for identification and reassembly reference. Remove rings from piston if necessary.

***NOTE: DO NOT mix pistons and pins within an engine set.***

**3)** Inspect piston(s) for excessive wear. Piston diameter can be determined from size group marking stamped on piston crown. Piston diameter is identified by a "0", "1", "2" or "3". See PISTONS, PINS & RINGS table under ENGINE SPECIFICATIONS at end of article. Ensure cylinder bore is within specification for piston being used.

**4)** For example, if piston diameter is identified as a "1", ensure cylinder diameter is also identified as a "1" to ensure proper piston clearance. Cylinder bore is measured 2.20" (56 mm) from top of cylinder. *See Fig. 13*. See CYLINDER table under ENGINE SPECIFICATIONS at end of article. If cylinder is not within specification, replace cylinder.

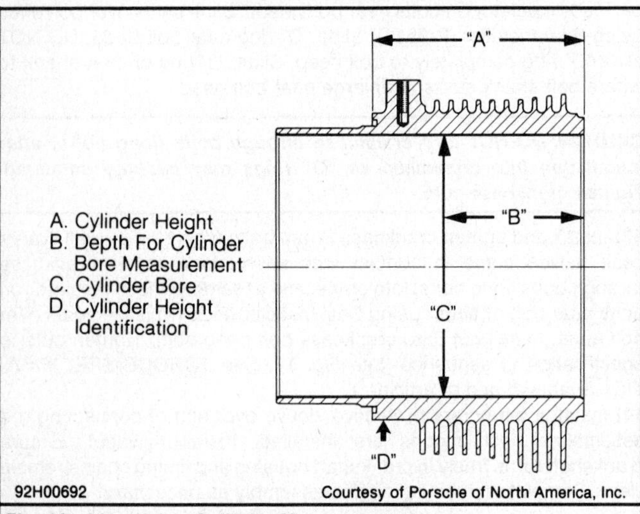


***Fig. 13: Identifying Cylinder Measurements***

**5)** To install, lubricate piston with oil. Using Piston Pin Circlip Installer (9500), install new piston pin circlip with opening facing up or down. Insert piston pin. Piston pin bore is offset .035" (.9 mm).

**6)** Piston pin is a press fit into piston. If piston pin can be inserted into piston while cold, a pin of larger diameter is necessary. Correct pin size is determined from color code (black or white) marked on inside of piston pin boss. See PISTONS, PINS & RINGS table under ENGINE SPECIFICATIONS at end of article.

**7)** Heat piston to approximately 176°F (80°C). Lubricate pin, and insert it into piston until it contacts circlip. Using piston pin circlip installer, install remaining circlip.

***NOTE: Cylinder bore is smaller by approximately .0012" (.030 mm) near top of cylinder because of varying thermal loads.***

**Fitting Pistons – 1)** Install piston with marking stamped on piston dome toward intake. Use only pistons from same manufacturer and of same weight class (with cylinders of same size). Maximum weight difference between one piston set (6) is .21 oz. (6 g).

**2)** Ensure no damage to Mahle or Nikasil cylinder surface coating is present. Cylinder surface coating is applied galvanically. Measure pistons and cylinders for wear and out-of-round. To measure piston diameter, measure piston at 90 degrees to piston pin, .591" (15 mm) from edge of piston skirt. See PISTONS, PINS & RINGS table under ENGINE SPECIFICATIONS at end of article.

**3)** Check cylinder out-of-round. Take one measurement in line with thrust face and another at 90 degrees to this measurement. See CYLINDER table under ENGINE SPECIFICATIONS at end of article. Replace cylinder if difference between 2 measurements is more than .0016" (.041 mm).

***CAUTION: Use only cylinders of same height class on any one side of engine.***

**4)** Identify cylinder height. Cylinder height is identified by a "5" or "6" stamped on cylinder opposite of knock sensor boss. *See Fig. 13*. When cylinder height is identified, measure cylinder bore. Cylinder bore is identified as a "0", "1", "2" or "3". Cylinder bore is measured 2.20" (56 mm) from top of cylinder. *See Fig. 13*. Measure cylinder sealing surface runout. See CYLINDER table under ENGINE SPECIFICATIONS at end of article. If cylinder is not within specifications, replace cylinder.

**Piston Rings –** Position rings onto piston. *See Fig. 14*. Ensure rings are positioned on pistons with end gaps staggered. Ensure oil scrapper ring end gap is facing top (as engine cylinder is flat in vehicle). Lightly oil cylinder bore. Using a piston ring compressor, compress rings. Remove ring compressor.

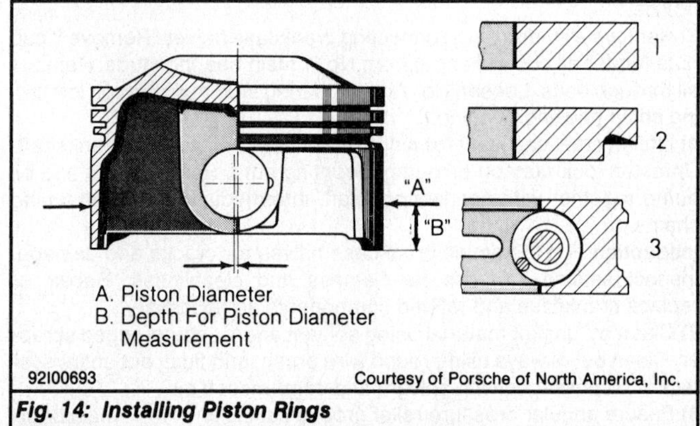


***Fig. 14: Installing Piston Rings***

## CRANKSHAFT MAIN BEARINGS

***NOTE: Main bearing bores in crankcase must be measured and resized, if necessary, whenever crankcase halves are disassembled for repair.***

**Main Bearing Bore Measurements – 1)** Attach left crankcase half to mount fixture. Assemble both crankcase halves without intermediate shaft. Lightly tighten all crankcase main bearing studs and two 8-mm nuts at main bearing No. 1.

**2)** Align both crankcase halves using a plastic mallet. Ensure main bearing No. 8 is not offset in relation to each half. Using an inside micrometer, cross-check No. 8 main bearing bore, and realign bore as needed.

**3)** Tighten all crankcase studs and both 8-mm nuts to proper torque. Measure all main bearing bores using an inside micrometer. Standard I.D. for all crankcase main bearing bores is 2.5591-2.5598" (65.000-65.019 mm).

**4)** If bores are too tight, ream bores to standard size. If bores are too large, ream light alloy crankcase bores (in 2 steps) to "B" bearing (oversize) of 2.5689-2.5696" (65.250-65.269 mm).

**5)** When reaming, use cutting oil on reamer, and make initial cut to 2.4468" (62.150 mm). When reaming pressure-cast crankcases, cut in one pass, without oil. Ream to oversize specification of 2.5689" (65.250 mm).

***NOTE: Main bearing first reground size is color-coded blue and second reground size is color-coded green.***

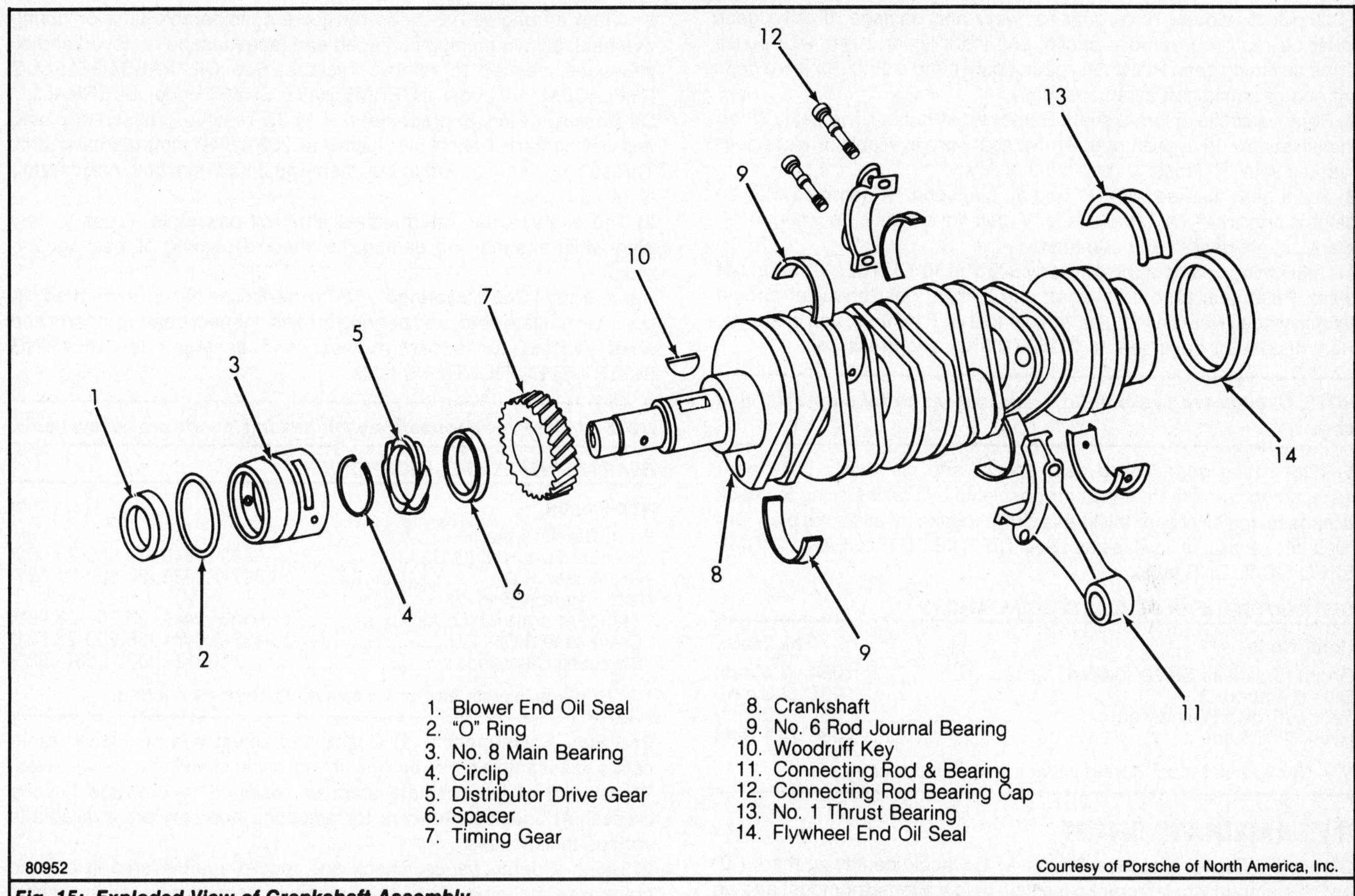


***Fig. 15: Exploded View of Crankshaft Assembly***

**Main Bearings – 1)** Main bearing No. 8 includes an external "O" ring and an internal oil seal. *See Fig. 15.* A steel dowel, pressed into crankcase, is used to locate No. 8 bearing and prevents it from turning. Crankshaft journals 1-7 are same size.

**2)** When inspecting crankshaft, check main bearing insert bores in crankcase for size and straightness. See MAIN BEARING BORE MEASUREMENTS under CRANKSHAFT MAIN BEARINGS. Using a bore gauge and micrometer (or Plastigage method), assemble crankcases with inserts installed.

**3)** Measure all main bearing inserts I.D. and crank journals O.D. to check insert-to-journal clearances. Maximum clearance is no more than .0033" (.083 mm). Grind crankshaft and replace bearing inserts as necessary. Main bearings are available in 3 sizes. See CRANKSHAFT, MAIN & CONNECTING ROD BEARINGS table under ENGINE SPECIFICATIONS at end of article.

## CRANKSHAFT & CONNECTING RODS

***CAUTION: Connecting rod stretch bolts should never be reused. Replace rod bolts whenever connecting rods are disassembled.***

**1)** Separate crankcase halves. Lift out crankshaft and connecting rods. *See Fig. 15.* Remove connecting rods. Inspect connecting rods for wear, damage and non-alignment.

**2)** Inspect connecting rod small end bushing for excessive wear and damage. Bushing is pressed into rod with interference fit of .0006-.0022" (.014-.055 mm). If interference fit is not maintained, replace bushing.

***CAUTION: Replacement connecting rods (without inserts) must have a weight difference of no more than .32 oz. (9 g).***

**3)** Check small end rod/bushing width and large end rod width. Check rod side clearance. Check rod center-to-center length. Repair or replace connecting rod if not within specifications. If a connecting rod is replaced, ensure replacement connecting rod is within same weight group. See CONNECTING RODS table under ENGINE SPECIFICATIONS at end of article.

**4)** If crankshaft is reground, plugs must be removed from oil passages. Thoroughly clean passages. Install and secure new plugs. Ensure all oilways are properly radiused and sharp edges chamfered.

***CAUTION: If bearing journals are reground, crankshaft must have a surface hardness treatment done to restore journals to proper hardness.***

**5)** After regrind, crankshaft must have a "Tenifer" treatment for 2 hours at 1060°F (570°C). After crankshaft heat treatment, polish all bearing journals. Magnaflux complete crankshaft to check for cracks. If crankshaft is rebalanced after regrinding, ensure balance is within 10 cmg.

**6)** Check crankshaft runout. Measure runout on bearing journals No. 4 and 8 with journals No. 1 and 7 on "V" blocks. See CRANKSHAFT, MAIN & CONNECTING ROD BEARINGS table under ENGINE SPECIFICATIONS at end of article. After "Tenifer" treatment, DO NOT attempt to straighten No. 3 and 5 bearing journals. All other main bearing journals may be straightened by applying pressure to bearing journal webs.

## DISTRIBUTOR DRIVE GEAR

***NOTE: Incorrect installation of distributor drive gear will cause initial ignition timing to be off by approximately 13 degrees. With distributor drive gear in place, distributor rotor will turn clockwise.***

# 1990-91 ENGINES
# 3.6L 6-Cylinder (Cont.)

**1)** Check distributor drive gear for wear and damage. If drive gear must be replaced, remove circlip, and install gear puller with puller arms on timing gear. Pull timing gear, spacer and distributor drive gear off end of crankshaft as an assembly.
**2)** Remove circlip on crankshaft. Remove distributor drive gear. When installing new drive gear, note 2 drive gears are available. Ensure gear marked with "P" faces "V" belt drive pulley.
**3)** For a gear marked with "P" and an additional "X" (scribed with an electric engraver), "X" should face "V" belt drive pulley. Location of "P" mark on this gear does not matter.
**4)** Heat timing gear to approximately 302°F (150°C) in oil bath or on hot plate. Push gear onto crankshaft end. Timing gear shoulder should face flywheel. Heat timing gear spacer to 212°F (100°C), and press on. Heat distributor drive gear to 212°F (100°C), and press on.

***NOTE: Circlips are available in 4 thicknesses to take up axial end play.***

**5)** With timing gear, timing gear spacer and distributor drive gear installed on crankshaft, select proper circlip by first installing to check thickness. Install proper thickness circlip to take up axial end play. Circlips are available in 4 sizes. See DISTRIBUTOR GEAR CIRCLIP SPECIFICATIONS table.

***DISTRIBUTOR GEAR CIRCLIP SPECIFICATIONS***

| Color Code | Thickness |
|---|---|
| Bright (Stainless Steel-Colored) | .094" (2.4 mm) |
| Blue (Tempered) [1] | .091" (2.3 mm) |
| Yellow/Brown (Tempered) | .087" (2.2 mm) |
| Black (Finished) | .083" (2.1 mm) |

[1] – Circlip used most during initial assembly at factory.

## INTERMEDIATE SHAFT

**Center-To-Center Distance Check – 1)** Check identifying mark ("0" or "1") stamped into left crankcase half, below alternator mount and on crankshaft gear and intermediate shaft gear. Gears and crankcase may be paired together only as indicated.
**2)** If crankcase is stamped with a "0", distance between shaft centers is 4.0935-4.0941" (103.975-103.990 mm). Install crankshaft gear with "0" and intermediate shaft gear with "0". Using dial indicator mounted to crankcase, ensure gear backlash is .0011-.0019" (.029-.049 mm).

***NOTE: DO NOT mix gears with different stamped number unless gear backlash falls within specification.***

**3)** If crankshaft gear is stamped with "1" and intermediate shaft gear is stamped "0", gear backlash must be .0006-.0016" (.016-.042 mm). If crankshaft gear is stamped "0" and intermediate shaft gear is stamped "1", gear backlash must be .0007-.0017" (.017-.043 mm).
**4)** If crankcase is stamped with a "1", distance between shaft centers is 4.0941-4.0945" (103.990-104.000 mm). Install crankshaft gear with "1" and intermediate shaft gear with "1". Ensure gear backlash is .0050-.0016" (.012-.041 mm).
**5)** If crankshaft gear is stamped with "0" and intermediate shaft gear is stamped "1", gear backlash must be .0010-.0019" (.025-.049 mm). If crankshaft gear is stamped "1" and intermediate shaft gear is stamped "0", gear backlash must be .0010-.0018" (.025-.048 mm).

***CAUTION: Bolt-on intermediate shaft gear is machined in position on shaft to avoid improper gear meshing or out-of-roundness. DO NOT replace just gear if worn. Replace both shaft and gear assembly.***

**Gear Inspection – 1)** With gear removed from intermediate shaft, place two .18" (4.5 mm) diameter steel rollers into gear teeth, 180 degrees apart from each other. Measure total O.D. distance of rollers and gear.
**2)** If measuring standard gear, distance must be no less than 5.374" (136.50 mm). If gear is stamped with "1", distance must be no less than 5.376" (136.55 mm). Replace crankshaft drive gear and intermediate shaft gear if not within specification.
**3)** When an engine has been run for a considerable time or during overhaul, aluminum plugs on shaft end face must be removed and oil passages cleaned to remove residue. See OIL PASSAGE PLUG REPLACEMENT under INTERMEDIATE SHAFT under OVERHAUL.

**Oil Passage Plug Replacement – 1)** To remove pressed-in plugs, drill out center of each plug using a .252" (6.40 mm) diameter drill. Thread plug using an 8-mm tap. Install an 8 x 65-mm bolt, and carefully turn out plug.
**2)** Thoroughly clean intermediate shaft oil passages. Press in new plug while ensuring no damage is done to bearing oil passages in plug.

**Intermediate Shaft Bearings –** With crankcase halves separated, lift out intermediate shaft and bearing inserts. Inspect bearing inserts and shaft journals for excessive wear and damage. See BEARING INSERT SPECIFICATIONS table.

***NOTE: Undersize intermediate shaft bearing inserts are not available.***

***BEARING INSERT SPECIFICATIONS*** [1]

| Application | In. (mm) |
|---|---|
| Front Blower Inserts | |
| Standard Journal (O.D.) | .9835-.9843 (24.980-25.000) |
| Crankcase (I.D.) | 1.0827-1.0835 (27.500-27.521) |
| Rear Flywheel End | |
| Standard Journal (O.D.) | .9436-.9441 (23.967-23.980) |
| Crankcase (I.D.) | 1.0433-1.0441 (26.500-26.521) |
| Standard Clearance | .0012-.0033 (.030-.084) |

[1] – Replace inserts and/or intermediate shaft as needed.

**End Play Adjustment – 1)** Check and adjust end play with crankcases reassembled but before timing chain housings are installed. Thrust end of intermediate shaft is designed to protrude beyond crankshaft housing. Spacers for adjusting end play are available in various thicknesses.
**2)** Using a depth gauge, check and record shaft overhang beyond crankcase housing. Use this measurement during timing chain alignment. Place a new "O" ring in groove on intermediate shaft cover, and install in crankshaft housing.
**3)** Install Dial Indicator Fixture (P-220) with probe positioned on face of intermediate shaft. Measure end play. End play should be .0016-.006" (.040-.16 mm). Replace intermediate shaft bearing inserts if beyond specification.
**4)** If necessary, adjust clearance by inserting proper size shim spacers. After end play check, set shaft cover and spacers aside for final assembly.

## THRUST BEARING

**Thrust Bearing End Play – 1)** Check size and end play at No. 1 main (thrust) bearing. Standard thrust bearing width is 1.1024-1.1047" (28.000-28.060 mm). With crankshaft and inserts installed and crankcases temporarily assembled, mount dial indicator with pointer positioned on crankshaft end.
**2)** Move crankshaft back and forth, and record end play. If necessary, replace No. 1 main bearing inserts and/or crankshaft. See CRANKSHAFT, MAIN & CONNECTING ROD BEARINGS table under ENGINE SPECIFICATIONS at end of article.

# ENGINE OILING

## ENGINE LUBRICATION SYSTEM

Lubrication is dry sump type. Two independent oil pumps (built into one pump body) provide pressure and suction to system. Pressure pump draws oil from externally mounted oil tank and forces it through an oil cooler to main, connecting rod and intermediate shaft bearings. *See Fig. 16.* Suction pump removes oil from sump (through strainer) and forces it through oil filter to oil tank.

Camshaft bearings are oiled by external oil lines leading to camshaft housing. Oil from camshaft housing is returned to crankcase by oil return pipes. Pressure is controlled by 4 separate valves. At temperatures below 176°F (80°C), a thermostatically controlled valve directs

# 1990-91 ENGINES
# 3.6L 6-Cylinder (Cont.)

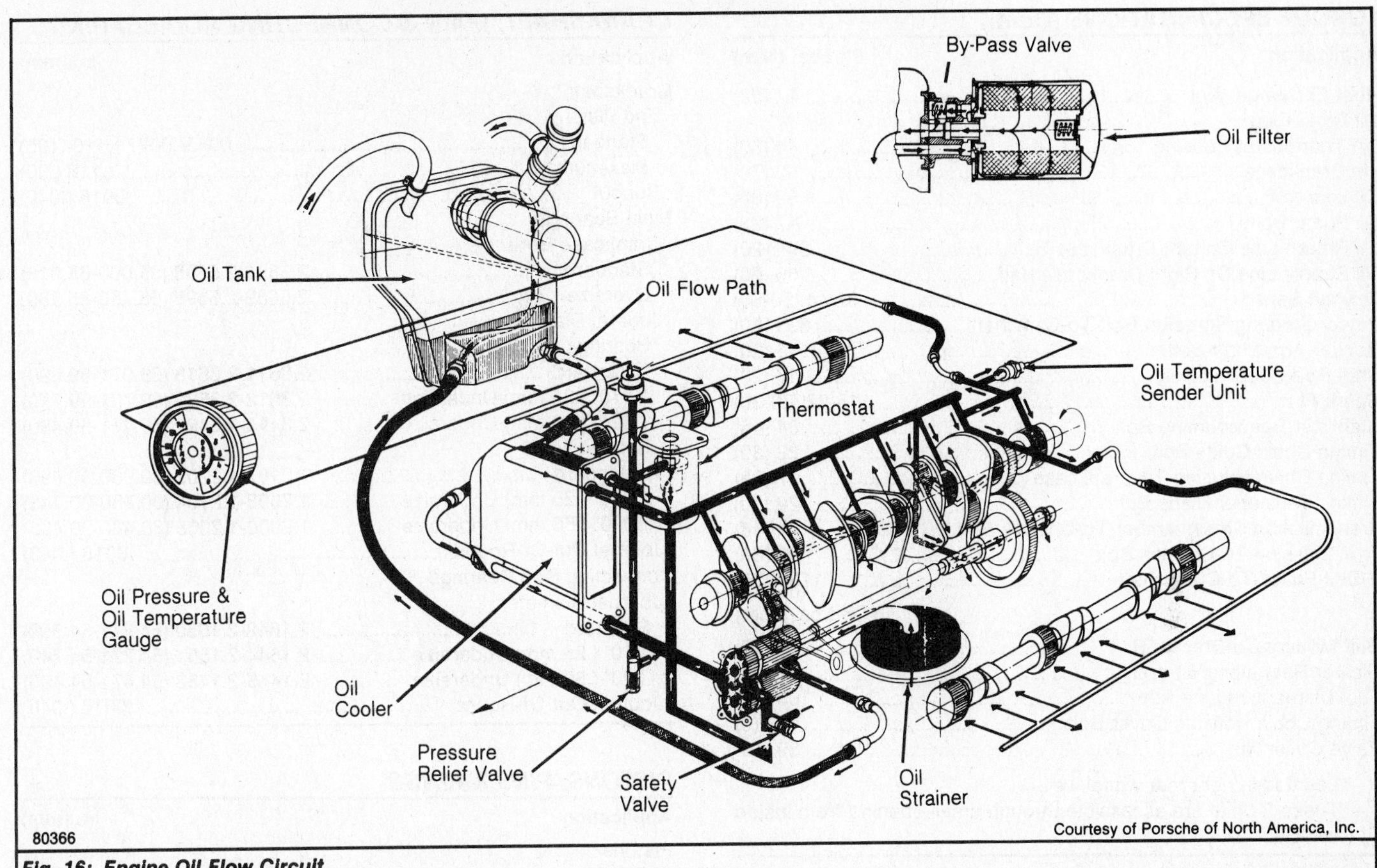


*Fig. 16: Engine Oil Flow Circuit*

oil to engine. At higher temperatures, oil first flows through cooler and then to bearings.

A pressure relief valve directs oil into crankcase if pressure rises to 76.9-99.6 psi (5.4-7.0 kg/cm²). Additional safety and by-pass valves are built into system to prevent damage from excessive pressure.

**Oil Capacity** – Standard oil capacity is 9.5 qts. (9L) when changing oil. Total engine capacity (with oil cooler) is 12.2 qts. (11.5L). Always check oil level with engine at idle speed and normal operating temperature. Difference between maximum and minimum marks on dipstick is approximately 1.9 qts. (1.8L).

**Oil Pressure** – Oil pressure should be 60 psi (4.2 kg/cm²) at 5000 RPM with an oil temperature of 194°F (90°C).

## PRESSURE RELIEF & SAFETY VALVES

**1)** Pressure release and safety valves use identically-constructed coil springs. Safety valve is set to operate at higher pressure than relief valve by greater compression of coil spring in its fitted position.

**2)** Spring for pressure release and safety valves is 2.75" (70 mm) long (in free length) with an O.D. of .48" (12.2 mm) and wire diameter of .055" (1.4 mm).

**3)** Fully compressed length is 1.31" (33.3 mm). Pressure exerted at length of 2.04" (52 mm) is 77 lbs. (342 N); at length of 1.81" (46 mm), pressure is 102 lbs. (454 N).

**4)** Pressure relief valve (in right crankcase half, across from thermostat) uses an aluminum washer and safety valve (located in horizontal position in left crankcase half) uses a copper washer.

## OIL PUMP

Engine oil pump may be removed only when crankcase halves are separated. See CRANKCASE HOUSING under OVERHAUL. DO NOT attempt to repair a defective oil pump assembly. Replace unit as an assembly.

When installing engine oil pump (with connecting shaft and intermediate shaft attached), new sealing ring must be installed in grooves in right crankcase half main oil passage. Ensure ring is not trapped between crankcase inlet passage and centering groove on oil pump.

## TORQUE SPECIFICATIONS

*TORQUE SPECIFICATIONS*

| Application | Ft. Lbs. (N.m) |
|---|---|
| Alternator Cooling Fan | 10 (14) |
| Alternator Pulley Nut | 33-41 (45-55) |
| Axle Shaft Bolt | |
| 8 mm | 31 (42) |
| 10 mm | 59 (80) |
| Belt Monitor Bracket-To-Crankcase Bolt | 11-15 (15-20) |
| Camshaft Housing-To-Cylinder Head Bolt | 17 (23) |
| Camshaft Sprocket Bolt | 89 (120) |
| Clamping Sleeve Allen Bolt | 55 (75) |
| Connecting Rod Nut | |
| Step 1 | 11 (15) |
| Step 2 | Angle Tighten 90 Degrees |
| Step 3 | Angle Tighten 90 Degrees |
| Crankcase Outer Bolt (Short Bolts) | 30 (40) |
| Crankcase Through Bolt (Long Bolts) | 37 (50) |
| Cylinder Head Nut | |
| Step 1 | 11 (15) |
| Step 2 | Angle Tighten 90 Degrees |
| Double Mass Flywheel-To-Crankshaft Bolt | 63 (85) |
| Drive Plate-To-Crankshaft Bolt | 66 (90) |
| Engine Mount Bolt | 63 (85) |
| Flywheel-To-Crankshaft Bolt | 66 (90) |

# 1990-91 ENGINES
# 3.6L 6-Cylinder (Cont.)

### TORQUE SPECIFICATIONS (Cont.)

| Application | Ft. Lbs. (N.m) |
|---|---|
| Heat Exchanger Nut | 17 (23) |
| Oil Drain Plug | |
| In Thermostat Housing | 44 (60) |
| In Crankcase | 52 (70) |
| Oil Line Nut | [1] 59 (80) |
| Oil Pump Bolts | 17 (23) |
| Oil Return Line On Left Crankcase Half | 89 (120) |
| Oil Supply Line On Right Crankcase Half | 66 (90) |
| Oxygen Sensor | 37-44 (50-60) |
| Power Steering Sprocket Bolt-To-Camshaft | 89 (120) |
| Rocker Arm Shaft Bolt | 15 (20) |
| Shift Rod Coupling Bolt | 17 (23) |
| Spark Plug | 15-22 (20-30) |
| Stabilizer Bar Mounting Bolt | 34 (46) |
| Timing Chain Guide Bolt | 22 (30) |
| Timing Chain Housing-To-Crankcase | 17 (23) |
| Timing Tensioner Blade Bolt | 22 (30) |
| Transmission Crossmember-To-Chassis Bolt | 34 (46) |
| Transmission-To-Chassis Bolt | [2] 63 (85) |
| V-Belt Pulley-To-Crankshaft | 173 (235) |
| | INCH Lbs. (N.m) |
| Belt Monitor-To-Bracket Bolt | 89 (10) |
| Blower Restraining Strap Nut | 71 (8) |
| Fuel Distribution Line Nut | 106 (12) |
| Timing Chain Housing Cover Bolt | 53 (6) |
| Valve Cover Nut | 89 (10) |

[1] – Located in right rear wheel well.
[2] – These 2 bolts are accessible through small opening from inside vehicle.

## ENGINE SPECIFICATIONS

### GENERAL SPECIFICATIONS

| Application | Specification |
|---|---|
| Displacement | 220 Cu. In. (3.6L) |
| Bore | 3.94" (100 mm) |
| Stroke | 3.01" (76.5 mm) |
| Compression Ratio | 11.3:1 |
| Fuel System | PFI |
| Horsepower @ RPM | 247 @ 6100 |
| Torque Ft. Lbs. @ RPM | 228 @ 4800 |

### CONNECTING RODS

| Application | Specification |
|---|---|
| Bushing Bore | .9843-.9851" (25.000-25.021 mm) |
| Pin Bushing | |
| Inside Diameter | .8669-.8674" (22.020-22.033 mm) |
| Outside Diameter | .9856-.9864" (25.035-25.055 mm) |
| Length | 5.031" (127.80 mm) |
| Width | |
| Small End | 1.0228-1.0236" (25.980-26.000 mm) |
| Large End | .9331-.9370" (23.70-23.80 mm) |
| Side Clearance | .008-.014" (.20-.35 mm) |
| Weight Groups [1] | |
| Group 3 (Code 53) [2] | 21.7-22.0 ozs. (615-624 g) |
| Group 4 (Code 54) [2] | 22.0-22.3 ozs. (624-633 g) |
| Group 5 (Code 55) [2] | 22.3-22.6 ozs. (633-642 g) |
| Group 6 (Code 56) [2] | 22.6-23.0 ozs. (642-651 g) |
| Group 7 (Code 57) [2] | 23.0-23.3 ozs. (651-660 g) |
| Group 8 (Code 58) [2] | 23.3-23.6 ozs. (660-669 g) |
| Group 9 (Code 59) [2] | 23.6-24.0 ozs. (669-678 g) |
| Group 10 (Code 60) [2] | 24.0-24.2 ozs. (678-687 g) |
| Group 11 (Code 61) [2] | 24.2-24.5 ozs. (687-696 g) |

[1] – Connecting rod weight is measured without inserts.
[2] – Last 2 digits of connecting rod part number identify code number.

### CRANKSHAFT, MAIN & CONNECTING ROD BEARINGS

| Application | In. (mm) |
|---|---|
| Crankshaft | |
| End Play | |
| Standard | .0043-.0077 (.110-.195) |
| Maximum | .118 (.30) |
| Runout | .0016 (.040) |
| Main Bearings | |
| Crankcase Bore | |
| Standard | 2.5591-2.5598 (65.000-65.019) |
| Oversize | 2.5689-2.5696 (65.250-65.269) |
| Journal Diameter | |
| Bearings No. 1-7 | |
| Standard | 2.3611-2.3618 (59.971-59.990) |
| .010" (.25 mm) Undersize | 2.3512-2.3520 (59.721-59.740) |
| .020" (.50 mm) Undersize | 2.3414-2.3421 (59.471-59.490) |
| Bearing No. 8 | |
| Standard | 1.2197-1.2202 (30.980-30.993) |
| .010" (.25 mm) Undersize | 1.2098-1.2104 (30.730-30.743) |
| .020" (.50 mm) Undersize | 1.2000-1.2005 (30.480-30.493) |
| Journal Out-Of-Round | .0016 (.040) |
| Connecting Rod Bearings | |
| Journal Diameter | |
| Standard | 2.1642-2.1650 (54.971-54.990) |
| .010" (.25 mm) Undersize | 2.1544-2.1551 (54.721-54.740) |
| .020" (.50 mm) Undersize | 2.1445-2.1453 (54.471-54.490) |
| Journal Out-Of-Round | .0016 (.040) |

### PISTONS, PINS & RINGS

| Application | In. (mm) |
|---|---|
| Pistons | |
| Diameter [1] | |
| Group T Diameter Stage 0 | 3.9358-3.9362 (99.970-99.980) |
| Group T Diameter Stage 1 | 3.9361-3.9365 (99.977-99.987) |
| Group T Diameter Stage 2 | 3.9363-3.9368 (99.984-99.994) |
| Group T Diameter Stage 3 | 3.9366-3.9370 (99.991-100.001) |
| Pins | |
| Diameter | |
| Black Color Code | .8659-.8660 (21.994-21.997) |
| White Color Code | .8661-.8666 (22.000-22.003) |
| Piston Fit | [2] |
| Rod Fit | .0008-.0015 (.020-.039) |
| Rings | |
| No. 1 | |
| End Gap | .004-.008 (.10-.20) |
| Side Clearance | .003-.004 (.07-.10) |
| No. 2 | |
| End Gap | .004-.008 (.10-.20) |
| Side Clearance | .002-.003 (.04-.07) |
| No. 3 (Oil) | |
| End Gap | .006-.012 (.15-.30) |
| Side Clearance | .0008-.0020 (.020-.050) |

[1] – Piston diameter is measured 90 degrees from piston pin, .591" (15 mm) from edge of piston skirt.
[2] – Interference fit.

# 1990-91 ENGINES
# 3.6L 6-Cylinder (Cont.)

## CYLINDER

| Application | In. (mm) |
|---|---|
| Cylinder Bore [1] | |
| Diameter | |
| Group T Diameter Stage 0 | 3.9370-3.9373 (100.000-100.007) |
| Group T Diameter Stage 1 | 3.9373-3.9376 (100.007-100.014) |
| Group T Diameter Stage 2 | 3.9376-3.9378 (100.014-100.021) |
| Group T Diameter Stage 3 | 3.9378-3.9381 (100.021-100.028) |
| Maximum Taper | [2] |
| Maximum Out-Of-Round | .002 (.04) |
| Cylinder Height | |
| Group 5 | 3.2579 (82.750) |
| Group 6 | 3.2587 (82.770) |

[1] – Cylinder bore is measured 2.20" (56 mm) from top of cylinder.
[2] – Cylinder bore is smaller by approximately .0012" (.030 mm) near top of cylinder because of varying thermal loads.

## VALVES & VALVE SPRINGS

| Application | Specification |
|---|---|
| Intake Valves | |
| Face Angle | 45° |
| Head Diameter | 1.93" (49 mm) |
| Length | 4.325-4.344" (109.85-110.35 mm) |
| Stem Diameter | .353" (8.97 mm) |
| Exhaust Valves | |
| Face Angle | 45° |
| Head Diameter | 1.67" (42.5 mm) |
| Length | 4.258-4.278" (108.15-108.65 mm) |
| Stem Diameter | .352-.353" (8.94-8.97 mm) |
| Valve Springs | |
| Installed Height [1] | |
| Intake | 1.35-1.37" (34.2-34.8 mm) |
| Exhaust | 1.31-1.33" (33.2-33.8 mm) |

[1] – *See Fig. 11.*

## CYLINDER HEAD

| Application | Specification |
|---|---|
| Maximum Warpage | .006" (.15 mm) |
| Valve Seats | |
| Seat Depth | 1.78-1.80" (45.2-45.8 mm) |
| Maximum Seat Runout | .002" (.05 mm) |
| Interference Fit | .0055-.0071" (.140-.180 mm) |
| Intake Valve | |
| Seat Angle | 45° |
| Seat Width | |
| Standard | 2.0339-2.0346" (51.661-51.680 mm) |
| Oversize | 2.0465-2.0472" (51.981-52.000 mm) |
| Seat Bore Diameter | |
| Standard | 2.0276-2.0287" (51.500-51.530 mm) |
| Oversize | 2.0401-2.0413" (51.820-51.850 mm) |
| Exhaust Valve | |
| Seat Angle | 45° |
| Seat Width | |
| Standard | 1.7395-1.7402" (44.184-44.200 mm) |
| Oversize | 1.7616-1.7622" (44.744-44.760 mm) |
| Seat Bore Diameter | |
| Standard | 1.7323-1.7333" (44.000-44.025 mm) |
| Oversize | 1.7543-1.7554" (44.560-44.588 mm) |
| Valve Guides | |
| Intake & Exhaust Valves | |
| I.D. | .0354-.3549" (9.000-9.015 mm) |
| O.D. | .5137-.5142" (13.049-13.060 mm) |
| Cylinder Head Bore | .5118-.5125" (13.000-13.018 mm) |
| Press Fit | |
| Standard | .0012-.0024" (.031-.060 mm) |
| Replacement | .0024-.0035" (.060-.090 mm) |
| Installed Height | .51-.52" (12.9-13.2 mm) |
| Valve Stem-To-Guide Oil Clearance | |
| Intake | .004-.006" (.10-.15 mm) |
| Exhaust | .004-.008" (.10-.20 mm) |

## CAMSHAFT

| Application | In. (mm) |
|---|---|
| Camshaft Runout | .0008 (.020) |
| Bore Diameter | 1.8490-1.8501 (46.965-46.992) |
| End Play | |
| Standard | .006-.008 (.15-.20) |
| Maximum | .016 (.40) |
| Journal Diameter | 1.8474-1.8481 (46.924-46.942) |
| Oil Clearance | |
| Standard | .0010-.0026 (.025-.066) |
| Maximum | .0040 (.102) |

## ROCKER ARM ASSEMBLY

| Application | In. (mm) |
|---|---|
| Rocker Arm Shaft Bore | |
| Diameter | .7087-.7094 (18.000-18.018) |
| Width | 1.0236-1.0295 (26.000-26.150) |
| Rocker Arm Shaft Diameter | .7083-.7087 (17.992-18.000) |
| Rocker Arm Bore | .7093-.7097 (18.016-18.027) |
| Rocker Arm Width | 1.0157-1.0197 (25.800-25.900) |
| Rocker Arm-To-Shaft Clearance | |
| Standard | .0006-.0014 (.016-.035) |
| Limit | .0031 (.080) |
| Rocker Arm-To-Camshaft Housing Clearance | |
| Limit | .020 (.50) |
| Rocker Arm Side Play | .004-.014 (.10-.35) |

# 1990-91 CLUTCHES AWD & RWD

## 911 Carrera 2/4

***CAUTION: DO NOT start engine with ground strap between transmission and chassis disconnected or Digital Motor Electronics (DME) control unit will be destroyed.***

## DESCRIPTION

Clutch assembly is a non-asbestos dry type with a rubber damped single disc and a diaphragm spring pressure plate. The clutch release mechanism is hydraulically operated by fluid received from the brake master cylinder.

## ADJUSTMENTS

System is automatically adjusted and requires no manual adjustment.

## FUEL PRESSURE RELEASE

Turn ignition off. Access fuse panel in luggage compartment. Remove fuel pump/oxygen sensor fuse. Start engine. Allow engine to run until it stalls. Crank engine to ensure residual fuel pressure is released.

## REMOVAL & INSTALLATION

### CLUTCH ASSEMBLY

**Removal** - Remove engine/transmission assembly from vehicle. See ENGINE under REMOVAL & INSTALLATION. Remove clutch release shaft bolt. Remove clutch release shaft from transmission. Mark pressure plate and flywheel for reassembly. Insert clutch alignment tool. Loosen bolts evenly in a diagonal pattern. Separate clutch assembly from engine.

**Inspection** - Check disc for loose rivets, worn springs and oil contamination. Inspect flywheel and pressure plate friction surfaces for burns, scoring and grooves. Resurface or replace flywheel and/or pressure plate as necessary. Mount disc on input shaft. Check disc hub splines for excessive wear. Hub must slide smoothly on input shaft splines.

**Installation** - **1)** Ensure marks on flywheel and clutch are aligned. Tighten pressure plate bolts evenly in a diagonal pattern. Use clutch alignment tool to center disc. If installing new clutch, balancing marks on clutch and flywheel should be offset 180 degrees.

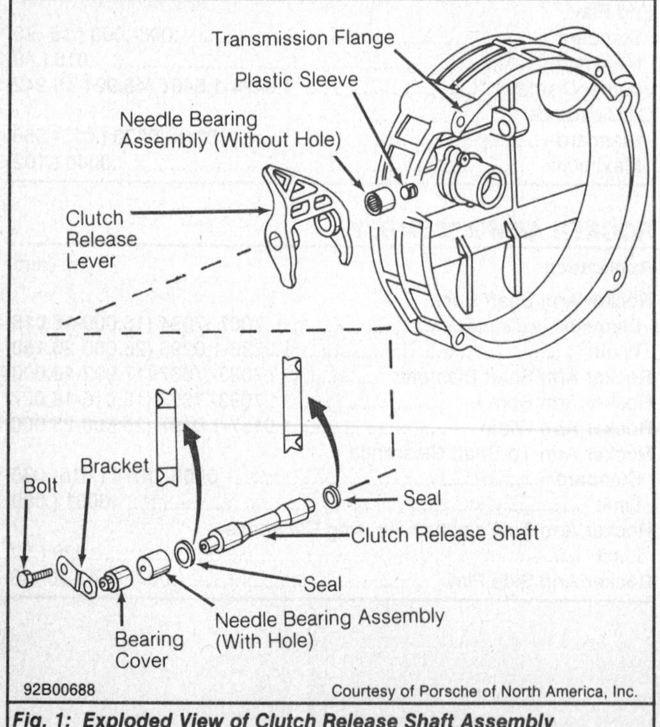


***Fig. 1: Exploded View of Clutch Release Shaft Assembly***

**2)** With transaxle installed, pull release lever away from engine. At least .78" (19.8 mm) clearance must exist between release lever and transaxle housing. Lubricate all sliding surfaces of clutch release mechanism and gear teeth of drive shaft with long-term grease. Position release fork in release bearing. Using adhesive tape, fix position of release fork. Mount transmission to engine.

**3)** Ensure seals are positioned properly on clutch release shaft. *See Fig. 1*. Guide clutch release shaft with sealing rings into release fork. Remove adhesive tape through assembly hole. Pack needle bearing cap with long-term grease. Install needle bearing cap and bracket onto clutch release shaft. Tighten bracket into place using bolt. To complete installation, reverse removal procedure.

### CLUTCH RELEASE BEARING

**Removal** - Bearing is removed with pressure plate. Remove by laying pressure plate on bearing and removing snap ring on flywheel side of clutch fingers. Remove bearing along with washers. Check bearing for roughness or noise by turning by hand in thrust direction.

**Installation** - Apply thin coat of lubricant to guide tube and friction surfaces. Complete installation by reversing removal procedure.

### ENGINE

***NOTE: Engine and transmission is removed as an assembly from underneath vehicle.***

**Removal & Installation (Carrera 2)** - **1)** Release fuel pressure. See FUEL PRESSURE RELEASE. Disconnect negative battery cable. Raise and support vehicle. Position supports for vehicle so transmission supports can be removed later. Remove rear wheels.

**2)** Disconnect 6 electrical connections at intake manifold assembly. Remove cable clip from airflow sensor. Remove hot air blower (electric fan) from engine.

**3)** On left side of engine compartment, disconnect carbon canister hose, brake booster vacuum hose, reference mark sensor electrical connector, knock sensor electrical connector, temperature sensor electrical connector, cruise control electrical connector, oxygen sensor connector and fuel return line. If fuel tank is full, connect an extra piece of fuel line to vehicle fuel return line. Pinch off extra fuel line connected to vehicle fuel return line to prevent fuel from leaking.

**4)** Remove cover for engine electrics board. Disconnect multiple electrical connectors. Disconnect ignition coil wires from distributor. Disconnect electrical connector from double distributor assembly. Disconnect belt monitoring device electrical connector.

**5)** On A/C-equipped vehicles, disconnect A/C compressor mounting bolts. Set A/C compressor aside with hoses attached. On all vehicles, remove air filter housing. Disconnect fuel supply line at fuel filter.

**6)** Remove power steering fluid from power steering pump reservoir. Remove top hose from power steering pump, and collect any remaining fluid. Remove lower hose from power steering pump, and collect any remaining fluid.

**7)** Disconnect throttle valve linkage. Remove engine and transmission covers from underside of vehicle. Drain engine oil at thermostat housing. If engine is being overhauled, also drain oil from crankcase.

**8)** Using Line Wrench (9501), disconnect oil line at right rear wheel housing. Disconnect oil line retaining clip. Disconnect and plug oil line. Disconnect axles from transmission at axle flange next to transmission. Support axles using wire.

**9)** Disconnect heating hoses at heat exchanger. Disconnect ground strap at bottom starter mounting. Disconnect starter cables. Disconnect throttle valve actuating linkage at underfloor assembly guide tube. Disconnect transmission selector lever cable at transmission.

**10)** Disconnect transmission selector lever cable holder at transmission. Disconnect electrical connector located next to transmission selector cable holder. Remove rear stabilizer bar from vehicle. Disconnect 2 remaining oil line connections at right rear wheel housing. Plug remaining oil line connections at right rear wheel housing.

**11)** Remove engine guard bracket. Reinstall bolts for engine guard bracket as bolts are a contact surface for engine mounting plate used in engine removal. Connect Engine Mounting Plate Adapter (9111/1),

Support Plate (9111/2) and Engine Mounting Plate (9111/3) to a jack. Position jack under engine. Attach mounting plates and adapter to engine. Slightly preload jack.

**12)** Remove transmission transverse crossmember bolts. Remove engine mounting bolts. Lower engine/transmission assembly approximately 4". Disconnect electrical connector at airflow meter. Disconnect electrical connector at transmission. Ensure all vacuum, oil, fuel and electrical lines leading from engine are disconnected. Slowly lower engine/transmission assembly from vehicle.

**13)** To separate engine from transmission, remove starter from transmission. Attach an overhead support to transmission. Slightly preload overhead support. Remove engine-to-transmission bolts. Separate transmission from engine. To install, reverse removal procedure.

**Removal (Carrera 4) – 1)** Release fuel pressure. See FUEL PRESSURE RELEASE. Disconnect negative battery cable. Raise and support vehicle. Position supports for vehicle so transmission supports can be removed later. Remove rear wheels.

**2)** Disconnect differential lock control/pump assembly electrical connector located in luggage compartment. Disconnect 5 electrical connections at intake manifold assembly. Remove cable clip from airflow sensor. Remove hot air blower (electric fan) from engine.

**3)** On left side of engine compartment, disconnect carbon canister hose, brake booster vacuum hose, reference mark sensor electrical connector, knock sensor electrical connector, temperature sensor electrical connector, cruise control electrical connector, oxygen sensor connector and fuel return line. If fuel tank is full, connect an extra piece of fuel line to vehicle fuel return line. Pinch off extra fuel line connected to vehicle fuel return line to prevent fuel from leaking.

**4)** Remove cover for engine electrics board. Disconnect multiple electrical connectors. Disconnect ignition coil wires from distributor. Disconnect electrical connector from double distributor assembly. Disconnect belt monitoring device electrical connector.

**5)** On A/C-equipped vehicles, disconnect A/C compressor mounting bolts. Set A/C compressor aside with hoses attached. On all vehicles, remove air filter housing. Disconnect fuel supply line at fuel filter.

**6)** Remove power steering fluid from power steering pump reservoir. Remove top hose from power steering pump, and collect any remaining fluid. Remove lower hose from power steering pump, and collect any remaining fluid.

**7)** From inside vehicle, remove rear tray console covering transmission tunnel. Remove a layer of PVC. Remove small access cover for 2 transmission-to-chassis bolts. If small access cover is difficult to remove, push cover out from under vehicle. Remove 2 transmission-to-chassis bolts.

**8)** Disconnect throttle valve linkage. Remove engine and transmission covers from underside of vehicle. Drain engine oil at thermostat housing. If engine is being overhauled, also drain oil from crankcase.

**9)** Using Line Wrench (9501), disconnect oil line at right rear wheel housing. Disconnect oil line retaining clip. Disconnect and plug oil line. Disconnect axles from transmission at axle flange next to transmission. Support axles using wire.

**10)** Disconnect heating hoses at heat exchanger. Disconnect ground strap at bottom starter mounting. Disconnect starter cables. Disconnect clutch slave cylinder with hydraulic line attached, and set aside. Remove rear stabilizer bar from vehicle.

**11)** Pull rubber sleeve forward over shift rod coupling. Remove shift rod coupling bolt. Remove 2 Allen bolts for center drive shaft clamping sleeve. Slide sleeve forward along central drive shaft. Disconnect throttle valve actuating linkage at guide tube of underfloor assembly.

**12)** Place a self-made support across center drive shaft assembly to keep center drive shaft from falling during engine removal. Remove wheel-to-wheel slave cylinder mounting bolts. Remove Allen bolt for interaxle differential lock slave cylinder. Without disconnecting hydraulic lines, hang both slave cylinders aside.

**13)** Disconnect remaining oil line connections at right rear wheel housing. Plug remaining oil line connections at right rear wheel housing. Remove engine guard bracket. Reinstall bolts for engine guard bracket as bolts are a contact surface for engine mounting plate used in engine removal.

**14)** Connect Engine Mounting Plate Adapter (9111/1), Support Plate (9111/2) and Engine Mounting Plate (9111/3) to a jack. Position jack under engine. Attach mounting plates and adapter to engine. Slightly preload jack.

**15)** Remove transmission transverse crossmember bolts. Remove engine mounting bolts. Slowly lower engine/transmission assembly until center drive shaft contacts self-made support. Disconnect electrical connector at airflow meter. Ensure all vacuum, oil, fuel and electrical lines leading from engine are disconnected. Pull engine/transmission assembly slightly to rear of vehicle. Slowly lower engine/transmission assembly from vehicle.

**16)** To separate engine from transmission, disconnect electrical connectors from starter and back-up light switch. Attach an overhead support to transmission. Slightly preload overhead support. Remove 4 engine-to-transmission bolts. Separate transmission from engine. Using Wrench (P119), remove upper mounting nut on starter.

**Installation (Carrera 4) –** During engine installation, ensure heat exchanger hoses are not pinched. Slide heat exchanger hoses onto heat exchangers just before engine/transmission assembly is in position. Ensure inner rubber seal on heat exchanger is seated correctly. To complete installation, reverse removal procedure.

## OVERHAUL

***NOTE: Manufacturer recommends replacement of faulty clutch master and release cylinders and does not provide overhaul procedures.***

## TORQUE SPECIFICATIONS

***TORQUE SPECIFICATIONS***

| Application | Ft. Lbs. (N.m) |
|---|---|
| Axle Shaft Bolt | |
| 8 mm | 31 (42) |
| 10 mm | 59 (80) |
| Clamping Sleeve Allen Bolt | 55 (75) |
| Clutch Cover Bolt | 18 (25) |
| Double Mass Flywheel-To-Crankshaft Bolt | 63 (85) |
| Drive Plate-To-Crankshaft Bolt | 66 (90) |
| Engine Mount Bolt | 63 (85) |
| Engine-To-Transmission Bolts | 32 (45) |
| Flywheel-To-Crankshaft Bolt | 66 (90) |
| Oil Line Nut | [1] 59 (80) |
| Oil Return Line On Left Crankcase Half | 89 (120) |
| Oil Supply Line On Right Crankcase Half | 66 (90) |
| Stabilizer Bar Mounting Bolt | 34 (46) |
| Transmission Crossmember-To-Chassis Bolt | 34 (46) |
| Transmission-To-Chassis Bolt | [2] 63 (85) |
| | **INCH Lbs. (N.m)** |
| Fuel Distribution Line Nut | 106 (12) |

[1] – Located in right rear wheelwell.

[2] – These 2 bolts are accessible through small opening from inside vehicle.

# 1990-91 DRIVE AXLES
# AWD Front Axle Shafts

**911 Carrera 4**

## DESCRIPTION & OPERATION

Front axle shafts transfer power from front differential to front wheels. All axle shafts consist of a shaft with a flexible Constant Velocity (CV) joint at each end. Inner tripod-type CV joint is bolted to differential. Outer CV joint is splined to hub assembly and secured by axle shaft nut.

Inner and outer CV joints are enclosed by CV joint boots. Boots maintain lubrication in the joint and prevent contaminants from entering joint. Boots must be replaced when signs of leakage or cracks are present. Inner tripod-type CV joint can be repaired, but outer CV joint and shaft must be replaced as an assembly.

## TROUBLE SHOOTING

***NOTE: See TROUBLE SHOOTING article in GENERAL INFORMATION.***

## REMOVAL, DISASSEMBLY, REASSEMBLY & INSTALLATION

### FRONT AXLE SHAFTS

**Removal** – Raise and support vehicle. Remove undercover. Remove wheel. Remove axle shaft nut. Remove inner CV joint bolts. Remove axle shaft from steering knuckle. If necessary, use appropriate puller to remove axle shaft from steering knuckle. DO NOT damage axle shaft threads. Remove axle shaft.

***CAUTION: DO NOT damage toothed wheel on outer CV Joint.***

**Disassembly** – **1)** Straighten bent end of boot clamps on inner boot of axle shaft. *See Fig. 1*. Loosen clamps with screwdriver or pliers, taking care not to damage boot. Slide boot from larger end of inboard joint. Remove CV joint cover and snap ring.

**2)** Wrap axle shaft splines with tape. Remove inboard joint, boot and clamps from shaft assembly. Remove outer boot clamps in same manner as previously described in step **1)**. Remove outer boot from inboard joint end of axle shaft.

***NOTE: DO NOT disassembly outboard CV joint. If outboard CV joint is defective, replace axle shaft as an assembly.***

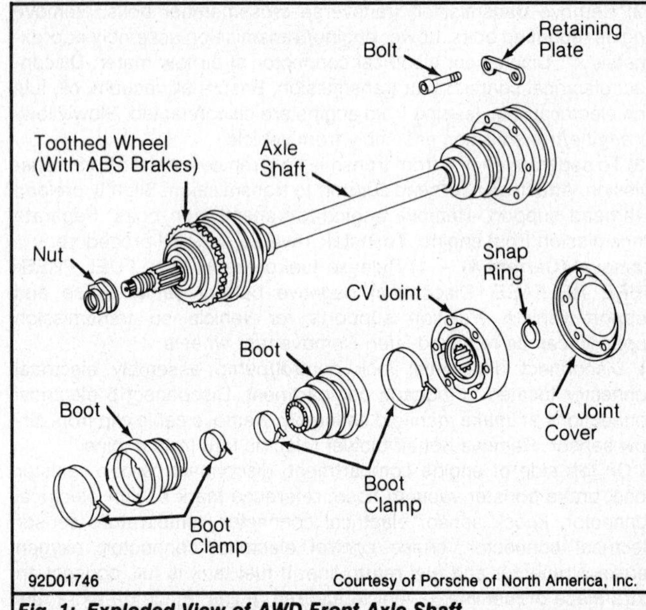


***Fig. 1: Exploded View of AWD Front Axle Shaft***

**Reassembly & Installation** – Clean all components and inspect for wear and/or damage. To reassemble axle shaft, reverse disassembly procedure. Pack CV boots with new grease supplied with boot kit. To complete installation, reverse removal procedure. Tighten nuts and bolts to specification. See TORQUE SPECIFICATIONS table.

## TORQUE SPECIFICATIONS

***TORQUE SPECIFICATIONS***

| Application | Ft. Lbs. (N.m) |
|---|---|
| Axle Shaft Hub Nut | 340 (460) |
| Axle Shaft-To-Differential Bolt | 31 (42) |
| Wheel Lug Nut | 96 (130) |

# 1990-91 DRIVE AXLES
# RWD Axle Shafts

## 911 Carrera 2/4

## DESCRIPTION & OPERATION

Rear axle shafts transfer power from transaxle to rear wheels. All axle shafts consist of a shaft with a flexible Constant Velocity (CV) joint at each end. Inner tripod-type CV joint is bolted to transaxle. Outer CV joint is splined to hub assembly and secured by axle shaft nut.

Inner and outer CV joints are enclosed by CV joint boots. Boots maintain lubrication in the joint and prevent contaminants from entering joint. Boots must be replaced when signs of leakage or cracks are present. Inner tripod-type CV joint can be repaired, but outer CV joint and shaft must be replaced as an assembly.

## TROUBLE SHOOTING

***NOTE: See TROUBLE SHOOTING in GENERAL INFORMATION.***

## REMOVAL, DISASSEMBLY, REASSEMBLY & INSTALLATION

### DRIVE AXLE SHAFTS

**Removal – 1)** Raise and support vehicle. Remove rear wheel. Remove axle shaft nut. Remove engine and transaxle covers from underside of vehicle. Remove inner CV joint bolts. Remove axle shaft from hub assembly.

**2)** If necessary, use appropriate puller to remove axle shaft from hub assembly. DO NOT damage axle shaft threads. Remove axle shaft.

**Disassembly – 1)** Straighten bent end of boot clamps on inner boot of axle shaft. *See Fig. 1*. Carefully loosen clamps with screwdriver or pliers; DO NOT damage boot. Slide boot from larger end of inboard joint. Remove CV joint cover and snap ring.

**2)** Wrap axle shaft splines with tape. Remove inboard joint, boot and clamps from shaft assembly. Remove outer boot clamps in same manner as described in step **1)**. Remove outer boot from inboard joint end of axle shaft.

***NOTE: DO NOT disassembly outboard CV joint. If outboard CV joint is defective, replace axle shaft as an assembly.***

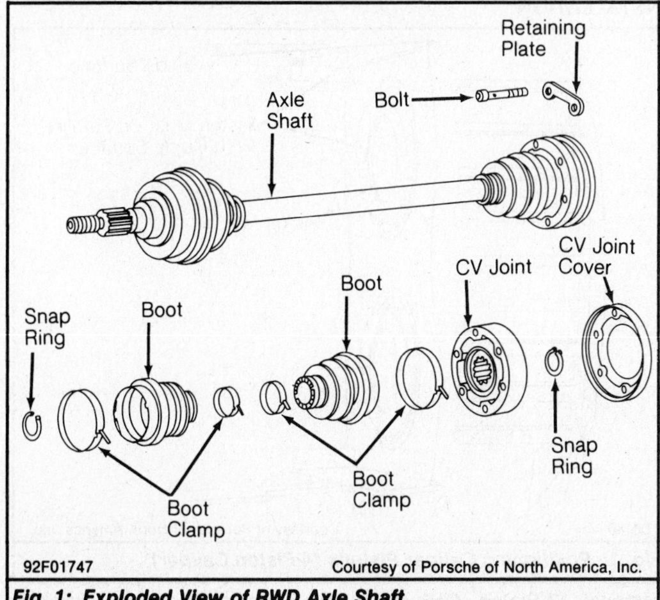


***Fig. 1: Exploded View of RWD Axle Shaft***

**Reassembly & Installation –** Clean all components and inspect for wear and/or damage. To reassemble axle shaft, reverse disassembly procedure. Pack CV boots with new grease supplied with boot kit. To complete installation, reverse removal procedure. Tighten nuts and bolts to specification. See TORQUE SPECIFICATIONS table at end of article.

### REAR HUB ASSEMBLY

**Removal & Disassembly – 1)** Raise and support vehicle. Remove rear wheel. Remove engine and transaxle covers from underside of vehicle. Remove drive axle shaft. See DRIVE AXLE SHAFTS. Disconnect stabilizer bar at stabilizer link.

**2)** Remove brake caliper, and wire caliper out of way. Remove brake rotor. Disconnect emergency brake cable. Remove speed sensor. Disconnect strut from control arm. Remove bolts attaching control arm to vehicle body. Remove control arm assembly. *See Fig. 2*.

**3)** Place control arm in soft-jawed vise. Drive hub out of wheel bearing assembly. Remove wheel bearing retaining plates. Remove wheel bearing assembly from control arm hub.

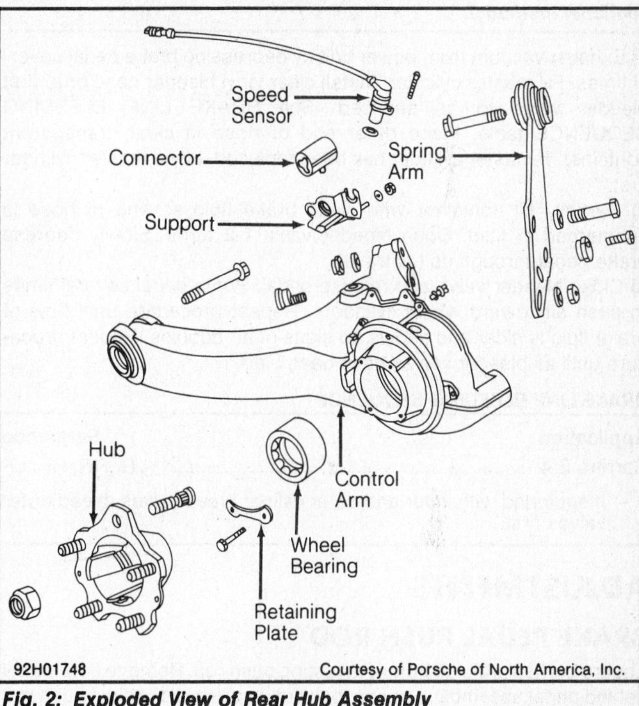


***Fig. 2: Exploded View of Rear Hub Assembly***

**Reassembly & Installation – 1)** Lubricate bearing surface of control arm and wheel bearing assembly. Install wheel bearing assembly into control arm hub. Install retaining plates. Install hub into wheel bearing assembly.

**2)** To complete installation, reverse removal procedure. Tighten nuts and bolts to specification. See TORQUE SPECIFICATIONS table.

## TORQUE SPECIFICATIONS

*TORQUE SPECIFICATIONS*

| Application | Ft. Lbs. (N.m) |
|---|---|
| Axle Shaft Hub Nut | 340 (460) |
| Axle Shaft-To-Transaxle Bolt | |
| 8 mm Bolt | 31 (42) |
| 10 mm Bolt | 59 (80) |
| Brake Caliper Bolt | 60 (82) |
| Control Arm Bolt | 148 (200) |
| Retaining Plate Bolt | 15 (20) |
| Stabilizer Bar-To-Stabilizer Link Nut | 34 (46) |
| Strut-To-Control Arm Bolt | 148 (200) |
| Wheel Lug Nut | 96 (130) |
| | INCH Lbs. (N.m) |
| Speed Sensor Bolt | 89 (10) |

# 1990-91 BRAKES
# Disc

## 911 Carrera 2/4

## DESCRIPTION

The brake system is hydraulically operated using a tandem master cylinder and power brake unit. All models are equipped with 4-wheel disc brakes. Rear drum parking brake is cable activated. Carrera 2 models are equipped with 4-piston calipers on front and 2-piston calipers on rear. Carrera 4 models are equipped with 4-piston calipers front and rear. On all vehicles, front and rear brake pads are monitored for wear.

## BLEEDING BRAKE SYSTEM

### BLEEDING PROCEDURES

***NOTE: Bleeding anti-lock brake portion of system, requires ABS Tester (9288). Conventional part of brake system can be bled using conventional methods.***

**1)** Exhaust vacuum from power unit by depressing brake pedal several times. Fill master cylinder. Install clear vinyl bleeder hose onto first bleeder valve to be serviced. See BRAKE LINE BLEEDING SEQUENCE table. Place other end of hose in clean transparent container. If master cylinder has been replaced, bleed master cylinder first.
**2)** Partially fill container with clean brake fluid so end of hose is submerged in fluid. Open bleeder valve 1-2 turns. Slowly depress brake pedal through its full travel.
**3)** Close bleeder valve and release pedal. Pump pedal several times to push air toward wheel cylinders. Repeat procedure until flow of brake fluid is clear and shows no signs of air bubbles. Repeat procedure until all bleeder valves have been bled.

***BRAKE LINE BLEEDING SEQUENCE***

| Application | Sequence |
|---|---|
| Carrera 2/4 | [1] LR, RR, RF, LF |

[1] - If equipped with inner and outer caliper bleed valves, bleed outer valves first.

## ADJUSTMENTS

### BRAKE PEDAL PUSH ROD

Ensure brakes are bled before adjusting push rod. Remove floor panel behind pedal assembly. Loosen lock nut on push rod. Adjust push rod length so brake pedal travels approximately .31" (8 mm) before brake application begins. Operate brake pedal by hand to check for proper travel. Push rod is adjusted correctly when brake pedal height is same as clutch pedal plus or minus .12" (3 mm). Check pedal height with no pressure applied to brake or clutch pedals.

### PARKING BRAKE

***NOTE: Parking brake requires adjustment if brake lever can be pulled up with medium force more than 4 teeth without brake application.***

**1)** Raise and support vehicle. Remove rear wheels. Release parking brake lever. Push caliper pistons and pads into caliper to allow rotor to turn freely. Remove access cover behind parking brake lever.
**2)** Loosen parking brake cable lock nuts until cable is slacked. Working through access hole, hand turn star wheel adjuster until rotor cannot be turned.
**3)** Turn star wheel adjuster until rotor can be turned easily again. Turn star wheel adjuster 2 more catches in loosing direction. Pull up parking brake lever 2 teeth. Tighten parking brake cable lock nuts until rotors are hard to turn by hand. Release parking brake lever. Ensure rotors are turn easily by hand.

### STOPLIGHT SWITCH

Stoplights should light when brake pedal travels .24-.63" (6-16 mm). Measure pedal travel from middle of brake pedal. Adjust stoplight switch as necessary so stoplights illuminate within specified pedal travel. If stoplight switch adjustment is not enough, ensure brake pedal push rod is adjusted properly.

## REMOVAL & INSTALLATION

### DISC BRAKE PADS

***NOTE: Mark disc pads and calipers before removal. If disc pads are to be reused, they must be installed in original position. If only one pad (front or rear) needs replacing, all disc pads on same axle must be replaced.***

**Removal (4-Piston Calipers)** – Raise and support vehicle. Remove wheel. Compress cross spring in middle, and remove spring from holder. DO NOT damage spring holder during spring removal. Pull out brake pad wear indicator contact. Using a putty knife or similar tool, separate damping plates from back of brake pads. *See Fig. 4*. Remove disc pads using Hazet Pad Remover (1966-2).

***CAUTION: If fluid level is too high in reservoir, overflow will result when pistons are pushed back into calipers.***

**Installation (4-Piston Calipers) – 1)** Push piston back into caliper using a wooden block. Clean all parts with alcohol.

***NOTE: Brake pad wear indicators can be reused if brake pads are replaced when pad thickness is .098" (2.5 mm). Brake pad wear indicators must be replaced if brake pads are replaced when pad thickness is .079" (2.0 mm).***

**2)** Inspect all parts for damage or wear. If brake pads were worn enough to illuminate brake pad wear indicator light, replace brake pad wear indicator assembly. If only plastic part of brake pad wear indicator is worn and brake pad wear indicator light did not illuminate, brake pad wear indicator may be reused.
**3)** Ensure pistons are parallel to guide surface. *See Fig. 1*. Install NEW damping plates. *See Fig. 4*. Remove protective sheet on damping plates prior to installation. DO NOT lubricate brake pad backplates. Install remaining parts in reverse order of removal, replacing parts as necessary. See BREAKING-IN BRAKE PADS under REMOVAL & INSTALLATION.

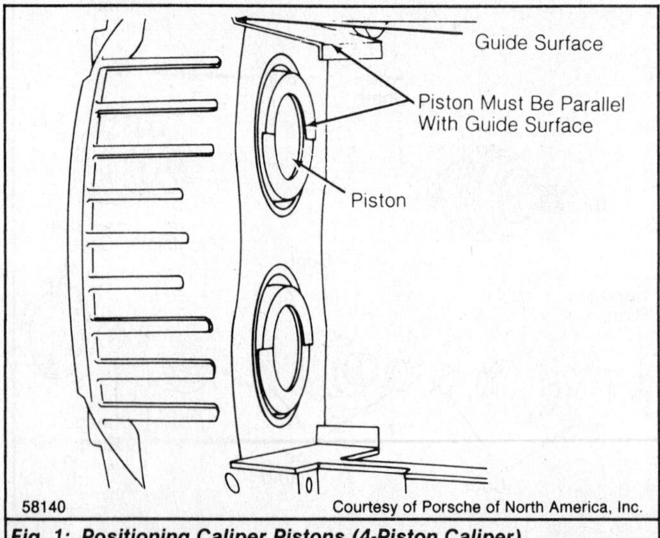


***Fig. 1: Positioning Caliper Pistons (4-Piston Caliper)***

**Removal (2-Piston Calipers) – 1)** Raise and support vehicle. Remove wheel. Remove retaining pin clips. Using a mandrel, remove retaining pins and spreader spring. Pull out brake pad wear indicator contact. Using a putty knife or similar tool, separate damping plates from back of brake pads. *See Fig. 5*.
**2)** Remove inner disc pad using Hazet Pad Remover (1966-2). Tab on sliding caliper frame guides outside disc pad. Push frame out away from rotor, and remove outer disc pad.

# 1990-91 BRAKES
# Disc (Cont.)

***CAUTION: If fluid level is too high in reservoir, overflow will result when pistons are pushed back into calipers.***

**Installation (2-Piston Calipers) – 1)** Push piston back into caliper using a wooden block. Clean all parts with alcohol.

***NOTE: Brake pad wear indicators can be reused if brake pads are replaced when pad thickness is .098" (2.5 mm). Brake pad wear indicators must be replaced if brake pads are replaced when pad thickness is .079" (2.0 mm).***

**2)** Inspect all parts for damage or wear. If brake pads were worn enough to illuminate brake pad wear indicator light, replace brake pad wear indicator assembly. If only plastic part of brake pad wear indicator is worn and brake pad wear indicator light did not illuminate, brake pad wear indicator may be reused.
**3)** Ensure stepped-down piston pressure surface is positioned at 20 degrees, using 20 Degree Gauge (P84). *See Fig. 2*. Install NEW damping plates. *See Fig. 5*. Remove protective sheet on damping plates prior to installation. DO NOT lubricate brake pad backplates. Install remaining parts in reverse order of removal, replacing parts as necessary. See BREAKING-IN BRAKE PADS under REMOVAL & INSTALLATION.

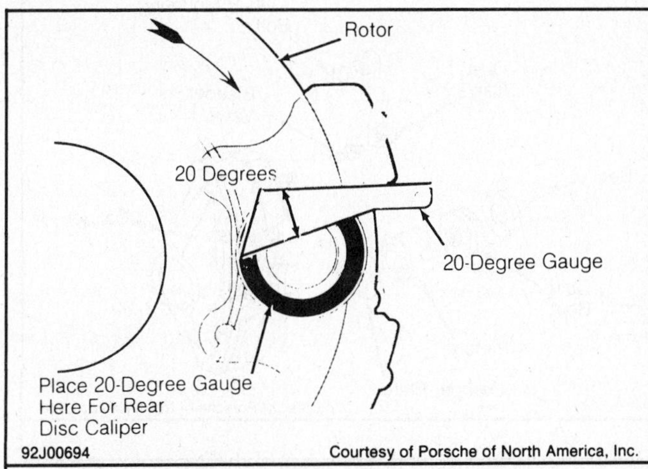


***Fig. 2: Positioning Caliper Piston (2-Piston Calipers)***

## BREAKING-IN BRAKE PADS

New brake pads reach their most favorable friction and wear value after 125 miles (200 km) of breaking-in time. Only then will brake pad fit correctly on disc. Initially high pedal force will go back to normal value and possible screeching should stop. Extreme braking during break-in time should be limited only to emergency situations.

## DISC BRAKE CALIPER

**Removal & Installation –** Raise and support vehicle. Remove brake pads. See DISC BRAKE PADS under REMOVAL & INSTALLATION. Disconnect and plug hydraulic line. Remove caliper. To install, reverse removal procedure. Bleed hydraulic system. See BLEEDING BRAKE SYSTEM.

## DISC BRAKE ROTOR

***CAUTION: Rotors must be installed in original position due to cooling holes and internal ventilation channels. These holes and channels are different for right and left sides.***

**Removal & Installation –** Remove brake caliper, and wire caliper out of way. DO NOT disconnect brake line unless caliper is being replaced. Mark rotor and hub for reassembly reference. Remove rotor-to-hub screws. Separate rotor from hub. To install, reverse removal procedure.

## PARKING BRAKE SHOES

**Removal –** Raise and support vehicle. Remove wheel. Remove wheel spacer (if equipped). Working through access hole, hand turn star wheel adjuster in "loosen" direction. Remove caliper. See DISC BRAKE CALIPER under REMOVAL & INSTALLATION. Remove brake rotor. See DISC BRAKE ROTOR under REMOVAL & INSTALLATION. Remove springs, adjuster and upper return spring. Remove parking brake shoes. *See Fig. 3*.
**Installation –** Lightly coat adjuster, operating lever shaft and sliding surfaces of parking brake shoes with grease. To install, reverse removal procedure. Ensure hooks of springs engage correctly in web of brake backing plate.

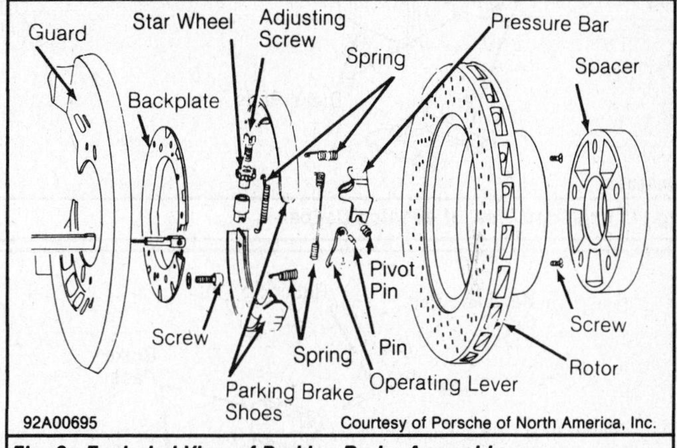


***Fig. 3: Exploded View of Parking Brake Assembly***

## MASTER CYLINDER

**Removal & Installation (Carrera 2) –** Raise and support vehicle. Drain brake fluid from reservoir. Remove cover from under front of vehicle to access master cylinder. Disconnect hydraulic lines from master cylinder. Remove master cylinder mounting bolts. Remove master cylinder. To install, reverse removal procedure. Install NEW gaskets and/or "O" rings as necessary. Bleed master cylinder.
**Removal & Installation (Carrera 4) –** Open trunk. Drain brake fluid from reservoir. Disconnect hydraulic lines from master cylinder. Remove master cylinder mounting bolts. Remove master cylinder. To install, reverse removal procedure. Install NEW gaskets and/or "O" rings as necessary. Bleed master cylinder.

## POWER BRAKE UNIT

**Removal (Carrera 2) –** Remove master cylinder. See MASTER CYLINDER under REMOVAL & INSTALLATION. Disconnect vacuum hose from power brake unit. Remove floor panel behind pedal assembly. Remove pin connecting power brake unit operating rod to brake pedal assembly. Remove power brake unit from vehicle.
**Installation (Carrera 2) –** To install, reverse removal procedure. Apply sealer to power brake unit mounting surface and vacuum line connections. Install NEW gaskets and/or "O" rings as necessary. Adjust pedal height. See BRAKE PEDAL PUSH ROD under ADJUSTMENTS. Check system for leaks.

## BRAKE SERVO

**Removal & Installation (Carrera 4) –** Remove master cylinder. See MASTER CYLINDER under REMOVAL & INSTALLATION. Remove floor panel behind pedal assembly. Remove brake pedal to push rod pin. Remove hydraulic lines to brake servo. Remove brake servo mount nuts. Remove brake servo. To install, reverse removal procedure. Install NEW gaskets and/or "O" rings as necessary. Adjust pedal height. See BRAKE PEDAL PUSH ROD under ADJUSTMENTS. Bleed brake system. See BLEEDING BRAKE SYSTEM. Check system for leaks.

# 1990-91 BRAKES
# Disc (Cont.)

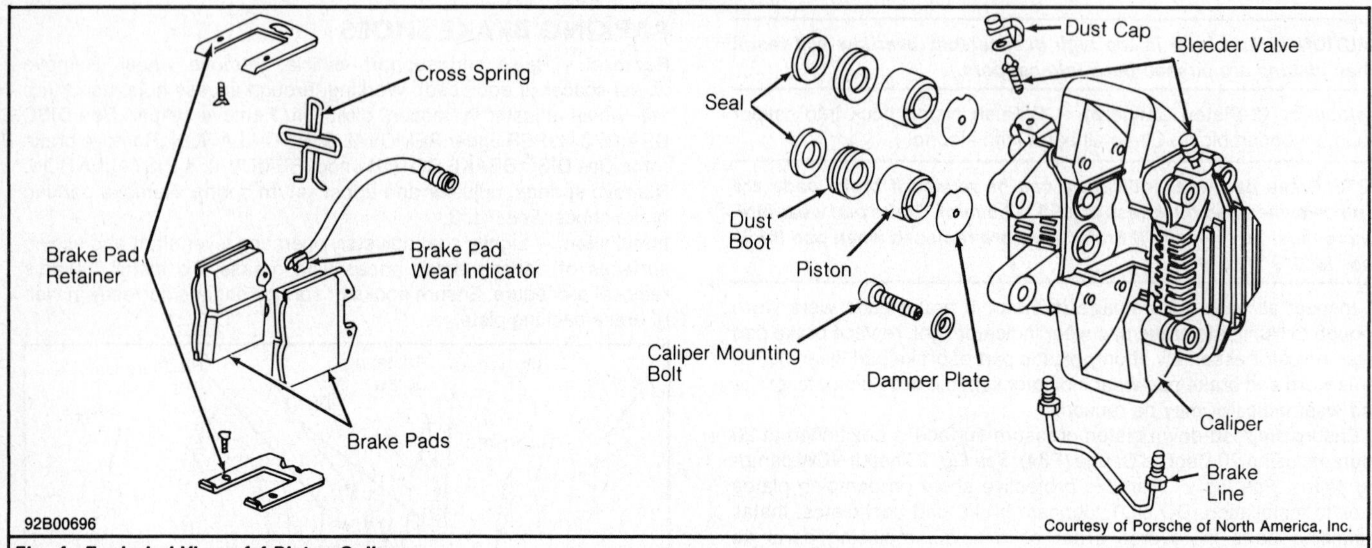


*Fig. 4: Exploded View of 4-Piston Caliper*

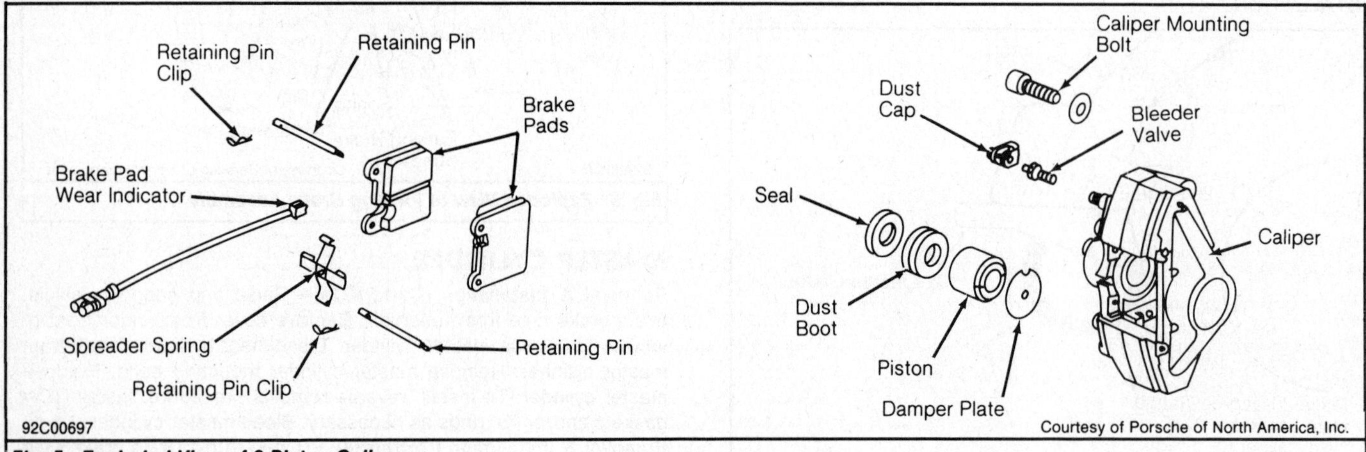


*Fig. 5: Exploded View of 2-Piston Caliper*

## OVERHAUL

***CAUTION: DO NOT separate caliper halves. If "O" ring seals are leaking, replace caliper assembly. When installing caliper pistons, ensure pistons are properly aligned. See Figs. 1 and 2.***

***NOTE: See Figs. 4 and 5 for exploded views of brake calipers. Manufacturer does not recommend overhaul of power brake unit. Replace complete assembly if defective. Overhaul procedures are not available for master cylinder assembly or brake servo.***

## TORQUE SPECIFICATIONS

***TORQUE SPECIFICATIONS***

| Application | Ft. Lbs. (N.m) |
|---|---|
| Caliper Mounting Bolt | 63 (85) |
| Wheel Lug Nut | 96 (130) |
| | **INCH Lbs. (N.m)** |
| Rotor-To-Hub Screw | 44 (5) |

## DISC BRAKE SPECIFICATIONS

***DISC BRAKE SPECIFICATIONS***

| Application | In. (mm) |
|---|---|
| Brake Pad | |
| Original Thickness | |
| Carrera 2 | |
| Front | .51 (13) |
| Rear | .40 (10) |

***DISC BRAKE SPECIFICATIONS (Cont.)***

| Application | In. (mm) |
|---|---|
| Carrera 4 | |
| Front & Rear | .51 (13) |
| Minimum Thickness | .08 (2) |
| Disc Diameter | |
| Front | 11.73 (298) |
| Rear | 11.77 (299) |
| Disc Thickness | |
| New | |
| Front | 1.10 (28) |
| Rear | .94 (24) |
| Minimum After Machining | |
| Front | 1.03 (26.6) |
| Rear | .89 (22.6) |
| Wear Limit | |
| Front | 1.02 (26) |
| Rear | .87 (22) |
| Lateral Runout | |
| Off Car | .002 (.05) |
| On Car | .004 (.10) |
| Parallelism | .002 (.02) |
| Parking Brake Drum Diameter | |
| Standard | 7.09 (180) |
| Wear Limit | 7.13 (181) |
| Parking Brake Liner Thickness | |
| New | .18 (4.5) |
| Wear Limit | .08 (2) |
| Parking Brake Shoe Width | .98 (25) |

# 1990-91 WHEEL ALIGNMENT
# Specifications & Procedures

## 911 Carrera 2/4

***NOTE: Before performing wheel alignment, perform preliminary visual and mechanical inspection of wheels, tires and suspension components. See PRE-ALIGNMENT INSTRUCTIONS in WHEEL ALIGNMENT THEORY & OPERATION article in GENERAL INFORMATION.***

## RIDING HEIGHT ADJUSTMENT

Before adjusting alignment, check riding height. Riding height must be checked with vehicle on level floor and tires properly inflated. Bounce vehicle several times, and allow suspension to settle.

Visually inspect vehicle for abnormal height from front to rear or side to side. Check passenger and luggage compartments for extra-heavy items, and remove if present. If riding height is not within specification, check, repair or replace suspension components.

For front riding height, measure distance "A" from head of cross-member rear body bolt to wheel road contact point. *See Fig. 1*. Measurement should be 6-7" (165-175 mm). For rear riding height, measure distance "B" from body end surface of lower control arm mount on vehicle to wheel road contact point. Measurement should be 10.75-11.00" (270-280 mm).

If body end surface of lower control arm mount on vehicle does not exist, measure distance "C" from lower control arm cast boss surface to wheel road contact point. *See Fig. 1*. Measurement should be 10.25-10.63" (258-268 mm).

Riding height is adjusted by turning adjusting nut located on bottom of each strut assembly. Turn nut clockwise to raise vehicle and counterclockwise to lower vehicle. Riding height between left and right sides of vehicle should vary less than 0.4" (10 mm).

## JACKING & HOISTING

Illustration indicates riding height measuring points. *See Fig. 1*. Illustration also shows areas of underbody and frame which may be used to raise and support vehicle, using either floor jack or hoist.

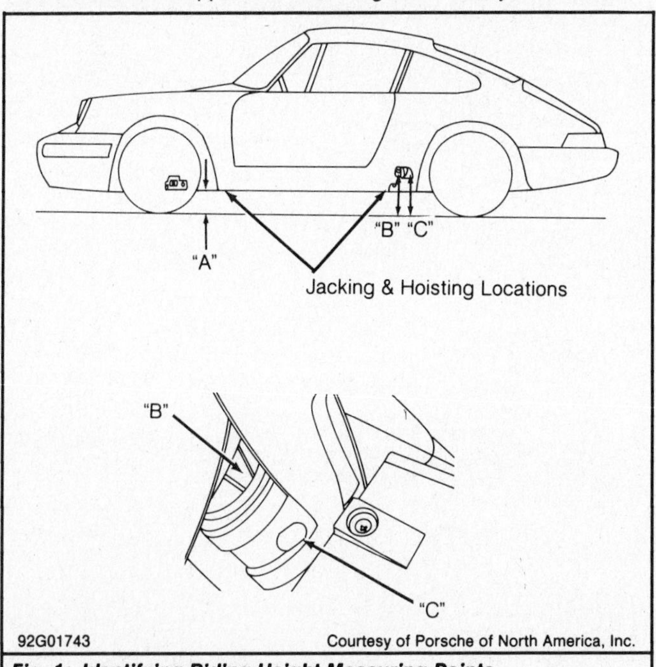


***Fig. 1: Identifying Riding Height Measuring Points & Jacking & Hoisting Locations***

## WHEEL ALIGNMENT PROCEDURES

### CAMBER ADJUSTMENT

**1)** Loosen 2 strut-to-steering knuckle mounting nuts. Turn upper mounting bolt until front camber is set to specification. See WHEEL ALIGNMENT SPECIFICATIONS table at end of article. Tighten strut-to-steering knuckle mounting nuts to specification. See TORQUE SPECIFICATIONS table at end of article.

**2)** To adjust rear camber, remove engine and transaxle covers from underside of vehicle. Loosen 2 spring arm bolts. Loosen camber lock nut, and turn camber eccentric until rear camber is set to specification. See WHEEL ALIGNMENT SPECIFICATIONS table. *See Fig. 2*. Tighten camber lock nut and spring arm bolts to specification. See TORQUE SPECIFICATIONS table.

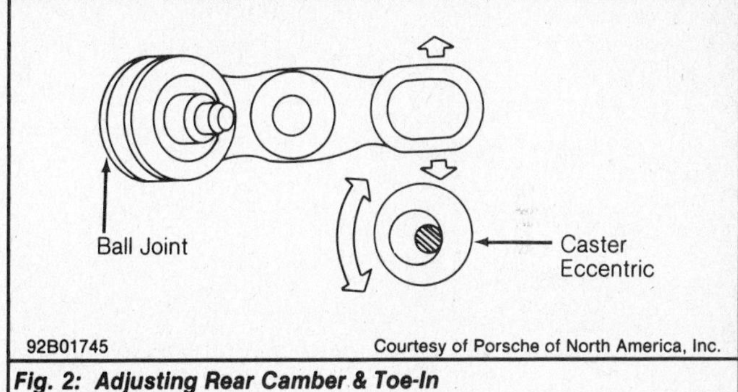


***Fig. 2: Adjusting Rear Camber & Toe-In***

### CASTER ADJUSTMENT

Loosen nut connecting caster eccentric to lower control arm. Rotate caster eccentric until front caster is set to specification. See WHEEL ALIGNMENT SPECIFICATIONS table at end of article. *See Fig. 3*. Tighten caster eccentric nut to specification. See TORQUE SPECIFICATIONS table at end of article.

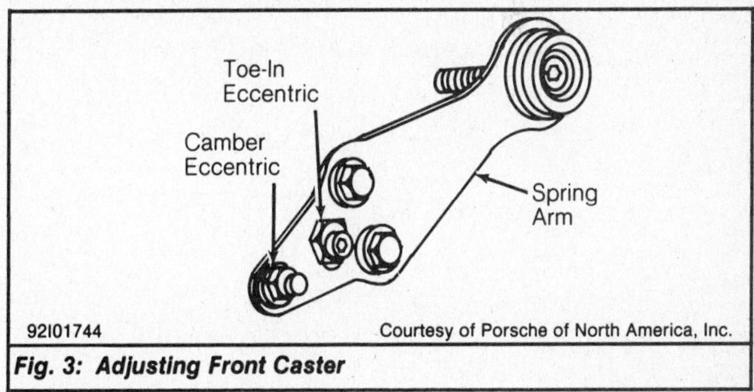


***Fig. 3: Adjusting Front Caster***

### TOE-IN ADJUSTMENT

**1)** Clamp steering wheel in centered position. Loosen tie rod lock nuts and adjust front toe-in by adjusting tie rod end length until toe-in is set to specification.

**2)** To adjust rear toe-in, remove engine and transaxle covers from underside of vehicle. Loosen 2 spring arm bolts. Loosen toe eccentric nut, and turn hexagon screw until rear toe-in is set to specification. See WHEEL ALIGNMENT SPECIFICATIONS table at end of article. *See Fig. 2*. Tighten eccentric nut and spring arm bolts to specification. See TORQUE SPECIFICATIONS table at end of article.

# 1990-91 WHEEL ALIGNMENT Specifications & Procedures (Cont.)

## TORQUE SPECIFICATIONS

*TORQUE SPECIFICATIONS*

| Application | Ft. Lbs. (N.m) |
|---|---|
| Ball Joint Nut | 48 (65) |
| Camber Lock Nut | 148 (200) |
| Caster Eccentric Nut | 34 (46) |
| Spring Arm Bolt | 148 (200) |
| Strut-To-Steering Knuckle Nut | 111 (150) |
| Tie Rod Lock Nut | 33 (45) |
| Toe-In Eccentric Nut | 43 (58) |
| Wheel Lug Nut | 96 (130) |

## WHEEL ALIGNMENT SPECIFICATIONS

*WHEEL ALIGNMENT SPECIFICATIONS*

| Application | Preferred | Range |
|---|---|---|
| **911 Carrera 2** | | |
| Camber [1] | | |
| Front | 0 | -5/32 To 5/32 |
| Rear | -11/32 | -1/2 To -5/32 |
| Caster [1] | 4 13/32 | 4 5/32 To 4 21/32 |
| Toe-In [2] | | |
| Front | 7/32 (5.5) | 5/32 To 1/4 (4 To 6.8) |
| Rear | 1/4 (6.5) | 5/32 To 11/32 (4 To 8.5) |
| Toe-In [1] | | |
| Front | 13/32 | 11/32 To 1/2 |
| Rear | 1/2 | 11/32 To 21/32 |
| **911 Carrera 4** | | |
| Camber [1] | | |
| Front | 0 | -5/32 To 5/32 |
| Rear | -11/32 | -1/2 To -5/32 |
| Caster [1] | 4 5/32 | 3 29/32 To 4 13/32 |
| Toe-In [2] | | |
| Front | 7/32 (5.5) | 5/32 To 1/4 (4 To 6.8) |
| Rear | 1/4 (6.5) | 5/32 To 11/32 (4 To 8.5) |
| Toe-In [1] | | |
| Front | 13/32 | 11/32 To 1/2 |
| Rear | 1/2 | 11/32 To 21/32 |

[1] – Measurement in degrees.

[2] – Measurement in inches (mm).

# 1990-91 SUSPENSION
# Front

## 911 Carrera 2/4

## DESCRIPTION

The independent MacPherson strut-type front suspension features strut assemblies attached to the vehicle body at the top and steering knuckle at bottom. Strut assemblies include an adjuster ring to adjust vehicle height. Steering knuckle is attached to a ball joint.

Ball joint is connected to lower control arm, which pivots on suspension bracket connected to body. A stabilizer bar is attached to stabilizer arms and suspension brackets. *See Fig. 1.*

## ADJUSTMENTS & INSPECTION

### WHEEL ALIGNMENT SPECIFICATIONS & PROCEDURES

***NOTE: See SPECIFICATIONS & PROCEDURES article in WHEEL ALIGNMENT.***

### WHEEL BEARING

Wheel bearing is not adjustable. Tighten hub nut to specification. If wheel bearing play exists, replace wheel bearing.

### RIDING HEIGHT

For riding height information, see RIDING HEIGHT ADJUSTMENT in SPECIFICATIONS & PROCEDURES article in WHEEL ALIGNMENT.

### BALL JOINT CHECKING

Check lower ball joints for any signs of unusual wear, damage or excessive play. Wear limits are not available from manufacturer.

## REMOVAL & INSTALLATION

### COIL SPRING & STRUT ASSEMBLY

**Removal – 1)** Raise and support vehicle. Remove wheel. Remove brake caliper and wire out of way. Remove rotor. Mark upper strut position for installation reference. Remove nuts attaching strut to vehicle body. Remove strut-to-steering knuckle nuts and bolts and remove strut assembly.

**2)** Secure strut in soft-jawed vise. Loosen but DO NOT remove piston rod nut. Install spring compressor on coil spring and compress spring. Remove piston rod nut. Remove mount support, spacer, spring upper support, rubber cushion, boot and coil spring. Remove strut adjuster ring and spring lower support (if necessary). *See Fig. 1.*

**3)** Inspect strut for leaks. If leak is discovered, replace strut. There should be no variation of pressure when pushing down or pulling up on piston rod.

**Installation –** To install, reverse removal procedure. Tighten nuts and bolts to specification. See TORQUE SPECIFICATIONS table at end of article. Lower vehicle and check riding height and wheel alignment. See SPECIFICATIONS & PROCEDURES article in WHEEL ALIGNMENT.

### HUB & KNUCKLE ASSEMBLY

***NOTE: Always replace wheel bearing assembly when hub has been removed.***

**Removal – 1)** Raise and support vehicle. Remove undercover. Remove wheel. Remove axle shaft nut. Remove brake caliper and wire out of way. Remove rotor. On AWD vehicles, remove axle shaft. See AWD FRONT AXLE SHAFTS article in DRIVE AXLES.

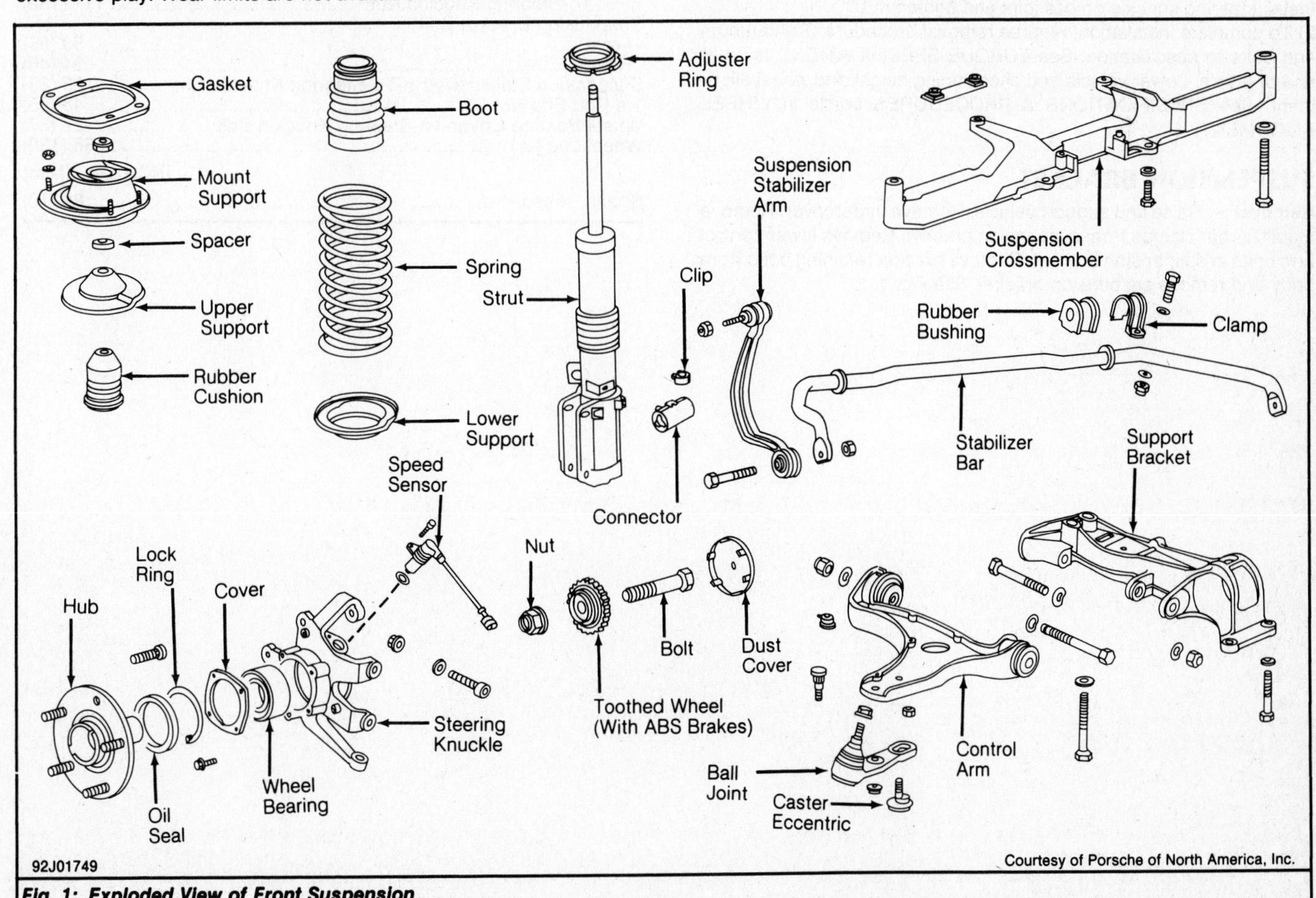


*Fig. 1: Exploded View of Front Suspension*

# 1990-91 SUSPENSION
# Front (Cont.)

**2)** On 2WD vehicles, remove dust cover, axle shaft bolt and toothed wheel from rear of steering knuckle. On all vehicles, remove tie rod nut and separate tie rod from steering knuckle. Remove ball joint nut and separate ball joint from steering knuckle. Remove speed sensor from steering knuckle. *See Fig. 1.*
**3)** Remove suspension stabilizer arm from steering knuckle. Remove strut-to-steering knuckle nuts and bolts. Remove steering knuckle from vehicle. Secure steering knuckle in a soft-jawed vise. Drive out hub assembly from wheel bearing assembly. Remove oil seal and lock ring (if equipped).
**4)** Remove wheel bearing cover bolts (if equipped) and remove wheel bearing assembly from steering knuckle. If wheel bearing assembly is pressed into steering knuckle, drive out wheel bearing assembly from steering knuckle.
**Installation** – To install, reverse removal procedure. Tighten nuts and bolts to specification. See TORQUE SPECIFICATIONS table at end of article. Lower vehicle and check riding height and wheel alignment. See SPECIFICATIONS & PROCEDURES article in WHEEL ALIGNMENT.

## LOWER CONTROL ARM & BALL JOINT

**Removal – 1)** Raise and support vehicle. Remove undercover. Remove wheel. Remove ball joint nut at steering knuckle. Separate ball joint from steering knuckle.
**2)** Remove bolts retaining lower control arm at suspension bracket. *See Fig. 1.* Remove lower control arm from vehicle. Secure control arm in soft-jawed vise.
**3)** Remove bolts attaching ball joint to lower control arm. Remove ball joint from control arm. Check sealing bellows on ball joint for damage or cracks and replace as necessary.
**Installation – 1)** Install ball joint in control arm. Place control arm in proper position in vehicle and tighten retaining bolts (front to rear). Install steering knuckle on ball joint and tighten nut.
**2)** To complete installation, reverse removal procedure. Tighten nuts and bolts to specification. See TORQUE SPECIFICATIONS table at end of article. Lower vehicle and check riding height and wheel alignment. See SPECIFICATIONS & PROCEDURES article in WHEEL ALIGNMENT.

## SUSPENSION BRACKET

**Removal** – Raise and support vehicle. Remove undercover. Remove stabilizer bar clamps from suspension bracket. Remove lower control arm bolts at suspension bracket. Remove bracket retaining bolts from body and remove suspension bracket. *See Fig. 1.*
**Installation** – To install, reverse removal procedure. Tighten nuts and bolts to specification. See TORQUE SPECIFICATIONS table at end of article. Lower vehicle and check riding height and wheel alignment. See SPECIFICATIONS & PROCEDURES article in WHEEL ALIGNMENT.

## STABILIZER BAR

**Removal & Installation – 1)** Raise and support vehicle. Remove undercover. Remove stabilizer bar clamps from suspension brackets. Remove stabilizer bar from suspension stabilizer arm. Remove stabilizer bar from vehicle. *See Fig. 1.*
**2)** Check all rubber bushings for signs of wear and replace if necessary. To install, reverse removal procedure. Tighten nuts and bolts to specification. See TORQUE SPECIFICATIONS table.

## WHEEL BEARING

For removal and installation of wheel bearing, see HUB & KNUCKLE ASSEMBLY under REMOVAL & INSTALLATION.

## TORQUE SPECIFICATIONS

***TORQUE SPECIFICATIONS***

| Application | Ft. Lbs. (N.m) |
|---|---|
| Axle Shaft Hub Nut | 340 (460) |
| Ball Joint Nut | 48 (65) |
| Caliper Mounting Bolt | 63 (85) |
| Control Arm Bolt | |
| Front | 81 (110) |
| Rear | 63 (85) |
| Stabilizer Bar-To-Suspension Bracket Bolt | 17 (23) |
| Stabilizer Bar-To-Suspension Stabilizer Arm Nut | 34 (46) |
| Strut Piston Rod Nut | 59 (80) |
| Strut-To-Body Nut | 17 (23) |
| Strut-To-Steering Knuckle Nut | 111 (150) |
| Suspension Bracket Bolt | |
| Front | 63 (85) |
| Rear | 34 (46) |
| Suspension Stabilizer Arm-To-Steering Knuckle Nut | 26 (35) |
| Tie Rod End Nut | 48 (65) |
| Wheel Bearing Cover-To-Steering Knuckle Bolt | 27 (37) |
| Wheel Lug Nut | 96 (130) |
| | **INCH Lbs. (N.m)** |
| Speed Sensor | 89 (10) |

### 911 Carrera 2/4

## DESCRIPTION

An independent MacPherson strut-type suspension is used. Strut assemblies are attached to vehicle body at top and lower control arm at bottom. Strut assembly includes adjuster ring to adjust vehicle height. Lower control arm is carrier for rear wheel bearing assembly.

Inside mount of lower control arm is attached to spring arm. Spring arm is attached to vehicle body. Outside mount of lower control arm is attached to vehicle body. A stabilizer bar is attached to stabilizer links and vehicle body. *See Fig. 1.*

## ADJUSTMENTS & INSPECTION

### WHEEL ALIGNMENT SPECIFICATIONS & PROCEDURES

***NOTE: See SPECIFICATIONS & PROCEDURES article in WHEEL ALIGNMENT.***

### WHEEL BEARING

Wheel bearing is not adjustable. Tighten hub nut to specification. If wheel bearing play exists, replace wheel bearing.

### RIDING HEIGHT

For riding height information, see RIDING HEIGHT ADJUSTMENT in SPECIFICATIONS & PROCEDURES article in WHEEL ALIGNMENT.

## REMOVAL & INSTALLATION

### COIL SPRING & STRUT ASSEMBLY

**Removal – 1)** Raise and support vehicle. Remove wheel. Remove brake caliper and wire out of way. Remove rotor. Mark upper strut position for installation reference. Remove nuts attaching strut to vehicle body. Remove strut bolt from lower control arm and remove strut assembly.

**2)** Secure strut in soft-jawed vise. Loosen but DO NOT remove piston rod nut. Install spring compressor on coil spring and compress spring. Remove piston rod nut. Remove strut mounting, mount support, protective tube, support ring, rubber cushion and coil spring. Remove stop washer, support cover, strut adjuster ring and adjuster sleeve. *See Fig. 1.*

**3)** Inspect strut for leaks. If leak is discovered, replace strut. There should be no variation of pressure when pushing down or pulling up on piston rod.

**Installation –** To install, reverse removal procedure. Tighten nuts and bolts to specification. See TORQUE SPECIFICATIONS table at end of article. Lower vehicle and check riding height and wheel alignment. See SPECIFICATIONS & PROCEDURES article in WHEEL ALIGNMENT.

### LOWER CONTROL ARM & HUB ASSEMBLY

**Removal & Disassembly – 1)** Raise and support vehicle. Remove rear wheel. Remove engine and transaxle covers from underside of vehicle. Remove drive axle shaft. See RWD AXLE SHAFTS article in DRIVE AXLES. Disconnect stabilizer bar at stabilizer link.

**2)** Remove brake caliper and wire out of way. Remove brake rotor. Disconnect emergency brake cable. Remove speed sensor. Disconnect strut from control arm. Remove bolts attaching control arm to vehicle body. Remove control arm assembly. *See Fig. 1.*

**3)** Place control arm in soft-jawed vise. Drive hub out of wheel bearing assembly. Remove wheel bearing retaining plates. Remove wheel bearing assembly from control arm hub.

**Reassembly & Installation – 1)** Lubricate bearing surface of control arm and wheel bearing assembly. Install wheel bearing assembly into control arm hub. Install retaining plates. Install hub into wheel bearing assembly.

**2)** To complete installation, reverse removal procedure. Tighten nuts and bolts to specification. See TORQUE SPECIFICATIONS table.

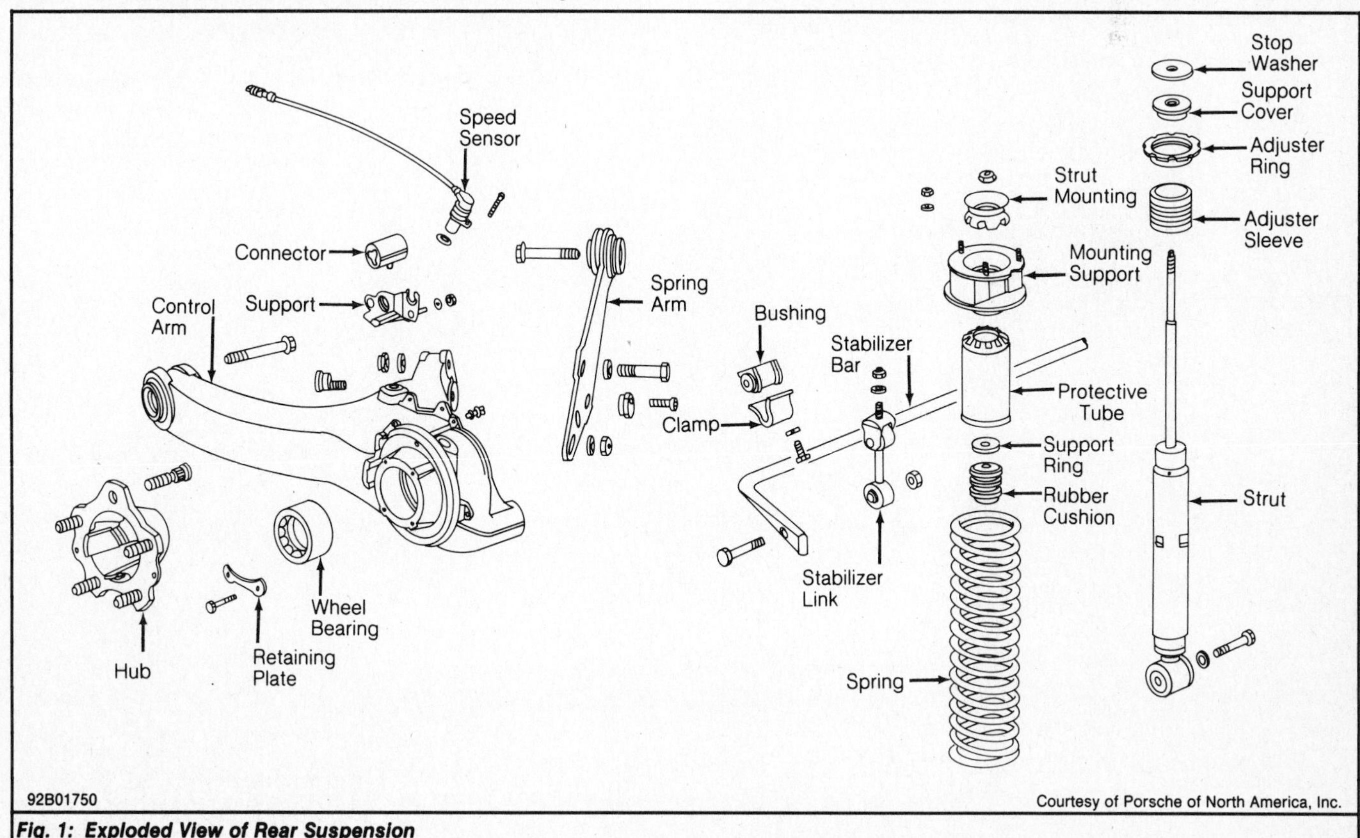


***Fig. 1: Exploded View of Rear Suspension***

# 1990-91 SUSPENSION
# Rear (Cont.)

## STABILIZER BAR

**Removal & Installation – 1)** Raise and support vehicle. Remove stabilizer bar clamps from vehicle body. Remove stabilizer bar from stabilizer links. *See Fig. 1.* Remove stabilizer bar from vehicle.

**2)** Check all rubber bushings for signs of wear and replace if necessary. To install, reverse removal procedure. Tighten nuts and bolts to specification. See TORQUE SPECIFICATIONS table.

## WHEEL BEARING

For removal and installation of wheel bearing, see LOWER CONTROL ARM & HUB ASSEMBLY.

## TORQUE SPECIFICATIONS

***TORQUE SPECIFICATIONS***

| Application | Ft. Lbs. (N.m) |
|---|---|
| Axle Shaft Hub Nut | 340 (460) |
| Axle Shaft-To-Transaxle Bolt | |
| 8 mm | 31 (42) |
| 10 mm | 60 (82) |
| Caliper Mounting Bolt | 60 (82) |
| Control Arm Bolt | 148 (200) |
| Stabilizer Bar-To-Body Bolt | 17 (23) |
| Stabilizer Bar-To-Stabilizer Link Nut | 34 (46) |
| Strut-To-Body Nut | 18 (25) |
| Strut-To-Control Arm Bolt | 148 (200) |
| Wheel Lug Nut | 96 (130) |
| | **INCH Lbs. (N.m)** |
| Speed Sensor Bolt | 89 (10) |

# 1990-91 STEERING
# Steering Columns

### 911 Carrera 2/4

## DESCRIPTION & OPERATION

Steering column is designed to be a energy-absorbing unit. A flexible joint and "U" joint connect steering column to steering gear. Cruise control, turn signal/headlight and wiper/washer switches are mounted on steering column. Switches can be serviced by removing steering wheel and steering column trim panel.

***WARNING: Vehicles are equipped with Supplemental Restraint System (SRS). Use extreme caution when servicing steering column. Air bag could deploy. Before any repairs are performed, disconnect and shield battery negative cable. Wait about 10 minutes to allow system to electrically discharge before attempting any repairs.***

## DISABLING & ACTIVATING AIR BAG SYSTEM

***WARNING: Wait about 10 minutes after disabling air bag system before servicing. Air bag system voltage is maintained for about 10 minutes after system is disabled. Servicing system before the 10-minute period may cause accidental air bag deployment and possible personal injury.***

To disable air bag system, turn ignition off. Disconnect and shield negative battery cable. To activate air bag system, reconnect negative battery cable. Turn ignition switch to ON position. Observe AIR BAG indicator light.

## REMOVAL & INSTALLATION

***WARNING: Vehicle is equipped with Supplemental Restraint System (SRS). Before working on steering column components, disable air bag system. See DISABLING & ACTIVATING AIR BAG SYSTEM.***

### STEERING WHEEL & HORN PAD

**Removal - 1)** Place wheels in straight-ahead position. Disable air bag system. See DISABLING & ACTIVATING AIR BAG SYSTEM. Remove Torx screws securing air bag module to steering wheel.

**2)** Disconnect air bag electrical connector and remove air bag module from steering wheel. *See Fig. 1*. Set air bag module aside with padded side facing upward. Remove steering wheel nut and spring washer. Mark position of steering wheel to steering shaft for installation reference. Use appropriate puller to remove steering wheel.

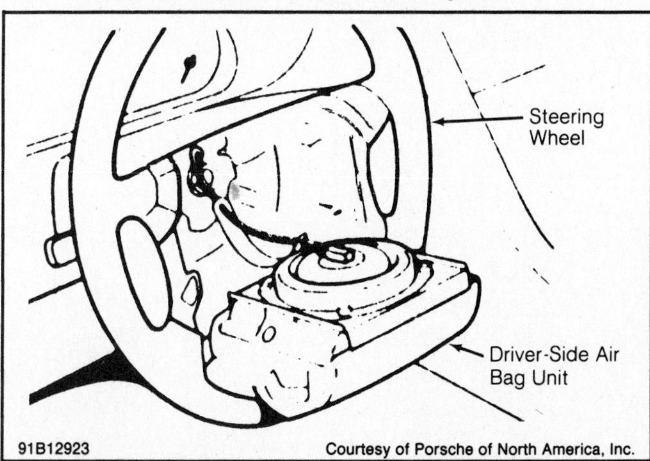


***Fig. 1: Removing Air Bag Unit***

**Installation - 1)** Align steering wheel to steering shaft. Ensure electrical wires are not pinched on installation of steering wheel. Install spring washer and nut.

**2)** Tighten nut to specification. See TORQUE SPECIFICATIONS table at end of article. To complete installation, reverse removal procedure. Install NEW Torx screws. Check horn operation. Activate air bag system and ensure system is operating properly. See DISABLING & ACTIVATING AIR BAG SYSTEM.

### COMBINATION SWITCH

**Removal - 1)** Ensure front wheels are in straight-ahead position. Disable air bag system. See DISABLING & ACTIVATING AIR BAG SYSTEM. Remove steering wheel. See STEERING WHEEL & HORN PAD under REMOVAL & INSTALLATION. Remove steering column trim panel.

**2)** Disconnect contact unit electrical connectors. Remove screws securing contact unit to combination switch and remove contact unit. *See Fig. 2*. Disconnect combination switch electrical connectors and remove combination switch from steering column.

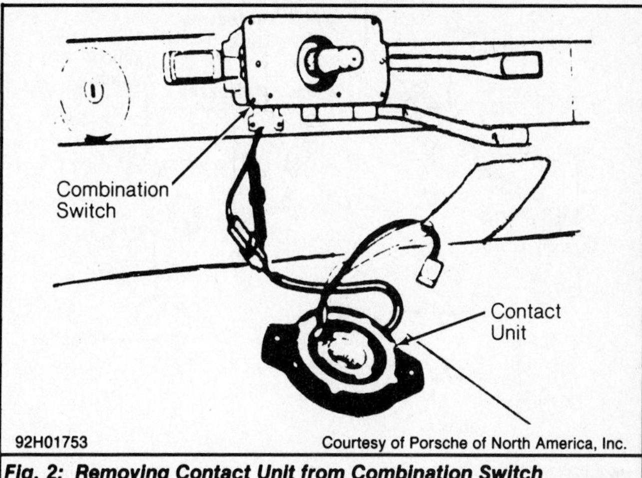


***Fig. 2: Removing Contact Unit from Combination Switch***

**Installation -** To install, reverse removal procedure. To center contact unit, move unit approximately 4 1/2 turns from left or right final stop before installation. Ensure arrows on contact unit are aligned. Tighten steering wheel nut to specification. See TORQUE SPECIFICATIONS table at end of article. Activate air bag system and ensure system is working properly. See DISABLING & ACTIVATING AIR BAG SYSTEM.

### IGNITION SWITCH

**Removal & Installation - 1)** Disable air bag system. See DISABLING & ACTIVATING AIR BAG SYSTEM. Remove ignition switch cover and washer. Remove reinforcement plate bolts. Remove light switch knob. Remove dash trim cover at ignition switch. Unplug ignition switch electrical connector.

**2)** Remove bolts attaching protective tube to dash. Disengage ignition switch from steering shaft. Remove ignition switch from protective tube and dash. *See Fig. 3*. To install, reverse removal procedure.

**3)** Install NEW bolts attaching reinforcement plate and protective tube. Activate air bag system and ensure system is working properly. See DISABLING & ACTIVATING AIR BAG SYSTEM.

### STEERING COLUMN

***CAUTION: Applying excessive pressure or causing impact to mainshaft during service, may cause the column to collapse.***

**Removal - 1)** Disable air bag system. See DISABLING & ACTIVATING AIR BAG SYSTEM. Remove steering wheel. See STEERING WHEEL & HORN PAD under REMOVAL & INSTALLATION. Remove floor panel from pedal assembly. Remove steering shaft "U" joint retaining bolt. Remove "U" joint from steering gear. *See Fig. 3*.

# 1990-91 STEERING
## Steering Columns (Cont.)

2) Disengage ignition switch from steering shaft. Remove protective tube clamp. Remove bolts attaching protective tube to dash. Remove protective tube from ignition switch. Ensure all wire connections are disconnected. Remove steering column assembly from vehicle.

**Installation** – To install, reverse removal procedure. Ensure ignition switch operates properly. Install NEW bolts attaching protective tube and reinforcement plate. Activate air bag system and ensure system is working properly. See DISABLING & ACTIVATING AIR BAG SYSTEM.

## OVERHAUL

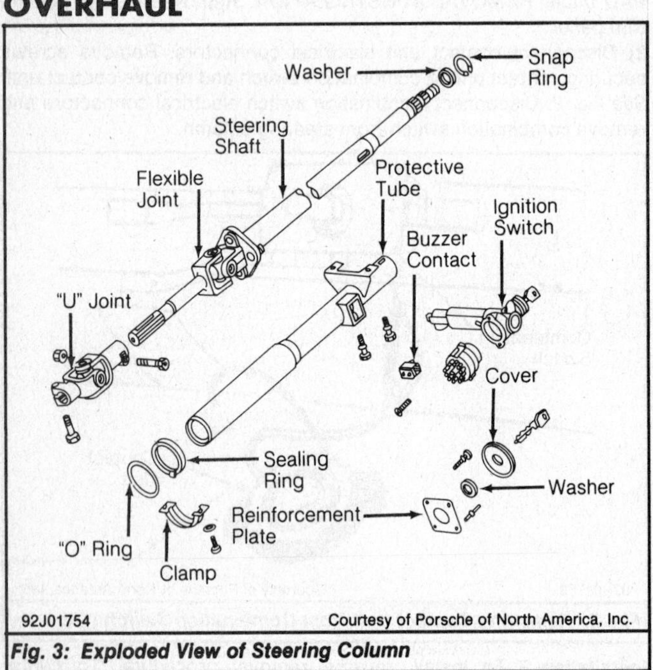


***Fig. 3: Exploded View of Steering Column***

## TORQUE SPECIFICATIONS

***TORQUE SPECIFICATIONS***

| Application | Ft. Lbs. (N.m) |
|---|---|
| "U" Joint-To-Steering Gear Bolt | 17 (23) |
| Steering Wheel Nut | 33 (45) |
| | **INCH Lbs. (N.m)** |
| Air Bag Module-To-Steering Wheel Screw | 90 (10) |

# 1990-91 STEERING
# Power Rack & Pinion

### 911 Carrera 2/4

## DESCRIPTION

Power steering system consists of a rack and pinion steering gear, steering pump, fluid reservoir and flexible connecting lines. *See Fig. 2.* Rack is protected from dirt by rubber bellows. Pinion and bearing are assembled as one unit and use an adjustable spring-loaded plunger. Tie rods connect steering rack to steering knuckles.

## LUBRICATION

### CAPACITY

Fluid capacity is approximately 1.0 qt. (1.0L).

### FLUID TYPE

Use Dexron-II ATF type fluid.

### FLUID LEVEL CHECK

Check fluid level when fluid is cold with engine off. Remove fluid level gauge from reservoir, and check fluid level. Fluid level should be between MIN and MAX marks on gauge dipstick. Add fluid through dipstick opening as needed, and recheck. DO NOT overfill.

### HYDRAULIC SYSTEM BLEEDING

**1)** To ensure system is filled to maximum capacity after a component has been repaired or replaced, fill reservoir with fluid to MAX mark on gauge dipstick. Start and immediately shut off engine several times. Check fluid level. Fluid level in reservoir will deplete rapidly.
**2)** Ensure reservoir is not drained during this procedure. If fluid level no longer drops when engine is started briefly, start engine, and let engine run at idle. Turn steering wheel rapidly from stop to stop several times so air can escape system.
**3)** DO NOT hold steering wheel to stop longer than 10 seconds. Observe fluid level. If fluid level drops, fill reservoir until fluid level remains constant and air bubbles do not appear in reservoir when steering wheel is turned from stop to stop. With engine off, ensure fluid level is between MIN and MAX marks on gauge dipstick.

## ADJUSTMENTS

### POWER STEERING PUMP BELT

Power steering pump belt tension is not adjustable. Power steering pump is driven by camshaft belt. *See Fig. 1.*

### PINION ROTATING FORCE & RACK SLIDING FORCE

Information is not available from manufacturer.

## TESTING

### HYDRAULIC SYSTEM PRESSURE TEST

**1)** Ensure fluid is at correct level. With engine idling, turn steering wheel to stop and hold for a maximum of 10 seconds. This procedure creates maximum system pressure. DO NOT hold steering wheel to stop longer than 10 seconds.
**2)** Release steering wheel and check system for leaks at steering gear, reservoir, pump and all hose connections. Repeat previous procedure if necessary. Repair as necessary.

### STEERING WHEEL TURNING FORCE

Information is not available from manufacturer.

## REMOVAL & INSTALLATION

### POWER STEERING PUMP

***NOTE: Torque specifications are not available from manufacturer.***

**Removal & Installation – 1)** Power steering pump is located on right side of engine, below air cleaner. Remove air cleaner assembly. Remove pump belt upper cover. *See Fig. 1.* Remove 3 pump gear bolts. Remove pump gear and belt from pump. Remove hoses from pump, and plug hoses to prevent fluid loss.
**2)** Remove nuts attaching pump to top mounting bracket, and remove bracket. Remove nuts attaching pump to rear mounting bracket. Remove power steering pump. To install, reverse removal procedure. Tighten nuts and bolts. Bleed hydraulic system. See HYDRAULIC SYSTEM BLEEDING under LUBRICATION.

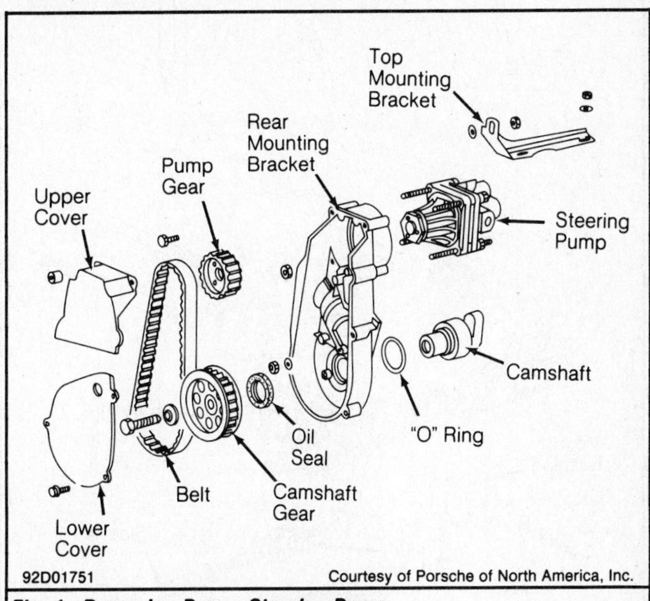


***Fig. 1: Removing Power Steering Pump***

### POWER RACK & PINION

**Removal – 1)** Position wheels in straight-ahead position. Remove floor panel from pedal assembly. Locate steering shaft "U" joint. Mark steering shaft-to-steering gear "U" joint position for installation reference. Remove "U" joint bolt, and disconnect steering shaft "U" joint from steering gear.
**2)** Raise and support vehicle. Remove undercover. Remove wheels. Remove tie rod nuts, and disconnect tie rods from steering knuckles. Mark power steering hoses for installation reference, and remove power steering hoses from steering gear. *See Fig. 2.* Drain fluid into drain pan.
**3)** Remove bolts connecting rack mounting clamps to suspension crossmember. Remove clamps and steering gear from vehicle. Install steering gear in a soft-jawed vise.
**4)** Remove clamps securing bellows to steering gear. Loosen tie rod lock nuts, and remove tie rod, lock nuts, sleeve and bellows from link fork. Replace parts as necessary.
**Installation –** To install, reverse removal procedure. Ensure equal amount of threads are screwed into each end of tie rod sleeve at link fork and tie rod. *See Fig. 2.* Tighten nuts and bolts to specification. See TORQUE SPECIFICATIONS table at end of article. Bleed hydraulic system. See HYDRAULIC SYSTEM BLEEDING under LUBRICATION. Check wheel alignment. See SPECIFICATIONS & PROCEDURES article in WHEEL ALIGNMENT.

# 1990-91 STEERING
# Power Rack & Pinion (Cont.)

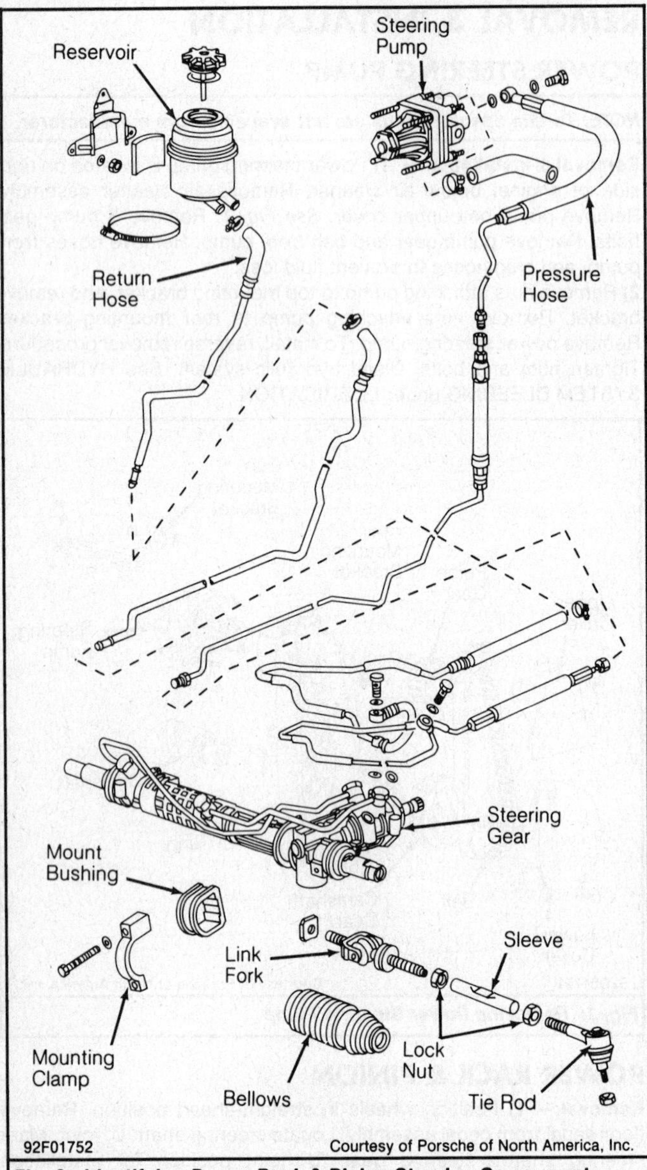


**Fig. 2: Identifying Power Rack & Pinion Steering Components**

## OVERHAUL

***NOTE: Overhaul procedures for rack and pinion assembly and power steering pump are not available from manufacturer. Manufacturer recommends rack and pinion assembly and power steering pump be replaced as an assembly if servicing is required.***

## TORQUE SPECIFICATIONS

***TORQUE SPECIFICATIONS***

| Application | Ft. Lbs. (N.m) |
|---|---|
| Pressure Hose-To-Steering Gear Bolt | 15 (20) |
| Return Hose-To-Steering Gear Bolt | 15 (20) |
| Steering Gear-To-Crossmember Bolt | 33 (45) |
| Tie Rod End Nut | 48 (65) |
| Tie Rod Lock Nut | 33 (45) |
| "U" Joint-To-Steering Gear Bolt | 17 (23) |
| Wheel Lug Nut | 96 (130) |

# 1990-91 TRANSMISSION SERVICING
# Automatic Transmission

## 911 Carrera 2

## IDENTIFICATION

*AUTOMATIC TRANSMISSION APPLICATION*

| Model | Transmission |
|---|---|
| 911 Carrera 2 | A50/01 |

## LUBRICATION

### SERVICE INTERVALS

Check fluid level at every engine oil change. Replace fluid and oil screen every 30,000 miles. Under severe conditions, replace fluid and screen every 15,000 miles.

### CHECKING FLUID LEVEL

**Transmission - 1)** Apply parking brake. Check fluid level with gear selector in Park position and engine idling at normal operating temperature. Raise and support vehicle. Remove vehicle undercover. Observe fluid level at sight tube on right side of transmission.

**2)** Fluid level should be between MIN and MAX level in sight tube. If level is not within specification, lower vehicle and turn engine off. Raise vehicle and add needed fluid at quick fill connector located next to sight tube. *See Fig. 1.* Recheck and ensure fluid level is filled to proper level.

**Final Drive -** Remove filler plug. Check fluid level at filler plug. Fluid level is okay if fluid drains out or fluid is even with bottom of fill hole. Add fluid as needed.

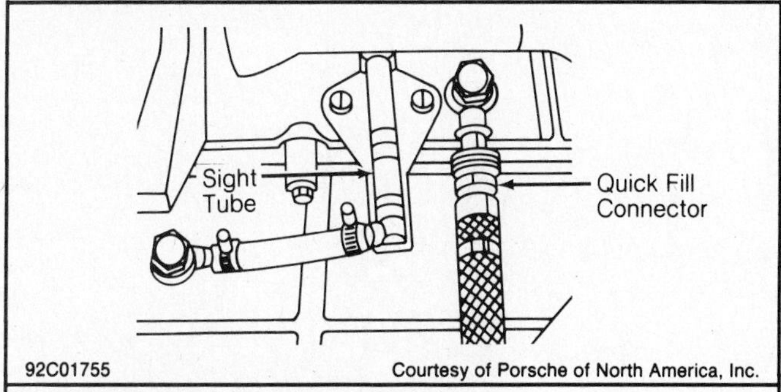


*Fig. 1: Checking Transmission Fluid Level*

### RECOMMENDED FLUID

**Transmission -** Use Dexron-II ATF type fluid.
**Final Drive -** Use API GL-5 75W/90 gear oil.

### FLUID CAPACITIES

*TRANSMISSION REFILL CAPACITIES*

| Application | Refill Qts. (L) | Dry Refill Qts. (L) |
|---|---|---|
| 911 Carrera 2 | 3.2 (3.0L) | 9.5 (9.0L) |

*FINAL DRIVE REFILL CAPACITY*

| Application | Pts. (L) |
|---|---|
| 911 Carrera 2 | 1.9 (0.9L) |

### DRAINING & REFILLING

**1)** Raise and support vehicle. Remove drain plug and drain fluid. Remove oil pan. Remove oil screen. Clean oil pan, magnet (if equipped) and oil screen in clean solvent and air dry. Replace screen if necessary.

**2)** Install pan with NEW pan gasket. Fill transmission. Start engine and run to normal operating temperature. Ensure fluid level is filled to correct level.

## ADJUSTMENTS

### GEARSHIFT CABLE

**1)** Place gear selector in "1" position in automatic shifting gate. Raise and support vehicle. Remove undercover. Disconnect fork head from neutral safety switch actuating lever. *See Fig. 2.* Move neutral safety switch to "1" position by pushing switch actuating lever to maximum forward position. Push gearshift cable forward.

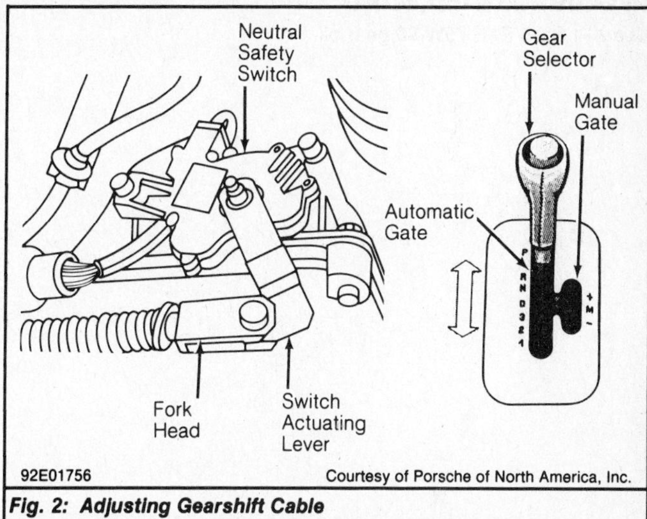


*Fig. 2: Adjusting Gearshift Cable*

**2)** Adjust position of fork head until bore holes of fork head and switch actuating lever are aligned. With fork head and switch actuating lever aligned, rotate fork head 2 additional turns onto cable threads. Connect fork head to switch actuating lever. Lower vehicle.

**3)** Check gearshift cable adjustment by shifting through all gears and confirming that proper gear selection is displayed at speedometer. Shift gear selector from "D" selection in automatic shift gate to "M" position in manual selection gate. Shift should occur with one smooth and straight movement. *See Fig. 2.* Readjust gearshift cable if necessary.

## TORQUE SPECIFICATIONS

*TORQUE SPECIFICATIONS*

| Application | Ft. Lbs. (N.m) |
|---|---|
| Gearshift Actuating Lever Nut | 11 (15) |
| | INCH Lbs. (N.m) |
| Neutral Safety Switch Bolt | 89 (10) |
| Transmission Pan Bolt | 71 (8) |

# 1990-91 TRANSMISSION SERVICING
# Manual Transmission

## 911 Carrera 2/4

## IDENTIFICATION

*PORSCHE MANUAL TRANSMISSION APPLICATIONS*

| Model | Transmission |
|---|---|
| 911 Carrera 2 | 5-Speed – G50.03 |
| 911 Carrera 4 | 5-Speed – G64.00 |

## LUBRICATION

### SERVICE INTERVALS

Check fluid level every 15,000 miles. Replace fluid every 60,000 miles.

### CHECKING FLUID LEVEL

Fluid should be level with bottom of fill hole on side of case.

### RECOMMENDED FLUID

Use API GL-5 SAE 75W-90 gear oil

## FLUID CAPACITIES

*TRANSMISSION REFILL CAPACITIES*

| Application | Qts. (L) |
|---|---|
| 911 Carrera 2 | 3.8 (3.6) |
| 911 Carrera 4 | 4.0 (3.8) |

## ADJUSTMENTS

### GEARSHIFT LINKAGE

Information is not available from manufacturer.

## TORQUE SPECIFICATIONS

*TORQUE SPECIFICATIONS*

| Application | Ft. Lbs. (N.m) |
|---|---|
| Drain Plug | 22 (30) |
| Fill Plug | 22 (30) |

# 1990-91 TRANSMISSION SERVICING
# Transmission Removal & Installation

## 911 Carrera 2/4

***CAUTION: DO NOT start engine with ground strap between transmission and chassis disconnected or Digital Motor Electronics (DME) control unit will be destroyed.***

## FUEL PRESSURE RELEASE

Turn ignition off. Access fuse panel in luggage compartment. Remove fuel pump/oxygen sensor fuse. Start engine. Allow engine to run until it stalls. Crank engine to ensure residual fuel pressure is released.

## MANUAL

***NOTE: For manual transmission/transaxle removal and installation procedures, see AWD & RWD article in CLUTCHES.***

## AUTOMATIC

***NOTE: Engine and transmission is removed as an assembly from underneath vehicle.***

**Removal & Installation (Carrera 2) – 1)** Release fuel pressure. See FUEL PRESSURE RELEASE. Disconnect negative battery cable. Raise and support vehicle. Position supports for vehicle so transmission supports can be removed later. Remove rear wheels.

**2)** Disconnect 6 electrical connections at intake manifold assembly. Remove cable clip from airflow sensor. Remove hot air blower (electric fan) from engine.

**3)** On left side of engine compartment, disconnect carbon canister hose, brake booster vacuum hose, reference mark sensor electrical connector, knock sensor electrical connector, temperature sensor electrical connector, cruise control electrical connector, oxygen sensor connector and fuel return line. If fuel tank is full, connect an extra piece of fuel line to vehicle fuel return line. Pinch off extra fuel line connected to vehicle fuel return line to prevent fuel from leaking.

**4)** Remove cover for engine electrics board. Disconnect multiple electrical connectors. Disconnect ignition coil wires from distributor. Disconnect electrical connector from double distributor assembly. Disconnect belt monitoring device electrical connector.

**5)** On A/C-equipped vehicles, disconnect A/C compressor mounting bolts. Set A/C compressor aside with hoses attached. On all vehicles, remove air filter housing. Disconnect fuel supply line at fuel filter.

**6)** Remove power steering fluid from power steering pump reservoir. Remove top hose from power steering pump, and collect any remaining fluid. Remove lower hose from power steering pump, and collect any remaining fluid.

**7)** Disconnect throttle valve linkage. Remove engine and transmission covers from underside of vehicle. Drain engine oil at thermostat housing. If engine is being overhauled, also drain oil from crankcase.

**8)** Using Line Wrench (9501), disconnect oil line at right rear wheel housing. Disconnect oil line retaining clip. Disconnect and plug oil line. Disconnect axles from transmission at axle flange next to transmission. Support axles using wire.

**9)** Disconnect heating hoses at heat exchanger. Disconnect ground strap at bottom starter mounting. Disconnect starter cables. Disconnect throttle valve actuating linkage at underfloor assembly guide tube. Disconnect transmission selector lever cable at transmission.

**10)** Disconnect transmission selector lever cable holder at transmission. Disconnect electrical connector located next to transmission selector cable holder. Remove rear stabilizer bar from vehicle. Disconnect 2 remaining oil line connections at right rear wheel housing. Plug remaining oil line connections at right rear wheel housing.

**11)** Remove engine guard bracket. Reinstall bolts for engine guard bracket as bolts are a contact surface for engine mounting plate used in engine removal. Connect Engine Mounting Plate Adapter (9111/1), Support Plate (9111/2) and Engine Mounting Plate (9111/3) to a jack. Position jack under engine. Attach mounting plates and adapter to engine. Slightly preload jack.

**12)** Remove transmission transverse crossmember bolts. Remove engine mounting bolts. Lower engine/transmission assembly approximately 4". Disconnect electrical connector at airflow meter. Disconnect electrical connector at transmission. Ensure all vacuum, oil, fuel and electrical lines leading from engine are disconnected. Slowly lower engine/transmission assembly from vehicle.

**13)** To separate engine from transmission, remove starter from transmission. Hang Torque Converter Holder (9325) behind starter ring gear. Attach brace for torque converter holder to starter mounting bolt holes. Torque converter holder will prevent torque converter from falling out during separation.

***CAUTION: Ensure Torque Converter Holder (9325) is positioned properly. If holder is not positioned properly, torque converter may fall out when transmission is separated from engine.***

**14)** Connect Transmission Holder (9324) to transmission mounting bores on sides of transmission case. Attach an overhead support to transmission holder. Slightly preload overhead support. Remove engine-to-transmission bolts. Separate transmission from engine. To install, reverse removal procedure.

## TORQUE SPECIFICATIONS

*TORQUE SPECIFICATIONS*

| Application | Ft. Lbs. (N.m) |
|---|---|
| Axle Shaft Bolt | |
| 8 mm | 31 (42) |
| 10 mm | 59 (80) |
| Clamping Sleeve Allen Bolt | 55 (75) |
| Double Mass Flywheel-To-Crankshaft Bolt | 63 (85) |
| Drive Plate-To-Crankshaft Bolt | 66 (90) |
| Engine Mount Bolt | 63 (85) |
| Engine-To-Transmission Bolts | 32 (45) |
| Flywheel-To-Crankshaft Bolt | 66 (90) |
| Oil Line Nut | [1] 59 (80) |
| Oil Return Line On Left Crankcase Half | 89 (120) |
| Oil Supply Line On Right Crankcase Half | 66 (90) |
| Stabilizer Bar Mounting Bolt | 34 (46) |
| Torque Converter Housing-To-Transmission Bolts | 34 (46) |
| Transmission Crossmember-To-Chassis Bolt | 34 (46) |
| Transmission-To-Chassis Bolt | [2] 63 (85) |
| | **INCH Lbs. (N.m)** |
| Fuel Distribution Line Nut | 106 (12) |

[1] – Located in right rear wheelwell.

[2] – These 2 bolts are accessible through small opening from inside vehicle.

# SAAB

# 1991 SAAB CONTENTS

## GENERAL INFORMATION [1]

### ALL MODELS



[1] – For all GENERAL INFORMATION, see front of Volume 1.

## ENGINE PERFORMANCE

### INTRODUCTION



### EMISSION APPLICATIONS



## ENGINE PERFORMANCE (Cont.)

### SERVICE & ADJUSTMENT SPECIFICATIONS



### ON-VEHICLE ADJUSTMENTS



### THEORY & OPERATION

# 1991 SAAB CONTENTS (Cont.)



## ENGINE PERFORMANCE (Cont.)

### BASIC DIAGNOSTIC PROCEDURES



### SELF-DIAGNOSTICS



### TROUBLE SHOOTING - NO CODES



### SYSTEM & COMPONENT TESTING



### SENSOR OPERATING RANGE CHARTS



## ENGINE PERFORMANCE (Cont.)

### WIRING DIAGRAMS



### VACUUM DIAGRAMS



### REMOVAL, OVERHAUL & INSTALLATION



## ELECTRICAL

### ALTERNATORS & REGULATORS



### STARTERS

# 1991 SAAB CONTENTS (Cont.)

## WIRING DIAGRAMS

### CHASSIS WIRING DIAGRAMS



## SAFETY EQUIPMENT

### AIR BAG RESTRAINT SYSTEM



### INSTRUMENT PANELS



### STEERING COLUMN SWITCHES



### WIPER/WASHER SYSTEMS



## ENGINES

### 2.0L, 2.1L & 2.3L 4-CYLINDER



## CLUTCHES

### FWD



## DRIVE AXLES

### FWD AXLE SHAFTS

# 1991 SAAB CONTENTS (Cont.)

## BRAKES

### DISC



### ANTI-LOCK



## WHEEL ALIGNMENT

### SPECIFICATIONS & PROCEDURES



## SUSPENSION

### FRONT



### REAR



## STEERING

### STEERING COLUMNS



### POWER RACK & PINION



## TRANSMISSION SERVICING

### AUTOMATIC TRANSMISSION



### MANUAL TRANSMISSION



### TRANSMISSION REMOVAL & INSTALLATION

# 1991 ENGINE PERFORMANCE
## Saab Introduction

### 1991 MODEL COVERAGE

| MODEL | BODY CODE | ENGINE [1] | ENGINE ID [2] | FUEL SYSTEM [3] | IGNITION SYSTEM [4] |
|---|---|---|---|---|---|
| 900/900S | 3 & 4 | 2.1L DOHC | D | PFI | Hall Sensor |
| 900 Turbo | 3, 4 & 7 | 2.0L DOHC Turbo | L | PFI | Hall Sensor |
| 900 Turbo SPG | 3 | 2.0L DOHC Turbo | L | PFI | Hall Sensor |
| 9000S | 4 & 5 | 2.3L DOHC | D | PFI | [5] DIS |
| 9000 Turbo | 5 | 2.3L DOHC Turbo | L | PFI | [5] DIS |
| 9000 Turbo CD | 4 | 2.3L DOHC Turbo | L | PFI | [5] DIS |

[1] – See illustrations for engine code and serial number location.
[2] – Engine ID is 8th character of Vehicle Identification Number (VIN), located on left front corner of instrument panel.
[3] – PFI is port fuel injection.
[4] – Computer controlled.
[5] – DIS is Direct Ignition System.

### VIN DEFINITION

**YS3CT54LXMY123456**
① ② ③ ④ ⑤ ⑥ ⑦ ⑧ ⑨ ⑩ ⑪ ⑫ ⑬ ⑭ ⑮ ⑯ ⑰

① ② Indicates Nation of Origin.
③ Indicates Manufacturer.
④ Indicates Model.
⑤ Indicates Vehicle Series.
⑥ Indicates Body Type.
⑦ Indicates Transmission Type.
⑧ **Indicates Engine Type.**
⑨ Indicates Check Digit.
⑩ **Indicates Model Year.**
⑪ Indicates Assembly Plant.
⑫⑬⑭⑮⑯⑰ Indicates Plant Sequential Number.

121813

***MODEL YEAR VIN CODE APPLICATION***

| VIN Code | Model Year |
|---|---|
| K | 1989 |
| L | 1990 |
| M | 1991 |

### ENGINE CODE LOCATION

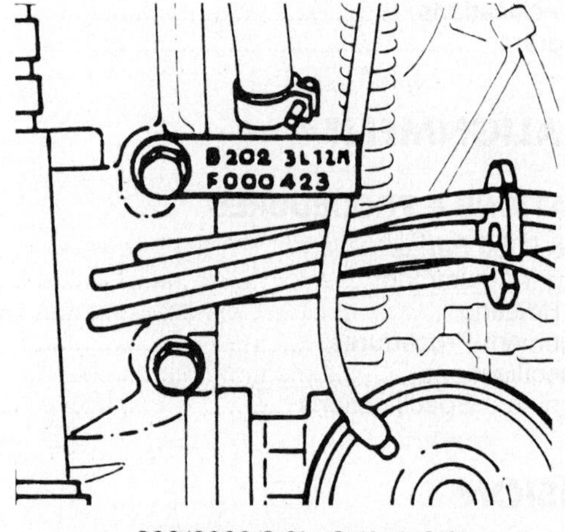


900/9000 2.0L, 2.1L & 2.3L

121471 Courtesy of Saab-Scania of America, Inc.

# Emission Applications

***1991 SAAB EMISSION SYSTEMS***

| Model, Engine & Fuel System | Emission Control Systems & Devices | Remarks |
|---|---|---|
| 900 & 9000 Series 2.0L, 2.1L & 2.3L 4-Cyl. (PFI) | **PCV, EVAP, TWC, [1] EGR, SPK, [2] PAS, $O_2$, CEC, CE,** DV, [3] EGR-SC, EGR-TVS, EVAP-PC, EVAP-VC, [4] SPK-VR, SPK-CC | [1] – Except 9000 turbo models. [2] – 9000 Series only. [3] – Turbo models only. [4] – 900 turbo models only. |

**NOTE:** Major emission control systems are listed in bold type; components are listed in light type.

**CE** – CHECK ENGINE Light
**CEC** – Computerized Engine Controls
**DV** – Decel Valve
**EGR** – Exhaust Gas Recirculation
**EGR-SC** – EGR Signal Converter
**EGR-TVS** – EGR Thermal Vacuum Switch
**EVAP** – Fuel Evaporative System
**EVAP-PC** – EVAP Purge Control
**EVAP-VC** – EVAP Vapor Canister
**$O_2$** – Oxygen Sensor
**PAS** – Pulse Air Injection System
**PCV** – Positive Crankcase Ventilation
**PFI** – Port Fuel Injection
**SPK** – Spark Control System
**SPK-CC** – SPK Computer Controlled
**SPK-VR** – SPK Vacuum Retard
**TWC** – Three-Way Catalyst

# 1991 ENGINE PERFORMANCE
# Service & Adjustment Specifications

### 900 Series, 9000 Series

## INTRODUCTION

Use this article to quickly find specifications related to servicing and on-vehicle adjustments. This is a quick reference for when you are familiar with an adjustment procedure and only need a specification.

## CAPACITIES

*BATTERY SPECIFICATIONS*

| Application | Amp Hr. Rating |
|---|---|
| All Models | 62 |

*FLUID CAPACITIES*

| Application | Quantity |
|---|---|
| Crankcase (Includes Filter) | |
| 900 Series | |
| Non-Turbo | 4.0 Qts. (3.8L) |
| Turbo | 4.5 Qts. (4.3L) |
| 9000 Series | 4.4 Qts. ((4.2L) |
| Cooling System (Includes Heater) | |
| 900 Series | 10.5 Qts. (10.5L) |
| 9000 Series | 9.5 Qts. (9.0L) |
| Man. Transaxle (SAE 10W-30 or 10W-40) | |
| 900 Series | 2.6 Qts. (2.5L) |
| 9000 Series | 2.6 Qts. (2.5L) |
| Auto. Transaxle [1] | |
| 900 Series (Ford M2C-33F/G) | 8.5 Qts. (8.0L) |
| 9000 Series (Dexron-II) | 8.7 Qts. (8.3L) |
| A/T Final Drive (SAE 10W-30) | |
| 900 Series | 1.3 Qts. (1.2L) |

[1] – Includes torque converter and cooler.

## QUICK-SERVICE

### SERVICE INTERVALS & SPECIFICATIONS

*REPLACEMENT INTERVALS*

| Component | Miles |
|---|---|
| Air Filter | 30,000 |
| Coolant | [1] 30,000 |
| Fuel Filter | 30,000 |
| Oil & Filter | [2] 7500 |
| Spark Plugs | 30,000 |

[1] – Interval is for first service. Change every 15,000 miles thereafter.
[2] – 3700 miles if vehicle is operated under severe conditions.

*BELT ADJUSTMENT*

| Application | Deflection – In. (mm) |
|---|---|
| 900 Series | |
| Alternator & A/C Compressor | [1] 3/16 (4.7) |
| Power Steering | [2] 3/16 (4.7) |
| 9000 Series [3] | |

[1] – Deflection is with 10 lbs. (4.5 kg) pressure applied midway on longest belt run.
[2] – Deflection is with 15 lbs. (6.8 kg) pressure applied midway on longest belt run.
[3] – Belt tension is controlled by an automatic tensioner.

## MECHANICAL CHECKS

### ENGINE COMPRESSION

Check engine compression at normal operating temperature with all spark plugs removed. To prevent damage to catalytic converter, make tests quickly and only when necessary.

*COMPRESSION SPECIFICATIONS* [1]

| Application | Specification |
|---|---|
| Compression Ratio | |
| 900 Non-Turbo | 10.1:1 |
| 900 Turbo | 9.0:1 |
| 9000 Non-Turbo | 10.1:1 |
| 9000 Turbo | 8.5:1 |

[1] – Compression pressure is not specified by manufacturer.

## VALVE CLEARANCE

***NOTE: All models are equipped with hydraulic lifters. No adjustments are required.***

## IGNITION SYSTEM

### IGNITION COIL

*IGNITION COIL RESISTANCE – Ohms @ 68°F (20°C)*

| Application | Primary | Secondary |
|---|---|---|
| 900 Series | .52-.76 | 7200-8200 |
| 9000 Series | [1] | [1] |

[1] – 9000 Series DIS coil specifications are not available from manufacturer.

### HIGH TENSION WIRE RESISTANCE

*HIGH TENSION WIRE RESISTANCE*

| Application | Ohms |
|---|---|
| Coil Wire | 500-1500 |
| Spark Plug Wires | 2000-4000 |

### SPARK PLUGS

*SPARK PLUG TYPE*

| Application | NGK |
|---|---|
| 900 Non-Turbo | BCP5ES |
| 900 Turbo | BCP7EV |
| 900 Turbo (City Driving) | BCP6EV |
| 9000 Non-Turbo | BCPR6ES |
| 9000 Turbo | BCPR7ES |

*SPARK PLUG SPECIFICATIONS*

| Application | Gap In. (mm) | Torque Ft. Lbs. (N.m) |
|---|---|---|
| 900 Series | .024-.028 (0.6-0.7) | 18.5-21.5 (25-29) |
| 9000 Series | .039-.047 (1.0-1.2) | 18.5-21.5 (25-29) |

### FIRING ORDER & TIMING MARKS

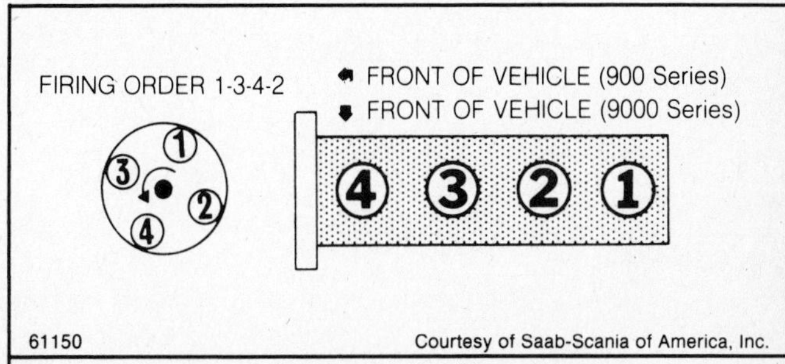


*Fig. 1: Firing Order & 900 Series Distributor Rotation*

# 1991 ENGINE PERFORMANCE
# Service & Adjustment Specifications (Cont.)

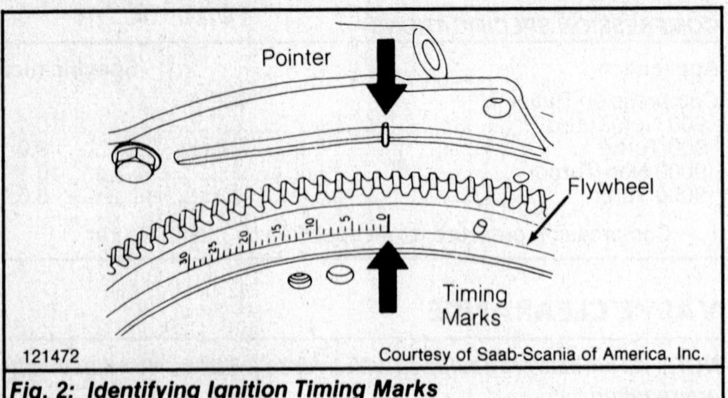


*Fig. 2: Identifying Ignition Timing Marks*

## IGNITION TIMING

*IGNITION TIMING (Degrees BTDC @ RPM)*

| Application | Man. Trans. | Auto. Trans. |
|---|---|---|
| Non-Turbo Models | 14 @ 850 | 14 @ 850 |
| Turbo Models | 16 @ 850 | 16 @ 850 |

## FUEL SYSTEM

### FUEL PUMP

***NOTE: Fuel pump performance is a measurement of fuel pressure and volume availability, not regulated fuel pressure.***

*FUEL PUMP PERFORMANCE*

| Application | Pressure psi (kg/cm²) | Min. Vol. in 30 Sec. Pts. (L) |
|---|---|---|
| 900 Non-Turbo | 44 (3.1) | 1.6 (.76) |
| 900 Turbo | 36 (2.5) | 1.6 (.76) |
| 9000 Series | 28-36 (2.0-2.5) | 1.9 (.90) |

*REGULATED FUEL PRESSURE*

| Application | At Idle w/o Vacuum psi (kg/cm²) | At Idle w/ Vacuum psi (kg/cm²) |
|---|---|---|
| 900 Non-Turbo | [1] | 43 (3.0) |
| 900 Turbo | [1] | 36 (2.5) |
| 9000 Series | 36-45 (2.5-3.2) | 28-36 (2.0-2.5) |

[1] – Information is not available from manufacturer.

## INJECTOR RESISTANCE

*INJECTOR RESISTANCE SPECIFICATIONS* [1]

| Application | Ohms |
|---|---|
| All Models | 16 |

[1] – Injector tested at 68°F (20°C).

## IDLE SPEED & MIXTURE

*IDLE SPEED & CO LEVEL*

| Application | Idle RPM | CO Level % |
|---|---|---|
| 900 Non-Turbo | 750-900 | .5-1.5 |
| 900 Turbo | 750-900 | .9-1.6 |
| 9000 Non-Turbo | 750-900 | 1-1.6 |
| 9000 Turbo | 800-900 | .5-1.5 |

## DASHPOT SPECIFICATION

Accelerate engine to 3000 RPM and measure time from release of throttle until engine reaches idle speed. If deceleration time is not 3-5 seconds, turn dashpot in toward stop to lengthen delay, or away from stop to shorten delay time.

## THROTTLE POSITION SENSOR

No adjustment is required.

# 1991 ENGINE PERFORMANCE On-Vehicle Adjustments

900 Series, 9000 Series

## ENGINE MECHANICAL

Before performing any on-vehicle adjustments to fuel or ignition systems, ensure engine mechanical condition is okay.

## VALVE CLEARANCE

***NOTE: All models use hydraulic lifters. No adjustments are required.***

## IGNITION TIMING

***NOTE: 9000 Series are equipped with Distributorless Ignition System (DIS). Timing is not adjustable.***

**900 Series** – Connect tachometer and timing light. Disconnect and plug vacuum advance hose (if equipped). Place transmission in Neutral. With engine at normal operating temperature, check ignition timing at specified RPM. See IGNITION TIMING table. Adjust ignition timing, if necessary, by loosening distributor hold-down bolt and turning distributor.

***IGNITION TIMING (Degrees BTDC @ RPM)***

| Application | Man. Trans. | Auto. Trans. |
|---|---|---|
| 900 Series | | |
| Non-Turbo | 14 @ 850 | 14 @ 850 |
| Turbo | 16 @ 850 | 16 @ 850 |

## IDLE SPEED & MIXTURE

### IDLE SPEED

**1)** Ensure engine is at normal operating temperature. Locate dashpot and Automatic Idle Control (AIC) valve on throttle body. Loosen air bleed screw lock nut. Loosen lock nut on throttle and lower dashpot to clear throttle lever. Pull back rubber boot on AIC connector and connect dwell meter to pins No. 2 and No. 3.

***NOTE: DO NOT make idle setting when radiator fan is operating.***

**2)** Start engine. Ensure all accessories are off. On models not equipped with air bleed adjusting screw, loosen throttle stop screw lock nut. Turn adjusting screw counterclockwise until screw does not touch throttle linkage.

**3)** On models equipped with air bleed adjusting screw, loosen throttle stop screw lock nut. Adjust throttle butterfly-to-housing clearance to .002" (.05 mm). Loosen air bleed screw lock nut and turn air bleed screw clockwise until fully seated.

**4)** On all models, dwell meter should indicate a minimum of 34 degrees. If dwell is not to specification, check for vacuum leaks. Turn adjusting screw/air bleed screw clockwise until engine idle speed is 850 RPM.

**5)** Dwell meter should indicate 31-33 degrees. Tighten lock nut on adjusting screw/air bleed screw. Turn engine off. Adjust throttle dashpot. See DASHPOT ADJUSTMENT.

### IDLE MIXTURE

***NOTE: Mixture adjustment is NOT a part of normal tune-up procedure and should not be performed unless mixture control unit is replaced or vehicle fails emissions testing.***

Start engine and warm to normal operating temperature. Using an exhaust analyzer, check CO level. If CO level is not within specification, turn CO adjusting screw clockwise to increase value. Turn adjusting screw counterclockwise to decrease value. See IDLE SPEED & CO LEVEL table. Remove test equipment and plug adjusting screw.

***IDLE SPEED & CO LEVEL***

| Application | Idle RPM | CO Level % |
|---|---|---|
| 900 Non-Turbo | 750-900 | .5-1.5 |
| 900 Turbo | 750-900 | .9-1.6 |
| 9000 Non-Turbo | 750-900 | 1-1.6 |
| 9000 Turbo | 800-900 | .5-1.5 |

## DASHPOT ADJUSTMENT

**1)** Bring engine to normal operating temperature. On Turbo models, disconnect and plug EGR hose (if equipped). On all other models, disconnect and plug vacuum advance (if equipped). Connect tachometer and check idle speed. Adjust if necessary.

**2)** Rotate throttle lever. Ensure dashpot rod strikes stop at 2500-2700 RPM on Turbo models or 2400-2600 RPM on all others. If not, adjust by turning dashpot.

**3)** Accelerate engine to 3000 RPM and measure time from release of throttle until engine reaches idle speed. Deceleration time should be 3-5 seconds. If not, turn dashpot in toward stop to lengthen delay, or away from stop to shorten delay time.

## PROGRAMMING ECU

***NOTE: If the power supply to the ECU has been interrupted, the system must be reprogrammed.***

**9000 Series** – To program system, accelerate vehicle at full throttle from 2000-4500 RPM. Because programming occurs at 2750-4500 RPM and requires 3 seconds to complete, the procedure should be performed in a gear that permits operation between those engine speeds.

**900 Series** – Drive vehicle for 10 minutes with engine at normal operating temperature.

## THROTTLE POSITION SENSOR

No adjustment is required. For testing procedure, refer to SYSTEM & COMPONENT TESTING article.

# 1991 ENGINE PERFORMANCE
# Theory & Operation

### 900 Series, 9000 Series

## INTRODUCTION

This article covers basic description and operation of engine performance-related systems and components. Read this article before diagnosing vehicles or systems with which you are not completely familiar.

## AIR INDUCTION SYSTEM

### TURBOCHARGERS

On turbo models, a turbocharger and wastegate assembly are mounted on the exhaust manifold. At idle and light throttle, the turbo engine operates like a standard engine. When more power is required, exhaust gases spin the impeller and turbine. Exhaust flow and turbocharger RPM increase as engine RPM increases. As turbocharger RPM increases, boost pressure also increases.

The wastegate is the safety valve of the system, preventing excessive boost pressure which can cause engine damage. A signal from the Automatic Performance Control system energizes a solenoid which opens the wastegate to control optimum boost pressure. In the event of control system failure, the wastegate will open automatically to limit boost pressure.

Turbocharger operation requires a supply of clean oil. Engine oil pressure provides lubrication to the system.

## COMPUTERIZED ENGINE CONTROLS

The computerized engine control system consists of 3 electronic control units (ECU's): a fuel injection ECU, an ignition ECU, and on turbo models, an automatic performance control (APC) ECU.

### CONTROL UNITS

**Fuel Injection ECU** – The fuel injection system ECU receives and processes data from various sensors. It then sends signals to fuel injectors for correct fuel delivery under all operating conditions. The fuel injection ECU is located on the right kick panel on 900 Series; in engine compartment on left side of firewall on 9000 Series. This unit also controls the Automatic Idle Control (AIC) system.

**Ignition ECU** – The ignition ECU is located in the engine compartment, forward of the left front wheel housing on 900 Series. On 9000 Series, the ignition ECU is under the driver's seat. It receives inputs from a detonation sensor, fuel injection ECU and the Hall Effect sensor. From these inputs it calculates and controls ignition timing.

**Automatic Performance Control (APC) ECU (Turbo)** – The APC system ECU is located under the dash, left of the steering column. It receives signals from a detonation sensor, pressure sensor and ignition system ECU. The APC ECU processes these signals and sends a signal to a solenoid valve at the turbocharger to control optimum boost pressure.

***NOTE: Components are grouped into 2 categories. The first category covers INPUT DEVICES, which control or produce voltage signals monitored by the control unit. The second category covers OUTPUT SIGNALS, which are components controlled by the control unit.***

### INPUT DEVICES

Vehicles are equipped with different combinations of input devices. Not all devices are used on all models. To determine the input device usage on a specific model, see appropriate wiring diagram in WIRING DIAGRAMS article. The available input signals include the following:

**A/C Switch** – When A/C switch is on, it sends a signal to the fuel injection ECU. The ECU sends a signal to the Automatic Idle Control (AIC) valve to increase idle speed to compensate for increased load.

**Coolant Temperature Sensor** – The coolant temperature sensor is located on the intake manifold flange. It transmits an engine temperature signal to the fuel injection ECU. If the ECU fails to receive this signal, it defaults to an assumed engine temperature of 113°F (45°C).

**Detonation Sensor** – This sensor is located in the engine block, below the intake manifold. When knocking occurs, it sends a signal to the ignition and APC ECU's.

**EGR Temperature Sensor** – See EXHAUST GAS RECIRCULATION (EGR) under EMISSION SYSTEMS.

**Gear Selector Switch** – Automatic transmission models are equipped with a switch that signals the fuel injection ECU whenever the transmission is in a range other than Park or Neutral. The ECU signals the Automatic Idle Control (AIC) valve to increase idle speed.

**Hall Effect Sensor** – This sensor transmits engine RPM and crankshaft position signals to the fuel injection, ignition and APC ECUs. On 900 Turbo it is located within the distributor. It is located on the crankshaft pulley on all others.

**Mass Airflow Meter** – This sensor measures mass airflow of air entering the engine intake system. It is located between the air cleaner and throttle body. After the engine is shut off, the fuel injection ECU sends a signal to the sensor filament to heat it for 4 seconds to burn off any deposits, provided that engine speed has been greater than 2000 RPM.

**Oxygen Sensor** – This sensor measures quantity of free oxygen in the exhaust gas. The fuel injection ECU uses a signal from this sensor to adjust fuel injection quantity. Sensor is threaded into the exhaust manifold.

**Throttle Position Sensor** – This sensor is located on the throttle body. It transmits throttle position to the fuel injection ECU.

**Vehicle Speed Sensor** – This sensor is located in the speedometer. It sends a signal to the fuel injection ECU to determine whether or not the vehicle is moving.

### OUTPUT SIGNALS

***NOTE: Vehicles are equipped with different combinations of computer-controlled components. Not all components listed below are used on every vehicle. For theory and operation on each output component, refer to the system indicated after component.***

**Airflow Meter Self-Cleaning** – See MASS AIRFLOW METER under INPUT DEVICES.

**Automatic Idle Control Valve** – See IDLE SPEED under FUEL SYSTEM.

**Canister Purge Solenoid** – See EVAPORATIVE EMISSIONS under EMISSION SYSTEMS.

**CHECK ENGINE Light** – See SELF-DIAGNOSTIC SYSTEM.

**Cold Start Injector** – See FUEL CONTROL under FUEL SYSTEM.

**EGR Control Solenoid Valve** – See EXHAUST GAS RECIRCULATION (EGR) under EMISSION SYSTEM.

**Fuel Pump Relay** – See FUEL DELIVERY under FUEL SYSTEM.

**Fuel Injectors** – See FUEL CONTROL under FUEL SYSTEM.

**Idle-Up Solenoid** – See IDLE SPEED under FUEL SYSTEM.

**Ignition Coil(s)** – See IGNITION SYSTEMS.

**Oxygen Sensor Heating Element** – See FUEL CONTROL under FUEL SYSTEM.

**Self-Diagnostics** – See SELF-DIAGNOSTIC SYSTEM.

**Wastegate Solenoid** – See TURBOCHARGERS under AIR INDUCTION SYSTEM.

## FUEL SYSTEM

### FUEL DELIVERY

The fuel system consists of a fuel tank, fuel pump, fuel lines, filter and a fuel pressure regulator. Fuel is supplied to each injector at a constant pressure.

**Fuel Pressure Regulator** – Fuel pressure regulator, located on fuel rail, maintains constant fuel pressure at fuel injectors. Excess fuel bypasses injectors and returns to fuel tank.

**Fuel Pump** – Fuel pump is located within the fuel tank. Fuel is strained through a mesh screen before entering pump. A check valve, located on outlet side of pump, maintains pressure within the fuel system when engine is off.

**Fuel Pump Relay** – Fuel pump relay supplies power to fuel pump. It is controlled by fuel injection ECU. Fuel pump relay is located on right kick panel on 900 Series, or behind glove box on 9000 Series.

## FUEL CONTROL

**Cold Start Injector** – On 900 Series, a signal from the fuel injection ECU opens a cold start injector to supply additional fuel under cold start conditions. This device is located at the throttle body.

**Fuel Injection ECU** – The fuel injection ECU processes pulses from the ignition ECU to determine basic fuel injection timing. It also processes signals from other sensors for calculating pulse duration to control fuel injector on time.

**Fuel Injectors** – Each fuel injector, located in the intake manifold, sprays atomized fuel directly toward the associated intake valve. All injectors are supplied with fuel from a common fuel manifold. Injection pulse duration is controlled by a signal from the fuel injection ECU. Injectors open simultaneously once per engine revolution, except during cold starting. During cold starting, injectors open twice per engine revolution.

**Oxygen Sensor Heating Element** – The fuel injection ECU sends a signal to the to a heating element in the oxygen sensor. The function of the heating element is to bring the sensing element to operating temperature more quickly.

## IDLE SPEED

**Automatic Idle Control (AIC) Valve** – The automatic idle control valve consists of an air control valve and integral solenoid. This system provides a more stable idle speed during warm and cold engine operation. The fuel injection ECU sends a signal to the AIC valve to control the amount of air that by-passes the throttle valve.

**Idle-Up Solenoid** – On 900 Series, the fuel injection ECU sends a signal to an idle-up solenoid to increase idle speed when the air conditioner is on. This solenoid is located in the by-pass hose at the throttle body.

# IGNITION SYSTEM

## DIRECT IGNITION SYSTEM (DIS)

**9000 Series** – The DIS system is a capacitive discharge type. Components of the DIS include an ignition cartridge, Hall Effect sensor and knock detector. There is a separate coil for each spark plug. Energy for the spark is stored in a capacitor and discharged through the ignition coil based upon a signal from the ignition ECU.

When the engine is cranking, the ignition ECU establishes firing order by signals sent from the crankshaft sensor. During difficult start conditions (less than 420 RPM), a continuous series of sparks (multi-sparking) occurs during 70 degrees of engine rotation in the cylinder pair whose pistons are approaching TDC. Multi-sparking continues until engine speed reaches 850 RPM, and will reoccur if engine speed drops to less then 420 RPM. If the engine fails to start, multi-sparking will occur in all cylinders to remove spark plug electrode deposits.

## ELECTRONIC IGNITION SYSTEM (DISTRIBUTOR TYPE)

**900 Series** – The ignition ECU receives a signal from the crankshaft position sensor. This signals is processed and sent to the ignition amplifier. The ignition amplifier sends a signal which opens the primary circuit of the ignition coil, thus generating a high voltage pulse which is directed to each spark plug by the distributor.

## IGNITION TIMING CONTROL SYSTEM

**9000 Series With DIS** – Ignition timing remains at base setting until engine speed reaches 850 RPM. At engine speeds greater than 850 RPM, the ignition ECU controls ignition timing. If the knock detector senses detonation, engine timing and boost pressure will be retarded. If detonation continues, the ignition ECU signals the fuel injectors to increase fuel delivery. No timing adjustment is possible on this system.

**900 Series** – Ignition advance is controlled by the ignition ECU. Inputs from the fuel injection ECU, Hall Effect sensor, and coil are used by the ECU to calculate advance. A sensor detects any knocking in the engine and sends a signal to the ECU, which then retards ignition timing. On 900 Series Turbo, a pressure signal from the air intake duct controls a distributor-mounted diaphragm which retards timing.

# EMISSION SYSTEMS

## AIR INJECTION

The pulse air injection system sends air to the exhaust manifold to reduce exhaust emissions (HC and CO). Components of the system include check valves, air injection manifolds, a nozzle by each exhaust valves and an air supply hose from the air cleaner. Filtered air from the air cleaner flows through the pulse air valves by means of exhaust manifold pressure variation. Check valves prevent exhaust gases from flowing back into the air cleaner.

## CATALYTIC CONVERTER

All vehicles are equipped with a 3-way catalytic converter. This device frees oxygen from oxides of nitrogen, and oxidizes hydrocarbons and carbon monoxide.

## EVAPORATIVE EMISSIONS

Fumes from the fuel tank are stored in a charcoal canister while the vehicle is not running. When the engine is started, intake manifold vacuum purges these fumes through a canister purge solenoid, based upon a signal from the ECU. The canister is located in the left front of the engine compartment on 900 Series; in the right front wheel housing on 9000 Series.

A rollover valve in the fuel evaporation line closes if the vehicle rolls over. It is located in the evaporation line, above the fuel tank. A vacuum relief valve in the fuel filler cap bleeds air into the fuel tank if the vent lines become plugged.

## EXHAUST GAS RECIRCULATION (EGR)

To lower oxides of nitrogen (NOx) exhaust gas emissions, a computer controlled exhaust gas recirculation system is used. Depending on engine operating temperature, the fuel injection ECU controls an EGR solenoid to control vacuum signal to EGR valve. Valve routes exhaust gases from the exhaust manifold into the intake manifold.

An EGR temperature sensor is used on some models. Sensor informs fuel injection ECU when EGR function is occurring. This enables ECU to determine if system is functioning as commanded.

## POSITIVE CRANKCASE VENTILATION

All vehicles have a completely closed crankcase ventilation system. Crankcase fumes are drawn into the intake manifold by manifold vacuum. When intake manifold vacuum is low, the fumes are diverted into the intake air duct ahead of the throttle body and turbocharger (if equipped).

# SELF-DIAGNOSTIC SYSTEM

All models are equipped with a self-diagnostic system that makes fault diagnosis possible by displaying error codes. When the system detects a malfunction, it sets a code in memory and sends a signal to the CHECK ENGINE warning light. Fault diagnosis can be performed using ISAT Scan tester, a proprietary device available from manufacturer. Error codes are also displayed by flashing of the CHECK ENGINE light.

# 1991 ENGINE PERFORMANCE
# Theory & Operation (Cont.)

## CHECK ENGINE LIGHT

All vehicles are equipped with a CHECK ENGINE light on the instrument panel. The light will come on when the ignition switch is turned to the ON position (bulb check), and when emission controls malfunction during normal operation. For additional information, see SELF-DIAGNOSTICS article.

## MISCELLANEOUS CONTROLS

***NOTE: Although not considered true engine performance-related systems, some controlled devices may affect driveability if they malfunction.***

## A/C CLUTCH

At full throttle, the fuel injection ECU opens the ground circuit to the A/C clutch to inhibit A/C operation.

## COOLING FAN

**Cooling Fan Motor** – The cooling fan is controlled by a temperature switch on the left side of the radiator. Failure of the fan to operate may result in overheating and detonation.

**Cooling Fan Control Relay** – The cooling fan relay is located in the power distribution box, on the left rear of the engine compartment. When the temperature switch closes, it grounds the relay coil. When the relay is energized, it supplies battery voltage to the fan motor. A signal from an A/C (if equipped) pressure switch also energizes the relay.

# 1991 ENGINE PERFORMANCE
# Basic Diagnostic Procedures



## 900 Series, 9000 Series

## INTRODUCTION

The following diagnostic steps will help prevent overlooking a simple problem. This is also where to begin diagnosis for a no start condition.

The first step in diagnosing any driveability problem is verifying the customer's complaint with a test drive under the conditions the problem reportedly occurred.

Before entering self-diagnostics, perform a careful and complete visual inspection. Most engine control problems result from mechanical breakdowns, poor electrical connections or damaged/misrouted vacuum hoses. Before condemning the computerized system, perform each test listed in this article.

***NOTE: Perform all voltage tests with a Digital Volt-Ohmmeter (DVOM) with a minimum 10-megohm input impedance, unless stated otherwise in test procedure.***

## PRELIMINARY INSPECTION & ADJUSTMENTS

### VISUAL INSPECTION

Perform a visual inspection of all electrical wiring. Look for chafed, stretched, cut or pinched wiring. Inspect electrical connectors and connections for tight fit and corrosion. Repair as necessary. Ensure all vacuum hoses are properly routed, and are not cut or pinched. See VACUUM DIAGRAMS article to verify routing and connections (if necessary). Inspect air induction system for possible vacuum leaks after the airflow meter.

### MECHANICAL INSPECTION

**Compression** – Check engine mechanical condition with a compression gauge, vacuum gauge, or an engine analyzer. See engine analyzer instruction manual for specific instructions.

***CAUTION: Use a remote starter to crank engine during compression test, NOT the ignition switch. The fuel injectors on many fuel injected models are triggered during the cranking mode. This could cause a fire hazard, flooding, crankcase contamination, hydrostatic lock, or lubrication to be washed off of cylinder walls.***

Check engine compression at normal operating temperature with all spark plugs removed. To prevent damage to catalytic converter, make tests quickly and only when necessary.

***ENGINE COMPRESSION*** [1]

| Application | Specification |
|---|---|
| Compression Ratio | |
| 900 Non-Turbo | 10.1:1 |
| 900 Turbo | 9.0:1 |
| 9000 Non-Turbo | 10.1:1 |
| 9000 Turbo | 8.5:1 |

[1] – Compression pressure is not specified by manufacturer.

**Exhaust System Backpressure** – The exhaust system can be checked with a vacuum or pressure gauge. Remove $O_2$ sensor. Connect a 0-10 psi gauge and run engine at 2500 RPM. If exhaust system backpressure is greater than 2 psi (.14 kg/cm²), exhaust system or catalytic converter is plugged.

If a vacuum gauge is used, connect it to intake manifold vacuum port and start engine. Observe vacuum gauge. Open throttle part way and hold steady. If vacuum gauge slowly drops after stabilizing, exhaust system should be checked for a restriction.

## FUEL SYSTEM

### FUEL PRESSURE

Basic diagnosis of fuel system should begin with determining fuel system pressure.

***WARNING: ALWAYS relieve fuel pressure before disconnecting any fuel injection-related component. DO NOT allow fuel to contact engine or electrical components.***

**Fuel Pressure – 1)** Turn ignition off. Disconnect banjo coupling at inlet to fuel injection manifold. Connect a fuel pressure gauge using existing seals. Ensure pressure gauge hangs vertically.

**2)** Remove fuse No. 30 on 900 models. Remove fuse No. 14 from 9000 models. Connect a jumper lead between fuse No. 27, 28, or 29 and slot of fuse No. 30 for 900 models. Connect the jumper between fuse No. 22 and slot of fuse No. 14 on 9000 models. This will provide current to the fuel pump. Turn ignition on.

**3)** Fuel pressure should increase to approximately 36 psi (2.5 kg/cm²). If fuel pressure is too high, go to next step. If fuel pressure is too low, go to step **5)**.

**4)** Turn ignition off. Disconnect fuel return line from pressure regulator and blow through line. If line is open, pressure regulator is defective and should be replaced. If line is blocked, remove blockage or replace with a new return line. Check one-way valve at tank and retest system.

**5)** Check fuel level; do not rely on fuel gauge. Check for fuel system leaks. Check fuel pressure regulator. See FUEL PRESSURE REGULATOR test. If proceeding to FUEL PRESSURE REGULATOR test, do not remove fuel pressure gauge.

**Fuel Pressure Regulator – 1)** If fuel pressure gauge is already attached, go to next step. If not, disconnect banjo coupling at inlet to fuel injection manifold. Connect fuel pressure gauge at this point, using existing seals. Ensure pressure gauge hangs vertically.

**2)** Connect Pressure Gauge (83 93 514), with "Y" connection, to vacuum port of fuel pressure regulator. Hang pressure gauge vertically. Connect cooling system pressure tester to "Y" connection.

**3)** Turn ignition off. Remove fuse No. 30 on 900 models. Remove fuses No. 14 and No. 22 from 9000 models. Connect a jumper lead between fuse No. 27, 28, or 29 and slot of fuse No. 30 for 900 models. Connect the jumper between fuse No. 22 and slot of fuse No. 14 on 9000 models. This will provide current to fuel pump. Turn ignition on.

**4)** Fuel pressure should increase to approximately 36 psi (2.5 kg/cm²). Using a cooling system pressure tester, increase system pressure as specified in APPLIED PRESSURE REGULATOR SPECIFICATIONS table, and compare fuel pressure to specification.

**5)** Remove cooling system pressure tester. Install vacuum pump to "Y" connection. Fuel pressure should be approximately 36 psi (2.5 kg/cm²). Use vacuum pump to reduce system pressures as specified in APPLIED VACUUM REGULATOR SPECIFICATIONS table, and compare fuel pressure to specification. Disconnect vacuum pump.

**6)** Turn ignition on to operate fuel pump. Verify fuel pressure of 36 psi (2.5 kg/cm²). Turn ignition off. Pressure should drop 1.4-2.8 psi (.1-.2 kg/cm²), and then hold steady for at least 10 minutes.

**7)** If pressure drops more than specified, check for leakage in pressure regulator and fuel pump non-return valve.

***APPLIED PRESSURE REGULATOR SPECIFICATIONS***

| Applied Pressure psi (kg/cm²) | Fuel Pressure psi (kg/cm²) |
|---|---|
| 0 (0) | 36.3 (2.5) |
| 2.9 (.2) | 39.2 (2.7) |
| 5.8 (.4) | 42.1 (2.9) |
| 8.6 (.6) | 44.9 (3.1) |

***APPLIED VACUUM REGULATOR SPECIFICATIONS***

| Applied Vacuum In. Hg | Fuel Pressure psi (kg/cm²) |
|---|---|
| 0 | 36.3 (2.5) |
| 5 | 33.4 (2.3) |
| 11 | 30.5 (2.1) |
| 16 | 27.5 (1.9) |

# 1991 ENGINE PERFORMANCE
# Basic Diagnostic Procedures (Cont.)

**Fuel Pump Delivery Pressure – 1)** Turn ignition off. Disconnect banjo coupling at inlet to fuel injection manifold. Connect a fuel pressure gauge using existing seals. Ensure pressure gauge hangs vertically. Turn ignition on. Pinch off fuel return line and check fuel pressure. When line is plugged, there should be an immediate increase in fuel pressure.

***CAUTION: DO NOT allow pressure to rise above 83 psi (5.8 kg/cm²).***

**2)** If fuel pressure does not increase, check for the following problems:

- At least 11.5 volts across fuel pump terminals
- Obstructed fuel lines
- Clogged fuel filter
- Fuel filter installed backward
- Defective relief valve in fuel pump

***NOTE: If fuel filter has been installed backward, it must be replaced.***

**3)** After checking fuel pump pressure, turn ignition off. Go to FUEL PUMP DELIVERY FLOW test procedure (do not disconnect pressure gauge).

**Fuel Pump Delivery Flow – 1)** Turn ignition off. Disconnect fuel return line at pressure regulator. Connect a section of test hose to return line at pressure regulator. Place other end of test hose in graduated container of about 2 quarts.

**2)** Activate fuel pump by turning ignition on. Run fuel pump for 30 seconds. Check volume of fuel flow and fuel pressure drop. Minimum acceptable volume is .95 qt. (.9 L), and maximum allowed fuel pressure drop is 1.4-2.8 psi (.1-.2 kg/cm²). If fuel volume or pressure drop does not meet specification, replace fuel pressure regulator.

**Fuel Pump Relay – 1)** Remove relay. Relay is located on passenger side kick panel on 900 Series; behind glove box on 9000 Series.

**2)** Connect ohmmeter across relay contact terminals (Red and Green/Red wires on mating connector). Ohmmeter should indicate no continuity.

**3)** Connect 12 volts across relay coil (Brown/Violet and Violet wires on 900 Series; Green/White and Violet wires on 9000 Series). Ohmmeter should indicate continuity.

## IGNITION CHECKS

### DIS IGNITION SYSTEM (9000 SERIES)

**Quick Check – 1)** Measure voltage at Red wire going into ignition cartridge. With ignition on, voltmeter should indicate battery voltage.

**2)** Turn ignition off. Remove No. 14 fuse (fuel pump). Remove ignition cartridge and spark plugs. Install spark plugs into ignition cartridge. Using jumper wires, connect negative electrodes of spark plugs together. Ground other ends of jumper wires.

**3)** With ignition key, crank engine and observe tachometer. Needle of tachometer should hunt. Ensure there is spark at all spark plugs. Release ignition key to RUN position for approximately 5 seconds. Ensure tachometer needle hunts and multiple sparks occur at spark plugs.

### EZK IGNITION SYSTEM (900 SERIES)

**Spark Test –** Check for spark at coil wire and each spark plug wire, using a spark tester. Check spark plug wire resistance on suspect wires. Resistance should be 2000-4000 ohms. Coil wire resistance should be 500-1500 ohms.

**Ignition Coil Power Source –** Turn ignition on. Using voltmeter, check voltage between Green/White wire at ignition coil and ground at ignition coil harness connector. Battery voltage should exist.

**Ignition Coil Resistance – 1)** Turn ignition switch off. Remove primary and secondary leads from ignition coil. Using ohmmeter, check primary resistance between positive and negative terminals of coil. Resistance should be as specified. See IGNITION COIL RESISTANCE table.

**2)** Check secondary resistance between tower and negative terminals of coil. See IGNITION COIL RESISTANCE table. Replace coil if readings are not within specification.

***IGNITION COIL RESISTANCE – Ohms @ 68°F (20°C)***

| Application | Primary | Secondary |
|---|---|---|
| 900 Series | .52-.76 | 7200-8200 |
| 9000 Series | [1] | [1] |

[1] – DIS coil specifications not available from manufacturer.

***NOTE: All voltage tests should be performed with a Digital Volt Ohmmeter (DVOM) with a minimum 10-megohm input impedance, unless specifically stated different in testing procedures.***

**Hall Effect Sensor – 1)** Make all checks at the back of electrical connectors for EZK Electronic Control Unit (ECU) with ignition on.

**2)** To test sensor supply voltage, connect voltmeter between terminal No. 10 and 4 of ECU. See WIRING DIAGRAMS article. Voltmeter reading should be battery voltage.

**3)** To test signal from Hall Effect sensor to ECU, connect voltmeter between terminals No. 10 and 24 of ECU. See WIRING DIAGRAMS article. Slowly turn engine by hand. Voltmeter indication should vary from 0.4-3.0 volts as Hall Effect sensor shutter opens and closes.

## PROGRAMMING ECU

***NOTE: If the power supply to the ECU has been interrupted, the system must be reprogrammed.***

**9000 Series –** To program system, accelerate vehicle at full throttle from 2000-4500 RPM. Because programming occurs at 2750-4500 RPM and requires 3 seconds to complete, the procedure should be performed in a gear that permits operation between those engine speeds.

**900 Series –** Drive vehicle for 10 minutes with engine at normal operating temperature.

## IDLE SPEED & IGNITION TIMING

Ensure idle speed and ignition timing are set to specification. For adjustment procedures, see ON-VEHICLE ADJUSTMENTS article.

## SUMMARY

If no faults were found while performing BASIC DIAGNOSTIC PROCEDURES, proceed to SELF-DIAGNOSTICS article. If no hard codes are found in self-diagnostics, or vehicle does not have a self-diagnostic system, proceed to TROUBLE SHOOTING – NO CODES article for diagnosis by symptom (i.e., ROUGH IDLE, NO START, etc.) or intermittent diagnostic procedures.

# 1991 ENGINE PERFORMANCE
# Self-Diagnostics

## 900 Series, 9000 Series

## INTRODUCTION

If no faults were found while performing BASIC DIAGNOSTIC PROCEDURES, proceed with self-diagnostics. If no fault codes or only pass codes are present after entering self-diagnostics, proceed to TROUBLE SHOOTING - NO CODES article for diagnosis by symptom (i.e.,ROUGH IDLE, NO-START, etc.).

## SELF-DIAGNOSTIC SYSTEM

**Hard Failures** - Hard failures cause CHECK ENGINE light to come on and remain on until the malfunction is repaired. If light comes on and remains on (light may flash) during vehicle operation, cause of malfunction must be determined using diagnostic code table. If a sensor fails, control unit will use a substitute value in its calculations to continue engine operation. In this condition, commonly known as limp-in mode, the vehicle runs but driveability will not be optimum.

**Intermittent Failures** - Intermittent failures may cause CHECK ENGINE light to flicker or light and go out after the intermittent fault goes away. The corresponding trouble code will be retained in ECU memory, however. If related fault does not reoccur within a certain time frame, related trouble code will be erased from ECU memory. Intermittent failures may be caused by sensor, connector or wiring related problems. See INTERMITTENTS in TROUBLE SHOOTING - NO CODES article.

## ENTERING SELF-DIAGNOSTICS

Using a switched jumper wire, connect one end to ground pin No. 3 of the 3 pin test socket on left side of engine compartment. *See Fig. 1.* Connect other end of switched jumper to ground (switch off). Turn ignition switch to ON position (CHECK ENGINE light will be on). You are now ready to retrieve codes.

## TROUBLE CODE DEFINITION

***DIAGNOSTIC CODES***

| Permanent Fault | Intermittent Fault | Malfunction Indicated |
|---|---|---|
| 42241 | 22241 | Voltage Higher Than 16 Volts |
| 42251 | 22251 | Less Than One Volt At ECU Pin No. 4 |
| 42252 | 22252 | Signal Voltage Less Than 10 Volts |
| 42291 | 22291 | Battery Voltage Less Than 10 Volts Or Higher Than 16 Volts |
| 42440 | 22440 | Rich Mixture: No Control By $O_2$ Sensor |
| 42441 | 22441 | Rich Idle Mixture |
| 42442 | 22442 | Rich Mixture |
| 42450 | 24250 | Lean Mixture: No Control By $O_2$ Sensor |
| 42451 | 22451 | Lean Idle Mixture |
| 42452 | 22452 | Lean Mixture |
| 42460 [1] | 22460 [1] | $O_2$ Sensor Signal Faulty |
| 42491 | 22491 | Incorrect Idle Mixture |
| 42492 | 22492 | Incorrect Mixture |
| 44221 | 24221 | Vehicle Speed Sensor Signal Absent |
| 44261 | 24621 | Vehicle Speed Sensor Signal Faulty |
| 44360 | 24360 | Crankshaft Sensor Signal Faulty |
| 44460 [1] | 24460 | Load Signal Faulty |
| 44461 | 24461 | ECU Programming Fault: Outside Limits |
| 44660 | 24660 | Pre-Ignition Fault |
| 44661 | 24661 | Knock Sensor Signal Faulty |
| 44671 | 24671 | Pre-Ignition Signal Longer Than 20 Seconds |
| 44662 | 24462 | Pre-Ignition Synchronization Signal Faulty |
| 45260 | 25260 | Throttle Potentiometer Signal Faulty |
| 45360 | 25360 | Brake Signal Faulty |
| 45641 [1] | 25641 [1] | Mass Airflow Meter Signal High |
| 45651 [1] | 25651 [1] | Mass Airflow Meter Signal Low |
| 45691 [1] | 25691 [1] | Mass Airflow Meter Signal Faulty |
| 45723 | 25723 | Transmission Range Signal/Function Faulty |
| 45771 [1] | 25771 | Throttle Position Sensor Signal Shorted |
| 45772 [1] | 25772 | Throttle Position Sensor Signal Indicates Idle And Full Throttle Simultaneously |
| 46221 [1] | 26221 | Temperature Sensor Circuit Open |
| 46261 | 26261 | Temperature Sensor Signal Indicates Constant Temperature |
| 46271 | 26271 | Temperature Sensor Circuit Shorted |
| 46391 | 26391 | EGR System Function Faulty |
| 58121 | 38121 | Mass Airflow Meter Burn-Off Function Absent |
| 58321 | 38321 | AIC Valve Function Faulty |
| 58322 [1] | 38322 | Canister Purge Valve Function Faulty |
| 58371 [1] | 38371 | Injector Faulty |
| 58372 [1] | 38372 | Canister Purge Valve Circuit Open Or Shorted To Ground |
| 53882 [1] | 38382 | Canister Purge Valve Circuit Shorted To Battery Voltage |
| 60000 | .... | Internal Monitoring |
| 60001 | .... | ECU Fault |
| 60002 | .... | ECU Fault |
| 67192 [1] | .... | ECU Fault |

[1] - CHECK ENGINE light will be on.

# 1991 ENGINE PERFORMANCE
## Self-Diagnostics (Cont.)

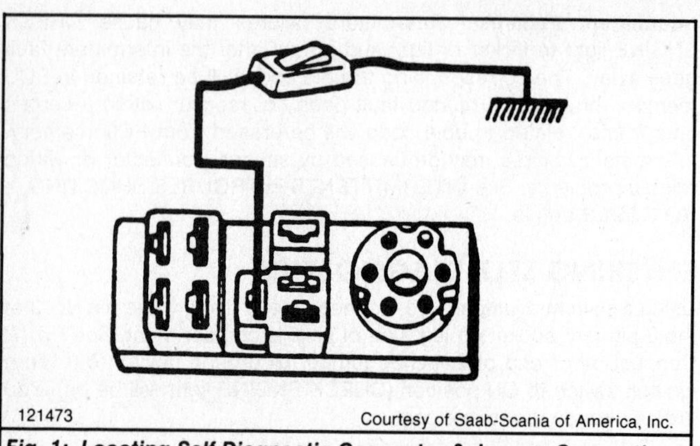

121473 Courtesy of Saab-Scania of America, Inc.

***Fig. 1: Locating Self-Diagnostic Connector & Jumper Connection***

## RETRIEVING CODES

Connect ISAT Scan tester (available from manufacturer) according to manufacturer's instructions. The diagnostic connector is under the right front seat, protected by a plastic cover. Follow instructions furnished with the tester to retrieve codes.

## CLEARING CODES

**1)** To erase codes, turn jumper switch on. After about 2.5 seconds, there will be 3 short flashes of CHECK ENGINE light. Immediately after third flash, turn jumper switch off.

**2)** Some faults can be classified as adaptation faults. Once the fault is corrected, the codes generated may not be erased until the system re-adapts to the new running conditions. See PROGRAMMING ECU.

## PROGRAMMING ECU

***NOTE: If the power supply to the ECU has been interrupted, the system must be reprogrammed.***

**9000 Series** – To program system, accelerate vehicle at full throttle from 2000-4500 RPM. Because programming occurs at 2750-4500 RPM and requires 3 seconds to complete, the procedure should be performed in a gear that permits operation between those engine speeds.

**900 Series** – Drive vehicle for 10 minutes with engine at normal operating temperature.

## ECU LOCATION

**900 Series** – The ignition ECU is located in the engine compartment, forward of the left wheel housing. The fuel injection ECU is located on the right kick panel. The automatic performance control ECU is located under the dash, left of the steering column.

**9000 Series** – The ECU's are under the left front seat.

## SUMMARY

If no hard fault codes (or only pass codes) are present, proceed to TROUBLE SHOOTING – NO CODES article for diagnosis by symptom (i.e., ROUGH IDLE, NO-START, etc.), or intermittent diagnostic procedures.

# 1991 ENGINE PERFORMANCE
# Trouble Shooting – No Codes

## 900 Series, 9000 Series

## INTRODUCTION

Before diagnosing symptoms or intermittent faults, perform steps in BASIC DIAGNOSTIC PROCEDURES and SELF-DIAGNOSTICS articles. Use this article to diagnose driveability problems existing when a hard fault code is not present.

***NOTE: Some driveability problems may have been corrected by manufacturer with a revised computer calibration chip or computer control unit. Check with manufacturer for latest chip or computer application.***

Symptom checks can direct the technician to malfunctioning component(s) for further diagnosis. A symptom should lead to a specific component, system test or an adjustment.

Use intermittent test procedures to locate driveability problems that DO NOT occur when the vehicle is being tested. These test procedures should also be used if a soft (intermittent) trouble code was present, but no problem was found during self-diagnostic testing.

***NOTE: For specific testing procedures, see SYSTEM & COMPONENT TESTING article. For specifications, see ON-VEHICLE ADJUSTMENTS or SERVICE & ADJUSTMENT SPECIFICATIONS article.***

## SYMPTOMS

### SYMPTOM DIAGNOSIS

Symptom checks cannot be used properly unless the problem occurs while the vehicle is being tested. To reduce diagnostic time, ensure steps in BASIC DIAGNOSTIC PROCEDURES and SELF-DIAGNOSTICS articles were performed before diagnosing a symptom. Symptoms available for diagnosis include:

- Engine Won't Start
- Engine Starts But Stops
- Rough or Unstable Idle
- Poor Response On Acceleration
- Engine Hesitates or Misses
- Poor Fuel Mileage
- Lack of Power

### ENGINE WON'T START

- Ensure electrical harness, connectors and wires are not broken or loose. Ensure battery voltage is at least 11.5 volts. Check system relay and fuel pump relay. On turbo models, check pressure switch. Check all ECU input signals.
- Using a spark tester, ensure that there is spark at the plugs.
- Ensure fuel pump is operating. Check fuel pressure and pressure regulator. Check for fuel line leaks or restrictions in return line.
- Check injector operation.
- Check induction system. Check for leaks downstream of throttle valve. Inspect duct between mass airflow meter and throttle body.
- Check coolant temperature sensor operation.
- Check Automatic Idle Control (AIC) valve.

### ENGINE STARTS BUT STOPS

- Ensure electrical harness, connectors and wires are not broken or loose. Ensure battery voltage is at least 11.5 volts. Check system relay and fuel pump relay. On turbo models, check pressure switch. Check all ECU input signals.
- Check coolant temperature sensor operation.
- Check induction system. Check for leaks downstream of throttle valve. Inspect duct between mass airflow meter and throttle body.
- CO too high or too low.
- Check throttle position sensor.
- Check Automatic Idle Control (AIC) valve.

### ROUGH OR UNSTABLE IDLE

- Check temperature sensor operation.
- Check for proper CO setting (if adjustable) on mass airflow meter. Check for broken mass airflow meter filament. Check mass airflow meter resistance.
- Check induction system. Check for vacuum leaks downstream of throttle valve. Inspect duct between mass airflow meter and throttle body.
- Check idle speed and EGR valve (if equipped) pulse ratio.
- Check injector operation and opening duration. Check injectors for leaks.
- Ensure fuel pump is okay. Check fuel pressure and pressure regulator. Check for leaks in fuel lines or restrictions in return line.
- Ensure electrical harness, connectors and wires are not broken or loose. Check all input signals to ECU.
- Check EGR valve (if equipped) for proper operation.
- Check oxygen sensor.

### POOR RESPONSE ON ACCELERATION

- Check for proper CO setting (if adjustable) on mass airflow meter and for broken filament. Check mass airflow meter resistance.
- Check induction system. Check for leaks downstream of throttle valve. Inspect duct between mass airflow meter and throttle body.
- On 900 Series vehicles, check idle speed and pulse ratio.
- Check injector operation and opening duration. Check injectors for leaks.
- Ensure fuel pump is okay. Check fuel pressure and pressure regulator. Check for leaks or restrictions.
- Ensure electrical harness, connectors and wires are not broken or loose. Check all input signals to ECU.
- Check temperature sensor.
- Check oxygen sensor.

### ENGINE HESITATES OR MISSES

- Ensure electrical harness, connectors and wires are not broken or loose. Check ECU connector pins No. 9, 11, 13, 17 and 25, and all input signals to ECU.
- Check charging system for low output and poor ground connections. Check all electrical connections for tightness.
- Check injector operation and opening duration. Check injectors for leaks.
- Check turbo and Automatic Performance Control (APC) systems for proper operation.
- Check throttle position sensor.
- Ensure mass airflow meter filament is not broken and burn-off function is working.
- Check induction system. Check for air leaks downstream of throttle valve. Inspect duct between mass airflow meter and throttle body.
- Ensure fuel pump is okay. Check fuel pressure and pressure regulator. Check for fuel leaks or restrictions in return line.
- Check temperature sensor.

### POOR FUEL MILEAGE

- Ensure fuel pump is okay. Check fuel pressure and pressure regulator. Check for fuel leaks or restrictions in return line.
- Check injector operation by unplugging connectors one at a time. Engine RPM should drop noticeably. Check opening duration. Check injectors for leaks.
- Check coolant temperature sensor.
- Check throttle position sensor.
- Ensure mass airflow meter filament is not broken and burn-off function is okay.
- Ensure electrical harness, connectors and wires are not broken or loose. Check all input signals to ECU.

# 1991 ENGINE PERFORMANCE
# Trouble Shooting – No Codes (Cont.)

### LACK OF POWER

- Check induction system. Check for air leaks downstream of throttle valve. Inspect duct between mass airflow meter and throttle body.
- Check throttle valve for binding and proper adjustment. Ensure throttle valve opens completely.
- Ensure fuel pump is okay. Check fuel pressure and pressure regulator. Check for leaks or restrictions in fuel line.
- Check injector operation by unplugging connectors one at a time. Engine RPM should drop noticeably. Check opening duration. Check injectors for leaks.
- Ensure mass airflow meter filament is not broken and burn-off function is working.
- Check turbo and Automatic Performance Control (APC) systems for proper operation.
- Check coolant temperature sensor operation.
- Ensure electrical harness, connectors and wires are not broken or loose. Check all input signals to ECU.

## INTERMITTENTS

### INTERMITTENT PROBLEM DIAGNOSIS

Intermittent fault testing requires reproducing circuit or component failure to identify the problem. These procedures may lead to the computer setting a fault code which may help in diagnosis.

Use a DVOM to pinpoint faults. When monitoring voltage, ensure ignition switch is in ON position or engine is running. Ensure ignition switch is in OFF position or negative battery cable is disconnected when monitoring circuit resistance. Status changes on DVOM during test procedures indicate area of fault.

### TEST PROCEDURES

**Intermittent Simulation** – To produce the conditions which create an intermittent fault so that it may be identified during testing, some of the following methods may be used:

- Lightly vibrate components.
- Heat a component.
- Wiggle or bend wiring harness.
- Spray component with water mist.
- Remove/apply vacuum supply source.

Monitor circuit/component voltage or resistance while attempting to reproduce an intermittent. If engine is running, monitor for self-diagnostic codes. Use the results of these tests to identify a faulty component or circuit.

## 900 Series, 9000 Series

## INTRODUCTION

Before testing separate components or systems, perform procedures in BASIC DIAGNOSTIC PROCEDURES article. Since many computer controlled and monitored components set a trouble code if they malfunction, also perform procedures in SELF-DIAGNOSTICS article.

***NOTE:** Testing of individual components does not isolate possible shorts or opens. Perform all voltage tests with a Digital Volt-Ohmmeter (DVOM) with a minimum 10-megohm input impedance, unless stated otherwise in testing procedures. Use ohmmeter to isolate wiring harness shorts or opens.*

Manufacturer recommends that trouble codes be retrieved, and diagnostic command codes be entered, with an ISAT Scan tester, a proprietary device available from manufacturer.

## AIR INDUCTION SYSTEMS

### TURBOCHARGER

**Pressure Transducer - 1)** Remove panel underneath dashboard (driver side). Unplug electrical connector from pressure transducer. Connect vacuum pump and pressure gauge to pressure transducer hose.
**2)** Measure resistance between transducer terminals (Black/White and Green/Red wires on mating connector). Resistance should be 8-13 ohms at atmospheric pressure.
**3)** Increase pressure to about 14.5 psi (1.0 kg/cm²) and then let it drop to 8.7 psi (0.6 kg/cm²), while tapping lightly on pressure transducer bracket. Resistance should be 83-93 ohms at 8.7 psi (0.6 kg/cm²). If resistance is not as specified, replace pressure transducer.
**Wastegate Solenoid Valve -** Test solenoid valve by connecting battery voltage to solenoid valve terminals. Valve should open when battery voltage is applied and close when power is removed. Replace wastegate solenoid valve if defective.

## COMPUTERIZED ENGINE CONTROLS

### FUEL INJECTION CONTROL UNIT

***NOTE:** On 900 Series, fuel injection control unit is located on right kick panel, behind trim. On 9000 Series, fuel injection control unit is located in engine compartment, on left side of firewall.*

**Ground Circuits - 1)** Turn ignition off. Connect negative lead of ohmmeter to ground. Using positive lead, backprobe ECU terminals No. 5 and No. 17 (Black wires). Resistance should be zero ohms. If not, repair open wire to ground.
**2)** Connect negative lead of DVOM to a good ground. Using positive lead, backprobe ECU terminals No. 5 and No. 17 (Black wires). With engine running, DVOM should indicate less than one volt. If higher than one volt, check for opens, corrosion, or loose connection on ground leads.
**Power Circuits - 1)** Check for battery voltage between ECU terminal No. 4 (Red wire) and ground. If battery voltage is not present, repair Red wire to main distribution terminal on battery bracket.
**2)** Turn ignition on. Check for battery voltage between ECU terminal No. 35 (Green/White wire) and ground. If battery voltage is not present, check fuse No. 14 on 900 Series, or fuse No. 13 on 9000 Series. Fuse panel is located in left side of engine compartment on 900 Series; behind panel inside glove compartment on 9000 Series. If fuse is okay, check for open Green/White wire between fuse box and ECU terminal No. 35, or check for a defective ignition switch.
**3)** Turn ignition on. Check for battery voltage between ECU terminal No. 9 and ground. If battery voltage is not present, check for open wire from ECU terminal No. 9 to main relay terminal No 2. On 900 Series, wire is Brown/White to fuel injector terminal block, and Blue/Red to main relay. On 9000 Series, wire is Gray/White to terminal block, and Blue/Red to main relay. If wire is okay, see MAIN RELAY.
**4)** Connect DVOM between ground and ECU terminal No. 1 (Blue wire). Turn ignition switch to START position. Voltage should be higher than 6.5 volts ONLY when ignition switch is in START position.
**5)** If voltage is not present, check for open Blue wire between terminal No. 1 of fuel injection ECU unit and terminal No. 29 of ignition ECU.

### EZK IGNITION CONTROL UNIT

**900 Series Ground Circuit - 1)** Turn ignition off. Locate ignition control unit in engine compartment, forward of left front wheel housing. Connect negative lead of ohmmeter to ground. Backprobe ECU terminal No. 20 (Black wire). Resistance should be zero ohms. If not, repair open to ground.
**2)** Connect negative lead of DVOM to a good ground. Backprobe ECU terminal No. 20. With vehicle running, DVOM should indicate less than one volt. If voltage is higher than one volt, check for open, corrosion or loose connection on ground lead.
**900 Series Power Circuit -** Turn ignition on. Check for battery voltage between ECU terminal No. 6 (Green/White wire) and ground. If battery voltage is not present, check fuse No. 3. Fuse panel is located in left side of engine compartment. If fuse is okay, check for open Green/White wire between fuse panel and ECU terminal No. 6, or for a defective ignition switch.

### DIS IGNITION CONTROL UNIT

**9000 Series Ground Circuit - 1)** Locate ignition control unit under driver's seat. Turn ignition off. Connect negative lead of ohmmeter to ground. Using positive lead, check for continuity between ECU terminal No. 13 (Black wire) and ground. Resistance should be zero ohms. If not, repair open to ground.
**2)** Connect negative lead of DVOM to a good ground. Backprobe ECU terminal No. 13 (Black wire). With vehicle running, DVOM should indicate less than one volt. If voltage is higher than one volt, check for open, corrosion, or loose connection on ground lead.
**9000 Series Power Circuit - 1)** Check for battery voltage between ECU terminal No. 22 (Red wire) and ground. If battery voltage is not present, check fuse No. 23 on power distribution panel behind glove box. If fuse is okay, repair Red wire to fuse No. 23, or Red wire from fuse panel to main distribution terminal on battery bracket.
**2)** Turn ignition on. Check for battery voltage between ECU terminal No. 35 (Green/Red wire) and ground. If battery voltage is not present, check for open Green/Red wire from ECU terminal No. 35 to main relay terminal No. 3. If wire is okay, check main relay. See MAIN RELAY.
**3)** Turn ignition on. Check for battery voltage between ECU terminal No. 21 (Green/White wire) and ground. If battery voltage is not present, check fuse No. 9 on fuse panel in engine compartment. If fuse is okay, check for open Green/White wire from ECU to fuse panel, open Green/White wire from ignition switch to fuse panel, or defective ignition switch.

## ENGINE SENSORS & SWITCHES

**Coolant Temperature Sensor -** Turn ignition off. Unplug sensor connector. Sensor is threaded into intake manifold. Measure resistance between sensor terminals. Replace sensor if resistance is not as specified in ENGINE COOLANT TEMPERATURE SENSOR RESISTANCE table.

***ENGINE COOLANT TEMPERATURE SENSOR RESISTANCE***

| Temperature - °F (°C) | Ohms |
|---|---|
| -4 (-20) | 14,000 |
| 32 ( 0) | 5800 |
| 68 (20) | 2600 |
| 86 (30) | 1700 |
| 176 (80) | 320 |

***WARNING:** To prevent engine from starting when checking Hall Effect sensor, disable ignition by disconnecting coil primary wires on 900 Series, or by unplugging connector to ignition cartridge on 9000 Series. DO NOT rotate engine more than necessary to check Hall Effect sensor.*

# 1991 ENGINE PERFORMANCE
# System & Component Testing (Cont.)

**Hall Effect Sensor – 1)** Turn ignition on. Connect DVOM between ignition ECU terminals No. 4 (Red wire) and No. 10 (Black wire) on 900 Series, or between terminals No. 6 (Red wire) and No. 15 (Black wire) on 9000 Series. Voltage should be at least 10 volts.
**2)** Connect DVOM between ignition ECU terminals No. 10 (Black wire) and No. 24 (Green/Red wire) on 900 Series, or between terminals No. 15 (Black wire) and No. 23 (Green/Red wire) on fuel injection ECU on 9000 Series. Slowly turn engine over by hand. Voltage should be less than 0.4 volt (shutter open) or higher than 3.0 volts (shutter closed).
**3)** If voltage is not as specified, check wiring harness and connectors. If wiring and connectors are okay, replace Hall Effect sensor, located behind crankshaft pulley.
**4)** If engine performance is poor, check ignition timing. If timing marks appear to move back and forth, inspect sensor for chips or a loosely mounted magnet. Repair or replace as necessary.
**Mass Airflow Meter – 1)** Check induction system from throttle body to engine for air/vacuum leaks. Connect ISAT Scan tester according to manufacturer's instructions. Diagnostic connector is under right front seat, protected by a plastic cover. Follow instructions furnished with tester to retrieve codes. Enter command code 22A. Go to step **2)** if tester does not display 802.2 at idle and 805.0 at full throttle.
**2)** Turn ignition off. Unplug connector from mass airflow meter. Check for continuity between harness connector terminal No. 1 and ground. If no continuity, repair Black wire between terminal No. 1 and ground terminal on intake manifold.
**3)** Reconnect wiring to mass airflow meter. Turn ignition on. Check for battery voltage at terminal No. 5 (Brown/White wire) on harness connector. If battery voltage is not present, repair Brown/White wire between connector and pin No. 87 of system relay.
**4)** Enter ISAT command code 22A. Check that signal varies between 2 and 5 volts (display varies between 802.0 and 805.0) depending on load. If not, check Orange/Green wire between mass airflow meter pin No. 3 and ECU pin No. 7.
**5)** Turn ignition off. Check for continuity between mass airflow harness connector pin No. 2 (Blue/White wire) and ECU pin No. 6. If no continuity, repair Blue/White wire.
**6)** Clear codes and drive vehicle. If code resets, try a known good mass airflow meter. If code still resets, try a known good ECU.
**Mass Airflow Meter Burn-Off Function – 1)** With mass airflow meter disconnected from air cleaner, but wiring still attached, start and warm engine to 158°F (70°C). Let engine idle. Increase engine speed to 2500 RPM, release throttle, and again let engine idle.
**2)** Turn engine off. After 4 seconds, filament should glow brightly for about one second. If filament does not glow, turn engine off and unplug mass airflow meter connector.
**3)** With ignition on, check for 12 volts between harness connector pin No. 5 (Brown/White wire) and ground. If no voltage, repair Brown/White wire from pin No. 5 to pin No. 87B of system relay.
**4)** Turn ignition off. Check for continuity between harness connector terminal No. 1 and ground. If no continuity, repair Black wire between pin No. 1 and ground terminal on intake manifold.
**5)** If malfunction persists, temporarily install a known good mass air flow meter. Clear codes and drive vehicle. If code appears again, reinstall original mass airflow meter and replace ECU.
**Oxygen ($O_2$) Sensor – 1)** Turn ignition off. Disconnect 2-wire $O_2$ sensor connector. Sensor is threaded into exhaust manifold. Measure resistance between 2 White wires. Resistance should be about 4 ohms.
**2)** Set DVOM to 2-volt DC scale. Connect DVOM leads between Black sensor wire and ground. Start engine. With sensor at operating temperature, voltage should fluctuate between 0.1-0.9 volt. Replace $O_2$ sensor if resistance or voltage is not as specified.
**Throttle Position Sensor – 1)** Connect ISAT Scan tester according to manufacturer's instructions. Diagnostic connector is under right front seat, protected by a plastic cover. Turn ignition on. Enter command code 279. With accelerator pedal in idle position, tester should display 80000. Tester should display 80085 with pedal in full throttle position. If not okay, go to step **2)**.
**2)** Turn ignition off. Unplug connector from throttle position sensor, located on throttle body. Connect ohmmeter to terminals No. 1 and No. 3 on sensor. At idle position, resistance should be 2600-3000 ohms. Resistance should be 1100-1500 ohms at full throttle. Replace throttle position sensor if resistance is not within specifications.
**3)** Turn ignition on. Measure voltage between terminal No. 1 (Green/Red wire) of throttle position sensor harness connector and a good engine ground. If voltage is not 5 volts, check Green/Red wire between harness connector and ECU pin No. 10 for opens or shorts to ground.
**4)** Turn ignition off. Check for continuity between terminal No. 2 (Black/White wire) of throttle position harness connector and a good ground. Repair Black/White wire if there is no continuity.
**5)** Reconnect wiring to sensor. Turn ignition on. Measure voltage between sensor terminal No. 2 (Black wire) and a good ground. At idle position, voltage should be about 0.2 volt.
**6)** Measure voltage between sensor terminal No. 2 (Black wire) and a good ground. With accelerator pedal in full throttle position, voltage should be about 4 volts. Replace throttle position sensor if voltage or resistance is not within specifications.
**Vehicle Speed Sensor (900 Series) – 1)** Ensure speedometer works. Disconnect ECU. Connect DVOM between fuel injection ECU harness connector pin No. 34 and ground. Turn ignition on. Rotate one front wheel. If voltage does not fluctuate between 0.5 and 5 volts, check fuse No. 22 and replace if defective.
**2)** Check Green wire between fuel injection ECU connector pin No. 34 and speed sensor behind speedometer. Check Black wire between sensor connector and ground. Check Green/White wire between sensor connector and fuse panel.
**3)** Temporarily install a known good speed sensor. Clear codes and drive vehicle. If code appears again, reinstall original sensor and replace ECU.
**Vehicle Speed Sensor (9000 Series) – 1)** Go to step **5)** if speedometer works. If not, unplug 2-pin connector from speedometer. Set DVOM to measure AC voltage. Connect DVOM to terminals on harness connector. Spin wheels with engine. Voltage should increase from zero to 5 volts as speed increases.
**2)** With wheels stopped, signal should be zero or 12 volts, depending on wheel position. If signal is absent or incorrect, check Green wire between speed sensor and ignition ECU pin No. 34. If signal is okay, install a known good ignition ECU.
**3)** With ignition on, check for battery voltage at pin No. 1 (Green/White wire) of speed sensor connector at speedometer. If not, repair Green/White wire from connector to ignition switch.
**4)** With ignition off, check for continuity between sensor harness connector terminal No. 3 (Black wire) and ground. If no continuity, repair Black wire between harness connector and ground.
**5)** Temporarily install a known good speed sensor. Clear codes and drive vehicle. If code appears again, reinstall original sensor and replace ECU.

## MODULES, RELAYS & SOLENOIDS

### MODULES

**Ignition Module** – See COMPUTERIZED ENGINE CONTROLS.

### RELAYS

***NOTE: For ECU and relay terminal numbers or location, refer to WIRING DIAGRAMS article.***

**A/C Clutch Relay** – See MISCELLANEOUS CONTROLS.
**Cooling Fan Control Relay** – See MISCELLANEOUS CONTROLS.
**Fuel Pump Relay – 1)** Turn ignition off. Unplug fuel injection ECU connector. Ground ECU harness connector harness terminals No. 20 (Yellow/White wire) and No. 21 (Violet wire). If fuel pump runs, fuel pump relay is okay. If fuel pump does not run, go to step **2)**.

# 1991 ENGINE PERFORMANCE
# System & Component Testing (Cont.)

**2)** Remove jumper wires. Remove fuel pump relay. Relay is located on right kick panel, behind trim. Check for voltage at relay socket terminal No. 86 (Brown/White wire). If no voltage, repair Brown/White wire to main relay, or go to MAIN RELAY.
**3)** Check for voltage at relay socket terminal No. 30 (Red wire). If no voltage, repair Red wire to main battery junction on battery bracket.
**4)** Reinstall relay. Connect DVOM to relay terminal No. 87B (Green/Red wire) and ground. Using a jumper wire, ground terminal No. 85 (Violet wire). Replace relay if DVOM does not indicate battery voltage.
**Main Relay - 1)** Turn ignition off. Unplug connector from fuel injection ECU. Connect DVOM to terminal No. 5 (Brown/White wire) at mass airflow meter and ground. Using a jumper wire, ground harness connector terminals No. 20 (Violet wire) and No. 21 (Yellow/White wire). If fuel pump runs and DVOM indicates battery voltage, main relay is okay. If not, go to step **2)**.
**2)** Remove jumper wires. Remove main relay. Relay is located on right kick panel, behind trim. Check for battery voltage at relay socket terminals No. 30 (Red wire) and No. 86 (Red wire). If no voltage, repair Red wires to main battery junction on battery bracket.
**3)** Reinstall relay. Connect DVOM to relay terminal No. 87B (single Blue/Red wire on 900 Series; Green/White wire on 9000 Series) and ground. Using a jumper wire, ground terminal No. 85 (Yellow/White wire). Replace relay if DVOM does not indicate battery voltage.
**4)** Leave jumper wire in place. Connect DVOM to relay terminal No. 87 (Blue/Red and Brown/White wires on 900 Series; Blue/Red wire on 9000 Series) and ground. Replace relay if DVOM does not indicate battery voltage.

### SOLENOIDS

**Canister Purge Solenoid** - See FUEL EVAPORATION under EMISSION SYSTEMS & SUB-SYSTEMS.
**Wastegate Solenoid Valve** - See AIR INDUCTION SYSTEMS.

## FUEL SYSTEM

### FUEL DELIVERY

***NOTE: For fuel system pressure testing, see BASIC DIAGNOSTIC PROCEDURES article.***

### FUEL CONTROL

**Fuel Injectors** - Unplug electrical connector. Measure resistance between injector terminals. Resistance should be 10-20 ohms with injector at 68°F (20°C). If resistance is not as specified, replace injector.

## IDLE CONTROL SYSTEM

**Automatic Idle Control (AIC) - 1)** Connect ISAT Scan tester according to manufacturer's instructions. Diagnostic connector is under right front seat, protected by a plastic cover. Turn ignition on. Enter command code 553. Listen for sound from AIC valve, located on intake manifold.
**2)** If no sound, leave ignition on. Check that battery voltage is available at pin No. 2 (Blue/Red wire) on AIC valve. If no voltage, repair Blue/Red and Green/White wires to pin No. 87 of main relay.
**3)** Turn ignition off. Unplug connector from AIC valve. Measure resistance between pins No. 1 and No. 2 (Blue/Red and Blue/White wires on mating connector).
**4)** Measure resistance between pins No. 2 and No. 3 (Gray/Red wire on 900 Series; Green/Gray wire on 9000 Series) and Blue/Red wires on mating connector. Replace AIC valve if resistance is not 10-15 ohms for each measurement.
**5)** With ignition off, check Blue/White wire between AIC valve connector and pin No. 33 on fuel injection ECU for open or short circuit. Repair wire if defective.
**6)** With ignition off, check Gray/Red (900 Series) or Green/Gray (9000 Series) wire between AIC valve connector and pin No. 15 on fuel injection ECU. Repair wire if it is shorted or open.

**Transmission Range Switch - 1)** Connect ISAT Scan tester according to manufacturer's instructions. Diagnostic connector is under right front seat, protected by a plastic cover. Turn ignition on. Enter command code 203. With transmission lever in Park or Neutral position, tester should display 8B003. Tester should display 8B103 in all other positions. If not, check fuse No. 13 on 900 Series, or fuse No. 9 on 9000 Series.
**2)** With ignition on, check for battery voltage at White wire at switch, located at base of transmission selector lever. If no voltage, repair White wire back to fuse panel.
**3)** Set transmission selector lever in turn to Park and Neutral positions. With ignition on, check that no voltage appears at Orange wire on switch with lever in either position. With lever in all other positions, battery voltage should appear at Orange wire. Replace switch if it does not meet specifications.
**4)** Connect DVOM to pin No. 30 (Orange wire) at fuel injection ECU. Battery voltage should appear with switch in all positions but Park or Neutral. Repair Orange wire between switch and ECU if voltage does not appear.

## IGNITION SYSTEM

***NOTE: For basic ignition checks, see BASIC DIAGNOSTIC PROCEDURES article.***

### TIMING CONTROL SYSTEMS

**Advance Components** - Timing advance is controlled by the ignition ECU on all models.
**Retard Components** - All models are equipped with a knock sensor. 900 Turbo vehicles are equipped with a retard cylinder on the distributor, which retards timing in response to increasing boost pressure. Except for those components, all retard functions are controlled by the ignition ECU. See KNOCK SENSOR and RETARD CYLINDER (900 TURBO).
**Knock Sensor - 1)** Connect timing light. With engine running at a fast idle, tap cylinder head with a plastic mallet. If timing retards, knock sensor is okay. If timing does not retard, turn ignition off. Go to step **2)** for 900 Series vehicles, or to step **4)** for 9000 Series vehicles.
**2)** Locate knock sensor under intake manifold. Unplug connectors from sensor and ignition ECU. Check Green wire for continuity between harness connector and ignition ECU pin No. 13. Also check Green wire for short to ground, to Brown wire, or to shield.
**3)** Check Brown wire for continuity between harness connector and ignition ECU pin No. 12. Also check Brown wire for short to ground, to Green wire, or to shield. Ensure there is continuity between shield and ground. Replace wire assembly if defective. Go to step **6)**.
**4)** Locate knock sensor under intake manifold. Unplug connectors from sensor and ignition ECU. Check Gray wire for continuity between harness connector and ignition ECU pin No. 11. Also check Gray wire for short to shield or to ground.
**5)** Check shield for continuity between sensor harness connector and ignition ECU pin No. 30. Check shield for short to ground. Replace wire assembly if defective.
**6)** Temporarily replace knock sensor with a known good one. Repeat step **1)**. If timing still does not retard, reinstall original sensor and replace ignition ECU.
**Retard Cylinder (900 Turbo)** - If timing does not retard as boost pressure increases, check hose from throttle body to distributor. If hose is okay, repair or replace distributor.

## EMISSION SYSTEMS & SUB-SYSTEMS

### EXHAUST GAS RECIRCULATION

**1)** Connect ISAT Scan tester according to manufacturer's instructions. Diagnostic connector is under right front seat, protected by a plastic cover. Turn ignition on. Enter command code 555. Listen for sound of modulation valve, located forward of left front wheel housing. If there is sound from valve, go to step **5)**. If there is no sound, go to step **2)**.

# 1991 ENGINE PERFORMANCE
# System & Component Testing (Cont.)

**2)** Turn ignition off. Unplug connector from modulation valve. Measure resistance between modulation valve terminals. If resistance is not about 30 ohms, replace valve.
**3)** Turn ignition on. Check for battery voltage at Green/White wire on modulation valve harness connector. If no voltage, repair Green/White and/or Blue/Red wires to pin No. 87 of fuel injection relay.
**4)** With ignition off, unplug fuel injection ECU. Check White and Yellow/White leads between modulation valve harness connector and ECU for open or short circuit. If valve and wiring are okay, replace fuel injection ECU.
**5)** Reconnect wiring to modulation valve and fuel injection ECU. Locate EGR temperature sensor. Temperature sensor is integral with EGR valve, located on intake manifold. Unplug connector from EGR temperature sensor.
**6)** Start engine. With engine idling, measure resistance between EGR sensor terminals. Resistance should be several megohms. Apply vacuum to valve by connecting vacuum pump to Red-marked hose. Sensor resistance should drop to several thousand ohms. Replace EGR valve if resistance is not as specified.
**7)** With ignition off, unplug fuel injection ECU connector. Check Yellow/White wire between EGR temperature sensor and fuel injector ECU terminal No. 23 for open or short to ground. Check Black wire between temperature sensor and ground.
**8)** If fault persists, disconnect Red-marked hose from modulation valve. Apply vacuum to hose. If engine RPM drops, EGR valve is okay. If not, check hoses, connections, and vacuum tank.

### FUEL EVAPORATION

**EVAP Canister** - The EVAP canister on 900 Series is located in the engine compartment, forward of the left wheel front housing. The EVAP canister on 9000 Series is forward of the right front wheel housing. On all models, EVAP solenoid valve is located atop the canister.
**EVAP Solenoid Valve** - **1)** Connect ISAT Scan tester according to manufacturer's instructions. Diagnostic connector is under right front seat, protected by a plastic cover. Turn ignition on. Enter command code 554. Listen for valve operation sound. If no sound, go to step **2)**.
**2)** With ignition on, check that battery voltage appears at EVAP solenoid valve pin No. 2. If not, check Green/White wire between harness connector and pin No. 87 of main relay.
**3)** Unplug connector from valve. Measure resistance between valve terminals. Replace valve if resistance is not 40-60 ohms.
**4)** With ignition off, unplug fuel injection ECU connector. Check Yellow/Red wire between valve harness connector and pin No. 27 of ECU connector. Repair Yellow/Red wire if it is open or shorted to ground. If valve and wiring are okay, replace fuel injection ECU.

## THROTTLE CONTROLS

**Dashpot** - **1)** Connect tachometer. Warm engine to normal operating temperature. Adjust idle speed to specification. See ON-VEHICLE ADJUSTMENTS article.
**2)** Increase engine speed to 3000 RPM. Release throttle, noting time between release of throttle and return to idle. Deceleration time should be 3-5 seconds from contact of plunger.

## MISCELLANEOUS CONTROLS

***NOTE: Although some of the controlled devices listed here are not technically engine performance components, they can affect driveability if they malfunction.***

### A/C CLUTCH

**A/C Clutch Relay (900 Non-Turbo)** - **1)** Remove relay from relay panel. Relay panel is located under hood, on left side.
**2)** Check for continuity between relay terminals No. 30 (Yellow wire on socket) and No. 87B (Red wire on socket). Replace relay if continuity exists.
**3)** Check for continuity between relay terminals No. 30 (Yellow wire on socket) and No. 87 (Green wire on socket). Replace relay if continuity exists.
**4)** Connect 12 volts to relay terminal No. 86 (Blue wire on socket). Connect terminal No. 85 (Black wire on socket) to ground. Relay should click.
**5)** Check for continuity between relay terminals No. 30 (Yellow wire on socket) and No. 87B (Red wire on socket). Replace relay if there is no continuity.
**6)** Check for continuity between relay terminals No. 30 (Yellow wire on socket) and No. 87 (Green wire on socket). Replace relay if there is no continuity.
**A/C Clutch Relay (900 Turbo)** - **1)** Remove relay from relay panel. Relay panel is located under hood, on left side. Measure and record resistance between relay terminals No. 5 and No. 3 (Black and Red wires on socket). Transpose ohmmeter leads, then measure resistance between same terminals. Replace relay if resistance is not high for one measurement and low for the other.
**2)** Check for continuity between relay terminals No. 30 (Yellow wire on socket) and No. 87B (Red wire on socket). Replace relay if continuity exists.
**3)** Check for continuity between relay terminals No. 30 (Yellow wire on socket) and No. 87 (Green wire on socket). Replace relay if continuity exists.
**4)** Connect one lead of ohmmeter to terminal No. 30 (Yellow wire on socket. Connect relay terminal No. 15 (Green/White wire on socket) to battery voltage. Connect terminal No. 31 (Black wire on socket) to ground.
**5)** Momentarily connect terminal No. 50 (Yellow wire on socket) to battery voltage. Connect terminal No. 86 (Blue/White wire on socket) to battery voltage. Relay should click in about 10 seconds.
**6)** Connect remaining ohmmeter lead in turn to terminals No. 87B (Red wire on socket) and No. 87 (Blue wire on socket). Ohmmeter should indicate continuity at both terminals.
**7)** Measure voltage between terminal No. 14 (Red/White wire on socket) and ground. DVOM should indicate battery voltage.
**8)** Measure voltage between terminal TK (Blue wire on socket) and ground. DVOM should indicate battery voltage. Replace relay if voltage or resistance measurements are not as specified.
**A/C Clutch Relay (9000 Series)** - **1)** Remove relay from relay panel. Relay panel is located behind glove box.
**2)** Check for continuity between relay terminals No. 30 (Yellow wire on socket) and No. 87B (Blue wire on socket). Replace relay if continuity exists.
**3)** Check for continuity between relay terminals No. 30 (Yellow wire on socket) and No. 87 (Green wire on socket). Replace relay if continuity exists.
**4)** Connect 12 volts to relay terminal No. 86 (Green/White wire on socket). Connect terminal No. 85 (Black wire on socket) to ground. Relay should click.
**5)** Check for continuity between relay terminals No. 30 (Yellow wire on socket) and No. 87B (Blue wire on socket). Replace relay if there is no continuity.
**6)** Check for continuity between relay terminals No. 30 (Yellow wire on socket) and No. 87 (Green wire on socket). Replace relay if there is no continuity.

### COOLING FAN

**Cooling Fan Motor (900 Series)** - Unplug connector from cooling fan. Apply 12 volts to one terminal of fan connector. Ground remaining fan connector terminal. Replace fan if it does not run.
**Cooling Fan Motor (9000 Series)** - **1)** For models without air conditioning, go to step **3)**. Unplug connector from cooling fan. Connect Green/White and White wires together at fan connector. Connect 12 volts to connection just made. Connect either Black wire to ground. Replace fan motor if it does not run at high speed.
**2)** Disconnect wiring installed in step **1)**. Connect 12 volts to Green wire. Connect remaining Black wire to ground. Replace fan motor if it does not run at low speed.
**3)** Unplug connector from cooling fan. Apply 12 volts to one terminal of fan connector. Ground remaining fan connector terminal. Replace fan if it doesn't run.

# 1991 ENGINE PERFORMANCE
# System & Component Testing (Cont.)

**Cooling Fan Control Relay (900 Series)** – On 900 Series, the cooling fan is controlled by the air conditioner clutch relay. See A/C CLUTCH RELAY.

**Cooling Fan Control Relay (9000 Series)** – **1)** For models with air conditioning, go to step **5)**. For models without air conditioning, go to step **2)**.

**2)** Remove relay from socket in panel behind glove box. Check that there is no continuity between terminals No. 30 (Yellow wire on socket) and No. 87 (Green wire on socket). Connect terminals No. 9 (Black wire on socket) and No. 5 (Blue wire on socket) to ground.

**3)** Apply 12 volts to terminal No. 15 (Gray wire on socket). Check that there is continuity between terminals No. 30 (Yellow wire on socket) and No. 87 (Green wire on socket).

**4)** Leave power connected. After about 10 minutes, relay should open. Check that there is again no continuity between terminals No. 30 (Yellow wire on socket) and No. 87 (Green wire on socket).

**5)** Models with air conditioning are equipped with 2 fan control relays. One relay controls high speed operation; the other low speed. To test high speed relay, go to step **6)**. Go to step **8)** to test low speed relay.

**6)** Remove relay from socket behind glove box. Check that there is no continuity between terminals No. 30 (Yellow/White wire on socket) and No. 87 (Green/White and White wires on socket).

**7)** Connect terminal No. 5 (Blue/White wire on socket) to ground. Connect 12 volts to terminal No. 4 (Gray wire on socket). Check that there is continuity between terminals No. 30 (Yellow/White wire on socket) and No. 87 (Green/White and White wires on socket).

**8)** Remove relay from socket in panel behind glove box. Check that there is no continuity between terminals No. 30 (Yellow wire on socket) and No. 87 (Green wire on socket). Connect terminals No. 9 (Black wire on socket) and No. 5 (Blue wire on socket) to ground.

**9)** Apply 12 volts to terminal No. 15 (Gray wire on socket). Check that there is continuity between terminals No. 30 (Yellow wire on socket) and No. 87 (Green wire on socket).

**10)** Leave power connected. After about 10 minutes, relay should open. Check that there is again no continuity between terminals No. 30 (Yellow wire on socket) and No. 87 (Green wire on socket).

# Sensor Operating Range Charts

## 900 Series, 9000 Series

## INTRODUCTION

Sensor operating range information can help determine if a sensor is out of calibration. An out-of-calibration sensor may not set a trouble code, but it may cause driveability problems.

***NOTE: Perform all voltage tests with a Digital Volt-Ohmmeter (DVOM) with a minimum 10-megohm input impedance, unless stated otherwise in test procedure.***

***COOLANT TEMPERATURE SENSOR RESISTANCE TEST*** [1]

| Temperature – °F (°C) | Ohms |
|---|---|
| 32 ( 0) | 5800 |
| 50 (10) | 3800 |
| 59 (15) | 3000 |
| 68 (20) | 2600 |
| 77 (25) | 2000 |
| 86 (30) | 1700 |
| 176 (80) | 320 |

[1] – Measure resistance across sensor terminals.

***OXYGEN SENSOR VOLTAGE TEST***

| Condition | [1] Volts |
|---|---|
| Lean | 0-.4 |
| Rich | .6-1.0 |

[1] – With engine running, measure voltage between pin No. 24 of fuel injection ECU and ground.

***THROTTLE POSITION SENSOR RESISTANCE TEST*** [1]

| Position | Ohms |
|---|---|
| Fully Closed | 2600-3000 |
| Fully Open | 1100-1500 |

[1] – Measure resistance between terminals No. 1 and 3.

***VEHICLE SPEED SENSOR VOLTAGE TEST*** [1]

| Application | Volts |
|---|---|
| 900 Series | [2] .5-5 |
| 9000 Series | [3] 0-5 |

[1] – Measure voltage between fuel injection ECU terminal No. 34 and ground.
[2] – With one front wheel rotating.
[3] – Rotate front wheels with engine. Voltage should increase with increasing wheel RPM.

# 1991 ENGINE PERFORMANCE
# Wiring Diagrams

## 900 Series, 9000 Series

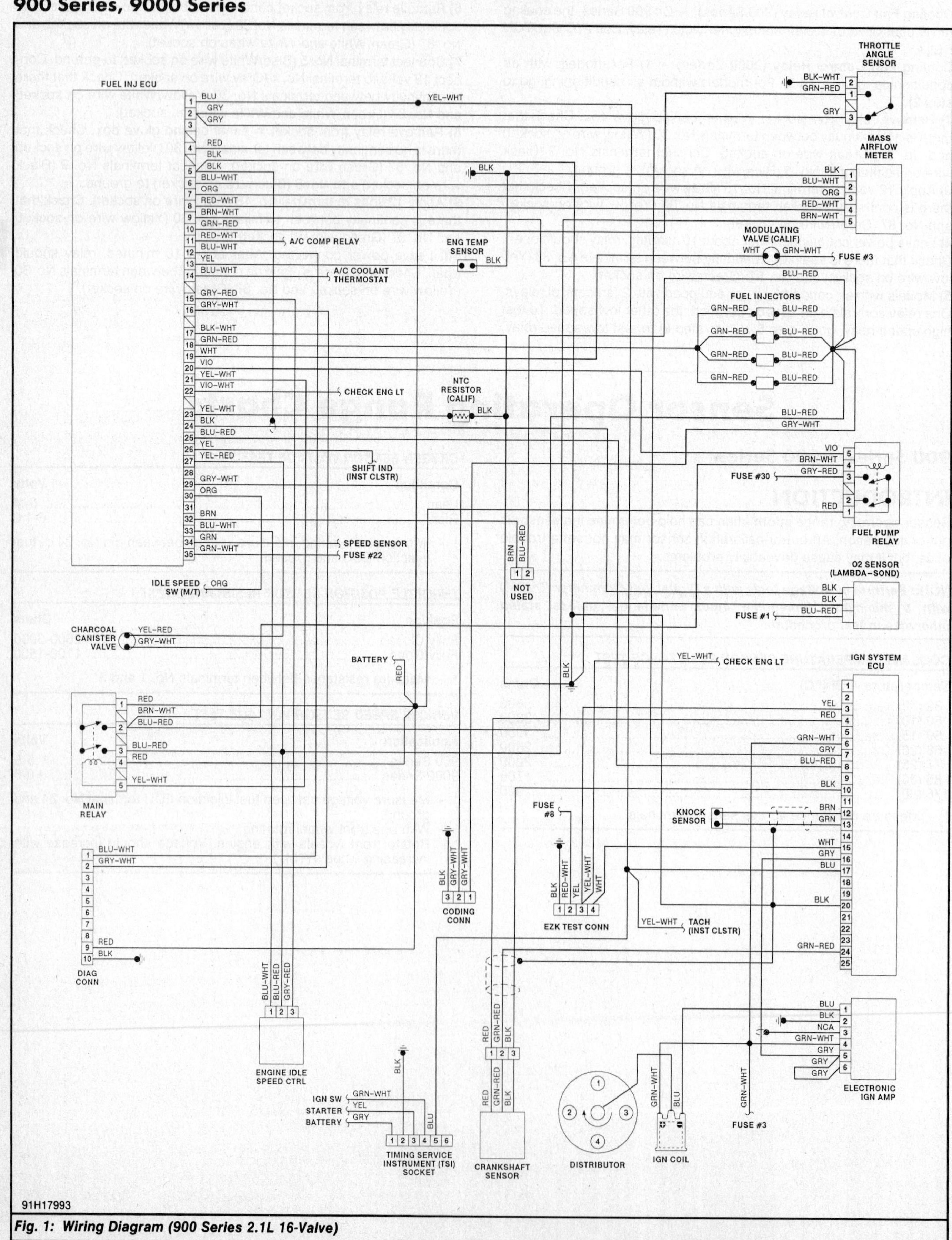


*Fig. 1: Wiring Diagram (900 Series 2.1L 16-Valve)*

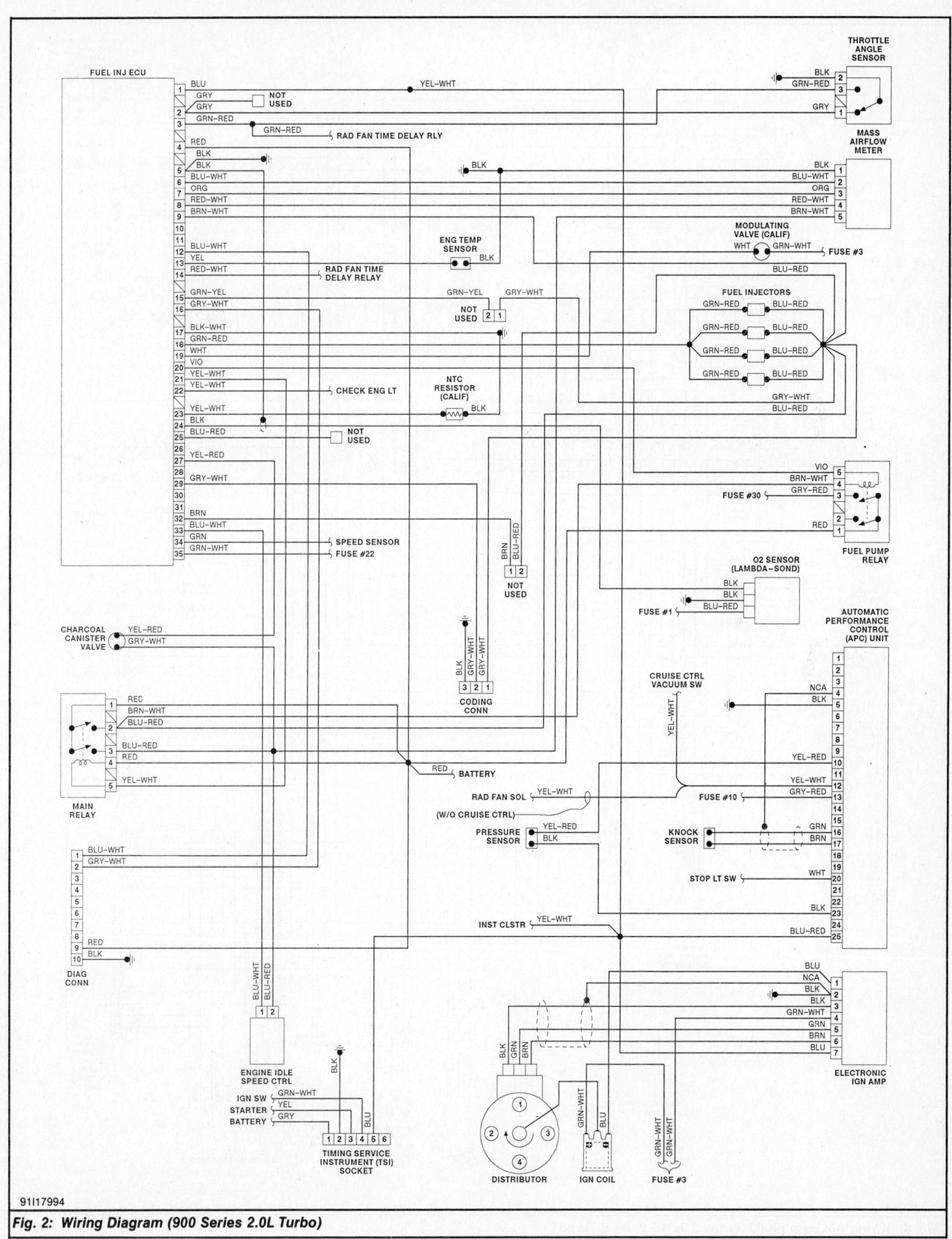


*Fig. 2: Wiring Diagram (900 Series 2.0L Turbo)*

# 1991 ENGINE PERFORMANCE
## Wiring Diagrams (Cont.)

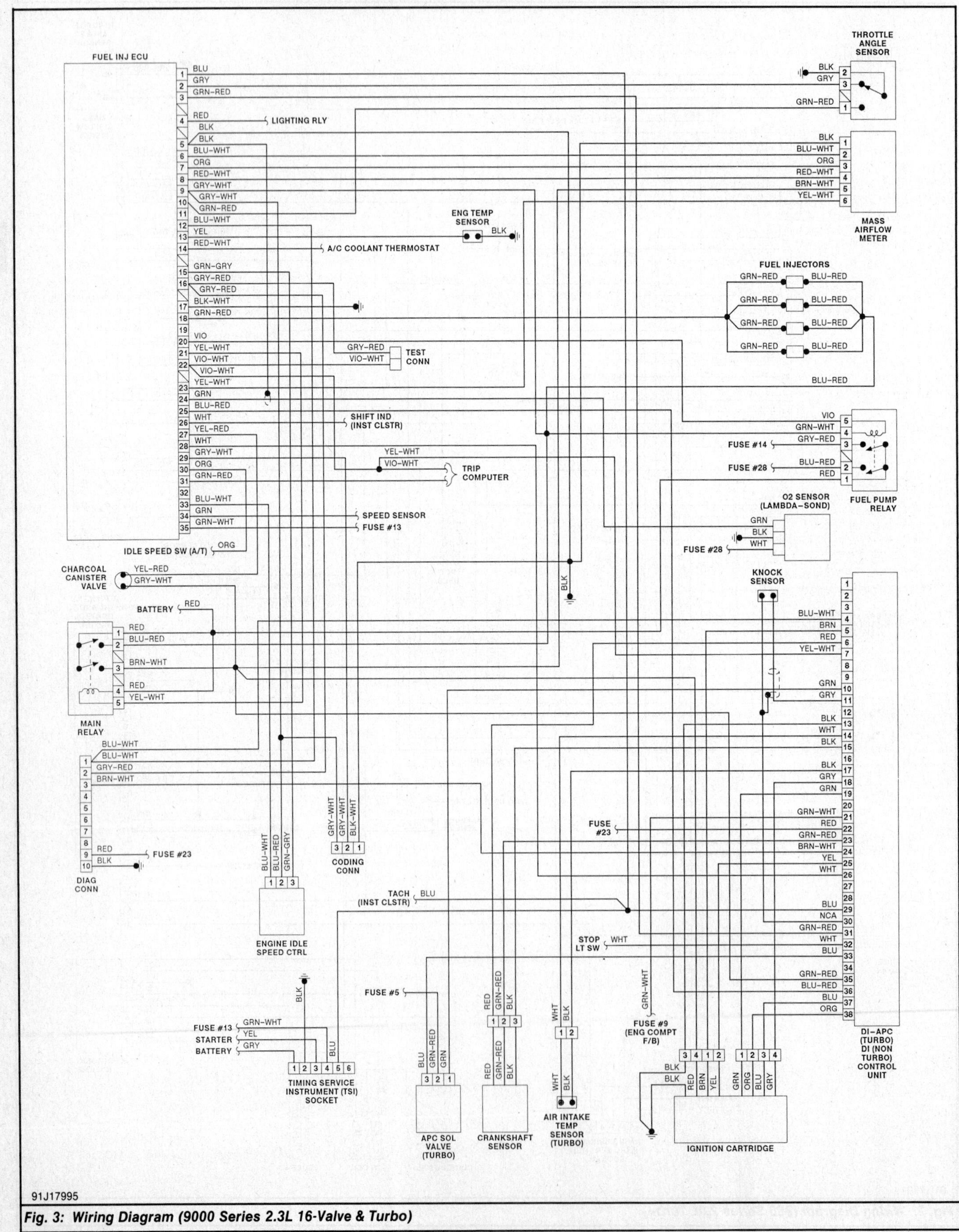


*Fig. 3: Wiring Diagram (9000 Series 2.3L 16-Valve & Turbo)*

# 1991 ENGINE PERFORMANCE
# Vacuum Diagrams

## 900 Series, 9000 Series

## INTRODUCTION

This article contains underhood views or schematics of vacuum hose routing. Use these vacuum diagrams during the visual inspection portion of BASIC DIAGNOSTIC PROCEDURES article. This will assist in identifying improperly routed vacuum hoses which may cause driveability and/or computer indicated malfunctions.

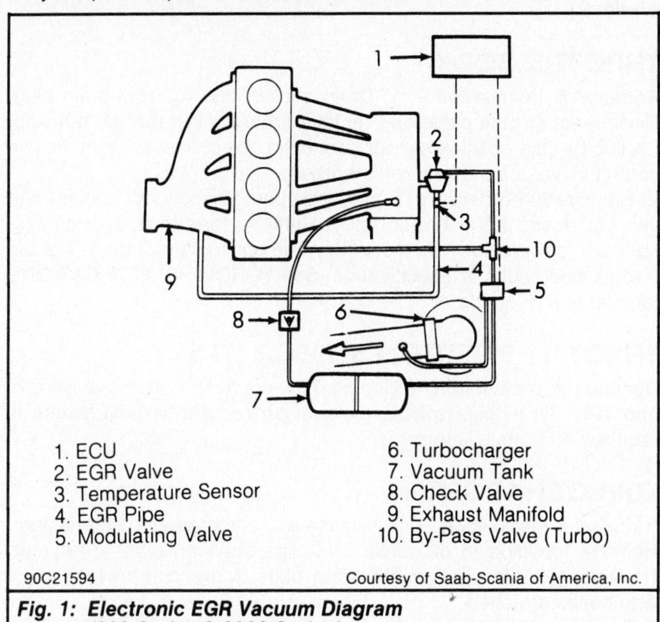


*Fig. 1: Electronic EGR Vacuum Diagram (900 Series & 9000 Series)*

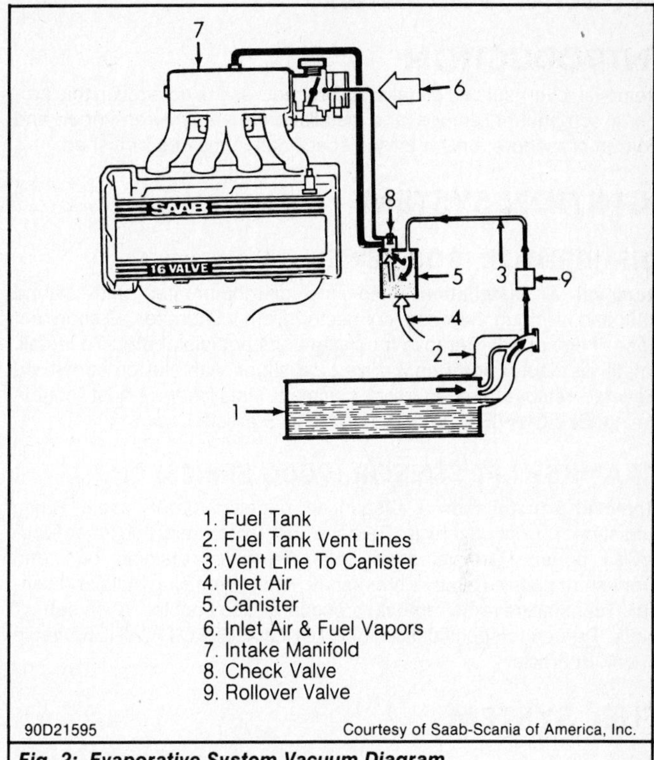


*Fig. 2: Evaporative System Vacuum Diagram (900 Series & 9000 Series)*

# 1991 ENGINE PERFORMANCE
# Removal, Overhaul & Installation

900 Series, 9000 Series

## INTRODUCTION

Removal, overhaul and installation procedures are covered in this article. If component removal and installation is primarily an unbolt and bolt-on procedure, only a torque specification may be furnished.

## IGNITION SYSTEM

### DISTRIBUTOR (900 SERIES)

**Removal & Installation** - Remove distributor cap with wiring attached. Unplug harness connector from distributor. Disconnect hose (if equipped). Remove mounting bolts and distributor. To install, rotate distributor shaft until drive tang aligns with slot on camshaft. Reverse removal procedure to complete installation. Adjust ignition timing. See ON-VEHICLE ADJUSTMENTS article.

### CRANKSHAFT SENSOR (9000 SERIES)

**Removal & Installation** - Disconnect negative battery cable. Raise and support front of vehicle. Remove right front wheel and inner fenderwell panel. Remove drive belts. Remove retaining bolt and crankshaft pulley. Remove crankshaft sensor retaining bolts and sensor. To install, reverse removal procedure. Use Loctite 270 on sensor bolts. Tighten to specification. See TORQUE SPECIFICATIONS table at end of article.

## FUEL SYSTEM

### FUEL SYSTEM PRESSURE RELEASE

***WARNING: ALWAYS relieve fuel pressure before disconnecting any fuel injection-related component. DO NOT allow fuel to contact engine or electrical components.***

To relieve fuel pressure, remove fuel pump fuse. On 900 Series, the fuse box is located on left side of engine compartment. Fuel pump fuse is No. 30. On 9000 Series, fuses are located behind panel inside the glove compartment. Fuel pump fuse is No. 14. Start engine and let run until engine stalls. Turn ignition off. Replace fuse.

### FUEL RAIL & INJECTORS

**Removal & Installation - 1)** Relieve fuel pressure. See FUEL SYSTEM PRESSURE RELEASE. Turn ignition off. Disconnect fuel supply line at banjo fitting and fuel return line at pressure regulator. Disconnect vacuum hose at fuel pressure regulator.

**2)** Unplug electrical connectors from injectors. Remove bolts from fuel rail, but leave injectors in place. Remove injector "O" ring seals from intake manifold.

**3)** Remove fuel rail and injectors as an assembly. Remove injector clips. Remove injectors from fuel rail. To install injectors, lubricate injector "O" ring with petroleum jelly and reinstall. To complete installation, reverse removal procedure.

### FUEL PRESSURE REGULATOR

**Removal & Installation** - Remove fuel rail. See FUEL RAIL & INJECTORS. Clean area around fuel pressure regulator. Disconnect vacuum hose from fuel pressure regulator. Remove retaining clip. Carefully pry fuel pressure regulator from fuel rail. To install, reverse removal procedure.

### OXYGEN SENSOR

**Removal & Installation - 1)** $O_2$ sensor is mounted on the exhaust pipe, below exhaust manifold. Ensure sensor is free of contaminants. Avoid using cleaning solvents of any type.

**2)** Disconnect wiring from sensor before removal. Sensor may be difficult to remove when engine temperature is less than 120°F (49°C). Always use anti-seize compound on threads before installation. Tighten to specification. See TORQUE SPECIFICATIONS table at end of article.

### THROTTLE BODY

**Removal & Installation - 1)** Drain coolant and reinstall drain plug. Disconnect throttle cable and remove bracket from throttle housing. Unplug throttle position sensor connector. Disconnect automatic idle control valve hose from throttle body.

**2)** Remove turbo delivery pipe (if equipped). Disconnect coolant and vacuum hoses from throttle body. Remove throttle body mounting bolts and throttle body. To install, reverse removal procedure. Tighten throttle body bolts to specification. See TORQUE SPECIFICATIONS table at end of article.

### THROTTLE POSITION SENSOR (TPS)

**Removal & Installation** - Unplug TPS connector. Remove screws and TPS. To install, reverse removal procedure. No adjustment is required after installation.

### TURBOCHARGER

**Removal & Installation - 1)** Release A/C compressor belt tensioner. Remove top pipe to oil cooler and clips securing pipe to radiator. Remove A/C compressor mounting bolts. Move compressor aside with hoses attached.

**2)** Remove solenoid valve mounted on radiator. Unplug fan electrical connectors and fan. Remove air intake hose to air cleaner, mass airflow meter and, turbocharger.

**3)** Disconnect turbo pressure pipe. Remove bolts securing oil pipe to turbo unit and cylinder head. Unbolt clutch slave cylinder. Disconnect oil line fitting from block and remove clip on inlet manifold. Remove exhaust pipe from turbocharger.

**4)** Unhook front rubber hangers to exhaust pipe. Remove bracket between turbocharger and oil pan. Remove and plug oil return line. Remove exhaust manifold and turbocharger as an assembly.

**5)** Separate turbocharger from exhaust manifold. Replace turbocharger mounting bolt and exhaust lock nuts. Tighten mounting nuts and bolts to specification. See TORQUE SPECIFICATIONS table. To complete installation, reverse removal procedure.

## TORQUE SPECIFICATIONS

*TORQUE SPECIFICATIONS*

| Applications | Ft. Lbs. (N.m) |
|---|---|
| Crankshaft Pulley Bolt | 140 (190) |
| Distributor Hold-Down Bolt | 15 (20) |
| Exhaust Manifold Bolt (Turbo) | 19 (26) |
| Oxygen Sensor | 25-30 (34-41) |
| Throttle Body Bolt | 13 (18) |
| Turbocharger Bolt | 30 (41) |
| Other Bolts | |
| 5 mm | 4 (5) |
| 6 mm | 7 (10) |
| 8 mm | 14 (20) |
| 10 mm | 24 (40) |

# 1991 ELECTRICAL
# Alternators & Regulators

### 900 Series, 9000 Series

## DESCRIPTION

Saab models use conventional 3-phase, 80-amp Bosch alternators with integral regulators.

## ADJUSTMENTS

### BELT TENSION

On 900 Series, adjust alternator belt tension until deflection at midpoint of longest run is 3/16" (5 mm) with 10 lbs. (4.5 kg) pressure applied to belt. On 9000 Series, drive belt is self-adjusting.

## TROUBLE SHOOTING

***NOTE: See TROUBLE SHOOTING article in GENERAL INFORMATION.***

## ON-VEHICLE TESTING

### WIRING CONTINUITY TEST

**1)** Connect a voltmeter between alternator B+ terminal and ground. Voltmeter should indicate battery voltage. If battery voltage is not present, check wiring between alternator and battery.
**2)** Turn ignition on and ensure alternator indicator light comes on. If light does not come on, check bulb and wiring between alternator and warning light.

### OUTPUT TEST

***NOTE: Ensure B+ connection (heavy Red wire) at alternator is tight and insulating sleeve is not pinched between nut and washer. Alternator output may be low if connection is loose.***

**1)** Ensure connections at battery, alternator, and starter are clean and tight. Ensure alternator, engine, and body are properly grounded. Ensure alternator drive belt is tight and in good condition.
**2)** Connect ammeter following manufacturer's instructions. Connect voltmeter leads to battery terminals. Start engine and run at 3000 RPM. Adjust carbon pile on tester to obtain maximum alternator output. DO NOT allow voltage to drop to less than 12.6 volts.
**3)** Output should equal alternator rating minus 16-20 amps. If output is more than 16-20 amps below alternator rating, replace regulator and retest. If output is still low, repair or replace alternator.

### REGULATOR CONTROL VOLTAGE TEST

**1)** Connect ammeter following manufacturer's instructions. Connect voltmeter leads to battery terminals. Start engine and run at 3000 RPM.
**2)** Run engine until voltage stops rising. Voltage should be 13.5-14.5 volts. If voltage is not within specification, remove regulator from alternator. Ensure brushes are longer than 7/32" (6 mm). Replace if necessary.
**3)** If brushes are okay and regulator fails to keep voltage within specified limits, replace regulator and retest. If voltage is still incorrect, repair or replace alternator.

## BENCH TESTING

### POSITIVE RECTIFIER DIODES

**1)** Connect negative terminal of ohmmeter or self-powered test light (40-volt maximum) to alternator B+ terminal. Measure resistance or continuity between terminal B+ and each diode stator terminal, one at a time, with stator leads disconnected. *See Fig. 1*. Test light should glow or ohmmeter should indicate low resistance when positive terminal of test light or ohmmeter is connected to each diode terminal.
**2)** Reverse ohmmeter or test light connections, and repeat each measurement. Test light should not glow or ohmmeter should indicate high resistance. Replace rectifier assembly if any diode is defective.

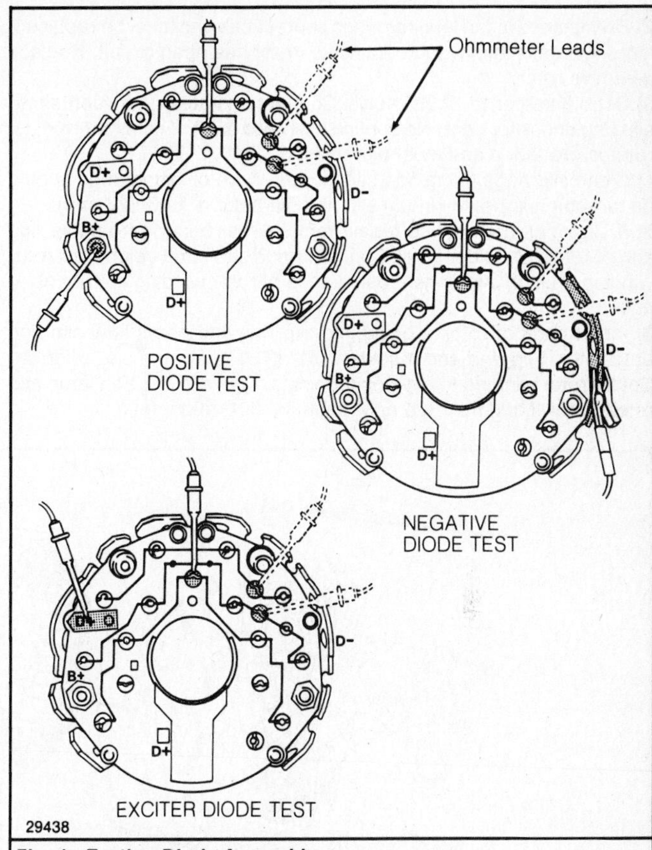

***Fig. 1: Testing Diode Assembly***

### NEGATIVE RECTIFIER DIODES

**1)** Connect positive terminal of ohmmeter or a self-powered test light (40-volt maximum) to alternator D- terminal. Measure resistance or continuity between terminal D- and each diode stator terminal, one at a time, with stator leads disconnected. *See Fig. 1*. Test light should glow or ohmmeter should indicate low resistance when negative terminal of test light or ohmmeter is connected to each diode terminal.
**2)** Reverse ohmmeter or test light connections, and repeat each measurement. Test light should not glow or ohmmeter should indicate high resistance. Replace rectifier assembly if any diode is defective.

### EXCITER DIODES

**1)** Connect negative terminal of ohmmeter or a self-powered test light (40-volt maximum) to alternator D+ terminal. Measure resistance or continuity between terminal D+ and each diode stator terminal, one at a time. *See Fig. 1*. Test light should glow or ohmmeter should indicate low resistance when positive terminal of test light or ohmmeter is connected to each diode stator terminal.
**2)** Reverse ohmmeter or test light connections, and repeat each measurement. Test light should not glow or ohmmeter should indicate high resistance. Replace diode assembly if any diode is defective.

### STATOR

**1)** Set ohmmeter on lowest scale. Connect ohmmeter across stator leads. Resistance between leads should be approximately .09-.11 ohm. If resistance is incorrect, stator has open or shorted windings and must be replaced.
**2)** Set ohmmeter to X1000 scale. Connect ohmmeter between stator core and stator lead. No continuity should exist. If continuity exists, stator is grounded and must be replaced.

### ROTOR

**1)** Set ohmmeter to lowest scale. Connect ohmmeter across slip rings. Resistance should be 2.7-2.9 ohms.

# 1991 ELECTRICAL
# Alternators & Regulators (Cont.)

**2)** If resistance is too low, rotor has short circuit and must be replaced. If resistance is infinity (no continuity), rotor has open circuit. Replace defective rotor.

**3)** Set ohmmeter to X1000 scale. Connect ohmmeter between either slip ring and rotor core. No continuity should exist. If continuity exists, rotor is grounded and must be replaced.

**4)** Clean slip rings using fine sandpaper. Worn or pitted rings should be turned on lathe. Minimum slip ring diameter is 1.06" (27 mm).

**5)** If slip rings are beyond repair, remove rear bearing from slip ring end of rotor. Unsolder wires from slip rings and bend up ends of rotor winding. Pull off slip rings. Ensure ends of rotor winding are not damaged.

**6)** Insert ends of rotor winding into slip ring and press new slip ring onto rotor. Slip ring end must be .141" (3.58 mm) from end of collar. Solder rotor winding to slip ring terminals. Turn slip rings on lathe and retest rotor. Maximum slip ring runout is .001" (.03 mm).

## BEARINGS

Always replace bearings when servicing alternator. If replacement bearing is sealed on one side only, open side must face rotor.

## BRUSHES

Ensure brushes are longer than .22" (5.6 mm). Replace if necessary. Unsolder brushes from voltage regulator. Solder new brushes into place. DO NOT allow solder to run into strands of brush leads. Brushes must be free to slide in brush holder with normal spring tension of 10-14 ozs. (283-397 g).

## OVERHAUL

***NOTE: Refer to illustration for alternator overhaul. See Fig. 2.***

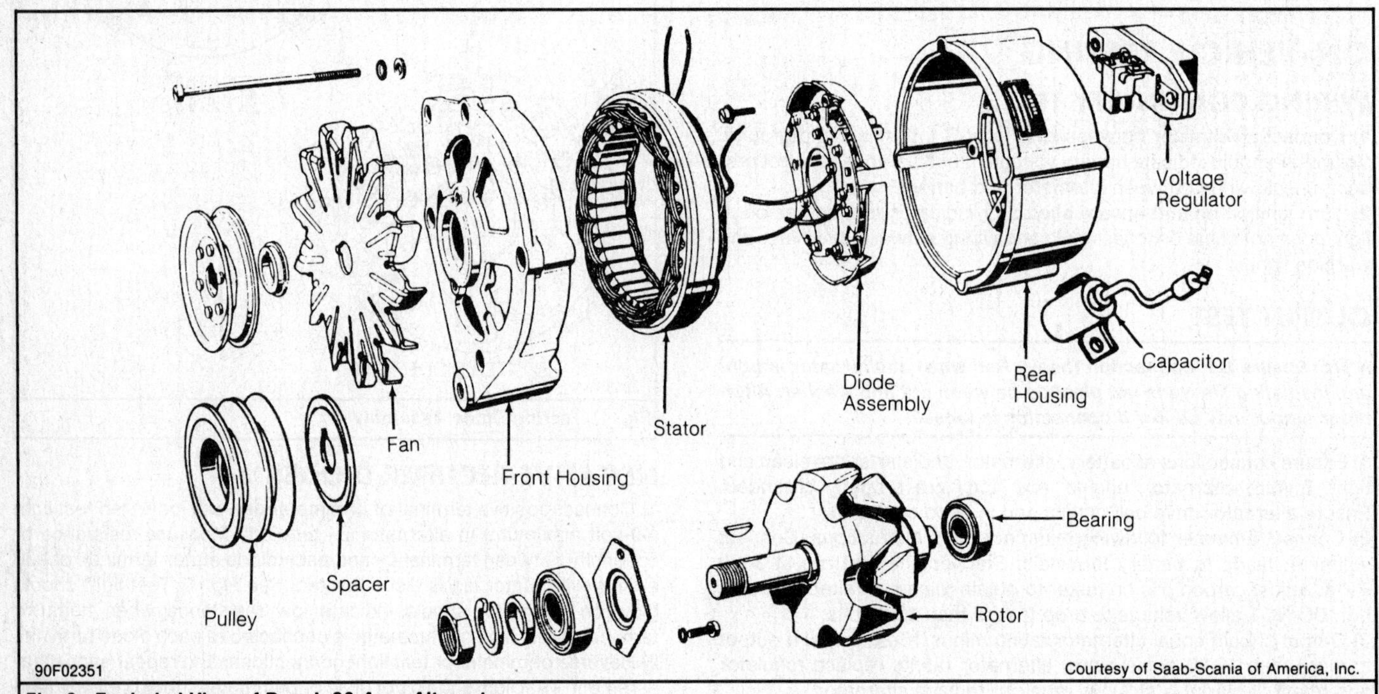


***Fig. 2: Exploded View of Bosch 80-Amp Alternator***

### 900 Series, 9000 Series

## DESCRIPTION

Starter is a brush-type, reduction gear electric motor with an overrunning clutch. Some models have permanent magnets in place of field coils. An attached solenoid engages the starter.

## TROUBLE SHOOTING

*NOTE: See TROUBLE SHOOTING article in GENERAL INFORMATION.*

## ON-VEHICLE TESTING

### CRANKING TEST

Connect starting system tester according to manufacturer's instructions. Operate starter. Starter current should not exceed 315 amps. Voltage should not be less than 9 volts.

### CIRCUIT TEST

Ensure voltage at solenoid terminal is at least 7 volts with battery charged and ignition switch in START position. If voltage is less than 7 volts, check wiring between solenoid and ignition switch. Also check neutral safety switch on vehicles with A/T.

## BENCH TESTING

### STARTER LOAD (LOCK) TEST

Place starter on test bench. Lock starter drive pinion. Energize starter and ensure voltage and amperage are within specification. See STARTER LOAD (LOCK) TEST SPECIFICATIONS table.

*STARTER LOAD (LOCK) TEST SPECIFICATIONS*

| Application | Volts | Amps |
|---|---|---|
| All Models | 4 | 650-750 |

### STARTER NO-LOAD TEST

Place starter on test bench. Operate starter and ensure voltage, amperage and RPM are within specification. See STARTER NO-LOAD TEST SPECIFICATIONS table.

*STARTER NO-LOAD TEST SPECIFICATIONS*

| Application | Volts | Amps | RPM |
|---|---|---|---|
| All Models | 12 | 70 | 3000 |

## OVERHAUL

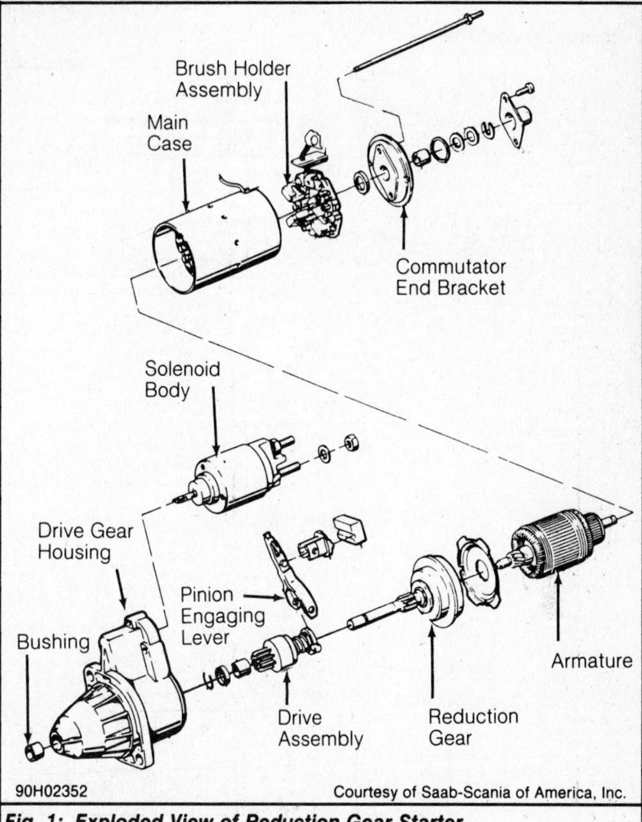


*Fig. 1: Exploded View of Reduction Gear Starter*

## TORQUE SPECIFICATIONS

*TORQUE SPECIFICATIONS*

| Application | Ft. Lbs. (N.m) |
|---|---|
| All Models | |
| 8-mm Bolts | 15 (20) |
| | INCH Lbs. (N.m) |
| Solenoid Mounting Bolts | 44 (5) |
| 6-mm Bolts | 89 (10) |

# 1991 WIRING DIAGRAMS
# 900 Series

**COMPONENT LOCATOR:**

| Component | Location |
|---|---|
| A/C COMP RELAY | B-C 27 |
| A/C COMP RELAY (NON TURBO) | A 24 |
| A/C CYCLING SW | A 25-26 |
| A/C RAD FAN RELAY (NON TURBO) | A 24 |
| A/C RECIRC SW | A 27 |
| A/C SW | A-B 27 |
| ABS FUSES | C 29-30 |
| AIRBAG ELECTRONIC CONTROL UNIT | E 29-30 |
| ALTERNATOR | A-B 3 |
| ANTENNA MOTOR | C 35 |
| ANTI-LOCK BRAKE SYSTEM (ABS) ELECTRONIC CONTROL UNIT | A 29-30 |
| AUTOMATIC PERFORMANCE CONTROL (APC) UNIT | C-D 7 |
| BACK-UP LT SW (A/T) | E 16 |
| BACK-UP LT SW (M/T) | E 18 |
| BURGLAR ALARM UNIT (CONVERTIBLE) | C-D 36 |
| BURGLAR ALARM UNIT (EX CONVERTIBLE) | C 40 |
| CIG LTR | D 18 |
| CONVERTIBLE TOP FUSE | B 37 |
| CONVERTIBLE TOP SW | B-C 38 |
| CRUISE CONTROL SYSTEM | A-B 36-39 |
| DEFOG RELAY (W/ TIME RELAY) | C-D 27 |
| DEFOG RELAY (W/O TIME RELAY) | D 24 |
| DEFOG SW (W/ TIME RELAY) | D 27 |
| DEFOG SW (W/O TIME RELAY) | C 24 |
| DIR SW | E 20 |
| DOOR LOCK CONTROLLER (CONVERTIBLE) | B-C 44 |
| DOOR LOCK CONTROLLER (EX CONVERTIBLE) | C 40 |
| DOOR SWS | E 41-43 |
| ELECTRONIC DISTRIBUTION BOX (EDB) | B-D 12-19 |
| ELECTRONIC IGN AMP (2.0L TURBO) | E 7 |
| EXTRA ELECTRONIC DISTRIBUTION BOX (EEDB) | A-B 21-22 |
| EZK TEST CONN | D 10 |
| FASTEN BELT IND | E 41 |
| FLASHER RELAY | D 21-22 |
| FOG LT RELAY | C 1-2 |
| FOG LT SW | A 16-17 |
| FUEL INJ ECU (2.0L TURBO) | A-C 4 |
| FUEL INJ ECU (2.1L) | A-C 8 |
| FUEL PUMP RELAY (2.0L TURBO) | B-C 7 |
| FUEL PUMP RELAY (2.1L) | B-C 11 |
| HAZARD SW | D-E 20 |
| HEADLT WIPER MOTOR | E 3 |
| HEATING PAD | D-E 44-45 |
| HEATING RHEOSTAT | C 44-45 |
| HORN RELAY | B-C 1-2 |
| HORN SW | E 14 |
| IGN COIL (2.0L TURBO) | E 6 |
| IGN COIL (2.1L) | E 10 |
| IGN KEY ILLUM LT | D 33 |
| IGN SW | A 12 |
| IGN SW RELAY #1 | A-B 12 |
| IGN SW RELAY #2 | C 20 |
| IGN SYSTEM ECU (2.1L) | C-D 11 |
| INHIBITOR SW | A 14 |
| INST CLSTR | A-D 32 |
| INTERIOR LT SW (CONVERTIBLE) | D-E 35 |
| INTERIOR LT SW (EX CONVERTIBLE) | D 32-33 |
| INTERIOR LT TIME DELAY RELAY (CONVERTIBLE) | D 35 |
| INTERIOR LT TIME DELAY RELAY (EX CONVERTIBLE) | E 32 |
| INTERMITTENT WIPER RELAY | E 23 |
| LIGHT SW | A 17-18 |
| LIGHTING RELAY | A 18-19 |
| MAIN RELAY (2.0L TURBO) | C-D 4 |
| MAIN RELAY (2.1L) | C-D 8 |
| O2 SENS (2.0L TURBO) | C 7 |
| PARK BRAKE SW | C 34 |
| POWER MIRROR SYSTEM | A-E 48-49 |
| POWER SEAT SYSTEM | B-E 47 |
| POWER WDO SW | A 44-47 |
| POWER WDO/SUNROOF SW | A 40-43 |
| RAD FAN TIME DELAY RELAY | D 3 |
| RAISING RELAY | B 36 |
| REAR WDO SWS | C 42-43 |
| SEAT BELT WARNING RELAY | E 40 |
| SPEED SENS | B 39 |
| STARTER | A 3 |
| STOP LT SW | A 39 |
| TIMING SERVICE INSTRUMENT (TSI) SOCKET (2.0L TURBO) | E 5 |
| TIMING SERVICE INSTRUMENT (TSI) SOCKET (2.1L) | E 9 |
| TRUNK LT (EX CONVERTIBLE) | D 42 |
| TRUNK LT SW (CONVERTIBLE) | E 39 |
| VACUUM SW | A 37-38 |
| VENT FAN MAIN SW | E 24-26 |
| WIPER MOTOR | C 3 |
| WIPER/WASHER SW | D 22-23 |

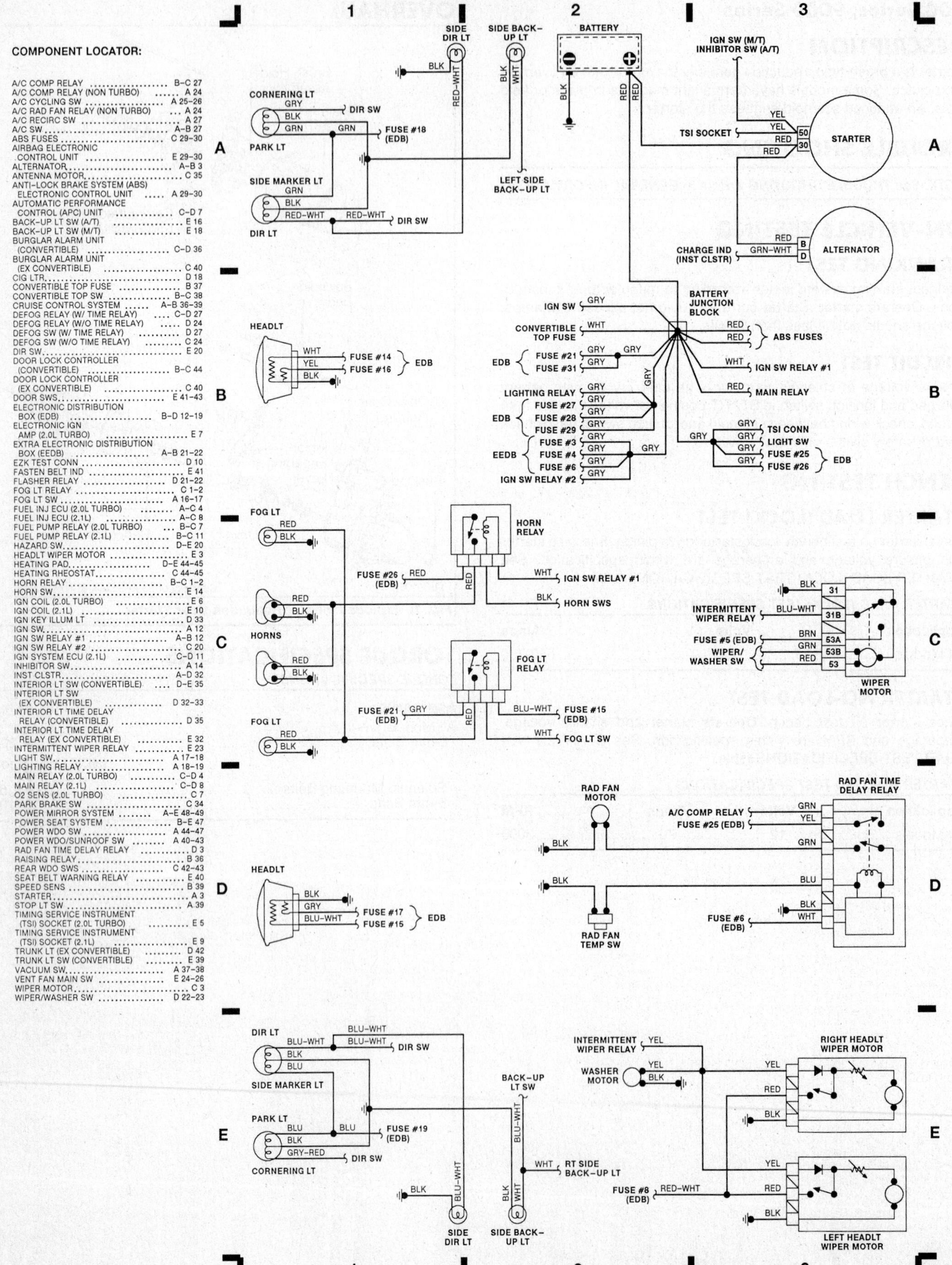

# 1991 WIRING DIAGRAMS
# 900 Series (Cont.)

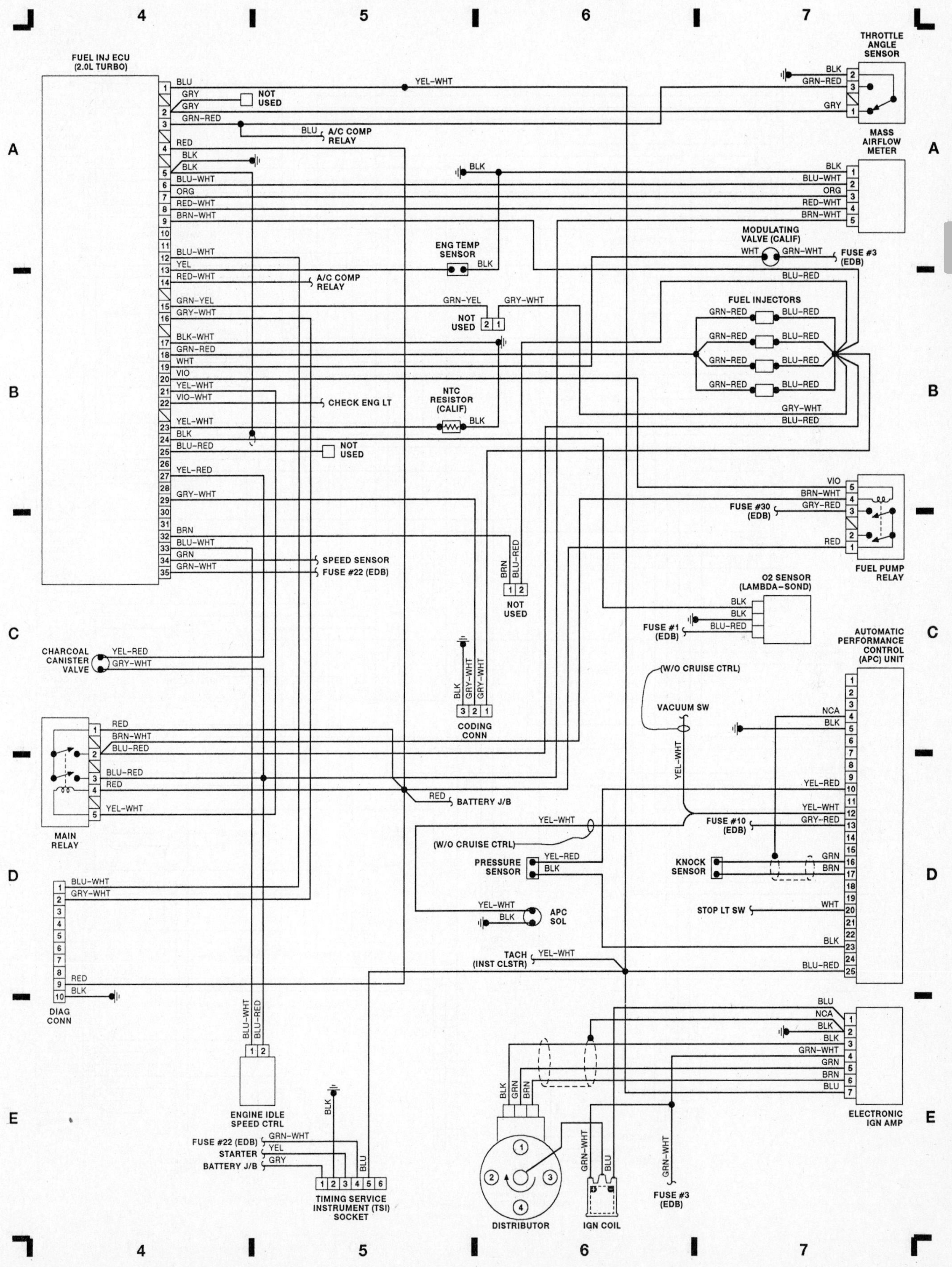

# 1991 WIRING DIAGRAMS
# 900 Series (Cont.)

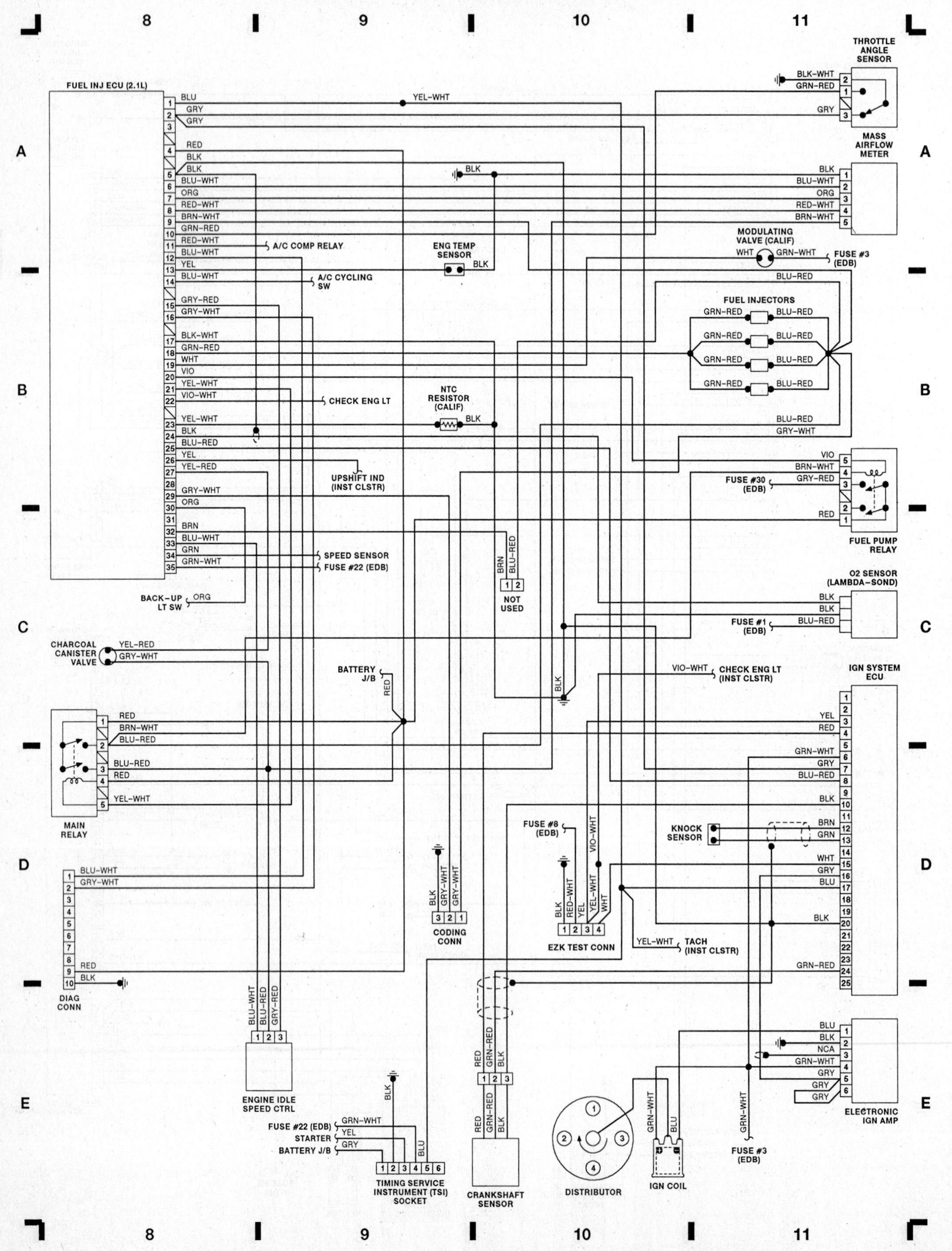

# 1991 WIRING DIAGRAMS
# 900 Series (Cont.)

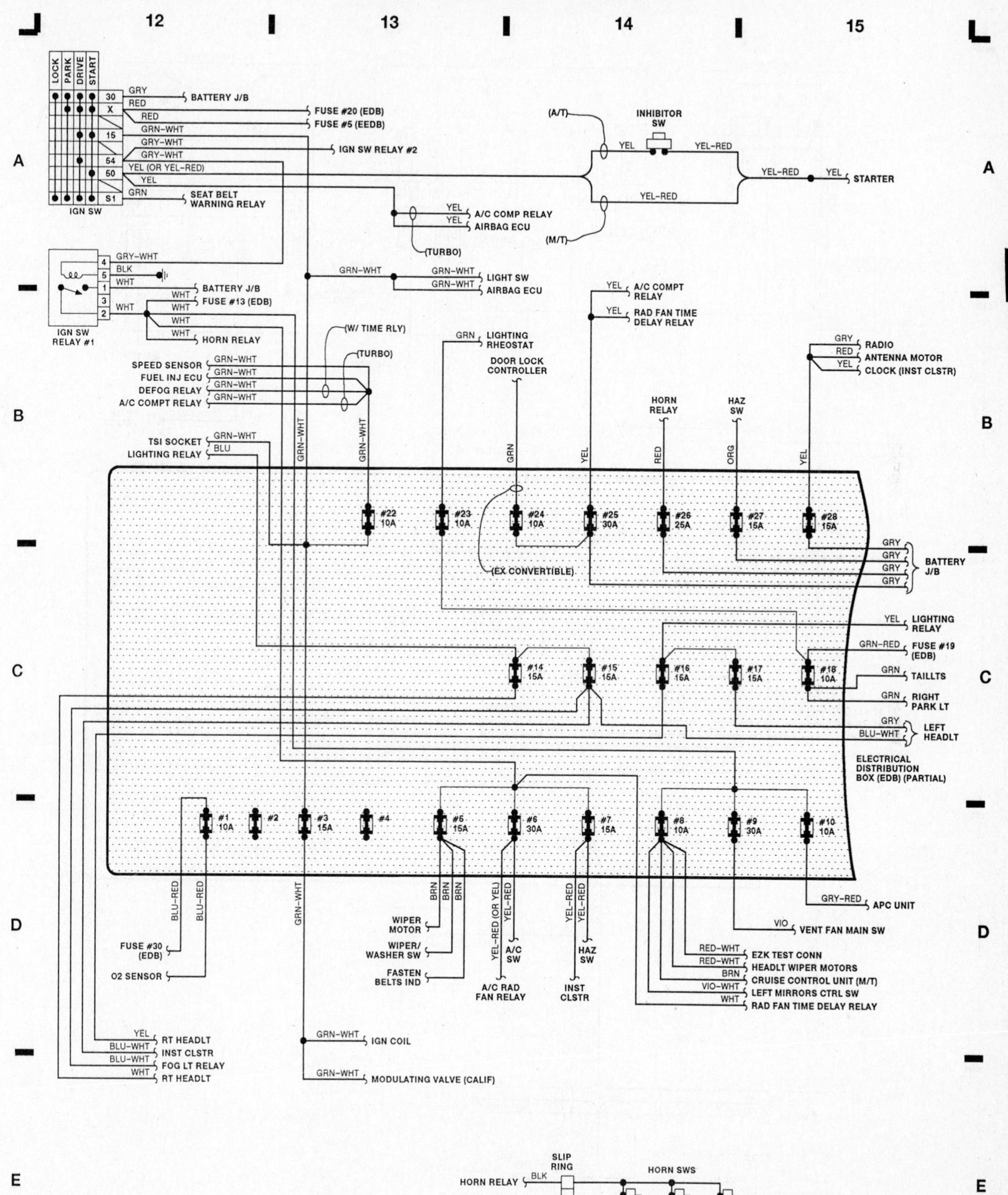


12 13 14 15

# 1991 WIRING DIAGRAMS
## 900 Series (Cont.)

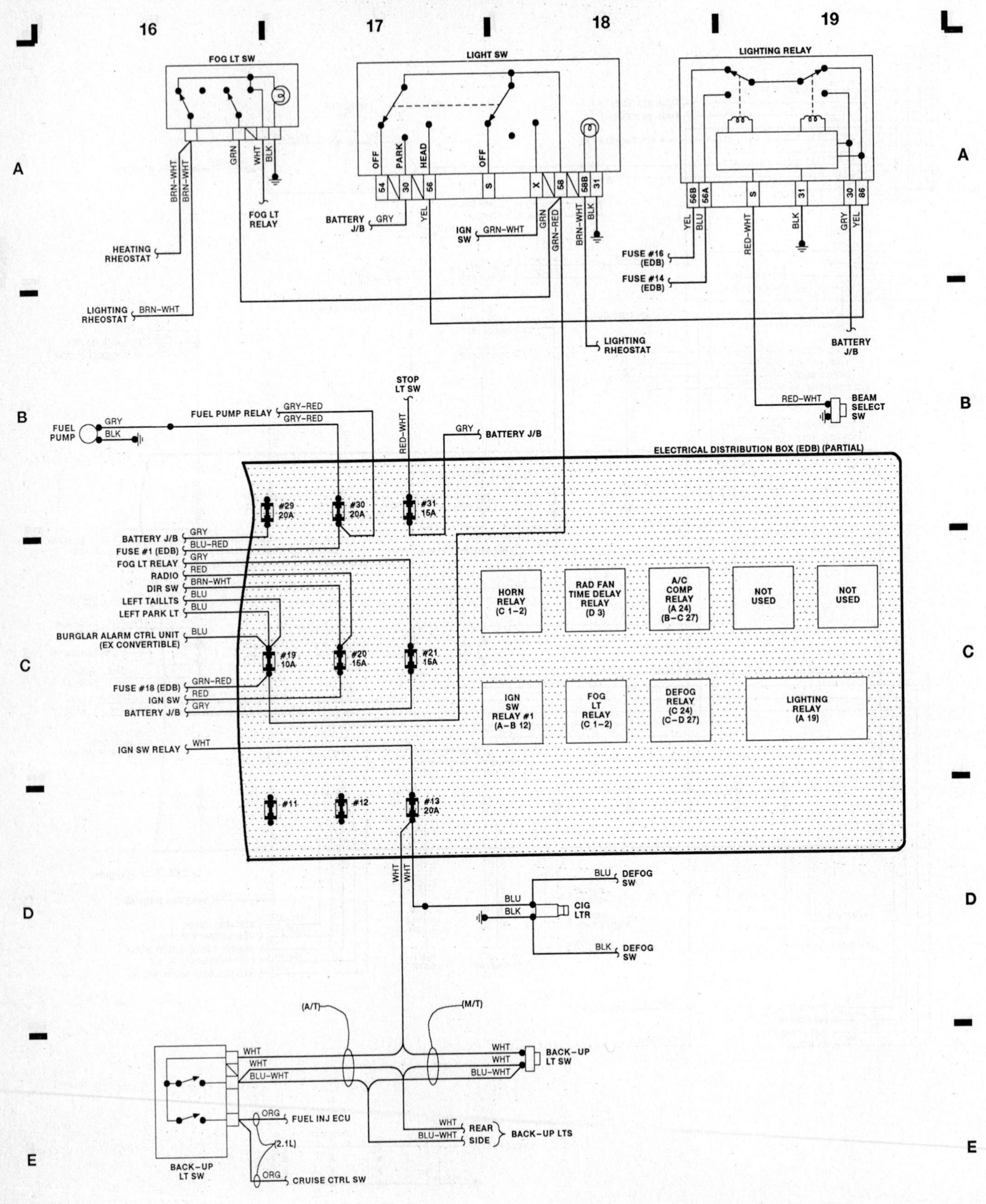

# 1991 WIRING DIAGRAMS
# 900 Series (Cont.)

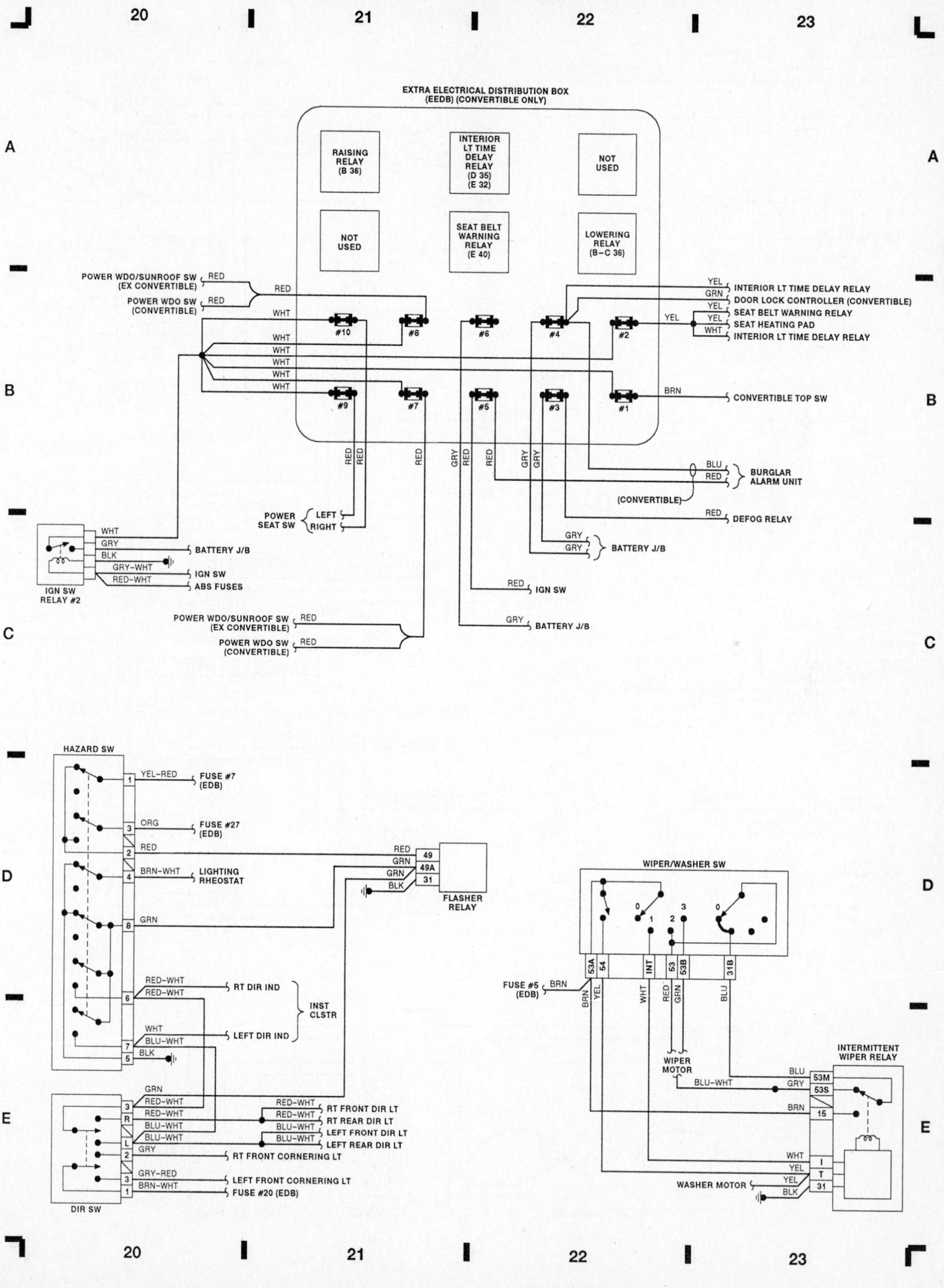

20 21 22 23

A

EXTRA ELECTRICAL DISTRIBUTION BOX
(EEDB) (CONVERTIBLE ONLY)

RAISING RELAY (B 36)
INTERIOR LT TIME DELAY RELAY (D 35) (E 32)
NOT USED
NOT USED
SEAT BELT WARNING RELAY (E 40)
LOWERING RELAY (B–C 36)

POWER WDO/SUNROOF SW (EX CONVERTIBLE) RED
POWER WDO SW (CONVERTIBLE) RED
RED
WHT
WHT
WHT
WHT
WHT
WHT
#10 #8 #6 #4 #2
#9 #7 #5 #3 #1
YEL INTERIOR LT TIME DELAY RELAY
GRN DOOR LOCK CONTROLLER (CONVERTIBLE)
YEL SEAT BELT WARNING RELAY
YEL YEL SEAT HEATING PAD
WHT INTERIOR LT TIME DELAY RELAY
BRN CONVERTIBLE TOP SW

B

RED RED RED GRY RED RED GRY GRY
BLU
RED
BURGLAR ALARM UNIT
(CONVERTIBLE)
RED DEFOG RELAY
GRY
GRY
BATTERY J/B
POWER SEAT SW LEFT RIGHT

WHT
GRY
BLK
GRY–WHT
RED–WHT
BATTERY J/B
IGN SW
ABS FUSES
IGN SW RELAY #2

RED IGN SW
GRY BATTERY J/B

C

POWER WDO/SUNROOF SW (EX CONVERTIBLE) RED
POWER WDO SW (CONVERTIBLE) RED

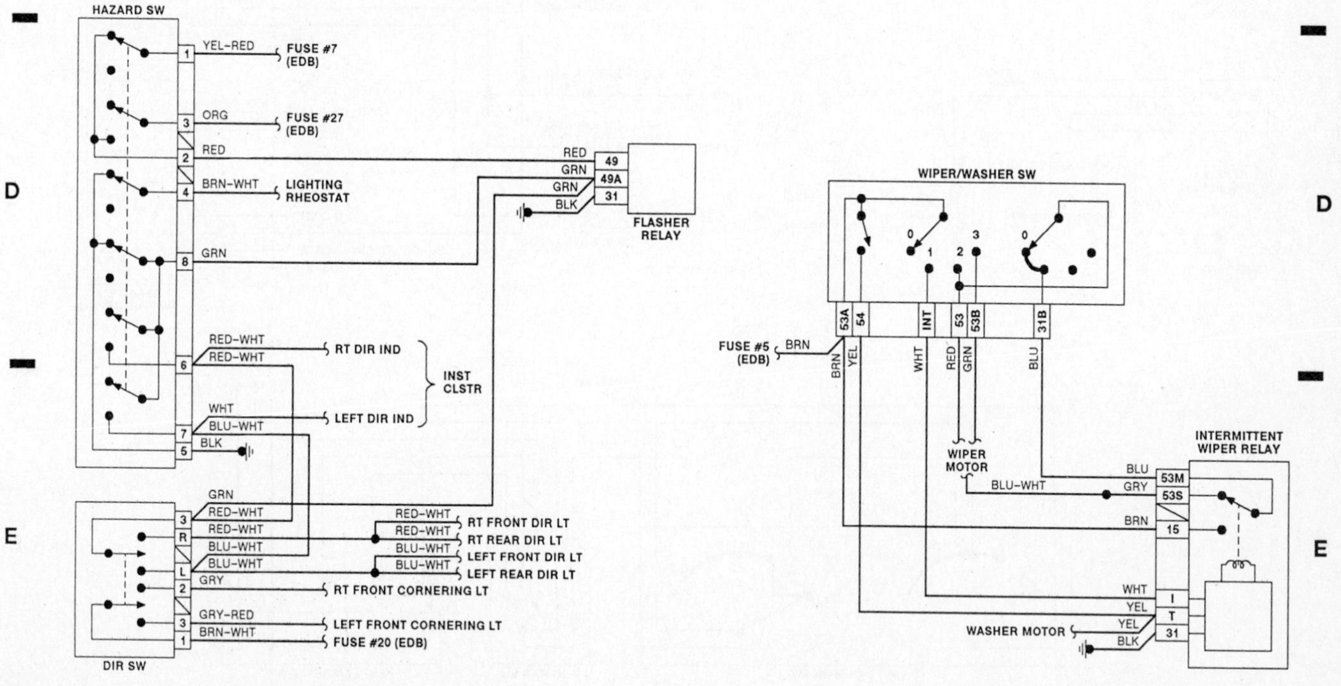


20 21 22 23

# 1991 WIRING DIAGRAMS
# 900 Series (Cont.)

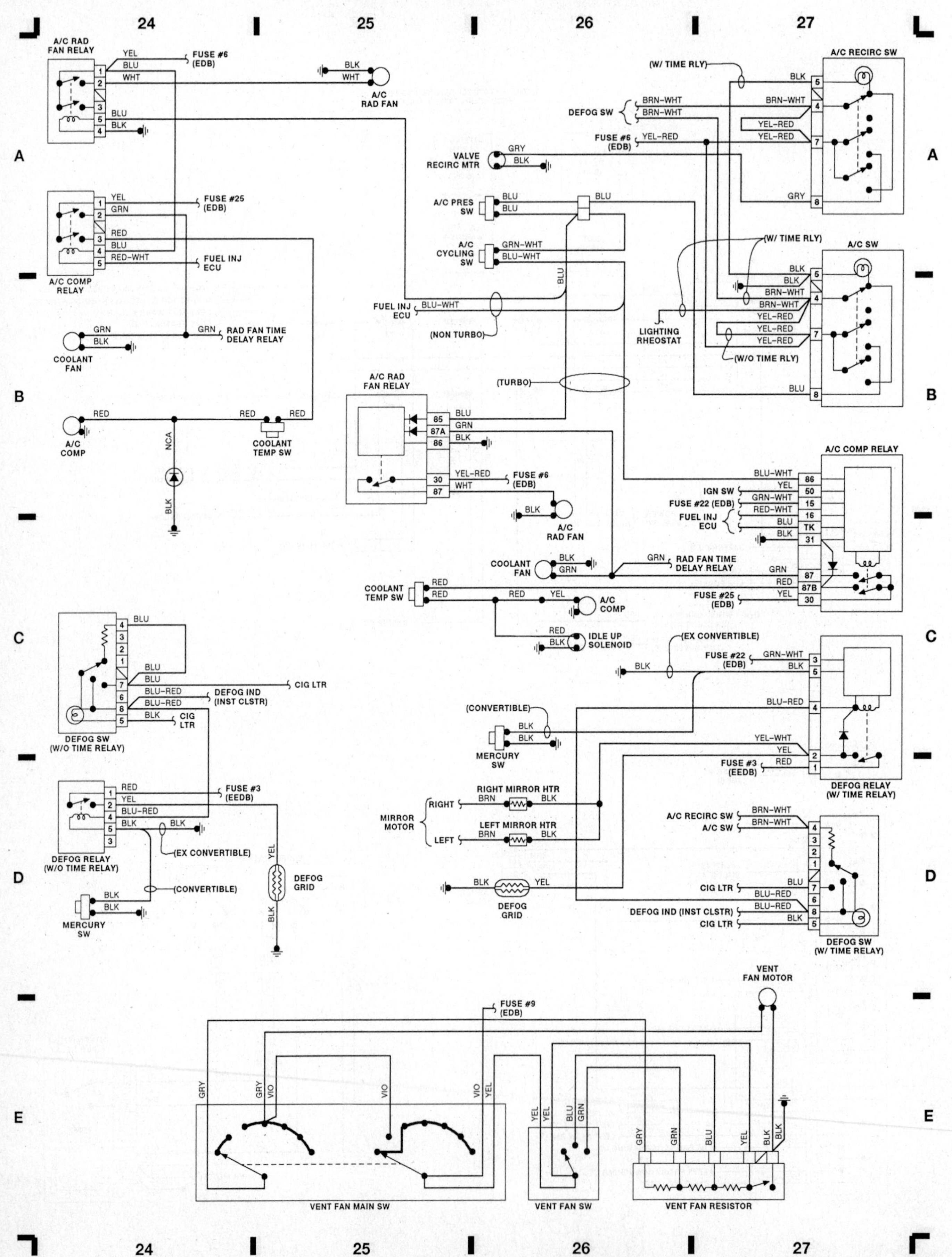

# 1991 WIRING DIAGRAMS
# 900 Series (Cont.)

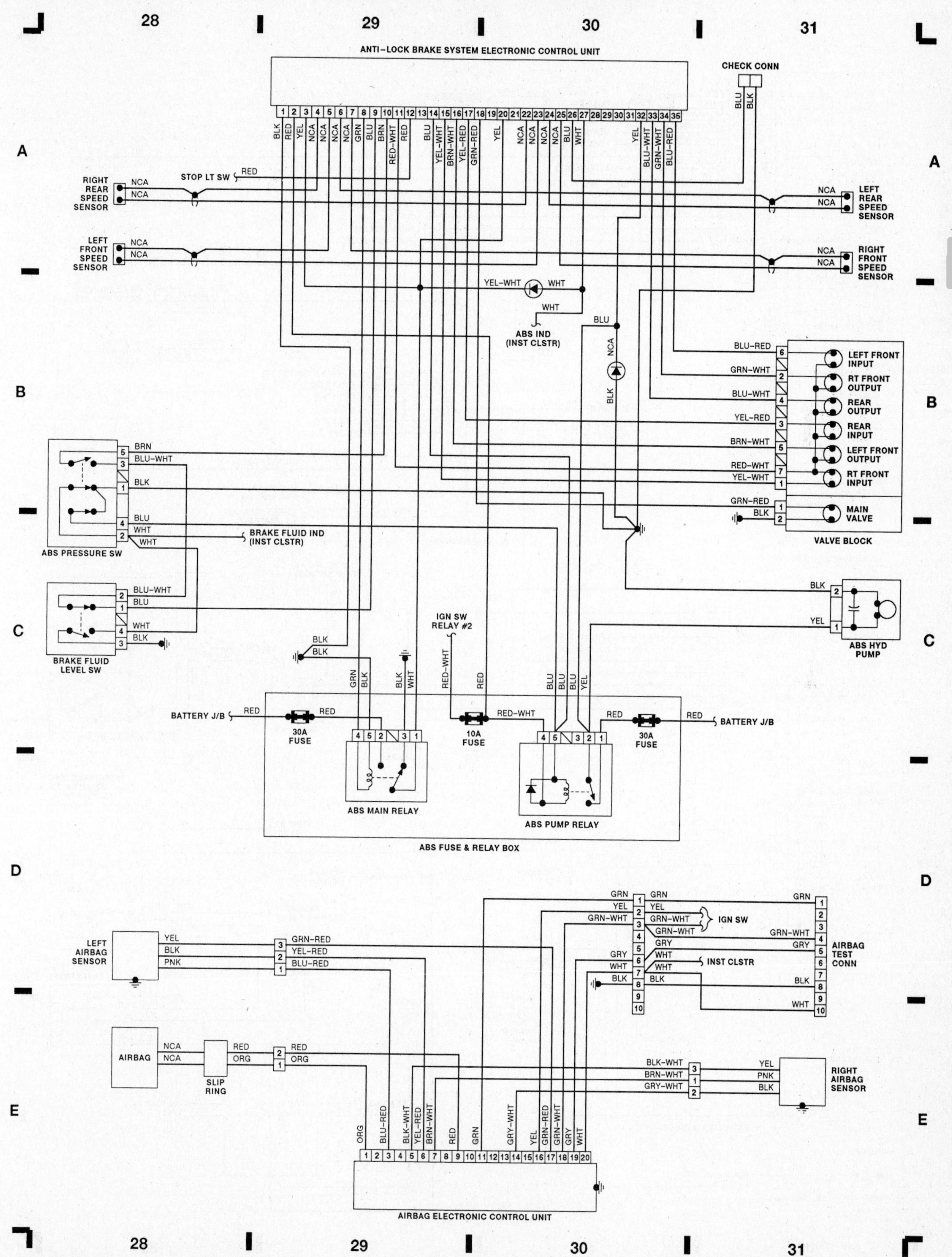

# 1991 WIRING DIAGRAMS
# 900 Series (Cont.)

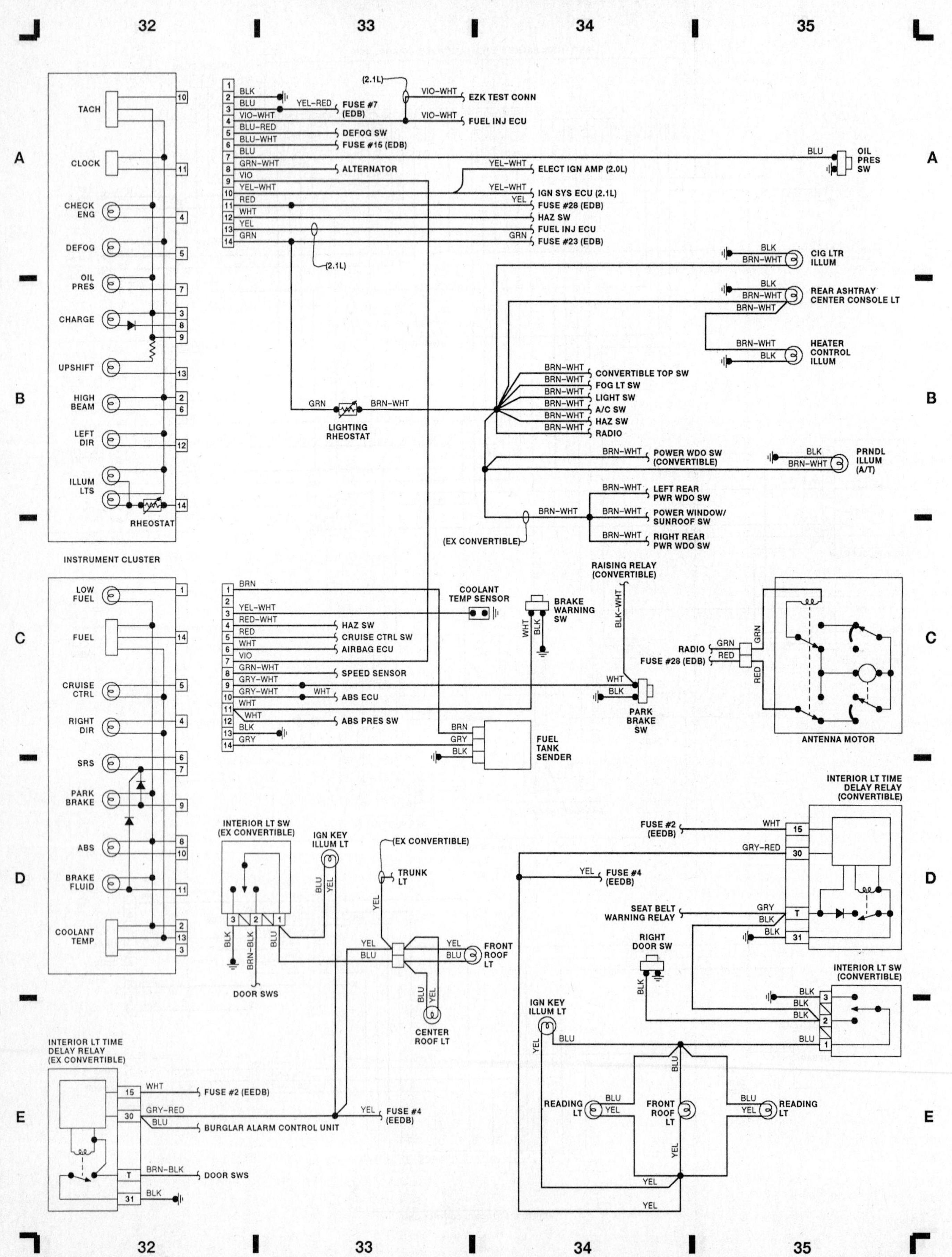

# 1991 WIRING DIAGRAMS
# 900 Series (Cont.)

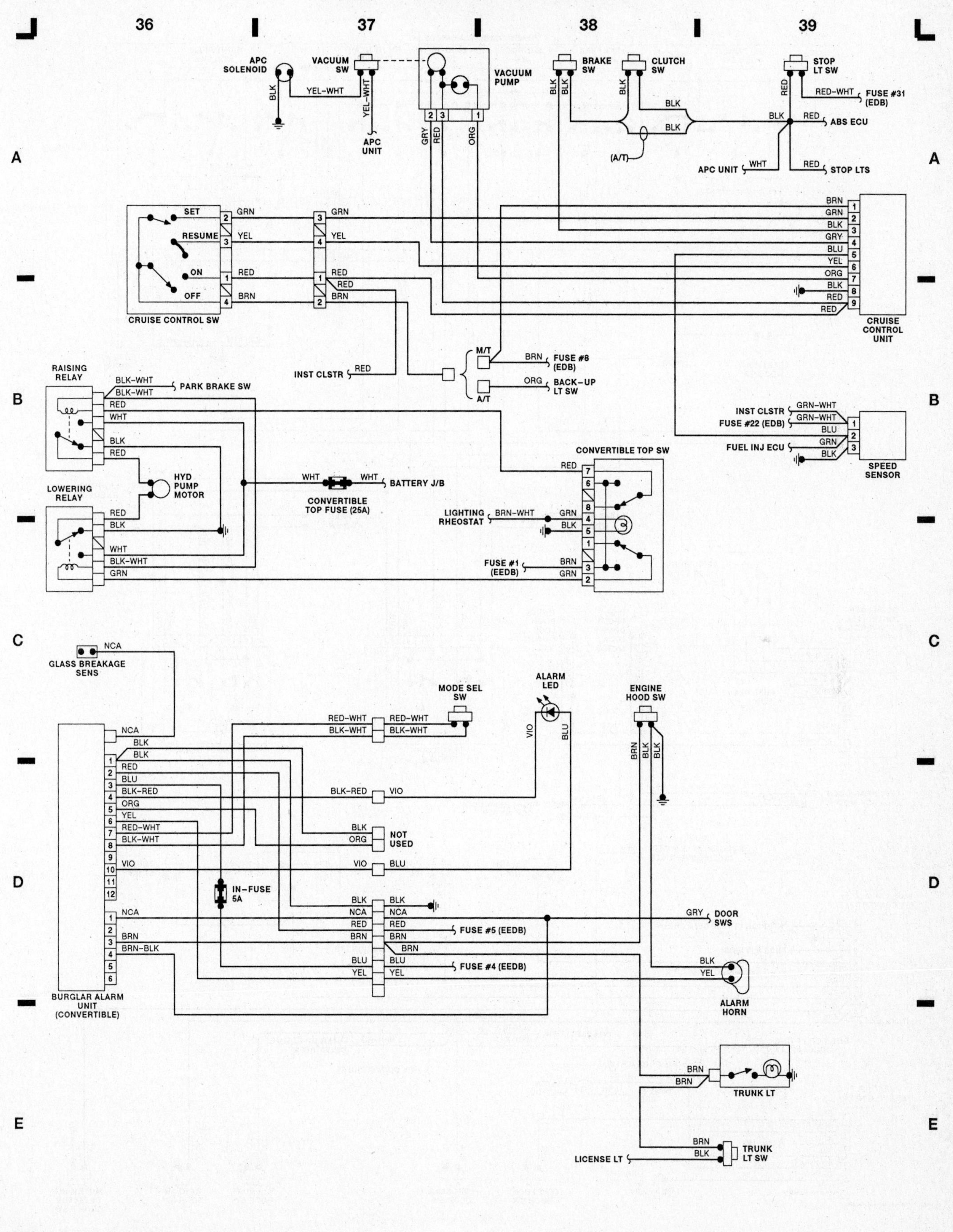

# 1991 WIRING DIAGRAMS
# 900 Series (Cont.)

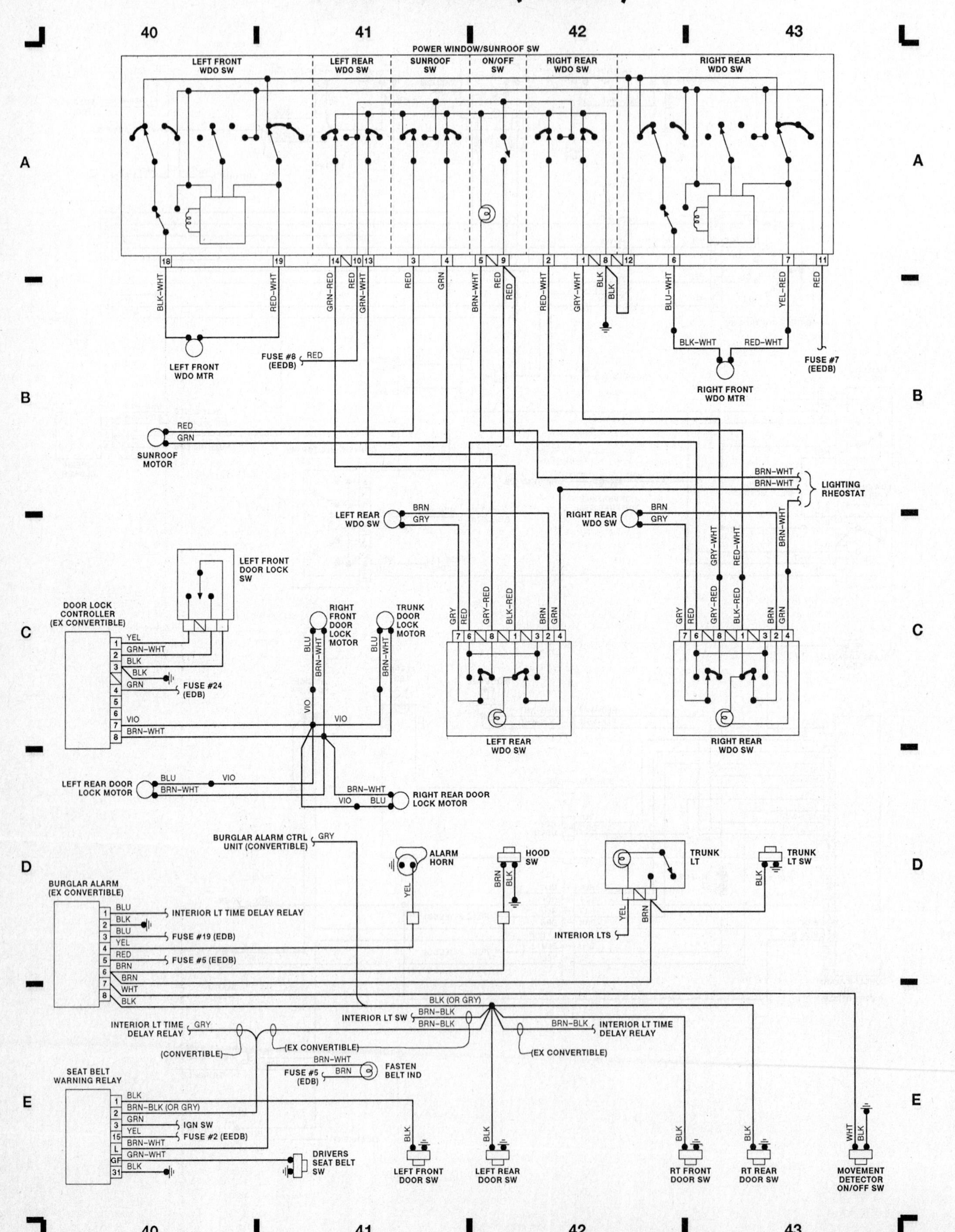

# 1991 WIRING DIAGRAMS
# 900 Series (Cont.)

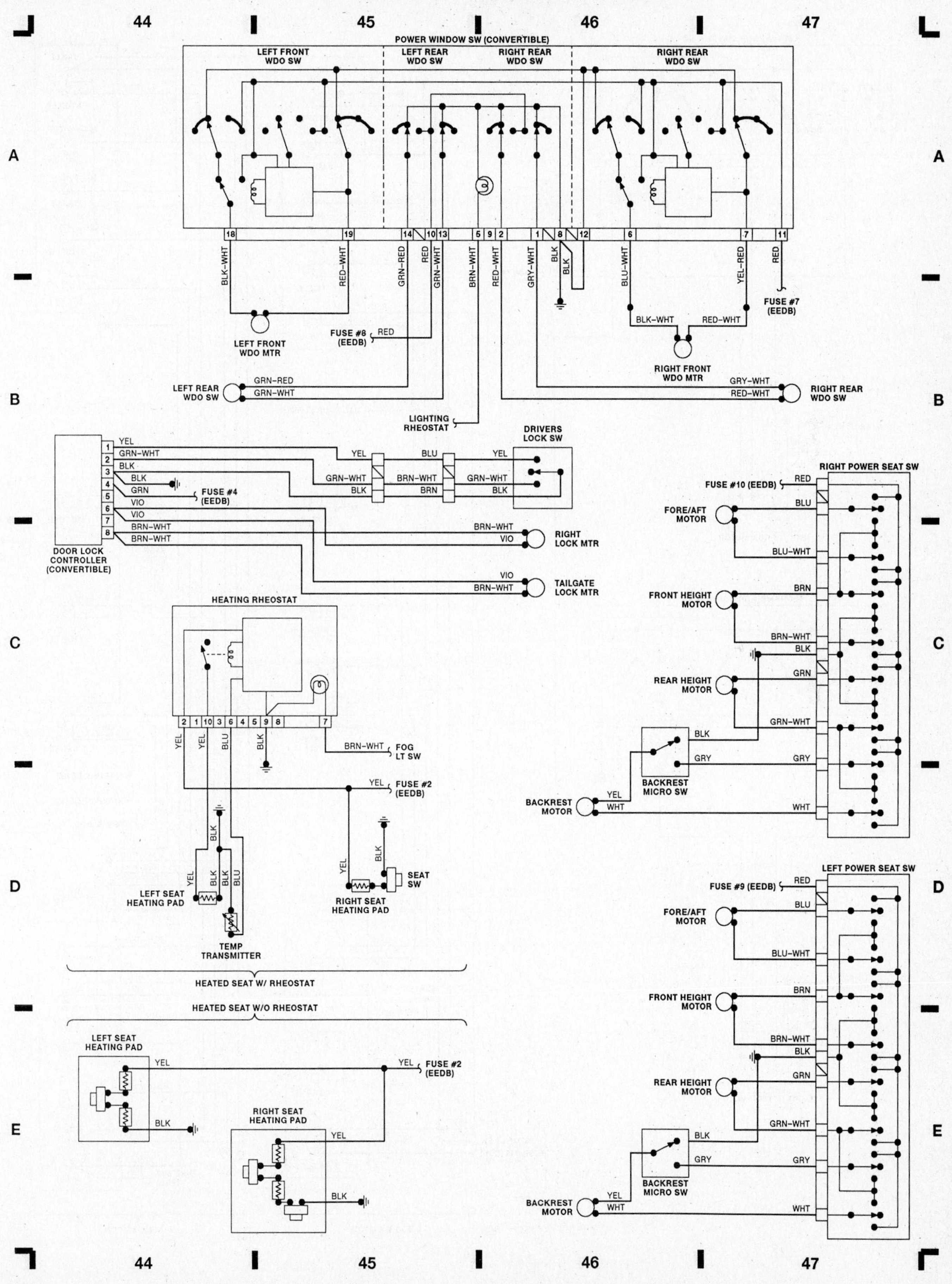

# 1991 WIRING DIAGRAMS
# 900 Series (Cont.)

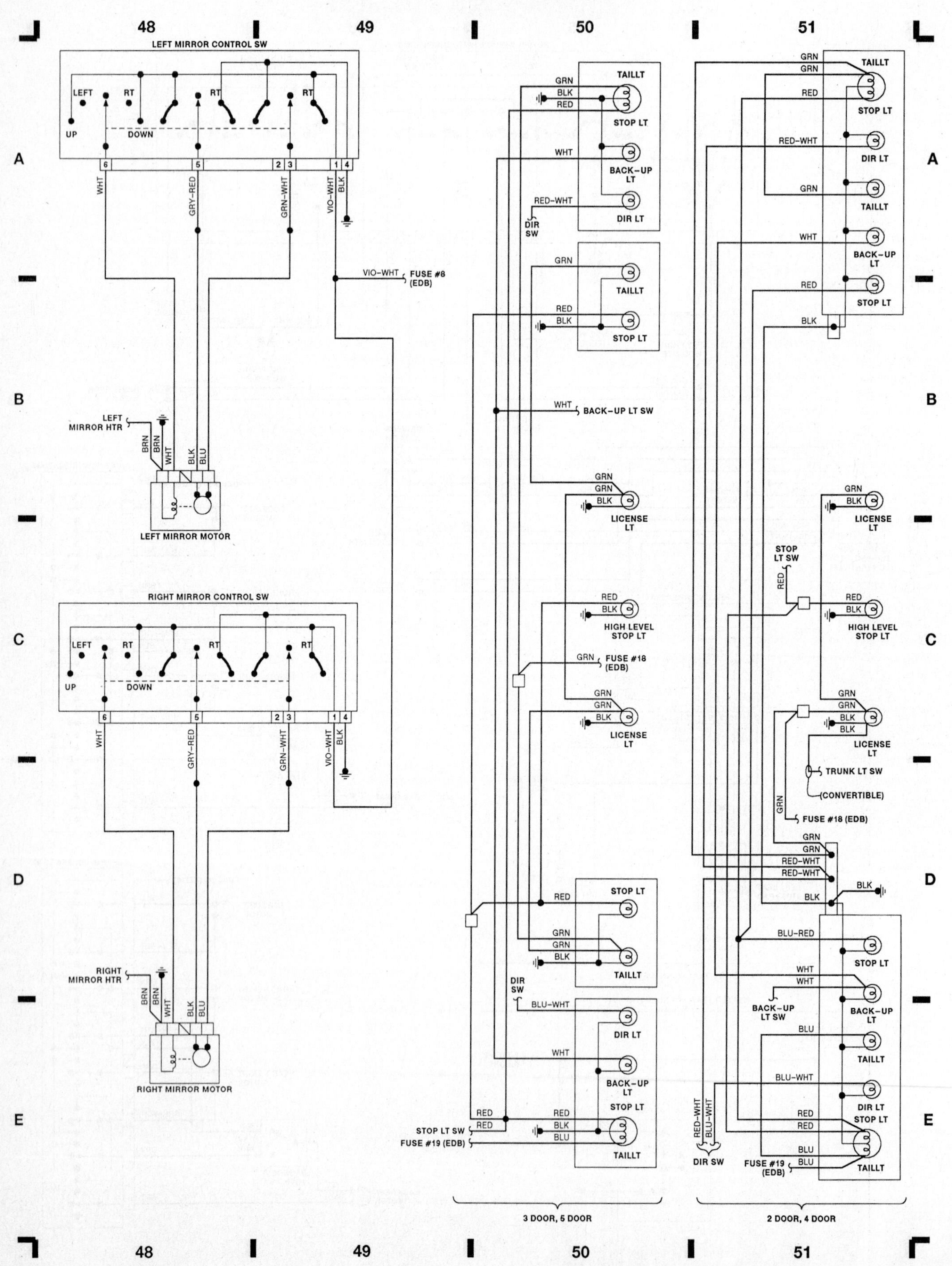

# 1991 WIRING DIAGRAMS
# 9000 Series

## COMPONENT LOCATOR:

| Component | Location |
|---|---|
| A/C PRES SW | B 23 |
| A/C RECIRC SW | C–D 22–23 |
| A/C SW | C 23 |
| A/C TIME DELAY RELAY | A 23 |
| ABS FUSES | C 25–26 |
| AIRBAG ELECTRONIC CONTROL UNIT (ECU) | E 25–26 |
| AIRBAG TEST CONN | D 27 |
| ALTERNATOR | A–B 3 |
| APC SOL VALVE (TURBO) | E 5 |
| APC VAC SW | E 22 |
| AUTOMATIC CLIMATE CONTROL (ACC) UNIT | A–D 20 |
| BACK-UP LT RELAY | E 12 |
| BACK-UP LT SW | D–E 13 |
| BATTERY JUNCTION BLOCK | B 2 |
| BRAKE FLUID LEVEL SW | C 24 |
| BRAKE SW | E 21 |
| BURGLAR ALARM CONTROL UNIT | C–D 36 |
| CIG LTR | E 13 |
| CLUTCH SW | E 21 |
| COURTESY LIGHTS | D–E 39 |
| CRUISE CONTROL SW | E 20 |
| CRUISE CONTROL UNIT | D–E 20 |
| DCC TRIP COMPUTER | B–C 28 |
| DEFOG RELAY (A/C) | C–D 44 |
| DEFOG RELAY (ACC) | D 44 |
| DEFOG SW | E 14–15 |
| DI CONTROL UNIT (NON TURBO) | C–E 7 |
| DI-APC CONTROL UNIT (TURBO) | C–E 7 |
| DIAG CONN | D 4 |
| DIR/HAZ SW | A–B 28 |
| DISTRIBUTION TERMINAL +15 | D 14 |
| DISTRIBUTION TERMINAL +30 | B 2 |
| DISTRIBUTION TERMINAL +54 | B 13 |
| DOOR LOCK CONTROLLER | A 44 |
| EDU TEST CONN | E 28–29 |
| EDU TRIP COMPUTER | C–E 28 |
| ELECTRICAL DISTRIBUTION BOX (EDB) | C 12–19 |
| ENGINE COMPARTMENT ELECTRICAL DISTRIBUTION (ECED) BOX | C–D 9–10 |
| FASTEN BELT IND | A 33 |
| FILAMENT MONITOR (ENGINE COMPT) | E 32 |
| FILAMENT MONITOR (GLOVE COMPT) | C–D 32 |
| FOG LT RELAY | D 1 |
| FOG LT SW | A 31 |
| FUEL INJ ECU | A–C 4 |
| FUEL PUMP RELAY | B 7 |
| GEAR SEL SW | D–E 12 |
| GLOVE BOX LT SW | E 37 |
| HEADLT WIPER MOTORS | E 3 |
| HORN RELAY | B 1 |
| HORN SWS | E 16–17 |
| IGM SW RELAY | B 12 |
| IGN SW | A 12 |
| INST CLSTR | A–D 35 |
| INTERIOR LT TIME DELAY RELAY | C–D 39 |
| INTERMITTENT WIPER RELAY | E 23 |
| LEFT REAR WINDOW SW | B 36–37 |
| LEFT SEAT HEATER SW | E 44 |
| LIGHT SW | A 18 |
| LIGHTING RELAY | A 19 |
| LIGHTING RHEOSTAT | B 31 |
| MAIN FAN SW | D 21 |
| MAIN RELAY | C–D 4 |
| PICTOGRAM | D–E 35 |
| POWER MIRROR SW | B 44–46 |
| POWER SEAT SYSTEM | A–E 40–43 |
| POWER WINDOW AND SUNROOF SW | A 36–39 |
| RAD FAN 2 SPEED RELAY | B–C 3 |
| RAD FAN TIME DELAY RELAY | C–D 3 |
| RIGHT FRONT READING LT | E 36 |
| RIGHT REAR WINDOW SW | B 39 |
| RIGHT SEAT HEATER SW | D 46 |
| SEAT BELT CONTROLLER | A 32 |
| SEAT BELT LOCK ILLUM | B 33 |
| SEAT BELT WARNING RELAY | A–B 32 |
| STARTER | A 3 |
| STOP LT SW | D 16 |
| STORAGE COMPT AND REAR ASHTRAY LT | E 37 |
| TIMING SERVICE INSTRUMENT (TSI) SOCKET | E 5 |
| TRAILER CONN | C–D 47 |
| WASHER MOTOR | E 2 |
| WIPER MOTOR | D 3 |
| WIPER/WASHER SW | D 23 |

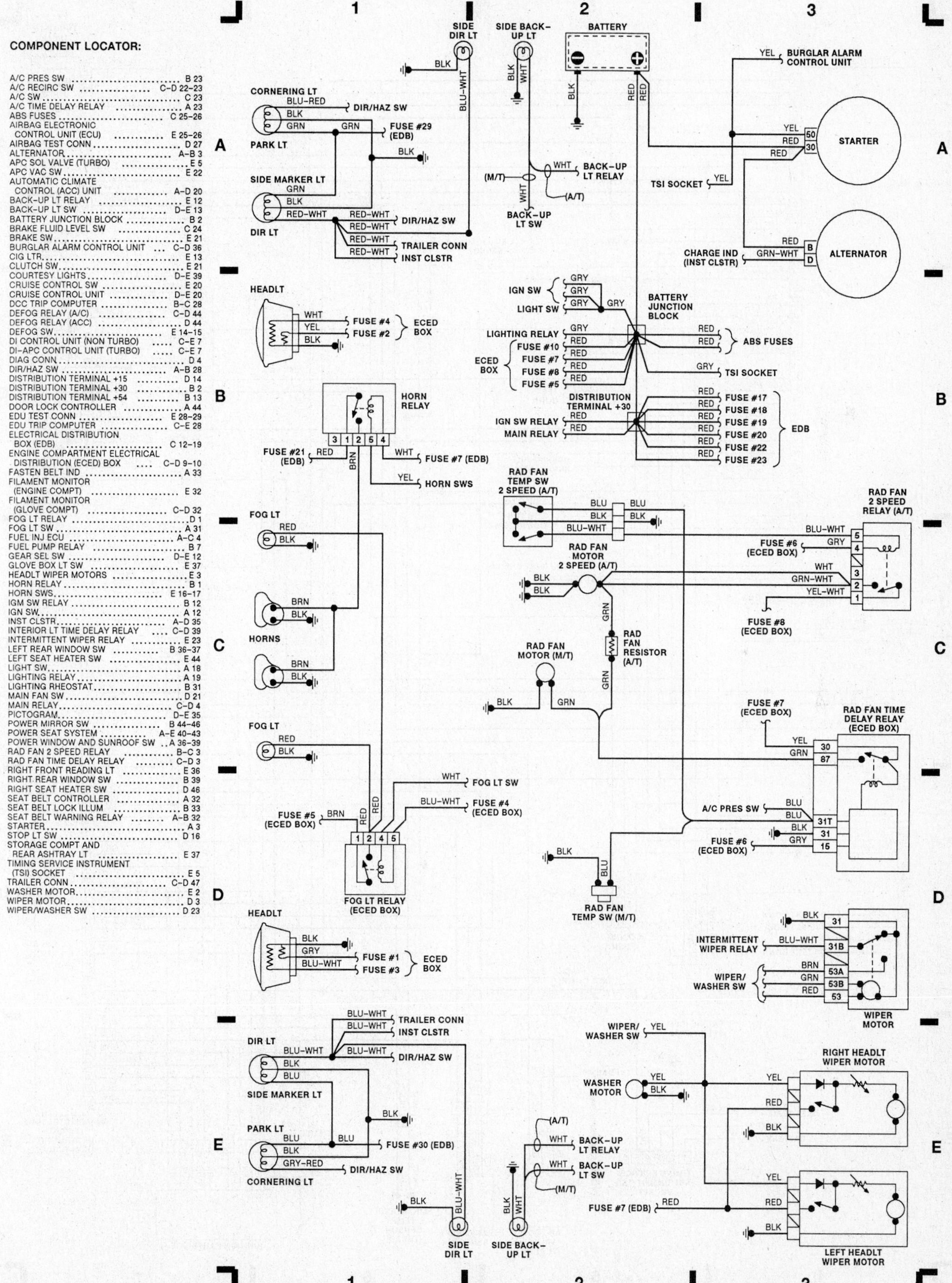

# 1991 WIRING DIAGRAMS
# 9000 Series (Cont.)

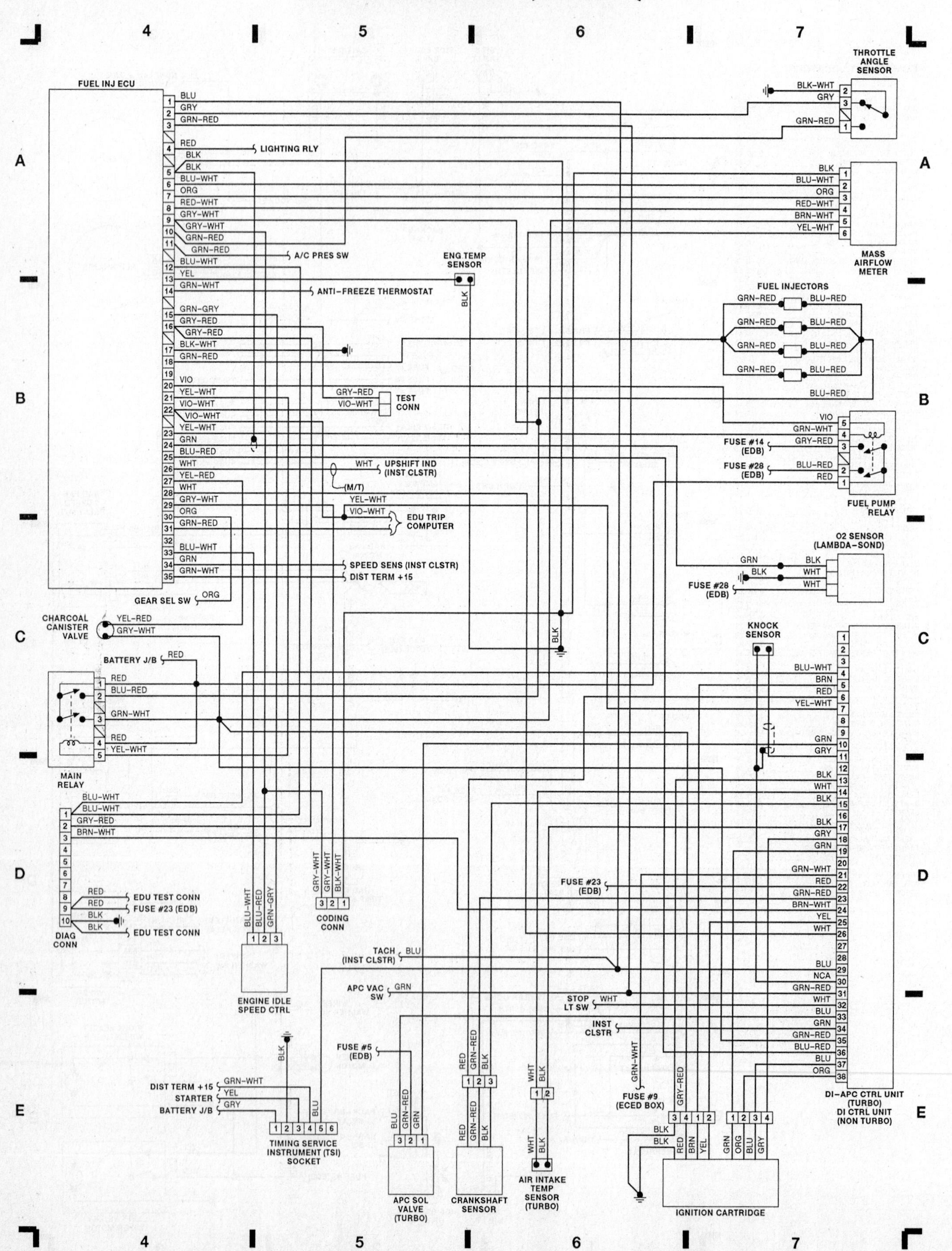

# 1991 WIRING DIAGRAMS
# 9000 Series (Cont.)

8 9 10 11

A

B

C

D

E

GLOVE COMPARTMENT RELAY JUNCTION BOX
INTERM WIPER RELAY E 23
INTERIOR LT TIME DELAY RELAY C–D 39
FLASHER RELAY A 30
NOT USED
MAIN RELAY C–D 4
FUEL PUMP RELAY B 7
SPARE
SPARE
DEFOG RELAY C–D 44
A/C TIME DELAY RELAY A 23
SPARE
IGN SW RELAY B 12
SEAT BELT WARNING RELAY A–B 32
FILAMENT MONITOR C–D 32
HORN RELAY B 1
+54 (B 13)
+30 (B 2)
+15 (D 14)
ENGINE COMPARTMENT ELECTRICAL DISTRIBUTION (ECED) BOX
FILAMENT MONITOR D–E 32
LIGHTING RELAY A 19
RAD FAN 2 SPEED RELAY B–C 3
RAD FAN TIME DELAY RELAY C–D 3
FOG LT RELAY D 1
#10 20A
#8 30A
#6 5A
#4 15A
#2 15A
#9 15A
#7 30A
#5 15A
#3 15A
#1 15A
BATTERY J/B RED RED
MOBILE PHONE CONN RED
IGN SW GRN–WHT
DI–APC CTRL UNIT (TURBO) DI CTRL UNIT (NON TURBO) GRN–WHT
BATTERY J/B RED
RAD FAN 2 SPEED RELAY YEL–WHT
RAD FAN TIME DELAY RELAY YEL GRY
RAD FAN 2 SPEED RELAY GRY (A/T)
GRY–WHT IGN SW
BLU–WHT FOG LT RELAY
WHT YEL GRY BLU–WHT HEADLTS
BLU–WHT INST CLSTR
GRY YEL BLU WHT FILAMENT MONITOR (ENG COMPT)
BRN FOG LT RELAY
RED BATTERY J/B

8 9 10 11

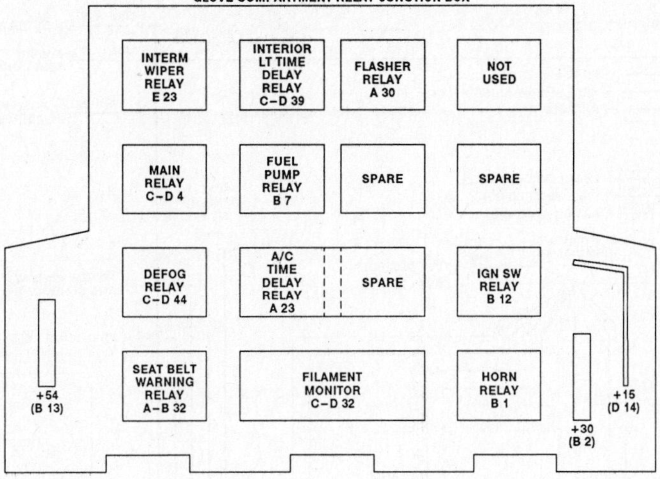

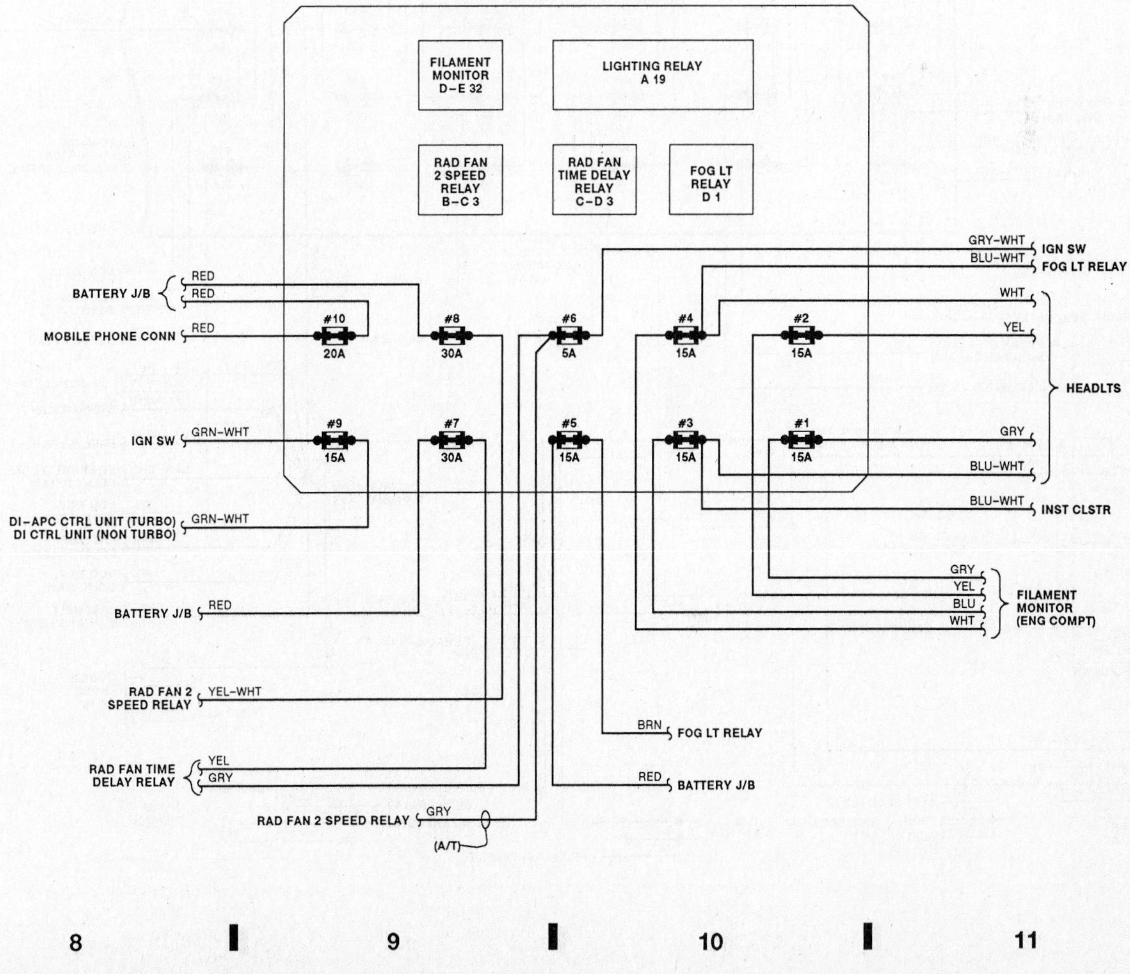

# 1991 WIRING DIAGRAMS
# 9000 Series (Cont.)

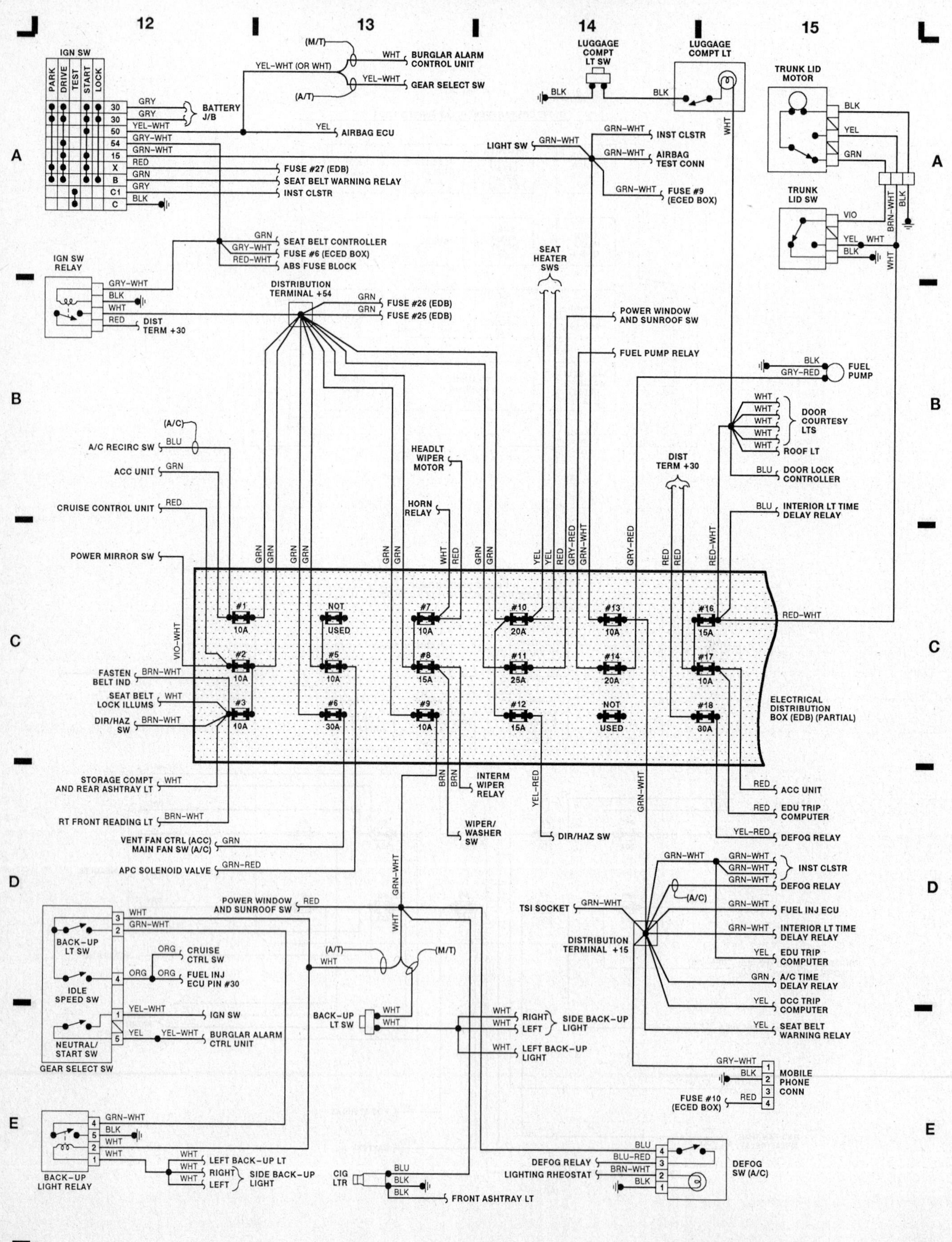

# 1991 WIRING DIAGRAMS
# 9000 Series (Cont.)

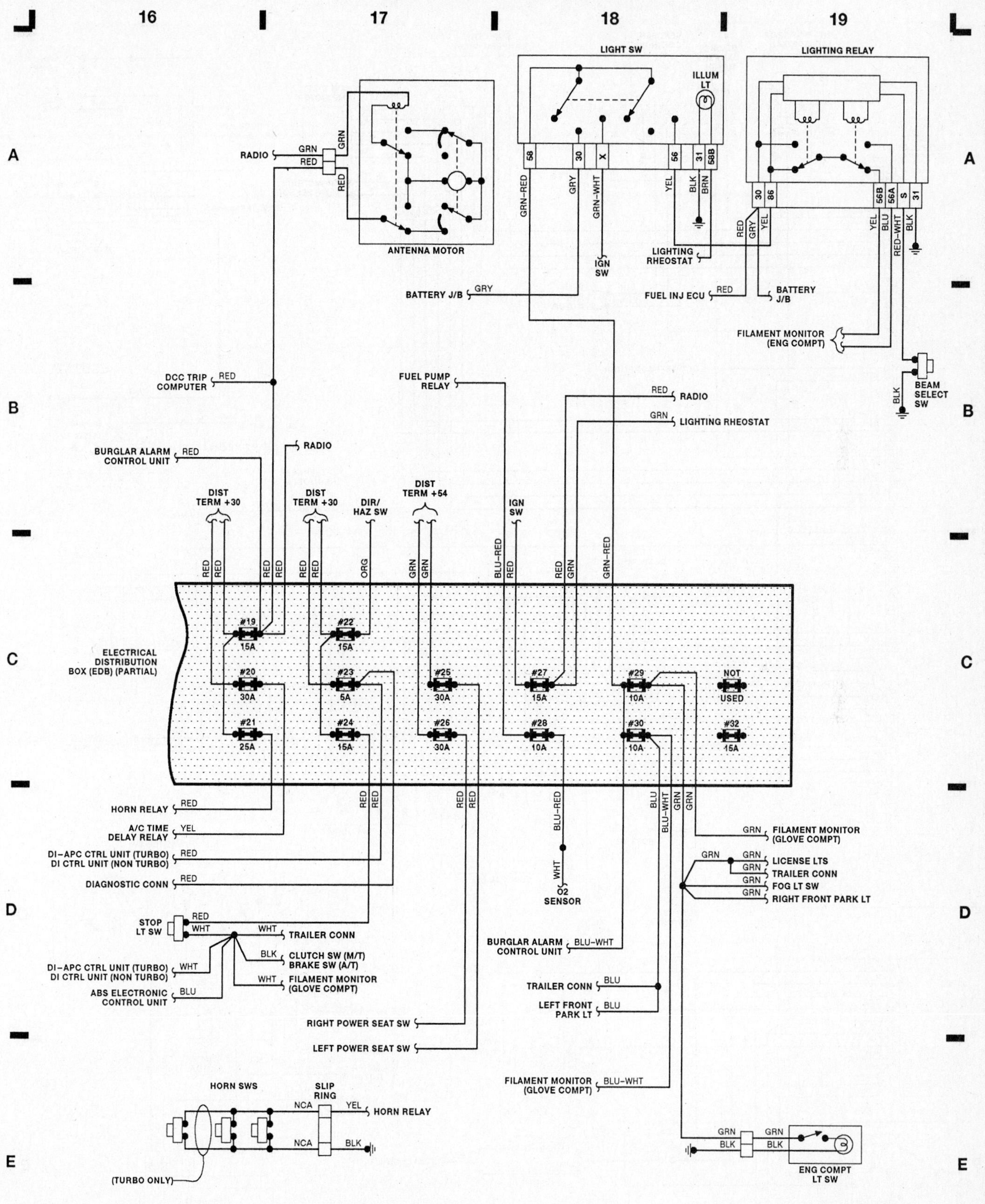

# 1991 WIRING DIAGRAMS
# 9000 Series (Cont.)

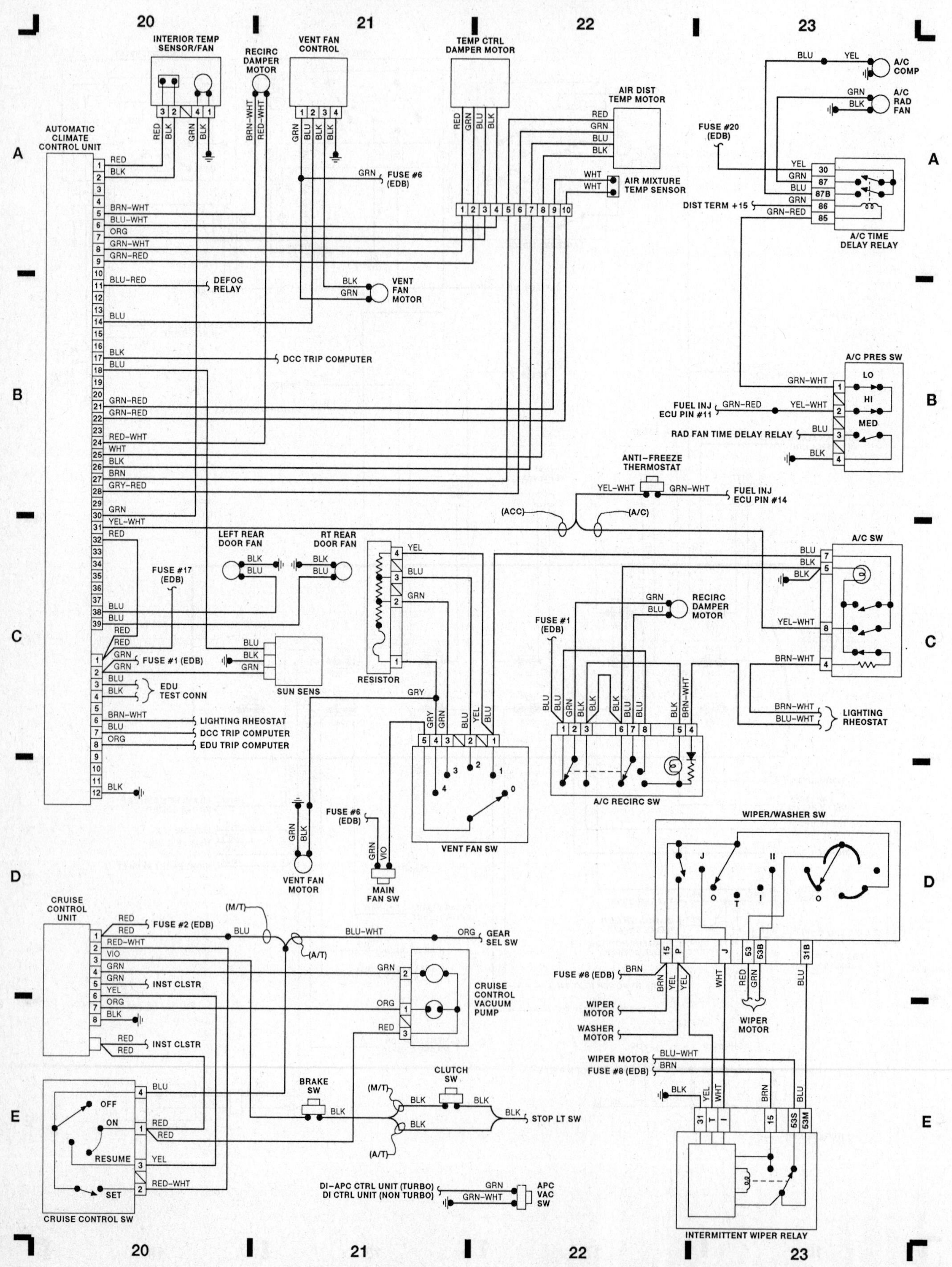

# 1991 WIRING DIAGRAMS
# 9000 Series (Cont.)

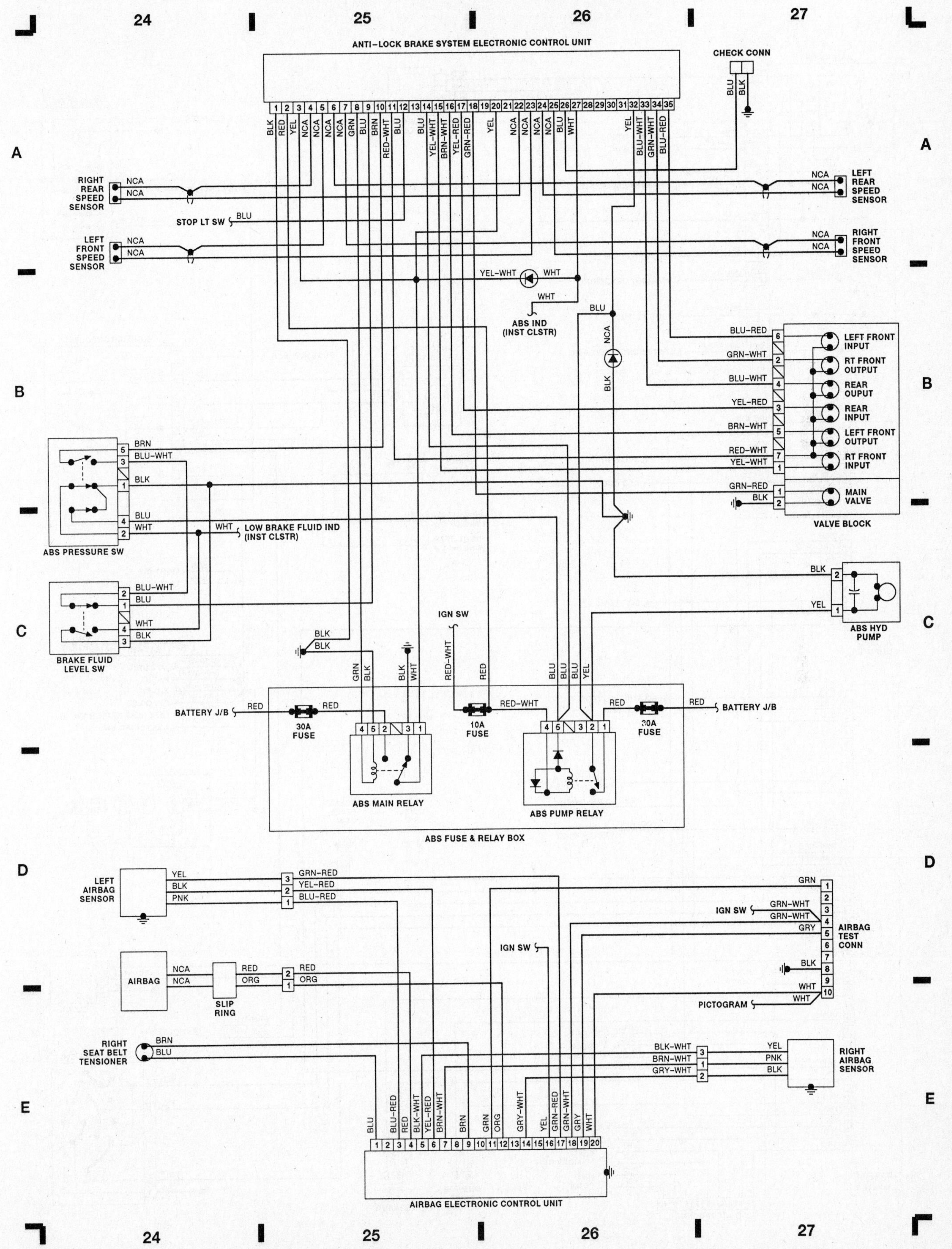

# 1991 WIRING DIAGRAMS
## 9000 Series (Cont.)

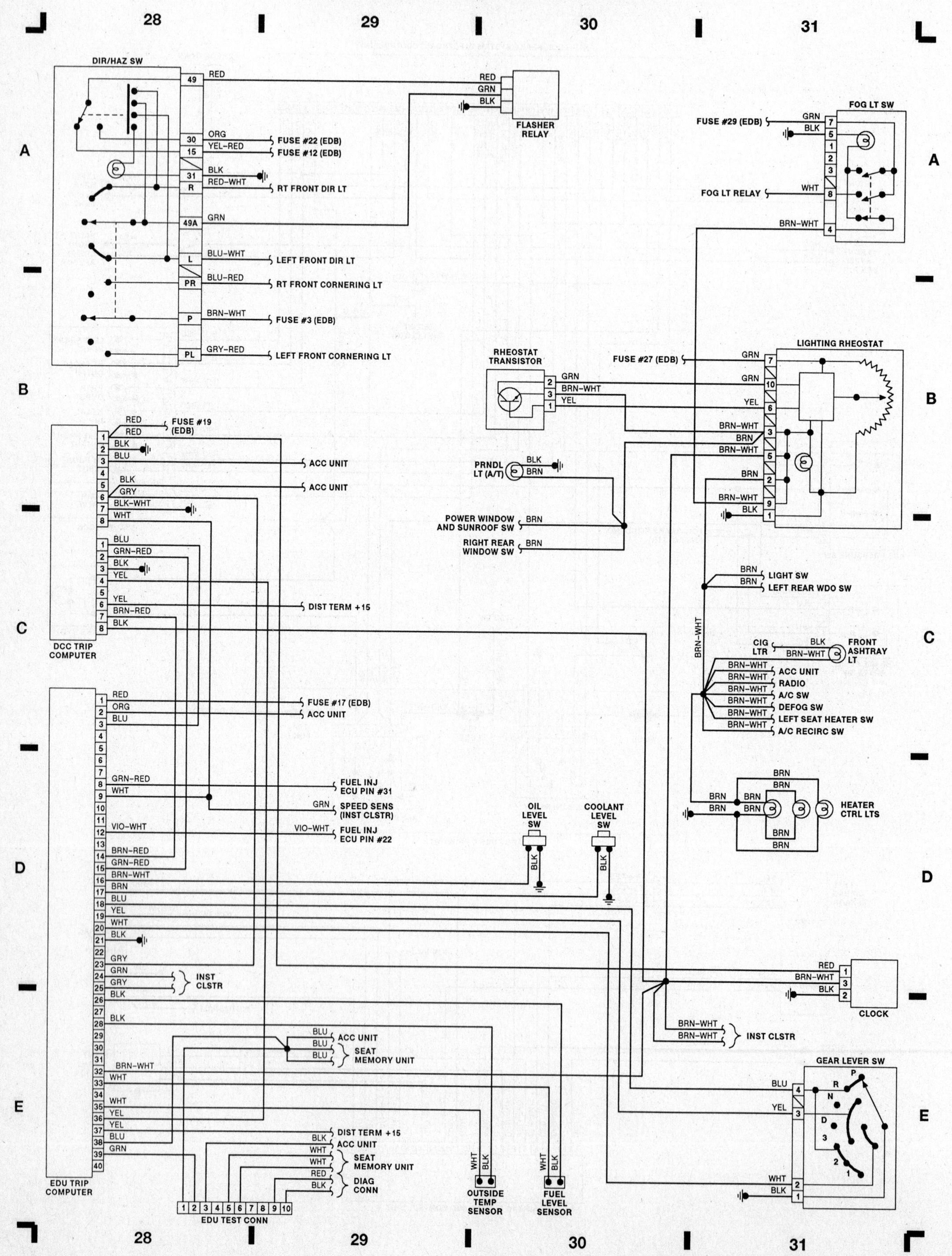

# 1991 WIRING DIAGRAMS
# 9000 Series (Cont.)

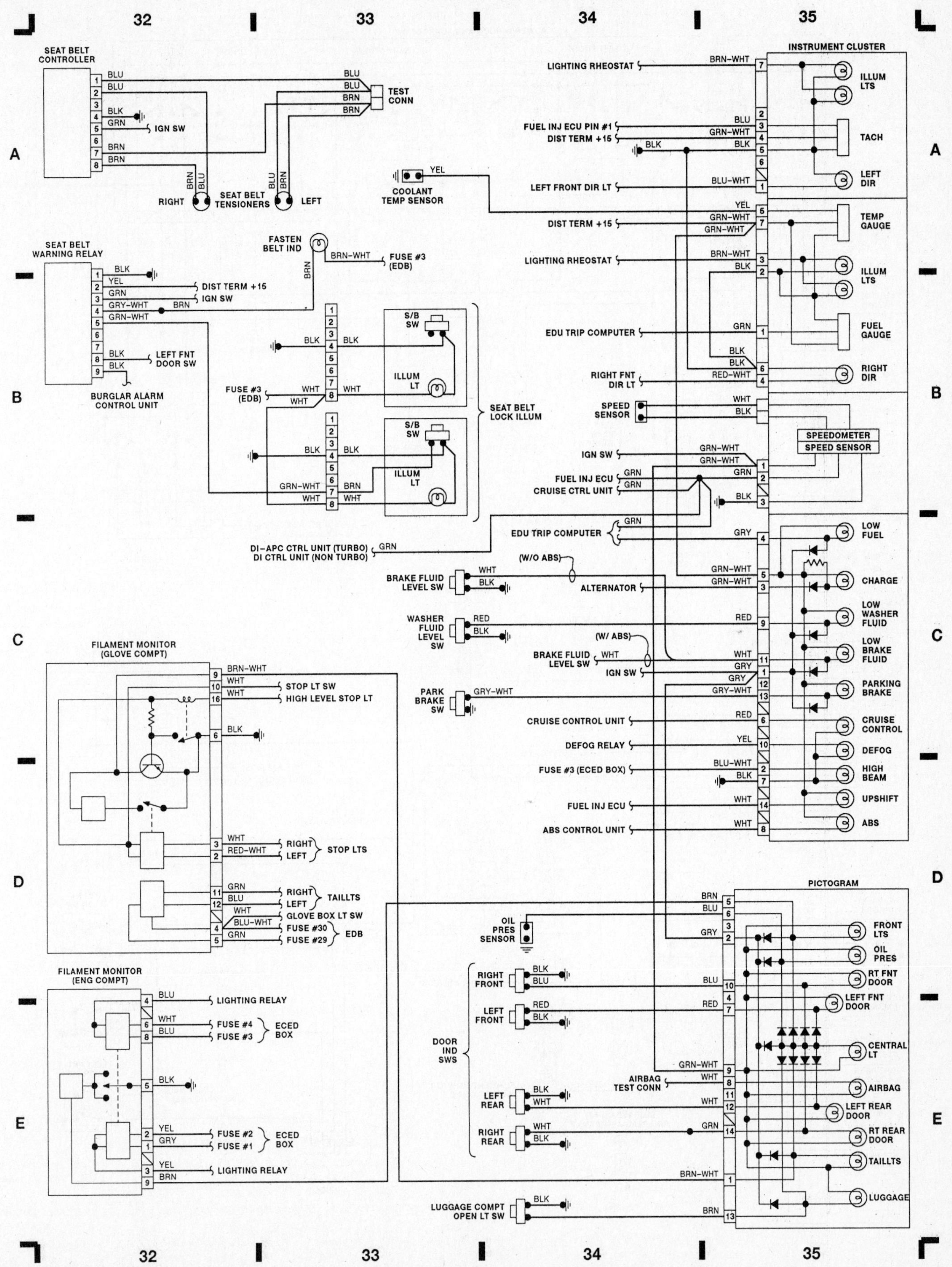

# 1991 WIRING DIAGRAMS
# 9000 Series (Cont.)

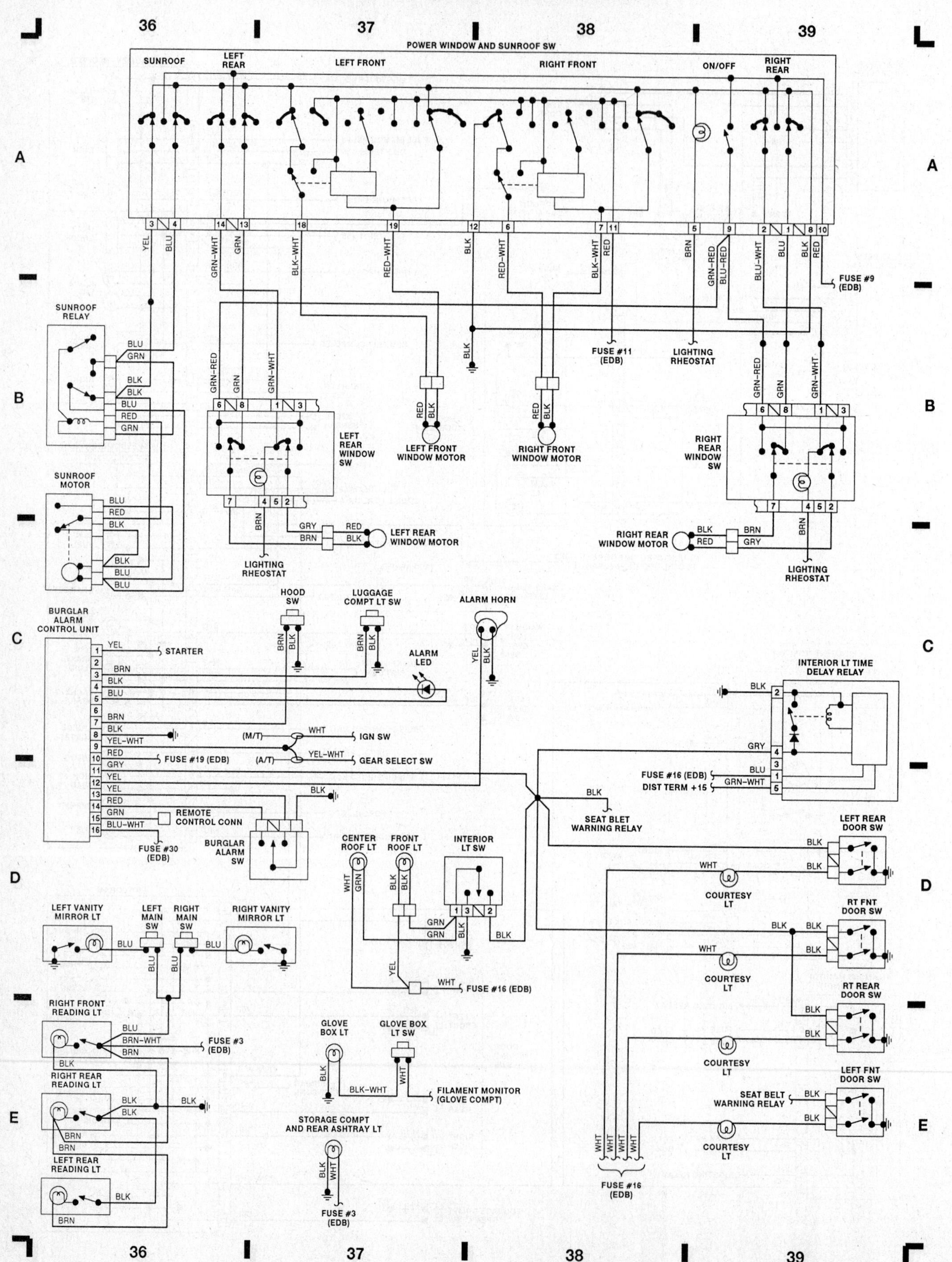

# 1991 WIRING DIAGRAMS
# 9000 Series (Cont.)

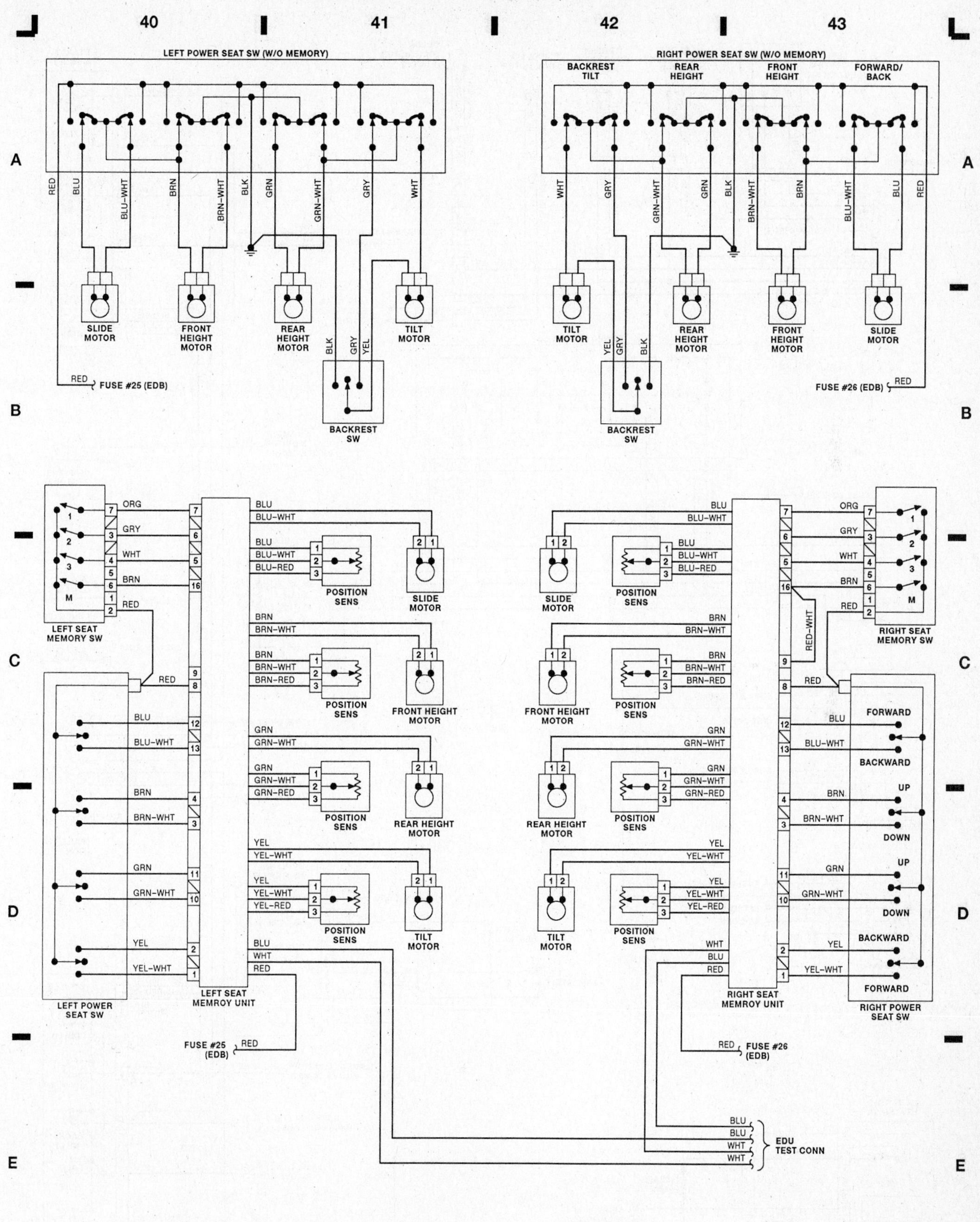

# 1991 WIRING DIAGRAMS
# 9000 Series (Cont.)

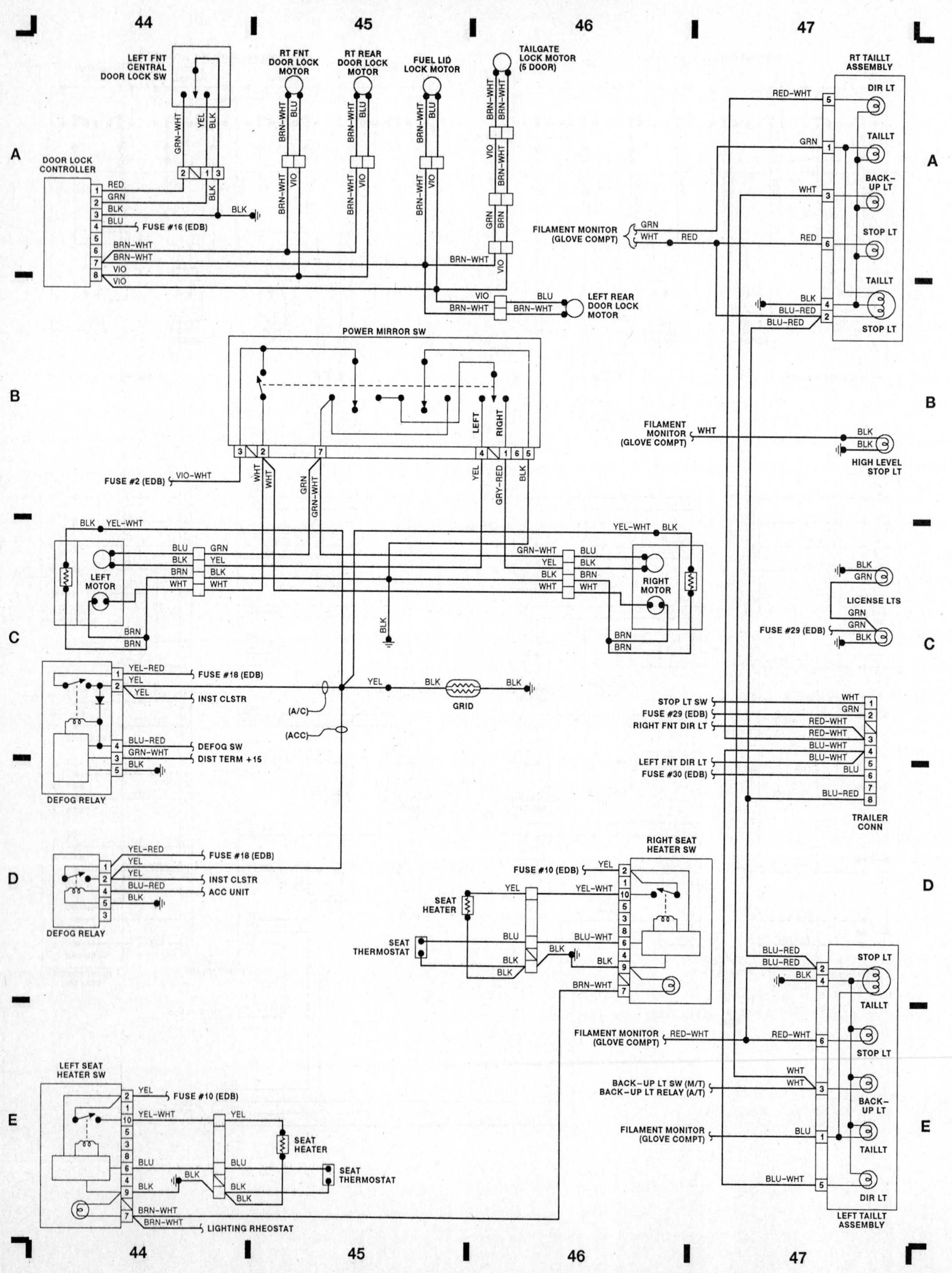

# 1991 SAFETY EQUIPMENT
# Air Bag Restraint System

## 900 Series, 9000 Series

*NOTE: For information on air bag DIAGNOSIS & TESTING or DISPOSAL PROCEDURES, see MITCHELL'S AIR BAG SERVICE & REPAIR MANUAL, DOMESTIC & IMPORTED MODELS.*

## DESCRIPTION & OPERATION

On vehicles equipped with air bag, Supplemental Restraint System (SRS) is marked on the steering wheel horn pad. The SRS consists of air bag module, Electronic Control Unit (ECU) with safety sensor, clockspring, 2 front sensors and an SRS warning light in instrument cluster. *See Fig. 1 or 2*. In addition, 9000 Series incorporate a passenger-side seat belt tensioner.

### FRONT SENSORS

Front sensors verify direction and severity of an impact. Front sensors contain an inertia switch, which completes an electrical circuit during impact. Front sensors are located under front fenders. *See Fig. 1 or 2.*

### AIR BAG MODULE

Air bag module is mounted in center of steering wheel. *See Fig. 1 or 2.* When a small amount of current from ECU is applied, inflator assembly produces nitrogen gas to fill air bag.

### ELECTRONIC CONTROL UNIT (ECU)

The ECU stores fault codes and provides system information to SRS warning light. A code will be stored whenever SRS warning light is activated. Safety sensor is an integral part of ECU.

### CLOCKSPRING

Clockspring connects air bag module to steering column wiring. Clockspring is a flat, ribbon-like tape of conductive material, which winds and unwinds during steering wheel movement.

## SYSTEM OPERATION CHECK

**1)** Turn ignition on. On 9000 Series with ECU part No. 9124074, engine must be allowed to idle approximately 15 minutes. On all other models, engine does not have to be running and there is no delay period.
**2)** On all models, if SRS warning light comes on for about 6 seconds then goes out, system is operating properly. If light remains on, a fault exists in the system.
**3)** If a fault occurs in the system while ignition switch is on, SRS warning light will flash for about 10 minutes and then stay lit. If air bag is deployed, SRS warning light will flash for about 5 seconds and then stay lit.

## SERVICE PRECAUTIONS

Observe these precautions when working with air bag systems:

- Disable SRS before servicing any SRS or steering column component. See DISABLING & ACTIVATING AIR BAG SYSTEM.
- Wait about 20 minutes after deactivating air bag system. System maintains air bag system voltage for about 20 minutes after battery is disconnected. Servicing air bag system before 20-minute period may cause accidental air bag deployment and possible personal injury.
- Because of critical operating requirements of system, DO NOT attempt to service air bag components. Corrections are made by replacement only.
- Always wear safety glasses when servicing or handling an air bag.
- Handle air bag components carefully. Avoid exposing components to impact, heat, moisture, etc.
- Air bag module must be installed immediately after it is taken out of storage. If work is interrupted, module must be returned to storage. Air bag modules must never be left unattended out of storage.
- Air bag module is a sealed unit. DO NOT attempt to dismantle or repair it.
- When placing a live air bag module on a bench or other surface, always face air bag and trim cover up, away from surface. This will reduce motion of module if accidentally deployed.
- After deployment, air bag surface may contain deposits of sodium hydroxide, which can irritate skin. Always wear safety glasses, rubber gloves and long-sleeved shirt during clean-up, and wash hands using mild soap and water. Follow correct disposal procedures.

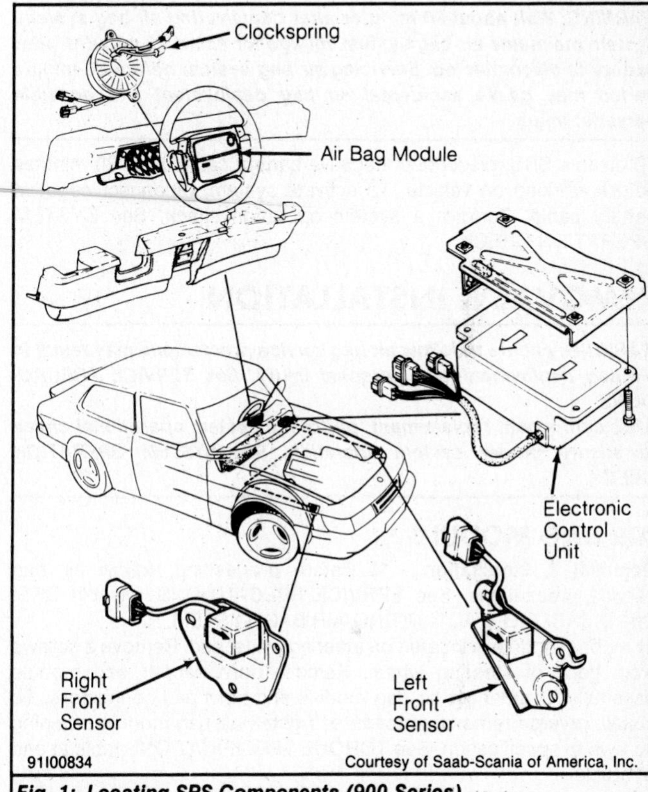


*Fig. 1: Locating SRS Components (900 Series)*

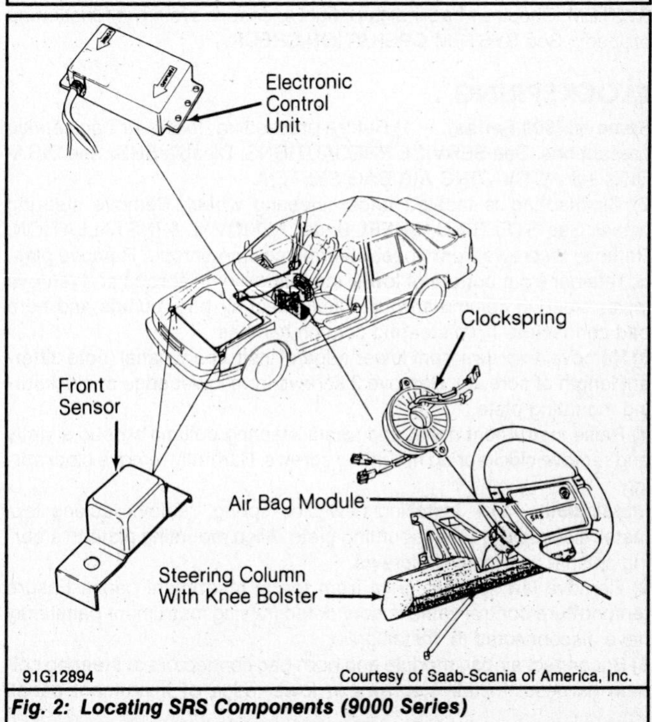


*Fig. 2: Locating SRS Components (9000 Series)*

# 1991 SAFETY EQUIPMENT
# Air Bag Restraint System (Cont.)

- NEVER allow any electrical source near inflator on the back of air bag module.
- When carrying a live air bag module, trim cover should be pointed away from your body to minimize injury in case of accidental deployment.
- Never apply grease to SRS system connectors.

## DISABLING & ACTIVATING AIR BAG SYSTEM

***WARNING: Wait about 20 minutes after deactivating air bag system. System maintains air bag system voltage for about 20 minutes after battery is disconnected. Servicing air bag system before 20-minute period may cause accidental air bag deployment and possible personal injury.***

To disable SRS, disconnect negative battery cable. Wait 20 minutes before working on vehicle. To activate system, reconnect negative battery cable. Perform a system operation check. See SYSTEM OPERATION CHECK.

## REMOVAL & INSTALLATION

***WARNING: Failure to follow air bag service precautions may result in air bag deployment and personal injury. See SERVICE PRECAUTIONS.***
***After component replacement, perform a system operational check to ensure proper system operation. See SYSTEM OPERATION CHECK.***

### AIR BAG MODULE

**Removal & Installation – 1)** Before proceeding, follow air bag service precautions. See SERVICE PRECAUTIONS. Disable SRS. See DISABLING & ACTIVATING AIR BAG SYSTEM.
**2)** Air bag module is located on steering wheel pad. Remove 2 screws from back of steering wheel. Remove horn pad/air bag module assembly. Disconnect air bag module and horn pad connectors. To install, reverse removal procedure. Tighten air bag module retaining screws to specification. See TORQUE SPECIFICATIONS table at end of article.
**3)** Reactivate SRS. See DISABLING & ACTIVATING AIR BAG SYSTEM. Check air bag indicator light to ensure system is functioning properly. See SYSTEM OPERATION CHECK.

### CLOCKSPRING

**Removal (900 Series) – 1)** Before proceeding, follow air bag service precautions. See SERVICE PRECAUTIONS. Disable SRS. See DISABLING & ACTIVATING AIR BAG SYSTEM.
**2)** Clockspring is located under steering wheel. Remove steering wheel. See STEERING WHEEL under REMOVAL & INSTALLATION. Remove 2 screws from upper steering column shroud. Remove plastic retainer from bottom of lower steering column shroud and remove lower steering column shroud. Disconnect air bag module and horn pad connectors from steering column harness.
**3)** Remove 4 screws from lower edge of instrument panel (note different length of screws). Remove 2 screws from lower edge of clockspring mounting plate.
**4)** Raise instrument panel and upper steering column shroud slightly and remove clockspring mounting screws. Carefully remove clockspring.
**Installation – 1)** If installing new clockspring, remove locking tab. Install clockspring onto mounting plate. Align mounting plate to steering column and install 2 screws.
**2)** Remove left speaker grille from top of instrument panel. Ensure temperature control cable is connected (raising instrument panel may have disconnected it). Install grille.
**3)** Reconnect air bag module and horn pad connectors at steering column harness. Install 4 screws in lower edge of instrument panel. Install lower steering column shroud. Ensure front wheels are in straight-ahead position.
**4)** Rotate clockspring clockwise until it stops. Rotate counterclockwise 3 1/2 turns to center clockspring. Install steering wheel. Tighten steering wheel nut to specification. See TORQUE SPECIFICATIONS table at end of article. Reactivate SRS. See DISABLING & ACTIVATING AIR BAG SYSTEM. Check air bag indicator light to ensure system is functioning properly. See SYSTEM OPERATION CHECK.
**Removal (9000 Series) – 1)** Before proceeding, follow air bag service precautions. See SERVICE PRECAUTIONS. Disable SRS. See DISABLING & ACTIVATING AIR BAG SYSTEM.
**2)** Clockspring is located under steering wheel. Remove steering wheel. See STEERING WHEEL under REMOVAL & INSTALLATION. Remove steering column covers. Disconnect horn connector. Remove 2 clockspring retaining screws. Disconnect connectors and remove clockspring.
**Installation – 1)** If installing new clockspring, remove locking tab. Connect clockspring and horn connectors. Install clockspring onto mounting plate. Align mounting plate to steering column and install 2 screws.
**2)** Install top and bottom steering column covers. Ensure clockspring wires are not pinched by middle retaining screw. Ensure front wheels are in straight-ahead position.
**3)** Rotate clockspring clockwise until it stops. Rotate counterclockwise 3 1/2 turns to center clockspring. Install steering wheel. Tighten steering wheel nut to specification. See TORQUE SPECIFICATIONS table at end of article. To install remaining components, reverse removal procedure. Reactivate SRS. See DISABLING & ACTIVATING AIR BAG SYSTEM. Check air bag indicator light to ensure system is functioning properly. See SYSTEM OPERATION CHECK.

### ELECTRONIC CONTROL UNIT (ECU)

**Removal & Installation (900 Series) – 1)** Before proceeding, follow air bag service precautions. See SERVICE PRECAUTIONS. Disable SRS. See DISABLING & ACTIVATING AIR BAG SYSTEM.
**2)** Electronic Control Unit (ECU) is located under center of instrument panel. Remove radio and radio housing (if equipped). Remove rubber bellows from between radio console and gearshift lever. Remove ashtray and ashtray housing.
**3)** Remove 4 screws from bottom of radio console. Pull console forward slightly and remove 2 screws, one from each side of console. Remove lower steering column shroud. Remove lower instrument panel trim and air duct (above knee level).
**4)** Remove 4 screws securing relay panel and cruise control module to instrument panel support. Allow relay panel and cruise control module to hang by their wiring harnesses.

***WARNING: ECU MUST be installed with arrow pointing toward front of vehicle.***

**5)** Disconnect clockspring connector (Orange connector) at steering column between clockspring and ECU. Remove 3 ECU bracket-to-instrument panel support screws. Lift out ECU. Label and unplug 3 connectors from ECU. To install, reverse removal procedure. Install ECU with arrow pointing toward front of vehicle. Ensure ground wire connections are clean.
**6)** Reactivate SRS. See DISABLING & ACTIVATING AIR BAG SYSTEM. Check air bag indicator light to ensure system is functioning properly. See SYSTEM OPERATION CHECK.
**Removal & Installation (9000 Series) – 1)** Before proceeding, follow air bag service precautions. See SERVICE PRECAUTIONS. Disable SRS. See DISABLING & ACTIVATING AIR BAG SYSTEM.
**2)** ECU is located above and behind glove box. Remove right sound baffle under instrument panel. Remove floor duct. Lower glove box door by prying out hinge arm to release stop cleats.
**3)** Remove 6 glove box retaining screws. Pull out glove box with right air vent register. Pry register carefully with a screwdriver. Disconnect glove box light wire. Disconnect ECU connectors. Remove ECU mounting screws and remove ECU.

# 1991 SAFETY EQUIPMENT
# Air Bag Restraint System (Cont.)

***WARNING: ECU MUST be installed with arrow pointing toward front of vehicle.***

**4)** To install, reverse removal procedure. Install ECU with arrow pointing toward front of vehicle. Ensure ground wire connections are clean. Reactivate SRS. See DISABLING & ACTIVATING AIR BAG SYSTEM. Check air bag indicator light to ensure system is functioning properly. See SYSTEM OPERATION CHECK.

## FRONT SENSORS

**Removal - 1)** Before proceeding, follow air bag service precautions. See SERVICE PRECAUTIONS. Disable SRS. See DISABLING & ACTIVATING AIR BAG SYSTEM.
**2)** Front sensors are located under front fenders. Disconnect negative battery cable. On 9000 Series, electrical distribution box must be moved to one side to remove left sensor. On all models, disconnect electrical connector from sensor(s). Remove sensor mounting screws and remove sensor(s).

***WARNING: Front sensor MUST be installed with arrow pointing to front of vehicle.***

**Installation - 1)** To install, reverse removal procedure. Clean mounting pad to ensure good electrical ground. Install sensor with arrow pointing toward front of vehicle. Tighten front sensor bolts to specification. See TORQUE SPECIFICATIONS table at end of article.
**2)** Reactivate SRS. See DISABLING & ACTIVATING AIR BAG SYSTEM. Check air bag indicator light to ensure system is functioning properly. See SYSTEM OPERATION CHECK.

## STEERING WHEEL

**Removal - 1)** Before proceeding, follow air bag service precautions. See SERVICE PRECAUTIONS. Disable SRS. See DISABLING & ACTIVATING AIR BAG SYSTEM.
**2)** Position front wheels in straight-ahead position. Disconnect negative battery cable. Remove 2 screws from back of steering wheel and remove horn pad/air bag module assembly. Disconnect air bag module and horn pad electrical connectors.
**3)** Place match marks on steering wheel and shaft. Remove steering wheel nut. Gently ease steering wheel off of shaft to prevent damage to air bag clockspring.
**Installation - 1)** To ensure clockspring is centered, set front wheels to straight-ahead position. Rotate clockspring clockwise until it stops, then rotate counterclockwise 3 1/2 turns. Maintain clockspring in this position.
**2)** Thread air bag module and horn wiring harnesses through hole in steering wheel. Slide steering wheel onto shaft. Align match marks on shaft and steering wheel, and align clockspring with hole in wheel.
**3)** Install steering wheel nut and tighten to specification. See TORQUE SPECIFICATIONS table at end of article. Connect air bag module and horn pad electrical connectors. Install air bag module. Install screws on back of steering wheel.
**4)** Reactivate SRS. See DISABLING & ACTIVATING AIR BAG SYSTEM. Check air bag indicator light to ensure system is functioning properly. See SYSTEM OPERATION CHECK.

# ADJUSTMENTS

## CLOCKSPRING CENTERING

Position front wheels in straight-ahead position. Rotate clockspring clockwise until it stops, then rotate counterclockwise 3 1/2 turns.

# TORQUE SPECIFICATIONS

***TORQUE SPECIFICATIONS***

| Application | Ft. Lbs. (N.m) |
|---|---|
| Steering Wheel Nut | 24-32 (33-43) |
| | **INCH Lbs. (N.m)** |
| Air Bag Module Screw | 48-60 (5-7) |
| Front Sensor Bolt | 49-92 (5.5-10.5) |

# WIRING DIAGRAMS

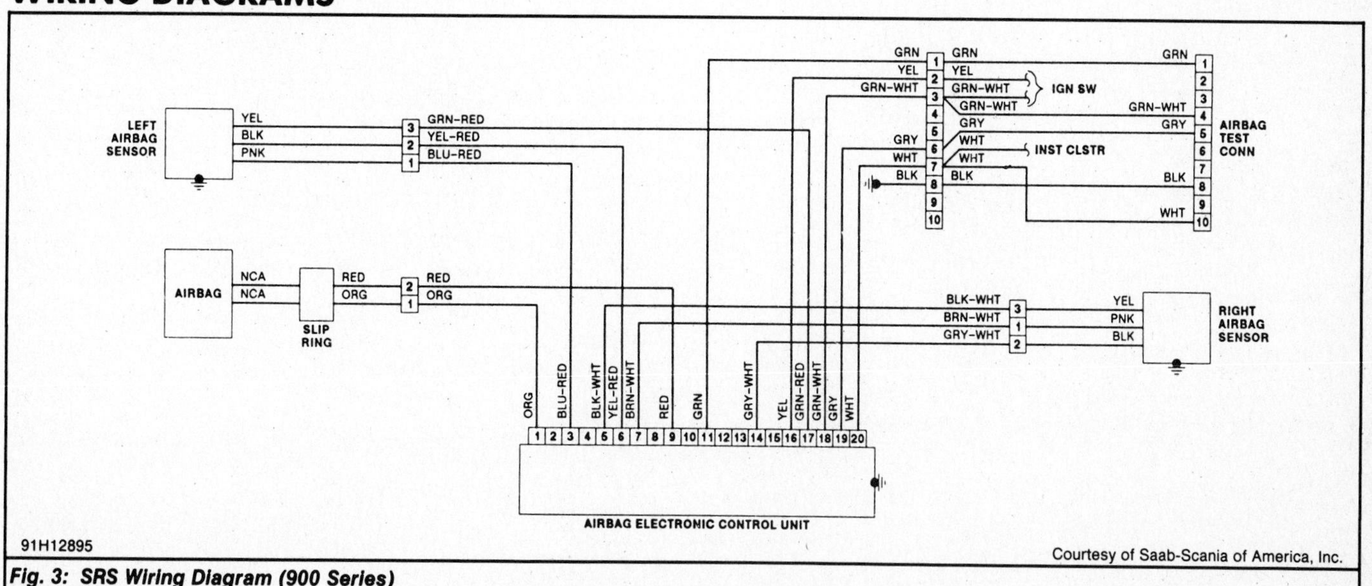


*Fig. 3: SRS Wiring Diagram (900 Series)*

# 1991 SAFETY EQUIPMENT
# Air Bag Restraint System (Cont.)

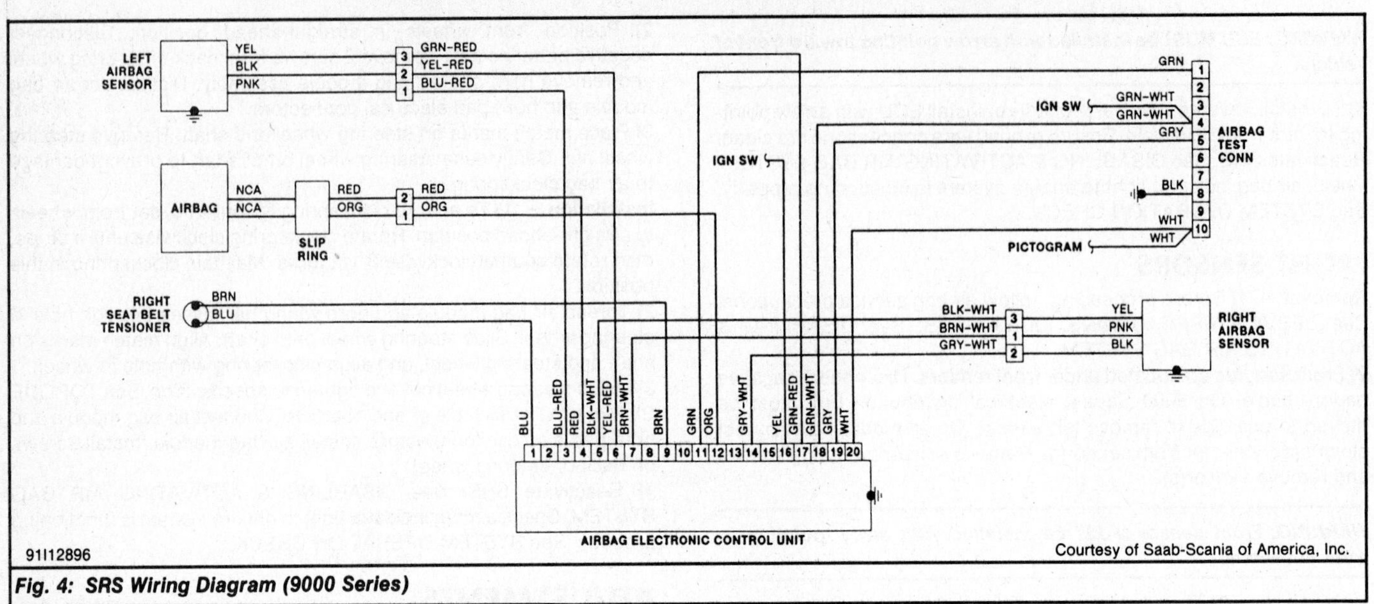


Fig. 4: SRS Wiring Diagram (9000 Series)

# 1991 SAFETY EQUIPMENT
# Instrument Panels

## 900 Series, 9000 Series

## DESCRIPTION & OPERATION

Instrument cluster contains a speedometer, tachometer, fuel gauge, temperature gauge, and clock. Saab 9000 models have a pictographic display which warns of any front or rear light failure, doors ajar, or low oil pressure. Turbo models have a boost gauge.

## TESTING

Manufacturer does not supply instrument panel testing.

## REMOVAL & INSTALLATION

### INSTRUMENT CLUSTER

**900 Series - 1)** Disconnect negative battery cable. Remove steering wheel. Remove 4 screws under edge of instrument panel. Tilt instrument panel back.

***CAUTION: Instrument panel retaining screws are different lengths. Note positions of screws for reassembly.***

**2)** Remove left speaker/defroster grille. Reach through opening and unplug wiring connectors. Disconnect speedometer cable and EGR wire. Remove instrument panel with switches. Remove instrument cluster retaining screws and instrument cluster. To install, reverse removal procedure.

**9000 Series - 1)** Disconnect negative battery cable. Remove left and right speaker grilles. Remove 7 upper instrument panel pad screws and instrument panel pad.

**2)** Remove air ducting. Disconnect speedometer cable and vacuum hose to turbo boost gauge (if equipped). Unplug instrument panel connectors. Remove 2 instrument cluster retaining screws. Remove instrument cluster from panel. To install, reverse removal procedure.

### INSTRUMENT PANEL LOWER PAD

Remove lower steering column cover. With hood open, remove nut at each end of lower pad. Remove ashtray. Remove screw inside ashtray opening and remove lower pad. To install, reverse removal procedure.

## WIRING DIAGRAMS

See appropriate chassis wiring diagram in WIRING DIAGRAMS.

# Steering Column Switches

## 900 Series, 9000 Series

***WARNING: If vehicle is equipped with driver's side air bag, use extreme caution while servicing steering column. Disconnect battery and wait at least 20 minutes before attempting any repair. To prevent inadvertent deployment of air bag, DO NOT apply electrical power to any component on steering column without disconnecting air bag electronic control unit.***

## TESTING

***NOTE: Testing information is not available from manufacturer.***

## REMOVAL & INSTALLATION

### STEERING WHEEL & HORN PAD

**Removal (With Air Bag) - 1)** Position front wheels straight ahead. Disconnect negative battery cable. Wait at least 20 minutes. Remove 2 screws from back of steering wheel. Remove air bag module/horn pad assembly. Unplug electrical connectors for air bag module and horn pad.

**2)** Match-mark steering wheel and shaft. Remove steering wheel nut. Gently ease steering wheel from shaft to prevent damage to air bag clockspring.

**Installation - 1)** To ensure clockspring is set in middle position, align front wheels to straight-ahead position. Rotate clockspring clockwise until it stops, then rotate counterclockwise 3 1/2 turns.

**2)** Thread air bag module and horn wiring harnesses through hole in steering wheel. Slide steering wheel onto shaft, aligning match marks on shaft and wheel and aligning clockspring with hole in wheel.

**3)** Install steering wheel nut and tighten to 24-32 ft. lbs. (33-43 N.m). Connect air bag module and horn pad electrical connectors. Install screws on back of steering wheel. Reconnect battery negative cable.

**4)** Start engine and ensure SRS warning light comes on for approximately 6 seconds, then goes off.

**Removal & Installation (Without Air Bag) - 1)** Disconnect battery ground cable. On standard steering wheels, remove 4 screws behind steering wheel to remove safety padding and horn switch. On sport type steering wheels, lift rubber flaps from steering wheel spokes to remove safety padding and horn switch.

**2)** Remove steering wheel nut. Using a steering wheel puller, pull steering wheel from steering column. Using 2 screwdrivers, pry turn signal canceling sleeve from steering wheel.

**3)** To install, reverse removal procedure. Ensure front wheels are in straight-ahead position. Tighten steering wheel nut to 19 ft. lbs. (26 N.m) on 900 Series or 21 ft. lbs. (28 N.m) on 9000 Series.

### IGNITION SWITCH

**Removal & Installation (9000 Series) -** Disconnect negative battery cable. Remove lower steering column bearing cover. Pull steering wheel out as far as it will go. Release spacer by unscrewing transverse bolt. Remove upper steering column cover. Remove retaining screws, connector, and ignition switch. To install, reverse removal procedure.

### TURN SIGNAL SWITCH

**Removal & Installation - 1)** Disconnect negative battery cable. Remove bearing cover from lower steering column. Release spacer by unscrewing transverse bolt. Pull steering wheel out as far as it will go. Remove upper steering column cover. Unplug upper connector.

**2)** Remove 2 turn signal switch retaining screws. Pull turn signal switch forward. Disconnect lower connector. Reverse removal procedure to install.

### WIPER SWITCH

**Removal & Installation -** Disconnect negative battery cable. Pull steering wheel out as far as it will go. Remove covers from steering column bearing bracket. Unplug wiper switch connector. Remove retaining screws and windshield wiper switch. Reverse removal procedure to install.

## TORQUE SPECIFICATIONS

***TORQUE SPECIFICATIONS***

| Application | Ft. Lbs. (N.m) |
|---|---|
| Steering Wheel Nut | |
| 900 Series | |
| With Air Bag | 24-32 (33-43) |
| Without Air Bag | 19 (26) |
| 9000 Series | 21 (28) |

# 1991 SAFETY EQUIPMENT
# Wiper/Washer Systems

### 900 Series, 9000 Series

## DESCRIPTION

All models are equipped with a 2-speed wiper motor. An intermittent control relay is located on the relay bracket under left side of dashboard, next to the turn signal flasher.

## TESTING

***NOTE: Testing information is not available from manufacturer.***

## REMOVAL & INSTALLATION

### WIPER MOTOR

**900 Series** - Lift wiper arm. Fold cap up and remove wiper shaft nut. Remove wiper arms and rubber shaft covers. Remove bolts at wiper bracket and one bolt at each shaft. Unplug connector. Remove wiper motor and bracket as an assembly. To install, reverse removal procedure. *See Fig. 1.*

**9000 Series** - Lift wiper arm covers. Remove nuts and wiper arms. Remove rubber grommets from wiper arm shafts. Remove 4 cowl panel bolts and cowl. Unplug motor connectors. Remove spindle nuts from wiper arm shafts. Remove wiper motor retaining bolts. Remove motor with bracket and linkage. To install, reverse removal procedure.

### WIPER SWITCH

**900 Series** - Disconnect negative battery cable. Remove steering column bearing bracket. Remove switch bracket. Remove wiper/washer switch. To install, reverse removal procedure.

**9000 Series** - Disconnect negative battery cable. Pull steering wheel back as far as it will go. Remove steering column bearing bracket cover. Unplug connector. Remove wiper/washer switch retaining screws and switch. To install, reverse removal procedure.

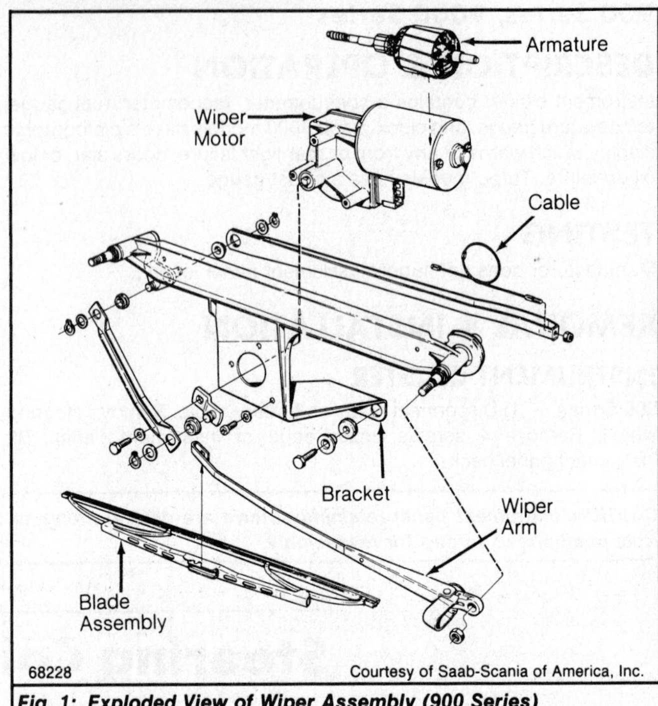


***Fig. 1: Exploded View of Wiper Assembly (900 Series)***

## WIRING DIAGRAMS

See appropriate chassis wiring diagram in WIRING DIAGRAMS.

# 1991 ENGINES
# 2.0L, 2.1L & 2.3L 4-Cylinder

## 900 Series, 9000 Series

***NOTE: For repair procedures not covered in this article, see ENGINE OVERHAUL PROCEDURES article in GENERAL INFORMATION.***

## ENGINE IDENTIFICATION

Vehicle Identification Number (VIN) is located on top left end of instrument panel, visible through windshield. Engine code is eighth character from left of VIN. See ENGINE IDENTIFICATION CODES table.

***ENGINE IDENTIFICATION CODES***

| Application | Code |
|---|---|
| 2.0L Turbo | D |
| 2.1L | E |
| 2.3L Non-Turbo | B |
| 2.3L Turbo | M |

## ADJUSTMENTS

### VALVE CLEARANCE ADJUSTMENT

All vehicles have hydraulic valve lifters. No adjustment is required.

## REMOVAL & INSTALLATION

***NOTE: For reassembly reference, label all electrical connectors, vacuum hoses, and fuel lines before removal. Also place mating marks on engine hood and other major assemblies before removal.***

### FUEL PRESSURE RELEASE

***WARNING: Residual fuel pressure may be present in fuel system when engine is off. To avoid fire hazard, wrap a shop towel around fuel fitting before disconnecting fuel lines.***

To release fuel pressure, disconnect fuel lines at fuel pressure regulator and fuel injection manifold.

### ENGINE

***NOTE: Remove engine and transaxle as a unit. On 900 Series, transaxle housing is attached to engine lower crankcase pan.***

**Removal (900 Series) – 1)** Disconnect windshield washer hoses. Remove hood. Install Spacer (83 93 209) between upper control arm and body. Remove battery. Disconnect exhaust pipe at manifold. Loosen right front wheel lug bolts. Drain power steering reservoir. Raise and support vehicle.

**2)** Disconnect shifter rod from transmission linkage. Disconnect speedometer cable at transaxle. Remove exhaust pipe bracket at transaxle. Disconnect CV joint boots at transaxle. Remove right front wheel. Lower control arm and anti-roll bar from ball joint.

**3)** Separate right drive axle from transmission. Disconnect pressure line from power steering pump. Remove A/C compressor drive belt. Drain engine coolant. Disconnect oil filler tube. Disconnect coolant hoses at intercooler, expansion tank, and thermostat housing.

**4)** Unplug all wiring connectors. Lift wiring harness from engine compartment and place it on A/C condenser. Remove turbo discharge duct (if equipped). Remove mass airflow meter and air cleaner. On turbo models, remove intercooler and air duct as an assembly. Cap turbocharger inlet. Remove top cover and baffle plate from side of intercooler on turbo models.

**5)** On all models, remove ignition coil and cooling fan. Disconnect coolant hose from bottom of radiator. Disconnect throttle cable. Disconnect all remaining wiring and vacuum hoses. Disconnect and plug end of line to clutch release cylinder (if equipped).

**6)** Release fuel pressure. See FUEL PRESSURE RELEASE. Disconnect fuel lines at fuel pressure regulator and fuel injection manifold. Remove A/C compressor and place it on A/C condenser. DO NOT disconnect A/C hoses. Remove engine mount bolts. Attach engine hoist and lifting sling.

**7)** Lift engine slightly. Disconnect remaining inboard drive axle joint. Remove return line from power steering pump. Remove oil pressure sensor and oil cooler lines at oil filter. Ensure all wiring, hoses, and other attachments have been removed from engine. Lift engine and transaxle from vehicle as an assembly. Cover CV joints at transaxle.

**Installation** – Pack CV joint cups with grease. Tilt engine forward slightly while lowering into position. To complete installation, reverse removal procedure. Tighten bolts to specification. See TORQUE SPECIFICATIONS table at end of article. Bleed clutch (if equipped).

**Removal (9000 Series) – 1)** Raise and support vehicle. Remove front wheels, inner panel from right front fender, and center panel under spoiler. Drain coolant. Remove battery. Disconnect ABS brace. Unplug wiring and disconnect battery cable from terminal block on battery tray. Remove battery tray.

**2)** Unplug connectors for ignition system and knock sensor. Disconnect upper radiator hose. Remove mass airflow meter, muffler, and elbow as an assembly. Remove washer fluid reservoir. Disconnect throttle cable.

**3)** Release fuel pressure. See FUEL PRESSURE RELEASE. Disconnect fuel return line at fuel pressure regulator, and fuel supply line at fuel rail. Remove cover over space between firewall and panel. Remove panel. Unplug engine wiring connector. Disconnect speedometer sensor wire at transaxle.

**4)** Disconnect heater hoses at cylinder head. Unplug connector at brake fluid reservoir. Apply sufficient upward tension to accessory drive belt to install Lock (83 94 488) to tensioner. Protect oil cooler and radiator crossmember. Remove A/C compressor and wire it to radiator crossmember. DO NOT disconnect hoses.

**5)** On models with A/T, disconnect cooler lines at transmission. Plug lines and transmission fittings. Disconnect kickdown cable clip at power steering pump. Remove nut from A/T shifter linkage. Pry shifter cable from clip.

**6)** On models with M/T, disconnect line from clutch release cylinder. Cap hose and release cylinder openings. Position gear selector in 4th gear. Separate rubber joint in shift linkage.

**7)** Disconnect hoses from expansion tank. Disconnect radiator hoses at water pump. Unplug connector at $O_2$ sensor. Remove torque strut. Disconnect exhaust pipe at manifold. Unplug connector at oil level sensor. Secure oil cooler to engine with wire.

**8)** Remove power steering reservoir retaining bolt. Lower reservoir. Siphon fluid from reservoir. Disconnect return hose. Place reservoir on firewall. Disconnect pressure line at power steering pump. Plug hose and pump openings. Remove clip from rear engine mount.

**9)** Remove right hand engine mount nuts. Remove clips from inboard drive axle joints. Remove upper and loosen lower shock absorber bolts. Pull steering knuckles outward to separate CV joints at transmission. Cover both halves of each joint.

**10)** Disconnect hood struts. Install Extensions (83 94 439) onto struts. Ensure all wiring, hoses, or other attachments have been removed from engine. Attach engine hoist and lifting sling. Carefully lift engine and transmission assembly from vehicle.

**Installation** – Pack CV joint cups with grease. Insert bolt through left-hand engine mount. To complete installation, reverse removal procedure. Tighten bolts to specification. See TORQUE SPECIFICATIONS table at end of article. Bleed clutch (if equipped).

### INTAKE MANIFOLD

**Removal & Installation (900 Series) – 1)** See FUEL PRESSURE RELEASE. Disconnect fuel lines at fuel pressure regulator and fuel injection manifold. Drain coolant. Disconnect coolant hose at thermostat housing. Remove fuel pressure regulator. Remove ground connections for fuel injection ECU.

**2)** Remove auxiliary air valve (if equipped). Unbolt A/C bracket from cylinder head. Remove intake manifold, fuel injectors, and fuel rail as an assembly. To install, reverse removal procedure.

**Removal & Installation (9000 Series) – 1)** Drain coolant. Disconnect negative battery cable. Remove rubber elbow from between throttle body and mass airflow meter. Unplug connector from throttle position sensor. Disconnect hoses from throttle body. Remove throttle body retaining bolts. Move throttle body aside.

# 1991 ENGINES
# 2.0L, 2.1L & 2.3L 4-Cylinder (Cont.)

**2)** Unplug connector from automatic idle control valve. Move AIC valve aside. See FUEL PRESSURE RELEASE. Disconnect fuel lines at fuel pressure regulator and rail. Disconnect wiring from fuel injectors. Remove fuel rail and injectors as an assembly.

**3)** Disconnect temperature sensor and ground points on intake manifold. Remove harness from clips under manifold. Disconnect EGR tube and Red-marked hose (if equipped). Remove retaining bolts and intake manifold. To install, reverse removal procedure. Tighten bolts to specification. See TORQUE SPECIFICATIONS table at end of article.

## EXHAUST MANIFOLD

**Removal** – Remove A/C compressor (if equipped). Remove pulse air unit and EGR tube. Remove exhaust manifold retaining nuts. Disconnect exhaust pipe from manifold. Remove manifold.

**Installation** – Always install NEW pulse air nozzles and ferrules. Ensure nozzles are perpendicular to flanges, and extend .6-.7" (15-18 mm) beyond face of flange. To complete installation, reverse removal procedure. To complete installation, reverse removal procedure. Tighten bolts to specification. See TORQUE SPECIFICATIONS table at end of article.

## CYLINDER HEAD

**Removal (900 Series)** – **1)** Remove intake manifold. See INTAKE MANIFOLD. Remove turbocharger (if equipped) and exhaust manifold. See EXHAUST MANIFOLD. Remove 2 timing cover-to-cylinder head bolts. Remove engine mount bolts from cylinder head.

**2)** Disconnect lead from temperature sender. Remove inspection panel from valve cover. Remove distributor cap and spark plug leads as an assembly. Remove valve cover. Disconnect crankcase ventilation hose. Remove split rubber plugs from cylinder head.

**3)** Align timing mark on flywheel with "0" mark on flywheel cover. Remove camshaft chain tensioner, camshaft chain and sprockets. Raise engine to permit removal of cylinder head from engine brace. Remove cylinder head bolts in reverse order of tightening sequence. *See Fig. 1*.

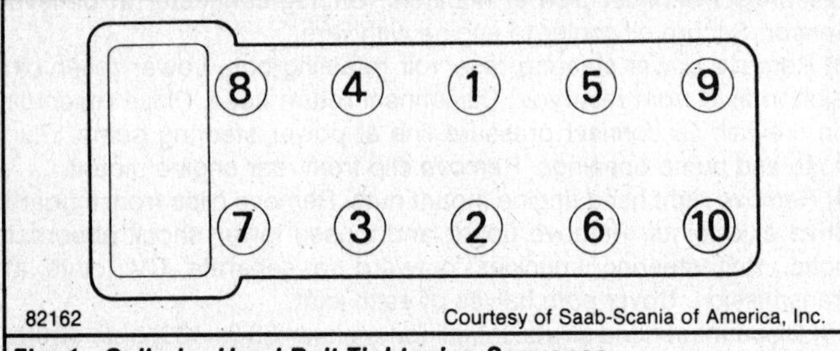


***Fig. 1: Cylinder Head Bolt Tightening Sequence***

**Installation** – **1)** Install guide pin into one bolt hole. Remove cylinder head. Ensure pivoting timing chain guide is not damaged.

**2)** Lubricate cylinder head bolts and washers before installation. Tighten cylinder head bolts in sequence shown. *See Fig. 1*. Tighten bolts to an initial torque of 44 ft. lbs. (60 N.m). Then tighten bolts to 59 ft. lbs. (80 N.m). Finally, tighten each bolt an additional 90 degrees.

**3)** Install 2 timing cover-to-cylinder head bolts. Install timing chain and camshaft sprockets, starting with exhaust valve camshaft. Keep chain taut between sprockets. Lightly tighten sprocket bolts.

**4)** Adjust chain tensioner by pressing piston and rotating tensioner into locked position. Install tensioner with piston under tension. Tighten bolt. Release tensioner by pressing pivoting guide firmly. Press pivoting guide against chain to release tension. Press pivoting guide to check tensioner operation.

**5)** Rotate crankshaft 2 complete turns clockwise. Check timing marks on crankshaft and camshafts. To complete installation, reverse removal procedure. Tighten bolts to specification. See TORQUE SPECIFICATIONS table at end of article.

**Removal (9000 Series)** – **1)** Remove turbocharger (if equipped) and exhaust manifold as an assembly. See EXHAUST MANIFOLD. Disconnect lead from temperature sender. Remove intake manifold. See INTAKE MANIFOLD. Remove engine mount bolts from cylinder head.

**2)** Disconnect hoses from valve cover. Remove ignition cartridge and valve cover. Rotate crankshaft to align "0" mark on flywheel with timing mark on flywheel cover. Remove camshaft sprockets and chain tensioner. Remove 2 timing cover-to-cylinder head bolts.

**3)** Detach starter lead from clip on thermostat housing. Remove cylinder head bolts. Install guide pin into top right corner of cylinder head. Ensure timing chain is positioned so that pivoting chain guide does not obstruct cylinder head. Lift cylinder head from engine.

**Inspection** – Check for cracks. Inspect valve seats and refinish as necessary. Check cylinder head height after resurfacing. See CYLINDER HEAD in ENGINE SPECIFICATIONS tables at end of article.

**Installation** – **1)** Place new gasket on cylinder block. Rotate crankshaft to TDC position of No. 1 piston. Align camshafts with their respective timing marks. Position timing chain in pivot guide.

**2)** Install guide pin into top right-hand corner of cylinder head. Lubricate cylinder head bolts and washers before installation. Tighten cylinder head bolts in sequence shown. *See Fig. 1*. Tighten bolts to an initial torque of 44 ft. lbs. (60 N.m). Then tighten bolts to 59 ft. lbs. (80 N.m). Finally, tighten each bolt an additional 90 degrees.

**3)** Install sprocket for intake camshaft first, then remaining sprocket. Ensure timing chain is positioned correctly between guides. To complete installation, reverse removal procedure. Tighten bolts to specification. See TORQUE SPECIFICATIONS table at end of article.

## FRONT COVER OIL SEAL

**Removal** – Remove drive belt. Remove drive pulley and vibration damper. Remove A/C pulley. Pry out old seal.

**Installation** – Grease sealing surface of new seal. Press seal into position with Seal Installer (83 93 349). Reverse removal procedure to complete installation. Tighten bolts to specification. See TORQUE SPECIFICATIONS table at end of article.

## TIMING CHAIN

**Removal (900 Series)** – **1)** Remove engine/transaxle from vehicle. See ENGINE. Rotate crankshaft until "0" mark on flywheel aligns with timing mark on flywheel cover. Remove inspection panel from valve cover. Disconnect ignition leads and vacuum hose (if equipped) from distributor. Remove distributor cap and valve cover.

**2)** Remove center bolts from camshaft sprockets. Ensure camshafts remain at correct timing settings. Remove chain tensioner and camshaft sprockets. Remove crankshaft pulley and oil pump. Remove water pump pulley and water pump. Remove cylinder head-to-timing cover bolts.

**3)** Remove timing cover bolts and cover. Note lengths and locations of retaining bolts. Remove timing chain and crankshaft sprocket.

**Removal (9000 Series)** – **1)** Disconnect negative battery cable. Using Locking Attachment (83 93 993), prevent flywheel from turning. Raise and support vehicle. Drain engine oil and coolant. Remove right front wheel and inner fender panel. Remove drive belt and belt tensioner.

**2)** Remove power steering pump retaining bolts. Lower pump onto subframe. Remove alternator mounting bolts. Place alternator inboard of rear engine mount. Remove power steering pump bracket. Remove lower bolts from upper engine mount. Remove torque strut. Remove remaining upper engine mount bolts.

**3)** Remove bolt from coolant pipe clip next to knock detector. Remove upper belt tensioner bracket. Remove A/C compressor and wire it to radiator crossmember. DO NOT disconnect hoses. Remove A/C compressor bracket. Remove water pump.

**4)** Remove crankshaft pulley. Move Hall Effect sensor aside. Disconnect coolant tube clip. Move coolant tube aside. Remove oil pan. See OIL PAN. Remove 2 timing cover-to-cylinder head bolts. Remove timing cover retaining bolts and timing cover. Note lengths and locations of retaining bolts.

5) Rotate crankshaft until "0" mark on flywheel aligns with timing mark on flywheel cover. Remove ignition cartridge. Remove inspection panel from valve cover. Remove camshaft sprocket retaining bolts.
6) Ensure camshafts remain at correct timing settings. On 2.3L engines, remove balance shaft chain. See BALANCE SHAFTS. On all engines, remove chain tensioner and camshaft sprockets. Remove timing chain and crankshaft sprocket.
**Installation (All Models) – 1)** Ensure No. 1 piston is in TDC position and camshafts are aligned with their respective timing marks. *See Fig. 2.* Position timing chain around crankshaft sprocket and through pivoting guide.
**2)** Install timing chain and camshaft sprockets, starting with exhaust valve camshaft. Keep chain taut between sprockets. Lightly tighten sprocket bolts. Adjust chain tensioner by fully bottoming and then rotating piston to locked position.
**3)** Install tensioner with piston under tension. Release tensioner by pressing pivoting guide firmly. Press pivoting guide to check tensioner operation.
**4)** Rotate crankshaft 2 complete turns clockwise. Check timing marks on crankshaft and camshafts. Tighten camshaft sprocket bolts to specification. See TORQUE SPECIFICATIONS table at end of article. Apply anaerobic sealant to timing cover sealing surface. Reverse removal procedure to complete installation.

## VALVE LASH ADJUSTER

**Removal & Installation –** See CYLINDER HEAD under OVERHAUL.

## CAMSHAFT

**Removal – 1)** Rotate crankshaft until "0" mark on flywheel aligns with timing mark on flywheel cover. Remove inspection panel from valve cover. On 900 Series, disconnect ignition leads and vacuum hose from distributor. Remove distributor (if equipped). On 9000 Series, remove ignition cartridge.
**2)** Remove valve cover. Remove camshaft sprocket retaining bolts. Remove chain tensioner, camshaft sprockets, and timing chain. Remove oil line and camshaft bearing caps. Remove camshafts.
**Installation – 1)** Ensure "0" mark on flywheel aligns with timing mark on flywheel cover. Install intake camshaft with bearing caps No. 1 through 5, and exhaust camshaft with bearing caps No. 6 through 10.
**2)** Tighten bearing cap bolts to specification. See TORQUE SPECIFICATIONS table at end of article. Rotate camshafts until they are aligned with their respective timing marks. *See Fig. 2.* Reverse removal procedure to complete installation.

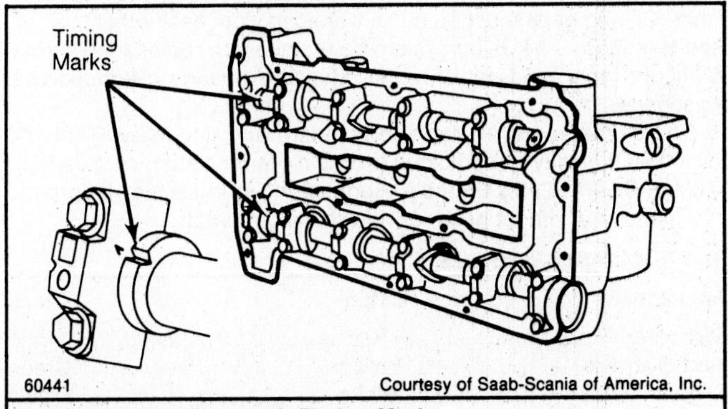


***Fig. 2: Locating Camshaft Timing Marks***

## BALANCE SHAFTS (2.3L)

**Removal –** Remove timing chain cover. See TIMING CHAIN. Remove upper chain guide, chain tensioner, and pivoting guide. Remove idler sprocket and balance shaft chain. Pull oil pump drive and balance chain drive sprocket from crankshaft. Carefully pull balance shafts from engine block.
**Inspection –** Inspect all parts for wear or damage. Replace bearings and/or balance shafts if bearing clearance exceeds .007" (.18 mm).
**Installation – 1)** Ensure "0" mark on flywheel aligns with timing mark on flywheel cover. Lubricate balance shaft journals and bearing housings. Carefully insert balance shafts into their respective bores. Shaft marked INL goes into intake side of engine. Ensure timing marks on balance shaft bearing housings and sprockets are aligned.
**2)** Install balance shaft chain and idler sprocket, leaving some slack in area of tensioner. Keep chain reasonably taut with upper chain guide. Press plunger on chain tensioner. Maintain plunger in position by inserting paper clip into hole in housing. Ensure plunger is turned to position in which spring acts fully upon it.
**3)** Install chain guides and tensioner. Remove paper clip to set tensioner. Rotate crankshaft several times. Ensure timing marks align. To complete installation, reverse removal procedure. Tighten bolts to specification. See TORQUE SPECIFICATIONS table at end of article.

## REAR CRANKSHAFT OIL SEAL

**Removal (900 Series M/T) –** Remove clutch. See CLUTCH under REMOVAL & INSTALLATION in CLUTCHES, FWD article. Remove flywheel. Pry out old seal.
**Removal (900 Series A/T)–** Remove engine. See ENGINE. Separate engine and transaxle. See TRANSMISSION SERVICING, REMOVAL & INSTALLATION. Remove torque converter and flexplate. Pry out old seal.
**Removal (9000 Series M/T) –** Remove clutch. See CLUTCH under REMOVAL & INSTALLATION in CLUTCHES, FWD article. Remove flywheel. Pry out old seal.
**Removal (9000 Series A/T) –** Remove transaxle and flexplate. See TRANSMISSION SERVICING, REMOVAL & INSTALLATION. Pry out old seal.
**Installation (All Models) –** Lubricate sealing surface of new seal with engine oil. Install into position with Seal Installer (83 92 540). Reverse removal procedure to complete installation. Tighten bolts to specification. See TORQUE SPECIFICATIONS table at end of article.

## WATER PUMP

**Removal (900 Series) –** Drain coolant. Remove drive belt. Remove pulley, water pump retaining bolts, and water pump.
**Removal (9000) Series) –** Raise and support front of vehicle. Remove right front wheel assembly. Drain coolant. Loosen drive belt. Remove water pump pulley. Unbolt oil and water line clips. Disconnect coolant hoses. Remove water pump.
**Installation (All Models) –** Clean gasket surfaces. Install new gasket. Install water pump, belt tensioner pulley, and drive belt. Reverse removal procedure to complete installation. Tighten bolts to specification. See TORQUE SPECIFICATIONS table at end of article.

## OIL PAN

**Removal – 1)** Remove dipstick. Stuff rag into opening. Raise and support of vehicle. Drain engine oil. Remove right front wheel and inner fender panel. Remove front and rear engine mount nuts, $O_2$ sensor, and front section of exhaust pipe. Remove torque strut through-bolt. Lift engine slightly. Remove lower oil pan-to-transaxle bolt.
**2)** Disconnect wiring from oil level sensor. Remove turbocharger brace and oil return line (if equipped). Fold down splash plate. Remove rubber plugs from transaxle housing to gain access to rear oil pan bolts. Remove oil pan retaining bolts. Tap guide sleeve into engine block. Remove oil pan. Remove guide sleeve.
**Installation –** Clean gasket surfaces. Apply silicone sealant to gasket surfaces. Install rubber seal for oil strainer into groove in oil pan. Reverse removal procedure to complete installation. Tighten bolts to specification. See TORQUE SPECIFICATIONS table at end of article.

# OVERHAUL

## CYLINDER HEAD

**Cylinder Head –** Measure cylinder head height after resurfacing. See CYLINDER HEAD table under ENGINE SPECIFICATIONS at end

# 1991 ENGINES
# 2.0L, 2.1L & 2.3L 4-Cylinder (Cont.)

of article. Cylinder head warpage information is not available from manufacturer.

**Valve Springs - 1)** Remove camshafts. Remove valve lifters with magnet. Install Lifter Bore Sleeves (83 93 746) to protect lifter bores. Position Valve Retainer Remover (83 94 181) squarely on valve head and tap firmly with hammer. Remove keepers with magnet. Remove springs and caps.

**2)** To assemble, install valve spring and cap over valve stem. Position retainers into groove in spring cap. Using Valve Retainer Remover (83 94 181) and Valve Retainer Installer Sleeve (83 94 207), carefully tap retainers into groove of valve stem. Length of valve spring when installed should be 1.46" (37 mm). To complete assembly, reverse disassembly procedure.

**Valve Stem Oil Seals -** Remove seals using Pliers (83 94 157) Ensure protective sleeves for lifter guides are in place. Install seals using Installer (83 93 803). Remove shank from installer. Insert seal into installer. Insert Installer into guide. Tap seal into position with plastic mallet.

**Valve Guides - 1)** To check for valve guide wear, pull valve approximately .12" (3.0 mm) from its seat and check side play with a dial indicator. If side play exceeds .020" (.50 mm), replace valve and/or valve guide.

**2)** To replace guide, flush hot water through head and pull valve guide from top of head using Guide Puller (83 93 811), Spacer (83 93 829), and Nut (83 93 845). To install, flush hot water through head and press in new valve guide from bottom side.

**Valve Seat -** Grind intake and exhaust valve seats to an angle of 45 degrees.

**Valves -** Grind intake valves to an angle of 44.5 degrees. DO NOT grind exhaust valve face. Use only lapping compound to finish face.

**Valve Seat Correction Angles -** Using a 75-degree cutter, adjust exhaust valve seat width so that valve contact surface extends to edge of head. Using a 75-degree cutter below, and an 11- or 12-degree cutter above, adjust intake valve seat contact area to center of valve head. Valve seat width should be approximately .06" (1.5 mm) after refinishing. *See Figs. 3 and 4.*

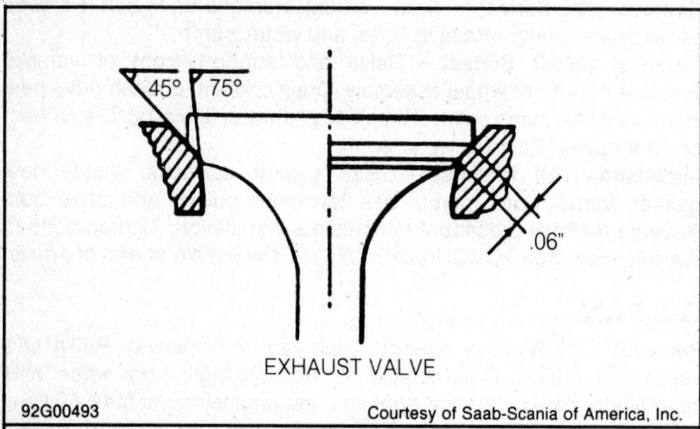


***Fig. 3: Refinishing Exhaust Valve Seat***

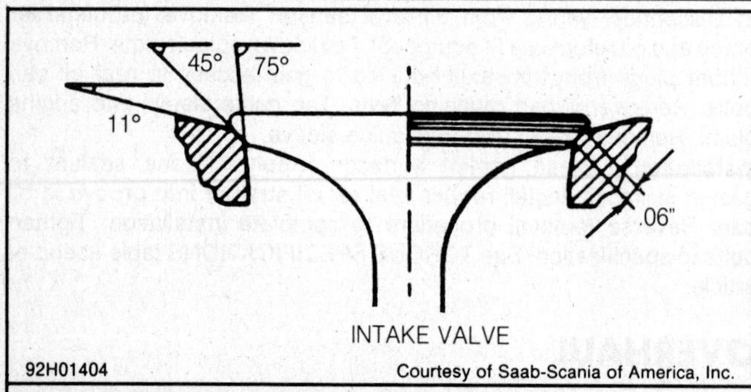


***Fig. 4: Refinishing Intake Valve Seat***

## VALVE TRAIN

**Lash Adjusters -** See CYLINDER HEAD under OVERHAUL.

## CYLINDER BLOCK ASSEMBLY

**Piston & Rod Assembly - 1)** Mark pistons for reassembly reference. Rod and cap for each cylinder are stamped with an identification number (1-4). Piston pins are retained by circlips. Remove circlips and press out piston pins. Check pins and bearings for wear or damage and replace as necessary.

**2)** Install piston and rod assembly with number on rod and cap facing exhaust side of engine. Install piston with notch on top of piston (at outer circumference) facing timing chain end of engine.

**Fitting Pistons - 1)** To fit pistons to cylinder bores, use a feeler gauge 1/2" (12.7 mm) wide and a spring scale. Oil cylinder lightly. Insert piston without rings. Attach spring scale to feeler gauge.

**2)** Insert feeler gauge between piston and cylinder wall at right angle to piston pin. When feeler gauge can be pulled out of cylinder with a force of 1.8-2.6 lbs. (.8-1.2 kg), piston clearance is equal to feeler gauge thickness. See PISTONS, PINS & RINGS table in ENGINE SPECIFICATIONS.

**3)** Repeat test at various bore depths. Standard and oversize pistons are available. See PISTON DIAMETER SPECIFICATIONS table.

***PISTON DIAMETER SPECIFICATIONS***

| Application | In. (mm) |
|---|---|
| 2.0L | |
| Standard AB | 3.5428-3.5431 (89.988-89.996) |
| Standard B | 3.5431-3.5435 (89.996-90.004) |
| Standard C | 3.5435-3.5441 (90.004-90.020) |
| 1st Oversize | 3.5623-3.5629 (90.482-90.497) |
| 2nd Oversize | 3.5820-3.5826 (90.982-90.997) |
| 2.1L | |
| Standard A | 3.6607-3.6611 (92.982-92.992) |
| Standard B | 3.6611-3.6615 (92.993-93.002) |
| Standard B+ | 3.6615-3.6619 (93.003-93.012) |
| 1st Oversize | 3.6804-3.6808 (93.482-93.492) |
| 2nd Oversize | 3.7001-3.7005 (93.982-93.992) |
| 2.3L | |
| Standard AB | 3.5425-3.5429 (89.980-89.989) |
| Standard B | 3.5429-3.5432 (89.989-89.997) |
| Standard C | 3.5432-3.5438 (89.997-90.013) |
| 1st Oversize | 3.5619-3.5625 (90.472-90.488) |
| 2nd Oversize | 3.5816-3.5822 (90.972-90.988) |

**Piston Rings - 1)** Check piston rings for end gap and side clearance. Use an inverted piston to push ring down into bore. On worn bores, measure at lower end of bore. See PISTONS, PINS & RINGS table under ENGINE SPECIFICATIONS at end of article.

**2)** Lubricate pistons and rings. Install rings onto pistons. Stagger ring gaps. Compression ring gaps must be located 180 degrees from each other. Oil ring gaps must be equally spaced from each other.

**Rod Bearings - 1)** Using a micrometer, measure rod bearing journal diameter, taper, and out-of-round. Measure bearing clearance with Plastigage.

**2)** Rod bearings are available in standard and undersize. Thin and thick bearings may be combined to obtain proper clearance. See ROD & MAIN BEARING SIZES table. Rod bearing journals may be ground one undersize without need for rehardening of shaft.

***ROD & MAIN BEARING SIZES***

| Application | Thin | Thick |
|---|---|---|
| Standard | Red | Blue |
| First Oversize | Yellow | Green |
| Second Oversize | White | Brown |

**Crankshaft & Main Bearings - 1)** Turn engine upside down to prevent weight of crankshaft from affecting measurements. Measure bearing clearance with Plastigage positioned to one side of journal centerline.

**2)** Main bearings are available in standard and undersize. Thin and thick bearings may be combined to obtain proper clearance. See ROD & MAIN BEARING SIZES table. Main bearing journals may be ground one undersize without need for rehardening of shaft.

**Thrust Bearing -** Center main bearing is thrust bearing. If crankshaft end play exceeds specification, install new thrust washer. Thrust washer oil grooves should face toward crankshaft. See CRANKSHAFT MAIN & CONNECTING ROD BEARINGS table under ENGINE SPECIFICATIONS at end of article.

**Cylinder Block** – Check each cylinder for wear, cracks, or damage. Ensure oil passages are clean. Ensure freeze plugs are in good condition.

## ENGINE OILING

### ENGINE LUBRICATION SYSTEM

The crankshaft drives an oil pump on the timing cover. Oil flows through a full flow filter to oil passages which feed main bearings, rod bearings, and valve train.

**Crankcase Capacity** – Oil capacity, including filter, is 4.0 qts. (3.8L) for 900 Series Non-Turbo, 4.5 qts. (4.3L) for 900 Series Turbo, and 4.4 qts. (4.2L) for 9000 Series.

**Oil Pressure** – Oil pressure is 43 psi (3.0 kg/cm²) at 2000 RPM.

### OIL PUMP

**Removal** – Clean area around pump. Attach Locking Device (83 92 987) to flywheel ring gear. Remove crankshaft pulley retaining bolt and pulley. Remove oil pump retaining bolts and pump.

**Installation** – Coat gears with oil. Ensure ring gear is installed with mark on visible face. Position NEW sealing ring into groove in pump body. Prime pump with oil and install on engine. Remove oil filter adapter casting and fill passage with oil. Install casting.

***NOTE: It may be necessary to pull pump gear out slightly to position gear on driving plate.***

## TORQUE SPECIFICATIONS

### *TORQUE SPECIFICATIONS*

| Application | Ft. Lbs. (N.m) |
|---|---|
| Camshaft Bearing Cap Bolt | 11 (15) |
| Camshaft Sprocket Bolt | 48 (65) |
| Crankshaft Pulley Bolt | 140 (190) |
| Cylinder Head Bolt [1] | |
| Step 1 | 44 (60) |
| Step 2 | 66 (90) |
| Step 3 | Additional 90° |
| Distributor Hold-Down Bolt | 15 (20) |
| Exhaust Manifold Bolt | 19 (26) |
| Flywheel Bolt | 44 (60) |
| Intake Manifold Bolt | 13 (18) |
| Knock Sensor | 11-19 (15-26) |
| Main Bearing Cap Bolt | 81 (110) |
| Oil Pan Bolt | 15 (20) |
| Rod Bearing Bolt | 41 (56) |
| Thermostat Housing Bolt | 13 (18) |
| Timing Chain Cover Bolt | 15 (20) |
| Timing Chain Tensioner Bolt | 48 (65) |
| Water Pump Bolt | 15 (20) |
| | **INCH Lbs. (N.m)** |
| Belt Tensioner Pulley | 71 (8) |
| Oil Pump Bolt | 71 (8) |

[1] – Tighten in sequence. *See Fig. 1.*

## ENGINE SPECIFICATIONS

### *GENERAL SPECIFICATIONS*

| Application | Specification |
|---|---|
| **2.0L** | |
| Displacement | 121 Cu. In. (2.0L) |
| Bore | 3.54" (90.0 mm) |
| Stroke | 3.07" (78.0 mm) |
| Compression Ratio | 9.0:1 |
| Fuel System | PFI |
| Horsepower @ RPM | |
| 900 Turbo | 160 @ 5500 |
| 900 Turbo SPG | 175 @ 5500 |
| Torque Ft. Lbs. | |
| 900 Turbo @ RPM | 188 @ 3000 |
| 900 Turbo SPG @ RPM | 195 @ 3000 |
| **2.1L** | |
| Displacement | 129 Cu. In. (2.1L) |
| Bore | 3.66" (93.0 mm) |
| Stroke | 3.07" (78.0 mm) |
| Compression Ratio | 10.1:1 |
| Fuel System | PFI |
| Horsepower @ RPM | 140 @ 6000 |
| Torque Ft. Lbs. @ RPM | 133 @ 2900 |
| **2.3L** | |
| Displacement | 140 Cu. In. (2.3L) |
| Bore | 3.54" (90.0 mm) |
| Stroke | 3.54" (90.0 mm) |
| Compression Ratio | |
| Non-Turbo | 9.0:1 |
| Turbo | 8.5:1 |
| Fuel System | PFI |
| Horsepower @ RPM | |
| Non-Turbo | 150 @ 5500 |
| Turbo | 200 @ 5000 |
| Torque Ft. Lbs. @ RPM | |
| Non-Turbo | 157 @ 3800 |
| Turbo | 244 @ 2000 |

### *CRANKSHAFT, MAIN & CONNECTING ROD BEARINGS*

| Application | In. (mm) |
|---|---|
| **2.0L, 2.1L & 2.3L** | |
| Crankshaft | |
| End Play | .003-.011 (.08-.28) |
| Runout | .002 (.050) |
| Main Bearing | |
| Journal Diameter | 2.2827-2.2835 (57.980-58.000) |
| Journal Out-of-Round | .002 (.050) |
| Journal Taper | .002 (.050) |
| Oil Clearance | .0008-.0024 (.020-.061) |
| Connecting Rod Bearings | |
| Journal Diameter | 2.046-2.047 (51.97-52.00) |
| Oil Clearance | .0008-.0024 (.020-.061) |

### *CONNECTING RODS*

| Application | In. (mm) |
|---|---|
| **2.0L, 2.1L & 2.3L** | |
| Bore Diameter | |
| Pin Bore | .9451-.9453 (24.006-24.011) |
| Crankpin Bore | 2.2047-2.2055 (56.000-56.020) |
| Center-To-Center Length | [1] |
| Maximum Bend | [1] |
| Maximum Twist | [1] |
| Side Play | [1] |

[1] – Information is not available from manufacturer.

# 1991 ENGINES
# 2.0L, 2.1L & 2.3L 4-Cylinder (Cont.)

## PISTONS, PINS & RINGS

| Application | In. (mm) |
|---|---|
| **2.0L** | |
| Pistons | |
| Clearance | .0008-.0020 (.020-.051) |
| Diameter | 3.542 (89.97) |
| Pins | |
| Diameter | .9447-.9449 (23.995-24.000) |
| Piston Fit | [1] .0002-.0006 (.005-.015) |
| Rod Fit | [1] .0002-.0006 (.005-.015) |
| Rings | |
| No. 1 | |
| End Gap | .014-.021 (.36-.53) |
| Side Clearance | .002-.003 (.05-.08) |
| No. 2 | |
| End Gap | .012-.018 (.30-.46) |
| Side Clearance | .002-.003 (.05-.08) |
| No. 3 (Oil) | |
| End Gap | .015-.055 (.38-1.40) |
| Side Clearance | [2] |
| **2.1L** | |
| Pistons | |
| Clearance | .0004-.0014" (.009-.035) |
| Diameter | 3.6607-3.6611 (92.982-92.992) |
| Pins | |
| Diameter | .9447-.9449 (23.995-24.000) |
| Piston Fit | [1] .0001-.0004 (.002-.011) |
| Rod Fit | [1] .0001-.0004 (.002-.011) |
| Rings | |
| No. 1 | |
| End Gap | .014-.021 (.36-.53) |
| Side Clearance | .002-.003 (.05-.08) |
| No. 2 | |
| End Gap | .012-.018 (.30-.46) |
| Side Clearance | .002-.003 (.05-.08) |
| No. 3 (Oil) | |
| End Gap | .015-.055 (.38-1.40) |
| Side Clearance | [2] |
| **2.3L** | |
| Pistons | |
| Clearance | .0002-.0016 (.006-.041) |
| Diameter | 3.542 (89.97) |
| Pins | |
| Diameter | .9447-.9449 (23.995-24.000) |
| Piston Fit | |
| Non-Turbo | [1] .0002-.0006 (.005-.015) |
| Turbo | [1] .0001-.0004 (.002-.011) |
| Rod Fit | |
| Non-Turbo | [1] .0002-.0006 (.005-.015) |
| Turbo | [1] .0001-.0004 (.002-.011) |
| Rings | |
| No. 1 | |
| End Gap | .012-.020 (.30-.50) |
| Side Clearance | .002-.003 (.05-.08) |
| No. 2 | |
| End Gap | .012-.018 (.30-.45) |
| Side Clearance | .002-.003 (.03-.07) |
| No. 3 (Oil) | |
| End Gap | .015-.055 (.38-1.40) |
| Side Clearance | [2] |

[1] – Sliding fit under gentle thumb pressure.
[2] – Information is not available from manufacturer.

## CYLINDER BLOCK

| Application | In. (mm) |
|---|---|
| **2.0L** | |
| Cylinder Bore | |
| Standard Diameter | 3.543-3.544 (90.00-90.01) |
| Maximum Taper | [1] |
| Maximum Out-Of-Round | [1] |
| **2.1L** | |
| Cylinder Bore | |
| Standard Diameter | 3.661-3.662 (93.00-93.01) |
| Maximum Taper | [1] |
| Maximum Out-Of-Round | [1] |
| **2.3L** | |
| Cylinder Bore | |
| Standard Diameter | 3.543-3.544 (90.000-90.01) |
| Maximum Taper | [1] |
| Maximum Out-Of-Round | [1] |

[1] - Information is not available from manufacturer.

## VALVES & VALVE SPRINGS

| Application | Specification |
|---|---|
| **2.0L, 2.1L & 2.3L** | |
| Intake Valves | |
| Face Angle | 44.5° |
| Head Diameter | 1.26" (32 mm) |
| Minimum Margin | [1] |
| Minimum Refinish Length | [1] |
| Stem Diameter | .274-.275" (6.96-6.99 mm) |
| Valve Tip Maximum Refinish | [1] |
| Exhaust Valves | |
| Face Angle | 44.5° |
| Head Diameter | 1.14" (29 mm) |
| Minimum Margin | [1] |
| Minimum Refinish Length | [1] |
| Stem Diameter | .274-.275" (6.96-6.99 mm) |
| Valve Tip Maximum Refinish | [1] |
| Valve Springs | |
| Free Length | 1.77" (45.00 mm) |
| Installed Height | 1.46" (37.0 mm) |
| Out-Of-Square | [1] |
| | **Lbs. @ In. (kg @ mm)** |
| Pressure | 132-145 lbs. @ 1.12" (60-66 kg @ 28.4 mm) |

[1] - Information is not available from manufacturer.

## CYLINDER HEAD

| Application | Specification |
|---|---|
| **2.0L, 2.1L & 2.3L** | |
| Cylinder Head Height (Minimum) | 5.51" (140 mm) |
| Maximum Warpage | [1] |
| Valve Seats | |
| Intake Valve | |
| Seat Angle | 45° |
| Seat Width | .06" (1.5 mm) |
| Maximum Seat Runout | [1] |
| Seat Bore Diameter | [1] |
| Exhaust Valve | |
| Seat Angle | 45° |
| Seat Width | .06" (1.5 mm) |
| Maximum Seat Runout | [1] |
| Seat Bore Diameter | [1] |
| Valve Guides | |
| Intake Valve | |
| Valve Guide Bore I.D. | .4724-.4731" (12.000-12.018) |
| Valve Guide I.D. | [1] |
| Valve Guide Installed Height | [1] |
| Valve Stem-to-Guide Oil Clearance | .002" (.05 mm) |
| Exhaust Valve | |
| Valve Guide Bore I.D. | .4724-.4731" (12.000-12.018) |
| Valve Guide I.D. | [1] |
| Valve Guide Installed Height | [1] |
| Valve Stem-to-Guide Oil Clearance | .002" (.05 mm) |
| Bore Diameter | .4724-.4731" (12.000-12.018 mm) |

[1] - Information is not available from manufacturer.

## CAMSHAFT

| Application | In. (mm) |
|---|---|
| **2.0L, 2.1L & 2.3L** | |
| Bore Diameter | [1] |
| End Play | .003-.014 (.08-.36) |
| Journal Diameter | 1.1387-1.1392 (28.923-28.936) |
| Journal Runout | [1] |
| Lobe Height | 1.024 (26.01) |
| Oil Clearance | [1] |
| Lobe Lift | .340 (8.64) |

[1] - Information is not available from manufacturer.

## VALVE LIFTERS

| Application | In. (mm) |
|---|---|
| **2.0L, 2.1L & 2.3L** | |
| Bore Diameter | 1.2992-1.2998 (33.000-33.016) |
| Lifter Diameter | 1.2976-1.2982 (32.959-32.975) |
| Oil Clearance | [1] |

[1] - Information is not available from manufacturer.

# 1991 CLUTCHES
# FWD - 900 Series

## DESCRIPTION

The clutch is a single dry plate, diaphragm spring type. Clutch operates hydraulically by a clutch master cylinder and a slave cylinder on the transaxle.

## ADJUSTMENTS

### CLUTCH PEDAL FREE PLAY AND HEIGHT

Clutch pedal free play and height are adjusted automatically by operation of hydraulic system.

## REMOVAL & INSTALLATION

### CLUTCH ASSEMBLY

**Inspection (On-Vehicle) - 1)** With clutch assembly installed, remove inspection plate on top of clutch cover and look through inspection hole. Measure distance between rear edge of plastic sleeve and front edge of machined surface on slave cylinder housing.

**2)** Replace clutch disc if distance is less than .08" (2 mm). Ensure compressed thickness of disc is within limits. See CLUTCH DISC SPECIFICATIONS table. Ensure unloaded disc-to-pressure plate clearance is within specification.

***CLUTCH DISC SPECIFICATIONS***

| Application | In. (mm) |
|---|---|
| Disc Compressed Thickness | |
| Non-Turbo | .28-.30 (7.1-7.6) |
| Turbo | .27-.29 (6.9-7.4) |
| Disc-to-Pressure Plate Clearance | |
| Unloaded | .050 (1.27) |

**Removal - 1)** Disconnect preheater hose. Remove clutch cover housing. Press clutch pedal to disengage clutch fully. Install Spacer Ring (83 90 023) between diaphragm spring fingers and pressure plate cover. Spacer ring must be used to keep clutch disengaged while removing components.

***NOTE: If clutch cannot be disengaged normally, compress diaphragm spring to install spacer ring.***

**2)** Unhook shaft cover spring clip. Remove input shaft cover. Unscrew plastic cross from end of shaft. Install 8-mm bolt in end of input shaft. Using Shaft Remover Fork (83 93 175) and a hammer, drive out input shaft as far as possible toward radiator. Input shaft will not come out completely.

**3)** Remove 3 slave cylinder mounting bolts. Remove pressure plate mounting bolts. Simultaneously lift out clutch disc, pressure plate assembly, slave cylinder, and release bearing. Ensure slave cylinder sleeve is not damaged by clutch during removal.

**Inspection (Off-Vehicle) - 1)** Check flywheel and pressure plate friction surfaces for burns, cracks, or scoring. Measure surface warpage. At pressure plate inner edge, maximum taper is .0012" (.030 mm). Resurface or replace pressure plate if necessary.

**2)** Ensure clutch release bearing turns freely. If bearing is noisy, rough, or dry, it must be replaced. DO NOT clean bearing with solvent.

**Installation - 1)** Before installing clutch, check input shaft seal condition. If necessary, replace seal. Reassemble clutch components and install as an assembly. Loosely install pressure plate mounting bolts.

**2)** Hardened side of release bearing must face clutch assembly. Lightly coat input shaft splines with molybdenum grease. Tap shaft into position. Ensure splined shaft engages with splines of disc and flywheel bearing. Apply Loctite to slave cylinder bolts. Install slave cylinder.

***NOTE: DO NOT press clutch pedal farther than necessary when removing spacer ring. Seal lip may overextend, causing hydraulic leak.***

**3)** Tighten pressure plate bolts evenly. Ensure plastic sleeve with circlip is installed with slave cylinder. Press clutch pedal and remove spacer ring. To complete installation, reverse removal procedure.

### CLUTCH MASTER CYLINDER

**Removal - 1)** Remove lower instrument panel. Panel attaching bolts are located behind ashtray, on each side of engine compartment. One of the side bolts is located near fuse panel. The other is located near plastic bottle inside right fenderwell.

**2)** Remove push rod pin at clutch pedal. Remove master cylinder mounting nuts from firewall. From inside engine compartment, remove fluid flex hose from reservoir to cylinder. Plug openings. Remove hydraulic line at rear of cylinder. Remove master cylinder.

**Installation -** To install, reverse removal procedure. Bleed hydraulic system.

### CLUTCH RELEASE CYLINDER

**Removal & Installation -** Release cylinder is removed and installed during removal and installation of clutch assembly. See CLUTCH ASSEMBLY under REMOVAL & INSTALLATION.

## OVERHAUL

***NOTE: DO NOT use mineral oil to clean cylinder components.***

### CLUTCH MASTER CYLINDER

**Disassembly - 1)** Pull back rubber cover. Remove circlip, push rod, and stop washer. *See Fig. 1.* Remove piston assembly, convex washer, rear piston seal, and return spring.

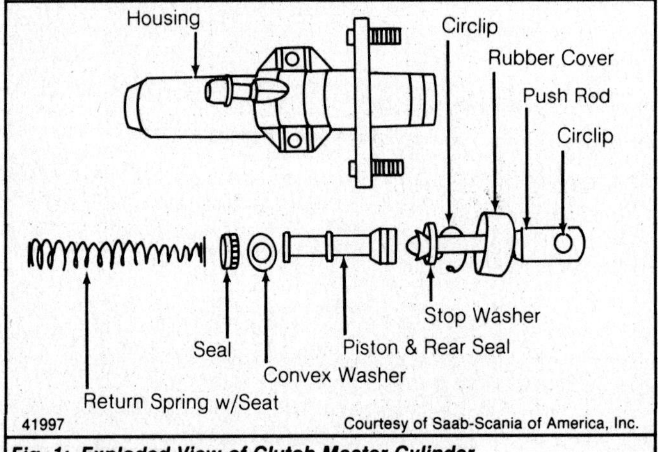


***Fig. 1: Exploded View of Clutch Master Cylinder***

**2)** Inspect cylinder bore and piston assembly. Replace complete master cylinder if bore or piston assembly shows signs of excessive wear or damage.

**Reassembly - 1)** Install return spring and retainer. Lubricate piston and seals with clean brake fluid. Install seals, convex washer, and piston. *See Fig. 2.*

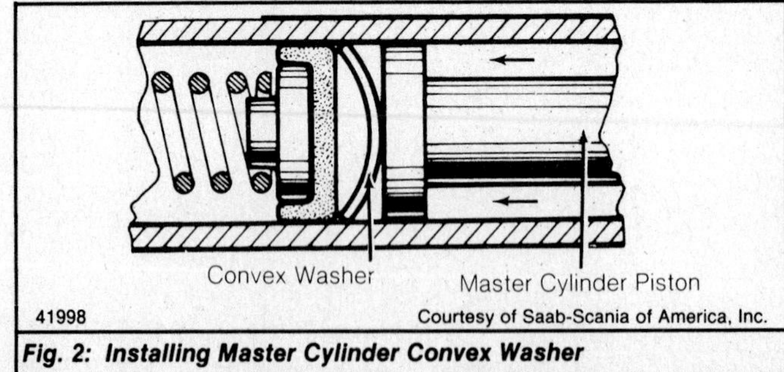


***Fig. 2: Installing Master Cylinder Convex Washer***

# 1991 CLUTCHES
# FWD – 900 Series (Cont.)

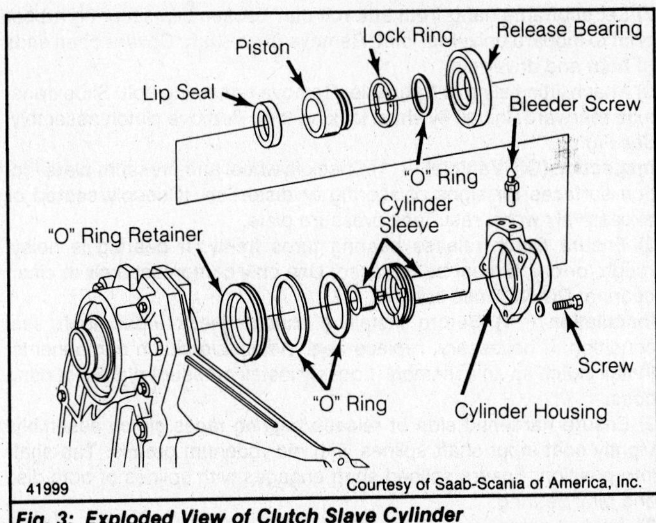


**Fig. 3: Exploded View of Clutch Slave Cylinder**

2) Convex side of washer must face master cylinder piston. Install push rod, washer, and circlip. Install rubber cover. Install cylinder and bleed system.

## CLUTCH RELEASE CYLINDER

***NOTE: Sleeve rides on machined surface of cylinder body and doubles as dust cover.***

**Disassembly – 1)** Remove clutch release bearing from slave cylinder. Position slave cylinder with release bearing end facing up. Press out cylinder sleeve. Remove "O" ring from sleeve flange. Remove piston, lip seal, and related components.

**2)** Clean and inspect slave cylinder bore, sleeve inner and outer surfaces, piston assembly, and all rubber components. Replace slave cylinder assembly if cylinder bore, sleeve, or piston assembly are excessively worn or damaged. *See Fig. 3*.

**Reassembly – 1)** Lightly coat lip seal and piston with rubber grease. DO NOT coat "O" ring with grease. Fit "O" ring to sleeve flange. Slide lip seal onto cylinder sleeve. Coat sleeve flange with brake fluid. Insert sleeve into cylinder housing. Push lip seal part way into cylinder.

**2)** Guide sleeve and cylinder together by pushing on piston until lock rings and "O" ring are in position. Place slave cylinder on support and seat sleeve into cylinder housing. Fit release bearing to piston. Install cylinder. Bleed system.

## TORQUE SPECIFICATIONS

***TORQUE SPECIFICATIONS***

| Applications | Ft. Lbs. (N.m) |
|---|---|
| Flywheel-To-Crankshaft Bolts | 43 (59) |
| Pressure Plate Bolts | 10-19 (14-26) |
| Slave Cylinder Retaining Nuts | 10 (14) |

# 1991 CLUTCHES
# FWD – 9000 Series

## DESCRIPTION

The clutch is a single dry plate, diaphragm spring type. Clutch operates hydraulically by a clutch master cylinder and a release cylinder within the clutch housing. *See Fig. 1.*

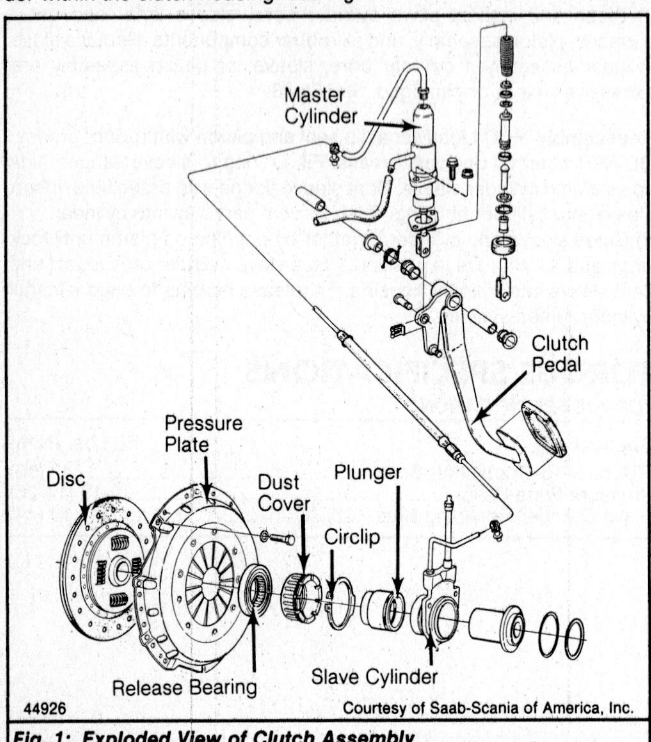


**Fig. 1: Exploded View of Clutch Assembly**

## ADJUSTMENTS

### CLUTCH PEDAL FREE PLAY AND HEIGHT

Clutch pedal free play and height are adjusted automatically. No service adjustment is required.

## REMOVAL & INSTALLATION

### CLUTCH ASSEMBLY

**Inspection (On-Vehicle)** – Remove inspection plate from top of clutch cover. Measure distance between rear edge of plastic sleeve and front edge of machined surface on release cylinder housing. Replace clutch disc if distance is less than .08" (2 mm).

**Removal – 1)** Raise and support front of vehicle. Remove battery and tray. Detach air intake duct from inner fender. Remove washer fluid reservoir. Disconnect positive lead from electrical terminal block. Remove fuel filter and terminal block.

**2)** Carefully remove air mass meter. Remove air cleaner intake duct. Remove cover and filter element from air cleaner. Remove air cleaner body. Remove turbo pressure duct (if equipped).

**3)** Disconnect battery ground and back-up light switch connector from transaxle. Remove and plug pressure line to release cylinder. Remove release cylinder line retaining clip. Loosen left engine mount. Support engine. Remove left front wheel and inner fender panel.

**4)** Separate control arm from ball joint. Disconnect speedometer sending unit wiring. Separate 2 halves of selector rod joint. Remove clip from dust cover on intermediate drive shaft. Remove brace from inlet manifold.

**5)** Remove starter. Move bracket aside. Support starter motor with wire. Leave one bolt in position between engine and transaxle. Remove other bolts and install Locating Dowels (8392128).

**6)** Loosen 2 subframe pivot mountings and 4 retaining bolts. Unbolt front and rear mounting bracket. Remove 4 retaining bolts at back of subframe. Remove bolts retaining lower attachment point for bracket in wheelhousing.

**7)** Let subframe hang from anti-roll bar. Loosen clip securing rubber boot to inboard universal joint. Remove drive shaft. Covers open ends of boot and driver cup.

**8)** Attach lifting sling to transaxle. Remove remaining bolt. Slide transaxle rearward. Install flywheel locking tool. Remove clutch assembly. *See Fig. 1.*

**Inspection (Off-Vehicle) – 1)** Check flywheel and pressure plate friction surfaces for signs of scoring or distortion. If deeply scored or excessively worn, resurface pressure plate.

**2)** Ensure clutch release bearing turns freely. If bearing is noisy, rough, or dry, it must be replaced. Use only compressed air to clean bearing; DO NOT use solvent.

**Installation – 1)** Before installing clutch, check input shaft seal condition. If necessary, replace seal. Assemble clutch components. Install clutch as an assembly. Loosely install pressure plate mounting bolts.

**2)** Ensure hardened side of release bearing faces clutch assembly. Lightly coat input shaft splines with molybdenum grease. Tap shaft into position. Ensure splined shaft engages with splines of both disc and pilot bearing.

**3)** Apply Loctite to release cylinder bolts. Install release cylinder. Tighten pressure plate bolts evenly to specification. Ensure plastic sleeve with circlip is installed with release cylinder. To complete installation, reverse removal procedure.

### CLUTCH MASTER CYLINDER

**Removal – 1)** From inside vehicle, remove trim panel above brake pedal. Spread protective covering under clutch pedal to shield carpet from clutch fluid spillage.

**2)** Remove clip and withdraw clevis pin from clutch master cylinder push rod. Remove cylinder supply hose from cylinder and plug. Detach pressure line from clutch master cylinder. Remove mounting bolts and lift out cylinder.

**Installation** – Position master cylinder and install mounting bolts. Check gasket between cylinder body and mounting surface. Connect fluid lines to clutch master cylinder. Tighten mounting bolts to specification. To complete installation, reverse removal procedure. Bleed system.

### CLUTCH RELEASE CYLINDER

**Removal** – Remove transaxle. See CLUTCH ASSEMBLY under REMOVAL & INSTALLATION. Remove release bearing. Disconnect pressure line and bleeder fitting. Loosen 3 mounting screws and remove release cylinder.

**Installation** – Install release cylinder into clutch housing. Tighten screws evenly in sequence to 72-89 INCH lbs. (8-10 N.m). Install release bearing. To complete installation, reverse removal procedure. Bleed system.

## OVERHAUL

### CLUTCH MASTER CYLINDER

**Disassembly – 1)** Remove clutch master cylinder. See CLUTCH MASTER CYLINDER under REMOVAL & INSTALLATION. Pull back dust cover. Remove circlip and push rod. Withdraw plunger assembly complete with spring. Remove spring, seal retainer, recuperating seal, and washer. *See Fig. 2.*

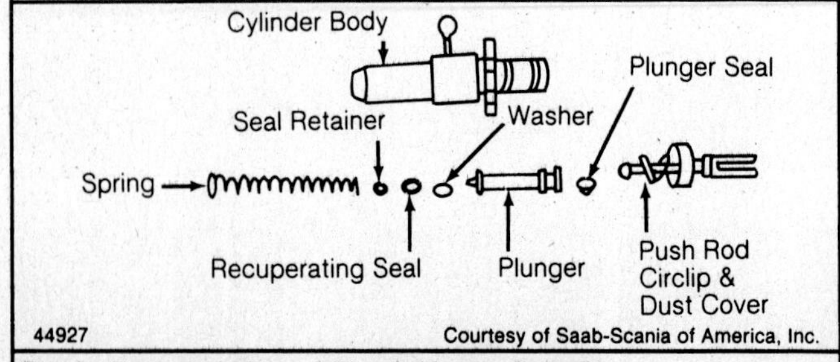


**Fig. 2: Exploded View of Clutch Master Cylinder**

# 1991 CLUTCHES
# FWD – 9000 Series (Cont.)

2) Carefully remove plunger seal. If cylinder has a smooth surface, free of scoring, replace seals only. Replace complete assembly if cylinder bore, sleeve, or piston is excessively worn or damaged.

**Reassembly** – Wash master cylinder in clean brake fluid before assembling. Lubricate plunger and seals with rubber grease. Install return spring and seal retainer. Install washer, plunger, and seals. Install push rod, circlip, and dust cover. Replace dust cover if damaged.

## CLUTCH RELEASE CYLINDER

**Disassembly** – Remove release bearing sleeve and tap out stuffing box. Push plunger out of bore and carefully remove 2 seals from plunger. Replace release cylinder assembly if cylinder bore, sleeve, or piston assembly is excessively worn or damaged. *See Fig. 3.*

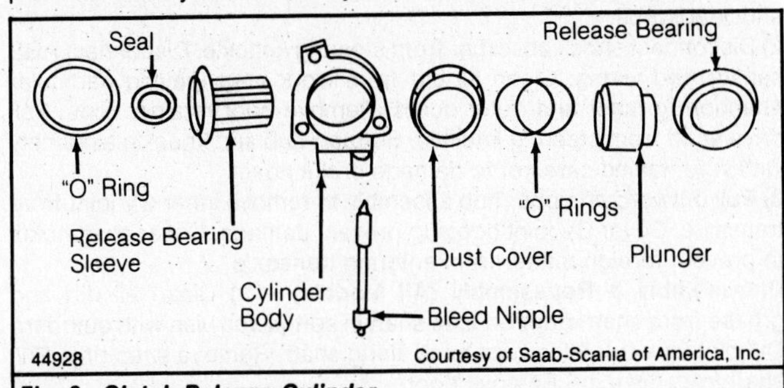


***Fig. 3: Clutch Release Cylinder***

**Reassembly** – Ensure release cylinder is clean. Install dust cover retainer .43" (11 mm) from the machined edge of cylinder body. Install new "O" rings on plunger and lubricate with brake fluid. Install plunger into bore so that release bearing flange is slightly forward of dust cover.

## TORQUE SPECIFICATIONS

***TORQUE SPECIFICATIONS***

| Applications | Ft. Lbs. (N.m) |
|---|---|
| Anti-Roll Bar Clamp Bolt | 30-40 (41-54) |
| Anti-Roll Bar End Nut | 30-40 (41-54) |
| Back-Up Light Switch Lock Nut | 15-18 (20-24) |
| Clutch Pedal Nut | 31 (42) |
| Engine Mounting Bolt | 36-67 (49-91) |
| Engine-To-Transaxle Bolt | 40-74 (54-100) |
| Flywheel-To-Crankshaft Bolt | 43 (58) |
| Master Cylinder Mounting Bolt | 16 (22) |
| Pressure Plate Bolt | 11-20 (15-27) |
| Starter Motor Bolt | 28-35 (38-47) |
| Subframe Mounting Bolt | 32-42 (43-57) |
| Suspension Arm-To-Ball Joint Nut | 15-20 (20-27) |
| | **INCH Lbs. (N.m)** |
| Clutch Release Cylinder Bolt | 72-89 (8-10) |

# 1991 DRIVE AXLES
# FWD Axle Shafts

### 900 Series, 9000 Series

## DESCRIPTION

Each axle shaft consists of a shaft and a Constant Velocity (CV) joint at each end. Outer CV joint is splined to hub assembly and secured by an axle shaft nut. Inner and outer CV joints are enclosed by boots.

## TROUBLE SHOOTING

***NOTE: See TROUBLE SHOOTING article in GENERAL INFORMATION.***

## REMOVAL, DISASSEMBLY, REASSEMBLY & INSTALLATION

### FWD AXLE SHAFT

***NOTE: Downward movement of control arms is limited by rubber buffer inside shock absorber. Install Spacer (8393209) before raising vehicle.***

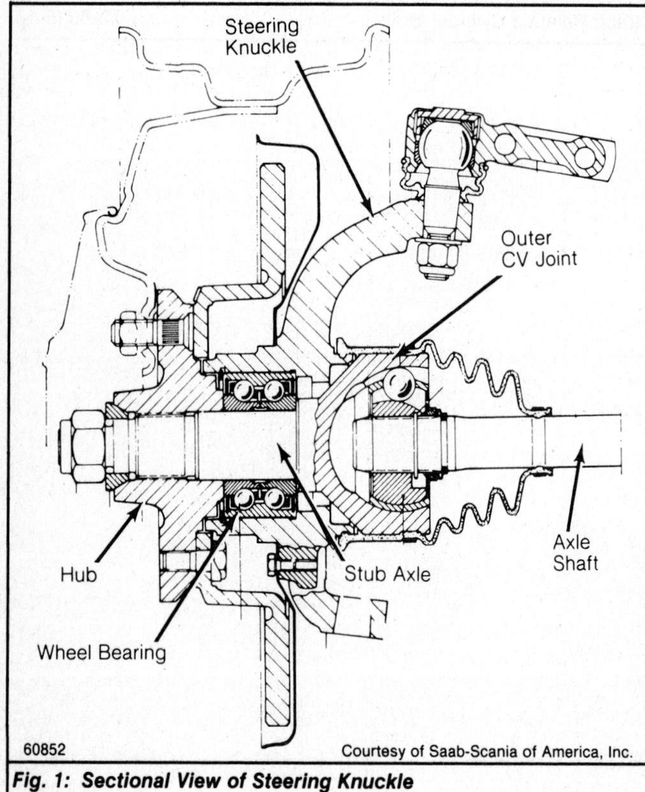


***Fig. 1: Sectional View of Steering Knuckle***

**Removal (900 Series) - 1)** Place Spacer (8393209) between underside of upper control arm and body. Disconnect upper end of shock absorber. Remove hub cap. Loosen axle shaft nut and wheel lugs. Raise and support vehicle. Remove wheels. Release boot clamps. Remove caliper mounting bolts. Hang caliper aside with wire, taking care not to damage brake hose. DO NOT disconnect hydraulic line.

**2)** Disconnect tie rod end from steering arm. Remove bolts from lower control arm bracket. *See Fig. 1.* Disconnect upper ball joint from control arm. Separate inner CV joint from axle flange. Remove axle shaft through wheelwell. Thoroughly clean axle assembly.

**Removal (9000 Series) - 1)** Raise and support vehicle. Remove wheel assembly. Remove and discard hub nut. Using Puller (8791287), Jaws (8791303), and Adapter (8791154), press axle shaft into hub assembly no more than .79" (20 mm). Disconnect brake hose from shock absorber.

**2)** Disconnect shock absorber from steering knuckle. Disconnect ABS sensor and wiring. Clean all dirt from work area, paying particular attention to inner and outer boots. Remove boot retainer clips. Pull drive shaft from steering knuckle. Support hub and knuckle assembly with wire, taking care not to damage brake hose.

**3)** Pull outward on upper hub assembly to remove inner CV joint from transaxle. Cover CV joint boots to prevent damage. Cover shaft holes to prevent foreign matter from entering transaxle.

**Disassembly & Reassembly (All Models) - 1)** Clean all dirt and grease from shaft. Support axle shaft in soft-jawed vise with outboard CV joint upward. Slide boot back along shaft. Remove snap ring. Pull shaft from CV joint. Remove boot.

**2)** Support axle shaft in soft-jawed vise with inboard joint upward. Remove snap ring. Note how spider is installed. Using a 3-jaw puller, remove spider from shaft. Remove boot.

**3)** Reverse disassembly procedure to assemble axle shaft. Press inboard joint spider onto shaft using a 27-mm socket. Ensure 45-degree bevel on spider is toward shaft. Pack approximately 2 ozs. (60 grams) grease into inboard joint, and approximately 2.8 ozs. (80 grams) grease into outboard joint when assembling.

**Installation (900 Series) -** To install axle shaft, reverse removal procedure. Tighten bolts to specification. See TORQUE SPECIFICATIONS table at end of article. Pump brake pedal several times to seat brake pads.

**Installation (9000 Series) -** Reverse removal procedure to install axle shaft. Apply Loctite 641 to outer 3/8" (10 mm) of axle shaft splines. Install NEW hub nut. Tighten bolts to specification. See TORQUE SPECIFICATIONS table.

## TORQUE SPECIFICATIONS

***TORQUE SPECIFICATIONS***

| Application | Ft. Lbs. (N.m) |
|---|---|
| Axle Shaft Hub Nut | 207-222 (280-300) |
| Brake Caliper Bolts | 51-65 (70-90) |
| Strut Lower Bolts | 56-75 (78-105) |
| Wheel Lug Bolts | 78-93 (105-125) |

# 1991 BRAKES
# Disc

## 900 Series, 9000 Series

## DESCRIPTION

Brake circuit is a diagonal system (right front/left rear and left front/right rear). Mechanical parking brake operates by cables to rear caliper assemblies. Tandem master cylinder contains a level sensor. Warning light, located on instrument panel, comes on if fluid level is low.

## BLEEDING BRAKE SYSTEM

***NOTE: Use DOT 4 brake fluid only. DO NOT use DOT 5 silicone brake fluid.***

***NOTE: If vehicle is equipped with anti-lock brake system, see ANTI-LOCK article in BRAKES for bleeding procedure.***

Connect pressure bleeder according to manufacturer's instructions. See HYDRAULIC BRAKE BLEEDING article in GENERAL INFORMATION. Bleed brakes in sequence specified in BRAKE LINE BLEEDING SEQUENCE table.

***BRAKE LINE BLEEDING SEQUENCE***

| Application | Sequence |
|---|---|
| 900 Series | LR, RF, RR, LF |
| 9000 Series | Any Order |

## ADJUSTMENTS

### PARKING BRAKE

***NOTE: If installing new cable(s), apply parking brake several times to stretch cable(s).***

**900 Series** – Lift rear seat. Using a screwdriver, pry adjuster apart. Insert .08" (2 mm) feeler gauge between brake lever and stop on brake caliper. Rotate lock nut against adjuster sleeve until feeler gauge drops out. Apply and release parking brake several times to settle adjuster. Ensure clearance between brake lever and stop is .02-.08" (.5-2 mm).

**9000 Series** – **1)** Slide seal from handbrake lever. Remove lock plate from adjusting nuts. Remove plug from adjuster screw. Bottom adjuster screw, then back off 1/4 - 1/2 turn. Ensure wheel rotates freely.

**2)** Insert .04" (1 mm) feeler gauge between brake lever and stop on caliper. Rotate adjuster nut, under handbrake lever inside vehicle, until feeler gauge slips out. Repeat for other wheel. Reinstall lock plate and seal.

## REMOVAL & INSTALLATION

### FRONT DISC BRAKE PADS

***NOTE: Resurface or replace rotors each time new brake pads are installed.***

**Removal & Installation (900 Series)** – Raise and support vehicle. Remove wheels. Using water pump pliers, press piston into bore. Remove lower guide pin. Swing caliper assembly upward. Remove brake pads. Reverse removal procedure to install pads. Pump brake pedal several times to position brake pads.

**Removal & Installation (9000 Series)** – Raise and support vehicle. Remove wheels. Remove dust caps and guide pins. Remove retaining clip. Separate hydraulic body from brake assembly. Remove brake pads. Reverse removal procedure to install pads. Pump brake pedal several times to position brake pads.

### FRONT BRAKE CALIPER

**Removal & Installation (900 Series)** – **1)** Raise and support vehicle. Remove wheels. Clean work area. Using pliers, retract brake pads. Pinch off brake hose. Disconnect brake hose. Plug openings. Remove brake hose bracket. Remove guide pin bolts and caliper.

**2)** To install caliper, reverse removal procedure. Tighten bolts to specification. See TORQUE SPECIFICATIONS table at end of article. Bleed system. See BLEEDING BRAKE SYSTEM. Pump brake pedal several times to position brake pads.

**Removal & Installation (9000 Series)** – **1)** Raise and support vehicle. Remove wheels. Loosen brake hose fitting at caliper. Remove lower guide pin bolt. Pivot caliper upward. Remove brake pads. Remove upper guide pin bolt. Rotate caliper to disconnect brake hose. Plug openings.

**2)** To install caliper, reverse removal procedure. Tighten bolts to specification. See TORQUE SPECIFICATIONS table at end of article. Bleed system. See BLEEDING BRAKE SYSTEM. Pump brake pedal several times to position brake pads.

### FRONT BRAKE ROTOR

***NOTE: Before removing wheels, check for excessive wheel bearing runout at outer edge of rim. Before removing rotor, check for excessive lateral runout. See DISC BRAKE SPECIFICATIONS table at end of article.***

**Removal & Installation** – **1)** Raise and support vehicle. Remove wheels. Loosen locating stud and retaining bolt. Using pliers, retract brake pads. Remove caliper retaining bolts and caliper assembly. Wire caliper to strut. Remove locating stud, retaining bolt, and brake rotor.

**2)** Ensure mating surfaces of hub and rotor are clean and free of burrs. Ensure rotor runout does not exceed .003" (.08 mm). To install, reverse removal procedure. Tighten bolts to specification. See TORQUE SPECIFICATIONS table at end of article. Pump brake pedal several times to position brake pads.

### REAR DISC BRAKE PADS

***NOTE: Resurface or replace rotors each time new brake pads are installed.***

**Removal & Installation (900 Series)** – **1)** Raise and support vehicle. Remove wheels. Disconnect parking brake cable at caliper. Remove plug from adjuster screw. Loosen adjuster screw until piston moves back against stop. Remove dust caps and guide pins. Remove retaining clip. Remove caliper assembly. Remove brake pads.

**2)** Wire-brush guide pins and mating surfaces of caliper and brake pads. Reverse removal procedure to install pads. Bottom adjuster screw, then back off 1/4 - 1/2 turn. Ensure wheel rotates freely. Pump brake pedal several times to position brake pads. Adjust parking brake.

**Removal & Installation (9000 Series)** – **1)** Raise and support vehicle. Remove wheels. Disconnect parking brake cable at caliper. Remove plug from adjuster screw. Loosen adjuster screw. Press piston back against stop. Remove dust caps and guide pins. Remove retaining clip. Separate hydraulic body from brake assembly. Remove brake pads.

**2)** Wire-brush guide pins and mating surfaces of caliper and brake pads. Lubricate guide pins. To complete installation, reverse removal procedure. Pump brake pedal several times to position brake pads. Adjust parking brake.

### REAR BRAKE CALIPER

**Removal & Installation (900 Series)** – **1)** Raise and support vehicle. Remove wheels. Disconnect parking brake cable at caliper. Remove plug from adjuster screw. Loosen adjuster screw. Pinch off brake hose. Loosen brake hose. Plug openings. Remove dust covers and guide pin bolts. Remove caliper assembly and brake pads. Rotate caliper to unscrew brake hose.

**2)** To install caliper, reverse removal procedure. Tighten bolts to specification. See TORQUE SPECIFICATIONS table at end of article. Bleed system. See BLEEDING BRAKE SYSTEM. Pump brake pedal several

# 1991 BRAKES
# Disc (Cont.)

times to position brake pads. Adjust parking brake. See PARKING BRAKE under ADJUSTMENTS.

**Removal & Installation (9000 Series) - 1)** Raise and support vehicle. Remove wheels. Disconnect parking brake cable at caliper. Loosen brake hose fitting at caliper. Remove dust covers and guide pin bolts. Remove retaining clip. Remove caliper. Remove brake pads. Rotate caliper to disconnect brake hose. Plug openings.

**2)** To install caliper, reverse removal procedure. Tighten bolts to specification. See TORQUE SPECIFICATIONS table at end of article. Bleed system. See BLEEDING BRAKE SYSTEM. Pump brake pedal several times to position brake pads. Adjust parking brake. See PARKING BRAKE under ADJUSTMENTS.

## REAR BRAKE ROTOR

**Removal & Installation (900 Series) - 1)** Raise and support vehicle. Remove wheels. Disconnect parking brake cable at caliper. Remove plug from adjuster screw. Loosen adjuster screw. Press piston back against stop. Remove backing plate and caliper retaining bolts. Wire caliper aside. Remove locating stud and brake rotor.

**2)** Ensure mating surfaces of hub and rotor are clean and free of burrs. Ensure rotor runout does not exceed .003" (.08 mm). To install, reverse removal procedure. Tighten bolts to specification. See TORQUE SPECIFICATIONS table at end of article. Pump brake pedal several times to position brake pads.

**Removal & Installation (9000 Series) - 1)** Raise and support vehicle. Remove wheels. Loosen locating stud and retaining bolt. Using pliers, retract brake pads. Remove backing plate and caliper retaining bolts. Wire caliper to strut. Remove locating stud, retaining bolt, and brake rotor.

**2)** Ensure mating surfaces of hub and rotor are clean and free of burrs. Ensure rotor runout does not exceed .003" (.08 mm). To install, reverse removal procedure. Tighten bolts to specification. See TORQUE SPECIFICATIONS table at end of article. Pump brake pedal several times to position brake pads.

## MASTER CYLINDER

**Removal & Installation (900 Series) - 1)** Disconnect wiring from reservoir. Remove vacuum hose and check valve at booster. Pinch off hose between reservoir and clutch master cylinder. Remove fluid from reservoir.

**2)** Connect hose to bleeder fitting at right front caliper. Open bleeder valve. Expel fluid from system by pressing brake pedal. Close bleeder valve when pedal reaches floor. Release brake pedal. Repeat procedure until one chamber of reservoir is empty.

**3)** Repeat step **2)** with hose connected to bleeder valve at left front caliper. Disconnect brake lines at master cylinder. Remove master cylinder retaining nuts and master cylinder.

**4)** To install, reverse removal procedure. Refill system with DOT 4 brake fluid. Bleed system. See BLEEDING BRAKE SYSTEM.

**Removal & Installation (9000 Series) -** Remove battery. Drain brake fluid reservoir. Disconnect hoses and brake lines at master cylinder. Remove retaining nuts and master cylinder. To install, reverse removal procedure. Refill system with DOT 4 brake fluid. Bleed system. See BLEEDING BRAKE SYSTEM.

## POWER BRAKE BOOSTER

***NOTE: If vehicle is equipped with anti-lock brake system, see ANTI-LOCK article in BRAKES.***

**Removal & Installation (900 Series) - 1)** Remove steering column bearing cover, ashtray, and central console upper screw (behind ashtray). Remove shift lever boot and switch assembly from center console.

**2)** Remove center console and safety padding from beneath dash. Remove lower air duct. Disconnect electrical leads, hydraulic lines, and vacuum hose from master cylinder and power brake unit. Pinch off fluid lines to prevent fluid loss. Siphon fluid from reservoir.

**3)** Connect hose to bleeder fitting at right front caliper. Open bleeder valve. Expel fluid from system by pressing brake pedal. Close bleeder valve when pedal reaches floor. Release brake pedal. Repeat procedure until reservoir is empty.

**4)** Disconnect hose from clutch master cylinder. Plug fitting on brake fluid reservoir. Disconnect brake lines from master cylinder. Remove master cylinder from brake booster. Remove brake booster retaining nuts and brake booster.

**5)** To install, reverse removal procedure. Refill system with DOT 4 brake fluid. Tighten bolts to specification. See TORQUE SPECIFICATIONS table at end of article. Bleed system. See BLEEDING BRAKE SYSTEM.

**Removal & Installation (9000 Series) - 1)** Remove battery. Move fuel filter aside. Remove battery tray. Connect hose to bleeder fitting at left front caliper. Open bleeder valve. Expel fluid from system by pressing brake pedal. Close bleeder valve when pedal reaches floor. Release brake pedal. Repeat procedure until reservoir is empty. Repeat procedure with hose connected to right front caliper.

**2)** Disconnect hoses and brake lines at master cylinder. Unbolt master cylinder from booster. Pull vacuum check valve together with vacuum hose from booster. Remove trim panel to gain access to brake pedal. Disconnect push rod linkage from brake pedal. Remove retaining nuts and brake booster.

**3)** Reverse removal procedure to install. Refill system with DOT 4 brake fluid. Tighten bolts to specification. See TORQUE SPECIFICATIONS table at end of article. Bleed system. See BLEEDING BRAKE SYSTEM.

***NOTE: Power brake unit is non-serviceable. Replace unit as an assembly if defective.***

## REAR AXLE HUB BEARINGS

**Removal & Installation - 1)** Raise and support vehicle. Remove wheel. Remove rotor and caliper. Wire caliper aside. See REAR BRAKE ROTOR and REAR BRAKE CALIPER. Pry out dust cap. Remove hub nut and washer. It may be necessary to use Puller (89 96 084) to remove hub.

**2)** Install hub washer and hub nut. Tighten bolts to specification. See TORQUE SPECIFICATIONS table at end of article. Using a round-nose drift, tap nut collar into groove in spindle to lock hub nut in position. Reverse removal procedure to complete installation.

***NOTE: If rear hub bearings are worn or damaged, replace hub as an assembly.***

# OVERHAUL

***NOTE: Refer to illustrations for overhaul. See Figs. 1-3.***

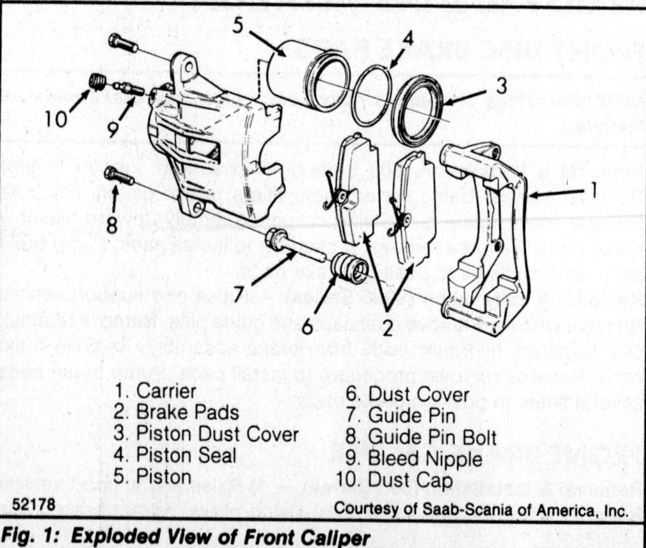


***Fig. 1: Exploded View of Front Caliper***

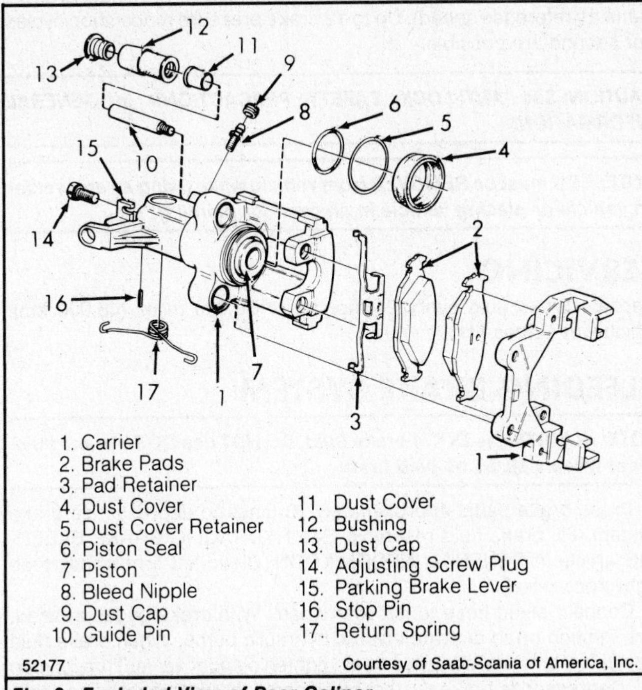


**Fig. 2: Exploded View of Rear Caliper**

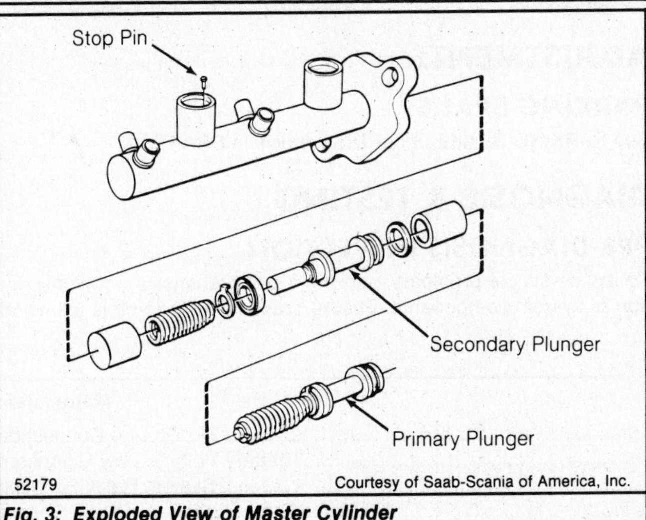


**Fig. 3: Exploded View of Master Cylinder**

## TORQUE SPECIFICATIONS

***TORQUE SPECIFICATIONS***

| Application | Ft. Lbs. (N.m) |
|---|---|
| Front Caliper Guide Pins | 18-22 (25-30) |
| Front Caliper Mounting Bolt | 52-81 (70-110) |
| Hub Nut | |
| 900 Series | 250-265 (340-360) |
| 9000 Series | 200-215 (270-290) |
| Rear Caliper Mounting Bolt | |
| 900 Series | 34-40 (40-45) |
| 9000 Series | (52-66 (70-90)) |
| Wheel Lug Nut | |
| 900 Series | 65-80 (88-108) |
| 9000 Series | 76-90 (103-122) |
| Other Bolts | |
| 5 mm | 4 (5) |
| 6 mm | 7 (10) |
| 8 mm | 15 (20) |
| 10 mm | 30 (40) |

## DISC BRAKE SPECIFICATIONS

***DISC BRAKE SPECIFICATIONS***

| Application | In. (mm) |
|---|---|
| **900 Series** | |
| Front | |
| Diameter | 10.9 (278.0) |
| Lateral Runout | .003 (.08) |
| Parallelism | .0006 (.015) |
| Original Thickness | .93 (23.5) |
| Minimum Refinish Thickness | [1] .87 (22.0) |
| Discard Thickness | .85 (21.5) |
| Rear | |
| Diameter | 10.2 (258) |
| Lateral Runout | .003 (.08) |
| Parallelism | .0006 (.015) |
| Original Thickness | .35 (9.0) |
| Minimum Refinish Thickness | [1] .31 (8.0) |
| Discard Thickness | .30 (7.5) |
| **9000 Series** | |
| Front | |
| Diameter | 11.0 (280) |
| Lateral Runout | .003 (.08) |
| Parallelism | .0006 (.015) |
| Original Thickness | .87 (22) |
| Minimum Refinish Thickness | .79 (20) |
| Discard Thickness | .77 (19.5) |
| Rear | |
| Diameter | 10.2 (258) |
| Lateral Runout | .003 (.08) |
| Parallelism | .0006 (.015) |
| Original Thickness | .35 (9) |
| Minimum Refinish Thickness | .30 (7.5) |
| Discard Thickness | .28 (7.0) |

[1] – Remove equal thickness from each side when refinishing.

# 1991 BRAKES
# Anti-Lock

**900 Series, 9000 Series**

## DESCRIPTION

The Anti-Lock Brake System (ABS) monitors front wheels individually, and rear wheels as a pair. The ABS system consists of 4 wheel sensors, relays, fuses, hydraulic unit, warning lights, and an Electronic Control Unit (ECU). Brake servo unit is hydraulically operated rather than vacuum operated. ECU provides self-diagnostic capability.

***NOTE: For more information on brakes, see DISC article in BRAKES.***

## OPERATION

Each time a sensor rotor tooth passes by the wheel speed sensor, a magnetic field is distorted, causing an electric signal to be generated. These signals, which are proportional to wheel speed, are transmitted to the Electronic Control Unit (ECU). ECU processes these signals and computes a value defined as reference speed. *See Fig. 1.*

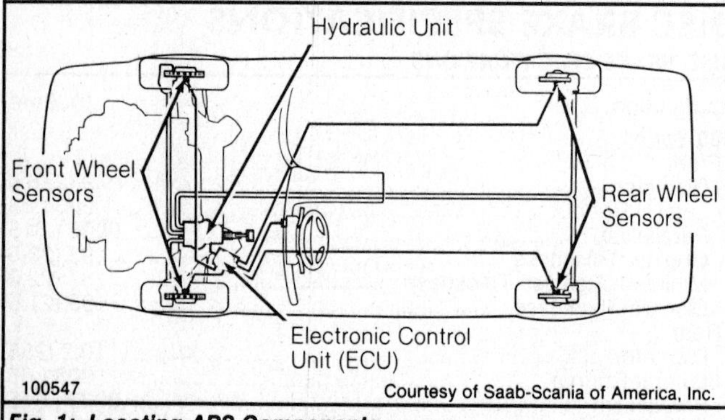


***Fig. 1: Locating ABS Components***

When a wheel is about to lock, the speed signal from that wheel will be different from reference speed. ECU detects this difference and modulates the solenoid valves. Solenoid valves regulate hydraulic brake pressure to the brake circuits.

ABS operation will continue until ECU detects that wheel speed is decreasing at the same rate for all wheels (all wheel speeds are the same as reference speed). Up to 12 brake pressure modulation cycles per second are possible.

***CAUTION: See ANTI-LOCK SAFETY PRECAUTIONS in GENERAL INFORMATION.***

***NOTE: ECU must be REMOVED from vehicle when using an arc welder on vehicle or placing vehicle in an oven for painting.***

## SERVICING

Replace brake fluid every 24 months or 30,000 miles (48,000 km), whichever comes first.

## BLEEDING BRAKE SYSTEM

***NOTE: ALWAYS use DOT 4 brake fluid. DO NOT use DOT 5 brake fluid. Front wheels MUST be bled first.***

**1)** Press brake pedal approximately 20 times to depressurize brake system. Fill brake fluid reservoir. See HYDRAULIC BRAKE BLEEDING article in GENERAL INFORMATION. Bleed left font wheel, then right front wheel.
**2)** Connect bleed hose to left rear wheel. With brake pedal pressed, turn ignition on to activate electric hydraulic pump. When brake fluid from left rear wheel contains no air, tighten bleeder valve. Turn ignition off. Depressurize brake system and bleed right rear wheel using same procedure.

## ADJUSTMENTS

### PARKING BRAKE

See PARKING BRAKE under DISC article in BRAKES.

## DIAGNOSIS & TESTING

### PRE-DIAGNOSIS INSPECTION

To isolate simple problems, perform a comprehensive visual inspection of system components. Ensure brake fluid reservoir is full when

***ABS TROUBLE CODES***

| Code | ECU Pin | Malfunction |
|---|---|---|
| E001 | 1 | No Ground Connection |
| E002 | 2 | Battery Voltage Low Or Absent |
| E320 | 3, 20 | System Relay Function |
| E422 | 4, 22 | No Signal From Right Rear Wheel Sensor |
| E523 | 5, 23 | No Signal From Left Front Wheel Sensor |
| E624 | 6, 24 | No Signal From Left Rear Wheel Sensor |
| E725 | 7, 25 | No Signal From Right Front Wheel Sensor |
| E008 | 8 | System Relay Control Signal Missing |
| E009 | 9 | Hydraulic Pressure Low Or Brake Fluid Low |
| E010 | 10 | ECU Defective |
| E011 | 11 | No Ground Connection |
| E014 | 14 | Pump Relay Or Pressure Switch Defective |
| E015 | 15 | Right Front Inlet Valve |
| E016 | 16 | Rear Outlet Valve |
| E017 | 17 | Rear Inlet Valve |
| E018 | 18 | Main Valve |
| EE22 | Sensor | Right Rear Sensor Wheel Runout |
| EE23 | Sensor | Left Front Sensor Wheel Runout |
| EE24 | Sensor | Left Rear Sensor Wheel Runout |
| EE25 | Sensor | Right Front Sensor Wheel Runout |
| E032 | 32 | Pump Relay Defective |
| E0132 | 1, 32 | Pump Running Continuously |
| E033 | 33 | Left Front Outlet Valve |
| E034 | 34 | Right Front Outlet Valve |
| E035 | 35 | Left Front Inlet Valve |
| PRES | EXT | Hydraulic Pressure To Pressure Switch Low |

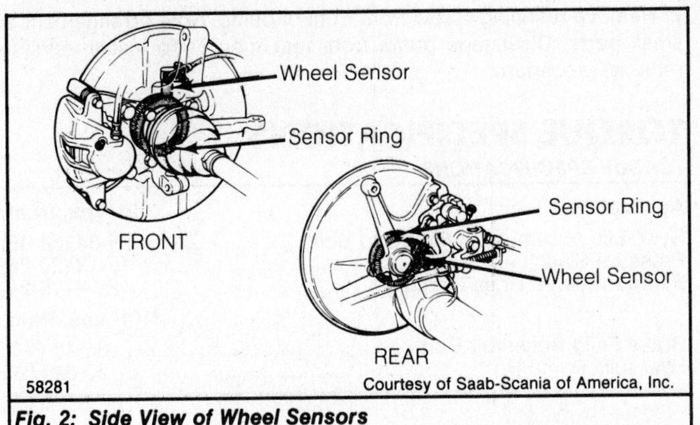


***Fig. 2: Side View of Wheel Sensors***

accumulator is fully charged. Ensure fuses in fuse box adjacent to ABS ECU are okay.

***NOTE: ABS Tester (89 96 514) and Extension Cable (89 96 589) are required for ABS testing.***

## RETRIEVING CODES

Connect ABS Tester (89 96 514) according to manufacturer's instructions. Follow manufacturer's test procedure to retrieve codes. See ABS TROUBLE CODES table.

## REMOVAL & INSTALLATION

***CAUTION: Before removing any ABS hydraulic brake component, press brake pedal approximately 20 times, with engine off, to depressurize brake system. Clean work area thoroughly to prevent entry of dirt.***

### ACCUMULATOR

**Removal & Installation (900 Series)** - Remove retaining bolt, then remove accumulator. To install, reverse removal procedure. Install NEW "O" ring and tighten bolt to specification. See TORQUE SPECIFICATIONS table at end of article.

**Removal & Installation (9000 Series)** - Remove battery. Move fuel filter aside. Remove hydraulic accumulator. To install, reverse removal procedure. Install new "O" ring and tighten bolts to specification. See TORQUE SPECIFICATIONS table at end of article.

### ELECTRONIC CONTROL UNIT

**Removal & Installation (900 Series)** - ABS ECU is located in engine compartment, on left side. Remove retaining screws. Unplug connector. Remove ECU. To install, reverse removal procedure.

**Removal & Installation (9000 Series)** - Remove left cover over space behind false firewall panel. Undo retaining clips. Unplug connector. To install, reverse removal procedure.

### HYDRAULIC CONTROL UNIT

**Removal (900 Series)** - **1)** Remove center console, trim panel below dash, heater duct, and acoustic insulation behind brake pedal. Disconnect left heater hose from heater box. Remove retaining clip and pin from hydraulic unit push rod. Remove air intake.

**2)** Move coolant expansion tank aside. Unplug electrical connectors from pressure switch, main valve, fluid level indicator, and pump motor. Unbolt bracket between hydraulic unit and front assembly. Disconnect ground lead. Unplug sensor connector. Move bracket and wiring aside.

**3)** Siphon fluid from reservoir. On M/T vehicles, disconnect hose for clutch cylinder. Plug hose opening. To avoid entry of air into clutch system, DO NOT allow fluid to drain from hose. Disconnect fluid lines. Plug openings. Remove hydraulic unit.

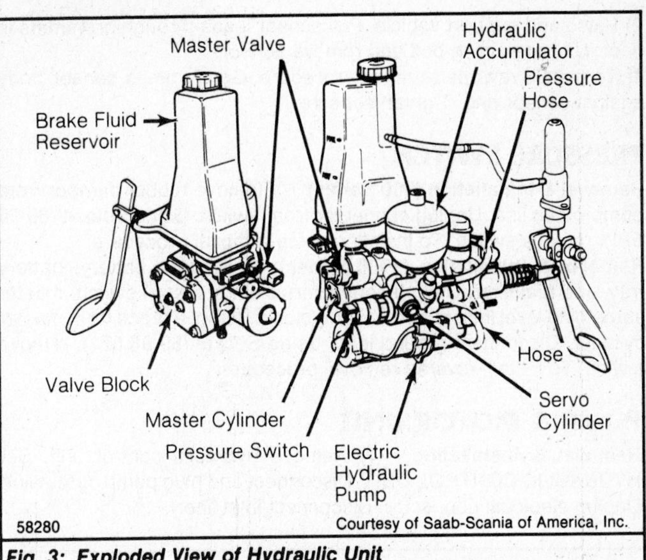


***Fig. 3: Exploded View of Hydraulic Unit***

**Installation** - To install, reverse removal procedure. Tighten bolts and fittings to specification. See TORQUE SPECIFICATIONS table at end of article. Refill reservoir. Bleed system. See BLEEDING BRAKE SYSTEM. Ensure brakes and clutch (if equipped) work properly.

**Removal (9000 Series)** - **1)** Remove battery. Clean work area thoroughly. Remove trim panel. Remove clevis pin securing brake pedal to push rod. Separate junction box from battery tray. Remove fuel filter and battery tray. Remove rubber intake duct.

**2)** Unplug brake fluid sensor, master valve, pressure switch, and valve block connectors. Remove brace from master cylinder. Remove ground lead. Raise and support vehicle. Remove left front wheel. Remove splash guard.

**3)** Unplug electrical connector from hydraulic pump. Disconnect brake lines from valve block. Plug all brake lines and ports. Remove hydraulic unit from vehicle.

**Installation** - To install, reverse removal procedure. Tighten bolts and fittings to specification. See TORQUE SPECIFICATIONS table at end of article. Refill reservoir. Bleed system. See BLEEDING BRAKE SYSTEM. Ensure brakes work properly.

### WHEEL SENSORS

**Removal (900 Series)** - **1)** Unplug sensor lead connectors. Connector for front sensors are located in engine compartment. Connectors for rear sensors are located under rear seat. Raise and support vehicle. Remove wheels. Pull front sensor leads through grommet in front fenderwell. Remove set screw and sensor.

**2)** On rear wheels, undo clip which secures handbrake cable to suspension arm. Note position of spacer. Pull rear sensor leads through grommets in floor. Separate sensor lead from guide on suspension arm. Remove set screw and sensor.

**Installation** - **1)** Install new wheel sensor into adjusting sleeve. Clean end of spacer with a wire brush. Wipe clean with dry cloth. Ensure there is no trace of old fiber spacer above sensor wheel. Rotate wheel to ensure sensor ring is okay. Glue new .026" (.65 mm) thick spacer onto end of sensor.

**2)** Position sensor. To prevent damage to sensor, DO NOT rotate wheel before tightening retaining screw. Ensure set screw bottoms on adjusting sleeve at a different location from original installation to avoid incorrect setting of sensor body. Position sensor and tighten retaining screw. Press sensor body gently against sensor ring. Tighten set screw. Reconnect sensor wiring.

**Removal & Installation (9000 Series)** - **1)** To remove rear sensors, go to step **2)** Unplug front sensor lead connectors. Connectors are under cover panel for space behind false firewall. Loosen false firewall panel retaining bolt enough to allow sensor lead to pass.

# 1991 BRAKES
# Anti-Lock (Cont.)

**2)** Raise and support vehicle. Pull sensor leads through grommets in floor. Undo retaining bolt and remove sensors.
**3)** To install, reverse removal procedure. Gently press sensor body against sensor ring. Tighten set screw.

## PRESSURE SWITCH

**Removal & Installation (900 Series)** – Remove rubber damper from pump outlet line. Unplug connector from switch. Using Socket (89 96 571), remove switch. To install, reverse removal procedure.

**Removal & Installation (9000 Series)** – Remove battery, battery tray, and fuel filter. Unplug connectors from pressure switch, master valve, fluid level indicator, and valve block. Remove brace from master cylinder. Disconnect ground lead. Using Socket (89 96 571), remove switch. To install, reverse removal procedure.

## PUMP & MOTOR UNIT

**Removal & Installation – 1)** Remove hydraulic control unit. See HYDRAULIC CONTROL UNIT. Disconnect and plug pump output line. Unplug electrical connector. Disconnect inlet line.

**2)** Remove retaining screw from front of pump. Note arrangement of small parts. Disengage pump from rear mount. To install, reverse removal procedure.

## TORQUE SPECIFICATIONS

*TORQUE SPECIFICATIONS*

| Application | Ft. Lbs. (N.m) |
|---|---|
| Hydraulic Accumulator Mounting Bolt | 25-34 (34-46) |
| Pressure Switch | 15-19 (20-26) |
| Pump Pressure Hose Fitting | 12-18 (16-24) |
| | **INCH Lbs. (N.m)** |
| Brake Fluid Reservoir Bolt | 36-48 (4-6) |
| Hydraulic Pump Bolt | 60-84 (7-9) |

## WIRING DIAGRAM

*See Fig. 4.* For additional diagrams, see appropriate chassis wiring diagram in WIRING DIAGRAMS.

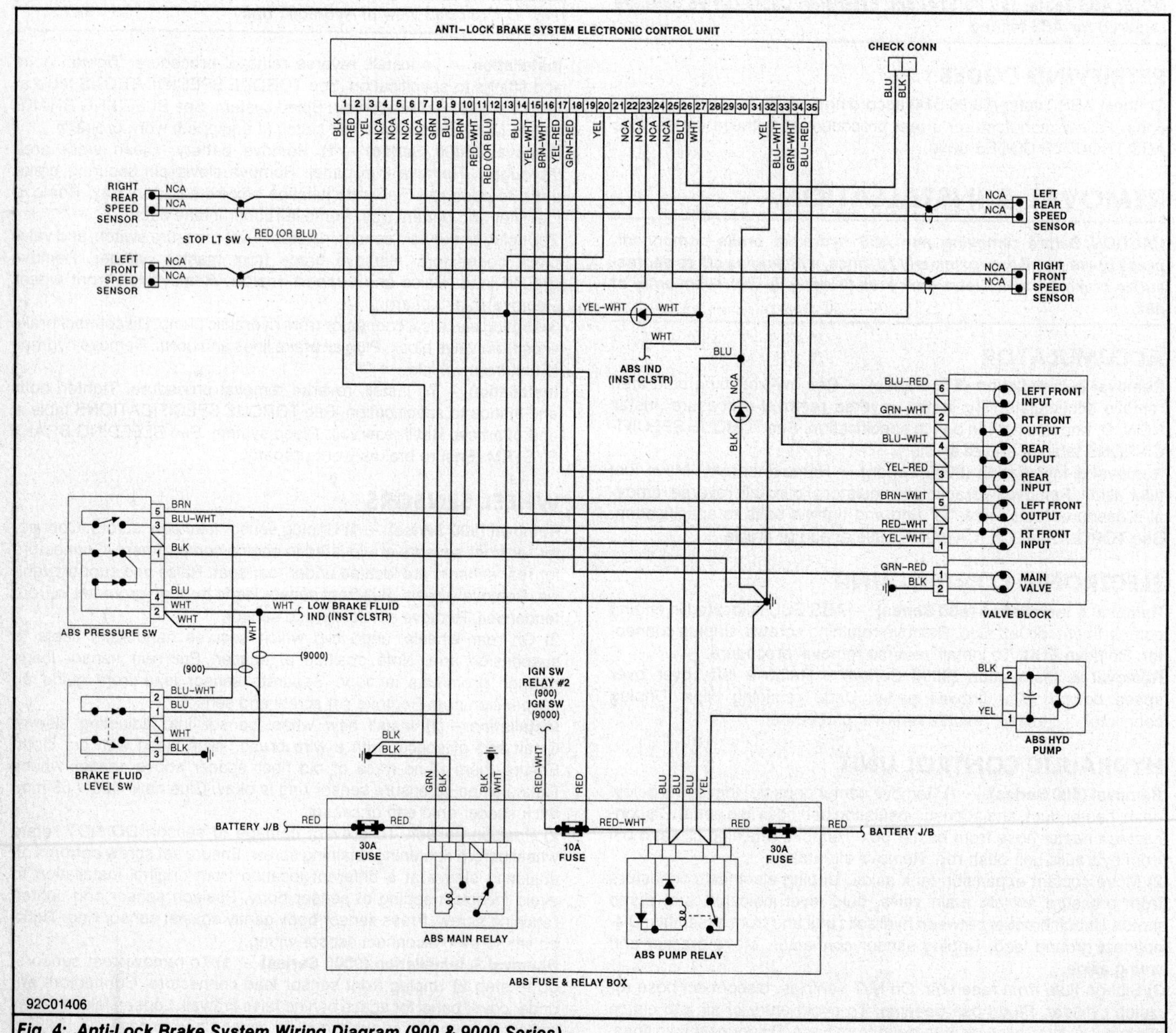


*Fig. 4: Anti-Lock Brake System Wiring Diagram (900 & 9000 Series)*

# 1991 WHEEL ALIGNMENT
# Specifications & Procedures

## 900 Series, 9000 Series

***NOTE:** Prior to performing wheel alignment, perform preliminary visual and mechanical inspection of wheels, tires and suspension components. See PRE-ALIGNMENT INSTRUCTIONS in WHEEL ALIGNMENT THEORY & OPERATION article in GENERAL INFORMATION.*

## RIDING HEIGHT ADJUSTMENT

Before adjusting alignment, check riding height. Riding height must be checked with vehicle on level floor and tires properly inflated. Bounce vehicle several times and allow suspension to settle.

Visually inspect vehicle for signs of abnormal height from front to rear or side to side. Check passenger and luggage compartments for extra heavy items and remove if present. Riding height between left and right side of vehicle should vary less than 1" (25.4 mm).

## JACKING & HOISTING

### FLOOR JACK

Using a floor jack or hoist, lift vehicle at points indicated by shaded areas on frame. *See Fig. 1.*

### EMERGENCY JACKING

The points on outline of body (indicated by dots) designate lifting points for manufacturer's supplied jack. *See Fig. 1.*

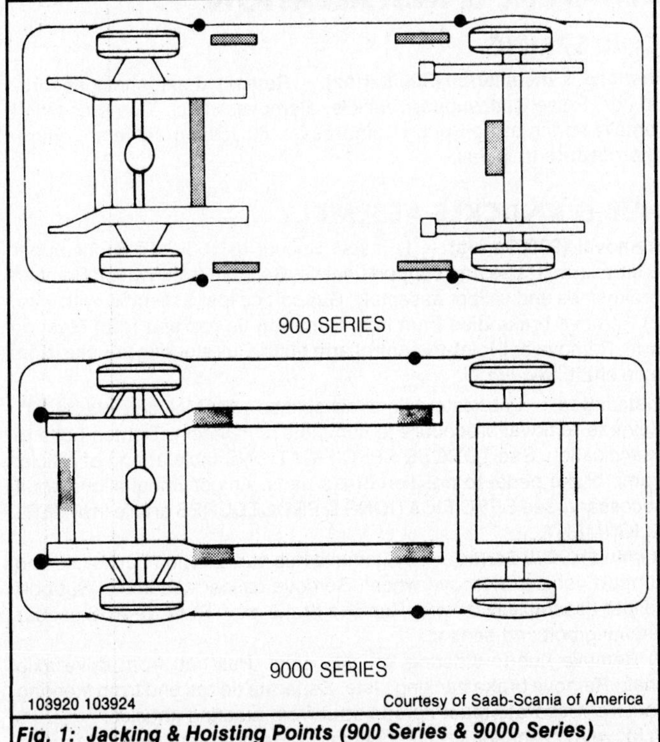


***Fig. 1: Jacking & Hoisting Points (900 Series & 9000 Series)***

## WHEEL ALIGNMENT PROCEDURES

### CAMBER ADJUSTMENT

Camber is not adjustable. Replace defective components if camber is not within specification.

### CASTER ADJUSTMENT

Caster is not adjustable. Replace defective components if caster is not within specification.

### TOE-IN ADJUSTMENT

Loosen outer of tie rod boot clips. Loosen tie rod end lock nuts. Turn tie rod to adjust toe-in. Ensure tie rod boot does not turn. Tighten tie rod lock nuts and boot clips. See TORQUE SPECIFICATIONS.

## TORQUE SPECIFICATIONS

*TORQUE SPECIFICATIONS*

| Application | Ft. Lbs. (N.m) |
|---|---|
| Tie Rod Lock Nut | 44-59 (60-80) |
| Wheel Lug Nut | |
| 900 Series | 65-80 (88-108) |
| 9000 Series | 76-90 (103-122) |

## WHEEL ALIGNMENT SPECIFICATIONS

*WHEEL ALIGNMENT SPECIFICATIONS*

| Application | Preferred | Range |
|---|---|---|
| **900 Series** | | |
| Camber [1] | | |
| Front | 1/2 | 0 To 1 |
| Rear | -1/2 | -3/4 To -1/4 |
| Caster [1] | 2 | 1 1/2 To 2 1/2 |
| Toe-In [2] | | |
| Front | 3/32 (2.5) | 1/32 To 5/32 (1 To 4) |
| Rear | 1/4 (6.5) | 1/8 To 3/8 (3 To 9) |
| Toe-In [1] | | |
| Front | 3/16 | 1/16 To 5/16 |
| Rear | 1/2 | 1/4 To 3/4 |
| Toe-Out On Turns [1] | | |
| Inner | 21 | ..... |
| Outer | 20 | ..... |
| **9000 Series** | | |
| Camber [1] | | |
| Front | -5/8 | -1 1/8 To -1/8 |
| Rear | -1/4 | -1/2 To 0 |
| Caster [1] | 1 5/8 | 1 1/8 To 2 1/8 |
| Toe-In [2] | | |
| Front | 3/32 (2.5) | 1/32 To 5/32 (1 To 4) |
| Rear | 3/16 (5) | 1/16 To 5/16 (1.5 To 8) |
| Toe-In [1] | | |
| Front | 3/16 | 1/16 To 5/16 |
| Rear | 3/8 | 1/8 To 5/8 |
| Toe-Out On Turns [1] | | |
| Inner | 21 | ..... |
| Outer | 20 | ..... |

[1] – Measurement in degrees.
[2] – Measurement in inches (mm).

# 1991 SUSPENSION
# Front

## 900 Series, 9000 Series

## DESCRIPTION

The 900 Series use upper and lower control arm front suspension with double-acting shock absorbers. Coil spring is mounted between upper control arm and wheel housing. *See Fig. 1*. The 9000 Series use MacPherson struts and an anti-roll bar. *See Fig. 2*.

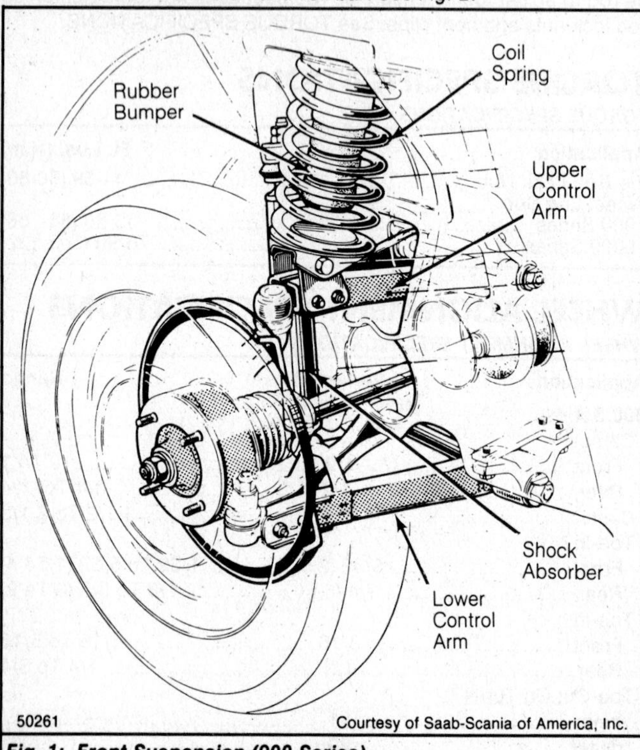


***Fig. 1: Front Suspension (900 Series)***

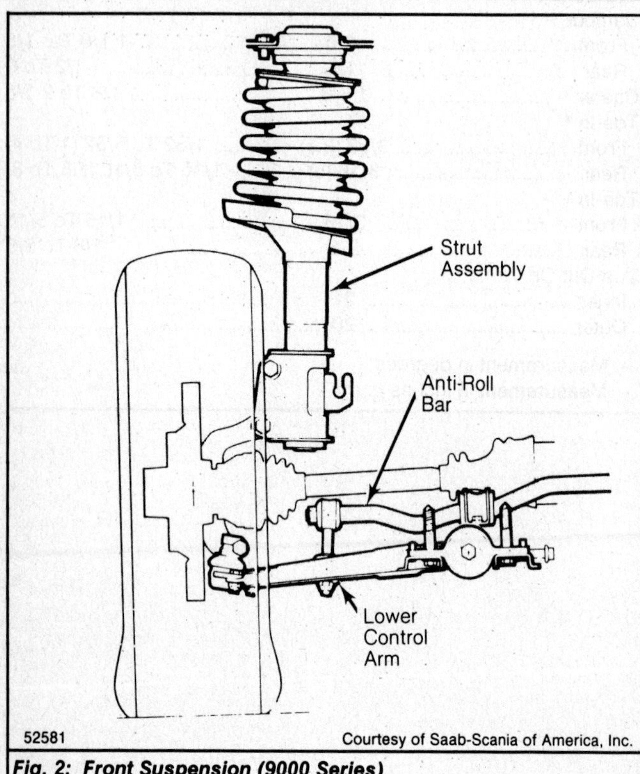


***Fig. 2: Front Suspension (9000 Series)***

## ADJUSTMENTS & INSPECTION

### WHEEL ALIGNMENT SPECIFICATIONS & PROCEDURES

***NOTE: See SPECIFICATIONS & PROCEDURES article in WHEEL ALIGNMENT.***

### WHEEL BEARING

Bearings are permanently lubricated and nonadjustable. With wheel installed, grasp wheel at top and bottom and try to move top toward center of vehicle and bottom away from vehicle. Measure distance wheel moves at edge of rim. If play exceeds .08" (2 mm), replace bearing or hub assembly.

### BALL JOINT CHECKING

***NOTE: On 900 Series, insert Spacer (83 93 209) under upper control arm to release tension from upper ball joint.***

**1)** Compress ball joint with water pump pliers. Replace ball joint if axial play exceeds .08" (2.0 mm).
**2)** To check radial play, apply pressure between lower control arm and vertical link. Replace ball joint if radial play exceeds .04" (1.0 mm). Check ball joint seals for wear and damage. Replace as necessary.

## REMOVAL & INSTALLATION

### COIL SPRING

**Removal & Installation (900 Series)** – Remove upper shock absorber nut. Raise and support vehicle. Remove wheel. Compress and remove spring using Spring Compressor (89 95 839). Reverse removal procedure to install.

### HUB & KNUCKLE ASSEMBLY

**Removal (900 Series)** – **1)** Install Spacer (83 93 209) under upper control arm. Raise and support vehicle. Remove front wheel. Remove brake pads and caliper assembly. Support caliper assembly with wire.
**2)** Remove brake disc from hub. Separate tie rod end from steering arm. Remove ball joint-to-control arm bolts. Pull steering knuckle from axle shaft. *See Fig. 3*.

**Installation** – Lubricate axle shaft splines with Molycote Paste "G". Reverse removal procedure to complete installation. Tighten bolts to specification. See TORQUE SPECIFICATIONS table at end of article. Pump brake pedal to position brake pads. Adjust wheel alignment if necessary. See SPECIFICATIONS & PROCEDURES article in WHEEL ALIGNMENT.

**Removal (9000 Series)** – **1)** Remove hub cap and hub nut. Raise and support vehicle. Remove wheel. Remove caliper assembly. Support caliper assembly with wire. Remove brake disc. Remove ABS sensor retaining bolt and sensor.
**2)** Remove hub-to-steering knuckle bolts. Pull hub from drive axle shaft. Remove brake backing plate. Separate tie rod end from steering knuckle. Separate MacPherson strut from steering knuckle.
**3)** Move ABS sensor lead bracket aside. Remove ball joint-to-steering knuckle bolt. Move steering knuckle aside. Support CV joint on control arm. Remove steering knuckle.

**Installation** – Clean end of drive axle shaft and hub. Apply Loctite 641 to exposed area of drive axle shaft after installing hub. Reverse removal procedure to complete installation. Tighten bolts to specification. See TORQUE SPECIFICATIONS table at end of article. Pump brake pedal to position brake pads. Adjust wheel alignment if necessary. See SPECIFICATIONS & PROCEDURES article in WHEEL ALIGNMENT.

### LOWER CONTROL ARM & BALL JOINT

**Removal (900 Series)** – Remove upper shock absorber retaining nut. Raise and support vehicle. Remove wheel assembly. Remove ball joint-to-lower control arm bolts. Remove lower control arm bracket

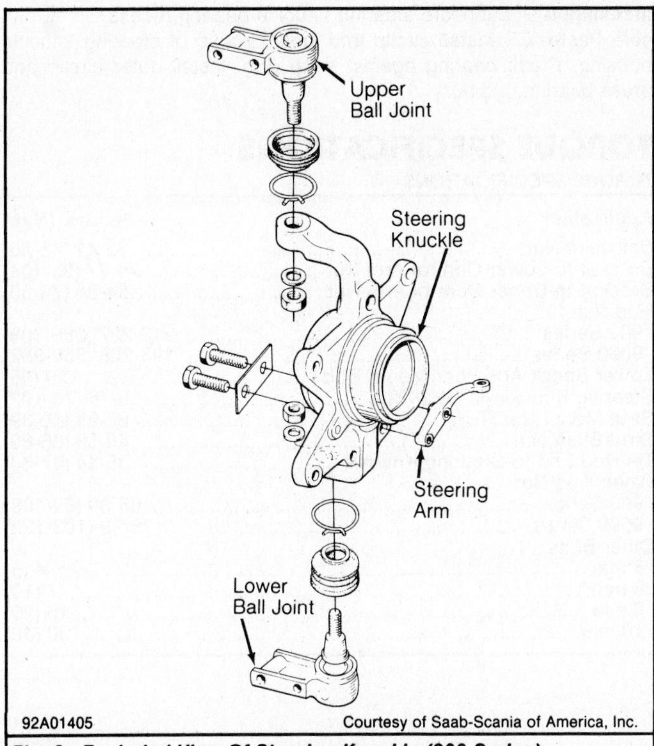


*Fig. 3: Exploded View Of Steering Knuckle (900 Series)*

bolts. Remove lower control arm. Remove ball joint retaining bolts and ball joint.

**Installation** – Attach bracket to lower control arm so angle between bracket and control arm is 16-20 degrees. *See Fig. 4.* Reverse removal procedure to complete installation. Tighten bolts to specification. See TORQUE SPECIFICATIONS table at end of article. Adjust wheel alignment if necessary. See SPECIFICATIONS & PROCEDURES article in WHEEL ALIGNMENT.

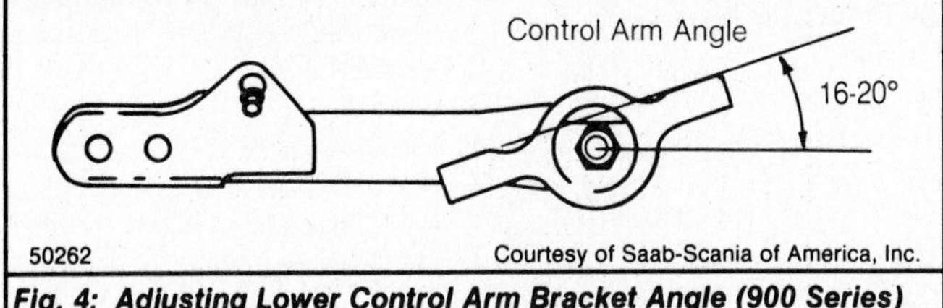


*Fig. 4: Adjusting Lower Control Arm Bracket Angle (900 Series)*

**Removal (9000 Series) – 1)** Raise and support vehicle. Remove wheel. Remove 3 ball joint retaining bolts. Remove nut which retains anti-roll bar to control arm. Loosen nut which retains anti-roll bar link to anti-roll bar. Move steering knuckle aside.

**2)** Separate anti-roll bar link from control arm. Remove 2 nuts which retain control arm to subframe. Push bolts toward engine as far as possible. Remove retaining bolts and reinforcement plate. Pry control arm toward steering knuckle to remove. Remove ball joint retaining bolt and ball joint.

***NOTE: To avoid damage to rubber bushing, DO NOT tighten rear control arm mounting nut for until car is on ground.***

**installation** – Place control arm into position. Support control arm weight by placing on ball joint. Reverse removal procedure to complete installation. Tighten bolts to specification. See TORQUE SPECIFICATIONS table at end of article. Adjust wheel alignment if necessary. See SPECIFICATIONS & PROCEDURES article in WHEEL ALIGNMENT.

## LOWER CONTROL ARM BUSHINGS

**Removal & Installation (900 Series)** – Remove lower control arm. See LOWER CONTROL ARM & BALL JOINT. Press out bushing. Press in new bushing using Installer (78 41 349). Use only soapy water for lubrication during installation. Assemble bracket and lower control arm so angle between them is 16-20 degrees. *See Fig. 4.*

**Removal & Installation (9000 Series)** – Remove lower control arm. See LOWER CONTROL ARM & BALL JOINT. Press out bushing. Press in new bushing using Sleeve (87 91 204). Use only petroleum jelly for lubrication during installation.

## ANTI-ROLL BAR

**Removal (900 Series)** – Install Spacer (83 93 209) under each upper control arms. Raise and support vehicle. Disconnect anti-roll bar from both lower control arms. Unbolt mountings at engine compartment floor. Disconnect steering gear and move it as far forward as possible. Remove anti-roll bar.

**Installation** – Reverse removal procedure to install. Tighten bolts to specification. See TORQUE SPECIFICATIONS table at end of article.

**Removal (9000 Series)** – Raise and support vehicle. Remove front wheels. Remove "U" clamps. Remove ball joint-to-control arm bolts. Remove anti-roll bar links. Remove anti-roll bar.

**Installation** – Reverse removal procedure to install. Tighten bolts to specification. See TORQUE SPECIFICATIONS table at end of article.

## STRUT ASSEMBLY

***WARNING: DO NOT remove nut from top center of strut assembly unless coil spring is compressed with spring compressor.***

**Removal (9000 Series)** – Raise and support vehicle. Remove wheel. Detach brake hose from clip on strut. Remove strut-to-steering knuckle bolt. Remove upper strut bolts. Remove cap from center nut. Remove strut.

**Installation** – To install, reverse removal procedure. Tighten bolts to specification. See TORQUE SPECIFICATIONS table at end of article. Adjust wheel alignment if necessary. See SPECIFICATIONS & PROCEDURES article in WHEEL ALIGNMENT.

## UPPER CONTROL ARM & BALL JOINT

**Removal (900 Series)** – If left control arm is to be removed, remove engine. See REMOVAL & INSTALLATION in appropriate ENGINES article. Remove spring. See COIL SPRING. Remove ball joint-to-control arm bolts. Support steering knuckle to prevent brake line damage. Remove control arm and brackets. Note locations of shims. Remove ball joint retaining bolts and ball joint.

**Installation** – Install shims into original locations. Reverse removal procedure to complete installation. Tighten bolts to specification. See TORQUE SPECIFICATIONS table at end of article. Adjust wheel alignment if necessary. See SPECIFICATIONS & PROCEDURES article in WHEEL ALIGNMENT.

## UPPER CONTROL ARM BUSHINGS

**Removal & Installation (900 Series)** – Remove lower control arm. See UPPER CONTROL ARM & BALL JOINT. Press out bushing. Press in new bushing using Installer 78 41 331. Use only soapy water for lubrication during installation. Assemble bracket and lower control arm so angle between them is 60-64 degrees. *See Fig. 5.*

## WHEEL BEARING

***NOTE: Front wheel bearings cannot be serviced on 9000 Series. Replace hub assembly if bearing is worn or defective.***

**Removal – (900 Series) 1)** Position Spacer (83 93 209) between upper control arm and body to release tension from upper ball joint. On all models, loosen hub nut. Raise and support vehicle. Remove wheel assembly. Align recess on rotor edge with brake pad assembly. Remove brake pads. Remove and support brake caliper. Remove disc brake rotor from hub.

# 1991 SUSPENSION
## Front (Cont.)

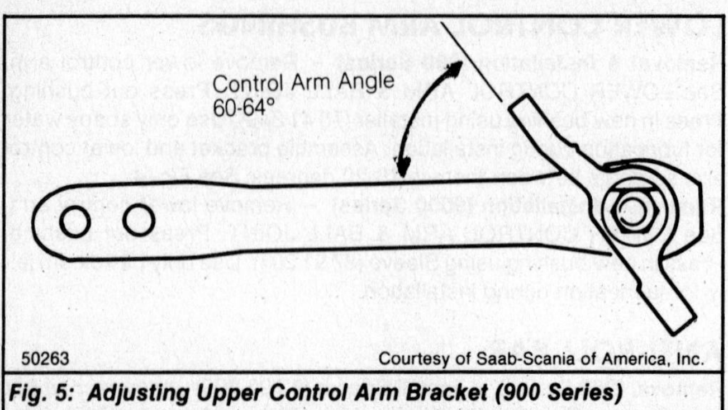


*Fig. 5: Adjusting Upper Control Arm Bracket (900 Series)*

**2)** Separate tie rod end from steering arm. Remove bolts holding upper and lower ball joints to control arms. Pull steering knuckle housing and hub from axle shaft and control arms.
**3)** Press hub out of steering knuckle assembly. Pull inner bearing race from hub. If no recess is present for puller, chisel race from hub. Remove circlips from steering knuckle assembly and press out bearing.

***NOTE: Pressing hub from steering knuckle assembly damages wheel bearing. ALWAYS replace bearing if it has been removed.***

**Installation** – Lubricate steering knuckle bearing recess with Molycote Paste "G". Install circlip into inner groove of steering knuckle housing. Press bearing against snap ring. Install outer circlip and press bearing into hub.

## TORQUE SPECIFICATIONS

***TORQUE SPECIFICATIONS***

| Application | Ft. Lbs. (N.m) |
|---|---|
| Ball Joint Nut | 32-41 (43-56) |
| Bracket-to-Lower Control Arm Nut | 70-77 (95-104) |
| Bracket-to-Upper Control Arm Nut | 54-66 (73-89) |
| Hub Nut | |
| 900 Series | 213-227 (289-308) |
| 9000 Series | 195-208 (264-282) |
| Lower Shock Absorber Mount Bolt | 70 (95) |
| Steering Knuckle-to-Strut Bolt | 56-75 (76-102) |
| Strut Mount Nut (Top) | 22-29 (30-39) |
| Strut Shaft Nut | 49-59 (66-80) |
| Tie Rod End-to-Steering Knuckle | 35-44 (47-60) |
| Wheel Lug Nut | |
| 900 Series | 65-80 (88-108) |
| 9000 Series | 76-90 (103-122) |
| Other Bolts | |
| 5 mm | 4 (5) |
| 6 mm | 7 (10) |
| 8 mm | 15 (20) |
| 10 mm | 30 (40) |

## 900 Series, 9000 Series

# DESCRIPTION

Rear suspension consists of a rigid axle, coil springs, and shock absorbers. The axle is a straight tube with mountings for spring links and hub carriers. A panhard rod prevents lateral movement. Torque arms and rear links prevent torsional movement. The 9000 series incorporates an anti-roll bar. *See Figs. 1 and 2.*

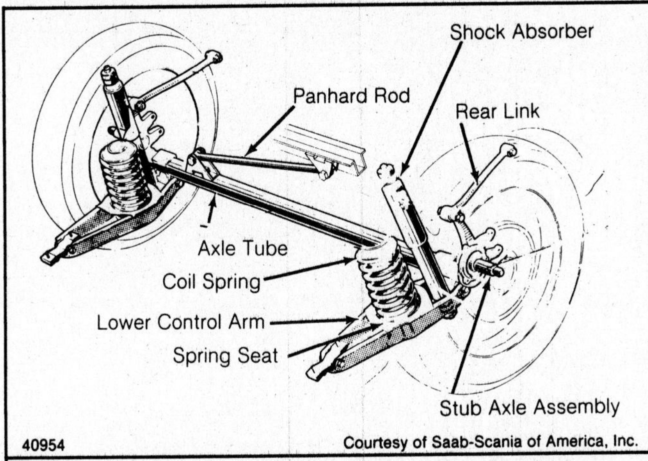


***Fig. 1: Identifying Rear Suspension Components (900 Series)***

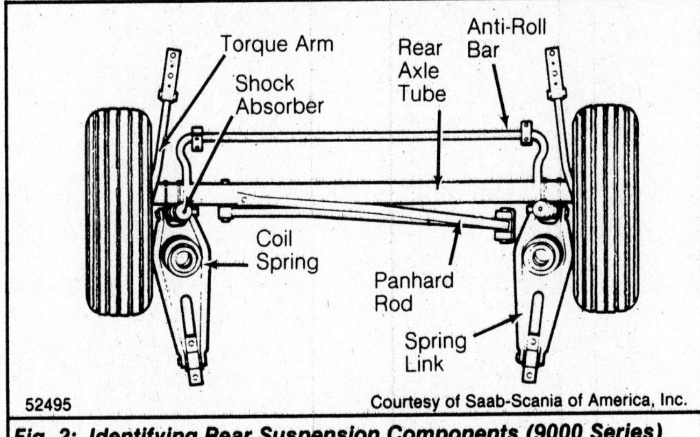


***Fig. 2: Identifying Rear Suspension Components (9000 Series)***

# ADJUSTMENTS & INSPECTION

## WHEEL ALIGNMENT

**Specifications & Procedures** - See SPECIFICATIONS & PROCEDURES article in WHEEL ALIGNMENT.

## WHEEL BEARING

With wheel installed, grasp wheel at top and bottom and try to move top toward center of vehicle and bottom away from vehicle. Measure distance wheel moves at edge of rim. If play exceeds .08" (2 mm), adjust or replace bearing or hub assembly.

**900 Series** - Tighten hub nut to 36 ft. lb (49 N.m). Loosen hub nut. Tighten hub nut to 1.5-3 ft. lb. (2 - 4 N.m). Lock hub nut by bending locking collar into slot.

**9000 Series** - Wheel bearings are part of wheel hub. Bearings are permanently lubricated and maintenance free.

# REMOVAL & INSTALLATION

## COIL SPRING

**Removal & Installation** - **1)** Apply parking brake. Loosen wheel lug nuts. Raise and support vehicle. Remove wheel. Release parking brake. On 9000 series, remove parking brake cable from bracket on spring link. On all models, support control arm with floor jack. Slightly raise arm and disconnect lower end of shock absorber.

**2)** Support rear axle with safety stand. Disconnect control arm from body. Carefully lower control arm and remove coil spring, coil spring support, and rubber spacer.

**3)** To install, reverse removal procedure. Use self-locking nuts to attach control arm to body.

## HUB ASSEMBLY

**Removal & Installation (900 Series)** - **1)** Raise and support vehicle. Remove brake caliper and wire it aside. Remove brake disc. Remove bearing dust cover.

**2)** Remove bearing nut and washer. Pull hub from axle. Reverse removal procedure to install. Adjust wheel bearing. See WHEEL BEARING under ADJUSTMENTS & INSPECTION.

**Removal & Installation (9000 Series)** - **1)** Clean work area to prevent entry of dirt into bearing. Raise and support vehicle. Remove brake caliper and wire it aside. Remove brake disc. Remove hub dust cover.

**2)** Remove hub nut and thrust washer. Pull hub from axle. Reverse removal procedure to install. Tighten hub nut to specification. See TORQUE SPECIFICATIONS table at end of article.

## ANTI-ROLL BAR

**Removal & Installation** - Raise and support rear of vehicle. Remove rear wheels. Using floor jacks at rear sill jacking points, raise vehicle sufficiently to relieve load on anti-roll bar. Disconnect anti-roll bar from links and remove from vehicle. Reverse removal procedure to install.

## SHOCK ABSORBER

***NOTE: Before installation, bleed air from shock absorber by holding shock upright and repeatedly working it through full cycle.***

**Removal & Installation** - **1)** Raise vehicle and support with safety stands. Remove wheel. Support axle with safety stand to prevent sudden drop of axle.

**2)** Raise control arm with floor jack under axle. Remove shock absorber retaining nuts. Remove control arm-to-rear axle mounting bolts. Lower control arm and remove shock.

**3)** On 9000 series, raise vehicle and support with safety stands under rear axle at spring links. Using a floor jack, raise vehicle to relieve tension on shock absorbers and anti-roll bar.

**4)** Remove bolt from bottom of shock absorber. Remove panel over spare tire and fold back carpet. Remove upper nut from shock absorber. Remove shock absorber. To install, reverse removal procedure.

***CAUTION: Used shock absorbers require special handling to prevent personal injury. Drill a .08" (2 mm) hole 3/8 - 5/8" (10-15 mm) from end of pressure chamber before discarding.***

## WHEEL BEARING

**Removal (900 Series)** - **1)** Raise and support vehicle. Remove wheel. Remove and support brake caliper. Remove disc brake rotor. Pry bearing dust cap from hub. Bend back locking collar and remove hub nut and washer.

**2)** Remove hub using Puller (89 96 084) if necessary. Remove seal ring using a screwdriver (seal ring cannot be removed intact). Remove inner bearing race. Drive outer bearing race from hub.

**Installation** - To install, reverse removal procedure. Replace seal ring. Adjust wheel bearings. See WHEEL BEARING under ADJUSTMENTS & INSPECTION in this article.

***NOTE: 9000 series wheel bearings are part of hub and cannot be replaced separately.***

# 1991 SUSPENSION
## Rear (Cont.)

## TORQUE SPECIFICATIONS

*TORQUE SPECIFICATIONS*

| Application | Ft. Lbs. (N.m) |
|---|---|
| Anti-Roll Bar-To-Anti-Roll Bar Link Bolt | 58-68 (79-92) |
| Caliper Retaining Bolt | 51-65 (69-88) |
| Hub Nut | 195-208 (264-282) |
| Shock Absorber Nut | 63 (85) |
| Wheel Lug Nut | |
| 900 Series | 65-80 (88-108) |
| 9000 Series | 76-90 (103-122) |
| Other Bolts | |
| 5 mm | 4 (5) |
| 6 mm | 7 (10) |
| 8 mm | 15 (20) |
| 10 mm | 30 (40) |

# 1991 STEERING
# Steering Columns

### 900 Series, 9000 Series

## DESCRIPTION & OPERATION

On vehicles equipped with air bag, Supplemental Restraint System (SRS) is marked on the steering wheel horn pad. The SRS consists of air bag module, Electronic Control Unit (ECU) with safety sensor, clockspring, 2 front sensors, and an SRS warning light in instrument cluster.

## REMOVAL & INSTALLATION

***WARNING: If vehicle is equipped with driver's side air bag, use extreme caution while servicing steering column. Disconnect battery and wait at least 20 minutes before attempting any repair. To prevent inadvertent air bag deployment, DO NOT apply electrical power to any component on steering column without disconnecting air bag electronic control unit.***

### STEERING WHEEL & HORN PAD

**Removal (With Air Bag) – 1)** Position front wheels straight ahead. Disconnect negative battery cable. Wait at least 20 minutes. Remove 2 screws from back of steering wheel. Remove air bag module/horn pad assembly. Unplug air bag module and horn pad electrical connectors.

**2)** Match-mark steering wheel and shaft! Remove steering wheel nut. Gently ease steering wheel from shaft to prevent damage to air bag clockspring.

**Installation – 1)** To ensure clockspring is set in middle position, align front wheels to straight-ahead position. Rotate clockspring clockwise until it stops, then rotate counterclockwise 3 1/2 turns.

**2)** Thread air bag module and horn wiring harnesses through hole in steering wheel. Slide steering wheel onto shaft, aligning match marks on shaft and wheel and aligning clockspring with hole in wheel.

**3)** Install steering wheel nut and tighten to 24-32 ft. lbs. (33-43 N.m). Connect air bag module and horn pad electrical connectors. Install screws on back of steering wheel. Reconnect battery negative cable.

**4)** Start engine and ensure SRS warning light comes on for approximately 6 seconds, then goes off.

**Removal & Installation (Without Air Bag) – 1)** Disconnect battery ground cable. On standard steering wheels, remove 4 screws behind steering wheel to remove safety padding and horn switch. On sport type steering wheels, lift rubber flaps from steering wheel spokes to remove safety padding and horn switch.

**2)** Remove steering wheel nut. Using a steering wheel puller, pull steering wheel from steering column. Using 2 screwdrivers, pry turn signal canceling sleeve from steering wheel.

**3)** To install, reverse removal procedure. Ensure front wheels are in straight-ahead position. Tighten steering wheel nut to 19 ft. lbs. (26 N.m) on 900 Series or 21 ft. lbs. (28 N.m) on 9000 Series.

### WINDSHIELD WIPER SWITCH

**Removal & Installation –** Disconnect negative battery cable. Pull steering wheel out as far as it will go. Remove covers from steering column bearing bracket. Unplug wiper switch connector. Remove retaining screws and windshield wiper switch. Reverse removal procedure to install.

### TURN SIGNAL SWITCH

**Removal & Installation – 1)** Disconnect negative battery cable. Remove bearing cover from lower steering column. Release spacer by unscrewing transverse bolt. Pull steering wheel out as far as it will go. Remove upper steering column cover. Unplug upper connector.

**2)** Remove 2 turn signal switch retaining screws. Pull turn signal switch forward. Disconnect lower connector. Reverse removal procedure to install.

### IGNITION SWITCH

**Removal & Installation (9000 Series) –** Disconnect negative battery cable. Remove lower steering column bearing cover. Pull steering wheel out as far as it will go. Release spacer by unscrewing transverse bolt. Remove upper steering column cover. Remove retaining screws, connector, and ignition switch. To install, reverse removal procedure.

### STEERING COLUMN

**Removal (900 Series) –** Remove steering wheel. See STEERING WHEEL & HORN PAD. Remove lock bolt at steering gear joint. Remove lower bearing cover and safety pad under instrument panel. Remove turn signal and windshield wiper switches. See TURN SIGNAL SWITCH and WINDSHIELD WIPER SWITCH. Remove rubber boot at dash panel. Remove 4 screws at bearing support. Pull steering column from vehicle.

**Installation –** Reverse removal procedure to install steering column. Ensure lock bolt at steering joint engages groove in shaft. Apply adhesive to groove in boot.

**Removal (9000 Series) – 1)** Disconnect negative battery cable. Position wheels to straight-ahead position. Remove steering wheel. See STEERING WHEEL & HORN PAD. Remove upper and lower steering column covers. Unplug connectors from windshield wiper and turn signal switches. Unplug harness connectors for air bag and horn.

**2)** Remove clockspring and steering column switch retainer. Remove sound baffle under instrument panel. Remove floor duct. Remove 2 bolts on universal joint between steering column shaft and intermediate shaft. Pull universal joint from steering column shaft splines.

**3)** Remove circlip from lower end of steering column. Remove transverse bolt, washers, and spacer from upper end of steering column. Push steering column shaft upward through lower bearing. Unplug connector from ignition switch. Pull shaft and steering lock from vehicle as an assembly.

***CAUTION: The 2 sections of the steering shaft are a matched set. DO NOT separate them under any circumstances.***

**Installation –** Ensure bolt in lower joint is below upper cleat at end of intermediate shaft. When installing shaft, adjust clearance between universal joint and column to .12-.20" (3-5 mm). Secure connectors and wiring for air bag and horn to steering column. Reverse removal procedure to complete installation.

## OVERHAUL

***NOTE: For exploded views of steering column assemblies, see Figs. 1 and 2.***

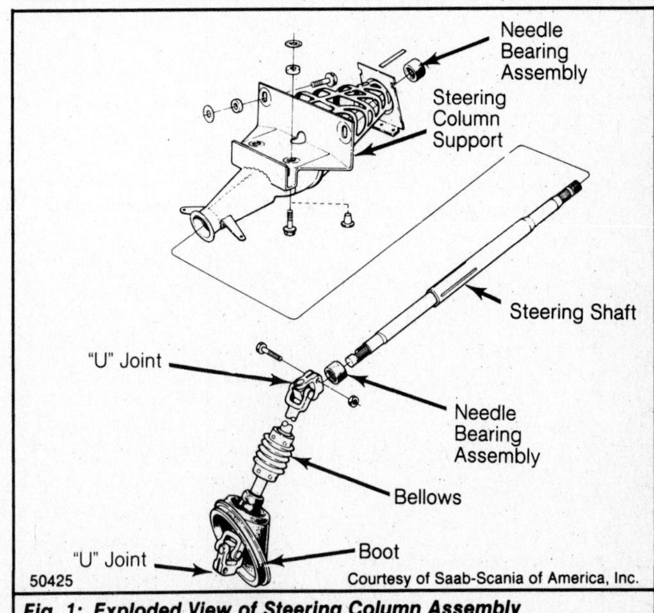


***Fig. 1: Exploded View of Steering Column Assembly (900 Series Without Air Bag)***

# 1991 STEERING
# Steering Columns (Cont.)

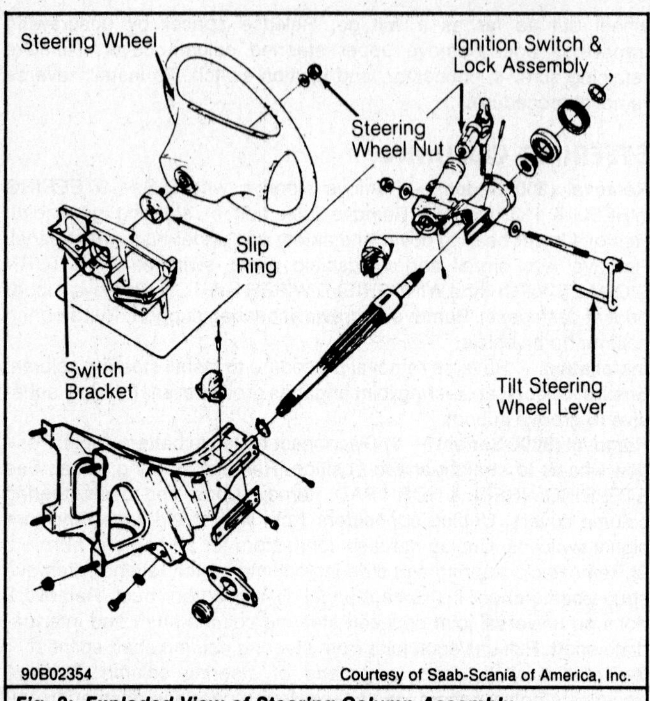


***Fig. 2: Exploded View of Steering Column Assembly (9000 Series)***

## TORQUE SPECIFICATIONS

| Application | Ft. Lbs. (N.m) |
|---|---|
| Steering Wheel Nut | |
| 900 Series | |
| With Air Bag | 24-32 (33-43) |
| Without Air Bag | 19 (26) |
| 9000 Series | 21 (28) |
| Steering Column Transverse Bolt | 15 (20) |
| Universal Joint Lock Bolt | 17-22 (23-30) |

# 1991 STEERING
# Power Rack & Pinion

### 900 Series, 9000 Series

## DESCRIPTION

All models have power rack and pinion power steering. A belt-driven pump provides hydraulic pressure. *See Fig. 1.*

## LUBRICATION

### FLUID TYPE

Use General Motors power steering fluid only. DO NOT use automatic transmission fluid.

### FLUID LEVEL CHECK

With engine at normal operating temperature, maintain fluid level between HOT and COLD marks on reservoir. If engine and fluid are cold, fluid level should be between COLD and ADD marks

## ADJUSTMENTS

### POWER STEERING PUMP BELT

**900 Series** – Adjust tension on new belts to 90-110 lb. (41-50 kg). Adjust tension on used bells to 65-75 lb. (29-34 kg).
**9000 Series** – Belt tension is adjusted automatically. No service adjustment is required.

## TESTING

***POWER STEERING TEST SPECIFICATIONS***

| Application | Specification |
|---|---|
| Steering Wheel Turning Torque [1] | 7-22 INCH lbs. (.8-2.5 N.m) |
| Pump Relief Valve Opens | 1000-1100 psi (70-77 kg/cm²) |
| Flow | 1.7-2.1 gal/min. (6.4-7.9 L/min.) |

[1] – Front wheels off ground.

## REMOVAL & INSTALLATION

### POWER STEERING PUMP

**Removal & Installation (900 Series) 1)** Drain fluid from system by disconnecting supply hose at reservoir. Disconnect negative battery cable. Remove alternator mounting bolts. Move alternator aside. Remove tensioner links for alternator and power steering pump.
**2)** Remove drive belt. Remove pump mounting bolts. Disconnect pressure hose. Remove pump. Reverse removal procedure to install. Tighten bolts to specification. See TORQUE SPECIFICATIONS table at end of article.

**Removal & Installation (9000 Series) 1)** Drain fluid from system by disconnecting supply hose at reservoir. Disconnect negative battery cable. Remove oil filler tube bracket. Remove torque strut. Disconnect supply hose to pump. Plug openings. Remove fluid reservoir.
**2)** Remove belt. Disconnect pressure hose at pump. Plug openings. On models with A/T, remove kickdown cable clip. Remove pump retaining bolts. One bolt is accessible through hole in pulley. Reverse removal procedure to install. Tighten bolts to specification. See TORQUE SPECIFICATIONS table at end of article.

### POWER RACK & PINION

**Removal (900 Series) – 1)** Clean area around hydraulic connections. Drain fluid from system by disconnecting supply hose at reservoir. Disconnect return and pressure lines from steering gear. Plug openings to prevent entry of dirt and loss of fluid.
**2)** Remove steering gear-to-intermediate shaft clamp bolt. Raise and support vehicle. Remove front wheels. Separate tie rods from steering knuckles.
**3)** Remove steering gear retaining bolts. Separate intermediate shaft "U" joint from steering gear. Lift steering gear to the side. Remove by guiding it diagonally downward through opening in engine compartment.

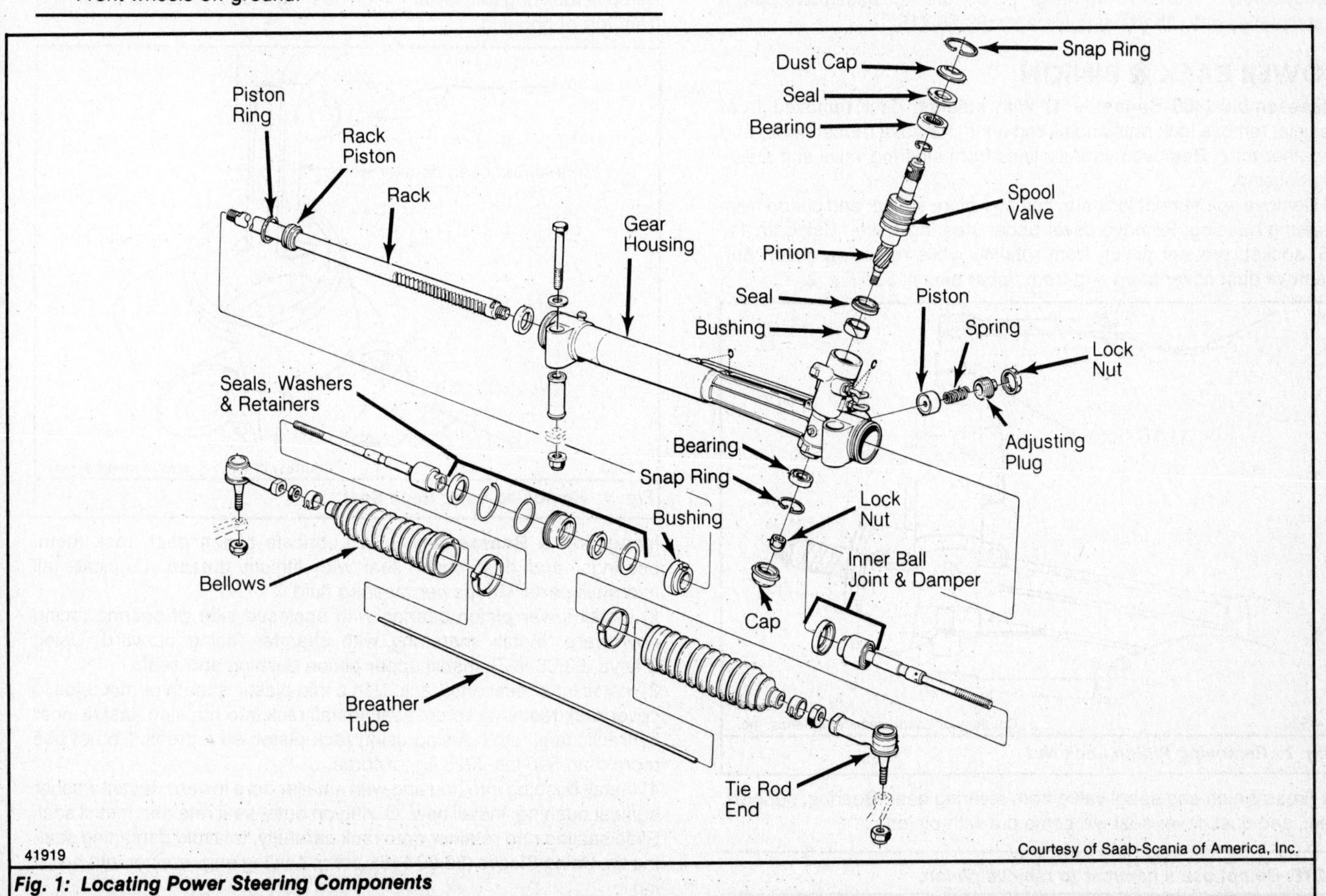


*Fig. 1: Locating Power Steering Components*

# 1991 STEERING
# Power Rack & Pinion (Cont.)

**Removal (9000 Series) – 1)** Clean areas around hydraulic connections. Drain fluid from system by disconnecting supply hose at reservoir. Loosen oil filler tube bracket. Move bracket aside. Disconnect pressure hose from pump. Plug openings.
**2)** Fold carpet back. Peel boot away from intermediate steering shaft. Remove both clamp bolts from "U" joints on intermediate steering shaft. Remove cover plate from firewall. Save gasket, seal, and plastic bushing.
**3)** Raise and support vehicle. Remove front wheels. Remove rear section of right fender liner. Measure and record distance between tie rod end and groove in rack. Loosen tie rod end lock nuts. Separate tie rod ends from steering knuckles.
**4)** Remove upper bolt for subframe brace on right side. Remove steering gear retaining bolts. Unbolt lower mount. Remove brace. Remove steering gear.
**Installation (All Models) –** To install, reverse removal procedure. DO NOT connect tie rod ends until rack and pinion assembly has been fully installed. Reverse removal procedure to install. Tighten bolts to specification. See TORQUE SPECIFICATIONS table at end of article. Adjust wheel alignment.

## OVERHAUL

### POWER STEERING PUMP

**Disassembly – 1)** Remove pulley using Puller (89 96 423). Press end cover inward. Insert screwdriver into hole in housing to start retaining ring from groove. Remove retaining ring. Tap pump against bench to remove end cover.
**2)** Remove rotor and vanes as an assembly. Remove pump ring and dowel pins. Remove end plate and end plate "O" ring. Remove spring and pin. Remove remaining "O" ring.
**Inspection –** Inspect all parts for wear or damage. Inspect vanes and housing for scoring. Replace any worn or defective parts.
**Reassembly –** Reverse removal procedure to assemble pump. Install pulley onto shaft using Installer (89 96 415).

### POWER RACK & PINION

**Disassembly (900 Series) – 1)** With steering gear removed from vehicle, remove lock nuts and tie rod ends. Remove rubber boots and breather tube. Remove hydraulic lines from steering valve and steering housing.
**2)** Remove adjustment lock nut, adjuster plug, spring, and piston from steering housing. Remove cover under steering valve . Using an 11/16" socket, prevent pinion from rotating while removing pinion nut. Remove dust cover snap ring from upper pinion. *See Fig. 2.*

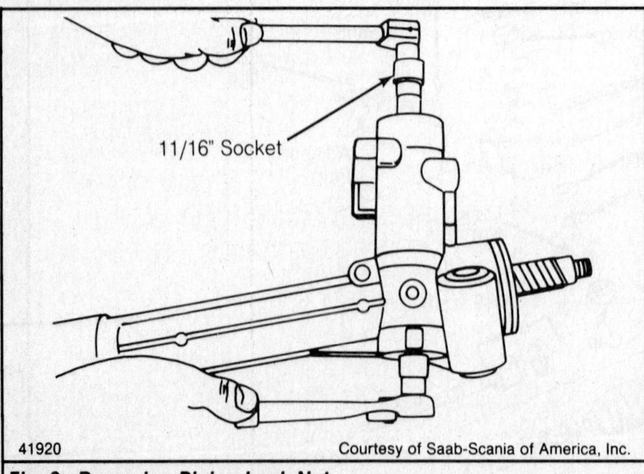


***Fig. 2: Removing Pinion Lock Nut***

**3)** Press pinion and spool valve from steering gear. Bearing, support, seal, and dust cover seal will come out with pinion.

***NOTE: Do not use a hammer to remove pinion.***

**4)** Remove inner ball joint farthest from pinion. Clamp rack in a soft-jawed vise. Move plastic sleeve out of the way. Unscrew ball joint.
**5)** Remove lock ring from end of housing. Push rack into gear housing as far as it will go. Install Removal/Installer Sleeve (89 96 407) over rack. Tighten inner ball joint to press seal housing inward. *See Fig. 3.*

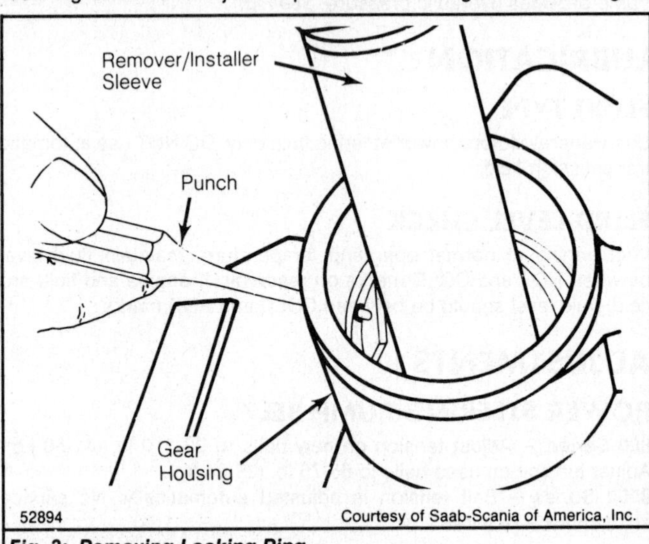


***Fig. 3: Removing Locking Ring***

**6)** Use a punch to start lock ring from its groove. then pry it from groove. Remove ball joint and special sleeve. Press out rack together with seal, washer, and bushing. Ensure there are no burrs on rack before removing seal and bushing.
**7)** Insert lips of Seal Remover/Installer (89 96 399) under seal. From opposite end of housing, drive out seal with long punch. *See Fig. 4.* Remove lock ring and lower pinion bearing. Remove seal and bushing from top of housing.

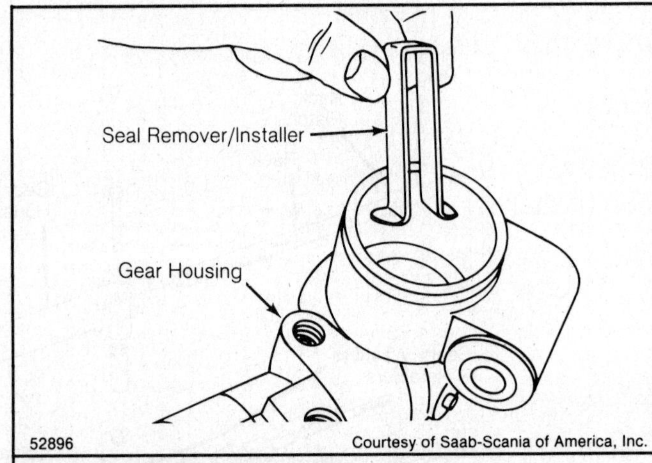


***Fig. 4: Removing Inner Rack Seal***

**Inspection & Reassembly – 1)** Lubricate pinion gear, rack teeth, bearings, and dust cover seal with lithium grease. Lubricate all hydraulic parts with power steering fluid.
**2)** Install lower pinion bearing with enclosed side of bearing facing downward. Install snap ring with chamfer facing outward. Using Sleeve (90 06 407), install upper pinion bushing and seal.
**3)** Install inner seal onto rack. Use a thin plastic sheath or metal foil to cover rack teeth to protect seal. Install rack into housing. Install inner hydraulic seal into housing using rack piston as a press. Do not use more than 500 lbs. (225 kg) of force.
**4)** Install bushing into housing with smaller bore inward. Install washer against bushing. Install new "O" ring on outer seal retainer. Install seal. Slide sealing ring retainer onto rack carefully, to avoid damaging sealing lip. Using Sleeve (83 90 148), press sealing ring retainer into housing.

# 1991 STEERING
# Power Rack & Pinion (Cont.)

**5)** Center rack. Rotate rack so teeth will mesh with pinion gear teeth when it is installed. Hold pinion gear with spool valve, so that groove in end of shaft points toward 9 o'clock position when pinion teeth engage rack teeth. *See Fig. 5.*
**6)** Insert pinion. Pinion should rotate so that groove in end of pinion points toward front (12 o'clock position), with rack centered. Install pinion lock nut. Tighten lock nut. Install cover.

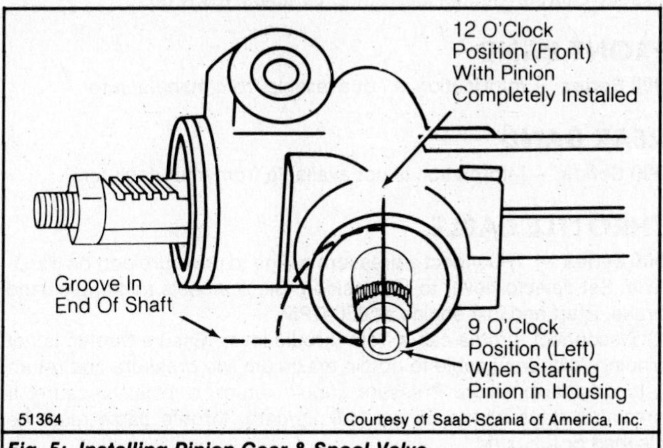


***Fig. 5: Installing Pinion Gear & Spool Valve***

**7)** Install washer, bearing, sealing ring, dust cover, and snap ring onto top of pinion gear (spool valve). Protect seal lips with tape or plastic sleeve over pinion splines. Install piston, spring, and adjuster plug into gear housing. Tighten adjuster plug until bearing piston contacts rack firmly. Back off adjuster plug 30-50 degrees. Install and tighten lock nut.
**8)** Assemble plastic sleeves, inner ball joints, and tie rods to rack ends. Hold rack in soft-jawed vise. Tighten ball joints. Lock inner ball joints by tapping tab on ball joint into rack. DO NOT hold pinion when loosening or tightening ball joints.
**9)** Install sealing ring retainer ring into housing. Turn pinion until inner ball joint presses against sealing ring retainer. Press in retainer. At the same time, install sealing ring into groove. Install rubber boots, breather tube, and hydraulic lines.
**Disassembly (9000 Series) – 1)** With steering gear removed from vehicle, measure and record distance between each tie rod lock nut and end of tie rod. Remove lock nuts and tie rod ends. Remove rubber boots and breather tube. Remove hydraulic lines from steering valve and steering housing.
**2)** Remove inner ball joint farthest from pinion. Clamp rack in a soft-jawed vise. Tap thrust washer down. Remove ball joint and thrust washer. DO NOT hold pinion when removing ball joint.
**3)** Press retaining ring inward, then remove it with wire hook. Remove remaining ball joint. Remove lock nut, adjuster plug, spring, and damper. Tap end cap from bottom of pinion housing. Hold pinion while removing lock nut.
**4)** Remove dust cap retaining ring at upper end of valve. Press out pinion, valve, seals, and bearings as an assembly. Remove rack, seal retainer, and bushing. Insert lips of Seal Remover/Installer (89 96 399) under seal. Drive out seal with long punch. *See Fig. 4*. Remove lock ring and lower pinion bearing. Remove seal and bushing from top of housing.

**Inspection & Reassembly – 1)** Inspect all parts for wear or damage. Ensure each Teflon ring on valve is split. If not, use a razor blade to cut a slit .20 to .28" (5 to 7 mm) deep across each ring. Cut rings by using pressure only; DO NOT use a sawing motion.
**2)** Lubricate pinion gear, rack teeth, bearings, and dust cover seal with lithium grease. Lubricate all hydraulic parts with power steering fluid.
**3)** Using Remover/Installer Sleeve (90 06 407), install upper pinion bushing. Install seal with chamfer upward. Tap in lower pinion, using a 19-mm socket. Install circlip.
**4)** Install seal onto rack. Use Seal Protector (89 95 946) to cover rack teeth to protect sealing lip of seal. Press rack into housing. Do not use more than 500 lbs. (225 kg) force.
**5)** Install new "O" ring onto outer seal retainer. Install seal. Slide seal and seal retainer onto rack. Center rack. Rotate rack so that rack teeth mesh with those on pinion. Install bearing and seals onto valve.
**6)** Hold valve with slot on end of shaft at 11 o'clock position. Slide valve in as far as it will go, then press it home with Sleeve (78 41 067). When installed, slot in shaft should be at 12 o'clock position. Install circlip. Install pinion shaft lock nut.
**7)** Tap end cap into position using Sleeve (78 41 067). Lubricate damper yoke with lithium grease. Install yoke, spring, adjuster plug, and lock nut. Center rack. Tighten adjuster plug to 6-11 ft. lbs. (8-15 N.m). Back off adjuster plug 50-60 degrees. Tighten lock nut.
**8)** Move rack to end of travel in direction of pinion. Mount assembly in soft-jawed vise. Install Spacer (89 46 360) onto end of shaft before installing inner ball joint. Install ball joint. DO NOT hold pinion while tightening ball joint.
**9)** Lock ball joint in position by tapping tabs onto 2 flats on rack. Press end stop into position. Install retaining ring into housing. To enable future removal, ensure end of retaining ring is opposite hole in housing.
**10)** Install Spacer (89 46 360) onto end of shaft before installing inner ball joint. Install remaining inner ball joint. DO NOT hold pinion while tightening ball joint. Lock ball joint in position by tapping tabs onto 2 flats on rack.
**11)** Reverse disassembly procedure to complete assembly. Tighten bolts to specification. See TORQUE SPECIFICATIONS table. Screw tie rod end lock nuts onto tie rods to distance recorded during removal.

## TORQUE SPECIFICATIONS

***TORQUE SPECIFICATIONS***

| Application | Ft. Lbs. (N.m) |
|---|---|
| Bearing Lock Nut | 48-55 (65-75) |
| Inner Ball Joint-To-Rack | 59-72 (80-98) |
| Pinion Gear Lower Lock Nut | 22-34 (30-46) |
| Rack & Pinion Mounting Bolts | 44-59 (60-80) |
| Steering Gear Clamp Bolt | 44-60 (60-81) |
| Tie Rod End Lock Nut | 37-44 (50-60) |
| Tie Rod End-To-Steering Knuckle | 35-44 (47-60) |
| Wheel Lug Nut | |
| 900 Series | 65-80 (88-108) |
| 9000 Series | 76-90 (103-122) |
| Other Bolts | |
| 5 mm | 4 (5) |
| 6 mm | 7 (10) |
| 8 mm | 15 (20) |
| 10 mm | 30 (40) |

# 1991 TRANSMISSION SERVICING
# Automatic Transmission

## 900 Series, 9000 Series

## IDENTIFICATION

*AUTOMATIC TRANSAXLE APPLICATIONS*

| Model | Transaxle |
|---|---|
| 900 Series | Borg-Warner Model 35 or 37 |
| 9000 Series | ZF 4HP 18 |

## LUBRICATION

### SERVICE INTERVALS

Check fluid level every 15,000 miles, change every 30,000 miles.

### CHECKING FLUID LEVEL

**Transaxle - 1)** Park vehicle on level surface. Apply hand brake. Allow engine to idle at normal operating temperature. Place selector lever in each gear position for at least 15 seconds. Return to "P" position.

**2)** Remove dipstick, wipe clean, and check fluid level. Fluid level should be between the MIN and MAX marks on dipstick. Use hot or cold markings on dipstick, depending on transmission fluid temperature. Do not overfill.

**Differential -** Fill plug hole is located on side of case. Fluid level should be to bottom of hole.

### RECOMMENDED FLUID

**Transaxle -** Use Ford specification M2C-33F/G automatic transmission fluid on 900 Series. Use Dexron II automatic transmission fluid on 9000 Series.

**900 Series Differential -** Use 10W-30 engine oil or SAE EP 80, API GL-4, or GL-5 gear lubricant.

### FLUID CAPACITY

*TRANSAXLE REFILL CAPACITIES*

| Application | Qts. (L) |
|---|---|
| 900 Series | |
| Transaxle | 8.4 (8.0) |
| Differential | 1.3 (1.2) |
| 9000 Series | 8.7 (8.2) |

*DIFFERENTIAL REFILL CAPACITY*

| Application | Qts. (L) |
|---|---|
| 900 Series | 1.3 (1.2) |

### DRAINING & REFILLING

**Transaxle (900 Series) - 1)** Remove transaxle drain plug. Remove oil pan if replacing filter or adjusting front band. Install oil pan and new gasket. Tighten oil pan bolts to 71-106 INCH lbs. (8-12 N.m).

**2)** Install drain plug and tighten to 44-71 ft. lbs. (5-8 N.m). Add fluid and check fluid level. DO NOT overfill.

**Final Drive (900 Series) -** Final drive has separate drain and fill plugs. Remove drain plug, drain fluid, and tighten drain plug securely. Fill final drive through fill hole until fluid comes out of hole. Tighten fill plug securely.

**Transaxle (9000 Series) -** Remove drain plug and drain fluid. Fill with required amount of fluid through filler tube on top of valve body cover.

**Filter (9000 Series) - 1)** Loosen 3 Torx retaining bolts from bottom filter cover and allow fluid to drain. Remove retaining bolts and cover. Withdraw filter element from bore.

**2)** Discard filter element "O" ring and cover "O" rings. Clean cover and filter. Fit new "O" ring onto filter and install into bore. Fit new "O" ring onto filter cover. Install cover. Tighten retaining bolts to 70 INCH lbs. (8 N.m).

## ADJUSTMENTS

### BRAKE BAND

**9000 Series -** Brake band adjusting screw is located on side of case near valve body cover. Loosen adjusting screw lock nut. Tighten adjusting screw to 89 INCH lbs. (10 N.m). Back off adjusting screw exactly 2 turns. Tighten lock nut to 59 ft. lbs. (80 N.m).

### FRONT BAND

**900 Series -** Information is not available from manufacturer.

### REAR BAND

**900 Series -** Information is not available from manufacturer.

### THROTTLE CABLE

**900 Series - 1)** Connect a pressure gauge to pressure port on transaxle. Set selector lever to "P" position. Block wheels and apply hand brake. Start and idle engine at 850 RPM.

**2)** Disconnect throttle cable from throttle lever. Ensure throttle is not binding. Withdraw cable to obtain maximum line pressure and return it to original position. Pressure should return to initial pressure. If pressure stays above 69 psi (4.9 kg/cm²), throttle cable must be cleaned or adjusted.

**3)** Connect throttle cable to throttle lever. Set selector lever to "D" position. Ensure cable is released to obtain lowest pressure.

**4)** Increase pressure to 1.4 psi (0.1 kg/cm²) by adjusting throttle cable. Adjust cable at bracket in engine compartment. Set selector lever to "P" position. Pressure should be 59-69 psi (4.1-4.9 kg/cm²).

**9000 Series - 1)** Measure distance between cable crimp and cable housing when throttle is opened to wide open position (just before kickdown on transmission cam). Distance should be 1.54" (39 mm).

**2)** With throttle in idle position, again measure distance between cable crimp and cable housing. Distance should be .098" (2.5 mm). Loosen both lock nuts on throttle housing bracket to adjust. Tighten lock nuts.

### SELECTOR LEVER

**900 Series - 1)** Set selector lever to "N" position. Press pawl button and move selector lever slightly back and forth. Increased resistance should be felt in both directions. Hold lever midway between positions in which resistance is felt.

**2)** Disconnect gear selector cable from lever. Release pawl button. Set lever to "N" position. Tighten gear selector cable set screw. *See Fig. 1.*

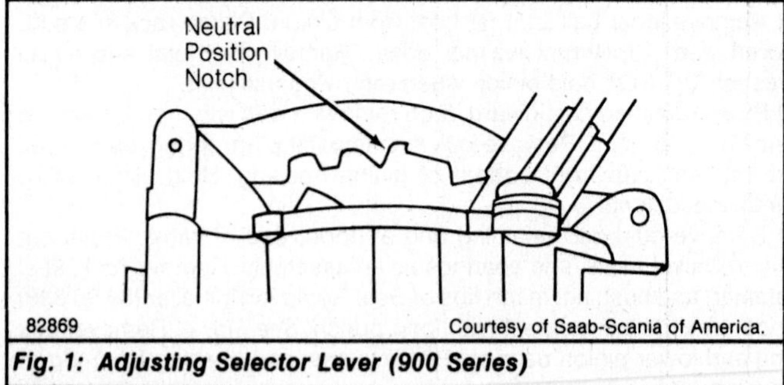


***Fig. 1: Adjusting Selector Lever (900 Series)***

**9000 Series -** Loosen nut on adjustment mechanism in front of selector lever. Set transmission lever to "N" position. Tighten adjustment nut to 53-88 INCH lbs. (6-10 N.m).

### NEUTRAL SAFETY SWITCH

Set selector lever to "N" position. Loosen switch retaining screws. Rotate switch housing to align lever with mark on switch housing. Tighten retaining screws.

# 1991 TRANSMISSION SERVICING
# Manual Transmission

## 900 Series, 9000 Series

## IDENTIFICATION

*SAAB MANUAL TRANSAXLE APPLICATIONS*

| Model | Transaxle |
|---|---|
| 900 & 900 Turbo | 5-Speed - GM 45606 |
| 900S | 5-Speed - GMT 5202 |
| 900S Turbo | 5-Speed - GM 55712 |
| 9000S | 5-Speed - GMT 5203 |
| 9000 Turbo | 5-Speed - GMT 5401 |

## LUBRICATION

### SERVICE INTERVALS

Check fluid level every 15,000 miles.

### CHECKING FLUID LEVEL

**900 Series** - Check oil level with dipstick, located on right side of engine. Oil level should be between MIN and MAX marks.

**9000 Series** - Check transaxle oil level with engine oil dipstick. Remove transaxle filler plug. Insert dipstick so that notch next to the word GEARBOX rests against the edge of filler plug hole. Level should be between marks.

### RECOMMENDED FLUID

Use SAE 10W-30 or 10W-40 engine oil.

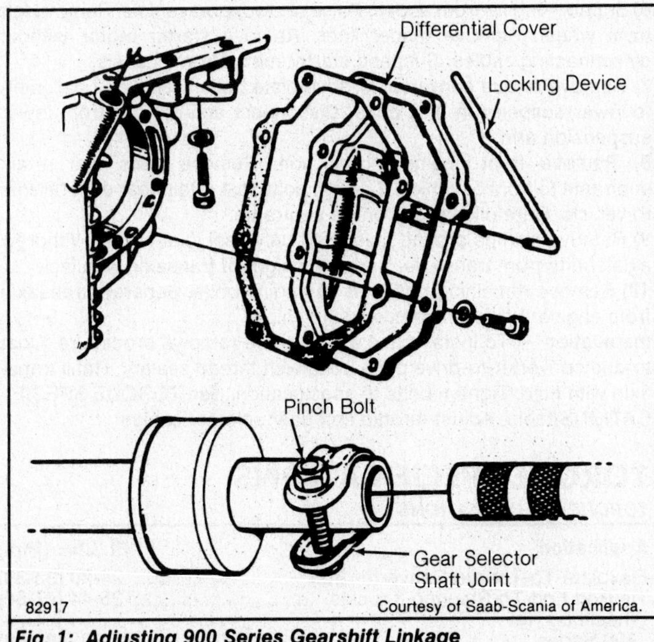


*Fig. 1: Adjusting 900 Series Gearshift Linkage*

## FLUID CAPACITY

*TRANSMISSION REFILL CAPACITIES*

| Application | Qts. (L) |
|---|---|
| 900 Series | 2.6 (2.5) |
| 9000 Series | 2.6 (2.5) |

## ADJUSTMENTS

### GEARSHIFT LINKAGE

**900 Series** - **1)** Place shift lever in 3rd gear position. Loosen pinch bolt at gear selector shaft joint on engine side of firewall. *See Fig. 1.*

**2)** Lock gearshift lever into 3rd gear position in gearshift housing with a .24" (6 mm) drift. It may be necessary to fold back carpeting in front of shift lever console for access to shift rod.

**3)** Slip Locking Device (87 91 576) into hole in shift lever input shaft and then into differential cover. *See Fig. 1.* This locks transaxle into 3rd gear. Tighten pinch bolt at gearshift joint to 22-26 ft. lbs. (20-35 N.m).

**9000 Series** - **1)** Working inside passenger compartment, pry up rubber boot around gearshift lever. Loosen pinch bolt securing selector rod to transaxle. Pinch bolt is on engine side of firewall above steering rack. *See Fig. 2.*

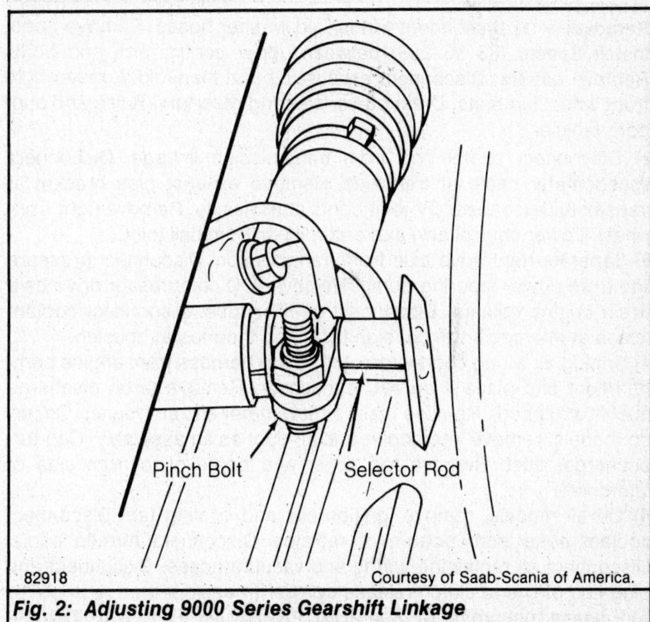


*Fig. 2: Adjusting 9000 Series Gearshift Linkage*

**2)** Lock gearshift lever in reverse gear by inserting a 4-mm drill bit through locating holes in gearshift lever and gearshift lever housing.

**3)** Ensure transaxle is in Reverse. Tighten pinch bolt on selector rod. Remove drill and reinstall rubber boot.

# 1991 TRANSMISSION SERVICING
# Transmission Removal & Installation

## 900 Series, 9000 Series

## MANUAL

***NOTE:** On 900 Series, transaxle and engine must be removed as an assembly. See ENGINES article. For manual transaxle removal and installation on 9000 Series, see appropriate article in CLUTCHES.*

## AUTOMATIC

### FUEL PRESSURE RELEASE

***WARNING:** Residual fuel pressure may be present in fuel system when engine is off. To avoid fire hazard, wrap a shop towel around fuel fitting before disconnecting fuel lines.*

To release fuel pressure, disconnect fuel lines at fuel pressure regulator and fuel injection manifold.

### 900 SERIES

***NOTE:** For reassembly reference, label all electrical connectors, vacuum hoses, and fuel lines before removal. Also place mating marks on engine hood and other major assemblies before removal.*

**Removal – 1)** Disconnect windshield washer hoses. Remove hood. Install Spacer (83 93 209) between upper control arm and body. Remove battery. Disconnect exhaust pipe at manifold. Loosen right front wheel lug bolts. Drain power steering reservoir. Raise and support vehicle.

**2)** Disconnect shifter rod from transmission linkage. Disconnect speedometer cable at transaxle. Remove exhaust pipe bracket at transaxle. Disconnect CV joint boots at transaxle. Remove right front wheel. Lower control arm and anti-roll bar from ball joint.

**3)** Separate right drive axle from transmission. Disconnect pressure line from power steering pump. Remove A/C compressor drive belt. Drain engine coolant. Disconnect oil filler tube. Disconnect coolant hoses at intercooler, expansion tank, and thermostat housing.

**4)** Unplug all wiring connectors. Lift wiring harness from engine compartment and place it on A/C condenser. Remove turbo discharge duct (if equipped). Remove mass airflow meter and air cleaner. On turbo models, remove intercooler and air duct as an assembly. Cap turbocharger inlet. Remove top cover and baffle plate from side of intercooler.

**5)** On all models, remove ignition coil and cooling fan. Disconnect coolant hose from bottom of radiator. Disconnect throttle cable. Disconnect all remaining wiring and vacuum hoses. Disconnect and plug end of line to clutch release cylinder (if equipped).

**6)** Release fuel pressure. See FUEL PRESSURE RELEASE. Disconnect fuel lines at fuel pressure regulator and fuel injection manifold. Remove A/C compressor and place it on A/C condenser. DO NOT disconnect A/C hoses. Remove engine mount bolts. Attach engine hoist and lifting sling.

**7)** Lift engine slightly. Disconnect remaining inboard drive axle joint. Remove return line from power steering pump. Remove oil pressure sensor and oil cooler lines at oil filter. Ensure all wiring, hoses, and other attachments have been removed from engine. Lift engine and transaxle from vehicle as an assembly. Cover CV joints at transaxle.

**8)** To separate transaxle from engine, drain engine oil and remove inspection cover. Remove starter. Disconnect throttle cable. Remove engine-to-transaxle bolts. Remove 4 converter-to-flexplate bolts. Turn flexplate until angles are horizontal. Unbolt engine from transaxle.

**Installation – 1)** Thoroughly clean mating surfaces for transaxle and engine. Use gasket sealer on new gasket when assembling transaxle and engine. Coat flexplate-to-converter bolts with thread sealer.

**2)** Tilt engine forward slightly while lowering into position. Pack inner universal joints with grease. To complete installation, reverse removal procedure. Adjust shift cable. Tighten bolts to specification. See TORQUE SPECIFICATIONS table at end of article. Check cooling system for leaks.

### 9000 SERIES

**Removal – 1)** Open hood. Remove battery and windshield washer fluid reservoir. Disconnect electrical cable from battery tray. Remove clamps for positive cable under the tray. Remove fuel filter. Remove battery tray.

**2)** Disconnect wiring from mass airflow meter. Remove mass airflow meter. Disconnect by-pass hose from turbocharger output duct (if equipped). Remove turbocharger outlet duct (if equipped).

**3)** Disconnect throttle cable from throttle body. Remove gear selector cable from transaxle lever. DO NOT separate ball joint. Disconnect oil cooler hose from top of transaxle.

**4)** Disconnect gear selector cable from transaxle. Disconnect oil cooler hose from front of transaxle. Remove turbocharger oil supply hose clamp (if equipped) from transaxle.

**5)** Remove negative battery cable. Disconnect speed sensor wiring from transaxle. Remove transaxle-to-engine bolts that are accessible from above. Remove upper starter retaining bolt. Disconnect starter brace.

**6)** Support engine from above. Raise and support vehicle. Remove left front wheel. Remove fender liner. Remove starter motor without disconnecting cables. Suspend starter motor from chassis.

**7)** Remove torque converter-to-drive plate bolts. Remove 2 ball joint-to-lower suspension arm bolts. Disconnect anti-roll bar from lower suspension arm.

**8)** Remove front engine mount bolt. Remove bolts that retain subframe to front of vehicle. Loosen bolts that retain rear of subframe to vehicle. Carefully lower front of subframe.

**9)** Remove clamps around axle shaft universal joint boots. Withdraw axle shafts from transaxle. Support weight of transaxle with jack.

**10)** Remove remaining transaxle-to-engine bolts. Separate transaxle from engine. Lower transaxle from vehicle.

**Installation –** To install transaxle, reverse removal procedure. Coat torque converter-to-drive plate bolts with thread sealant. Refill transaxle with fluid. Tighten bolts to specification. See TORQUE SPECIFICATIONS table. Adjust throttle and gear selector cables.

## TORQUE SPECIFICATIONS

***TORQUE SPECIFICATIONS***

| Application | Ft. Lbs. (N.m) |
|---|---|
| Flexplate-To-Torque Converter Bolt | 24-29 (33-39) |
| Tie Rod End-To-Steering Knuckle | 35-44 (47-60) |
| Wheel Lug Nut | |
| 900 Series | 65-80 (88-108) |
| 9000 Series | 76-90 (103-122) |
| Other Bolts | |
| 5 mm | 4 (5) |
| 6 mm | 7 (10) |
| 8 mm | 15 (20) |
| 10 mm | 30 (40) |

# SUBARU

# 1991 SUBARU CONTENTS

## GENERAL INFORMATION [1]

### ALL MODELS



[1] – For all GENERAL INFORMATION, see front of Volume 1.

## ENGINE PERFORMANCE

### INTRODUCTION



### EMISSION APPLICATIONS



### SERVICE & ADJUSTMENT SPECIFICATIONS



## ENGINE PERFORMANCE (Cont.)

### ON-VEHICLE ADJUSTMENTS



### THEORY & OPERATION



### BASIC DIAGNOSTIC PROCEDURES



### SELF-DIAGNOSTICS

# 1991 SUBARU CONTENTS (Cont.)

## ENGINE PERFORMANCE (Cont.)



## ELECTRICAL



## WIRING DIAGRAMS

# 1991 SUBARU CONTENTS (Cont.)

## SAFETY EQUIPMENT

### INSTRUMENT PANELS



### POWER MIRRORS



### REAR WINDOW DEFOGGER



### STEERING COLUMN SWITCHES



### WIPER/WASHER SYSTEMS



## ENGINES

### 1.2L 3-CYLINDER



### 1.8L 4-CYLINDER



### 2.2L 4-CYLINDER



### 2.7L 6-CYLINDER

# 1991 SUBARU CONTENTS (Cont.)

## CLUTCHES



## DRIVE AXLES



## BRAKES



## WHEEL ALIGNMENT

# 1991 SUBARU CONTENTS (Cont.)

## SUSPENSION



## STEERING



## STEERING (Cont.)



## TRANSMISSION SERVICING

# 1991 ENGINE PERFORMANCE
# Subaru Introduction

## 1991 MODEL COVERAGE

| MODEL | BODY CODE | ENGINE | ENGINE ID | FUEL SYSTEM | IGNITION [1] SYSTEM |
|---|---|---|---|---|---|
| Justy | A & D | 1.2L 3-Cylinder | [2] 7 | Carbureted | Magnetic |
| | | 1.2L 3-Cylinder | [2] 7 | PFI | Magnetic |
| Legacy | | | | | |
| Sedan | C | 2.2L 4-Cylinder | 6 | PFI | DIS |
| Station Wagon | J | 2.2L 4-Cylinder | 6 | PFI | DIS |
| Touring Wagon | F | 2.2L 4-Cylinder | 6 | PFI | DIS |
| Loyale | | | | | |
| Sedan | C | 1.8L 4-Cylinder | [3] 4 | [4] PFI | Optical |
| 3-Door Coupe | G | 1.8L 4-Cylinder | [3] 4 | [4] PFI | Optical |
| Station Wagon | N | 1.8L 4-Cylinder | [3] 4 | [4] PFI | Optical |
| Touring Wagon | K | 1.8L 4-Cylinder | [3] 4 | [4] PFI | Optical |
| XT | X | 1.8L 4-Cylinder | [5] 4 | PFI | Optical |
| XT6 | X | 2.7L 6-Cylinder | [6] 8 | PFI | Optical |

[1] - Computer Controlled Ignition.
[2] - Engine VIN is 7 for 2WD and 8 for 4WD.
[3] - Engine VIN is 4 for 2WD and 5 for 4WD.
[4] - Non-turbo models are equipped with Throttle Body Injection (TBI).
[5] - Engine VIN is 4 without air suspension and 7 with air suspension.
[6] - Engine VIN is 8 without air suspension and 9 with air suspension.

## VIN DEFINITION

**JF1BC632XMB00001**

① ② ③ ④ ⑤ ⑥ ⑦ ⑧ ⑨ ⑩ ⑪ ⑫ ⑬ ⑭ ⑮ ⑯ ⑰

① Indicates Nation of Origin.
② Indicates Manufacturer & Make.
③ Indicates Type of Vehicle.
④ Indicates Line.
⑤ Indicates Body Type.
⑥ **Indicates Engine.**
⑦ Indicates Model.
⑧ Indicates Weight Class & Restraint Type.
⑨ Indicates Check Digit.
⑩ **Indicates Model Year.**
⑪ Indicates Assembly Plant & Transmission Type.
⑫ ⑬ ⑭ ⑮ ⑯ ⑰ Indicates Production Sequence.

91D17080

***MODEL YEAR VIN CODE APPLICATION***

| VIN Code | Model Year |
|---|---|
| J | 1988 |
| K | 1989 |
| L | 1990 |
| M | 1991 |

## ENGINE CODE LOCATION

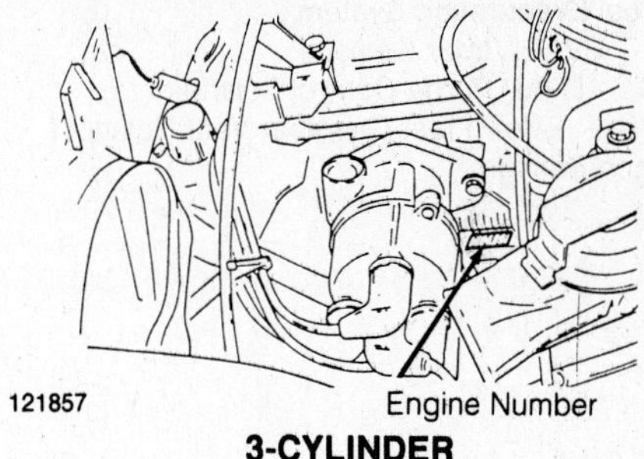


121857
**3-CYLINDER**

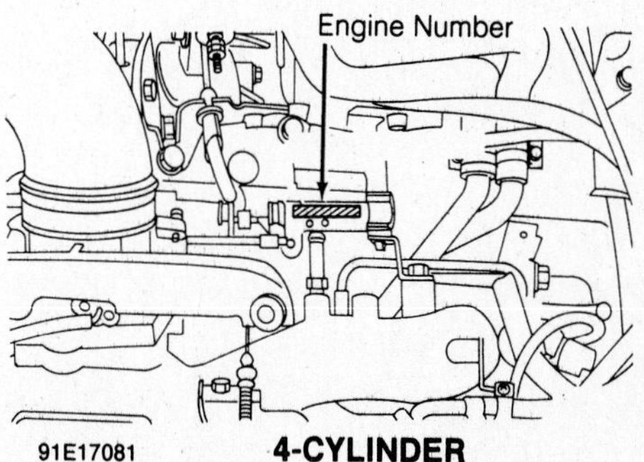


91E17081
**4-CYLINDER**

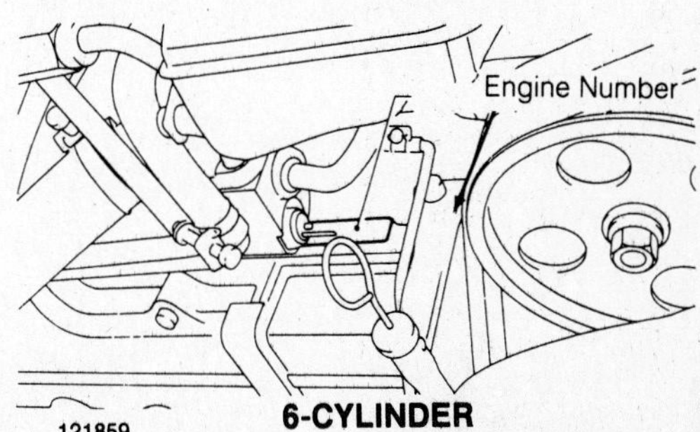


121859
**6-CYLINDER**

Courtesy of Subaru of America, Inc.

# 1991 ENGINE PERFORMANCE
# Emission Applications

*1991 SUBARU EMISSION SYSTEMS*

| Model, Engine & Fuel System | Emission Control Systems & Devices | Remarks |
|---|---|---|
| Justy<br>1.2L (2-Bbl.) | **PCV, TAC, EVAP, TWC/OC, EGR, SPK, PAS, $O_2$, CEC, CE,**<br>EVAP-VC, EVAP-PCS, EVAP-FCVS,<br>EGR-SOL, PAS-ASV, SPK-CC | |
| 1.2L (PFI) | **PCV, EVAP, TWC/OC, SPK, $O_2$, CEC, CE,**<br>EVAP-VC, EVAP-PCS, SPK-CC | |
| Legacy 2.2L (PFI) Turbo &<br>Non-Turbo | **PCV, EVAP, TWC, SPK, $O_2$, CEC, CE,**<br>EVAP-VC, EVAP-PCS, SPK-CC | |
| Loyale 1.8L (TBI) &<br>1.8L (PFI) Turbo | **PCV, EVAP, TWC/OC, [1] EGR, SPK, [2] $O_2$, CEC, CE,**<br>EVAP-VC, EVAP-PCS, EGR-SOL, [3] EGR-TS, SPK-CC | [1] - TBI only.<br>[2] - California uses heated sensor.<br>[3] - California only. |
| XT 1.8L (PFI) &<br>XT6 2.7L (PFI) | **PCV, EVAP, TWC/OC, SPK, $O_2$, CEC, CE,**<br>EVAP-VC, EVAP-PCS, SPK-CC | |

**NOTE:** Major emission control systems are listed in bold type; components are listed in light type.

**CE** - CHECK ENGINE Light
**CEC** - Computerized Engine Control
**EGR** - Exhaust Gas Recirculation
**EGR-SOL** - EGR Solenoid
**EGR-TS** - EGR Temperature Sensor
**EVAP** - Fuel Evaporation System
**EVAP-VC** - EVAP Vapor Canister
**EVAP-PCS** - EVAP Purge Control Solenoid
**EVAP-FCVS** - EVAP Float Chamber Vent Solenoid
**$O_2$** - Oxygen Sensor
**PAS** - Pulse Air System
**PAS-ASV** - PAS Air Suction Valve
**PCV** - Positive Crankcase Ventilation
**PFI** - **Port Fuel Injection**
**SPK** - Spark Control System
**SPK-CC** - SPK Computer Controlled
**TAC** - Thermostatic Air Cleaner
**TBI** - **Throttle Body Injection**
**TWC** - Three-Way Catalyst
**TWC/OC** - Three-Way Catalyst/Oxidation Catalyst

# 1991 ENGINE PERFORMANCE
# Service & Adjustment Specifications

**Justy, Legacy, Loyale, XT, XT6**

## INTRODUCTION

Use this article to quickly find specifications related to servicing and on-vehicle adjustments. This is a quick-reference article to use when you are familiar with an adjustment procedure and only need a specification.

## CAPACITIES

***BATTERY SPECIFICATIONS***

| Application | Amp Hr. Rating |
|---|---|
| 1.2L | 52 |
| 1.8L & 2.2L | 78 or 111 |
| 2.7L | 99 or 111 |

***FLUID CAPACITIES***

| Application | Quantity |
|---|---|
| **1.2L** | |
| Cooling System (Including Heater) | 4.5 qts. (4.3L) |
| Crankcase (Includes Filter) | 3.0 qts. (2.8L) |
| ECVT Transaxle (Dexron-II) | 3.6 qts. (3.4L) |
| Manual Transaxle (SAE 85W-90) | |
| FWD | 2.4 qts. (2.3L) |
| 4WD | 3.5 qts. (3.3L) |
| Power Steering | 1.5 pts. (.7L) |
| Rear Differential (4WD) | 1.7 pts. (.8L) |
| **1.8L** | |
| Automatic Transaxle (Dexron-II) | |
| FWD | |
| Loyale | 6.6 qts. (6.2L) |
| XT | 9.8 qts. (9.3L) |
| 4WD | 7.0 qts. (6.6L) |
| Automatic Transaxle Differential | 2.5 pts. (1.2L) |
| Cooling System (Including Heater) | 5.8 qts. (5.5L) |
| Crankcase (Includes Filter) | 4.2 qts. (4.0L) |
| Manual Transaxle (SAE 85W-90) | |
| FWD | 2.7 qts. (2.6L) |
| 4WD | 3.5 qts. (3.3L) |
| Power Steering | 1.5 pts. (.7L) |
| Rear Differential (4WD) | 1.7 pts. (.8L) |
| **2.2L** | |
| Automatic Transaxle (Dexron-II) | |
| Non-Turbo | 8.8 qts. (8.3L) |
| Turbo | 9.4 qts. (8.9L) |
| Automatic Transaxle Differential | 1.5 qts. (1.4L) |
| Cooling System (Including Heater) | |
| Non-Turbo | 6.3 qts. (6.0L) |
| Turbo | 7.2 qts. (7.0L) |
| Crankcase (Includes Filter) | |
| Lower Level | 3.7 qts. (3.5L) |
| Upper Level | 4.8 qts. (4.5L) |
| Manual Transaxle (SAE 85W-90) | |
| FWD | 3.5 qts. (3.3L) |
| 4WD | 3.7 qts. (3.5L) |
| Power Steering | 1.5 pts. (.7L) |
| Rear Differential (4WD) | 1.7 pts. (.8L) |
| **2.7L** | |
| Automatic Transmission | |
| FWD | 9.8 qts. (9.3L) |
| 4WD | 10.0 qts. (9.5L) |
| Automatic Transmission Differential | 1.7 pts. (.8L) |
| Cooling System (Including Heater) | 7.2 qts. (7.0L) |
| Crankcase (Including Filter) | 5.3 qts. (5.0L) |
| Manual Transmission | 3.7 qts. (3.5L) |
| Power Steering | 1.5 pts. (.7L) |
| Rear Differential (4WD) | 1.7 pts. (.8L) |

## QUICK-SERVICE

### SERVICE INTERVALS & SPECIFICATIONS

***REPLACEMENT INTERVALS***

| Component | Interval (Miles) |
|---|---|
| Air Filter | 30,000 |
| Camshaft Timing Belt | 60,000 |
| Coolant (Radiator) | 30,000 |
| ECVT Fluid | 30,000 |
| Fuel Filter | 30,000 |
| Oil & Filter | 7500 |
| Spark Plugs | 30,000 |

***BELT ADJUSTMENT***

| Application | Deflection In. (mm) |
|---|---|
| Alternator Belt | |
| Except XT | .35-.39 (9-10) |
| XT | .35-.43 (9-11) |
| Power Steering Belt | |
| Except XT | .35-.43 (9-11) |
| XT | .28-.35 (7-9) |
| A/C Belt | |
| Except XT | .43-.47 (11-12) |
| XT | .40-.47 (10-12) |
| A/C & P/S Equipped Models | |
| Except XT | .30-.33 (7.5-8.5) |
| XT | .24-.31 (6-8) |

## MECHANICAL CHECKS

### ENGINE COMPRESSION

***COMPRESSION SPECIFICATIONS***

| Application | Specification |
|---|---|
| **1.2L** | |
| Compression Ratio | 9.1:1 |
| Compression Pressure | 135-156 psi (9.5-11.0 kg/cm²) |
| Maximum Variation Between Cylinders | 28 psi (2.0 kg/cm²) |
| **1.8L** | |
| Compression Ratio | |
| Non-Turbo | 9.5:1 |
| Turbo | 7.7:1 |
| Compression Pressure | |
| Non-Turbo | 168 psi (11.8 kg/cm²) |
| Turbo | 145 psi (10.2 kg/cm²) |
| Maximum Variation Between Cylinders | 28 psi (2.0 kg/cm²) |
| **2.2L** | |
| Compression Ratio | |
| Non-Turbo | 9.5:1 |
| Turbo | 8.0:1 |
| Compression Pressure | |
| Non-Turbo | 156-185 psi (11.0-13.0 kg/cm²) |
| Turbo | 142-171 psi (10-12 kg/cm²) |
| Maximum Variation Between Cylinders | 28 psi (2.0 kg/cm²) |
| **2.7L** | |
| Compression Ratio | 9.5:1 |
| Compression Pressure | 139-168 psi (9.8-11.8 kg/cm²) |
| Maximum Variation Between Cylinders | 28 psi (2.0 kg/cm²) |

### VALVE CLEARANCE

***NOTE: All 1.8L, 2.2L and 2.7L engines are equipped with hydraulic lash adjusters. No adjustments are required.***

***VALVE CLEARANCE SPECIFICATIONS***

| Application | [1] In. (mm) |
|---|---|
| 1.2L | |
| Intake | .006 (.15) |
| Exhaust | .010 (.25) |

[1] – Adjust valves with engine cold.

# 1991 ENGINE PERFORMANCE
# Service & Adjustment Specifications (Cont.)

## IGNITION SYSTEM

### IGNITION COIL

*IGNITION COIL RESISTANCE – OHMS @ 68°F (20°C)*

| Application | Primary | Secondary |
|---|---|---|
| 1.2L | .81-.99 | 8500-11,000 |
| 1.8L & 2.7L | .84-1.02 | 8000-12,000 |
| 2.2L | | |
| Automatic Transaxle | .63-.77 | 10,400-15,600 |
| Manual Transaxle | .62-.76 | 17,900-24,500 |

### DISTRIBUTOR SENSORS

***NOTE:*** *Information on distributor sensors is not available from manufacturer. See IGNITION CHECKS in appropriate BASIC DIAGNOSTIC PROCEDURES article for test procedures.*

### HIGH TENSION WIRE RESISTANCE

*JUSTY HIGH TENSION WIRE RESISTANCE*

| Application | Ohms |
|---|---|
| No. 1 | 458-10,680 |
| No. 2 | 411-959 |
| No. 3 | 290-676 |
| Coil | 459-10,710 |

*LEGACY HIGH TENSION WIRE RESISTANCE*

| Application | Ohms | Wire Length In. (mm) |
|---|---|---|
| No. 1 | 495-11,560 | 21.25 (540) |
| No. 2 | 486-11,330 | 21.65 (550) |
| No. 3 | 495-11,560 | 21.25 (540) |
| No. 4 | 524-12,230 | 23.62 (600) |

*LOYALE HIGH TENSION WIRE RESISTANCE*

| Application | Ohms (PFI) | Ohms (TBI) |
|---|---|---|
| No. 1 | 243-567 | 243-567 |
| No. 2 | 948-22,130 | 838-19,560 |
| No. 3 | 958-22,360 | 790-18,440 |
| No. 4 | 241-562 | 241-562 |

*XT & XT6 HIGH TENSION WIRE RESISTANCE*

| Application | Ohms (1.8L) | Ohms (2.7L) |
|---|---|---|
| No. 1 | 243-567 | 243-567 |
| No. 2 | 947-23,030 | 10,860-25,330 |
| No. 3 | 958-22,360 | 11,240-26,230 |
| No. 4 | 241-562 | 452-10,550 |
| No. 5 | ..... | 11,430-26,680 |
| No. 6 | ..... | 260-607 |

## SPARK PLUGS

*SPARK PLUG TYPE*

| Application | NGK | Nippondenso |
|---|---|---|
| 2.2L | [1] BKR6E-11 | [2] K20PUR-11 |
| All Other Engines | [3] BPR6ES-11 | [4] W20EPR-U11 |

[1] - Spark Plug No. BKR5E-11 or BKR7E-11 may also be used.
[2] - Spark Plug No. K16PUR-11 or K22PUR-11 may also be used.
[3] - Spark Plug No. BPR5ES-11 or BPR7ES-11 may also be used.
[4] - Spark Plug No. W16EPR-U11 or W22EPR-U11 may also be used.

*SPARK PLUG SPECIFICATIONS*

| Application | Gap In. (mm) | Torque Ft. Lbs. (N.m) |
|---|---|---|
| All Engines | .039-.043 (1.0-1.1) | 15 (20) |

## FIRING ORDER & TIMING MARKS

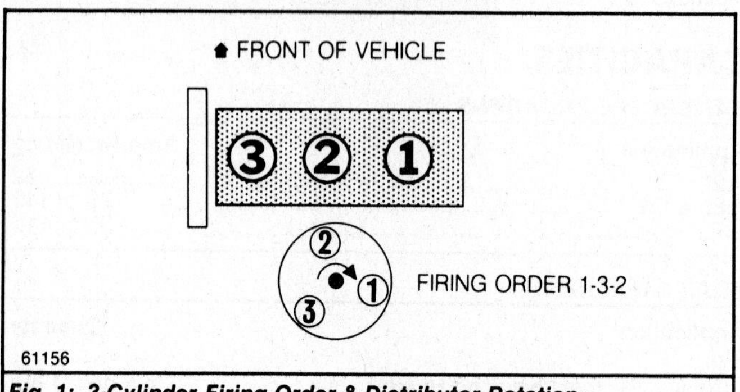


*Fig. 1: 3-Cylinder Firing Order & Distributor Rotation*

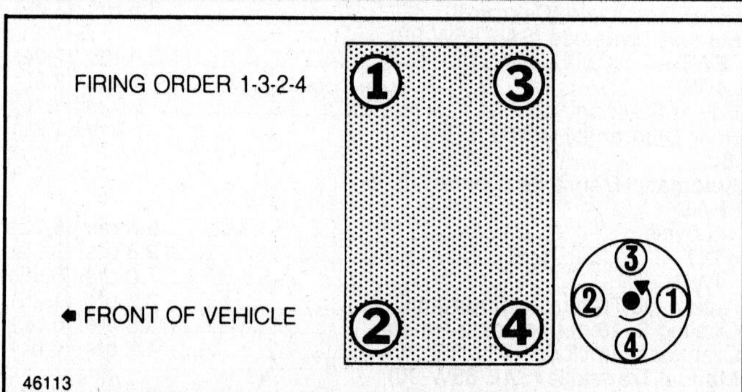


*Fig. 2: 4-Cylinder Firing Order & Distributor Rotation*

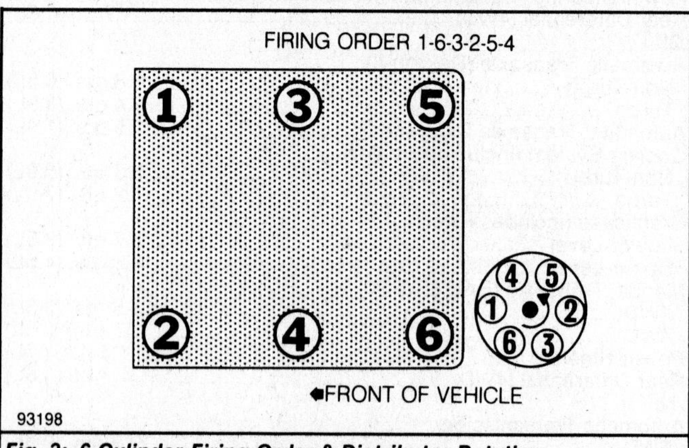


*Fig. 3: 6-Cylinder Firing Order & Distributor Rotation*

*IGNITION TIMING (Degrees BTDC @ RPM)*

| Application | Man. Trans. | Auto. Trans. |
|---|---|---|
| 1.2L | [1] 5 @ 800 | [1] 5 @ 850 |
| 1.8L | | |
| Non-Turbo | 20 @ 700 | 20 @ 700 |
| Turbo | 20 @ 800 | 20 @ 800 |
| 2.2L | | |
| Non-Turbo | 18-22 @ 700 | 12-28 @ 700 |
| Turbo | 7-23 @ 700 | 7-23 @ 700 |
| 2.7L | 20 @ 750 | 20 @ 750 |

[1] – With test mode connector connected.

# 1991 ENGINE PERFORMANCE
# Service & Adjustment Specifications (Cont.)

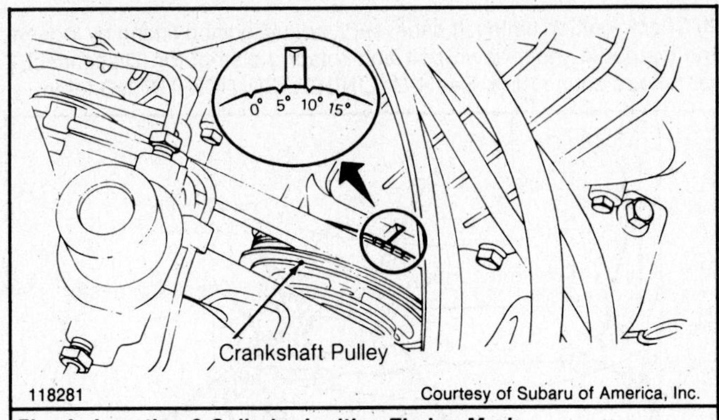


*Fig. 4: Locating 3-Cylinder Ignition Timing Mark*

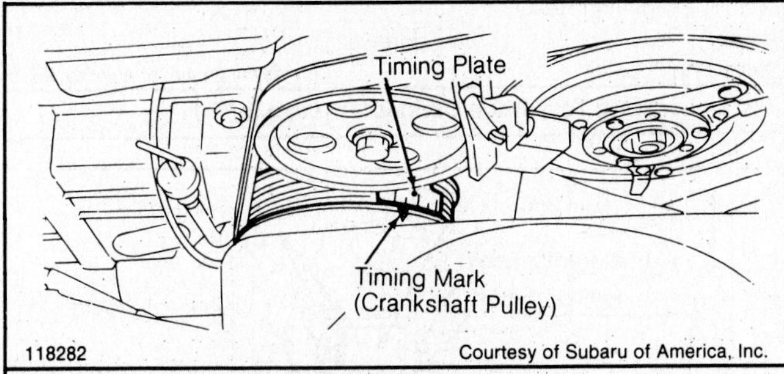


*Fig. 5: Locating 4-Cylinder Ignition Timing Mark*

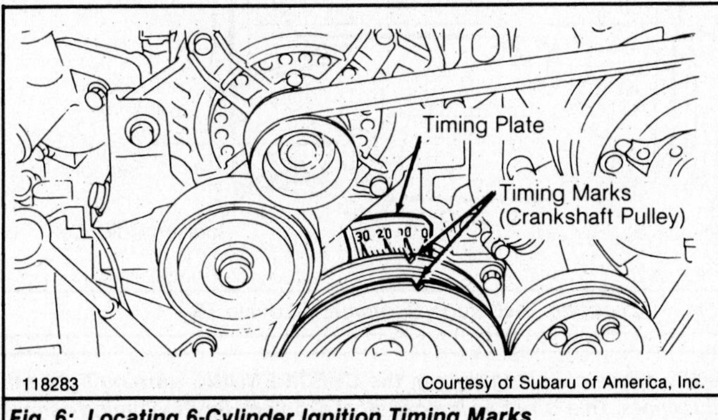


*Fig. 6: Locating 6-Cylinder Ignition Timing Marks*

## DISTRIBUTOR SPECIFICATIONS

***NOTE: All models use electronic ignition with spark timing controlled by emission system control unit.***

*PICK-UP COIL AIR GAP*

| Application | In. (mm) |
|---|---|
| 1.2L | .008-.016 (0.2-0.4) |

# FUEL SYSTEM

## FUEL PUMP

***NOTE: Fuel pump performance measures fuel pressure and volume availability, not regulated fuel pressure.***

*FUEL PUMP PERFORMANCE*

| Application | Pressure psi (kg/cm²) | Min. Vol. in 30 sec. Pts. (L) |
|---|---|---|
| 1.2L 2-Bbl. | 1.3-2.0 (.09-.14) | .35 (.17) |
| 1.2L PFI | [1] | [1] |
| 1.8L | | |
| Loyale | | |
| PFI | 61-71 (4.3-5.0) | 1.7 (.8) |
| TBI | 36-50 (2.5-3.5) | 1.4 (.7) |
| XT | 36 (2.5) | 1.4 (.7) |
| 2.2L | 36 (2.5) | 1.4 (.7) |
| 2.7L | 37 (2.6) | 1.7 (.8) |

[1] – Information is not available from manufacturer.

*REGULATED FUEL PRESSURE*

| Application | At Idle psi (kg/cm²) |
|---|---|
| Except Justy | 36 (2.6) |
| Justy | 31-34 (2.2-2.4) |

## INJECTOR RESISTANCE

*INJECTOR RESISTANCE SPECIFICATIONS*

| Application | Ohms |
|---|---|
| 1.2L | 10.0-18.0 |
| 1.8L | |
| PFI | 2.0-3.0 |
| TBI | 0.5-2.0 |
| 2.2L | 11.0-12.0 |
| 2.7L | 13.0-14.5 |

## IDLE SPEED & MIXTURE

*IDLE SPEED SPECIFICATIONS*

| Application | RPM |
|---|---|
| 1.2L [1] | |
| 2-Bbl. | 750-850 |
| PFI | 650-750 |
| 1.8L PFI | |
| Non-Turbo | 600-800 |
| Turbo | 700-900 |
| 1.8L TBI | 500-600 |
| 2.2L | |
| With Accessories Off | 600-800 |
| With Accessories On | 800-900 |
| 2.7L | 650-850 |

[1] – With test mode and read memory connector connected.

## FAST IDLE SPEED

***NOTE: Fast idle speed is not available from manufacturer. See REMOVAL, OVERHAUL & ADJUSTMENT article for FAST IDLE ADJUSTMENT procedure.***

## THROTTLE POSITION SENSOR

***NOTE: Refer to ON-VEHICLE ADJUSTMENTS article for Throttle Position Sensor (TPS) adjustment procedures.***

# 1991 ENGINE PERFORMANCE
# On-Vehicle Adjustments

### Justy, Legacy, Loyale, XT, XT6

## ENGINE MECHANICAL

Before performing any on-vehicle adjustments to fuel or ignition system, ensure engine mechanical condition is okay.

## VALVE CLEARANCE

***NOTE: All 1.8L, 2.2L and 2.7L engines are equipped with hydraulic lash adjusters. No adjustment is required.***

### 3-CYLINDER VALVE CLEARANCE

**Justy - 1)** Place cylinder to be adjusted to top dead center position of compression stroke. Insert thickness gauge between valve and valve rocker arm, and check valve clearance. Adjust valves when engine is cold. Use Valve Clearance Adjuster (498767000) and adjust to specification. See VALVE CLEARANCE SPECIFICATIONS table.
**2)** After adjustment, rotate crankshaft several turns and recheck valve clearance.

***3-CYLINDER VALVE CLEARANCE SPECIFICATIONS***

| Application | [1] Clearance In. (mm) |
|---|---|
| Intake | .006 (.15) |
| Exhaust | .010 (.25) |

[1] - Adjust valves with engine cold.

## IGNITION TIMING

### 3-CYLINDER IGNITION TIMING

**Justy - 1)** Warm engine to normal operating temperature. Place transmission in Neutral and turn off all accessories. Disconnect test mode and read memory connectors. *See Fig. 1.*
**2)** Start engine and check ignition timing. If necessary, loosen distributor hold-down bolt and adjust ignition timing by rotating distributor. Reconnect test mode and read memory connectors.

***3-CYLINDER IGNITION TIMING***

| Application | [1] Degrees BTDC @ RPM |
|---|---|
| M/T | 5 @ 800 |
| A/T | 5 @ 850 |

[1] - With test mode connector connected.

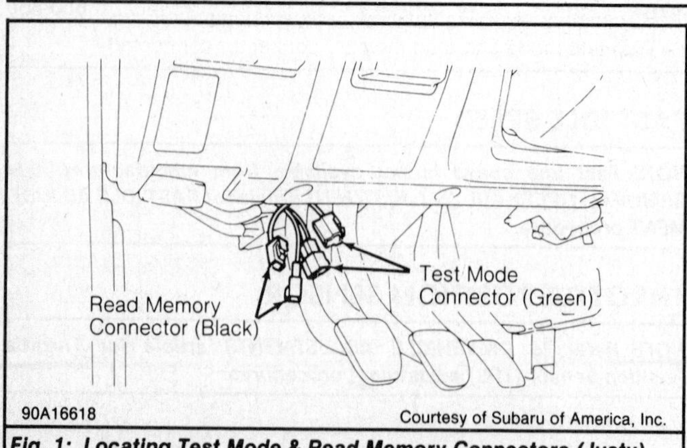


***Fig. 1: Locating Test Mode & Read Memory Connectors (Justy)***

### 4-CYLINDER IGNITION TIMING

**Loyale & XT - 1)** Ensure engine is at normal operating temperature and idle speed is correct. Place transaxle in Neutral (M/T), or Park (A/T).
**2)** Ensure throttle valve is closed and throttle position sensor is correctly adjusted. Connect 2 test mode connectors together. *See Figs. 2-4.*

**3)** Check ignition timing. If necessary, adjust ignition timing by loosening distributor hold-down bolt and rotating distributor. Disconnect 2 test mode connectors. See 4-CYLINDER IGNITION TIMING table.

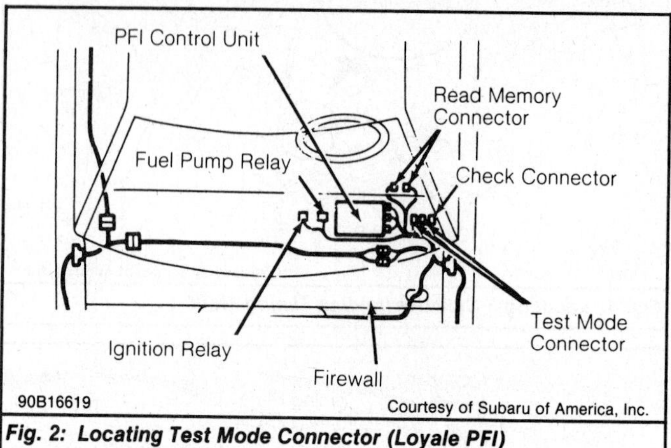


***Fig. 2: Locating Test Mode Connector (Loyale PFI)***

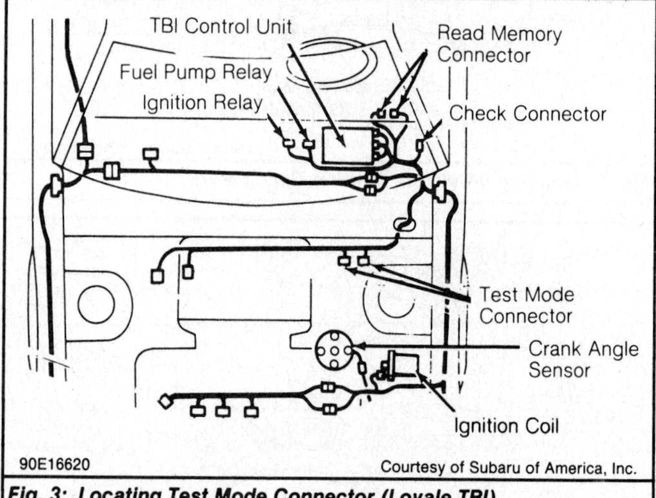


***Fig. 3: Locating Test Mode Connector (Loyale TBI)***

***NOTE: When checking timing, the CHECK ENGINE warning light will illuminate. This is not an indication of problem. Ignition timing cannot be set if idle contacts in TPS are open and test mode connector is not plugged in.***

**Legacy - 1)** Ensure engine is at normal operating temperature and idle speed is correct. Place transaxle in Neutral (M/T), or Park (A/T). Attach timing light to No. 1 spark plug wire.
**2)** Check timing mark located on crankshaft pulley. If timing is not as specified in 4-CYLINDER IGNITION TIMING table, check self-diagnostic system for trouble code(s) and repair as necessary. See SELF-DIAGNOSTICS article.

***4-CYLINDER IGNITION TIMING***

| Application | Degrees BTDC @ RPM |
|---|---|
| 1.8L Non-Turbo | 20 @ 700 |
| 1.8L Turbo | 20 @ 800 |
| 2.2L M/T | 18-22 @ 700 |
| 2.2L A/T | 12-28 @ 700 |

### 6-CYLINDER IGNITION TIMING

**XT6 - 1)** Ensure engine is at normal operating temperature and idle speed is correct. Place transaxle in Neutral (M/T) or Park (A/T).
**2)** Ensure throttle valve is closed and throttle position sensor is correctly adjusted. Plug in 2 test mode connector wires. *See Fig. 4.*

# 1991 ENGINE PERFORMANCE
# On-Vehicle Adjustments (Cont.)

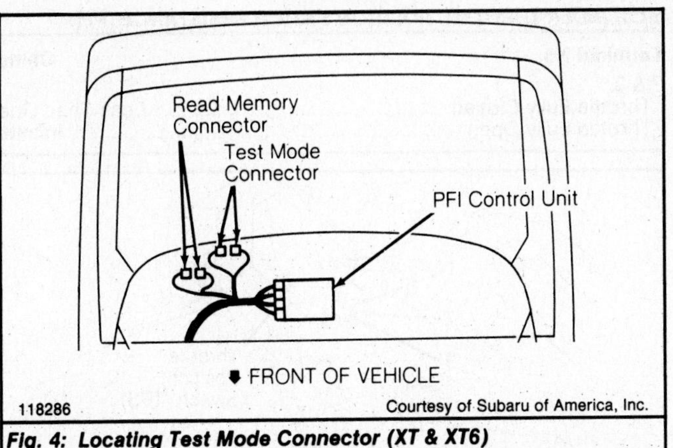


*Fig. 4: Locating Test Mode Connector (XT & XT6)*

**3)** Check ignition timing. Timing marks are on crankshaft pulley. If necessary, adjust ignition timing by loosening distributor hold-down bolt and rotating distributor.

***NOTE: When checking timing, the CHECK ENGINE warning light will come on; this is not an indication of problem. Ignition timing cannot be set if idle contacts in TPS are open and test mode connector is not plugged in.***

***6-CYLINDER IGNITION TIMING***

| Application | Degrees BTDC @ RPM |
|---|---|
| XT6 | 20 @ 750 |

## IDLE SPEED & MIXTURE

***NOTE: Mixture adjustment is NOT a part of normal tune-up procedure and should not be performed unless mixture control unit is replaced, or vehicle fails emissions testing. Idle mixture is electronically controlled on fuel injected models; adjustments are not necessary.***

## COLD (FAST) IDLE

***NOTE: Fast idle on TBI engines is controlled by air control valve. On PFI engines, fast idle is controlled by auxiliary air valve. Adjustment is not necessary on either system.***

**Justy (Carbureted)** – Fast idle is adjusted by measuring throttle valve opening. Measure clearance between throttle valve and bore of carburetor. On M/T models, clearance should be .030" (.77 mm). On A/T models, clearance should be .034" (.86 mm).

## DASHPOT

**Justy (PFI) & XT – 1)** While slowly returning throttle valve from fully open position, read engine RPM when dashpot lever comes in contact with dashpot.
**2)** On Justy, ensure engine speed is 2200-2400 RPM when dashpot lever contacts dashpot. On XT, ensure engine speed is 2800-3400 RPM when dashpot lever contacts dashpot.
**3)** If engine speed is not to specification, loosen lock nut and turn adjusting screw to obtain correct adjustment.

## 3-CYLINDER IDLE SPEED

**Justy – 1)** Ensure ignition timing is correct. Ensure vacuum hoses, blow-by hoses, rocker arm cover, oil cap and other components connected to intake system are securely attached.
**2)** Warm engine and oxygen sensor by operating engine at 2500 RPM for about one minute after engine reaches normal operating temperature. Disconnect and plug canister purge hose at check valve (near intake manifold).
**3)** Connect the test mode and read memory connectors. *See Fig. 1.* Place transaxle in Neutral (M/T) or Park (A/T) position. Start engine and use idle speed screw to adjust idle speed to specification. See 3-CYLINDER IDLE SPEED SPECIFICATIONS table. Disconnect test mode and read memory connector.

***3-CYLINDER IDLE SPEED SPECIFICATIONS***

| Application | [1] RPM |
|---|---|
| Carbureted | 750-850 |
| PFI | 650-750 |

[1] – With test mode and read memory connector connected.

## 3-CYLINDER IDLE MIXTURE

***NOTE: Idle mixture on fuel injected models is electronically controlled; adjustments are not necessary.***

**Justy (Carbureted – 1)** Warm engine to operating temperature. Connect dwell meter to Yellow/Red wire of Pink 6-pin check connector located on left inner fender panel. Set dwell meter on 4-cylinder scale and observe needle movement with engine at idle. If needle fluctuates in proper range (mixture solenoid duty cycle is correct), no other action is necessary.
**2)** If needle fluctuates out of normal range, raise engine speed to 2000-3000 RPM for 2-3 minutes. Return engine to idle and set idle speed. If needle still fluctuates outside range, check spark plugs and ignition timing.
**3)** If spark plugs and ignition timing are okay, check vacuum hose routing, air cleaner element and carburetor. Adjust idle mixture screw until mixture solenoid duty ratio (at idle) is correct. See MIXTURE SOLENOID DUTY RATIO table.

***3-CYLINDER MIXTURE SOLENOID DUTY RATIO [1]***

| Altitude | Degrees | Allowable Variation (Degrees) |
|---|---|---|
| Sea Level | 36.0 | 4.5 |
| 5250 Ft. | 67.5 | 4.5 |

[1] – Adjustment is made at idle.

***NOTE: If correct duty ratio cannot be obtained, see CARBURETOR in REMOVAL, OVERHAUL & INSTALLATION article.***

## 4-CYLINDER IDLE SPEED

**Loyale (PFI) & XT – 1)** Ensure vacuum hoses, blow-by hoses, rocker arm cover, oil cap and other components connected to intake system are securely attached. Warm engine and oxygen sensor by operating engine at 2500 RPM for one minute after engine reaches normal operating temperature.
**2)** Plug canister purge hose after disconnecting it from intake manifold. Ensure auxiliary air valve is completely closed. Place transaxle in Neutral (M/T) or Park (A/T) position. To adjust idle speed, rotate idle adjusting screw on throttle body, at base of air induction hose. *See Fig. 6.* See 1.8L IDLE SPEED & CO LEVEL table.
**Loyale (TBI) – 1)** Warm engine to normal operating temperature. Turn engine off. Disconnect electrical connector for air control valve. Start engine.
**2)** Turn idle adjustment screw and adjust idle speed to 500-600 RPM. *See Fig. 5.* Reconnect electrical connector for air control valve. Ensure idle speed is within specification. See 1.8L IDLE SPEED & CO LEVEL table.

***1.8L IDLE SPEED & CO LEVEL (LOYALE & XT)***

| Application | Idle RPM | CO Level |
|---|---|---|
| PFI | | |
| Non-Turbo | 600-800 | [1] .1% |
| Turbo | 700-900 | [1] .1% |
| TBI | 500-600 | [1] |

[1] – Idle mixture is computer controlled; adjustment is not necessary.

# 1991 ENGINE PERFORMANCE
# On-Vehicle Adjustments (Cont.)

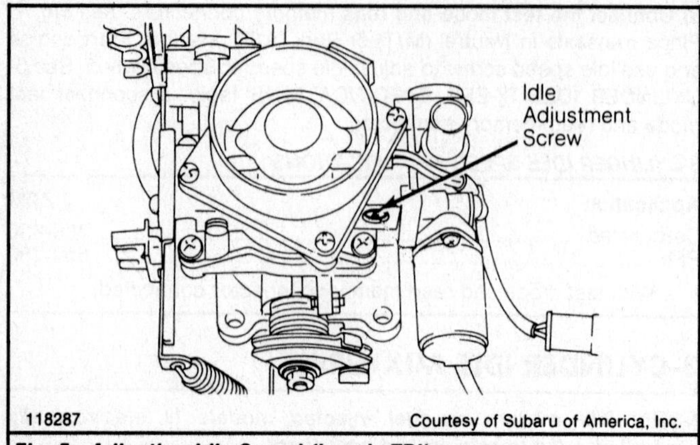


***Fig. 5: Adjusting Idle Speed (Loyale TBI)***

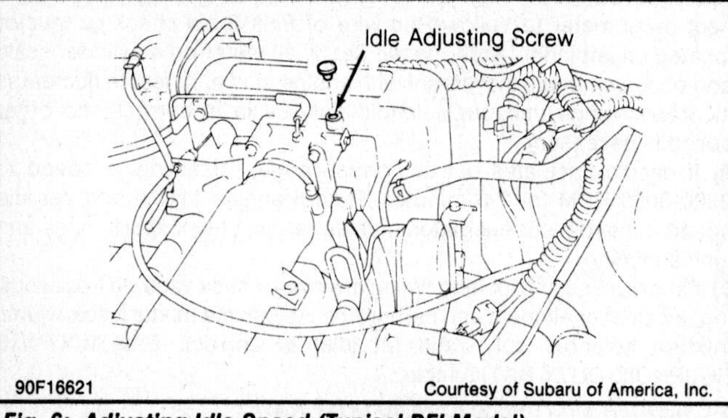


***Fig. 6: Adjusting Idle Speed (Typical PFI Model)***

**Legacy – 1)** Ensure air filter is clean, vacuum hoses are properly routed, and timing is correct. Warm engine to operating temperature and attach inductive pick-up tachometer to No. 1 spark plug wire.

***NOTE: Because spark plugs No. 1 and No. 2 fire simultaneously, some tachometers may register twice the actual engine speed.***

**2)** Check idle speed with all accessories off, then check with all accessories on. If idle speed is not specified in 2.2L IDLE SPEED SPECIFICATIONS table, check self-diagnostic system for trouble code(s) and repair as necessary. See SELF-DIAGNOSTICS article.

***2.2L IDLE SPEED SPECIFICATIONS (LEGACY)***

| Application | RPM |
|---|---|
| Accessories Off | 600-800 |
| Accessories On | 800-900 |

## 6-CYLINDER IDLE SPEED ADJUSTMENT

Idle speed is electronically controlled; adjustment is not necessary.

***6-CYLINDER IDLE SPEED SPECIFICATIONS***

| Application | RPM |
|---|---|
| XT6 | 650-850 |

# THROTTLE POSITION SENSOR/SWITCH

## 3-CYLINDER THROTTLE POSITION SWITCH

**Justy (PFI) – 1)** With ignition off, disconnect Throttle Position Switch (TPS) connector. Using an ohmmeter, measure resistance between terminals No. 2 and 3 with throttle fully closed, then measure with throttle fully open. *See Fig. 7.* Record reading.

**2)** Ensure readings are as specified. See 3-CYLINDER THROTTLE POSITION SWITCH RESISTANCE (PFI) table. If necessary, loosen attaching screws and rotate TPS until correct resistance is obtained. Replace TPS if resistance cannot be adjusted to specification.

***3-CYLINDER THROTTLE POSITION SWITCH RESISTANCE (PFI)***

| Terminal No. | Ohms |
|---|---|
| 2 & 3 | |
| Throttle Fully Closed | Less Than One |
| Throttle Fully Open | Infinite |

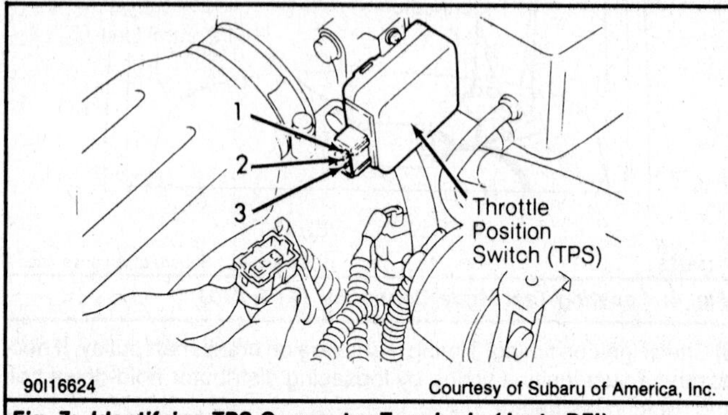


***Fig. 7: Identifying TPS Connector Terminals (Justy PFI)***

## 4-CYLINDER THROTTLE POSITION SENSOR

***NOTE: All testing procedures are performed with engine at normal operating temperature.***

**Legacy – 1)** With engine off, disconnect TPS connector. Using an ohmmeter, measure resistance between terminals No. 2 and 3. *See Fig. 8.* Record reading. Measure resistance between terminals No. 2 and 4 with throttle fully closed, then measure with throttle fully open. Record readings. Ensure readings are as specified. See 4-CYLINDER THROTTLE POSITION SENSOR RESISTANCE table.

**2)** If adjustment is necessary, loosen attaching screws. Check continuity by inserting a .028" (0.7 mm) feeler gauge between throttle lever and stopper screw. Continuity should exist. Continuity should not exist when gauge thickness is changed to .035" (0.9 mm). Rotate TPS until correct resistance is obtained. Tighten attaching screws. Replace TPS if resistance cannot be adjusted to specification.

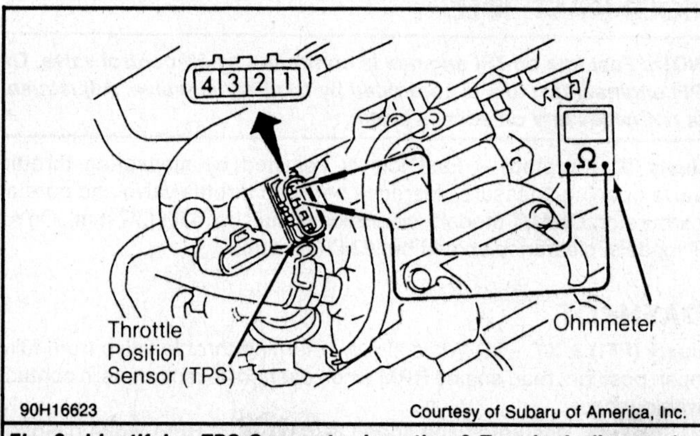


***Fig. 8: Identifying TPS Connector Location & Terminals (Legacy)***

**Loyale (PFI) – 1)** With engine off, disconnect TPS connector. Using an ohmmeter, measure resistance between terminals No. 1 and 3. *See Fig. 9.* Record reading. Measure resistance between terminals No. 1 and 2 with throttle fully closed, then measure with throttle fully open. Record readings.

**2)** Ensure readings are as specified. See 4-CYLINDER THROTTLE POSITION SENSOR RESISTANCE table. If necessary, loosen attaching screws and rotate TPS until correct resistance is obtained. Replace TPS if resistance cannot be adjusted to specification.

**Loyale (TBI) – 1)** With ignition off, disconnect TPS connector. Using an ohmmeter, measure resistance between terminals "B" and "D". *See Fig. 9.* Record reading. Measure resistance between terminals "B" and "C" with throttle fully closed, then measure with throttle fully open. Record readings.

# 1991 ENGINE PERFORMANCE
# On-Vehicle Adjustments (Cont.)

**2)** Ensure readings are as specified. See 4-CYLINDER THROTTLE POSITION SENSOR RESISTANCE table. If necessary, loosen attaching screws and rotate TPS until correct resistance is obtained. Replace TPS if resistance cannot be adjusted to specification.

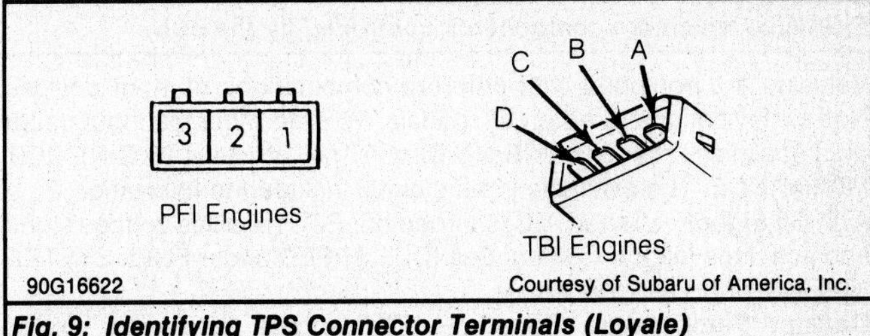


***Fig. 9: Identifying TPS Connector Terminals (Loyale)***

***4-CYLINDER THROTTLE POSITION SENSOR RESISTANCE***

| Terminal No. | Ohms |
|---|---|
| **Legacy** | |
| No. 2 & 3 | 12,000 |
| No. 2 & 4 | |
| Throttle Fully Closed | 10,000-12,000 |
| Throttle Fully Open | 3000-5000 |
| **Loyale (PFI)** | |
| No. 1 & 3 | 6000-18,000 |
| No. 1 & 2 | |
| Throttle Fully Closed | 5800-17,800 |
| Throttle Fully Open | 1500-5100 |
| **Loyale (TBI)** | |
| "B" & "D" | 3500-6500 |
| "B" & "C" | |
| Throttle Fully Closed | Less Than 1000 |
| Throttle Fully Open | Greater Than 2400 |

**XT – 1)** Disconnect connector from Throttle Position Sensor (TPS). Ensure throttle valve is fully closed. Using ohmmeter, check continuity between Black wire and Blue/White wire at TPS terminals. Continuity should exist.

**2)** Insert a .021" (.55 mm) feeler gauge between stopper screw of throttle chamber and stopper. Ensure continuity exists between Black wire and Blue/White wire at TPS terminals.

**3)** Ensure continuity is NOT present when thickness of gauge is changed to .036" (.92 mm). To adjust, loosen screws securing TPS until continuity is as specified. Replace TPS if proper adjustment cannot be made.

## 6-CYLINDER THROTTLE POSITION SENSOR

***NOTE: All testing procedures are performed with engine at normal operating temperature.***

**1)** Disconnect TPS electrical connector. Insert a .014" (.35 mm) feeler gauge between throttle lever and throttle screw. Connect an ohmmeter between Black wire and Gray wire at TPS terminals. Maximum resistance should be 5000 ohms. Remove feeler gauge.

**2)** Insert a .030" (.75 mm) feeler gauge between throttle lever and throttle screw. Ohmmeter should indicate infinity. Remove feeler gauge. Connect ohmmeter between Black/White wire and Black wire. Ohmmeter should indicate 3000-7000 ohms.

**3)** Connect ohmmeter between Green/Black wire and Black wire. With throttle valve closed, ohmmeter should read 4200-15,000 ohms. Open throttle valve to wide open throttle position. Ohmmeter should indicate 100-11,000 ohms.

**4)** Close throttle valve. With ohmmeter connected to Green/Black wire and Black wire, slowly open throttle. Ohmmeter reading should change smoothly as throttle goes from idle to wide open position.

# 1991 ENGINE PERFORMANCE
# Theory & Operation

**Justy, Legacy, Loyale, XT, XT6**

## INTRODUCTION

This article covers basic description and operation of engine performance-related systems and components. Read this article before diagnosing vehicles or systems with which you are not completely familiar.

## AIR INDUCTION SYSTEM

### TURBOCHARGERS

Legacy and Loyale use a water-cooled turbocharger mounted on the exhaust crossover pipe. A wastegate assembly is attached to rear of turbine housing. The turbocharger consists of a turbine/compressor assembly, oil supply system, wastegate valve, and wastegate control solenoid valve. Other components include impellers, impeller shaft, bearings and impeller housings.

If intake boost pressure exceeds safe limits, engine damage may result. To prevent excessive intake boost pressure, the system uses a pressure-actuated wastegate valve as a limiting device. The wastegate valve opens when intake pressure exceeds a predetermined limit, allowing exhaust gases to by-pass the compressor.

Turbocharger operation requires a large quantity of clean oil to prevent bearing failure. Engine oil pressure provides constant lubrication to the system.

**Wastegate Control Solenoid Valve** – Located in pressure line between intake manifold and wastegate valve, this duty solenoid compensates for reduced intake air volume due to high altitude. When Electronic Control Unit (ECU) energizes solenoid, valve closes. This restricts pressure line, eliminating the wastegate valve by-pass function. Boost pressure is then unregulated (full volume). This maintains maximum allowable boost under high altitude conditions.

## COMPUTERIZED ENGINE CONTROLS

**Carbureted** – Electronic Fuel Control (EFC) system is a computerized fuel, ignition and emission control system designed to maintain fuel economy and reduce vehicle emissions. An Electronic Control Unit (ECU) monitors data from various sensors and controls such functions as carburetor air/fuel mixture ratio, ignition timing and emission control devices.

**Port Fuel Injection (PFI)** – PFI system is a computerized fuel, ignition and emission control system designed to maintain fuel economy and reduce vehicle emissions. Fuel is metered to intake system through a separate injector, mounted in intake manifold next to intake valve, for each cylinder. An Electronic Control Unit (ECU) monitors data from various sensors and controls such functions as fuel injector pulse width ("on" time), ignition timing and emission control devices.

**Throttle Body Injection (TBI)** – TBI system is a computerized fuel, ignition and emission control system designed to maintain fuel economy and reduce vehicle emissions. Fuel is metered to intake system through a single fuel injector, mounted to a throttle body on the intake manifold. An Electronic Control Unit (ECU) monitors data from various sensors and controls such functions as fuel injector pulse width ("on" time), ignition timing and emission control devices.

### ENGINE CONTROL UNIT (ECU)

**All Systems** – If a system fault (malfunction) occurs, a built-in fail-safe mechanism within the ECU controls fuel and ignition system functions according to preprogrammed values. This allows the vehicle to be driven, but driving performance may not be optimal.

A self-diagnostic function allows the ECU to store trouble codes in its memory. If a system fault occurs, CHECK ENGINE light will come on to inform the driver of system problems, and trouble code will be stored. For further self-diagnostic system information, see SELF-DIAGNOSTICS article.

### INPUT DEVICES (CARBURETED)

*NOTE: Components are grouped into 2 categories. The first category covers INPUT DEVICES, which control or produce voltage signals monitored by the ECU. The second category covers OUTPUT SIGNALS, which are components controlled by the ECU.*

Vehicles are equipped with different combinations of input devices. Not all devices are used on all models. To determine the input usage on a specific model, see WIRING DIAGRAMS article in ENGINE PERFORMANCE. The available input signals include the following:

**A/C-On Signal** – When A/C is turned on, ECU receives voltage signal and activates idle-up system. See IDLE SPEED under FUEL SYSTEM (CARBURETED) in this article.

**Coolant Temperature Sensor** – ECU applies reference voltage signal to this thermistor. Resistance value of sensor changes with variations in coolant temperature, causing reference voltage to increase or decrease. Sensor is equipped with 2 terminals. One terminal is used for ECU; the other is used for temperature gauge.

**Crank Angle Sensor (Engine Speed Sensor)** – Crank angle sensor is a magnetic pick-up coil sensing mechanism located in distributor. Sensor provides crankshaft angle and engine RPM inputs to ECU.

**Electrical Loads** – When headlights, heater blower or rear defogger are turned on, ECU receives voltage signal and activates idle-up system. See IDLE SPEED under FUEL SYSTEM (CARBURETED).

**Oxygen ($O_2$) Sensor** – Sensor generates voltage according to exhaust gas oxygen content. Voltage increases when oxygen content is low (rich), and decreases when oxygen content is high (lean). ECU determines air/fuel ratio based on voltage generated.

**Vacuum/Pressure Sensor & Vacuum Line Control (VLC) Solenoid Valve** – Detect changes in intake manifold vacuum and atmospheric pressure. Solenoid valve, located in line between intake manifold and vacuum/pressure sensor, receives voltage signal from ECU. With no voltage applied to solenoid valve, sensor monitors intake manifold vacuum. With voltage applied to solenoid valve, sensor monitors atmospheric pressure.

**Vehicle Speed Sensor** – ECU supplies voltage signal to one side of a tiny reed switch located in speedometer assembly. Speedometer cable revolutions open and close reed switch, providing ECU with CONTINUITY/NO CONTINUITY input. ECU converts this signal to vehicle speed.

### OUTPUT SIGNALS (CARBURETED)

*NOTE: Vehicles are equipped with different combinations of computer-controlled components. Not all components listed below are used on every vehicle. For theory and operation on each output component, refer to the system indicated after component.*

**Canister Purge Control (CPC) Solenoid Valve** – See FUEL EVAPORATION SYSTEM under EMISSION SYSTEMS.

**CHECK ENGINE Light** – See SELF-DIAGNOSTICS.

**Coasting Fuel Cut (CFC) Solenoid** – See FUEL CONTROL under FUEL SYSTEM (CARBURETED).

**Duty Solenoid Valve (DSV)** – See FUEL CONTROL under FUEL SYSTEM (CARBURETED).

**EGR Control Solenoid Valve** – See EXHAUST GAS RECIRCULATION (EGR) under EMISSION SYSTEMS.

**Float Chamber Ventilation (FCV) Solenoid Valve** – See FUEL EVAPORATION SYSTEM under EMISSION SYSTEMS.

**Fuel Pump Relay** – See FUEL DELIVERY under FUEL SYSTEM (CARBURETED).

**High Altitude Compensator (HAC) Solenoid Valve (Federal)** – See FUEL CONTROL under FUEL SYSTEM (CARBURETED).

**Idle-Up Control Solenoid Valve (ICSV)** – See IDLE SPEED under FUEL SYSTEM (CARBURETED).

**Power Transistor** – See IGNITION SYSTEMS.

**Self-Diagnostics** – See SELF-DIAGNOSTICS.

**Vacuum/Pressure Sensor & Vacuum Line Control (VLC) Solenoid Valve** – See INPUT DEVICES (CARBURETED).

## INPUT DEVICES (FUEL INJECTION)

***NOTE:** Components are grouped into 2 categories. The first category covers INPUT DEVICES, which control or produce voltage signals monitored by the ECU. The second category covers OUTPUT SIGNALS, which are components controlled by the ECU.*

Vehicles are equipped with different combinations of input devices. Not all devices are used on all models. To determine the input usage on a specific model, see WIRING DIAGRAMS article in ENGINE PERFORMANCE. The available input signals include the following:

**A/C Switch** – Signals ECU of A/C operation.

**Airflow Meter (Except Justy)** – Hot-wire type airflow meter uses heat transfer between incoming air and a heating resistor (hot wire), located in air intake, to convert air flowing into engine to an electric signal.

**Air Temperature Sensor (Justy)** – ECU applies reference voltage signal to the air-temperature sensitive thermistor installed on air cleaner housing. Reference voltage increases and decreases with variations in air temperature.

**Atmospheric Pressure Sensor** – Sensor is a component part of ECU. ECU uses this signal to compensate for variations in altitude, which affect air/fuel mixture ratios.

**Cam Angle Sensor (Legacy)** – Sensor is located on camshaft support, on left cylinder bank. Pick-up coil acts as triggering device. Based on signals received from triggering device, ECU distinguishes No. 1 cylinder from other cylinders. ECU then uses these signals to trigger distributorless ignition system and fuel injectors.

**Coolant Temperature Sensor** – ECU applies reference voltage signal to thermistor. Resistance value of sensor changes with variations in coolant temperature, causing reference voltage to increase or decrease.

**Crank Angle Sensor (Legacy)** – Sensor is installed on oil pump, at front center of cylinder block. Pick-up coil acts as triggering device. Based on signals received from triggering device, ECU determines crankshaft angle. Based on these signals, ECU triggers distributorless ignition system and fuel injectors.

**Crank Angle & TDC (Cylinder Identification) Sensor Assembly (Except Legacy)** – Assembly is located in distributor. On Justy, pick-up coil acts as triggering device. On Loyale, optical sensing unit (light emitting diode) acts as triggering device. Based on signals received from triggering device, ECU determines crankshaft angle and identifies No. 1 cylinder. Based on these signals, ECU triggers ignition system and fuel injector(s).

**Detonation (Knock) Sensor** – Installed on cylinder block, this sensor responds to cylinder block vibrations resulting from detonation. If detonation occurs, a voltage is generated and sent to ECU. Based on the voltage received, ECU retards spark timing until detonation stops.

**Idle Switch** – Switch signals ECU of closed throttle condition.

**Inhibitor Switch (A/T)** – Switch signals ECU of transmission gear position.

**Neutral & Park Switches** – Switch signals ECU of transmission gear position.

**Oxygen ($O_2$) Sensor** – Sensor generates voltage according to exhaust gas oxygen content. Voltage increases when oxygen content is low (rich), and decreases when oxygen content is high (lean). ECU determines air/fuel ratio based on voltage generated.

**Pressure Switch (Turbo)** – Mounted in front of body strut mount, this switch closes when intake manifold vacuum reaches approximately 2 in. Hg. This causes TURBO indicator light to illuminate, indicating turbocharging operation is in effect.

**Throttle Sensor (Except Justy)** – Throttle sensor contains a potentiometer (variable resistor) and an idle switch. Throttle position sensor sends ECU a potentiometer output signal corresponding to opening of throttle valve. Idle switch signal occurs when throttle is near idle position. ECU uses these signals to control air/fuel ratio during acceleration, deceleration and idling.

**Throttle Switch (Justy)** – This switch, attached to end of throttle shaft, informs ECU that throttle valve is closed, wide open (at least 50 degrees), or neither. This is NOT a variable resistor.

**Vehicle Speed Sensor** – ECU supplies voltage signal to one side of a tiny reed switch located in speedometer assembly. Speedometer cable revolutions open and close reed switch, providing ECU with CONTINUITY/NO CONTINUITY input. ECU converts this signal to vehicle speed.

## OUTPUT SIGNALS (FUEL INJECTION)

***NOTE:** Vehicles are equipped with different combinations of computer-controlled components. Not all components listed below are used on every vehicle. For theory and operation on each output component, refer to the system indicated after component.*

**Auxiliary Air Valve** – See IDLE SPEED under FUEL SYSTEM (FUEL INJECTION).

**By-Pass Air Control Valve** – See IDLE SPEED under FUEL SYSTEM (FUEL INJECTION).

**Canister Purge Control (CPC) Solenoid Valve** – See FUEL EVAPORATION SYSTEM under EMISSION SYSTEMS.

**CHECK ENGINE Light** – See SELF-DIAGNOSTICS.

**Detonation (Knock) Sensor** – See IGNITION TIMING CONTROL SYSTEM under IGNITION SYSTEMS.

**EGR Control Solenoid Valve** – See EXHAUST GAS RECIRCULATION (EGR) under EMISSION SYSTEMS.

**Fast Idle Control Device (FICD) Solenoid Valve** – See IDLE SPEED under FUEL SYSTEM (FUEL INJECTION).

**Fuel Injector Resistor Pack** – See FUEL CONTROL (PFI) under FUEL SYSTEM (FUEL INJECTION).

**Fuel Injector(s)** – See FUEL CONTROL (TBI) or FUEL CONTROL (PFI) under FUEL SYSTEM (FUEL INJECTION).

**Fuel Pump Relay** – See FUEL DELIVERY under FUEL SYSTEM (FUEL INJECTION).

**Power Transistor** – See IGNITION SYSTEMS.

**Self-Diagnostics** – See SELF-DIAGNOSTICS.

# FUEL SYSTEM (CARBURETED)

## FUEL DELIVERY

**Fuel Pump** – Electric fuel pump is located on crossmember, under center of floor. Flow rate of fuel changes as pressure varies on delivery side. This controls required quantity of fuel delivered.

**Fuel Pump Relay** – ECU provides power supply and ground for control circuit in fuel pump relay. When ignition is turned on with engine off, ECU energizes fuel pump relay for 3 seconds, activating fuel pump. After 3 seconds, unless ECU receives crank angle signal, it will stop energizing fuel pump relay.

## FUEL CONTROL

**Coasting Fuel Cut (CFC) Solenoid** – Located in carburetor, this solenoid responds to voltage signal from ECU to adjust air/fuel mixture through idle circuit during deceleration. This prevents rich air/fuel mixtures during deceleration.

**Duty Solenoid Valve (DSV)** – Located in carburetor, this ECU-controlled solenoid cycles on and off to control air/fuel mixture ratio entering slow speed and main metering passages.

**Electric Choke** – When fuel pump relay is energized, voltage is applied to electric choke heater element. Voltage is applied to choke heater under same conditions as fuel pump. See FUEL PUMP RELAY under FUEL DELIVERY of FUEL SYSTEM (CARBURETED).

**High Altitude Compensator (HAC) Solenoid Valve (Federal)** – To compensate for richer air/fuel mixtures at higher altitudes (26.38 in. Hg or less), HAC admits air into main metering passage. When vacuum/pressure sensor indicates barometric pressure has reached predetermined specification, ECU energizes HAC solenoid. This opens valve, admitting more air into main metering passage.

**Hot Idle Compensator** – Bimetallic heat sensor, located inside air filter housing, allows more idle air through idle circuit at high engine temperatures.

# 1991 ENGINE PERFORMANCE
# Theory & Operation (Cont.)

### IDLE SPEED

**Idle-Up Control Solenoid Valve (ICSV)** – ICSV compensates for decrease in engine RPM due to the following conditions: cold engine temperatures, increased electrical load (alternator loading), and A/C operation. See INPUT DEVICES (CARBURETED).

When ECU receives input signals indicating engine RPM has dropped, ECU energizes ICSV. ICSV controls vacuum supply to throttle opener diaphragm. When vacuum is applied to throttle opener diaphragm, throttle plate opens to compensate for decrease in engine RPM.

## FUEL SYSTEM (FUEL INJECTION)

### FUEL DELIVERY

**Fuel Pump** – Impeller-type pump is used. On Justy and Legacy, fuel pump is located in fuel tank. On Loyale, XT and XT6, fuel pump is mounted to underbody, near fuel tank.

On all models, fuel pump pressurizes fuel through in-line filter, to fuel injector rail. Fuel pump receives battery power through fuel pump relay.

**Fuel Pump Relay** – ECU energizes fuel pump relay based on inputs from ignition switch and ignition coil. During cranking, ignition switch cranking circuit supplies current to energize fuel pump relay. After engine starts and key is released to RUN position, ECU provides fuel pump relay ground. This activates fuel pump.

**Fuel Pressure Regulator** – Regulator maintains constant fuel system pressure by bleeding off fuel at injector rail back to fuel tank. Intake manifold vacuum acts on regulator diaphragm to control position of bleed-off valve in regulator.

**Fuel Pulsation Damper (Justy)** – This device, located on fuel injector rail, absorbs fuel pressure pulsations.

### FUEL CONTROL (TBI)

**Fuel Injectors** – Fuel is supplied to engine through a single throttle body injector valve mounted to intake manifold. ECU controls injectors' energized time (pulse width), which affects amount of fuel metered through injectors. ECU triggers injectors based on signals received from crank angle sensor.

### FUEL CONTROL (PFI)

**Fuel Injectors** – Fuel is supplied to engine through injector valves located at intake manifold, near intake valve opening. ECU controls injectors' energized time (pulse width), which affects amount of fuel metered through injectors. ECU triggers injectors based on signals received from crank angle sensor.

**Fuel Injector Resistor Pack (Loyale PFI & XT)** – Positioned in series between fuel injector power source and ground, resistor pack regulates current flow through fuel injectors.

### IDLE SPEED

**Auxiliary Air Valve (Loyale PFI & XT)** – Valve increases idle air volume when engine ambient temperatures are low. Valve consists of a coiled bimetallic spring, a shutter valve, and an electric heater element. Shutter valve closes gradually to decrease airflow. Current to heater is supplied by fuel pump relay circuit.

**By-Pass Air Control Valve (Legacy)** – Valve consists of coolant temperature-sensitive bimetallic valve and ECU-controlled duty solenoid. Bimetallic valve compensates for varying engine temperatures. ECU cycles duty solenoid on and off, regulating amount of air by-passing throttle valve. System compensates for idle speed decreases due to the following conditions: cold engine temperatures, A/C operation and electrical loads (alternator loading). System also provides dashpot function to prevent rich air/fuel mixture ratios during deceleration.

**By-Pass Air Control Valve (Loyale TBI & XT6)** – An air passage by-passing throttle valve is provided to control idle air intake volume. ECU cycles duty solenoid on and off, regulating amount of air by-passing throttle valve. System compensates for idle speed changes due to cold engine temperatures, A/C operation, and varying altitude.

**Fast Idle Control Device (FICD) Solenoid Valve (Justy)** – Valve is located in line between air filter housing and intake manifold. When A/C is turned on, ECU energizes solenoid valve. Solenoid valve will open, allowing fresh air to by-pass throttle valve through solenoid valve, into intake manifold.

**Idle Speed Control (ISC) Solenoid Valve (Justy)** – Valve is mounted on air filter housing, in line between air filter housing and intake manifold. At idle, ECU opens and closes solenoid valve. This allows fresh air to by-pass throttle valve through solenoid valve, into intake manifold.

**Thermal Air Valve (Justy)** – Coolant temperature-sensitive wax pellet valve allows idle air to by-pass throttle valve. This increases idle RPM during cold engine conditions.

## IGNITION SYSTEMS

The power transistor acts as primary current switching device for ignition system. When ECU signals power transistor base, primary current is allowed to flow to ground.

### DISTRIBUTOR (MAGNETIC)

**Justy** – Magnetic pick-up coil sensing mechanism (crank angle sensor) in distributor signals ECU of crankshaft angle, and distinguishes between No. 1 cylinder and other cylinders. Based on these inputs, ECU signals power transistor base, allowing primary current to flow to ground through ignition coil.

On carbureted engines, ignition coil receives battery voltage from ignition switch. On PFI engines, ignition coil receives battery voltage from ignition relay. Ignition relay is energized with ignition switch in ON or START position.

### DISTRIBUTOR (OPTICAL)

**Loyale, XT & XT6** – Optical sensing unit (crank angle sensor) in distributor signals ECU of crankshaft angle and identifies No. 1 cylinder. System consists of distributor (crank angle sensor), ignition coil and power transistor.

Based on input from crank angle sensor, ECU signals base of power transistor. This allows primary current flow to ground. Ignition coil receives primary power supply when ignition coil relay is energized.

### DISTRIBUTORLESS (OPTICAL)

**Legacy** – Distributorless ignition system is controlled by ECU. System consists of 2 ignition coils and a power transistor assembly. Power transistor assembly consists of 2 transistors, which control primary current path to ground for each ignition coil. One transistor controls primary path to ground for ignition coil, which fires cylinders No. 1 and 2. The other transistor controls primary path to ground for ignition coil, which fires cylinders No. 3 and 4.

Although each coil fires 2 plugs at the same time, ignition takes place in only one cylinder, since the other cylinder is on its exhaust stroke when plug fires. Based on input from crankshaft and camshaft angle sensors, ECU signals base of appropriate power transistor. This allows primary current flow to ground. Ignition coils receive primary power supply when ignition coil relay is energized.

### IGNITION TIMING CONTROL SYSTEM

**Detonation Retard Operation** – When engine knock (detonation) is present, a signal is generated by knock sensor and is sent to ECU. ECU retards spark timing until engine knocking stops, then gradually advances spark timing.

**Ignition Timing Advance Control** – On all models, ignition timing advance is controlled by ECU. Based on sensor input signals, ECU adjusts ignition timing to the preprogrammed advance and retard specifications.

# 1991 ENGINE PERFORMANCE
# Theory & Operation (Cont.)

## EMISSION SYSTEMS

### AIR INJECTION SYSTEM

The air injection system reduces exhaust emissions by oxidizing hydrocarbons (HC) and carbon monoxide (CO). System is composed of a one-way air suction valve (pulse air valve), air cleaner, various hoses and tubing.

Negative pressure from exhaust pulsation reaches suction valve through a suction pipe. This causes reeds in suction valve to draw open. Secondary (fresh) air from air cleaner is drawn into exhaust passages. When positive pressure is present in exhaust, reeds are closed to prevent reverse flow of exhaust gas.

### EXHAUST GAS RECIRCULATION (EGR)

EGR lowers oxides of nitrogen (NOx) exhaust emissions by admitting exhaust gases back into intake system. Exhaust gases lower peak combustion temperatures, which lowers NOx emissions.

**EGR Control Solenoid Valve** – EGR valve diaphragm receives operating vacuum through EGR control solenoid valve. ECU controls operation of EGR control solenoid valve.

### FUEL EVAPORATION SYSTEM

**Canister Purge Control (CPC) Solenoid Valve** – On models with Canister Purge Valve (CPV), CPC solenoid valve is located in vacuum signal line between CPV and ported vacuum source. See CANISTER PURGE VALVE (CPV). Under certain conditions, ECU energizes CPC solenoid valve. This allows ported vacuum signal to CPV.

On models without CPV, CPC solenoid valve is located in purge line between canister and ported vacuum source. Under certain conditions, ECU energizes CPC solenoid valve, allowing ported vacuum to purge the canister.

**Canister Purge Valve (CPV)** – Located on top of canister, this vacuum-controlled valve opens and closes purge line between intake manifold and canister. CPV valve remains closed at idle because ported vacuum activates its control diaphragm. When vacuum activates the control diaphragm, purge line is opened, and stored vapors are free to be drawn into intake manifold.

**Float Chamber Ventilation (FCV) Solenoid Valve** – When ignition is off, this solenoid valve remains open to allow float bowl vapor to escape to canister. When ignition switch is in ON or START position, ECU energizes FCV solenoid valve, blocking off passage between float bowl and canister passage.

### POSITIVE CRANKCASE VENTILATION (PCV)

PCV system draws crankcase blow-by, vapors and gases into combustion system rather than allowing them to escape into atmosphere. Crankcase gases mix with air/fuel mixture, and are burned in combustion chamber. When engine is running, manifold vacuum pulls PCV valve open, allowing crankcase fumes to enter intake manifold. If engine backfires, PCV valve is forced closed, stopping any flow of gases. This prevents ignition of fumes in crankcase.

### THERMOSTATIC AIR CLEANER (CARBURETED)

Thermostatic air cleaner reduces exhaust emissions by maintaining a uniform intake air temperature. System consists of an air cleaner housing, air stove on exhaust pipe, and air intake hose between air cleaner and manifold stove. Air cleaner housing contains an air control diaphragm, air control valve, temperature sensor valve, flame arrester, and connecting tubes and hoses.

## SELF-DIAGNOSTICS

### CHECK ENGINE LIGHT

All vehicles are equipped with a CHECK ENGINE light on instrument panel. Light illuminates when ignition switch is turned to ON position (bulb check), and when system malfunctions occur. For additional information, see SELF-DIAGNOSTICS article.

# 1991 ENGINE PERFORMANCE
# Basic Diagnostic Procedures

### Justy, Legacy, Loyale, XT, XT6

## INTRODUCTION

The following diagnostic steps help prevent overlooking a simple problem. This is also where to begin diagnosis for a no-start condition. The first step in diagnosing any driveability problem is verifying the customer's complaint with a test drive under the conditions the problem reportedly occurred.

Before entering self-diagnostics, perform a careful and complete visual inspection. Most engine control problems result from mechanical breakdowns, poor electrical connections or damaged/misrouted vacuum hoses. Before condemning the computerized system, perform each test listed in this article.

***NOTE: Perform all voltage tests with a Digital Volt-Ohmmeter (DVOM) with a minimum 10-megohm input impedance, unless stated otherwise in test procedure.***

## PRELIMINARY INSPECTION & ADJUSTMENTS

### VISUAL INSPECTION

Visually inspect all electrical wiring for chafed, stretched, cut or pinched wiring. Ensure electrical connectors fit tightly and are not corroded. Ensure vacuum hoses are properly routed and are not pinched or cut. See VACUUM DIAGRAMS article to verify routing and connections (if necessary). Inspect air induction system for possible vacuum leaks.

### MECHANICAL INSPECTION

**Compression** – Check engine mechanical condition with a compression gauge, vacuum gauge or an engine analyzer. See engine analyzer manual for specific instructions.

***WARNING: DO NOT use ignition switch during compression tests on fuel injected vehicles. Use a remote starter to crank engine. Fuel injectors on many models are triggered by ignition switch during cranking mode, which can create a fire hazard or contaminate the engine's oiling system.***

**Exhaust System Backpressure – 1)** The exhaust system can be checked with a vacuum or pressure gauge. Remove $O_2$ sensor or air injection check valve (if equipped).

**2)** Connect a 1-10 psi pressure gauge and operate engine at 2500 RPM. If exhaust system backpressure is greater than 1 3/4 - 2 psi, exhaust system or catalytic converter is plugged.

**3)** If a vacuum gauge is used, connect vacuum gauge hose to intake manifold vacuum port and start engine. Observe vacuum gauge. Open throttle part way and hold it steady. If vacuum gauge reading slowly drops after stabilizing, check exhaust system for restriction.

## FUEL SYSTEM

### FUEL PRESSURE

Basic diagnosis of fuel system should begin with determining fuel system pressure. If fuel pump is inoperative, see appropriate FUEL PUMP CIRCUIT TEST chart.

***WARNING: ALWAYS relieve fuel pressure before disconnecting any fuel injection-related component. DO NOT allow fuel to contact engine or electrical components. If connecting fuel pressure gauge to fuel system without using a "T" connector, DO NOT operate fuel pump for more than a few seconds. Operating fuel pump for longer than a few seconds under this condition damages fuel pump.***

**Carbureted** – Disconnect fuel pressure hose from carburetor, and install pressure gauge using "T" connector. Turn ignition on. Fuel pump should run for 3 seconds and stop. See REGULATED FUEL PRESSURE table.

**Fuel-Injected – 1)** Disconnect fuel pump connector. Crank engine for at least 5 seconds. If engine starts, let it run until it stops. Disconnect fuel hose at pressure regulator, and install fuel pressure gauge using "T" connector.

**2)** Start engine and check fuel pressure at idle. Se REGULATED FUEL PRESSURE table. Ensure fuel pressure increases as engine speed increases.

***REGULATED FUEL PRESSURE***

| Application | psi (kg/cm²) |
|---|---|
| Justy | 41.3 (2.9) |
| Legacy, Loyale PFI, XT & XT6 | 26-30 (1.8-2.1) |
| Loyale TBI | 20-24 (1.4-1.7) |

## IGNITION CHECKS

***NOTE: For additional ignition system testing procedures, see appropriate IGNITION CONTROL SYSTEM TEST chart.***

### SPARK

Check for spark at spark plug wires using a spark tester. Check resistance of each spark plug wire. Replace wire if resistance is not within specification. See appropriate HIGH TENSION WIRE RESISTANCE table.

***HIGH TENSION WIRE RESISTANCE (JUSTY)***

| Application | Ohms |
|---|---|
| No. 1 | 458-10,680 |
| No. 2 | 411-959 |
| No. 3 | 290-676 |
| Coil | 459-10,710 |

***HIGH TENSION WIRE RESISTANCE (LEGACY)***

| Application | Ohms | Wire Length In. (mm) |
|---|---|---|
| No. 1 | 495-11,560 | 21.25 (540) |
| No. 2 | 486-11,330 | 21.65 (550) |
| No. 3 | 495-11,560 | 21.25 (540) |
| No. 4 | 524-12,230 | 23.62 (600) |

***HIGH TENSION WIRE RESISTANCE (LOYALE)***

| Application | Ohms (PFI) | Ohms (TBI) |
|---|---|---|
| No. 1 | 243-567 | 243-567 |
| No. 2 | 948-22,130 | 838-19,560 |
| No. 3 | 958-22,360 | 790-18,440 |
| No. 4 | 241-562 | 241-562 |

***HIGH TENSION WIRE RESISTANCE (XT & XT6)***

| Application | Ohms (1.8L) | Ohms (2.7L) |
|---|---|---|
| No. 1 | 243-567 | 243-567 |
| No. 2 | 947-23,030 | 10,860-25,330 |
| No. 3 | 958-22,360 | 11,240-26,230 |
| No. 4 | 241-562 | 452-10,550 |
| No. 5 | ..... | 11,430-26,680 |
| No. 6 | ..... | 260-607 |

## IGNITION COIL RESISTANCE

**Justy (Carbureted) – 1)** Disconnect 4-wire connector at ignition coil/ power transistor assembly. Check primary resistance between terminals No. 2 and 3. *See Fig. 1*. If resistance is not .81-.99 ohm, replace coil.

**2)** To check secondary resistance, connect ohmmeter between coil secondary tower and terminal No. 3 of 4-wire connector. If resistance is not 8500-11,000 ohms, replace coil.

**Legacy – 1)** Disconnect 3-wire connector from ignition coil assembly. Using an ohmmeter, check primary resistance between terminals No. 1 and 2 for one coil. *See Fig. 2*.

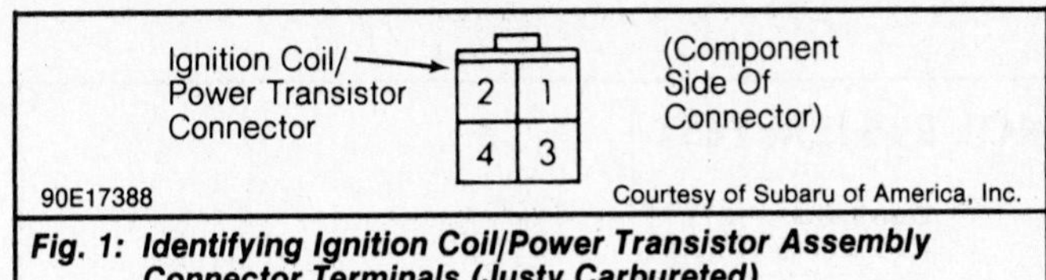


*Fig. 1: Identifying Ignition Coil/Power Transistor Assembly Connector Terminals (Justy Carbureted)*

**2)** Check primary resistance between terminals No. 2 and 3 for remaining coil. If resistance is not .62-.76 ohm (M/T) or .63-.77 ohm (A/T) for each coil, replace ignition coil assembly.
**3)** To test secondary resistance, connect one ohmmeter lead to tower at one end of coil. Connect remaining ohmmeter lead to tower at opposite end of same coil. Repeat test for other coil.
**4)** If resistance of each coil is not about 17.9-24.5 k/ohms (M/T) or 10.4-15.6 k/ohms (A/T), replace ignition coil assembly.

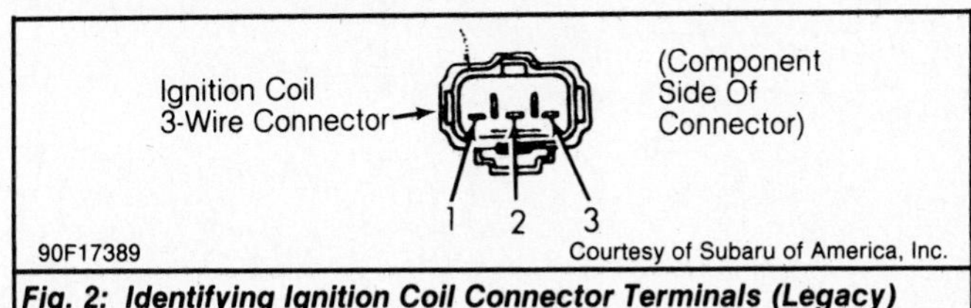


*Fig. 2: Identifying Ignition Coil Connector Terminals (Legacy)*

**Justy PFI, Loyale, XT & XT6 - 1)** On Justy PFI, disconnect ignition coil 2-wire connector. On Loyale, XT and XT6, disconnect the round 2-wire connectors at ignition coil.
**2)** On all models, check primary resistance between terminals. If resistance is not .84-1.02 ohms, replace coil.
**3)** To check secondary resistance, connect ohmmeter between coil secondary tower and White/Black wire terminal of 2-wire connector. If resistance is not 8000-12,000 ohms, replace coil.

## CRANK ANGLE & TDC SENSOR SIGNALS

***NOTE: For crank angle and TDC sensor signal testing, see SELF-DIAGNOSTICS article.***

## IDLE SPEED & IGNITION TIMING

Ensure idle speed and ignition timing are set to specification. For adjustment procedures, see ON-VEHICLE ADJUSTMENTS article.

***IDLE SPEED SPECIFICATIONS***

| Application | RPM |
|---|---|
| 1.2L [1] | |
| 2-Bbl. | 750-850 |
| PFI | 650-750 |
| 1.8L PFI | |
| Non-Turbo | 600-800 |
| Turbo | 700-900 |
| 1.8L TBI | 500-600 |
| 2.2L | |
| Accessories Off | 600-800 |
| Accessories On | 800-900 |
| 2.7L | 650-850 |

[1] - With test mode and read memory connector connected.

***IGNITION TIMING (Degrees BTDC @ RPM)***

| Application | Man. Trans. | Auto. Trans. |
|---|---|---|
| 1.2L | [1] 5 @ 800 | [1] 5 @ 850 |
| 1.8L | | |
| Non-Turbo | 20 @ 700 | 20 @ 700 |
| Turbo | 20 @ 800 | 20 @ 800 |
| 2.2L | | |
| Non-Turbo | 18-22 @ 700 | 12-28 @ 700 |
| Turbo | 7-23 @ 700 | 7-23 @ 700 |
| 2.7L | 20 @ 750 | 20 @ 750 |

[1] - With test mode connector connected.

## SUMMARY

If no faults were found while performing BASIC DIAGNOSTIC PROCEDURES, proceed to SELF-DIAGNOSTICS article. If no hard codes are found in self-diagnostics, go to TROUBLE SHOOTING - NO CODES article for diagnosis by symptom (i.e., ROUGH IDLE, NO START, etc.), or intermittent diagnostic procedures.

# 1991 ENGINE PERFORMANCE
# Basic Diagnostic Procedures (Cont.)

## IGNITION CONTROL SYSTEM TESTS

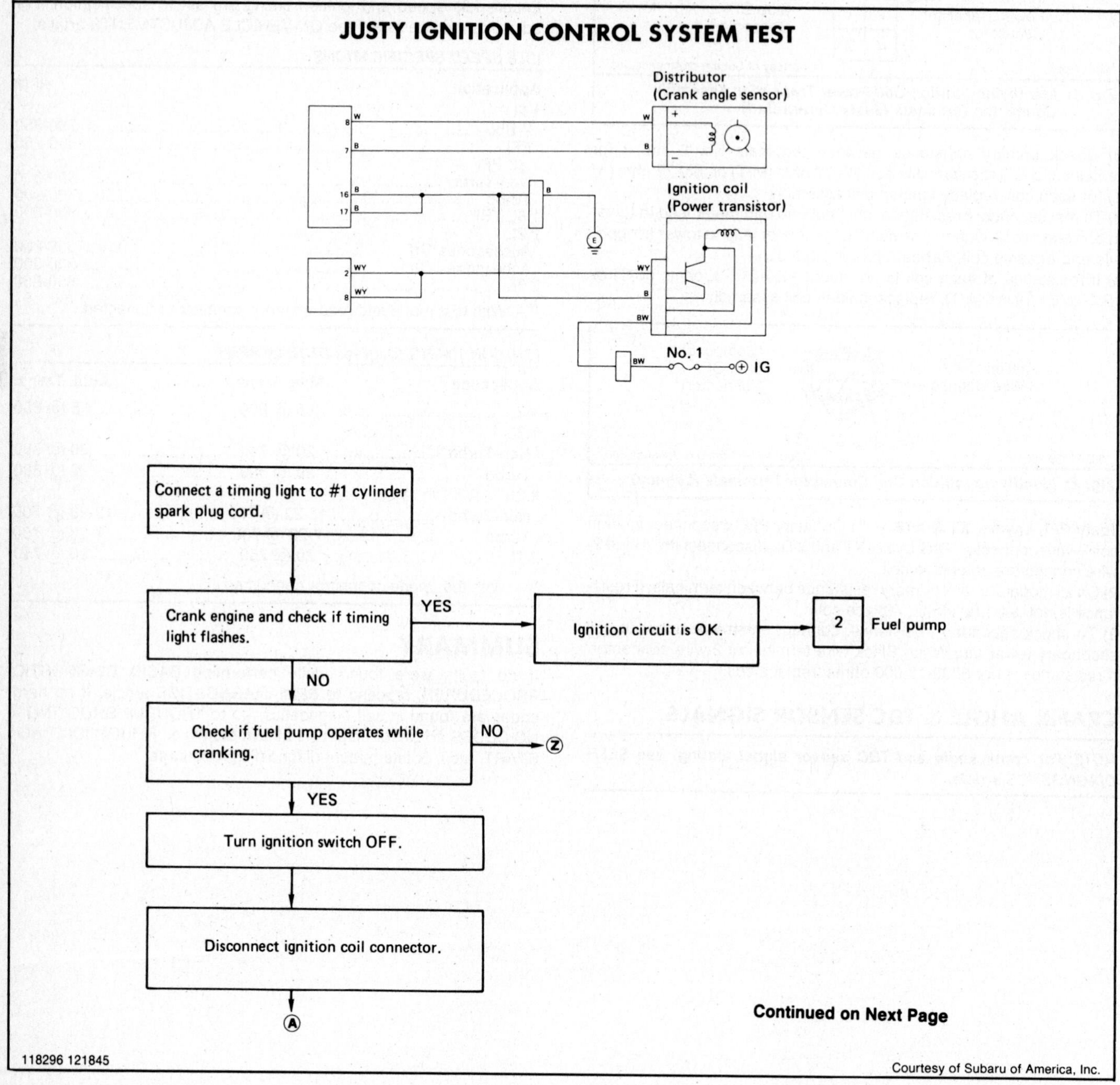
JUSTY IGNITION CONTROL SYSTEM TEST
Distributor
(Crank angle sensor)
Ignition coil
(Power transistor)
No. 1
IG
Connect a timing light to #1 cylinder spark plug cord.
Crank engine and check if timing light flashes.
YES
Ignition circuit is OK.
2
Fuel pump
NO
Check if fuel pump operates while cranking.
NO
Z
YES
Turn ignition switch OFF.
Disconnect ignition coil connector.
YES
A
Continued on Next Page
118296 121845
Courtesy of Subaru of America, Inc.

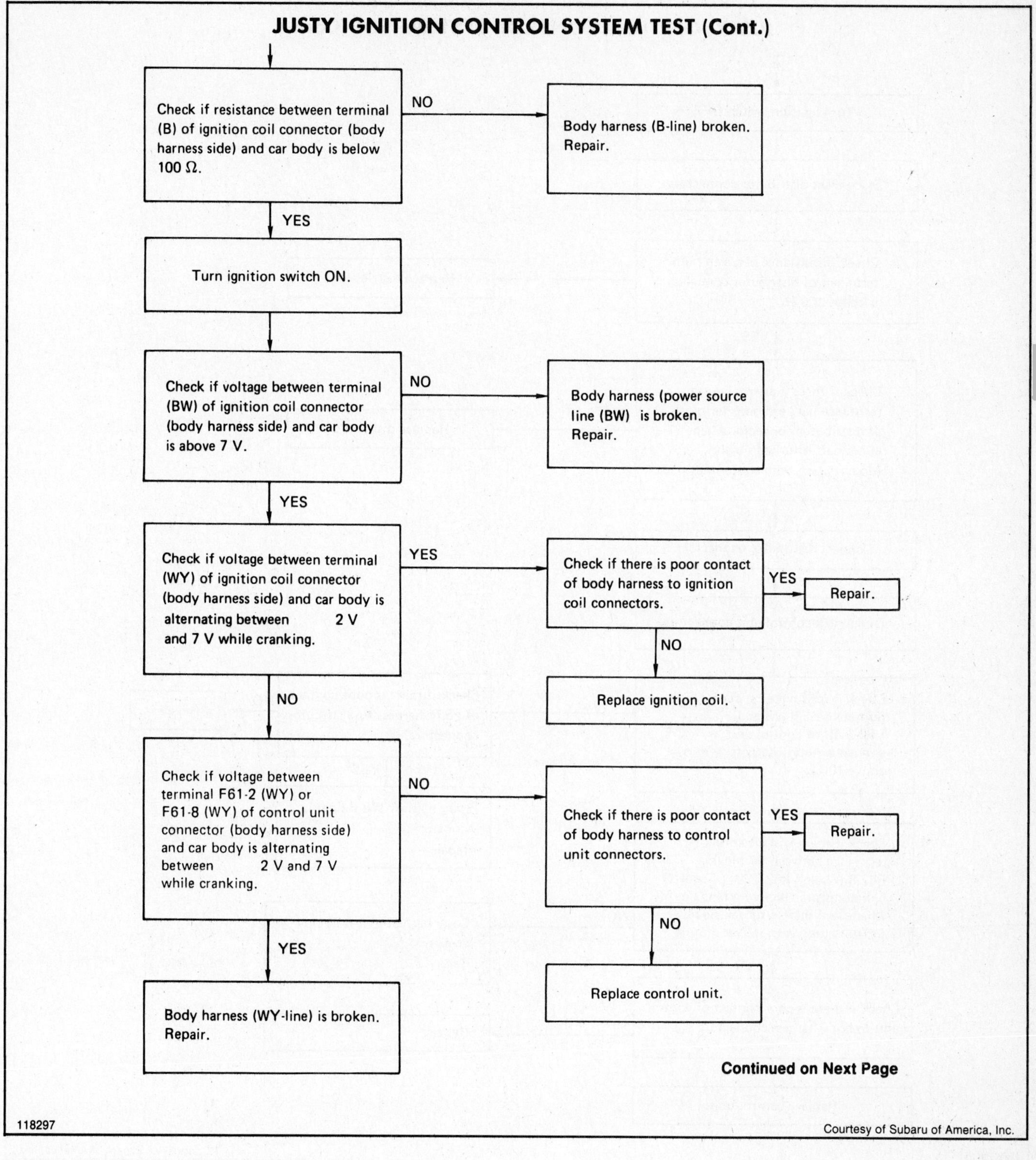
JUSTY IGNITION CONTROL SYSTEM TEST (Cont.)
Check if resistance between terminal (B) of ignition coil connector (body harness side) and car body is below 100 Ω.
NO
Body harness (B-line) broken. Repair.
YES
Turn ignition switch ON.
Check if voltage between terminal (BW) of ignition coil connector (body harness side) and car body is above 7 V.
NO
Body harness (power source line (BW) is broken. Repair.
YES
Check if voltage between terminal (WY) of ignition coil connector (body harness side) and car body is alternating between 2 V and 7 V while cranking.
YES
Check if there is poor contact of body harness to ignition coil connectors.
YES
Repair.
NO
Replace ignition coil.
NO
Check if voltage between terminal F61-2 (WY) or F61-8 (WY) of control unit connector (body harness side) and car body is alternating between 2 V and 7 V while cranking.
NO
Check if there is poor contact of body harness to control unit connectors.
YES
Repair.
NO
Replace control unit.
YES
Body harness (WY-line) is broken. Repair.
Continued on Next Page
118297
Courtesy of Subaru of America, Inc.

# 1991 ENGINE PERFORMANCE
# Basic Diagnostic Procedures (Cont.)

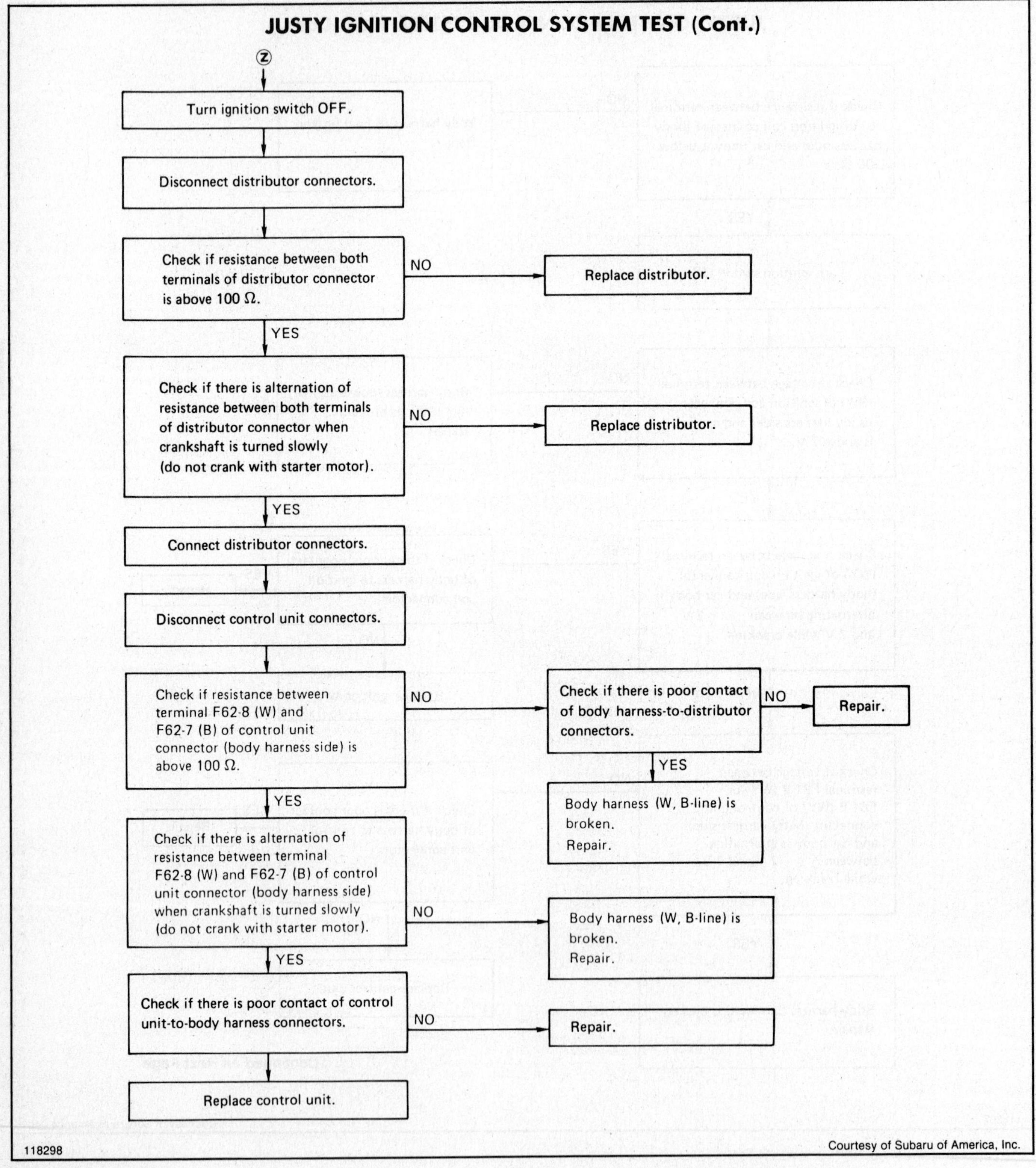

JUSTY IGNITION CONTROL SYSTEM TEST (Cont.)
Z
Turn ignition switch OFF.
Disconnect distributor connectors.
Check if resistance between both terminals of distributor connector is above 100 Ω.
NO
Replace distributor.
YES
Check if there is alternation of resistance between both terminals of distributor connector when crankshaft is turned slowly (do not crank with starter motor).
NO
Replace distributor.
YES
Connect distributor connectors.
Disconnect control unit connectors.
Check if resistance between terminal F62-8 (W) and F62-7 (B) of control unit connector (body harness side) is above 100 Ω.
NO
Check if there is poor contact of body harness-to-distributor connectors.
NO
Repair.
YES
Body harness (W, B-line) is broken. Repair.
YES
Check if there is alternation of resistance between terminal F62-8 (W) and F62-7 (B) of control unit connector (body harness side) when crankshaft is turned slowly (do not crank with starter motor).
NO
Body harness (W, B-line) is broken. Repair.
YES
Check if there is poor contact of control unit-to-body harness connectors.
NO
Repair.
Replace control unit.
118298
Courtesy of Subaru of America, Inc.

# 1991 ENGINE PERFORMANCE
## Basic Diagnostic Procedures (Cont.)

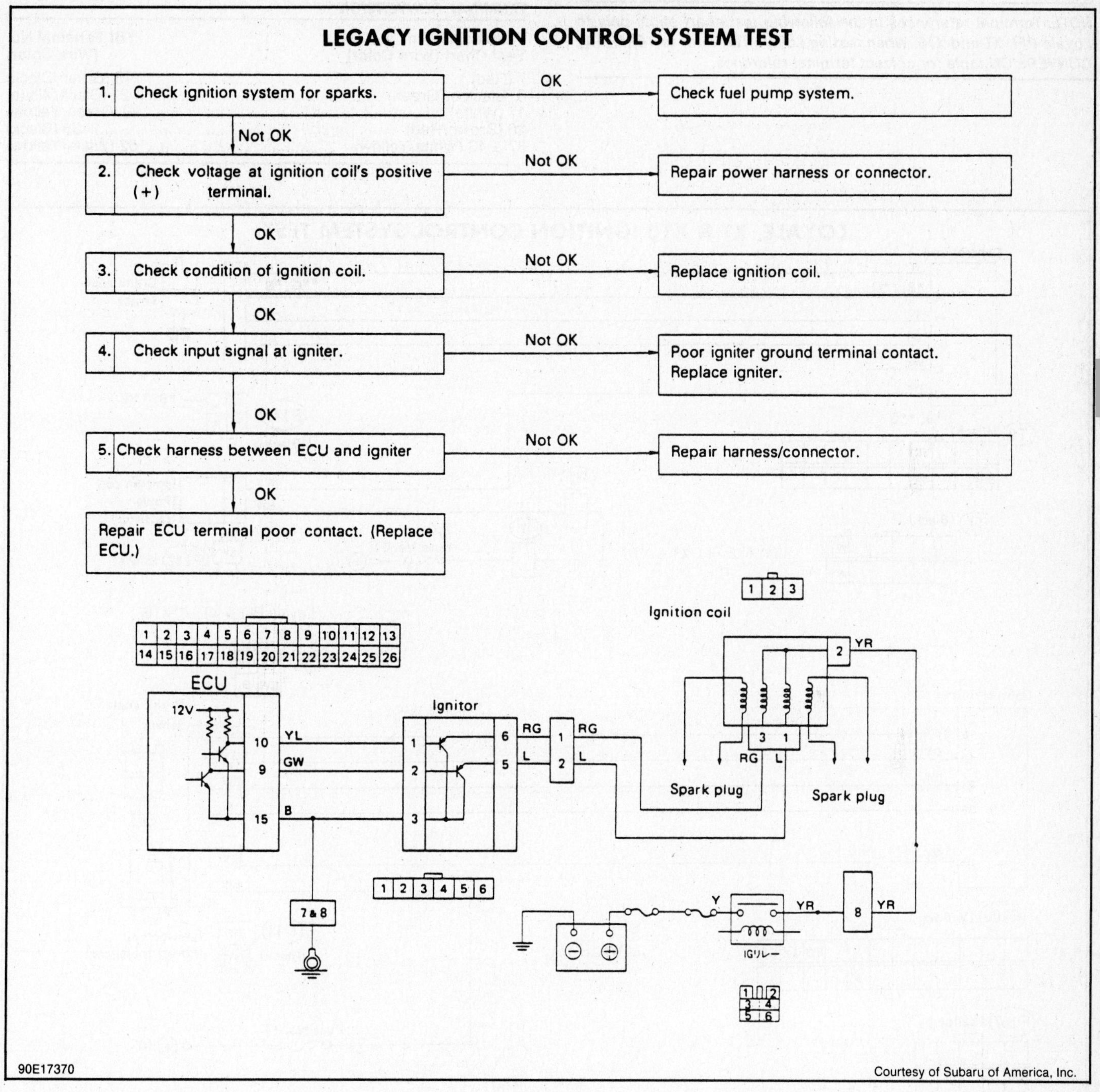
LEGACY IGNITION CONTROL SYSTEM TEST
1. Check ignition system for sparks.
OK
Check fuel pump system.
Not OK
2. Check voltage at ignition coil's positive (+) terminal.
Not OK
Repair power harness or connector.
OK
3. Check condition of ignition coil.
Not OK
Replace ignition coil.
OK
4. Check input signal at igniter.
Not OK
Poor igniter ground terminal contact. Replace igniter.
OK
5. Check harness between ECU and igniter
Not OK
Repair harness/connector.
OK
Repair ECU terminal poor contact. (Replace ECU.)
1 2 3 4 5 6 7 8 9 10 11 12 13
14 15 16 17 18 19 20 21 22 23 24 25 26
ECU
12V
10
9
15
YL
GW
B
Ignitor
1
2
3
6
5
RG
L
1
2
RG
L
1 2 3 4 5 6
7 & 8
1 2 3
Ignition coil
2
YR
3 1
RG L
Spark plug
Spark plug
Y
YR
8
YR
IGリレー
1 2
3 4
5 6
90E17370
Courtesy of Subaru of America, Inc.

# 1991 ENGINE PERFORMANCE
## Basic Diagnostic Procedures (Cont.)

***NOTE:** Terminal references in the following test chart apply only to Loyale PFI, XT and XT6. When testing Loyale TBI, refer to TERMINAL CONVERSION table for correct terminal reference.*

*TERMINAL CONVERSION*

| Terminal No. In Test Chart (Wire Color) | TBI Terminal No. (Wire Color) |
|---|---|
| 7 (Red) | 19 (Green/Black) |
| 8 (Black or Green) | 21 (Black/White) |
| 17 (White) | 20 (Green/Yellow) |
| 20 (Brown/Red) | 35 (Black) |
| 37 & 43 (White/Yellow) | 52 (White/Yellow) |

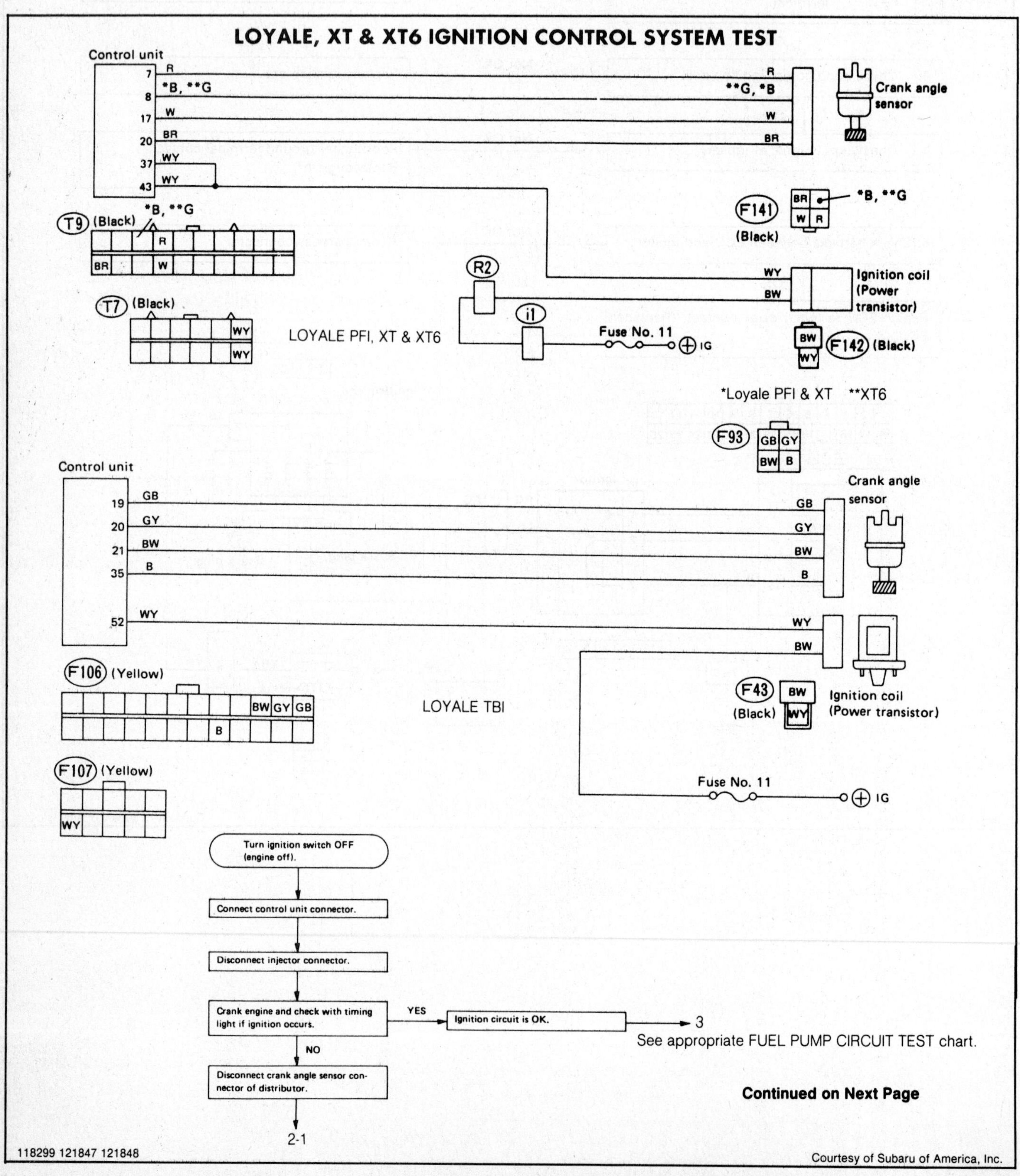


See appropriate FUEL PUMP CIRCUIT TEST chart.

Continued on Next Page

118299 121847 121848

## LOYALE, XT & XT6 IGNITION CONTROL SYSTEM TEST (Cont.)

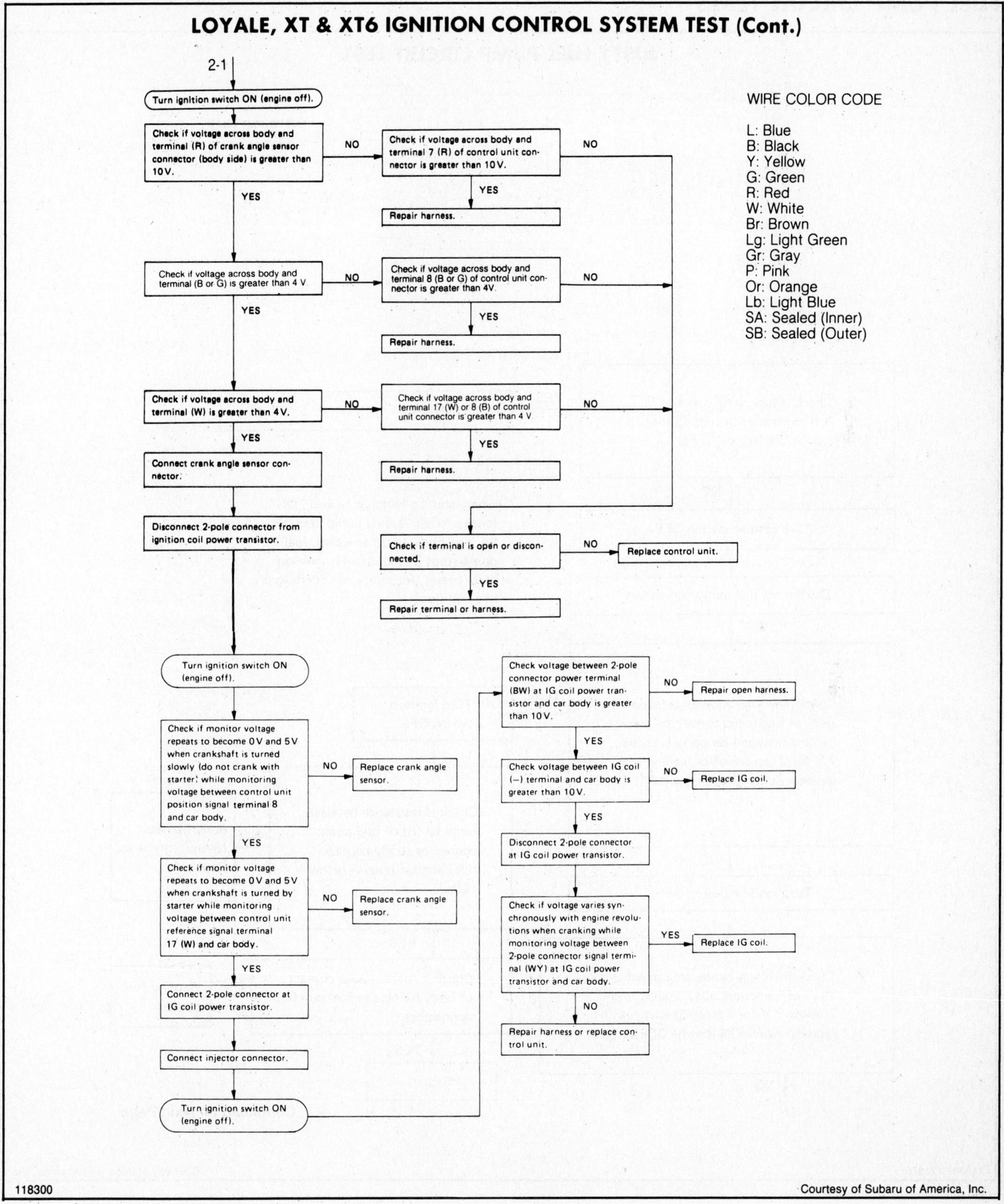

2-1
Turn ignition switch ON (engine off).
Check if voltage across body and terminal (R) of crank angle sensor connector (body side) is greater than 10V.
NO
Check if voltage across body and terminal 7 (R) of control unit connector is greater than 10V.
YES
Repair harness.
YES
Check if voltage across body and terminal (B or G) is greater than 4 V.
NO
Check if voltage across body and terminal 8 (B or G) of control unit connector is greater than 4V.
YES
Repair harness.
YES
Check if voltage across body and terminal (W) is greater than 4V.
NO
Check if voltage across body and terminal 17 (W) or 8 (B) of control unit connector is greater than 4 V
YES
Repair harness.
YES
Connect crank angle sensor connector.
Disconnect 2-pole connector from ignition coil power transistor.
Check if terminal is open or disconnected.
NO
Replace control unit.
YES
Repair terminal or harness.
Turn ignition switch ON (engine off).
Check if monitor voltage repeats to become 0V and 5V when crankshaft is turned slowly (do not crank with starter) while monitoring voltage between control unit position signal terminal 8 and car body.
NO
Replace crank angle sensor.
YES
Check if monitor voltage repeats to become 0V and 5V when crankshaft is turned by starter while monitoring voltage between control unit reference signal terminal 17 (W) and car body.
NO
Replace crank angle sensor.
YES
Connect 2-pole connector at IG coil power transistor.
Connect injector connector.
Turn ignition switch ON (engine off).
Check voltage between 2-pole connector power terminal (BW) at IG coil power transistor and car body is greater than 10V.
NO
Repair open harness.
YES
Check voltage between IG coil (−) terminal and car body is greater than 10V.
NO
Replace IG coil.
YES
Disconnect 2-pole connector at IG coil power transistor.
Check if voltage varies synchronously with engine revolutions when cranking while monitoring voltage between 2-pole connector signal terminal (WY) at IG coil power transistor and car body.
YES
Replace IG coil.
NO
Repair harness or replace control unit.
WIRE COLOR CODE
L: Blue
B: Black
Y: Yellow
G: Green
R: Red
W: White
Br: Brown
Lg: Light Green
Gr: Gray
P: Pink
Or: Orange
Lb: Light Blue
SA: Sealed (Inner)
SB: Sealed (Outer)
118300
Courtesy of Subaru of America, Inc.

# 1991 ENGINE PERFORMANCE
# Basic Diagnostic Procedures (Cont.)

## FUEL PUMP CIRCUIT TESTS

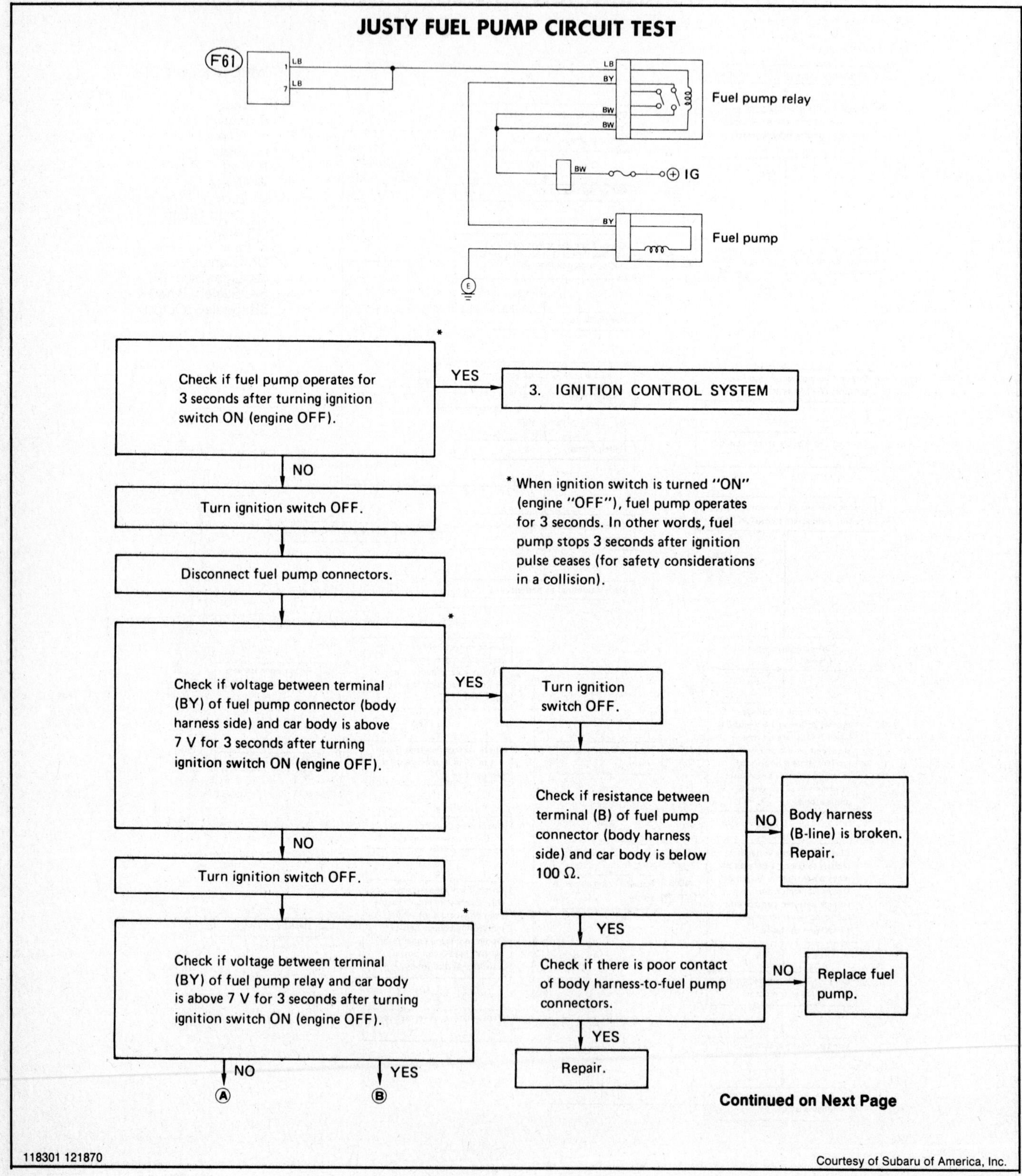
JUSTY FUEL PUMP CIRCUIT TEST
F61
LB
LB
LB
BY
BW
BW
Fuel pump relay
BW
IG
BY
Fuel pump
E
Check if fuel pump operates for 3 seconds after turning ignition switch ON (engine OFF). *
YES
3. IGNITION CONTROL SYSTEM
NO
Turn ignition switch OFF.
Disconnect fuel pump connectors.
* When ignition switch is turned "ON" (engine "OFF"), fuel pump operates for 3 seconds. In other words, fuel pump stops 3 seconds after ignition pulse ceases (for safety considerations in a collision).
Check if voltage between terminal (BY) of fuel pump connector (body harness side) and car body is above 7 V for 3 seconds after turning ignition switch ON (engine OFF). *
YES
Turn ignition switch OFF.
Check if resistance between terminal (B) of fuel pump connector (body harness side) and car body is below 100 Ω.
NO
Body harness (B-line) is broken. Repair.
YES
Check if there is poor contact of body harness-to-fuel pump connectors.
NO
Replace fuel pump.
YES
Repair.
NO
Turn ignition switch OFF.
Check if voltage between terminal (BY) of fuel pump relay and car body is above 7 V for 3 seconds after turning ignition switch ON (engine OFF). *
NO
A
YES
B
118301 121870
Courtesy of Subaru of America, Inc.

Continued on Next Page

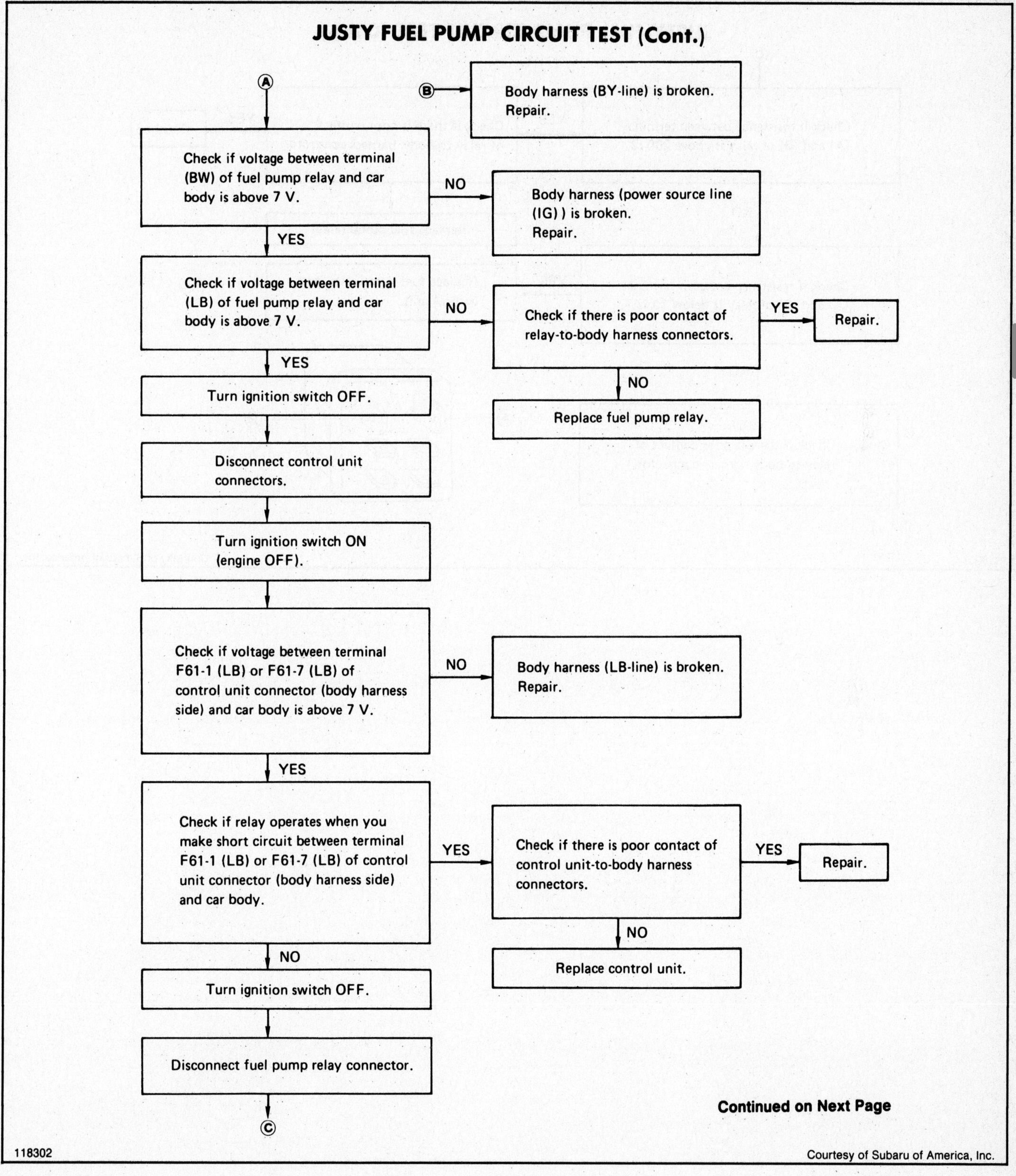

JUSTY FUEL PUMP CIRCUIT TEST (Cont.)
A
B
Body harness (BY-line) is broken. Repair.
Check if voltage between terminal (BW) of fuel pump relay and car body is above 7 V.
NO
Body harness (power source line (IG) ) is broken. Repair.
YES
Check if voltage between terminal (LB) of fuel pump relay and car body is above 7 V.
NO
Check if there is poor contact of relay-to-body harness connectors.
YES
Repair.
NO
Replace fuel pump relay.
YES
Turn ignition switch OFF.
Disconnect control unit connectors.
Turn ignition switch ON (engine OFF).
Check if voltage between terminal F61-1 (LB) or F61-7 (LB) of control unit connector (body harness side) and car body is above 7 V.
NO
Body harness (LB-line) is broken. Repair.
YES
Check if relay operates when you make short circuit between terminal F61-1 (LB) or F61-7 (LB) of control unit connector (body harness side) and car body.
YES
Check if there is poor contact of control unit-to-body harness connectors.
YES
Repair.
NO
Replace control unit.
NO
Turn ignition switch OFF.
Disconnect fuel pump relay connector.
C
Continued on Next Page
118302
Courtesy of Subaru of America, Inc.

# 1991 ENGINE PERFORMANCE
# Basic Diagnostic Procedures (Cont.)

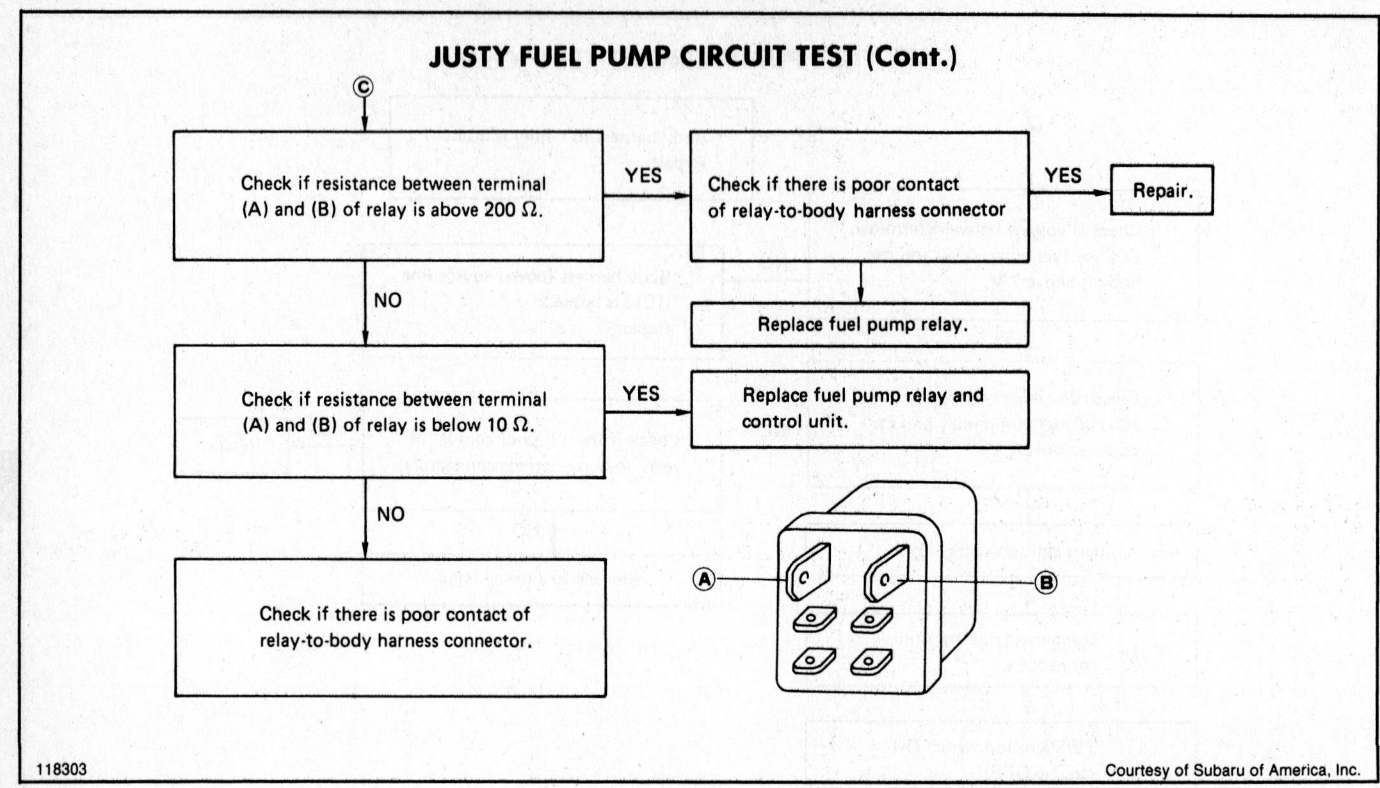
JUSTY FUEL PUMP CIRCUIT TEST (Cont.)
C
Check if resistance between terminal (A) and (B) of relay is above 200 Ω.
YES
Check if there is poor contact of relay-to-body harness connector
YES
Repair.
Replace fuel pump relay.
NO
Check if resistance between terminal (A) and (B) of relay is below 10 Ω.
YES
Replace fuel pump relay and control unit.
NO
Check if there is poor contact of relay-to-body harness connector.
A
B
118303
Courtesy of Subaru of America, Inc.

# 1991 ENGINE PERFORMANCE
## Basic Diagnostic Procedures (Cont.)

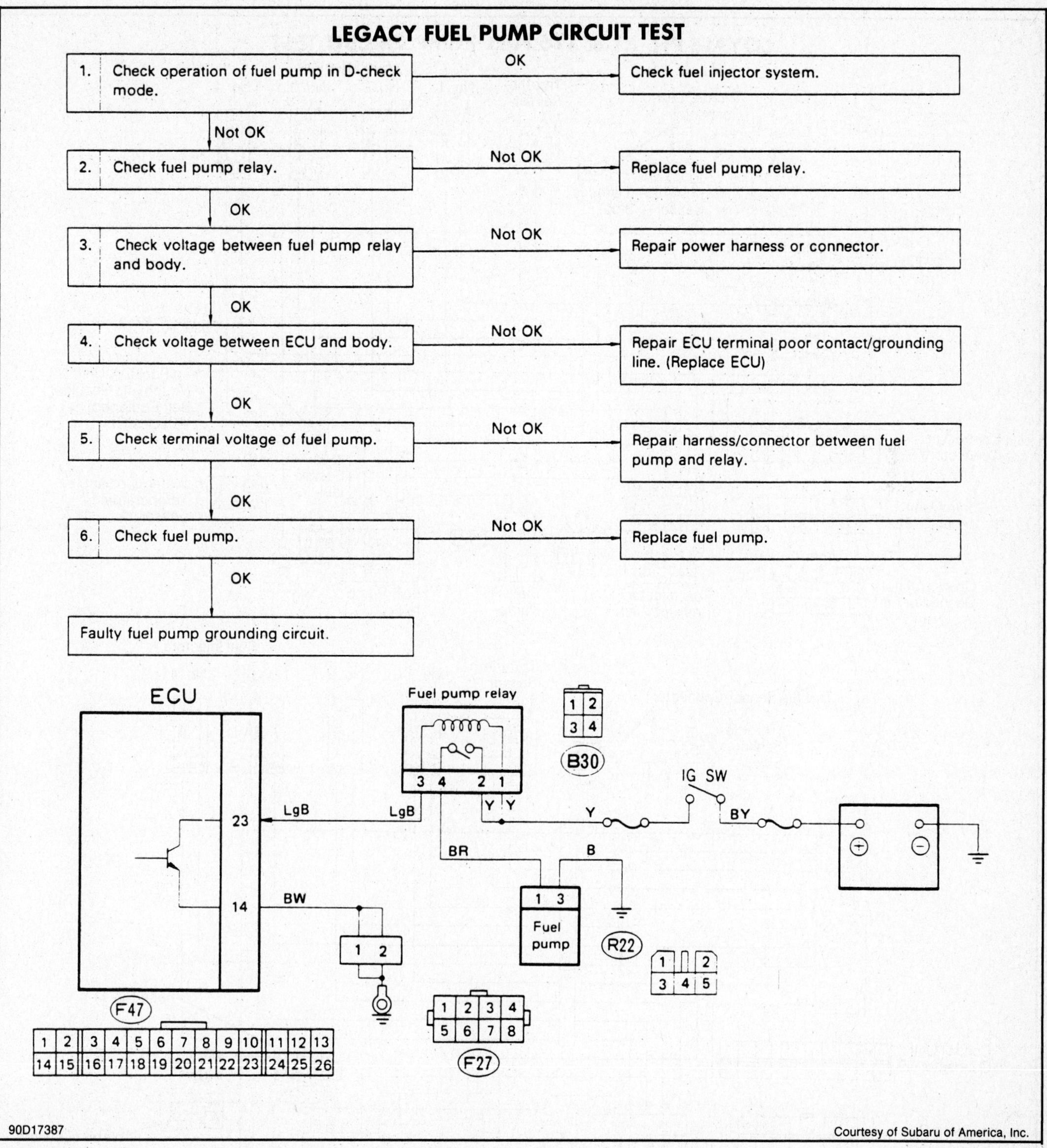
LEGACY FUEL PUMP CIRCUIT TEST
1. Check operation of fuel pump in D-check mode.
OK
Check fuel injector system.
Not OK
2. Check fuel pump relay.
Not OK
Replace fuel pump relay.
OK
3. Check voltage between fuel pump relay and body.
Not OK
Repair power harness or connector.
OK
4. Check voltage between ECU and body.
Not OK
Repair ECU terminal poor contact/grounding line. (Replace ECU)
OK
5. Check terminal voltage of fuel pump.
Not OK
Repair harness/connector between fuel pump and relay.
OK
6. Check fuel pump.
Not OK
Replace fuel pump.
OK
Faulty fuel pump grounding circuit.
ECU
Fuel pump relay
B30
IG SW
23
14
LgB
LgB
Y
Y
Y
BY
BR
B
BW
Fuel pump
R22
F47
F27
90D17387
Courtesy of Subaru of America, Inc.

# 1991 ENGINE PERFORMANCE
## Basic Diagnostic Procedures (Cont.)

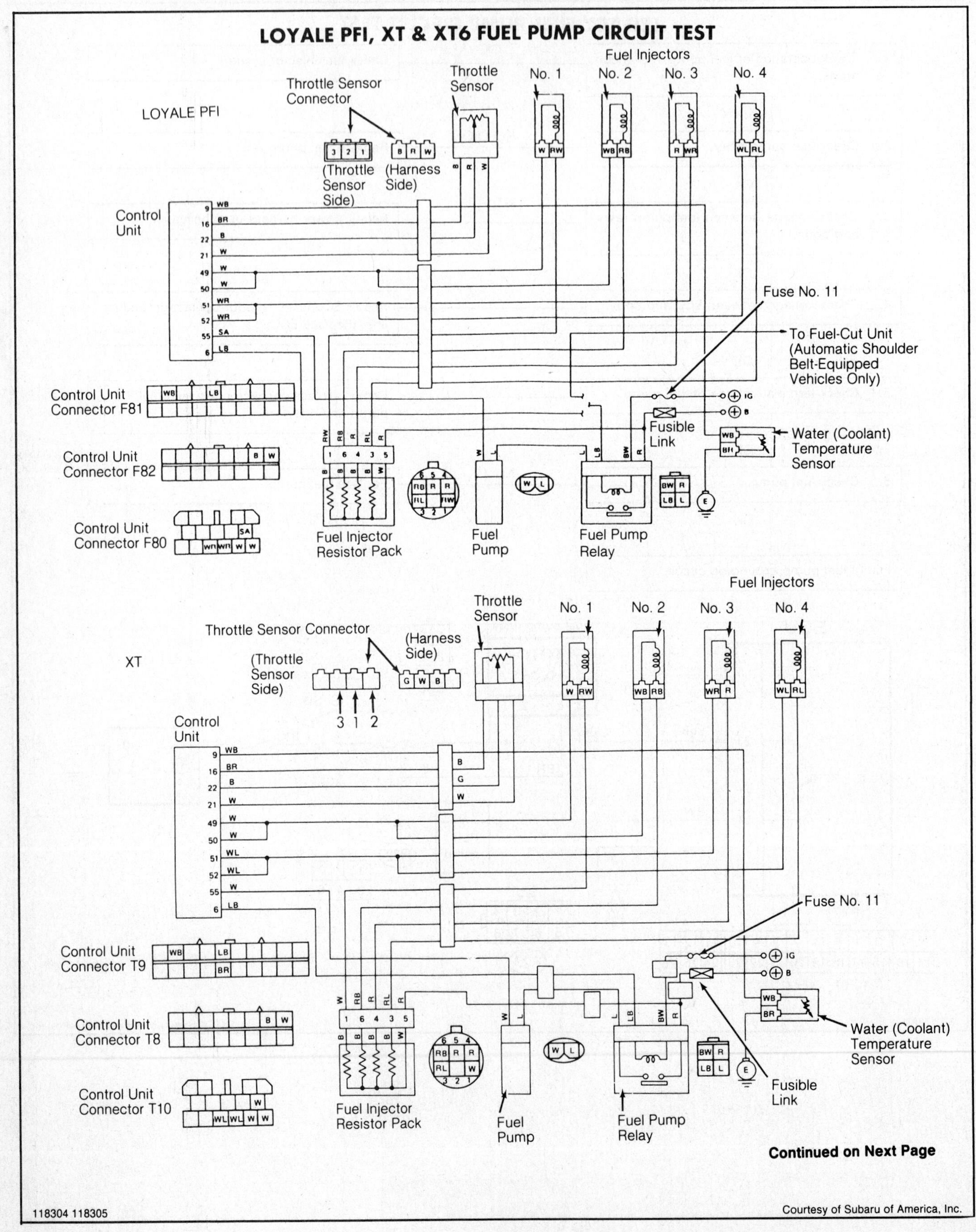


Continued on Next Page

118304 118305

Courtesy of Subaru of America, Inc.

## LOYALE PFI, XT & XT6 FUEL PUMP CIRCUIT TEST (Cont.)

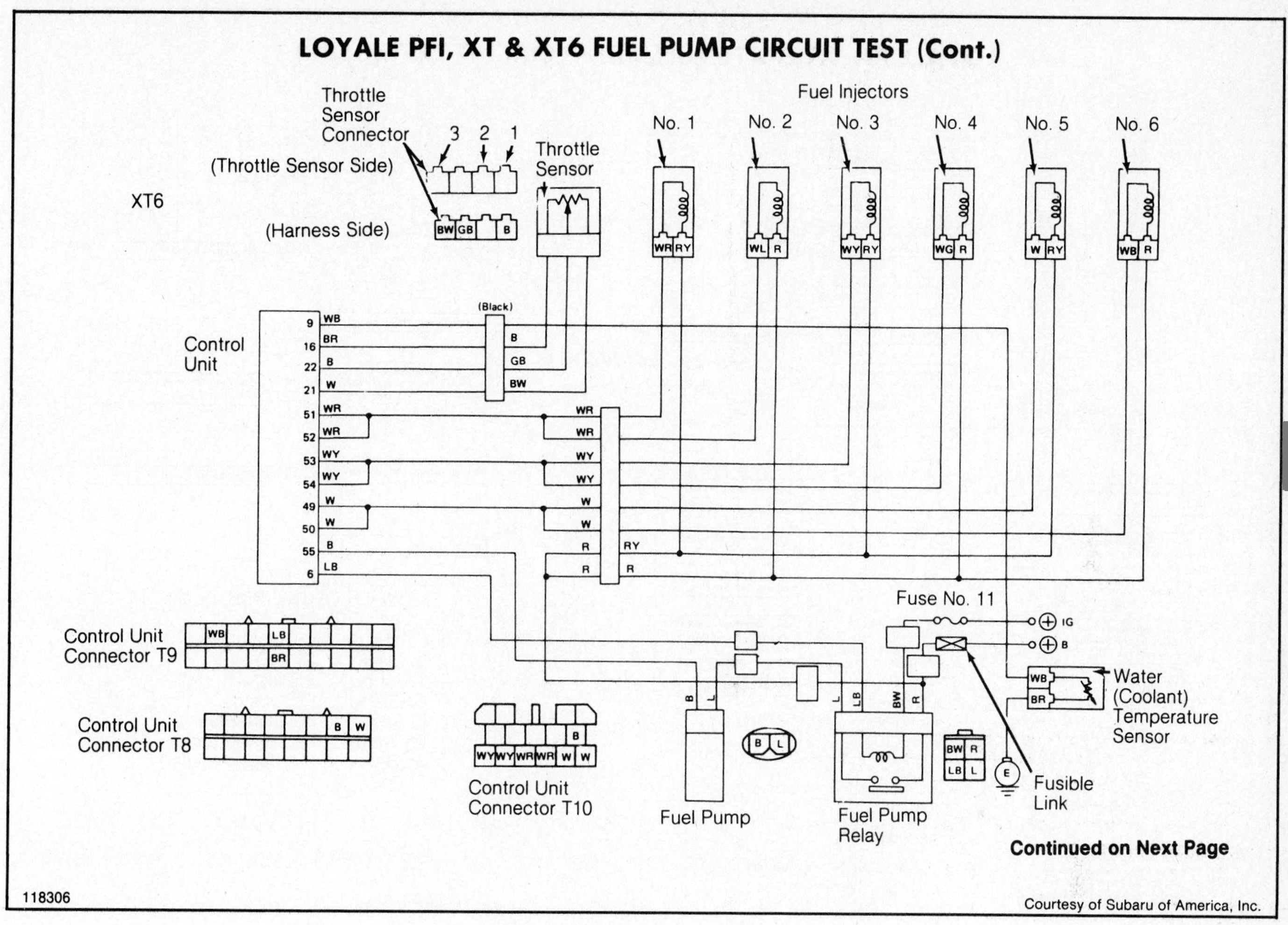


Continued on Next Page

118306

Courtesy of Subaru of America, Inc.

# 1991 ENGINE PERFORMANCE
## Basic Diagnostic Procedures (Cont.)

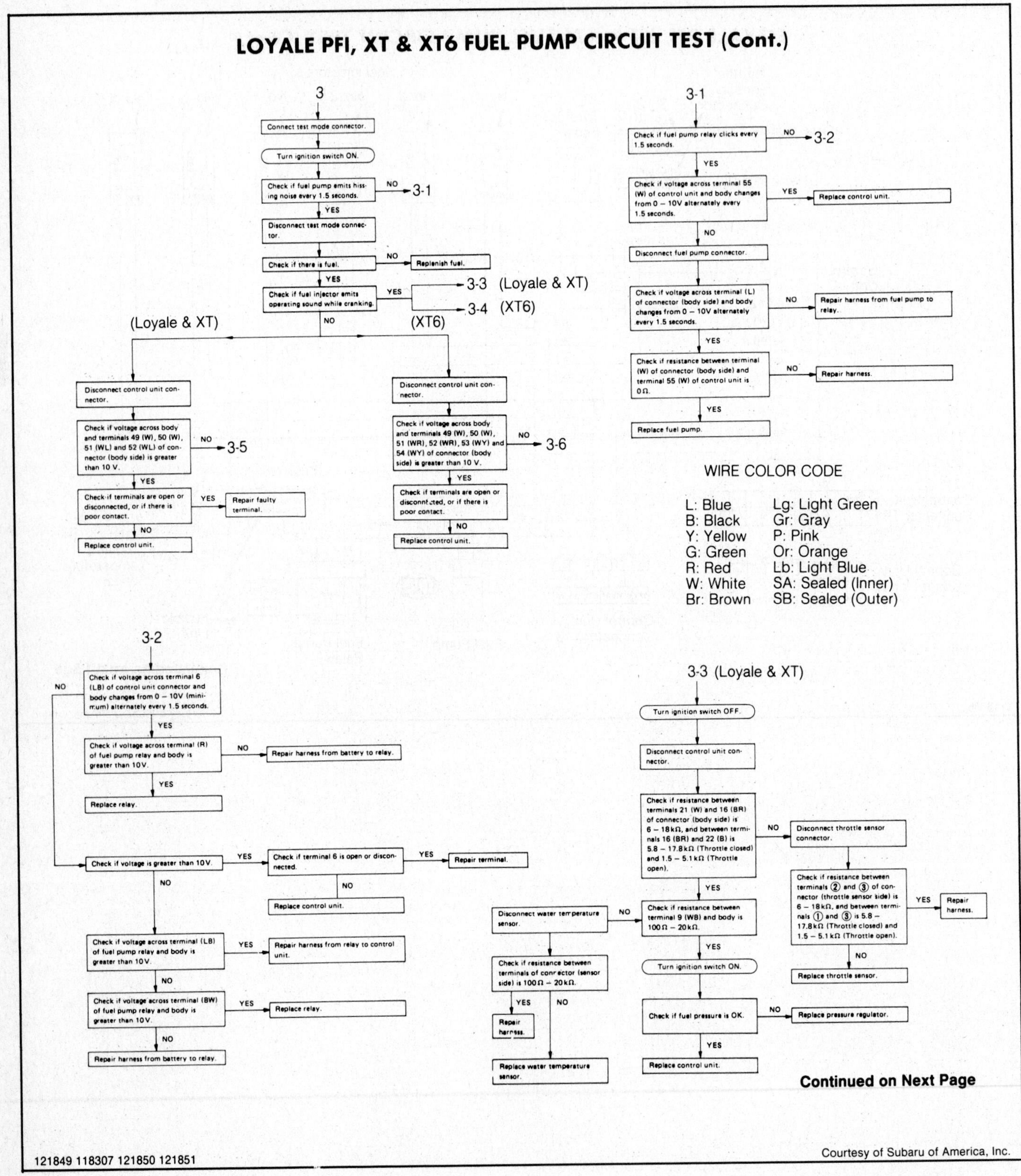

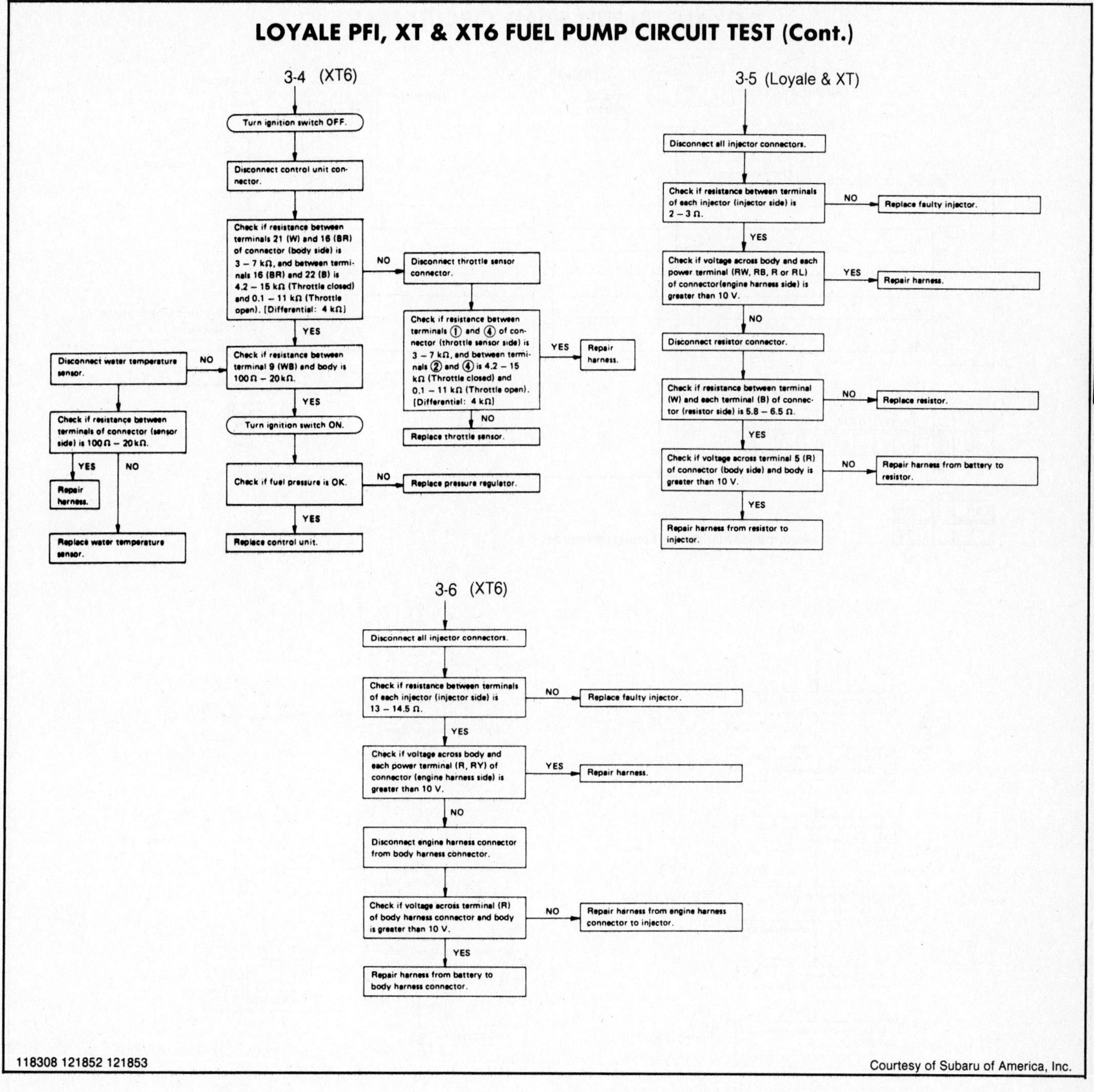
LOYALE PFI, XT & XT6 FUEL PUMP CIRCUIT TEST (Cont.)
3-4 (XT6)
Turn ignition switch OFF.
Disconnect control unit connector.
Check if resistance between terminals 21 (W) and 16 (BR) of connector (body side) is 3 – 7 kΩ, and between terminals 16 (BR) and 22 (B) is 4.2 – 15 kΩ (Throttle closed) and 0.1 – 11 kΩ (Throttle open). [Differential: 4 kΩ]
NO
Disconnect throttle sensor connector.
Check if resistance between terminals ① and ④ of connector (throttle sensor side) is 3 – 7 kΩ, and between terminals ② and ④ is 4.2 – 15 kΩ (Throttle closed) and 0.1 – 11 kΩ (Throttle open). [Differential: 4 kΩ]
YES
Repair harness.
NO
Replace throttle sensor.
YES
Check if resistance between terminal 9 (WB) and body is 100Ω – 20kΩ.
NO
Disconnect water temperature sensor.
Check if resistance between terminals of connector (sensor side) is 100Ω – 20kΩ.
YES
Repair harness.
NO
Replace water temperature sensor.
YES
Turn ignition switch ON.
Check if fuel pressure is OK.
NO
Replace pressure regulator.
YES
Replace control unit.
3-5 (Loyale & XT)
Disconnect all injector connectors.
Check if resistance between terminals of each injector (injector side) is 2 – 3 Ω.
NO
Replace faulty injector.
YES
Check if voltage across body and each power terminal (RW, RB, R or RL) of connector (engine harness side) is greater than 10 V.
YES
Repair harness.
NO
Disconnect resistor connector.
Check if resistance between terminal (W) and each terminal (B) of connector (resistor side) is 5.8 – 6.5 Ω.
NO
Replace resistor.
YES
Check if voltage across terminal 5 (R) of connector (body side) and body is greater than 10 V.
NO
Repair harness from battery to resistor.
YES
Repair harness from resistor to injector.
3-6 (XT6)
Disconnect all injector connectors.
Check if resistance between terminals of each injector (injector side) is 13 – 14.5 Ω.
NO
Replace faulty injector.
YES
Check if voltage across body and each power terminal (R, RY) of connector (engine harness side) is greater than 10 V.
YES
Repair harness.
NO
Disconnect engine harness connector from body harness connector.
Check if voltage across terminal (R) of body harness connector and body is greater than 10 V.
NO
Repair harness from engine harness connector to injector.
YES
Repair harness from battery to body harness connector.
118308 121852 121853
Courtesy of Subaru of America, Inc.

# 1991 ENGINE PERFORMANCE
## Basic Diagnostic Procedures (Cont.)

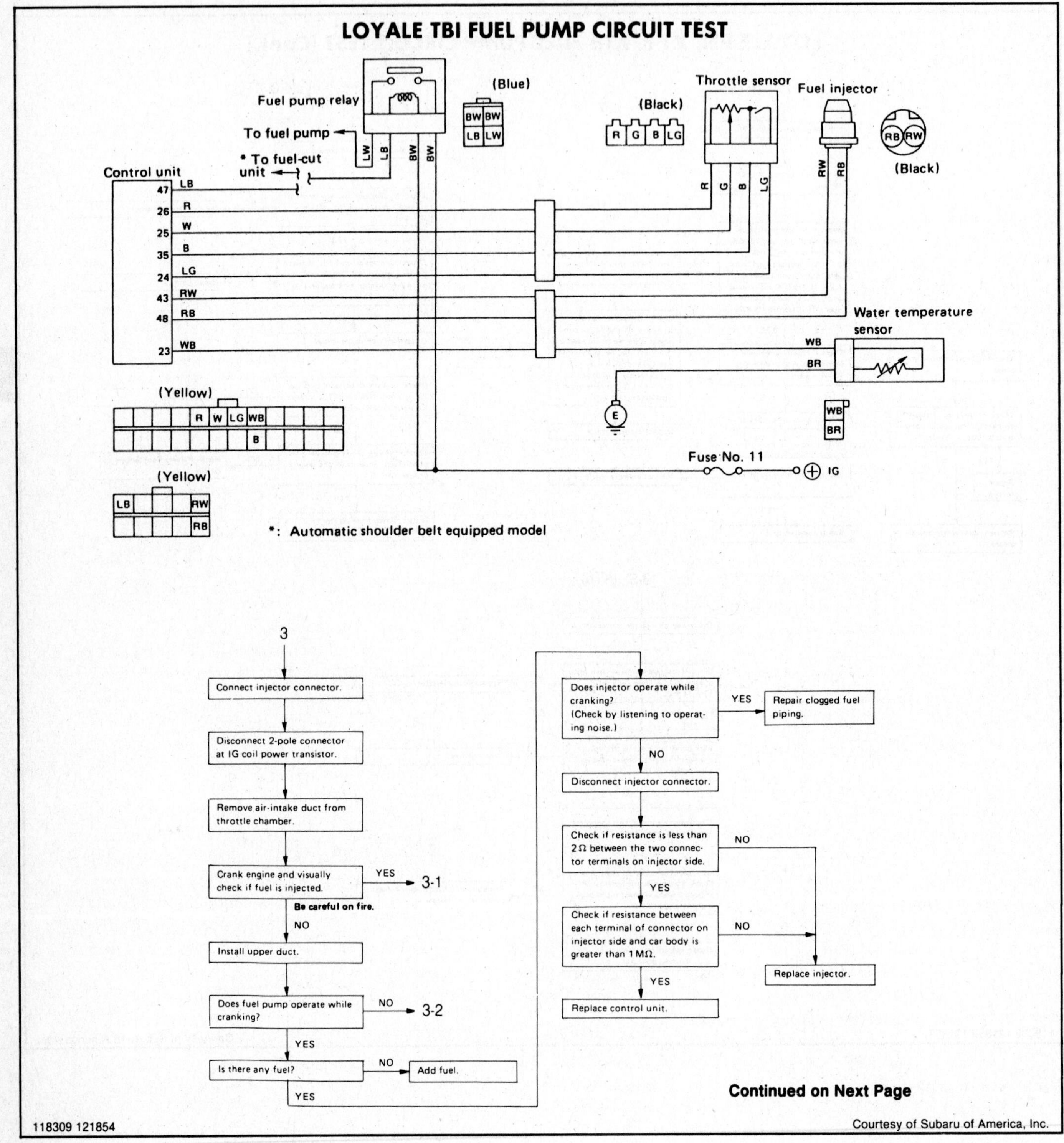
LOYALE TBI FUEL PUMP CIRCUIT TEST
Fuel pump relay
(Blue)
To fuel pump
* To fuel-cut unit
Control unit
Throttle sensor
(Black)
Fuel injector
(Black)
Water temperature sensor
(Yellow)
(Yellow)
Fuse No. 11
IG
*: Automatic shoulder belt equipped model
3
Connect injector connector.
Disconnect 2-pole connector at IG coil power transistor.
Remove air-intake duct from throttle chamber.
Crank engine and visually check if fuel is injected.
YES
3-1
Be careful on fire.
NO
Install upper duct.
Does fuel pump operate while cranking?
NO
3-2
YES
Is there any fuel?
NO
Add fuel.
YES
Does injector operate while cranking? (Check by listening to operating noise.)
YES
Repair clogged fuel piping.
NO
Disconnect injector connector.
Check if resistance is less than 2 Ω between the two connector terminals on injector side.
NO
YES
Check if resistance between each terminal of connector on injector side and car body is greater than 1 MΩ.
NO
Replace injector.
YES
Replace control unit.
Continued on Next Page
118309 121854
Courtesy of Subaru of America, Inc.

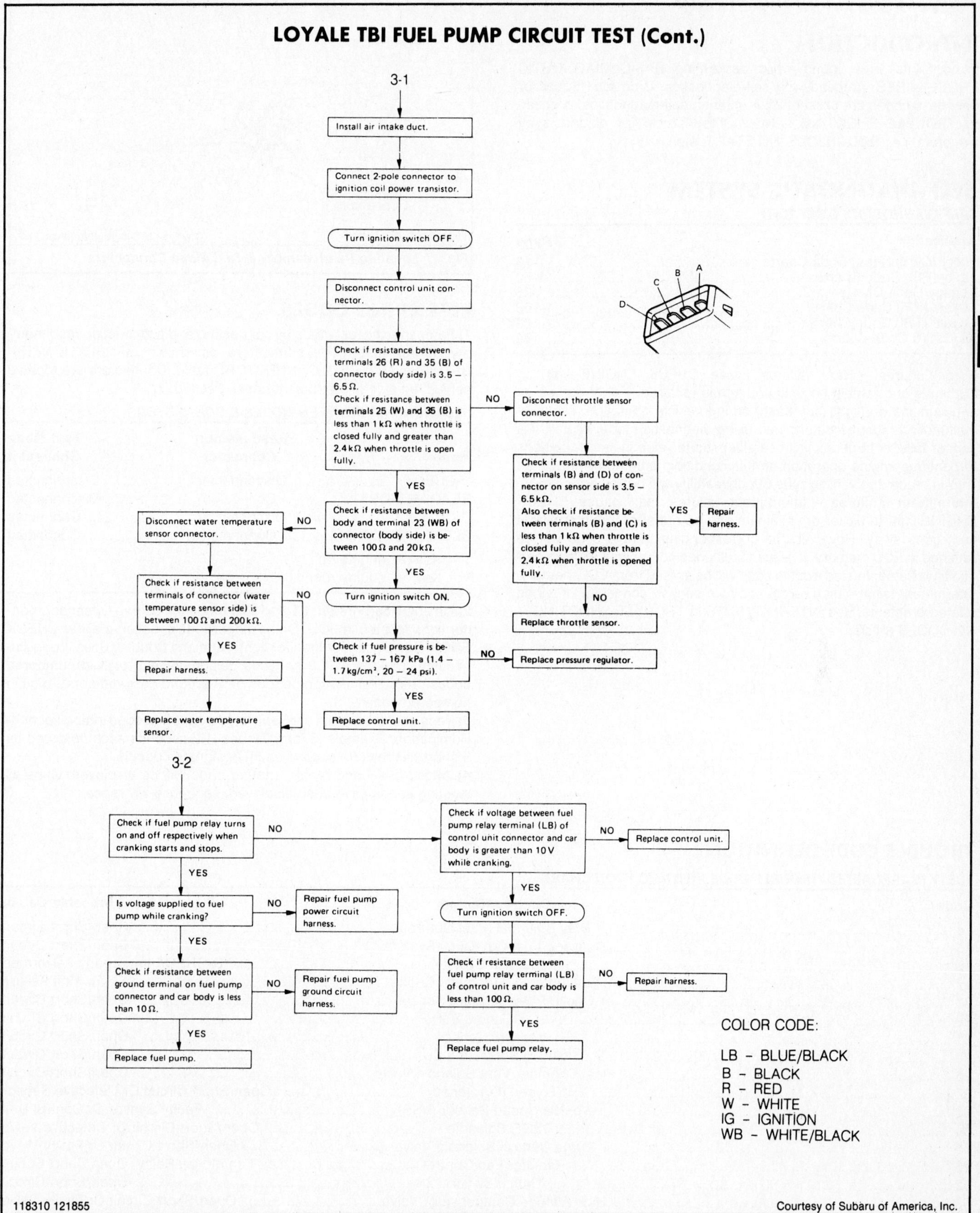
LOYALE TBI FUEL PUMP CIRCUIT TEST (Cont.)
3-1
Install air intake duct.
Connect 2-pole connector to ignition coil power transistor.
Turn ignition switch OFF.
Disconnect control unit connector.
Check if resistance between terminals 26 (R) and 35 (B) of connector (body side) is 3.5 – 6.5 Ω.
Check if resistance between terminals 25 (W) and 35 (B) is less than 1 kΩ when throttle is closed fully and greater than 2.4 kΩ when throttle is open fully.
NO
Disconnect throttle sensor connector.
Check if resistance between terminals (B) and (D) of connector on sensor side is 3.5 – 6.5 kΩ.
Also check if resistance between terminals (B) and (C) is less than 1 kΩ when throttle is closed fully and greater than 2.4 kΩ when throttle is opened fully.
YES
Repair harness.
NO
Replace throttle sensor.
A
B
C
D
YES
Check if resistance between body and terminal 23 (WB) of connector (body side) is between 100 Ω and 20 kΩ.
NO
Disconnect water temperature sensor connector.
Check if resistance between terminals of connector (water temperature sensor side) is between 100 Ω and 200 kΩ.
NO
YES
Repair harness.
Replace water temperature sensor.
YES
Turn ignition switch ON.
Check if fuel pressure is between 137 – 167 kPa (1.4 – 1.7 kg/cm², 20 – 24 psi).
NO
Replace pressure regulator.
YES
Replace control unit.
3-2
Check if fuel pump relay turns on and off respectively when cranking starts and stops.
NO
Check if voltage between fuel pump relay terminal (LB) of control unit connector and car body is greater than 10 V while cranking.
NO
Replace control unit.
YES
Turn ignition switch OFF.
Check if resistance between fuel pump relay terminal (LB) of control unit and car body is less than 100 Ω.
NO
Repair harness.
YES
Replace fuel pump relay.
YES
Is voltage supplied to fuel pump while cranking?
NO
Repair fuel pump power circuit harness.
YES
Check if resistance between ground terminal on fuel pump connector and car body is less than 10 Ω.
NO
Repair fuel pump ground circuit harness.
YES
Replace fuel pump.
COLOR CODE:
LB - BLUE/BLACK
B - BLACK
R - RED
W - WHITE
IG - IGNITION
WB - WHITE/BLACK
118310 121855
Courtesy of Subaru of America, Inc.

# 1991 ENGINE PERFORMANCE
# Self-Diagnostics

**Justy, Legacy, Loyale, XT, XT6**

## INTRODUCTION

If no faults were found while performing BASIC DIAGNOSTIC PROCEDURES, proceed with self-diagnostics. If no fault codes or only pass codes are present after entering self-diagnostics, proceed to TROUBLE SHOOTING - NO CODES article for diagnosis by symptom (i.e., ROUGH IDLE, NO START, etc.).

## SELF-DIAGNOSTIC SYSTEM

***SELF-DIAGNOSTICS DIRECTORY***



**Hard Failures -** Hard failures cause CHECK ENGINE light to illuminate and remain on until problem is repaired. If light comes on and remains on (light may flash) during vehicle operation, cause of malfunction must be determined using diagnostic (code) charts. If a sensor fails, control unit will use a substitute value in its calculations to continue engine operation. In this condition, commonly known as limp-in mode, the vehicle runs but driveability will not be optimum.

**Intermittent Failures -** Intermittent failures may cause CHECK ENGINE light to flicker or illuminate and go out after the intermittent fault goes away. However, the corresponding trouble code will be retained in ECU memory. If related fault does not reoccur within a certain time frame, related trouble code will be erased from ECU memory. Intermittent failures may be caused by a sensor, connector or wiring related problems. See INTERMITTENTS in TROUBLE SHOOTING - NO CODES article.

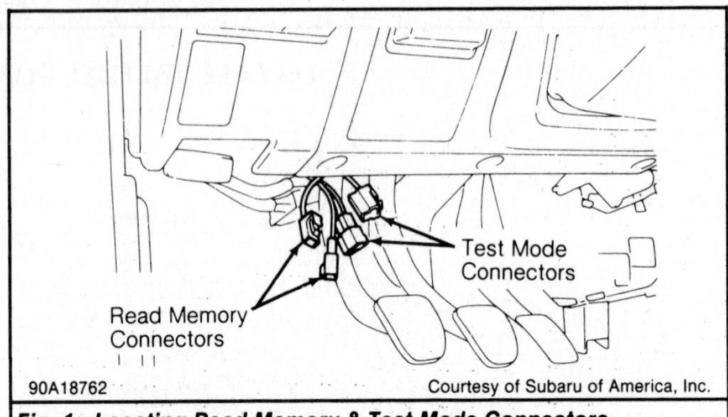


***Fig. 1: Locating Read Memory & Test Mode Connectors***

## RETRIEVING CODES

**1)** Enter specific test mode by connecting or disconnecting read memory and/or test mode connectors as shown in RELATIONSHIP BETWEEN MODES & CONNECTORS table. Connectors are located behind left side of instrument panel. *See Fig. 1.*

***RELATIONSHIP BETWEEN MODES & CONNECTORS***

| Mode | Read Memory Connector | Test Mode Connector |
|---|---|---|
| U-CHECK [1] | Disconnected | Disconnected |
| READ MEMORY [1] | Connected | Disconnected |
| D-CHECK [1] | Disconnected | Connected |
| CLEAR MEMORY [2] | Connected | Connected |

[1] - Key on, engine off.
[2] - Key on, engine running.

**2)** On Justy carbureted, XT and XT6 models, observe $O_2$ sensor monitor light, located in ECU. On all other models, observe either CHECK ENGINE or $O_2$ sensor monitor light. Note any trouble codes. Long illumination periods of 1.2 seconds designate tens digit in numbered codes. Short illumination periods of .2 second designate ones digit in numbered codes.

**3)** Tens and ones digits are separated by a .03-second interval of non-illumination. Example: 3 long flashes (1.2 seconds each) followed by 5 short flashes (.02 second each) designate code 35.

**4)** After a 2-second break, another code will be displayed. Once all existing codes have been displayed, sequence will repeat.

## TROUBLE CODE DEFINITION

***JUSTY (CARBURETED) TROUBLE CODE IDENTIFICATION CHART***

| Code | Circuit Affected | Probable Cause |
|---|---|---|
| 14 | Duty Solenoid (Fuel Control) | Open/Short Circuit |
| 15 | Coasting Fuel-Cut (CFC) System | Open/Short Circuit |
| 16 | Feedback System | D-CHECK Improperly Performed |
| 17 | Fuel Pump & Automatic Choke | Unit Failure |
| 21 | Coolant Temperature Sensor | Open/Short Circuit |
| 22 | [1] VLC Solenoid Valve | Open/Short Circuit |
| 23 | Pressure Sensor | Open/Short Circuit |
| 24 | Idle-Up Solenoid Valve | Open/Short Circuit |
| 25 | Float Chamber Vent Solenoid Valve | Open/Short Circuit |
| 32 | Oxygen ($O_2$) Sensor | Open/Short Circuit Or Defective Sensor |
| 33 | Vehicle Speed Sensor (VSS) | Faulty Sensor Or Control Unit |
| 34 | EGR Solenoid | Open/Short Circuit Or Defective Valve |
| 35 | Purge Control Solenoid Valve | Open/Short Circuit Or Faulty Valve |
| 46 | Radiator Fan Control | Fan Motor, Relay, Open/Short Circuit |
| 52 | Clutch Switch | Open/Short Circuit |
| 53 | High Altitude Compensator Valve | Open/Short Circuit Or Faulty Valve |
| 62 | Idle-Up System (1) | Faulty Headlight/Defogger Switch |
| 63 | Idle-Up System (2) | Faulty Fan/Radiator Switch |

[1] - Vacuum/Pressure Sensor Line Control (VLC) solenoid valve.

# 1991 ENGINE PERFORMANCE
# Self-Diagnostics (Cont.)

***JUSTY (PFI) TROUBLE CODE IDENTIFICATION CHART***

| Code | Circuit Affected | Probable Cause |
|---|---|---|
| 11 | Crank Angle Sensor | No Reference Signal |
| 12 | Starter Switch | Open/Short Circuit |
| 13 | TDC Sensor | No Reference Signal |
| 14 | Injector No. 1 | Inoperative Injector |
| 15 | Injector No. 2 | Inoperative Injector |
| 16 | Injector No. 3 | Inoperative Injector |
| 21 | Coolant Temperature Sensor | Open/Short Circuit |
| 23 | Pressure Sensor | Open/Short Circuit |
| 24 | ISC Solenoid Valve | Open/Short Circuit |
| 26 | Air Temperature Sensor | Open/Short Circuit |
| 32 | Oxygen ($O_2$) Sensor | Inoperative $O_2$ Sensor |
| 33 | Vehicle Speed Sensor | No Reference Signal |
| 35 | Purge Control Solenoid Valve | Open/Short Circuit |
| 36 | Ignitor Circuit | Open/Short Circuit |
| 41 | Air/Fuel Ratio Control System | Faulty Learning Control Function |
| 42 | Idle Switch | Open/Short Circuit |
| 43 | Throttle Switch | Open/Short Circuit |
| 45 | Atmospheric Pressure Sensor | No Signal |
| 52 | [1] Clutch Switch | Open/Short Circuit |
| 62 | Electric Load Signal | Open/Short Circuit |
| 63 | Blower Fan Switch | Open/Short Circuit |
| 65 | Vacuum Pressure Sensor | Abnormal Signal |

[1] – FWD manual transmission or ECVT models only.

***LEGACY TROUBLE CODE IDENTIFICATION CHART***

| Code | Circuit Affected | Probable Cause |
|---|---|---|
| 11 | Crank Angle Sensor | No Reference Signal |
| 12 | Starter Switch | Open/Short Circuit |
| 13 | Cam Angle Sensor | No Reference Signal |
| 14 | Fuel Injector No. 1 | Inoperative Fuel Injector |
| 15 | Fuel Injector No. 2 | Inoperative Fuel Injector |
| 16 | Fuel Injector No. 3 | Inoperative Fuel Injector |
| 17 | Fuel Injector No. 4 | Inoperative Fuel Injector |
| 21 | Coolant Temperature Sensor | Open/Short Circuit |
| 22 | Knock Sensor | Open/Short Circuit |
| 23 | Airflow Sensor Circuit | Open/Short Circuit |
| 24 | Air Control Valve | Inoperative Air Control Valve |
| 31 | Throttle Position Sensor | Open/Short Circuit |
| 32 | Oxygen ($O_2$) Sensor | Abnormal Sensor Signal |
| 33 | Vehicle Speed Sensor | No Reference Signal |
| 35 | Purge Control Solenoid Valve | Open/Short Circuit |
| 41 | Air/Fuel Ratio Control System | Faulty Learning Control Function |
| 42 | Idle Switch | Abnormal Reference Signal |
| 44 | Wastegate Duty Solenoid (Turbo) | Open/Short Circuit |
| 45 | Atmospheric Pressure Sensor (Non-Turbo) | Faulty Sensor |
| 45 | Pressure Sensor Duty Solenoid | Valve Inoperative |
| 49 | Airflow Sensor | Use Of Improper Airflow Sensor |
| 51 | Neutral Safety Switch (M/T) | Open/Short Circuit |
| 51 | Inhibitor Switch (A/T) | Open/Short Circuit |
| 52 | Parking Brake Switch (A/T) | Open/Short Circuit |

# 1991 ENGINE PERFORMANCE
# Self-Diagnostics (Cont.)

***LOYALE (PFI) TROUBLE CODE IDENTIFICATION CHART***

| Code | Circuit Affected | Probable Cause |
|---|---|---|
| 11 | Crank Angle Sensor | No Reference Signal |
| 12 | Starter Switch | Open/Short Circuit |
| 13 | Crank Angle Sensor | No Position Pulse |
| 14 | Fuel Injectors No. 1 & 2 | Abnormal Injector Output |
| 15 | Fuel Injectors No. 3 & 4 | Abnormal Injector Output |
| 21 | Coolant Temperature Sensor | Open/Short Circuit |
| 22 | Knock Sensor | Open/Short Circuit |
| 23 | Airflow Meter Circuit | Open/Short Circuit |
| 31 | Throttle Position Sensor | Open/Short Circuit |
| 32 | Oxygen ($O_2$) Sensor | Abnormal Sensor Signal |
| 33 | Vehicle Speed Sensor | No Reference Signal |
| 35 | Purge Control Solenoid Valve | Open/Short Circuit |
| 41 | System Too Lean | Check Fuel Pressure Or Vacuum Leak |
| 42 | Idle Switch | Abnormal Reference Signal |
| 44 | Wastegate Duty Solenoid (Turbo) | Open/Short Circuit |

***LOYALE (TBI) TROUBLE CODE IDENTIFICATION CHART***

| Code | Circuit Affected | Probable Cause |
|---|---|---|
| 11 | Crank Angle Sensor | No Reference Signal |
| 12 | Starter Switch | Open/Short Circuit |
| 13 | Crank Angle Sensor | No Position Pulse |
| 14 | Fuel Injector | Abnormal Injector Output |
| 21 | Coolant Temperature Sensor | Open/Short Circuit |
| 23 | Airflow Meter Circuit | Open/Short Circuit |
| 24 | Air Control Valve | Open/Short Circuit |
| 31 | Throttle Position Sensor | Open/Short Circuit |
| 32 | Oxygen ($O_2$) Sensor | Abnormal Sensor Signal |
| 33 | Vehicle Speed Sensor | No Reference Signal |
| 34 | EGR Valve Solenoid | Open/Short Circuit Or EGR System |
| 35 | Purge Control Solenoid Valve | Open/Short Circuit |
| 42 | Idle Switch | Abnormal Reference Signal |
| 45 | Kickdown Control Relay | Open/Short Circuit |
| 51 | Neutral Switch (A/T & M/T) | Short Circuit |
| 55 [1] | EGR Temperature Sensor | Open/Short Circuit |
| 61 | Parking Brake Switch (A/T) | Open/Short Circuit |

[1] – California models only.

***XT & XT6 TROUBLE CODE IDENTIFICATION CHART***

| Code | Circuit Affected | Probable Cause |
|---|---|---|
| 11 | Crank Angle Sensor | No Reference Signal |
| 12 | Starter Switch | Open/Short Circuit |
| 13 | Crank Angle Sensor | No Position Pulse |
| 14 | Fuel Injectors No. 1 & 2 (XT) | Abnormal Injector Output |
| 14 | Fuel Injectors No. 5 & 6 (XT6) | Abnormal Injector Output |
| 15 | Fuel Injectors No. 3 & 4 (XT) | Abnormal Injector Output |
| 15 | Fuel Injectors No. 1 & 2 (XT6) | Abnormal Injector Output |
| 21 | Coolant Temperature Sensor | Open/Short Circuit |
| 22 | Knock Sensor (XT6) | Open/Short Circuit |
| 23 | Airflow Meter Circuit | Open/Short Circuit |
| 24 | By-Pass Air Control Valve (XT6) | Open/Short Circuit |
| 25 | Fuel Injectors No. 3 & 4 (XT6) | Abnormal Injector Output |
| 31 | Throttle Position Sensor | Open/Short Circuit |
| 32 | Oxygen ($O_2$) Sensor | Abnormal Sensor Signal |
| 33 | Vehicle Speed Sensor | No Reference Signal |
| 35 | Purge Control Solenoid Valve | Open/Short Circuit |
| 41 | Fuel System | Fuel System Too Lean |
| 42 | Idle Switch | Abnormal Reference Signal |
| 51 | Neutral Switch | No Signal Present |

# 1991 ENGINE PERFORMANCE
# Self-Diagnostics (Cont.)

## SPECIFICATION CODES

Specification codes are codes accessed with trouble code(s) from ECU. These codes determine transmission and vehicle emissions application. Specification code is not available on carbureted models.

*JUSTY (PFI) SPECIFICATION CODES* [1]

| Code | Application |
|---|---|
| 01 | FWD (M/T), Canada & Federal |
| 02 | FWD (ECVT), Canada & Federal |
| 03 | 4WD (M/T), Canada & Federal |
| 04 | 4WD (ECVT), Canada & Federal |
| 10 | FWD (M/T), California |
| 20 | FWD (ECVT), California |
| 30 | 4WD (M/T), California |
| 40 | 4WD (ECVT), California |

[1] – Specification codes are accessed with trouble codes through CHECK ENGINE or $O_2$ monitor light.

*LEGACY SPECIFICATION CODES* [1]

| Code | Application |
|---|---|
| 01 | M/T (Non-Turbo), Canada & Federal |
| 02 | M/T (Non-Turbo), California |
| 03 | A/T (Non-Turbo), Canada & Federal |
| 04 | A/T (Non-Turbo), California |
| 05 | M/T (Turbo), Canada & Federal |
| 06 | M/T (Turbo), California |
| 07 | A/T (Turbo), Canada & Federal |
| 08 | A/T (Turbo), California |

[1] – Specification codes are accessed with trouble codes through CHECK ENGINE or $O_2$ monitor light.

*LOYALE (PFI) SPECIFICATION CODES* [1]

| Code | Application |
|---|---|
| 01 | M/T, Canada & Federal |
| 02 | M/T, California |
| 03 | A/T, Canada & Federal |
| 04 | A/T, California |

[1] – Specification codes are accessed with trouble codes through CHECK ENGINE or $O_2$ monitor light.

*LOYALE (TBI) SPECIFICATION CODES* [1]

| Code | Application |
|---|---|
| 05 | M/T, Canada & Federal |
| 06 | M/T, California |
| 07 | A/T, Canada & Federal |
| 08 | A/T, California |

[1] – Specification codes are accessed with trouble codes through CHECK ENGINE or $O_2$ monitor light.

*XT & XT6 SPECIFICATION CODES* [1]

| Code | Application |
|---|---|
| 01 | M/T (2.7L), Canada & Federal |
| 02 | M/T (2.7L), California |
| 03 | A/T (1.8L 4WD & 2.7L), Canada & Federal |
| 04 | A/T (1.8L 4WD & 2.7L), California |
| 05 | M/T (1.8L FWD/4WD & 2.7L), Canada & Federal |
| 06 | M/T (1.8L FWD/4WD & 2.7L), California |
| 07 | A/T (1.8L), Canada & Federal |
| 08 | A/T (1.8L), California |

[1] – Specification codes are accessed with trouble codes through CHECK ENGINE or $O_2$ monitor light.

## CLEARING CODES

After malfunction has been corrected, trouble code will clear from memory when CLEAR MEMORY mode is accessed. Unless all items check okay in D-CHECK mode, memory will not be cleared. See RELATIONSHIP BETWEEN MODES & CONNECTORS table.

## ECM LOCATION

*ECM LOCATION*

| Application | Location |
|---|---|
| Justy, Legacy & Loyale | Behind Left Dash Panel |
| XT & XT6 | Behind Center of Dash |

## SUMMARY

If no hard fault codes (or only pass codes) are present, driveability symptoms exist or intermittent codes exist, proceed to TROUBLE SHOOTING – NO CODES article for diagnosis by symptom (i.e., ROUGH IDLE, NO START, etc.) or intermittent diagnostic procedures.

*WIRE COLOR ABBREVIATIONS USED IN CODE CHARTS*

| Abbreviation | Color |
|---|---|
| BR | Black/Red |
| BW | Black/White |
| BY | Black/Yellow |
| G | Green |
| GB | Green/Black |
| GL | Green/Blue |
| GR | Green/Red |
| GW | Green/White |
| GY | Green/Yellow |
| Lg | Light Green |
| LgB | Light Green/Black |
| LR | Blue/Red |
| LW | Blue/White |
| LY | Blue/Yellow |
| RY | Red/Yellow |
| W | White |
| WB | White/Black |
| WR | White/Red |
| WY | White/Yellow |
| Y | Yellow |
| YL | Yellow/Blue |
| YR | Yellow/Red |
| YW | Yellow/White |

***NOTE: The following diagnostic flow charts and mini-schematics are courtesy of Subaru of America, Inc.***

# 1991 ENGINE PERFORMANCE
# Self-Diagnostics – Justy – Carbureted

## JUSTY (CARBURETED) CODE CHARTS

### BASIC OPERATION OF SELF-DIAGNOSTIC SYSTEM

**NO TROUBLE**

○ : CONNECT   X : DISCONNECT

| Engine | Read memory connector | Test mode connector | CHECK ENGINE light | $O_2$ monitor lamp | Remarks |
|---|---|---|---|---|---|
| ON | X | X | OFF | $O_2$ monitor | |
| ON | ○ | X | Blinking | OFF | |
| ON | X | ○ | Blinking | Vehicle specification code | |
| OFF (Ignition switch ON) | X | X | ON | Vehicle specification code | Before starting the engine, the self-diagnosis system assumes the engine to be in NO TROUBLE condition. |
| OFF (Ignition switch ON) | ○ | X | Blinking | OFF | |
| OFF (Ignition switch ON) | X | ○ | * ON → Blinking | Vehicle specification code | |

**TROUBLE**

| Engine | Read memory connector | Test mode connector | CHECK ENGINE light | $O_2$ monitor lamp | Remarks |
|---|---|---|---|---|---|
| ON | X | X | ON | Trouble code | |
| ON | ○ | X | ON | Trouble code (memory) | |
| ON | X | ○ | * OFF → ON | Trouble code | Vehicle specification code is outputted when CHECK ENGINE light is OFF. |
| OFF (Ignition switch ON) | X | X | ON | Trouble code | |
| OFF (Ignition switch ON) | ○ | X | ON | Trouble code (memory) | |
| OFF (Ignition switch ON) | X | ○ | ON | * Vehicle specification code → Trouble code | |

*** : The indication is not changed until engine is operated at speed greater than 1,500 rpm for at least 39 seconds.**

90B18763

# 1991 ENGINE PERFORMANCE
# Self-Diagnostics – Justy – Carbureted (Cont.)

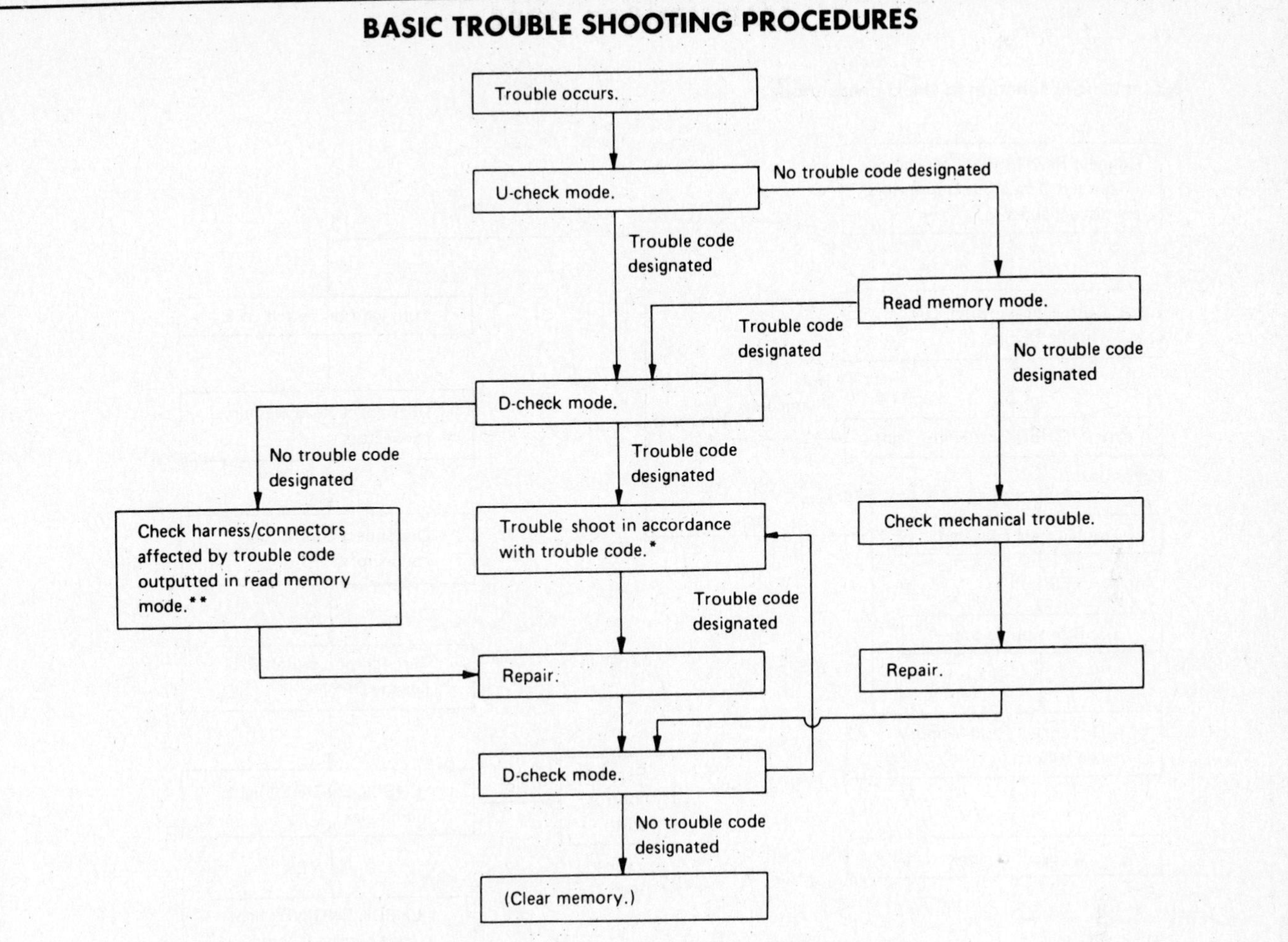


* When more than one trouble code is outputted, begin trouble shooting with the smallest trouble code number and proceed to the next higher code.
After correcting each problem, conduct the D-check and ensure that the corresponding trouble code no longer appears.

** When more than one trouble code is outputted, check all related harness connectors, starting with that corresponding to the smallest trouble code number and proceeding to the next higher code.

95062

# 1991 ENGINE PERFORMANCE
# Self-Diagnostics – Justy – Carbureted (Cont.)

## READ MEMORY MODE

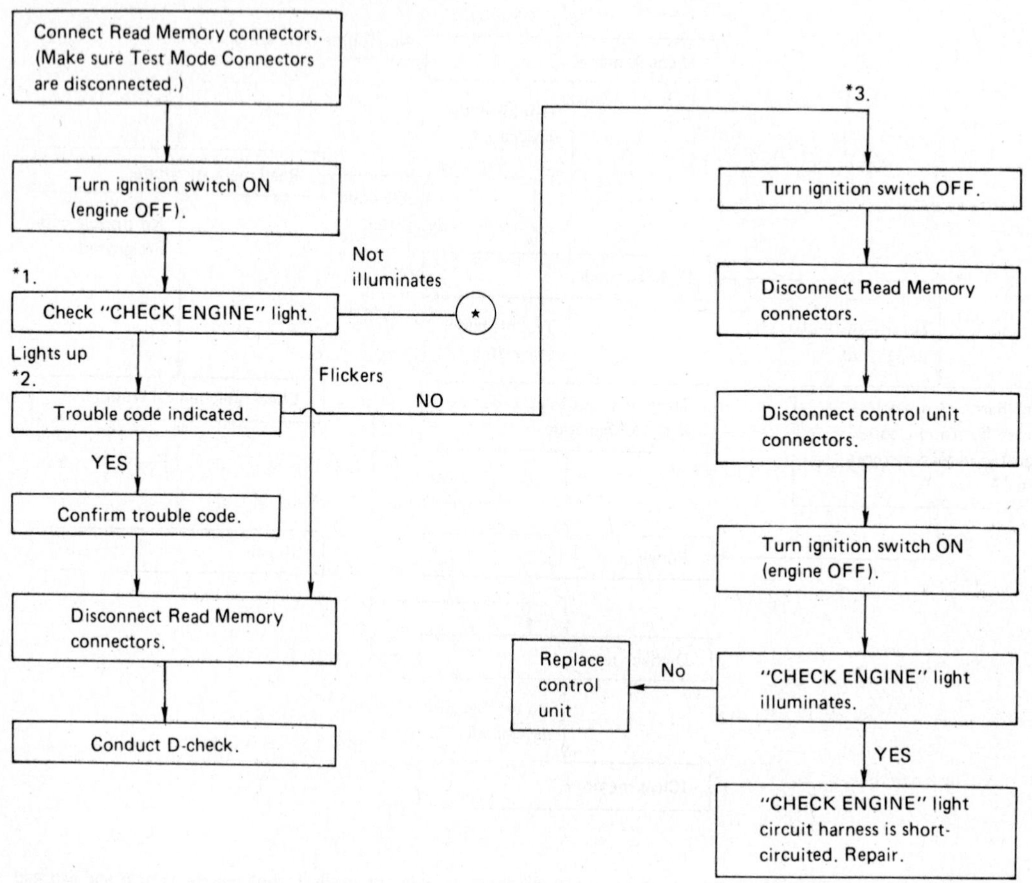
[N.G. memory function in the U-check mode.]
Connect Read Memory connectors. (Make sure Test Mode Connectors are disconnected.)
Turn ignition switch ON (engine OFF).
*1.
Check "CHECK ENGINE" light.
Not illuminates
*
Lights up
*2.
Flickers
Trouble code indicated.
NO
YES
Confirm trouble code.
Disconnect Read Memory connectors.
Conduct D-check.
*3.
Turn ignition switch OFF.
Disconnect Read Memory connectors.
Disconnect control unit connectors.
Turn ignition switch ON (engine OFF).
"CHECK ENGINE" light illuminates.
No
Replace control unit
YES
"CHECK ENGINE" light circuit harness is short-circuited. Repair.

*1. Check engine light illuminates and indicates trouble codes are stored in memory. However, trouble codes may not be shown at *2 in chart due to malfunctioning lamp circuit or control unit which is not a problem related to self-diagnostic functions. Such a problem can be checked at *3.
*2. Check engine light flickers and no trouble codes stored in memory means no problem has occured in the past when checked in "U-check" mode. For this reason, "D-check" must be performed after items are checked in the "U-check" mode as indicated by the arrow in the chart.
*3. Check engine light remains off. This rarely occurs under normal circumstances, except for malfunctioning check engine light circuit.

★ See "G" in D-CHECK MODE (Cont.) Chart

118312

# 1991 ENGINE PERFORMANCE
# Self-Diagnostics – Justy – Carbureted (Cont.)

## D-CHECK MODE

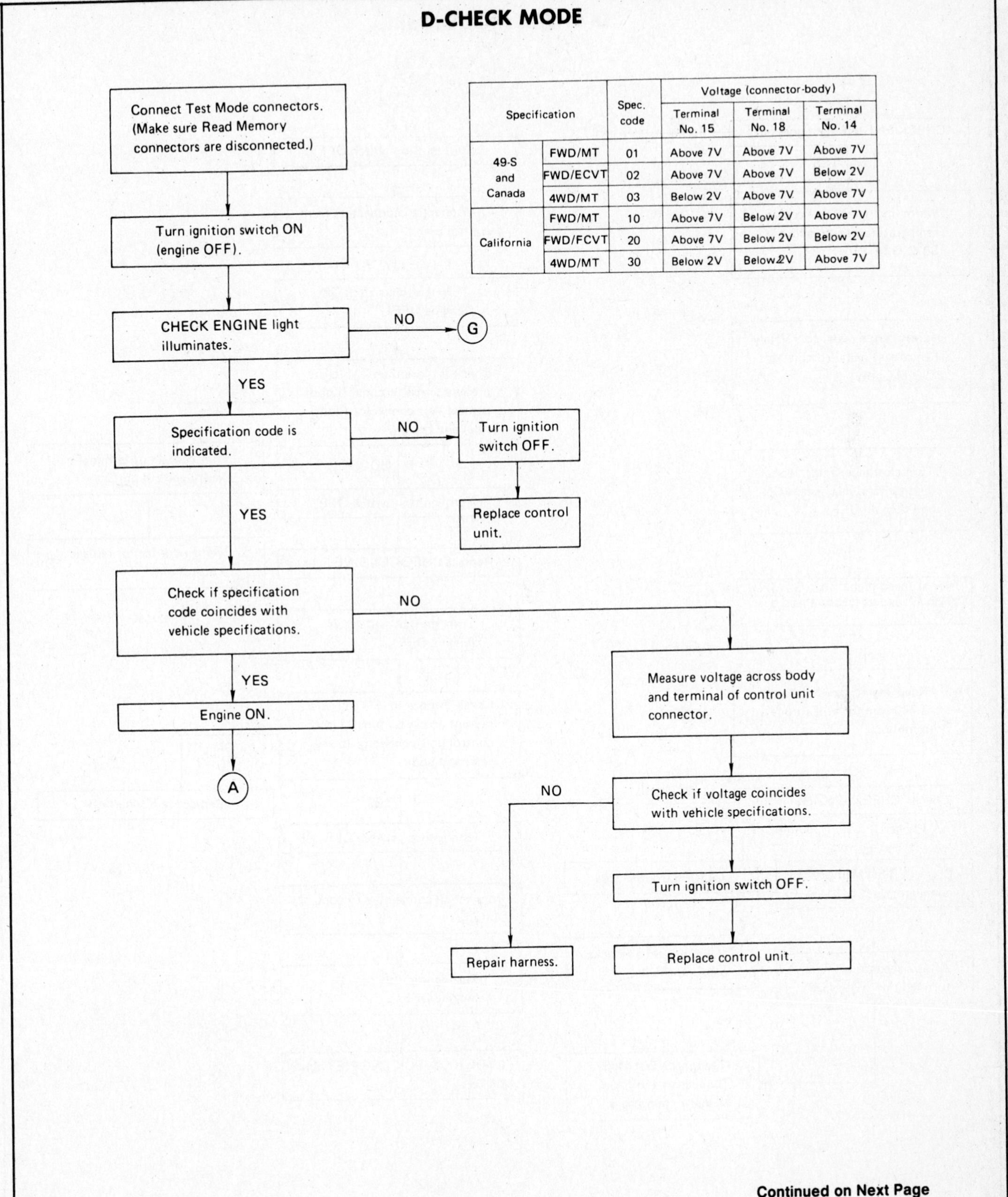

| Specification | | Spec. code | Voltage (connector-body) | | |
|---|---|---|---|---|---|
| | | | Terminal No. 15 | Terminal No. 18 | Terminal No. 14 |
| 49-S and Canada | FWD/MT | 01 | Above 7V | Above 7V | Above 7V |
| | FWD/ECVT | 02 | Above 7V | Above 7V | Below 2V |
| | 4WD/MT | 03 | Below 2V | Above 7V | Above 7V |
| California | FWD/MT | 10 | Above 7V | Below 2V | Above 7V |
| | FWD/FCVT | 20 | Above 7V | Below 2V | Below 2V |
| | 4WD/MT | 30 | Below 2V | Below 2V | Above 7V |

Connect Test Mode connectors. (Make sure Read Memory connectors are disconnected.)
Turn ignition switch ON (engine OFF).
CHECK ENGINE light illuminates.
NO
G
YES
Specification code is indicated.
NO
Turn ignition switch OFF.
Replace control unit.
YES
Check if specification code coincides with vehicle specifications.
NO
YES
Engine ON.
A
Measure voltage across body and terminal of control unit connector.
Check if voltage coincides with vehicle specifications.
NO
Turn ignition switch OFF.
Repair harness.
Replace control unit.

Continued on Next Page

118313

# 1991 ENGINE PERFORMANCE
# Self-Diagnostics – Justy – Carbureted (Cont.)

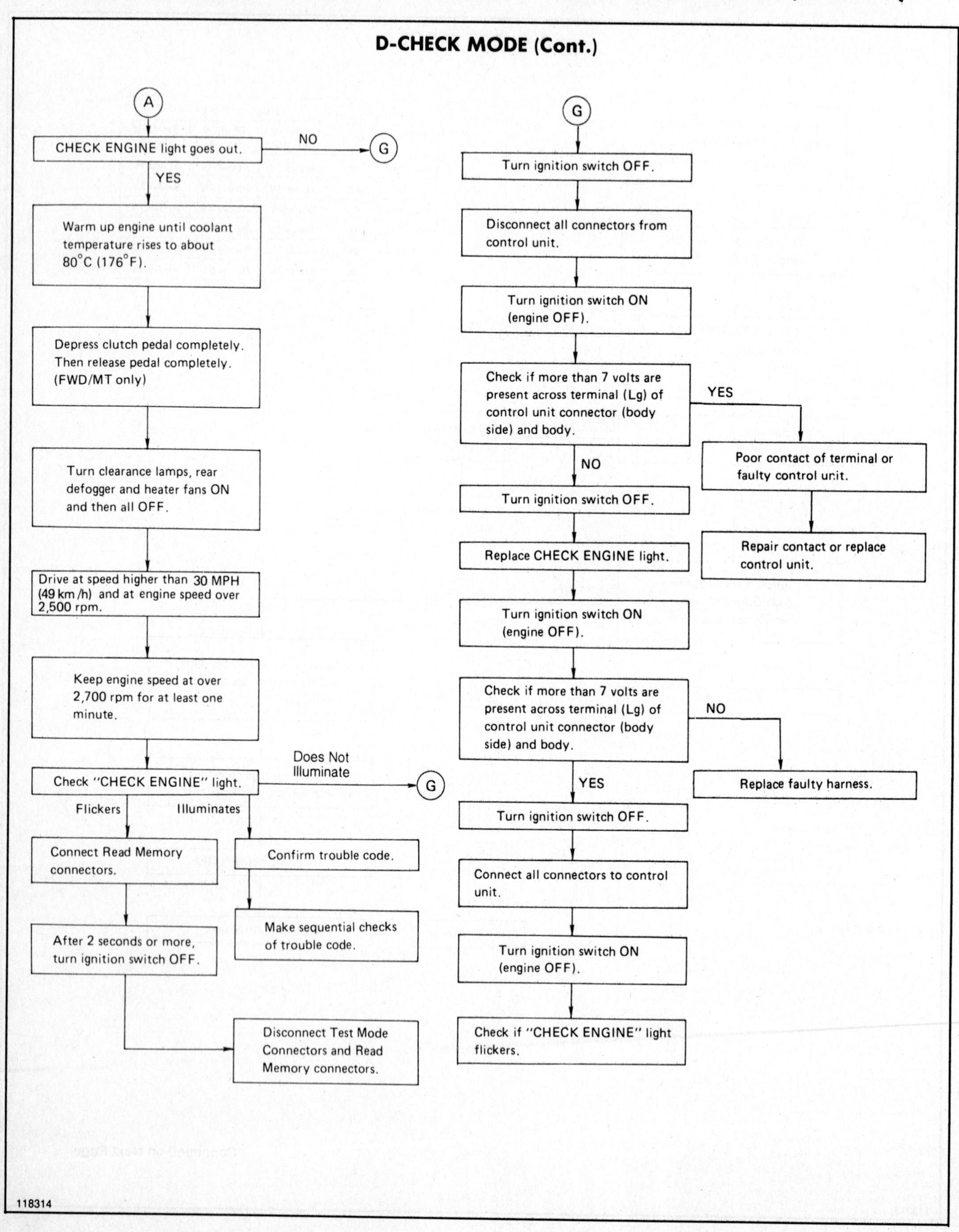
D-CHECK MODE (Cont.)
A
CHECK ENGINE light goes out.
NO
G
YES
Warm up engine until coolant temperature rises to about 80°C (176°F).
Depress clutch pedal completely. Then release pedal completely. (FWD/MT only)
Turn clearance lamps, rear defogger and heater fans ON and then all OFF.
Drive at speed higher than 30 MPH (49 km/h) and at engine speed over 2,500 rpm.
Keep engine speed at over 2,700 rpm for at least one minute.
Check "CHECK ENGINE" light.
Does Not Illuminate
G
Flickers
Illuminates
Connect Read Memory connectors.
Confirm trouble code.
After 2 seconds or more, turn ignition switch OFF.
Make sequential checks of trouble code.
Disconnect Test Mode Connectors and Read Memory connectors.
G
Turn ignition switch OFF.
Disconnect all connectors from control unit.
Turn ignition switch ON (engine OFF).
Check if more than 7 volts are present across terminal (Lg) of control unit connector (body side) and body.
YES
Poor contact of terminal or faulty control unit.
Repair contact or replace control unit.
NO
Turn ignition switch OFF.
Replace CHECK ENGINE light.
Turn ignition switch ON (engine OFF).
Check if more than 7 volts are present across terminal (Lg) of control unit connector (body side) and body.
NO
Replace faulty harness.
YES
Turn ignition switch OFF.
Connect all connectors to control unit.
Turn ignition switch ON (engine OFF).
Check if "CHECK ENGINE" light flickers.
118314

# 1991 ENGINE PERFORMANCE
# Self-Diagnostics – Justy – Carbureted (Cont.)

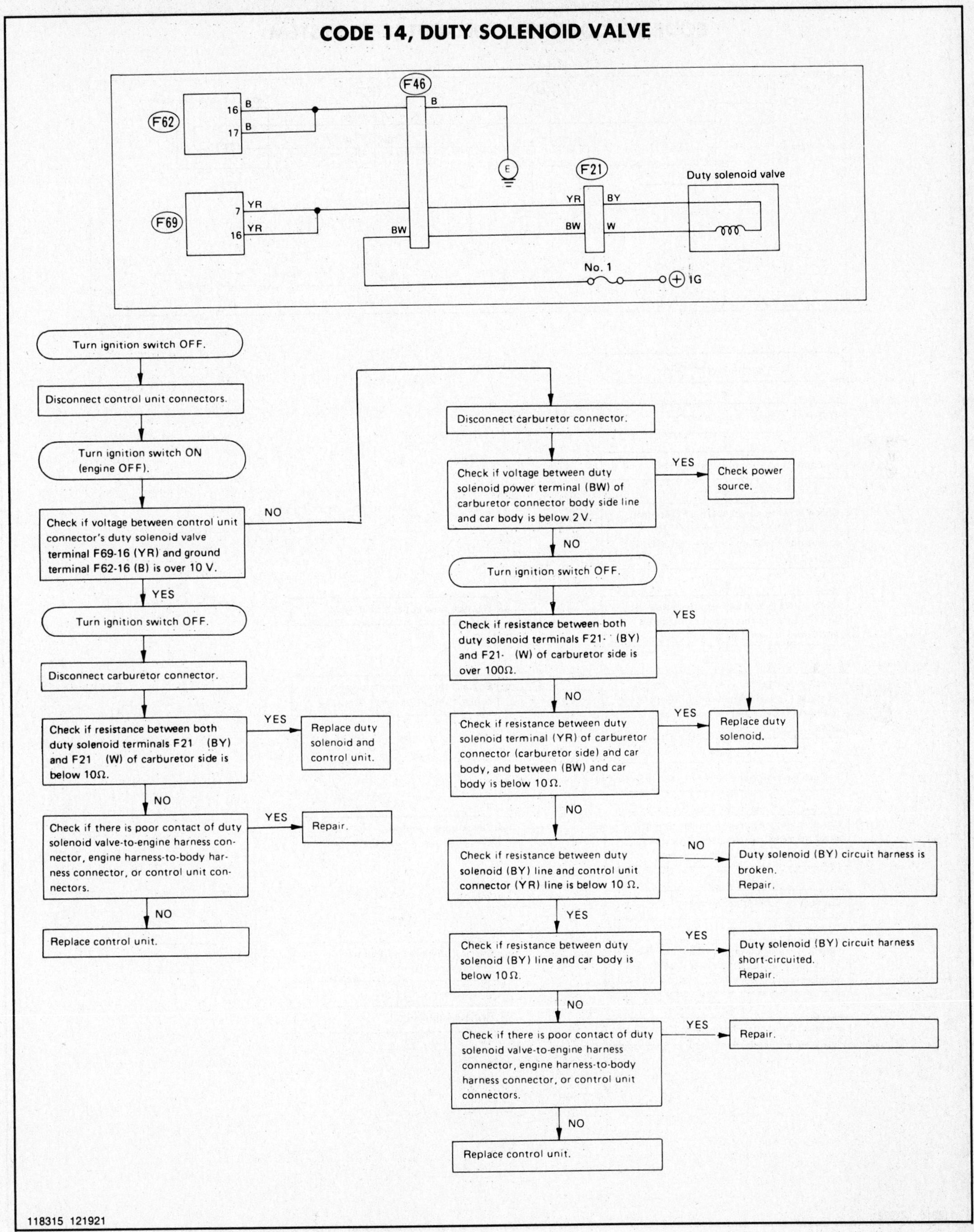

CODE 14, DUTY SOLENOID VALVE
F62
16
17
B
B
F46
B
E
F69
7
16
YR
YR
BW
F21
YR
BY
BW
W
Duty solenoid valve
No. 1
IG
Turn ignition switch OFF.
Disconnect control unit connectors.
Turn ignition switch ON (engine OFF).
Check if voltage between control unit connector's duty solenoid valve terminal F69-16 (YR) and ground terminal F62-16 (B) is over 10 V.
NO
YES
Turn ignition switch OFF.
Disconnect carburetor connector.
Check if resistance between both duty solenoid terminals F21 (BY) and F21 (W) of carburetor side is below 10Ω.
YES
Replace duty solenoid and control unit.
NO
Check if there is poor contact of duty solenoid valve-to-engine harness connector, engine harness-to-body harness connector, or control unit connectors.
YES
Repair.
NO
Replace control unit.
Disconnect carburetor connector.
Check if voltage between duty solenoid power terminal (BW) of carburetor connector body side line and car body is below 2 V.
YES
Check power source.
NO
Turn ignition switch OFF.
Check if resistance between both duty solenoid terminals F21- (BY) and F21- (W) of carburetor side is over 100Ω.
YES
NO
Check if resistance between duty solenoid terminal (YR) of carburetor connector (carburetor side) and car body, and between (BW) and car body is below 10 Ω.
YES
Replace duty solenoid.
NO
Check if resistance between duty solenoid (BY) line and control unit connector (YR) line is below 10 Ω.
NO
Duty solenoid (BY) circuit harness is broken. Repair.
YES
Check if resistance between duty solenoid (BY) line and car body is below 10 Ω.
YES
Duty solenoid (BY) circuit harness short-circuited. Repair.
NO
Check if there is poor contact of duty solenoid valve-to-engine harness connector, engine harness-to-body harness connector, or control unit connectors.
YES
Repair.
NO
Replace control unit.
118315 121921

# 1991 ENGINE PERFORMANCE
## Self-Diagnostics – Justy – Carbureted (Cont.)

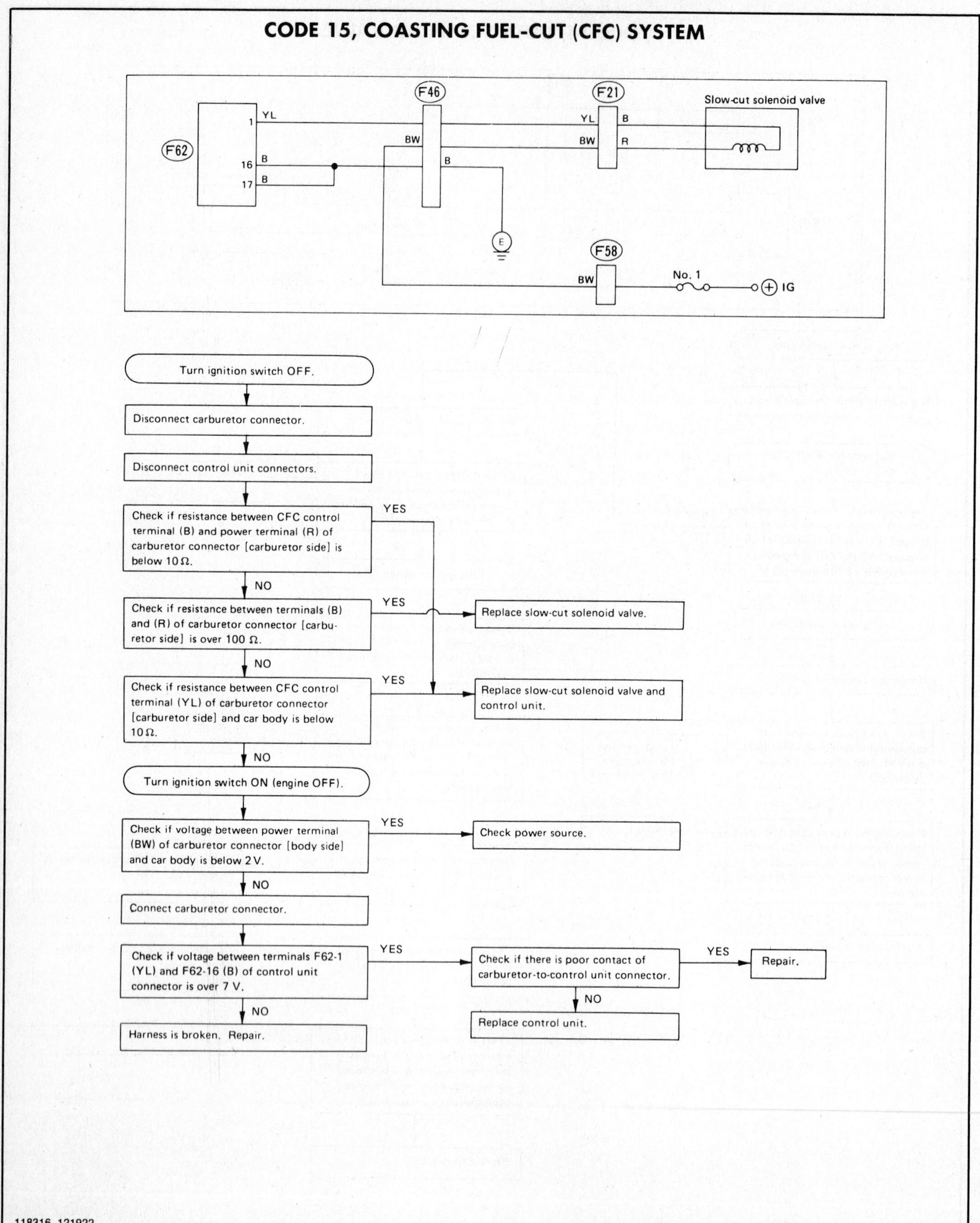

# 1991 ENGINE PERFORMANCE
# Self-Diagnostics – Justy – Carbureted (Cont.)

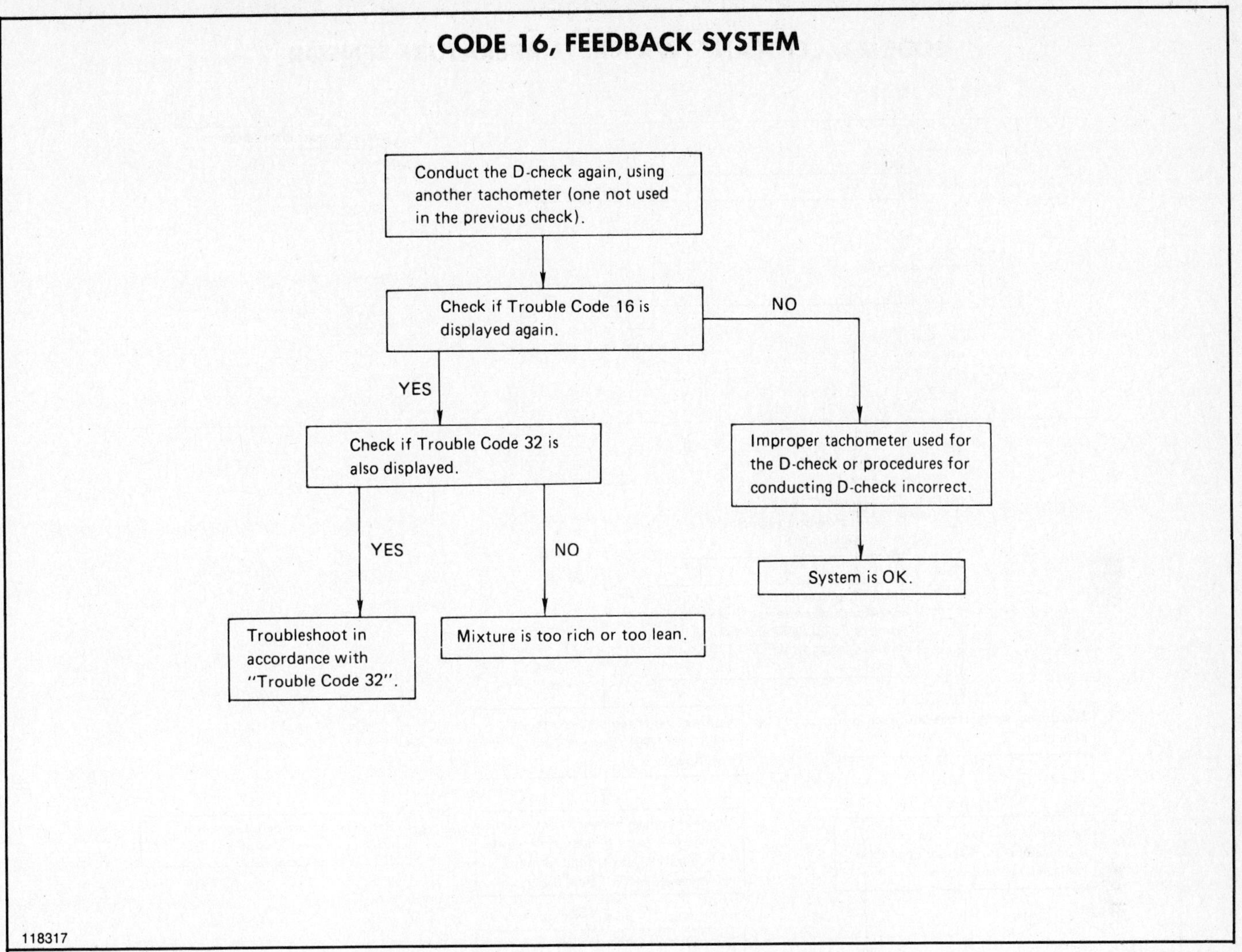


## CODE 17, FUEL PUMP & AUTOMATIC CHOKE

When trouble Code 17 appears, replace fuel pump and automatic choke unit.

## CODE 21, COOLANT (WATER) TEMPERATURE SENSOR

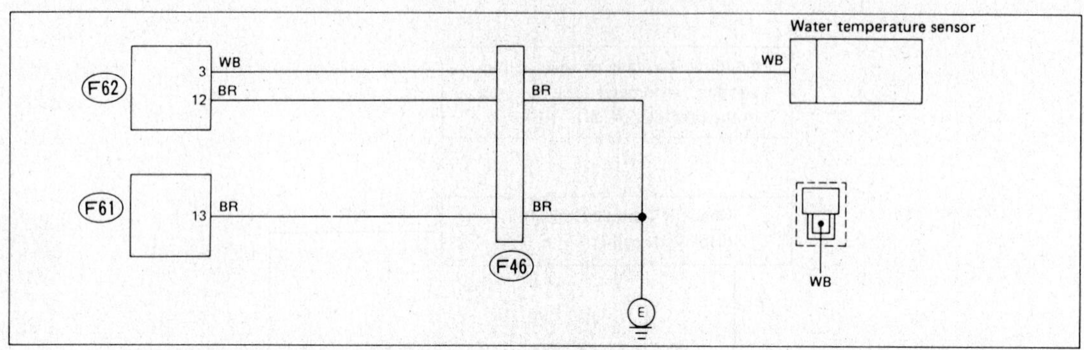


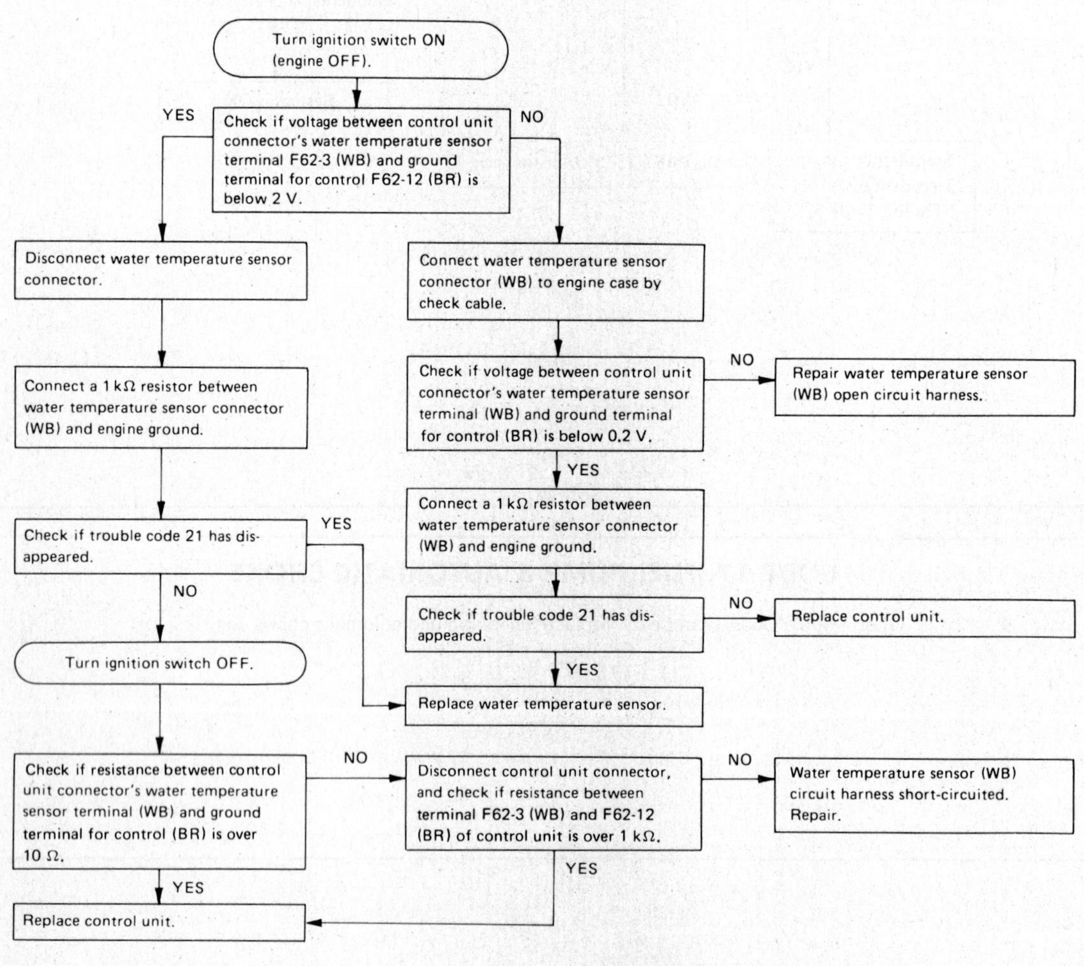


118318 121923

# 1991 ENGINE PERFORMANCE
# Self-Diagnostics – Justy – Carbureted (Cont.)

## CODE 22, VLC SOLENOID VALVE

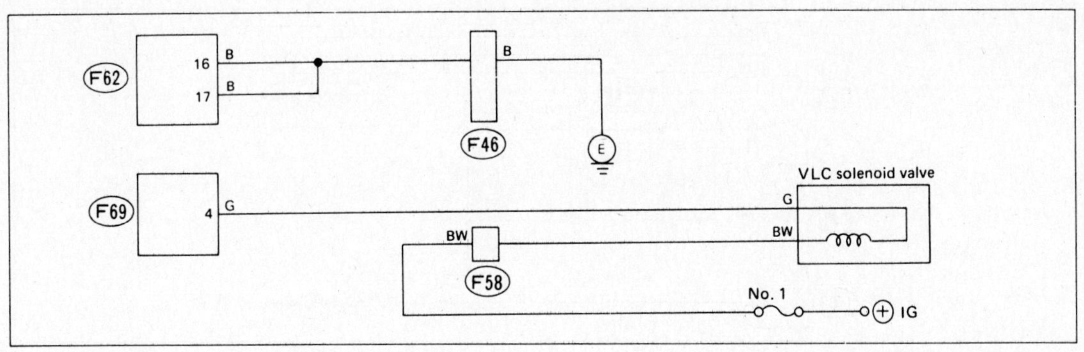


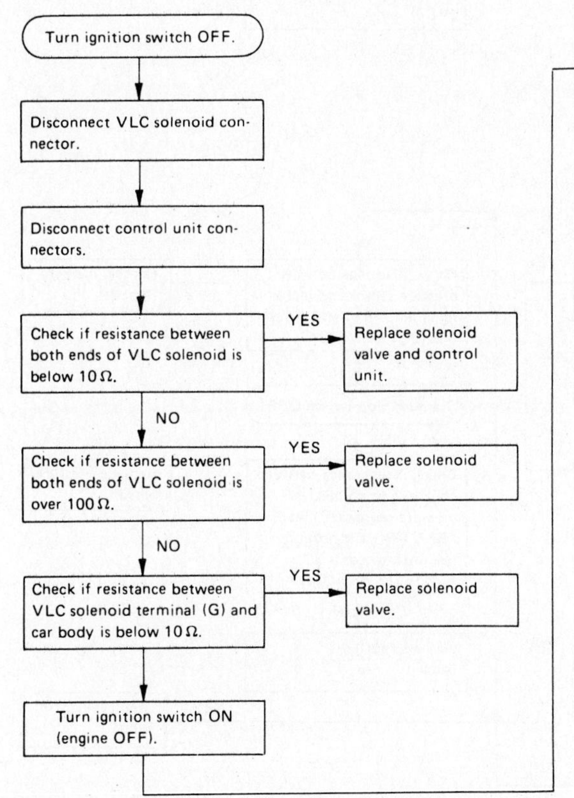


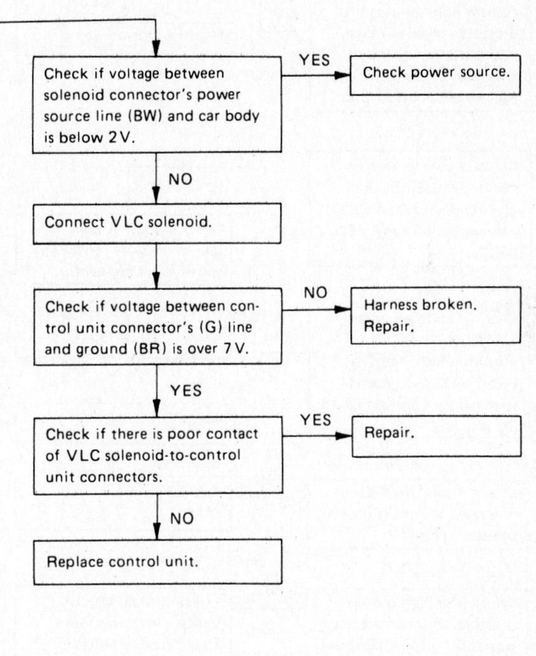


118319 121924

# 1991 ENGINE PERFORMANCE
## Self-Diagnostics – Justy – Carbureted (Cont.)

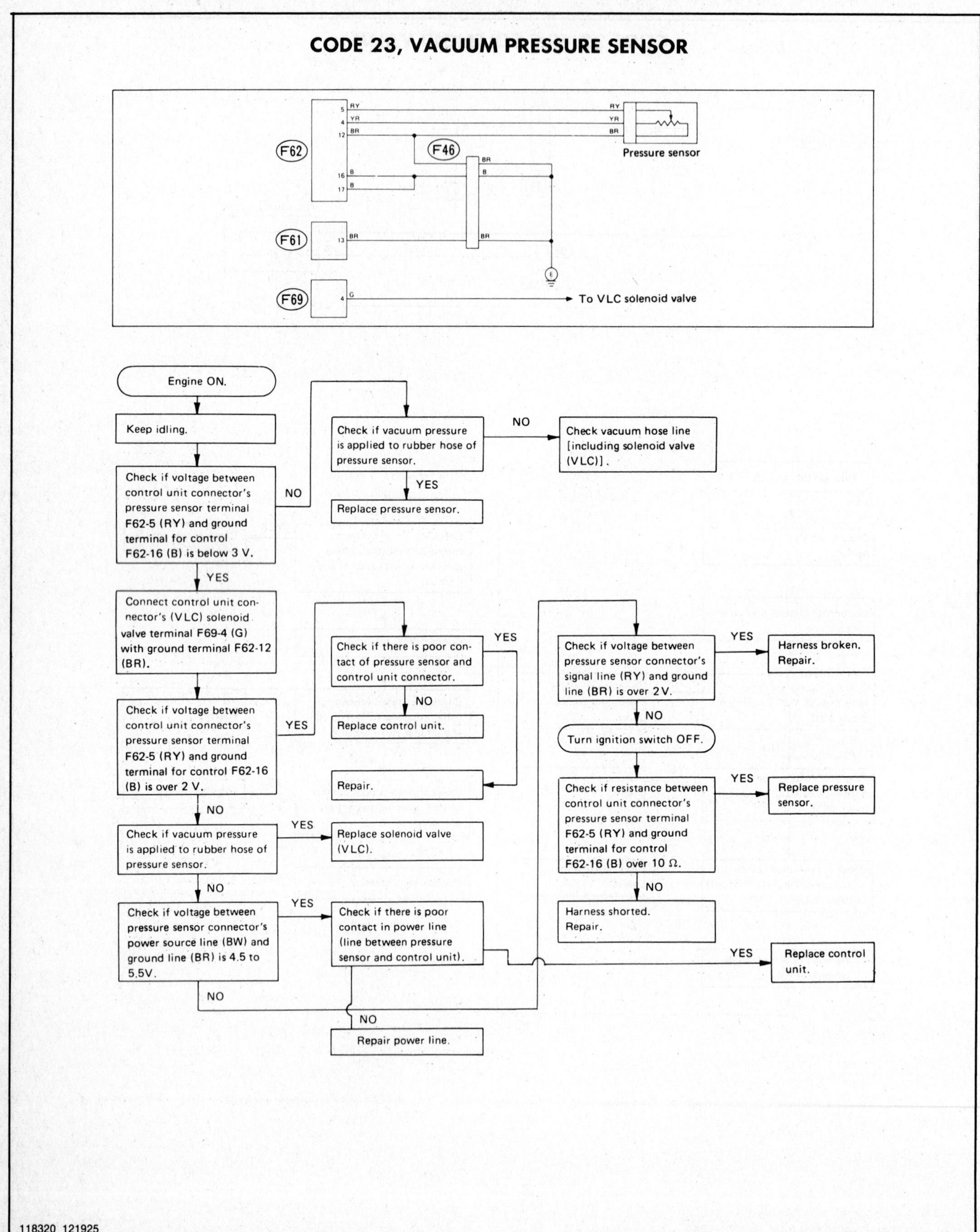

# 1991 ENGINE PERFORMANCE
## Self-Diagnostics – Justy – Carbureted (Cont.)

### CODE 24, IDLE-UP SOLENOID

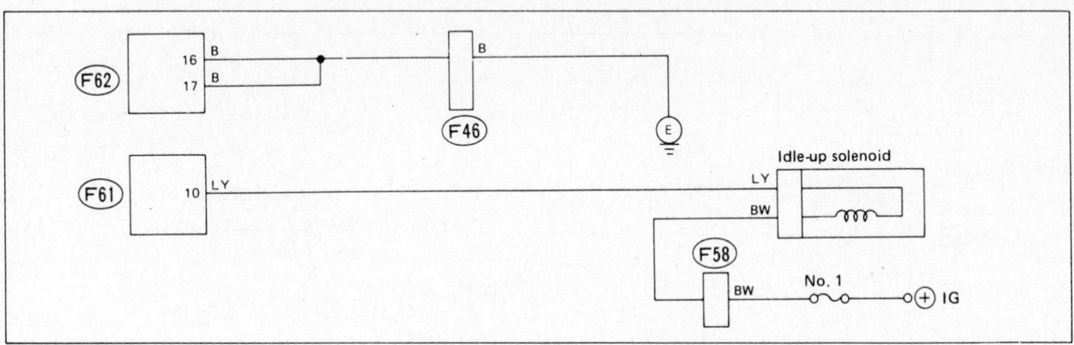


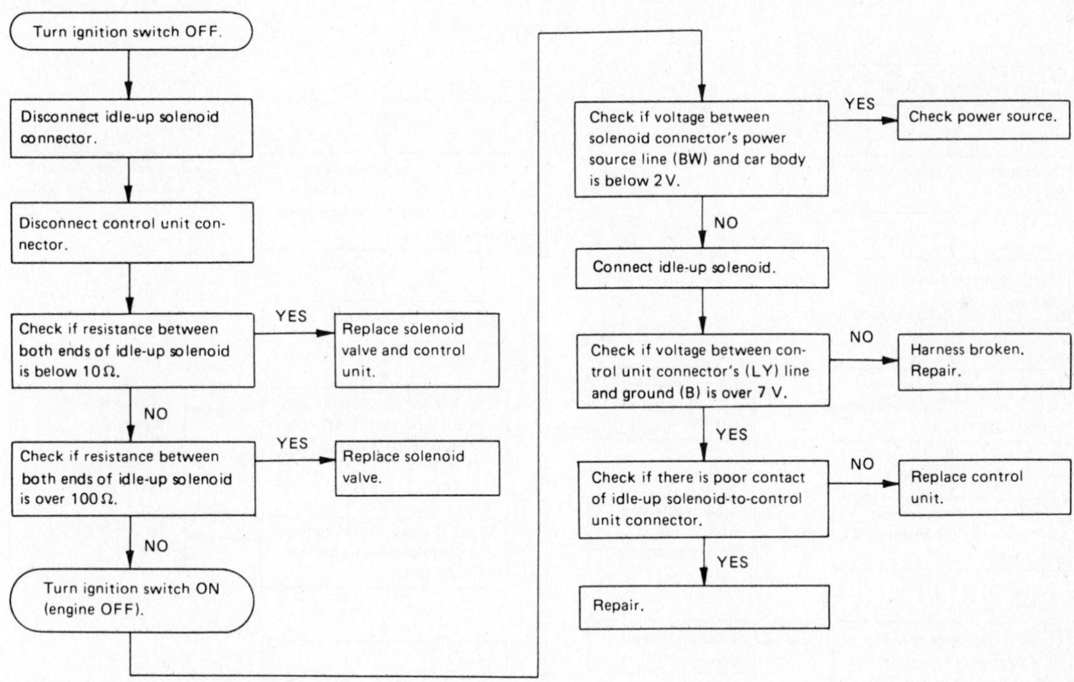


118321 121926

## CODE 25, FLOAT CHAMBER VENT (FCV) SOLENOID VALVE

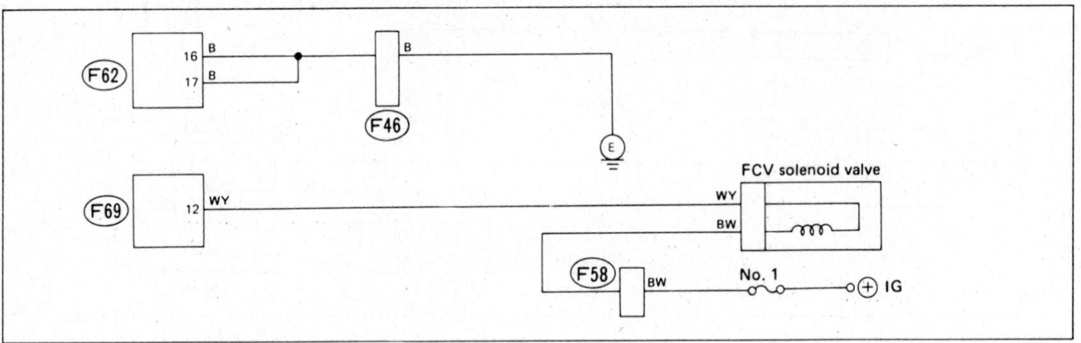


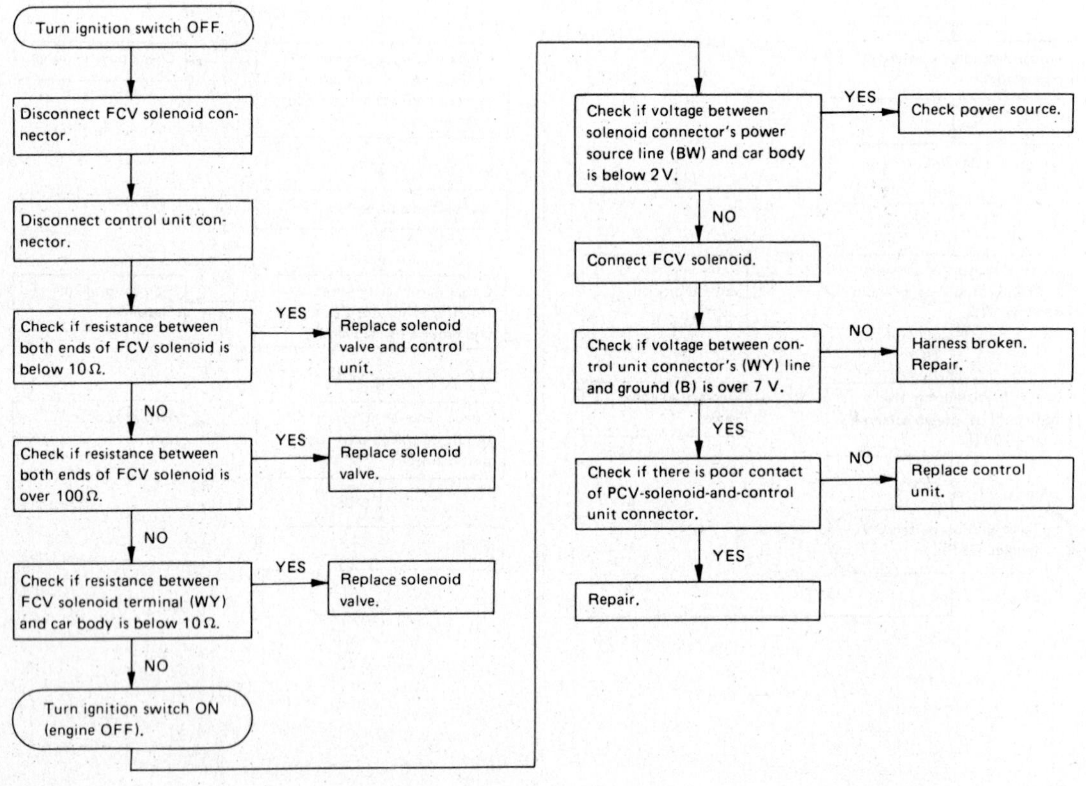


118322 121927

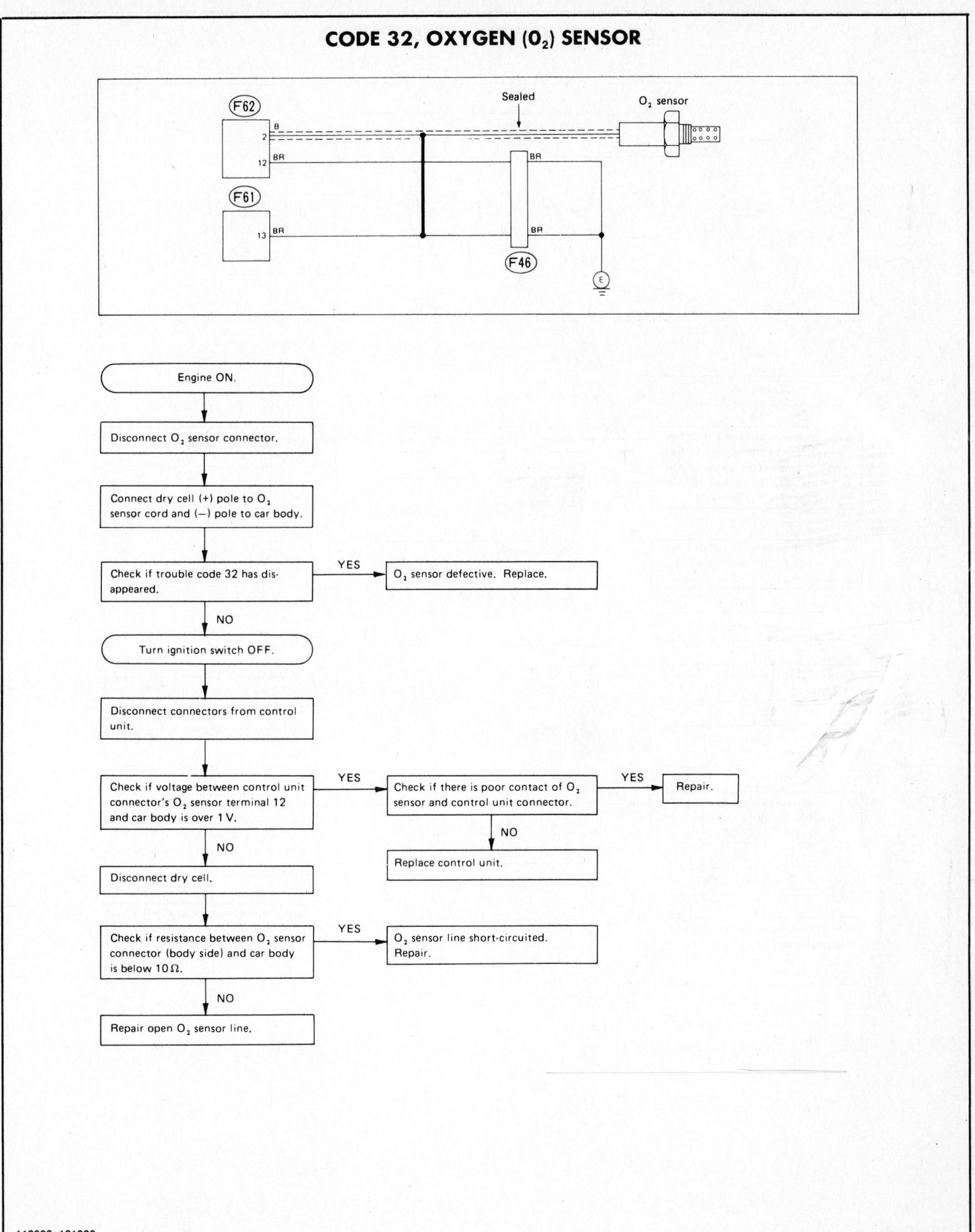

CODE 32, OXYGEN ($0_2$) SENSOR
Sealed
$O_2$ sensor
F62
B
2
12
BR
BR
F61
13
BR
BR
F46
E
Engine ON.
Disconnect $O_2$ sensor connector.
Connect dry cell (+) pole to $O_2$ sensor cord and (–) pole to car body.
Check if trouble code 32 has disappeared.
YES
$O_2$ sensor defective. Replace.
NO
Turn ignition switch OFF.
Disconnect connectors from control unit.
Check if voltage between control unit connector's $O_2$ sensor terminal 12 and car body is over 1 V.
YES
Check if there is poor contact of $O_2$ sensor and control unit connector.
YES
Repair.
NO
Replace control unit.
NO
Disconnect dry cell.
Check if resistance between $O_2$ sensor connector (body side) and car body is below 10 Ω.
YES
$O_2$ sensor line short-circuited. Repair.
NO
Repair open $O_2$ sensor line.
118323 121928

# 1991 ENGINE PERFORMANCE
## Self-Diagnostics – Justy – Carbureted (Cont.)

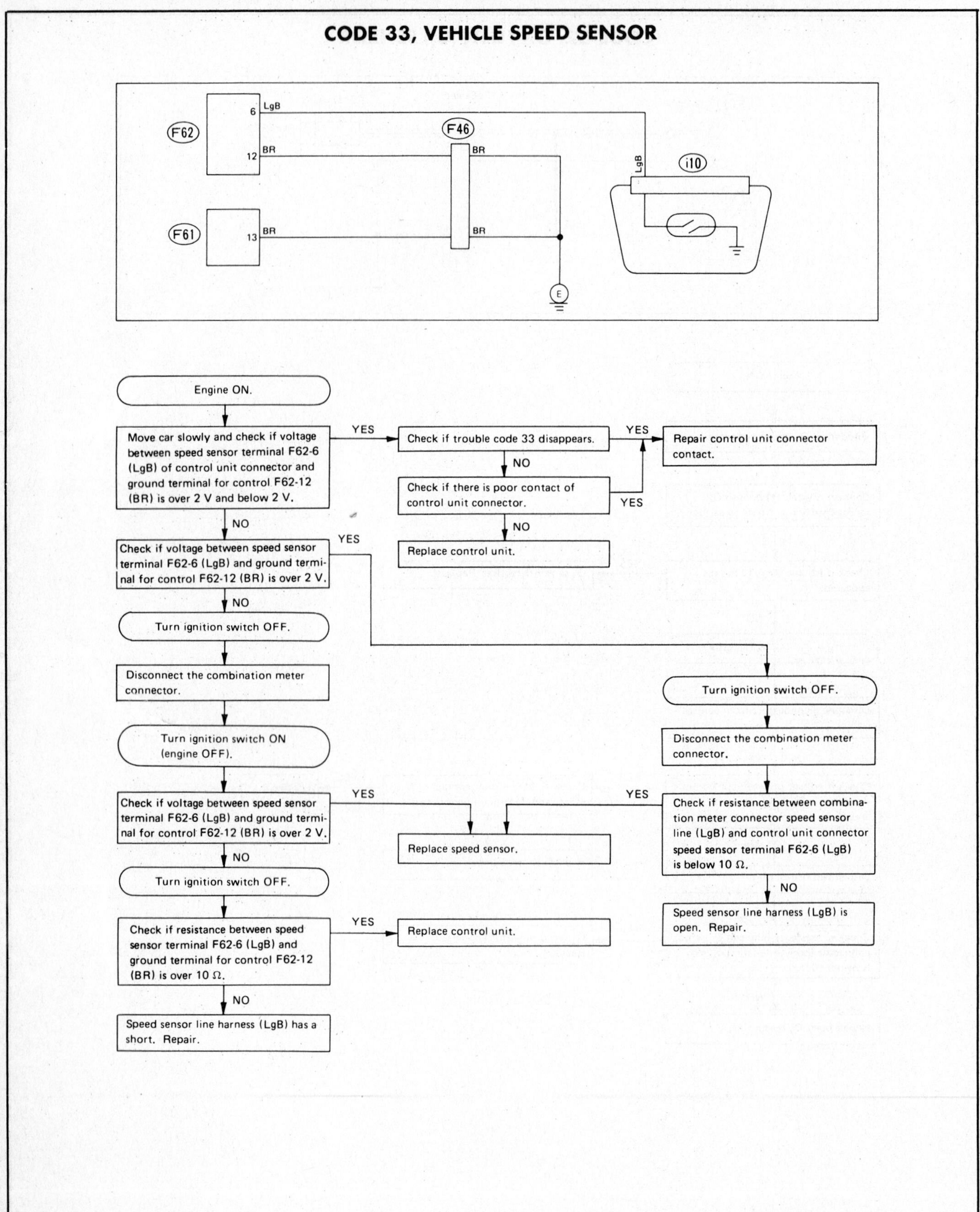

# 1991 ENGINE PERFORMANCE
# Self-Diagnostics – Justy – Carbureted (Cont.)

## CODE 34, EGR SOLENOID VALVE

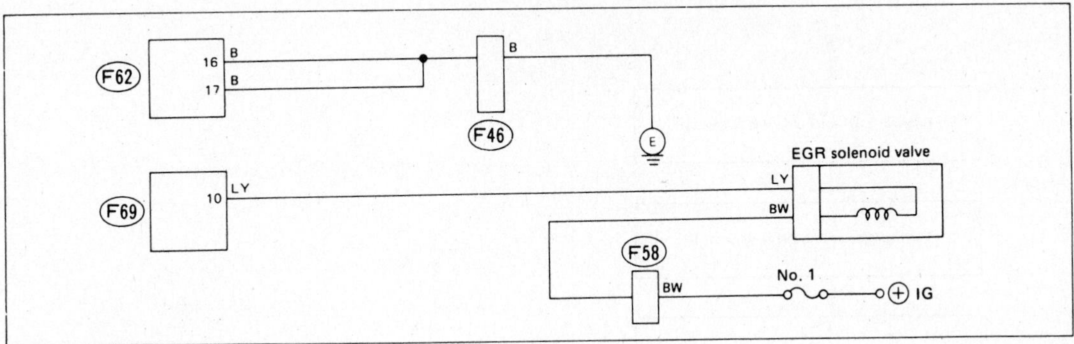
F62
16
17
B
B
F46
B
E
F69
10
LY
EGR solenoid valve
LY
BW
F58
BW
No. 1
IG

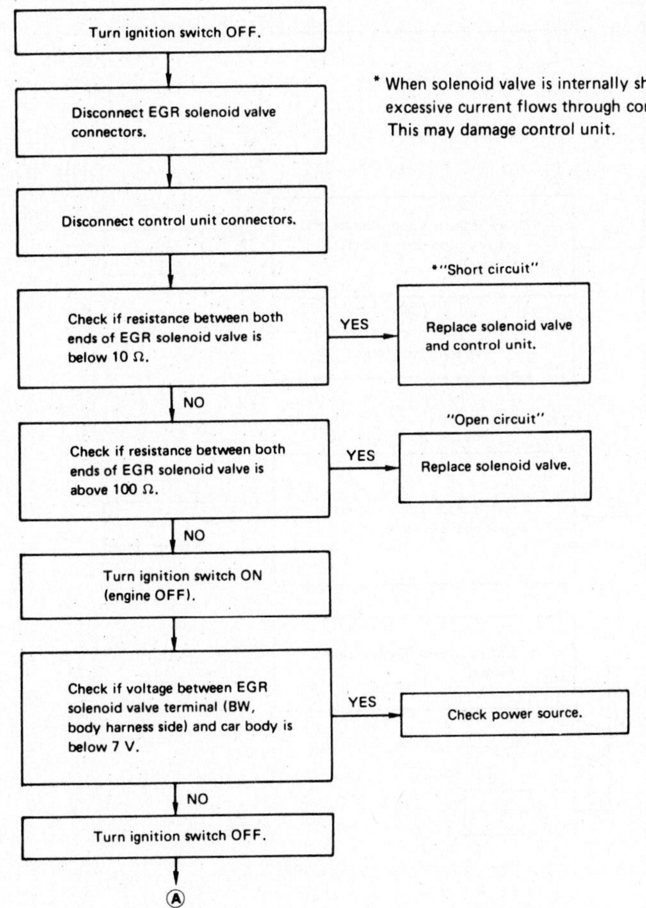
Turn ignition switch OFF.
Disconnect EGR solenoid valve connectors.
Disconnect control unit connectors.
Check if resistance between both ends of EGR solenoid valve is below 10 Ω.
YES
*"Short circuit"
Replace solenoid valve and control unit.
NO
Check if resistance between both ends of EGR solenoid valve is above 100 Ω.
YES
"Open circuit"
Replace solenoid valve.
NO
Turn ignition switch ON (engine OFF).
Check if voltage between EGR solenoid valve terminal (BW, body harness side) and car body is below 7 V.
YES
Check power source.
NO
Turn ignition switch OFF.
A

* When solenoid valve is internally shortcircuited, excessive current flows through control unit. This may damage control unit.

Continued on Next Page

118325 121935

# 1991 ENGINE PERFORMANCE
## Self-Diagnostics – Justy – Carbureted (Cont.)

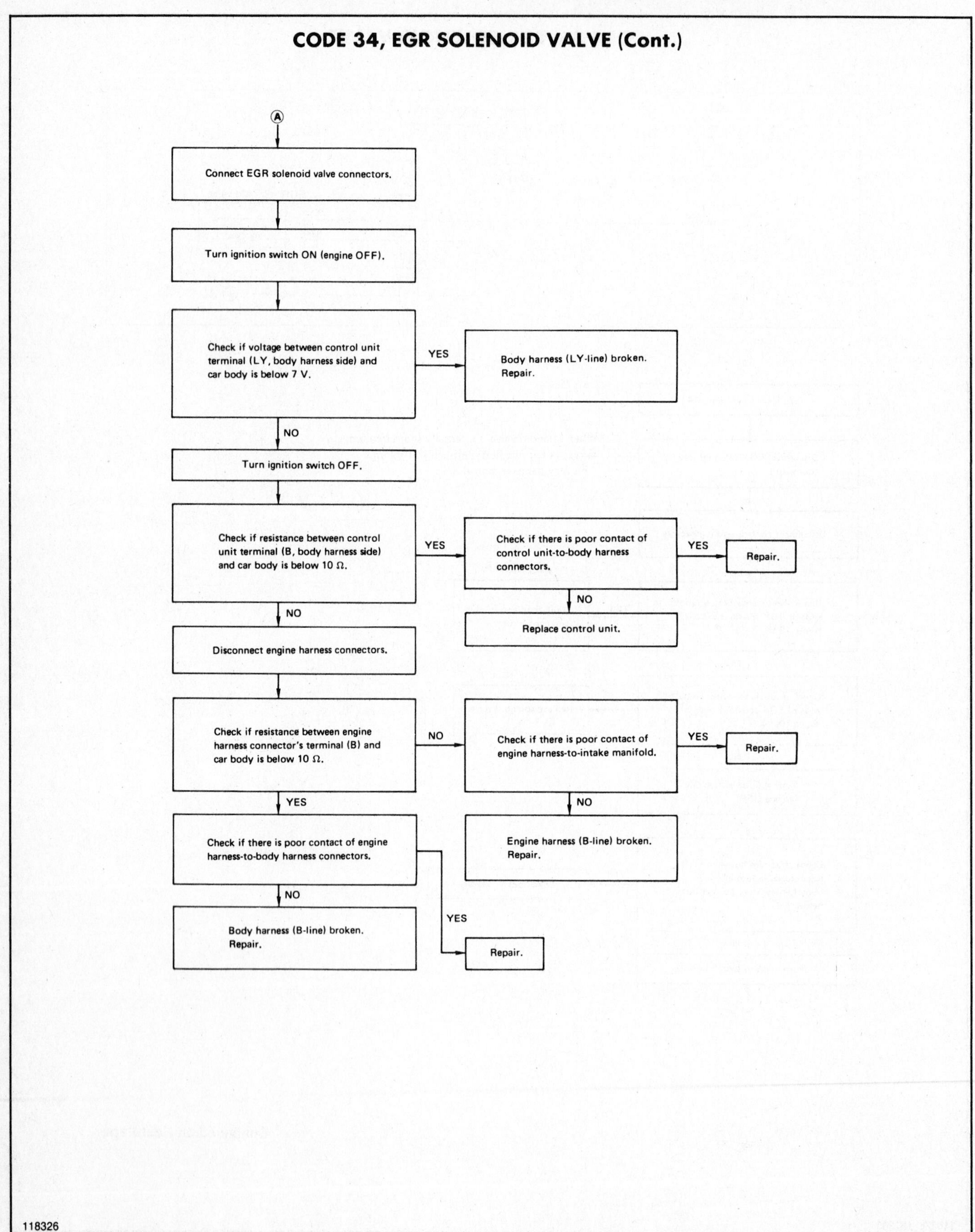
CODE 34, EGR SOLENOID VALVE (Cont.)
A
Connect EGR solenoid valve connectors.
Turn ignition switch ON (engine OFF).
Check if voltage between control unit terminal (LY, body harness side) and car body is below 7 V.
YES
Body harness (LY-line) broken. Repair.
NO
Turn ignition switch OFF.
Check if resistance between control unit terminal (B, body harness side) and car body is below 10 Ω.
YES
Check if there is poor contact of control unit-to-body harness connectors.
YES
Repair.
NO
Replace control unit.
NO
Disconnect engine harness connectors.
Check if resistance between engine harness connector's terminal (B) and car body is below 10 Ω.
NO
Check if there is poor contact of engine harness-to-intake manifold.
YES
Repair.
NO
Engine harness (B-line) broken. Repair.
YES
Check if there is poor contact of engine harness-to-body harness connectors.
NO
Body harness (B-line) broken. Repair.
YES
Repair.
118326

## CODE 35, CANISTER PURGE CONTROL (CPC) SOLENOID VALVE

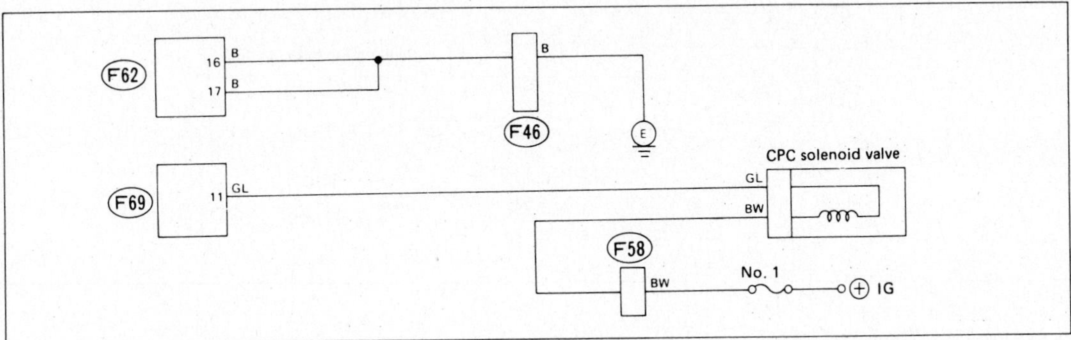


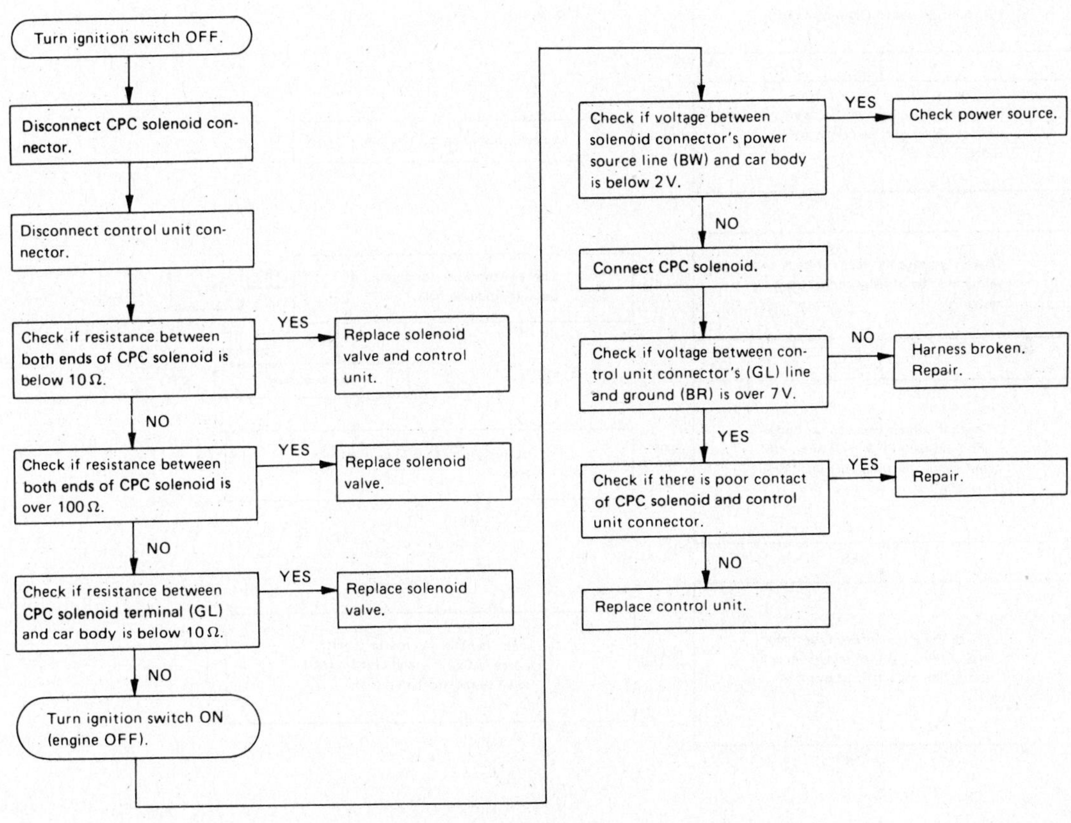


118327 121936

# 1991 ENGINE PERFORMANCE
# Self-Diagnostics – Justy – Carbureted (Cont.)

## CODE 46, RADIATOR FAN CONTROL SYSTEM

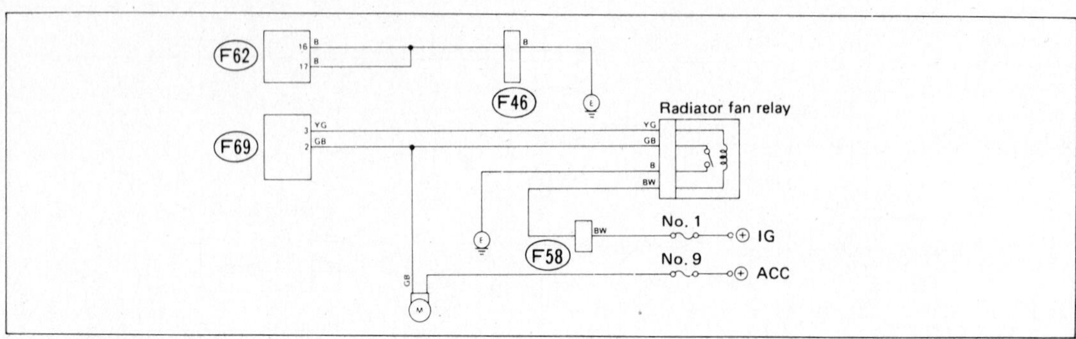
F62
16
17
B
B
F46
B
Radiator fan relay
F69
3
2
YG
GB
YG
GB
B
BW
No. 1
IG
F58
BW
No. 9
ACC
GB
M

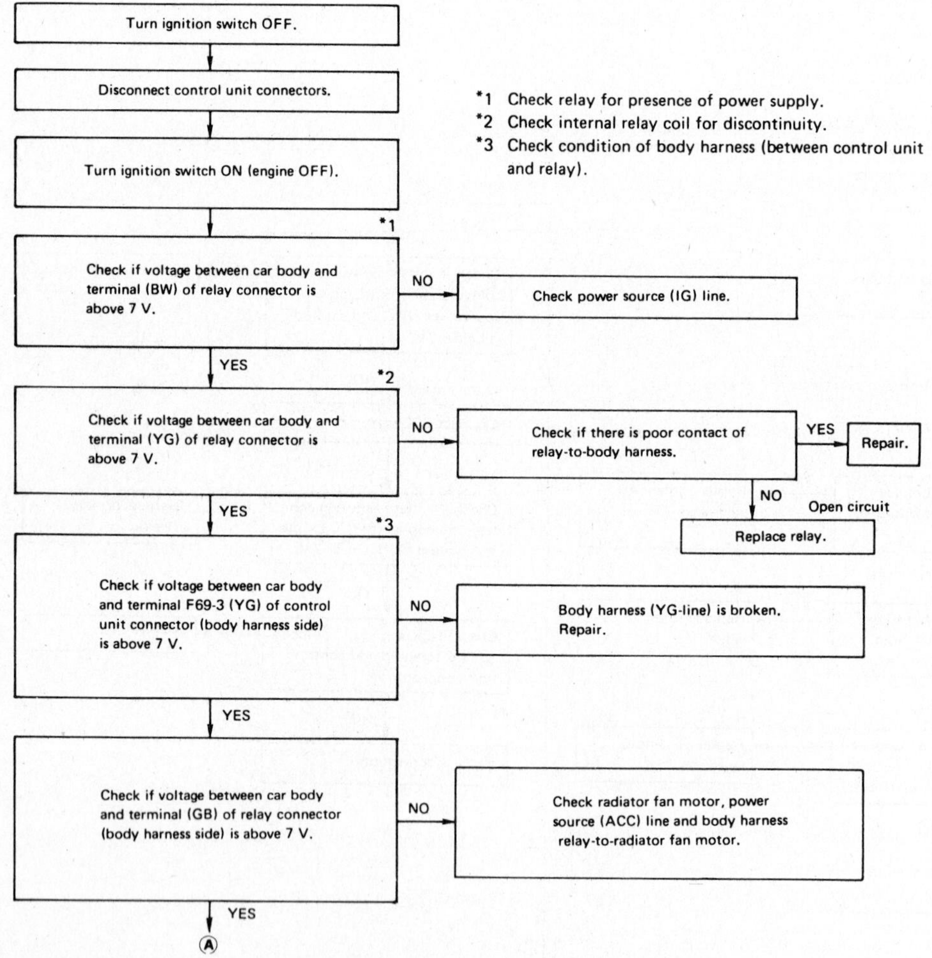
Turn ignition switch OFF.
Disconnect control unit connectors.
Turn ignition switch ON (engine OFF).
*1
Check if voltage between car body and terminal (BW) of relay connector is above 7 V.
NO
Check power source (IG) line.
YES
*2
Check if voltage between car body and terminal (YG) of relay connector is above 7 V.
NO
Check if there is poor contact of relay-to-body harness.
YES
Repair.
NO
Open circuit
Replace relay.
YES
*3
Check if voltage between car body and terminal F69-3 (YG) of control unit connector (body harness side) is above 7 V.
NO
Body harness (YG-line) is broken. Repair.
YES
Check if voltage between car body and terminal (GB) of relay connector (body harness side) is above 7 V.
NO
Check radiator fan motor, power source (ACC) line and body harness relay-to-radiator fan motor.
YES
A
*1 Check relay for presence of power supply.
*2 Check internal relay coil for discontinuity.
*3 Check condition of body harness (between control unit and relay).

Continued on Next Page

121937

# 1991 ENGINE PERFORMANCE
## Self-Diagnostics – Justy – Carbureted (Cont.)

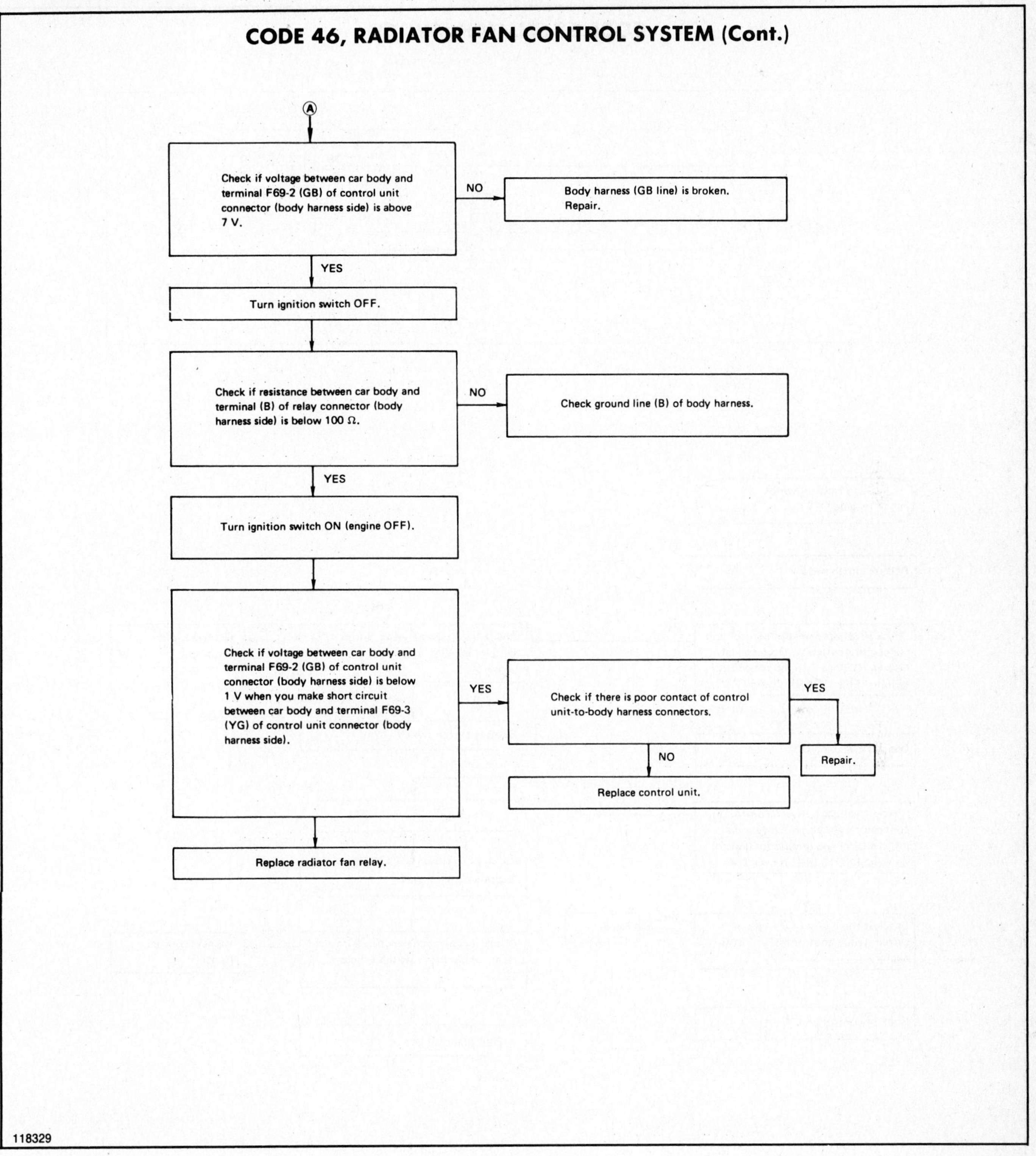
CODE 46, RADIATOR FAN CONTROL SYSTEM (Cont.)
A
Check if voltage between car body and terminal F69-2 (GB) of control unit connector (body harness side) is above 7 V.
NO
Body harness (GB line) is broken. Repair.
YES
Turn ignition switch OFF.
Check if resistance between car body and terminal (B) of relay connector (body harness side) is below 100 Ω.
NO
Check ground line (B) of body harness.
YES
Turn ignition switch ON (engine OFF).
Check if voltage between car body and terminal F69-2 (GB) of control unit connector (body harness side) is below 1 V when you make short circuit between car body and terminal F69-3 (YG) of control unit connector (body harness side).
YES
Check if there is poor contact of control unit-to-body harness connectors.
YES
Repair.
NO
Replace control unit.
Replace radiator fan relay.
118329

# 1991 ENGINE PERFORMANCE
## Self-Diagnostics – Justy – Carbureted (Cont.)

### CODE 52, CLUTCH SWITCH

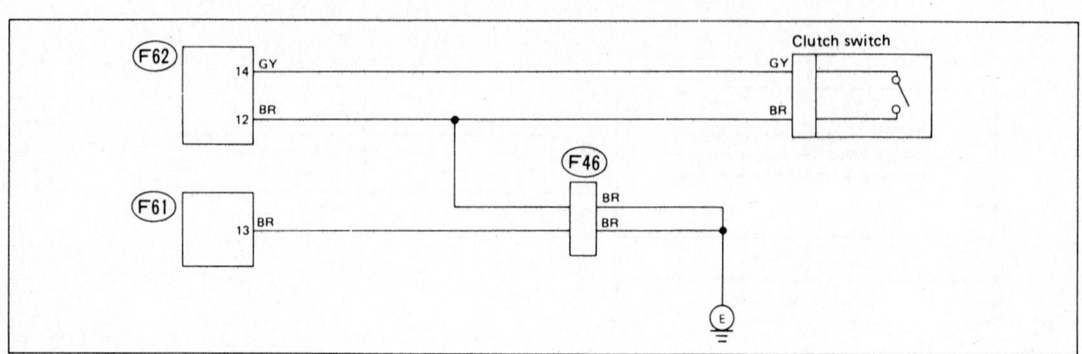


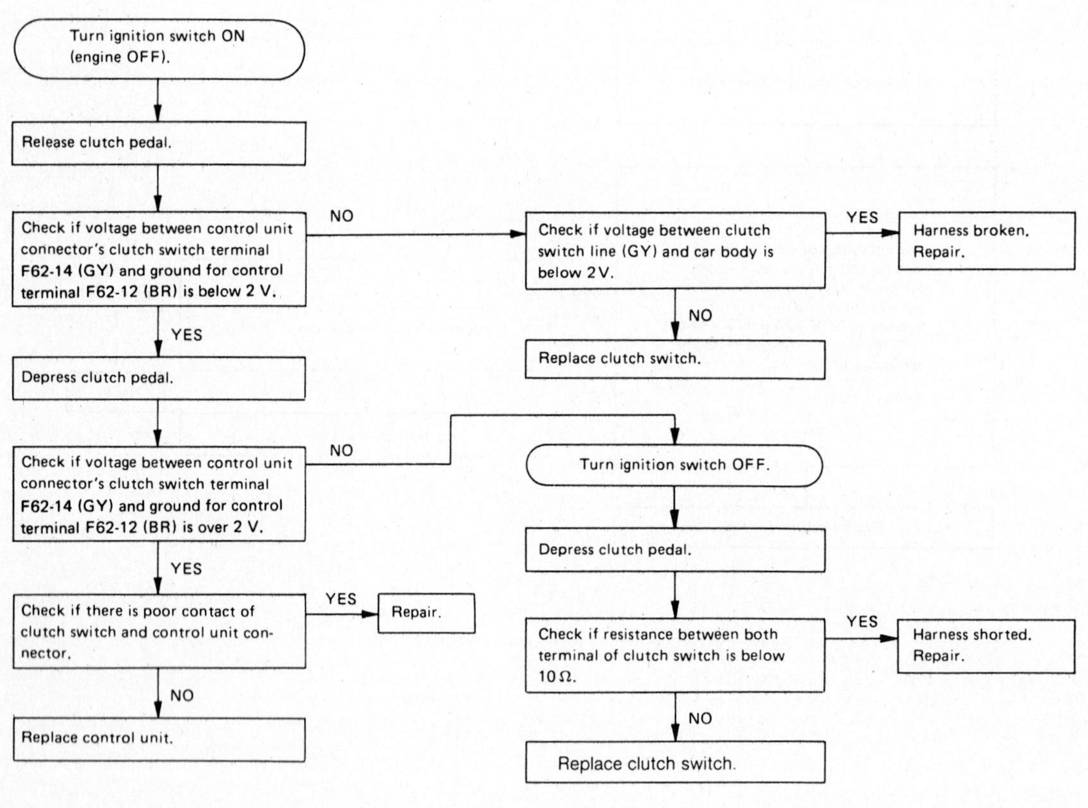


118330 121929

## CODE 53, HIGH ALTITUDE COMPENSATOR (HAC) SOLENOID VALVE

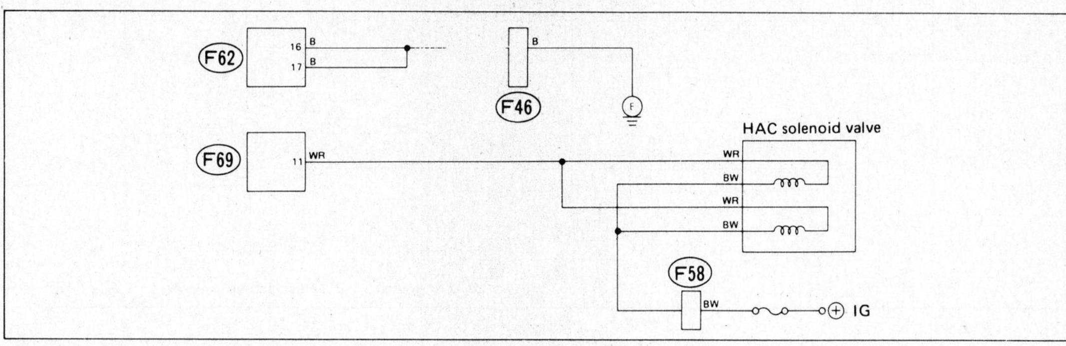


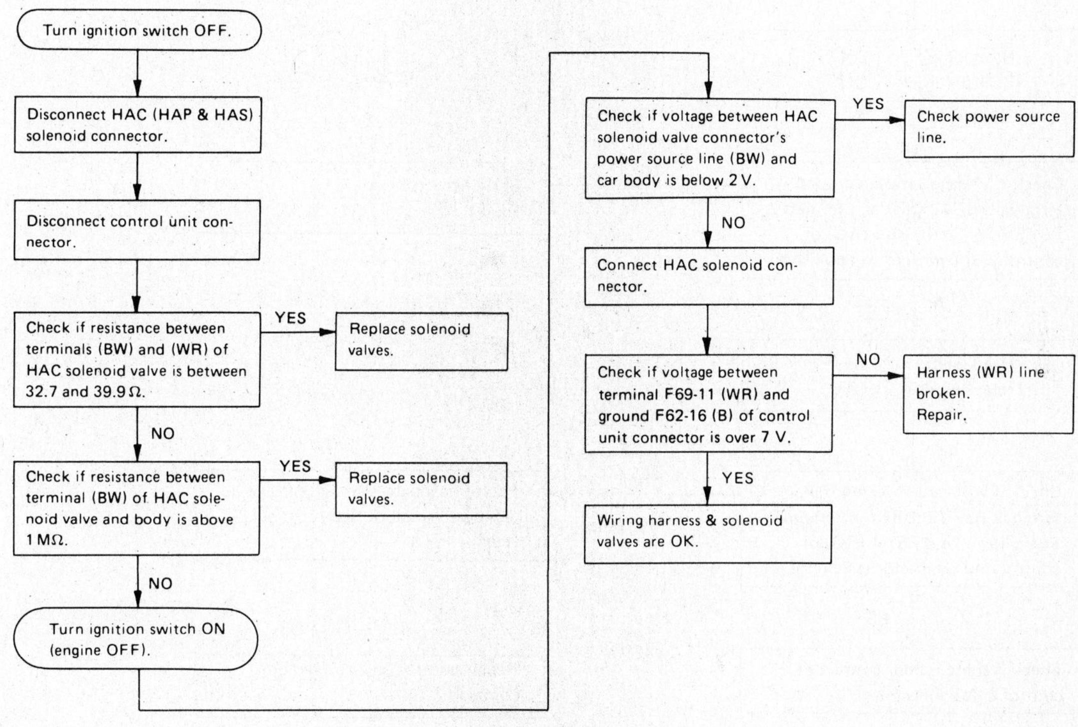


118331 121930

# 1991 ENGINE PERFORMANCE
## Self-Diagnostics – Justy – Carbureted (Cont.)

### CODE 62, IDLE-UP SYSTEM (1)

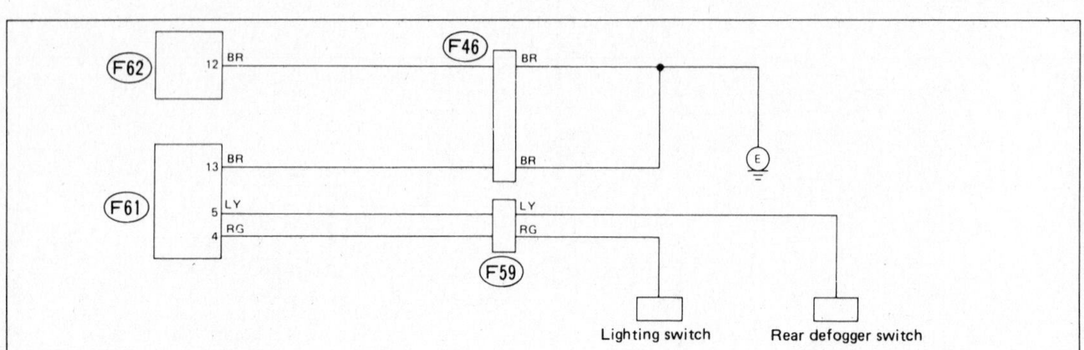


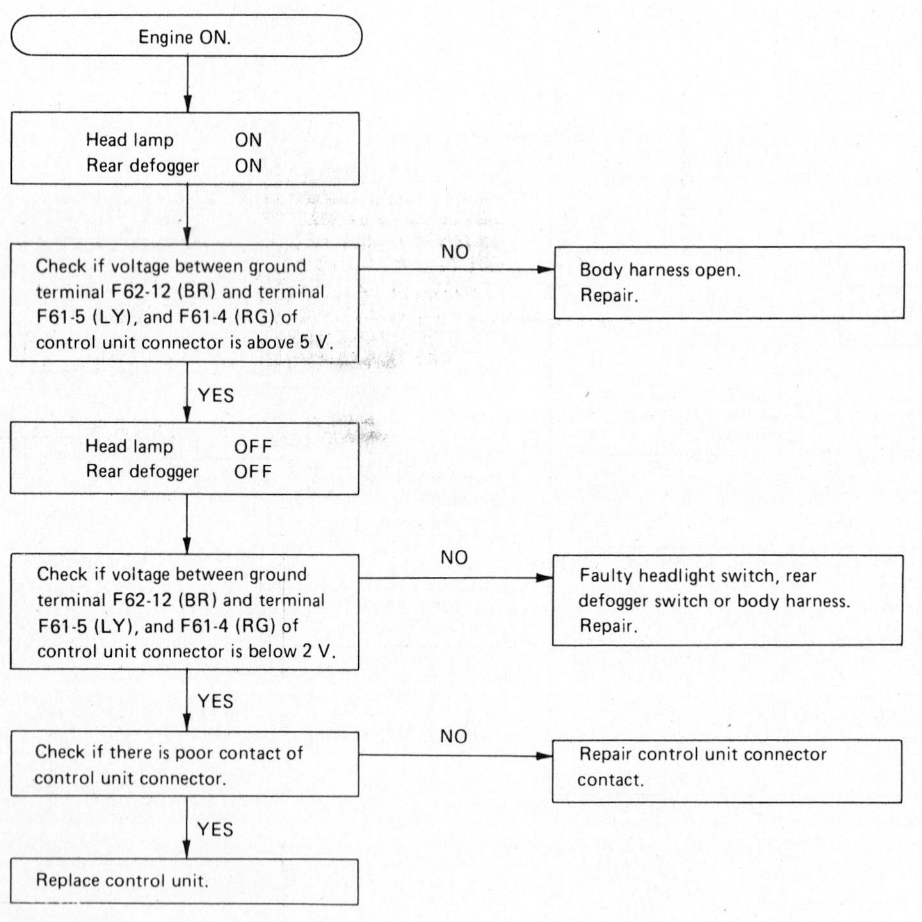


118334 121932

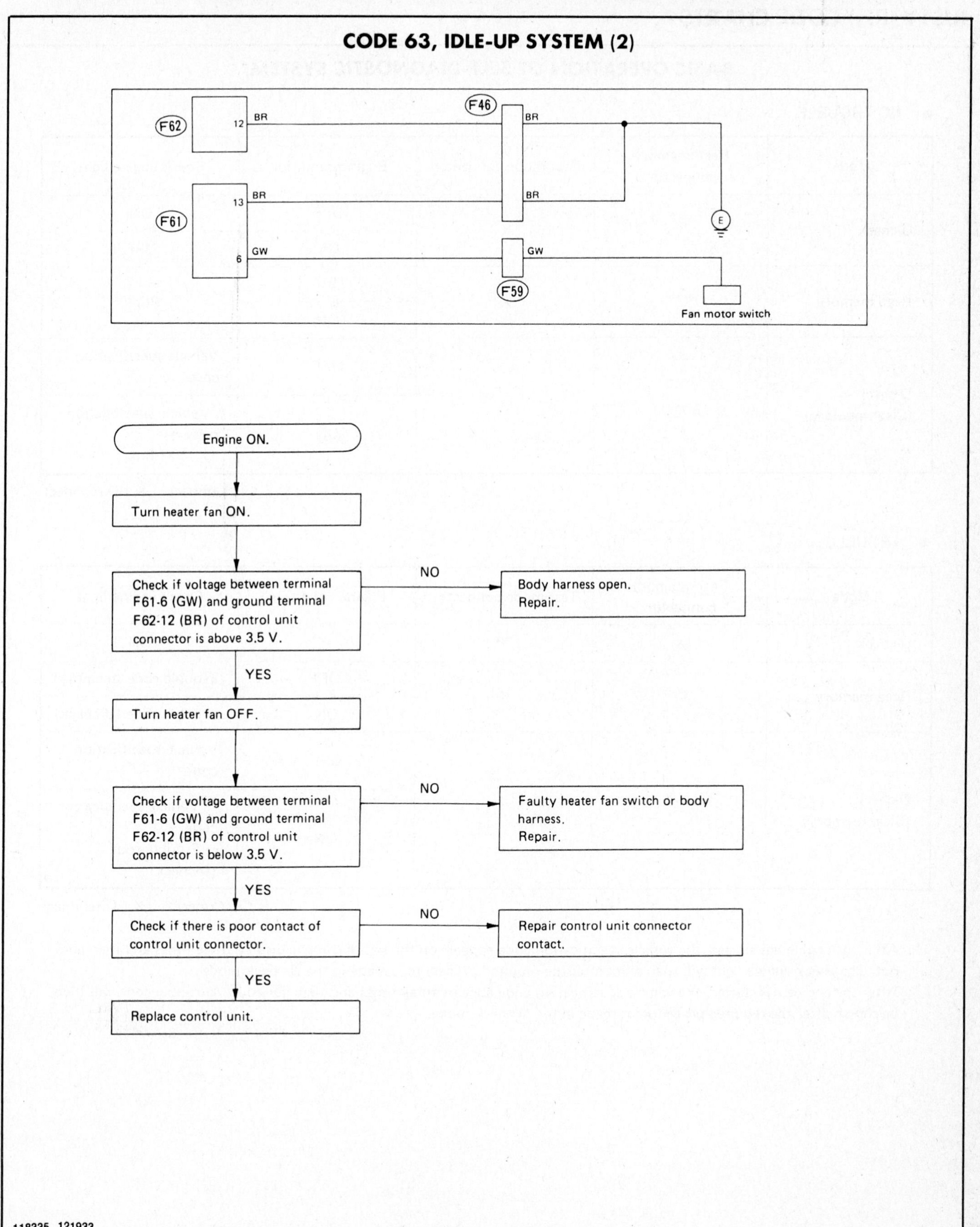
CODE 63, IDLE-UP SYSTEM (2)
F62
12
BR
F46
BR
F61
13
BR
BR
E
6
GW
GW
F59
Fan motor switch
Engine ON.
Turn heater fan ON.
Check if voltage between terminal F61-6 (GW) and ground terminal F62-12 (BR) of control unit connector is above 3.5 V.
NO
Body harness open. Repair.
YES
Turn heater fan OFF.
Check if voltage between terminal F61-6 (GW) and ground terminal F62-12 (BR) of control unit connector is below 3.5 V.
NO
Faulty heater fan switch or body harness. Repair.
YES
Check if there is poor contact of control unit connector.
NO
Repair control unit connector contact.
YES
Replace control unit.
118335 121933

## JUSTY (PFI) CODE CHARTS

### BASIC OPERATION OF SELF-DIAGNOSTIC SYSTEM

● NO TROUBLE

| Mode | Read memory connector | Test mode connector | Engine condition | Check engine light |
|---|---|---|---|---|
| U-check | X | X | OFF | ON |
| | | | ON | OFF |
| Read memory | O | X | OFF | Blink |
| | | | ON | |
| D-check (Clear memory) | – | O | OFF | Vehicle specification code |
| | | | ON | *Vehicle specification code → → Blink |

O: Connect X: Disconnect

● TROUBLE

| Mode | Read memory connector | Test mode connector | Engine condition | Check engine light |
|---|---|---|---|---|
| U-check | X | X | – | ON |
| Read memory | O | X | OFF | Trouble code (memory) |
| | | | ON | Trouble code (U-check) |
| D-check (Clear memory) | – | O | OFF | Vehicle specification code |
| | | | ON | **Vehicle specification code → → Trouble code (D-check) |

O: Connect X: Disconnect

*: After the engine has started, the vehicle specification code appears on the self-diagnostic display three times and then goes out. The check engine light will then blink after the required procedure is made in the D-check mode.

**: After the engine has started, the vehicle specification code appears three times and then goes out. A trouble code will then be shown after the required procedure is made in the D-check mode.

90C18764

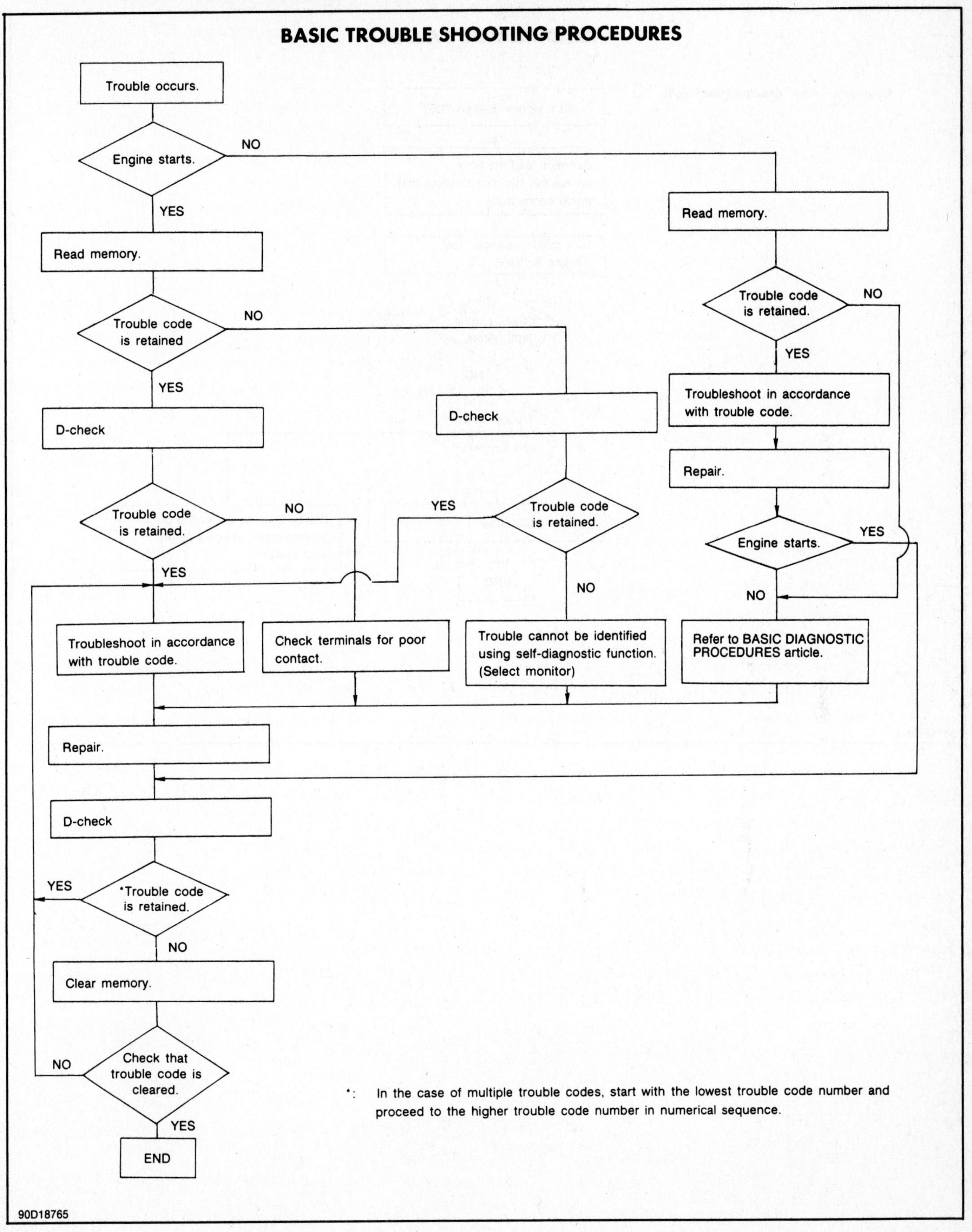
BASIC TROUBLE SHOOTING PROCEDURES
Trouble occurs.
Engine starts.
NO
YES
Read memory.
Read memory.
Trouble code is retained
NO
YES
Trouble code is retained.
NO
YES
Troubleshoot in accordance with trouble code.
D-check
D-check
Repair.
Trouble code is retained.
NO
YES
Trouble code is retained.
Engine starts.
YES
YES
NO
NO
Troubleshoot in accordance with trouble code.
Check terminals for poor contact.
Trouble cannot be identified using self-diagnostic function. (Select monitor)
Refer to BASIC DIAGNOSTIC PROCEDURES article.
Repair.
D-check
YES
*Trouble code is retained.
NO
Clear memory.
NO
Check that trouble code is cleared.
YES
END
*: In the case of multiple trouble codes, start with the lowest trouble code number and proceed to the higher trouble code number in numerical sequence.
90D18765

# 1991 ENGINE PERFORMANCE
# Self-Diagnostics – Justy – PFI (Cont.)

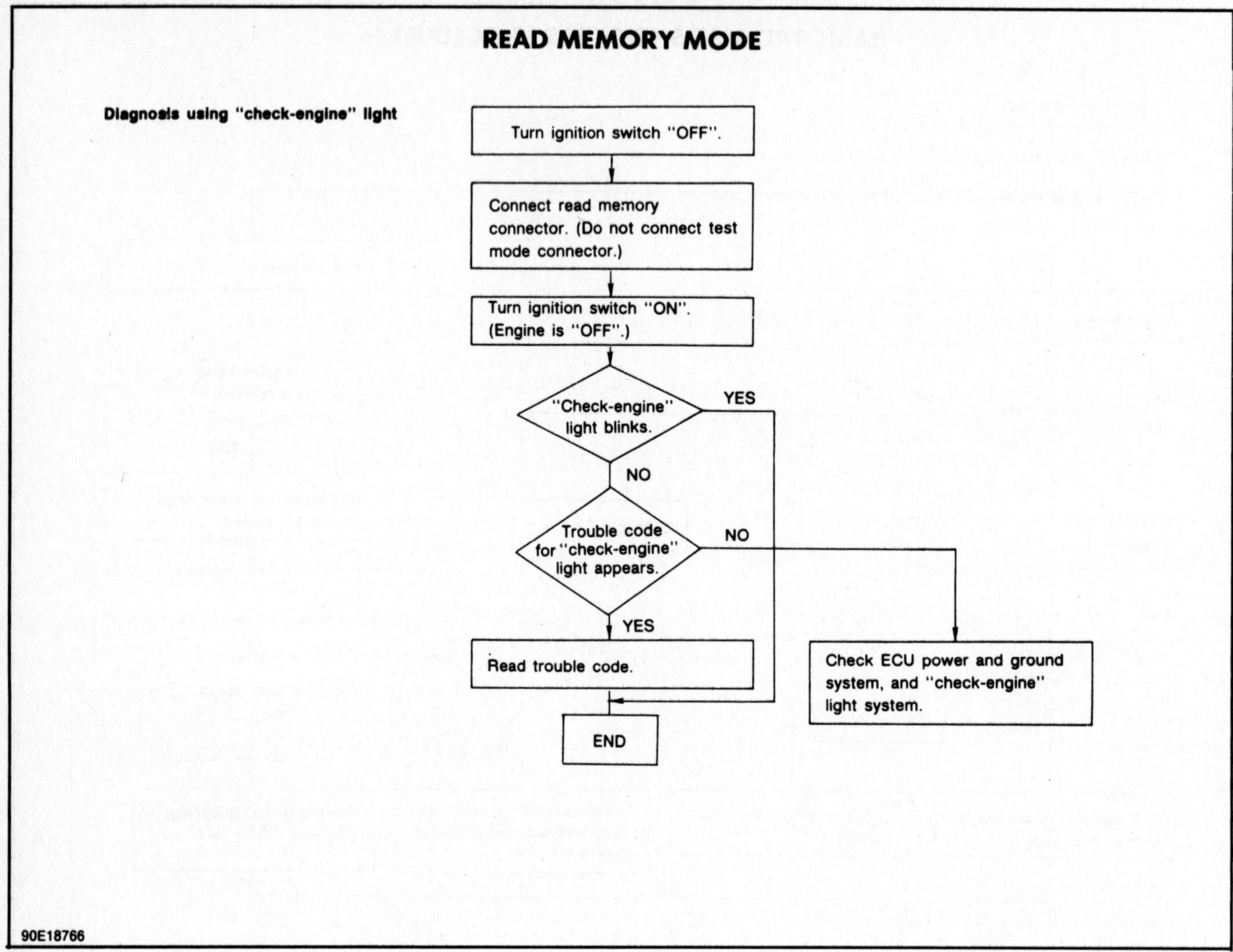

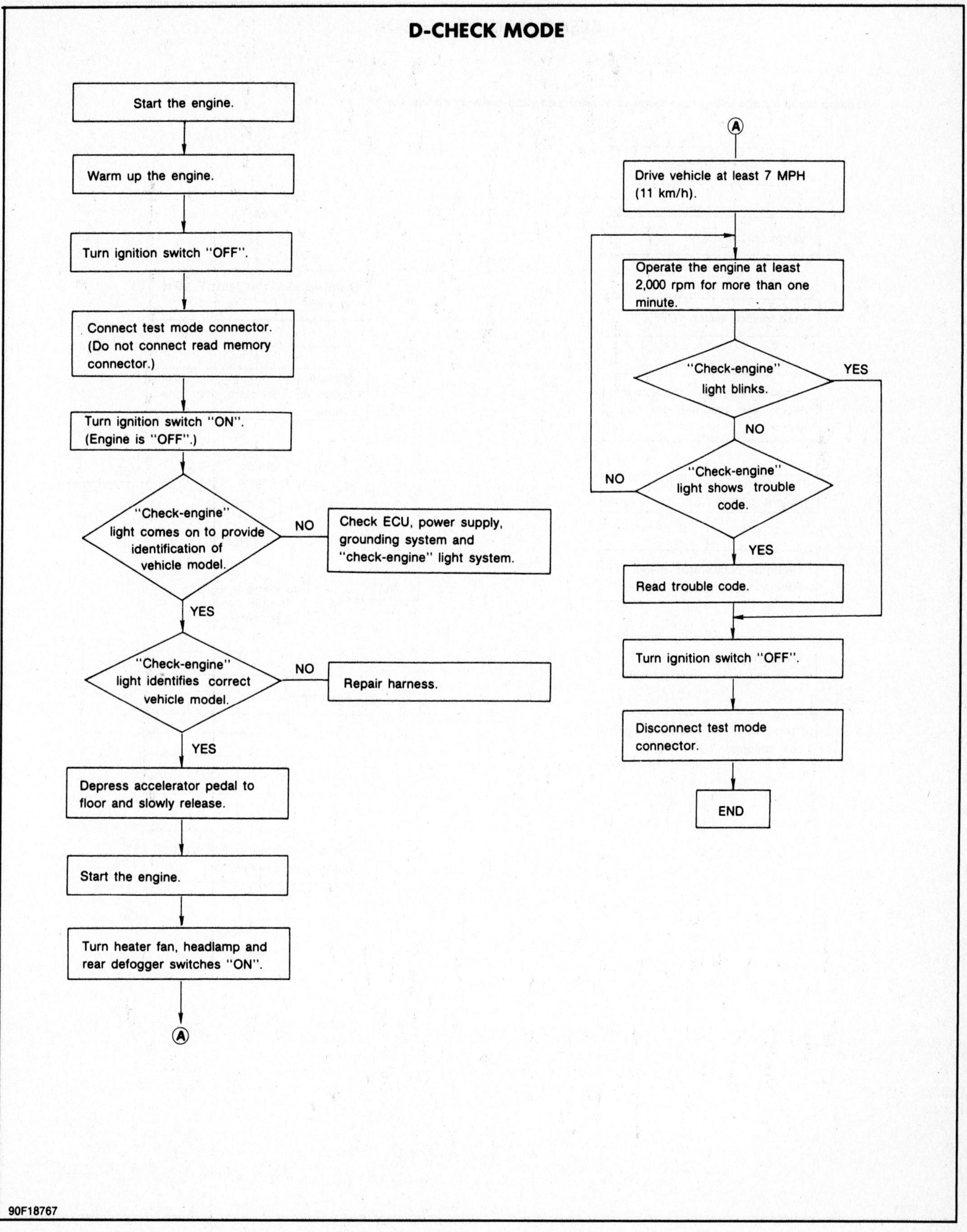

D-CHECK MODE
Start the engine.
Warm up the engine.
Turn ignition switch "OFF".
Connect test mode connector. (Do not connect read memory connector.)
Turn ignition switch "ON". (Engine is "OFF".)
"Check-engine" light comes on to provide identification of vehicle model.
NO
Check ECU, power supply, grounding system and "check-engine" light system.
YES
"Check-engine" light identifies correct vehicle model.
NO
Repair harness.
YES
Depress accelerator pedal to floor and slowly release.
Start the engine.
Turn heater fan, headlamp and rear defogger switches "ON".
A
A
Drive vehicle at least 7 MPH (11 km/h).
Operate the engine at least 2,000 rpm for more than one minute.
"Check-engine" light blinks.
YES
NO
"Check-engine" light shows trouble code.
NO
YES
Read trouble code.
Turn ignition switch "OFF".
Disconnect test mode connector.
END
90F18767

# 1991 ENGINE PERFORMANCE
# Self-Diagnostics – Justy – PFI (Cont.)

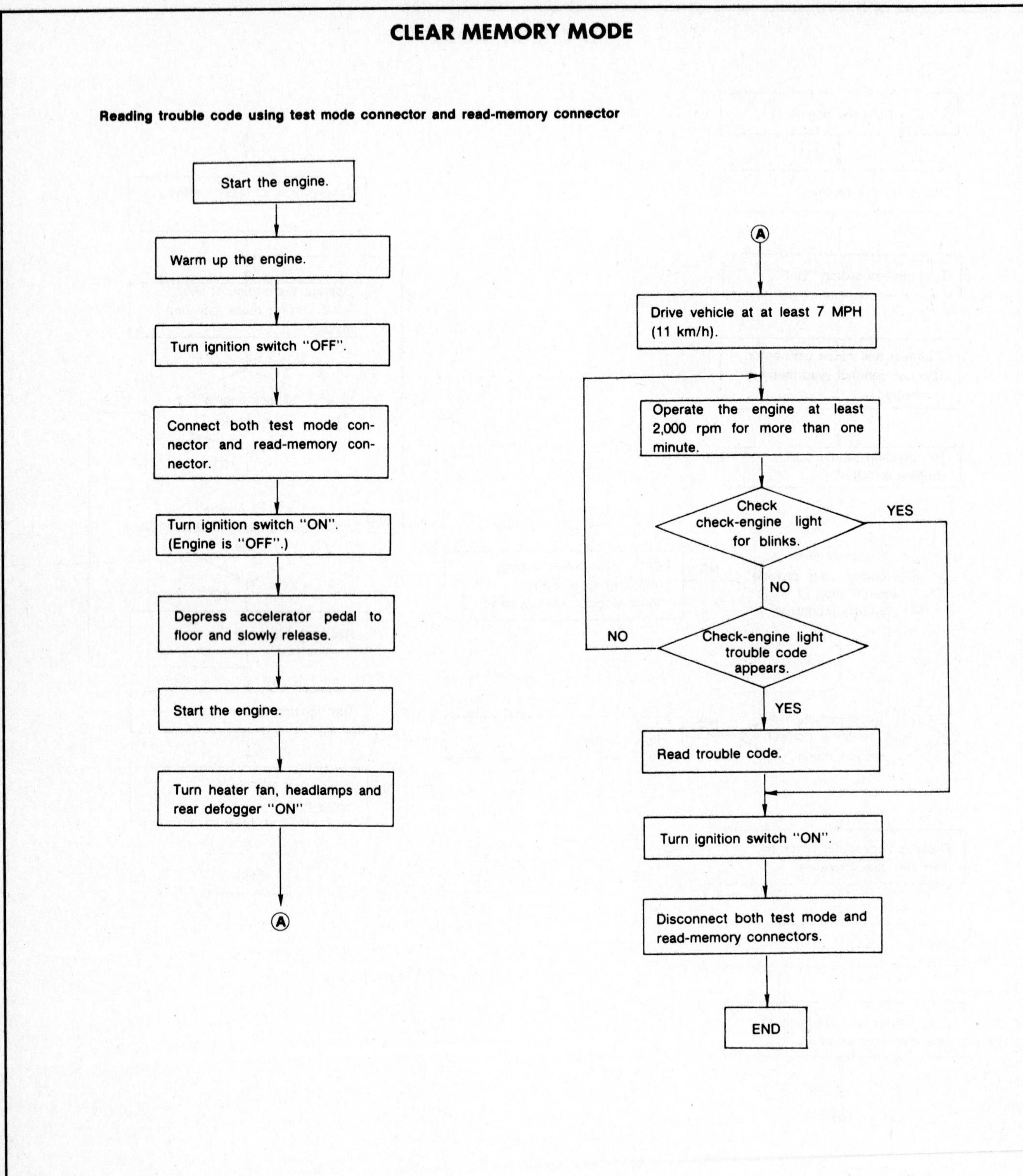

# 1991 ENGINE PERFORMANCE
## Self-Diagnostics – Justy – PFI (Cont.)

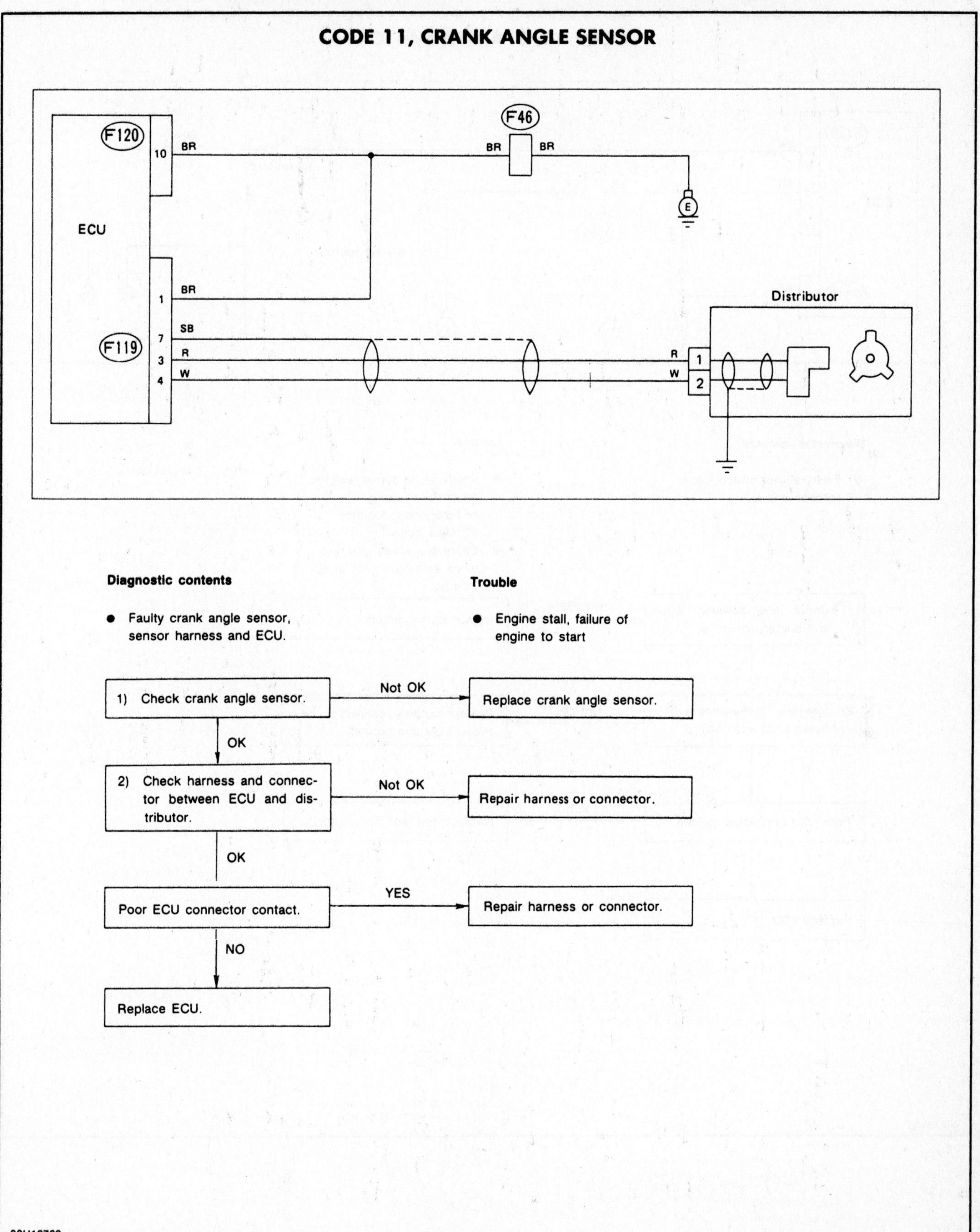
CODE 11, CRANK ANGLE SENSOR
F120
10
BR
F46
BR
BR
E
ECU
1
BR
SB
F119
7
R
3
W
4
Distributor
R
1
W
2
Diagnostic contents
● Faulty crank angle sensor, sensor harness and ECU.
Trouble
● Engine stall, failure of engine to start
1) Check crank angle sensor.
Not OK
Replace crank angle sensor.
OK
2) Check harness and connector between ECU and distributor.
Not OK
Repair harness or connector.
OK
Poor ECU connector contact.
YES
Repair harness or connector.
NO
Replace ECU.
90H18769

# 1991 ENGINE PERFORMANCE
# Self-Diagnostics – Justy – PFI (Cont.)

## CODE 12, STARTER SWITCH

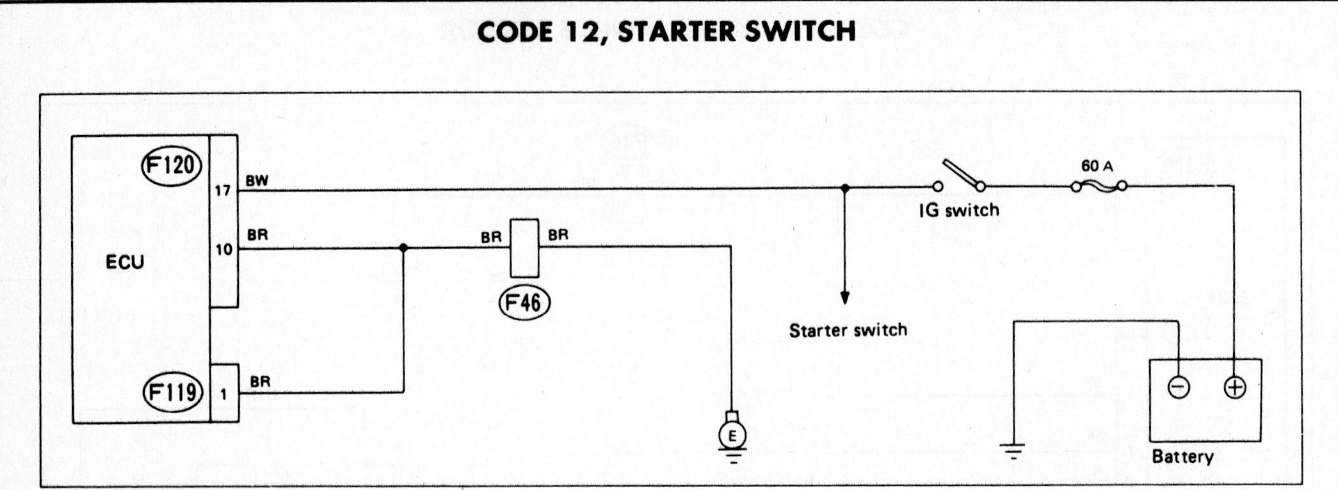


**Diagnostic contents**

- Faulty starter switch signal, harness and ECU

**Trouble**

- Crank angle sensor cannot be checked using self-diagnostic function. (Trouble code 11)
- Spark plugs wet with fuel when starting engine at full throttle.

1) Check line between ECU and starter circuit. — Not OK → Repair starter circuit.

↓ OK

2) Measure resistance between ECU and body. — Not OK → Repair harness connector between ECU and ground.

↓ OK

Poor ECU connector contact. — YES → Replace harness connector.

↓ NO

Replace ECU.

90A18770

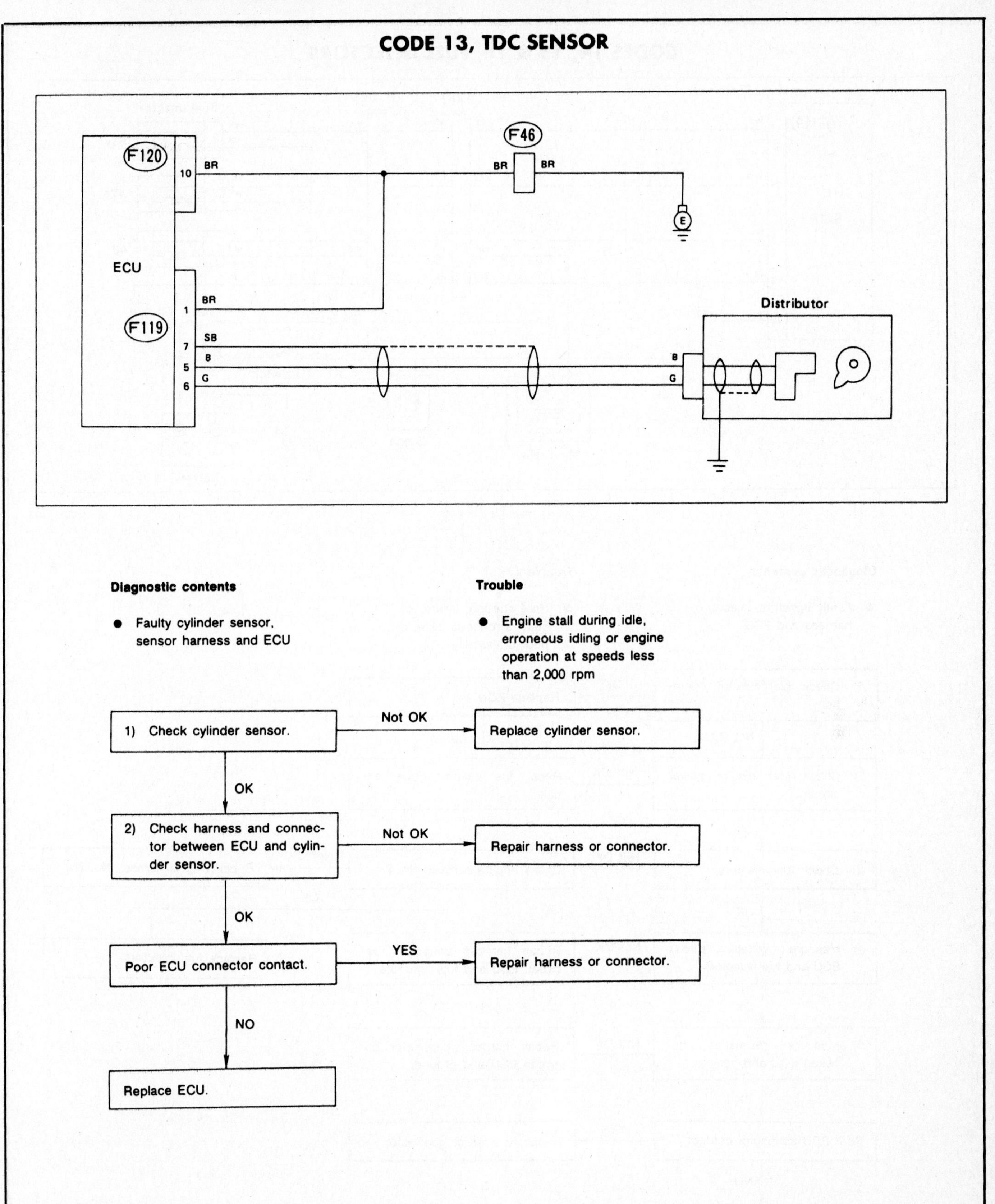

CODE 13, TDC SENSOR
F120
F46
BR
BR
BR
10
E
ECU
1
BR
F119
Distributor
7
SB
B
5
G
6
B
G
Diagnostic contents
● Faulty cylinder sensor, sensor harness and ECU
Trouble
● Engine stall during idle, erroneous idling or engine operation at speeds less than 2,000 rpm
1) Check cylinder sensor.
Not OK
Replace cylinder sensor.
OK
2) Check harness and connector between ECU and cylinder sensor.
Not OK
Repair harness or connector.
OK
Poor ECU connector contact.
YES
Repair harness or connector.
NO
Replace ECU.
90B18771

# 1991 ENGINE PERFORMANCE
## Self-Diagnostics – Justy – PFI (Cont.)

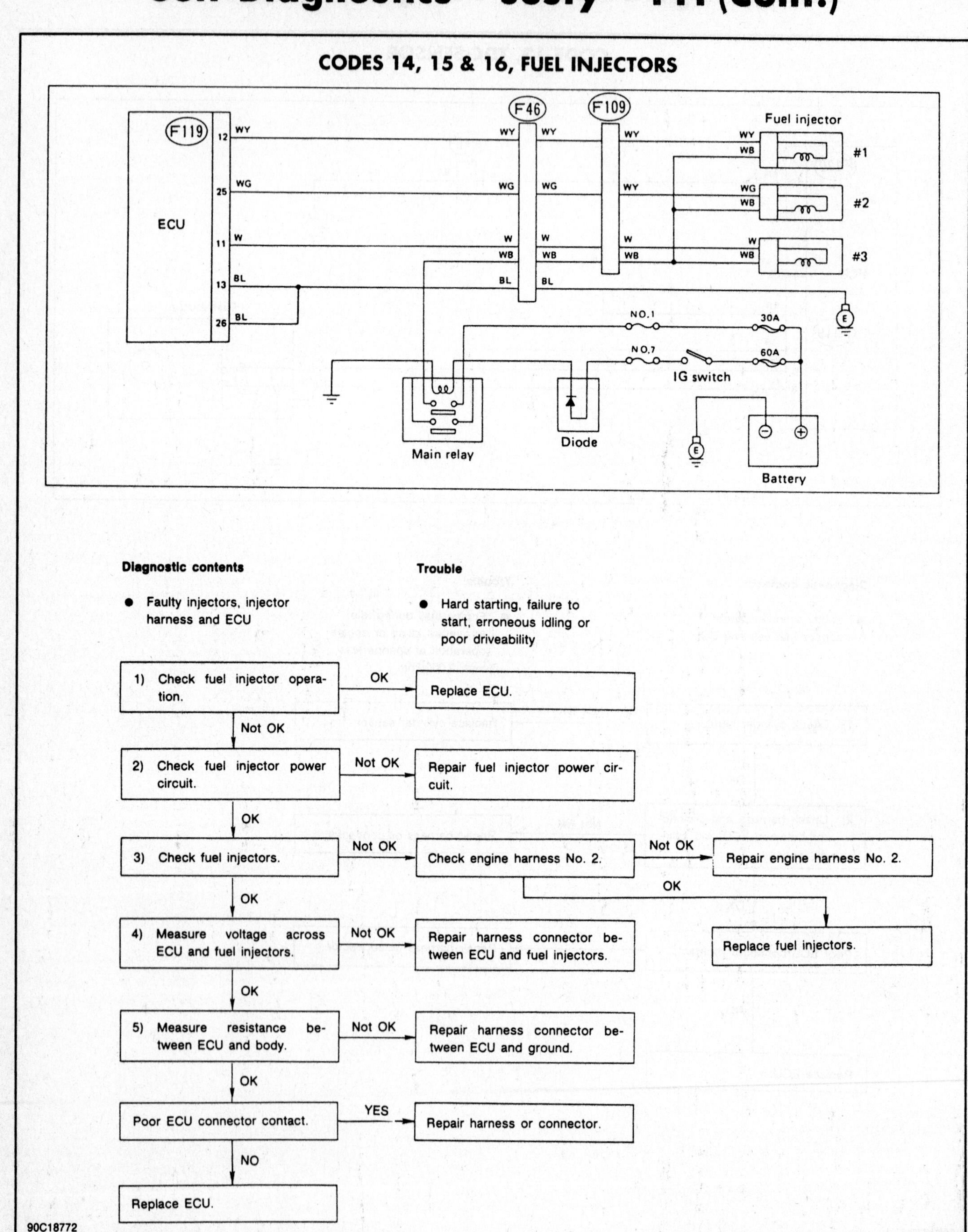
CODES 14, 15 & 16, FUEL INJECTORS
F119
ECU
12 WY
25 WG
11 W
13 BL
26 BL
F46
F109
WY
WG
W
WB
BL
Fuel injector
#1
#2
#3
NO.1
30A
NO.7
60A
IG switch
Main relay
Diode
Battery
E
Diagnostic contents
Faulty injectors, injector harness and ECU
Trouble
Hard starting, failure to start, erroneous idling or poor driveability
1) Check fuel injector operation.
OK
Replace ECU.
Not OK
2) Check fuel injector power circuit.
Not OK
Repair fuel injector power circuit.
OK
3) Check fuel injectors.
Not OK
Check engine harness No. 2.
Not OK
Repair engine harness No. 2.
OK
Replace fuel injectors.
OK
4) Measure voltage across ECU and fuel injectors.
Not OK
Repair harness connector between ECU and fuel injectors.
OK
5) Measure resistance between ECU and body.
Not OK
Repair harness connector between ECU and ground.
OK
Poor ECU connector contact.
YES
Repair harness or connector.
NO
Replace ECU.
90C18772

## CODE 21, COOLANT (WATER) TEMPERATURE SENSOR

F120 10 BR
F121 5 WB 1 BG 2 BG
ECU
F119 1 BR
F46 WB BG BR
Water temperature sensor WB BG
E

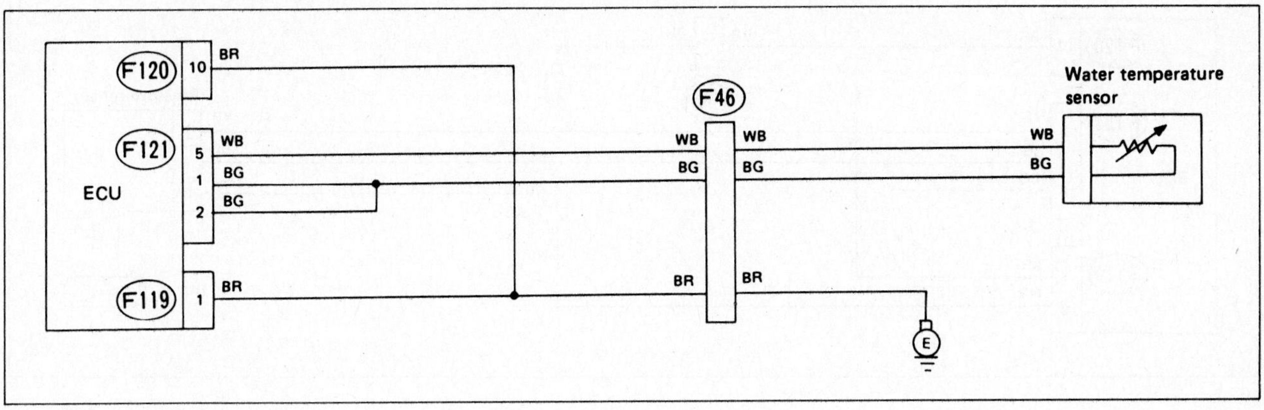

**Diagnostic contents**

- Shorted signal system Faulty water temperature sensor

**Trouble**

- Hard starting, failure to start, erroneous idling, poor driveability, etc.

1) Measure voltage across ECU and body. → OK → Poor ECU connector contact. → YES → Repair harness or connector. / NO → Replace ECU.

↓ Not OK

2) Check water temperature sensor. → Not OK → Replace water temperature sensor.

↓ OK

3) Check harness and connector between ECU and water temperature sensor. → Not OK → Repair harness or connector.

↓ OK

Poor ECU connector contact. → YES → Repair harness or connector.

↓ NO

Replace ECU.

90D18773

# 1991 ENGINE PERFORMANCE
## Self-Diagnostics – Justy – PFI (Cont.)

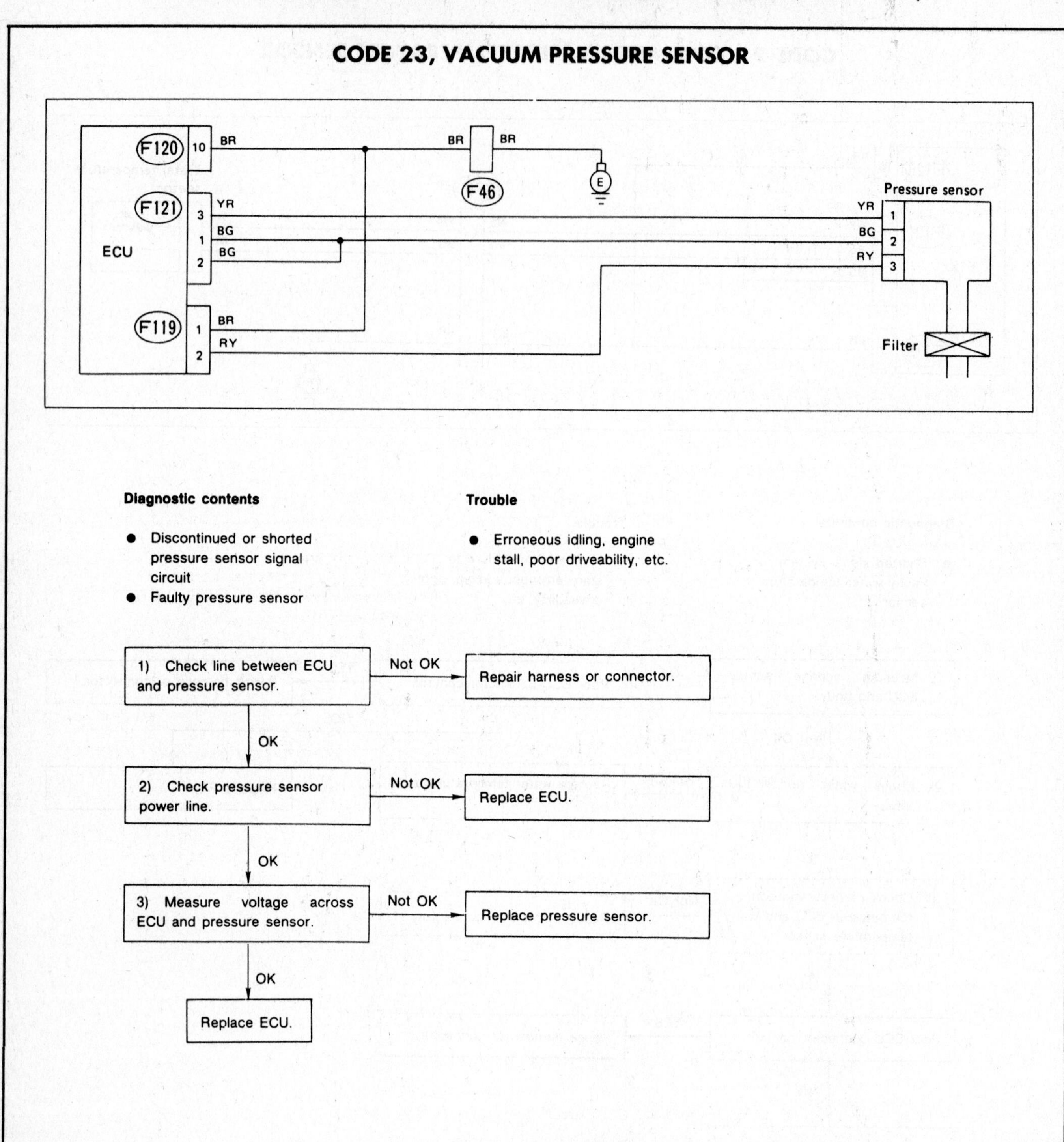

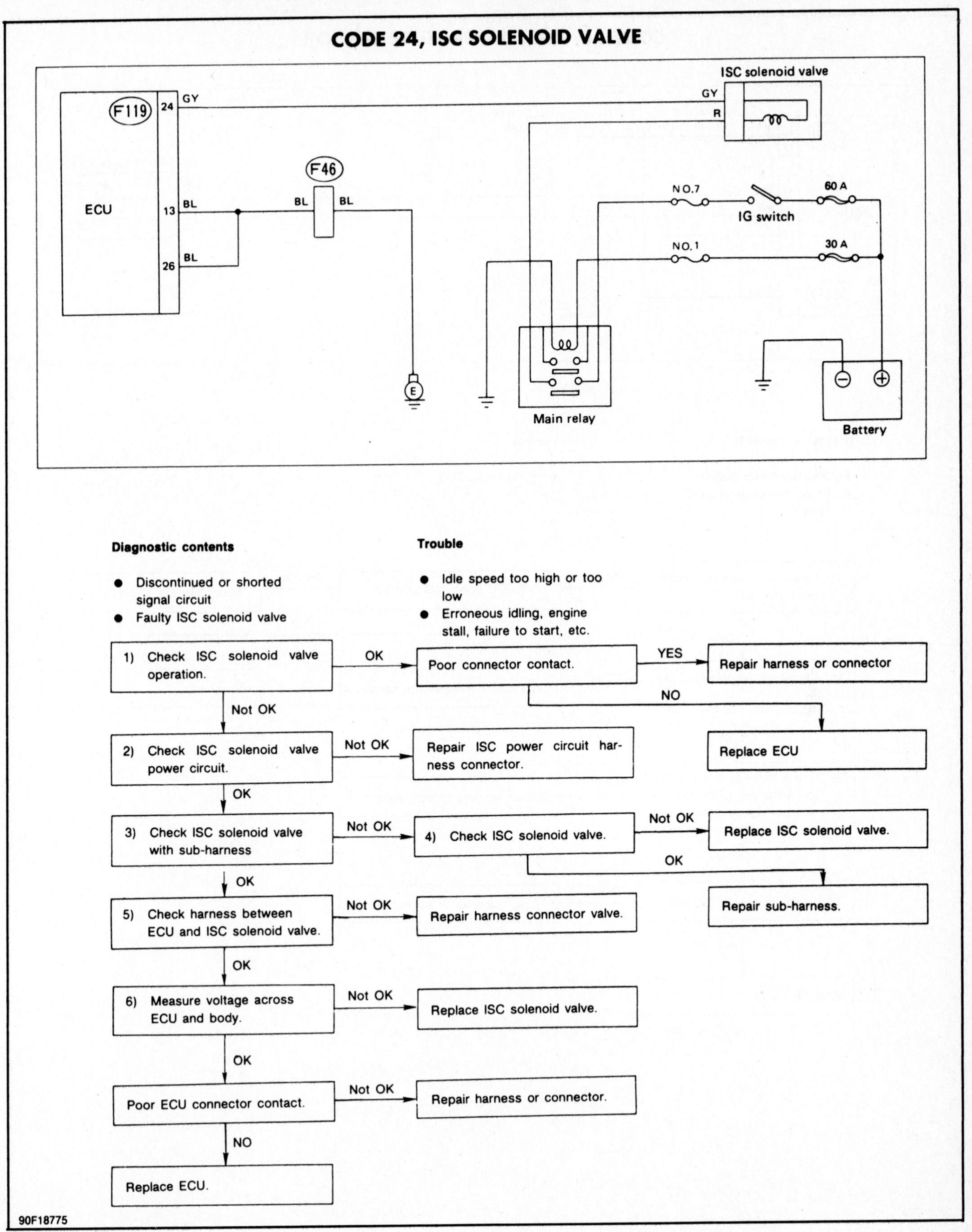
CODE 24, ISC SOLENOID VALVE
ISC solenoid valve
F119
24
GY
GY
R
ECU
F46
13
BL
BL
BL
26
BL
NO.7
60 A
IG switch
NO.1
30 A
E
Main relay
Battery
Diagnostic contents
Discontinued or shorted signal circuit
Faulty ISC solenoid valve
Trouble
Idle speed too high or too low
Erroneous idling, engine stall, failure to start, etc.
1) Check ISC solenoid valve operation.
OK
Poor connector contact.
YES
Repair harness or connector
NO
Replace ECU
Not OK
2) Check ISC solenoid valve power circuit.
Not OK
Repair ISC power circuit harness connector.
OK
3) Check ISC solenoid valve with sub-harness
Not OK
4) Check ISC solenoid valve.
Not OK
Replace ISC solenoid valve.
OK
Repair sub-harness.
OK
5) Check harness between ECU and ISC solenoid valve.
Not OK
Repair harness connector valve.
OK
6) Measure voltage across ECU and body.
Not OK
Replace ISC solenoid valve.
OK
Poor ECU connector contact.
Not OK
Repair harness or connector.
NO
Replace ECU.
90F18775

# 1991 ENGINE PERFORMANCE
## Self-Diagnostics – Justy – PFI (Cont.)

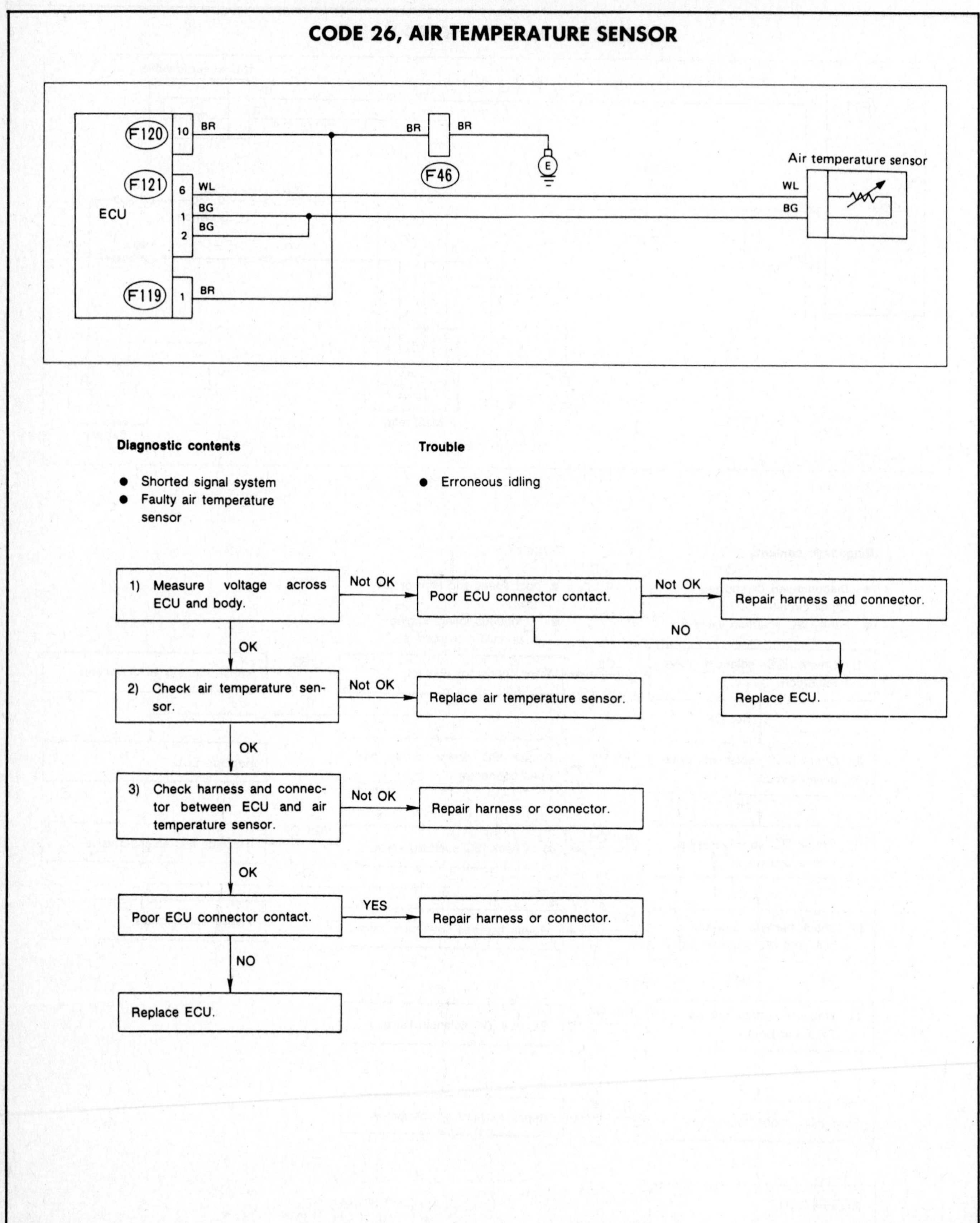
CODE 26, AIR TEMPERATURE SENSOR
F120
10
BR
BR
BR
F46
E
Air temperature sensor
F121
6
WL
WL
BG
BG
ECU
1
2
BG
F119
1
BR
Diagnostic contents
Shorted signal system
Faulty air temperature sensor
Trouble
Erroneous idling
1) Measure voltage across ECU and body.
Not OK
Poor ECU connector contact.
Not OK
Repair harness and connector.
NO
Replace ECU.
OK
2) Check air temperature sensor.
Not OK
Replace air temperature sensor.
OK
3) Check harness and connector between ECU and air temperature sensor.
Not OK
Repair harness or connector.
OK
Poor ECU connector contact.
YES
Repair harness or connector.
NO
Replace ECU.
90G18776

# 1991 ENGINE PERFORMANCE
## Self-Diagnostics – Justy – PFI (Cont.)

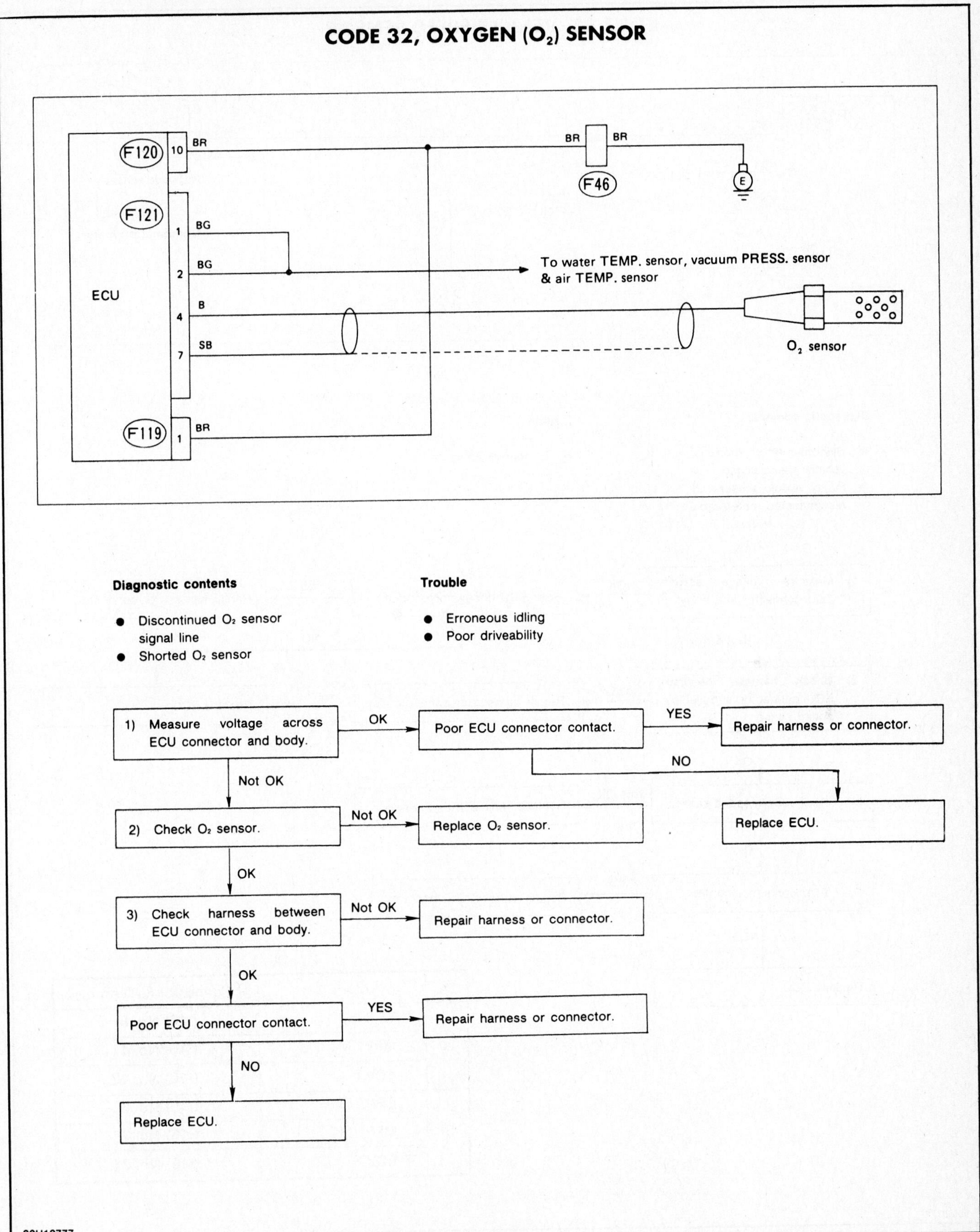
CODE 32, OXYGEN ($O_2$) SENSOR
F120
10
BR
BR
BR
F46
E
F121
1
BG
2
BG
To water TEMP. sensor, vacuum PRESS. sensor & air TEMP. sensor
ECU
4
B
7
SB
$O_2$ sensor
F119
1
BR
Diagnostic contents
● Discontinued $O_2$ sensor signal line
● Shorted $O_2$ sensor
Trouble
● Erroneous idling
● Poor driveability
1) Measure voltage across ECU connector and body.
OK
Poor ECU connector contact.
YES
Repair harness or connector.
NO
Replace ECU.
Not OK
2) Check $O_2$ sensor.
Not OK
Replace $O_2$ sensor.
OK
3) Check harness between ECU connector and body.
Not OK
Repair harness or connector.
OK
Poor ECU connector contact.
YES
Repair harness or connector.
NO
Replace ECU.
90H18777

# 1991 ENGINE PERFORMANCE
## Self-Diagnostics – Justy – PFI (Cont.)

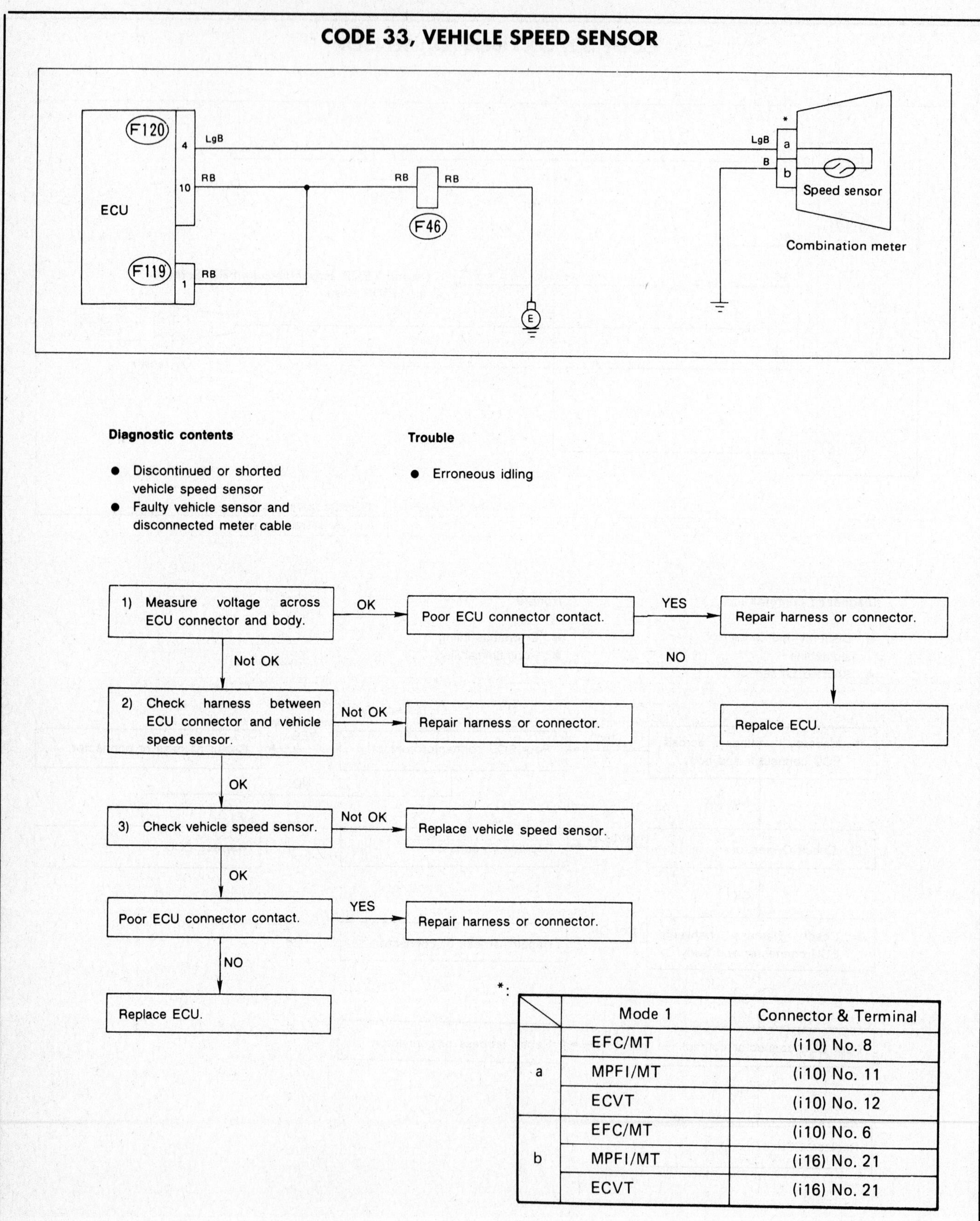
CODE 33, VEHICLE SPEED SENSOR
F120
4
LgB
10
RB
ECU
F119
RB
1
RB
F46
RB
E
LgB
B
a
b
*
Speed sensor
Combination meter
Diagnostic contents
Discontinued or shorted vehicle speed sensor
Faulty vehicle sensor and disconnected meter cable
Trouble
Erroneous idling
1) Measure voltage across ECU connector and body.
OK
Poor ECU connector contact.
YES
Repair harness or connector.
NO
Repalce ECU.
Not OK
2) Check harness between ECU connector and vehicle speed sensor.
Not OK
Repair harness or connector.
OK
3) Check vehicle speed sensor.
Not OK
Replace vehicle speed sensor.
OK
Poor ECU connector contact.
YES
Repair harness or connector.
NO
Replace ECU.
*:
90I18778

| | Mode 1 | Connector & Terminal |
|---|---|---|
| a | EFC/MT | (i10) No. 8 |
| | MPFI/MT | (i10) No. 11 |
| | ECVT | (i10) No. 12 |
| b | EFC/MT | (i10) No. 6 |
| | MPFI/MT | (i16) No. 21 |
| | ECVT | (i16) No. 21 |

# 1991 ENGINE PERFORMANCE
## Self-Diagnostics – Justy – PFI (Cont.)

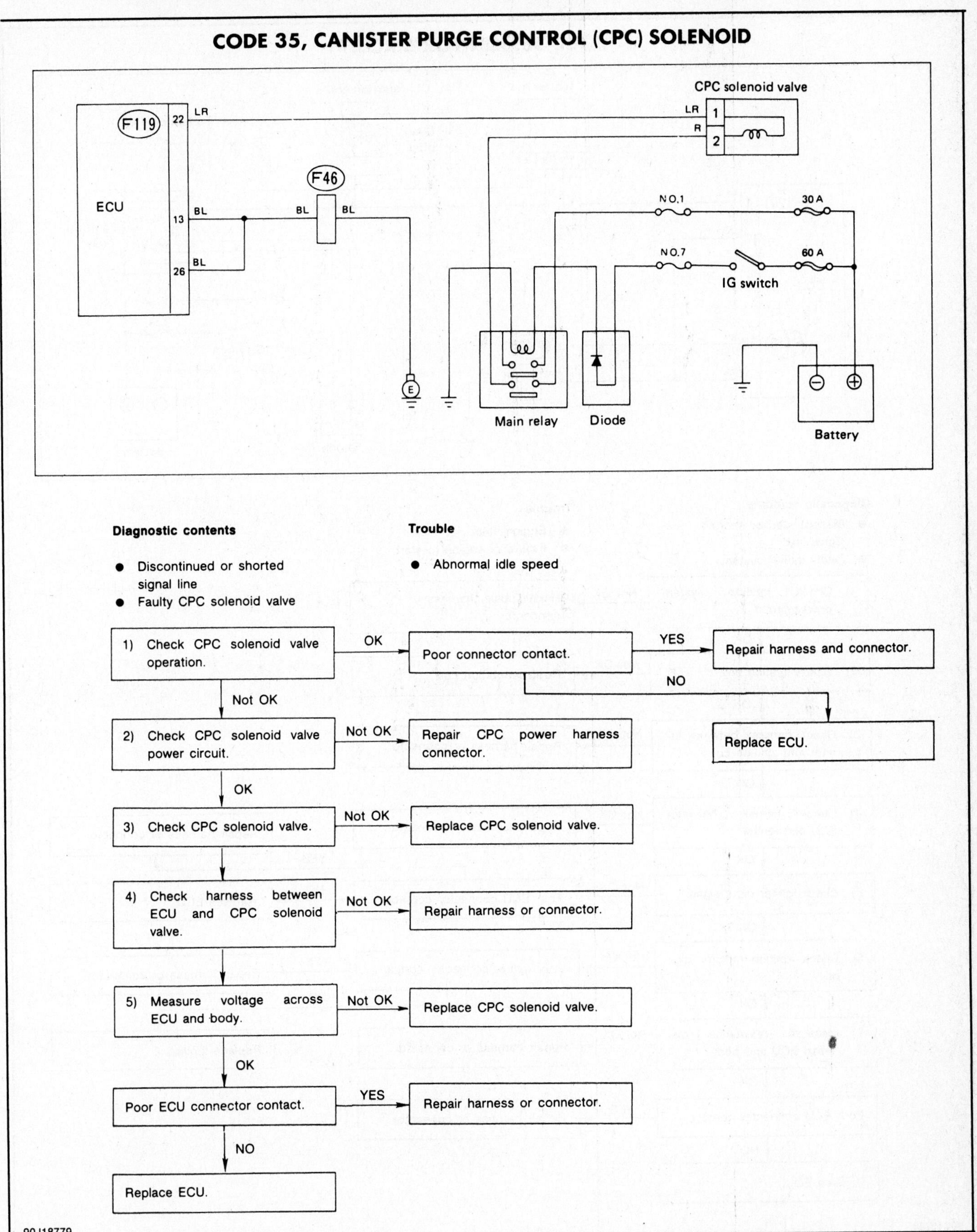
CODE 35, CANISTER PURGE CONTROL (CPC) SOLENOID
CPC solenoid valve
F119
22
LR
LR
1
R
2
F46
ECU
13
BL
BL
BL
26
BL
NO.1
30 A
NO.7
60 A
IG switch
E
Main relay
Diode
Battery
Diagnostic contents
Discontinued or shorted signal line
Faulty CPC solenoid valve
Trouble
Abnormal idle speed
1) Check CPC solenoid valve operation.
OK
Poor connector contact.
YES
Repair harness and connector.
NO
Replace ECU.
Not OK
2) Check CPC solenoid valve power circuit.
Not OK
Repair CPC power harness connector.
OK
3) Check CPC solenoid valve.
Not OK
Replace CPC solenoid valve.
4) Check harness between ECU and CPC solenoid valve.
Not OK
Repair harness or connector.
5) Measure voltage across ECU and body.
Not OK
Replace CPC solenoid valve.
OK
Poor ECU connector contact.
YES
Repair harness or connector.
NO
Replace ECU.
90J18779

# 1991 ENGINE PERFORMANCE
## Self-Diagnostics – Justy – PFI (Cont.)

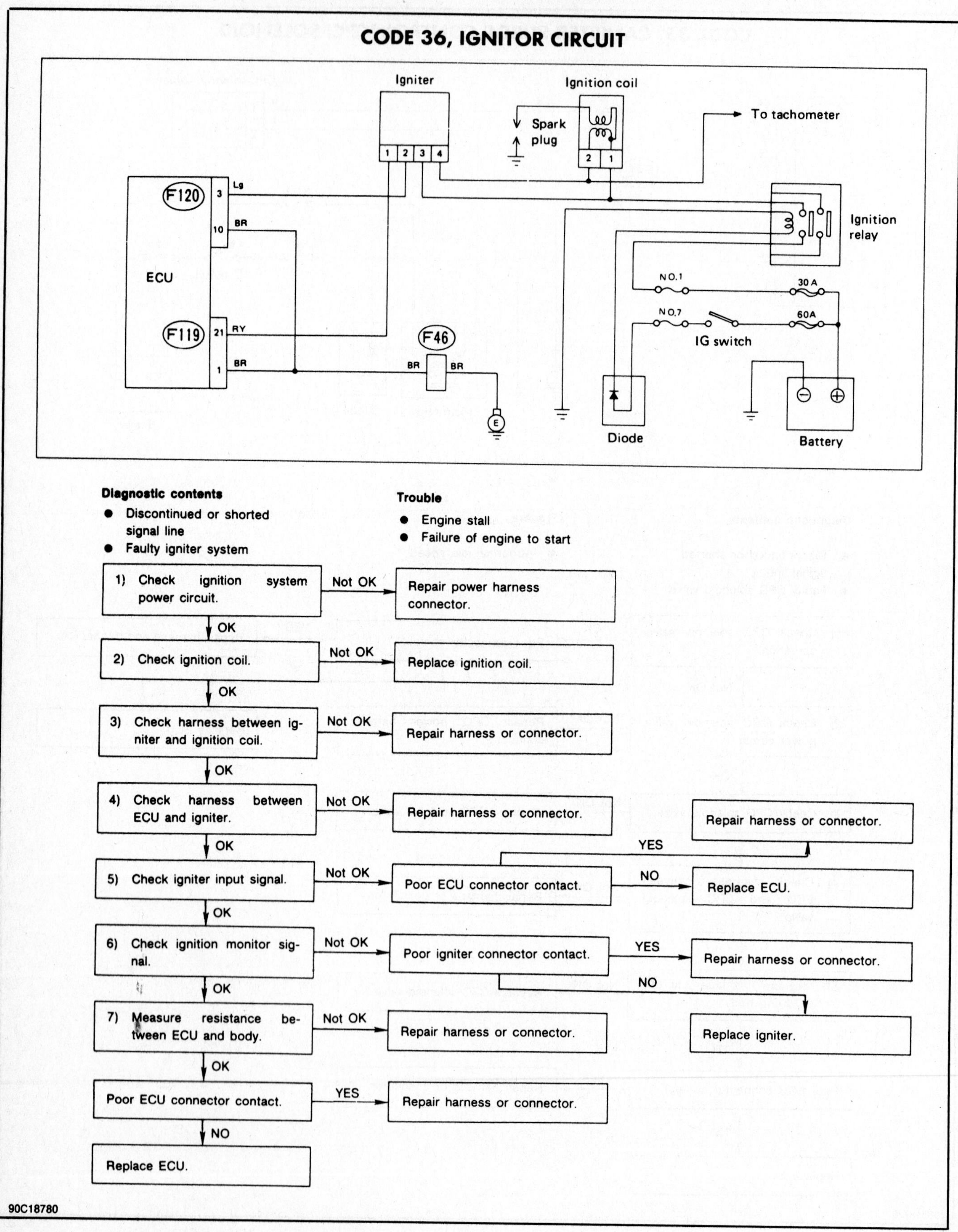
CODE 36, IGNITOR CIRCUIT
Igniter
Ignition coil
Spark plug
To tachometer
Ignition relay
ECU
F120
F119
F46
Lg
BR
RY
NO.1
NO.7
30 A
60A
IG switch
Diode
Battery
Diagnostic contents
● Discontinued or shorted signal line
● Faulty igniter system
Trouble
● Engine stall
● Failure of engine to start
1) Check ignition system power circuit.
Not OK
Repair power harness connector.
OK
2) Check ignition coil.
Not OK
Replace ignition coil.
OK
3) Check harness between igniter and ignition coil.
Not OK
Repair harness or connector.
OK
4) Check harness between ECU and igniter.
Not OK
Repair harness or connector.
OK
5) Check igniter input signal.
Not OK
Poor ECU connector contact.
YES
Repair harness or connector.
NO
Replace ECU.
OK
6) Check ignition monitor signal.
Not OK
Poor igniter connector contact.
YES
Repair harness or connector.
NO
Replace igniter.
OK
7) Measure resistance between ECU and body.
Not OK
Repair harness or connector.
OK
Poor ECU connector contact.
YES
Repair harness or connector.
NO
Replace ECU.
90C18780

# 1991 ENGINE PERFORMANCE
# Self-Diagnostics – Justy – PFI (Cont.)

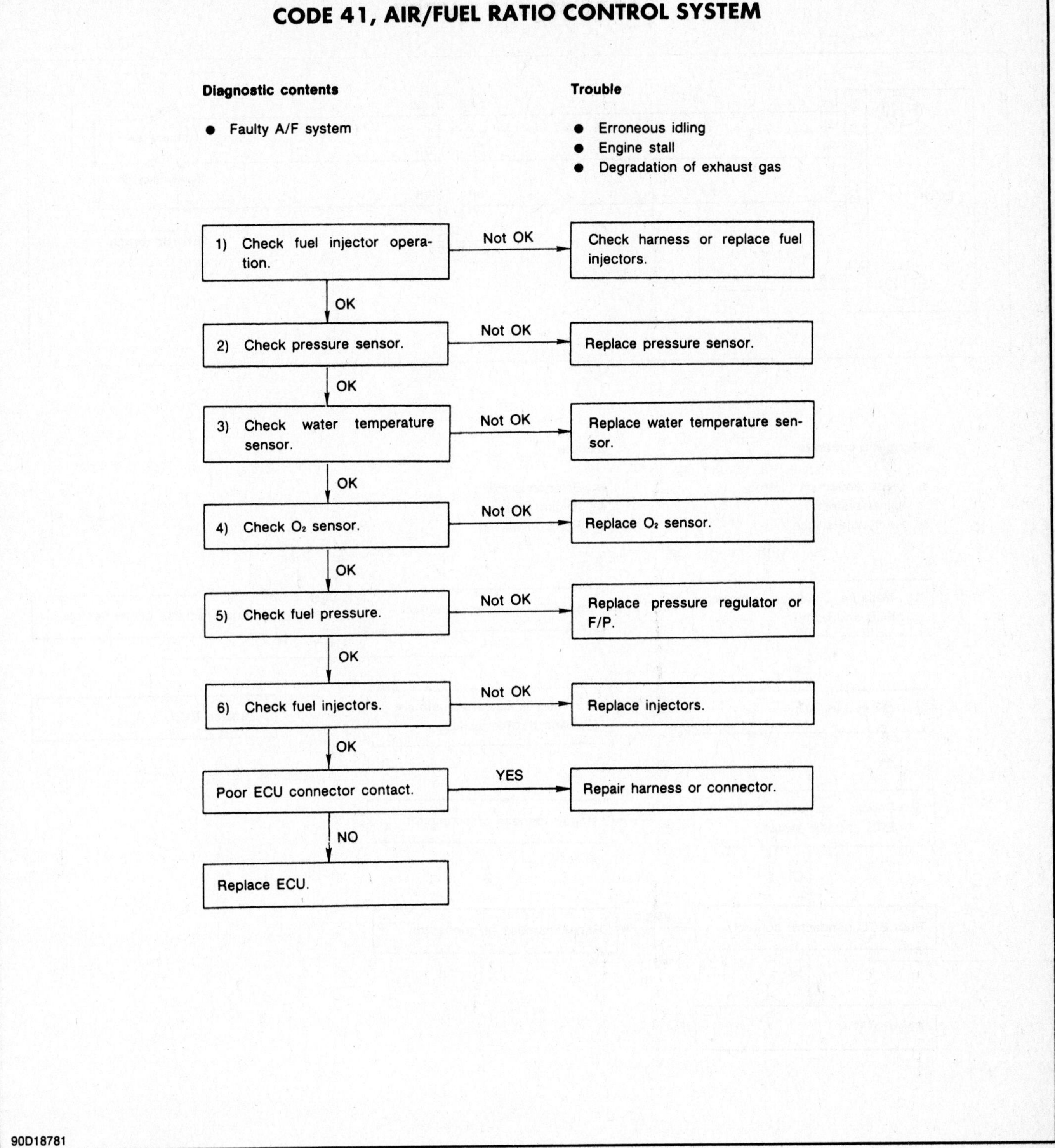
CODE 41, AIR/FUEL RATIO CONTROL SYSTEM
Diagnostic contents
• Faulty A/F system
Trouble
• Erroneous idling
• Engine stall
• Degradation of exhaust gas
1) Check fuel injector operation.
Not OK
Check harness or replace fuel injectors.
OK
2) Check pressure sensor.
Not OK
Replace pressure sensor.
OK
3) Check water temperature sensor.
Not OK
Replace water temperature sensor.
OK
4) Check $O_2$ sensor.
Not OK
Replace $O_2$ sensor.
OK
5) Check fuel pressure.
Not OK
Replace pressure regulator or F/P.
OK
6) Check fuel injectors.
Not OK
Replace injectors.
OK
Poor ECU connector contact.
YES
Repair harness or connector.
NO
Replace ECU.
90D18781

# 1991 ENGINE PERFORMANCE
# Self-Diagnostics – Justy – PFI (Cont.)

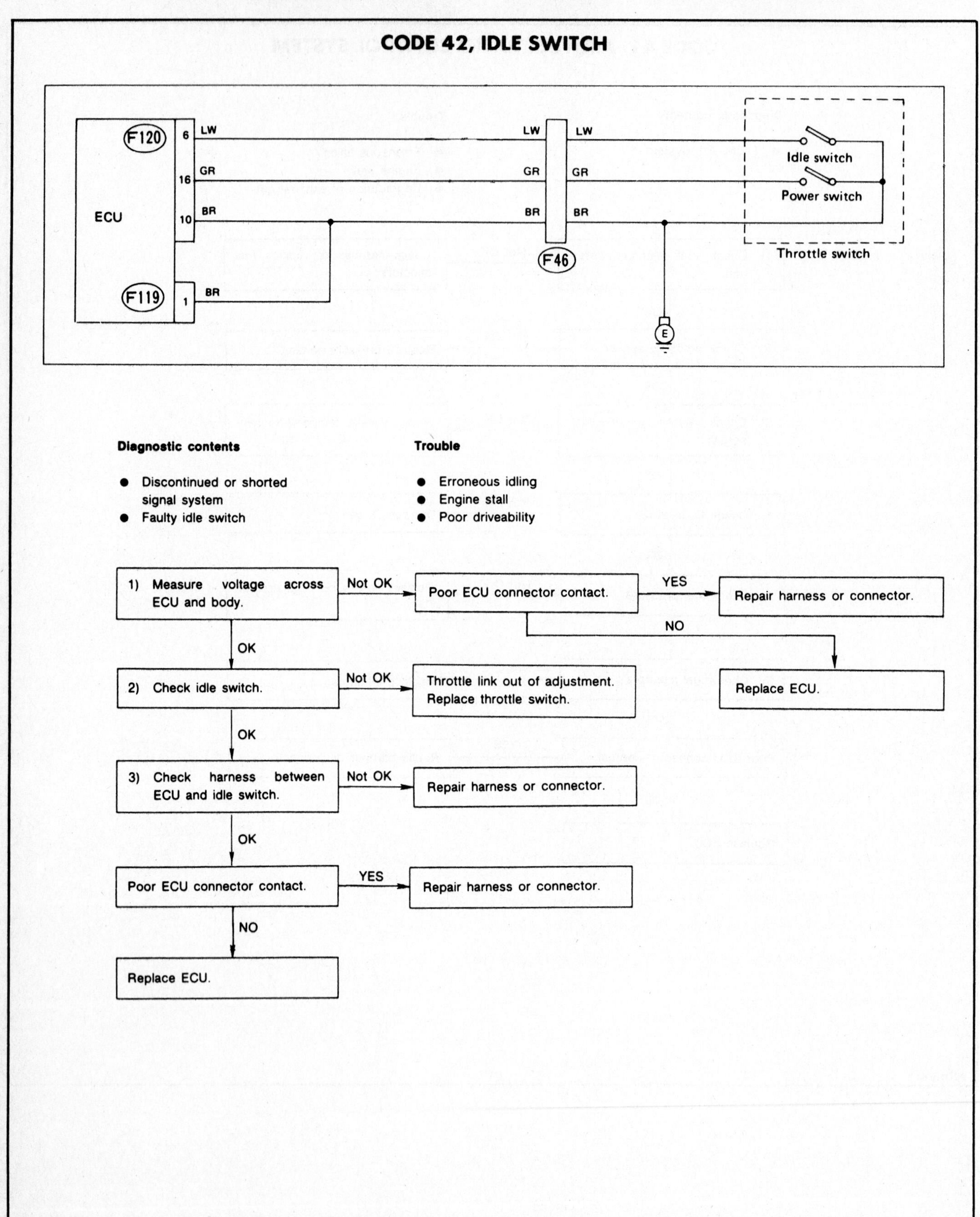
CODE 42, IDLE SWITCH
F120
6
LW
16
GR
10
BR
ECU
F119
1
BR
LW
LW
GR
GR
BR
BR
F46
E
Idle switch
Power switch
Throttle switch
Diagnostic contents
Discontinued or shorted signal system
Faulty idle switch
Trouble
Erroneous idling
Engine stall
Poor driveability
1) Measure voltage across ECU and body.
Not OK
Poor ECU connector contact.
YES
Repair harness or connector.
NO
Replace ECU.
OK
2) Check idle switch.
Not OK
Throttle link out of adjustment. Replace throttle switch.
OK
3) Check harness between ECU and idle switch.
Not OK
Repair harness or connector.
OK
Poor ECU connector contact.
YES
Repair harness or connector.
NO
Replace ECU.
90E18782

# 1991 ENGINE PERFORMANCE
## Self-Diagnostics – Justy – PFI (Cont.)

### CODE 43, THROTTLE SWITCH

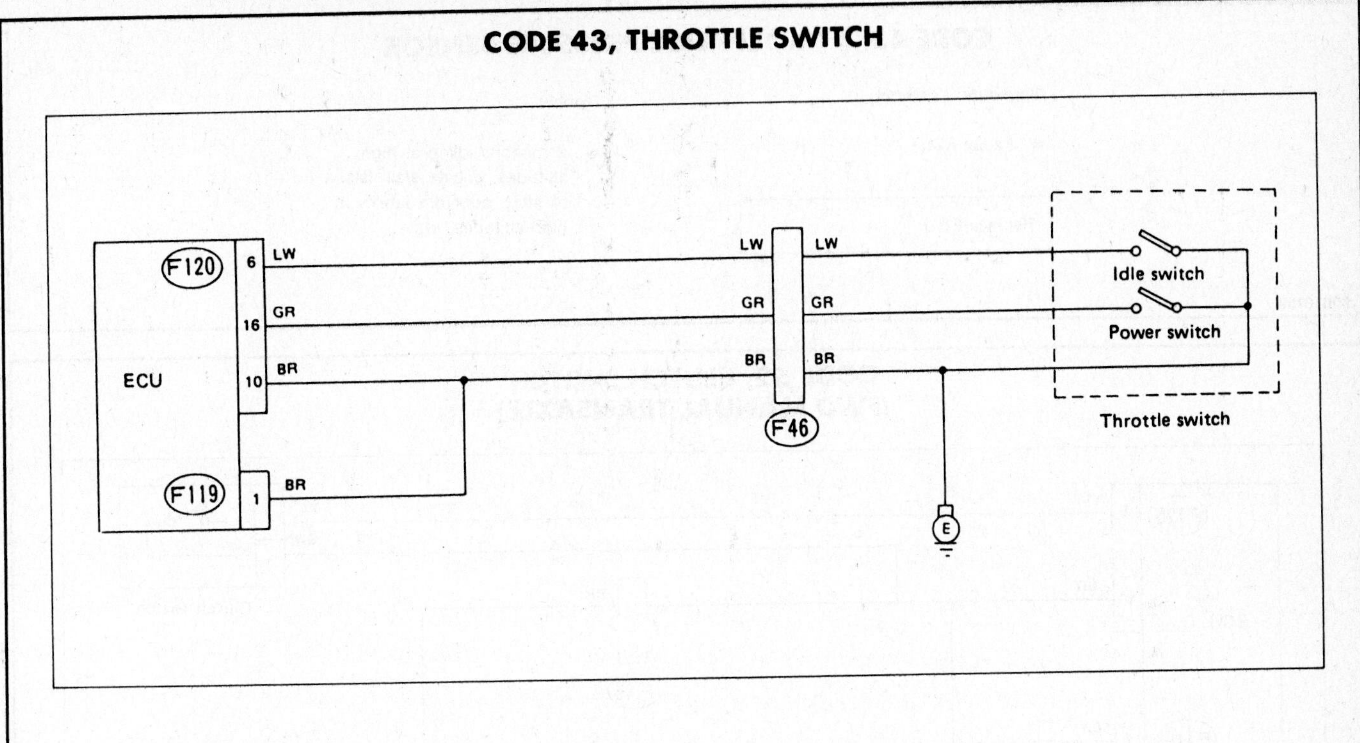
ECU
F120
6
LW
16
GR
10
BR
F119
1
BR
LW
LW
GR
GR
BR
BR
F46
E
Idle switch
Power switch
Throttle switch

**Diagnostic contents**

- Discontinued or shorted signal circuit
- Faulty power switch

**Trouble**

- Poor driveability

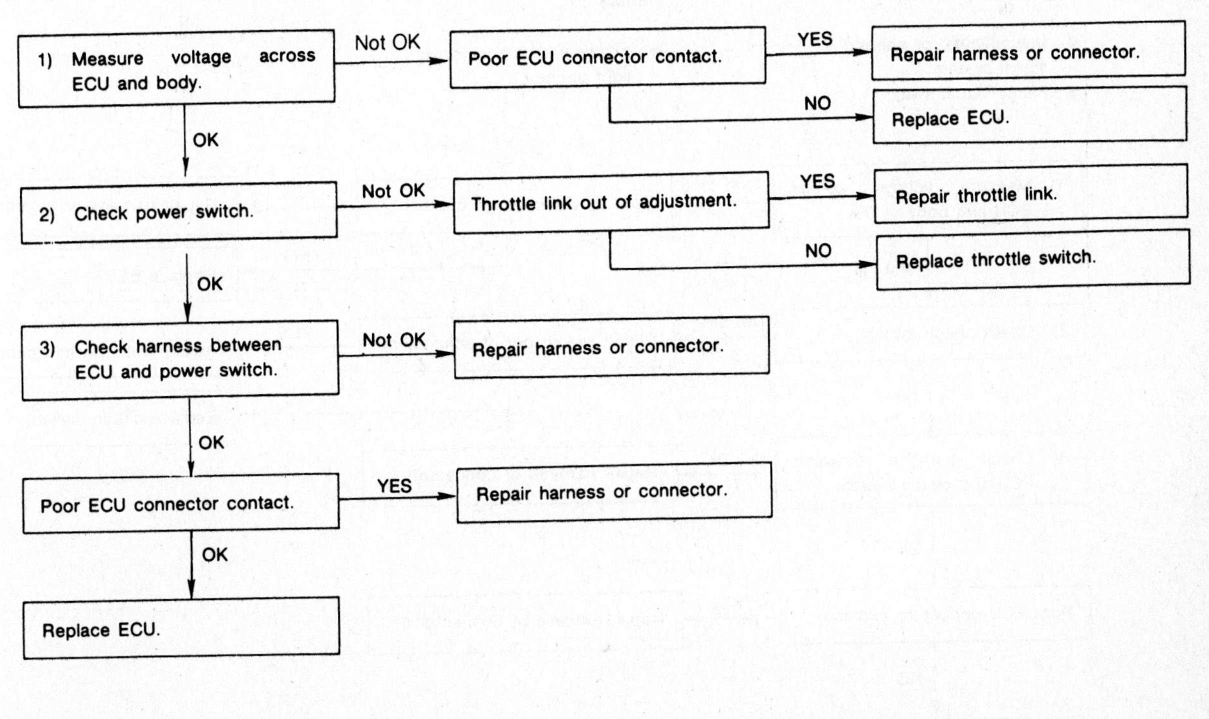
1) Measure voltage across ECU and body.
Not OK
Poor ECU connector contact.
YES
Repair harness or connector.
NO
Replace ECU.
OK
2) Check power switch.
Not OK
Throttle link out of adjustment.
YES
Repair throttle link.
NO
Replace throttle switch.
OK
3) Check harness between ECU and power switch.
Not OK
Repair harness or connector.
OK
Poor ECU connector contact.
YES
Repair harness or connector.
OK
Replace ECU.

90F18783

# 1991 ENGINE PERFORMANCE
## Self-Diagnostics – Justy – PFI (Cont.)

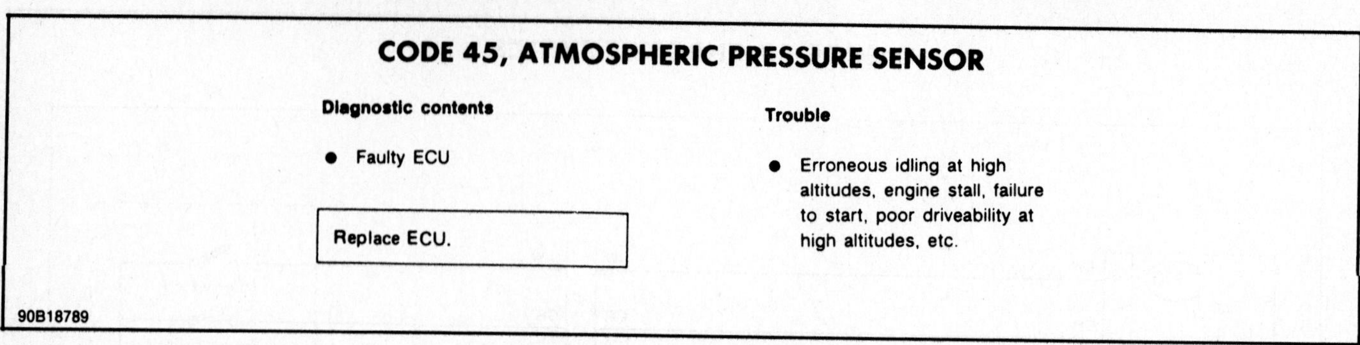

### CODE 45, ATMOSPHERIC PRESSURE SENSOR

**Diagnostic contents**

- Faulty ECU

Replace ECU.

**Trouble**

- Erroneous idling at high altitudes, engine stall, failure to start, poor driveability at high altitudes, etc.

90B18789

### CODE 52, CLUTCH SWITCH (FWD MANUAL TRANSAXLE)

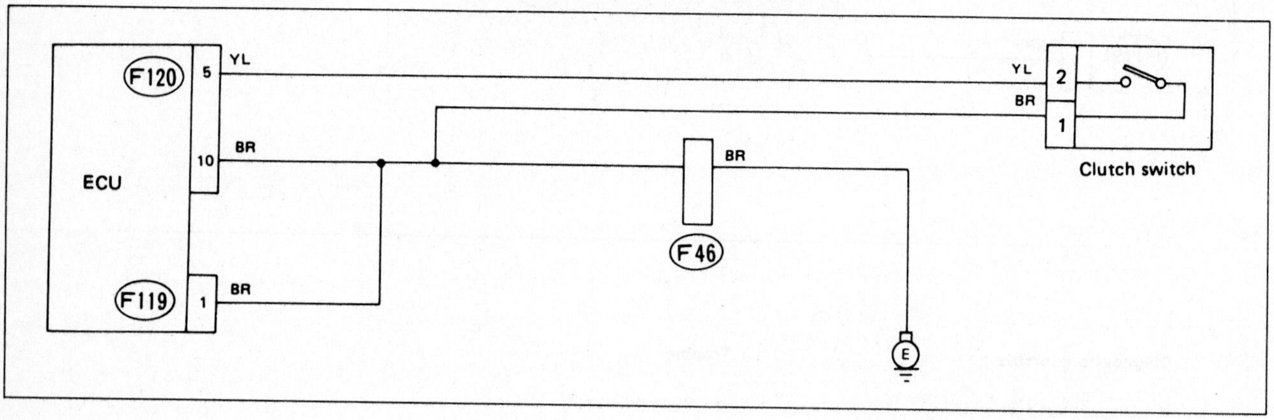

F120
5
YL
10
BR
ECU
F119
1
BR
BR
F46
E
YL
BR
2
1
Clutch switch

**Diagnostic contents**

- Discontinued or shorted signal system
- Faulty clutch switch

**Trouble**

- Erroneous shift indicator light operation

1) Measure voltage across ECU and body.
- OK → Poor ECU connector contact.
  - YES → Repair harness or connector.
  - NO → Replace ECU.
- Not OK → 2) Check clutch switch.

2) Check clutch switch.
- Not OK → Clutch switch out of adjustment
  - YES → Adjust clutch switch contact.
  - NO → Replace clutch switch.
- OK → 3) Check harness between ECU and clutch switch.

3) Check harness between ECU and clutch switch.
- Not OK → Repair harness or connector.
- OK → Poor ECU connector contact.
  - YES → Repair harness or connector.
  - NO → Replace ECU.

Continued on Next Page

90G18784

## CODE 52, CLUTCH SWITCH (Cont.)
## (ECVT)

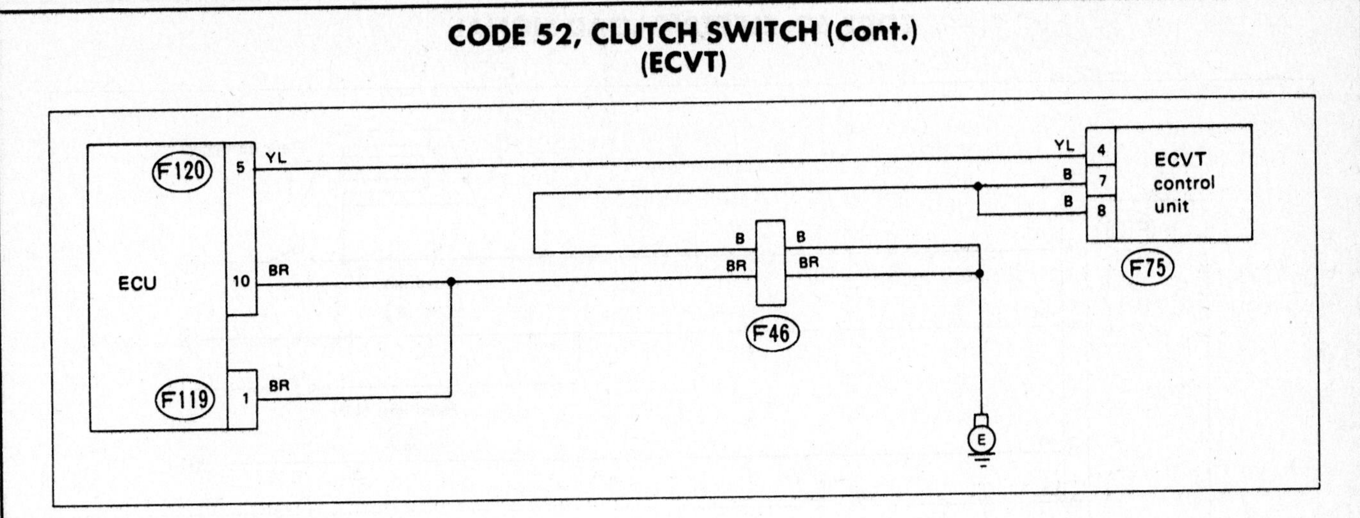


**Diagnostic contents**

- Discontinued or shorted signal circuit

**Trouble**

- Engine stall or erroneous idling

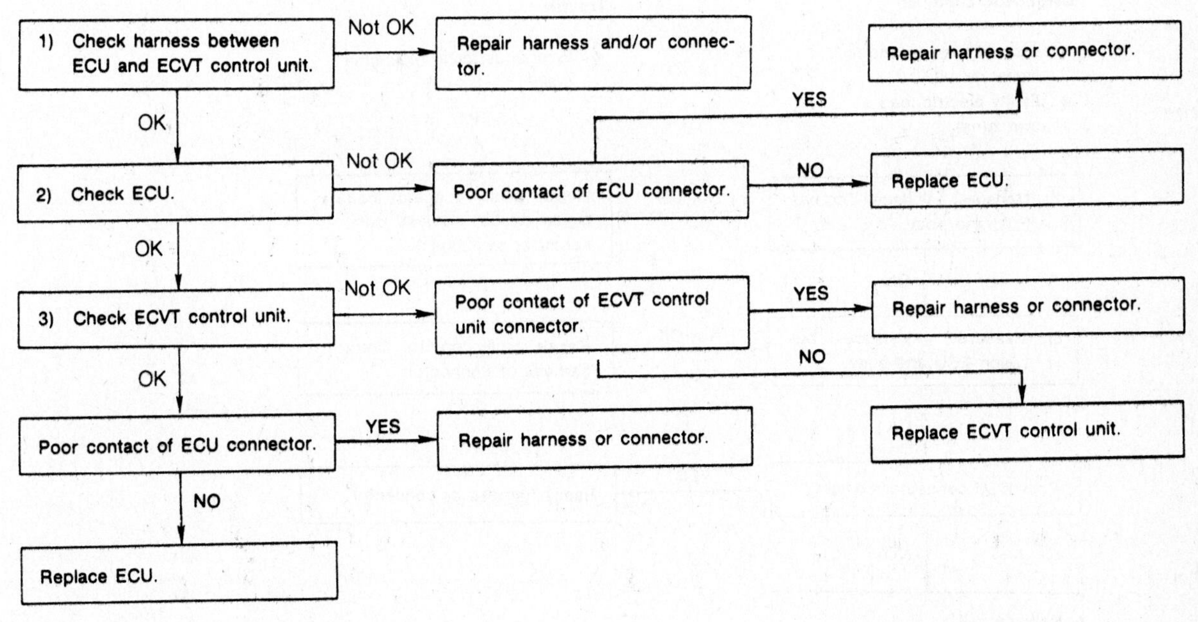


90H18785

# 1991 ENGINE PERFORMANCE
# Self-Diagnostics – Justy – PFI (Cont.)

## CODE 62, ELECTRIC LOAD SIGNAL

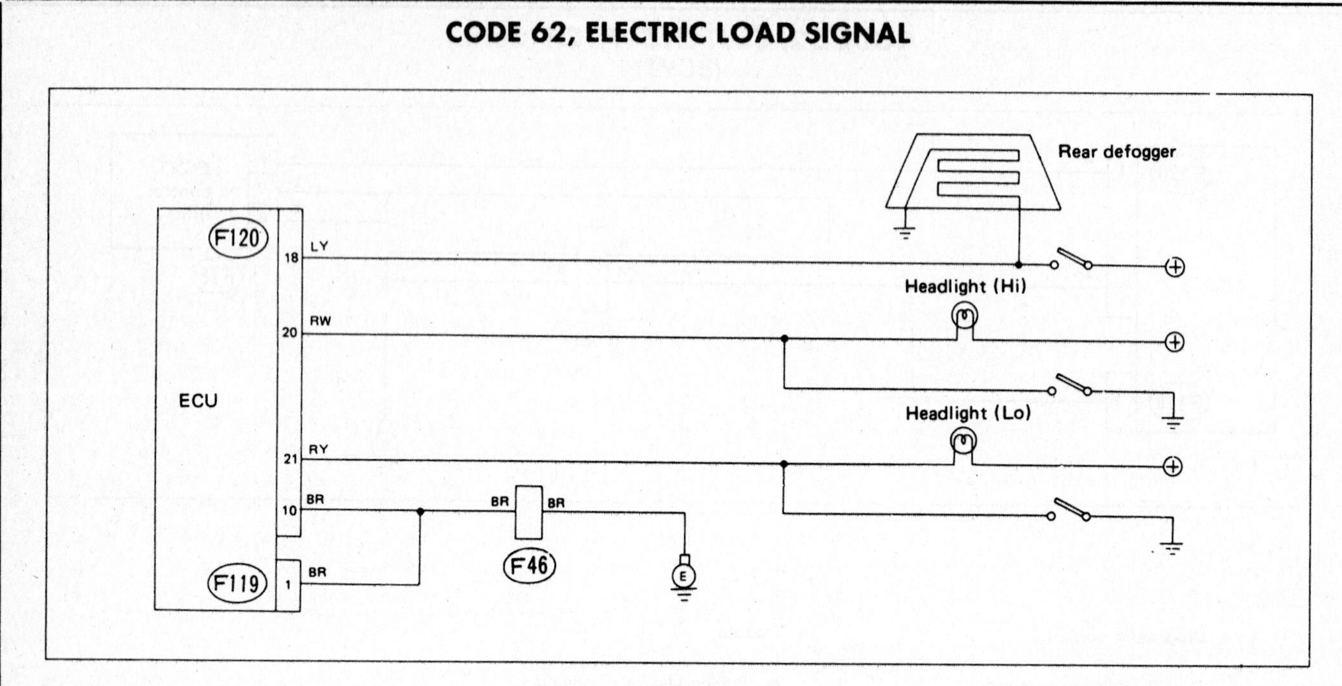


**Diagnostic contents**

- Discontinued or shorted signal circuit
- Faulty electric load switch(es)

**Trouble**

- Erroneous idling or engine stall

1) Measure voltage across ECU and body.
   - Not OK → Repair faulty electric load signal circuit, harness connector or switches.
   - OK ↓

2) Measure resistance between ECU and body.
   - Not OK → Repair faulty control body harness or connector.
   - OK ↓

Poor ECU connector contact.
   - YES → Repair harness or connector.
   - NO ↓

Replace ECU.

90I18786

## CODE 63, BLOWER FAN SWITCH

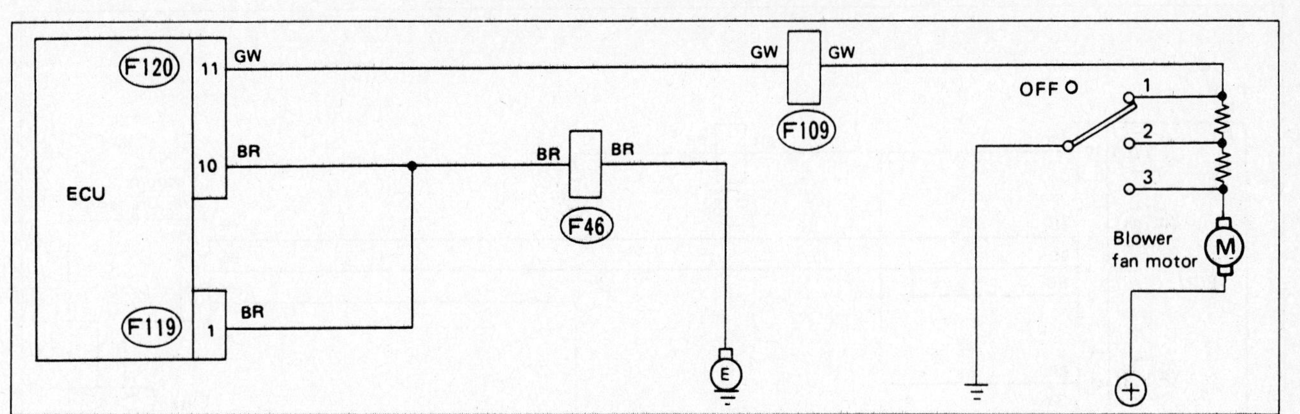


**Diagnostic contents**

- Discontinued or shorted signal circuit
- Faulty heater fan switch

**Trouble**

- Erroneous idling or engine stall
- Failure of air conditioning system to turn "ON"

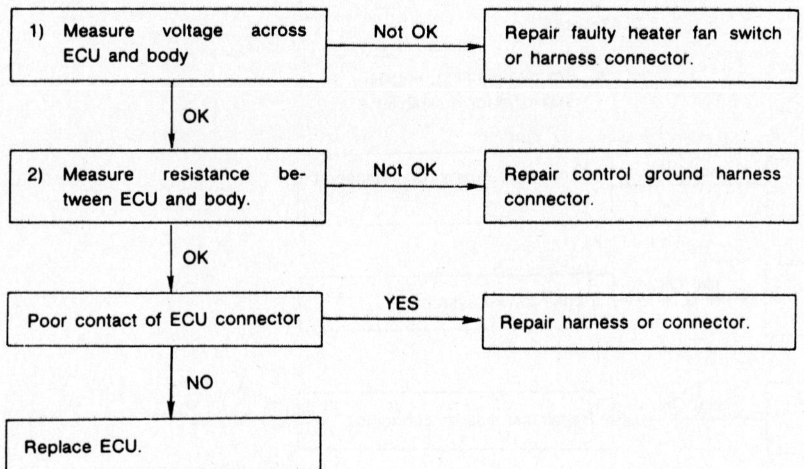


90J18787

# 1991 ENGINE PERFORMANCE
## Self-Diagnostics – Justy – PFI (Cont.)

### CODE 65, VACUUM PRESSURE SENSOR

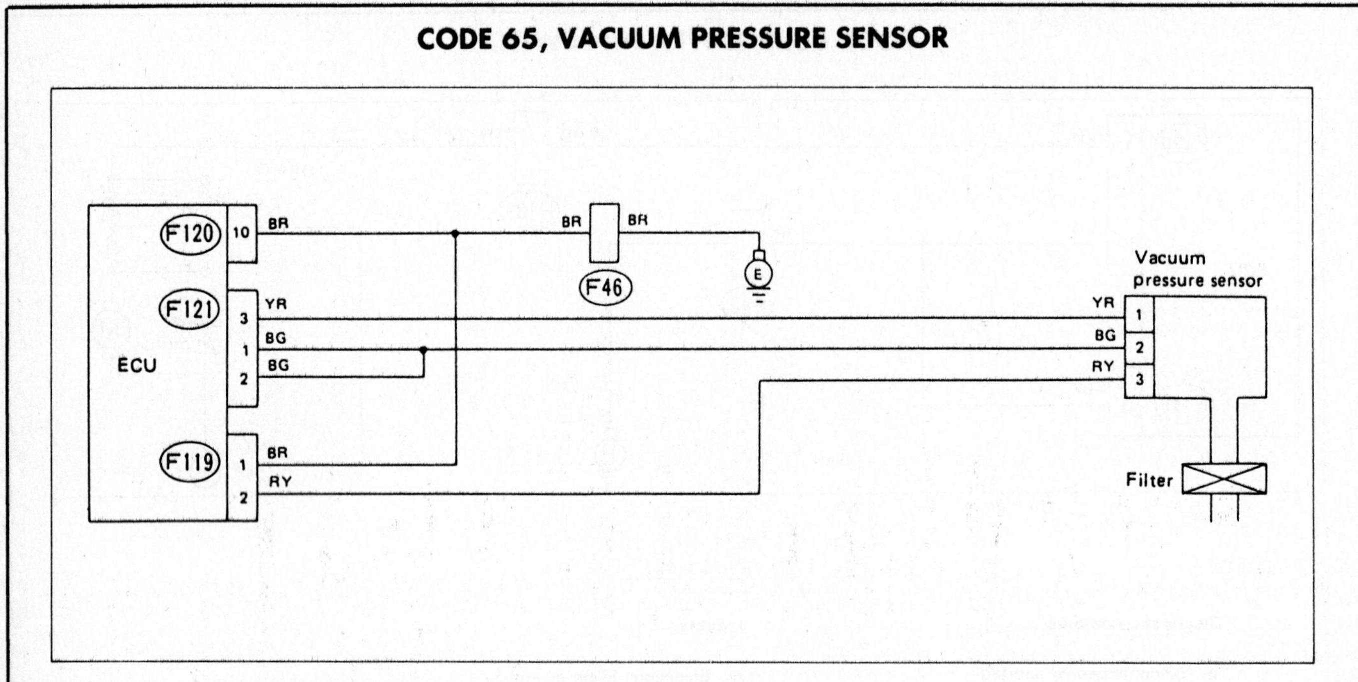


**Diagnostic contents**

- Disconnected pressure sensor hose

**Trouble**

- Erroneous idling, engine stall or poor driveability

1) Check pressure sensor. — Not OK → Connect properly or replace if faulty.
↓ OK
2) Check intake manifold vacuum pressure. — Not OK → Repair intake system.
↓ OK
3) Check line between ECU and pressure sensor. — Not OK → Repair harness or connector.
↓ OK
4) Check pressure sensor power supply line. — Not OK → Replace ECU.
↓ OK
5) Measure voltage across ECU and pressure sensor. — Not OK → Replace pressure sensor.
↓ OK

Replace ECU.

90A18788

## LEGACY CODE CHARTS

### BASIC OPERATION OF SELF-DIAGNOSTIC SYSTEM

O = Connect X = Disconnect

| Mode | Read memory connector | Test mode connector | Condition | CHECK ENGINE light |
|---|---|---|---|---|
| U-check | X | X | Ignition switch ON (Engine OFF) | ON |
| | | | Engine ON | OFF |
| Read memory | O | X | Ignition switch ON (Engine OFF) | Blink |
| | | | Engine ON | |
| D-check | X | O | Ignition switch ON (Engine OFF) | ON |
| | | | Engine ON | Vehicle specification code → Blink* |
| Clear memory | O | O | Ignition switch ON (Engine OFF) | ON |
| | | | Engine ON | Vehicle specification code → Blink |

- **TROUBLE**

| Mode | Read memory connector | Test mode connector | Condition | CHECK ENGINE light |
|---|---|---|---|---|
| U-check | X | X | Ignition switch ON | ON |
| Read memory | O | X | Ignition switch ON | Trouble code (memory) |
| D-check | X | O | Engine ON | Trouble code** |
| Clear memory | O | O | Engine ON | Trouble code** |

* When the engine operates at a speed greater than 2,000 rpm for more than 40 seconds, the check engine light blinks. However, when all check items check out "O.K.'," even before the 40 seconds is reached, the check engine light blinks.

** When the engine operates at a speed greater than 2,000 rpm for more than 40 seconds, a trouble code is emitted.

91A17574

### READ MEMORY MODE

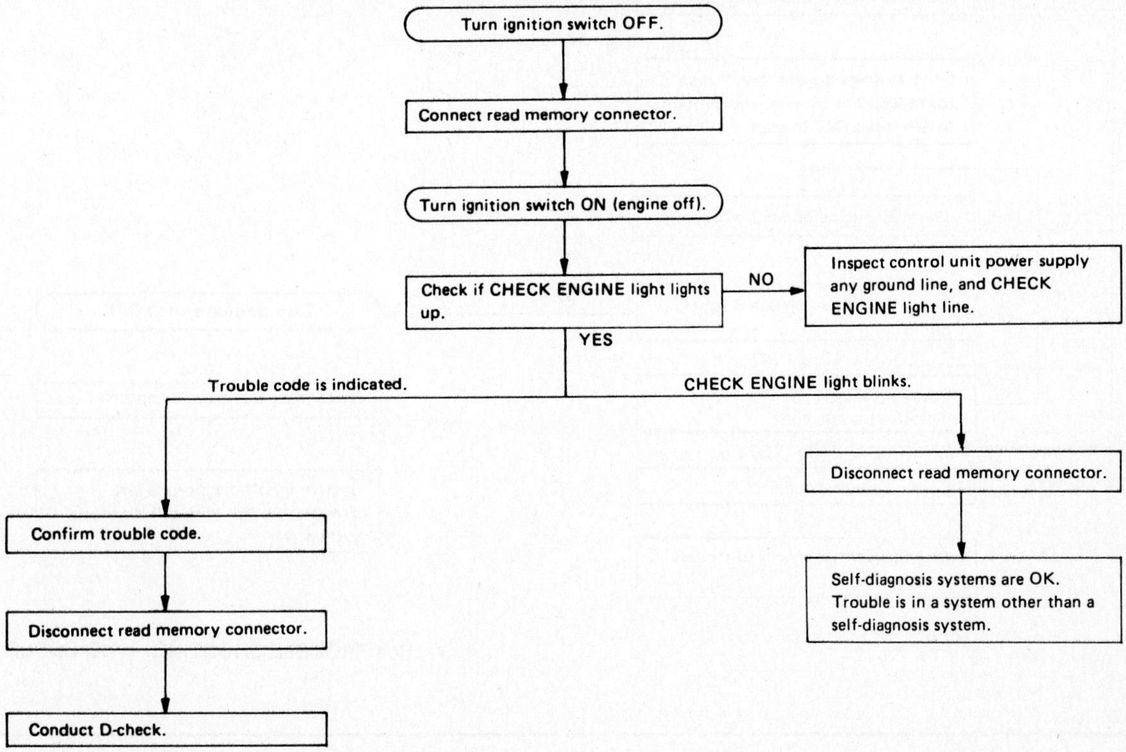

Turn ignition switch OFF.

↓

Connect read memory connector.

↓

Turn ignition switch ON (engine off).

↓

Check if CHECK ENGINE light lights up.

- NO → Inspect control unit power supply any ground line, and CHECK ENGINE light line.
- YES:
  - Trouble code is indicated. → Confirm trouble code. → Disconnect read memory connector. → Conduct D-check.
  - CHECK ENGINE light blinks. → Disconnect read memory connector. → Self-diagnosis systems are OK. Trouble is in a system other than a self-diagnosis system.

91F17587

# 1991 ENGINE PERFORMANCE
## Self-Diagnostics – Legacy (Cont.)

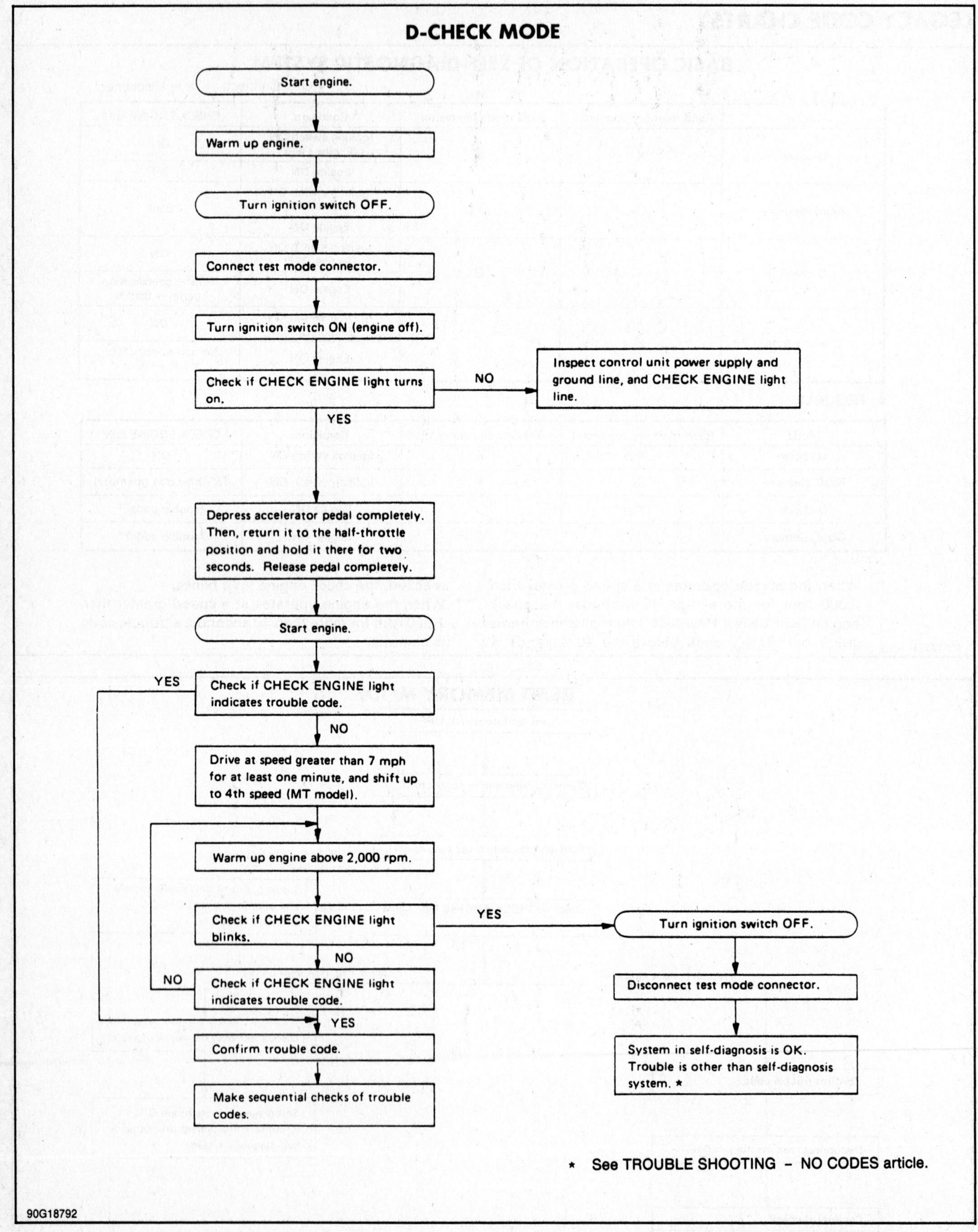
D-CHECK MODE
Start engine.
Warm up engine.
Turn ignition switch OFF.
Connect test mode connector.
Turn ignition switch ON (engine off).
Check if CHECK ENGINE light turns on.
NO
Inspect control unit power supply and ground line, and CHECK ENGINE light line.
YES
Depress accelerator pedal completely. Then, return it to the half-throttle position and hold it there for two seconds. Release pedal completely.
Start engine.
YES
Check if CHECK ENGINE light indicates trouble code.
NO
Drive at speed greater than 7 mph for at least one minute, and shift up to 4th speed (MT model).
Warm up engine above 2,000 rpm.
Check if CHECK ENGINE light blinks.
YES
Turn ignition switch OFF.
Disconnect test mode connector.
System in self-diagnosis is OK. Trouble is other than self-diagnosis system. *
NO
NO
Check if CHECK ENGINE light indicates trouble code.
YES
Confirm trouble code.
Make sequential checks of trouble codes.
* See TROUBLE SHOOTING – NO CODES article.
90G18792

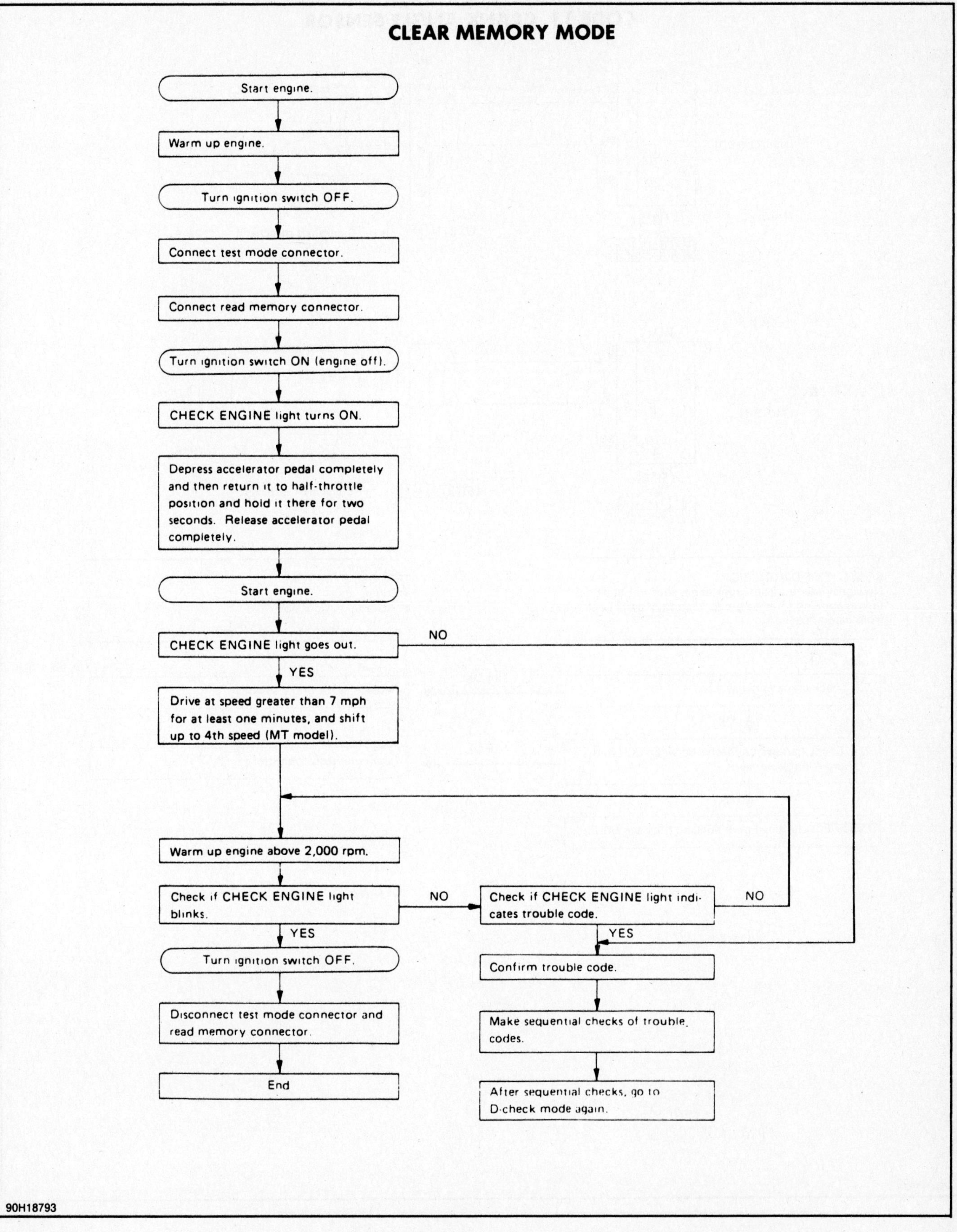
CLEAR MEMORY MODE
Start engine.
Warm up engine.
Turn ignition switch OFF.
Connect test mode connector.
Connect read memory connector.
Turn ignition switch ON (engine off).
CHECK ENGINE light turns ON.
Depress accelerator pedal completely and then return it to half-throttle position and hold it there for two seconds. Release accelerator pedal completely.
Start engine.
CHECK ENGINE light goes out.
NO
YES
Drive at speed greater than 7 mph for at least one minutes, and shift up to 4th speed (MT model).
Warm up engine above 2,000 rpm.
Check if CHECK ENGINE light blinks.
NO
Check if CHECK ENGINE light indicates trouble code.
NO
YES
YES
Turn ignition switch OFF.
Confirm trouble code.
Disconnect test mode connector and read memory connector.
Make sequential checks of trouble codes.
End
After sequential checks, go to D-check mode again.
90H18793

# 1991 ENGINE PERFORMANCE
## Self-Diagnostics – Legacy (Cont.)

### CODE 11, CRANK ANGLE SENSOR

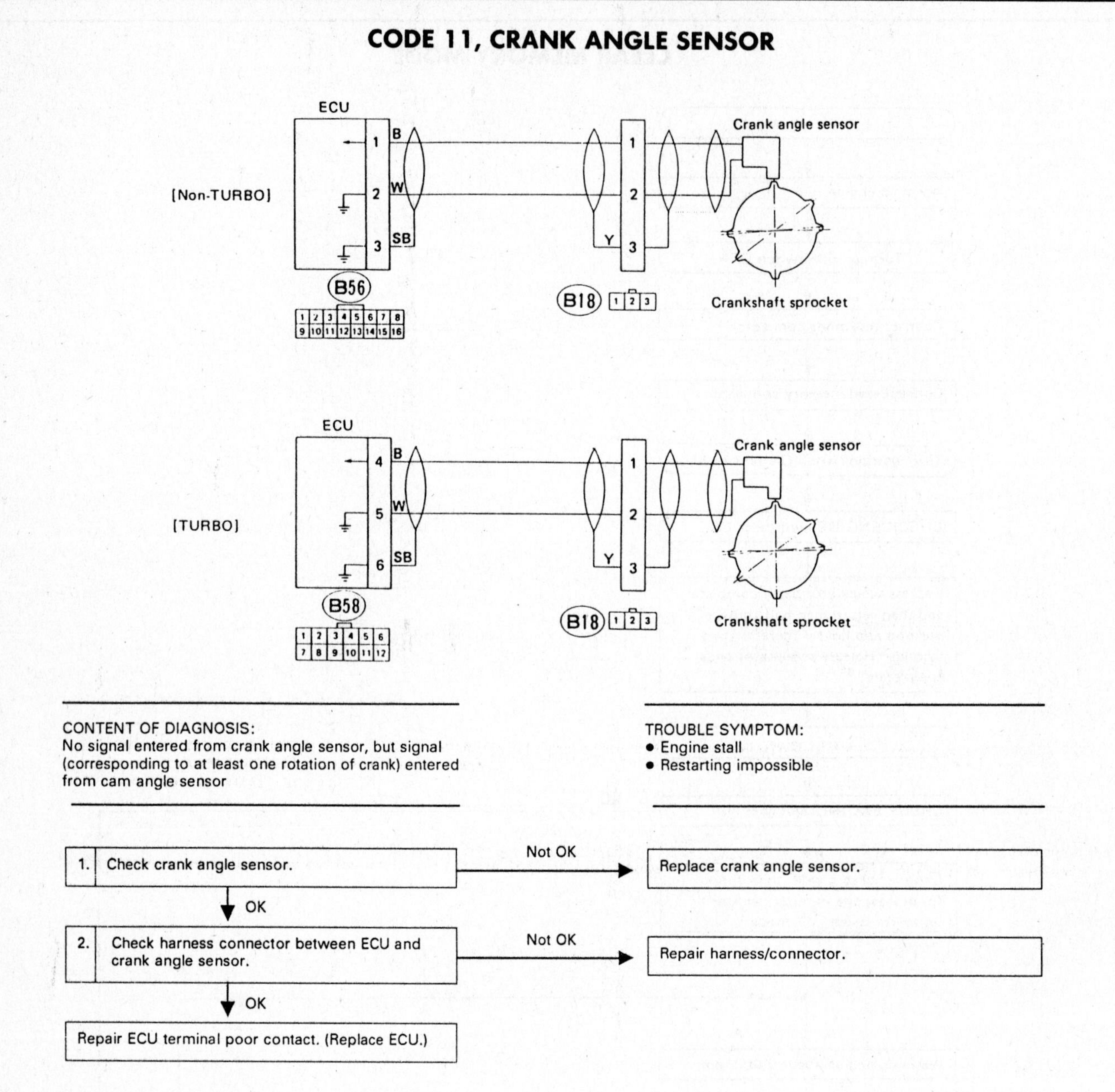


CONTENT OF DIAGNOSIS:
No signal entered from crank angle sensor, but signal (corresponding to at least one rotation of crank) entered from cam angle sensor

TROUBLE SYMPTOM:
- Engine stall
- Restarting impossible

1. Check crank angle sensor. — Not OK → Replace crank angle sensor.

↓ OK

2. Check harness connector between ECU and crank angle sensor. — Not OK → Repair harness/connector.

↓ OK

Repair ECU terminal poor contact. (Replace ECU.)

91B17575

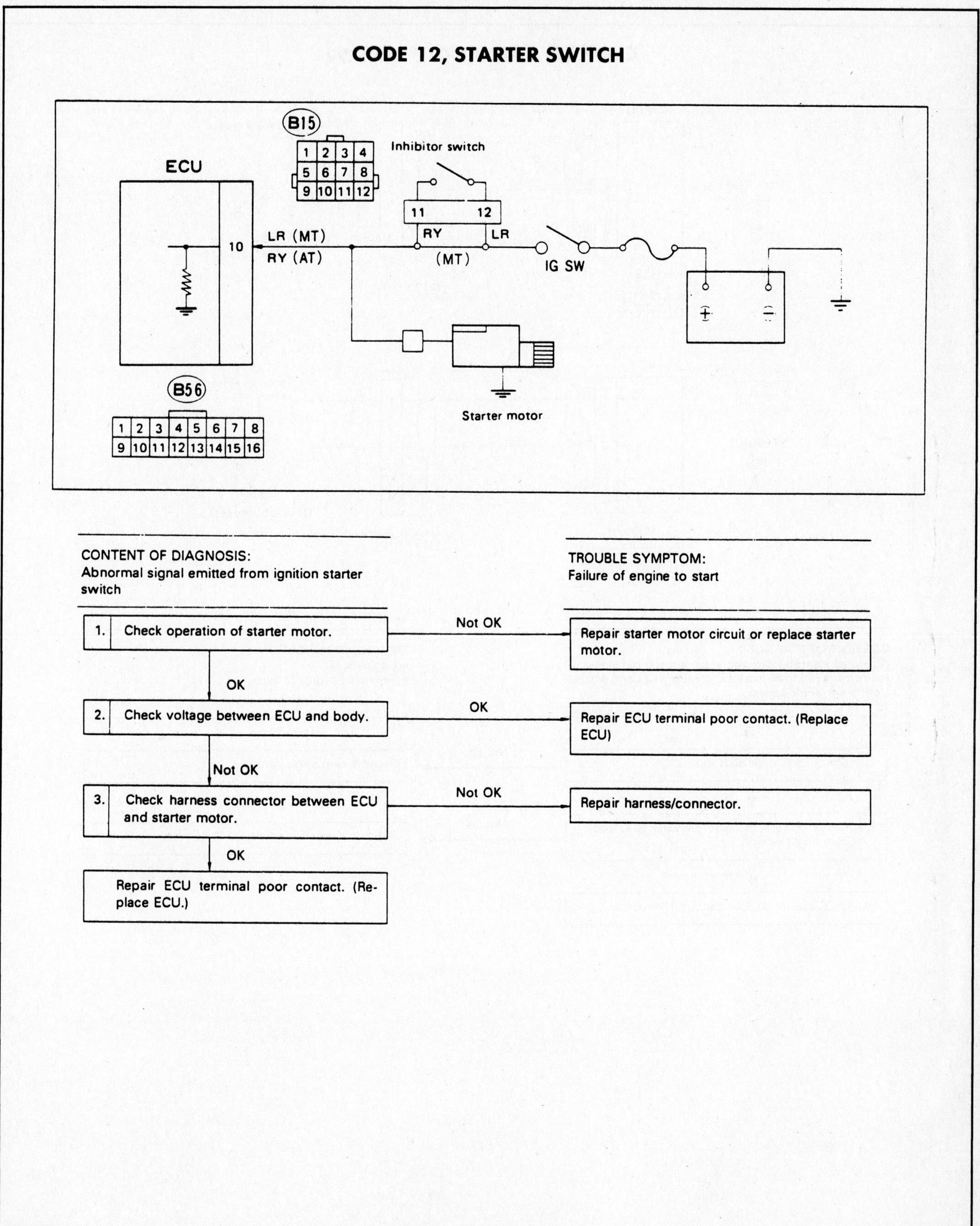


CONTENT OF DIAGNOSIS:
Abnormal signal emitted from ignition starter switch

TROUBLE SYMPTOM:
Failure of engine to start

1. Check operation of starter motor.
   - Not OK → Repair starter motor circuit or replace starter motor.
   - OK → 2.

2. Check voltage between ECU and body.
   - OK → Repair ECU terminal poor contact. (Replace ECU)
   - Not OK → 3.

3. Check harness connector between ECU and starter motor.
   - Not OK → Repair harness/connector.
   - OK → Repair ECU terminal poor contact. (Replace ECU.)

90J18795

# 1991 ENGINE PERFORMANCE
## Self-Diagnostics – Legacy (Cont.)

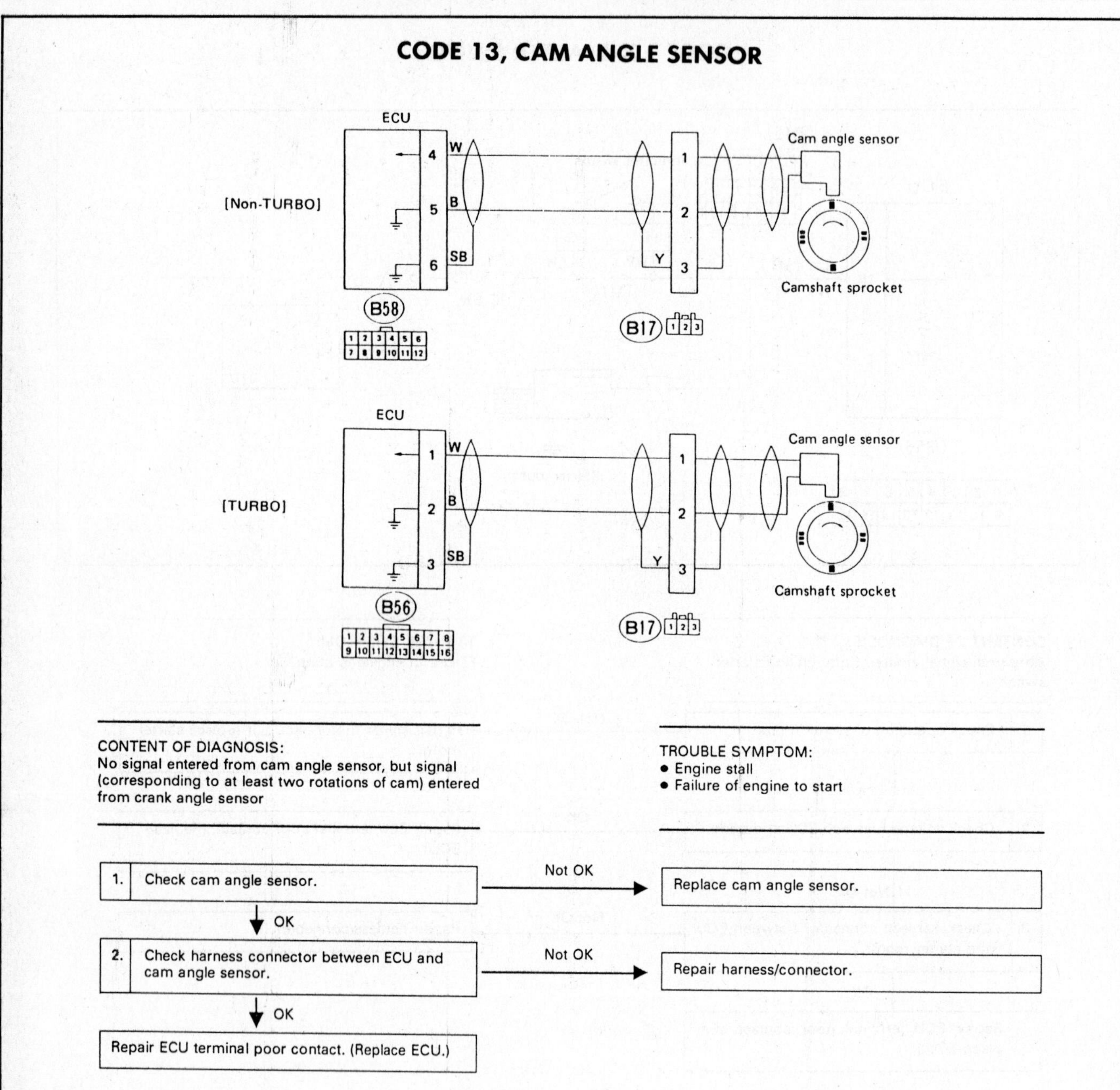

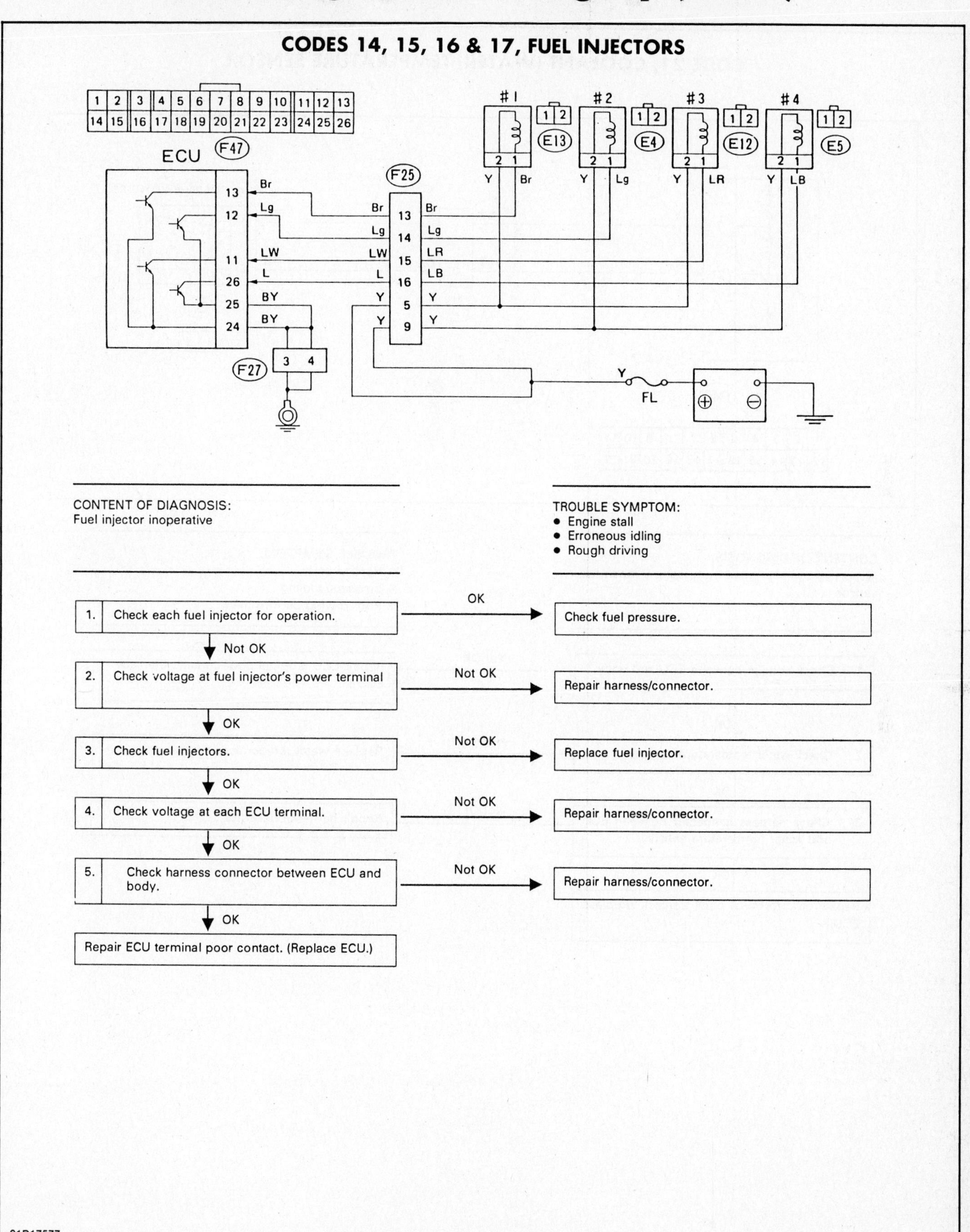

CODES 14, 15, 16 & 17, FUEL INJECTORS
ECU
F47
F25
F27
#1
#2
#3
#4
E13
E4
E12
E5
FL
CONTENT OF DIAGNOSIS:
Fuel injector inoperative
TROUBLE SYMPTOM:
• Engine stall
• Erroneous idling
• Rough driving
1. Check each fuel injector for operation.
OK
Check fuel pressure.
Not OK
2. Check voltage at fuel injector's power terminal
Not OK
Repair harness/connector.
OK
3. Check fuel injectors.
Not OK
Replace fuel injector.
OK
4. Check voltage at each ECU terminal.
Not OK
Repair harness/connector.
OK
5. Check harness connector between ECU and body.
Not OK
Repair harness/connector.
OK
Repair ECU terminal poor contact. (Replace ECU.)
91D17577

# 1991 ENGINE PERFORMANCE
## Self-Diagnostics – Legacy (Cont.)

### CODE 21, COOLANT (WATER) TEMPERATURE SENSOR

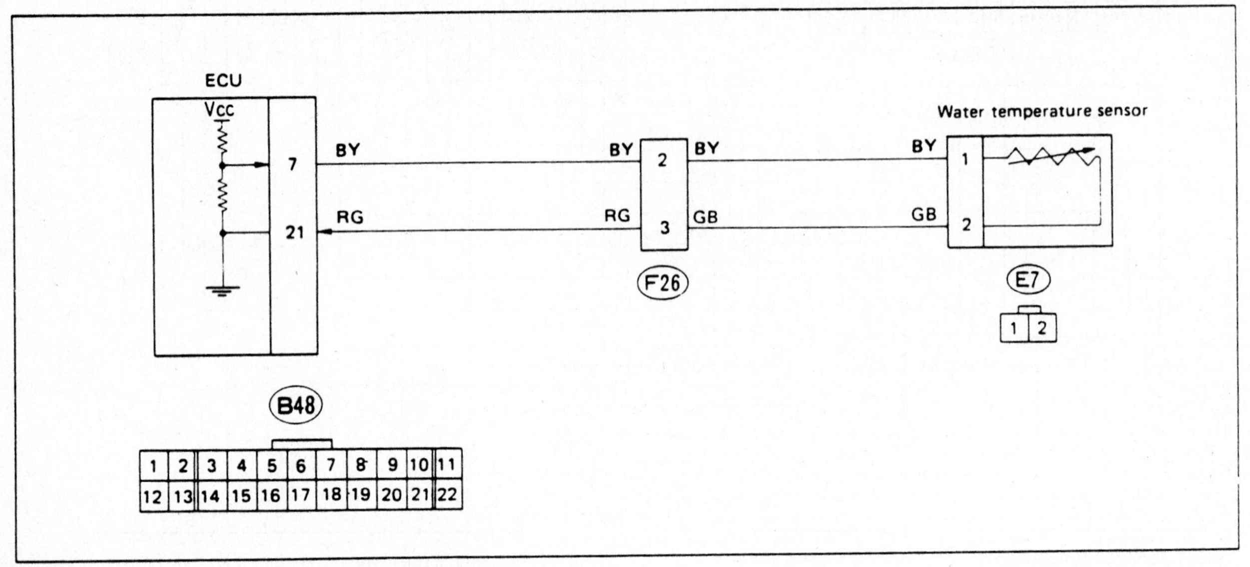
ECU
Vcc
7
21
BY
RG
BY
RG
2
3
BY
GB
F26
Water temperature sensor
BY
GB
1
2
E7
1 2
B48
1 2 3 4 5 6 7 8 9 10 11
12 13 14 15 16 17 18 19 20 21 22

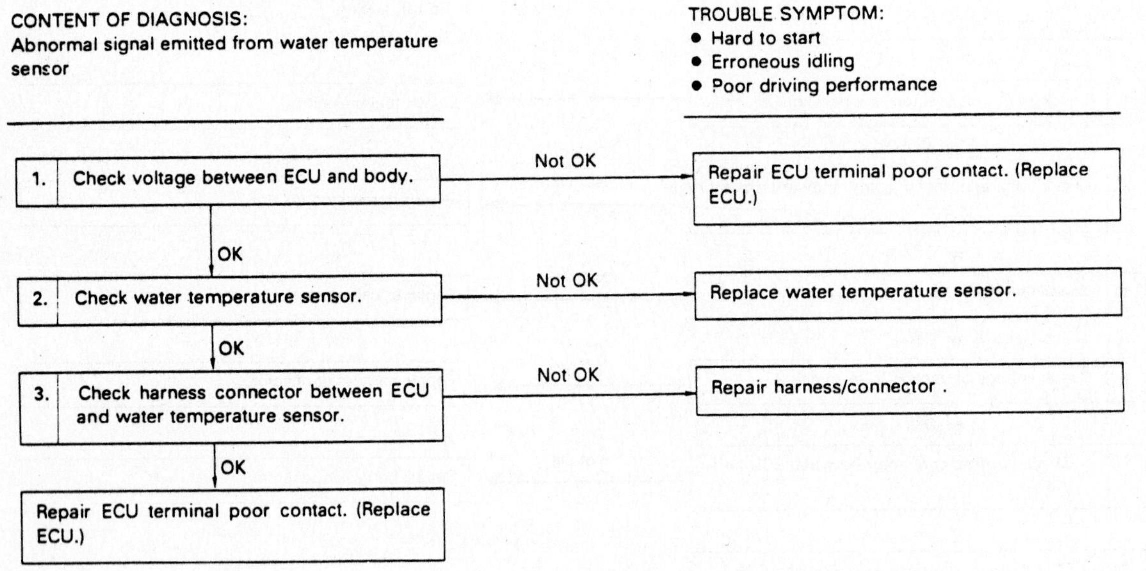
CONTENT OF DIAGNOSIS:
Abnormal signal emitted from water temperature sensor
TROUBLE SYMPTOM:
● Hard to start
● Erroneous idling
● Poor driving performance
1. Check voltage between ECU and body.
Not OK
Repair ECU terminal poor contact. (Replace ECU.)
OK
2. Check water temperature sensor.
Not OK
Replace water temperature sensor.
OK
3. Check harness connector between ECU and water temperature sensor.
Not OK
Repair harness/connector .
OK
Repair ECU terminal poor contact. (Replace ECU.)

90A21840

# 1991 ENGINE PERFORMANCE
# Self-Diagnostics – Legacy (Cont.)

## CODE 22, KNOCK SENSOR

ECU
5
4
W
SB
B19
Knock sensor
A56
1 2 3 4 5 6 7 8
9 10 11 12 13 14 15 16

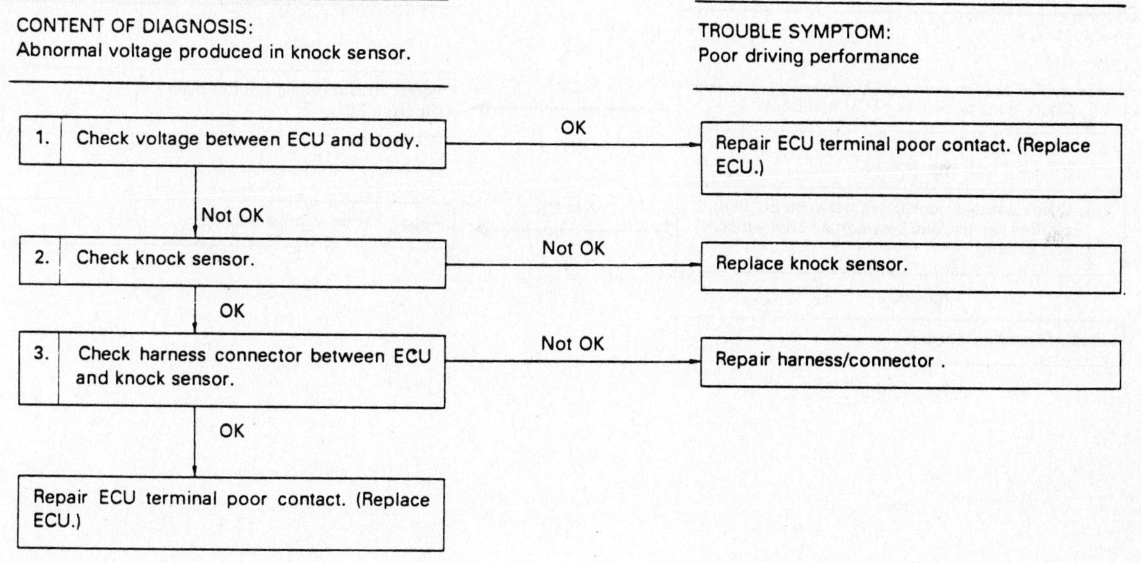
CONTENT OF DIAGNOSIS:
Abnormal voltage produced in knock sensor.
TROUBLE SYMPTOM:
Poor driving performance
1. Check voltage between ECU and body.
OK
Repair ECU terminal poor contact. (Replace ECU.)
Not OK
2. Check knock sensor.
Not OK
Replace knock sensor.
OK
3. Check harness connector between ECU and knock sensor.
Not OK
Repair harness/connector .
OK
Repair ECU terminal poor contact. (Replace ECU.)

90B21841

# 1991 ENGINE PERFORMANCE
# Self-Diagnostics – Legacy (Cont.)

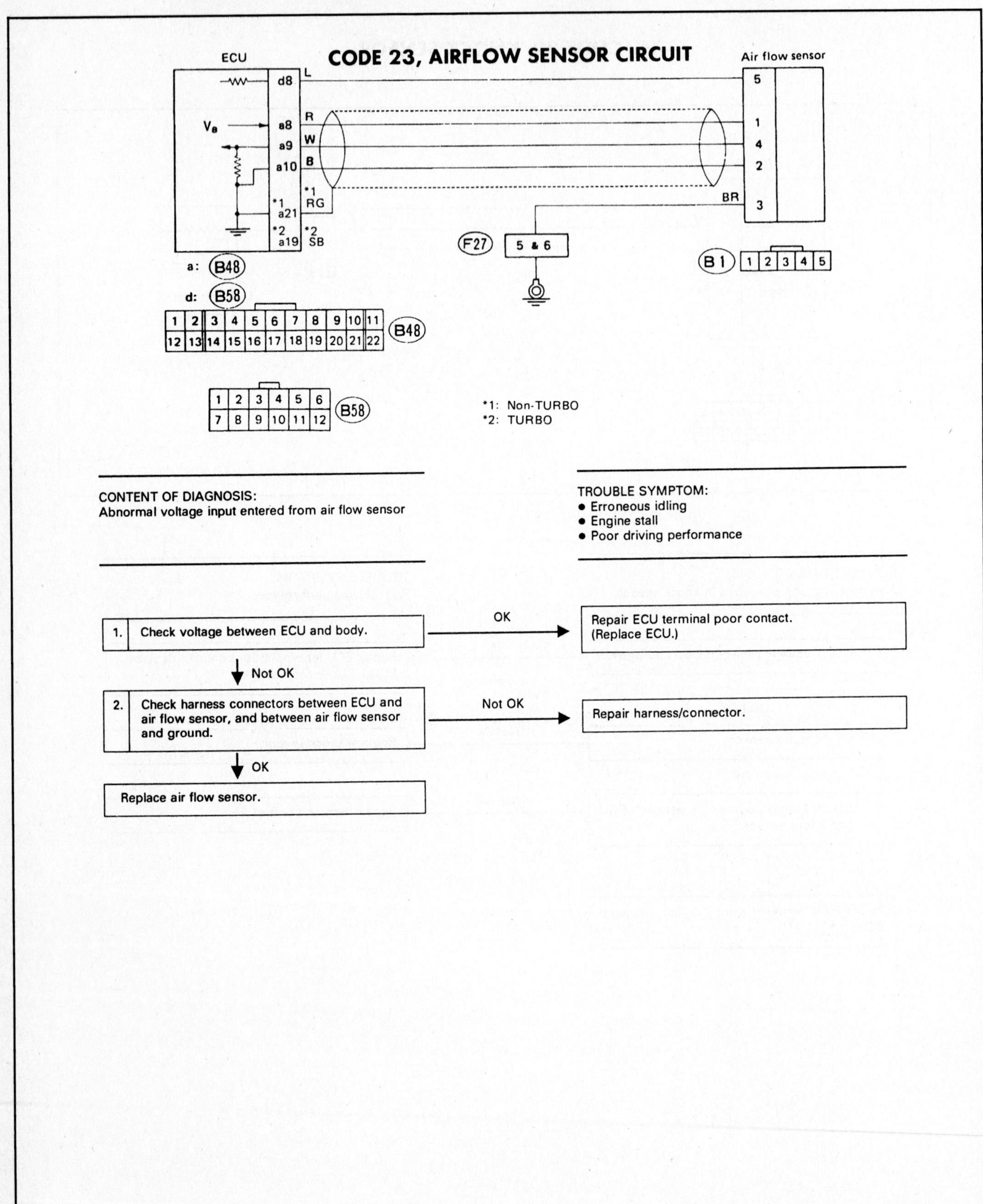

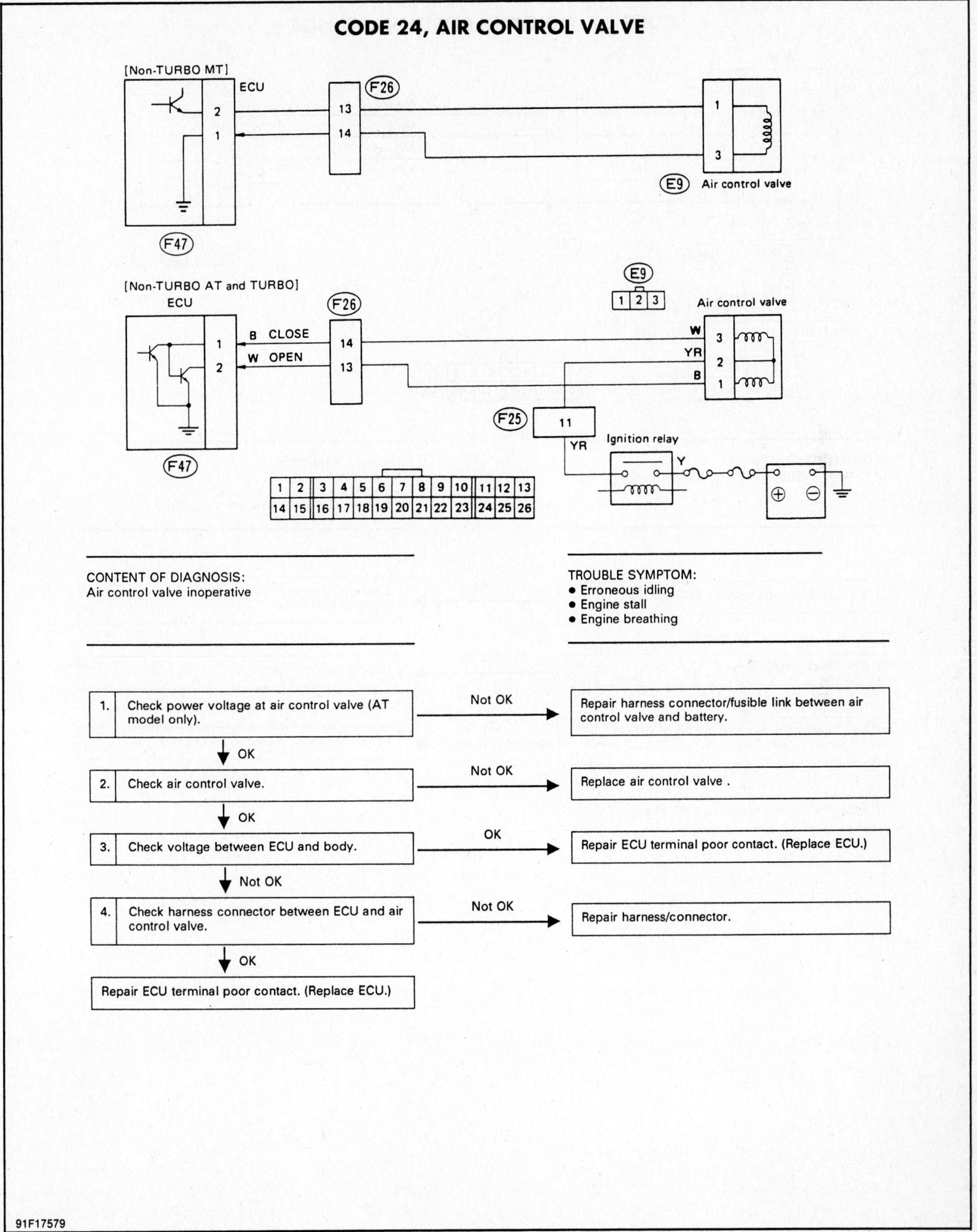
CODE 24, AIR CONTROL VALVE
[Non-TURBO MT]
ECU
F26
2
1
13
14
1
3
E9
Air control valve
F47
[Non-TURBO AT and TURBO]
ECU
F26
B CLOSE
W OPEN
1
2
14
13
E9
1 2 3
Air control valve
W
YR
B
3
2
1
F25
11
YR
Ignition relay
Y
F47
1 2 3 4 5 6 7 8 9 10 11 12 13
14 15 16 17 18 19 20 21 22 23 24 25 26
CONTENT OF DIAGNOSIS:
Air control valve inoperative
TROUBLE SYMPTOM:
• Erroneous idling
• Engine stall
• Engine breathing
1. Check power voltage at air control valve (AT model only).
Not OK
Repair harness connector/fusible link between air control valve and battery.
OK
2. Check air control valve.
Not OK
Replace air control valve .
OK
3. Check voltage between ECU and body.
OK
Repair ECU terminal poor contact. (Replace ECU.)
Not OK
4. Check harness connector between ECU and air control valve.
Not OK
Repair harness/connector.
OK
Repair ECU terminal poor contact. (Replace ECU.)
91F17579

# 1991 ENGINE PERFORMANCE
# Self-Diagnostics – Legacy (Cont.)

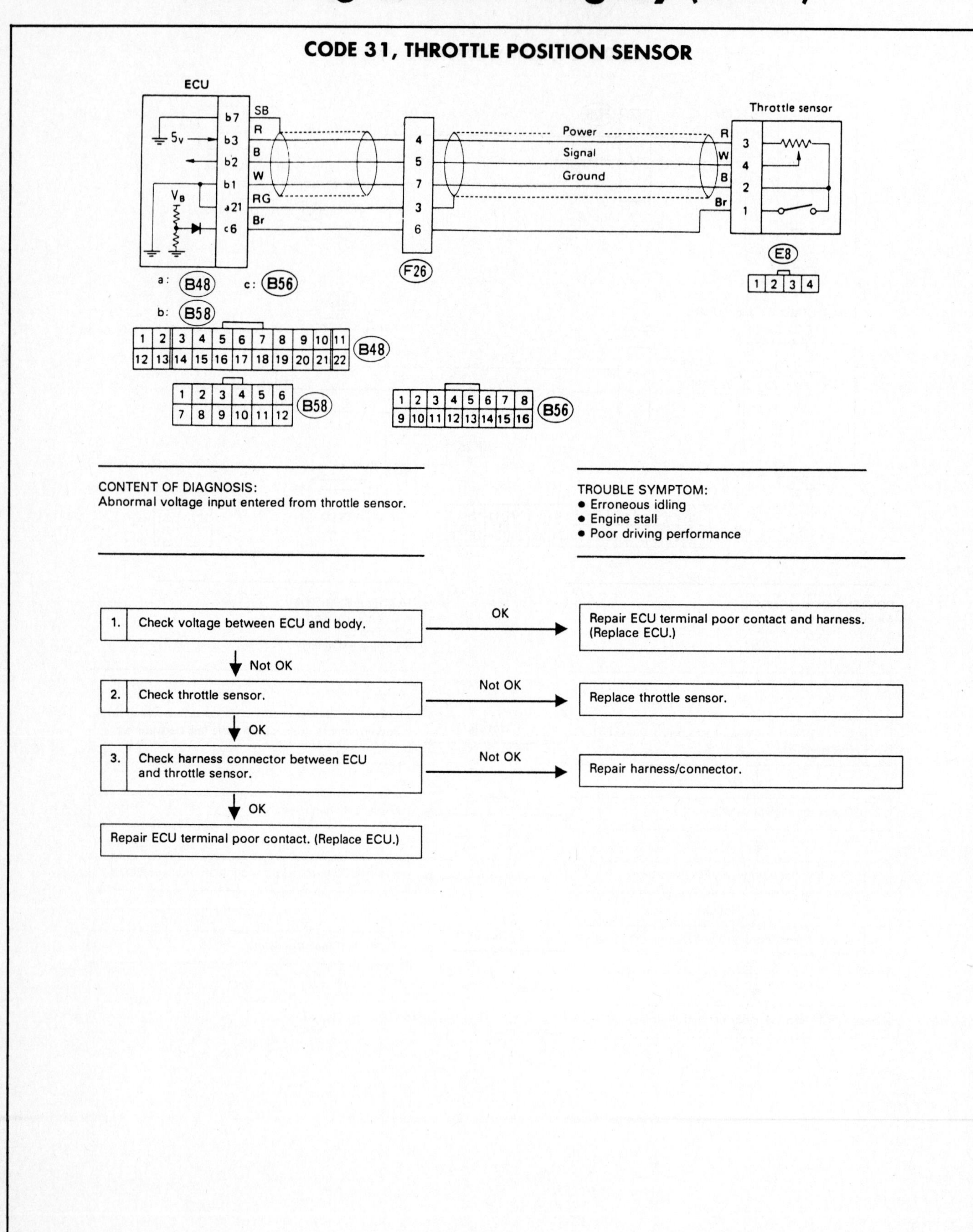

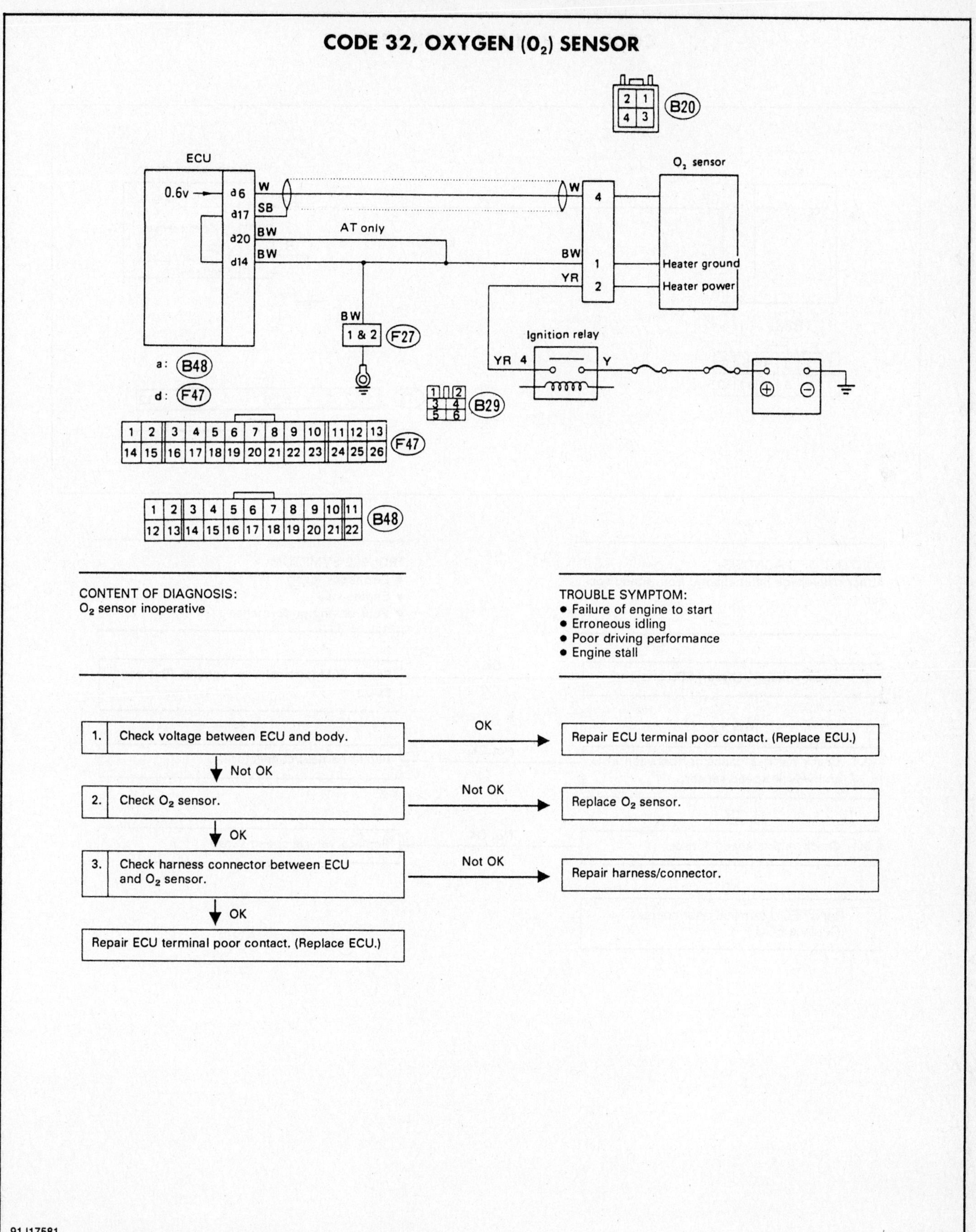


CONTENT OF DIAGNOSIS:
$O_2$ sensor inoperative

TROUBLE SYMPTOM:
- Failure of engine to start
- Erroneous idling
- Poor driving performance
- Engine stall

1. Check voltage between ECU and body. — OK → Repair ECU terminal poor contact. (Replace ECU.)
   ↓ Not OK
2. Check $O_2$ sensor. — Not OK → Replace $O_2$ sensor.
   ↓ OK
3. Check harness connector between ECU and $O_2$ sensor. — Not OK → Repair harness/connector.
   ↓ OK

Repair ECU terminal poor contact. (Replace ECU.)

91J17581

# 1991 ENGINE PERFORMANCE
# Self-Diagnostics – Legacy (Cont.)

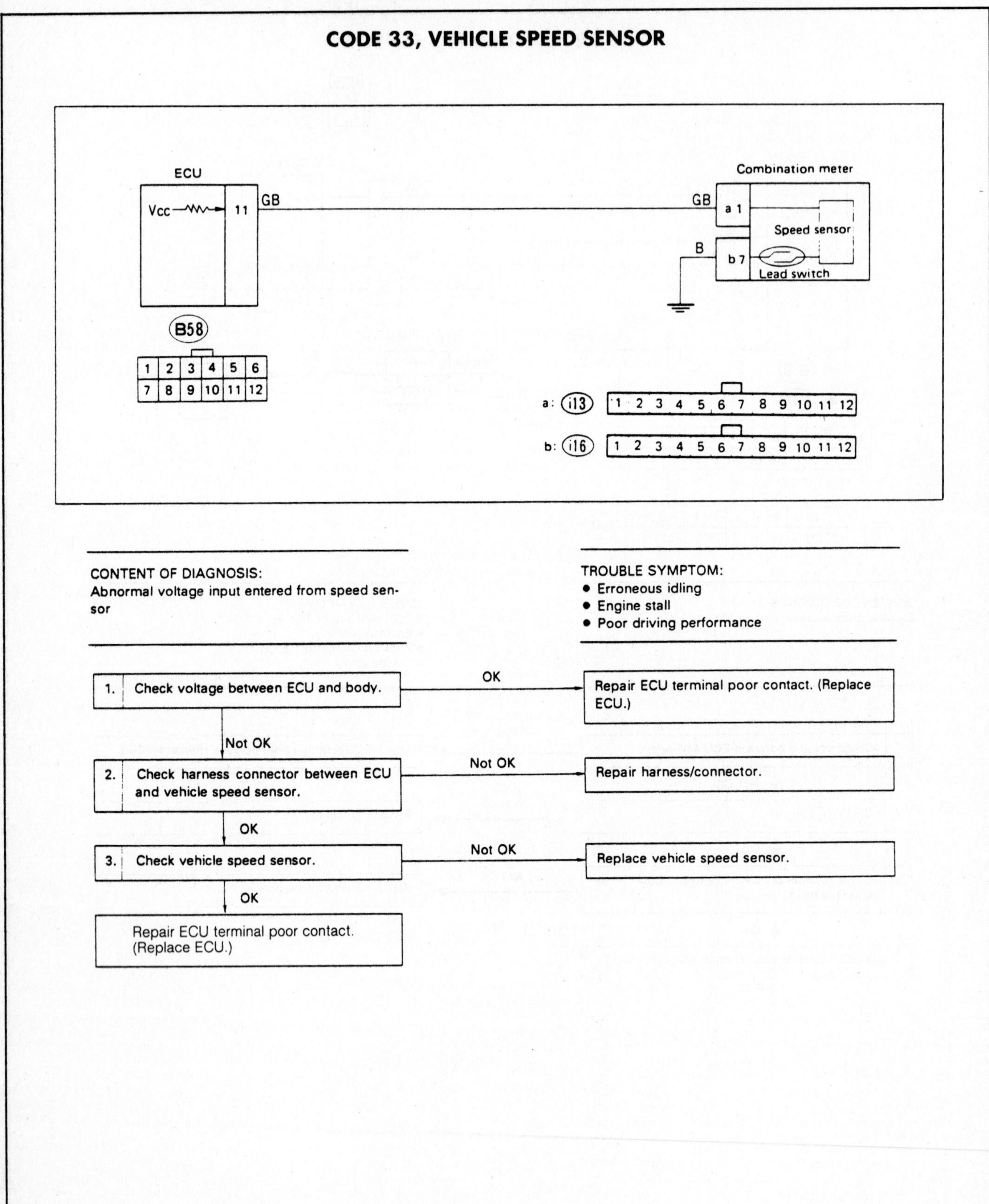

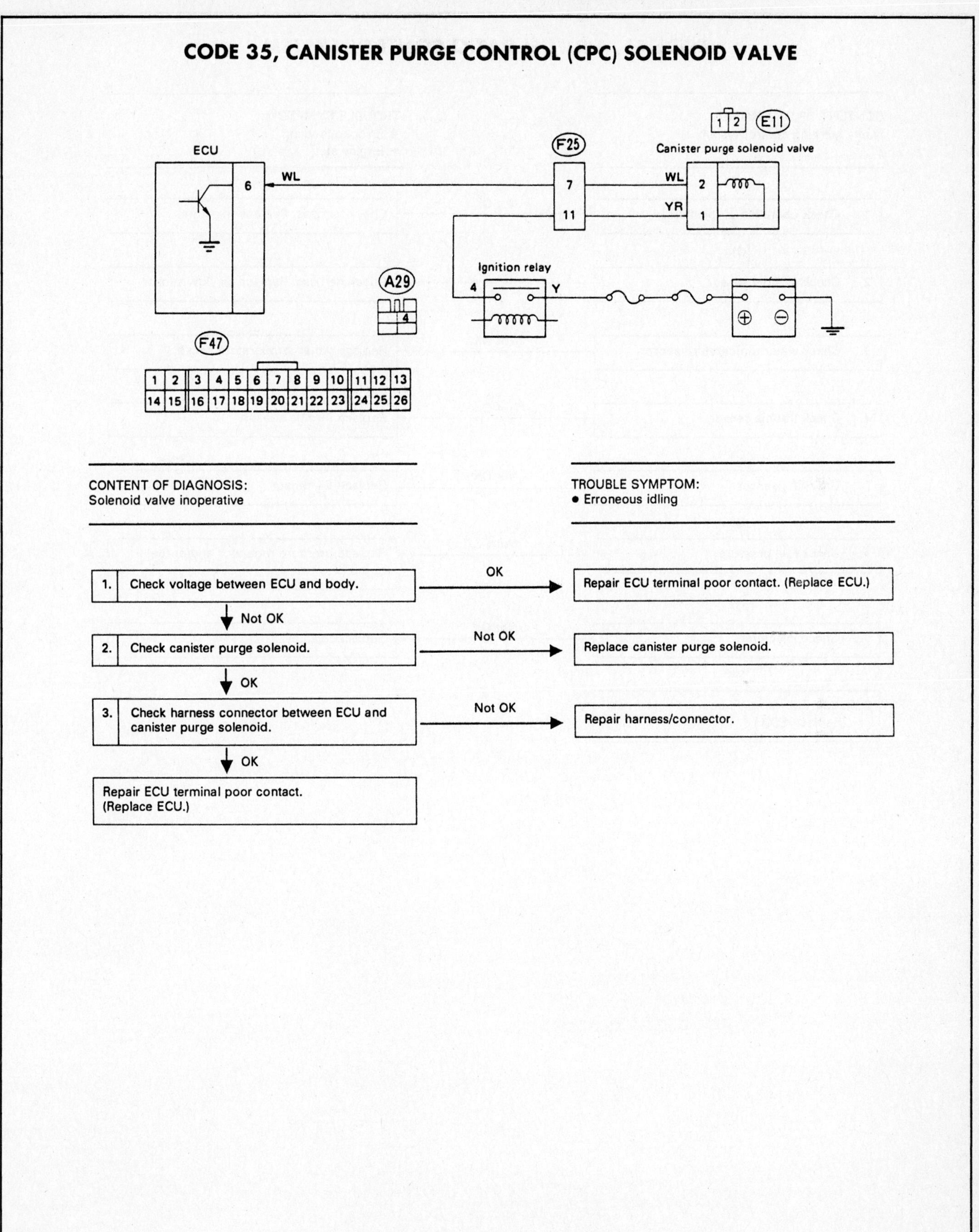
CODE 35, CANISTER PURGE CONTROL (CPC) SOLENOID VALVE
ECU
6
WL
F25
7
11
E11
1 2
Canister purge solenoid valve
WL
2
YR
1
Ignition relay
4
Y
A29
4
F47
1 2 3 4 5 6 7 8 9 10 11 12 13
14 15 16 17 18 19 20 21 22 23 24 25 26
CONTENT OF DIAGNOSIS:
Solenoid valve inoperative
TROUBLE SYMPTOM:
• Erroneous idling
1. Check voltage between ECU and body.
OK
Repair ECU terminal poor contact. (Replace ECU.)
Not OK
2. Check canister purge solenoid.
Not OK
Replace canister purge solenoid.
OK
3. Check harness connector between ECU and canister purge solenoid.
Not OK
Repair harness/connector.
OK
Repair ECU terminal poor contact.
(Replace ECU.)
91A17582

# 1991 ENGINE PERFORMANCE
## Self-Diagnostics – Legacy (Cont.)

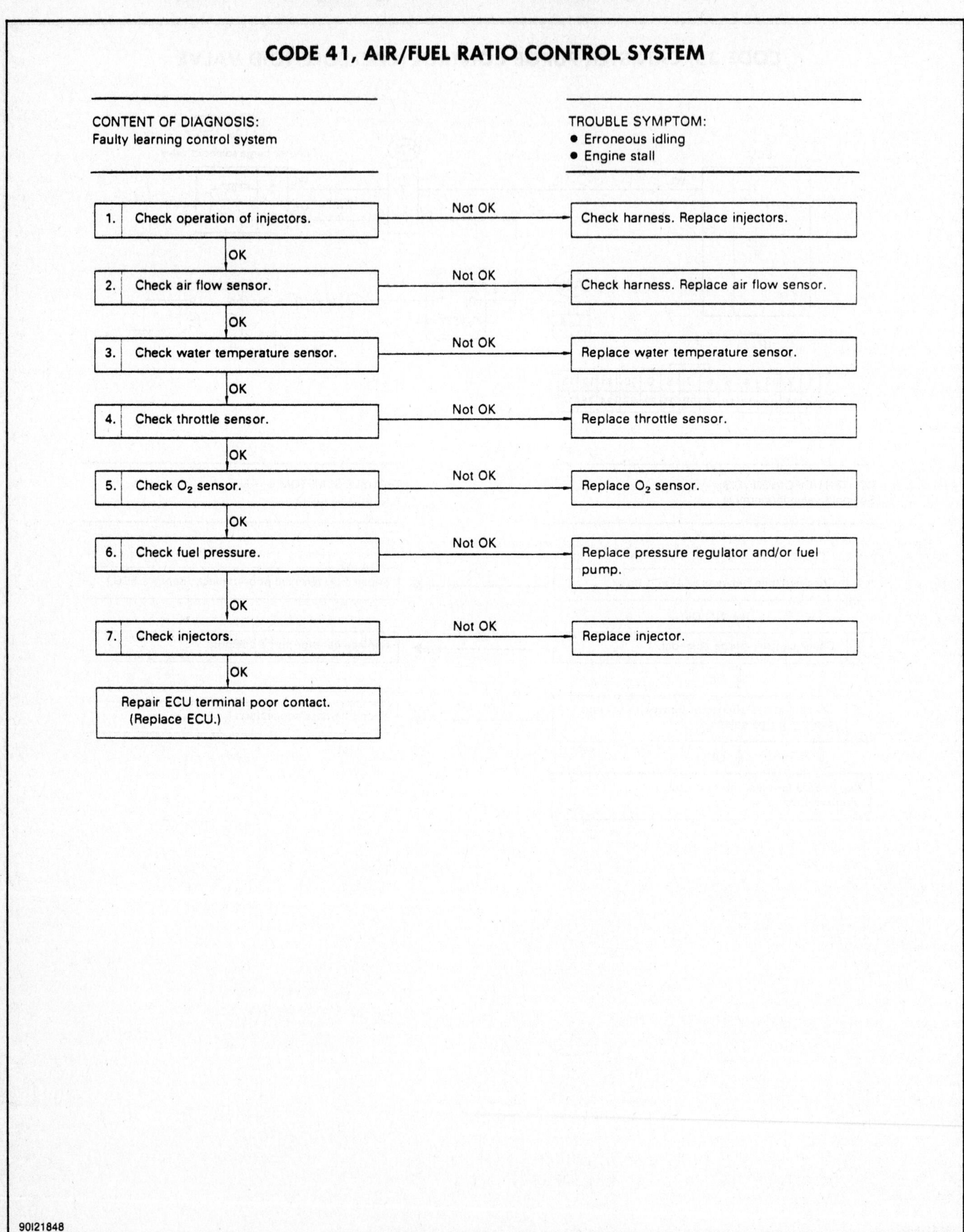

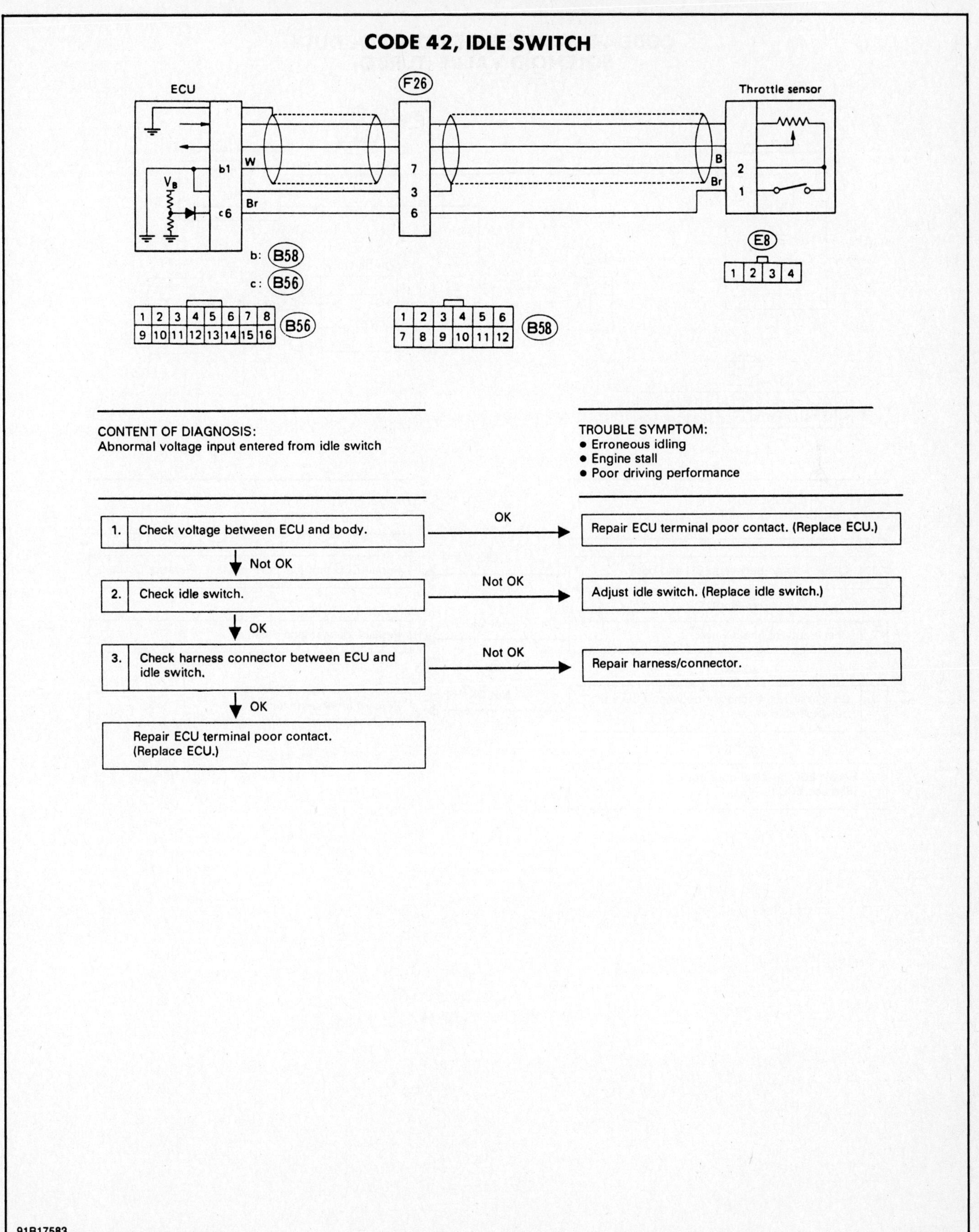
CODE 42, IDLE SWITCH
ECU
F26
Throttle sensor
b1
c6
W
Br
B
Br
7
3
6
2
1
E8
b: B58
c: B56
B56
B58
CONTENT OF DIAGNOSIS:
Abnormal voltage input entered from idle switch
TROUBLE SYMPTOM:
● Erroneous idling
● Engine stall
● Poor driving performance
1. Check voltage between ECU and body.
OK
Repair ECU terminal poor contact. (Replace ECU.)
Not OK
2. Check idle switch.
Not OK
Adjust idle switch. (Replace idle switch.)
OK
3. Check harness connector between ECU and idle switch.
Not OK
Repair harness/connector.
OK
Repair ECU terminal poor contact. (Replace ECU.)
91B17583

# 1991 ENGINE PERFORMANCE
## Self-Diagnostics – Legacy (Cont.)

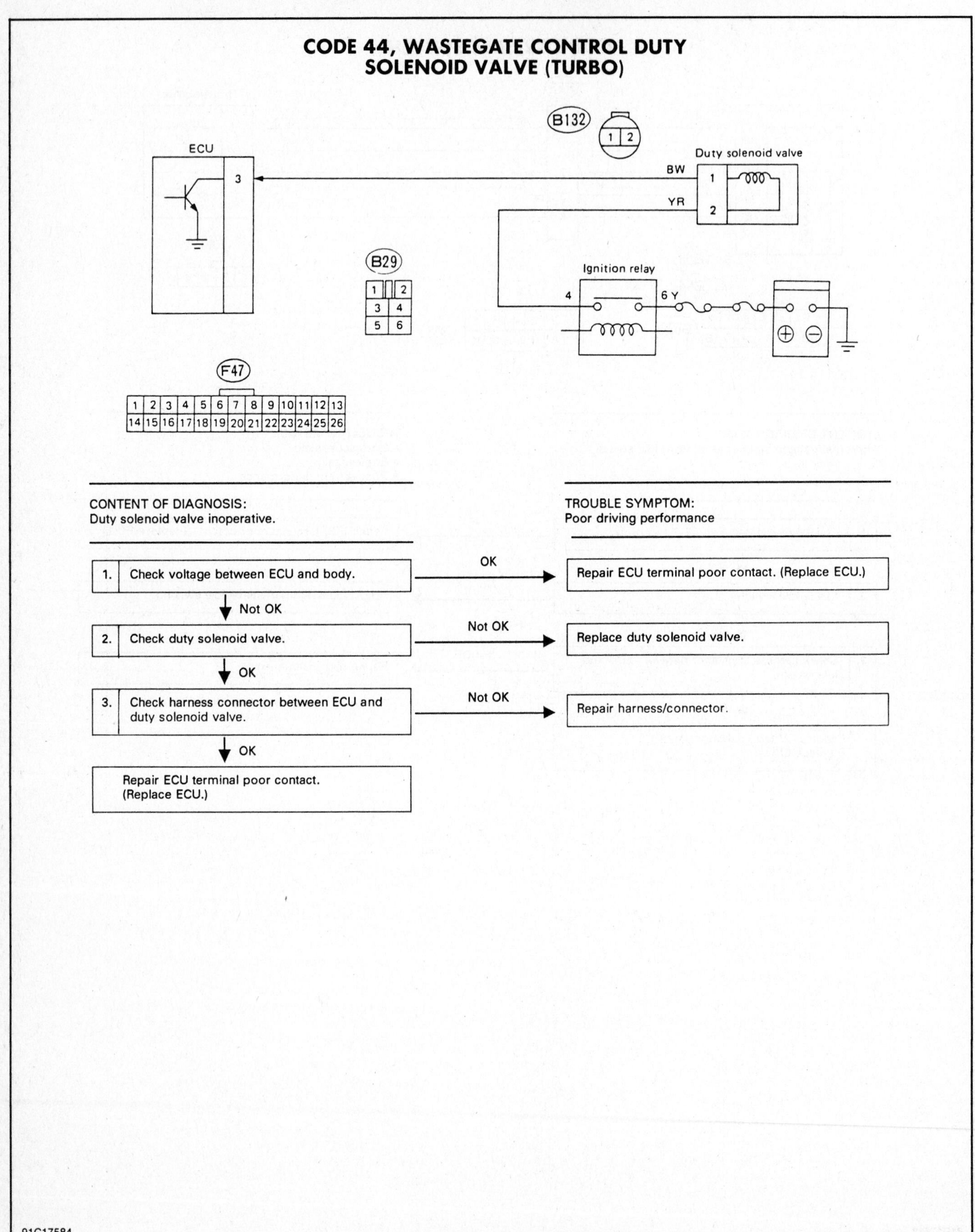

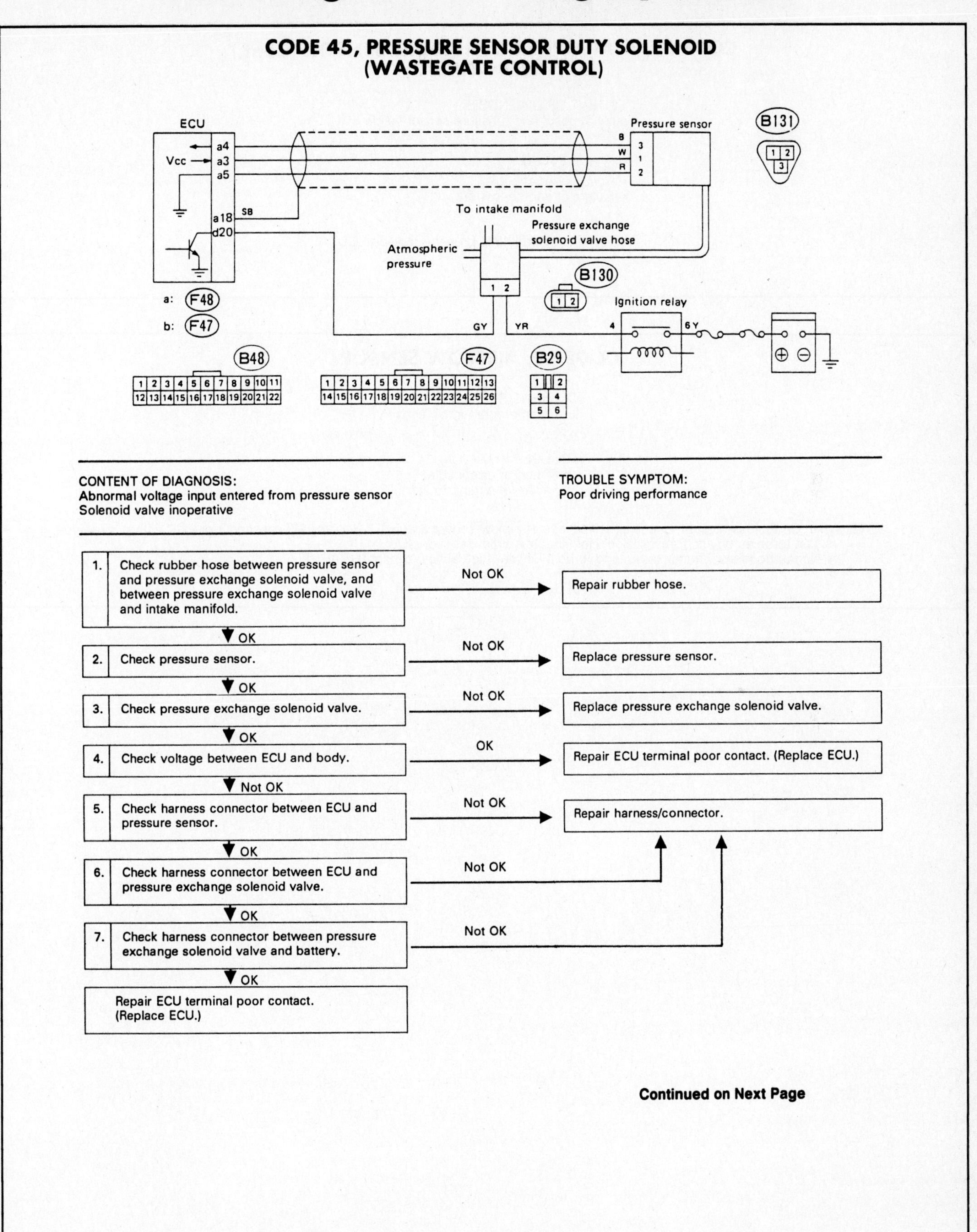

CODE 45, PRESSURE SENSOR DUTY SOLENOID
(WASTEGATE CONTROL)
ECU
Vcc
a4
a3
a5
a18
d20
SB
a:
F48
b:
F47
Pressure sensor
B131
B
W
R
3
1
2
To intake manifold
Pressure exchange
solenoid valve hose
Atmospheric
pressure
B130
Ignition relay
GY
YR
4
6Y
B48
F47
B29
CONTENT OF DIAGNOSIS:
Abnormal voltage input entered from pressure sensor
Solenoid valve inoperative
TROUBLE SYMPTOM:
Poor driving performance
1. Check rubber hose between pressure sensor and pressure exchange solenoid valve, and between pressure exchange solenoid valve and intake manifold.
Not OK
Repair rubber hose.
OK
2. Check pressure sensor.
Not OK
Replace pressure sensor.
OK
3. Check pressure exchange solenoid valve.
Not OK
Replace pressure exchange solenoid valve.
OK
4. Check voltage between ECU and body.
OK
Repair ECU terminal poor contact. (Replace ECU.)
Not OK
5. Check harness connector between ECU and pressure sensor.
Not OK
Repair harness/connector.
OK
6. Check harness connector between ECU and pressure exchange solenoid valve.
Not OK
OK
7. Check harness connector between pressure exchange solenoid valve and battery.
Not OK
OK
Repair ECU terminal poor contact.
(Replace ECU.)
Continued on Next Page
91E17586

# 1991 ENGINE PERFORMANCE
## Self-Diagnostics – Legacy (Cont.)

### CODE 45, ATMOSPHERIC PRESSURE SENSOR (Cont.)
### (NON-TURBO)

CONTENT OF DIAGNOSIS:
Faulty atmospheric pressure sensor inside ECU.

TROUBLE SYMPTOM:
- Rough or erratic idle.
- Failure of engine to start.

NOTE: When Code 45 is present, replace ECU.

### CODE 49, AIRFLOW SENSOR

CONTENT OF DIAGNOSIS:
Use of improper airflow sensor.

TROUBLE SYMPTOM:
- Rough or erratic idle.
- Failure of engine to start.

NOTE: When Code 49 is present, check specifications of airflow sensor and ECU. Replace airflow sensor or ECU with proper type.
- Non-turbo automatic transmission: Hot film type airflow sensor (JECS).
- Non-turbo manual transmission and turbo: Hot wire type airflow sensor (HITACHI).

### CODE 51
### NEUTRAL SAFETY SWITCH (M/T)

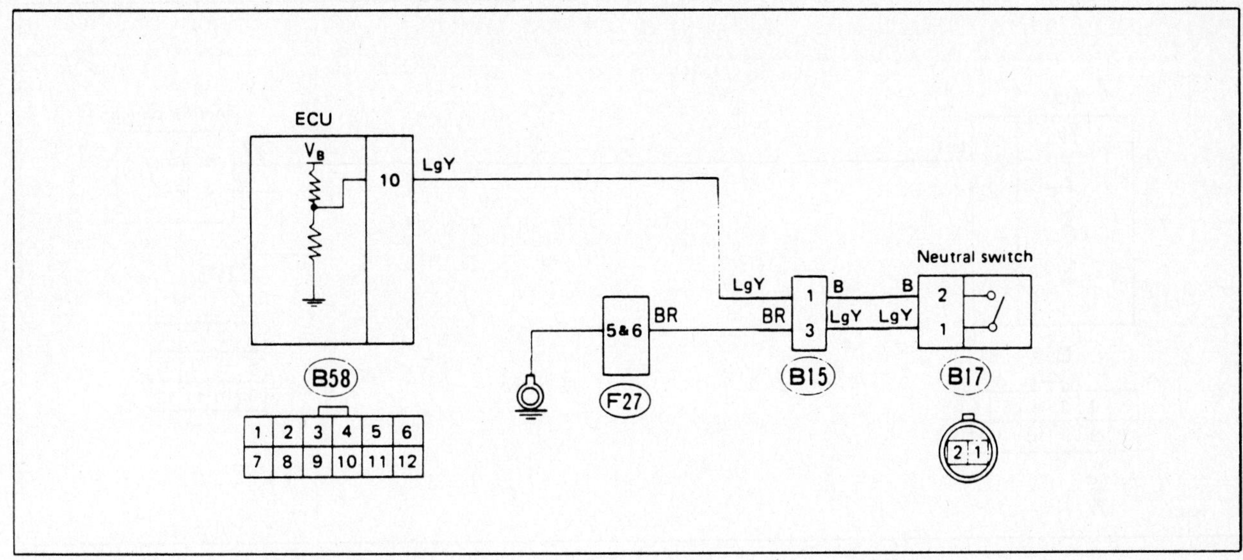
ECU
$V_B$
10
LgY
LgY
B
B
Neutral switch
2
1
BR
BR
5&6
1
3
LgY
LgY
B58
F27
B15
B17
1 2 3 4 5 6
7 8 9 10 11 12
2 1

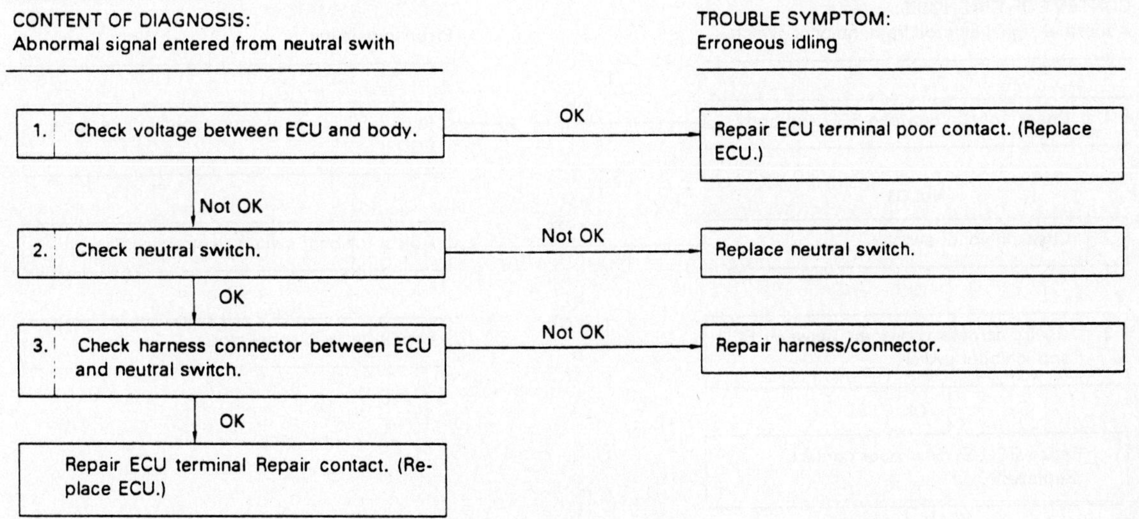
CONTENT OF DIAGNOSIS:
Abnormal signal entered from neutral swith
TROUBLE SYMPTOM:
Erroneous idling
1. Check voltage between ECU and body.
OK
Repair ECU terminal poor contact. (Replace ECU.)
Not OK
2. Check neutral switch.
Not OK
Replace neutral switch.
OK
3. Check harness connector between ECU and neutral switch.
Not OK
Repair harness/connector.
OK
Repair ECU terminal Repair contact. (Replace ECU.)

**Continued on Next Page**

90D21850

# 1991 ENGINE PERFORMANCE
## Self-Diagnostics – Legacy (Cont.)

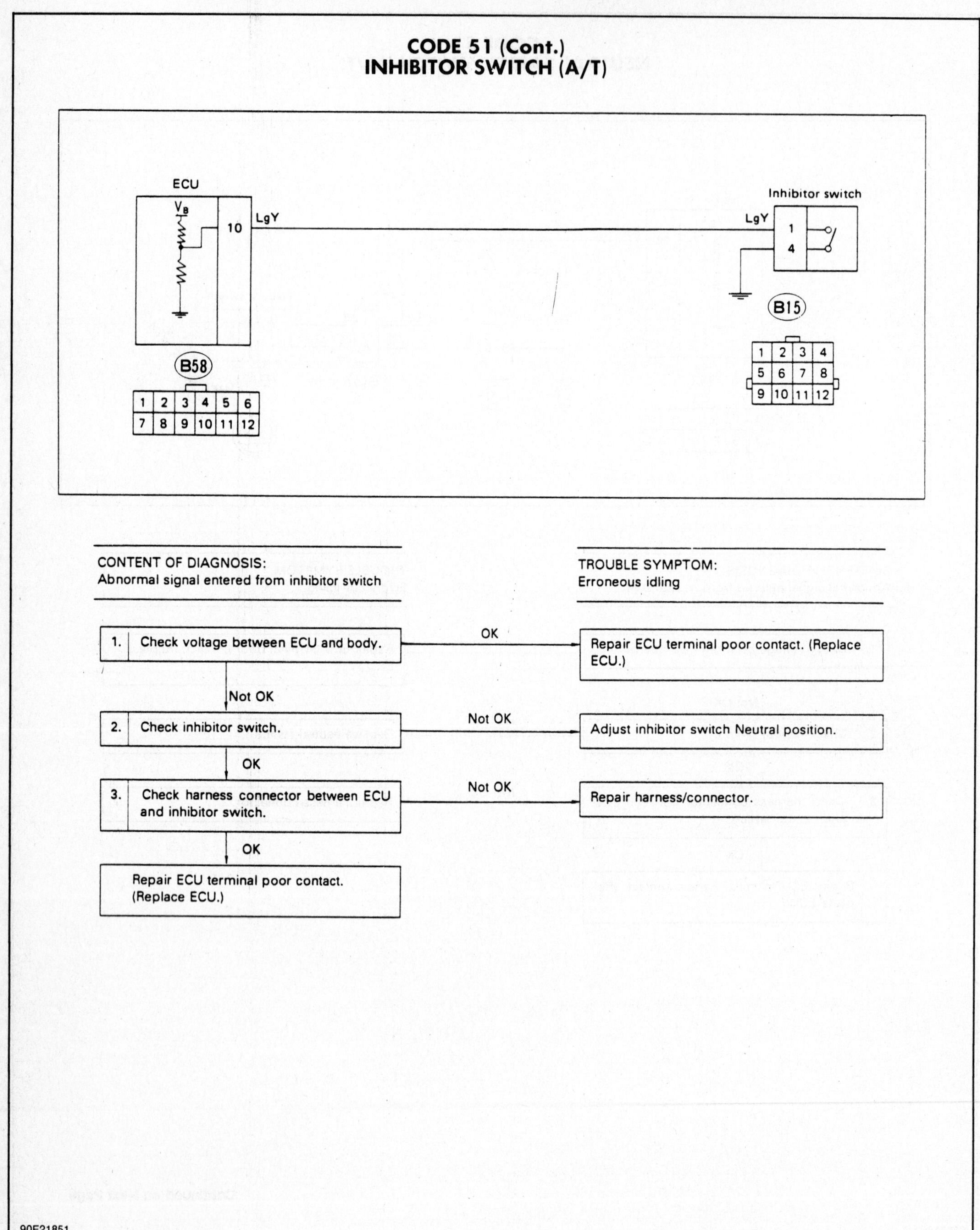
CODE 51 (Cont.)
INHIBITOR SWITCH (A/T)
ECU
$V_B$
10
LgY
LgY
Inhibitor switch
1
4
B15
1 2 3 4
5 6 7 8
9 10 11 12
B58
1 2 3 4 5 6
7 8 9 10 11 12
CONTENT OF DIAGNOSIS:
Abnormal signal entered from inhibitor switch
TROUBLE SYMPTOM:
Erroneous idling
1. Check voltage between ECU and body.
OK
Repair ECU terminal poor contact. (Replace ECU.)
Not OK
2. Check inhibitor switch.
Not OK
Adjust inhibitor switch Neutral position.
OK
3. Check harness connector between ECU and inhibitor switch.
Not OK
Repair harness/connector.
OK
Repair ECU terminal poor contact. (Replace ECU.)
90E21851

# 1991 ENGINE PERFORMANCE
# Self-Diagnostics – Legacy (Cont.)

## CODE 52, PARKING BRAKE SWITCH (A/T)

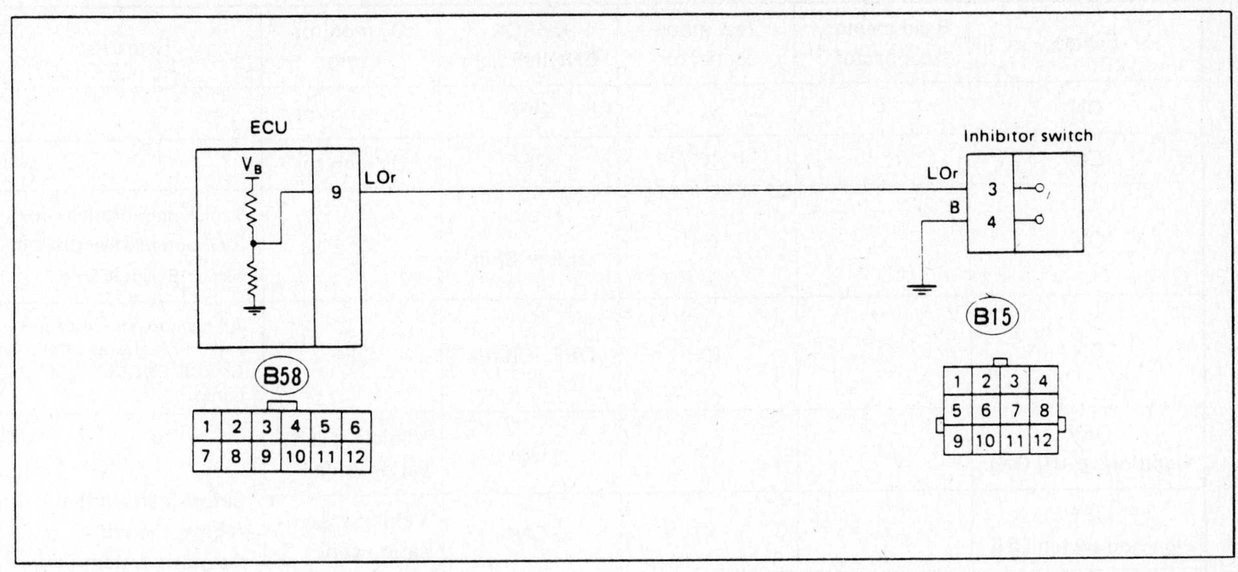
ECU
$V_B$
9
LOr
Inhibitor switch
LOr
B
3
4
B58
1 2 3 4 5 6
7 8 9 10 11 12
B15
1 2 3 4
5 6 7 8
9 10 11 12

CONTENT OF DIAGNOSIS:
Abnormal signal entered from parking switch

TROUBLE SYMPTOM:
- Erroneous idling
- Poor warm-up performance with select lever in "P."

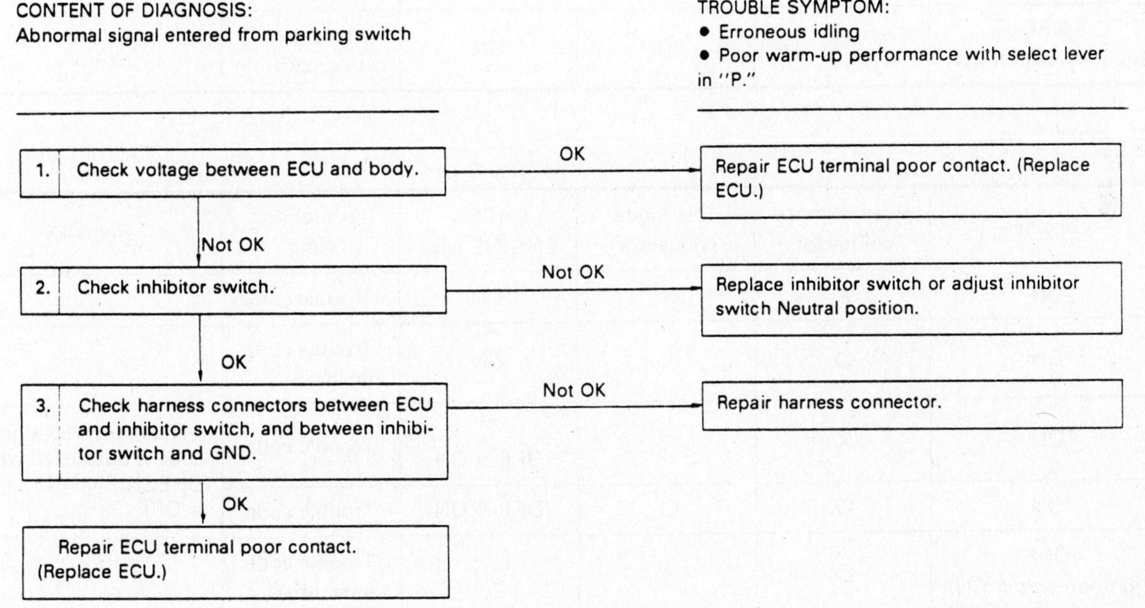
1. Check voltage between ECU and body.
OK
Repair ECU terminal poor contact. (Replace ECU.)
Not OK
2. Check inhibitor switch.
Not OK
Replace inhibitor switch or adjust inhibitor switch Neutral position.
OK
3. Check harness connectors between ECU and inhibitor switch, and between inhibitor switch and GND.
Not OK
Repair harness connector.
OK
Repair ECU terminal poor contact. (Replace ECU.)

90F21852

# 1991 ENGINE PERFORMANCE
# Self-Diagnostics – Loyale – PFI

## LOYALE (PFI) CODE CHARTS

### BASIC OPERATION OF SELF-DIAGNOSTIC SYSTEM

**NO TROUBLE**

O : CONNECT X : DISCONNECT

| Engine | Read memory connector | Test mode connector | CHECK ENGINE light | $O_2$ monitor lamp | Remarks |
|---|---|---|---|---|---|
| ON | X | X | OFF | $O_2$ monitor | |
| ON | O | X | OFF | $O_2$ monitor | |
| *ON | X | O | ** OFF → Blink | OFF | Vehicle specification code is outputted when CHECK ENGINE light is OFF. |
| *ON | O | O | OFF → Blink | OFF | All memory stored in control unit is cleared after CHECK ENGINE light blinks. |
| OFF (Ignition switch ON) | O | X | ON | Vehicle specification code | Before starting the engine, the self-diagnosis system assumes the engine to be in a NO TROUBLE condition. |
| OFF (Ignition switch ON) | X | X | ON | Vehicle specification code | |
| OFF (Ignition switch ON) | X | O | ON | Vehicle specification code | |
| OFF (Ignition switch ON) | O | O | ON | Vehicle specification code | |

**TROUBLE**

| Engine | Read memory connector | Test mode connector | CHECK ENGINE light | $O_2$ monitor lamp | Remarks |
|---|---|---|---|---|---|
| ON | X | X | ON | Trouble code | |
| ON | O | X | ON | Trouble code (memory) | |
| *ON | X | O | ** OFF → ON | Trouble code | Vehicle specification code is outputted when CHECK ENGINE light is OFF. |
| *ON | O | O | OFF → ON | Trouble code | |
| OFF (Ignition switch ON) | O | X | ON | Trouble code (memory) | |
| STALL (Ignition switch ON) | X | X | ON | Trouble code | |
| STALL (Ignition switch ON) | X | O | ON | Trouble code | |
| STALL (Ignition switch ON) | O | O | ON | Trouble code | |

***: Ignition timing is set to 20° BTDC (when the engine is on, test mode connector is connected, and idle switch is ON).**
****: CHECK ENGINE light remains off until engine is operated at speed greater than 2,000 rpm for at least 40 seconds.**

90J21880

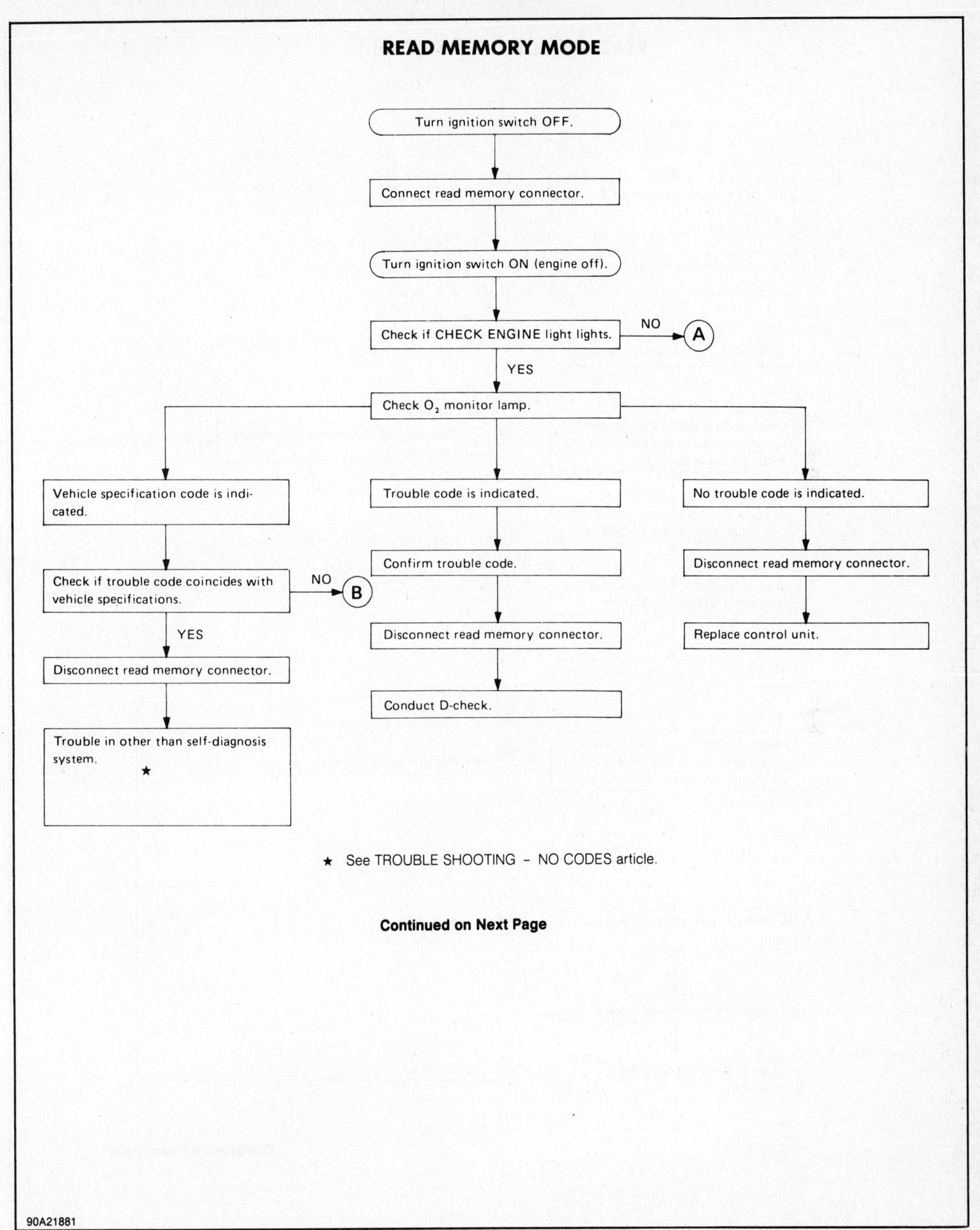
READ MEMORY MODE
Turn ignition switch OFF.
Connect read memory connector.
Turn ignition switch ON (engine off).
Check if CHECK ENGINE light lights.
NO
A
YES
Check O2 monitor lamp.
Vehicle specification code is indicated.
Trouble code is indicated.
No trouble code is indicated.
Check if trouble code coincides with vehicle specifications.
NO
B
Confirm trouble code.
Disconnect read memory connector.
YES
Disconnect read memory connector.
Replace control unit.
Disconnect read memory connector.
Conduct D-check.
Trouble in other than self-diagnosis system. ★
★ See TROUBLE SHOOTING – NO CODES article.
Continued on Next Page
90A21881

# 1991 ENGINE PERFORMANCE
## Self-Diagnostics – Loyale – PFI (Cont.)

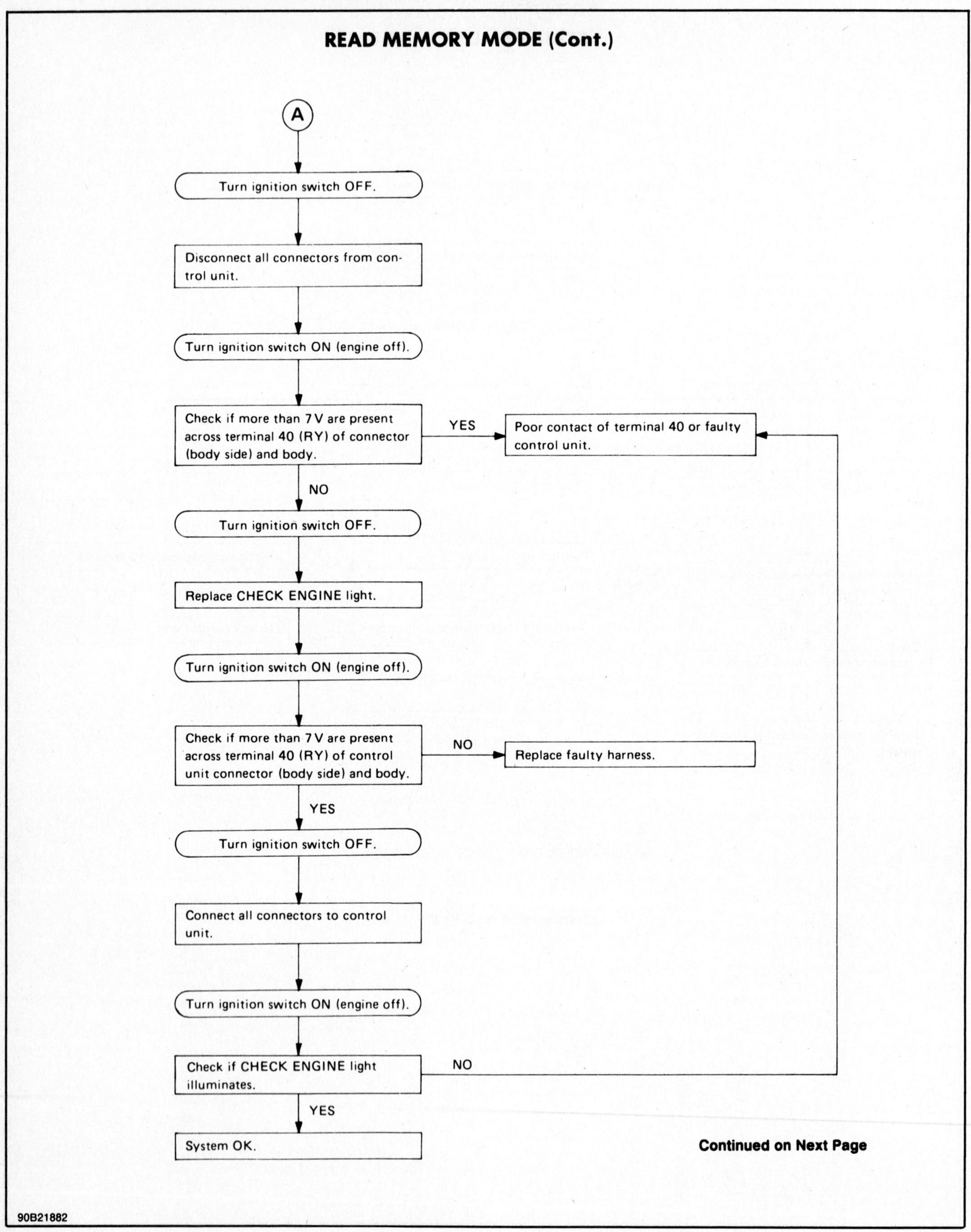
READ MEMORY MODE (Cont.)
A
Turn ignition switch OFF.
Disconnect all connectors from control unit.
Turn ignition switch ON (engine off).
Check if more than 7 V are present across terminal 40 (RY) of connector (body side) and body.
YES
Poor contact of terminal 40 or faulty control unit.
NO
Turn ignition switch OFF.
Replace CHECK ENGINE light.
Turn ignition switch ON (engine off).
Check if more than 7 V are present across terminal 40 (RY) of control unit connector (body side) and body.
NO
Replace faulty harness.
YES
Turn ignition switch OFF.
Connect all connectors to control unit.
Turn ignition switch ON (engine off).
Check if CHECK ENGINE light illuminates.
NO
YES
System OK.
Continued on Next Page
90B21882

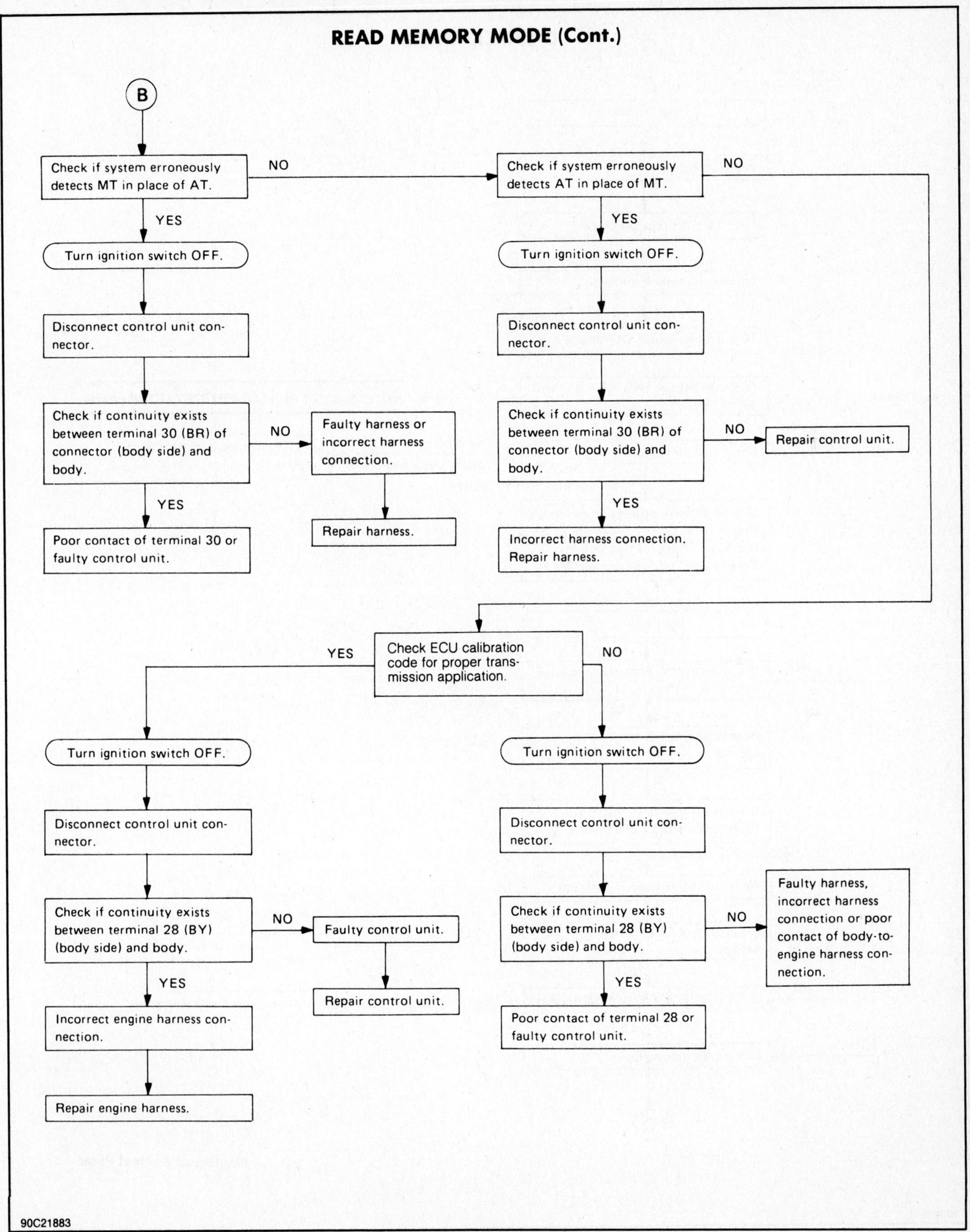
READ MEMORY MODE (Cont.)
B
Check if system erroneously detects MT in place of AT.
NO
YES
Turn ignition switch OFF.
Disconnect control unit connector.
Check if continuity exists between terminal 30 (BR) of connector (body side) and body.
NO
Faulty harness or incorrect harness connection.
Repair harness.
YES
Poor contact of terminal 30 or faulty control unit.
Check if system erroneously detects AT in place of MT.
NO
YES
Turn ignition switch OFF.
Disconnect control unit connector.
Check if continuity exists between terminal 30 (BR) of connector (body side) and body.
NO
Repair control unit.
YES
Incorrect harness connection. Repair harness.
Check ECU calibration code for proper transmission application.
YES
NO
Turn ignition switch OFF.
Disconnect control unit connector.
Check if continuity exists between terminal 28 (BY) (body side) and body.
NO
Faulty control unit.
Repair control unit.
YES
Incorrect engine harness connection.
Repair engine harness.
Turn ignition switch OFF.
Disconnect control unit connector.
Check if continuity exists between terminal 28 (BY) (body side) and body.
NO
Faulty harness, incorrect harness connection or poor contact of body-to-engine harness connection.
YES
Poor contact of terminal 28 or faulty control unit.
90C21883

# 1991 ENGINE PERFORMANCE
# Self-Diagnostics – Loyale – PFI (Cont.)

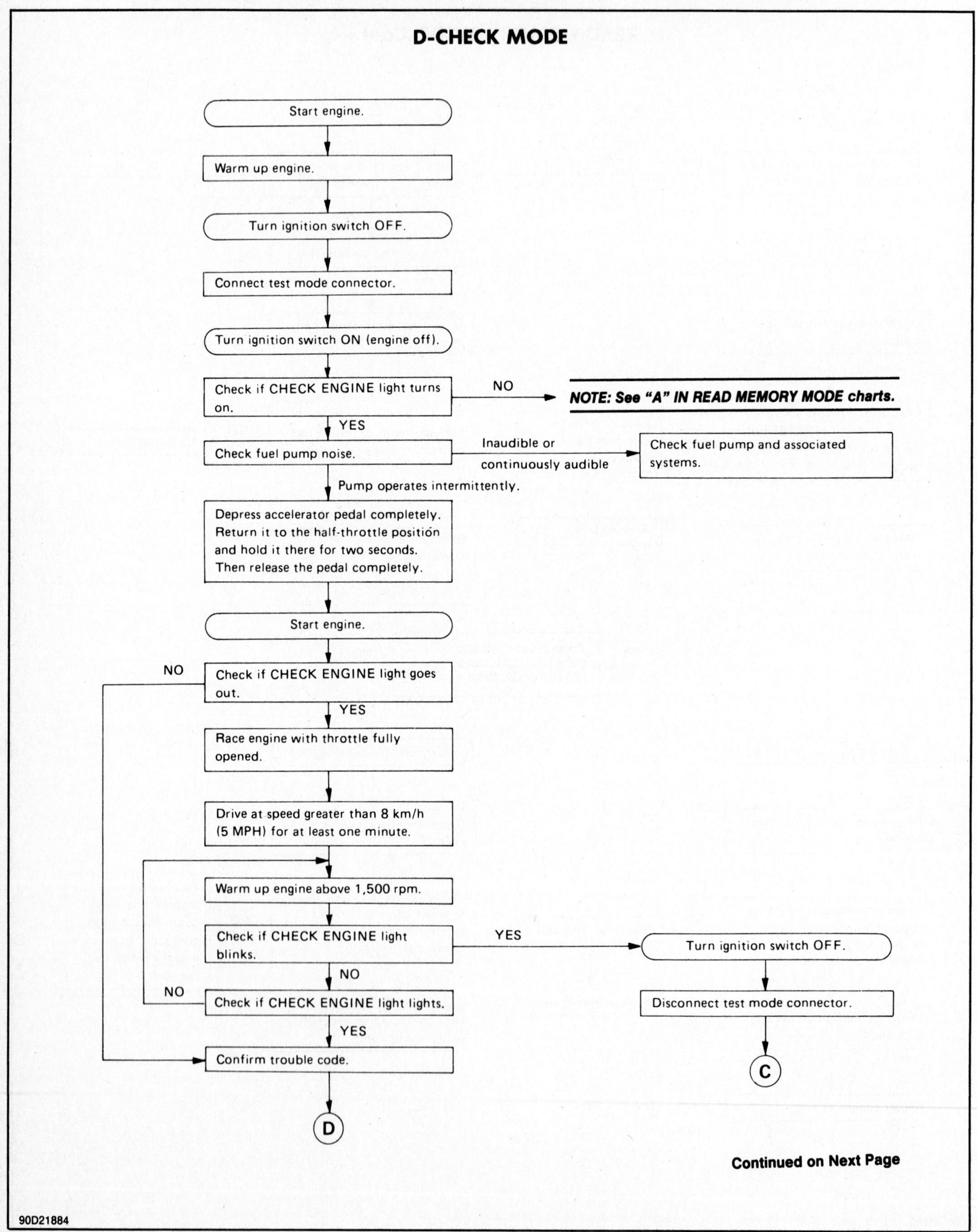
D-CHECK MODE
Start engine.
Warm up engine.
Turn ignition switch OFF.
Connect test mode connector.
Turn ignition switch ON (engine off).
Check if CHECK ENGINE light turns on.
NO
NOTE: See "A" IN READ MEMORY MODE charts.
YES
Check fuel pump noise.
Inaudible or continuously audible
Check fuel pump and associated systems.
Pump operates intermittently.
Depress accelerator pedal completely. Return it to the half-throttle position and hold it there for two seconds. Then release the pedal completely.
Start engine.
NO
Check if CHECK ENGINE light goes out.
YES
Race engine with throttle fully opened.
Drive at speed greater than 8 km/h (5 MPH) for at least one minute.
Warm up engine above 1,500 rpm.
Check if CHECK ENGINE light blinks.
YES
Turn ignition switch OFF.
Disconnect test mode connector.
C
NO
NO
Check if CHECK ENGINE light lights.
YES
Confirm trouble code.
D
Continued on Next Page
90D21884

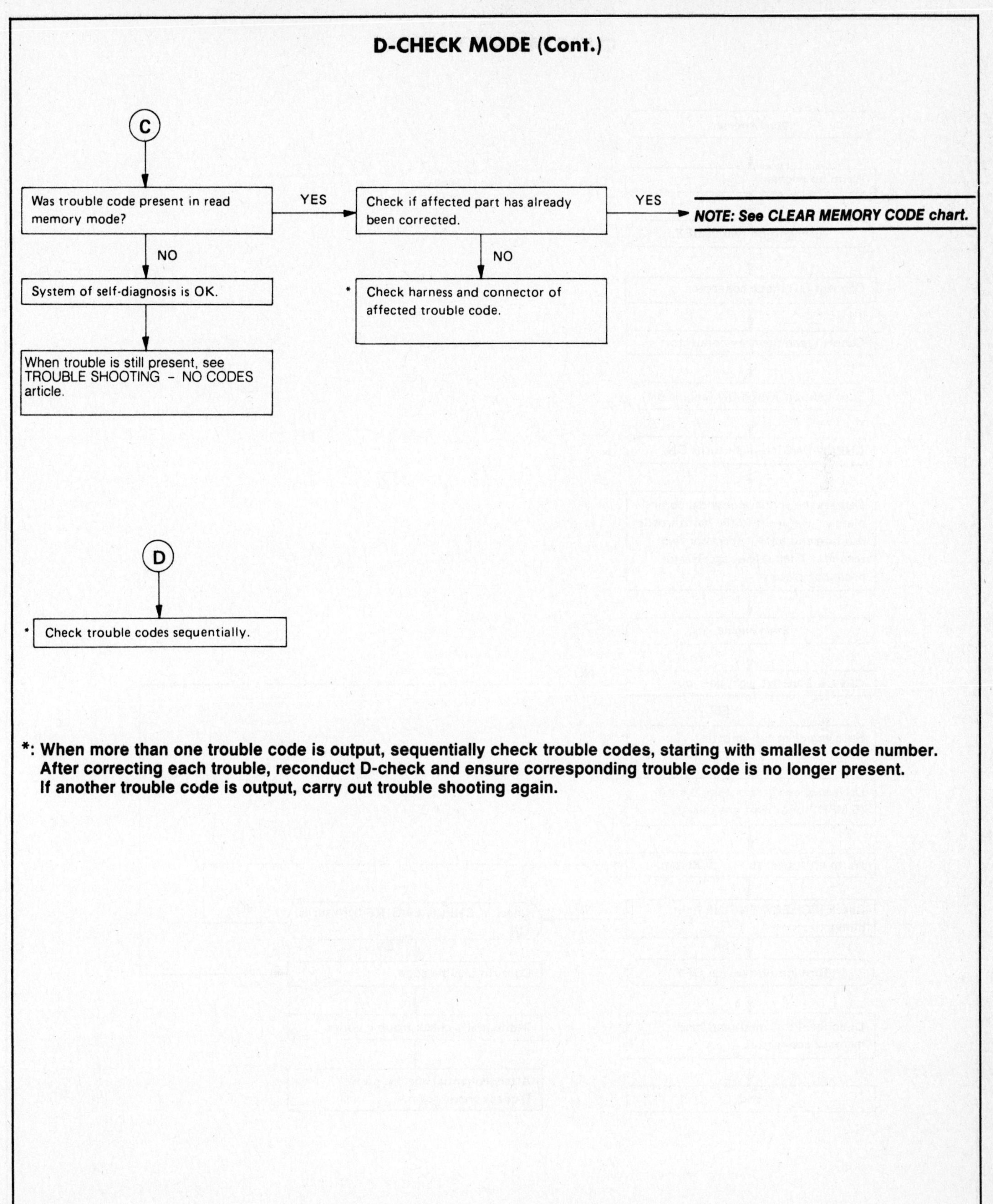
D-CHECK MODE (Cont.)
C
Was trouble code present in read memory mode?
YES
Check if affected part has already been corrected.
YES
NOTE: See CLEAR MEMORY CODE chart.
NO
System of self-diagnosis is OK.
When trouble is still present, see TROUBLE SHOOTING – NO CODES article.
NO
* Check harness and connector of affected trouble code.
D
* Check trouble codes sequentially.
*: When more than one trouble code is output, sequentially check trouble codes, starting with smallest code number.
After correcting each trouble, reconduct D-check and ensure corresponding trouble code is no longer present.
If another trouble code is output, carry out trouble shooting again.
90E21885

# 1991 ENGINE PERFORMANCE
# Self-Diagnostics – Loyale – PFI (Cont.)

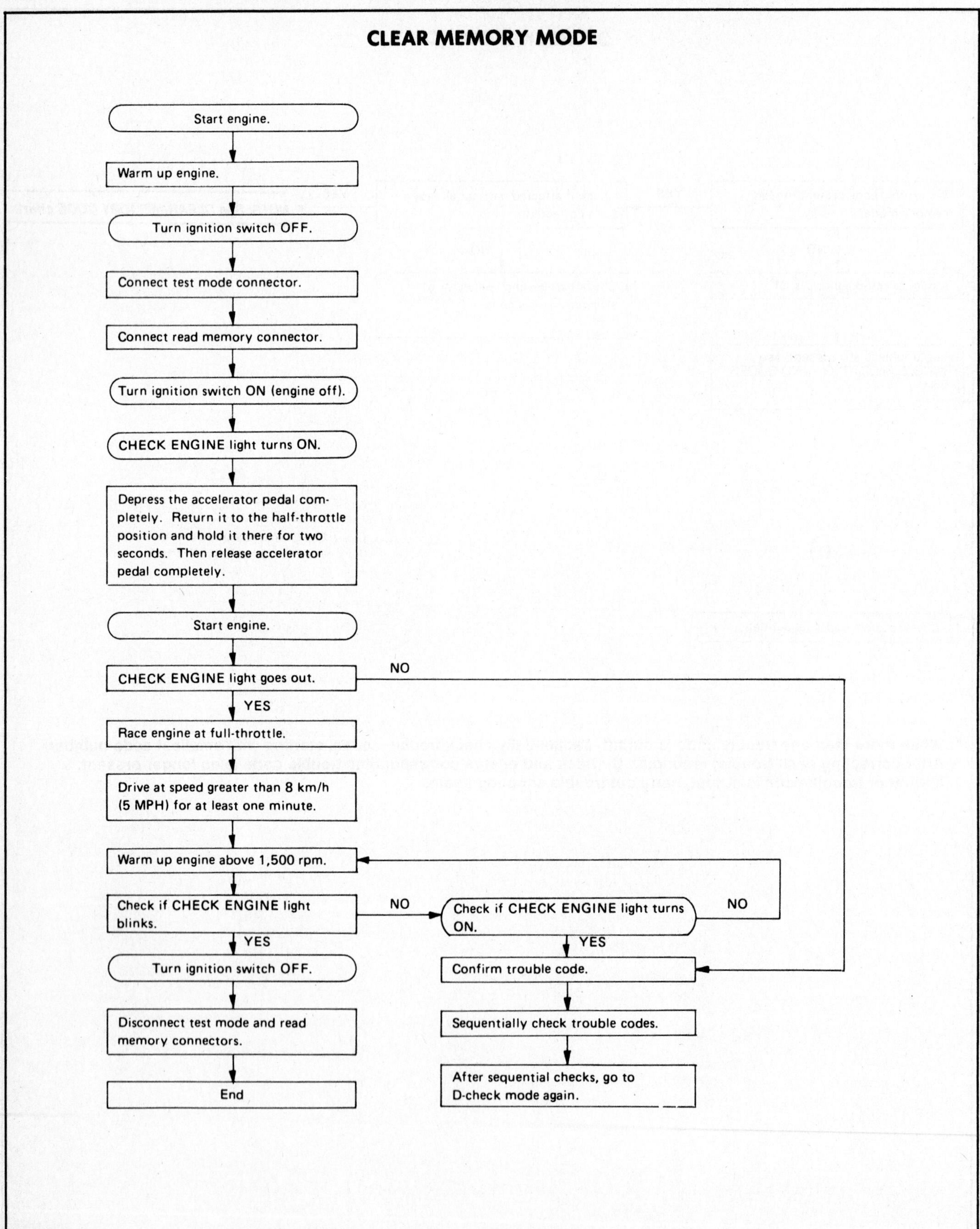
CLEAR MEMORY MODE
Start engine.
Warm up engine.
Turn ignition switch OFF.
Connect test mode connector.
Connect read memory connector.
Turn ignition switch ON (engine off).
CHECK ENGINE light turns ON.
Depress the accelerator pedal completely. Return it to the half-throttle position and hold it there for two seconds. Then release accelerator pedal completely.
Start engine.
CHECK ENGINE light goes out.
NO
YES
Race engine at full-throttle.
Drive at speed greater than 8 km/h (5 MPH) for at least one minute.
Warm up engine above 1,500 rpm.
Check if CHECK ENGINE light blinks.
NO
Check if CHECK ENGINE light turns ON.
NO
YES
YES
Turn ignition switch OFF.
Confirm trouble code.
Disconnect test mode and read memory connectors.
Sequentially check trouble codes.
End
After sequential checks, go to D-check mode again.
90F21886

# 1991 ENGINE PERFORMANCE
# Self-Diagnostics – Loyale – PFI (Cont.)

## CODE 11, CRANK ANGLE SENSOR
## NO REFERENCE SIGNAL

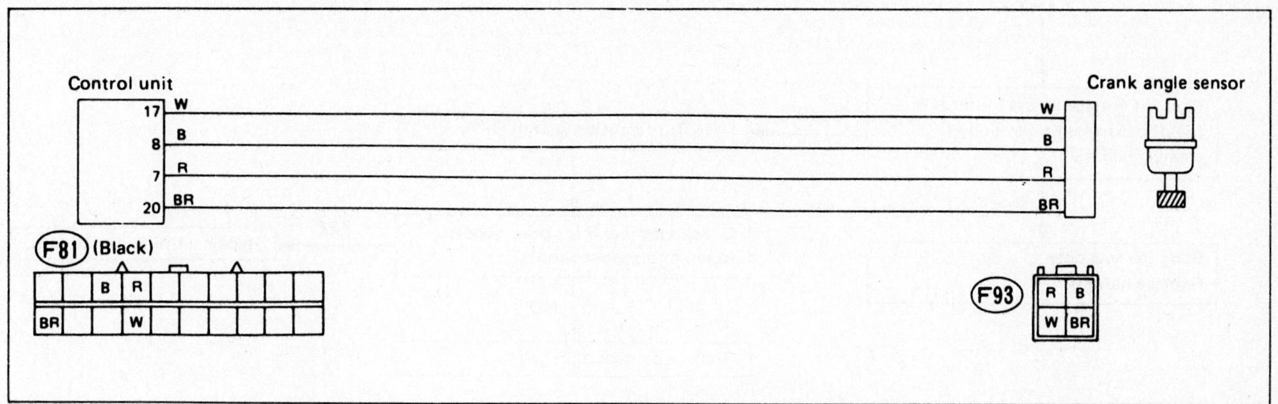


Check if trouble code is output in D-check mode. — NO → Check terminals of control unit connector.

YES ↓

Turn ignition switch OFF (engine off).

↓

Disconnect test mode connector.

↓

Check if engine starts. — YES → Check terminals 7, 8 and 20 of control unit connector for poor contact.

NO ↓

Turn ignition switch OFF.

↓

Disconnect crank angle sensor connector.

↓

Turn ignition switch ON (engine off).

↓

Check if voltage across terminal (B) of crank angle sensor connector (body side) and body is greater than 4 V. — NO → **11-1**

YES ↓

Check if voltage across terminal (R) of connector (body side) and body is greater than 10 V. — NO → **11-2**

YES ↓

Check if continuity exists between terminal (BR) of connector (body side) and body. — NO → **11-3**

YES ↓

Check if female terminal of connector (body side) is open. — YES → Repair terminal or replace body harness.

NO ↓

Replace crank angle sensor.

**Continued on Next Page**

90G21887

# 1991 ENGINE PERFORMANCE
## Self-Diagnostics – Loyale – PFI (Cont.)

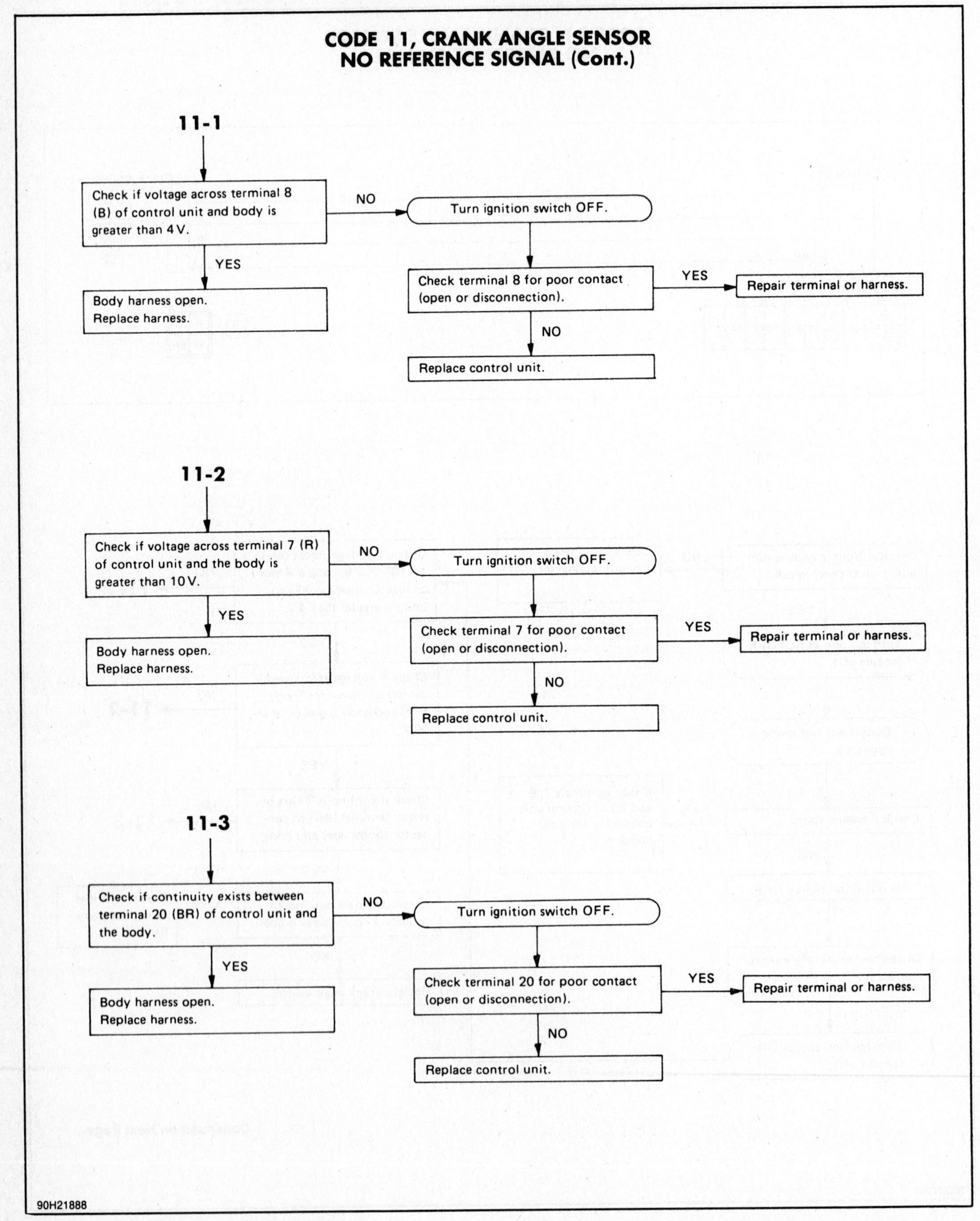
CODE 11, CRANK ANGLE SENSOR
NO REFERENCE SIGNAL (Cont.)
11-1
Check if voltage across terminal 8 (B) of control unit and body is greater than 4 V.
NO
Turn ignition switch OFF.
YES
Body harness open. Replace harness.
Check terminal 8 for poor contact (open or disconnection).
YES
Repair terminal or harness.
NO
Replace control unit.
11-2
Check if voltage across terminal 7 (R) of control unit and the body is greater than 10 V.
NO
Turn ignition switch OFF.
YES
Body harness open. Replace harness.
Check terminal 7 for poor contact (open or disconnection).
YES
Repair terminal or harness.
NO
Replace control unit.
11-3
Check if continuity exists between terminal 20 (BR) of control unit and the body.
NO
Turn ignition switch OFF.
YES
Body harness open. Replace harness.
Check terminal 20 for poor contact (open or disconnection).
YES
Repair terminal or harness.
NO
Replace control unit.
90H21888

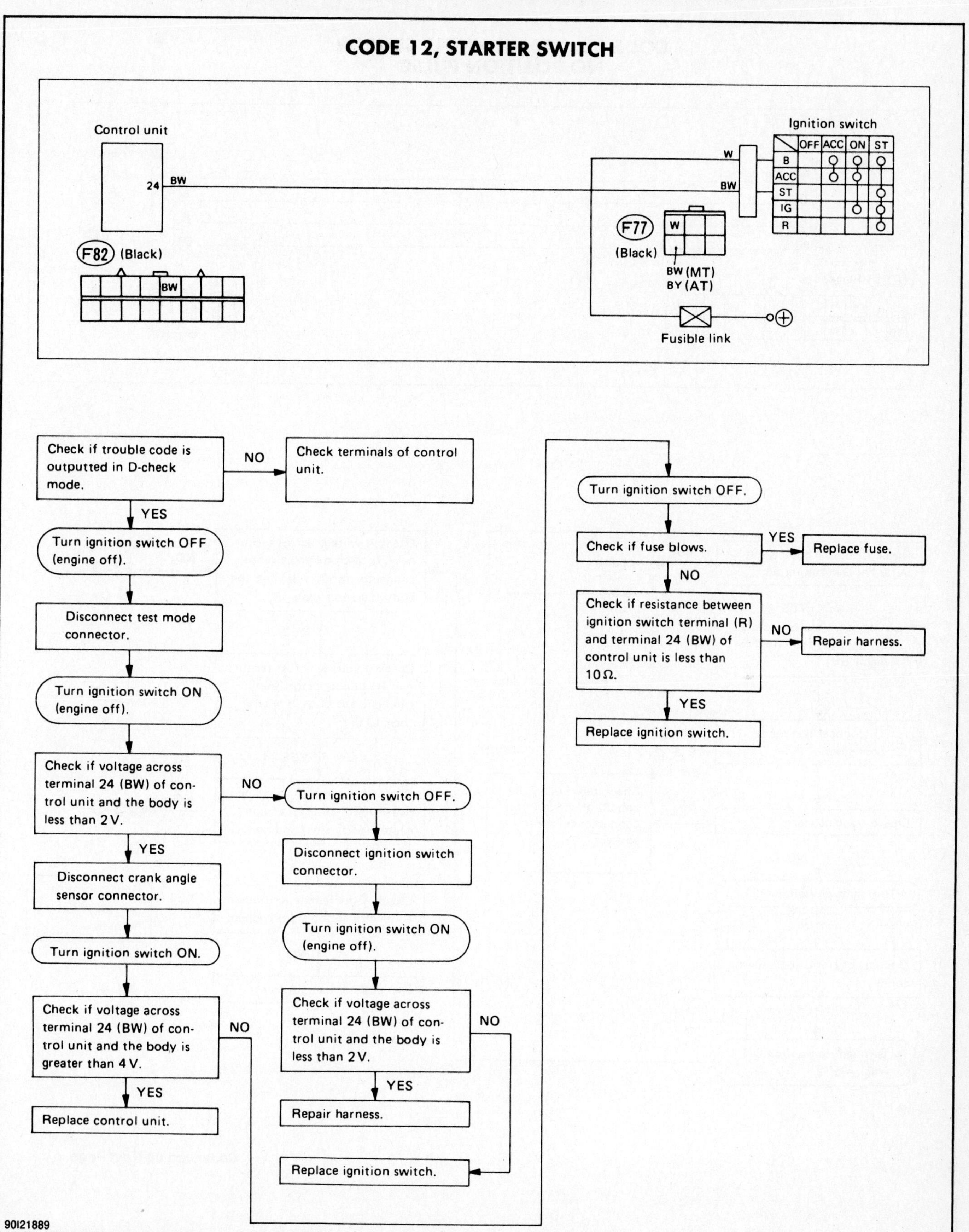
CODE 12, STARTER SWITCH
Control unit
24
BW
F82 (Black)
BW
Ignition switch
OFF
ACC
ON
ST
B
ACC
ST
IG
R
W
BW
F77
(Black)
W
BW (MT)
BY (AT)
Fusible link
Check if trouble code is outputted in D-check mode.
NO
Check terminals of control unit.
YES
Turn ignition switch OFF (engine off).
Disconnect test mode connector.
Turn ignition switch ON (engine off).
Check if voltage across terminal 24 (BW) of control unit and the body is less than 2 V.
NO
Turn ignition switch OFF.
Disconnect ignition switch connector.
Turn ignition switch ON (engine off).
Check if voltage across terminal 24 (BW) of control unit and the body is less than 2 V.
NO
YES
Repair harness.
Replace ignition switch.
YES
Disconnect crank angle sensor connector.
Turn ignition switch ON.
Check if voltage across terminal 24 (BW) of control unit and the body is greater than 4 V.
NO
YES
Replace control unit.
Turn ignition switch OFF.
Check if fuse blows.
YES
Replace fuse.
NO
Check if resistance between ignition switch terminal (R) and terminal 24 (BW) of control unit is less than 10 Ω.
NO
Repair harness.
YES
Replace ignition switch.
90I21889

# 1991 ENGINE PERFORMANCE
# Self-Diagnostics – Loyale – PFI (Cont.)

## CODE 13, CRANK ANGLE SENSOR NO POSITION PULSE

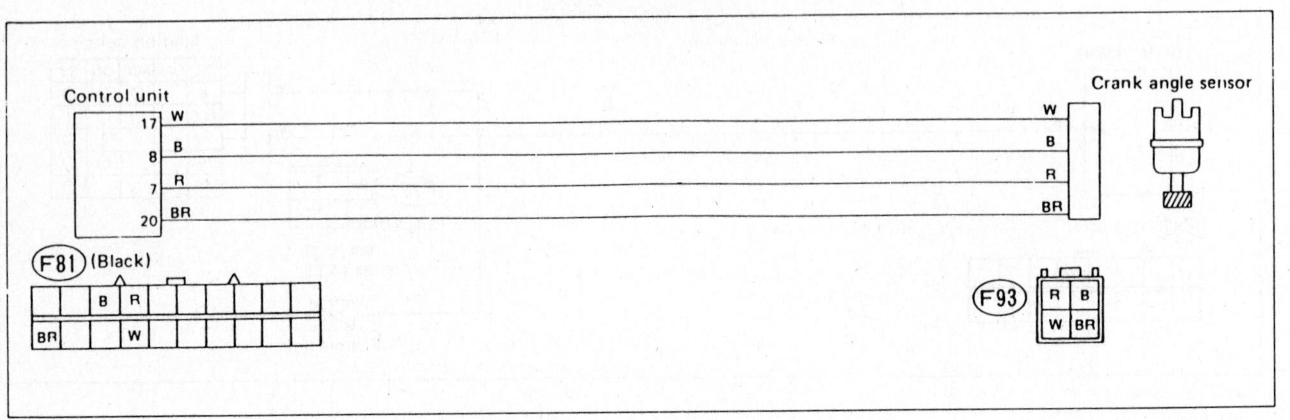


Check if trouble code is outputted in D-check mode.
- NO → Check terminals of control unit.
- YES → Turn ignition switch OFF (engine off).

Disconnect test mode connector.

Check if engine starts.
- YES → Check terminals 7, 8 and 20 of control unit connector for poor contact.
- NO → Turn ignition switch OFF.

Disconnect crank angle sensor connector.

Turn ignition switch ON (engine off).

Check if voltage across terminal (W) of crank angle sensor connector (body side) and the body is greater than 4 V.
- NO → **13-1**
- YES → Check if voltage across terminal (R) of connector (body side) and the body is greater than 10 V.
  - NO → **13-2**
  - YES → Check if continuity exists between terminal (BR) of connector (body side) and body.
    - NO → **13-3**
    - YES → Check if the female terminal of connector (body side) is open.
      - YES → Repair terminal or replace body harness.
      - NO → Replace crank angle sensor.

**Continued on Next Page**

90B21890

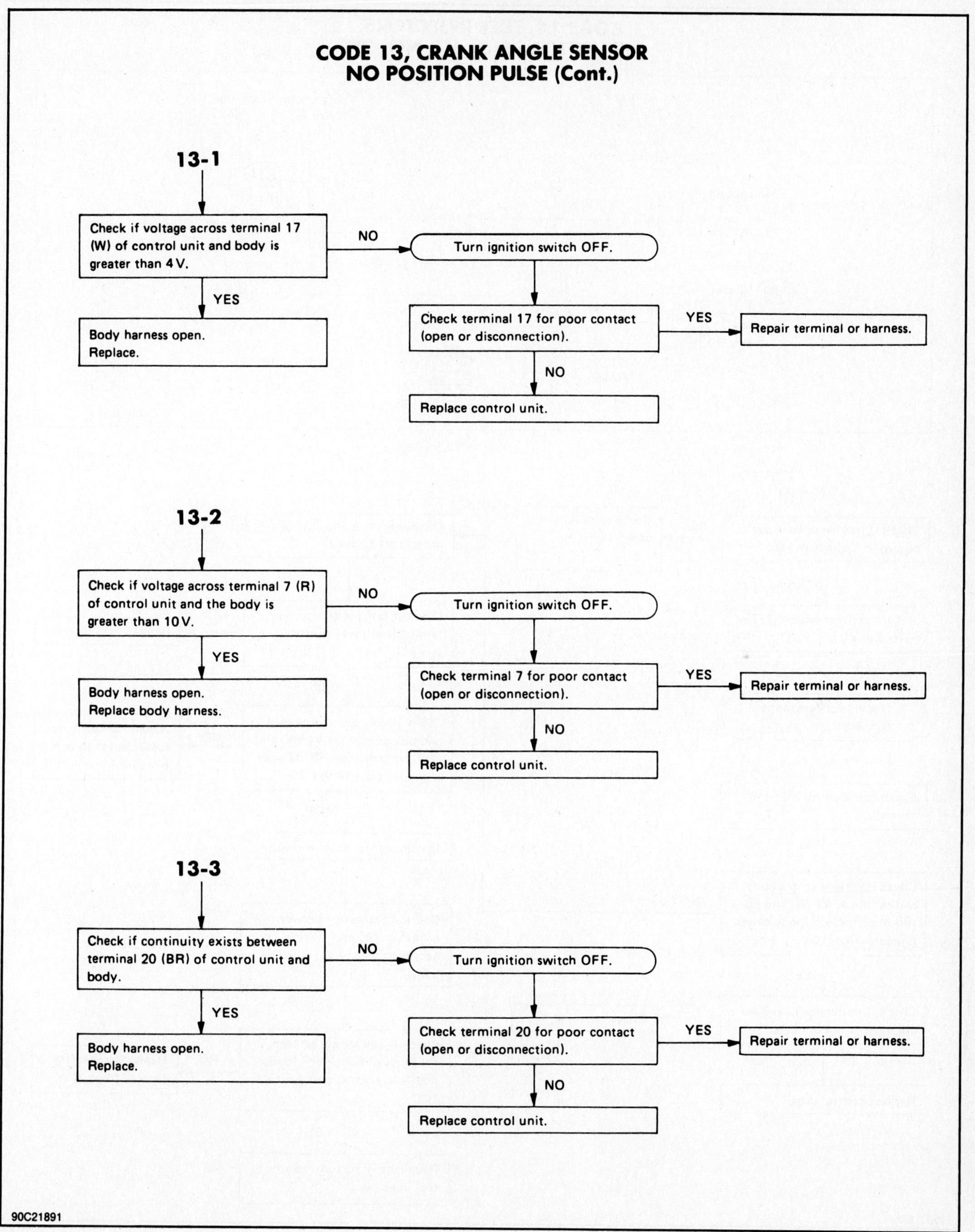
CODE 13, CRANK ANGLE SENSOR
NO POSITION PULSE (Cont.)
13-1
Check if voltage across terminal 17 (W) of control unit and body is greater than 4 V.
NO
Turn ignition switch OFF.
YES
Body harness open. Replace.
Check terminal 17 for poor contact (open or disconnection).
YES
Repair terminal or harness.
NO
Replace control unit.
13-2
Check if voltage across terminal 7 (R) of control unit and the body is greater than 10 V.
NO
Turn ignition switch OFF.
YES
Body harness open. Replace body harness.
Check terminal 7 for poor contact (open or disconnection).
YES
Repair terminal or harness.
NO
Replace control unit.
13-3
Check if continuity exists between terminal 20 (BR) of control unit and body.
NO
Turn ignition switch OFF.
YES
Body harness open. Replace.
Check terminal 20 for poor contact (open or disconnection).
YES
Repair terminal or harness.
NO
Replace control unit.
90C21891

# 1991 ENGINE PERFORMANCE
## Self-Diagnostics – Loyale – PFI (Cont.)

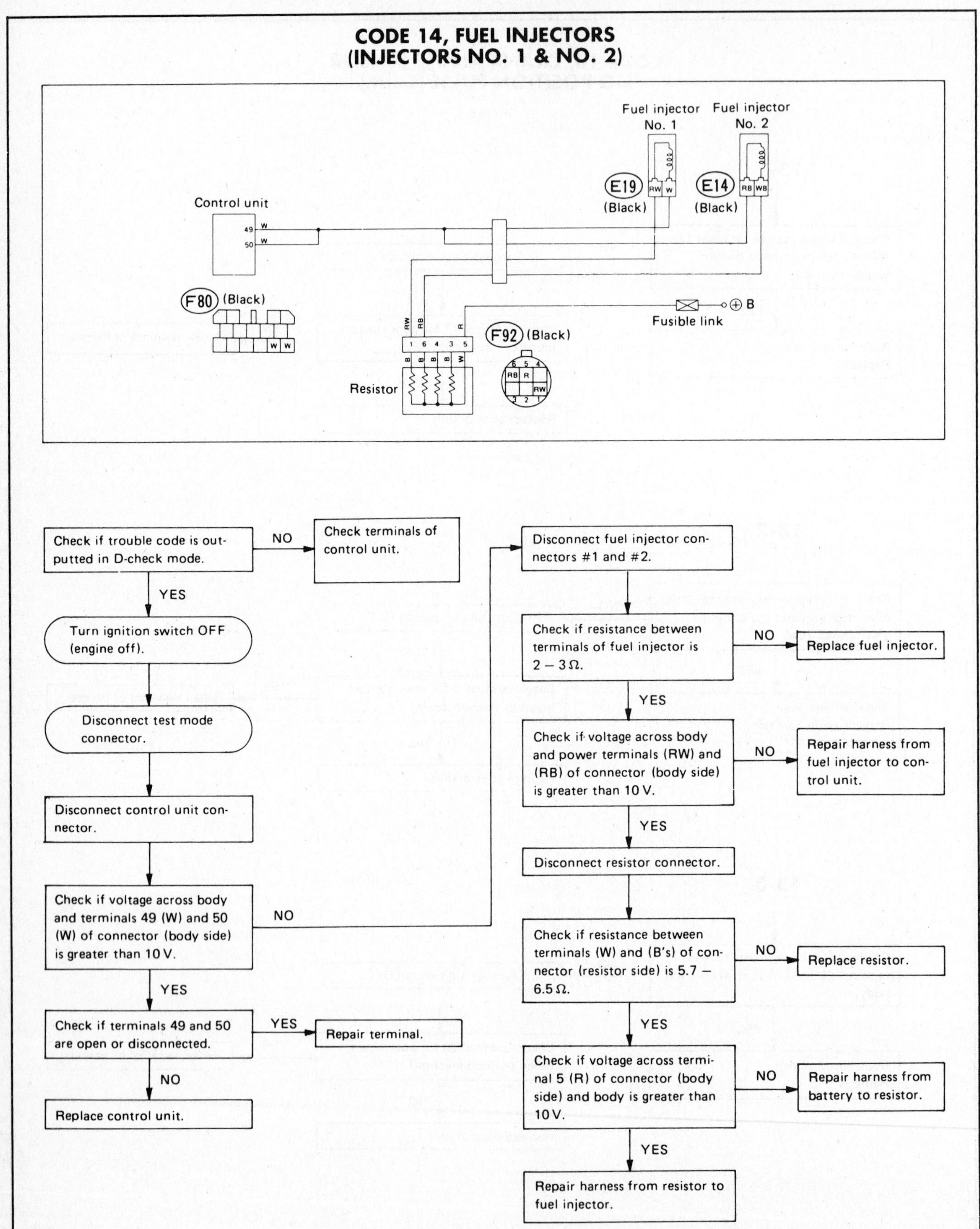

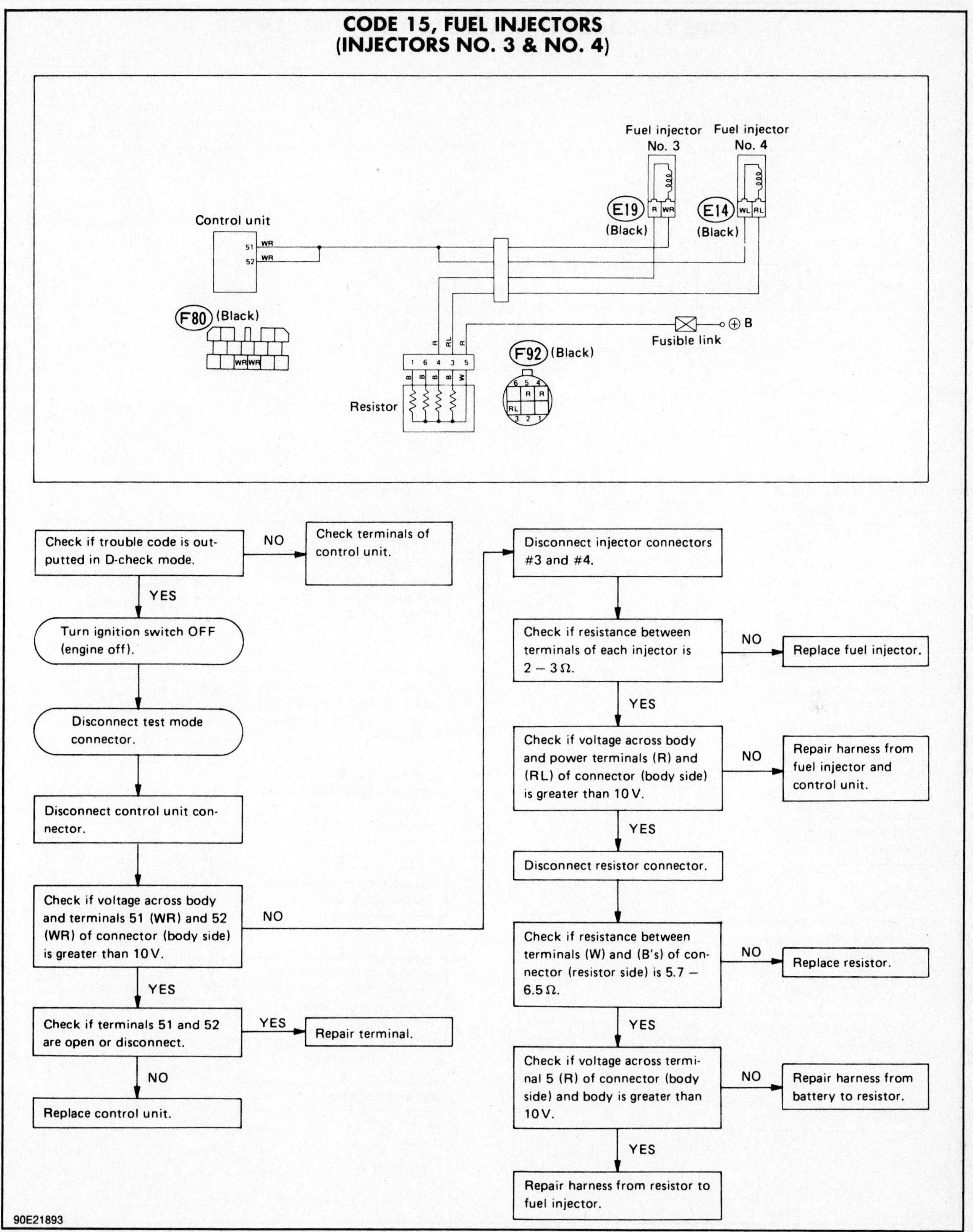

CODE 15, FUEL INJECTORS
(INJECTORS NO. 3 & NO. 4)
Fuel injector No. 3
Fuel injector No. 4
E19
(Black)
R
WR
E14
(Black)
WL
RL
Control unit
51
52
WR
WR
F80 (Black)
WR
WR
Fusible link
⊕ B
R
RL
R
1 6 4 3 5
B B B B W
Resistor
F92 (Black)
6 5 4
R R
RL
3 2 1
Check if trouble code is outputted in D-check mode.
NO
Check terminals of control unit.
YES
Turn ignition switch OFF (engine off).
Disconnect test mode connector.
Disconnect control unit connector.
Check if voltage across body and terminals 51 (WR) and 52 (WR) of connector (body side) is greater than 10 V.
NO
YES
Check if terminals 51 and 52 are open or disconnect.
YES
Repair terminal.
NO
Replace control unit.
Disconnect injector connectors #3 and #4.
Check if resistance between terminals of each injector is 2 – 3 Ω.
NO
Replace fuel injector.
YES
Check if voltage across body and power terminals (R) and (RL) of connector (body side) is greater than 10 V.
NO
Repair harness from fuel injector and control unit.
YES
Disconnect resistor connector.
Check if resistance between terminals (W) and (B's) of connector (resistor side) is 5.7 – 6.5 Ω.
NO
Replace resistor.
YES
Check if voltage across terminal 5 (R) of connector (body side) and body is greater than 10 V.
NO
Repair harness from battery to resistor.
YES
Repair harness from resistor to fuel injector.
90E21893

# 1991 ENGINE PERFORMANCE
## Self-Diagnostics – Loyale – PFI (Cont.)

### CODE 21, COOLANT (WATER) TEMPERATURE SENSOR

Control unit
9 WB
WB WB
Water temperature sensor
WB
BR
E12
WB BR
F81 (Black)
WB
F41 (Black)
WB
Intermediate connector
E EG

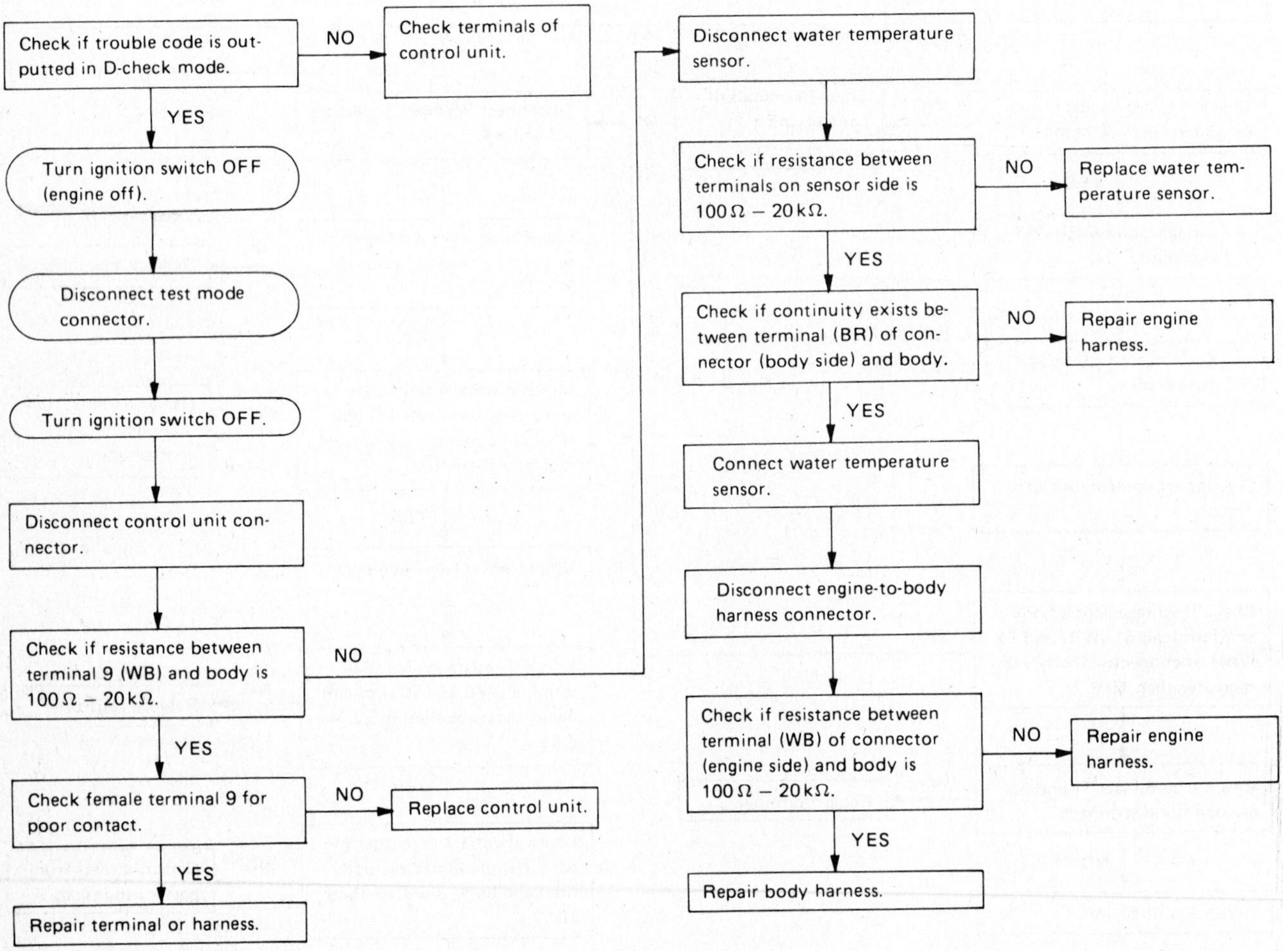

Check if trouble code is outputted in D-check mode.
- NO → Check terminals of control unit.
- YES ↓

Turn ignition switch OFF (engine off).
↓
Disconnect test mode connector.
↓
Turn ignition switch OFF.
↓
Disconnect control unit connector.
↓
Check if resistance between terminal 9 (WB) and body is 100 Ω – 20 kΩ.
- NO → Disconnect water temperature sensor.
- YES ↓

Check female terminal 9 for poor contact.
- NO → Replace control unit.
- YES → Repair terminal or harness.

Disconnect water temperature sensor.
↓
Check if resistance between terminals on sensor side is 100 Ω – 20 kΩ.
- NO → Replace water temperature sensor.
- YES ↓

Check if continuity exists between terminal (BR) of connector (body side) and body.
- NO → Repair engine harness.
- YES ↓

Connect water temperature sensor.
↓
Disconnect engine-to-body harness connector.
↓
Check if resistance between terminal (WB) of connector (engine side) and body is 100 Ω – 20 kΩ.
- NO → Repair engine harness.
- YES → Repair body harness.

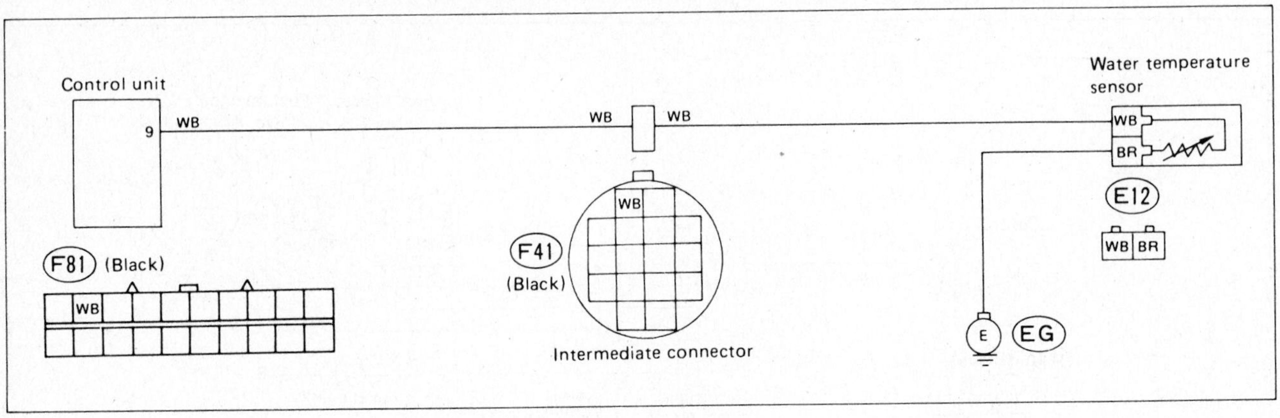

90F21894

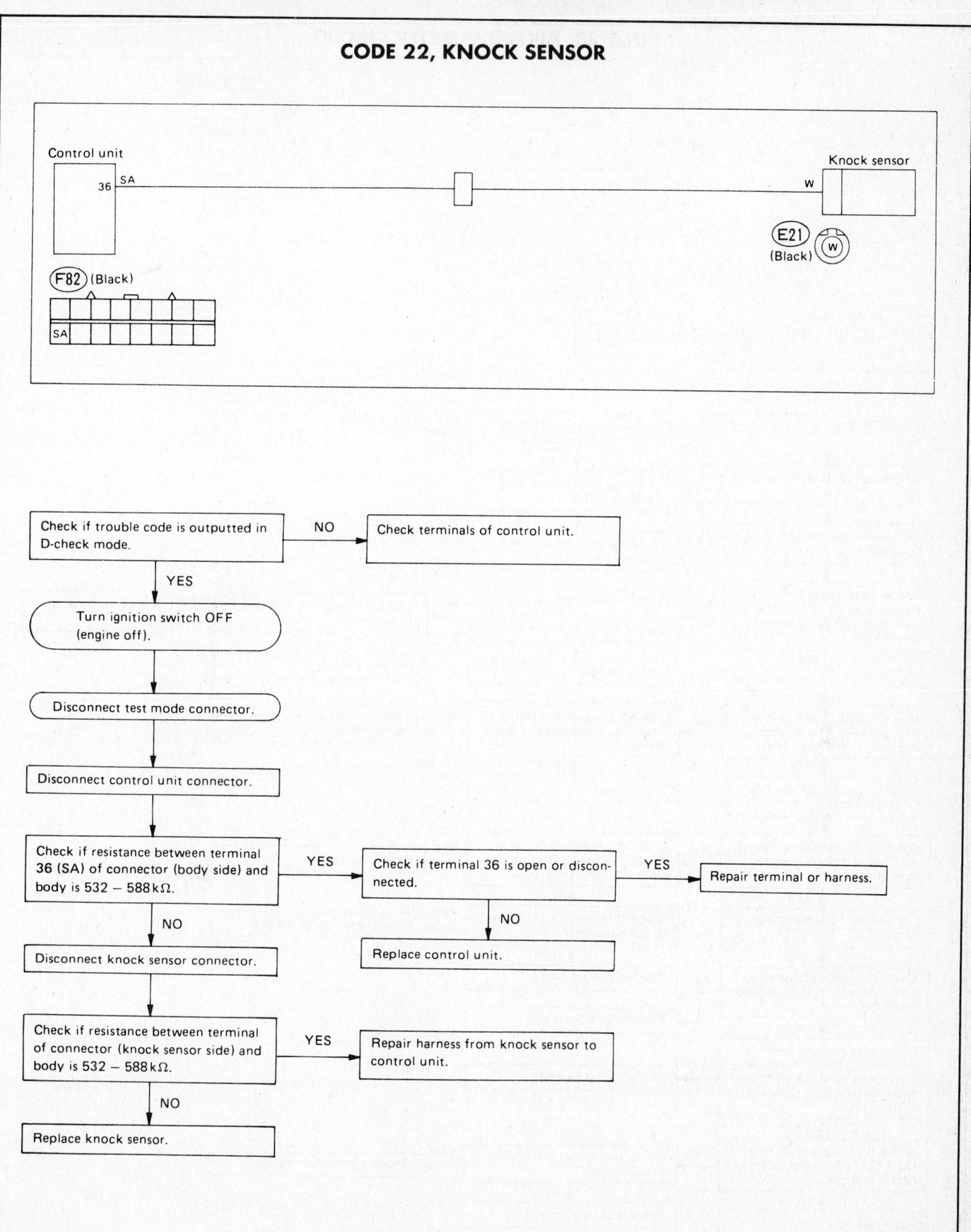
CODE 22, KNOCK SENSOR
Control unit
36
SA
Knock sensor
W
E21
(Black)
W
F82 (Black)
SA
Check if trouble code is outputted in D-check mode.
NO
Check terminals of control unit.
YES
Turn ignition switch OFF (engine off).
Disconnect test mode connector.
Disconnect control unit connector.
Check if resistance between terminal 36 (SA) of connector (body side) and body is 532 – 588 kΩ.
YES
Check if terminal 36 is open or disconnected.
YES
Repair terminal or harness.
NO
Replace control unit.
NO
Disconnect knock sensor connector.
Check if resistance between terminal of connector (knock sensor side) and body is 532 – 588 kΩ.
YES
Repair harness from knock sensor to control unit.
NO
Replace knock sensor.
90G21895

# 1991 ENGINE PERFORMANCE
## Self-Diagnostics – Loyale – PFI (Cont.)

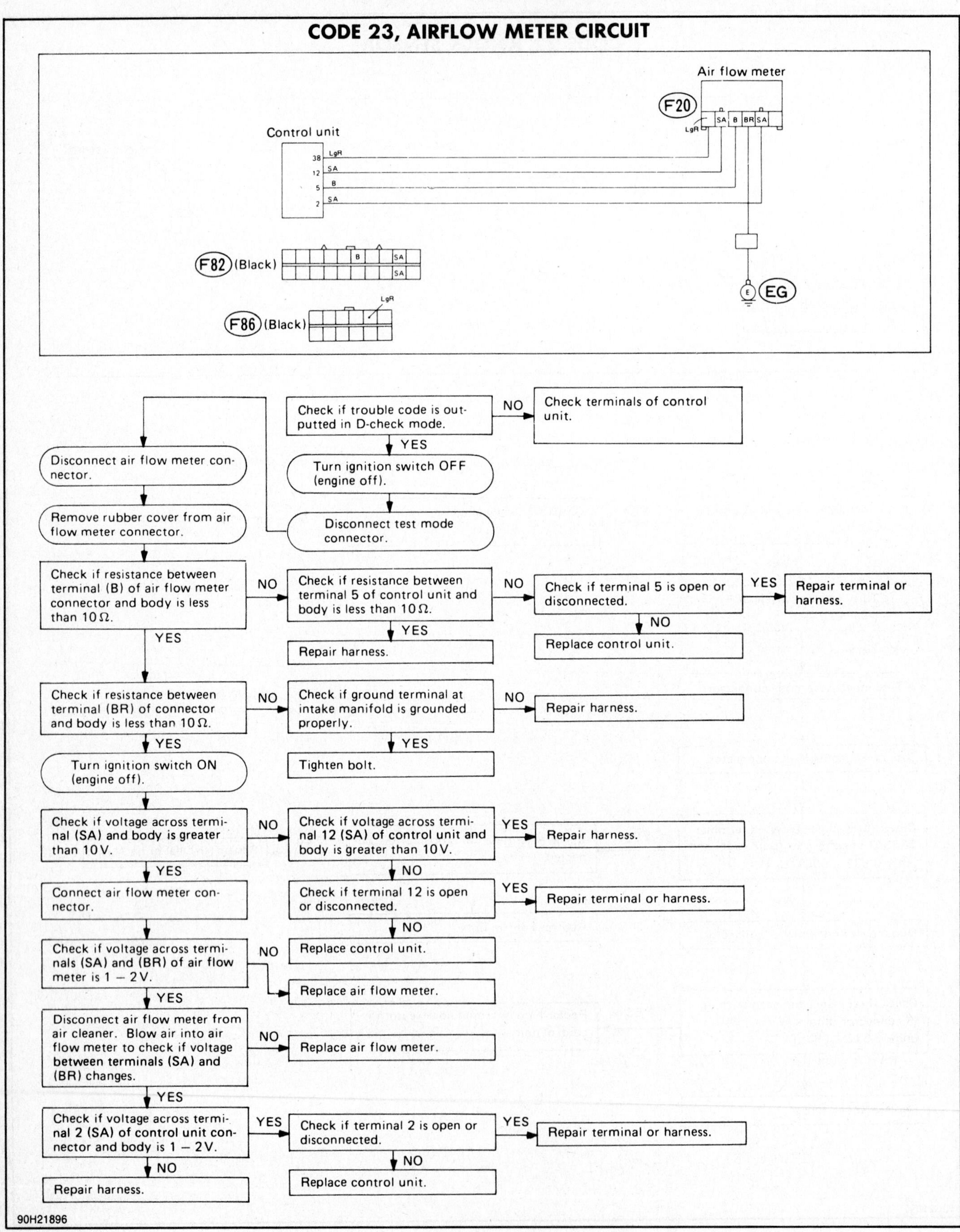

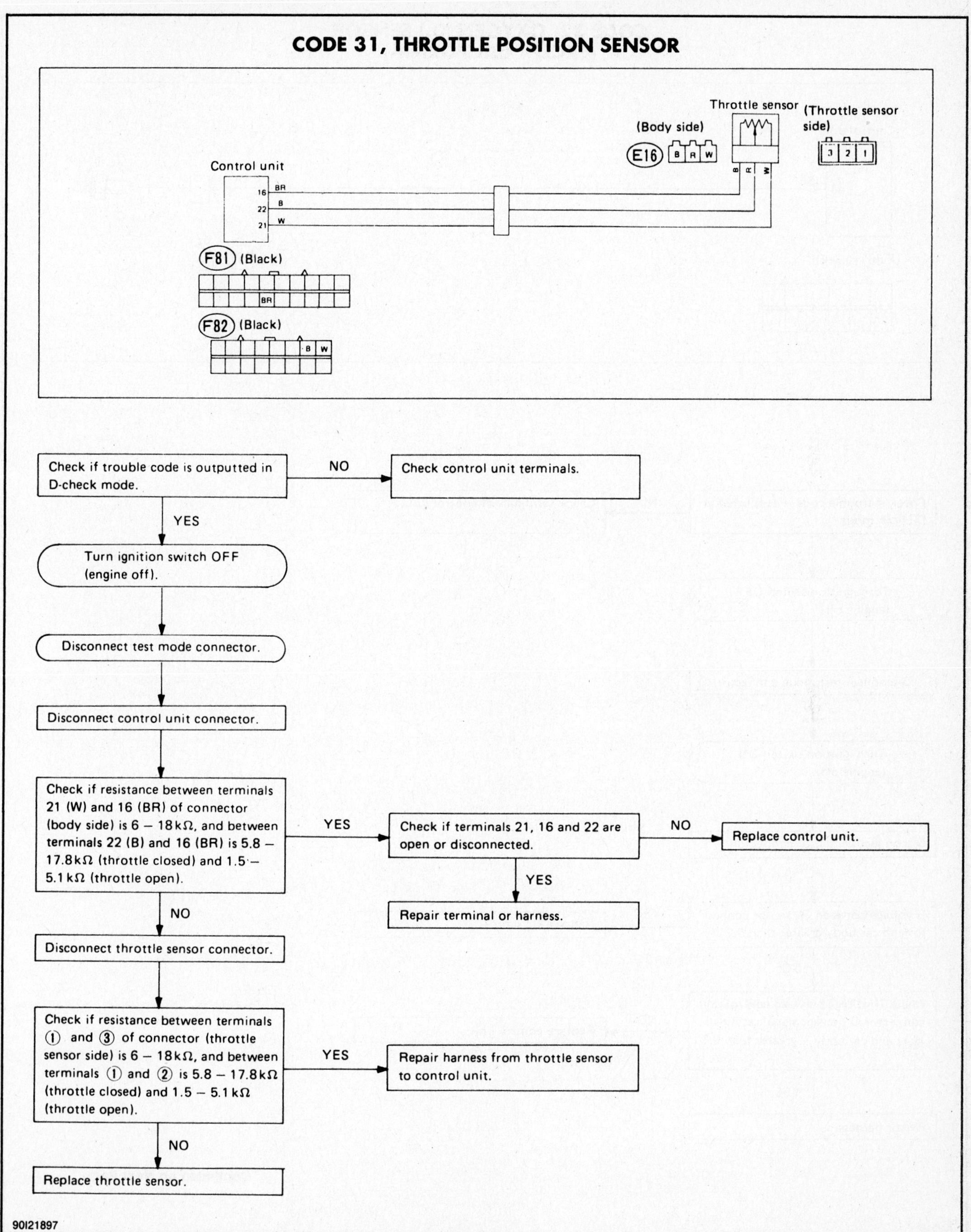
CODE 31, THROTTLE POSITION SENSOR
Throttle sensor
(Throttle sensor side)
(Body side)
E16
B R W
3 2 1
Control unit
16 BR
22 B
21 W
F81 (Black)
BR
F82 (Black)
B W
Check if trouble code is outputted in D-check mode.
NO
Check control unit terminals.
YES
Turn ignition switch OFF (engine off).
Disconnect test mode connector.
Disconnect control unit connector.
Check if resistance between terminals 21 (W) and 16 (BR) of connector (body side) is 6 – 18 kΩ, and between terminals 22 (B) and 16 (BR) is 5.8 – 17.8 kΩ (throttle closed) and 1.5 – 5.1 kΩ (throttle open).
YES
Check if terminals 21, 16 and 22 are open or disconnected.
NO
Replace control unit.
YES
Repair terminal or harness.
NO
Disconnect throttle sensor connector.
Check if resistance between terminals ① and ③ of connector (throttle sensor side) is 6 – 18 kΩ, and between terminals ① and ② is 5.8 – 17.8 kΩ (throttle closed) and 1.5 – 5.1 kΩ (throttle open).
YES
Repair harness from throttle sensor to control unit.
NO
Replace throttle sensor.
90I21897

# 1991 ENGINE PERFORMANCE
# Self-Diagnostics – Loyale – PFI (Cont.)

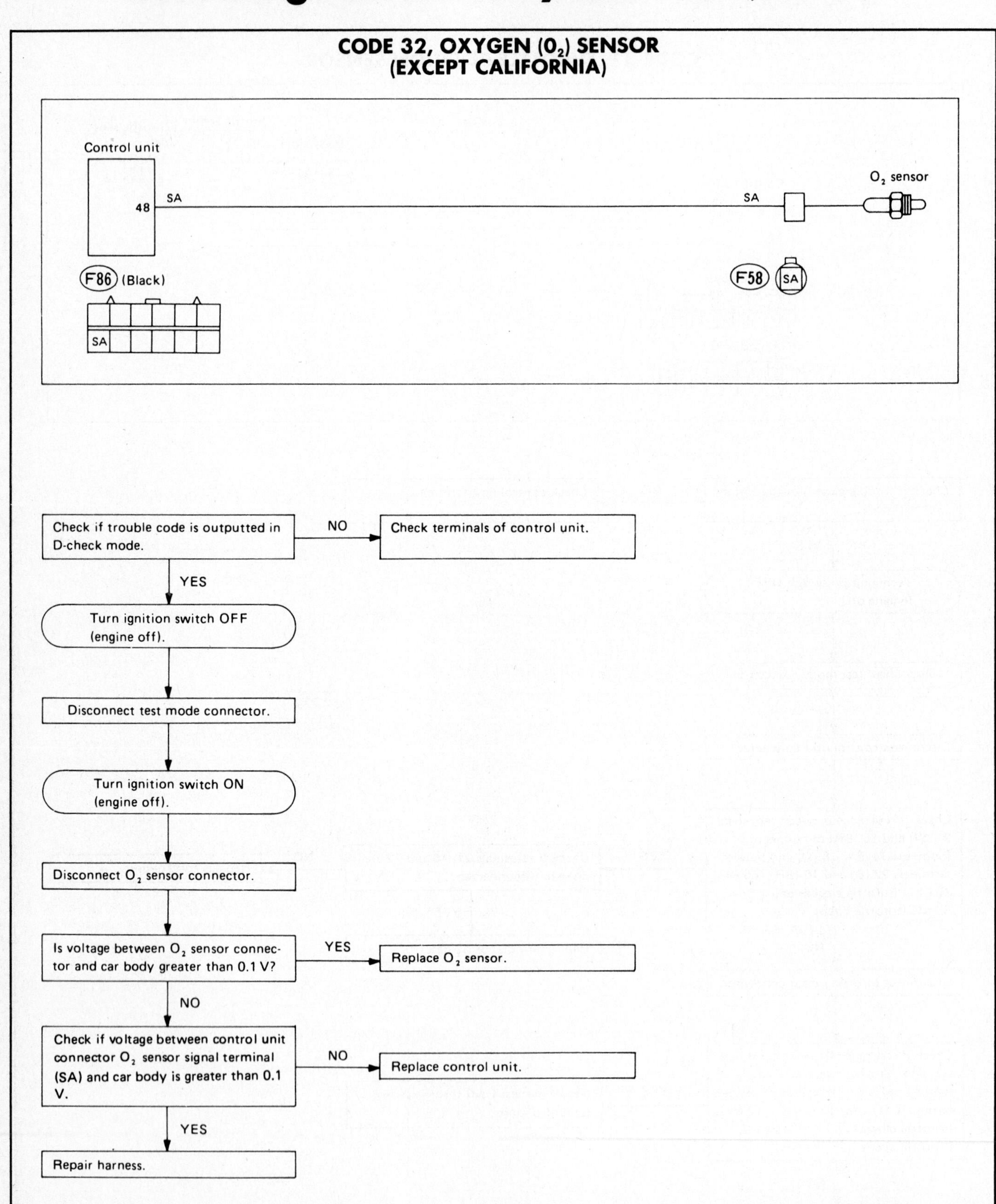

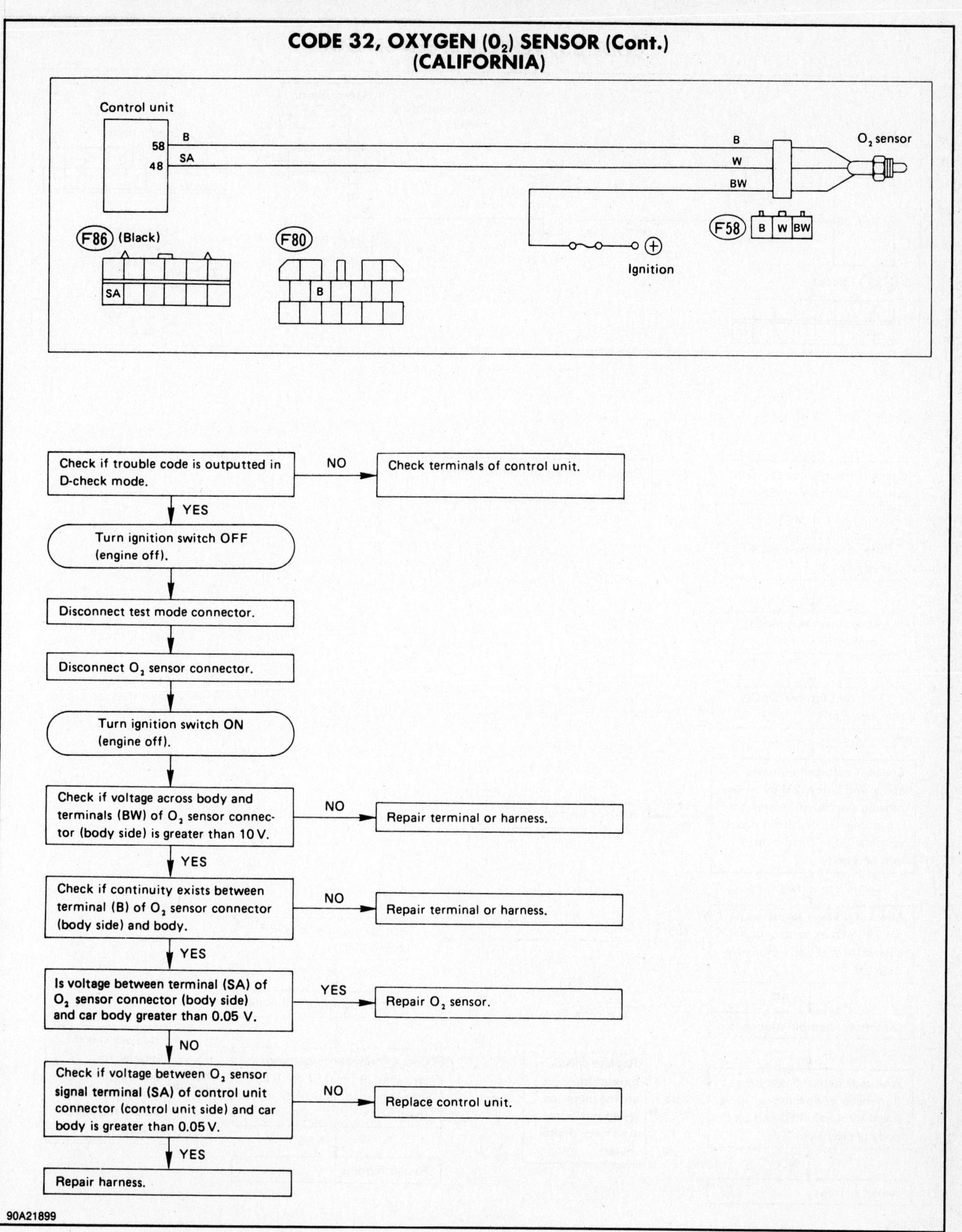
CODE 32, OXYGEN ($O_2$) SENSOR (Cont.)
(CALIFORNIA)
Control unit
58
48
B
SA
B
W
BW
$O_2$ sensor
F58
B W BW
F86 (Black)
SA
F80
B
Ignition
Check if trouble code is outputted in D-check mode.
NO
Check terminals of control unit.
YES
Turn ignition switch OFF (engine off).
Disconnect test mode connector.
Disconnect $O_2$ sensor connector.
Turn ignition switch ON (engine off).
Check if voltage across body and terminals (BW) of $O_2$ sensor connector (body side) is greater than 10 V.
NO
Repair terminal or harness.
YES
Check if continuity exists between terminal (B) of $O_2$ sensor connector (body side) and body.
NO
Repair terminal or harness.
YES
Is voltage between terminal (SA) of $O_2$ sensor connector (body side) and car body greater than 0.05 V.
YES
Repair $O_2$ sensor.
NO
Check if voltage between $O_2$ sensor signal terminal (SA) of control unit connector (control unit side) and car body is greater than 0.05 V.
NO
Replace control unit.
YES
Repair harness.
90A21899

# 1991 ENGINE PERFORMANCE
## Self-Diagnostics – Loyale – PFI (Cont.)

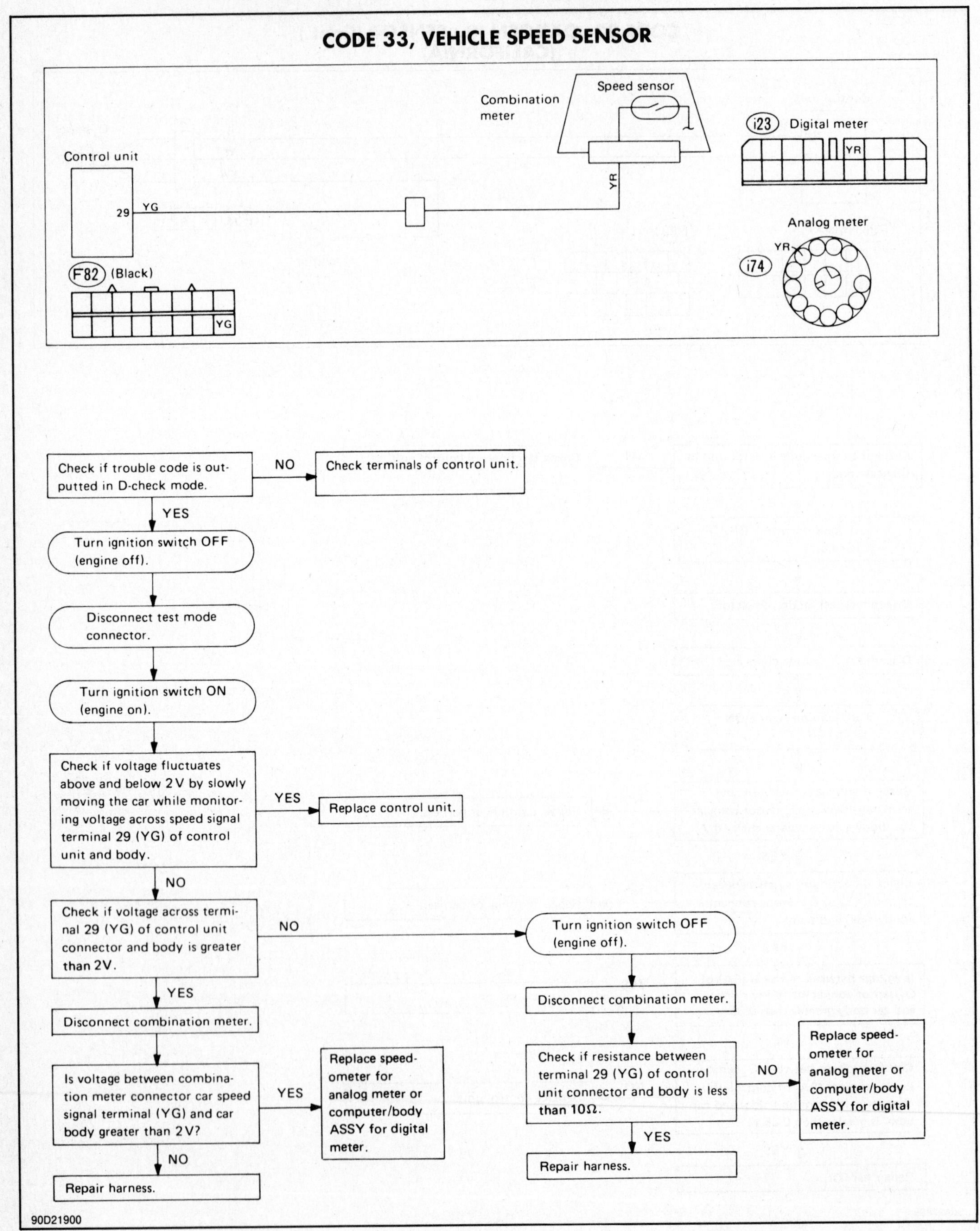

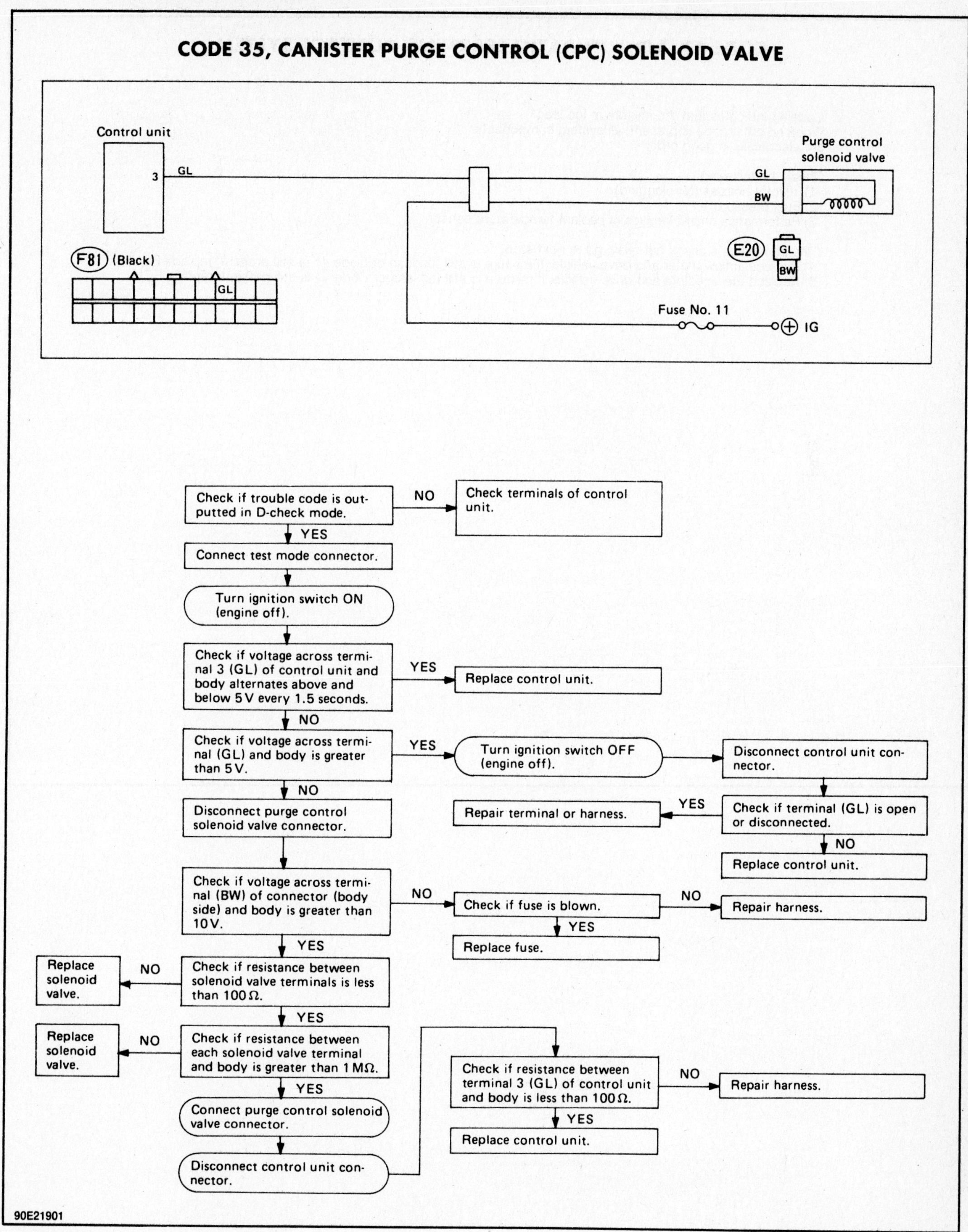

CODE 35, CANISTER PURGE CONTROL (CPC) SOLENOID VALVE
Control unit
3
GL
Purge control solenoid valve
GL
BW
F81 (Black)
GL
E20
GL
BW
Fuse No. 11
IG
Check if trouble code is outputted in D-check mode.
NO
Check terminals of control unit.
YES
Connect test mode connector.
Turn ignition switch ON (engine off).
Check if voltage across terminal 3 (GL) of control unit and body alternates above and below 5 V every 1.5 seconds.
YES
Replace control unit.
NO
Check if voltage across terminal (GL) and body is greater than 5 V.
YES
Turn ignition switch OFF (engine off).
Disconnect control unit connector.
Check if terminal (GL) is open or disconnected.
YES
Repair terminal or harness.
NO
Replace control unit.
NO
Disconnect purge control solenoid valve connector.
Check if voltage across terminal (BW) of connector (body side) and body is greater than 10 V.
NO
Check if fuse is blown.
NO
Repair harness.
YES
Replace fuse.
YES
Check if resistance between solenoid valve terminals is less than 100 Ω.
NO
Replace solenoid valve.
YES
Check if resistance between each solenoid valve terminal and body is greater than 1 MΩ.
NO
Replace solenoid valve.
YES
Connect purge control solenoid valve connector.
Disconnect control unit connector.
Check if resistance between terminal 3 (GL) of control unit and body is less than 100 Ω.
NO
Repair harness.
YES
Replace control unit.
90E21901

# 1991 ENGINE PERFORMANCE
# Self-Diagnostics – Loyale – PFI (Cont.)

## CODE 41, AIR/FUEL RATIO LEARNING CONTROL SYSTEM

Code 41 indicates that the mixture is too lean.
When no other code is present, all system components are electrically in good order.

Check the following:

1) Injector nozzles (for clogging).
2) Fuel pressure.
3) Performance characteristics of coolant temperature sensor.

If the above steps check out okay, go to next step.

4) Replace airflow meter and drive vehicle. If mixture is still too lean or Code 41 is still present, replace ECU.
5) Replace fuel injectors and drive vehicle. If mixture is still too lean or Code 41 is still present, replace ECU.

## CODE 42, IDLE SWITCH

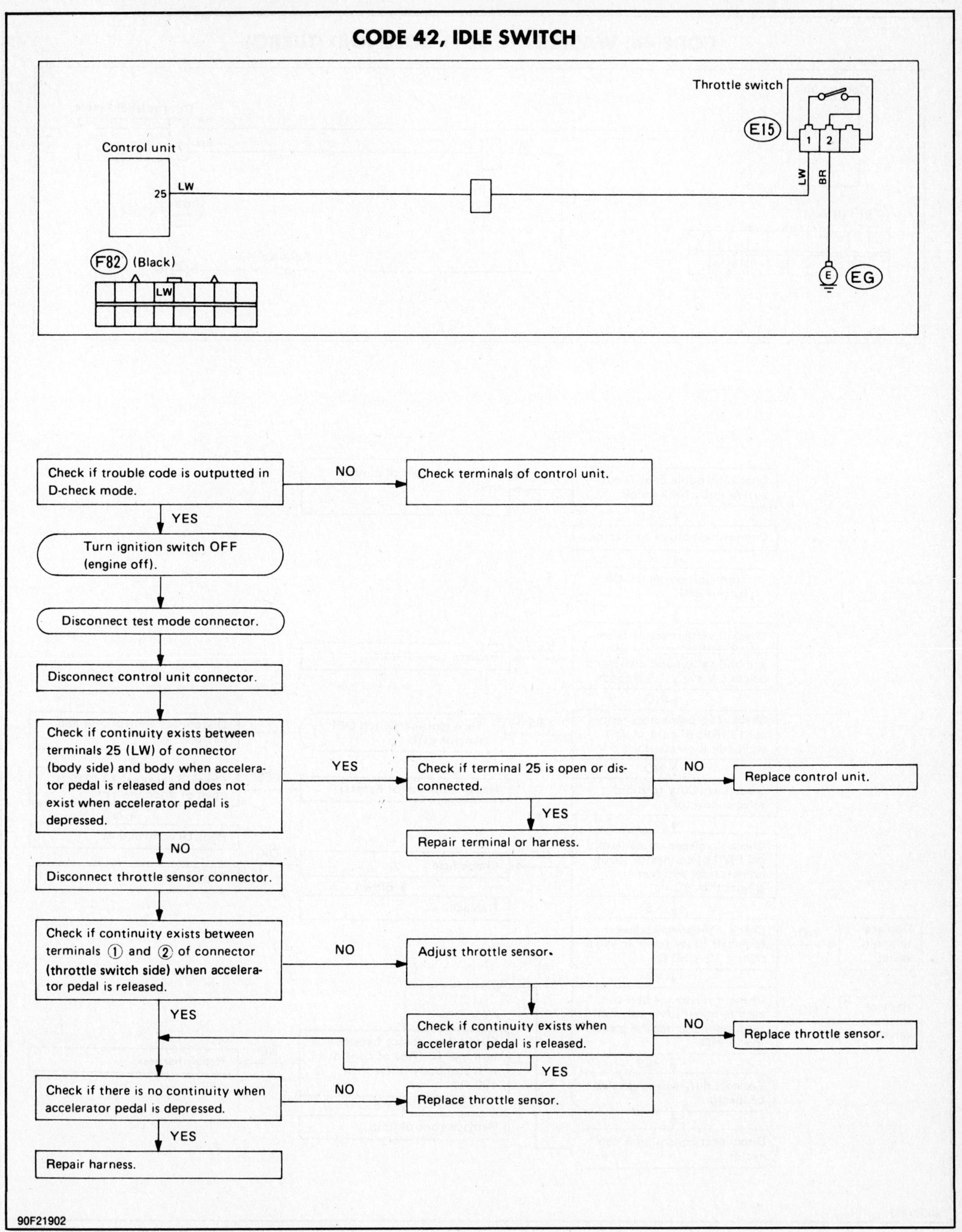

# 1991 ENGINE PERFORMANCE
## Self-Diagnostics – Loyale – PFI (Cont.)

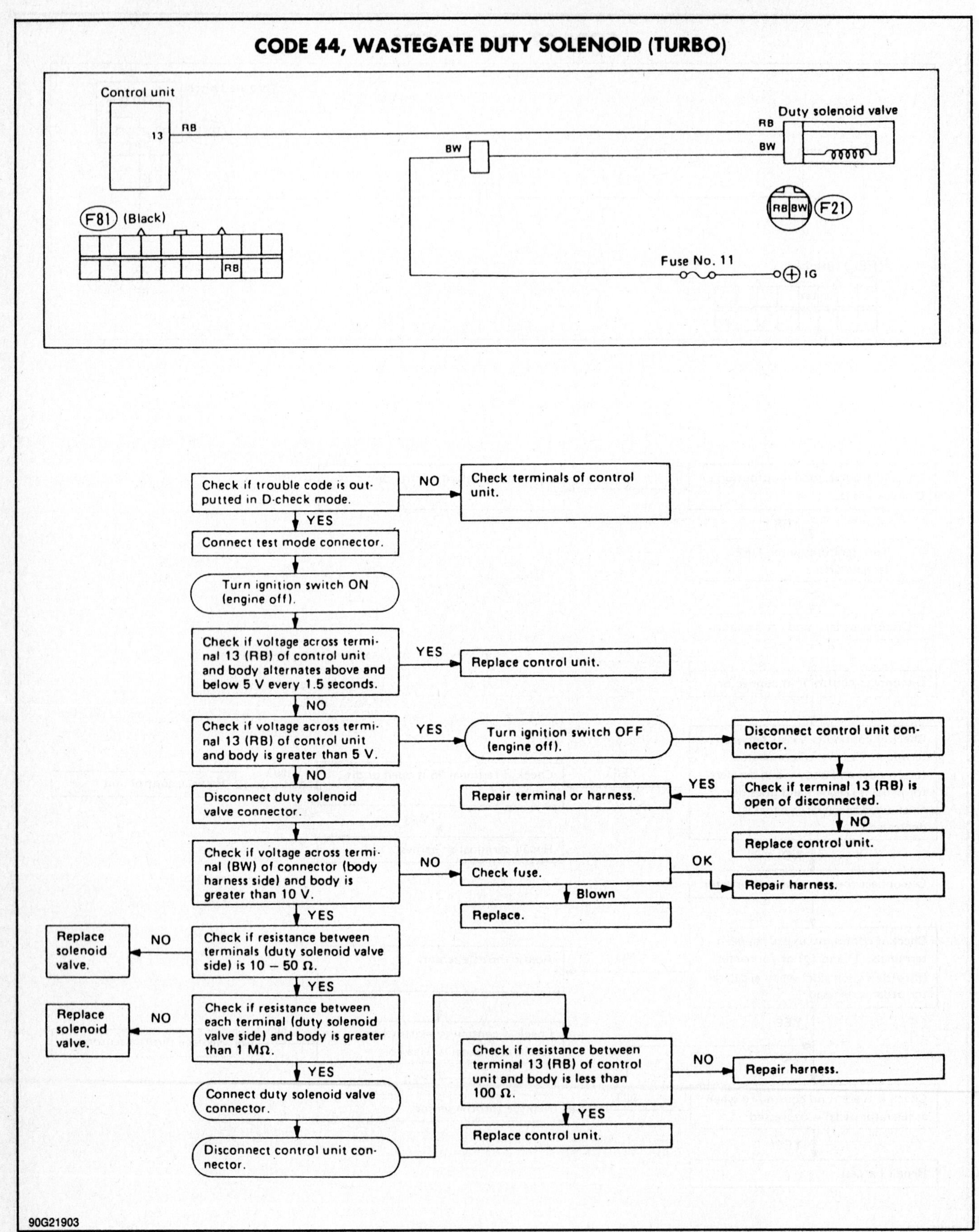

## LOYALE (TBI) CODE CHARTS

### BASIC OPERATION OF SELF-DIAGNOSTIC SYSTEM

**NO TROUBLE**

O : CONNECT    X : DISCONNECT

| Engine | Read memory connector | Test mode connector | CHECK ENGINE light | $O_2$ monitor lamp | Remarks |
|---|---|---|---|---|---|
| ON | X | X | OFF | $O_2$ monitor | |
| ON | O | X | OFF | $O_2$ monitor | |
| *ON | X | O | ** OFF → Blink | OFF | Vehicle specification code is outputted when CHECK ENGINE light is OFF. |
| *ON | O | O | OFF → Blink | OFF | All memory stored in control unit is cleared after CHECK ENGINE light blinks. |
| OFF (Ignition switch ON) | O | X | ON | Vehicle specification code | Before starting the engine, the self-diagnosis system assumes the engine to be in a NO TROUBLE condition. |
| OFF (Ignition switch ON) | X | X | ON | Vehicle specification code | |
| OFF (Ignition switch ON) | X | O | ON | Vehicle specification code | |
| OFF (Ignition switch ON) | O | O | ON | Vehicle specification code | |

**TROUBLE**

| Engine | Read memory connector | Test mode connector | CHECK ENGINE light | $O_2$ monitor lamp | Remarks |
|---|---|---|---|---|---|
| ON | X | X | ON | Trouble code | |
| ON | O | X | ON | Trouble code (memory) | |
| *ON | X | O | ** OFF → ON | Trouble code | Vehicle specification code is outputted when CHECK ENGINE light is OFF. |
| *ON | O | O | OFF → ON | Trouble code | |
| OFF (Ignition switch ON) | O | X | ON | Trouble code (memory) | |
| STALL (Ignition switch ON) | X | X | ON | Trouble code | |
| STALL (Ignition switch ON) | X | O | ON | Trouble code | |
| STALL (Ignition switch ON) | O | O | ON | Trouble code | |

***: Ignition timing is set to 20° BTDC (when the engine is on, test mode connector is connected, and idle switch is ON).**
****: CHECK ENGINE light remains off until engine is operated at speed greater than 2,000 rpm for at least 40 seconds.**

90G21853

# 1991 ENGINE PERFORMANCE
## Self-Diagnostics – Loyale – TBI (Cont.)

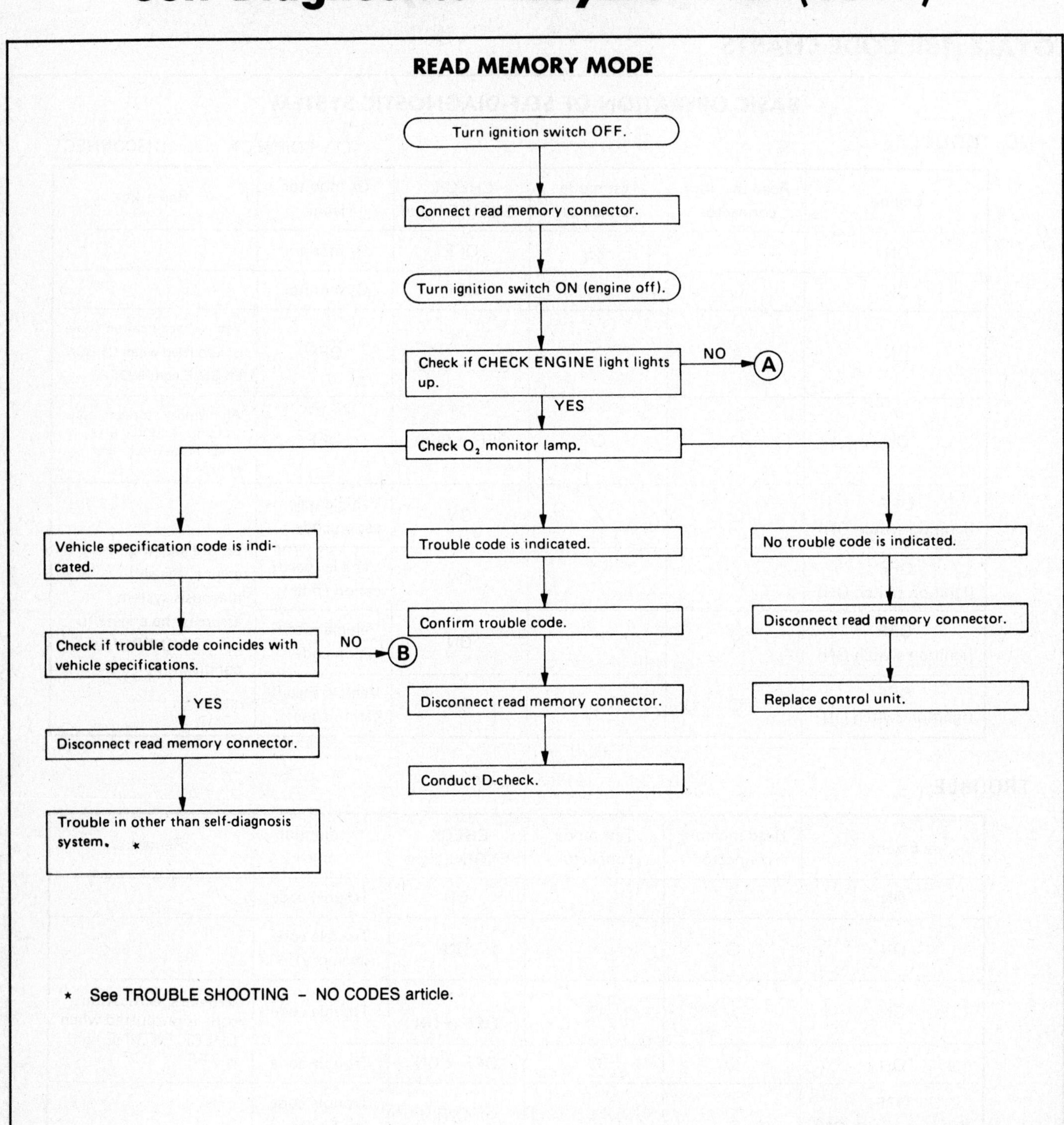


Continued on Next Page

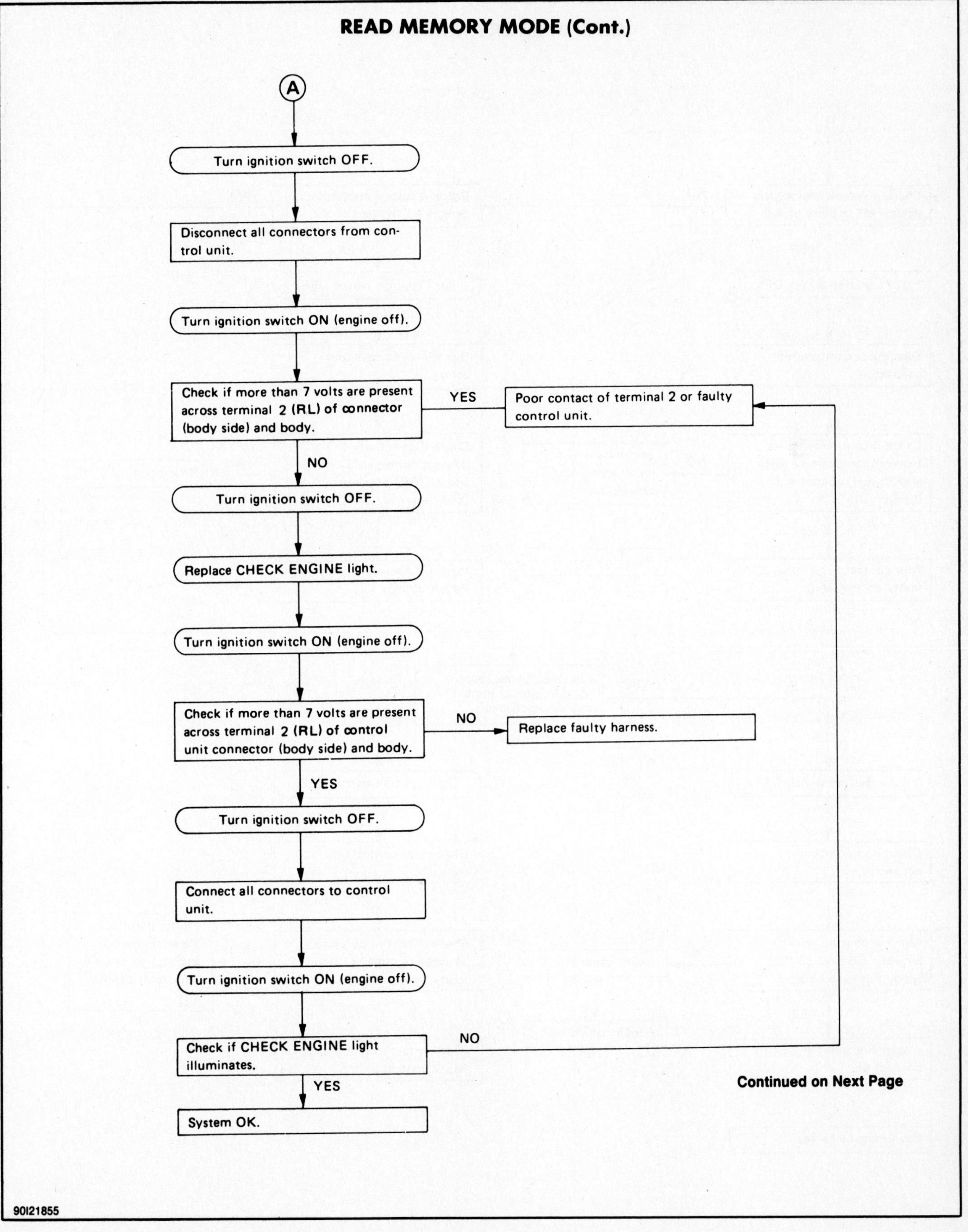
READ MEMORY MODE (Cont.)
A
Turn ignition switch OFF.
Disconnect all connectors from control unit.
Turn ignition switch ON (engine off).
Check if more than 7 volts are present across terminal 2 (RL) of connector (body side) and body.
YES
Poor contact of terminal 2 or faulty control unit.
NO
Turn ignition switch OFF.
Replace CHECK ENGINE light.
Turn ignition switch ON (engine off).
Check if more than 7 volts are present across terminal 2 (RL) of control unit connector (body side) and body.
NO
Replace faulty harness.
YES
Turn ignition switch OFF.
Connect all connectors to control unit.
Turn ignition switch ON (engine off).
Check if CHECK ENGINE light illuminates.
NO
YES
System OK.
Continued on Next Page
90I21855

# 1991 ENGINE PERFORMANCE
## Self-Diagnostics – Loyale – TBI (Cont.)

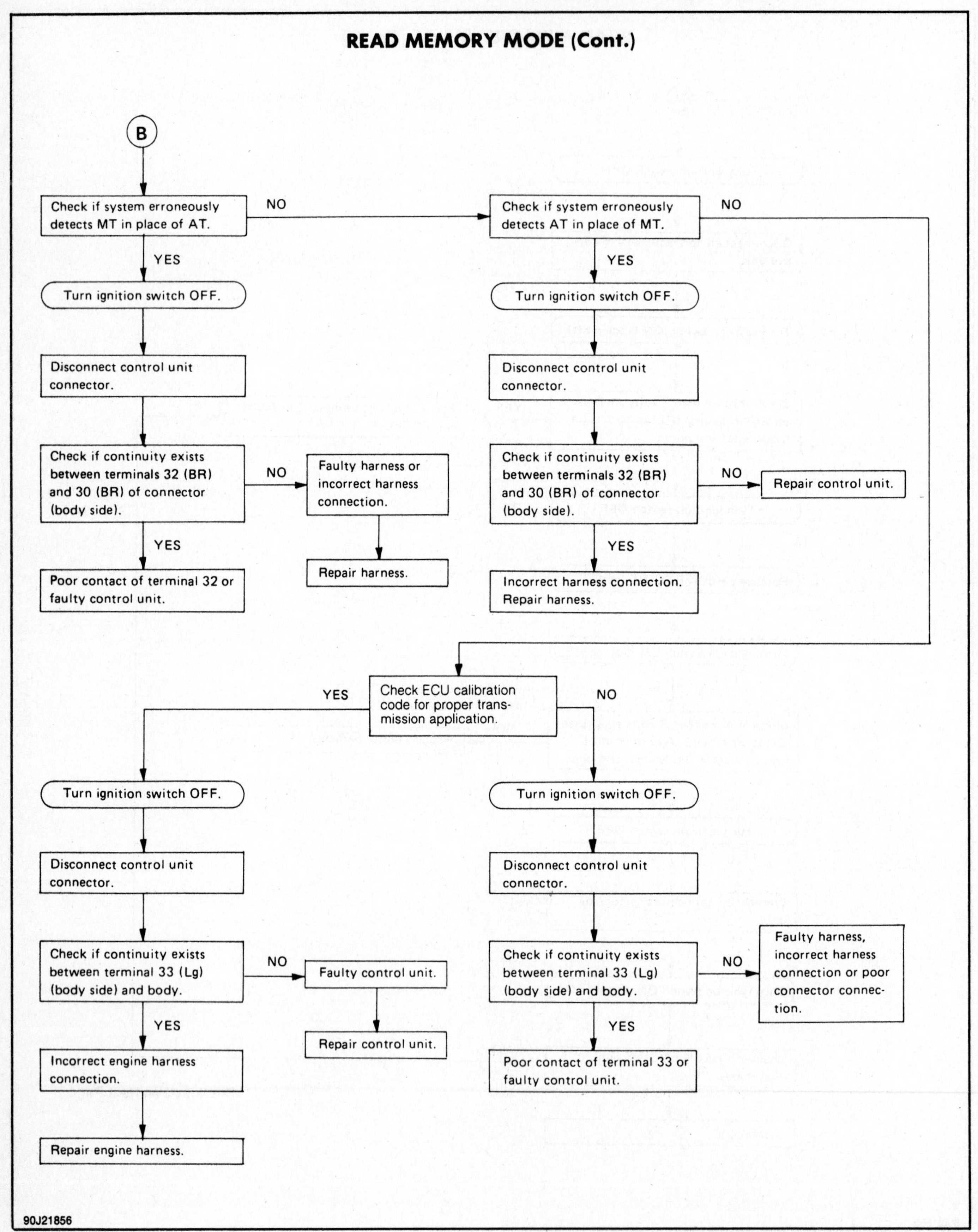

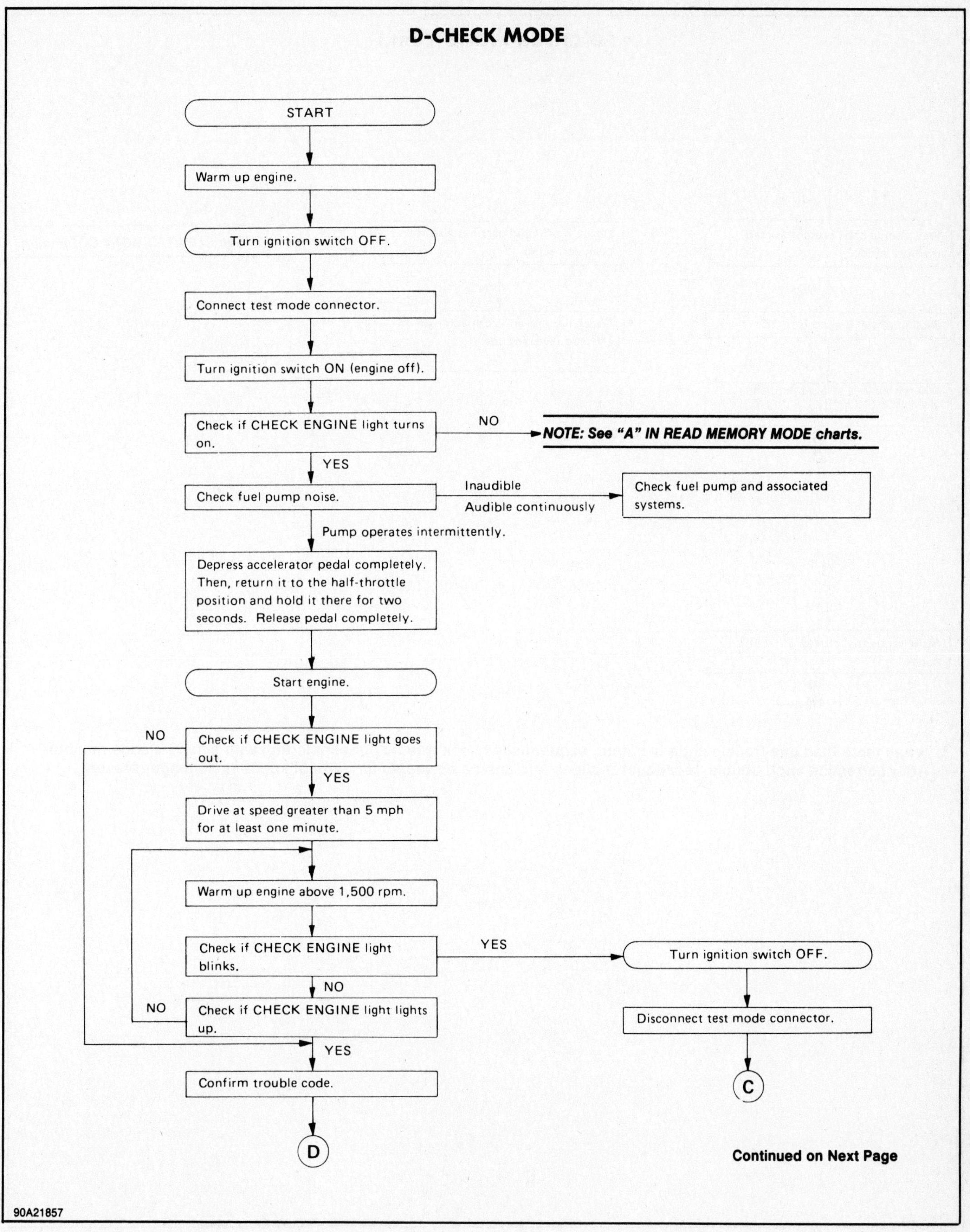

D-CHECK MODE
START
Warm up engine.
Turn ignition switch OFF.
Connect test mode connector.
Turn ignition switch ON (engine off).
Check if CHECK ENGINE light turns on.
NO
NOTE: See "A" IN READ MEMORY MODE charts.
YES
Check fuel pump noise.
Inaudible
Audible continuously
Check fuel pump and associated systems.
Pump operates intermittently.
Depress accelerator pedal completely. Then, return it to the half-throttle position and hold it there for two seconds. Release pedal completely.
Start engine.
NO
Check if CHECK ENGINE light goes out.
YES
Drive at speed greater than 5 mph for at least one minute.
Warm up engine above 1,500 rpm.
Check if CHECK ENGINE light blinks.
YES
Turn ignition switch OFF.
Disconnect test mode connector.
C
NO
NO
Check if CHECK ENGINE light lights up.
YES
Confirm trouble code.
D
Continued on Next Page
90A21857

# 1991 ENGINE PERFORMANCE
## Self-Diagnostics – Loyale – TBI (Cont.)

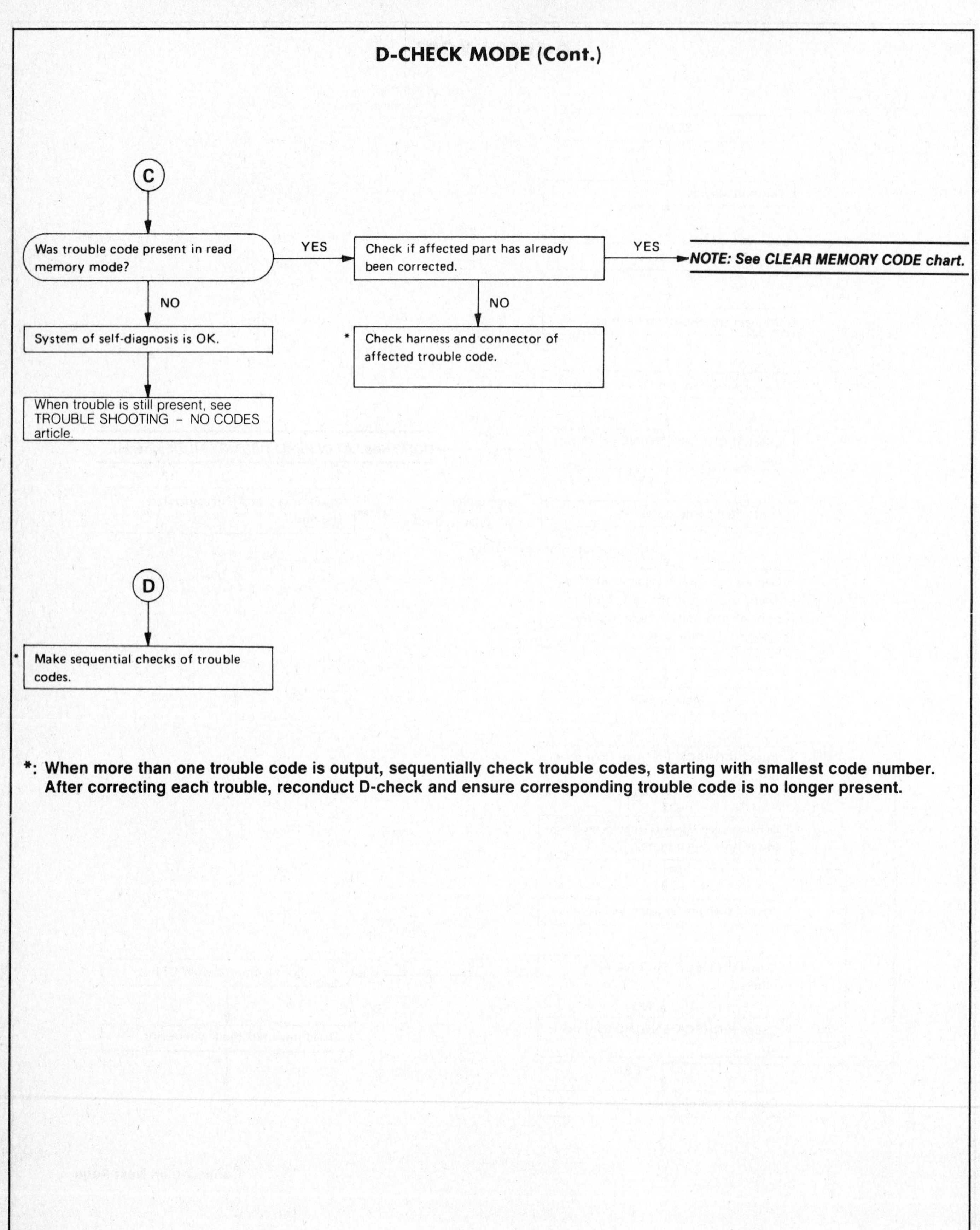
D-CHECK MODE (Cont.)
C
Was trouble code present in read memory mode?
YES
Check if affected part has already been corrected.
YES
NOTE: See CLEAR MEMORY CODE chart.
NO
System of self-diagnosis is OK.
When trouble is still present, see TROUBLE SHOOTING - NO CODES article.
NO
* Check harness and connector of affected trouble code.
D
* Make sequential checks of trouble codes.
*: When more than one trouble code is output, sequentially check trouble codes, starting with smallest code number. After correcting each trouble, reconduct D-check and ensure corresponding trouble code is no longer present.
90B21858

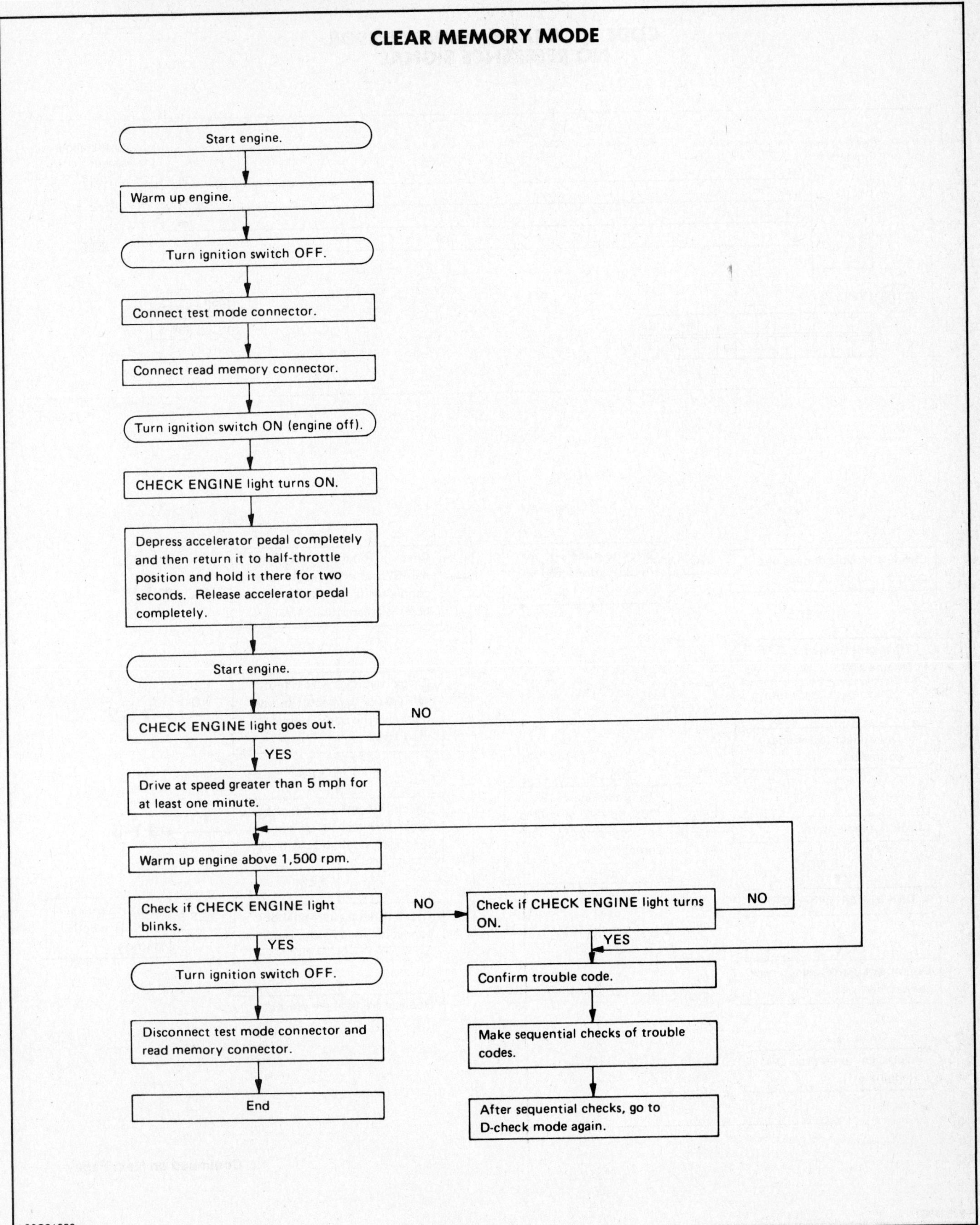
CLEAR MEMORY MODE
Start engine.
Warm up engine.
Turn ignition switch OFF.
Connect test mode connector.
Connect read memory connector.
Turn ignition switch ON (engine off).
CHECK ENGINE light turns ON.
Depress accelerator pedal completely and then return it to half-throttle position and hold it there for two seconds. Release accelerator pedal completely.
Start engine.
CHECK ENGINE light goes out.
NO
YES
Drive at speed greater than 5 mph for at least one minute.
Warm up engine above 1,500 rpm.
Check if CHECK ENGINE light blinks.
NO
Check if CHECK ENGINE light turns ON.
NO
YES
YES
Turn ignition switch OFF.
Disconnect test mode connector and read memory connector.
End
Confirm trouble code.
Make sequential checks of trouble codes.
After sequential checks, go to D-check mode again.
90C21859

# 1991 ENGINE PERFORMANCE
# Self-Diagnostics – Loyale – TBI (Cont.)

## CODE 11, CRANK ANGLE SENSOR NO REFERENCE SIGNAL

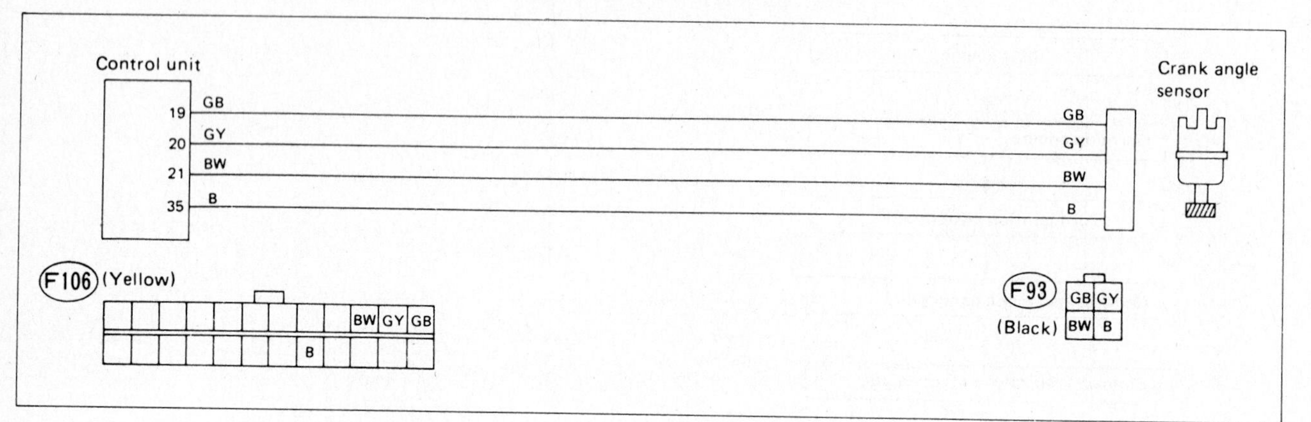


- Check if trouble code is outputted in D-check mode.
  - NO → Check terminals of control unit connector.
  - YES → Turn ignition switch OFF (engine off).
- Disconnect test mode connector.
- Check if engine starts.
  - YES → Check terminals (19), (20) and (35) of control unit connector for poor contact.
  - NO → Turn ignition switch OFF.
- Disconnect crank angle sensor connector.
- Turn ignition switch ON (engine off).
- Check if voltage across terminal (BW) of crank angle sensor connector (body side) and the body is greater than 4 V.
  - NO → **11-1**
  - YES → next step.
- Check if voltage across terminal (GB) or connector (body side) and the body is greater than 10 V.
  - NO → **11-2**
  - YES → next step.
- Check if continuity exists between terminal (B) of connector (body side) and the body.
  - NO → **11-3**
  - YES → next step.
- Check if female terminal of connector (body side) is open.
  - YES → Repair terminal or replace body harness.
  - NO → Replace crank angle sensor.

**Continued on Next Page**

90F21860

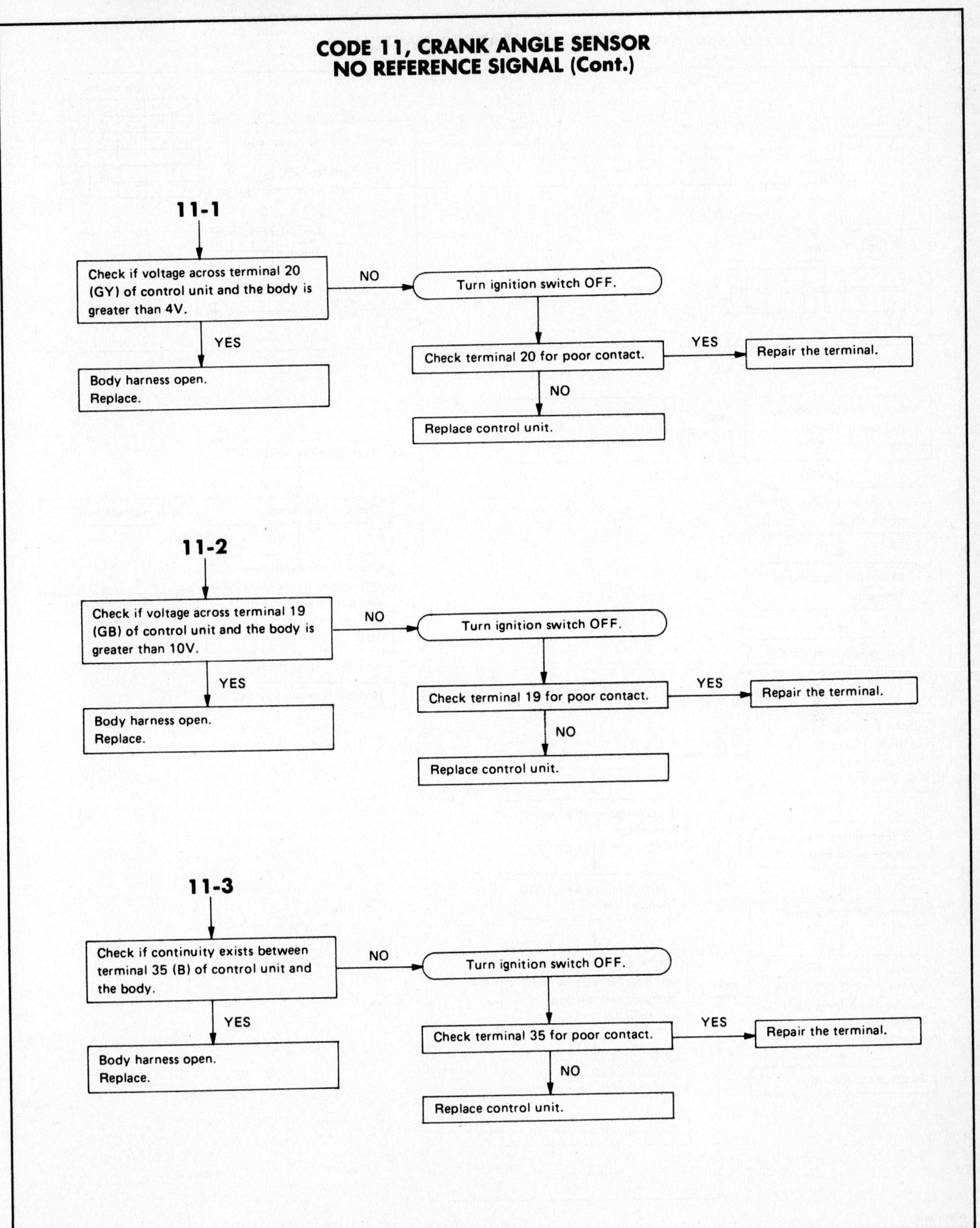
CODE 11, CRANK ANGLE SENSOR
NO REFERENCE SIGNAL (Cont.)
11-1
Check if voltage across terminal 20 (GY) of control unit and the body is greater than 4V.
NO
Turn ignition switch OFF.
YES
Body harness open. Replace.
Check terminal 20 for poor contact.
YES
Repair the terminal.
NO
Replace control unit.
11-2
Check if voltage across terminal 19 (GB) of control unit and the body is greater than 10V.
NO
Turn ignition switch OFF.
YES
Body harness open. Replace.
Check terminal 19 for poor contact.
YES
Repair the terminal.
NO
Replace control unit.
11-3
Check if continuity exists between terminal 35 (B) of control unit and the body.
NO
Turn ignition switch OFF.
YES
Body harness open. Replace.
Check terminal 35 for poor contact.
YES
Repair the terminal.
NO
Replace control unit.
90G21861

# 1991 ENGINE PERFORMANCE
## Self-Diagnostics – Loyale – TBI (Cont.)

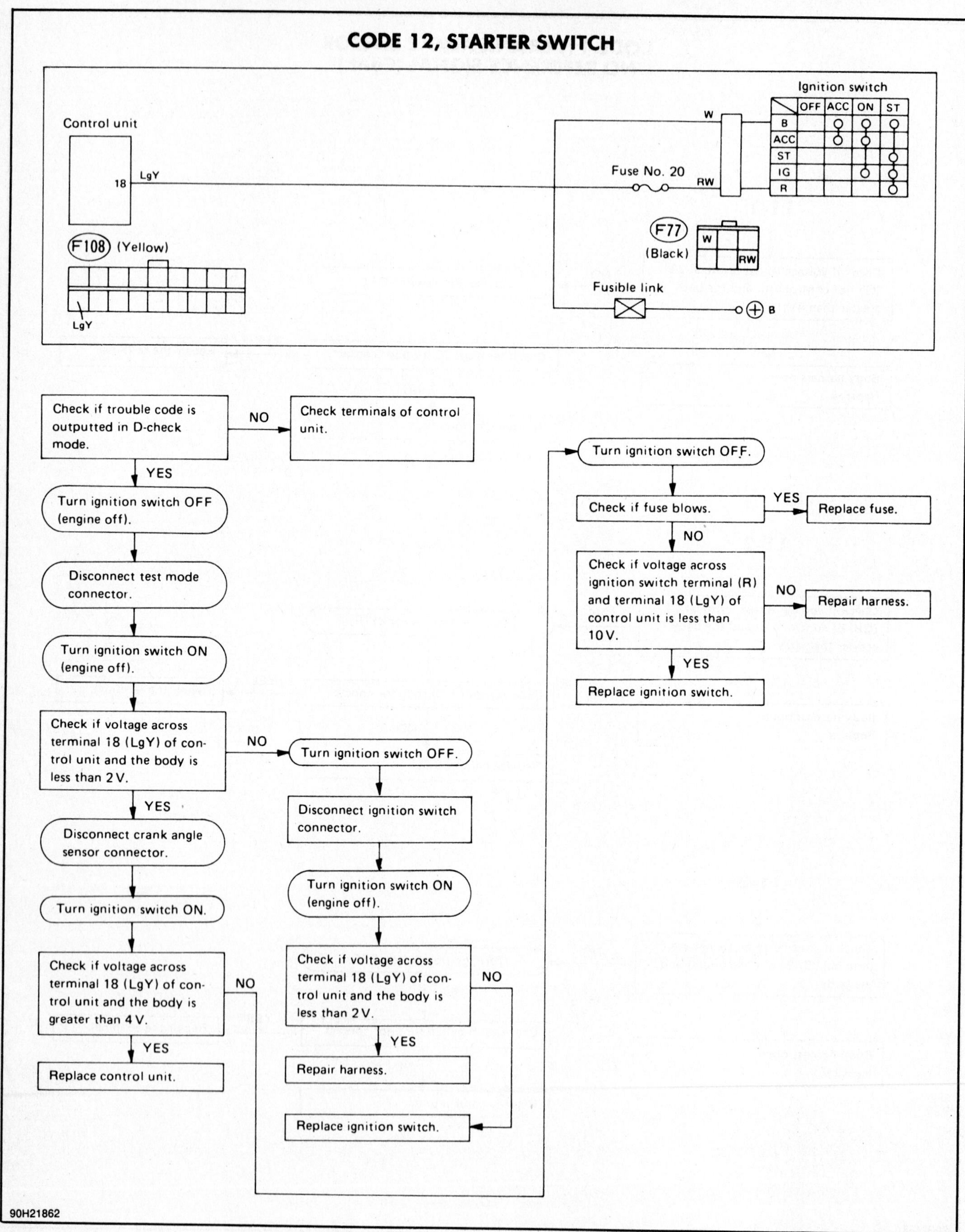

# 1991 ENGINE PERFORMANCE
# Self-Diagnostics – Loyale – TBI (Cont.)

## CODE 13, CRANK ANGLE SENSOR NO POSITION PULSE

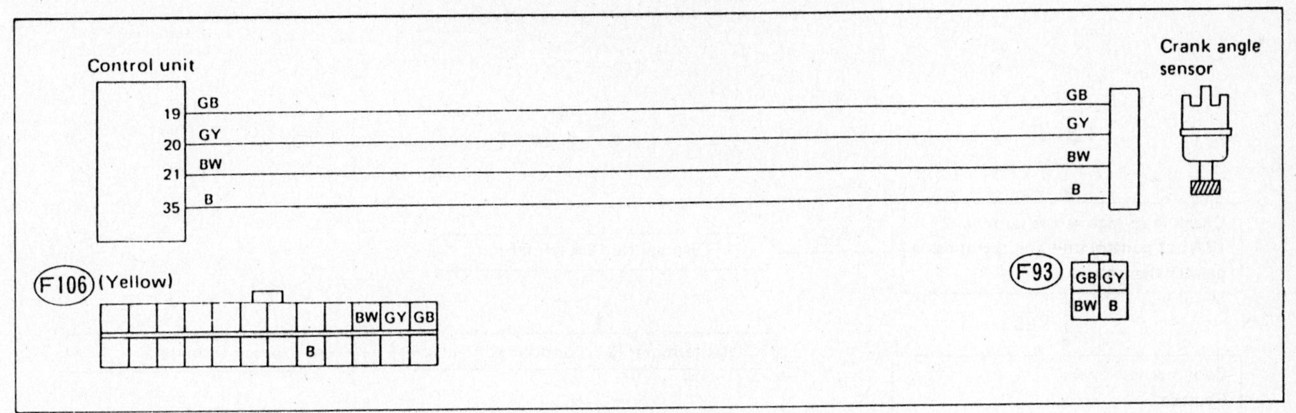


Check if trouble code is outputted in D-check mode.
- NO → Check terminals of control unit.
- YES ↓

Turn ignition switch OFF (engine off).

↓

Disconnect test mode connector.

↓

Check if engine starts.
- YES → Check terminals (19), (21) and (35) of control unit connector for poor contact.
- NO ↓

Turn ignition switch OFF.

↓

Disconnect crank angle sensor connector.

↓

Turn ignition switch ON (engine off).

↓

Check if voltage across terminal (BW) of crank angle sensor connector (body side) and the body is greater than 4 V.
- NO → **13-1**
- YES ↓

Check if voltage across terminal (GB) of connector (body side) and the body is greater than 10V.
- NO → **13-2**
- YES ↓

Check if continuity exists between terminal (B) of connector (body side) and the body.
- NO → **13-3**
- YES ↓

Check if the female terminal of connector (body side) is open.
- YES → Repair terminal or replace body harness.
- NO ↓

Replace crank angle sensor.

Continued on Next Page

90I21863

# 1991 ENGINE PERFORMANCE
## Self-Diagnostics – Loyale – TBI (Cont.)

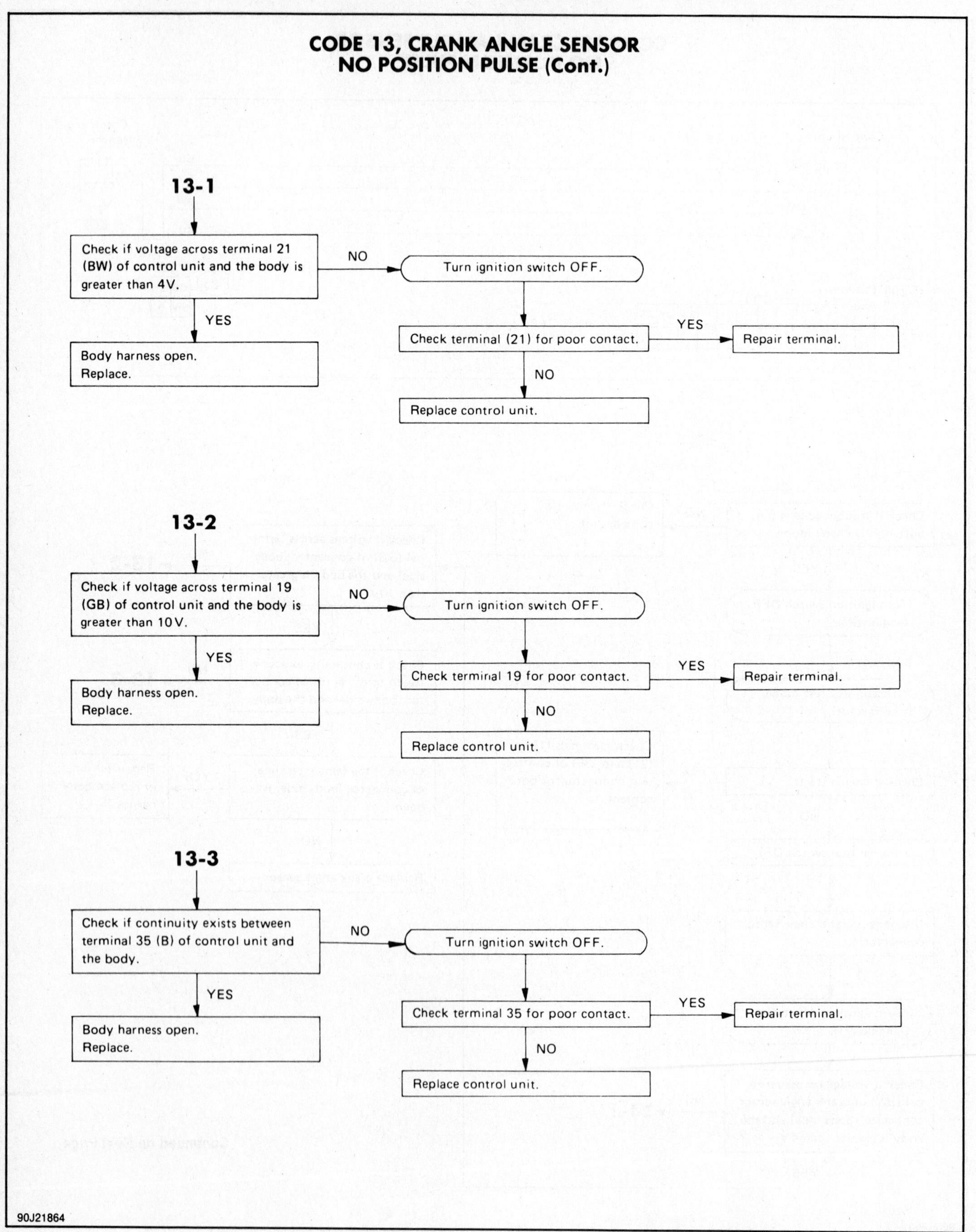
CODE 13, CRANK ANGLE SENSOR
NO POSITION PULSE (Cont.)
13-1
Check if voltage across terminal 21 (BW) of control unit and the body is greater than 4V.
NO
Turn ignition switch OFF.
Check terminal (21) for poor contact.
YES
Repair terminal.
NO
Replace control unit.
YES
Body harness open. Replace.
13-2
Check if voltage across terminal 19 (GB) of control unit and the body is greater than 10V.
NO
Turn ignition switch OFF.
Check terminal 19 for poor contact.
YES
Repair terminal.
NO
Replace control unit.
YES
Body harness open. Replace.
13-3
Check if continuity exists between terminal 35 (B) of control unit and the body.
NO
Turn ignition switch OFF.
Check terminal 35 for poor contact.
YES
Repair terminal.
NO
Replace control unit.
YES
Body harness open. Replace.
90J21864

# 1991 ENGINE PERFORMANCE
## Self-Diagnostics – Loyale – TBI (Cont.)

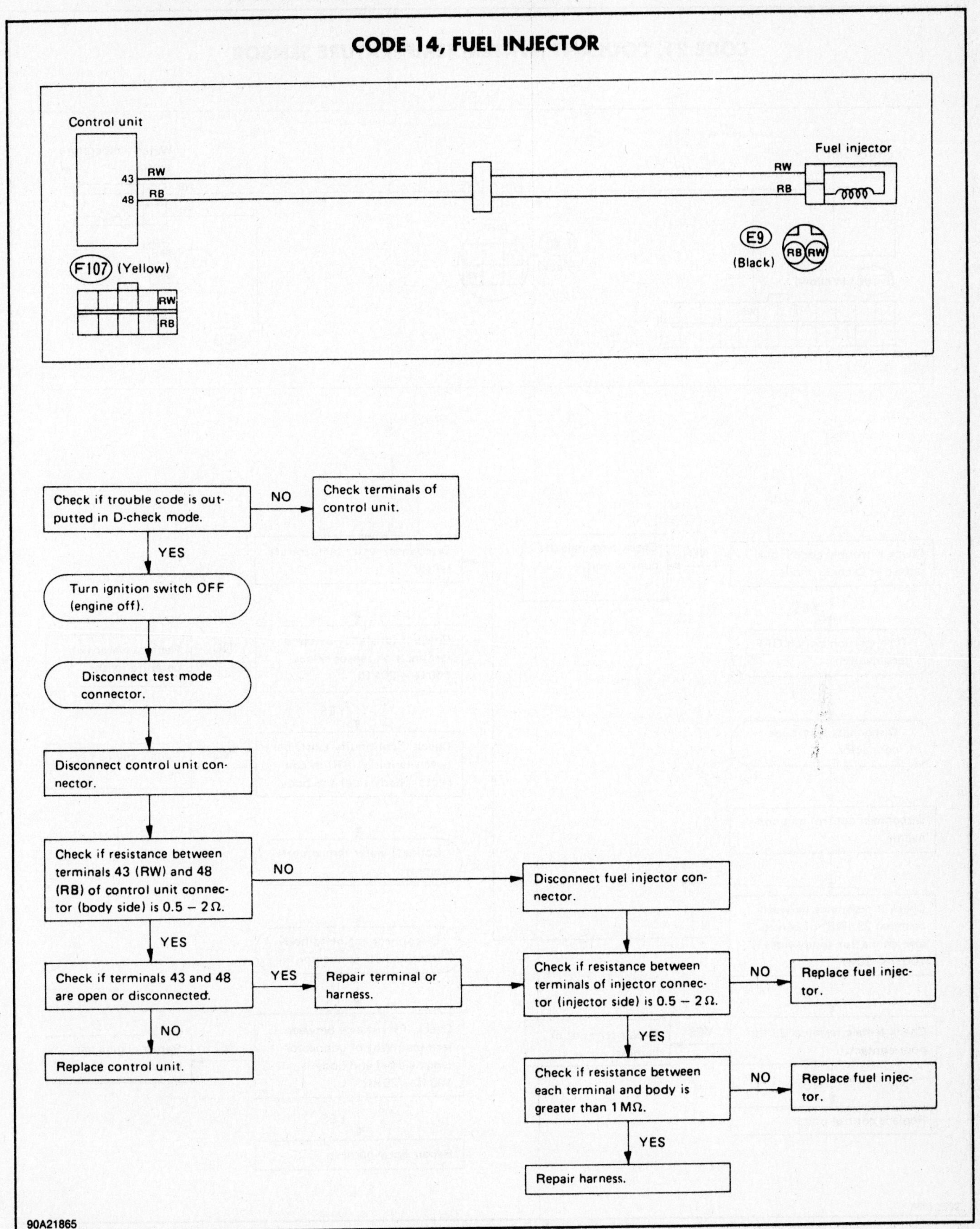

# 1991 ENGINE PERFORMANCE
## Self-Diagnostics – Loyale – TBI (Cont.)

### CODE 21, COOLANT (WATER) TEMPERATURE SENSOR

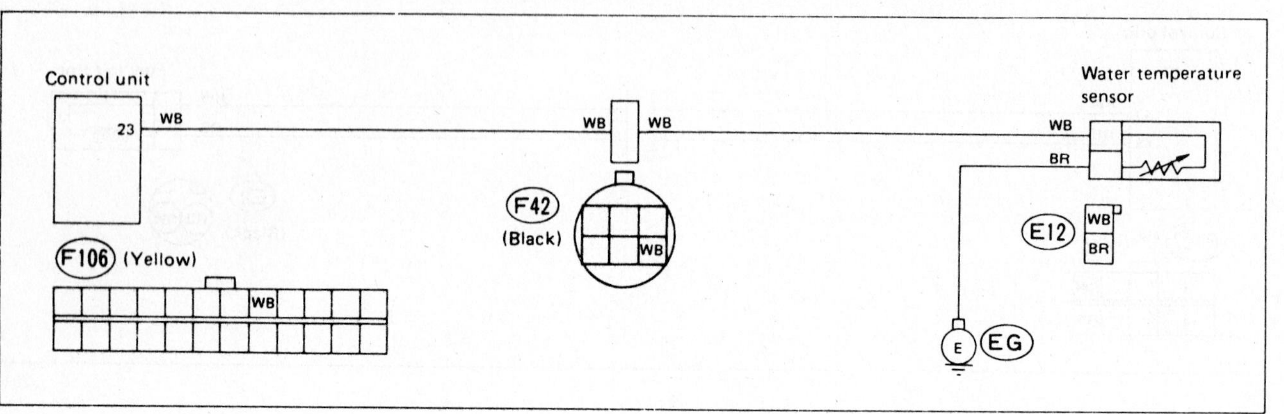


Check if trouble code is outputted in D-check mode.
- NO → Check terminals of control unit.
- YES → Turn ignition switch OFF (engine off).

Disconnect test mode connector.

Disconnect control unit connector.

Check if resistance between terminal 23 (WB) of control unit connector (body side) is 100Ω – 20kΩ.
- NO → Disconnect water temperature sensor.
- YES → Check female terminal 23 for poor contact.

Check female terminal 23 for poor contact.
- YES → Repair terminal or harness.
- NO → Replace control unit.

Disconnect water temperature sensor.

Check if resistance between terminals on sensor side is 100Ω – 20kΩ.
- NO → Replace water temperature sensor.
- YES → Check if continuity exists between terminal (BR) of connector (body side) and body.

Check if continuity exists between terminal (BR) of connector (body side) and body.
- NO → Repair engine harness.
- YES → Connect water temperature sensor.

Connect water temperature sensor.

Disconnect engine-to-body intermediate connector.

Check if resistance between terminal (WB) of connector (engine side) and body is 100Ω – 20kΩ.
- NO → Repair engine harness.
- YES → Repair body harness.

90B21866

## CODE 23, AIRFLOW METER CIRCUIT

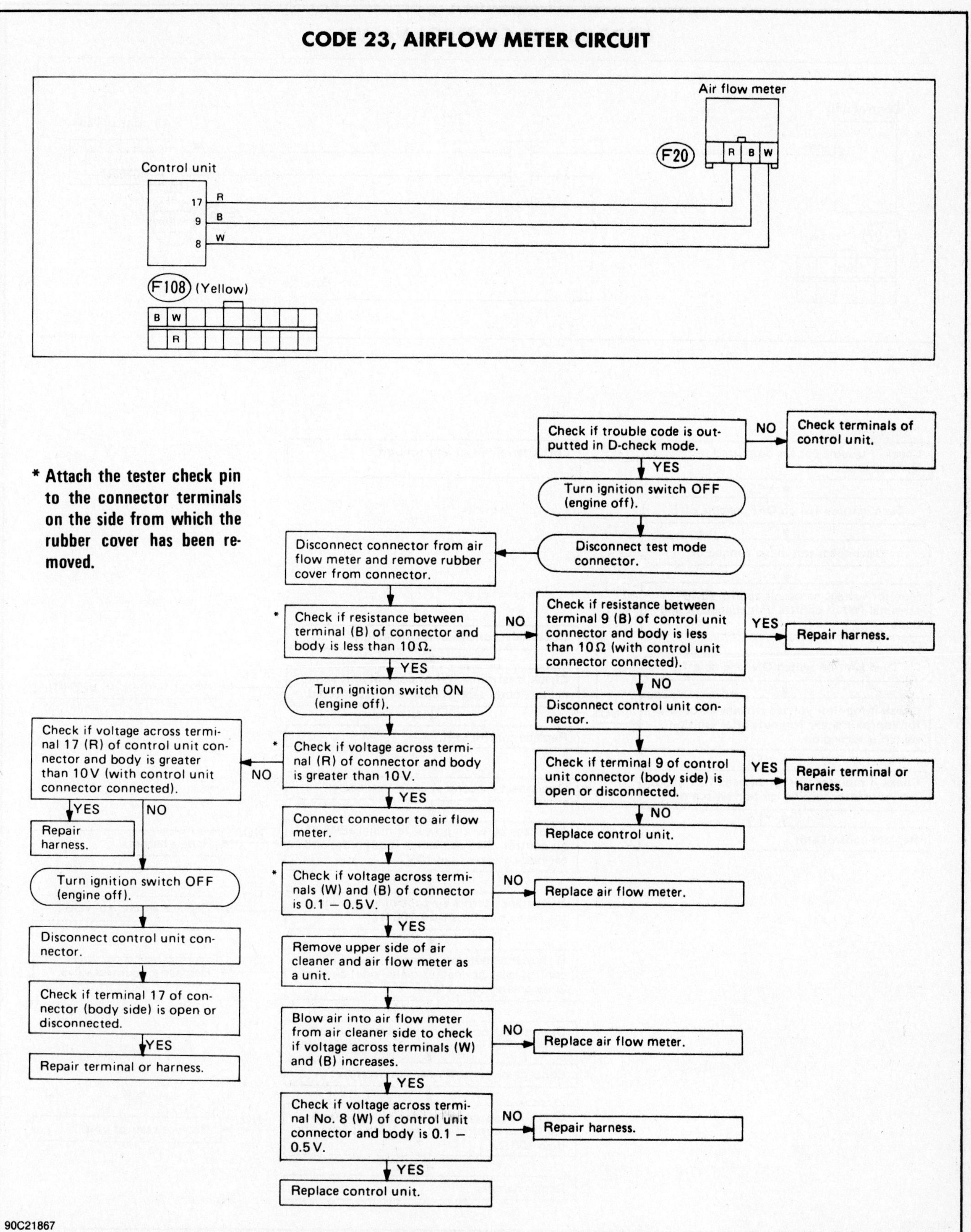


*** Attach the tester check pin to the connector terminals on the side from which the rubber cover has been removed.**

# 1991 ENGINE PERFORMANCE
## Self-Diagnostics – Loyale – TBI (Cont.)

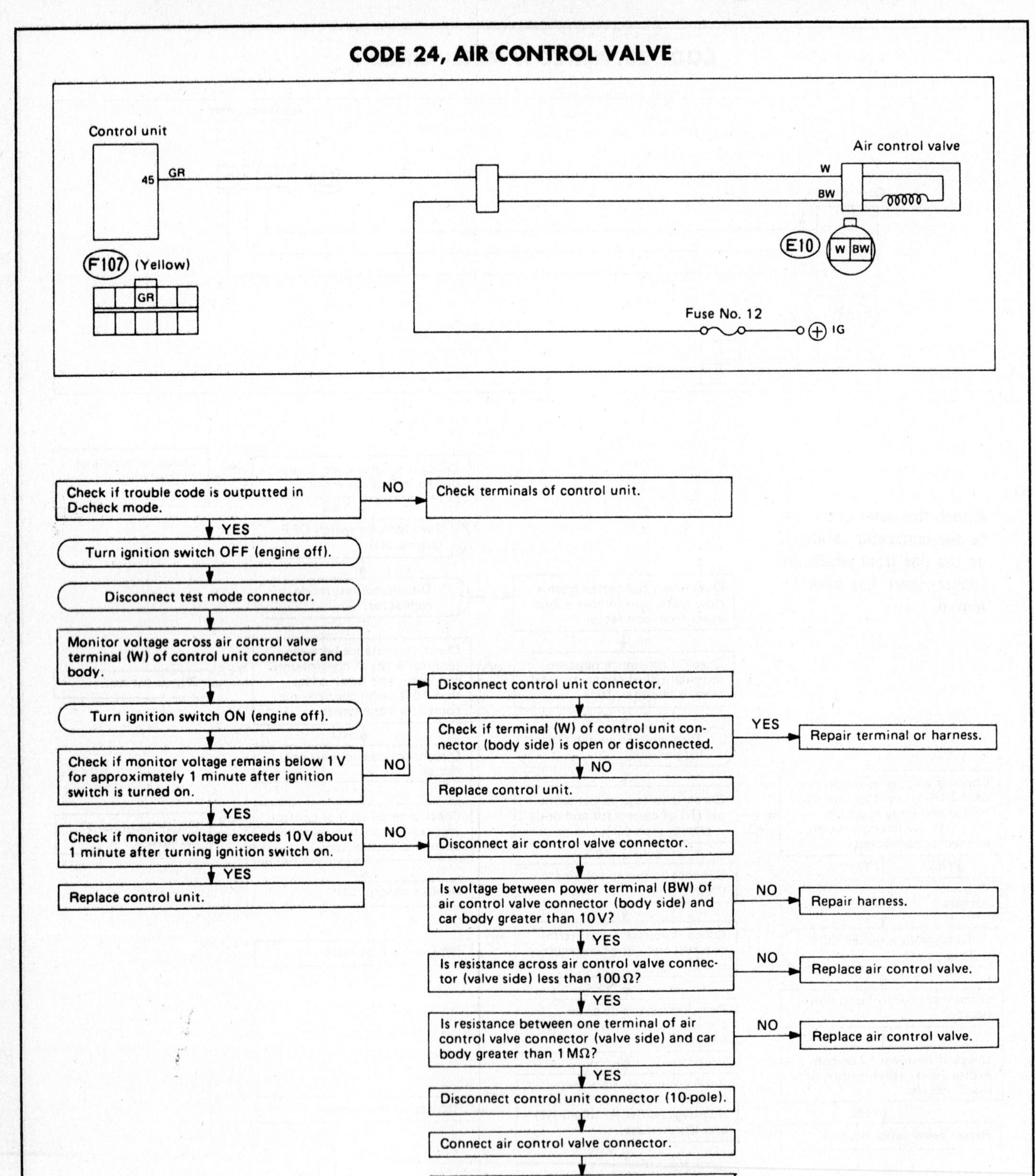

CODE 24, AIR CONTROL VALVE
Control unit
45
GR
F107 (Yellow)
GR
Air control valve
W
BW
E10
W BW
Fuse No. 12
IG
Check if trouble code is outputted in D-check mode.
NO
Check terminals of control unit.
YES
Turn ignition switch OFF (engine off).
Disconnect test mode connector.
Monitor voltage across air control valve terminal (W) of control unit connector and body.
Turn ignition switch ON (engine off).
Check if monitor voltage remains below 1 V for approximately 1 minute after ignition switch is turned on.
NO
Disconnect control unit connector.
Check if terminal (W) of control unit connector (body side) is open or disconnected.
YES
Repair terminal or harness.
NO
Replace control unit.
YES
Check if monitor voltage exceeds 10 V about 1 minute after turning ignition switch on.
NO
Disconnect air control valve connector.
YES
Replace control unit.
Is voltage between power terminal (BW) of air control valve connector (body side) and car body greater than 10 V?
NO
Repair harness.
YES
Is resistance across air control valve connector (valve side) less than 100 Ω?
NO
Replace air control valve.
YES
Is resistance between one terminal of air control valve connector (valve side) and car body greater than 1 MΩ?
NO
Replace air control valve.
YES
Disconnect control unit connector (10-pole).
Connect air control valve connector.
Check if resistance between air valve terminal (W) of control unit and body is less than 100 Ω.
NO
Replace control unit.
YES
Repair harness.
90D21868

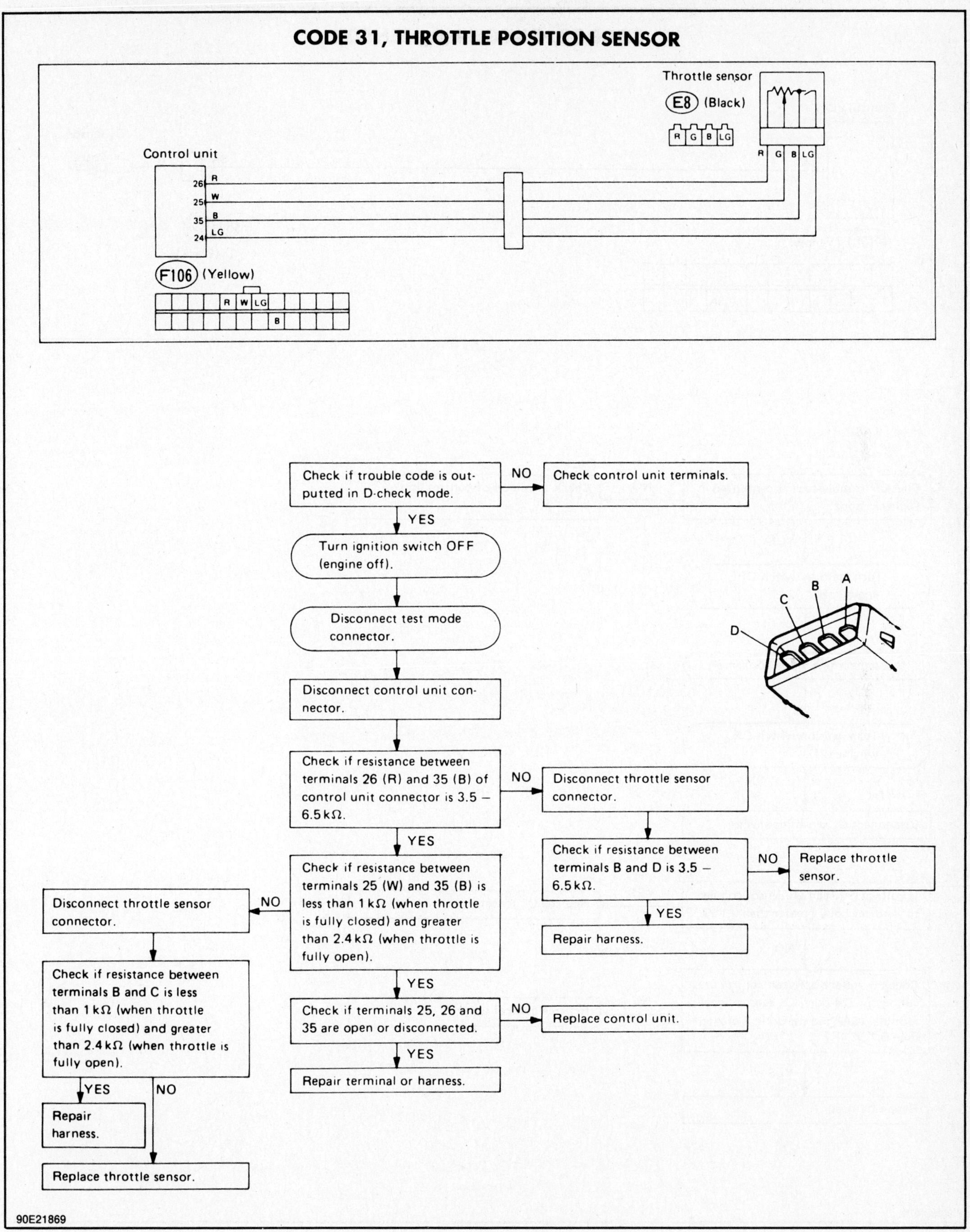
CODE 31, THROTTLE POSITION SENSOR
Throttle sensor
E8 (Black)
R G B LG
Control unit
26 R
25 W
35 B
24 LG
F106 (Yellow)
R W LG
B
Check if trouble code is outputted in D-check mode.
NO
Check control unit terminals.
YES
Turn ignition switch OFF (engine off).
Disconnect test mode connector.
Disconnect control unit connector.
Check if resistance between terminals 26 (R) and 35 (B) of control unit connector is 3.5 – 6.5 kΩ.
NO
Disconnect throttle sensor connector.
Check if resistance between terminals B and D is 3.5 – 6.5 kΩ.
NO
Replace throttle sensor.
YES
Repair harness.
YES
Check if resistance between terminals 25 (W) and 35 (B) is less than 1 kΩ (when throttle is fully closed) and greater than 2.4 kΩ (when throttle is fully open).
NO
Disconnect throttle sensor connector.
Check if resistance between terminals B and C is less than 1 kΩ (when throttle is fully closed) and greater than 2.4 kΩ (when throttle is fully open).
YES
Repair harness.
NO
Replace throttle sensor.
YES
Check if terminals 25, 26 and 35 are open or disconnected.
NO
Replace control unit.
YES
Repair terminal or harness.
A
B
C
D
90E21869

# 1991 ENGINE PERFORMANCE
## Self-Diagnostics – Loyale – TBI (Cont.)

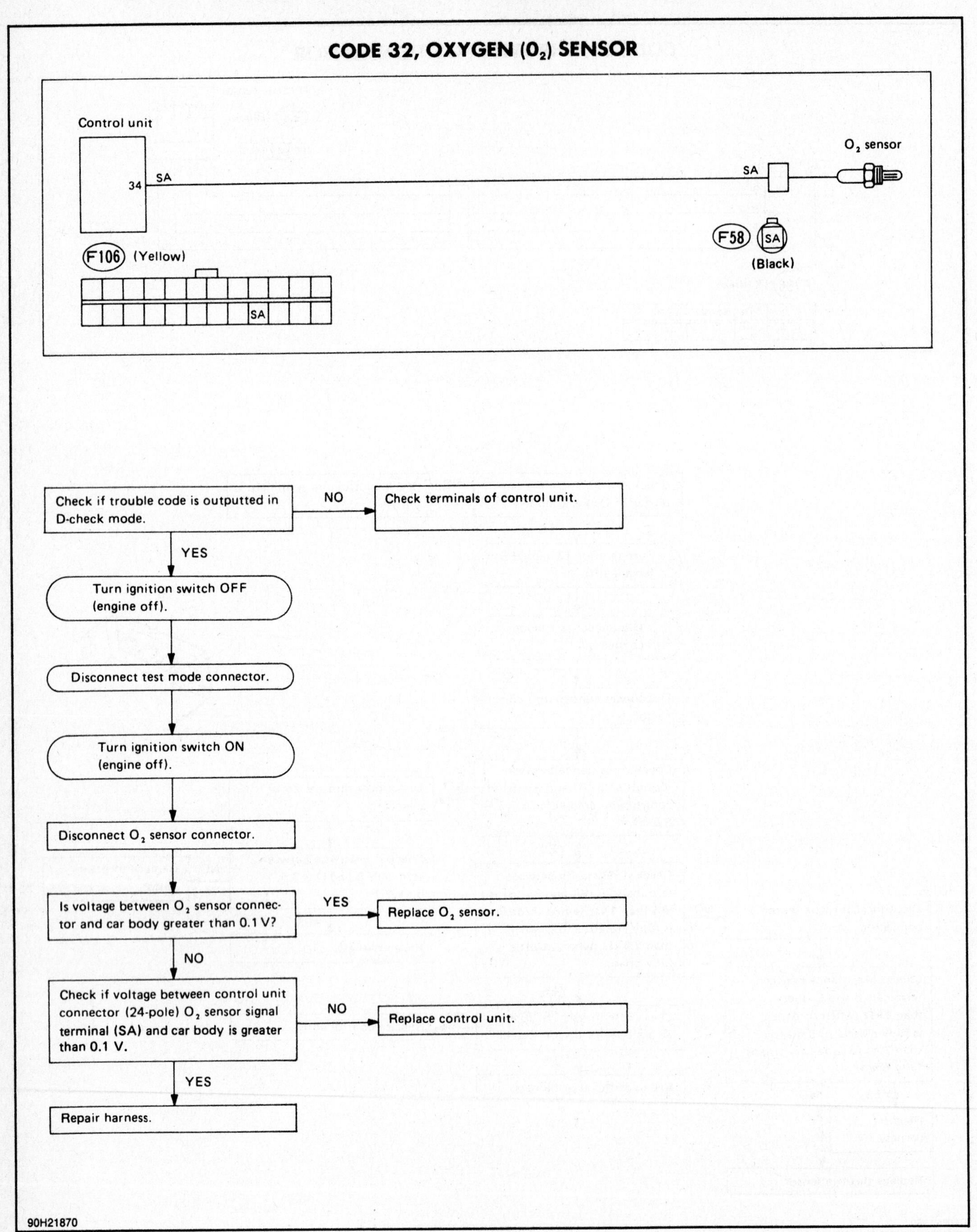

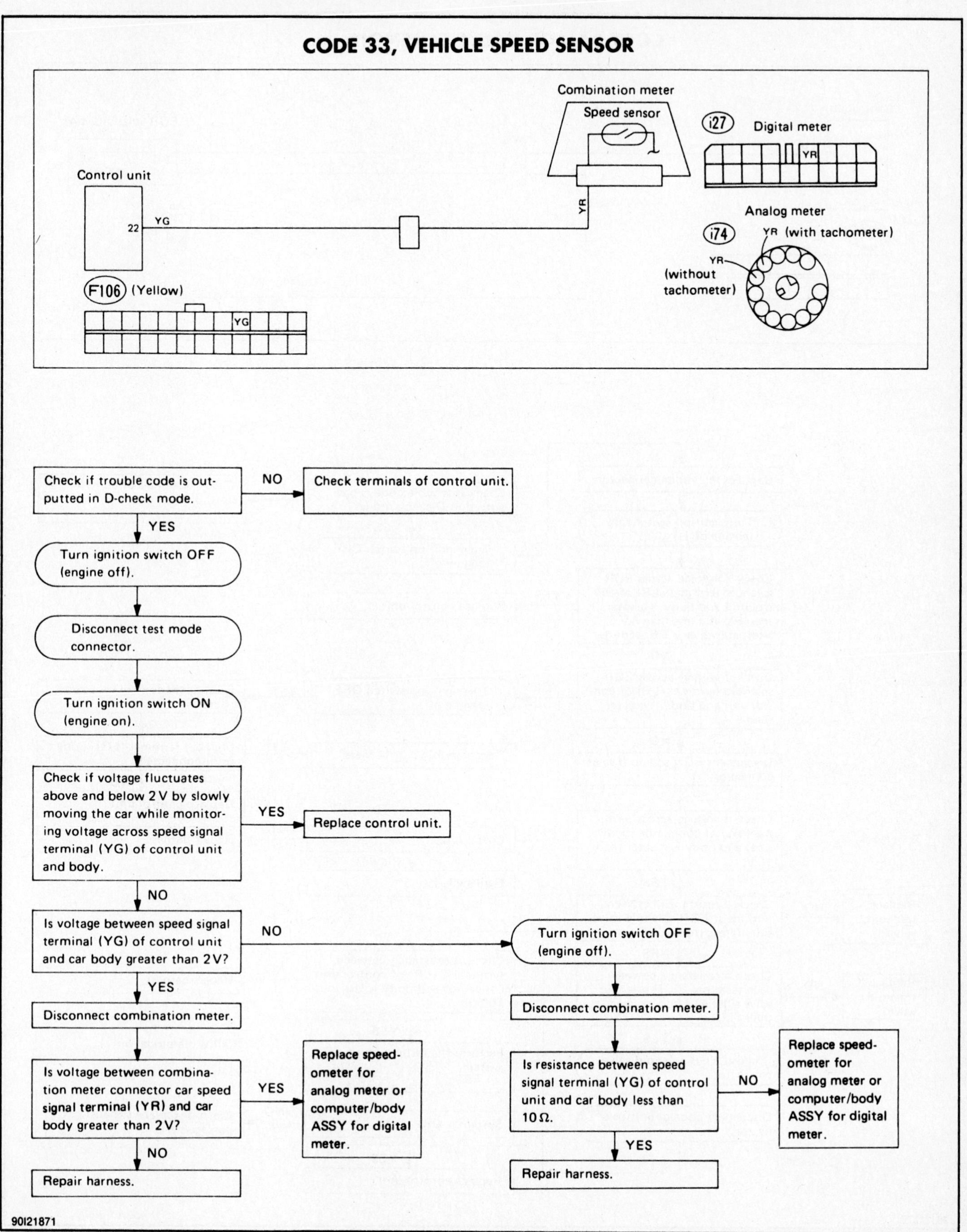
CODE 33, VEHICLE SPEED SENSOR
Combination meter
Speed sensor
i27
Digital meter
YR
Control unit
22
YG
YR
Analog meter
i74
YR (with tachometer)
YR
(without tachometer)
F106 (Yellow)
YG
Check if trouble code is outputted in D-check mode.
NO
Check terminals of control unit.
YES
Turn ignition switch OFF (engine off).
Disconnect test mode connector.
Turn ignition switch ON (engine on).
Check if voltage fluctuates above and below 2 V by slowly moving the car while monitoring voltage across speed signal terminal (YG) of control unit and body.
YES
Replace control unit.
NO
Is voltage between speed signal terminal (YG) of control unit and car body greater than 2 V?
NO
Turn ignition switch OFF (engine off).
YES
Disconnect combination meter.
Disconnect combination meter.
Is voltage between combination meter connector car speed signal terminal (YR) and car body greater than 2 V?
YES
Replace speedometer for analog meter or computer/body ASSY for digital meter.
NO
Repair harness.
Is resistance between speed signal terminal (YG) of control unit and car body less than 10 Ω.
NO
Replace speedometer for analog meter or computer/body ASSY for digital meter.
YES
Repair harness.
90I21871

# 1991 ENGINE PERFORMANCE
## Self-Diagnostics – Loyale – TBI (Cont.)

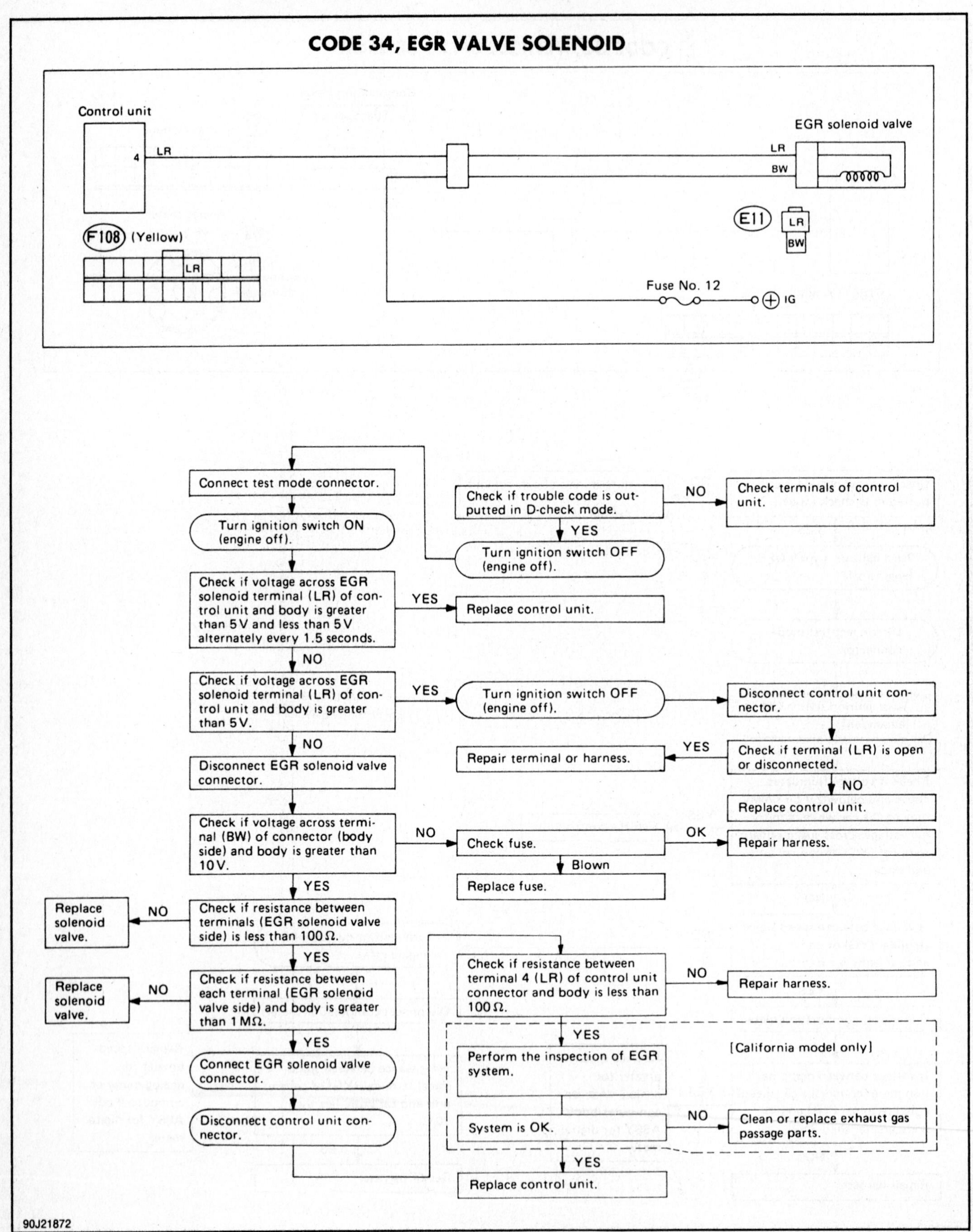

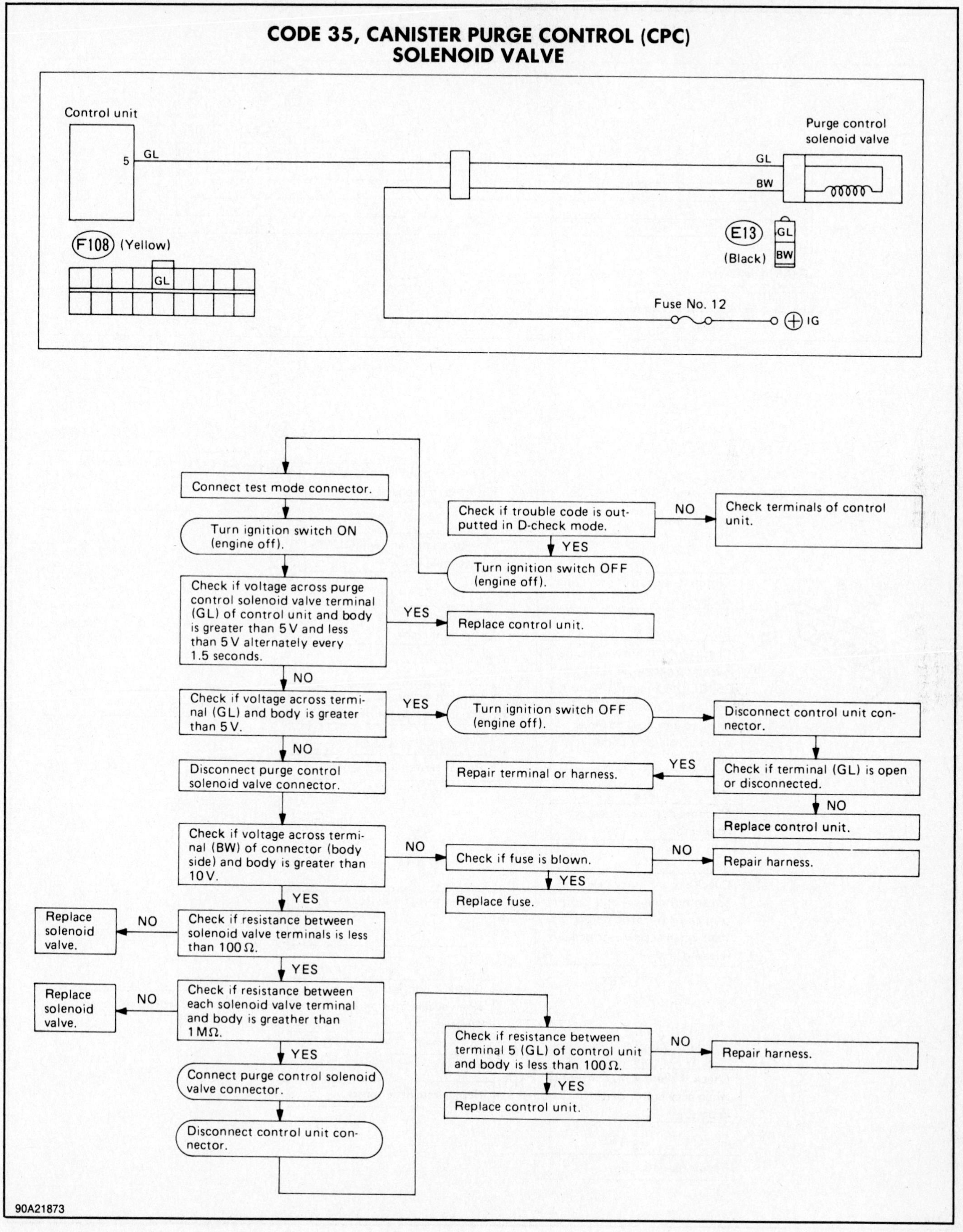

CODE 35, CANISTER PURGE CONTROL (CPC)
SOLENOID VALVE
Control unit
5
GL
Purge control solenoid valve
GL
BW
E13
(Black)
GL
BW
F108
(Yellow)
GL
Fuse No. 12
IG
Connect test mode connector.
Turn ignition switch ON (engine off).
Check if voltage across purge control solenoid valve terminal (GL) of control unit and body is greater than 5 V and less than 5 V alternately every 1.5 seconds.
YES
Replace control unit.
NO
Check if voltage across terminal (GL) and body is greater than 5 V.
YES
Turn ignition switch OFF (engine off).
Disconnect control unit connector.
Check if terminal (GL) is open or disconnected.
YES
Repair terminal or harness.
NO
Replace control unit.
NO
Disconnect purge control solenoid valve connector.
Check if voltage across terminal (BW) of connector (body side) and body is greater than 10 V.
NO
Check if fuse is blown.
NO
Repair harness.
YES
Replace fuse.
YES
Check if resistance between solenoid valve terminals is less than 100 Ω.
NO
Replace solenoid valve.
YES
Check if resistance between each solenoid valve terminal and body is greather than 1 MΩ.
NO
Replace solenoid valve.
YES
Connect purge control solenoid valve connector.
Disconnect control unit connector.
Check if resistance between terminal 5 (GL) of control unit and body is less than 100 Ω.
NO
Repair harness.
YES
Replace control unit.
Check if trouble code is outputted in D-check mode.
NO
Check terminals of control unit.
YES
Turn ignition switch OFF (engine off).
90A21873

# 1991 ENGINE PERFORMANCE
## Self-Diagnostics – Loyale – TBI (Cont.)

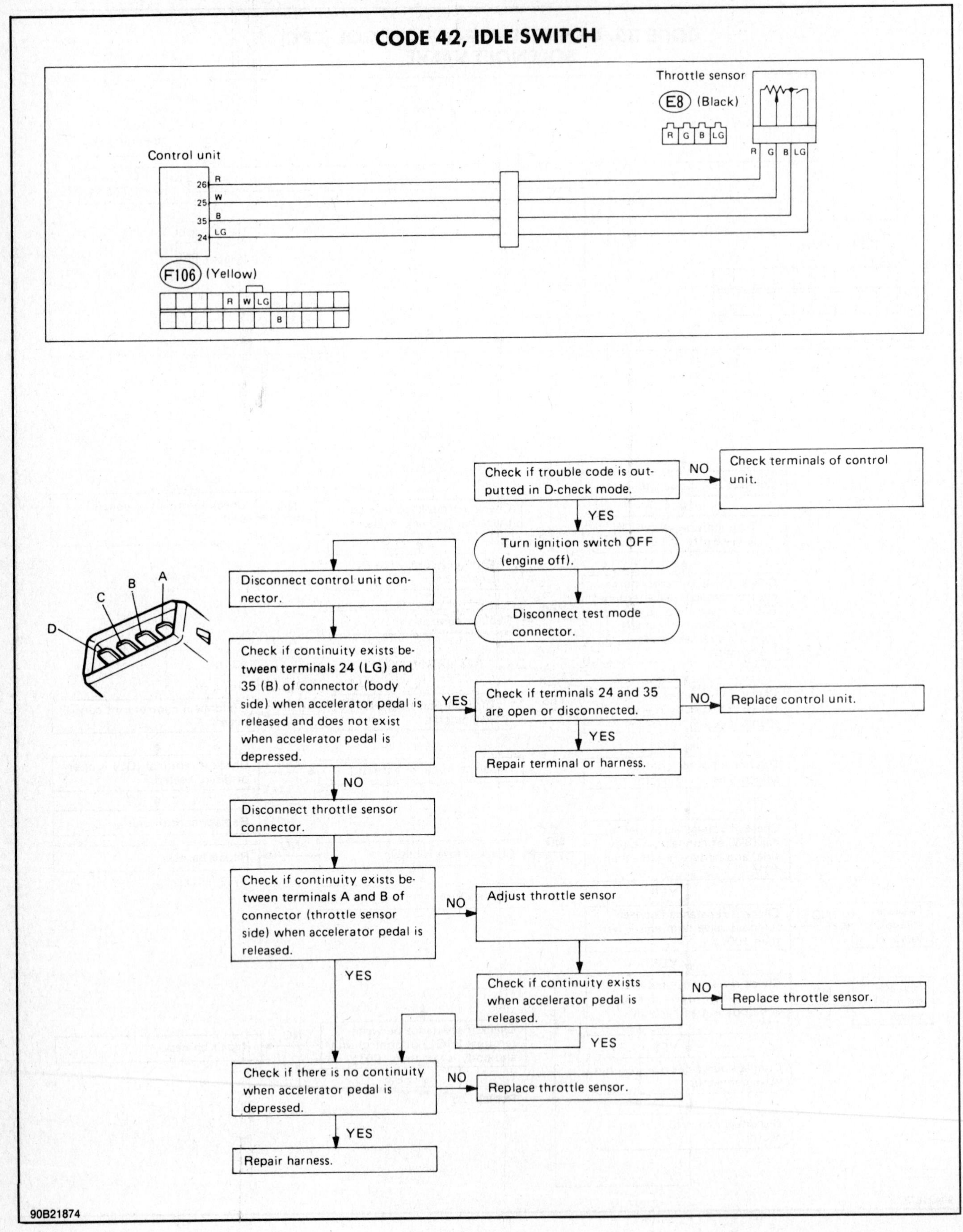

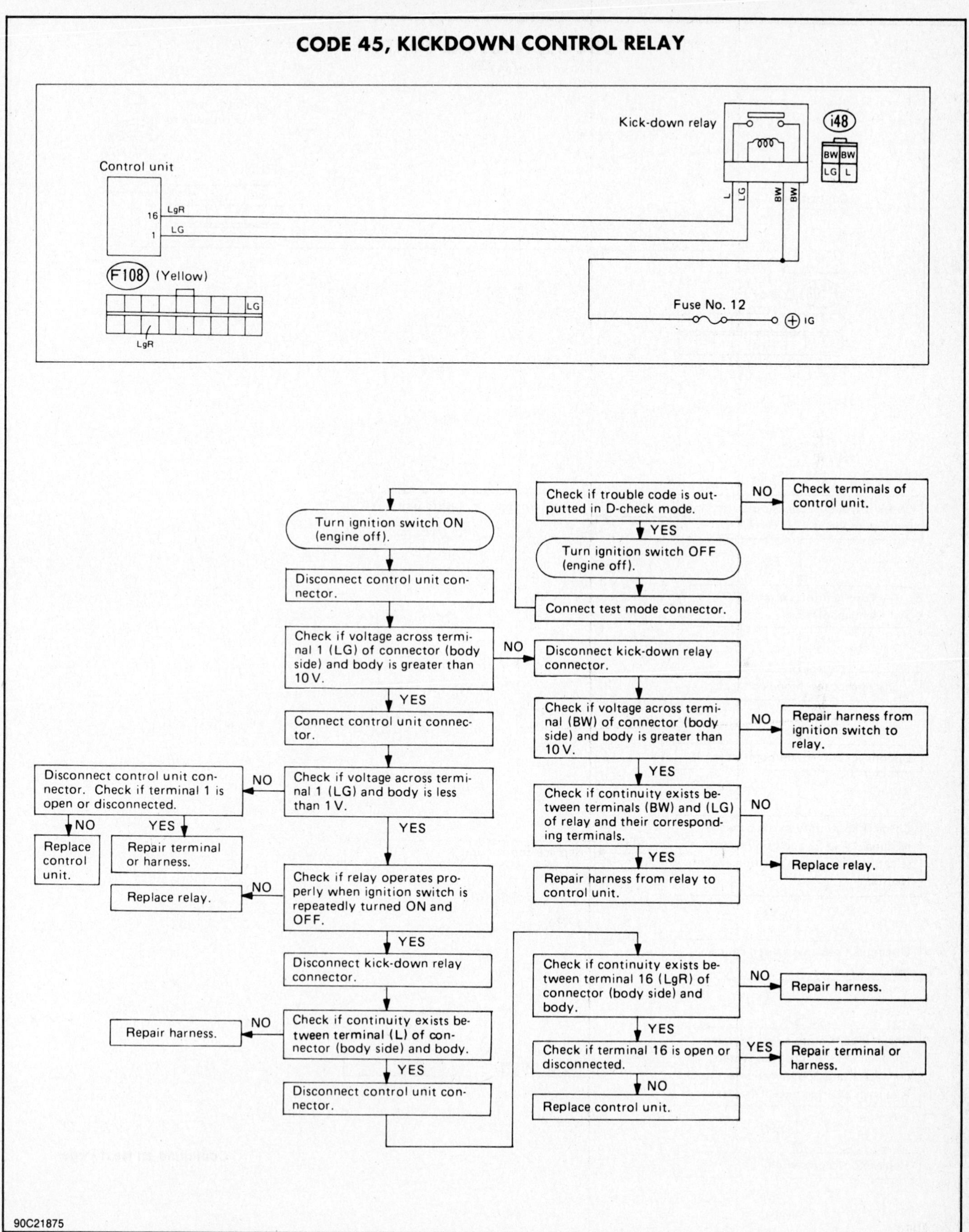

CODE 45, KICKDOWN CONTROL RELAY
Kick-down relay
i48
BW BW
LG L
Control unit
16 LgR
1 LG
L
LG
BW
BW
F108 (Yellow)
LG
LgR
Fuse No. 12
IG
Check if trouble code is outputted in D-check mode.
NO
Check terminals of control unit.
YES
Turn ignition switch OFF (engine off).
Connect test mode connector.
Turn ignition switch ON (engine off).
Disconnect control unit connector.
Check if voltage across terminal 1 (LG) of connector (body side) and body is greater than 10 V.
NO
Disconnect kick-down relay connector.
Check if voltage across terminal (BW) of connector (body side) and body is greater than 10 V.
NO
Repair harness from ignition switch to relay.
YES
Check if continuity exists between terminals (BW) and (LG) of relay and their corresponding terminals.
NO
Replace relay.
YES
Repair harness from relay to control unit.
YES
Connect control unit connector.
Check if voltage across terminal 1 (LG) and body is less than 1 V.
NO
Disconnect control unit connector. Check if terminal 1 is open or disconnected.
NO
Replace control unit.
YES
Repair terminal or harness.
YES
Check if relay operates properly when ignition switch is repeatedly turned ON and OFF.
NO
Replace relay.
YES
Disconnect kick-down relay connector.
Check if continuity exists between terminal (L) of connector (body side) and body.
NO
Repair harness.
YES
Disconnect control unit connector.
Check if continuity exists between terminal 16 (LgR) of connector (body side) and body.
NO
Repair harness.
YES
Check if terminal 16 is open or disconnected.
YES
Repair terminal or harness.
NO
Replace control unit.
90C21875

# 1991 ENGINE PERFORMANCE
## Self-Diagnostics – Loyale – TBI (Cont.)

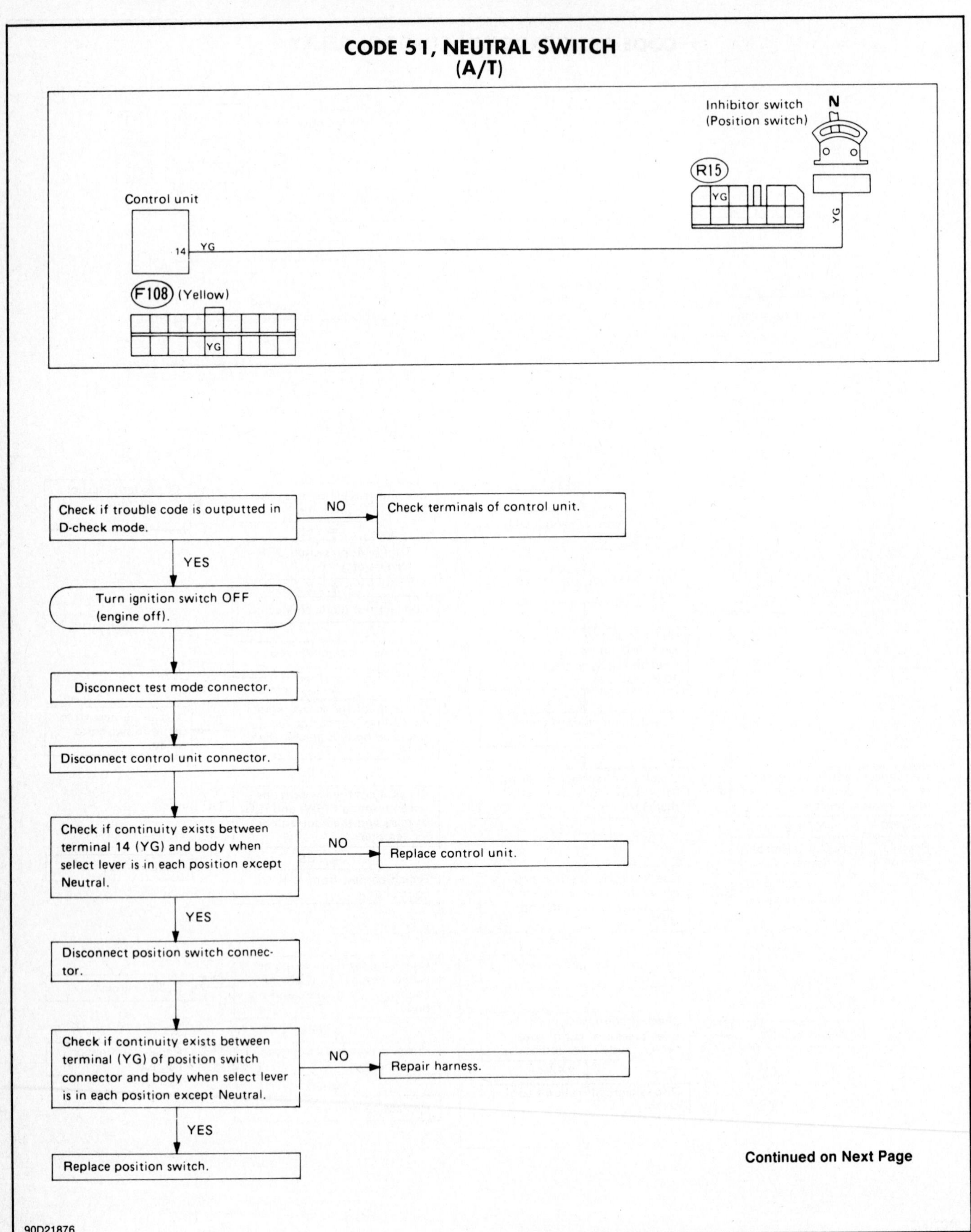

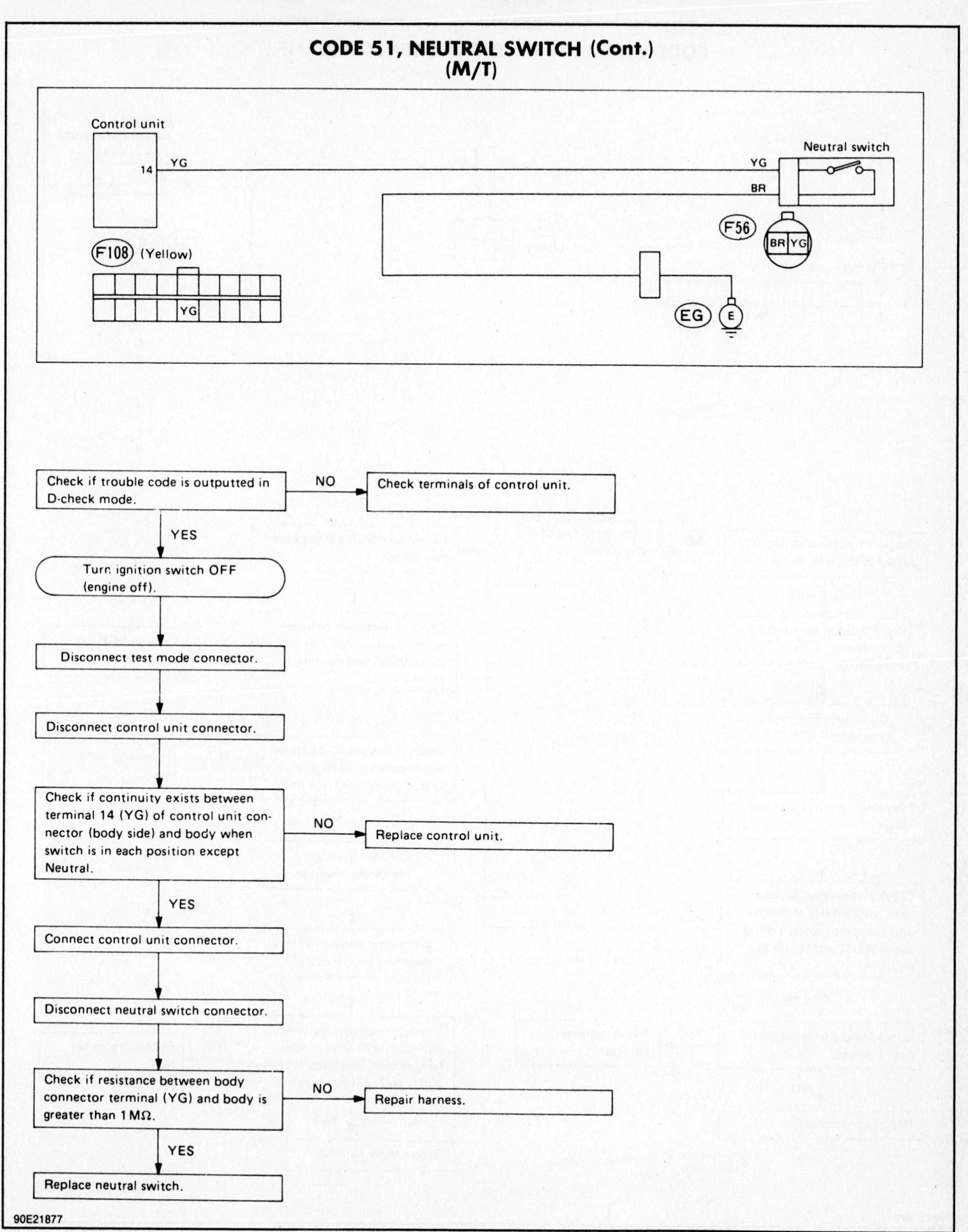

CODE 51, NEUTRAL SWITCH (Cont.)
(M/T)
Control unit
14
YG
Neutral switch
YG
BR
F56
BR
YG
F108
(Yellow)
YG
EG
E
Check if trouble code is outputted in D-check mode.
NO
Check terminals of control unit.
YES
Turn ignition switch OFF (engine off).
Disconnect test mode connector.
Disconnect control unit connector.
Check if continuity exists between terminal 14 (YG) of control unit connector (body side) and body when switch is in each position except Neutral.
NO
Replace control unit.
YES
Connect control unit connector.
Disconnect neutral switch connector.
Check if resistance between body connector terminal (YG) and body is greater than 1 MΩ.
NO
Repair harness.
YES
Replace neutral switch.
90E21877

# 1991 ENGINE PERFORMANCE
## Self-Diagnostics – Loyale – TBI (Cont.)

### CODE 55, EGR TEMPERATURE SENSOR (CALIF.)

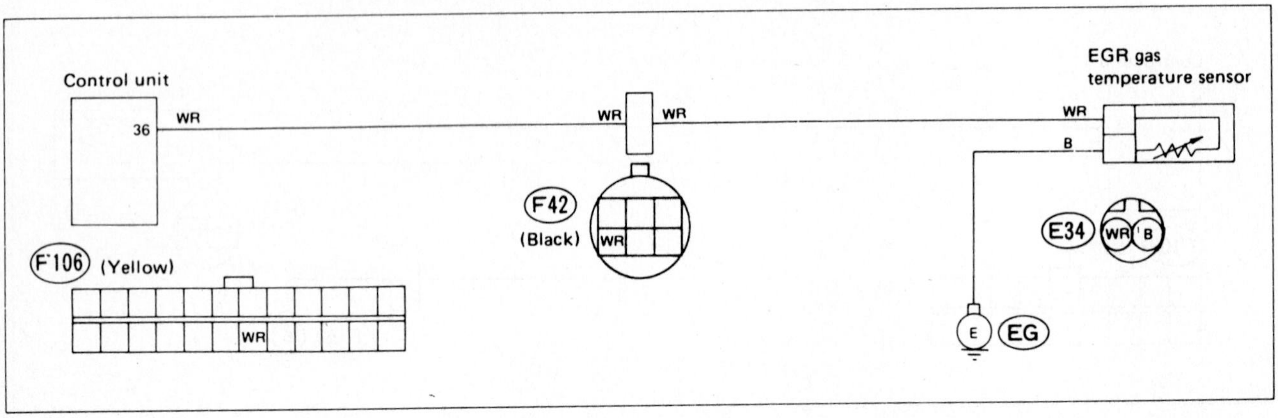

Check if trouble code is outputted in D-check mode.
- NO → Check terminals of control unit.
- YES → Turn ignition switch OFF (engine off).

Disconnect test mode connector.

Disconnect control unit connector.

Check if resistance between terminal 36 (WR) of control unit connector (body side) is above 250 Ω and continuity exists.
- YES → Check female terminal 36 for poor contact.
  - YES → Repair terminal or harness.
  - NO → Replace control unit.
- NO → Disconnect EGR gas temperature sensor.

Check if resistance between terminals on sensor side is above 250 Ω and continuity exists.
- NO → Replace EGR gas temperature sensor.
- YES → Check if continuity exists between terminal (BR) of connector (body side) and body.
  - NO → Repair engine harness.
  - YES → Connect EGR gas temperature sensor.

Disconnect engine-to-body intermediate connector.

Check if resistance between terminal (WR) of connector (engine side) and body is above 250 Ω and continuity exists.
- NO → Repair engine harness.
- YES → Repair body harness.

90F21878

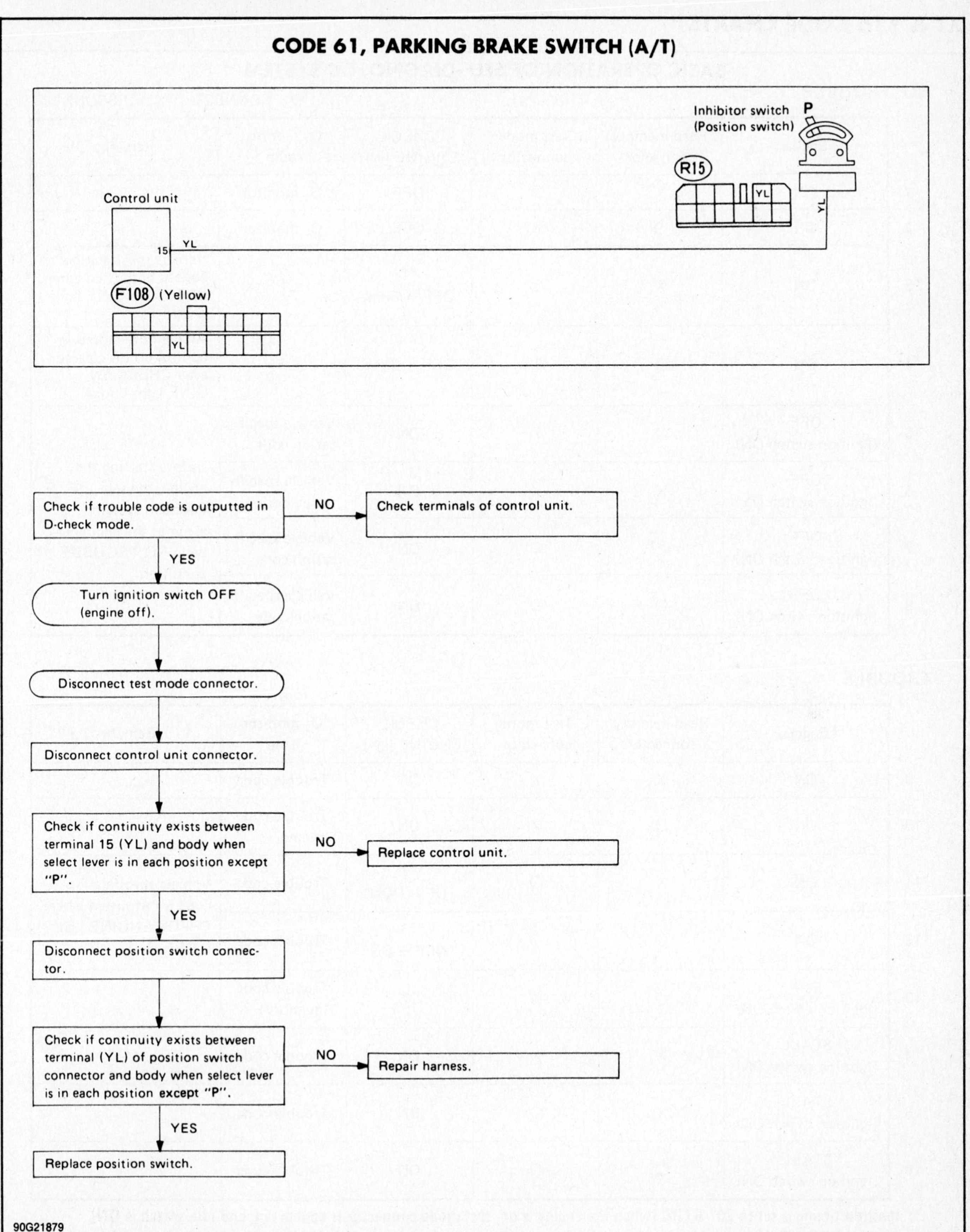
CODE 61, PARKING BRAKE SWITCH (A/T)
Inhibitor switch
(Position switch)
P
R15
YL
Control unit
15
YL
F108 (Yellow)
YL
Check if trouble code is outputted in D-check mode.
NO
Check terminals of control unit.
YES
Turn ignition switch OFF (engine off).
Disconnect test mode connector.
Disconnect control unit connector.
Check if continuity exists between terminal 15 (YL) and body when select lever is in each position except "P".
NO
Replace control unit.
YES
Disconnect position switch connector.
Check if continuity exists between terminal (YL) of position switch connector and body when select lever is in each position except "P".
NO
Repair harness.
YES
Replace position switch.
90G21879

# 1991 ENGINE PERFORMANCE
# Self-Diagnostics – XT & XT6

## XT & XT6 CODE CHARTS

### BASIC OPERATION OF SELF-DIAGNOSTIC SYSTEM

NO TROUBLE

○ : CONNECT X : DISCONNECT

| | Engine | Read memory connector | Test mode connector | CHECK ENGINE light | $O_2$ monitor lamp | Remarks |
|---|---|---|---|---|---|---|
| 1 | ON | X | X | OFF | $O_2$ monitor | |
| 2 | ON | ○ | X | OFF | $O_2$ monitor | |
| *3 | ON | X | ○ | ** OFF → Blink | OFF | Vehicle specification code is outputted when CHECK ENGINE light is OFF. |
| *4 | ON | ○ | ○ | OFF → Blink | OFF | All memory stored in control unit is cleared after CHECK ENGINE light blinks. |
| 5 | OFF (Ignition switch ON) | ○ | X | ON | Vehicle specification code | Before starting the engine, the self-diagnosis system assumes the engine to be in NO TROUBLE condition. |
| 6 | OFF (Ignition switch ON) | X | X | ON | Vehicle specification code | |
| 7 | OFF (Ignition switch ON) | X | ○ | ON | Vehicle specification code | |
| 8 | OFF (Ignition switch ON) | ○ | ○ | ON | Vehicle specification code | |

TROUBLE

| | Engine | Read memory connector | Test mode connector | CHECK ENGINE light | $O_2$ monitor lamp | Remarks |
|---|---|---|---|---|---|---|
| 9 | ON | X | X | ON | Trouble code | |
| 10 | ON | ○ | X | ON | Trouble code (memory) | |
| *11 | ON | X | ○ | ** OFF → ON | Trouble code | Vehicle specification code is outputted when CHECK ENGINE light is OFF. |
| *12 | ON | ○ | ○ | ** OFF → ON | Trouble code | |
| 13 | OFF (Ignition switch ON) | ○ | X | ON | Trouble code (memory) | |
| 14 | STALL (Ignition switch ON) | X | X | ON | Trouble code | |
| 15 | STALL (Ignition switch ON) | X | ○ | ON | Trouble code | |
| 16 | STALL (Ignition switch ON) | ○ | ○ | ON | Trouble code | |

*: Ignition timing is set to 20° BTDC (when the engine is on, test mode connector is connected, and idle switch is ON).
**: CHECK ENGINE light remains off until engine is operated at speed greater than 2,000 rpm for at least 40 seconds.

118371

## READ MEMORY MODE

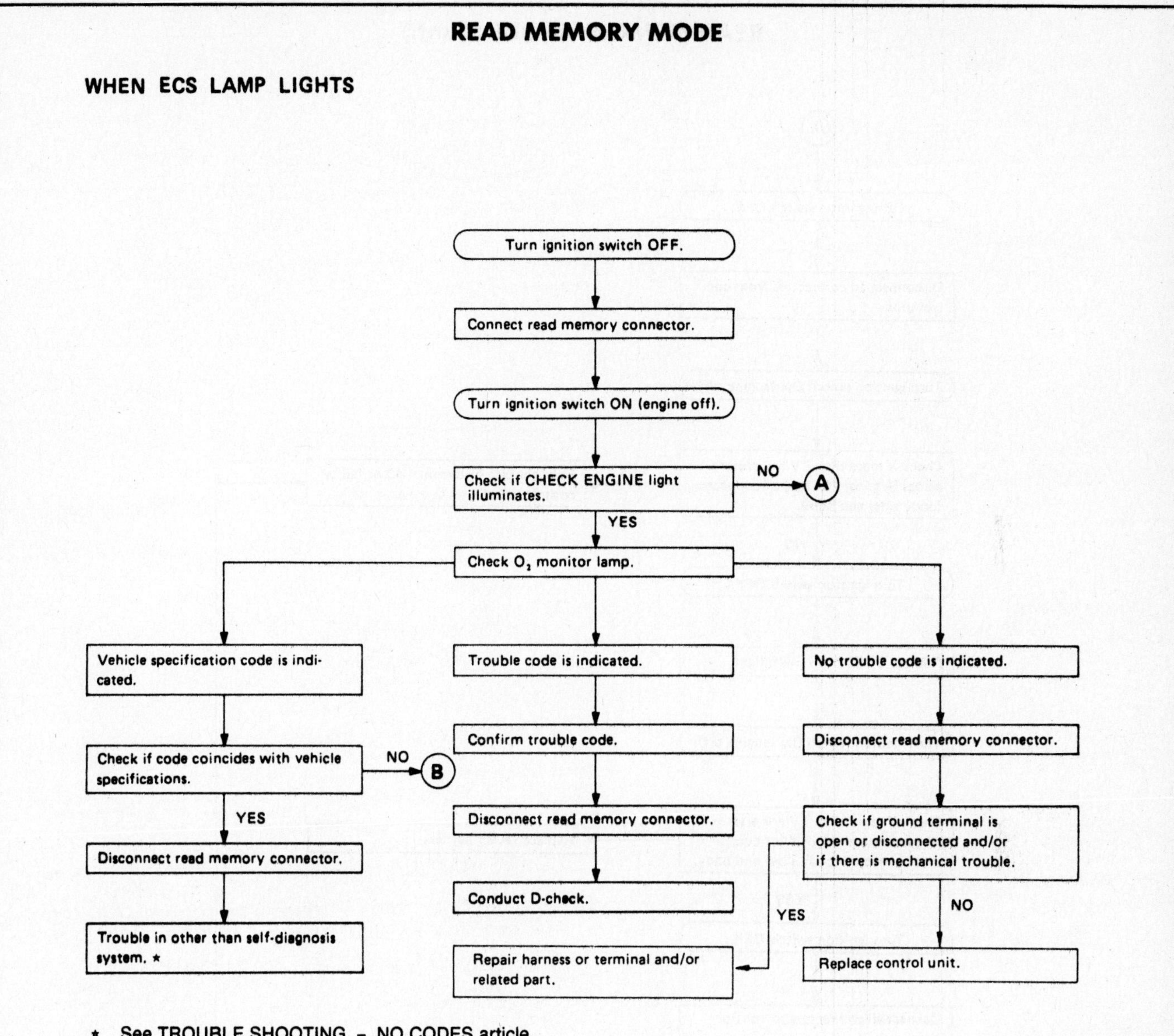


* See TROUBLE SHOOTING – NO CODES article.

Continued on Next Page

118374

# 1991 ENGINE PERFORMANCE
# Self-Diagnostics – XT & XT6 (Cont.)

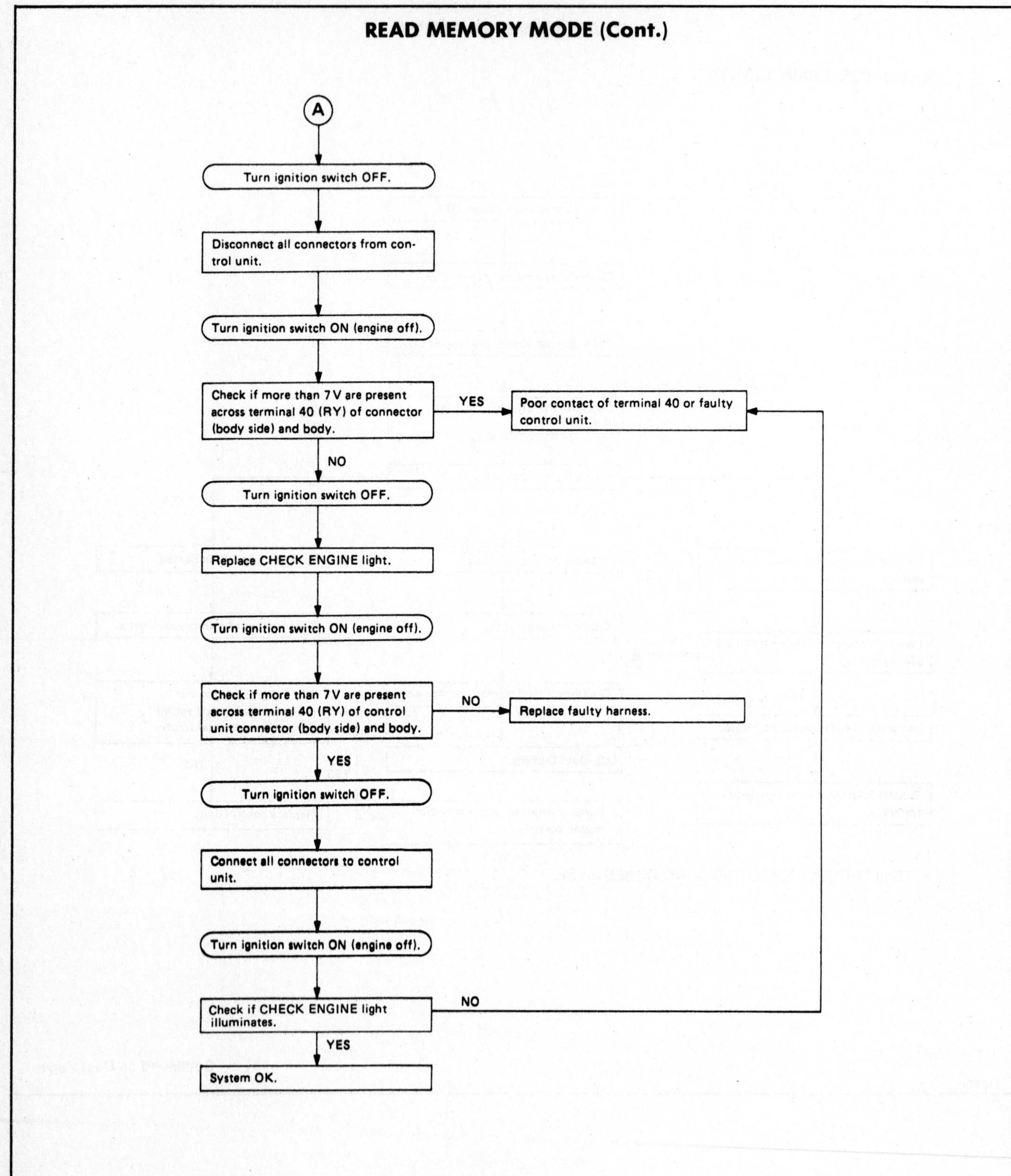
READ MEMORY MODE (Cont.)
A
Turn ignition switch OFF.
Disconnect all connectors from control unit.
Turn ignition switch ON (engine off).
Check if more than 7 V are present across terminal 40 (RY) of connector (body side) and body.
YES
Poor contact of terminal 40 or faulty control unit.
NO
Turn ignition switch OFF.
Replace CHECK ENGINE light.
Turn ignition switch ON (engine off).
Check if more than 7 V are present across terminal 40 (RY) of control unit connector (body side) and body.
NO
Replace faulty harness.
YES
Turn ignition switch OFF.
Connect all connectors to control unit.
Turn ignition switch ON (engine off).
Check if CHECK ENGINE light illuminates.
NO
YES
System OK.

Continued on Next Page

118375

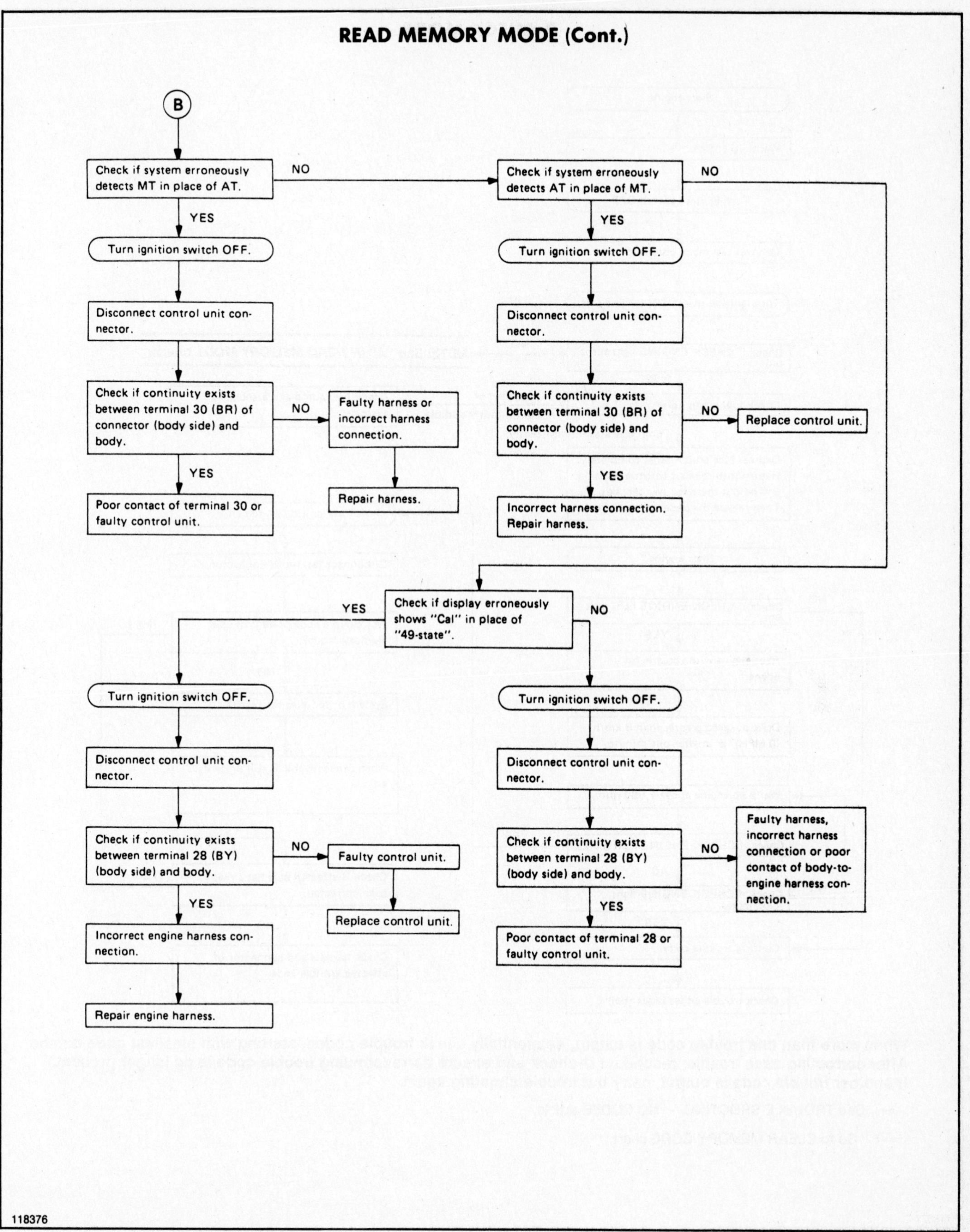
READ MEMORY MODE (Cont.)
B
Check if system erroneously detects MT in place of AT.
NO
YES
Turn ignition switch OFF.
Disconnect control unit connector.
Check if continuity exists between terminal 30 (BR) of connector (body side) and body.
NO
Faulty harness or incorrect harness connection.
Repair harness.
YES
Poor contact of terminal 30 or faulty control unit.
Check if system erroneously detects AT in place of MT.
NO
YES
Turn ignition switch OFF.
Disconnect control unit connector.
Check if continuity exists between terminal 30 (BR) of connector (body side) and body.
NO
Replace control unit.
YES
Incorrect harness connection. Repair harness.
Check if display erroneously shows "Cal" in place of "49-state".
YES
NO
Turn ignition switch OFF.
Disconnect control unit connector.
Check if continuity exists between terminal 28 (BY) (body side) and body.
NO
Faulty control unit.
Replace control unit.
YES
Incorrect engine harness connection.
Repair engine harness.
Turn ignition switch OFF.
Disconnect control unit connector.
Check if continuity exists between terminal 28 (BY) (body side) and body.
NO
Faulty harness, incorrect harness connection or poor contact of body-to-engine harness connection.
YES
Poor contact of terminal 28 or faulty control unit.
118376

# 1991 ENGINE PERFORMANCE
# Self-Diagnostics – XT & XT6 (Cont.)

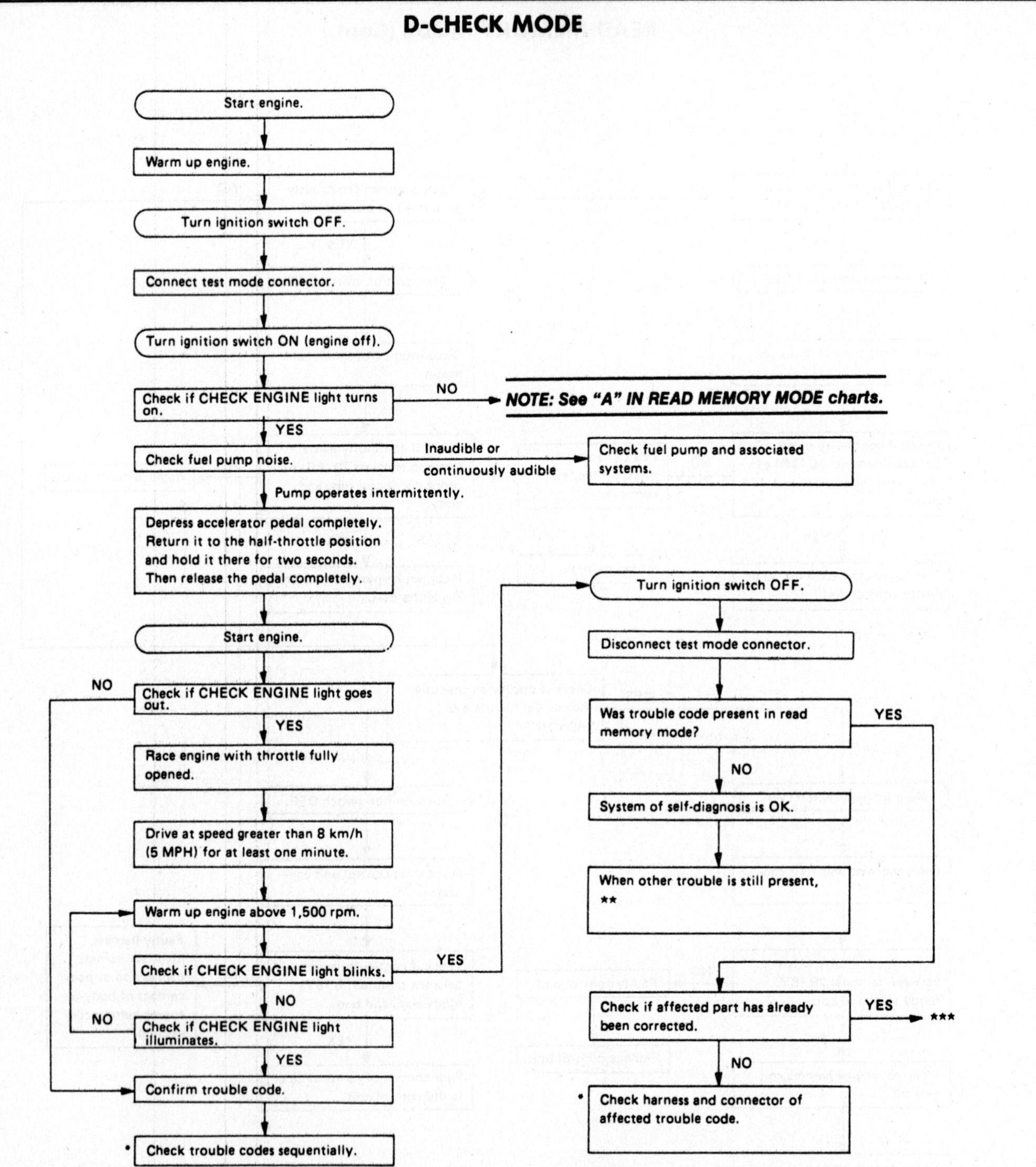
D-CHECK MODE
Start engine.
Warm up engine.
Turn ignition switch OFF.
Connect test mode connector.
Turn ignition switch ON (engine off).
Check if CHECK ENGINE light turns on.
NO
NOTE: See "A" IN READ MEMORY MODE charts.
YES
Check fuel pump noise.
Inaudible or continuously audible
Check fuel pump and associated systems.
Pump operates intermittently.
Depress accelerator pedal completely. Return it to the half-throttle position and hold it there for two seconds. Then release the pedal completely.
Start engine.
NO
Check if CHECK ENGINE light goes out.
YES
Race engine with throttle fully opened.
Drive at speed greater than 8 km/h (5 MPH) for at least one minute.
Warm up engine above 1,500 rpm.
Check if CHECK ENGINE light blinks.
YES
NO
NO
Check if CHECK ENGINE light illuminates.
YES
Confirm trouble code.
* Check trouble codes sequentially.
Turn ignition switch OFF.
Disconnect test mode connector.
Was trouble code present in read memory mode?
YES
NO
System of self-diagnosis is OK.
When other trouble is still present, **
Check if affected part has already been corrected.
YES
***
NO
* Check harness and connector of affected trouble code.

**When more than one trouble code is output, sequentially check trouble codes, starting with smallest code number. After correcting each trouble, reconduct D-check and ensure corresponding trouble code is no longer present. If another trouble code is output, carry out trouble shooting again.**

** See TROUBLE SHOOTING – NO CODES article.

*** Go to CLEAR MEMORY CODE chart.

118377

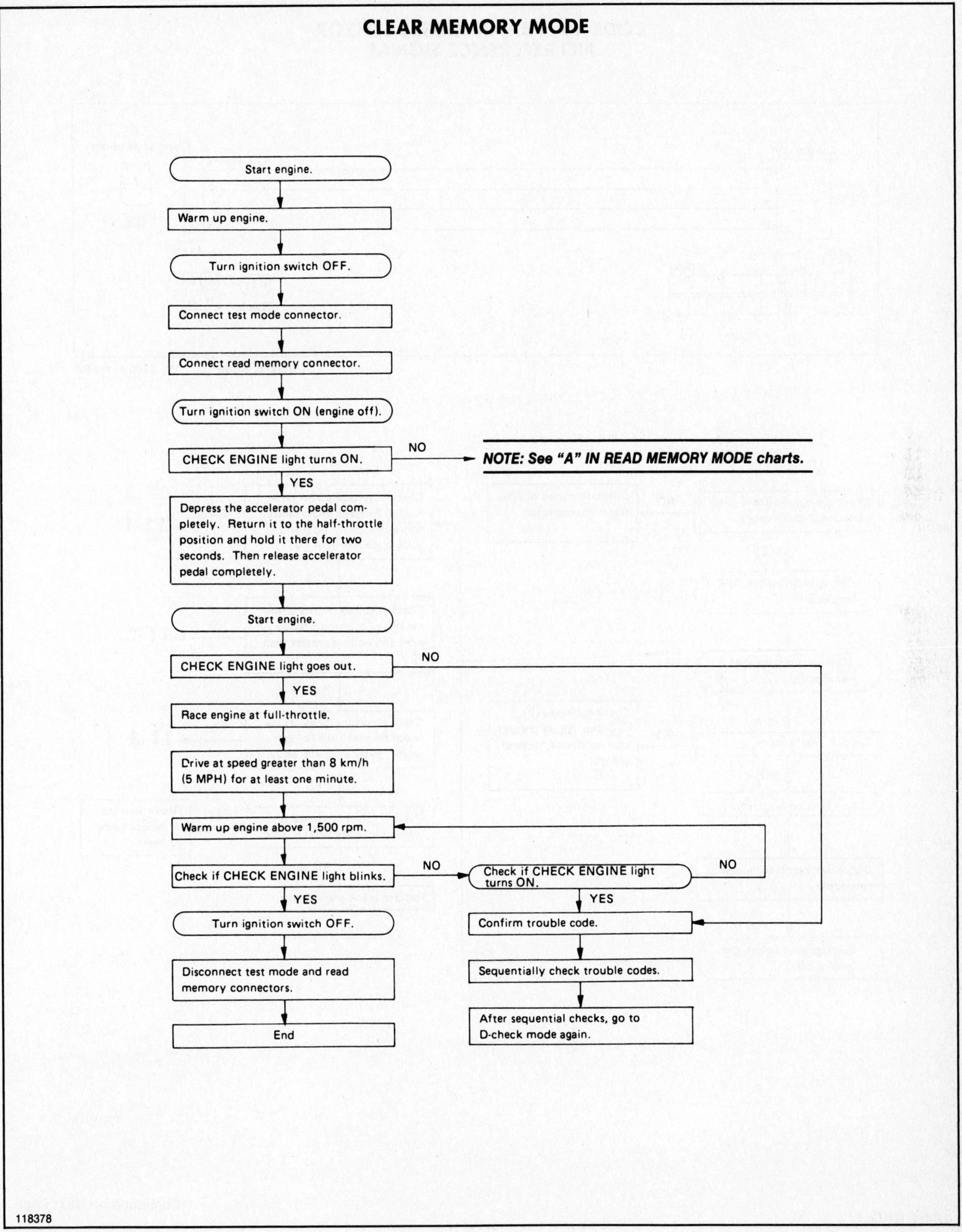
CLEAR MEMORY MODE
Start engine.
Warm up engine.
Turn ignition switch OFF.
Connect test mode connector.
Connect read memory connector.
Turn ignition switch ON (engine off).
CHECK ENGINE light turns ON.
NO
NOTE: See "A" IN READ MEMORY MODE charts.
YES
Depress the accelerator pedal completely. Return it to the half-throttle position and hold it there for two seconds. Then release accelerator pedal completely.
Start engine.
CHECK ENGINE light goes out.
NO
YES
Race engine at full-throttle.
Drive at speed greater than 8 km/h (5 MPH) for at least one minute.
Warm up engine above 1,500 rpm.
Check if CHECK ENGINE light blinks.
NO
Check if CHECK ENGINE light turns ON.
NO
YES
Turn ignition switch OFF.
YES
Confirm trouble code.
Disconnect test mode and read memory connectors.
Sequentially check trouble codes.
End
After sequential checks, go to D-check mode again.
118378

# 1991 ENGINE PERFORMANCE
# Self-Diagnostics – XT & XT6 (Cont.)

## CODE 11, CRANK ANGLE SENSOR
## NO REFERENCE SIGNAL

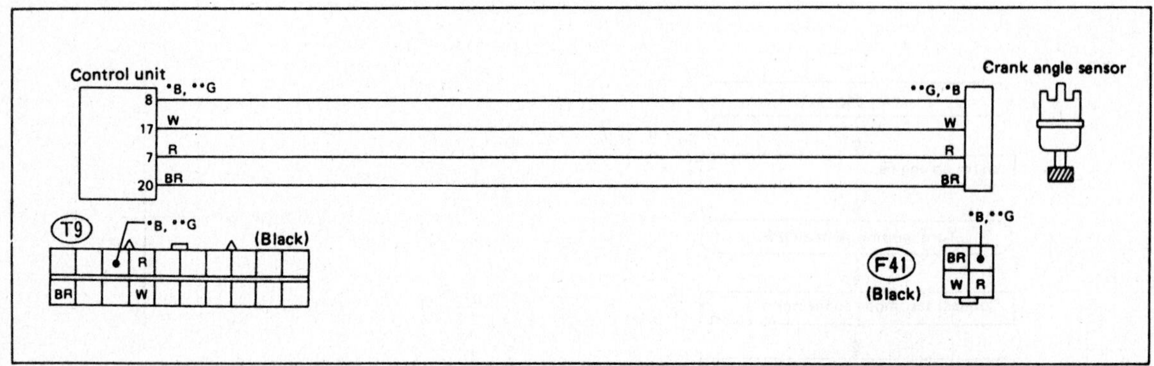


*: 1800 cc model **: 2700 cc model

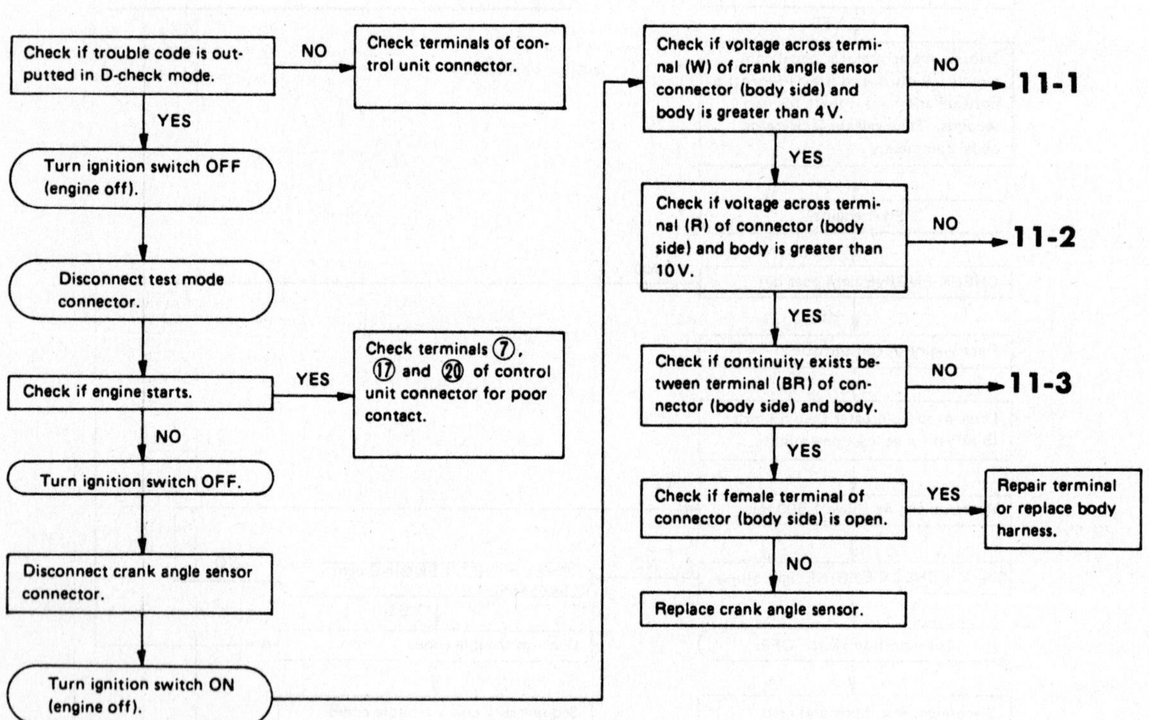


Continued on Next Page

118380 121902

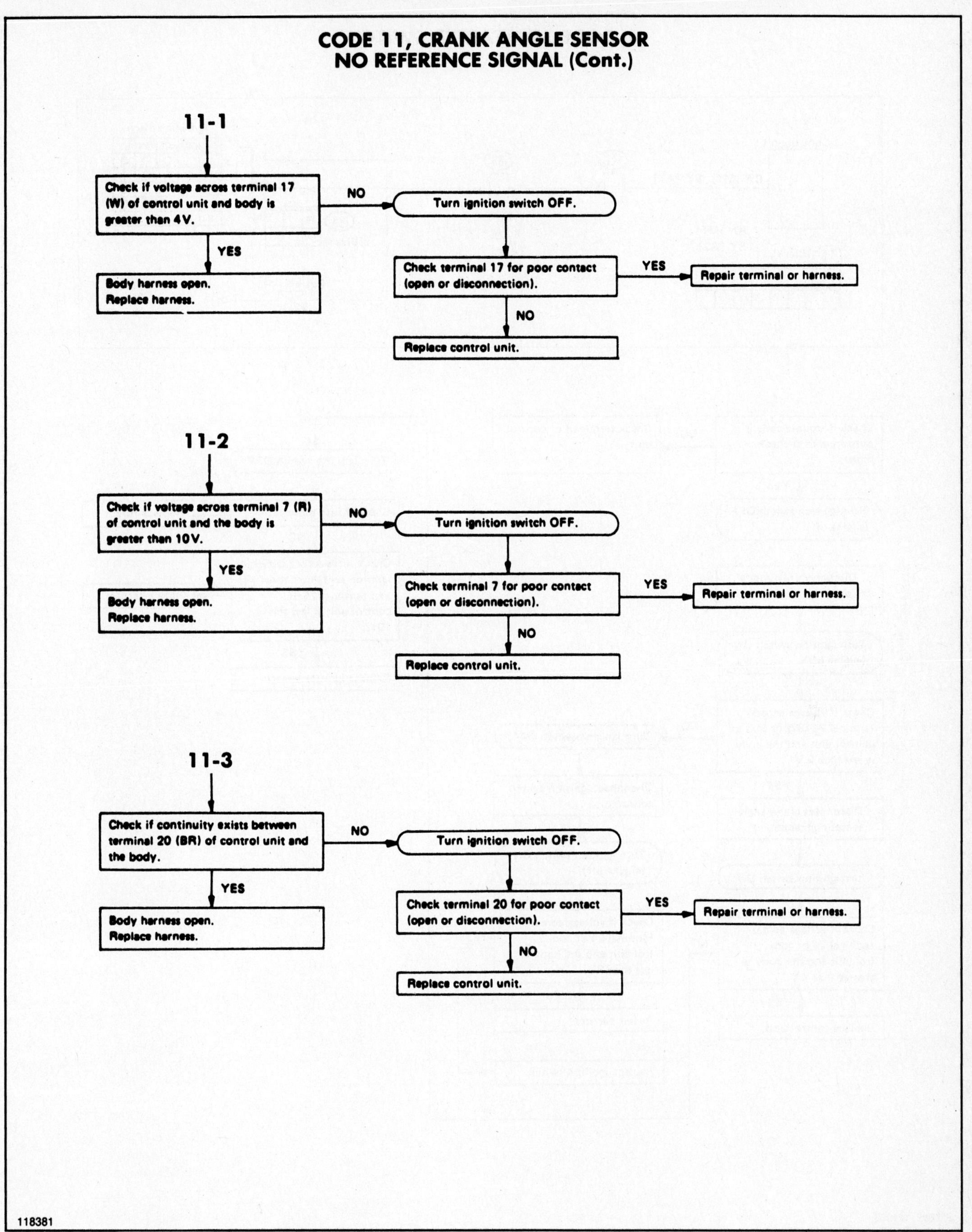
CODE 11, CRANK ANGLE SENSOR
NO REFERENCE SIGNAL (Cont.)
11-1
Check if voltage across terminal 17 (W) of control unit and body is greater than 4V.
NO
Turn ignition switch OFF.
YES
Body harness open. Replace harness.
Check terminal 17 for poor contact (open or disconnection).
YES
Repair terminal or harness.
NO
Replace control unit.
11-2
Check if voltage across terminal 7 (R) of control unit and the body is greater than 10V.
NO
Turn ignition switch OFF.
YES
Body harness open. Replace harness.
Check terminal 7 for poor contact (open or disconnection).
YES
Repair terminal or harness.
NO
Replace control unit.
11-3
Check if continuity exists between terminal 20 (BR) of control unit and the body.
NO
Turn ignition switch OFF.
YES
Body harness open. Replace harness.
Check terminal 20 for poor contact (open or disconnection).
YES
Repair terminal or harness.
NO
Replace control unit.
118381

# 1991 ENGINE PERFORMANCE
# Self-Diagnostics – XT & XT6 (Cont.)

## CODE 12, STARTER SWITCH

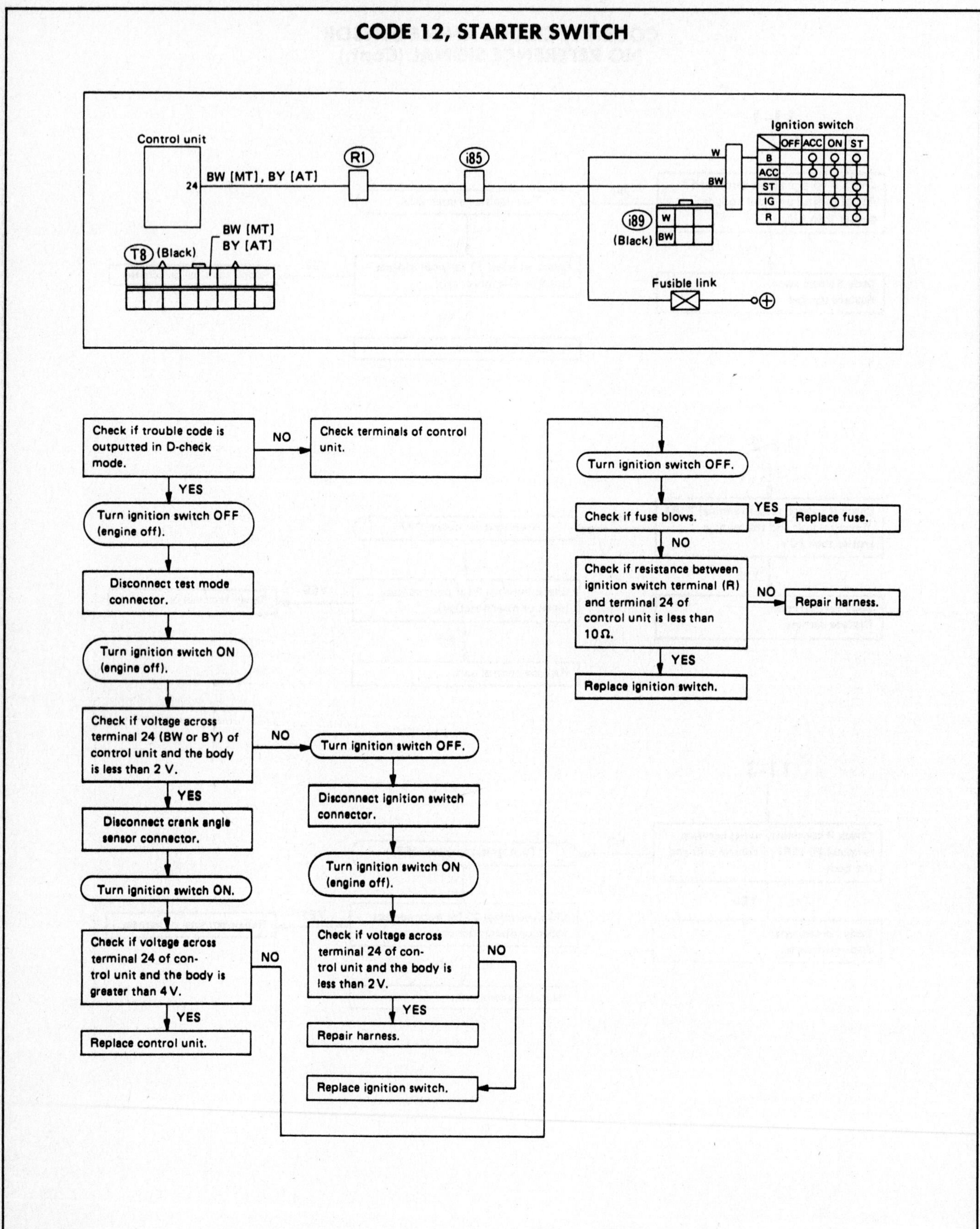

## CODE 13, CRANK ANGLE SENSOR NO POSITION PULSE

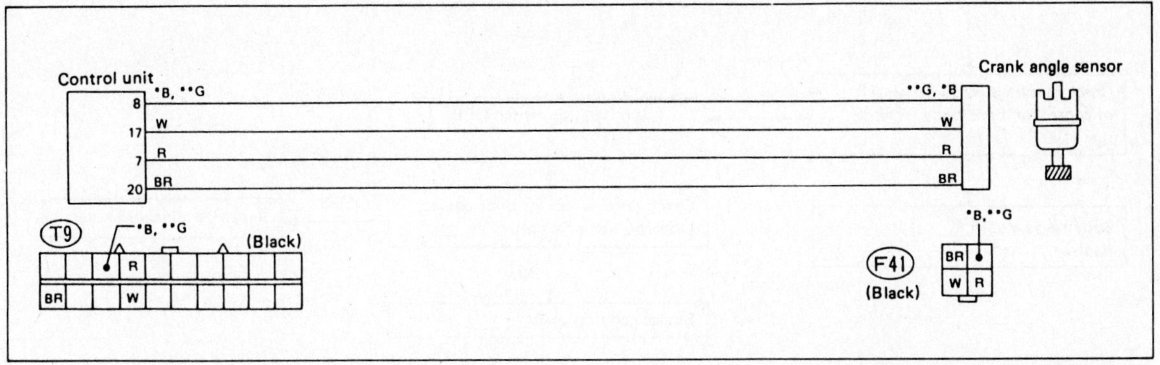


*: 1800 cc model **: 2700 cc model

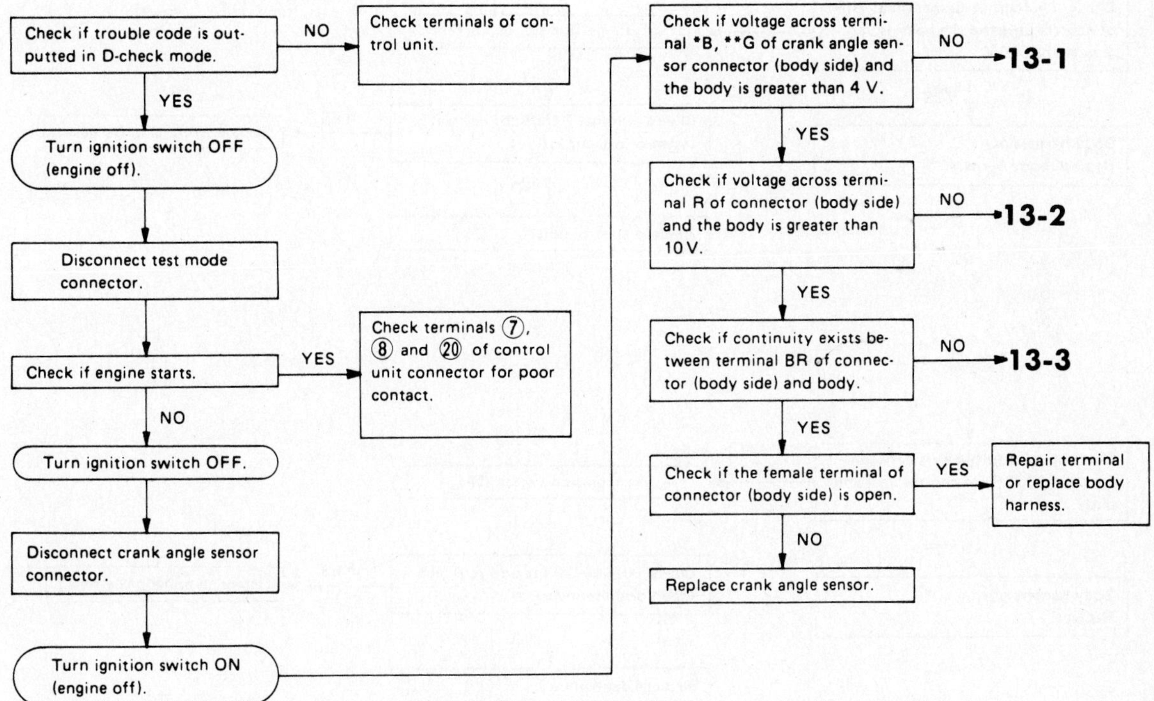


Continued on Next Page

118383 121904

# 1991 ENGINE PERFORMANCE
## Self-Diagnostics – XT & XT6 (Cont.)

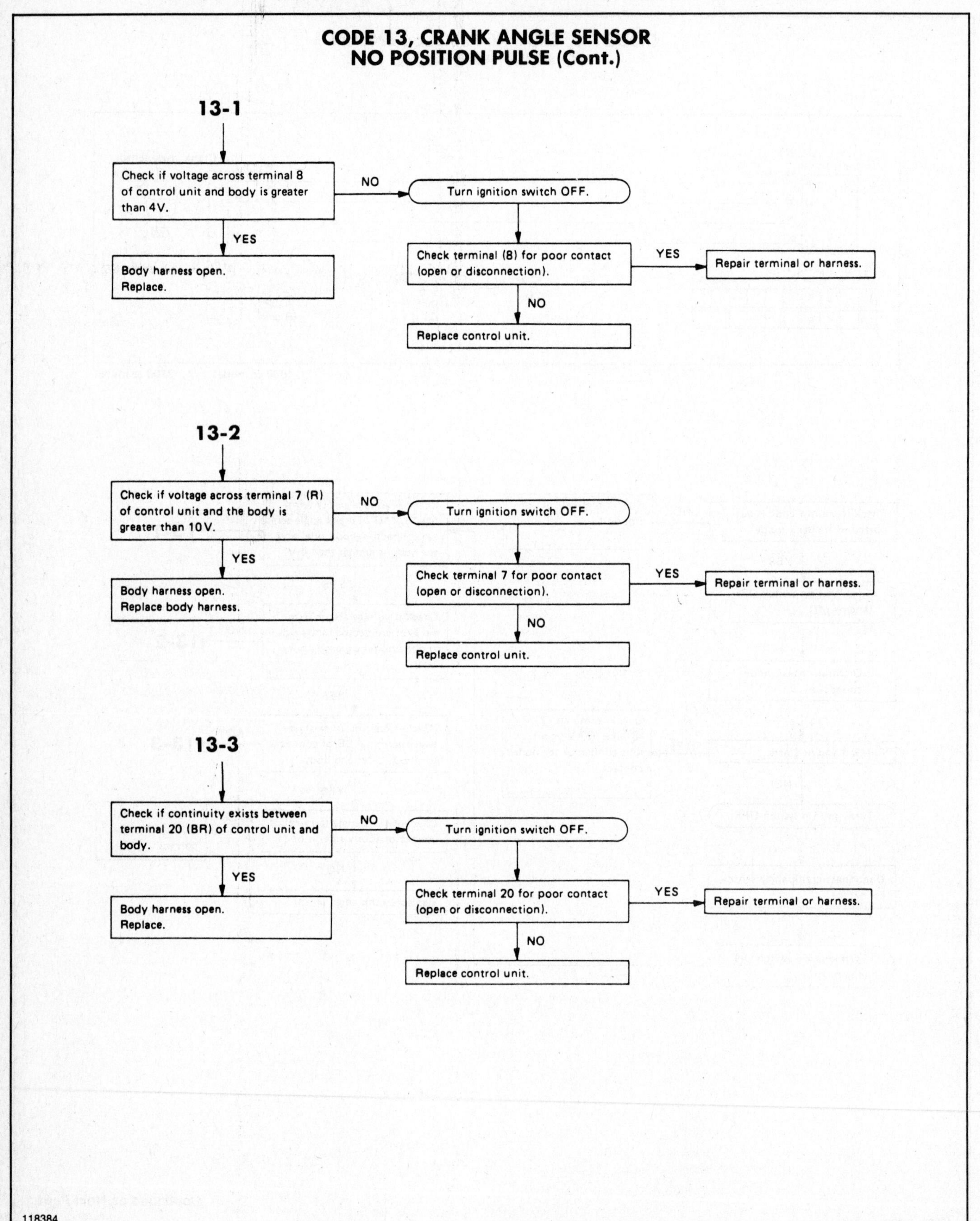
CODE 13, CRANK ANGLE SENSOR
NO POSITION PULSE (Cont.)
13-1
Check if voltage across terminal 8 of control unit and body is greater than 4V.
NO
Turn ignition switch OFF.
YES
Body harness open. Replace.
Check terminal (8) for poor contact (open or disconnection).
YES
Repair terminal or harness.
NO
Replace control unit.
13-2
Check if voltage across terminal 7 (R) of control unit and the body is greater than 10V.
NO
Turn ignition switch OFF.
YES
Body harness open. Replace body harness.
Check terminal 7 for poor contact (open or disconnection).
YES
Repair terminal or harness.
NO
Replace control unit.
13-3
Check if continuity exists between terminal 20 (BR) of control unit and body.
NO
Turn ignition switch OFF.
YES
Body harness open. Replace.
Check terminal 20 for poor contact (open or disconnection).
YES
Repair terminal or harness.
NO
Replace control unit.
118384

# 1991 ENGINE PERFORMANCE
# Self-Diagnostics – XT & XT6 (Cont.)

## CODE 14
## FUEL INJECTORS NO. 1 & 2 (XT)

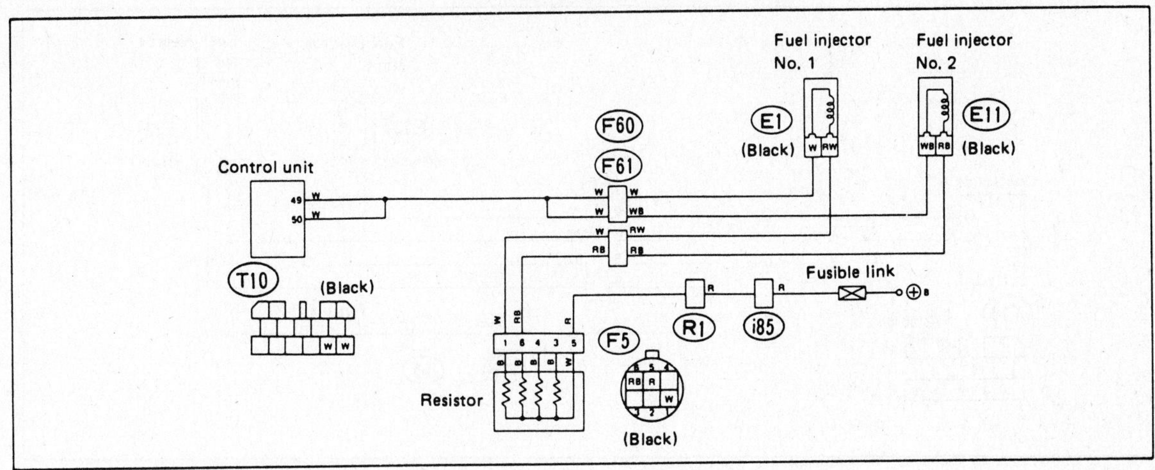

Check if trouble code is outputted in D-check mode.
- NO → Check terminals of control unit.
- YES ↓

Turn ignition switch OFF (engine off).

↓

Disconnect test mode connector.

↓

Disconnect control unit connector.

↓

Check if voltage across body and terminals 49 (W) and 50 (W) of connector (body side) is greater than 10 V.
- NO → Disconnect fuel injector connectors #1 and #2.
- YES ↓

Check if terminals 49 and 50 are open or disconnected.
- YES → Repair terminal.
- NO ↓

Replace control unit.

---

Disconnect fuel injector connectors #1 and #2.

↓

Check if resistance between terminals of fuel injector is 2 – 3 Ω.
- NO → Replace fuel injector.
- YES ↓

Check if voltage across body and power terminals (RW) and (RB) of connector (body side) is greater than 10 V.
- NO → Repair harness from fuel injector to control unit.
- YES ↓

Disconnect resistor connector.

↓

Check if resistance between terminals (W) and (B's) of connector (resistor side) is 5.7 – 6.5 Ω.
- NO → Replace resistor.
- YES ↓

Check if voltage across terminal 5 (R) of connector (body side) and body is greater than 10 V.
- NO → Repair harness from battery to resistor.
- YES ↓

Repair harness from resistor to fuel injector.

Continued on Next Page

# 1991 ENGINE PERFORMANCE
# Self-Diagnostics – XT & XT6 (Cont.)

## CODE 14 (Cont.)
## FUEL INJECTORS NO. 5 & 6 (XT6)

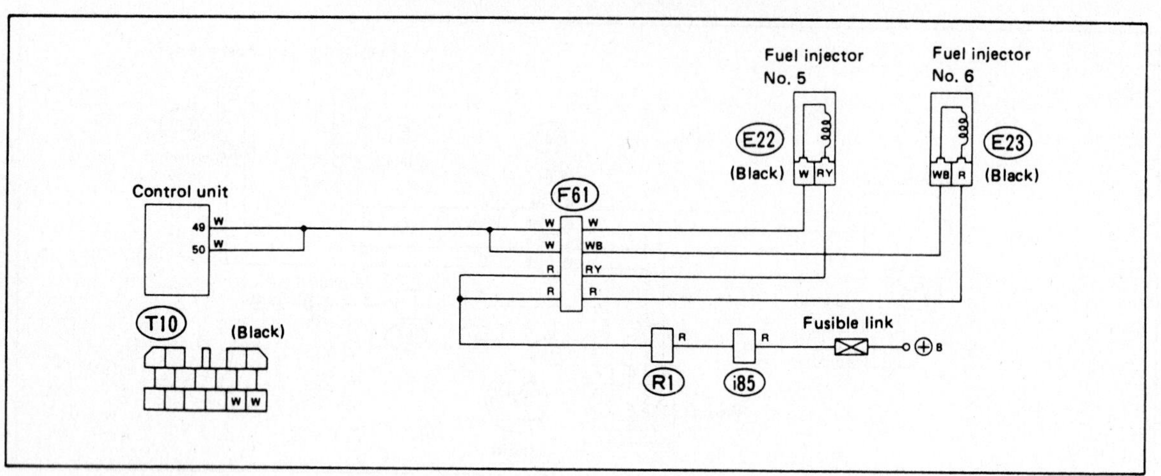


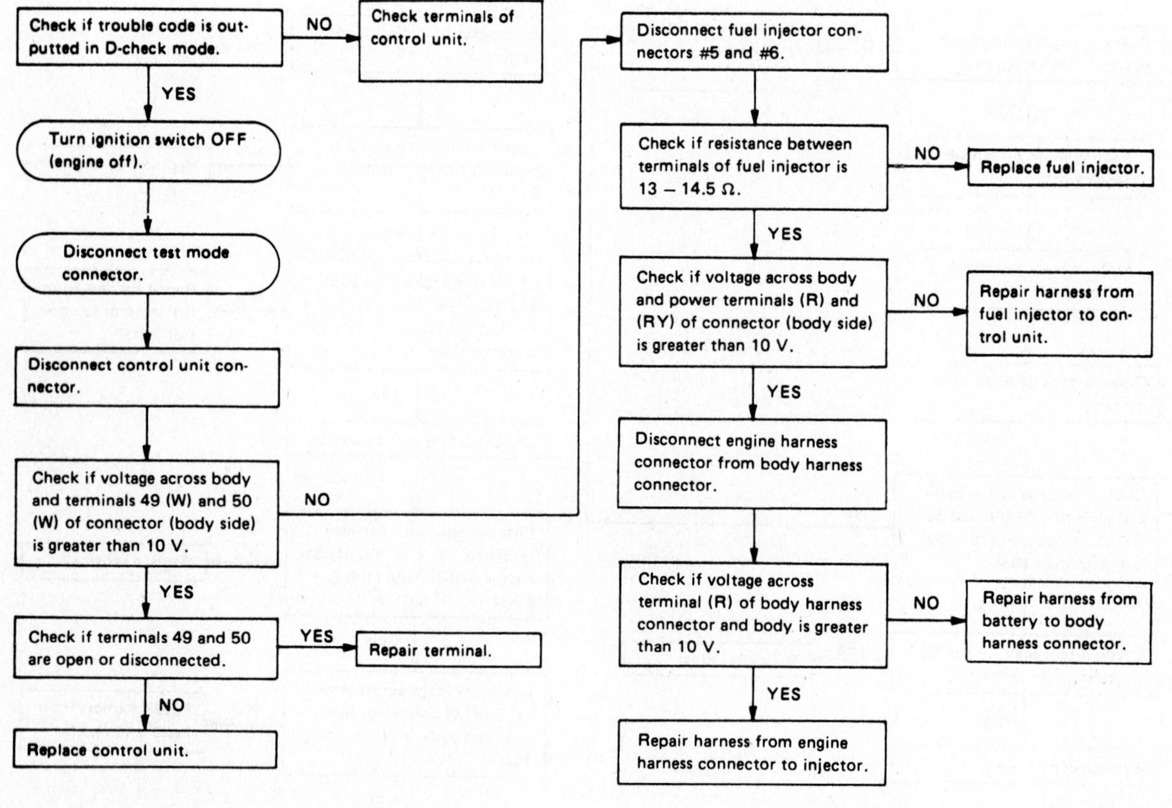


118386 121906

# 1991 ENGINE PERFORMANCE
# Self-Diagnostics – XT & XT6 (Cont.)

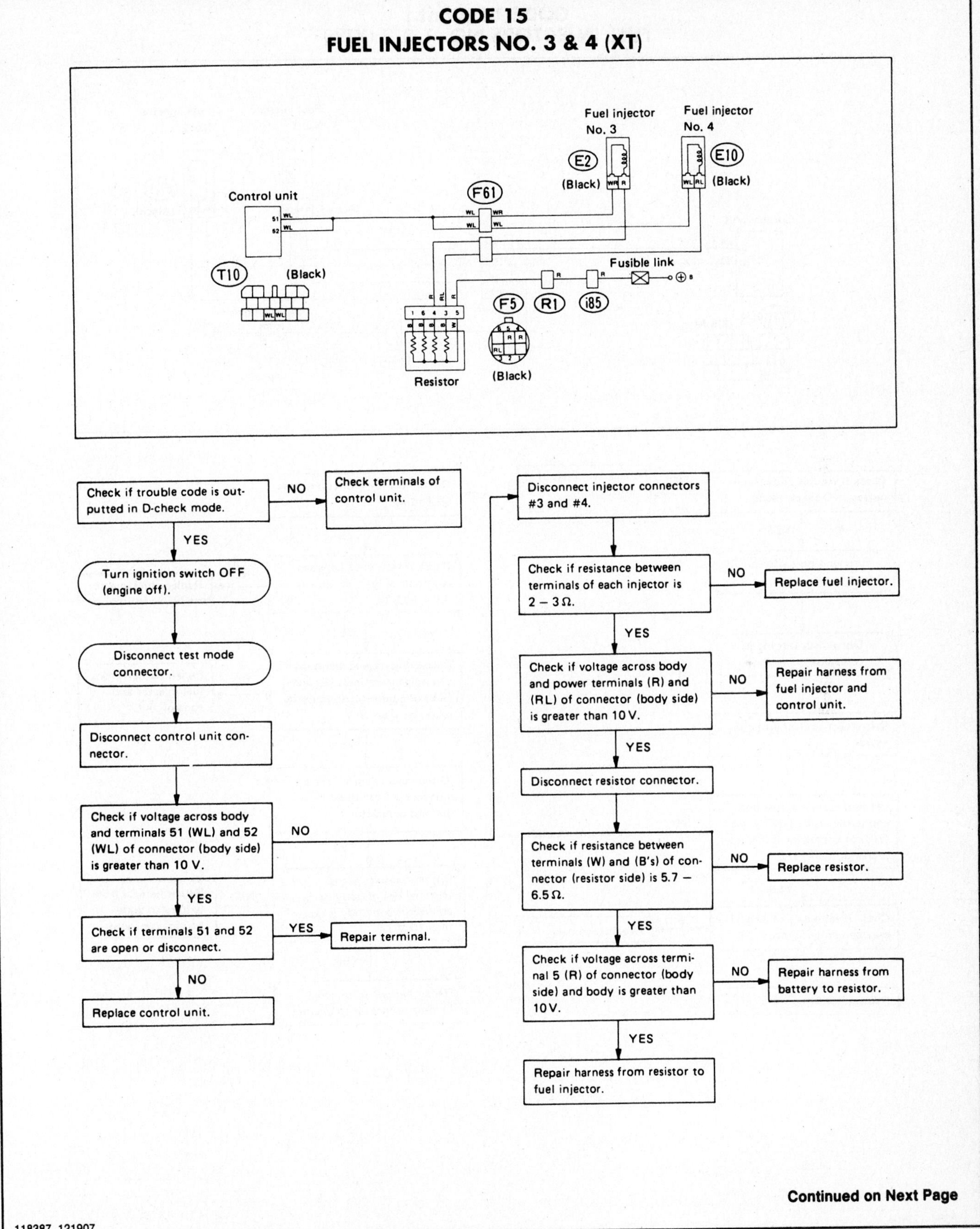

# 1991 ENGINE PERFORMANCE
# Self-Diagnostics – XT & XT6 (Cont.)

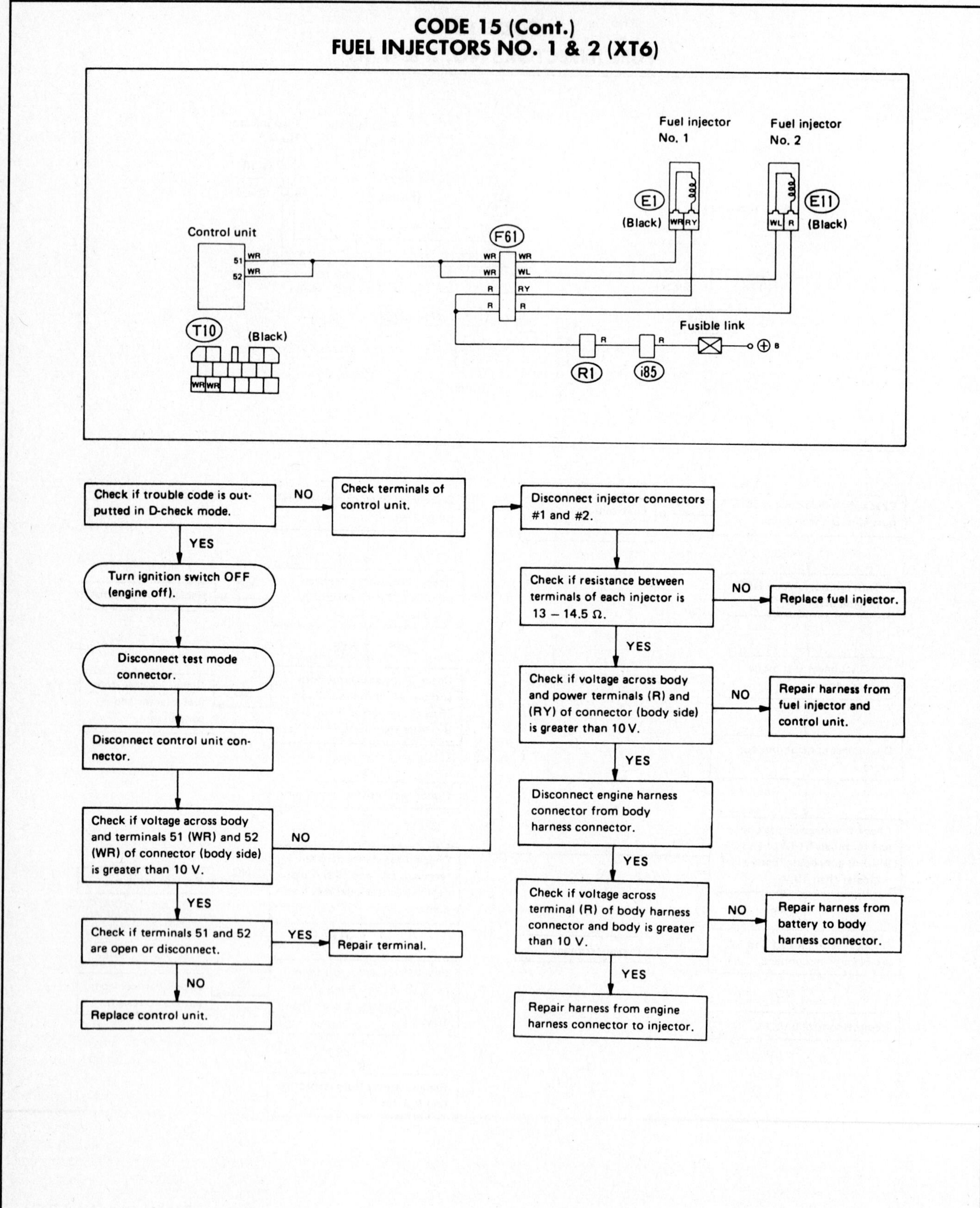

### CODE 21, COOLANT (WATER) TEMPERATURE SENSOR

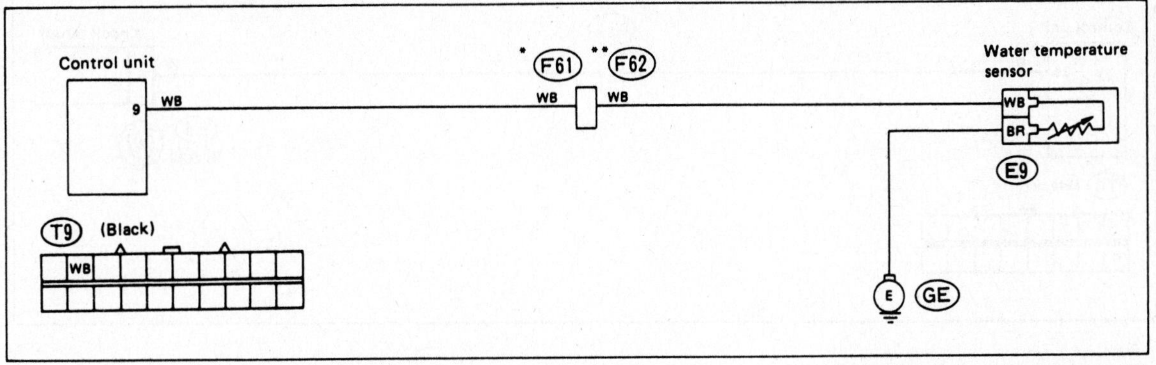


*: 1800 cc model **: 2700 cc model

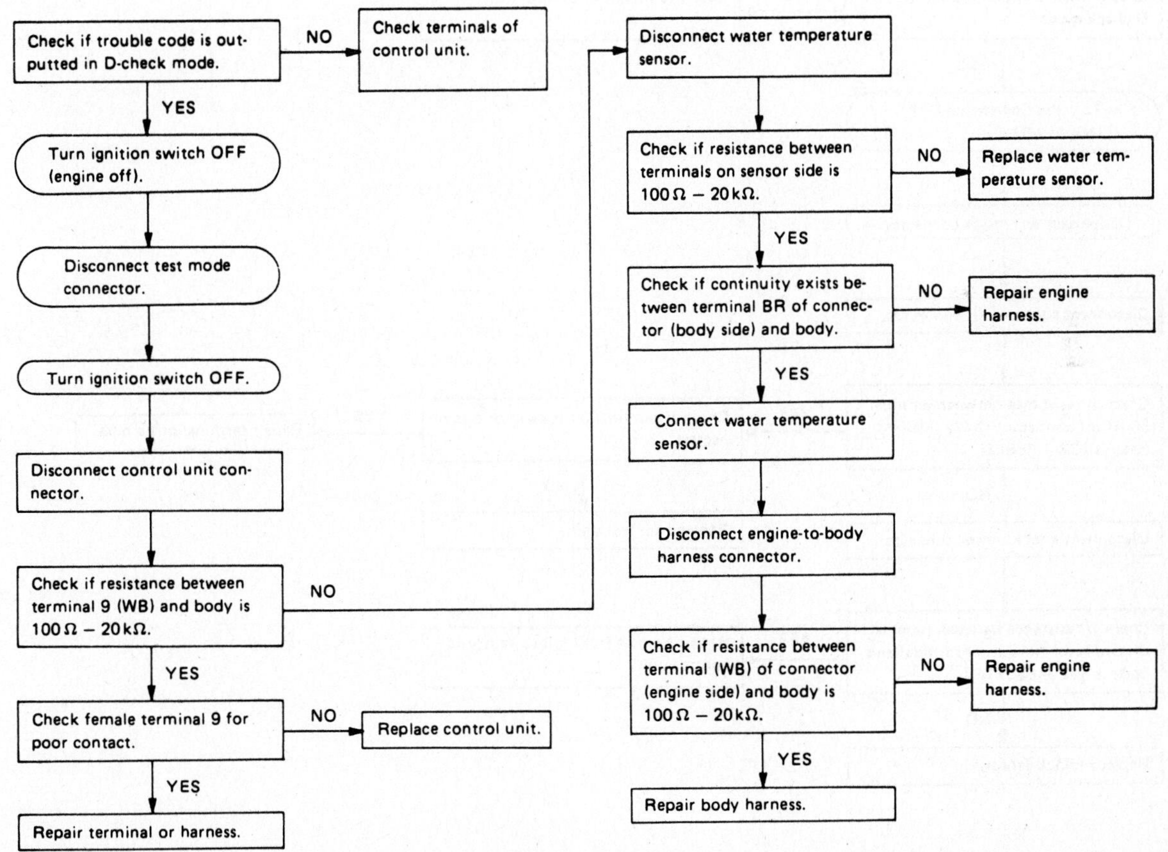


118389 121909

# 1991 ENGINE PERFORMANCE
## Self-Diagnostics – XT & XT6 (Cont.)

### CODE 22, KNOCK SENSOR (XT6)

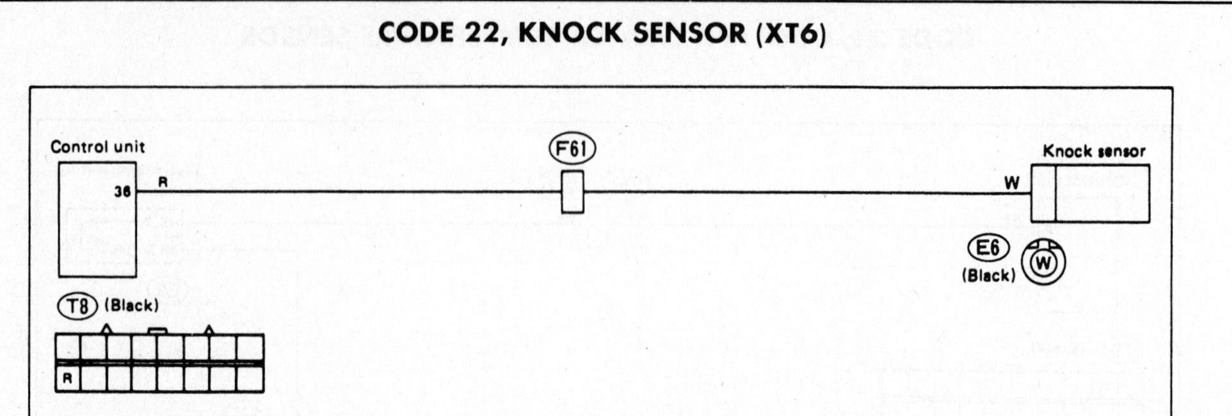


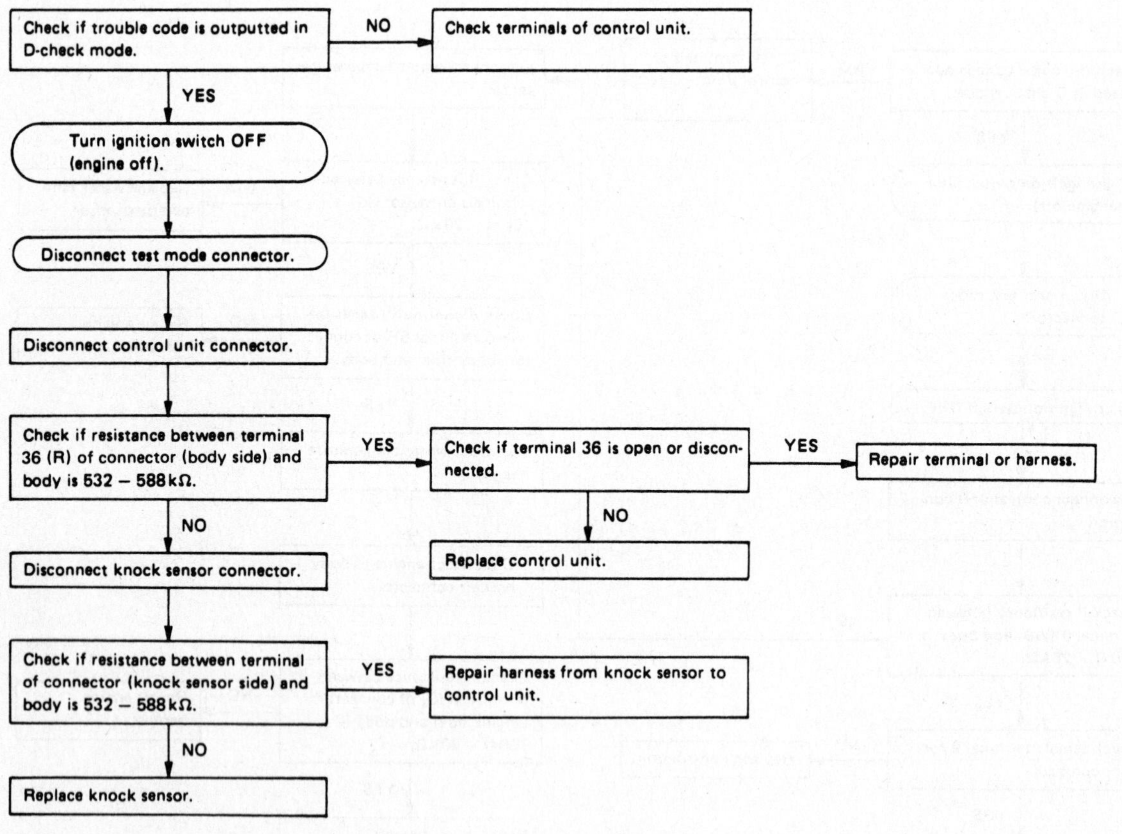


118390 121910

# 1991 ENGINE PERFORMANCE
# Self-Diagnostics – XT & XT6 (Cont.)

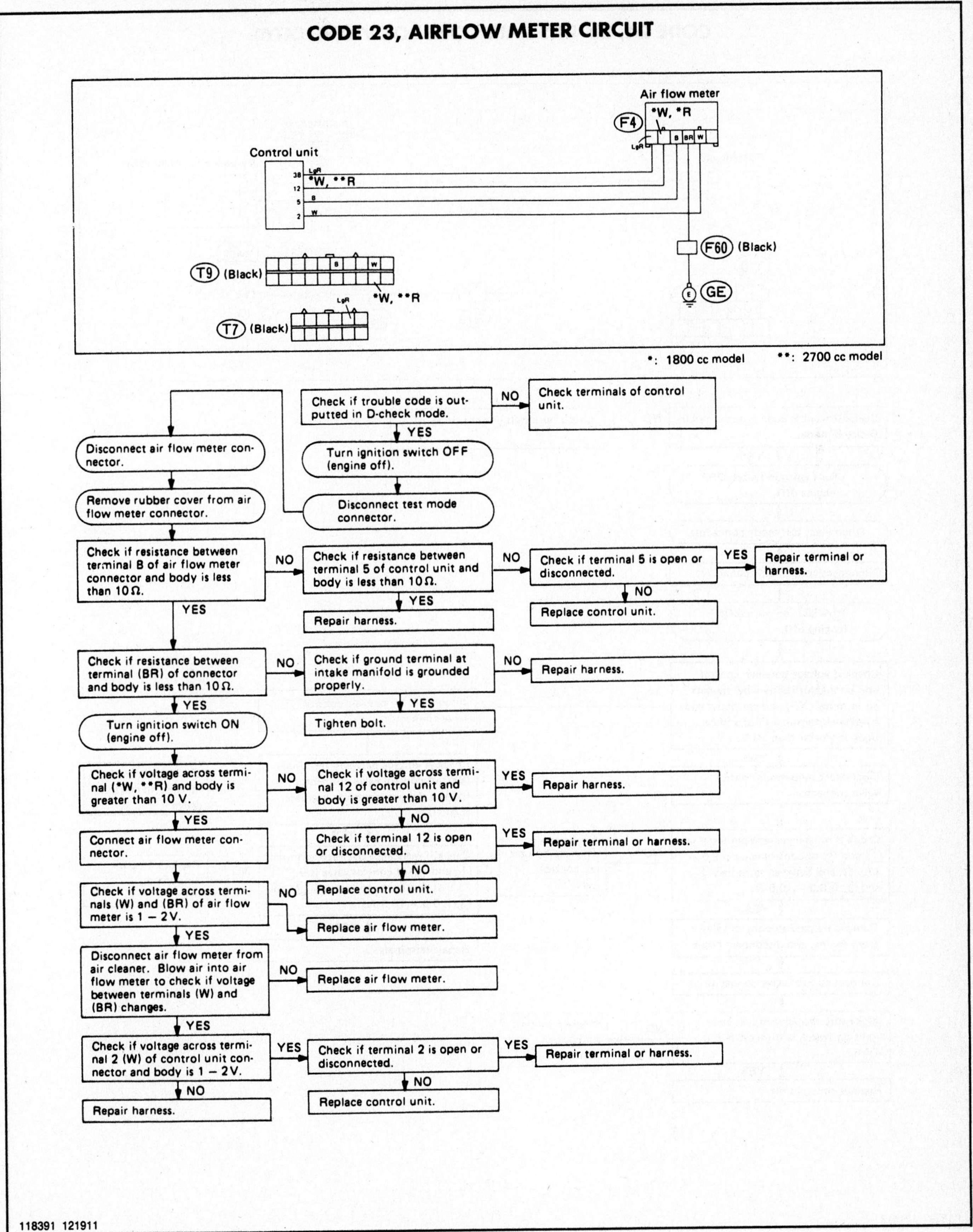

CODE 23, AIRFLOW METER CIRCUIT
Air flow meter
F4
*W, *R
LgR
B
BR
W
Control unit
38
12
5
2
LgR
*W, **R
B
W
F60 (Black)
GE
T9 (Black)
*W, **R
T7 (Black)
*: 1800 cc model
**: 2700 cc model
Check if trouble code is outputted in D-check mode.
NO
Check terminals of control unit.
YES
Turn ignition switch OFF (engine off).
Disconnect test mode connector.
Disconnect air flow meter connector.
Remove rubber cover from air flow meter connector.
Check if resistance between terminal B of air flow meter connector and body is less than 10 Ω.
NO
Check if resistance between terminal 5 of control unit and body is less than 10 Ω.
NO
Check if terminal 5 is open or disconnected.
YES
Repair terminal or harness.
NO
Replace control unit.
YES
Repair harness.
YES
Check if resistance between terminal (BR) of connector and body is less than 10 Ω.
NO
Check if ground terminal at intake manifold is grounded properly.
NO
Repair harness.
YES
Tighten bolt.
YES
Turn ignition switch ON (engine off).
Check if voltage across terminal (*W, **R) and body is greater than 10 V.
NO
Check if voltage across terminal 12 of control unit and body is greater than 10 V.
YES
Repair harness.
NO
Check if terminal 12 is open or disconnected.
YES
Repair terminal or harness.
NO
Replace control unit.
YES
Connect air flow meter connector.
Check if voltage across terminals (W) and (BR) of air flow meter is 1 – 2V.
NO
Replace air flow meter.
YES
Disconnect air flow meter from air cleaner. Blow air into air flow meter to check if voltage between terminals (W) and (BR) changes.
NO
Replace air flow meter.
YES
Check if voltage across terminal 2 (W) of control unit connector and body is 1 – 2V.
YES
Check if terminal 2 is open or disconnected.
YES
Repair terminal or harness.
NO
Replace control unit.
NO
Repair harness.
118391 121911

# 1991 ENGINE PERFORMANCE
# Self-Diagnostics – XT & XT6 (Cont.)

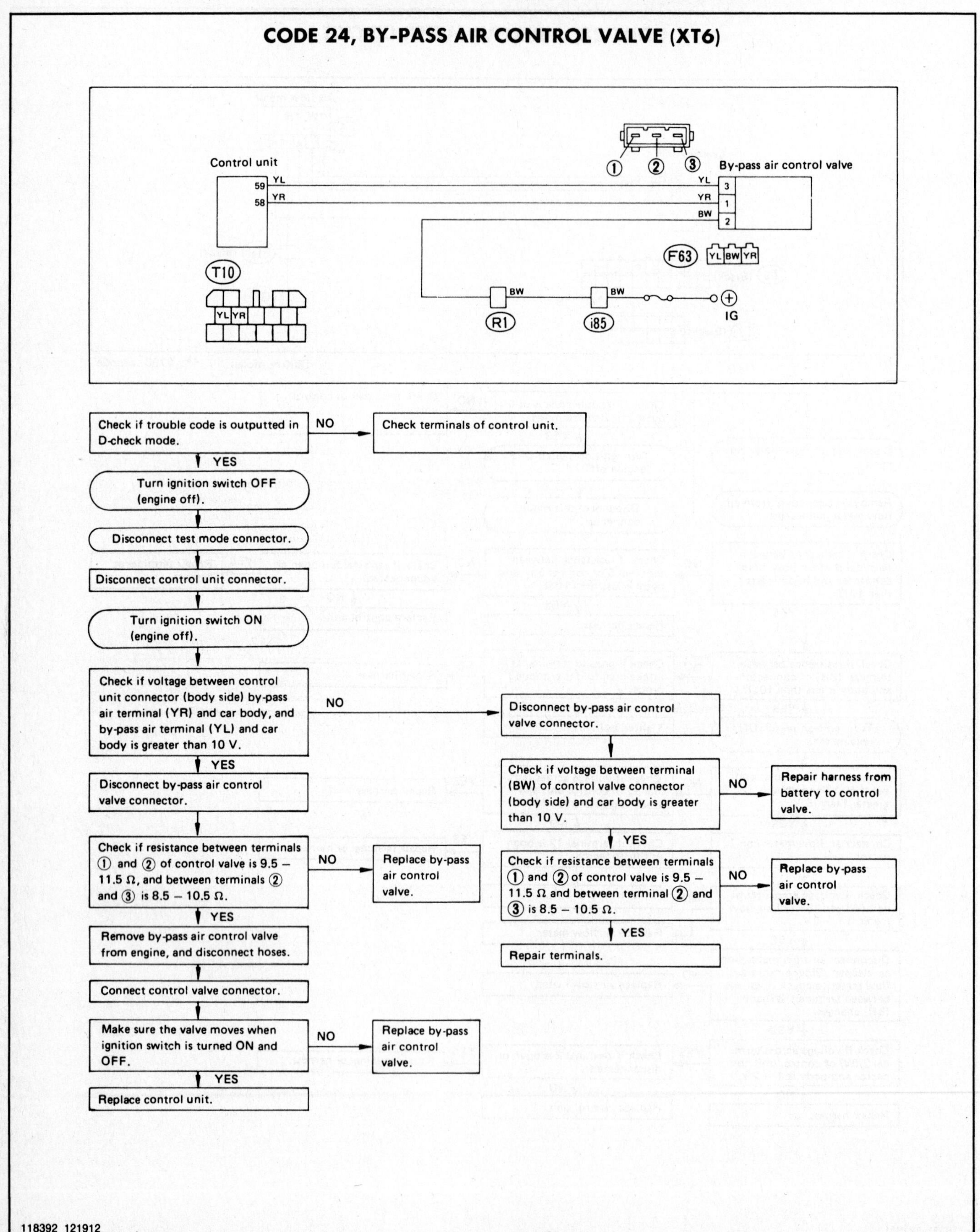

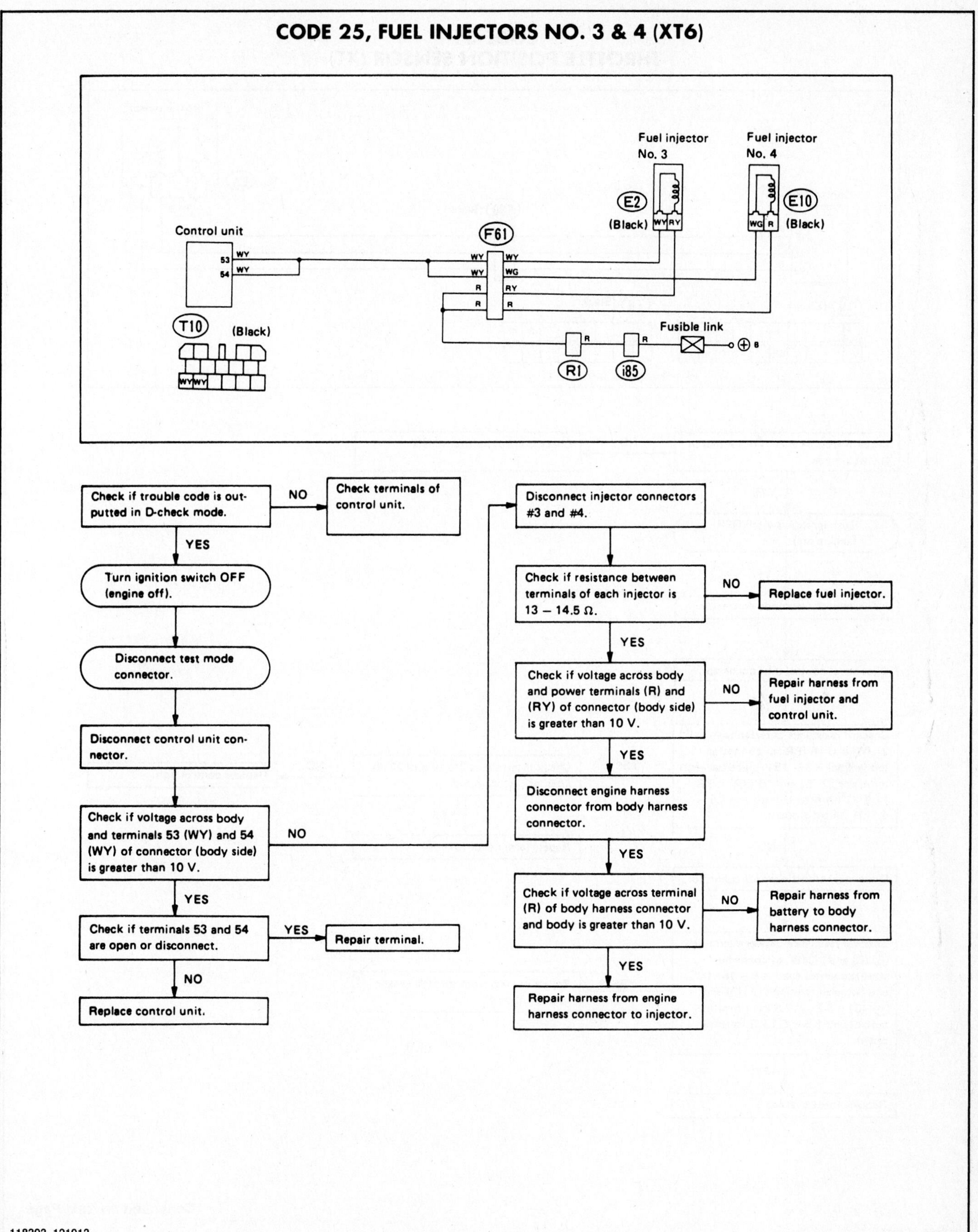
CODE 25, FUEL INJECTORS NO. 3 & 4 (XT6)
Fuel injector No. 3
Fuel injector No. 4
E2
(Black)
E10
(Black)
Control unit
53
54
WY
F61
WG
RY
R
T10
(Black)
Fusible link
R1
i85
Check if trouble code is outputted in D-check mode.
NO
Check terminals of control unit.
YES
Turn ignition switch OFF (engine off).
Disconnect test mode connector.
Disconnect control unit connector.
Check if voltage across body and terminals 53 (WY) and 54 (WY) of connector (body side) is greater than 10 V.
Check if terminals 53 and 54 are open or disconnect.
Repair terminal.
Replace control unit.
Disconnect injector connectors #3 and #4.
Check if resistance between terminals of each injector is 13 – 14.5 Ω.
Replace fuel injector.
Check if voltage across body and power terminals (R) and (RY) of connector (body side) is greater than 10 V.
Repair harness from fuel injector and control unit.
Disconnect engine harness connector from body harness connector.
Check if voltage across terminal (R) of body harness connector and body is greater than 10 V.
Repair harness from battery to body harness connector.
Repair harness from engine harness connector to injector.
118393 121913

# 1991 ENGINE PERFORMANCE
# Self-Diagnostics – XT & XT6 (Cont.)

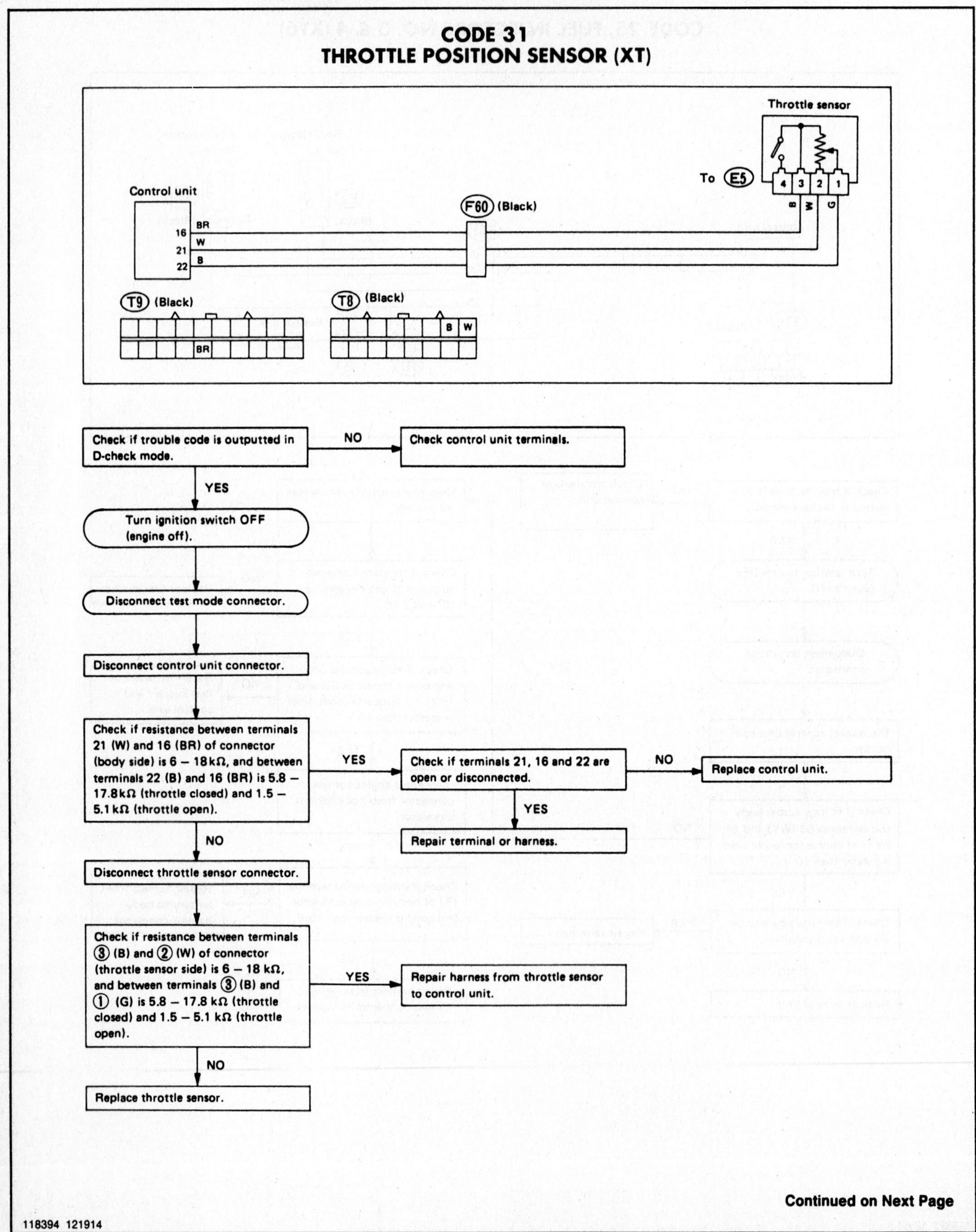


Continued on Next Page

118394 121914

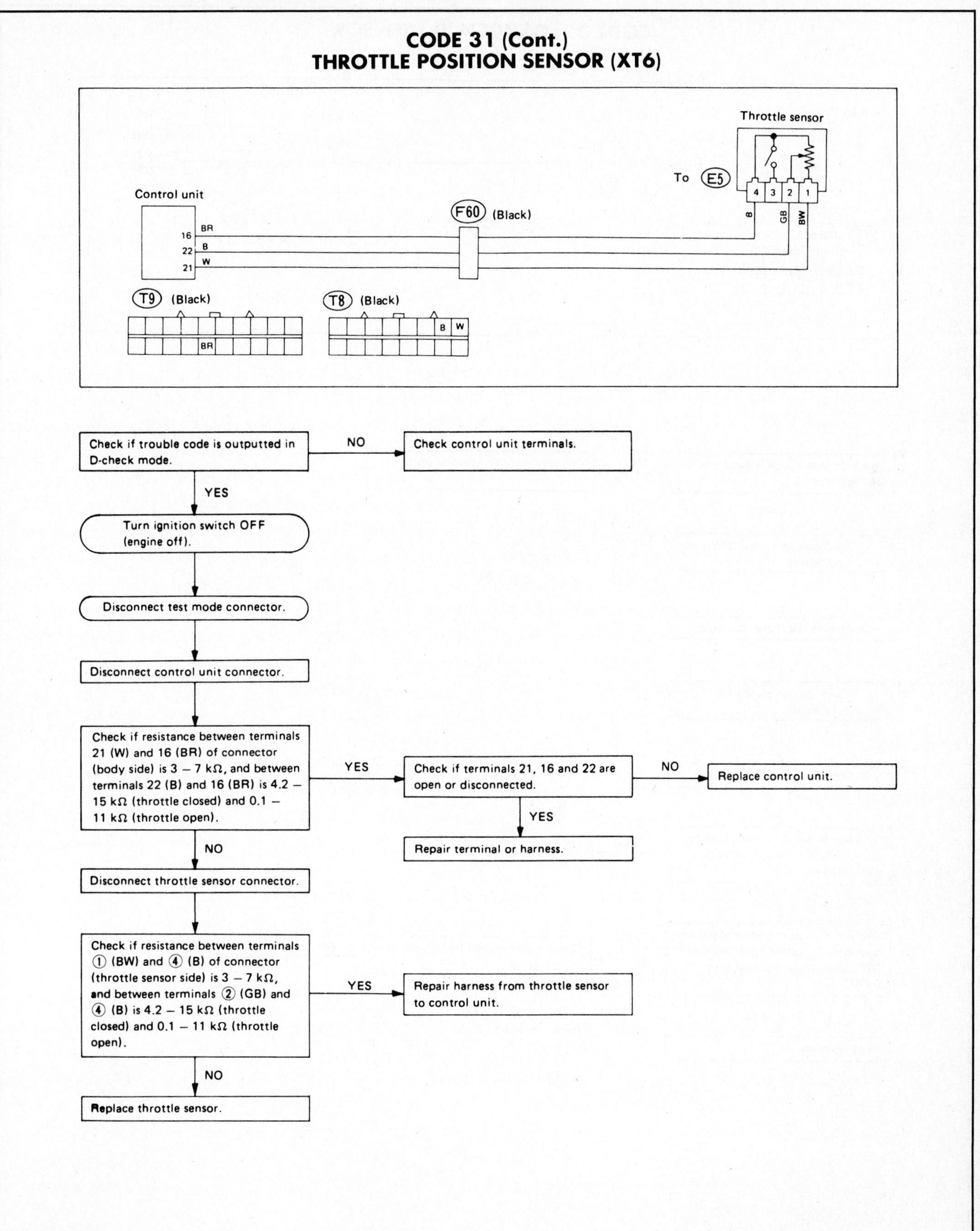
CODE 31 (Cont.)
THROTTLE POSITION SENSOR (XT6)
Throttle sensor
To E5
4 3 2 1
Control unit
F60 (Black)
16 BR
22 B
21 W
B GB BW
T9 (Black)
BR
T8 (Black)
B W
Check if trouble code is outputted in D-check mode.
NO
Check control unit terminals.
YES
Turn ignition switch OFF (engine off).
Disconnect test mode connector.
Disconnect control unit connector.
Check if resistance between terminals 21 (W) and 16 (BR) of connector (body side) is 3 – 7 kΩ, and between terminals 22 (B) and 16 (BR) is 4.2 – 15 kΩ (throttle closed) and 0.1 – 11 kΩ (throttle open).
YES
Check if terminals 21, 16 and 22 are open or disconnected.
NO
Replace control unit.
YES
Repair terminal or harness.
NO
Disconnect throttle sensor connector.
Check if resistance between terminals ① (BW) and ④ (B) of connector (throttle sensor side) is 3 – 7 kΩ, and between terminals ② (GB) and ④ (B) is 4.2 – 15 kΩ (throttle closed) and 0.1 – 11 kΩ (throttle open).
YES
Repair harness from throttle sensor to control unit.
NO
Replace throttle sensor.
118395 121915

# 1991 ENGINE PERFORMANCE
# Self-Diagnostics – XT & XT6 (Cont.)

## CODE 32, OXYGEN ($O_2$) SENSOR

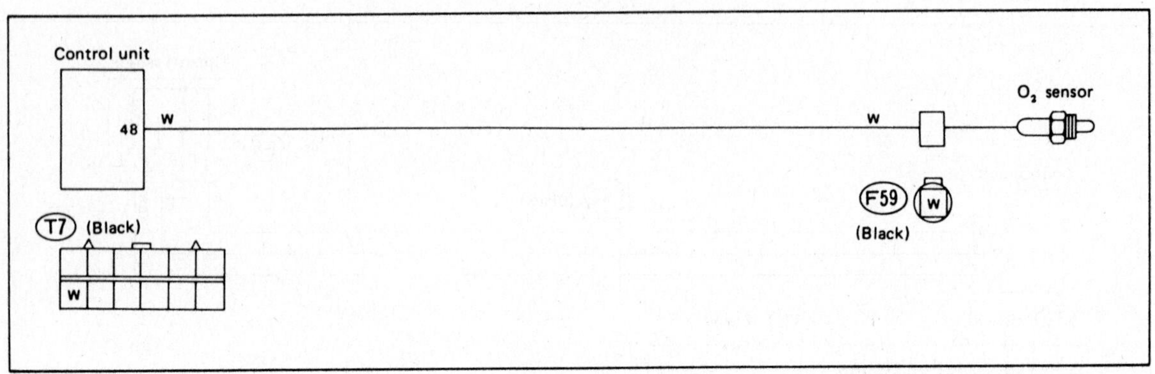


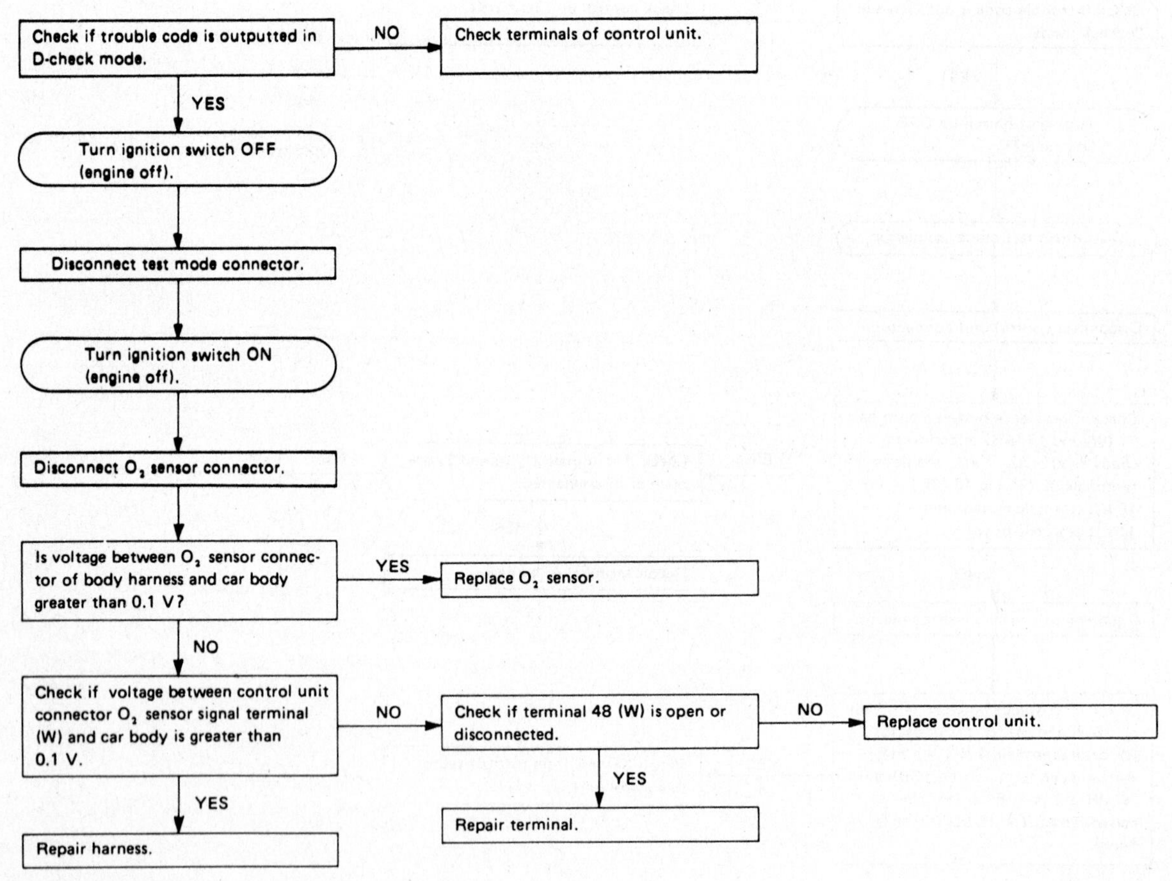


118396 121916

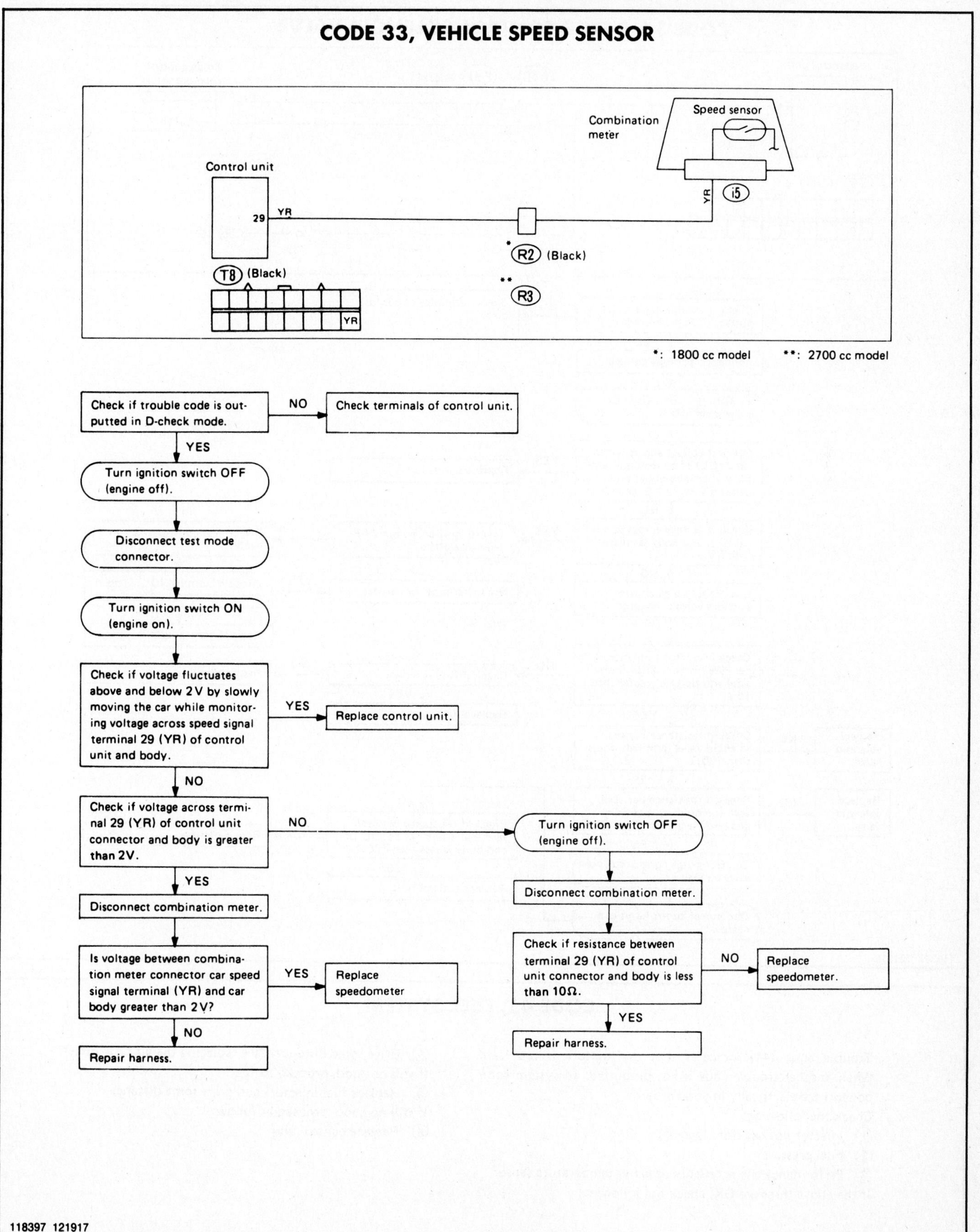
CODE 33, VEHICLE SPEED SENSOR
Combination meter
Speed sensor
Control unit
29
YR
YR
i5
* R2 (Black)
** R3
T8 (Black)
YR
*: 1800 cc model
**: 2700 cc model
Check if trouble code is outputted in D-check mode.
NO
Check terminals of control unit.
YES
Turn ignition switch OFF (engine off).
Disconnect test mode connector.
Turn ignition switch ON (engine on).
Check if voltage fluctuates above and below 2 V by slowly moving the car while monitoring voltage across speed signal terminal 29 (YR) of control unit and body.
YES
Replace control unit.
NO
Check if voltage across terminal 29 (YR) of control unit connector and body is greater than 2V.
NO
Turn ignition switch OFF (engine off).
Disconnect combination meter.
Check if resistance between terminal 29 (YR) of control unit connector and body is less than 10Ω.
NO
Replace speedometer.
YES
Repair harness.
YES
Disconnect combination meter.
Is voltage between combination meter connector car speed signal terminal (YR) and car body greater than 2 V?
YES
Replace speedometer
NO
Repair harness.
118397 121917

# 1991 ENGINE PERFORMANCE
## Self-Diagnostics – XT & XT6 (Cont.)

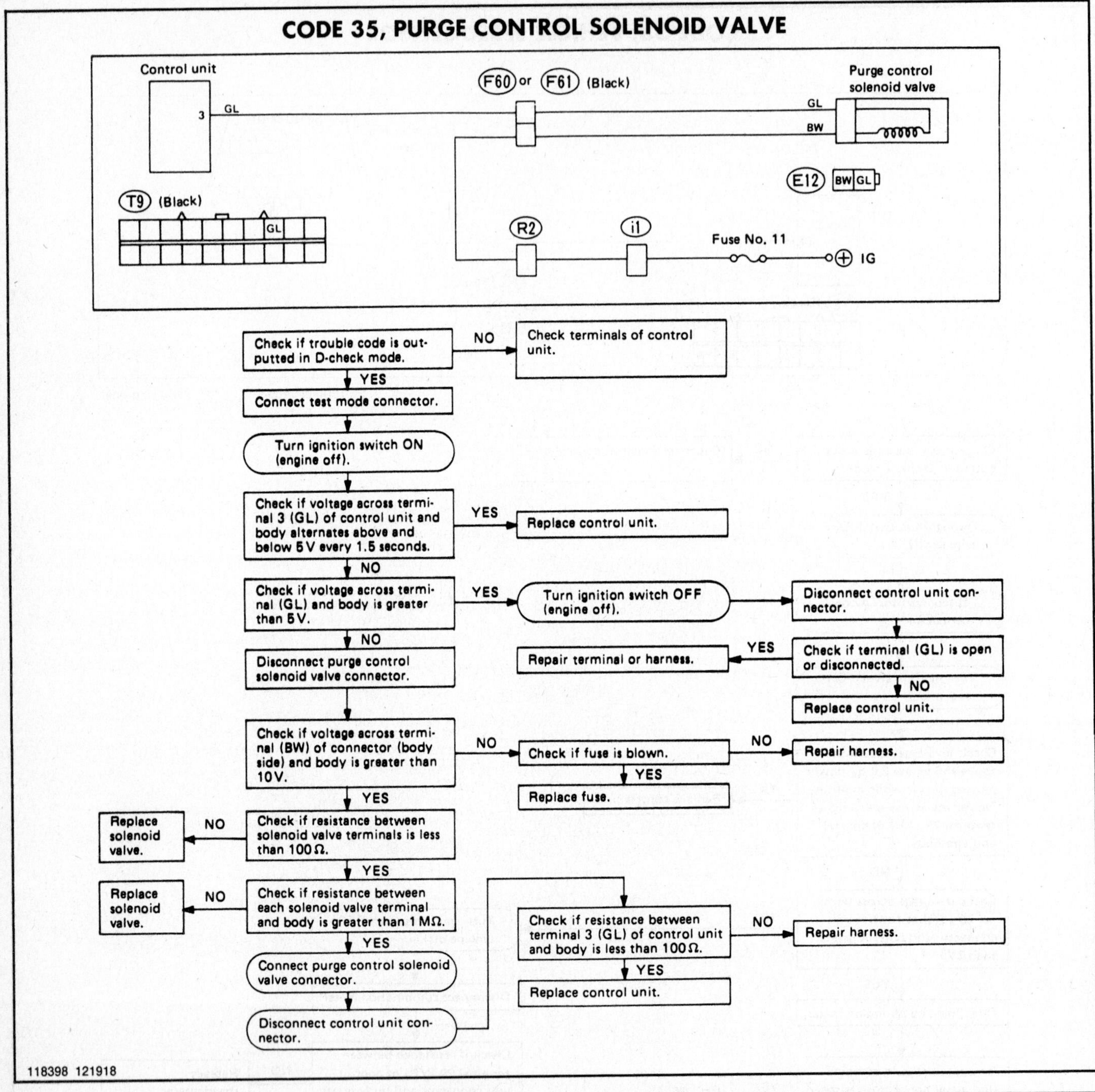


## CODE 41, FUEL SYSTEM

Trouble code (41) indicates that the mixture is too lean. When another trouble code is not outputted, all system components are electrically in good order.

Check the following:

① Injector nozzles (for clogging)
② Fuel pressure
③ Performance characteristics of water temperature sensor

If the above three are OK, check the following:

④ Drive some distance after replacing the air flow meter.

If still no good, proceed to ⑤.

⑤ Replace fuel injectors and drive some distance.

If still no good, proceed as follow:

⑥ Replace control unit.

## CODE 42, IDLE SWITCH

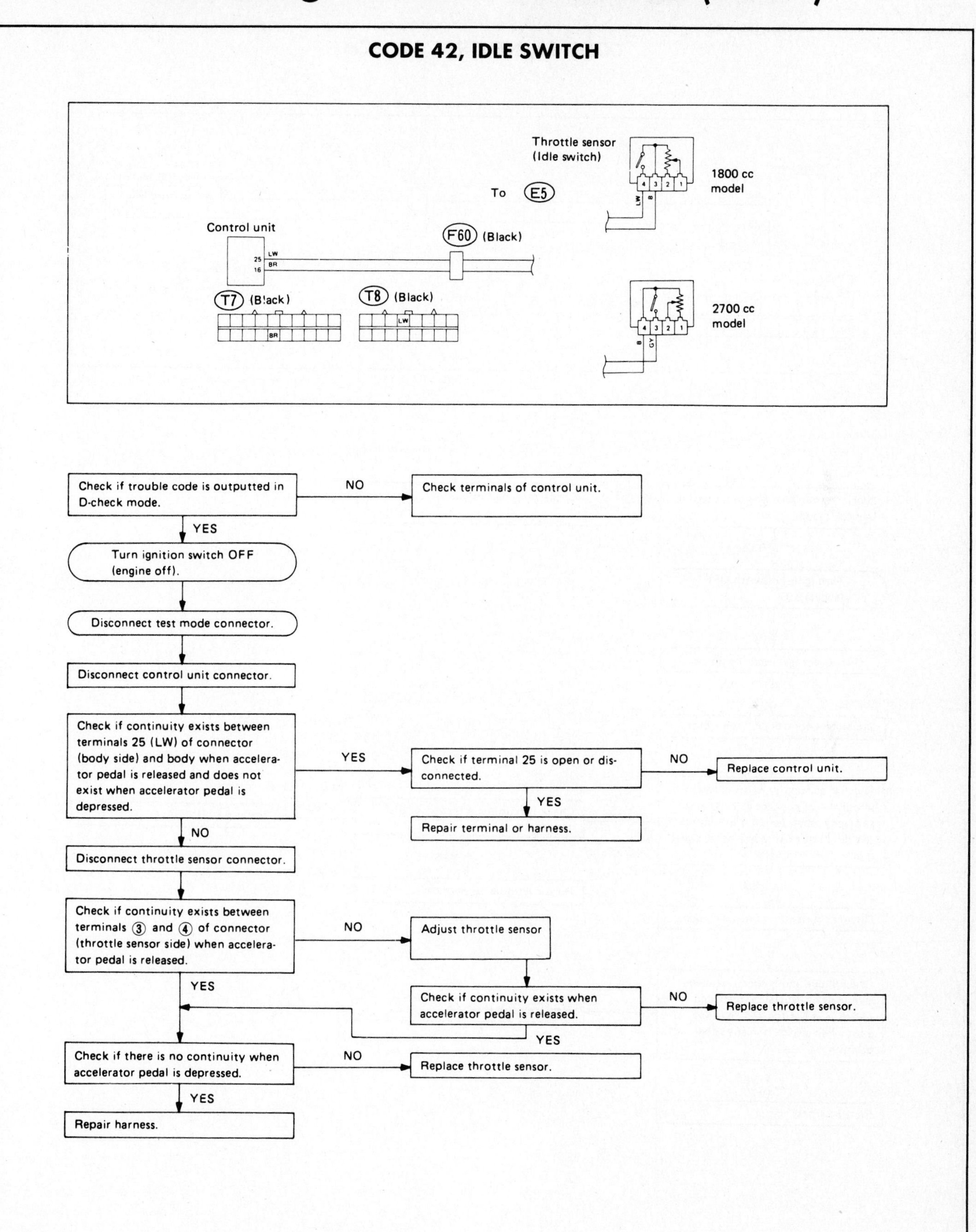


118399 121919

# 1991 ENGINE PERFORMANCE
# Self-Diagnostics – XT & XT6 (Cont.)

## CODE 51, NEUTRAL SWITCH

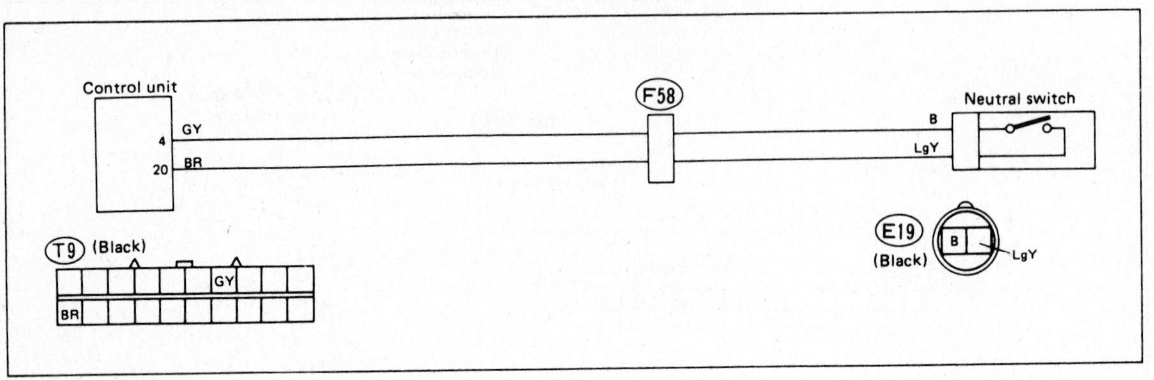


Check if trouble code is outputted in D-check mode.
- NO → Check terminals of control unit.
- YES → Turn ignition switch OFF (engine off).

↓

Disconnect test mode connector.

↓

Disconnect control unit connector.

↓

Check if continuity exists between terminal 4 of connector (body side) and body when switch is in Neutral and does not exist in any other position.
- YES → Check if terminal 4 is open or disconnected.
  - NO → Replace control unit.
  - YES → Repair terminal or harness.
- NO → Disconnect neutral switch connector.

↓

Check if continuity exists between terminals of neutral switch when switch is in Neutral and does not exist when switch is in any other position.
- → Replace neutral switch.
- YES → Repair harness.

118400 121920

# 1991 ENGINE PERFORMANCE
# Trouble Shooting – No Codes

### Justy, Legacy, Loyale, XT, XT6

## INTRODUCTION

Before diagnosing symptoms or intermittent faults, perform steps in BASIC DIAGNOSTIC PROCEDURES and SELF-DIAGNOSTICS articles. Use this article to diagnose driveability problems existing when a hard fault code is not present.

***NOTE: Some driveability problems may have been corrected by manufacturer with a revised computer calibration chip or computer control unit. Check with manufacturer for latest chip or computer application.***

Symptom checks can direct the technician to malfunctioning component(s) for further diagnosis. A symptom should lead to a specific component, system test or adjustment.

Use intermittent test procedures to locate driveability problems that DO NOT occur when the vehicle is being tested. These test procedures should also be used if a soft (intermittent) trouble code was present, but no problem was found during self-diagnostic testing.

***NOTE: For specific testing procedures, see SYSTEM & COMPONENT TESTING article. For specifications, see ON-VEHICLE ADJUSTMENTS or SERVICE & ADJUSTMENT SPECIFICATIONS article.***

## SYMPTOMS

### SYMPTOM DIAGNOSIS (JUSTY CARBURETED)

Symptom checks cannot be used properly unless the problem occurs while the vehicle is being tested. To reduce diagnostic time, perform steps in BASIC DIAGNOSTIC PROCEDURES and SELF-DIAGNOSTICS articles before diagnosing a symptom. The following symptoms are available for diagnosis.

- Does Not Start - Cold
- Does Not Start - Warm
- Rough Or Unstable Idle
- Idle Speed Too High
- Engine Stalls
- Poor Fuel Mileage
- Engine Afterburn Occurs
- Engine Backfires
- Engine Knocks

### DOES NOT START – COLD

- Ensure sufficient secondary spark is available.
- Ensure ignition and valve timing are correct.
- Verify choke valve is closed.
- Ensure fuel level is at specified mark on carburetor sight glass.
- Ensure fuel system pressure is correct.
- Check for contaminated fuel.
- Ensure correct vacuum hose routing.
- Check slow fuel-cut solenoid valve operation. A click from solenoid valve should be heard as ignition switch is cycled on and off.
- Check charcoal canister operation by clamping hose(s) shut. If problem discontinues, check vacuum hose routing.
- Ensure exhaust system is not restricted.

### DOES NOT START – WARM

- Ensure sufficient secondary spark is available.
- Ensure ignition and valve timing are correct.
- Verify choke valve is open.
- Ensure fuel level is at specified mark on carburetor sight glass.
- Ensure fuel system pressure is correct.
- Check for contaminated fuel.
- Check for clogged fuel return hose.
- Check for loose or clogged carburetor jets.
- Check for fuel percolation.
- Ensure vacuum hose routing is correct.
- Check operation of float chamber vent solenoid.
- Check slow fuel-cut solenoid valve operation. A click from solenoid valve should be heard as ignition switch is cycled on and off.
- Check charcoal canister operation by clamping hose(s) shut. If problem stops, check vacuum hose routing.
- Ensure exhaust system is not restricted.

### ROUGH OR UNSTABLE IDLE

- Ensure there are no vacuum leaks.
- Verify vacuum hose routing is correct.
- Ensure idle adjustment is correct.
- Ensure fast idle adjustment is correct.
- Check choke vacuum break diaphragm.
- Check choke valve operation.
- Ensure fuel level is at specified mark on carburetor sight glass.
- Check for fuel percolation.
- Check PCV system operation.
- Check EGR operation.
- Verify ignition timing is correct.
- Try to isolate problem by individually removing each spark plug wire briefly.
- Check thermostatic air cleaner operation.

### IDLE SPEED TOO HIGH

- Check idle-up actuator vacuum hose routing.
- Check fast idle cam for binding.
- Check linkage for binding.
- Check choke adjustment and operation.
- Check throttle cable adjustment.
- Check ignition timing.

### ENGINE STALLS

- Verify correct operation of air cleaner intake control door.
- Ensure correct choke adjustment and operation.
- Check idle compensator operation.
- Check idle mixture adjustment.
- Ensure there are no vacuum leaks.
- Check PCV system operation.
- Check EGR valve operation.

### POOR FUEL MILEAGE

- Ensure there are no vacuum leaks.
- Ensure ignition and valve timing are correct.
- Verify choke valve is open (engine warm).
- Ensure fuel level is at specified mark on carburetor sight glass.
- Ensure fuel system pressure and volume are correct.
- Verify base timing is correct, and timing advance system is functional.
- Ensure sufficient secondary spark is available.
- Check canister purge control valve operation.
- Ensure engine has sufficient compression.
- Ensure exhaust system is not plugged.
- Check carburetor mixture-control duty cycle using dwell meter.
- Check engine for overheating or overcooling.

### ENGINE AFTERBURN OCCURS

- Ensure idle adjustment is correct.
- Ensure automatic choke operation is correct.
- Check for clogged carburetor main air bleed.
- Ensure ignition timing is correct.
- Check spark plug cables for poor contact.

### ENGINE BACKFIRES

- Ensure air injection system operation is correct.
- Ensure automatic choke setting is correct.
- Check for clogged carburetor main jet.
- Ensure air cleaner is installed properly.
- Ensure ignition timing is correct.
- Check carburetor mixture-control duty cycle using dwell meter.

# 1991 ENGINE PERFORMANCE
# Trouble Shooting – No Codes (Cont.)

## ENGINE KNOCKS

- Check for clogged carburetor main jet.
- Ensure operation of ignition control unit is correct.
- Check EGR valve operation.
- Ensure ignition timing is correct.
- Check for poor or contaminated fuel.
- Check for carbon in combustion chamber.
- Check engine for overheating.

## SYMPTOM DIAGNOSIS (JUSTY PFI, LOYALE PFI, XT & XT6)

*: The CHECK ENGINE light blinks.
*1: The CHECK ENGINE light blinks when contact is resumed during inspection (although poor contact is present in the D-check).
*2: The CHECK ENGINE light lights when the mixture is leaner than that specified and does not light (U-check) or blink (D-check) when the mixture is richer.
*3: The CHECK ENGINE light lights when abnormality is detected in the D-check mode if the idle switch persistently remains off with the accelerator pedal released.

Symbols shown in the table refer to the degree of possibility of the reason for the trouble ("Very often" to "Rarely").
◎ : Very often
○ : Sometimes
△ : Rarely
☆ : Occurs only in extremely low temperatures

| No. | TROUBLE | |
|---|---|---|
| 1 | Engine will not start | No initial combustion |
| 2 | | Initial combustion occurs. |
| 3 | | Engine stalls after initial combustion. |
| 4 | Rough idle and engine stall | |
| 5 | Inability to drive at constant speed | |
| 6 | Inability to accelerate and decelerate | |
| 7 | Engine does not return to idle. | |
| 8 | Afterburning in exhaust system | |
| 9 | Knocking | |
| 10 | Excessive fuel consumption | |
| 11 | | |
| U | CHECK ENGINE light operation | U-check mode & read memory mode |
| D | | D-check mode |

| 1 | 2 | 3 | 4 | 5 | 6 | 7 | 8 | 9 | 10 | 11 | CHECK ENGINE light U | CHECK ENGINE light D | POSSIBLE CAUSE |
|---|---|---|---|---|---|---|---|---|---|---|---|---|---|
| | | | | | | | | | | | | | AIR FLOW METER |
| | | ☆ | ◎ | | | | △ | △ | ○ | | ON | ON | • Connector not connected |
| | | △ | ◎ | ◎ | ◎ | | ◎ | ○ | △ | | ON | *1 | • Poor contact of terminal |
| | | ☆ | ◎ | | | | △ | ○ | △ | | ON | ON | • Short circuit |
| | | ☆ | ◎ | | | | △ | △ | ○ | | ON | ON | • Discontinuity of wiring harness |
| | | ○ | ○ | ○ | ○ | | △ | ◎ | ○ | | *2 | *2 | • Performance characteristics unusual |
| | | | | | | | | | | | | | COOLANT THERMOSENSOR |
| | ☆ | ○ | ☆ | | ○ | | ○ | ○ | ○ | | ON | ON | • Connector not connected |
| | △ | △ | ◎ | ○ | ○ | | ◎ | △ | ○ | | ON | *1 | • Poor contact of terminal |
| | ☆ | ○ | ☆ | | ○ | | ○ | ○ | ○ | | ON | ON | • Short circuit |
| | ☆ | ○ | ☆ | | ○ | | ○ | ○ | ○ | | ON | ON | • Discontinuity of wiring harness |
| | ☆ | ○ | ☆ | | ○ | | ◎ | ◎ | ◎ | | *2 | *2 | • Performance characteristics unusual |
| | | | | | | | | | | | | | IDLE SWITCH OF THROTTLE SENSOR |
| | | | | ○ | ◎ | | ◎ | | | | OFF | ON | • Connector not connected |
| | | | | ○ | | | ○ | | | | ON | *1 | • Poor contact of terminal |
| | | | | ○ | △ | | ○ | | | | ON | ON | • Short circuit |
| | | | | | △ | | ○ | | | | OFF | ON | • Discontinuity of wiring harness |
| | | | | | | | ○ | | | | OFF | *3 | • Improper adjustment |
| | | | | | | | | | | | | | THROTTLE SENSOR |
| | | | | | ◎ | | ◎ | | | | ON | ON | • Connector not connected |
| | | | | ◎ | ◎ | | ◎ | | | | ON | *1 | • Poor contact of terminal |
| △ | | | | | ◎ | | ◎ | | | | ON | ON | • Short circuit |
| | | | | | ◎ | | ◎ | | | | ON | ON | • Discontinuity of wiring harness |
| | ○ | ○ | △ | ○ | ◎ | | ◎ | | | | OFF | * | • Performance characteristics unusual |
| | | | | | | | | | | | | | PRESSURE REGULATOR |
| | ○ | ○ | ◎ | ◎ | ◎ | ○ | | △ | | | *2 | *2 | • Sensing hose not connected |
| | △ | | | | ○ | | ○ | | ◎ | | OFF | * | • Fuel pressure too high |
| ○ | ○ | ○ | ◎ | ◎ | ◎ | | ◎ | | | | *2 | *2 | • Fuel pressure too low |

| 1 | 2 | 3 | 4 | 5 | 6 | 7 | 8 | 9 | 10 | 11 | CHECK ENGINE light U | CHECK ENGINE light D | POSSIBLE CAUSE |
|---|---|---|---|---|---|---|---|---|---|---|---|---|---|
| | | | | | | | | | | | | | FUEL INJECTOR |
| | ◎ | ◎ | ○ | ○ | ○ | | ○ | ○ | | | ON | *1 | • Connector not connected |
| | ○ | ○ | ○ | ◎ | ◎ | | ○ | | | | ON | ON | • Poor contact of terminal |
| | ◎ | ◎ | ○ | ○ | ○ | | ○ | | | | ON | ON | • Short circuit |
| | ◎ | ◎ | ○ | ○ | ○ | | ○ | ○ | | | ON | ON | • Discontinuity of wiring harness |
| | △ | ○ | ○ | △ | ○ | | ○ | △ | ○ | | *2 | *2 | • Performance characteristics unusual |
| | △ | ○ | △ | △ | ○ | | ○ | △ | | | *2 | *2 | • Clogged filter |
| | △ | ○ | ○ | ○ | ○ | | ○ | △ | | | *2 | *2 | • Clogged nozzle |
| ○ | | | | | | | | | | | OFF | * | • Stuck open |
| | | | ○ | | | | ○ | | ○ | | OFF | * | • Slight leakage from seat |
| | | | | | | | | | | | | | CRANK ANGLE SENSOR |
| ◎ | | | | | | | | | | | ON | ON | • Connector disconnected |
| | ○ | ○ | ◎ | ◎ | ◎ | | ○ | ○ | | | ON | *1 | • Poor contact of terminal |
| ◎ | | | | | | | | | | | ON | ON | • Short circuit |
| ◎ | | | | | | | | | | | ON | ON | • Discontinuity of wiring harness |
| | | | | | | | | | | | | | POWER TRANSISTOR OF IGNITION COIL |
| ◎ | | | | | | | | | | | OFF | * | • Connector not connected |
| | ○ | ○ | ◎ | ◎ | ◎ | | ○ | | | | OFF | * | • Poor contact of terminal |
| ◎ | | | | | | | | | | | OFF | * | • Short circuit |
| ◎ | | | | | | | | | | | OFF | * | • Discontinuity of wiring harness |
| | | | | | | | | | | | | | AIR REGULATOR |
| | | | | | | ◎ | | | | | OFF | * | • Connector not connected |
| | ○ | ◎ | ○ | | | | | | | | OFF | * | • Short circuit |
| | | | | | | ◎ | | | | | OFF | * | • Discontinuity of wiring harness |
| | | | | | | | | | | | | | KNOCK SENSOR |
| | | | | | | | | ◎ | | | ON | ON | • Connector not connected |
| | | | | ○ | ○ | | | | | | ON | ON | • Short circuit |
| | | | | | | | | ◎ | | | ON | ON | • Discontinuity of wiring harness |
| | | | | | | | | | | | | | DUTY SOLENOID |
| | | | | | △ | | | | | | OFF | * | • Connector disconnected |
| | | | | | | | | | | | OFF | * | • Poor contact of terminal |
| | | | | | | | | ○ | | | OFF | * | • Short circuit |
| | | | | | △ | | | | | | OFF | * | • Discontinuity of wiring harness |
| | | | ○ | ○ | ○ | ○ | ○ | ○ | | | OFF | * | • Disconnected or cracked hose |
| | | | | | | | | | | | | | AIR CONTROL VALVE [2700 cc model only] |
| | ○ | △ | ◎ | | | | | | | | ON | ON | • Connector not connected |
| | △ | ○ | ◎ | | | | | | | | ON | *1 | • Poor contact of terminal |
| | | | ○ | | | | ○ | | | | ON | ON | • Short circuit |
| | ○ | △ | ◎ | | | | | | | | ON | ON | • Discontinuity of wiring harness |
| | | | ◎ | | | ◎ | | | | | OFF | * | • IAS improperly adjusted |
| | | | | | ◎ | ◎ | | | | | ON | * | • Stuck open |
| | ○ | ○ | ◎ | | | | | | | | OFF | * | • Stuck closed |
| | | | | | | | | | | | | | ENGINE GROUNDING |
| ○ | | | | | | | | | | | ON | | • Disconnecting of engine grounding terminal at intake manifold |
| ◎ | ◎ | ○ | ◎ | ◎ | ◎ | | | | | | ON | *1 | • Poor contact of engine grounding terminal |
| ○ | | | | | | | | | | | ON | | • Discontinuity of wiring harness for engine grounding |

118401 121830 121832

Courtesy of Subaru of America, Inc.

### SYMPTOM DIAGNOSIS (LOYALE TBI)

***:** The CHECK ENGINE light blinks.
***1:** The CHECK ENGINE light blinks when contact is resumed during inspection (although poor contact is present in the D-check).
***2:** The CHECK ENGINE light lights when the mixture is leaner than that specified and does not light (U-check) or blink (D-check) when the mixture is richer.
***3:** The CHECK ENGINE light lights when abnormality is detected in the D-check mode if the idle switch persistently remains off with the accelerator pedal released.

**Symbols shown in the table refer to the degree of possibility of the reason for the trouble ("Very often" to "Rarely").**
- ◎ : Very often
- ○ : Sometimes
- △ : Rarely
- ☆ : Occurs only in extremely low temperatures

| | TROUBLE | |
|---|---|---|
| 1 | Engine will not start. | No initial combustion |
| 2 | | Initial combustion occur. |
| 3 | | Engine stalls after initial combustion. |
| 4 | Rough idle and engine stall. | |
| 5 | Inability to drive at constant speed | |
| 6 | Inability to accelerate and decelerate | |
| 7 | Engine does not return to idle. | |
| 8 | Afterburning in exhaust system | |
| 9 | Knocking | |
| 10 | Excessive fuel consumption | |
| 11 | Inability to "kick-down" and upshift | |
| U | ECS lamp operation | U-check mode & read memory mode |
| D | | D-check mode |

| TROUBLE No. | | | | | | | | | | | ECS lamp | | POSSIBLE CAUSE |
|---|---|---|---|---|---|---|---|---|---|---|---|---|---|
| 1 | 2 | 3 | 4 | 5 | 6 | 7 | 8 | 9 | 10 | 11 | U | D | |
| | | | | | | | | | | | | | AIR FLOW METER |
| | | ☆ | ◎ | | | | △ | △ | ○ | | ON | ON | • Connector not connected |
| | | △ | ◎ | ◎ | ◎ | | ◎ | ○ | △ | | ON | *1 | • Poor contact of terminal |
| | | ☆ | ◎ | | | | △ | ○ | △ | | ON | ON | • Short circuit |
| | | ☆ | ◎ | | | | △ | △ | ○ | | ON | ON | • Discontinuity of wiring harness |
| | | ○ | ○ | ○ | ○ | | △ | ◎ | ○ | | OFF | | • Performance characteristics unusual |
| | | | | | | | | | | | | | COOLANT THERMOSENSOR |
| | ☆ | ○ | ☆ | | ○ | | ○ | ○ | ○ | | ON | ON | • Connector not connected |
| | △ | △ | ◎ | ○ | ○ | △ | ◎ | ◎ | ○ | | ON | *1 | • Poor contact of terminal |
| | ☆ | ○ | ☆ | | ○ | | ○ | ○ | ○ | | ON | ON | • Short circuit |
| | ☆ | ○ | ☆ | | ○ | | ○ | ◎ | ○ | | ON | ON | • Discontinuity of wiring harness |
| | ☆ | ○ | ○ | △ | ○ | ○ | ◎ | ◎ | ◎ | △ | OFF | | • Performance characteristics unusual |
| | | | | | | | | | | | | | IDLE SWITCH OF THROTTLE SENSOR |
| | | | ◎ | ○ | ◎ | ◎ | ◎ | | | | ON | ON | • Connector not connected |
| | | | ◎ | ○ | | ◎ | ◎ | | | | ON | *1 | • Poor contact of terminal |
| | | | ◎ | ◎ | △ | | ◎ | | | | ON | ON | • Short circuit |
| | | | ◎ | | △ | ◎ | ◎ | | | | ON | ON | • Discontinuity of wiring harness |
| | | | ◎ | | | ◎ | ◎ | | | | OFF | *2 | • Improper adjustment |
| | | | | | | | | | | | | | THROTTLE SENSOR |
| | | | | ◎ | ◎ | | ◎ | | | ○ | ON | *1 | • Poor contact of terminal |
| △ | | | ◎ | | ◎ | | ◎ | | | ◎ | ON | ON | • Short circuit |
| | | | △ | | ◎ | | ◎ | | | ◎ | ON | ON | • Discontinuity of wiring harness |
| | ○ | ○ | △ | ○ | ◎ | | ◎ | | | ◎ | OFF | *3 | • Performance characteristics unusual |
| | | | | | | | | | | | | | PRESSURE REGULATOR |
| | | | | | | | | △ | | | OFF | | • Sensing hose cracked or disconnected |
| | △ | | | | ○ | | ○ | | | | OFF | | • Fuel pressure too high |
| ○ | ○ | ○ | ◎ | ◎ | ◎ | | ◎ | | | | OFF | | • Fuel pressure too low |
| | | | | | | | | | | | | | FUEL INJECTOR |
| ○ | | | | | | | | | | | ON | ON | • Connector not connected |
| | ○ | ○ | ◎ | ◎ | ◎ | | ○ | | | | ON | *1 | • Poor contact of terminal |
| ○ | | | | | | | | | | | ON | ON | • Short circuit |
| ○ | | | | | | | | | | | ON | ON | • Discontinuity of wiring harness |
| | ○ | ○ | ◎ | ◎ | ◎ | | ◎ | | ◎ | | OFF | | • Performance characteristics unusual |
| | ○ | ○ | ○ | ○ | ○ | | | | | | OFF | | • Clogged filter |
| ○ | △ | | | | | | | | | | OFF | | • Stuck open |
| | | | ○ | | | | ○ | | ○ | | OFF | | • Slight leakage from seat |
| | | | | | | | | | | | | | AIR CONTROL VALVE |
| | ○ | △ | ◎ | | | | | | | | ON | ON | • Connector not connected |
| | △ | ○ | ◎ | | | | | | | | ON | *1 | • Poor contact of terminal |
| | | | ○ | | | | ○ | | | | ON | ON | • Short circuit |
| | ○ | △ | ◎ | | | | | | | | ON | ON | • Discontinuity of wiring harness |
| | | | ◎ | | | ◎ | | | | | OFF | | • IAS improperly adjusted |
| | | | | | | ◎ | | | | | OFF | | • Stuck open |
| | ○ | ○ | ◎ | | | | | | | | OFF | | • Stuck closed |

118402 121831

Courtesy of Subaru of America, Inc.

# 1991 ENGINE PERFORMANCE
# Trouble Shooting – No Codes (Cont.)

## SYMPTOM DIAGNOSIS (LEGACY)

| Parts to check | ECU power supply | Air flow sensor | Water temperature sensor | Idle switch | Throttle sensor | Fuel pump | Pressure regulator | Fuel injector | Igniter (power transistor) | Ignition coil | Spark plug | Knock sensor | Cam angle sensor | Crank angle sensor | Air control valve | $O_2$ sensor | Duty solenoid valve (Waste gate control) |
|---|---|---|---|---|---|---|---|---|---|---|---|---|---|---|---|---|---|
| Symptom – Failure of engine to start – Initial combustion does not occur. | 1 | 10 | 11 | | | 5 | 6 | 7 | 2 | 3 | 4 | | 8 | 9 | | | |
| Symptom – Failure of engine to start – Initial combustion occurs. | 1 | | 10 | | | 2 | 3 | 4 | 5 | 6 | 7 | | 8 | 9 | 11 | | |
| Symptom – Failure of engine to start – Engine stalls after initial combustion. | 1 | 2 | 7 | | 8 | 4 | 5 | 6 | 11 | 12 | 13 | | 9 | 10 | 3 | | |
| Symptom – Rough idling | 1 | 3 | 12 | 8 | 7 | 4 | 5 | 6 | 9 | 10 | 11 | | 13 | 14 | 2 | 15 | 16 |
| Symptom – Hard to drive at constant speed | 1 | 4 | 6 | 8 | 7 | 3 | 2 | 9 | 12 | 13 | 14 | | 10 | 11 | | 5 | 15 |
| Symptom – Poor acceleration/ deceleration | 1 | 2 | 6 | 7 | 8 | 3 | 4 | 5 | 13 | 14 | 15 | 9 | 11 | 12 | 10 | | 2 |
| Symptom – Poor return to idle | | | 3 | 2 | | | | | | | | | | | 1 | | |
| Symptom – Backfire | | | 3 | 4 | 5 | | 6 | 7 | | | | | 2 | 1 | | | |
| Symptom – Knocking | | 1 | 2 | | | | 4 | 5 | | | | 3 | | 6 | | | 7 |
| Symptom – Excessive fuel consumption | | 3 | 4 | | | | 1 | 2 | | | | | | | | | |
| Symptom – Shocks while driving | 1 | 8 | | | | | | 7 | 4 | 5 | 6 | | 2 | 3 | | | |
| Symptom – Poor engine revving | | 2 | 3 | 4 | 5 | | 1 | | | | | | | | | | |
| Remarks | Include engine gro unding circuit. | | | | | | | | | | | | | | Check hoses. | | Check hoses. |

91G17596

Courtesy of Subaru of America, Inc.

# INTERMITTENTS

## INTERMITTENT PROBLEM DIAGNOSIS

Intermittent fault testing requires duplicating circuit or component failure to identify problem. These procedures may lead to the computer setting a fault code, which may help in diagnosis.

If problem vehicle does not produce fault codes, monitor voltage or resistance values using a DVOM while attempting to reproduce the conditions causing intermittent fault. A status change on DVOM indicates a fault has been located.

Use a DVOM to pinpoint faults. When monitoring voltage, ensure ignition switch is in ON position or engine is running. Ensure ignition switch is in OFF position or negative battery cable is disconnected when monitoring circuit resistance. Status changes on DVOM during test procedures indicate area of fault.

## TEST PROCEDURES

**Intermittent Simulation** – To reproduce the conditions creating an intermittent fault, use the following methods:

- Lightly vibrate component.
- Heat component.
- Wiggle or bend wiring harness.
- Spray component with water.
- Remove/apply vacuum source.

Monitor circuit/component voltage or resistance while simulating intermittent. If engine is running, monitor for self-diagnostic codes. Use test results to identify a faulty component or circuit.

# 1991 ENGINE PERFORMANCE
# System & Component Testing

## Justy, Legacy, Loyale, XT, XT6

## INTRODUCTION

Before testing separate components or systems, perform procedures in BASIC DIAGNOSTIC PROCEDURES article. Since many computer-controlled and monitored components set a trouble code if they malfunction, also perform procedures in SELF-DIAGNOSTICS article.

***NOTE: Testing individual components does not isolate shorts or opens. Perform all voltage tests with a Digital Volt-Ohmmeter (DVOM) with a minimum 10-megohm input impedance, unless stated otherwise in test procedure. Use ohmmeter to isolate wiring harness shorts or opens.***

## AIR INDUCTION SYSTEMS

### TURBOCHARGER TROUBLE SHOOTING

**High Boost Pressure –** If turbocharger fails, excessive boost pressures can cause engine knock and overheating. Check wastegate operation, electrical circuits between wastegate duty solenoid and ECU, and ECU problems.

**Low Boost Pressure –** Low boost pressure can cause the following: lack of power, poor acceleration and increased fuel consumption. Check for leaks in the intake and exhaust system, incorrect ignition timing, electrical circuits between wastegate duty solenoid and ECU, and ECU problems.

**Oil Leaks – 1)** Worn turbocharger oil seals can cause excessive oil consumption and White smoke from the exhaust. Remove center exhaust pipe and examine the turbocharger from the exhaust side. If there is excessive carbon deposits on the turbine exhaust side, oil is leaking from the turbine.

**2)** The turbocharger is not necessarily defective when oil is present on the blower side. Oil most likely has come from oil vapors contained in blow-by gases present in the intake system or defective PCV system.

**3)** If intake side contains oil and a rattle is present, remove the turbocharger. Check the end play and side play.

### TURBOCHARGER COMPONENT TESTING

***NOTE: Replace turbocharger if found to be defective. Manufacturer does not provide turbocharger disassembly or adjustment procedures.***

**Boost Pressure – 1)** Disconnect wastegate duty solenoid connector. Engine must be at normal operating temperature. Disconnect rubber hose from pressure switch. Using a "T" fitting, connect an air pressure gauge. Use enough hose so that gauge may be carried inside passenger compartment.

**2)** Boost pressure should be checked at 4600 RPM (Legacy) or 2400 RPM (Loyale) with a wide open throttle. On Legacy, normal pressure is 6.2-7.3 psi (4.3-5.1 kg/cm²). On Loyale, normal pressure is 7.2-8.3 psi (5.0-5.8 kg/cm²). Reconnect wastegate duty solenoid.

**3)** If boost pressure is too high, check the rubber hose that connects the intake manifold to the wastegate valve. Replace hose if defective. If wastegate valve is not operating and remains closed, replace the turbocharger. If boost pressure is too low, replace the turbocharger.

**Wastegate Duty Solenoid –** Disconnect wastegate duty solenoid connector. Using an ohmmeter, measure solenoid resistance. If resistance is not 17-21 ohms, replace solenoid. Check solenoid terminals for a short to ground. Also see SELF-DIAGNOSTICS article.

**End Play & Side Play –** The maximum end play on the turbine shaft is .0035" (.09 mm). Maximum side play is .0067" (.17 mm). Side play is checked by moving intake and exhaust side of shaft at the same time.

## COMPUTERIZED ENGINE CONTROLS

### CONTROL UNIT

**Ground Circuits – 1)** Turn ignition off. Using an ohmmeter, touch negative lead to ground. Using positive lead, backprobe each control unit ground terminal. See CONTROL UNIT GROUND TERMINAL IDENTIFICATION table. Resistance should be zero ohms. If resistance is not zero ohms, repair open to ground.

**2)** Using a DVOM, touch negative lead of voltmeter to a good ground. Touch positive lead of voltmeter to each ground terminal. With vehicle running, voltmeter should indicate less than one volt. If voltmeter reading is greater than one volt, check for open, corrosion or loose connection on ground lead.

***CONTROL UNIT GROUND TERMINAL IDENTIFICATION***

| Application | Wire Color |
|---|---|
| **Justy** | |
| Carbureted | |
| Terminal No. 12 | Black/Red |
| Terminal No. 16 | Black |
| Terminal No. 17 | Black |
| PFI | |
| Terminal No. 1 | Black/Red |
| Terminal No. 1 | Black/Green |
| Terminal No. 2 | Black/Green |
| Terminal No. 10 | Black/Red |
| Terminal No. 13 | Black/Blue |
| Terminal No. 26 | Black/Blue |
| **Legacy** | |
| Terminal No. 11 | Black/Red |
| Terminal No. 14 | Black/White |
| Terminal No. 15 | Black |
| Terminal No. 22 | Black/Red |
| Terminal No. 24 | Black/Yellow |
| Terminal No. 25 | Black/Yellow |
| **Loyale** | |
| TBI | |
| Terminal No. 9 | Black |
| Terminal No. 30 | Black/Red |
| Terminal No. 35 | Black |
| Terminal No. 42 | Black/Red |
| Terminal No. 44 | Black/Red |
| Terminal No. 50 | Black/Yellow |
| Terminal No. 51 | Black |
| PFI | |
| Terminal No. 5 | Black |
| Terminal No. 10 | Black/Red |
| Terminal No. 16 | Black/Red |
| Terminal No. 20 | Black/Red |
| Terminal No. 56 | Black |
| Terminal No. 57 | Black |
| Terminal No. 60 | Black/Red |
| Terminal No. 61 | Black/Red |
| **XT & XT6** | |
| Terminal No. 5 | Black |
| Terminal No. 10 | Black/Red |
| Terminal No. 16 | Black/Red |
| Terminal No. 20 | Black/Red |
| Terminal No. 56 | Black |
| Terminal No. 57 | Black |
| Terminal No. 60 | Black/Red |
| Terminal No. 61 | Black/Red |

**Power Circuits (Ignition Off) –** Turn ignition off. Using a voltmeter, check for battery voltage between control unit power terminals and ground. See CONTROL UNIT POWER TERMINAL IDENTIFICATION table. If battery voltage is not present, check fuse or fusible link. If fuse or fusible link is okay, check for an open in wire between fuse/fusible link and control unit.

**Power Circuits (Ignition On) –** Turn ignition switch to ON position. Using a voltmeter, check for battery voltage between control unit power terminals and ground. See CONTROL UNIT POWER TERMINAL IDENTIFICATION table. If battery voltage is not present, check fuse. If fuse is okay, check for an open in wire or a defective ignition switch.

***NOTE: The following procedure does not apply to Justy carbureted.***

**Power Circuits (Ignition Cranking) – 1)** Connect voltmeter between ground and control unit terminal. See CONTROL UNIT POWER TER-

# 1991 ENGINE PERFORMANCE
# System & Component Testing (Cont.)

MINAL IDENTIFICATION table. Turn ignition switch to START position. Battery voltage should be present between control unit terminal and ground ONLY when ignition switch is in START position.
**2)** If voltage is not present, check fusible link. If fusible link is okay, check for an open wire between fusible link and control unit terminal, or check for a defective ignition switch.

***CONTROL UNIT POWER TERMINAL IDENTIFICATION***

| Application | Wire Color |
|---|---|
| **Justy** | |
| Carbureted | |
| Ignition Off [1] | |
| Terminal No. 6 | White/Blue |
| Terminal No. 15 | White/Blue |
| Ignition On [2] | |
| Terminal No. 8 | White/Green |
| Terminal No. 9 | Black/White |
| PFI | |
| Ignition Off [1] | |
| Terminal No. 1 | Red |
| Ignition On [3] | |
| Terminal No. 2 | White/Blue |
| Terminal No. 12 | Red |
| Ignition Cranking | |
| Terminal No. 17 | Black/White |
| **Legacy** | |
| Ignition Off [4] | |
| Terminal No. 15 | Yellow/Red |
| Ignition On [5] | |
| Terminal No. 2 | Yellow/Red |
| Terminal No. 12 | Yellow |
| Terminal No. 13 | Yellow/Red |
| Ignition Cranking | |
| Terminal No. 10 | |
| Auto. Trans. | Blue/Red |
| Man. Trans. | Red/Yellow |
| **Loyale** | |
| TBI | |
| Ignition Off [6] | |
| Terminal No. 27 | Black/White |
| Ignition On [7] | |
| Terminal No. 29 | White |
| Terminal No. 38 | Red/Blue |
| Terminal No. 41 | White |
| Terminal No. 49 | Red/Blue |
| Ignition Cranking [8] | |
| Terminal No. 18 | Lt. Green/Yellow |
| PFI | |
| Ignition Off [9] | |
| Terminal No. 62 | Red |
| Ignition On [10] | |
| Terminal No. 19 | Black/White |
| Terminal No. 27 | White/Red |
| Terminal No. 35 | White/Red |
| Terminal No. 39 | Green/White |
| Ignition Cranking | |
| Terminal No. 24 | Black/White |
| **XT & XT6** | |
| Ignition Off [9] | |
| Terminal No. 62 | Red |
| Ignition On [10] | |
| Terminal No. 19 | Black/White |
| Terminal No. 27 | White/Red |
| Terminal No. 35 | White/Red |
| Terminal No. 39 | Green/White |
| Ignition Cranking | |
| Terminal No. 24 | |
| Auto. Trans. | Black/Yellow |
| Man. Trans. | Black/White |

[1] – Check fuse No. 2.
[2] – Check fuse No. 1.
[3] – Check fuses No. 1, 2 and 7.
[4] – Check fuse No. 14.
[5] – Check fuses No. 14 and 16.
[6] – Check fuse No. 5.
[7] – Check fuses No. 5 and 12.
[8] – Check fuse No. 20.
[9] – Check fusible link.
[10] – Check fusible link and fuse No. 11.

## ENGINE SENSORS & SWITCHES

**A/C Switch** – See WIRING DIAGRAMS article in ENGINE PERFORMANCE, and test switch and circuits as necessary.

**Airflow Meter** – Remove rubber cover from electrical connector on airflow meter. Leave connector connected. Connect volt/ohmmeter between terminals and record readings. See AIRFLOW METER SPECIFICATIONS table. If readings are not to specifications, check electrical wiring. If wiring is okay, replace airflow sensor.

***NOTE: DO NOT start engine unless specified. Place the ignition switch in the OFF or ON position as indicated.***

***NOTE: Airflow meter test specifications for Justy are not available from manufacturer.***

***AIRFLOW METER SPECIFICATIONS***

| Ign. Switch | Wire Colors | Readings |
|---|---|---|
| Legacy | | |
| Key On | Red & Black/Red | 10-13 Volts |
| Engine On | Red & Black/Red | 13-14 Volts |
| Key On | Black & Black/Red | 0-0.3 Volt |
| Engine On | Black & Black/Red | 0.8-1.2 Volts |
| Key On | White & Black/Red | Zero Volts |
| Engine On | White & Black/Red | Zero Volts |
| Loyale PFI | | |
| Off | Black & Black/Red | 0-10 Ohms |
| Off | Black/Red & Ground | 0-10 Ohms |
| On | Power Wire & Black/Red | 10 Volts Min. |
| On | Signal Wire & Ground | [1] 1-2 Volts |
| Loyale TBI | | |
| Key Off | Black & Ground | 0-10 Ohms |
| Key On | Red & Ground | 10 Volts Min. |
| Key On | White & Black | [1] .1-.5 Volt |
| XT & XT6 | | |
| Key Off | Black & Black/Red | 0-10 Ohms |
| Key Off | Black/Red & Ground | 0-10 Ohms |
| Key On | | |
| 1.8L Engine | White & Black/Red | 10 Volts Min. |
| 2.7L Engine | Red & Black/Red | 10 Volts Min. |
| 2.7L Engine | White & Black/Red | [1] 1-2 Volts |

[1] – Voltage should be higher when blowing air from air cleaner side.

**Atmospheric Pressure Sensor (Justy & Legacy)** – See HIGH ALTITUDE COMPENSATOR.

**Clutch Switch (Justy)** – See WIRING DIAGRAMS article in ENGINE PERFORMANCE and test switch and circuits as necessary.

**Coolant Temperature Sensor** – Disconnect coolant temperature sensor connector. Connect ohmmeter leads between sensor terminals. See COOLANT TEMPERATURE SENSOR RESISTANCE table.

***COOLANT TEMPERATURE SENSOR RESISTANCE***

| Application [1] | Temperature | Ohms |
|---|---|---|
| Justy 1.2L PFI & Legacy | 68°F (20°C) | 2000-3000 |
| | 176°F (80°C) | 270-330 |
| All Others | 14°F (-10°C) | 7000-11,500 |
| | 68°F (20°C) | 2000-3000 |
| | 122°F (50°C) | 700-1000 |

[1] – Information not available for Justy 1.2L carbureted.

**Crank Angle Sensor** – For testing information, see SELF-DIAGNOSTICS article.

**EGR Temperature Sensor (Loyale – Calif.)** – See SELF-DIAGNOSTICS and WIRING DIAGRAMS articles.

**Electrical Load Sensors (Justy)** – See WIRING DIAGRAMS article in ENGINE PERFORMANCE and test switch and circuits as necessary.

**Oxygen Sensor** - For testing procedures, see appropriate trouble code(s) for rich or lean running in SELF-DIAGNOSTICS and WIRING DIAGRAMS articles.

**P/N Switch (Except Justy)** - See SELF-DIAGNOSTICS and WIRING DIAGRAMS articles and test switch and circuits as necessary.

**Throttle Position Sensor (Or Switch)** - For testing and adjustments, see ON-VEHICLE ADJUSTMENTS article.

**Pressure Sensor** - For testing, see SELF-DIAGNOSTICS and WIRING DIAGRAMS articles.

**Vehicle Speed Sensor** - For testing, see SELF-DIAGNOSTICS and WIRING DIAGRAMS articles.

## RELAYS & SOLENOIDS

### CARBURETED

**EGR Solenoid** - See EXHAUST GAS RECIRCULATION (EGR) under EMISSION SYSTEMS & SUB-SYSTEMS and SELF-DIAGNOSTICS article for appropriate trouble code.

**Float Bowl Control Solenoid** - See FUEL EVAPORATION under EMISSION SYSTEMS & SUB-SYSTEMS.

**Fuel Pump Relay** - For testing procedures, see BASIC DIAGNOSTIC PROCEDURES and WIRING DIAGRAMS articles.

**High Altitude Compensator Solenoids** - See HIGH ALTITUDE COMPENSATOR under EMISSION SYSTEMS & SUB-SYSTEMS and SELF-DIAGNOSTICS article for appropriate trouble code.

**Main Relay** - For testing procedures, see BASIC DIAGNOSTIC PROCEDURES and WIRING DIAGRAMS articles.

**Purge Control Solenoid** - See FUEL EVAPORATION under EMISSION SYSTEMS & SUB-SYSTEMS.

**Vacuum Line Control (VLC) Solenoid** - See HIGH ALTITUDE COMPENSATOR under EMISSION SYSTEMS & SUB-SYSTEMS and SELF-DIAGNOSTICS article for appropriate trouble code(s).

### FUEL INJECTION

**EGR Solenoid** - See EXHAUST GAS RECIRCULATION (EGR) under EMISSION SYSTEMS & SUB-SYSTEMS and SELF-DIAGNOSTICS article for appropriate trouble code.

**Fuel Injector(s)** - **1)** Connect tachometer to engine. Start engine and run at idle. Remove harness connector from injectors one at a time. Engine idle speed should drop 100-300 RPM as each injector is disconnected. If engine idle speed does not drop, check the wiring connector, injector resistance or injection signal from the computer.

**2)** Turn ignition off. Disconnect electrical connector from each injector. Measure injector resistance. See INJECTOR RESISTANCE SPECIFICATIONS table. If injector is not to specification, replace injector.

***INJECTOR RESISTANCE SPECIFICATIONS***

| Application | Ohms |
|---|---|
| 1.2L PFI | 10-18 |
| 1.8L PFI Turbo & Non-Turbo (Injector) | 2-3 |
| 1.8L PFI Turbo & Non-Turbo (Resistor) | 5.8-6.5 |
| 1.8LTBI | 0.5-2 |
| 2.2L PFI | 11-12 |
| 2.7L PFI | 13.8 |

**Fuel Injector Resistor (1.8L PFI)** - Disconnect resistor block. Measure resistance between terminals "W" (Red wire) and "B" (Red/Black, Red/Blue and/or Red wire). If reading is not 5.8-6.5 ohms, replace resistor block.

**Kickdown Relay Control (TBI)** - For testing procedures, see SELF-DIAGNOSTICS article.

**Fuel Pump Relay** - For testing procedures, see BASIC DIAGNOSTIC PROCEDURES and WIRING DIAGRAMS articles.

**Main Relay** - For testing procedures see BASIC DIAGNOSTIC PROCEDURES and WIRING DIAGRAMS articles.

**Purge Control Solenoid** - See FUEL EVAPORATION under EMISSION SYSTEMS & SUB-SYSTEMS in this article and SELF-DIAGNOSTICS article for appropriate trouble code.

## FUEL SYSTEM

### FUEL DELIVERY

***NOTE: For fuel system pressure testing, see BASIC DIAGNOSTIC PROCEDURES article.***

### FUEL CONTROL

**Duty Solenoid (Carbureted)** - Disconnect harness and measure resistance between solenoid terminals. Ensure resistance is 10-100 ohms. If resistance is not 10-100 ohms, replace solenoid(s). Also see appropriate trouble code(s) in SELF-DIAGNOSTICS article.

**Feedback System** - Manufacturer recommends performing complete inspection of self-diagnostic system. This includes checking mechanical condition of engine, available fuel to carburetor or injectors and ignition. Repair or replace components as required, and test drive vehicle.

### IDLE CONTROL SYSTEM

**System Inspection** - Check self-diagnostic system for any trouble codes. See SELF-DIAGNOSTICS article.

**Auxiliary Air Valve (1.2L PFI & 1.8L)** - **1)** With engine running, pinch hose between Auxiliary Air Valve (AAV) and intake manifold. Engine speed should drop (about 100 RPM with engine warm, more with engine cold). Release hose. Ensure engine speed returns to previous speed.

**2)** If RPM is not as specified, turn ignition off. Check AAV resistance. If reading is either zero or infinity, replace AAV. Check AAV solenoid for any short to ground. If short is present, replace solenoid.

**3)** Check for voltage at harness connector. Ensure 12 volts are available at Blue wire of AAV electrical connector. If 12 volts are not available, check main relay, fuses and power source.

**By-Pass Air Control Valve (2.7L PFI)** - **1)** Disconnect By-Pass Air Control Valve (BACV) harness connector. Connect ohmmeter leads between terminals No. 1 (Yellow/Red wire) and No. 2 (Black/White wire). Resistance should be 9.5-11.5 ohms.

**2)** Measure resistance between terminals No. 2 (Black/White wire) and No. 3 (Yellow/Blue wire). Resistance should be 8.5-10.5 ohms. Ensure terminals are not shorted to ground. If BACV does not test as described, replace BACV.

**By-Pass Air Control Valve (TBI)** - **1)** With engine running, disconnect electrical connector. Engine speed should drop (slightly with engine warm, significantly with engine cold). Reconnect electrical connector. Ensure engine speed returns to previous speed.

**2)** If engine does not return to previous speed, turn engine off. Turn ignition switch to ON position. Ensure 10-12 volts are available at Black/White wire of air control valve electrical connector.

**3)** Turn ignition off. Ensure resistance of Air Control Valve (ACV) is 7.3-13 ohms at -4 to 176°F (-20 to 80°C). If resistance is not as specified, replace ACV. Check ACV solenoid for any short to ground. If short is present, replace ACV.

**4)** Attach electrical connector to ACV. Disconnect connector at ECU. Turn ignition on. Ensure 10-12 volts are present at terminal No. 45 (Green/Red wire) of ECU. If voltage reading is not as specified, check harness between ACV and ECU.

**5)** Turn ignition off and reconnect ECU connector. Turn ignition on. Backprobe terminal No. 45 (Green/Red wire) of ECU. There should be one volt or less for about one minute after ignition switch is turned to ON position. After one minute, there should be at least 10 volts. If voltage reading is not as specified, check for a bad ground, problem with ECU circuits (sensors) or ECU.

**Dashpot (Justy PFI & XT)** - To check and adjust dashpot, see ON-VEHICLE ADJUSTMENTS article.

**Fast Idle & Idle-Up Control Device (Justy PFI)** - Using a hand vacuum pump, check to see if control device will hold vacuum. On models equipped with A/C, ensure idle speed increases when A/C is turned on. On models without A/C, idle speed should increase when headlights, rear defogger or heater blower is turned on. *See Fig. 1.*

# 1991 ENGINE PERFORMANCE
# System & Component Testing (Cont.)

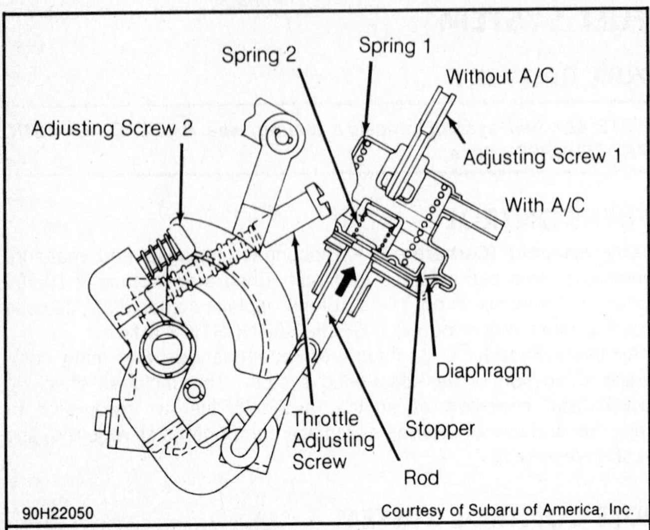


*Fig. 1: FICD Control Actuator*

**Idle Compensator (Justy Carbureted)** – Remove top of air cleaner. With engine running, apply a source of heated air to warm up idle compensator. Ensure idle compensator opens and idle speeds up. Allow idle compensator to cool (compensator should close). If idle compensator does not test as described, replace.

**Idle-Up Solenoid (Justy Carbureted)** – Disconnect harness and measure resistance between solenoid terminals. Ensure resistance is 33-40 ohms. *See Fig. 2.* If resistance is not as specified, replace solenoid. Also see appropriate trouble code(s) in SELF-DIAGNOSTICS article.

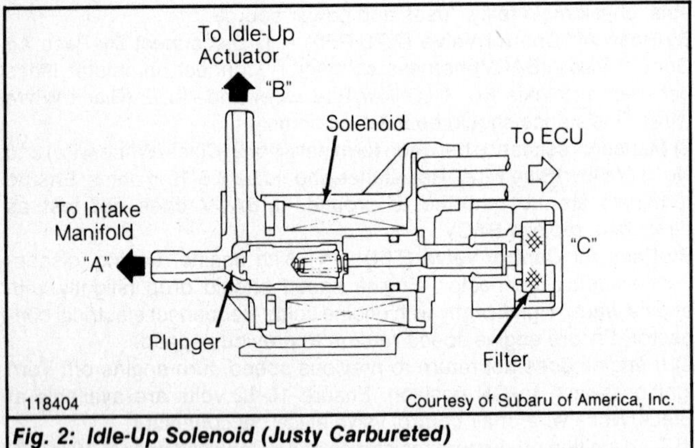


*Fig. 2: Idle-Up Solenoid (Justy Carbureted)*

## IGNITION SYSTEM

***NOTE:*** ***For basic ignition checks (coil, wires, crank angle sensor), see SELF-DIAGNOSTICS article.***

## TIMING CONTROL SYSTEMS

**Electronic Advance** – For testing, see ON-VEHICLE ADJUSTMENTS article.

**Knock Sensor (Legacy, Loyale Turbo & XT6)** – For testing, see SELF-DIAGNOSTICS and WIRING DIAGRAMS articles.

## EMISSION SYSTEMS & SUB-SYSTEMS

### AIR INJECTION (JUSTY)

**Suction Valve** – **1)** Blow air through suction valve air inlet section. Air should flow smoothly through to valve outlet. *See Figs. 3 and 4.* If air does not flow through smoothly, reed valve is stuck closed. Replace reed valve.

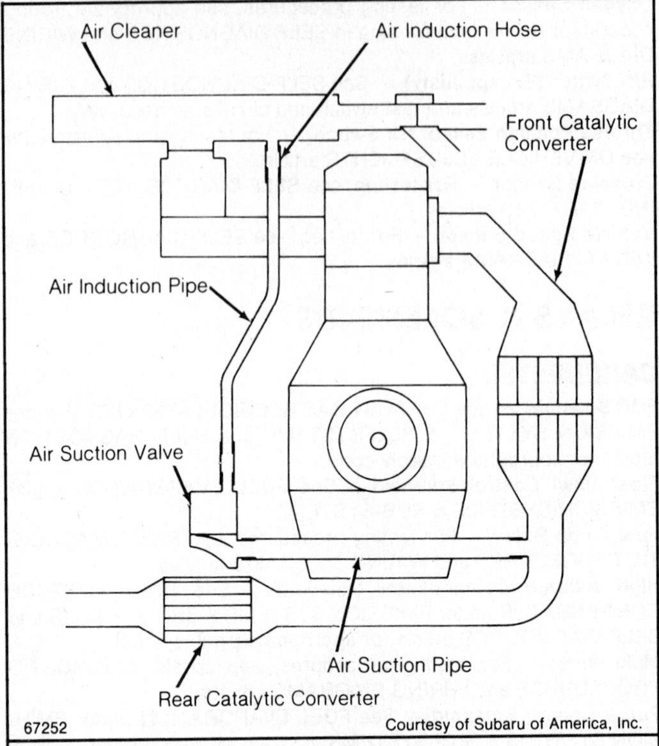


*Fig. 3: Air Injection System (Justy)*

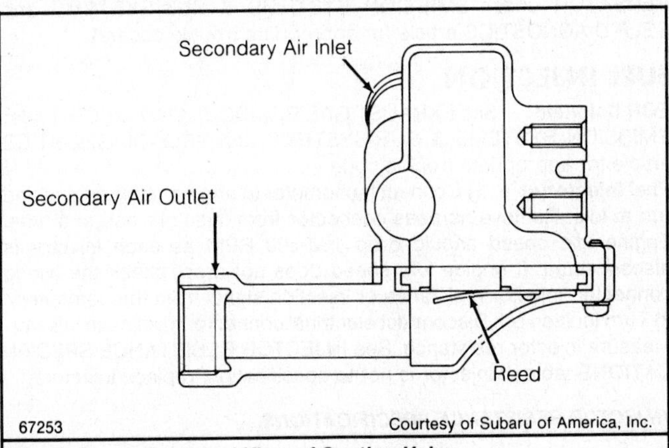


*Fig. 4: Cross-Sectional View of Suction Valve*

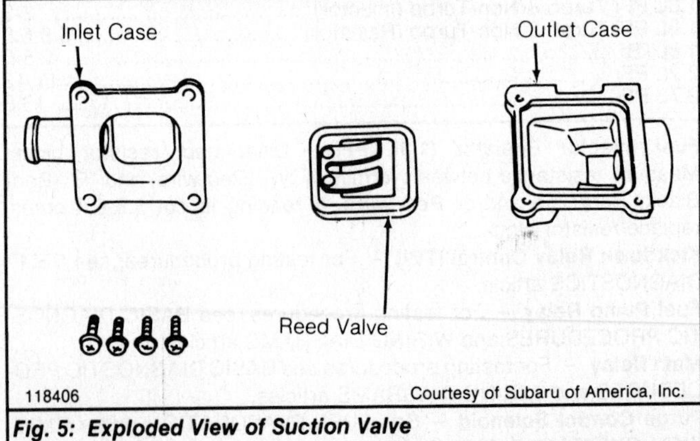


*Fig. 5: Exploded View of Suction Valve*

**2)** Blow air through valve outlet. If air flows out inlet, reed valve is broken or stuck open. Replace reed valve.

**3)** Open suction valve. Inspect gasket, inlet case and outlet case for damage (cracks). Clean reed valve with gasoline and inspect for waves, cracks or dents in reed valve seat. Inspect for broken or cracked point of reed valve, or rusted stopper. Replace as required. *See Fig. 5.*

## EXHAUST GAS RECIRCULATION (EGR)

**EGR System (Justy Carbureted & Loyale TBI) - 1)** Apply about 8 in. Hg to EGR valve with hand vacuum pump. With engine warmed up, either rough idling or engine stall should occur. *See Figs. 6 and 7.*
**2)** If engine idle does not change, check EGR pipe and gas passages for clogging and leaks. Clean or replace if necessary. When cleaning, inspect exhaust gas inlet to intake manifold for presence of deposits. Inspect EGR inlet pipe for exhaust deposits.

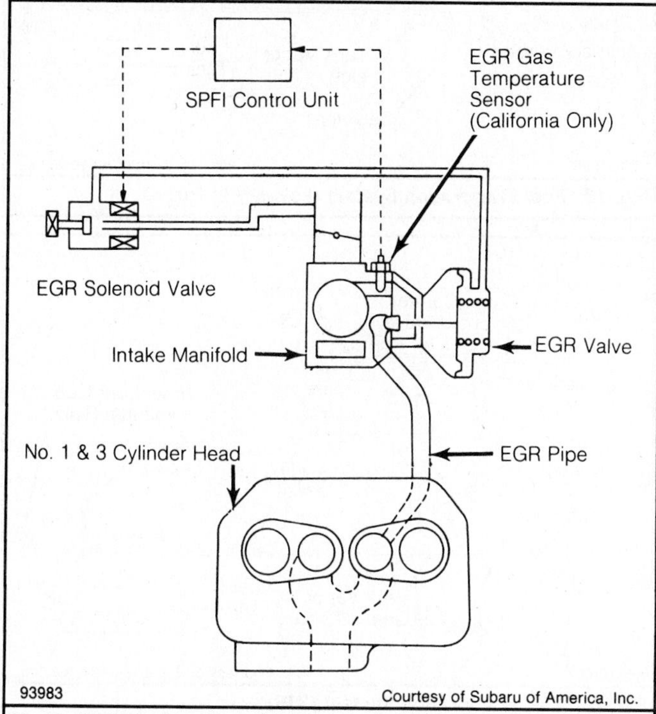


*Fig. 6: EGR System (Loyale TBI)*

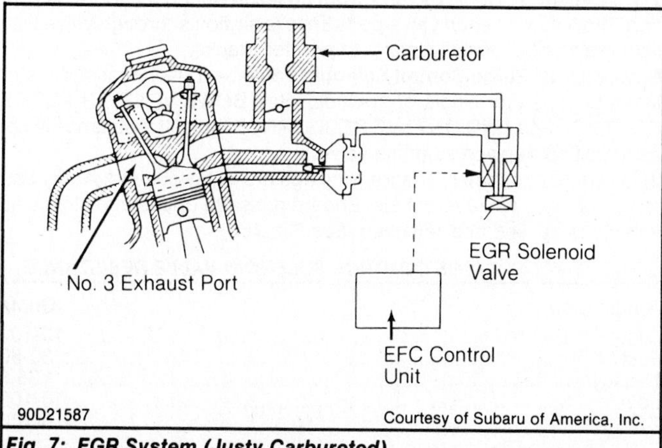


*Fig. 7: EGR System (Justy Carbureted)*

**EGR Valve - 1)** Look through opening in EGR valve body. Warm engine to normal operating temperature. Increase engine speed and check if valve shaft moves when engine reaches 3500-4000 RPM under no-load condition.
**2)** If shaft does not move, remove valve and manually check valve movement. If valve appears okay, check vacuum lines for leaks. If valve does not operate, clean or replace.

***NOTE: When cleaning EGR valve, DO NOT wash in solvent or degreaser, or permanent damage to the valve diaphragm will result.***

**3)** Depress valve diaphragm and inspect valve seat area. Inspect valve inlet and outlet for deposits and clean as necessary. Blow clean with compressed air. Recheck valve operation by applying 8 in. Hg with a hand vacuum pump. Install unit using a new gasket.
**EGR Solenoid Valve (Justy Carbureted & Loyale TBI) - 1)** Remove connector from solenoid valve. Measure resistance of solenoid valve. Resistance should be 33-40 ohms. If resistance is not 33-40 ohms, replace solenoid valve.
**2)** Measure resistance between solenoid valve terminal leads and body ground. If solenoid is shorted, replace solenoid valve.
**3)** Check vacuum passage for opening and closing operation. When EGR solenoid is not energized, passage between "A" and "B" should be closed and passage between "B" and "C" should be open. *See Fig. 8.* When solenoid is energized, passage between "A" and "B" should be open and passage between "B" and "C" should be closed.

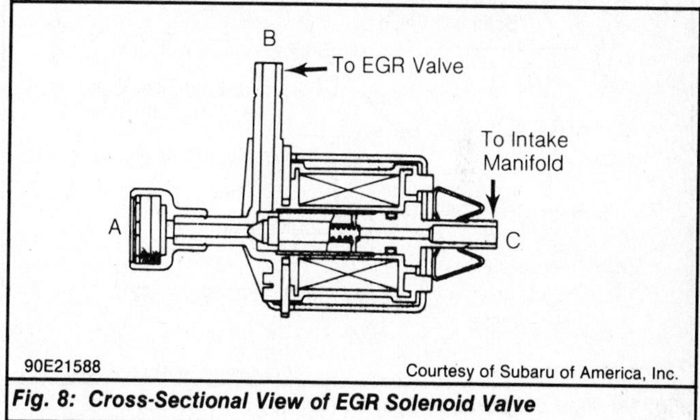


*Fig. 8: Cross-Sectional View of EGR Solenoid Valve*

## FUEL EVAPORATION

***CAUTION: DO NOT inhale fuel vapor when blowing into fuel evaporation hoses.***

**System Test -** Remove fuel filler cap. Disconnect vent hose between charcoal canister and fuel tank. Blow air toward canister. Ensure air flows freely into canister. Blow air toward fuel tank. Ensure air flows into tank with a slight resistance from 2-way valve. *See Figs. 9-14.*

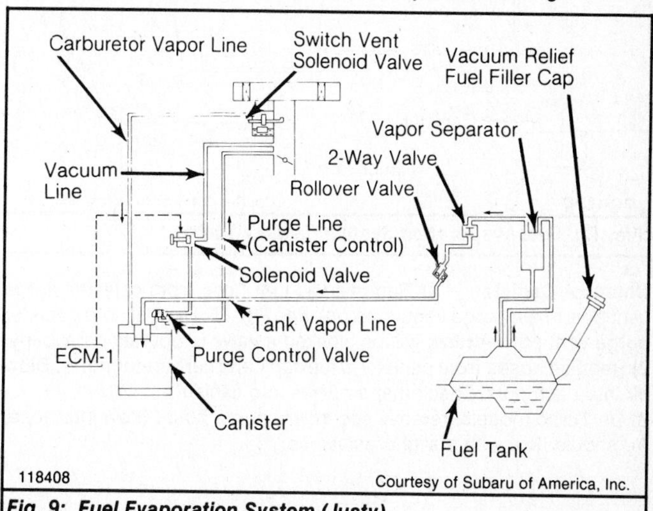


*Fig. 9: Fuel Evaporation System (Justy)*

# 1991 ENGINE PERFORMANCE
## System & Component Testing (Cont.)

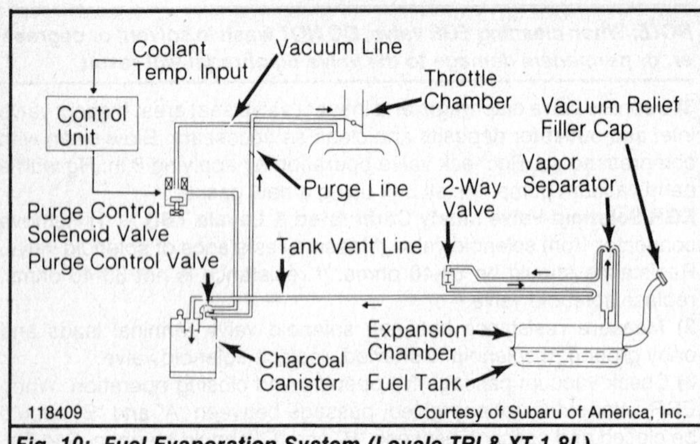


*Fig. 10: Fuel Evaporation System (Loyale TBI & XT 1.8L)*

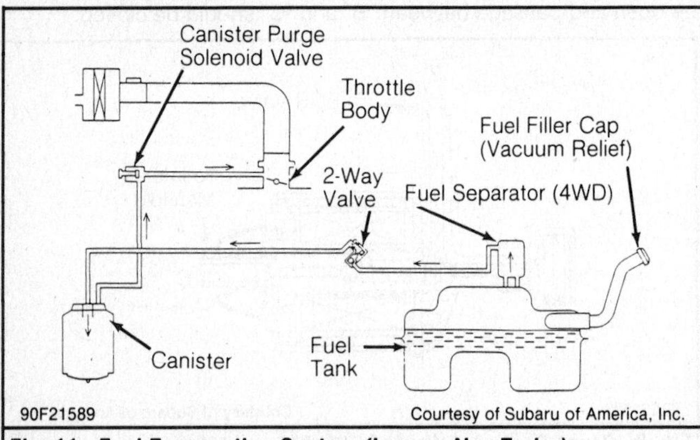


*Fig. 11: Fuel Evaporation System (Legacy Non-Turbo)*

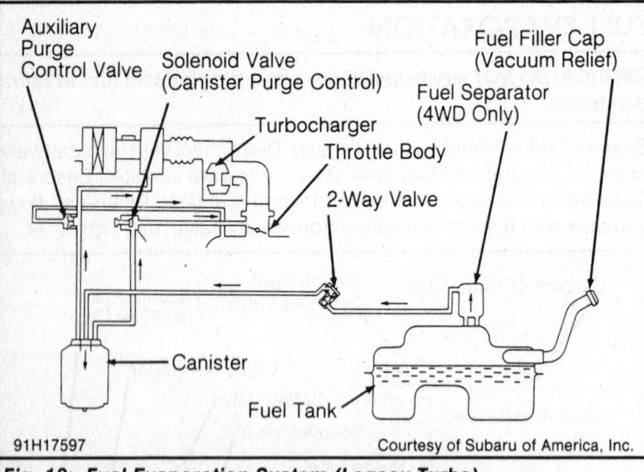


*Fig. 12: Fuel Evaporation System (Legacy Turbo)*

**Charcoal Canister – 1)** Remove vacuum hose from canister purge vent port (main purge vent on turbo). *See Fig. 15.* Blow air into canister purge vent port. Airflow will be blocked if valve is operating properly.
**2)** Remove hoses from canister's fuel tank and carburetor ports. Blow air into each port. Check that air flows into canister.
**3)** On Turbo models, remove secondary purge hose. Blow into hose. Air should flow with a slight resistance.

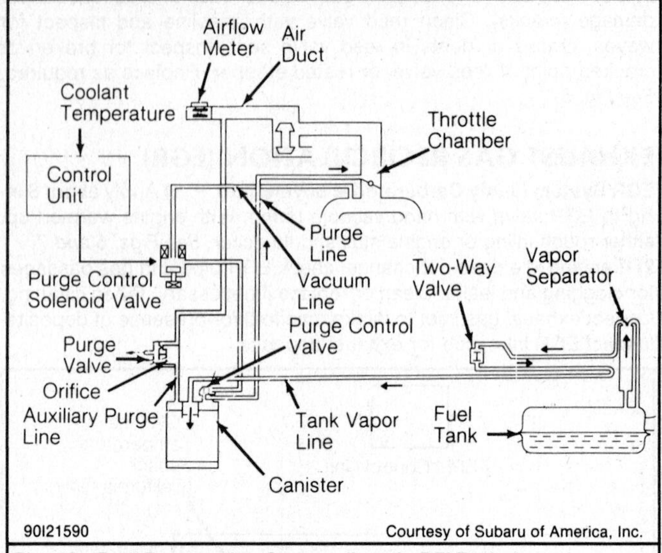


*Fig. 13: Fuel Evaporation System (Loyale PFI Turbo)*

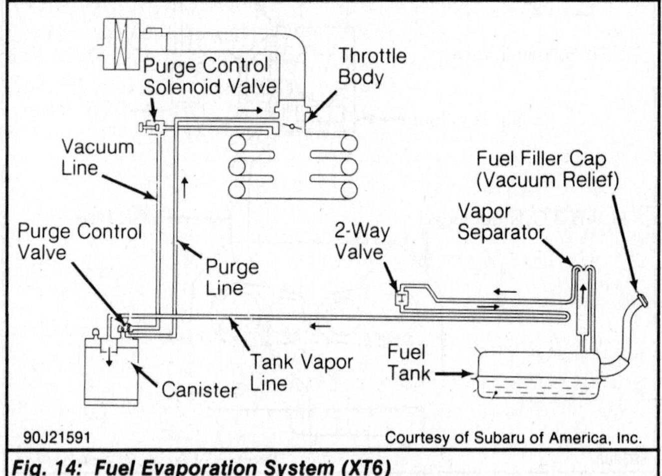


*Fig. 14: Fuel Evaporation System (XT6)*

**2-Way Valve –** Remove valve from hoses. Mark hoses for reinstallation. Blow air into each valve port. Ensure air flows through valve with light resistance. Visually inspect valve for cracks.
**Bowl Vent Or Purge Control Solenoid Valve – 1)** Connect ohmmeter leads between terminals of solenoid. See BOWL VENT OR PURGE CONTROL SOLENOID VALVE RESISTANCE table. If resistance is not as specified, replace solenoid valve.
**2)** Using an ohmmeter, ensure windings are not grounded. Apply battery voltage to valve terminals. Ensure passage opens and closes as voltage is applied and removed. *See Fig. 16.*

***BOWL VENT OR PURGE CONTROL SOLENOID VALVE RESISTANCE***

| Application | Ohms |
|---|---|
| Justy Carbureted | 10-100 |
| Justy PFI | 30-50 |
| Legacy | [1] 35.5 |
| Loyale | 10-100 |
| XT & XT6 | 0-100 |

[1] – At 68°F (20°C).

# 1991 ENGINE PERFORMANCE
# System & Component Testing (Cont.)

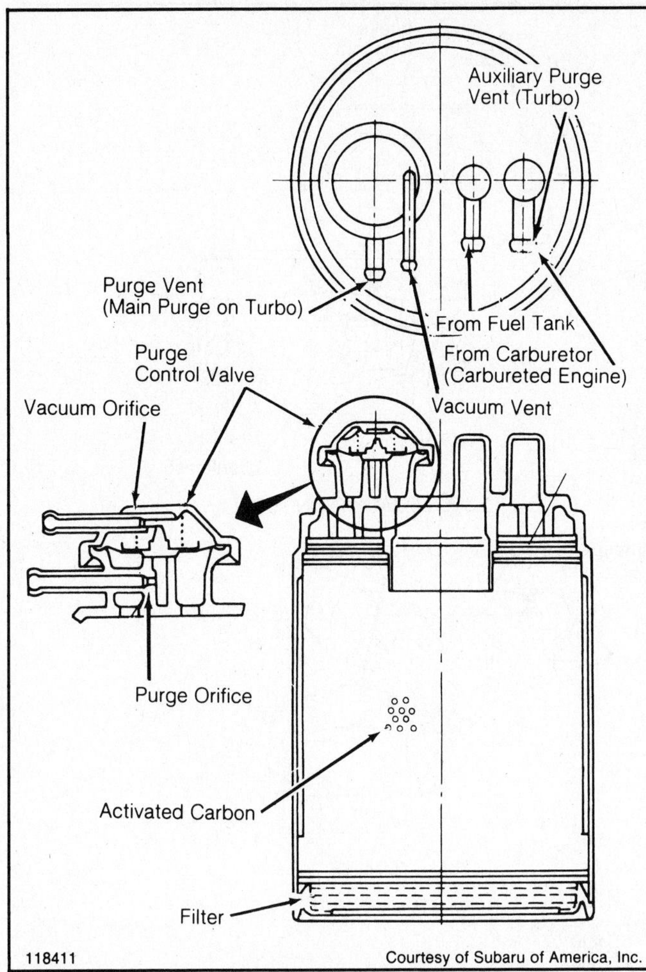


118411 Courtesy of Subaru of America, Inc.

***Fig. 15: Identifying Charcoal Canister Hose***

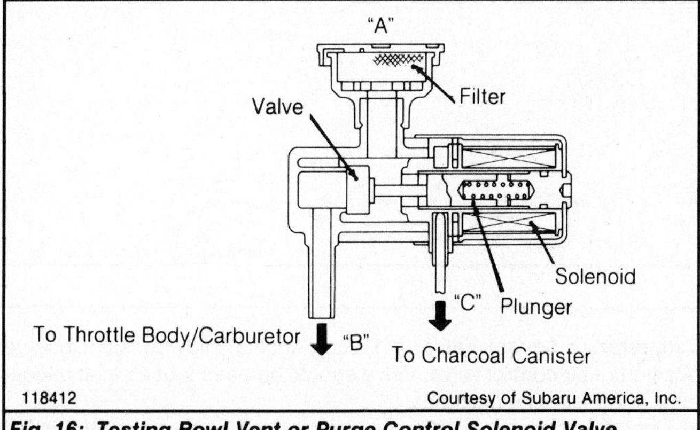


118412 Courtesy of Subaru America, Inc.

***Fig. 16: Testing Bowl Vent or Purge Control Solenoid Valve***

## HIGH ALTITUDE COMPENSATOR

**Atmospheric Pressure Sensor (Justy PFI & Legacy)** – Atmospheric pressure sensor is located in ECU. If appropriate trouble code appears, replace ECU.

**High Altitude Compensator Solenoids (Justy Carbureted)** – **1)** Connect ohmmeter leads between terminals of Black/White and White/Red wires of solenoid. If resistance is not 33-40 ohms, replace solenoid valve.

**2)** Ensure windings are not grounded. Apply battery voltage to valve terminals. Ensure vacuum passage opens and closes as voltage is applied and removed.

**3)** When solenoid is not energized, passage between "A" and "B" should be closed. *See Fig. 17*. When solenoid is energized, passage between "A" and "B" should be open. If solenoid valve does not operate properly, replace solenoid valve.

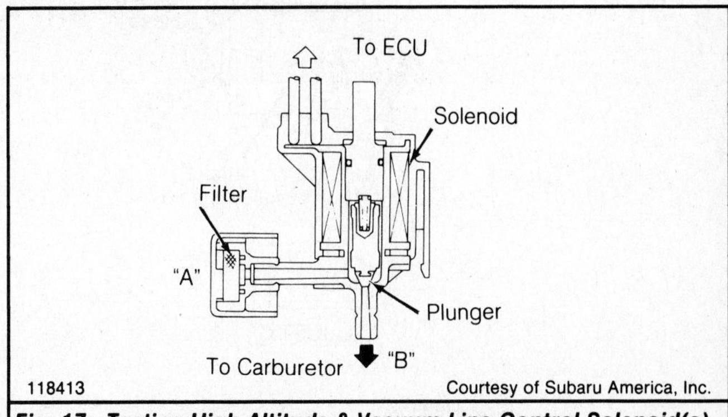


118413 Courtesy of Subaru America, Inc.

***Fig. 17: Testing High Altitude & Vacuum Line Control Solenoid(s)***

**Vacuum Line Control Solenoid Valve (Justy Carbureted) – 1)** Connect ohmmeter leads between terminals of solenoid. If resistance is not 10-100 ohms, replace solenoid valve.

**2)** Using an ohmmeter, ensure windings are not grounded. Apply battery voltage to valve terminals. Ensure passage opens and closes as voltage is applied and removed.

**3)** When solenoid is not energized, passage between "A" and "B" should be closed and open between "B" and "C". *See Fig. 17*. When solenoid is energized, passage between "A" and "B" should be open and closed between "B" and "C". If solenoid valve does not operate properly, replace solenoid valve.

## PCV

***NOTE: For information on PCV systems, see Fig. 19.***

## THERMOSTATIC AIR CLEANER (JUSTY)

**Air Control Diaphragm & Valve – 1)** In warm weather, it may be difficult to find a malfunction in hot air control system. In cold weather, vacuum leaks or faulty air control valve will result in engine stalling or hesitation, increased fuel consumption and/or lack of power.

**2)** Check vacuum hoses for cracks and proper connections. Inspect air control diaphragm (vacuum motor) with engine stopped. *See Fig. 18*.

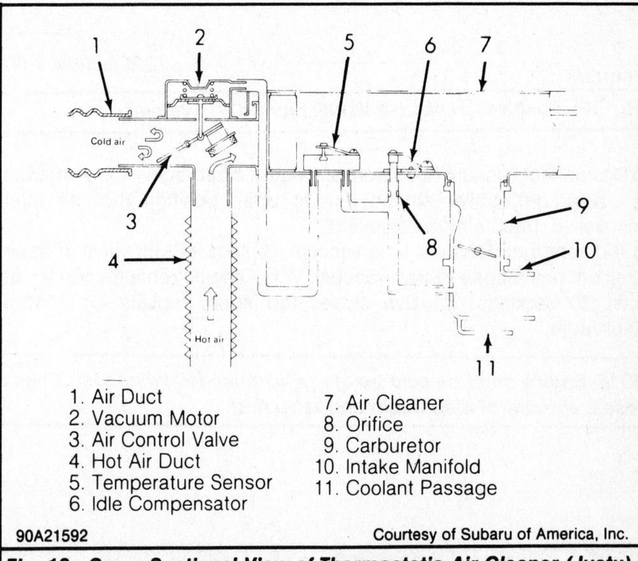


90A21592 Courtesy of Subaru of America, Inc.

***Fig. 18: Cross-Sectional View of Thermostatic Air Cleaner (Justy)***

# 1991 ENGINE PERFORMANCE
## System & Component Testing (Cont.)

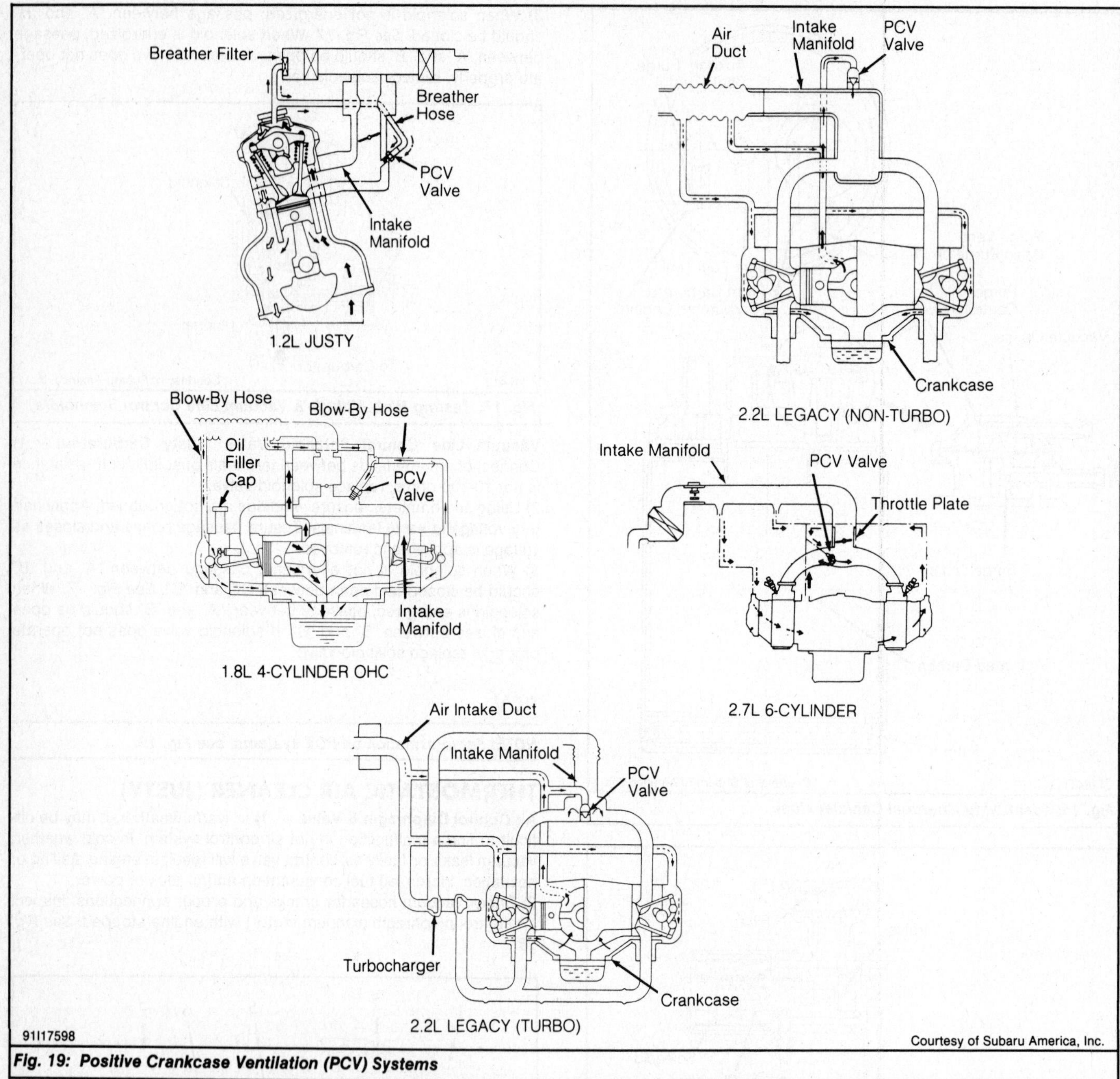


*Fig. 19: Positive Crankcase Ventilation (PCV) Systems*

**3)** Disconnect vacuum hose from air control diaphragm. Apply vacuum to diaphragm. Valve should rise to open position (hot air inlet uncovered, fresh air inlet blocked).

**4)** If diaphragm does not hold vacuum, replace it. With valve in open position, pinch hose to trap vacuum. Valve should remain open for at least 30 seconds. If valve closes too soon, replace air control diaphragm.

***NOTE: Engine must be cold before performing following test. Check hoses, air control diaphragm and valve first.***

**Temperature Sensor Valve – 1)** Start engine, allow to idle. Observe position of air control valve. Valve should be open (hot air inlet uncovered, fresh air inlet blocked).

**2)** Continue to observe valve as engine warms up. Air control valve should gradually move to closed position (hot air inlet blocked). If valve does not move to closed position, replace temperature sensor valve assembly.

# 1991 ENGINE PERFORMANCE
# Pin Voltage Charts

## Justy, Legacy, Loyale, XT, XT6

## INTRODUCTION

Pin voltage charts are supplied to reduce diagnostic time. Checking pin voltages at the ECU determines whether it is receiving and transmitting proper voltage signals. Charts may also help determine if ECU harness is shorted or opened.

***NOTE: All voltage tests should be performed with a Digital Volt-Ohmmeter (DVOM) with a minimum 10-megohm input impedance, unless stated otherwise in testing procedures. Voltage readings may vary slightly due to battery condition or charging rate.***

## JUSTY

**1)** ECU circuits are checked at the ECU connector under one or more of the following conditions: ignition off, ignition on and engine off, or ignition on and engine running. Test between indicated terminal No. and body ground. Use wire color to help identify terminal. See appropriate ECU PIN SPECIFICATIONS table. To test pin voltage, carefully backprobe terminal at harness side of ECU connector. *See Figs. 1 and 2.*

**2)** If resistance or voltage is not as specified, test and repair, or replace, circuit or affected component. Retest circuit to verify repair has been made. Unless stated otherwise, perform all tests with ECU harness connected.

F62 YELLOW

| 1 | 2 | 3 | 4 | 5 | | 6 | 7 | 8 | 9 | 10 |
|---|---|---|---|---|---|---|---|---|---|---|
| 11 | 12 | 13 | 14 | 15 | 16 | 17 | 18 | 19 | 20 | 21 | 22 |

F69 YELLOW

| 1 | 2 | 3 | 4 | | 5 | 6 | 7 |
|---|---|---|---|---|---|---|---|
| 8 | 9 | 10 | 11 | 12 | 13 | 14 | 15 | 16 |

F61 YELLOW

| 1 | 2 | 3 | | 4 | 5 | 6 |
|---|---|---|---|---|---|---|
| 7 | 8 | 9 | 10 | 11 | 12 | 13 | 14 |

F62

| | | |
|---|---|---|
| 1 | YL | CFC monitor |
| 2 | B | $O_2$ sensor (sealed) |
| 3 | WB | Water temperature sensor |
| 4 | YR | Pressure sensor |
| 5 | RY | 5 volts output (for pressure sensor) |
| 6 | LgB | Car speed sensor |
| 7 | B | Crank angle sensor |
| 8 | W | Crank angle sensor |
| 9 | LR | Serial communication |
| 10 | GR | Serial communication |
| 11 | – | |
| 12 | BR | Ground (control) |
| 13 | – | |
| 14 | GY | Clutch switch |
| 15 | – | |
| 16 | B | Ground (drive) |
| 17 | B | Ground (drive) |
| 18 | – | |
| 19 | – | |
| 20 | BW | Power (Ignition) |
| 21 | LgW | Read memory connector |
| 22 | GW | Test mode connector |

F69

| | | |
|---|---|---|
| 1 | BY | A/Con. signal |
| 2 | GB | Radiator fan monitor |
| 3 | YG | Radiator fan signal |
| 4 | G | VLC solenoid valve |
| 5 | GW | A/Con. cut |
| 6 | RG | Power (Battery) |
| 7 | Y | Duty solenoid valve |
| 8 | WG | Control unit power |
| 9 | BW | Power (Ignition) |
| 10 | LY | EGR solenoid valve |
| 11 | GL | CPC solenoid valve |
| 12 | WY | E/CV solenoid valve |
| 13 | YL | CFC |
| 14 | – | |
| 15 | RG | Power (Battery) |
| 16 | Y | Duty solenoid valve |

F61

| | | |
|---|---|---|
| 1 | LB | Fuel pump & Auto choke relay |
| 2 | WY | Ignition output (power transistor) |
| 3 | Lg | CHECK ENGINE Light |
| 4 | RG | Idle-up signal (Lighting switch) |
| 5 | LY | Idle-up signal (R. defogger switch) |
| 6 | GW | Idle-up signal (Heater fan switch) |
| 7 | LB | Fuel pump & Auto choke relay |
| 8 | WY | Ignition output (power transistor) |
| 9 | R | Trouble code |
| 10 | LY | Idle-up solenoid valve |
| 11 | WR | HAC solenoid valve |
| 12 | BrW | UIL |
| 13 | BR | Ground (control) |
| 14 | – | |

90D16629 90G16630 90H16631 90I16632

Courtesy of Subaru of America, Inc.

*Fig. 1: Identifying ECU Connector Terminals (Justy Carbureted)*

# 1991 ENGINE PERFORMANCE
# Pin Voltage Charts (Cont.)

### *ECU PIN SPECIFICATIONS (JUSTY CARBURETED)*

| ECU Terminal No. (Wire Color) | Condition | Volts or Ohms |
|---|---|---|
| **Connector F62** | | |
| 1 (Yellow/Blue) [1] | Ign. On | 7-12V |
| 2 (Black) | Eng. On | .1-1.0V |
| 3 (White/Black) | Ign. On | .1-2V |
| 5 (Red/Yellow) | Eng. On | .1-3.0V |
| 5 (Red/Yellow) | Ign. On | 2.0-5.0V |
| 6 (Lt. Green/Black) | Eng. On | [2] 1-3V |
| 12 (Brown/Red) [1] | Ign. Off | 2-10 Ohms |
| 14 (Green/Yellow) | | |
| Release Clutch | Ign. On | 0-2V |
| Depress Clutch | Ign. On | 2-12V |
| 16 (Black) [1] | Ign. Off | 2-10 Ohms |
| 17 (Black) [1] | Ign. Off | 2-10 Ohms |
| 20 (Black/White) [1] | Ign. On | 7-12V |
| **Connector F61** | | |
| 1 (Blue/Black) [1] | Ign. On | 7-12V |
| 2 (White/Yellow) | Ign. On | [3] .1-7V |
| 4 (Red/Green) | Eng. On | [4] 5-12V |
| 5 (Blue/Yellow) | Eng. On | [4] 5-12V |
| 6 (Green/White) | Eng. On | [5] 3.5-10V |
| 7 (Blue/Black) [1] | Ign. On | 7-12V |
| 8 (White/Yellow) | Ign. On | [3] .1-7V |
| 10 (Blue/Yellow) [1] | Ign. On | 7-12V |
| 11 (White/Red) [1] | Ign. On | 7-12V |
| 13 (Brown/Red) [1] | Ign. Off | Zero Ohm |

### *ECU PIN SPECIFICATIONS (JUSTY CARBURETED – Cont.)*

| ECU Terminal No. (Wire Color) | Condition | Volts or Ohms |
|---|---|---|
| **Connector F69** | | |
| 2 (Green/Black) [1] | Ign. On | 7-12V |
| 3 (Yellow/Green) [1] | Ign. On | 7-12V |
| 4 (Green) [1] | Ign. On | 7-12V |
| 6 (Red/Green) [1] | Ign. Off | 9-12V |
| 7 (Yellow Or Yellow/Red) [1] | Ign. On | 10-12V |
| 9 (Black/White) [1] | Ign. On | 7-12V |
| 10 (Blue/Yellow) [1] | Ign. On | 7-12V |
| 11 (Green/Blue) [1] | Ign. On | 7-12V |
| 12 (White/Yellow) [1] | Ign. On | 7-12V |
| 15 (Red/Green) [1] | Ign. Off | 9-12V |
| 16 (Yellow Or Yellow/Red) [1] | Ign. On | 10-12V |

[1] – ECU harness disconnected.
[2] – Fluctuates around 2 volts while driving vehicle.
[3] – Fluctuates below 2 volts to 7 volts while cranking with starter.
[4] – With defogger and headlight switch on.
[5] – With heater fan on.

### *ECU PIN SPECIFICATIONS – CONNECTOR F119 [1] (JUSTY PFI)*

| ECU Terminal No. (Wire Color) | Circuit | Condition | Volts or Ohms |
|---|---|---|---|
| 1 (Black/Red) | Ground | Ignition Off | [2] 10 Ohms Or Less |
| 2 (Red/Yellow) | Vacuum Pressure Sensor | .... | .... |
| 3 (Red) | Crank Angle Signal (+) | Ignition Off | [2] Infinite |
| 3 (Red) | Crank Angle Signal (+) | Engine Cranking | 1-3V |
| 4 (White) | Crank Angle Signal (–) | Ignition Off | [2] Infinite |
| 5 (Black) | Cylinder Distinction Signal (+) | Ignition Off | [2] Infinite |
| 6 (Green) | Cylinder Distinction Signal (–) | Ignition Off | [2] Infinite |
| 7 (Shield) | Crank Angle/Cyl. Distinction | Ignition Off | 10 Ohms Or Less |
| 8 (White/Red) | High Altitude Signal [3] | .... | .... |
| 9 (Brown/Black) | Torque Signal [3] | .... | .... |
| 10 (Brown/White) | Coolant Temp. Signal [3] | .... | .... |
| 11 (White) | Injector No. 3 | Ignition On | 8V or More |
| 12 (White/Yellow) | Injector No. 1 | Ignition On | 8V or More |
| 13 (Black/Blue) | Ground | Ignition Off | [2] 10 Ohms Or Less |
| 14 | .... | .... | .... |
| 15 (Green/White) | A/C Cut Signal | .... | .... |
| 16 | .... | .... | .... |
| 17 | .... | .... | .... |
| 18 (Blue/Black) | Fuel Pump | .... | .... |
| 19 (Light Green) | Check Engine Light | Ignition On | 9V Or More |
| 20 (Orange) | Shift Indicator Light [4] | .... | .... |
| 21 (Yellow/White) | Ignition Signal | Ignition Off | [2] Infinite |
| 21 (Yellow/White) | Ignition Signal | Engine Cranking | 1-3V |
| 22 (Blue/Red) | Canister Purge Control | Ignition Off | [2] Infinite |
| 22 (Blue/Red) | Canister Purge Control | Ignition On | 2.5-8V (Alternating) |
| 23 (Brown/Red) | A/C Compressor | .... | .... |
| 24 (Green/Yellow) | ISC Signal | Ignition Off | [2] Infinite |
| 24 (Green/Yellow) | ISC Signal | Ignition On | 8V Or More |
| 25 (White/Green) | Injector No. 2 | Ignition On | 8V Or More |
| 26 (Black/Blue) | Ground | Ignition Off | [2] 10 Ohms Or Less |

[1] – Measure between test terminal and ground.
[2] – With ECU harness connector disconnected.
[3] – On automatic transmission vehicles only.
[4] – On manual transmission vehicles only.

# 1991 ENGINE PERFORMANCE
# Pin Voltage Charts (Cont.)

***ECU PIN SPECIFICATIONS – CONNECTOR F120 [1] (JUSTY PFI)***

| ECU Terminal No. (Wire Color) | Circuit | Condition | Volts or Ohms |
|---|---|---|---|
| 1 (Red) | Power | Ignition On | [2] 9V Or More |
| 2 (White/Blue) | Memory Back-Up Power | Ignition On | [2] 9V Or More |
| 3 (Light Green) | Ignition Monitor | Engine Cranking | 1-3V |
| 3 (Light Green) | Ignition Monitor | Ignition Off | Infinite |
| 4 (Light Green/Blue) | Speed Sensor | Ignition On | 0.25-2.5V (Alternating) |
| 5 (Yellow/Blue) | Clutch Switch | Ignition Off | Infinite |
| 5 (Yellow/Blue) | Clutch Switch [3] | Ignition On. | 8V Or More (Gear Select In "N") |
| 5 (Yellow/Blue) | Clutch Switch [3] | Ignition On. | 2.5V Or More (Gear Select In "D") |
| 5 (Yellow/Blue) | Clutch Switch [4] | Ignition On | 8V Or More |
| 5 (Yellow/Blue) | Clutch Switch [4] | Ignition On | 1V Or Less (Clutch Released) |
| 5 (Yellow/Blue) | Clutch Switch [4] | Ignition On. | 8V Or More (Clutch Applied) |
| 6 (Blue/White) | Idle Switch | Ignition Off | [2] Infinite |
| 6 (Blue/White) | Idle Switch | Ignition On | 1V Or Less |
| 7 (Blue/Green) | Serial Monitor RX | ..... | ..... |
| 8 (Yellow) | Serial Monitor Clock | ..... | ..... |
| 9 (Green/Blue) | Serial Monitor TX | ..... | ..... |
| 10 (Black/Red) | Ground | Ignition Off | 10 Ohms Or Less |
| 11 (Green/White) | Blower Fan Signal | Ignition On | 8V Or More (Fan Off) |
| 11 (Green/White) | Blower Fan Signal | Ignition On | 8V Or More (Fan In 3rd Position) |
| 12 (Red) | Power | Ignition On | 9V Or More |
| 13 | ..... | ..... | ..... |
| 14 (Blue) | A/C Signal | ..... | ..... |
| 15 (Green/Black) | Radiator Fan Signal | Ignition Off | Infinite |
| 15 (Green/Black) | Radiator Fan Signal | Ignition On | 1V Or Less (Fan On) |
| 15 (Green/Black) | Radiator Fan Signal | Ignition On | 8V Or More (Fan Off) |
| 16 (Green/Red) | Power Switch | Ignition Off | [2] Infinite |
| 16 (Green/Red) | Power Switch | Ignition On | [2] 8V (Throttle Fully Closed) |
| 16 (Green/Red) | Power Switch | Ignition On | [2] 1V (Throttle Fully Open) |
| 17 (Black/White) | Starter Switch | Engine Cranking | [2] 8V Or More |
| 18 (Blue/Yellow) | Rear Defogger Switch | Ignition On | 2V Or Less (Rear Defogger Off) |
| 18 (Blue/Yellow) | Rear Defogger Switch | Ignition On | 8V Or More (Rear Defogger On) |
| 19 | ..... | ..... | ..... |
| 20 (Blue/White) | Headlight: High Signal | Ignition On | 8V Or More (Headlights Off) |
| 20 (Blue/White) | Headlight: High Signal | Ignition On | 8V Or More (Headlights High) |
| 21 (Red/Yellow) | Headlight: Low Signal | Ignition On | 8V Or More (Headlights Off) |
| 21 (Red/Yellow) | Headlight: Low Signal | Ignition On | 8V Or Less (Headlights Low) |
| 22 | ..... | ..... | ..... |

[1] – Measure between test terminal and ground.
[2] – With ECU harness connector disconnected.
[3] – On automatic transmission vehicles only.
[4] – On manual transmission vehicles only.

# 1991 ENGINE PERFORMANCE
# Pin Voltage Charts (Cont.)

***ECU PIN SPECIFICATIONS – CONNECTOR F121 [1] (JUSTY PFI)***

| ECU Terminal No. (Wire Color) | Circuit | Condition | Volts or Ohms |
|---|---|---|---|
| 1 (Black/Green) | Ground | Ignition Off | 10 Ohms Or Less |
| 2 (Black/Green) | Ground | Ignition Off | 10 Ohms Or Less |
| 3 (Yellow/Red) | Vacuum Pressure Sensor | ..... | ..... |
| 4 (Black) | Oxygen Sensor | Engine Idling | 0.5-4.5 (Alternating) |
| 5 (White/Black) | Coolant Temperature Sensor | Ignition Off | [2] Infinite |
| 6 (White/Blue) | Air Temperature Sensor | Ignition Off | [2] Infinite |
| 7 (Shield) | Oxygen Sensor | ..... | ..... |
| 8 (Yellow/Black) | High Altitude Signal [3] | ..... | ..... |
| 9 (Light Green/White) | Read Memory Connector | Ignition Off | [4] One Ohm |
| 9 (Light Green/White) | Read Memory Connector | Ignition Off | [5] Infinite |
| 10 (Brown) | Test Mode Connector | Ignition Off | [4] One Ohm |
| 10 (Brown) | Test Mode Connector | Ignition Off | [5] Infinite |
| 11 (Black/Red) | Transmision Identification | Ignition Off | One Ohm Or Less (Auto. Trans.) |
| 11 (Black/Red) | Transmision Identification | Ignition Off | Infinite (Man. Trans.) |
| 12 (Black/Blue) | Vehicle Identification | Ignition Off | One Ohm Or less (Calif. Models) |
| 12 (Black/Blue) | Vehicle Identification | Ignition Off | Infinite (Federal Models) |
| 13 | ..... | ..... | ..... |
| 14 (Black/Red) | FWD Vehicle Identification | Ignition Off | Infinite (FWD Models) |
| 14 (Black/Red) | 4WD Vehicle Identification | Ignition Off | One Ohm Max. (4WD Models) |
| 15 | ..... | ..... | ..... |
| 16 | ..... | ..... | ..... |

[1] – Measure between test terminal and ground.
[2] – With ECU harness connector disconnected.
[3] – On automatic transmission vehicles only.
[4] – With connector connected.
[5] – With connector disconnected.

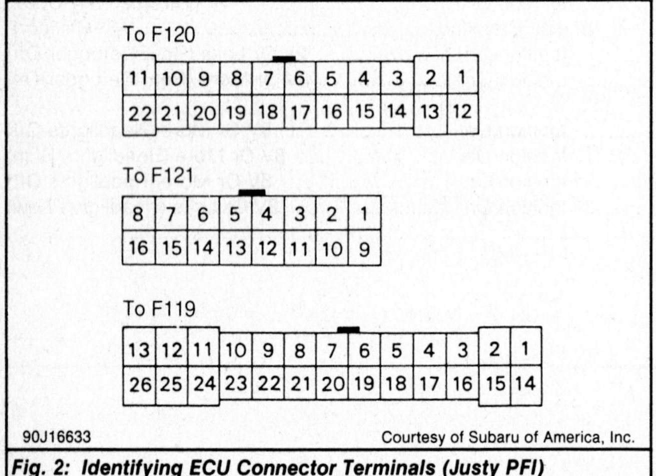

***Fig. 2: Identifying ECU Connector Terminals (Justy PFI)***

## LEGACY

**1)** ECU circuits are checked at the ECU connector under one or more the following conditions: ignition off, ignition on and engine off, or ignition on and engine running. *See Figs. 3-5.*

Test between indicated terminal No. and body ground. When testing pin voltage, carefully backprobe terminal at harness side of ECU connector.

**2)** If voltage is not as specified, test and repair, or replace, circuit or affected component. Retest circuit to verify repair has been made. Unless stated otherwise, perform all tests with ECU harness connected.

13 12 11 10 9 8 7 6 5 4 3 2 1
26 25 24 23 22 21 20 19 18 17 16 15 14
To F47

8 7 6 5 4 3 2 1
16 15 14 13 12 11 10 9
To B56

6 5 4 3 2 1
12 11 10 9 8 7
To B58

11 10 9 8 7 6 5 4 3 2 1
22 21 20 19 18 17 16 15 14 13 12
To B48

90A16634
Courtesy of Subaru of America, Inc.

***Fig. 3: Identifying ECU Connector Terminals (Legacy)***

# 1991 ENGINE PERFORMANCE
# Pin Voltage Charts (Cont.)

| Content | | | Connector No. | Terminal No. | Signal (V) | | | Note |
|---|---|---|---|---|---|---|---|---|
| | | | | | Ig SW | | Engine ON (Idling) | |
| | | | | | OFF | ON (Engine OFF) | | |
| Crank angle sensor | Non-TURBO | Signal (+) | B56 | 1 | — | 0 | * | *Sensor output waveform |
| | | Signal (−) | B56 | 2 | — | 0 | 0 | |
| | | Shield | B56 | 3 | — | 0 | 0 | |
| | TURBO | Signal (+) | B58 | 4 | — | 0 | * | *Sensor output waveform |
| | | Signal (−) | B58 | 5 | — | 0 | 0 | |
| | | Shield | B58 | 6 | — | 0 | 0 | |
| Cam angle sensor | Non-TURBO | Signal (+) | B58 | 4 | — | 0 | * | *Sensor output waveform |
| | | Signal (−) | B58 | 5 | — | 0 | 0 | |
| | | Shield | B58 | 6 | — | 0 | 0 | |
| | TURBO | Signal (+) | B56 | 1 | — | 0 | * | *Sensor output waveform |
| | | Signal (−) | B56 | 2 | — | 0 | 0 | |
| | | Shield | B56 | 3 | — | 0 | 0 | |
| Air flow sensor | | Power supply | B48 | 8 | — | 10 - 13 | 13 - 14 | — |
| | | Signal | B48 | 9 | — | 0 - 0.3 | 0.8 - 1.2 | — |
| | | GND | B48 | 10 | — | 0 | 0 | — |
| Throttle sensor | | Signal | B58 | 2 | — | Fully closed: 4.7<br>Fully opened: 1.6 | Fully closed: 4.7<br>Fully opened: 1.6 | — |
| | | Power supply | B58 | 3 | — | 5 | 5 | — |
| | | GND | B58 | 1 | — | 0 | 0 | — |
| $O_2$ sensor | Non-TURBO | Signal | B48 | 6 | — | (AT) 0.6<br>(MT) 0 | Rich mixture: 0.7 (AT), 1.0 (MT)<br>Lean mixture: 0 (AT), 0.2 (MT) | |
| | | Shield | B48 | 17 | — | 0 | 0 | — |
| | TURBO | Signal | B48 | 6 | — | 0 | Rich mixture: 1.0<br>Lean mixture: 0.2 | |
| | | Shield | B48 | 17 | — | 0 | 0 | — |
| Knock sensor | | Signal | B56 | 5 | — | 3 - 4 | 3 - 4 | — |
| | | Shield | B56 | 4 | — | 0 | 0 | — |
| Water temperature sensor | | | B48 | 7 | 0 | 0.7 - 1.0 | 0.7 - 1.0 | After warm-up |
| Vehicle speed sensor | | | B58 | 11 | — | 0 or 5 | 0 or 5 | "5" and "0" are repeatedly displayed when vehicle is driven. |

91E17594

Courtesy of Subaru of America, Inc.

***Fig. 4: Identifying ECU Circuits (Legacy – 1 of 2)***

# 1991 ENGINE PERFORMANCE
# Pin Voltage Charts (Cont.)

| Content | | | Connector No. | Terminal No. | Signal (V) | | | Note |
|---|---|---|---|---|---|---|---|---|
| | | | | | Ig SW | | Engine ON (Idling) | |
| | | | | | OFF | ON (Engine OFF) | | |
| Pressure sensor (TURBO only) | Signal | | B48 | 4 | — | 10 - 13 | 2.4 ↔ 2.7 | — |
| | Power supply | | B48 | 3 | — | 5 | 5 | — |
| | GND | | B48 | 5 | — | 0 | 0 | — |
| Idle switch | | | B56 | 6 | — | ON:0, OFF:4.6 | ON:0, OFF:4.6 | — |
| 49-state and Canada/ California identification | | | B56 | 11 | — | — | — | 49-state and Canada:12 California:0 |
| Starter switch | | | B56 | 10 | — | 0 | 0 | Cranking: 10 to 14 |
| Air conditioner switch | | | B56 | 9 | — | ON:10 - 13, OFF:0 | ON:13 - 14, OFF:0 | — |
| Ignition switch | | | B58 | 12 | 0 | 10 - 13 | 13 - 14 | — |
| Neutral switch | | | B58 | 10 | — | [AT] N Range: 0 Other: 8, min. [MT] N Position: 8, min. Other: 0 | [AT] N Range: 0 Other: 8, min. [MT] N Position: 8, min. Other: 0 | |
| Parking switch [AT] | | | B58 | 9 | — | P Range: 0 Other: 8, min. | P Range: 0 Other: 8, min. | — |
| Test mode connector | Non-TURBO | | B56 | 13 | — | [AT] 10 - 13 [MT] 5 | [AT] 13 - 14 [MT] 5 | [AT] When connected: 0 |
| | TURBO | | B56 | 13 | — | 5 | 5 | When connected: 0 |
| Read memory connector | Non-TURBO | | B56 | 12 | — | [AT] 10 - 13 [MT] 5 | [AT] 13 - 14 [MT] 5 | [AT] When connected: 0 |
| | TURBO | | B56 | 12 | — | 5 | 5 | When connected: 0 |
| AT/MT identification | Non-TURBO | | B48 | 20 | — | [AT] 0 [MT] 5 | [AT] 0 [MT] 5 | — |
| | TURBO | | B48 | 20 | — | 5 | 5 | — |
| Back-up power supply | | | B48 | 15 | 10 - 13 | 10 - 13 | 13 - 14 | — |
| Control unit power supply | | | B48 | 2 | 0 | 10 - 13 | 13 - 14 | |
| | | | B48 | 13 | 0 | 10 - 13 | 13 - 14 | — |
| Ignition control | Non-TURBO | #1, #2 | F47 | 10 | — | [AT] 0.01 [MT] 0 | — | — |
| | | #3, #4 | F47 | 9 | — | [AT] 0.01 [MT]0 | — | — |
| | TURBO | #1, #2 | F47 | 10 | — | 0 | — | — |
| | | #3, #4 | F47 | 9 | — | 0 | — | — |
| Fuel injector | | #1 | F47 | 13 | 10 - 13 | 10 - 13 | 13 - 14 | — |
| | | #2 | F47 | 12 | 10 - 13 | 10 - 13 | 13 - 14 | — |
| | | #3 | F47 | 11 | 10 - 13 | 10 - 13 | 13 - 14 | — |
| | | #4 | F47 | 26 | 10 - 13 | 10 - 13 | 13 - 14 | — |
| Air control valve | Non-TURBO | OPEN end | F47 | 2 | — | [AT] 7 [MT] 12 → * 0 | — | *1 min. after ignition switch ON. |
| | | CLOSE end | F47 | 1 | — | [AT] 6 [MT] 0 | — | — |
| | TURBO | OPEN end | F47 | 2 | — | 0 → *12 | — | *1 min. after ignition switch ON. |
| | | CLOSE end | F47 | 1 | — | 12 → *0 | — | |
| Fuel pump relay control | | | F47 | 23 | — | ON: 0 OFF: 10 - 13 | 0 | — |
| Air conditioner cut relay control | | | F47 | 22 | — | ON: 0 Off: 10 - 13 | ON: 0 OFF: 13 - 14 | — |
| Radiator fan control | | | F47 | 17 | — | ON: 0 OFF: 10 - 13 | ON: 0 OFF: 13 - 14 | — |
| Self-shutoff control | | | F47 | 5 | — | 10 - 13 | 13 - 14 | — |
| Wastegate control (TURBO only) | | | F47 | 3 | — | 10 - 13 | 13 - 14 | — |
| Trouble code output | | | B56 | 15 | — | — | — | — |
| CHECK ENGINE light | | | F47 | 19 | — | — | — | Light "ON": 1, max. Light "OFF": 10 - 14 |
| Pressure exchange solenoid valve (TURBO only) | | | F47 | 20 | — | ON: 0 OFF: 10 - 13 | ON: 0 OFF: 13 - 14 | — |
| Engine tachometer output | | | B56 | 16 | — | — | — | — |
| TI monitor * | | | F47 | 18 | — | — | — | — |
| Canister purge control | | | F47 | 6 | — | ON: 0 OFF: 10 - 13 | ON: 0 OF: 13 - 14 | — |
| Atmospheric pressure sensor (Non-TURBO only) | | | B48 | 16 | — | — | — | — |
| GND (sensors) | | | B48 | 21 | — | 0 | 0 | — |
| GND (injectors) | | | F47 | 24 | — | 0 | 0 | — |
| | | | F47 | 25 | — | 0 | 0 | — |
| GND (ignition system) | | | F47 | 15 | — | 0 | 0 | — |
| GND (power supply) | | | F47 | 14 | — | 0 | 0 | — |
| GND (control systems) | | | B48 | 11 | — | 0 | 0 | — |
| | | | B48 | 22 | — | 0 | 0 | — |
| Select Monitor Signal | | | B56 | 8 | — | — | — | — |
| | | | B56 | 7 | — | — | — | — |

91F17595

Courtesy of Subaru of America, Inc.

***Fig. 5: Identifying ECU Circuits (Legacy – 2 of 2)***

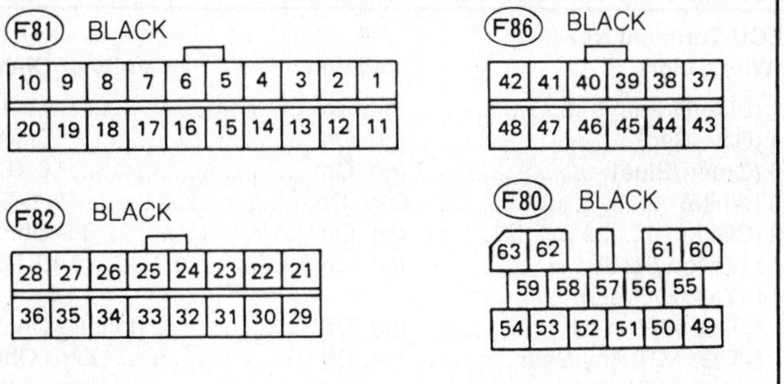

# 1991 ENGINE PERFORMANCE
# Pin Voltage Charts (Cont.)

(F81) BLACK

10 9 8 7 6 5 4 3 2 1
20 19 18 17 16 15 14 13 12 11

(F86) BLACK

42 41 40 39 38 37
48 47 46 45 44 43

(F82) BLACK

28 27 26 25 24 23 22 21
36 35 34 33 32 31 30 29

(F80) BLACK

63 62 61 60
59 58 57 56 55
54 53 52 51 50 49

118419 Courtesy of Subaru of America, Inc.

*Fig. 6: Identifying ECU Connector Terminals (Loyale PFI)*

## LOYALE

**1)** ECU circuits are checked at the ECU connector under one or more of the following conditions: ignition off, ignition on and engine off, or ignition on and engine running. Test between indicated terminal No. and body ground. Use wire color to help identify terminal. See ECU PIN SPECIFICATIONS (LOYALE PFI) table. To test pin voltage, carefully backprobe terminal at harness side of ECU connector. *See Figs. 6-9.*

**2)** If resistance or voltage is not as specified, test and repair, or replace, circuit or affected component. Retest circuit to verify repair has been made. Unless stated otherwise, perform all tests with ECU harness connected.

***WIRING COLOR CODE***

| Color Code | Wire Color |
|---|---|
| B | Black |
| Br | Brown |
| G | Green |
| Gr | Gray |
| L | Blue |
| Lg | Light Green |
| R | Red |
| W | White |
| Y | Yellow |

| | | | | | |
|---|---|---|---|---|---|
| 1 | YR | Check connector (used at line end only) | 33 | LgW | Read-memory connector |
| 2 | SA | Air flow meter (signal) | 34 | – | ——— |
| 3 | GL | Purge control solenoid | 35 | WR | Control unit power (input) |
| 4 | YL | Neutral switch (MT) | 36 | SA | Knock sensor |
| 5 | B | Air flow meter (ground) | 37 | WY | Ignition output (power transistor) |
| 6 | LB | Fuel pump relay | 38 | LgR | Air flow meter (burn-off output) |
| 7 | R | Crank angle sensor (power) | 39 | GW | Self-shutoff output |
| 8 | W | Crank angle sensor (reference) | 40 | RY | ECS lamp output |
| 9 | WB | Water temperature sensor | | | |
| 10 | BR | Ground | 42 | BrB | Kick down relay (3AT) |
| 11 | – | ——— | 43 | WY | Ignition output (power transistor) |
| 12 | SA | Air flow meter (power) | 44 | RL | Check connector |
| 13 | RB | Duty solenoid (waste gate control) | 45 | GB | Check connector |
| 14 | YW | Inhibitor switch | 46 | L | Check connector |
| 15 | GY | Inhibitor switch | 47 | R | Check connector (used at line end only) |
| 16 | BR | Throttle sensor (ground) | 48 | SA | $O_2$ sensor |
| 17 | W | Crank angle sensor (position) | 49 | W | Fuel injector #1 |
| 18 | – | ——— | 50 | W | Fuel injector #2 |
| 19 | BW | Ignition switch signal | 51 | WR | Fuel injector #3 |
| 20 | BR | Ground | 52 | WR | Fuel injector #4 |
| 21 | W | Throttle sensor (power supply) | 53 | – | ——— |
| 22 | B | Throttle sensor (signal) | 54 | – | ——— |
| 23 | LY | Air conditioner signal | 55 | SA | Fuel pump control |
| 24 | BW | Starter signal | 56 | B | Ground |
| 25 | LW | Idle switch signal | 57 | B | Ground |
| 26 | – | ——— | 58 | – | ——— |
| 27 | WR | Control unit power (input) | 59 | L | A/C cut relay (3AT) |
| 28 | BY | Identification of specifications | 60 | BR | Ground |
| 29 | YG | Car-speed sensor | 61 | BR | Ground |
| 30 | BR | Identification of AT | 62 | R | Power (input) |
| 31 | – | ——— | 63 | – | ——— |
| 32 | Br | Test mode connector | | | |

118418 Courtesy of Subaru of America, Inc.

*Fig. 7: Identifying ECU Circuits (Loyale PFI)*

# 1991 ENGINE PERFORMANCE
# Pin Voltage Charts (Cont.)

*NOTE: NCA stands for No Color Available.*

## *ECU PIN SPECIFICATIONS (LOYALE PFI)*

| ECU Terminal No. (Wire Color) | Condition | Volts or Ohms |
|---|---|---|
| 2 (NCA) | Ign. On | 1-2V |
| 3 (Green/Blue) | Ign. On | [2] 0-10V |
| 4 (Yellow/Blue) [1] | Ign. Off | Zero Ohm in "N" |
| 6 (Blue/Black) | Ign. On | [2] 0-10V |
| 7 (Red) | Ign. On | 10-12V |
| 8 (Black) | Ign. On | [3] .1 or 4-5V |
| 9 (White/Black) [1] | Ign. Off | 100-20,000 Ohms |
| 10 (Brown/Red) [1] | Ign. Off | Zero Ohm |
| 12 (NCA) | Ign. On | 10-12V |
| 13 (Red/Black) | Ign. On | [2] 0-10V |
| 17 (White) | Ign. On | [4] .1 or 4-5V |
| 19 (Black/White) [1] | Ign. On | 10-12V |
| 20 (Brown/Red) [1] | Ign. Off | Zero Ohm |
| 24 (Black/White) | Ign. On | [5] 10-12V |
| 25 (Blue/White) [1] | | |
| Closed Throttle | Ign. Off | Zero Ohm |
| Open Throttle | Ign. Off | Infinity |
| 27 (White/Red) [1] | Ign. On | 10-12V |
| 29 (Yellow/Green) | Eng. On | [6] 1-3V |
| 35 (White/Red) [1] | Ign. On | 10-12V |
| 36 (NCA) [1] | Ign. Off | 532-588 K/Ohms |
| 48 (NCA) | Eng. On | .1-1.0V |
| 49 (White) [1] | Ign. On | 10-12V |
| 50 (White) [1] | Ign. On | 10-12V |
| 51 (White/Red) [1] | Ign. On | 10-12V |
| 52 (White/Red) [1] | Ign. On | 10-12V |
| 55 (NCA) | Ign. On | [2] 0-10V |
| 56 (Black) [1] | Ign. Off | Zero Ohm |
| 57 (Black) [1] | Ign. Off | Zero Ohm |
| 60 (Brown/Red) [1] | Ign. Off | Zero Ohm |
| 61 (Brown/Red) [1] | Ign. Off | Zero Ohm |
| 62 (Red) [1] | Ign. On | 10-12V |

[1] – ECU harness disconnected.
[2] – Fluctuates every 1.5 seconds with test connectors attached.
[3] – Fluctuates 0-5 volts while cranking with starter.
[4] – Fluctuates 0-5 volts while slowly turning crankshaft hub nut with wrench.
[5] – 10-12 volts with ignition in START position.
[6] – Fluctuates around 2 volts while driving vehicle.

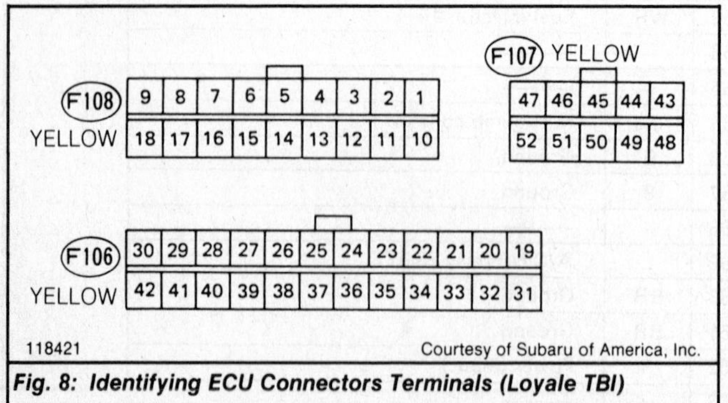


*Fig. 8: Identifying ECU Connectors Terminals (Loyale TBI)*

## *ECU PIN SPECIFICATIONS (LOYALE TBI)*

| ECU Terminal No. (Wire Color) | Condition | Volts or Ohms |
|---|---|---|
| 1 (Blue/Green) [1] | Ign. On | 0-1V |
| 4 (Blue/Red) | Ign. On | [2] 0-10V |
| 5 (Green/Blue) | Ign. On | [2] 0-10V |
| 8 (White) | Eng. On | .1-.5V |
| 9 (Black) [1] | Ign. Off | 0-9 Ohms |
| 13 (Yellow/Red) | Ign. On | [3] 10-12V |
| 14 (Yellow/Green) [1] | | |
| A/T Or M/T in "N" | Ign. Off | Infinite Ohms |
| A/T Or M/T Any Gear | Ign. Off | Zero Ohm |
| 15 (Yellow/Blue) [1] | Ign. Off | Infinity in "N" |
| 15 (Yellow/Blue) [1] | Ign. Off | Zero Ohm in Any Gear |
| 17 (Red) | Ign. On | 10-12V |
| 19 (Green/Black) [1] | Ign. On | 10-12V |
| 20 (Green/Yellow) | Ign. On | [4] .1 or 4-5V |
| 21 (Black/White) | Ign. On | [5] .1 or 4-5V |
| 22 (Yellow/Green) | Eng. On | [6] 1-3V |
| 23 (White/Black) [1] | Ign. Off | 100-20,000 Ohms |
| 24 (Blue/Green) [1] | | |
| Closed Throttle | Ign. Off | Zero Ohm |
| Open Throttle | Ign. Off | Infinity |
| 27 (Black/White) [1] | Ign. On | 10-12V |
| 29 (White) [1] | Ign. On | 10-12V |
| 30 (Brown/Red) [1] | Ign. Off | Zero Ohm |
| 33 (Lt. Green) [1] | Ign. Off | Zero Ohm |
| 36 (White/Red) [1] | Ign. Off | Over 250 Ohms |
| 41 (White) [1] | Ign. On | 10-12V |
| 42 (Brown/Red) [1] | Ign. Off | Zero Ohm |
| 44 (Brown/Red) [1] | Ign. Off | Zero Ohm |
| 45 (Green/Red) | Ign. On | [7] 0-1V |
| 48 (NCA) | Eng. On | .1-1.0V |
| 49 (Red/Blue) [1] | Ign. On | 10-12V |
| 51 (Black) [1] | Ign. Off | Zero Ohm |

[1] – ECU harness disconnected.
[2] – Fluctuates every 1.5 seconds with test connectors attached.
[3] – 10-12 volts with ignition in START position.
[4] – Fluctuates 0-5 volts while slowly turning crankshaft hub nut with wrench.
[5] – Fluctuates 0-5 volts while cranking with starter.
[6] – Fluctuates around 2 volts while driving vehicle.
[7] – After ignition is turned on, 0-1 volt for one minute and over 10 volts after one minute.

# 1991 ENGINE PERFORMANCE
# Pin Voltage Charts (Cont.)

| 1 | LG | Kick-down control | 27 | BW | Power (input) |
|---|---|---|---|---|---|
| 2 | RL | CHECK ENGINE light | 28 | GW | Self-shutoff signal |
| 3 | R | Test 4 | 29 | W | Power (input) |
| 4 | LR | EGR solenoid (control) | 30 | BR | GND |
| 5 | GL | Purge control solenoid | 31 | Br | Test mode connector (used at line end only) |
| 6 | LY | Air conditioner signal | 32 | BR | Test mode connector (used at line end only) |
| 7 | – | ——— | 33 | Lg | 49-state/Cal identification |
| 8 | W | Air flow meter (signal) | 34 | SA | $O_2$ sensor |
| 9 | B | Air flow meter (GND) | 35 | B | GND |
| 10 | Y | Line end cord output | 36 | WR | EGR monitor |
| 11 | L | Line end cord output | 37 | LgR | Test mode connector (used at line end only) |
| 12 | RL | Line end cord output | 38 | RL | Ignition switch |
| 13 | YR | Inhibitor switch (AT models only) | 39 | LgW | Clear memory |
| 14 | YG | Neutral switch | 40 | – | ——— |
| 15 | YL | Parking switch (AT models only) | 41 | W | Power (input) |
| 16 | LgR | Kick-down monitor | 42 | BR | GND |
| 17 | R | Air flow meter power (output) | 43 | RW | Injector ⊕ |
| 18 | LgY | Starter switch | 44 | BR | GND |
| 19 | GB | Crank angle sensor power (output) | 45 | GR | Air control valve |
| 20 | GY | Crank angle sensor signal (reference) | 46 | GY | A/C control |
| 21 | BW | Crank angle sensor signal (position) | 47 | LB | Fuel pump |
| 22 | YG | Car-speed sensor | 48 | RB | Injector ⊖ |
| 23 | WB | Water temperature sensor | 49 | RL | Power (input) |
| 24 | LG | Idle switch | 50 | BY | GND |
| 25 | W | Throttle sensor (signal) | 51 | B | GND |
| 26 | R | Throttle sensor power (output) | 52 | WY | Ignition control |

118420

Courtesy of Subaru of America, Inc.

*Fig. 9: Identifying ECU Circuits (Loyale TBI)*

## XT & XT6

**1)** ECU circuits are checked at the ECU connector under one or more of the following conditions: ignition switch off, ignition on and engine off, or ignition on and engine running.

**2)** To test pin voltage, carefully backprobe terminal at harness side of ECU connector. Test between indicated terminal No. and body ground. *See Figs. 10-12*. Use wire color to help identify terminal. See WIRING COLOR CODE table.

**3)** If resistance or voltage is not as specified, test and repair, or replace, circuit or affected component. See ECU PIN SPECIFICATIONS (XT & XT6) table. Retest circuit to verify repair has been made. Unless stated otherwise, perform all tests with ECU harness connected.

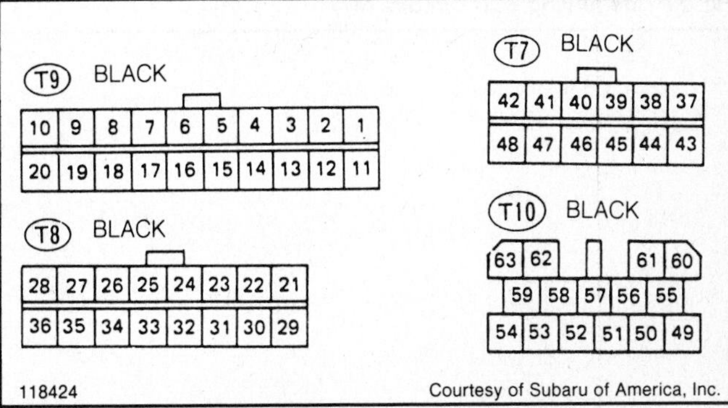


*Fig. 10: Identifying ECU Connectors Terminals (XT & XT6)*

# 1991 ENGINE PERFORMANCE
# Pin Voltage Charts (Cont.)

| | | | | | |
|---|---|---|---|---|---|
| 1 | YR | Check connector | 32 | Br | Test mode connector |
| 2 | W | Air flow meter (signal) | 33 | LgW | Read-memory connector |
| 3 | GL | Purge control solenoid | 34 | – | – |
| 4 | GY | Neutral switch (MT) | 35 | WR | Control unit power (input) |
| | YL | Inhibitor switch (AT) | 36 | – | – |
| 5 | B | Air flow meter (ground) | 37 | WY | Ignition output (power transistor) |
| 6 | LB | Fuel pump relay | 38 | LgR | Air flow meter (burn-off output) |
| 7 | R | Crank angle sensor (power) | 39 | GW | Self-shutoff output |
| 8 | B | Crank angle sensor (reference) | 40 | RY | CHECK ENGINE light |
| 9 | WB | Water temperature sensor | 41 | – | – |
| 10 | BR | Ground | 42 | RB | A/C cut control |
| 11 | – | – | 43 | WY | Ignition output (power transistor) |
| 12 | W | Air flow meter (power) | 44 | RL | Check connector |
| 13 | – | – | 45 | GB | Check connector |
| 14 | | | 46 | L | Check connector |
| 15 | Lg | Inhibitor switch (AT) | 47 | R | Trouble code output |
| 16 | BR | Throttle sensor (ground) | 48 | W | $O_2$ sensor |
| 17 | W | Crank angle sensor (position signal) | 49 | W | Fuel injector #1, #2 |
| 18 | – | – | 50 | W | Fuel injector #1, #2 |
| 19 | BW | Ignition switch signal | 51 | WL | Fuel injector #3, #4 |
| 20 | BR | Ground | 52 | WL | Fuel injector #3, #4 |
| 21 | W | Throttle sensor (power supply) | 53 | – | – |
| 22 | B | Throttle sensor (signal) | 54 | – | – |
| 23 | L | Air conditioner signal | 55 | W | Fuel pump control |
| 24 | BW (MT)<br>BY (AT) | Starter signal | 56 | B | Ground (ignition) |
| 25 | LW | Idle switch signal | 57 | B | Ground (ignition) |
| 26 | – | – | 58 | – | – |
| 27 | WR | Control unit power (input) | 59 | G | Auxiliary air valve control |
| 28 | BY | Specification code | 60 | BR | Ground (fuel injector) |
| 29 | YR | Car-speed sensor | 61 | BR | Ground (fuel injector) |
| 30 | BR | Identification of AT and MT | 62 | R | Power (fuel injector) |
| 31 | – | – | 63 | – | – |

118422

Courtesy of Subaru of America, Inc.

*Fig. 11: Identifying ECU Circuits (XT)*

# 1991 ENGINE PERFORMANCE
# Pin Voltage Charts (Cont.)

| | | | | | |
|---|---|---|---|---|---|
| 1 | YR | Check connector | 32 | Br | Test mode connector |
| 2 | W | Air flow meter (signal) | 33 | LgW | Read-memory connector |
| 3 | GL | Purge control solenoid | 34 | – | – |
| 4 | GY | Neutral switch (MT) | 35 | WR | Control unit power (input) |
| | YL | Inhibitor switch (AT) | 36 | R | Knock sensor |
| 5 | B | Air flow meter (ground) | 37 | WY | Ignition output (power transistor) |
| 6 | LB | Fuel pump relay | 38 | LgR | Air flow meter (burn-off output) |
| 7 | R | Crank angle sensor (power) | 39 | GW | Self-shutoff output |
| 8 | G | Crank angle sensor (position signal) | 40 | RY | CHECK ENGINE light |
| 9 | WB | Water temperature sensor | 41 | – | – |
| 10 | BR | Ground | 42 | RB | A/C cut control |
| 11 | – | – | 43 | WY | Ignition output (power transistor) |
| 12 | R | Air flow meter (power) | 44 | RL | Check connector |
| 13 | – | – | 45 | GB | Check connector |
| 14 | YW | Inhibitor switch (AT) | 46 | L | Check connector |
| 15 | Lg | Inhibitor switch (AT) | 47 | R | Trouble code output |
| 16 | BR | Throttle sensor (ground) | 48 | W | $O_2$ sensor |
| 17 | W | Crank angle sensor (reference) | 49 | W | Fuel injector #5, #6 |
| 18 | – | – | 50 | W | Fuel injector #5, #6 |
| 19 | BW | Ignition switch signal | 51 | WR | Fuel injector #1, #2 |
| 20 | BR | Ground | 52 | WR | Fuel injector #1, #2 |
| 21 | W | Throttle sensor (power supply) | 53 | WY | Fuel injector #3, #4 |
| 22 | B | Throttle sensor (signal) | 54 | WY | Fuel injector #3, #4 |
| 23 | L | Air conditioner signal | 55 | B | Fuel pump control |
| 24 | BW (MT)<br>BY (AT) | Starter signal | 56 | B | Ground (ignition) |
| 25 | LW | Idle switch signal | 57 | B | Ground (ignition) |
| 26 | – | – | 58 | YR | By-pass air control |
| 27 | WR | Control unit power (input) | 59 | YL | By-pass air control |
| 28 | – | – | 60 | BR | Ground (fuel injector) |
| 29 | YR | Car-speed sensor | 61 | BR | Ground (fuel injector) |
| 30 | BR | Identification of AT and MT | 62 | R | Power (fuel injector) |
| 31 | LB | Specification code | 63 | Br | Power steering control |

118423

Courtesy of Subaru of America, Inc.

*Fig. 12: Identifying ECU Circuits (XT6)*

# 1991 ENGINE PERFORMANCE
# Pin Voltage Charts (Cont.)

***ECU PIN SPECIFICATIONS (XT & XT6)***

| ECU Terminal No. (Wire Color) | Condition | Volts or Ohms |
|---|---|---|
| 2 (White) | Ign. On | 1-2V |
| 3 (Green/Blue) | Ign. On | [1] 0-10V |
| 4 (Yellow/Blue Or Green/Yellow) [2] | Ign. Off | Zero Ohm in "N" |
| 6 (Blue/Black) | Ign. On | [1] 0-10V |
| 7 (Red) | Ign. On | 10-12V |
| 8 | | |
| XT (Black) | Ign. On | [3] .1 or 4-5V |
| XT6 (Green) | Ign. On | [3] .1 or 4-5V |
| 9 (White/Black) [2] | Ign. Off | 100-20,000 Ohms |
| 10 (Brown/Red) [2] | Ign. Off | Zero Ohm |
| 12 | | |
| XT (White) | Ign. On | 10-12V |
| XT6 (Red) | Ign. On | 10-12V |
| 17 (White) | Ign. On | [4] .1 or 4-5V |
| 19 (Black/White) | Ign. On | [5] 10-12V |
| 20 (Brown/Red) [2] | Ign. Off | Zero Ohm |
| 24 | | |
| A/T (Black/White) | Ign. On | [6] 10-12V |
| M/T (Black/Yellow) | Ign. On | [6] 10-12V |
| 25 (Blue/White) [2] | | |
| Closed Throttle | Ign. Off | Zero Ohm |
| Open Throttle | Ign. Off | Infinity |
| 27 (White/Red) | Ign. On | 10-12V |
| 29 (Yellow/Red) | Eng. On | [7] 1-3V |
| 35 (White/Red) | Ign. On | 10-12V |
| 36 (Red - XT6) [2] | Ign. Off | 532-588 K/Ohms |
| 48 (White) | Eng. On | .1-1.0V |
| 49 (White) [2] | Ign. On | 10-12V |
| 50 (White) [2] | Ign. On | 10-12V |
| 51 [2] | | |
| XT (White/Blue) | Ign. On | 10-12V |
| XT6 (White/Red) | Ign. On | 10-12V |
| 52 [2] | | |
| XT (White/Blue) | Ign. On | 10-12V |
| XT6 (White/Red) | Ign. On | 10-12V |
| 53 (White/Yellow - XT6) [2] | Ign. On | 10-12V |
| 54 (White/Yellow - XT6) [2] | Ign. On | 10-12V |
| 55 | | |
| XT (White) | Ign. On | [1] 0-10V |
| XT6 (Black) | Ign. On | [1] 0-10V |
| 56 (Black) [2] | Ign. Off | Zero Ohm |
| 57 (Black) [2] | Ign. Off | Zero Ohm |
| 58 (Yellow/Red - XT6) [2] | Ign. On | 10-12V |
| 59 [2] | | |
| XT (Green) | Ign. On | 10-12V |
| XT6 (Yellow/Blue) | Ign. On | 10-12V |
| 60 (Brown/Red) [2] | Ign. Off | Zero Ohm |
| 61 (Brown/Red) [2] | Ign. Off | Zero Ohm |
| 62 (Red) | Ign. On | 10-12V |

[1] - Fluctuates every 1.5 seconds while Green test connectors (in trunk) are joined together.
[2] - ECU harness disconnected.
[3] - Fluctuates 0-5 volts while cranking with starter.
[4] - Fluctuates 0-5 volts while slowly turning crankshaft hub nut with wrench.
[5] - With airflow meter disconnected.
[6] - 10-12 volts with ignition in START position.
[7] - Fluctuates around 2 volts while driving vehicle.

# 1991 ENGINE PERFORMANCE
# Sensor Operating Range Charts

## Justy, Legacy, Loyale, XT, XT6

## INTRODUCTION

Sensor operating range information can help determine if a sensor is out of calibration. An out-of-calibration sensor may not set a trouble code, but it may cause driveability problems.

***NOTE: Unless stated otherwise in test procedure, perform all voltage tests using a Digital Volt-Ohmmeter (DVOM) with a minimum 10-megohm input impedance.***

### *AIRFLOW METER VOLTAGE*

| Application | [1] Volts |
|---|---|
| Justy | [2] |
| Legacy | |
| ECU Pin No. 8 & Ground [3] | |
| Engine Off | 0-13 |
| At Idle | 13-14 |
| ECU Pin No. 9 & Ground [3] | |
| Engine Off | 0-.3 |
| At Idle | .8-1.2 |
| ECU Pin No. 10 & Ground [3] | |
| Engine Off | Zero |
| At Idle | Zero |
| Loyale PFI [4] | 1.0-2.0 |
| Loyale TBI | |
| White Wire & Black Wire Terminals [3] | 0.1-0.5 |
| XT & XT6 | |
| White Wire & Black/Red Wire Terminals [3] | 1.0-2.0 |

[1] – Voltage should be higher when blowing air through inlet side of airflow meter.
[2] – Justy does not have airflow meter.
[3] – Connect voltmeter between these 2 terminals of airflow meter connector.
[4] – Connect voltmeter between Black/Red wire terminal and sealed wire terminal next to unused terminal.

### *AIRFLOW SENSOR RESISTANCE (LEGACY)* [1]

| Terminal | Specification |
|---|---|
| Red Wire & Ground | One Megohm (Min.) |
| White Wire & Ground | One Megohm (Min.) |
| Black Wire & Ground | One Megohm (Min.) |
| Black/Red Wire & Ground | Zero Ohm |

[1] – Measure resistance between indicated terminal of airflow sensor connector and ground.

### *AIR TEMPERATURE SENSOR RESISTANCE (JUSTY CARB.)* [1]

| Temperature | Ohms |
|---|---|
| 68°F (20°C) | 2000-3000 |
| 176°F (80°C) | 270-370 |

[1] – Measure resistance between air temperature sensor connector terminals.

**Atmospheric Pressure Sensor** – See SELF-DIAGNOSTICS article for testing information.

### *CAM ANGLE SENSOR VOLTAGE (LEGACY)*

| Wire Colors | [1] Volts |
|---|---|
| Black & White | .1 (Minimum) |

[1] – Turn ignition on. Voltage will vary with each engine revolution.

### *COOLANT TEMPERATURE SENSOR RESISTANCE*

| Application [1] | Temperature | Ohms |
|---|---|---|
| Justy PFI & Legacy | 68°F (20°C) | 2000-3000 |
| | 176°F (80°C) | 270-330 |
| All Others | 14°F (-10°C) | 7000-11,500 |
| | 68°F (20°C) | 2000-3000 |
| | 122°F (50°C) | 700-1000 |

[1] – Information is not available for Justy carbureted.

### *CRANK ANGLE SENSOR VOLTAGE*

| Application | Wires Colors | [1] Volts |
|---|---|---|
| Legacy | Black & White | .1 (Minimum) |
| Loyale PFI | Black & Ground | 4 (Minimum) |
| | White & Ground | 4 (Minimum) |
| | Red & Ground | 10 (Minimum) |

[1] – Turn ignition on. Voltage will vary with each engine revolution. For testing information on other models, see SELF-DIAGNOSTICS article.

### *CYLINDER DISTINCTION (TDC) SENSOR VOLTAGE (JUSTY PFI)*

| Distributor Terminals | [1] Volts |
|---|---|
| Black Wire & Green Wire | 0-.5 |

[1] – Measure voltage between distributor terminal (sensor side) while cranking engine. Voltage should vary while cranking engine.

### *CYLINDER DISTINCTION (TDC) SENSOR RESISTANCE (JUSTY PFI)*

| ECU/Distributor Terminals | [1] Ohms |
|---|---|
| No. 5 & Black Wire | One Or Less |
| No. 6 & Green Wire | One Or Less |
| No. 5 & Ground | Infinity |
| No. 6 & Ground | Infinity |

[1] – Measure resistance between ECU pin No. and distributor terminal (sensor side).

### *DETONATION (KNOCK) SENSOR RESISTANCE* [1]

| Application | Ohms |
|---|---|
| All Models | 532,000-588,000 |

[1] – Measure resistance between ground and connector terminal.

**EGR Temperature Sensor (Loyale TBI)** – For testing information, see SELF-DIAGNOSTICS article.

### *OXYGEN SENSOR VOLTAGE*

| Application | Volts |
|---|---|
| Loyale (California) | |
| Black/White Wire & Ground | 10 Or Less |
| White Wire & Ground | .05 Or More |
| All Others | [1] 0.1-0.9 |

[1] – Measure voltage between oxygen sensor connector terminal and ground.

### *TURBOCHARGER PRESSURE SENSOR VOLTAGE (LEGACY)* [1]

| Terminals | Voltage |
|---|---|
| Sensor Connector | |
| Red Wire & Black Wire | [2] 3.1 |
| Red Wire & Black Wire | [3] 2.6 |
| Red Wire & Black Wire | [4] 2.1 |

[1] – Apply 5 volts across terminals No. 1 (White wire) and 2 (Red wire), then connect terminal No. 1 to positive voltage and terminal No. 2 to negative voltage. Install vacuum pump to pressure sensor hose fitting. Measure voltage across indicated terminals when pressure is applied to pressure sensor.
[2] – With 7.87 in. Hg applied to pressure sensor.
[3] – With Zero in. Hg applied to pressure sensor.
[4] – With -7.87 in. Hg applied to pressure sensor.

### *TURBOCHARGER PRESSURE SENSOR RESISTANCE (LEGACY)*

| ECU Connector [1] | Sensor Connector | Ohms |
|---|---|---|
| Pin No. 3 | White Wire | 1 |
| Pin No. 4 | Black Wire | 3 |
| Pin No. 5 | Red Wire | 2 |

[1] – Disconnect ECU and pressure sensor connectors. Measure resistance between indicated pins and terminals of connectors.

# 1991 ENGINE PERFORMANCE
# Sensor Operating Range Charts (Cont.)

### *THROTTLE POSITION SENSOR (TPS) RESISTANCE*

| Application [1] | TPS Connector [2] Terminals | Ohms |
|---|---|---|
| **Total Resistance** | | |
| Legacy | Black Wire & Red Wire | 12,000 |
| Loyale PFI | Black Wire & White Wire | 6000-18,000 |
| Loyale TBI | Black Wire & Red Wire | 3500-6500 |
| XT & XT6 | Black Wire & White Wire | 6000-18,000 |
| **Variable Resistance** | | |
| Legacy | | |
| Throttle Closed | Black Wire & White Wire | 1000 |
| Throttle Open | Black Wire & White Wire | 4300 |
| Loyale PFI | | |
| Throttle Closed | Black Wire & Red Wire | 5800-17,800 |
| Throttle Open | Black Wire & Red Wire | 1500-5100 |
| Loyale TBI | | |
| Throttle Closed | Black Wire & Green Wire | 1000 Or Less |
| Throttle Open | Black Wire & Red Wire | 2400 Or More |
| XT | | |
| Throttle Closed | Black Wire & Brown Wire | 5800-17,800 |
| Throttle Open | Black Wire & Brown Wire | 1500-5100 |
| XT6 | | |
| Throttle Closed | Black Wire & Brown Wire | 4200-15,000 |
| Throttle Open | Black Wire & Brown Wire | 100-1100 |

[1] – Justy is not equipped with TPS.

[2] – Disconnect TPS connector. At component side of connector, connect ohmmeter between the indicated terminals.

### *THROTTLE SWITCH (IDLE SWITCH) CONTINUITY*

| Application [1] | [2] Terminals |
|---|---|
| Justy 1.2L PFI | [3] Blue/White Wire & Black/Red Wire |
| Legacy | Brown Wire & Black Wire |
| Loyale PFI | Blue/White Wire & Black/Red Wire |
| Loyale TBI | Light Green Wire & Black Wire |
| XT | Blue/White Wire & Black Wire |
| XT6 | Green/Yellow Wire & Black Wire |

[1] – Justy carbureted models do not have throttle switch.

[2] – On all models except Loyale PFI, disconnect TPS connector. On Loyale PFI, disconnect throttle switch connector. On all models, check continuity between indicated terminals of connector. There should be continuity with throttle closed and no continuity with throttle open.

[3] – In addition to idle switch function, throttle switch also contains wide open throttle switch function. To test wide open throttle switch function, check continuity between Green/Red wire and Black/Red wire terminals of throttle switch connector. There should be continuity with throttle fully open (at least 50 degrees) and no continuity with throttle closed.

**Vacuum/Pressure Sensor (Justy Carbureted)** – See HIGH ALTITUDE COMPENSATOR in SYSTEM & COMPONENT TESTING article. Also, check for possible trouble codes. See SELF-DIAGNOSTICS article.

### *VEHICLE SPEED SENSOR VOLTAGE [1]*

| Application | ECU Connector Pin No. | Wire Color |
|---|---|---|
| Justy Carb. | 6 (22-Pin) | LT GRN/BLK |
| Justy PFI | 4 (22-Pin) | LT GRN/BLK |
| Legacy | 11 (12-Pin) | GRN/BLK |
| Loyale PFI | 29 (16-Pin) | YEL/GRN |
| Loyale TBI | 22 (24-Pin) | YEL/GRN |
| XT & XT6 | 29 (16-Pin) | YEL/RED |

[1] – Turn ignition on. Connect voltmeter between indicated terminal and ground. Slowly rotate drive wheels. Voltage should fluctuate between zero and approximately 5 volts (Legacy) or 2 volts (all others).

# 1991 ENGINE PERFORMANCE
# Wiring Diagrams

## Justy, Legacy, Loyale, XT, XT6

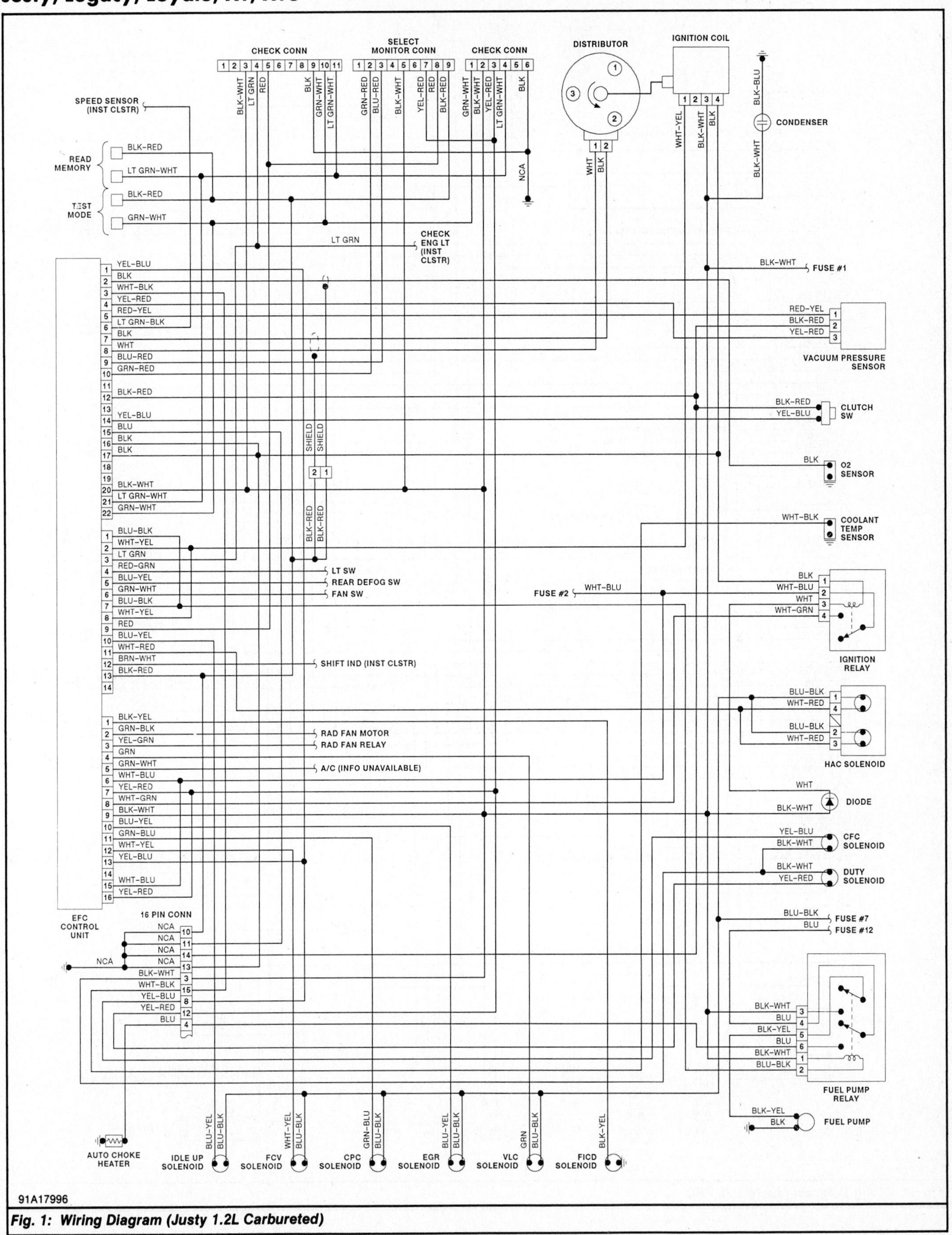


*Fig. 1: Wiring Diagram (Justy 1.2L Carbureted)*

# 1991 ENGINE PERFORMANCE
## Wiring Diagrams (Cont.)

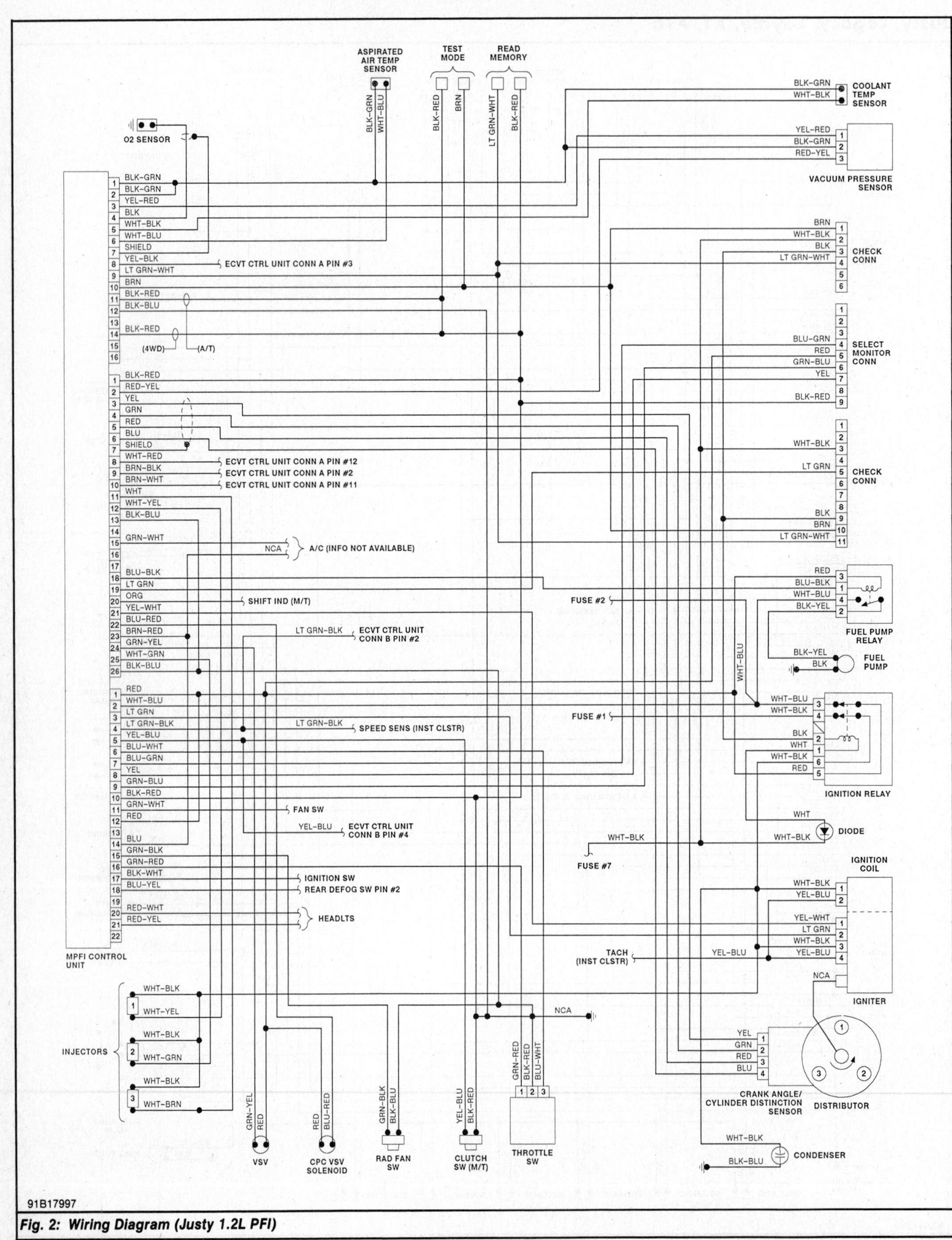


*Fig. 2: Wiring Diagram (Justy 1.2L PFI)*

# 1991 ENGINE PERFORMANCE
## Wiring Diagrams (Cont.)

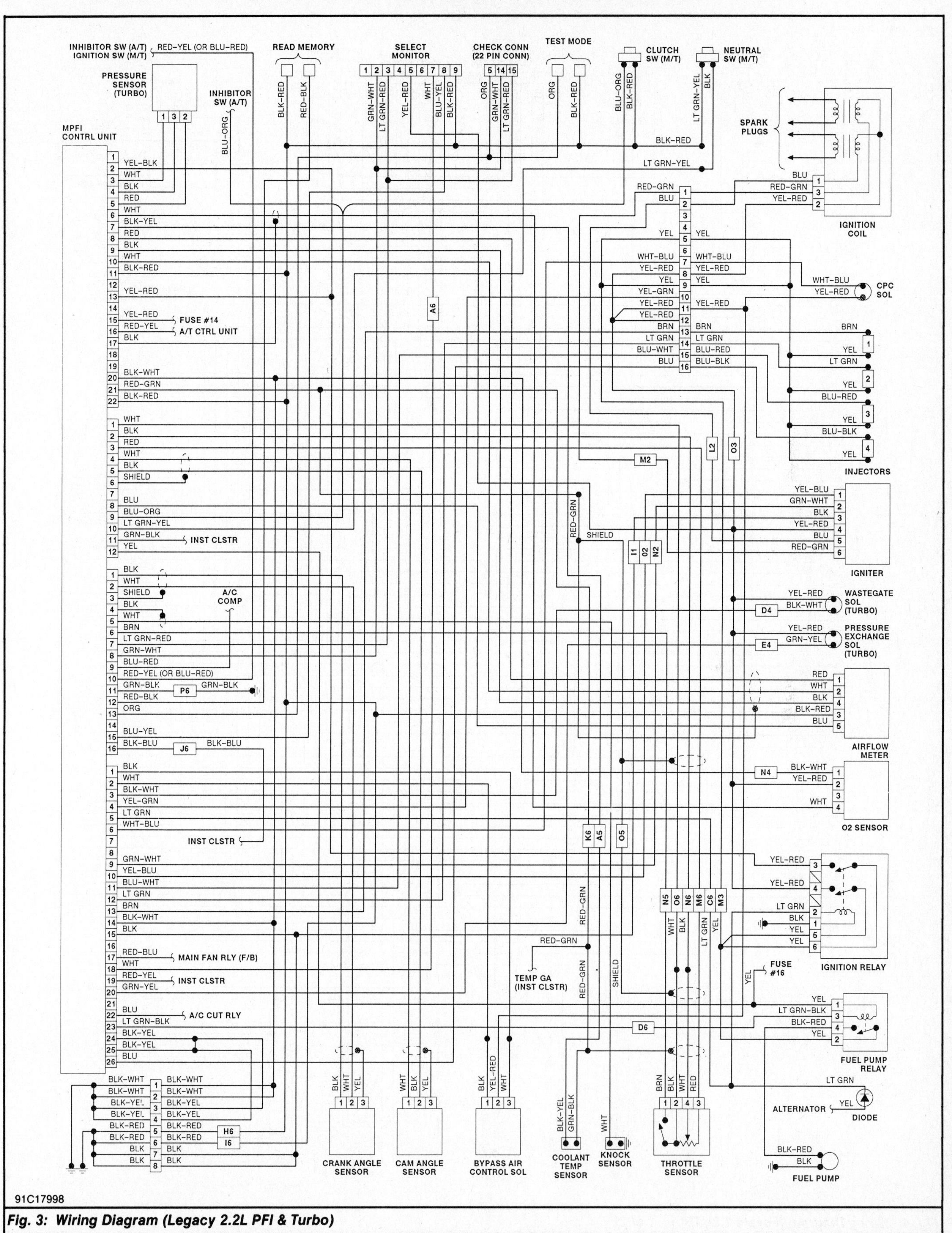


*Fig. 3: Wiring Diagram (Legacy 2.2L PFI & Turbo)*

# 1991 ENGINE PERFORMANCE
## Wiring Diagrams (Cont.)

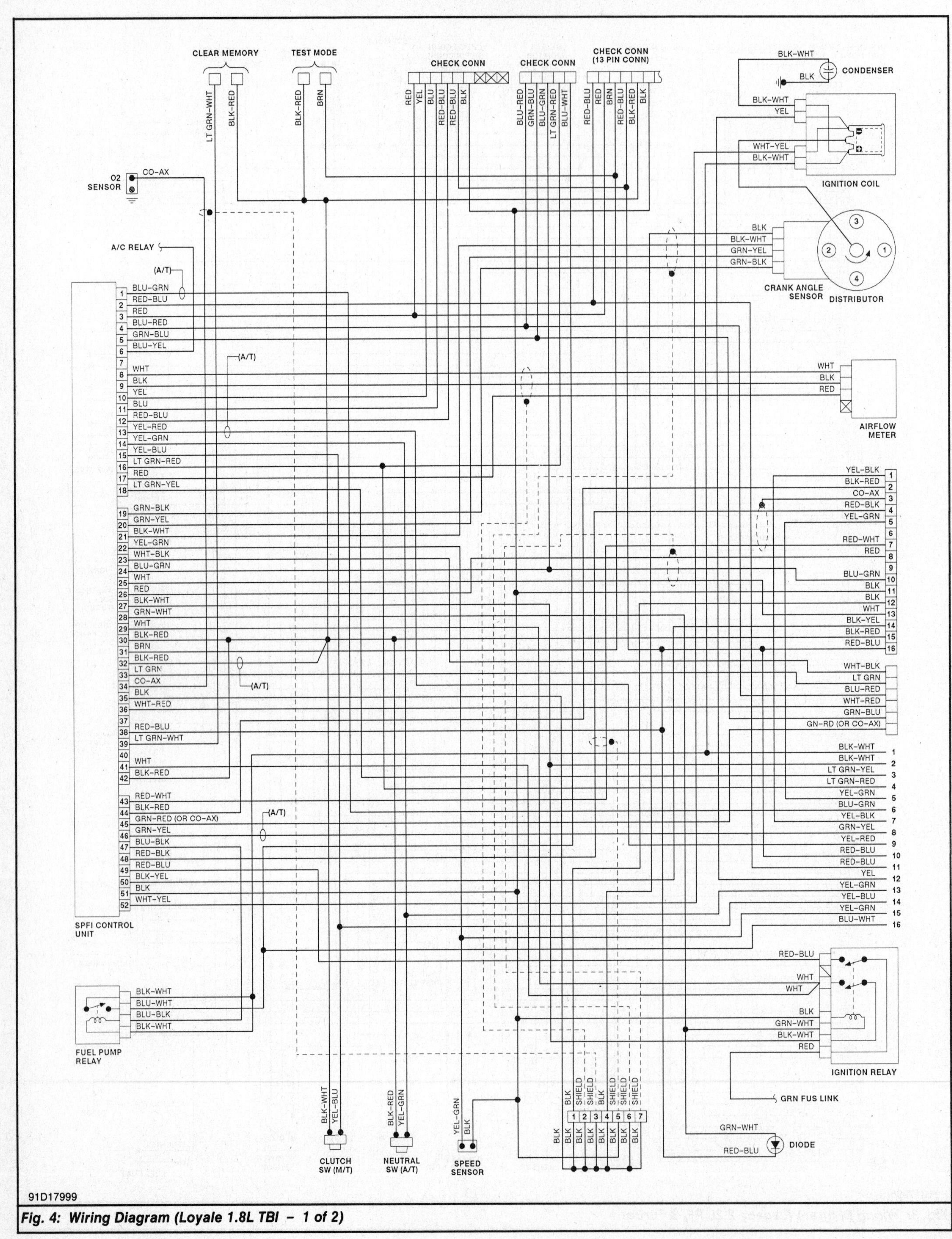

*Fig. 4: Wiring Diagram (Loyale 1.8L TBI – 1 of 2)*

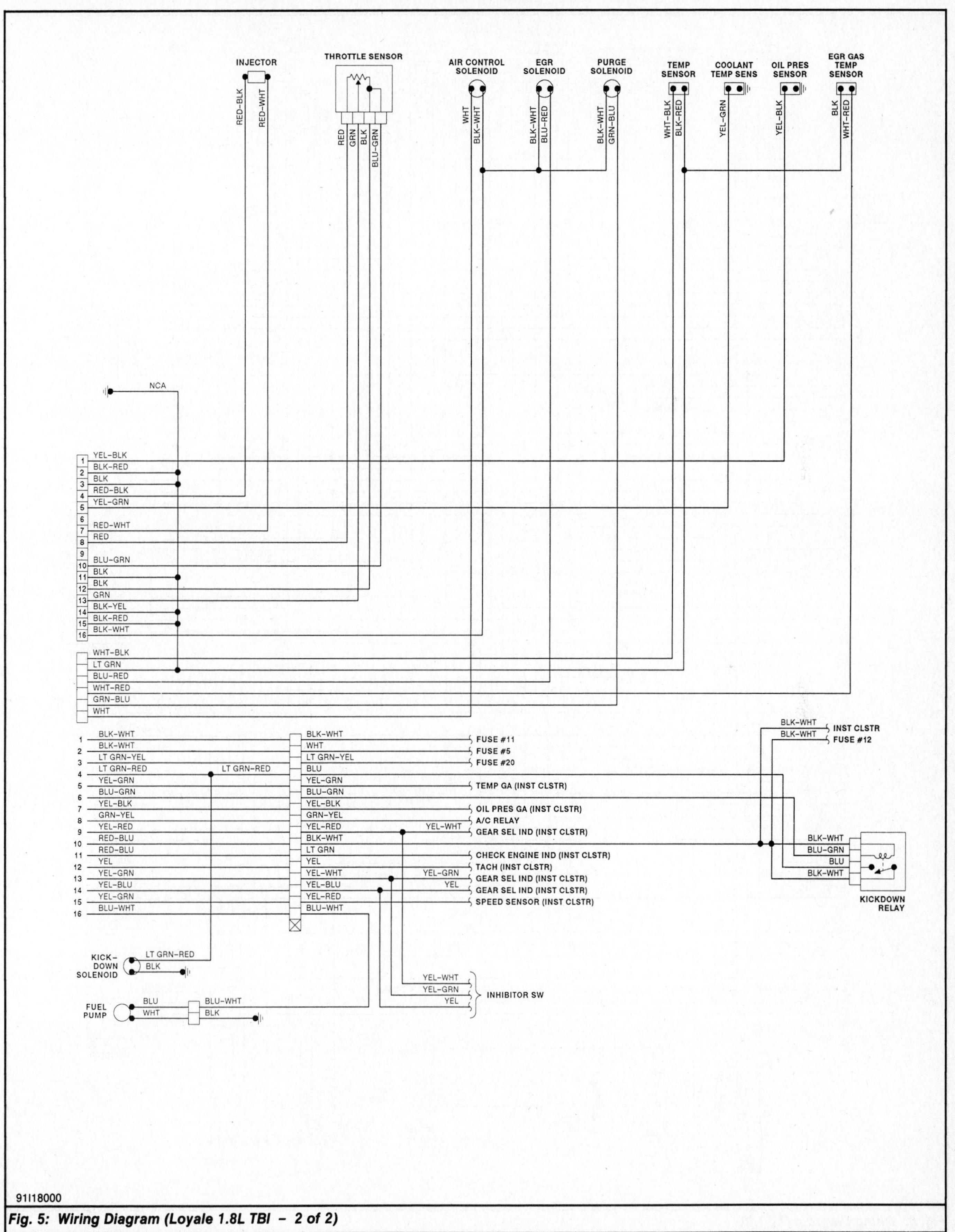


*Fig. 5: Wiring Diagram (Loyale 1.8L TBI – 2 of 2)*

# 1991 ENGINE PERFORMANCE
## Wiring Diagrams (Cont.)

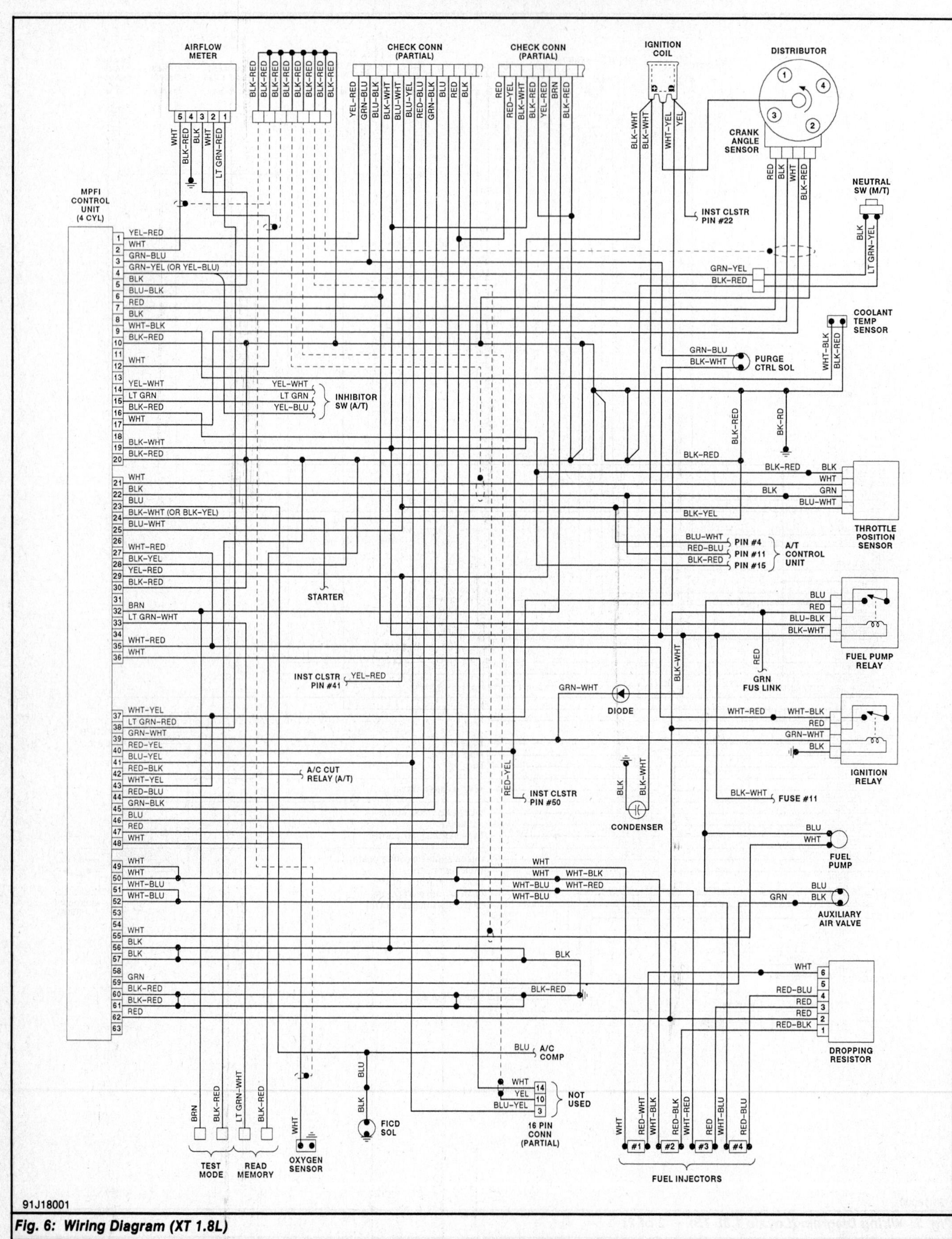


*Fig. 6: Wiring Diagram (XT 1.8L)*

# 1991 ENGINE PERFORMANCE
# Wiring Diagrams (Cont.)

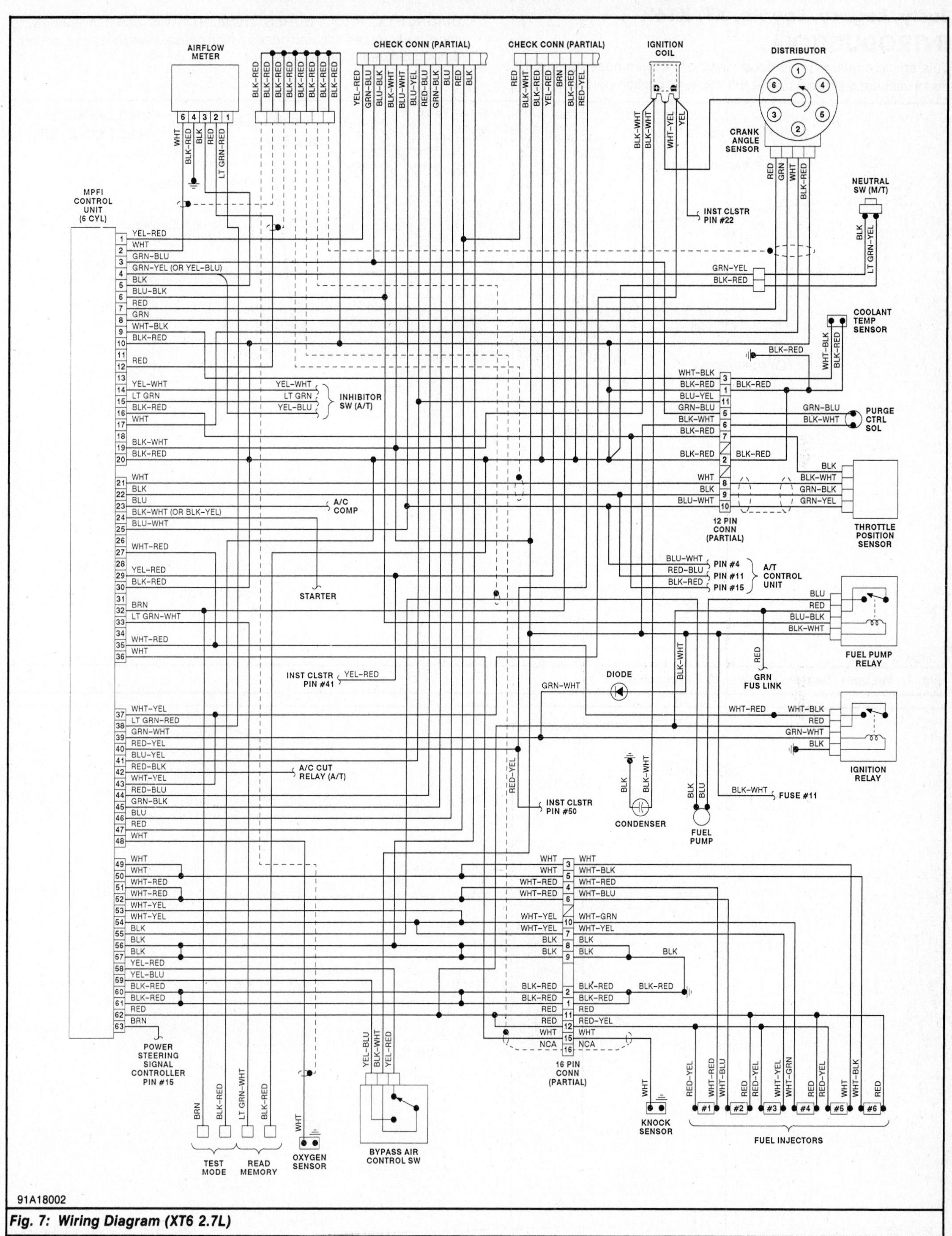


*Fig. 7: Wiring Diagram (XT6 2.7L)*

# 1991 ENGINE PERFORMANCE
# Vacuum Diagrams

## Justy, Legacy, Loyale, XT, XT6

## INTRODUCTION

This article contains underhood views of vacuum hose routing. Use these vacuum diagrams during the visual inspection portion of BASIC DIAGNOSTIC PROCEDURES article. This will assist in identifying improperly routed vacuum hoses which cause driveability and/or computer-indicated malfunctions.

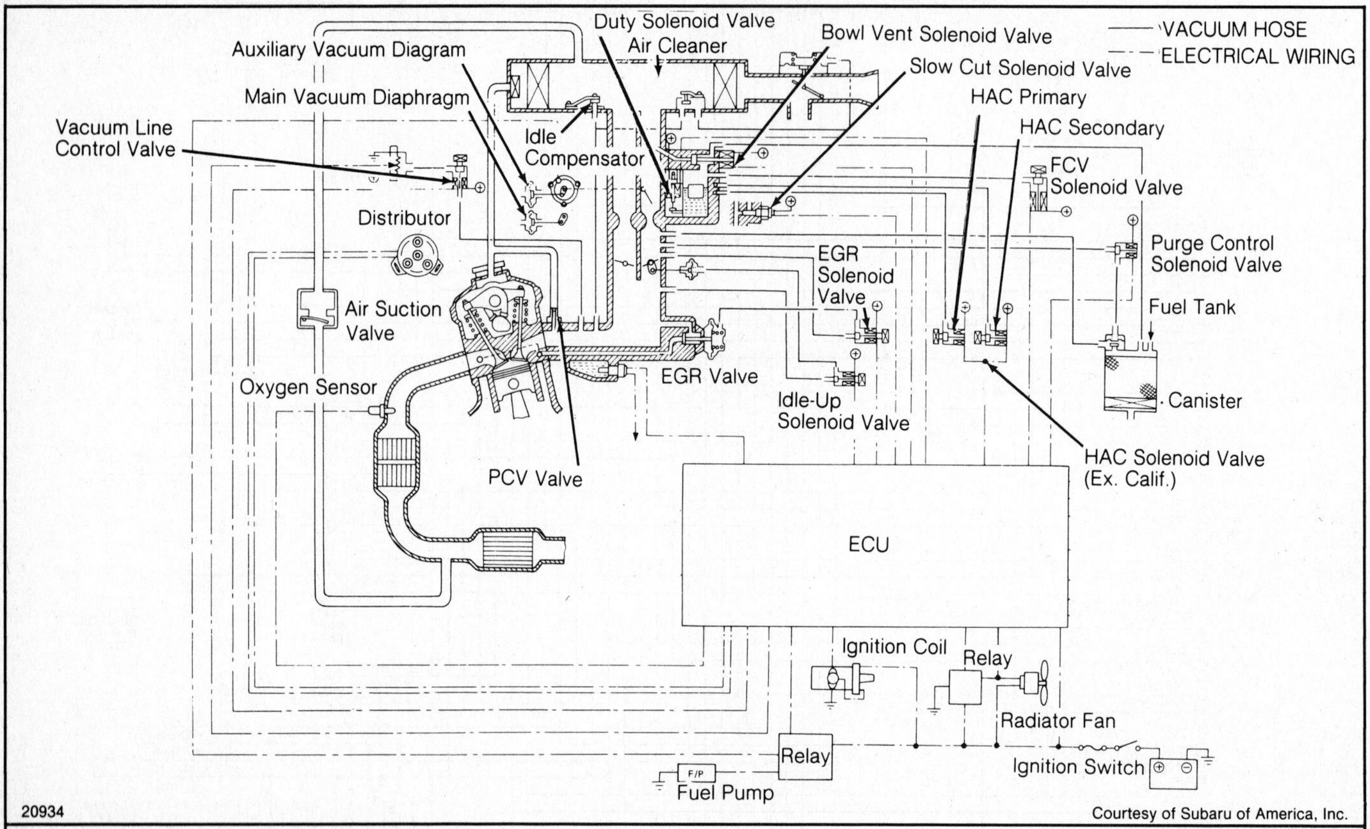

*Fig. 1: Vacuum Diagram (Justy 1.2L Carbureted)*

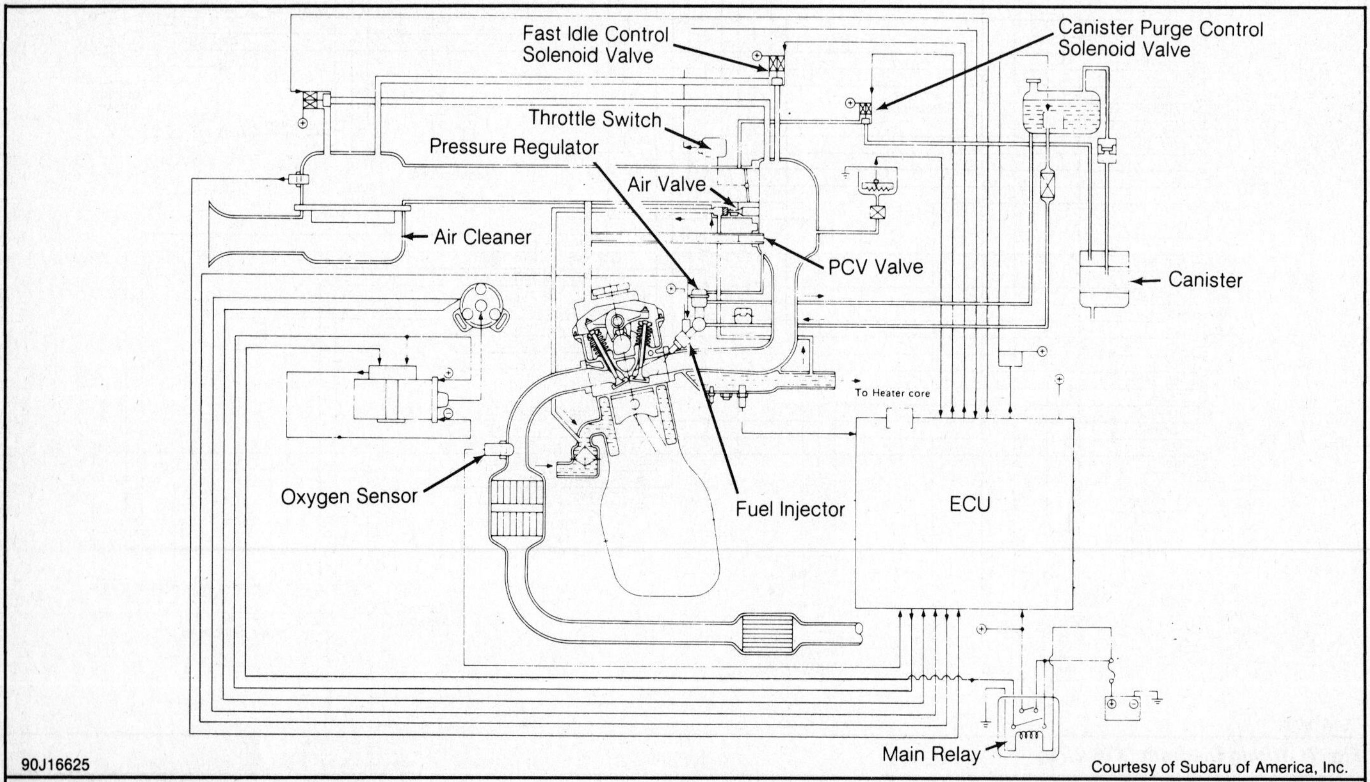

*Fig. 2: Vacuum Diagram (Justy 1.2L PFI)*

# 1991 ENGINE PERFORMANCE
# Vacuum Diagrams (Cont.)

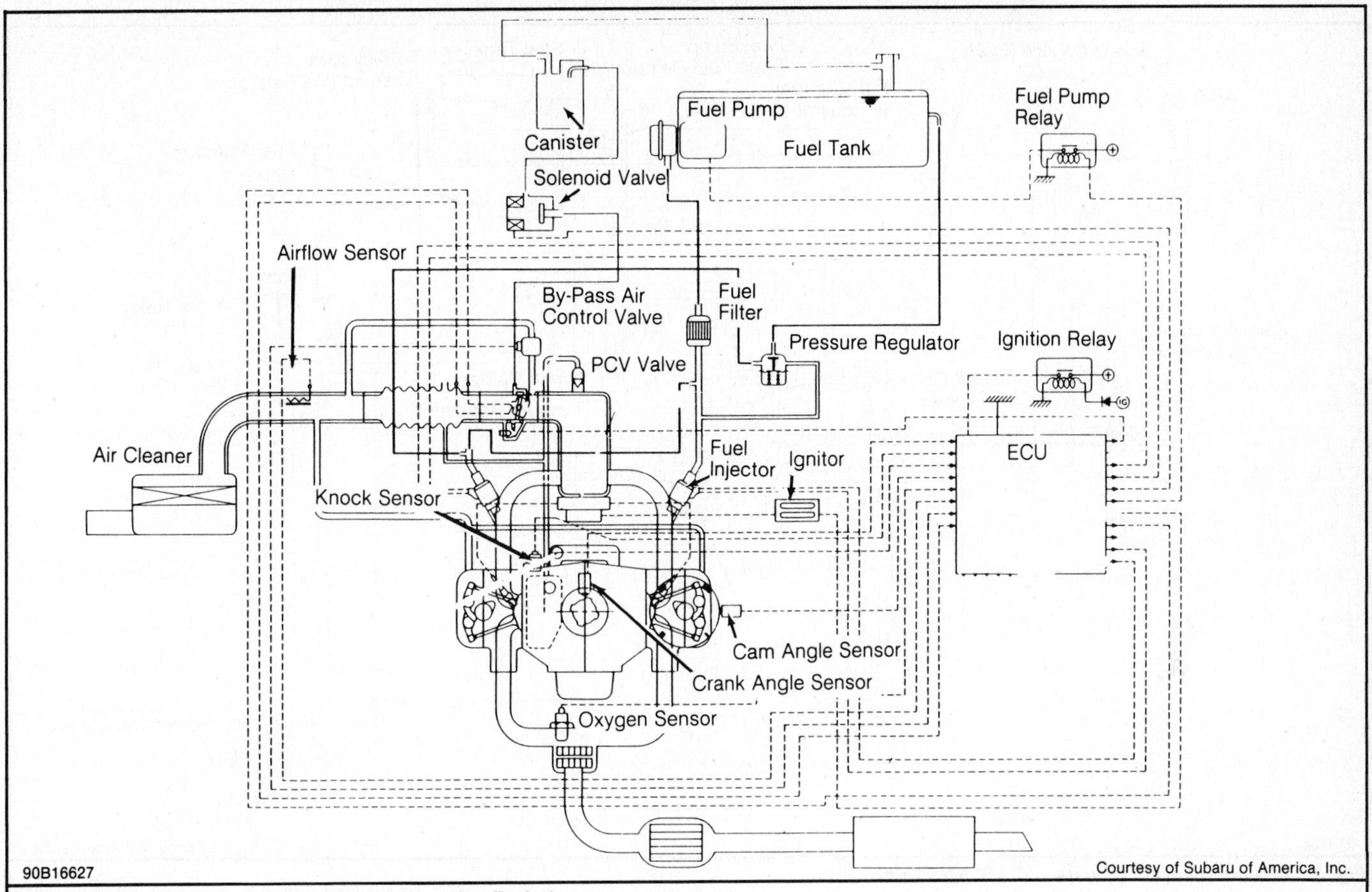

Courtesy of Subaru of America, Inc.

***Fig. 3: Vacuum Diagram (Legacy 2.2L PFI - Non-Turbo)***

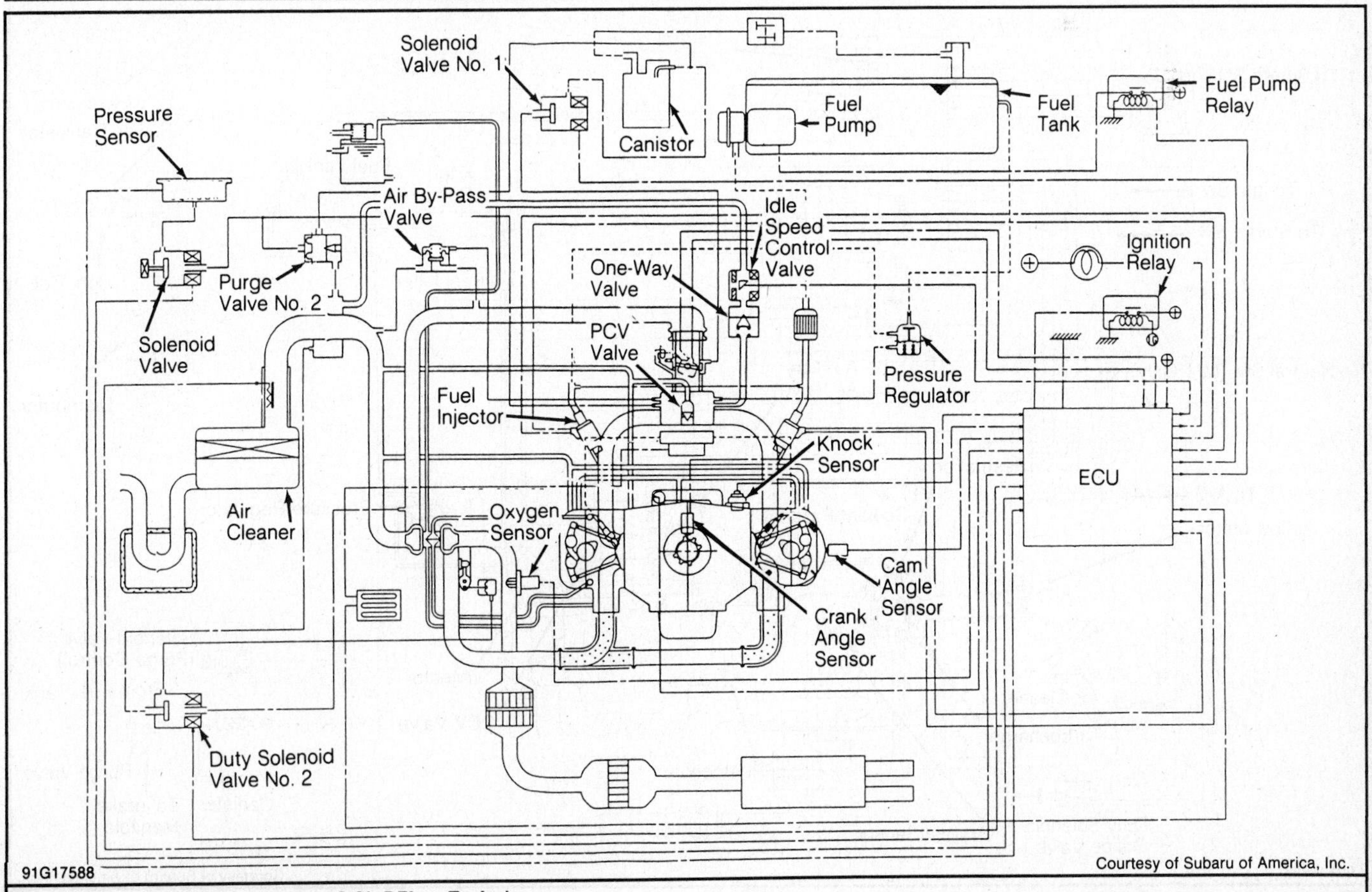

Courtesy of Subaru of America, Inc.

***Fig. 4: Vacuum Diagram (Legacy 2.2L PFI - Turbo)***

# 1991 ENGINE PERFORMANCE
## Vacuum Diagrams (Cont.)

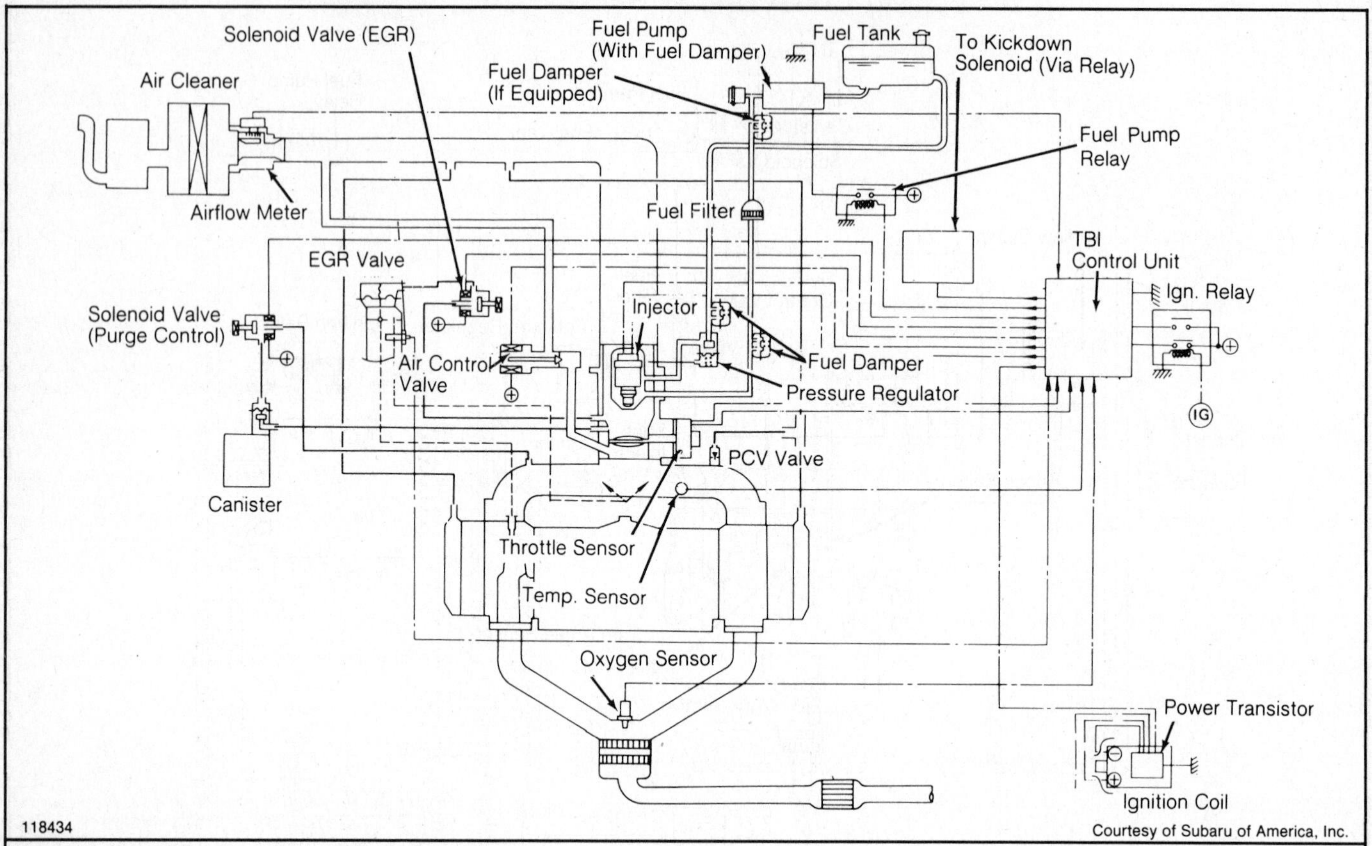

Courtesy of Subaru of America, Inc.

*Fig. 5: Vacuum Diagram (Loyale 1.8L TBI Non-Turbo)*

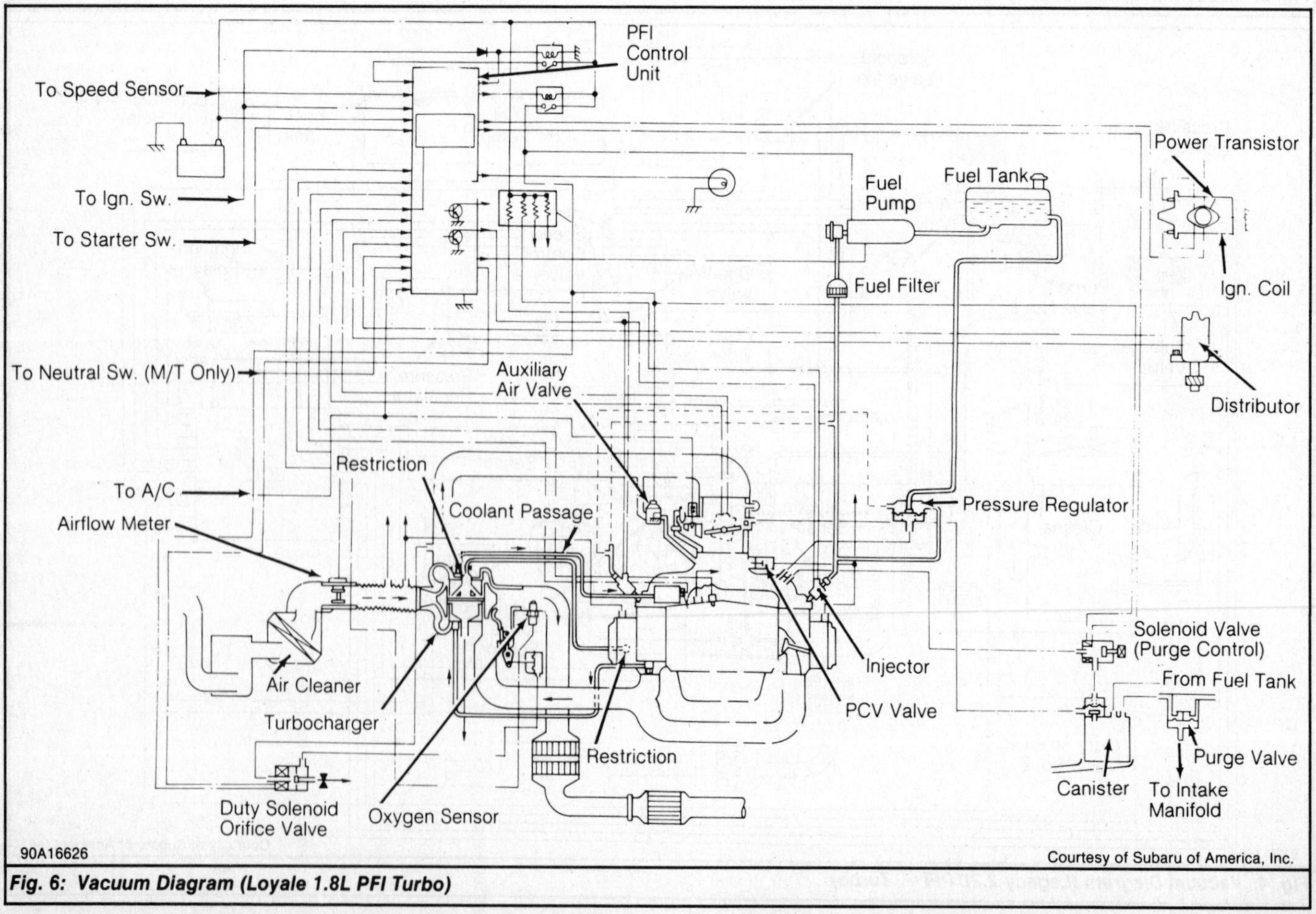

Courtesy of Subaru of America, Inc.

*Fig. 6: Vacuum Diagram (Loyale 1.8L PFI Turbo)*

# 1991 ENGINE PERFORMANCE
# Vacuum Diagrams (Cont.)

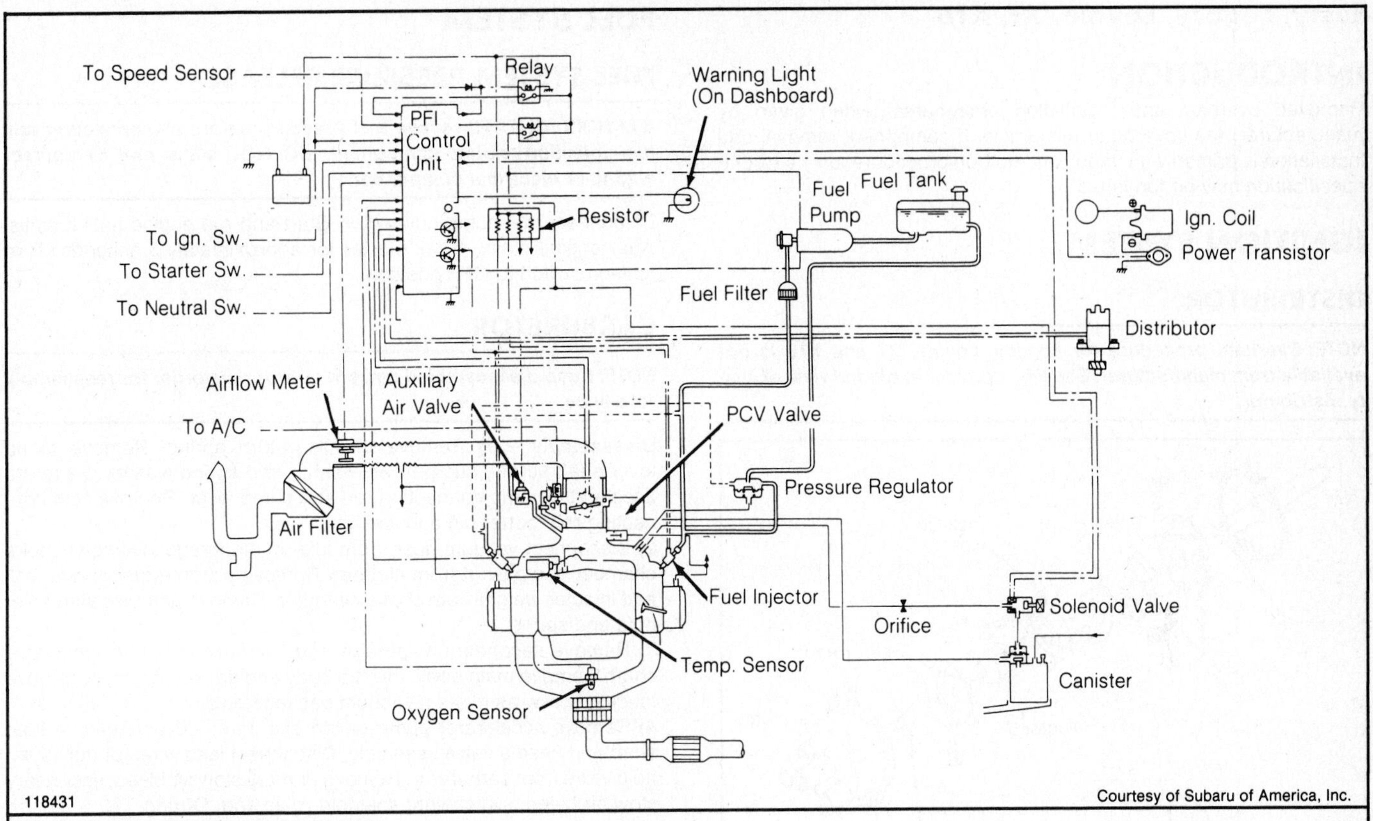


**Fig. 7: Vacuum Diagram (XT 1.8L PFI)**

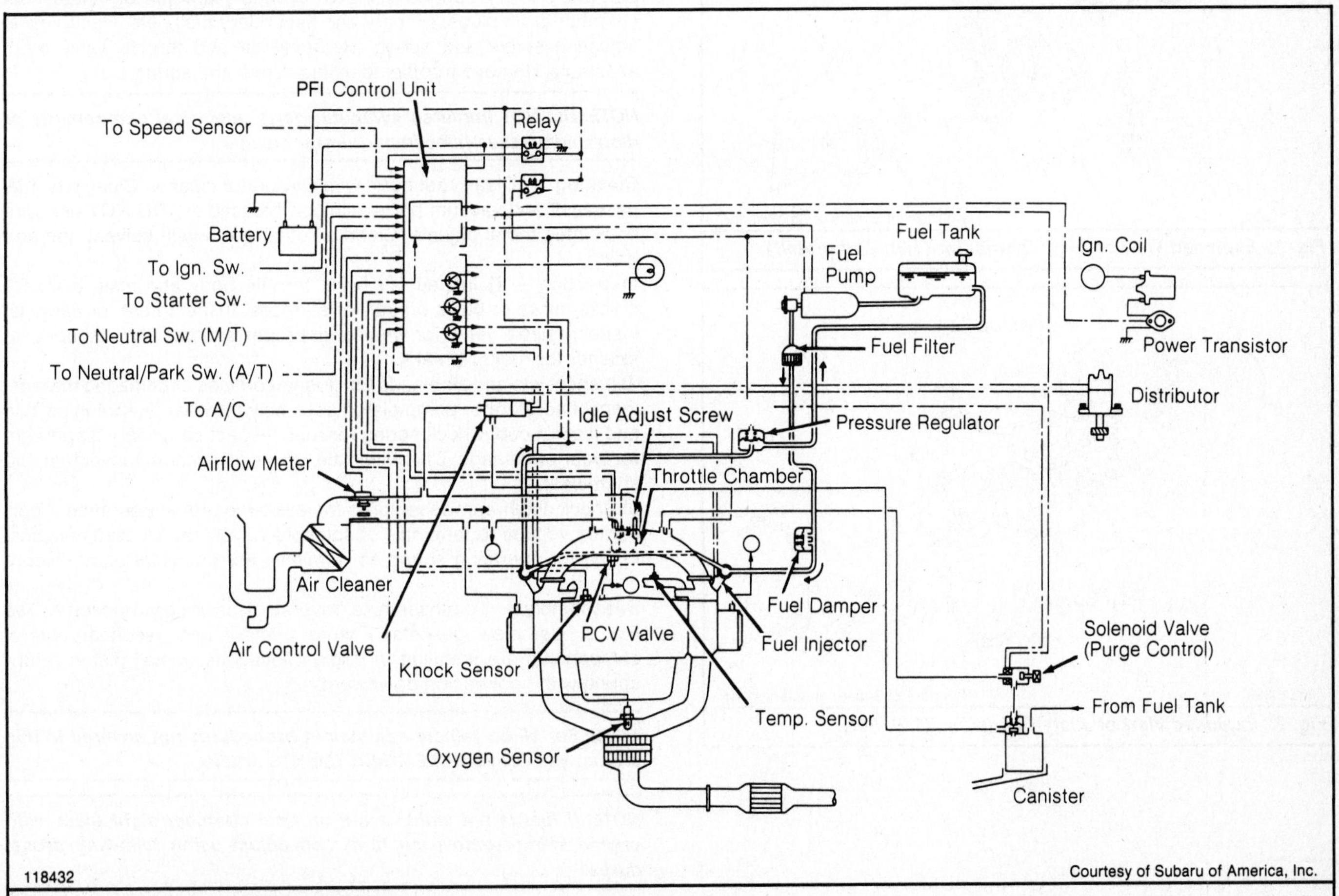


**Fig. 8: Vacuum Diagram (XT6 2.7L PFI)**

# 1991 ENGINE PERFORMANCE
# Removal, Overhaul & Installation

**Justy, Legacy, Loyale, XT, XT6**

## INTRODUCTION

Removal, overhaul and installation procedures (when given by manufacturer) are covered in this article. If component removal and installation is primarily an unbolt and bolt-on procedure, only a torque specification may be furnished.

## IGNITION SYSTEM

### DISTRIBUTOR

***NOTE: Overhaul procedure for Legacy, Loyale, XT and XT6 is not available from manufacturer. See Fig. 1 or 2 for exploded view of Justy distributor.***

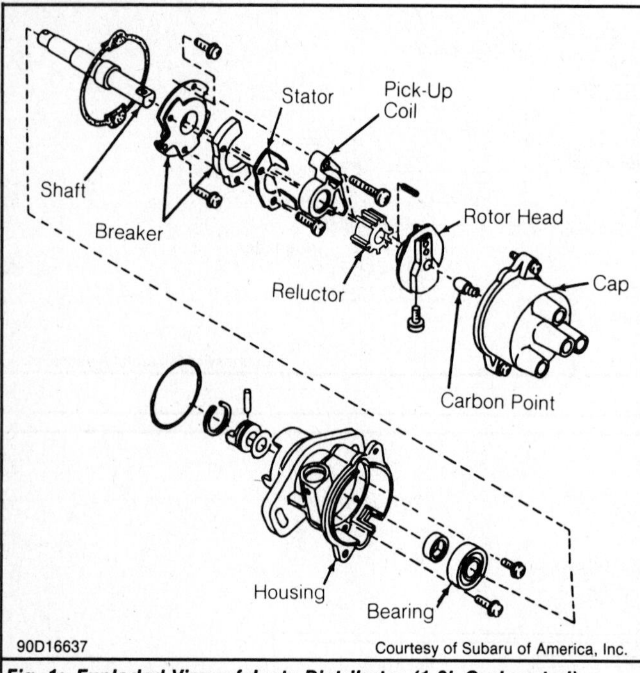


***Fig. 1: Exploded View of Justy Distributor (1.2L Carbureted)***

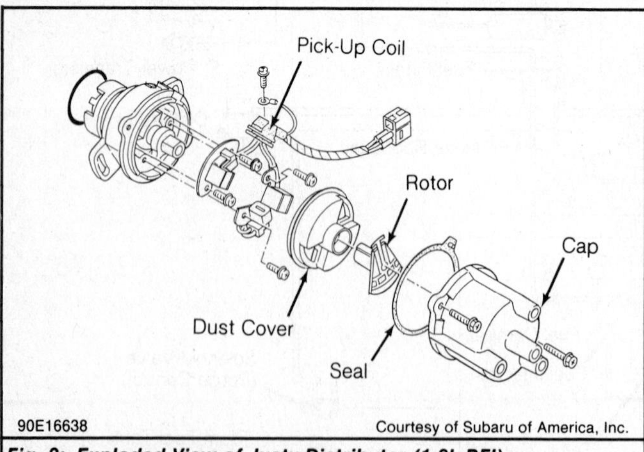


***Fig. 2: Exploded View of Justy Distributor (1.2L PFI)***

## FUEL SYSTEM

### FUEL SYSTEM PRESSURE RELEASE

***WARNING: ALWAYS relieve fuel pressure before disconnecting any fuel injection-related component. DO NOT allow fuel to contact engine or electrical components.***

Disconnect fuel pump connector. Start and run engine until it stalls. After engine stalls, crank starter for approximately 5 seconds. Turn ignition switch to OFF position.

### CARBURETOR

***NOTE: Keep disassembled parts in appropriate order for reassembly reference.***

**Disassembly – 1)** Remove throttle return spring. Remove pump lever shaft screw, pump lever, washer and spring washer. Separate accelerator pump connecting rod and pump lever. Remove cam connecting rod, cotter pin and washer.

**2)** Disconnect vacuum hose from idle-up diaphragm. Remove choke chamber and gasket from air horn. Remove piston return spring, ball and injector weight from choke chamber. Remove anti-dieseling solenoid and spring.

**3)** Remove secondary diaphragm rod from secondary throttle valve shaft. Remove main body, throttle body and gasket. Carefully remove longest screw as it has a vacuum passage hole.

**4)** Remove accelerator pump piston and pump cover. Remove float shaft and needle valve assembly. Disconnect lead wires of duty solenoid valve from carburetor. Remove primary slow air bleed, secondary slow air bleed, switch vent solenoid valve and "O" ring.

**5)** Remove primary main air bleed, secondary main air bleed, primary plug and primary slow jet. Remove secondary slow jet, lock plate, float chamber drain plugs, primary and secondary main jets. Remove idle adjusting screw and spring. Remove nut and throttle valve shaft assembly. Remove throttle adjusting screw and spring.

***NOTE: DO NOT immerse synthetic parts, electrical components or diaphragm assemblies in carburetor cleaner.***

**Cleaning –** Clean cast parts with carburetor cleaner. Clean jets, fuel passages and vacuum ports with compressed air. DO NOT use wire or pointed metal objects. Clean all other parts with solvent and soft brush.

**Inspection – 1)** Inspect air horn, throttle body and main body for cracks, nicks or burrs on gasket surfaces. Inspect float for damage. Inspect needle valve for wear or improper seating, and inspect seat strainer for rust or breaks.

**2)** Inspect jets and air bleeds for clogged orifices or damaged threads. Inspect accelerator pump piston assembly for wear on sliding portion and leather cup. Check spring for rust. Inspect secondary diaphragm for wear or damage. Check throttle valves for smooth movement and shaft wear.

**3)** Check diaphragm assemblies for leaks and proper operation. Apply battery voltage to terminals of solenoid valves and electric switches. Listen for operating sound as terminals are connected and disconnected.

**Reassembly –** To reassemble, reverse disassembly procedure. *See Fig. 3.* Use new gaskets. Ensure primary and secondary barrel components are installed in original locations. Install piston return spring with hook facing downward.

***NOTE: For all on-vehicle adjustment procedures not covered in this article, see ON-VEHICLE ADJUSTMENTS article.***

***NOTE: If fuel is not within mark on float chamber sight glass with engine idling, remove air horn and adjust using following procedures.***

# 1991 ENGINE PERFORMANCE
## Removal, Overhaul & Installation (Cont.)

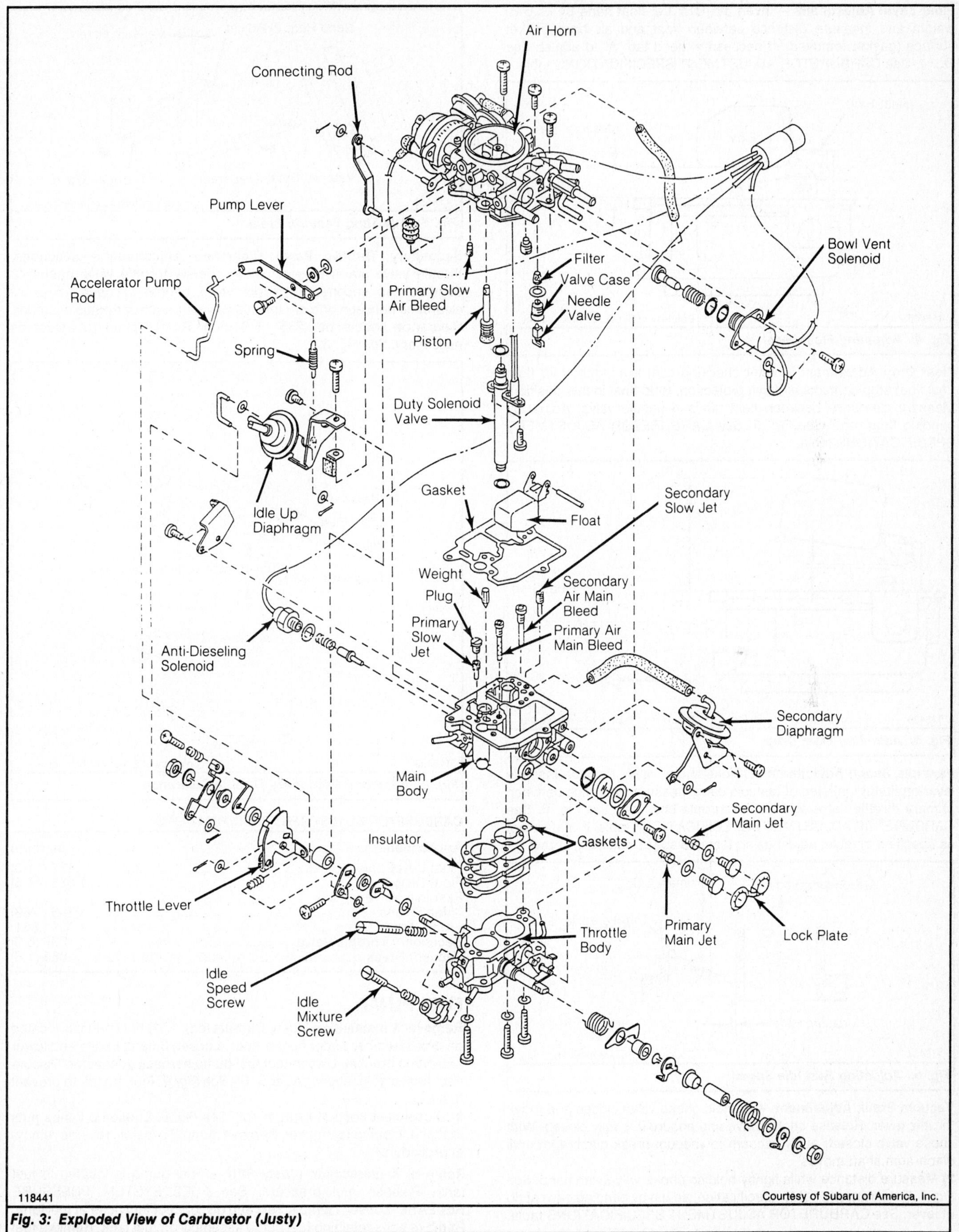


*Fig. 3: Exploded View of Carburetor (Justy)*

# 1991 ENGINE PERFORMANCE
## Removal, Overhaul & Installation (Cont.)

**Float Level Adjustment** - Invert air horn. Let float hang by its own weight and measure distance between float and air horn gasket surface (gasket removed). If necessary, bend tab "A" to adjust. *See Fig. 4.* See CARBURETOR ADJUSTMENT SPECIFICATIONS table.

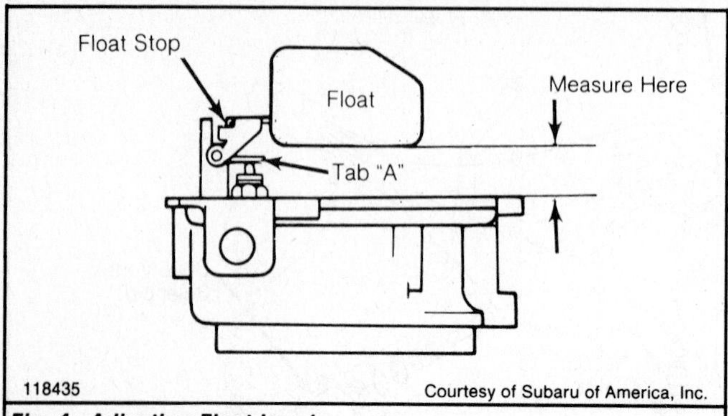


*Fig. 4: Adjusting Float Level*

**Float Drop Adjustment** - After checking float level, gently lift float until float stop contacts air horn projection. Hold float in this position. Measure clearance between float tab and needle valve. Adjust by bending float stop. *See Fig. 5.* See CARBURETOR ADJUSTMENT SPECIFICATIONS table.

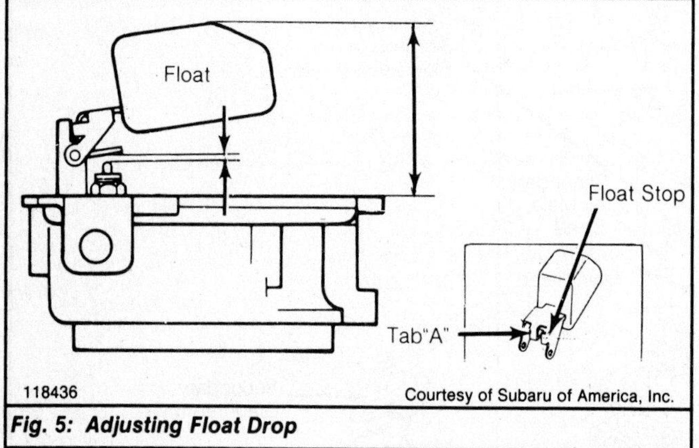


*Fig. 5: Adjusting Float Drop*

**Fast Idle Bench Adjustment** - Close choke valve. Position fast idle lever on first (high) step of fast idle cam. Measure clearance between primary throttle valve and wall of throttle chamber. *See Fig. 6.* See CARBURETOR ADJUSTMENT SPECIFICATIONS table. If value is not as specified in table, adjust using fast idle speed adjusting screw.

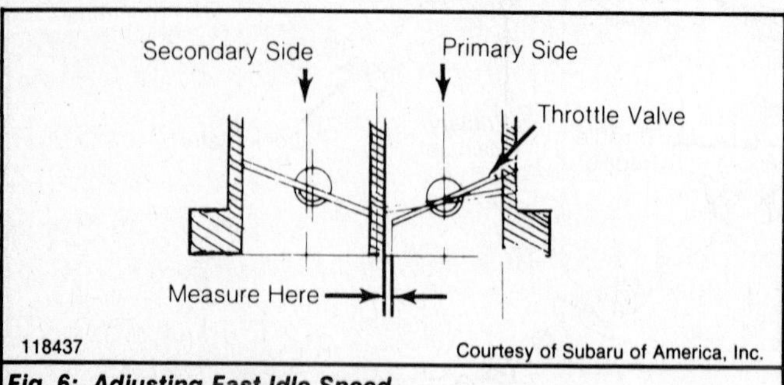


*Fig. 6: Adjusting Fast Idle Speed*

**Vacuum Break Adjustment** - **1)** Hold choke valve closed and move throttle lever. Release choke valve and ensure it is fully closed. With choke valve closed, apply vacuum to vacuum break diaphragm until diaphragm shaft moves.

**2)** Measure distance while lightly holding choke valve with hand. *See Fig. 7.* If clearance is not to specification, adjust by bending pawl at tip of lever. See CARBURETOR ADJUSTMENT SPECIFICATIONS table.

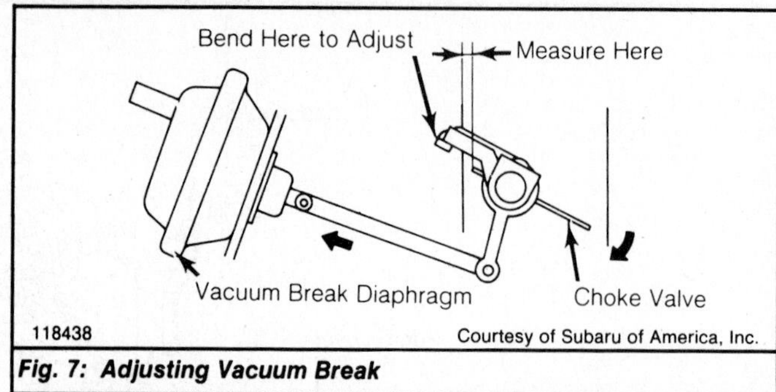


*Fig. 7: Adjusting Vacuum Break*

**Secondary Throttle Valve Clearance Adjustment** - Secondary throttle valve starts to open when primary throttle valve opens 43 degrees. As secondary throttle valve begins to open, measure clearance between primary throttle valve and wall of throttle chamber. Clearance should be .236" (6.0 mm). Rotate plate to adjust as necessary. *See Fig. 8.*

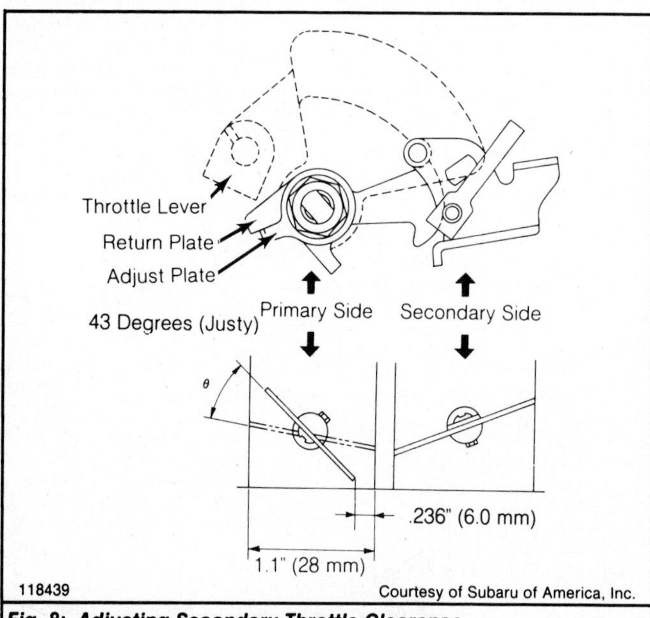


*Fig. 8: Adjusting Secondary Throttle Clearance*

***CARBURETOR ADJUSTMENT SPECIFICATIONS***

| Application | In. (mm) |
|---|---|
| Float Level | .437 (11.0) |
| Float Drop | 1.836 (46.6) |
| Fast Idle Valve | |
| Man. Trans. | .0303 (.789) |
| Auto. Trans. | .0339 (.861) |
| Secondary Throttle Valve | .236 (6.0) |
| Vacuum Break | .063 (1.6) |

## FUEL PUMP

**Removal & Installation (Justy Carbureted)** - **1)** Fuel pump is located on crossmember under center floor. Loosen 3 flange bolts and lower fuel pump bracket. Disconnect fuel pump harness connector. Disconnect hoses at locations "A" and "B". *See Fig. 9.* Plug hoses to prevent fuel loss.

**2)** Disconnect hose at location "C". *See Fig. 9.* Loosen 3 flange nuts that attach pump to bracket. Remove pump. To install, reverse removal procedure.

**Removal & Installation (Justy PFI)** - Fuel pump is located in fuel tank. Release fuel pressure. See FUEL SYSTEM PRESSURE RELEASE. Loosen clamp screw and disconnect fuel hose at fuel tank. Remove bolts retaining fuel pump assembly on fuel tank. Remove fuel pump. To install, reverse removal procedure.

# 1991 ENGINE PERFORMANCE
# Removal, Overhaul & Installation (Cont.)

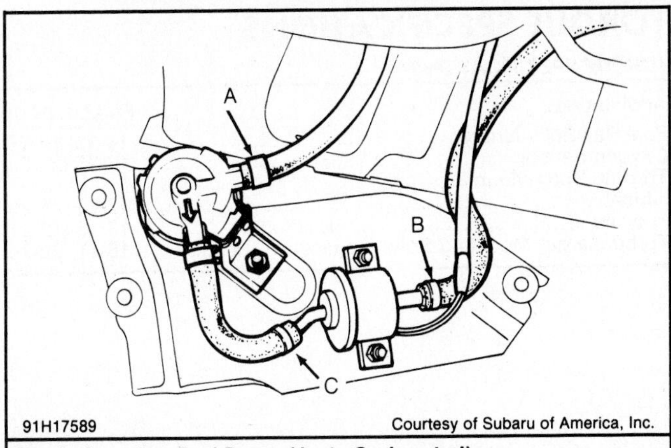


*Fig. 9: Locating Fuel Pump (Justy Carbureted)*

**Removal & Installation (Legacy)** – Fuel pump is located in fuel tank. Release fuel pressure. See FUEL SYSTEM PRESSURE RELEASE. Remove floor mat from luggage compartment. Remove access hole lid. Disconnect fuel pump harness. Remove 8 nuts. Remove fuel pump assembly. *See Fig. 10.* To install, reverse removal procedure.

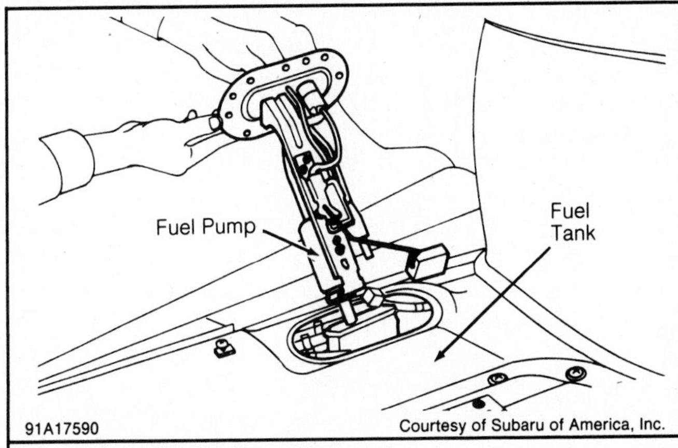


*Fig. 10: Locating Fuel Pump (Legacy)*

**Removal & Installation (Loyale, XT & XT6)** – Fuel pump is located under rear of vehicle. *See Fig. 11.* Release fuel pressure. See FUEL SYSTEM PRESSURE RELEASE. Raise and support vehicle. To avoid fuel flowing from fuel tank, clamp middle portion of thick hose between pipe coupling and fuel pump.

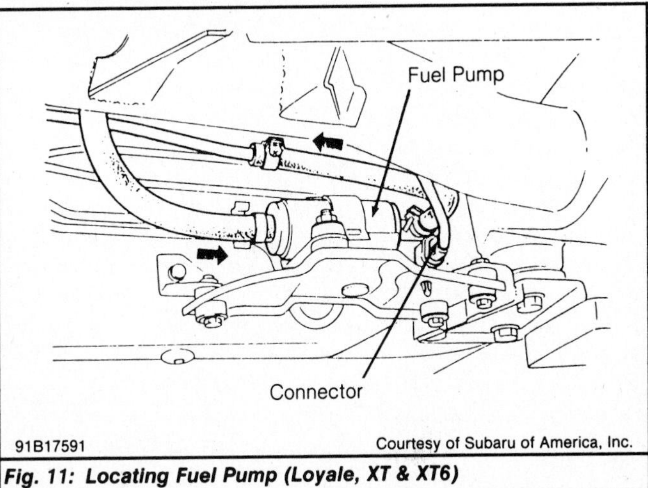


*Fig. 11: Locating Fuel Pump (Loyale, XT & XT6)*

## INJECTORS (TBI)

**Removal & Installation** – Remove injector cap and gasket. Hold injector with pliers and pull out injector from chamber. Remove injector and "O" ring from chamber assembly. DO NOT damage nozzle on injector point. To install, reverse removal procedure.

## OXYGEN ($O_2$) SENSOR

**Removal** – If $O_2$ sensor is difficult to remove, use rust penetrant to avoid damaging exhaust threads.
**Installation** – If old sensor is reused, apply anti-seize compound to sensor threads. Ensure anti-seize compound is kept away from sensor body. New sensors are coated with anti-seize compound. DO NOT remove anti-seize compound from sensor. Tighten to 18-25 ft. lbs. (24-34 N.m).

## THROTTLE POSITION SENSOR/SWITCH

**Removal & Installation** – Remove 2 throttle position sensor-to-throttle chamber screws. Remove throttle position sensor by pulling it in axial direction of throttle shaft. Note "O" ring attached to the throttle sensor mounting face of throttle chamber. To install, reverse removal procedure.

## TURBOCHARGER

**Removal & Installation** – During turbocharger removal and installation, do not allow dirt and dust to enter inlet and outlet openings of turbine and blower. If foreign matter is allowed to enter, turbine and blower blades will be damaged. Turbocharger cannot be disassembled or adjusted. *See Fig. 12 or 13.*

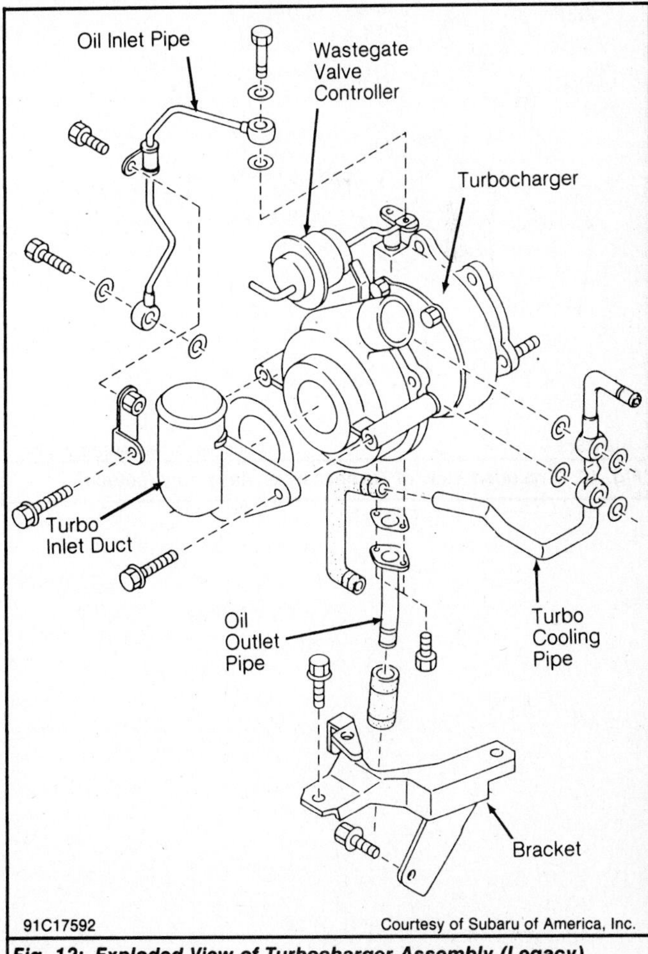


*Fig. 12: Exploded View of Turbocharger Assembly (Legacy)*

# 1991 ENGINE PERFORMANCE
# Removal, Overhaul & Installation (Cont.)

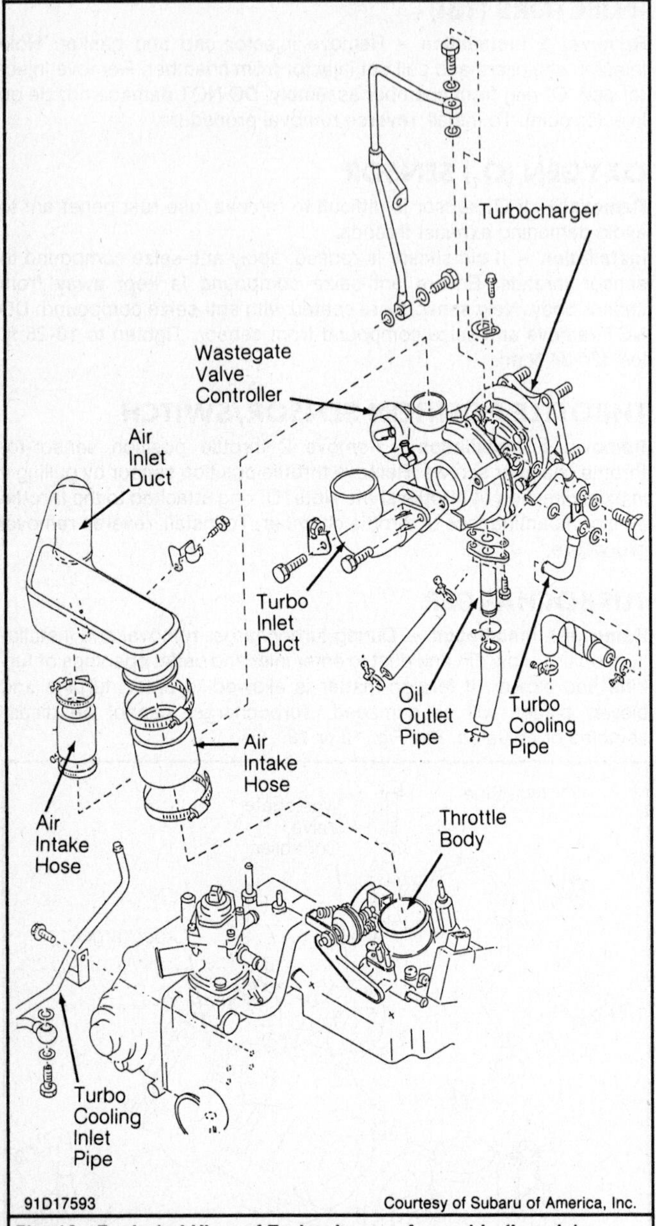


*Fig. 13: Exploded View of Turbocharger Assembly (Loyale)*

## TORQUE SPECIFICATIONS

*TORQUE SPECIFICATIONS*

| Application | Ft. Lbs. (N.m) |
|---|---|
| Fuel Rail Bolts (Justy) | 10-13 (14-17) |
| Oxygen Sensor | 17-25 (24-34) |
| Throttle Body Mounting Bolts | |
| Justy | 17-20 (24-26) |
| Loyale | 13-15 (18-21) |
| Turbocharger Mounting Bolts (Legacy) | 16-17 (22-24) |

# 1991 ELECTRICAL
# Alternators & Regulators – Hitachi

## Justy, Legacy, Loyale, XT

## DESCRIPTION

***NOTE: For information on alternator used on XT6, see ALTERNATORS & REGULATORS - MITSUBISHI article.***

Hitachi alternators are conventional rotating field, 3-phase, self-rectifying type alternators. Four positive and 4 negative diodes are used to rectify current. All models are equipped with Integrated Circuit (IC) voltage regulators. When charge indicator light voltage and alternator output voltage are about equal, charge indicator light is turned off.

## TROUBLE SHOOTING

***NOTE: See TROUBLE SHOOTING article in GENERAL INFORMATION.***

## ADJUSTMENTS

### BELT TENSION

***BELT ADJUSTMENT***

| Application | [1] Deflection - In. (mm) |
|---|---|
| Alternator Belt | |
| XT [2] | |
| New (Without A/C) [3] | .24-.28 (6-7) |
| Used (Without A/C) [3] | .28-.35 (7-9) |
| New & Used [4] | .24-.31 (6-8) |
| Except XT | .35-.39 (9-10) |
| Power Steering Belt | |
| Except XT | .35-.43 (9-11) |
| A/C Belt | |
| Except XT | .43-.47 (11-12) |
| A/C & Power Steering | |
| Except XT | .30-.33 (7.5-8.5) |

[1] - Deflection is measured with gauge applied force of 22 lbs. (10 kg) at belt longest run.
[2] - XT models use a serpentine belt.
[3] - Deflection is measured between power steering pulley and alternator pulley.
[4] - Equipped with P/S and A/C. Deflection is measured between crankshaft pulley and power steering pulley.

## ON-VEHICLE TESTING

***NOTE: On-vehicle testing is not available for Justy.***

### LEGACY, LOYALE & XT

**Regulated Voltage Test – 1)** Connect test equipment to alternator as per appropriate illustration. Connect an ammeter, voltmeter, 0-.25 ohm/1 KW variable resistor, 2 single-pole switches (SW 1 and SW 2), .25 ohm/25 watt resistor and a 12-volt test light. *See Fig. 1, 2 or 3.*

**2)** Open switch SW 1 and close SW 2. Turn alternator at 5000-6000 RPM. If output voltage is approximately 14.1-14.8 volts, alternator and voltage regulator are okay. If voltage is not within specification, replace voltage regulator.

***ALTERNATOR OUTPUT SPECIFICATIONS***

| Application | Amps |
|---|---|
| Legacy | |
| 1500 RPM | 33 Or More |
| 3000 RPM | 66 Or More |
| 6000 RPM | 80 Or More |
| Loyale | |
| 1250 RPM | 18 Or More |
| 2500 RPM | 49 Or More |
| 5000 RPM | 58 Or More |
| XT | |
| 1600 RPM | 22 Or More |
| 3000 RPM | 53 Or More |
| 5000 RPM | 63 Or More |

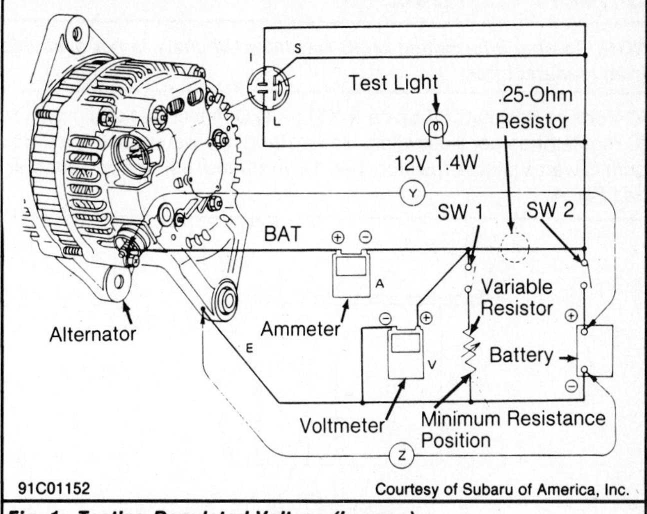


***Fig. 1: Testing Regulated Voltage (Legacy)***

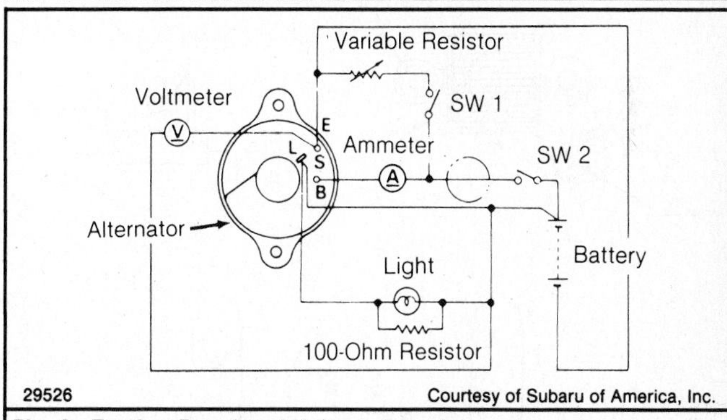


***Fig. 2: Testing Regulated Voltage (Loyale)***

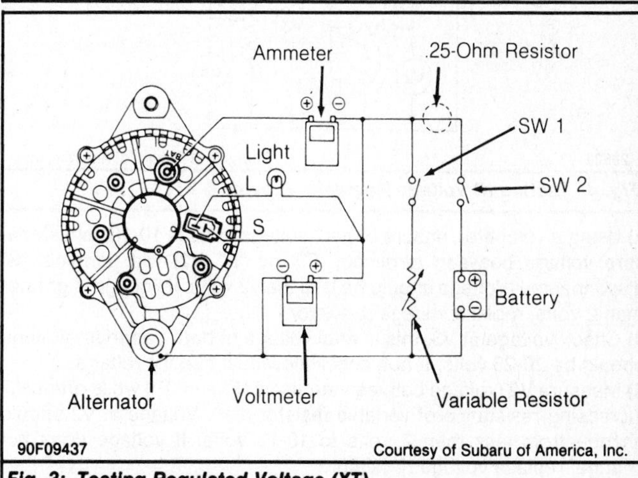


***Fig. 3: Testing Regulated Voltage (XT)***

**Alternator Output Test – 1)** Connect test equipment to alternator according to appropriate illustration. Connect an ammeter, voltmeter, 0-.25 ohm/1 KW variable resistor, 2 single-pole switches (SW 1 and SW 2), .25 ohm/25 watt resistor and a 12-volt test light. *See Fig. 1, 2 or 3.*

**2)** Set variable resistor to minimum resistance position. Close switches SW 1 and SW 2. Keep voltage constant by adjusting variable resistor while raising alternator RPM. Alternator output should measure as shown in ALTERNATOR OUTPUT SPECIFICATIONS table.

# 1991 ELECTRICAL
# Alternators & Regulators – Hitachi (Cont.)

## BENCH TESTING

***NOTE: Testing information on IC regulator for Justy is not available from manufacturer.***

**IC Voltage Regulator (Loyale & XT) – 1)** Connect test equipment to IC regulator as per illustration. Use a 10-ohm/3-watt resistor, a 0-300 ohm/3-watt variable resistor, two 12-volt batteries, and a voltmeter. *See Fig. 4.*

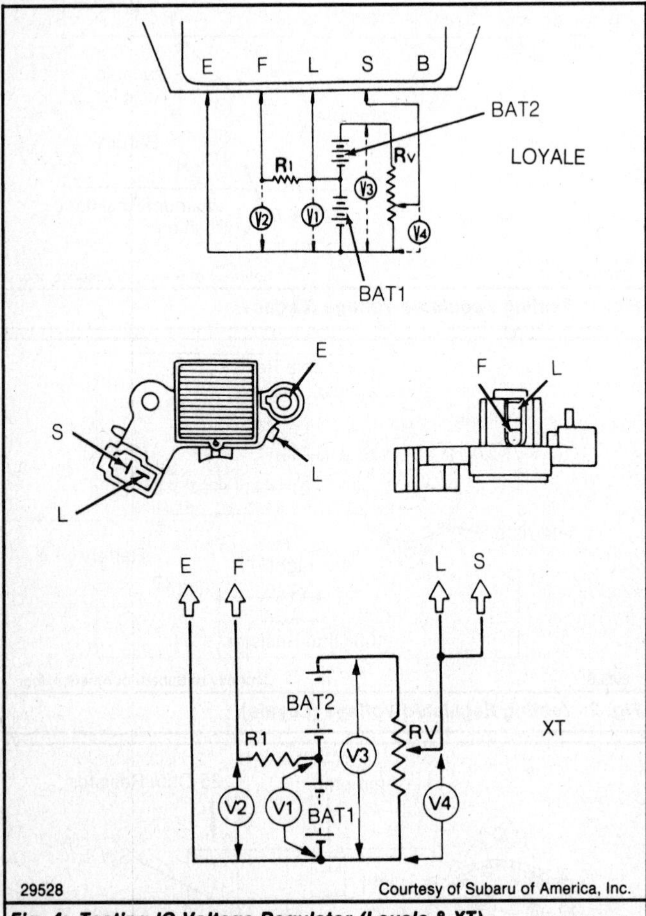


***Fig. 4: Testing IC Voltage Regulator (Loyale & XT)***

**2)** Using a voltmeter, ensure battery voltage at V1 is 10-13 volts. Measure voltage between terminals "F" and "E" (V2) with terminal "S" disconnected. Voltage should be less than 2 volts. If voltage is greater than 2 volts, replace voltage regulator.

**3)** Check voltage at V3, this is total voltage of both batteries. Voltage should be 20-26 volts. If not, check individual battery voltage.

**4)** Measure V2 (voltage between terminals "F" and "E") while gradually increasing resistance of variable resistor (RV). Voltage at V2 should change from less than 2 volts to 10-13 volts. If voltage does not change, replace voltage regulator.

**5)** Check voltage V4 (voltage between center tap of variable resistor RV and terminal "E") With variable resistor RV fixed at "0", V4 voltage should be 14.1-14.8 volts. If voltage is not as specified, replace voltage regulator.

**IC Voltage Regulator (Legacy) – 1)** Connect test equipment to IC regulator. Use a variable DC voltage power source with a capacity of at least 15 volts, two 12-volt 1.4 watt light bulbs, two 12-volt switches and a 0-50 volt voltmeter. *See Fig. 5.*

**2)** Open switches SW1 and SW2. Set power supply to 12 volts. Close SW1 and note L1 and L2 bulb conditions. L1 bulb should be bright, L2 bulb should be dim. With SW 1 closed, close SW 2 and note L1 and L2 bulb conditions. L1 should be off, L2 should be bright.

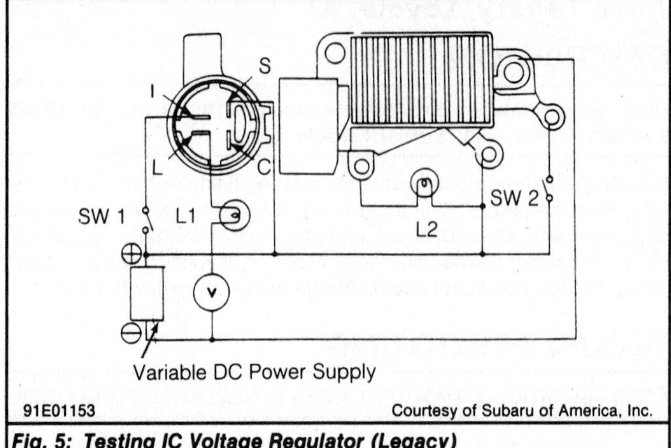


***Fig. 5: Testing IC Voltage Regulator (Legacy)***

**3)** Close both switches, gradually increase voltage supply to 14.1-14.7 volts. Note L1 and L2 bulb conditions. Both bulbs should be off. If any of these test results are not as specified, replace IC regulator.

**Rotor – 1)** Measure slip ring outer wear. If worn more than .04" (1.0 mm), replace rotor. Standard diameter is 1.063" (27 mm). Wear limit is 1.024" (26 mm). Inspect slip rings for contamination or roughness. Polish with No. 500 or 600 emery paper or crocus cloth.

**2)** Check continuity between rotor slip rings. See ROTOR SLIP RING RESISTANCE table. If continuity or proper resistance does not exist, replace rotor. Connect ohmmeter between each slip ring and rotor core, individually. If continuity exists, replace rotor assembly. Check rotor bearing for noise and ease of rotation when turning. Replace as necessary.

***ROTOR SLIP RING RESISTANCE***

| Model | Ohms |
|---|---|
| Justy | 2.1-2.7 |
| Loyale | 4-5 |
| Legacy | [1] |
| XT | [1] |

[1] – Information is not available from manufacturer.

**Stator** – Using an ohmmeter, check for continuity between stator core leads. If continuity does not exist between any 2 leads, replace stator. Connect ohmmeter between stator core and each stator lead, individually. If continuity does not exist, stator is good. If continuity exists, stator is grounded and must be replaced.

**Diode Assembly – 1)** To check diode assembly, remove it from rear cover. Using ohmmeter, check each diode for continuity in one direction only.

**2)** If resistance or continuity is shown in both directions, diode is bad. If any diodes are defective, replace complete rectifier assembly.

**3)** Diode trio is good if all tests show continuity to exist in one direction only. If continuity exists in both directions, replace diode trio.

**Brushes** – Inspect brushes for freedom of movement in holder (no binding). Clean brush holder and springs if necessary. Check brushes for cracks and wear. Check brush springs for corrosion or damage. Replace brushes if worn near to or beyond limit line. See BRUSH WEAR LIMIT table.

***BRUSH WEAR LIMIT***

| Application | In. (mm) |
|---|---|
| Justy | .315 (8.0) |
| Legacy | .059 (1.5) |
| Loyale | [1] |
| XT | .236 (6.0) |

[1] – Information is not available from manufacturer.

## OVERHAUL

To remove a stuck rear cover after removing case bolts, use soldering iron/gun to heat rear cover bearing housing to about 122-140°F (50-

60°C). This action will expand housing enough to slide cover off rear rotor bearing. Use care not to lose spring washer located in rear cover bearing bore. See Figs. 6-9.

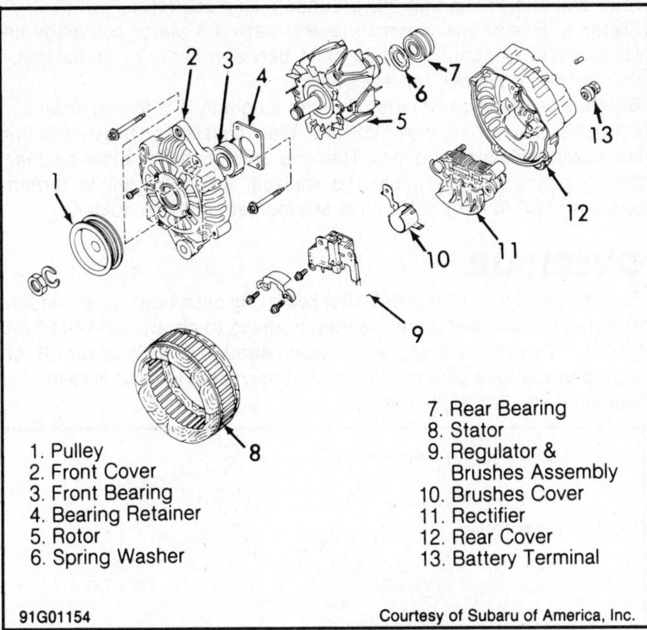


91G01154 Courtesy of Subaru of America, Inc.

**Fig. 6: Identifying Alternator Components (Justy)**

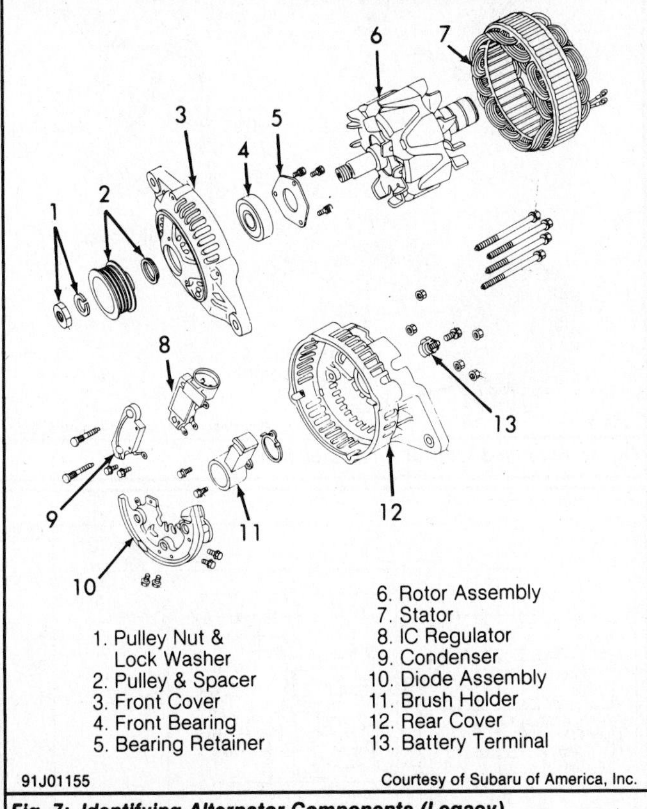


91J01155 Courtesy of Subaru of America, Inc.

**Fig. 7: Identifying Alternator Components (Legacy)**

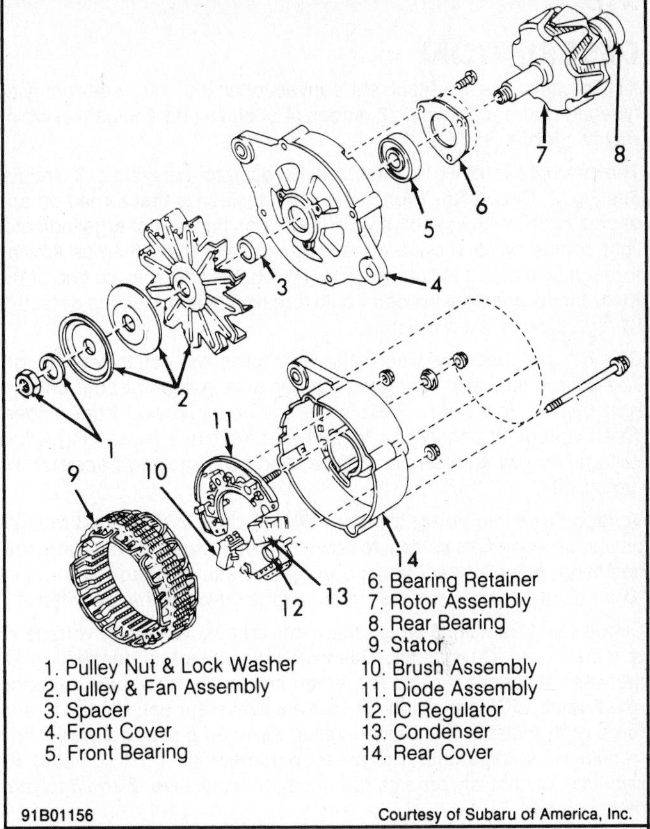


91B01156 Courtesy of Subaru of America, Inc.

**Fig. 8: Identifying Alternator Components (Loyale)**

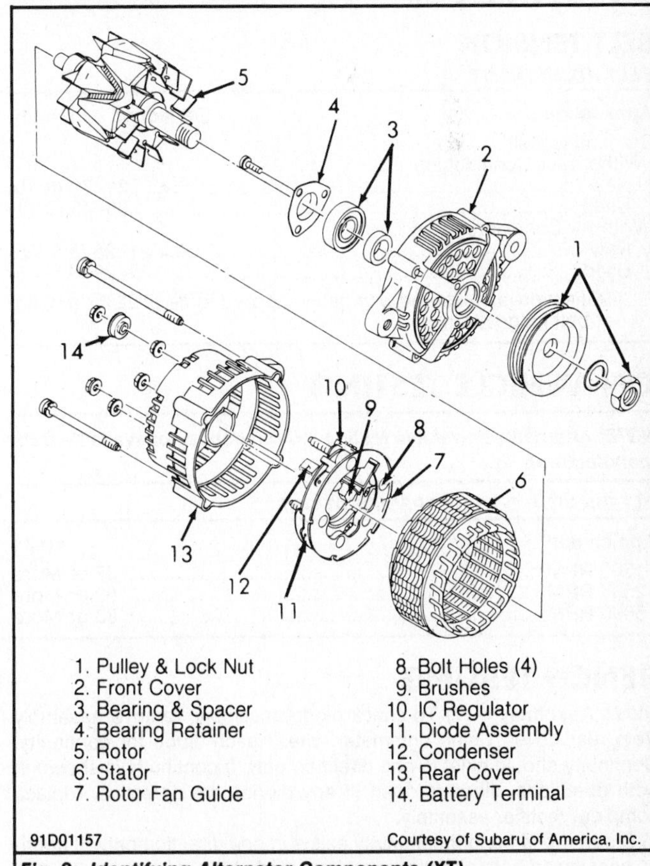


91D01157 Courtesy of Subaru of America, Inc.

**Fig. 9: Identifying Alternator Components (XT)**

# 1991 ELECTRICAL
# Alternators & Regulators – Mitsubishi

## XT6

## DESCRIPTION

XT6 models use a Mitsubishi conventional 3-phase, self-rectifying type alternator, containing 8 diodes (4 positive and 4 negative) which rectify current. *See Fig. 1.*

The internal circuitry of a Mitsubishi IC regulator consists of 3 circuits. *See Fig. 2.* Circuit No. 1 functions when ignition is first turned on and engine is off. With ignition switch in ON position, the charge indicator light comes on to show a current flow of less than .5 amps flowing through field coil. If indicator light is not on, the fault may be one of the following: burned out indicator bulb, break in field coil wiring defective IC regulator, or worn brushes.

Circuit No. 2 functions when alternator turns and generates voltage. The charge indicator light goes out because voltage at both ends of light bulb is now equal. Field current is now supplied from diodes. When voltage at connection "a" (between resistors Rv and $R_1$) is low voltage, no voltage flows into Zener diode Dz, keeping transistor $Tr_1$ turned off.

Voltage flows into power transistor, (large circle in diagram) turning it on and allowing field current to flow through it, creating voltage. In this condition, when current voltage exceeds battery voltage at terminal "B" of IC regulator, excess current voltage flows to charge battery.

Circuit No. 3 functions when alternator creates too much voltage at terminal "L" of IC regulator. This increases voltage at connection "a" (between resistors Rv and $R_1$). When increased "a" voltage exceeds rated value of Zener diode Dz, current flows through diode Dz and turns on transistor $Tr_1$. This condition turns off power transistor and "regulates" voltage output to preset parameters (14.0-15.0 volts). IC regulator continually repeats operation of circuits No. 2 and 3 to regulate voltage.

## ADJUSTMENTS

### BELT TENSION

***BELT ADJUSTMENT***

| Application | [1] Deflection – In. (mm) |
|---|---|
| Serpentine Belt | |
| Without Air Conditioning | |
| New | .31-.39 (8-10) |
| Used | .35-.43 (9-11) |
| With Air Conditioning | |
| New | .21-.25 (5.5-6.5) |
| Used | .25-.29 (6.5-7.5) |

[1] – Deflection is measured with gauge applied force of 22 lbs. (10 kg) at belt longest run.

## ON-VEHICLE TESTING

***NOTE: Alternator on-vehicle testing information is not available from manufacturer.***

***ALTERNATOR OUTPUT SPECIFICATIONS***

| Application | Amps |
|---|---|
| 1500 RPM | 27 or More |
| 2500 RPM | 62 or More |
| 5000 RPM | 83 or More |

## BENCH TESTING

**Diode Assembly – 1)** To check diode assembly, remove assembly from rear cover. Using ohmmeter, check each diode for continuity. Continuity should exist in one direction only. If continuity is shown in both directions, diode is open. If any diodes are defective, replace complete rectifier assembly.

**2)** Diode trio is good if continuity exists in one direction only. If continuity exists in both directions, replace diode trio.

**Rotor –** Continuity across rotor slip rings should be 3-3.5 ohms. If continuity does not exist, replace rotor. Check continuity between each slip ring and rotor core/shaft, individually. If any continuity exists, rotor coil and/or slip ring are grounded. Replace rotor.

**Stator –** Ensure no continuity exists between stator coil leads and stator core. Continuity should exist between leads of stator coil. If there is no continuity, replace stator.

**Brushes –** Replace brushes if brush length is .31" (8mm) or less, or if brushes are worn to wear limit line. Wear limit line on brush is bottom line of Mitsubishi symbol box. Remove brushes from holder by unsoldering pigtail from terminal. To replace, solder pigtail to terminal ensuring 1/4" (6 mm) of brush is still located in brush holder.

## OVERHAUL

To remove a stuck rear cover after removing case bolts, use soldering iron/gun to heat rear cover bearing housing to about 122-140 F° (50-60 C°). This action will expand housing enough to slide cover off rear rotor bearing. Use care not to lose spring washer located in rear cover bearing bore. *See Figs. 1 and 2.*

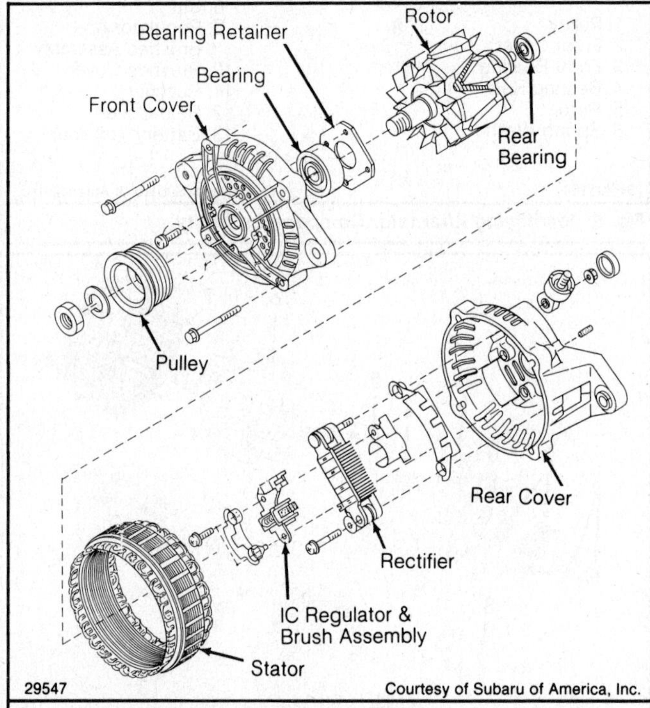


***Fig. 1: Exploded View of Alternator (XT6)***

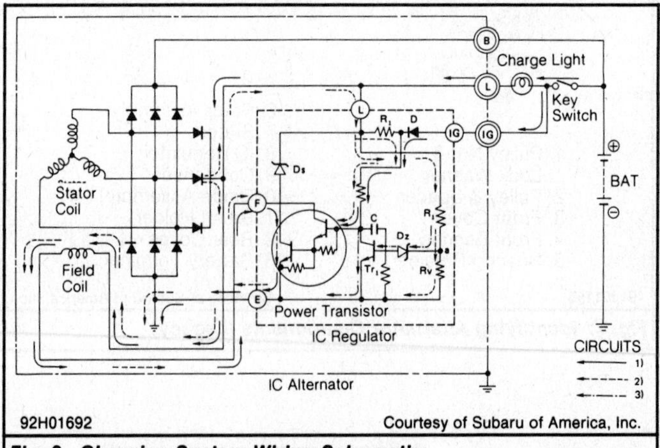


***Fig. 2: Charging System Wiring Schematic***

# 1991 ELECTRICAL
# Starters – Direct Drive

## Justy

## DESCRIPTION

Justy models use a conventional Nippondenso 12-volt, 4-brush, direct drive starter. Integral solenoid is attached to gear case. When starter is energized, solenoid engages shift lever which engages overrunning clutch pinion drive to engage flywheel ring gear. Overrunning clutch pinion drive is mounted directly on drive end of armature shaft.

## ON-VEHICLE TESTING

### CRANKING TEST

**1)** Ensure vehicle has fully charged battery. Connect voltmeter to battery terminals and ammeter to battery cables as per each meter's instructions. Disable distributor from firing spark plugs.

**2)** Crank engine for less than 30 seconds. When cranking engine, note and record voltmeter reading (voltage drop) and ammeter reading (current draw). Average starter cranking voltage should exceed 8 volts, with a current draw of 200 amps or less.

### CIRCUIT TEST

**Automatic Transmission – 1)** If voltage does not exist in any of the following circuit tests, check wiring for opens or shorts, or replace faulty component.

**2)** Turn ignition switch to START position. Check for near battery voltage at ignition switch "S" terminal (Black/Yellow wire). If voltage exists, check for near battery voltage at Black/Yellow wire terminal of transmission inhibitor switch. Inhibitor switch is located on drivers gear select lever, under console.

**3)** If voltage exists at Black/Yellow wire terminal of transmission inhibitor switch, check for voltage at inhibitor switch's Black/White wire terminal when gear select lever is in Park or Neutral position.

**4)** If voltage exists at inhibitor switch's Black/White wire terminal, check for near battery voltage at Black/White wires of ECVT unit harness connector. ECVT unit is located behind drivers left dash panel, above EFC/MPFI control unit.

**5)** If voltage exists at both Black/White wires, check for near battery voltage at starter "S" terminal (Black/White wire). If voltage exists at starter solenoid, start circuit is good. Problem is with starter.

***NOTE: No information is available for testing inhibitor switch or ECVT unit.***

**Manual Transmission – 1)** If voltage does not exist in any of the following circuit tests, check wiring for opens or shorts, or replace faulty component.

**2)** Turn ignition switch to START position. Check for near battery voltage at ignition switch "S" terminal (Black/Yellow wire). If voltage exists, check for near battery voltage at both Black/Yellow wire terminals of starter interlock relay.

**3)** Interlock relay has a Blue, 4-terminal connector and is located below EFC/MPFI control unit and to far left of unit. EFC/MPFI control unit is located behind drivers left dash panel.

**4)** Clutch switch, located at top of clutch pedal arm, grounds interlock relays Blue wire, energizing interlock relay. Press clutch pedal to floor and check interlock relay's Black/White wire terminal for near battery voltage.

**5)** If voltage exists, check for near battery voltage at starter solenoid "S" terminal (Black/White wire). If voltage exists at starter solenoid, start circuit is good. Problem is with starter.

### STARTER INTERLOCK RELAY TEST

**1)** Interlock relay has a Blue, 4-terminal connector and is located below EFC/MPFI control unit and to far left of unit. EFC/MPFI control unit is located behind drivers left dash panel. Locate and unplug interlock relay.

**2)** Connect test light to Black/White wire terminal of interlock relay. Using jumper wire, apply 12 volts to both Black/Yellow wires terminals of interlock relay.

**3)** Using another jumper wire connected to ground, momentarily touch jumper wire to Blue wire terminal of interlock relay. Test light should illuminate. If not, replace interlock relay.

### IGNITION SWITCH TEST

**Start Circuit Test – 1)** Remove lower instrument panel below steering wheel. Remove air duct. Remove harness connector from rear of ignition switch.

**2)** Using jumper wire, apply 12 volts to switch terminal "B". Connect test light to switch terminal "S". Turn ignition switch to START position. Test light should illuminate. If not, replace ignition switch.

**Continuity Tests –** Ensure continuity exists between terminals indicated in table, when ignition switch is in specified position. See IGNITION SWITCH CONTINUITY SPECIFICATIONS table. *See Fig. 1.* Repair or replace as necessary.

***IGNITION SWITCH CONTINUITY SPECIFICATIONS***

| Switch Position | Continuity Between Terminals |
|---|---|
| Lock | No Continuity |
| OFF | No Continuity |
| ACC | A & B |
| ON | A, B & IG |
| START | B, IG, R & S |

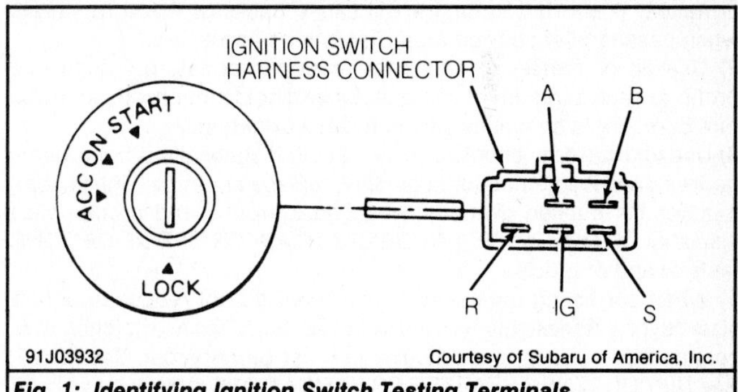


***Fig. 1: Identifying Ignition Switch Testing Terminals***

## BENCH TESTING

***CAUTION: Perform tests in less than 30 seconds to prevent solenoid coil and armature damage.***

### NO-LOAD TEST

**1)** Clamp starter to test bench or in vise. Set up test equipment as shown in illustration. *See Fig. 2.* Close switch to engage starter. Measure current draw, rotating speed, and voltage drop. See NIPPONDENSO STARTER SPECIFICATIONS table at end of article.

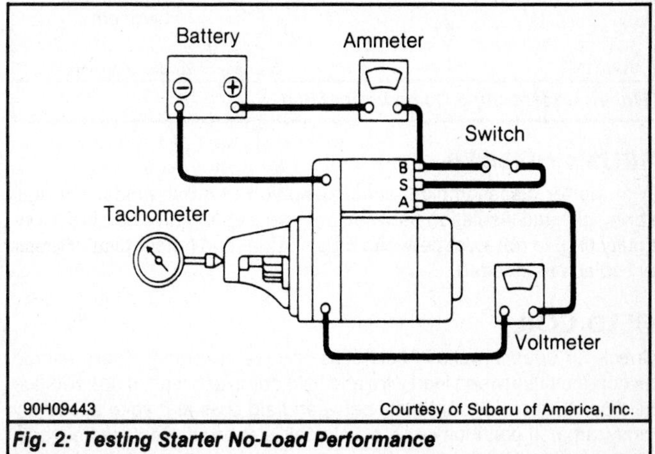


***Fig. 2: Testing Starter No-Load Performance***

**2)** Low rotating speed or excessive current draw may be caused by high friction rotating resistance caused by worn bushings or improper assembly.

# 1991 ELECTRICAL
# Starters – Direct Drive (Cont.)

## LOAD TEST

**1)** Using proper starter bench tester, apply 3.5 ft. lbs. (4.7 N.m) load to starter. Engage tester switch for less than 30 seconds. Note and record voltage drop and current draw.
**2)** Voltage should not fall below 8 volts. Current draw should be less that 200 amps. Starter should spin at 1200 RPM or more.

## LOCK TEST

**1)** Using proper starter bench tester, connect test equipment and lock starter armature. Engage tester momentarily, while measuring starter torque, current draw and voltage drop.
**2)** Voltage should not drop more than 5 volts from voltage at beginning of test. Current draw should be less than 400 amps. Starter should produce minimum torque of 6.5 ft. lbs. (9 N.m).
**3)** Low current draw and no torque during lock test may be caused by excessive resistance between brushes and commutator. Normal current draw, but low torque speed, may be caused by a shorted commutator and/or poor insulation.

## ARMATURE TEST

**1)** With starter disassembled, check armature for shorts using a growler. Hold hacksaw blade against armature while slowly rotating armature. A shorted armature will cause hacksaw blade to vibrate when passed over shorted area. Replace as necessary.
**2)** Use an ohmmeter to check for grounded armature. Touch one probe to each segment of commutator and hold other probe to armature core. If any continuity exists, replace armature.
**3)** Use ohmmeter to check for open circuit. If continuity is not present between any 2 commutator segments, replace armature. Check commutator for outside diameter wear, out-of-round and proper mica insulation depth. See NIPPONDENSO STARTER SPECIFICATIONS table at end of article.
**4)** When correcting out-of-round condition, do not reduce armature size beyond specification. If mica insulation is even or higher than commutator surface, mica insulation must be undercut. *See Fig. 3.* See NIPPONDENSO STARTER SPECIFICATIONS table at end of article.

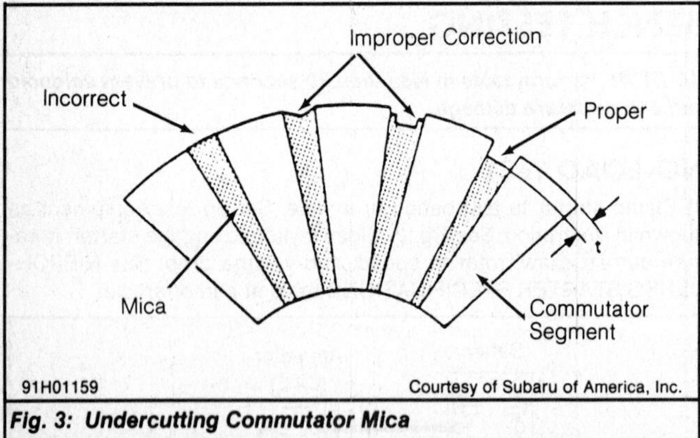


***Fig. 3: Undercutting Commutator Mica***

## BRUSH HOLDER

With starter disassembled, check condition of brush holder springs, spring clip and insulation between positive and negative holders. Continuity should not exist between brush holder and holder plate. Repair or replace as needed.

## FIELD COIL

Check for open circuits in field coils of yoke assembly. There should be continuity between lead wire and field coil brush lead. If not, replace field coil. Check for continuity between field coils and yoke assembly (end frame). If continuity exists, field coil is shorted. Replace field coil.

## OVERRUNNING CLUTCH

Ensure that pinion rotates smoothly in direction of rotation. Pinion should not rotate in opposite direction. Inspect teeth for excessive wear or damage. Replace as necessary.

## STARTER SOLENOID

**Shunt Coil Test –** Ensure continuity exists between solenoid start "S" terminal and solenoid body (ground). Ensure continuity exists between "M" and "S" solenoid terminals. If continuity does not exist, solenoid is open and requires replacement. *See Fig. 4.*

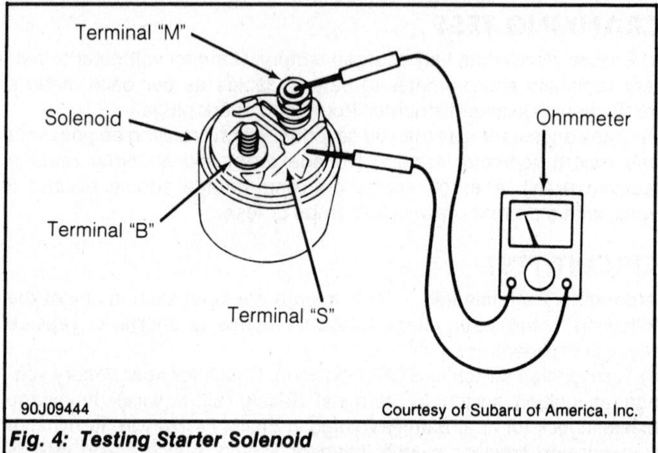


***Fig. 4: Testing Starter Solenoid***

**Contact Continuity Test –** Remove solenoid from starter. Continuity should exist between "M" terminal and "B" terminal with solenoid plunger pushed in. If continuity does not exist, replace solenoid.

# OVERHAUL

***NOTE: See Figs. 5 and 6 for exploded views of starters.***

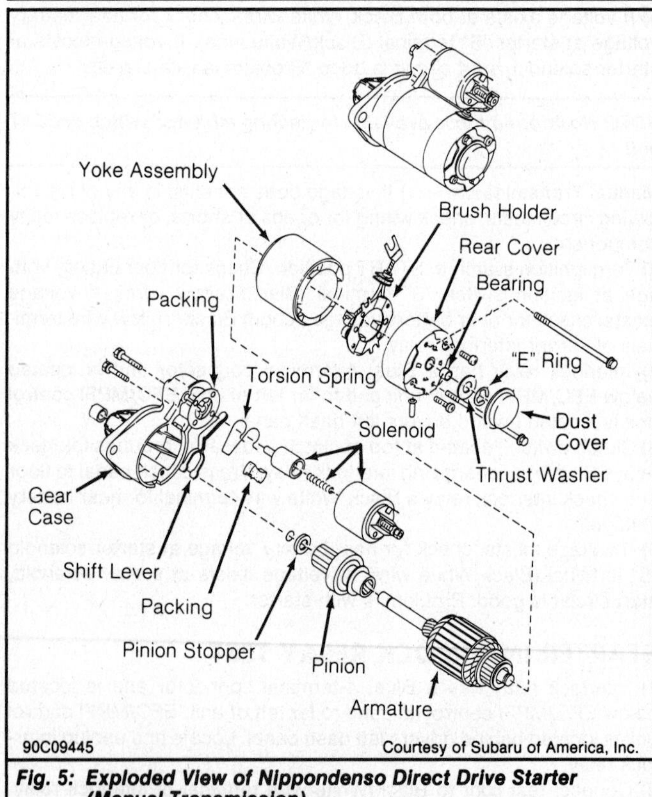


***Fig. 5: Exploded View of Nippondenso Direct Drive Starter (Manual Transmission)***

# 1991 ELECTRICAL
# Starters – Direct Drive (Cont.)

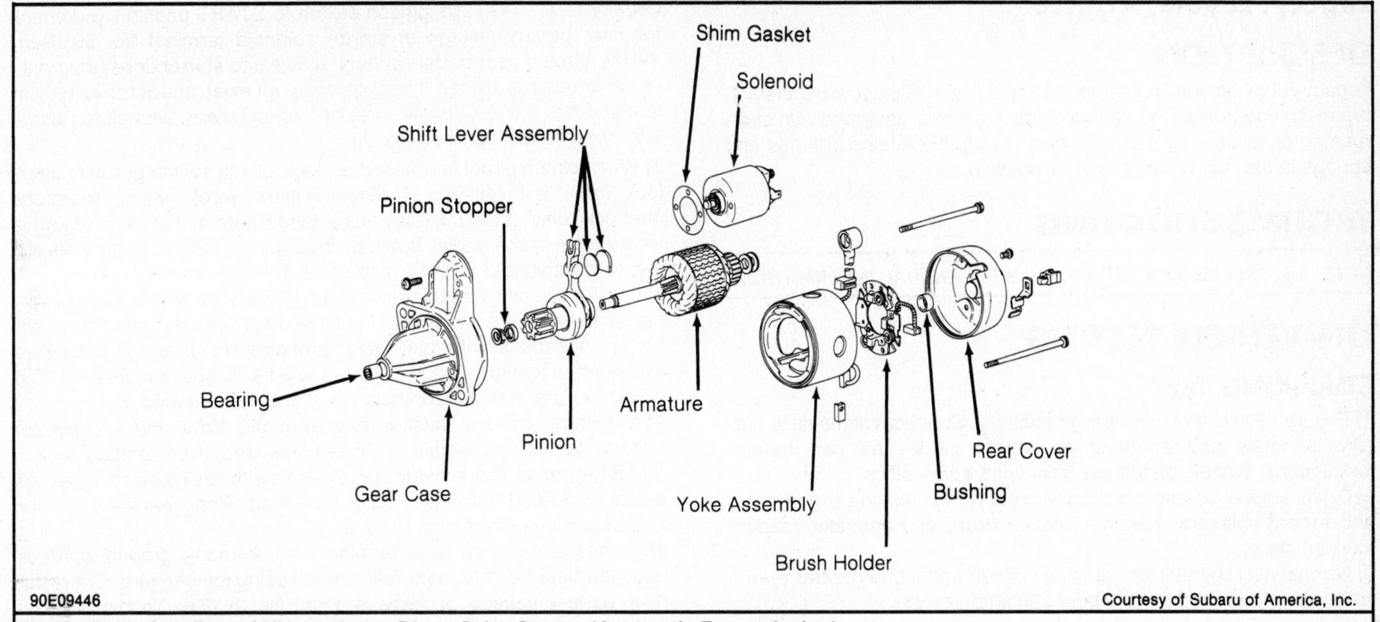


*Fig. 6: Exploded View of Nippondenso Direct Drive Starter (Automatic Transmission)*

## STARTER SPECIFICATIONS

*NIPPONDENSO STARTER SPECIFICATIONS*

| Application | Specification |
|---|---|
| Armature | |
| Out-Of-Round | |
| Standard | .002" (.05 mm) |
| Limit | .004" (.10 mm) |
| Carbon Brushes | |
| Brush Standard Length | .55" (14 mm) |
| Brush Minimum Length | .43" (11 mm) |
| Commutator | |
| Outside Diameter | |
| Standard | 1.30" (33 mm) |
| Limit | 1.26" (32 mm) |
| Mica Depth | |
| Standard | .02-.03" (.5-.8 mm) |
| Limit | .008" (.20 mm) |
| No-Load Test At 11.5 Volts | |
| Automatic Transmission | |
| Maximum Amps | 160 |
| Minimum RPM | 6600 |
| Manual Transmission | |
| Maximum Amps | 45 |
| Minimum RPM | 5500 |
| Pinion Gap | .012-.098" (.3-2.5 mm) |

## TORQUE SPECIFICATIONS

*TORQUE SPECIFICATIONS*

| Application | Ft. Lbs. (N.m) |
|---|---|
| Starter Bolts | [1] |
| | **INCH Lbs. (N.m)** |
| Long Through Bolts | 43-57 (4.9-6.4) |
| Rear Cover Screws | 15-21 (1.7-2.4) |
| Solenoid Bolts | 57-69 (6.4-7.8) |

[1] – Information is not available from manufacturer.

# 1991 ELECTRICAL
# Starters – Reduction Gear

### Legacy, Loyale, XT, XT6

## DESCRIPTION

Legacy & Loyale use Nippondenso and XT and XT6 use Mitsubishi 4-brush, solenoid-actuated, reduction gear starters, equipped with overrunning clutches. The 4-brush holder assembly retains brushes and springs in the rear cover of starter housing.

## TROUBLE SHOOTING

***NOTE:** See TROUBLE SHOOTING article in GENERAL INFORMATION.*

## ON-VEHICLE TESTING

### CRANKING TEST

**1)** Ensure vehicle has fully charged battery. Connect voltmeter to battery terminals and ammeter to battery cables as per meters' instructions. Disable distributor from firing spark plugs.
**2)** Crank engine for less than 30 seconds. When cranking engine, note and record voltmeter reading (voltage drop) and ammeter reading (current draw).
**3)** Normal average starter cranking voltage should be greater than 8 volts with a current draw of about 200 amps or less.

### CIRCUIT TEST

**Legacy A/T – 1)** Turn ignition switch to START position and check for near battery voltage at starter solenoid terminal No. 50 (Red/Yellow wire). If near battery voltage exists and starter does not crank, repair or replace starter. If voltage does not exist, check for voltage at inhibitor switch Red/Yellow wire terminal.
**2)** Inhibitor switch is located on gear select lever, under console. Ensure lever is in Park or Neutral. If voltage exists at inhibitor switch Red/Yellow wire terminal, check for open or short in wiring to starter. If low or no voltage exists at inhibitor switch, check inhibitor switch Blue/Red wire for input voltage when ignition switch is turned to START position.
**3)** If voltage exists at inhibitor switch Blue/Red wire terminal, replace inhibitor switch. If voltage does not exist at inhibitor switch Blue/Red wire terminal, check for near battery voltage at ignition switch "S" terminal (Blue/Red wire) when ignition switch is turned to START position. If voltage does not exist at ignition switch Blue/Red wire, check for battery voltage to ignition switch. If battery voltage exists at battery terminal (BAT) of switch, replace ignition switch.

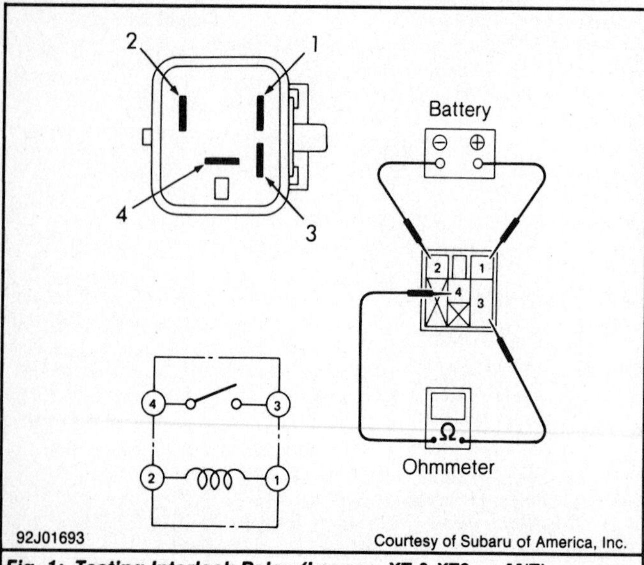


***Fig. 1:** Testing Interlock Relay (Legacy, XT & XT6 – M/T)*

**Legacy M/T – 1)** Turn ignition switch to START position and check for near battery voltage at starter solenoid terminal No. 50 (Red/Yellow wire). If near battery voltage exists and starter does not crank, repair or replace starter. If voltage does not exist, check for voltage at terminal No. 3 (Red/Yellow wire) of interlock relay with clutch pedal fully pressed to floor. *See Fig. 1.*
**2)** When clutch pedal is pressed to floor, clutch switch grounds interlock relay terminal No. 1 (Green/Yellow wire), which energizes interlock relay. Interlock relay has a Blue 4-terminal connector and is located on brake pedal bracket, next to brakelight switch. Clutch switch is located at top of clutch pedal arm.
**3)** If voltage exists at relay terminal No. 3 (Red/Yellow wire), repair wiring between relay and starter. If voltage does not exist, check for near battery voltage at interlock relay terminals No. 2 and 4 (Blue/Red wires) when ignition switch is turned to START position. *See Fig. 1.* If voltage exists at relay terminals No. 2 and 4, go to step **5)**.
**4)** If voltage does not exist at relay terminals No. 2 and 4, check for voltage to ignition switch BAT terminal and from ignition switch START terminal. Repair wiring or replace switch as required. If voltage exists at START terminal, repair Blue/Red wiring between ignition switch and relay terminals No. 2 and 4.
**5)** If voltage exists at relay terminals No. 2 and 4, ground interlock relay terminal No. 1 (Green/Yellow wire) using jumper wire. Check for near battery voltage at relay terminal No. 3 (Red/Yellow wire). If voltage exists, replace clutch switch. If voltage does not exist, replace relay.

**Loyale A/T – 1)** Ensure gear select lever is in Park or Neutral. Turn ignition switch to START position and check for near battery voltage at starter solenoid terminal No. 50 (Black/White wire). If near battery voltage exists and starter does not crank, repair or replace starter. If voltage does not exist, check for voltage at inhibitor switch Black/White wire terminal.
**2)** Inhibitor switch for models equipped with 3AT transmission is located on gear select lever, under console. Inhibitor switch for models equipped with 4AT transmission is located on transmission lever. If near battery voltage exists at inhibitor switch Black/White wire terminal, repair wiring between inhibitor switch and starter.
**3)** If voltage does not exist at inhibitor switch Black/White wire terminal, check for voltage at Black/Yellow wire terminal of transmission inhibitor switch. If voltage does not exist at inhibitor switch Black/Yellow wire terminal, check for voltage to ignition switch BAT terminal and from ignition switch START terminal to inhibitor switch Black/Yellow wire terminal. If voltage does not exist, repair wiring as required or replace ignition switch.

**Loyale M/T – 1)** Turn ignition switch to START position, press clutch pedal to floor and check for near battery voltage at starter solenoid terminal No. 50 (Black/White wire). If near battery voltage exists and starter does not crank, repair or replace starter. If voltage does not exist, check for voltage at clutch switch Black/White wire terminal when clutch pedal is pressed to floor.
**2)** Clutch switch is located at top of clutch pedal arm. If voltage exists at Black/White wire terminal of clutch switch, repair wiring between clutch switch and starter. If voltage does not exist, check for voltage at Black/Yellow wire terminal of clutch switch. If voltage exists, replace clutch switch.
**3)** If voltage does not exist at Black/Yellow wire terminal of clutch switch, check for near battery voltage at ignition switch "S" terminal (Black/Yellow wire). If voltage exists, repair Black/Yellow wire between ignition switch and clutch switch.
**4)** If voltage does not exist at ignition switch "S" terminal (Black/Yellow wire), check for battery voltage at ignition switch battery terminal. If voltage does not exist, replace ignition switch.

**XT & XT6 (A/T) – 1)** Ensure gear select lever is in Park or Neutral. Turn ignition switch to START position and check for near battery voltage at starter solenoid "S" terminal (Black/Yellow wire). If near battery voltage exists and starter does not crank, repair or replace starter. If voltage does not exist, check for voltage at inhibitor switch Black/Yellow wire terminal.

# 1991 ELECTRICAL
# Starters – Reduction Gear (Cont.)

**2)** Inhibitor switch is located on transmission lever. If voltage exists at inhibitor switch Black/Yellow wire terminal, repair wiring to starter. If voltage does not exist, check for voltage from ignition switch to inhibitor switch Black/White wire terminal.
**3)** If voltage exists at inhibitor switch Black/White wire terminal, replace inhibitor switch. If voltage does not exist, check for voltage at ignition switch "S" terminal (Black/White wire). If voltage exists here, repair Black/White wire between ignition switch and inhibitor switch. If voltage does not exist at ignition switch "S" terminal, replace ignition switch.
**XT & XT6 (M/T) – 1)** Turn ignition switch to START position, press clutch pedal to floor and check for near battery voltage at starter solenoid "S" terminal (Black/Red wire). If near battery voltage exists and starter does not crank, repair or replace starter. If voltage does not exist, check for voltage at interlock relay terminal No. 3 (Black/Red wire). *See Fig. 1.*
**2)** Interlock relay has a Blue 4-terminal connector and is located behind center console, above radio. When clutch pedal is pressed to floor, clutch switch grounds interlock relay terminal No. 1 (Green/Yellow wire), which energizes interlock relay. Clutch switch is located at top of clutch pedal arm.
**3)** If voltage exists at interlock relay terminal No. 3 (Black/Red wire), repair wiring to starter. If voltage does not exist, check for near battery voltage at interlock relay terminals No. 2 and 4 (Black/White wires) when ignition switch is turned to START position. *See Fig. 1.* If voltage exists at relay terminals No. 2 and 4, go to step **5)**.
**4)** If voltage does not exist at relay terminals No. 2 and 4, check for voltage to ignition switch BAT terminal and from ignition switch START terminal. Repair wiring or replace switch as required. If voltage exists at START terminal, repair Black/White wiring between ignition switch and interlock relay terminals No. 2 and 4.
**5)** If voltage exists at relay terminals No. 2 and 4, ground interlock relay terminal No. 1 (Green/Yellow wire) using jumper wire. Check for near battery voltage at relay terminal No. 3 (Black/Red wire). If voltage exists, replace clutch switch. If voltage does not exist, replace relay.

## STARTER INTERLOCK RELAY TEST

**Legacy M/T – 1)** Interlock relay has a Blue 4-terminal connector and is located on brake pedal bracket, next to brakelight switch. Locate and unplug relay.
**2)** Connect test light to terminal No. 3 (Red/Yellow wire) of interlock relay. *See Fig. 1.* Using jumper wire, apply 12 volts to terminals No. 2 and 4 (Blue/Red wires) of relay. Using another jumper wire, connected to ground, momentarily touch terminal No. 1 (Green/Yellow wire) of relay. If test light does not illuminate, replace relay.
**XT M/T – 1)** Interlock relay has a Blue 4-terminal connector and is located behind center console, above radio. Clutch switch is located at top of clutch pedal arm.
**2)** Connect test light to terminal No. 3 (Black/Red wire) of interlock relay. *See Fig. 1.* Using jumper wire, apply 12 volts to terminals No. 2 and 4 (Black/White wires) of relay. Using another jumper wire, connected to ground, momentarily touch terminal No. 1 (Green/Yellow wire) of relay. Test light should illuminate. If test light does not illuminate, replace relay.

## IGNITION SWITCH TEST

**Start Circuit Test – 1)** Remove lower instrument panel below steering wheel. Remove air duct. Remove harness connector from rear of ignition switch.
**2)** Using jumper wire, apply 12 volts to ignition switch terminal "B". Connect test light to switch terminal "S". Turn ignition switch to START position. If test light does not illuminate, replace relay.
**Continuity Test –** Ensure continuity is as specified. See IGNITION SWITCH CONTINUITY SPECIFICATIONS table. *See Fig. 2.* Repair or replace as necessary.

*IGNITION SWITCH CONTINUITY SPECIFICATIONS*

| Switch Position | Continuity Between Terminals |
|---|---|
| Lock | No Continuity |
| OFF | No Continuity |
| ACC | A & B |
| ON | A, B & IG |
| START | B, IG, [1] R & S |

[1] – XT & XT6 models do not have terminal "R".

Ignition Switch Harness Connector
A B
START ON ACC LOCK
R IG S

91J03932 Courtesy of Subaru of America, Inc.

*Fig. 2: Identifying Ignition Switch Testing Terminals*

## BENCH TESTING

***CAUTION: Perform tests in less than 30 seconds to prevent solenoid coil and armature damage.***

## NO-LOAD TEST

**1)** Clamp starter in bench tester or in vise. Connect test equipment to starter. *See Fig. 3.* Close switch to engage starter. Measure current draw, rotating speed and voltage drop. See STARTER SPECIFICATIONS table at end of article.
**2)** Low rotating speed or excessive current draw may be caused by high friction rotating resistance caused by worn bushings or improper assembly.

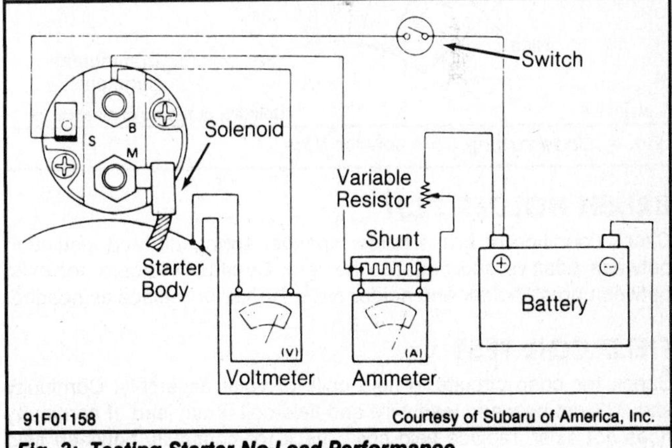


*Fig. 3: Testing Starter No-Load Performance (XT Shown; Others Are Similar)*

## LOAD TEST

**1)** Using proper starter bench tester, connect test equipment and apply specified load to starter. See STARTER SPECIFICATIONS table at end of article. Engage tester switch for less than 30 seconds. Note and record voltage drop and current draw.
**2)** Voltage should not drop to less than 8 volts. On A/T models, current draw should be less than 370 amps and rotating speed should be greater than 880 RPM. On M/T models, see STARTER SPECIFICATIONS table.

# 1991 ELECTRICAL
# Starters – Reduction Gear (Cont.)

## LOCK TEST

**1)** Using proper starter bench tester, connect test equipment and lock starter armature. Engage tester momentarily while measuring starter torque, current draw and voltage drop.

**2)** Check specifications for minimum torque, voltage drop (minimum volts) and current draw (maximum amps). See STARTER SPECIFICATIONS table at end of article.

**3)** Low current draw and no torque during lock test may be caused by excessive resistance between brushes and commutator. Normal current draw but low torque speed may be caused by a shorted commutator and/or poor insulation.

## ARMATURE TEST

**1)** With starter disassembled, check armature for shorts using a growler. Hold hacksaw blade against armature while slowly rotating armature. A shorted armature will cause hacksaw blade to vibrate when passed over shorted area. Replace as necessary.

**2)** Use an ohmmeter to check for grounded armature. Touch one probe to each segment of commutator and hold other probe to armature core. If continuity exists, replace armature.

**3)** Use ohmmeter to check for open circuit. If continuity is not present between any 2 commutator segments, replace armature. Check commutator for outside diameter wear, runout and mica insulation depth. See STARTER SPECIFICATIONS table at end of article.

**4)** If correcting runout condition, DO NOT reduce armature size beyond specification. Undercut mica insulation if it is even or higher than commutator surface. *See Fig. 4*. See STARTER SPECIFICATIONS table.

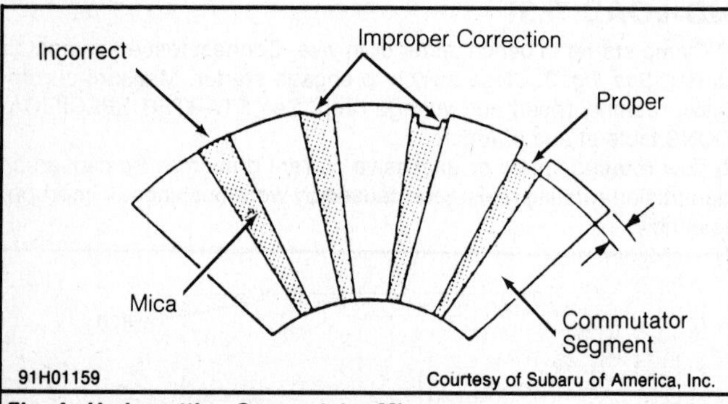


***Fig. 4: Undercutting Commutator Mica***

## BRUSH HOLDER TEST

Check condition of brush holder springs, spring clip and insulation between positive and negative holders. Continuity should not exist between brush holder and holder plate. Repair or replace as needed.

## FIELD COIL TEST

Check for open circuits in field coils of yoke assembly. Continuity should exist between lead wire and field coil brush lead. If continuity does not exist, replace field coil. Check for continuity between field coils and yoke assembly (end frame). If continuity exists, field coil is shorted to ground. Replace field coil.

## OVERRUNNING CLUTCH TEST

Ensure pinion rotates smoothly in direction of rotation. Pinion should not rotate in opposite direction. Inspect teeth for excessive wear and damage. Replace as necessary.

## SOLENOID TESTS

**Shunt Coil Test (XT & XT6)** – Ensure continuity exists between solenoid terminal "S" and solenoid body (ground). Ensure continuity exists between solenoid terminals "M" and "S". If continuity does not exist, solenoid is open and requires replacement.

**Contact Continuity Test (XT & XT6)** – Continuity should exist between terminal "M" and terminal "B" with solenoid plunger pushed in. If continuity does not exist, replace solenoid.

**Solenoid Pull-In Test (Legacy & Loyale)** – Connect 2 jumper wires from negative terminal of 12-volt battery to starter solenoid case and to terminal "C". *See Fig. 5*. Pinion should extend when jumper wire from battery positive terminal is connected to solenoid terminal No. 50. If pinion does not extend as specified, replace starter.

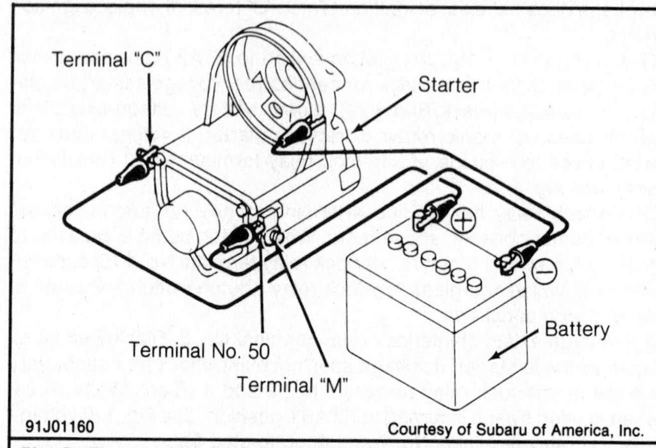


***Fig. 5: Testing Starter Solenoid Pull-In & Hold-In Windings (Legacy & Loyale)***

**Solenoid Hold-In Test (Legacy & Loyale)** – Disconnect jumper wire from solenoid terminal "C" with pinion extended. Pinion should remain extended. If pinion does not remain extended, replace starter.

**Pinion Gear Return Test (Legacy & Loyale)** – Connect 2 jumper wires from negative terminal of 12-volt battery to starter solenoid case and to terminal No. 50. *See Fig. 6*. Momentarily touch positive jumper wire to terminal "C". Pinion gear should return immediately. If pinion gear does not return immediately, replace starter.

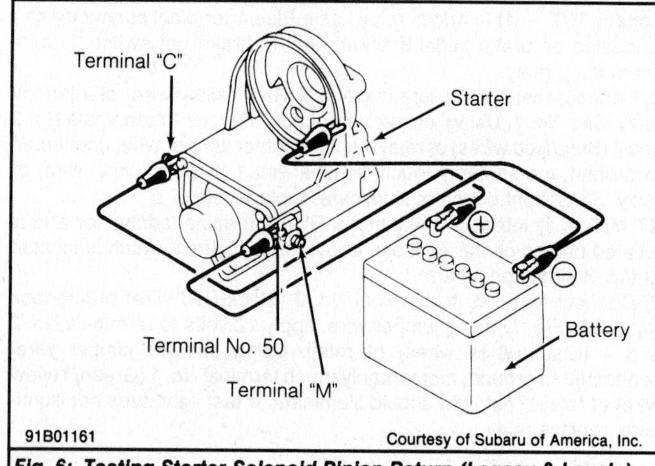


***Fig. 6: Testing Starter Solenoid Pinion Return (Legacy & Loyale)***

## OVERHAUL

***NOTE: For exploded view of starter, see Fig. 7, 8 or 9.***

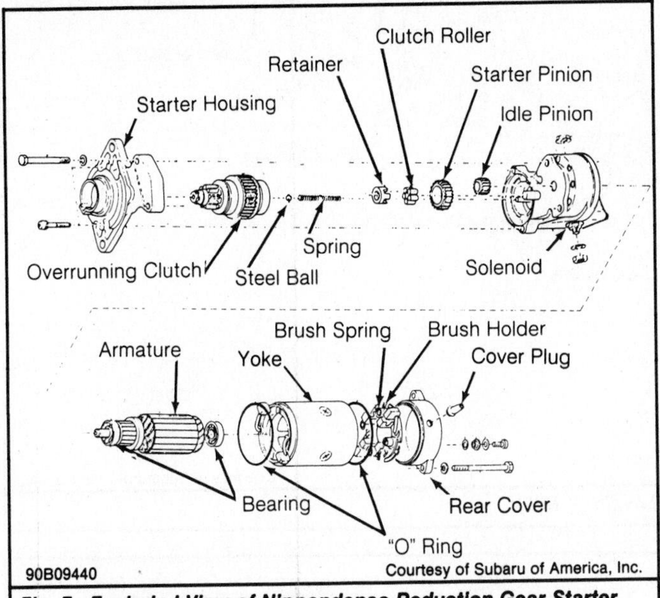


***Fig. 7: Exploded View of Nippondenso Reduction Gear Starter (Legacy & Loyale – A/T)***

## STARTER SPECIFICATIONS

*STARTER SPECIFICATIONS*

| Application | Specification |
|---|---|
| Carbon Brushes | |
| Legacy A/T & Loyale | |
| Minimum Length | .39" (10.0 mm) |
| Standard Length | .59" (15.0 mm) |
| Legacy M/T | |
| Minimum Length | .34" (8.5 mm) |
| Standard Length | .51" (13.0 mm) |
| XT & XT6 | |
| A/T | |
| Minimum Length | .47" (12.0 mm) |
| Standard Length | .69" (17.5 mm) |
| M/T | |
| Minimum Length | .45" (11.5 mm) |
| Standard Length | .67" (17.0 mm) |
| Commutator | |
| Runout | |
| Legacy & Loyale | |
| Limit | .002" (.050 mm) |
| Standard | .0008" (.020 mm) |
| XT & XT6 | |
| Limit | .0039" (.100 mm) |
| Standard | .002" (.05 mm) |
| Outside Diameter | |
| Limit | 1.14" (29.0 mm) |
| Standard | 1.18" (30.0 mm) |
| Mica Depth | |
| Limit | .008" (.20 mm) |
| Standard | .020-.031" (.50-.80 mm) |

*STARTER SPECIFICATIONS (Cont.)*

| Application | Specification |
|---|---|
| No-Load Test | |
| Legacy | |
| Maximum Amps | 90 Amps |
| Minimum RPM | |
| A/T | 3350 RPM |
| M/T | 3000 RPM |
| Voltage Drop (Minimum) | 11 Volts |
| Loyale | |
| Maximum Amps | 90 Amps |
| Minimum RPM | |
| A/T | 4000 RPM |
| M/T | 3000 RPM |
| Voltage Drop (Minimum) | 11 Volts |
| XT & XT6 | |
| Maximum Amps | 90 Amps |
| Minimum RPM | |
| A/T | 2900 RPM |
| M/T | 3000 RPM |
| Voltage Drop (Minimum) | 11 Volts |
| Load Test | |
| Legacy | |
| Load | 7 Ft. Lbs. (10 N.m) |
| Maximum Amps (M/T) | 280 Amps |
| Minimum RPM (M/T) | 900 RPM |
| Voltage Drop (Minimum) | 8 Volts |
| Loyale | |
| Load | 4.7 Ft. Lbs. (6.4 N.m) |
| Maximum Amps (M/T) | 230 Amps |
| Minimum RPM (M/T) | 1180 RPM |
| Voltage Drop (Minimum) | 8 Volts |
| XT & XT6 | |
| Load | 6.3 Ft. Lbs. (8.5 N.m) |
| Maximum Amps (M/T) | 280 Amps |
| Minimum RPM (M/T) | 980 RPM |
| Voltage Drop (Minimum) | 8 Volts |
| Lock Test | |
| Legacy | |
| Minimum Voltage | 5 Volts |
| Maximum Amps | |
| A/T | 735 Amps |
| M/T | 800 Amps |
| Minimum Torque | 20 Ft. Lbs. (27 N.m) |
| Loyale | |
| A/T | |
| Minimum Voltage | 5 Volts |
| Maximum Amps | 735 Amps |
| Minimum Torque | 20 Ft. Lbs. (27 N.m) |
| M/T | |
| Minimum Voltage | 2.5 Volts |
| Maximum Amps | 300 Amps |
| Minimum Torque | 5.1 Ft. Lbs. (7 N.m) |
| XT & XT6 | |
| A/T | |
| Minimum Voltage | 4 Volts |
| Maximum Amps | 980 Amps |
| Minimum Torque | 19 Ft. Lbs. (25 N.m) |
| M/T | |
| Minimum Voltage | 4 Volts |
| Maximum Amps | 780 Amps |
| Minimum Torque | 13 Ft. Lbs. (18 N.m) |

## TORQUE SPECIFICATIONS

*TORQUE SPECIFICATIONS*

| Application | Ft. Lbs. (N.m) |
|---|---|
| Starter Bolts | [1] |

[1] – Information is not available from manufacturer.

# 1991 ELECTRICAL
## Starters – Reduction Gear (Cont.)

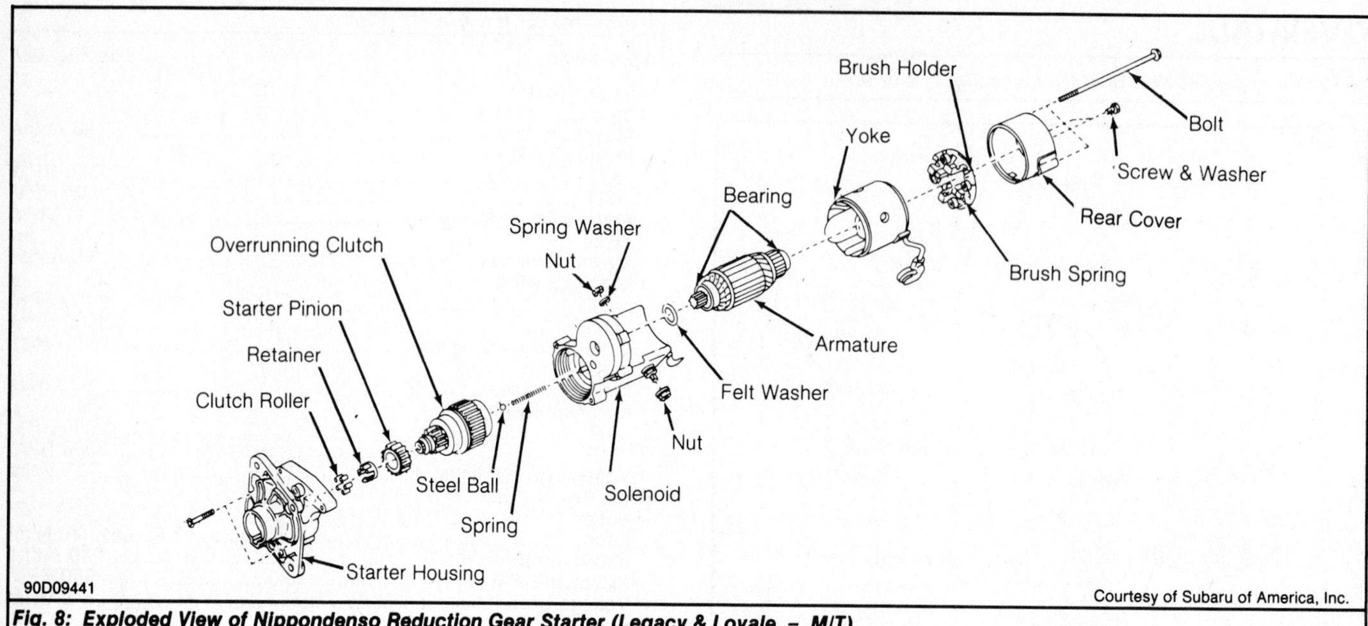


***Fig. 8:* Exploded View of Nippondenso Reduction Gear Starter (Legacy & Loyale – M/T)**

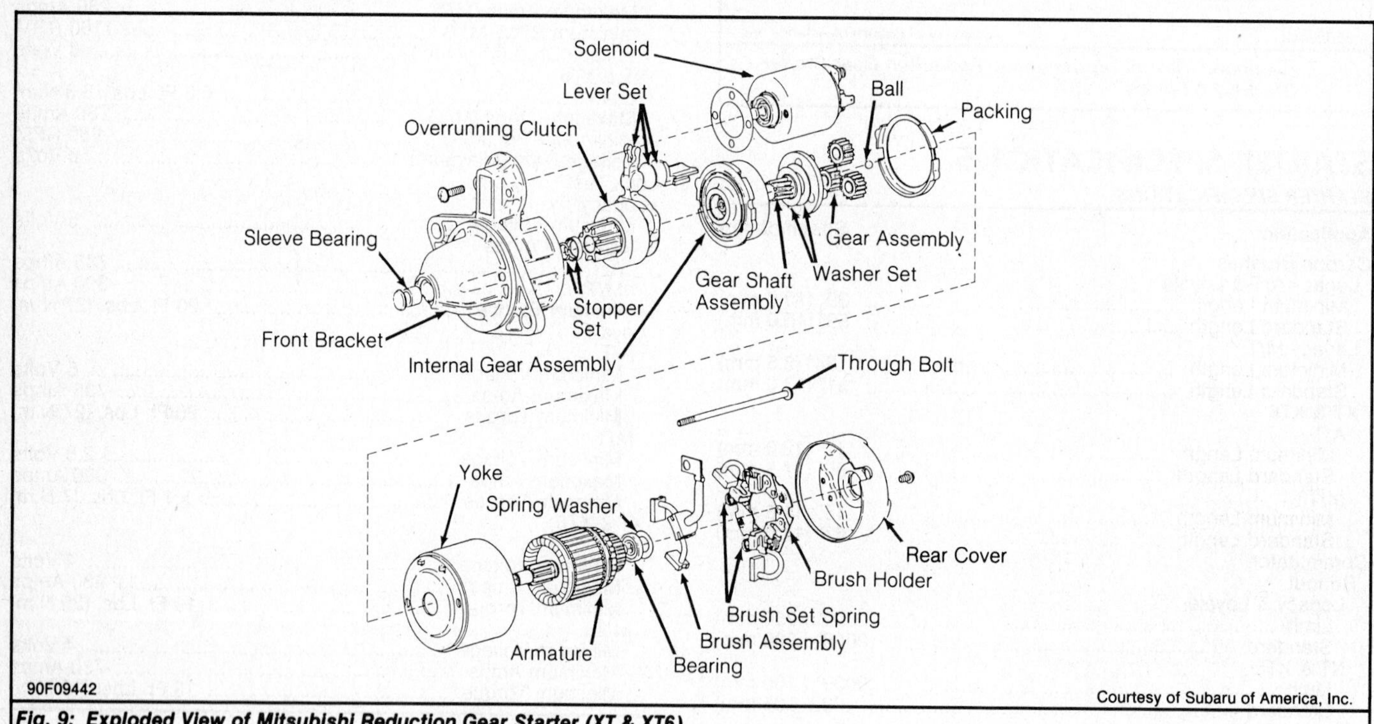


***Fig. 9:* Exploded View of Mitsubishi Reduction Gear Starter (XT & XT6)**

# 1991 WIRING DIAGRAMS
## Justy

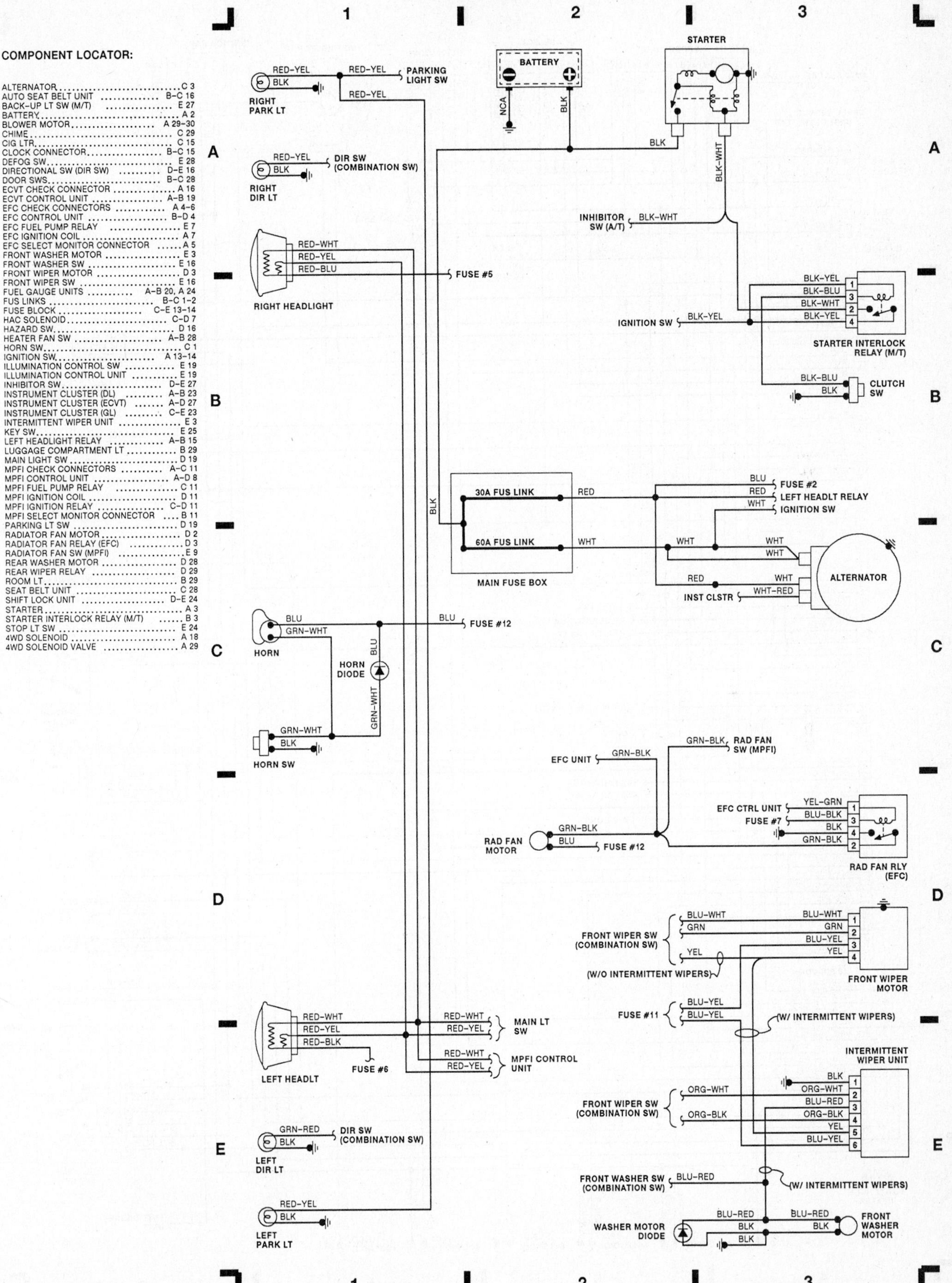
COMPONENT LOCATOR:
ALTERNATOR .......... C 3
AUTO SEAT BELT UNIT .......... B-C 16
BACK-UP LT SW (M/T) .......... E 27
BATTERY .......... A 2
BLOWER MOTOR .......... A 29-30
CHIME .......... C 29
CIG LTR .......... C 15
CLOCK CONNECTOR .......... B-C 15
DEFOG SW .......... E 28
DIRECTIONAL SW (DIR SW) .......... D-E 16
DOOR SWS .......... B-C 28
ECVT CHECK CONNECTOR .......... A 16
ECVT CONTROL UNIT .......... A-B 19
EFC CHECK CONNECTORS .......... A 4-6
EFC CONTROL UNIT .......... B-D 4
EFC FUEL PUMP RELAY .......... E 7
EFC IGNITION COIL .......... A 7
EFC SELECT MONITOR CONNECTOR .......... A 5
FRONT WASHER MOTOR .......... E 3
FRONT WASHER SW .......... E 16
FRONT WIPER MOTOR .......... D 3
FRONT WIPER SW .......... E 16
FUEL GAUGE UNITS .......... A-B 20, A 24
FUS LINKS .......... B-C 1-2
FUSE BLOCK .......... C-E 13-14
HAC SOLENOID .......... C-D 7
HAZARD SW .......... D 16
HEATER FAN SW .......... A-B 28
HORN SW .......... C 1
IGNITION SW .......... A 13-14
ILLUMINATION CONTROL SW .......... E 19
ILLUMINATION CONTROL UNIT .......... E 19
INHIBITOR SW .......... D-E 27
INSTRUMENT CLUSTER (DL) .......... A-B 23
INSTRUMENT CLUSTER (ECVT) .......... A-D 27
INSTRUMENT CLUSTER (GL) .......... C-E 23
INTERMITTENT WIPER UNIT .......... E 3
KEY SW .......... E 25
LEFT HEADLIGHT RELAY .......... A-B 15
LUGGAGE COMPARTMENT LT .......... B 29
MAIN LIGHT SW .......... D 19
MPFI CHECK CONNECTORS .......... A-C 11
MPFI CONTROL UNIT .......... A-D 8
MPFI FUEL PUMP RELAY .......... C 11
MPFI IGNITION COIL .......... D 11
MPFI IGNITION RELAY .......... C-D 11
MPFI SELECT MONITOR CONNECTOR .......... B 11
PARKING LT SW .......... D 19
RADIATOR FAN MOTOR .......... D 2
RADIATOR FAN RELAY (EFC) .......... D 3
RADIATOR FAN SW (MPFI) .......... E 9
REAR WASHER MOTOR .......... D 28
REAR WIPER RELAY .......... D 29
ROOM LT .......... B 29
SEAT BELT UNIT .......... C 28
SHIFT LOCK UNIT .......... D-E 24
STARTER .......... A 3
STARTER INTERLOCK RELAY (M/T) .......... B 3
STOP LT SW .......... E 24
4WD SOLENOID .......... A 18
4WD SOLENOID VALVE .......... A 29
1
2
3
A
B
C
D
E
RED-YEL
BLK
RIGHT PARK LT
PARKING LIGHT SW
BATTERY
NCA
STARTER
BLK-WHT
DIR SW (COMBINATION SW)
RIGHT DIR LT
INHIBITOR SW (A/T)
RED-WHT
RED-BLU
FUSE #5
RIGHT HEADLIGHT
BLK-YEL
BLK-BLU
IGNITION SW
STARTER INTERLOCK RELAY (M/T)
CLUTCH SW
30A FUS LINK
60A FUS LINK
MAIN FUSE BOX
RED
WHT
BLU
FUSE #2
LEFT HEADLT RELAY
IGNITION SW
ALTERNATOR
WHT-RED
INST CLSTR
GRN-WHT
FUSE #12
HORN
HORN DIODE
HORN SW
GRN-BLK
RAD FAN SW (MPFI)
EFC UNIT
EFC CTRL UNIT
YEL-GRN
BLU-BLK
FUSE #7
RAD FAN MOTOR
RAD FAN RLY (EFC)
FRONT WIPER SW (COMBINATION SW)
BLU-WHT
GRN
BLU-YEL
YEL
(W/O INTERMITTENT WIPERS)
FRONT WIPER MOTOR
FUSE #11
(W/ INTERMITTENT WIPERS)
RED-BLK
MAIN LT SW
MPFI CONTROL UNIT
FUSE #6
LEFT HEADLT
INTERMITTENT WIPER UNIT
ORG-WHT
ORG-BLK
BLU-RED
GRN-RED
LEFT DIR LT
LEFT PARK LT
FRONT WASHER SW (COMBINATION SW)
WASHER MOTOR DIODE
FRONT WASHER MOTOR

# 1991 WIRING DIAGRAMS
## Justy (Cont.)

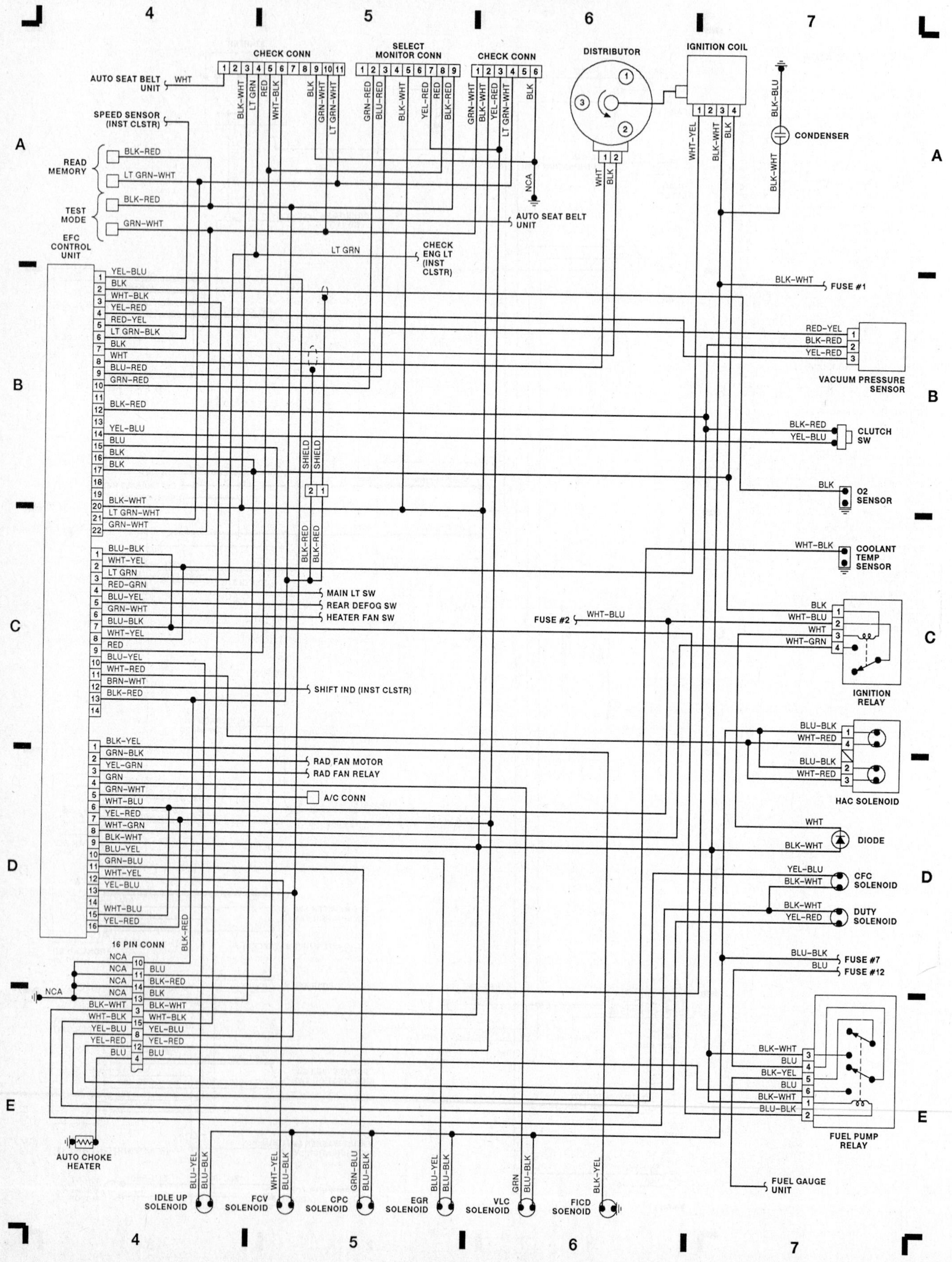

# 1991 WIRING DIAGRAMS
## Justy (Cont.)

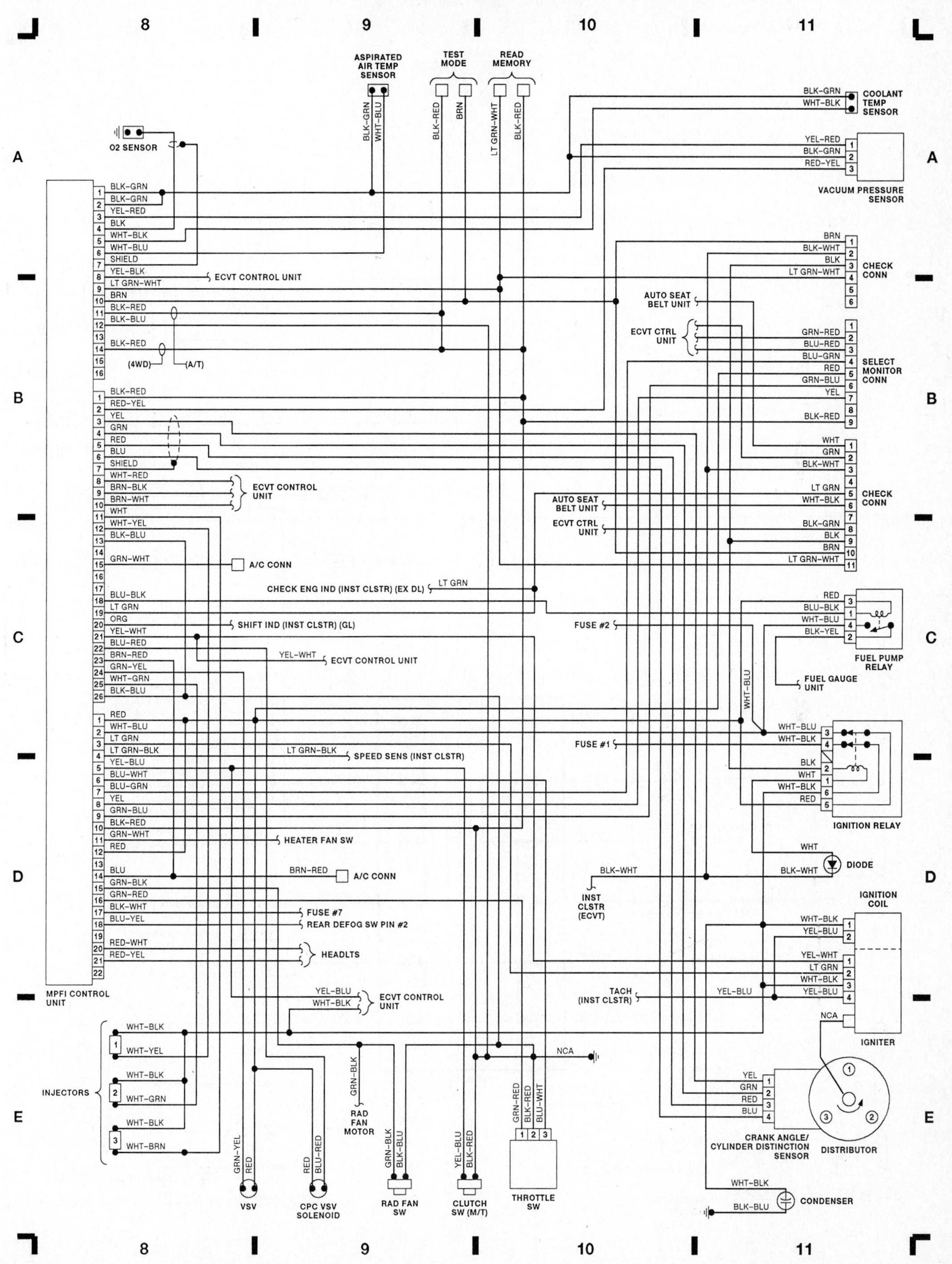

# 1991 WIRING DIAGRAMS
## Justy (Cont.)

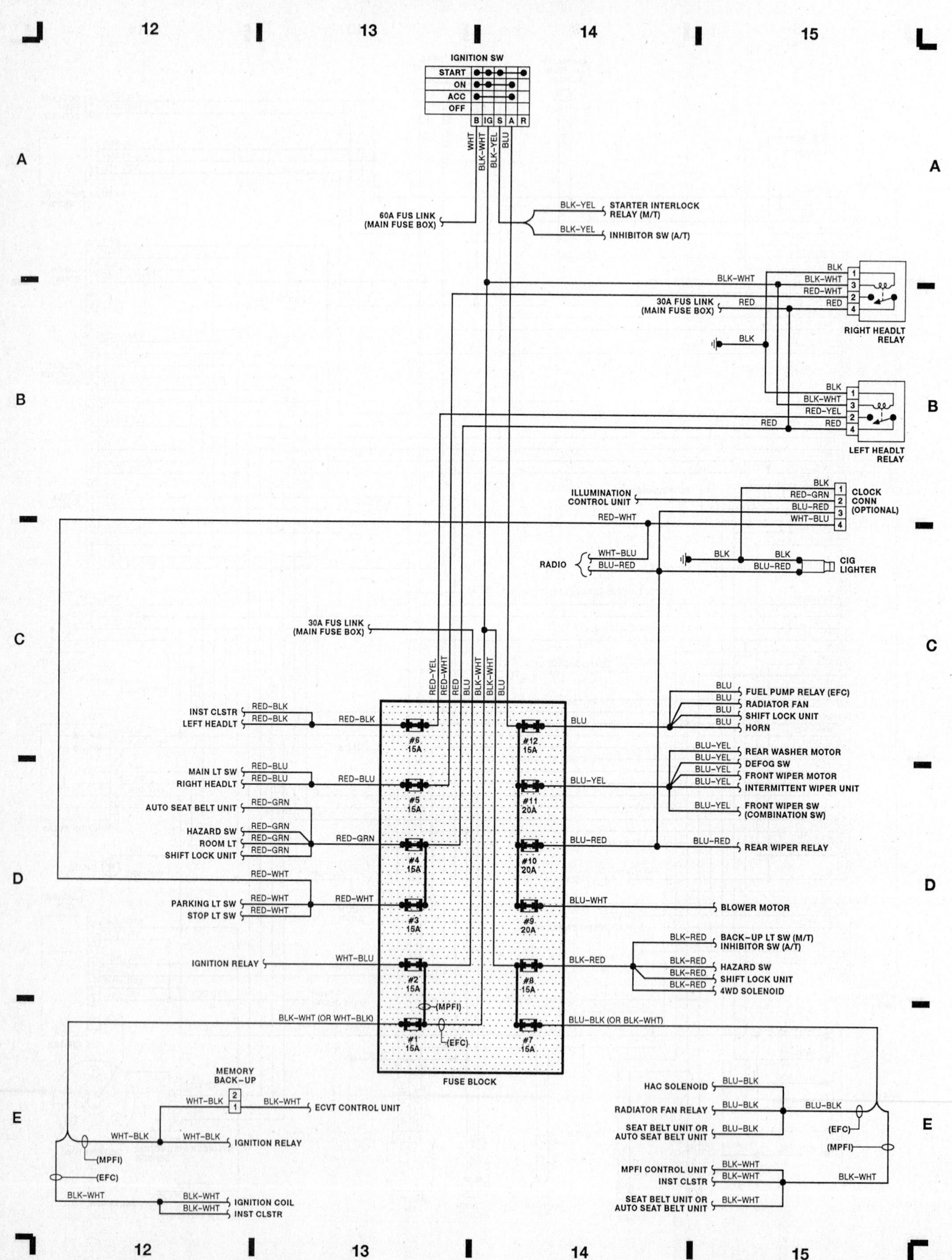

# 1991 WIRING DIAGRAMS
## Justy (Cont.)

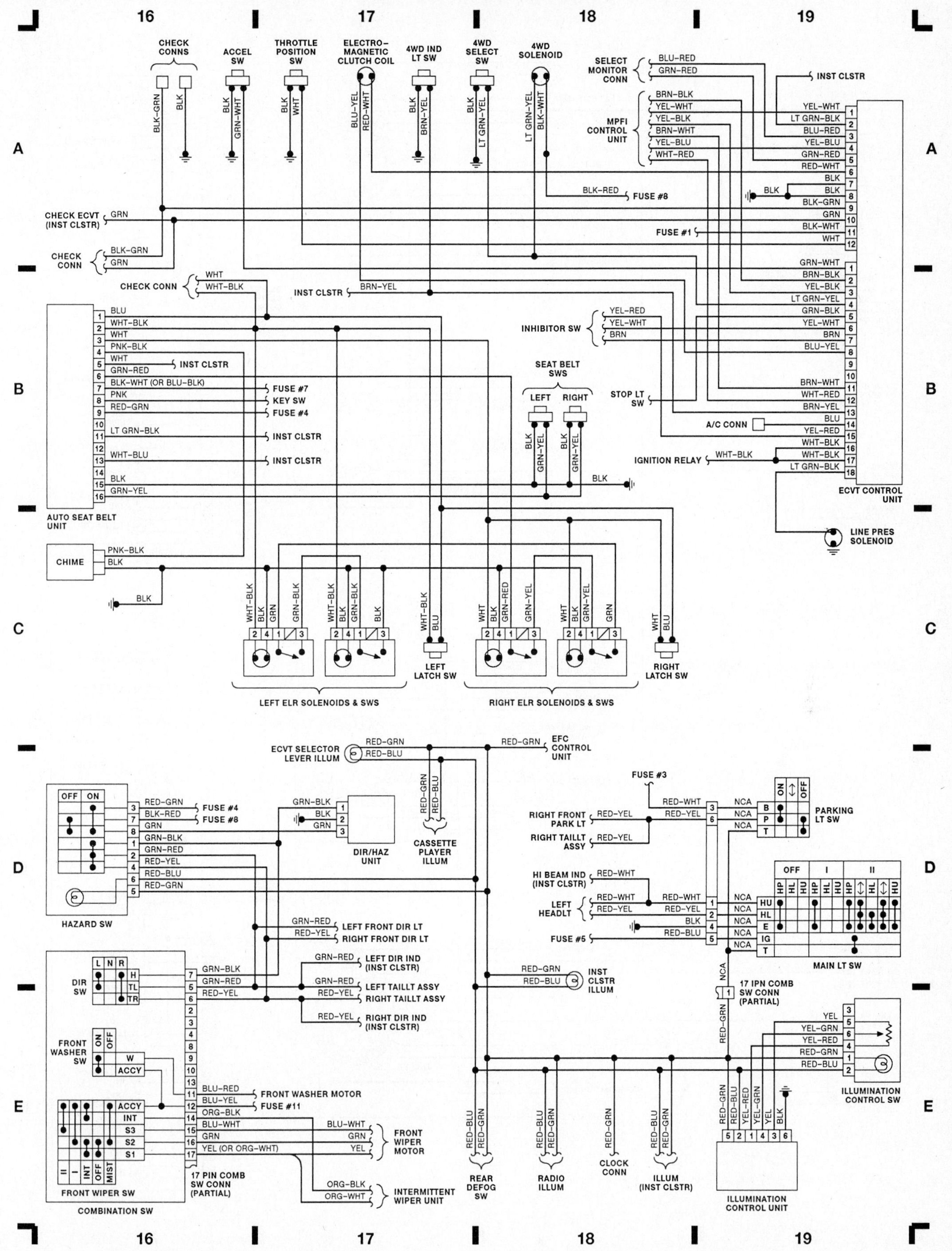

# 1991 WIRING DIAGRAMS
## Justy (Cont.)

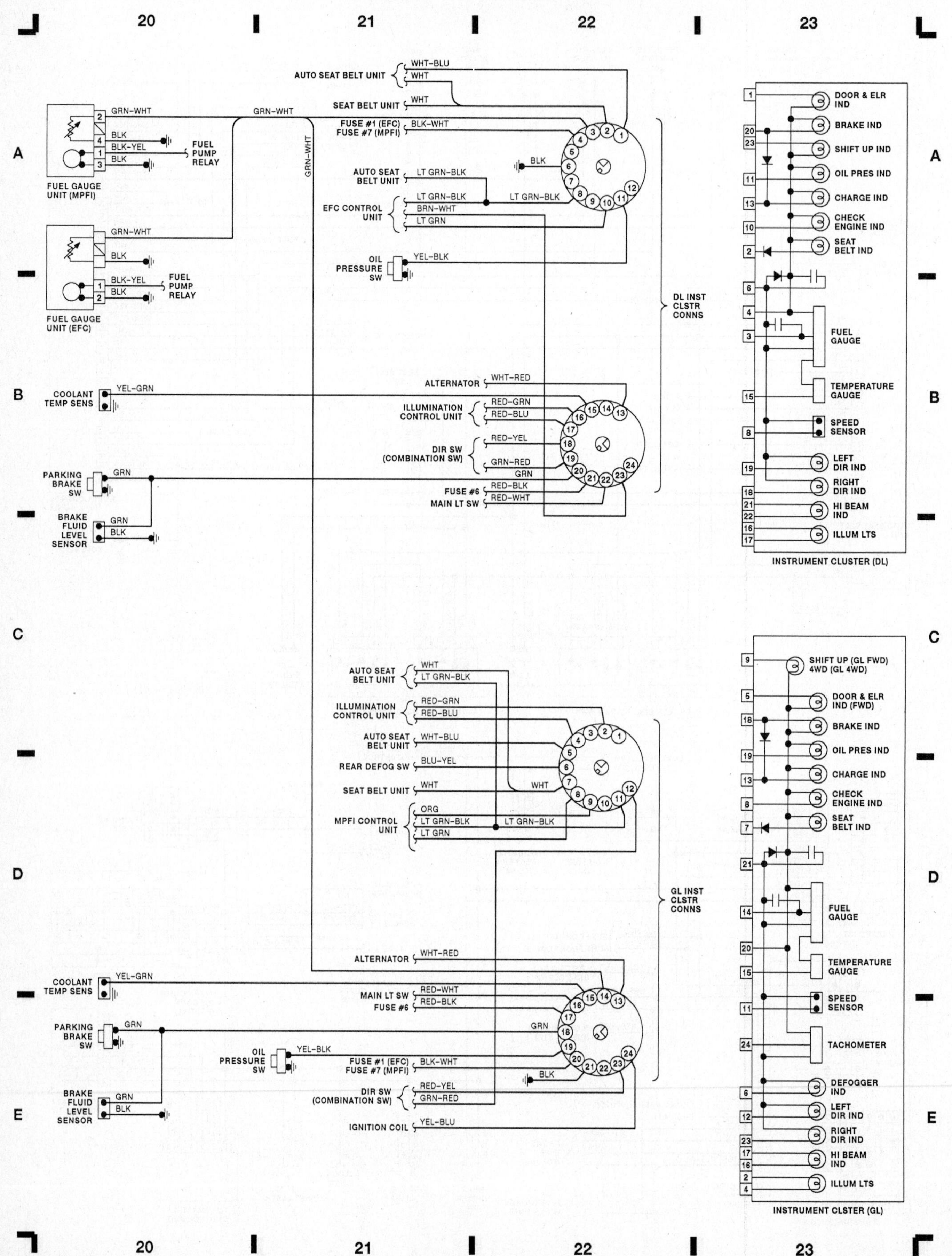

# 1991 WIRING DIAGRAMS
## Justy (Cont.)

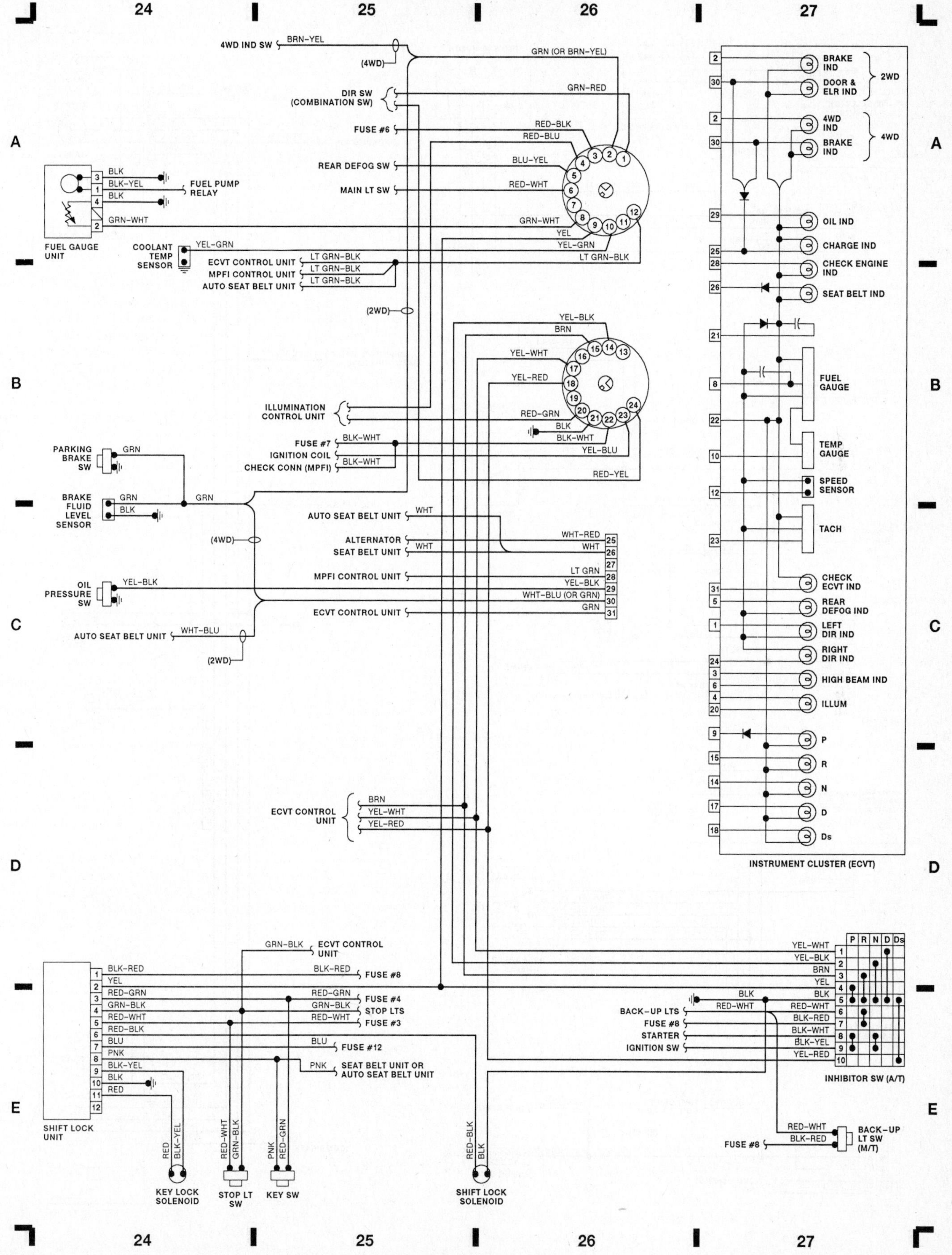

# 1991 WIRING DIAGRAMS
## Justy (Cont.)

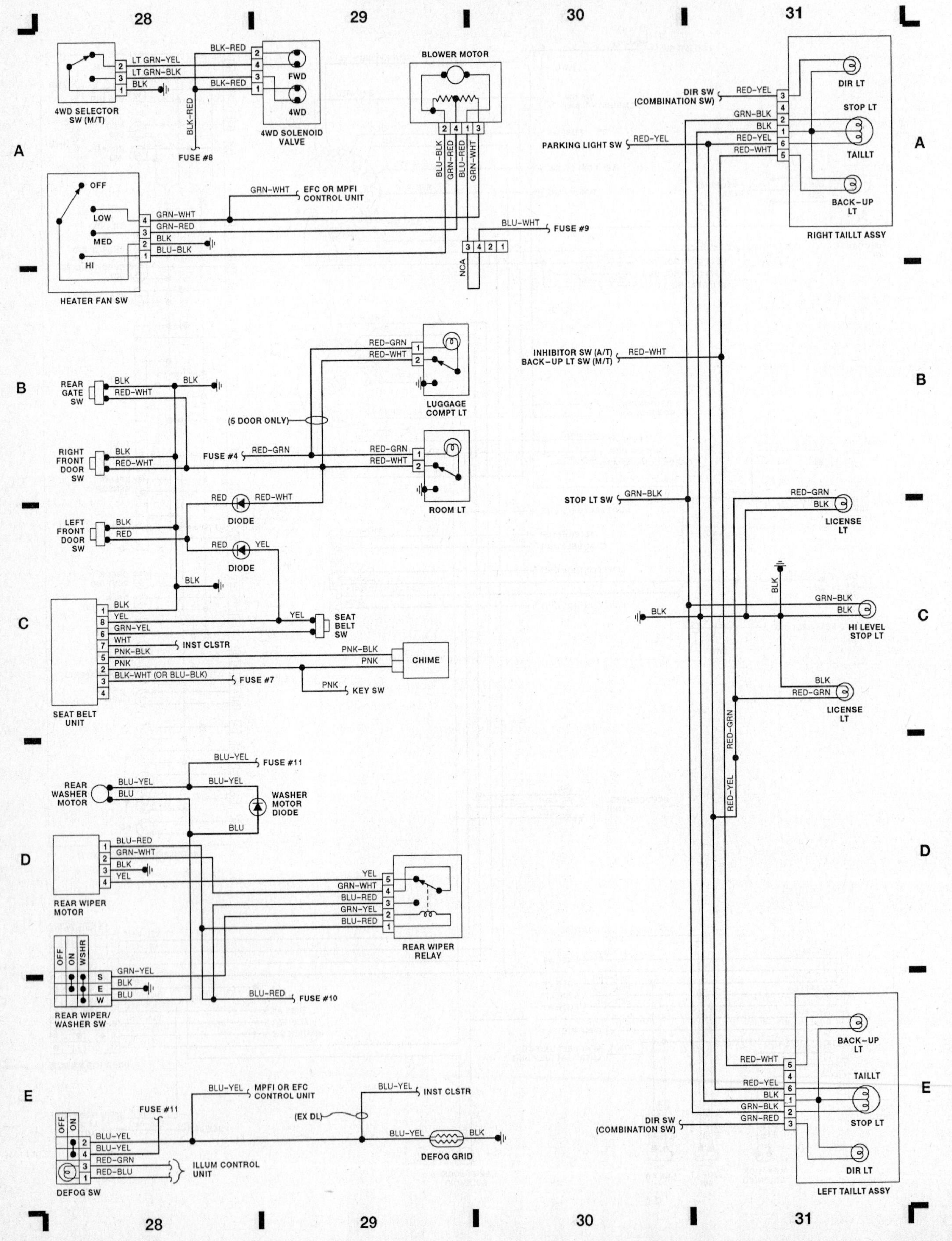

# 1991 WIRING DIAGRAMS
## Legacy

**COMPONENT LOCATOR:**

| | |
|---|---|
| A/C AUTO CONTROL UNIT | A–C 28 |
| A/C CUT RELAY | D–E 31 |
| A/C RELAY BOX | C–E 28 |
| A/T CONTROL UNIT | A–C 16 |
| ABS HYDRAULIC UNIT | C–D 23 |
| AIR SUSP COMP & DISCHARGE SOLENOID | D 24 |
| AIR SUSP COMP RELAY | D 27 |
| AIR SUSP SOLENOIDS | D–E 27 |
| ALTERNATOR | D 3 |
| ANTI–LOCK BRAKE CONTROL UNIT | C–E 20 |
| AUTO SHOULDER BELT CONTROL UNIT | A 41–42 |
| BACK–UP LT SW (M/T) | D 19 |
| BATTERY | A 2 |
| BLOWER MOTOR | B 35 |
| BLOWER RELAY | D 31 |
| CHECK CONNECTOR | A–B 11 |
| CIG LTR | C 15 |
| COOLANT TEMP SENSOR | E 6 |
| CRUISE CONTROL DIODE | A–B 20 |
| CRUISE CONTROL MAIN SW | B 21 |
| CRUISE CONTROL SUB SW | B–C 23 |
| CRUISE CONTROL UNIT | A 21–22 |
| DELAY AMP (4WD) | E 45 |
| DIAGNOSTIC CONNECTOR | A 22 |
| DIMMER/PASSING SW | D 32 |
| DIODE | E 7 |
| DIR SW | C 32 |
| DOME LT | C–D 39 |
| DOOR SWS | B–C 39 |
| EVAP TEMP SW | A 31 |
| FAN SW | A 35 |
| FRESH/RECIRC ACTUATOR | B 35 |
| FRONT WASHER MOTOR | A 34 |
| FUEL PUMP | E 7 |
| FUEL PUMP RELAY | E 7 |
| FUEL TANK UNIT | E 44 |
| FUSE/RELAY BOX (F/B) | C–E 12–15 |
| HAZARD SW | C 32 |
| HEIGHT CONTROL SW | C 24 |
| HEIGHT CONTROL UNIT | A–B 24 |
| HORN RELAY & SW | D 1 |
| IGNITION COIL | E 8 |
| IGNITION RELAY | D 7 |
| IGNITION SW | A 12 |
| ILLUMINATION LTS CONTROL UNIT | D 35 |
| INHIBITOR SW | C–D 19 |
| INSTRUMENT CLUSTER | A–E 36 |
| KEY WARNING SW | |
| LEFT FRONT DOOR LOCK SW | C–D 40–43 |
| LIGHT SW | D 32 |
| MAIN FAN A/C RELAY | D 28 |
| MAIN FAN MOTOR | E 28 |
| MAIN FAN RELAY | D 12 |
| MAIN FUSE BOX (MAIN F/B) | B–C 2–3 |
| MODE CONTROL PANEL | C–D 35 |
| MPFI CONTROL UNIT | A–E 4 |
| PARKING SW | E 32 |
| POWER ANTENNA MOTOR | D 47 |
| POWER MIRROR SW | A 44 |
| POWER WINDOW RELAY | D 40 |
| PRESSURE SW | C 31 |
| REAR DEFOG RELAY | D 12 |
| REAR DEFOG SW | D 44 |
| RIGHT & LEFT HEADLIGHT RELAY | C 3 |
| SELECT MONITOR | A 11 |
| SHIFT LOCK CONTROL UNIT | E 19 |
| STARTER | A 3 |
| STARTER INTERLOCK RELAY (M/T) | A 3 |
| STOP LT SW (CRUISE CONTROL) | B 20 |
| STOP LT SW (W/O CRUISE CTRL) | C–D 45 |
| SUB FAN DIODE | E 29 |
| SUB FUS LINKS | D 3 |
| SUNROOF RELAY | D 46 |
| TAILLIGHT/ILLUMINATION RELAY | C–D 12 |
| THROTTLE SENSOR | E 6–7 |
| TRUNK LT | C 47 |
| WIPER/WASHER SYSTEM (FRONT) | A–B 32 |
| WIPER/WASHER SYSTEM (REAR) | B–C 44–46 |

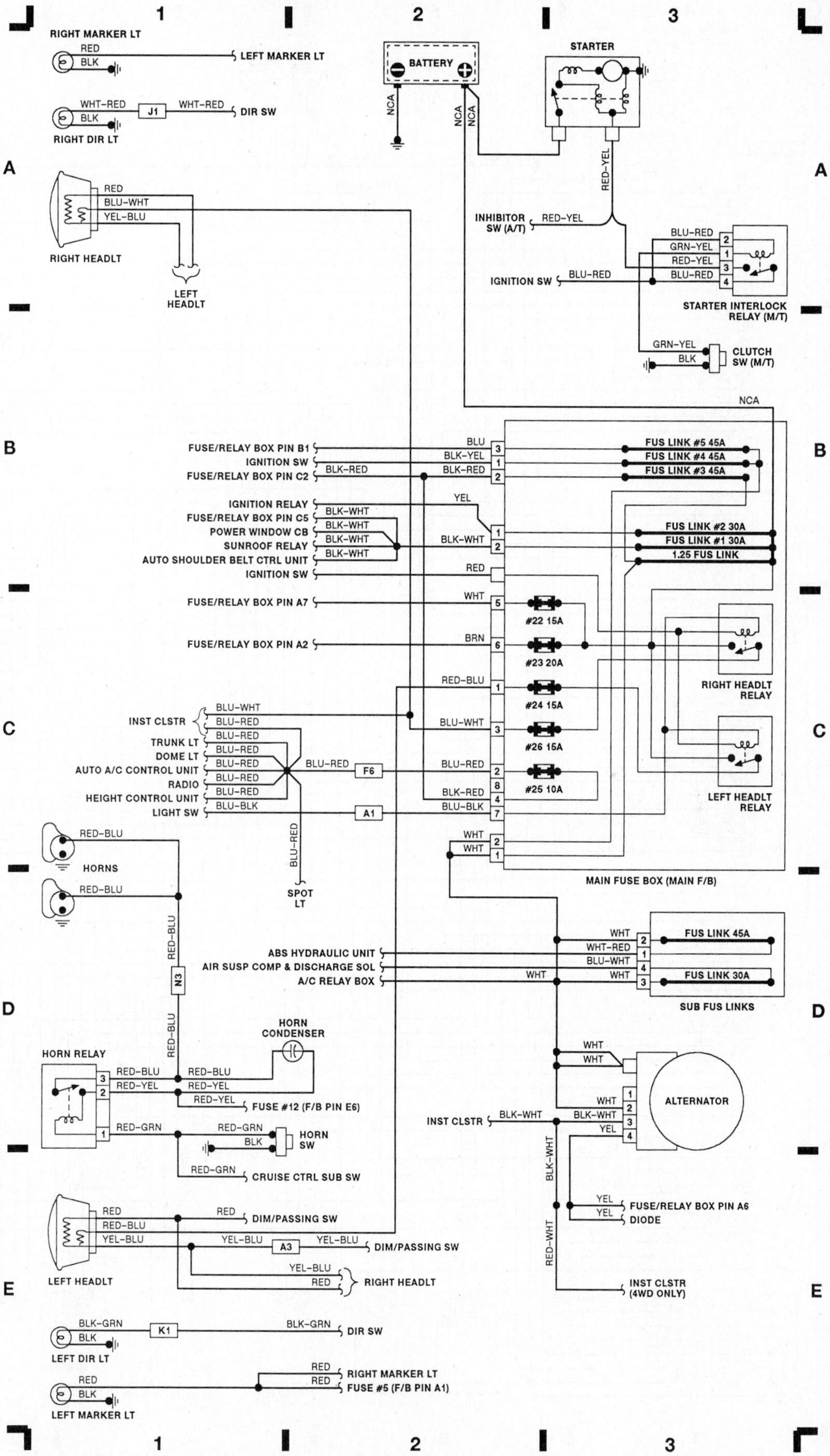

RIGHT MARKER LT
RED
BLK
LEFT MARKER LT
WHT–RED
J1
DIR SW
RIGHT DIR LT
RED
BLU–WHT
YEL–BLU
RIGHT HEADLT
LEFT HEADLT
BATTERY
NCA
STARTER
RED–YEL
INHIBITOR SW (A/T)
BLU–RED
GRN–YEL
IGNITION SW
STARTER INTERLOCK RELAY (M/T)
CLUTCH SW (M/T)

FUSE/RELAY BOX PIN B1
IGNITION SW
FUSE/RELAY BOX PIN C2
BLU
BLK–YEL
BLK–RED
FUS LINK #5 45A
FUS LINK #4 45A
FUS LINK #3 45A
IGNITION RELAY
FUSE/RELAY BOX PIN C5
POWER WINDOW CB
SUNROOF RELAY
AUTO SHOULDER BELT CTRL UNIT
IGNITION SW
BLK–WHT
YEL
FUS LINK #2 30A
FUS LINK #1 30A
1.25 FUS LINK
FUSE/RELAY BOX PIN A7
FUSE/RELAY BOX PIN A2
WHT
BRN
#22 15A
#23 20A
#24 15A
#26 15A
#25 10A
RIGHT HEADLT RELAY
LEFT HEADLT RELAY
INST CLSTR
TRUNK LT
DOME LT
AUTO A/C CONTROL UNIT
RADIO
HEIGHT CONTROL UNIT
LIGHT SW
BLU–WHT
BLU–RED
BLU–BLK
F6
A1
RED–BLU
SPOT LT
HORNS
MAIN FUSE BOX (MAIN F/B)

ABS HYDRAULIC UNIT
AIR SUSP COMP & DISCHARGE SOL
A/C RELAY BOX
WHT–RED
FUS LINK 45A
FUS LINK 30A
SUB FUS LINKS
N3
HORN CONDENSER
HORN RELAY
RED–YEL
FUSE #12 (F/B PIN E6)
RED–GRN
HORN SW
CRUISE CTRL SUB SW
ALTERNATOR
INST CLSTR
YEL
FUSE/RELAY BOX PIN A6
DIODE
RED–WHT
INST CLSTR (4WD ONLY)

RED–BLU
DIM/PASSING SW
A3
DIM/PASSING SW
RIGHT HEADLT
LEFT HEADLT
BLK–GRN
K1
DIR SW
LEFT DIR LT
RIGHT MARKER LT
FUSE #5 (F/B PIN A1)
LEFT MARKER LT

# 1991 WIRING DIAGRAMS
## Legacy (Cont.)

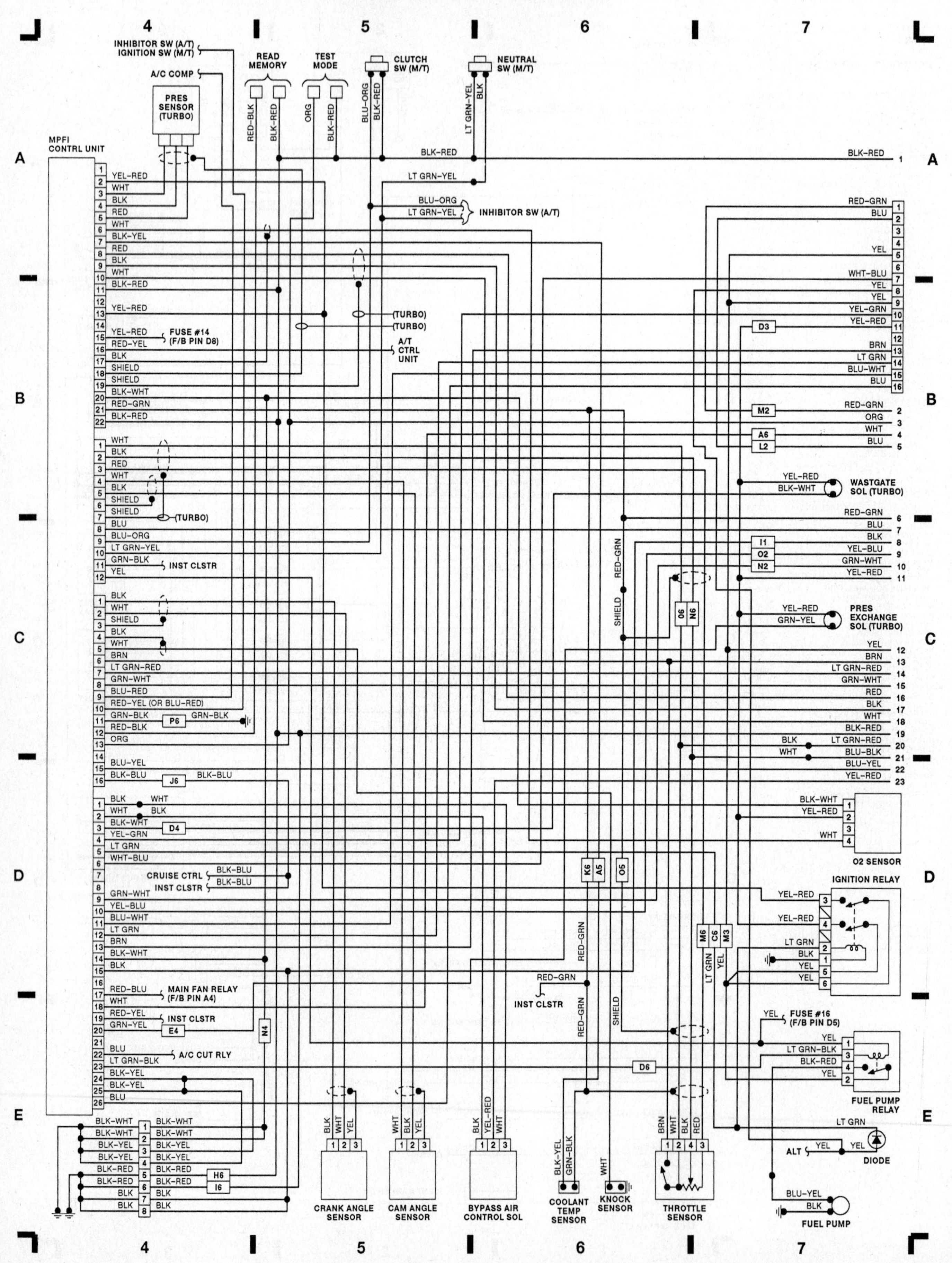

# 1991 WIRING DIAGRAMS
## Legacy (Cont.)

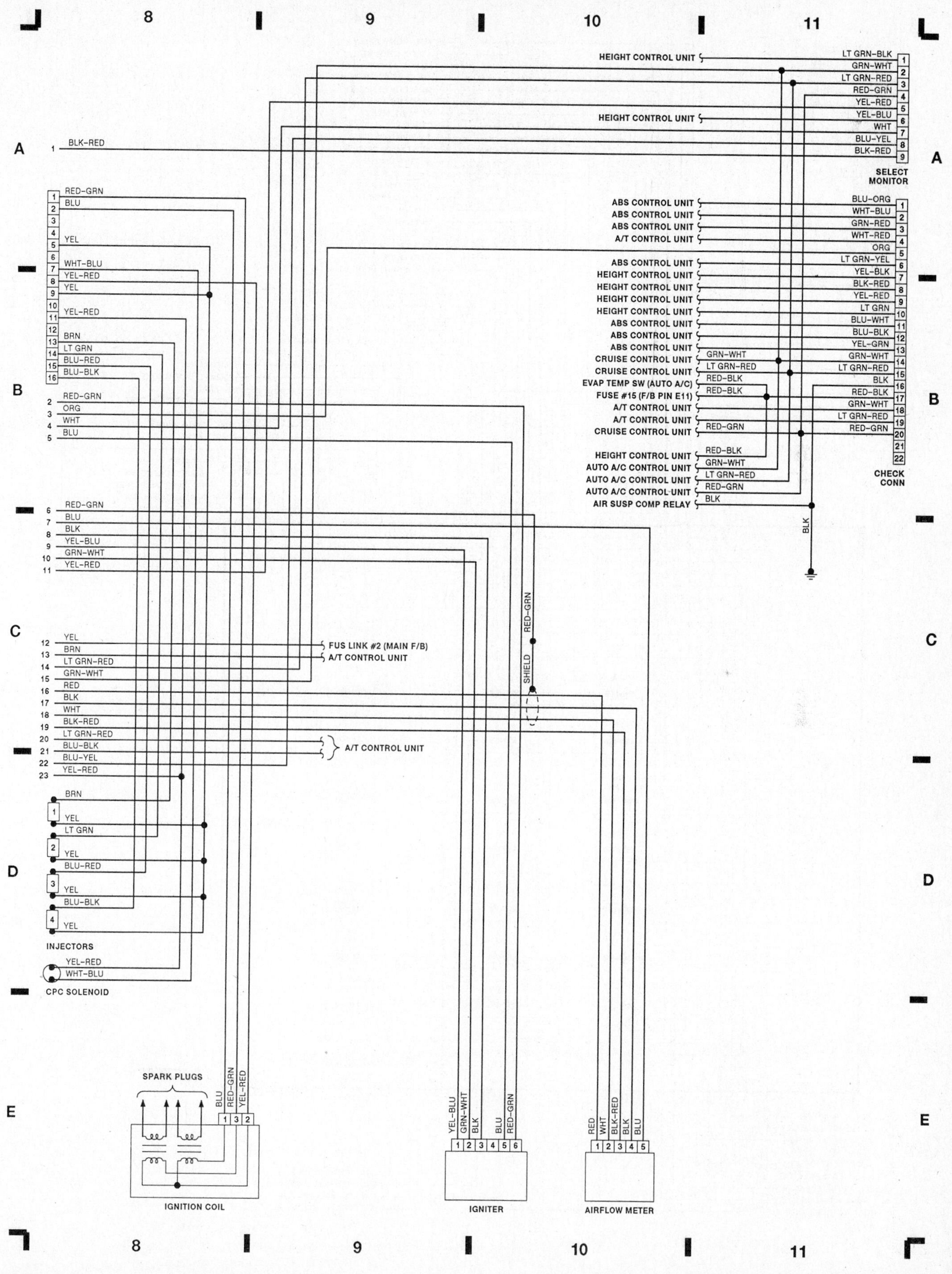

# 1991 WIRING DIAGRAMS
## Legacy (Cont.)

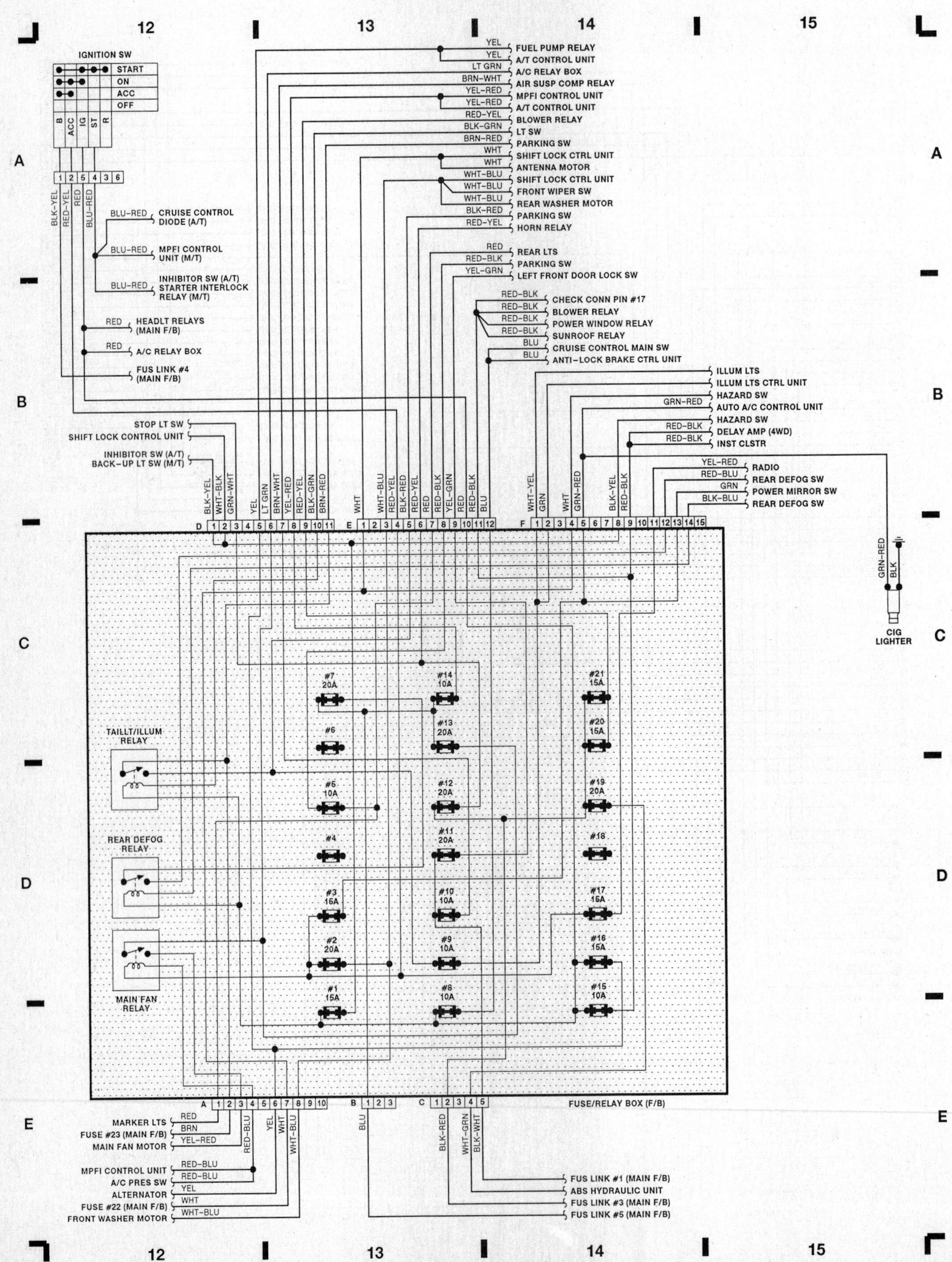

# 1991 WIRING DIAGRAMS
## Legacy (Cont.)

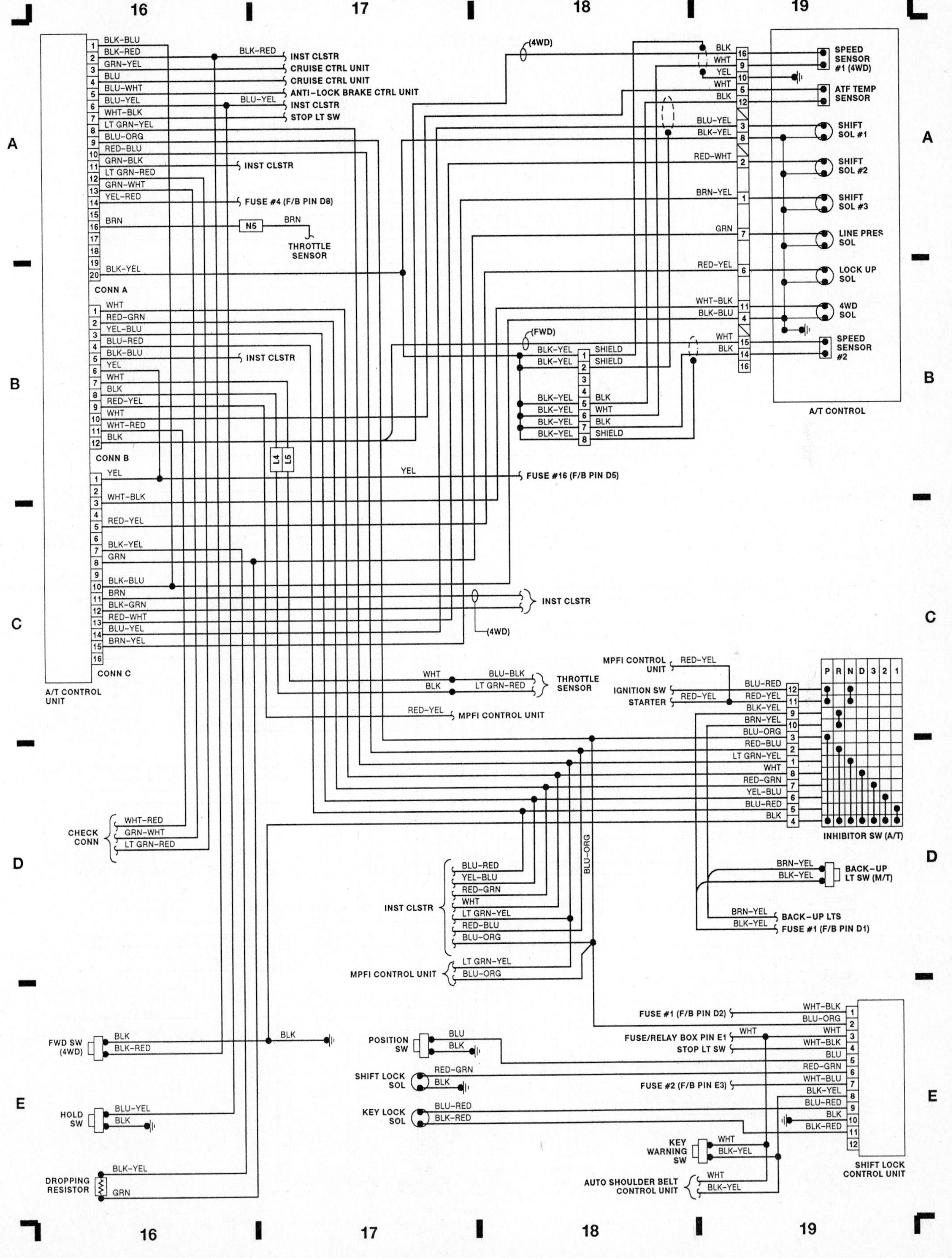

# 1991 WIRING DIAGRAMS
## Legacy (Cont.)

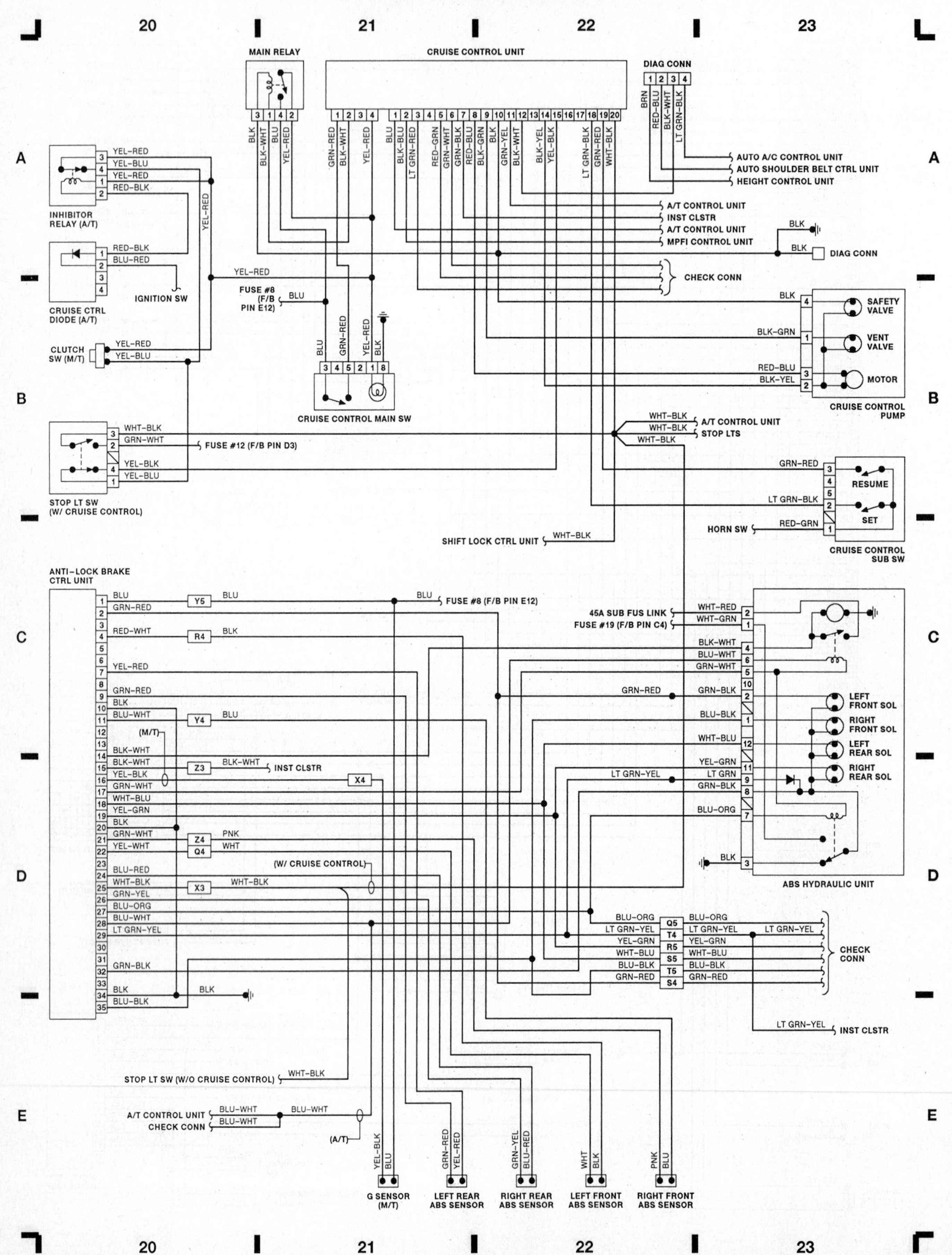

# 1991 WIRING DIAGRAMS
## Legacy (Cont.)

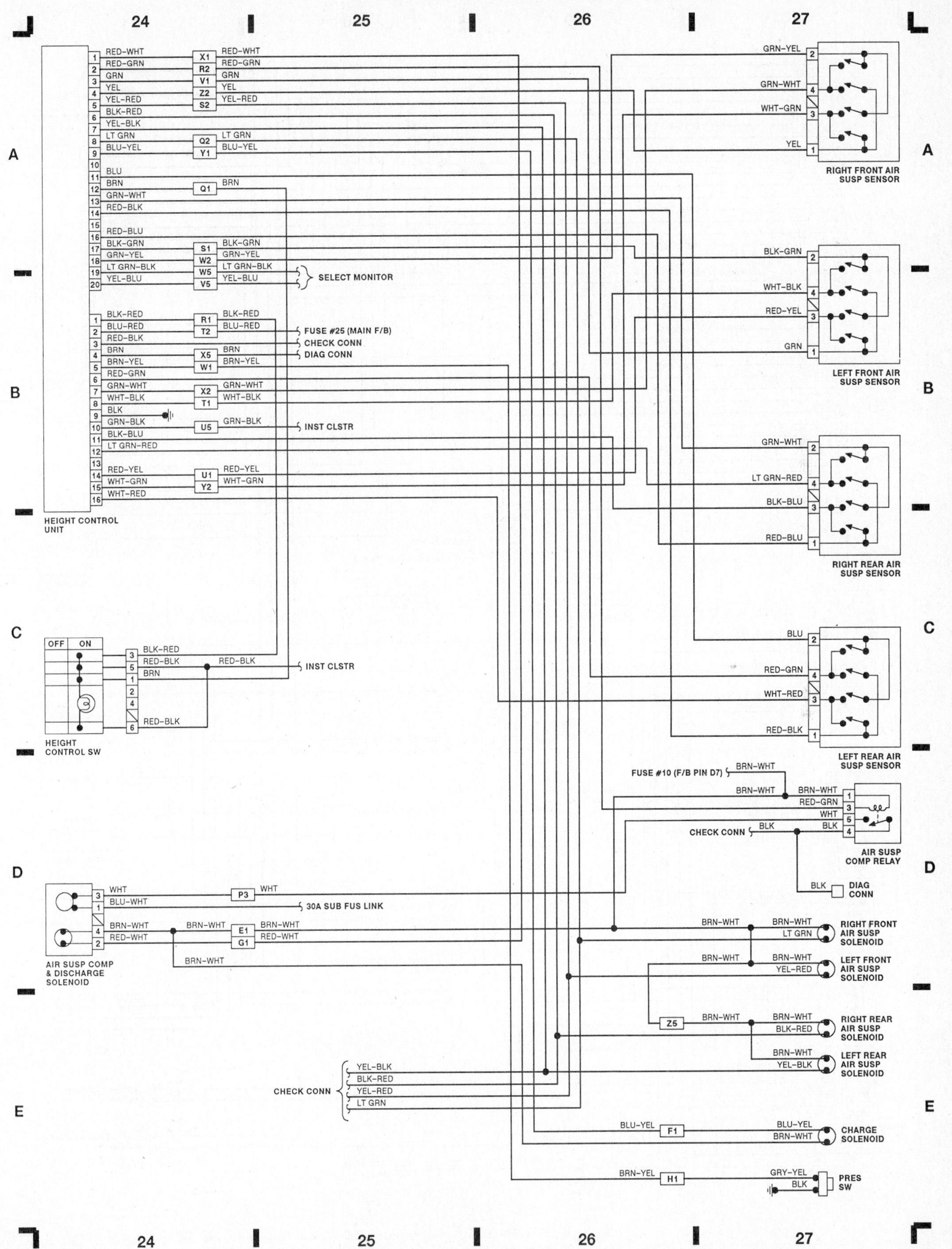

# 1991 WIRING DIAGRAMS
## Legacy (Cont.)

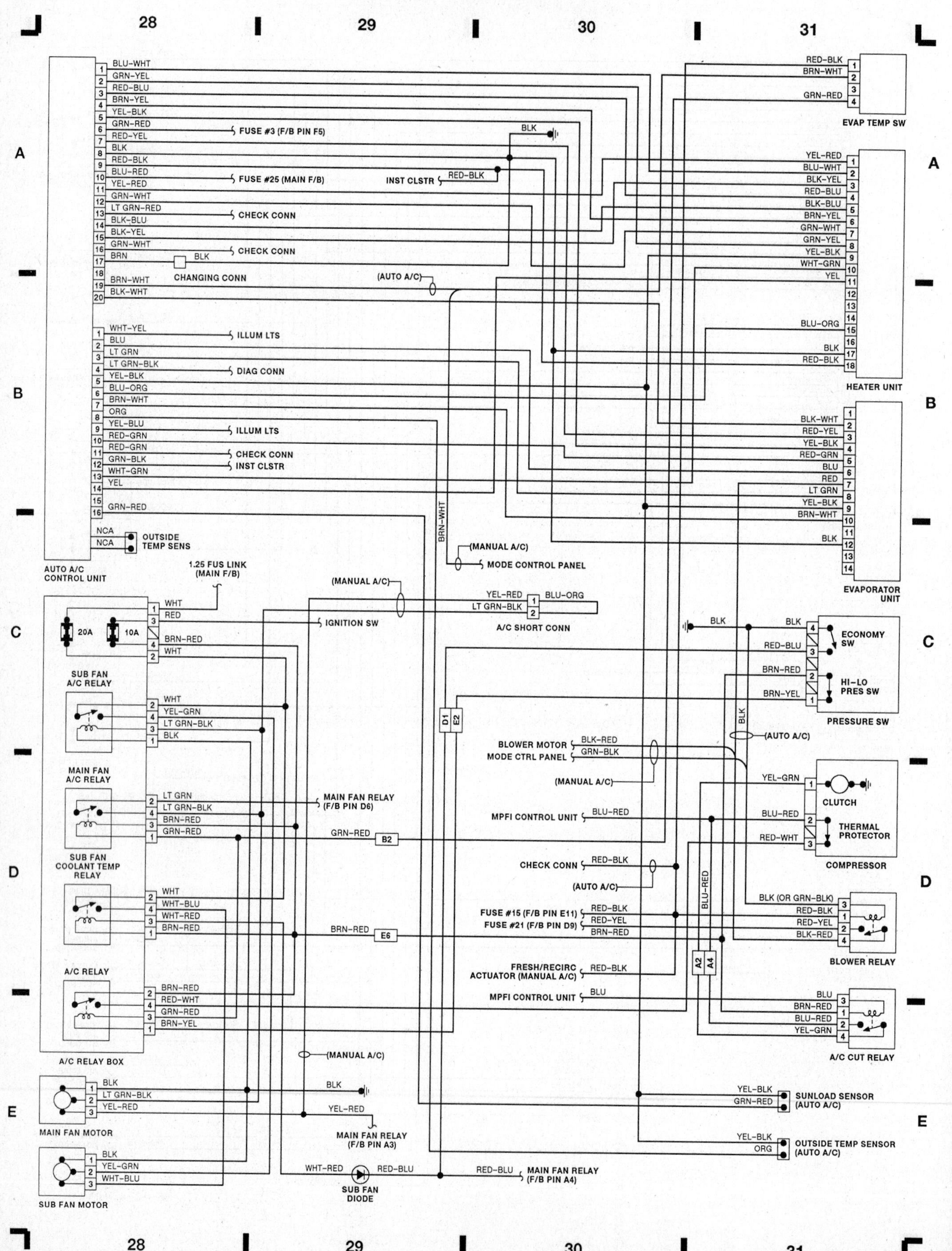

# 1991 WIRING DIAGRAMS
## Legacy (Cont.)

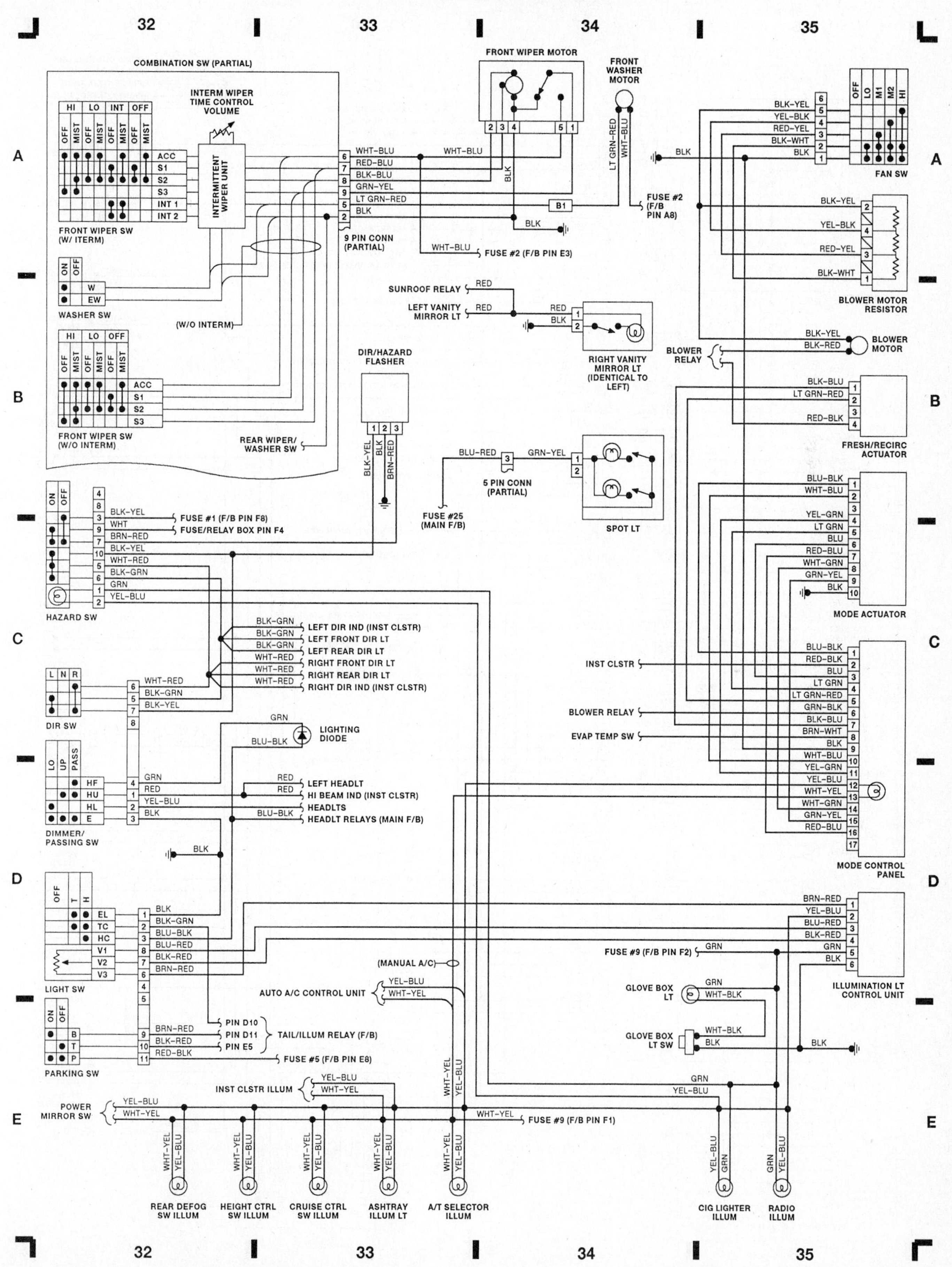

# 1991 WIRING DIAGRAMS
## Legacy (Cont.)

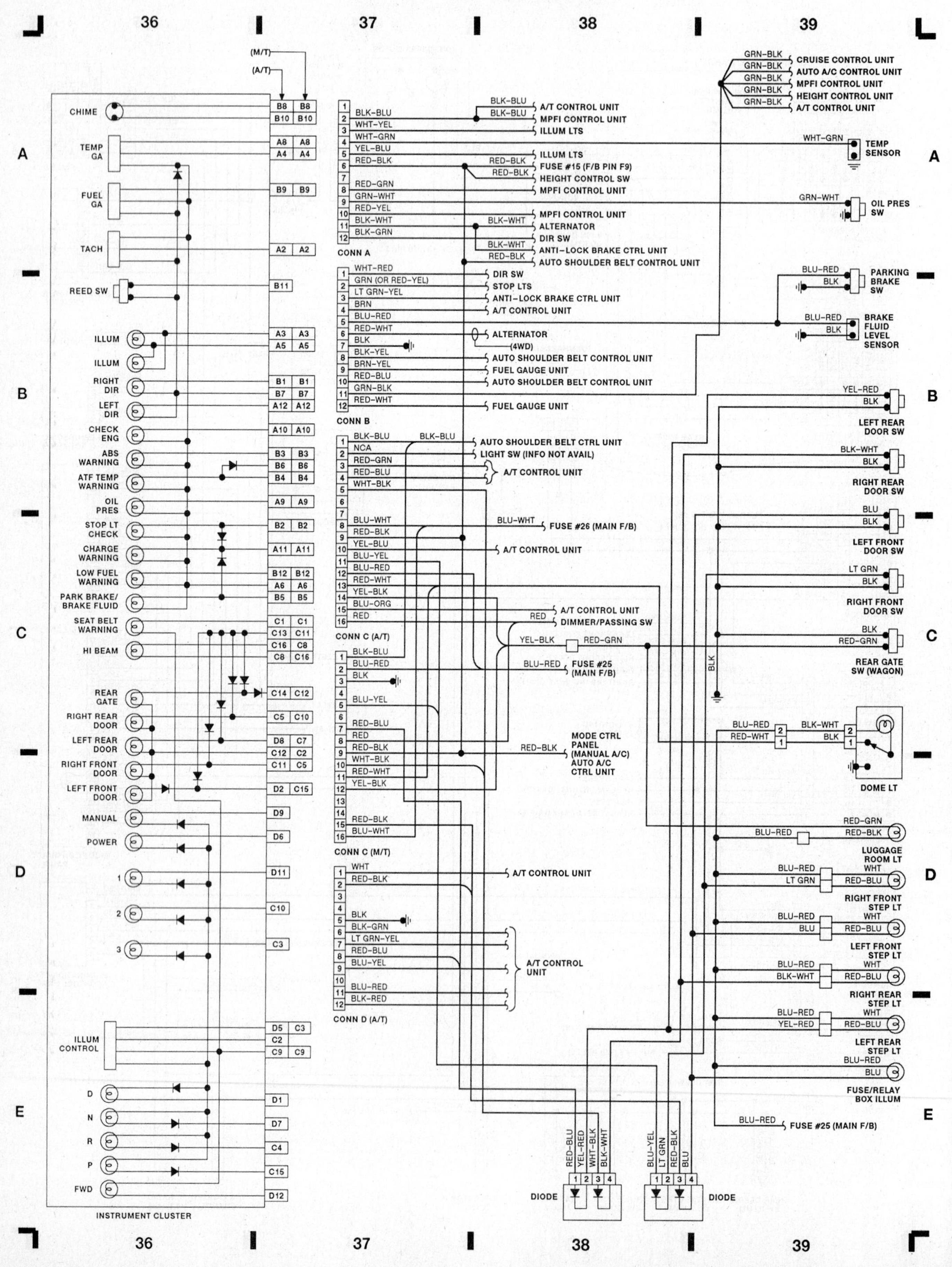

# 1991 WIRING DIAGRAMS
## Legacy (Cont.)

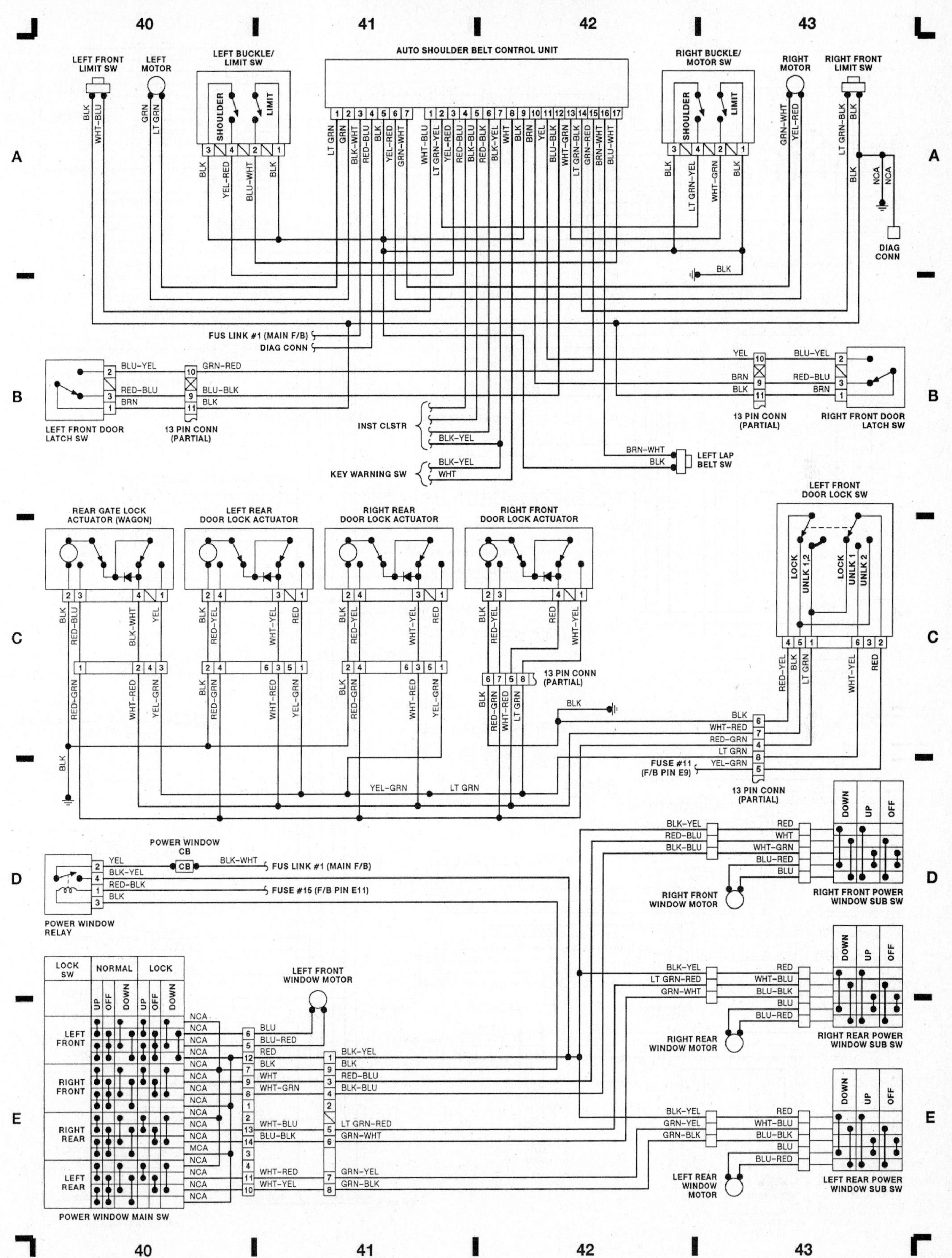

# 1991 WIRING DIAGRAMS
## Legacy (Cont.)

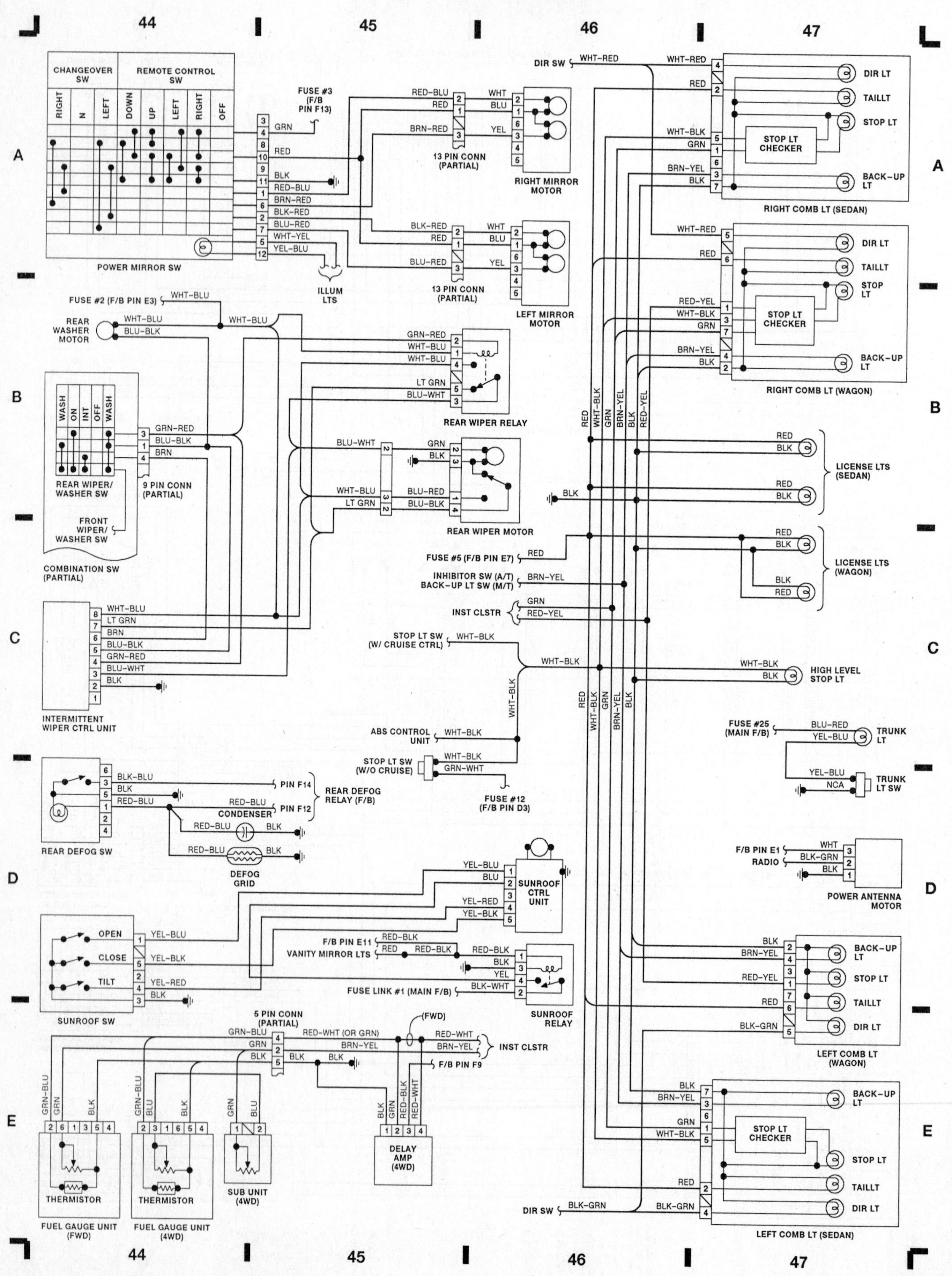

# 1991 WIRING DIAGRAMS
## Loyale

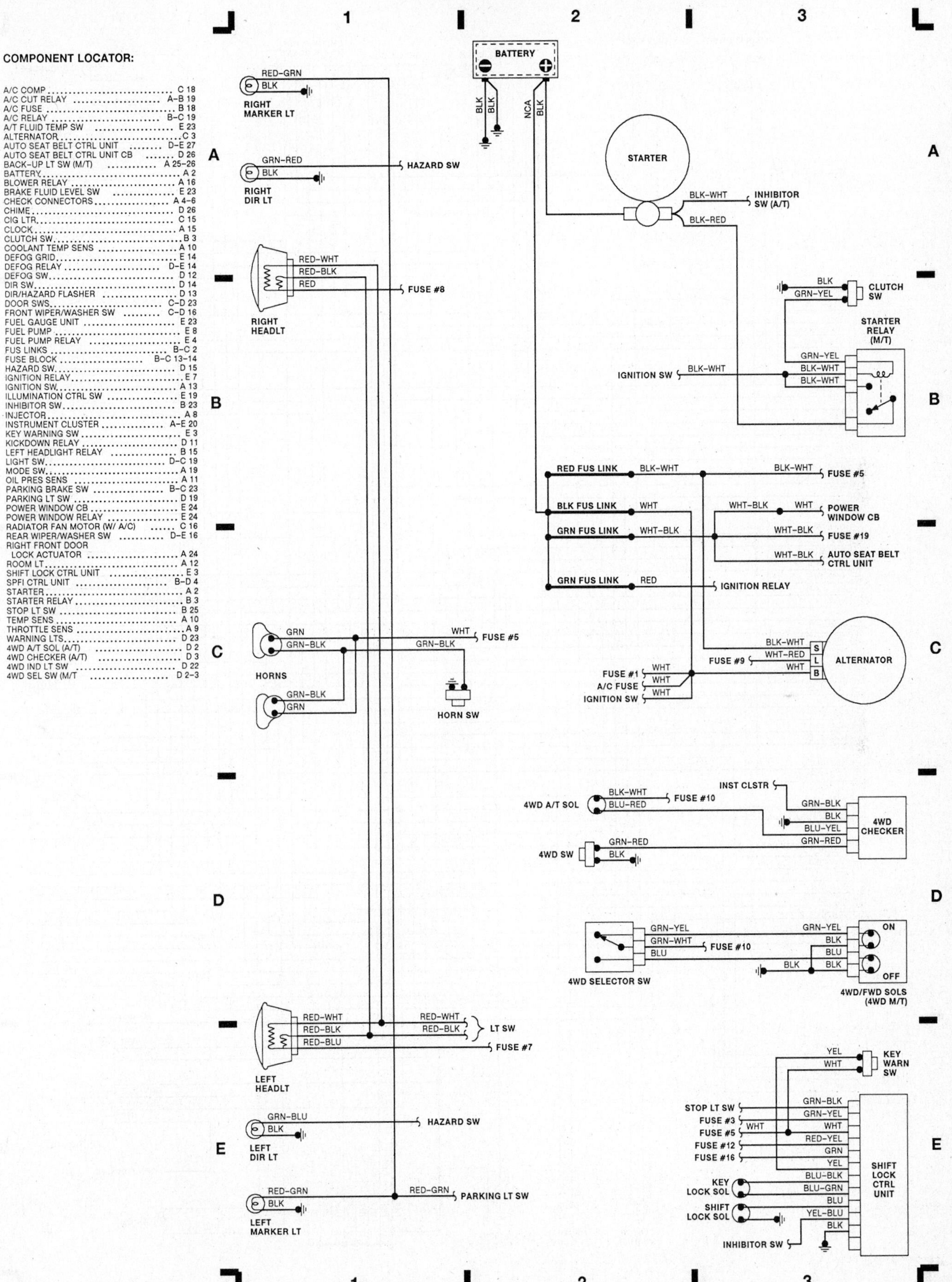

# 1991 WIRING DIAGRAMS
## Loyale (Cont.)

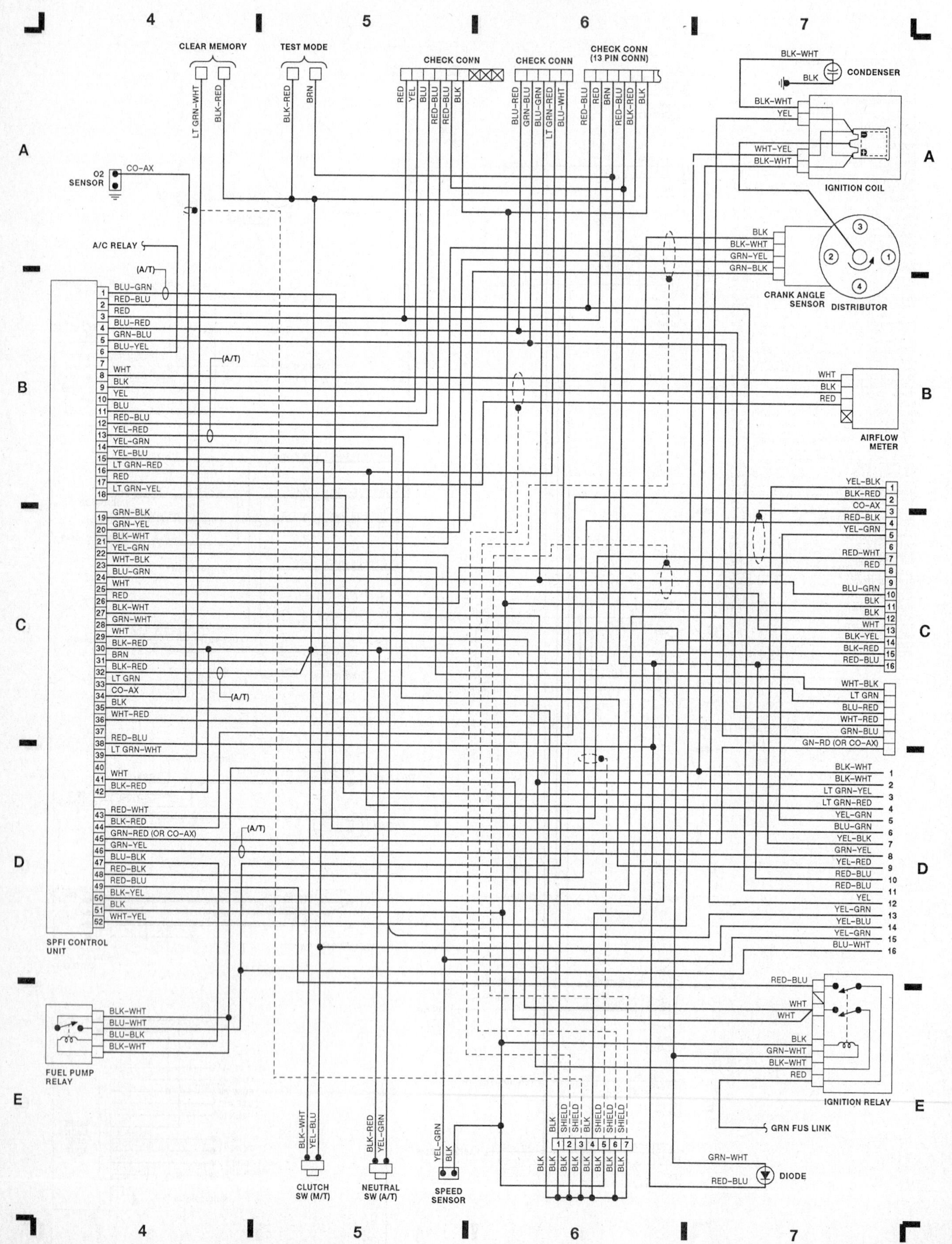

# 1991 WIRING DIAGRAMS
## Loyale (Cont.)

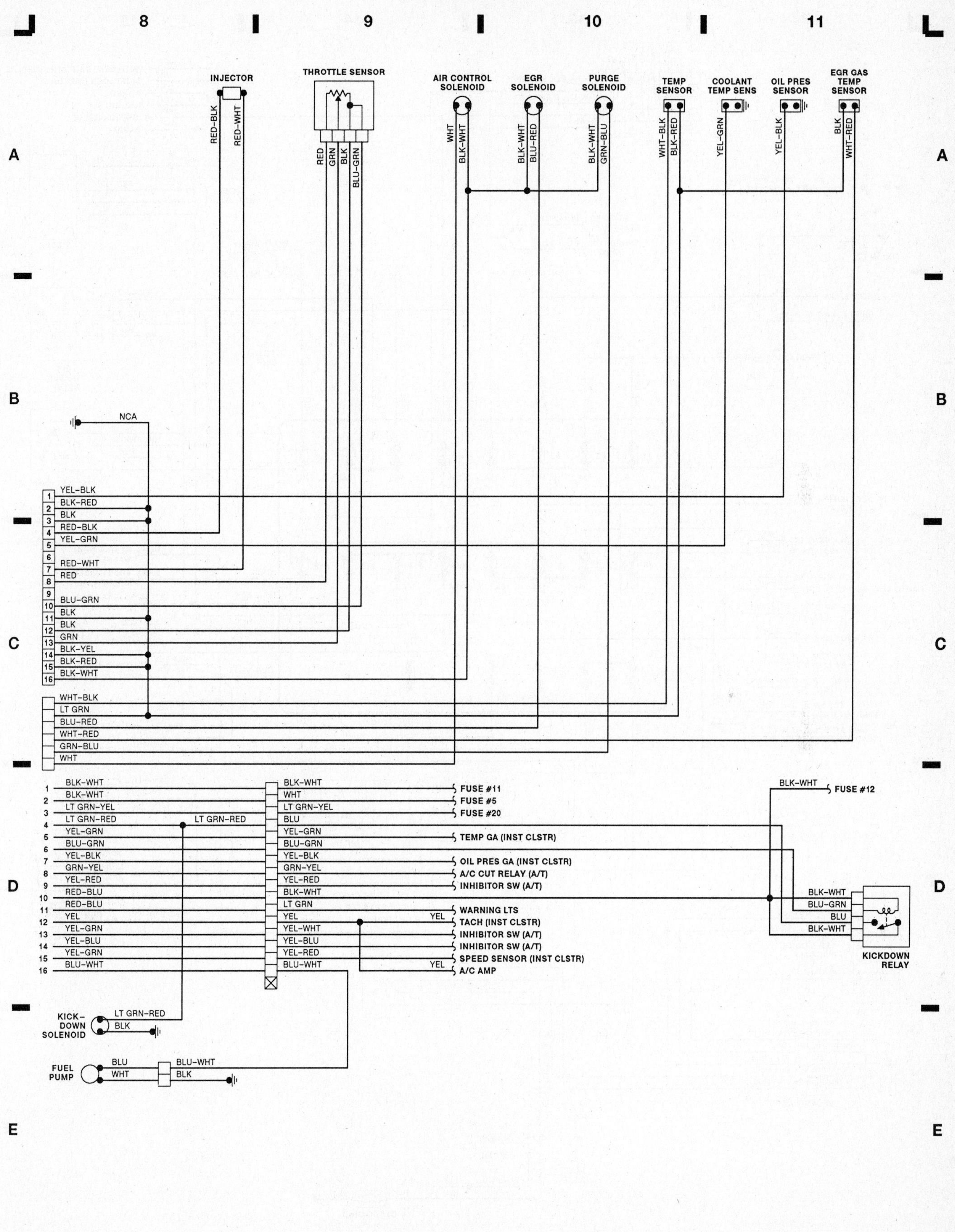

# 1991 WIRING DIAGRAMS
## Loyale (Cont.)

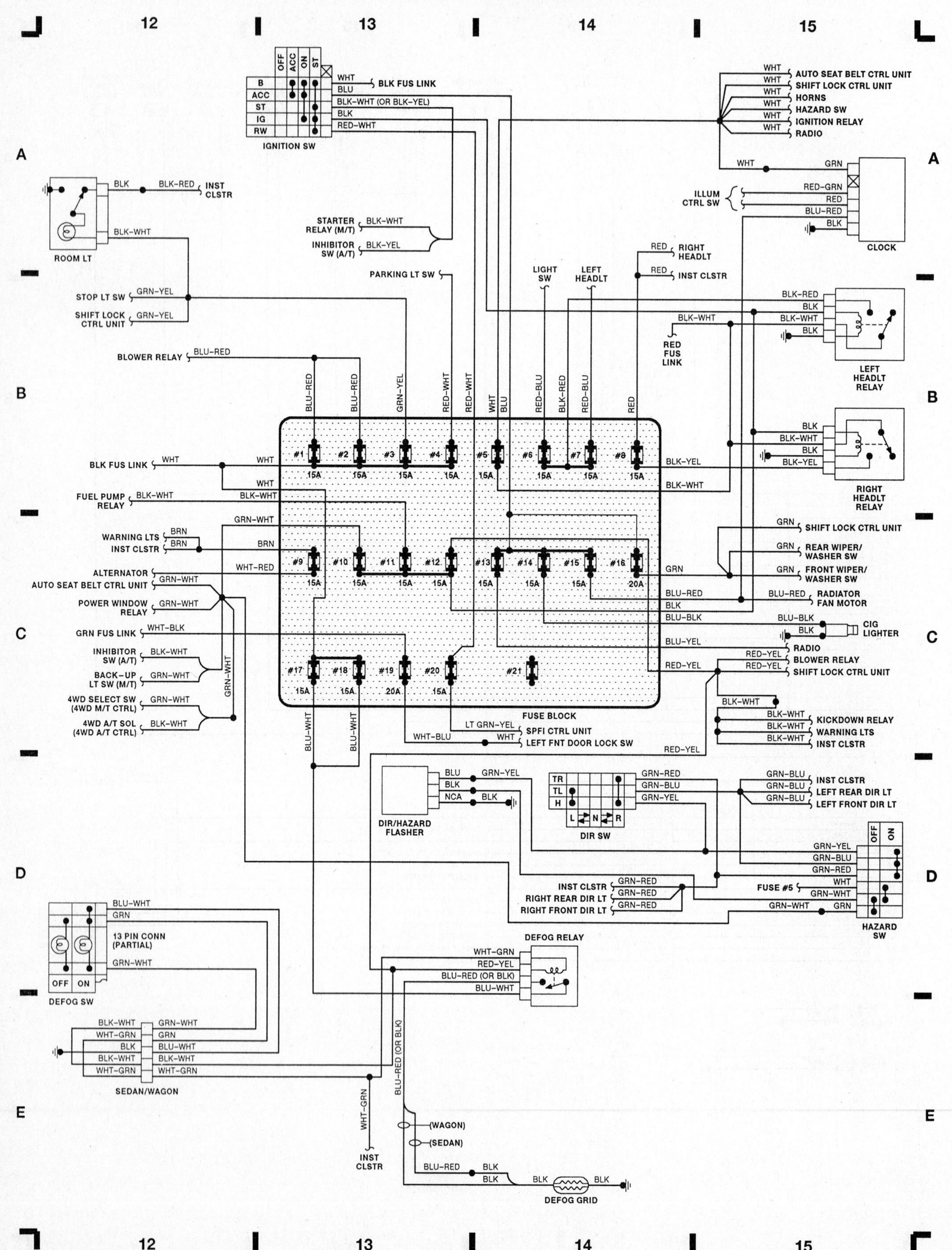

# 1991 WIRING DIAGRAMS
## Loyale (Cont.)

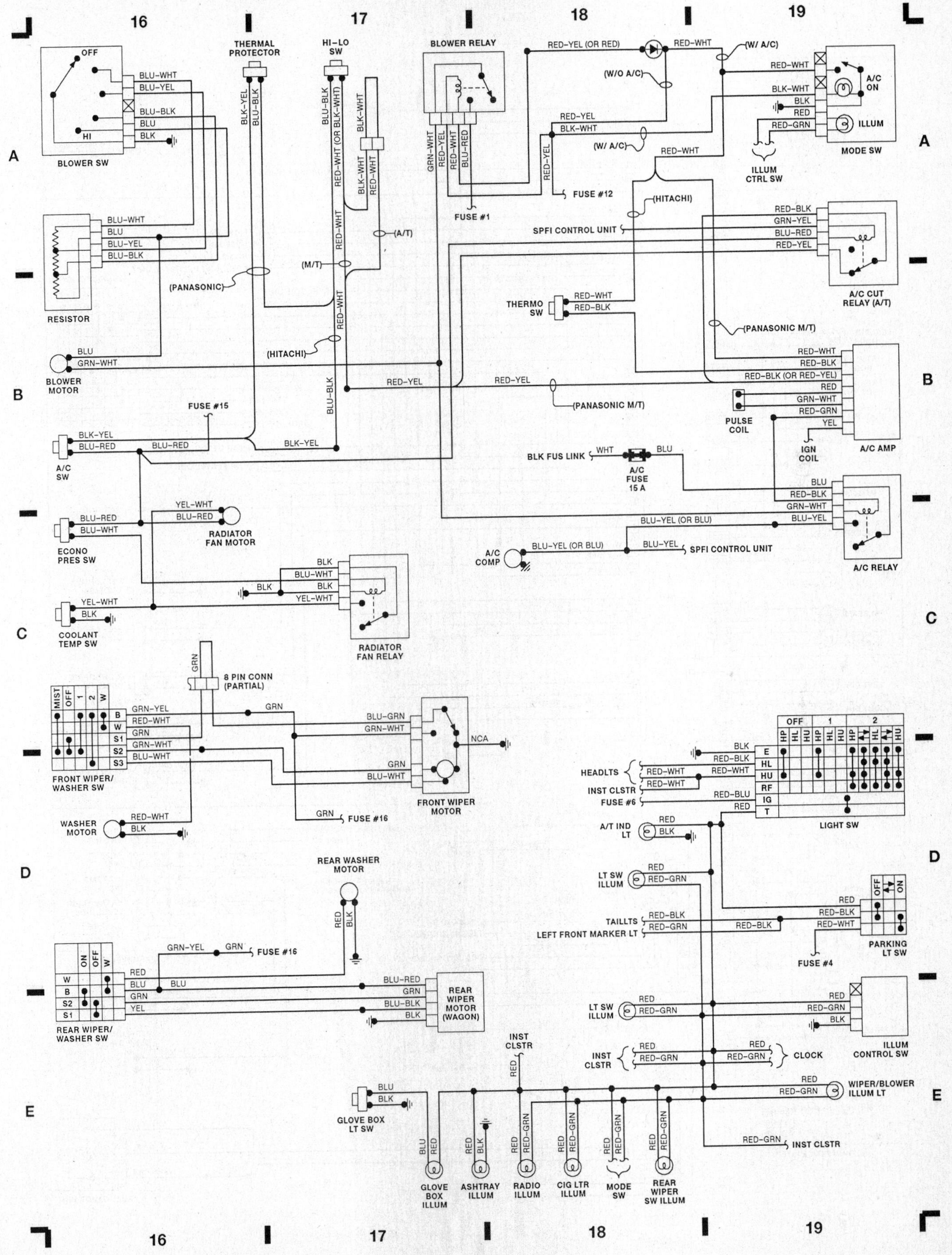

# 1991 WIRING DIAGRAMS
## Loyale (Cont.)

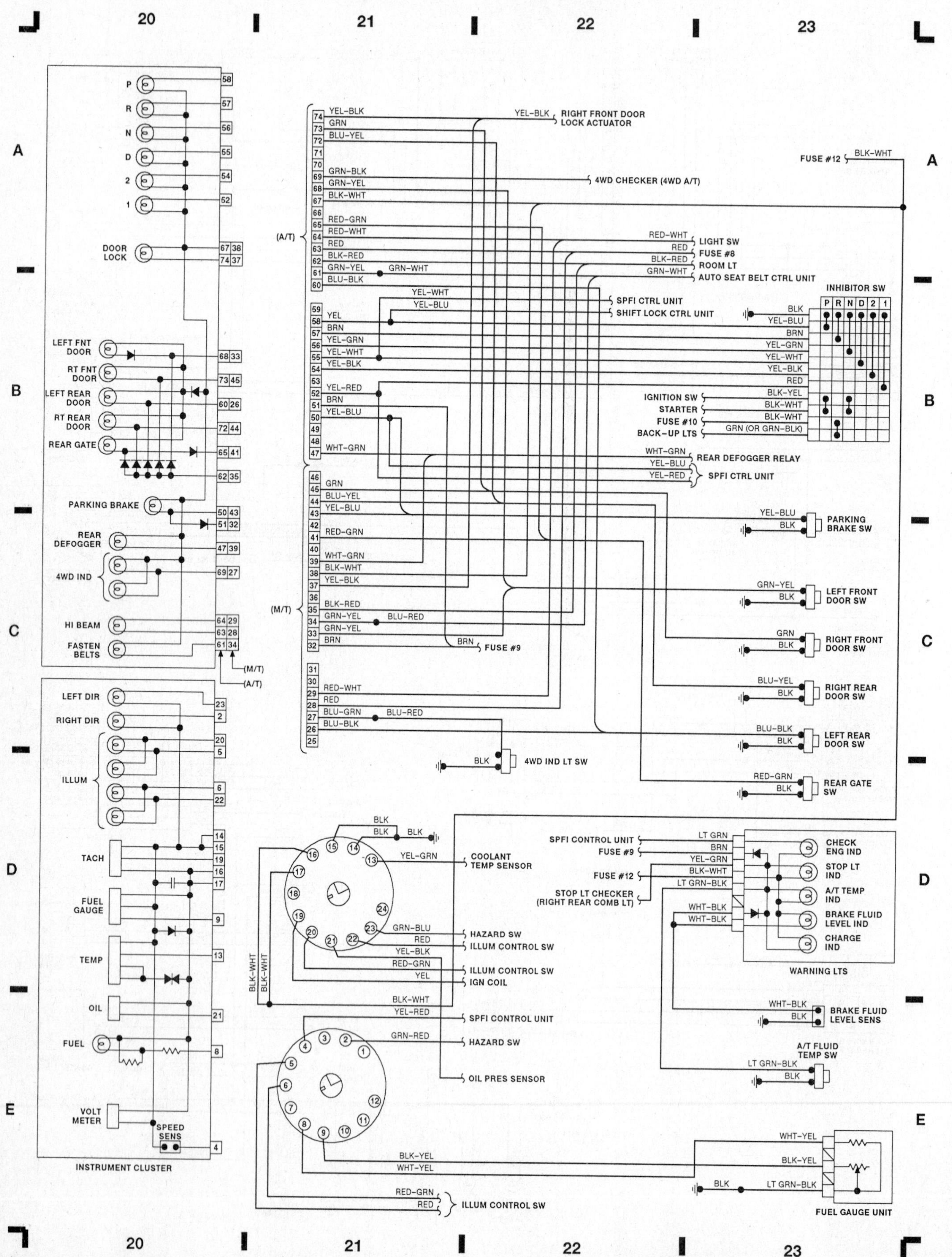

# 1991 WIRING DIAGRAMS
## Loyale (Cont.)

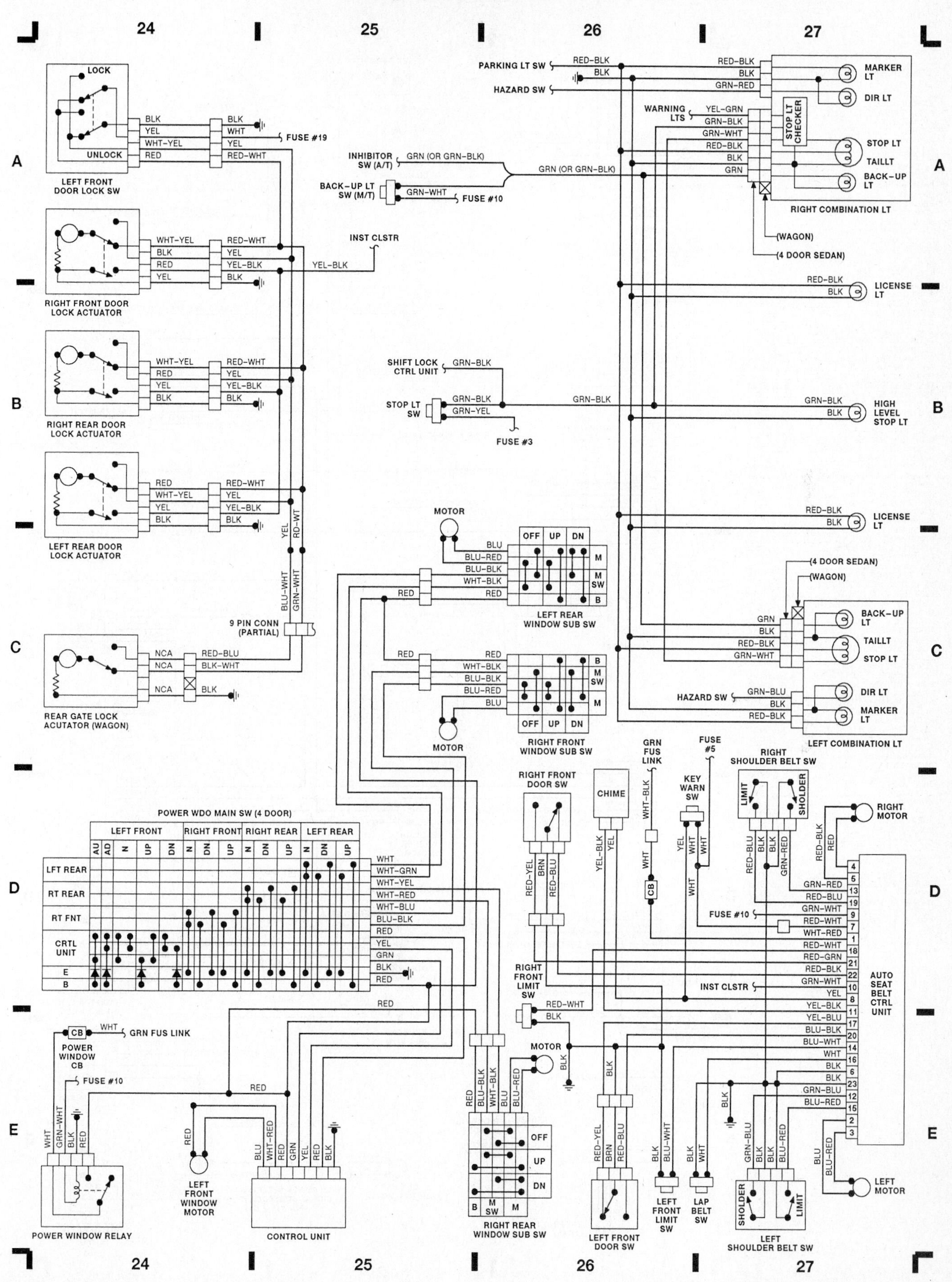

# 1991 WIRING DIAGRAMS
# XT/XT6

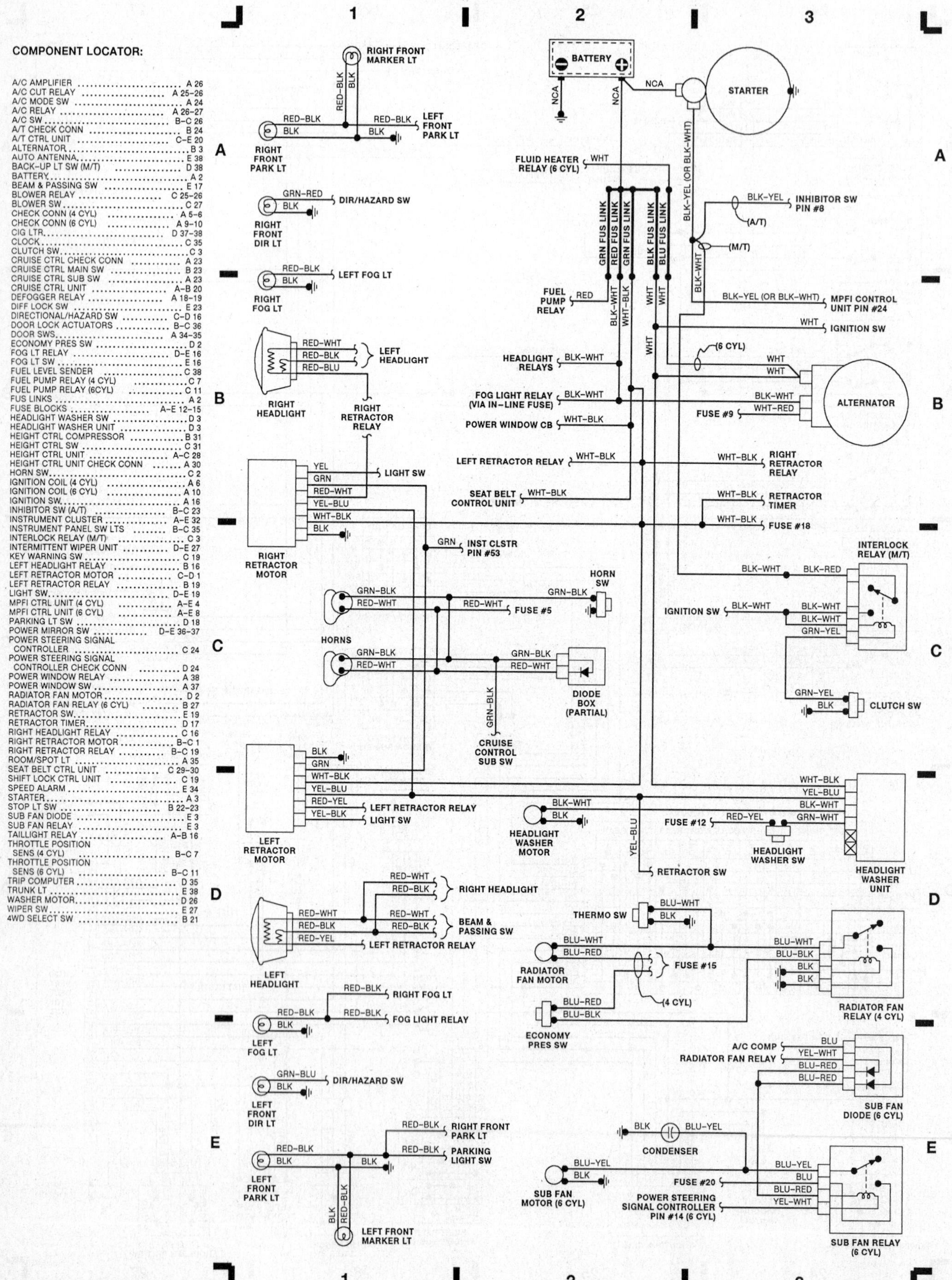


**COMPONENT LOCATOR:**

| | |
|---|---|
| A/C AMPLIFIER | A 26 |
| A/C CUT RELAY | A 25–26 |
| A/C MODE SW | A 24 |
| A/C RELAY | A 26–27 |
| A/C SW | B–C 26 |
| A/T CHECK CONN | B 24 |
| A/T CTRL UNIT | C–E 20 |
| ALTERNATOR | B 3 |
| AUTO ANTENNA | E 38 |
| BACK-UP LT SW (M/T) | D 38 |
| BATTERY | A 2 |
| BEAM & PASSING SW | E 17 |
| BLOWER RELAY | C 25–26 |
| BLOWER SW | C 27 |
| CHECK CONN (4 CYL) | A 5–6 |
| CHECK CONN (6 CYL) | A 9–10 |
| CIG LTR | D 37–38 |
| CLOCK | C 35 |
| CLUTCH SW | C 3 |
| CRUISE CTRL CHECK CONN | A 23 |
| CRUISE CTRL MAIN SW | B 23 |
| CRUISE CTRL SUB SW | A 23 |
| CRUISE CTRL UNIT | A–B 20 |
| DEFOGGER RELAY | A 18–19 |
| DIFF LOCK SW | E 23 |
| DIRECTIONAL/HAZARD SW | C–D 16 |
| DOOR LOCK ACTUATORS | B–C 36 |
| DOOR SWS | A 34–35 |
| ECONOMY PRES SW | D 2 |
| FOG LT RELAY | D–E 16 |
| FOG LT SW | E 16 |
| FUEL LEVEL SENDER | C 38 |
| FUEL PUMP RELAY (4 CYL) | C 7 |
| FUEL PUMP RELAY (6CYL) | C 11 |
| FUS LINKS | A 2 |
| FUSE BLOCKS | A–E 12–15 |
| HEADLIGHT WASHER SW | D 3 |
| HEADLIGHT WASHER UNIT | D 3 |
| HEIGHT CTRL COMPRESSOR | B 31 |
| HEIGHT CTRL SW | C 31 |
| HEIGHT CTRL UNIT | A–C 28 |
| HEIGHT CTRL UNIT CHECK CONN | A 30 |
| HORN SW | C 2 |
| IGNITION COIL (4 CYL) | A 6 |
| IGNITION COIL (6 CYL) | A 10 |
| IGNITION SW | A 16 |
| INHIBITOR SW (A/T) | B–C 23 |
| INSTRUMENT CLUSTER | A–E 32 |
| INSTRUMENT PANEL SW LTS | B–C 35 |
| INTERLOCK RELAY (M/T) | C 3 |
| INTERMITTENT WIPER UNIT | D–E 27 |
| KEY WARNING SW | C 19 |
| LEFT HEADLIGHT RELAY | B 16 |
| LEFT RETRACTOR MOTOR | C–D 1 |
| LEFT RETRACTOR RELAY | B 19 |
| LIGHT SW | D–E 19 |
| MPFI CTRL UNIT (4 CYL) | A–E 4 |
| MPFI CTRL UNIT (6 CYL) | A–E 8 |
| PARKING LT SW | D 18 |
| POWER MIRROR SW | D–E 36–37 |
| POWER STEERING SIGNAL CONTROLLER | C 24 |
| POWER STEERING SIGNAL CONTROLLER CHECK CONN | D 24 |
| POWER WINDOW RELAY | A 38 |
| POWER WINDOW SW | A 37 |
| RADIATOR FAN MOTOR | D 2 |
| RADIATOR FAN RELAY (6 CYL) | B 27 |
| RETRACTOR SW | E 19 |
| RETRACTOR TIMER | D 17 |
| RIGHT HEADLIGHT RELAY | C 16 |
| RIGHT RETRACTOR MOTOR | B–C 1 |
| RIGHT RETRACTOR RELAY | B–C 19 |
| ROOM/SPOT LT | A 35 |
| SEAT BELT CTRL UNIT | C 29–30 |
| SHIFT LOCK CTRL UNIT | C 19 |
| SPEED ALARM | E 34 |
| STARTER | A 3 |
| STOP LT SW | B 22–23 |
| SUB FAN DIODE | E 3 |
| SUB FAN RELAY | E 3 |
| TAILLIGHT RELAY | A–B 16 |
| THROTTLE POSITION SENS (4 CYL) | B–C 7 |
| THROTTLE POSITION SENS (6 CYL) | B–C 11 |
| TRIP COMPUTER | D 35 |
| TRUNK LT | E 38 |
| WASHER MOTOR | D 26 |
| WIPER SW | E 27 |
| 4WD SELECT SW | B 21 |

# 1991 WIRING DIAGRAMS
# XT & XT6

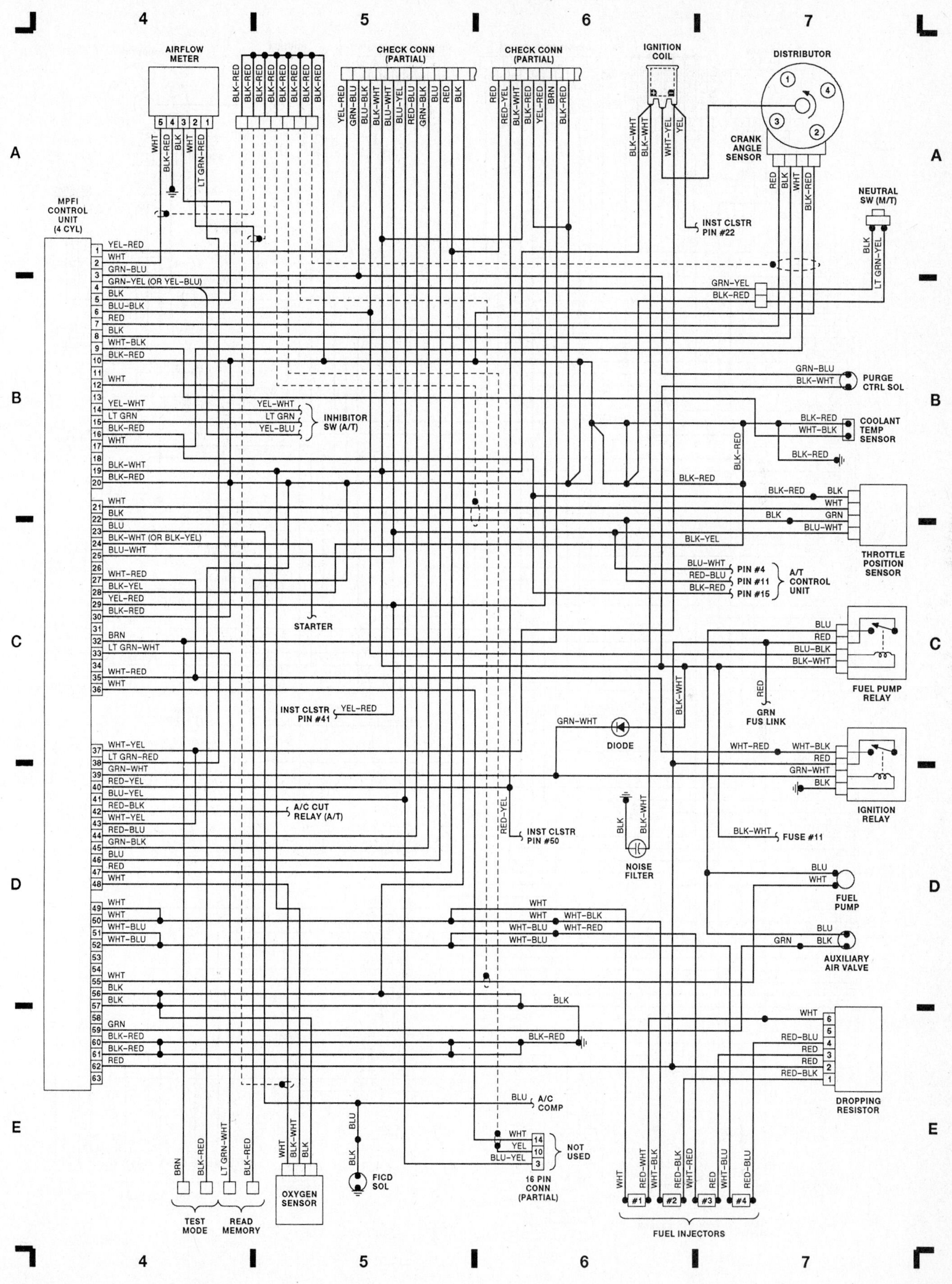

# 1991 WIRING DIAGRAMS
# XT & XT6 (Cont.)

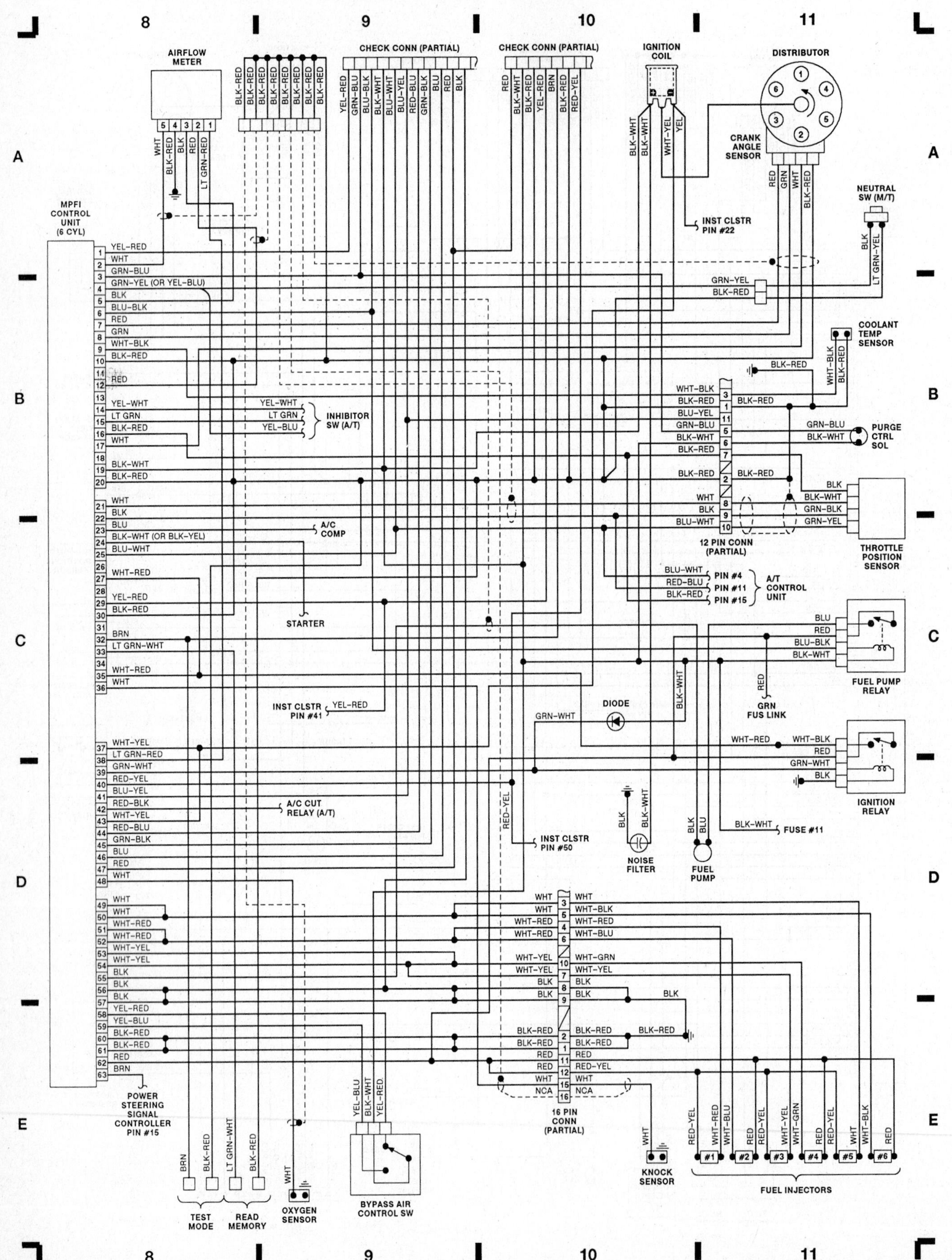

# 1991 WIRING DIAGRAMS
# XT & XT6 (Cont.)

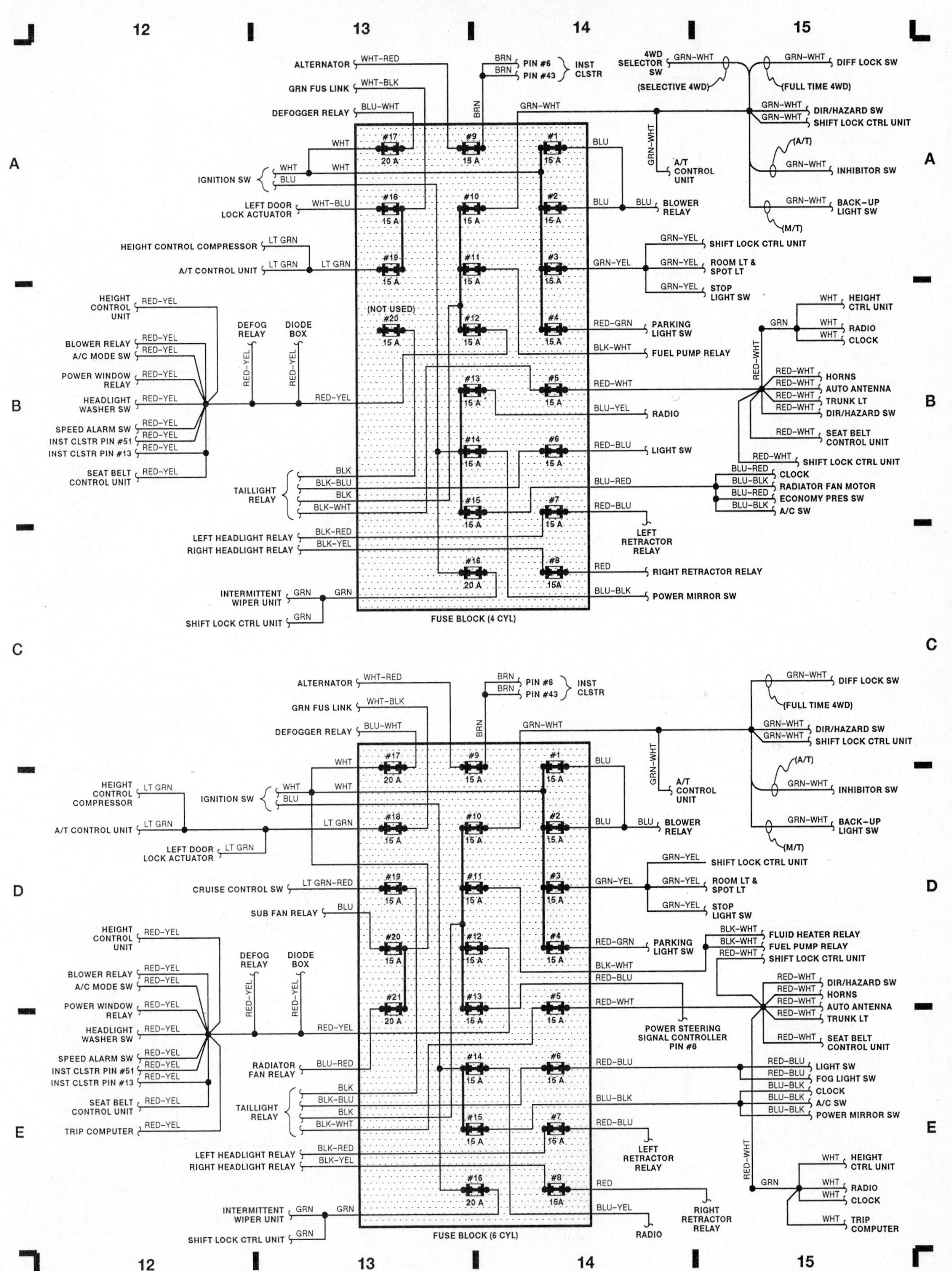

# 1991 WIRING DIAGRAMS
# XT & XT6 (Cont.)

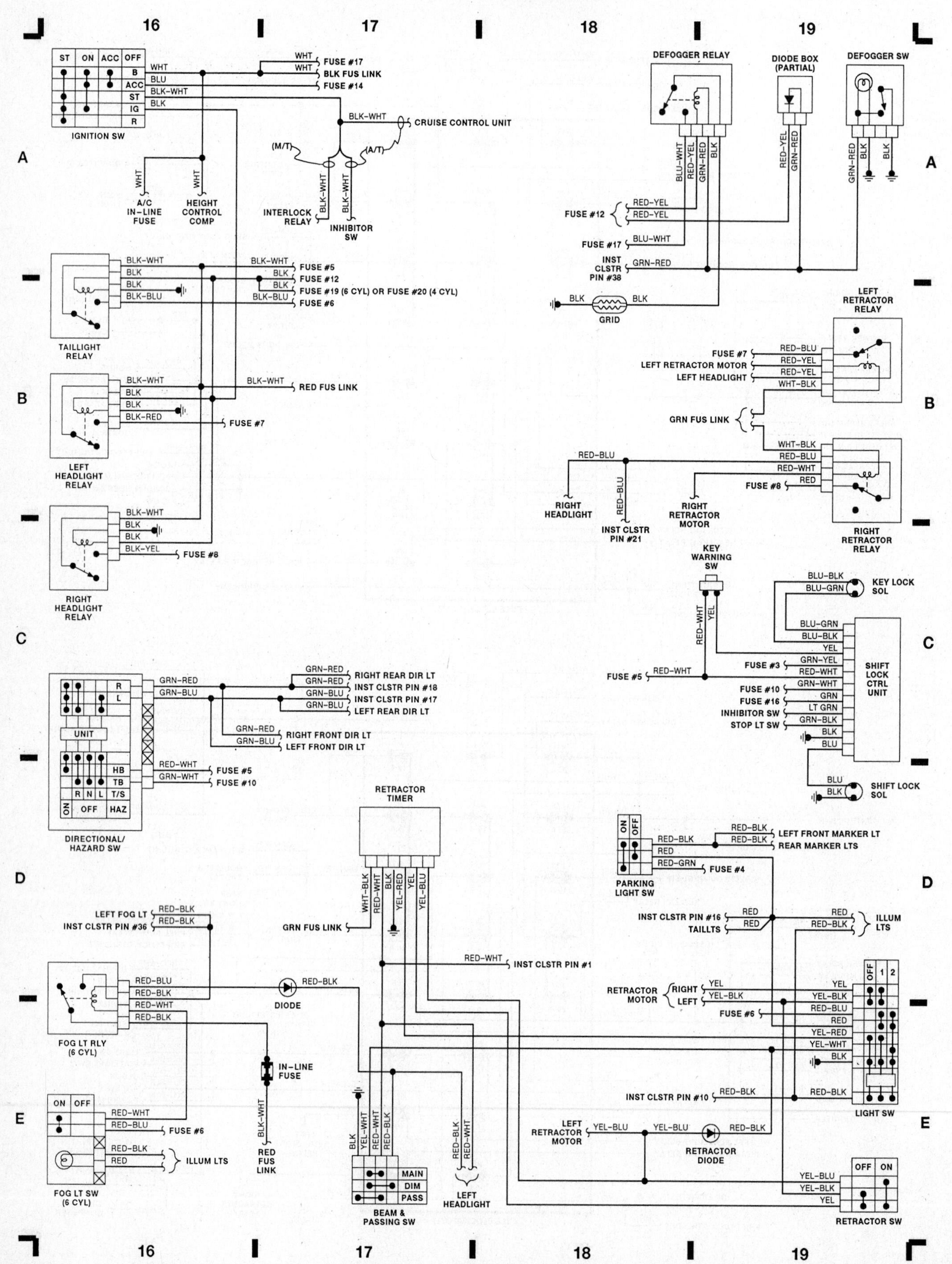

# 1991 WIRING DIAGRAMS
# XT & XT6 (Cont.)

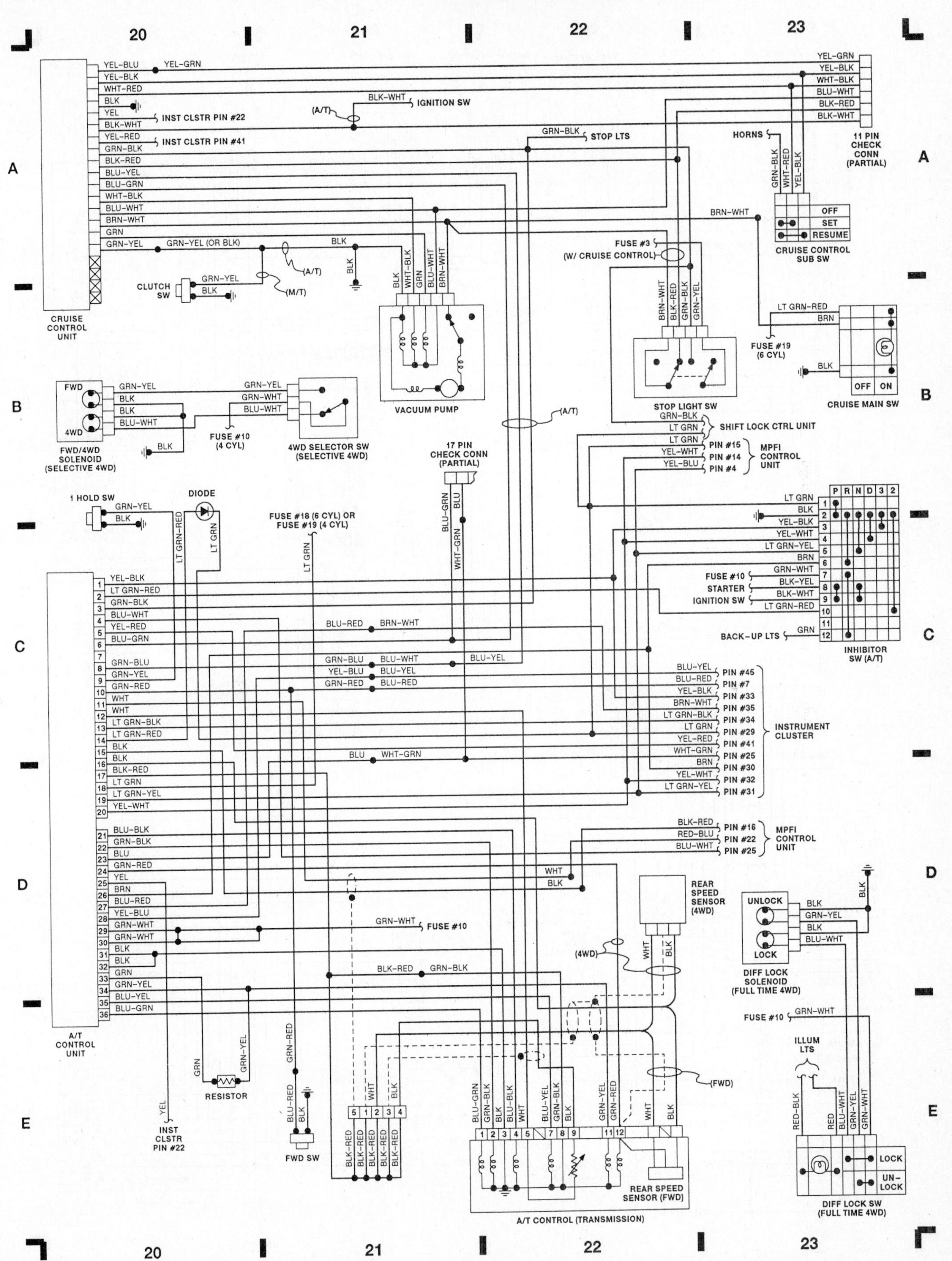

# 1991 WIRING DIAGRAMS
# XT & XT6 (Cont.)

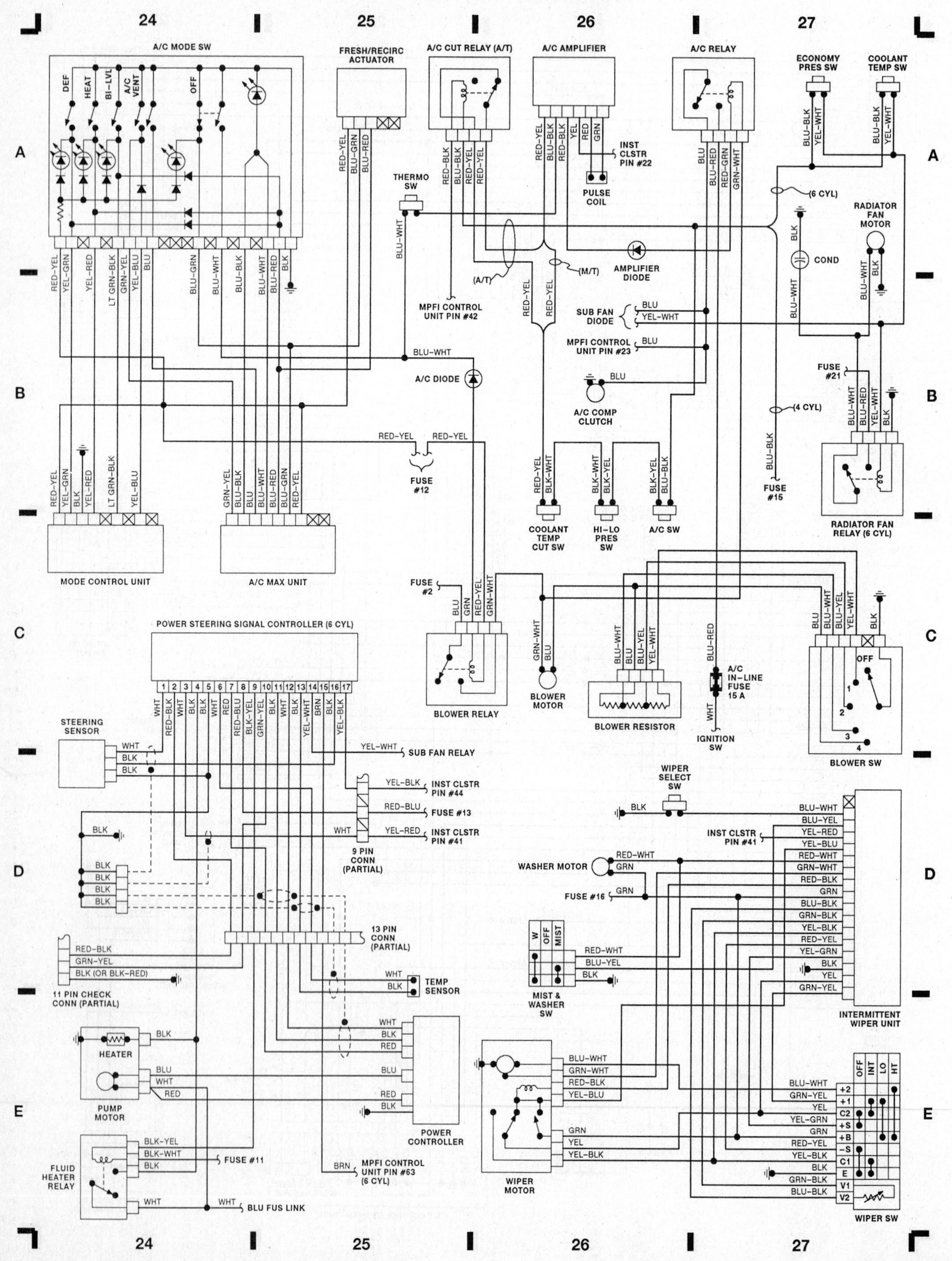

# 1991 WIRING DIAGRAMS
# XT & XT6 (Cont.)

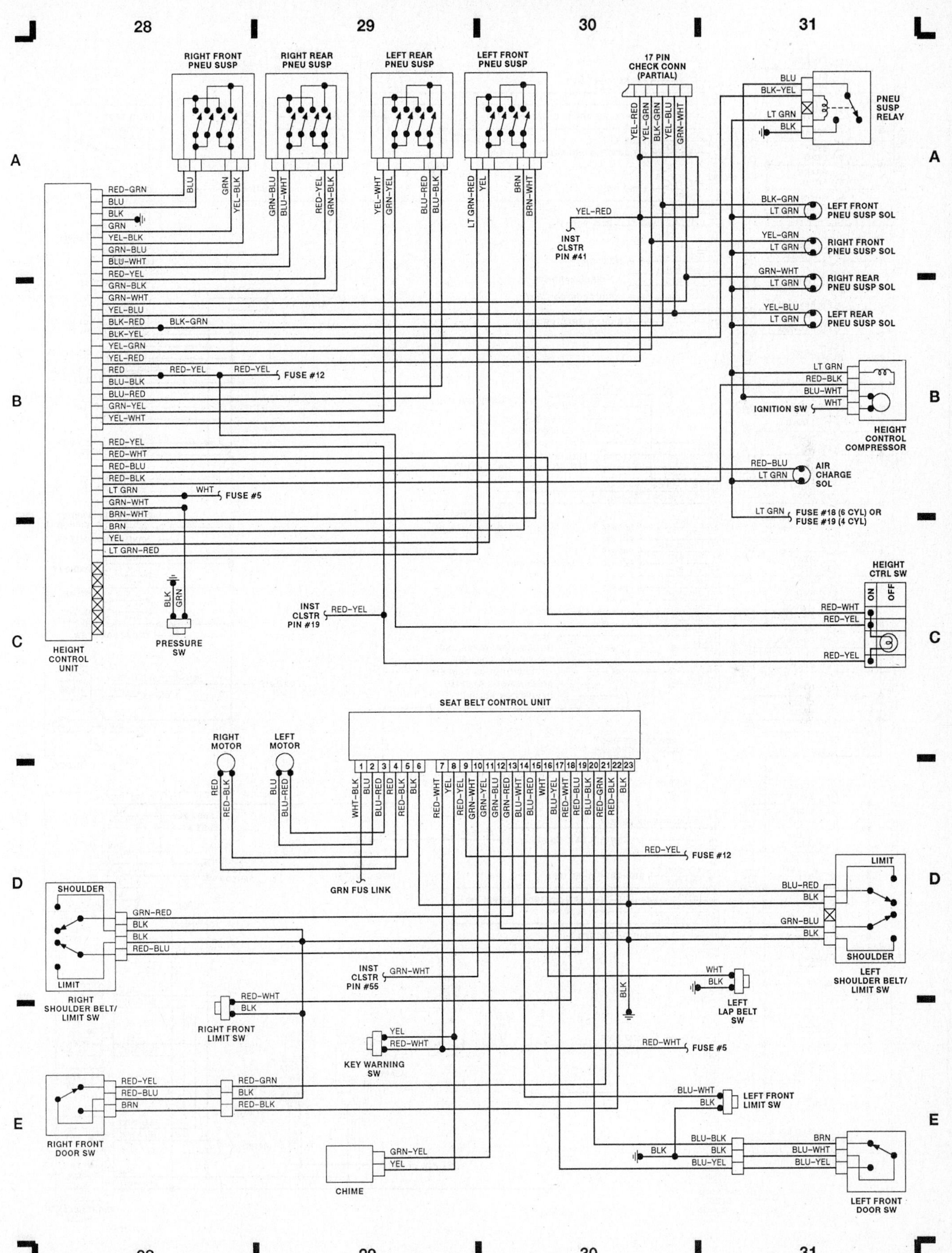

# 1991 WIRING DIAGRAMS
# XT & XT6 (Cont.)

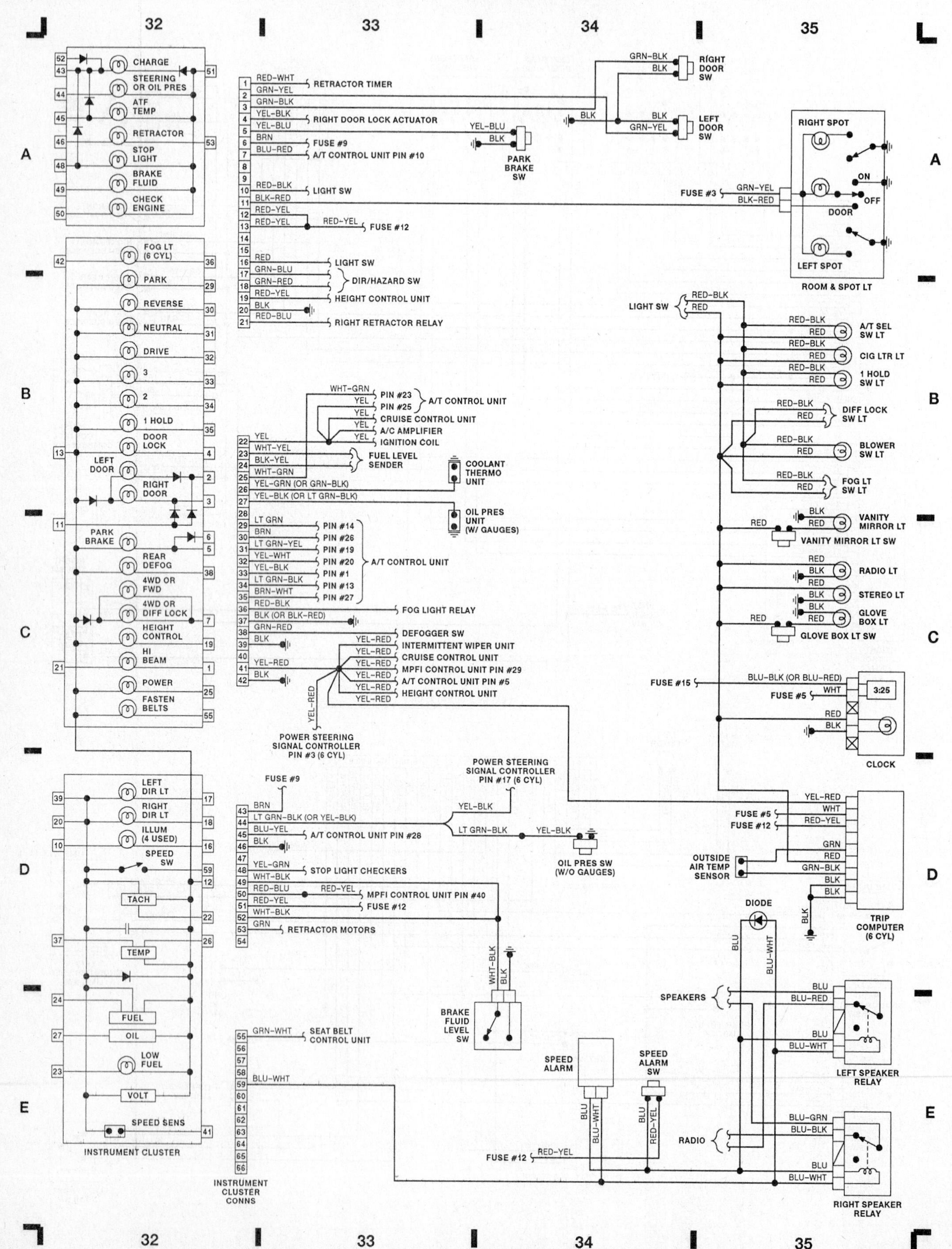

# 1991 WIRING DIAGRAMS
# XT & XT6 (Cont.)



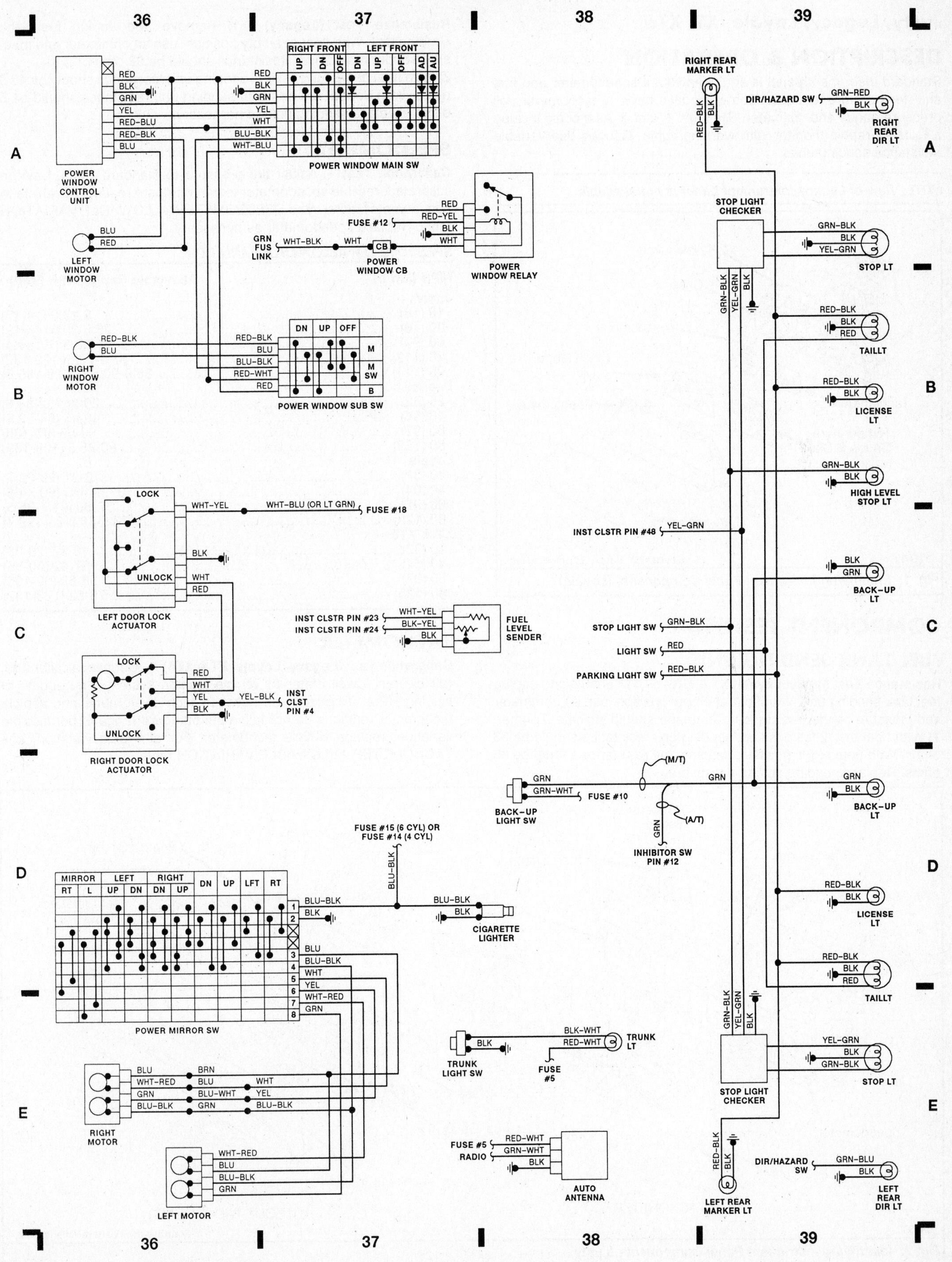

# 1991 SAFETY EQUIPMENT
# Instrument Panels

## Justy, Legacy, Loyale, XT, XT6

## DESCRIPTION & OPERATION

Standard instrument panel is equipped with a speedometer and fuel and temperature gauges. Some models have a tachometer, oil pressure gauge and voltmeter. *See Figs. 1, 2 or 3.* All models include a telltale graphic monitor with warning lights. Gauges use variable resistance sending units.

***NOTE: View of Legacy instrument panel is not available.***

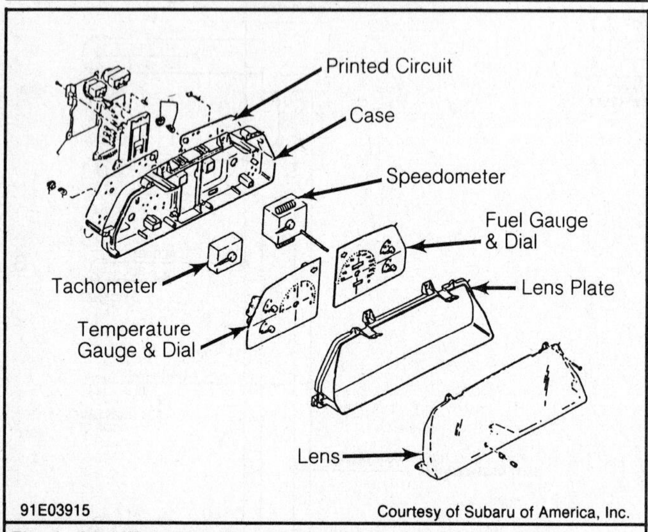


***Fig. 1: Identifying Instrument Panel Components (Loyale)***

## COMPONENT TESTING

### FUEL TANK SENDING UNIT

**Resistance Test (Justy, Loyale, XT & XT6) - 1)** Remove and unplug fuel tank sending unit. With float at empty position, use an ohmmeter and measure sender resistance. Ohmmeter should indicate 7 ohms.
**2)** With float at 1/2 full position, sending unit resistance should be 33 ohms. With float at full position, sending unit resistance should be 95 ohms. Replace sending unit as necessary.

**Resistance Test (Legacy) - 1)** Remove and unplug fuel tank sending unit. With float at empty position, use an ohmmeter and measure sender resistance. Resistance should be 92 ohms.
**2)** With float at 1/2 full position, sending unit resistance should be 48.5 ohms. With float at full position, sending unit resistance should be 5 ohms. Replace sending unit as necessary.

### SPEEDOMETER

**Calibration Test** - Adjust tire pressure to standard value. Using a calibrated, reliable speedometer tester, compare reading of vehicle to speedometer tester. See SPEEDOMETER ALLOWABLE VARIATION table. Replace speedometer as necessary.

***SPEEDOMETER ALLOWABLE VARIATION***

| MPH (km/h) | Allowable Range MPH (km/h) |
|---|---|
| **Justy** | |
| 10 (16) | 9-10.6 (14-17) |
| 30 (48) | 28.6-30.6 (46-49) |
| 60 (97) | 48-50.6 (77-81.4) |
| 70 (112) | 67.5-70.6 (122-132) |
| 90 (144) | 86.9-90.5 (139.8-145.6) |
| **Legacy** | |
| 20 (32) | 20-24 (32-38.6) |
| 40 (64) | 40-45 (64-72.4) |
| 60 (97) | 60-66 (97-106) |
| 80 (129) | 80-86.5 (129-139) |
| **Loyale** | |
| 20 (32) | 18-21 (29-33.7) |
| 40 (64) | 37.5-40.5 (60.3-65) |
| 60 (97) | 57-60 (91.7-96.5) |
| 80 (129) | 76.5-80 (123-128.7) |
| **XT & XT6** | |
| 20 (32) | 18-22 (29-35) |
| 40 (64) | 37-42 (60-68) |
| 60 (97) | 56-62 (90-100) |
| 80 (129) | 76-82 (122-132) |

### TACHOMETER

**Calibration Test (Legacy, Loyale, XT & XT6) -** Connect a calibrated, reliable tach-dwell meter to vehicle ignition system. Run engine at varying RPM. If comparison between tach-dwell meter and vehicle tachometer readings do not fall in the standard range of permissible variation, replace vehicle tachometer. For allowable variation, see TACHOMETER ALLOWABLE VARIATION table.

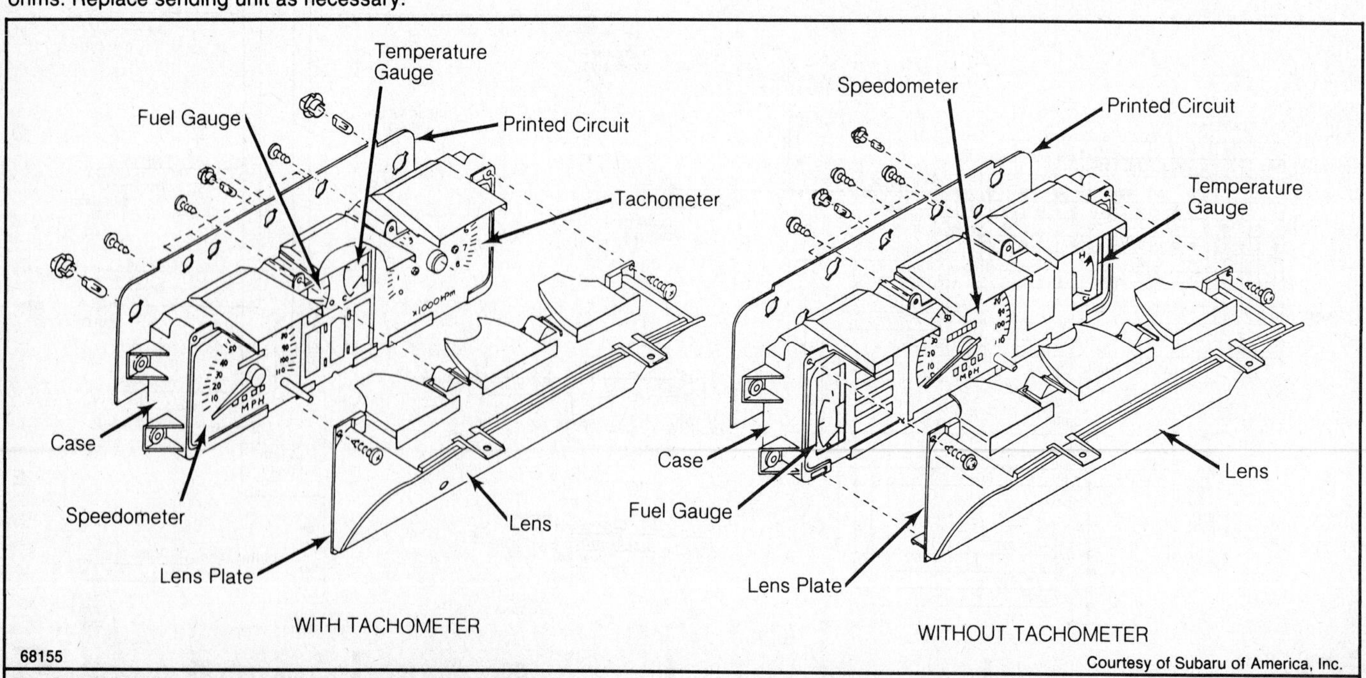


***Fig. 2: Identifying Instrument Panel Components (Justy)***

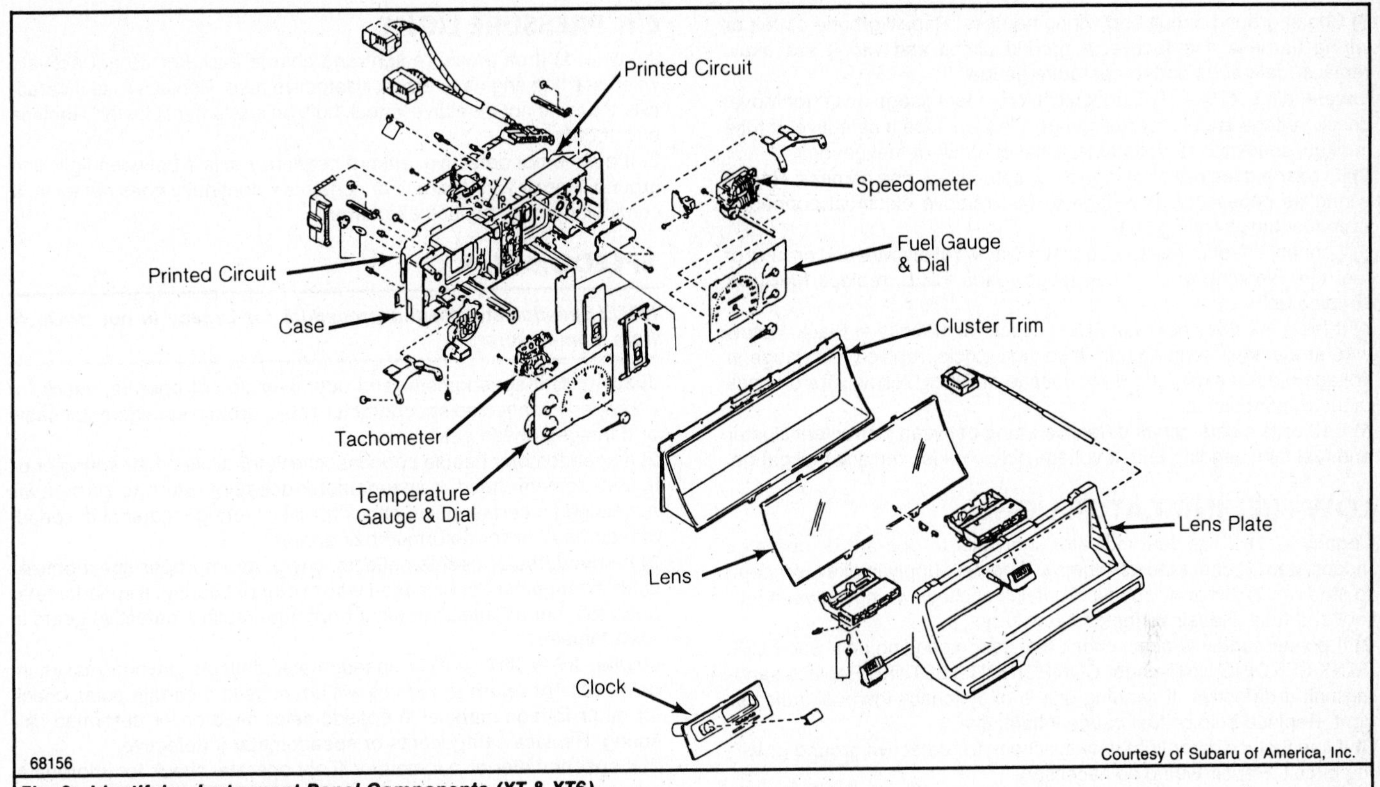


*Fig. 3: Identifying Instrument Panel Components (XT & XT6)*

***TACHOMETER ALLOWABLE VARIATION***

| Engine RPM | Tachometer RPM Range |
|---|---|
| **Legacy** | |
| 1000 | 925-1075 |
| 2000 | 1890-2145 |
| 3000 | 2890-3180 |
| 4000 | 3890-4220 |
| 5000 | 4900-5255 |
| 6000 | 5900-6290 |
| **Loyale, XT & XT6** | |
| 1000 | 940-1090 |
| 2000 | 1955-2145 |
| 3000 | 2970-3200 |
| 4000 | 3980-4250 |
| 5000 | 4990-5305 |
| 6000 | 6000-6360 |

## TEMPERATURE GAUGE

**Resistance Test (Loyale, XT & XT6) –** Temperature gauge standard resistance should be 45 ohms. Replace gauge as necessary.

## TEMPERATURE GAUGE SENDING UNIT

**Resistance Test –** With engine coolant at specified temperatures, resistances of sending unit should be as listed in SENDING UNIT RESISTANCE table. Replace sending unit as necessary.

***SENDING UNIT RESISTANCE***

| Application Gauge Reading °F (°C) | Coolant Temp. °F (°C) | Ohms |
|---|---|---|
| **Justy** | | |
| 122 (50) | N/A | 154 |
| 187 (86) | 167-186 (75-85.5) | 52 |
| 239 (115) | 211-228 (99.5-109) | 23.6 |
| 266 (130) | N/A | 12.4 |
| **Legacy** | | |
| 122 (50) | 115-129 (46-54) | 187.6 |
| 248 (120) | 241-255 (116-124) | 19 |
| **Loyale, XT & XT6** | | |
| 158 (70) | 144-169 (62-76) | 72 |
| 248 (120) | 243-253 (117-123) | 16.1 |

## VOLTMETER

**Calibration Test (Loyale, XT & XT6) –** Connect a test voltmeter to vehicle voltmeter circuits. Compare vehicle voltmeter to test voltmeter. See VOLTMETER ALLOWABLE VARIATION table. Replace vehicle voltmeter if not within specified range.

***VOLTMETER ALLOWABLE VARIATION***

| Test Gauge (Volts) | Allowable Range (Volts) |
|---|---|
| 8 | 7-8 |
| 12 | 11.4-12.6 |
| 16 | 15-17 |

# SYSTEM TESTING

## FUEL GAUGE & SENDING UNIT

**Justy – 1)** Turn ignition switch to ACC position. Note if fuel gauge indicates below empty. If fuel gauge does not indicate below EMPTY, replace fuel gauge.

**2)** If fuel gauge indicates below EMPTY, turn ignition on. Ensure voltage exists at the fuse. If voltage exists, proceed to step **3)**. If fuse is blown, replace fuse and check for shorts in wiring. If no voltage exists, check for broken wiring harness between battery and fuse box. Repair wiring as necessary.

**3)** Ensure 12 volts exists between Green/White wire and ground at back of combination meter connector. If voltage exists, proceed to step **4)**. If voltage did not exist, check for open in wiring between fuse box and combination meter. Repair wiring as necessary.

**4)** Connect 17-ohm resistor between fuel tank sending unit Green/White wire and ground. If gauge reads FULL, replace fuel tank sending unit.

**Legacy – 1)** If fuel gauge does not move, check voltage supply for fuel gauge. If voltage supply is okay, proceed to step **2)**. If voltage supply is defective, check for defective fuse or wiring between battery and fuse.

**2)** Check fuel tank sending unit. See FUEL TANK SENDING UNIT under COMPONENT TESTING. Replace sending unit if defective. If sending unit is okay, proceed to step **3)**.

# 1991 SAFETY EQUIPMENT
# Instrument Panels (Cont.)

**3)** Check ground circuit and wiring harness. Repair ground circuit or wiring harness if defective. If ground circuit and wiring are okay, replace fuel gauge and temperature gauge.
**Loyale, XT & XT6 - 1)** Turn ignition on. If fuel gauge does not move, check voltage supply for fuel gauge. Replace fuse if defective. If fuse is okay, check for 12 volts at terminal on back of fuel gauge.
**2)** If voltage does not exist, check for defective wiring harness. Repair wiring as necessary. If voltage exists, remove electrical connector from fuel tank sending unit.
**3)** Connect a 7-ohm resistor between Black/Yellow wire and ground of fuel tank sending unit. If fuel gauge reads FULL, replace fuel tank sending unit.
**4)** If fuel tank does not read FULL, check for 12 volts at Black/Yellow wire at fuel tank sending unit. If voltage exists, replace fuel gauge. If voltage did not exist, check for voltage at Black/Yellow wire on back of instrument cluster.
**5)** If 12 volts exists, repair defective wiring between instrument cluster and fuel tank sending unit. If voltage did not exist, replace fuel gauge.

## LOW FUEL INDICATOR LIGHT

**Legacy - 1)** If low fuel indicator light fails to operate or operates inconsistently, check power supply. If power supply is okay, proceed to step No. **2)**. If power supply is defective, check wiring between battery and fuse. Repair wiring as necessary.
**2)** If power supply is okay, check fuel gauge sending unit. See FUEL TANK SENDING UNIT under COMPONENT TESTING. Replace sending unit if defective. If sending unit is okay, check low fuel indicator light. Replace bulb or fuel gauge if defective.
**3)** If low fuel indicator light is okay, check for defective ground or wiring circuit. Repair wiring as necessary.
**Loyale, XT & XT6 - 1)** If low fuel indicator light fails to operate or activates inconsistently, ensure fuse is okay. Replace fuse if defective. If fuse is okay, turn ignition on.
**2)** Check fuel gauge and temperature gauge operation. If fuel gauge and temperature gauge do not operate, repair Black/White wire (Loyale) or Red/Yellow wire (XT & XT6) between fuse and instrument cluster. If fuel gauge and temperature gauge operate, proceed to step **3)**.
**3)** Remove fuel tank sending unit connector. Ground White/Yellow lead and note if low fuel indicator light activates. If low fuel indicator light activates, proceed to step **4)**. If light does not activate, check for defective bulb. If bulb is okay, repair White/Yellow wire circuit between instrument cluster and fuel tank sending unit.
**4)** If low fuel indicator light activated, check for improper connection at fuel tank sending unit or improper ground on fuel gauge. If connections and ground on gauge are okay, replace fuel tank sending unit.

## OIL PRESSURE GAUGE

**Loyale, XT & XT6 - 1)** Replace oil pressure gauge if gauge reading does not lower with ignition off. Turn ignition on. If gauge reading does not increase, check for defective fuse. Replace fuse if defective. If fuse is not defective, proceed to step **2)**. If gauge reading increases, proceed to step **4)**.
**2)** Ensure 12 volts exists on Yellow/Black wire of 12-pin connector (Loyale) or Light Green/Black wire of 21-pin connector (XT and XT6) at rear of instrument cluster. If 12 volts exists, repair defective wiring between oil pressure gauge and oil pressure sending unit.
**3)** If 12 volts does exist, in step **2)**, check for 12 volts on Black/White wire of 12-pin connector (Loyale) or Red/Yellow wire of 21-pin connector (XT and XT6) at rear of instrument cluster. If voltage exists, replace oil pressure gauge. If voltage does exist, check for defective power supply to instrument cluster from ignition.
**4)** If oil pressure gauge operates, remove connector from oil pressure sending unit. Connect a 140-ohm resistor between oil pressure sending unit connector and ground.
**5)** Oil pressure gauge should now read 57 psi (4 kg/cm$^2$)). If reading is correct, replace oil pressure sending unit. If reading is not correct, replace oil pressure gauge.

## OIL PRESSURE LIGHT

**Justy - 1)** If oil pressure light and charge indicator do not activate when starting engine, check for defective fuse. Replace fuse if defective. If fuse is not defective, check bulb on instrument cluster. Replace bulb if defective.
**2)** If bulb is not defective, ensure continuity exists between light and ground. Repair wiring circuit or contacts if continuity does not exist. If continuity exists, replace alternator.

## SPEEDOMETER

***NOTE: Speedometer testing procedure for Legacy is not available from manufacturer.***

**Justy - 1)** If speedometer and odometer do not operate, check for improperly connected speedometer cable, broken speedometer cable or damaged driven gear.
**2)** If speedometer needle bounces, check for broken hair spring or oil in speedometer head. If speedometer does not return to zero or will not exceed a certain point, check for oil or foreign material in speedometer head or for deformed hair spring.
**3)** If speedometer needle deflects, check for improper speedometer cable arrangement or damaged worm rotor or bearing. If speedometer operates, but odometer does not operate, replace defective gears in speedometer.
**Loyale, XT & XT6 - 1)** If speedometer deflects beyond maximum point, will not return to zero or will not exceed a certain point, check for oil or foreign material in speedometer head or for deformed hair spring. Replace components or speedometer if defective.
**2)** If speedometer or odometer will not operate, check for improperly connected speedometer cable, broken speedometer cable or damaged driven gear. Replace defective components.
**3)** If speedometer deflects erratically, check for improper cable routing or defective cable. If speedometer operates but odometer or trip meter does not operate, check for defective gear in speedometer. Replace defective components.

## TACHOMETER

**Loyale, XT & XT6 - 1)** If tachometer does not operate, check for defective fuse. Replace fuse if defective. If fuse is not defective, check for power to tachometer and proper ground. If defective, repair as necessary.
**2)** If power and ground are okay with ignition off, check continuity between tachometer terminal of instrument cluster and (-) terminal of ignition coil. Repair wiring if no continuity exists. If wiring circuit is okay, replace tachometer.
**3)** If tachometer needle deflects beyond maximum point, will not return to zero, or will not exceed a certain point, replace tachometer.

## TEMPERATURE GAUGE & SENDING UNIT

**Justy - 1)** If temperature gauge indicates below COLD with ignition switch in ACC position, replace temperature gauge. If temperature gauge indicates below COLD with ignition on, ensure fuse is okay.
**2)** Replace fuse if defective. If fuse is not defective, check for defective wiring harness between battery and fuse box. Repair as necessary.
**3)** If fuse is not defective, check for 12 volts between Yellow/Red wire and ground at electrical connector on back of instrument panel. If 12 volts does not exist, check for broken wiring between fuse box and instrument panel. Repair wiring as necessary.
**4)** If voltage does exist, connect a 18.5-ohm resistor between Yellow/Red wire and ground at temperature gauge sending unit. If temperature gauge indicates 240°F (115°C), replace sending unit. If temperature gauge does not indicate 240°F (115°C), replace temperature gauge.
**Legacy - 1)** If temperature gauge does not operate, check power supply. If power supply is defective, check and repair wiring between battery and fuse. If power supply is okay, check temperature gauge sending unit. See TEMPERATURE GAUGE SENDING UNIT under COMPONENT TESTING. Replace sending unit if defective.

**2)** If sending unit is okay, check ground circuit and wiring harness. Repair ground circuit if defective. If ground circuit is okay, replace temperature gauge.

**Loyale, XT & XT6 - 1)** Turn ignition off. Replace temperature gauge if gauge indicates below COLD. Turn ignition on. Note if fuel gauge is operating correctly. If fuel gauge is operating correctly, proceed to step **3)**.

**2)** If fuel gauge is not operating correctly, check for defective fuse. Replace fuse if defective. If fuse is okay, check for 12 volts on temperature gauge terminal on back of instrument cluster. If voltage does not exist, repair wiring to instrument cluster. If voltage exists, replace temperature gauge.

**3)** If fuel gauge operates correctly, connect a 42-ohm resistor between Yellow/Green wire and ground at temperature gauge sending unit. If temperature gauge indicates 187°F (86°C), replace sending unit.

**4)** If temperature gauge does not indicate 187°F (86°C), ensure 7 volts exists on Yellow/Green wire at sending unit. If 7 volts exists, replace temperature gauge.

**5)** If 7 volts does not exist at sending unit, check for 7 volts on Yellow/Green wire of 12-pin connector (Loyale) or Yellow/Green wire of 21-pin connector (XT and XT6) at rear of instrument cluster.

**6)** If 7 volts does not exist at instrument cluster, replace temperature gauge. If 7 volts does exist, check wiring between instrument cluster and sending unit. Repair as necessary.

### VOLTMETER

**Loyale, XT & XT6 - 1)** If voltmeter needle will not lower with ignition off, replace voltmeter. Turn ignition on. If voltmeter operates, proceed to step **3)**. If voltmeter does not operate, check for defective fuse. Replace fuse if defective.

**2)** If fuse is okay, ensure 12 volts exists on Black/White wire of 12-pin connector (Loyale) or Red/Yellow wire of 21-pin connector (XT and XT6) at rear of instrument cluster. If voltage does not exist, check for defective wiring to instrument cluster. Replace voltmeter if voltage exists.

**3)** Ensure battery is fully charged. Turn headlights and all accessories on and note voltmeter reading. Voltmeter should read 11.5 to 12.5 volts. Replace voltmeter is voltage reading is incorrect.

## REMOVAL & INSTALLATION

### INSTRUMENT PANELS & SWITCHES

**Removal & Installation (Justy) - 1)** Disconnect negative battery cable. Remove 4 clips, one screw, choke knob and nut retaining cluster cover. Remove cluster cover. Remove 4 cluster retaining screws.

**2)** Pull cluster forward and disconnect wiring and speedometer cable from rear of cluster. Remove instrument cluster. To install, reverse removal procedure.

**Removal & Installation (Legacy) - 1)** Disconnect negative battery cable. Remove steering column bracket bolts and lower column. Remove ventilation grille from visor. Disconnect and remove switches. Remove cup holder. Remove visor.

**2)** Remove cluster retaining screws. Pull cluster forward and disconnect wiring and speedometer cable from rear of cluster. Remove cluster. To install, reverse removal procedure.

**Removal & Installation (Loyale) - 1)** Disconnect negative battery cable. Remove steering column bracket bolts and lower column. Remove screws retaining cluster cover. *See Fig. 4*. Disconnect wire connectors and remove cover.

**2)** Remove cluster retaining screws. Pull cluster forward and disconnect wiring and speedometer cable from rear of cluster. Remove cluster. To install, reverse removal procedure.

**Removal & Installation (XT & XT6) - 1)** Disconnect negative battery cable. Disconnect steering column universal joint. Remove lower panel and ventilation duct. Remove protector. Disconnect wiring harness connectors for steering sensor, ignition switch, combination switch, control wing switch, and instrument cluster.

**2)** Remove harness retaining screws. Disconnect speedometer cable. Raise steering wheel and remove cable. Push steering wheel down and lock. Tighten tilt lock bolt beneath column bracket. *See Fig. 5*.

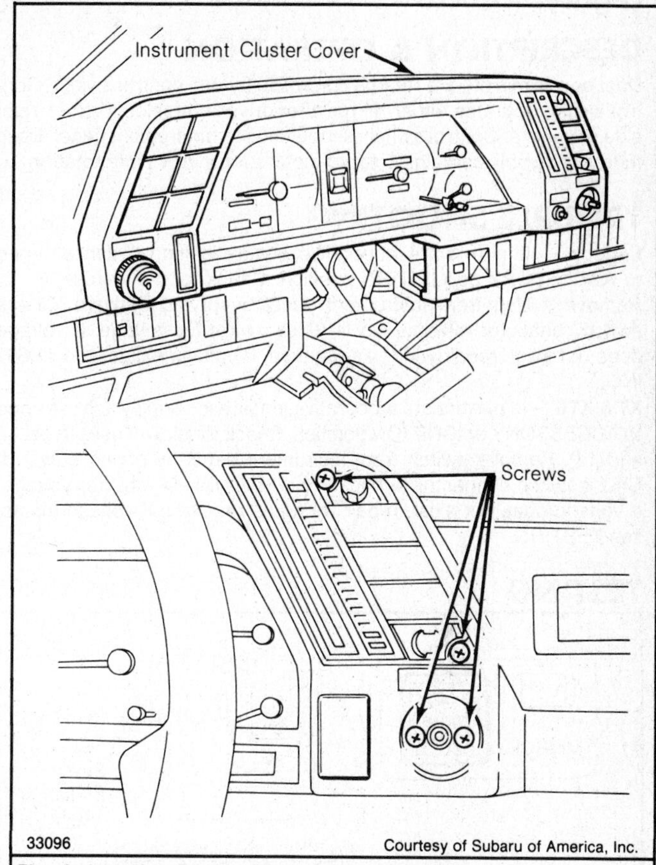


***Fig. 4: Locating Cluster Cover Screws (Loyale)***

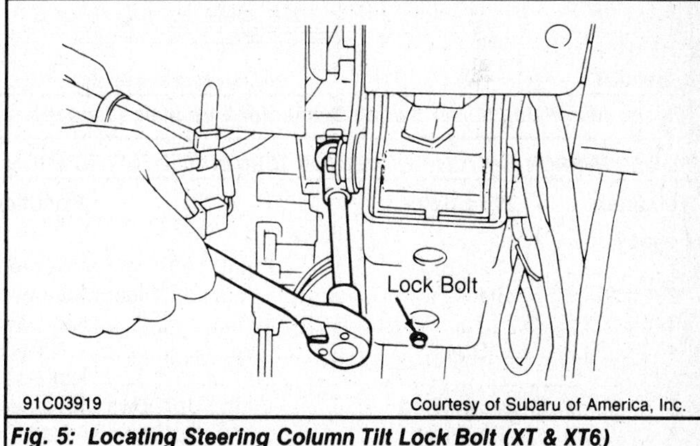


***Fig. 5: Locating Steering Column Tilt Lock Bolt (XT & XT6)***

**3)** Remove steering column bracket bolts. Remove steering shaft assembly with instrument cluster. Remove nut on cluster bracket of steering column. Remove cluster and covers. Remove screws and disconnect control wings. To install, reverse removal procedure.

***NOTE: To remove switch knob, push pawl inside knob with a pin and pull knob out.***

## WIRING DIAGRAMS

See appropriate chassis wiring diagram in WIRING DIAGRAMS.

# 1991 SAFETY EQUIPMENT
## Power Mirrors

### Legacy, XT, XT6

## DESCRIPTION & OPERATION

Dual power mirrors are remote controlled by one control switch. Control switch operates either mirror after driver pre-selects left or right side of vehicle. Control switch is mounted into instrument panel. Each mirror assembly contains 2 servo motors for mirror plate rotation.

## TROUBLE SHOOTING

**Legacy** – If mirrors are inoperative, ensure ignition switch is turned to ACCESSORY or IGNITION position. Check for blown fuse No. 3. Remove switch from instrument panel by prying outward. Check switch connector terminal No. 4 (Green wire) for voltage. If voltage does not exist, repair wiring as required. If voltage exists, see TESTING.

**XT & XT6** – If mirrors are inoperative, ensure ignition switch is turned to ACCESSORY or IGNITION position. Check for blown fuses (Nos. 13 and 14). Remove switch from instrument panel by prying outward. Check switch connector terminal No. 1 (Blue/Black wire) for voltage. If voltage does not exist, repair wiring as required. If voltage exists, see TESTING.

## TESTING

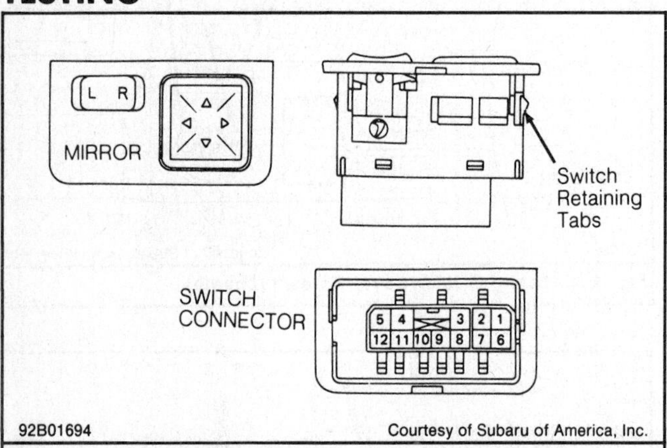


*Fig. 1: Identifying Mirror Switch Connector Terminals (Legacy)*

***POWER MIRROR SWITCH CONNECTOR TERMINAL IDENTIFICATION***

| Terminal | Wire Color | Function |
|---|---|---|
| **Legacy** | | |
| 1 | Red/Blue | Right, Left/Right Movement |
| 2 | Black/Red | Left, Left/Right Movement |
| 3 | | Not Used |
| 4 | Green | Power |
| 5 | | Not Used |
| 6 | Brown/Red | Right, Up/Down Movement |
| 7 | Blue/Red | Left, Up/Down Movement |
| 8 | | Not Used |
| 9 | | Not Used |
| 10 | Red | [1] Both Motors |
| 11 | Black | Out To Ground |
| 12 | | Not Used |
| **XT & XT6** | | |
| 1 | Blue/Black | Power |
| 2 | Black | Ground |
| 3 | Blue | Either, Left & Right Movement |
| 4 | Blue/White | Either, Up/Down Movement |
| 5 | White | Right, Left/Right Movement |
| 6 | Yellow | Right, Up/Down Movement |
| 7 | Brown | Left, Left/Right Movement |
| 8 | Green | Left, Up/Down Movement |

[1] – This particular switch wire is connected to both left and right mirror's motors. It is used for sending power to motor, or used for a ground for motor depending on switch position.

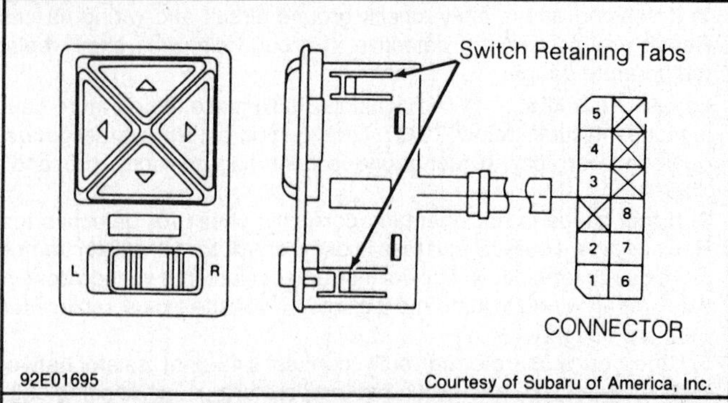


*Fig. 2: Identifying Mirror Switch Connector Terminals (XT & XT6)*

## POWER MIRROR MOTOR TEST

**Legacy** – Remove door panel. Unplug mirror motor 6-pin harness connector. Using 12-volt power supply and 2 jumper wires, apply voltage to specified terminal and ground other specified terminal as per table. See POWER MIRROR MOTOR TEST table. *See Fig. 3.*

***POWER MIRROR MOTOR TEST***

| Function | Battery Terminal | Ground Terminal |
|---|---|---|
| Up | 1 | 3 |
| Down | 3 | 1 |
| Right | 3 | 2 |
| Left | 2 | 3 |

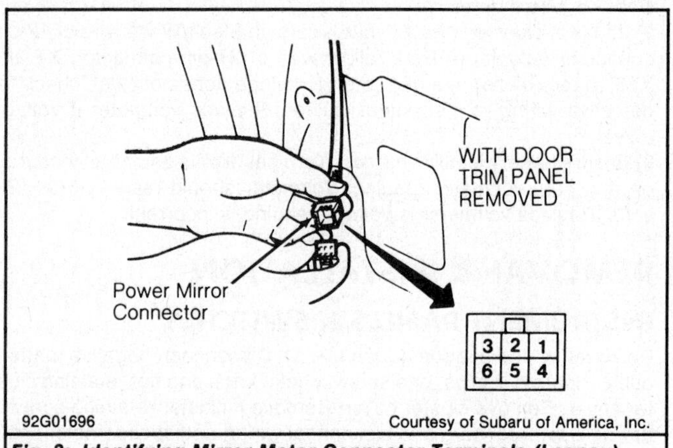


*Fig. 3: Identifying Mirror Motor Connector Terminals (Legacy)*

## POWER MIRROR SWITCH TEST

**Legacy – 1)** Remove mirror switch from instrument panel. Unplug switch harness connector. Press desired position button on switch, while checking switch connector terminal continuity. See POWER MIRROR SWITCH CONTINUITY TEST table. *See Fig. 1.*

**2)** If continuity testing results for all switch positions are correct, check for faulty ground wire connection.

**XT & XT6 – 1)** Remove mirror switch from instrument panel. Unplug switch harness connector. Press desired position button on switch, while checking switch connector terminal continuity. See POWER MIRROR SWITCH CONTINUITY TEST table. *See Fig. 2.*

**2)** XT models have capability of oblique movements. By pressing 2 adjacent position buttons at same time, mirror plate will move diagonally. If continuity testing results for all switch positions are correct, check for faulty ground wire connection.

# 1991 SAFETY EQUIPMENT
# Power Mirrors (Cont.)

*POWER MIRROR SWITCH CONTINUITY TEST*

| Application | Terminals |
|---|---|
| **Legacy** [1] | |
| Left Mirror | |
| Up | 4 & 7, 10 & 11 |
| Down | 4 & 10, 7 & 11 |
| Left | 2 & 4, 10 & 11 |
| Right | 4 & 10, 2 & 11 |
| Right Mirror | |
| Up | 4 & 6, 10 & 11 |
| Down | 4 & 10, 6 & 11 |
| Left | 1 & 4, 10 & 11 |
| Right | 4 & 10, 1 & 11 |
| **XT & XT6** [2] | |
| Left Mirror | |
| Up | 1 & 8, 4 & 2 |
| Down | 1 & 4, 8 & 2 |
| Left | 1 & 3, 7 & 2 |
| Right | 1 & 7, 3 & 2 |
| Up/Left Diagonally | 1, 3 & 8; 4, 7 & 2 |
| Down/Left Diagonally | 1, 3 & 4; 7, 8 & 2 |
| Up/Right Diagonally | 1, 7 & 8; 3, 8 & 2 |
| Down/Right Diagonally | 1, 4 & 7; 3, 8 & 2 |
| Right Mirror | |
| Up | 1 & 6, 4 & 2 |
| Down | 1 & 4, 6 & 2 |
| Left | 1 & 3, 5 7 2 |
| Right | 1 & 5, 3 & 2 |
| Up/Left Diagonally | 1, 3 & 6; 4, 5 & 2 |
| Down/Left Diagonally | 1, 3 & 4; 5, 6 & 2 |
| Up/Right Diagonally | 1, 5 & 6; 3, 4 & 2 |
| Down/Right Diagonally | 1, 4 & 5; 3, 6 & 2 |

[1] – Legacy connector terminal No. 11 is ground.
[2] – XT connector terminal No. 2 is ground.

## REMOVAL & INSTALLATION

### POWER MIRROR SWITCH

**1)** Using small flat blade screwdriver, remove switch from instrument panel by prying side edges outward to release switch retaining tabs on sides of switch. There are 2 retaining tabs per side of switch. *See Figs. 1 and 2*. Be careful not to damage instrument panel.

**2)** Remove switch and unplug harness connector. To install, plug harness connector into switch. Push switch into panel until it snaps into position or until switch bezel is flush with panel.

### POWER MIRROR ASSEMBLY

**1)** Remove door trim panel by first removing top of trim panel gusset cover. Remove door pull handle screws and window regulator handle. Remove trim panel using Clip Puller (925580000) to remove retaining clips surrounding door trim panel.

**2)** Remove sealing cover with care, in order that it may be reused. Unplug mirror motor harness connector. Hold outside mirror while removing mirror mounting screws to keep mirror from damaging body. Remove mirror and harness from body.

## WIRING DIAGRAMS

See appropriate chassis wiring diagram in WIRING DIAGRAMS.

# 1991 SAFETY EQUIPMENT
# Rear Window Defogger

## Justy, Legacy, Loyale, XT, XT6

## TROUBLE SHOOTING

### REAR DEFOGGER INOPERATIVE

**Indicator Light On (Legacy)** – If rear defogger will not come on but indicator light comes on, check the following:

- Slow-blow fuse No. 5 in main fuse box, located in engine compartment.
- Fuse No. 7 in passenger compartment fuse box, located under left side of dash.
- Rear defogger relay in passenger compartment fuse box.
- Open grid wire.
- Poor ground connection.
- Open in wiring harness.

**Indicator Light Off (Legacy)** – If rear defogger and indicator light will not come on, check the following:

- Fusible link in main fuse box, located in engine compartment.
- Slow-blow fuse No. 4 in main fuse box, located in engine compartment.
- Ignition switch.
- Fuse No. 7 in passenger compartment fuse box, located under left side of dash.
- Rear defogger relay in passenger compartment fuse box.
- Indicator light bulb.
- Open grid wire.
- Poor ground connection.
- Open in harness.

**Defogger Inoperative (Loyale, XT & XT6)** – **1)** Turn ignition on. Ensure harness-to-grid connector is tight. With rear defogger switch on, 12 volts should be present at harness-to-grid connector.

**2)** If 12 volts is not present, check circuit between rear defogger relay and grid for open or poor connection. If 12 volts is present, check circuit between grid harness and ground for poor connection.

### DEFOGGER INDICATOR LIGHT INOPERATIVE

**Legacy** – If rear defogger operates properly but indicator light does not come on, check the following:

- Indicator light bulb.
- Poor ground connection.
- Open in harness.

**Loyale, XT & XT6** – **1)** If rear defogger operates properly but indicator light does not come on, turn ignition on. Check fuse No. 12 and replace as necessary. If fuse blows again, search for short circuit. If fuse is okay, ensure voltage is not present on White/Green wire circuit (Loyale) or on Green/Red wire circuit (XT & XT6) with defogger switch on.

**2)** With defogger switch off, 12 volts should be present on White/Green wire circuit. If voltage is present on White/Green wire circuit with defogger switch on and 12 volts is not present on White/Green circuit with switch off, check circuit between switch and ground or replace switch.

**3)** If there is no voltage on White/Green wire circuit with defogger switch on and 12 volts is present on White/Green circuit with switch off, check indicator light bulb. Replace as necessary. If bulb is okay, check for poor connection between instrument cluster and switch.

## TESTING

### DEFOGGER SWITCH TEST

***NOTE: Information on testing rear defogger switch for XT and XT6 is not available from manufacturer.***

**Justy, Legacy & Loyale** – Ensure continuity is present between indicated terminals. *See Fig. 1, 2 or 3.*

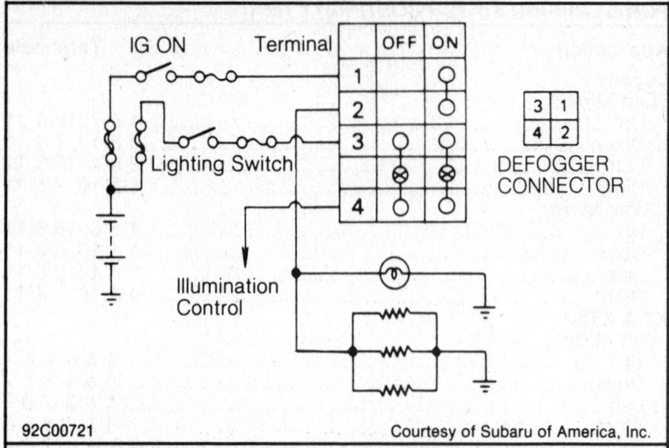


***Fig. 1: Testing Rear Defogger Switch (Justy)***

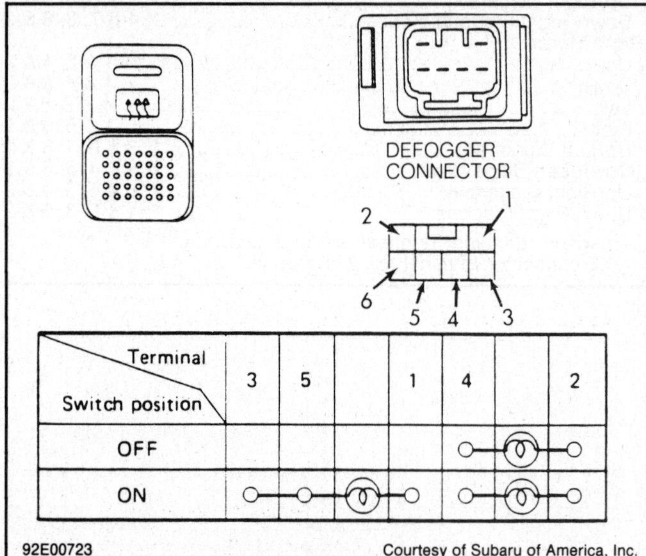


***Fig. 2: Testing Rear Defogger Switch (Legacy)***

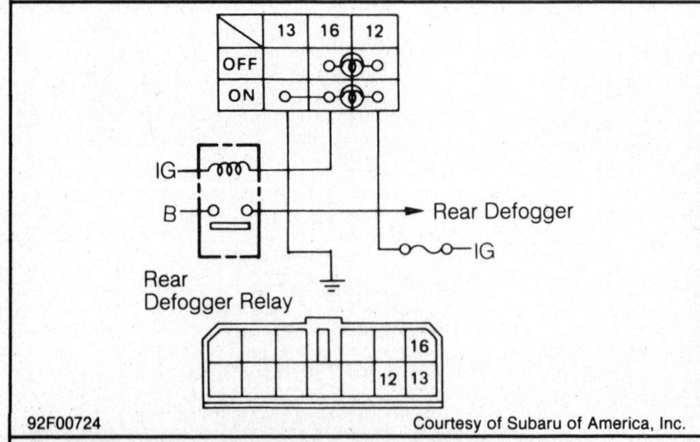


***Fig. 3: Testing Rear Defogger Switch (Loyale)***

### GRID FILAMENT TEST

**1)** Start engine and turn rear defogger switch on. Check each grid line at center point with DVOM. If DVOM reads either 12 volts or zero, grid line being tested is broken.

**2)** An unbroken grid line will read 6 volts. To find broken section, move positive DVOM lead along suspected grid line until sudden change in voltage is seen.

# 1991 SAFETY EQUIPMENT
# Rear Window Defogger (Cont.)

## ON-VEHICLE SERVICE

### GRID FILAMENT REPAIR

**1)** Clean broken area of grid line with alcohol. Place masking tape along both sides of grid line area to be repaired. *See Fig. 4*.

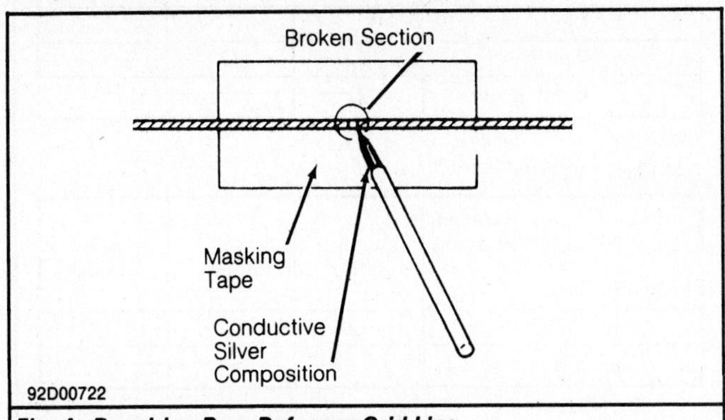


***Fig. 4: Repairing Rear Defogger Grid Line***

**2)** Thoroughly mix small amount of repair agent (Dupont paste No. 4817). Apply agent to grid line break area, overlapping each end of line about 3/4". After a few minutes drying time, carefully remove tape from line edges. DO NOT touch repaired area for 24 hours.

## REMOVAL & INSTALLATION

### DEFOGGER SWITCH

**1)** On Justy and Legacy, use small screwdriver to pry defogger switch out of dash panel. On Loyale, pry off switch knobs and remove screws holding switch panel to dash panel. On XT and XT6, remove combination switch.

**2)** See COMBINATION SWITCH under REMOVAL & INSTALLATION in STEERING COLUMN SWITCHES article. Remove fixing bolts and detach control wing. Remove screws and separate switch cases from control wing. To install, reverse removal procedure.

***NOTE: To remove switch knob, use a pin to lightly depress pawl inside knob. Remove knob. When installing sliding switch knobs and volume control knob, hold rear of control with finger and mesh knob with control.***

***CAUTION: Do not allow wiring harness to become pinched between forward and rear switch cases during installation.***

## WIRING DIAGRAMS

See appropriate chassis wiring diagram in WIRING DIAGRAMS.

# 1991 SAFETY EQUIPMENT
# Steering Column Switches

### Justy, Legacy, Loyale, XT, XT6

## TESTING

### COMBINATION SWITCH

***NOTE: For testing of wiper switch, see appropriate WIPER/WASHER SYSTEMS article in SAFETY EQUIPMENT. For testing of XT and XT6 headlight switch, see HEADLIGHT SWITCH under TESTING in this article.***

**Continuity Tests** – Ensure continuity is present between terminals as indicated in appropriate figure. *See Figs. 1-4*. Repair or replace as necessary.

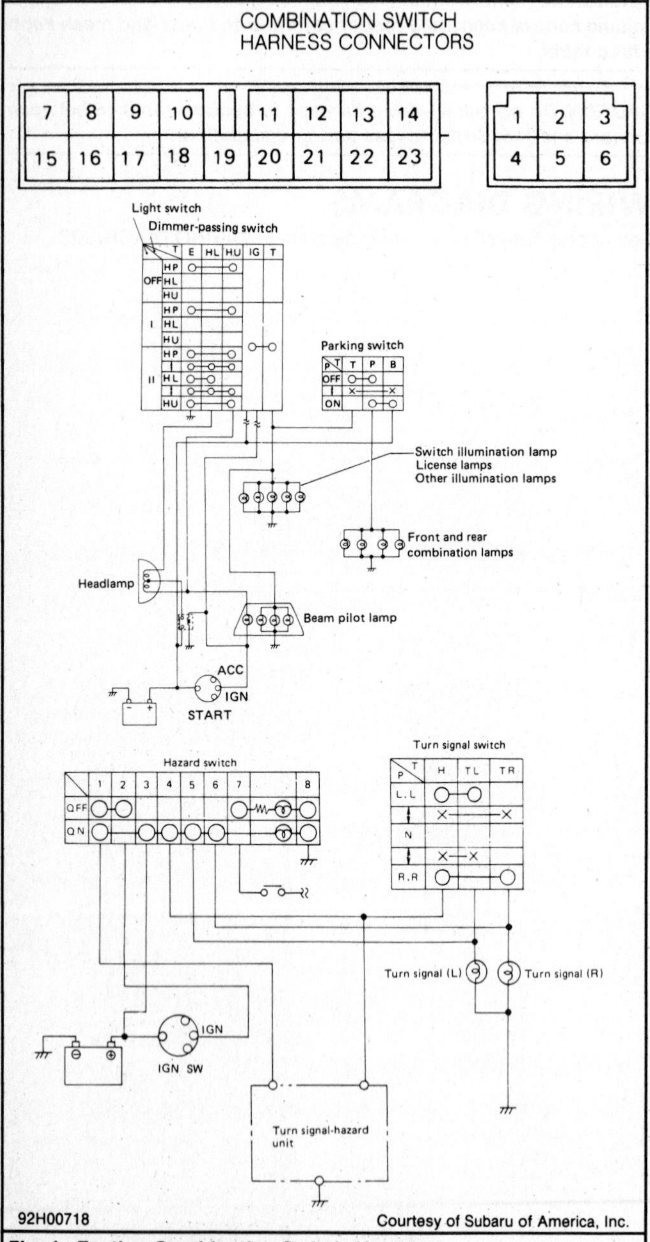


Courtesy of Subaru of America, Inc.

*Fig. 1: Testing Combination Switch (Justy)*

LIGHTING SWITCH

| Switch position \ Terminal (Wire color) | c-1 (W) | c-2 (W) | c-3 (R) |
|---|---|---|---|
| OFF | | | |
| Tail | O— | —O | |
| Head | O— | —O— | —O |

PARKING SWITCH

| Switch position \ Terminal (Wire color) | c-10 (R) | c-11 (RG) | c-9 (RW) |
|---|---|---|---|
| OFF | O— | —O | |
| ON | | O— | —O |

DIMMER & PASSING SWITCH

| Switch position \ Terminal (Wire color) | a-3 (B) | a-2 (RB) | a-1 (RY) | a-4 (YR) |
|---|---|---|---|---|
| Flash | O— | —— | —O— | —O |
| Low beam | O— | —O | | |
| High beam | O— | —— | —O | |

TURN SIGNAL SWITCH

| Switch position \ Terminal (Wire color) | | a-5 (GY) | a-7 (G) | a-b (GR) |
|---|---|---|---|---|
| Turn | L·L' | O— | —O | |
| | | x— | —— | —x |
| | N | | | |
| | | x— | —— | —x |
| | R·R' | | O— | —O |

COMBINATION SWITCH
HARNESS CONNECTORS

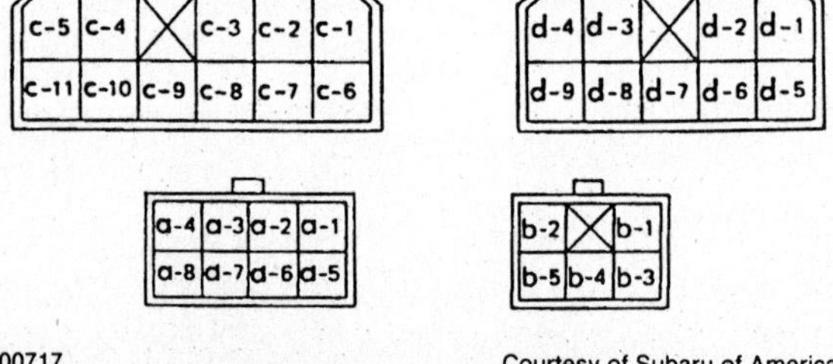


92G00717 Courtesy of Subaru of America, Inc.

*Fig. 2: Testing Combination Switch (Legacy)*

### HAZARD SWITCH

***NOTE: For testing of hazard switch for XT and XT6, see COMBINATION SWITCH under TESTING. Hazard switch on Justy, Legacy and Loyale is located on instrument panel. See INSTRUMENT PANELS article in SAFETY EQUIPMENT.***

### HEADLIGHT SWITCH

***NOTE: For all models except XT & XT6, see COMBINATION SWITCH under TESTING for headlight switch testing procedures.***

**Continuity Tests (XT & XT6)** – Ensure continuity is present between terminals as indicated. *See Fig. 5*. Replace as necessary.

### IGNITION SWITCH

**Continuity Tests** – Ensure continuity is present between terminals as indicated. See IGNITION SWITCH CONTINUITY SPECIFICATIONS table. *See Fig. 6*. Replace as necessary.

# 1991 SAFETY EQUIPMENT
# Steering Column Switches (Cont.)

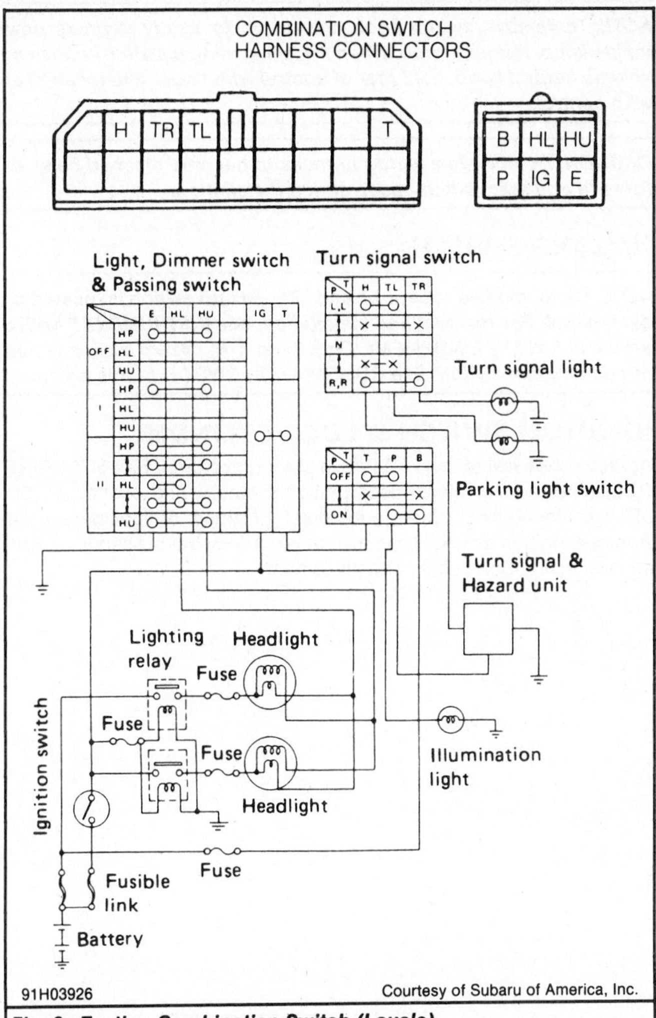

Courtesy of Subaru of America, Inc.

*Fig. 3: Testing Combination Switch (Loyale)*

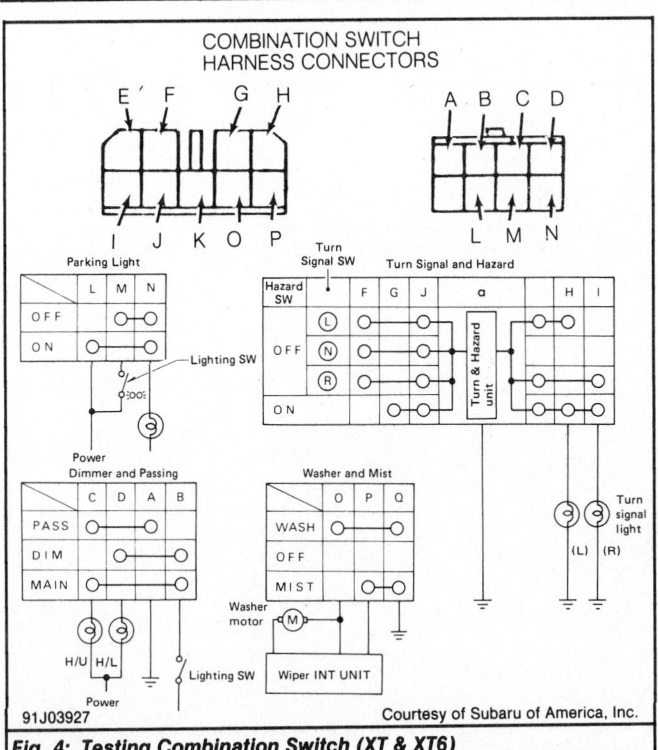

Courtesy of Subaru of America, Inc.

*Fig. 4: Testing Combination Switch (XT & XT6)*

***IGNITION SWITCH CONTINUITY SPECIFICATIONS***

| Switch Position | Continuity Between Terminals |
|---|---|
| Lock | No Continuity |
| OFF (Justy) | No Continuity |
| ACC | A & B |
| ON | A, B & IG |
| START | B, IG, [1] R & S |

[1] – XT & XT6 models do not have terminal "R".

## TURN SIGNAL SWITCH

See COMBINATION SWITCH under TESTING.

## WIPER SWITCHES

See appropriate WIPER/WASHER SYSTEMS article in SAFETY EQUIPMENT.

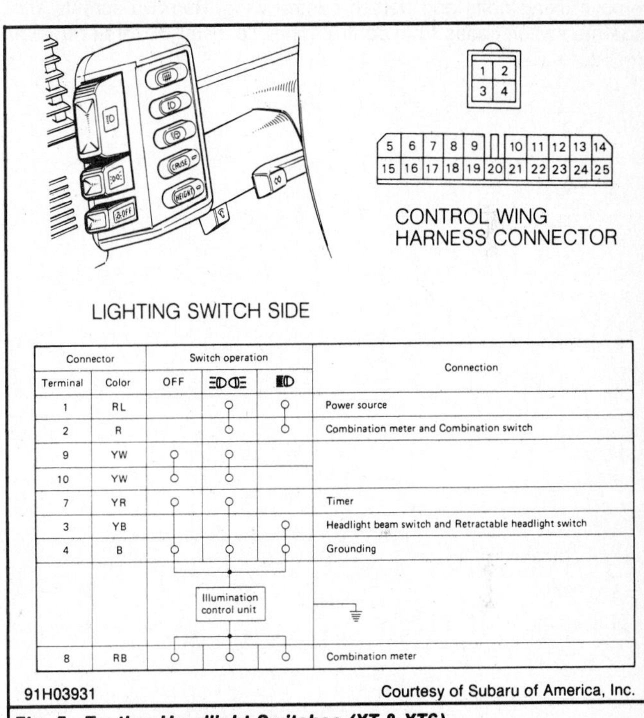


| Connector Terminal | Color | Switch operation OFF | Switch operation ≡D○≡ | Switch operation ■D | Connection |
|---|---|---|---|---|---|
| 1 | RL | | O | O | Power source |
| 2 | R | | O | O | Combination meter and Combination switch |
| 9 | YW | O | O | | |
| 10 | YW | O | O | | |
| 7 | YR | O | O | | Timer |
| 3 | YB | | | O | Headlight beam switch and Retractable headlight switch |
| 4 | B | O | O | O | Grounding |
| 8 | RB | O | O | O | Combination meter |

Courtesy of Subaru of America, Inc.

*Fig. 5: Testing Headlight Switches (XT & XT6)*

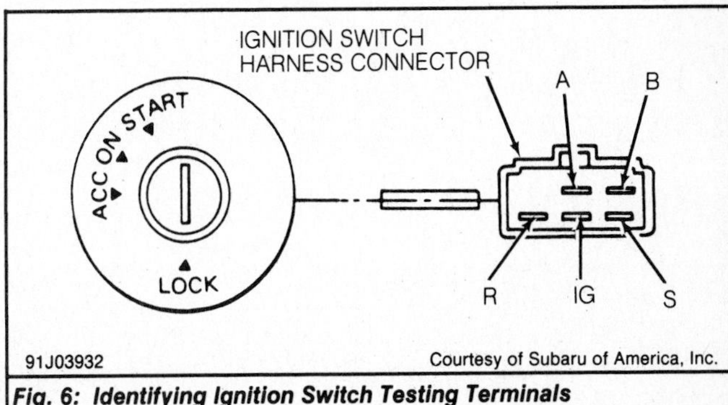

Courtesy of Subaru of America, Inc.

*Fig. 6: Identifying Ignition Switch Testing Terminals*

# REMOVAL & INSTALLATION

## COMBINATION SWITCH

**Removal & Installation (Justy) – 1)** Remove steering column bracket bolts and pull down steering column. Remove screws from backside of steering wheel. Disconnect wires from horn switch connector.

**2)** Remove horn pad and steering wheel. Remove steering column cover screws. Unplug wiring connectors. Remove combination switch. To install, reverse removal procedure.

# 1991 SAFETY EQUIPMENT
# Steering Column Switches (Cont.)

**Removal & Installation (Legacy & Loyale) - 1)** Remove lower instrument panel cover. Remove column covers. Disconnect wires from horn switch connector.

**2)** Remove horn pad. Remove steering wheel using puller. Unplug wiring connectors. Remove combination switch. To install, reverse removal procedure.

**Removal & Installation (XT & XT6) - 1)** Remove lower instrument panel cover. Remove column covers. Remove steering wheel cover. Remove steering wheel with a steering wheel puller.

**2)** Disconnect wiring harness from steering column. Disconnect wiring connectors. Remove combination switch from control wing. To install, reverse removal procedure.

## CONTROL WING

**Removal & Installation (XT & XT6) -** Remove combination switch. See COMBINATION SWITCH under REMOVAL & INSTALLATION. Remove fixing bolts and detach control wing. Remove screws and separate switch cases from control wing. To install, reverse removal procedure.

***NOTE: To remove switch knob, use a pin to lightly depress pawl inside knob. Remove knob. When installing sliding switch knobs and volume control knob, hold rear of control with finger and mesh knob with control.***

***CAUTION: Do not allow wiring harness to become pinched between forward and rear switch cases during installation.***

## HAZARD SWITCH

***NOTE: On all models except XT and XT6, hazard switch is located on dash panel. For removal and installation, see INSTRUMENT PANELS article in SAFETY EQUIPMENT. On XT and XT6, hazard switch is part of combination switch. See COMBINATION SWITCH in this article.***

## IGNITION SWITCH & LOCK CYLINDER

**Removal & Installation -** Remove steering column. See STEERING COLUMNS article. Disconnect ignition switch wiring connector. Cut off bolt connecting upper and lower portions of ignition switch. Remove ignition switch. To install, reverse removal procedure. Tighten connecting bolts until heads twists off.

# 1991 SAFETY EQUIPMENT
# Wiper/Washer Systems – Except Legacy

## Justy, Loyale, XT, XT6

## DESCRIPTION

Wiper/washer systems include a 2-speed motor, separate washer pump and a switch. An intermittent wiper system is optional. Some models are equipped with a rear window wiper/washer.

## ADJUSTMENTS

### WASHER ADJUSTMENT

Adjust washer nozzles so that washer fluid sprays at correct points on windshield or liftgate glass. *See Figs. 1-3.*

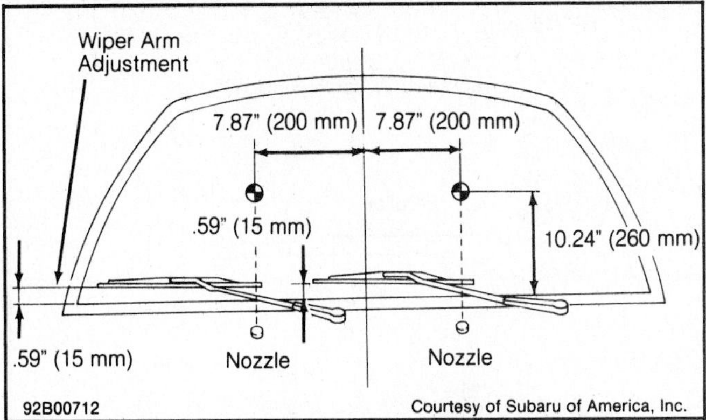


***Fig. 1: Adjusting Front Wiper Arms & Washer Points (Justy)***

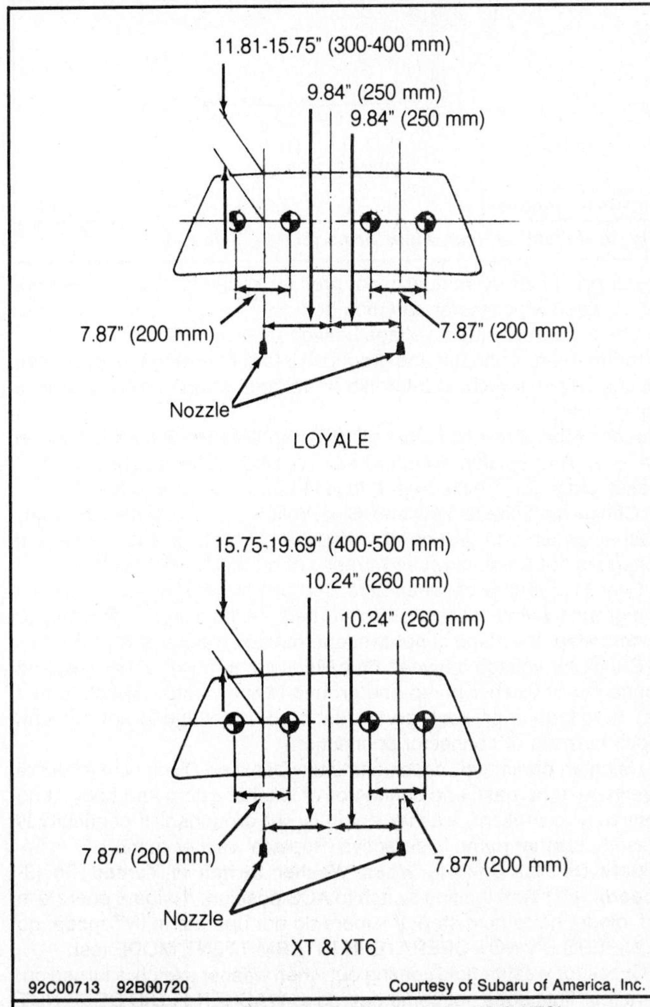


***Fig. 2: Adjusting Front Washer Points (Loyale, XT & XT6)***

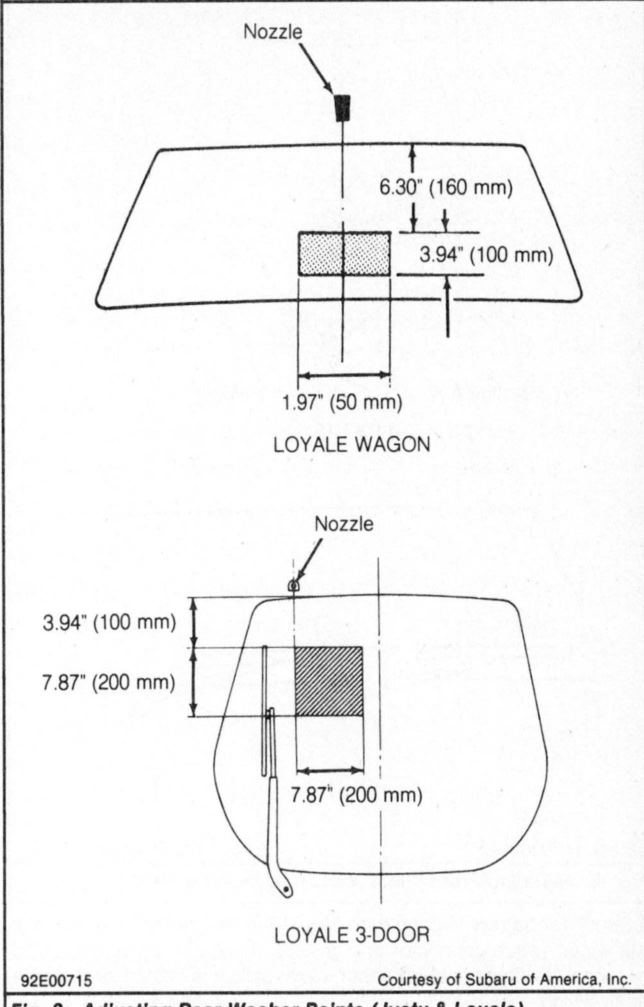


***Fig. 3: Adjusting Rear Washer Points (Justy & Loyale)***

### WIPER ADJUSTMENT

If wiper arms have been replaced or are out of adjustment, set arms back into proper position. *See Figs. 1, 4 and 5.*

## TESTING

***NOTE: System testing information for XT and XT6 is not available from manufacturer.***

### WIPER SWITCHES

**Front Wiper Switch** – Ensure continuity is present between terminals as indicated in appropriate figure. *See Figs. 6 and 7.* Repair or replace as necessary.

**Rear Wiper Switch (Justy & Loyale)** – **1)** Ensure continuity is present between terminals as indicated in appropriate figure. *See Fig. 6.*

**2)** With switch in ON position, continuity should be present between terminals ER and RS. With switch in WASH position, continuity should be present between terminals ER, RS and RW. Replace switch if continuity is not as described.

### WIPER SYSTEM (JUSTY)

**Wipers Do Not Operate** – **1)** Turn ignition switch to ACC position and set wiper switch to LO position. Check for battery voltage between Blue/Yellow wire terminal of harness side connector of wiper switch and ground. If battery voltage is present, go to next step. If battery voltage is not present, check fuse. If fuse is okay, check for improper connector contact, a defective harness or faulty ignition switch.

# 1991 SAFETY EQUIPMENT
# Wiper/Washer Systems – Except Legacy (Cont.)

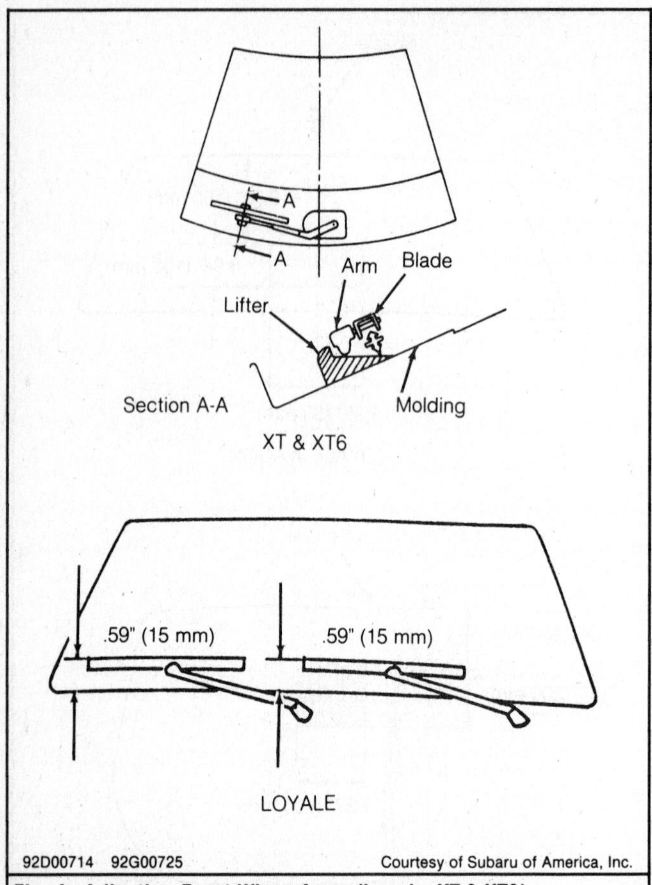


***Fig. 4: Adjusting Front Wiper Arms (Loyale, XT & XT6)***

**2)** Check for battery voltage between Green wire terminal of harness side wiper switch connector and ground. If voltage is present, go to next step. If voltage is not present, wiper switch is defective. Replace wiper switch.

**3)** Check for battery voltage between Green wire terminal of wiper motor connector and ground. If voltage is present, go to next step. If voltage is not present, repair harness between wiper switch and wiper motor.

**4)** Using an ohmmeter, check continuity between Black wire (ground) of wiper motor and body. If no continuity is present, wiper motor and/ or ground wire is not grounded. If continuity is present, wiper motor is defective. Replace wiper motor.

**Wipers Do Not Operate In Intermittent Mode** – Turn ignition switch to ACC position. If wipers operate in LO mode, switch is defective. If wipers do not operate in any mode, go to WIPERS DO NOT OPERATE test. If wipers operate continuously when switch is set to INT, replace intermittent wiper unit.

**Wipers Do Not Stop Automatically (2-Speed) – 1)** Turn ignition switch to ACC position and set wiper switch to LO position. If battery voltage is present between Blue/Yellow wire terminal of wiper motor 4-pin connector and ground, go to next step. If voltage is not present, repair harness or connector between wiper motor and fuse block.

**2)** Check for intermittent voltage between Yellow wire terminal of wiper motor 4-pin connector and ground. If intermittent voltage is present, go to next step. If intermittent voltage is not present, replace wiper motor.

**3)** Check for intermittent voltage between Yellow wire terminal of wiper switch 17-pin connector and ground. If intermittent voltage is not present, repair harness. If intermittent voltage is present, replace wiper switch.

**Wipers Do Not Stop Automatically (3-Speed) – 1)** Turn ignition switch to ACC position and set wiper switch to LO position. Check if battery voltage is present between Blue/Yellow wire terminal of wiper motor 4-pin connector and ground. If battery voltage is present, go to

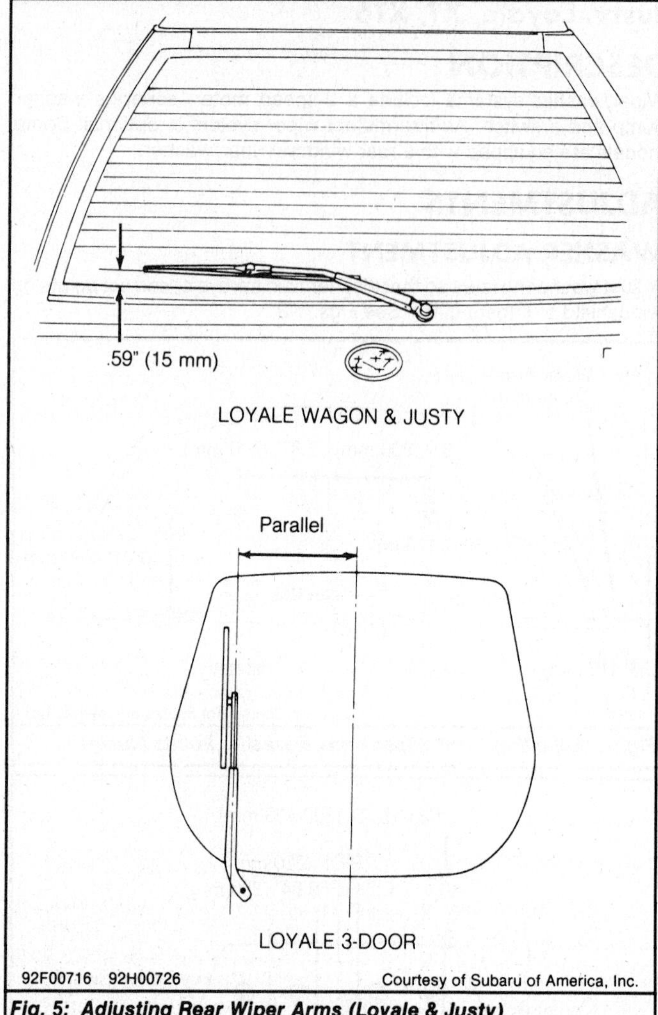


***Fig. 5: Adjusting Rear Wiper Arms (Loyale & Justy)***

next step. If battery voltage is not present, repair harness or connector between wiper motor and fuse box.

**2)** Check for intermittent voltage between Yellow wire terminal of wiper motor 4-pin connector and ground. If intermittent voltage is present, replace wiper switch. If intermittent voltage is not present, replace wiper motor.

**Washer Fluid Does Not Come Out When Washer Switch Is Turned On – 1)** Turn ignition switch to ACC position. Check fuse No. 11. If fuse is okay, go to next step. If fuse is blown, replace fuse.

**2)** Check for voltage between Blue/Yellow wire terminal or wiper/ washer switch and ground. If voltage is present, go to next step. If voltage is not present, repair harness or connector connection.

**3)** Check for voltage between Blue/Red wire terminal of washer switch and ground. (when washer switch turned on). If voltage is present, go to next step. If voltage is not present, replace washer switch.

**4)** Check for voltage between Blue/Red wire terminal of harness end connector of washer pump and ground (when washer switch turned on). If voltage is present, go to next step. If voltage is not present, repair harness or connector connections.

**5)** Using an ohmmeter, check continuity between Black wire (ground) terminals of harness end connector of washer pump and body. If no continuity is present, washer pump is not grounded. If continuity is present, washer pump is defective. Replace washer pump.

**Wipers Do Not Operate When Washer Switch Is Turned On (3-Speed) – 1)** Turn ignition switch to ACC position. If wipers operate in INT mode, go to next step. If wipers do not operate in INT mode, go to WIPERS DO NOT OPERATE IN INTERMITTENT MODE test.

**2)** Check for washer fluid coming out when washer switch is turned on. If washer fluid does not come out, go to WASHER FLUID DOES NOT

# 1991 SAFETY EQUIPMENT
## Wiper/Washer Systems – Except Legacy (Cont.)

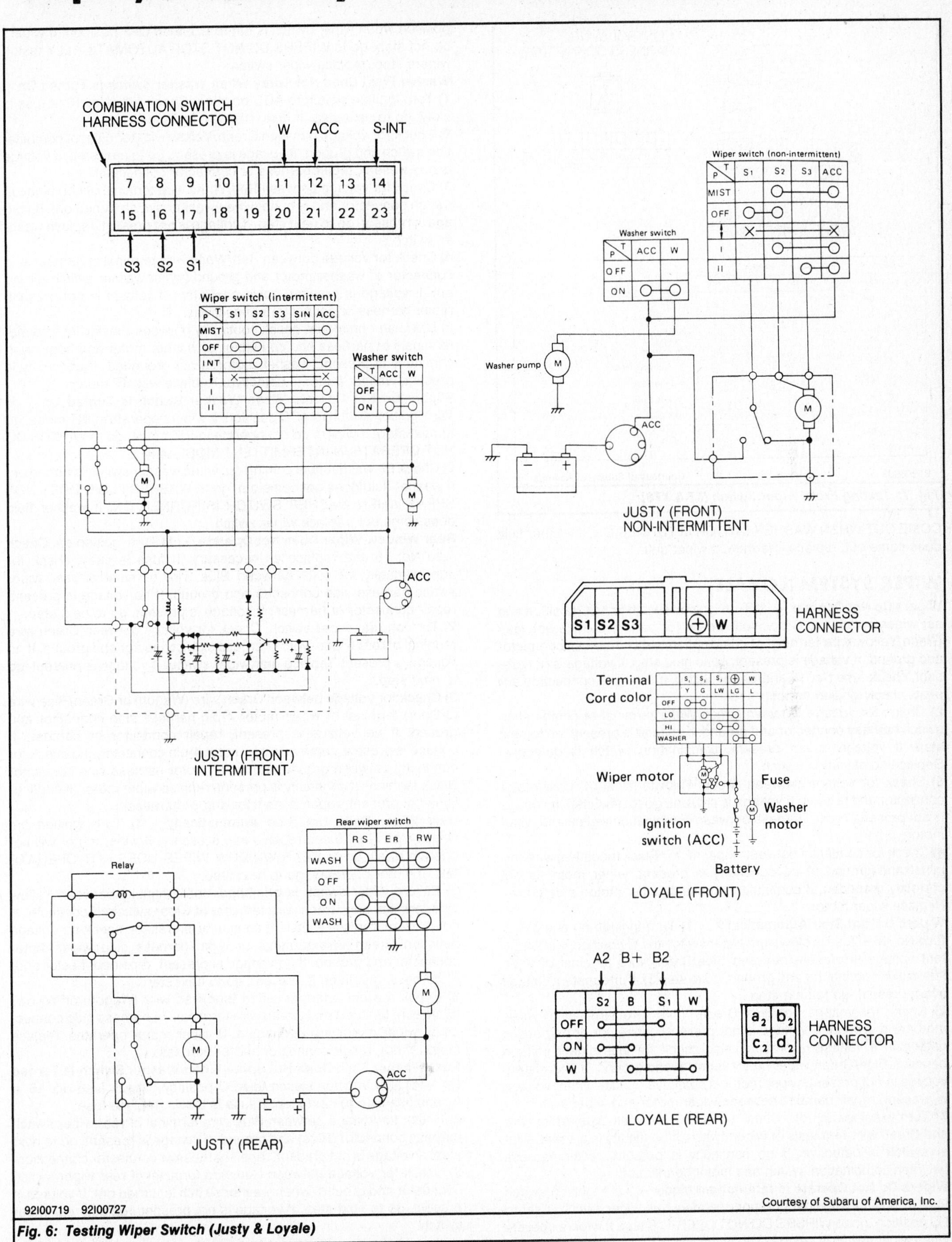


*Fig. 6: Testing Wiper Switch (Justy & Loyale)*

# 1991 SAFETY EQUIPMENT

## Wiper/Washer Systems – Except Legacy (Cont.)

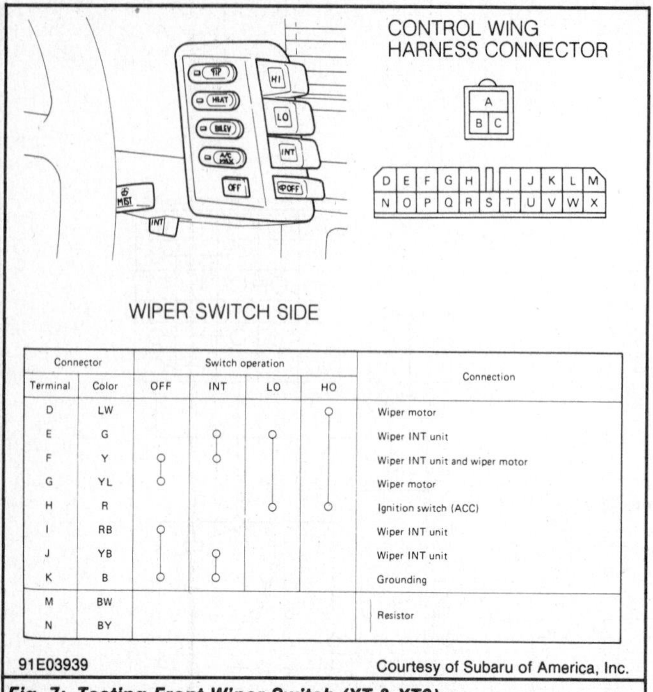


| Connector | | Switch operation | | | | Connection |
|---|---|---|---|---|---|---|
| Terminal | Color | OFF | INT | LO | HO | |
| D | LW | | | | O | Wiper motor |
| E | G | | O | O | | Wiper INT unit |
| F | Y | O | O | | | Wiper INT unit and wiper motor |
| G | YL | O | | | | Wiper motor |
| H | R | | | O | O | Ignition switch (ACC) |
| I | RB | O | | | | Wiper INT unit |
| J | YB | | O | | | Wiper INT unit |
| K | B | O | O | | | Grounding |
| M | BW | | | | | Resistor |
| N | BY | | | | | |

***Fig. 7: Testing Front Wiper Switch (XT & XT6)***

COME OUT WHEN WASHER SWITCH IS TURNED ON. If washer fluid does come out, replace intermittent wiper unit.

## WIPER SYSTEM (LOYALE)

**Wipers Do Not Operate – 1)** Turn ignition switch to ACC position and set wiper switch to LO position. Check for battery voltage between Green/Yellow wire terminal of combination switch harness connector and ground. If voltage is present, go to next step. If voltage is not present, check fuse No. 16 and/or connector. If fuse and connection are okay, check ignition switch.

**2)** Check for voltage between Green/White terminal of combination switch harness connector and ground. If voltage is present, go to next step. If voltage is not present, combination switch is defective. Replace combination switch.

**3)** Check for voltage between Green/White terminal of wiper motor connector and ground. If voltage is present, go to next step. If voltage is not present, repair harness between combination switch and wiper motor.

**4)** Check for continuity between wiper motor Black (negative) wire terminal and ground. If no continuity is present, wiper motor is not correctly grounded. If continuity is present, wiper motor is defective. Replace wiper motor.

**Wipers Do Not Stop Automatically – 1)** Turn ignition on and check fuse No. 16. If fuse is okay, turn wiper switch to LO position. If intermittent voltage is present between Blue/Green wire terminal of 8-pin interval unit connector and ground, go to step **3)**. If intermittent voltage is not present, go to next step.

**2)** Check for voltage between Green/White wire terminal of wiper motor and ground. If voltage is not present, connector or harness is defective. If voltage is present, also check for intermittent voltage between Blue/Green wiper motor terminal and ground. If intermittent voltage is not present, wiper motor is defective. If intermittent voltage is present, repair harness between wiper motor and wiper switch.

**3)** Turn wiper switch off. Check continuity between Blue/White wire and Green wire terminals of wiper switch. If continuity is present, wiper switch is defective. If no continuity is present, repair harness between combination switch and motor connection.

**Wipers Do Not Operate In Intermittent Mode –** Turn ignition switch to ACC position. If wipers do not operate when wiper switch is set to LO position, go to WIPERS DO NOT OPERATE test. If wipers operate when wiper switch is set to LO position, check if wipers stop at original position when wiper switch is set to LO, then OFF position. If wipers do not stop, go to WIPERS DO NOT STOP AUTOMATICALLY test. If wipers stop, replace wiper switch.

**Washer Fluid Does Not Spray When Washer Switch Is Turned On – 1)** Turn ignition switch to ACC position. Check fuse No. 16. If fuse is okay, go to next step. If fuse is blown, replace fuse.

**2)** Check for voltage between Green/Yellow wire terminal of combination switch and ground. If voltage is present, go to next step. If voltage is not present, repair harness or connector connection.

**3)** Check for voltage between Red/White wire terminal of combination switch connector and ground (when washer switch turned on). If voltage is present, go to next step. If voltage is not present, replace washer switch.

**4)** Check for voltage between Red/White wire terminal of harness end connector of washer motor and ground (when washer switch turned on). If voltage is present, go to next step. If voltage is not present, repair harness or connector connections.

**5)** Using an ohmmeter, check continuity between Black wire (ground) terminals of harness end connector of washer motor and body. If no continuity is present, washer motor is not grounded. If continuity is present, washer motor is defective. Replace washer motor.

**Wipers Do Not Operate When Washer Switch Is Turned On – 1)** Turn ignition switch to ACC position. If wipers operate in INT mode, go to next step. If wipers do not operate in INT mode, go to WIPERS DO NOT OPERATE IN INTERMITTENT MODE test.

**2)** Check for washer fluid coming out when washer switch is turned on. If washer fluid does not come out, go to WASHER FLUID DOES NOT SPRAY WHEN WASHER SWITCH IS TURNED ON. If washer fluid does come out, replace wiper switch.

**Rear Window Wiper Does Not Operate – 1)** Turn ignition on. Check fuse No. 16 and replace as necessary. If fuse is okay, check for approximately 12 volts between Blue wire terminal of rear wiper switch harness side connector and ground. If no voltage is present, repair connector or harness. If voltage is present, go to next step.

**2)** Turn on rear wiper switch. Check for voltage between Green wire terminal of rear wiper switch harness side connector and ground. If no voltage is present, replace rear wiper switch. If voltage is present, go to next step.

**3)** Check for voltage between Green wire (Wagon) or Green/Blue wire (3-Door) terminal of wiper motor 4-pin harness side connector and ground. If no voltage is present, repair connector or harness. If voltage is present, remove wiper motor 4-pin connector and check for continuity between ground and wiper motor harness side connector Black terminal. If continuity is present, replace wiper motor. If continuity is not present, repair connector and/or harness.

**Rear Wiper Does Not Stop Automatically – 1)** Turn ignition on. Check fuse No. 16 and replace as necessary. If wiper motor will not operate at all, go to REAR WINDOW WIPER DOES NOT OPERATE test. If motor operates, go to next step.

**2)** Ensure wiper switch is off. Check for continuity between Yellow wire terminal and Green wire terminal of wiper switch. If continuity is not present, replace switch. If continuity is present, check for voltage between Green wire terminal of 4-pin harness side wiper motor connector and ground. If no voltage is present, repair connector and/or harness. If voltage is present, go to next step.

**3)** Check if wiper operates when Blue/Red wire (Wagon) or Yellow/White wire (3-Door) and Green wire terminals of harness side connector of wiper motor are connected. If wiper motor operates, replace motor. If not, repair connector and/or harness.

**Rear Washer Fluid Does Not Spray When Washer Switch Is Turned On – 1)** Turn ignition switch to ACC position. Check fuse No. 16. If fuse is okay, go to next step. If fuse is blown, replace fuse.

**2)** Check for voltage between Blue wire terminal of rear wiper switch harness connector (Blue) and ground. If voltage is present, go to next step. If voltage is not present, repair harness or connector connection.

**3)** Check for voltage between Red wire terminal of rear wiper switch connector and ground (when washer switch is turned on). If voltage is present, go to next step. If voltage is not present, replace rear wiper switch.

# 1991 SAFETY EQUIPMENT
# Wiper/Washer Systems – Except Legacy (Cont.)

**4)** Check for voltage between Red wire terminal of washer motor harness connector and ground (when washer switch is turned on). If voltage is present, go to next step. If voltage is not present, repair harness or connector connections.

**5)** Using an ohmmeter, check continuity between Black wire (ground) terminal of washer motor harness connector and body. If no continuity is present, repair connections or harness. If continuity is present, washer motor is defective. Replace washer motor.

## REMOVAL & INSTALLATION

### FRONT WIPER ASSEMBLY

**Removal & Installation (Justy) – 1)** Remove negative battery cable. Disconnect wiper motor electronic connector. Remove 3 wiper motor mounting bolts and separate wiper link from motor. *See Fig. 8.*

**2)** Remove cowl panel screws and cowl panel. Remove link mounting bolts and link. To install, reverse removal procedure. Ensure blades stop about .6" (15 mm) above bottom of glass.

**Removal & Installation (Loyale) – 1)** Remove weatherstrip and debris screen. Disconnect electric connector, and remove motor mounting bolts. *See Fig. 8.*

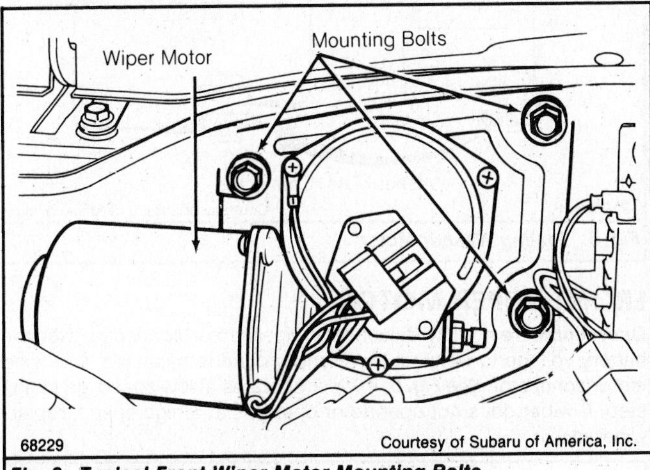


***Fig. 8: Typical Front Wiper Motor Mounting Bolts***

**2)** Remove nut securing motor link on back side of motor. Remove nuts fixing sleeve units. Remove rods along with sleeve units. To install, reverse removal procedure. Ensure blades stop about .6" (15 mm) above bottom of glass.

**Removal & Installation (XT & XT6) –** Remove molding. Disconnect electrical connector. Remove mounting bolts and motor assembly. Disconnect linkage wheel from motor. To install, reverse removal procedure.

### REAR WIPER ASSEMBLY

**Removal & Installation –** Remove wiper arm nut cover. Remove shaft nut and wiper arm. Remove inside trim from hatch or tailgate. Disconnect wiring connector and remove wiper motor. To install, reverse removal procedure.

### WASHER RESERVOIR

**Removal & Installation (Front) –** On Loyale, XT and XT6, detach right side mud guard. On XT and XT6, remove air cleaner. On all models, disconnect electrical connectors. Disconnect hose from washer reservoir and nozzle. Remove drain hose. Remove reservoir mounting screws and reservoir. To install, reverse removal procedure.

**Removal & Installation (Rear) –** Remove trim and attaching screws. Disconnect hose from washer reservoir and nozzle. Disconnect wiring connector from washer pump. Lift out washer reservoir. To install, reverse removal procedure.

## WIRING DIAGRAMS

See appropriate chassis wiring diagram in WIRING DIAGRAMS.

# 1991 SAFETY EQUIPMENT
# Wiper/Washer Systems – Legacy

## DESCRIPTION

Wiper/washer system includes a 2-speed motor for the front wipers, a single-speed motor for the rear wiper, separate washer motors and a single combination front and rear wiper switch. Wagon models are equipped with rear wiper/washer systems.

## ADJUSTMENTS

### WASHER ADJUSTMENT

**Washer Points** – Adjust washer nozzles so that washer fluid sprays at correct points on windshield or liftgate glass. *See Fig. 1 or 2.*

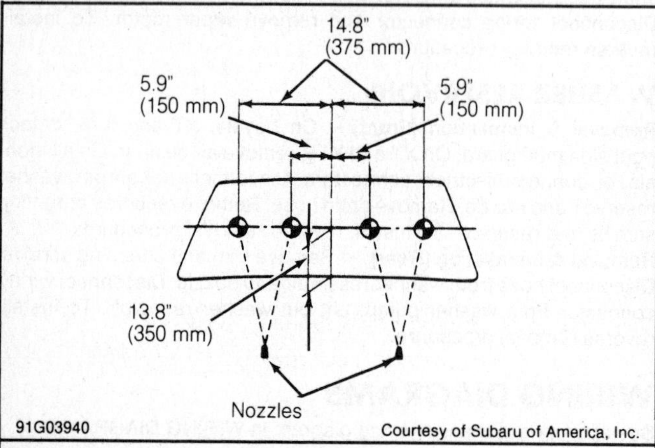


***Fig. 1: Adjusting Front Washer Points***

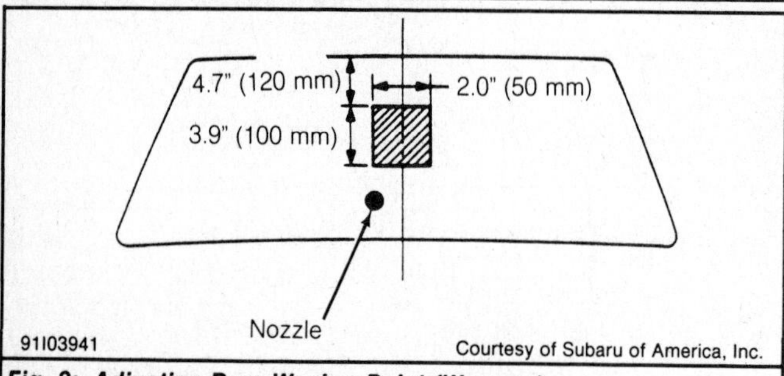


***Fig. 2: Adjusting Rear Washer Point (Wagons)***

### WIPER ADJUSTMENT

**Wiper Arms** – With wiper switch in OFF position, adjust wiper arm during installation to set blade(s) in correct position. *See Fig. 3 or 4.*

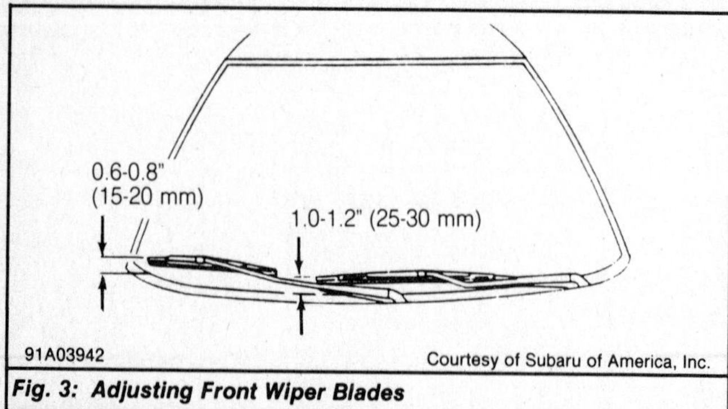


***Fig. 3: Adjusting Front Wiper Blades***

## TESTING

### FRONT WASHER MOTOR

**Operational Test** – Disconnect washer motor harness connector. Apply battery voltage to terminal No. 2 and ground to terminal No. 1 of

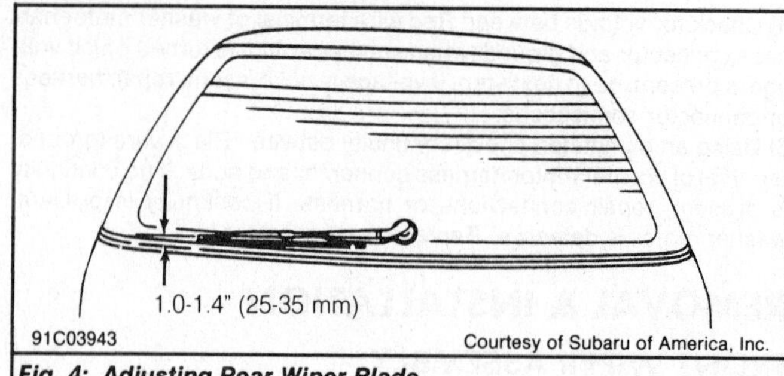


***Fig. 4: Adjusting Rear Wiper Blade***

washer motor connector. *See Fig. 5.* If motor does not operate, replace washer motor.

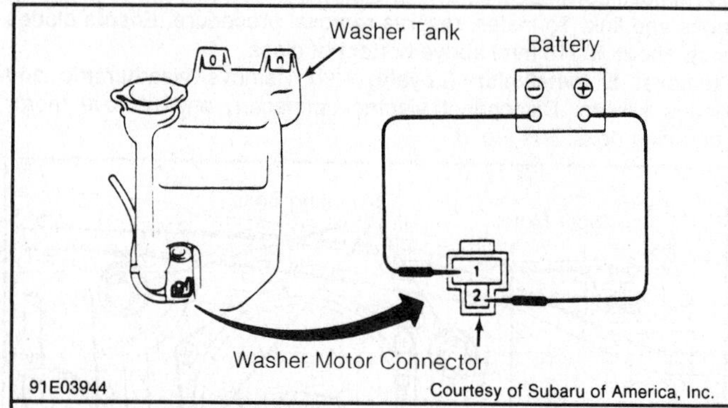


***Fig. 5: Testing Washer Motor***

### FRONT WIPER MOTOR

**Operational Test** – **1)** Disconnect wiper motor connector. Connect battery voltage to terminal No. 2 and ground terminal No. 4 of wiper motor connector. *See Fig. 6.* If wiper operates at low speed, go to next step. If wiper does not operate or operates at a high speed, replace wiper motor.

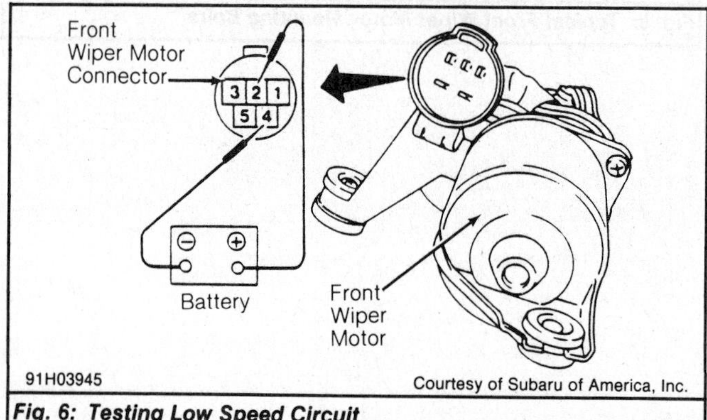


***Fig. 6: Testing Low Speed Circuit***

**2)** Connect battery voltage to terminal No. 3 and ground terminal No. 4 of wiper motor connector. *See Fig. 6.* If wiper operates at a faster speed than in step **1)**, go to next step. If wiper motor does not operate or operates at the same speed as in step **1)**, replace wiper motor.

**3)** Connect battery voltage to terminal No. 2 and ground terminal No. 4. After operating motor at low speed, disconnect battery voltage from terminal No. 2. to stop motor. Reconnect battery to terminal No. 5 and ground No. 4. Connect a jumper wire between terminals No. 1 and 2. Motor should operate then automatically stop.

### FRONT WIPER SWITCH

**Wiper Switch Continuity Test** – **1)** Remove instrument panel lower cover. Remove lower column cover. Unfasten hold-down clip securing harness.

**2)** Disconnect combination switch harness connectors from body harness. Ensure continuity is present between terminals as indicated. *See Fig. 7*. Repair or replace as necessary.

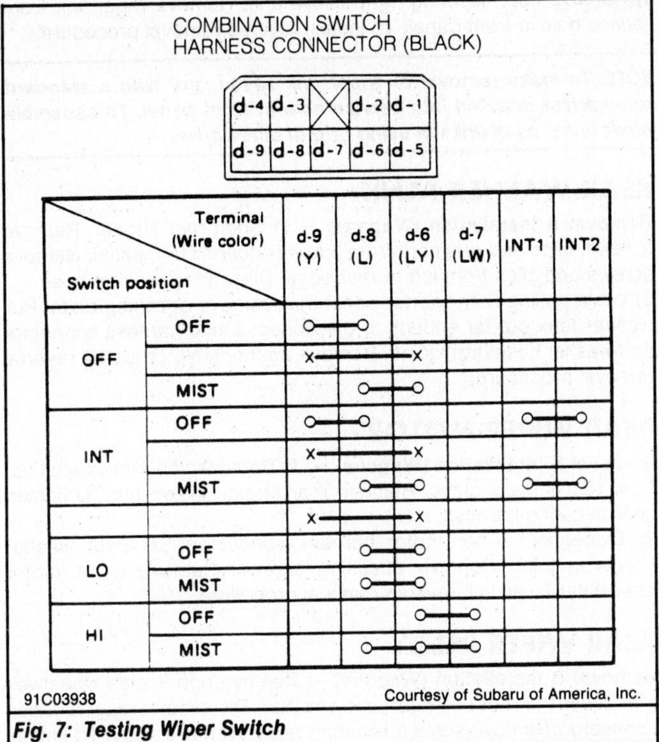


| Switch position | | d-9 (Y) | d-8 (L) | d-6 (LY) | d-7 (LW) | INT1 | INT2 |
|---|---|---|---|---|---|---|---|
| OFF | OFF | O | O | | | | |
| | | X | | X | | | |
| | MIST | | O | O | | | |
| INT | OFF | O | O | | | O | O |
| | | X | | X | | | |
| | MIST | | O | O | | O | O |
| | | X | | X | | | |
| LO | OFF | | O | O | | | |
| | MIST | | O | O | | | |
| HI | OFF | | | O | O | | |
| | MIST | | O | O | O | | |

91C03938 Courtesy of Subaru of America, Inc.

*Fig. 7: Testing Wiper Switch*

**Washer Switch Continuity Test – 1)** Check continuity between terminals d-2 (White wire) and d-5 (Black wire) of combination switch connector. *See Fig. 7*.

**2)** Continuity should be present with washer switch turned on. Continuity should not be present when washer switch is turned off. Repair or replace as necessary.

## REAR WASHER MOTOR

**Operational Test (Wagons) –** Disconnect washer motor harness connector. Remove motor (if necessary). See REAR WASHER MOTOR under REMOVAL & INSTALLATION in this article. Apply battery voltage to terminal No. 2 and ground terminal No. 1 of washer motor connector. *See Fig. 5*. If washer motor does not operate, replace washer motor.

## REAR WIPER MOTOR

**Operational Test (Wagons) – 1)** Disconnect wiper motor connector. Connect battery voltage to terminal No. 2 and ground terminal No. 3 of wiper motor connector. *See Fig. 8*. If wiper motor operates, go to next step. If wiper motor does not operate, replace wiper motor.

**2)** Connect battery voltage to terminal No. 1 and ground terminal No. 3 of wiper motor connector. Using a jumper wire, connect terminals No. 2 and 4. Motor should operate. Remove jumper wire and ensure that motor stops at auto-stop position after operating.

## REAR WIPER RELAY

**Continuity Tests (Wagons) – 1)** Remove rear wiper relay. See REAR WIPER RELAY under REMOVAL & INSTALLATION in this article. Using an ohmmeter, check continuity between relay terminals No. 3 and 5. *See Fig. 9*. If continuity exists, go to next step. If continuity does not exist, replace relay.

**2)** Check continuity between relay terminals No. 1 and 2 and between terminals No. 3 and No. 4. If continuity does not exist in either case, go to next step. If continuity exists in either case, replace relay.

**3)** Connect battery voltage to relay terminal No. 1 and ground to terminal No. 2. Using an ohmmeter, check continuity between relay terminals No. 3 and 5. If continuity does not exist, go to next step. If continuity exists, replace relay.

**4)** With battery voltage still applied, check continuity between relay terminals No. 3 and 4. If continuity exists, relay is operating correctly. If continuity does not exist, replace relay.

## REAR WIPER SWITCH

**Continuity Test (Wagons) – 1)** Remove instrument panel lower cover. Remove lower column cover. Unfasten hold-down clip securing harness. Disconnect combination switch harness connectors from body harness.

**2)** With rear wiper switch in OFF position, there should be no continuity between combination switch connector terminals d-1, d-2 and d-3. *See Fig. 7*. With rear wiper switch in ON position, continuity should be present between terminals d-2 and d-3.

**3)** With rear wiper switch in WASH position, continuity should be present between terminals d-1, d-2 and d-3. Replace switch if continuity is not as described.

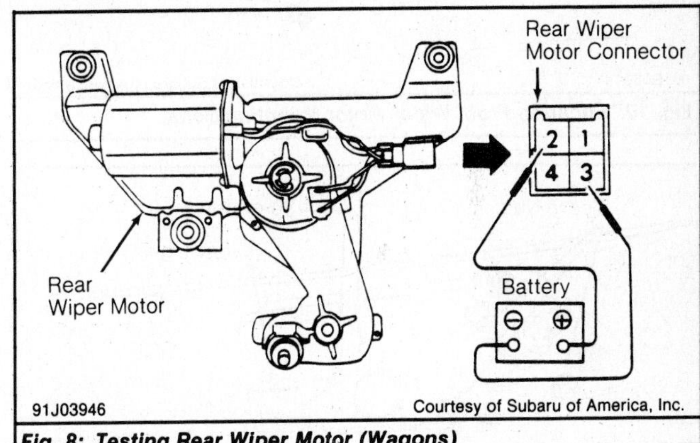


91J03946 Courtesy of Subaru of America, Inc.

*Fig. 8: Testing Rear Wiper Motor (Wagons)*

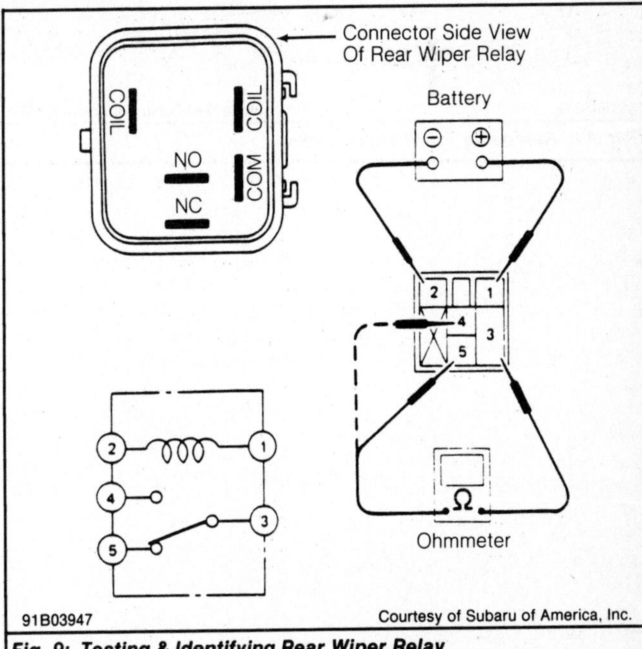


91B03947 Courtesy of Subaru of America, Inc.

*Fig. 9: Testing & Identifying Rear Wiper Relay*

# REMOVAL & INSTALLATION

## FRONT WASHER TANK

**Removal & Installation –** Remove washer tank attaching bolts. Pull washer tank far enough to disconnect wiring harness connector and washer hose. Remove washer tank. To install, reverse removal procedure.

# 1991 SAFETY EQUIPMENT
# Wiper/Washer Systems – Legacy (Cont.)

## FRONT WIPER MOTOR & LINK

**Removal & Installation – 1)** Detach weatherstrip and cowl net. Apply silicone oil or soapy water to both sides of cowl net to facilitate removal. Disconnect electrical connector. Remove motor attaching bolts. *See Fig. 10.*

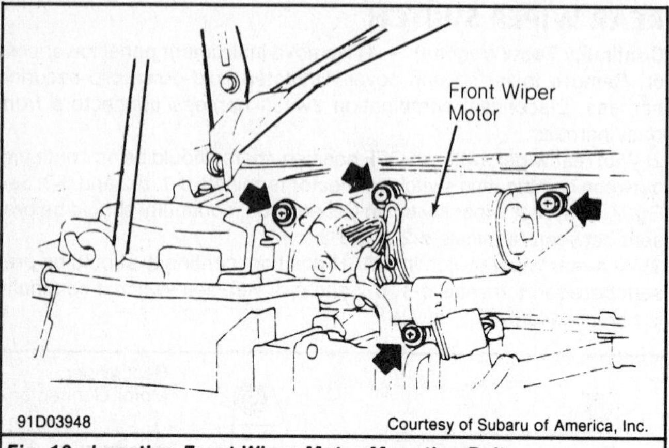


**Fig. 10: Locating Front Wiper Motor Mounting Bolts**

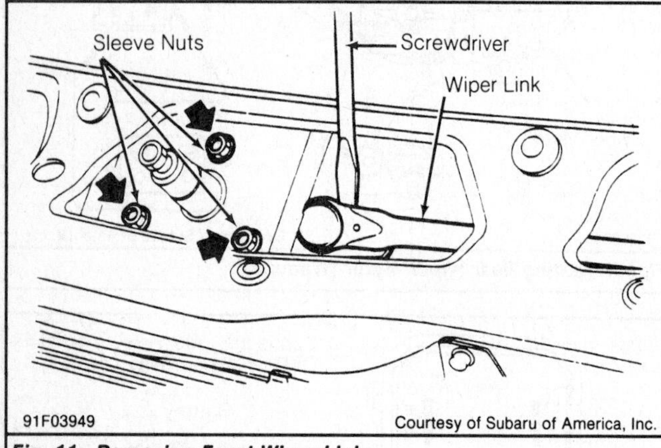


**Fig. 11: Removing Front Wiper Links**

**2)** Remove nut securing motor link on back side of motor and remove motor. Remove nuts securing left sleeve unit. Separate left and right wiper links at center joint. *See Fig. 11.*

**3)** Remove nuts securing right sleeve unit. Remove wiper link from service hole in front panel. To install, reverse removal procedure.

***NOTE: To make removal of wiper link easier, pry with a standard screwdriver inserted into service hole in front panel. To assemble wiper links, push links in using grip of screwdriver.***

## REAR WASHER TANK

**Removal & Installation (Wagons) – 1)** Open rear liftgate. Remove screws, clips and retainers from left rear quarter trim panel. Remove screws and clips from left of rear edge. Disconnect washer hose.

**2)** While pulling rear quarter panel trim, remove attaching bolts. Pull washer tank out far enough to disconnect wiring harness connector and washer hose (from joint). Remove washer tank. To install, reverse removal procedure.

## REAR WIPER MOTOR

**Removal & Installation (Wagons) – 1)** Remove cap and special nut from rear liftgate glass. Remove rear liftgate inside trim. Unfasten clips securing harness.

**2)** Disconnect wiper motor harness connector. Separate washer hoses at joint. Remove attaching screws. Remove wiper motor assembly. To install, reverse removal procedure.

## REAR WIPER RELAY

**Removal & Installation (Wagons) –** Remove right inside wheelwell trim cover that houses right rear speaker. Disconnect relay harness connector. Remove screws securing relay. Remove relay. To install, reverse removal procedure.

## WIPER SWITCH

**Removal & Installation – 1)** Remove steering wheel using steering wheel puller. Remove lower steering column cover. Remove bracket cover. Disconnect harness connectors.

**2)** Unfasten hold-down band. Remove combination switch from steering column. Remove slip ring from combination switch. Remove wiper/washer assembly from combination switch. To install, reverse removal procedure.

## WIRING DIAGRAMS

See appropriate chassis wiring diagram in WIRING DIAGRAMS.

# 1991 ENGINES
# 1.2L 3-Cylinder



## Justy

***NOTE: For repair procedures not covered in this article, see ENGINE OVERHAUL PROCEDURES article in GENERAL INFORMATION.***

## ENGINE IDENTIFICATION

Vehicle Identification Number (VIN) is stamped on metal plate located near lower left corner of windshield. Engine can be identified by 6th character in VIN. Engine serial number is stamped on cylinder block below distributor.

***ENGINE IDENTIFICATION CODES***

| Application | VIN Code |
|---|---|
| 2WD | 7 |
| 4WD | 8 |

## ADJUSTMENTS

### VALVE CLEARANCE ADJUSTMENT

**1)** Position cylinder to be adjusted on TDC of compression stroke. Ensure piston is at TDC and valves are closed. Using Valve Adjuster (498767000), adjust valve clearance to specification. *See Fig. 1.*

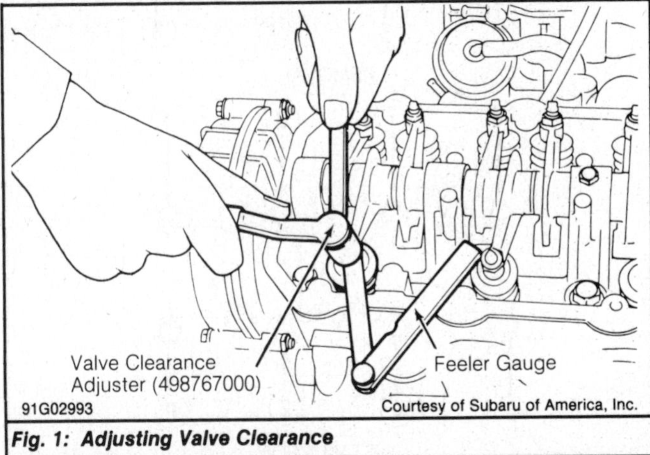


***Fig. 1: Adjusting Valve Clearance***

**2)** See VALVE CLEARANCE SPECIFICATIONS table. Tighten lock nut to specification. Repeat procedure on remaining cylinders. Rotate engine several revolutions after completing valve adjustment. Recheck valve clearance.

***VALVE CLEARANCE SPECIFICATIONS***

| Application | In. (mm) |
|---|---|
| Intake | .005-.006 (.13-.17) |
| Exhaust | .009-.010 (.23-.27) |

## REMOVAL & INSTALLATION

### FUEL PRESSURE RELEASE

Remove rear seat. Remove cover from fuel pump connector. Unplug connector. Start and run engine until it stalls. After engine stalls, operate starter for 5 seconds to complete fuel pressure release.

### ENGINE

***NOTE: For reassembly reference, label all electrical connectors, vacuum hoses and fuel lines before removal. Also place mating marks on engine hood and other major assemblies before removal.***

**Removal – 1)** Position hood in widest open position. Disconnect negative battery cable and cooling fan connections. Drain cooling system and remove radiator. Remove front bumper and grille.

**2)** Disconnect hood release cable. Remove radiator support member. Remove air cleaner and air intake duct. On carbureted models, disconnect and mark hoses to carburetor. On PFI models, release fuel pressure and remove fuel line. See FUEL PRESSURE RELEASE. On all models, remove hose from brake booster.

**3)** Remove heater hoses. Disconnect clutch and accelerator cable. Disconnect speedometer cable from transmission. Remove support arm from engine to firewall. Disconnect and mark wiring at alternator, distributor and starter.

**4)** Raise and support vehicle. Remove lower engine covers. Disconnect exhaust pipes. Disconnect gearshift rod at transmission. Disconnect gearshift support rod at cylinder block.

**5)** Remove transverse link. *See Fig. 2.* Remove spring pin from axle shaft. Separate front axle shaft. *See Fig. 3.*

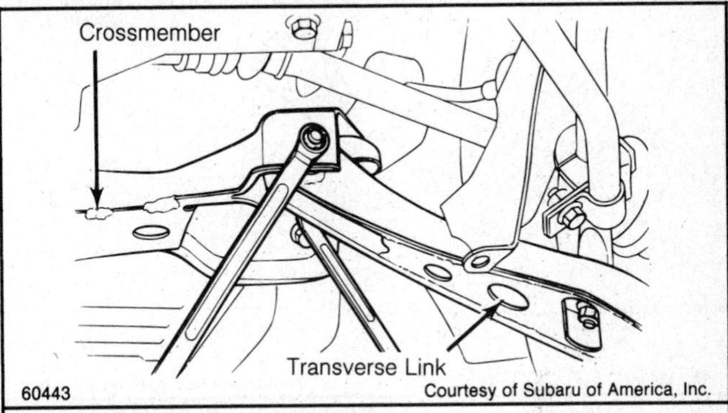


***Fig. 2: Removing Transverse Link***

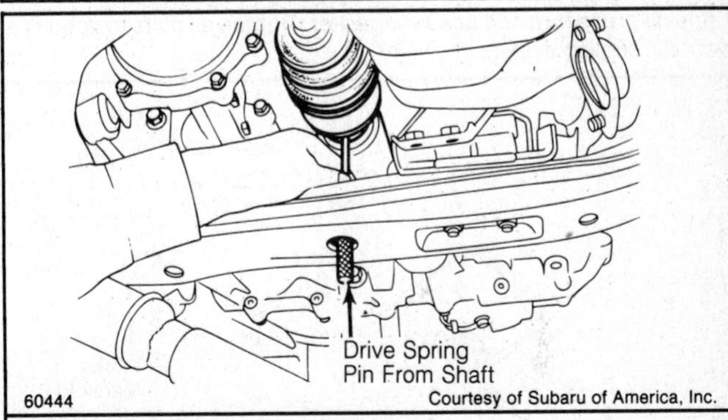


***Fig. 3: Removing Axle Shaft Spring Pin***

**6)** Remove engine and transmission mounting brackets. Install chain and raise engine slightly. Remove lower front engine mount bolts. Remove crossmember. Ensure all components are disconnected. Remove engine and transaxle.

**Installation –** To install reverse removal procedure. Adjust clutch cable. Adjust fluid levels. Tighten bolts to specification.

***CAUTION: Transverse link-to-crossmember bolt must be tightened to specification with vehicle at operating height and no additional load.***

### INTAKE MANIFOLD

**Removal & Installation (Carbureted) – 1)** Drain cooling system. Remove air cleaner. Remove heater and radiator hoses. Disconnect electrical connectors. Remove accelerator cable. Mark and disconnect vacuum hoses.

**2)** Remove air suction pipe. Remove intake manifold retaining bolts and nuts. *See Fig. 4.* Remove intake manifold and carburetor. To install, reverse removal procedure and use new gasket. Tighten all bolts to specification. Fill cooling system.

**Removal & Installation (PFI) – 1)** Drain cooling system. Remove air duct and PCV hose. Release fuel pressure and remove fuel line. See FUEL PRESSURE RELEASE. Remove throttle body hose, heater and radiator hoses. Disconnect electrical connectors. Remove accelerator cable. Mark and disconnect vacuum hoses.

**2)** Remove throttle body from collector chamber. Remove collector chamber. Remove intake manifold. *See Fig. 5.* To install, reverse

# 1991 ENGINES
# 1.2L 3-Cylinder (Cont.)

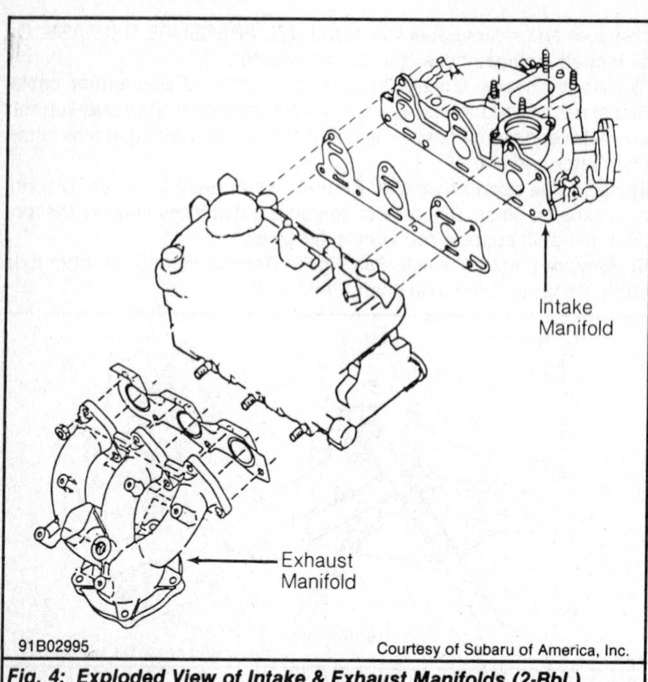


*Fig. 4: Exploded View of Intake & Exhaust Manifolds (2-Bbl.)*

removal procedure and use new gasket. Tighten all bolts to specification. Fill cooling system.

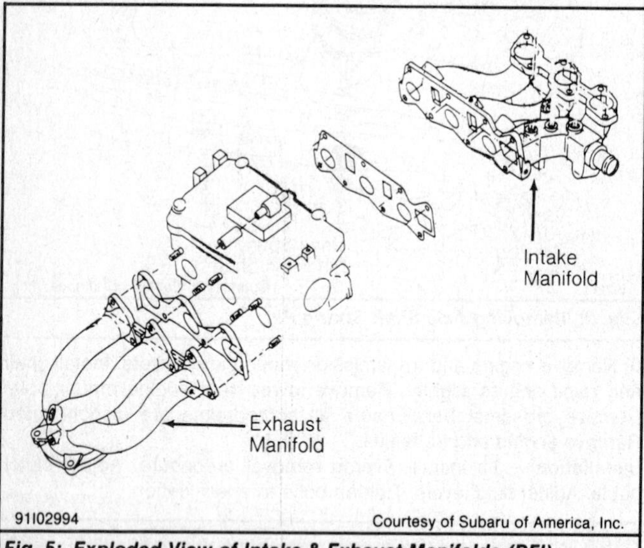


*Fig. 5: Exploded View of Intake & Exhaust Manifolds (PFI)*

## EXHAUST MANIFOLD

**Removal & Installation** – Remove exhaust manifold-to-flange bolts. Remove exhaust manifold retaining nuts. Remove exhaust manifold. To install, reverse removal procedure; use new gasket. Tighten all bolts to specification. *See Figs. 4 and 5.*

***NOTE: Exhaust manifold retaining nuts are stainless steel. DO NOT use any other type of nut.***

## CYLINDER HEAD

**Removal** – **1)** Remove front bumper and grille. Drain cooling system. Remove air duct. Remove exhaust manifold. Remove accelerator cable.

**2)** Disconnect radiator and heater hoses. Mark and disconnect air cleaner and carburetor hoses. Disconnect wiring from distributor. Remove alternator drive belt. Remove air suction pipe from crankcase and intake manifold.

**3)** Using Pulley Holder (499205500), remove crankshaft pulley bolts. Remove crankshaft pulley. Remove timing belt. See TIMING BELT under CAMSHAFT. Remove camshaft sprocket retaining bolts. Remove camshaft sprocket. Remove timing belt tensioner. Remove inner timing belt cover.

**4)** Remove PCV hose from valve cover. Remove valve cover. Remove cylinder head bolts in proper sequence. *See Fig. 6.* Remove cylinder head.

***CAUTION: Cylinder head bolts must be removed in proper sequence to prevent cylinder head damage.***

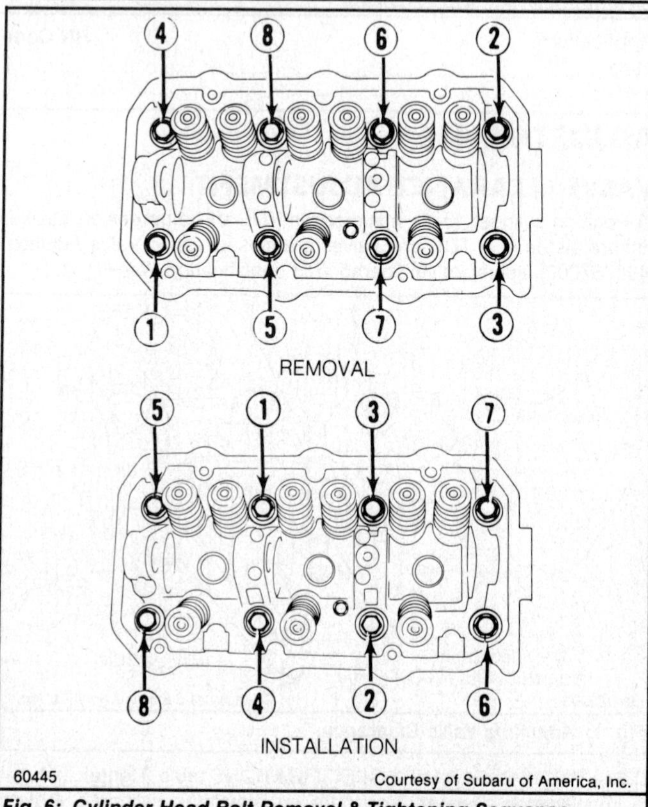


*Fig. 6: Cylinder Head Bolt Removal & Tightening Sequence*

**Inspection** – **1)** Inspect cylinder head for cracks or damage. Check cylinder head warpage. Resurface if warped beyond specification.

**2)** Measure cylinder head thickness. Cylinder head thickness must not be less than minimum specification after resurfacing. See CYLINDER HEAD table under ENGINE SPECIFICATIONS at end of article. Replace cylinder head if thickness is less than specification.

***CAUTION: Cylinder head must be retorqued COLD, after engine has been run at normal operating temperature.***

**Installation** – **1)** Ensure mating surfaces are clean. Install head gasket. Install cylinder head. Install head bolts and washers. Head bolts must be tightened in proper sequence. *See Fig. 6.* Tighten head bolts in 3 steps to specification. See TORQUE SPECIFICATIONS table at end of article.

**2)** After ensuring correct valve timing, install and adjust timing belt. Reverse removal procedure for remaining components. Tighten all bolts to specification. Fill cooling system.

## FRONT COVER OIL SEAL

**Removal** – **1)** Drain engine oil and coolant. Remove oil level gauge and oil level guide. Disconnect alternator connector, remove alternator and "V" belt.

**2)** Remove crankshaft pulley with Pulley Holder (499205500). Remove cam belt cover. Remove cam belt tensioner spring and drive belt. Remove camshaft drive plate and drive belt.

**NOTE: Before removing, mark belt indicating direction of rotation. Camshaft belt MUST be installed in original direction of rotation.**

**3)** Remove camshaft pulley. Remove cam belt cover and cover mount. Remove flywheel housing. Remove oil pan, oil pan plate and oil strainer. Remove air suction manifold bracket from air suction manifold and crankcase cover. Remove crankcase cover.
**4)** With a press and suitable drift, press out crankshaft oil seal. Inspect all surfaces for damage.
**Installation** - With press and suitable drift, press in new oil seal. *See Fig. 7.* To complete installation, reverse removal procedure.

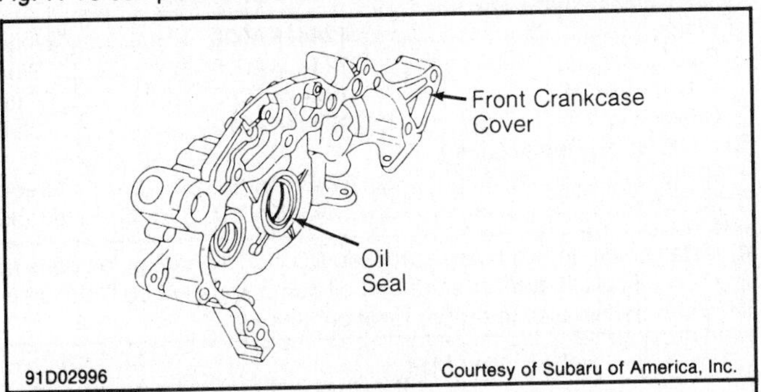


***Fig. 7: Installing Front Cover Oil Seal***

## TIMING BELT

**Removal - 1)** Remove alternator drive belt. Using Pulley Holder (499205500), loosen crankshaft pulley bolts. Rotate engine until No. 3 piston is at TDC. Remove crankshaft pulley retaining bolts using access hole in fenderwell housing.
**2)** Remove outer timing belt cover. Loosen tensioner retaining bolts. Move tensioner toward outside of engine. Tighten bolts to hold tensioner.
**3)** Mark timing belt for direction of rotation. Install belt in original direction of rotation. Remove crankshaft belt drive sprocket plate and timing belt.
**Inspection** - Inspect timing belt for wear on rounded edges of drive teeth. Inspect belt for signs of oil contamination. Replace belt if damaged or contaminated. Inspect all drive sprockets for wear in drive belt area. Inspect tensioner for noise or grease leakage. Replace as necessary.
**Installation - 1)** Using Pulley Holder (499205500), rotate camshaft to align camshaft sprocket mark with alignment mark on timing belt cover. *See Fig. 8.* Install crankshaft belt drive sprocket with flanged side facing inward (if removed). Rotate crankshaft so crankshaft belt drive sprocket aligns with crankcase alignment mark.
**2)** Remove valve cover (if not previously removed). Loosen valve adjusting screws to gain rocker arm free play. Install timing belt. Ensure timing belt is installed in original direction of rotation.
**3)** Loosen tensioner retaining bolts. Apply tension to timing belt. Tighten inner then outer tensioner retaining bolt. Ensure all timing marks are aligned.
**4)** Install crankshaft belt drive sprocket plate. Reverse removal procedure for remaining components. Tighten all bolts to specification. Adjust valve clearance. See VALVE CLEARANCE ADJUSTMENT under ADJUSTMENTS.

## CAMSHAFT

***NOTE: Check camshaft end play before removing camshaft. See CAMSHAFT END PLAY.***

**Removal - 1)** Remove valve cover. Remove rocker arm assembly. See ROCKER ARM SHAFT ASSEMBLY. Remove timing belt. See TIMING BELT. Using Pulley Holder (499205500), remove camshaft drive pulley.
**2)** Mark distributor wires. Remove distributor. Remove camshaft retaining breaker case. Remove camshaft using care not to damage lobes and journals.

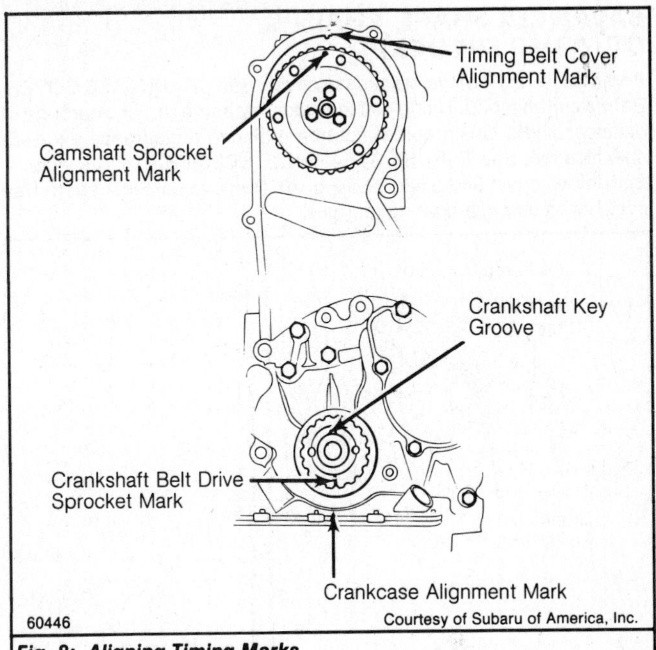


***Fig. 8: Aligning Timing Marks***

**Inspection - 1)** Measure camshaft lobe height. Replace if not within specification. See CAMSHAFT table under ENGINE SPECIFICATIONS at end of article.
**2)** Clean camshaft journals and cylinder head journal surfaces. Inspect journal areas for wear. Replace camshaft and or cylinder head if excessively worn.
**Installation - 1)** Coat camshaft with ample amount of camshaft lubricant. Install camshaft in cylinder head. Install camshaft retainer breaker case. Check camshaft end play. See CAMSHAFT END PLAY. Reverse removal procedure for remaining components. Tighten bolts to specification.
**2)** Adjust valve clearance. See VALVE CLEARANCE ADJUSTMENT under ADJUSTMENTS. Install valve cover and new gasket. Tighten bolts to specification.
**3)** Install distributor. Distributor and camshaft contain an offset coupling. Ensure coupling offset of camshaft and distributor are on same side. Tighten retaining bolt.

## CAMSHAFT END PLAY

Using dial indicator, check camshaft end play. End play must be within specification. See CAMSHAFT table under ENGINE SPECIFICATIONS at end of article. If not within specification, grind retainer breaker case surface of cylinder head until end play is within specification. *See Fig. 9.*

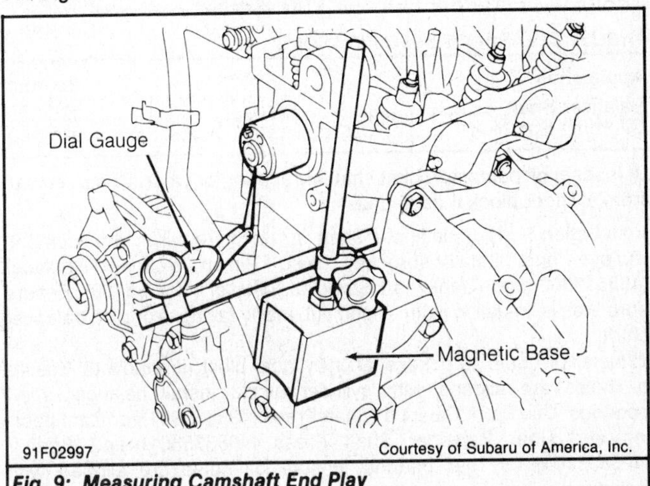


***Fig. 9: Measuring Camshaft End Play***

# 1991 ENGINES
# 1.2L 3-Cylinder (Cont.)

## BALANCER SHAFT, CHAIN & OIL PUMP SPROCKET

**Removal** – **1)** Remove crankcase cover. See CRANKCASE COVER. Remove crankshaft. Using dial indicator, measure thrust clearance of balancer shaft. Chain guide must be replaced if clearance exceeds specification. See THRUST CLEARANCE SPECIFICATIONS table.
**2)** Remove chain and guide. *See Fig. 10.* Remove balancer shaft. Use care not to damage bearing journals.

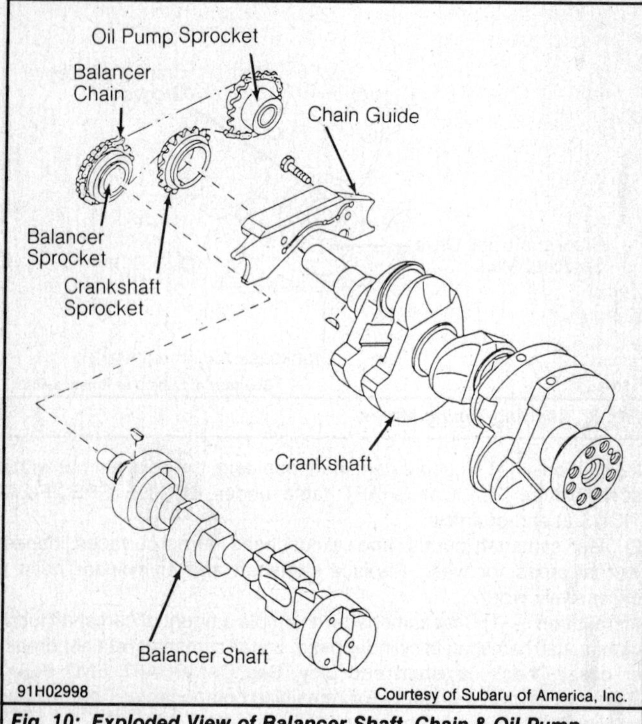


***Fig. 10: Exploded View of Balancer Shaft, Chain & Oil Pump Sprocket***

**3)** Inspect balancer shaft bearings for scoring or wear. If front bearing requires removal, use Front Balancer Shaft Press (498835901) and hydraulic press. Press front bearing from cylinder block.
**4)** Remove plug from rear of cylinder block. Using Rear Balancer Shaft Press (498835801) and hydraulic press, remove bearing from block.
**Inspection** – **1)** Inspect balancer shaft for scoring or wear in bearing journals. Inspect all sprockets for damage in chain drive area. Inspect chain and guide for damage and wear.
**2)** Place dial indicator on cylinder block with tip resting against oil pump sprocket. Check thrust clearance of oil pump sprocket. Replace oil pump sprocket if thrust clearance exceeds specification. See THRUST CLEARANCE SPECIFICATIONS table.

***THRUST CLEARANCE SPECIFICATIONS***

| Application | In. (mm) |
|---|---|
| Balancer Shaft | .020 (.50) |
| Oil Pump Sprocket | .016 (.40) |

**3)** Inspect oil pump sprocket shaft for scoring or wear. Remove shaft from cylinder block if damaged.

**Installation** – **1)** If balancer shaft sprocket requires replacement, remove and install sprocket using Pinion Bearing Replacer (498517000) and Crankshaft Sprocket Installer (499585400). Ensure sprocket is installed with alignment mark facing front of balancer shaft.
**2)** Install oil pump sprocket shaft in cylinder block (if removed). Ensure oil holes are aligned with cylinder block. Install balancer shaft bearings. Use Front Balancer Shaft Press (498835901) for front bearing and Rear Balancer Shaft Press (498835801) and Spacer (498835803) for rear bearing. Ensure oil holes are aligned with cylinder block.
**3)** Using rear balancer shaft press, install rear plug in cylinder block. Lubricate balancer shaft with engine oil. Install balancer shaft in cylinder block. Proper chain must be installed when different components are replaced. Determine proper components to be used when installing chain and guide. See CHAIN & GUIDE APPLICATION table.

***CHAIN & GUIDE APPLICATION***

| Guide/Color Code | Chain Part No. | Color Code |
|---|---|---|
| Chain Replacement Only | | |
| White | 12430KA060 | Green |
| Blue | 12430KA060 | Green |
| Guide Replacement Only | | |
| White | 12441KA000 | White |
| Blue | 12441KA010 | Blue |
| Green | 12441KA000 | White |
| Green | 12441KA010 | Blue |
| Chain & Guide Replacement | | |
| White | 12430KA060 | Green |
| Blue | 12430KA060 | Green |

**4)** Install guide and oil pump sprocket. DO NOT tighten guide bolts at this time. Rotate balancer shaft and oil pump sprocket so Gold chain links can be installed in proper location. *See Fig. 11.*

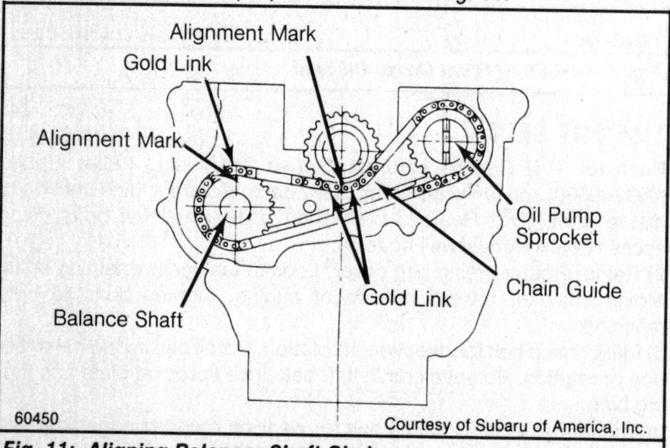


***Fig. 11: Aligning Balancer Shaft Chain***

**5)** Install chain. Install crankshaft. Once crankshaft is installed, tighten guide retaining bolts to specification. Ensure all alignment marks are aligned with Gold links. Reverse removal procedure for remaining components. Tighten bolts to specification. See TORQUE SPECIFICATIONS table at end of article.

## REAR CRANKSHAFT OIL SEAL

**Removal & Installation** – **1)** Remove flywheel. Pry seal from cylinder block. Note direction of seal lips. Ensure seal surfaces are free of burrs. Lubricate seal lips with engine oil.
**2)** Install Crank Seal Guide (498725500) on rear of crankshaft. Using Seal Press (498725600), install seal. Install flywheel. Tighten bolts to specification. See TORQUE SPECIFICATIONS table at end of article.

## WATER PUMP

**Removal** – **1)** Drain engine oil and coolant. Remove dipstick and guide. Disconnect negative battery cable. Remove connector from alternator. Remove alternator drive belt and alternator.
**2)** Remove crankshaft pulley and outer timing belt cover. Remove timing belt. See TIMING BELT. Remove camshaft drive sprocket. Remove inner timing belt cover.
**3)** Remove flywheel cover. Remove oil pan. See OIL PAN. Remove water pump cover. Install screwdriver against balancer shaft to hold balancer shaft from turning.
**4)** Remove impeller retaining bolt and impeller. *See Fig. 12.* Remove crankcase cover retaining bolts. Remove crankcase cover.
**Disassembly** – Position crankcase cover in hydraulic press. Using Mechanical Seal Remover (499715400) and Plate (499685510), press mechanical seal from crankcase cover.

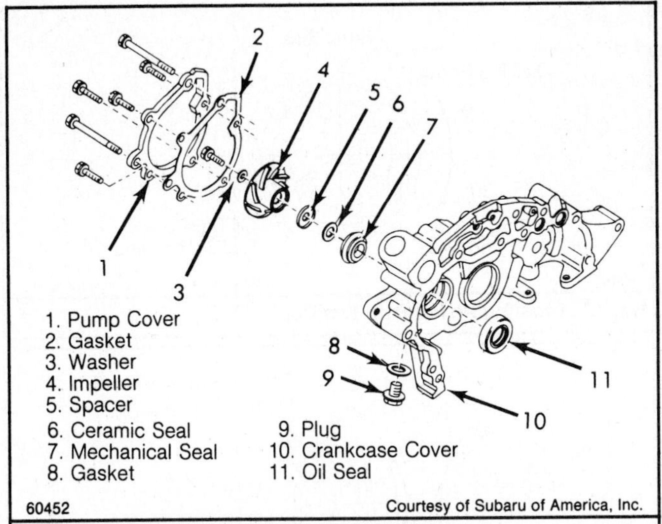


*Fig. 12: Exploded View of Water Pump*

**Inspection** - Inspect ceramic seal for cracks. Inspect mechanical seal and ceramic seal contact areas for wear or damage. Inspect impeller for corrosion or damage. Inspect oil seal for damage.

***NOTE: When replacing impeller, mechanical seal must also be replaced.***

**Reassembly** - Coat mechanical seal-to-cover surface with Three Bond (No. 1303). Using Mechanical Seal Installer (499795400) and hydraulic press, install mechanical seal.

***CAUTION: Coat impeller seal with coolant prior to installation.***

**Installation - 1)** Install crankcase cover on cylinder block. Coat impeller with coolant and install. When installing new impeller, add one or 2 spacers and measure tip clearance.

**2)** Manually press impeller against balancer shaft and measure tip clearance. Tip clearance must be within specification. See WATER PUMP TIP CLEARANCE table.

***WATER PUMP TIP CLEARANCE***

| Application | In. (mm) |
|---|---|
| Standard | .012-.035 (.30-.88) |
| Service Limit | .043 (1.09) |

**3)** Install impeller retaining bolt. Tighten to specification. Install new gasket and pump cover. Tighten retaining bolts. Reverse removal procedure for remaining components. Use new gaskets and tighten all bolts to specification. Fill cooling system and engine oil. See TORQUE SPECIFICATIONS table at end of article.

## OIL PAN

**Removal - 1)** Raise and support vehicle. Drain engine oil. Remove exhaust manifold cover. Remove lower engine covers. Disconnect header pipe from tailpipe.

**2)** Disconnect tailpipe hanger from engine mount. Install chain and slightly raise engine. DO NOT raise excessively. Engine must be supported for crossmember removal.

**3)** Remove support arm from engine to firewall. Remove crossmember from body and transaxle. Remove stabilizer bar from body. Remove transmission center mount. Remove flywheel cover. Disconnect air suction pipe. Remove oil pan and gasket.

**Installation** - To install reverse removal procedure using new gasket. Tighten all bolts to specification. See TORQUE SPECIFICATIONS table at end of article. Fill with engine oil.

# OVERHAUL

## CYLINDER HEAD

**1)** Disassemble cylinder head. Measure valve stem diameter. Replace valves not within specification. See VALVES & VALVE SPRINGS table under ENGINE SPECIFICATIONS at end of article.

**2)** Measure valve margin. Replace valves if valve margin is not within specification. See VALVES & VALVE SPRINGS table under ENGINE SPECIFICATIONS at end of article. Remeasure valve margin after grinding valves.

## VALVE GUIDE

**Inspection** - Measure valve stem-to-guide clearance. Replace valves and valve guides not within specification. See CYLINDER HEAD table under ENGINE SPECIFICATIONS at end of article. Valve guide I.D. can be measured using telescopic gauge. Replace guides not within specification. See CYLINDER HEAD table under ENGINE SPECIFICATIONS at end of article.

**Removal & Installation - 1)** Using Valve Guide Remover (399762103), drive valve guide from cylinder head. Use oversize valve guide when replacing valve guide.

**2)** Using Valve Guide Reamer (399762104), ream cylinder head for oversize valve guide. Using Valve Guide Installer (499765400), install valve guide. Check valve guide installed height. Ensure valve guide is located at specified height. See CYLINDER HEAD table under ENGINE SPECIFICATIONS at end of article.

## VALVE SEAT

Grind valve seats to proper seat angle. Check valve seat width after grinding. Adjust seat width to specification. See CYLINDER HEAD table under ENGINE SPECIFICATIONS at end of article.

## VALVE STEM OIL SEALS

When installing valve stem oil seals, ensure valve seals are proper height for valve application. See VALVE STEM OIL SEAL APPLICATION table. Use Valve Stem Installer (398852100) for seal installation.

***VALVE STEM OIL SEAL APPLICATION***

| Application | Seal Height - In. (mm) |
|---|---|
| Intake | .512 (13.00) |
| Exhaust | .425 (10.79) |

## VALVE SPRINGS

**1)** Measure free length of valve springs. Check spring tension at specified height. Replace springs if not within specification. See VALVES & VALVES SPRINGS table under ENGINE SPECIFICATIONS at end of article.

**2)** Measure valve spring retainer thickness from spring contact area to top of retainer. Replace if not within specification. See VALVE SPRING RETAINER SPECIFICATIONS table.

***VALVE SPRING RETAINER SPECIFICATIONS***

| Application | In. (mm) |
|---|---|
| Standard | .1102 (2.799) |
| Service Limit | .0906 (2.301) |

## ROCKER ARM SHAFT ASSEMBLY

***CAUTION: Rocker arm shaft assembly components must be marked for location prior to removal. Components must be installed in original location.***

**Removal & Disassembly - 1)** Remove valve cover. Position No. 1 piston on TDC. Loosen rocker arm adjusting screw lock nuts. Loosen adjusting screw until measurement from bottom of rocker arm to bottom of adjusting screw is .039" (1.0 mm).

**2)** Repeat procedure on remaining cylinders and rocker arms. Remove rocker arm shaft retaining bolt. Note location of all components. Carefully remove rocker arm shaft. DO NOT allow components to fall.

# 1991 ENGINES
# 1.2L 3-Cylinder (Cont.)

**3)** Remove rocker arms and spring washers. Mark components for location. Rocker Arm Shaft Guide (498005400) can be used in assisting in shaft removal if shaft is snug fit.

**Inspection** - Measure and record shaft O.D. in each rocker arm operating area. Using dial bore gauge, measure rocker arm I.D. and out-of-round. Subtract shaft reading from corresponding rocker arm. Replace rocker arm and or shaft if clearance exceeds specification. See ROCKER ARM SPECIFICATIONS table.

***ROCKER ARM SPECIFICATIONS***

| Application | In. (mm) |
|---|---|
| Oil Clearance | .0006-.0022 (.015-.050) |

**Reassembly & Installation - 1)** To reassemble, reverse removal procedure. Ensure components are installed in original location. Ensure rocker arm shaft is aligned with retaining bolt. Tighten rocker arm shaft retaining bolt.

**2)** Adjust valve clearance. See VALVE CLEARANCE ADJUSTMENTS under ADJUSTMENTS. Install valve cover and new gasket. Tighten bolts to specification.

## CYLINDER BLOCK ASSEMBLY

Inspect cylinder block for cracks, warpage, bore diameter, taper, out-of-round and deck height. Replace or repair cylinder block if not within specification. See CYLINDER BLOCK table under ENGINE SPECIFICATIONS at end of article.

## CRANKCASE COVER

**Removal - 1)** Disconnect negative battery cable. Drain engine oil and cooling system. Remove oil dipstick and guide. Disconnect and mark alternator wiring. Remove alternator drive belt and alternator.

**2)** Using Pulley Holder (499205500), remove crankshaft pulley. Remove outer timing belt cover. Remove timing belt. See TIMING BELT. Remove belt tensioner and camshaft sprocket.

**3)** Remove inner timing belt cover. Remove flywheel cover, oil pan and gasket. Remove air suction tube bracket. Remove water pump cover and water pump impeller. See WATER PUMP. Remove crankcase cover retaining bolts. Remove crankcase cover.

**Installation** - To install, reverse removal procedure. Replace all gaskets and "O" rings. Tighten bolts to specification. Fill crankcase and cooling system. *See Fig. 7.*

## PISTON & ROD ASSEMBLY

**Removal - 1)** Remove cylinder head. See CYLINDER HEAD. Remove oil pan. Ensure cylinder ridge is removed. Mark connecting rod and cap for cylinder identification.

**2)** Note direction of recess areas in piston. Remove rod cap. Remove piston assembly.

**Installation - 1)** Ensure piston ring end gap and side clearance are within specification. Install rings on piston. Ensure R1 or R2 mark for top and second ring is toward top of piston. Lubricate piston, rings and cylinder bore with engine oil.

**2)** Properly space ring end gaps on piston. *See Fig. 13.* Install piston and rod into cylinder bore. Ensure piston and connecting rod are properly positioned. Recess areas on piston must face intake manifold side. *See Fig. 14.*

**3)** Check bearing clearance using Plastigage method. Tighten rod cap nuts to specification. See TORQUE SPECIFICATIONS table at end of article. Ensure rod moves freely on crankshaft. Check connecting rod side play. Replace connecting rod if not within specification.

## FITTING PISTONS

Measure cylinder bore and piston skirt diameter. Piston skirt diameter should be measured at 90 degree angle to piston pin. Measure at 1.673" (42.49 mm) from top of piston with normal temperature of 68°F (20°C). Clearance between piston and cylinder bore must be within specification. See PISTONS, PINS & RINGS table under ENGINE SPECIFICATIONS at end of article.

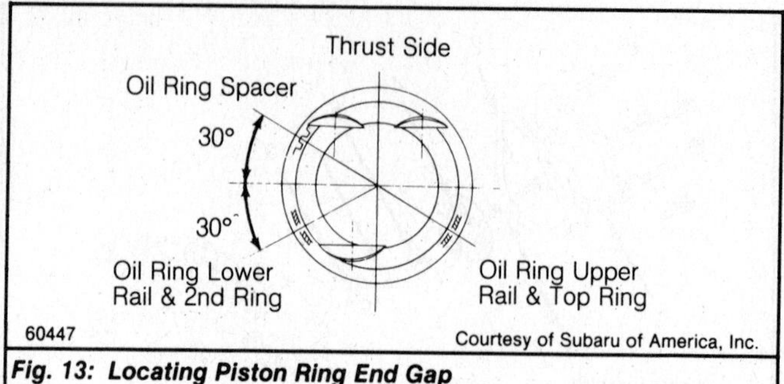


***Fig. 13: Locating Piston Ring End Gap***

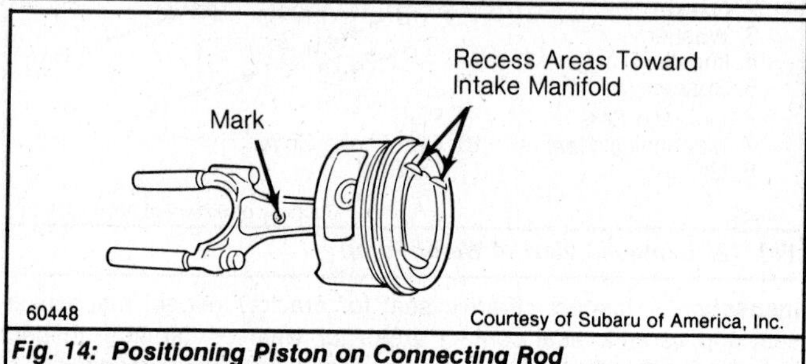


***Fig. 14: Positioning Piston on Connecting Rod***

## PISTON PIN REPLACEMENT

**Removal - 1)** Note piston location in reference to mark on connecting rod. *See Fig. 14.* Use Piston Pin Press (499015400) for pin removal. Install spring and attachment in base. *See Fig. 15.*

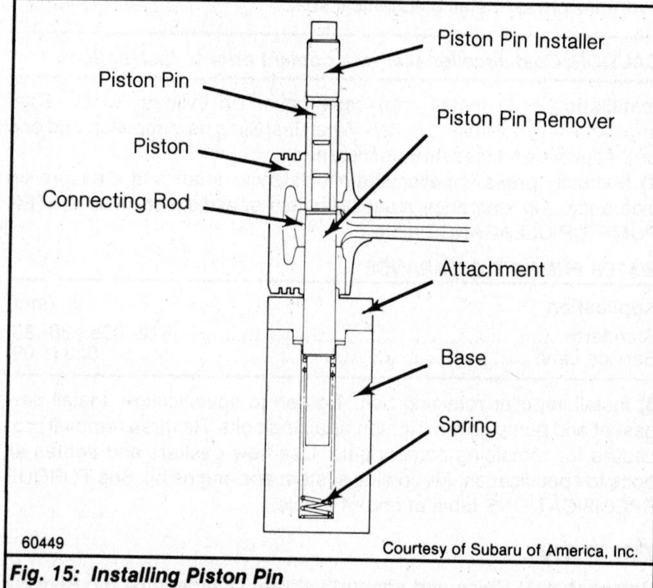


***Fig. 15: Installing Piston Pin***

**2)** Lubricate attachment guide hole, piston pin remover and piston pin installer with engine oil. Position piston pin installer in guide hole of attachment.

**3)** Position piston on attachment. Alignment mark on attachment must align with piston head direction. Install piston pin remover on piston pin. Using hydraulic press, remove piston pin.

**Inspection - 1)** Inspect piston for cracks or damage in ring areas. Check ring side clearance. Replace piston if not within specification. See PISTONS, PINS & RINGS table under ENGINE SPECIFICATIONS at end of article.

**2)** Measure piston skirt diameter. Piston skirt diameter should be measured at 90 degree angle to piston pin. Measure at 1.673" (42.49 mm) from top of piston with normal temperature of 68°F (20°C). Replace piston if not within specification. See PISTON DIAMETER SPECIFICATIONS table.

***PISTON DIAMETER SPECIFICATIONS***

| Application | In. (mm) |
|---|---|
| Standard | 3.0690-3.0694 (77.952-77.962) |
| .020" Oversize | 3.0887-3.0890 (78.452-78.462) |
| .039" Oversize | 3.1083-3.1087 (78.952-78.962) |

**3)** Measure piston pin bore I.D. Clearance between piston and pin must be within specification. Measure clearance between connecting rod and piston pin. Clearance must be within specification. See PISTONS, PINS & RINGS table under ENGINE SPECIFICATIONS at end of article.
**4)** Check connecting rod for bend or twist. Replace connecting rod if beyond specification. See CONNECTING ROD table under ENGINE SPECIFICATIONS at end of article.

***CAUTION: Ensure piston is installed with recess areas aligned with connecting rod mark.***

**Installation - 1)** Position piston on connecting rod. Ensure piston recess areas are installed in accordance with connecting rod mark. *See Fig. 14.* Lubricate attachment guide hole, piston pin remover, piston pin and piston pin bores of piston and connecting rod with engine oil.
**2)** Install piston pin installer on piston pin. Place assembly on base. *See Fig. 15.* Using press, install piston pin until piston pin remover bottoms in base.

### MAIN BEARINGS

**Removal - 1)** Ensure connecting rod and main bearing caps are marked for location. Remove connecting rod caps and bearings. Remove main bearing caps.
**2)** Ensure all components are placed in correct order. Note alignment marks for balancer shaft chain prior to removing crankshaft. *See Fig. 11.* Remove crankshaft. Remove main bearings from cylinder block. Mark bearings for location.
**Inspection -** Inspect crankshaft for cracks, damaged sprocket or threads. Measure journal diameters. Check crankshaft for runout, out-of-round, and taper. Replace or repair crankshaft if not within specification. See CRANKSHAFT, MAIN & CONNECTING ROD BEARINGS table under ENGINE SPECIFICATIONS at end of article. Replace sprocket if damaged.
**Installation - 1)** On crankshafts with main journal diameter of 1.6525-1.6529" (41.974-41.985 mm), note letter code stamped on oil pan mating surface of cylinder block. Select proper replacement bearing using letter code. See MAIN BEARING SELECTION table.

***MAIN BEARING SELECTION***

| Letter Code | Bearing Color Code |
|---|---|
| A or B | Black |
| C or D | Green |

**2)** Install upper main bearings in cylinder block. Ensure oil hole is aligned and bearing is properly seated. Lubricate bearings with engine oil. Install crankshaft in block.
**3)** Ensure crankshaft sprocket is properly aligned with Gold link of balancer shaft chain. Check all alignment marks and Gold links for proper alignment. *See Fig. 11.*

***CAUTION: Main bearing caps must be installed in original location with arrow facing front of engine.***

**4)** Install bearings in main bearing caps. Check oil clearance using Plastigage method. Main bearing caps must be installed in original location with arrow pointing toward front of engine.
**5)** Tighten bolts to specification. Remove main bearing caps. Clearance must be within specification. If oil clearance exceeds specification, replace bearing with new or undersized bearing.
**6)** Recheck oil clearance. Ensure crankshaft rotates freely with all main bearing caps installed. Check crankshaft end play. See CRANKSHAFT, MAIN & CONNECTING ROD BEARINGS table under ENGINE SPECIFICATIONS at end of article.
**7)** Torque chain guide retaining bolts to specification (if loosened). Install connecting rod caps and bearings. Torque to specification. Ensure connecting rods move freely on crankshaft. Install remaining components. Torque bolts to specification.

### CONNECTING ROD BEARINGS

**1)** Ensure bearing cap and connecting rod are marked for location. Remove connecting rod caps and bearings. Install replacement bearings. Check bearing clearance using Plastigage method. Torque nuts to specification.
**2)** Clearance must be within specification. Replace connecting rod bearing assembly if oil clearance is incorrect. Recheck oil clearance. Ensure connecting rod will move freely after cap is torqued to specification. Check connecting rod side clearance after proper clearance oil is obtained.

### CRANKSHAFT END PLAY

If not within specification, inspect thrust bearing or crankshaft for damage. Replace damaged components. See CRANKSHAFT, MAIN & CONNECTING ROD BEARINGS table under ENGINE SPECIFICATIONS at end of article.

## ENGINE OILING

### ENGINE OILING SYSTEM

Rotor-type oil pump provides oil pressure. Oil pump is driven by crankshaft through drive sprocket and chain. Oil pressure is delivered to main and connecting rod bearings. Pressure relief valve is located in crankcase cover.

### CRANKCASE CAPACITY

Crankcase capacity is 3.0 qts. (2.8L) with filter replacement.

### NORMAL OIL PRESSURE

Minimum oil pressure at 1500 RPM should be 30 psi (2.1 kg/cm²) and 47 psi (3.3 kg/cm²) at 3000 RPM with oil temperature at 172-180°F (78-82°C).

### OIL PUMP

***NOTE: Oil pump clearances can be checked without removing oil pump. Remove oil pump cover and perform clearance inspection. See INSPECTION under OIL PUMP.***

**Removal - 1)** Drain engine oil and coolant. Remove dipstick and guide. Disconnect negative battery cable. Mark and remove wiring from alternator. Remove alternator drive belt and alternator.
**2)** Remove crankshaft pulley and outer timing belt cover. Remove timing belt. See TIMING BELT. Remove camshaft drive sprocket. Remove inner timing belt cover.
**3)** Remove flywheel cover. Remove oil pan. See OIL PAN under REMOVAL & INSTALLATION. Remove crankcase cover. See CRANKCASE COVER. Remove oil pump cover and "O" ring. Remove inner and outer rotor from crankcase cover.
**Inspection - 1)** Inspect rotors, pump shaft and pump housing for scoring or damage. *See Fig. 16.*
**2)** Ensure relief valve slides freely in bore. Measure O.D of rotors and crankcase cover I.D. Replace components not within specification. See OIL PUMP SPECIFICATIONS table.

# 1991 ENGINES
# 1.2L 3-Cylinder (Cont.)

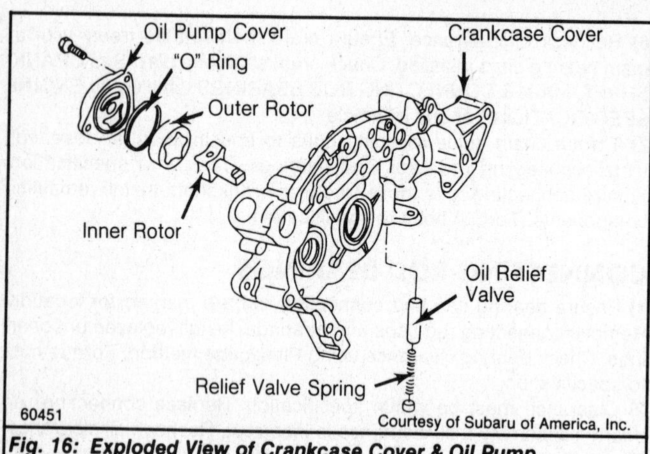


*Fig. 16: Exploded View of Crankcase Cover & Oil Pump*

### OIL PUMP SPECIFICATIONS

| Application | In. (mm) |
|---|---|
| Case-to-Rotor | [1] .0059-.0083 (.149-.210) |
| Inner Rotor O.D. | 1.1693-1.1709 (29.700-29.740) |
| Outer Rotor O.D. | 1.5957-1.5968 (40.530-40.558) |
| Rotor Tip Clearance | [2] .0008-.0059 (.020-.149) |
| Rotor-to-Cover Side Clearance | [3] .0020-.0063 (.050-.160) |

[1] – Service limit is .0098" (.248 mm).
[2] – Service limit is .0079" (.200 mm).
[3] – Service limit is .0071" (.180 mm).

**3)** Install rotors in crankcase cover. Check clearance between tip of inner and outer rotor. Replace rotors as matched set if not within specification. Check clearance between outer rotor and crankcase cover. Replace rotor or crankcase cover if not within specification.
**4)** Place straightedge across crankcase cover. Check clearance between inner pump rotor and straightedge. Replace parts as necessary if not within specification.
**Installation** – To install, reverse removal procedure. Use new gaskets and "O" rings. Torque bolts to specification. Fill cooling system and engine oil.

## TORQUE SPECIFICATIONS

### TORQUE SPECIFICATIONS

| Application | Ft. Lbs. (N.m) |
|---|---|
| Connecting Rod Nut | 29-33 (39-45) |
| Crankshaft Pulley Bolt | 58-72 (78-98) |
| Cylinder Head Bolt [1] | |
| Step 1 | 29 (39) |
| Step 2 | 54 (73) |
| Step 3 | 51-57 (70-77) |
| Engine Mount-To-Body Bolt | 27-49 (37-66) |
| Exhaust Flange-To-Pipe Nut | 34-64 (46-87) |
| Exhaust Manifold Nut | 14-22 (19-30) |
| Exhaust Manifold-To-Flange Bolt | 12-19 (16-25) |
| Flywheel Bolt | 65-71 (88-96) |
| Intake Manifold Bolt | 14-22 (19-30) |
| Main Bearing Cap Bolt | 30-35 (41-47) |
| Transmission Mount-To-Body Bolt | 27-49 (37-66) |
| Transverse Link-To-Crossmember | 54-69 (73-94) |
| Valve Adjusting Screw Nut | 12-17 (16-23) |
| | **INCH Lbs. (N.m)** |
| Camshaft Sprocket Bolt | 100-108 (11-12) |
| Chain Guide Bolt | 51-61 (5.7-6) |
| Oil Pan Bolt | 40-48 (4-5) |
| Shift Rod-To-Transmission Bolt | 84-132 (9-15) |
| Valve Cover Bolt | 61-70 (6-8) |
| Water Pump Impeller Bolt | 83-91 (9-10) |

[1] – Before step No. 3, back off head bolts 90 degrees then perform step No. 3. Tighten in sequence. *See Fig. 3.*

## ENGINE SPECIFICATIONS

### GENERAL SPECIFICATIONS

| Application | Specification |
|---|---|
| Displacement | 73 Cu. In. (1.2L) |
| Bore | 3.07" (77.9 mm) |
| Stroke | 3.27" (83 mm) |
| Compression Ratio | |
| Carbureted | 9.0:1 |
| PFI | 9.1:1 |
| Fuel System | 2-Bbl., PFI |
| Horsepower @ RPM | |
| Carbureted | 66 @ 3600 |
| PFI | 73 @ 5600 |
| Torque Ft. Lbs. @ RPM | |
| Carbureted | 70 @ 3600 |
| PFI | 71 @ 3600 |

### CRANKSHAFT, MAIN & CONNECTING ROD BEARINGS

| Application | In. (mm) |
|---|---|
| Crankshaft | |
| End Play | .0031-.0070 (.078-.179) |
| Runout | .0012 (.030) |
| Main Bearings | |
| Journal Diameter | 1.6525-1.6529 (41.974-41.985) |
| Journal Out-Of-Round | .0012 (.030) |
| Journal Taper | .0008 (.020) |
| Oil Clearance | .0006-.0018 (.015-.045) |
| Connecting Rod Bearings | |
| Journal Diameter | 1.6531-1.6535 (41.989-41.998) |
| Journal Out-Of-Round | .0012 (.030) |
| Journal Taper | .0008 (.020) |
| Grinding Limit | .0098 (.248) |
| Oil Clearance | .0006-.0018 (.015-.045) |

### CYLINDER HEAD

| Application | Specification |
|---|---|
| Cylinder Head Height | 4.39" (111.5 mm) |
| Maximum Warpage | .002" (.05 mm) |
| Valve Seats | |
| Intake Valve | |
| Seat Angle | 45° |
| Seat Width | .039" (1.0 mm) |
| Maximum Seat Runout | [1] |
| Seat Bore Diameter | [1] |
| Exhaust Valve | |
| Seat Angle | 45° |
| Seat Width | .051" (1.3 mm) |
| Maximum Seat Runout | [1] |
| Seat Bore Diameter | [1] |
| Valve Guides | |
| Intake Valve | |
| Valve Guide Cylinder Head Bore I.D. [2] | [1] |
| Valve Guide I.D. | .2756-.2762 (7.000-7.015 mm) |
| Valve Guide Installed Height | .807" (20.5 mm) |
| Valve Stem/Guide Oil Clearance | .0008-.0020" (.020-.050 mm) |
| Exhaust Valve | |
| Valve Guide Cylinder Head Bore I.D. [2] | [1] |
| Valve Guide I.D. | .2756-.2762" (7.000-7.015 mm) |
| Valve Guide Installed Height | .807" (20.5 mm) |
| Valve Stem-To-Guide | |
| Oil Clearance | .0016-.0028" (.040-.070 mm) |

[1] – Information not available from manufacturer.
[2] – Valve guide requires .0012-.0024" (.031-.060 mm) interference fit with cylinder head.

# 1991 ENGINES
# 1.2L 3-Cylinder (Cont.)

## PISTONS, PINS & RINGS

| Application | In. (mm) |
|---|---|
| Pistons [1] | |
| Clearance | .0015-.0024 (.038-.062) |
| Diameter | 3.0690-3.0694 (77.592-77.962) |
| Pins | |
| Diameter | .7084-.7087 (17.994-18.000) |
| Piston Fit | .0005-.0007 (.012-.018) |
| Rod Fit | .0007-.0016 (.018-.041) |
| Rings | |
| No. 1 | |
| End Gap | .0079-.0138 (.200-.350) |
| Side Clearance | .0014-.0030 (.035-.075) |
| No. 2 | |
| End Gap | .0079-.0138 (.200-.350) |
| Side Clearance | .001-.0026 (.025-.065) |
| No. 3 (Oil) | |
| End Gap | .0012-.035 (.30-.90) |
| Side Clearance | [2] |

[1] – Two oversize pistons are available. See PISTON PIN REPLACEMENT.
[2] – Information is not available from manufacturer.

## CONNECTING RODS

| Application | In. (mm) |
|---|---|
| Bore Diameter | |
| Pin Bore | 0.7079-0.7082 (17.981-17.988) |
| Crankpin Bore | 1.7116-1.7124 (43.475-43.495) |
| Center-To-Center Length | [1] |
| Maximum Bend | .004 (.10) |
| Maximum Twist | .004 (.10) |
| Side Play | .0028-.0118 (.071-.299) |

[1] – Information is not available from manufacturer.

## CAMSHAFT

| Application | In. (mm) |
|---|---|
| Bore Diameter | [1] |
| End Play | .0012-.0015 (.030-.038) |
| Journal Diameter | [1] |
| Journal Runout | [1] |
| Lobe Height | 1.4520-1.4528 (36.88-36.90) |
| Lobe Lift | .1920-.1928 (4.88-4.90) |
| Oil Clearance | [1] |

[1] – Information is not available from manufacturer.

## CYLINDER BLOCK

| Application | In. (mm) |
|---|---|
| Cylinder Bore | |
| Standard Diameter | 3.0709-3.0718 (78.000-78.024) |
| Maximum Boring Limit | .039 (.99) |
| Maximum Taper | .0020 (.050) |
| Maximum Out-Of-Round | .0020 (.050) |
| Minimum Deck Height | 7.862 (199.8) |
| Maximum Deck Warpage | .0020 (.050) |
| Warpage Grind Limit | .008 (.20) |

## VALVES & VALVE SPRINGS

| Application | Specification |
|---|---|
| Intake Valves | |
| Face Angle | 45° |
| Head Diameter | [1] |
| Minimum Margin | .020" (.50 mm) |
| Minimum Refinish Length | 4.22" (107.7 mm) |
| Stem Diameter | .2742-.2748" (6.964-6.979 mm) |
| Valve Tip Maximum Refinish | [1] |
| Exhaust Valves | |
| Face Angle | 45° |
| Head Diameter | [1] |
| Minimum Margin | .020" (.50 mm) |
| Minimum Refinish Length | 4.25" (108 mm) |
| Stem Diameter | .2734-.2740" (6.945-6.960 mm) |
| Valve Tip Maximum Refinish | [1] |
| Valve Springs | |
| Free Length | 1.83" (46.50 mm) |
| Installed Height | 1.248" (31.7 mm) |
| Out-Of-Square | [1] |
| | **Lbs. @ In. (kg @ mm)** |
| Pressure | |
| Valve Open | [1] |
| Valve Closed | 112.7-129.7 @ 1.25 (51-59 @ 32) |

[1] – Information is not available from manufacturer.

## Loyale, XT

***NOTE: For repair procedures not covered in this article, see ENGINE OVERHAUL PROCEDURES article in GENERAL INFORMATION.***

## ENGINE IDENTIFICATION

Engine can be identified by sixth character of Vehicle Identification Number (VIN). The VIN is stamped on a metal plate located on front right side of firewall. Identification number of engine is stamped on a machined pad on right front of engine cylinder block.

***ENGINE IDENTIFICATION CODES***

| Application | Code |
|---|---|
| Loyale | |
| 1.8L 2WD | 4 |
| 1.8L 4WD | 5 |
| XT | |
| 1.8L 2WD | 4 |
| 1.8L 4WD Air Suspension | 7 |

## ADJUSTMENTS

### VALVE CLEARANCE ADJUSTMENT

Valve adjustment is not required.

## REMOVAL & INSTALLATION

### FUEL PRESSURE RELEASE

Disconnect fuel pump wiring connector. Start engine and operate until engine stalls. Crank engine for an additional 5 seconds. With ignition off, reconnect fuel pump wiring connector.

### ENGINE

***NOTE: Removal procedure is with transaxle remaining in vehicle.***

**Removal – 1)** Release fuel pressure. See FUEL PRESSURE RELEASE under REMOVAL & INSTALLATION. Drain cooling system. Disconnect upper and lower radiator hoses and heater hoses, and remove radiator. Disconnect electrical connectors, vacuum hoses and fuel lines.

**2)** Disconnect accelerator cable, cruise control cable (if equipped) and hill holder cable (M/T) at clutch release fork. Remove accessory drive belts. Remove power steering pump with hoses attached. Discharge A/C system and disconnect hoses.

**3)** On turbo models, remove upper and lower turbo covers. Disconnect exhaust pipe and necessary lines at turbo. On all models, remove center exhaust pipe and heat shield. Remove air cleaner case and hoses.

**4)** On A/T models, remove timing hole plug. Remove torque converter to drive plate bolts. Ensure bolts do not fall into housing. Remove engine stabilizer.

**5)** On all models, remove upper bolts attaching engine to transaxle. Attach hoist to engine and support. Remove engine-to-crossmember bolts. Remove remaining engine-to-transaxle bolts. Support transaxle with a floor jack. Remove engine.

**Installation –** To install, reverse removal procedure. Adjust all control cables. Adjust fluid levels.

## INTAKE MANIFOLD

***NOTE: Fuel pressure must be released if fuel lines or fuel system components are removed.***

**Removal & Installation –** Release fuel pressure. See FUEL PRESSURE RELEASE under REMOVAL & INSTALLATION. Drain cooling system. Remove air cleaner and duct. Mark intake manifold components for reassembly reference. Remove intake manifold and components. *See Figs. 1-3.* To install, reverse removal procedure. Replace all "O" rings.

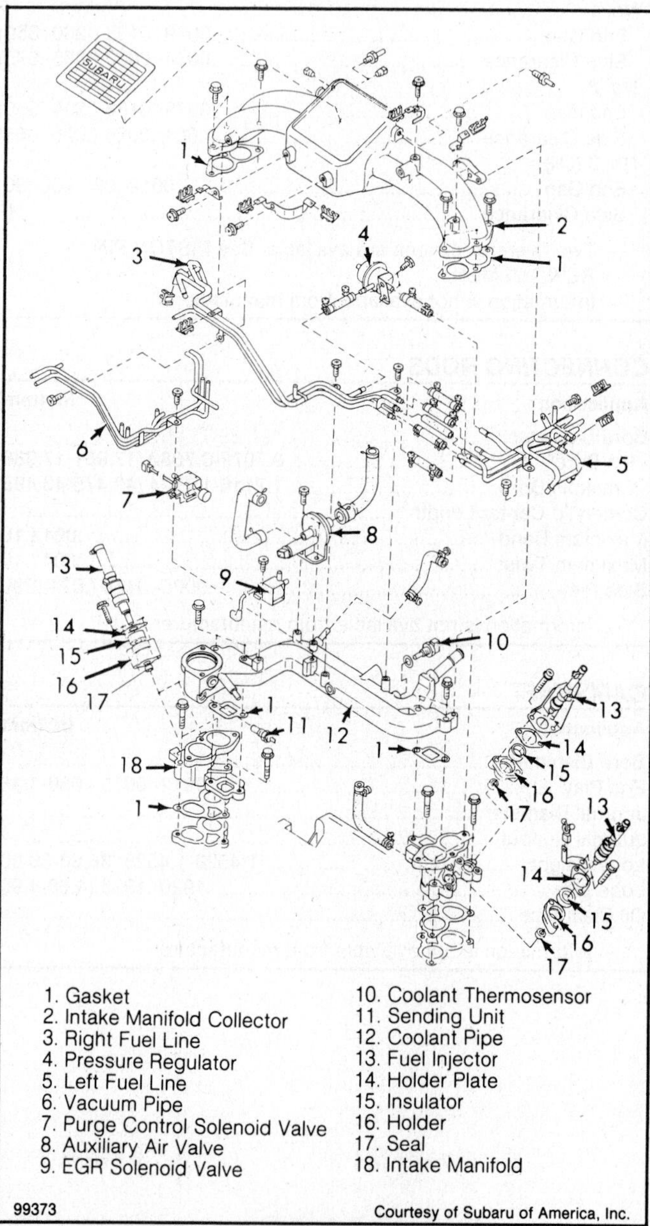


***Fig. 1: Exploded View of Intake Manifold (XT PFI)***

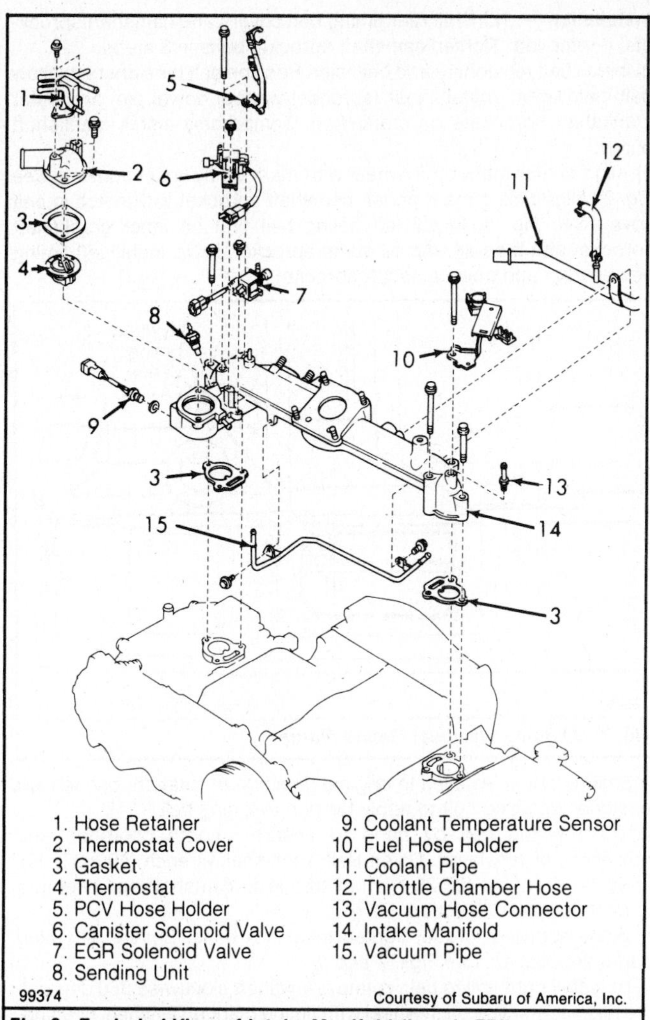


*Fig. 2: Exploded View of Intake Manifold (Loyale TBI)*

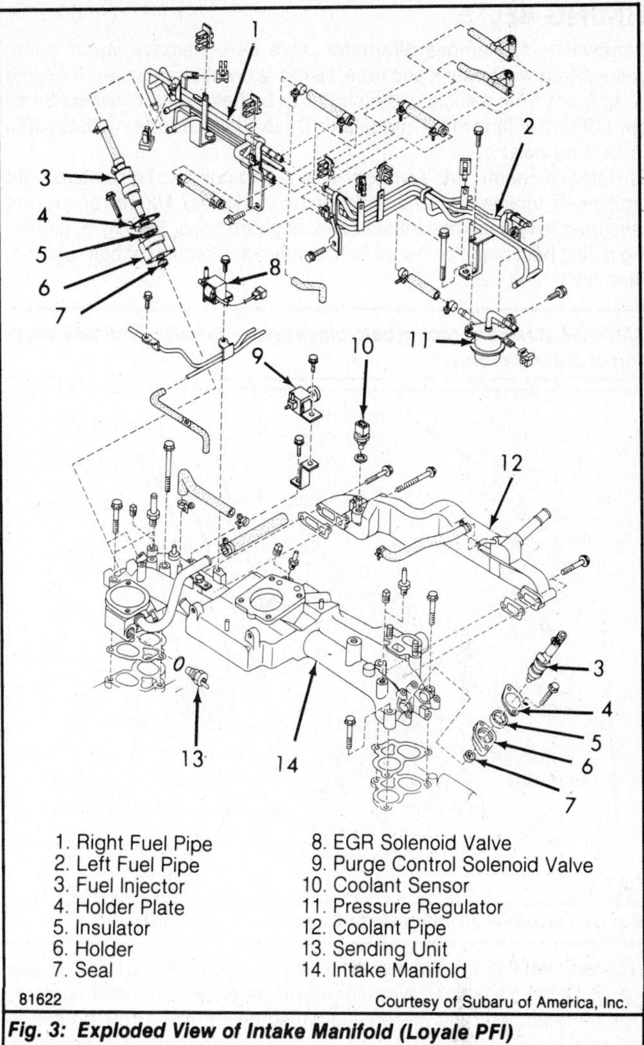


*Fig. 3: Exploded View of Intake Manifold (Loyale PFI)*

## EXHAUST MANIFOLD

***NOTE: Exhaust manifold is integral with cylinder head.***

## CYLINDER HEAD

**Removal – 1)** Remove timing belts. See TIMING BELTS. On turbo models, remove turbo coolant line from cylinder head. On all models, remove camshaft and components. See CAMSHAFT.

**2)** Remove alternator and mounting bracket. Remove A/C compressor (if equipped). Remove adjusting bar-to-cylinder head bolt (except A/C models). Remove intake manifold. Disconnect exhaust pipe from cylinder head. Remove coolant by-pass pipe bracket at cylinder head. Remove spark plugs. Remove cylinder head bolts, cylinder head and gasket.

**Inspection** – Check cylinder head warpage and height. Resurface head if warpage exceeds specification. See CYLINDER HEAD table under ENGINE SPECIFICATIONS at end of article. Replace cylinder head if not within specification after resurfacing.

**Installation – 1)** Ensure mating surfaces are clean and dry. Install head gasket. Coat head bolt threads with oil. Tighten bolts to specification using proper sequence. *See Fig. 4.* See TORQUE SPECIFICATIONS table at end of article.

**2)** To install remaining components, reverse removal procedure. Tighten bolts to specification.

***CAUTION: After initial start-up, recheck cylinder head bolt torque after reaching operating temperature. Ensure engine is COLD while retorquing head bolts.***

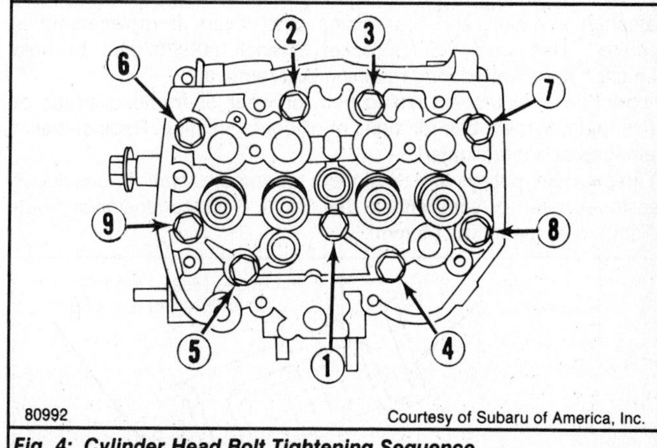


*Fig. 4: Cylinder Head Bolt Tightening Sequence*

## FRONT CRANKSHAFT OIL SEAL

**Removal & Installation – 1)** Remove timing belts and crankshaft sprockets. See TIMING BELTS. Pry seal from cylinder block.

**2)** To install, apply oil to outside surface of seal and grease on seal lip. Using Seal Installer (499567000), install seal in cylinder block. Install remaining components. Tighten bolts to specification. See TORQUE SPECIFICATIONS table at end of article.

# 1991 ENGINES
# 1.8L 4-Cylinder (Cont.)

## TIMING BELTS

**Removal - 1)** Remove alternator drive belt. Remove water pump pulley. Remove dipstick and tube. Remove crankshaft pulley. If engine is removed from vehicle, crankshaft can be held using Flywheel Stopper (498277000) for M/T models or Drive Plate Stopper (498497000) for A/T models.

**2)** Remove center, left and right timing belt covers. To remove right timing belt, loosen tensioner bolts on No. 1 cylinder 1/2 turn and rotate tensioner to release belt tension and retighten bolts. *See Fig. 5.* If reusing timing belt, place arrow on belt to indicate direction of belt rotation. Remove timing belt.

***CAUTION: If reusing timing belt, place arrow on belt to indicate direction of belt rotation.***

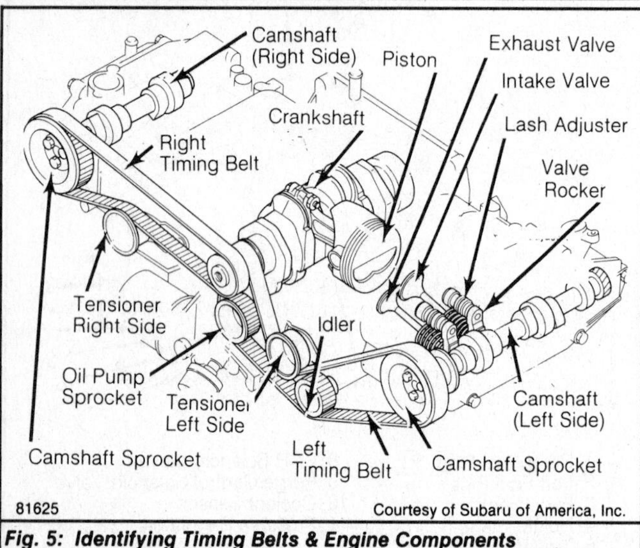


***Fig. 5: Identifying Timing Belts & Engine Components***

**3)** Loosen left timing belt tensioner bolts 1/2 turn on No. 2 cylinder. *See Fig. 5.* Using Tensioner Wrench, rotate tensioner until belt is slack. Tighten mounting bolts. If reusing timing belt, place arrow on belt to indicate direction of belt rotation. Remove outer crankshaft sprocket.

**4)** Remove timing belt and inner crankshaft sprocket. Remove camshaft sprocket and rear timing belt covers if replacement is required. Use Camshaft Sprocket Wrench (499207000) to hold camshaft sprockets during retaining bolt removal.

**Inspection - 1)** Inspect timing belt for wear or rounded edges of drive teeth. Inspect belt for signs of oil contamination. Replace belt if damaged or contaminated.

**2)** Inspect idler pulleys and tensioners for smooth rotation. Check belt tensioner roller for squareness. *See Fig. 6.* Replace tensioner if out-of-square exceeds .02" (.5 mm).

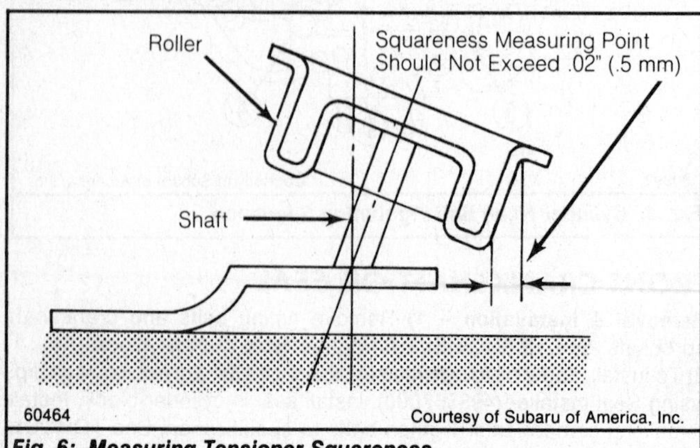


***Fig. 6: Measuring Tensioner Squareness***

**Installation - 1)** Install rear timing belt covers and camshaft sprockets, if removed. Tighten camshaft sprocket bolts in 3 steps.

**2)** Install belt tensioners and belt idler. Position belt tensioners to allow belt installation. Install inner (sprocket without dowel pin) and outer crankshaft sprockets on crankshaft. Temporarily install crankshaft pulley.

**3)** Align center mark on flywheel with mark on flywheel housing. *See Fig. 7.* Align timing mark on left camshaft sprocket with notch in belt cover. *See Fig. 8.* Install left timing belt first on inner crankshaft sprocket and then around oil pump sprocket. Next, install left timing belt on idler and then camshaft sprocket.

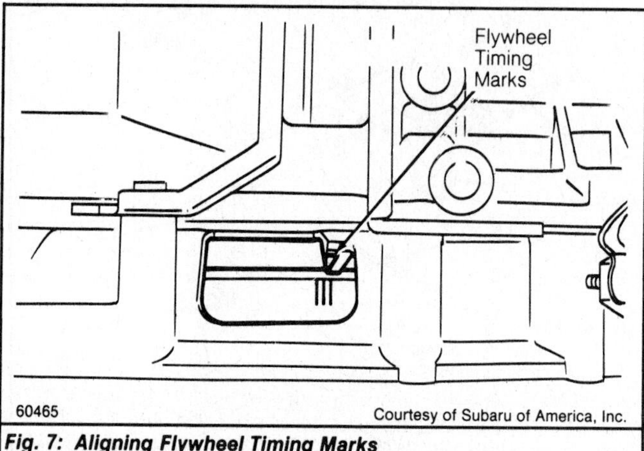


***Fig. 7: Aligning Flywheel Timing Marks***

**4)** Ensure belt is installed in original direction of rotation. Loosen left tensioner retaining bolt to apply tension to timing belt.

**5)** Push timing belt by hand to ensure smooth operation and movement of tensioner. Using Belt Tensioner Wrench (499437000), apply 17-19 ft. lbs. (23-26 N.m) of torque to camshaft sprocket in a counterclockwise direction.

**6)** While applying torque, tighten tensioner bolts. Ensure all timing marks are aligned. *See Figs. 7 and 8.*

**7)** To install right timing belt, rotate crankshaft clockwise 360 degrees and align center line on flywheel with timing mark on flywheel housing. Align camshaft sprocket timing mark with notch in housing. *See Fig. 8.*

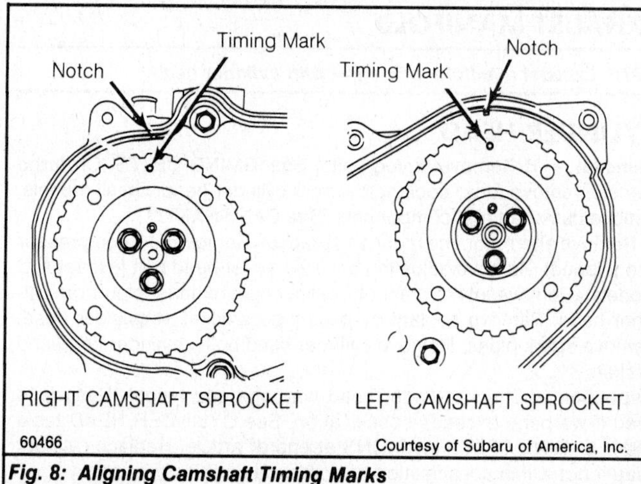


***Fig. 8: Aligning Camshaft Timing Marks***

**8)** Install right timing belt over crankshaft and camshaft sprockets, keeping slack out of side opposite tensioner. Ensure belt is installed in original direction of rotation.

**9)** Loosen inner tensioner bolt and allow tensioner to apply belt tension. Using Belt Tension Wrench (499437000), apply 17-19 ft. lbs. (23-26 N.m) of torque, while turning camshaft sprocket in counterclockwise direction.

**10)** While applying torque, tighten inner and then outer tensioner retaining bolts. Ensure all timing marks are aligned. To install remaining components, reverse removal procedure.

# 1991 ENGINES
# 1.8L 4-Cylinder (Cont.)

## VALVE LASH ADJUSTERS

***NOTE: For information on valve lash adjusters, see VALVE TRAIN under OVERHAUL.***

## CAMSHAFT

**Removal - 1)** Remove valve covers. Remove distributor cap. Attach dial indicator to case with stem resting against gear of distributor. Rotate distributor and note backlash between distributor gear and distributor gear of camshaft.

**2)** Camshaft distributor gear should be replaced if backlash is not within specification. See CAMSHAFT table under ENGINE SPECIFICATIONS at end of article. Remove distributor. Remove timing belt and camshaft sprockets. See TIMING BELTS under REMOVAL & INSTALLATION. Remove coolant pipe.

**3)** Remove oil filler. On turbo models, remove EGR pipe. On all models, remove camshaft case bolts. Remove camshaft case and camshaft as a unit. Ensure valve rockers do not fall from cylinder head during case removal.

**4)** Remove valve rockers and valve lash adjusters from cylinder head. Mark components for location and keep valve lash adjusters upright. Remove camshaft support. Remove camshaft.

***CAUTION: Carefully remove camshaft case as valve rockers may fall during removal. Mark components for location. DO NOT place valve lash adjusters upside-down or on their sides.***

**Inspection - 1)** Clean camshaft journals and case surfaces. Inspect components for damage. Measure camshaft journals. Replace camshaft if not within specification. See CAMSHAFT table under ENGINE SPECIFICATIONS at end of article.

**2)** Measure camshaft lobe height and runout at center camshaft journal. Measure I.D. of case journal bores. Replace components if not within specification.

**Installation - 1)** Coat camshaft journals and case bores with oil and install camshaft. Install camshaft support and new "O" ring. Tighten bolts to specification. See TORQUE SPECIFICATIONS table at end of article. Position camshaft dowel pin upward toward the camshaft support retaining bolt.

**2)** With valve lash adjusters upright, press pivot area downward to ensure no air exists in adjuster. Install valve lash adjusters in original location of cylinder head. Coat spherical surface and sliding surface of valve rocker with grease and install in original location.

***CAUTION: Valve lash adjusters and valve rockers must be installed in original location. On new valve lash adjusters, pin located on side of adjuster must be removed before to installation.***

**3)** Apply a bead of Three Bond (1207B) sealant to grooves of camshaft case and install case on cylinder head. Install bolts and tighten to specification. See TORQUE SPECIFICATIONS table at end of article. Apply engine oil to valve rockers and camshaft.

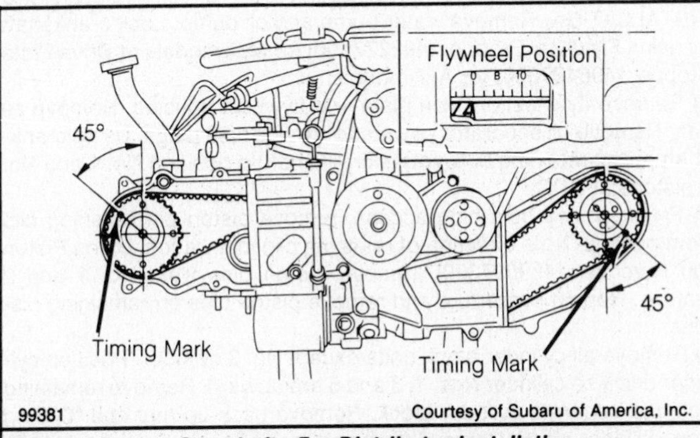


***Fig. 9: Aligning Camshafts For Distributor Installation***

**4)** To install remaining components, reverse removal procedure. Tighten bolts to specification. Before installing distributor, rotate engine to bring No. 1 cylinder at TDC of compression stroke so camshaft mark is properly positioned. *See Fig. 9.*

**5)** Align marks on distributor housing with mark on distributor gear. Install distributor.

## REAR CRANKSHAFT OIL SEAL

**Removal & Installation - 1)** Remove flywheel or drive plate. It may be necessary to remove oil separator plate to access oil seal. Pry oil seal from cylinder block.

**2)** To install seal, apply oil to outside surface of seal and apply grease to seal lip. Using Seal Installer (499587000), install seal in cylinder block. Install remaining components. Tighten bolts to specification. See TORQUE SPECIFICATIONS table at end of article.

## WATER PUMP

**Removal & Installation -** Drain coolant. Disconnect radiator hose and by-pass hose from water pump. Loosen water pump pulley nuts. Remove alternator drive belt. Remove front timing belt cover. To install, reverse removal procedure.

## OIL PAN

**Removal & Installation -** Drain oil. Remove oil pan bolts. Remove oil pan and gasket. To install, reverse removal procedure using new gasket. Tighten bolts to specification. See TORQUE SPECIFICATIONS table at end of article.

# OVERHAUL

## CYLINDER HEAD

**Cylinder Head -** Check cylinder head warpage and height. Resurface head if warpage exceeds specification. See CYLINDER HEAD in ENGINE SPECIFICATIONS tables at end of article. Check for cracks. Inspect valve seats and grind as necessary. Replace cylinder head if not within specification after resurfacing.

**Valve Springs -** Measure free length of valve springs. Check spring tension at specified height. Check valve spring for squareness. See VALVES & VALVE SPRINGS table under ENGINE SPECIFICATIONS at end of article. Replace springs if not within specification.

**Valve Stem Oil Seals -** With valves removed, remove oil seals from cylinder head. Note location of oil seals. Intake valve stem seal is Black with White spring. Exhaust valve stem seal is Brown with White spring. Coat seals with oil. Using Valve Stem Oil Seal Guide (498857100), install valve stem oil seal.

**Valve Guides - 1)** Check clearance between valve guide and stem by measuring outside diameter of valve stem and inside diameter of valve guide using an outside and inside micrometer. See CYLINDER HEAD in ENGINE SPECIFICATIONS table at end of article.

**2)** If clearance is not within specification, replace valve guide. To replace valve guide, position cylinder head with combustion chamber facing upward. Insert Valve Guide Remover (499767200) into valve guide and press down to remove valve guide.

**3)** Turn cylinder head upside down and place Valve Guide Adjuster (4997670000) onto valve guide. Coat new valve guide with engine oil. Insert Valve Guide Remover (499767200) into new valve guide. Press in until valve guide upper end is flush with upper surface of Valve Guide Adjuster (499767200).

**4)** Check valve guide protrusion. Valve guide protrusion should be .69-.71" (17.5-18.0 mm). Ream inside of valve guide using Valve Guide Reamer (499767400). Clean all chips or metal particles from valve guide. Recheck contact between valve and valve seat after replacing valve guide.

**Valve Seats -** Inspect intake and exhaust valve seats. If valve seats are defective, correct contact surfaces with valve seat cutter when replacing valve guides. See CYLINDER HEAD table under ENGINE SPECIFICATIONS at end of article.

# 1991 ENGINES
# 1.8L 4-Cylinder (Cont.)

**Valves** – Disassemble cylinder head. Measure valve stem diameter, valve margin and overall length. Replace valves if not within specification. See VALVES & VALVE SPRINGS table under ENGINE SPECIFICATIONS at end of article. Recheck valve margin after grinding valves.

## VALVE TRAIN

**Valve Lash Adjuster** – With adjuster set in an upright position, push adjuster pivot piston down hard and quickly by hand. If pivot piston can be depressed more than .020" (.50 mm), put adjuster in a container of light oil and move pivot piston up and down until adjuster is within specification. If adjuster is still not within specification, replace adjuster.

## CYLINDER BLOCK ASSEMBLY

**Crankshaft & Connecting Rods** – **1)** Remove intake manifold and cylinder head. See INTAKE MANIFOLD and CYLINDER HEAD under REMOVAL & INSTALLATION. Remove water pump, oil pump and oil pan. Remove oil separator cover. Remove 14-mm Allen head service hole plugs from crankcase.

**2)** Using crankshaft pulley retaining bolt, rotate crankshaft and position No. 1 and No. 2 pistons at BDC. Access piston pins No. 1 and No. 2 through front service hole plugs. Access No. 3 and No. 4 pins through rear service hole plugs. From service hole plug access, remove piston pin retaining clip from the pistons. Note direction of retaining clip installation.

**3)** Using Piston Pin Remover (399094310), remove piston pins from No. 1 and 2 pistons. Repeat procedure and remove piston pins on remaining pistons. Remove all cylinder block bolts except 10 mm bolt at center journal.

**4)** Position cylinder block so cylinders No. 1 and No. 3 are upward. Remove remaining bolt and separate cylinder block. Remove back-up ring and "O" ring from cylinder block. Remove crankshaft and connecting rods.

***CAUTION: DO NOT allow connecting rods to fall and damage cylinder block while separating cylinder block.***

**5)** Inspect crankshaft for cracks. Check crankshaft runout at center journal and journal out-of-round. Repair or replace if not within specification. See CRANKSHAFT, MAIN & CONNECTING ROD BEARINGS table under ENGINE SPECIFICATIONS at end of article.

**6)** Check connecting rod for bend or twist. Measure crankpin and piston pin bore I.D. Replace if not within specification. See CONNECTING RODS table under ENGINE SPECIFICATIONS at end of article.

**7)** Lubricate and install bearings in connecting rod. Install connecting rod in proper cylinder location with identification mark toward the front of crankshaft with matching numbers aligned. *See Fig. 11.*

***CAUTION: Connecting rods must be installed so identification mark is toward front of crankshaft. See Fig. 11.***

**8)** Apply oil to connecting rod bolt threads before tightening nut. Check oil clearance using Plastigage method. Replace bearings to obtain correct clearance. See CRANKSHAFT, MAIN & CONNECTING ROD BEARINGS table under ENGINE SPECIFICATIONS at end of article.

**9)** Install main bearings in cylinder block. Install crankshaft in left side of cylinder block. Using feeler gauge, measure end play between center bearing and crankshaft.

**10)** Replace bearing if end play is not within specification. See CRANKSHAFT, MAIN & CONNECTING ROD BEARINGS table under ENGINE SPECIFICATIONS at end of article. Install right side of cylinder block to check oil clearance using Plastigage method.

**11)** Tighten bolts to specification. See TORQUE SPECIFICATIONS table at end of article. Check oil clearance. Replace bearings to obtain correct clearance. See CRANKSHAFT, MAIN & CONNECTING ROD BEARINGS table under ENGINE SPECIFICATIONS at end of article. Reassemble cylinder block.

**Pistons & Rings** – **1)** Remove crankshaft and rod assembly. See CYLINDER BLOCK ASSEMBLY under OVERHAUL. Note direction of piston installation and cylinder location. Using soft hammer, drive pistons from cylinder block. Inspect piston for cracks or damage in ring areas.

**2)** Check ring side clearance. Replace piston if not within specification. See PISTONS, PINS & RINGS table at end of article. Measure piston diameter at temperature of 68°F (20°C). Measure piston diameter at 90 degree angle to piston pin at .787" (19.98 mm) from bottom of piston skirt on XT and non-turbo Loyale models and 1.059" (26.90 mm) on from bottom of piston skirt on turbo models.

**3)** To determine piston fit of pin, measure piston pin O.D. and subtract from piston pin bore I.D. See PISTONS, PINS & RINGS table under ENGINE SPECIFICATIONS at end of article. Replace piston if piston fit is not within specification. Ensure piston pin can be installed in piston at 68°F (20°C). Replace components if piston pin cannot be installed at given temperature.

**4)** Ensure piston ring end gap and side clearance are within specification. See PISTONS, PINS & RINGS table under ENGINE SPECIFICATIONS at end of article. Install rings on piston with "R" or "N" mark toward top of piston. Lubricate piston, rings and cylinder bore with engine oil.

**5)** Properly space ring end gaps on piston. Bend over pawl of upper rail and install in piston hole. *See Fig. 10.* Install piston into cylinder bore.

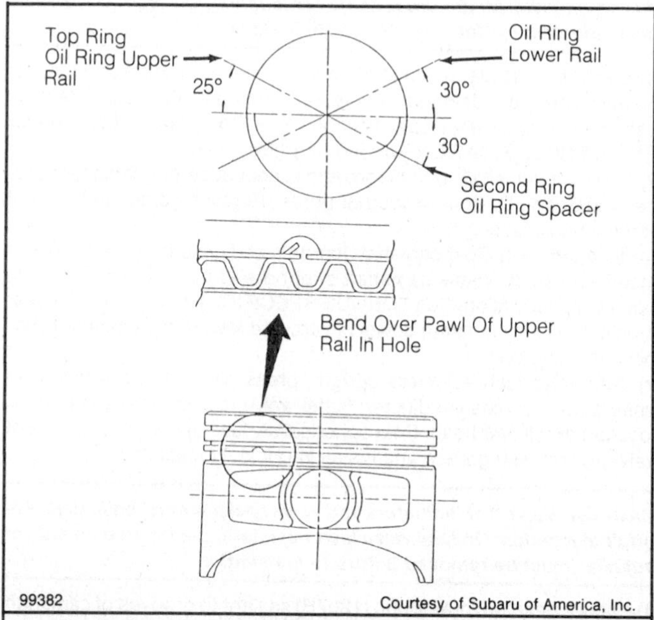


*Fig. 10: Positioning Piston Rings*

**Cylinder Block** – **1)** Remove intake manifold and cylinder head. See INTAKE MANIFOLD and CYLINDER HEAD under REMOVAL & INSTALLATION. Remove water pump and oil pump. Lock crankshaft by using Flywheel Stopper (498277000) for M/T models or Drive Plate Stopper (498497000) for A/T models.

**2)** Remove flywheel or drive plate and flywheel housing. Remove oil pan. Remove oil separator cover and service hole plugs. Using crankshaft pulley retaining bolt, rotate crankshaft to position No. 1 and No. 2 pistons at BDC.

**3)** From service hole plug access, remove piston pin retaining clip from pistons. Note direction of retaining clip installation. Using Piston Pin Remover (499097300), remove piston pins from No. 1 and 2 pistons. Repeat procedure and remove piston pins on remaining pistons.

**4)** Remove all cylinder block bolts except No. 3 cylinder. Position cylinder block so cylinder Nos. 1, 3 and 5 are upward. Remove remaining bolt and separate cylinder block. Remove back-up ring and "O" ring from cylinder block. Remove front and rear oil seals from crankshaft. Remove crankshaft, connecting rods and pistons.

# 1991 ENGINES
# 1.8L 4-Cylinder (Cont.)

**CAUTION: DO NOT allow connecting rods to fall and damage cylinder block while separating cylinder block.**

**5)** Inspect cylinder block for cracks, warpage, bore taper and out-of-round. Replace or repair cylinder block if not within specification. See CYLINDER BLOCK table under ENGINE SPECIFICATIONS at end of article.

**6)** Measure cylinder bore and piston skirt diameter with temperature of 68°F (20°C). Piston skirt diameter should be measured at 90 degree angle to piston pin. Measure piston diameter 1.0618" (26.697 mm) from bottom of piston skirt. Clearance between piston and cylinder bore must be within specification. See PISTONS, PINS & RINGS table under ENGINE SPECIFICATIONS at end of article.

**7)** Install main bearings, crankshaft and connecting rods. *See Fig. 11.* Ensure all crankshaft bearings are installed in cylinder block. Install "O" ring and back-up ring on cylinder block. Ensure "O" ring properly fits in groove.

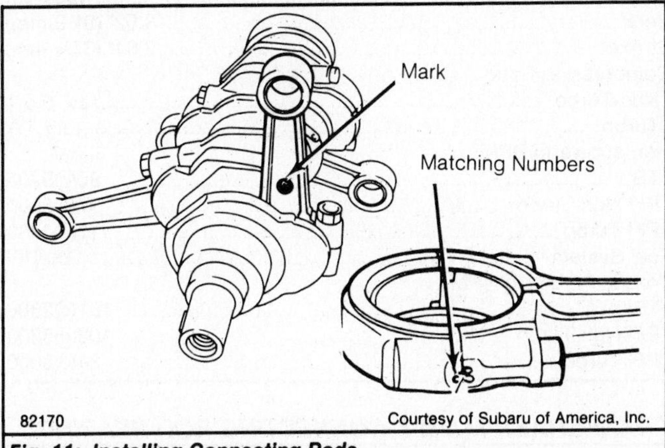


***Fig. 11: Installing Connecting Rods***

**8)** Clean all sealing surfaces of cylinder block. Apply Three Bond (1215) to sealing surface on one side of cylinder block.

***CAUTION: Ensure sealant does not enter oil and coolant passages of cylinder block.***

**9)** With left cylinder block facing downward, install right cylinder block. Install right side of cylinder block. Ensure "O" ring fits properly in groove. Temporarily install cylinder block bolts. Lay cylinder block down and tighten bolts to specification. See TORQUE SPECIFICATIONS table at end of article.

**10)** With cylinder No. 3 and No. 4 facing downward, rotate crankshaft so No. 1 and 2 cylinder connecting rods are at BDC.

**11)** Lubricate piston, rings and cylinder wall. Ensure piston rings are properly positioned. Install piston Nos. 1 and 2 using Piston Guide (398744300).

**12)** Use Piston Pin Guide (399284300) to align service hole, piston pin hole and connecting rod hole. Install piston pin retaining clips with end of clip away from piston pin. Install piston pin and circlip through service hole.

***CAUTION: Piston pin retaining clips must be installed with end of clip positioned away from piston pin.***

**13)** Repeat procedure on remaining cylinders. Ensure all piston pin retaining clips are properly installed. Apply Three Bond (1205) to service hole plugs. Install plugs and tighten to specification. See TORQUE SPECIFICATIONS table at end of article. To reassemble remaining components, reverse removal procedure. Tighten bolts to specification.

## ENGINE OILING

### ENGINE LUBRICATION SYSTEM

Oil pressure is provided by a Trochoid-type pump driven by the timing belt. Pressure relief valve is located in the oil pump body.

### CRANKCASE CAPACITY

Crankcase capacity with filter replacement is 4.2 qts. (4.0L) at the upper level mark and 3.2 qts. (3.0L) at the lower level mark.

### NORMAL OIL PRESSURE

Oil pressure should be 14 psi (1.0 kg/cm²) at 550 RPM and 43 psi (3.0 kg/cm²) at 5000 RPM with engine at normal operating temperature.

### OIL PUMP

**Removal – 1)** Disconnect negative battery cable. Remove lower undercovers. Remove radiator shroud assembly. It may be necessary to remove A/C condenser fan shroud. Remove oil dipstick and tube.

**2)** Remove drive belts. It may be necessary to remove A/C compressor (if equipped). Remove water pump pulley. Loosen oil pump pulley retaining bolts. Remove timing belts. See TIMING BELTS under REMOVAL & INSTALLATION.

**3)** Remove left camshaft sprocket. Remove left timing belt rear covers. Remove oil pump assembly and gasket.

**Disassembly & Inspection – 1)** Disassemble pump. Measure O.D. of inner rotor shaft and outer rotor shaft. Measure clearance between outer rotor and cylinder block housing.

**2)** Measure case projection height H1 plus inner and outer rotors H2. *See Fig. 12.* Measure housing bore depth "L" of cylinder block. To determine side clearance "C", use the following formula: "C" = "L"-(H1 + H2).

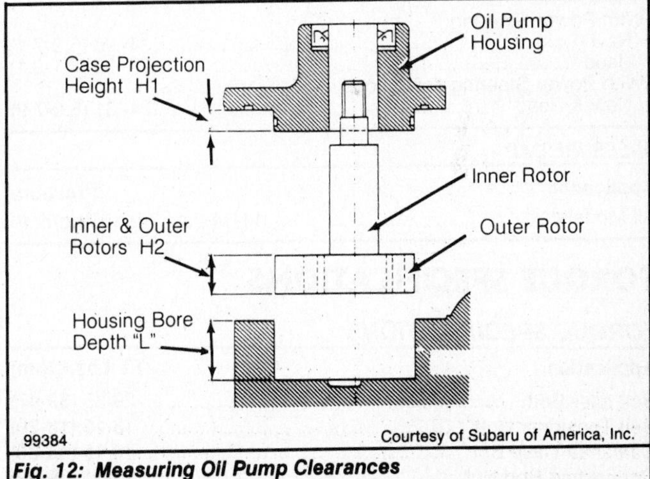


***Fig. 12: Measuring Oil Pump Clearances***

**3)** Side clearance must be within specification. See OIL PUMP SPECIFICATIONS table.

***OIL PUMP SPECIFICATIONS***

| Application | In. (mm) |
|---|---|
| Case Projection Height H1 | .3138-.3150 (7.971-8.001) |
| Outer Rotor-to-Cylinder Block | [1] .0039-.0071 (.099-.180) |
| Relief Valve Spring Free Length | 1.854 (47.092) |
| Rotor Housing Depth "L" | .8646-.8677 (21.961-22.039) |
| Rotor O.D | |
| Inner Rotor | 1.4035-1.4055 (35.649-35.699) |
| Outer Rotor | 1.9665-1.9685 (44.949-49.999) |
| Side Clearance "C" | [2] .0020-.0063 (.051-.160) |

[1] – Wear limit is .0087" (.221 mm).
[2] – Wear limit is .0071" (.180 mm).

# 1991 ENGINES
# 1.8L 4-Cylinder (Cont.)

**4)** If side clearance is not within specification, replace inner and outer rotors with proper rotors. See ROTOR SPECIFICATIONS table. Check relief valve spring free length. Replace components if not within specification. See OIL PUMP SPECIFICATIONS table.

***ROTOR SPECIFICATIONS***

| Identification Mark | Height - In. (mm) |
|---|---|
| A | .5468-.5476 (13.889-13.909) |
| B | .5472-.5480 (13.899-13.919) |
| C | .5476-.5484 (13.909-13.929) |

**Reassembly & Installation** - To reassemble and install, reverse removal procedure using new gaskets and "O" rings. Tighten bolts to specification.

## ENGINE COOLING

### ENGINE COOLING SPECIFICATIONS

***COOLANT SYSTEM CAPACITY***

| Application | Quantity |
|---|---|
| Loyale | |
| Non-Turbo | 5.8 qts. (5.5L) |
| Turbo | 6.3 qts. (6.0L) |
| XT | 5.8 qts. (5.5L) |

***BELT TENSION***

| Application | Deflection - In. (mm) |
|---|---|
| Loyale | |
| With Power Steering | |
| New | .28-.35 (7.1-9.1) |
| Used | .35-.43 (9.1-11.11) |
| With Power Steering & Air Cond. | |
| New & Used | .295-.335 (7.5-8.7) |
| XT | |
| With Power Steering | |
| New | .24-.28 (5.9-7.1) |
| Used | .28-.35 (7.1-9.1) |
| With Power Steering & Air Cond. | |
| New & Used | .24-.31 (5.9-7.9) |

***PRESSURE CAP***

| Application | Pressure |
|---|---|
| All Models | 11-14 psi (.75-1.05 kg/cm²) |

## TORQUE SPECIFICATIONS

***TORQUE SPECIFICATIONS***

| Application | Ft. Lbs. (N.m) |
|---|---|
| Belt Idler Bolt | 29-35 (39-47) |
| Belt Tensioner Bolt | 13-15 (18-20) |
| Camshaft Case Bolt | 13-15 (18-20) |
| Connecting Rod Nut | 29-31 (39-42) |
| Crankshaft Pulley Bolt [1] | 66-79 (90-107) |
| Cylinder Block Bolt | |
| 8 mm | 17-20 (23-27) |
| 10 mm | 29-35 (39-47) |
| Cylinder Head Bolt | |
| Step 1 | 22 (30) |
| Step 2 | 43 (58) |
| Step 3 | 47 (64) |
| Drive Plate Bolt | 51-55 (69-75) |
| Flywheel Bolt | 51-55 (69-75) |
| Flywheel Housing Bolt | 25-30 (34-41) |
| Intake Manifold Bolt | 13-16 (18-22) |
| Oil Pump Pulley Nut | 13-15 (18-20) |
| Oil Relief Valve Plug | 23-27 (31-37) |
| Service Hole Plug | 46-56 (62-76) |
| Turbo Coolant Pipe-To-Head Bolt | 16-18 (22-24) |

[1] - Coat bolt threads with oil before installation.

***TORQUE SPECIFICATIONS (Cont.)***

| Application | INCH Lbs. (N.m) |
|---|---|
| Camshaft Sprocket Bolt | 80-92 (9-10) |
| Camshaft Support Bolt | 52-61 (6-7) |
| Oil Pan Bolt | 40-48 (4-5) |
| Oil Separator Cover Bolt | 40-48 (4-5) |
| Timing Belt Cover Bolt | 40-48 (4-5) |
| Valve Cover Bolt | 40-48 (4-5) |
| Water Pump Pulley Bolt | 80-92 (9-10) |

## ENGINE SPECIFICATIONS

***GENERAL SPECIFICATIONS***

| Application | Specification |
|---|---|
| Displacement | 109 (1.8) |
| Bore | 3.62" (91.9 mm) |
| Stroke | 2.64" (67.1 mm) |
| Compression Ratio | |
| Non-Turbo | 9.5:1 |
| Turbo | 7.7:1 |
| Horsepower@RPM | |
| TBI | 90@5200 |
| PFI Non-Turbo | 97@5200 |
| PFI Turbo | 15@4800 |
| Fuel System | TBI, PFI |
| Torque Ft. Lbs.@RPM | |
| TBI | 101@2800 |
| PFI Non-Turbo | 103@3200 |
| PFI Turbo | 134@2800 |

***CRANKSHAFT, MAIN & CONNECTING ROD BEARINGS***

| Application | In. (mm) |
|---|---|
| Crankshaft | |
| End Play | [1] .0004-.0037 (.010-.095) |
| Runout | .0014 (.035) |
| Main Bearings | |
| Journal Diameter | |
| Front Journal | 2.1637-2.1643 (54.957-54.972) |
| Center Journal | 2.1635-2.1642 (54.954-54.970) |
| Rear Journal | 2.1636-2.1642 (54.955-54.970) |
| Journal Out-Of-Round | .0012 (.030) |
| Journal Taper | .0028 (.070) |
| Oil Clearance | [2] .0001-.0014 (.003-.036) |
| Connecting Rod Bearings | |
| Journal Diameter | 1.7715-1.7720 (44.995-45.010) |
| Oil Clearance | [3] .0004-.0021 (.010-.054) |

[1] - End play limit is .0118" (.3 mm).

[2] - Specification is for front and rear bearing. Center bearing oil clearance is .0003-.0011" (.008-.027 mm) with a limit of .0018" (.045 mm). Maximum front and rear bearing oil clearance is .0022" (.055 mm).

[3] - Maximum oil clearance is .0039" (.10 mm).

***CONNECTING RODS***

| Application | In. (mm) |
|---|---|
| Bore Diameter | |
| Pin Bore | .8268-.8274 (21.000-21.016) |
| Crankpin Bore | 1.8898-1.8905 (48.00-48.019) |
| Center-To-Center Length | 4.6043-4.6083 (116.95-117.05) |
| Maximum Bend | [1] .0039 (.10) |
| Side Play | [2] .0028-.0130 (.070-.330) |

[1] - Limit of bend per 3.94" (100 mm).

[2] - Maximum clearance is .0039" (.10 mm)

# 1991 ENGINES
# 1.8L 4-Cylinder (Cont.)

## PISTONS, PINS & RINGS

| Application | In. (mm) |
|---|---|
| Pistons | |
| Clearance | |
| Non-Turbo | [1] .0006-.0014 (.015-.035) |
| Turbo | .0004-.0012 (.010-.030) |
| Diameter | |
| Non-Turbo | 3.6209-3.6213 (91.970-91.981) |
| Turbo | 3.6211-3.6214 (91.975-91.983) |
| Pins | |
| Diameter | .8265-.8268 (20.994-21.000) |
| Piston Fit | .00004-.00059 (.001-.015) |
| Rod Fit | 0-.0009 (0-.022) |
| Rings | |
| No. 1 | |
| End Gap | [2] .0079-.0138 (.200-.350) |
| Side Clearance | [3] .0016-.0031 (.040-.080) |
| No. 2 | |
| End Gap | [2] .0079-.0138 (.200-.350) |
| Side Clearance | [3] .0012-.0028 (.030-.070) |
| No. 3 (Oil) | |
| End Gap | .012-.035 (.300-.900) |

[1] – Maximum clearance for non-turbo is .0024" (.060 mm). Maximum clearance for turbo is .002" (.050 mm).
[2] – Maximum clearance is .059" (1.5 mm).
[3] – Maximum clearance is .0059" (.15 mm).

## VALVES & VALVE SPRINGS

| Application | Specification |
|---|---|
| Intake Valves | |
| Face Angle | 45° |
| Minimum Margin | .031" (.80 mm) |
| Overall Length | 4.2354" (107.58 mm) |
| Stem Diameter | .2736-.2742" (6.950-6.965 mm) |
| Exhaust Valves | |
| Face Angle | 45° |
| Minimum Margin | |
| Non-Turbo | .031" (.80 mm) |
| Turbo | .051" (1.30 mm) |
| Overall Length | |
| Non-Turbo | 4.2354" (107.58 mm) |
| Turbo | 4.256" (108.10 mm) |
| Stem Diameter | .2734-.2740" (6.945-6.960 mm) |
| Valve Springs | |
| Free Length | |
| Inner Spring | 1.980" (50.30 mm) |
| Outer Spring | 1.996" (50.70 mm) |
| Out-Of-Square | .087" (2.20 mm) |
| | Lbs @ In. (kg @ mm) |
| Pressure | |
| Valve Closed | |
| Outer Spring | 46-54@1.63 (21-24@41.5) |
| Inner Spring | 20-23@1.516 (9-10 kg@38.5) |
| Valve Open | |
| Outer Spring | 113-130@1.24 (51-59@31.5) |
| Inner Spring | 45-52@1.122 (21-24@28.5) |

## CYLINDER BLOCK

| Application | In. (mm) |
|---|---|
| Cylinder Bore | |
| Standard Diameter | 3.6214-3.6226 (91.985-92.015) |
| Maximum Taper | .002 (.05) |
| Maximum Out-Of-Round | .002 (.05) |
| Bore Limit | .012 (.30) |
| Maximum Warpage | .002 (.05) |
| Surface Grinding Limit | .016 (.400) |

## CYLINDER HEAD

| Application | In. (mm) |
|---|---|
| Cylinder Head Height | 3.567 (90.6) |
| Surface Grinding Limit | .012 (.300) |
| Warpage Limit | .002 (.050) |
| Valve Seats | |
| Refacing Angle | 45° |
| Wear Limit | .020 (.50) |
| Contacting Width | |
| Intake | .047-.071 (1.2-1.8) |
| Exhaust | .059-.079 (1.5-2.0) |
| Valve Guide | |
| Inner Diameter | .2756-.2762 (7.000-7.015) |
| Protrusion Above Head | .689-.728 (17.5-18.5) |
| Oil Clearance | |
| Intake | .0014-.0026 (.035-.065) |
| Exhaust | .0016-.0028 (.040-.070) |

## CAMSHAFT

| Application | In. (mm) |
|---|---|
| Maximum Runout | .0010 (.025) |
| Thrust Clearance | .0012-.0102 (.030-.260) |
| Minimum Lobe Height | .0059 (.150) |
| Journal Diameter | |
| Front | 1.4946-1.4953 (37.964-37.980) |
| Center | 1.9080-1.9087 (48.464-48.480) |
| Rear | 1.8883-1.8890 (47.964-47.980) |
| Oil Clearance | |
| Standard | .0008-.0021 (.020-.054) |
| Limit | .0028 (.070) |

## VALVE LIFTERS

| Application | In. (mm) |
|---|---|
| Outer Diameter | .8417-.8422 (21.380-21.393) |
| Inside Diameter | .8430-.8453 (21.413-21.470) |
| Oil Clearance | |
| Standard | .0008-.0035 (.020-.090) |
| Limit | .004 (.100) |

# 1991 ENGINES
# 2.2L 4-Cylinder

## Legacy

***NOTE: For repair procedures not covered in this article, see ENGINE OVERHAUL PROCEDURES article in GENERAL INFORMATION.***

## ENGINE IDENTIFICATION

Engine can be identified by sixth character of Vehicle Identification Number (VIN). The VIN is stamped on a metal plate located on front right side of firewall. Identification number of engine is stamped on a machined pad on right front of engine cylinder block.

***ENGINE IDENTIFICATION CODES***

| Application | Code |
|---|---|
| 2.2L | 6 |

## ADJUSTMENTS

### VALVE CLEARANCE ADJUSTMENT

Engine uses hydraulic lifters. Valve adjustment is not required.

## REMOVAL & INSTALLATION

### FUEL PRESSURE RELEASE

To release fuel pressure, disconnect fuel pump wiring connector. Start engine and operate until engine stalls. Crank engine for an additional 5 seconds. With ignition off, reconnect fuel pump wiring connector.

### ENGINE

***NOTE: Removal procedure is with transaxle remaining in vehicle.***

**Removal - 1)** Release fuel pressure. Drain cooling system. Disconnect battery cable and remove battery. Disconnect upper and lower radiator hoses, heater hoses and remove radiator. Disconnect electrical connectors, vacuum hoses and fuel lines.

**2)** Disconnect accelerator cable, cruise control cable (if equipped) and hill holder cable (manual transmission) at clutch release fork. Remove accessory drive belts. Remove power steering pump with hoses attached. Discharge A/C system and disconnect hoses.

**3)** Remove center exhaust pipe and heat shield. Remove air cleaner case and hoses. Disconnect engine mount from front crossmember. Remove nuts attaching lower engine to transmission. Remove timing hole cover.

**4)** Disconnect drive plate from torque converter. Remove pitching stopper rod. Attach engine hoist to engine. Support transmission. Remove bolts attaching upper side of engine to transmission. Remove engine.

**Installation -** To install, reverse removal procedure. Adjust all control cables. Check all fluid levels.

### INTAKE MANIFOLD

***NOTE: Fuel pressure must be released if fuel lines or fuel system components are removed. See FUEL PRESSURE RELEASE.***

**Removal & Installation - 1)** Release fuel pressure. Disconnect fuel pump wiring connector. Start engine and operate until it stalls. Crank engine for an additional 5 seconds. With ignition off, reconnect fuel pump wiring connector.

**2)** Remove "V" belt. Remove power steering pump. Remove alternator and bracket. Disconnect PCV and blow-by hoses. Disconnect spark plug caps. Remove crank angle and cam angle sensors. Disconnect oil pressure switch connector. Remove knock sensor. Remove intake manifold. To install, reverse removal procedure. Replace all "O" rings.

### EXHAUST MANIFOLD

***NOTE: Exhaust manifold is integral with cylinder head.***

### CYLINDER HEAD

**Removal -** Drain coolant. Remove timing belts and camshaft sprocket. See TIMING BELT under REMOVAL & INSTALLATION. Remove intake manifold and exhaust pipe. Remove cylinder head bolts in reverse of tightening sequenco. *See Fig. 1.* Remove cylinder head and gasket.

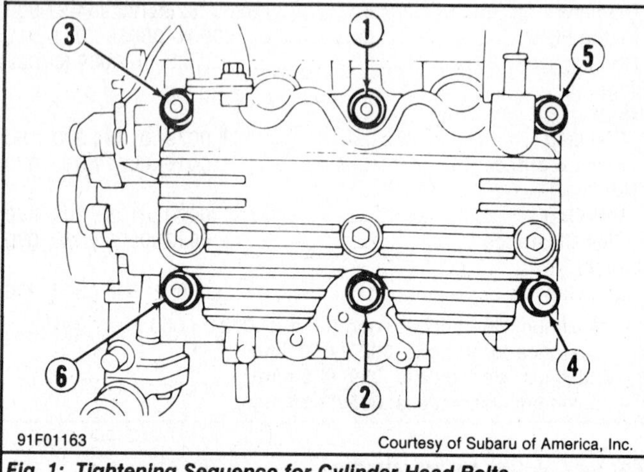


***Fig. 1: Tightening Sequence for Cylinder Head Bolts***

**Inspection -** Check cylinder head warpage and height. Resurface head if warpage exceeds specification. See CYLINDER HEAD under ENGINE SPECIFICATIONS at end of article. Replace cylinder head if not within specification after resurfacing.

**Installation - 1)** Ensure mating surfaces are clean and dry. Install head gasket. Coat head bolt threads with oil. Tighten bolts to specification using proper sequence. *See Fig. 1.* See TORQUE SPECIFICATIONS table at end of article.

**2)** To install remaining components, reverse removal procedure. Tighten bolts to specification. See TORQUE SPECIFICATIONS table at end of article.

***CAUTION: After initial start-up, cylinder head bolt torque should be rechecked after engine reaches operating temperature. Ensure engine is COLD while retorquing head bolts.***

### TIMING BELT

**Removal - 1)** Remove alternator drive belt. Remove crankshaft pulley bolt. Remove crankshaft pulley. If engine is removed from vehicle, crankshaft can be held using Flywheel Stopper (498277000) for manual transmission models or Drive Plate Stopper (498497000) for automatic transmission models.

**2)** Remove center, left and right timing belt covers. If timing belt is to be reused, place arrow on belt to indicate direction of belt rotation before removal. Use Crankshaft Socket (499987500) to turn crankshaft pulley.

**3)** Align crankshaft and camshaft timing marks with corresponding marks on timing cover and engine block. Use White paint to mark timing belt in relation to sprocket marks. Loosen tensioner adjuster mounting bolts. Remove belt idler. Remove belt idler No. 2. Remove timing belt. *See Figs. 2-4.*

**Inspection - 1)** Inspect timing belt for wear on rounded edges of drive teeth. Inspect belt for signs of oil contamination. Replace belt if damaged or contaminated. Inspect belt tension adjuster oil seals for leaks, and rod ends for abnormal wear or scratches. Timing belt bend radius must be greater than 2.36" (60 mm). *See Fig. 5.*

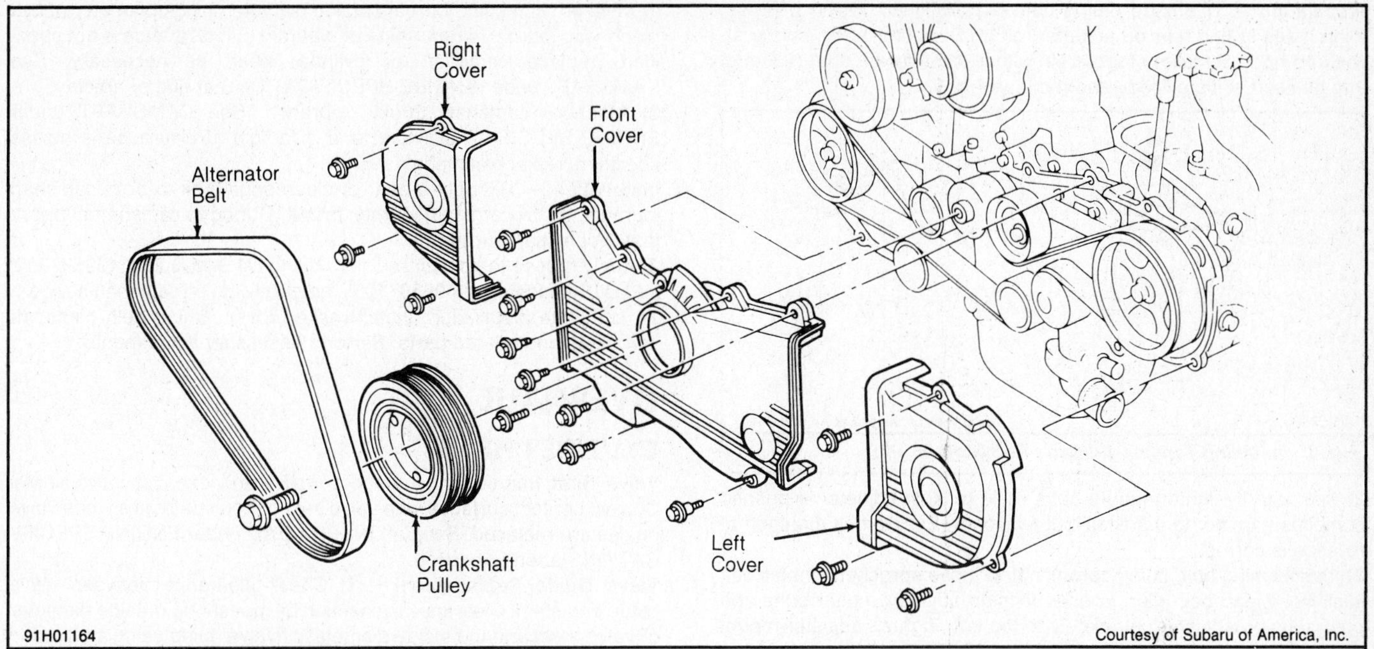


***Fig. 2: Removing Front, Right & Left Timing Belt Covers***

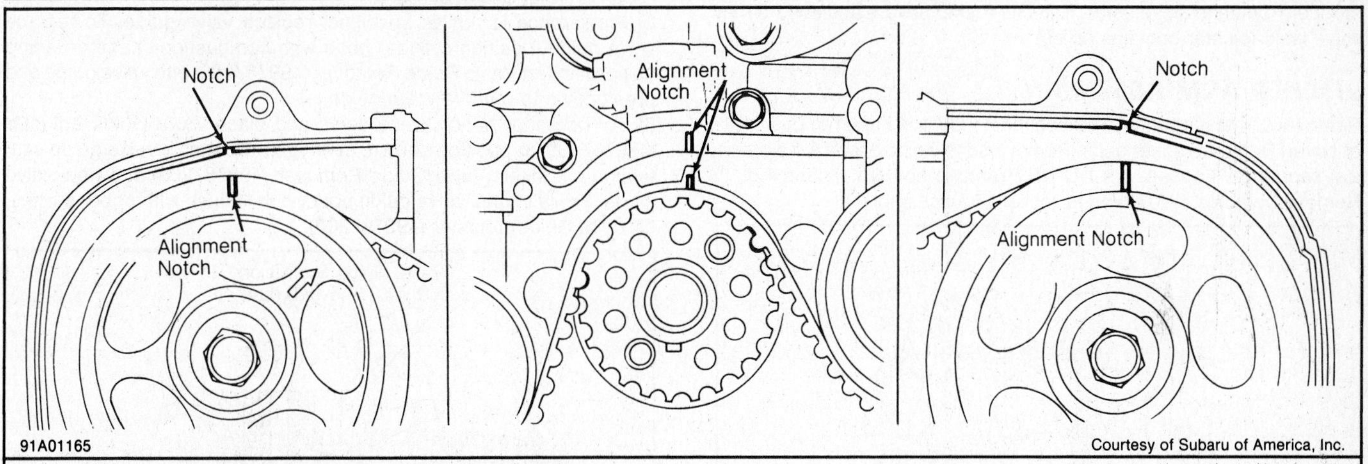


***Fig. 3: Aligning Camshaft & Crankshaft Pulley Timing Marks***

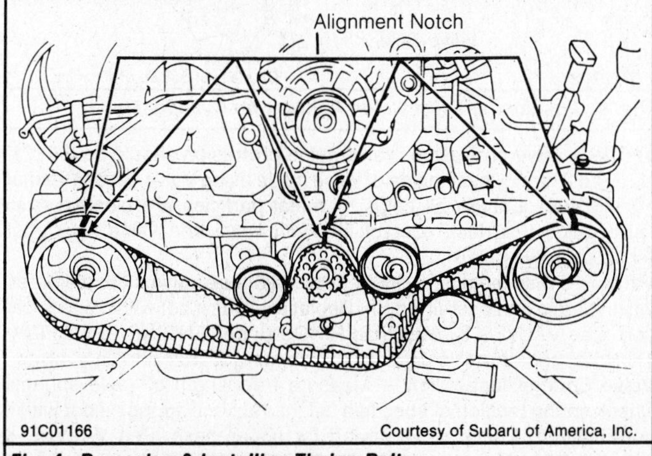


***Fig. 4: Removing & Installing Timing Belt***

**2)** Slight traces of oil at rod oil seal does not indicate a problem. While holding tensioner with both hands, push the rod section against floor or wall with a force of 33-110 lbs. (15-50 kg) to ensure that the rod section does not move.

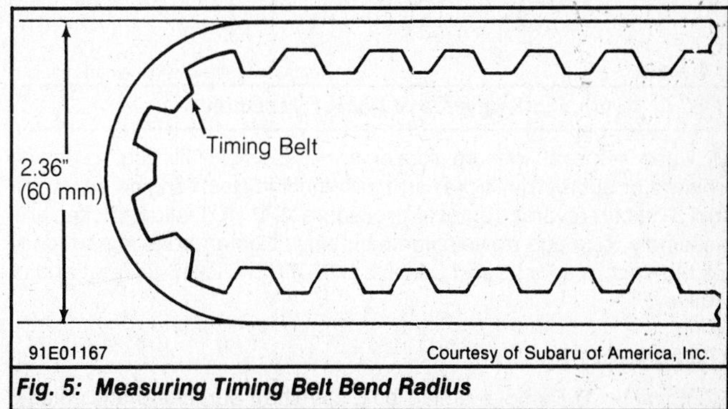


***Fig. 5: Measuring Timing Belt Bend Radius***

**3)** If rod section moves, replace tension adjuster with a new one. Measure the extension of rod beyond the body. Rod extension should be .606-.646" (15.4-16.4 mm). Replace belt tension adjuster if extension of the rod is not as specified. Inspect belt tensioner and belt adjuster rod mating surface. Check spacer and tensioner bushing.

***CAUTION: DO NOT allow press pressure to exceed 2205 lbs. (992 kg). DO NOT release pressure until stopper pin is completely installed.***

# 1991 ENGINES
# 2.2L 4-Cylinder (Cont.)

**Installation – 1)** Ensure timing marks are aligned. Using a press, align holes in belt tension adjuster rod and adjuster body, and push rod into body. Install a stopper pin with a diameter of .059" (1.5 mm) into holes in adjuster body and rod. *See Fig. 6.*

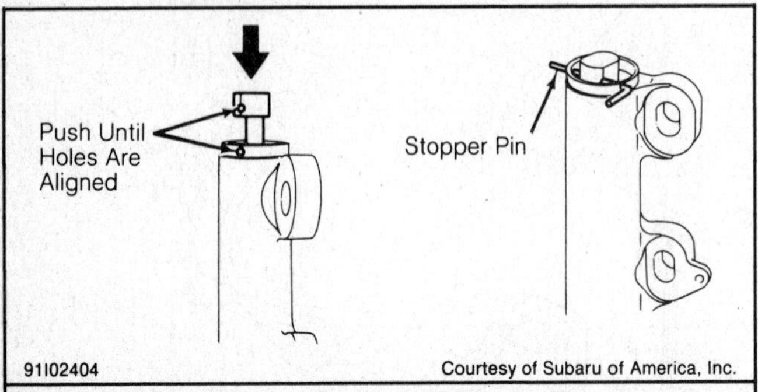


*Fig. 6: Installing Tension Adjuster Rod Stopper Pin*

**2)** Temporarily tighten mount bolts while tension adjuster is pushed completely to the right. Install belt tensioner. Ensure belt direction of rotation is correct.

**3)** Install timing belt, being careful not to move sprockets. Install belt idler No. 2 and belt idler. Loosen tension adjuster mount bolts and push tension adjuster completely to the left. Tighten adjuster mount bolts.

**4)** Ensure marks on timing belt and sprockets are aligned. Remove stopper from tension adjuster. Remove rocker covers and ensure that valve lash adjuster contains no air.

## ROCKER ARM ASSEMBLY

**Removal & Installation – 1)** Disconnect PCV hose and remove rocker cover. Remove rocker bolts. Remove bolts No. 2, 3, and 4 in numerical sequence. Loosen, but DO NOT remove bolt No. 1. *See Fig. 7.* Remove bolts No. 5-8. Remove rocker arm assembly.

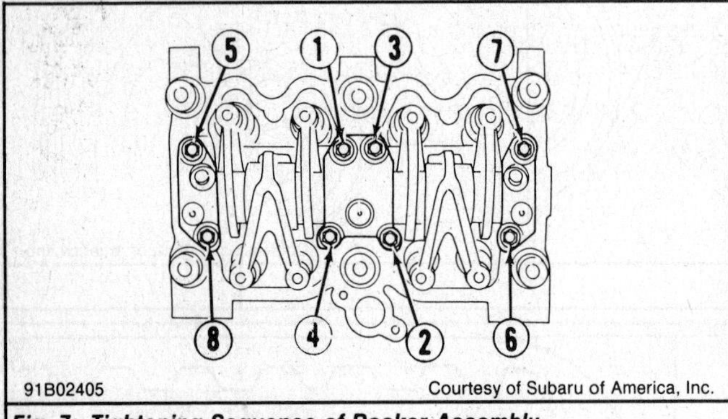


*Fig. 7: Tightening Sequence of Rocker Assembly*

**2)** Upon removal, ensure rocker arm assembly air vent is facing upward or submerge rocker arm assembly in clean engine oil.

**3)** To install, reverse removal procedure. DO NOT allow rocker arm assembly to gouge dowel/alignment pins. Tighten bolts in sequence and to specification. See TORQUE SPECIFICATIONS table at end of article.

## CAMSHAFT

**Removal – 1)** Remove timing belt, camshaft sprockets and related parts. Refer to TIMING BELT under REMOVAL & INSTALLATION. On left camshaft, remove cam angle sensor and oil gauge guide mounting bolt. Remove left camshaft support and "O" ring. Remove left camshaft.

**2)** On right camshaft, remove oil seal only if necessary. Remove camshaft.

**Inspection – 1)** Measure bend. Bend limit is .001" (.03 mm). Check cam face condition and remove minor burrs by grinding with oil stone. Check cam height and journal for damage wear.

**2)** Measure camshaft journal outside diameter inside diameter of cylinder head journal to determine oil clearance. If clearance is not specified, replace camshaft or cylinder head as necessary. See CAMSHAFT under ENGINE SPECIFICATIONS at end of article.

**3)** Measure camshaft thrust clearance. See CAMSHAFT under ENGINE SPECIFICATIONS at end of article. If clearance is not as specified, replace camshaft support.

**Installation – 1)** Apply a coat of clean engine oil to both camshaft journals. Install camshaft journal. Install "O" ring to camshaft support. Install camshaft support.

**2)** Apply grease to new oil seal lips. Using Oil Seal Guide (499597000) and Oil Seal Installer (499587100), install oil seal on camshaft support. To complete installation, install rocker cover, timing belt, camshaft sprockets and related parts. Perform necessary adjustments.

# OVERHAUL

## CYLINDER HEAD

**Valve Seat Inspection –** Inspect intake and exhaust valve seats. Correct contact surfaces with valve seat cutter if defective when valve guides are replaced. See CYLINDER HEAD under ENGINE SPECIFICATIONS at end of article.

**Valve Guide Replacement – 1)** Check clearance between valve guide and stem. Clearance is checked by measuring outside diameter of valve stem and the inside diameter of valve guide using an outside and inside micrometer. See CYLINDER HEAD under ENGINE SPECIFICATIONS at end of article.

**2)** If clearance is not as specified, replace valve guide. To replace valve guide, position cylinder head with combustion chamber facing upward. Insert Valve Guide Remover (499767200) into valve guide and press down to remove valve guide.

**3)** Turn cylinder head upside down and place Valve Guide Adjuster (499767000) in position shown. *See Fig. 8.* Coat new valve guide with engine oil. Insert Valve Guide Remover (499767200) into new valve guide. Press in until valve guide upper end is flush with upper surface of Valve Guide Adjuster (499767200).

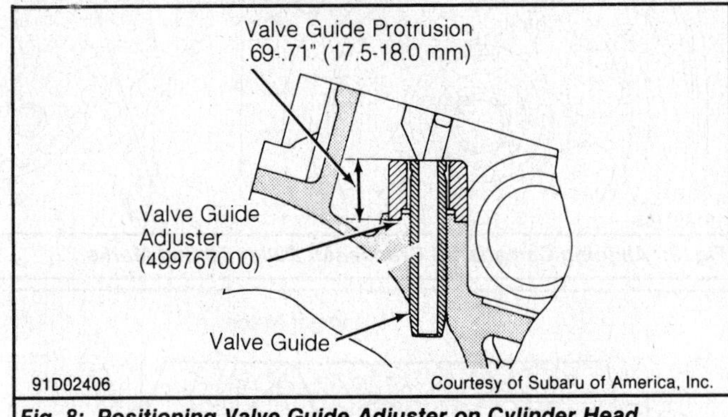


*Fig. 8: Positioning Valve Guide Adjuster on Cylinder Head*

**4)** Check valve protrusion. Valve guide protrusion should be .69-.71" (17.5-18.0 mm). Ream inside of valve guide using Valve Guide Reamer (499767400). Ensure all chips or metal particles are cleaned from valve guide. Recheck contact between valve and valve seat after replacing valve guide.

**Valves –** Disassemble cylinder head. Measure valve stem diameter, valve margin and overall length. Replace valves if not within specification. See VALVES & VALVE SPRINGS under ENGINE SPECIFICATIONS at end of article. Recheck valve margin after grinding valves.

**Valve Springs Inspection –** Measure free length of valve springs. Check spring tension at specified height. Replace springs if not within specification. Check valve spring for squareness. See VALVES & VALVE SPRINGS under ENGINE SPECIFICATIONS at end of article.

**Valve Stem Oil Seals Replacement –** With valves removed, remove oil seals from cylinder head. Note location of oil seals. Intake valve stem seal is Black with White spring. Exhaust valve stem seal is Brown with White spring. Coat seals with oil. Using Valve Stem Oil Seal Guide (498857100), install valve stem oil seal.

# 1991 ENGINES
# 2.2L 4-Cylinder (Cont.)

## VALVE TRAIN

**Valve Lash Adjuster Inspection - 1)** Dip valve lash adjuster in engine oil. Push check ball in using a .08" (2 mm) diameter round bar. With check ball pushed in, manually move plunger up and down at one second interval until air bubbles disappears.

**2)** After air bubbles disappear, remove bar and quickly push plunger in to ensure it is locked. If plunger does not lock properly, replace valve lash adjuster. Always leave valve lash adjuster in engine oil until it is ready for installation.

**Rocker Arm Inspection -** Check oil clearance between valve rocker arm and shaft. Oil clearance should be .0008-.0032" (.020-.081 mm) with a limit of .004" (.10 mm). Replace valve rocker or shaft if clearance is not as specified.

## CYLINDER BLOCK ASSEMBLY

**Cylinder Block Disassembly - 1)** Set up cylinder block so that cylinders No. 1 and 3 are on upper side. Remove cylinder block connecting bolts. Separate left and right cylinder blocks. DO NOT allow connecting rod to fall and damage block.

**2)** Remove rear oil seal. Remove crankshaft together with connecting rod. Remove crankshaft bearings from cylinder block using hammer handle. Ensure bearings are marked for proper location. Draw out each piston from cylinder block.

**Crankshaft & Connecting Rod Removal - 1)** Separate cylinder block. See CYLINDER BLOCK DISASSEMBLY. Remove connecting rod cap. Remove connecting rod bearing. Note connecting rod cap and bearing location.

**2)** Remove piston rings and oil ring and mark for proper order/location. Remove circlip from piston pin. Remove piston pin. Separate piston from connecting rod.

**Crankshaft & Connecting Rod Inspection - 1)** Inspect crankshaft for cracks. Check crankshaft runout at center journal and journal out-of-round. Repair or replace crankshaft if not within specification. See CRANKSHAFT, MAIN & CONNECTING ROD BEARINGS under ENGINE SPECIFICATIONS at end of article.

**2)** Check connecting rod for bend or twist. Measure crankpin and piston pin bore inside diameter. Replace if not within specification. See CONNECTING RODS under ENGINE SPECIFICATIONS at end of article.

**Crankshaft & Connecting Rod Installation - 1)** Lubricate and install bearings in connecting rod. Install connecting rod in proper cylinder location with identification mark toward the front of crankshaft with matching numbers aligned.

**2)** Apply oil to connecting rod bolt threads prior to tightening nut. Check oil clearance using Plastigage method. Replace bearings to obtain correct clearance. See CRANKSHAFT, MAIN & CONNECTING ROD BEARINGS under ENGINE SPECIFICATIONS at end of article.

**3)** Install main bearings in cylinder block. Install crankshaft in left side of cylinder block. Using feeler gauge, measure crankshaft end play between center bearing and crankshaft.

**4)** Replace bearing if clearance is not within specification. See CRANKSHAFT, MAIN & CONNECTING ROD BEARINGS under ENGINE SPECIFICATIONS at end of article. Install right side of cylinder block to check oil clearance using Plastigage method.

**5)** Tighten bolts to specification. See TORQUE SPECIFICATIONS table at end of article. Check oil clearance. Replace bearings to obtain correct clearance. See CRANKSHAFT, MAIN & CONNECTING ROD BEARINGS under ENGINE SPECIFICATIONS at end of article. Reassemble cylinder block.

**Piston & Rod Assembly Removal -** Remove crankshaft and rod assembly. See CRANKSHAFT & CONNECTING ROD (REMOVAL). Note direction of piston installation and cylinder location. Using soft hammer, drive pistons from cylinder block.

**Piston & Rod Assembly Inspection - 1)** Inspect piston for cracks or damage in ring areas. Check ring side clearance. Replace piston if not within specification. See PISTONS, PINS & RINGS under ENGINE SPECIFICATIONS at end of article.

**2)** Measure piston pin O.D. and piston pin bore I.D. Replace piston if not within specification. Ensure piston pin can be installed in piston at 68°F (20°C). Replace components if piston pin cannot be installed.

**Piston & Rod Assembly Installation - 1)** Ensure piston ring end gap and side clearance are within specification. Install rings on piston with "R" mark toward top of piston. Lubricate piston, rings and cylinder bore with engine oil.

**2)** Properly space ring end gaps on piston. *See Fig. 9.* Bend pawl of upper rail over and install in piston hole. Install piston into cylinder bore.

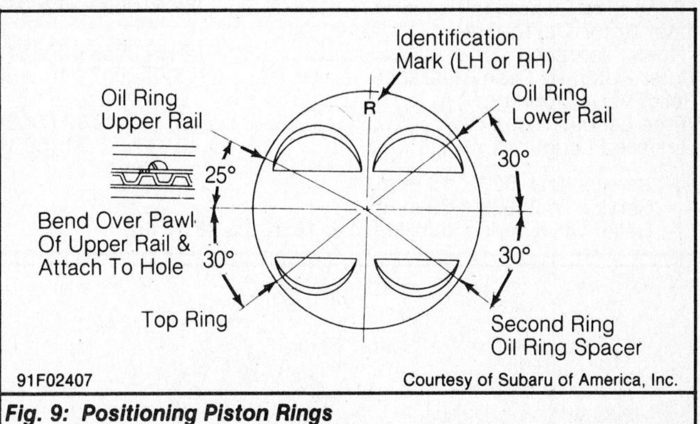


***Fig. 9: Positioning Piston Rings***

**Piston & Piston Pin Inspection - 1)** Check piston, piston pins and piston ring grooves for damage, cracks and wear. Replace as necessary. Measure piston-to-cylinder clearance. See PISTONS, PINS & RINGS under ENGINE SPECIFICATIONS at end of article.

**2)** If clearance is not as specified, replace piston or rebore cylinder and use an oversized piston. Ensure piston pin can be inserted into piston hole with thumb pressure at 68°F (20°C). Replace if defective.

**Piston & Piston Pin Installation - 1)** Turn cylinder block so that cylinders No. 1 and 2 are facing up. Turn crankshaft so cylinders No. 1 and 2 connecting rods are set at bottom dead center. Apply engine oil to pistons and cylinders. Insert pistons into cylinders.

**2)** Coat Piston Pin Guide (498747100) with oil and insert into service hole to align piston pin hole with connecting rod small end. Coat piston pin with oil and insert piston pin into piston and connecting rod through service hole. Install circlip. Install service hole plug and gasket.

**3)** Turn cylinder block over so that cylinders No. 3 and 4 are facing up. Turn crankshaft so cylinders No. 3 and 4 connecting rods are set at bottom dead center. Apply engine oil to pistons and cylinders. To complete installation, repeat step **2)**.

# ENGINE OILING

## ENGINE LUBRICATION SYSTEM

Oil pressure is provided by a trochoid type pump driven by the timing belt. Pressure relief valve is located in the oil pump body.

**Crankcase Capacity -** Crankcase capacity is 5.0 qts. (4.7L) with filter replacement.

**Normal Oil Pressure -** Oil pressure should be 14 psi (1.0 kg/cm²) at 600 RPM and 43 psi (3.0 kg/cm²) at 5000 RPM with engine at normal operating temperature.

## OIL PAN

**Removal & Installation -** Drain oil. Remove oil pan bolts. Remove oil pan and gasket. To install, reverse removal procedure using new gasket. Tighten bolts to specification. See TORQUE SPECIFICATIONS table at the end of article.

## OIL PUMP

**Removal -** Disconnect negative battery cable. Drain engine oil. Remove timing belt covers, drive belt and related parts. See TIMING BELT under REMOVAL & INSTALLATION. Remove belt tensioner bracket. Remove water pump. Remove oil pump assembly and gasket.

# 1991 ENGINES
# 2.2L 4-Cylinder (Cont.)

**Disassembly & Inspection - 1)** Disassemble pump. *See Fig. 10.* Measure tip clearance of rotors. See OIL PUMP SPECIFICATIONS table. If clearance is not as specified, replace rotors as a matched set.

### OIL PUMP SPECIFICATIONS

| Application | In. (mm) |
|---|---|
| Inner Rotor-To-Pump Case Side Clearance | .0008-.0028 (.02-.07) |
| Inner Rotor Tip-To-Outer Rotor Clearance | [1] .0016-.0055 (.04-.14) |
| Outer Rotor-To-Case Clearance | [2] .004-.007 (.10-.18) |
| Relief Valve Spring [3] | |
| Free Length | 2.92 (74.2) |
| Installed Length | 2.21 (56.1) |

[1] - Service limit .007" (.18 mm).
[2] - Service limit .008" (.20 mm).
[3] - Relief valve spring installed load 18.32 lbs. (8.31 kg)

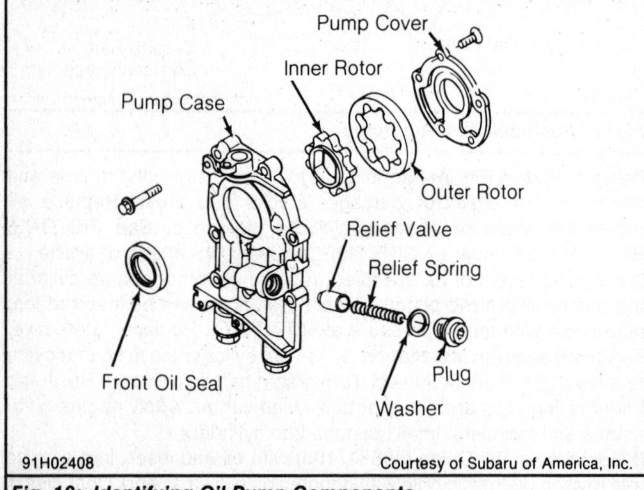


*Fig. 10: Identifying Oil Pump Components*

**2)** Measure clearance between outer rotor and oil pump cylinder block rotor housing. If case clearance is not as specified, replace rotor. See OIL PUMP SPECIFICATIONS table.

**3)** Measure clearance between oil pump inner rotor and pump cover. If clearance is not as specified, replace rotor or pump body. See OIL PUMP SPECIFICATIONS table.

**4)** Check oil relief valve and relief spring for wear or damage. Check oil pump case for worn shaft hole, clogged oil passage, worn rotor chamber or cracks. Check oil seal lips for deformation, hardening or wear. Replace components as necessary.

**Installation -** Install front oil seal using Oil Seal Installer (499587100). Install inner and outer rotors, oil relief valve, relief spring and oil pump cover. *See Fig. 10.* To complete installation, reverse removal procedure. Replace "O" ring.

## TORQUE SPECIFICATIONS

### TORQUE SPECIFICATIONS

| Application | Ft. Lbs. (N.m) |
|---|---|
| Camshaft Sprocket Bolt | 54-61 (74-83) |
| Camshaft Support Bolt | 12 (16) |
| Connecting Rod Cap Nut | 32-34 (43-46) |
| Crankshaft Pulley Bolt | 69-76 (93-103) |
| Cylinder Block Bolt (LH-To-RH) | 17-20 (23-27) |
| Cylinder Block Service Hole Plug | 46-56 (62-76) |

### TORQUE SPECIFICATIONS (Cont.)

| Application | Ft. Lbs. (N.m) |
|---|---|
| Cylinder Head Bolt [1] | 33-37 (45-50) |
| Drive Plate Reinforcement Bolt | 51-55 (69-75) |
| Flywheel Bolt | 51-55 (69-75) |
| Timing Belt Idler Bolt | 26-32 (35-43) |
| Timing Belt Tension Adjuster Bolt | 17-20 (23-27) |
| Timing Belt Tensioner Bracket Bolt | 17-20 (23-27) |
| | **INCH Lbs. (N.m)** |
| Oil Pan Bolt | 43 (5) |
| Oil Pump Bolt | 56 (6.4) |
| Rocker Cover Bolt | 43 (5) |
| Rocker Shaft Support Bolt (Long) | 108 (12.2) |
| Rocker Shaft Support Bolt (Short) | 43 (5) |
| Timing Belt Cover Bolt | 43 (5) |
| Water Pump Bolt | 84-120 (10-14) |

[1] - First, torque head bolts to 22 ft. lbs. (29 N.m); then, to 51 ft. lbs. (69 N.m). Back out head bolts 180 degrees; then another 180 degrees. On non-turbo engines, torque bolts No. 1 and 2 to 25 ft. lbs. (34 N.m). Torque bolts No. 3, 4, 5 and 6 to 11 ft. lbs. (15 N.m). On turbo engines, torque bolts No. 1 and 2 to 27 ft. lbs. (36 N.m). Torque bolts No. 3, 4, 5, and 6 to 14 ft. lbs. (20 N.m). On all engines, torque bolts an additional 180 degrees in 80-90 degree steps.

## ENGINE SPECIFICATIONS

### GENERAL SPECIFICATIONS

| Application | Specification |
|---|---|
| Displacement | 135 Cu. In. (2.2L) |
| Bore | 3.82" (97 mm) |
| Stroke | 2.95" (75 mm) |
| Compression Ratio | |
| Non-Turbo | 9.5:1 |
| Turbo | 8.0 |
| Fuel System | PFI |
| Horsepower @ RPM | |
| Non-Turbo | 130 @ 5600 |
| Turbo | 160 @ 5600 |
| Torque Ft. Lbs. @ RPM | |
| Non-Turbo | 137 @ 4400 |
| Turbo | 181 @ 2800 |

### CYLINDER BLOCK

| Application | In. (mm) |
|---|---|
| Cylinder Bore | |
| Standard Diameter | |
| A | 3.8151-3.8155 (96.904-96.914) |
| B | 3.8148-3.8151 (96.895-96.904) |
| C | 3.8144-3.8148 (96.885-96.896) |
| Maximum Taper | .002 (.05) |
| Maximum Deck Warpage | .002 (.05) |
| Maximum Reboring Limit | .020 (.5) |
| Out-Of-Round | |
| Standard | .0004 (.010) |
| Service Limit | .002 (.050) |

### CONNECTING RODS

| Application | In. (mm) |
|---|---|
| Bore Diameter | |
| Crankpin Bore | 2.047 (52.00) |
| Pin Bore | .9053-.9055 (22.99-23.00) |
| Side Play | |
| Standard | .003-.013 (.08-.33) |
| Service Limit | .016 (.41) |

# 1991 ENGINES
# 2.2L 4-Cylinder (Cont.)

## CRANKSHAFT MAIN & CONNECTING ROD BEARINGS

| Application | In. (mm) |
|---|---|
| Crankshaft | |
| End Play | |
| Standard | .001-.005 (.03-.13) |
| Service Limit | .009 (.23) |
| Runout | |
| Standard | .001 (.03) |
| Service Limit | .010 (.25) |
| Main Bearings | |
| Journal Diameter | 2.3616-2.3622 (59.985-60.000) |
| Journal Out-of-Round | |
| Standard | .0012 (.031) |
| Service Limit | .0010 (.248) |
| Journal Taper | |
| Standard | .0002 (.005) |
| Service Limit | .0004 (.010) |
| Oil Clearance | |
| No. 1 & No. 5 Journal | |
| Standard | .0004-.0012 (.010-.031) |
| Service Limit | .0016 (.041) |
| All Others | |
| Standard | .0004-.0012 (.010-.031) |
| Service Limit | .0014 (.036) |
| Connecting Rod Bearings | |
| Journal Diameter | 2.0466-2.0472 (51.984-52.000) |
| Journal Out-of-Round | |
| Standard | .0012 (.031) |
| Service Limit | .001 (.248) |
| Journal Taper | |
| Service Limit | .0028 (.071) |
| Oil Clearance | |
| Non-Turbo | |
| Standard | .0006-.0017 (.015-.048) |
| Service Limit | .002 (.05) |
| Turbo | |
| Standard | .001-.0021 (.025-.053) |
| Service Limit | .0024 (.06) |

## VALVES & VALVE SPRINGS

| Application | Specification |
|---|---|
| Intake Valves | |
| Face Angle | 45° |
| Head Diameter | [1] |
| Minimum Margin | |
| Standard | .039" (1.00 mm) |
| Service Limit | .031" (0.79 mm) |
| Stem Diameter | |
| Standard | .2343-.2348" (5.951-5.964 mm) |
| Exhaust Valves | |
| Face Angle | 45° |
| Head Diameter | [1] |
| Minimum Margin | |
| Standard | .047" (1.19 mm) |
| Service Limit | .031" (0.79 mm) |
| Stem Diameter | |
| Standard | .2341-.2346" (5.946-5.960 mm) |
| Valve Springs | |
| Free Length | |
| Intake & Exhaust | |
| Standard | 1.8173" (42.99 mm) |

[1] – Information is not available from manufacturer.

## PISTONS, PINS & RINGS

| Application | In. (mm) |
|---|---|
| Pistons | |
| Clearance | .0004-.0012 (.0100-.0300) |
| Diameter [1] | |
| Standard | |
| A | 3.8144-3.8148 (96.885-96.895) |
| B | 3.8140-3.8144 (96.875-96.885) |
| C | 3.8136-3.8140 (96.865-96.875) |
| Pins | |
| Diameter | .9053-.9055 (22.990-23.000) |
| Piston Fit | [2] |
| Rings | |
| No. 1 | |
| Non-Turbo | |
| End Gap | .008-.014 (.20-.36) |
| Service Limit | .039 (1.0) |
| Side Clearance | .0016-.0031 (.041-.079) |
| Service Limit | .0059 (.15) |
| Turbo | |
| End Gap | .0079-.0098 (.20-.25) |
| Service Limit | .035 (.9) |
| Side Clearance | .0016-.0031 (.041-.079) |
| Service Limit | .0059 (.15) |
| No. 2 | |
| End Gap | .0146-.0205 (.37-.52) |
| Service Limit | .039 (1.0) |
| Side Clearance | .0012-.0028 (.031-.071) |
| Service Limit | .0059 (.15) |
| No. 3 (Oil) | |
| End Gap | .008-.028 (.20-.71) |
| Service Limit | .059 (1.5) |

[1] – Measure at .59" (15 mm) from bottom of skirt.
[2] – Thumb press fit.

## CAMSHAFT

| Application | In. (mm) |
|---|---|
| End Play | |
| Standard | .0012-.0102 (.031-.260) |
| Service Limit | .0014 (.036) |
| Journal Runout | [1] |
| Oil Clearance | |
| Standard | .002-.004 (.05-.10) |
| Service Limit | .004 (.10) |
| Lobe Height | |
| Standard | 1.2752-1.2791 (32.390-32.489) |

[1] – Information is not available from manufacturer.

# 1991 ENGINES
# 2.2L 4-Cylinder (Cont.)

## CYLINDER HEAD

| Application | Specification |
|---|---|
| Cylinder Head | |
| Height | 3.870" (98.3 mm) |
| Maximum Warpage | [1] .002" (.05 mm) |
| Valve Seats | |
| Intake Valve | |
| Seat Angle | 45° |
| Seat Width | |
| Standard | .028 (.71) |
| Service Limit | .055" (1.40 mm) |
| Exhaust Valve | |
| Seat Angle | 45° |
| Seat Width | |
| Standard | .047" (1.19 mm) |
| Service Limit | .071" (1.80 mm) |
| Valve Guides | |
| Intake | |
| Valve Guide I.D. | |
| Standard | .2362-.2367" (6.000-6.012 mm) |
| Valve Guide Installed Height | .69-.78" (17.5-20.0 mm) |
| Valve Stem-To-Guide Oil Clearance | |
| Standard | .0014-.0024" (.036-.061 mm) |
| Service Limit | .006" (.15 mm) |
| Exhaust Valve | |
| Valve Guide I.D. | |
| Standard | .2362-.2367" (6.000-6.012 mm) |
| Valve Guide Installed Height | .69-.78" (17.5-20.0 mm) |
| Valve Stem-To-Guide Oil Clearance | |
| Standard | .0016-.0026" (.041-.066 mm) |
| Service Limit | .006" (.15 mm) |

[1] – Maximum resurface limit is .012" (.31 mm).

# 1991 ENGINES
# 2.7L 6-Cylinder

## XT6

***NOTE: For repair procedures not covered in this article, see ENGINE OVERHAUL PROCEDURES article in GENERAL INFORMATION.***

## ENGINE IDENTIFICATION

Engine can be identified by sixth character of Vehicle Identification Number (VIN). The VIN is stamped on a metal plate, located on front right side of engine compartment. Engine serial number is stamped on a machined pad on right front of cylinder block.

***ENGINE IDENTIFICATION CODES***

| Application | VIN Code |
|---|---|
| 2.7L 2WD Without Air Suspension | 8 |
| 2.7L 4WD With Air Suspension | 9 |

## ADJUSTMENTS

### VALVE CLEARANCE ADJUSTMENT

No adjustment is required. Hydraulic lifter preload is automatically adjusted.

## REMOVAL & INSTALLATION

***NOTE: For reassembly reference, label all electrical connectors, vacuum hoses and fuel lines before removal. Also place mating marks on engine hood and other major assemblies before removal.***

### FUEL PRESSURE RELEASE

Disconnect fuel pump wiring connector. Start engine and operate until engine stalls. Crank engine for approximately 5 seconds. With ignition off, reconnect fuel pump wiring connector.

### ENGINE

**Removal - 1)** Release fuel pressure. See FUEL PRESSURE RELEASE. Drain cooling system and remove coolant hoses and radiator. Disconnect negative battery cable.

**2)** Disconnect fuel lines. Mark and disconnect vacuum hoses and electrical connectors. Disconnect accelerator and cruise control cables.

**3)** Disconnect exhaust pipe at cylinder head and rear exhaust pipe and remove. Remove air intake and air cleaner. Discharge A/C system. Remove and plug lines at A/C compressor.

**4)** On A/T models, remove torque converter bolts. These bolts can be reached through the timing hole plug. On all models, remove bolts from support rod-to-engine at the frame. Remove engine mount-to-crossmember bolts.

**5)** Support engine and remove engine-to-transaxle bolts. Support transaxle and remove engine.

**Installation -** To install, reverse removal procedure. On M/T models, apply small amount of grease to transaxle mainshaft splines before installing engine.

### INTAKE MANIFOLD

**Removal & Installation - 1)** Release fuel pressure. See FUEL PRESSURE RELEASE. Drain cooling system. Remove air cleaner and duct. Mark intake manifold components for reassembly reference. Remove intake manifold and components. *See Fig. 1.*

**2)** To install, reverse removal procedure. Replace all "O" rings. Tighten bolts to specification. See TORQUE SPECIFICATIONS table at end of article.

### EXHAUST MANIFOLD

***NOTE: Exhaust manifold is integral with cylinder head.***

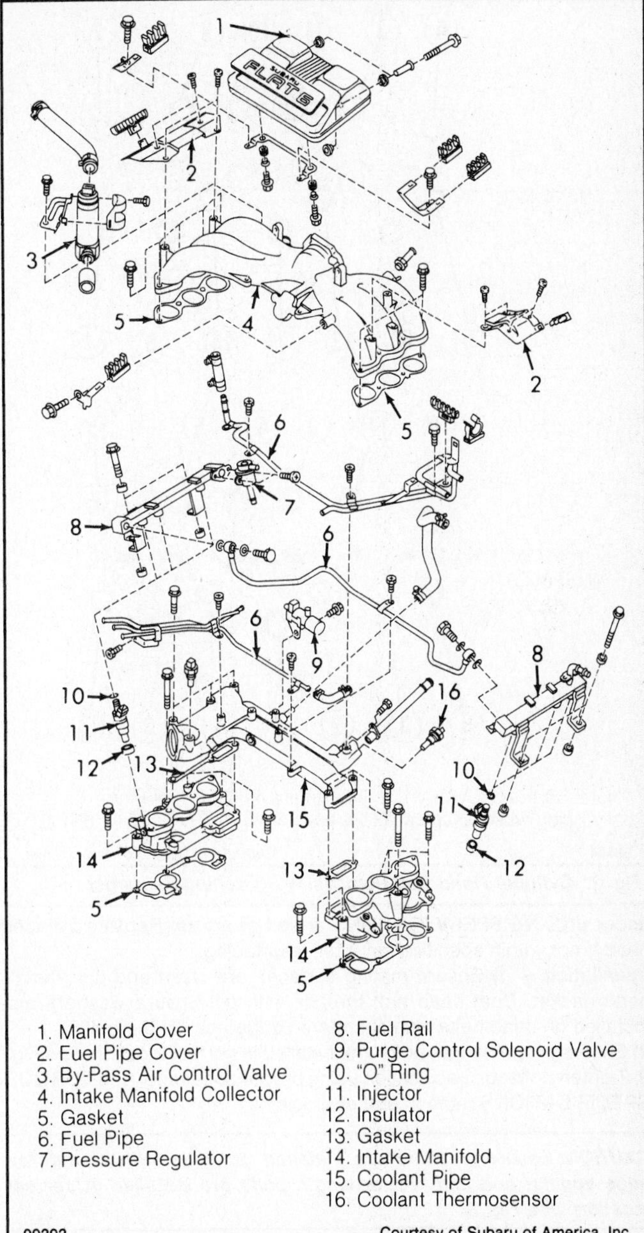


***Fig. 1: Exploded View of Intake Manifold & Components***

### CYLINDER HEAD

**Removal - 1)** Remove timing belts. See TIMING BELT under REMOVAL & INSTALLATION. Remove camshaft and components. See CAMSHAFT under REMOVAL & INSTALLATION. Remove alternator and mounting bracket. Remove A/C compressor (if equipped).

**2)** Remove intake manifold collector. *See Fig. 1.* Disconnect exhaust pipe at cylinder head. Remove coolant by-pass pipe. Remove spark plugs. Loosen cylinder head bolts in 2 steps using proper sequence.

***CAUTION: Loosen cylinder head bolts in 2 steps using proper sequence to prevent cylinder head warpage or cracking. Note bolt length and location.***

**3)** Remove cylinder head bolts. Note bolt length, location and direction of washer installation on bolt. Remove cylinder head.

**Inspection -** Check cylinder head warpage and height. Resurface head if warpage exceeds specification. See CYLINDER HEAD table

# 1991 ENGINES
# 2.7L 6-Cylinder (Cont.)

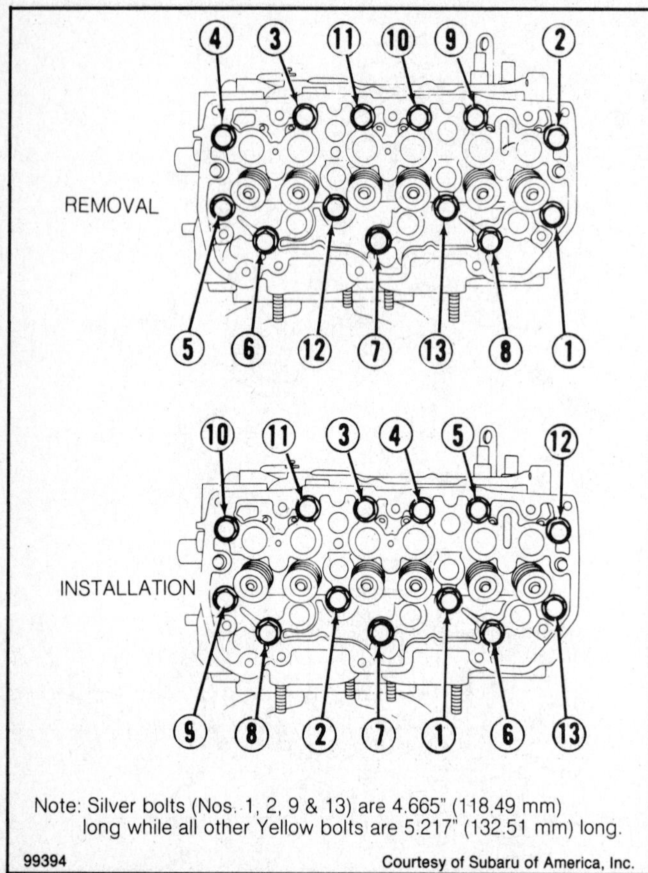


***Fig. 2: Cylinder Head Bolt Removal & Tightening Sequence***

under ENGINE SPECIFICATIONS at end of article. Replace cylinder head if not within specification after resurfacing.

**Installation – 1)** Ensure mating surfaces are clean and dry. Install head gasket. Coat head bolt threads with oil. Ensure washers are installed on head bolts with chamfered edge against the bolt.

**2)** Ensure proper length bolts are installed in correct location. *See Fig. 2*. Tighten bolts to specification using proper sequence. See TORQUE SPECIFICATIONS table at end of article.

***CAUTION: Ensure washers are installed on bolts with chamfered edge against bolt and proper length bolts are installed in correct location. See Fig. 2.***

**3)** To install remaining components, reverse removal procedure. Tighten bolts to specification. See TORQUE SPECIFICATIONS table at end of article.

## TIMING BELT

**Removal – 1)** Loosen water pump pulley and alternator mounting bolts. Loosen tensioner pulley lock nut and release belt tension. Ensure adjuster bolt is turned fully counterclockwise and remove alternator belt.

**2)** Remove water pump pulley. Remove crankshaft pulley. With engine removed from vehicle, crankshaft can be held using Flywheel Stopper (498277000) for M/T models or using Drive Plate Stopper (498497000) for A/T models.

**3)** Remove oil pressure switch connector. Remove oil level gauge and guide. *See Fig. 3*. Remove center, left and right timing belt covers.

**4)** To remove right timing belt, loosen tensioner bolts on No. 1 cylinder 1/2 turn and rotate tensioner to release belt tension and retighten bolts. *See Fig. 4*. If timing belt is to be reused, place arrow on belt to indicate direction of belt rotation. Remove timing belt.

***CAUTION: If reusing timing belt, mark belt rotation direction.***

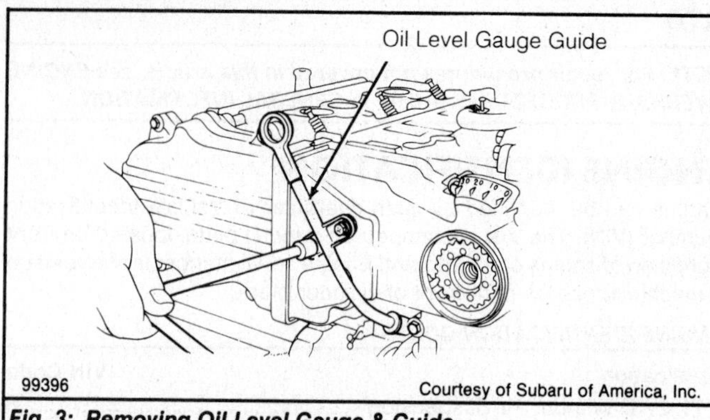


***Fig. 3: Removing Oil Level Gauge & Guide***

**5)** Remove tensioner for right timing belt. Remove crankshaft sprocket. To remove left timing belt, remove idler pulley. *See Fig. 4*. Remove plug rubber located below belt tension adjuster. *See Fig. 5*.

**6)** Remove plug from bottom of belt tension adjuster. Insert screwdriver in bottom of belt tension adjuster and rotate screw clockwise to release belt tension. Install Belt Adjuster Stopper (13082AA000) on tension adjuster. *See Fig. 5*.

**7)** Remove left belt tensioner. If timing belt is to be reused, place arrow on belt to indicate direction of belt rotation. Remove timing belt, crankshaft No. 2 sprocket, idler pulley and belt tension adjuster.

**8)** Reinstall plug in bottom of belt tension adjuster. Remove camshaft sprocket and rear timing belt covers if replacement is required.

**Inspection – 1)** Inspect timing belt for wear on rounded edges of drive teeth. Inspect belt for signs of oil contamination. Replace belt if damaged or contaminated.

**2)** Inspect idler pulleys and tensioners for smooth rotation. Check belt tensioner roller for squareness. *See Fig. 6*. Replace tensioner if out-of-square exceeds .020" (.51 mm).

**Installation – 1)** Install rear timing belt covers and camshaft sprockets, if removed. Tighten bolts to specification. See TORQUE SPECIFICATIONS table at end of article. To install left timing belt, remove plug from belt tension adjuster. Turn screw clockwise to compress rubber boot if belt adjuster stopper is not installed. Install Belt Adjuster Stopper (13082AA000) on top of belt tension adjuster.

**2)** Using syringe, add engine oil through vent hole on top of rubber boot. Add oil until it overflows. Install plug and new gasket. Install belt tension adjuster. Tighten bolts to specification. See TORQUE SPECIFICATIONS table at end of article. Install plug rubber.

**3)** Install idler pulley. Tighten bolt to specification. See TORQUE SPECIFICATIONS table at end of article. Install No. 2 crankshaft sprocket. Align center line of the 3 lines on flywheel or drive plate with mark on housing. Align left camshaft sprocket timing mark with notch in housing. *See Fig. 7*.

**4)** Install timing belt. Ensure belt is installed in original direction of rotation. Install tensioner. Tighten bolt to specification. See TORQUE SPECIFICATIONS table at end of article. Ensure tensioner moves smoothly. Remove belt adjuster stopper from belt tension adjuster.

***CAUTION: Ensure tensioner arm contacts top of belt tension adjuster and all timing marks align.***

**5)** To install right timing belt, rotate crankshaft clockwise 360 degrees and align center line with timing mark on housing. Align camshaft sprocket timing mark with notch in housing. *See Fig. 7*.

**6)** Install tensioner and temporarily tighten inner bolt with tensioner pushed toward the bottom of case. Install crankshaft sprocket. Install timing belt. Ensure belt is installed in original direction of rotation.

**7)** Loosen inner tensioner bolt and allow tensioner to apply belt tension. Install Belt Tension Wrench (499437100) on right camshaft sprocket.

**8)** Using torque wrench and belt tension wrench, apply 17-19 ft. lbs. (23-26 N.m) torque to camshaft sprocket. While applying torque, temporarily tighten inner and then outer tensioner retaining bolts.

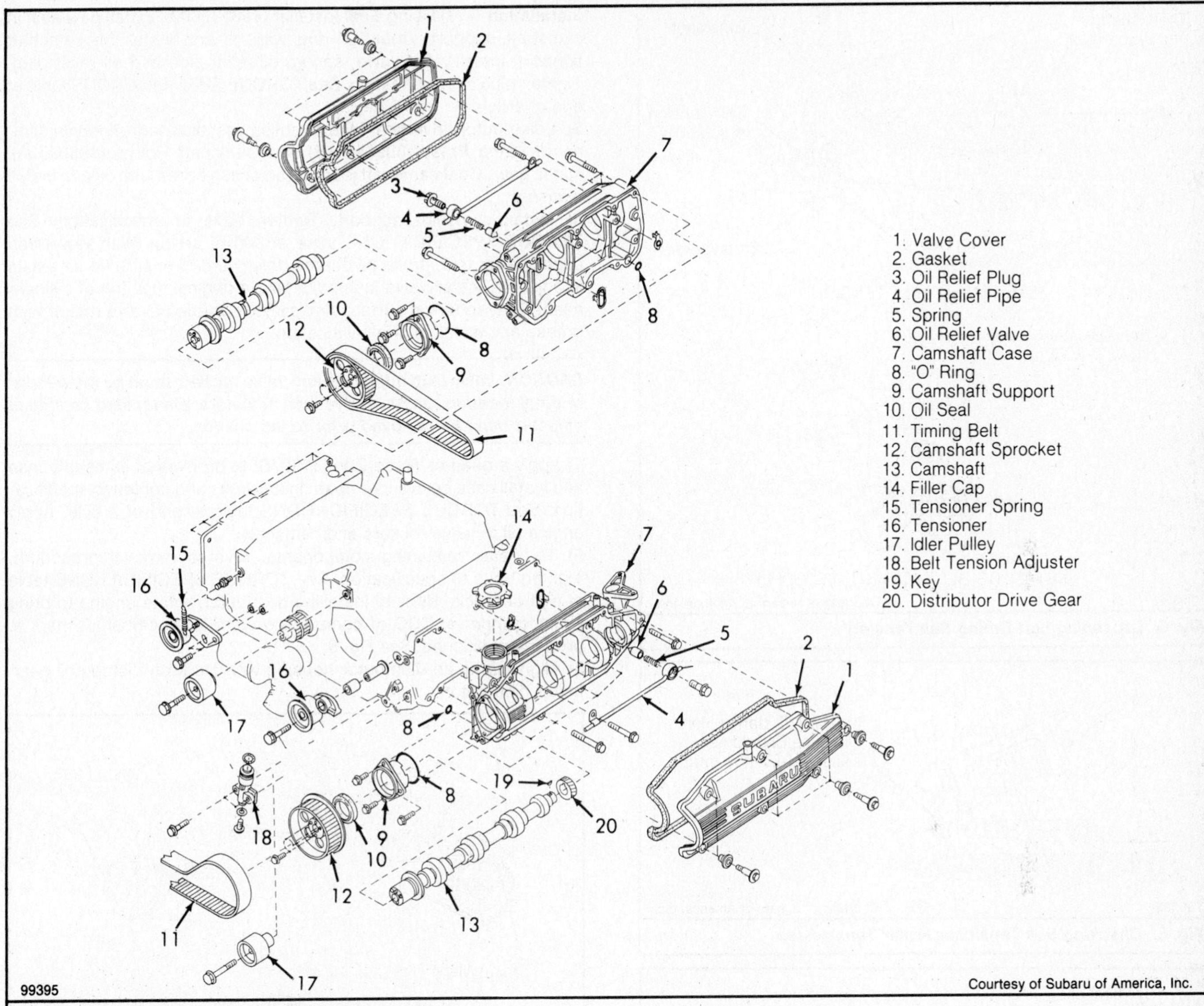


**Fig. 4: Exploded View of Timing Belt Components**

**9)** Check belt tension. Belt tension should be 33-55 lbs. (15-25 kg). With proper belt tension, tighten inner then outer tension bolts to specification. See TORQUE SPECIFICATIONS table at end of article. Ensure all timing marks are aligned.

**10)** To install remaining components, reverse removal procedure. Coat crankshaft pulley bolt with oil prior to installation. Tighten bolts to specification. Tighten alternator belt so belt tension is 143-165 lbs. (65-75 kg) on new belt or 99-143 lbs. (45-65 kg) on used belts.

***CAUTION: Readjust new alternator belt after 5 minutes of operation.***

## CAMSHAFT

**Removal – 1)** Remove valve covers. Remove distributor cap. Attach dial indicator to case with stem resting against gear of distributor. Rotate distributor and note backlash between distributor gear and distributor gear of camshaft.

**2)** Camshaft distributor gear should be replaced if backlash is not within specification. See CAMSHAFT table under ENGINE SPECIFICATIONS at end of article. Remove distributor. Remove timing belt and camshaft sprockets. See TIMING BELT under REMOVAL & INSTALLATION. Remove coolant pipe.

**3)** Remove camshaft case bolts. *See Fig. 4*. Remove camshaft case and camshaft as a unit. Ensure valve rockers do not fall from cylinder head during case removal. Remove valve rockers and valve lash adjusters from cylinder head. Mark components for location and keep valve lash adjusters upright.

***CAUTION: Use care when removing camshaft case as valve rockers may fall during removal. Mark components for location. DO NOT place valve lash adjusters upside down or on their side.***

**4)** Using feeler gauge, measure clearance between camshaft and camshaft support. Replace camshaft support if end play is not within specification. See CAMSHAFT table under ENGINE SPECIFICATIONS at end of article.

**5)** Remove camshaft support and camshaft. Remove oil relief plug, oil relief pipe, spring and relief valve. *See Fig. 4*.

**Inspection – 1)** Clean camshaft journals and case surfaces. Inspect components for damage. Measure camshaft journals. Front journal is referred to as No. 1, while No 5 is the rear of camshaft. Replace camshaft if not within specification. See CAMSHAFT table under ENGINE SPECIFICATIONS at end of article.

**2)** Measure camshaft lobe height and runout at center camshaft journal. Measure I.D. of case journal bores. Camshaft support is referred to as No. 1, while No. 5 is at the rear of the case. Replace components if not within specification. See CAMSHAFT table under ENGINE SPECIFICATIONS at end of article.

# 1991 ENGINES
# 2.7L 6-Cylinder (Cont.)

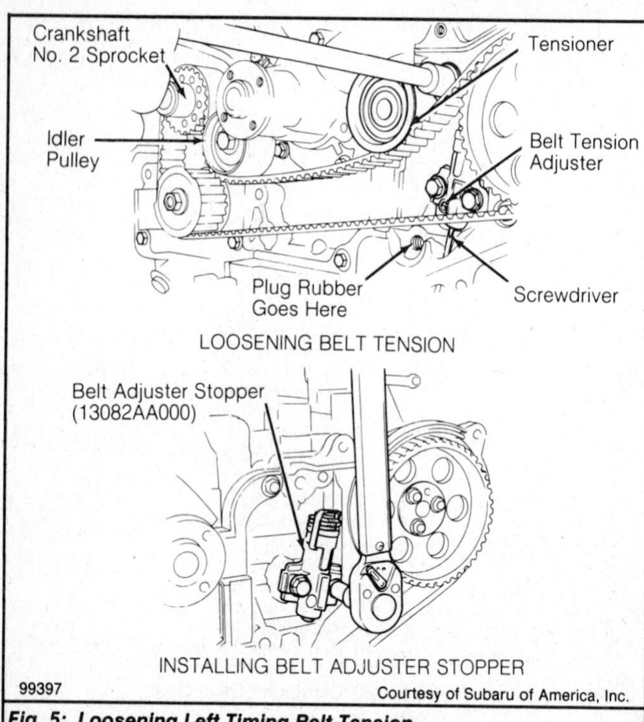


*Fig. 5: Loosening Left Timing Belt Tension*

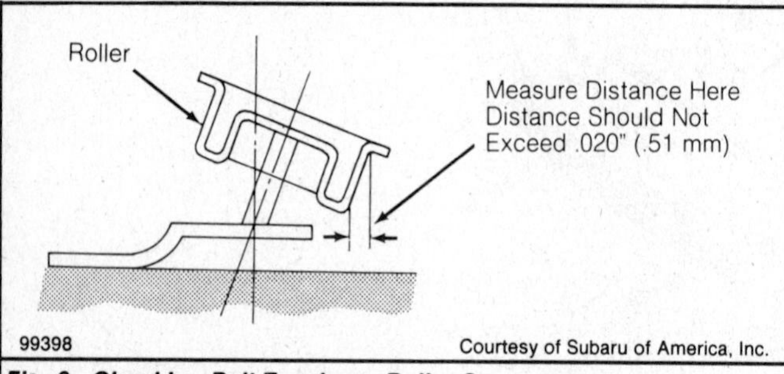


*Fig. 6: Checking Belt Tensioner Roller Squareness*

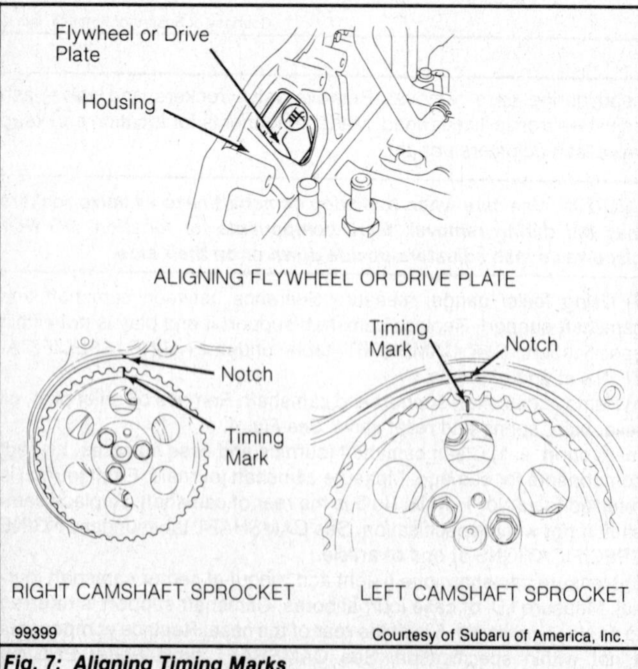


*Fig. 7: Aligning Timing Marks*

**Installation - 1)** Using Seal Installer (498037000), install new seal in camshaft support. Coat "O" ring with oil and install on camshaft support. Install relief valve, spring, oil relief pipe and oil relief plug. Tighten plug to specification. See TORQUE SPECIFICATIONS table at end of article.

**2)** If distributor drive gear was removed, install Woodruff key in camshaft. Using Press (899754112) and Camshaft Holder (49802700), install gear. Coat camshaft journals and case bores with oil and install camshaft.

**3)** Install camshaft support. Tighten bolts to specification. See TORQUE SPECIFICATIONS table at end of article. With valve lash adjusters upright, press pivot area downward to ensure no air exists in adjuster. Install valve lash adjusters in original location of cylinder head. Coat spherical surface and sliding surface of valve rocker with grease and install in original location.

***CAUTION: Valve lash adjusters and valve rockers must be installed in original location. On new valve lash adjusters, pin located on side of adjuster must be removed prior to installation.***

**4)** Apply a bead of Three Bond (1207B) to grooves of camshaft case and install case on cylinder head. Install bolts and tighten to specification. See TORQUE SPECIFICATIONS table at end of article. Apply engine oil to valve rockers and camshaft.

**5)** To install remaining components, reverse removal procedure. Tighten bolts to specification. See TORQUE SPECIFICATIONS table at end of article. Prior to installing distributor, rotate engine to bring No. 1 cylinder at TDC of compression stroke so camshaft mark is properly positioned. *See Fig. 8.*

**6)** Align marks on distributor housing with mark on distributor gear. Install distributor.

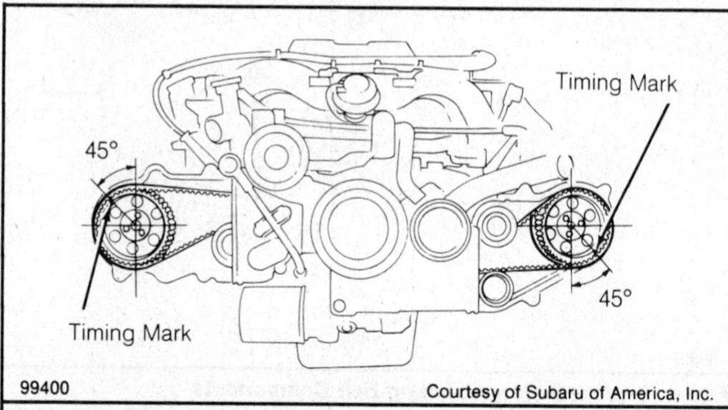


*Fig. 8: Aligning Camshafts for Distributor Installation*

## FRONT CRANKSHAFT OIL SEAL

**Removal & Installation - 1)** Remove timing belts and crankshaft sprockets. See TIMING BELT under REMOVAL & INSTALLATION. Pry seal from cylinder block.

**2)** To install, apply oil to outside surface of seal and grease on seal lip. Using Seal Installer (499567100), install seal in cylinder block. Install remaining components. Tighten bolts to specification. See TORQUE SPECIFICATIONS table at end of article.

## REAR CRANKSHAFT OIL SEAL

**Removal & Installation - 1)** Remove flywheel or drive plate. It may be necessary to remove oil separator plate to gain access to oil seal. Pry oil seal from cylinder block.

**2)** To install, apply oil to outside surface of seal and grease on seal lip. Using Seal Installer (499587000), install seal in cylinder block. Install remaining components. Tighten bolts to specification. See TORQUE SPECIFICATIONS table at end of article.

## WATER PUMP

**Removal - 1)** Drain cooling system. Disconnect negative battery cable. Remove radiator hose, coolant by-pass hose, air vent hose and coolant pipe. Loosen water pump pulley bolts.

**2)** Loosen belt tensioner pulley. Remove water pump drive belt and pulley. Remove A/C compressor, alternator and bracket. Remove crankshaft pulley and front timing belt covers. Remove water pump bolts, water pump and gasket.

***CAUTION: DO NOT allow coolant to spill on timing belts.***

**Installation** – To install, reverse removal procedure using new gasket. Coat crankshaft pulley bolt with oil prior to installation. Tighten bolts to specification. See TORQUE SPECIFICATIONS table at end of article.

***NOTE: For further information on cooling systems, see ENGINE COOLING article.***

## OVERHAUL

### CYLINDER HEAD

**Valves** – Disassemble cylinder head. Measure valve stem diameter, valve margin and overall length. Replace valves if not within specification. See VALVES table under ENGINE SPECIFICATIONS at end of article. Recheck valve margin after grinding valves.

**Valve Guide (Inspection)** – Measure clearance between valve stem and guide. Insert valve in guide and move left or right. If tip moves more than specification, replace guide. See CYLINDER HEAD table under ENGINE SPECIFICATIONS at end of article.

**Valve Guide (Removal & Installation)** – **1)** Using Valve Guide Remover/Installer (399762103), drive valve guide out from the combustion chamber side of cylinder head.

**2)** Position cylinder head with combustion chamber downward. Place Valve Guide Adjuster (899768603) over valve guide bore of cylinder head.

**3)** Coat valve guide with oil. Using valve guide remover/installer, install valve guide until upper end of valve guide is even with upper surface of valve guide adjuster.

**4)** Check valve guide protrusion. Valve guide protrusion should be .67-.71" (17.0-18.0 mm) above valve spring seat. Ream valve guide to obtain proper clearance.

**Valve Stem Oil Seals (Removal & Installation)** – With valves removed, remove oil seals from cylinder head. Note height and location of oil seals. Intake valve seal height is .512" (13.00 mm) and exhaust seal height is .425" (10.79 mm). Coat seals with oil. Using Valve Stem Oil Seal Installer (398852100), install valve stem oil seal.

**Valve Springs (Inspection)** – Measure free length of valve springs. Check spring tension at specified height. Replace springs if not within specification. Check valve spring for squareness. See VALVES & VALVE SPRINGS table under ENGINE SPECIFICATIONS at end of article.

### VALVE TRAIN

**Lash Adjusters (Removal & Installation)** – **1)** To remove lash adjusters, remove camshaft. See CAMSHAFT under REMOVAL & INSTALLATION. With valve lash adjusters upright, press pivot area downward to ensure no air exists in each adjuster.

**2)** Measure valve lash O.D. and cylinder head bore. Determine oil clearance. Replace components if not within specification. See VALVE LASH ADJUSTERS table under ENGINE SPECIFICATIONS at end of article.

### CYLINDER BLOCK ASSEMBLY

**Crankshaft & Connecting Rod (Removal)** – **1)** Separate cylinder block. See CYLINDER BLOCK (DISASSEMBLY). Using feeler gauge, measure crankshaft end play clearance between center bearing and crankshaft.

**2)** Replace bearing if clearance is not within specification. See CRANKSHAFT, MAIN & CONNECTING ROD BEARINGS table under ENGINE SPECIFICATIONS at end of article. Remove front and rear oil seals. Lift crankshaft and connecting rod assembly from cylinder block.

**3)** Using feeler gauge, measure connecting rod side clearance. Replace connecting rod if not within specification. See CRANKSHAFT, MAIN & CONNECTING ROD BEARINGS table under ENGINE SPECIFICATIONS at end of article.

**4)** Note direction and location of connecting rod installation. Remove connecting rod cap and bearing. Remove connecting rod.

**Inspection** – **1)** Inspect crankshaft for cracks. Check crankshaft runout at center journal and journal out-of-round. Repair or replace if not within specification. See CRANKSHAFT, MAIN & CONNECTING ROD BEARINGS table under ENGINE SPECIFICATIONS at end of article.

**2)** Check connecting rod for bend or twist. Measure crankpin and piston pin bore I.D. Replace if not within specification. See CONNECTING RODS table.

**Installation** – **1)** Lubricate and install bearings in connecting rod. Install connecting rod in proper cylinder location with identification mark toward the front of crankshaft with matching numbers aligned. *See Fig. 9.*

***CAUTION: Connecting rods must be installed so identification mark is toward the front of crankshaft. See Fig. 9.***

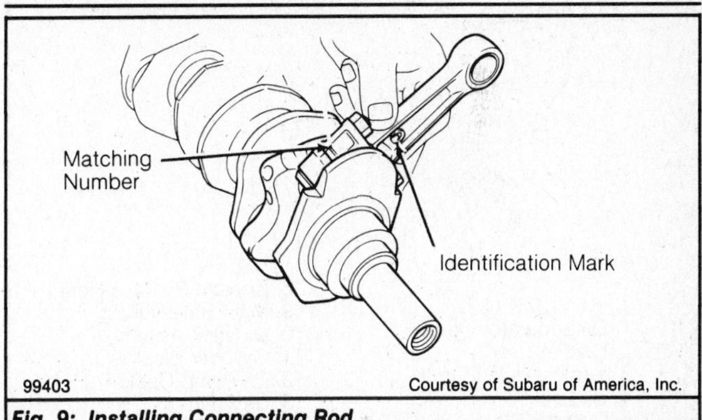


***Fig. 9: Installing Connecting Rod***

**2)** Apply oil to connecting rod bolt threads before tightening nut. Check oil clearance using Plastigage method. Replace bearings to obtain correct clearance. See CRANKSHAFT, MAIN & CONNECTING ROD BEARINGS table under ENGINE SPECIFICATIONS at end of article.

**3)** Install main bearings in cylinder block. Install crankshaft in left side of cylinder block. Using feeler gauge, measure crankshaft end play between center bearing and crankshaft.

**4)** Replace bearing if clearance is not within specification. See CRANKSHAFT, MAIN & CONNECTING ROD BEARINGS table under ENGINE SPECIFICATIONS at end of article. Install right side of cylinder block to check oil clearance using Plastigage method.

**5)** Tighten bolts to specification. See TORQUE SPECIFICATIONS table at end of article. Check oil clearance. Replace bearings to obtain correct clearance. See CRANKSHAFT, MAIN & CONNECTING ROD BEARINGS table under ENGINE SPECIFICATIONS at end of article. Reassemble cylinder block.

**Cylinder Block (Disassembly)** – **1)** Remove distributor. Remove intake manifold and cylinder head. See INTAKE MANIFOLD and CYLINDER HEAD under REMOVAL & INSTALLATION.

**2)** Remove water pump and oil pump. Lock crankshaft by using Flywheel Stopper (498277000) for M/T models or Drive Plate Stopper (498497000) for A/T models.

**3)** Remove flywheel or drive plate and flywheel housing. Remove oil pan. Remove oil separator cover and service hole plugs. *See Fig. 10.*

**4)** Using crankshaft pulley retaining bolt, rotate crankshaft and position No. 1 and No. 2 pistons at BDC. From service hole plug access, remove piston pin retaining clip from pistons. Note direction of retaining clip installation.

**5)** Using Piston Pin Remover (499097300), remove piston pins from No. 1 and 2 pistons. Repeat procedure and remove piston pins on remaining pistons. Remove all cylinder block bolts except No. 3 cylinder.

# 1991 ENGINES
# 2.7L 6-Cylinder (Cont.)

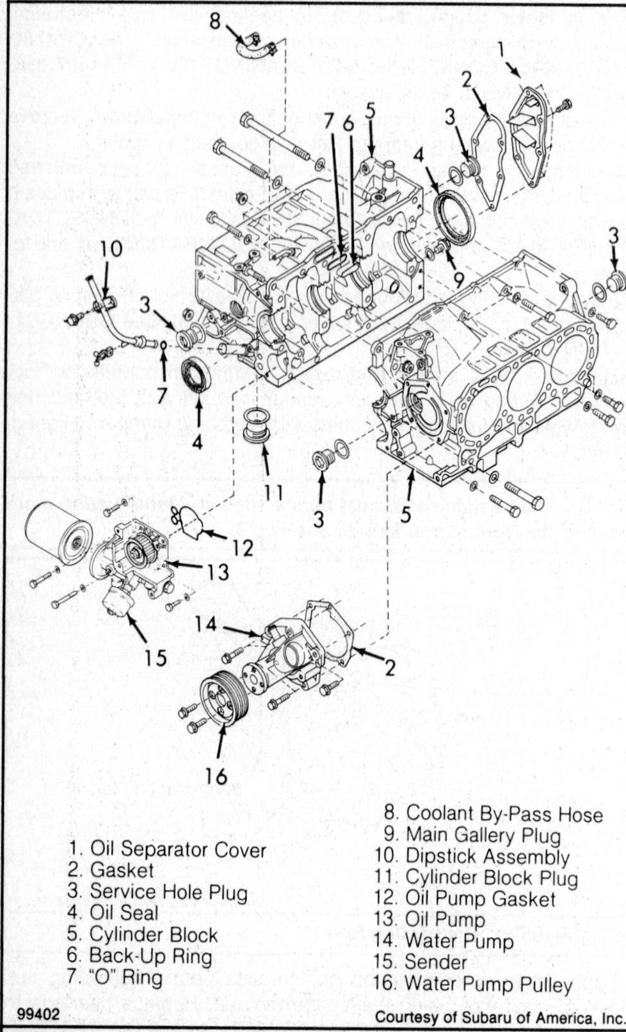


***Fig. 10: Exploded View of Cylinder Block Assembly***

**6)** Position cylinder block so cylinders No. 1, 3 and 5 are upward. Remove remaining bolt and separate cylinder block. Remove back-up ring and "O" ring from cylinder block. *See Fig. 10*. Remove crankshaft, connecting rods and pistons. See CYLINDER BLOCK under OVERHAUL.

***CAUTION: DO NOT allow connecting rods to fall and damage cylinder block while separating cylinder block.***

**Inspection – 1)** Inspect cylinder block for cracks, warpage, bore taper and out-of-round. Replace or repair cylinder block if not within specification. See CYLINDER BLOCK table under ENGINE SPECIFICATIONS at end of article.

**2)** Measure cylinder bore and piston skirt diameter with temperature of 68°F (20°C). Piston skirt diameter should be measured at 90 degree angle to piston pin. Measure piston diameter 1.0618" (26.697 mm) from bottom of piston skirt. Clearance between piston and cylinder bore must be within specification. See PISTONS, PINS & RINGS table under ENGINE SPECIFICATIONS at end of article.

**Reassembly – 1)** Install main bearings, crankshaft and connecting rods. Ensure all crankshaft bearings are installed in cylinder block. Install "O" ring and back-up ring on cylinder block. Ensure "O" ring properly fits in groove.

**2)** Clean all sealing surfaces of cylinder block. Apply Three Bond (1215) to sealing surface on one side of cylinder block.

***CAUTION: Ensure sealant does not enter oil and coolant passages of cylinder block.***

**3)** Position cylinder block with left cylinder block downward. Install right side of cylinder block. Ensure "O" ring fits properly in groove. Temporarily install cylinder block bolts.

**4)** Lay cylinder block down and tighten bolts to specification. See TORQUE SPECIFICATIONS table at end of article. With cylinders No. 5 and 6 facing downward, rotate crankshaft so No. 3 and 4 cylinder connecting rods are at BDC.

**5)** Lubricate piston, rings and cylinder wall. Ensure piston rings are properly positioned. *See Fig. 11*. Install No. 4 cylinder piston. Using Piston Pin Guide (499017000), align connecting rod and piston pin holes.

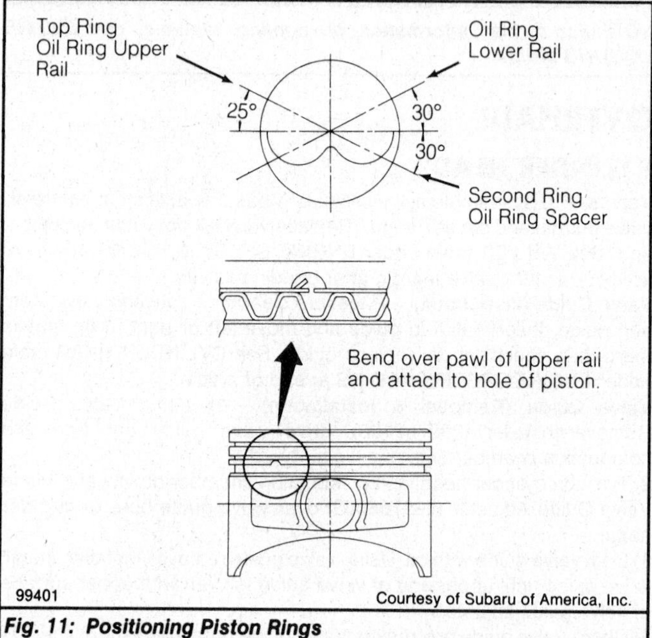


***Fig. 11: Positioning Piston Rings***

**6)** Install piston pin. Install piston pin retaining clips with end of clip away from piston pin.

***CAUTION: Piston pin retaining clips must be installed with end of clip positioned away from piston pin.***

**7)** Repeat procedure on remaining cylinders in the following sequence: No. 3, 1, 2, 5 and 6 cylinders. Ensure all piston pin retaining clips are properly installed. Apply Three Bond (1205) to service hole plugs. Install plugs and tighten to specification. See TORQUE SPECIFICATIONS table at end of article. To reassemble remaining components, reverse removal procedure. Tighten bolts to specification.

**Piston & Rod Assembly (Removal)** – Remove crankshaft and rod assembly. See CYLINDER BLOCK ASSEMBLY under OVERHAUL. Note direction of piston installation and cylinder location. Using soft hammer, drive pistons from cylinder block.

**Inspection – 1)** Inspect piston for cracks or damage in ring areas. Check ring side clearance. Replace piston if not within specification. See PISTONS, PINS & RINGS table under ENGINE SPECIFICATIONS at end of article.

**2)** Measure piston pin O.D. and piston pin bore I.D. Replace piston if not within specification. Ensure piston pin can be installed in piston at 68°F (20°C). Replace components if piston pin cannot be installed.

**Installation – 1)** Ensure piston ring end gap and side clearance are within specification. Install rings on piston with "R" mark toward top of piston. Lubricate piston, rings and cylinder bore with engine oil.

**2)** Properly space ring end gaps on piston. Bend pawl of upper rail over and install in piston hole. *See Fig. 11*. Install piston into cylinder bore.

# 1991 ENGINES
# 2.7L 6-Cylinder (Cont.)

## ENGINE OILING

### ENGINE LUBRICATION SYSTEM

Oil pressure is provided by a rotor-type pump, driven by timing belt. Pressure relief valve is located in oil pump body.

**Crankcase Capacity** – Crankcase capacity is 5.3 qts. (5.0L) with filter replacement.

**Oil Pressure** – Oil pressure should be 55-71 psi (3.9-5.0 kg/cm²) at 2000 RPM and 70-82 psi (4.9-5.8 kg/cm²) at 3000 RPM with engine at normal operating temperature.

### OIL PAN

**Removal & Installation** – Drain oil. Remove oil pan bolts. Remove oil pan and gasket. To install, reverse removal procedure using new gasket. Tighten bolts to specification. See TORQUE SPECIFICATIONS table at end of article.

### OIL PUMP

**Removal – 1)** Disconnect negative battery cable. Remove radiator shroud assembly. Remove A/C condenser fan shroud (if necessary). Drain engine oil.

**2)** Loosen oil pump pulley retaining bolts. Remove timing belts. See TIMING BELT under REMOVAL & INSTALLATION. Remove oil pump assembly and gasket.

**Disassembly & Inspection – 1)** Disassemble pump. *See Fig. 12.* Measure O.D. of inner rotor shaft portion and outer rotor O.D. Measure clearance between outer rotor and cylinder block housing.

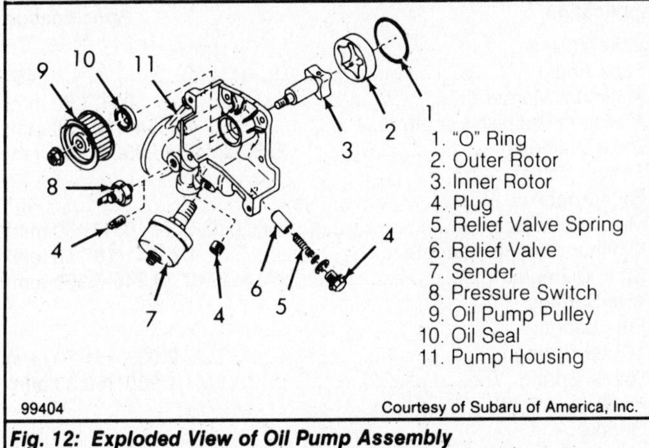


***Fig. 12: Exploded View of Oil Pump Assembly***

**2)** Measure case projection height H1 plus inner and outer rotors H2. *See Fig. 13.* Measure housing bore depth "L" of cylinder block. To determine side clearance "C", use following formula: "C" = "L"-(H1 + H2).

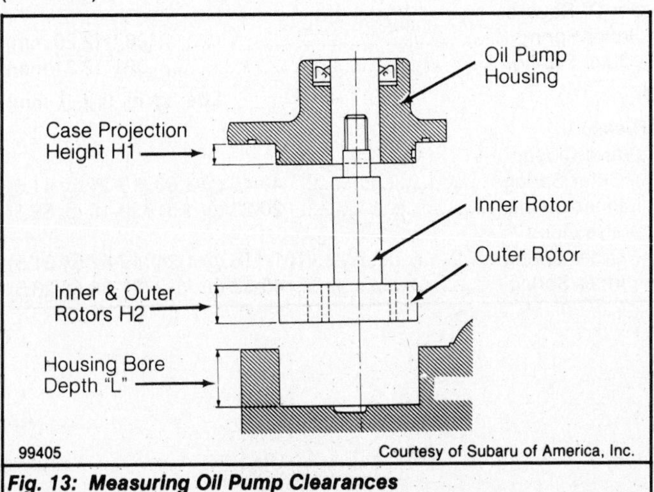


***Fig. 13: Measuring Oil Pump Clearances***

**3)** Side clearance must be within specification. See OIL PUMP SPECIFICATIONS table.

***OIL PUMP SPECIFICATIONS***

| Application | In. (mm) |
|---|---|
| Case Projection Height H1 | [1] .1169-.1181 (2.969-2.999) |
| Outer Rotor-to-Cylinder Block | [2] .0039-.0071 (.099-.180) |
| Relief Valve Spring Free Length | 2.055 (52.197) |
| Rotor Housing Depth "L" | [1] .8646-.8677 (21.961-22.039) |
| Rotor O.D. | |
| Inner | 1.4035-1.4055 (35.649-35.699) |
| Outer | 1.9665-1.9685 (44.949-49.999) |
| Side Clearance "C" | [1 3] .0020-.0063 (.051-.160) |

[1] – *See Fig. 13.*
[2] – Wear limit is .0087" (.221 mm).
[3] – Wear limit is .0071" (.180 mm).

**4)** If side clearance is not within specification, replace inner and outer rotors with proper rotors. See ROTOR SPECIFICATIONS table. Check relief valve spring free length. Replace components if not within specification. See OIL PUMP SPECIFICATIONS table.

***ROTOR SPECIFICATIONS***

| Identification Mark | Height – In. (mm) |
|---|---|
| A | .7437-.7445 (18.889-18.910) |
| B | .7441-.7449 (18.900-18.920) |
| C | .7445-.7453 (18.910-18.931) |

**Reassembly & Installation** – Replace gaskets and "O" rings. To reassemble, reverse disassembly procedure. To install, reverse removal procedure. Tighten bolts to specification. See TORQUE SPECIFICATIONS table.

## TORQUE SPECIFICATIONS

***TORQUE SPECIFICATIONS***

| Application | Ft. Lbs. (N.m) |
|---|---|
| Belt Idler Bolt | 29-35 (39-47) |
| Belt Tension Adjuster Bolt | 17-20 (23-27) |
| Camshaft Case Bolt | 13-15 (18-20) |
| Connecting Rod Nut | 29-31 (39-42) |
| Crankshaft Pulley Bolt [1] | 66-79 (90-107) |
| Cylinder Block | |
| 8-mm Bolt | 17-20 (23-27) |
| 10-mm Bolt | 29-35 (39-47) |
| Cylinder Block Nut | 13-15 (18-20) |
| Cylinder Head Bolt | |
| Step 1 | 29 (39) |
| Step 2 | 47 (64) |
| Step 3 | Loosen 90 Degrees |
| Step 4 | 44-50 (60-68) |
| Drive Plate Bolt | 51-55 (69-75) |
| Flywheel Bolt | 51-55 (69-75) |
| Flywheel Housing Bolt | 25-30 (34-41) |
| Intake Manifold Bolt | 13-16 (18-22) |
| Oil Relief Plug | 17-20 (23-27) |
| Service Hole Plug | 46-56 (62-76) |
| Tensioner Bolt | |
| Left Tensioner | 29-35 (39-47) |
| Right Tensioner | 17-20 (23-27) |
| | **INCH Lbs. (N.m)** |
| Camshaft Sprocket Bolt | 96-108 (11-12) |
| Camshaft Support Bolt | 52-61 (6-7) |
| Oil Level Gauge Guide Bolt | 40-48 (4-5) |
| Oil Pan Bolt | 40-48 (4-5) |
| Oil Separator Cover Bolt | 40-48 (4-5) |
| Timing Belt Cover Bolt | 40-48 (4-5) |
| Valve Cover Bolt | 40-48 (4-5) |
| Water Pump Pulley Bolt | 80-92 (9-10) |

[1] – Coat bolt threads with oil before installation.

# 1991 ENGINES
# 2.7L 6-Cylinder (Cont.)

## ENGINE SPECIFICATIONS

### GENERAL SPECIFICATIONS

| Application | Specification |
|---|---|
| Displacement | 163 Cu. In. |
| Bore | 3.62" (91.9 mm) |
| Stroke | 2.64" (67.1 mm) |
| Compression Ratio | 9.5:1 |
| Fuel System | PFI |
| Horsepower @ RPM | 145 @ 5200 |
| Torque Ft. Lbs. @ RPM | 156 @ 4000 |

### CRANKSHAFT, MAIN & CONNECTING ROD BEARINGS

| Application | In. (mm) |
|---|---|
| Crankshaft | |
| End Play | |
| Standard | .0004-.0037 (.010-.095) |
| Limit | .0118 (.300) |
| Runout | .0014 (.036) |
| Main Bearings | |
| Journal Diameter | |
| Front | 2.1637-2.1642 (54.957-54.970) |
| Center | 2.1635-2.1642 (54.954-54.970) |
| Rear | 2.1636-2.1642 (54.955-54.970) |
| Journal Out-Of-Round | .0012 (.030) |
| Journal Taper | .0028 (.070) |
| Oil Clearance | |
| Front & Rear Bearings | |
| Standard | .0001-.0014 (.003-.036) |
| Limit | .0022 (.055) |
| Center Bearings | |
| Standard | .0003-.0011 (.008-.027) |
| Limit | .0018 (.045) |
| Connecting Rod Bearings | |
| Journal Diameter | 1.7715-1.7720 (44.995-45.010) |
| Journal Out-Of-Round | .0012 (.030) |
| Journal Taper | .0028 (.070) |
| Oil Clearance | |
| Standard | .0004-.0021 (.010-.054) |
| Limit | .0039 (.099) |

### CONNECTING RODS

| Application | In. (mm) |
|---|---|
| Bore Diameter | |
| Pin Bore | .8268-.8274 (21.000-21.016) |
| Crankpin Bore | 1.8898-1.8905 (48.000-48.019) |
| Center-To-Center Length | 4.6043-4.6083 (116.95-117.05) |
| Maximum Bend | [1] .0039 (.099) |
| Maximum Twist | .0039 (.099) |
| Side Play | |
| Standard | .0028-.0130 (.070-.330) |
| Limit | .0039 (.099) |

[1] – Limit of bend per 3.94" (100 mm).

### CYLINDER BLOCK

| Application | In. (mm) |
|---|---|
| Cylinder Bore | |
| Standard Diameter | 3.6214-3.6226 (91.985-92.015) |
| Maximum Out-Of-Round & Taper | .002 (.05) |
| Boring Limit | .020 (.50) |
| Maximum Deck Grinding Limit | .016 (.41) |
| Maximum Deck Warpage | .0030 (.075) |

### PISTONS, PINS & RINGS

| Application | In. (mm) |
|---|---|
| Pistons | |
| Clearance | |
| Standard | .0006-.0014 (.015-.035) |
| Limit | .0024 (.60). |
| Diameter | 3.6209-3.6213 (91.975-91.985) |
| Pins | |
| Diameter | .8267-.8268 (20.994-21.001) |
| Piston Fit | .00004-.00059 (.001-.015) |
| Rod Fit | 0-.0009 (0-.022) |
| Rings | |
| No. 1 | |
| End Gap | [1] .0079-.0138 (.200-.350) |
| Side Clearance | [2] .0016-.0031 (.040-.080) |
| No. 2 | |
| End Gap | [1] .0079-.0138 (.200-.350) |
| Side Clearance | [2] .0012-.0028 (.030-.070) |
| No. 3 (Oil) | |
| End Gap | [3] .012-.035 (.30-.90) |
| Side Clearance | 0 (0) |

[1] – Maximum clearance is .059" (1.5 mm).
[2] – Maximum clearance is .0059" (.15 mm).
[3] – Maximum clearance is .079" (2.01 mm).

### VALVES & VALVE SPRINGS

| Application | Specification |
|---|---|
| Intake Valves | |
| Face Angle | 45° |
| Minimum Margin | .031" (.80 mm) |
| Minimum Refinish Length | 4.2354" (107.58 mm) |
| Stem Diameter | .2736-.2742" (6.950-6.965 mm) |
| Exhaust Valves | |
| Face Angle | 45° |
| Minimum Margin | .031" (.80 mm) |
| Minimum Refinish Length | 4.2354" (107.58 mm) |
| Stem Diameter | .2734-.2740" (6.945-6.960 mm) |
| Valve Springs | |
| Free Length | |
| Outer Spring | 2.035" (51.70 mm) |
| Inner Spring | 1.980" (50.30 mm) |
| Installed Height | |
| Intake | |
| Inner Spring | 1.516" (38.5 mm) |
| Outer Spring | 1.634" (41.5 mm) |
| Exhaust | |
| Inner Spring | 1.122" (28.5 mm) |
| Outer Spring | 1.240" (31.5 mm) |
| Out-Of-Square | |
| Inner Spring | .087" (2.20 mm) |
| Outer Spring | .091" (2.31 mm) |
| | **Lbs. @ In. (kg @ mm)** |
| Pressure | |
| Valve Closed | |
| Outer Spring | 40-46 @ 1.63 (18-21 @ 41.5) |
| Inner Spring | 20-23 @ 1.516 (9-10 @ 38.5) |
| Valve Open | |
| Outer Spring | 101-116 @ 1.24 (46-52 @ 31.5) |
| Inner Spring | 45-52 @ 1.12 (21-24 @ 28.5) |

# 1991 ENGINES
# 2.7L 6-Cylinder (Cont.)

## CYLINDER HEAD

| Application | Specification |
|---|---|
| Cylinder Head Height | 3.567" (90.60 mm) |
| Grinding Limit | .012 (.3mm) |
| Maximum Warpage | .0030" (.075 mm) |
| Valve Seats | |
| Intake Valve | |
| Seat Angle | 45° |
| Seat Width | .047-.071" (1.19-1.80 mm) |
| Maximum Seat Runout | .020" (.50 mm) |
| Exhaust Valve | |
| Seat Angle | 45° |
| Seat Width | .059-.079" (1.5-2.0 mm) |
| Maximum Seat Runout | .020" (.50 mm) |
| Valve Guides | |
| Intake Valve | |
| Valve Guide I.D. | .2756-.2762" (7.000-7.015 mm) |
| Valve Guide Installed Height | [1] .67-.71" (17-18 mm) |
| Valve Stem-To-Guide Oil Clearance | [2] .0014-.0026" (.035-.065 mm) |
| Exhaust Valve | |
| Valve Guide I.D. | .2756-.2762" (7.000-7.015 mm) |
| Valve Guide Installed Height | [1] .67-.71" (17-18 mm) |
| Valve Stem-To-Guide Oil Clearance | [2] .0016-.0028" (.040-.070 mm) |

[1] – Protrusion above head.
[2] – Maximum clearance is .0059" (.15 mm).

## CAMSHAFT

| Application | In. (mm) |
|---|---|
| Bearing Bore Diameter | |
| No. 1 | 1.4961-1.4968 (38.000-38.018) |
| No. 2 | 1.9094-1.9102 (48.500-48.518) |
| No. 3 | 1.8898-1.8905 (48.000-48.018) |
| No. 4 | 1.8701-1.8711 (47.500-47.525) |
| No. 5 (Left) | 1.5354-1.5359 (39.000-39.013) |
| Distributor Gear Backlash | |
| Standard | .0006-.0050 (.015-.127) |
| Limit | .0071 (.180) |
| End Play | |
| Standard | .0012-.0102 (.030-.260) |
| Limit | .0138 (.350) |
| Journal Diameter | |
| No. 1 | 1.4946-1.4953 (37.964-37.980) |
| No. 2 | 1.9080-1.9087 (48.464-48.480) |
| No. 3 | 1.8883-1.8890 (47.964-47.980) |
| No. 4 | 1.8687-1.8693 (47.464-47.480) |
| No. 5 (Left) | 1.5340-1.5346 (38.964-38.980) |
| Journal Runout | .0010 (.025) |
| Lobe Height | |
| Standard | 1.5606-1.5646 (39.64-39.74) |
| Minimum Limit | 1.5547 (39.49) |
| Oil Clearance | |
| Standard | .0008-.0021 (.020-.054) |
| Limit | .0028 (.070) |

## VALVE LASH ADJUSTERS

| Application | In. (mm) |
|---|---|
| Bore Diameter | .8425-.8441 (21.400-21.440) |
| Lash Adjuster Diameter | .8417-.8422 (21.380-21.393) |
| Oil Clearance | |
| Standard | .0003-.0024 (.007-.061) |
| Limit | .004 (.10) |

# 1991 CLUTCHES FWD & 4WD

## Justy, Legacy, Loyale, XT, XT6

## DESCRIPTION

Clutch is single, dry disc type using a diaphragm spring pressure plate. Release bearing is a self-aligning design. System is controlled by either a cable running from pedal assembly to clutch release lever, or a hydraulic clutch master cylinder and clutch release cylinder.

## ADJUSTMENTS

***NOTE: Adjustment information is not available from manufacturer for vehicles with hydraulic clutch system.***

### CLUTCH RELEASE FORK FREE PLAY

**1)** Remove release lever return spring from lever. Rotate adjustment nut so that free play is as specified. *See Fig. 1.*

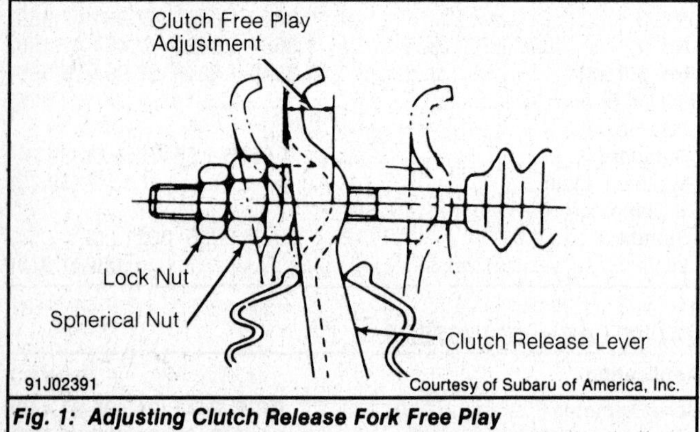


***Fig. 1: Adjusting Clutch Release Fork Free Play***

**2)** See CLUTCH RELEASE FORK FREE PLAY SPECIFICATIONS table. DO NOT twist cable during adjustment. Tighten lock nut. Install return spring on lever. Depress pedal to ensure correct operation.

***CLUTCH RELEASE FORK FREE PLAY SPECIFICATIONS***

| Application | In. (mm) |
|---|---|
| Justy | .08-.16 (2.1-4.1) |
| Legacy | .12-.16 (3.0-4.1) |
| Loyale, XT & XT6 | |
| 2WD | .08-.12 (2.0-3.0) |
| 4WD | .12-.16 (3.0-4.1) |

## REMOVAL & INSTALLATION

### CLUTCH ASSEMBLY

**Removal (Legacy, Loyale, XT & XT6) – 1)** Disconnect negative battery cable. Remove spare tire and tire support. Remove hill-holder cable, lock nut and clips. Remove clutch cable return spring, lock nut, adjusting nut and clips.

**2)** Remove speedometer cable and clip. Label and disconnect wiring and hoses connected to transaxle. Disconnect $O_2$ sensor wire connector. Remove air cleaner. Remove mount support rod from engine and vehicle body. Install Engine Supporter (926610000) between engine and vehicle body.

**3)** Remove starter. Raise vehicle. Remove front and rear exhaust pipe. Remove front crossmember (if equipped). On 4WD vehicles, mark propeller shaft for installation reference and remove propeller shaft.

**4)** Plug opening at rear of extension housing. Remove select rod from transfer rail. On vehicles with hydraulic clutch, remove clutch release cylinder from transaxle and wire out of way. On all vehicles, disconnect spring, gearshift rod and brace from transaxle.

**5)** Using a pin punch, drive out each axle shaft roll pin. Remove stabilizer bar from transverse link. Remove hand brake cable bracket from transverse link. Remove transverse link bolt at crossmember. Separate axle shafts from transaxle.

**6)** Remove engine-to-transaxle mounting bolts/nuts. Support transaxle with transmission jack. Remove rear cushion mounting nuts and remove rear crossmember. Separate transaxle from engine.

**7)** Remove transaxle from vehicle. Remove pressure plate and clutch disc from flywheel. Remove release bearing, bearing holder and clutch release lever from transaxle.

**Removal (Justy) – 1)** Disconnect negative battery cable. Disconnect hoses and cables from air cleaner. Remove air cleaner. Remove starter. Disconnect speedometer cable and back-up light switch. Remove transaxle ground strap. Disconnect clutch cable from transaxle. Remove clutch cable bracket.

**2)** Attach lifting device to transaxle lifting bracket. Remove mount support assembly attaching transaxle to vehicle body. Mount Engine Supporter (921540000), between radiator body mount and engine. Mount another supporter, between engine and removed transaxle mount.

**3)** Lift up transaxle slightly. Remove undercovers. Disconnect rear exhaust pipe from front exhaust pipe and vehicle body. Remove center crossmember. Remove transverse link. Using a pin punch, drive out each axle shaft roll pin. Separate axle shafts from transaxle.

**4)** Remove transaxle mounting bracket. Disconnect gearshift rod and brace from transaxle. On 4WD vehicles, mark propeller shaft for installation reference and remove propeller shaft. Plug opening at rear of extension housing. Remove bolts mounting transaxle to engine and separate.

**5)** Lift transaxle up and out of vehicle. Remove release bearing, release bearing fork and seal from transaxle. Remove pressure plate and clutch disc from flywheel.

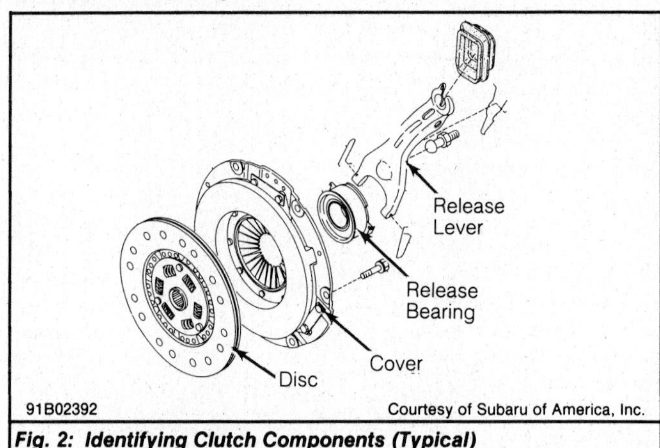


***Fig. 2: Identifying Clutch Components (Typical)***

**Inspection (All Models) – 1)** Check disc runout by mounting disc on Clutch Disc Guide (499747000 for 2WD models of Loyale, XT and XT6; 499745000 for Justy; or 499747100 for 2WD/4WD Legacy and 4WD models of Loyale, XT and XT6). Mount dial indicator with plunger against disc face.

**2)** Measure runout 3.7" (95 mm) from hub center for 2WD models of Loyale, XT and XT6; 6.7" (170 mm) for Justy; and 4.2" (107 mm) for 2WD/4WD Legacy and 4WD models of Loyale, XT and XT6. On all models, maximum runout is .03" (.7 mm) or less. Check clutch disc for wear. Minimum height of lining above rivet heads is .012" (.3 mm).

**3)** Check clutch release bearing for damage or rough rotation. Replace if defective. Inspect pressure plate and flywheel. Light roughness may be dressed with fine emery cloth. If surfaces are deeply scored, replace defective parts.

**Installation (All Models) – 1)** Install clutch release lever and release bearing holder. Lubricate inner groove of release bearing holder, transaxle mainshaft spline and contact surfaces of release lever with a light coat of molybdenum disulphide grease.

**2)** Use clutch alignment tool to position clutch disc against flywheel. Position clutch cover against disc. Tighten cover bolts in a crisscross pattern. Install transaxle in vehicle.

**3)** Ensure NEW roll pins are installed in axle shafts. To complete installation, reverse removal procedure. Tighten nuts and bolts to specification. See TORQUE SPECIFICATIONS table at end of article. Adjust free play. See CLUTCH RELEASE FORK FREE PLAY under ADJUSTMENTS.

## CLUTCH MASTER CYLINDER

**Removal & Installation (Legacy)** – Remove snap pin and separate push rod of master cylinder from clutch pedal. Remove and plug hose from master cylinder. Remove master cylinder nuts and remove master cylinder. To install, reverse removal procedure. Tighten nuts to specification. See TORQUE SPECIFICATIONS table at end of article. Bleed hydraulic system.

## CLUTCH RELEASE CYLINDER

**Removal & Installation (Legacy)** – Remove and plug hose from release cylinder. Remove bolts attaching release cylinder to transaxle and remove release cylinder. To install, reverse removal procedure. Tighten bolts to specification. See TORQUE SPECIFICATIONS table at end of article. Bleed hydraulic system.

## OVERHAUL

***NOTE: Manufacturer recommends replacement of faulty clutch master and release cylinders and does not provide overhaul procedures.***

## TORQUE SPECIFICATIONS

***TORQUE SPECIFICATIONS***

| Application | Ft. Lbs. (N.m) |
|---|---|
| Clutch Cover Bolt | |
| Legacy, Loyale, XT & XT6 | 11-13 (15-18) |
| Clutch Hose Bolt | 11-15 (15-20) |
| Clutch Master Cylinder Nut | 9-17 (12-23) |
| Clutch Release Cylinder Bolt | 25-30 (34-40) |
| Exhaust Pipe Support Bracket Bolt | 18-25 (25-34) |
| Exhaust Pipe-To-Engine Nut | 18-25 (25-34) |
| Flywheel Bolt | |
| Justy | 65-71 (88-96) |
| Legacy, Loyale, XT & XT6 | 51-55 (69-75) |
| Front Crossmember Bolt | 35-63 (48-86) |
| Mount Support Assembly Nut | |
| To Body | 35-51 (47-69) |
| To Engine | 32-40 (44-54) |
| Propeller Shaft Center Bearing Support Bolt | 25-32 (34-44) |
| Propeller Shaft-To-Differential Nut | |
| Except XT & XT6 | 13-20 (17-27) |
| XT & XT6 | 17-24 (23-32) |
| Rear Crossmember Cushion Nut | 20-35 (27-47) |
| Rear Crossmember Front Bolt | |
| Legacy | 87-116 (118-157) |
| Loyale, XT & XT6 | 65-87 (88-118) |
| Rear Crossmember Rear Bolt | |
| Legacy | 40-61 (54-83) |
| Loyale, XT & XT6 | 27-49 (37-66) |
| Stabilizer Bar-To-Transverse Link Bolt | 14-22 (19-30) |
| Starter Bolt | |
| Upper | 34-40 (46-54) |
| Lower | 22-27 (30-37) |
| Transaxle-To-Engine Bolt/Nut | 34-40 (46-54) |
| Transverse Link-To-Crossmember Nut | 43-51 (58-69) |
| | **INCH Lbs. (N.m)** |
| Clutch Cover Bolts | |
| Justy | 84-96 (9-11) |

# 1991 DRIVE AXLES
# FWD Axle Shafts

**Justy, Legacy, Loyale, XT, XT6**

## DESCRIPTION & OPERATION

Axle shafts transfer power from transaxle to driving wheels. All axle shafts consist of a shaft with a flexible Constant Velocity (CV) joint at each end. Inner tripod type CV joint is attached to transaxle by a roll pin. Outer CV joint is splined to hub assembly and secured by axle shaft nut.

Inner and outer CV joints are enclosed by CV joint boots. Boots maintain lubrication in the joint and prevents contaminants from entering joint. Boots must be replaced when signs of leakage or cracks are present. Inner tripod type CV joint can be repaired, but outer CV joint and shaft must be replaced as an assembly.

## TROUBLE SHOOTING

***NOTE: See TROUBLE SHOOTING article in GENERAL INFORMATION.***

## REMOVAL, DISASSEMBLY, REASSEMBLY & INSTALLATION

***NOTE: For information on rear axle shafts for 4WD vehicles, see 4WD REAR AXLE SHAFTS article.***

### FWD AXLE SHAFT

**Removal – 1)** Apply parking brake. Remove front hub cap and axle shaft cotter pin. Loosen axle shaft nut. Raise and support vehicle. Remove front wheels. Remove brake caliper assembly from steering knuckle without disconnecting hydraulic line. Wire caliper out of way.
**2)** Remove axle shaft nut, conical washer, and center piece from axle shaft. Remove brake rotor. On inboard side of axle shaft, drive out roll pin securing axle shaft to transaxle.
**3)** Remove tie rod cotter pin and nut. Using a puller, disconnect tie rod end from steering knuckle. Remove steering knuckle-to-strut retaining bolt(s). Remove pinch bolt and separate ball joint from lower control arm.
**4)** Remove steering knuckle and axle shaft as a unit. Remove axle shaft from steering knuckle by using Adapter (922493000) and Remover (921122000). *See Fig. 1.*

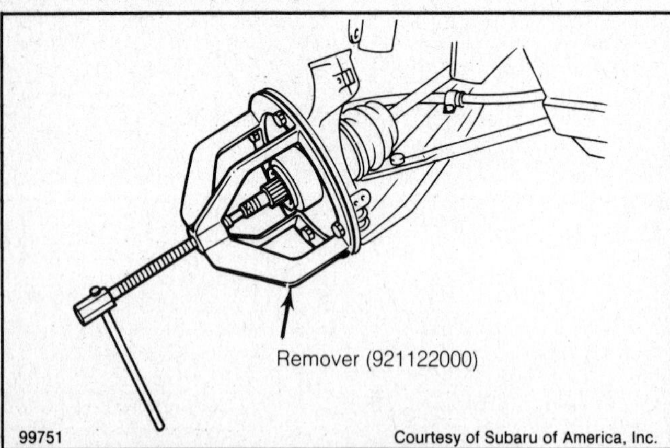


***Fig. 1: Removing Axle Shaft From Steering Knuckle***

**Disassembly – 1)** Straighten bent end of boot clamps on inner boot of axle shaft. Loosen clamps with screwdriver or pliers, taking care not to damage boot.
**2)** Slide boot from larger end of inboard joint. Pry out and remove round snap ring located at neck of outer race of inboard joint. *See Fig. 2.* Slide outer race from shaft assembly.
**3)** Wipe off grease and remove balls. Move cage to boot side. Remove inner race snap ring and slide off inner race. Remove cage from shaft. Wrap axle shaft splines with tape and remove inner boot.

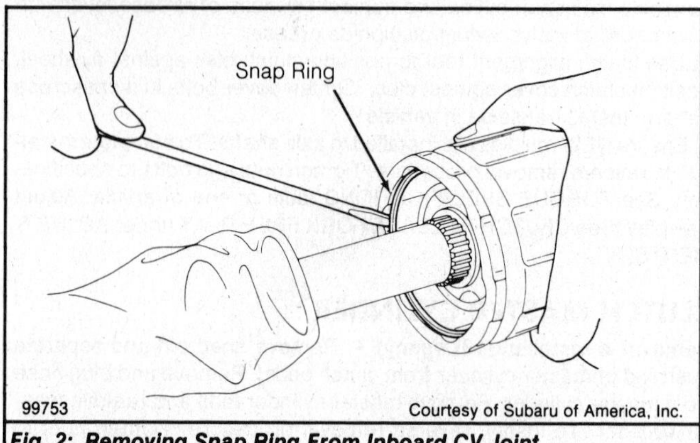


***Fig. 2: Removing Snap Ring From Inboard CV Joint***

**4)** Remove outer boot clamps in same manner as previously described in step **1)**. Remove outer boot from inboard joint end of axle shaft.

***NOTE: DO NOT disassemble outboard CV joint. If outboard CV joint is defective, replace axle shaft as an assembly.***

**Reassembly – 1)** To reassemble axle shaft, reverse disassembly procedure. Use Molylex No. 2 grease on CV joint. Ensure cage is installed onto shaft with cut-out side facing end of shaft. *See Fig. 3.*

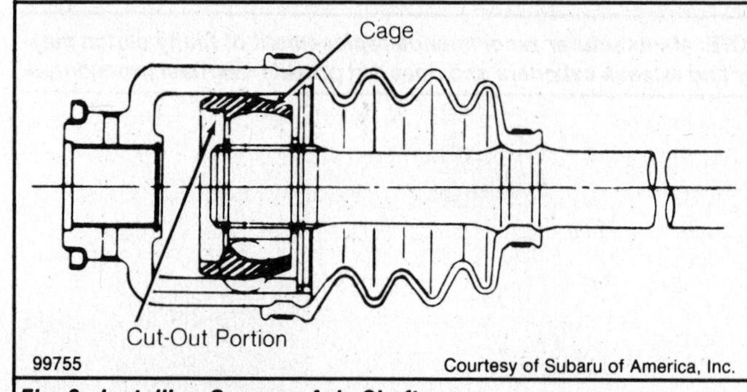


***Fig. 3: Installing Cage on Axle Shaft***

**2)** When installing cage over inner race, align inner race protrusions with tracks on cage, then rotate cage one-half turn. *See Fig. 4.*

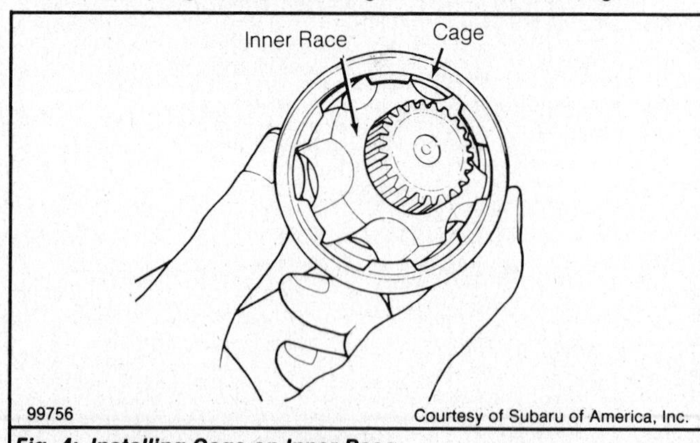


***Fig. 4: Installing Cage on Inner Race***

**3)** Before tightening inner boot clamps, ensure inboard joint is at center of its travel. On Justy, boot setting length should be 2.99" (76 mm). *See Fig. 5.*
**4)** On all other models, measure distance between inner and outer boots. See DISTANCE BETWEEN INNER & OUTER BOOTS table. *See Fig. 5.*

# 1991 DRIVE AXLES
# FWD Axle Shafts (Cont.)

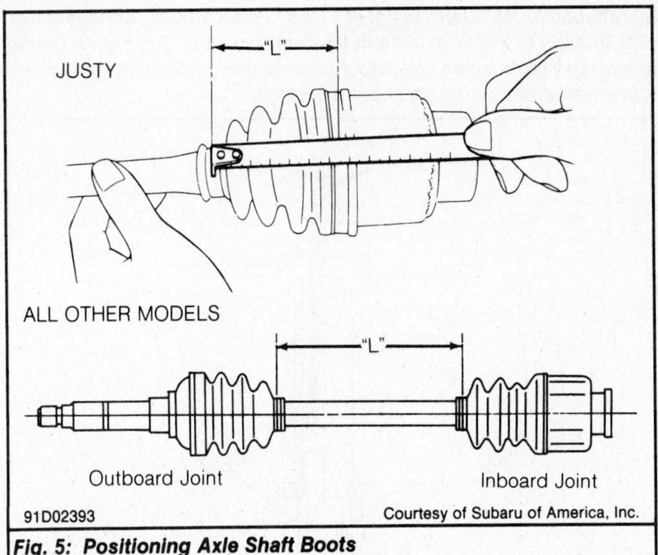


*Fig. 5: Positioning Axle Shaft Boots*

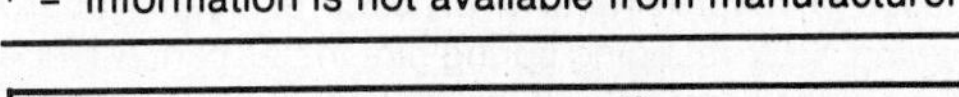

***DISTANCE BETWEEN INNER & OUTER BOOTS***

| Application | In. (mm) |
|---|---|
| Legacy | |
| 87AC-25 | 10.91 (277) |
| 95AC-25 | 10.28 (261) |
| Loyale | |
| Non-Turbo | |
| 82AC | 10.43 (265) |
| 87AC | 10.12 (257) |
| Turbo | |
| 95AC-23 | 9.53 (242) |
| 95AC-25 | 9.53 (242) |
| XT & XT6 | [1] |

[1] – Information is not available from manufacturer.

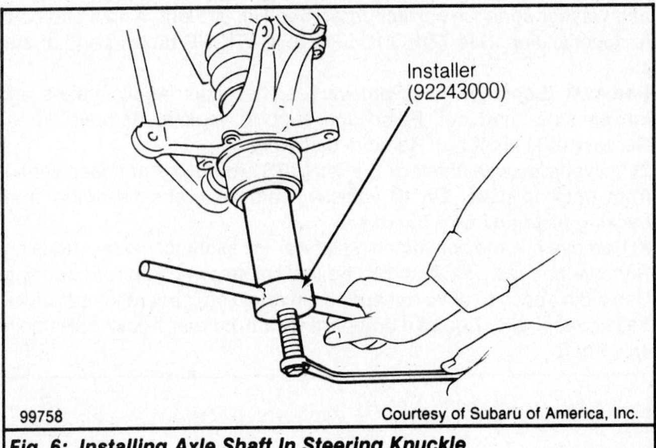


*Fig. 6: Installing Axle Shaft In Steering Knuckle*

**Installation – 1)** To install axle shaft, insert outboard end of shaft in steering knuckle. Use Installer (92243000) to insert shaft through knuckle. *See Fig. 6.*

**2)** To complete installation, reverse removal procedure. Check seals at both ends of axle shaft and replace prior to installation, if necessary. Lubricate transaxle seal lip with transaxle oil.

**3)** Install a NEW retaining roll pin on inboard side of axle. Ensure conical washer and center piece are installed correctly. *See Fig. 7.*

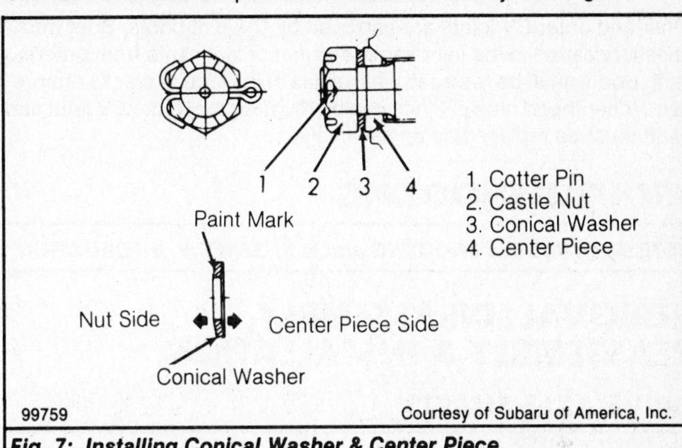


*Fig. 7: Installing Conical Washer & Center Piece*

**4)** Apply brakes and tighten axle shaft hub nut to specification. See TORQUE SPECIFICATIONS table. If hub nut needs to be aligned with cotter pin hole, nut may be tightened up to an additional 30 degrees of rotation.

## TORQUE SPECIFICATIONS

***TORQUE SPECIFICATIONS***

| Application | Ft. Lbs. (N.m) |
|---|---|
| Axle Shaft Hub Nut | |
| Justy, Loyale, XT & XT6 | 145 (196) |
| Legacy | 137 (186) |
| Ball Joint Pinch Bolt | |
| Justy | 25-32 (34-44) |
| Legacy, Loyale & XT6 | 28-37 (38-50) |
| XT | 21-29 (29-39) |
| Brake Caliper Bolt | |
| Justy | 38-49 (52-66) |
| Legacy, Loyale, XT & XT6 | 36-51 (49-69) |
| Strut-to-Steering Knuckle Bolt | |
| Justy | 25-33 (34-44) |
| Legacy | 97-120 (132-162) |
| Loyale | 28-37 (38-50) |
| XT | 22-29 (29-39) |
| XT6 | 47-61 (64-83) |
| Tie Rod Nut | 18-22 (25-29) |
| Wheel Lug Nut | 58-72 (78-98) |

# 1991 DRIVE AXLES
# 4WD Rear Axle Shafts

### Justy, Legacy, Loyale, XT, XT6

## DESCRIPTION & OPERATION

Axle shafts transfer power from rear differential to rear wheels. Axle shafts consist of a shaft with a flexible Constant Velocity (CV) joint at each end. Inner tripod type CV joint is attached to differential by a spring pin. Outer CV joint is attached to spindle by a spring pin or splined to hub assembly and secured by axle shaft nut.

Inner and outer CV joints are enclosed by CV joint boots. Boot maintains lubrication in the joint and prevents contaminants from entering joint. Boots must be replaced when signs of leakage or cracks are present. Inner tripod type CV joint can be repaired, but outer CV joint and shaft must be replaced as an assembly.

## TROUBLE SHOOTING

***NOTE: See TROUBLE SHOOTING article in GENERAL INFORMATION.***

## REMOVAL, DISASSEMBLY, REASSEMBLY & INSTALLATION

### DRIVE AXLE SHAFTS

***NOTE: Disassembly and reassembly procedures for rear axle shafts are same as front shafts. See FWD AXLE SHAFTS article.***

**Removal (Justy) – 1)** Remove rear hub cap, center cap and cotter pin. Apply brakes and loosen castle nut. Raise and support vehicle. Remove wheel. Remove castle nut, washer spring and center piece.
**2)** Remove brake drum. Remove brake line bracket from rear housing. Remove brake assembly and wire out of way. Use a pin punch to drive out spring pin retaining inboard joint to differential. *See Fig. 1*.

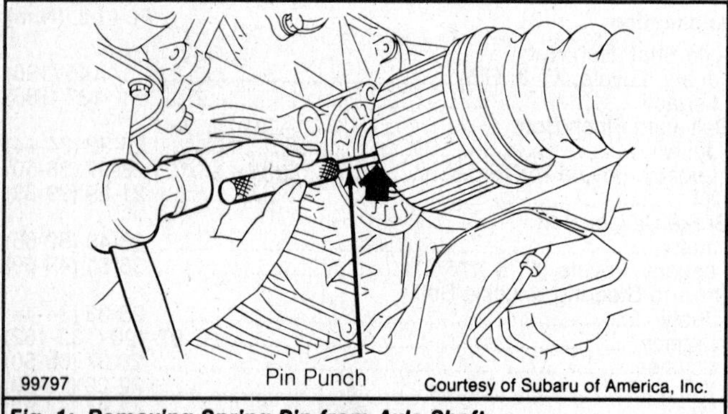


***Fig. 1: Removing Spring Pin from Axle Shaft***

**3)** Remove strut, lower arm and trailing link from rear housing. Remove rear housing and axle shaft as a unit. Using Removers (922493000 and 921122000), remove axle shaft from rear housing. *See Fig. 2*.

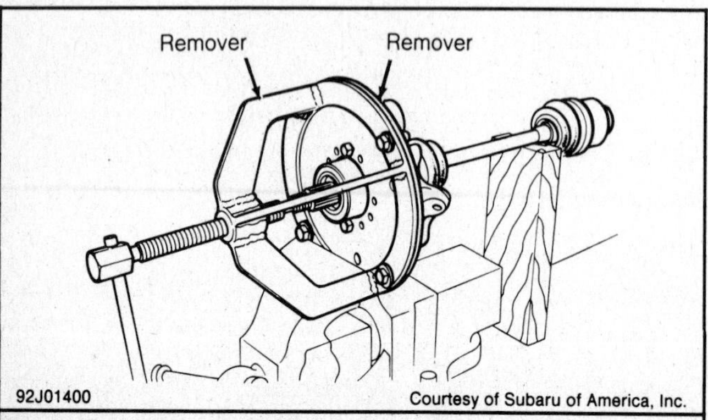


***Fig. 2: Removing Axle Shaft from Rear Housing (Justy)***

**Installation – 1)** Use Installer Cap (922320000) and Installer (921360000) to install axle shaft into rear housing. *See Fig. 3*. Clamp axle shaft in soft-jawed vise. Mount rear housing onto axle shaft. Position installer cap onto hub bearing surface.

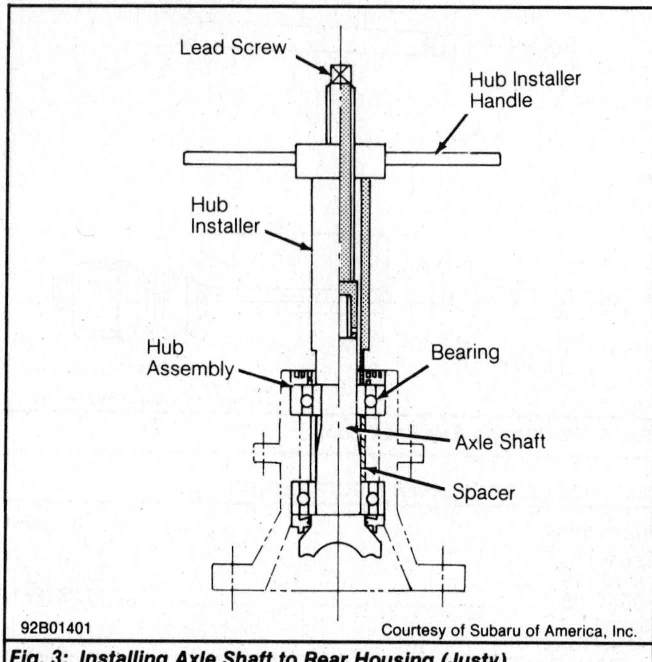


***Fig. 3: Installing Axle Shaft to Rear Housing (Justy)***

**2)** Screw lead screw into axle shaft. Install handle to lead screw. Hold lead screw with wrench to prevent lead screw from turning. Press housing onto axle shaft by turning handle. Ensure that excessive load is not applied to outer seal during press procedure.
**3)** To complete installation, reverse removal procedure. Install inboard joint to differential using NEW retaining spring pin. Install center piece and washer spring in correct order. *See Fig. 8*. Tighten nuts and bolts to specification. See TORQUE SPECIFICATIONS table at end of article.
**Removal (Legacy) – 1)** Remove rear hub cap. Apply brakes and loosen axle shaft nut. Raise and support vehicle. Remove wheel. Remove axle shaft nut. Remove disc rotor.
**2)** On vehicles with anti-lock brakes (ABS), remove rear speed sensor from backing plate. On all vehicles, remove brake assembly from backing plate and wire out of way.
**3)** Remove nut and bolt attaching lateral link assembly to rear housing. Remove nut and bolt attaching trailing link assembly to rear housing. Use a pin punch to drive out spring pin retaining inboard joint to differential. *See Fig. 1*. Remove outboard joint from rear housing. Remove axle shaft.

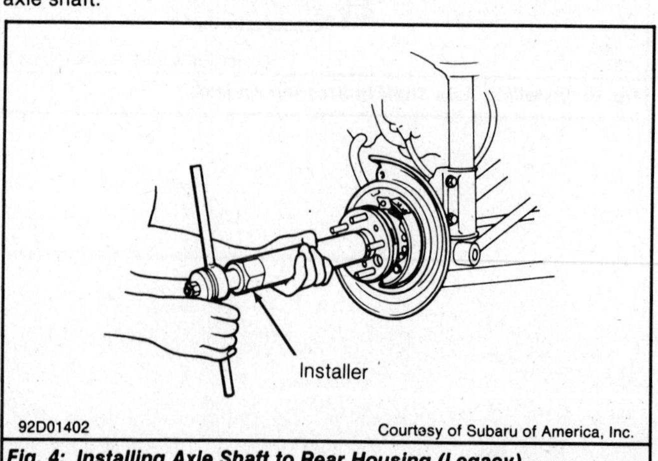


***Fig. 4: Installing Axle Shaft to Rear Housing (Legacy)***

# 1991 DRIVE AXLES
# 4WD Rear Axle Shafts (Cont.)

**Installation - 1)** Using Installer (9224310000) and Adapter (927390000), install outboard joint into rear housing. *See Fig. 4*. Install, but DO NOT tighten new axle shaft nut. Install inboard joint to differential using NEW retaining spring pin.

**2)** To complete installation, reverse removal procedure. Tighten all nuts and bolts to specification. See TORQUE SPECIFICATIONS table at end of article.

**Removal (Loyale, XT & XT6) - 1)** Raise and support vehicle. Remove wheel. Remove lower strut bolt from inner trailing arm. Loosen outer arm-to-inner trailing arm lock bolts.

**2)** On inboard and outboard joints, use pin punch to drive out spring pins retaining axle shaft to differential and outer spindle. *See Fig. 1*. Lower inner trailing arm and remove outboard joint from spindle. Remove axle shaft from differential.

**Installation - 1)** To install, reverse removal procedure. DO NOT install axle shaft backward. Inboard axle shaft flange has a smaller diameter. Position axle splines so spring pin holes will be aligned.

**2)** Install NEW spring pins. Tighten nuts and bolts to specification. See TORQUE SPECIFICATIONS table at end of article. Check rear wheel alignment. See SPECIFICATIONS & PROCEDURES article in WHEEL ALIGNMENT.

## REAR HUB ASSEMBLY

**Removal & Disassembly (Justy) -** Remove axle shaft. See DRIVE AXLE SHAFTS under REMOVAL, DISASSEMBLY, REASSEMBLY & INSTALLATION. With rear housing removed, move spacer inside housing in radial direction. Using a brass drift, drive outer bearing, race and oil seal out of housing. Remove spacer. Drive inner bearing, race and oil seal out of housing. *See Fig. 5*.

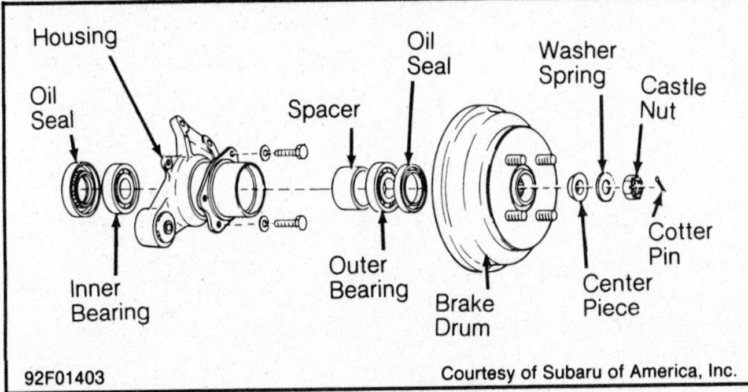


**Fig. 5: Exploded View of 4WD Rear Hub Assembly (Justy)**

**Reassembly & Installation - 1)** Clean rear housing and spacer. Check for deformation or damage to housing and spacer. Install new bearings and oil seals. Pack bearings with grease. Use appropriate press to install inner bearing and oil seal into housing.

**2)** Apply grease to inner housing. Install spacer into housing. Press outer bearing and oil seal into housing. Install rear housing onto axle shaft. See DRIVE AXLE SHAFTS.

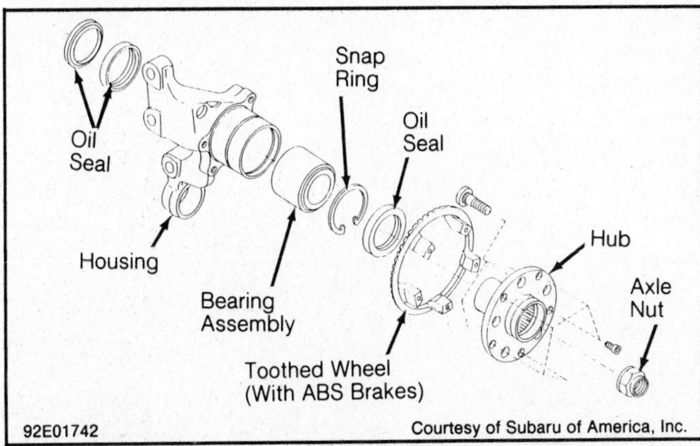


**Fig. 6: Exploded View of 4WD Rear Hub Assembly (Legacy)**

**Removal & Disassembly (Legacy) - 1)** Remove axle shaft. See DRIVE AXLE SHAFTS under REMOVAL, DISASSEMBLY, REASSEMBLY & INSTALLATION. Remove nuts and bolts attaching lower strut assembly to rear housing. Remove rear housing.

**2)** Remove backing plate from rear housing. Press hub from rear housing. Use a screwdriver to remove inner and outer oil seals. Remove snap ring from rear housing. *See Fig. 6*. Press bearing assembly out of rear housing.

***CAUTION: On vehicles with anti-lock brakes (ABS), DO NOT damage toothed wheel.***

**Reassembly & Installation -** Clean housing before installing bearing assembly. Lubricate and install new bearing assembly and oil seals. Ensure snap ring fits properly into groove. To complete reassemble, reverse disassembly procedure. Tighten nuts and bolts to specification. See TORQUE SPECIFICATIONS table at end of article.

**Removal (Loyale, XT & XT6) - 1)** Remove rear hub cap. Remove cotter pin and loosen castle nut. Raise and support vehicle. Remove axle shaft. See DRIVE AXLE SHAFTS under REMOVAL, DISASSEMBLY, REASSEMBLY & INSTALLATION. Remove castle nut, washer spring and center piece from center of rear hub.

**2)** Disconnect and plug brake line at inner trailing arm bracket. Remove brake assembly from inner trailing arm. Remove inner trailing arm mounting bolts and remove arm from vehicle.

**Disassembly - 1)** Mount inner trailing arm in bench vise. Straighten staked portion of ring nut. *See Fig. 7*. Remove ring nut with Socket (925550000).

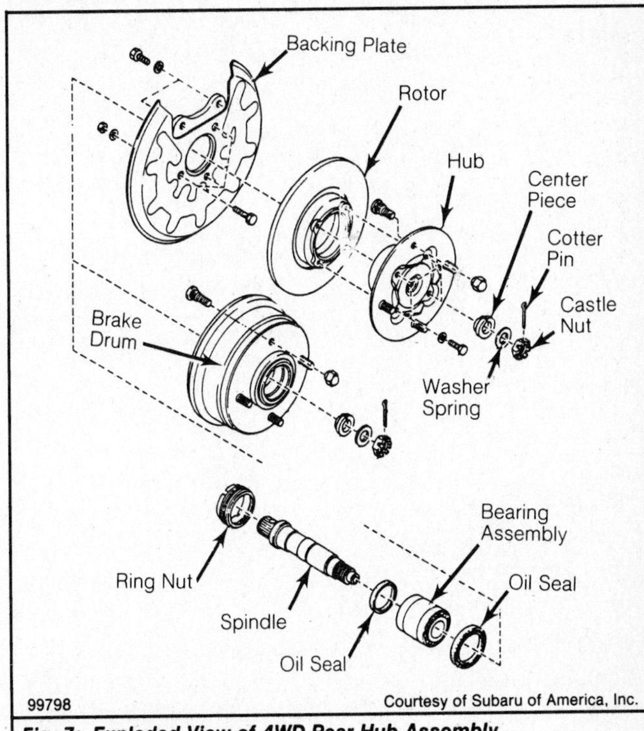


**Fig. 7: Exploded View of 4WD Rear Hub Assembly (Loyale, XT & XT6)**

**2)** Using a plastic hammer, tap spindle out of hub. Remove oil seal from inner arm housing. Press bearings from spindle and housing.

**Reassembly & Installation - 1)** Replace oil seals. After lubricating thoroughly with grease, press bearings onto spindle and into housing. Install spindle into housing.

**2)** Install and tighten ring nut. Stake ring nut. Install inner trailing arm on vehicle. Install brake assembly. Tighten ring nut and brake backing plate bolts to specification. See TORQUE SPECIFICATIONS table.

**3)** Install spindle castle nut, washer spring and center piece in correct order. *See Fig. 8*. Tighten nuts and bolts to specification. See TORQUE SPECIFICATIONS table. Castle nut may be tightened an additional 30 degrees to align cotter pin slots. Bleed brake system.

# 1991 DRIVE AXLES
# 4WD Rear Axle Shafts (Cont.)

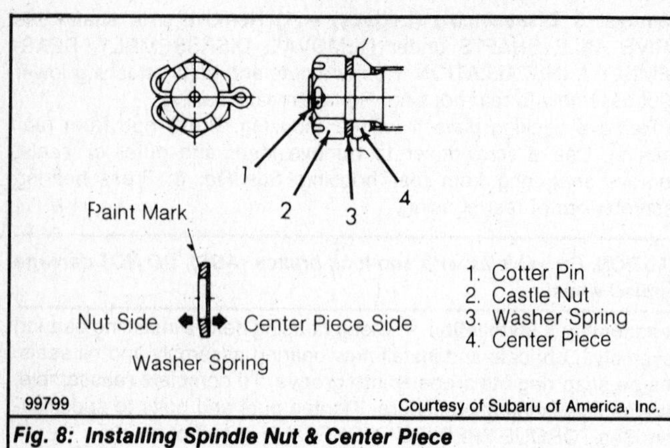


**Fig. 8: Installing Spindle Nut & Center Piece**

## TORQUE SPECIFICATIONS

*TORQUE SPECIFICATIONS*

| Application | Ft. Lbs. (N.m) |
|---|---|
| Axle Shaft Castle Nut [1] | |
| Justy | 108 (147) |
| Legacy | 123-152 (167-206) |
| Loyale, XT & XT6 | 107 (145) |
| Brake Backing Plate Bolt | |
| Justy | 13-23 (18-31) |
| Loyale, XT & XT6 | 34-43 (46-58) |
| Brake Caliper Bolt | 34-43 (46-58) |
| Brake Line Bracket Bolt | 10-17 (13-23) |
| Lateral Arm Nut | 87-101 (118-137) |
| Lower Arm Nut | 55-69 (74-93) |
| Lower Strut Bolt | |
| Justy | 72-87 (98-118) |
| Legacy | 97-127 (132-172) |
| Loyale, XT & XT6 | 65-87 (88-118) |
| Rear Axle Ring Nut | 127-163 (172-221) |
| Trailing Arm Nut | 72-94 (98-127) |
| Trailing Link Nut | 44-51 (59-69) |
| Wheel Lug Nut | 58-72 (78-98) |

[1] – If necessary, tighten an additional 30 degrees to align cotter pin holes.

# 1991 DRIVE AXLES
# 4WD Differential

## Justy, Legacy, Loyale, XT, XT6

## DESCRIPTION

Rear axle assembly on all 4WD models is a hypoid type with integral carrier housing. A limited slip differential is available on some models.

## AXLE RATIO & IDENTIFICATION

All 4WD models use one basic type of rear axle assembly. An identification mark is painted on top front of differential. An identification tag is attached to differential cover. To determine axle ratio, divide number of ring gear teeth by number of pinion teeth.

***REAR AXLE IDENTIFICATION***

| Application | Mark | Ratio |
|---|---|---|
| Justy | ..... | 3.70:1 |
| Legacy | ..... | 4.10:1 |
| Loyale & XT | | |
| Non-Turbo | WP | 3.90:1 |
| Turbo | WL, WM [1] | 3.70:1 |
| XT6 | WP, WR [1] | 3.90:1 |

[1] - Limited slip differential.

## LUBRICATION

### CAPACITY

Fluid capacity is approximately .8 qts. (0.8L).

### FLUID TYPE

Use API GL4 75W/80 gear oil. Use limited slip gear oil on vehicles with limited slip differential,.

## TROUBLE SHOOTING

See TROUBLE SHOOTING article in GENERAL INFORMATION.

## REMOVAL & INSTALLATION

***NOTE: For models with independent rear suspension, see FWD AXLE SHAFTS article for axle shaft overhaul.***

### AXLE SHAFT & BEARING

See 4WD REAR AXLE SHAFTS article in DRIVE AXLES.

### PROPELLER SHAFT

***NOTE: If propeller shaft is defective, replace as an assembly. If only center bearing is defective, disassemble propeller shaft and replace center bearing.***

**Removal - 1)** Remove rear exhaust pipe (if necessary). Remove front cover of rear differential mount (if equipped). Mark propeller shaft for installation reference.

**2)** Remove bolts attaching propeller shaft to pinion flange. Remove bolts attaching center bearing to body. Remove propeller shaft from transaxle. Plug opening at rear of extension housing.

**Disassembly - 1)** Mark front and rear propeller shaft for reassembly reference. Remove bolts attaching front and rear propeller shaft. Install companion flange in a soft-jawed vise. Remove self locking nut and washer.

**2)** Mark companion flange and rear propeller shaft for reassembly reference. Use appropriate press to remove companion flange from rear propeller shaft. Using a soft-faced hammer, drive rear propeller shaft from center bearing. DO NOT damage shaft threads.

**Reassembly -** Mount center bearing onto propeller shaft. Apply grease to both sides of washer and attach washer to center bearing end face. With reference marks aligned, install companion flange onto rear propeller shaft. Install washer and new self locking nut.

**Installation -** To install, reverse removal procedure. Tighten nut and bolts to specification. See TORQUE SPECIFICATIONS table at end of article.

### PINION FLANGE & OIL SEAL

**Removal -** Drain gear oil from differential. Raise and support rear of vehicle. Disconnect propeller shaft from pinion flange. Measure and record rotating torque of pinion shaft. Remove pinion nut. Remove pinion flange with puller. Remove oil seal.

**Installation -** Apply grease to oil seal lip. Install oil seal. Install pinion flange. Tighten flange nut until pinion shaft rotating torque is same as recorded before removal. Tighten pinion flange nut to specification. See TORQUE SPECIFICATIONS table at end of article. Stake lock nut. To complete installation, reverse removal procedure.

### DIFFERENTIAL ASSEMBLY

***NOTE: Dismount inner arm of trailing arm from body before removing and installing rear axle.***

**Removal & Installation - 1)** Raise and support rear of vehicle. Drain gear oil. Remove 2 upper shock mounting bolts. Remove wheel. Remove spring pins from inner DOJ and outer BJ. Completely lower trailing arm assembly. Remove outer BJ from spindle on trailing arm.

**2)** Remove inner DOJ from differential. Match mark and remove drive axle shafts. Remove propeller shaft. Plug opening in transaxle. Support differential assembly with a jack.

**3)** Remove 2 bolts at center of differential carrier. Remove 4 differential-to-bracket mounting bolts. Lower jack and remove differential assembly. To install, reverse removal procedure. Install NEW spring pins. Fill differential with gear oil.

## OVERHAUL

### DIFFERENTIAL ASSEMBLY

***NOTE: Manufacturer does not recommend overhauling limited slip differential assembly.***

**Disassembly - 1)** Remove rear cover and inspect differential before disassembly. Check gear tooth contact, drive gear-to-pinion backlash, ring gear runout and drive pinion rotating preload before disassembly.

***NOTE: Mark bearing side retainers and shim positions for reassembly reference. Left and right retainers are not interchangeable.***

**2)** Using Wrench (92560000), remove spindles. Remove rear differential cover. Mark right and left side bearing retainer for reassembly reference. Using puller and Adapter (398457700), remove side retainer and shims. Remove differential case assembly from carrier.

**3)** Remove side bearing races from differential case with puller. Remove side bearing from carrier housing. Remove ring gear. Unstake pinion shaft lock pin. Drive pin out from flange side. Remove pinion shaft, pinion gears, side gears and thrust washer. *See Fig. 2.*

**4)** Keep thrust washers, pinion gears and side gears in order for reassembly reference. Remove pinion nut. Remove pinion flange with puller. Press drive pinion from carrier. Remove rear bearing inner race, bearing spacer and adjusting washer.

**Cleaning & Inspection -** Wash all parts in solvent. Check gear teeth for cracks, scoring or excessive wear. Replace ring gear and drive pinion as a set, if necessary. Check bearings for wear or dragging during rotation. Check thrust washer contacting surface for wear. Replace parts as necessary.

**Reassembly & Adjustments - 1)** Assemble pinion gears, side gears and thrust washers in original positions in differential case. Fit pinion shaft to differential case aligning lock pin holes with holes in case.

**2)** Adjust clearance between differential case and back of side gear to .004-.008" (.10-.20 mm) by selecting proper thrust washer. Thrust washers are available in the following sizes: .030-.032" (.75-.80 mm), .032-.034" (.80-.85 mm), and .034-.036" (.85-.90 mm).

# 1991 DRIVE AXLES
# 4WD Differential (Cont.)

3) Install pinion shaft lock pin and lock in place on both sides. Apply gear oil to gear tooth surface and thrust surfaces and ensure gears rotate smoothly. Install ring gear on differential case. Install bolts and new lock washers.

***NOTE: Tighten ring gear bolts in a crisscross pattern while tapping bolt heads with a hammer.***

4) When replacing side bearings, measure bearing width by using a Weight Block (398227700). *See Fig. 1.* Rotate bearing several times before measuring. Standard bearing width is .787" (20 mm). If measurement varies greatly when rotating, replace bearing.

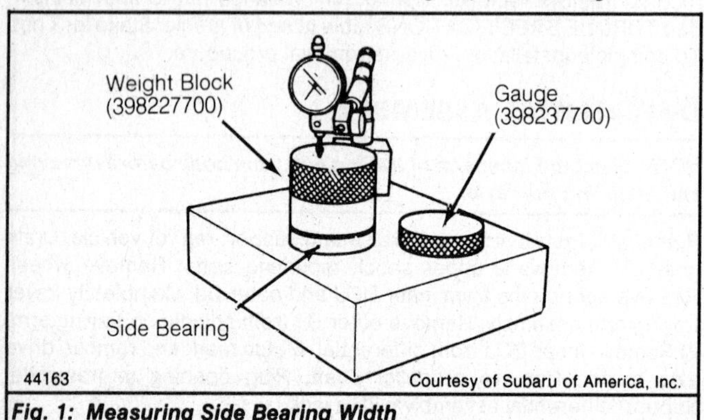


***Fig. 1: Measuring Side Bearing Width***

5) Press side bearing inner race onto differential case and bearing outer race into side bearing retainer. Install new oil seal on side bearing retainer. Apply grease to cavity between seal lips.

**Drive Pinion Bearing Preload Adjustment – 1)** Press front and rear bearing outer races into carrier. Install Dummy Shaft (398507702) with rear bearing and pinion depth washer into case. *See Fig. 3.*

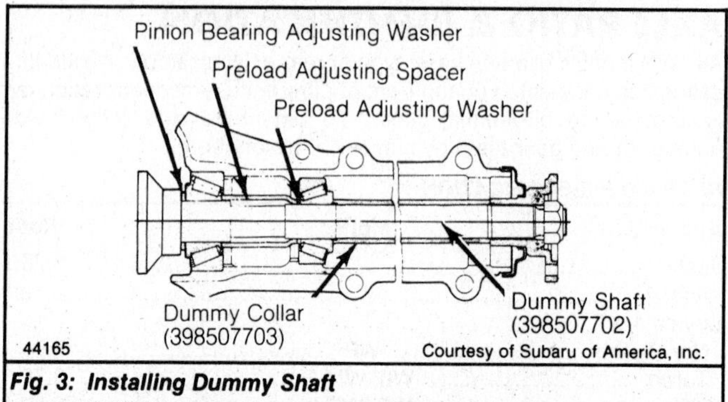


***Fig. 3: Installing Dummy Shaft***

2) Install preload adjusting spacer and washer, front bearing, Dummy Collar (398507703), companion flange, washer and nut onto dummy shaft. DO NOT install oil seal at this time. Rotate pinion by hand until it is seated.

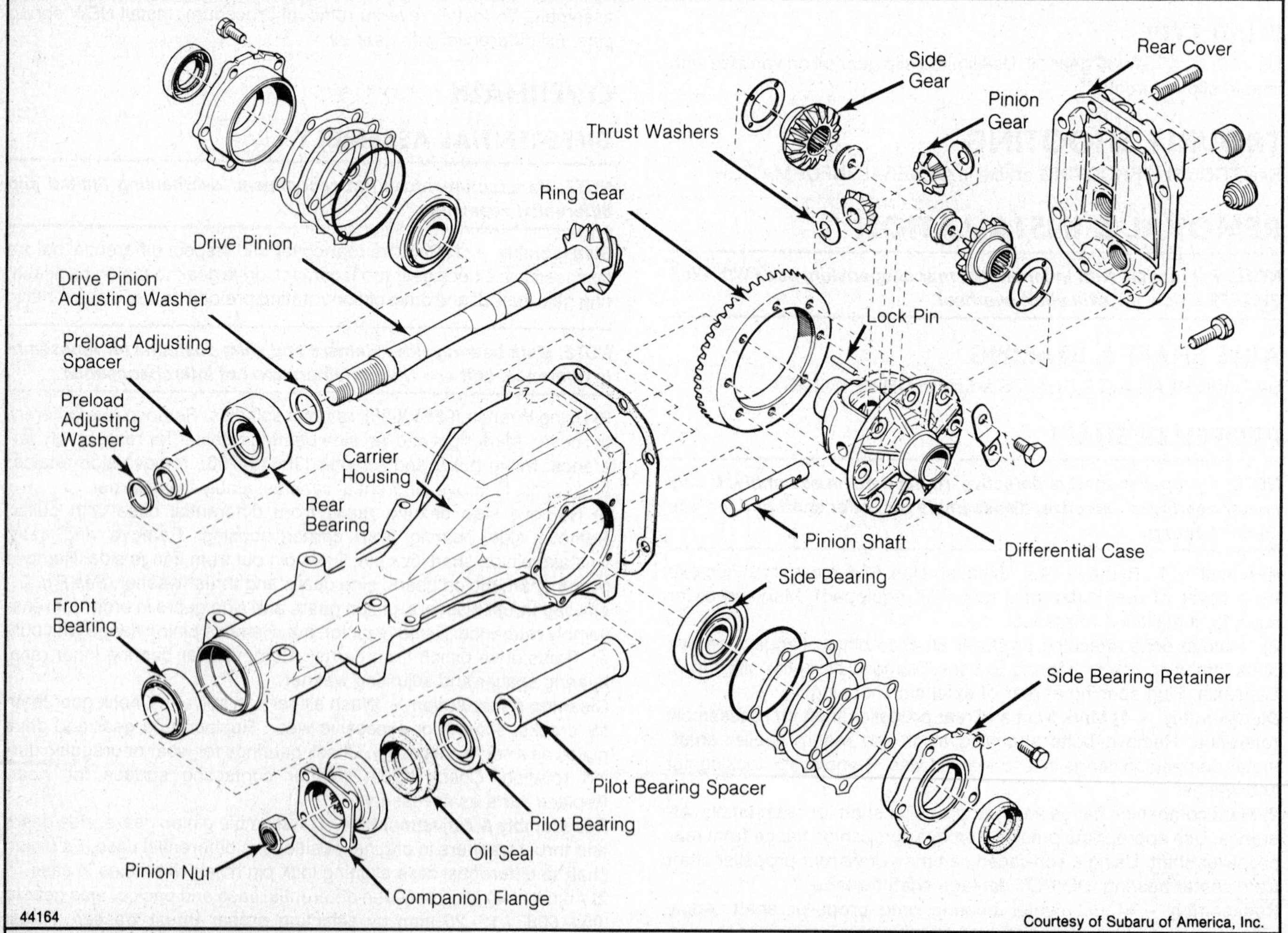

44164 Courtesy of Subaru of America, Inc.

***Fig. 2: Identifying 4WD Differential Components***

# 1991 DRIVE AXLES
# 4WD Differential (Cont.)

***NOTE: Do not exceed specified preload torque during preload adjustment.***

**3)** Using a torque wrench, check rotating torque of pinion shaft. Tighten pinion nut to specification. Using a spring scale, preload should be 4.4-6.4 lbs. (1.99-2.90 kg) with new bearings or 1.87-3.75 lbs. (.84-1.70 kg) with used bearings. If not, install correct washer and spacer to obtain proper preload.

**4)** Spacers are available in lengths of 2.213-2.252" (56.21-57.20 mm) in increments of .008" (.20 mm). Washers are available in thicknesses of .091-.102" (2.31-2.59 mm) in increments of .0008" (.020 mm).

**Drive Pinion Gear Installed Height – 1)** Leave dummy pinion shaft installed, and install Pinion Height Gauge (398507701). Using a feeler gauge, measure clearance (N) between end of pinion gear head and height gauge. *See Fig. 4.* Determine thickness of pinion height adjusting washer to be installed using the following formula.

***NOTE: Formula values are given in millimeters.***

**T = To + N - (H x .01) - .20**

**T = Thickness of adjusting washer needed.**
**To = Thickness of washer temporarily installed.**
**N = Clearance between gauge and dummy shaft.**
**H = Figure marked on drive pinion head.**

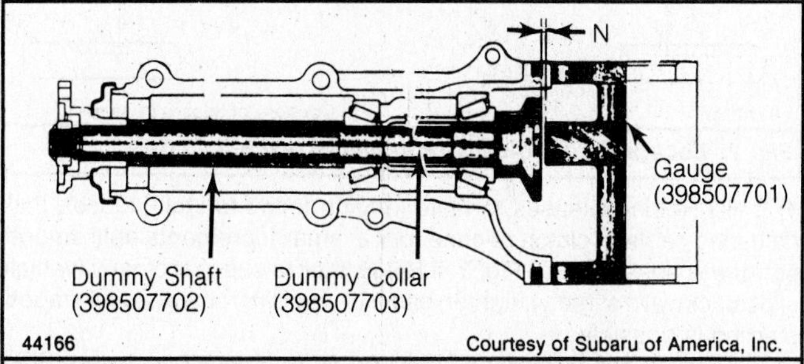


***Fig. 4: Measuring Drive Pinion Gear Installed Height***

**2)** After determining correct thickness of required pinion height adjusting washer, remove dummy shaft and height gauge. Adjusting washers are available in thicknesses of .1217-.1441" (3.091-3.660 mm), in .0012" (.030 mm). Install selected pinion height adjusting washer on drive pinion. Press rear bearing onto shaft.

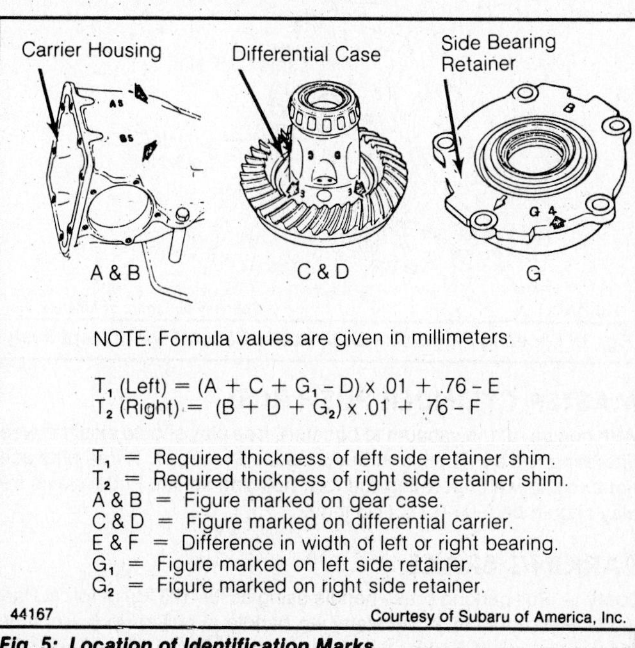


***Fig. 5: Location of Identification Marks***

**3)** Insert drive pinion into carrier housing. Install previously selected preload adjusting spacer, washer, oil seal, companion flange and pinion nut. Tighten pinion nut. Using a torque wrench, check pinion rotating preload and record.

**Side Bearing Preload – 1)** Determine proper thickness of left and right side retainer shims. *See Fig. 5.* If identification mark is not present, regard it as zero.

**2)** Install differential case assembly into carrier housing in reverse order of disassembly. Fit selected shims and "O" ring on side bearing retainer. On limited slip differential models, apply locking sealant to bolt threads. On all models, install side bearing retainers in carrier with arrow pointing toward uppermost bolt. *See Fig. 6.*

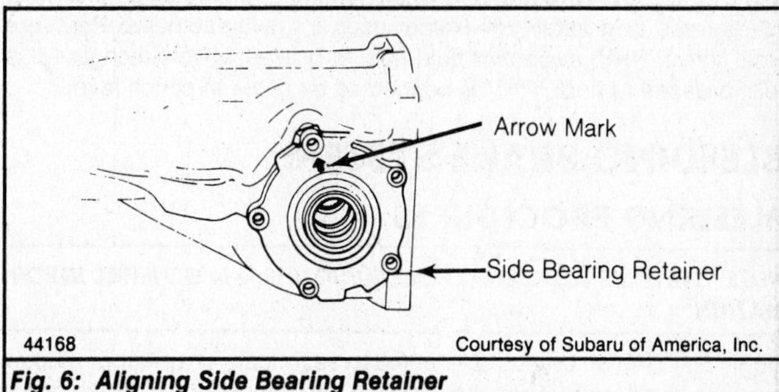


***Fig. 6: Aligning Side Bearing Retainer***

**3)** Measure ring gear-to-drive pinion backlash. If backlash is not .0039-.0079" (.099-.201 mm), correct by decreasing shim thickness on one side and increasing shim thickness on other side the same amount. Total shim thickness must be the same to maintain proper bearing preload. Using a torque wrench, measure pinion rotating torque. Compare reading with reading in step **3)** of DRIVE PINION GEAR INSTALLED HEIGHT procedure.

**4)** If reading does not increase .90-5.2 INCH lbs. (.10-.59 N.m), readjust side bearing retainer shims. Recheck all readings if shim thickness is changed. Check tooth contact of drive gear. If tooth contact is incorrect, recheck shim measurements.

## TORQUE SPECIFICATIONS

***TORQUE SPECIFICATIONS***

| Application | Ft. Lbs. (N.m) |
|---|---|
| Center Bearing Bolt | |
| Justy | 27-49 (37-67) |
| Legacy | 35-42 (47-57) |
| Loyale, XT & XT6 | 25-32 (34-44) |
| Front Carrier Mounting Nut | 33-40 (45-54) |
| Front Carrier Mounting Through Bolt | 51-58 (69-79) |
| Pinion Flange Nut | 123-145 (167-196) |
| Propeller Shaft Flange Bolt | 17-24 (23-33) |
| Propeller Shaft Self-Locking Nut | |
| Justy | 173-203 (235-275) |
| Legacy, Loyale, XT & XT6 | 181-217 (245-294) |
| Rear Carrier Mounting Bracket Bolt | 29-36 (39-49) |
| Rear Carrier Mounting Nut | 51-58 (69-79) |
| Rear Cover Bolt | 14-18 (19-25) |
| Ring Gear Bolt | 69-83 (94-113) |
| | **INCH Lbs. (N.m)** |
| Side Bearing Retaining Bolt | 80-106 (9-12) |

# 1991 BRAKES
# Disc & Drum

### Justy, Legacy, Loyale, XT, XT6

## DESCRIPTION & OPERATION

All models are equipped with front disc brakes. Rear brakes are either disc or drum. On Justy and Legacy, parking brake is cable actuated on rear drum brakes. On Loyale, XT and XT6, parking brake is cable actuated on front disc brakes.

M/T models (except Justy) are equipped with Hill-Holder system. Incorporated in the primary brake line from the master cylinder, Hill-Holder system permits easy uphill acceleration during take-off from a standing/stopped position. Hill-Holder is activated when both brake and clutch pedals are pressed when coming to a stop on an incline of 10 degrees or greater. Hill-Holder uses a gravity-actuated Pressure Hold Valve (PHV) to control fluid flow to brakes while clutch pedal is fully pressed to floor. PHV is connected by cable to clutch lever.

## BLEEDING BRAKE SYSTEM

### BLEEDING PROCEDURES

***NOTE: See HYDRAULIC BRAKE BLEEDING article in GENERAL INFORMATION.***

Begin bleeding on brakes connected to secondary chamber of master cylinder. Time interval between release and depression of brake pedal during bleeding should be 3-4 seconds. Open brake cylinder bleeder screw for 1-2 seconds on every pressure stroke.

***BRAKE LINE BLEEDING SEQUENCE***

| Application | Sequence |
|---|---|
| Justy | Longest Line First |
| Legacy | RF, LR, LF, RR |
| Loyale, XT & XT6 | LF, RR, RF, LR |

## ADJUSTMENTS

### BRAKE PEDAL FREE PLAY

**1)** Ensure brake operating rod free play is correct before proceeding. See MASTER CYLINDER PUSH ROD under ADJUSTMENTS.
**2)** Adjust brake pedal free play using stoplight switch. On Justy, adjust free play to .20-.43" (5-11 mm). On all others, adjust free play to .020-.098" (.51-2.49 mm). Tighten stoplight switch lock nut. *See Fig. 1.*

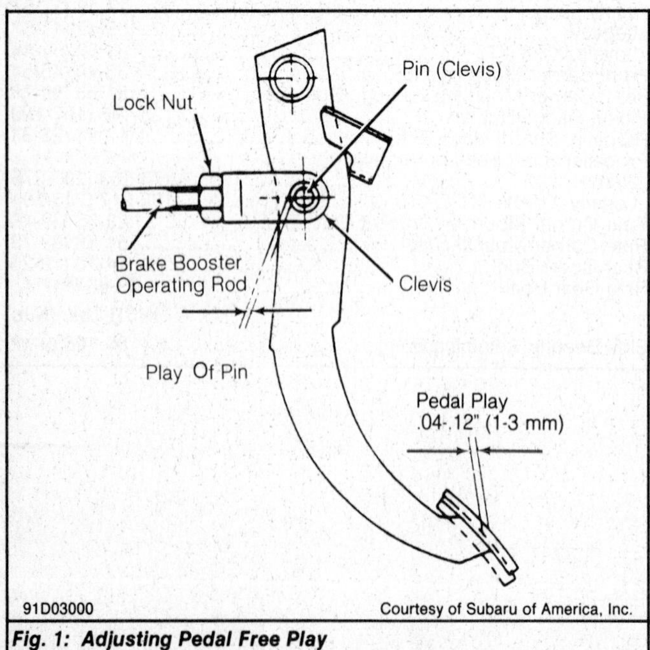


***Fig. 1: Adjusting Pedal Free Play***

### HILL-HOLDER BRAKE

**Except Justy – 1)** Before adjusting Hill-Holder PHV cable, ensure clutch pedal free play is within specification. Free play at clutch pedal should be .39-.79" (10-20 mm).
**2)** Free play at clutch fork should be .12-.16" (3-4 mm). If free play is not within specification, adjust clutch free play by turning adjusting nut on engine side of clutch cable release fork.
**3)** Check stopping and starting performance by activating Hill-Holder on an uphill road with more than 3 degree incline. If vehicle does not stop, tighten PHV cable at PHV. *See Fig. 2*

***NOTE: Hill-Holder may not activate on a very slight incline.***

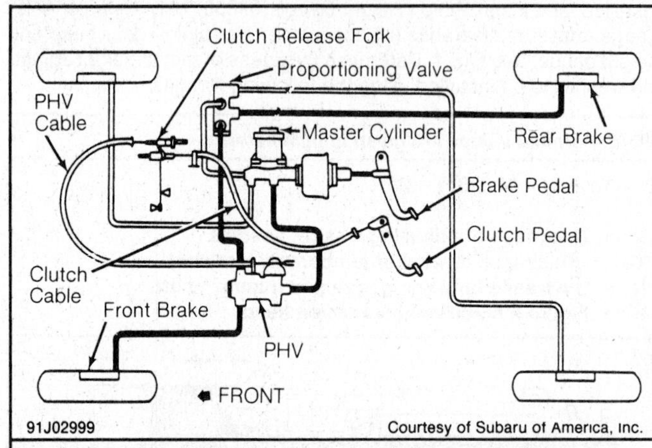


***Fig. 2: Locating Hill-Holder Components (except Justy)***

**4)** If Hill-Holder releases too late (engine tends to stall), loosen PHV adjusting cable at clutch release fork in small increments until smooth starting is possible. *See Fig. 3.* If Hill-Holder releases too early (vehicle slips backward slightly), tighten cable in small increments until smooth starting is possible.
**5)** To adjust Hill-Holder to apply on a slight incline, insert Shim (725807000) between side frame and PHV support bracket (raising front of PHV). Shims are .024" (.6 mm) thick and will increase PHV angle 1/2 degree. DO NOT raise front of PHV excessively. Never insert more than one shim at a time.

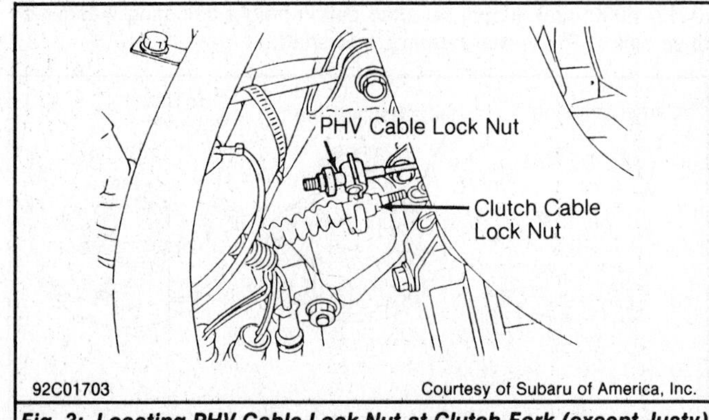


***Fig. 3: Locating PHV Cable Lock Nut at Clutch Fork (except Justy)***

### MASTER CYLINDER PUSH ROD

With engine off (no vacuum to booster), free play should exist between operating rod clevis pin and brake pedal. *See Fig. 1.* If free play does not exist, loosen operating rod lock nut, and adjust. Pedal clevis free play should be 0.04-0.12" (1-3 mm).

### PARKING BRAKE

**Justy** – Pull parking brake handle using 55 lbs. (25 kg) of force. Parking brake should lock wheels when handle is pulled up 6-7 notches (11 maximum). If parking brake does not lock wheels as specified,

# 1991 BRAKES
# Disc & Drum (Cont.)

raise vehicle and tighten parking brake cable until correct adjustment (6-7 notches) is obtained. Ensure wheels rotate freely with parking brake released.

**Legacy - 1)** Remove adjusting hole cover from rear wheel backing plate. Using flat blade screwdriver, turn brake adjusting screw star wheel until shoes make snug contact with drum surface of rotor and wheel will not turn. Back off adjusting screw star wheel 3-4 notches.
**2)** Turn wheel to ensure brake shoes do not drag. If shoes drag, back off shoe adjustment a few more notches. Install adjusting hole cover to rear wheel backing plate.
**3)** With service brakes properly adjusted, pull parking brake lever 3-5 notches. Raise vehicle on hoist. Loosen lock nut at parking brake cable equalizer. Turn adjusting nut until clearance is 0-.02" (0-.5 mm). *See Fig. 4*. Hold adjusting nut, and tighten lock nut.
**4)** Lower vehicle, but keep tires off ground. Release parking brake lever. Rotate front wheels and pull parking brake lever using 55 lbs. (25 kg) of force. Wheels should lock when handle is pulled up 3-4 notches. Readjust if needed.

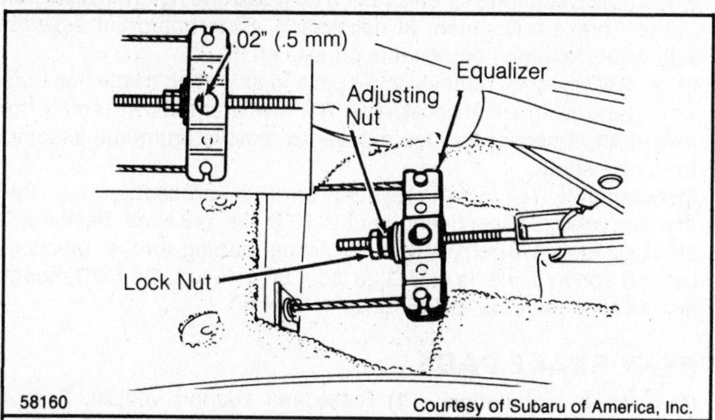


***Fig. 4: Adjusting Parking Brake (except Justy)***

**Loyale, XT & XT6 - 1)** With service brakes properly adjusted, pull parking brake lever 3-5 notches. Raise vehicle on hoist. Loosen lock nut at parking brake cable equalizer. Turn adjusting nut until clearance is 0-.02" (0-.5 mm). *See Fig. 4*. Hold adjusting nut, and tighten lock nut.
**2)** Lower vehicle, but keep tires off ground. Release parking brake lever. Rotate front wheels and pull parking brake lever using 55 lbs. (25 kg) of force. Wheels should lock when handle is pulled up 3-5 notches. Readjust if needed.

### REAR DRUM BRAKE SHOES

***NOTE: Rear brakes on Justy and 4WD models are self-adjusting.***

**Loyale & XT -** Raise and support vehicle. Turn adjuster wedge until wheel locks. Back off adjusting wedge 180 degrees. Clearance between drum and shoes should be .004-.006" (.10-.15 mm). Wheel should rotate easily by hand.

## TESTING

### POWER BRAKE UNIT

**1)** With engine off, depress brake pedal several times and hold pedal down. Start engine. Pedal should move slightly toward floor. Continue to hold brake pedal down and turn off engine.
**2)** Continue to hold brake pedal down longer than 30 seconds. Brake pedal height should not change. If pedal goes slowly downward, a vacuum leak exists in power brake system. Inspect brake vacuum check valve for proper operation. If check valve is okay, replace power brake unit.

## REMOVAL & INSTALLATION

### FRONT & REAR BRAKE CALIPER

**Removal - 1)** Raise and support vehicle. Remove wheel. Disconnect brake line from caliper, and plug openings. Remove parking brake cable from front caliper.
**2)** Remove brake caliper guide pin bolts from brake caliper support bracket. Remove caliper. DO NOT remove pads or support bracket unless rotor is being removed.
**Installation -** Apply silicone grease to guide pin, boot and guide pin bolt. Install caliper assembly, pads and parking brake cable. Install brake line. Bleed hydraulic system. See BLEEDING BRAKE SYSTEM.

### FRONT BRAKE PADS

***NOTE: DO NOT disconnect hydraulic line from caliper. DO NOT press on brake pedal after caliper has been removed.***

**Removal & Installation (Justy) - 1)** Raise and support vehicle. Remove wheel. Remove brake caliper from brake caliper support bracket on steering knuckle, and wire aside. Remove brake pads from caliper support bracket, noting positions of pad clips and shims.
**2)** Minimum pad thickness, including metal backing plate, is .295" (7.49 mm). Open caliper bleeder screw, and press piston into caliper. To install, reverse removal procedure. Before test driving vehicle, pump brake pedal a few times to push caliper piston against pads to set proper pad-to-rotor clearance. Recheck brake fluid in reservoir.
**Removal (Except Justy) -** Raise and support vehicle. Remove wheel. Remove parking brake cable from caliper. Remove lower caliper guide pin bolt. Rotate caliper body up and away from disc. Remove pads, clips and shims from caliper support bracket. Minimum pad thickness, including metal backing plate, is .295" (7.49 mm).
**Installation - 1)** Using piston wrench, turn piston clockwise to seat piston in caliper bore and position caliper notches to align with raised tab on installed pads. *See Fig. 5*. After turning and seating piston, check piston boot for twist.
**2)** Install shim on outer pad only (if required). Install pad clips to support bracket, and install pads. Rotate caliper body down, aligning piston notches with pad tabs. Install lower caliper guide pin bolt. Reconnect parking brake cable. Depress brake pedal several times to set pad-to-rotor clearance.

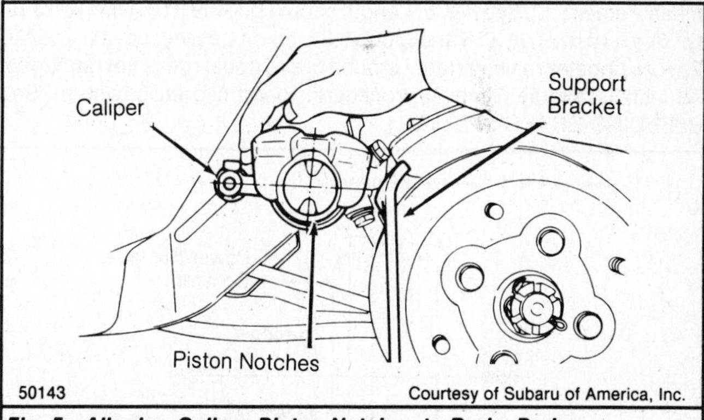


***Fig. 5: Aligning Caliper Piston Notches to Brake Pads***

### FRONT ROTOR

**Removal - 1)** Raise and support vehicle. Remove wheel. Remove caliper assembly, and wire aside. Disconnecting brake line or parking brake cable from caliper is not necessary. Remove caliper support bracket with attached disc pads from steering knuckle.
**2)** Remove cotter pin and nut from axle shaft. On Justy, remove center piece wedge using a screwdriver. Lightly tap screwdriver into center piece slot to spread wedge, and remove it from axle.
**3)** On all models, remove rotor and hub assembly from axle shaft using a puller. Separate rotor from hub.
**Installation - 1)** To install, reverse removal procedure. Tighten hub-to-rotor bolts evenly and to specification. See TORQUE SPECIFICATIONS table at end of article.
**2)** On Justy, tighten wheel bearing/axle nut to 130 ft. lbs. (177 N.m). On all other models, tighten axle shaft nut to 145 ft. lbs. (196 N.m). Depress brake pedal several times to seat pads.

# 1991 BRAKES
# Disc & Drum (Cont.)

## HILL-HOLDER PRESSURE HOLD VALVE (PHV)

**Removal (Except Justy)** – Siphon brake fluid from master cylinder. Disconnect PHV adjusting cable at PHV. *See Fig. 2.* Disconnect brake lines from PHV. Remove PHV from support bracket. Plug all lines and fittings.

**Inspection** – Inspect boots of PHV cable for damage and corrosion. Inspect return spring for damage and corrosion. Listen for internal check ball rolling sound when PHV valve is tilted. Inspect PHV lever for smooth rotation operation.

***NOTE: If PHV is defective, replace complete PHV assembly. DO NOT disassemble PHV; PHV is not rebuildable.***

**Installation** – To install, reverse removal procedure. Apply grease to hook of return spring, cable end portion of lever and cable end portion of clutch release fork. Bleed hydraulic system, and adjust PHV cable. See BLEEDING BRAKE SYSTEM. See HILL-HOLDER BRAKE under ADJUSTMENTS.

## MASTER CYLINDER

**Removal & Installation** – Siphon brake fluid from reservoir. Disconnect warning light fluid level connection. Remove hydraulic lines. Remove master cylinder from power brake unit. To install, reverse removal procedure. Bleed hydraulic system. See BLEEDING BRAKE SYSTEM.

## POWER BRAKE UNIT

**Removal – 1)** From inside vehicle, remove brake pedal clevis pin snap pin and clevis pin. Remove power brake retaining nuts from firewall inside vehicle. Remove master cylinder. See MASTER CYLINDER under REMOVAL & INSTALLATION.

**2)** Disconnect vacuum hose at power brake unit. Remove power brake unit without damaging hydraulic lines.

**Installation** – Check booster-to-master cylinder push rod length at measurement "L". *See Fig. 6.* Length should be .409" (10.4 mm) on Justy, .394" (10 mm) on XT6 and .366" (9.3 mm) on Legacy, Loyale and XT. Ensure booster resin material around brake pedal rod is not damaged. To install, reverse removal procedure. Bleed hydraulic system. See BLEEDING BRAKE SYSTEM.

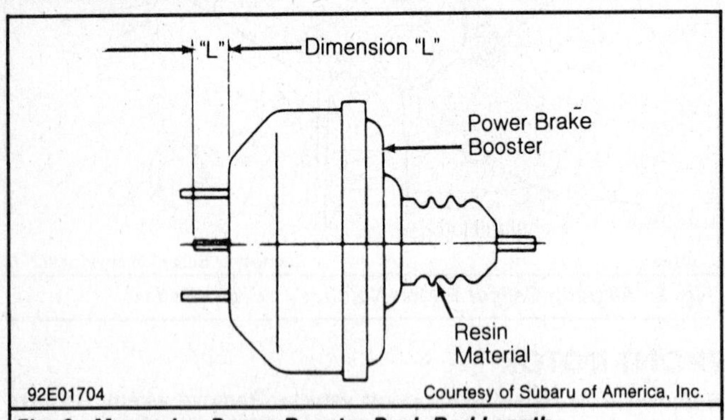


***Fig. 6: Measuring Power Booster Push Rod Length***

## REAR BRAKE DRUM

**Removal (Justy) – 1)** Raise and support vehicle. Remove wheel. On 2WD models, remove hub dust cap and nut from axle shaft. Remove center piece wedge using a screwdriver. Lightly tap screwdriver into center piece slot to spread wedge, and remove it from axle.

**2)** Loosen parking brake cable. Loosen brake shoe adjustment by inserting a screwdriver through backing plate access hole to push adjuster lever to initial position. *See Fig. 7.* Slide hub/drum assembly with wheel bearing components off axle shaft.

**Installation** – To install, reverse removal procedure. On 2WD models, tighten wheel bearing nut to 29 ft. lbs. (39 N.m). Back nut off, and then tighten nut until hub rotating starting torque, measured using a spring scale, is 3.1-4.4 lbs. (1.4-2.0 kg). On 4WD models, tighten axle nut to 108 ft. lbs. (147 N.m).

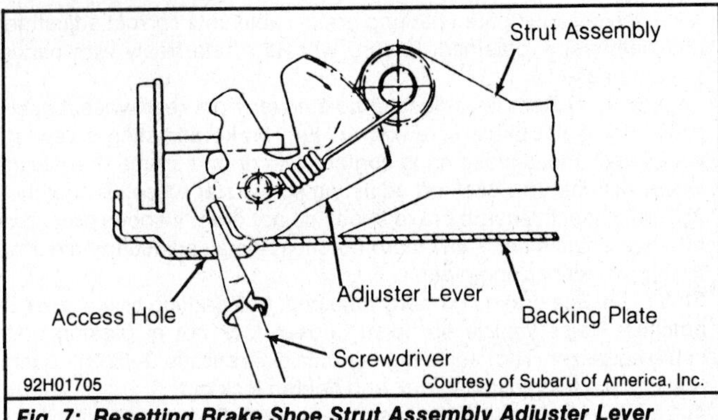


***Fig. 7: Resetting Brake Shoe Strut Assembly Adjuster Lever (Justy)***

**Removal (Loyale & XT) – 1)** Raise and support vehicle. Remove wheel. On 2WD models, remove hub dust cap and nut from axle shaft. Loosen brake adjustment (if necessary). Slide hub/drum assembly with wheel bearing components off axle shaft.

**2)** On 4WD models, remove cotter pin and axle shaft castle nut. Loosen brake adjustment (if necessary). Remove drum/hub assembly from axle shaft. If necessary, use a puller to remove drum/hub assembly from axle shaft.

**Installation** – To install, reverse removal procedure. On 2WD models, tighten wheel bearing nut to 36 ft. lbs. (49 N.m). Back nut off approximately 1/8 turn until hub rotating starting torque, measured using a spring scale, is 1.87-3.20 lbs. (.85-1.45 kg). On 4WD models, tighten axle shaft nut to 145 ft. lbs. (196 N.m).

## REAR BRAKE PADS

**Removal & Installation – 1)** Raise and support vehicle. Remove wheel. Remove lower guide pin bolt. Rotate caliper upward, and wire aside. Remove brake pads from support bracket, noting positions of shims and clips.

**2)** Minimum pad thickness, including metal backing plate, is .315" (8 mm) on XT6 and .256" (6.5 mm) on all others. To install, reverse removal procedure. Open caliper bleeder screw and press piston back into caliper bore. Bleed brake system (if necessary). See BLEEDING BRAKE SYSTEM.

## REAR BRAKE ROTOR

**Removal & Installation (Legacy) – 1)** Raise and support vehicle. Remove wheel. Remove rear caliper from support bracket, and wire aside. Remove pads and support bracket from rear axle housing. Pull rotor from hub (outboard type rotor).

**2)** To remove disc rotor from hub, loosen parking brake shoe adjustment by inserting a screwdriver through backing plate access hole to turn adjusting star wheel. Remove disc rotor/drum from hub. To install, reverse removal procedure. Tighten bolts to specification. See TORQUE SPECIFICATIONS table at end of article.

**Removal & Installation (2WD Except Legacy) – 1)** Raise and support vehicle. Remove wheel. Remove caliper from support bracket, and wire aside. Remove pads and support bracket from rear axle housing. Remove hub dust cap and nut from rear axle shaft. Slide hub/rotor assembly with wheel bearing components off axle shaft.

**2)** To install, reverse removal procedure. Tighten wheel bearing nut to 36 ft. lbs. (49 N.m). Back nut off approximately 1/8 turn until hub rotating starting torque, measured using a spring scale, is 1.87-3.20 lbs. (.85-1.45 kg). Bend over lock washer and install dust cap.

**Removal & Installation (4WD Except Legacy)** – Raise and support vehicle. Remove wheel. Remove caliper from support bracket, and wire aside. Remove pads and support bracket from rear axle housing. Remove hub/rotor assembly from axle shaft using puller. To install, reverse removal procedure. Tighten bolts to specification. See TORQUE SPECIFICATIONS table at end of article.

## REAR BRAKE SHOES

**Removal (Justy) – 1)** Remove brake drum. See REAR BRAKE DRUM under REMOVAL & INSTALLATION. To aid in removing brake drum, insert a screwdriver through backplate access hole to push strut assembly adjuster lever to initial position. *See Fig. 7*.

**2)** Remove hold-down spring clips and strut assembly springs to release shoe tension. Remove lower return spring from shoes. Remove parking brake arm from shoe. Remove brake shoes.

**Installation** - Ensure strut assembly is not damaged or worn. Ensure yellow strut assembly is on right side of vehicle and white strut assembly is on left side. Preset strut assembly adjuster to 3.78" (96 mm). *See Fig. 8*. To install, reverse removal procedure. *See Fig. 9*.

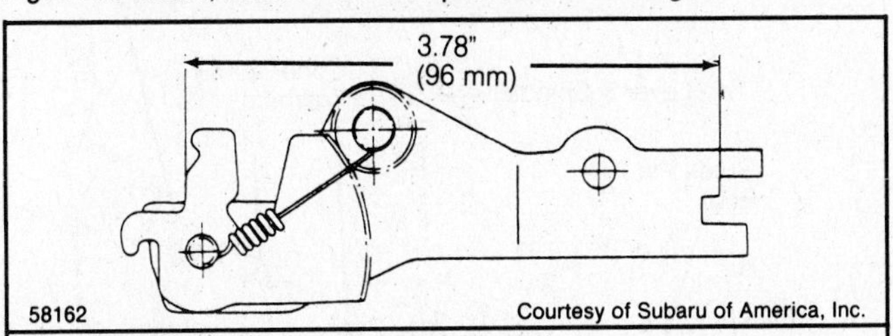


***Fig. 8: Presetting Brake Shoe Strut Assembly Adjuster Lever (Justy)***

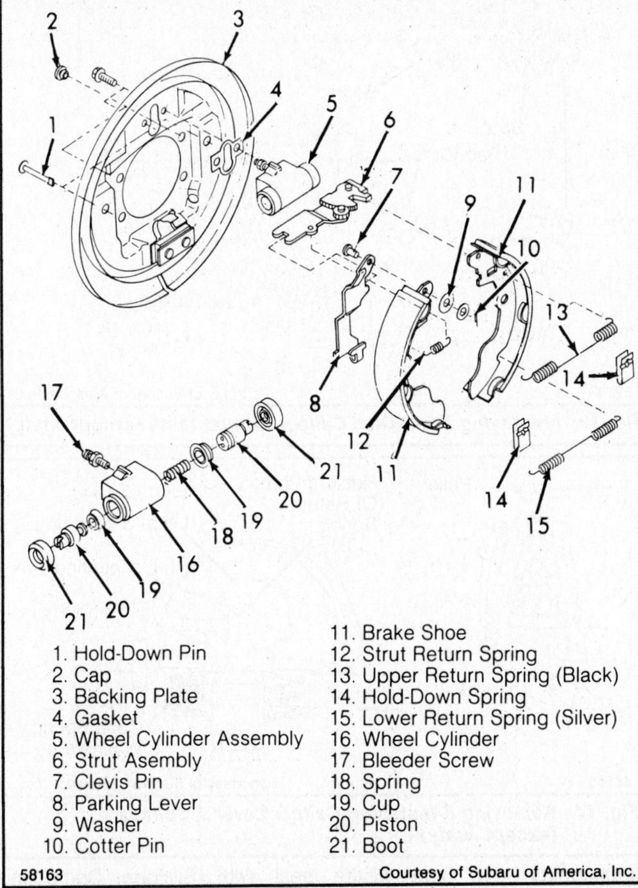


***Fig. 9: Identifying Rear Drum Brake Components (Justy)***

**Removal & Installation (Legacy)** - **1)** Remove rear caliper from support, and wire aside. To remove disc rotor from hub, loosen parking brake shoe adjustment by inserting a screwdriver through backing plate access hole to turn adjusting star wheel. Remove disc rotor/drum from hub.

**2)** Remove front shoe return springs and shoe hold-down spring. Remove center strut and spring from between shoes. Remove adjuster star wheel assembly. Remove rear shoe return springs and shoe hold-down spring. Remove parking brake cable from lever. Remove lever from shoe. To install, reverse removal procedure. Adjust parking brake. See PARKING BRAKE under ADJUSTMENTS.

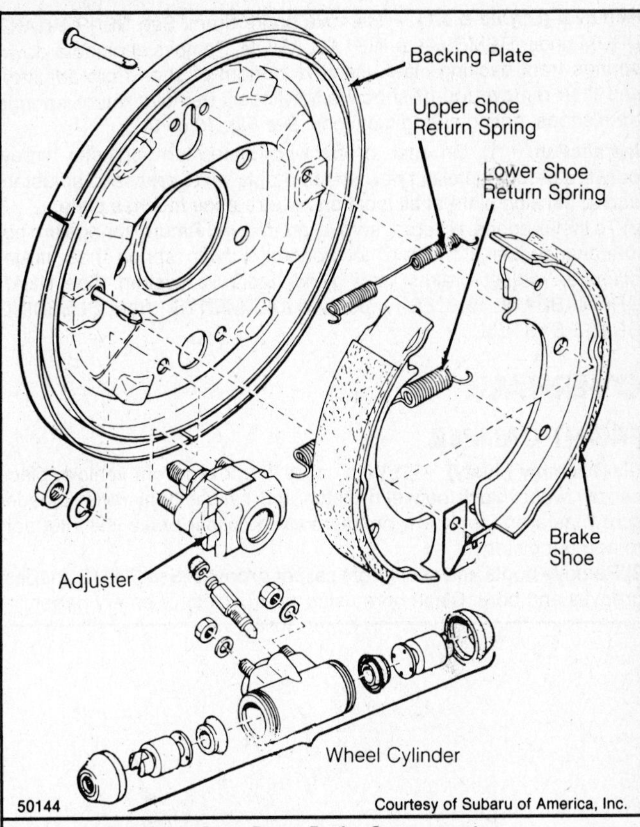


***Fig. 10: Identifying Rear Drum Brake Components (Loyale & XT - 2WD)***

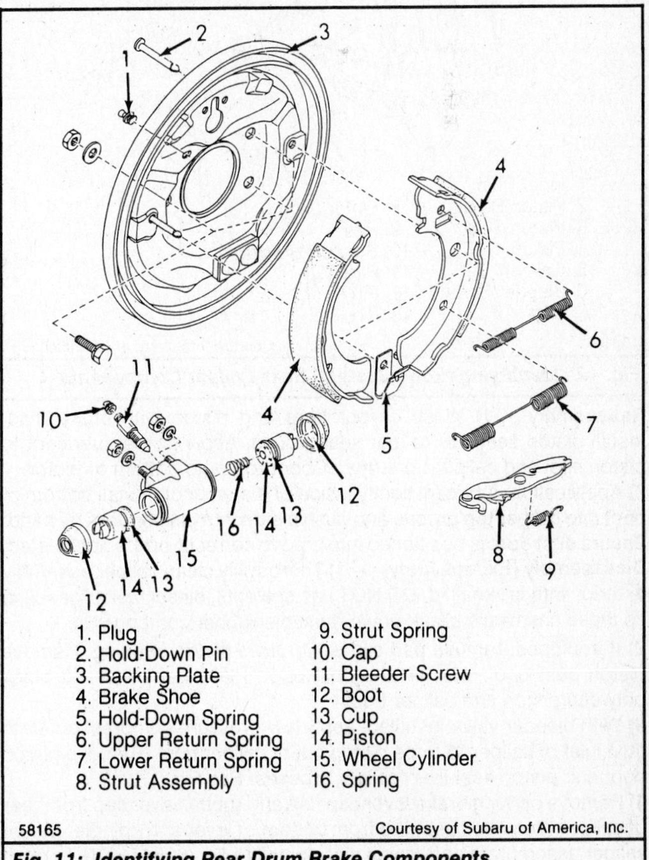


***Fig. 11: Identifying Rear Drum Brake Components (Loyale & XT - 4WD)***

**Removal (Loyale & XT)** – Remove brake drum. See REAR BRAKE DRUM under REMOVAL & INSTALLATION. Remove shoe hold-down springs from backing plate. Remove bottom of shoe from adjuster, and then remove top of shoe from cylinder. Remove return springs from shoes, noting spring locations. *See Fig. 10 or 11.*

**Installation** – **1)** On rear of backing plate, turn adjuster screw outward before installing new shoes. Apply white grease to adjusters and to backing plate at all locations where shoe touches plate.

**2)** To install shoes, reverse removal procedure. Return springs are not interchangeable from top to bottom. Lower spring has larger diameter. Adjust brakes, and bleed hydraulic system. See REAR DRUM BRAKE SHOES under ADJUSTMENTS. See BLEEDING BRAKE SYSTEM.

## OVERHAUL

### FRONT CALIPER

**Disassembly (Justy)** – **1)** With caliper removed from vehicle, place narrow wood block between piston and caliper body. With bleeder screw installed, apply low-pressure air to caliper brake line inlet port to pop out piston.

**2)** Remove boots and seals from caliper grooves. *See Fig. 12.* Inspect grooves and bore. Clean bore using crocus cloth or emery paper.

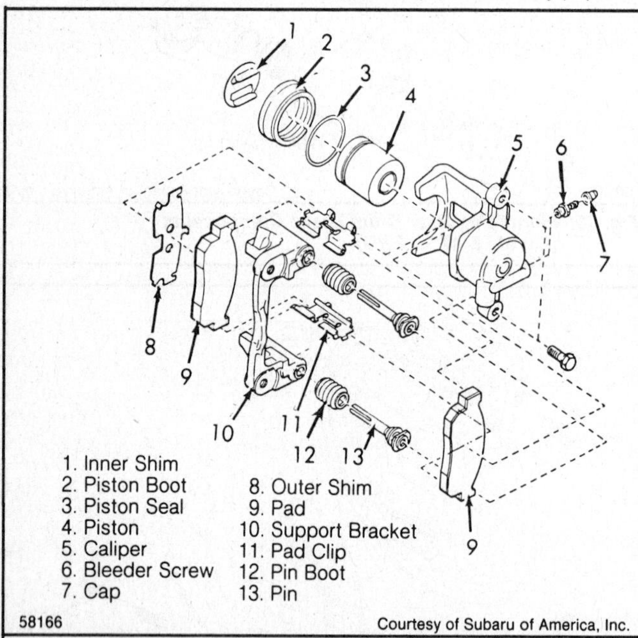


*Fig. 12: Identifying Front (Justy) & Rear Caliper Components*

**Reassembly** – **1)** Wash caliper bore and piston with brake fluid. Install piston seal into caliper seal groove. Apply caliper lubricant to piston seal and caliper bore. Install boot top onto bottom of piston.

**2)** Apply caliper lubricant lightly inside of piston boot. Install bottom of boot into caliper top groove and push piston into caliper bore by hand. Ensure dust boot is positioned into groove correctly and is not twisted.

**Disassembly (Except Justy)** – **1)** Thoroughly clean caliper assembly exterior with brake fluid. DO NOT use solvents, diesel fuel or gasoline as these chemicals break down reusable rubber components.

**2)** If equipped, remove pad clip (shim) from piston opening. Remove piston dust boot retainer and dust boot. Place narrow wood block between piston and caliper body.

**3)** With bleeder valve installed, apply low pressure compressed air to fluid inlet of caliper to force piston out of caliper bore. Remove piston boot and piston seal from caliper grooves. *See Fig. 13.*

**4)** Remove parking brake lever cap ring and rubber lever cap from rear of caliper. Remove snap ring from bottom of lever and spindle. Mount caliper assembly in soft-jawed vise. Install Puller (925471000) to push down on spring washer to release cone spring tension. *See Fig. 14.*

**5)** With spring tension released, pull out lever and spindle. Remove puller, and remove connecting link, return spring, spindle and cone spring.

***NOTE: When overhauling caliper, DO NOT remove mounting bracket. Loosen or remove mounting bracket only if mounting bracket is being replaced.***

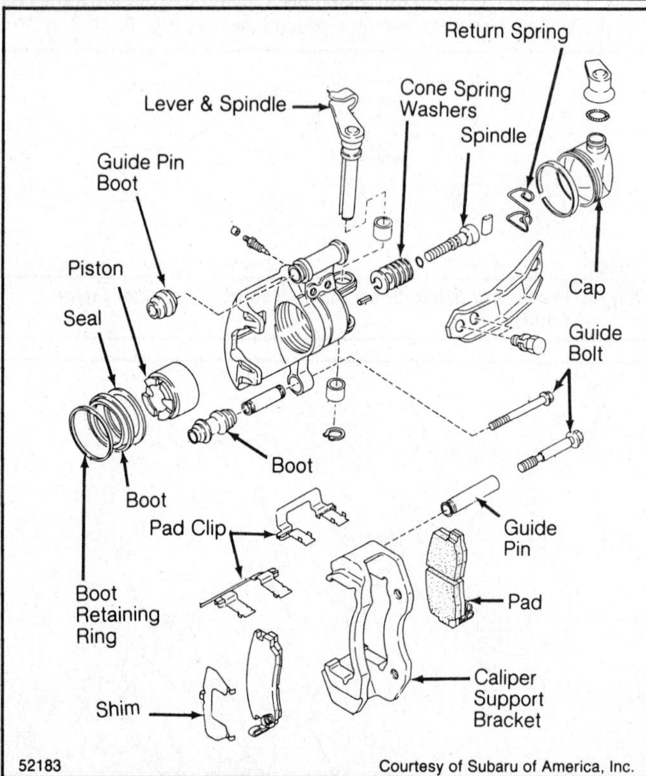


*Fig. 13: Identifying Front Disc Caliper Components (except Justy)*

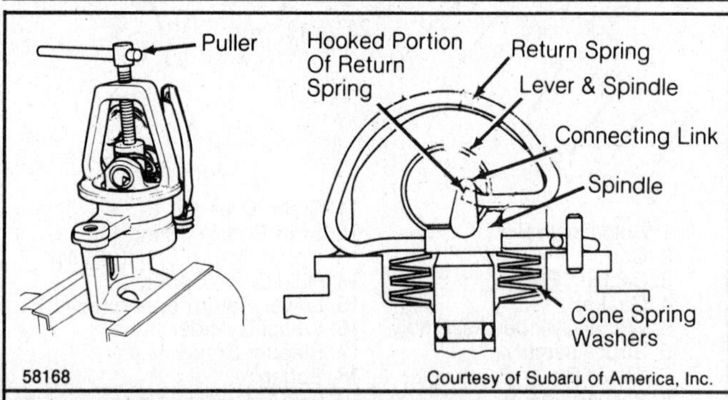


*Fig. 14: Removing & Installing Caliper Lever & Spindle (except Justy)*

**Reassembly** – **1)** Coat piston seal with Silicone Compound (725191050), and install into caliper groove. Coat piston, inside of piston boot and caliper bore with brake fluid. Insert piston into caliper bore. Using hand pressure, push piston inward until bottomed. Install boot and boot retainer.

**2)** Install cone spring washers to spindle in order. *See Fig. 14.* Position Adapter Sleeve (925600000) onto spindle, and install "O" ring seal to spindle. *See Fig. 15.* Lightly coat spindle shaft spline and "O" ring with silicone grease.

**3)** Install spindle with attached spring washers into caliper, and compress using Puller (925471000). Lubricate and install connecting link to spindle (thick side toward spindle head slot). *See Fig. 14.*

**4)** Install lever and spindle assembly. Ensure hooked portion of return spring is installed into groove of lever and spindle. Install snap ring at end of lever and spindle.

# 1991 BRAKES
# Disc & Drum (Cont.)

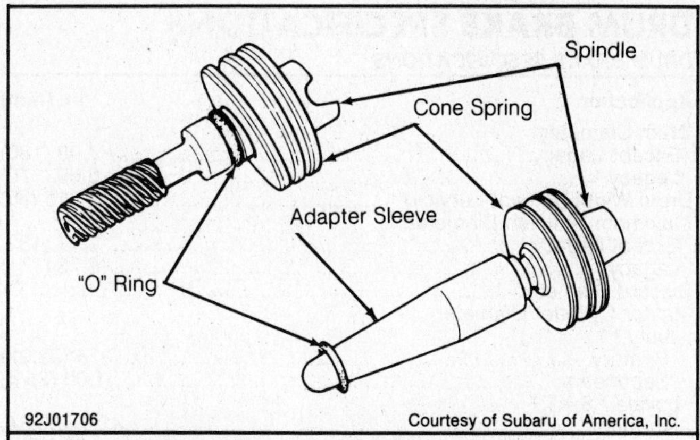


*Fig. 15: Installing Spindle "O" Ring Using Adapter Sleeve (except Justy)*

**5)** Remove puller. Install lever cap and cap retainer ring. Clean holes for guide pins in caliper body. Evenly tap new guide pin boots into caliper hole. *See Fig. 13*. Ensure boot is not damaged.

***NOTE: Always replace guide pin boot with a new one.***

## HILL-HOLDER PRESSURE HOLD VALVE (PHV)

Manufacturer does not recommend overhaul of this unit. Replace as complete assembly.

## MASTER CYLINDER

**Disassembly - 1)** Remove warning light level indicators and filters from reservoir, and siphon fluid. Push primary piston into cylinder bore, and remove stop bolt and/or primary piston circlip.

**2)** Remove stop washer, gasket, primary and secondary piston assemblies. Remove check valve plug and valve assembly.

***NOTE: DO NOT disassemble piston assemblies. Piston cup replacement requires replacement of piston assemblies. Removal of fluid reservoir requires installation of new reservoir and gaskets.***

**Cleaning & Inspection -** Clean all components in brake fluid. Inspect cylinder bore for smoothness and roundness. Replace cylinder if scored, corroded or out of round. DO NOT hone cylinder. Piston-to-cylinder clearance should not exceed .004" (.10 mm).

**Reassembly -** To reassemble master cylinder, reverse disassembly procedure. Bleed brake system. See BLEEDING BRAKE SYSTEM.

## POWER BRAKE UNIT

Manufacturer does not recommend overhaul of this unit. Replace as complete assembly.

## REAR CALIPER

**Disassembly - 1)** If equipped, remove pad clip (shim) from piston opening. Place narrow wood block between piston and caliper body.

**2)** With bleeder screw installed, apply low-pressure compressed air to fluid hose inlet of caliper to force piston out of caliper bore. Remove piston boot and piston seal from caliper grooves. *See Fig. 12*.

**Reassembly - 1)** Wash caliper bore and piston with brake fluid. Install piston seal into caliper seal groove, ensuring seal is not twisted. Apply caliper lubricant to piston seal and caliper bore. Install boot top onto bottom of piston.

**2)** Apply caliper lubricant lightly inside of piston boot. Install bottom of boot into caliper top groove and push piston into caliper bore by hand. Ensure dust boot is positioned into groove correctly and is not twisted.

## REAR WHEEL CYLINDER

**Disassembly -** Remove end cap boots, pistons with cups and spring. *See Fig. 9, 10 or 11*. DO NOT separate rubber cup seal from piston unless replacement is available.

**Cleaning & Inspection -** Clean all parts in brake fluid only. If cylinder is out of round, burred or corroded, replace cylinder as an assembly. DO NOT hone.

**Reassembly -** To reassemble, reverse disassembly procedure. Ensure piston cup is not installed on piston in reverse direction.

# TORQUE SPECIFICATIONS

***TORQUE SPECIFICATIONS***

| Application | Ft. Lbs. (N.m) |
|---|---|
| Backing Plate Mounting Bolts | |
| Except Justy | 34-43 (46-58) |
| Justy | 14-22 (19-30) |
| Booster Mounting Nut | 9-17 (12-23) |
| Brake Line-To-Caliper | 12-14 (16-19) |
| Brake Line-To-Master Cylinder | 10-13 (14-18) |
| Brake Line-To-Wheel Cylinder | 10-13 (14-18) |
| Caliper Guide Pin (Front) | 33-40 (45-54) |
| Caliper Pin Bolt | |
| Except Justy | 23-30 (31-41) |
| Justy | 16-23 (22-31) |
| Caliper-To-Support Bolt (Rear) | 16-23 (22-31) |
| Hub-To-Rotor Bolt | 33-42 (45-57) |
| Master Cylinder Mounting Nut | 7-13 (10-18) |
| Support Bracket Mounting Bolts | |
| Front | 36-51 (49-69) |
| Rear | 34-43 (46-58) |
| Wheel Bearing Nut | |
| Front | |
| Except Justy | 145 (196) |
| Justy | 131 (177) |
| Rear | |
| 2WD | |
| Except Legacy | [1] |
| Legacy | 123-152 (167-206) |
| 4WD | |
| Justy | 108 (147) |
| Legacy | 123-152 (167-206) |
| Loyale, XT & XT6 | 145 (196) |
| Wheel Lug Nut | 58-72 (79-98) |
| | **INCH Lbs. (N.m)** |
| Master Cylinder Stop Bolt | 12-24 (1.4-2.7) |

[1] - See REAR BRAKE DRUM or REAR BRAKE ROTOR under REMOVAL & INSTALLATION.

# 1991 BRAKES
# Disc & Drum (Cont.)

## DISC BRAKE SPECIFICATIONS

*DISC BRAKE SPECIFICATIONS*

| Application | In. (mm) |
|---|---|
| Disc Diameter | |
| Justy | 8.35 (212) |
| Legacy, Loyale & XT | |
| Front | 9.53 (242) |
| Rear | 8.90 (226) |
| XT6 | 10.31 (262) |
| Lateral Runout | |
| Except Justy | .004 (.10) |
| Justy | .006 (.15) |
| Parallelism | [1] |
| Original Thickness | |
| Justy | .71 (18) |
| Legacy, Loyale & XT | |
| Front | .71 (18) |
| Rear | .39 (10) |
| XT6 | .39 (10) |
| Minimum Refinish Thickness | |
| Justy | .61 (15.5) |
| Legacy, Loyale & XT | |
| Front | .63 (16) |
| Rear | .335 (8.5) |
| XT6 | .335 (8.5) |
| Discard Thickness | [1] |
| Master Cylinder Diameter | |
| Justy [2] | |
| Primary | .875 (22.22) |
| Secondary | 1.00 (25.4) |
| Loyale [2] & XT [2] | |
| Primary | .8126 (20.64) |
| Secondary | 1.00 (25.4) |
| XT6 [2] | |
| Primary & Secondary | .937 (23.81) |
| Legacy | |
| Primary & Secondary (With ABS) | 1.059 (26.9) |
| Primary & Secondary (Without ABS) | 1.00 (25.4) |

[1] – Information is not available from manufacturer.
[2] – Dual master cylinder.

## DRUM BRAKE SPECIFICATIONS

*DRUM BRAKE SPECIFICATIONS*

| Application | In. (mm) |
|---|---|
| Drum Diameter | |
| Except Legacy | 7.09 (180) |
| Legacy [1] | 6.69 (170) |
| Drum Width (Except Legacy) | 1.18 (30) |
| Maximum Refinish Diameter | |
| Except Legacy | 7.17 (182) |
| Legacy [1] | 6.73 (171) |
| Discard Diameter | [2] |
| Master Cylinder Diameter | |
| Justy [3] | |
| Primary | .875 (22.22) |
| Secondary | 1.00 (25.4) |
| Loyale [3] & XT [3] | |
| Primary | .8126 (20.64) |
| Secondary | 1.00 (25.4) |
| Wheel Cylinder Diameter | |
| Justy | .750 (19.05) |
| Loyale & XT | .687 (17.45) |

[1] – Legacy has parking brake drum inside of rear disc.
[2] – Any diameter greater than maximum refinish diameter.
[3] – Dual master cylinder.

## Legacy

## DESCRIPTION

Anti-Lock Brake System (ABS) is designed to prevent wheel lock-up during heavy braking. Reducing chance of wheel lock-up allows driver to maintain better steering control of the vehicle. ABS system consists of 4 wheel speed sensors, 4 tone rings, ABS Electronic Control Unit (ECU), hydraulic control unit, "G" sensor (on 4WD models) and "ABS" warning light. *See Fig. 1.*

***NOTE: For more information on brake system, see DISC & DRUM article in BRAKES.***

## OPERATION

As vehicle is driven, each wheel speed sensor sends an AC signal to ABS ECU. As brake pedal is depressed, ABS ECU starts to monitor vehicle rate of deceleration. If rate of deceleration is greater than preprogrammed amount, ABS ECU signals hydraulic control unit solenoid valves to regulate brake hydraulic pressure. Solenoid valves increase or decrease hydraulic pressure to each front wheel and/or to both rear wheels. This action will slow each wheel at a preprogrammed rate to prevent wheel lock-up, allowing driver to maintain steering control.

If ABS system malfunction occurs, "ABS" warning light will come on in instrument cluster panel. ABS ECU will then deactivate ABS system, leaving conventional braking system intact. ABS ECU also has ability to self-diagnose ABS system during each ignition cycle (OFF-ON-OFF). If an ABS system fault has been detected, ABS ECU will store a trouble code to assist technician in diagnosing ABS system.

***CAUTION: See ANTI-LOCK BRAKE SAFETY PRECAUTIONS article in GENERAL INFORMATION.***

## BLEEDING BRAKE SYSTEM

***NOTE: Use DOT 3 or 4 brake fluid only. When bleeding secondary air bleeders, cone screw must be replaced by bleeder screw.***

## ABS BLEEDING PROCEDURES

1) Disconnect negative battery terminal. Using conventional manual brake bleeding method (using tubing and bottle, with foot pressure on

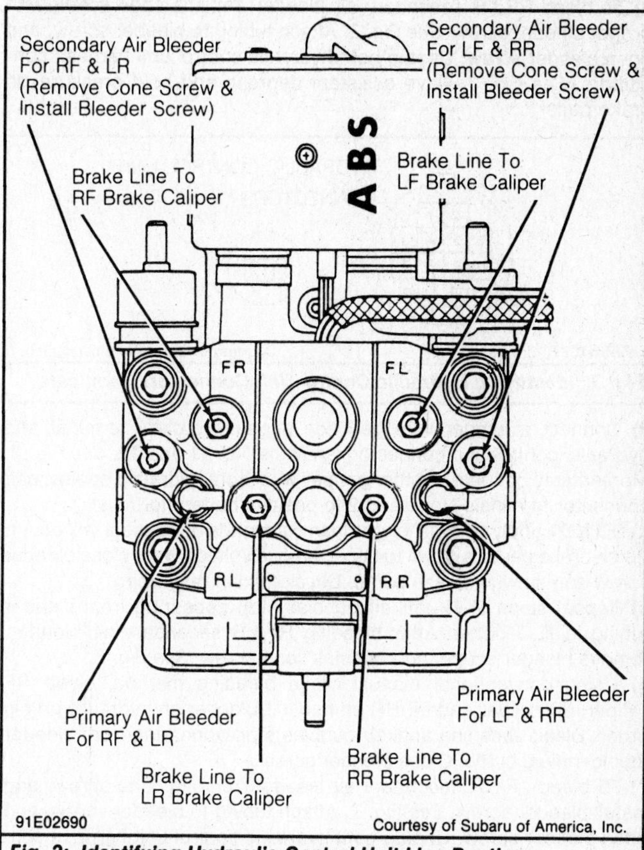


***Fig. 2: Identifying Hydraulic Control Unit Line Routing & Bleeding Ports***

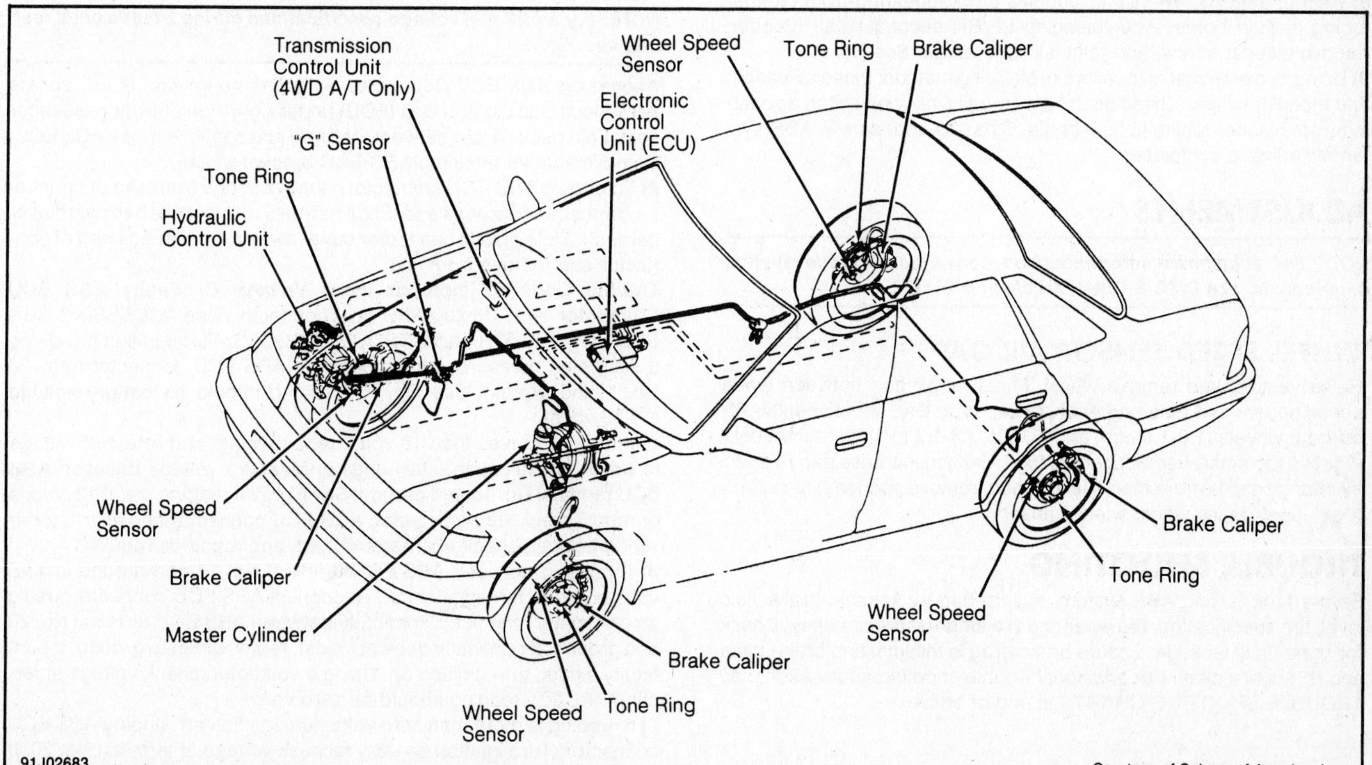

91J02683

Courtesy of Subaru of America, Inc.

***Fig. 1: Locating ABS Components***

brake pedal), bleed RF/LR primary air bleeder on hydraulic control unit. *See Fig. 2.* Bleed until air bubbles stop appearing from bleeder tubing in fluid bottle. Close bleeder screw.
**2)** To bleed RF/LR secondary air bleeder, replace cone screw with proper bleeder screw. *See Fig. 2.* Attach tubing to bleeder screw, and open bleeder screw. Unplug both hydraulic control unit harness connectors. *See Fig. 3.* Have assistant depress and hold pressure on brake pedal.

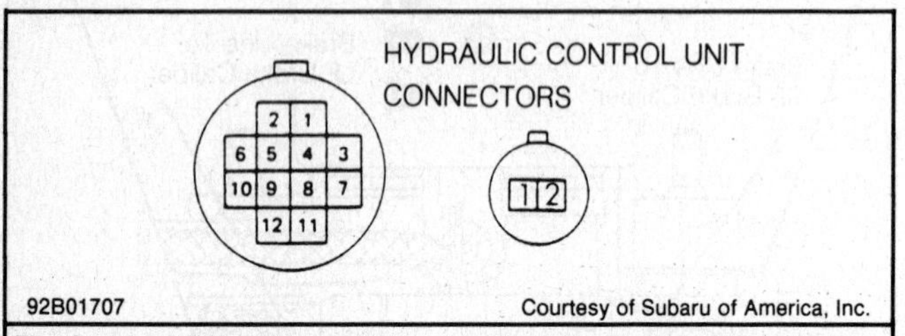


***Fig. 3: Identifying Hydraulic Control Unit Connectors Terminals***

**3)** Connect a jumper wire between negative battery terminal and hydraulic control unit connector terminals No. 11 and 12. *See Fig. 3.* Momentarily connect another jumper wire from hydraulic control unit connector terminals No. 1 and 2 to positive battery terminal.
**4)** DO NOT apply voltage longer than 5 seconds or damage will occur. When brake pedal is down to floor, remove voltage wire, close bleeder screw and slowly release pedal. Check fluid in reservoir.
**5)** Repeat steps **3)-4)** until air bubbles stop appearing from bleeder tubing in fluid bottle. After bleeding RF/LR secondary air bleeder, remove bleeder screw, and reinstall cone screw. *See Fig. 2.*
**6)** Using conventional manual brake bleeding method, bleed RF caliper, LR caliper and LF/RR primary air bleeder on hydraulic unit in order. Bleed each line until air bubbles stop appearing from bleeder tubing in fluid bottle. Close bleeder screw.
**7)** To bleed LF/RR secondary air bleeder, remove cone screw, and install bleeder screw. *See Fig. 2.* Attach tubing to bleeder screw, and open bleeder screw. Unplug both hydraulic control unit harness connectors. *See Fig. 3.* Have assistant depress and hold pressure on brake pedal.
**8)** Repeat steps **3)-4)** until air bubbles stop appearing from bleeder tubing in fluid bottle. After bleeding LF/RR secondary air bleeder, remove bleeder screw, and reinstall cone screw. *See Fig. 2.*
**9)** Using conventional manual brake bleeding method, bleed LF caliper and then RR caliper. Bleed each caliper until air bubbles stop appearing from bleeder tubing in fluid bottle. Close bleeder screw. ABS system bleeding is completed.

# ADJUSTMENTS

***NOTE: For adjustment information on conventional brake system components, see DISC & DRUM article in BRAKES.***

## WHEEL SPEED SENSOR AIR GAP

Raise vehicle, and remove wheel. Measure air gap between wheel speed sensor and tone ring, rear of disc rotor. Gap should be .04-.06" on front wheels (1.0-1.5 mm) and .03-.05" (.8-1.3 mm) on rear wheels. If gap is too small, use Spacer (26755AA000) to increase gap to specification. If gap is more than specification, remove spacer(s) or replace tone ring or faulty wheel speed sensor.

## TROUBLE SHOOTING

Before fault testing ABS system, ensure battery voltage, brake fluid level, tire specification, tire wear and tire air pressure are okay. Check for brake fluid leakage. Ensure brake drag is minimal and brake pads and rotors are okay. For additional trouble shooting information, see TROUBLE SHOOTING CHARTS at end of article.

# DIAGNOSIS & TESTING

***NOTE: Resistance readings of 1 megohm are same as readings of infinity.***

## RETRIEVING CODES

**1)** ABS system has ability to store trouble codes when system fault is detected. To retrieve trouble codes, locate ABS electronic control unit (ECU) under right side of front passenger seat. Fold back carpet between door sill and seat to expose ABS ECU. *See Fig. 4.*
**2)** Turn ignition on. An ABS ECU LED light will start to flash if a trouble code is stored. *See Fig. 5.* ABS ECU is capable of displaying one code at a time. If more than one code is stored, lowest number code will be displayed first. If necessary, drive vehicle after repairing first code to store and read any additional codes.

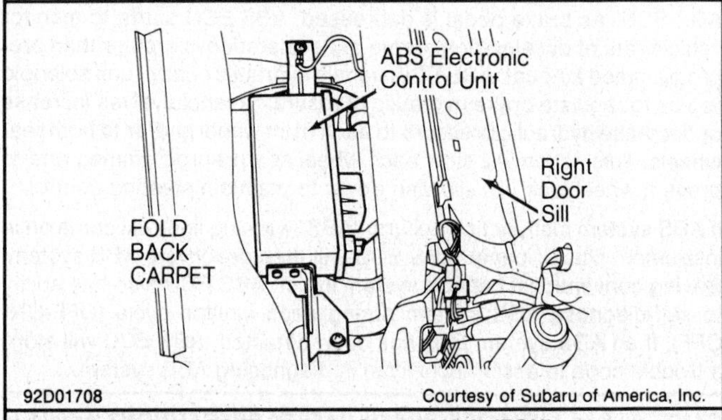


***Fig. 4: Locating ABS Electronic Control Unit (ECU)***

## TROUBLE CODES

***NOTE: For ABS ECU terminal identification, see Fig. 7. For check connector terminal identification, see Fig. 8. For other connectors terminal identification, see Figs. 2 and 16.***

***NOTE: For additional voltage specifications during trouble code testing, see Fig. 6.***

**Accessing ABS ECU Connector – 1)** Ensure ignition is off. Locate ABS Electronic Control Unit (ECU) under right side of front passenger seat. Fold back carpet between door sill and seat to expose ABS ECU. Remove screws retaining ABS ECU bracket to floor.
**2)** To unplug ABS ECU connector, remove screw from end of connector opposite of harness end. Slide harness rubber boot backward over harness. Slide plastic connector cover away from harness end of connector and remove from unit.
**Trouble Code 0: Improper Input Voltage Or Faulty ABS ECU Connector – 1)** Unplug ABS ECU connector. See ACCESSING ABS ECU CONNECTOR under TROUBLE CODES. Turn ignition on. Using a voltmeter, measure voltage between ABS ECU connector terminal No. 1 and ground. *See Fig. 7.* Reading should be battery voltage (10-13 volts).
**2)** If reading is less than 10 volts, repair wiring, and retest. If voltage is within specification, start engine. Measure voltage between ABS ECU terminal No. 15 and ground. *See Fig. 7.* If reading is not 13.5 volts or more, check wiring between ABS ECU connector and alternator. If wiring is okay, check alternator output, and repair as required.
**3)** If reading between ABS ECU terminal No. 15 and ground is 13.5 volts or more, turn ignition off. Reconnect ABS ECU connector. Using an ohmmeter, check for continuity between ABS ECU terminal No. 20 and ground. If continuity does not exist, repair wiring to ground. If continuity exists, turn ignition on. Using a voltmeter, check voltage at terminal No. 20. Reading should be zero volts.
**4)** If reading is more than zero volts, turn ignition off. Unplug ABS ECU connector. Turn ignition on, and recheck voltage at terminal No. 20. If reading is now zero volts, replace ABS ECU. If reading is more than zero volts, wiring is shorted to voltage.

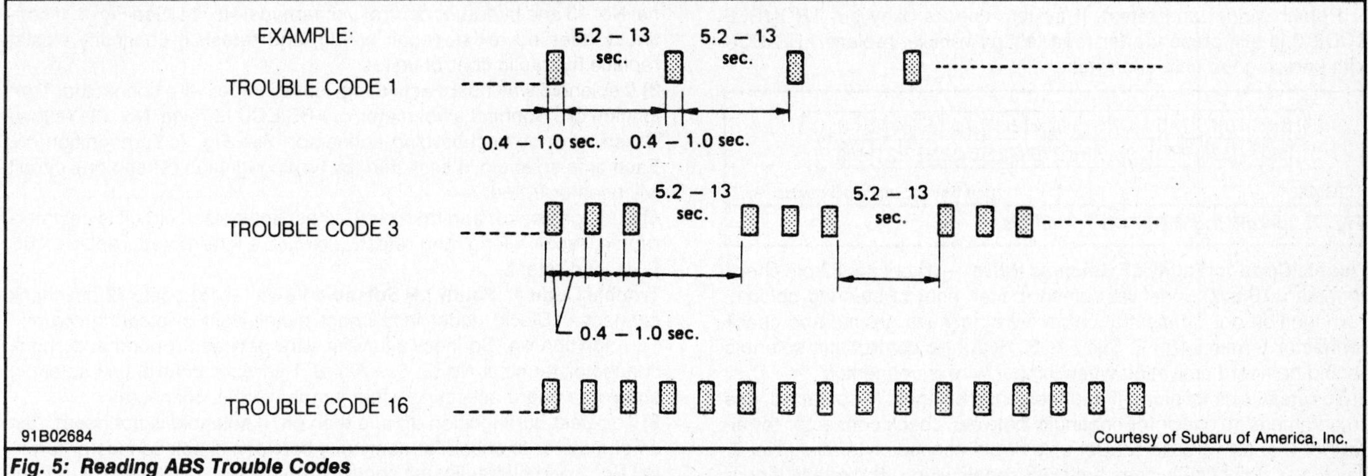


*Fig. 5: Reading ABS Trouble Codes*

| Contents | | | ECU Terminal No. | With engine idling | Input/output signals | |
|---|---|---|---|---|---|---|
| | | | | | Measured value | Measuring conditions |
| Wheel speed sensors | Left front wheel<br>GND | | 22<br>4 | 0 V | 200 – 300 mV (AC Range) | • No. 22 – No. 4<br>• Vehicle speed 2.75 km/h (1.7 MPH) |
| | Right front wheel<br>GND | | 11<br>21 | 0 V | 200 – 300 mV (AC Range) | • No. 11 – No. 21<br>• Vehicle speed 2.75 km/h (1.7 MPH) |
| | Left rear wheel<br>GND | | 7<br>9 | 0 V | 200 – 300 mV (AC Range) | • No. 7 – No. 9<br>• Vehicle speed 2.75 km/h (1.7 MPH) |
| | Right rear wheel<br>GND | | 24<br>26 | 0 V | 200 – 300 mV (AC Range) | • No. 24 – No. 26<br>• Vehicle speed 2.75 km/h (1.7 MPH) |
| G senor | | | 16 | 13 – 14 V | 0 V | |
| Stop light switch | | | 25 | 0 V | 13 – 14 V | When brake pedal is depressed. |
| Motor monitoring | | | 14 | 0 V | 13 – 14 V | When motor operates. |
| Valve power-supply monitoring | | | 32 | 13 – 14 V | 13 – 14 V | – |
| Hydraulic unit | Solenoid | Left front wheel | 2 | 13 – 14 V | 0 V | When solenoid is energized to produce output. |
| | | Right front wheel | 35 | 13 – 14 V | 0 V | |
| | | Left rear wheel | 18 | 13 – 14 V | 0 V | |
| | | Right rear wheel | 19 | 13 – 14 V | 0 V | |
| | Valve relay coil | | 27 | 0 V | 0 V | – |
| | Motor relay coil | | 28 | 13 – 14 V | 0 V | When motor operates to produce output |
| Warning light | | | 29 | 70 mV | 0 V | When warning activates to produce output or when valve relay is OFF |
| Power supply | Alternator | | 15 | 13 – 14 V | 1.7 V | Ignition switch ON (Engine OFF) |
| | Battery | | 1 | 13 – 14 V | 13 – 14 V | – |
| | Relay coil (valve, motor, etc) | | 17 | 13 – 14 V | 13 – 14 V | – |

91E02685

Courtesy of Subaru of America, Inc.

*Fig. 6: ABS ECU Pin Voltage Chart*

# 1991 BRAKES
## Anti-Lock (Cont.)

**5)** Repair wiring, and retest. If system checks okay but TROUBLE CODE 0 is still present after road testing vehicle, replace ABS ECU with known good unit, and retest.

| 18 | 17 | 16 | 15 | 14 | 13 | 12 | 11 | 10 | 9 | 8 | 7 | 6 | 5 | 4 | 3 | 2 | 1 |
|---|---|---|---|---|---|---|---|---|---|---|---|---|---|---|---|---|---|
| 35 | 34 | 33 | 32 | 31 | 30 | 29 | 28 | 27 | 26 | 25 | 24 | 23 | 22 | 21 | 20 | 19 | |

91G02686 Courtesy of Subaru of America, Inc.

***Fig. 7: Identifying ABS ECU Terminals***

**Trouble Code 1: Faulty LF Solenoid Valve - 1)** Locate 22-pin check connector (Black) under instrument panel, right of steering column. Turn ignition on. Connect a jumper wire between ground and check connector terminal No. 3. *See Fig. 8.* Hydraulic control unit solenoid should be heard activating when jumper wire is connected.

**2)** To retest, turn ignition off and then on. If solenoid is not heard, use an ohmmeter to check for continuity between check connector terminal No. 3 and hydraulic control unit 12-pin connector terminal No. 2. *See Fig. 3.* If continuity does not exist, repair wiring, and retest. If continuity exists, solenoid is faulty. Replace hydraulic control unit.

**3)** If solenoid was heard activating, leave jumper wire connected. Turn ignition off. Connect a voltmeter to ABS ECU terminal No. 2 (Green/Red wire) by backprobing connector. *See Fig. 7.* Turn ignition on. Each time solenoid is activated (by turning ignition off and on), circuit will be interrupted.

**4)** Turn ignition off and then on to retest solenoid. If circuit is not interrupted, repair wiring, and retest. If circuit is interrupted, replace ABS ECU, and retest.

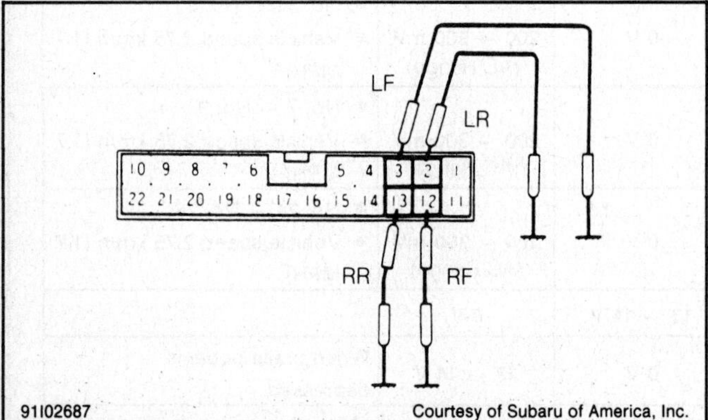


91I02687 Courtesy of Subaru of America, Inc.

***Fig. 8: Identifying Check Connector Terminals***

**Trouble Code 2: Faulty RF Solenoid Valve - 1)** Locate 22-pin check connector (Black) under instrument panel, right of steering column. Turn ignition on. Connect a jumper wire between ground and check connector terminal No. 12. *See Fig. 8.* Hydraulic control unit solenoid should be heard activating when jumper wire is connected.

**2)** To retest, turn ignition off and then on. If solenoid is not heard, use an ohmmeter to check for continuity between check connector terminal No. 12 and hydraulic control unit 12-pin connector terminal No. 1. *See Fig. 3.* If continuity does not exist, repair wiring, and retest. If continuity exists, replace hydraulic control unit.

**3)** If solenoid was heard activating, leave jumper wire connected. Turn ignition off. Connect a voltmeter to ABS ECU terminal No. 35 (Blue/Black wire) by backprobing connector. *See Fig. 7.* Turn ignition on. Each time solenoid is activated (by turning ignition off and on), circuit will be interrupted.

**4)** Turn ignition off and then on to retest solenoid. If circuit is not interrupted, repair wiring, and retest. If circuit is interrupted, replace ABS ECU, and retest.

**Trouble Code 3: Faulty RR Solenoid Valve - 1)** Locate 22-pin check connector (Black) under instrument panel, right of steering column. Turn ignition on. Connect a jumper wire between ground and check connector terminal No. 13. *See Fig. 8.* Hydraulic control unit solenoid should be heard activating when jumper wire is connected.

**2)** To retest, turn ignition off and then on. If solenoid is not heard, use an ohmmeter to check for continuity between check connector terminal No. 13 and hydraulic control unit terminal No. 11. *See Fig. 3.* If continuity does not exist, repair wiring, and retest. If continuity exists, replace hydraulic control unit.

**3)** If solenoid was heard activating, leave jumper wire connected. Turn ignition off. Connect a voltmeter to ABS ECU terminal No. 19 (Yellow/Green wire) by backprobing connector. *See Fig. 7.* Turn ignition on. Each time solenoid is activated (by turning ignition off and on), circuit will be interrupted.

**4)** Turn ignition off and then on to retest solenoid. If circuit is not interrupted, repair wiring, and retest. If circuit is interrupted, replace ABS ECU, and retest.

**Trouble Code 4: Faulty LR Solenoid Valve - 1)** Locate 22-pin check connector (Black) under instrument panel, right of steering column. Turn ignition on. Connect a jumper wire between ground and check connector terminal No. 2. *See Fig. 8.* Hydraulic control unit solenoid should be heard activating when jumper wire is connected.

**2)** To retest, turn ignition off and then on. If solenoid is not heard, use an ohmmeter to check for continuity between check connector terminal No. 2 and hydraulic unit control terminal No. 12. *See Fig. 3.* If continuity does not exist, repair wiring, and retest. If continuity exists, replace hydraulic control unit.

**3)** If solenoid was heard activating, leave jumper wire connected. Turn ignition off. Connect a voltmeter to ABS ECU terminal No. 18 (White/Blue wire) by backprobing connector. *See Fig. 7.* Turn ignition on. Each time solenoid is activated (by turning ignition off and on), circuit will be interrupted.

**4)** Turn ignition off and then on to retest solenoid. If circuit is not interrupted, repair wiring, and retest. If circuit is interrupted, replace ABS ECU, and retest.

**Trouble Code 5: Faulty LF Wheel Speed Sensor - 1)** Unplug ABS ECU connector. See ACCESSING ABS ECU CONNECTOR under TROUBLE CODES. Connect a voltmeter (AC range) between ABS ECU connector terminals No. 4 and 22. *See Fig. 7.* Raise and support vehicle.

**2)** Rotate LF wheel faster than 2 MPH and measure voltage. If reading is 200-300 millivolts, measure sensor and wiring resistance by connecting ohmmeter between ABS ECU connector terminal No. 22 and ground. If resistance is infinity, speed sensor and wiring are good. Replace ABS ECU.

**3)** If reading is not 200-300 millivolts, measure speed sensor wiring resistance by connecting ohmmeter between ABS ECU connector terminal No. 22 and ground. If resistance is infinity, speed sensor wiring is good. Check speed sensor in step **4)**. If resistance is less than infinity, repair wiring between speed sensor and ABS ECU connector and replace speed sensor.

**4)** Unplug wheel speed sensor connector (in engine compartment). Measure resistance across speed sensor connector terminals. If resistance is less than 800-1300 ohms, replace speed sensor. If resistance is 800-1300 ohms, measure resistance between speed sensor connector terminal No. 1 (Yellow/White wire) and ground.

**5)** If resistance is infinity, speed sensor is good. Repair wiring, and retest system. If resistance is less than infinity, replace speed sensor and repair wiring. Retest system.

**Trouble Code 6: Faulty RF Wheel Speed Sensor - 1)** Unplug ABS ECU connector. See ACCESSING ABS ECU CONNECTOR under TROUBLE CODES. Connect a voltmeter (AC range) between ABS ECU connector terminals No. 11 and 21. *See Fig. 7.* Raise and support vehicle.

**2)** Rotate RF wheel faster than 2 MPH and measure voltage. If reading is 200-300 millivolts, measure speed sensor and wiring resistance by connecting ohmmeter between ABS ECU connector terminal No. 21 and ground. If resistance is infinity, speed sensor and wiring are good. Replace ABS ECU.

**3)** If reading is not 200-300 millivolts, measure speed sensor wiring resistance by connecting ohmmeter between ABS ECU connector terminal No. 21 and ground. If resistance is infinity, speed sensor wiring is good. Check speed sensor in step **4)**. If resistance is less than infinity, repair wiring between speed sensor and ABS ECU connector and replace speed sensor.

**4)** Unplug wheel speed sensor connector (in engine compartment). Measure resistance across speed sensor connector terminals. If

# 1991 BRAKES
# Anti-Lock (Cont.)

resistance is less than 800-1300 ohms, replace speed sensor. If resistance is 800-1300 ohms, measure resistance between speed sensor connector terminal No. 1 (Blue/White wire) and ground.

**5)** If resistance is infinity, speed sensor is good. Repair wiring, and retest system. If resistance is less than infinity, replace speed sensor and repair wiring. Retest system.

**Trouble Code 7: Faulty RR Wheel Speed Sensor – 1)** Unplug ABS ECU connector. See ACCESSING ABS ECU CONNECTOR under TROUBLE CODES. Connect a voltmeter (AC range) between ABS ECU connector terminals No. 24 and 26. *See Fig. 7.* Raise and support vehicle.

**2)** Rotate RR wheel faster than 2 MPH and measure voltage. If reading is 200-300 millivolts, measure speed sensor and wiring resistance by connecting ohmmeter between ABS ECU connector terminal No. 26 and ground. If resistance is infinity, speed sensor and wiring are good. Replace ABS ECU.

**3)** If reading is not 200-300 millivolts, measure speed sensor wiring resistance by connecting ohmmeter between ABS ECU connector terminal No. 26 and ground. If resistance is infinity, speed sensor wiring is good. Check speed sensor in step **4)**. If resistance is less than infinity, repair wiring between speed sensor and ABS ECU connector and replace speed sensor.

**4)** Unplug wheel speed sensor connector. Measure resistance across speed sensor connector terminals. If resistance is less than 800-1300 ohms, replace speed sensor. If resistance is 800-1300 ohms, measure resistance between speed sensor connector terminal No. 1 (Blue/Red wire) and ground.

**5)** If resistance is infinity, speed sensor is good. Repair wiring, and retest system. If resistance is less than infinity, replace speed sensor and repair wiring. Retest system.

**Trouble Code 8: Faulty LR Wheel Speed Sensor – 1)** Unplug ABS ECU connector. See ACCESSING ABS ECU CONNECTOR under TROUBLE CODES. Connect a voltmeter (AC range), between ABS ECU connector terminals No. 7 and 9. *See Fig. 7.* Raise and support vehicle.

**2)** Rotate LR wheel faster than 2 MPH and measure voltage. If reading is 200-300 millivolts, measure speed sensor and wiring resistance by connecting ohmmeter between ABS ECU connector terminal No. 9 and ground. If resistance is infinity, speed sensor and wiring are good. Replace ABS ECU.

**3)** If reading is not 200-300 millivolts, measure speed sensor wiring resistance by connecting ohmmeter between ABS ECU connector terminal No. 9 and ground. If resistance is infinity, speed sensor wiring is good. Check speed sensor in step **4)**. If resistance is less than infinity, repair wiring between speed sensor and ABS ECU connector and replace speed sensor.

**4)** Unplug wheel speed sensor connector. Measure resistance across speed sensor connector terminals. If resistance is less than 800-1300 ohms, replace speed sensor. If resistance is 800-1300 ohms, measure resistance between speed sensor connector terminal No. 1 (Yellow/Red wire) and ground.

**5)** If resistance is infinity, speed sensor is good. Repair wiring, and retest system. If resistance is less than infinity, replace speed sensor and repair wiring. Retest system.

**Trouble Code 9: Faulty Hydraulic Motor Or Motor Relay – 1)** Turn ignition off. Unplug ABS ECU connector. See ACCESSING ABS ECU CONNECTOR under TROUBLE CODES. Using an ohmmeter, measure resistance between ABS ECU connector terminals No. 17 and 28. If reading is 45-55 ohms, go to step **6)**.

**2)** If reading is not 45-55 ohms, unplug hydraulic control unit connectors. Measure resistance between hydraulic control unit terminals No. 5 and 6. *See Fig. 3.* If reading is 45-55 ohms, go to step **4)**. If reading is not 45-55 ohms, remove "ABS" cover on hydraulic control unit, and remove motor relay (4-terminal relay).

**3)** Connect ohmmeter to relay terminals No. 87 and 30. *See Fig. 9.* Apply 12 volts to relay terminals No. 85 and 86 (86 is ground). Ohmmeter should indicate zero ohms. Remove 12 volts from relay; ohmmeter reading should be infinity. If either reading is not as specified, replace relay and repair connectors and wiring between ABS ECU and hydraulic control unit. If relay readings are as specified, replace hydraulic control unit.

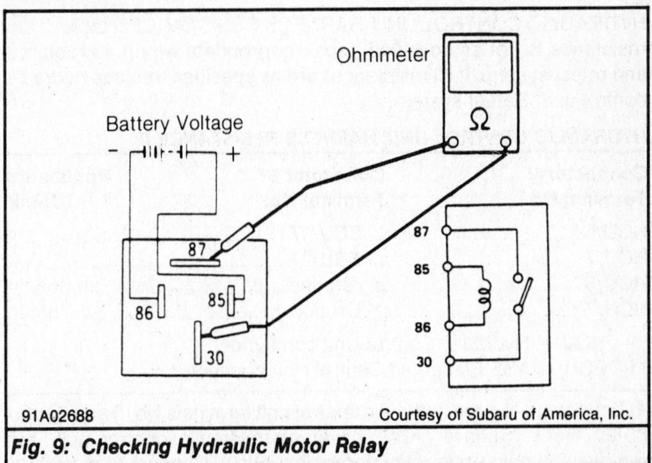


*Fig. 9: Checking Hydraulic Motor Relay*

**4)** If reading between hydraulic control unit terminals No. 5 and 6 is 45-55 ohms, ensure ABS ECU connector and hydraulic control unit connectors are unplugged. Use ohmmeter to measure wiring resistances between each unit's connector terminals and from unit connector terminal to ground. See HYDRAULIC CONTROL UNIT HARNESS RESISTANCE I table.

***HYDRAULIC CONTROL UNIT HARNESS RESISTANCE I***

| Connector [1] Terminal No. | Connector [2] Terminal No. | Resistance (Ohms) |
|---|---|---|
| HCU/6 | ECU/28 | 0 |
| HCU/5 | ECU/17 | 0 |
| HCU/6 | Ground | Infinity |
| HCU/4 | Ground | Infinity |

[1] – HCU = Hydraulic Control Unit connector.
[2] – ECU = ABS Electronic Control Unit connector.

**5)** If any resistance is not as specified, repair appropriate wiring as required, and retest system. If all resistances are as specified, replace hydraulic control unit, and retest system.

**6)** If reading was 45-55 ohms in step **1)**, unplug both connectors from hydraulic control unit. Using an ohmmeter, measure resistance between hydraulic control unit 2-pin connector terminal No. 2 (White/Red wire) and hydraulic control unit 12-pin connector terminal No. 4. *See Fig. 3.*

**7)** If reading is less than infinity, remove motor relay. Go to step **9)**. If reading is infinity, motor relay is good: check and repair voltage input wiring to hydraulic control unit. To check voltage input wiring to hydraulic control unit, turn ignition on.

**8)** Measure voltage between hydraulic control unit 2-pin connector terminal No. 2 (White/Red wire) and ground. Reading should be 10-12 volts. Repair as required. *See Fig. 16.*

**9)** To remove motor relay, remove "ABS" cover on hydraulic control unit, and remove motor relay (4-terminal relay). Connect ohmmeter to relay terminals No. 87 and 30. *See Fig. 9.* Apply 12 volts to relay terminals No. 85 and 86 (86 is ground). Ohmmeter should indicate zero ohms.

**10)** Remove 12 volts from relay. Ohmmeter reading should be infinity. If either reading is not as specified, replace relay. If relay readings are as specified, replace hydraulic control unit.

**Trouble Code 10: Faulty Solenoid Valve Relay Or System Interruption – 1)** Turn ignition off. Unplug ABS ECU connector. See ACCESSING ABS ECU CONNECTOR under TROUBLE CODES. Using an ohmmeter, measure resistance between ABS ECU connector terminals No. 17 and 27. If reading is 80-90 ohms, go to step **6)**.

**2)** If reading is not 80-90 ohms, unplug hydraulic control unit connectors. Measure resistance between hydraulic control unit terminals No. 5 and 7. *See Fig. 3.* If reading is not 80-90 ohms, go to step **4)**. If reading is 80-90 ohms, ensure ABS ECU connector and hydraulic control unit connectors are unplugged.

**3)** Use ohmmeter to measure wiring resistances between units' connector terminals and from unit connector terminal to ground. See

# 1991 BRAKES
# Anti-Lock (Cont.)

HYDRAULIC CONTROL UNIT HARNESS RESISTANCE II table. If any resistance is not as specified, repair appropriate wiring as required, and retest system. If all resistances are as specified, replace hydraulic control unit. Retest system.

***HYDRAULIC CONTROL UNIT HARNESS RESISTANCE II***

| Connector [1]/ Terminal No. | Connector [2]/ Terminal No. | Resistance (Ohms) |
|---|---|---|
| HCU/5 | ECU/17 | 0 |
| HCU/7 | ECU/27 | 0 |
| HCU/5 | Ground | Infinity |
| HCU/7 | Ground | Infinity |

[1] - HCU = Hydraulic Control Unit connector.
[2] - ECU = ABS Electronic Control Unit connector.

**4)** If reading between hydraulic control unit terminals No. 5 and 7 is not 80-90 ohms, remove "ABS" cover on hydraulic control unit, and remove solenoid valve relay (5-terminal relay). Connect ohmmeter to relay terminals No. 87 and 30. *See Fig. 10.* Apply 12 volts to relay terminals No. 85 and 86 (86 is ground). Ohmmeter should indicate zero ohms. Remove 12 volts from relay; ohmmeter reading should be infinity.

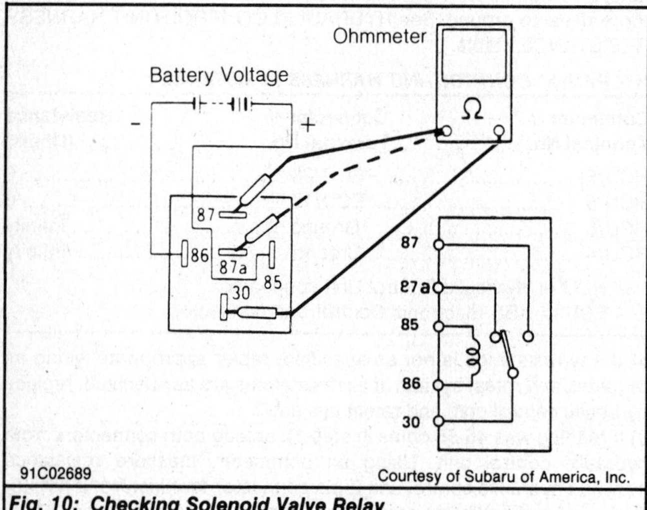

Courtesy of Subaru of America, Inc.

***Fig. 10: Checking Solenoid Valve Relay***

**5)** Connect ohmmeter to relay terminals No. 87a and 30. *See Fig. 10.* Apply 12 volts to relay terminals No. 85 and 86 (86 is ground). Ohmmeter reading should be infinity. Remove 12 volts from relay; ohmmeter should indicate zero ohms. If any readings are not as specified, replace relay and repair connectors and wiring between ABS ECU and hydraulic control unit. If all relay readings are as specified, replace hydraulic control unit.

**6)** Unplug both hydraulic control unit connectors. Using an ohmmeter, measure resistance between hydraulic control unit 2-pin connector terminal No. 1 (White/Green wire) and hydraulic control unit 12-pin connector terminal No. 8. If reading is less than infinity, go to step **8)**. If reading is infinity, solenoid valve relay is good: check and repair voltage input wiring to hydraulic control unit. *See Fig. 16.*

**7)** To check voltage input wiring to hydraulic control unit, turn ignition on. Measure voltage between hydraulic control unit 2-pin connector terminal No. 1 (White/Green wire) and ground. Reading should be 10-12 volts. If reading is less than 10 volts, check fuse No. 19 and/or wiring between connector and fuse block. Repair as required. *See Fig. 16.*

**8)** To remove solenoid valve relay, remove "ABS" cover on hydraulic control unit, and remove solenoid valve relay (5-terminal relay). Connect ohmmeter to relay terminals No. 87 and 30. *See Fig. 10.* Apply 12 volts to relay terminals No. 85 and 86 (86 is ground). Ohmmeter should indicate zero ohms. Remove 12 volts from relay; ohmmeter reading should be infinity.

**9)** Connect ohmmeter to relay terminals No. 87a and 30. *See Fig. 10.* Apply 12 volts to relay terminals No. 85 and 86 (86 is ground). Ohmmeter reading should be infinity. Remove 12 volts from relay; ohmmeter should indicate zero ohms. If any readings are not as specified, replace relay and repair connectors and wiring between ABS ECU and hydraulic control unit. If all ohmmeter readings are as specified, replace hydraulic control unit.

**Trouble Code 16: Faulty ABS ECU Or "G" Sensor - 1)** Position vehicle on a flat surface. Unplug ABS ECU connector. See ACCESSING ABS ECU CONNECTOR under TROUBLE CODES. Using an ohmmeter, measure resistance between ABS ECU connector terminals No. 1 and 16. If reading is 550-670 ohms, check ABS ECU input power supply at connector terminal No. 1 for battery voltage. If power supply is okay, replace ABS ECU, and retest.

**2)** If reading is not 550-670 ohms between ABS ECU connector terminals No. 1 and 16, unplug "G" sensor connector. "G" sensor is located in engine compartment, below right shock tower, on frame rail. *See Fig. 11.* Measure resistance between "G" sensor terminals. Ensure "G" sensor is mounted horizontally and vehicle is horizontal. If reading is not 550-670 ohms, replace "G" sensor.

**3)** If reading is 550-670 ohms between "G" sensor terminals, check wiring between "G" sensor and ABS ECU by plugging in "G" sensor connector and turning ignition on. Using voltmeter, backprobe "G" sensor connector terminal No. 1 and ground, and note reading. Using voltmeter, backprobe ABS ECU connector terminal No. 16 to ground, and note reading.

**4)** Both readings should be 10-12 volts. If readings are not as specified, repair wiring as required. If both readings are 10-12 volts, replace ABS ECU. Drive vehicle, and retest system for any other trouble codes.

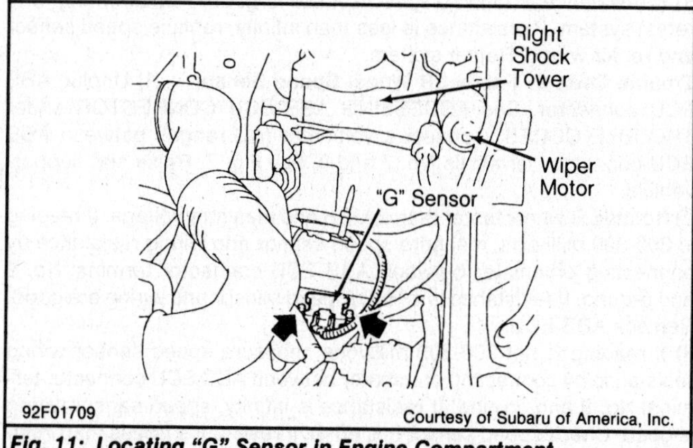

Courtesy of Subaru of America, Inc.

***Fig. 11: Locating "G" Sensor In Engine Compartment***

## "G" SENSOR

**1)** "G" sensor is located in engine compartment, below right shock tower, on frame rail. *See Fig. 11.* With "G" sensor removed from vehicle and horizontal, measure resistance between "G" sensor terminals. *See Fig. 12.* If reading is not 550-670 ohms, replace "G" sensor.

**2)** If reading is 550-670 ohms, tilt sensor forward 14-21°. *See Fig. 12.* Using an ohmmeter, check for continuity between "G" sensor connector terminals. Continuity should be greater than 100,000 ohms. Replace "G" sensor if continuity is not as specified.

# REMOVAL & INSTALLATION

## ELECTRONIC CONTROL MODULE

**Removal & Installation - 1)** Ensure ignition is off. Locate ABS electronic control unit (ECU) under right side of front passenger seat. Fold back carpet between door sill and seat to expose ABS ECU. *See Fig. 4.* Remove screws retaining ABS ECU bracket to floor.

**2)** To unplug ABS ECU connector, remove screw from end of connector opposite of harness end. Slide harness rubber boot backward over harness. Slide plastic connector cover away from harness end of connector, and remove. To install, reverse removal procedure.

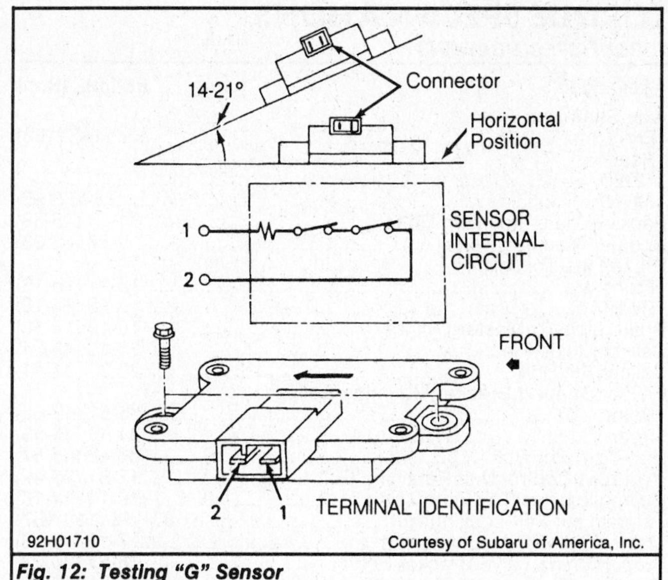

*Fig. 12: Testing "G" Sensor*

## "G" SENSOR

**Removal & Installation** – "G" sensor is located in engine compartment, below right shock tower, on frame rail. *See Fig. 11.* Unplug harness connector. Remove bolts retaining "G" Sensor. To install, reverse removal procedure. Ensure "G" sensor is mounted horizontally and top arrow points forward. *See Fig. 12.*

***NOTE: If "G" sensor is tilted backwards or is not mounted horizontally, sensor will not function properly.***

## HYDRAULIC CONTROL UNIT

***NOTE: DO NOT place hydraulic control unit upside-down or on its side during removal or installation procedure.***

**Removal & Installation** – Remove carbon canister from engine compartment. Disconnect hydraulic lines from hydraulic control unit. Plug all line openings. Remove "ABS" cover from hydraulic control unit. Remove bolts retaining hydraulic control unit. To install, reverse removal procedure. When installing a new control unit, apply Rust Preventive Wax (Nippeco LT or GB) to retaining bolts after tightening.

## PROPORTIONING VALVE

***NOTE: DO NOT disassemble or adjust proportioning valve. Valve must be replaced as an assembly.***

**Removal & Installation** – Valve is located near master cylinder, mounted to shock tower. *See Fig. 13.* Remove all brake lines, and plug all openings. Remove valve from bracket. To install, reverse removal procedure. Tighten valve-to-bracket bolts to 15-21 ft. lbs. (20-29 N.m). Bleed system. See BLEEDING BRAKE SYSTEM.

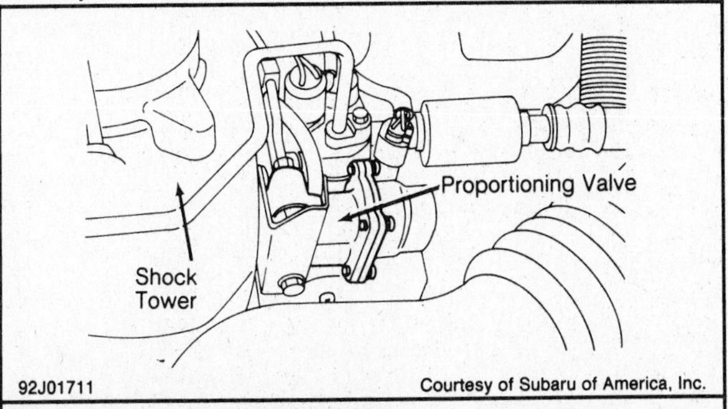

*Fig. 13: Locating Proportioning Valve*

## TONE RING

**Removal & Installation (Front) – 1)** Raise and support vehicle. Remove front wheel. Remove disc brake caliper, and wire aside. Unplug wheel speed sensor connector, and remove speed sensor from hub assembly. *See Fig. 15.* Mark rotor-to-hub location, and remove brake rotor. Remove axle shaft nut. Remove stabilizer.

**2)** Loosen transverse link ball joint nut, and separate ball joint from wheel hub assembly. Drive out spring pin retaining inner CV joint to transaxle spline. Remove drive shaft from vehicle. Disconnect tie rod and ball joints from wheel hub assembly. Remove bolts retaining strut assembly to wheel hub assembly.

**3)** Remove wheel hub assembly from vehicle. Remove hub from wheel hub assembly using press. Remove bolts retaining tone ring to hub flange. *See Fig. 14.* Remove tone ring. To install, reverse removal procedure. Use new inner axle joint spring pin and new outer axle shaft nut.

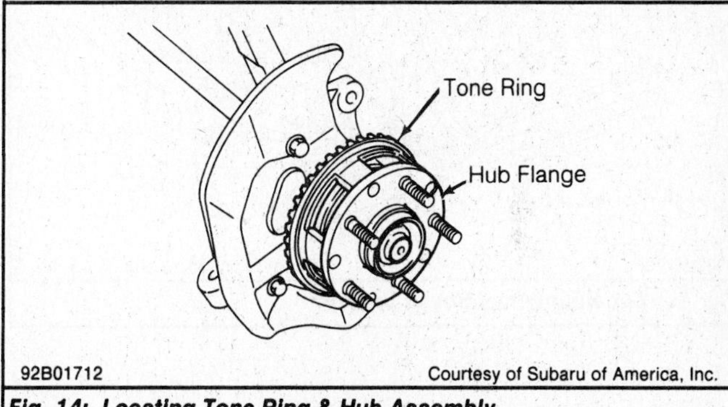

*Fig. 14: Locating Tone Ring & Hub Assembly*

**Removal & Installation (Rear) – 1)** Raise and support vehicle. Remove rear wheel. Remove disc brake caliper, and wire aside. Unplug wheel speed sensor connector, and remove speed sensor from hub assembly. *See Fig. 15.* Mark rotor-to-hub location, and remove brake rotor. Disconnect parking brake adjuster cable.

**2)** Remove axle shaft nut. Remove lateral link and trailing link retaining bolts. Drive out spring pin retaining inner CV joint to drive axle case. Remove drive shaft from vehicle. Remove bolts retaining strut assembly to wheel hub assembly.

**3)** Remove wheel hub assembly. Remove hub from wheel hub assembly using press. Remove bolts retaining tone ring to hub flange. *See Fig. 14.* Remove tone ring. To install, reverse removal procedure. Use new spring pin, axle shaft nut, and training link and lateral link self-locking nuts.

## WHEEL SPEED SENSOR

***NOTE: Use care when removing and installing wheel speed sensor to prevent damage to sensor tip.***

**Removal & Installation (Front)** – Unplug front wheel speed sensor connector. Remove bolt retaining wheel speed sensor and wiring harness. Remove wheel speed sensor. *See Fig. 15.* To install, reverse removal procedure. See TORQUE SPECIFICATIONS table at end of article. See WHEEL SPEED SENSOR AIR GAP under ADJUSTMENTS.

**Removal & Installation (Rear)** – Remove rear seat. Unplug rear wheel speed sensor connector. From underneath vehicle, remove wheel speed sensor retaining bolt. Remove wheel speed sensor. *See Fig. 15.* To install, reverse removal procedure. See TORQUE SPECIFICATIONS table at end of article. See WHEEL SPEED SENSOR AIR GAP under ADJUSTMENTS.

# 1991 BRAKES
# Anti-Lock (Cont.)

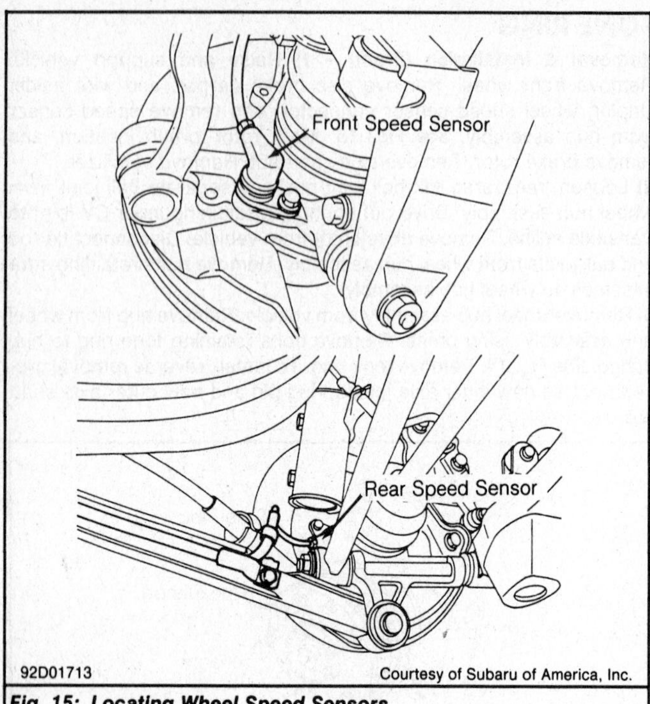


***Fig. 15: Locating Wheel Speed Sensors***

## TORQUE SPECIFICATIONS

***TORQUE SPECIFICATIONS***

| Application | Ft. Lbs. (N.m) |
|---|---|
| Axle Shaft Nut | |
| Front | 145 (196) |
| Rear | |
| 2WD | [1] |
| 4WD | 145 (196) |
| Backing Plate Mounting Bolts | 34-43 (46-58) |
| Booster Mounting Nuts | 9-17 (12-23) |
| Brake Line-To-Caliper | |
| Front | 12-14 (16-19) |
| Rear | 10-13 (14-18) |
| Brake Line-To-Master Cylinder | 10-13 (14-18) |
| Caliper Guide Pin | 33-40 (45-54) |
| Caliper Pin Bolt | 23-30 (31-41) |
| Caliper Support Bracket Mounting Bolts | |
| Front | 36-51 (49-69) |
| Rear | 34-43 (46-58) |
| Hub-To-Rotor Bolt | 33-42 (45-57) |
| Hydraulic Control Unit Retaining Bolt | 17-31 (23-42) |
| Hydraulic Lines-To-Control Unit | 10-13 (14-18) |
| Lateral Link Self-Locking Nut | 87-116 (118-157) |
| Master Cylinder Mounting Nut | 7-13 (10-18) |
| Proportioning Valve Bracket Bolts | 15-21 (20-29) |
| Stabilizer-To-Crossmember | 15-21 (20-29) |
| Stabilizer Link-To-Front Transverse Link | 14-22 (19-30) |
| Strut Lower Retaining Bolts | 98-119 (133-162) |
| Tie Rod Ball Joint Nut | 18-22 (24-30) |
| Trailing Link Self-Locking Nut | 72-94 (98-128) |
| Transverse Link Ball Joint Nut | 28-37 (38-50) |
| Wheel Lug Nut | 58-72 (79-98) |
| Wheel Speed Sensor Harness Bracket Bolt | 7-12 (10-16) |
| Wheel Speed Sensor Retaining Bolt | 17-31 (23-42) |
| | **INCH Lbs. (N.m)** |
| Hydraulic Control Unit "ABS" Cover | 11-13 (1.2-1.5) |

[1] – See procedures in DISC & DRUM article in BRAKES.

## TROUBLE SHOOTING CHARTS

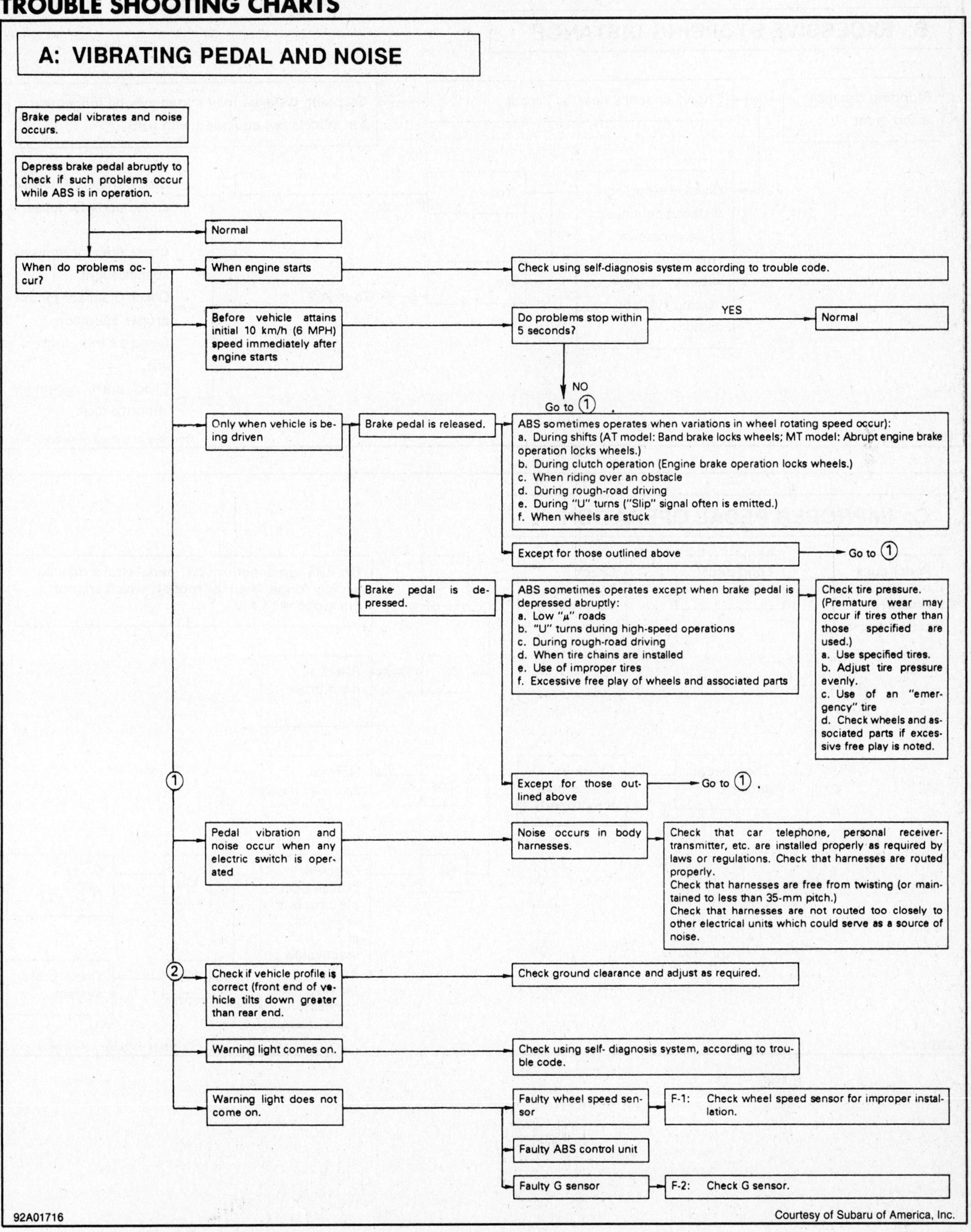

# 1991 BRAKES
## Anti-Lock (Cont.)

### B: EXCESSIVE STOPPING DISTANCE

Stopping distance is too great.
Snowy or sandy (low "μ") roads
Stopping distance may sometimes be longer than for models not equipped with ABS.
Check if stopping distance continues to be excessive when ABS is inactivated by disconnecting H/U connector.
Yes
No
Go to A②
Check wheels and associated parts for looseness.
Check tires for improper specifications.
Check G sensor for improper operation.
Bleed air from brake line.
Check brake system for abnormalities.

92C01717

Courtesy of Subaru of America, Inc.

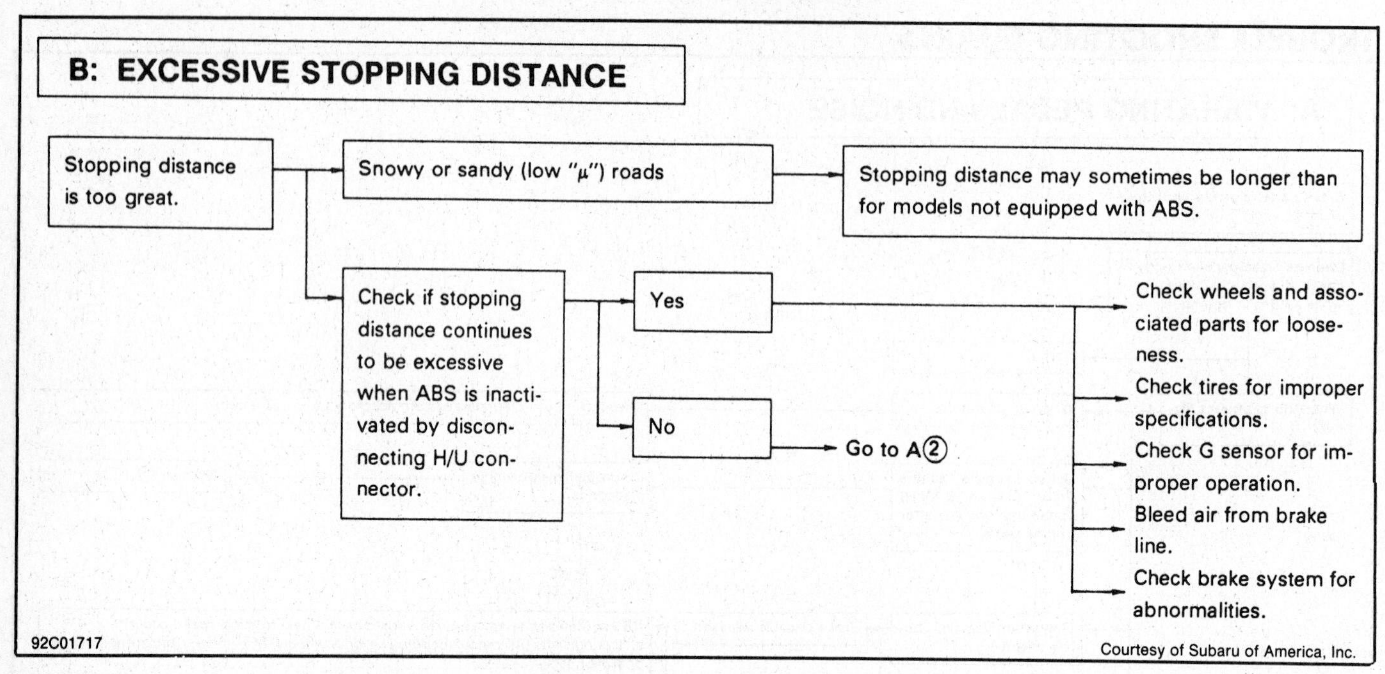

### C: IMPROPER PEDAL OPERATION

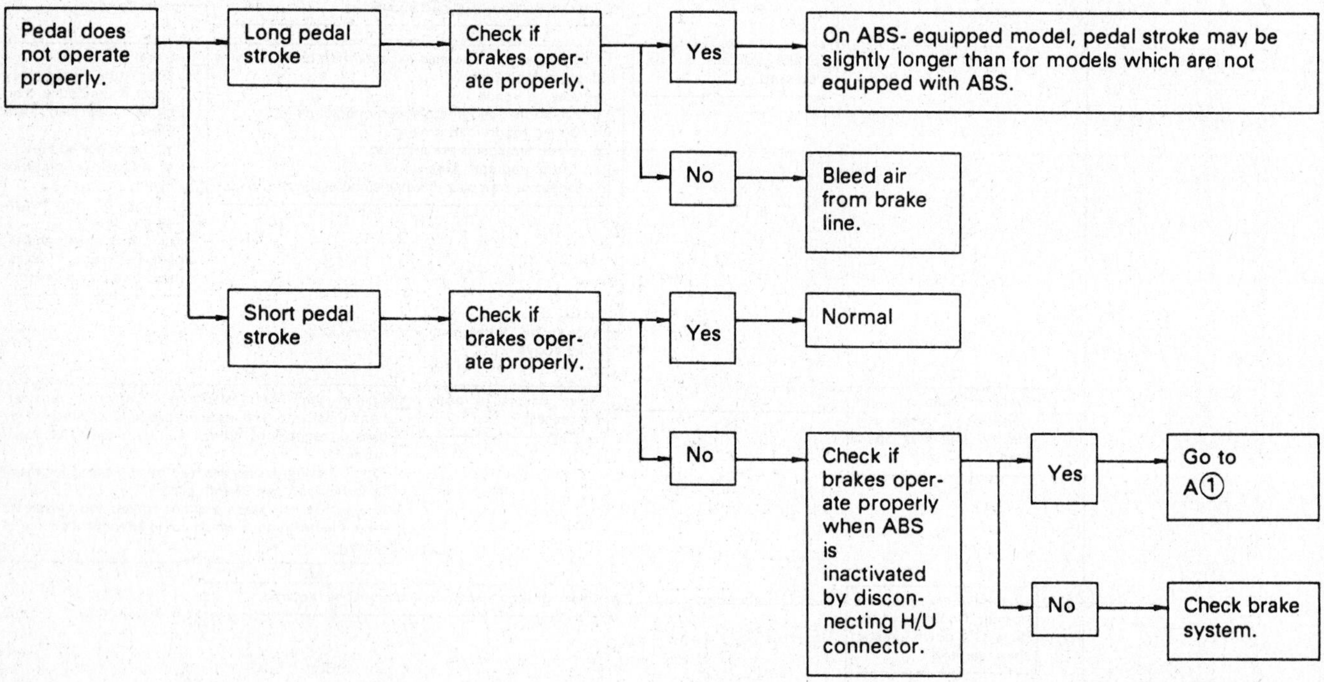

Pedal does not operate properly.
Long pedal stroke
Check if brakes operate properly.
Yes
On ABS- equipped model, pedal stroke may be slightly longer than for models which are not equipped with ABS.
No
Bleed air from brake line.
Short pedal stroke
Check if brakes operate properly.
Yes
Normal
No
Check if brakes operate properly when ABS is inactivated by disconnecting H/U connector.
Yes
Go to A①
No
Check brake system.

92E01718

Courtesy of Subaru of America, Inc.

## WIRING DIAGRAM

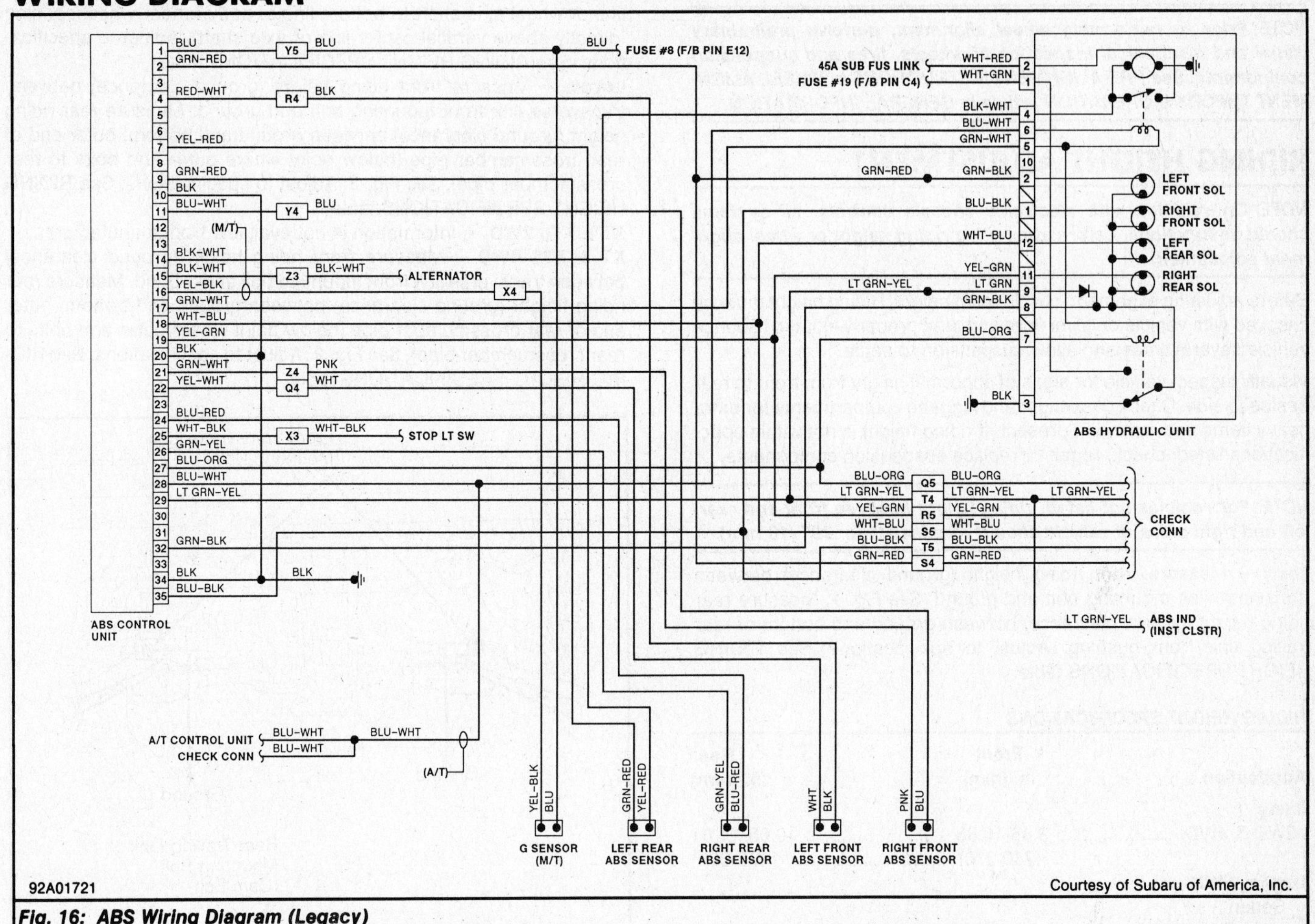


*Fig. 16: ABS Wiring Diagram (Legacy)*

# 1991 WHEEL ALIGNMENT
# Specifications & Procedures

## Justy, Legacy, Loyale, XT & XT6

***NOTE: Prior to performing wheel alignment, perform preliminary visual and mechanical inspection of wheels, tires and suspension components. See PRE-ALIGNMENT INSTRUCTIONS in WHEEL ALIGNMENT THEORY & OPERATION article in GENERAL INFORMATION.***

## RIDING HEIGHT ADJUSTMENT

***NOTE: On vehicles with electronic chassis controls, all systems should be functional before attempting riding height or wheel alignment adjustment.***

Before adjusting alignment, check riding height. Riding height must be checked with vehicle on level floor and tires properly inflated. Bounce vehicle several times and allow suspension to settle.

Visually inspect vehicle for signs of abnormal height from front to rear or side to side. Check passenger and luggage compartments for extra heavy items and remove if present. If riding height is not within specifications listed, check, repair or replace suspension components.

***NOTE: For vehicles not listed, riding height between front and rear, left and right sides of vehicle should vary less than .39" (10 mm).***

**Justy** – Measure front riding height (ground clearance) between transverse link mounting bolt and ground. *See Fig. 1.* Measure rear riding height (ground clearance) between ground and bottom of rear trailing link front bushing. Adjust to specifications. See RIDING HEIGHT SPECIFICATIONS table.

***RIDING HEIGHT SPECIFICATIONS***

| Application | Front In. (mm) | Rear In. (mm) |
|---|---|---|
| **Justy** | | |
| 2WD & 4WD | 9.45-10.63 (240-270) | 10.63-11.81 (270-300) |
| **Legacy 2WD** | | |
| Sedan | | |
| Coil Suspension | 14.69-15.47 (373-393) | 13.55-14.33 (344-364) |
| Air Suspension | 14.89-15.28 (378-388) | 14.14-14.92 (359-379) |
| Wagon | 14.69-15.47 (373-393) | 14.14-14.92 (359-379) |
| **Legacy 4WD** | | |
| Sedan | | |
| Coil Suspension | 15.08-15.86 (383-403) | 13.94-14.72 (354-374) |
| Air Suspension | 14.89-15.28 (378-388) | 14.14-14.92 (359-379) |
| Wagon | 14.69-15.47 (373-393) | 14.53-15.31 (369-389) |
| **Loyale 2WD** | | |
| 3-Door | 8.42-9.76 (214-248) | 7.75-8.93 (197-227) |
| Wagon | 8.66-10.00 (220-254) | 8.54-9.72 (217-247) |
| **Loyale 4WD** | | |
| 3 Door | 9.6-10.94 (244-278) | 9.64-10.82 (245-275) |
| Wagon | 9.76-11.10 (248-282) | 10.59-11.37 (269-289) |
| **XT 4WD** [1] | 9.17-10.51 (233-267) | 9.05-10.23 (230-260) |
| **XT6 4WD** [1] | 9.09-10.43 (231-265) | 8.97-10.15 (228-258) |

[1] – XT & XT6 2WD riding height information is not available.

**Legacy** – Measure front and rear riding height from horizontal center line of wheel axle shaft to bottom line of body/fender wheel opening (directly above vertical center line of axle shaft). Adjust to specifications. See RIDING HEIGHT SPECIFICATIONS table.

**Loyale** – Measure front riding height (ground clearance) between transverse link front mounting bolt and ground. Measure rear riding height (ground clearance) between ground and bottom, outer end of rear crossmember pipe (below point where outer arm bolts to rear crossmember pipe). *See Fig. 2.* Adjust to specifications. See RIDING HEIGHT SPECIFICATIONS table.

**XT & XT6 2WD** – Information is not available from manufacturer.

**XT & XT6 4WD** – Measure front riding height (ground clearance) between transverse link front mounting bolt and ground. Measure rear riding height (ground clearance) between ground and bottom, outer end of rear crossmember pipe (below point where outer arm bolts to rear crossmember pipe). *See Fig. 2.* Adjust to specifications. See RIDING HEIGHT SPECIFICATIONS table.

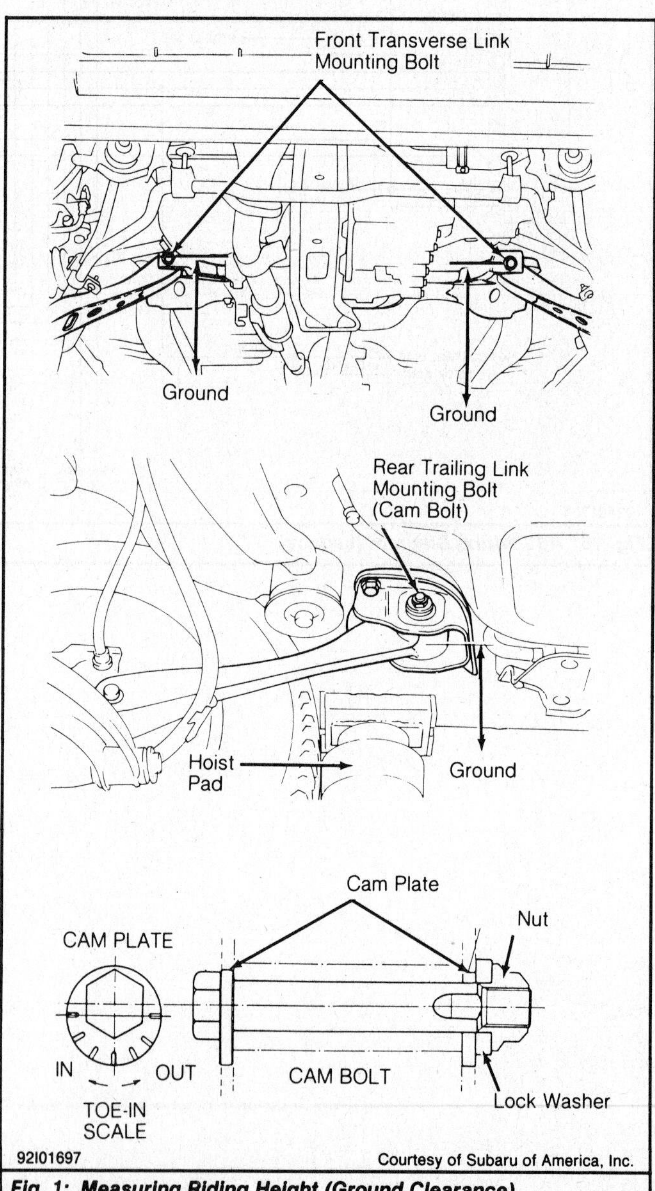


***Fig. 1: Measuring Riding Height (Ground Clearance) & Adjusting Rear Toe-In (Justy)***

# 1991 WHEEL ALIGNMENT
# Specifications & Procedures (Cont.)

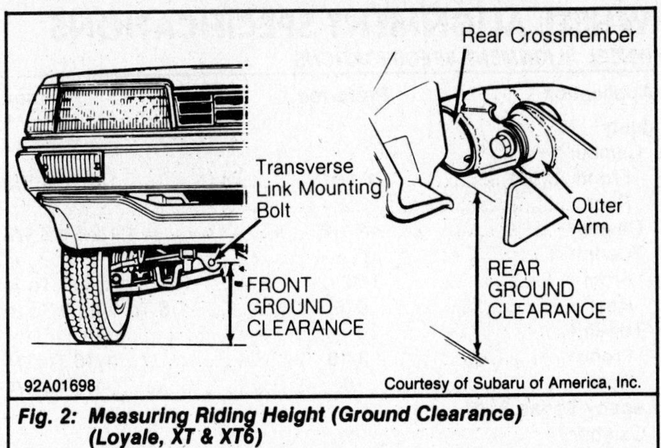


*Fig. 2: Measuring Riding Height (Ground Clearance) (Loyale, XT & XT6)*

## JACKING & HOISTING

### FLOOR JACK

Using a garage-type floor jack, vehicles can be lifted at following points: under rear differential case on 4WD models, under center of rear crossmember on 2WD models and under engine center support crossmember (if equipped).

### HOIST/LIFT & EMERGENCY JACKING

Lower body seam areas indicated in illustration by circles, are specifically designed to facilitate use of vehicle's own jack. *See Fig. 3.* These jacking points are also to be used by hoist/lift pads. If floor jack is used at these points, extreme care should be taken to avoid damaging outer body shell.

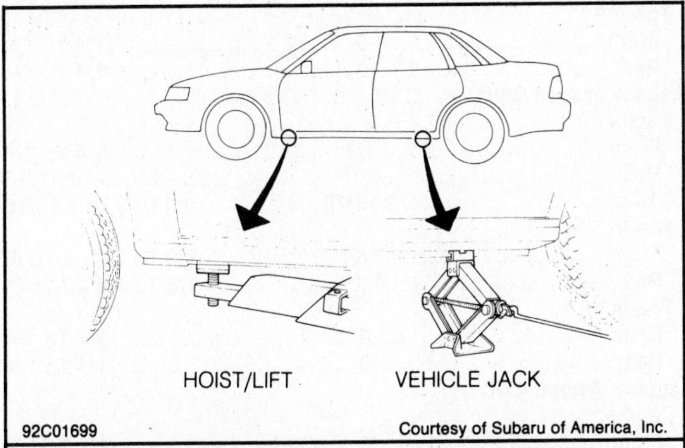


*Fig. 3: Locating Hoisting/Lifting Points on Lower Body Seam*

## WHEEL ALIGNMENT PROCEDURES

### CAMBER ADJUSTMENT

**Justy (Front & Rear)** - Camber and caster are not adjustable. If measurements are not within specifications, check for frame damage, transverse link damage, or worn out components (struts/springs, ball joint, etc.).

**Legacy (Front)** - Loosen both lower strut mounting bolts so strut can rotate. *See Fig. 4.* Turn strut adjusting bolt to adjust camber. Strut adjusting bolt has eccentric cam head to force strut to positive or negative camber adjustment. Tighten bolts to specification. See TORQUE SPECIFICATIONS table at end of article.

**Legacy (Rear)** - Camber is not adjustable. If camber measurement is not within specification, check for frame damage, lateral link damage or worn out components (struts/springs, joints, etc.).

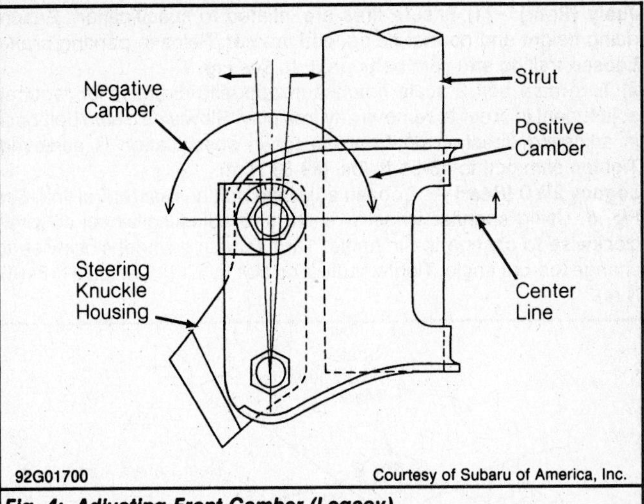


*Fig. 4: Adjusting Front Camber (Legacy)*

**Loyale (Front)** - Camber and caster are not adjustable. If measurements are not within specifications, check for frame damage, transverse link damage, or worn out components (struts/springs, ball joint, etc.).

**Loyale, XT & XT6 (Rear)** - **1)** Remove wheel. Remove lower shock bolt at inner arm (if necessary). Loosen outer arm mounting bolts. *See Fig. 5.* If camber angle measurement is too positive, use a lever to increase angle "0" between inner arm and outer arm. *See Fig. 5.*

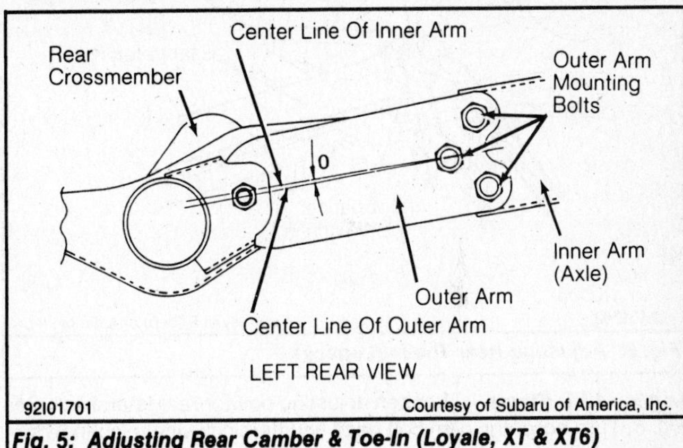


*Fig. 5: Adjusting Rear Camber & Toe-In (Loyale, XT & XT6)*

**2)** If camber angle measurement is too negative, use lever to decrease angle "0" between inner arm and outer arm. Changing camber angle will change toe-in measurement. Changing toe-in will change camber angle. Tighten outer arm mounting bolts to 94-108 ft. lbs. (127-147 N.m).

**XT & XT6 (Front)** - Camber and caster are not adjustable. If measurements are not within specifications, check for frame damage, transverse link damage or worn out components (struts/springs, ball joint, etc.).

### CASTER ADJUSTMENT

**All Models (Front)** - Caster is not adjustable. If measurement is not within specification, check for frame damage, transverse link damage, or worn out components (struts, ball joint, etc.).

### TOE-IN ADJUSTMENT

**All Models (Front)** - **1)** Ensure tires are inflated to specification. Ensure riding height and normal riding load are set. Lock steering wheel to straight-ahead center position.

**2)** Loosen both tie rod lock nuts. Turn both tie rods equal amounts until within toe-in specifications. See WHEEL ALIGNMENT SPECIFICATIONS table at end of article. Tighten lock nuts to specification. See TORQUE SPECIFICATIONS table at end of article.

# 1991 WHEEL ALIGNMENT
# Specifications & Procedures (Cont.)

**Justy (Rear) - 1)** Ensure tires are inflated to specification. Ensure riding height and normal riding load are set. Release parking brake. Loosen trailing arm cam bolt one turn. *See Fig. 1.*

**2)** Turn cam bolt 2 scale notches in opposite direction of required adjustment in order to remove any free play. Slowly turn cam bolt back in adjusting direction until correct toe-in specification is achieved. Tighten cam bolt to 43-51 ft. lbs. (59-69 N.m).

**Legacy 2WD (Rear) -** Loosen adjusting bolt on rear lateral link. *See Fig. 6.* Using spanner wheel wrench, turn adjusting wheel counterclockwise to change toe-in angle. Turn adjusting wheel clockwise to change toe-out angle. Tighten adjusting bolt to 87-116 ft. lbs. (118-157 N.m).

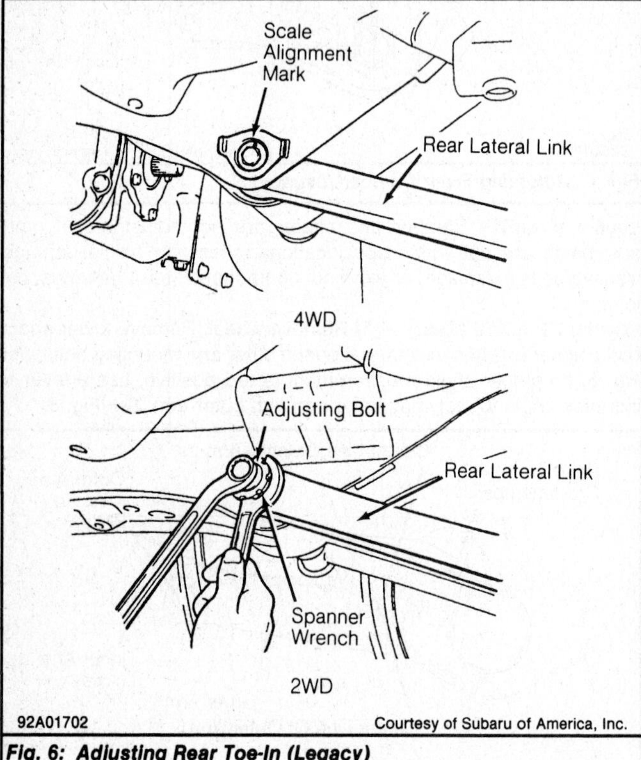


***Fig. 6: Adjusting Rear Toe-In (Legacy)***

**Legacy 4WD (Rear) -** Loosen adjusting bolt for rear lateral link. *See Fig. 6.* Turn eccentric cam bolt head counterclockwise to change toe-out angle. Turn eccentric cam bolt head clockwise to change toe-in angle. Tighten adjusting bolt to 61-83 ft. lbs. (83-113 N.m).

**Loyale, XT & XT6 (Rear) - 1)** Remove wheel. Loosen outer arm mounting bolts. *See Fig. 5.* If toe-in is excessive, push/pull rear axle toward rear of vehicle while tightening outer arm mounting bolts.

**2)** If toe-out is excessive, push/pull rear axle toward front of vehicle while tightening outer arm mounting bolts. Changing toe-in will change camber angle. Changing camber angle will change toe-in measurement. Tighten outer arm mounting bolts to 94-108 ft. lbs. (127-147 N.m).

## TORQUE SPECIFICATIONS

*TORQUE SPECIFICATIONS*

| Application | Ft. Lbs. (N.m) |
|---|---|
| Front Strut Camber Adjusting Bolts (Legacy) | 97-127 (132-172) |
| Rear Trailing Link Cam Bolt (Justy) | 44-51 (59-69) |
| Tie Rod Lock Nuts | |
| Justy | 36-47 (49-64) |
| Loyale, Legacy, XT & XT6 | 58-65 (78-88) |
| Wheel Lug Nuts (All) | 58-72 (79-98) |

## WHEEL ALIGNMENT SPECIFICATIONS

*WHEEL ALIGNMENT SPECIFICATIONS*

| Application | Preferred | Range |
|---|---|---|
| **Justy** | | |
| Camber [1] | | |
| Front | 1 1/16 | -1/4 To 1 5/8 |
| Rear | ..... | ...... |
| Caster [1] | 2 1/2 | 1 1/2 To 3 1/2 |
| Toe-In [1] | | |
| Front | 3/32 (2) | 1/32 To 1/8 (1 To 3) |
| Rear | 0 (0) | -1/8 To 1/8 (-3 To 3) |
| Toe-In [2] | | |
| Front | 3/16 | 1/16 To 1/4 |
| Rear | 0 | -1/4 To 1/4 |
| **Legacy Sedan 2WD** | | |
| Camber [1] | | |
| Front | -1/4 | -3/4 To 1/4 |
| Rear | 1/2 | -1 1/2 To 1/2 |
| Caster [1] | 3 1/16 | 2 1/16 To 4 1/16 |
| Toe-In [1] | | |
| Front | 0 (0) | -1/8 To 1/8 (-3 To 3) |
| Rear | 0 (0) | -1/8 To 1/8 (-3 To 3) |
| Toe-In [2] | | |
| Front | 0 | 1/4 To 1/4 |
| Rear | 0 | -1/4 To 1/4 |
| **Legacy Sedan 4WD** | | |
| Camber [1] | | |
| Front | 0 | -1/2 To 1/2 |
| Rear | -1/2 | -1 To 0 |
| Caster [1] | 3 | 2 To 4 |
| Toe-In [1] | | |
| Front | 0 (0) | -1/8 To 1/8 (-3 To 3) |
| Rear | 0 (0) | -1/8 To 1/8 (-3 To 3) |
| Toe-In [2] | | |
| Front | 0 | -1/4 To 1/4 |
| Rear | 0 | -1/4 To 1/4 |
| **Legacy Wagon 2WD** | | |
| Camber [1] | | |
| Front | -1/4 | -3/4 To 1/4 |
| Rear | -5/16 | -1 5/16 To 11/16 |
| Caster [1] | 2 13/16 | 1 13/16 To 3 13/16 |
| Toe-In [1] | | |
| Front | 0 (0) | -1/8 To 1/8 (-3 To 3) |
| Rear | 0 (0) | -1/8 To 1/8 (-3 To 3) |
| Toe-In [2] | | |
| Front | 0 | -1/4 To 1/4 |
| Rear | 0 | -1/4 To 1/4 |
| **Legacy Wagon 4WD** | | |
| Camber [1] | | |
| Front | 0 | -1/2 To 1/2 |
| Rear | -5/16 | -1 5/16 To 11/16 |
| Caster [1] | 2 3/4 | 1 3/4 To 3 3/4 |
| Toe-In [1] | | |
| Front | 0 (0) | -1/8 To 1/8 (-3 To 3) |
| Rear | 0 (0) | -1/8 To 1/8 (-3 To 3) |
| Toe-In [2] | | |
| Front | 0 | -1/4 To 1/4 |
| Rear | 0 | -1/4 To 1/4 |
| **Loyale 2WD** | | |
| Camber [1] | | |
| Front | 3/4 | 0 To 1 1/2 |
| Rear | 0 | -1/2 To 1/2 |
| Caster [1] | 2 1/2 | 1 3/4 To 3 1/4 |
| Toe-In [1] | | |
| Front | 1/16 (2) | 1/32 To 1/8 (1 To 3) |
| Rear | 0 (0) | -1/16 To 1/16 (-2 To 2) |

[1] - Measurement in degrees.
[2] - Measurement in inches (mm).

# 1991 WHEEL ALIGNMENT
# Specifications & Procedures (Cont.)

***WHEEL ALIGNMENT SPECIFICATIONS (Cont.)***

| Application | Preferred | Range |
|---|---|---|
| **Loyale 2WD (Cont.)** | | |
| Toe-In [2] | | |
| Front | 1/8 | 1/16 To 1/8 |
| Rear | 0 | -1/8 To 1/8 |
| **Loyale 4WD** | | |
| Camber [1] | | |
| Front | 1 11/16 | 15/16 To 2 7/16 |
| Rear | 0 | -1/2 To 1/2 |
| Caster [1] | .... | .... |
| Toe-In [1] | | |
| Front | 3/16 (5) | 5/32 To 1/4 (4 To 6) |
| Rear | 0 (0) | -1/16 To 1/16 (-2 To 2) |
| Toe-In [2] | | |
| Front | 1/4 | 3/16 To 5/16 |
| Rear | 0 | -1/8 To 1/8 |
| **Loyale Wagon 2WD** | | |
| Camber [1] | | |
| Front | 1 | 1/4 To 1 3/4 |
| Rear | 0 | -1/2 To 1/2 |
| Caster [1] | 2 1/16 | 1 5/16 To 2 13/16 |
| Toe-In [1] | | |
| Front | 1/16 (2) | 1/32 To 1/8 (1 To 3) |
| Rear | 0 (0) | -1/16 To 1/16 (-2 To 2) |
| Toe-In [2] | | |
| Front | 1/8 | 1/16 To 1/8 |
| Rear | 0 | -1/8 To 1/8 |
| **Loyale Wagon 4WD** | | |
| Camber [1] | | |
| Front | 1 3/4 | 1 To 2 1/2 |
| Rear | 0 | -1/2 To 1/2 |
| Caster [1] | .... | .... |
| Toe-In [1] | | |
| Front | 3/16 (5) | 5/32 To 1/4 (4 To 6) |
| Rear | 0 (0) | -1/16 To 1/16 (-2 To 2) |
| Toe-In [2] | | |
| Front | 1/4 | 3/16 To 5/16 |
| Rear | 0 | -1/8 To 1/8 |
| **XT & XT6 2WD** | | |
| Camber [1] | | |
| Front | 0 | -3/4 To 3/4 |
| Rear | 0 | -3/4 To 3/4 |
| Caster [1] | 4 1/16 | 3 5/16 To 4 13/16 |
| Toe-In [1] | | |
| Front | 0 (0) | -1/32 To 1/32 (-1 To 1) |
| Rear | 0 (0) | -3/32 To 3/32 (-2 To 2) |
| Toe-In [2] | | |
| Front | 0 | -1/16 To 1/16 |
| Rear | 0 | -1/8 To 1/8 |
| **XT & XT6 4WD** | | |
| Camber [1] | | |
| Front | 13/16 | 1/16 To 1 9/16 |
| Rear | -3/16 | -15/16 To 9/16 |
| Caster [1] | 3 1/2 | 2 3/4 To 4 1/4 |
| Toe-In [1] | | |
| Front | -3/16 (-5) | -1/4 To -5/32 (-6 To -4) |
| Rear | 0 (0) | -3/32 To 3/32 (-2 To 2) |
| Toe-In [2] | | |
| Front | -1/4 | -5/16 To -3/16 |
| Rear | 0 | -1/8 To 1/8 |

[1] – Measurement in degrees.
[2] – Measurement in inches (mm).

# 1991 SUSPENSION
# Front

## Justy, Legacy, Loyale, XT, XT6

## DESCRIPTION

Front suspension is a MacPherson strut type, consisting of lower control arms, leading rods, knuckle housings and a stabilizer bar. Leading rods are mounted between lower control arms and brackets on body.

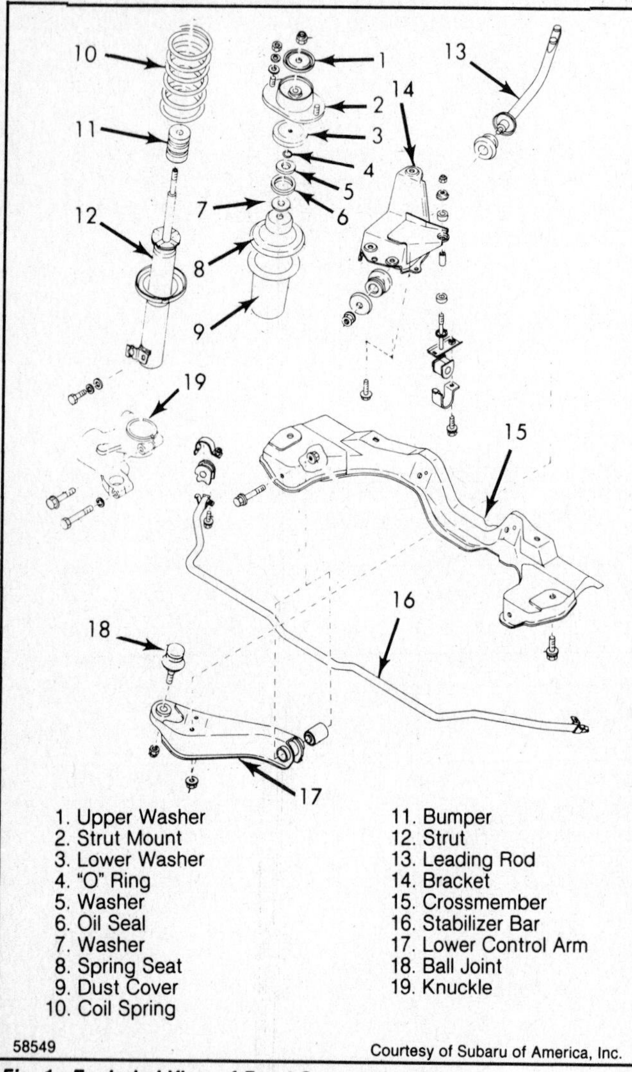


*Fig. 1: Exploded View of Front Suspension (Justy)*

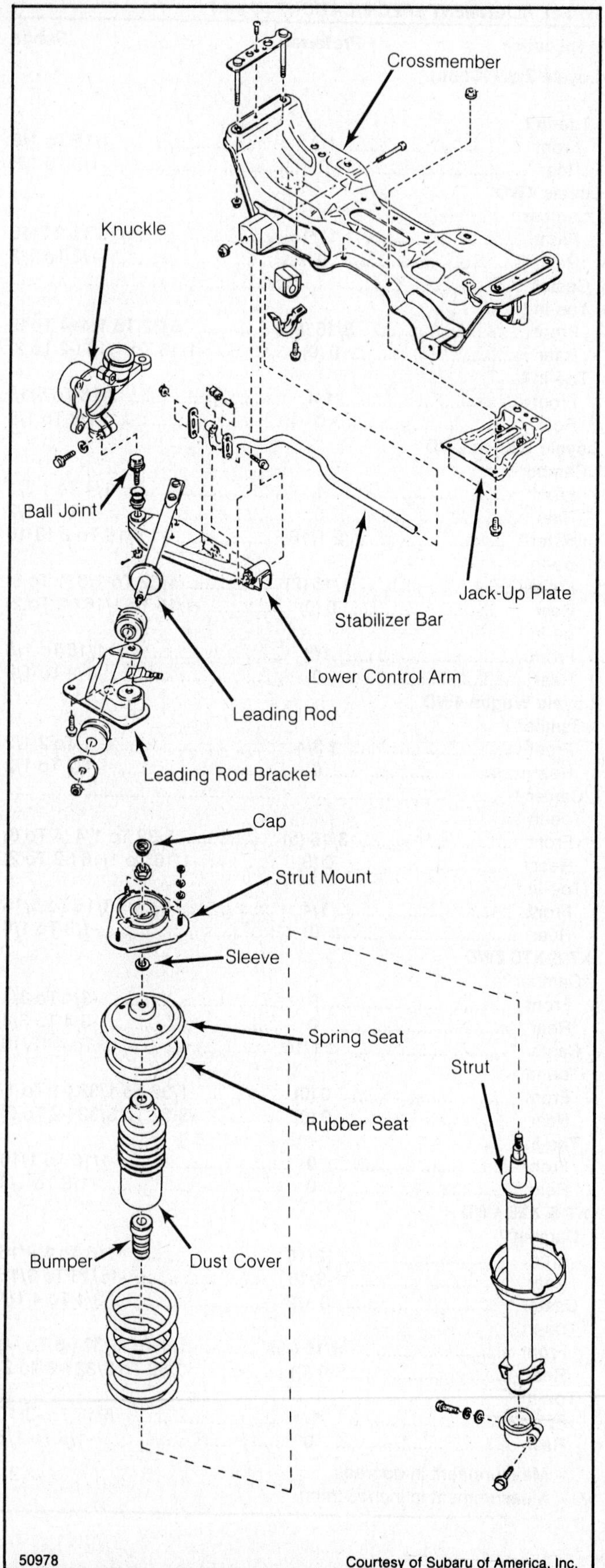

50978
Courtesy of Subaru of America, Inc.

*Fig. 2: Exploded View of Front Suspension (Loyale & XT; Legacy is Similar)*

## ADJUSTMENTS & INSPECTION

### WHEEL ALIGNMENT SPECIFICATIONS & PROCEDURES

***NOTE:** See SPECIFICATIONS & PROCEDURES article in WHEEL ALIGNMENT.*

### WHEEL BEARING

Front wheel bearings do not require periodic adjustment, but should be inspected at 60,000 mile intervals for proper lubrication.

### BALL JOINT CHECKING

Load ball joint stud with 154 lbs. (69 kg). On Justy, vertical play should not exceed .016" (.40 mm). On all other models, vertical play should not exceed .012" (.30 mm). Replace ball joint if play is excessive.

# 1991 SUSPENSION
# Front (Cont.)

## REMOVAL & INSTALLATION

### KNUCKLE & WHEEL BEARING ASSEMBLY

**Removal & Installation (Loyale & XT) - 1)** Apply parking brake. Loosen axle nut and lug nuts. Raise and support vehicle. Remove wheel assembly. Release parking brake. *See Fig. 3*. Pull parking brake cable outer clip from caliper. Remove parking brake cable end from caliper lever.

**2)** Remove caliper assembly and wire aside. Remove bolts connecting knuckle to strut. Disconnect tie rod from knuckle. Pull strut from knuckle. DO NOT spread housing slit more than .16" (4 mm).

**3)** Remove castle nut, spring washer and center piece on axle shaft. Remove hub and disc assembly. Remove disc cover. Use Puller (926470000) to pull knuckle from axle shaft. Disconnect ball joint from knuckle and remove knuckle. To install, reverse removal procedure.

**Removal & Installation (Justy) - 1)** Pull parking brake lever. Loosen axle nut and lug nuts. Raise and support vehicle. Remove wheel assembly. Remove brake caliper assembly and axle nut. Remove brake rotor from axle shaft. Remove disc cover from knuckle.

**2)** Drive out spring pin attaching axle shaft to differential. DO NOT reuse old spring pin. Disconnect tie-rod from knuckle. Remove bolt attaching knuckle to strut. Disconnect ball joint from control arm. Remove knuckle and axle as a unit. Use Remover (922493000 and 921122000) to separate knuckle and axle. To install, reverse removal procedure. *See Fig. 3*.

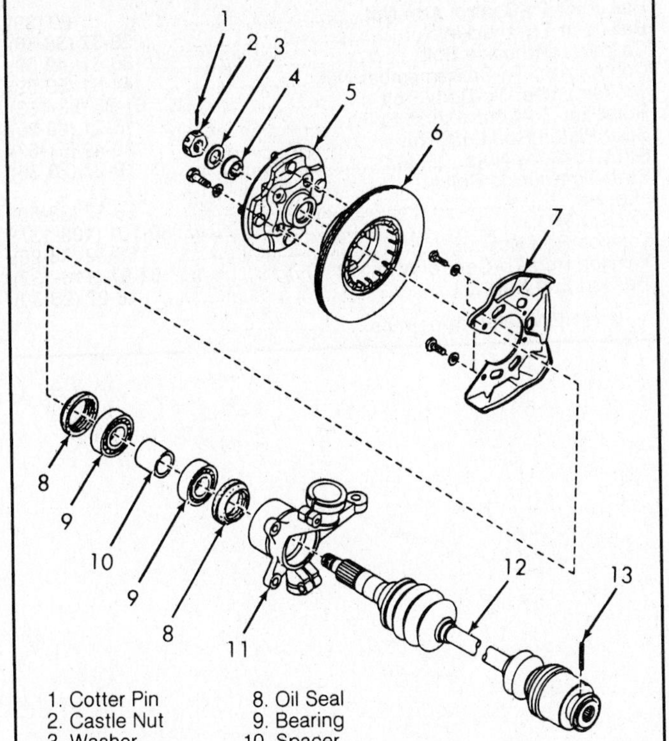

1. Cotter Pin
2. Castle Nut
3. Washer
4. Center Piece
5. Hub
6. Brake Rotor
7. Disc Cover
8. Oil Seal
9. Bearing
10. Spacer
11. Knuckle
12. Axle Shaft Assembly
13. Spring Pin

91F02394 Courtesy of Subaru of America, Inc.

*Fig. 3: Exploded View of Front Axle Hub (Typical)*

**Removal & Installation (Legacy) -** Raise and support vehicle. Remove stabilizer bar from crossmember. Remove axle shaft. Remove brake caliper and rotor from knuckle. Disconnect tie-rod from knuckle. Disconnect ball joint from control arm. Remove front speed sensor from knuckle. Disconnect knuckle from strut. To install, reverse removal procedure. *See Fig. 3*.

### LOWER CONTROL ARM & BALL JOINT

**Removal - 1)** Raise vehicle and support. Remove front wheels. Disconnect stabilizer bar and leading rod from control arm. On Loyale, XT and XT6, disconnect parking brake cable mounting bracket from lower control arm. *See Fig. 1 or 2*.

**2)** On all models, remove bolt and separate control arm from front crossmember. Remove ball joint pinch bolt and separate ball joint from knuckle housing. Without damaging CV joint boot, carefully use a screwdriver to spread knuckle (if necessary). DO NOT spread housing slit more than .16" (4 mm).

**3)** Remove control arm from vehicle. Remove ball joint nut and remove ball joint from control arm.

**Installation -** To install, reverse removal procedure. Check bushing for wear or damage. Replace if necessary. Install NEW cotter pin. Tighten control arm to crossmember bolt after vehicle has been lowered to ground.

### STRUT ASSEMBLY

**Removal - 1)** Raise vehicle and support. Remove wheel assembly. Disconnect brake line from caliper. Disconnect brake hose from strut bracket. Remove knuckle to strut retaining bolts.

**2)** Separate knuckle from strut by pushing knuckle down. On Loyale, XT and XT6, without damaging CV joint boot, carefully use a screwdriver to spread knuckle if necessary. DO NOT spread housing slit more than .16" (4 mm). Remove upper strut retaining nuts. On all models, remove strut from vehicle.

**Disassembly -** Compress coil spring with Compressor (926110000) until upper seat is separated from coil spring. On Justy, hold strut rod with an Allen wrench and remove self-locking nut. On all models, use Spanner (926510000) to hold spring seat while removing self-locking nut. Remove components from strut. On Justy, note position of thrust washers and washers for reassembly reference.

**Inspection -** Check all parts for wear or damage. Replace if necessary. Check rod deflection. Fully extend rod and mount a dial indicator .4" (10 mm) from end of rod. Apply a load of 4 lbs. (1.8 kg) to end of rod and measure play. Maximum side play is .031" (.80 mm). Replace strut if play exceeds specification. Strut cannot be disassembled. Check action of rod for abnormal noise or resistance.

**Reassembly & Installation - 1)** To reassemble, reverse disassembly procedure. Use NEW self-locking nut. On Justy, coat thrust washer with grease. Ensure projection on dust cover fits into notch on upper spring seat.

**2)** Ensure groove in washer for "O" ring faces up. Ensure notch in thrust washer aligns with notch in upper spring seat. Ensure notches in upper and lower spring seats are aligned.

**3)** On all other models, ensure flat side of coil spring is up when assembling strut. To install, reverse removal procedure. Bleed brakes.

### STABILIZER BAR

**Removal & Installation -** Raise vehicle and support with safety stands. Remove brackets securing stabilizer bar to lower control arm. Remove brackets attaching stabilizer bar to crossmember. Remove jack-up plate of crossmember and remove stabilizer. To install, reverse removal procedure. Tighten bolts after vehicle has been lowered to ground.

### CROSSMEMBER

**Removal & Installation (Justy) -** Raise and support vehicle. Support engine at front and rear with Engine Support (921540000). Remove engine splash shield. Remove engine mount center member. Remove exhaust system with muffler attached. Remove lower control arm from crossmember. Remove engine mount nut from crossmember. Remove crossmember from vehicle. To install, reverse removal procedure.

# 1991 SUSPENSION
# Front (Cont.)

**Removal & Installation (Except Justy)** – **1)** Raise and support vehicle. Remove wheels. Remove spare tire, air cleaner assembly, and pitching stopper rod. Cover throttle body to keep out dust.

**2)** Remove parking brake cable bracket from lower control arm. Disconnect tie rod end from knuckle housing. Remove front exhaust pipe. Remove lower control arm from crossmember.

**3)** Remove nuts attaching engine mounts to crossmember. Remove nuts connecting steering torque rod and pinion shaft. Lift engine assembly .40" (10 mm). Support crossmember with jack. Remove nuts and remove crossmember along with steering box.

**4)** To install, reverse removal procedure. Tighten crossmember nuts and lower control arm-to-crossmember bolt with vehicle on ground and suspension unloaded.

## TORQUE SPECIFICATIONS

*TORQUE SPECIFICATIONS*

| Application [1] | Ft. Lbs. (N.m) |
|---|---|
| **Justy** | |
| Ball Joint-To-Control Arm Nut | 29 (39) |
| Ball Joint-To-Knuckle Nut | 25-40 (34-54) |
| Caliper-To-Knuckle Bolt | 38-49 (52-66) |
| Control Arm-To-Crossmember Nut | 44-58 (59-78) |
| Crossmember-To-Body Bolt | 44-51 (59-69) |
| Stabilizer-To-Control Arm Bolt | 15-22 (20-30) |
| Strut Piston Rod Lock Nut | 43-51 (59-69) |
| Strut-To-Body Nuts | 29-44 (39-59) |
| Strut-To-Knuckle Bolt | 25-40 (34-55) |
| Tension Rod Nut | 40-55 (54-74) |
| Tension Rod-To-Control Arm Nut | 55-69 (74-93) |
| Tie Rod End Nut | 18-22 (25-30) |
| **Legacy** | |
| Ball Joint-To-Control Arm Nut | 29 (39) |
| Ball Joint-To-Knuckle Nut | 28-37 (38-50) |
| Caliper-To-Knuckle Bolt | 36-51 (49-69) |
| Control Arm-To-Crossmember Nut | 61-83 (83-113) |
| Crossmember-To-Body Bolt | 61-83 (83-113) |
| Stabilizer-To-Control Arm Bolt | 15-21 (21-28) |
| Strut Piston Rod Lock Nut | 36-51 (49-69) |
| Strut-To-Body Nuts | 10-18 (14-25) |
| Strut-To-Knuckle Bolt | 97-120 (132-162) |
| Tension Rod Nut | 40-55 (54-74) |
| Tension Rod-To-Control Arm Nut | 55-69 (74-93) |
| Tie Rod End Nut | 18-22 (25-30) |
| **Loyale, XT & XT6** | |
| Ball Joint-To-Control Arm Nut | 29 (39) |
| Ball Joint-To-Knuckle Nut | 28-37 (38-50) |
| Caliper-To-Knuckle Bolt | 36-51 (49-69) |
| Control Arm-To-Crossmember Nut | 44-51 (59-69) |
| Crossmember-To-Body Bolt | 61-83 (83-113) |
| Stabilizer-To-Control Arm Bolt | 15-21 (20-29) |
| Strut Piston Rod Lock Nut | 38-49 (51-67) |
| Strut-To-Body Nuts | 19-27 (26-36) |
| Strut-To-Knuckle Bolt | |
| Loyale | 28-37 (38-50) |
| XT & XT6 | 80-101 (108-137) |
| Tension Rod Nut | 58-72 (78-98) |
| Tension Rod-To-Control Arm Nut | 83-97 (113-132) |
| Tie Rod End Nut | 18-22 (25-30) |

[1] – Use NEW self-locking nuts.

# 1991 SUSPENSION
# Rear - Except Justy

## Legacy, Loyale, XT, XT6

## DESCRIPTION

Rear suspension is a semi-trailing arm, independent type. Crossmember is mounted to body frame with brackets at both ends via bushings. *See Figs. 1 and 2.*

One end of trailing arm is bolted to crossmember through a bushing, and other end is mounted to body through shock absorber. An outer arm is bolted on one end to crossmember through a bushing, and other end is directly bolted to trailing arm.

***NOTE: For information on rear axle shafts for 4WD vehicles, see 4WD REAR AXLE SHAFTS article in DRIVE AXLES.***

## ADJUSTMENTS & INSPECTION

### WHEEL ALIGNMENT

***NOTE: See SPECIFICATIONS & PROCEDURES article in WHEEL ALIGNMENT.***

### WHEEL BEARING (2WD)

***NOTE: Information on adjustment and inspection of Legacy models is not provided by manufacturer. A general inspection should be performed, however. Clean parts and check for wear, damage and corrosion.***

**Adjustment (Except Legacy)** - Tighten hub nut to 36 ft. lbs. (49 N.m). Rotate hub several times to seat bearings. Check starting torque using spring scale. Correct starting torque is 1.9-3.2 lbs. (8.3-14.2 N). Adjust starting torque by loosening nut 1/8 - 1/10 turn.

**Inspection (Except Legacy)** - When inspecting grease, a general inspection of bearings should be performed. If grease has diminished in quantity or has turned white, remove bearings and races. Inspect for wear, damage or corrosion. Replace grease every 60,000 miles.

### WHEEL BEARING (4WD)

***NOTE: No periodic adjustment of rear wheel bearings is required.***

**Inspection (Legacy)** - **1)** With rear of vehicle raised, move top and bottom of tire in and out to check bearing free play. Remove rear wheel. If bearing free play exists, attach a dial indicator to wheel hub. Measure axial hub play by pulling hub straight out.

**2)** Axial play should be no more than .002" (.05 mm). Turn hub back and forth to check for noise or binding. If axial play is excessive or if bearings are noisy or binding, disassemble hub assembly and check condition of bearings and seals.

**Inspection (Except Legacy)** - When inspecting grease, a general inspection of bearings should be performed. If grease has diminished in quantity or has turned white, remove bearings from hub/housing, clean, inspect and repack. Inspect for wear, damage or corrosion. Replace grease every 60,000 miles.

## REMOVAL & INSTALLATION

### WHEEL BEARING

***NOTE: Information on rear wheel bearing removal for Legacy 2WD is not available from manufacturer.***

**Removal (2WD - Loyale, XT & XT6)** - Raise and support vehicle. Remove wheel assembly. Remove brake drum, inner race and bearing, outer race and oil seal together. Remove spacer and inner

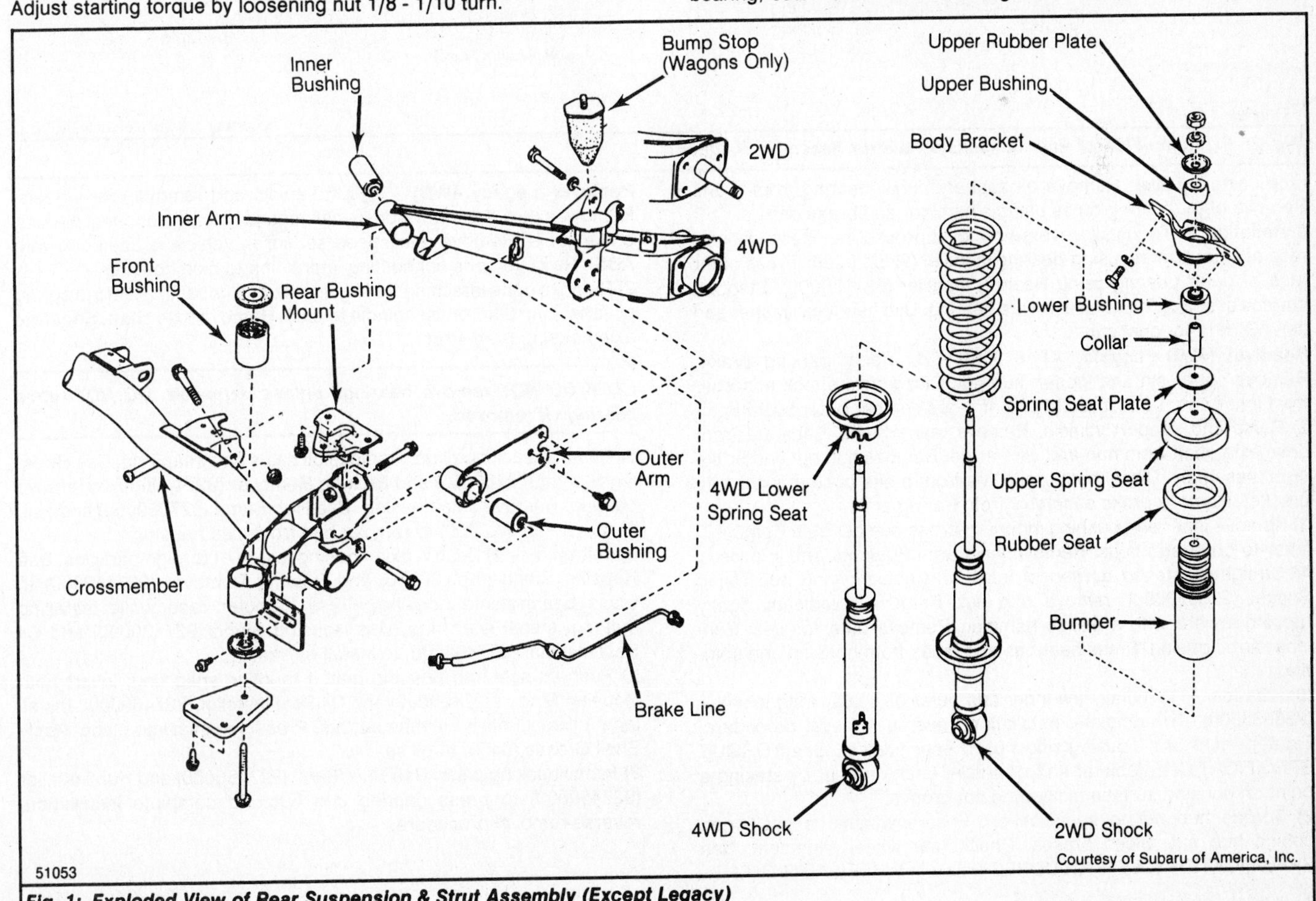


*Fig. 1: Exploded View of Rear Suspension & Strut Assembly (Except Legacy)*

# 1991 SUSPENSION
## Rear – Except Justy (Cont.)

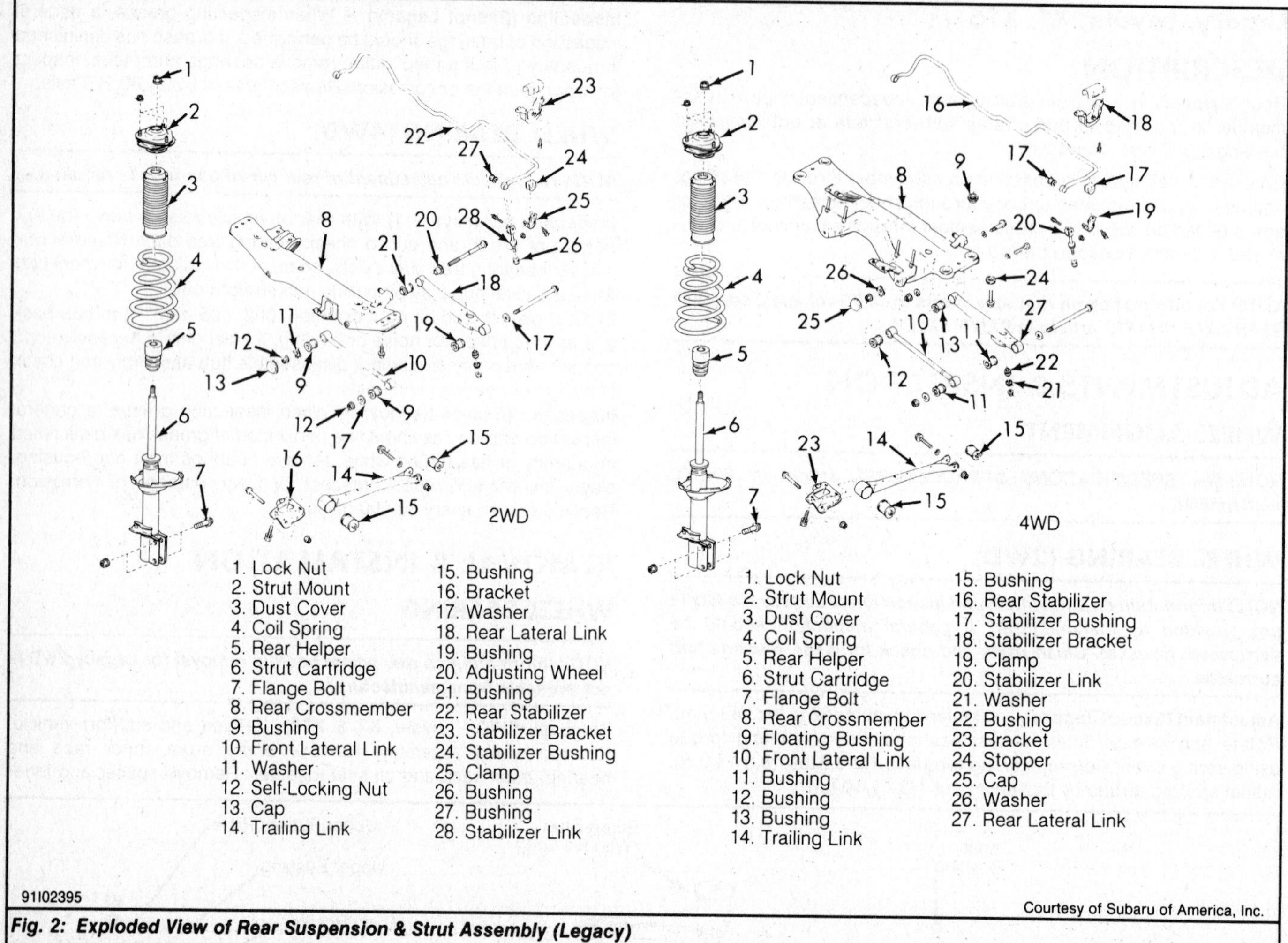


**Fig. 2: Exploded View of Rear Suspension & Strut Assembly (Legacy)**

race using a puller. Remove oil seal and inner bearing from drum. Remove outer bearing races using a hammer and brass drift.

**Installation** – To install, reverse removal procedure. Press in outer race of inner bearing using Bearing Installer (925220000). Press outer race of outer bearing using Bearing Installer (921130000). Stepped surface of spacer must face toward bearing. Use new lock washer and new "O" ring for dust cap.

**Removal (4WD – Loyale, XT & XT6) – 1)** Apply parking brake. Remove cotter pin and loosen hub nut. Disconnect shock absorber from inner arm. Loosen lock bolts of crossmember outer bushing.

**2)** Raise and support vehicle. Remove rear wheels. Separate front drive axle shaft from hub and wire aside. Remove hub nut and brake drum assembly. Disconnect brake line from brake hose at inner arm bracket. Remove brake assembly from trailing arm.

**3)** Remove inner arm bushing mount-to-crossmember bolt. Remove 3 inner-to-outer arm bolts. Remove inner arm. Put inner arm in a vise.

**4)** Straighten staked portion of inner arm housing ring nut. Using Socket (925550000), remove ring nut. Remove spindle by lightly tapping inward with a plastic hammer. Remove outer oil seal from inner arm housing. Press bearings and races from housing and spindle.

**Installation – 1)** Install new inner and outer oil seals using Installer (925530000). To complete installation, reverse removal procedure. Tighten inner arm housing ring nut to specification. See TORQUE SPECIFICATIONS table at end of article. Lock ring nut by staking a point on housing surface facing ring nut groove.

**2)** Torque hub nut to specification. Ensure washer is positioned behind hub nut. Bleed brakes. Check rear wheel alignment. See SPECIFICATIONS & PROCEDURES article in WHEEL ALIGNMENT.

**Removal (Legacy 4WD) – 1)** Lift vehicle and remove rear wheels. Remove axle nut. Remove brake caliper and rotor. Disconnect parking brake cable. Remove rear speed sensor (if vehicle is equipped with ABS). Remove bolts connecting lateral link to axle housing.

**2)** Remove bolts attaching trailing arm to axle housing. Remove spring pin attaching differential spindle to axle. Remove axle shaft. Separate axle housing from strut.

***NOTE: DO NOT remove bearings unless damaged. DO NOT reuse bearings if removed.***

**3)** Remove backing plate. Remove oil seals and snap ring. Use Housing Stand (927430000) and Bearing Remover (927440000) to remove bearing. Remove axle housing. Use Hub Stand (927080000) and Hub Remover (927420000) to remove hub from axle housing.

**Installation – 1)** Ensure axle housing is free of foreign particles. Use Housing Stand (927430000) and Bearing Remover (927440000) to press bearing into housing. Press in outer race while installing bearing. Install snap ring. Use Housing Stand (927430000) and Oil Seal Installer (927460000) to install oil seal.

**2)** Push oil seal into housing until it touches snap ring. Invert both Housing Stand (927430000) and Oil Seal Installer (927460000). Install inner oil seal until it touches bottom. Press sub seal into place. Apply Shell Grease (6459) to oil seal lip.

**3)** Install backing plate. Use Hub Stand (927080000) and Hub Installer (927450000) to press bearing into hub. To complete installation, reverse removal procedure.

# 1991 SUSPENSION
# Rear – Except Justy (Cont.)

## REAR SUSPENSION ASSEMBLY

***NOTE: Information on rear suspension assembly removal and installation for Legacy is not available from manufacturer.***

**Removal (Loyale, XT & XT6) – 1)** Remove shock absorber-to-body mounting bolts. Raise and support vehicle. Remove wheel assembly. On 4WD models, remove drive shafts. Separate drive axle shaft from hub and wire aside. Disconnect propeller shaft from differential. Slowly pull propeller shaft out of transmission. Plug hole in transmission to prevent oil spills.

**2)** Support differential with floor jack. Remove 2 center differential nuts and 4 differential-to-crossmember nuts. Remove differential from vehicle.

**3)** On all models, remove all exhaust system parts interfering with access to rear suspension. Disconnect brake hoses at inner arm brackets. Support crossmember at center with floor jack. Remove crossmember-to-body bolts and slowly lower rear suspension assembly to floor.

**Inspection** – Check for any damage or wear to bushings. Press out and replace bushings if necessary. Check for deformation or cracks on trailing arm, outer arm and crossmember. Replace components as necessary.

**Installation** – To install, reverse removal procedure. Tighten bolts and rear bushing mounts with vehicle unloaded. See TORQUE SPECIFICATIONS table. Bleed brake system. Check wheel alignment. See SPECIFICATIONS & PROCEDURES article in WHEEL ALIGNMENT.

## STRUT ASSEMBLY

**Removal & Disassembly (Legacy)** – Remove rear seat cushion and rear seat backrest. Raise and support vehicle. Remove rear wheels. Remove brake caliper if necessary. Remove upper and lower mounting bolts and remove strut from vehicle. Use Coil Spring Compressor (926110000) to compress coil spring. Remove double nuts and disassemble shock. Note position of coil spring in relation to upper bracket. *See Fig. 1 or 2.*

**Inspection** – Check shock absorber for oil leaks. Check action of piston rod for abnormal noise or resistance.

**Reassembly & Installation** – To reassemble, reverse removal procedure. Mount coil spring with flat end down. To install, reverse removal procedure.

## TORQUE SPECIFICATIONS

***TORQUE SPECIFICATIONS***

| Application | Ft. Lbs. (N.m) |
|---|---|
| Legacy | |
| Backing Plate-To-Inner Arm Bolt | 34-43 (46-58) |
| Crossmember-To-Body | 80-108 (108-147) |
| Differential-To-Crossmember Nut (4WD) | 41-53 (56-72) |
| Hub Nut (4WD) | 123-152 (167-206) |
| Propeller Shaft Bolt (4WD) | 18-29 (24-39) |
| Stabilizer Bracket-To-Inner Arm Bolt | 13-16 (18-22) |
| Strut Piston Rod Lock Nut | 36-51 (49-69) |
| Strut-To-Axle Housing Bolt | 92-127 (132-172) |
| Strut-To-Body Bolt | 10-18 (14-25) |
| Loyale, XT & XT6 | |
| Backing Plate-To-Inner Arm Bolt | 34-43 (46-58) |
| Crossmember-To-Body | 58-72 (78-98) |
| Differential-To-Crossmember Nut (4WD) | 51-58 (69-78) |
| Hub Nut (4WD) | 145 (196) |
| Inner Arm-To-Crossmember Bolt | 51-65 (69-88) |
| Inner-To-Outer Arm Bolt | 94-108 (127-147) |
| Outer Arm-To-Crossmember Bolt | 94-108 (127-147) |
| Propeller Shaft Bolt (4WD) | 18-24 (24-32) |
| Shock Bracket-To-Body Bolt | 65-94 (88-127) |
| Shock Piston Rod Lock Nut | 13-18 (18-25) |
| Shock-To-Inner Arm Bolt | 65-87 (88-118) |

# 1991 SUSPENSION
# Rear – Justy

## DESCRIPTION

Rear suspension assembly consists of a crossmember, trailing links, lower control arms, strut assemblies, coil springs and spindle housings. Spindle housing is bolted to strut, trailing link and lower arm. Coil spring mounts between crossmember and lower control arm.

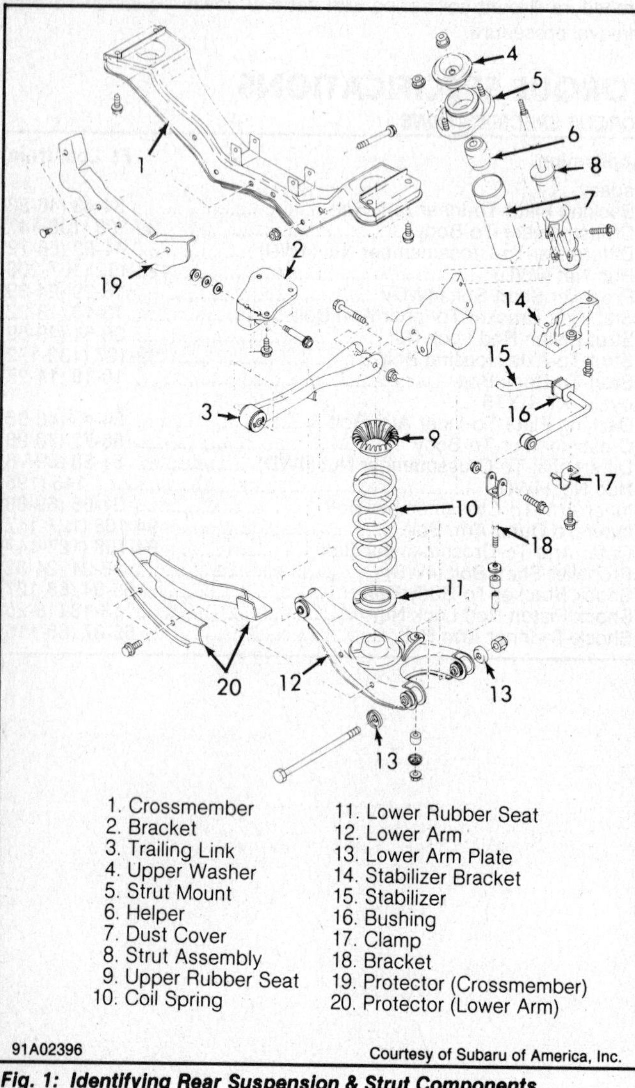


*Fig. 1: Identifying Rear Suspension & Strut Components*

## ADJUSTMENTS & INSPECTION

### WHEEL ALIGNMENT & RIDE HEIGHT SPECIFICATIONS & PROCEDURES

*NOTE: See SPECIFICATIONS & PROCEDURES article in WHEEL ALIGNMENT.*

### WHEEL BEARING

*NOTE: Rear wheel bearings on 4WD models are not adjustable.*

On 2WD models, tighten spindle nut to 29 ft. lbs. (39 N.m). Rotate drum several times to seat bearings. Loosen nut. Check starting torque of drum using spring scale attached to wheel lug nut. Starting torque should be 3.1-4.4 lbs. (1.4-2.0 kg). Tighten spindle nut until proper starting torque is obtained.

## REMOVAL & INSTALLATION

### WHEEL BEARING

**Removal (2WD)** – Raise and support vehicle. Remove wheel assembly. Remove grease cap (do not damage "O" ring), spindle nut, lock washer and washer. Remove brake drum with outer bearing. Remove spacer, oil seal and inner bearing. Drive out bearing outer races using brass bar and hammer.

**Installation** – **1)** Inspect brake drum, races and spindle for wear, cracks or damage. Press bearing outer races into drum using Installer (922111000). Pack bearings with grease and install. Press oil seal in using installer.

**2)** To complete installation, reverse removal procedure. Ensure spacer is installed with chamfered side facing in. Use NEW lock washer. Adjust wheel bearing.

**Removal (4WD)** – **1)** Remove wheel and remove hub nut. Remove brake drum. Remove spring pin attaching axle shaft to differential. Remove strut, lower link and trailing link. Remove axle housing together with axle shaft.

**2)** Use Removers (921122000 and 922490000) to separate axle housing from axle shaft. Drive inner and outer bearings and races from axle housing. Remove spacer.

**Inspection** – Clean all parts. Check all parts for cracks, wear and heat damaged. Replace as necessary.

**Installation** – **1)** Pack wheel bearings with grease. Use Hub Bearing Installer (921350000) to install bearing. Apply grease to oil seal. Press seal into housing until it contacts bearing. Install spacer. Use Hub Bearing Installer (921350000) to install other bearing.

**2)** Coat oil seal with grease and install. Use Hub Installer Cap (922320000), lead screw and handle from Hub Installer (92136000) to install axle shaft into axle housing. To complete installation, reverse removal procedure.

### REAR SUSPENSION ASSEMBLY

**Removal & Installation** – **1)** Raise and support vehicle. Remove wheel assembly. Disconnect brake hose at frame bracket. Disconnect muffler from rear exhaust pipe. Remove rear exhaust pipe from hanger. Remove exhaust pipe heat protector rear bolt.

**2)** Remove equalizer at center of parking brake cable. Remove rod from support and separate inner cable. Remove clamp bolt from parking brake outer cable.

**3)** On 4WD models, remove bolts mounting drive shaft to rear differential. Remove spring pins and separate both axles from differential. Discard spring pins. On all models, remove bolts attaching trailing link bracket to body. Remove bolt attaching lower arm to crossmember. Remove coil spring.

**4)** Raise and support lower arms. Remove trim cover on upper part of strut. Remove nuts attaching strut to body. Remove suspension assembly from vehicle.

**5)** To install, reverse removal procedure. On 4WD models, use NEW spring pins when installing axle shafts. On all models, install new exhaust pipe gasket. Tighten lower arm-to-crossmember bolt with vehicle on ground and suspension unloaded.

### CROSSMEMBER

**Removal & Installation** – **1)** Raise and support vehicle. Remove wheel assembly. Disconnect strut from spindle housing. Push lower arm down and remove coil spring. Disconnect lower arm from crossmember. On 4WD models, jack up rear differential.

**2)** Disconnect rear differential from crossmember. Disconnect crossmember from body. Remove muffler from hanger and push down. Remove crossmember from vehicle. To install, reverse removal procedure.

### STRUT ASSEMBLY & COIL SPRING

**Removal & Disassembly** – **1)** Raise and support vehicle. Remove wheel assembly. Remove trim cover on top of strut. Remove nuts attaching strut to body. Push lower arm down and pull out coil spring. *See Fig. 1.*

# 1991 SUSPENSION
# Rear – Justy (Cont.)

**2)** Remove bolts attaching strut to spindle housing. Remove strut from vehicle. Clamp strut in vise. Loosen strut rod lock nut while holding rod with Allen wrench. Remove components from strut.

**Inspection – 1)** Inspect strut mount for damage. Check bolt threads for damage. Inspect helper, dust cover and upper and lower coil spring seats for cracks or damage. Check strut rod for binding or unusual noise. Check strut for oil leakage, deformed outer shell or deformed or cracked bracket.

**2)** Check rod side play. Fully extend rod and mount a dial indicator .4" (10 mm) from end of rod. Apply a load of 4 lbs. (20 N) to end of rod and measure play. Maximum side play is .031" (.80 mm).

**3)** Check diameter of piston rod. Standard diameter is .71" (18 mm) and should not exceed .7067" (17.95 mm). Replace strut if play exceeds specification. Strut cannot be disassembled.

**Reassembly & Installation –** To reassemble, reverse disassembly procedure. Ensure helper is installed with small end up. Use NEW strut rod lock nut. To install, reverse removal procedure. Ensure coil spring fits properly in upper and lower rubber seats.

## TORQUE SPECIFICATIONS

***TORQUE SPECIFICATIONS***

| Application | Ft. Lbs. (N.m) |
|---|---|
| Bracket-To-Body Bolt | 36-51 (49-69) |
| Crossmember-To-Body Bolt | 36-51 (49-69) |
| Drive Shaft-To-Rear Differential Bolt | 18-24 (24-32) |
| Lower Arm-To-Crossmember Bolt | 44-58 (59-78) |
| Lower Arm-To-Housing Bolt | 55-69 (74-93) |
| Strut Piston Rod Lock Nut | 43-51 (59-69) |
| Strut-To-Body Nut | 40-55 (54-74) |
| Strut-To-Housing Bolt | 72-87 (98-118) |
| Trailing Link-To-Bracket Bolt | 36-51 (49-69) |
| Trailing Link-To-Housing Bolt | 44-58 (59-78) |

# 1991 SUSPENSION
# Electronic

## Legacy, XT, XT6

## DESCRIPTION

Major components of electronic height control suspension system include an air compressor, air tank, air shocks, pressure switch, solenoid valves, drier, and system control unit. *See Figs. 1 and 2.* System responds to commands from control switch and from an automatic override feature, which functions at higher vehicle speeds. System incorporates self-diagnostic capabilities.

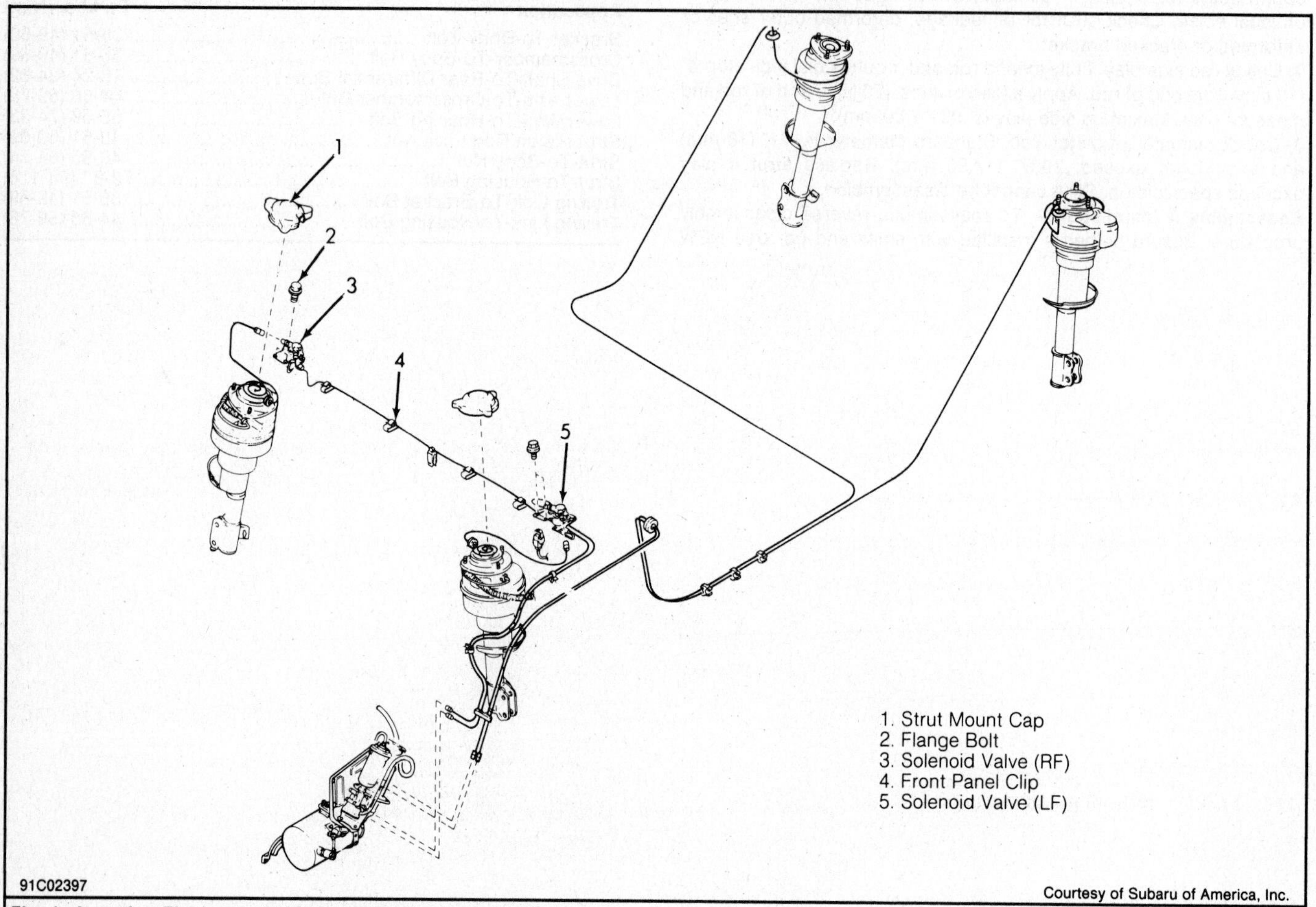

1
2
3
4
5
1. Strut Mount Cap
2. Flange Bolt
3. Solenoid Valve (RF)
4. Front Panel Clip
5. Solenoid Valve (LF)
91C02397
Courtesy of Subaru of America, Inc.

***Fig. 1: Locating Electronic Air Suspension Components (Legacy)***

Solenoid Valve
Rear Air
Suspension
Solenoid Valve
Front Air
Suspension
Control Unit
Compressor
Drier
Air Tank
91E02398
Courtesy of Subaru of America, Inc.

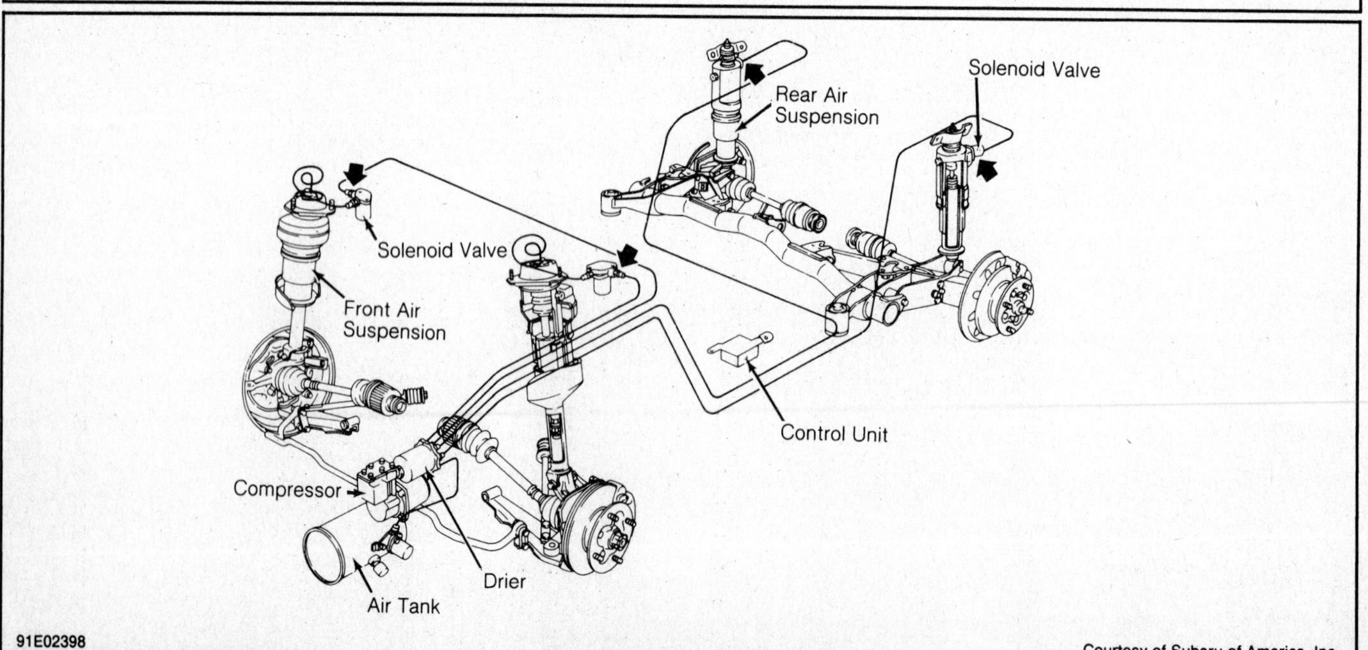

***Fig. 2: Locating Electronic Air Suspension Components (XT & XT6)***

# 1991 SUSPENSION
# Electronic (Cont.)

## OPERATION

Vehicle height can be adjusted by driver, using switch located on instrument panel. At speeds greater than about 55 MPH, with switch in HIGH position, vehicle height reverts automatically to NORMAL. If speed drops to less than 40 MPH, vehicle height returns automatically to HIGH position. At speeds less than 55 MPH, vehicle height is completely under driver control.

On Legacy, vehicle height in HIGH position is approximately 1.6" (40 mm) higher than in NORMAL position. On XT and XT6, vehicle height is approximately 1.2" (30 mm) higher at front end, and 1.4" (35 mm) higher at rear.

## GENERAL PRECAUTIONS

**1)** Before raising vehicle for service, ensure vehicle height control switch is in NORMAL position and indicator light is off. Disconnect negative battery cable to avoid accidental activation of system.
**2)** When welding near height control system components, ensure components are sufficiently protected. Never apply undercoating to system components. DO NOT allow battery acid to contact air tubes.

## TESTING & DIAGNOSIS

***NOTE: Diagnose electronic suspension system using self-diagnostic system or Subaru Select Monitor.***

## SELF-DIAGNOSTIC SYSTEM

***NOTE: When a malfunction is present, auto leveler and vehicle height controls become non-operational.***

**Retrieving Trouble Codes (Legacy) – 1)** Turn ignition off. Connect jumper from diagnostic connector terminal No. 1 (located under instrument panel lower cover) to ground terminal. *See Fig. 3*. Turn ignition on.

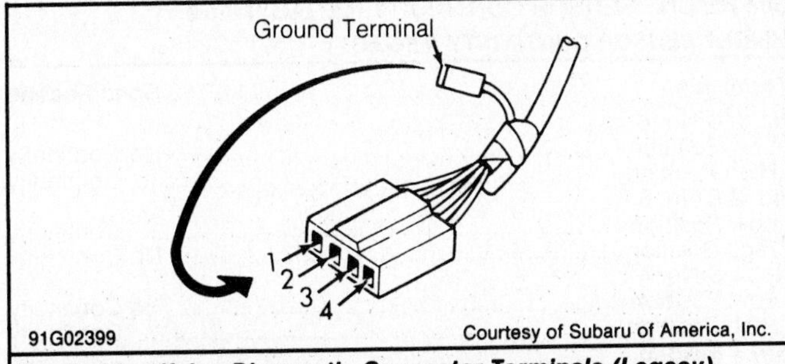


***Fig. 3: Identifying Diagnostic Connector Terminals (Legacy)***

**2)** Codes are displayed by indicator light flashes. Codes are separated by a 1.2-second pause between .3-second flashes of trouble code. For trouble code explanation, see TROUBLE CODES and DIAGNOSING CODES under TESTING & DIAGNOSIS. When no trouble codes are present, indicator light displays a .6-second flash and a .6-second pause.
**3)** Codes will flash until ignition is turned off. To clear codes, turn off ignition and remove No. 25 fuse or disconnect negative battery cable.
**Retrieving Trouble Codes (XT & XT6) – 1)** Complete steps **1)** and **3)** within one minute. Turn ignition off. Set height selector switch to HIGH. Turn ignition on.
**2)** Turn ignition off. Set height selector switch to OFF. Turn ignition on. Turn ignition off. Set height selector switch to HIGH.
**3)** Turn ignition on. System will now be in self-diagnostic mode. Codes are indicated by flashes of indicator light.
**4)** Trouble codes are separated by 1.5-second pauses between .5-second flashes of trouble code. For trouble code explanation, see TROUBLE CODES and DIAGNOSING CODES under TESTING & DIAGNOSIS. If no trouble code is present, indicator light will flash for 1.3 seconds and pause for 1.3 seconds.
**5)** Codes will flash until ignition is turned off. To clear codes, turn ignition off and then on, or disconnect negative battery terminal. DO NOT disconnect battery terminal until all checks are completed.

## TROUBLE CODES

***Trouble Codes***

| Code | Fault |
|---|---|
| 1 | RF Height Sensor |
| 2 | LF Height Sensor |
| 3 | RR Height Sensor |
| 4 | LR Height Sensor |
| 5 | RF Solenoid Valve |
| 6 | LF Solenoid Valve |
| 7 | RR Solenoid Valve |
| 8 | LR Solenoid Valve |
| 9 | Compressor Relay Output |
| 10 [1] | Discharge Solenoid Valve |

[1] – Code 10 appears with Code 5, 6, 7, or 8

## DIAGNOSING CODES

**Codes 1-4 –** Unplug harness connectors from suspension control unit and affected height sensor. Ensure there is continuity between each end of harness. Measure resistance between each connector terminal and ground, and between each pair of terminals. Resistance should be at least one megohm. Repair or replace harness if resistance is not as specified. See HEIGHT SENSOR under COMPONENT TESTING if wiring is okay.
**Codes 5-8 –** Unplug harness connectors from suspension control unit and affected solenoid valve. Check wiring between solenoid valve and battery and between solenoid valve and suspension control unit. See WIRING DIAGRAMS. If wiring is okay, see SOLENOID VALVE under COMPONENT TESTING.
**Code 9 –** Check wiring between compressor relay and battery and between compressor relay and suspension control unit. See WIRING DIAGRAMS. If wiring is okay, see COMPRESSOR RELAY under COMPONENT TESTING.
**Code 10 –** Unplug harness connector from discharge solenoid valve. Check wiring between discharge solenoid valve and battery and between discharge solenoid valve and suspension control unit. See WIRING DIAGRAMS.

## POWER SUPPLY & GROUND CIRCUIT

**Suspension Control Unit (Legacy) – 1)** Suspension control unit is located under driver's seat. Measure voltage between suspension control unit 16-pin connector (P34) terminal No. 2 and ground. *See Fig. 4*. If voltage is not 10-12 volts, repair defective wiring between suspension control unit and battery. If voltage is 10-12 volts, go to step **2)**.
**2)** Turn ignition on. Measure voltage between suspension control unit 16-pin connector terminal No. 3 and ground. *See Fig. 4*. If voltage is not 10-12 volts, repair defective wiring back to ignition switch. If voltage is 10-12 volts, go to step **3)**.
**3)** Unplug P34 connector. Check for continuity between connector terminal No. 9 and ground. If no continuity, repair ground wire between terminal No. 9 and ground.

**Suspension Control Unit (XT & XT6) – 1)** Suspension control unit is located under driver's seat. Measure voltage between suspension control unit 16-pin R13 connector Light Green wire and ground. See WIRING DIAGRAMS. If voltage is not 10-12 volts, repair defective wiring between suspension control unit and battery. If voltage is 10-12 volts, go to step **2)**.
**2)** Turn ignition on. Measure voltage between suspension control unit 21-pin R12 connector terminal No. 3 and ground. See WIRING DIAGRAMS. Voltage should be 10-12 volts. If voltage is not as specified, repair defective wiring back to ignition switch. If voltage is 10-12 volts, go to step **3)**.
**3)** Unplug R12 connector. Check for continuity between connector Black wire and ground. If continuity is not present, repair Black wire to ground.

# 1991 SUSPENSION
# Electronic (Cont.)

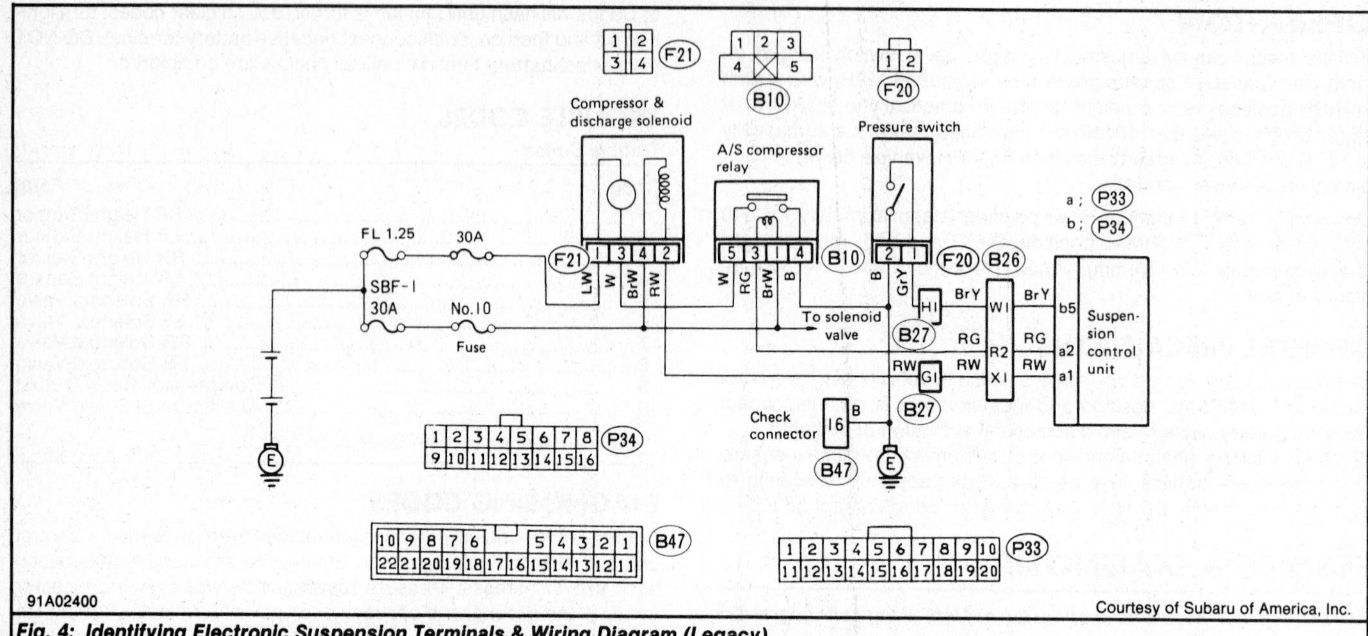


91A02400

Courtesy of Subaru of America, Inc.

***Fig. 4: Identifying Electronic Suspension Terminals & Wiring Diagram (Legacy)***

## COMPONENT TESTING

### COMPRESSOR

Unplug connector from compressor. Connect a jumper wire from compressor terminal No. 3 (Blue/White wire) to ground. Connect 12 volts to terminal No. 1 (White wire). Replace compressor if it does not run.

### COMPRESSOR RELAY

**1)** Unplug harness connector from compressor relay, located on left side, forward of firewall. Apply 12 volts to relay terminal "B". Ground terminal "A". Check continuity between terminals "C" and "D". *See Fig. 5*. Continuity should exist.

**2)** Disconnect power from terminal "B". Continuity should not be present at terminals "C" and "D". If results are not as specified, replace compressor relay.

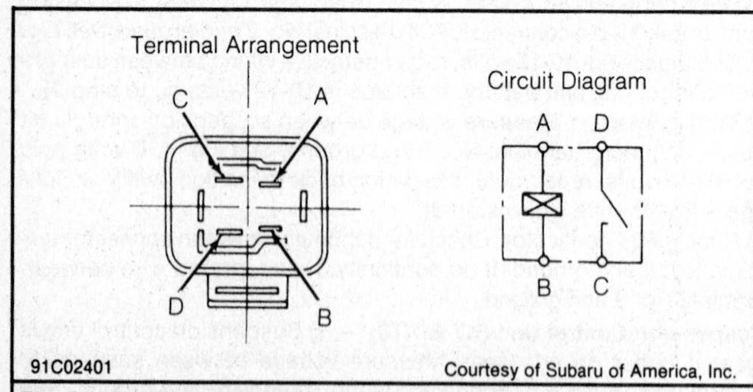


91C02401

Courtesy of Subaru of America, Inc.

***Fig. 5: Identifying Compressor Relay Terminals***

### DISCHARGE SOLENOID VALVE

Discharge solenoid is located next to compressor. Measure resistance between solenoid valve terminals No. 2 and 4. Resistance should be 25-35 ohms. Apply 12 volts to solenoid terminals. Listen for sound from valve. If there is no sound, discharge solenoid valve is defective.

### HEIGHT SENSOR

**Legacy – 1)** Remove solenoid valve and air hose from strut assembly. Bleed air from strut. Unplug height control connector. Connect ohmmeter between height sensor terminals specified in HEIGHT SENSOR CONTINUITY (LEGACY) table. *See Fig. 4*.

**2)** Position jack under crossmember. Gradually raise vehicle. Check for continuity between height sensor terminals. Continuity should be as specified. Replace height sensor if continuity is not as specified. See HEIGHT SENSOR CONTINUITY (LEGACY) table.

***HEIGHT SENSOR CONTINUITY (LEGACY)***

| Terminals | Specification |
|---|---|
| No. 2 & No. 4 | |
| Low Position | No Continuity |
| High Position | Continuity |
| No. 2 & No. 3 | |
| Low Position | Continuity |
| High Position | No Continuity |
| No. 1 & No. 4 | |
| Low Position | No Continuity |
| High Position | Continuity |
| No. 1 & No. 3 | |
| Low Position | Continuity |
| High Position | No Continuity |

**XT & XT6 –** Bleed air from strut. Unplug height control connector. Connect ohmmeter between height sensor terminals specified in HEIGHT SENSOR CONTINUITY (XT & XT6) table. See WIRING DIAGRAMS. Extend and compress each strut. Continuity should be as specified in HEIGHT SENSOR CONTINUITY (XT & XT6) table.

***HEIGHT SENSOR CONTINUITY (XT & XT6)***

| Terminals | Specification |
|---|---|
| A & B | |
| Compressed | No Continuity |
| Extended | Continuity |
| B & D | |
| Compressed | Continuity |
| High Position | No Continuity |
| A & C | |
| Compressed | No Continuity |
| Extended | Continuity |
| C & D | |
| Compressed | Continuity |
| Extended | No Continuity |

## SOLENOID VALVE

Unplug harness connector from solenoid valve, located near strut. Measure resistance between solenoid valve terminals No. 1 and 2. *See Fig. 4*. See WIRING DIAGRAMS. Resistance should be 24-35 ohms. Apply 12 volts to solenoid terminals. Listen for sound from valve. If there is no sound, solenoid valve is defective.

# REMOVAL & INSTALLATION

## AIR COMPRESSOR & DRIER

**Removal** - Remove left front wheel and front half of mud guard. Use Air Hose Remover (926520000) to disconnect all air hoses from drier. *See Fig. 6*. Remove couplers. Remove compressor and drier assembly as a unit.

**Disassembly & Reassembly** - Compressor and drier may be separated; however, service is limited to unit replacement. Ensure "O" rings are clean and lubricated prior to assembly.

**Installation** - To install, reverse removal procedure. Ensure all connections are clean and tight.

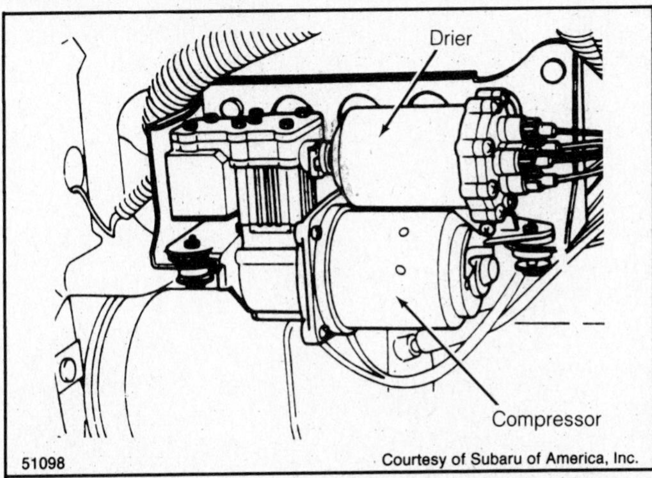


***Fig. 6: Locating Air Compressor & Drier Assembly (XT & XT6)***

## AIR TANK

***CAUTION: Carefully discharge air pressure from tank before removing pressure switch or solenoid.***

**Removal & Installation** - **1)** Use Air Hose Remover (926520000) to separate hoses from solenoid valve. Remove solenoid valve coupler. On XT and XT6, remove left signal light assembly from front bumper. On all models, remove air tank retaining bolts/nuts. Remove air tank assembly. *See Fig. 7*.

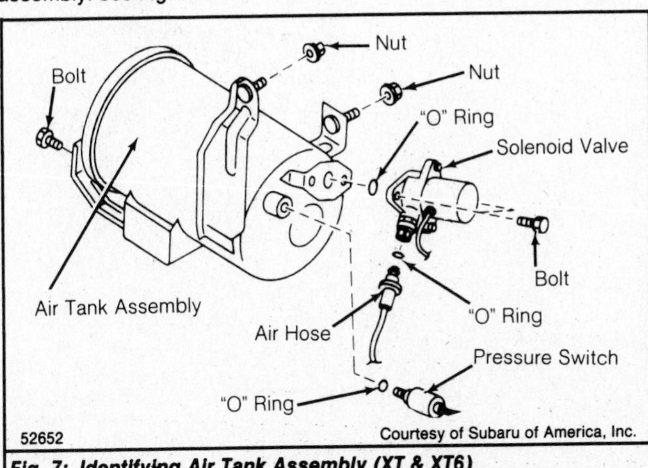


***Fig. 7: Identifying Air Tank Assembly (XT & XT6)***

**2)** To install, reverse removal procedure. Clean and lubricate "O" rings before installation. Handle "O" rings carefully to avoid damage. Apply grease to pressure switch threads before installation.

## FRONT STRUT ASSEMBLY

**Removal & Installation (Legacy)** - **1)** Raise and support vehicle. Remove front wheels. Remove union bolts. Remove clamp securing brake hose to strut. Disconnect brake hose. Cap brake hose to prevent brake fluid from leaking.

**2)** Scribe alignment mark on camber adjustment bolt. Remove strut-to-housing bolts. Remove ABS sensor bolts (if equipped). Disconnect air line from solenoid valve.

**3)** Unplug solenoid valve connector. Remove strut cap. Remove upper strut mount nuts and front strut assembly. Position strut assembly on Coil Spring Compressor (926110000) mounted on vise.

**4)** Ensure air pressure is discharged from air spring. Place Spanner (927750000) under strut mount to hold assembly while removing tower unit. *See Fig. 8*. Avoid damaging diaphragm. To install, reverse removal procedure. Ensure air lines are routed properly.

**Removal (XT & XT6)** - **1)** Remove air hose and mud guard. Remove height sensor harness clip and harness coupler. Remove strut assembly as a unit. Position strut assembly in support tool.

**2)** Before removing strut mount, ensure air pressure is discharged from air spring. Place Spanner (926510000) under strut mount to hold assembly while removing tower nut. *See Fig. 8*. Avoid damage to diaphragm.

**Installation** - To install, reverse removal procedure. Attach sensor harness clip 8.3" (210 mm) from strut assembly to prevent twisting. *See Fig. 9 or 10*. Position new "O" ring in unit before inserting air hose. Install air hose .5" (13 mm) into fitting.

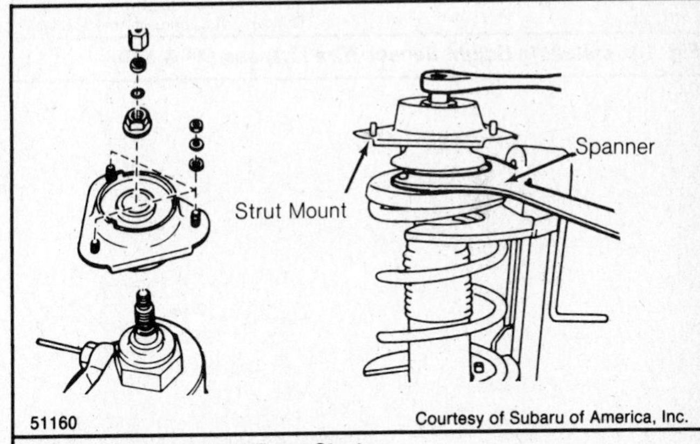


***Fig. 8: Disassembling Front Strut***

## REAR STRUT ASSEMBLY

**Removal & Installation (Legacy)** - **1)** Remove brake hose and rear strut-to-housing bolt. Remove stereo cover from upper side of rear quarter trim panel. Remove rear solenoid valve from rear suspension assembly.

**2)** Using Air Pipe Remover (926520000), disconnect air pipe. Pull out vehicle height sensor harness through access hole. Disconnect coupler. Remove rear strut from body. To install, reverse removal procedure. Ensure hoses and harness are routed correctly. *See Figs. 9 and 10*.

**Removal & Installation (XT & XT6)** - **1)** Remove rear apron protector. Remove rear solenoid valve. Support solenoid valve away from work area. Remove height sensor harness from access hole. Detach harness coupler.

**2)** Carefully remove strut assembly as a unit. Discharge air pressure from strut assembly if it is to be disassembled. To install, reverse removal procedure. *See Figs. 9 and 10*.

# 1991 SUSPENSION
# Electronic (Cont.)

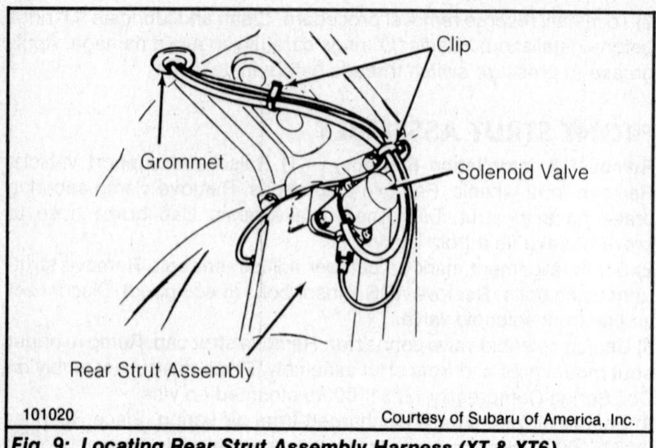


**Fig. 9: Locating Rear Strut Assembly Harness (XT & XT6)**

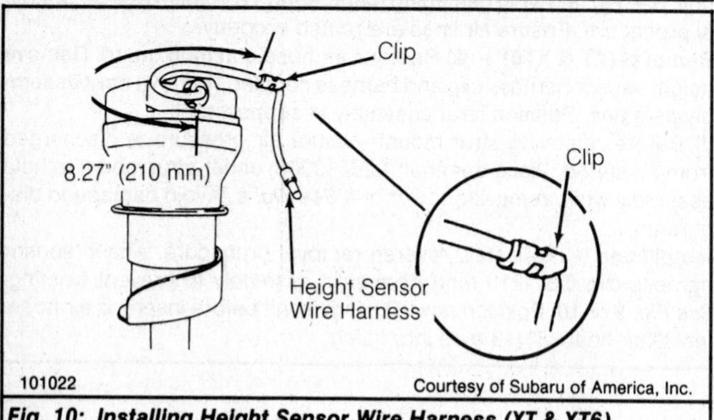


**Fig. 10: Installing Height Sensor Wire Harness (XT & XT6)**

## TORQUE SPECIFICATIONS

***TORQUE SPECIFICATIONS***

| Application | Ft. Lbs. (N.m) |
|---|---|
| ABS Sensor Bolt | 15-29 (20-39) |
| Strut-To-Body Nuts | 10-18 (14-25) |
| Strut-To-Housing Bolts | |
| Front | 91-112 (123-152) |
| Rear | 97-120 (132-162) |
| | **INCH Lbs. (N.m)** |
| Air Compressor | 53-62 (6-7) |
| Air Compressor-To-Drier Bolts | |
| Large | 44-71 (5-8) |
| Small | 27-44 (3-5) |
| Air Tank Bolt | 89-159 (10-18) |

# 1991 SUSPENSION
# Electronic (Cont.)

## WIRING DIAGRAMS

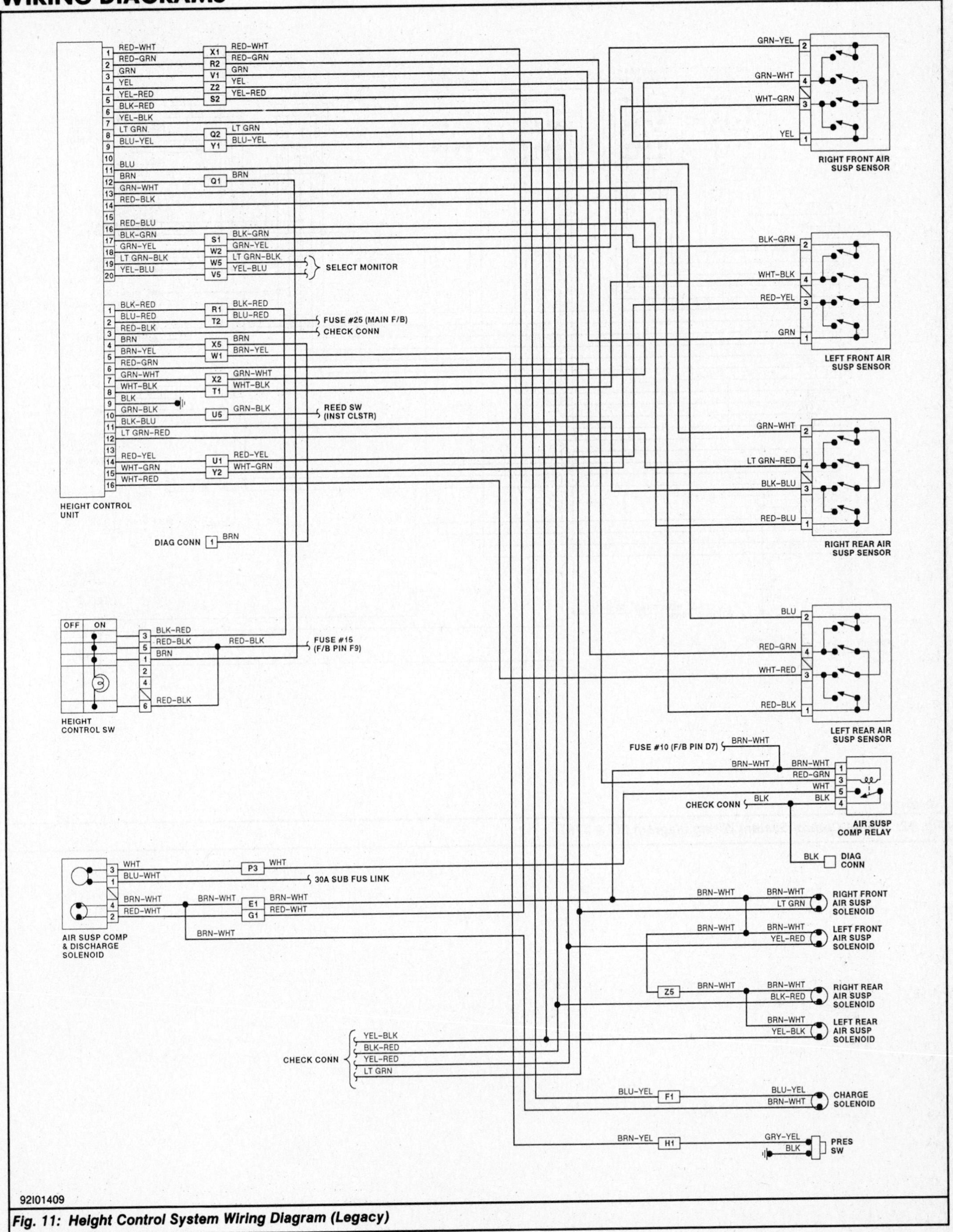


*Fig. 11: Height Control System Wiring Diagram (Legacy)*

# 1991 SUSPENSION
## Electronic (Cont.)

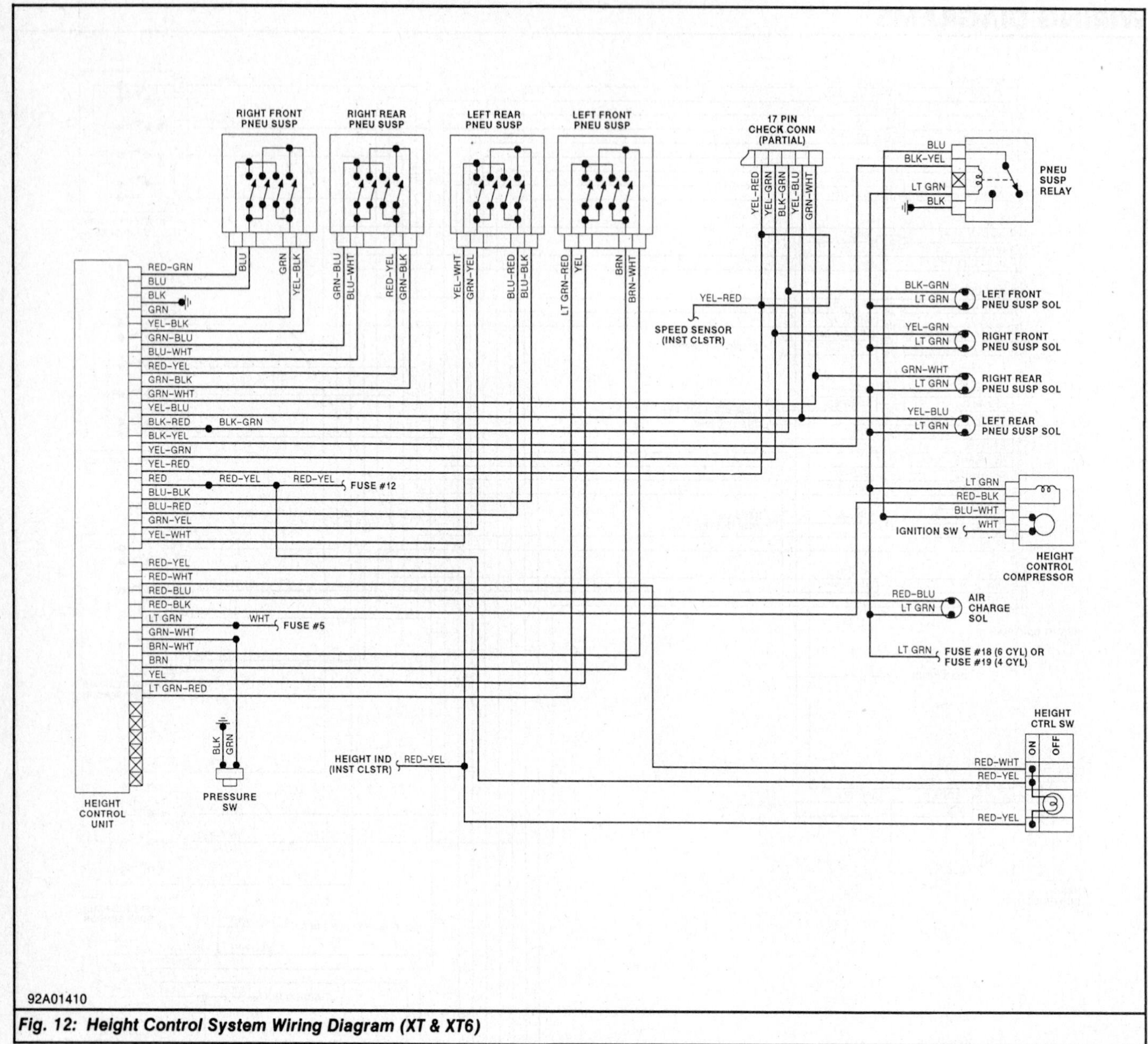


*Fig. 12: Height Control System Wiring Diagram (XT & XT6)*

# 1991 STEERING
# Steering Columns

### Justy, Legacy, Loyale, XT, XT6

## DESCRIPTION

Collapsible steering columns are used on all models. Column lower end is connected to steering gear pinion flange with a "U" joint.

## ADJUSTMENTS

### TILT TIGHTENING FORCE (XT & XT6)

Adjust tilt lever so lever knob is parallel with center of column.

### TELESCOPING OPERATING EFFORT (XT & XT6)

Turn adjusting screw until it makes contact. Back off adjusting screw 20-30 degrees. Tighten lock nut while holding adjusting screw in place.

## REMOVAL & INSTALLATION

### STEERING WHEEL & HORN PAD

**Removal & Installation (Justy)** – Pull off horn pad by hand. Remove steering wheel nut. Using a puller, remove steering wheel. To install, reverse removal procedure.

**Removal & Installation (Legacy – Rigid Column)** – Remove horn pad bolts, disconnect horn connector and remove horn pad. Remove steering wheel nut, and withdraw wheel from shaft using steering wheel puller. To install, reverse removal procedure.

**Removal & Installation (Legacy – Memory Function Column)** – Remove horn pad lower screw, slide horn pad assembly forward and disconnect horn connector. Remove horn pad by pulling it. Remove steering wheel nut, and withdraw wheel from shaft using steering wheel puller. To install, reverse removal procedure.

**Removal & Installation (Loyale)** – Remove horn pad lower screws, slide horn pad assembly forward and disconnect horn connector. Remove horn pad by pulling it. Remove steering wheel nut, and withdraw wheel from shaft using steering wheel puller. To install, reverse removal procedure.

**Removal & Installation (XT & XT6)** – Remove screws from rear of steering wheel and loosen telescopic lever. Hold concave portion of pad by hand, and pull it toward you. Loosen nut on top of steering shaft and remove telescopic lever. Using a puller, remove steering wheel. To install, reverse removal procedure.

### COMBINATION SWITCH

**Removal & Installation (Justy)** – **1)** Remove steering column bracket bolts and pull down steering column. Disconnect wires from horn switch connector.

**2)** Remove horn pad and steering wheel. Remove steering column cover screws. Unplug wiring connectors. Remove combination switch. To install, reverse removal procedure.

**Removal & Installation (Legacy & Loyale)** – **1)** Remove lower instrument panel cover. Remove column covers. Disconnect wires from horn switch connector.

**2)** Remove horn pad. Remove steering wheel using puller. Unplug wiring connectors. Remove combination switch. To install, reverse removal procedure.

**Removal & Installation (XT & XT6)** – **1)** Remove lower instrument panel cover. Remove column covers. Remove steering wheel cover. Remove steering wheel using a steering wheel puller.

**2)** Disconnect wiring harness from steering column. Disconnect wiring connectors. Remove combination switch from control wing. To install, reverse removal procedure.

### IGNITION SWITCH & LOCK CYLINDER

**Removal & Installation** – Remove steering column. See STEERING COLUMN under REMOVAL & INSTALLATION. Disconnect ignition switch wiring connector. Cut off bolt connecting upper and lower portions of ignition switch. Remove ignition switch. To install, reverse removal procedure. Tighten connecting bolts until heads twists off.

### STEERING COLUMN

***CAUTION: DO NOT apply excessive pressure or impact to mainshaft. This may cause column to collapse.***

**Removal** – **1)** Disconnect battery ground cable. Remove "U" joint clamp bolt. Remove trim panel and air duct from under instrument panel. Separate shaft from "U" joint.

**2)** Unplug ignition switch and combination switch connectors. Remove upper and lower bracket bolts. Remove steering column toward passenger compartment.

**Installation** – **1)** Insert column through floorboard into "U" joint. Install and tighten upper bracket bolt into instrument panel. Install air duct and trim panel.

**2)** Install and tighten lower column bolts. Connect electrical connectors. Tighten "U" joint clamp bolt. Check operation of steering wheel and switches.

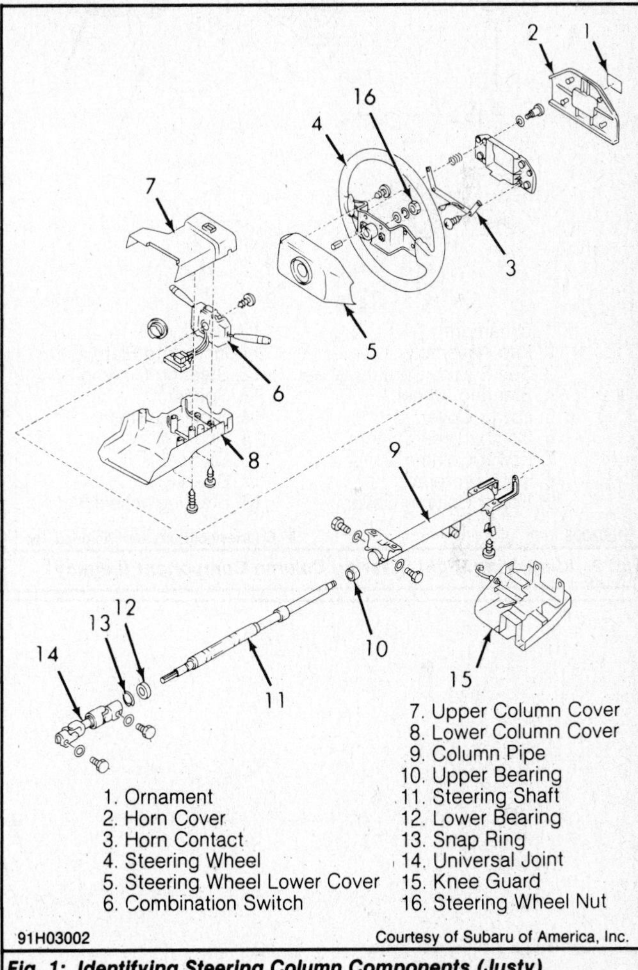


*Fig. 1: Identifying Steering Column Components (Justy)*

## OVERHAUL

### STEERING COLUMN

***NOTE: Refer to illustrations during overhaul. See Figs. 1-5.***

**Disassembly** – **1)** Remove horn pad retaining screw (2-spoke wheel) or screws (4-spoke wheel) from behind wheel. Pull horn pad to remove. On soft-type steering wheel, lift up horn pad from front.

**2)** Remove steering wheel. Remove column covers, combination switch and horn brush. Remove lower bearing screws. Pull shaft with bearing downward. Remove snap ring, washer, "O" ring and bearing.

# 1991 STEERING
## Steering Columns (Cont.)

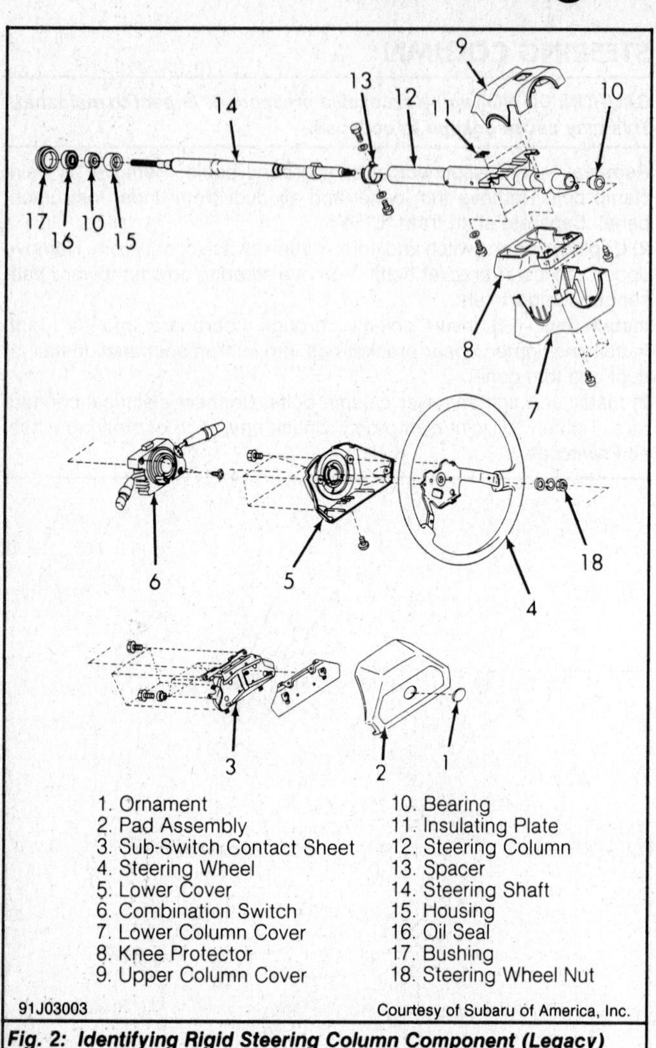


**Fig. 2: Identifying Rigid Steering Column Component (Legacy)**

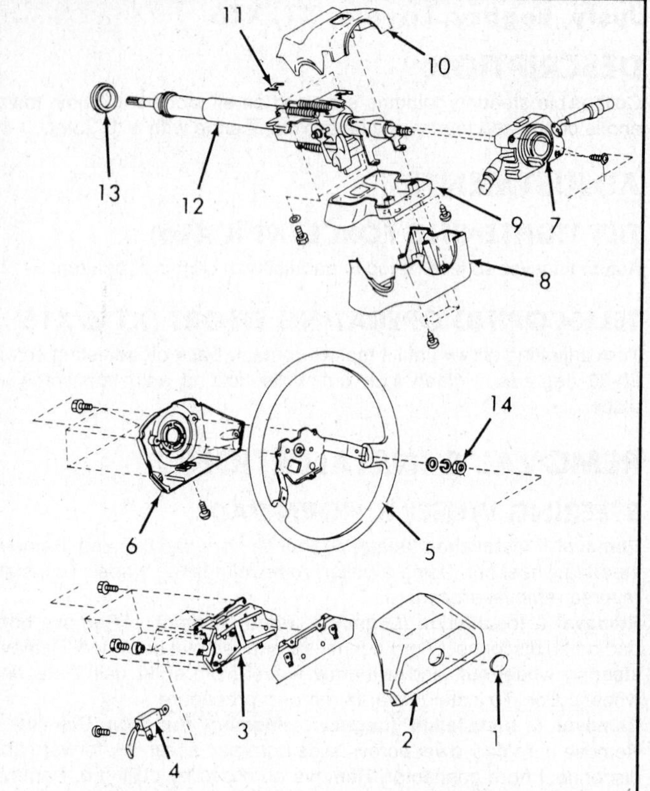

1. Ornament
2. Pad Assembly
3. Sub-Switch Contact Sheet
4. Cruise Control Sub-Switch
5. Steering Wheel
6. Lower Cover
7. Combination Switch
8. Lower Column Cover
9. Knee Protector
10. Upper Column Cover
11. Insulating Plate
12. Steering Column
13. Bushing
14. Steering Wheel Nut

91F03001

Courtesy of Subaru of America, Inc.

**Fig. 4: Identifying Tilt Steering Column Component (Legacy)**

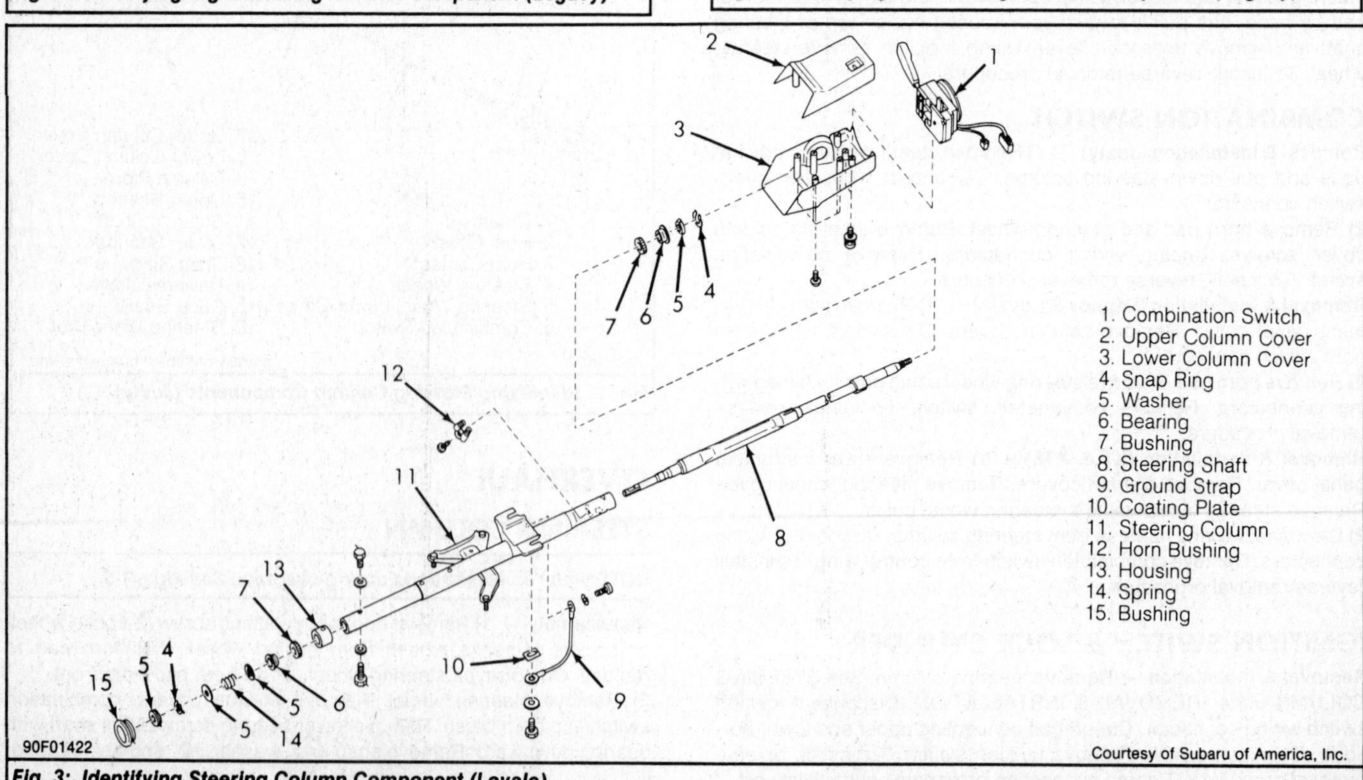


**Fig. 3: Identifying Steering Column Component (Loyale)**

# 1991 STEERING
## Steering Columns (Cont.)

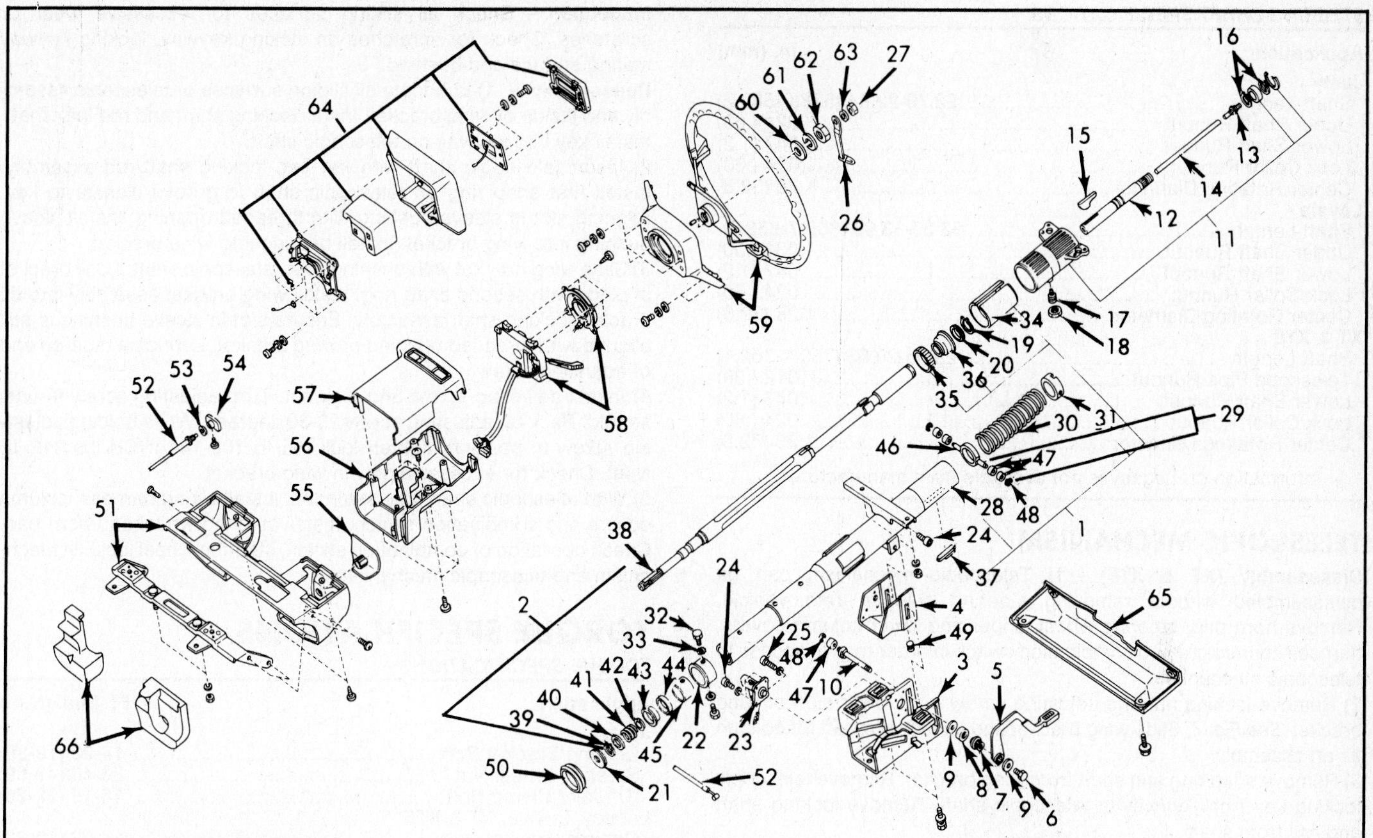

1. Column Assembly
2. Shaft Assembly
3. Tilt Column Mounting Bracket
4. Inner Tilt Bracket
5. Tilt Lever
6. Bolt
7. Tilt Adjusting Screw
8. Bearing
9. Washer
10. Tilt Bolt
11. Wing Bracket Assembly
12. Telescopic Shaft
13. Locking Shaft
14. Rod
15. Telescopic Locking Key
16. Snap Ring
17. Telescopic Adjusting Screw
18. Nut
19. Snap Ring
20. Washer
21. Dust Seal
22. Spacer
23. Memory Pin Assembly
24. Bolt
25. Bolt
26. Telescopic Lever
27. Nut
28. Column Tube
29. Pin Assembly
30. Tilt Spring
31. Boss
32. Bolt
33. Lock Washer
34. Telescopic Sleeve Bushing
35. Bearing Bushing
36. Bearing
37. Telescopic Guide
38. Steering Shaft
39. Snap Ring
40. Washer
41. Shaft Spring
42. Washer
43. Bearing
44. Bearing Bushing
45. Housing
46. Tilt Pin
47. Bearing
48. Clip
49. Stopper
50. Floorboard Bushing
51. Lower Cover Assembly
52. Pop-Up Cable Assembly
53. Nut
54. Knob
55. Cap
56. Lower Column Cover
57. Upper Column Cover
58. Combination Switch
59. Steering Wheel
60. Washer
61. Spring Washer
62. Nut
63. Spring Washer
64. Horn Pad Assembly
65. Cover
66. Knee Pads

58905 Courtesy of Subaru of America, Inc.

*Fig. 5: Identifying Steering Column Components (XT & XT6)*

**Inspection – 1)** Ensure "U" joint has no play. Flex "U" joint and check for binding. On Justy, replace "U" joint if torque required to turn exceeds 3 INCH lbs. (.4 N.m). On all others, replace "U" joint if torque required to turn exceeds 4 INCH lbs. (.58 N.m).

**2)** Check plastic washer for damage, and serration for wear. Check steering shaft dimensions. See STEERING SHAFT SPECIFICATIONS table. *See Fig. 6.* Replace steering shaft if not within specifications. Check bearings for damage. Replace any worn bearings.

**Reassembly – 1)** To reassemble, reverse disassembly procedure. Lubricate shaft sliding section at lower and upper bearing and horn brush.

**2)** With steering wheel in place, check clearance between steering wheel and cover. If clearance exceeds .04-.12" (1.0-3.0 mm), loosen column cover screws to adjust.

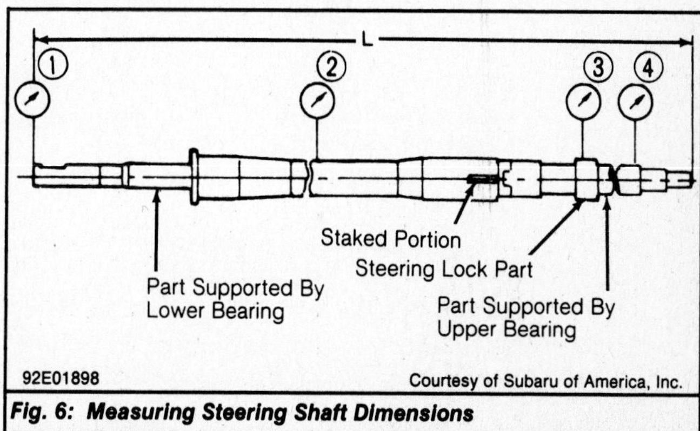


*Fig. 6: Measuring Steering Shaft Dimensions*

# 1991 STEERING
# Steering Columns (Cont.)

*STEERING SHAFT SPECIFICATIONS*

| Application [1] | In. (mm) |
|---|---|
| **Justy** | |
| Shaft Length | 22.76-22.84 (578.2-580.2) |
| Upper Shaft Runout | .024 (.60) |
| Lower Shaft Runout | .047 (1.2) |
| Lock Collar Runout | .024 (.60) |
| Center Rotating Diameter | 1.28 (32.6) |
| **Loyale** | |
| Shaft Length | 33.89-33.96 (860.7-862.7). |
| Upper Shaft Runout | .031 (.60) |
| Lower Shaft Runout | .047 (1.2) |
| Lock Collar Runout | .024 (.60) |
| Center Rotating Diameter | 1.28 (32.6) |
| **XT & XT6** | |
| Shaft Length | 29.55-29.63 (750.1-752.1) |
| Telescope Pipe Runout | .012 (.30) |
| Lower Shaft Runout | .047 (1.2) |
| Lock Collar Runout | .024 (.60) |
| Center Rotating Diameter | 1.28 (32.6) |

[1] - Information on Legacy is not available from manufacturer.

## TELESCOPIC MECHANISM

**Disassembly (XT & XT6) - 1)** Telescopic mechanism can be disassembled without removing steering column from vehicle. Remove horn pad, steering wheel, upper and lower column covers, harness connectors and combination switch in order to gain access to telescopic mechanism.

**2)** Remove locking nut and adjusting screw from lower side of wing bracket. *See Fig. 7.* Slide wing bracket and telescopic shaft off column as an assembly.

**3)** Remove snap ring and shaft from wing bracket. Remove telescopic locking key from keyway in telescopic shaft. Remove locking shaft and rod from shaft.

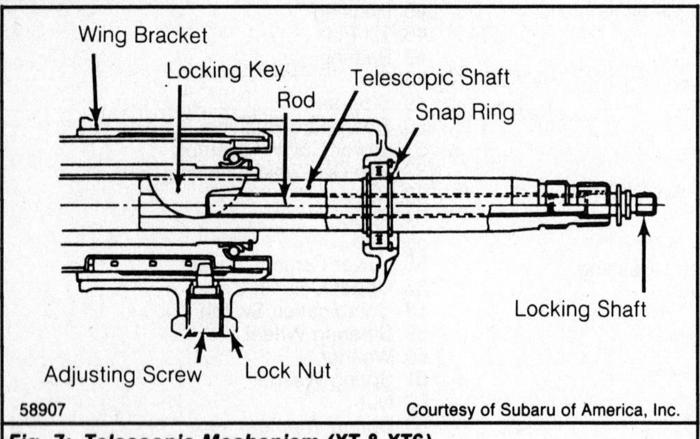


*Fig. 7: Telescopic Mechanism (XT & XT6)*

**Inspection** - Check all sliding surfaces for excessive wear or scratches. Check for scratches on locking keyway, locking keyway mating surface and bushing.

**Reassembly - 1)** Lubricate all sliding surfaces of telescopic assembly and inside of wing bracket. Install locking shaft and rod into shaft. Install key into keyway on telescopic shaft.

**2)** Insert telescopic shaft with key into locking shaft/rod assembly. Install first snap ring on telescopic shaft in groove closest to key. Aligning slot in sleeve bushing with threaded opening, install sleeve bushing into wing bracket. Install bearing into wing bracket.

**3)** Slide wing bracket with bushing over telescopic shaft. Lock bracket in place with second snap ring. Install wing bracket assembly into tilt bracket/locking shaft assembly. Ensure slot in sleeve bushing is still aligned with threaded opening of wing bracket. Lubricate tapered end of adjusting screw.

**4)** Install adjusting screw and lock nut. Turn adjusting screw in until seated. Back off adjusting screw 20-30 degrees. While holding adjusting screw in position, tighten lock nut to 108-144 INCH lbs. (12-16 N.m). Check for excessive play in wing bracket.

**5)** With telescopic shaft fully extended, install wiring harness, column covers and combination switch. Install steering wheel and horn pad. Check operation of combination switch, steering wheel lock, tilt mechanism and telescopic mechanism.

## TORQUE SPECIFICATIONS

*TORQUE SPECIFICATIONS*

| Application | Ft. Lbs. (N.m) |
|---|---|
| Justy | |
| Column Bracket Bolt | 14-22 (19-30) |
| Steering Wheel Nut | 36-43 (49-59) |
| "U" Joint Clamp Bolt | 16-19 (22-26) |
| Legacy, Loyale, XT & XT6 | |
| Column Bracket Bolt | 14-22 (19-30) |
| Steering Wheel Nut | 22-29 (29-39) |
| "U" Joint Clamp Bolt | 15-20 (21-26) |
| | **INCH Lbs. (N.m)** |
| Tilt Lock Nut | 108-144 (12-16) |

# 1991 STEERING
# Manual Rack & Pinion

## Justy, Loyale

## DESCRIPTION

Steering gear is rack and pinion type. Pinion shaft connects to steering shaft with a universal joint. Outer ends of tie rods connect to steering knuckles with ball joints.

## ADJUSTMENTS

Adjustment is made during overhaul. See OVERHAUL.

## REMOVAL & INSTALLATION

### RACK & PINION

**Removal (Justy)** – Raise and support vehicle. Remove "U" joint coupling bolts, dust seal and front wheels. Separate tie rod ends from steering knuckles. Remove steering gear retaining bolts. Remove steering gear through tie rod opening on left side of vehicle.

**Removal (Loyale)** – **1)** Disconnect battery ground cable. Raise and support vehicle. Remove both front wheels. Separate tie rod ends from steering knuckles.

**2)** Disconnect "U" joint from pinion shaft. Remove exhaust manifold. Pull manifold down out of way. Remove pinion shaft rubber boot. Remove steering mounting bolts. Lower steering gear until pinion shaft separates from "U" joint. Rotate steering gear to rear. Remove steering gear.

**Installation (Justy & Loyale)** – Reverse removal procedure to install. Tighten bolts to specification. See TORQUE SPECIFICATIONS table at end of article. Adjust toe-in.

## OVERHAUL

### STEERING GEAR

**Disassembly** – **1)** Measure and record pinion shaft turning torque. Note and record angular position of adjusting screw. Place steering gear in a soft-jawed vise. Loosen tie rod end lock nuts. Remove tie rod ends. Remove boot retaining clips. Remove boots. *See Fig. 1.*

**2)** Straighten tab on inner tie rod joint lock washer. Separate tie rod from rack. Repeat procedure for other tie rod. Remove adjusting screw lock nut, adjusting screw, "O" ring, plunger spring and sleeve.

**3)** Remove pinion gear oil seal from steering gear housing. Remove large pinion gear snap ring from housing. Remove pinion gear and bearing as a unit.

**4)** From pinion side, pull rack from housing. Remove small snap ring from pinion gear. Press bearing from pinion gear.

**5)** Remove clip from housing. Using an aluminum drift, remove adapter "A" from end of housing.

**Inspection** – **1)** Place rack ends in "V" blocks. Position dial indicator so plunger rests on center of rack. Rotate rack while noting deflection of dial indicator.

**2)** Maximum deflection should be .008" (.20 mm). Replace rack if not within specification. Check all other components for wear and damage. Replace components as necessary.

**Reassembly** – **1)** Press adapter "A" into housing. Install clip. Grease bushing and adapter "B". If pinion was disassembled, press on new bearing. Install new snap ring.

**2)** Grease toothed and sliding portions of rack. Install rack into housing from pinion side. Position rack so an equal length of rack protrudes from each end of housing.

**3)** Grease pinion gear teeth. Install pinion into steering gear housing. Install large pinion gear snap ring into housing. Check pinion gear end play. End play should be less than .012" (.30 mm).

**4)** If end play is not to specification, check for worn snap rings, bearing and steering gear housing. Replace components as necessary. End play adjustment snap rings are available in 8 thicknesses for Justy.

**5)** With pinion gear end play correct, press oil seal into steering gear housing. Grease rack plunger cavity. Install rack sleeve, plunger spring, adjusting screw and lock nut.

**6)** Adjust rack plunger preload. Turn adjusting screw in until torque increases sharply. Back adjusting screw off 15 degrees. Tighten lock

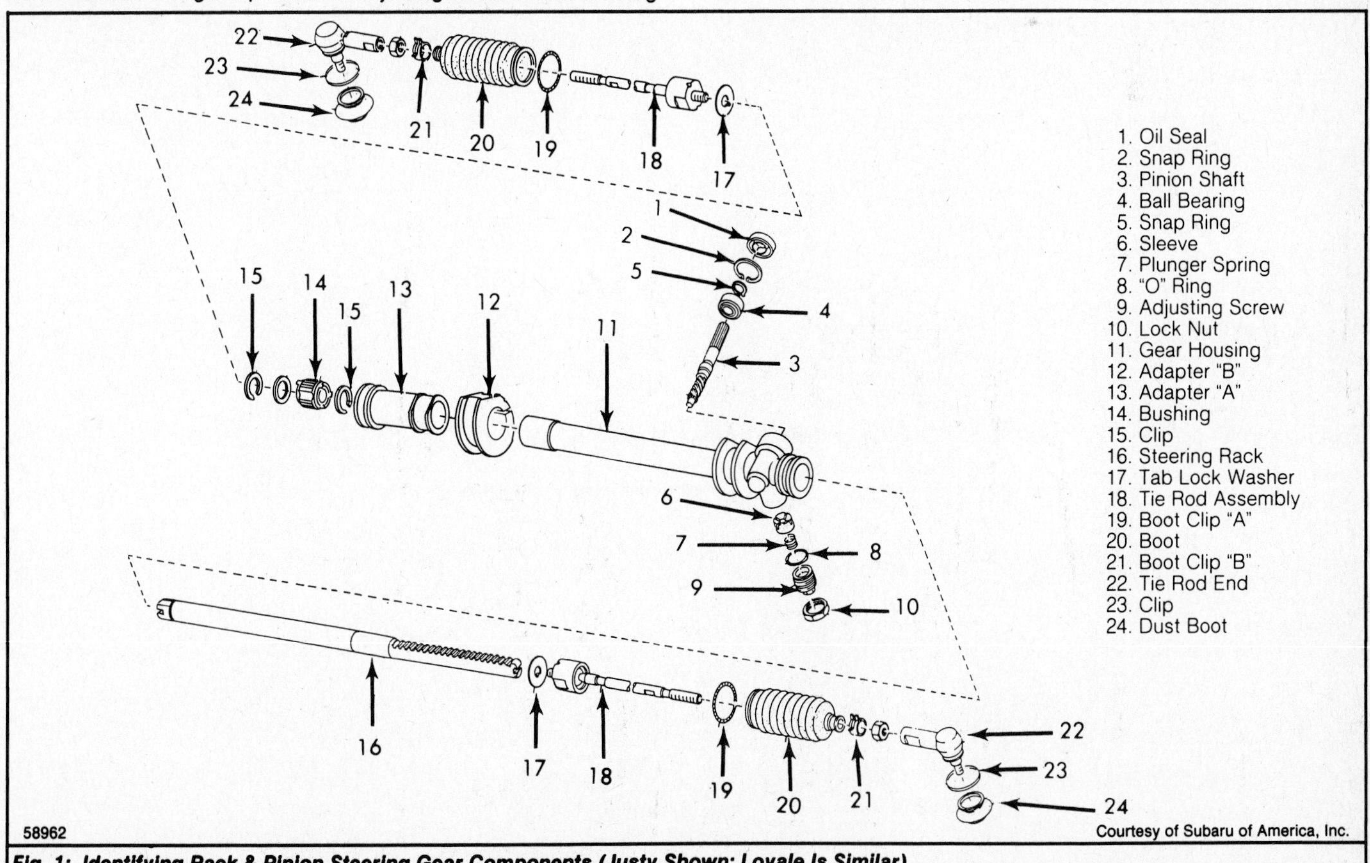


**Fig. 1: Identifying Rack & Pinion Steering Gear Components (Justy Shown; Loyale Is Similar)**

# 1991 STEERING
# Manual Rack & Pinion (Cont.)

nut to 22-36 ft. lbs. (29-49 N.m). Install tie rod inner lock washer. Grease inner tie rod.

**7)** Install tie rods. Tighten inner tie rod to 58 ft. lbs. (79 N.m). Bend lock washer over flat area on inner tie rod. Grease inside lip of large end of rubber boot. Slide boots onto housing.

**8)** Install boot clips. Install lock nuts and tie rod ends. Ensure tie rod ends are installed on correct end of steering gear. Left tie rod end is marked LH; right tie rod end is marked RH.

**9)** Ensure steering gear operates smoothly. Check pinion turning torque at 30 degrees in each direction from straight-ahead position. Turning torque should be 9.5-13.0 INCH lbs. (1.0-1.5 N.m) for Justy and 8.4-12.0 INCH lbs. (.9-1.4 N.m) for Loyale.

**10)** If turning torque is not within specification, loosen lock nut. Turn adjusting screw clockwise to increase or counterclockwise to lower turning torque. Hold adjusting screw while tightening lock nut. See TORQUE SPECIFICATIONS table at end of article.

## TORQUE SPECIFICATIONS

***TORQUE SPECIFICATIONS***

| Application | Ft. Lbs. (N.m) |
|---|---|
| Adjuster Screw Lock Nut | 22-36 (30-49) |
| Steering Mounting Bolts | |
| Justy | 43-54 (58-73) |
| Loyale | 35-52 (47-71) |
| Tie Rod End Castle Nuts | 18-22 (24-30) |
| Tie Rod End Lock Nuts | |
| Justy | 36-47 (49-64) |
| Loyale | 51-65 (69-88) |
| Tie Rod Inner Ball Joint-To-Rack | 58 (79) |
| "U" Joint-To-Pinion Clamp Bolts | |
| Justy | 16-19 (22-26) |
| Loyale | 15-20 (20-27) |

# 1991 STEERING
# Power Rack & Pinion

## Legacy, Loyale, XT, XT6

***NOTE: For information on XT6 electronic power steering, see ELECTRONIC POWER STEERING article.***

## DESCRIPTION

System consists of a fluid reservoir, power steering pump, pressure and return fluid lines, control valve and rack and pinion assembly. *See Fig. 1.*

## LUBRICATION

### CAPACITY

Total capacity is .75 qt. (.7L). Reservoir capacity is .3 qt. (.28L).

### FLUID TYPE

Power steering fluid type is Dexron-II ATF.

### FLUID LEVEL CHECK

Remove reservoir cap. Start engine, and let it idle. Ensure fluid level is up to top mark on dipstick.

## HYDRAULIC SYSTEM BLEEDING

Fluid level should be approximately 1.6" (40 mm) below mouth of reservoir tank. Turn steering wheel slowly from lock to lock until bubbles stop appearing in tank. Ensure tank fluid is maintained at correct level. Start engine, and run it at idle. Again turn steering wheel slowly from lock to lock until bubbles stop appearing in tank. Ensure reservoir tank fluid is at correct level.

## ADJUSTMENTS

### BELT TENSION

Belt tension is checked by measuring deflection between power steering pump and alternator pulleys. *See Fig. 2.* On Legacy and Loyale, deflection should be 9/32-3/8" (7-9 mm) for a new belt and 3/8-7/16" (9-11 mm) for an existing belt. On XT and XT6, deflection should be 1/4-9/32" (6-7 mm) for new belt and 9/32-3/8" (7-9 mm) for used belt.

### RACK & PINION BACKLASH

**1)** On Legacy, XT and XT6, ensure sleeve is in contact with rack assembly. *See Fig. 1.* Loosen adjusting screw lock nut. Tighten adjusting screw to 44 INCH lbs. (5 N.m). Loosen adjusting screw 180 degrees. Turn adjusting screw until turning torque increases. Loosen adjusting screw 30 degrees.

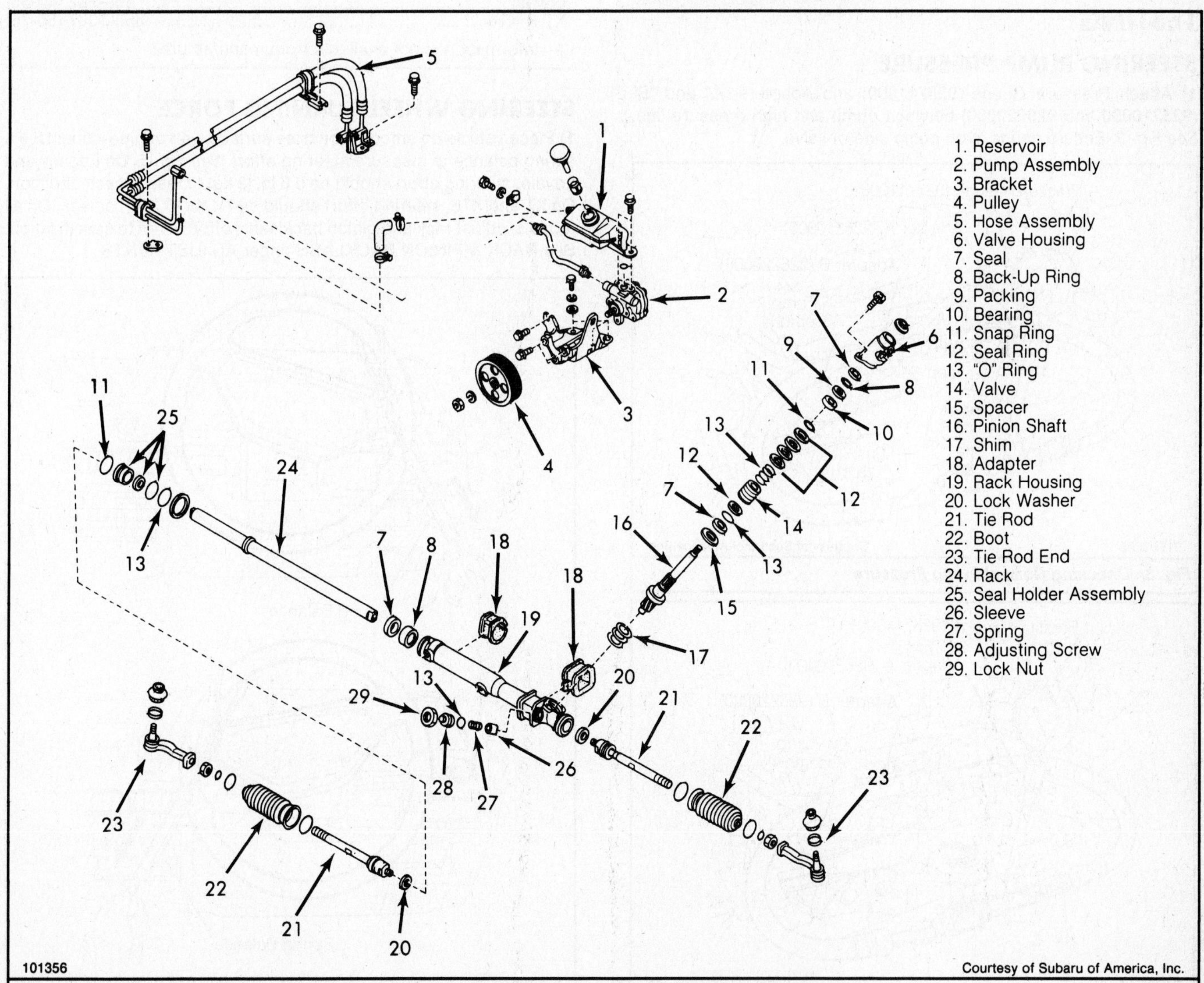


***Fig. 1: Exploded View of Power Steering System (XT & XT6 Shown; Legacy & Loyale Are Similar)***

# 1991 STEERING
# Power Rack & Pinion (Cont.)

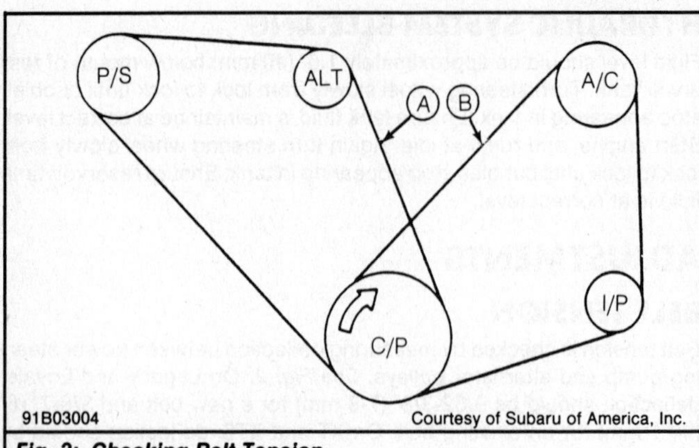


**Fig. 2: Checking Belt Tension (Legacy Shown; Loyale, XT & XT6 Are Similar)**

**2)** On Loyale, loosen adjusting screw lock nut. Tighten adjusting screw to 65 INCH lbs. (7.4 N.m). Loosen adjusting screw 180 degrees. Turn adjusting screw until turning torque increases. Loosen adjusting screw 25 degrees. Tighten adjusting screw lock nut to 22-36 ft. lbs. (30-49 N.m).

## TESTING

### STEERING PUMP PRESSURE

**1)** Attach Pressure Gauge (925711000) and Adapters "A" and "B" (926210000 and 926220000) between pump and high pressure line. *See Fig. 3.* Ensure gauge is on pump side of valve.

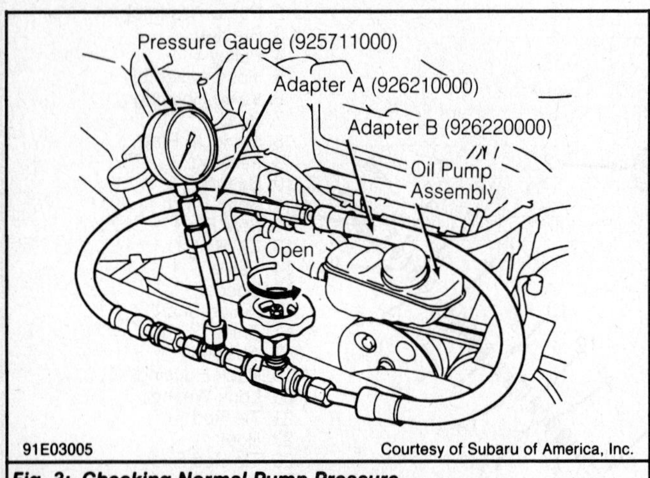


**Fig. 3: Checking Normal Pump Pressure**

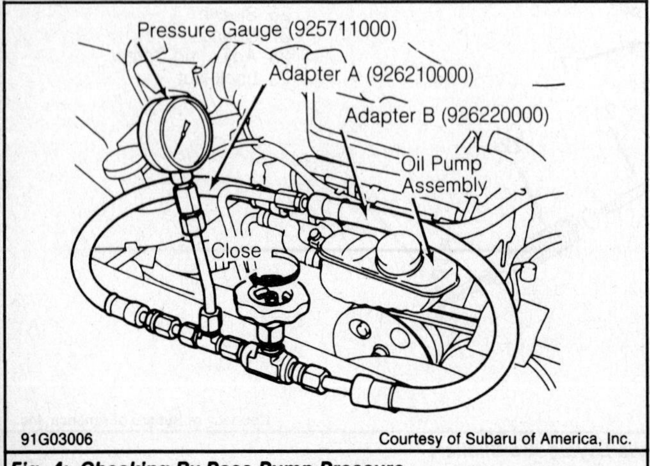


**Fig. 4: Checking By-Pass Pump Pressure**

**2)** With engine idling and valve open, pressure should be as specified. See STEERING PUMP PRESSURE SPECIFICATIONS table. If pressure is not within specification, check for flattened, leaking or blocked lines.

**3)** With engine idling and valve closed, pressure should be as specified. See STEERING PUMP PRESSURE SPECIFICATIONS table. *See Fig. 4.* If pressure is not as specified, check for faulty relief valve, fluid leak inside pump and excessive wear of vane mechanism in pump.

***CAUTION: DO NOT leave valve closed or steering wheel at full lock longer than 5 seconds; otherwise, pump damage could occur.***

***STEERING PUMP PRESSURE SPECIFICATIONS***

| Application | psi (kg/cm²) |
|---|---|
| Normal (Open Valve) | 142 (10) |
| By-Pass (Closed Valve) | |
| Legacy | 1067-1138 (75-80) |
| Loyale | |
| Non-Turbo | 569-782 (40-55) |
| Turbo | 853-1067 (60-75) |
| XT | 569-782 (40-55) |
| XT6 | 853-1067 (60-75) |
| Working Pressure | |
| Legacy | [1] |
| Loyale | 569-782 (40-55) |
| XT & XT6 | 853-1067 (60-75) |

[1] – Information is not available from manufacturer.

### STEERING WHEEL TURNING FORCE

**1)** Place vehicle on smooth concrete surface with engine idling. Use a spring balance to measure steering effort. *See Fig. 5.* On Legacy and Loyale, steering effort should be 6.6 lb. (3 kg) or less in each direction. On XT and XT6, steering effort should be 7.1 lb. (3.2 kg) or less. On all models, adjust rack and pinion backlash if effort is not to specification. See RACK & PINION BACKLASH under ADJUSTMENTS.

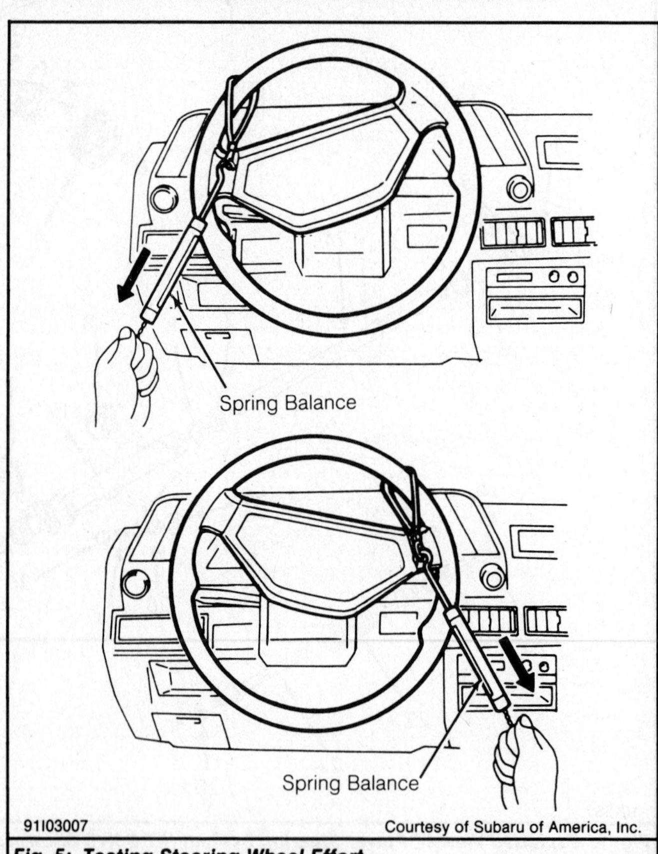


**Fig. 5: Testing Steering Wheel Effort**

# 1991 STEERING
# Power Rack & Pinion (Cont.)

**2)** Turn engine off. On Loyale, use spring balance to measure steering effort. Steering effort should be 20.9 lb. (9.5 kg) or less in each direction. If effort is not to specification, adjust rack and pinion backlash, and retest.

**3)** If effort is still not to specification, disconnect universal joint from steering column. With joint removed, steering effort should be 0.51 lb. (0.23 kg) or less in each direction. If effort is within specification, inspect tie rod ends and ball joints for wear and looseness. Ensure folding force of universal joint is within specification. *See Fig. 6.*

**4)** On all models, measure rotating and sliding resistance of gear box assembly. *See Fig. 7.* On Legacy and Loyale, rotating resistance should be 2.51 lb. (1.14 kg) around center position and 3.55 lb. (1.61 kg) or less in all other positions, with a 20 percent difference between clockwise and counterclockwise. Sliding resistance should be 68 lb. (31 kg) or less, with 20 percent difference between left and right directions.

**5)** On XT and XT6, rotating resistance should be 1.76 lb. (.80 kg) around center position and 2.27 lb. (1.03 kg) or less in all other

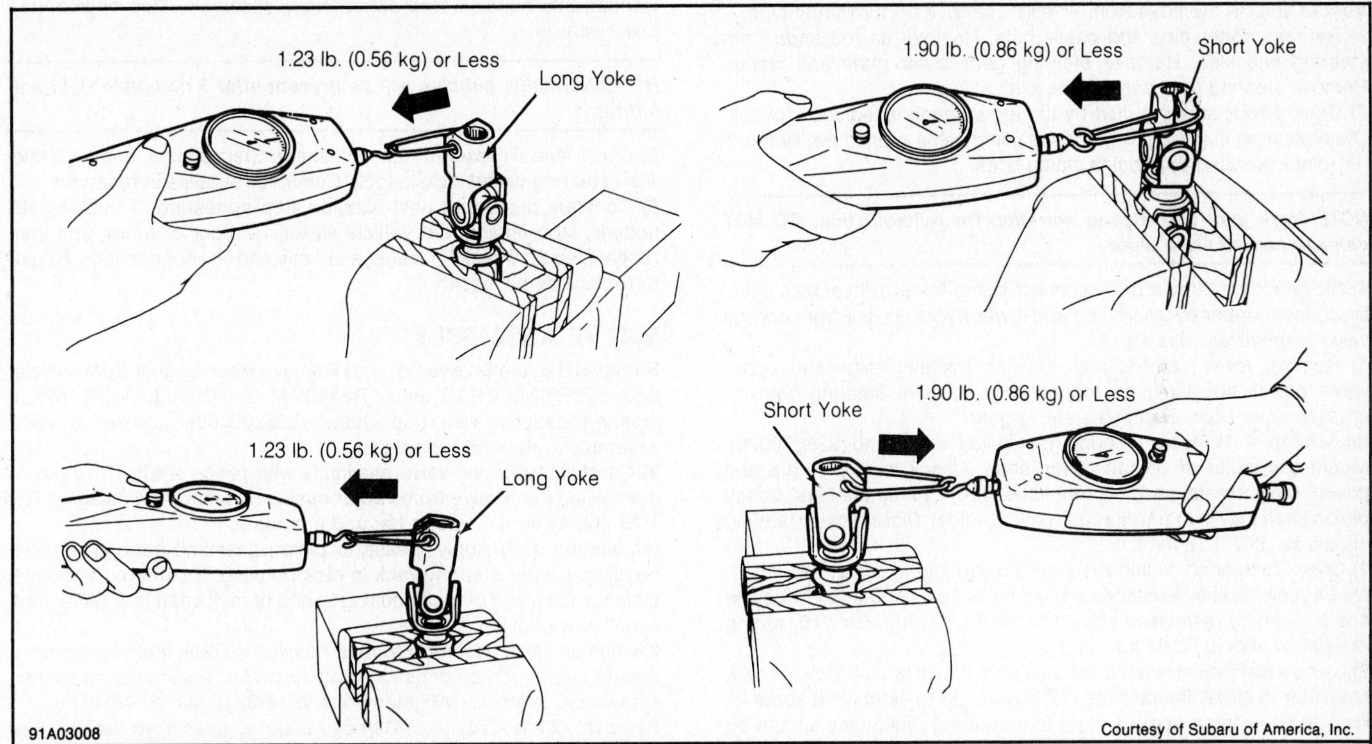


***Fig. 6: Testing Universal Joint***

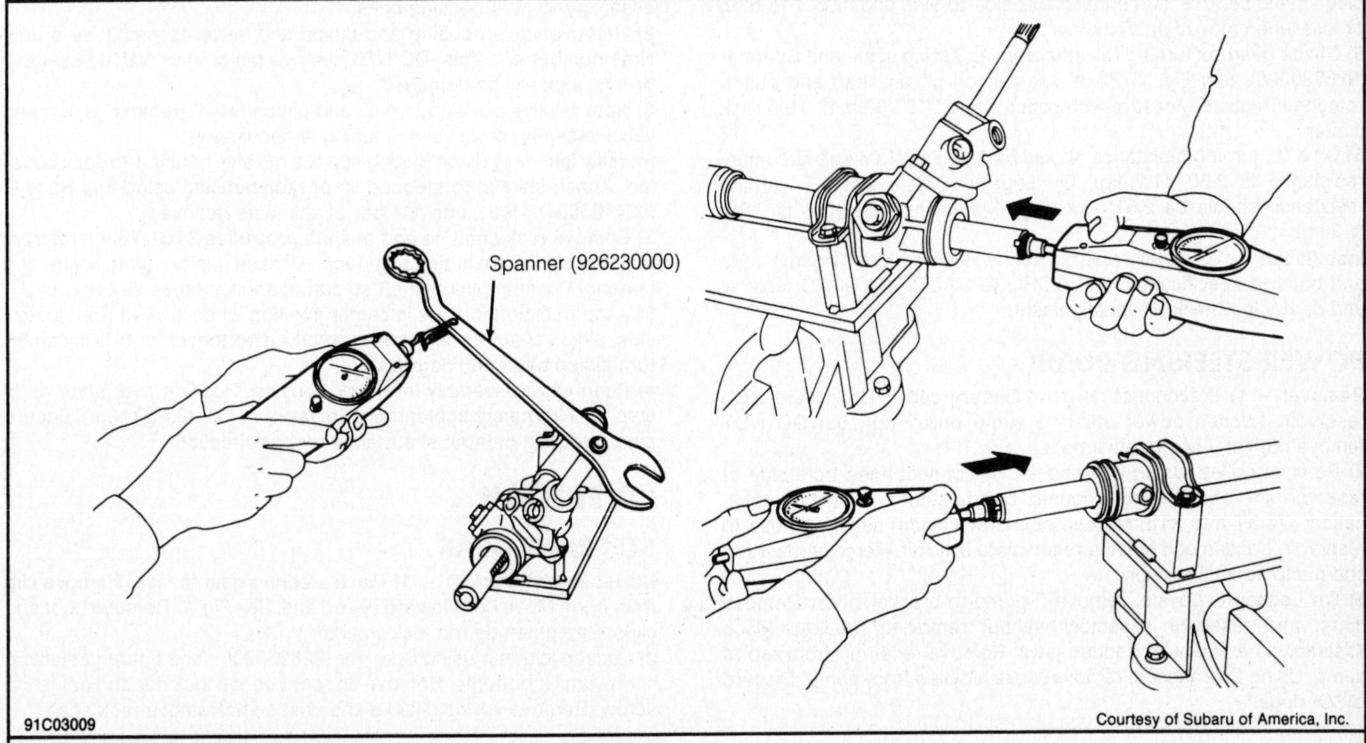


***Fig. 7: Checking Steering Gear Box***

positions, with a 20 percent difference between clockwise and counterclockwise. Sliding resistance should be 55 lb. (25 kg) or less, with 20 percent difference between left and right directions.

# REMOVAL & INSTALLATION

## STEERING GEAR

**Removal - 1)** Disconnect negative battery cable. Remove spare tire and support. Disconnect thermosensor connector. Raise and support front of vehicle. Remove front wheels. Remove front exhaust pipe.
**2)** Remove cotter pins and castle nuts. Remove tie rod ends from steering knuckles. Remove steering gear lower plate and clamp. Remove steering gear center pipe joint.
**3)** Drain power steering fluid by turning steering wheel lock-to-lock. Drain steering fluid from other pipes using same procedure. Remove "U" joint lower and upper side clamp bolts.

***NOTE: Mark joint and mating serration for reinstallation. DO NOT damage control valve pipes.***

**4)** Move "U" joint upward. Disconnect pump-to-valve hydraulic lines. Disconnect upper hydraulic line and lower hydraulic line from control valve respectively. *See Fig. 1.*
**5)** Remove lower valve-to-rack housing hydraulic pipe and upper valve-to-rack housing pipe respectively. Remove steering gear-to-crossmember bolts. Remove steering gear.
**Inspection - 1)** Mount steering gear in vise and Stand (926200000). Mount dial indicator on top pinion shaft. Check axial play (up and down). Dial indicator reading should be .004" (.10 mm) or less. Check pinion shaft play in radial direction (side-to-side). Dial indicator reading should be .007" (.18 mm).
**2)** Check rack shaft sliding resistance using spring scale. *See Fig. 7.* On Legacy, sliding resistance should be 54 lbs. (24.5 kg). On Loyale and XT, sliding resistance should be 68 lbs. (31 kg). On XT6, sliding resistance should be 64 lbs. (29 kg).
**3)** Using a dial indicator mounted near end of rack housing, check rack shaft play in radial direction (up and down/side-to-side). With about 22 lbs. (30 N) of force applied, right turn steering radial play should be .006" (.15 mm) or less.
**4)** With about 22 lbs. (30 N) of force applied, left turn steering radial play should be .012" (.30 mm) or less side-to-side and .006" (.15 mm) or less when moved up and down.
**5)** Check gearbox turning resistance using spring scale and Spanner (926230000). *See Fig. 7.* Place spanner on pinion shaft and pull in rotating direction. Measure with pinion shaft 1.18" (30 mm) from rack center.
**6)** On XT6, turning resistance should be 2.29 lbs. (1.04 kg). Maximum resistance is 2.60" (1.2 kg). On Legacy, Loyale and XT, turning resistance should be 2.51" (1.14 kg). Maximum resistance is 2.90" (1.3 kg).
**Installation -** To install, reverse removal procedure. Tighten nuts and bolts to specification. See TORQUE SPECIFICATIONS table at end of article. Check wheel alignment.

## POWER STEERING PUMP

**Removal - 1)** Disconnect negative battery cable. Drain fluid from reservoir. Loosen power steering pump pulley nut, but DO NOT remove nut yet. Loosen drive belts.
**2)** Remove pulley. Using 2 wrenches, disconnect hose from side of reservoir and power steering pump. Cap hoses to prevent contamination. On XT and XT6, remove hold-down clamp securing hose to reservoir. Loosen bolt holding reservoir to bracket. Remove reservoir and pump as an assembly.
**3)** On Legacy & Loyale, remove 3 pump-to-bracket bolts. Remove pump and reservoir assembly without removing bracket. Place assembly in a vise with padded jaws. Remove reservoir from top of pump. Using 2 wrenches, remove hydraulic pipe from pump. Discard all "O" rings.

**Installation - 1)** Install bracket on engine (if removed). Using 2 wrenches, install hydraulic pipe on pump. Install a new "O" ring on reservoir. Install reservoir on pump.
**2)** To complete installation, reverse removal procedure. Fill reservoir with fluid. Attach negative battery cable. Raise and support vehicle. Slowly turn steering wheel lock-to-lock.
**3)** Repeat procedure until bubbles stop appearing in reservoir. Maintain fluid level during this procedure.
**4)** Start and idle engine. Slowly turn steering wheel lock-to-lock. Repeat until bubbles stop appearing in reservoir. Stop engine, and lower vehicle.

***NOTE: Normally, bubbles will be present after 3 complete right and left turns.***

**5)** Check and fill reservoir as necessary. Start engine, and let it idle. Turn steering wheel lock-to-lock. Check for bubbles in reservoir.
**6)** Continue procedure until bubbles stop appearing. If bubbles still appear, stop engine. Let vehicle sit for 1/2 hour or more, and then repeat step **5)**. Check for leakage at hose and line connections. Repair or replace as necessary.

## VALVE ASSEMBLY

**Removal (Loyale & Legacy) - 1)** Remove steering gear from vehicle. See STEERING GEAR under REMOVAL & INSTALLATION. Mount steering gear in vise and Stand (926200000). Loosen 2 valve assembly-to-rack housing bolts.
**2)** Carefully withdraw valve assembly with pinion shaft. Drive pinion shaft with pinion valve from valve housing (if necessary) using a 1.65-1.73" (42-44 mm) diameter bar and a press.
**Installation - 1)** Apply grease to pinion gear and bearing of valve housing. Center steering rack in rack housing. If centered correctly, distance from end of rack housing to end of rack shaft is 3" (76.2 mm). Install new packing.
**2)** Position valve assembly to rack housing so rack teeth face pinion. Ensure cutout portion of pinion shaft serration faces toward adjusting screw hole. Alternately tighten bolts to 14-22 ft. lbs. (20-29 N.m).
**Removal (XT & XT6) - 1)** Remove steering gear from vehicle. See STEERING GEAR under REMOVAL & INSTALLATION. Mount steering gear in vise and Stand (926200000). Loosen 2 control valve assembly-to-rack housing bolts.
**2)** Remove valve housing and pinion and valve assembly as a unit. Note number of shims. DO NOT remove pinion from valve assembly or dust seal will be damaged.
**3)** Note relative position of rack and pinion teeth. Remove pinion and valve assembly from valve housing (if necessary).
**Installation - 1)** Clean mating surface of valve housing-to-rack housing. Attach shim(s) to stepped lip of rack housing using Fuji Bond C (004403004). Use same number of shims as removed.
**2)** Remove rack shaft so end of shaft protrudes 3.03" (76.9 mm) from pinion side of rack housing face. Grease pinion gear teeth and bearing. Position pinion shaft so cutout section faces sleeve boss.
**3)** If top of pinion tooth is in center position when viewed from sleeve side, pinion shaft is positioned correctly. If bottom of tooth is in center, turn pinion shaft 180 degrees.
**4)** Push valve assembly into rack housing. Position rack shaft as in step **2)**. Alternately tighten bolts to 14-22 ft. lbs. (20-29 N.m). Ensure cutout section of input shaft faces proper direction.

# OVERHAUL

## STEERING GEAR

**Disassembly (Loyale) - 1)** Place steering gear in vise. Remove clip from boot. Move boot toward tie rod end. *See Fig. 1.* Remove boot and clips. Straighten tie rod lock washer.
**2)** Loosen lock nut using Spanner (926230000), and tighten adjusting screw until it bottoms. Remove tie rod. Loosen lock nut and adjusting screw. Remove spring, sleeve and dust seal. Remove rack shaft.

# 1991 STEERING
# Power Rack & Pinion (Cont.)

**3)** Push rack into steering gear. Using chisel, straighten tie rod lock washer. Using Wrench (925700000) and Spanner (926230000), loosen inner tie rods. Remove valve assembly and pinion shaft.

**4)** Remove tie rod from rack assembly. Remove spring, sleeve, dust seal and dust cover (if equipped).

**Inspection** - Clean all parts. Replace any worn or damaged parts. If water is found inside of steering gear, replace boot, clips, input shaft, shaft dust seal and adjusting screw "O" ring.

**Reassembly** - **1)** Apply grease to rack teeth, sliding portion of rack shaft, sleeve insertion hole, dust seal and dust cover hole. Press dust seal into steering gear. Maximum distance between end of rack housing and top of dust seal is .08" (2.0 mm).

***NOTE: Move rack shaft back and forth full stroke to squeeze grease which accumulates on both ends. Remove grease to prevent clogging of air passage hole.***

**2)** Apply grease to sliding surface of sleeve and spring seat. Insert sleeve into pinion housing. Insert spring into adjusting screw. Pack grease inside screw. Install screw.

**3)** Rotate pinion shaft until rack shaft extends 1.57" (40 mm) beyond end of rack housing. Tighten backlash adjusting screw until it bottoms. Screw left and right side tie rods onto rack shaft. Left tie rod is grooved for identification and should be installed on pinion end of rack shaft.

**4)** Bend each lock washer in 2 places. Tighten backlash adjusting screw to 43 INCH lbs. (5 N.m), and then loosen. Repeat this procedure twice. Retighten adjusting screw to 43 INCH lbs. (5 N.m), then back off 30 degrees. Tighten adjusting screw lock nut. Install tie rod boots.

**Disassembly (Legacy)** - **1)** Slide mount bushing off to expose rack stopper. Use Wrench (926340001) to rotate rack stopper clockwise. Rotate until end of circlip comes out of stopper, and then rotate stopper in opposite direction and pull out circlip.

**2)** Pull rack shaft from cylinder side of rack housing. Pull out rack bushing and rack stopper together with rack shaft.

**Inspection** - Clean all parts. Replace any worn or damaged parts. If water is found inside of steering gear, replace boot, clips, input shaft, shaft dust seal and adjusting screw "O" ring.

**Reassembly** - **1)** Place rack housing on Stand (926200000). Apply grease to teeth of rack shaft. Install cover from Cover and Remover Set (926390001) onto toothed section of rack shaft. Check air passage hole for excessive grease, and unclog if necessary.

**2)** Apply Dexron-II ATF to cover and rack shaft piston ring. Insert rack shaft into rack housing from cylinder end of housing. Remove cover after rack shaft has passed completely through oil seal. Fit Guide (927660000) over end of rack shaft, dip rack bushing assembly in Dexron-II ATF and install rack bushing assembly.

**3)** Install rack stopper into rack housing and wrap circlip into position using Wrench (926340001). Fit mount bushing onto rack housing. Rotate wrench an additional 90-180 degrees after end of circlip has been wrapped into housing.

**Disassembly (XT & XT6)** - **1)** Use Remover (926260000) to remove seal snap ring. Place remover onto snap ring through hole in dust boot groove on cylinder end rack housing. Lightly tap remover to drive out snap ring. Push rack shaft out from valve end of rack housing.

**2)** Insert Remover (926330000) into valve end of rack housing, and push back-up ring and oil seal out of cylinder end. Remove rack shaft.

**Inspection** - Clean all parts. Replace any worn or damaged parts. If water is found inside of steering gear, replace boot, clips, input shaft, shaft dust seal and adjusting screw "O" ring.

**Reassembly** - **1)** Place rack housing on Stand (926200000). Oil Seal Installer (926240000) consists of 3 pieces: "A", "B" and "C". *See Fig. 8.* Using installers "B" and "C", attach oil seal to installer "A". Insert installer "A" with oil seal into rack housing from gear side.

**2)** Remove oil seal near rack shaft piston, and then remove Installer (926240000). Apply a coat of grease to rack teeth, sliding portion of sleeve and pistons sealing side. Install rack shaft into rack housing from cylinder end. Attach Guide (926250000) to cylinder end of rack shaft.

**3)** Apply a thin coat of grease to entire exposed surface of guide and rack shaft. Apply a coat of grease to inner surface of back-up ring and "O" ring. Install snap ring into groove in rack housing. Attach Installer (926320000) to cylinder end of rack shaft and drive back-up ring and oil seal into place using a press.

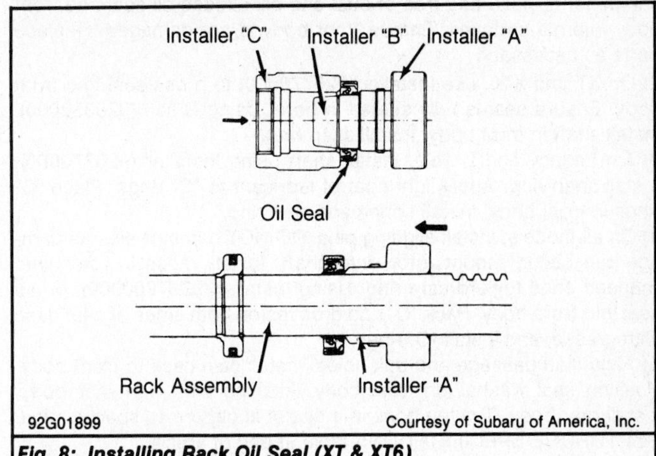


***Fig. 8: Installing Rack Oil Seal (XT & XT6)***

## POWER STEERING PUMP

**Disassembly** - **1)** Place pump in a soft-jawed vise. Remove reservoir and pipe from pump. Remove adapter and "O" ring. *See Fig. 9.*

**2)** Tilt pump assembly. Remove adapter, "O" ring, pressure valve and spring. DO NOT drop pressure valve. Remove rear body-to-front body bolts. Separate rear body from front body. On Legacy and Loyale, remove seal washer.

**3)** On XT and XT6, remove cam case and "O" ring. Remove snap ring, and detach spacer. Remove pins. Carefully remove rotor and cam ring as an assembly. Remove "O" ring from cam ring and vanes from rotor. Remove shaft and seal from front body.

**4)** On Legacy and Loyale, remove side plate, spring and "O" rings. Remove shaft from front body. Press bearing from shaft. Using a

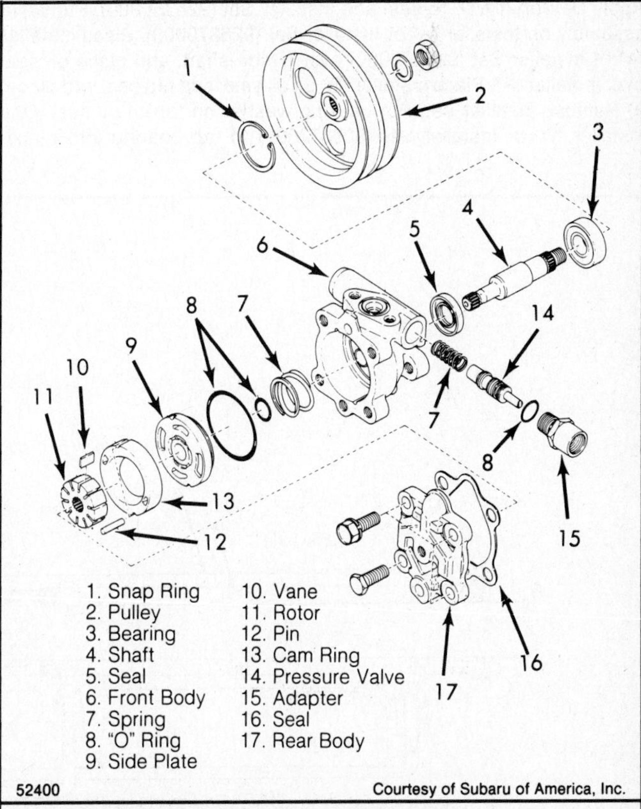


***Fig. 9: Exploded View of Power Steering Pump (Loyale, XT & XT6 Shown; Legacy Is Similar)***

# 1991 STEERING
# Power Rack & Pinion (Cont.)

screwdriver, remove seal from front body. Discard seal. DO NOT damage front body during seal removal.

**Reassembly - 1)** Replace all "O" rings, seals and snap rings. Keep components clean and free of dust and oil. Grease oil seal and front body internal surfaces. Ensure front body is not damaged. Replace parts as necessary.

**2)** On XT and XT6, use Installer (926770000) to press seal into front body. Ensure seal is fully seated in bore. Using Guide (926830000), install shaft in front body. Install snap ring.

**3)** On Legacy and Loyale, install shaft using Installer (926770000). Install snap ring. Apply light coat of lubricant to "O" rings. Place "O" rings in front body. Install spring and cam ring.

**4)** On all models, install aligning pins. DO NOT hammer pins as damage can occur. Mount rotor onto shaft. Install vanes in rotor with rounded ends toward cam ring. Using Installer (9267900000), press seal into front body. Pack "O" ring grooves on both sides of cam case with grease, and install "O" rings.

**5)** Align fluid passage and bolt holes. Install cam case to front body. Position seal washer on front body. Aligning pins with rear body, install rear body. Tighten bolts in a diagonal pattern to specification. See TORQUE SPECIFICATIONS table at end of article.

**6)** Lightly lubricate pressure valve. Install spring and pressure valve. Ensure pressure valve moves smoothly. Apply light coating of grease to adapter "O" ring. Install adapter and "O" ring. Tighten adapter. Ensure shaft turns smoothly without excessive play. Install reservoir on pump. Install pipe to pump.

## VALVE ASSEMBLY

**Disassembly (Loyale & Legacy) - 1)** With valve assembly removed from rack assembly, press out pinion shaft and valve assembly using a 1.65-1.73" (42-44 mm) pipe. *See Fig. 10.* To replace valve housing oil seal, pry off dust cover. Remove snap ring. Pry out oil seal.

**2)** To remove low pressure oil seal from pinion shaft, remove snap ring. Use 1.46-1.50" (37-38 mm) pipe to press off pinion bearing. DO NOT reuse bearing. Remove oil seal.

**Reassembly - 1)** Fit pinion and valve assembly onto valve housing. Apply Dexron-II ATF to seal and Installer Set (926360000). Put valve assembly on Installer "A" of Installer Set (926370000). Place installer "A" of Installer Set (926360000) over pinion shaft, and place oil seal over installer "A". Place installer "B" on oil seal, and tap seal into place.

**2)** Remove installer set. Put backing washer on top of oil seal. Use installer "B" of Installer Set (926370000) to tap bearing into place. Install snap ring. Apply Dexron-II ATF to pinion housing oil seal, and press in housing using Installer (926350000).

**3)** Install snap ring and dust cover. Apply Dexron-II ATF to outer surface of pinion shaft and valve body "O" ring.

**Disassembly (XT & XT6) -** Remove dust cover. Push pinion and valve assembly from valve housing. *See Fig. 10.* Use press if necessary. DO NOT allow serrated edges of input shaft to contact "Y" packing. Using Remover (926290000), drive dust seal, back-up ring, "Y" packing and bearing from housing.

**Reassembly - 1)** Apply grease to inside of valve housing, back-up ring and "Y" packing. Apply grease to mating surface of Installer (926300000). Drive dust seal into place. Ensure seal faces proper direction. Drive in "Y" packing and back-up ring. Ensure "Y" packing faces proper direction.

**2)** Use Remover (926290000) to press bearing into place. Fill dust seal with grease. Apply grease to Guide (926310000) and input shaft. Install guide over end of input shaft. Insert pinion and valve assembly into valve housing until lip of pinion oil seal touches valve housing. Push valve housing in until pinion and valve assembly fits.

**3)** Apply grease to lip of dust cover. Install cover until it butts up against graded section of input shaft. Ensure no more than 0-.02" (0-.5 mm) clearance exists between dust cover lip and end of housing.

## TORQUE SPECIFICATIONS

***TORQUE SPECIFICATIONS***

| Application | Ft. Lbs. (N.m) |
|---|---|
| Front Pump Body-To-Rear Pump Body Bolt | |
| Legacy | 10-13 (14-18) |
| Loyale | 28-38 (38-52) |
| XT & XT6 | 36-44 (49-59) |
| Outlet Connector | |
| Legacy & Loyale | 51-58 (69-78) |
| XT & XT6 | 22-29 (29-39) |
| Pulley Retaining Nut | 31-46 (42-62) |
| Pump Bracket-To-Engine Bolt | 13-16 (18-22) |
| Pump Bracket-To-Pump Bolt | |
| Legacy | 13-17 (18-23) |
| Loyale, XT & XT6 | 22-36 (29-49) |
| Rack Mounting Bolts | 35-52 (47-71) |
| Reservoir Mounting Bolt | |
| Legacy | 13-17 (18-23) |
| Loyale, XT & XT6 | 15-22 (20-29) |
| Tie Rod End Castle Nut | 18-22 (25-29) |
| Tie Rod End Lock Nut | 58-65 (78-88) |
| Tie Rod-To-Steering Rack | 51-65 (69-88) |
| Valve Housing Bolt | 15-22 (20-29) |

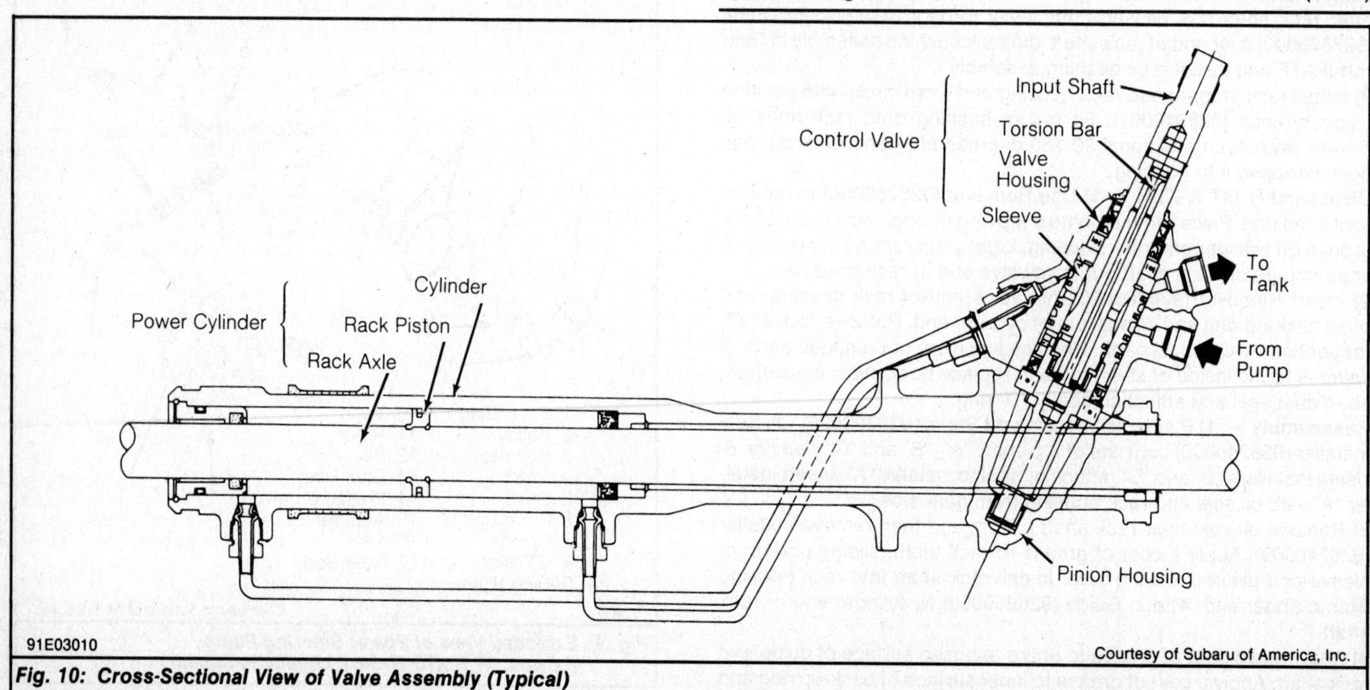


*Fig. 10: Cross-Sectional View of Valve Assembly (Typical)*

# 1991 STEERING
# Electronic Power Steering

## XT6

## DESCRIPTION

***NOTE: For information on steering rack and linkage, see POWER RACK & PINION article in STEERING.***

The electronic power steering system senses vehicle speed and frequency of steering operation. System activates motor to supply required amount of fluid to vary assist force according to vehicle speed. Components in system include: motor, pump, steering angle sensor, speed sensor, signal controller and power controller. *See Fig. 1.*

As vehicle speed increases, power steering system assist is reduced. System automatically selects one of 4 driving modes depending on average vehicle speed and frequency of steering operation. These modes include: high speed driving, suburban driving, winding road driving and city driving. Motor will not activate when vehicle speed is less than 6 MPH.

The electronic control logic configuration includes both an initial diagnostic function and a normal processing function to monitor input and output signals transmitted by various components. System includes self-diagnostic and fail safe functions.

## LUBRICATION

### CAPACITY

Fluid capacity is .7 qts. (.65L). Reservoir capacity is .30 qts. (.25L).

### FLUID TYPE

Fluid type is Special Power Steering Fluid (K0209A0080).

### FLUID LEVEL CHECK

With engine cold, ensure fluid level is between arrow marks on COLD side of dipstick.

## TROUBLE SHOOTING

See SELF-DIAGNOSTIC PROCEDURE under SELF-DIAGNOSTIC CHARTS at end of article. To trouble shoot sub-fan problems, see FAULTY SUB-FAN CONTROL CIRCUIT charts under SELF-DIAGNOSTIC CHARTS at end of article.

## TESTING

### HYDRAULIC SYSTEM PRESSURE TEST

**1)** Check fluid level. Disconnect high pressure line at pump. Connect Pressure Gauge (925711000) between shutoff valve and pump. *See Fig. 2.* Open shutoff valve.

**2)** Check fluid level. Start engine and turn steering wheel lock-to-lock several times to expel air from system.

***NOTE: DO NOT hold steering wheel at lock position or shutoff valve closed for more than 5 seconds, or system damage may occur.***

**3)** With shutoff valve open, check system pressure. Pressure should be 142 psi (10 kg/cm²) or less. Close shutoff valve and check pump relief pressure. Pressure should be 853-1067 psi (60-75 kg/cm²).

**4)** With shutoff valve open, turn steering wheel left-to-right to check working pressure. Pressure should be 853-1067 psi (60-75 kg/cm²).

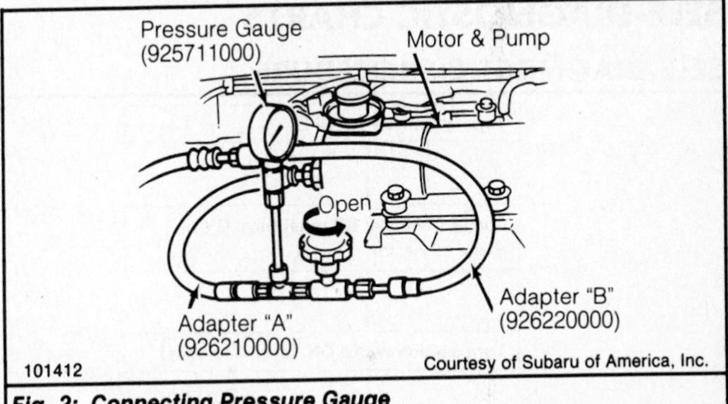


***Fig. 2: Connecting Pressure Gauge***

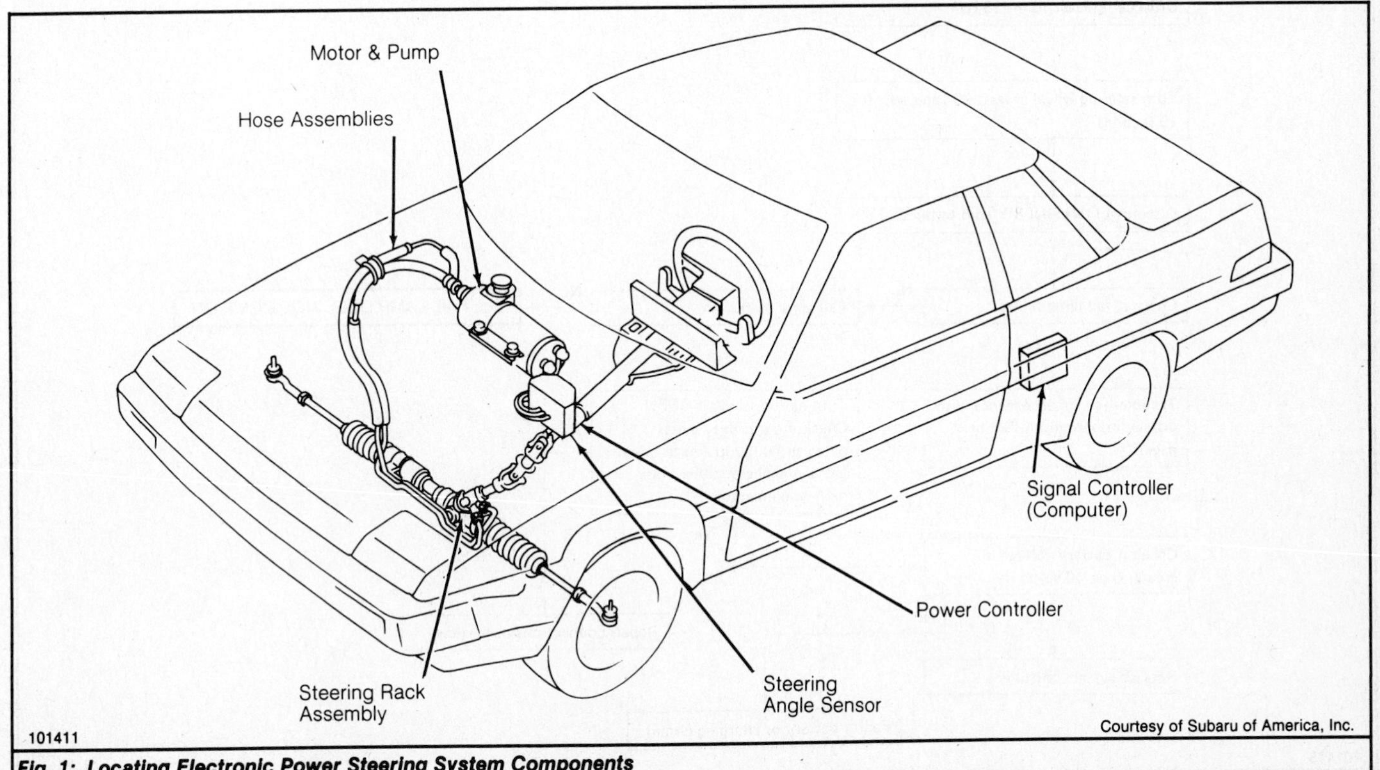


***Fig. 1: Locating Electronic Power Steering System Components***

# 1991 STEERING
# Electronic Power Steering (Cont.)

## OVERHAUL

***NOTE:* See Fig. 3 for exploded view of electronic power steering pump.**

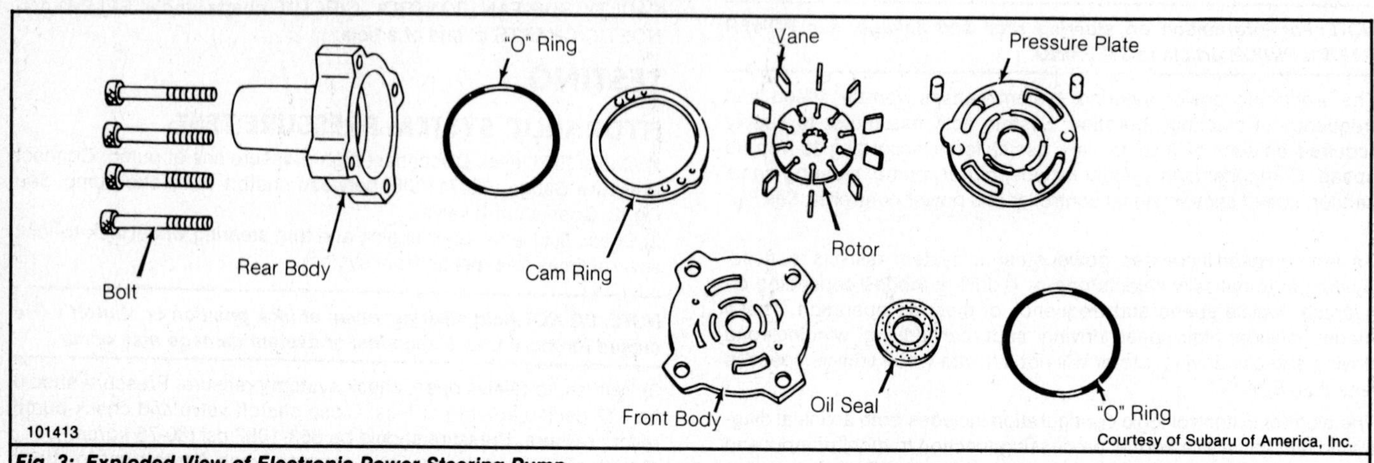


***Fig. 3: Exploded View of Electronic Power Steering Pump***

## SELF-DIAGNOSTIC CHARTS

### SELF-DIAGNOSTIC PROCEDURE

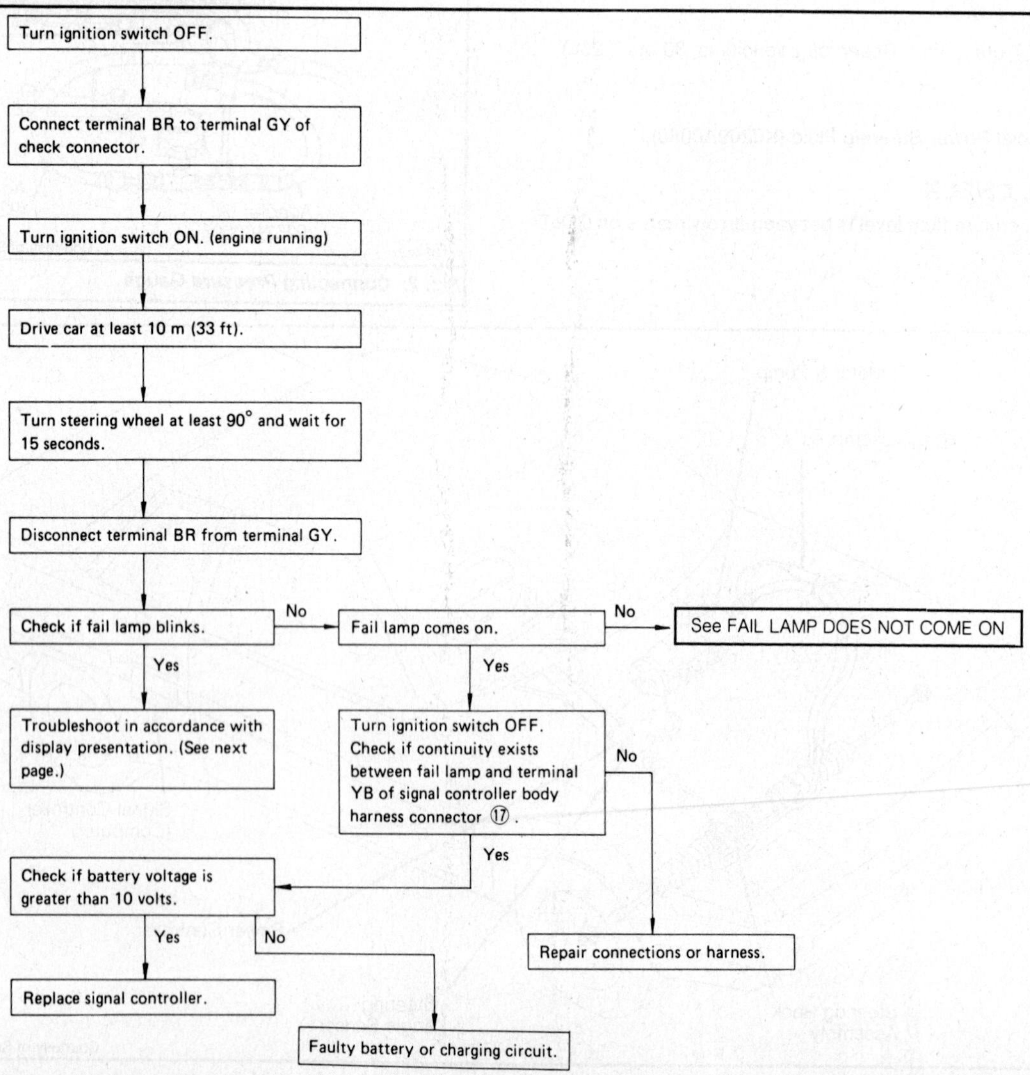

Turn ignition switch OFF.

↓

Connect terminal BR to terminal GY of check connector.

↓

Turn ignition switch ON. (engine running)

↓

Drive car at least 10 m (33 ft).

↓

Turn steering wheel at least 90° and wait for 15 seconds.

↓

Disconnect terminal BR from terminal GY.

↓

Check if fail lamp blinks.
- Yes → Troubleshoot in accordance with display presentation. (See next page.)
- No → Fail lamp comes on.
  - No → See FAIL LAMP DOES NOT COME ON
  - Yes → Turn ignition switch OFF. Check if continuity exists between fail lamp and terminal YB of signal controller body harness connector ⑰.
    - No → Repair connections or harness.
    - Yes → Check if battery voltage is greater than 10 volts.
      - Yes → Replace signal controller.
      - No → Faulty battery or charging circuit.

101415

Courtesy of Subaru of America, Inc.

# 1991 STEERING
# Electronic Power Steering (Cont.)

## DISPLAY PRESENTATION

| Display presentation | Cause - See flow chart listed |
|---|---|
| | SYSTEM OPERATES PROPERLY |
| Lamp remains off. | FAIL LAMP DOES NOT COME ON |
| | FAULTY SPEED SENSOR CIRCUIT |
| | FAULTY STEERING SENSOR CIRCUIT |
| | FAULTY TEMPERATURE SENSOR CIRCUIT |
| | FAULTY POWER STEERING FLUID HEATER CIRCUIT |
| | FAULTY PUMP MOTOR DRIVE CIRCUIT (PART 1) |
| | FAULTY PUMP MOTOR DRIVE CIRCUIT (PART 2) |
| | FAULTY SIGNAL CONTROLLER LINE VOLTAGE |
| | FAULTY POWER CONTROLLER CONTROL |

Example:

- All systems operate properly.

1 second — Start pulse alone is emitted.

1 second — 1 second — ..... Waveform pattern is repeated.

- Faulty car-speed pulse circuit.

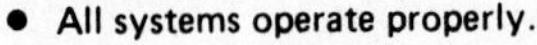
..... Waveform pattern is repeated.
Start pulse
Car-speed sensor circuit is N.G.

- Both car-speed pulse circuit and pump motor circuits are faulty.

..... Waveform pattern is repeated.

Start pulse — Car-speed sensor circuit is N.G. — Pump motor circuit is faulty.

101416

# 1991 STEERING
# Electronic Power Steering (Cont.)

## FAIL LAMP DOES NOT COME ON

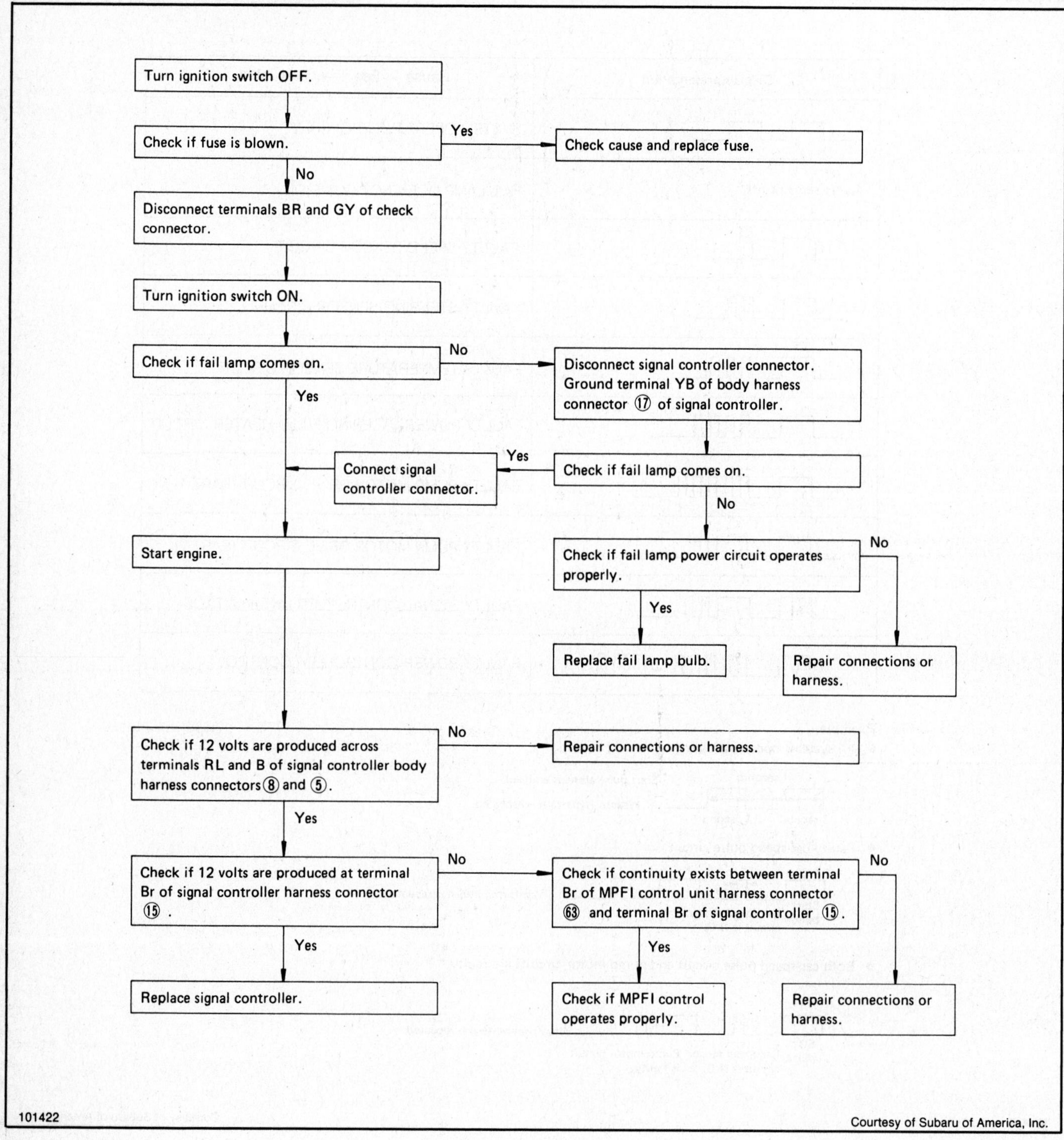
Turn ignition switch OFF.
Check if fuse is blown.
Yes
Check cause and replace fuse.
No
Disconnect terminals BR and GY of check connector.
Turn ignition switch ON.
Check if fail lamp comes on.
No
Disconnect signal controller connector. Ground terminal YB of body harness connector ⑰ of signal controller.
Yes
Yes
Connect signal controller connector.
Check if fail lamp comes on.
No
Start engine.
Check if fail lamp power circuit operates properly.
No
Yes
Replace fail lamp bulb.
Repair connections or harness.
Check if 12 volts are produced across terminals RL and B of signal controller body harness connectors ⑧ and ⑤.
No
Repair connections or harness.
Yes
Check if 12 volts are produced at terminal Br of signal controller harness connector ⑮ .
No
Check if continuity exists between terminal Br of MPFI control unit harness connector ⑥③ and terminal Br of signal controller ⑮.
No
Yes
Yes
Replace signal controller.
Check if MPFI control operates properly.
Repair connections or harness.
101422
Courtesy of Subaru of America, Inc.

# 1991 STEERING
# Electronic Power Steering (Cont.)

## FAULTY SPEED SENSOR CIRCUIT

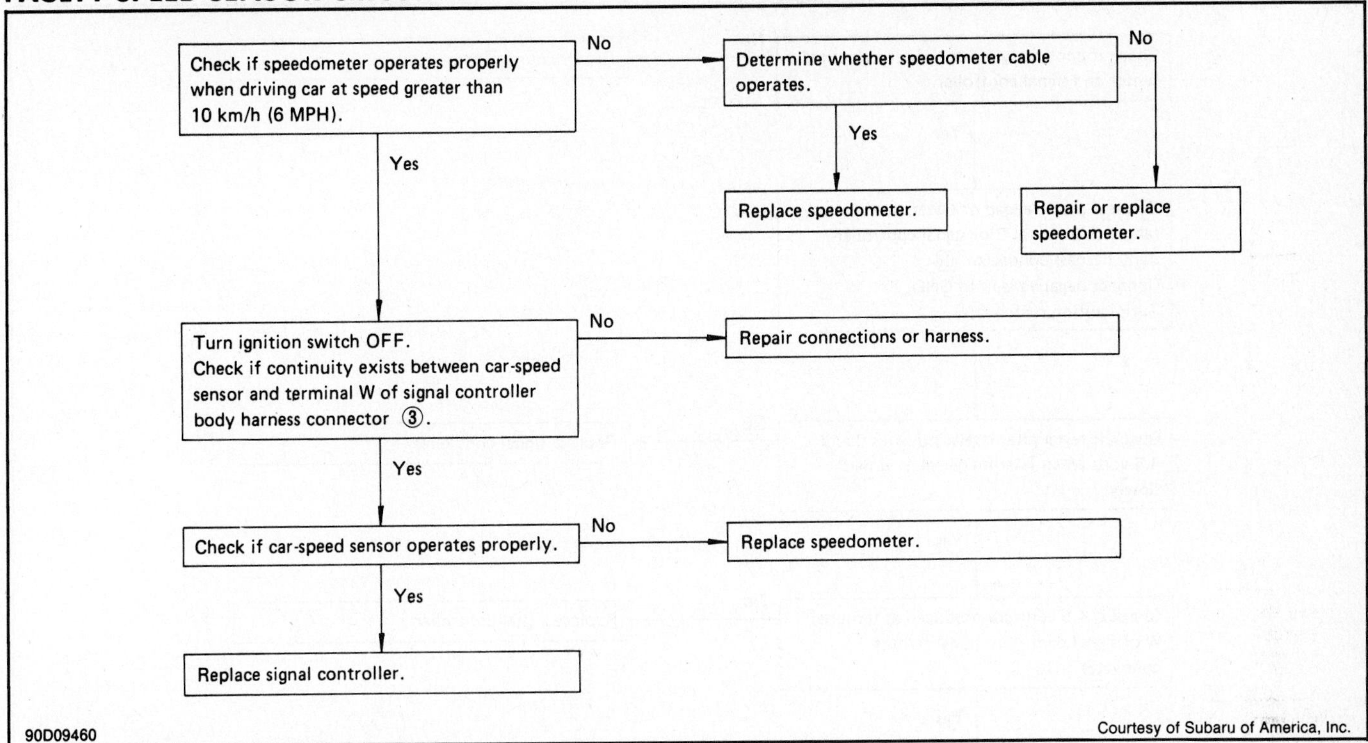
Check if speedometer operates properly when driving car at speed greater than 10 km/h (6 MPH).
No
Determine whether speedometer cable operates.
No
Yes
Replace speedometer.
Repair or replace speedometer.
Yes
Turn ignition switch OFF.
Check if continuity exists between car-speed sensor and terminal W of signal controller body harness connector ③.
No
Repair connections or harness.
Yes
Check if car-speed sensor operates properly.
No
Replace speedometer.
Yes
Replace signal controller.
90D09460
Courtesy of Subaru of America, Inc.

## FAULTY TEMPERATURE SENSOR CIRCUIT

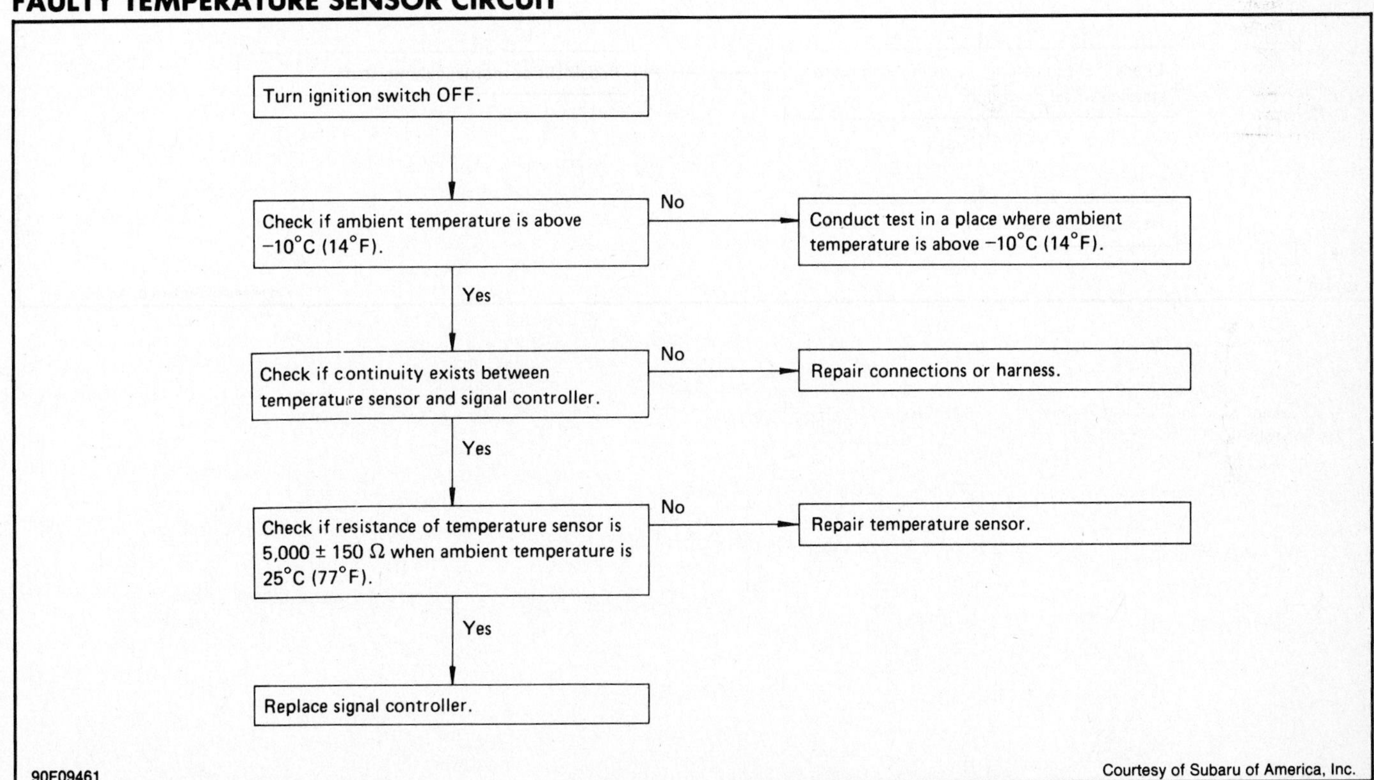
Turn ignition switch OFF.
Check if ambient temperature is above −10°C (14°F).
No
Conduct test in a place where ambient temperature is above −10°C (14°F).
Yes
Check if continuity exists between temperature sensor and signal controller.
No
Repair connections or harness.
Yes
Check if resistance of temperature sensor is 5,000 ± 150 Ω when ambient temperature is 25°C (77°F).
No
Repair temperature sensor.
Yes
Replace signal controller.
90F09461
Courtesy of Subaru of America, Inc.

# 1991 STEERING
# Electronic Power Steering (Cont.)

## FAULTY STEERING SENSOR CIRCUIT

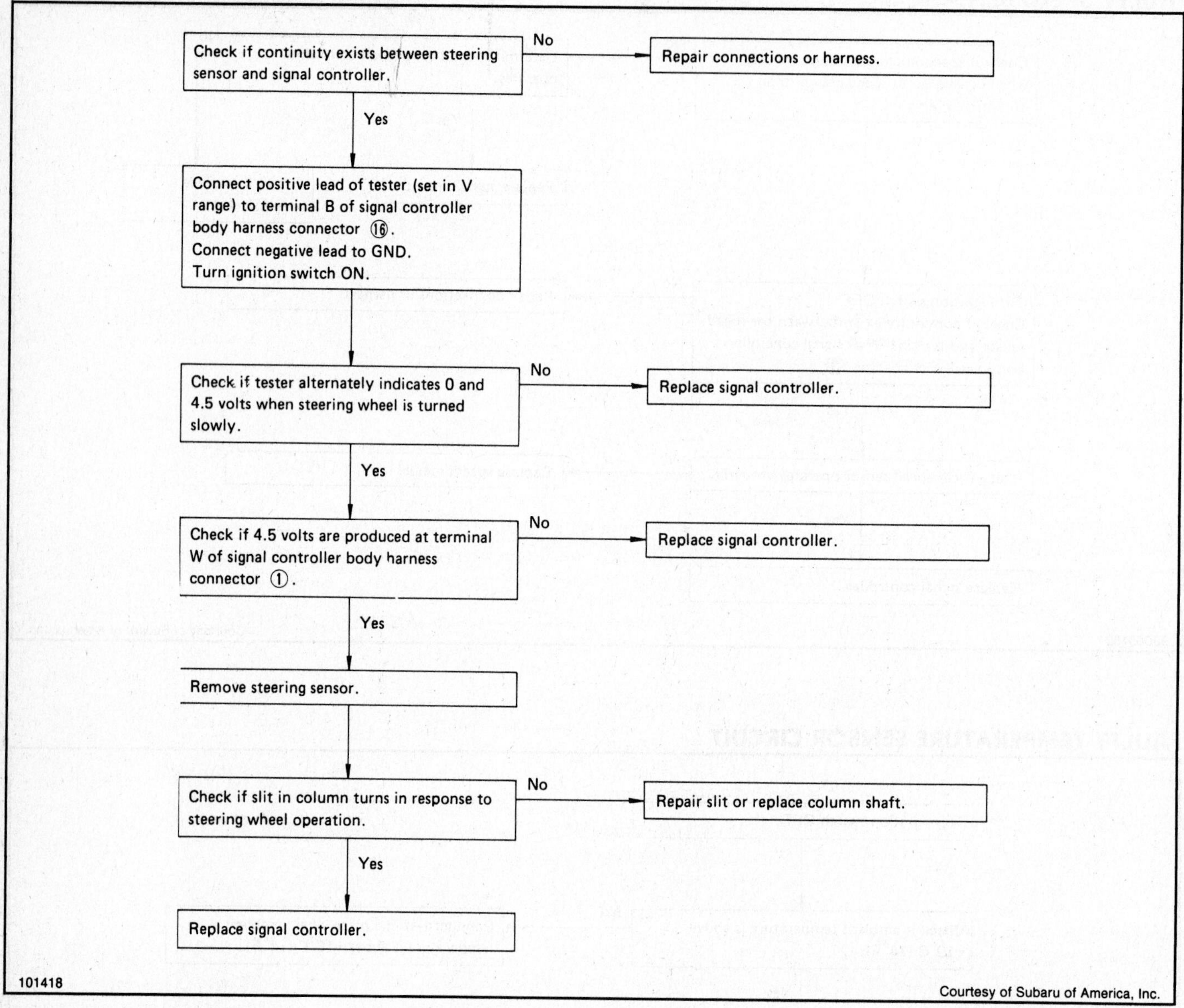

Check if continuity exists between steering sensor and signal controller.
No
Repair connections or harness.
Yes
Connect positive lead of tester (set in V range) to terminal B of signal controller body harness connector ⑯.
Connect negative lead to GND.
Turn ignition switch ON.
Check if tester alternately indicates 0 and 4.5 volts when steering wheel is turned slowly.
No
Replace signal controller.
Yes
Check if 4.5 volts are produced at terminal W of signal controller body harness connector ①.
No
Replace signal controller.
Yes
Remove steering sensor.
Check if slit in column turns in response to steering wheel operation.
No
Repair slit or replace column shaft.
Yes
Replace signal controller.
101418
Courtesy of Subaru of America, Inc.

## FAULTY POWER STEERING FLUID HEATER CIRCUIT

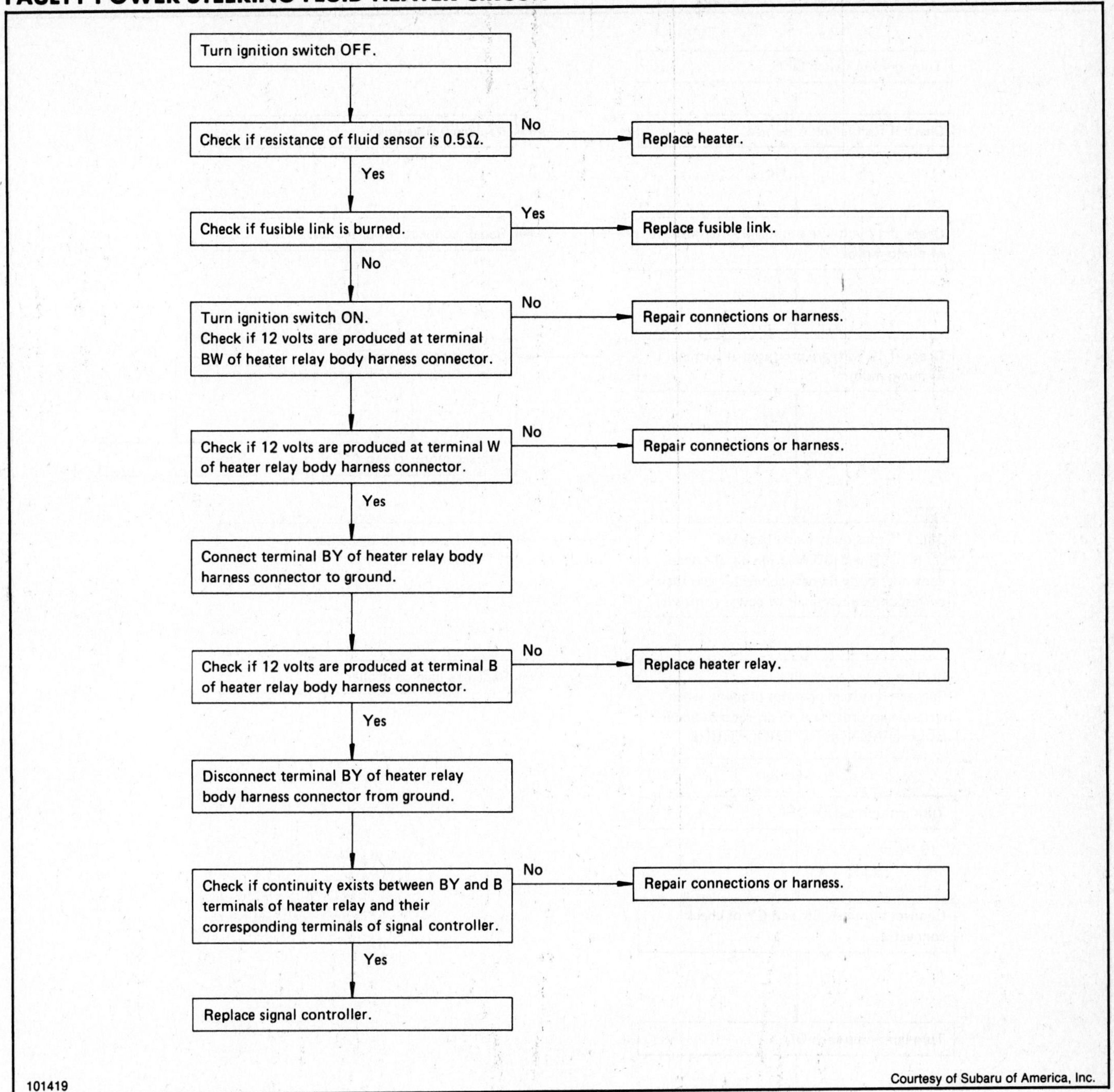

Turn ignition switch OFF.
Check if resistance of fluid sensor is 0.5Ω.
No
Replace heater.
Yes
Check if fusible link is burned.
Yes
Replace fusible link.
No
Turn ignition switch ON.
Check if 12 volts are produced at terminal BW of heater relay body harness connector.
No
Repair connections or harness.
Check if 12 volts are produced at terminal W of heater relay body harness connector.
No
Repair connections or harness.
Yes
Connect terminal BY of heater relay body harness connector to ground.
Check if 12 volts are produced at terminal B of heater relay body harness connector.
No
Replace heater relay.
Yes
Disconnect terminal BY of heater relay body harness connector from ground.
Check if continuity exists between BY and B terminals of heater relay and their corresponding terminals of signal controller.
No
Repair connections or harness.
Yes
Replace signal controller.
101419
Courtesy of Subaru of America, Inc.

# 1991 STEERING
# Electronic Power Steering (Cont.)

## FAULTY PUMP MOTOR DRIVE CIRCUIT

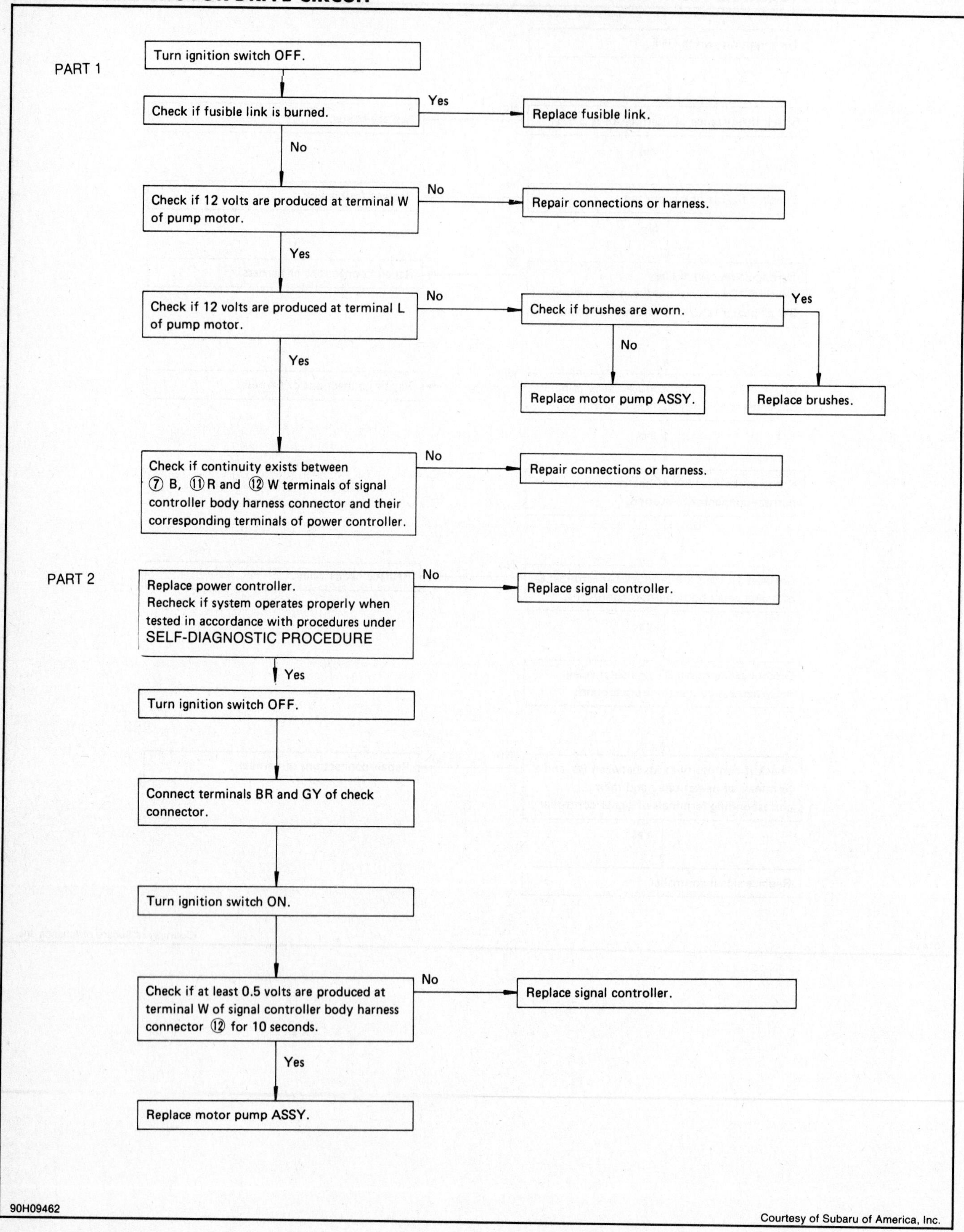

PART 1
Turn ignition switch OFF.
Check if fusible link is burned.
Yes
Replace fusible link.
No
Check if 12 volts are produced at terminal W of pump motor.
No
Repair connections or harness.
Yes
Check if 12 volts are produced at terminal L of pump motor.
No
Check if brushes are worn.
Yes
Replace brushes.
No
Replace motor pump ASSY.
Yes
Check if continuity exists between ⑦ B, ⑪ R and ⑫ W terminals of signal controller body harness connector and their corresponding terminals of power controller.
No
Repair connections or harness.
PART 2
Replace power controller.
Recheck if system operates properly when tested in accordance with procedures under SELF-DIAGNOSTIC PROCEDURE
No
Replace signal controller.
Yes
Turn ignition switch OFF.
Connect terminals BR and GY of check connector.
Turn ignition switch ON.
Check if at least 0.5 volts are produced at terminal W of signal controller body harness connector ⑫ for 10 seconds.
No
Replace signal controller.
Yes
Replace motor pump ASSY.
90H09462


Courtesy of Subaru of America, Inc.

# 1991 STEERING
# Electronic Power Steering (Cont.)

## FAULTY POWER CONTROLLER CONTROL

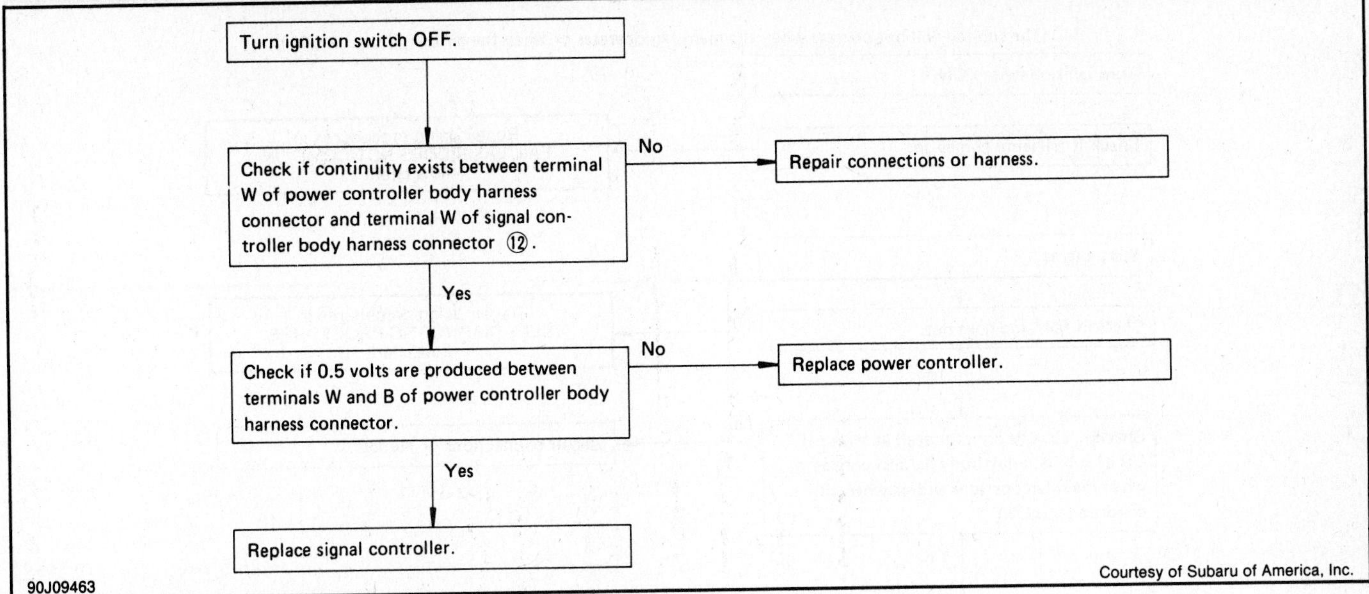
Turn ignition switch OFF.
Check if continuity exists between terminal W of power controller body harness connector and terminal W of signal controller body harness connector ⑫.
No
Repair connections or harness.
Yes
Check if 0.5 volts are produced between terminals W and B of power controller body harness connector.
No
Replace power controller.
Yes
Replace signal controller.
90J09463
Courtesy of Subaru of America, Inc.

## FAULTY SIGNAL CONTROLLER LINE VOLTAGE

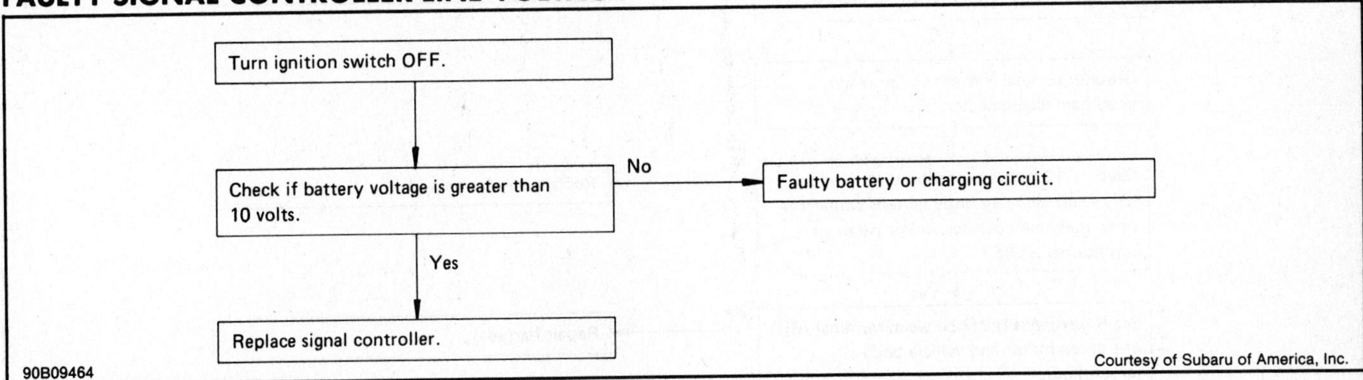
Turn ignition switch OFF.
Check if battery voltage is greater than 10 volts.
No
Faulty battery or charging circuit.
Yes
Replace signal controller.
90B09464
Courtesy of Subaru of America, Inc.

## FAULTY SUB-FAN CONTROL CIRCUIT (PART 1)

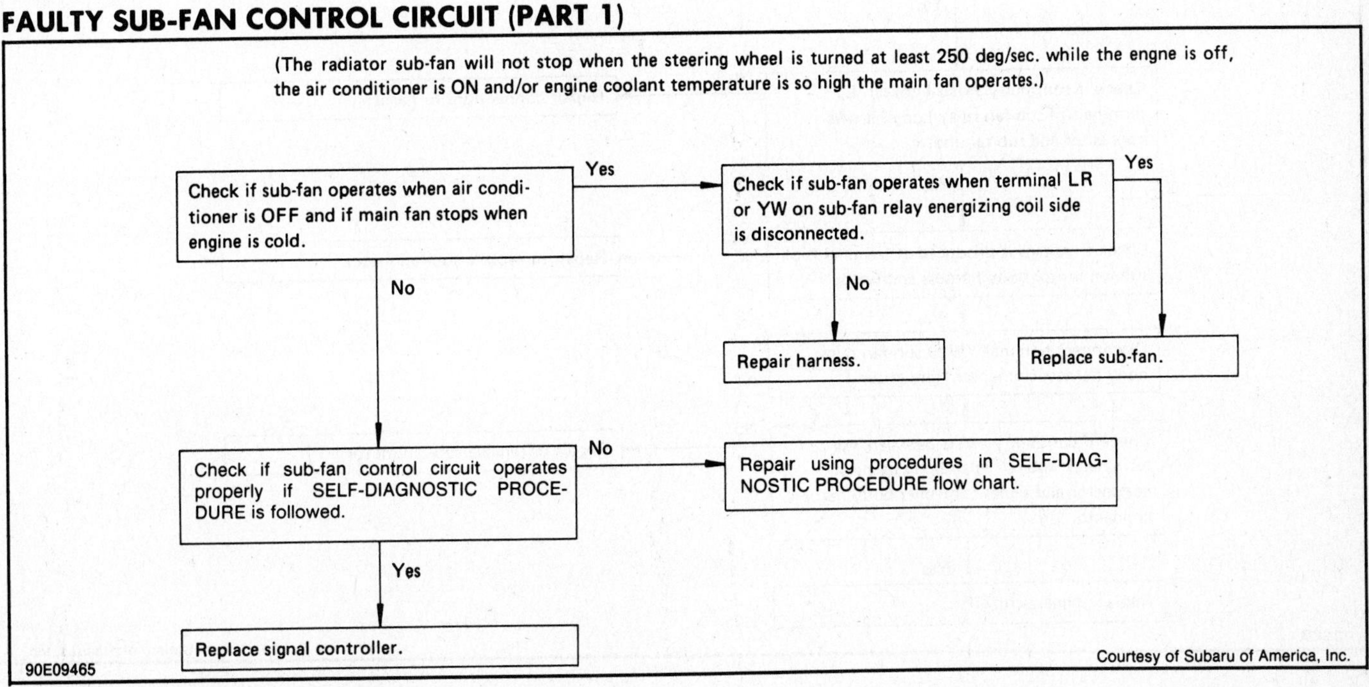
(The radiator sub-fan will not stop when the steering wheel is turned at least 250 deg/sec. while the engne is off, the air conditioner is ON and/or engine coolant temperature is so high the main fan operates.)
Check if sub-fan operates when air conditioner is OFF and if main fan stops when engine is cold.
Yes
Check if sub-fan operates when terminal LR or YW on sub-fan relay energizing coil side is disconnected.
Yes
Replace sub-fan.
No
Repair harness.
No
Check if sub-fan control circuit operates properly if SELF-DIAGNOSTIC PROCEDURE is followed.
No
Repair using procedures in SELF-DIAGNOSTIC PROCEDURE flow chart.
Yes
Replace signal controller.
90E09465
Courtesy of Subaru of America, Inc.

# 1991 STEERING
# Electronic Power Steering (Cont.)

## FAULTY SUB-FAN CONTROL CIRCUIT (PART 2)

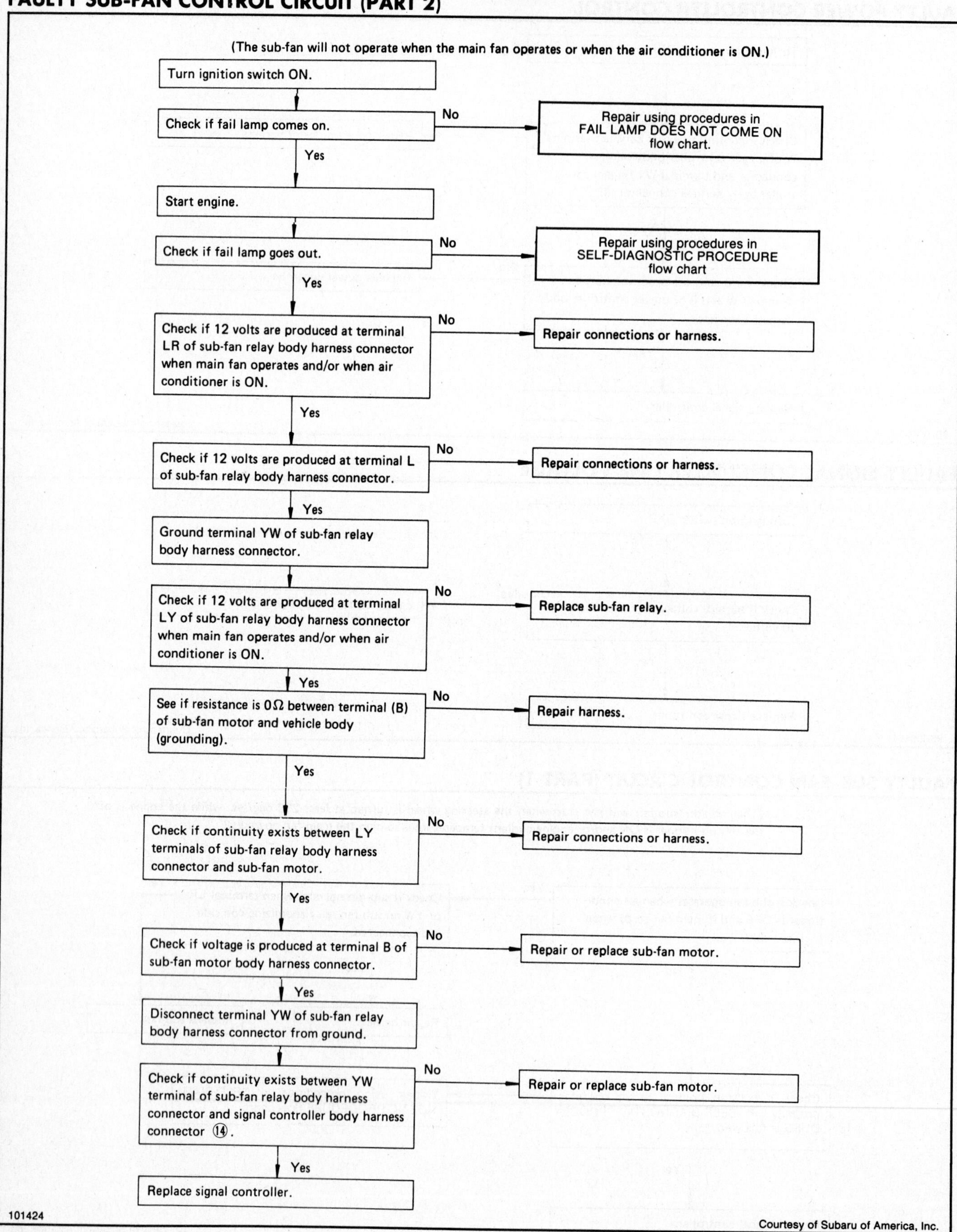

(The sub-fan will not operate when the main fan operates or when the air conditioner is ON.)
Turn ignition switch ON.
Check if fail lamp comes on.
No
Repair using procedures in FAIL LAMP DOES NOT COME ON flow chart.
Yes
Start engine.
Check if fail lamp goes out.
No
Repair using procedures in SELF-DIAGNOSTIC PROCEDURE flow chart
Yes
Check if 12 volts are produced at terminal LR of sub-fan relay body harness connector when main fan operates and/or when air conditioner is ON.
No
Repair connections or harness.
Yes
Check if 12 volts are produced at terminal L of sub-fan relay body harness connector.
No
Repair connections or harness.
Yes
Ground terminal YW of sub-fan relay body harness connector.
Check if 12 volts are produced at terminal LY of sub-fan relay body harness connector when main fan operates and/or when air conditioner is ON.
No
Replace sub-fan relay.
Yes
See if resistance is 0Ω between terminal (B) of sub-fan motor and vehicle body (grounding).
No
Repair harness.
Yes
Check if continuity exists between LY terminals of sub-fan relay body harness connector and sub-fan motor.
No
Repair connections or harness.
Yes
Check if voltage is produced at terminal B of sub-fan motor body harness connector.
No
Repair or replace sub-fan motor.
Yes
Disconnect terminal YW of sub-fan relay body harness connector from ground.
Check if continuity exists between YW terminal of sub-fan relay body harness connector and signal controller body harness connector ⑭.
No
Repair or replace sub-fan motor.
Yes
Replace signal controller.
101424

# 1991 STEERING
# Electronic Power Steering (Cont.)

## WIRING DIAGRAM

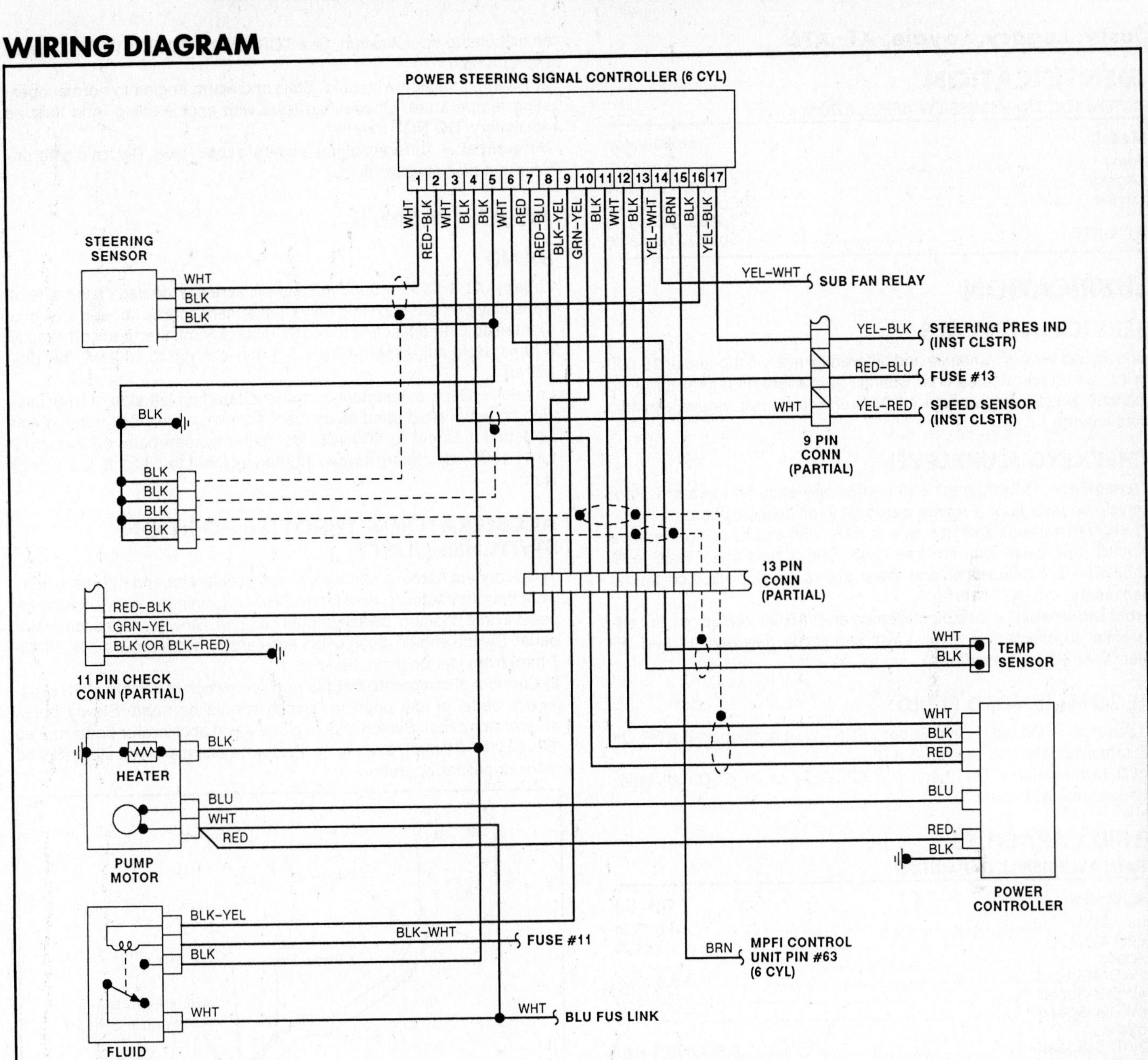


*Fig. 4: Electronic Power Steering Pump Wiring Diagram (XT6)*

# 1991 TRANSMISSION SERVICING
## Automatic Transmission

**Justy, Legacy, Loyale, XT, XT6**

## IDENTIFICATION

*AUTOMATIC TRANSMISSION APPLICATION*

| Model | Transmission |
|---|---|
| Justy | ECVT |
| Legacy | 4-Speed Transaxle |
| Loyale | 3-Speed Transaxle |
| | 4-Speed Transaxle |
| XT & XT6 | 4-Speed Transaxle |

## LUBRICATION

### SERVICE INTERVALS

Check fluid level in transaxle and differential every 5 months or 15,000 miles, whichever comes first. Change fluid every 30,000 miles or 30 months, whichever comes first. Differentials do not require periodic fluid change.

### CHECKING FLUID LEVEL

**Transaxle - 1)** Bring engine to normal operating temperature. Park vehicle on level floor. Engage transaxle in all gear positions.

**2)** Set transmission selector lever in Park with engine idling. Remove dipstick and clean with lint-free cloth. Check fluid level. Fluid level should be between upper and lower marks on dipstick. Add fluid if necessary. DO NOT overfill.

**Front Differential -** Use dipstick marked DIFF OIL on top of front differential to check fluid level. Level should be between "L" and "F" marks. Add fluid if necessary.

### RECOMMENDED FLUID

**Transaxle -** On Justy, use Subaru ECVT fluid or Dexron-II ATF. On all other models, use Dexron-II ATF.

**4WD Differential -** On Justy, use API GL-4 or GL-5. On all other models, use API GL-5.

### FLUID CAPACITIES

*TRANSAXLE REFILL CAPACITIES*

| Application | [1] Qts. (L) |
|---|---|
| Justy 2WD | 3.5 (3.3) |
| Justy 4WD | 4.5 (4.2) |
| Legacy | |
| 2WD 3-Speed | 6.6 (6.2) |
| 4WD 3-Speed [2] | 6.9 (6.5) |
| 4WD 4-Speed [2] | 10.0 (9.5) |
| Loyale | |
| 2WD 3-Speed | 6.5-7.0 (6.1-6.6) |
| 2WD & 4WD 4-Speed | 10.0 (9.5) |
| 4WD 3-Speed | 6.9-7.1 (6.5-6.7) |
| XT & XT6 | |
| 2WD | 9.9 (9.3) |
| 4WD [2] | 10.0 (9.5) |

[1] - Dry fill capacities.
[2] - Includes transfer case.

*DIFFERENTIAL CAPACITIES*

| Application | Qts. (L) |
|---|---|
| Justy | 0.7 (0.7) |
| Legacy | |
| 2WD | 1.3 (1.2) |
| 4WD | 0.7 (0.7) |
| Loyale | |
| 2WD | 1.3 (1.2) |
| 4WD | 0.7 (0.7) |
| XT & XT6 | 1.5 (1.4) |

## DRAINING & REFILLING

**Transaxle - 1)** Remove drain plug to drain fluid. If cleaning oil screen, remove oil pan. Install new gaskets when reassembling. Tighten all bolts to specification. See TORQUE SPECIFICATIONS table at end of article.

**2)** Fill transmission with fluid. Start and warm engine to normal operating temperature. Check fluid level with engine idling. Add fluid as necessary. DO NOT overfill.

**Differential -** Differential has separate drain plug. Remove differential drain plug to drain fluid.

## ADJUSTMENTS

### BAND

**Legacy, XT & XT6 -** Band adjustment screw is located on left side of transmission housing. Hold band adjustment screw. Loosen lock nut. Tighten adjustment screw to 80 INCH lbs (9 N.m), then back off exactly 3 turns. Hold adjustment screw. Tighten lock nut to 18-21 ft. lbs. (25-28 N.m).

**Loyale -** Band adjustment screw is located on left side of transmission housing. Hold band adjustment screw. Loosen lock nut. Tighten adjustment screw to 80 INCH lbs. (9 N.m), then back off exactly 2 turns. Hold adjustment screw. Tighten lock nut to 18-21 ft. lbs. (25-28 N.m).

### ACCELERATOR & THROTTLE POSITION SWITCHES (JUSTY)

**1)** Disconnect harness connector from accelerator and throttle switch. Connect ohmmeter to accelerator switch terminals. With accelerator pedal in idle position, switch should be open. Slowly press accelerator pedal. Switch should close when accelerator pedal moves .12-.28" (3-7 mm) from idle position. *See Fig. 1.*

**2)** Connect ohmmeter to throttle position switch terminals. With accelerator pedal in idle position, switch should be open. Slowly press accelerator pedal. Switch should close when accelerator pedal moves .63-.94" (16-24 mm). *See Fig. 1.* Perform necessary adjustments and recheck proper operation.

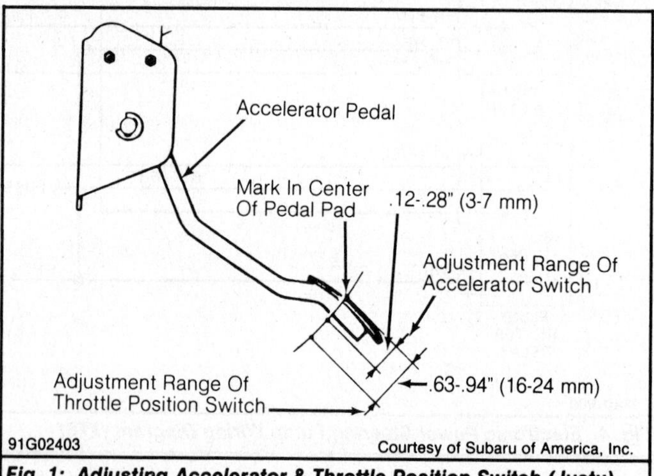


***Fig. 1: Adjusting Accelerator & Throttle Position Switch (Justy)***

### KICKDOWN SWITCH & DOWNSHIFT SOLENOID

**Justy - 1)** Ensure shift control lever on transmission side turns fully when throttle valve is fully opened. Ensure throttle valve opens or closes fully. To adjust cable, fully open throttle valve and lightly pull transmission control cable to measure free play.

**2)** Transmission control cable free play should be .02-.06" (.5-1.5 mm). If free play is not as specified, adjust cable. To adjust, loosen lock nut on cable. One rotation of lock nut changes free play by .04" (1.0 mm). Tighten lock nut and recheck adjustment.

**Legacy & Loyale - 1)** With ignition on, press accelerator pedal to stop. A click should be heard just as accelerator bottoms. If adjustment is necessary, loosen adjustment nut and adjust switch position for proper operation. Tighten nut.

# 1991 STEERING
# Electronic Power Steering (Cont.)

## FAIL LAMP DOES NOT COME ON

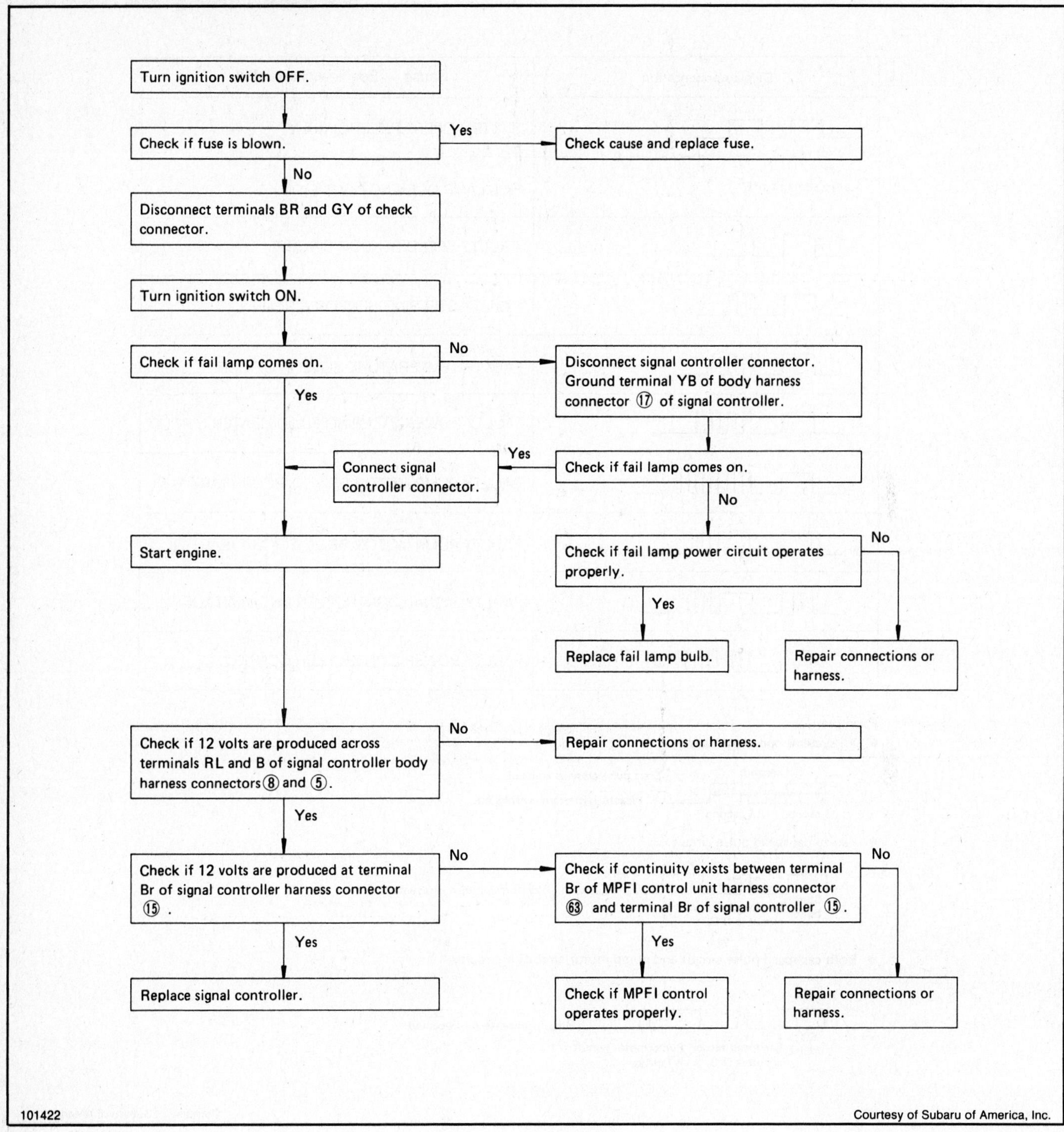

## DISPLAY PRESENTATION

| Display presentation | Cause - See flow chart listed |
|---|---|
| | SYSTEM OPERATES PROPERLY |
| Lamp remains off. | FAIL LAMP DOES NOT COME ON |
| | FAULTY SPEED SENSOR CIRCUIT |
| | FAULTY STEERING SENSOR CIRCUIT |
| | FAULTY TEMPERATURE SENSOR CIRCUIT |
| | FAULTY POWER STEERING FLUID HEATER CIRCUIT |
| | FAULTY PUMP MOTOR DRIVE CIRCUIT (PART 1) |
| | FAULTY PUMP MOTOR DRIVE CIRCUIT (PART 2) |
| | FAULTY SIGNAL CONTROLLER LINE VOLTAGE |
| | FAULTY POWER CONTROLLER CONTROL |

Example:

- All systems operate properly.

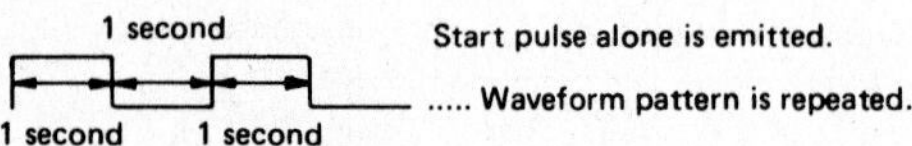

1 second
Start pulse alone is emitted.
..... Waveform pattern is repeated.
1 second
1 second

- Faulty car-speed pulse circuit.

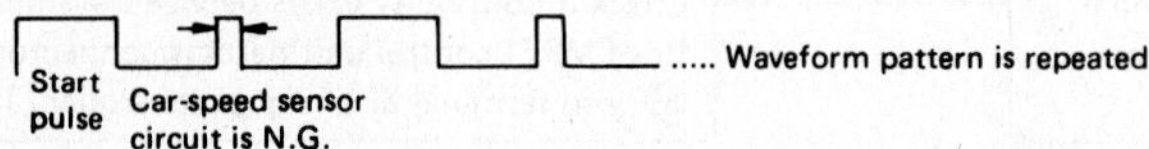

..... Waveform pattern is repeated.
Start pulse
Car-speed sensor circuit is N.G.

- Both car-speed pulse circuit and pump motor circuits are faulty.

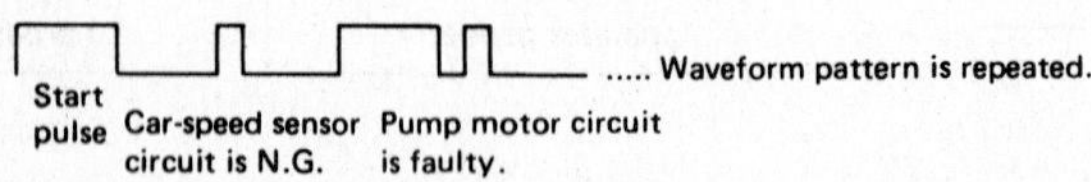

..... Waveform pattern is repeated.
Start pulse
Car-speed sensor circuit is N.G.
Pump motor circuit is faulty.

101416

Courtesy of Subaru of America, Inc.

# 1991 TRANSMISSION SERVICING
## Automatic Transmission (Cont.)

**2)** If kickdown failure occurs infrequently, solenoid may be malfunctioning because of contamination. Remove and clean inside of solenoid while moving push rod. After cleaning, carefully check solenoid operation. Install with new "O" ring.

## NEUTRAL SAFETY SWITCH

**1)** Loosen neutral safety switch mounting bolts. Move gear selector lever to Neutral.

**2)** On Justy, match locator-to-bracket hole and movable plate pin-to-arm hole. On all other models, insert Stopper Pin (499267300) as vertically as possible into holes in neutral safety switch lever and switch body. *See Fig. 2.* On all models, tighten mounting bolts and recheck adjustment.

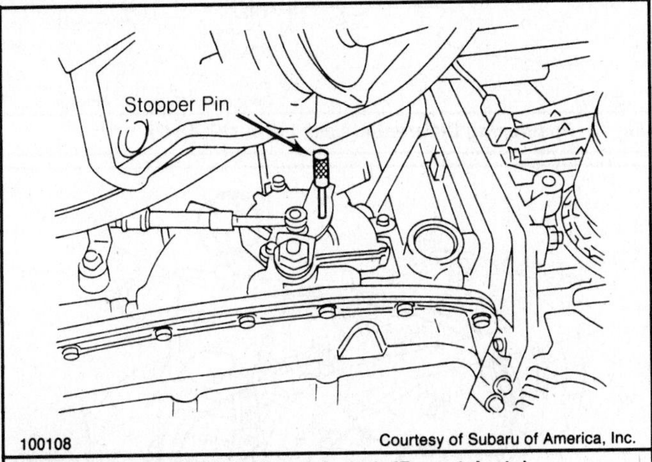


***Fig. 2: Adjusting Neutral Safety Switch (Except Justy)***

## SHIFT LINKAGE

**Legacy & Loyale – 1)** Move selector lever through all gear positions. Lever should go into each position with a corresponding click from transaxle when engaged. At each position, ensure selector needle indicates proper gear position.

**2)** If linkage is out of adjustment, move selector lever to Neutral. Loosen linkage adjuster nut at transaxle lever. With transaxle lever in Neutral position, lever should align between 2 raised bosses on case. *See Fig. 3.*

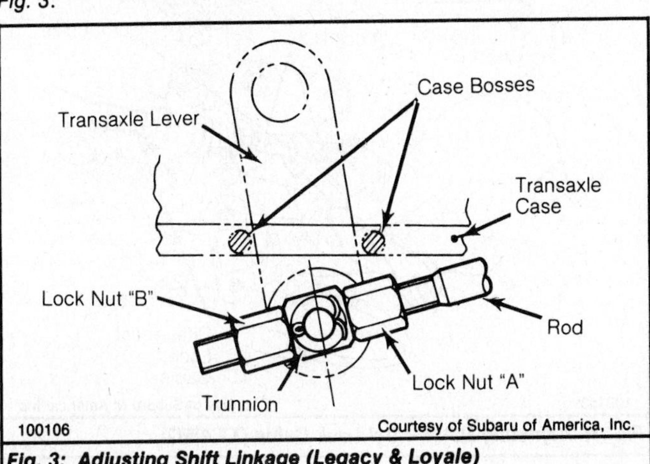


***Fig. 3: Adjusting Shift Linkage (Legacy & Loyale)***

**3)** Turn lock nut "A" until it contacts trunnion. Tighten lock nut "B" to 89-159 INCH lbs. (10-18 N.m). If indicator needle is not aligned with guide plate marking, remove console box. Loosen mounting screws and adjust as required.

**Justy, XT & XT6 – 1)** Adjust shift cable at lower end of selector lever. Set selector lever in Neutral. Loosen lock nuts on both sides of inner cable. *See Fig. 4.*

**2)** Lightly push selector lever away from lock nut "B". Tighten lock nut "A" until it contacts selector lever trunnion. Tighten lock nut "B" to 9-17 ft. lbs. (13-23 N.m).

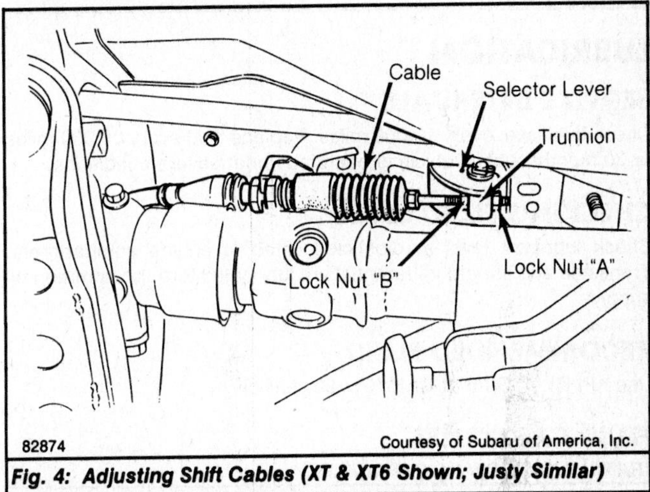


***Fig. 4: Adjusting Shift Cables (XT & XT6 Shown; Justy Similar)***

## TORQUE SPECIFICATIONS

***TORQUE SPECIFICATIONS***

| Application | Ft. Lbs. (N.m) |
|---|---|
| Band Adjustment Lock Nut | 18-21 (25-28) |
| Drain Plug | 18 (25) |
| | **INCH Lbs. (N.m)** |
| Oil Pan Bolt | 30-39 (3.4-4.4) |
| Oil Screen Retaining Bolt | |
| Justy & Legacy | 71-80 (8-9) |
| Loyale | 53-71 (6-8) |
| XT & XT6 | 30-39 (3.4-4.4) |
| Shift Linkage Adjusting Nut "B" | |
| Legacy & Loyale | 89-159 (10-18) |
| Justy, XT & XT6 | 80-151 (9-17) |

# 1991 TRANSMISSION SERVICING
## Manual Transmission

### Justy, Legacy, Loyale, XT, XT6

## IDENTIFICATION

*SUBARU MANUAL TRANSMISSION APPLICATIONS*

| Model | Transaxle |
|---|---|
| Justy | 2WD & 4WD 5-Speed |
| Legacy | 2WD & 4WD 5-Speed |
| Loyale | 2WD & 4WD 5-Speed |
| XT | 2WD & Selective 4WD 5-Speed |
| XT6 | Full Time 4WD 5-Speed |

## LUBRICATION

### SERVICE INTERVALS

Check fluid level every 15,000 miles. Replace fluid every 30,000 miles or 30 months when vehicle is operated under severe conditions.

### CHECKING FLUID LEVEL

Check lubricant level at dipstick located in engine compartment. Transaxle and integral differential are lubricated through common oil supply.

### RECOMMENDED FLUID

Use API GL-4, GL-5 or SAE 75W-90 gear oil..

### FLUID CAPACITIES

*TRANSMISSION REFILL CAPACITIES*

| Application | [1] Qts. (L) |
|---|---|
| Justy | |
| 2WD | 2.4 (2.3) |
| 4WD | 3.5 (3.3) |
| Legacy | |
| 2WD | 3.5 (3.3) |
| 4WD | 3.7 (3.5) |
| Loyale | |
| 2WD | 2.7 (2.6) |
| 4WD | 3.5 (3.3) |
| XT | |
| 2WD | 2.8 (2.6) |
| Selective 4WD | 3.5 (3.3) |
| XT6 | 3.7 (3.5) |

[1] - Dry fill capacities.

## ADJUSTMENTS

### VACUUM-CONTROLLED DIFFERENTIAL LOCK CABLE

**XT 4WD - 1)** Loosen differential lock lever cable adjustment lock nuts. Remove clevis pin from differential lock lever. Move differential lock lever to LOCK position. *See Fig. 1.*

**2)** Disconnect outer vacuum hose from vacuum actuator. Connect vacuum pump to actuator. *See Fig. 2.* Apply 7.8-9.8 in. Hg to actuator to pull cable forward. Vacuum must keep actuator in applied position when adjusting cable.

**3)** Rotate turnbuckle to align differential lock lever bore with hole at end of cable. *See Fig. 3.* Install clevis pin and snap ring. Back off turnbuckle 180 degrees. Tighten lock nuts to 44 INCH lbs. (5 N.m).

**4)** Check operation of transfer shifter rod when 7.8-9.8 in. Hg is alternately applied to each side of vacuum actuator. Shifter rod should move smoothly from LOCK to UNLOCK position, and vice versa.

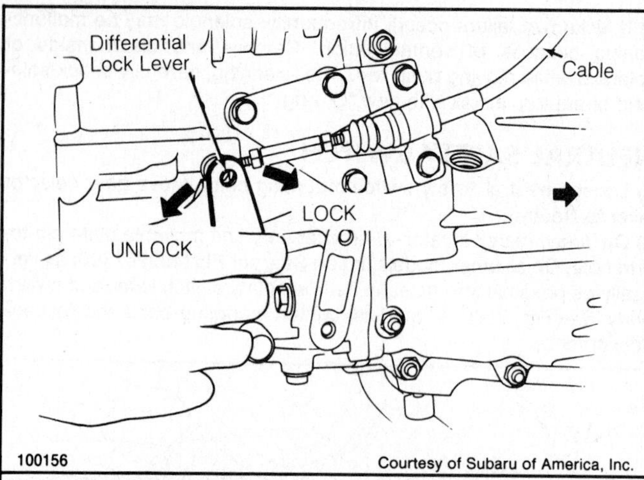


**Fig. 1: Positioning Differential Lock Lever (XT 4WD)**

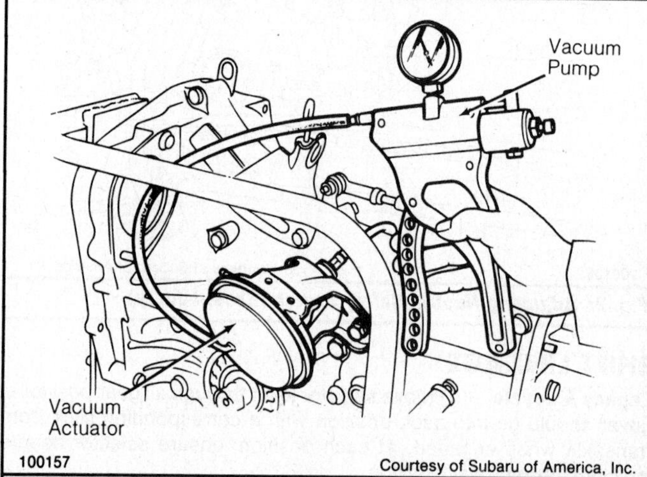


**Fig. 2: Applying Vacuum to Actuator (XT 4WD)**

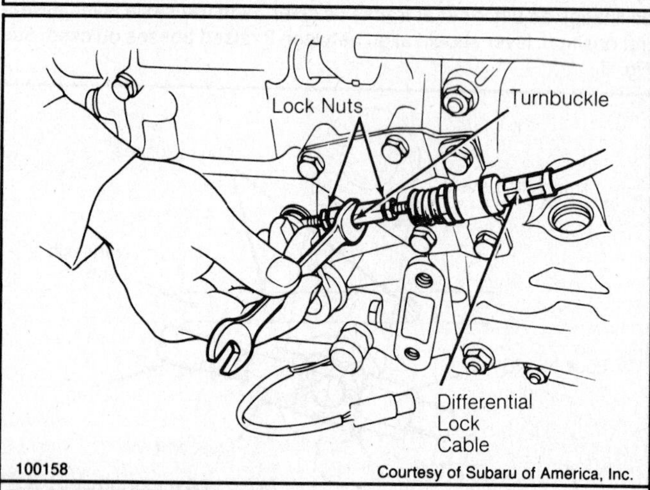


**Fig. 3: Adjusting Differential Lock Cable (XT 4WD)**

# 1991 TRANSMISSION SERVICING
# Transmission Removal & Installation

### Justy, Legacy, Loyale, XT, XT6

## MANUAL

***NOTE:** For manual transmission/transaxle replacement procedures, see appropriate CLUTCHES article.*

## AUTOMATIC

### JUSTY

***NOTE:** To prevent damage to oil pump shaft, engine and transaxle must be removed as a unit. Tag all wiring and hoses for reassembly reference.*

**Removal — 1)** Remove rear seat. Remove fuel pump connector cover. Unplug connector. Start and run engine until it stalls. After engine stalls, operate starter for 5 seconds to complete fuel pressure release.
**2)** Open hood. Adjust support so hood opens fully. Remove battery. Drain coolant. Disconnect accelerator and transaxle control cables. On models with fuel injection, remove intake air duct, blow-by hose, and air filter housing. On models with carburetor, remove air filter. Cover carburetor to prevent entry of foreign material.
**3)** On all models, remove grille and radiator. Disconnect hood release cable. Remove upper radiator support. Disconnect horn. Disconnect hoses from carburetor or collector chamber, heater hoses, and vacuum hose to brake booster. Disconnect accelerator cable from carburetor or throttle body. Disconnect cable between coil and distributor.
**4)** Disconnect speedometer cable at transaxle. Disconnect vacuum hoses at 4WD changeover cylinder. Disconnect selector cable from transaxle. Disconnect torque strut from bracket. Remove hanger strap from rear of transaxle.
**5)** Disconnect starter cable. Unplug all engine wiring harness connectors. Disconnect engine and transaxle ground straps. Unplug brush holder connector.
**6)** Raise and support vehicle. Remove under covers. Remove stabilizer bar. Remove front and rear exhaust pipes. Disconnect propeller shaft at transaxle. Plug transaxle opening. Remove transverse link. Drive out roll pins, then separate front axle shafts.
**7)** Remove engine and transaxle mounting brackets. Attach lifting sling. Raise engine and transaxle slightly. Remove center support and crossmember. Ensure all wiring and other attachments have been removed from engine and transaxle. Remove engine and transaxle from vehicle.
**8)** Remove starter. Remove brush holder. Disconnect shift control cable from bracket. Separate transaxle from engine.
**Installation –** To install transaxle, reverse removal procedure. Always use new roll pins when installing axle shafts. Tighten bolts to specification. See TORQUE SPECIFICATIONS table at end of article.

### LEGACY & LOYALE

**Removal – 1)** Disconnect negative battery cable. Remove spare tire and mount from engine compartment (if equipped). Disconnect oxygen sensor connector. Raise and support vehicle. Disconnect speedometer cable, electrical connectors, and vacuum hoses from transaxle.
**2)** Lower vehicle. Remove torque strut and replace with Engine Support (926610000). Remove starter harness and starter. Remove timing hole plug and 4 drive plate-to-converter bolts.
**3)** On non-turbo models, raise and support vehicle. Disconnect front exhaust pipe from engine, leaving one nut in place to temporarily hold exhaust pipe. Disconnect front-to-rear exhaust pipe connection. Remove front exhaust pipe.
**4)** On turbo models, remove upper turbo heat shield. Raise and support vehicle. Loosen 2 bolts at front exhaust pipe. Lower vehicle. Remove lower turbo heat shield. Disconnect center exhaust pipe from turbocharger. Raise and support vehicle. Remove center exhaust pipe.
**5)** On all models, drain transaxle fluid. On 4WD models, remove rear drive shaft. On all models, disconnect shift linkage from transaxle. Disconnect stabilizer bar and parking brake cables from lower control arms.
**6)** Remove bolts attaching lower control arms to crossmember. Drop lower control arms. Remove roll pins and separate both axles from transaxle. Discard roll pins.
**7)** Remove engine-to-transaxle mounting bolts. Disconnect and plug ATF cooler hoses. Place jack under transaxle. Remove rear transaxle mounting nuts and rear crossmember. Pull transaxle away from engine and lower from vehicle.
**Installation –** To install transaxle, reverse removal procedure. Always use new roll pins when installing axle shafts. Tighten bolts to specification. See TORQUE SPECIFICATIONS table at end of article.

### XT & XT6

**Removal – 1)** Disconnect negative battery cable. Disconnect oxygen sensor connector. Raise and support vehicle. Disconnect speedometer cable and all electrical connectors at transaxle.
**2)** Label and disconnect all vacuum hoses from transaxle. Remove starter harness and starter. Lower vehicle. Remove air intake duct. Remove timing hole plug. Remove 4 drive plate-to-converter bolts.
**3)** Remove torque strut. Remove right side engine-to-transaxle mounting bolt. Raise and support vehicle. Remove torque strut. Attach Engine Support Bracket (927160000) to body side torque strut bracket. Install Engine Support (927150000)
**4)** Disconnect front exhaust pipe from engine, leaving one nut in place to temporarily hold exhaust pipe. Disconnect front-to-rear exhaust pipe connection. Remove front exhaust pipe.
**5)** On all models, drain transaxle fluid. On 4WD models, remove rear drive shaft. On all models, disconnect shift linkage from transaxle. Disconnect stabilizer bar and parking brake cables from lower control arms.
**6)** Remove lower control arms-to-crossmember bolts. Drop lower control arms. Remove roll pins and separate both axles from transaxle. Discard roll pins.
**7)** Remove engine-to-transaxle mounting bolts. Disconnect and plug ATF cooler hoses. Place jack under transaxle. Remove rear transaxle mounting nuts and rear crossmember. Pull transaxle away from engine and lower from vehicle.
**Installation –** To install transaxle, reverse removal procedure. Always use new roll pins when installing axle shafts. Tighten bolts to specification. See TORQUE SPECIFICATIONS table at end of article.

## TORQUE SPECIFICATIONS

***TORQUE SPECIFICATIONS***

| Application | Ft. Lbs. (N.m) |
|---|---|
| Crossmember Bolts | 27-49 (37-67) |
| Engine Mount Bracket Bolts | 27-49 (37-67) |
| Engine Mount-To-Body Bolts | 27-49 (37-66) |
| Lower Control Arm-To-Crossmember Bolts | |
| Legacy & Loyale | 61-83 (83-113) |
| XT & XT6 | 43-51 (59-69) |
| Torque Converter-To-Drive Plate Bolts | 17-20 (23-27) |
| Torque Strut Bolt | 31-46 (42-62) |
| Transaxle-To-Engine Bolts | 34-40 (46-54) |
| Transaxle Mount-To-Body Bolts | 27-49 (37-66) |
| Transverse Link-To-Crossmember | 54-69 (73-94) |

# SUZUKI

# 1991 SUZUKI CONTENTS

## GENERAL INFORMATION [1]



[1] – For all GENERAL INFORMATION, see front of Volume 1.

## ENGINE PERFORMANCE



## ENGINE PERFORMANCE (Cont.)

# 1991 SUZUKI CONTENTS (Cont.)



## ENGINE PERFORMANCE (Cont.)

### PIN VOLTAGE CHARTS



### SENSOR OPERATING RANGE CHARTS



### WIRING DIAGRAMS



### VACUUM DIAGRAMS



### REMOVAL, OVERHAUL & INSTALLATION



## ELECTRICAL

### ALTERNATORS & REGULATORS



### STARTERS



## WIRING DIAGRAMS

### CHASSIS WIRING DIAGRAMS



## SAFETY EQUIPMENT

### INSTRUMENT PANELS



### REAR WINDOW DEFOGGER



### STEERING COLUMN SWITCHES



### WIPER/WASHER SYSTEMS



## ENGINES

### 1.3L & 1.6L 4-CYLINDER



## ENGINE COOLING

### SPECIFICATIONS & ELECTRIC COOLING FANS

# 1991 SUZUKI CONTENTS (Cont.)

## CLUTCHES



## DRIVE AXLES



## BRAKES



## WHEEL ALIGNMENT



## SUSPENSION

# 1991 SUZUKI CONTENTS (Cont.)

## STEERING

### STEERING COLUMNS



### MANUAL RACK & PINION



### MANUAL RECIRCULATING BALL



### POWER RECIRCULATING BALL



## TRANSMISSION SERVICING

### AUTOMATIC TRANSMISSION



### MANUAL TRANSMISSION



### TRANSMISSION REMOVAL & INSTALLATION

# 1991 ENGINE PERFORMANCE
## Suzuki Introduction

### 1991 MODEL COVERAGE

| MODEL | BODY CODE | ENGINE | ENGINE ID [1] | FUEL SYSTEM | IGNITION SYSTEM |
|---|---|---|---|---|---|
| Samurai | C | 1.3L (SOHC) | 3 | TBI | Magnetic [2] |
| Sidekick | C | 1.6L (SOHC) | 0 | TBI | Magnetic [2] |
| Swift | S | 1.3L (SOHC) | 3 | TBI | Magnetic |
| Swift GT | S | 1.3L (DOHC) | 3 | PFI | Magnetic [2] |

[1] - Engine ID is sixth digit of Vehicle Identification Number, located on left corner of instrument panel.
[2] - Computer controlled.

### VIN DEFINITION

**JS3TA 01C7M4100001**
① ② ③ ④ ⑤ ⑥ ⑦ ⑧ ⑨ ⑩ ⑪ ⑫ ⑬ ⑭ ⑮ ⑯ ⑰

① Indicates Nation of Origin.
② Indicates Manufacturer.
③ Indicates Vehicle Type.
④ Indicates Model.
⑤ Indicates Series (Samurai & Swift).
⑤ Indicates Gross Vehicle Weight (Sidekick).
⑥ **Indicates Engine Type.**
⑦ Indicates Design Sequence.
⑧ Indicates Body Type.
⑨ Indicates Check Digit.
⑩ **Indicates Model Year.**
⑪ Indicates Assembly Plant.
⑫ ⑬ ⑭ ⑮ ⑯ ⑰ Indicates Plant Sequential Number.

91I17267

### ENGINE CODE LOCATION

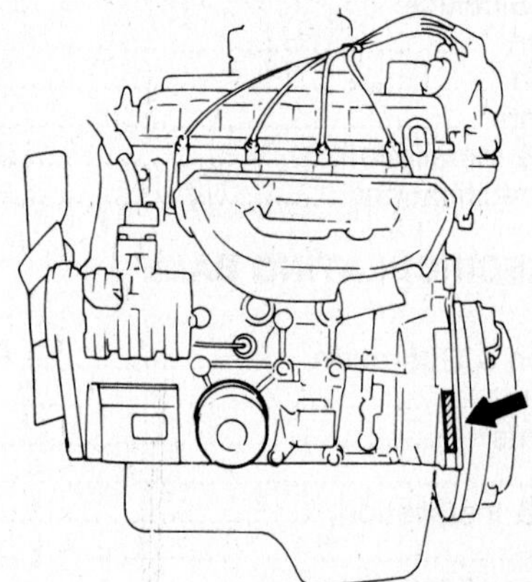

SAMURAI & SWIFT 1.3L & SIDEKICK 1.6L (SOHC)

119661 Courtesy of Suzuki of American Corp.

***MODEL YEAR VIN CODE APPLICATION***

| VIN Code | Model Year |
|---|---|
| K | 1989 |
| L | 1990 |
| M | 1991 |

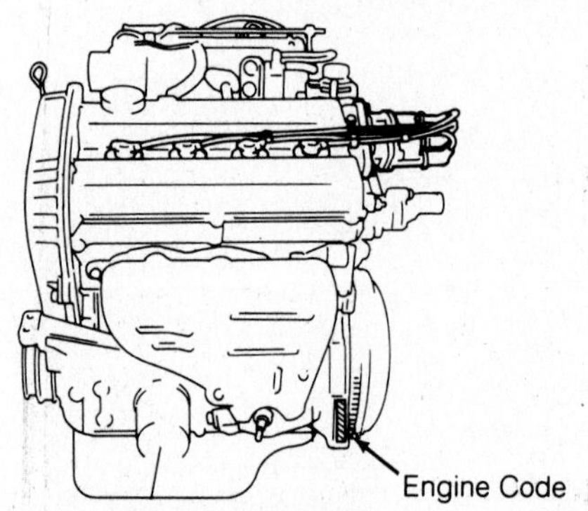


SWIFT 1.3L (DOHC)

119662 Courtesy of Suzuki of American Corp.

# 1991 ENGINE PERFORMANCE
# Emission Applications

### *1991 SUZUKI EMISSION SYSTEMS*

| Model, Engine & Fuel System | Emission Control Systems & Devices | Remarks |
|---|---|---|
| Samurai 1.3L 4-CYL (TBI) | **PCV, EVAP, TWC, EGR, SPK, $O_2$, CEC, CE,** EGR-MOD, EGR-VSV, EGR-TS [1], EVAP-BVSV, EVAP-FVS, EVAP-VC | [1] - California only. |
| Sidekick 1.6L 4-CYL (TBI) | **PCV, EVAP, TWC, EGR, SPK, $O_2$, CEC, CE,** EGR-MOD, EGR-VSV, EGR-TS [1], EVAP-FVS, EVAP-VC, EVAP-CPVSV | |
| Swift 1.3L DOHC 4-CYL (PFI) | **PCV, EVAP, TWC, EGR [1], SPK, $O_2$, CEC, CE,** EGR-VSV [1], EGR-MOD [1], EGR-TS [1], EVAP-VC, EVAP-CPVSV, | |
| Swift 1.3L SOHC 4-CYL (TBI) | **PCV, EVAP, TWC, EGR [1], $O_2$, CEC, CE,** EGR-VSV [1], EGR-MOD [1], EVAP-VC, EVAP-CPCV, EVAP-BVSV, | |

**NOTE:** Major emission control systems are listed in bold type; components are listed in light type.

**CE** - CHECK ENGINE Light
**CEC** - Computerized Engine Controls
**DOHC** - Dual Overhead Cam
**EGR** - Exhaust Gas Recirculation
**EGR-MOD** - EGR Modulator (Backpressure Transducer)
**EGR-TS** - EGR Temperature Sensor
**EGR-VSV** - EGR Vacuum Switching Valve
**EVAP** - Fuel Evaporative System
**EVAP-BVSV** - EVAP Bimetallic Vacuum Switching Valve
**EVAP-CPCV** - EVAP Canister Purge Control Valve
**EVAP-CPVSV** - EVAP Canister Purge Vacuum Switching Valve
**EVAP-FVS** - EVAP Fuel Vapor Separator
**EVAP-VC** - EVAP Vapor Canister
**$O_2$** - Oxygen Sensor
**PCV** - Positive Crankcase Ventilation
**PFI** - Port Fuel Injection
**SOHC** - Single Overhead Cam
**SPK** - Spark Control System
**TBI** - Throttle Body Injection
**TWC** - Three-Way Catalyst

# 1991 ENGINE PERFORMANCE
# Service & Adjustment Specifications

## Samurai, Sidekick, Swift

## INTRODUCTION

Use this article to quickly find specifications related to servicing and on-vehicle adjustments. This is a quick-reference article for when you are familiar with an adjustment procedure and only need a specification.

## CAPACITIES

*BATTERY SPECIFICATIONS*

| Application (Group) | Amp Hr. Rating |
|---|---|
| All Models | 38 |

*FLUID CAPACITIES*

| Application | Quantity |
|---|---|
| **Auto. Transaxle (Dexron-II)** | |
| Swift (DOHC & SOHC) | |
| Drain & Refill | 3.7 Qts. (3.5L) |
| Dry Refill | 5.2 Qts. (4.9L) |
| **Auto. Transmission (Dexron-II)** | |
| Sidekick | |
| Drain & Refill | 3.0 Qts. (2.8L) |
| Dry Refill | 5.4 Qts. (5.1L) |
| **Crankcase (Includes Filter)** | |
| Samurai | 3.7 Qts. (3.5L) |
| Sidekick | 4.7 Qts. (4.5L) |
| Swift (DOHC & SOHC) | 3.5 Qts. (3.3L) |
| **Cooling System (Includes Heater)** | |
| Samurai | 5.1 Qts. (4.8L) |
| Sidekick | |
| Auto. Transmission | 5.5 Qts. (5.2L) |
| Man. Transmission | 5.6 Qts. (5.3L) |
| Swift (DOHC & SOHC) | 4.9 Qts. (4.7L) |
| **Differential (SAE 75W-90 API GL-5 Gear Oil)** | |
| Samurai | |
| Front | 2.1 Qts. (2.0L) |
| Rear | 1.6 Qts. (1.5L) |
| Sidekick | |
| Front | 1.1 Qts. (1.0L) |
| Rear | 2.3 Qts. (2.2L) |
| **Man. Transaxle (SAE 75W-90 API GL-5 Gear Oil)** | |
| Swift (DOHC & SOHC) | 2.5 Qts. (2.4L) |
| **Man. Transmission (SAE 75W-90 API GL-5 Gear Oil)** | |
| Samurai | 1.4 Qts. (1.3L) |
| Sidekick | 1.6 Qts. (1.5L) |
| **Transfer Case (SAE 75W-90 API GL-4 Gear Oil)** | |
| Samurai | [1] |
| Sidekick | 1.8 Qts. (1.7LL) |

[1] – Capacity is 1.7 pts. (.8L).

## QUICK-SERVICE

### SERVICE INTERVALS & SPECIFICATIONS

*REPLACEMENT INTERVALS*

| Component | Miles |
|---|---|
| **Samurai & Sidekick** | |
| Air Filter | 30,000 |
| Auto. Transmission Fluid | |
| Sidekick | |
| Normal Service | 100,000 |
| Severe Service [1] | 15,000 |
| Brake Fluid | 60,000 |
| Catalytic Converter [2] | 100,000 |
| Charcoal Canister | 100,000 |
| Coolant | 30,000 |
| Differential Oil | [3] |
| Distributor Cap & Rotor [2] | 60,000 |
| EGR System [2] | 50,000 |
| Fan Belt | 60,000 |
| Fuel Filter | 30,000 |
| Man. Transmission Oil | [3] |
| Oil & Filter | |
| Normal Service | 7500 |
| Severe Service [1] | 3000 |

*REPLACEMENT INTERVALS (Cont.)*

| Component | Miles |
|---|---|
| **Samurai & Sidekick (Cont.)** | |
| Oxygen Sensor | 80,000 |
| PCV Valve | 50,000 |
| Spark Plugs | 30,000 |
| Spark Plug Wires | 60,000 |
| Timing Belt [2] | 60,000 |
| Transfer Case Oil | [3] |
| **Swift (DOHC & SOHC)** | |
| Air Filter | 30,000 |
| Auto. Transaxle Fluid | |
| Normal Service | 100,000 |
| Severe Service [1] | 12,000 |
| Brake Fluid | 60,000 |
| Coolant | 30,000 |
| Man. Transaxle Oil | |
| Normal Service | 15,000 |
| Severe Service [1] | 12,000 |
| Oil & Filter | |
| DOHC | |
| Normal Service | 5000 |
| Severe Service [1] | 3000 |
| SOHC | |
| Normal Service | 7500 |
| Severe Service [1] | 3000 |
| Spark Plugs | 30,000 |
| Spark Plug Wires | 60,000 |

[1] – Severe service is driving on rough dusty roads, repeated short trips, or towing a trailer.
[2] – Inspect and replace if required.
[3] – Change at 7500 miles and then every 30,000 miles under normal service. Under severe service, change at 7500 miles and then every 15,000 miles.

*ADJUSTMENT INTERVALS*

| Application | Miles |
|---|---|
| **Valve Clearance** | |
| Samurai & Sidekick | 15,000 |
| Swift | |
| DOHC | [1] |
| SOHC | 15,000 |

[1] – Hydraulic lash adjusters are used and no adjustment is required.

*BELT ADJUSTMENT (NEW BELT)*

| Application | [1] Deflection – In. (mm) |
|---|---|
| **Samurai** | |
| Water Pump Belt | .24-.35 (6.1-8.9) |
| **Sidekick** | |
| A/C Belt | .20-.25 (5.1-6.4) |
| Power Steering Belt | .24-.35 (6.1-8.9) |
| Water Pump Belt | .24-.32 (6.1-8.1) |
| **Swift (DOHC & SOHC)** | |
| A/C Belt | .20-.25 (5.1-6.4) |
| Water Pump Belt | .24-.32 (6.1-8.1) |

[1] – Deflection is checked with 22 lbs. (10 kg) pressure applied midway on longest belt run.

## MECHANICAL CHECKS

### ENGINE COMPRESSION

*COMPRESSION SPECIFICATIONS*

| Application | Specification |
|---|---|
| **Compression Ratio** | |
| Samurai | 9.5:1 |
| Sidekick | 8.9:1 |
| Swift | |
| DOHC | 10.0:1 |
| SOHC | 9.5:1 |

# 1991 ENGINE PERFORMANCE
# Service & Adjustment Specifications (Cont.)

*COMPRESSION SPECIFICATIONS (Cont.)*

| Application | Specification |
|---|---|
| **Compression Pressure** | |
| Samurai & Sidekick | |
| Standard | 199 psi (14.0 kg/cm²) |
| Limit | [1] 170 psi (11.9 kg/cm²) |
| Swift | |
| DOHC | |
| Standard | 206 psi (14.5 kg/cm²) |
| Limit | [1] 156 psi (10.9 kg/cm²) |
| SOHC | |
| Standard | 199 psi (14.0 kg/cm²) |
| Limit | [1] 156 psi (10.9 kg/cm²) |

[1] – Maximum variation between cylinders is 14.2 psi (.9 kg/cm²).

## VALVE CLEARANCE

*VALVE CLEARANCE SPECIFICATIONS*

| Application | In. (mm) |
|---|---|
| **Samurai, Sidekick & Swift SOHC** | |
| Engine Cold | |
| Intake | .005-.007 (.13-.18) |
| Exhaust | .006-.008 (.15-.20) |
| Engine Hot | |
| Intake | .009-.011 (.23-.28) |
| Exhaust | .010-.012 (.25-.30) |
| **Swift DOHC** | [1] |

[1] – Hydraulic lash adjusters are used and no adjustment is required.

## VALVE ARRANGEMENT

*NOTE: Right and left sides refer to engine, as viewed from flywheel.*

**Right Side** – All intake.
**Left Side** – All exhaust.

## IGNITION SYSTEM

### IGNITION COIL

*IGNITION COIL RESISTANCE – Ohms @ 68°F (20°C)*

| Application | Primary | Secondary |
|---|---|---|
| Samurai | .90-1.10 | 10,200-13,800 |
| Sidekick | 1.35-1.65 | 11,000-14,500 |
| Swift | | |
| DOHC | .72-.88 | 10,200-14,000 |
| SOHC | 1.12-1.38 | 11,400-15,600 |

### DISTRIBUTOR SENSORS

*PICK-UP COIL AIR GAP*

| Application | In. (mm) |
|---|---|
| Samurai | [1] |
| Sidekick | [1] |
| Swift | |
| DOHC [2] | .008-.012 (.20-.30) |
| SOHC | .008-.016 (.20-.41) |

[1] – Not adjustable.
[2] – Also referred to as crank angle sensor air gap.

*PICK-UP COIL RESISTANCE – Ohms @ 68°F (20°C)*

| Application | Ohms |
|---|---|
| Samurai | [1] |
| Sidekick | [1] |
| Swift | |
| DOHC [2] | 588-882 |
| SOHC | 130-190 |

[1] – Information not available from manufacturer.
[2] – Also referred to as crank angle sensor.

## HIGH TENSION WIRE RESISTANCE

*HIGH TENSION WIRE RESISTANCE*

| Application | Ohms |
|---|---|
| Samurai & Swift DOHC & SOHC | 3000-6700 per foot (10,000-22,000 per meter) |
| Sidekick | [1] |

[1] - Information not available from manufacturer.

## SPARK PLUGS

*SPARK PLUG TYPE*

| Application | Nippondenso | NGK |
|---|---|---|
| Samurai | W20EPR-U | BPR5ES |
| Sidekick | W16EXR-U | BPR5ES |
| Swift | | |
| DOHC | W20EPR-U | BPR6ES |
| SOHC | W20EPR-U11 | BPR6ES-11 |

*SPARK PLUG SPECIFICATIONS*

| Application | Gap In. (mm) | Torque Ft. Lbs. (N.m) |
|---|---|---|
| Samurai | .027-.031 (.69-.79) | 18-22 (24-30) |
| Sidekick | .027-.031 (.69-.79) | 15-22 (20-30) |
| Swift | | |
| DOHC | .027-.031 (.69-.79) | 18-22 (24-30) |
| SOHC | .039-.043 (.99-1.09) | 18-22 (24-30) |

## FIRING ORDER & TIMING MARKS

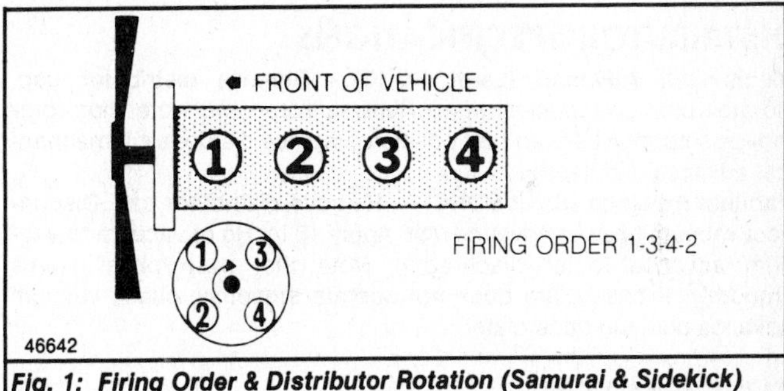

*Fig. 1: Firing Order & Distributor Rotation (Samurai & Sidekick)*

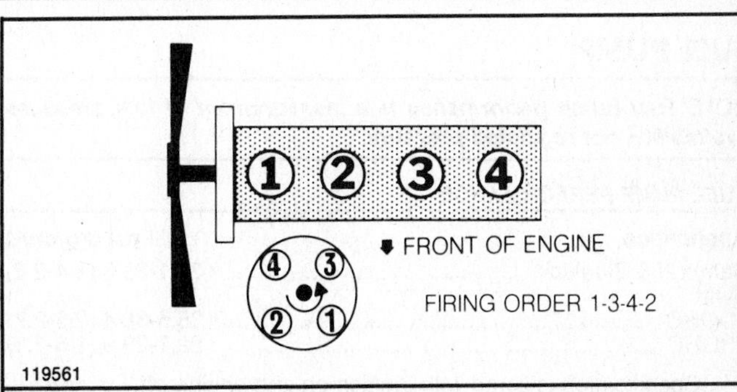

*Fig. 2: Firing Order & Distributor Rotation (Swift DOHC & SOHC)*

*IGNITION TIMING (Degrees BTDC @ RPM)*

| Application | Man. Trans. | Auto. Trans. |
|---|---|---|
| Samurai | [1] 7-9 @ 800 | N/A |
| Sidekick | 8 @ 750-850 | 8 @ 750-850 |

# 1991 ENGINE PERFORMANCE
# Service & Adjustment Specifications (Cont.)

*IGNITION COIL RESISTANCE (Cont.) - Ohms @ 68°F (20°C)*

| Application | Primary | Secondary |
|---|---|---|
| Swift | | |
| DOHC | [2] 5-7 @ 800-900 | [2] 5-7 @ 800-900 |
| SOHC | [3] 5-7 @ 600-700 | [3] 5-7 @ 700-800 |

[1] - With jumper wire installed between Blue wire and Black/Green wire of test connector, located near battery.
[2] - With jumper wire installed between Black wire and Violet/Green wire of test connector, located near ignition coil.
[3] - With vacuum hose disconnected from distributor. With hose connected, timing should be 11-13 degrees BTDC.

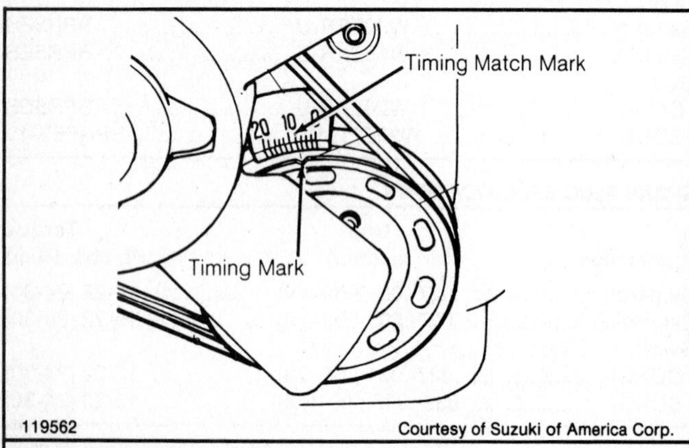

*Fig. 3: Typical Ignition Timing Mark Location*

## DISTRIBUTOR SPECIFICATIONS

**Mechanical Advance (Swift SOHC)** - Remove distributor cap. Rotate rotor counterclockwise. Release rotor and note that rotor moves smoothly back to rest position. Replace distributor if mechanical advance is defective.

**Vacuum Advance (Swift SOHC)** - Remove distributor cap. Disconnect vacuum hose at advance unit. Apply 15 in. Hg of vacuum to vacuum advance (outer diaphragm). Note that base plate moves smoothly. If base plate does not operate smoothly, check vacuum advance unit and base plate.

# FUEL SYSTEM

## FUEL PUMP

***NOTE: Fuel pump performance is a measurement of fuel pressure availability, not regulated pressure.***

*FUEL PUMP PERFORMANCE*

| Application | [1] psi (kg/cm²) |
|---|---|
| Samurai & Sidekick | [2] 34.1-39.8 (2.4-2.8) |
| Swift | |
| DOHC | [3] 35.5-38.4 (2.5-2.7) |
| SOHC | [4] 22.7-29.9 (1.6-2.1) |

[1] - Specification is listed with ignition on and engine off.
[2] - Pressure should remain at 21.3 psi (1.5 kg/cm²) for one minute after fuel pump is turned off.
[3] - Pressure should remain at 25.6 psi (1.8 kg/cm²) for one minute after fuel pump is turned off.
[4] - Pressure should remain at 12.8 psi (.9 kg/cm²) for one minute after fuel pump is turned off.

*REGULATED FUEL PRESSURE*

| Application | [1] psi (kg/cm²) |
|---|---|
| Samurai | [2] 24.2-29.9 (1.7-2.1) |
| Sidekick | [2] [3] |
| Swift | |
| DOHC | [4] 25.6-29.9 (1.8-2.1) |
| SOHC | [5] 12.8-20.0 (.9-1.4) |

*REGULATED FUEL PRESSURE (Cont.)*

[1] - Specification is listed with engine idling.
[2] - Pressure should remain at 21.3 psi (1.5 kg/cm²) for one minute after fuel pump is turned off.
[3] - Information is not available from manufacturer.
[4] - Pressure should remain at 25.6 psi (1.8 kg/cm²) for one minute after fuel pump is turned off.
[5] - Pressure should remain at 12.8 psi (.9 kg/cm²) for one minute after fuel pump is turned off.

## INJECTOR RESISTANCE

*INJECTOR RESISTANCE SPECIFICATIONS*

| Application | Ohms |
|---|---|
| Samurai & Sidekick | .8-1.8 |
| Swift | |
| DOHC | 1.5-2.2 |
| SOHC | .5-1.5 |

## IDLE SPEED

*IDLE SPEED SPECIFICATIONS [1]*

| Application | Idle RPM |
|---|---|
| Samurai | |
| With A/C Off | 750-850 |
| With A/C On | [2] 950-1050 |
| Sidekick | 750-850 |
| Swift | |
| DOHC | |
| With A/C Off | 800-900 |
| With A/C On | [2] 850-950 |
| SOHC | |
| With A/C Off | |
| Auto. Transaxle | 800-900 |
| Man. Transaxle | 700-800 |
| With A/C On | |
| Auto. Transaxle | [2] 800-900 |
| Man. Transaxle | [2] 850-950 |

[1] - Idle speed specification is with transaxle or transmission in Neutral or Park.
[2] - A/C idle speed is adjusted by rotating adjusting screw on A/C Vacuum Switching Valve (VSV).

## THROTTLE OPENER

*THROTTLE OPENER SPECIFICATIONS*

| Application | [1] RPM |
|---|---|
| Samurai | 2150-2250 |
| Sidekick | 2100-2300 |

[1] - Idle speed specification is with transaxle or transmission in Neutral or Park with vacuum hose disconnected and plugged at throttle opener.

## THROTTLE POSITION SENSOR (TPS)

***NOTE: Throttle position sensor is used on automatic transaxle models. Throttle switch is used only on Swift SOHC models with manual transaxle.***

*THROTTLE POSITION SENSOR (TPS) RESISTANCE*

| Application | Ohms |
|---|---|
| **Samurai** | |
| Between Terminals "C" & "D" | |
| With .008" (.20 mm) Clearance At Stop Screw | 0-550 |
| With .016" (.41 mm) Clearance At Stop Screw | Infinity |
| Between Terminals "A" & "D" | 3500-6500 |
| Between Terminals "B" & "D" | |
| At Idle [1] | 0-2000 |
| At Wide Open Throttle [2] | 2000-6500 |

# 1991 ENGINE PERFORMANCE
# Service & Adjustment Specifications (Cont.)

***THROTTLE POSITION SENSOR (TPS) RESISTANCE (Cont.)***

| Application | Ohms |
|---|---|
| **Sidekick** | |
| Between Terminals "C" & "D" | |
| At Idle [1] | 0-500 |
| At Wide Open Throttle | Infinity |
| Between Terminals "A" & "D" | 3500-6500 |
| Between terminals "B" & "D" | |
| At Idle [1] | 300-2000 |
| At Wide Open Throttle [2] | 2000-6500 |
| **Swift (DOHC)** | |
| Between Terminals "C" & "D" | |
| With .012" (.30 mm) Clearance At Stop Screw | 0-500 |
| With .035" (.89 mm) Clearance At Stop Screw | Infinity |
| Between Terminals "C" & "A" | 3500-6500 |
| Between Terminals "C" & "B" | |
| At Idle | 0-500 |
| At Wide Open Throttle | 3500-6500 |
| **Swift (SOHC)** [3] | |
| Between Terminals "A" & "B" | |
| With .012" (.30 mm) Clearance At Stop Screw | 0 |
| With .035" (.89 mm) Clearance At Stop Screw | Infinity |
| Between Terminals "A" & "D" | 4370-8130 |
| Between Terminals "A" & "C" | |
| At Idle | 240-1140 |
| At Wide Open Throttle | 3170-6600 |

1 - To obtain idle position, apply 19 in. Hg vacuum to throttle opener.
2 - There should be more than 2000 ohms difference between idle and wide open throttle readings.
3 - Throttle position sensor is used only on auto. transaxle, as man. transaxle uses a throttle switch.

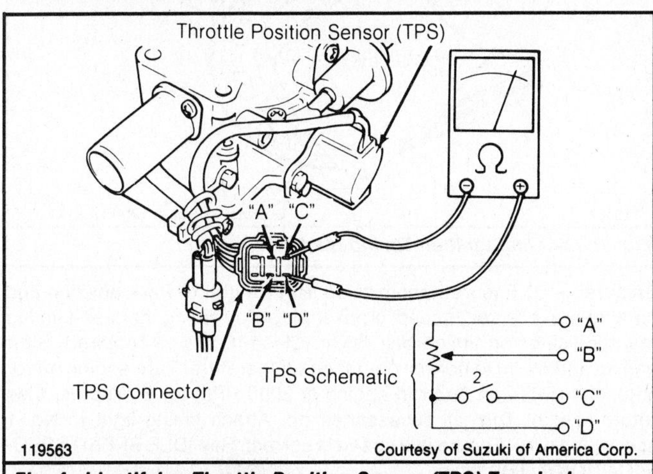


***Fig. 4: Identifying Throttle Position Sensor (TPS) Terminals (Samurai & Sidekick)***

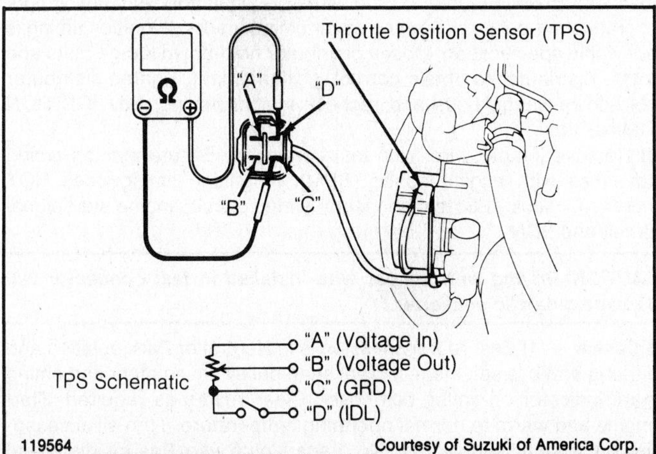


***Fig. 5: Identifying Throttle Position Sensor (TPS) Terminals (Swift DOHC)***

## THROTTLE SWITCH

***NOTE: Throttle switch is used only on Swift SOHC models with manual transaxle. Throttle position sensor is used on automatic transaxle models.***

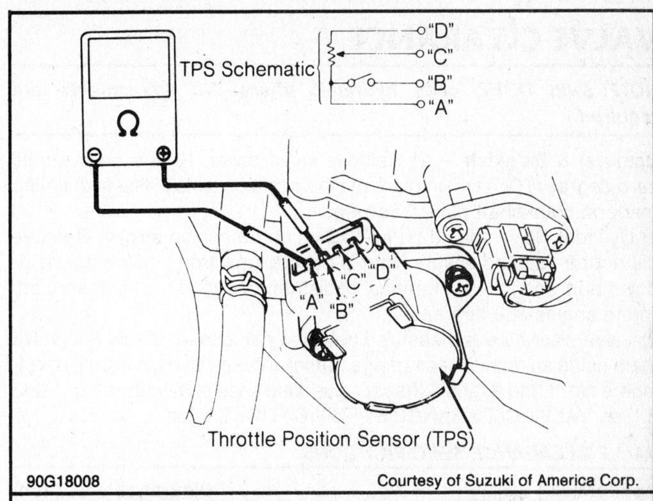


***Fig. 6: Identifying Throttle Position Sensor (TPS) Terminals (Swift SOHC Auto. Transaxle)***

***THROTTLE SWITCH CONTINUITY***

| Application | Specification |
|---|---|
| **Swift (SOHC)** | |
| Between Terminals "A" & "B" | |
| With .012" (.30 mm) Clearance At Stop Screw | Continuity |
| With .035" (.89 mm) Clearance At Stop Screw | No Continuity |
| With Throttle Wide Open | No Continuity |
| Between Terminals "B" & "C" | |
| With .012" (.30 mm) Clearance At Stop Screw | No Continuity |
| With .035" (.89 mm) Clearance At Stop Screw | No Continuity |
| With Throttle Wide Open | Continuity |
| Between Terminals "A" & "C" | |
| With .012" (.30 mm) Clearance At Stop Screw | No Continuity |
| With .035" (.89 mm) Clearance At Stop Screw | No Continuity |
| With Throttle Wide Open | No Continuity |

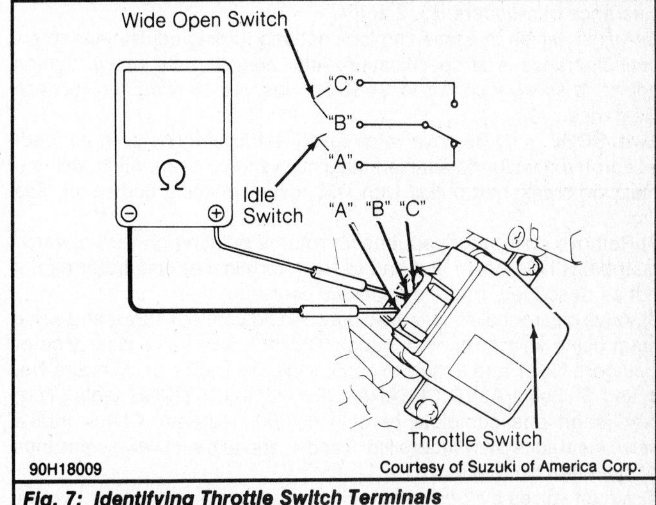


***Fig. 7: Identifying Throttle Switch Terminals (Swift SOHC Man. Transaxle)***

# 1991 ENGINE PERFORMANCE
# On-Vehicle Adjustments

## Samurai, Sidekick, Swift

## ENGINE MECHANICAL

Before performing any on-vehicle adjustments to fuel or ignition systems, ensure engine mechanical condition is okay.

## VALVE CLEARANCE

***NOTE: Swift DOHC uses hydraulic lifters. No adjustments are required.***

**Samurai & Sidekick - 1)** Remove valve cover. Rotate engine until zero degree (TDC) timing mark of timing belt cover is in line with timing mark on crankshaft pulley. *See Fig. 1.*

**2)** Cylinder No. 1 should be at TDC on compression stroke. Remove distributor cap and ensure rotor is pointed upward at distributor hold-down bolt, and to No. 1 terminal of distributor cap. If not as described, rotate engine 360 degrees.

**3)** Valve clearance is measured between adjustment screw and valve stem using shim thickness gauge. Check intake valve clearance of cylinders No. 1 and 2, and exhaust valve clearance of cylinders No. 1 and 3. See VALVE CLEARANCE SPECIFICATIONS table.

***VALVE CLEARANCE SPECIFICATIONS***

| Application | Clearance - In. (mm) |
|---|---|
| **Samurai & Sidekick** | |
| Engine Cold | |
| Intake | .005-.007 (.13-.17) |
| Exhaust | .006-.008 (.15-.20) |
| Engine Hot | |
| Intake | .009-.011 (.23-.27) |
| Exhaust | .010-.012 (.25-.30) |
| **Swift DOHC** | [1] |
| **Swift SOHC** | |
| Engine Cold | |
| Intake | .005-.007 (.13-.17) |
| Exhaust | .006-.008 (.15-.20) |
| Engine Hot | |
| Intake | .009-.011 (.23-.27) |
| Exhaust | .010-.012 (.25-.30) |

[1] - Hydraulic valve lash adjusters are used and no adjustment is required.

**4)** Turn crankshaft one complete revolution (360 degrees). Check intake valve clearance of cylinders No. 3 and 4, and exhaust valve clearance of cylinders No. 2 and 4.

**5)** Adjust valves by loosening lock nut and turning adjustment screw until clearance is at specification. After adjusting clearance, tighten adjusting screw lock nut to 11-13.5 ft. lbs. (15-18 N.m) and recheck clearance.

**Swift SOHC - 1)** Remove valve cover. Remove right side inner fender apron extension to enable timing marks to be seen. Align timing mark on crankshaft pulley with TDC mark on timing belt cover. *See Fig. 1.*

**2)** Remove distributor cap, ensure rotor is pointing upward toward distributor hold-down bolt and to No. 1 terminal of distributor cap. If not as described, rotate engine 360 degrees.

**3)** Valve clearance is measured between adjustment screw and valve stem using shim thickness gauge. Check intake valve clearance of cylinders No. 1 and 2, and exhaust valve clearance of cylinders No. 1 and 3. See VALVE CLEARANCE SPECIFICATIONS table. Turn crankshaft one complete revolution (360 degrees). Check intake valve clearance of cylinders No. 3 and 4, and exhaust valve clearance of cylinders No. 2 and 4.

**4)** Adjust valves by loosening lock nut and turning adjustment screw until clearance is at specification. Hold adjustment screw while tightening lock nut to 11-13.5 ft. lbs. (15-18 N.m). Recheck clearance.

## IGNITION TIMING

***IGNITION TIMING (Degrees BTDC @ RPM)***

| Application | Man. Trans. | Auto. Trans. |
|---|---|---|
| Samurai | [1] 7-9 @ 800 | ..... |
| Sidekick | [2] 7-9 @ 850 | [2] 7-9 @ 800 |
| Swift DOHC | [3] 5-7 @ 800-900 | [3] 5-7 @ 800-900 |
| Swift SOHC | [4] 5-7 @ 600-700 | [4] 5-7 @ 700-800 |

[1] - Specification listed is with jumper wire installed between terminals "C" and "D" (Black/Green and Blue wires) of test connector, located near the battery. *See Fig. 2.*

[2] - Specification listed is with jumper wire installed between terminals "C" and "D" (Black and Violet wires) of test connector, located near ignition coil. *See Fig. 2.*

[3] - Specification listed is with jumper wire installed between terminals "C" and "D" (Black and Violet/Green wires) of test connector, located near ignition coil. *See Fig. 2.*

[4] - Specification listed is with vacuum hose disconnected from distributor. With hose connected, timing should be 11-13 degrees BTDC.

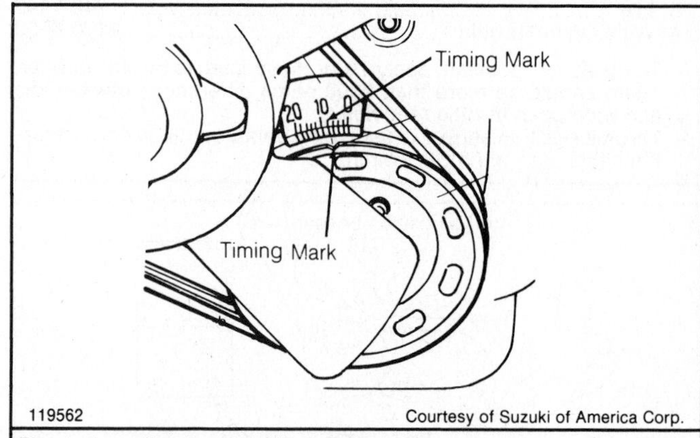


***Fig. 1: Locating Ignition Timing Mark***

**Samurai - 1)** Ensure transmission is in Neutral or Park position and parking brake is set. Inspect crankshaft pulley timing mark and timing mark indicator on timing belt cover. Clean marks as required. Start engine and warm to normal operating temperature. Turn engine off for 5 seconds. Restart and run engine at 2000 RPM for 5 minutes, then return to idle. Turn all accessories off. Attach timing light to No. 1 spark plug wire. Ensure idle speed is correct. See IDLE SPEED SPECIFICATIONS (TBI) table.

**2)** Remove protective cap from test connector located beside battery. *See Fig. 2.* Connect jumper wire between terminals "C" and "D" (between Black/Green and Blue wires of connector). Aim timing light at crankshaft pulley and timing cover timing marks. If ignition timing is not within specification, loosen distributor hold-down flange bolts and rotate distributor to obtain correct ignition timing. Tighten distributor hold-down flange bolts and recheck ignition timing. See IGNITION TIMING table.

**3)** Remove jumper wire from test connector. Ensure ignition timing advances with engine speed (RPM). If ignition timing does NOT increase, check TPS, test connector wiring circuit, engine start signal circuit and ECM.

***CAUTION: Driving with jumper wire installed in test connector will damage catalytic converter.***

**Sidekick - 1)** Ensure transmission is in Neutral or Park position and parking brake is set. Inspect crankshaft pulley timing mark and timing mark indicator on timing belt cover. Clean marks as required. Start engine and warm to normal operating temperature. Turn all accessories off. Attach timing light to No. 1 spark plug wire. Ensure idle speed is correct. See IDLE SPEED SPECIFICATIONS (TBI) table.

**2)** Aim timing light at crankshaft pulley and timing cover timing marks. If ignition timing is not within specification, loosen distributor hold-down bolt and rotate distributor to obtain correct ignition timing. Tighten distributor hold-down bolt and recheck timing. See IGNITION TIMING table.

**Swift SOHC - 1)** Ensure transmission is in Neutral or Park position and parking brake is set. Inspect crankshaft pulley timing mark and timing mark indicator on timing belt cover. *See Fig. 1.* Clean marks as required. Start engine and warm to normal operating temperature. Turn all accessories off. Attach timing light to No. 1 spark plug wire. Ensure idle speed is correct. See IDLE SPEED SPECIFICATIONS (TBI) table.

**2)** Disconnect vacuum advance vacuum hose at intake manifold filter fitting and plug fitting. Aim timing light at crankshaft pulley and timing cover timing marks. If ignition timing is not within specification, loosen distributor hold-down bolt and rotate distributor to obtain correct ignition timing. See IGNITION TIMING table.

**3)** Tighten distributor hold-down bolt and recheck ignition timing. Reconnect vacuum hose to intake manifold filter fitting. Check ignition timing to ensure vacuum advanced ignition timing is within specification. See IGNITION TIMING table.

**Swift DOHC - 1)** Ensure transmission is in Neutral or Park position and parking brake is set. Inspect crankshaft pulley timing mark and timing mark indicator on timing belt cover. *See Fig. 1.* Clean marks as required. Start engine and warm to normal operating temperature. Turn all accessories off. Attach timing light to No. 1 spark plug wire. Ensure idle speed is correct. See IDLE SPEED SPECIFICATIONS (PFI) table.

**2)** Remove protective cap from test connector located near ignition coil. *See Fig. 2.* Connect jumper wire between terminals "C" and "D" (between Black and Violet/Green wires of test connector). Aim timing light at crankshaft pulley and timing cover timing marks. If ignition timing is not within specification, loosen distributor hold-down bolt and rotate distributor to obtain correct ignition timing. Tighten distributor hold-down bolt and recheck ignition timing. See IGNITION TIMING table.

**3)** Remove jumper wire from test connector. Ensure ignition timing advances with engine speed (RPM). If ignition timing does not increase, check TPS, test connector wiring circuit, engine start signal circuit and ECM.

***CAUTION: Driving with jumper wire installed in test connector will damage catalytic converter.***

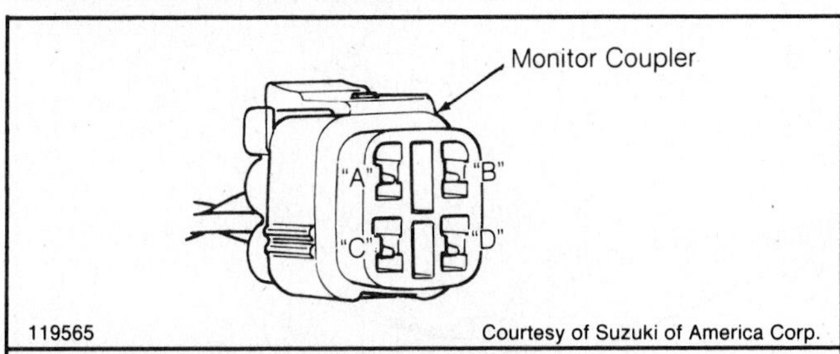


***Fig. 2: Identifying Test Connector Terminals***

## PICK-UP COIL AIR GAP

**1)** Remove distributor cap and rotor. Using non-magnetic shim thickness gauge, measure air gap between reluctor tooth and pick-up coil. See PICK-UP COIL AIR GAP table. If adjustment is required, loosen pick-up coil plate hold-down screws.

**2)** Using blade screwdriver, move pick-up coil plate to adjust air gap to specification. See PICK-UP COIL AIR GAP table. Tighten screws and recheck air gap. Ensure there are no metal particles on pick-up coil tooth.

***PICK-UP COIL AIR GAP***

| Application | Clearance - In. (mm) |
|---|---|
| Samurai | [1] |
| Sidekick | [1] |
| Swift DOHC [2] | .008-.012 (.20-.30) |
| Swift SOHC | .008-.016 (.20-.41) |

[1] - Not adjustable.
[2] - Also referred to as crank angle sensor air gap.

## IDLE SPEED & MIXTURE

***NOTE: Mixture is NOT adjustable. Mixture is controlled by ECM from various sensor inputs.***

## COLD (FAST) IDLE

***NOTE: Cold start or fast idle speed is not adjustable. Air valve operation supplies by-pass air for cold starting.***

## IDLE SPEED (TBI)

**Samurai - 1)** Start engine and warm to normal operating temperature. Install spare fuse into diagnosis terminal of fuse box and ensure CHECK ENGINE light indicates Code 12. *See Fig. 3.*

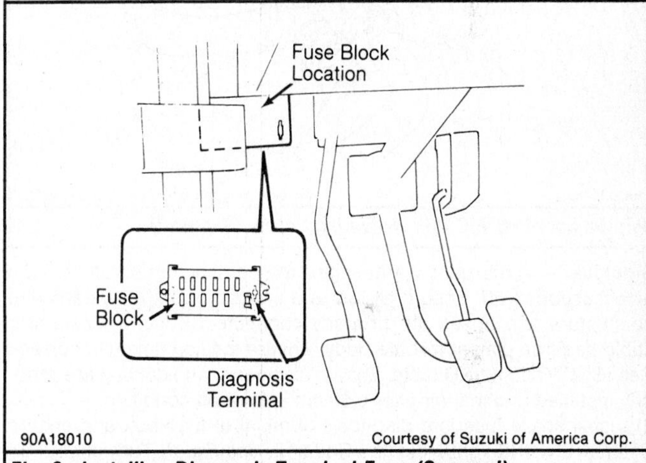


***Fig. 3: Installing Diagnosis Terminal Fuse (Samurai)***

**2)** Turn engine off and connect Duty Meter (99963-00006) to test connector terminals "A" (Violet wire) and "C" (ground terminal-Black/Green wire). Test connector is located near battery. Turn ignition on and wait 5 seconds. *See Fig. 2.*

**3)** Start engine, run at 2000 RPM for 5 minutes, then return to idle. Using Duty Meter (99963-00006), ensure idle speed and ISC duty percentage are within specification. See IDLE SPEED SPECIFICATIONS (TBI) table. If idle speed and/or ISC duty percentage require adjustment, remove idle speed adjusting screw protective cap on throttle body. Turn idle speed adjusting screw to adjust idle to specification. *See Fig. 4.*

**4)** When idle speed and ISC duty percentage are within specification and vehicle is A/C equipped, proceed to step **5)**. If vehicle is not A/C equipped, reinstall idle speed adjusting screw protective cap to throttle body and remove spare fuse from diagnosis terminal. Remove duty meter from test connector and reinstall cap.

**5)** Turn A/C on and set fan switch to LOW position. Check idle speed and ISC duty percentage. See IDLE SPEED SPECIFICATIONS (TBI) table. If idle speed and/or ISC duty percentage is not within specification, turn A/C VSV adjusting screw to adjust idle to specification. *See Fig. 5.*

# 1991 ENGINE PERFORMANCE
# On-Vehicle Adjustments (Cont.)

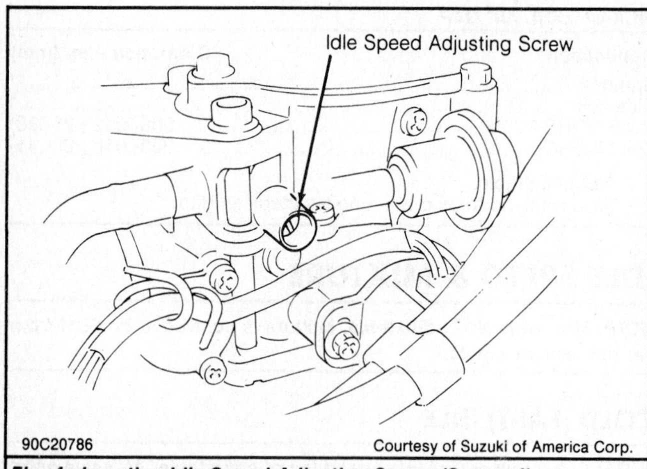


*Fig. 4: Locating Idle Speed Adjusting Screw (Samurai)*

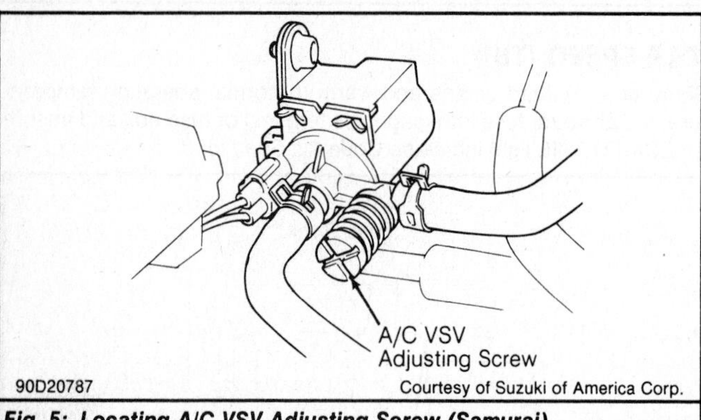


*Fig. 5: Locating A/C VSV Adjusting Screw (Samurai)*

**Sidekick – 1)** Start and warm engine to operating temperature. Turn all accessories off. Ensure all fuel and emission control system wire connectors and hoses are properly connected. Ensure accelerator cable has free play at throttle body. Ensure ignition timing is correct. See IGNITION TIMING table. Ensure air cleaner and ducting are properly installed and that air filter element is in good condition.

**2)** Install spare fuse into diagnosis terminal of fuse box and ensure CHECK ENGINE light indicates Code 12. *See Fig. 3.* Turn engine off and connect Duty Meter (99963-00006) to test connector terminals "A" (Violet wire) and "C" (ground terminal-Black/Green wire). Test connector is located near battery. Turn ignition on and wait 5 seconds. *See Fig. 2.*

**3)** Start engine, run at 2000 RPM for 5 minutes, then return to idle. Ensure idle speed and ISC duty percentage are within specification. See IDLE SPEED SPECIFICATIONS (TBI) table. If idle speed and/or ISC duty percentage require adjustment, remove idle speed adjusting screw protective cap on throttle body. Turn idle speed adjusting screw to adjust idle to specification. *See Fig. 6.*

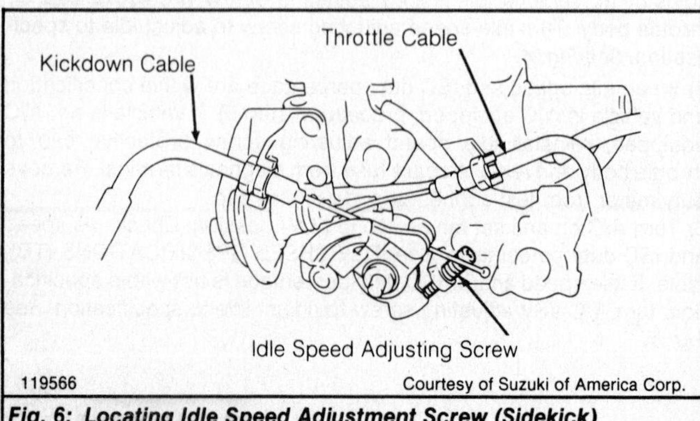


*Fig. 6: Locating Idle Speed Adjustment Screw (Sidekick)*

**4)** When idle speed and ISC duty percentage are within specification and vehicle is A/C equipped, proceed to step **5)**. If vehicle is not A/C equipped, reinstall idle speed adjusting screw protective cap to throttle body and remove spare fuse from diagnosis terminal. Remove duty meter from test connector and reinstall cap.

**5)** Turn A/C on and set fan switch to LOW position. Check idle speed and ISC duty percentage to be within specification with A/C on. See IDLE SPEED SPECIFICATIONS (TBI) table. If idle speed and/or ISC duty percentage is not within specification, turn A/C VSV adjusting screw to adjust idle to specification. *See Fig. 5.*

***NOTE: DO NOT adjust idle speed in areas above 8200 ft. elevation.***

**Swift SOHC – 1)** Idle speed is controlled by ECM using the ISC solenoid valve and requires NO adjustments under normal conditions. If conditions require idle speed to be adjusted, start and warm engine to operating temperature and turn all accessories off. Ensure all fuel and emission control system wire connectors and hoses are properly connected. Ensure accelerator cable has free-play. Ensure air cleaner and ducting are properly installed and air filter element is in good condition.

**2)** Ensure ignition timing is correct. See IGNITION TIMING table. Install spare fuse in diagnosis terminal in fuse box (CHECK ENGINE light should indicate Code 12). *See Fig. 7.* Attach tachometer to negative coil terminal (Brown/White wire) using adapter or attach an inductive pick-up type tachometer. Remove idle speed adjustment screw cap from side of throttle body just above throttle lever. Turn idle speed adjustment screw to obtain correct idle RPM. See IDLE SPEED SPECIFICATIONS (TBI) table.

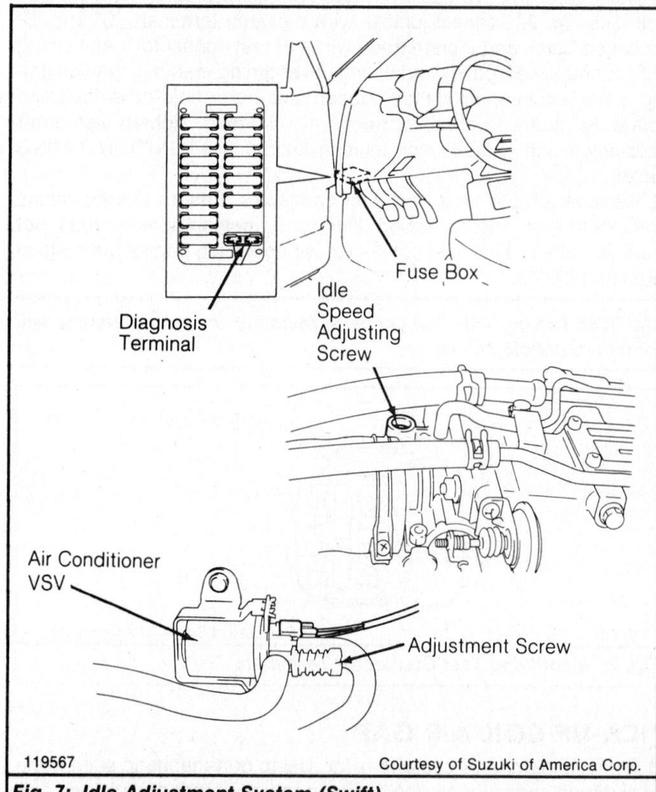


*Fig. 7: Idle Adjustment System (Swift)*

**3)** On vehicles equipped with A/C, turn A/C switch on and set fan switch to LOW position. With A/C operating correctly, verify idle speed is 850-950 RPM. If adjustment is required, turn A/C Vacuum Solenoid Valve (VSV) adjustment screw to obtain correct idle. *See Fig. 5.* See IDLE SPEED SPECIFICATIONS (TBI) table.

**4)** Reinstall protective cap to throttle body and remove spare fuse from diagnosis terminal.

***IDLE SPEED SPECIFICATIONS (TBI)*** [1]

| Application | Idle RPM |
|---|---|
| Samurai | |
| With A/C Off | [2] 750-850 |
| With A/C On | [2][3] 950-1050 |
| Sidekick | [2] 800-900 |
| Swift SOHC | |
| With A/C Off | |
| Auto. Transaxle | 800-900 |
| Man. Transaxle | 700-800 |
| With A/C On | |
| Auto. Transaxle | [3] 800-900 |
| Man. Transaxle | [3] 850-950 |

[1] - Idle speed specification is with transaxle or transmission in Neutral or Park.
[2] - ISC duty percentage should be 50% on Duty Meter (99963-00006).
[3] - The A/C idle speed is adjusted by rotating adjusting screw on the A/C Vacuum Switching Valve (VSV). *See Fig. 5.*

## IDLE SPEED (PFI)

**Swift DOHC - 1)** Idle speed is controlled by the ISC solenoid valve and should not require adjustment. If idle speed needs to be changed, start and warm engine to operating temperature and turn all accessories off. Ensure all fuel and emission control system wire connectors and hoses are properly connected. Ensure accelerator cable has free-play. Ensure air cleaner and ducting are properly installed and air filter element is in good condition.

**2)** Ensure ignition timing is correct. See IGNITION TIMING table. Install spare fuse in diagnosis terminal in fuse box (CHECK ENGINE should indicate Code 12). Attach tachometer to negative coil terminal (Brown/White wire) using adapter or attach an inductive pick-up type tachometer. Remove idle speed adjustment screw protective cap from top of throttle body. *See Fig. 7.* Turn idle speed adjustment screw to obtain correct idle RPM. See IDLE SPEED SPECIFICATIONS (PFI) table.

**3)** On vehicles equipped with A/C, turn A/C switch on and set fan switch to LOW position. With A/C operating correctly, verify idle is 850-950 RPM. If adjustment is required, turn A/C Vacuum Solenoid Valve (VSV) adjustment screw to obtain correct idle. See IDLE SPEED SPECIFICATIONS (PFI) table.

**4)** Reinstall protective cap to throttle body and remove spare fuse from diagnosis terminal.

***IDLE SPEED SPECIFICATIONS (PFI)*** [1]

| Application | Idle RPM |
|---|---|
| Swift DOHC | |
| With A/C Off | 800-900 |
| With A/C On | [2] 850-950 |

[1] - Idle speed specification is with transaxle or transmission in Neutral or Park.
[2] - The A/C idle speed is adjusted by rotating adjusting screw on the A/C Vacuum Switching Valve (VSV). *See Fig. 5.*

## THROTTLE CABLE

**Samurai - 1)** Ensure throttle cable has 0.4-0.6" (10-15 mm) free play. Hold exposed portion of cable at center and move cable up and down to measure play. Use lock nuts on cable bracket to adjust free play. *See Fig. 8.*

**2)** If hand vacuum pump is used to close throttle opener, ensure cable free play is 0.12-0.20" (3-5 mm). Use lock nuts on cable bracket to adjust free play.

**Sidekick - 1)** Ensure cable has 0.4-0.6" (10-15 mm) free play. Hold exposed portion of cable at center and move cable up and down to measure play. Use lock nut and adjusting nut on cable bracket to adjust free play. *See Fig. 8.*

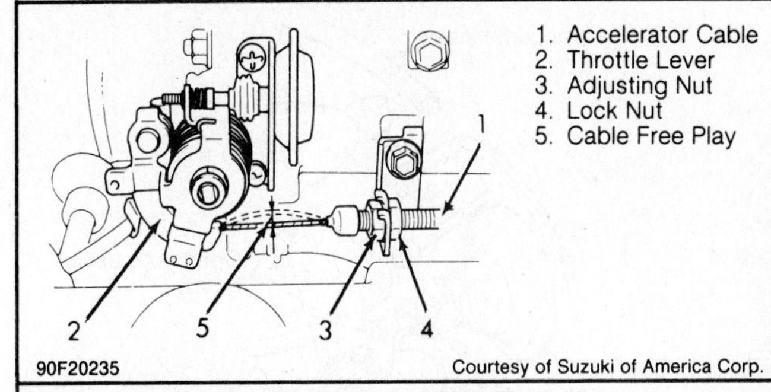


***Fig. 8: Adjusting Accelerator Cable Play (Typical)***

**2)** After throttle cable adjustment is complete, transmission kickdown cable must be adjusted. Loosen and back-off kickdown lock nut and adjusting nut considerably. With accelerator pedal fully depressed, pull on kickdown cable housing to remove cable free play. With free play removed, ensure there is 0.039" (1 mm) clearance between kickdown cable bracket and upper lock nut. Adjust upper lock nut to achieve this clearance.

**3)** Holding upper lock nut position on kickdown cable, release accelerator pedal. While holding upper lock nut position, securely tighten lower adjusting nut to bracket.

**Swift DOHC -** Ensure cable has .12-.20" (3.0-5.0 mm) free play. Hold exposed portion of cable at center and move cable up and down to measure free play. Use lock nut and adjusting nut on cable bracket to adjust free play. *See Fig. 8.*

## DASHPOT

**Swift DOHC - 1)** Ensure transmission is in Park or Neutral and parking brake is set. Start and warm engine to operating temperature. Turn all accessories off. Ensure idle speed is within specification. See IDLE SPEED SPECIFICATIONS table.

**2)** Operate throttle lever to increase and decrease engine RPM while noting RPM at which dashpot rod contacts throttle lever. Adjust dashpot adjusting screw to specified RPM at which dashpot rod should contact throttle lever. *See Figs. 8 and 12.* See DASHPOT ADJUSTMENT table.

***DASHPOT ADJUSTMENT***

| Application | [1] RPM |
|---|---|
| Swift DOHC | 3000-3400 |

[1] - Engine speed when throttle lever contacts dashpot rod after deceleration.

## THROTTLE OPENER

**Samurai - 1)** Ensure transmission is in Neutral or Park. Set parking brake. Turn ignition ON for 5 seconds, then start engine. Run engine at 2,000 RPM for 5 minutes to warm engine to operating temperature, then return engine to idle speed. Turn all accessories off. Disconnect and plug vacuum hose from throttle opener on throttle body.

**2)** Engine speed should increase to 2150-2250 RPM when vacuum hose is removed from throttle opener. If engine speed is not within specification, adjust by turning throttle opener adjusting screw. *See Fig. 9.* Reconnect vacuum hose when adjustment is within specification. See THROTTLE OPENER SPECIFICATIONS table.

***THROTTLE OPENER SPECIFICATIONS***

| Application | [1] RPM |
|---|---|
| Samurai | 2150-2250 |
| Sidekick | 2100-2300 |

[1] - Idle speed specification is with transaxle or transmission in Neutral or Park, and vacuum hose disconnected and plugged at throttle opener.

# 1991 ENGINE PERFORMANCE
# On-Vehicle Adjustments (Cont.)

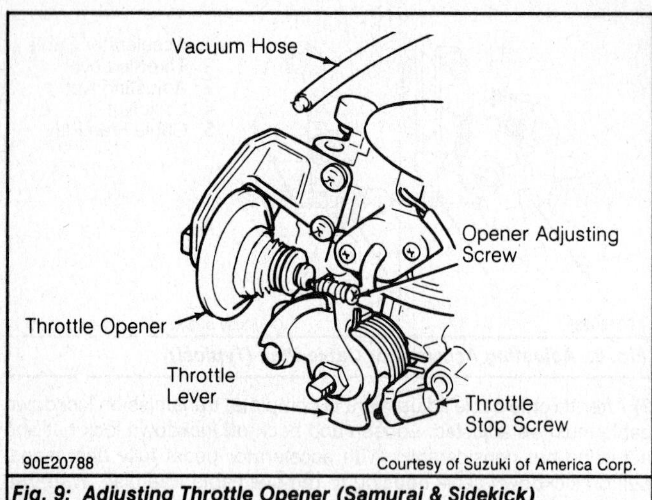


*Fig. 9: Adjusting Throttle Opener (Samurai & Sidekick)*

**Sidekick – 1)** Ensure transmission is in Neutral or Park and set parking brake. Warm engine to operating temperature. Turn all accessories off. Disconnect and plug vacuum hose from throttle opener on throttle body.

**2)** Engine speed should increase to 2100-2300 RPM when vacuum hose is removed from throttle opener. If engine speed is not within specification, adjust by turning throttle opener adjusting screw. *See Fig. 9.* Reconnect vacuum hose when adjustment is within specification. See THROTTLE OPENER SPECIFICATIONS table.

## THROTTLE POSITION SENSOR (TPS)

***CAUTION: DO NOT adjust Samurai throttle stop screw to adjust idle. Throttle stop screw is factory set and is used as zero reference point for all other adjustments.***

**TPS Inspection (Samurai) – 1)** Disconnect TPS connector. Move throttle lever to idle position by using hand vacuum pump and applying 15 in. Hg vacuum to throttle opener. Using ohmmeter, check continuity between upper and lower terminals of TPS connector with proper shim thickness gauge inserted between throttle valve lever and stop screw. *See Fig. 9.* See THROTTLE POSITION SENSOR (TPS) RESISTANCE table.

**2)** If TPS inspection results between terminals "C" and "D" are not within table specifications, adjust TPS. If any of TPS inspection results between terminals "C" and "D", "A" and "D" and "B" and "D" cannot be adjusted to be within specifications, replace TPS.

**TPS Adjustment (Samurai) – 1)** Disconnect TPS harness connector and throttle opener vacuum hose. Using hand vacuum pump, apply 15 in. Hg vacuum to throttle opener to move throttle lever to idle position. Insert .012" (.30 mm) shim thickness gauge between throttle lever and throttle stop screw. *See Fig. 9.*

**2)** Connect ohmmeter between terminals "C" (Black/Green wire) and "D" (Blue wire) of TPS connector. *See Fig. 10.* Loosen TPS mounting bolts and turn TPS fully clockwise, then turn TPS counterclockwise slowly to find position ohmmeter reading changes from infinity to zero ohms. Tighten TPS mounting bolts at that position.

**3)** Ensure there is NO continuity between terminals "C" and "D" when 0.016" (0.4 mm) shim thickness gauge is inserted between throttle lever and throttle stop screw.

**4)** Ensure there is continuity between terminals "C" and "D" when 0.008" (0.2 mm) shim thickness gauge is inserted between throttle lever and throttle stop screw.

**5)** If steps **3)** and **4)** DO NOT result as indicated, TPS zero adjustment is incorrect, start adjustment sequence again. If second adjustment results are the same after readjusting, replace TPS.

**6)** After final adjustment is completed, reconnect TPS connector and vacuum hose to throttle opener.

*THROTTLE POSITION SENSOR (TPS) RESISTANCE*

| Application | Ohms |
|---|---|
| **Samurai** | |
| Between Terminals "C" & "D" | |
| With .008" (.20 mm) Clearance At Stop Screw | 0-550 |
| With .016" (.41 mm) Clearance At Stop Screw | Infinity |
| Between Terminals "A" & "D" | 3500-6500 |
| Between Terminals "B" & "D" | |
| At Idle [1] | 0-2000 |
| At Wide Open Throttle [2] | 2000-6500 |
| **Sidekick** | |
| Between Terminals "C" & "D" | |
| At Idle [1] | 0-500 |
| At Wide Open Throttle [2] | Infinity |
| Between Terminals "A" & "D" | 3500-6500 |
| Between terminals "B" & "D" | |
| At Idle [1] | 300-2000 |
| At Wide Open Throttle [2] | 2000-6500 |
| **Swift DOHC** | |
| Between Terminals "C" & "D" | |
| With .012" (.30 mm) Clearance At Stop Screw | 0-500 |
| With .035" (.89 mm) Clearance At Stop Screw | Infinity |
| Between Terminals "C" & "A" | 3500-6500 |
| Between Terminals "C" & "B" | |
| At Idle | 0-500 |
| At Wide Open Throttle | 3500-6500 |
| **Swift SOHC** [3] | |
| Between Terminals "A" & "B" | |
| With .012" (.30 mm) Clearance At Stop Screw | 0 |
| With .035" (.89 mm) Clearance At Stop Screw | Infinity |
| Between Terminals "A" & "D" | 4370-8130 |
| Between Terminals "A" & "C" | |
| At Idle | 240-1140 |
| At Wide Open Throttle | 3170-6600 |

[1] – To obtain idle position, use hand vacuum pump to apply 19 in. Hg of vacuum to throttle opener.
[2] – There should be more than 2000 ohms difference between idle and wide open throttle readings.
[3] – Throttle position sensor is used only on SOHC auto. transaxle, SOHC manual transaxle uses throttle switch.

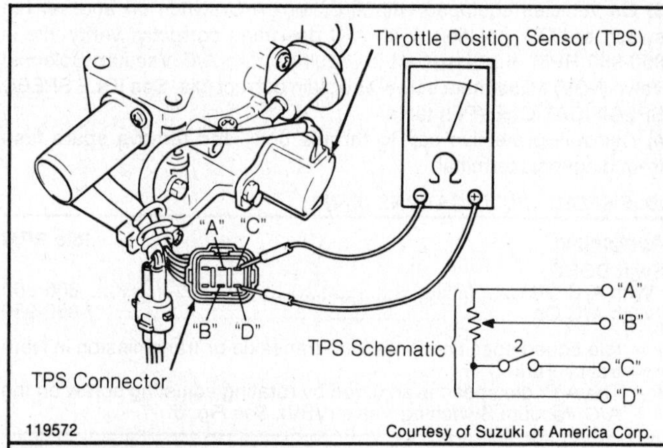


*Fig. 10: Identifying Throttle Position Sensor (TPS) Terminals (Samurai & Sidekick)*

**TPS Inspection (Sidekick) – 1)** Disconnect TPS harness connector and throttle opener vacuum hose. Using hand vacuum pump, apply 15 in. Hg vacuum to throttle opener to move throttle lever to idle position.

**2)** Using ohmmeter, check continuity between upper and lower terminals. *See Fig. 10.* See THROTTLE POSITION SENSOR (TPS) RESISTANCE table. If TPS cannot be adjusted to obtain the correct values at idle, replace TPS.

**TPS Adjustment (Sidekick) – 1)** Disconnect TPS harness connector and throttle opener vacuum hose. Using hand vacuum pump, apply 15 in. Hg vacuum to throttle opener to move throttle lever to idle position. Counting number of turns, loosen idle speed adjusting screw until clearance is obtained between throttle lever and adjusting screw. Record number of turns. Connect ohmmeter between terminals "C" and "D". *See Figs. 6 and 10.*

# 1991 ENGINE PERFORMANCE
# On-Vehicle Adjustments (Cont.)

**2)** Place a .016" (.40 mm) shim thickness gauge between idle speed adjusting screw and throttle lever. Loosen TPS mounting screws. Turn TPS fully clockwise then slowly rotate TPS counterclockwise to locate position where ohmmeter readings changes from infinity to zero ohms. Holding TPS at this position, tighten mounting screws to 30 INCH lbs. (3.4 N.m). Repeat TPS INSPECTION (SIDEKICK) to verify correct adjustment and operation.

**3)** After verifying adjustment, reconnect TPS harness connector and throttle opener vacuum hose. Turn idle speed adjusting screw inward the number of turns previously recorded. It may be necessary to readjust idle speed. See IDLE SPEED (TBI) in this article.

***CAUTION: DO NOT adjust Swift DOHC throttle stop screw to adjust idle. Throttle stop screw is factory set and is used as zero reference point for all other adjustments.***

**TPS Inspection (Swift DOHC)** – Unplug TPS connector. Using ohmmeter, check continuity with selected shim thickness gauges between throttle stop screw and throttle lever. *See Figs. 11 and 12.* See THROTTLE POSITION SENSOR (TPS) RESISTANCE table. If TPS cannot be adjusted to obtain the correct values at terminals "C" and "D", replace TPS.

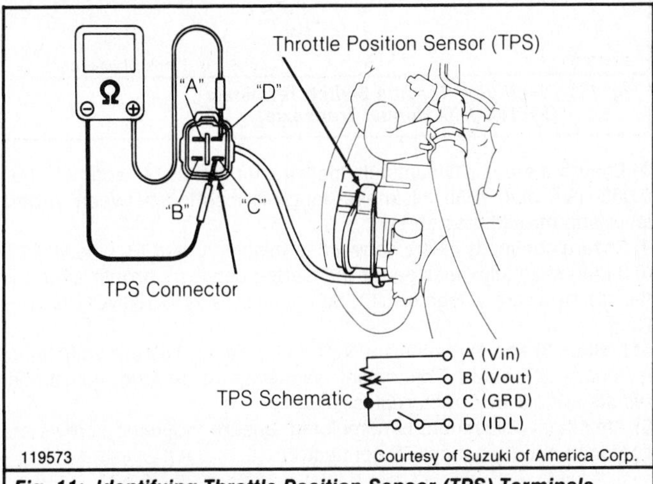


***Fig. 11: Identifying Throttle Position Sensor (TPS) Terminals (Swift DOHC)***

**TPS Adjustment (Swift DOHC)** – **1)** Unplug TPS connector and loosen TPS mounting screws. Place a .025" (.63 mm) shim thickness gauge between throttle lever and throttle stop screw. *See Fig. 12.*

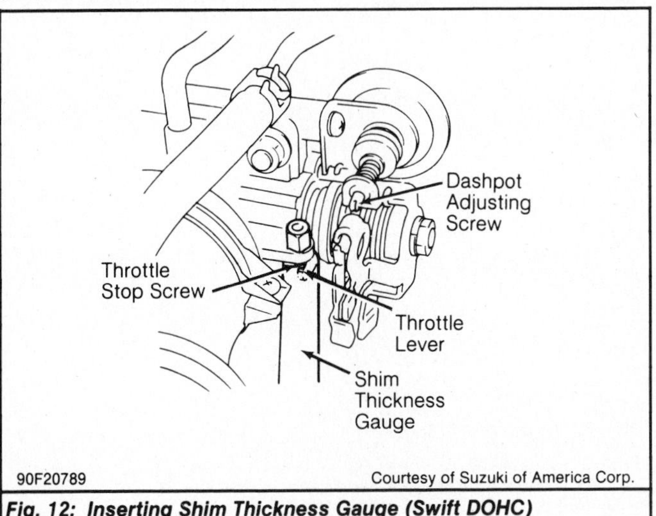


***Fig. 12: Inserting Shim Thickness Gauge (Swift DOHC)***

**2)** Connect ohmmeter between terminals "C" and "D". *See Fig. 11.* Turn TPS fully clockwise then slowly rotate TPS counterclockwise to locate position that ohmmeter reading changes from zero to infinity. Holding TPS at that position, tighten mounting screws snug-tight.

**3)** Ensure there is NO continuity between terminals "C" and "D" when 0.035" (0.9 mm) shim thickness gauge is inserted between throttle lever and throttle stop screw.

**4)** Ensure continuity exists between terminals "C" and "D" when 0.012" (0.3 mm) shim thickness gauge is inserted between throttle lever and throttle stop screw. Tighten TPS mounting screws to 30 INCH lbs. (3.4 N.m).

**5)** If steps **3)** and **4)** results are NOT as indicated, TPS zero adjustment is incorrect, start adjustment sequence again. If results are the same after readjusting, replace TPS. After final adjustment is completed, reconnect TPS connector.

***CAUTION: DO NOT adjust Swift SOHC throttle stop screw to adjust idle. Throttle stop screw is factory-set and is used as zero reference point for all other adjustments.***

**TPS Inspection (Swift SOHC)** – Unplug TPS connector. Using ohmmeter, check continuity between terminals of TPS connector with proper shim thickness gauge inserted between throttle lever and throttle stop screw. See THROTTLE POSITION SENSOR (TPS) RESISTANCE table. *See Figs. 13 and 14.*

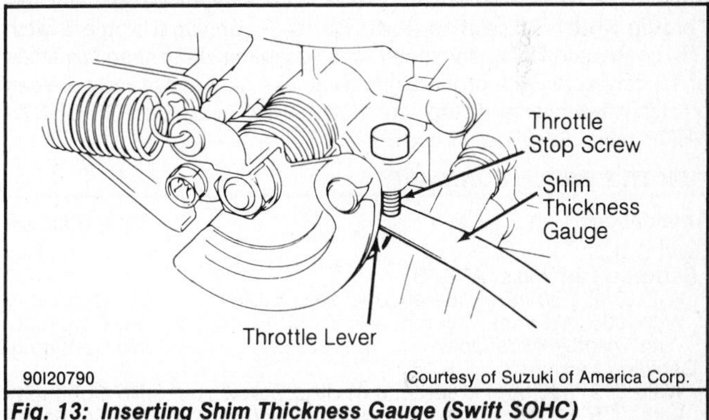


***Fig. 13: Inserting Shim Thickness Gauge (Swift SOHC)***

**TPS Adjustment (Swift SOHC)** – **1)** Unplug TPS connector and loosen TPS mounting screws. Insert .024" (.6 mm) shim thickness gauge between throttle lever and throttle stop screw. Connect ohmmeter between TPS terminals "A" and "B". *See Figs. 13 and 14.*

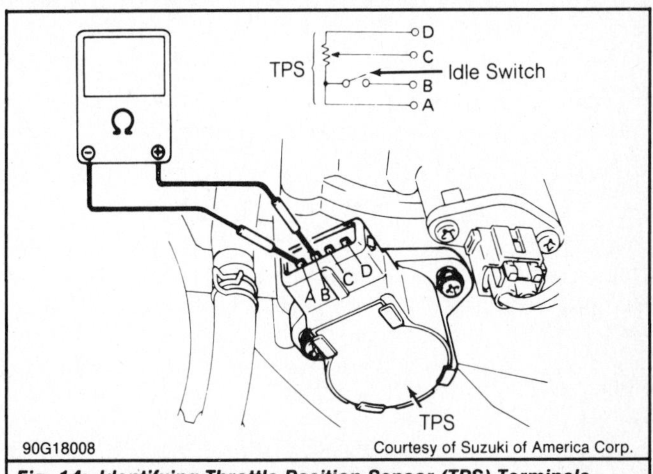


***Fig. 14: Identifying Throttle Position Sensor (TPS) Terminals (Swift SOHC Auto. Transaxle)***

# 1991 ENGINE PERFORMANCE
# On-Vehicle Adjustments (Cont.)

**2)** Turn TPS fully counterclockwise, then turn TPS clockwise to locate position that ohmmeter reading changes from zero to infinity. Holding TPS at that position, tighten TPS mounting screws snug-tight.
**3)** Ensure there is NO continuity between terminals "A" and "B" when 0.035" (0.9 mm) shim thickness gauge is inserted between throttle lever and throttle stop screw.
**4)** Ensure continuity exists between terminals "A" and "B" when 0.012" (0.3 mm) shim thickness gauge is inserted between throttle lever and throttle stop screw. Tighten TPS mounting screws to 18 INCH lbs. (2.0 N.m).
**5)** If steps **3)** and **4)** results are NOT as indicated, TPS zero adjustment is incorrect, start adjustment sequence again. If results are the same after readjusting, replace TPS. After final adjustment is completed, reconnect TPS connector.

## THROTTLE SWITCH (TS)

***NOTE: Throttle switch is used ONLY on Swift SOHC models with manual transaxle. Throttle position sensor is used on automatic transaxle models.***

***CAUTION: DO NOT adjust Swift SOHC throttle stop screw to adjust idle. Throttle stop screw is factory-set and is used as zero reference point for all other adjustments.***

**Throttle Switch Inspection (Swift SOHC)** – Unplug Throttle Switch (TS) connector. Using ohmmeter, check continuity between terminals of TS connector with proper shim thickness gauge inserted between throttle valve lever and stop screw. See THROTTLE SWITCH CONTINUITY table. *See Figs. 13 and 15.*

***THROTTLE SWITCH CONTINUITY***

| Application | Specification |
|---|---|
| Swift SOHC | |
| Between Terminals "A" & "B" | |
| With .012" (.30 mm) Clearance At Stop Screw | Continuity |
| With .035" (.89 mm) Clearance At Stop Screw | No Continuity |
| With Throttle Wide Open | No Continuity |
| Between Terminals "B" & "C" | |
| With .012" (.30 mm) Clearance At Stop Screw | No Continuity |
| With .035" (.89 mm) Clearance At Stop Screw | No Continuity |
| With Throttle Wide Open | Continuity |
| Between Terminals "A" & "C" | |
| With .012" (.30 mm) Clearance At Stop Screw | No Continuity |
| With .035" (.89 mm) Clearance At Stop Screw | No Continuity |
| With Throttle Wide Open | No Continuity |

**Throttle Switch Adjustment (Swift SOHC) – 1)** Unplug Throttle Switch (TS) connector. Insert .024" (.06 mm) shim thickness gauge between throttle lever and throttle stop screw. Loosen TS mounting screws. *See Fig. 13.*
**2)** Connect ohmmeter between "A" and "B" terminals. *See Fig. 15.* Turn TS fully counterclockwise, then turn TS clockwise slowly to locate position that ohmmeter reading changes from zero continuity to infinity. Hold TS at that position, snug-tighten mounting screws.

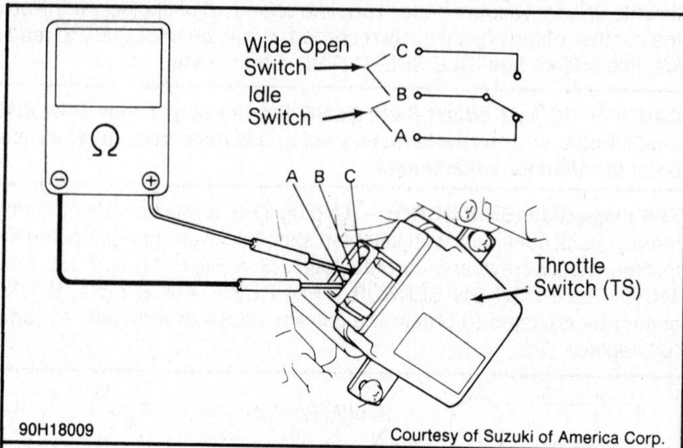


***Fig. 15: Identifying Throttle Switch Terminals (Swift SOHC Manual Transaxle)***

**3)** Ensure there is NO continuity between terminals "A" and "B" when 0.035" (0.9 mm) shim thickness gauge is inserted between throttle lever and throttle stop screw.
**4)** Ensure continuity exists between terminals "A" and "B" when 0.012" (0.3 mm) shim thickness gauge is inserted between throttle lever and throttle stop screw. Tighten TPS mounting screws to 18 INCH lbs. (2.0 N.m).
**5)** If steps **3)** and **4)** results are NOT as indicated, TS zero adjustment is incorrect, restart adjustment sequence. If second adjustment results are still incorrect, replace TS.
**6)** After final adjustment is completed, ensure mounting screws are tightened and reconnect TS connector.

# 1991 ENGINE PERFORMANCE
# Theory & Operation

## Samurai, Sidekick, Swift

## INTRODUCTION

This article covers basic description and operation of engine performance-related systems and components. Read this article before diagnosing vehicles or systems with which you are not completely familiar.

## COMPUTERIZED ENGINE CONTROLS

Computerized engine control system consists of various input devices which detect vehicle operating conditions. On all models, the Electronic Control Module (ECM) monitors input signals received from input devices and sends output signals to regulate air/fuel mixture and other engine control operations. This lowers exhaust emissions, while maintaining fuel economy and driveability.

System incorporates a self-diagnostic system, built-in fail-safe mechanism and back-up power. Self-diagnostic system provides capability of recognizing a system fault and storing a related trouble code in ECM memory for diagnostic purposes. Fail-safe mechanism substitutes preprogrammed sensor values to the ECM if a sensor fails, thus providing a certain level of engine performance. If ECM fails to operate properly, back-up power to ECM controls operation of fuel injectors based on signals from Manifold Absolute Pressure (MAP) sensor.

### CONTROL UNIT

**Samurai** – The ECM is located under glove box. ECM distributes power to all sensors except oxygen and speed sensor, which generate their own voltage signal. ECM power (ECM terminals B1 and B7) is received from the EFI main relay. ECM back-up power (ECM terminal B9) is supplied from fuse box 15-amp fuse No. 7.

**Sidekick** – The ECM is located under left side of dash. ECM distributes power to sensors (except oxygen sensor) and switches, and controls ground circuits of solenoids. ECM power (ECM terminals B1 and B7) is received from the control relay. ECM back-up power (ECM terminal B9) is received from fuse box 15-amp fuse No. 3.

**Swift (DOHC)** – The ECM is located under left side of dash. ECM distributes power to all sensors except oxygen and speed sensor, which generate a voltage signal of their own. ECM power (ECM terminals A1 and A2) is received from the EFI main relay. ECM back-up power (ECM terminal A16) is received from main fuse.

**Swift (SOHC)** – The ECM is located under left side of dash. ECM distributes power to all sensors except oxygen and speed sensor, which generate a voltage signal of their own. ECM power (ECM terminal B1) is received from EFI main relay. ECM back-up power (ECM terminal B7) is received from 15-amp taillight fuse.

***NOTE: Components are grouped into 2 categories. The first category covers INPUT DEVICES, which control or produce voltage signals monitored by the control unit. The second category covers OUTPUT SIGNALS, which are components controlled by the control unit.***

### INPUT DEVICES

**A/C Signal** – See MISCELLANEOUS CONTROLS.

**Air Temperature Sensor (Samurai, Sidekick & Swift SOHC)** – On Samurai and Sidekick, air temperature sensor is located on side of intake manifold. On Swift SOHC, air temperature sensor is located on side of air filter.

Air temperature sensor thermistor changes resistance with respect to temperature. High temperature causes low resistance. Low temperature causes high resistance. A reference voltage (supplied and monitored by ECM) is modified by sensor resistance. ECM uses this information to help determine control (output) signals to injector.

**Airflow Meter (Swift DOHC)** – Airflow meter, located between air cleaner and airflow meter outlet hose, consists of an airflow sensor and body. Airflow meter detects the amount of air drawn into engine and sends a voltage signal to ECM. ECM uses this signal to control fuel injectors.

**Clutch Switch (Samurai)** – Clutch switch is located above clutch pedal. Switch turns on when clutch pedal is depressed and off when released. ECM uses this signal to help determine control of fuel injector.

**Coolant (Water) Temperature Sensor** – On Samurai and Sidekick, coolant temperature sensor is located on side of intake manifold. On Swift DOHC, sensor is located on side of cylinder head. On Swift SOHC, sensor is located on side of throttle body.

Coolant temperature sensor thermistor changes resistance with respect to temperature. High temperature causes low resistance. Low temperature causes high resistance. A reference voltage (supplied and monitored by ECM) is modified by sensor resistance. ECM uses this information to help determine control (output) signals to injector(s), emission components and timing devices (Samurai and Swift DOHC).

**Crank Angle Sensor (Samurai)** – Engine speed signal is generated (4 pulses per revolution) by the pick-up coil and reluctor assembly located in the distributor. ECM uses these pulses to calculate engine speed, and to help determine control of fuel injector and ignition timing.

**Crank Angle Sensor (Swift DOHC)** – Engine speed signal is generated (12 pulses per revolution) by the pick-up coil and reluctor assembly located in the distributor. By providing 3 distinctive pulses for each cylinder, ECM is capable of more precisely timing engine control functions.

**EGR Temperature Sensor (Samurai, Sidekick & Swift DOHC – Calif.)** – The EGR temperature sensor is located in EGR passage on intake manifold. Sensor is used on California models only. Sensor's thermistor changes resistance with respect to exhaust gas temperature. High temperature causes low resistance. Low temperature causes high resistance. A reference voltage (supplied and monitored by ECM) is modified by sensor resistance. ECM uses EGR temperature sensor signal to determine if EGR action is occurring when requested by ECM.

**Engine Start Signal** – This signal is sent from starter circuit to ECM terminal B11 (terminal C1 on Swift DOHC or A1 on Swift SOHC). On Samurai and Sidekick, ECM uses signal to determine whether engine is cranking, to control fuel injection timing, injection time, Idle Speed Control (ISC) solenoid operation, throttle opener vacuum switching valve operation, and mixture heater operation (Sidekick A/T). On Swift DOHC, ECM uses this signal to determine whether engine is cranking and to control ignition timing. On Swift SOHC, ECM uses this signal to determine whether engine is cranking and to control fuel injector and fuel pump relay.

**Gear Position Switch (Samurai – Fed. & Sidekick M/T)** –Gear position switch is also known as 5th Gear Switch. Gear position is sensed when switch closes as transmission is shifted into 5th gear. Switch is open in all other gear positions. ECM uses on/off signal from gear position switch to control EGR vacuum switching valve.

**Idle Switch** – Idle switch is an integral part of throttle position sensor. Idle switch signals ECM of closed throttle condition. Switch is closed to ground at closed throttle (idle) and open at any position except closed throttle.

**Ignition Signal (Samurai)** – Ignition signal is sent from ignitor to ECM terminal A6. ECM uses this signal to help determine control of fuel injector.

**Ignition Signal (Sidekick & Swift)** – Ignition signal is sent to ECM terminal A1 (terminal A12 on Swift DOHC or B2 on Swift SOHC) from ignition coil. On Sidekick and Swift SOHC, ECM detects engine speed through this signal and uses it to control various actuators. On Swift DOHC, ECM uses this signal to detect if ignition spark is emitted and stops injector operation when signal is not received.

**Oxygen ($O_2$) Sensor** – The $O_2$ sensor is mounted in the exhaust manifold, where it comes in contact with exhaust gases as they enter the exhaust system. The $O_2$ sensor generates voltage according to the oxygen content of exhaust gases. This voltage will vary from .1 volt (lean condition) to as high as 1.0 volt (rich condition). Sensor will not generate a voltage signal until it has reached operating temperature. Until sensor is warmed up, ECM will adjust air/fuel mixture based upon preprogrammed tables in ECM's memory.

# 1991 ENGINE PERFORMANCE
# Theory & Operation (Cont.)

**Park/Neutral (Shift) Switch (Sidekick A/T)** – Park/neutral switch signals ECM on terminal B12 when transmission is in Park or Neutral. This input signal is used by ECM to help determine control of Idle Speed Control (ISC) solenoid.

**Park/Neutral Switch (Swift A/T)** – Automatic transmission ECM monitors park/neutral switch and relays a voltage signal to engine ECM when transmission is in Park or Neutral. This on/off input signal is used by ECM to help determine control of fuel injector(s) and Idle Speed Control (ISC) solenoid.

**Power Steering Oil Pressure Switch (Sidekick)** – ECM applies and monitors a reference voltage to power steering pressure switch from ECM terminal A13. When steering wheel is turned, pressure switch closes. This pulls reference voltage low. ECM uses this signal to help determine control of Idle Speed Control (ISC) solenoid.

**Pressure Sensor (Samurai, Sidekick & Swift SOHC)** – Pressure sensor is also known as Manifold Absolute Pressure (MAP) sensor. MAP sensor is connected to ECM by a 3-wire harness and to engine by a manifold vacuum hose. ECM applies a 5-volt reference signal from ECM terminal A23 (terminal A5 on Swift SOHC) to MAP sensor. MAP sensor has an internal mechanical resistor which varies resistance based on changes in engine load (manifold vacuum). As internal resistance varies, return voltage signal varies at ECM terminal A22 (terminal A4 on Swift SOHC). ECM interprets this voltage change as changes in engine load and uses this signal to help determine control of fuel injectors, Idle Speed Control (ISC) solenoid and EGR system.

**Throttle Position Sensor (Samurai, Sidekick, Swift DOHC & Swift SOHC A/T)** – ECM supplies throttle position sensor with a 5-volt reference signal. Sensor contains both a potentiometer (variable resistor) and an idle switch. Throttle position sensor sends ECM a potentiometer output signal corresponding to throttle valve opening and idle switch signal that turns on only when throttle is in idle position. ECM uses these signals to help determine control of air/fuel ratio during acceleration, deceleration and idle.

**Throttle Switch (Swift SOHC M/T)** – Throttle switch consists of 2-contact points (idle switch and wide open switch) connected to throttle valve shaft on throttle body and detects throttle valve opening. Throttle opening during idle is detected by idle switch which turns on at idle. Wide open throttle is detected by wide open throttle switch which turns on during wide open throttle. By monitoring on/off signals, ECM detects throttle valve opening. ECM uses on/off signals from throttle switch to help determine control of fuel injector, Idle Speed Control (ISC) solenoid, shift-up indicator light and EGR vacuum switching valve.

**Vehicle Speed Sensor** – Vehicle speed sensor is a P/M generator and switching transistor located in speedometer head. ECM supplies and monitors a voltage signal to speed sensor. As P/M generator rotates (vehicle moving), switching transistor in speed sensor grounds and ungrounds reference voltage signal from ECM terminal A10 (A11 on Swift SOHC). ECM uses this signal to help determine control of Idle Speed Control (ISC) solenoid and shift-up indicator light (Swift SOHC).

## OUTPUT SIGNALS

***NOTE: Vehicles are equipped with different combinations of computer-controlled components. Not all components listed below are used on every vehicle. For theory and operation on each output component, refer to the system indicated after component.***

**Canister Purge Vacuum Switching Valve** – See EMISSION SYSTEMS.
**CHECK ENGINE Light** – See SELF-DIAGNOSTIC SYSTEM.
**EGR Vacuum Switching Valve** – See EMISSIONS SYSTEMS.
**Fuel-Cut System** – See FUEL CONTROL.
**Fuel Injector(s)** – See FUEL CONTROL.
**Fuel Pump Relay** – See FUEL DELIVERY.
**Idle Speed Control (ISC) Solenoid** – See IDLE SPEED.
**Ignition Advance Control** – **See IGNITION SYSTEM.**
**Lock-Up Solenoid Relay** – See MISCELLANEOUS CONTROLS.
**Throttle Opener Vacuum Switching Valve** – See IDLE SPEED.

## FUEL SYSTEM

### FUEL DELIVERY

**Fuel Pump** – Electric fuel pump is located in fuel tank. Fuel pump receives power when ECM provides ground to fuel pump relay. When power is supplied to fuel pump, motor and impeller inside pump turn. This causes a pressure difference to occur between both sides of impeller. When fuel is drawn through fuel pump inlet port, pressure is increased and discharged through outlet port.

The fuel pump also incorporates a relief valve to prevent excessive rise of discharge pressure and a check valve to keep residual pressure in fuel feed line when fuel pump is not activated.

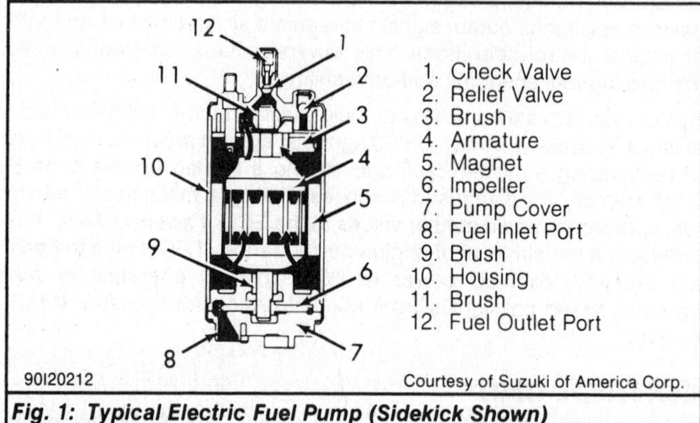


*Fig. 1: Typical Electric Fuel Pump (Sidekick Shown)*

**Fuel Pump Relay** – Fuel pump relay is energized based upon ignition switch and RPM inputs. Power for fuel pump is supplied by EFI main relay, which receives its power from main fuse. EFI main relay is energized by ECM when the ignition is turned on.

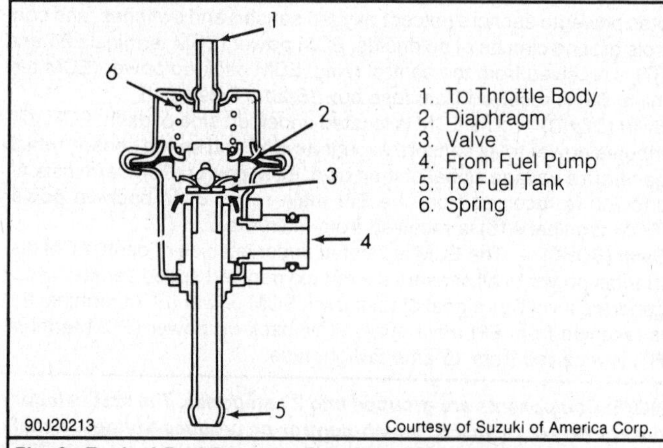


*Fig. 2: Typical Fuel Pressure Regulator (Sidekick Shown)*

**Fuel Pressure Regulator** – Fuel pressure regulator is a spring/vacuum operated diaphragm-type relief valve which maintains a constant regulated fuel pressure under all vehicle operating modes.

When manifold vacuum is high (low fuel requirements), diaphragm is drawn in, counteracting spring pressure. In this condition, excess fuel is routed back to fuel tank. When manifold vacuum drops (engine load), spring pressure overcomes vacuum, closing off fuel tank return line. This maintains pressure and volume to injector(s).

### FUEL CONTROL

**Fuel Injector(s)** – Samurai, Sidekick and Swift SOHC utilize Throttle Body Injection (TBI), which incorporates a single fuel injector in the throttle body unit. Swift DOHC utilizes Port Fuel Injection (PFI), which incorporates 4 fuel injectors mounted in a fuel rail assembly.

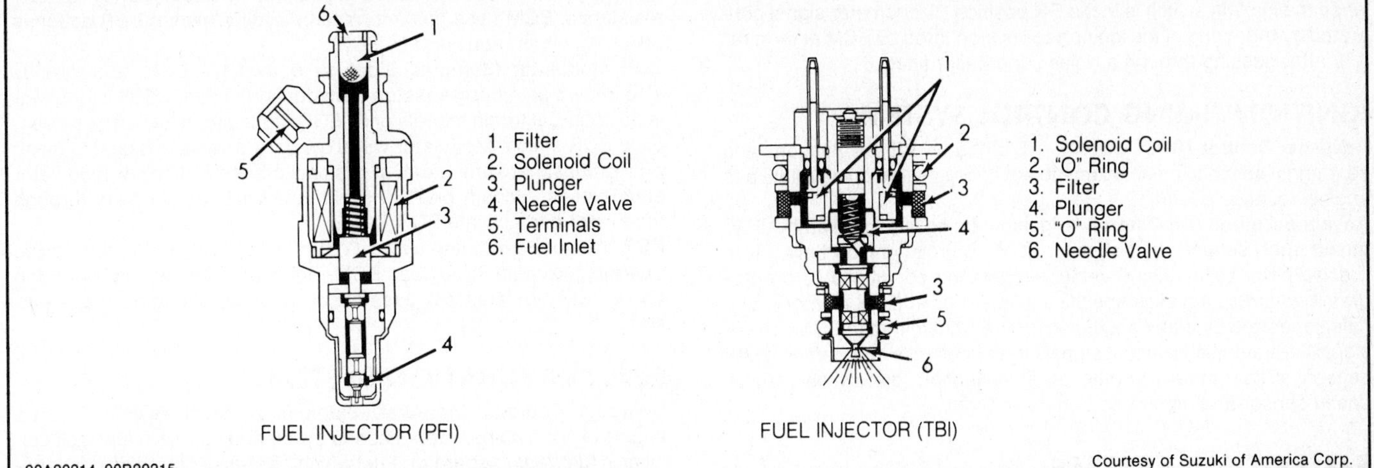


*Fig. 3: Typical Fuel Injector (Swift DOHC PFI & Sidekick TBI Shown)*

When the solenoid coil of injector is energized by ECM, coil becomes an electromagnet. This lifts injector plunger, allowing fuel under pressure to be injected into intake manifold (Samurai, Sidekick & Swift SOHC) or cylinder head (Swift DOHC). Since fuel pressure is relatively constant, air/fuel mixtures are controlled solely by injector pulse width ("on" time). ECM determines proper pulse width based upon input signals received from various sensors and switches.

Timing of injector firing is determined by ECM based upon RPM signals received from either distributor P/M generator (Swift) or ignition coil (Samurai, Sidekick and Swift SOHC). On Swift SOHC, ECM also monitors ignition coil signal. Since ECM interprets coil signals as an indication of spark presence, fuel injector triggering will cease if ignition coil signal is lost.

**Battery Voltage Compensation** – A drop in battery voltage directly affects the pulse width of injector(s). As battery voltage drops, pulse width tends to decrease. This would cause a leaner air/fuel mixture than desired. To compensate for this, the ECM monitors battery voltage. If battery voltage drops, ECM will increase injector pulse width.

**Fuel-Cut System** – The fuel-cut system will stop fuel injection during deceleration to prevent excess fuel build-up during periods when oxygen is insufficient for combustion (i.e. closed throttle deceleration).

Fuel-cut system will also deactivate injectors when engine speed exceeds 7200 RPM (Sidekick), 7500 RPM (Swift DOHC) or 6800 RPM (Samurai and Swift SOHC). This is done to prevent engine damage due to excessive engine speed. As engine speed drops to less than 6800 RPM (Sidekick), 7460 RPM (Swift DOHC), 6500 (Samurai) or 6600 (Swift SOHC), injection will once again occur.

## IDLE SPEED

**Air Valve (Swift DOHC)** – Air valve is located on intake manifold. Air valve is used to increase idle speed (airflow) when engine is started at a low ambient temperature. Air valve consists of a thermowax pellet, spring and plunger. Water from cooling system passes through valve, directly across thermowax pellet.

When coolant temperature is low, thermowax pellet is contracted, allowing air to pass under end of plunger and into intake manifold. This air by-passes throttle plate, increasing idle speed for improved cold engine driveability. As coolant temperature increases, thermowax pellet expands, gradually blocking off by-passed air and decreasing idle speed.

**Idle Speed Control (ISC) Solenoid** – An air passage by-passing the throttle valve is provided to route filtered air directly into intake manifold. The flow of air through this passage is regulated by ECM energized ISC solenoid valve. Solenoid is located on side of throttle body.

Air is allowed to pass through ISC solenoid valve when it is energized. Solenoid is energized whenever idle speed drops to less than desired RPM due to engine load (i.e. electrical, A/C, P/S, auto. trans. in Drive, etc.). ISC solenoid valve is also energized each time engine is started, or during periods of deceleration (to compensate for rich mixtures caused by a fully closed throttle). Duration of ISC solenoid valve operation is dependent on coolant temperature.

**Throttle Opener Control System (Samurai & Sidekick)** – When vehicle is first started, ECM energizes throttle opener Vacuum Switching Valve (VSV). This blocks manifold vacuum which normally draws throttle opener diaphragm and linkage rod to base idle position.

Once vehicle is started, ECM will de-energize VSV. This allows manifold vacuum to pass through VSV to throttle opener diaphragm. Diaphragm will then retract, allowing throttle linkage to return to normal base idle position.

**Throttle Opener Vacuum Switching Valve (Samurai & Sidekick)** – Throttle opener is controlled by Vacuum Switching Valve (VSV) which opens and closes vacuum passage to throttle opener. ECM controls throttle opener VSV according to engine, starter and coolant (water) temperature sensor signals.

# IGNITION SYSTEM

## ELECTRONIC IGNITION SYSTEM

**Samurai, Sidekick & Swift SOHC** – The electronic ignition system consists of a distributor which utilizes a pick-up coil and reluctor to produce ignition pulses through the ignitor. Ignitor is also located within the distributor.

Power for ignition coil and ignitor is provided from fuse box 15-amp fuse (20-amp on Swift SOHC), which receives power when the ignition switch is in the ON position. Ground circuit for ignition coil is regulated by the ignitor. As the rotating reluctor passes pick-up coil pole piece, an alternating current is produced. The ignitor uses this alternating signal to determine when to ground and open primary ignition circuit.

When ignitor opens ground circuit for primary ignition, the magnetic field around ignition coil windings collapses, producing an induced high voltage surge which is used to fire spark plugs.

**Swift DOHC** – The ignition system consists of an ignition coil, a distributor containing a P/M generator crank angle sensor, trigger wheel and rotor, and an ignition power unit which opens and closes ignition coil primary circuit based upon signals from ECM. When power unit removes the ground circuit from primary ignition, the magnetic field around ignition coil windings collapse. This produces an induced high voltage surge which is used to fire spark plugs.

# 1991 ENGINE PERFORMANCE
# Theory & Operation (Cont.)

Power for ignition coil is provided from fuse box 20-amp ignition fuse when the ignition switch is in the ON position. Tachometer signal generated by triggering of the ignition coil is monitored by ECM at terminal A12 after passing through a noise suppressor filter.

## IGNITION TIMING CONTROL SYSTEM

**Advance Control (Swift SOHC)** – Distributor utilizes vacuum and centrifugal advance mechanisms to advance ignition timing relative to engine speed and load.

**Advance Control (All Others)** – Ignition timing is controlled by ECM based upon sensor input signals. ECM controls ignition timing to a precise point by matching vehicles operating conditions to preprogrammed timing advance specifications stored in ECM memory. Signals generated by crank angle sensor are transmitted to ECM. These signals are modified by input signals from coolant (water) temperature sensor, airflow meter, throttle position sensor, idle switch, vehicle speed sensor and monitored battery voltage.

# EMISSION SYSTEMS

For additional information, see EMISSION APPLICATIONS and VACUUM DIAGRAMS articles.

## EXHAUST GAS RECIRCULATION (EGR)

To lower oxides of nitrogen (NOx) exhaust gas emissions, an EGR system is used. The EGR system introduces exhaust gases into intake system. The exhaust gases are noncombustible gases which, when combined with incoming air/fuel mixture, lower peak combustion chamber temperatures.

EGR valve receives ported operating vacuum through an ECM-regulated EGR Vacuum Switching Valve (VSV). ECM regulates VSV based upon input signals from various sensors. Control vacuum is further regulated by an EGR modulator, located in vacuum line between EGR valve and EGR solenoid.

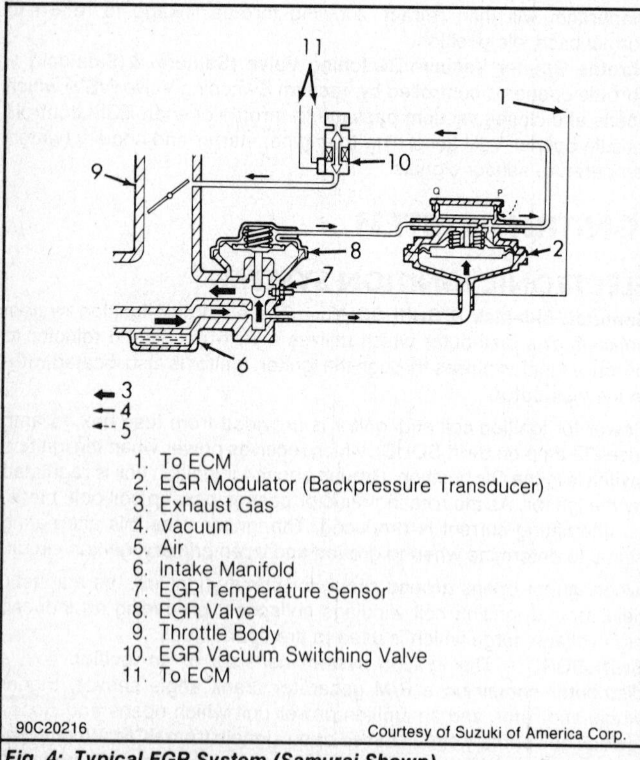


*Fig. 4: Typical EGR System (Samurai Shown)*

**EGR Temperature Sensor (Samurai, Sidekick & Swift DOHC – California)** – The EGR temperature sensor is located in EGR passage on intake manifold. Sensor's thermistor changes resistance with respect to exhaust gas temperature. High temperature causes low resistance. Low temperature causes high resistance. A reference voltage (supplied and monitored by ECM) is modified by sensor resistance. ECM uses this information to determine if EGR action is occurring when requested by ECM.

**EGR Modulator (Samurai, Sidekick & Swift)** – EGR Modulator is also known as a backpressure transducer. On Swift, EGR modulator is used on California models only. EGR modulator is used to help regulate EGR action. Modulator will allow ported vacuum signal to bleed off to atmosphere until exhaust gas backpressure in hollow modulator stem closes vacuum bleed. At this time vacuum will pass through modulator and activate EGR valve.

**EGR Vacuum Switching Valve (VSV)** – EGR valve receives ported operating vacuum through an ECM-regulated EGR vacuum switching valve. ECM regulates VSV based upon input signals from various sensors.

## FUEL EVAPORATION SYSTEM

**Charcoal Canister (Samurai, Sidekick & Swift DOHC)** – When engine is not running, vapor caused by expanding fuel in fuel tank collects in fuel vapor separator. Fuel which condenses in fuel vapor separator returns to fuel tank. Fuel vapor flows from fuel vapor separator and into charcoal canister where it is contained by activated charcoal. When engine is started, ported vacuum causes fresh air to be drawn in through bottom of canister. This pulls stored fuel vapor into the combustion chamber for burning.

On Swift DOHC, fuel vapor purge line is regulated by ECM operated canister purge vacuum switching valve. Vacuum switching valve allows purge to occur only under the following conditions:

- Coolant temperature greater than 140°F (60°C)
- Engine speed greater than 1500 RPM
- Throttle switch off (not idling)
- When engine is under load.

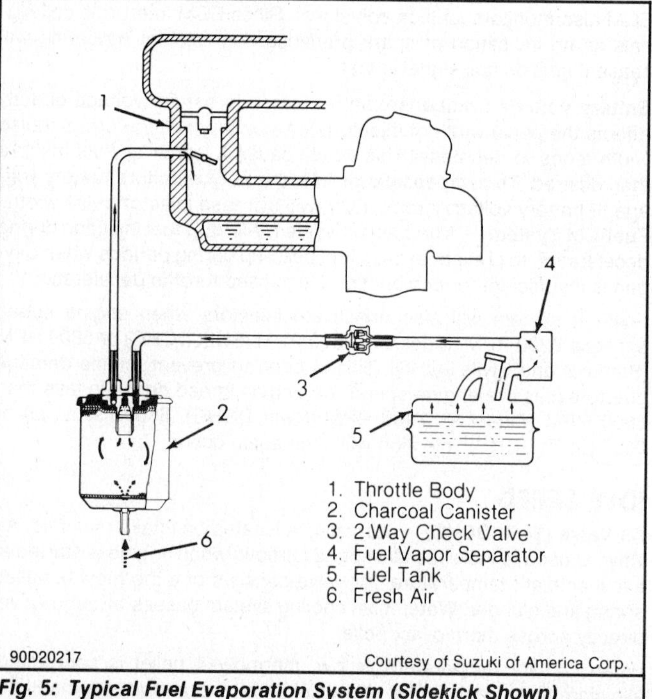


*Fig. 5: Typical Fuel Evaporation System (Sidekick Shown)*

**Charcoal Canister (Swift SOHC)** – The vapors generated in fuel tank pass through a 2-way check valve and enter charcoal canister where charcoal absorbs and stores fuel vapors. Canister is purged or cleaned by air drawn through the filter at bottom of canister and sucked into intake manifold through purge control valve and purge line. Throttle body vacuum is applied to canister purge control valve to open valve under the following conditions:

- Engine is running
- Engine is at operating temperature
- Throttle valve opens larger than idle position.

When engine coolant temperature is low, Bimetallic Vacuum Switching Valve (BVSV) opens to atmosphere, causing throttle body vacuum not to be applied to purge control valve, therefore closing purge control valve and not allowing vapors to purge into intake manifold.

**Canister Purge Vacuum Switching Valve (Swift DOHC) –** Canister purge Vacuum Switching Valve (VSV) is controlled by ECM according to signals from various sensors. When VSV is signalled by ECM, fuel vapors flow from charcoal canister into combustion chambers for burning.

**Fuel Vapor Separator (Samurai, Sidekick & Swift DOHC) –** When engine is not running, vapor from expanding fuel in fuel tank collects in fuel vapor separator. Fuel which condenses in fuel vapor separator returns to fuel tank. Fuel vapor flows from fuel vapor separator into charcoal canister where it is contained by activated charcoal. When engine is started, ported vacuum purges stored vapors from canister.

## POSITIVE CRANKCASE VENTILATION (PCV)

PCV system consists of PCV valve, 3-way joint and crankcase hoses from air cleaner and rocker cover, teeing at PCV valve. PCV system draws crankcase blow-by gases (hydrocarbons) into the air induction system rather than allowing then to escape to the atmosphere. Crankcase gases are mixed with air/fuel mixture and burned in combustion chamber.

# SELF-DIAGNOSTIC SYSTEM

When a system fault occurs, CHECK ENGINE light on dash will illuminate to inform driver a problem exists. Light will remain on until fault goes away or system is serviced. If fault goes away (system parameter returns to normal operation) before it is serviced, CHECK ENGINE light will go out. Related fault code will still remain in ECM memory until cleared. Stored codes may later be accessed and identified by counting flashes of CHECK ENGINE light.

## CHECK ENGINE LIGHT

All vehicles are equipped with a CHECK ENGINE light located on the instrument panel. CHECK ENGINE light will illuminate when ignition switch is turned to the ON position (bulb check) and engine is not running. Light should not flash at this time and go out when engine is started.

**Samurai & Sidekick (Federal) –** The CHECK ENGINE light will automatically flash at 50,000, 80,000 and 100,000 miles on a warmed up running vehicle. This is not an indication of a system fault; however, it is an indication that system inspection and/or system component replacement is required. After necessary services have been performed, turn off CHECK ENGINE light by moving cancel switch to opposite position. Cancel switch is located below steering column lower trim panel.

- At 50,000 Miles – Replace PCV valve, inspect EGR system.
- At 80,000 Miles – Replace $O_2$ sensor.
- At 100,000 Miles – Replace PCV valve, inspect catalytic converter for plugging, inspect EGR system, replace $O_2$ sensor, replace charcoal canister, inspect ECM and related sensors.

# MISCELLANEOUS CONTROLS

***NOTE: Although not considered true engine performance-related systems, some controlled devices may affect driveability if they malfunction.***

## A/C SIGNAL

This signal is sent from A/C amplifier to ECM terminal A2 (Samurai and Sidekick), A18 (Swift DOHC) or A10 (Swift SOHC). ECM uses this signal to detect when A/C is operating and sends a signal to Idle Speed Control (ISC) solenoid to increase idle speed.

## TRANSMISSION CONTROL

**Lock-Up Solenoid (Sidekick A/T) –** When ECM senses conditions are correct for energizing lock-up solenoid in automatic transmission, ECM will energize lock-up relay. Relay, in turn, energizes lock-up solenoid. When energized, the lock-up solenoid provides a feedback signal to ECM, indicating lock-up signal has been received. This is not a true indication that physical lock-up has occurred.

**Lock-Up Solenoid Relay (Sidekick A/T) –** Battery voltage is supplied to lock-up relay Light Green/Red wire from control relay terminal "E". Battery voltage is supplied to lock-up relay White/Red wire through the stoplight switch. Voltage through stoplight switch should drop to zero volts when the brake pedal is depressed. When ECM senses conditions are correct for energizing lock-up solenoid in automatic transmission, ECM will energize lock-up relay by providing a ground on ECM terminal A11. Relay, in turn, energizes lock-up solenoid. When energized, the lock-up solenoid will provide a feedback signal to the ECM, indicating lock-up signal has been received.

**Throttle Valve Output Signal (Swift DOHC A/T) –** Engine ECM converts throttle valve input signals into simple on and off signals which it transmits to the automatic transmission ECM. When gear selector is in "D" or "2", automatic transmission ECM uses these signals to determine proper gear selection. When gear selector is in D, transmission will select and shift transmission into 1st, 2nd or 3rd gear. When gear selector is in "2" position, ECM will select and shift between 1st or 2nd gear.

# 1991 ENGINE PERFORMANCE
# Basic Diagnostic Procedures

## Samurai, Sidekick, Swift

## INTRODUCTION

The following diagnostic steps will help prevent overlooking a simple problem. This is also where to begin diagnosis for a no-start condition.

The first step in diagnosing any driveability problem is verifying the customer's complaint with a test drive under the conditions the problem reportedly occurred.

Before entering self-diagnostics, perform a careful and complete visual inspection. Most engine control problems result from mechanical breakdowns, poor electrical connections or damaged/misrouted vacuum hoses. Before condemning the computerized system, perform each test listed in this article.

***NOTE: Perform all voltage tests with a Digital Volt-Ohmmeter (DVOM) with a minimum 10-megohm Input Impedance, unless stated otherwise in test procedure.***

## PRELIMINARY INSPECTION & ADJUSTMENTS

### VISUAL INSPECTION

Visually inspect all electrical wiring, looking for chafed, stretched, cut or pinched wiring. Ensure electrical connectors fit tightly and are not corroded. Ensure vacuum hoses are properly routed and not pinched or cut. See VACUUM DIAGRAMS article to verify routing and connections (if necessary). Inspect air induction system for vacuum leaks.

### MECHANICAL INSPECTION

**Compression -** Check engine mechanical condition with a compression gauge, vacuum gauge, or an engine analyzer. See engine analyzer instruction manual for specific instructions.

***WARNING: DO NOT use ignition switch during compression tests on fuel injected vehicles. Use a remote starter to crank engine. Fuel injectors on many models are triggered by ignition switch during cranking mode, which can create a fire hazard or contaminate the engine's oiling system.***

***COMPRESSION SPECIFICATIONS***

| Application | Specification |
|---|---|
| **Compression Ratio** | |
| Samurai | 9.5:1 |
| Sidekick | 8.9:1 |
| Swift | |
| DOHC | 10.0:1 |
| SOHC | 9.5:1 |
| **Compression Pressure** | |
| Samurai & Sidekick | |
| Standard | 199 psi (14.0 kg/cm²) |
| Limit | [1] 170 psi (11.9 kg/cm²) |
| Swift | |
| DOHC | |
| Standard | 206 psi (14.5 kg/cm²) |
| Limit | [1] 156 psi (10.9 kg/cm²) |
| SOHC | |
| Standard | 199 psi (14.0 kg/cm²) |
| Limit | [1] 156 psi (10.9 kg/cm²) |

[1] - Maximum variation between cylinders is 14.2 psi (.9 kg/cm²).

**Exhaust System Backpressure - 1)** Check exhaust system with vacuum gauge or pressure gauge. Remove $O_2$ sensor or air injection check valve (if equipped). Connect a 1-10 psi pressure gauge and run engine at 2500 RPM. If exhaust system backpressure is greater than 1 3/4-2 psi (.12-.14 kg/cm²), exhaust system or catalytic converter is plugged.

**2)** If a vacuum gauge is used, connect vacuum gauge hose to intake manifold vacuum port and start engine. Observe vacuum gauge. Open throttle part way and hold steady. If vacuum gauge reading slowly drops after stabilizing, exhaust system should be checked for a restriction.

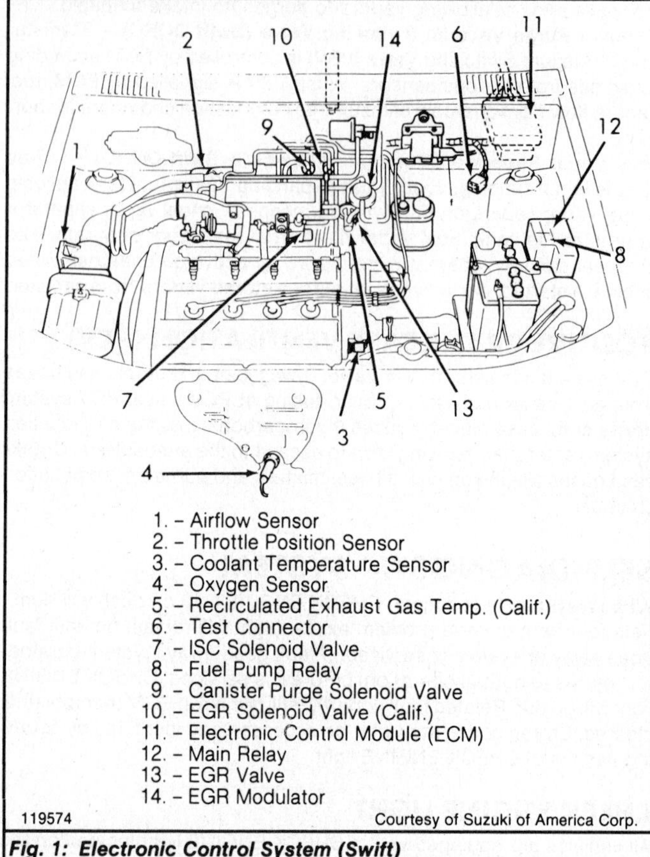


***Fig. 1: Electronic Control System (Swift)***

## FUEL SYSTEM

***WARNING: ALWAYS relieve fuel pressure before disconnecting any fuel injection-related component. DO NOT allow fuel to contact engine or electrical components.***

### FUEL SYSTEM PRESSURE RELEASE

**Samurai - 1)** Place transmission in Neutral or Park and set parking brake. Loosen fuel tank filler cap to relieve tank vapor pressure. Remove harness connector from fuel pump relay which is located under extreme right side of dash, mounted at the top front of ECM. See FUEL PUMP RELAY LOCATION table.

**2)** Start engine and let idle until engine dies. Crank engine 2-3 times to ensure fuel pressure is dissipated from system. Turn ignition off and remove key. Fuel system may now be opened safely. When loosening fuel line, hose or fitting, cover with shop towel to absorb leaking fuel. When repair is completed, reconnect relay.

***FUEL PUMP RELAY LOCATION***

| Model | Location |
|---|---|
| Samurai | Under Far Right Side Dash, Above ECM |
| Sidekick | Under Far Left Side Dash, Left of ECM |
| Swift | In Engine Fuse/Relay Box, Behind battery |

**Sidekick - 1)** Place transmission in Neutral or Park and set parking brake. Disconnect 4-wire connector from fuel pump control relay located under left side of dash, to left of ECM. See FUEL PUMP RELAY LOCATION table. *See Fig. 2.*

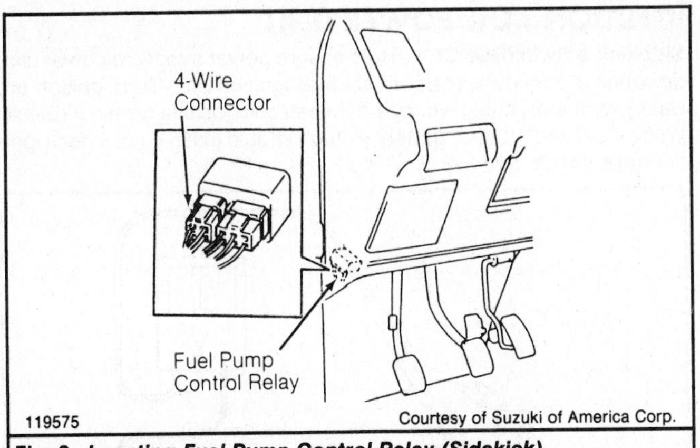


*Fig. 2: Locating Fuel Pump Control Relay (Sidekick)*

**2)** Loosen fuel tank filler cap to release tank vapor pressure. Start engine and let idle until engine dies. Crank engine 2-3 more times to ensure fuel pressure is dissipated from system. Turn ignition off and remove key. Fuel system may now be opened safely. When loosening fuel line, hose or fitting, cover with shop towel to absorb leaking fuel. When repair is completed, reconnect relay.

**Swift - 1)** Place transmission in Neutral or Park and set parking brake. Remove fuse/relay box cover located in engine compartment, behind battery. Remove coolant reservoir from bracket.

**2)** Disengage harness connector from fuel pump relay from underneath fuse/relay box. See FUEL PUMP RELAY LOCATION table. *See Fig. 4*. Loosen fuel tank filler cap to release tank vapor pressure. Start engine and let idle until engine dies. Crank engine 2-3 more times to ensure fuel pressure is dissipated from system. Fuel system may now be opened safely. Cover fuel line, hose or fitting with shop towel to absorb leaking fuel when loosening. When repair is completed, reconnect relay.

## FUEL SYSTEM PRESSURE

**Fuel Pressure Test (Samurai & Sidekick) - 1)** Start engine and warm to normal operating temperature. Release fuel system pressure. See FUEL SYSTEM PRESSURE RELEASE under FUEL SYSTEM. Attach Pressure Gauge Set (09912-58412) at fuel filter inlet union. *See Fig. 3*. Start engine and ensure there is no leakage at pressure gauge connection, turn engine off.

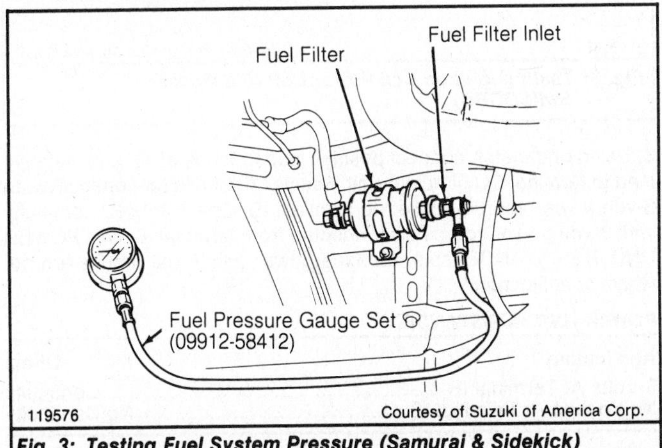


*Fig. 3: Testing Fuel System Pressure (Samurai & Sidekick)*

**2)** To operate fuel pump with engine off, wire Pink/Black and Black/White fuel pump relay wires together. See FUEL PUMP RELAY LOCATION table. Turn ignition on. Measure and record fuel pressure with pump operating and engine off. Turn ignition off, and allow one minute for fuel pressure to reduce. Measure and record minimum (rest) fuel pressure. See FUEL PUMP PERFORMANCE table.

**3)** Remove jumper wire from fuel pump relay and start engine. Measure and record fuel pressure with pump operating and engine running at idle. Turn ignition off, and allow one minute for fuel pressure to reduce. Measure and record minimum (rest) fuel pressure. See REGULATED FUEL PRESSURE table.

**4)** If pressures are not within specification, check for defective fuel pump, pressure regulator or restriction in fuel system. Repair as required. Remove fuel pressure gauge and start engine to ensure that no fuel leakage exists.

**Fuel Pressure Test (Swift) - 1)** Release fuel system pressure. See FUEL SYSTEM PRESSURE RELEASE under FUEL SYSTEM. Verify battery voltage is at least 11 volts.

**2)** On DOHC models, remove ISC solenoid valve and EGR modulator bracket (if equipped). *See Fig. 1*

**3)** Separate fuel feed hose from fuel delivery pipe near fuel rail. Install fuel pressure gauge and 3-way connector between fuel feed hose and fuel return hose. *See Fig. 4*.

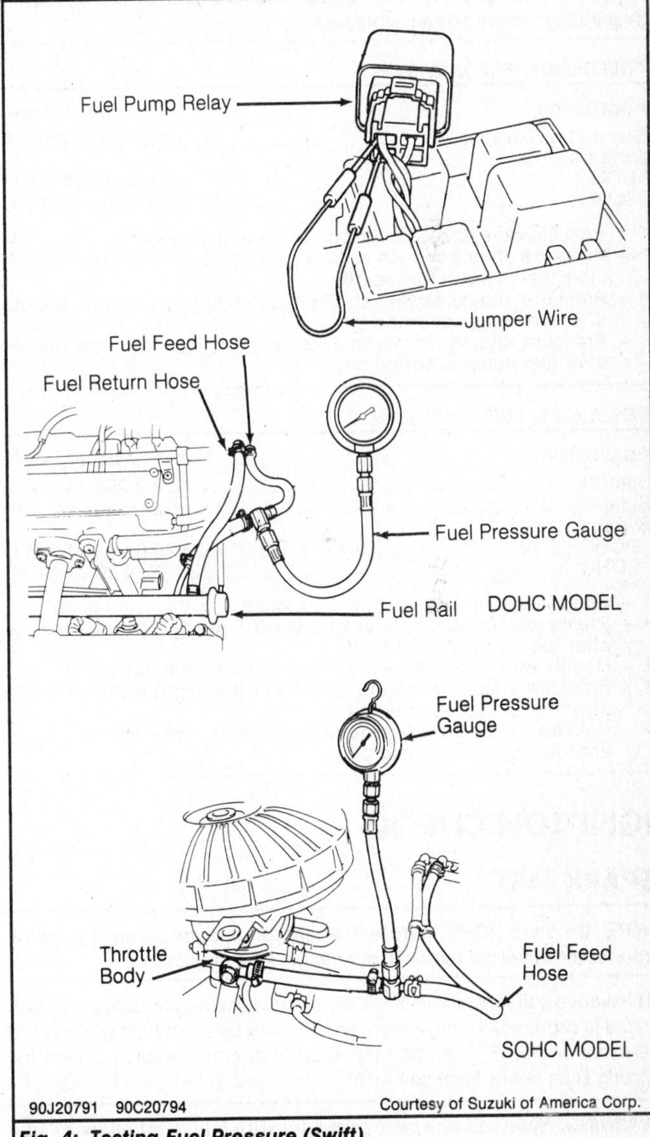


*Fig. 4: Testing Fuel Pressure (Swift)*

**4)** On SOHC models, remove air cleaner. Disconnect fuel feed hose from throttle body. Install fuel pressure gauge and 3-way connector between fuel feed hose and throttle body. Install air cleaner.

**5)** To jumper fuel pump relay on all models, remove fuel pump relay from fuse/relay box with harness connector installed. Fuse relay box is located in engine compartment, behind battery. Using jumper wire, connect Pink wire terminal to White/Blue wire terminal.

# 1991 ENGINE PERFORMANCE
# Basic Diagnostic Procedures (Cont.)

**6)** Turn ignition on. Fuel pressure should be within specification. See FUEL PUMP PERFORMANCE table. Turn ignition off and recheck pressure after one minute. Fuel pressure should be within specification.

**7)** Remove jumper wire. Install ISC solenoid valve on DOHC models. On all models, start engine and warm to normal operating temperature. Note fuel pressure with engine idling. Fuel pressure should be within specification.

**8)** If pressure is not within specification, check for defective fuel pump, pressure regulator or restriction in fuel system. Repair as required. Release fuel pressure and remove fuel pressure gauge. Reconnect fuel hoses and check for leaks.

**Fuel Pump Circuit** – Turn ignition on; leave engine off. Fuel pump should operate for 2 seconds. If fuel pump does not operate, check fuses, fuel pump control relay, fuel pump, all electrical connections and ECM. See SYSTEM & COMPONENT TESTING article.

***NOTE: Fuel pump performance is a measurement of fuel pressure availability, not regulated pressure.***

***FUEL PUMP PERFORMANCE***

| Application | [1] psi (kg/cm²) |
|---|---|
| Samurai & Sidekick | [2] 34.1-39.8 (2.4-2.8) |
| Swift | |
| DOHC | [3] 35.5-38.4 (2.5-2.7) |
| SOHC | [4] 22.7-29.9 (1.6-2.1) |

[1] – Specification listed is with ignition on and engine off.
[2] – Pressure should remain at 21.3 psi (1.5 kg/cm²) for one minute after fuel pump is turned off.
[3] – Pressure should remain at 25.6 psi (1.8 kg/cm²) for one minute after fuel pump is turned off.
[4] – Pressure should remain at 12.8 psi (.9 kg/cm²) for one minute after fuel pump is turned off.

***REGULATED FUEL PRESSURE***

| Application | [1] psi (kg/cm²) |
|---|---|
| Samurai | [2] 24.2-29.9 (1.7-2.1) |
| Sidekick | [2] [3] |
| Swift | |
| DOHC | [4] 25.6-29.9 (1.8-2.1) |
| SOHC | [5] 12.8-20.0 (.9-1.4) |

[1] – Specification is listed with engine idling.
[2] – Pressure should remain at 21.3 psi (1.5 kg/cm²) for one minute after fuel pump is turned off.
[3] – Regulated fuel pressure not available from manufacturer.
[4] – Pressure should remain at 25.6 psi (1.8 kg/cm²) for one minute after fuel pump is turned off.
[5] – Pressure should remain at 12.8 psi (.9 kg/cm²) for one minute after fuel pump is turned off.

## IGNITION CHECKS

### SPARK TEST

***NOTE: On Swift DOHC, before cranking engine, disconnect injector connector at wiring harness near engine oil dipstick.***

**1)** Remove coil wire from distributor cap. Have a helper depress clutch pedal (if required). Using a high output spark tester or holding coil wire terminal end 5/16" from an engine ground, crank engine. Check for strong Blue spark from coil wire.

***WARNING: Hold coil or spark plug wire with insulated pliers or use high output spark tester to prevent electrical shock.***

**2)** If spark does not exist, continue with ignition checks. If spark exists at coil wire, check for spark from each spark plug wire. If spark exists on one or more plug wires, check plug wire resistance. Using ohmmeter, ensure resistance of each plug wire is 3000-6700 ohms per 12" (10,000-22,000 ohms per meter). Replace any plug wire that does not test as specified.

### IGNITION COIL POWER UNIT

**Sidekick & Swift (DOHC)** – **1)** To ensure power supply to power unit, disconnect primary wires connector at ignition coil. Turn ignition on. Using voltmeter, check voltage between coil positive terminal (Black/White wire) and ground. Battery voltage should exist. If not, check ignition fuse circuit. *See Fig. 5.*

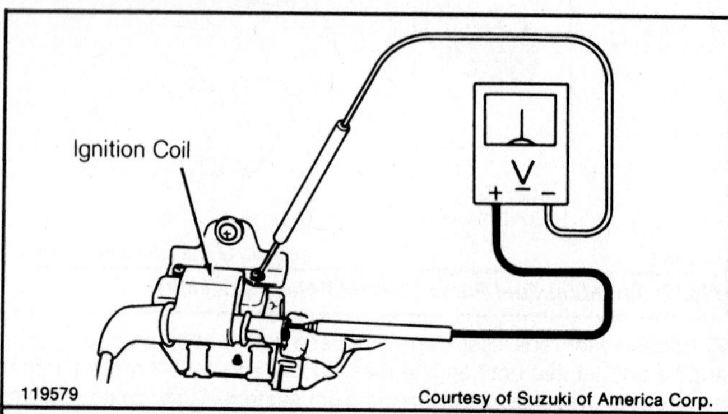


***Fig. 5: Testing Ignition Coil Power Supply (Sidekick & Swift DOHC)***

**2)** To check power unit resistance, turn ignition off. Remove power unit from under ignition coil. Tape together two 1.5-volt batteries in series to create a 3-volt power source. Install leads to 3-volt power source. Apply negative lead to "G" terminal and positive lead to terminal IB of power unit. *See Fig. 6.*

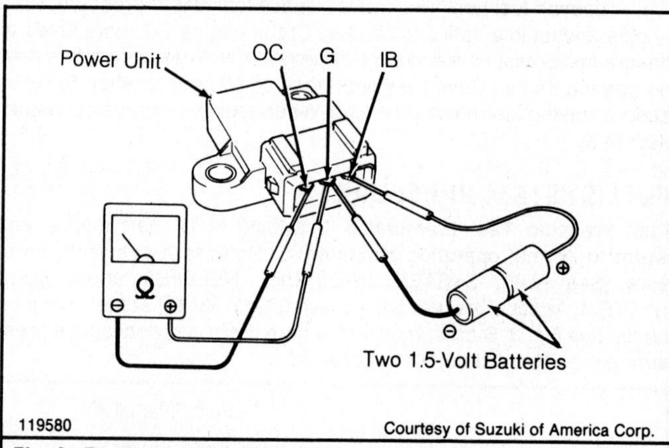


***Fig. 6: Testing Ignition Coil Power Unit (Sidekick & Swift DOHC)***

**3)** Using ohmmeter, connect positive lead to terminal "G" and negative lead to terminal OC of power unit. *See Fig. 6.* Check for continuity with 3-volt power source applied to terminal IB. Check for NO continuity with 3-volt power source disconnected from terminal IB. See POWER UNIT RESISTANCE table. Replace power unit if test results are not within specification.

***POWER UNIT RESISTANCE***

| Application | Ohms |
|---|---|
| 3-Volts At Terminal IB | Continuity |
| No Voltage At Terminal IB | No Continuity |

### IGNITION COIL RESISTANCE

**Samurai** – Disconnect secondary cable/wire from coil. Remove primary wire connector from ignition coil. Using ohmmeter, check coil resistances between primary terminals and secondary terminal of coil. *See Fig. 7.* See IGNITION COIL RESISTANCE table. Replace coil if readings are not within specifications.

# 1991 ENGINE PERFORMANCE
# Basic Diagnostic Procedures (Cont.)

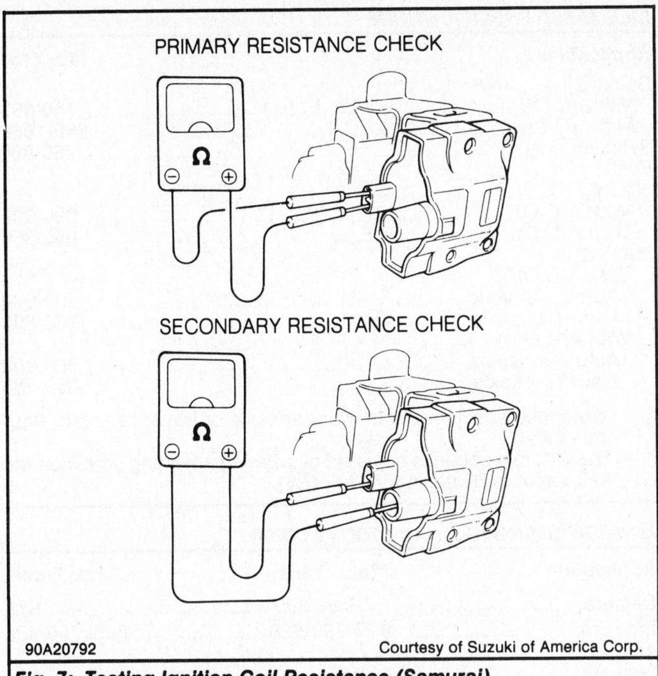


***Fig. 7: Testing Ignition Coil Resistance (Samurai)***

**Sidekick - 1)** Disconnect secondary cable/wire from coil. Remove primary leads from ignition coil. Using ohmmeter, check resistance between primary terminals of coil. See IGNITION COIL RESISTANCE table.

***IGNITION COIL RESISTANCE - Ohms @ 68°F (20°C)***

| Application | Primary | Secondary |
|---|---|---|
| Samurai | .90-1.10 | 10,200-13,800 |
| Sidekick | .72-.88 | 10,200-14,000 |
| Swift | | |
| DOHC | .72-.88 | 10,200-14,000 |
| SOHC | 1.12-1.38 | 11,400-15,600 |

**2)** Check secondary resistance between coil secondary terminal and primary positive terminal. Replace coil if readings are not within specifications.

**Swift -** Remove secondary coil wire and primary wire connector from coil. Using ohmmeter, check coil resistances using primary and secondary terminals. *See Fig. 8.* Replace coil if not within specification. See IGNITION COIL RESISTANCE table.

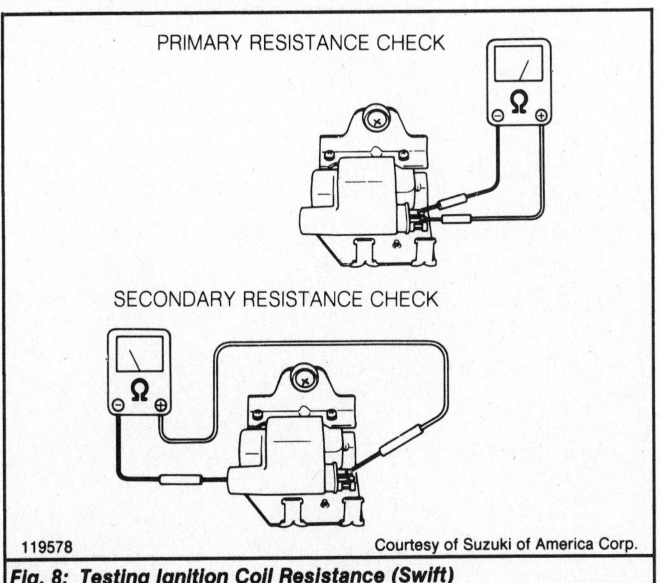


***Fig. 8: Testing Ignition Coil Resistance (Swift)***

## NOISE SUPPRESSOR

Disconnect harness connector from noise suppressor, located near ignitor/coil assembly. Using ohmmeter, ensure there is no continuity between terminals "A" and "B". Ensure there is approximately 2200 ohms resistance between terminals "B" and "C". If either test results are not within specification, replace noise suppressor. *See Fig. 9.*

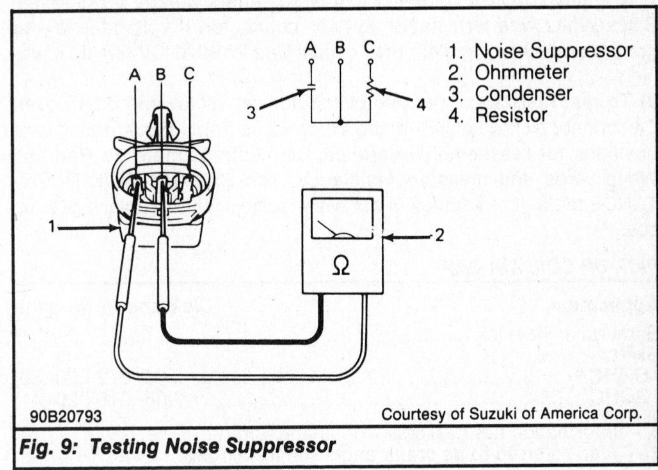


***Fig. 9: Testing Noise Suppressor***

## PICK-UP COIL

***NOTE: Samurai, Sidekick and Swift DOHC utilize an integral crank angle sensor within pick-up coil.***

**Samurai & Sidekick - 1)** With ignition off, disconnect Yellow ECM connector. Using voltmeter, backprobe positive lead to terminal B1 of ECM Green connector (still connected to ECM). Backprobe negative lead to terminal A13 of disconnected Yellow ECM connector.

**2)** Remove distributor cap, rotor, and shield cover. Check voltmeter reading when reluctor "window" is between magnet and Hall Effect pick-up coil. Voltmeter reading should be zero volts.

**3)** Turn reluctor so that window is not between magnet and Hall Effect pick-up coil, thus breaking magnetic field. Voltmeter reading should be battery voltage.

**4)** If results are not as indicated, inspect wiring and connections and repair as required. If wiring is okay, replace Hall Effect pick-up coil (crank angle sensor).

**Swift DOHC - 1)** Disconnect pick-up coil connector at distributor. Using ohmmeter, measure resistance between 2 upper terminals. *See Fig. 10.* See PICK-UP COIL RESISTANCE table. Replace pick-up coil if resistance is not within specification. If resistance is within specification, go to next step.

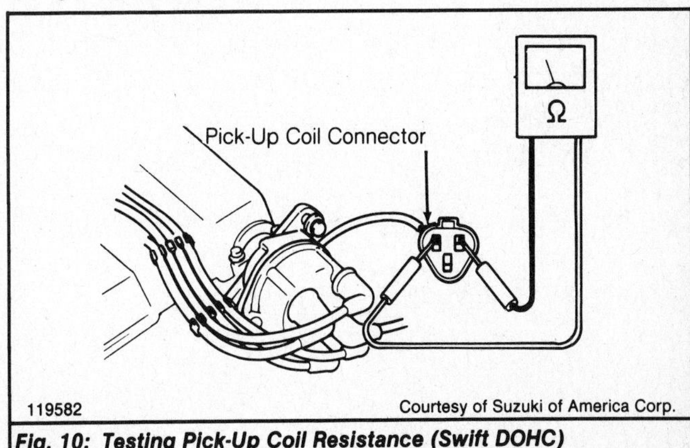


***Fig. 10: Testing Pick-Up Coil Resistance (Swift DOHC)***

**2)** Ensure pick-up coil has battery voltage. Disconnect pick-up coil connector at distributor. With ignition on and using voltmeter, ensure there is battery voltage at Brown/White wire terminal of connector. If voltage is not present, check wiring and connections to ECM and

# 1991 ENGINE PERFORMANCE
# Basic Diagnostic Procedures (Cont.)

check ECM power supply. Repair as required. Ensure ignition coil has power, see IGNITION COIL POWER UNIT under IGNITION CHECKS.
**3)** If ignition coil and pick-up coil test okay, recheck for spark. If spark is still not available, go to SELF-DIAGNOSTICS article to retrieve stored codes.
**Swift SOHC - 1)** Disconnect pick-up coil connector at distributor. With ignition on, use voltmeter to ensure battery voltage is present at Black/White wire terminal of harness connector. If voltage is low or not present, check ignition fuse circuit. See WIRING DIAGRAMS article.
**2)** To test resistance, remove distributor cap, rotor and dust cover. Disconnect pick-up coil Red and White wires from ignitor, noting wire positions for reassembly reference. Connect ohmmeter to Red and White wires and measure resistance. See PICK-UP COIL RESISTANCE table. If resistance is not within specification, replace pick up coil.

***PICK-UP COIL AIR GAP***

| Application | Clearance - In. (mm) |
|---|---|
| Samurai & Sidekick | [1] |
| Swift | |
| DOHC [2] | .008-.012 (.20-.30) |
| SOHC | .008-.016 (.20-.41) |

[1] - Information not available from manufacturer.
[2] - Also referred to as crank angle sensor air gap.

***PICK-UP COIL RESISTANCE - Ohms @ 68°F (20°C)***

| Application | Ohms |
|---|---|
| Samurai & Sidekick | [1] |
| Swift | |
| DOHC [2] | 588-882 |
| SOHC | 130-190 |

[1] - Information not available from manufacturer.
[2] - Also referred to as crank angle sensor.

## IDLE SPEED & IGNITION TIMING

Ensure idle speed and base ignition timing are set to specification. If necessary, see ON-VEHICLE ADJUSTMENTS article.

***IDLE SPEED SPECIFICATIONS*** [1]

| Application | Idle RPM |
|---|---|
| Samurai | |
| With A/C Off | 750-850 |
| With A/C On | [2] 950-1050 |
| Sidekick | 750-850 |
| Swift | |
| DOHC | |
| With A/C Off | 800-900 |
| With A/C On | [2] 850-950 |
| SOHC | |
| With A/C Off | |
| Auto. Transaxle | 800-900 |
| Man. Transaxle | 700-800 |
| With A/C On | |
| Auto. Transaxle | [2] 800-900 |
| Man. Transaxle | [2] 850-950 |

[1] - Idle speed specification is with transaxle or transmission in Neutral or Park.
[2] - The A/C idle speed is adjusted by rotating adjusting screw on the A/C Vacuum Switching Valve (VSV).

***IGNITION TIMING (Degrees BTDC @ RPM)***

| Application | Man. Trans. | Auto. Trans. |
|---|---|---|
| Samurai | [1] 7-9 @ 800 | N/A |
| Sidekick | 8 @ 750-850 | 8 @ 750-850 |
| Swift | | |
| DOHC | [2] 5-7 @ 800-900 | [2] 5-7 @ 800-900 |
| SOHC | [3] 5-7 @ 600-700 | [3] 5-7 @ 700-800 |

[1] - Specification is listed with jumper wire installed between terminals "C" and "D" (Black/Green and Blue wires) of test connector, located near the battery.
[2] - Specification is listed with jumper wire installed between terminals "C" and "D" (Black and Violet/Green wires) of test connector, located near ignition coil.
[3] - Specification is listed with vacuum hose disconnected from distributor. With hose connected, timing should be 11-13 degrees BTDC.

## SUMMARY

If no faults were found while performing BASIC DIAGNOSTIC PROCEDURES, proceed to SELF-DIAGNOSTICS article. If no hard codes are found in self-diagnostics, or vehicle does not have a self-diagnostic system, proceed to TROUBLE SHOOTING - NO CODES article for diagnosis by symptom (i.e., ROUGH IDLE, NO START, etc.) or intermittent diagnostic procedures.

# 1991 ENGINE PERFORMANCE
# Self-Diagnostics

## Samurai, Sidekick, Swift

## INTRODUCTION

If no faults were found while performing BASIC DIAGNOSTIC PROCEDURES, proceed with self-diagnostics. If no fault codes or only pass codes are present after entering self-diagnostics, proceed to TROUBLE SHOOTING - NO CODES article for diagnosis by symptom (i.e., ROUGH IDLE, NO START, etc.).

## SELF-DIAGNOSTIC SYSTEM

***SELF-DIAGNOSTICS DIRECTORY***



**Hard Failures** - Hard failures cause CHECK ENGINE light to illuminate and remain on until problem is repaired. If light comes on and remains on (light may flash) during vehicle operation, cause of malfunction must be determined using diagnostic (code) charts. If a sensor fails, Electronic Control Module (ECM) will use a substitute value in its calculations to continue engine operation. In this condition, commonly known as limp-in mode, the vehicle runs but driveability will not be optimum.

**Intermittent Failures** - Intermittent failures may cause CHECK ENGINE light to flicker or illuminate and go out after the intermittent fault goes away. However, the corresponding trouble code will be retained in Electronic Control Module (ECM) memory. If related fault does not reoccur within a certain time frame, related trouble code will be erased from ECM memory. Intermittent failures may be caused by sensor, connector or wiring related problems. See INTERMITTENTS in TROUBLE SHOOTING - NO CODES article.

## CHECK ENGINE LIGHT RESET PROCEDURE

**Samurai & Sidekick (Federal Models)** - CHECK ENGINE light will automatically flash at 50,000, 80,000 and 100,000 mile intervals, indicating system inspection and/or system component replacement is required. After necessary services have been performed, turn off CHECK ENGINE light by moving cancel switch to opposite position. Cancel switch is located below steering column lower trim panel.

- At 50,000 Miles - Replace PCV valve and inspect EGR system.
- At 80,000 Miles - Replace $O_2$ sensor.
- At 100,000 Miles - Replace PCV valve, $O_2$ sensor and charcoal canister. Inspect catalytic converter for plugging, EGR system, ECM and related sensors.

## RETRIEVING CODES

**1)** CHECK ENGINE light will come on when ignition is on and engine is not running. When engine is started, CHECK ENGINE light should go off. If light remains on while engine is running, a trouble code is present.

**2)** If light does not come on with key on and engine off, check CHECK ENGINE light circuit before continuing. See appropriate INITIAL DIAGNOSTIC PROCEDURE chart at beginning of code charts for each model. See SELF-DIAGNOSTICS DIRECTORY.

**3)** To retrieve codes, turn ignition off. Install fuse in diagnostic terminal on fuse block, located behind left side of instrument panel. *See Fig. 1.* Turn ignition on and count flashes of CHECK ENGINE light.

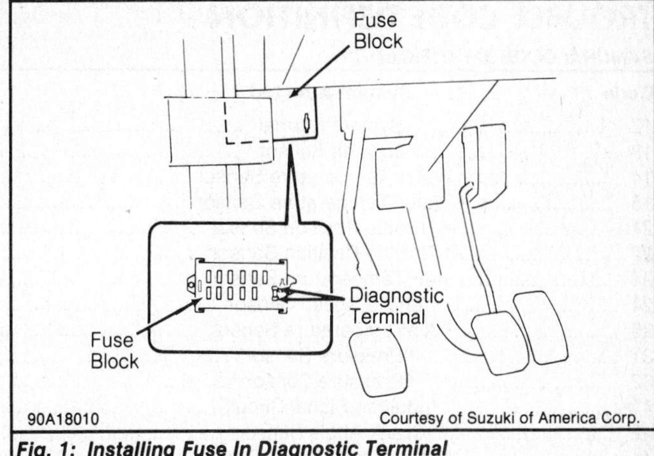


***Fig. 1: Installing Fuse In Diagnostic Terminal***

**4)** For example, a Code 21 would be identified by a flash, flash, pause and flash. After a long pause, Code 21 would be repeated twice more. *See Fig. 2.* Each individual code is repeated 3 times, and then next code is displayed.

**5)** If system is operating properly (with no codes), a Code 12 should exist with ignition on and engine off. This indicates diagnostic system is capable of storing codes.

**6)** Once all codes are displayed, codes will be repeated. Remove fuse from diagnostic terminal in fuse block after stored codes are recorded.

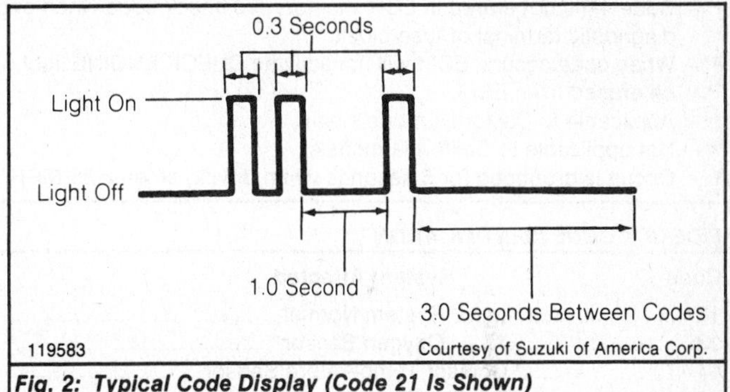


***Fig. 2: Typical Code Display (Code 21 Is Shown)***

## CLEARING CODES

***CAUTION: Ensure ignition is off when disconnecting or reconnecting power supply for ECM.***

After repairs are performed, clear ECM memory of all stored trouble codes. To clear memory, turn ignition off. Disconnect negative battery cable for at least 20 seconds (Samurai and Sidekick), 30 seconds (Swift DOHC) or 60 seconds (Swift SOHC).

## ECM LOCATION

***ECM LOCATION***

| Model | Location |
|---|---|
| Samurai | Near Glove Box |
| Sidekick & Swift | Upper Left Corner of Instrument Panel |

## SUMMARY

If no hard fault codes (or only pass codes) are present, driveability symptoms exist or intermittent codes exist, proceed to TROUBLE SHOOTING - NO CODES article for diagnosis by symptom (i.e., ROUGH IDLE, NO START, etc.) or intermittent diagnostic procedures.

# 1991 ENGINE PERFORMANCE
# Self-Diagnostics (Cont.)

## TROUBLE CODE DEFINITION

### SAMURAI CODE IDENTIFICATION

| Code | System Affected | Probable Cause |
|---|---|---|
| 12 | System Normal | System Normal |
| 13 | Oxygen Sensor | Sensor or Circuit, ECM |
| 14 | [1] Water Temperature Sensor | Sensor or Circuit, ECM |
| 15 | [2] Water Temperature Sensor | Sensor or Circuit, ECM |
| 21 | [3] Throttle Position Sensor | Sensor or Circuit, ECM |
| 22 | [4] Throttle Position Sensor | Sensor or Circuit, ECM |
| 23 | [1] Air Temperature Sensor | Sensor or Circuit, ECM |
| 24 | Vehicle Speed Sensor | Sensor or Circuit, ECM |
| 25 | [2] Air Temperature Sensor | Sensor or Circuit, ECM |
| 31 | [3] Pressure Sensor | Sensor or Circuit, ECM |
| 32 | [4] Pressure Sensor | Sensor or Circuit, ECM |
| 41 | [5] Ignition Signal Circuit | Ignition Coil, Ignitor, Wiring Circuit, ECM |
| 42 | Crank Angle Sensor | Sensor, Wiring, ECM |
| 44 | [6] Idle Switch Circuit Open | TPS, Wiring, ECM |
| 45 | [6] Idle Switch Circuit Shorted | TPS, Wiring, ECM |
| 51 | [1] EGR System | EGR, Wiring, ECM, Vacuum Switching Valve |
| 53 [7] | [6] ECM Ground Circuit Open | Wiring, ECM |
| 54 [8] | [6] Gear Position (5th Switch) | 5th Switch, Wiring, ECM |
| 71 [7] | [9] Test Switch Circuit | Wiring, ECM |

[1] – Low temperature is indicated.
[2] – High temperature is indicated.
[3] – High voltage is indicated.
[4] – Low voltage is indicated.
[5] – Code 41 is not stored in ECM memory. To check code when engine fails to start, crank engine, and then, with ignition still on, install fuse in diagnostic terminal of fuse block.
[6] – When code occurs, ECM will not activate CHECK ENGINE light while engine is running. When problem is fixed, memory of defective area will be erased from ECM.
[7] – Applicable to California models only.
[8] – Not applicable to California models.
[9] – Circuit is grounded for 5 seconds when driving at least 25 MPH.

### SIDEKICK CODE IDENTIFICATION

| Code | System Affected | Probable Cause |
|---|---|---|
| 12 | System Normal | System Normal |
| 13 | Oxygen Sensor | Sensor or Circuit, ECM |
| 14 | [1] Coolant Temperature Sensor | Sensor or Circuit, ECM |
| 15 | [2] Coolant Temperature Sensor | Sensor or Circuit, ECM |
| 21 | [3] Throttle Position Sensor | Sensor or Circuit, ECM |
| 22 | [4] Throttle Position Sensor | Sensor or Circuit, ECM |
| 23 | [1] Air Temperature Sensor | Sensor or Circuit, ECM |
| 24 | Vehicle Speed Sensor | Sensor or Circuit, ECM |
| 25 | [2] Air Temperature Sensor | Sensor or Circuit, ECM |
| 31 | [3] Pressure Sensor | Sensor or Circuit, ECM |
| 32 | [4] Pressure Sensor | Sensor or Circuit, ECM |
| 41 [5] | Ignition Signal Circuit | Ignition Coil, Ignitor, Wiring Circuit, ECM |
| 42 [6] | Crank Angle Sensor | Sensor, Wiring, ECM |
| 44 [6] | Idle Switch Circuit Open | TPS, Wiring, ECM |
| 45 | Idle Switch Circuit Shorted | TPS, Wiring, ECM |
| 51 [7] | EGR System | ECM, EGR, Modulator, Wiring, EGR Temperature Sensor, Vacuum Switching Valve |
| 53 [7] | ECM Ground Circuit | Wiring, ECM |

[1] – Low temperature is indicated.
[2] – High temperature is indicated.
[3] – High voltage is indicated.
[4] – Low voltage is indicated.
[5] – Code 41 is not stored in ECM memory. To check code when engine fails to start, crank engine, and then, with ignition still on, install fuse in diagnostic terminal of fuse block.
[6] – When code occurs, ECM will not activate CHECK ENGINE light while engine is running. When problem is fixed, memory of defective area will automatically be erased from ECM.
[7] – Applicable to California models only.

# 1991 ENGINE PERFORMANCE
# Self-Diagnostics (Cont.)

***SWIFT (DOHC) CODE IDENTIFICATION***

| Code | System Affected | Probable Cause |
|---|---|---|
| 12 | System Normal | System Normal |
| 13 | Oxygen Sensor | Sensor or Circuit, ECM |
| 14 | [1] Coolant Temperature Sensor | Sensor or Circuit, ECM |
| 15 | [2] Coolant Temperature Sensor | Sensor or Circuit, ECM |
| 21 | [3] Throttle Position Sensor | Sensor or Circuit, ECM |
| 22 | [4] Throttle Position Sensor | Sensor or Circuit, ECM |
| 24 | Speed Sensor | Sensor or Circuit, ECM |
| 33 | [3] Airflow Sensor | Sensor or Circuit, ECM |
| 34 | [4] Airflow Sensor | Sensor or Circuit, ECM |
| 41 [5] | Ignition Signal Circuit | Ignition System, ECM Noise Suppressor, Wiring Circuit, ECM |
| 42 | Crank Angle Sensor | Sensor or Circuit, ECM |
| 51 [6] | EGR System | ECM, EGR, Modulator, Wiring, EGR Temperature Sensor, Vacuum Switching Valve |
| 52 [6] | Fuel Injector | Fuel Injector, ECM |

[1] - Low temperature is indicated.
[2] - High temperature is indicated.
[3] - High voltage is indicated.
[4] - Low voltage is indicated.
[5] - Code 41 is not stored in ECM memory. To check code when engine fails to start, crank engine, and then, with ignition still on, install fuse in diagnostic terminal of fuse block.
[6] - Applicable to California models only.

***SWIFT (SOHC) CODE IDENTIFICATION***

| Code | System Affected | Probable Cause |
|---|---|---|
| 12 | System Normal | System Normal |
| 13 | Oxygen Sensor | Sensor or Circuit, ECM |
| 14 | [1] Water Temperature Sensor | Sensor or Circuit, ECM |
| 15 | [2] Water Temperature Sensor | Sensor or Circuit, ECM |
| 21 | Throttle Switch (M/T) | Switch or Circuit, ECM |
| 21 | [3] Throttle Position Sensor (A/T) | Sensor or Circuit, ECM |
| 22 | [4] Throttle Position Sensor (A/T) | Sensor or Circuit, ECM |
| 23 | [1] Air Temperature Sensor | Sensor or Circuit, ECM |
| 24 | Speed Sensor | Sensor or Circuit, ECM |
| 25 | [2] Air Temperature Sensor | Sensor or Circuit, ECM |
| 31 | [4] Pressure Sensor | Sensor or Circuit, ECM |
| 32 | [3] Pressure Sensor | Sensor or Circuit, ECM |
| 41 | Ignition Signal Circuit | Ignition System, ECM |
| 51 [5] | EGR System | ECM, EGR, Modulator, Wiring, EGR Temperature Sensor, Vacuum Switching Valve |

[1] - Low temperature is indicated.
[2] - High temperature is indicated.
[3] - High voltage is indicated.
[4] - Low voltage is indicated.
[5] - Applicable to California models only.

# 1991 ENGINE PERFORMANCE
# Self-Diagnostics (Cont.)

## CODE CHARTS

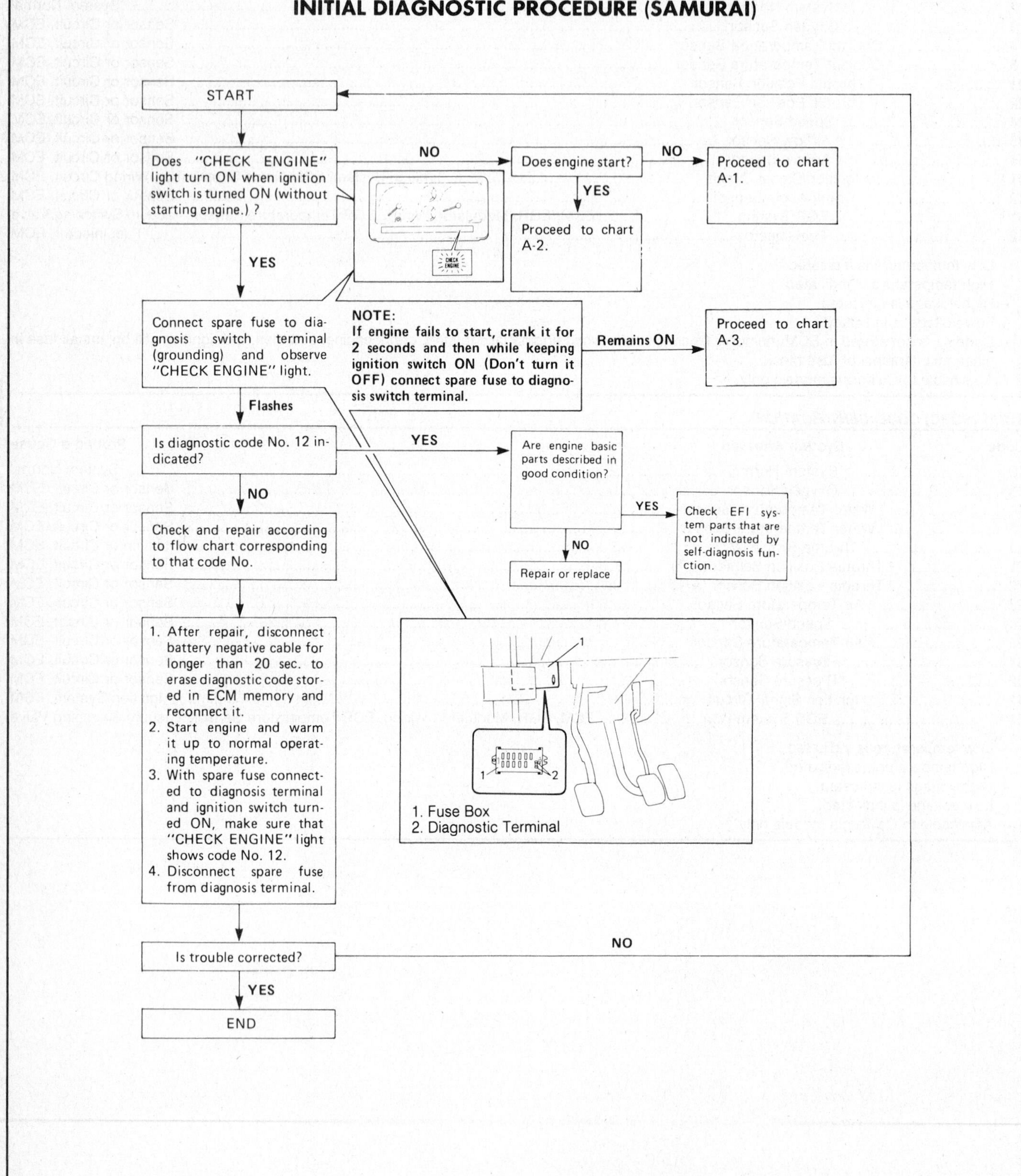
INITIAL DIAGNOSTIC PROCEDURE (SAMURAI)
START
Does "CHECK ENGINE" light turn ON when ignition switch is turned ON (without starting engine.) ?
NO
Does engine start?
NO
Proceed to chart A-1.
YES
Proceed to chart A-2.
YES
Connect spare fuse to diagnosis switch terminal (grounding) and observe "CHECK ENGINE" light.
NOTE:
If engine fails to start, crank it for 2 seconds and then while keeping ignition switch ON (Don't turn it OFF) connect spare fuse to diagnosis switch terminal.
Remains ON
Proceed to chart A-3.
Flashes
Is diagnostic code No. 12 indicated?
YES
Are engine basic parts described in good condition?
YES
Check EFI system parts that are not indicated by self-diagnosis function.
NO
Repair or replace
NO
Check and repair according to flow chart corresponding to that code No.
1. After repair, disconnect battery negative cable for longer than 20 sec. to erase diagnostic code stored in ECM memory and reconnect it.
2. Start engine and warm it up to normal operating temperature.
3. With spare fuse connected to diagnosis terminal and ignition switch turned ON, make sure that "CHECK ENGINE" light shows code No. 12.
4. Disconnect spare fuse from diagnosis terminal.
Is trouble corrected?
NO
YES
END
1. Fuse Box
2. Diagnostic Terminal

90B18011

Courtesy of Suzuki of America Corp.

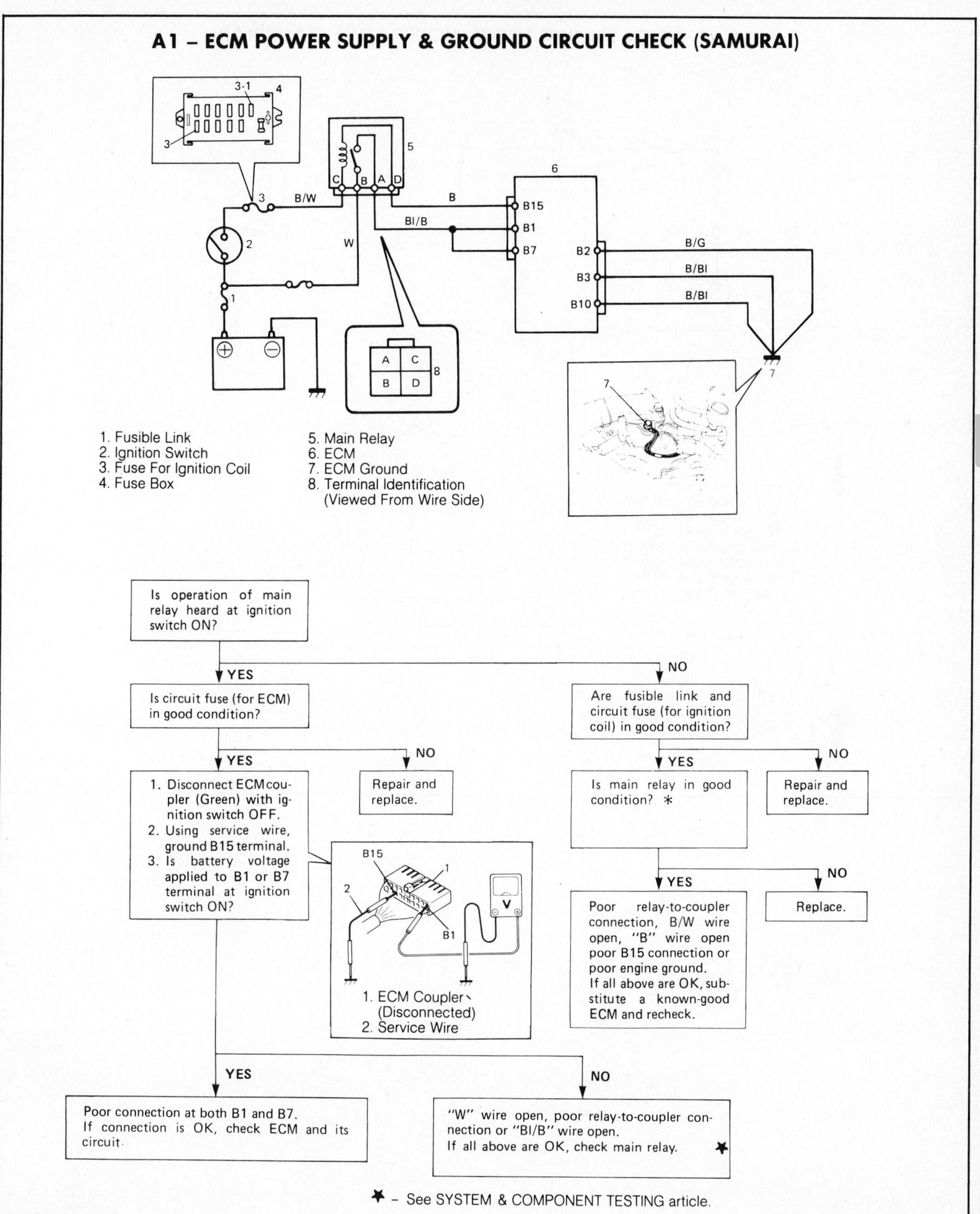

A1 – ECM POWER SUPPLY & GROUND CIRCUIT CHECK (SAMURAI)
3-1
4
3
5
6
B/W
B
Bl/B
W
B15
B1
B7
B2
B3
B10
B/G
B/Bl
B/Bl
A C
B D
7
8
1. Fusible Link
2. Ignition Switch
3. Fuse For Ignition Coil
4. Fuse Box
5. Main Relay
6. ECM
7. ECM Ground
8. Terminal Identification (Viewed From Wire Side)
Is operation of main relay heard at ignition switch ON?
YES
NO
Is circuit fuse (for ECM) in good condition?
Are fusible link and circuit fuse (for ignition coil) in good condition?
YES
NO
Repair and replace.
1. Disconnect ECM coupler (Green) with ignition switch OFF.
2. Using service wire, ground B15 terminal.
3. Is battery voltage applied to B1 or B7 terminal at ignition switch ON?
YES
NO
Is main relay in good condition? *
Repair and replace.
YES
NO
Poor relay-to-coupler connection, B/W wire open, "B" wire open poor B15 connection or poor engine ground.
If all above are OK, substitute a known-good ECM and recheck.
Replace.
B15
1
2
B1
V
1. ECM Coupler (Disconnected)
2. Service Wire
YES
NO
Poor connection at both B1 and B7.
If connection is OK, check ECM and its circuit.
"W" wire open, poor relay-to-coupler connection or "Bl/B" wire open.
If all above are OK, check main relay. *
* – See SYSTEM & COMPONENT TESTING article.
90C18012 90D18013
Courtesy of Suzuki of America Corp.

# 1991 ENGINE PERFORMANCE
## Self-Diagnostics (Cont.)

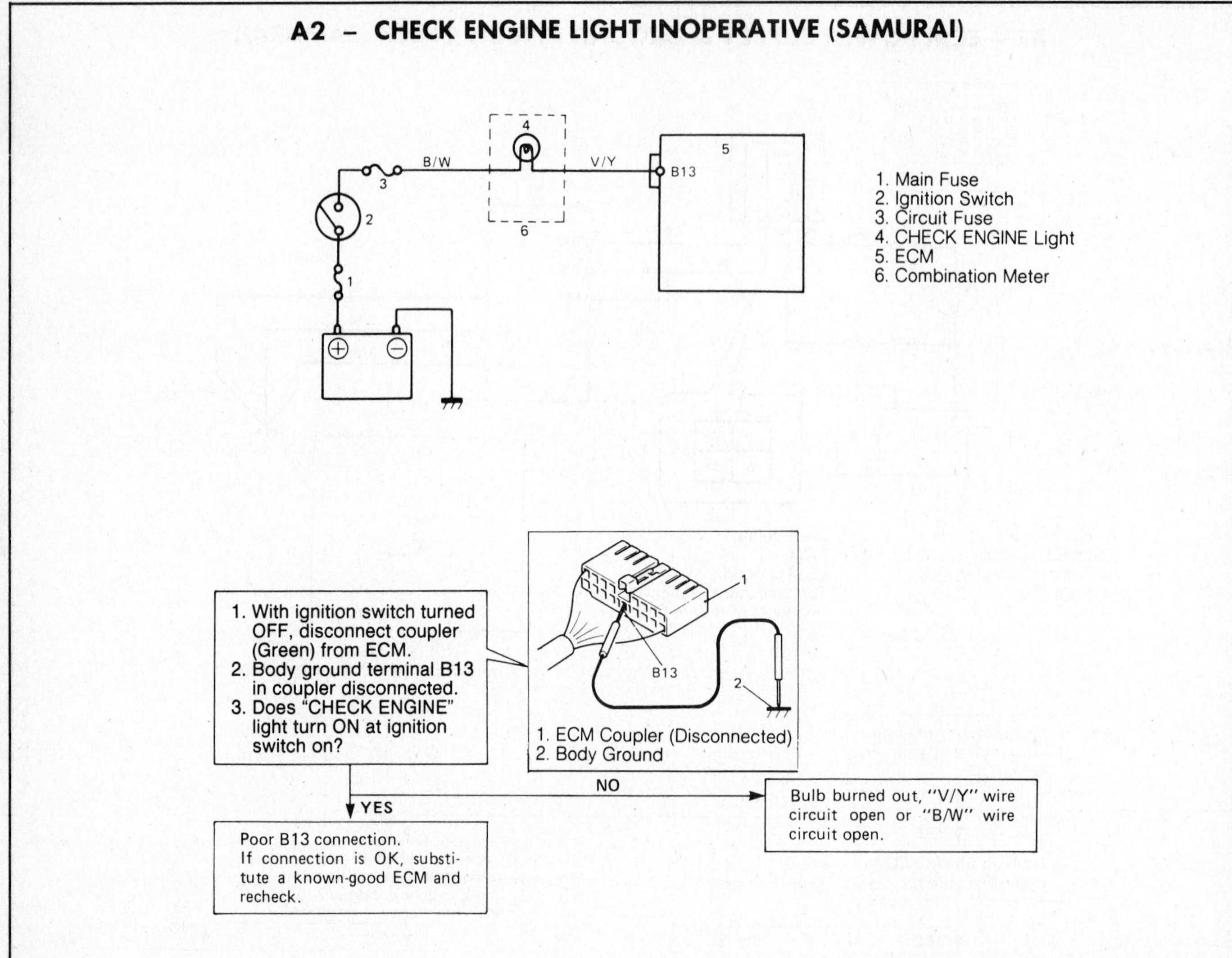
A2 – CHECK ENGINE LIGHT INOPERATIVE (SAMURAI)
B/W
V/Y
B13
1. Main Fuse
2. Ignition Switch
3. Circuit Fuse
4. CHECK ENGINE Light
5. ECM
6. Combination Meter
1. With ignition switch turned OFF, disconnect coupler (Green) from ECM.
2. Body ground terminal B13 in coupler disconnected.
3. Does "CHECK ENGINE" light turn ON at ignition switch on?
1. ECM Coupler (Disconnected)
2. Body Ground
NO
Bulb burned out, "V/Y" wire circuit open or "B/W" wire circuit open.
YES
Poor B13 connection. If connection is OK, substitute a known-good ECM and recheck.
90E18014
Courtesy of Suzuki of America Corp.

# 1991 ENGINE PERFORMANCE
## Self-Diagnostics (Cont.)

### A3 – CHECK ENGINE LIGHT STAYS ON – WON'T FLASH (SAMURAI)

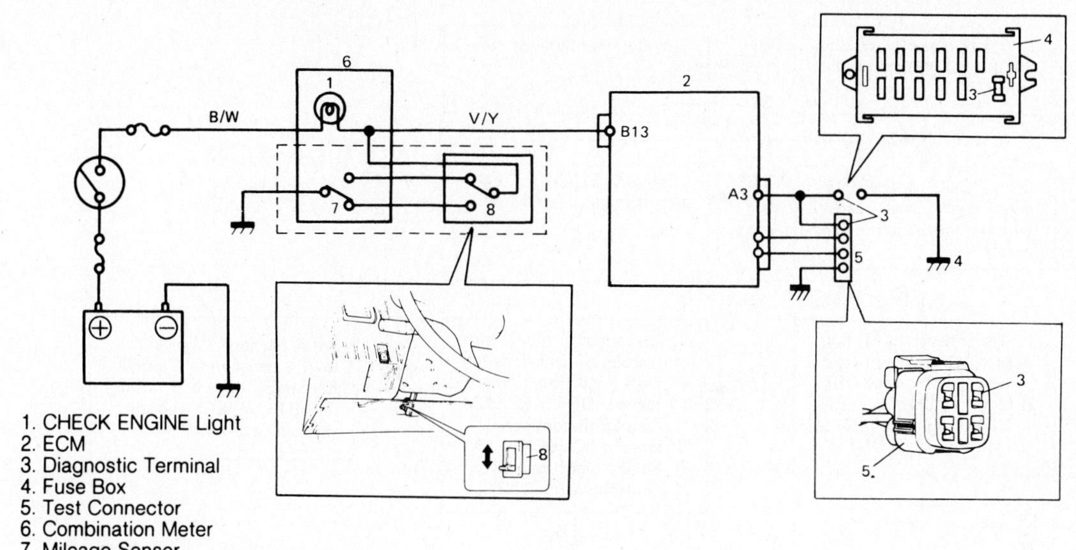


1. CHECK ENGINE Light
2. ECM
3. Diagnostic Terminal
4. Fuse Box
5. Test Connector
6. Combination Meter
7. Mileage Sensor
8. Cancel Switch (Federal Models Only)

**CALIFORNIA & CANADIAN MODELS**

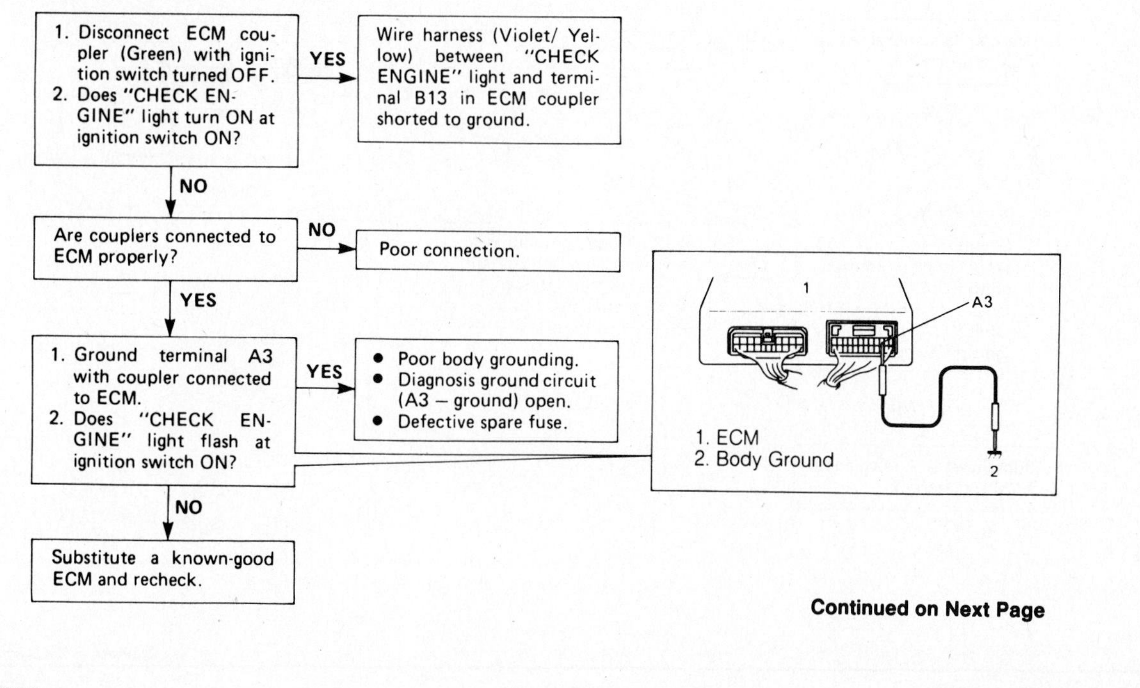

1. Disconnect ECM coupler (Green) with ignition switch turned OFF.
2. Does "CHECK ENGINE" light turn ON at ignition switch ON?

YES → Wire harness (Violet/ Yellow) between "CHECK ENGINE" light and terminal B13 in ECM coupler shorted to ground.

NO ↓

Are couplers connected to ECM properly?

NO → Poor connection.

YES ↓

1. Ground terminal A3 with coupler connected to ECM.
2. Does "CHECK ENGINE" light flash at ignition switch ON?

YES →
- Poor body grounding.
- Diagnosis ground circuit (A3 – ground) open.
- Defective spare fuse.

NO ↓

Substitute a known-good ECM and recheck.



1. ECM
2. Body Ground

**Continued on Next Page**

90F18015 90G18016

# 1991 ENGINE PERFORMANCE
## Self-Diagnostics (Cont.)

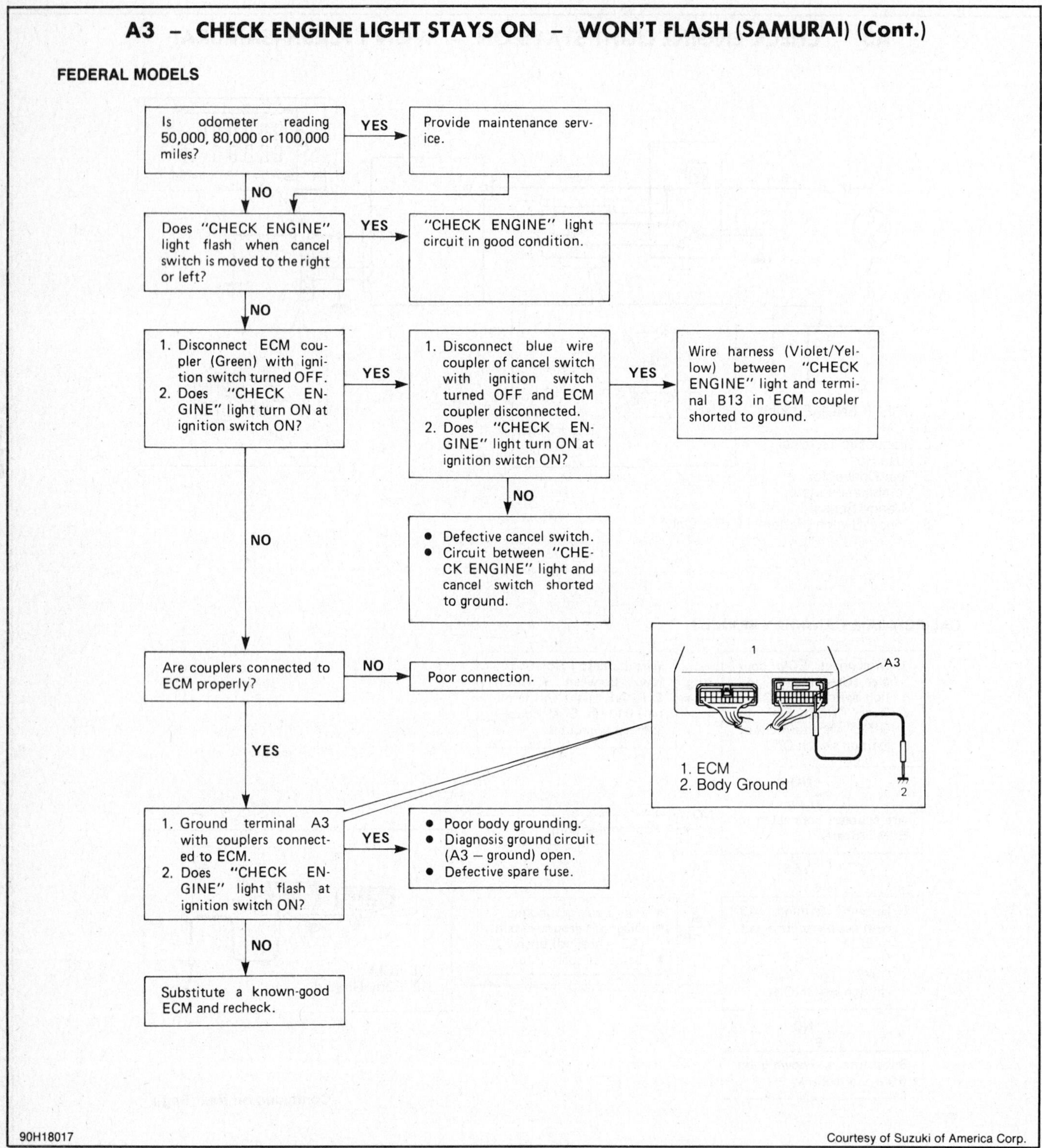
A3 – CHECK ENGINE LIGHT STAYS ON – WON'T FLASH (SAMURAI) (Cont.)
FEDERAL MODELS
Is odometer reading 50,000, 80,000 or 100,000 miles?
YES
Provide maintenance service.
NO
Does "CHECK ENGINE" light flash when cancel switch is moved to the right or left?
YES
"CHECK ENGINE" light circuit in good condition.
NO
1. Disconnect ECM coupler (Green) with ignition switch turned OFF.
2. Does "CHECK ENGINE" light turn ON at ignition switch ON?
YES
1. Disconnect blue wire coupler of cancel switch with ignition switch turned OFF and ECM coupler disconnected.
2. Does "CHECK ENGINE" light turn ON at ignition switch ON?
YES
Wire harness (Violet/Yellow) between "CHECK ENGINE" light and terminal B13 in ECM coupler shorted to ground.
NO
• Defective cancel switch.
• Circuit between "CHECK ENGINE" light and cancel switch shorted to ground.
NO
Are couplers connected to ECM properly?
NO
Poor connection.
YES
1. Ground terminal A3 with couplers connected to ECM.
2. Does "CHECK ENGINE" light flash at ignition switch ON?
YES
• Poor body grounding.
• Diagnosis ground circuit (A3 – ground) open.
• Defective spare fuse.
NO
Substitute a known-good ECM and recheck.
1
A3
2
1. ECM
2. Body Ground
90H18017
Courtesy of Suzuki of America Corp.

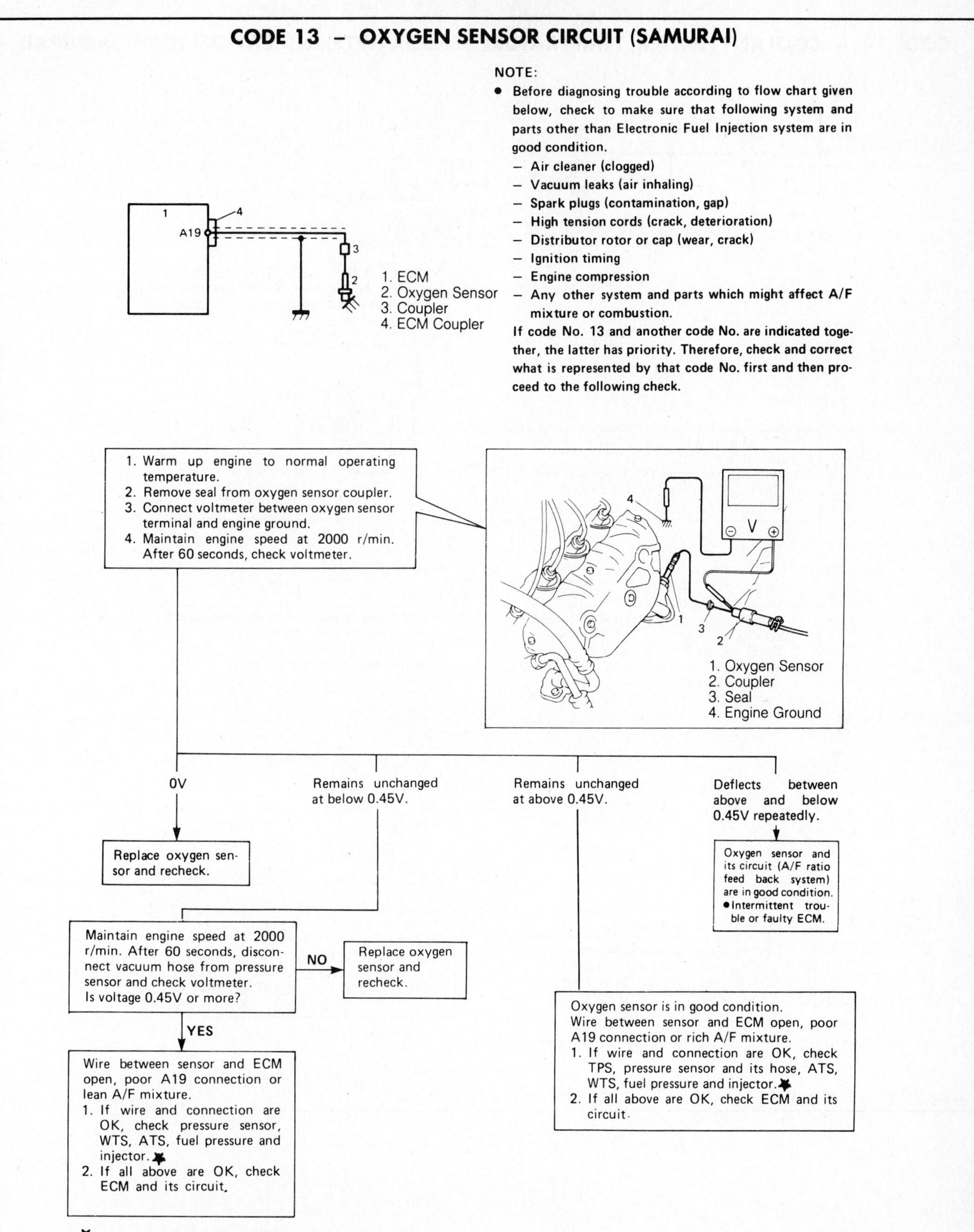
CODE 13 – OXYGEN SENSOR CIRCUIT (SAMURAI)
NOTE:
• Before diagnosing trouble according to flow chart given below, check to make sure that following system and parts other than Electronic Fuel Injection system are in good condition.
– Air cleaner (clogged)
– Vacuum leaks (air inhaling)
– Spark plugs (contamination, gap)
– High tension cords (crack, deterioration)
– Distributor rotor or cap (wear, crack)
– Ignition timing
– Engine compression
– Any other system and parts which might affect A/F mixture or combustion.
If code No. 13 and another code No. are indicated together, the latter has priority. Therefore, check and correct what is represented by that code No. first and then proceed to the following check.
A19
1. ECM
2. Oxygen Sensor
3. Coupler
4. ECM Coupler
1. Warm up engine to normal operating temperature.
2. Remove seal from oxygen sensor coupler.
3. Connect voltmeter between oxygen sensor terminal and engine ground.
4. Maintain engine speed at 2000 r/min. After 60 seconds, check voltmeter.
V
1. Oxygen Sensor
2. Coupler
3. Seal
4. Engine Ground
0V
Remains unchanged at below 0.45V.
Remains unchanged at above 0.45V.
Deflects between above and below 0.45V repeatedly.
Replace oxygen sensor and recheck.
Oxygen sensor and its circuit (A/F ratio feed back system) are in good condition.
• Intermittent trouble or faulty ECM.
Maintain engine speed at 2000 r/min. After 60 seconds, disconnect vacuum hose from pressure sensor and check voltmeter. Is voltage 0.45V or more?
NO
Replace oxygen sensor and recheck.
YES
Wire between sensor and ECM open, poor A19 connection or lean A/F mixture.
1. If wire and connection are OK, check pressure sensor, WTS, ATS, fuel pressure and injector.*
2. If all above are OK, check ECM and its circuit.
Oxygen sensor is in good condition.
Wire between sensor and ECM open, poor A19 connection or rich A/F mixture.
1. If wire and connection are OK, check TPS, pressure sensor and its hose, ATS, WTS, fuel pressure and injector.*
2. If all above are OK, check ECM and its circuit.
*– See SYSTEM & COMPONENT TESTING article.
90I18018
Courtesy of Suzuki of America Corp.

# 1991 ENGINE PERFORMANCE
# Self-Diagnostics (Cont.)

## CODE 14 – COOLANT (WATER) TEMPERATURE SENSOR (WTS) INDICATION LOW (SAMURAI)

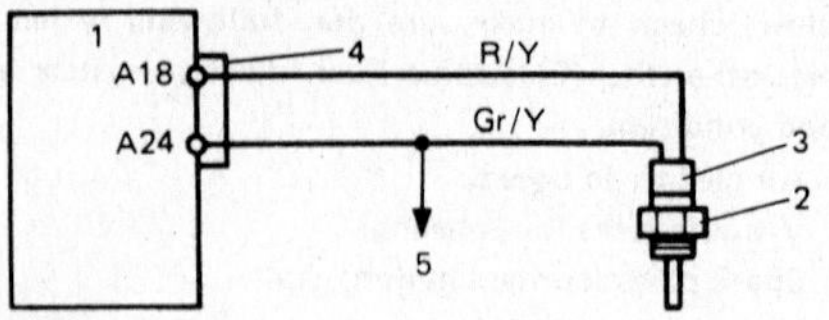

1
A18
A24
4
R/Y
Gr/Y
3
2
5

1. ECM
2. Coolant (Water) Temperature Sensor (WTS)
3. Coupler
4. ECM Coupler
5. To Other Sensors

NOTE: When Code No. 14, 21, 23, 31 and 44 are indicated together, "GR/Y" wire may be open or terminal A24 connection may be defective.

1. Disconnect WTS coupler with ignition switch OFF.
2. With ignition switch ON, check voltage at "R/Y" wire terminal of WTS coupler. Is it about 4 – 5V?

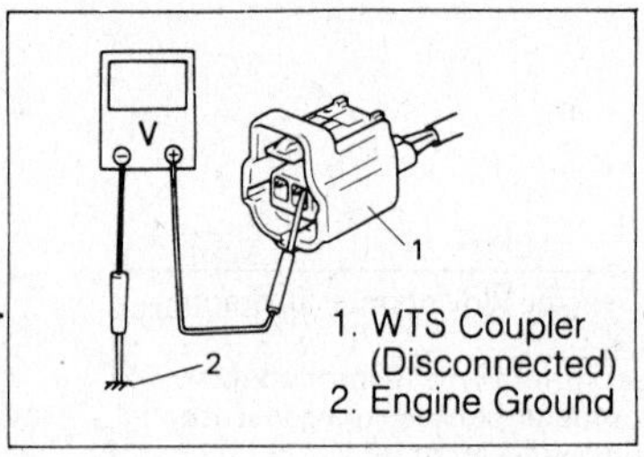

V
1
2
1. WTS Coupler (Disconnected)
2. Engine Ground

YES

1. Using service wire, connect WTS coupler terminals.
2. Check voltage at "R/Y" wire terminal of WTS coupler with ignition switch ON. Is it below 0.15V?

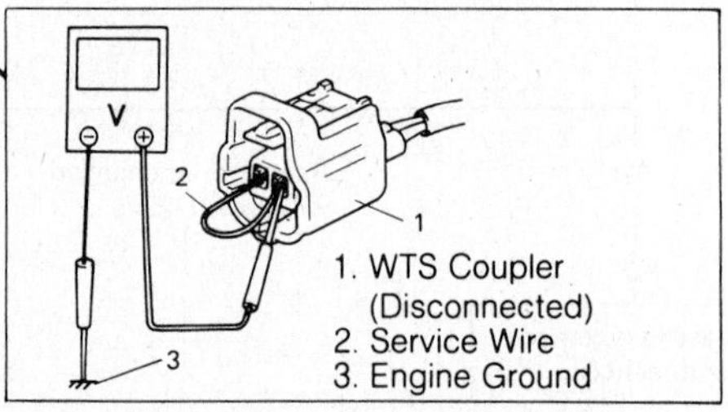

V
2
1
3
1. WTS Coupler (Disconnected)
2. Service Wire
3. Engine Ground

NO

"R/Y" wire open, poor A18 connection or "R/Y" wire shorted to power circuit. If wire and connection are OK, substitute a known-good ECM and recheck.

NO

"Gr/Y" wire open or poor A24 connection. If wire and connection are OK, faulty ECM. Substitute a known-good ECM and recheck.

YES

Poor WTS-to-WTS coupler connection or faulty WTS. If connection and WTS are OK, intermittent trouble or faulty ECM. See INTERMITTENTS in TROUBLE SHOOTING – NO CODES.

90J18019

Courtesy of Suzuki of America Corp.

## CODE 15 – COOLANT (WATER) TEMPERATURE SENSOR (WTS) INDICATION HIGH (SAMURAI)

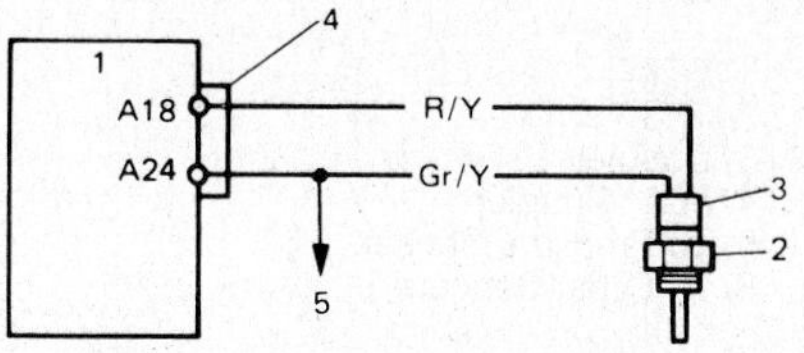

1
A18
A24
R/Y
Gr/Y
3
2
4
5

1. ECM
2. Coolant (Water) Temperature Sensor (WTS)
3. Coupler
4. ECM Coupler
5. To Other Sensors

1. Disconnect WTS coupler with ignition switch OFF.
2. With ignition switch ON, is voltage applied to "R/Y" wire terminal of WTS coupler 4V or more?

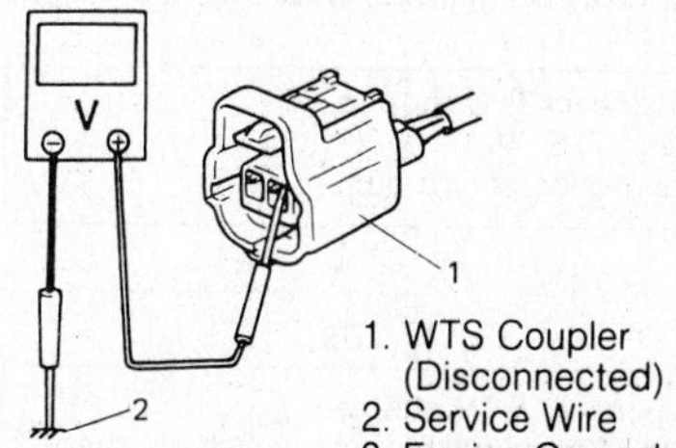

V
1
2

1. WTS Coupler (Disconnected)
2. Service Wire
3. Engine Ground

YES → Check WTS ✱ Is it in good condition?

NO → "R/Y" wire shorted to "Gr/Y" wire or ground circuit. If wire is OK, substitute a known-good ECM and recheck.

YES → Intermittent trouble or faulty ECM. See INTERMITTENTS in TROUBLE SHOOTING – NO CODES.

NO → Faulty WTS.

✱ – See SYSTEM & COMPONENT TESTING article.

90C18020

Courtesy of Suzuki of America Corp.

# 1991 ENGINE PERFORMANCE
## Self-Diagnostics (Cont.)

### CODE 21 – THROTTLE POSITION SENSOR CIRCUIT INDICATION HIGH (SAMURAI)

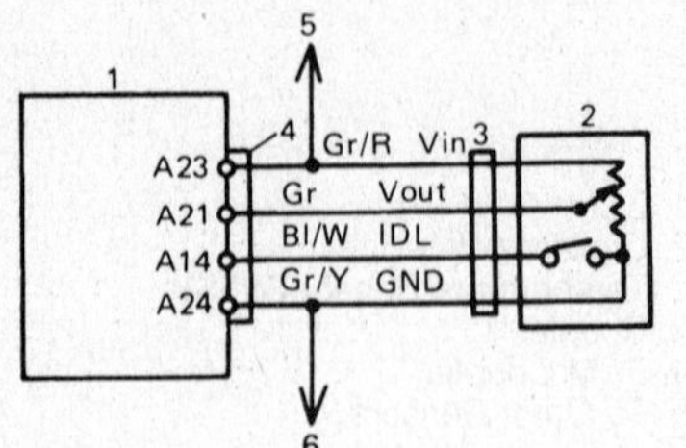
5
1
4
Gr/R Vin
3
2
A23
Gr Vout
A21
Bl/W IDL
A14
Gr/Y GND
A24
6

1. ECM
2. TPS
3. Coupler
4. ECM Coupler
5. To Pressure Sensor
6. To Other Sensors

**NOTE:**
**Be sure to turn OFF ignition switch for this check.**

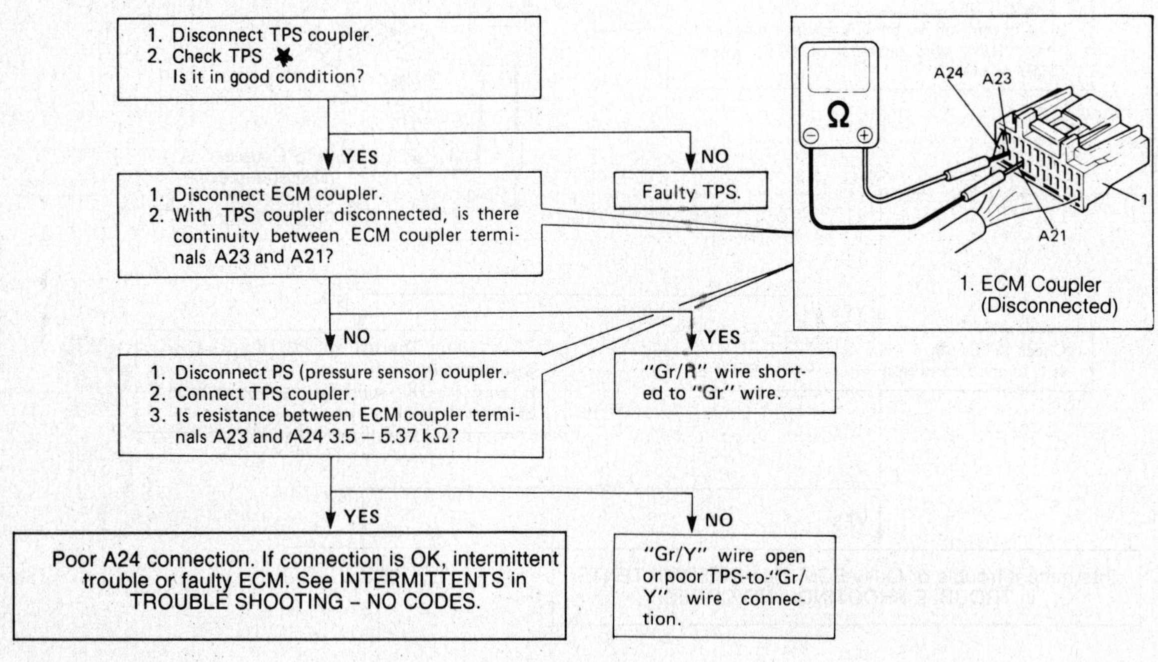
1. Disconnect TPS coupler.
2. Check TPS ✱
Is it in good condition?
YES
NO
Faulty TPS.
1. Disconnect ECM coupler.
2. With TPS coupler disconnected, is there continuity between ECM coupler terminals A23 and A21?
NO
YES
"Gr/R" wire shorted to "Gr" wire.
1. Disconnect PS (pressure sensor) coupler.
2. Connect TPS coupler.
3. Is resistance between ECM coupler terminals A23 and A24 3.5 – 5.37 kΩ?
YES
NO
Ω
A24
A23
A21
1
1. ECM Coupler (Disconnected)

Poor A24 connection. If connection is OK, intermittent trouble or faulty ECM. See INTERMITTENTS in TROUBLE SHOOTING – NO CODES.

"Gr/Y" wire open or poor TPS-to-"Gr/Y" wire connection.

✱ – See SYSTEM & COMPONENT TESTING article.

90D18021 90E18022

## CODE 22 – THROTTLE POSITION SENSOR CIRCUIT INDICATION LOW (SAMURAI)

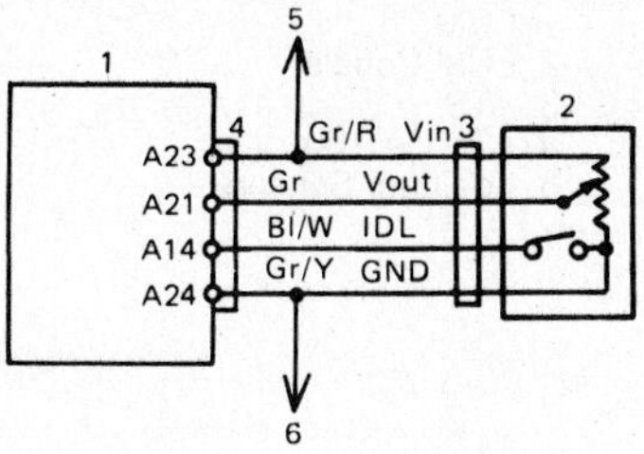

A23 4 Gr/R Vin 3 2
A21 Gr Vout
A14 Bl/W IDL
A24 Gr/Y GND
5
6

1. ECM
2. TPS
3. Coupler
4. ECM Coupler
5. To Pressure Sensor
6. To Other Sensors

1. Disconnect TPS coupler with ignition switch OFF.
2. With ignition switch ON, is voltage applied to "Gr/R" wire terminal of TPS coupler about 4 – 5V?

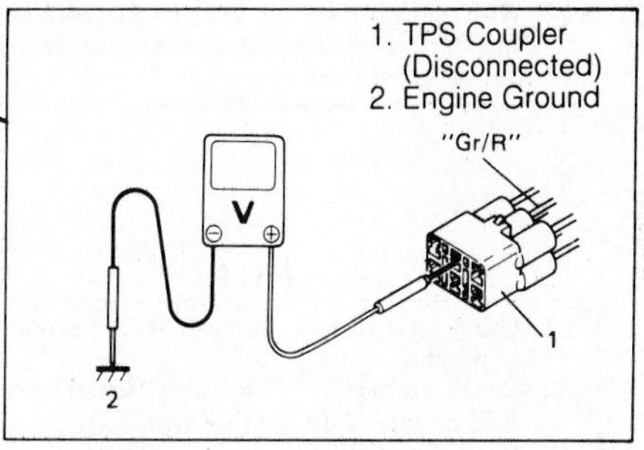

1. TPS Coupler (Disconnected)
2. Engine Ground

"Gr/R"
V

YES: Check TPS.✱ Is it in good condition?

NO: "Gr/R" wire open, "Gr/R" wire shorted to ground circuit or "Gr/Y" wire, or poor A23 connection. If wire and connection are OK, substitute a known-good ECM and recheck.

YES: "Gr" wire open. "GR" wire shorted to ground circuit, poor connection at TPS coupler or poor A21 connection. If wire and connections are OK, intermittent trouble or faulty ECM. See INTERMITTENTS in TROUBLE SHOOTING – NO CODES.

NO: Faulty TPS.

✱ – See SYSTEM & COMPONENT TESTING article.

90D18021 90F18023

Courtesy of Suzuki of America Corp.

# 1991 ENGINE PERFORMANCE
## Self-Diagnostics (Cont.)

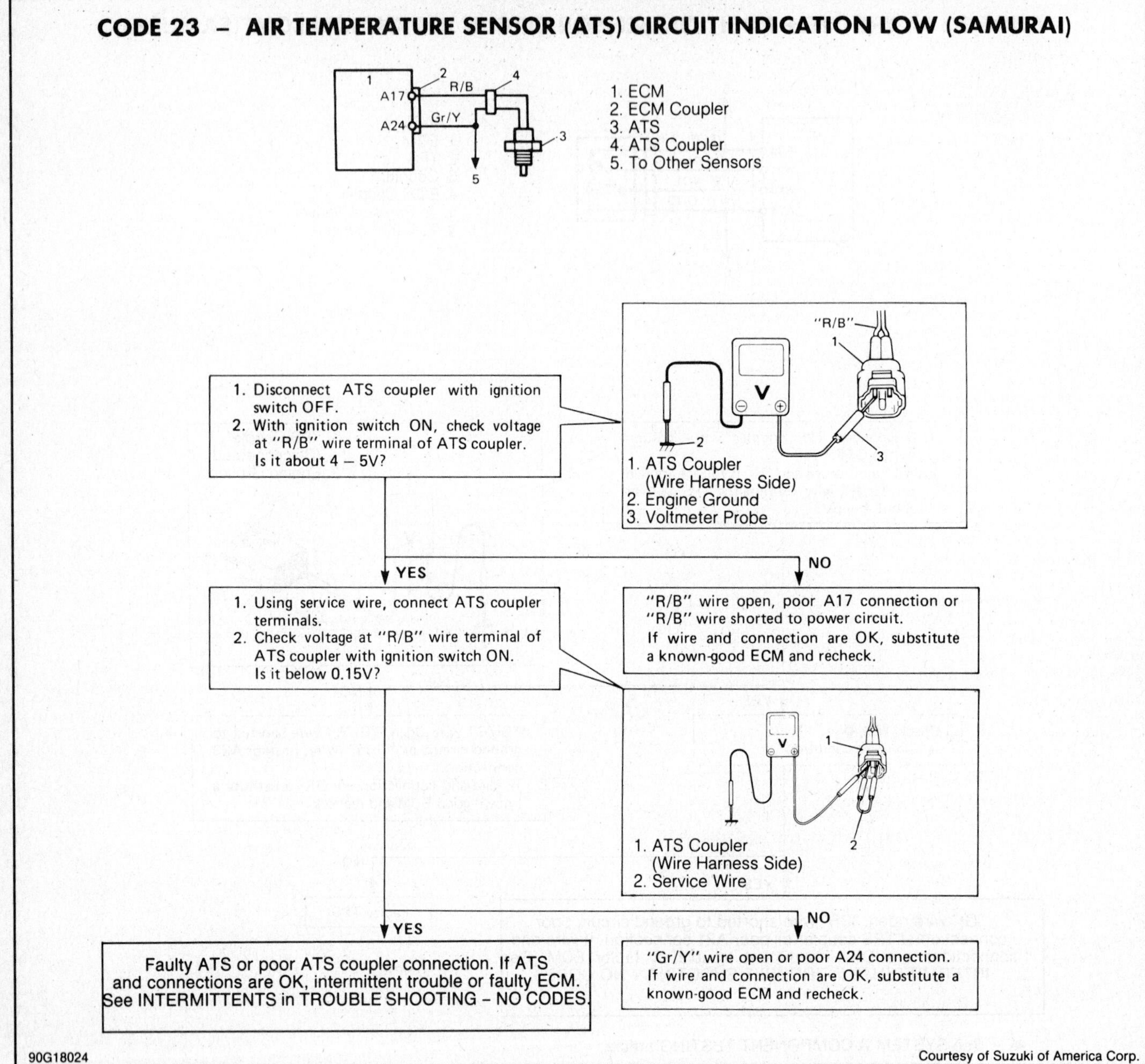

CODE 23 – AIR TEMPERATURE SENSOR (ATS) CIRCUIT INDICATION LOW (SAMURAI)
1
2
4
A17
R/B
A24
Gr/Y
3
5
1. ECM
2. ECM Coupler
3. ATS
4. ATS Coupler
5. To Other Sensors
1. Disconnect ATS coupler with ignition switch OFF.
2. With ignition switch ON, check voltage at "R/B" wire terminal of ATS coupler.
Is it about 4 – 5V?
"R/B"
V
1. ATS Coupler (Wire Harness Side)
2. Engine Ground
3. Voltmeter Probe
YES
NO
1. Using service wire, connect ATS coupler terminals.
2. Check voltage at "R/B" wire terminal of ATS coupler with ignition switch ON.
Is it below 0.15V?
"R/B" wire open, poor A17 connection or "R/B" wire shorted to power circuit.
If wire and connection are OK, substitute a known-good ECM and recheck.
1. ATS Coupler (Wire Harness Side)
2. Service Wire
YES
NO
Faulty ATS or poor ATS coupler connection. If ATS and connections are OK, intermittent trouble or faulty ECM. See INTERMITTENTS in TROUBLE SHOOTING - NO CODES.
"Gr/Y" wire open or poor A24 connection.
If wire and connection are OK, substitute a known-good ECM and recheck.
90G18024
Courtesy of Suzuki of America Corp.

## CODE 24 – VEHICLE SPEED SENSOR (SAMURAI)

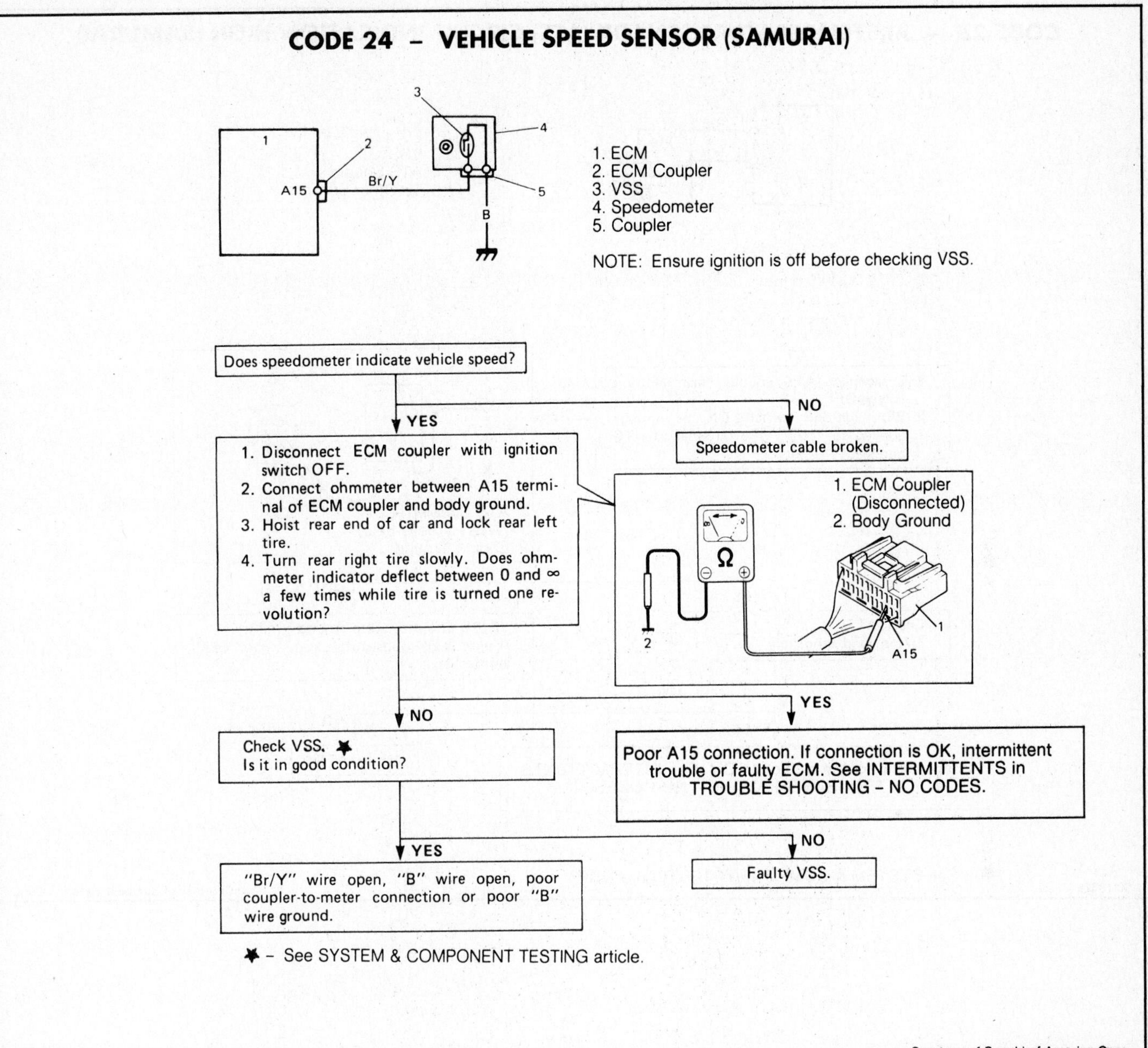

1
2
3
4
5
A15
Br/Y
B
1. ECM
2. ECM Coupler
3. VSS
4. Speedometer
5. Coupler
NOTE: Ensure ignition is off before checking VSS.
Does speedometer indicate vehicle speed?
YES
NO
Speedometer cable broken.
1. Disconnect ECM coupler with ignition switch OFF.
2. Connect ohmmeter between A15 terminal of ECM coupler and body ground.
3. Hoist rear end of car and lock rear left tire.
4. Turn rear right tire slowly. Does ohmmeter indicator deflect between 0 and ∞ a few times while tire is turned one revolution?
1. ECM Coupler (Disconnected)
2. Body Ground
Ω
A15
NO
YES
Check VSS. ✱
Is it in good condition?
Poor A15 connection. If connection is OK, intermittent trouble or faulty ECM. See INTERMITTENTS in TROUBLE SHOOTING - NO CODES.
YES
NO
"Br/Y" wire open, "B" wire open, poor coupler-to-meter connection or poor "B" wire ground.
Faulty VSS.
✱ - See SYSTEM & COMPONENT TESTING article.
90H18025
Courtesy of Suzuki of America Corp.

# 1991 ENGINE PERFORMANCE
## Self-Diagnostics (Cont.)

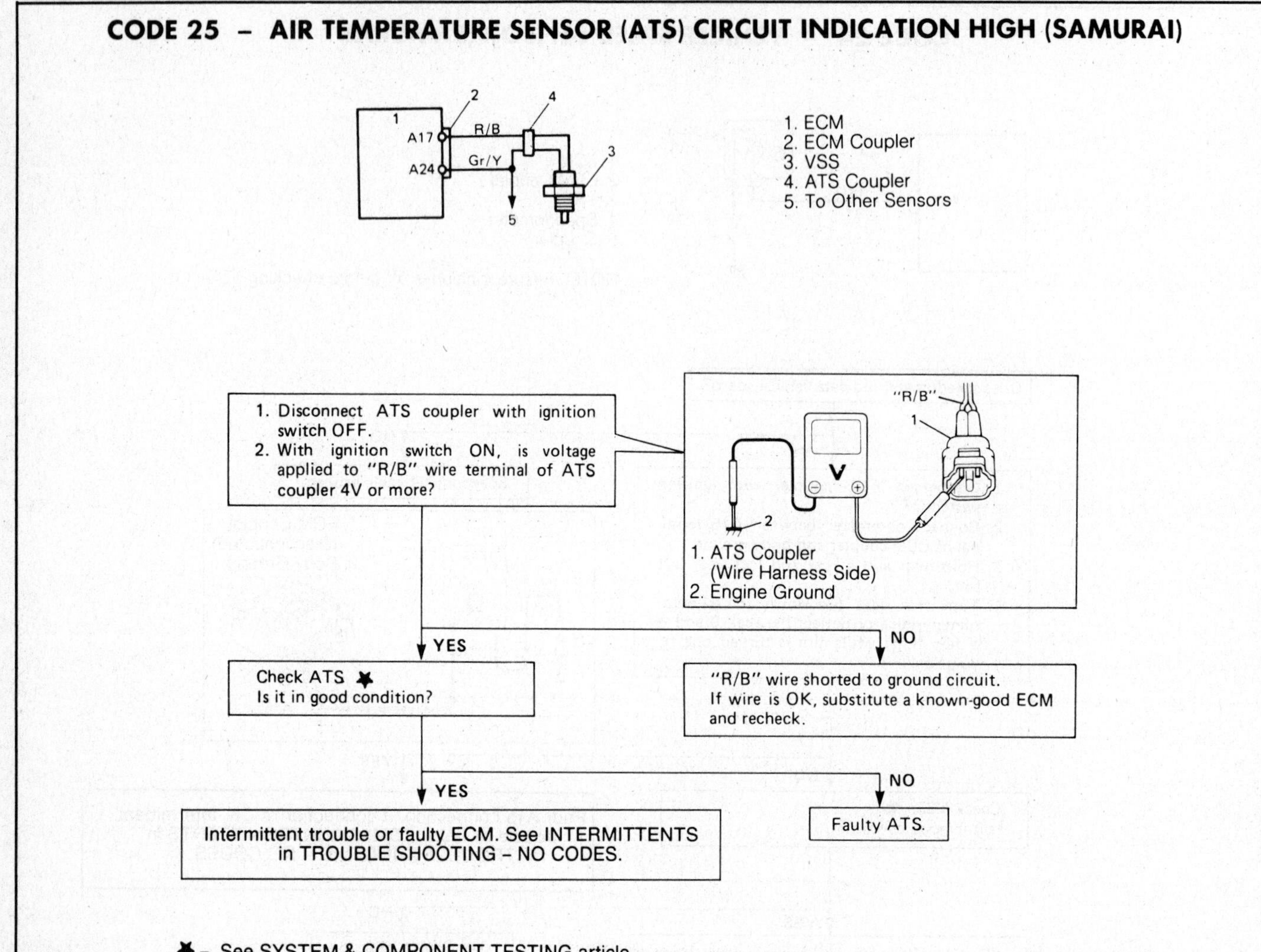

CODE 25 – AIR TEMPERATURE SENSOR (ATS) CIRCUIT INDICATION HIGH (SAMURAI)
A17
A24
R/B
Gr/Y
1. ECM
2. ECM Coupler
3. VSS
4. ATS Coupler
5. To Other Sensors
1. Disconnect ATS coupler with ignition switch OFF.
2. With ignition switch ON, is voltage applied to "R/B" wire terminal of ATS coupler 4V or more?
"R/B"
V
1. ATS Coupler (Wire Harness Side)
2. Engine Ground
YES
NO
Check ATS ✱
Is it in good condition?
"R/B" wire shorted to ground circuit.
If wire is OK, substitute a known-good ECM and recheck.
YES
NO
Intermittent trouble or faulty ECM. See INTERMITTENTS in TROUBLE SHOOTING – NO CODES.
Faulty ATS.
✱ – See SYSTEM & COMPONENT TESTING article.
90I18026
Courtesy of Suzuki of America Corp.

## CODE 31 – PRESSURE SENSOR (PS) CIRCUIT VOLTAGE HIGH (SAMURAI)

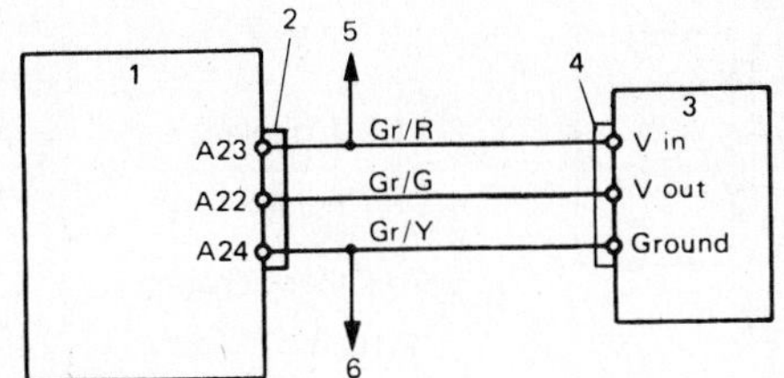
1
2
5
4
3
A23
A22
A24
Gr/R
Gr/G
Gr/Y
V in
V out
Ground
6

1. ECM
2. ECM Coupler
3. PS
4. PS Coupler
5. To TPS
6. To Other Sensors

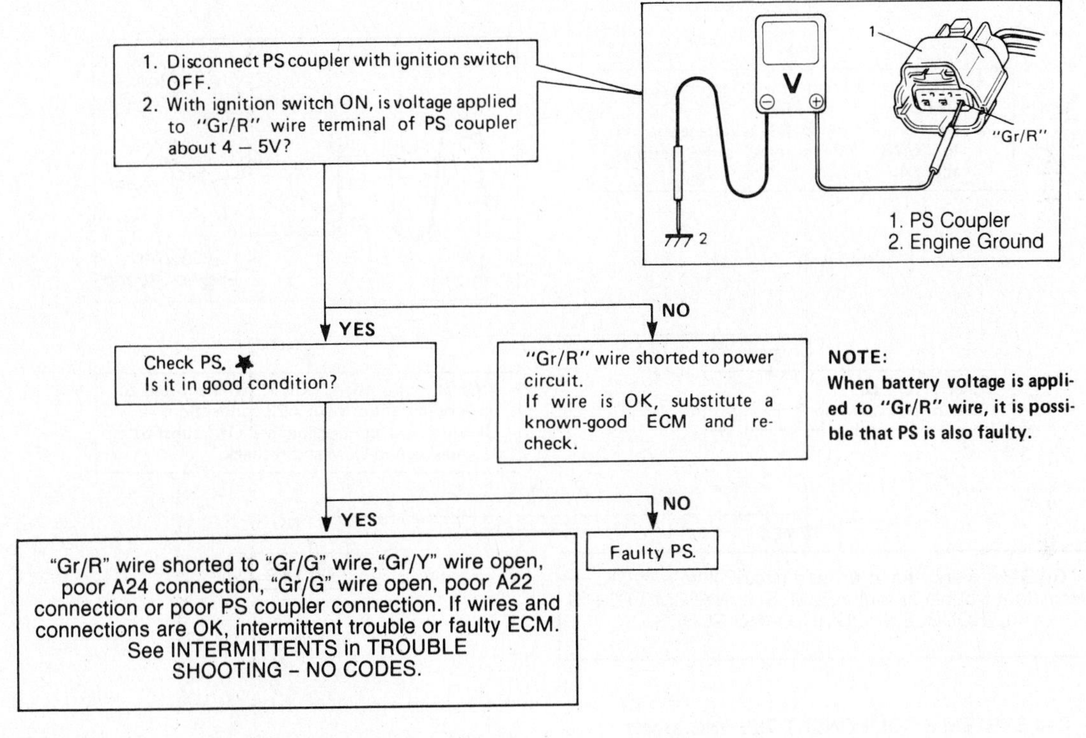
1. Disconnect PS coupler with ignition switch OFF.
2. With ignition switch ON, is voltage applied to "Gr/R" wire terminal of PS coupler about 4 – 5V?
V
"Gr/R"
1. PS Coupler
2. Engine Ground
YES
NO
Check PS. ✱
Is it in good condition?
"Gr/R" wire shorted to power circuit.
If wire is OK, substitute a known-good ECM and re-check.
YES
NO
Faulty PS.

**NOTE:**
**When battery voltage is applied to "Gr/R" wire, it is possible that PS is also faulty.**

"Gr/R" wire shorted to "Gr/G" wire, "Gr/Y" wire open, poor A24 connection, "Gr/G" wire open, poor A22 connection or poor PS coupler connection. If wires and connections are OK, intermittent trouble or faulty ECM. See INTERMITTENTS in TROUBLE SHOOTING - NO CODES.

✱ - See SYSTEM & COMPONENT TESTING article.

90J18027 90A18028

Courtesy of Suzuki of America Corp.

# 1991 ENGINE PERFORMANCE
# Self-Diagnostics (Cont.)

## CODE 32 – PRESSURE SENSOR (PS) CIRCUIT VOLTAGE LOW (SAMURAI)

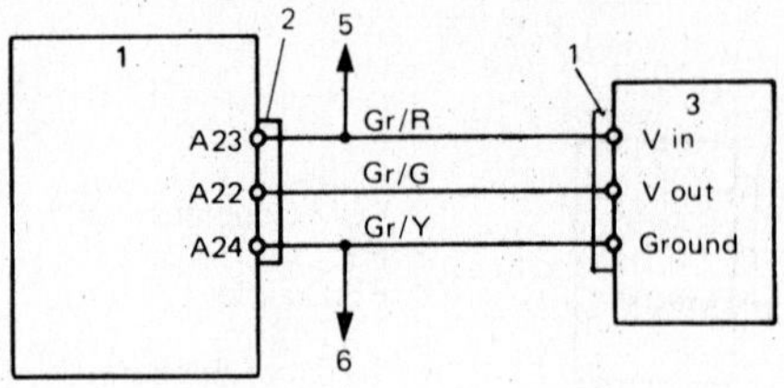

1 2 5 1 3
A23 Gr/R V in
A22 Gr/G V out
A24 Gr/Y Ground
6

1. ECM
2. ECM Coupler
3. PS
4. PS Coupler
5. To TPS
6. To Other Sensors

1. Disconnect PS coupler with ignition switch OFF.
2. With ignition switch ON, is voltage applied to "Gr/R" wire terminal of PS coupler about 4 – 5V?

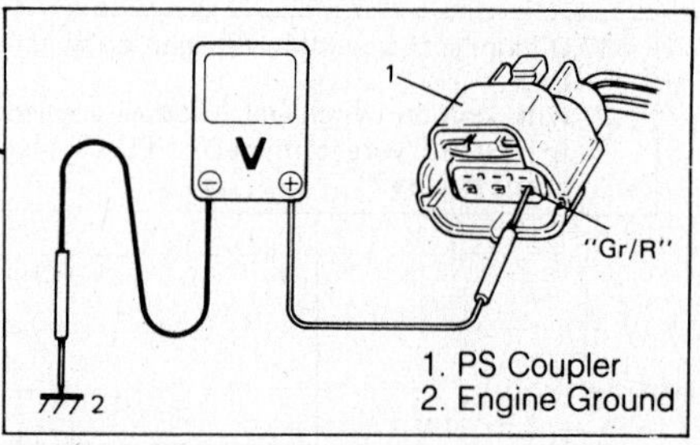

V
1
"Gr/R"
2

1. PS Coupler
2. Engine Ground

YES → Check PS. ✱ Is it in good condition?

NO → "Gr/R" wire open, "Gr/R" wire shorted to ground circuit or poor A23 connection. If wire and connection are OK, substitute a known-good ECM and recheck.

YES → "Gr/G" wire shorted to ground circuit. If wire is OK, intermittent trouble or faulty ECM. See INTERMITTENTS in TROUBLE SHOOTING – NO CODES.

NO → Faulty PS.

✱ – See SYSTEM & COMPONENT TESTING article.

90J18027 90B18029

Courtesy of Suzuki of America Corp.

# 1991 ENGINE PERFORMANCE
## Self-Diagnostics (Cont.)

### CODE 41 – NO IGNITION SIGNAL (SAMURAI)

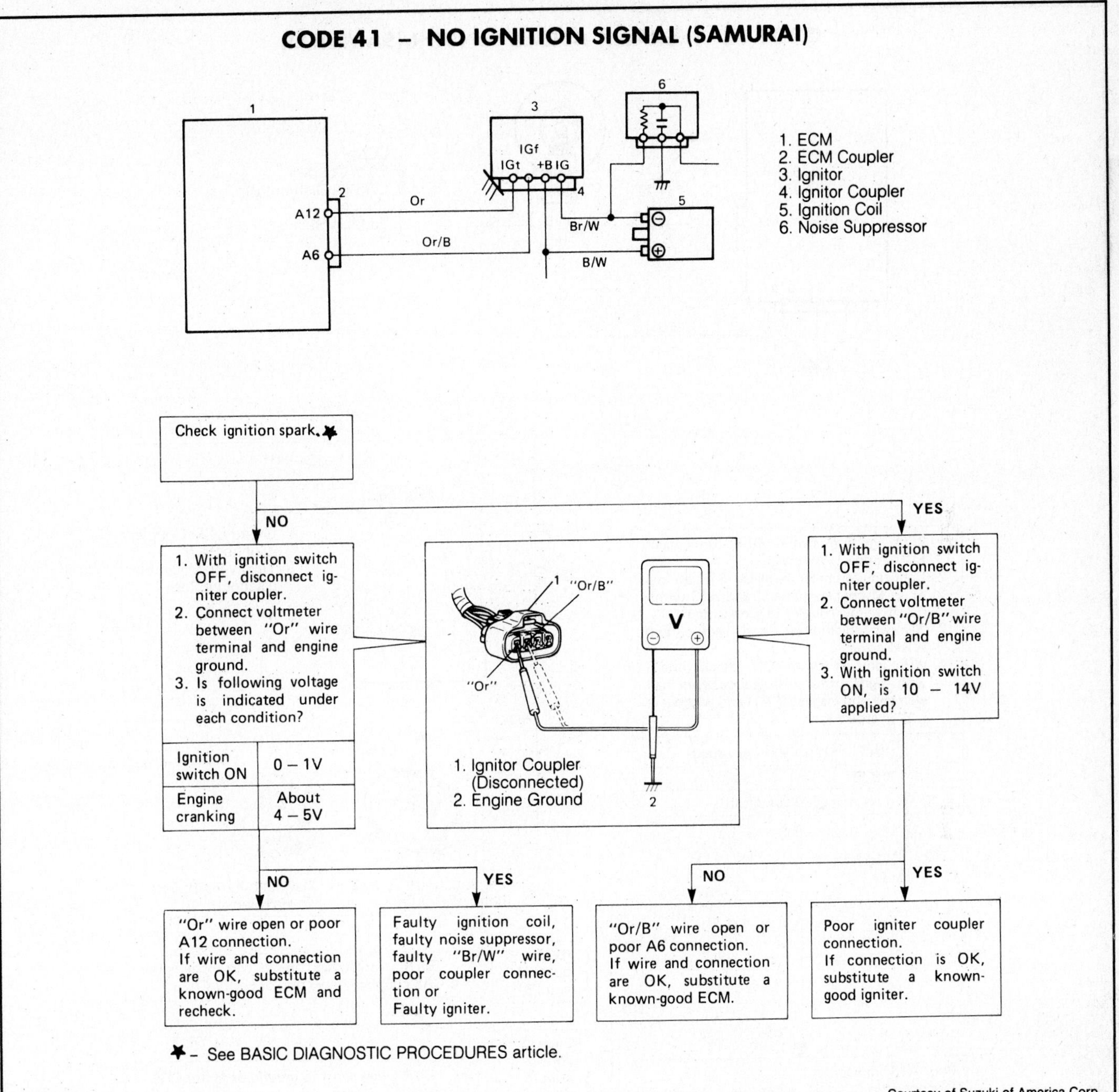

1
2
3
4
5
6
IGf
IGt
+B
IG
A12
A6
Or
Or/B
Br/W
B/W
1. ECM
2. ECM Coupler
3. Ignitor
4. Ignitor Coupler
5. Ignition Coil
6. Noise Suppressor
Check ignition spark.✱
NO
YES
1. With ignition switch OFF, disconnect igniter coupler.
2. Connect voltmeter between "Or" wire terminal and engine ground.
3. Is following voltage is indicated under each condition?
Ignition switch ON | 0 – 1V
Engine cranking | About 4 – 5V
"Or/B"
"Or"
V
1. Ignitor Coupler (Disconnected)
2. Engine Ground
1. With ignition switch OFF, disconnect igniter coupler.
2. Connect voltmeter between "Or/B" wire terminal and engine ground.
3. With ignition switch ON, is 10 – 14V applied?
NO
YES
NO
YES
"Or" wire open or poor A12 connection. If wire and connection are OK, substitute a known-good ECM and recheck.
Faulty ignition coil, faulty noise suppressor, faulty "Br/W" wire, poor coupler connection or Faulty igniter.
"Or/B" wire open or poor A6 connection. If wire and connection are OK, substitute a known-good ECM.
Poor igniter coupler connection. If connection is OK, substitute a known-good igniter.
✱ – See BASIC DIAGNOSTIC PROCEDURES article.


90E18030 90F18031

Courtesy of Suzuki of America Corp.

# 1991 ENGINE PERFORMANCE
## Self-Diagnostics (Cont.)

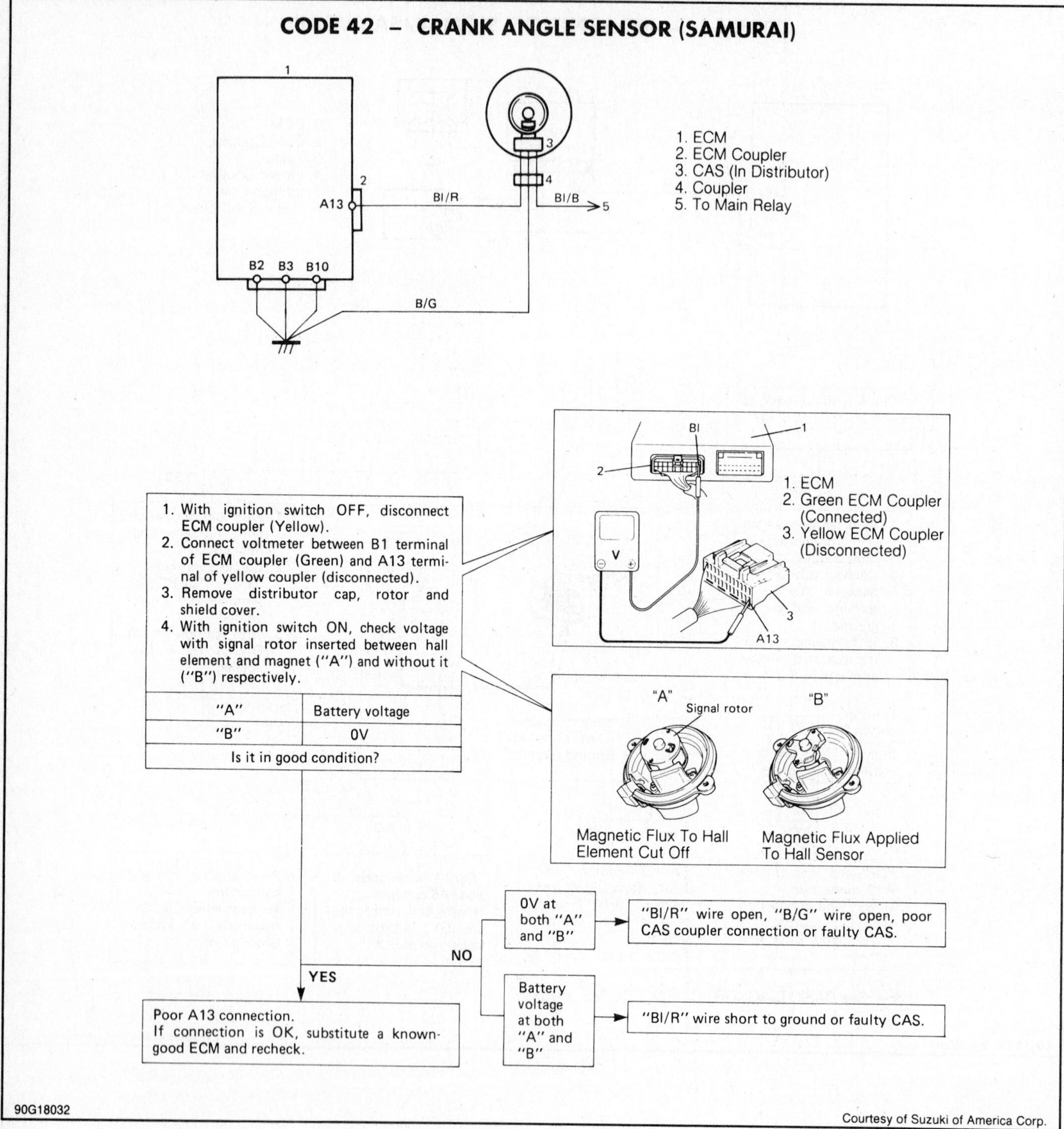
CODE 42 – CRANK ANGLE SENSOR (SAMURAI)
1
2
3
4
A13
Bl/R
Bl/B
5
B2 B3 B10
B/G
1. ECM
2. ECM Coupler
3. CAS (In Distributor)
4. Coupler
5. To Main Relay
Bl
1
2
V
3
A13
1. ECM
2. Green ECM Coupler (Connected)
3. Yellow ECM Coupler (Disconnected)
1. With ignition switch OFF, disconnect ECM coupler (Yellow).
2. Connect voltmeter between B1 terminal of ECM coupler (Green) and A13 terminal of yellow coupler (disconnected).
3. Remove distributor cap, rotor and shield cover.
4. With ignition switch ON, check voltage with signal rotor inserted between hall element and magnet ("A") and without it ("B") respectively.
"A" Battery voltage
"B" 0V
Is it in good condition?
"A"
Signal rotor
"B"
Magnetic Flux To Hall Element Cut Off
Magnetic Flux Applied To Hall Sensor
YES
NO
0V at both "A" and "B"
"Bl/R" wire open, "B/G" wire open, poor CAS coupler connection or faulty CAS.
Battery voltage at both "A" and "B"
"Bl/R" wire short to ground or faulty CAS.
Poor A13 connection.
If connection is OK, substitute a known-good ECM and recheck.

90G18032

Courtesy of Suzuki of America Corp.

## CODE 44 – IDLE SWITCH CIRCUIT OPEN OR MISADJUSTED (SAMURAI)

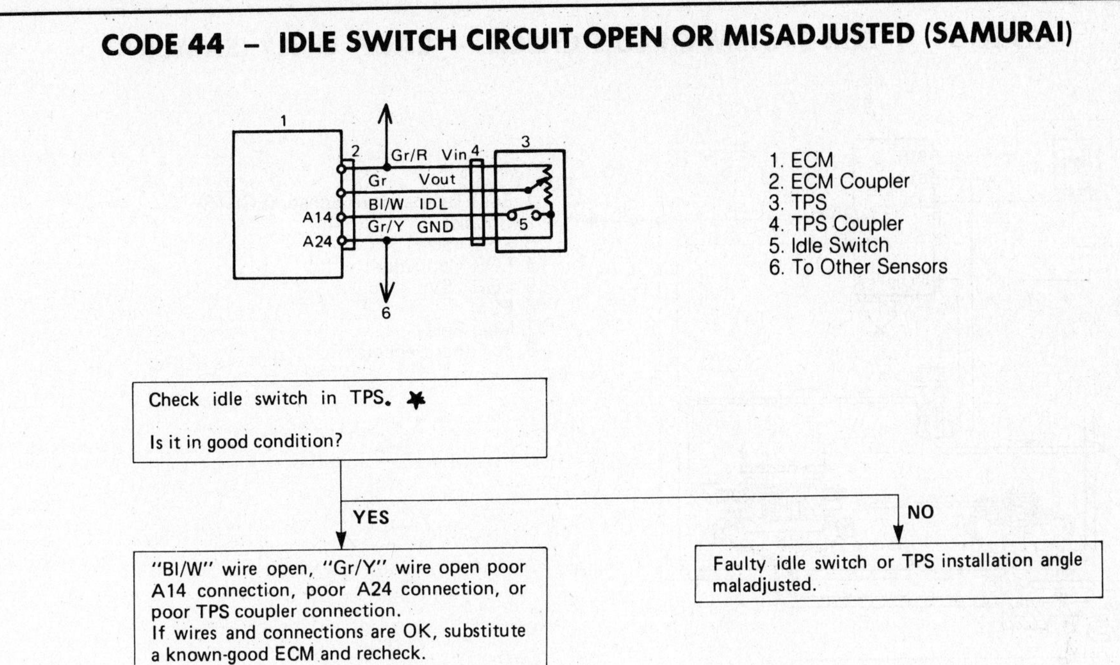
1
2
Gr/R Vin
4
3
Gr Vout
Bl/W IDL
A14
Gr/Y GND
A24
5
6
1. ECM
2. ECM Coupler
3. TPS
4. TPS Coupler
5. Idle Switch
6. To Other Sensors
Check idle switch in TPS. ✱
Is it in good condition?
YES
NO
"Bl/W" wire open, "Gr/Y" wire open poor A14 connection, poor A24 connection, or poor TPS coupler connection.
If wires and connections are OK, substitute a known-good ECM and recheck.
Faulty idle switch or TPS installation angle maladjusted.

✱ - See SYSTEM & COMPONENT TESTING article.

## CODE 45 – IDLE SWITCH CIRCUIT SHORTED OR MISADJUSTED (SAMURAI)

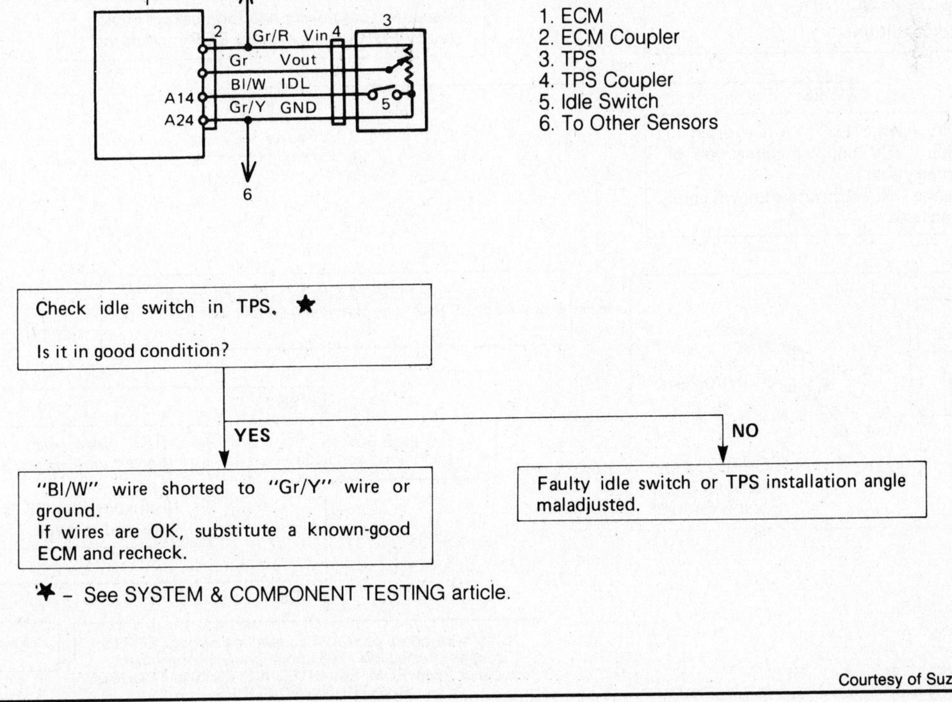
1
2
Gr/R Vin
4
3
Gr Vout
Bl/W IDL
A14
Gr/Y GND
A24
5
6
1. ECM
2. ECM Coupler
3. TPS
4. TPS Coupler
5. Idle Switch
6. To Other Sensors
Check idle switch in TPS. ★
Is it in good condition?
YES
NO
"Bl/W" wire shorted to "Gr/Y" wire or ground.
If wires are OK, substitute a known-good ECM and recheck.
Faulty idle switch or TPS installation angle maladjusted.
✱ - See SYSTEM & COMPONENT TESTING article.

90H18023 90I18034

Courtesy of Suzuki of America Corp.

# 1991 ENGINE PERFORMANCE
## Self-Diagnostics (Cont.)

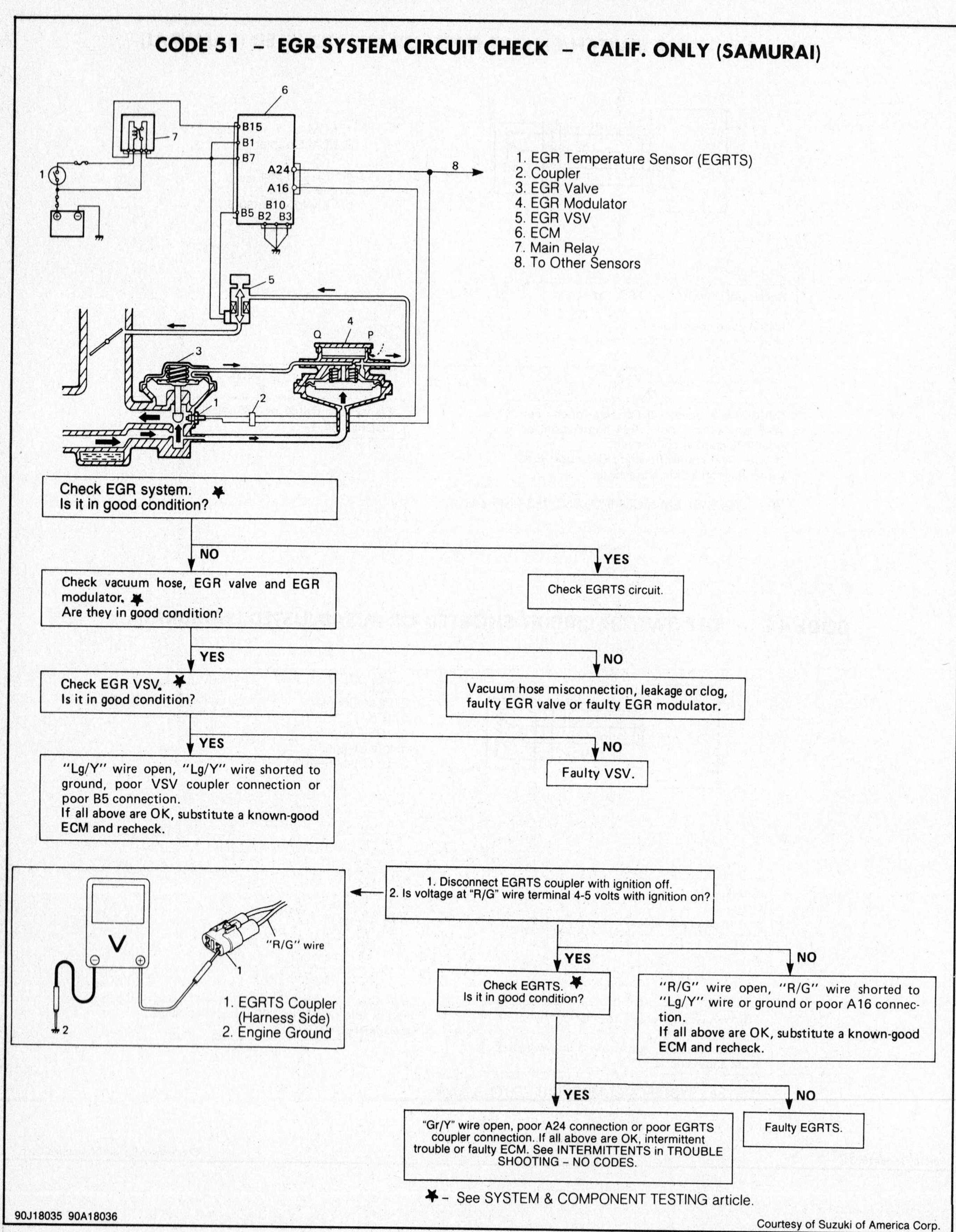

CODE 51 – EGR SYSTEM CIRCUIT CHECK – CALIF. ONLY (SAMURAI)
B15
B1
B7
A24
A16
B10
B5 B2 B3
1. EGR Temperature Sensor (EGRTS)
2. Coupler
3. EGR Valve
4. EGR Modulator
5. EGR VSV
6. ECM
7. Main Relay
8. To Other Sensors
Q
P
Check EGR system. ✱
Is it in good condition?
NO
YES
Check vacuum hose, EGR valve and EGR modulator. ✱
Are they in good condition?
Check EGRTS circuit.
YES
NO
Check EGR VSV. ✱
Is it in good condition?
Vacuum hose misconnection, leakage or clog, faulty EGR valve or faulty EGR modulator.
YES
NO
"Lg/Y" wire open, "Lg/Y" wire shorted to ground, poor VSV coupler connection or poor B5 connection.
If all above are OK, substitute a known-good ECM and recheck.
Faulty VSV.
V
"R/G" wire
1. EGRTS Coupler (Harness Side)
2. Engine Ground
1. Disconnect EGRTS coupler with ignition off.
2. Is voltage at "R/G" wire terminal 4-5 volts with ignition on?
YES
NO
Check EGRTS. ✱
Is it in good condition?
"R/G" wire open, "R/G" wire shorted to "Lg/Y" wire or ground or poor A16 connection.
If all above are OK, substitute a known-good ECM and recheck.
YES
NO
"Gr/Y" wire open, poor A24 connection or poor EGRTS coupler connection. If all above are OK, intermittent trouble or faulty ECM. See INTERMITTENTS in TROUBLE SHOOTING - NO CODES.
Faulty EGRTS.
✱ - See SYSTEM & COMPONENT TESTING article.
90J18035 90A18036
Courtesy of Suzuki of America Corp.

## CODE 53 – ECM GROUND CIRCUIT CHECK – CALIF. ONLY (SAMURAI)

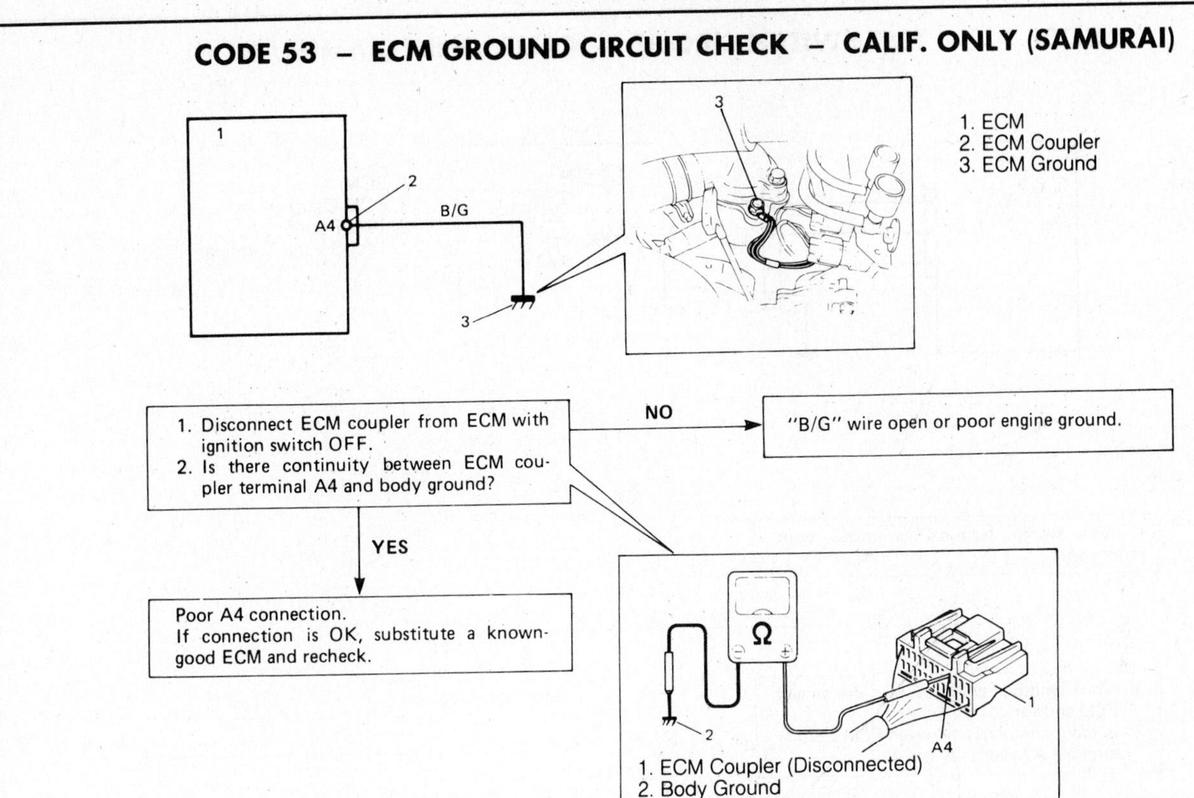

1
2
A4
B/G
3
1. ECM
2. ECM Coupler
3. ECM Ground
1. Disconnect ECM coupler from ECM with ignition switch OFF.
2. Is there continuity between ECM coupler terminal A4 and body ground?
NO
"B/G" wire open or poor engine ground.
YES
Poor A4 connection.
If connection is OK, substitute a known-good ECM and recheck.
Ω
A4
1. ECM Coupler (Disconnected)
2. Body Ground


## CODE 54 – GEAR POSITION (5TH SWITCH) CIRCUIT GROUNDED (SAMURAI)

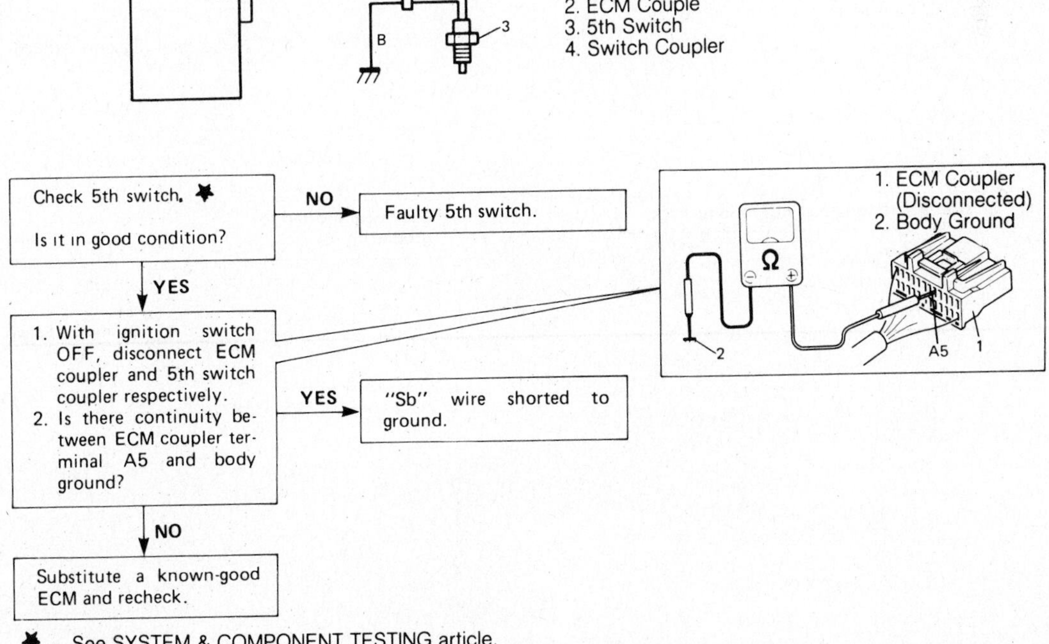

A5
Sb
B
1. ECM
2. ECM Couple
3. 5th Switch
4. Switch Coupler
Check 5th switch. ✱
Is it in good condition?
NO
Faulty 5th switch.
YES
1. With ignition switch OFF, disconnect ECM coupler and 5th switch coupler respectively.
2. Is there continuity between ECM coupler terminal A5 and body ground?
YES
"Sb" wire shorted to ground.
NO
Substitute a known-good ECM and recheck.
Ω
A5
1. ECM Coupler (Disconnected)
2. Body Ground


✱ – See SYSTEM & COMPONENT TESTING article.

Courtesy of Suzuki of America Corp.

90B18037 90C18038

# 1991 ENGINE PERFORMANCE
## Self-Diagnostics (Cont.)

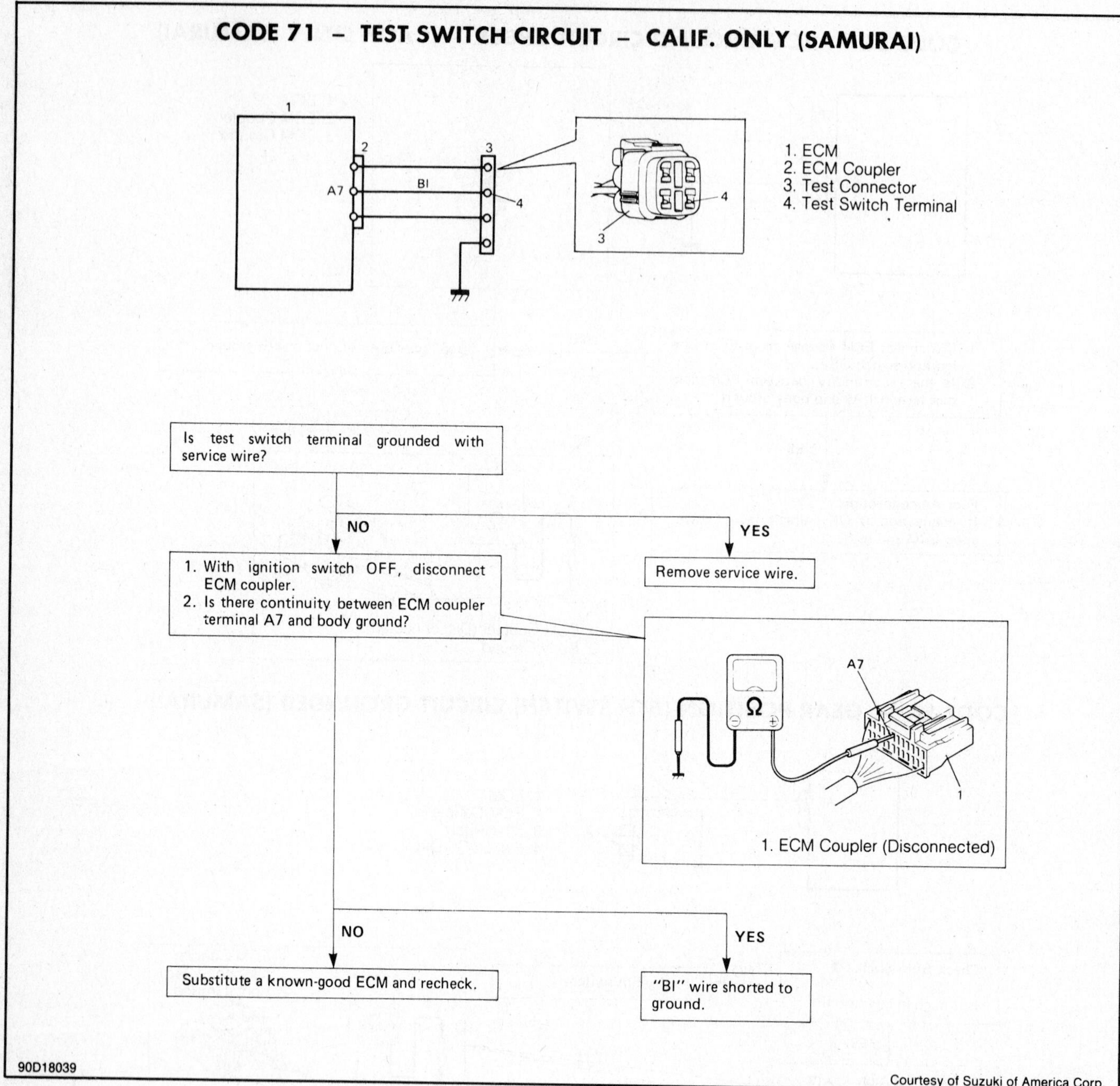
CODE 71 – TEST SWITCH CIRCUIT – CALIF. ONLY (SAMURAI)
1
2
3
A7
Bl
4
3
4
1. ECM
2. ECM Coupler
3. Test Connector
4. Test Switch Terminal
Is test switch terminal grounded with service wire?
NO
YES
Remove service wire.
1. With ignition switch OFF, disconnect ECM coupler.
2. Is there continuity between ECM coupler terminal A7 and body ground?
A7
Ω
1
1. ECM Coupler (Disconnected)
NO
YES
Substitute a known-good ECM and recheck.
"Bl" wire shorted to ground.
90D18039
Courtesy of Suzuki of America Corp.

# 1991 ENGINE PERFORMANCE
# Self-Diagnostics (Cont.)

## INITIAL DIAGNOSTIC PROCEDURE (SIDEKICK)

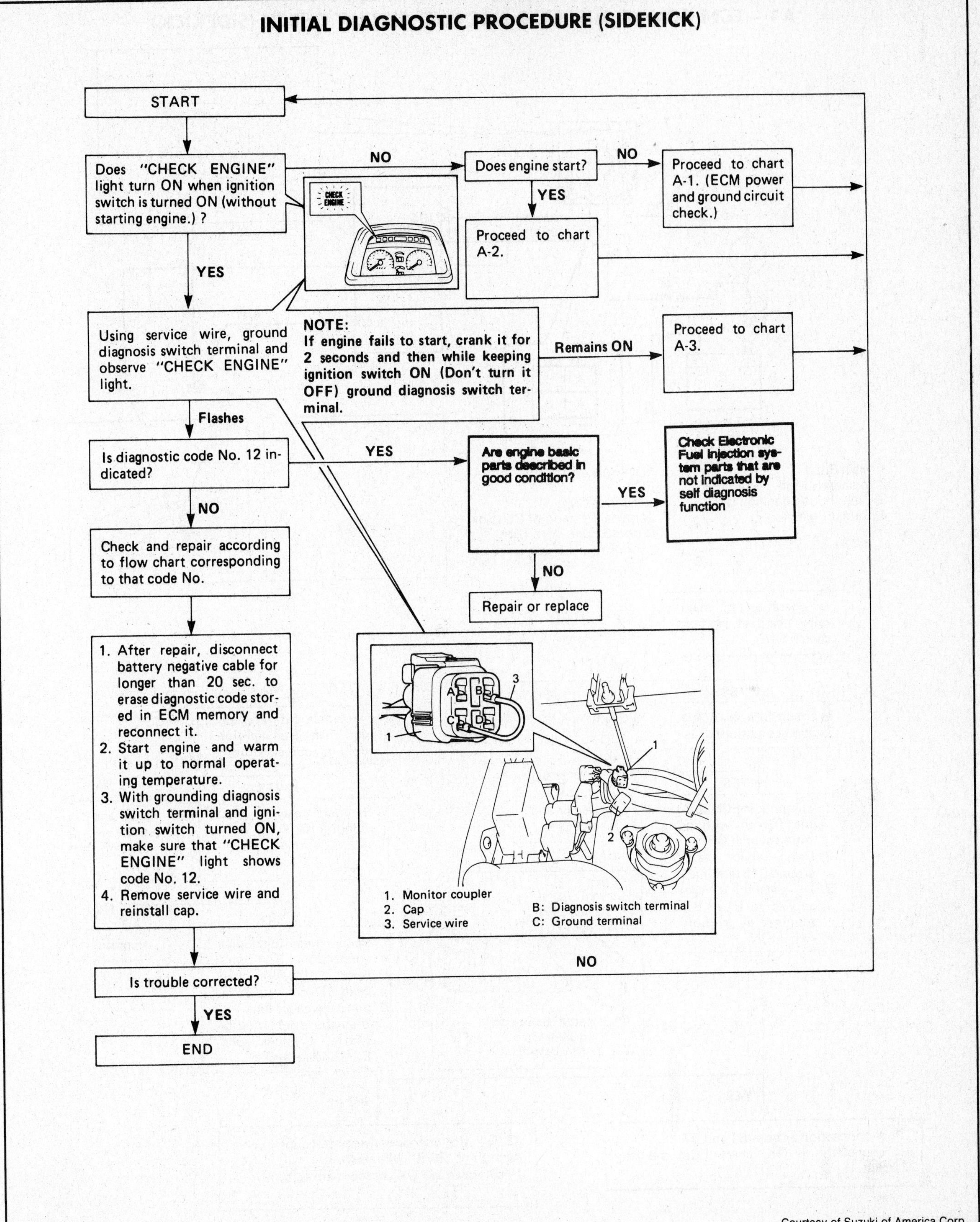

START
Does "CHECK ENGINE" light turn ON when ignition switch is turned ON (without starting engine.) ?
NO
Does engine start?
NO
Proceed to chart A-1. (ECM power and ground circuit check.)
YES
Proceed to chart A-2.
CHECK ENGINE
YES
Using service wire, ground diagnosis switch terminal and observe "CHECK ENGINE" light.
NOTE:
If engine fails to start, crank it for 2 seconds and then while keeping ignition switch ON (Don't turn it OFF) ground diagnosis switch terminal.
Remains ON
Proceed to chart A-3.
Flashes
Is diagnostic code No. 12 indicated?
YES
Are engine basic parts described in good condition?
YES
Check Electronic Fuel Injection system parts that are not indicated by self diagnosis function
NO
Repair or replace
NO
Check and repair according to flow chart corresponding to that code No.
1. After repair, disconnect battery negative cable for longer than 20 sec. to erase diagnostic code stored in ECM memory and reconnect it.
2. Start engine and warm it up to normal operating temperature.
3. With grounding diagnosis switch terminal and ignition switch turned ON, make sure that "CHECK ENGINE" light shows code No. 12.
4. Remove service wire and reinstall cap.
A
B
C
D
1
2
3
1. Monitor coupler
2. Cap
3. Service wire
B: Diagnosis switch terminal
C: Ground terminal
NO
Is trouble corrected?
YES
END
91H17415


Courtesy of Suzuki of America Corp.

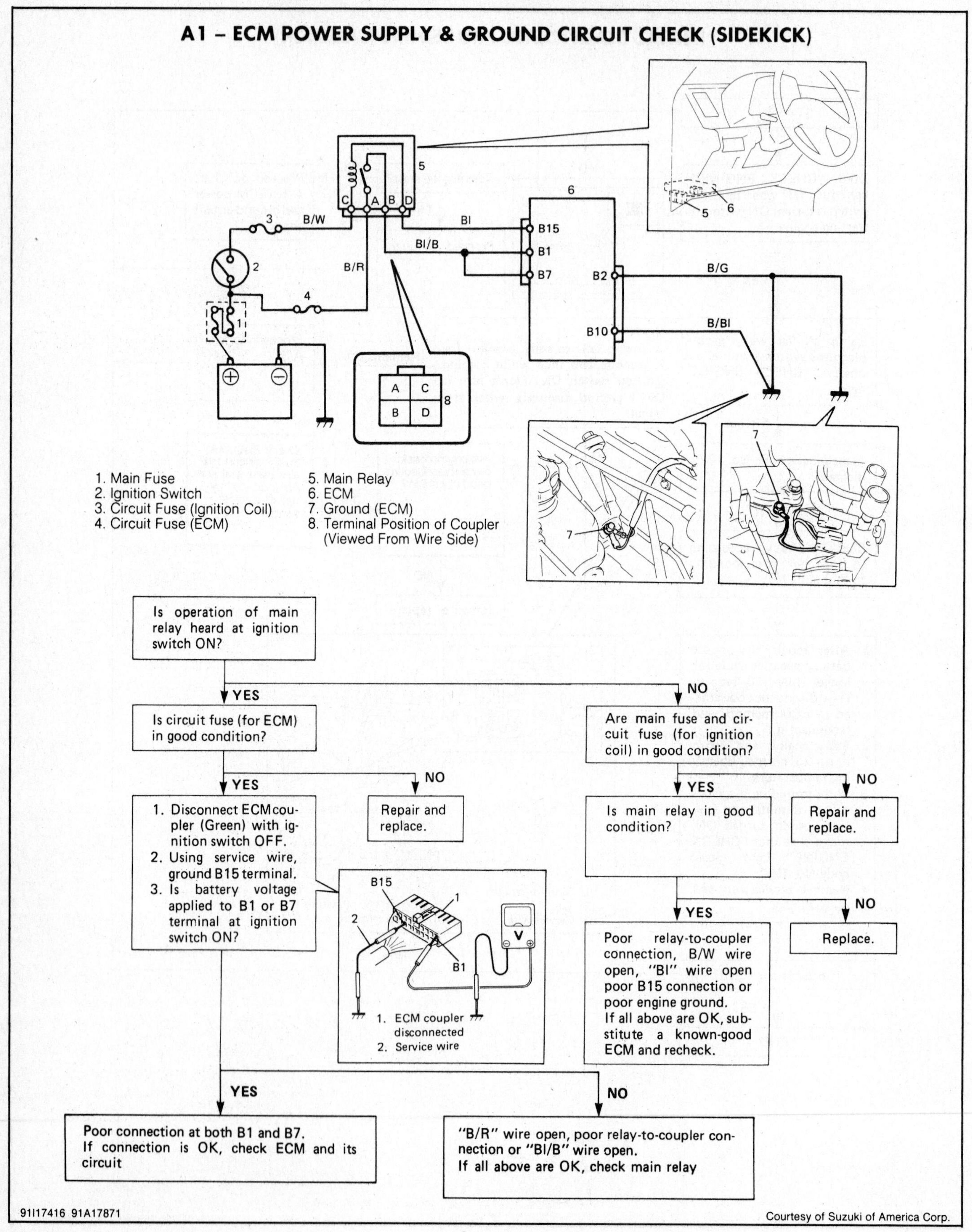
A1 – ECM POWER SUPPLY & GROUND CIRCUIT CHECK (SIDEKICK)
5
C A B D
3
B/W
Bl
6
B15
Bl/B
B1
2
B/R
B7
B2
B/G
4
1
B10
B/Bl
A C
B D
8
7
1. Main Fuse
2. Ignition Switch
3. Circuit Fuse (Ignition Coil)
4. Circuit Fuse (ECM)
5. Main Relay
6. ECM
7. Ground (ECM)
8. Terminal Position of Coupler (Viewed From Wire Side)
Is operation of main relay heard at ignition switch ON?
YES
NO
Is circuit fuse (for ECM) in good condition?
YES
NO
1. Disconnect ECM coupler (Green) with ignition switch OFF.
2. Using service wire, ground B15 terminal.
3. Is battery voltage applied to B1 or B7 terminal at ignition switch ON?
Repair and replace.
B15
1
2
V
B1
1. ECM coupler disconnected
2. Service wire
Are main fuse and circuit fuse (for ignition coil) in good condition?
YES
NO
Is main relay in good condition?
Repair and replace.
YES
NO
Poor relay-to-coupler connection, B/W wire open, "Bl" wire open poor B15 connection or poor engine ground.
If all above are OK, substitute a known-good ECM and recheck.
Replace.
YES
NO
Poor connection at both B1 and B7.
If connection is OK, check ECM and its circuit
"B/R" wire open, poor relay-to-coupler connection or "Bl/B" wire open.
If all above are OK, check main relay
91I17416 91A17871
Courtesy of Suzuki of America Corp.

# 1991 ENGINE PERFORMANCE
# Self-Diagnostics (Cont.)

## A2 – CHECK ENGINE LIGHT INOPERATIVE (SIDEKICK)

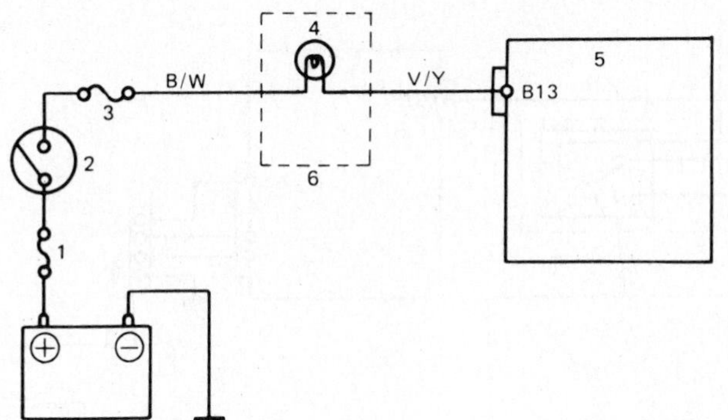
4
5
B/W
V/Y
B13
3
2
6
1

1. Main Fuse
2. Ignition Switch
3. Circuit Fuse
4. CHECK ENGINE Light
5. ECM
6. Combination Meter

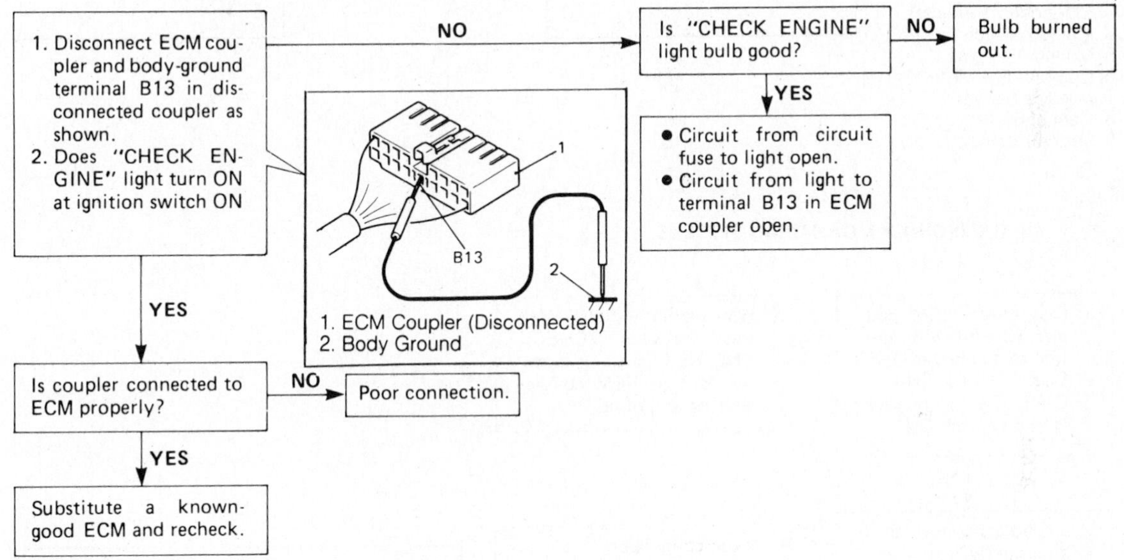
1. Disconnect ECM coupler and body-ground terminal B13 in disconnected coupler as shown.
2. Does "CHECK ENGINE" light turn ON at ignition switch ON
NO
Is "CHECK ENGINE" light bulb good?
NO
Bulb burned out.
YES
● Circuit from circuit fuse to light open.
● Circuit from light to terminal B13 in ECM coupler open.
1
B13
2
1. ECM Coupler (Disconnected)
2. Body Ground
YES
Is coupler connected to ECM properly?
NO
Poor connection.
YES
Substitute a known-good ECM and recheck.

119587

Courtesy of Suzuki of America Corp.

# 1991 ENGINE PERFORMANCE
## Self-Diagnostics (Cont.)

### A3 – CHECK ENGINE LIGHT STAYS ON – WON'T FLASH (SIDEKICK)

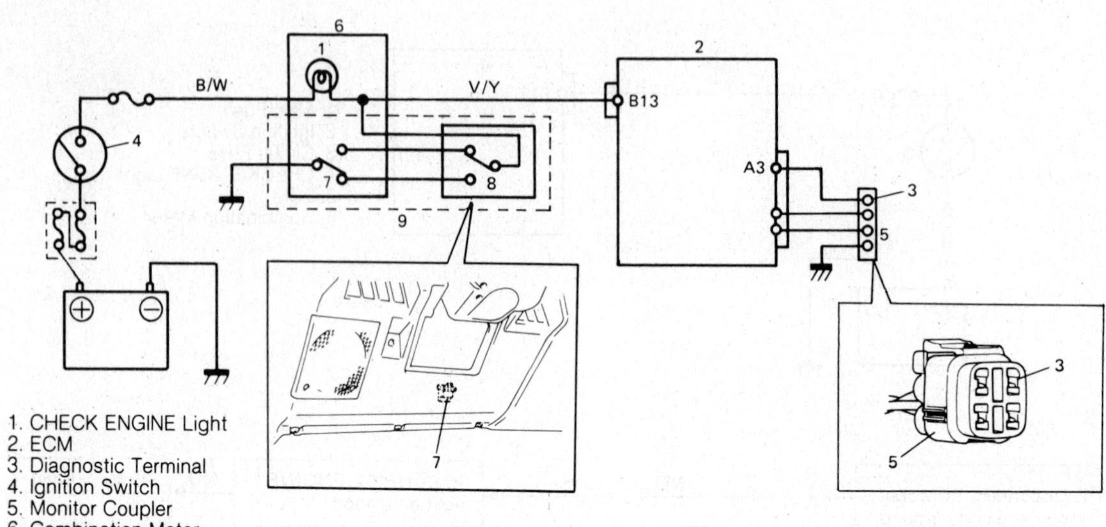
6
1
2
B/W
V/Y
B13
4
A3
3
7
8
5
9
3
7
5

1. CHECK ENGINE Light
2. ECM
3. Diagnostic Terminal
4. Ignition Switch
5. Monitor Coupler
6. Combination Meter
7. Mileage Sensor
8. Cancel Switch
9. Federal Vehicles Only

**CALIFORNIA & CANADIAN MODELS**

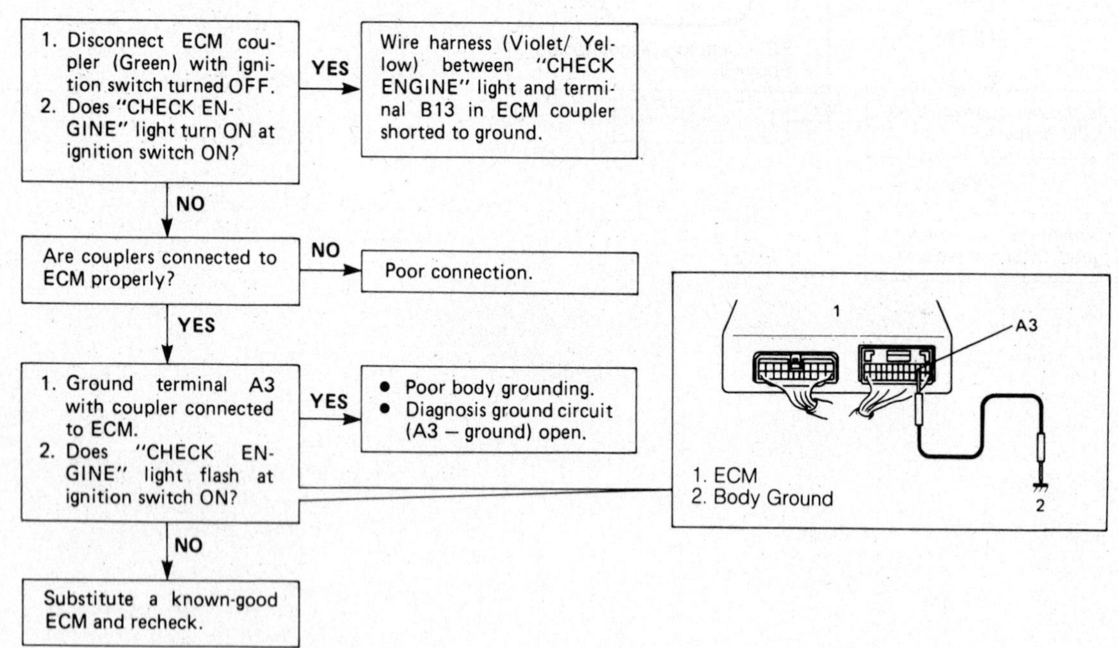
1. Disconnect ECM coupler (Green) with ignition switch turned OFF.
2. Does "CHECK ENGINE" light turn ON at ignition switch ON?
YES
Wire harness (Violet/ Yellow) between "CHECK ENGINE" light and terminal B13 in ECM coupler shorted to ground.
NO
Are couplers connected to ECM properly?
NO
Poor connection.
YES
1. Ground terminal A3 with coupler connected to ECM.
2. Does "CHECK ENGINE" light flash at ignition switch ON?
YES
• Poor body grounding.
• Diagnosis ground circuit (A3 – ground) open.
NO
Substitute a known-good ECM and recheck.
1
A3
1. ECM
2. Body Ground
2

**Continued on Next Page**

91J17417

Courtesy of Suzuki of America Corp.

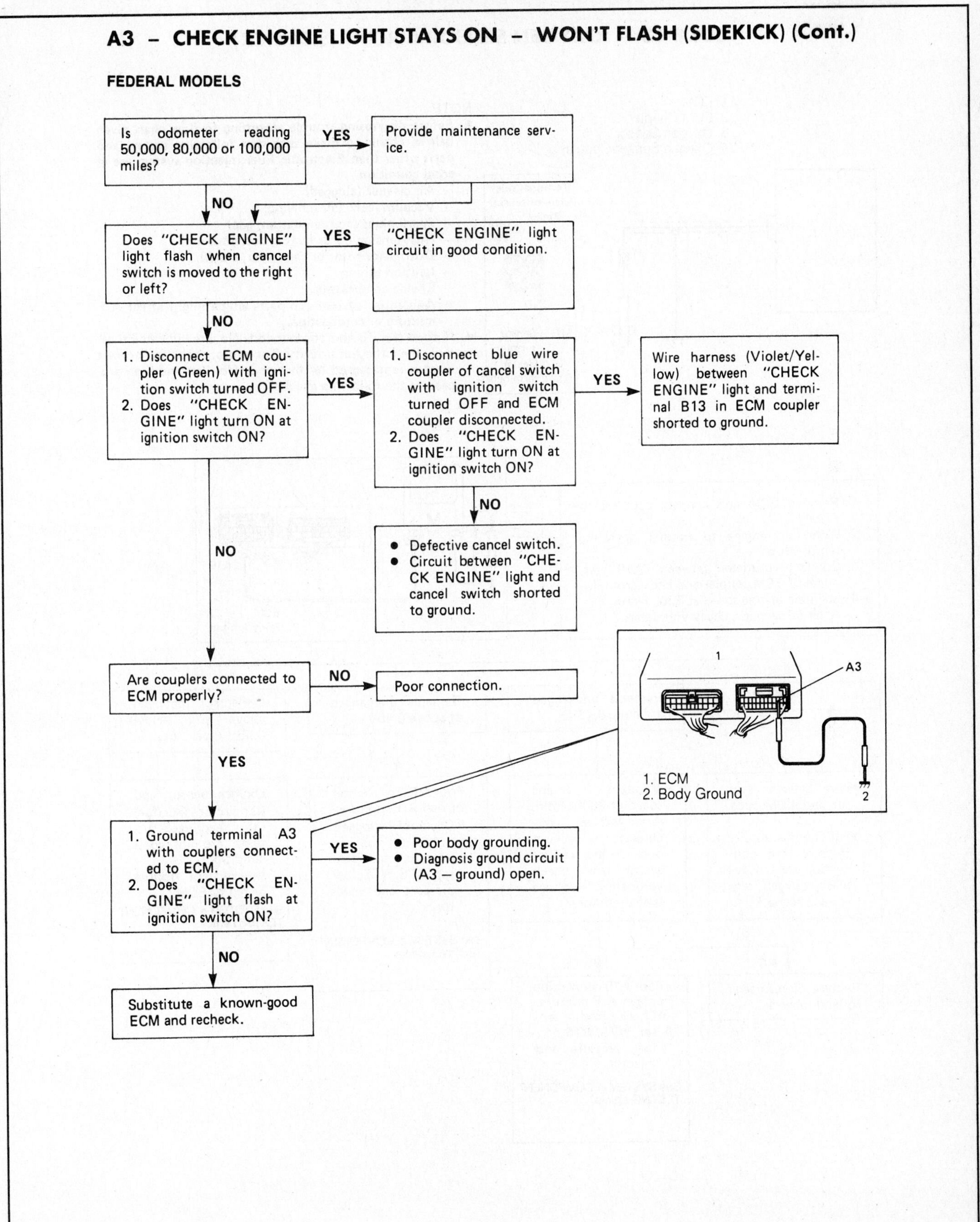

A3 – CHECK ENGINE LIGHT STAYS ON – WON'T FLASH (SIDEKICK) (Cont.)
FEDERAL MODELS
Is odometer reading 50,000, 80,000 or 100,000 miles?
YES
Provide maintenance service.
NO
Does "CHECK ENGINE" light flash when cancel switch is moved to the right or left?
YES
"CHECK ENGINE" light circuit in good condition.
NO
1. Disconnect ECM coupler (Green) with ignition switch turned OFF.
2. Does "CHECK ENGINE" light turn ON at ignition switch ON?
YES
1. Disconnect blue wire coupler of cancel switch with ignition switch turned OFF and ECM coupler disconnected.
2. Does "CHECK ENGINE" light turn ON at ignition switch ON?
YES
Wire harness (Violet/Yellow) between "CHECK ENGINE" light and terminal B13 in ECM coupler shorted to ground.
NO
• Defective cancel switch.
• Circuit between "CHECK ENGINE" light and cancel switch shorted to ground.
NO
Are couplers connected to ECM properly?
NO
Poor connection.
YES
1. Ground terminal A3 with couplers connected to ECM.
2. Does "CHECK ENGINE" light flash at ignition switch ON?
YES
• Poor body grounding.
• Diagnosis ground circuit (A3 – ground) open.
NO
Substitute a known-good ECM and recheck.
1
A3
2
1. ECM
2. Body Ground
91B17872
Courtesy of Suzuki of America Corp.

# 1991 ENGINE PERFORMANCE
## Self-Diagnostics (Cont.)

### CODE 13 – OXYGEN SENSOR CIRCUIT (SIDEKICK)

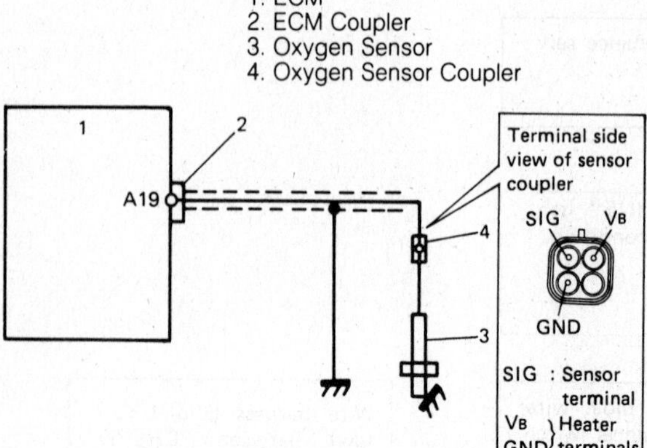


**NOTE:**

- **Before diagnosing trouble according to flow chart given below, check to make sure that following system and parts other than Electronic Fuel Injection system are in good condition.**
  - **Air cleaner (clogged)**
  - **Vacuum leaks (air inhaling)**
  - **Spark plugs (contamination, gap)**
  - **High-tension cords (crack, deterioration)**
  - **Distributor rotor or cap (wear, crack)**
  - **Ignition timing**
  - **Engine compression**
  - **Any other system and parts which might affect A/F mixture or combustion.**
- **If code No. 13 and another code No. are indicated together, the latter has priority. Therefore, check and correct what is represented by that code No. first and then proceed to the following check.**

1. Remove ECM and connect couplers to ECM.
2. Warm up engine to normal operating temperature.
3. Connect voltmeter between "A19" terminal of ECM coupler and body ground.
4. Maintain engine speed at 2000 r/min. After 60 seconds, check voltmeter.

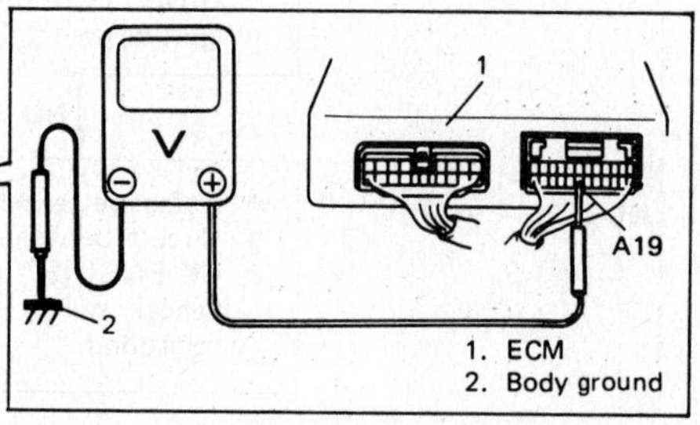

(Illustration labels: V; 1; A19; 2; 1. ECM; 2. Body ground)

| Result | Action |
|---|---|
| 0V | • Wire between sensor and ECM open or • Poor connection. If wire and connection are OK, replace oxygen sensor and recheck. |
| Remains unchanged at below 0.45V. | Maintain engine speed at 2000 r/min. After 60 sec., disconnect vacuum hose from pressure sensor and check voltmeter. Is voltage 0.45V or more? **NO:** Replace oxygen sensor and recheck. **YES:** Poor A19 connection or lean A/F mixture. • Check pressure sensor, WTS, ATS, fuel pressure and injector. See SYSTEM & COMPONENT TESTING article. |
| Remains unchanged at above 0.45V. | Poor A19 connection or rich A/F mixture. • Check TPS, clogged pressure sensor hose, pressure sensor, ATS, WTS, fuel pressure and injector. See SYSTEM & COMPONENT TESTING article. |
| Deflects between above and below 0.45V repeatedly. | Oxygen sensor and its circuit (Air/fuel ratio feed back system) are in good condition. Intermittent trouble or faulty ECM. See SYSTEM & COMPONENT TESTING article. |

91H17860 91C17873

Courtesy of Suzuki of America Corp.

## CODE 14 – COOLANT TEMPERATURE SENSOR (CTS) INDICATION LOW (SIDEKICK)

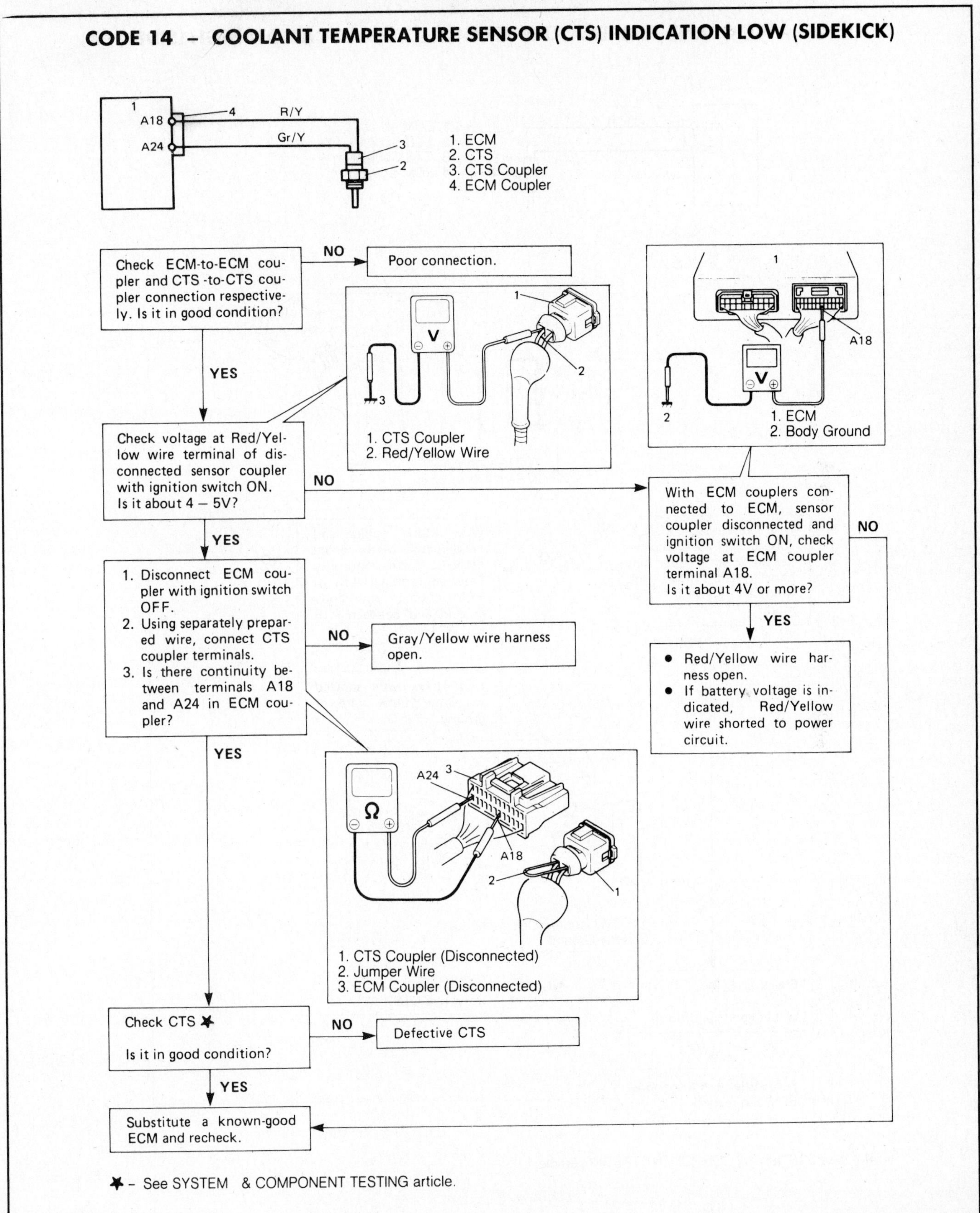

1
A18
A24
4
R/Y
Gr/Y
3
2
1. ECM
2. CTS
3. CTS Coupler
4. ECM Coupler
Check ECM-to-ECM coupler and CTS-to-CTS coupler connection respectively. Is it in good condition?
NO
Poor connection.
YES
1
V
2
3
1. CTS Coupler
2. Red/Yellow Wire
Check voltage at Red/Yellow wire terminal of disconnected sensor coupler with ignition switch ON. Is it about 4 – 5V?
NO
1
A18
V
2
1. ECM
2. Body Ground
With ECM couplers connected to ECM, sensor coupler disconnected and ignition switch ON, check voltage at ECM coupler terminal A18. Is it about 4V or more?
NO
YES
1. Disconnect ECM coupler with ignition switch OFF.
2. Using separately prepared wire, connect CTS coupler terminals.
3. Is there continuity between terminals A18 and A24 in ECM coupler?
NO
Gray/Yellow wire harness open.
YES
• Red/Yellow wire harness open.
• If battery voltage is indicated, Red/Yellow wire shorted to power circuit.
YES
Ω
A24
3
A18
2
1
1. CTS Coupler (Disconnected)
2. Jumper Wire
3. ECM Coupler (Disconnected)
Check CTS ✱
Is it in good condition?
NO
Defective CTS
YES
Substitute a known-good ECM and recheck.
✱ - See SYSTEM & COMPONENT TESTING article.


119592

Courtesy of Suzuki of America Corp.

# 1991 ENGINE PERFORMANCE
## Self-Diagnostics (Cont.)

### CODE 15 – COOLANT TEMPERATURE SENSOR (CTS) INDICATION HIGH (SIDEKICK)

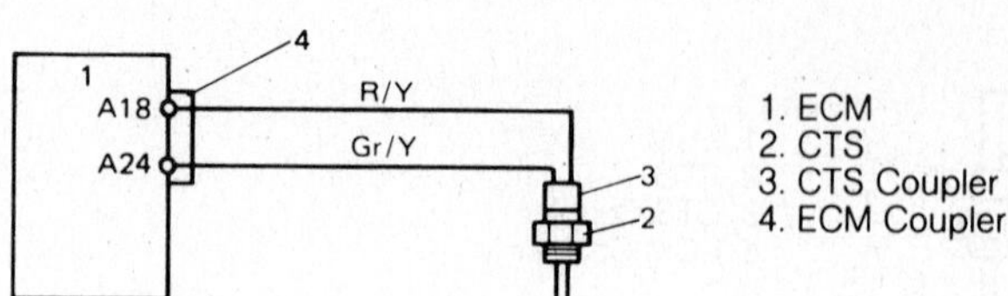


V

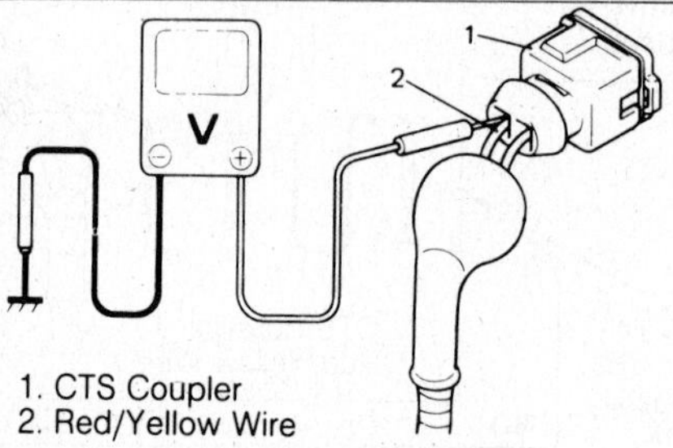

1. CTS Coupler
2. Red/Yellow Wire

With ignition switch ON, is voltage applied to disconnected sensor coupler terminal (Red/Yellow wire terminal) about 4V or more?

NO → With ECM coupler and WTS coupler disconnected each, is there continuity between terminal A18 of ECM coupler and body ground and between A18 and A24?

- YES → Red/Yellow wire shorted to Gray/Yellow wire or ground.
- NO → Substitute a known-good ECM and recheck.

Ω
A24
A18

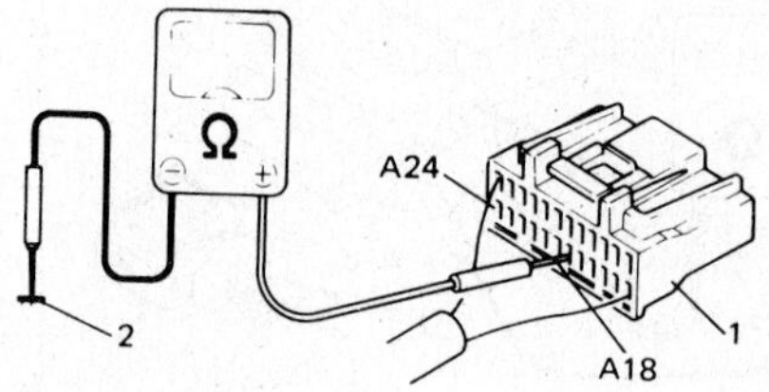

1. ECM Coupler (Disconnected)
2. Body Ground

YES → Check CTS ✱
Is it in good condition?

- NO → Defective CTS.
- YES → Substitute a known-good ECM and recheck.

✱ - See SYSTEM & COMPONENT TESTING article.

119593

Courtesy of Suzuki of America Corp.

## CODE 21 – THROTTLE POSITION SENSOR CIRCUIT INDICATION HIGH (SIDEKICK)

1
4
3
2
A23
A21
A14
A24
Gr/R
Gr
Bl/W
Gr/Y

1. ECM
2. TPS
3. TPS Coupler
4. ECM Coupler

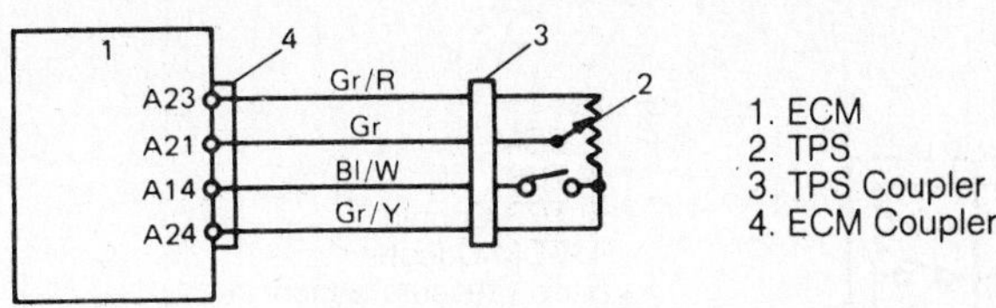

Check ECM-to-ECM coupler and TPS coupler-to-coupler connection respectively. Is it in good condition?
- NO → Poor connection.
- YES ↓

Check TPS ✱ Is it in good condition?
- NO → Defective TPS.
- YES ↓

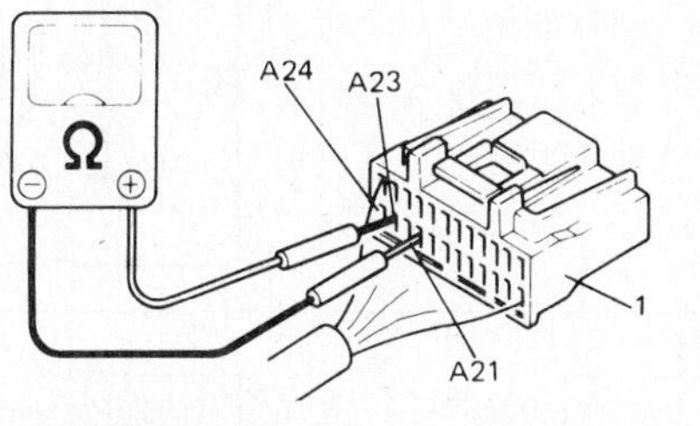

Ω
A24
A23
A21
1
1. ECM Coupler (Disconnected)

1. Disconnect ECM coupler with ignition switch OFF.
2. With TPS coupler disconnected, is there continuity between ECM coupler terminals A23 and A21?
- YES → Gray/Red wire shorted to Gray wire.
- NO ↓

1. Disconnect PS coupler.
2. Connect TPS coupler.
3. Is resistance between ECM coupler terminals A23 and A24 3.5 – 6.5 kΩ?
- NO → Gray/Yellow wire open.
- YES ↓

Substitute a known-good ECM and recheck.

1. PS - Pressure Sensor
2. TPS - Throttle Position Sensor

✱ - See SYSTEM & COMPONENT TESTING article.

119594

Courtesy of Suzuki of America Corp.

# 1991 ENGINE PERFORMANCE
# Self-Diagnostics (Cont.)

## CODE 22 – THROTTLE POSITION SENSOR CIRCUIT INDICATION LOW (SIDEKICK)

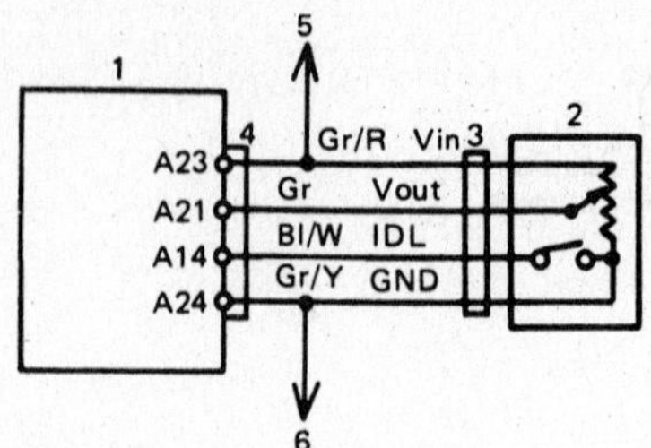


1. ECM
2. TPS
3. TPS Coupler
4. ECM Coupler
5. To Pressure Sensor
6. To Other Sensors

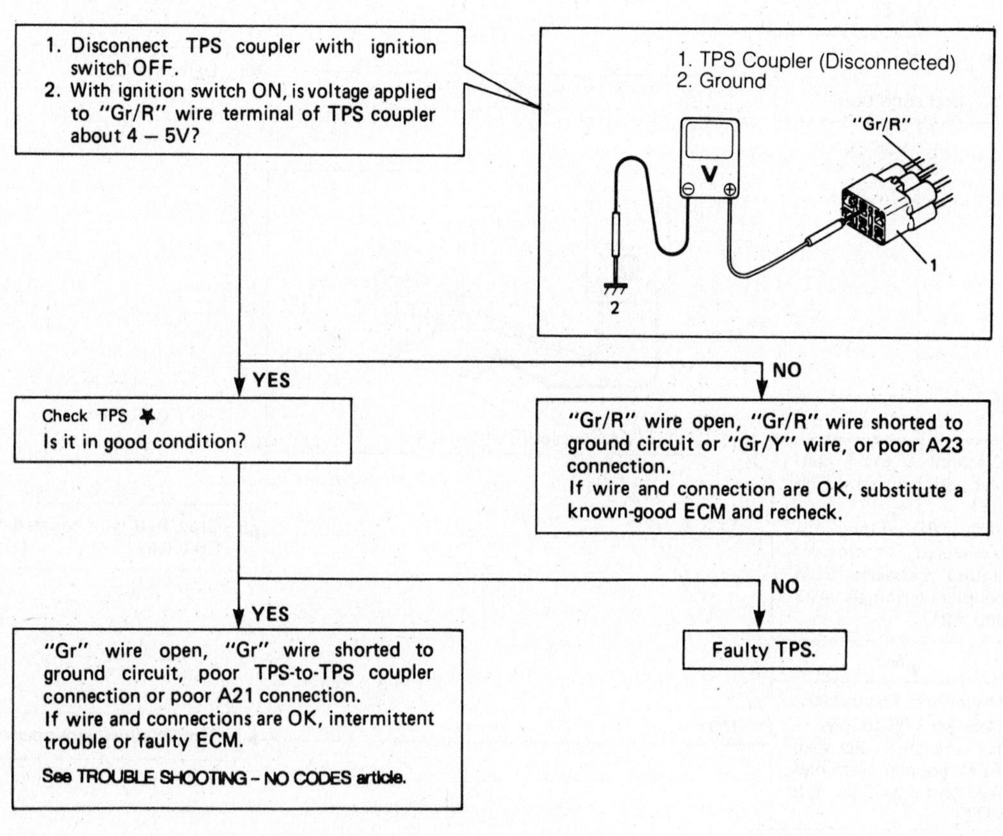


1. Disconnect TPS coupler with ignition switch OFF.
2. With ignition switch ON, is voltage applied to "Gr/R" wire terminal of TPS coupler about 4 – 5V?

**YES** → Check TPS ✱
Is it in good condition?

- **YES** → "Gr" wire open, "Gr" wire shorted to ground circuit, poor TPS-to-TPS coupler connection or poor A21 connection.
If wire and connections are OK, intermittent trouble or faulty ECM.
**See TROUBLE SHOOTING – NO CODES article.**
- **NO** → Faulty TPS.

**NO** → "Gr/R" wire open, "Gr/R" wire shorted to ground circuit or "Gr/Y" wire, or poor A23 connection.
If wire and connection are OK, substitute a known-good ECM and recheck.

✱ – See SYSTEM & COMPONENT TESTING article.

91I17861

Courtesy of Suzuki of America Corp.

# 1991 ENGINE PERFORMANCE
# Self-Diagnostics (Cont.)

## CODE 23 – AIR TEMPERATURE SENSOR (ATS) CIRCUIT INDICATION LOW (SIDEKICK)

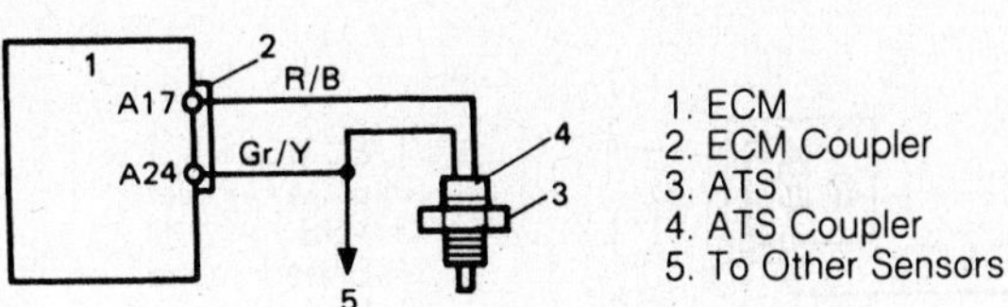
1
2
R/B
A17
A24
Gr/Y
4
3
5
1. ECM
2. ECM Coupler
3. ATS
4. ATS Coupler
5. To Other Sensors

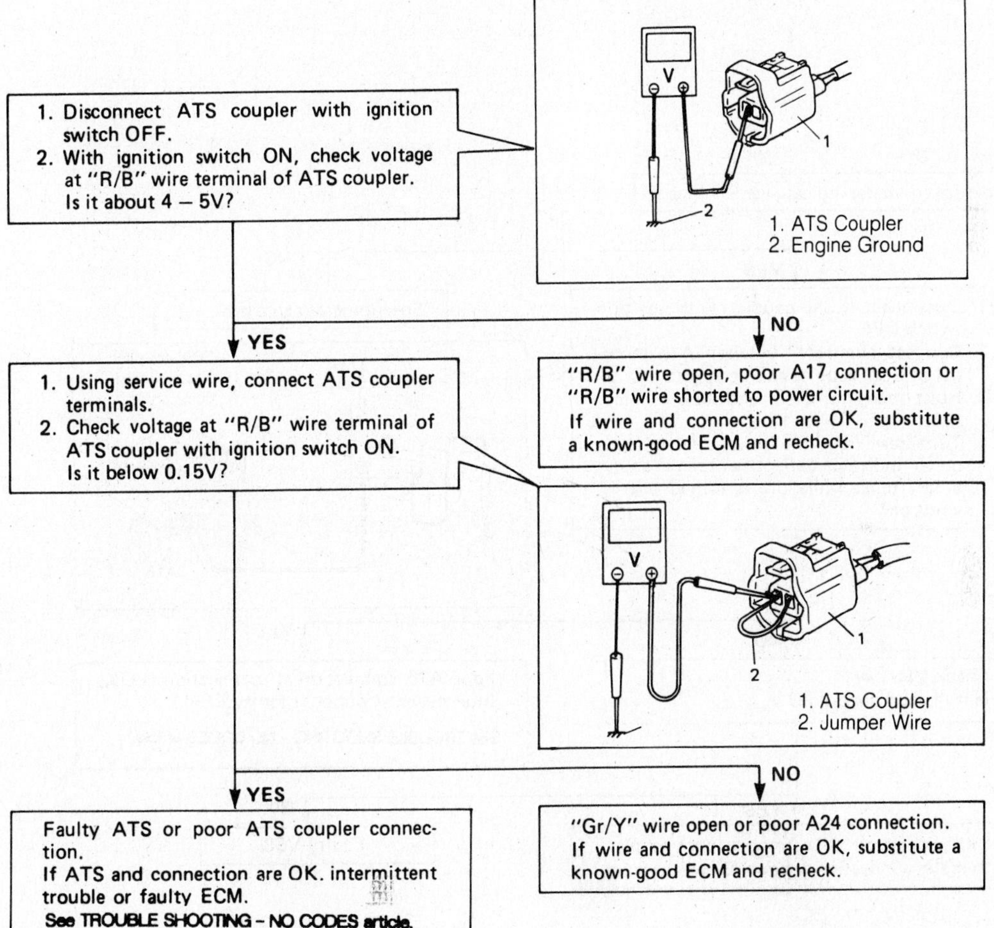
1. Disconnect ATS coupler with ignition switch OFF.
2. With ignition switch ON, check voltage at "R/B" wire terminal of ATS coupler.
Is it about 4 – 5V?
V
1
2
1. ATS Coupler
2. Engine Ground
YES
NO
"R/B" wire open, poor A17 connection or "R/B" wire shorted to power circuit.
If wire and connection are OK, substitute a known-good ECM and recheck.
1. Using service wire, connect ATS coupler terminals.
2. Check voltage at "R/B" wire terminal of ATS coupler with ignition switch ON.
Is it below 0.15V?
V
1
2
1. ATS Coupler
2. Jumper Wire
YES
NO
Faulty ATS or poor ATS coupler connection.
If ATS and connection are OK. intermittent trouble or faulty ECM.
See TROUBLE SHOOTING – NO CODES article.
"Gr/Y" wire open or poor A24 connection.
If wire and connection are OK, substitute a known-good ECM and recheck.

91J17862

Courtesy of Suzuki of America Corp.

# 1991 ENGINE PERFORMANCE
## Self-Diagnostics (Cont.)

### CODE 24 – VEHICLE SPEED SENSOR (SIDEKICK)

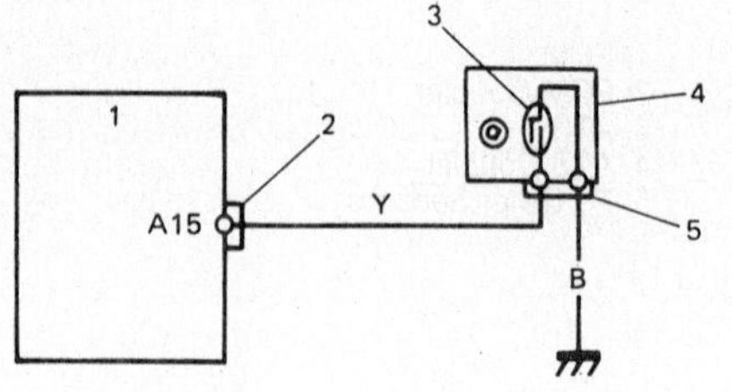
1
2
3
4
5
A15
Y
B

1. ECM
2. ECM Coupler
3. VSS
4. Speedometer
5. VSS Coupler

**NOTE:**
**Be sure to turn OFF ignition switch for this check.**

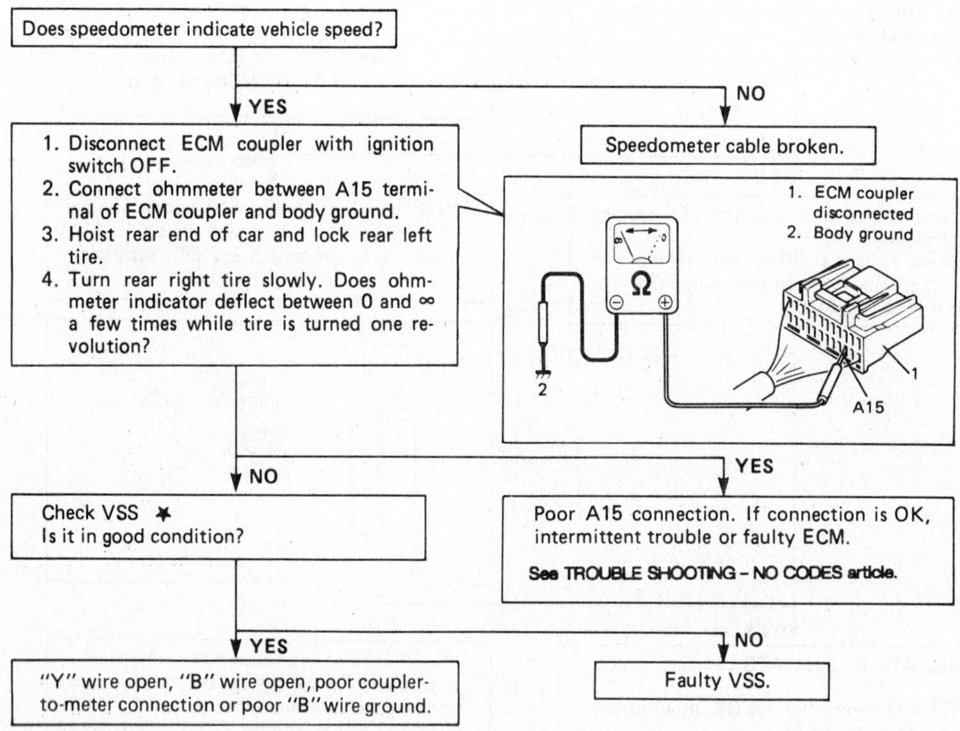
Does speedometer indicate vehicle speed?
YES
NO
Speedometer cable broken.
1. Disconnect ECM coupler with ignition switch OFF.
2. Connect ohmmeter between A15 terminal of ECM coupler and body ground.
3. Hoist rear end of car and lock rear left tire.
4. Turn rear right tire slowly. Does ohmmeter indicator deflect between 0 and ∞ a few times while tire is turned one revolution?
1. ECM coupler disconnected
2. Body ground
Ω
2
1
A15
NO
YES
Check VSS ✱
Is it in good condition?
Poor A15 connection. If connection is OK, intermittent trouble or faulty ECM.
See TROUBLE SHOOTING - NO CODES article.
YES
NO
"Y" wire open, "B" wire open, poor coupler-to-meter connection or poor "B" wire ground.
Faulty VSS.

✱- See SYSTEM & COMPONENT TESTING article.

91B17864

Courtesy of Suzuki of America Corp.

### CODE 25 – AIR TEMPERATURE SENSOR (ATS) CIRCUIT INDICATION HIGH (SIDEKICK)

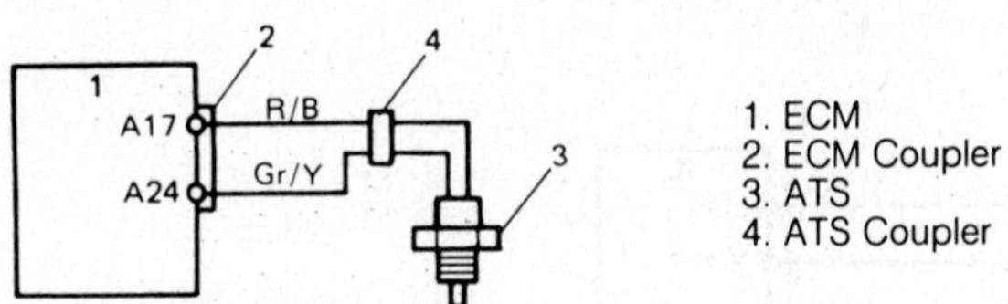


1. ECM
2. ECM Coupler
3. ATS
4. ATS Coupler

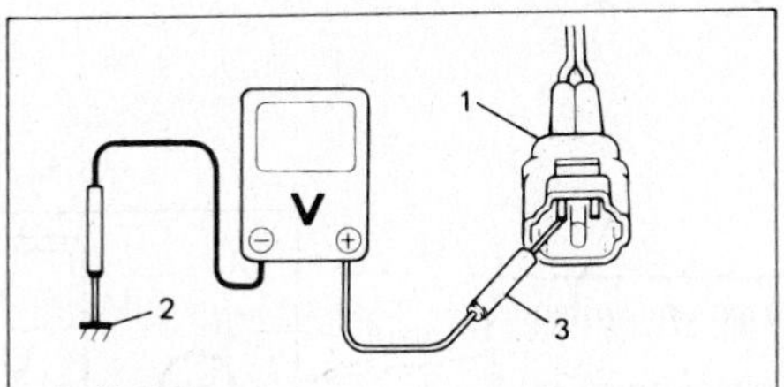

V

1. ATS Coupler
2. Engine Ground
3. Voltmeter Probe

With ignition switch ON, is voltage applied to Red/Black wire terminal on wire harness side of disconnected ATS coupler 4 – 5V?

- NO → With ECM coupler and ATS coupler disconnected each, is there continuity between ECM coupler terminal A17 and body ground and between A17 and A24?
  - YES → Red/Black wire shorted to Gray/Yellow wire or ground.
  - NO → Substitute a known-good ECM and recheck.
- YES → Check ATS ✱ Is it in good condition?
  - NO → Defective ATS.
  - YES → Substitute a known-good ECM and recheck.

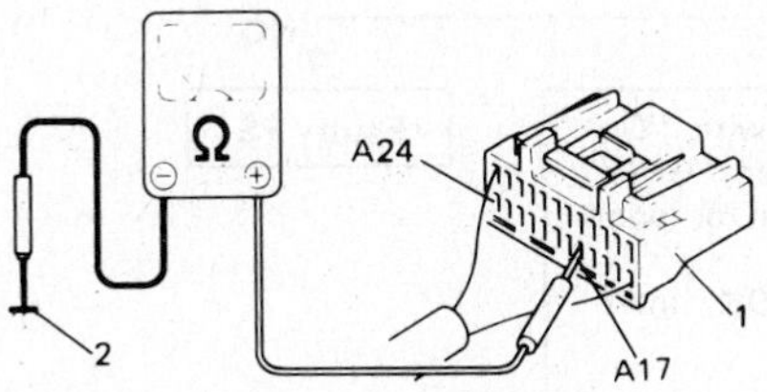

Ω
A24
A17

1. ECM
2. Body Ground

✱ - See SYSTEM & COMPONENT TESTING article.

119597

Courtesy of Suzuki of America Corp.

# 1991 ENGINE PERFORMANCE
## Self-Diagnostics (Cont.)

### CODE 31 – PRESSURE SENSOR (PS) CIRCUIT VOLTAGE HIGH (SIDEKICK)

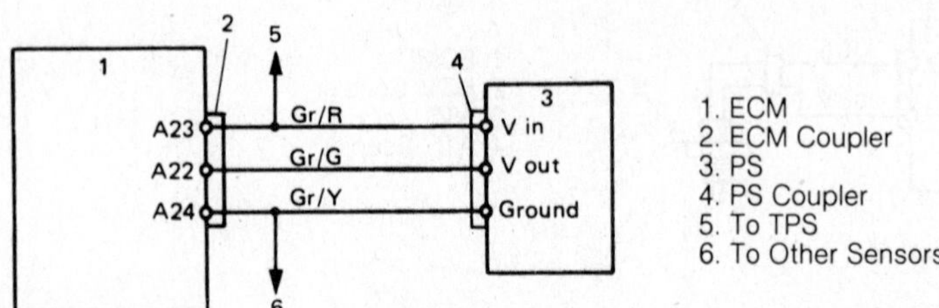
1
2
3
4
5
6
A23
A22
A24
Gr/R
Gr/G
Gr/Y
V in
V out
Ground
1. ECM
2. ECM Coupler
3. PS
4. PS Coupler
5. To TPS
6. To Other Sensors

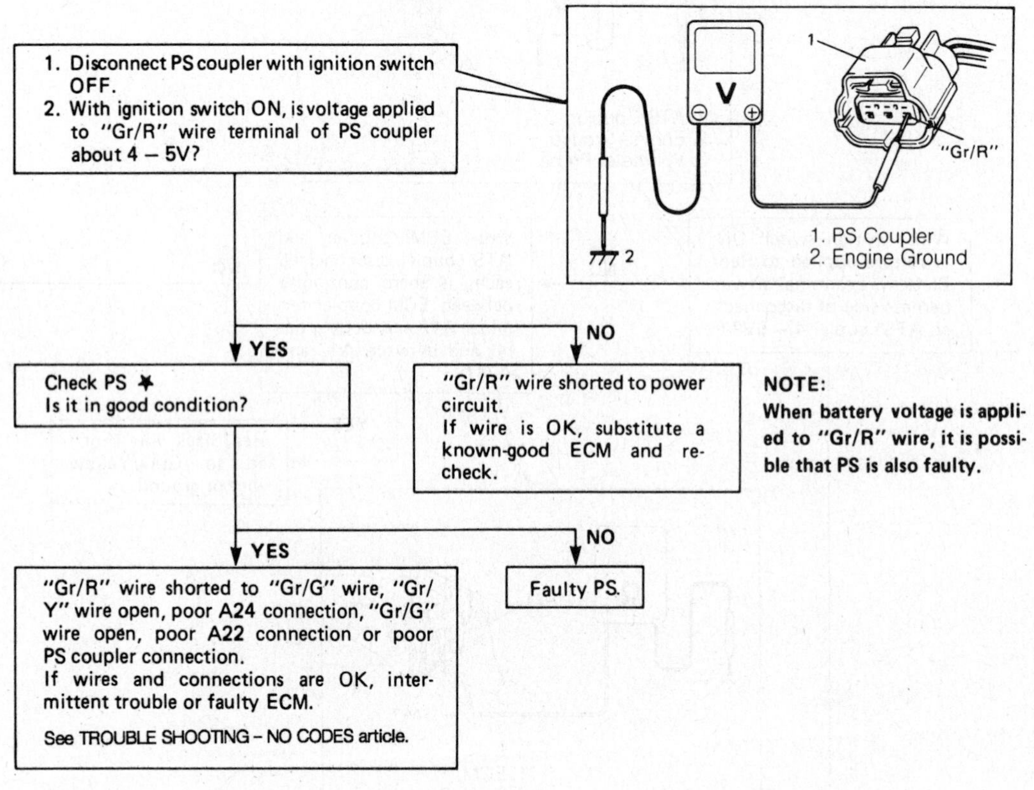
1. Disconnect PS coupler with ignition switch OFF.
2. With ignition switch ON, is voltage applied to "Gr/R" wire terminal of PS coupler about 4 – 5V?
V
"Gr/R"
1. PS Coupler
2. Engine Ground
YES
NO
Check PS ✱
Is it in good condition?
"Gr/R" wire shorted to power circuit.
If wire is OK, substitute a known-good ECM and recheck.
NOTE:
When battery voltage is applied to "Gr/R" wire, it is possible that PS is also faulty.
YES
NO
"Gr/R" wire shorted to "Gr/G" wire, "Gr/Y" wire open, poor A24 connection, "Gr/G" wire open, poor A22 connection or poor PS coupler connection.
If wires and connections are OK, intermittent trouble or faulty ECM.
See TROUBLE SHOOTING – NO CODES article.
Faulty PS.

✱- See SYSTEM & COMPONENT TESTING article.

91C17865

Courtesy of Suzuki of America Corp.

## CODE 32 – PRESSURE SENSOR (PS) CIRCUIT VOLTAGE LOW (SIDEKICK)

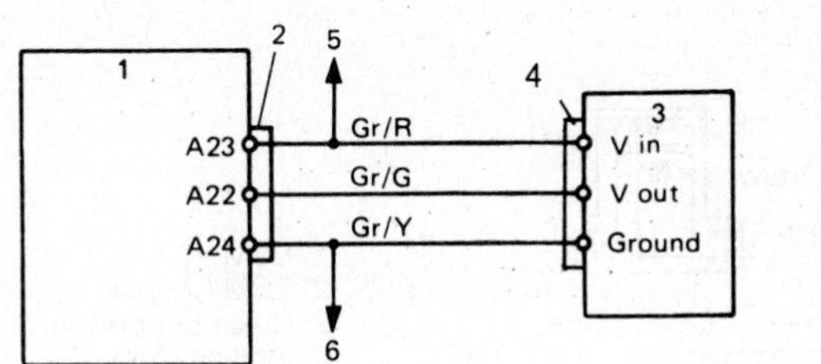


1. ECM
2. ECM Coupler
3. PS
4. PS Coupler
5. To TPS
6. To Other Sensors

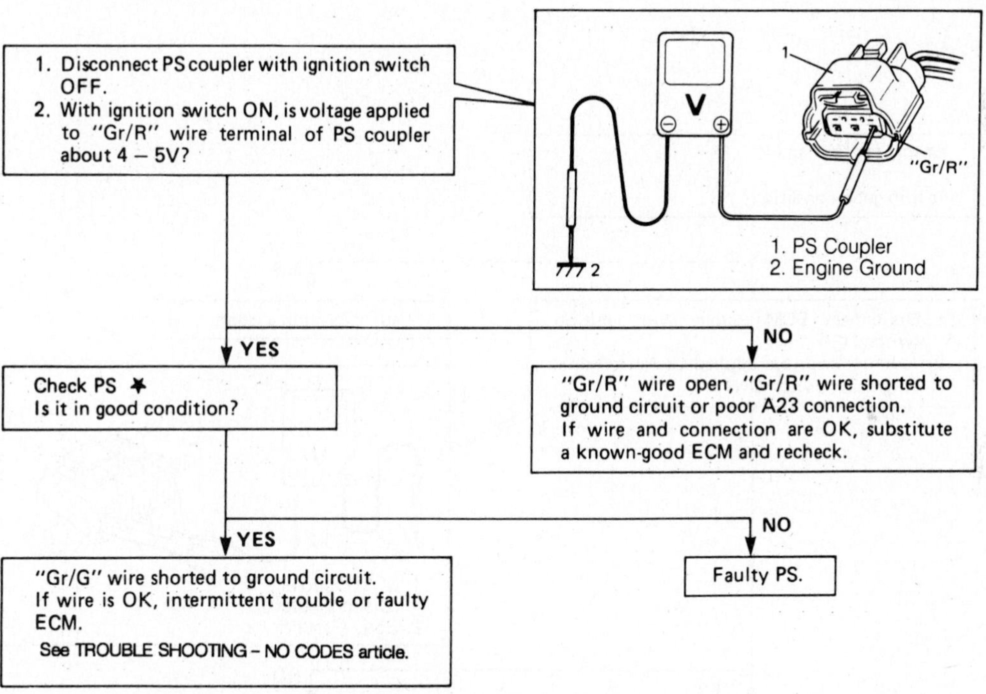


1. Disconnect PS coupler with ignition switch OFF.
2. With ignition switch ON, is voltage applied to "Gr/R" wire terminal of PS coupler about 4 – 5V?

**YES** → Check PS ✱ Is it in good condition?

- **YES** → "Gr/G" wire shorted to ground circuit. If wire is OK, intermittent trouble or faulty ECM. See TROUBLE SHOOTING – NO CODES article.
- **NO** → Faulty PS.

**NO** → "Gr/R" wire open, "Gr/R" wire shorted to ground circuit or poor A23 connection. If wire and connection are OK, substitute a known-good ECM and recheck.

✱ – See SYSTEM & COMPONENT TESTING article.

91D17866

Courtesy of Suzuki of America Corp.

# 1991 ENGINE PERFORMANCE
# Self-Diagnostics (Cont.)

## CODE 41 – NO IGNITION SIGNAL (SIDEKICK)

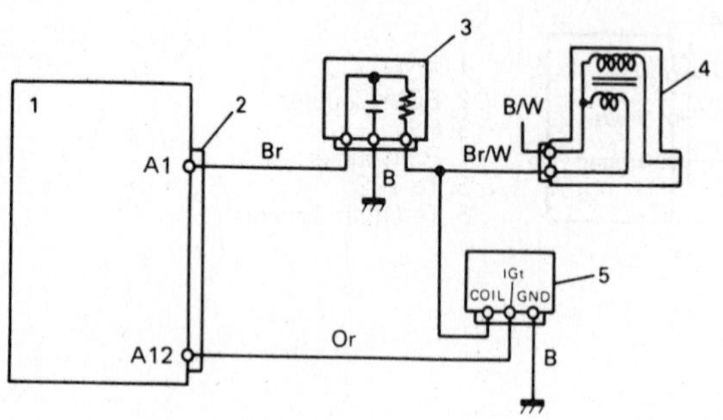


1. ECM
2. ECM Coupler
3. Noise Suppressor
4. Ignition Coil
6. Ignitor

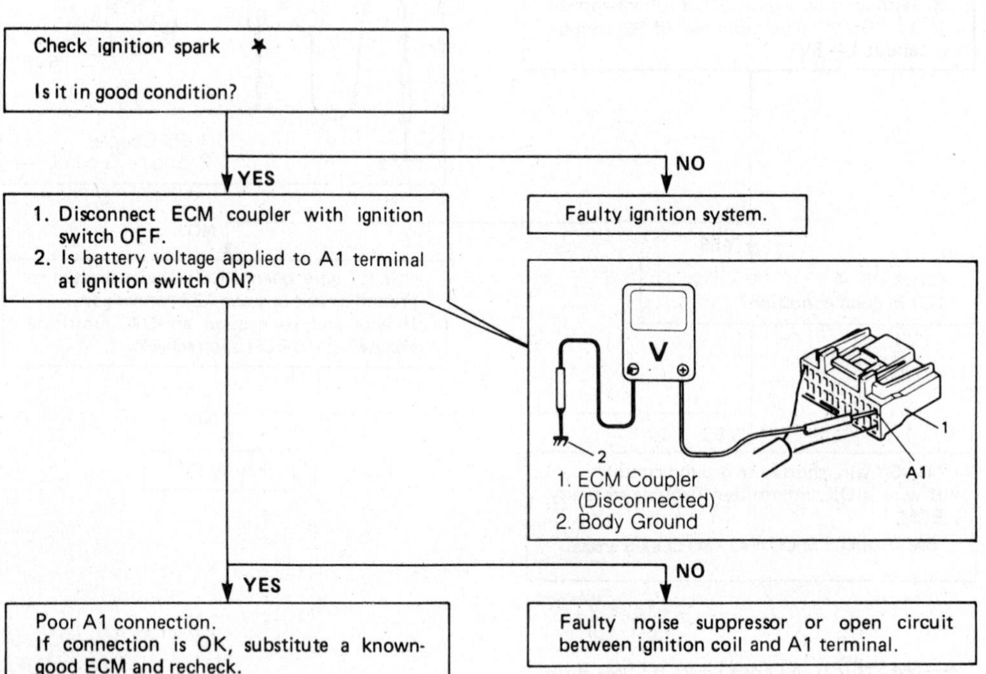

Check ignition spark ✱
Is it in good condition?
YES
NO
Faulty ignition system.
1. Disconnect ECM coupler with ignition switch OFF.
2. Is battery voltage applied to A1 terminal at ignition switch ON?
V
1
2
A1
1. ECM Coupler (Disconnected)
2. Body Ground
YES
NO
Poor A1 connection.
If connection is OK, substitute a known-good ECM and recheck.
Faulty noise suppressor or open circuit between ignition coil and A1 terminal.


✱ – See BASIC DIAGNOSTIC PROCEDURES article.

91E17867

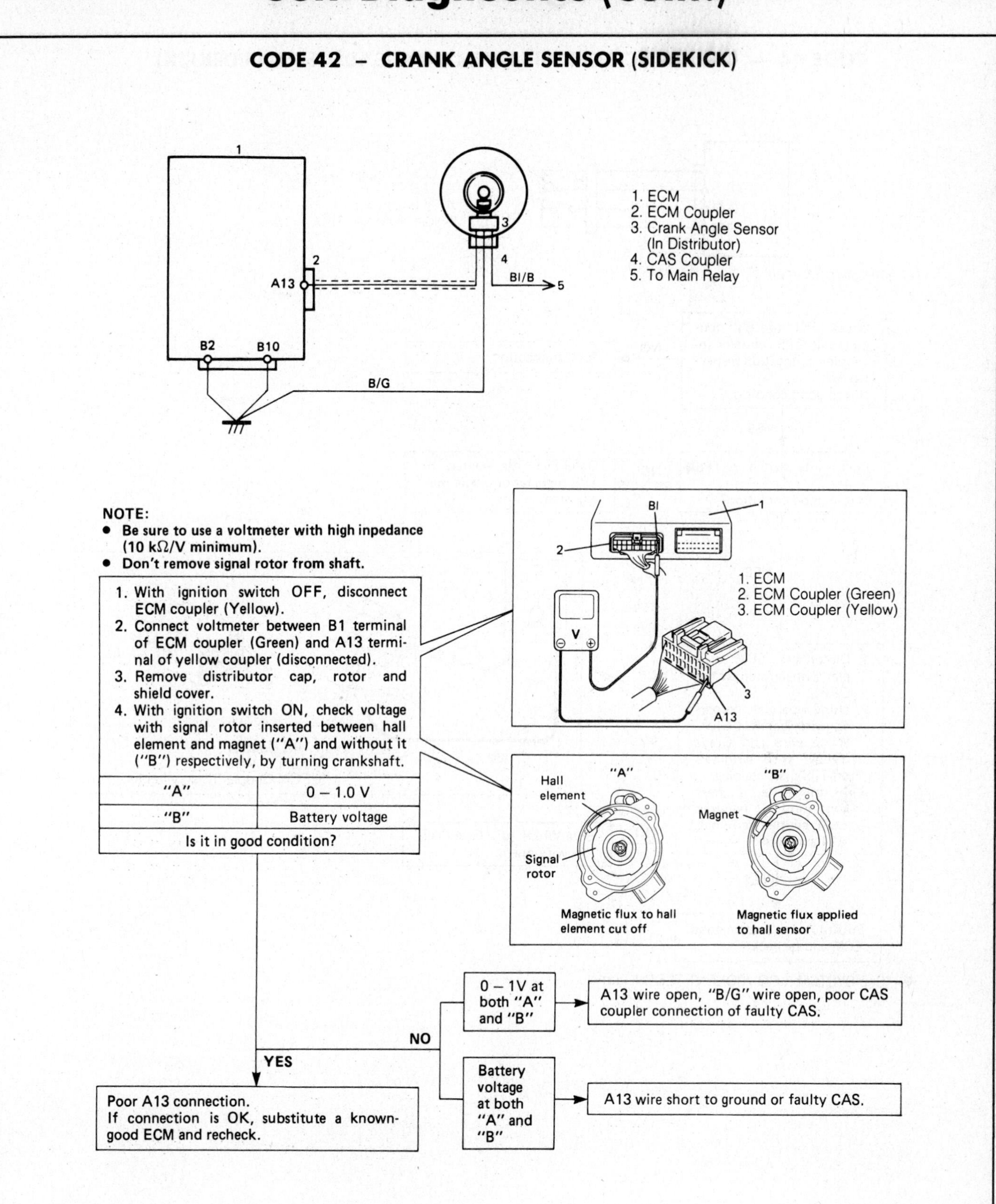
CODE 42 – CRANK ANGLE SENSOR (SIDEKICK)
1
2
3
4
A13
BI/B
5
B2
B10
B/G
1. ECM
2. ECM Coupler
3. Crank Angle Sensor
(In Distributor)
4. CAS Coupler
5. To Main Relay
NOTE:
• Be sure to use a voltmeter with high inpedance (10 kΩ/V minimum).
• Don't remove signal rotor from shaft.
1. With ignition switch OFF, disconnect ECM coupler (Yellow).
2. Connect voltmeter between B1 terminal of ECM coupler (Green) and A13 terminal of yellow coupler (disconnected).
3. Remove distributor cap, rotor and shield cover.
4. With ignition switch ON, check voltage with signal rotor inserted between hall element and magnet ("A") and without it ("B") respectively, by turning crankshaft.
"A" 0 – 1.0 V
"B" Battery voltage
Is it in good condition?
Bl
1
2
V
3
A13
1. ECM
2. ECM Coupler (Green)
3. ECM Coupler (Yellow)
"A"
"B"
Hall element
Signal rotor
Magnet
Magnetic flux to hall element cut off
Magnetic flux applied to hall sensor
YES
NO
0 – 1V at both "A" and "B"
A13 wire open, "B/G" wire open, poor CAS coupler connection of faulty CAS.
Battery voltage at both "A" and "B"
A13 wire short to ground or faulty CAS.
Poor A13 connection.
If connection is OK, substitute a known-good ECM and recheck.
91F17868
Courtesy of Suzuki of America Corp.

# 1991 ENGINE PERFORMANCE
# Self-Diagnostics (Cont.)

## CODE 44 – IDLE SWITCH CIRCUIT OPEN OR MISADJUSTED (SIDEKICK)

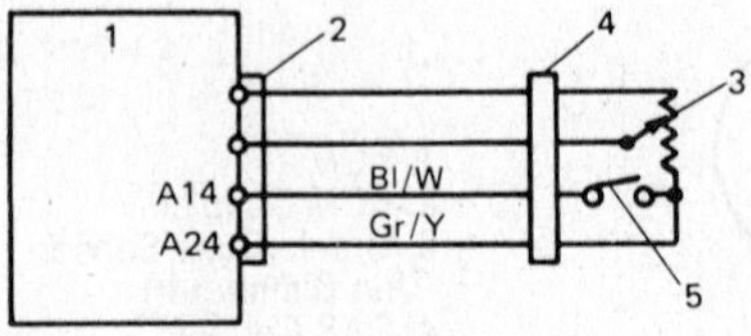


1. ECM
2. ECM Coupler
3. TPS
4. TPS Coupler
5. Idle Switch In TPS

*Idle Switch Circuit*

Check ECM-to-ECM coupler and TPS coupler-to-coupler connection respectively. Is it in good condition?

- **NO** → Poor connection.
- **YES** ↓

Check idle switch in TPS✱. Is it in good condition?

- **NO** → Defective idle switch or TPS installation angle maladjusted.
- **YES** ↓

1. Disconnect ECM coupler with ignition switch OFF.
2. Using separately prepared wire, connect Blue/White wire and Gray/Yellow wire terminals on TPS male coupler.
3. In this state, is there continuity between ECM coupler terminals A14 and A24?

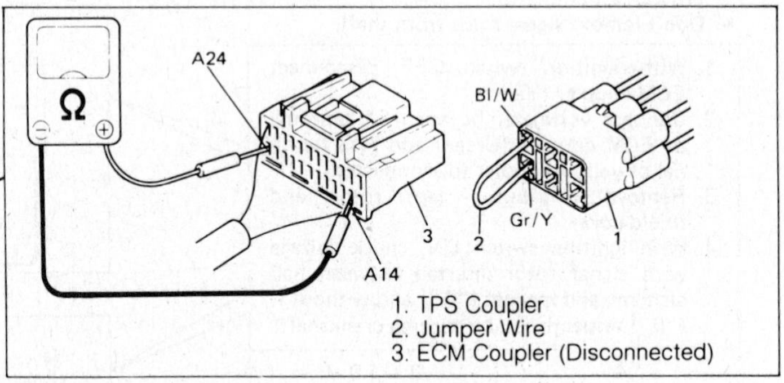


- **NO** → Blue/White or Gray/Yellow wire open.
- **YES** ↓

Substitute a known-good ECM and recheck.

✱- See SYSTEM & COMPONENT TESTING article.

119603

Courtesy of Suzuki of America Corp.

# 1991 ENGINE PERFORMANCE
# Self-Diagnostics (Cont.)

## CODE 45 – IDLE SWITCH CIRCUIT SHORTED OR MISADJUSTED (SIDEKICK)

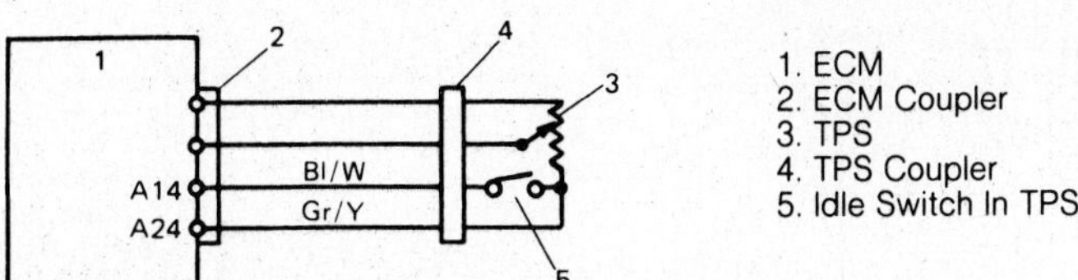


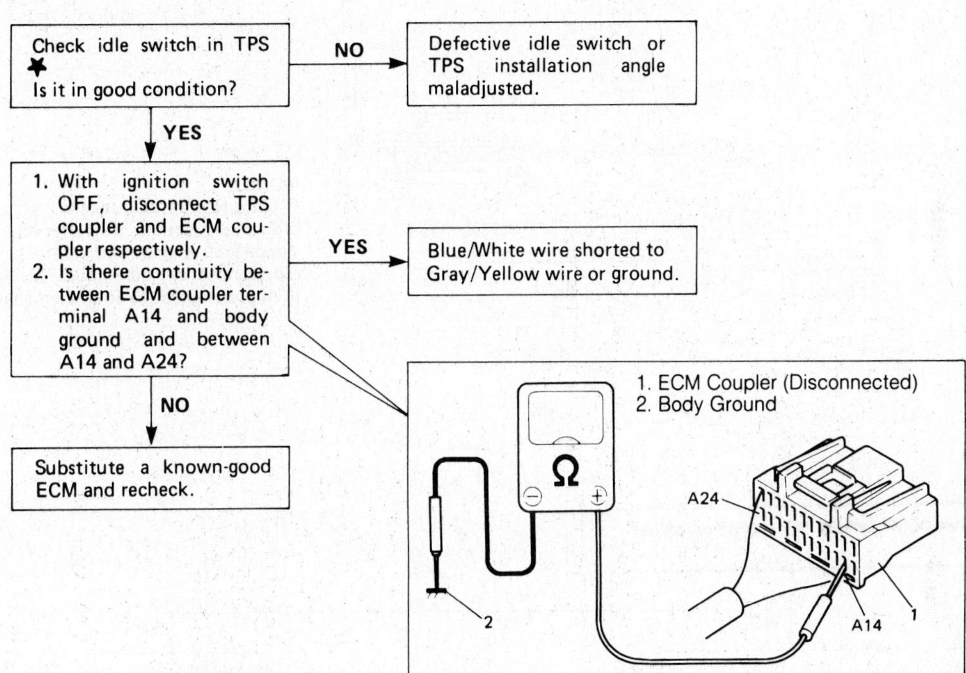

Check idle switch in TPS ✱
Is it in good condition?
NO
Defective idle switch or TPS installation angle maladjusted.
YES
1. With ignition switch OFF, disconnect TPS coupler and ECM coupler respectively.
2. Is there continuity between ECM coupler terminal A14 and body ground and between A14 and A24?
YES
Blue/White wire shorted to Gray/Yellow wire or ground.
NO
Substitute a known-good ECM and recheck.
1. ECM Coupler (Disconnected)
2. Body Ground
Ω
A24
A14
1
2


✱ - See SYSTEM & COMPONENT TESTING article.

119604

Courtesy of Suzuki of America Corp.

# 1991 ENGINE PERFORMANCE
# Self-Diagnostics (Cont.)

## CODE 51 – EGR SYSTEM CIRCUIT CHECK – CALIF. ONLY (SIDEKICK)

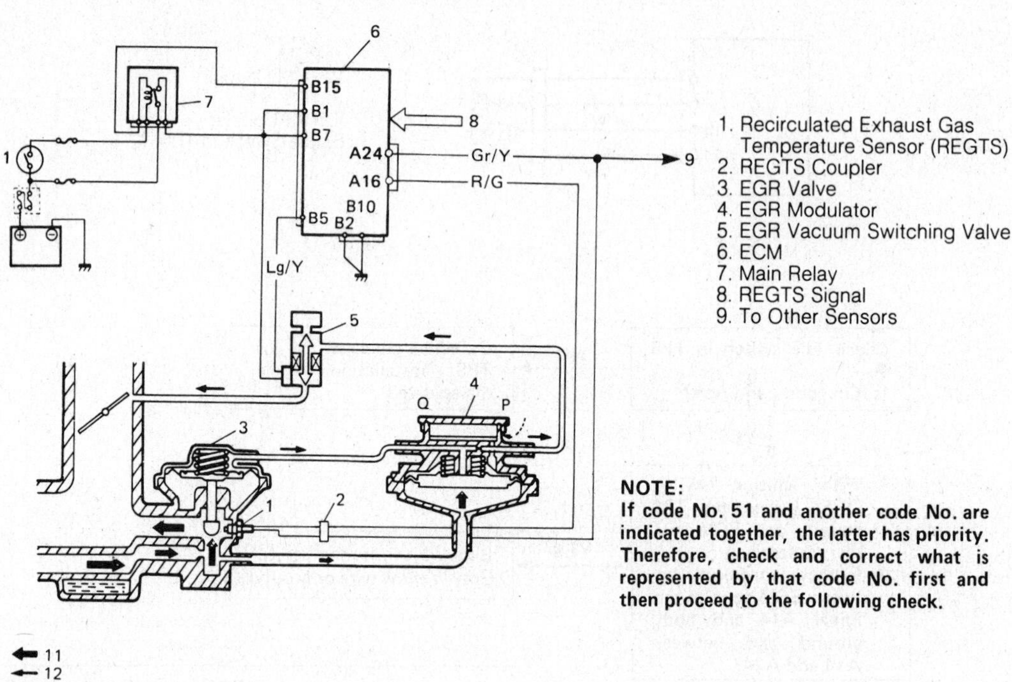
6
7
B15
B1
B7
8
A24
A16
Gr/Y
R/G
9
B10
B5
B2
Lg/Y
5
4
Q
P
3
2
1
11
12
13

1. Recirculated Exhaust Gas Temperature Sensor (REGTS)
2. REGTS Coupler
3. EGR Valve
4. EGR Modulator
5. EGR Vacuum Switching Valve
6. ECM
7. Main Relay
8. REGTS Signal
9. To Other Sensors

**NOTE: If code No. 51 and another code No. are indicated together, the latter has priority. Therefore, check and correct what is represented by that code No. first and then proceed to the following check.**

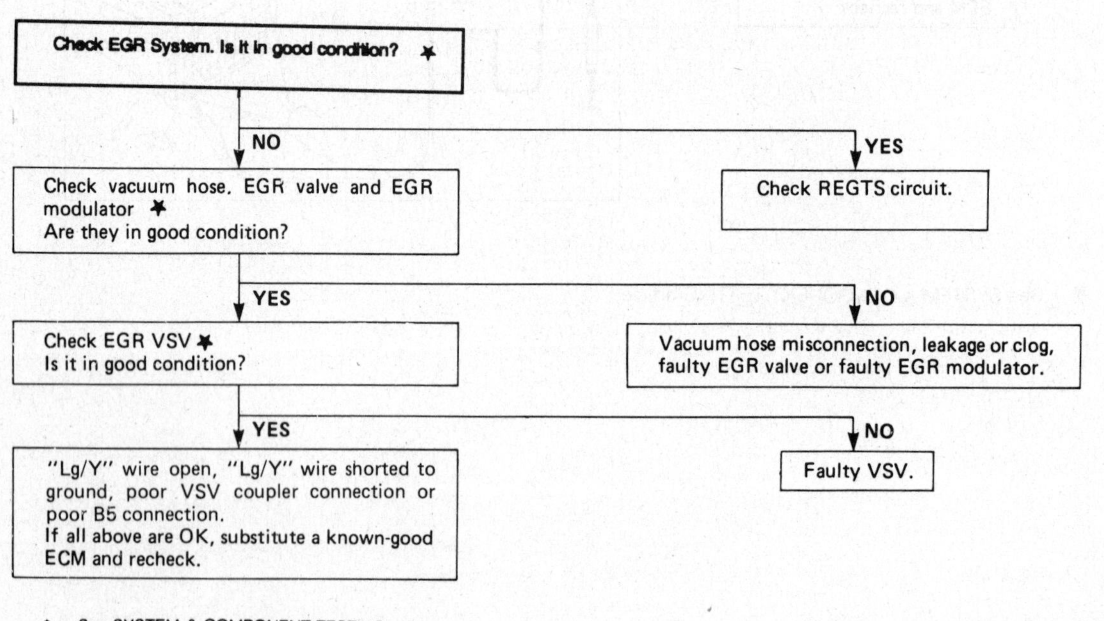
Check EGR System. Is it in good condition? *
NO
YES
Check vacuum hose, EGR valve and EGR modulator * Are they in good condition?
Check REGTS circuit.
YES
NO
Check EGR VSV * Is it in good condition?
Vacuum hose misconnection, leakage or clog, faulty EGR valve or faulty EGR modulator.
YES
NO
"Lg/Y" wire open, "Lg/Y" wire shorted to ground, poor VSV coupler connection or poor B5 connection. If all above are OK, substitute a known-good ECM and recheck.
Faulty VSV.

* – See SYSTEM & COMPONENT TESTING article.

**Continued on Next Page**

91G17869

Courtesy of Suzuki of America Corp.

### CODE 51 – EGR SYSTEM CIRCUIT CHECK – CALIF. ONLY (SIDEKICK – Cont.)

REGTS circuit check.

1. Disconnect REGTS coupler with ignition switch OFF.
2. Is voltage at "R/G" wire terminal about 4 – 5V at ignition switch ON?

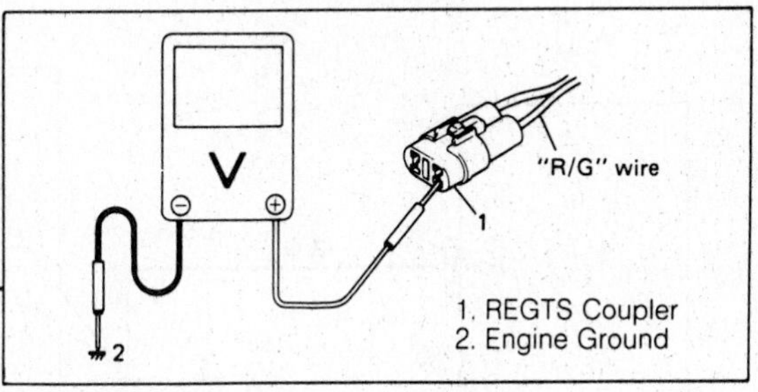

**YES** → Check REGTS ✱
Is it in good condition?

**NO** → "R/G" wire open, "R/G" wire shorted to "Lg/Y" wire or ground or poor A16 connection.
If all above are OK, substitute a known-good ECM and recheck.

**YES** → "Gr/Y" wire open, poor A24 connection or poor REGTS coupler connection.
If all above are OK, intermittent trouble or faulty ECM. ●

**NO** → Faulty REGTS.

✱ – See SYSTEM & COMPONENT TESTING article.

● – See TROUBLE SHOOTING – NO CODES article.

91J17870

Courtesy of Suzuki of America Corp.

# 1991 ENGINE PERFORMANCE
## Self-Diagnostics (Cont.)

### CODE 53 – ECM GROUND CIRCUIT CHECK – CALIF. ONLY (SIDEKICK)

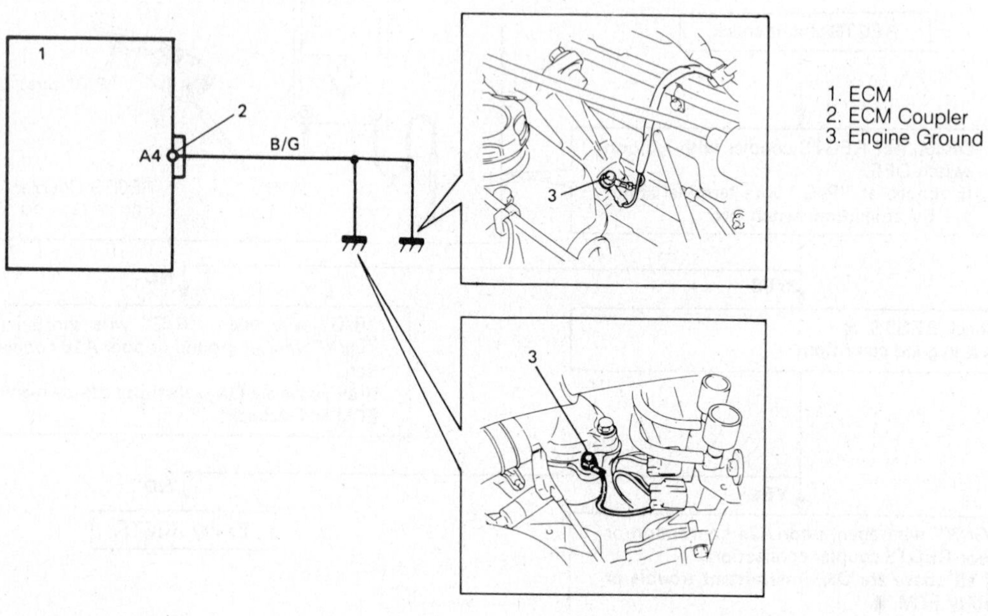


1. Disconnect ECM coupler from ECM with ignition switch OFF.
2. Is there continuity between ECM coupler terminal A4 and body ground?

NO → Black/Green wire open or poor engine ground.

YES → Poor A4 connection. If connection is OK, substitute a known-good ECM and recheck.

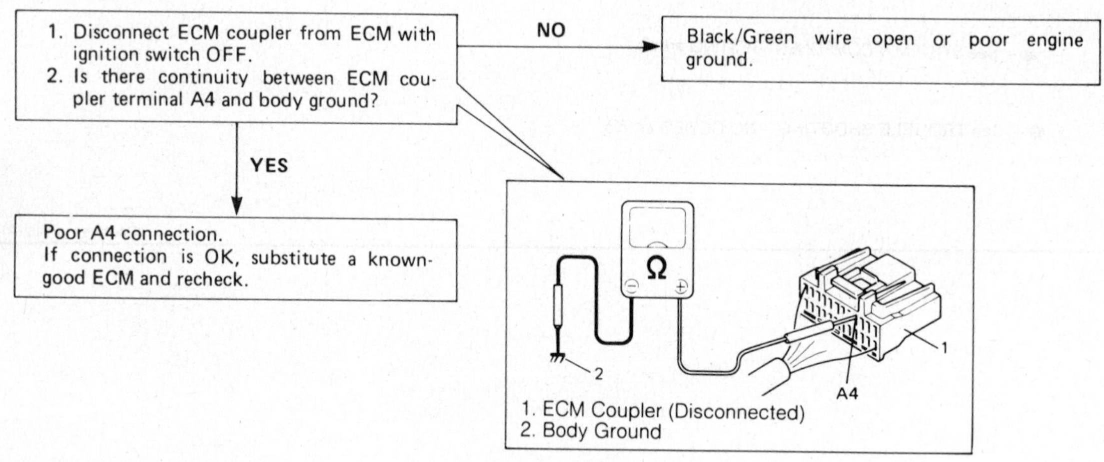


91A17871

Courtesy of Suzuki of America Corp.

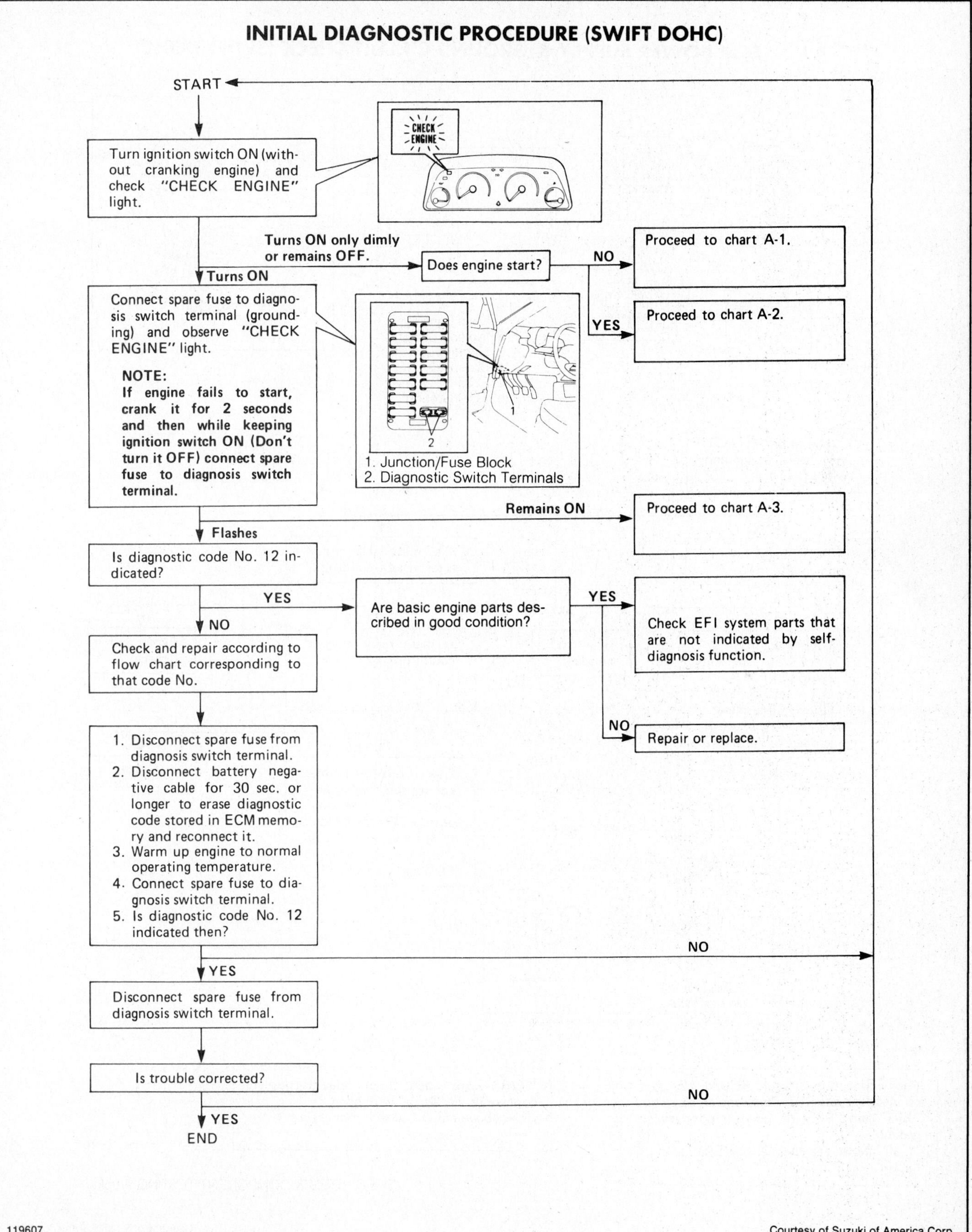
INITIAL DIAGNOSTIC PROCEDURE (SWIFT DOHC)
START
Turn ignition switch ON (without cranking engine) and check "CHECK ENGINE" light.
CHECK ENGINE
Turns ON only dimly or remains OFF.
Does engine start?
NO
Proceed to chart A-1.
YES
Proceed to chart A-2.
Turns ON
Connect spare fuse to diagnosis switch terminal (grounding) and observe "CHECK ENGINE" light.
NOTE:
If engine fails to start, crank it for 2 seconds and then while keeping ignition switch ON (Don't turn it OFF) connect spare fuse to diagnosis switch terminal.
1
2
1. Junction/Fuse Block
2. Diagnostic Switch Terminals
Remains ON
Proceed to chart A-3.
Flashes
Is diagnostic code No. 12 indicated?
YES
Are basic engine parts described in good condition?
YES
Check EFI system parts that are not indicated by self-diagnosis function.
NO
Repair or replace.
NO
Check and repair according to flow chart corresponding to that code No.
1. Disconnect spare fuse from diagnosis switch terminal.
2. Disconnect battery negative cable for 30 sec. or longer to erase diagnostic code stored in ECM memory and reconnect it.
3. Warm up engine to normal operating temperature.
4. Connect spare fuse to diagnosis switch terminal.
5. Is diagnostic code No. 12 indicated then?
NO
YES
Disconnect spare fuse from diagnosis switch terminal.
Is trouble corrected?
NO
YES
END
119607
Courtesy of Suzuki of America Corp.

# 1991 ENGINE PERFORMANCE
## Self-Diagnostics (Cont.)

### A1 – ECM POWER SUPPLY & GROUND CIRCUIT CHECK (SWIFT DOHC)

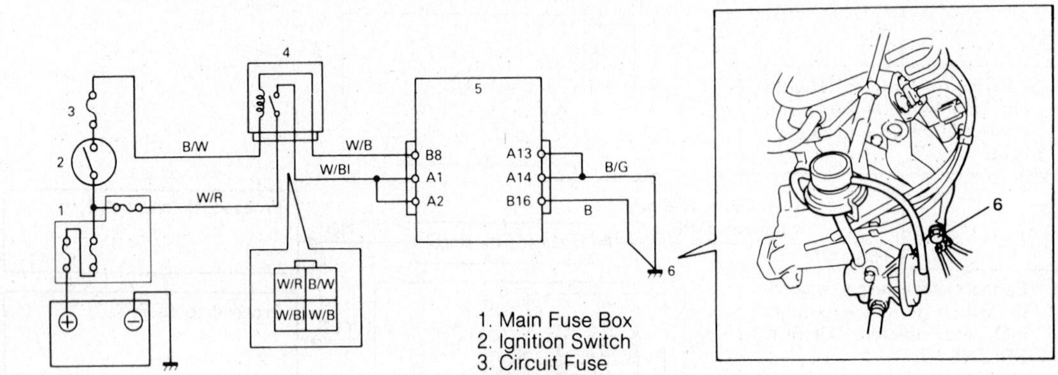

1. Main Fuse Box
2. Ignition Switch
3. Circuit Fuse
4. Main Relay
5. ECM
6. ECM Ground

Is operation of main relay heard at ignition switch ON?

- **YES** → Is 15A main fuse in good condition?
  - **YES** →
    1. Disconnect ECM couplers with ignition switch OFF.
    2. Using service wire, ground B8 terminal.
    3. Is battery voltage applied to A1 or A2 terminal at ignition switch ON?
    - **YES** → Poor connection at both A1 and A2, poor connection at A13, A14 and A16, both "B/G" and "B" wires open or poor engine ground. If all above are OK, check ECM and its circuit
    - **NO** → "W/R" wire open, poor relay-to-coupler connection or "W/Bl" wire open. If all above are OK, check main relay. *
  - **NO** → Repair and replace.
- **NO** → Are main and circuit fuses in good condition?
  - **YES** → Is main relay in good condition? *
    - **YES** → Poor relay-to-coupler connection, B/W wire open, W/B wire open or poor B8 connection. If all above are OK, substitute a known-good ECM and recheck.
    - **NO** → Replace.
  - **NO** → Repair and replace.

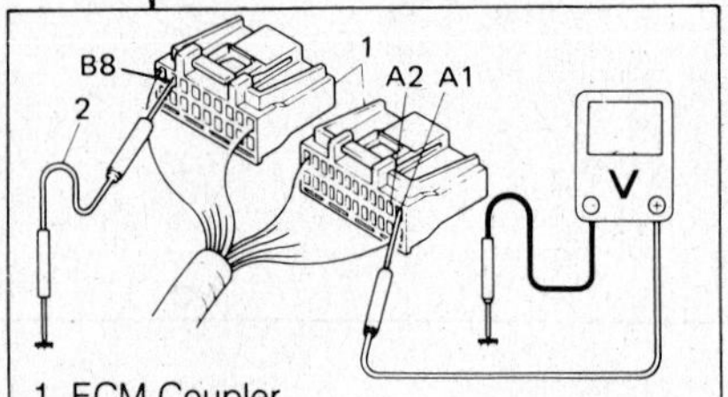

1. ECM Coupler
2. Service Wire

* – See SYSTEM & COMPONENT TESTING article.

119608

Courtesy of Suzuki of America Corp.

## A2 – CHECK ENGINE LIGHT INOPERATIVE (SWIFT DOHC)

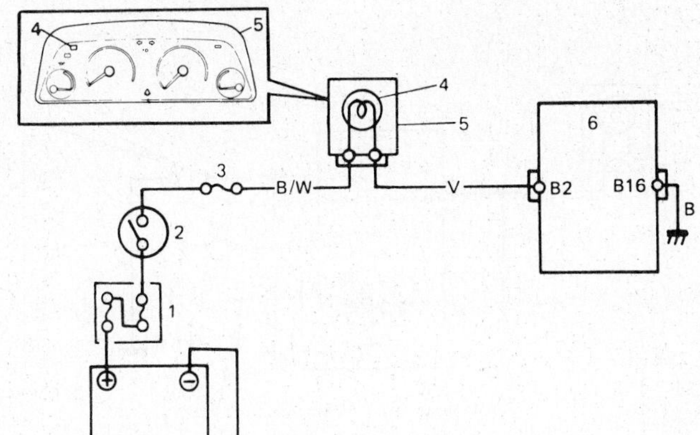


1. With ignition switch turned OFF, disconnect coupler "B" from ECM.
2. Body-ground terminal B2 in couper disconnected.
3. Does "CHECK ENGINE" light turn ON at ignition switch ON?

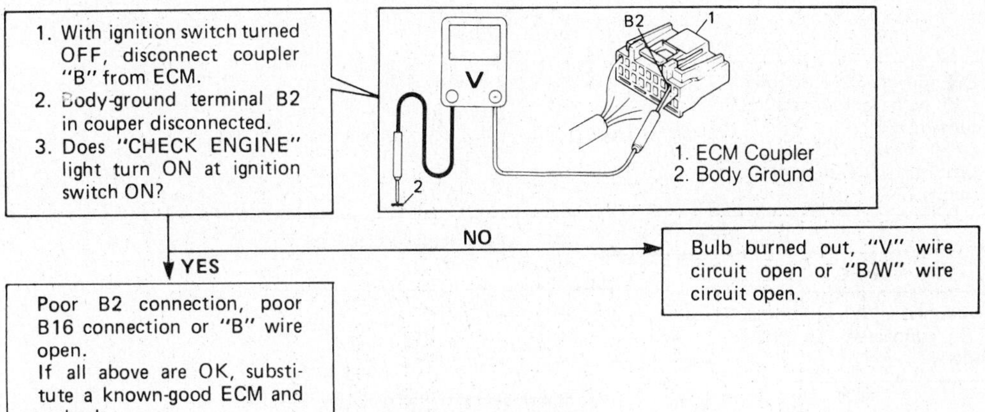


NO → Bulb burned out, "V" wire circuit open or "B/W" wire circuit open.

YES → Poor B2 connection, poor B16 connection or "B" wire open.
If all above are OK, substitute a known-good ECM and recheck.

119609

Courtesy of Suzuki of America Corp.

# 1991 ENGINE PERFORMANCE
# Self-Diagnostics (Cont.)

## A3 – CHECK ENGINE LIGHT STAYS ON – WON'T FLASH (SWIFT DOHC)

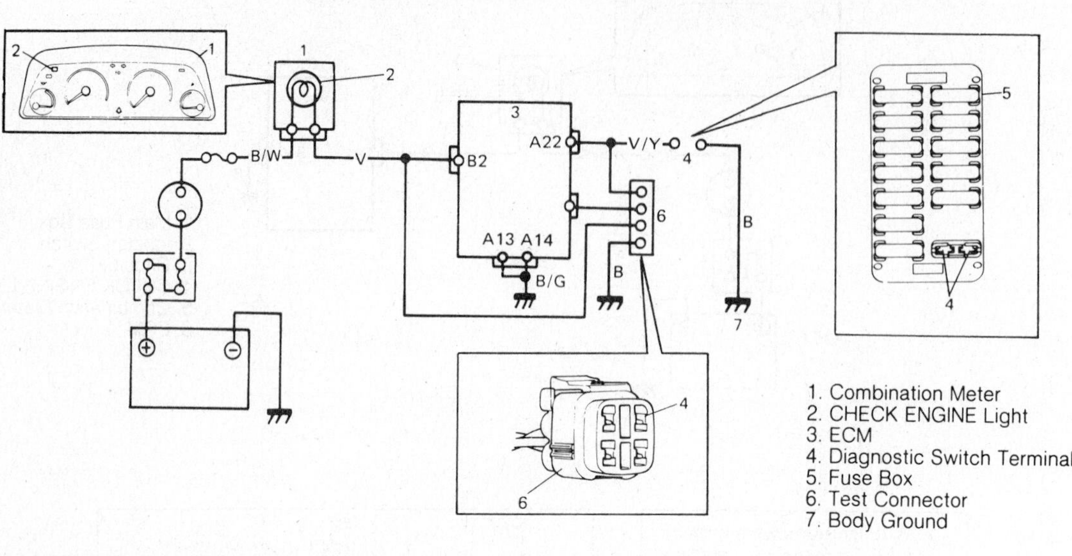


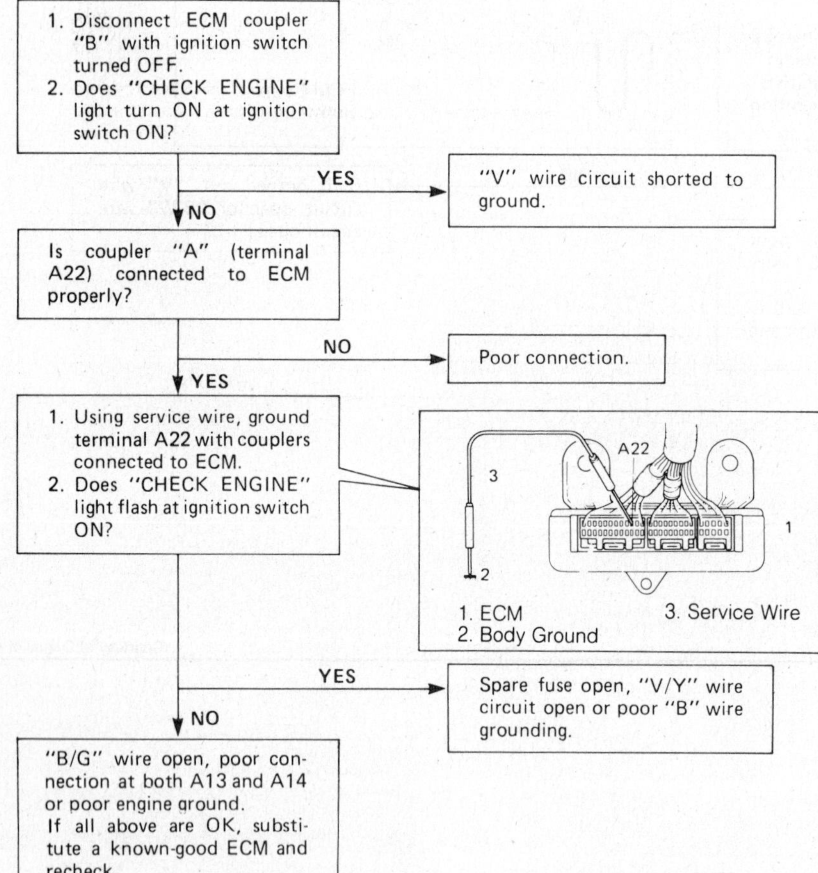

1. Disconnect ECM coupler "B" with ignition switch turned OFF.
2. Does "CHECK ENGINE" light turn ON at ignition switch ON?

YES → "V" wire circuit shorted to ground.

NO ↓

Is coupler "A" (terminal A22) connected to ECM properly?

NO → Poor connection.

YES ↓

1. Using service wire, ground terminal A22 with couplers connected to ECM.
2. Does "CHECK ENGINE" light flash at ignition switch ON?



YES → Spare fuse open, "V/Y" wire circuit open or poor "B" wire grounding.

NO ↓

"B/G" wire open, poor connection at both A13 and A14 or poor engine ground.
If all above are OK, substitute a known-good ECM and recheck.

119610

# 1991 ENGINE PERFORMANCE
# Self-Diagnostics (Cont.)

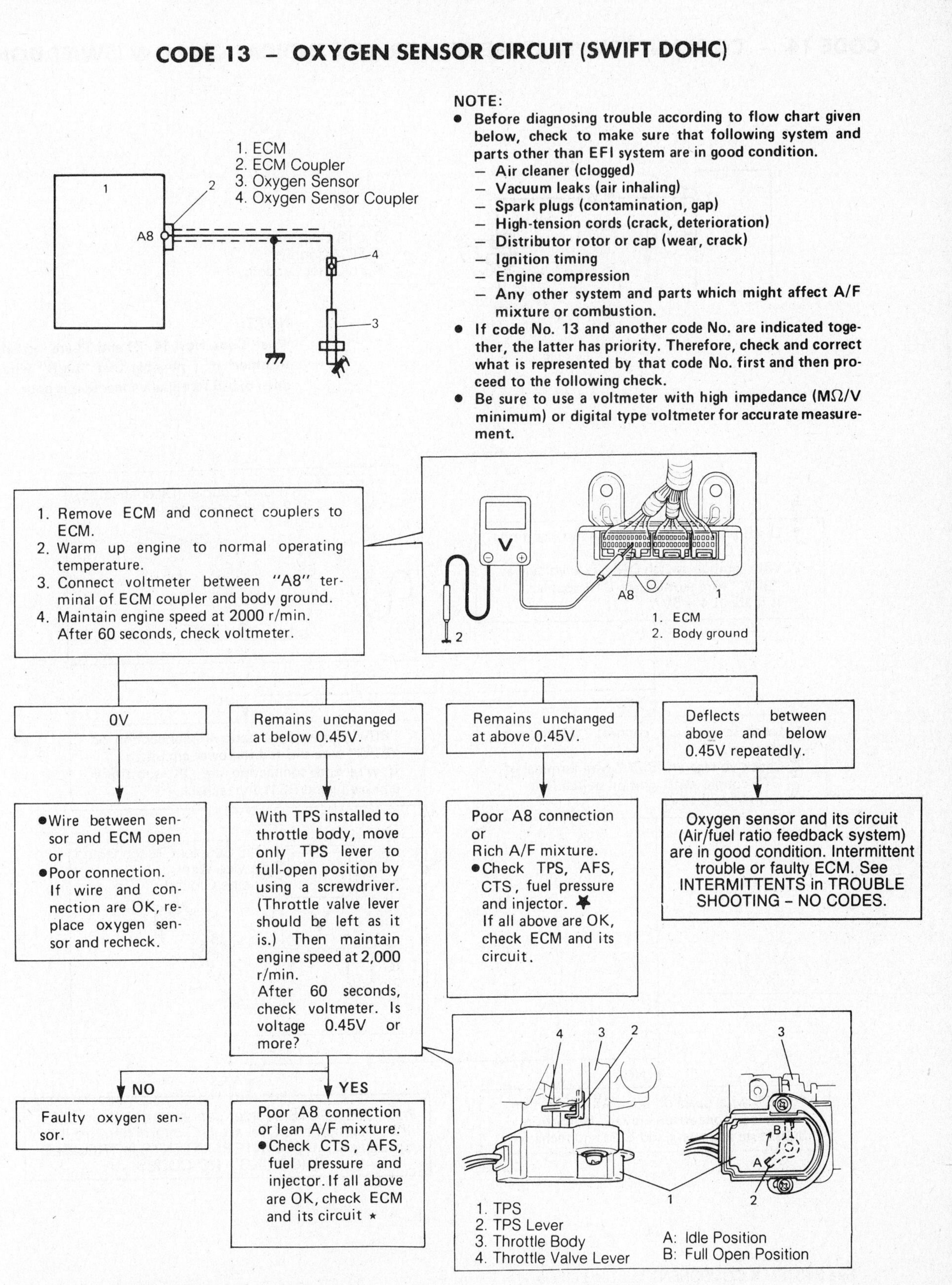
CODE 13 – OXYGEN SENSOR CIRCUIT (SWIFT DOHC)
1. ECM
2. ECM Coupler
3. Oxygen Sensor
4. Oxygen Sensor Coupler
A8
NOTE:
• Before diagnosing trouble according to flow chart given below, check to make sure that following system and parts other than EFI system are in good condition.
– Air cleaner (clogged)
– Vacuum leaks (air inhaling)
– Spark plugs (contamination, gap)
– High-tension cords (crack, deterioration)
– Distributor rotor or cap (wear, crack)
– Ignition timing
– Engine compression
– Any other system and parts which might affect A/F mixture or combustion.
• If code No. 13 and another code No. are indicated together, the latter has priority. Therefore, check and correct what is represented by that code No. first and then proceed to the following check.
• Be sure to use a voltmeter with high impedance (MΩ/V minimum) or digital type voltmeter for accurate measurement.
1. Remove ECM and connect couplers to ECM.
2. Warm up engine to normal operating temperature.
3. Connect voltmeter between "A8" terminal of ECM coupler and body ground.
4. Maintain engine speed at 2000 r/min. After 60 seconds, check voltmeter.
V
A8
1. ECM
2. Body ground
0V
Remains unchanged at below 0.45V.
Remains unchanged at above 0.45V.
Deflects between above and below 0.45V repeatedly.
•Wire between sensor and ECM open or
•Poor connection. If wire and connection are OK, replace oxygen sensor and recheck.
With TPS installed to throttle body, move only TPS lever to full-open position by using a screwdriver. (Throttle valve lever should be left as it is.) Then maintain engine speed at 2,000 r/min. After 60 seconds, check voltmeter. Is voltage 0.45V or more?
Poor A8 connection or Rich A/F mixture.
•Check TPS, AFS, CTS, fuel pressure and injector. *
If all above are OK, check ECM and its circuit.
Oxygen sensor and its circuit (Air/fuel ratio feedback system) are in good condition. Intermittent trouble or faulty ECM. See INTERMITTENTS in TROUBLE SHOOTING - NO CODES.
NO
Faulty oxygen sensor.
YES
Poor A8 connection or lean A/F mixture.
•Check CTS, AFS, fuel pressure and injector. If all above are OK, check ECM and its circuit *
1. TPS
2. TPS Lever
3. Throttle Body
4. Throttle Valve Lever
A: Idle Position
B: Full Open Position
* - See SYSTEM & COMPONENT TESTING article.
119611
Courtesy of Suzuki of America Corp.

# 1991 ENGINE PERFORMANCE
## Self-Diagnostics (Cont.)

### CODE 14 – COOLANT TEMPERATURE SENSOR (CTS) INDICATION LOW (SWIFT DOHC)

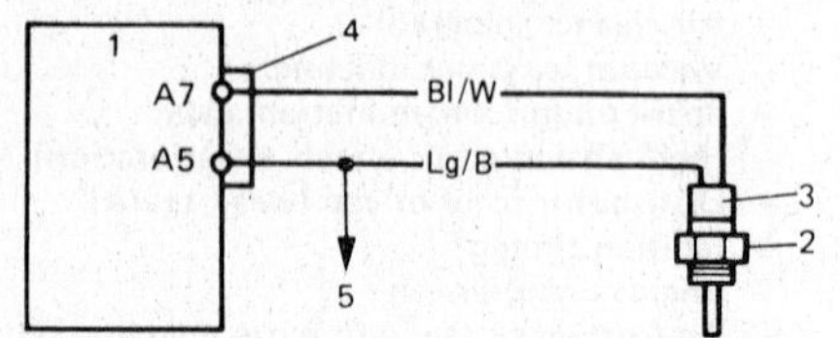


1. ECM
2. CTS
3. CTS Coupler
4. ECM Coupler
5. To Other Sensors

**NOTE:**
**When Code Nos. 14, 21 and 33 are indicated together, it is possible that "Lg/B" wire is open or A5 terminal connection is poor.**

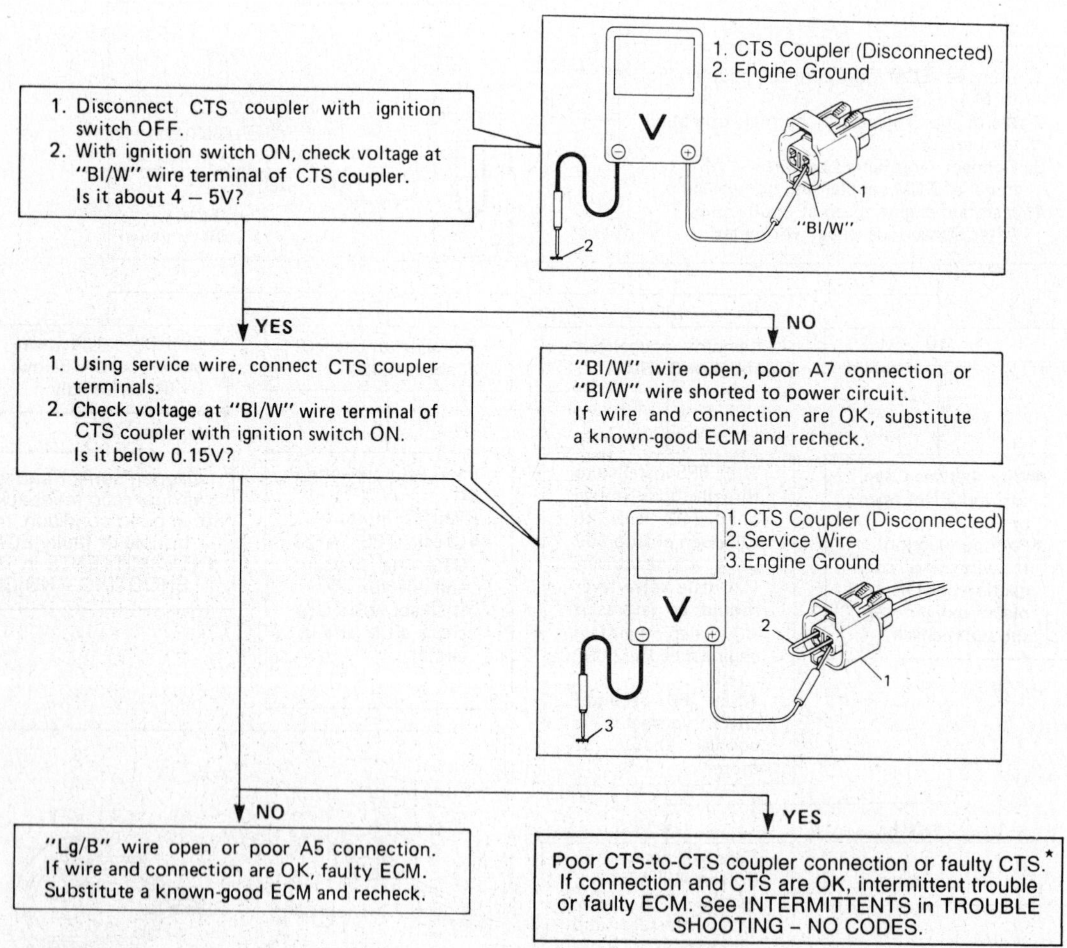

1. Disconnect CTS coupler with ignition switch OFF.
2. With ignition switch ON, check voltage at "Bl/W" wire terminal of CTS coupler.
Is it about 4 – 5V?
1. CTS Coupler (Disconnected)
2. Engine Ground
V
"Bl/W"
YES
NO
1. Using service wire, connect CTS coupler terminals.
2. Check voltage at "Bl/W" wire terminal of CTS coupler with ignition switch ON.
Is it below 0.15V?
"Bl/W" wire open, poor A7 connection or "Bl/W" wire shorted to power circuit.
If wire and connection are OK, substitute a known-good ECM and recheck.
1. CTS Coupler (Disconnected)
2. Service Wire
3. Engine Ground
NO
YES
"Lg/B" wire open or poor A5 connection.
If wire and connection are OK, faulty ECM.
Substitute a known-good ECM and recheck.
Poor CTS-to-CTS coupler connection or faulty CTS.*
If connection and CTS are OK, intermittent trouble or faulty ECM. See INTERMITTENTS in TROUBLE SHOOTING – NO CODES.


* – See SYSTEM & COMPONENT TESTING article.

119612

Courtesy of Suzuki of America Corp.

## CODE 15 – COOLANT TEMPERATURE SENSOR (CTS) INDICATION HIGH (SWIFT DOHC)

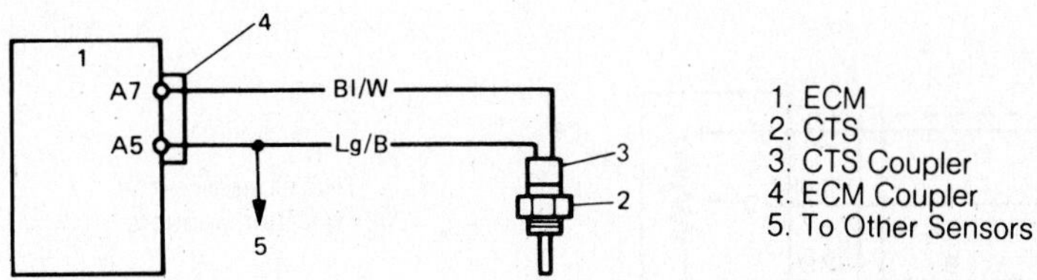
1
A7
A5
Bl/W
Lg/B
4
3
2
5
1. ECM
2. CTS
3. CTS Coupler
4. ECM Coupler
5. To Other Sensors

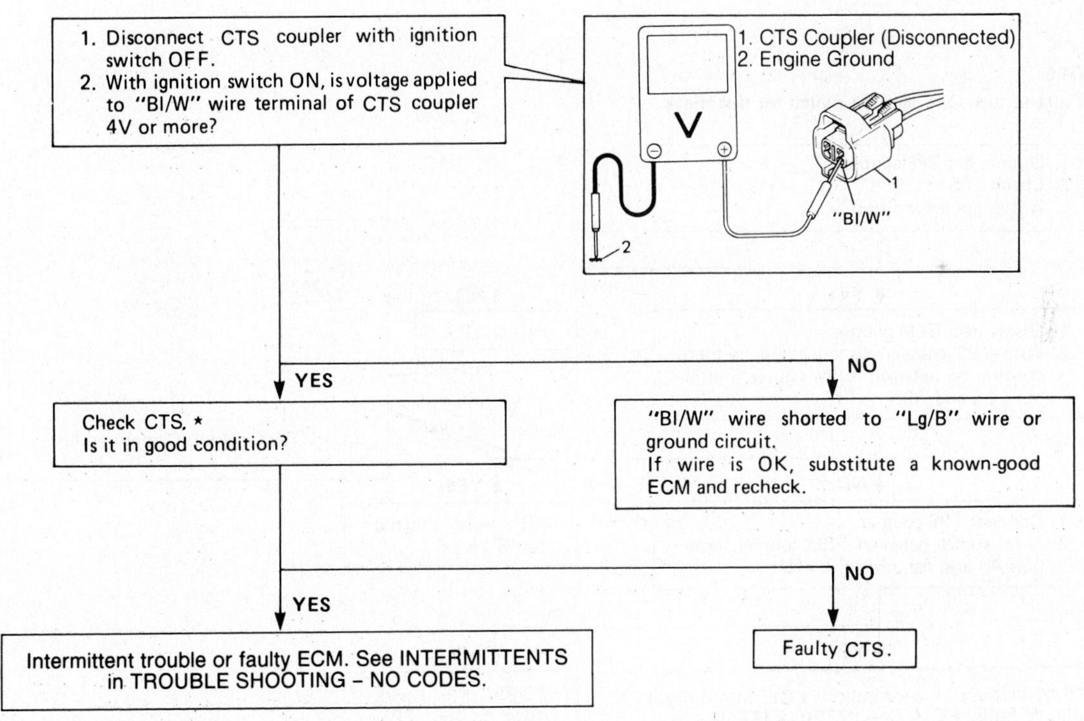
1. Disconnect CTS coupler with ignition switch OFF.
2. With ignition switch ON, is voltage applied to "Bl/W" wire terminal of CTS coupler 4V or more?
1. CTS Coupler (Disconnected)
2. Engine Ground
V
"Bl/W"
YES
NO
Check CTS. *
Is it in good condition?
"Bl/W" wire shorted to "Lg/B" wire or ground circuit.
If wire is OK, substitute a known-good ECM and recheck.
YES
NO
Intermittent trouble or faulty ECM. See INTERMITTENTS in TROUBLE SHOOTING – NO CODES.
Faulty CTS.

* – See SYSTEM & COMPONENT TESTING article.

119613

Courtesy of Suzuki of America Corp.

# 1991 ENGINE PERFORMANCE
# Self-Diagnostics (Cont.)

## CODE 21 – THROTTLE POSITION SENSOR VOLTAGE HIGH (SWIFT DOHC)

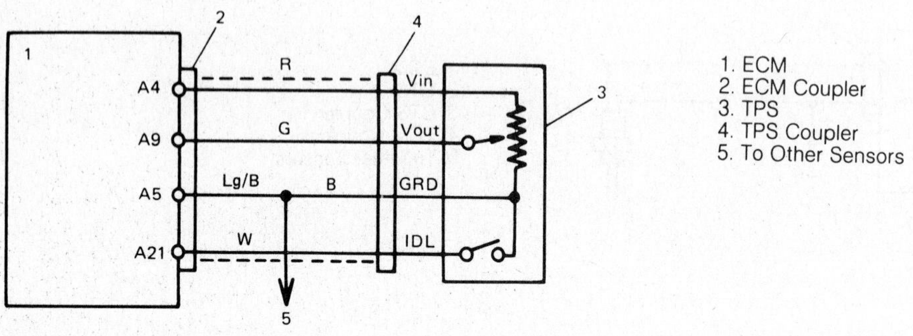


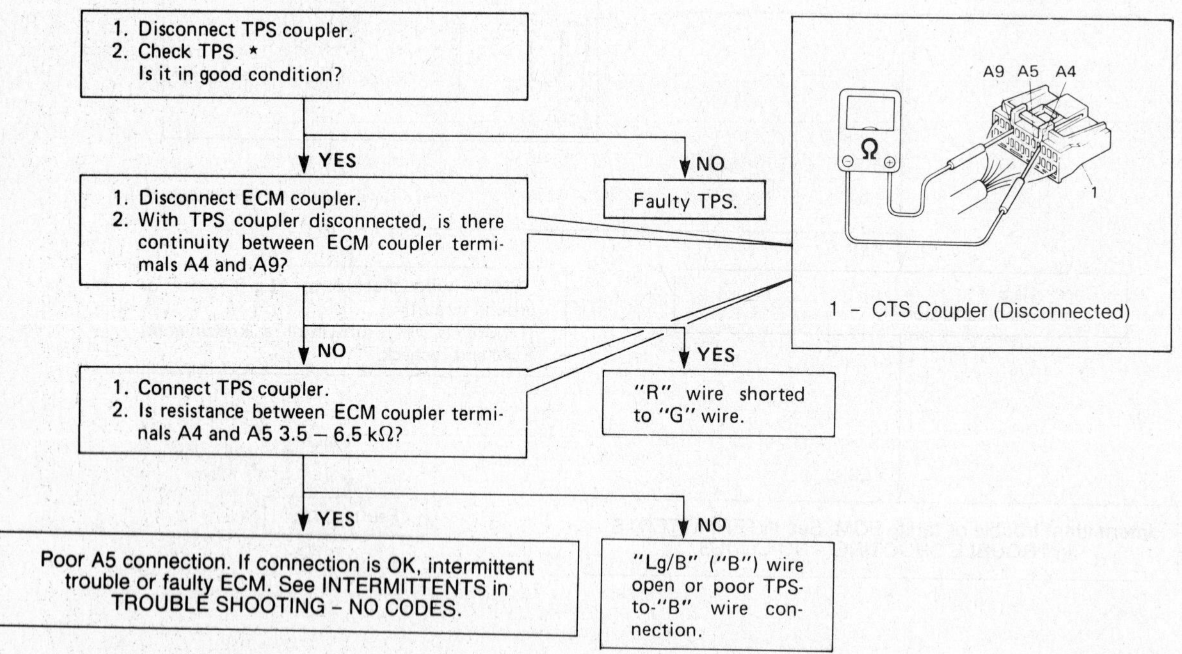

NOTE:
Be sure to turn OFF ignition switch for this check.
1. Disconnect TPS coupler.
2. Check TPS. *
Is it in good condition?
YES
NO
Faulty TPS.
1. Disconnect ECM coupler.
2. With TPS coupler disconnected, is there continuity between ECM coupler terminals A4 and A9?
NO
YES
"R" wire shorted to "G" wire.
1. Connect TPS coupler.
2. Is resistance between ECM coupler terminals A4 and A5 3.5 – 6.5 kΩ?
YES
NO
Poor A5 connection. If connection is OK, intermittent trouble or faulty ECM. See INTERMITTENTS in TROUBLE SHOOTING – NO CODES.
"Lg/B" ("B") wire open or poor TPS-to-"B" wire connection.
A9 A5 A4
Ω
1
1 – CTS Coupler (Disconnected)


* – See SYSTEM & COMPONENT TESTING article.

119614

# 1991 ENGINE PERFORMANCE
## Self-Diagnostics (Cont.)

### CODE 22 – THROTTLE POSITION SENSOR VOLTAGE LOW (SWIFT DOHC)

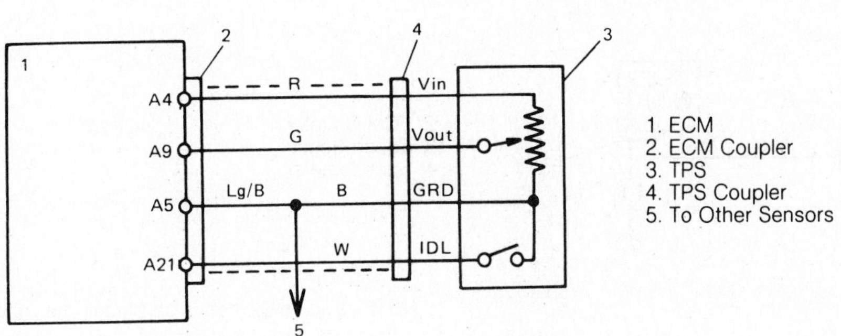
1
2
4
3
A4
A9
A5
A21
R
G
Lg/B
B
W
Vin
Vout
GRD
IDL
5
1. ECM
2. ECM Coupler
3. TPS
4. TPS Coupler
5. To Other Sensors

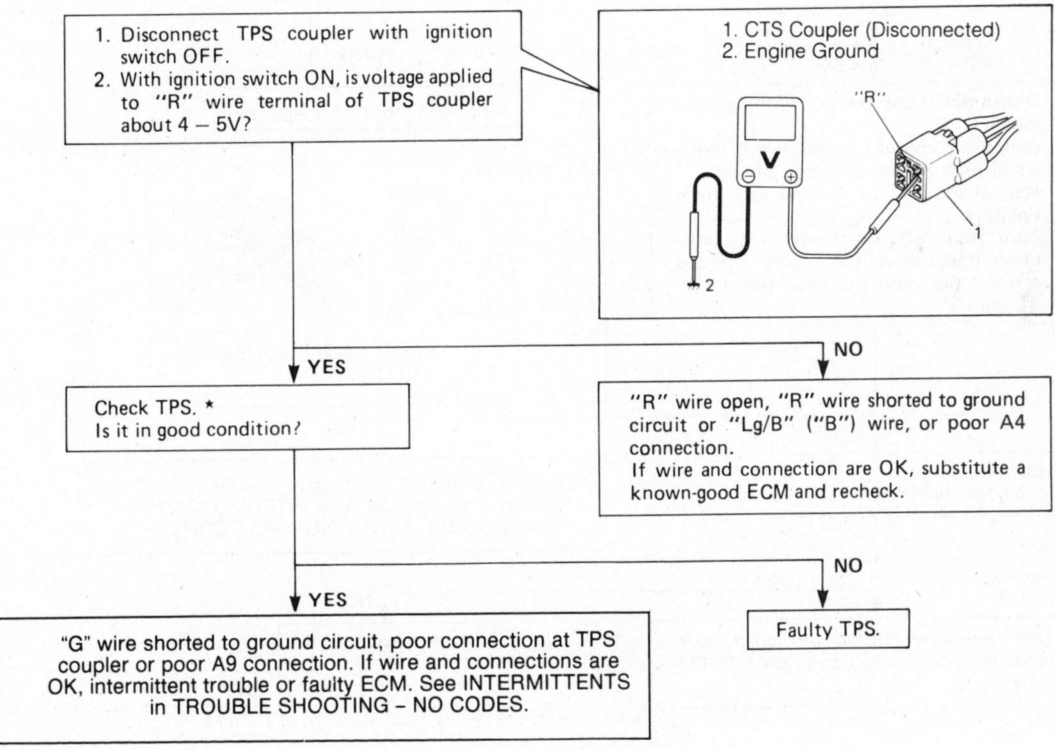
1. Disconnect TPS coupler with ignition switch OFF.
2. With ignition switch ON, is voltage applied to "R" wire terminal of TPS coupler about 4 – 5V?
1. CTS Coupler (Disconnected)
2. Engine Ground
"R"
V
1
2
YES
NO
Check TPS. *
Is it in good condition?
"R" wire open, "R" wire shorted to ground circuit or "Lg/B" ("B") wire, or poor A4 connection.
If wire and connection are OK, substitute a known-good ECM and recheck.
YES
NO
"G" wire shorted to ground circuit, poor connection at TPS coupler or poor A9 connection. If wire and connections are OK, intermittent trouble or faulty ECM. See INTERMITTENTS in TROUBLE SHOOTING – NO CODES.
Faulty TPS.

* – See SYSTEM & COMPONENT TESTING article.

119615

# 1991 ENGINE PERFORMANCE
# Self-Diagnostics (Cont.)

## CODE 24 – SPEED SENSOR CIRCUIT CHECK (SWIFT DOHC)

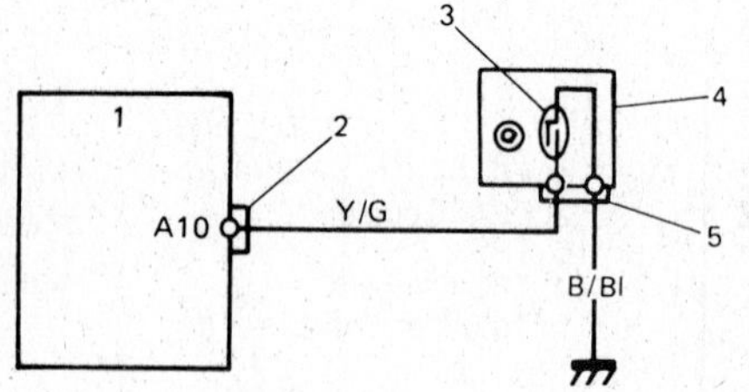


1. ECM
2. ECM Coupler
3. Speed Sensor
4. Speedometer

NOTE: Ensure ignition is off before checking VSS.

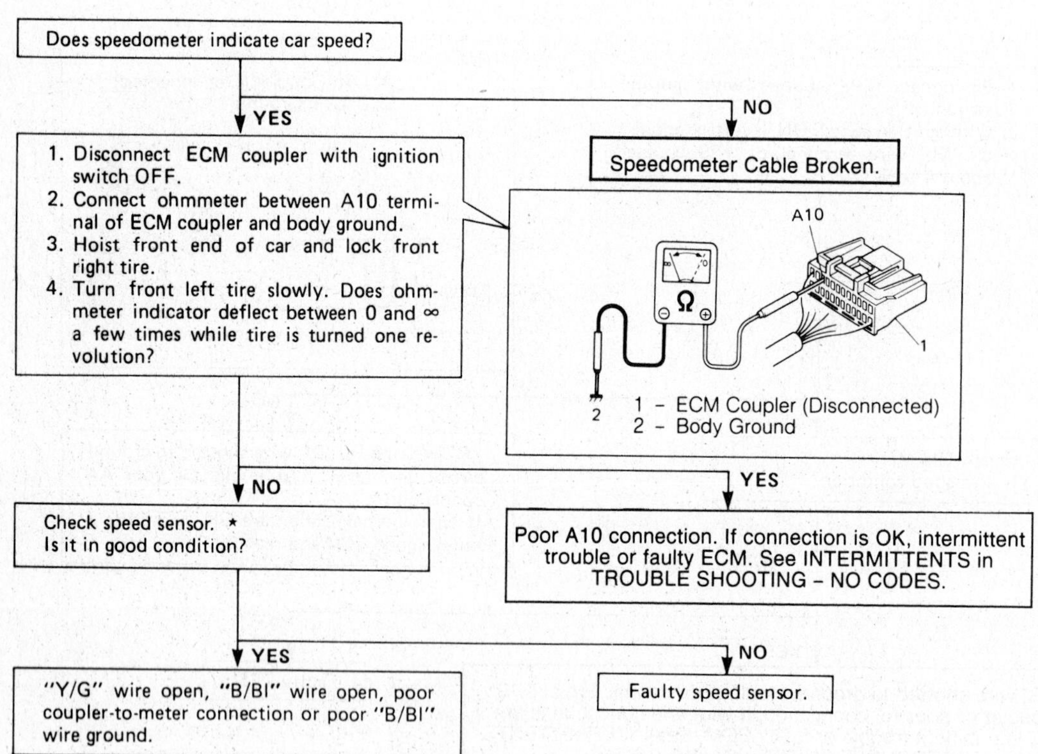

Does speedometer indicate car speed?
YES
NO
Speedometer Cable Broken.
1. Disconnect ECM coupler with ignition switch OFF.
2. Connect ohmmeter between A10 terminal of ECM coupler and body ground.
3. Hoist front end of car and lock front right tire.
4. Turn front left tire slowly. Does ohmmeter indicator deflect between 0 and ∞ a few times while tire is turned one revolution?
A10
Ω
1 – ECM Coupler (Disconnected)
2 – Body Ground
NO
YES
Check speed sensor. *
Is it in good condition?
Poor A10 connection. If connection is OK, intermittent trouble or faulty ECM. See INTERMITTENTS in TROUBLE SHOOTING – NO CODES.
YES
NO
"Y/G" wire open, "B/BI" wire open, poor coupler-to-meter connection or poor "B/BI" wire ground.
Faulty speed sensor.


* – See SYSTEM & COMPONENT TESTING article.

119616

Courtesy of Suzuki of America Corp.

## CODE 33 – AIRFLOW SENSOR (AFS) CIRCUIT SIGNAL VOLTAGE HIGH (SWIFT DOHC)

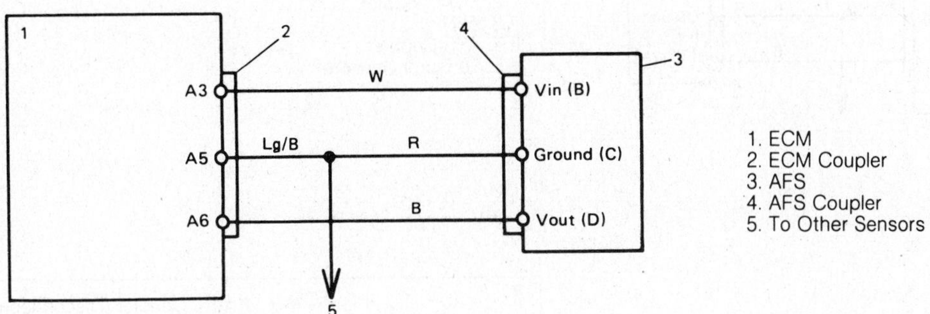


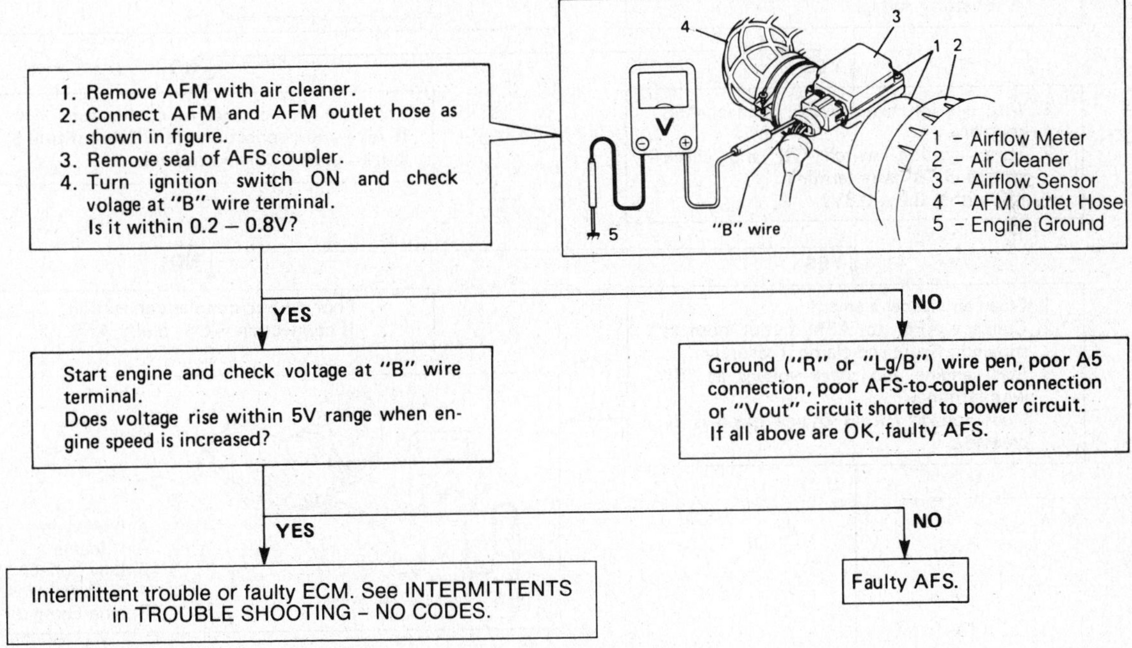

1. Remove AFM with air cleaner.
2. Connect AFM and AFM outlet hose as shown in figure.
3. Remove seal of AFS coupler.
4. Turn ignition switch ON and check volage at "B" wire terminal.
Is it within 0.2 – 0.8V?
4
3
1 2
V
5
"B" wire
1 - Airflow Meter
2 - Air Cleaner
3 - Airflow Sensor
4 - AFM Outlet Hose
5 - Engine Ground
YES
NO
Start engine and check voltage at "B" wire terminal.
Does voltage rise within 5V range when engine speed is increased?
Ground ("R" or "Lg/B") wire pen, poor A5 connection, poor AFS-to-coupler connection or "Vout" circuit shorted to power circuit.
If all above are OK, faulty AFS.
YES
NO
Intermittent trouble or faulty ECM. See INTERMITTENTS in TROUBLE SHOOTING - NO CODES.
Faulty AFS.


119617

Courtesy of Suzuki of America Corp.

# 1991 ENGINE PERFORMANCE
## Self-Diagnostics (Cont.)

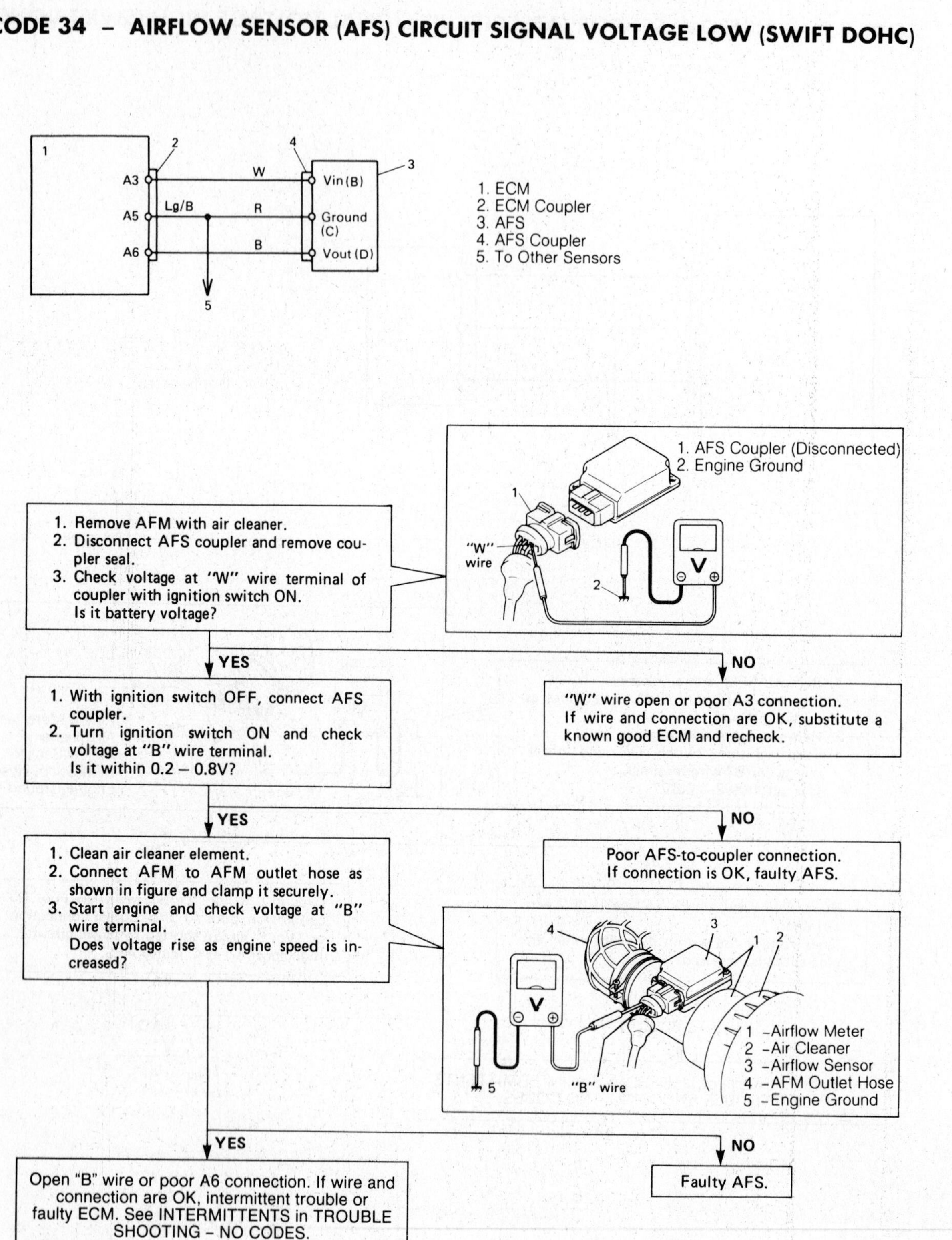

CODE 34 – AIRFLOW SENSOR (AFS) CIRCUIT SIGNAL VOLTAGE LOW (SWIFT DOHC)
1
2
4
3
A3
A5
A6
W
Lg/B
R
B
Vin (B)
Ground (C)
Vout (D)
5
1. ECM
2. ECM Coupler
3. AFS
4. AFS Coupler
5. To Other Sensors
1. AFS Coupler (Disconnected)
2. Engine Ground
"W" wire
V
1. Remove AFM with air cleaner.
2. Disconnect AFS coupler and remove coupler seal.
3. Check voltage at "W" wire terminal of coupler with ignition switch ON.
Is it battery voltage?
YES
NO
"W" wire open or poor A3 connection.
If wire and connection are OK, substitute a known good ECM and recheck.
1. With ignition switch OFF, connect AFS coupler.
2. Turn ignition switch ON and check voltage at "B" wire terminal.
Is it within 0.2 – 0.8V?
YES
NO
Poor AFS-to-coupler connection.
If connection is OK, faulty AFS.
1. Clean air cleaner element.
2. Connect AFM to AFM outlet hose as shown in figure and clamp it securely.
3. Start engine and check voltage at "B" wire terminal.
Does voltage rise as engine speed is increased?
"B" wire
1 -Airflow Meter
2 -Air Cleaner
3 -Airflow Sensor
4 -AFM Outlet Hose
5 -Engine Ground
YES
NO
Open "B" wire or poor A6 connection. If wire and connection are OK, intermittent trouble or faulty ECM. See INTERMITTENTS in TROUBLE SHOOTING - NO CODES.
Faulty AFS.
119618
Courtesy of Suzuki of America Corp.

## CODE 41 – NO IGNITION SIGNAL (SWIFT DOHC)

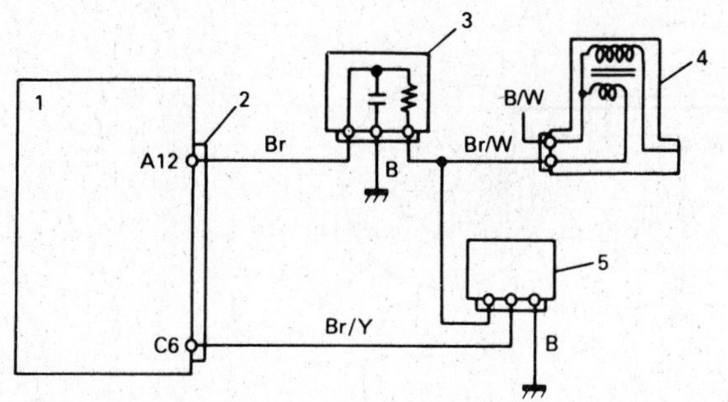


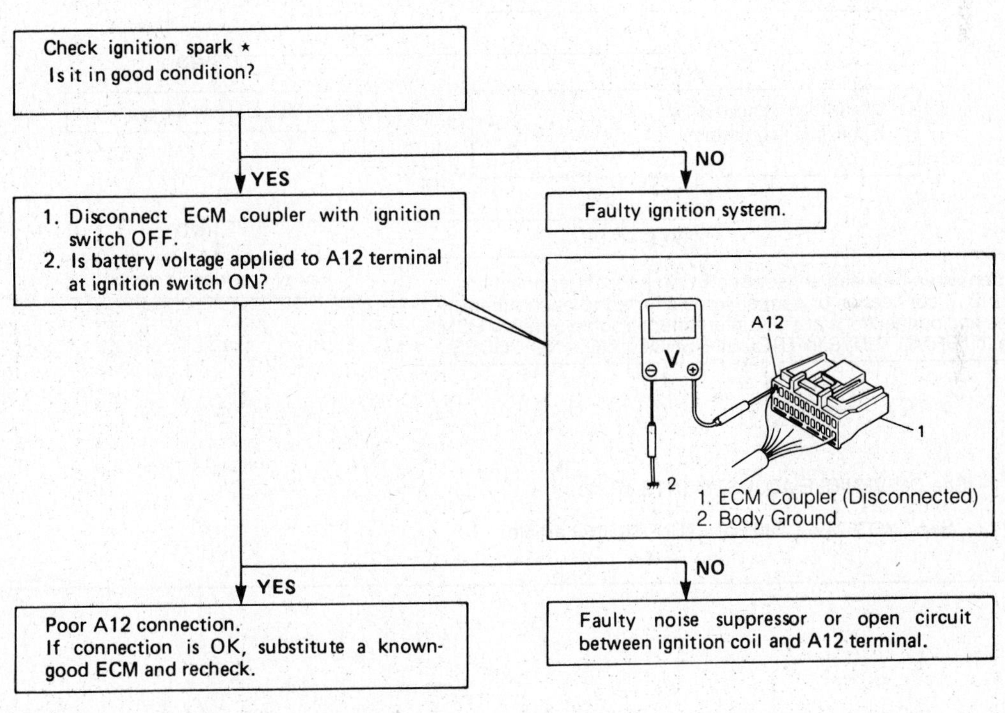

Check ignition spark *
Is it in good condition?
YES
NO
Faulty ignition system.
1. Disconnect ECM coupler with ignition switch OFF.
2. Is battery voltage applied to A12 terminal at ignition switch ON?
V
A12
1
2
1. ECM Coupler (Disconnected)
2. Body Ground
YES
NO
Poor A12 connection.
If connection is OK, substitute a known-good ECM and recheck.
Faulty noise suppressor or open circuit between ignition coil and A12 terminal.


* – See BASIC DIAGNOSTIC PROCEDURES article.

119619

Courtesy of Suzuki of America Corp.

# 1991 ENGINE PERFORMANCE
## Self-Diagnostics (Cont.)

### CODE 42 – CRANK ANGLE SENSOR (CAS) CIRCUIT CHECK (SWIFT DOHC)

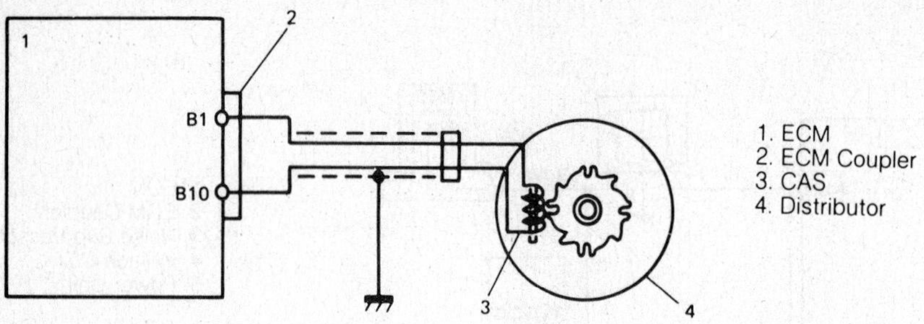
1
2
B1
B10
3
4
1. ECM
2. ECM Coupler
3. CAS
4. Distributor

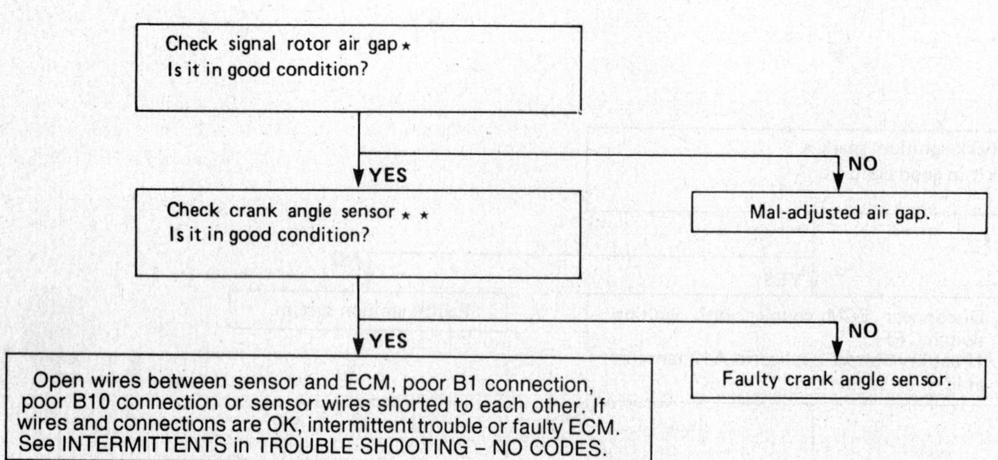
Check signal rotor air gap *
Is it in good condition?
YES
NO
Mal-adjusted air gap.
Check crank angle sensor * *
Is it in good condition?
YES
NO
Faulty crank angle sensor.
Open wires between sensor and ECM, poor B1 connection, poor B10 connection or sensor wires shorted to each other. If wires and connections are OK, intermittent trouble or faulty ECM. See INTERMITTENTS in TROUBLE SHOOTING – NO CODES.

* – See ON-VEHICLE ADJUSTMENTS article.

** – See SYSTEM & COMPONENT TESTING article.

119620

Courtesy of Suzuki of America Corp.

## CODE 51 – EGR SYSTEM CIRCUIT CHECK – CALIF. ONLY (SWIFT DOHC)

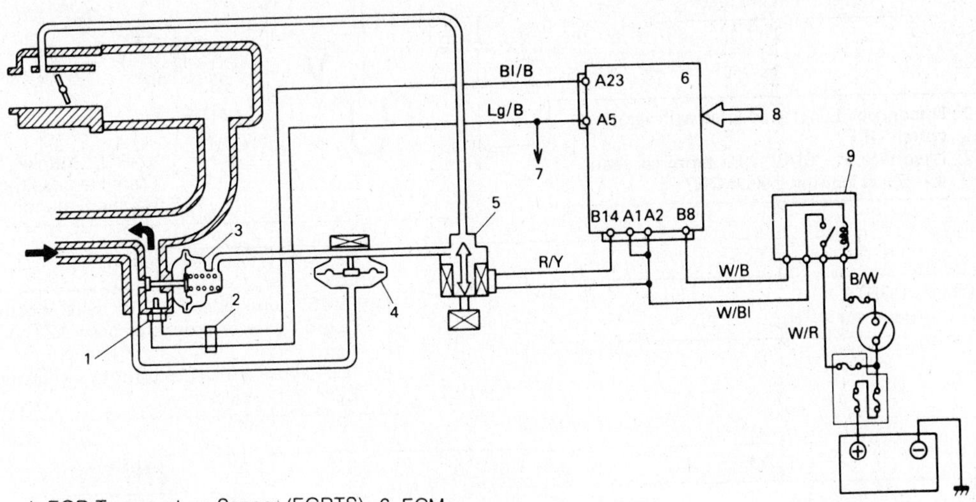


1. EGR Temperature Sensor (EGRTS)
2. EGRTS Coupler
3. EGR Valve
4. EGR Modulator
5. EGR VSV
6. ECM
7. To Other Sensors
8. Sensor Input
9. Main Relay

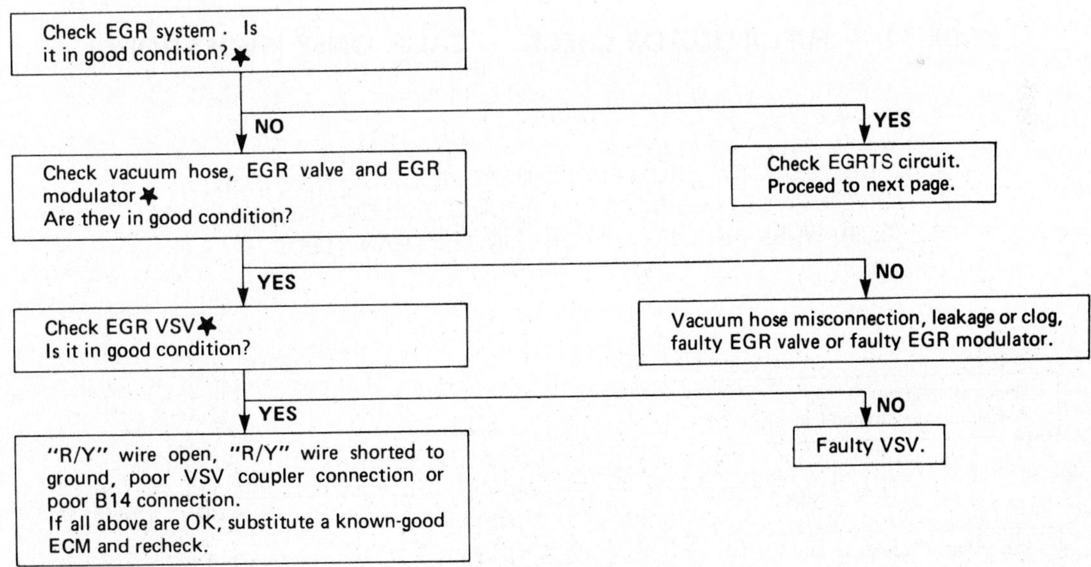

Check EGR system. Is it in good condition? *
NO
YES
Check EGRTS circuit. Proceed to next page.
Check vacuum hose, EGR valve and EGR modulator * Are they in good condition?
YES
NO
Vacuum hose misconnection, leakage or clog, faulty EGR valve or faulty EGR modulator.
Check EGR VSV * Is it in good condition?
YES
NO
Faulty VSV.
"R/Y" wire open, "R/Y" wire shorted to ground, poor VSV coupler connection or poor B14 connection.
If all above are OK, substitute a known-good ECM and recheck.


Continued on Next Page

* – See SYSTEM & COMPONENT TESTING article.

119621

Courtesy of Suzuki of America Corp.

# 1991 ENGINE PERFORMANCE
## Self-Diagnostics (Cont.)

### CODE 51 – EGR SYSTEM CIRCUIT CHECK – CALIF. ONLY (SWIFT DOHC) (Cont.)

EGRTS circuit check.

1. Disconnect EGRTS coupler with ignition switch OFF.
2. Is voltage at "Bl/B" wire terminal about 4 – 5V at ignition switch ON?

V
"Bl/B" wire
1. EGRTS Coupler (Wire Harness Side)
2. Engine Ground

**YES**

Check EGRTS *
Is it in good condition?

**NO**

"Bl/B" wire open, "Bl/B" wire shorted to "Lg/B" wire or ground or poor A23 connection.
If all above are OK, substitute a known-good ECM and recheck.

**YES**

"Lg/B" wire open, poor A5 connection or poor EGRTS coupler connection. If wires and connections are OK, intermittent trouble or faulty ECM. See INTERMITTENTS in TROUBLE SHOOTING - NO CODES.

**NO**

Faulty EGRTS

### CODE 52 – FUEL INJECTOR CHECK – CALIF. ONLY (SWIFT DOHC)

(FUEL LEAKAGE FROM FUEL INJECTOR, OXYGEN SENSOR OUTPUT VOLTAGE DOES NOT REDUCE TO LOWER THAN 0.35V WHEN FUEL IS CUT FOR LONGER THAN 1 SEC.)

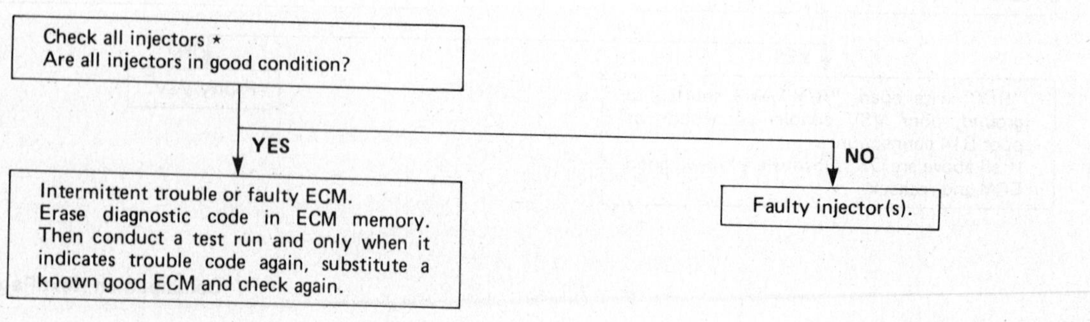

Check all injectors *
Are all injectors in good condition?
YES
NO
Intermittent trouble or faulty ECM.
Erase diagnostic code in ECM memory.
Then conduct a test run and only when it indicates trouble code again, substitute a known good ECM and check again.
Faulty injector(s).


* – See SYSTEM & COMPONENT TESTING article.

119622 119623

# 1991 ENGINE PERFORMANCE
## Self-Diagnostics (Cont.)

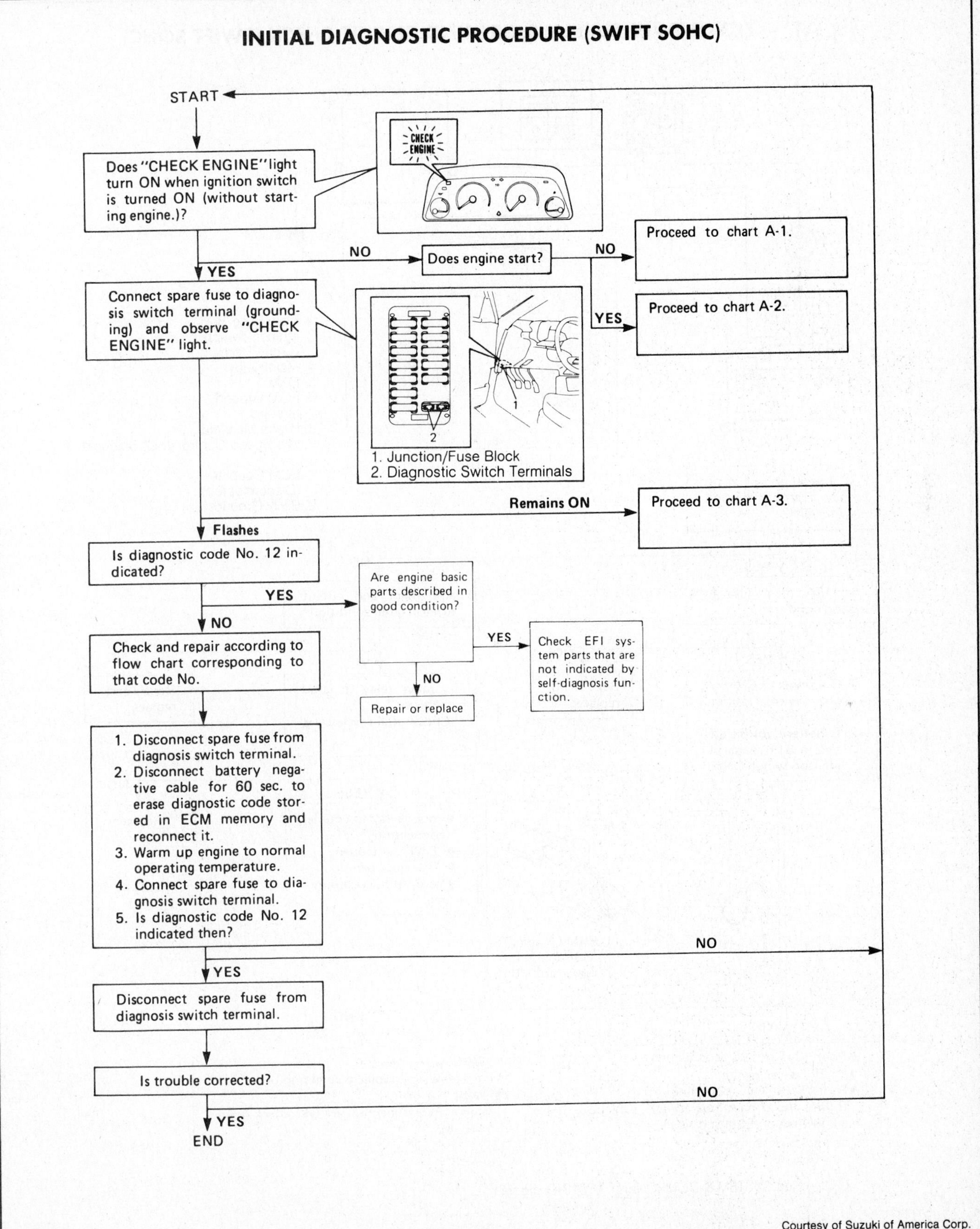
INITIAL DIAGNOSTIC PROCEDURE (SWIFT SOHC)
START
Does "CHECK ENGINE" light turn ON when ignition switch is turned ON (without starting engine.)?
CHECK ENGINE
NO
Does engine start?
NO
Proceed to chart A-1.
YES
Proceed to chart A-2.
YES
Connect spare fuse to diagnosis switch terminal (grounding) and observe "CHECK ENGINE" light.
1
2
1. Junction/Fuse Block
2. Diagnostic Switch Terminals
Remains ON
Proceed to chart A-3.
Flashes
Is diagnostic code No. 12 indicated?
YES
Are engine basic parts described in good condition?
YES
Check EFI system parts that are not indicated by self-diagnosis function.
NO
Repair or replace
NO
Check and repair according to flow chart corresponding to that code No.
1. Disconnect spare fuse from diagnosis switch terminal.
2. Disconnect battery negative cable for 60 sec. to erase diagnostic code stored in ECM memory and reconnect it.
3. Warm up engine to normal operating temperature.
4. Connect spare fuse to diagnosis switch terminal.
5. Is diagnostic code No. 12 indicated then?
NO
YES
Disconnect spare fuse from diagnosis switch terminal.
Is trouble corrected?
NO
YES
END
90G18040
Courtesy of Suzuki of America Corp.

# 1991 ENGINE PERFORMANCE
## Self-Diagnostics (Cont.)

### A1 – ECM POWER SUPPLY & GROUND CIRCUIT CHECK (SWIFT SOHC)

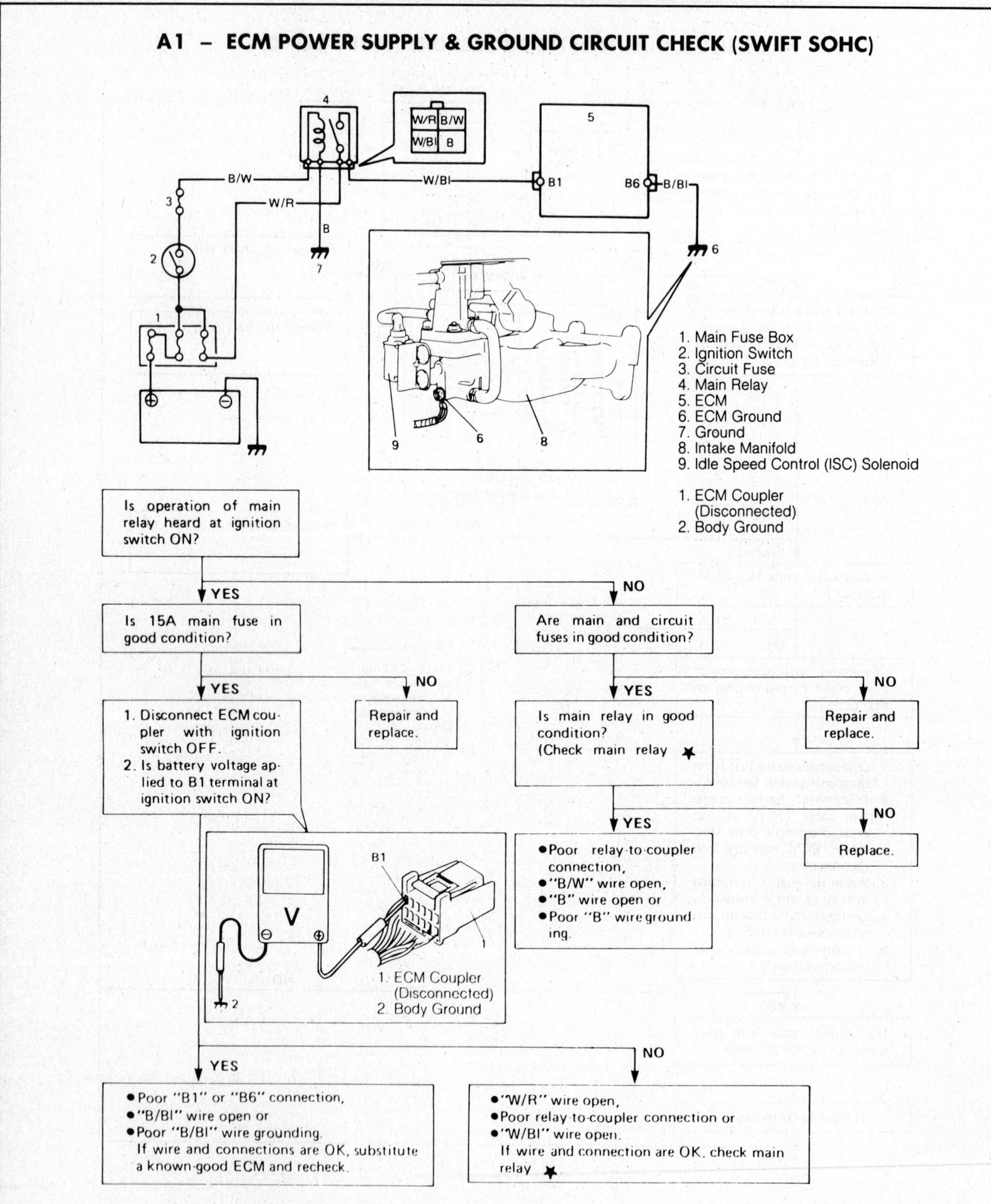

W/R
B/W
W/BI
B
B/W
W/R
W/BI
B1
B6
B/BI
1. Main Fuse Box
2. Ignition Switch
3. Circuit Fuse
4. Main Relay
5. ECM
6. ECM Ground
7. Ground
8. Intake Manifold
9. Idle Speed Control (ISC) Solenoid
1. ECM Coupler (Disconnected)
2. Body Ground
Is operation of main relay heard at ignition switch ON?
YES
NO
Is 15A main fuse in good condition?
Are main and circuit fuses in good condition?
YES
NO
Repair and replace.
1. Disconnect ECM coupler with ignition switch OFF.
2. Is battery voltage aplied to B1 terminal at ignition switch ON?
YES
NO
Repair and replace.
Is main relay in good condition? (Check main relay ★
YES
NO
Replace.
• Poor relay-to-coupler connection,
• "B/W" wire open,
• "B" wire open or
• Poor "B" wire grounding.
B1
V
1. ECM Coupler (Disconnected)
2. Body Ground
YES
NO
• Poor "B1" or "B6" connection,
• "B/BI" wire open or
• Poor "B/BI" wire grounding.
If wire and connections are OK, substitute a known-good ECM and recheck.
• "W/R" wire open,
• Poor relay-to-coupler connection or
• "W/BI" wire open.
If wire and connection are OK, check main relay ★
* – See SYSTEM & COMPONENT TESTING article.


90H18041 90I18042

Courtesy of Suzuki of America Corp.

## A2 – CHECK ENGINE LIGHT INOPERATIVE (SWIFT SOHC)

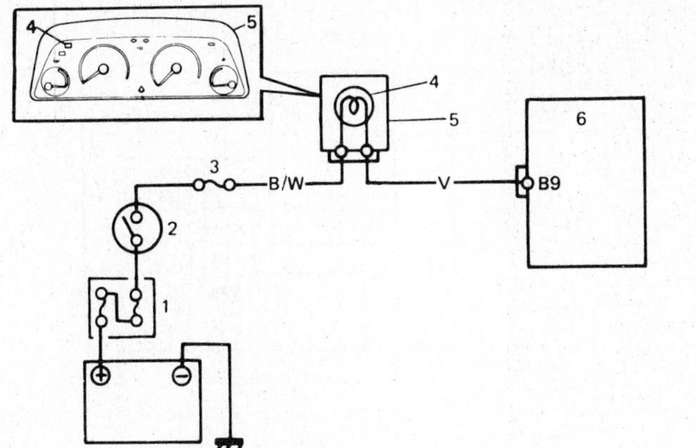


1. Main Fuse Box
2. Ignition Switch
3. Circuit Fuse
4. CHECK ENGINE Light
5. Combination Meter
6. ECM

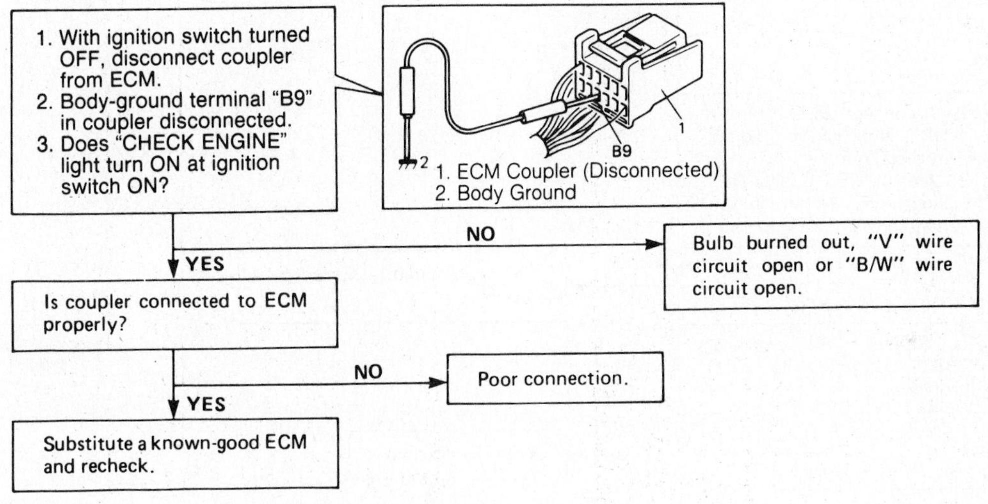


1. With ignition switch turned OFF, disconnect coupler from ECM.
2. Body-ground terminal "B9" in coupler disconnected.
3. Does "CHECK ENGINE" light turn ON at ignition switch ON?

1. ECM Coupler (Disconnected)
2. Body Ground

NO → Bulb burned out, "V" wire circuit open or "B/W" wire circuit open.

YES ↓

Is coupler connected to ECM properly?

NO → Poor connection.

YES ↓

Substitute a known-good ECM and recheck.

90J18043

Courtesy of Suzuki of America Corp.

# 1991 ENGINE PERFORMANCE
## Self-Diagnostics (Cont.)

### A3 – CHECK ENGINE LIGHT STAYS ON – WON'T FLASH (SWIFT SOHC)

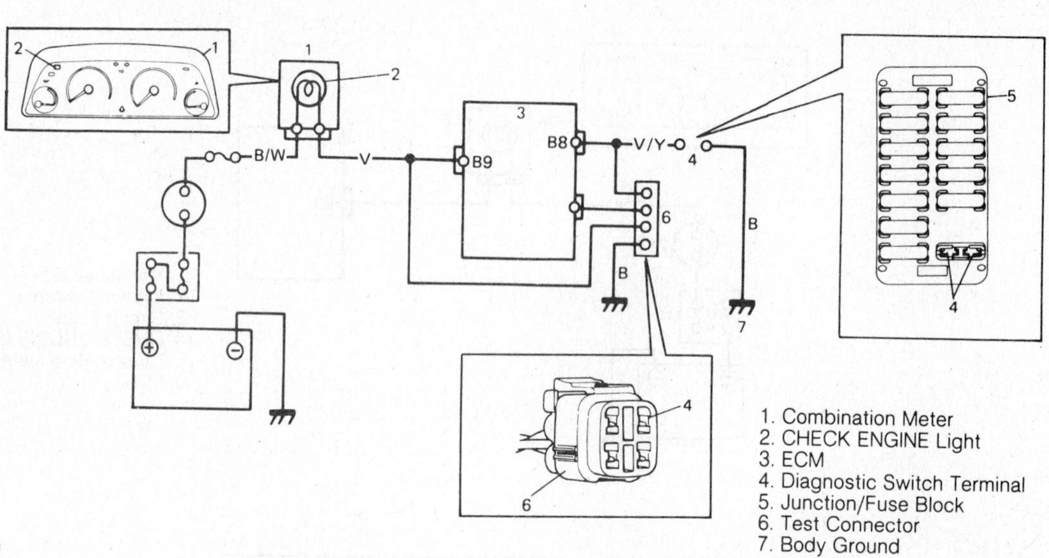


1. Disconnect ECM coupler "B" with ignition switch turned OFF.
2. Does "CHECK ENGINE" light turn ON at ignition switch ON?

YES → "V" wire circuit shorted to ground.

NO ↓

Is coupler "B" (terminal "B8") connected to ECM properly?

NO → Poor connection.

YES ↓

1. Using service wire, ground terminal "B8" with coupler connected to ECM.
2. Does "CHECK ENGINE" light flash at ignition switch ON?

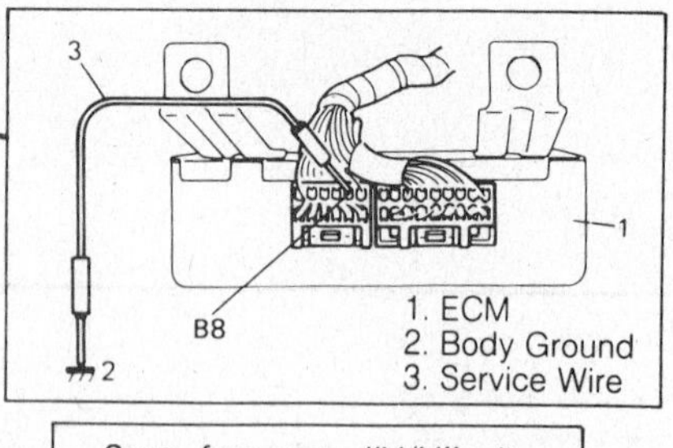

B8
1. ECM
2. Body Ground
3. Service Wire

YES → Spare fuse open, "V/Y" wire circuit open or poor "B" wire grounding.

NO ↓

Substitute a known-good ECM and recheck.

90A18044 90B18045

Courtesy of Suzuki of America Corp.

## CODE 13 – OXYGEN SENSOR CIRCUIT (SWIFT SOHC)

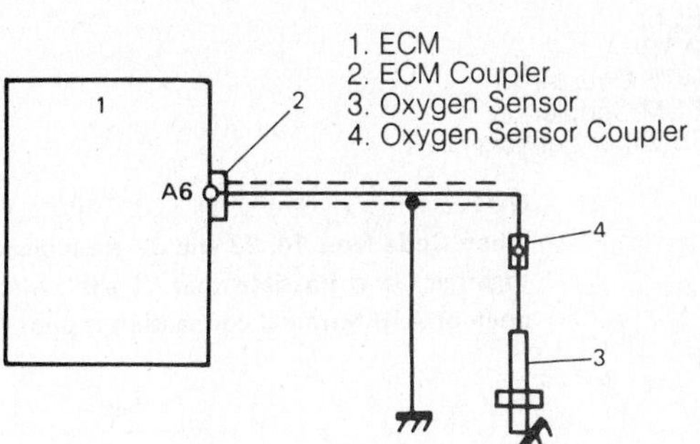


NOTE:

- Before diagnosing trouble according to flow chart given below, check to make sure that following system and parts other than Electronic Fuel Injection system are in good condition.
  - Air cleaner (clogged)
  - Vacuum leaks (air inhaling)
  - Spark plugs (contamination, gap)
  - High-tension cords (crack, deterioration)
  - Distributor rotor or cap (wear, crack)
  - Ignition timing
  - Engine compression
  - Any other system and parts which might affect A/F mixture or combustion.
- If code No. 13 and another code No. are indicated together, the latter has priority. Therefore, check and correct what is represented by that code No. first and then proceed to the following check.
- Be sure to use a voltmeter with high impedance (MΩ/V minimum) or digital type voltmeter for accurate measurement.

1. Remove ECM and connect couplers to ECM.
2. Warm up engine to normal operating temperature.
3. Connect voltmeter between "A6" terminal of ECM coupler and body ground.
4. Maintain engine speed at 2000 r/min. After 60 seconds, check voltmeter.

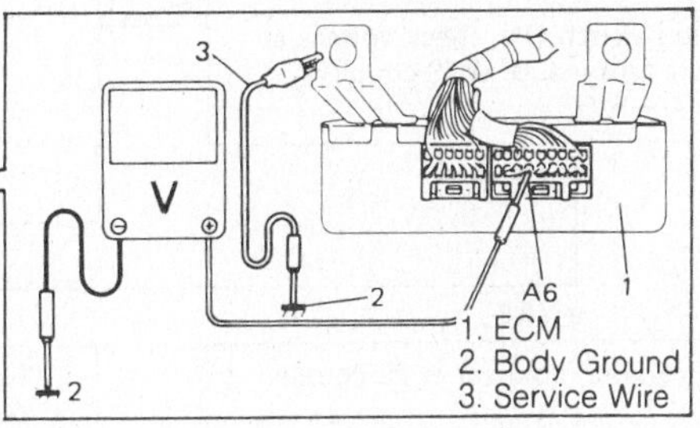

3
V
A6
1
2
2
1. ECM
2. Body Ground
3. Service Wire

**0V** →
- Wire between sensor and ECM open or
- Poor connection.
  If wire and connection are OK, replace oxygen sensor and recheck.

**Remains unchanged at below 0.45V.** →
Maintain engine speed at 2000 r/min. After 60 sec., disconnect vacuum hose from pressure sensor and check voltmeter. Is voltage 0.45V or more?

- **NO** → Faulty oxygen sensor.
- **YES** → Poor A6 connection or lean A/F mixture.
  - Check pressure sensor, WTS, ATS, fuel pressure and injector. *
  If all above are OK, check ECM and its circuit.

**Remains unchanged at above 0.45V.** →
Poor A6 connection or rich A/F mixture.
- Check TS (TPS for A/T model), clogged pressure sensor hose, pressure sensor, ATS, WTS, fuel pressure and injector. *
If all above are OK, check ECM and its circuit.

**Deflects between above and below 0.45V repeatedly.** →
Oxygen sensor and its circuit (Air/fuel ratio feedback system) are in good condition. Intermittent trouble or faulty ECM. See INTERMITTENTS in TROUBLE SHOOTING - NO CODES.

* - See SYSTEM & COMPONENT TESTING article.

90C18046

Courtesy of Suzuki of America Corp.

# 1991 ENGINE PERFORMANCE
## Self-Diagnostics (Cont.)

### CODE 14 – COOLANT (WATER) TEMPERATURE SENSOR (WTS) INDICATION LOW (SWIFT SOHC)

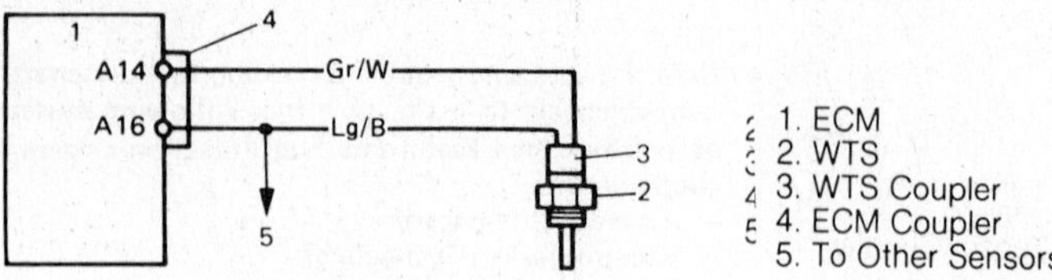


**NOTE:**
**When Code Nos. 14, 23 and 32 are indicated together, it is possible that "Lg/B" wire is open or A16 terminal connection is poor.**

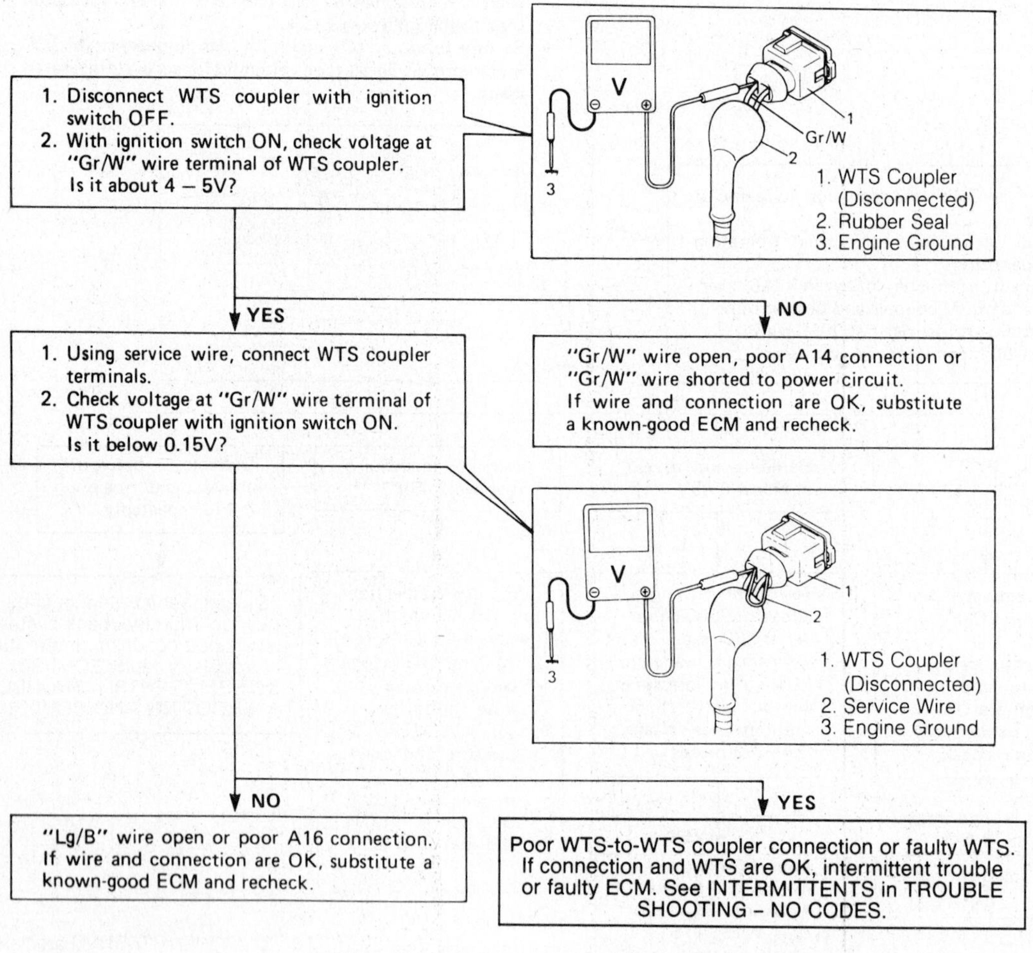


1. Disconnect WTS coupler with ignition switch OFF.
2. With ignition switch ON, check voltage at "Gr/W" wire terminal of WTS coupler. Is it about 4 – 5V?

**YES**

1. Using service wire, connect WTS coupler terminals.
2. Check voltage at "Gr/W" wire terminal of WTS coupler with ignition switch ON. Is it below 0.15V?

**NO**

"Gr/W" wire open, poor A14 connection or "Gr/W" wire shorted to power circuit. If wire and connection are OK, substitute a known-good ECM and recheck.

(From below 0.15V check:)

**NO**

"Lg/B" wire open or poor A16 connection. If wire and connection are OK, substitute a known-good ECM and recheck.

**YES**

Poor WTS-to-WTS coupler connection or faulty WTS. If connection and WTS are OK, intermittent trouble or faulty ECM. See INTERMITTENTS in TROUBLE SHOOTING - NO CODES.

90D18047 90E18048

Courtesy of Suzuki of America Corp.

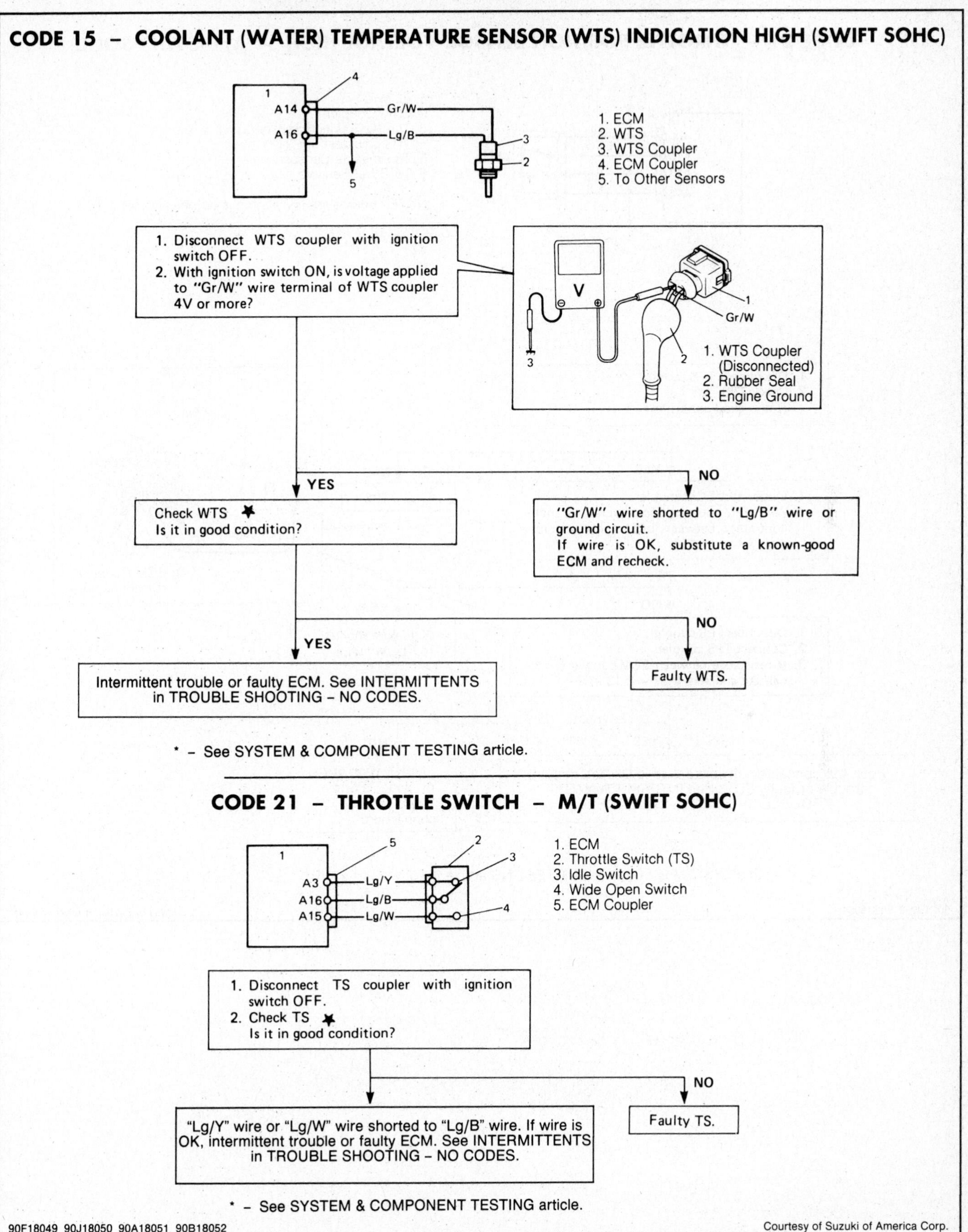
CODE 15 – COOLANT (WATER) TEMPERATURE SENSOR (WTS) INDICATION HIGH (SWIFT SOHC)
A14
A16
Gr/W
Lg/B
1. ECM
2. WTS
3. WTS Coupler
4. ECM Coupler
5. To Other Sensors
1. Disconnect WTS coupler with ignition switch OFF.
2. With ignition switch ON, is voltage applied to "Gr/W" wire terminal of WTS coupler 4V or more?
V
Gr/W
1. WTS Coupler (Disconnected)
2. Rubber Seal
3. Engine Ground
YES
NO
Check WTS *
Is it in good condition?
"Gr/W" wire shorted to "Lg/B" wire or ground circuit.
If wire is OK, substitute a known-good ECM and recheck.
YES
NO
Intermittent trouble or faulty ECM. See INTERMITTENTS in TROUBLE SHOOTING – NO CODES.
Faulty WTS.
* – See SYSTEM & COMPONENT TESTING article.
CODE 21 – THROTTLE SWITCH – M/T (SWIFT SOHC)
A3
A16
A15
Lg/Y
Lg/B
Lg/W
1. ECM
2. Throttle Switch (TS)
3. Idle Switch
4. Wide Open Switch
5. ECM Coupler
1. Disconnect TS coupler with ignition switch OFF.
2. Check TS *
Is it in good condition?
NO
"Lg/Y" wire or "Lg/W" wire shorted to "Lg/B" wire. If wire is OK, intermittent trouble or faulty ECM. See INTERMITTENTS in TROUBLE SHOOTING – NO CODES.
Faulty TS.
* – See SYSTEM & COMPONENT TESTING article.
90F18049 90J18050 90A18051 90B18052
Courtesy of Suzuki of America Corp.

# 1991 ENGINE PERFORMANCE
## Self-Diagnostics (Cont.)

### CODE 21 – THROTTLE POSITION SENSOR VOLTAGE HIGH – A/T (SWIFT SOHC)

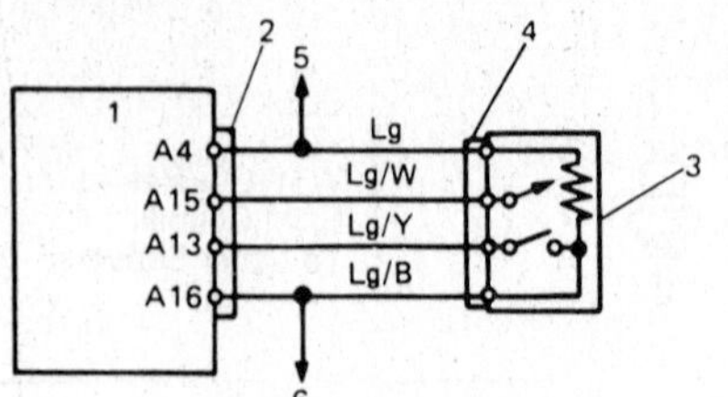


1. ECM
2. ECM Coupler
3. Throttle Position Sensor (TPS)
4. TPS Coupler
5. To Pressure Sensor
6. To Other Sensors

NOTE: Ensure ignition switch is off before testing TPS.

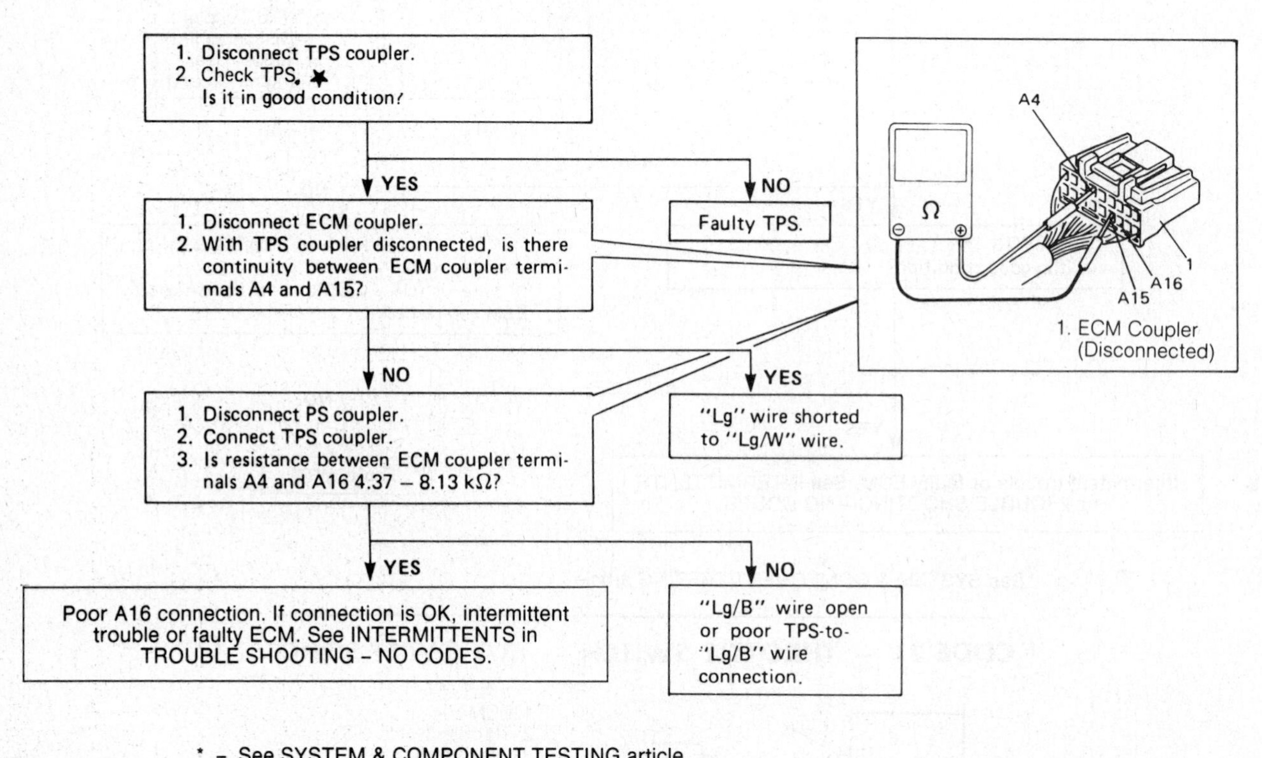

1. Disconnect TPS coupler.
2. Check TPS.*
Is it in good condition?
YES
NO
Faulty TPS.
1. Disconnect ECM coupler.
2. With TPS coupler disconnected, is there continuity between ECM coupler terminals A4 and A15?
NO
YES
"Lg" wire shorted to "Lg/W" wire.
1. Disconnect PS coupler.
2. Connect TPS coupler.
3. Is resistance between ECM coupler terminals A4 and A16 4.37 – 8.13 kΩ?
YES
NO
Poor A16 connection. If connection is OK, intermittent trouble or faulty ECM. See INTERMITTENTS in TROUBLE SHOOTING – NO CODES.
"Lg/B" wire open or poor TPS-to-"Lg/B" wire connection.
A4
Ω
A16
A15
1
1. ECM Coupler (Disconnected)


* – See SYSTEM & COMPONENT TESTING article.

90C18053 90D18054

Courtesy of Suzuki of America Corp.

## CODE 22 – THROTTLE POSITION SENSOR VOLTAGE LOW – A/T (SWIFT SOHC)

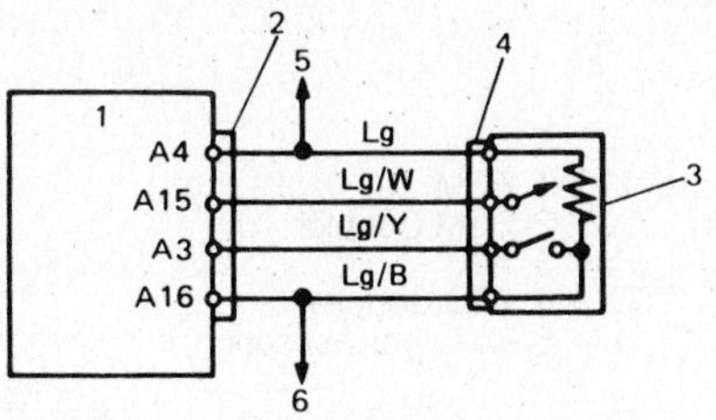

1. ECM
2. ECM Coupler
3. Throttle Position Sensor (TPS)
4. TPS Coupler
5. To Pressure Sensor
6. To Other Sensors

1. Disconnect TPS coupler with ignition switch OFF.
2. With ignition switch ON, is voltage applied to "Lg" wire terminal of TPS coupler about 4 – 5V?

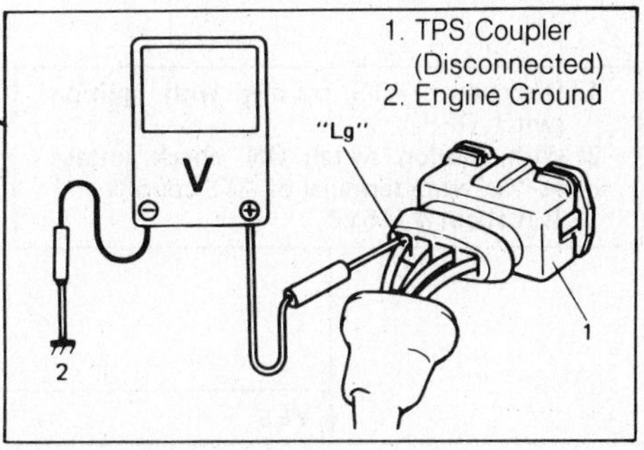

YES

Check TPS *
Is it in good condition?

NO

"Lg" wire open, "Lg" wire shorted to ground circuit or "Lg/B" wire or poor A4 connection.
If wire and connection are OK, substitute a known-good ECM and recheck.

YES

"Lg" wire open, "Lg/W" wire shorted to ground circuit, poor connection at TPS coupler or poor A15 connection. If wire and connections are OK, intermittent trouble or faulty ECM. See INTERMITTENTS in TROUBLE SHOOTING – NO CODES.

NO

Faulty TPS.

* – See SYSTEM & COMPONENT TESTING article.

90C18053 90E18055

# 1991 ENGINE PERFORMANCE
## Self-Diagnostics (Cont.)

### CODE 23 – AIR TEMPERATURE SENSOR (ATS) CIRCUIT INDICATION LOW (SWIFT SOHC)

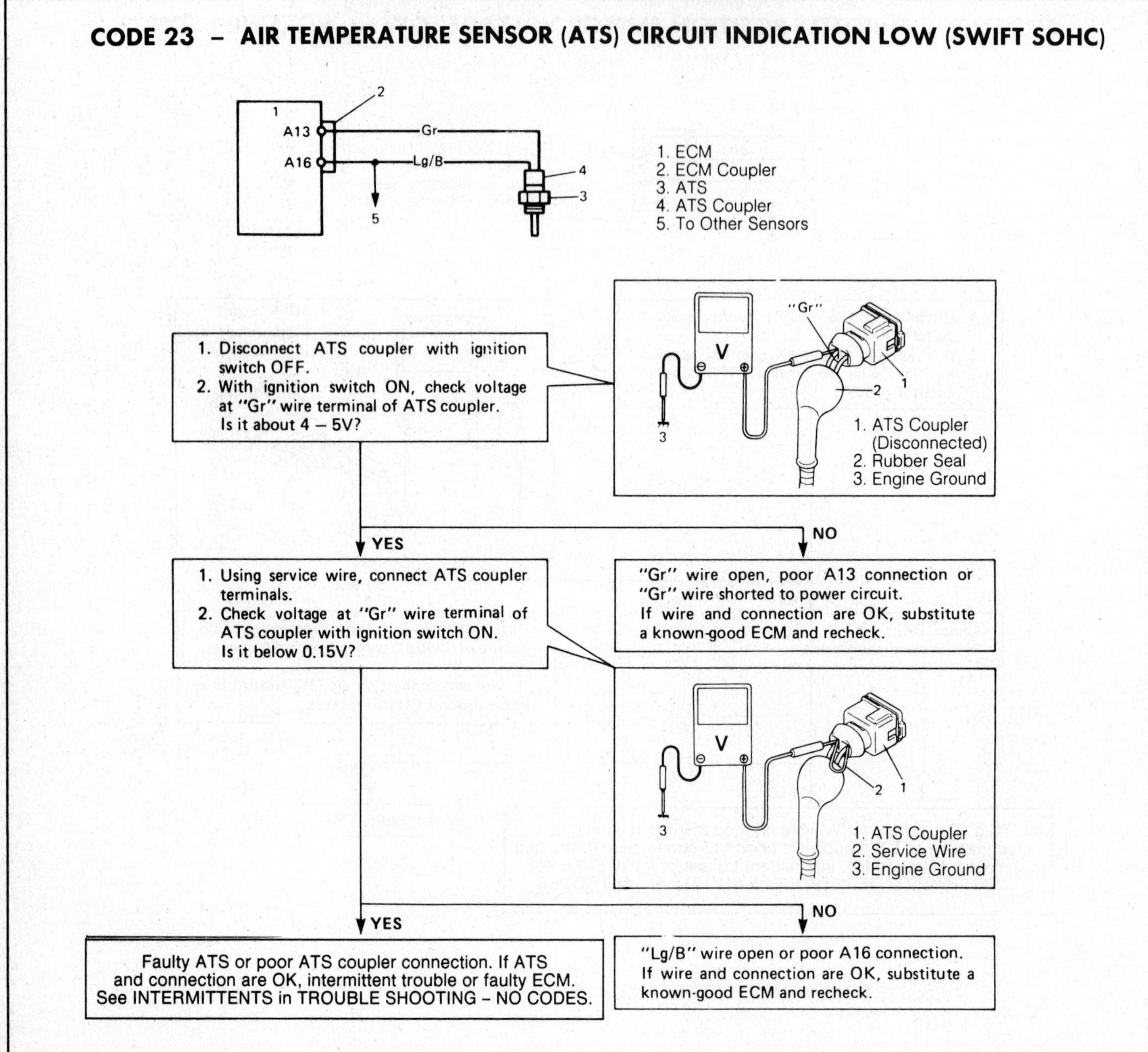
A13
A16
Gr
Lg/B
1. ECM
2. ECM Coupler
3. ATS
4. ATS Coupler
5. To Other Sensors
1. Disconnect ATS coupler with ignition switch OFF.
2. With ignition switch ON, check voltage at "Gr" wire terminal of ATS coupler.
Is it about 4 – 5V?
"Gr"
V
1. ATS Coupler (Disconnected)
2. Rubber Seal
3. Engine Ground
YES
NO
1. Using service wire, connect ATS coupler terminals.
2. Check voltage at "Gr" wire terminal of ATS coupler with ignition switch ON.
Is it below 0.15V?
"Gr" wire open, poor A13 connection or "Gr" wire shorted to power circuit.
If wire and connection are OK, substitute a known-good ECM and recheck.
V
1. ATS Coupler
2. Service Wire
3. Engine Ground
YES
NO

Faulty ATS or poor ATS coupler connection. If ATS and connection are OK, intermittent trouble or faulty ECM. See INTERMITTENTS in TROUBLE SHOOTING - NO CODES.

"Lg/B" wire open or poor A16 connection. If wire and connection are OK, substitute a known-good ECM and recheck.

90F18056 90G18057

## CODE 24 – SPEED SENSOR CIRCUIT CHECK (SWIFT SOHC)

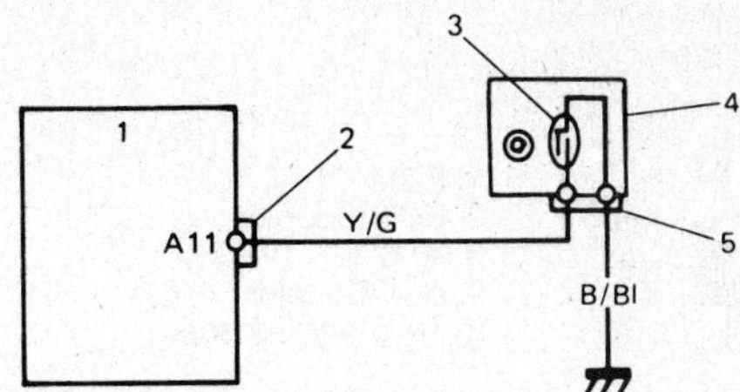
3
4
1
2
A11
Y/G
5
B/Bl

1. ECM
2. ECM Coupler
3. Speed Sensor
4. Speedometer
5. Coupler

NOTE: Ensure ignition is off before checking VSS.

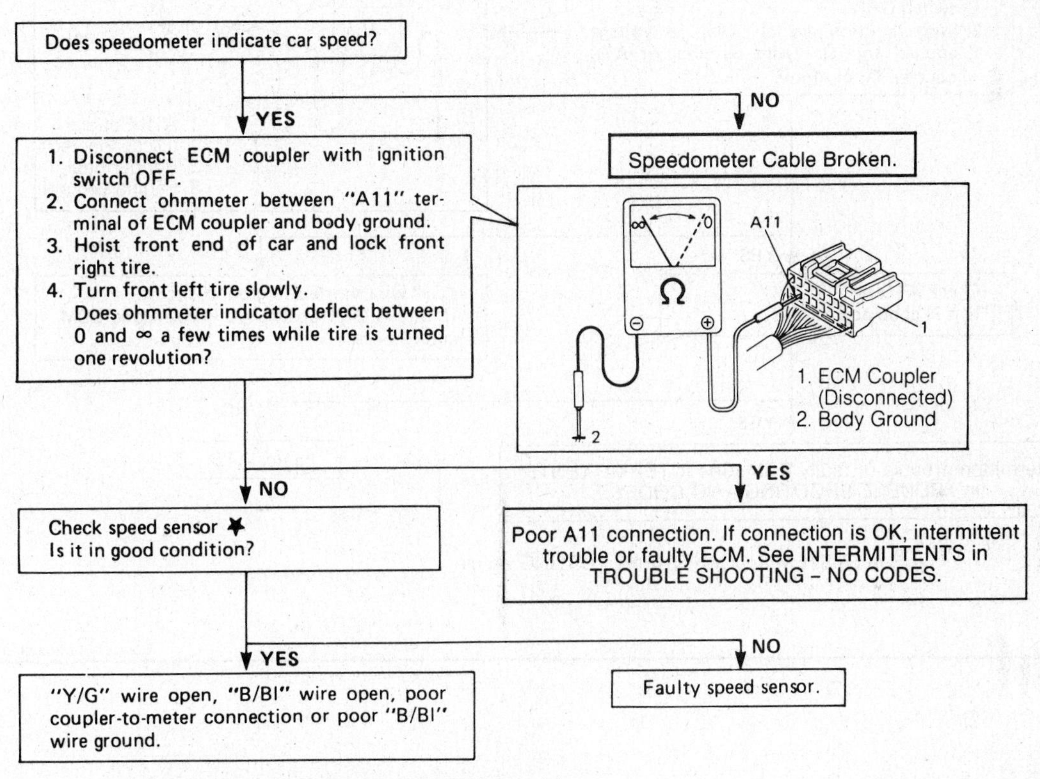
Does speedometer indicate car speed?
YES
NO
Speedometer Cable Broken.
1. Disconnect ECM coupler with ignition switch OFF.
2. Connect ohmmeter between "A11" terminal of ECM coupler and body ground.
3. Hoist front end of car and lock front right tire.
4. Turn front left tire slowly.
Does ohmmeter indicator deflect between 0 and ∞ a few times while tire is turned one revolution?
∞
0
A11
Ω
1
2
1. ECM Coupler (Disconnected)
2. Body Ground
NO
YES
Check speed sensor *
Is it in good condition?
Poor A11 connection. If connection is OK, intermittent trouble or faulty ECM. See INTERMITTENTS in TROUBLE SHOOTING - NO CODES.
YES
NO
"Y/G" wire open, "B/Bl" wire open, poor coupler-to-meter connection or poor "B/Bl" wire ground.
Faulty speed sensor.

* – See SYSTEM & COMPONENT TESTING article.

90H18058

Courtesy of Suzuki of America Corp.

# 1991 ENGINE PERFORMANCE
## Self-Diagnostics (Cont.)

### CODE 25 – AIR TEMPERATURE SENSOR (ATS) CIRCUIT INDICATION HIGH (SWIFT SOHC)

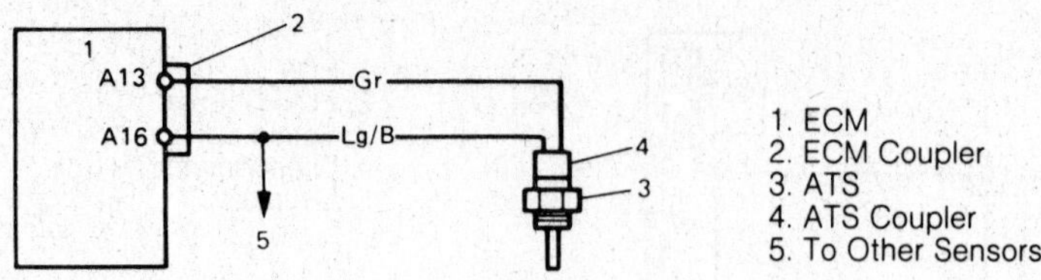


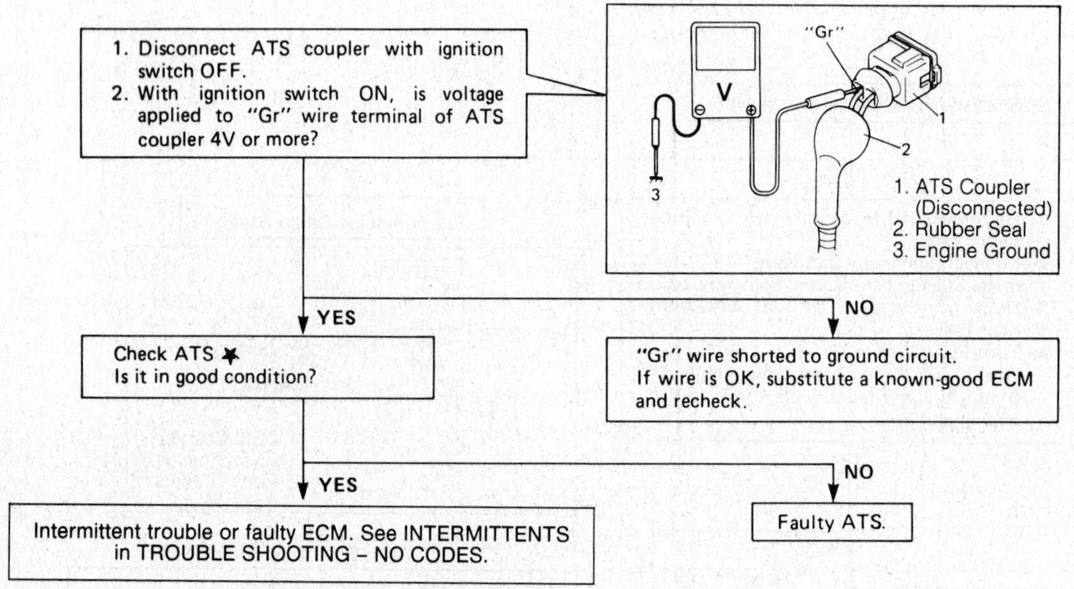


1. Disconnect ATS coupler with ignition switch OFF.
2. With ignition switch ON, is voltage applied to "Gr" wire terminal of ATS coupler 4V or more?

**YES** → Check ATS *. Is it in good condition?

- **YES** → Intermittent trouble or faulty ECM. See INTERMITTENTS in TROUBLE SHOOTING – NO CODES.
- **NO** → Faulty ATS.

**NO** → "Gr" wire shorted to ground circuit. If wire is OK, substitute a known-good ECM and recheck.

* – See SYSTEM & COMPONENT TESTING article.

90F18056 90I18059

Courtesy of Suzuki of America Corp.

# 1991 ENGINE PERFORMANCE
# Self-Diagnostics (Cont.)

## CODE 31 – PRESSURE SENSOR (PS) SIGNAL VOLTAGE LOW (SWIFT SOHC)

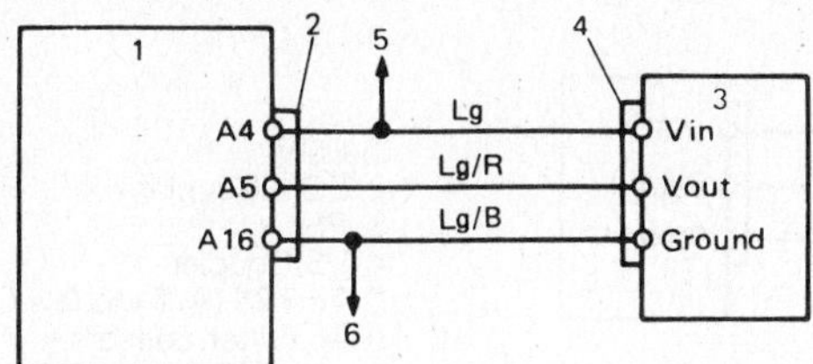


1. ECM
2. ECM Coupler
3. PS
4. PS Coupler
5. To TPS (A/T Models Only)
6. To Other Sensors

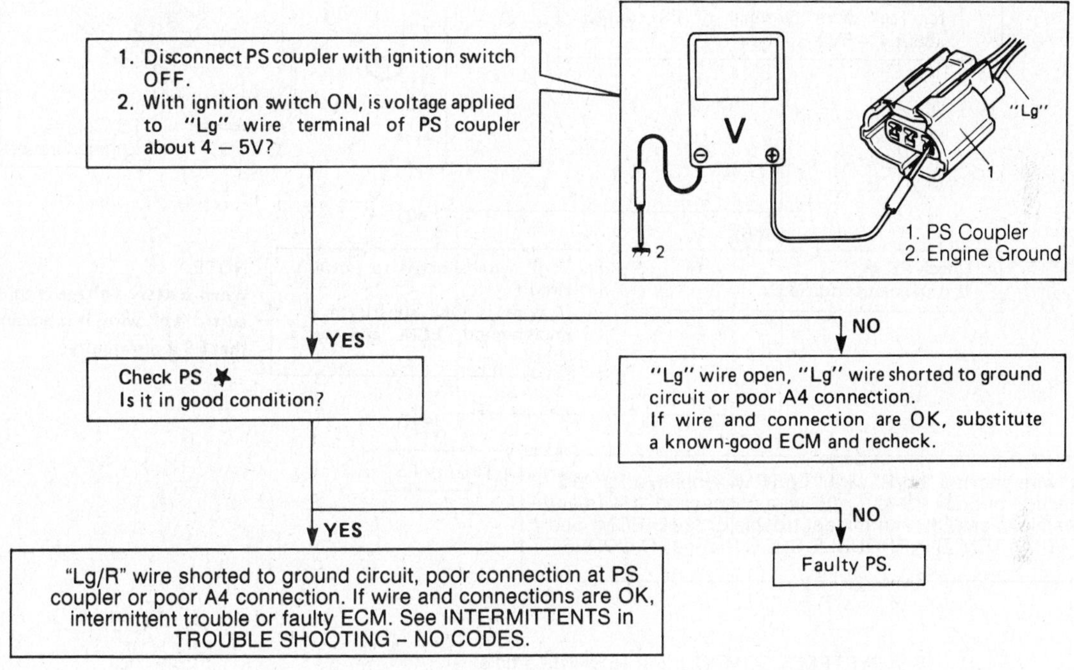


1. Disconnect PS coupler with ignition switch OFF.
2. With ignition switch ON, is voltage applied to "Lg" wire terminal of PS coupler about 4 – 5V?

YES → Check PS *
Is it in good condition?

NO → "Lg" wire open, "Lg" wire shorted to ground circuit or poor A4 connection.
If wire and connection are OK, substitute a known-good ECM and recheck.

Check PS – YES → "Lg/R" wire shorted to ground circuit, poor connection at PS coupler or poor A4 connection. If wire and connections are OK, intermittent trouble or faulty ECM. See INTERMITTENTS in TROUBLE SHOOTING - NO CODES.

Check PS – NO → Faulty PS.

* - See SYSTEM & COMPONENT TESTING article.

90B18060 90C18061

Courtesy of Suzuki of America Corp.

# 1991 ENGINE PERFORMANCE
## Self-Diagnostics (Cont.)

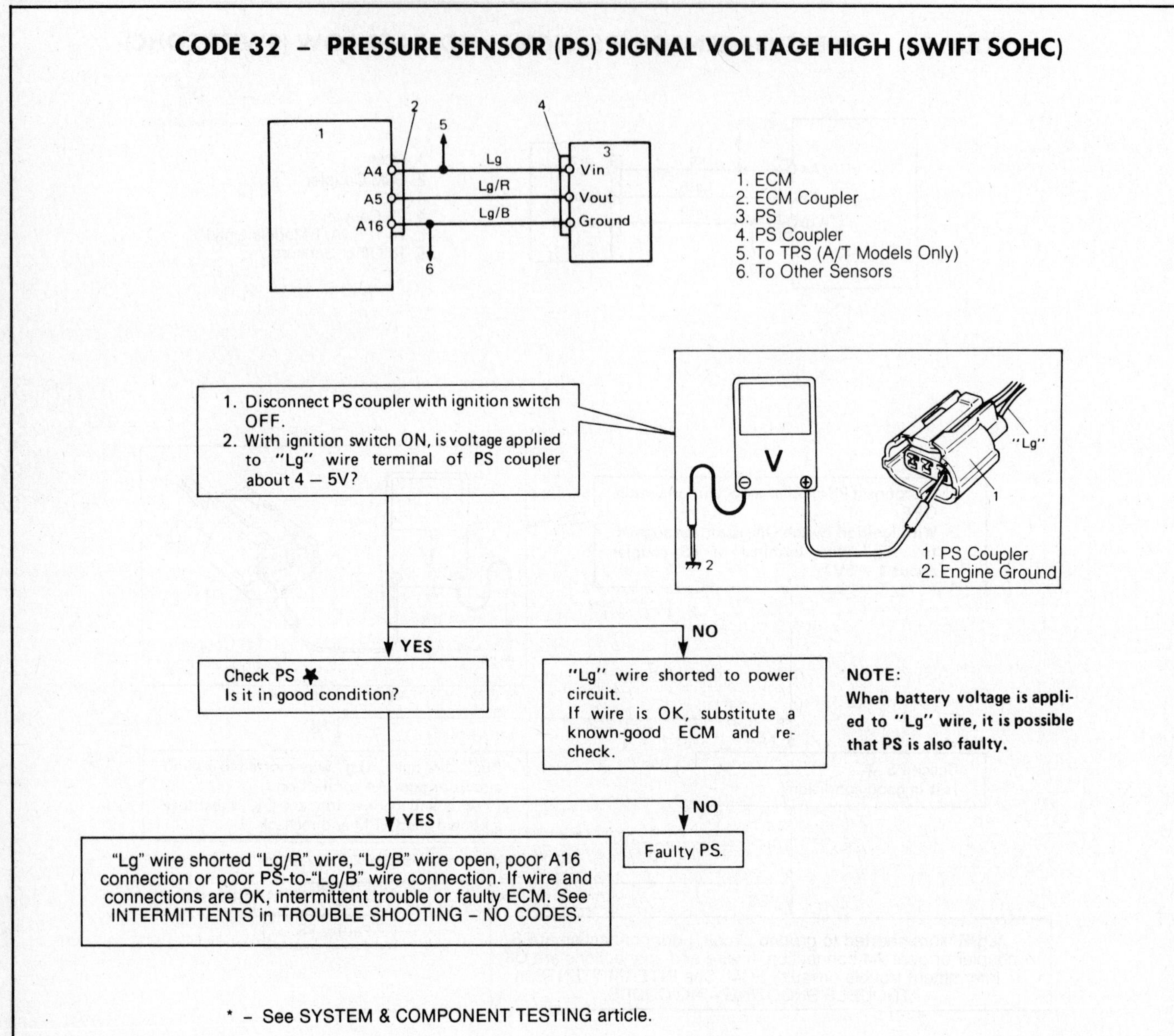
CODE 32 – PRESSURE SENSOR (PS) SIGNAL VOLTAGE HIGH (SWIFT SOHC)
1
2
3
4
5
6
A4
A5
A16
Lg
Lg/R
Lg/B
Vin
Vout
Ground
1. ECM
2. ECM Coupler
3. PS
4. PS Coupler
5. To TPS (A/T Models Only)
6. To Other Sensors
1. Disconnect PS coupler with ignition switch OFF.
2. With ignition switch ON, is voltage applied to "Lg" wire terminal of PS coupler about 4 – 5V?
V
"Lg"
1. PS Coupler
2. Engine Ground
YES
NO
Check PS ✱
Is it in good condition?
"Lg" wire shorted to power circuit.
If wire is OK, substitute a known-good ECM and re-check.
NOTE:
When battery voltage is applied to "Lg" wire, it is possible that PS is also faulty.
YES
NO
"Lg" wire shorted "Lg/R" wire, "Lg/B" wire open, poor A16 connection or poor PS-to-"Lg/B" wire connection. If wire and connections are OK, intermittent trouble or faulty ECM. See INTERMITTENTS in TROUBLE SHOOTING - NO CODES.
Faulty PS.

* – See SYSTEM & COMPONENT TESTING article.

90B18060 90D18062

Courtesy of Suzuki of America Corp.

# 1991 ENGINE PERFORMANCE
# Self-Diagnostics (Cont.)

## CODE 41 – NO IGNITION SIGNAL (SWIFT SOHC)

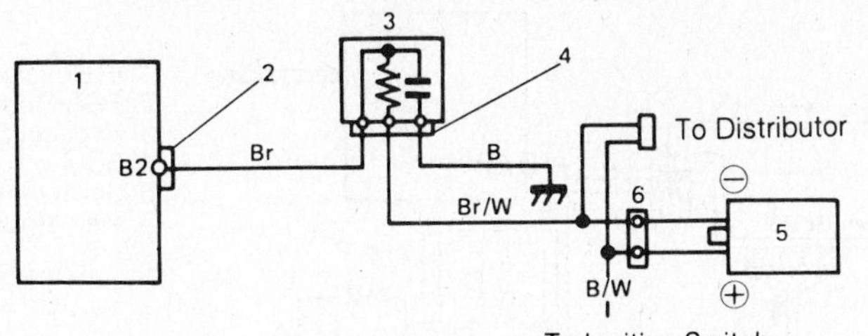
To Distributor
B2
Br
B
Br/W
B/W
To Ignition Switch
1. ECM
2. ECM Coupler
3. Noise Suppressor
4. Coupler
5. Ignition Coil
6. Coupler

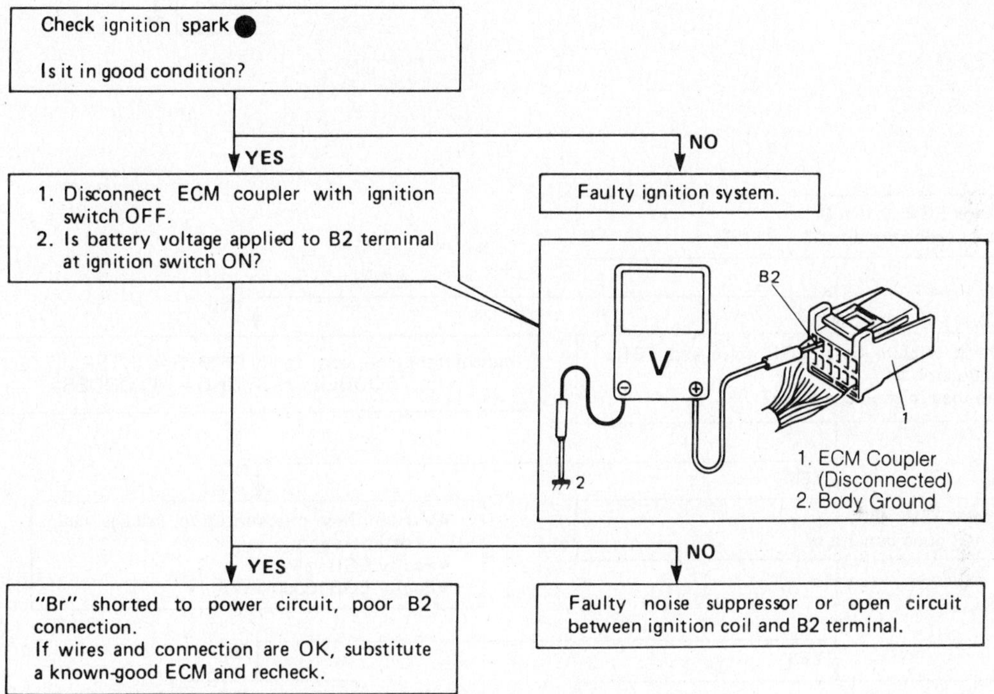
Check ignition spark ●
Is it in good condition?
YES
NO
Faulty ignition system.
1. Disconnect ECM coupler with ignition switch OFF.
2. Is battery voltage applied to B2 terminal at ignition switch ON?
B2
V
1. ECM Coupler (Disconnected)
2. Body Ground
YES
NO
"Br" shorted to power circuit, poor B2 connection.
If wires and connection are OK, substitute a known-good ECM and recheck.
Faulty noise suppressor or open circuit between ignition coil and B2 terminal.

● – See BASIC DIAGNOSTICS PROCEDURES article.

90E18063 90F18064

Courtesy of Suzuki of America Corp.

# 1991 ENGINE PERFORMANCE
## Self-Diagnostics (Cont.)

### CODE 51 – EGR SYSTEM CIRCUIT CHECK – CALIF. ONLY (SWIFT SOHC)

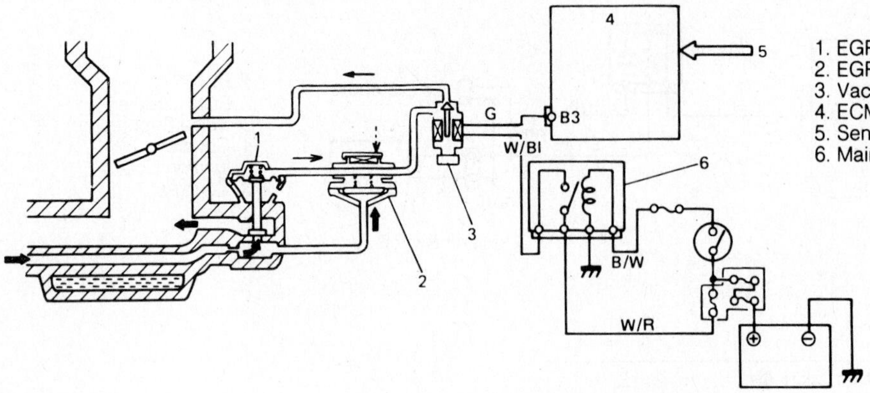

1. EGR Valve
2. EGR Modulator
3. Vacuum Switching Valve (VSV)
4. ECM
5. Sensor Information
6. Main Relay

G, B3, W/Bl, B/W, W/R

Check EGR system *
Is it in good condition?

- YES → Intermittent trouble or faulty ECM. See INTERMITTENTS in TROUBLE SHOOTING – NO CODES.
- NO → Check vacuum hose, EGR valve and EGR modulator *
  Are they in good condition?
  - NO → ● Vacuum hose misconnection, leakage, clog or deterioration,
    ● Faulty EGR valve or
    ● Faulty EGR modulator.
  - YES → Check VSV *
    Is it in good condition?
    - NO → Faulty VSV.
    - YES → ● "G" wire open,
      ● "G" wire shorted to ground,
      ● Poor VSV coupler connection or
      ● Poor B3 connection.
      If wire and connection are OK, substitute a known-good ECM and recheck.

* – See SYSTEM & COMPONENT TESTING article.

90G18065 90H18066

# 1991 ENGINE PERFORMANCE
# Trouble Shooting – No Codes

**Samurai, Sidekick, Swift**

## INTRODUCTION

Before diagnosing symptoms or intermittent faults, perform steps in BASIC DIAGNOSTIC PROCEDURES and SELF-DIAGNOSTICS articles. Use this article to diagnose driveability problems existing when a hard fault code is not present or vehicle is not equipped with a self-diagnostic system.

***NOTE: Some driveability problems may have been corrected by manufacturer with a revised computer calibration chip or computer control unit. Check with manufacturer for latest chip or computer application.***

Symptom checks can direct the technician to malfunctioning component(s) for further diagnosis. A symptom should lead to a specific component, system test or an adjustment.

Use intermittent test procedures to locate driveability problems that DO NOT occur when the vehicle is being tested. These test procedures should also be used if a soft (intermittent) trouble code was present, but no problem was found during self-diagnostic testing.

***NOTE: For specific testing procedures, see SYSTEM & COMPONENT TESTING article. For specifications, see ON-VEHICLE ADJUSTMENTS or SERVICE & ADJUSTMENT SPECIFICATIONS articles.***

## SYMPTOMS

### SYMPTOM DIAGNOSIS

Symptom checks cannot be used properly unless the problem occurs while the vehicle is being tested. To reduce diagnostic time, ensure steps in BASIC DIAGNOSTIC PROCEDURES and SELF-DIAGNOSTICS articles were performed before diagnosing a symptom. Symptoms available for diagnosis include:

- Difficult Or No Start (Cranks Okay)
- Engine Misfires Or Has Lack Of Power
- Rough Or Unstable Idle
- Engine Hesitates
- Engine Surges
- Spark Knock/Detonation
- Poor Fuel Mileage
- Fails Emission Test

### DIFFICULT OR NO START (CRANKS OKAY)

- Check for dirty or clogged fuel filter.
- Check fuel pressure and volume.
- Check for vacuum leaks.
- Check for poor compression.
- Check for contaminated fuel.
- Check for blown ignition coil fuse.
- Check for cracked distributor cap or rotor.
- Check ignition and valve timing.
- Check spark plugs.
- Check EGR system.
- Check pick-up coil air gap (if equipped).
- Check for faulty ignitor (if equipped).
- Check for faulty pick-up coil (if equipped).
- Check for faulty coolant (water) temperature sensor.
- Check for faulty air temperature sensor (if equipped).
- Check for faulty airflow sensor (if equipped).
- Check for faulty noise suppressor (if equipped).
- Check for faulty air valve (if equipped).
- Check for faulty ignition coil.
- Check for faulty throttle opener (if equipped).
- Check for faulty power unit (if equipped).
- Check for faulty crank angle sensor (if equipped).
- Check for lack of fuel in tank.
- Check for malfunctioning ECM.
- Check for malfunctioning PCV valve.
- Check for malfunctioning electronic fuel injection system.
- Check for slipped or broken timing belt.
- Check for adequate spark with a spark tester.

### ENGINE MISFIRES OR HAS LACK OF POWER

- Check ignition and valve timing.
- Check spark plugs.
- Check cooling system.
- Check for dirty or clogged fuel filter.
- Check for low compression.
- Check for clogged air filter.
- Check for vacuum leaks.
- Check for worn distributor terminals.
- Check for contaminated fuel.
- Check for malfunctioning distributor mechanical or vacuum advance (if equipped).
- Check for malfunctioning electronic fuel injection system.
- Check for malfunctioning EGR valve.
- Check for adequate spark with a spark tester.

### ROUGH OR UNSTABLE IDLE

- Check for play in throttle cable.
- Check for contaminated fuel.
- Check for clogged air filter.
- Check for vacuum leaks.
- Check cooling system.
- Check compression.
- Check spark plugs.
- Check idle speed.
- Check fuel pressure.
- Check for cracked distributor cap.
- Check ignition and valve timing.
- Clogged MAP sensor (pressure sensor) vacuum hose (if equipped).
- Check for faulty ECM.
- Check for faulty air valve (if equipped).
- Check for faulty coolant (water) temperature sensor.
- Check for faulty air temperature sensor (if equipped).
- Check for faulty A/C vacuum switching valve (if equipped).
- Check for faulty Idle Speed Control (ISC) solenoid valve (if equipped).
- Check for faulty throttle opener system (if equipped).
- Check for malfunctioning EGR valve.
- Check for malfunctioning PCV valve.
- Check for malfunctioning electronic fuel injection system.
- Check for worn distributor terminals.
- Check for adequate spark with a spark tester.

### ENGINE HESITATES

- Check fuel pressure.
- Check ignition and valve timing.
- Check spark plugs.
- Check for contaminated fuel.
- Check cooling system.
- Check for low compression.
- Check for vacuum leaks.
- Check throttle position sensor (if equipped).
- Check for clogged fuel filter.
- Check for clogged air filter.
- Check for clogged MAP sensor (pressure sensor) vacuum hose (if equipped).
- Check for faulty ECM.
- Check for faulty coolant (water) temperature sensor.
- Check for malfunctioning electronic fuel injection system.
- Check for malfunctioning EGR valve.
- Check for adequate spark with a spark tester.

# 1991 ENGINE PERFORMANCE
# Trouble Shooting – No Codes (Cont.)

## ENGINE SURGES

- Check spark plugs.
- Check fuel pressure.
- Check for vacuum leaks.
- Check for cracked distributor cap or rotor.
- Check ignition and valve timing.
- Check for clogged fuel filter.
- Check for faulty ECM.
- Check for malfunctioning electronic fuel injection system.
- Check for malfunctioning EGR valve.
- Check for malfunctioning distributor mechanical or vacuum advance (if equipped).
- Check for adequate spark with a spark tester.

## SPARK KNOCK/DETONATION

- Check cooling system.
- Check fuel pressure.
- Check spark plugs.
- Check ignition and valve timing.
- Check for clogged fuel filter.
- Check for vacuum leaks.
- Check for excessive combustion chamber deposits.
- Check for faulty throttle position sensor (if equipped).
- Check for faulty coolant (water) temperature sensor.
- Check for faulty MAP (pressure) sensor (if equipped).
- Check for malfunctioning electronic fuel injection system.
- Check for malfunctioning EGR valve.
- Check for adequate spark with a spark tester.

## POOR FUEL MILEAGE

- Check for fuel leaks.
- Check for clogged air filter.
- Check compression.
- Check fuel pressure.
- Check cooling system.
- Check ignition and valve timing.
- Check spark plugs.
- Check for faulty throttle position sensor (if equipped).
- Check for faulty coolant (water) temperature sensor.
- Check for faulty ECM.
- Check for high idle RPM.
- Check for malfunctioning electronic fuel injection system.
- Check for malfunctioning distributor mechanical or vacuum advance (if equipped).
- Check for malfunctioning EGR valve.
- Check for adequate spark with a spark tester.

## FAILS EMISSION TEST

- Check for clogged air filter.
- Check for engine not at normal operating temperature.
- Check for fuel leakage from injectors.
- Check for fuel pressure out of specification.
- Check for faulty coolant (water) temperature sensor.
- Check for faulty air temperature sensor (if equipped).
- Check for faulty ECM.
- Check for faulty EGR system.
- Check for improper ignition timing.
- Check for lead contamination in catalytic converter.
- Check for malfunctioning ignition system.
- Check for misrouted vacuum hoses.
- Check for poor compression.
- Check for vacuum leaks.

# INTERMITTENTS

## INTERMITTENT PROBLEM DIAGNOSIS

Intermittent fault testing requires duplicating circuit or component failure to identify the problem. These procedures may lead to the computer setting a fault code (on some systems) which may help in diagnosis.

If problem vehicle does not produce fault codes, monitor voltage or resistance values using a DVOM while attempting to reproduce conditions causing intermittent fault. A status change on DVOM indicates a fault has been located.

Use a DVOM to pinpoint faults. When monitoring voltage, ensure ignition switch is in ON position or engine is running. Ensure ignition switch is in OFF position or negative battery cable is disconnected when monitoring circuit resistance. Status changes on DVOM during test procedures indicate area of fault.

## TEST PROCEDURES

**Intermittent Simulation** – To reproduce the conditions creating an intermittent fault, use the following methods:

- Lightly vibrate component.
- Heat component.
- Wiggle or bend wiring harness.
- Spray component with water mist.
- Remove/apply vacuum source.

Monitor circuit/component voltage or resistance while simulating intermittent. If engine is running, monitor for self-diagnostic codes. Use test results to identify a faulty component or circuit.

# 1991 ENGINE PERFORMANCE
# System & Component Testing

## Samurai, Sidekick, Swift

## INTRODUCTION

Before testing separate components or systems, perform procedures in BASIC DIAGNOSTIC PROCEDURES article. Since many computer-controlled and monitored components set a trouble code if they malfunction, also perform procedures in SELF-DIAGNOSTICS article.

***NOTE: Testing individual components does not isolate shorts or opens. Perform all voltage tests with a Digital Volt-Ohmmeter (DVOM) with a minimum 10-megohm input impedance, unless stated otherwise in test procedure. Use ohmmeter to isolate wiring harness shorts or opens.***

## COMPUTERIZED ENGINE CONTROLS

### ELECTRONIC CONTROL MODULE (ECM)

***NOTE: For identification of ECM connectors and terminals, see WIRING DIAGRAMS or PIN VOLTAGE CHARTS article.***

***ECM LOCATION***

| Application | Location |
|---|---|
| Samurai | Under glove box |
| Sidekick & Swift | Under Left Side of Dash |

**Power Circuits** - Turn ignition on. Check for battery voltage between ground and indicated ECM connector terminal. See ECM POWER & GROUND CIRCUITS table. If battery voltage is not indicated, check EFI main relay or control relay (Sidekick) operation. See RELAYS & SOLENOIDS.

**Ground Circuits** - Disconnect ECM connector. Check continuity between ground and indicated ECM connector terminal. See ECM POWER & GROUND CIRCUITS table. If continuity does not exist, repair appropriate wire between ECM connector and ground.

***ECM POWER & GROUND CIRCUITS***

| Application | ECM Connector Terminal No. |
|---|---|
| **Power Circuits** | |
| Samurai | B1 & B7 |
| Sidekick | B1 & B7 |
| Swift DOHC | A1, A2 & A16 |
| Swift SOHC | B1 & B7 |
| **Ground Circuits** | |
| Samurai | A4, B2, B3 & B10 |
| Sidekick | A4, B2, B3 & B10 |
| Swift DOHC | A13, A14 & B16 |
| Swift SOHC | A7 & B6 |

## ENGINE SENSORS & SWITCHES

**Airflow Meter (Swift DOHC)** - **1)** Turn ignition switch to ON position. Without disconnecting airflow meter connector, slide back connector seal for access to terminals. Turn ignition on. Using a DVOM with a minimum 10-megohm input impedance, backprobe between White and Red wire terminals of connector.

**2)** If battery voltage is present, go to next step. If battery voltage is not present, check continuity of White and Red wire circuits between ECM and airflow meter connector.

**3)** Measure voltage between Black and Red wire terminals of airflow meter connector. If voltage is not 0.2-0.8 volt, check continuity of Black and Red wire circuits between ECM and airflow meter connector.

**4)** Start engine. Airflow meter voltage signal should increase as engine RPM increases. If airflow meter does not test as described, check airflow meter connections. If connections are okay, replace airflow meter.

**Air Temperature Sensor (Samurai, Sidekick & Swift SOHC)** - **1)** Disconnect air temperature sensor connector. Turn ignition on. Check voltage between Red/Black wire (Samurai and Sidekick) or Gray wire (Swift SOHC) terminals and ground. If voltage is not 4-5 volts, check sensor resistance or wiring harness for open or short.

**2)** Remove air temperature sensor and place it in water with a thermometer. Heat water to specified temperature and check resistance. See AIR TEMPERATURE SENSOR RESISTANCE table. Replace air temperature sensor if resistance is not within specification.

***AIR TEMPERATURE SENSOR RESISTANCE***

| Application | Ohms |
|---|---|
| Sidekick & Samurai | |
| 68°F (20°C) | 2280-2870 |
| 176°F (80°C) | 290-390 |
| Swift SOHC | |
| 68°F (20°C) | 2210-2690 |
| 176°F (80°C) | 290-350 |

**Coolant (Water) Temperature Sensor** - Remove sensor from intake manifold and place in water with a thermometer. Heat water to specified temperature and check resistance. See COOLANT (WATER) TEMPERATURE SENSOR RESISTANCE table. Replace sensor if resistance is not within specification.

***COOLANT (WATER) TEMPERATURE SENSOR RESISTANCE***

| Application | Ohms |
|---|---|
| Samurai, Sidekick & Swift SOHC | |
| 68°F (20°C) | 2210-2690 |
| 176°F (80°C) | 290-350 |
| Swift DOHC | |
| 68°F (20°C) | 2100-2900 |
| 176°F (80°C) | 290-350 |

**Crank Angle Sensor (Samurai, Sidekick & Swift DOHC)** - For testing, see Code 42 in SELF-DIAGNOSTICS article.

**EGR Temperature Sensor (Samurai, Sidekick & Swift DOHC - Calif.)** - See EXHAUST GAS RECIRCULATION (EGR) under EMISSION SYSTEMS & SUB-SYSTEMS.

**Idle Switch** - See THROTTLE POSITION SENSOR or THROTTLE SWITCH under ENGINE SENSORS & SWITCHES.

**Oxygen Sensor** - **1)** Start and warm engine to operating temperature. Pull back seal at oxygen sensor connector. Using a DVOM with at least a 10-megohm input impedance, backprobe oxygen sensor connector.

**2)** Increase engine speed to 2000 RPM and hold for approximately one minute while watching voltmeter. Reading should fluctuate between zero and one volt, without being constantly high or low. If voltage is not as specified, see Code 13 in SELF-DIAGNOSTICS article.

**Park/Neutral Switch (Sidekick A/T)** - **1)** Disconnect negative battery cable. Disconnect connector at park/neutral switch on right side of transmission. Connect ohmmeter between Black/Yellow and Black/Red wire terminals of switch connector. With gear selector in Park or Neutral, continuity should exist. With gear selector in any other position, continuity should not exist.

**2)** Connect ohmmeter between Yellow and Red wire terminals of switch connector. With gear selector in Reverse, continuity should exist. With gear selector in any other position, continuity should not exist. Replace park/neutral switch if it does not test as described.

**Park/Neutral Switch (Swift A/T)** - **1)** Engine ECM receives park/neutral gear selection information from automatic transmission ECM terminal A17. Check input signal by measuring voltage between ground and automatic transmission ECM terminal A17.

**2)** With ignition on and transmission in Park or Neutral, voltmeter should indicate less than 2 volts. With transmission in any other gear, voltmeter should indicate battery voltage. Replace park/neutral switch if it does not test as described.

**Power Steering (P/S) Pressure Switch (Sidekick)** - **1)** Disconnect wire connector from P/S pressure switch on P/S pump. Start engine. Connect ohmmeter between ground and switch terminal. With steering wheel in straight-ahead position, there should be no continuity.

# 1991 ENGINE PERFORMANCE
## System & Component Testing (Cont.)

*PRESSURE SENSOR OUTPUT VOLTAGE (ON-VEHICLE)*

| Altitude (Ft.) | Vacuum (In. Hg) | [1] [2] Output Voltage |
|---|---|---|
| **Samurai & Sidekick** | | |
| 0 | 30 | 3.6-4.4 |
| 1000 | 29 | 3.5-4.2 |
| 2000 | 28 | 3.4-4.1 |
| 3000 | 27 | 3.2-4.0 |
| 4000 | 26 | 3.1-3.8 |
| 5000 | 25 | 3.0-3.7 |
| 6000 | 24 | 2.9-3.6 |
| 7000 | 23 | 2.8-3.4 |
| 8000 | 22 | 2.7-3.3 |
| 9000 | 21 | 2.6-3.2 |
| 10,000 | 20 | 2.5-3.1 |
| **Swift SOHC** | | |
| 0 | 30 | 3.5-4.1 |
| 1000 | 29 | 3.4-4.0 |
| 2000 | 28 | 3.2-3.8 |
| 3000 | 27 | 3.1-3.7 |
| 4000 | 26 | 3.0-3.6 |
| 5000 | 25 | 2.9-3.5 |
| 6000 | 24 | 2.8-3.3 |
| 7000 | 23 | 2.7-3.2 |
| 8000 | 22 | 2.6-3.1 |
| 9000 | 21 | 2.5-3.0 |
| 10,000 | 20 | 2.4-2.9 |

[1] – Pressure sensor output voltage is tested at ECM connector. See ECM LOCATION table. Before testing pressure sensor output voltage, ensure ECM supply voltage is 4.75-5.52 volts at A23 Gray/Red wire (Samurai and Sidekick) or A5 Light Green wire (Swift SOHC) terminals of ECM connector.

[2] – Output voltage is checked at A22 Gray/Green wire (Samurai and Sidekick) or A5 Light Green/Red wire (Swift SOHC) terminals of ECM connector.

*PRESSURE SENSOR OUTPUT VOLTAGE (OFF-VEHICLE)*

| Altitude (Ft.) | Vacuum (in. Hg) | [1] [2] Output Voltage |
|---|---|---|
| **Samurai & Sidekick** | | |
| 0 | 30 | 3.4-3.8 |
| 1000 | 29 | 3.3-3.7 |
| 2000 | 28 | 3.1-3.6 |
| 3000 | 27 | 3.0-3.5 |
| 4000 | 26 | 2.9-3.3 |
| 5000 | 25 | 2.8-3.2 |
| 6000 | 24 | 2.7-3.1 |
| 7000 | 23 | 2.6-3.0 |
| 8000 | 22 | 2.5-2.9 |
| 9000 | 21 | 2.4-2.8 |
| 10,000 | 20 | 2.3-2.7 |
| **Swift SOHC** | | |
| 0-2000 | 28-30 | 2.9-4.2 |
| 2001-5000 | 25-28 | 2.7-4.0 |
| 5001-8000 | 22-25 | 2.5-3.8 |
| 8001-10,000 | 20-22 | 2.0-3.3 |

[1] – Pressure sensor output voltage is tested with three 1.5-volt batteries connected in series. Positive lead is connected to Gray/Red wire terminal (Samurai and Sidekick) or Light Green wire terminal (Swift SOHC). Connect negative lead to Gray/Yellow wire terminal (Samurai and Sidekick) or Light Green/Black wire terminal (Swift SOHC).

[2] – Output voltage is checked at Gray/Green wire terminal (Samurai and Sidekick) or Light Green/Red wire terminal (Swift SOHC) of pressure sensor connector.

**2)** Turn steering wheel. As steering pressure increases, there should be continuity. If there is no continuity when steering wheel is turned or if there is continuity with steering wheel in straight-ahead position, replace P/S switch.

**Pressure Sensor (Samurai, Sidekick & Swift SOHC – 1)** Sensor is mounted to right center of firewall. To test pressure sensor on vehicle, turn ignition on. Connect voltmeter between ground and indicated ECM connector terminal (backprobe ECM terminal). See PRESSURE SENSOR OUTPUT VOLTAGE (ON-VEHICLE) table.

**2)** If voltage is not within specification, see Code 31 or 32 in SELF-DIAGNOSTICS article. To test pressure sensor off vehicle, see PRESSURE SENSOR OUTPUT VOLTAGE (OFF-VEHICLE) table. If voltage is not within specification, replace pressure sensor.

***NOTE: Swift SOHC with manual transaxle uses throttle switch to detect throttle position. All other models use throttle position sensor.***

**Throttle Position Sensor (TPS – Except Swift SOHC With M/T) – 1)** Disconnect negative battery cable and TPS connector. *See Fig. 1, 2 or 3.*

**2)** Using ohmmeter, check resistance between indicated terminals. See THROTTLE POSITION SENSOR (TPS) RESISTANCE table. If resistance is not as specified, adjust TPS. See ON-VEHICLE ADJUSTMENTS article. If resistance is not as specified after adjustment, replace TPS. For further diagnostic procedures, see SELF-DIAGNOSTICS article.

*THROTTLE POSITION SENSOR (TPS) RESISTANCE*

| Application | Ohms |
|---|---|
| **Samurai** | |
| Between Terminals "C" & "D" | |
| With .008" (.20 mm) Clearance At Stop Screw | 0-550 |
| With .016" (.41 mm) Clearance At Stop Screw | Infinity |
| Between Terminals "A" & "D" | 3500-6500 |
| Between Terminals "B" & "D" | |
| At Idle [1] | 0-2000 |
| At Wide Open Throttle [2] | 2000-6500 |
| **Sidekick** | |
| Between Terminals "C" & "D" | |
| At Idle [1] | 0-500 |
| At Wide Open Throttle | Infinity |
| Between Terminals "A" & "D" | 3500-6500 |
| Between terminals "B" & "D" | |
| At Idle [1] | 300-2000 |
| At Wide Open Throttle [2] | 2000-6500 |
| **Swift DOHC** | |
| Between Terminals "C" & "D" | |
| With .012" (.30 mm) Clearance At Stop Screw | 0-500 |
| With .035" (.89 mm) Clearance At Stop Screw | Infinity |
| Between Terminals "C" & "A" | 3500-6500 |
| Between Terminals "C" & "B" | |
| At Idle | 0-500 |
| At Wide Open Throttle | 3500-6500 |
| **Swift SOHC With A/T** [3] | |
| Between Terminals "A" & "B" | |
| With .012" (.30 mm) Clearance At Stop Screw | 0 |
| With .035" (.89 mm) Clearance At Stop Screw | Infinity |
| Between Terminals "A" & "D" | 4370-8130 |
| Between Terminals "A" & "C" | |
| At Idle | 240-1140 |
| At Wide Open Throttle | 3170-6600 |

[1] – To obtain idle position, apply 19 in. Hg to throttle opener.

[2] – There should be more than 2000 ohms difference between idle and wide open throttle readings.

[3] – TPS is not used on Swift SOHC with manual transmission. For testing Swift SOHC with manual transmission, see THROTTLE SWITCH (SWIFT SOHC WITH M/T) under ENGINE SENSORS & SWITCHES.

**Throttle Switch (Swift SOHC With M/T) – 1)** Disconnect negative battery cable. Disconnect throttle switch connector. *See Fig. 4.* Using an ohmmeter, check continuity between indicated terminals. See THROTTLE SWITCH CONTINUITY table.

**2)** If resistance is not as specified, adjust throttle switch. See ON-VEHICLE ADJUSTMENTS article. If resistance is not as specified after adjustment, replace throttle switch.

# 1991 ENGINE PERFORMANCE
# System & Component Testing (Cont.)

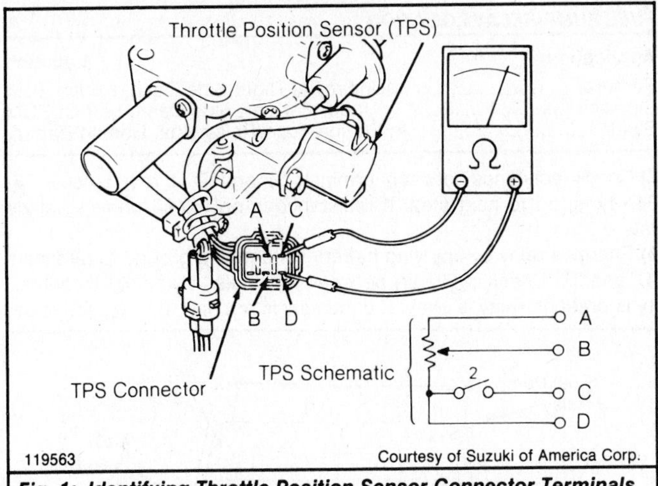


***Fig. 1: Identifying Throttle Position Sensor Connector Terminals (Samurai & Sidekick)***

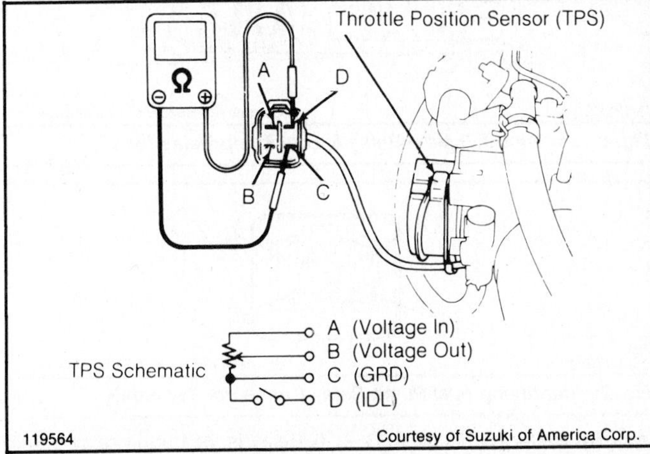


***Fig. 2: Identifying Throttle Position Sensor Connector Terminals (Swift DOHC)***

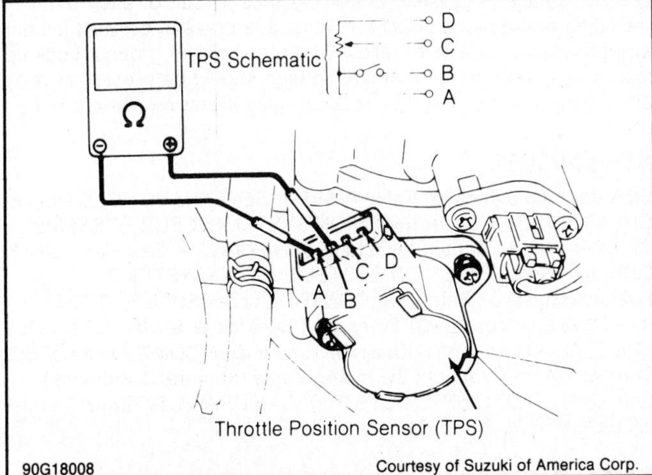


***Fig. 3: Identifying Throttle Position Sensor Connector Terminals (Swift SOHC With A/T)***

**Vehicle Speed Sensor - 1)** Disconnect negative battery cable. Remove instrument cluster. Connect ohmmeter between RSW and GND terminals on back of instrument cluster. Insert screwdriver into speedometer cable connector and rotate screwdriver. *See Fig. 5.*

**2)** Ohmmeter reading should alternate between zero and infinity 4 times for each revolution of speedometer cable. Replace speedometer if vehicle speed sensor does not test as described.

***THROTTLE SWITCH CONTINUITY***

| Application | Specification |
|---|---|
| **Swift SOHC With M/T** | |
| Between Terminals "A" & "B" | |
| With .012" (.30 mm) Clearance At Stop Screw | Continuity |
| With .035" (.89 mm) Clearance At Stop Screw | No Continuity |
| With Throttle Wide Open | No Continuity |
| Between Terminals "B" & "C" | |
| With .012" (.30 mm) Clearance At Stop Screw | No Continuity |
| With .035" (.89 mm) Clearance At Stop Screw | No Continuity |
| With Throttle Wide Open | Continuity |
| Between Terminals "A" & "C" | |
| With .012" (.30 mm) Clearance At Stop Screw | No Continuity |
| With .035" (.89 mm) Clearance At Stop Screw | No Continuity |
| With Throttle Wide Open | No Continuity |

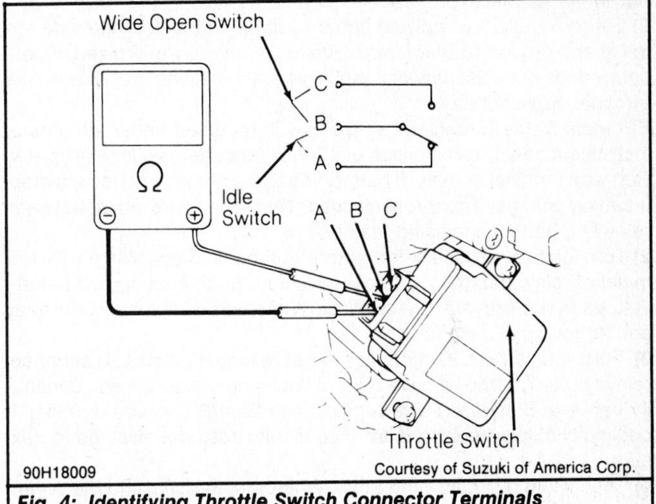


***Fig. 4: Identifying Throttle Switch Connector Terminals (Swift SOHC With M/T)***

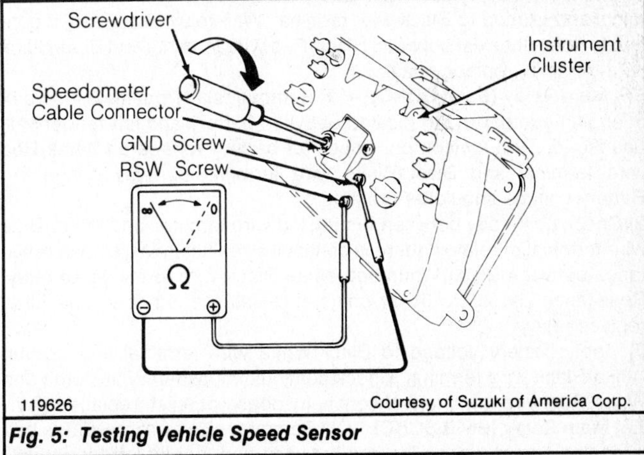


***Fig. 5: Testing Vehicle Speed Sensor***

**5th Gear Switch (Samurai M/T) -** Disconnect 2-wire connector, near ignition coil. Connect ohmmeter between Light Blue and Black/Green wire terminals of connector. With shift lever in 5th gear position, continuity should exist. With shift lever in any other position, continuity should not exist.

## RELAYS & SOLENOIDS

***NOTE: For relay terminal and circuit identification, see WIRING DIAGRAMS article.***

### RELAYS

**EFI Main Relay (Samurai) - 1)** Relay is mounted to ECM, under glove compartment. Turn ignition off. Check for battery voltage on

# 1991 ENGINE PERFORMANCE
# System & Component Testing (Cont.)

White wire terminal of relay. If battery voltage is present, go to next step. If battery voltage is not present, check White wire circuit between relay and battery, including fuse No. 7.
**2)** Turn ignition on. Check for battery voltage on Black/White wire terminal of relay. If battery voltage is present, go to next step. If battery voltage is not present, check Black/White wire circuit between relay and battery, including fuse No. 8.
**3)** Turn ignition off. Disconnect negative battery cable. Disconnect relay connector and remove relay. At relay side of connector, check continuity between White wire terminal and Blue/Black wire terminal. If continuity exists, replace relay. If continuity does not exist, go to next step.
**4)** Check continuity between Black/White wire terminal and Black wire terminal. If resistance is 56-84 ohms, go to next step. If resistance is not within specification, replace relay.
**5)** Energize relay by applying battery voltage to Black/White wire terminal and ground to Black wire terminal. With relay energized, if continuity does not exist between White wire terminal and Blue/Black wire terminal, replace relay.

**EFI Main Relay (Sidekick) – 1)** Relay is mounted under left side of instrument panel. Turn ignition off. Check for battery voltage on Black/Red wire terminal of relay. If battery voltage is present, go to next step. If battery voltage is not present, check Black/Red wire circuit between relay and battery, including fuse No. 14.
**2)** Turn ignition on. Check for battery voltage on Black/White wire terminal of relay. If battery voltage is present, go to next step. If battery voltage is not present, check Black/White wire circuit between relay and battery, including fuse No. 8.
**3)** Turn ignition off. Disconnect negative battery cable. Disconnect relay connector and remove relay. At relay connector, check continuity between Black/Red wire terminal and Blue/Black wire terminal. If continuity exists, replace relay. If continuity does not exist, go to next step.
**4)** Check continuity between Black/White wire terminal and Black wire terminal. If resistance is 56-84 ohms, go to next step. If resistance is not within specification, replace relay.
**5)** Energize relay by applying battery voltage to Black/White wire terminal and ground to Black wire terminal. With relay energized, if continuity does not exist between Black/Red wire terminal and Blue/Black wire terminal, replace relay.

**EFI Main Relay (Swift DOHC) – 1)** Remove relay from main fuse box in engine compartment, located between battery and left fenderwell. *See Fig. 6*. Turn ignition on. Check for battery voltage on White/Red wire terminal and Black/White wire terminal of relay connector. Battery voltage should be present.
**2)** Check continuity between White/Red wire terminal and White/Blue wire terminal of relay. If there is continuity, replace relay. Check resistance between Black/White and White/Black wire terminals of relay. Resistance should be 56-84 ohms. If resistance is not as specified, replace relay.
**3)** Apply battery voltage to Black/White wire terminal and ground White/Black wire terminal. Check continuity between White/Blue and White/Red wire terminals. If continuity does not exist, replace relay.

**EFI Main Relay (Swift SOHC) – 1)** Remove relay from main fuse box in engine compartment, located between battery and left fenderwell. *See Fig. 6*. Turn ignition on. Check for battery voltage on White/Red wire terminal and Black/White wire terminal of relay connector. Battery voltage should be present.
**2)** Check continuity between White/Red wire terminal and White/Blue wire terminal of relay. If there is continuity, replace relay. Check resistance between Black/White and White/Black wire terminals of relay. Resistance should be 56-84 ohms. If resistance is not as specified, replace relay.
**3)** Apply battery voltage to Black/White wire terminal and ground Black wire terminal. Check continuity between White/Blue and White/Red wire terminals. If continuity does not exist, replace relay.

**Fuel Pump Relay – 1)** Turn ignition off. Disconnect negative battery cable. Disconnect relay connector and remove relay. Using an ohmmeter, check continuity between terminals "A" and "B". *See Figs. 6 and 7*. If continuity is not present, go to next step. If continuity is present, replace relay.

***FUEL PUMP RELAY LOCATION***

| Application | Location |
|---|---|
| Samurai | Under Far Right Side Dash, Above ECM |
| Sidekick | Under Far Left Side Dash, Left Of ECM |
| Swift | In Engine Fuse/Relay Box, Behind Battery |

**2)** Check resistance between terminals "C" and "D". If resistance is 56-84 ohms, go to next step. If resistance is not 56-84 ohms, replace relay.
**3)** Energize relay by applying battery voltage and ground to terminals "C" and "D". Check continuity between terminals "A" and "B". If continuity is present, relay is okay. If continuity is not present, replace relay.

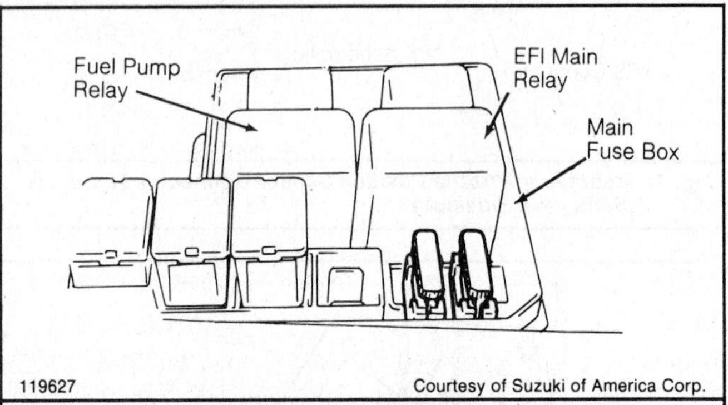


***Fig. 6: Locating EFI Main Relay & Fuel Pump Relay (Swift)***

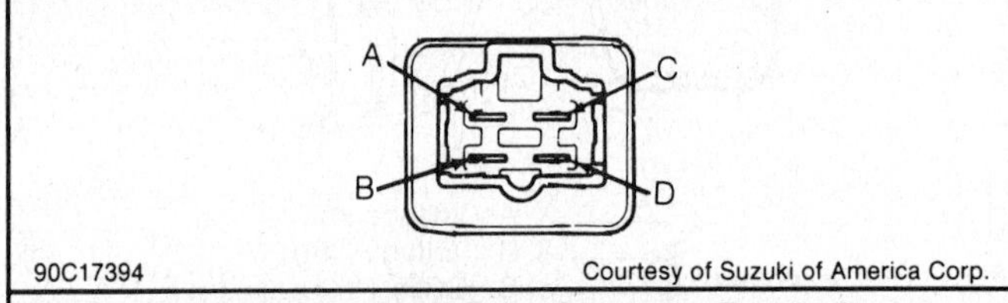


***Fig. 7: Identifying Fuel Pump Relay Connector Terminals***

**Lock-Up Relay (Sidekick A/T) – 1)** Relay is located in relay panel, near right shock tower in engine compartment. Turn ignition on. Check for battery voltage at lock-up relay White/Red and Blue/Black wire terminals. DO NOT depress brake pedal.
**2)** If no voltage is present, check electrical circuit of each terminal (including brake pedal switch). If voltage is present, connect jumper wire between relay White/Yellow wire terminal and ground. Lock-up relay should operate and battery voltage should be present at relay White wire terminal. Replace lock-up relay if test results are not as specified.

## SOLENOIDS

**EGR Vacuum Switching Valve (VSV) –** See EXHAUST GAS RECIRCULATION (EGR) under EMISSION SYSTEMS & SUB-SYSTEMS.
**Canister Purge Vacuum Switching Valve (VSV) –** See FUEL EVAPORATION under EMISSION SYSTEMS & SUB-SYSTEMS.
**Fuel Injector(s) –** See FUEL CONTROL under FUEL SYSTEM.
**Idle Speed Control (ISC) Solenoid (Sidekick & Swift) –** See IDLE SPEED CONTROL (ISC) SOLENOID under IDLE CONTROL SYSTEM.
**Throttle Opener Vacuum Switching Valve (Samurai & Sidekick) –** See THROTTLE OPENER SYSTEM (SAMURAI & SIDEKICK) under IDLE CONTROL SYSTEM.

# FUEL SYSTEM

## FUEL DELIVERY

**Fuel Pump Relay –** See FUEL PUMP RELAY under RELAYS.
**Fuel Pressure Regulator (Except Swift SOHC) – 1)** Regulator is mounted to throttle body, above TPS (Samurai and Sidekick) or at end of fuel rail closest to distributor (Swift DOHC).

**2)** Start and idle engine. Disconnect vacuum hose from regulator. If vacuum is present, go to next step. If no vacuum is present, check for blocked hose between regulator and intake manifold.

**3)** Check fuel pressure with engine running and vacuum hose connected to regulator. Disconnect vacuum hose from fuel pressure regulator. If fuel pressure does not increase, replace fuel pressure regulator.

***NOTE: For fuel system pressure testing and specifications, see BASIC DIAGNOSTIC PROCEDURES article.***

**Fuel Pressure Regulator (Swift SOHC) –** Regulator is mounted on top of throttle body. If fuel pressure is not within specification, check fuel pump unregulated pressure. If unregulated pressure is within specification, check for clogged vacuum passage between intake manifold and fuel pressure regulator. If passage is clear, replace regulator.

**Fuel Pump Circuit Test (Samurai) – 1)** When ignition switch is first turned on with engine off, fuel pump should operate for 2 seconds. If fuel pump does not operate, connect Pink/Blue and Blue/Black wires of fuel pump relay harness using jumper wire. See FUEL PUMP RELAY LOCATION table under RELAYS. If fuel pump operates, go to next step. If fuel pump DOES NOT operate, go to step **4)**.

**2)** If fuel pump operates, check for power at Black/White wire terminal of fuel pump relay. If power is not present, check fuse No. 7 and Black/White wiring circuit to fuel pump relay and repair as required. If power is present at Black/White wire terminal of fuel pump relay, check Pink wire ground circuit from fuel pump relay to ECM.

**3)** To test fuel pump relay and/or ground circuit, ground Pink wire terminal of fuel pump relay and listen for fuel pump operation. If fuel pump operates, relay is okay. Check Pink wire ground circuit to ECM and repair as required. If ground circuit is okay, replace ECM. If fuel pump does not operate and there is power at Blue/Black and Black/White wire terminals, replace relay.

**4)** If fuel pump did not operate in step **1)**, check for power at Blue/Black wire terminal of relay. If relay terminal has power, check for power at Pink/Blue wire terminal of fuel pump connector. If wire terminal does not have power, repair Pink/Blue wiring circuit to fuel pump. If fuel pump does have power, check ground wire circuit. If ground wire circuit is okay, replace fuel pump.

**Fuel Pump Circuit Test (Sidekick) – 1)** When ignition switch is first turned on with engine off, fuel pump should operate for 3 seconds. If fuel pump operates, fuel pump and main relay circuits are functioning properly. If fuel pump does not operate, disconnect fuel pump relay connector. Using jumper wire, connect Pink/Black and Blue/Black wires of fuel pump relay harness. See FUEL PUMP RELAY LOCATION table. If fuel pump operates, go to next step. If fuel pump does not operate, go to step **5)**.

**2)** If fuel pump operates with jumper wire installed, check for power at Black/Red and Black/White wire terminals of EFI main relay with ignition switch in the ON position. If power is NOT present, check for blown 15-amp fuse(s) in fuse box (fuses No. 8 and 14). If fuses are okay, check wiring between ignition switch and main relay.

**3)** If power is present at Black/Red and Black/White wire terminals, Turn ignition off. Connect test light to battery voltage. Probe Pink wire of fuel pump relay with test light. Turn ignition switch to ON position. Test light should illuminate for 3 seconds after ignition is turned on. If test light does not illuminate, go to step **4)**. If test light illuminates for 3 seconds, test fuel pump relay. See FUEL PUMP RELAY under RELAYS.

**4)** If test light does not illuminate for 3 seconds, check for open in Pink wire between ECM and fuel pump relay harness connector. If wire is okay, check for poor connection of Pink wire at ECM, or faulty ECM. See appropriate WIRING DIAGRAMS article.

**5)** If fuel pump did not operate in step **1)**, disconnect main relay connector. Using a jumper wire, connect Black/Red and Blue/Black wires of main relay harness connector together. If power is now available at Blue/Black wire of fuel pump relay harness, test main relay. If power is not available at Blue/Black wire of fuel pump relay harness, check for blown 15-amp fuse (No. 14) in fuse box. If fuse is okay, repair open in Black/Red wire between fuse box and main relay.

**Fuel Pump Circuit Test (Swift DOHC) – 1)** Turn ignition on. Operating sound of fuel pump should be heard for 3 seconds. If fuel pump operating sound is heard, fuel pump circuit is okay. If fuel pump operating sound is not heard, go to next step.

**2)** Remove fuel pump relay with connector from main fuse box, located near battery. *See Fig. 6*. With fuel pump relay connected, ensure voltage exists at White/Blue wire. If not, check EFI main relay. See EFI MAIN RELAY (SWIFT) under RELAYS & SOLENOIDS. With ignition on and engine off, install a jumper wire between fuel pump relay Pink and White/Blue wires. Fuel pump should activate.

**3)** If fuel pump activates, go to next step. If fuel pump does not activate, check fuel pump relay connector for poor connection and fuel pump relay Pink wire for an open. If okay, check for faulty fuel pump. See BASIC DIAGNOSTIC PROCEDURES article.

**4)** If fuel pump activates when fuel pump relay is jumpered, check ignition fuse. If ignition fuse is okay, check for faulty fuel pump relay. See FUEL PUMP RELAY (SAMURAI & SWIFT) under RELAYS & SOLENOIDS. If fuel pump relay is okay, check for open or poor connection between ECM and fuel pump relay Pink/White wire. If wire is okay, substitute a known good ECM and retest.

**Fuel Pump Circuit Test (Swift SOHC) – 1)** With ignition on and engine off, listen for operating sound of fuel pump. Pump should run for 2 seconds after switch is turned on.

**2)** If operating sound is not heard, go to next step. If operating sound is heard, fuel pump circuit is okay. Check fuel pressure to ensure pump is operating at full volume. See BASIC DIAGNOSTIC PROCEDURES article.

**3)** Remove fuel pump relay. See FUEL PUMP RELAY LOCATION table under RELAYS & SOLENOIDS. *See Fig. 6*. Apply battery voltage to Pink wire terminal (harness side of connector) and ground to body.

**4)** If pump operates, go to next step. If pump does not operate, check continuity of Pink wire between fuel pump relay and pump (in tank). If there is continuity, replace pump. If there is no continuity, repair circuit.

**5)** Turn ignition on. Check for battery voltage on Black/White and White/Blue wire terminals of fuel pump relay connector. If battery voltage is present on both terminals, go to next step. If battery voltage is not present on one or both terminals, check appropriate fuses and feed circuits.

**6)** Check fuel pump relay. See FUEL PUMP RELAY (SAMURAI & SWIFT) under RELAYS & SOLENOIDS. If fuel pump relay is okay, check continuity of Pink/White wire between fuel pump relay and ECM connector terminal B10. If circuit is okay, replace ECM.

## FUEL CONTROL

**Fuel Injector(s) – 1)** If engine does not run, go to step **3)**. If engine runs, listen for operational noise from fuel injector(s). Cycling of injectors should increase and decrease with engine speed.

**2)** On TBI models, if fuel is not injected in a conical-shaped pattern while engine is cranking or running, replace injector. Turn ignition off. If fuel leaks from injector at a rate of more than 1 drop per minute with ignition off, replace injector.

**3)** On all models, turn ignition off. Disconnect injector connector. Measure resistance across injector terminals. At 68°F (20°C), resistance should be as specified in FUEL INJECTOR RESISTANCE table.

***FUEL INJECTOR RESISTANCE***

| Application | Ohms |
|---|---|
| Samurai & Sidekick | 0.8-1.8 |
| Swift DOHC | 1.5-2.2 |
| Swift SOHC | 0.5-1.5 |

**Fuel Injector Resistor (Swift SOHC) –** Disconnect 2-wire connector from resistor, mounted on left end of firewall. Check resistance between terminals. If resistance is not 1.9-2.1 ohms, replace resistor.

***NOTE: For fuel system pressure testing and specifications, see BASIC DIAGNOSTIC PROCEDURES article.***

# 1991 ENGINE PERFORMANCE
# System & Component Testing (Cont.)

**Fuel Injector Circuit Test (Samurai & Sidekick) – 1)** Ensure fuel pressure is within specification. See BASIC DIAGNOSTIC PROCEDURES article. If fuel pressure is not within specification, see appropriate FUEL PUMP CIRCUIT TEST under FUEL DELIVERY.
**2)** Check fuel injector operation. See FUEL INJECTOR(S) under FUEL CONTROL. Turn ignition off. Disconnect injector connector and measure resistance between injector connector terminals. Resistance should be 0.8-1.8 ohms at 68°F (20°C). If resistance is not as specified, replace injector. If resistance is within specification, go to next step.
**3)** Disconnect ECM connector "B" from ECM. Measure resistance between connector terminals B8 (Red Wire) and B17 (Yellow wire). Resistance should be 0.8-1.8 ohms at 68°F (20°C). If resistance is not as specified, check Red and Yellow wires for short, open or poor connections.
**Fuel Injector Circuit Test (Swift DOHC) – 1)** Crank engine and check operating sound of each fuel injector. If operating sound can be heard from all 4 fuel injectors, fuel injector circuit is okay. If no operating sound is heard from any of the fuel injectors, go to next step. If one or more fuel injector(s) makes no operating sound, go to step **6)**.
**2)** If no operating sound is heard from any of the fuel injectors, turn ignition off. Disconnect ECM 10-pin connector. *See Fig. 8*.
**3)** Using an ohmmeter, check for continuity between ECM 10-pin connector terminals C3 and C8. If continuity does not exist, check for open between terminals C3 and C8 or poor connections at fuel injector. Check for continuity between terminal C5 and ground. If continuity does not exist, check C5 wire for open or poor ground.
**4)** Disconnect ohmmeter. Turn ignition on. Using a voltmeter, check for battery voltage between ECM terminal C2 and ground. If battery voltage is not present, check for open circuit. Check EFI main relay. See EFI MAIN RELAY (SWIFT) under RELAYS & SOLENOIDS. If ohmmeter and voltmeter readings are okay, go to next step.
**5)** If ohmmeter and voltmeter readings are okay, check connections at ECM 10-pin connector terminal C3 to C4, C8 to C9, C5 to C10 and C2 to C7. *See Fig. 9*. If connections are okay, substitute a known good ECM and retest.
**6)** If one or more fuel injector(s) makes no operating sound, check each fuel injector connector for poor connection. If okay, check fuel injectors. See FUEL INJECTOR(S) under FUEL CONTROL.

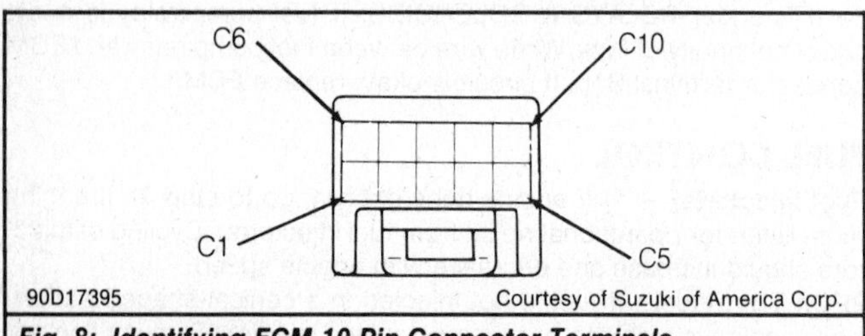


*Fig. 8: Identifying ECM 10-Pin Connector Terminals (Swift DOHC)*

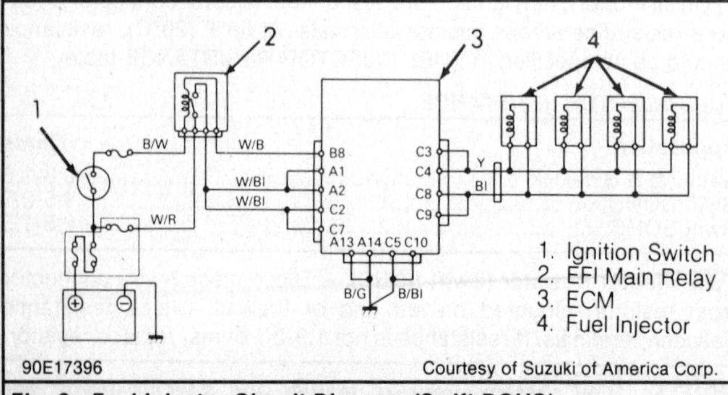


*Fig. 9: Fuel Injector Circuit Diagram (Swift DOHC)*

**Fuel Injector Circuit Test (Swift SOHC) – 1)** Turn ignition on. If fuel is NOT injected from injector when ignition is turned on (without cranking engine), go to step **3)**. If fuel is injected from injector when ignition is turned on (without cranking engine), go to next step.
**2)** Check for short to ground in Yellow/Black wire between injector and ECM. If wire is okay, check fuel injector and fuel injector resistor. See FUEL INJECTOR(S) and FUEL INJECTOR RESISTOR under FUEL CONTROL. If fuel injector and fuel injector resistor are okay, replace ECM.
**3)** Crank engine. If fuel is NOT injected during cranking, go to step **4)**. If fuel is injected during cranking turn ignition off and check fuel injector for leaks. See FUEL INJECTOR(S) under FUEL CONTROL. If fuel injector leaks, replace fuel injector. If fuel injector does not leak, fuel injector circuit is okay.
**4)** Listen for operating sound of fuel injector while cranking engine. If operating sound is NOT heard, go to next step. If operating sound is heard, check fuel pump. See appropriate FUEL PUMP CIRCUIT TEST under FUEL DELIVERY.
**5)** Turn ignition off. Disconnect fuel injector connector. Check resistance between fuel injector connector terminals. If resistance is 0.5-1.5 ohms at 68°F (20°C), go to step **7)**. If resistance is NOT within specification, check for open sub-wires (short section of wires between fuel injector and connector).
**6)** If sub-wires are okay, check for poor connection at sub-wire connector. If connection is okay, replace fuel injector.
**7)** Check fuel injector resistor. See FUEL INJECTOR RESISTOR under FUEL CONTROL. Replace fuel injector resistor if not within specification. If fuel injector resistor is okay, turn ignition off. Connect fuel injector and fuel injector resistor connectors.
**8)** Disconnect 12-pin ECM connector. Turn ignition on. If battery voltage is present on ECM terminal B5, go to next step. If battery voltage is not present, repair open in circuit between EFI main relay and ECM.
**9)** Check for poor connection at ECM connector terminal B5. If connection is good, replace ECM.

## IDLE CONTROL SYSTEM

### AIR VALVE

***CAUTION: DO NOT allow water to contact any other portion of throttle body when immersing air valve in water.***

**Samurai & Sidekick – 1)** For exploded view of throttle body showing air valve, see THROTTLE BODY in REMOVAL, OVERHAUL & INSTALLATION article. To check air valve, turn engine off. Remove air valve cap.
**2)** When coolant temperature is less than 140°F (60°C), air valve should be open. When coolant temperature is greater than 158°F (70°C), air valve should be closed. Install new air valve cap gasket when installing air valve cap.
**Swift DOHC –** Air valve is bolted to intake manifold. To check air valve on vehicle, turn engine off. Remove air valve cap at end of air valve. With coolant temperature less than 140°F (60°C), air valve should be open. With temperature greater than 158°F (70°C), air valve should be closed. Install new air valve cap gasket when installing air valve cap.
**Swift SOHC –** Remove throttle body. See THROTTLE BODY in REMOVAL, OVERHAUL & INSTALLATION article. Immerse air valve portion of throttle body in water. Ensure air valve closes gradually as water temperature rises. Air valve should be fully closed at approximately 176°F (80°C).

## IDLE SPEED CONTROL (ISC) SYSTEM

**Samurai – 1)** Warm engine to normal operating temperature. See if Code 12 is present in self-diagnostics. See SELF-DIAGNOSTICS article. If Code 12 is present, proceed to step **2)**. If Code 12 is not present, see INITIAL DIAGNOSTIC PROCEDURE in SELF-DIAGNOSTICS article.
**2)** Ensure idle speed and ISC duty are within specification. See ON-VEHICLE ADJUSTMENTS article. If idle speed and ISC duty are correct, system is operating correctly. If idle speed is correct, but ISC duty is not correct, go to step **3)**. If idle speed is high, go to step **4)**. If idle speed is low, go to step **7)**.

# 1991 ENGINE PERFORMANCE
# System & Component Testing (Cont.)

**3)** If idle speed is correct, but ISC duty is incorrect, adjust ISC duty. See ON-VEHICLE ADJUSTMENTS article.

***NOTE: When ISC is almost closed, check air intake system for vacuum leaks. If no vacuum leaks are present, adjust ISC duty. If ISC duty remains unchanged when adjusting screw is rotated, check wiring circuit of duty check terminal. For information on duty check terminal, see SELF-DIAGNOSTICS article.***

**4)** If idle speed is high, pinch upper hose on ISC solenoid closed. *See Fig. 10.* The ISC solenoid is located on right side of engine, near valve cover. Note if engine speed decreases. If engine speed did not decrease, go to step **6)**. If engine speed decreased, go to step **5)**.
**5)** Turn ignition off. Disconnect electrical connector from ISC solenoid. Using ohmmeter, check resistance between ISC solenoid terminals. Resistance should be 30-33 ohms. Replace ISC if defective. If resistance was okay, check for short in Light Green/Black wire. *See Fig. 10.* If wiring is okay, substitute a known good ECM and recheck.
**6)** Ensure no vacuum leaks are present in the air intake system and/or A/C Vacuum Switching Valve (VSV). Adjust idle speed and ISC duty. See ON-VEHICLE ADJUSTMENTS article. If idle speed cannot be adjusted, check air valve. See AIR VALVE under IDLE CONTROL SYSTEM.
**7)** If idle speed is low, disconnect ISC solenoid hose from air cleaner. Note if air is being drawn into the hose. If no air is being drawn in, go to step **8)**. If air is being drawn in, adjust idle speed and ISC duty. See ON-VEHICLE ADJUSTMENTS article.
**8)** Turn ignition off. Disconnect electrical connector from ISC solenoid. Using ohmmeter, check resistance between ISC solenoid terminals. Resistance should be 30-33 ohms. Replace ISC if defective. If resistance was okay, go to next step.
**9)** Check for open in Light Green/Black wire, defective wiring connections or clogged hoses to ISC solenoid. *See Fig. 10.* If all are okay, substitute a known good ECM and recheck operation.

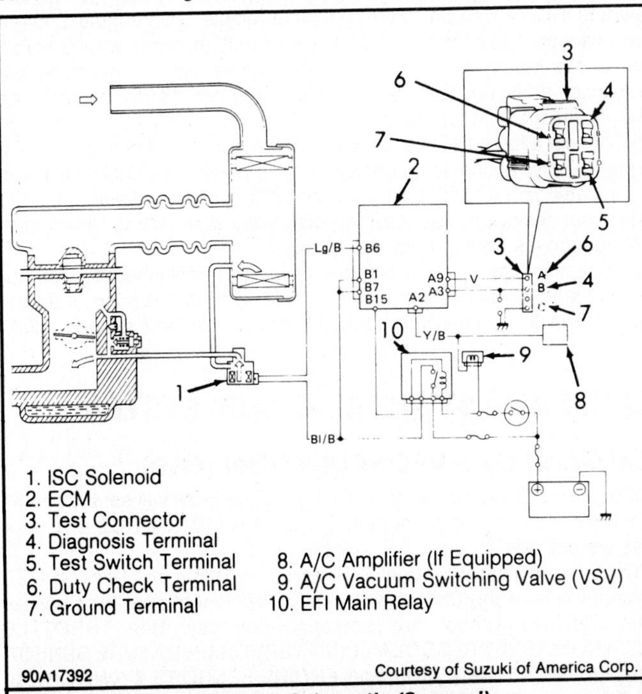


***Fig. 10: ISC Solenoid Wiring Schematic (Samurai)***

**Sidekick – 1)** Warm engine to normal operating temperature. Using a jumper wire, ground diagnosis terminal of test connector. *See Fig. 10.* Observe CHECK ENGINE light. If Code 12 flashes, go to next step. If Code 12 does not flash, see INITIAL DIAGNOSTIC PROCEDURE (SIDEKICK) chart in SELF DIAGNOSTICS article.
**2)** Check ISC duty and idle speed. If idle speed is within specification but duty is not, adjust idle speed screw to obtain proper duty. See IDLE SPEED in ON-VEHICLE ADJUSTMENTS article. If idle speed is high, proceed to next step. If idle speed is low, proceed to step **5)**.
**3)** Using an ohmmeter, check ISC resistance. Reading should be 11-14 ohms. If resistance reading is not within specification, replace ISC solenoid. If reading is within specification, observe duty meter. Reading should be less than 28 percent, (greater than 72 percent for OFF duty meter).
**4)** If reading is not as specified, check Light Green/Black wire for short to ground. See WIRING DIAGRAMS article. If wire is okay, substitute known good ECM and recheck. If reading is okay, check intake system for vacuum leaks. If system is okay, adjust idle speed screw to obtain correct idle. If idle will not set to specification, check air valve.
**5)** Using an ohmmeter, check ISC resistance. Reading should be 11-14 ohms. If resistance reading is not within specification, replace ISC solenoid. If reading is within specification, observe duty meter. Reading should be approximately 100 percent, (approximately zero percent for OFF duty meter).
**6)** If reading is as specified, adjust idle speed and duty. If reading is not as specified, check Light Green/Black wire for open condition. If wire is okay, substitute known good ECM and recheck.
**Swift DOHC – 1)** Warm engine to normal operating temperature. With engine running, use stethoscope and check for operating sound at ISC solenoid. ISC solenoid is mounted on intake manifold, between valve covers.
**2)** If operating sound is heard, go to step **4)**. If no operating sound is heard, check ISC solenoid. See appropriate IDLE SPEED CONTROL (ISC) SOLENOID under IDLE CONTROL SYSTEM. Replace ISC solenoid if defective. If ISC solenoid is okay, go to next step.
**3)** Check for open or short in Red/White wire between ECM and ISC solenoid. Check for defective connection at ISC solenoid and ECM. If wiring and connections are okay, substitute ECM and recheck.
**4)** With engine idling, pinch upper hose on ISC solenoid closed. Note if engine speed decreases. If engine speed decreases, go to step **5)**. If engine speed does not decrease, check for restricted air passages on ISC solenoid.
**5)** Ensure idle speed is within specification. See ON-VEHICLE ADJUSTMENTS article. With idle speed correct, ensure the following conditions are present:

- Idle speed remains at 800-900 RPM with headlights on.
- Ensure ISC solenoid does not operate (operating sound is not heard) for only a few seconds after warm engine is started.
- Increase engine speed to 4000 RPM, quickly close throttle valve and ensure ISC solenoid does not operate (operating sound is not heard) for only a few seconds.

If all conditions are met, system is operating correctly. If all conditions are not met, substitute a known good ECM and recheck.
**Swift SOHC – 1)** Warm engine to normal operating temperature. See if Code 12 is present in self-diagnostics. See SELF-DIAGNOSTICS article. If Code 12 is present, proceed to step **2)**. If Code 12 is not present, see SELF-DIAGNOSTICS article.
**2)** Turn ignition switch on. Using stethoscope, check for operating sound at ISC solenoid. The ISC solenoid is mounted near air cleaner. If operating sound is heard, go to step **4)**. If no operating sound is heard, check ISC solenoid. See IDLE SPEED CONTROL (ISC) SOLENOID under IDLE CONTROL SYSTEM. Replace ISC solenoid if defective. If ISC solenoid is okay, go to next step.
**3)** Check for open or short in Red/White wire between ECM and ISC solenoid. Check for defective connection at ISC solenoid and ECM. If wiring and connections are okay, substitute a known good ECM and recheck.
**4)** With engine idling, disconnect ISC solenoid hose from air cleaner. Note if air is being drawn into the hose. If no air is being drawn in, check for clogged air passages. If air is being drawn in, system is operating correctly.

## IDLE SPEED CONTROL (ISC) SOLENOID

**1)** Turn ignition off. Disconnect electrical connector from ISC solenoid.
**2)** Using ohmmeter, check resistance between ISC solenoid terminals. Resistance should be 30-33 ohms (11-14 ohms on Sidekick). Replace ISC solenoid if defective.

# 1991 ENGINE PERFORMANCE
# System & Component Testing (Cont.)

**3)** Warm engine to normal operating temperature. With running and electrical connector removed from ISC solenoid, disconnect ISC solenoid hose from lower port on ISC solenoid.
**4)** No air should be drawn into the hose. Connect battery voltage and ground to ISC solenoid terminals. Air should now be drawn into the hose. Replace ISC solenoid if defective. Reinstall hose.

***CAUTION: DO NOT apply battery voltage to ISC solenoid for more than one second. Wait 10 seconds before reconnecting battery voltage to ISC solenoid.***

## THROTTLE OPENER SYSTEM (SAMURAI & SIDEKICK)

***NOTE: For throttle opener system vacuum and wiring schematic, see Fig. 11.***

**System Test - 1)** Warm engine to normal operating temperature. Turn engine off. Ensure throttle opener slightly opens throttle valve with engine off and while engine is cranking. If throttle valve opens, go to step **3)**.
**2)** If throttle valve does not open, check throttle opener diaphragm. See THROTTLE OPENER DIAPHRAGM under THROTTLE OPENER SYSTEM (SAMURAI & SIDEKICK). Replace throttle opener if defective. If throttle opener is okay, adjust throttle opener. See ON-VEHICLE ADJUSTMENTS article.
**3)** Note if throttle opener rod retracts within one second after engine starts. If rod retracts, check throttle opener adjustment. See ON-VEHICLE ADJUSTMENTS article. Adjust as necessary. If rod does not retract, go to next step.
**4)** Check vacuum hoses to throttle opener. If vacuum hoses are okay, check throttle opener diaphragm. See THROTTLE OPENER DIAPHRAGM under THROTTLE OPENER SYSTEM (SAMURAI & SIDEKICK). Replace components as necessary. If components are okay, go to next step.
**5)** Check throttle opener vacuum switching valve. See appropriate THROTTLE OPENER VACUUM SWITCHING VALVE (VSV) under THROTTLE OPENER SYSTEM (SAMURAI & SIDEKICK). If VSV is okay, go to next step. Replace VSV if defective.
**6)** Turn ignition on. Check for battery voltage between ground and ECM terminal B14 (Light Green/White wire). ECM is located near glove box on Samurai or upper left corner of instrument panel on Sidekick.
**7)** If battery voltage is present, go to next step. If battery voltage is not present, check for defective connection at VSV, defective wiring between ECM and VSV or defective wiring between VSV and EFI main relay (Samurai) or control relay (Sidekick). If wiring and connections are okay, replace ECM and recheck operation.
**8)** While cranking engine, check for voltage on ECM connector terminal B14 (Light Green/White wire). If voltage is not present, ECM is okay. If voltage is present, go to next step.
**9)** While cranking engine, check for battery voltage on ECM connector terminal B11 (Black/Yellow wire). If battery voltage is present, go to next step. If battery voltage is not present, check for open or short to ground in Black/Yellow wire between ECM and starter.
**10)** Check for defective connection at ECM. If connection is okay, replace ECM and recheck system operation.
**Throttle Opener Diaphragm -** Disconnect vacuum hose from throttle opener diaphragm. Using a hand-held vacuum pump and gauge, apply 20 in. Hg to diaphragm. Ensure opener rod moves freely and remains in position. Replace throttle opener if defective.
**Throttle Opener Vacuum Switching Valve (Samurai & Sidekick) - 1)** Vacuum Switching Valve (VSV) is Brown and located on right side of valve cover, near front of engine. Turn ignition off. Disconnect electrical connector from VSV.
**2)** Using ohmmeter, check resistance between VSV terminals. Replace VSV if resistance is not 33-39 ohms. If resistance is okay, go to next step.
**3)** Disconnect vacuum hoses from VSV. Blow air through upper port. Air should exit from lower port and not from the filter. Replace VSV if air exits from filter. If air exits from lower port, go to next step.
**4)** Energize VSV by applying battery voltage to Blue/Black wire terminal and ground to other terminal. Blow air through upper port. Air should exit from filter and not from lower port. Replace VSV if defective. Reconnect vacuum hoses and electrical connector.

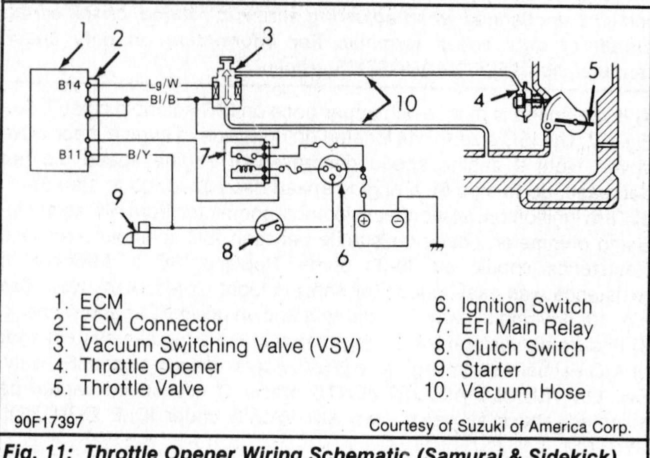


***Fig. 11: Throttle Opener Wiring Schematic (Samurai & Sidekick)***

## IGNITION SYSTEM

***NOTE: For basic ignition checks, see BASIC DIAGNOSTIC PROCEDURES article.***

### TIMING CONTROL SYSTEMS

**Samurai, Sidekick & Swift DOHC -** Ignition timing is controlled by ECM based upon various sensor input signals.
**Swift SOHC - 1)** Connect timing light to vehicle. Start engine. Disconnect vacuum hose from vacuum advance unit. Increase engine speed while monitoring timing marks with timing light. Timing should advance. If timing does not advance, inspect distributor advance weight mechanism for binding.
**2)** Connect a hand-held vacuum pump to vacuum advance diaphragm. Slowly apply vacuum to diaphragm while monitoring timing with timing light. Timing should advance as vacuum is applied. If timing does not advance, check for diaphragm-to-distributor plate linkage binding. If linkage moves freely, replace diaphragm.
**3)** Apply vacuum to retard diaphragm (diaphragm closest to distributor). Timing should retard as vacuum is applied. If timing does not retard, check for diaphragm-to-distributor plate linkage binding. If linkage moves freely, replace diaphragm.

## EMISSION SYSTEMS & SUB-SYSTEMS

### EXHAUST GAS RECIRCULATION (EGR)

**EGR System Test (Samurai - Calif.) -** The ECM will set a Code 51 if EGR system failure is present. See SELF-DIAGNOSTICS article for system diagnosis.
**EGR System Test (Samurai - Federal) - 1)** Before checking EGR system, ensure throttle position sensor, coolant temperature sensor and pressure sensor are operating correctly. See THROTTLE POSITION SENSOR, COOLANT (WATER) TEMPERATURE SENSOR and PRESSURE SENSOR under ENGINE SENSORS & SWITCHES.
**2)** Ensure no 5th gear switch signal is applied to ECM. The ECM is located behind glove box. To check 5th gear switch signal, check for voltage at terminal A5 (Light Blue wire) of ECM. If voltage is present, check 5th gear switch circuit. See WIRING DIAGRAMS article.
**3)** To check EGR system, place transmission in Neutral. Apply parking brake. With coolant temperature less than 127°F (53°C), start engine and operate at high RPM. EGR diaphragm should not move.
**4)** Warm engine to normal operating temperature. Operate engine at high RPM. EGR valve diaphragm should move up during acceleration.

# 1991 ENGINE PERFORMANCE
# System & Component Testing (Cont.)

**5)** If EGR valve does not operate as specified, check for misrouted, restricted, clogged or deteriorated vacuum hoses. If vacuum hoses are okay, check EGR valve and EGR modulator (backpressure transducer). See EGR VALVE and EGR MODULATOR (BACKPRESSURE TRANSDUCER) under EXHAUST GAS RECIRCULATION (EGR).

**6)** If EGR valve and EGR modulator (backpressure transducer) are okay, check EGR Vacuum Switching Valve (VSV). See EGR VACUUM SWITCHING VALVE (VSV) under EXHAUST GAS RECIRCULATION (EGR).

**7)** If VSV is okay, check for open or short in wiring circuit. *See Fig. 12.* Check for defective connections at ECM and VSV. If connections are okay, check EFI main relay. See EFI MAIN RELAY under RELAYS & SOLENOIDS. If all components and wiring are okay, substitute a known good ECM and recheck.

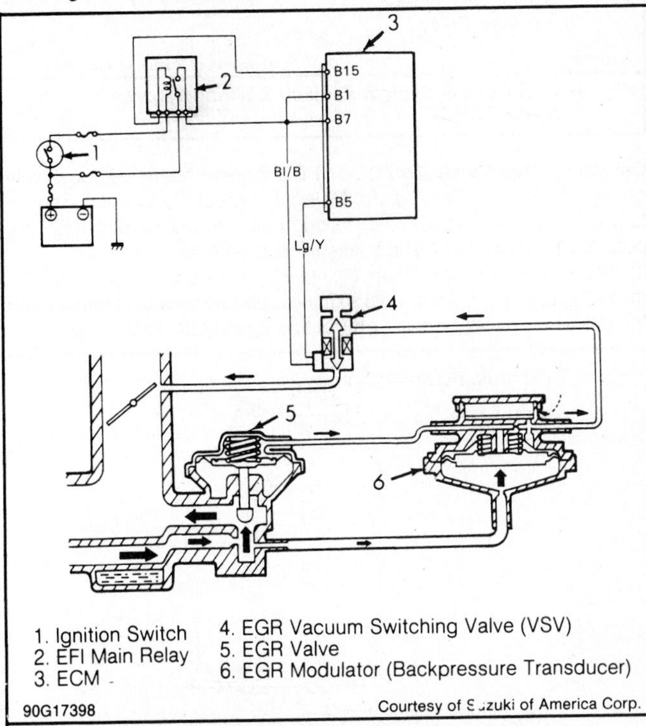


***Fig. 12: EGR Control System Wiring & Vacuum Diagram (Samurai & Sidekick)***

**EGR System Test (Sidekick - Calif.)** - The ECM will set a Code 51 if EGR system failure is present. See SELF-DIAGNOSTICS article for system diagnosis.

**EGR System Test (Sidekick - Federal) - 1)** Before checking EGR system, ensure pressure sensor is operating correctly. See PRESSURE SENSOR under ENGINE SENSORS & SWITCHES. Ensure no lock-up signal (A/T) is applied to ECM. The ECM is located at upper left corner of instrument panel.

**2)** On A/T models to check lock-up signal, check for voltage at terminal A11 (White/Yellow wire) of ECM. If voltage is present, check lock-up solenoid circuit. See WIRING DIAGRAMS article.

**3)** Place transmission in Park (A/T) or Neutral (M/T). Apply parking brake. With coolant temperature less than 118°F (48°C), start engine and operate at high RPM. EGR valve diaphragm should not move.

**4)** Warm engine to normal operating temperature. Operate engine at high RPM. EGR valve diaphragm should move up.

**5)** If EGR valve does not operate as specified, check for misrouted, restricted, clogged or deteriorated vacuum hoses. If vacuum hoses are okay, check EGR valve and EGR modulator (backpressure transducer). See EGR VALVE and EGR MODULATOR (BACKPRESSURE TRANSDUCER) under EXHAUST GAS RECIRCULATION (EGR).

**6)** If EGR valve and EGR modulator (backpressure transducer) are okay, check EGR Vacuum Switching Valve (VSV). See EGR VACUUM SWITCHING VALVE (VSV) under EXHAUST GAS RECIRCULATION (EGR).

**7)** If VSV is okay, disconnect 18-pin connector from ECM. Turn ignition on. Check for battery voltage on terminal B5 (Light/Green Yellow wire) of ECM connector. If battery voltage is present, go to step **10)**.

**8)** If battery voltage is not present, check for open in Blue/Black wire to VSV. *See Fig. 12.* Check for open or short in Blue/Black wire. If wiring is okay, check control relay. See CONTROL RELAY under RELAYS & SOLENOIDS. Repair as necessary.

**9)** If battery voltage is present as described in step **8)**, install connector on ECM. With engine running, check for battery voltage on terminal B5 (Light Green/Yellow wire) of ECM connector.

**10)** With coolant temperature less than 140°F (60°C), no voltage should be present. If no voltage is present, ECM is okay. If voltage is present, check coolant temperature sensor. See COOLANT (WATER) TEMPERATURE SENSOR under ENGINE SENSORS & SWITCHES.

**11)** Replace coolant temperature sensor if defective. If coolant temperature sensor is okay, check for proper connections at ECM. If connections are okay, substitute a known good ECM and recheck.

**EGR System Test (Swift - Calif.) - 1)** To check system operation, place transaxle in Park (A/T) or Neutral (M/T). Apply parking brake.

**2)** With coolant temperature less than 122°F (50°C) on DOHC models or 104 °F (40°C) on SOHC models, start engine and operate at high RPM. EGR valve diaphragm should not move.

**3)** Warm engine to normal operating temperature. Operate engine at high RPM. EGR valve diaphragm should move up.

**4)** If EGR valve does not operate as specified, check for misrouted, restricted, clogged or deteriorated vacuum hoses. If vacuum hoses are okay, check EGR valve and EGR modulator (backpressure transducer). See EGR VALVE and EGR MODULATOR (BACKPRESSURE TRANSDUCER) under EXHAUST GAS RECIRCULATION (EGR).

**5)** If EGR valve and EGR modulator (backpressure transducer) are okay, check EGR Vacuum Switching Valve (VSV). See EGR VACUUM SWITCHING VALVE (VSV) under EXHAUST GAS RECIRCULATION (EGR).

**6)** If VSV is okay, check wiring and ECM. The ECM will set a Code 51 if EGR system failure is present. See SELF-DIAGNOSTICS article for system diagnosis.

**7)** To check for clogged passages, allow engine to idle. Open EGR valve by hand. Engine RPM should decrease. If no decrease in engine speed occurs, check for clogged EGR passages.

**EGR Temperature Sensor (Samurai, Sidekick & Swift DOHC - Calif.) - 1)** Sensor is threaded into EGR valve. Disconnect negative battery cable. Disconnect 2-wire connector from sensor and remove sensor. Position sensor threads in container of water with thermometer. Connect ohmmeter leads to sensor terminals.

**2)** Apply heat to container until water reaches specified temperature. See EGR TEMPERATURE SENSOR RESISTANCE table. Replace sensor if resistance is not within specification.

***EGR TEMPERATURE SENSOR RESISTANCE***

| Temperature | Ohms |
|---|---|
| 68°F (20°C) | 214,000-313,800 |
| 176°F (80°C) | 21,100-26,500 |

**EGR Valve - 1)** Disconnect EGR vacuum hose and attach a hand-held vacuum pump to vacuum hose port. Apply approximately 8 in. Hg to EGR valve while checking for smooth operation of diaphragm. Ensure diaphragm maintains position without loosing vacuum.

**2)** With engine at idle, apply vacuum to EGR diaphragm. Engine should idle rough and/or stall. If diaphragm moves and engine RPM does not change, remove EGR valve and check for plugged passages.

**EGR Modulator (Backpressure Transducer) - 1)** For EGR modulator location, see appropriate vacuum diagram in VACUUM DIAGRAMS article. Remove upper cap from modulator. Remove filter and clean with compressed air. Install upper cap. Remove EGR modulator.

**2)** Plug one upper vacuum hose port while applying LOW PRESSURE air to opposite vacuum hose port. Air should flow freely through filter housing.

**3)** Connect hand-held vacuum pump to one upper vacuum hose port. Connect vacuum gauge to opposite vacuum hose port. Apply LOW

# 1991 ENGINE PERFORMANCE
# System & Component Testing (Cont.)

PRESSURE air to bottom port while applying vacuum with vacuum pump. Vacuum should be indicated on gauge. When low pressure air application stops at bottom port, vacuum gauge indicator should return to zero. Replace EGR modulator if operation is not as specified.

**EGR Vacuum Switching Valve – 1)** Turn ignition off. Disconnect Green ECM connector and VSV connector. Vacuum Switching Valve (VSV) is Blue and is mounted near right side of valve cover, at front of engine on Samurai and Sidekick. On Swift DOHC, solenoid is mounted behind engine, near center of firewall. On Swift SOHC, solenoid is located between distributor and EGR modulator. Turn ignition on.

**2)** Check for battery voltage on appropriate wire terminal at VSV connector. See EGR VACUUM SWITCHING VALVE POWER TERMINAL IDENTIFICATION. If battery voltage is present, go to next step. If battery voltage is not present, check circuit between VSV and EFI main/control relay. If circuit is okay, check EFI main relay. See EFI MAIN RELAY under RELAYS.

***EGR VACUUM SWITCHING VALVE POWER TERMINAL IDENTIFICATION***

| Application | Wire Color |
|---|---|
| Samurai & Sidekick | Blue/Black |
| Swift | White/Blue |

**3)** Turn ignition off. Check resistance between solenoid terminals. If resistance is not 33-39 ohms, replace solenoid. Disconnect upper and lower hoses from VSV. Connect short section of hose to lower horizontal port of solenoid. Blow air through hose connected to solenoid. Air should exit through filter.

**4)** If air does not exit through filter, replace solenoid. If air exits through filter, energize solenoid by applying battery voltage to appropriate wire terminal and ground to other terminal. See EGR VACUUM SWITCHING VALVE POWER TERMINAL IDENTIFICATION table. Solenoid should click. Blow air through hose connected to solenoid. Air should now exit through other port and not through filter. If test is not as specified, replace solenoid.

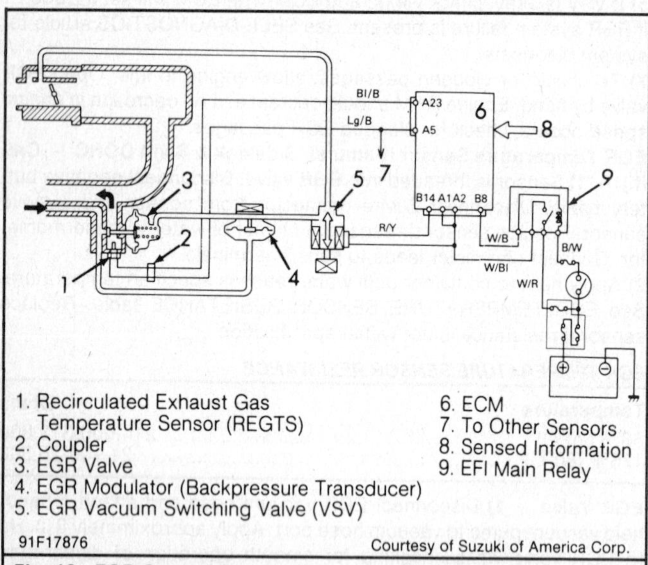


***Fig. 13: EGR Control System Vacuum & Wiring Diagram (Swift DOHC)***

## FUEL EVAPORATION

**Bimetallic Vacuum Switching Valve (Samurai)** – Disconnect both vacuum hoses from valve, located under intake manifold. When engine coolant is cold, ensure passageway between valve ports is closed. When engine coolant is warm, ensure passageway between valve ports is open.

**Bimetallic Vacuum Switching Valve (Swift)** – Disconnect vacuum hose from valve, located under intake manifold. Connect a hose to port on valve. Blow through hose. With engine coolant temperature less than 113°F (45°C), air should exit through filter on valve. With engine coolant temperature greater than 140°F (60°C), air should not exit through filter.

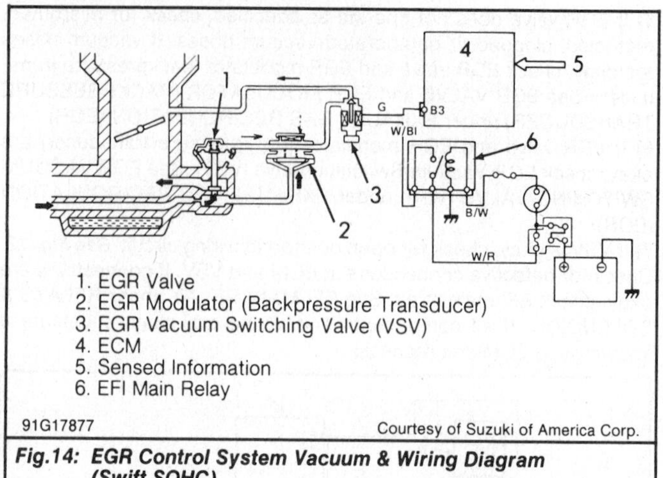


***Fig.14: EGR Control System Vacuum & Wiring Diagram (Swift SOHC)***

**Canister Purge Valve (Swift) – 1)** Disconnect hoses at purge valve on top of canister. *See Fig. 15.* Using low pressure air, blow through fuel tank port. Air should exit through air vent. Blow through purge port. No air should exit and pressure should hold.

**2)** While applying more than 3.1 in. Hg to throttle body port, blow through purge port. Air should exit through fuel tank port and air vent. If canister purge valve does not test as specified, replace canister.

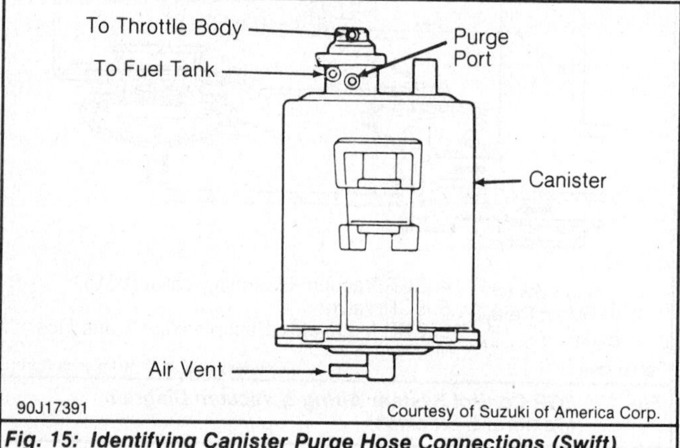


***Fig. 15: Identifying Canister Purge Hose Connections (Swift)***

**Canister Purge Vacuum Switching Valve (Swift DOHC) – 1)** Turn ignition off. Using ohmmeter, check resistance between terminals of Vacuum Switching Valve (VSV) connector. If resistance is not 33-39 ohms, replace VSV. Disconnect vacuum hoses from VSV. Connect short section of hose to either port of VSV. Blow through hose. Air should not pass through VSV.

**2)** Apply battery voltage to White/Blue wire terminal and ground to other wire terminal. Blow through hose. Air should pass through VSV. If VSV does not respond as described, replace VSV.

## POSITIVE CRANKCASE VENTILATION (PCV)

**PCV Valve** – Valve is located in intake manifold. Start engine. Remove valve from intake manifold. Place finger over valve. Vacuum should be present. Remove finger from PCV valve. Valve should snap back.

## MISCELLANEOUS CONTROLS

### TRANSMISSION

***NOTE: Although the lock-up relay system is not technically an engine performance system, it can affect driveability if it malfunctions.***

# 1991 ENGINE PERFORMANCE
# System & Component Testing (Cont.)

**Lock-Up Relay System (Sidekick) – 1)** Lock-up relay system is used on A/T models only. Disconnect negative battery terminal. Remove ECM from holder. Disconnect ECM harness connector. Install harness coupler between ECM and ECM harness connector. Connect negative battery terminal.

**2)** Start and warm engine to normal operating temperature. Connect DVOM between ECM coupler terminal A6 and ground. With engine running, shift transaxle to Drive and release brake pedal. DVOM should read zero volt at this time.

**3)** On a flat road, drive vehicle with transaxle in Drive at speed greater than 42 MPH. Maintain speed for at least 4 seconds, with throttle valve open at less than 70 percent of the way. Voltage at ECM terminal A6 should indicate battery voltage when lock-up relay transmits an engine signal to solenoid.

**4)** If battery voltage was not indicated, check wiring harness, lock-up relay, solenoid, brake pedal switch or oil pressure switch. To check lock-up relay, see LOCK-UP RELAY under RELAYS & SOLENOIDS. If system check out okay, replace faulty ECM.

# 1991 ENGINE PERFORMANCE
# Pin Voltage Charts

## Samurai, Sidekick, Swift

## INTRODUCTION

Pin voltage charts are supplied to reduce diagnostic time. Checking pin voltages at the Electronic Control Module (ECM) determines whether it's receiving and transmitting proper voltage signals. Charts may also help determine if ECM harness is shorted or opened.

***NOTE: Perform all voltage tests with a Digital Volt-Ohmmeter (DVOM) with a minimum 10-megohm input impedance, unless stated otherwise in test procedure. Voltage readings may vary slightly due to battery condition or charging rate.***

## PIN VOLTAGE DIAGNOSIS

***CAUTION: DO NOT connect voltmeter to ECM with ECM connectors disconnected.***

**1)** Ensure battery has a minimum of 11 volts with ignition switch in the ON position. Turn ignition off and remove ECM.

**2)** On all models except Samurai, ECM is located under left side of dash. On Samurai, ECM is located under glove box. Ground ECM case. With wiring harness connectors connected, use voltmeter to confirm correct voltage at each terminal. *See Figs. 1 through 10.*

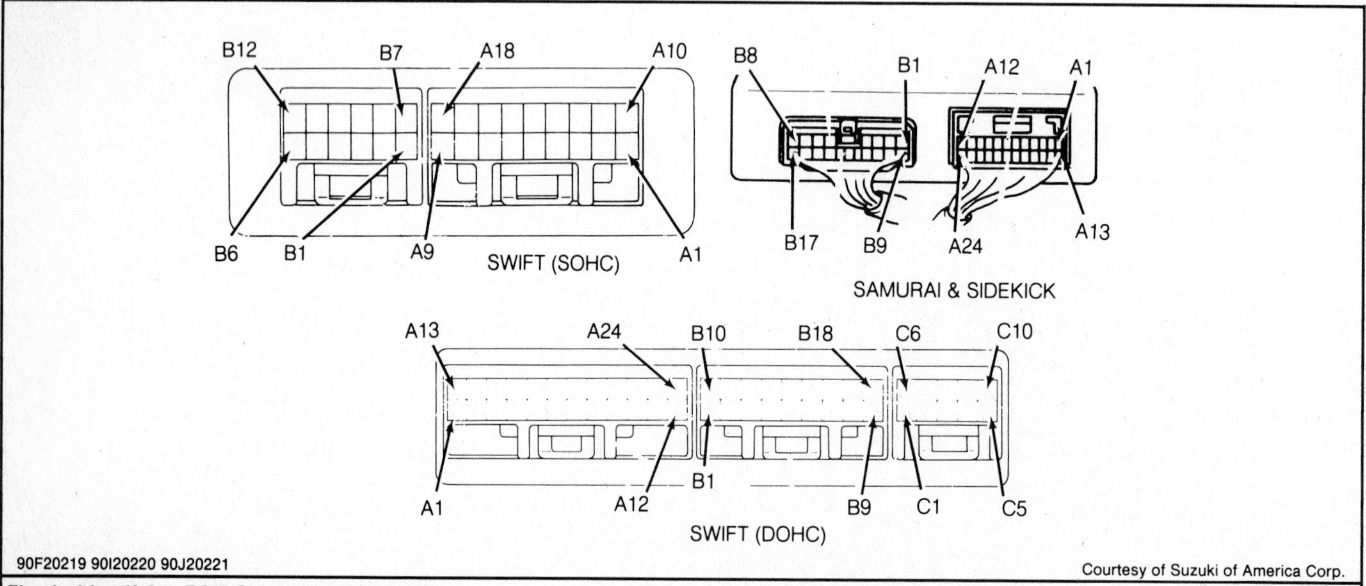


Courtesy of Suzuki of America Corp.

***Fig. 1: Identifying ECM Connector Terminals***

| TERMINAL | CIRCUIT | NORMAL VOLTAGE | CONDITION |
|---|---|---|---|
| A1 | Blank | —— | —— |
| A2 | Air-conditioner circuit (if equipped) | 10 – 14V | Ignition switch ON |
| | | 0 – 1V | Ignition switch ON<br>Air-conditioner ON |
| A3 | Diagnosis switch terminal | 10 – 14V | Ignition switch ON |
| | | 0V | Ignition switch ON<br>Diagnosis switch terminal grounded (with spare fuse connected to diagnosis switch terminals) |
| A4 | Ground (for California spec. only) | —— | —— |
| A5 | 5th switch (Not for California spec. model) | 10 – 14V | Ignition switch ON<br>Gear sihft lever at any other position than 5th gear position |
| | | 0V | Ignition switch ON<br>Gear shift lever at 5th gear position |
| A6 | Ignition (fail safe) signal | 3 – 5V | While engine cranking |
| | | 0V | Ignition switch ON |
| A7 | Test switch terminal | 10 – 14V | Ignition switch ON |
| | | 0V | Ignition switch ON<br>Test switch terminal grounded |
| A8 | Blank | —— | —— |
| A9 | Duty check terminal | —— | —— |
| A10 | Blank | —— | —— |

Continued on Next Page

90A20222

Courtesy of Suzuki of America Corp.

***Fig. 2: Pin Voltage Chart (Samurai – 1 of 2)***

# 1991 ENGINE PERFORMANCE
# Pin Voltage Charts (Cont.)

| TERMINAL | CIRCUIT | NORMAL VOLTAGE | CONDITION |
|---|---|---|---|
| A11 | Blank | ——— | ——— |
| A12 | Ignition output signal | 0V | Ignition switch ON |
| | | 2 – 4V | While engine cranking |
| A13 | CAS | Indicator deflection repeated between 0V and about 5V | Ignition switch ON<br>Crankshaft turned slowly |
| A14 | Idle switch of TPS | 0 – 1V | Ignition switch ON<br>Throttle valve is at idle position (with throttle opener rod drawn in by vacuum pump gauge) |
| | | 3 – 5V | Ignition switch ON<br>Throttle valve opens larger than idle position |
| A15 | VSS | Indicator deflection repeated between 0V and 3 – 5V | Ignition switch ON<br>Rear right tire turned slowly with rear left tire locked |
| A16 | REGTS | 3.8 – 4.5V | Ignition switch ON<br>Sensor ambient temperature: 20°C (68°F) |
| A17 | ATS | 2.2 – 3.0V | Ignition switch ON<br>Sensor ambinet temperature: 20°C (68°F) |
| A18 | WTS | 0.5 – 0.9V | Ignition switch ON<br>Cooling water temperature: 80°C (176°F) |
| A19 | Oxygen sensor | Refer to Diagnostic Flow Chart for Code No. 13 | |
| A20 | Blank | ——— | ——— |
| A21 | TPS | 0.5 – 1.2V | Ignition switch ON<br>Throttle valve at idle position (with throttle opener rod drawn in by vacuum gauge) |
| | | 3.4 – 4.7V | Ignition switch ON<br>Throttle valve at full open position |
| A22 | Pressure sensor | 3.6 – 4.4V | Ignition switch ON<br>Barometric pressure: 760 mmHg |
| A23 | Power source of sensors | 4.75–5.25V | Ignition switch ON |
| A24 | Ground of sensors | ——— | ——— |
| B1 | Power source | 10 – 14V | Ignition switch ON |
| B2 | Ground | ——— | ——— |
| B3 | Ground | ——— | ——— |
| B4 | Blank | ——— | ——— |
| B5 | EGR VSV | 10 – 14V | Ignition switch ON |
| B6 | ISC solenoid valve | 10 – 14V | Ignition switch ON |
| B7 | Power source | 10 – 14V | Ignition switch ON |
| B8 | Injector ⊕ | ——— | ——— |
| B9 | Power source for back-up circuit | 10 – 14V | Ignition switch OFF and ON |
| B10 | Ground | ——— | ——— |
| B11 | Engine start switch (Engine start signal) | 6 – 10V | While engine cranking |
| | | 0V | Other than above |
| B12 | Clutch switch | 0V | Ignition switch ON<br>Clutch pedal depressed |
| | | 10 – 14V | Ignition switch ON<br>Clutch pedal released |
| B13 | "CHECK ENGINE" light | 0 – 1V | Ignition switch ON |
| | | 10 – 14V | When engine running |
| B14 | Throttle opener VSV | 10 – 14V | Ignition switch ON |
| B15 | Main relay ground | 0 – 2V | Ignition switch ON |
| B16 | Fuel pump relay ground | 0 – 4V | For 3 sec. after ignition switch ON |
| | | 10 – 14V | When over 3 sec. after ignition switch ON |
| B17 | Injector ⊖ | ——— | ——— |

ATS - Air Temperature Sensor
CAS - Crank Angle Sensor
ISC - Idle Speed Control Solenoid
REGTS - EGR Gas Temperature Sensor
TPS - Throttle Position Sensor
VSS - Vehicle Speed Sensor
VSV - Vacuum Switching Valve

Courtesy of Suzuki of America Corp.

90B20223 90C20224

***Fig. 3: Pin Voltage Chart (Samurai – 2 of 2)***

# 1991 ENGINE PERFORMANCE
# Pin Voltage Charts (Cont.)

| TER-MINAL | CIRCUIT | NORMAL VOLTAGE | CONDITION |
|---|---|---|---|
| A1 | Ignition (fail safe) signal | 10 – 14V | Ignition switch ON |
| A2 | Air-conditioner circuit (if equipped) | 10 – 14V | Ignition switch ON |
| | | 0 – 1V | With engine running Air-conditioner ON |
| A3 | Diagnosis switch terminal | 10 – 14V | Ignition switch ON |
| | | 0V | Ignition switch ON Diagnosis switch terminal grounded |
| A4 | Ground (for California spec. only) | —— | —— |
| A5 | Blank | —— | —— |
| A6 | Power steering pressure switch (if equipped) | 10 – 14V | Ignition switch ON |
| | | 0 – 1V | With engine running at idle speed, turning steering wheel to the right and left as far as it stops, repeating it a few times |
| A7 | Test switch terminal | 10 – 14V | Ignition switch ON |
| | | 0V | Ignition switch ON Test switch terminal grounded |
| A8 | Canister purge VSV | 10 – 14V | Ignition switch ON |
| A9 | Duty check terminal | —— | —— |
| A10 | Blank | —— | —— |
| A11 | Lock-up relay for A/T | 10 – 14V | Ignition switch ON |
| | | 0 – 1V | With "D" range position, driving vehicle at 67 km/h (42 mile/h) on flat road and keeping it for 4 seconds or more |
| A12 | Ignition output signal | 0V | Ignition switch ON |
| | | 0.5 – 3V | While engine cranking |
| A13 | CAS | Indicator deflection repeated between 0V and about 5V | Ignition switch ON Crankshaft turned slowly |
| A14 | Idle switch of TPS | 0 – 1V | Ignition switch ON Throttle valve is at idle position (with throttle opener rod drawn in by vacuum pump gauge) |
| | | 3 – 5V | Ignition switch ON Throttle valve opens larger than idle position |
| A15 | VSS | Indicator deflection repeated between 0V and 3 – 5V | Ignition switch ON Rear left tire turned slowly with rear right tire locked |
| A16 | REGTS | 3.8 – 4.5V | Ignition switch ON Sensor ambient temperature: 20°C (68°F) |
| A17 | ATS | 2.2 – 3.0V | Ignition switch ON Sensor ambient temperature: 20°C (68°F) |
| A18 | WTS | 0.5 – 0.9V | Ignition switch ON Cooling water temperature: 80°C (176°F) |
| A19 | Oxygen sensor | Refer to Diagnostic Flow Chart for Code No. 13 | |
| A20 | Serial data terminal | 3 – 5V | Ignition switch ON |
| A21 | TPS | 0.5 – 1.2V | Ignition switch ON Throttle valve at idle position (with throttle opener rod drawn in by vacuum gauge) |
| | | 3.4 – 4.7V | Ignition switch ON Throttle valve at full open position |
| A22 | Pressure sensor | 3.6 – 4.4V | Ignition switch ON Barometric pressure: 760 mmHg |
| A23 | Power source of sensors | 4.75–5.25V | Ignition switch ON |
| A24 | Ground of sensors | —— | —— |
| B1 | Power source | 10 – 14V | Ignition switch ON |
| B2 | Ground | —— | —— |
| B3 | Blank | —— | —— |
| B4 | Blank | —— | —— |
| B5 | EGR VSV | 10 – 14V | Ignition switch ON |

ATS – Air Temperature Sensor
CAS – Crank Angle Sensor
REGTS – EGR Gas Temperature Sensor
TPS – Throttle Position Sensor
VSS – Vehicle Speed Sensor
VSV – Vacuum Switching Valve
WTS – Water (Coolant) Temperature Sensor

**Continued on Next Page**

91G17406 91H17407

Courtesy of Suzuki of America Corp.

***Fig. 4: Pin Voltage Chart (Sidekick – 1 of 2)***

# 1991 ENGINE PERFORMANCE
# Pin Voltage Charts (Cont.)

| TER-MINAL | CIRCUIT | NORMAL VOLTAGE | CONDITION |
|---|---|---|---|
| B6 | ISC solenoid valve | ——— | ——— |
| B7 | Power source | 10 – 14V | Ignition switch ON |
| B8 | Injector ⊕ | ——— | ——— |
| B9 | Power source for back-up circuit | 10 – 14V | Ignition switch OFF and ON |
| B10 | Ground | ——— | ——— |
| B11 | Engine start switch (Engine start signal) | 6 – 10V | While engine cranking |
| | | 0V | Other than above |
| B12 | Clutch switch (M/T only) | 0 – 1V | Ignition switch ON<br>Clutch pedal depressed |
| | | 10 – 14V | Ignition switch ON<br>Clutch pedal released |
| | Shift switch (A/T only) | 0 – 1V | Ignition switch ON<br>Selector lever in "P" or "N" range |
| | | 10 – 14V | Ignition switch ON<br>Selector lever in any other range than "P" and "N" |
| B13 | "CHECK ENGINE" light | 0 – 1V | Ignition switch ON |
| | | 10 – 14V | When engine running |
| B14 | Throttle opener VSV | 10 – 14V | Ignition switch ON |
| B15 | Main relay ground | 0 – 2V | Ignition switch ON |
| B16 | Fuel pump relay ground | 0 – 4V | For 3 sec. after ignition switch ON |
| | | 10 – 14V | When over 3 sec. after ignition switch ON |
| B17 | Injector ⊖ | ——— | ——— |

ISC - Idle Speed Control Solenoid
VSV - Vacuum Switching Valve

Courtesy of Suzuki of America Corp.

91I17408

**Fig. 5: Pin Voltage Chart (Sidekick - 2 of 2)**

| TERMINAL | CIRCUIT | STANDARD VOLTAGE | CONDITION |
|---|---|---|---|
| A1<br>A2 | Power source | 10 – 14V | Ignition switch ON |
| A3 | Power source of AFS | 10 – 14V | Ignition switch ON |
| A4 | Power source of TPS | 4.0 – 5.5V | Ignition switch ON |
| A5 | Sensor ground | ——— | ——— |
| A6 | AFS signal | 0.2 – 0.8V | Ignition switch ON |
| A7 | WTS | 1.0 – 3.0V | Ignition switch ON<br>Engine cooling water temp.: 80°C (176°F) |
| A8 | Oxygen sensor | Indicator deflection repeated between over and under 0.45V | While engine running at 2000 r/min for 1 minute or longer after warmed up |
| A9 | TPS signal | 0 – 1V | Ignition switch ON<br>Throttle valve at idle position |
| | | 3.0 – 5.0V | Ignition switch ON<br>Throttle valve at full open position |
| A10 | Speed sensor signal | Indicator deflection repeated between 0V and 3 – 5V | Ignition switch ON<br>Front left tire turned slowly with front right tire locked |
| A11<br>A20<br>B4<br>(A/T model only) | Throttle valve opening output signal (A/T control module) | 10 – 14V | Ignition switch ON<br>Throttle valve at idle position |
| | | 0 – 1V<br>↕<br>10 – 14V | Ignition switch ON<br>Opening throttle valve slowly causes voltage to vary as given at the left. |
| A12 | Ignition signal | 10 – 14V | Ignition switch ON |
| A13<br>A14 | Ground | ——— | ——— |
| A15 | ——— | ——— | ——— |
| A16 | Power source for back up circuit | 10 – 14V | Ignition switch ON and OFF |
| A17<br>(A/T model only) | "R", "D", "2" or "L" range signal (A/T control module) | 0 – 2V | Ignition switch ON, Selector lever in "P" or "N" range position |
| | | 10 – 14V | Ignition switch ON, Selector lever in "R", "D", "2" or "L" range position |
| A18 | Air-conditioner ON/OFF signal (if equipped) | 8 – 14V | Ignition switch ON |
| | | 0 – 2V | While engine running at idle speed, Air-conditioner ON |

AFS - Airflow Sensor
TPS - Throttle Position Sensor
WTS - Water (Coolant) Temperature Sensor

**Continued on Next Page**

Courtesy of Suzuki of America Corp.

90G20228 90H20229

**Fig. 6: Pin Voltage Chart (Swift DOHC - 1 of 3)**

# 1991 ENGINE PERFORMANCE
# Pin Voltage Charts (Cont.)

| TERMINAL | CIRCUIT | STANDARD VOLTAGE | CONDITION |
|---|---|---|---|
| A19 | Test switch terminal | 10 – 14V | Ignition switch ON |
| | | 0 – 1V | Ignition switch ON<br>Test switch terminal grounded |
| A21 | Idle switch (in TPS) | 0 – 1V | Ignition switch ON<br>Throttle valve at idle position |
| | | 3.0 – 5.0V | Ignition switch ON<br>Throttle valve opens larger than idle position |
| A22 | Diagnosis switch terminal | 10 – 14V | Ignition switch ON |
| | | 0 – 1V | Ignition switch ON<br>Diagnosis switch terminal grounded |
| A23 (California spec. model only) | REGTS | 4.0 – 5.0V | Ignition switch ON<br>Sensor ambient temp.: 20°C (68°F) |
| A24 | ——— | —— | ——— |
| | | | |
| B1 | CAS (positive) | —— | ——— |
| B2 | "CHECK ENGINE" light | 0 – 3V | Ignition switch ON<br>Diagnosis switch terminal ungrounded |
| | | 10 – 14V | Engine running<br>Diagnosis switch terminal ungrounded |
| | | Indicator deflection within 1.2V – 14V | Diagnosis switch terminal grounded<br>Test switch terminal grounded, while engine running at 2000 r/min after warmed up |
| B3 | ——— | —— | ——— |
| B5 | Canister purge VSV | 10 – 14V | Ignition switch ON |
| B6<br>B7 | ——— | —— | ——— |
| B8 | Main relay ground | 0 – 2V | Ignition switch ON |
| B9 | ——— | —— | ——— |
| B10 | CAS (negative) | —— | ——— |
| B11<br>B12 | ——— | | ——— |
| B13 | Fuel pump relay ground | 0 – 4V | For 3 seconds after ignition switch ON |
| | | 10 – 14V | When over 3 seconds after ignition switch ON |
| B14 (California spec. modle only) | EGR VSV | 10 – 14V | Ignition switch ON |
| B15 | ——— | —— | ——— |

CAS – Crank Angle Sensor
REGTS – EGR Gas Temperature Sensor
TPS – Throttle Position Sensor
VSV – Vacuum Switching Valve

**Continued on Next Page**

90A20230

Courtesy of Suzuki of America Corp.

***Fig. 7: Pin Voltage Chart (Swift DOHC – 2 of 3)***

# 1991 ENGINE PERFORMANCE
# Pin Voltage Charts (Cont.)

| TERMINAL | CIRCUIT | STANDARD VOLTAGE | CONDITION |
|---|---|---|---|
| B16 | Ground | ——— | ——— |
| B17 | ——— | ——— | ——— |
| B18 | ISC solenoid valve | 10 – 14V | Ignition switch ON |
| | | | |
| C1 | Engine start signal (Engine start switch) | 6 – 12V | While engine cranking |
| | | 0 – 1V | Other than above |
| C2<br>C7 | Power source for injector | 10 – 14V | Ignition switch ON |
| C3<br>C4 | Injector (positive) | ——— | ——— |
| | | ——— | ——— |
| C5<br>C10 | Ground for injector | ——— | ——— |
| C6 | Ignition output signal | 0V | Ignition switch ON |
| | | 1 – 3V | While engine cranking |
| C8<br>C9 | Injector (negative) | ——— | ——— |
| | | ——— | ——— |

ISC - Idle Speed Control Solenoid

Courtesy of Suzuki of America Corp.

90B20231

*Fig. 8: Pin Voltage Chart (Swift DOHC - 3 of 3)*

# 1991 ENGINE PERFORMANCE
# Pin Voltage Charts (Cont.)

| TERMINAL | CIRCUIT | NORMAL VOLTAGE | CONDITION |
|---|---|---|---|
| A1 | Engine start switch (Engine start signal) | 6 – 12V | While engine cranking |
| | | 0V | Other than above |
| A2 (M/T model only) | Electric load signal | 0V | Ignition switch ON, Headlight, small (or clearance) light, Heater fan, Radiator fan, stop light and rear window defogger all turned OFF. |
| | | 0V – 14V | Ignition switch ON, Headlight, small (or clearance) light, Heater fan, Radiator fan, stop light and rear window defogger all turned ON. |
| A2 (A/T model only) | A/T control module ("R", "D", "2" or "L" range signal) | 0V | Ignition switch ON, Selector lever in "P" or "N" range position |
| | | 10 – 14V | Ignition switch ON, Selector lever in "R", "D", "2" or "L" range position |
| A3 | Idle switch (in TS or TPS) | 0V | Ignition switch ON<br>Throttle valve at idle position |
| | | 4 – 5V | Ignition switch ON<br>Throttle valve opens larger than idle position |
| A4 | Power source of sensor (PS and TPS) | 4.75–5.25V | Ignition switch ON |
| A5 | Pressure sensor | 3.5 – 4.1V | Ignition switch ON<br>Barometric pressure: 760 mmHg |
| A6 | Oxygen sensor | Indicator deflection repeated between over and under 0.45V | While engine running at 2,000 r/min after warmed up and kept running at 2,000 r/min for 1 minute |
| A7 | Circuit ground | 0V | Ignition switch ON |
| A8 | Shift-up indicator light (if equipped) | 1 – 2V | Ignition switch ON |
| | | 10 – 14V | While engine running at idle speed |
| A8 | ——— | ——— | ——— |
| A9 (A/T model only) | A/T control module (Throttle valve opening signal) | 10 – 14V | Ignition switch ON, Throttle valve at idle position |
| | | 10 – 14V ↕ 0.2 – 0.4V | Ignition switch ON, Voltage varies as specified at the left while throttle valve is opened gradually. |
| A10 | Air conditioner circuit (If equipped) | 10 – 14V | Ignition switch ON |
| | | 0 – 0.6V | While engnie running at idle speed<br>Air-conditioner ON |

PS – Pressure (MAP) Sensor
TS – Throttle Switch
TPS – Throttle Position Sensor

**Continued on Next Page**

91J17409

Courtesy of Suzuki of America Corp.

***Fig. 9: Pin Voltage Chart (Swift SOHC – 1 of 2)***

# 1991 ENGINE PERFORMANCE
# Pin Voltage Charts (Cont.)

| TER-MINAL | CIRCUIT | NORMAL VOLTAGE | CONDITION |
|---|---|---|---|
| A11 | Speed sensor | Indicator deflection repeated between 0V and 4 – 5V | Ignition switch ON, front left tire turned slowly with front right tire locked. |
| A12 | Test switch terminal | 4 – 5V | Ignition switch ON |
| | | 0V | Ignition switch ON, Test switch terminal grounded |
| A13 | ATS | 2.0 – 2.7V | Ignition switch ON<br>Sensor ambient temp (Intake air temp.): 20°C (68°F) |
| A14 | WTS | 0.45–0.80V | Ignition switch ON<br>Engine cooling water temp.: 80°C (176°F) |
| A15 (M/T model only) | Wide open switch (in TS) | 4 – 5V | Ignition switch ON<br>Throttle valve at idle position |
| | | 0V | Ignition switch ON<br>Throttle valve at full open position |
| A15 (A/T model only) | TPS | 0.25–0.85V | Ignition switch ON<br>Throttle valve at idle position |
| | | 3.3 – 4.5V | Ignition switch ON<br>Throttle valve at full open position |
| A16 | Ground of sensors | 0V | Ignition switch ON |
| A17 (A/T model only) | A/T control module (Throttle valve opening signal) | 10 – 14V | Ignition switch ON, Throttle valve at idle position |
| | | 10 – 14V ↕ 0.2 – 0.4V | Ignition switch ON<br>Voltage varies as specified at the left while throttle valve is opened gradually. (Refer to Fig. 6E1-157 for relations between opening and voltage.) |
| A17 | ——— | —— | ——— |
| A18 (A/T model only) | A/T control module (Throttle valve opening signal) | 10 – 14V | Ignition switch ON, Throttle valve at idle position |
| | | 10 – 14V ↕ 0.2 – 0.4V | Ignition switch ON<br>Voltage varies as specified at the left while throttle valve is opened gradually. (Refer to Fig. 6E1-157 for relations between opening and voltage.) |
| B1 | Power source | 10 – 14V | Ignition switch ON |
| B2 | Ignition coil (Ignition signal) | 10 – 14V | Ignition switch ON |
| B3 (California spec. model only) | EGR VSV | 10 – 14V | Ignition switch ON |
| B4 | ISC solenoid valve | 0.9 – 1.5V | Ignition switch ON<br>Diagnosis switch terminal ungrounded |
| | | 10 – 13V | Ignition switch ON<br>Diagnosis switch terminal grounded |
| B5 | Injector | 10 – 14V | Ignition switch ON |
| B6 | Ground | 0V | Ignition switch ON |
| B7 | Power source for back-up circuit | 10 – 14V | Ignition switch ON and OFF |
| B8 | Diagnosis switch terminal | 4 – 5V | Ignition switch ON |
| | | 0V | Ignition switch ON, Diagnosis switch terminal grounded |
| B9 | "CHECK ENGINE" light | 1.2 – 2.0 V | Ignition switch ON<br>Diagnosis switch terminal ungrounded |
| | | 10 – 14V | When engine running<br>Diagnosis switch terminal ungrounded |
| B10 | Fuel pump relay | 1.2 – 1.8V | For 2 seconds after ignition switch ON |
| | | 10 – 14V | When over 2 seconds after ignition switch ON |
| B11 | ——— | —— | ——— |
| B12 (A/T model only) | Electric load signal | 3.5 – 5.5V | Ignition switch ON or Engine running<br>Headlight, small (or clearance) light, Heator fan, Radiator fan, stop light, and rear window defogger all turned OFF |
| | | 0.0 – 1.0V | Ignition switch ON or Engine running<br>Only headlight turned ON. |

ATS - Air Temperature Sensor
ISC - Idle Speed Control Solenoid
TPS - Throttle Position Sensor
TS - Throttle Switch
VSV - Vacuum Switching Valve
WTS - Water (Coolant) Temperature Sensor

Courtesy of Suzuki of America Corp.

91C17410 91D17411

***Fig. 10: Pin Voltage Chart (Swift SOHC – 2 of 2)***

# 1991 ENGINE PERFORMANCE
# Sensor Operating Range Charts

## Samurai, Sidekick, Swift

## INTRODUCTION

Sensor operating range information can help determine if a sensor is out of calibration. An out-of-calibration sensor may not set a trouble code, however, it may cause driveability problems.

***NOTE: Unless stated otherwise in test procedure, perform all voltage tests using a Digital Volt-Ohmmeter (DVOM) with a minimum 10-megohm input impedance.***

### *AIR TEMPERATURE SENSOR RESISTANCE*

| Application - °F (°C) | Ohms |
|---|---|
| **Samurai & Sidekick** | |
| 32 (0) | 5400-6600 |
| 68 (20) | 2280-2870 |
| 104 (40) | 1060-1360 |
| 140 (60) | 530-700 |
| 176 (80) | 290-390 |
| 212 (100) | 160-230 |
| **Swift (SOHC)** | |
| 32 (0) | 5880 |
| 68 (20) | 2210-2690 |
| 104 (40) | 1140 |
| 140 (60) | 580 |
| 176 (80) | 290-350 |

### *COOLANT (WATER) TEMPERATURE SENSOR RESISTANCE*

| Application - °F (°C) | Ohms |
|---|---|
| **Samurai, Sidekick & Swift (SOHC)** | |
| 32 (0) | 5880 |
| 68 (20) | 2210-2690 |
| 104 (40) | 1140 |
| 140 (60) | 580 |
| 176 (80) | 290-350 |
| **Swift (DOHC)** | |
| 14 (-14) | 7000-11,400 |
| 68 (20) | 2100-2900 |
| 122 (50) | 680-1000 |
| 176 (80) | 290-350 |

### *EGR TEMPERATURE SENSOR RESISTANCE* [1]

| Application - °F (°C) | Ohms |
|---|---|
| **Samurai, Sidekick & Swift (DOHC)** | |
| 68 (20) | 214,000-313,800 |
| 104 (40) | 90,900-125,700 |
| 140 (60) | 42,100-55,500 |
| 176 (80) | 21,100-26,500 |
| 212 (100) | 11,200-13,600 |

[1] - Used on California models only.

### *PRESSURE SENSOR VOLTAGE OUTPUT (ON-VEHICLE)*

| Altitude (Feet) | Vacuum (In. Hg) | [1] [2] Output (Volts) |
|---|---|---|
| **Samurai & Sidekick** | | |
| 0 | 30 | 3.6-4.4 |
| 1000 | 29 | 3.5-4.2 |
| 2000 | 28 | 3.4-4.1 |
| 3000 | 27 | 3.2-4.0 |
| 4000 | 26 | 3.1-3.8 |
| 5000 | 25 | 3.0-3.7 |
| 6000 | 24 | 2.9-3.6 |
| 7000 | 23 | 2.8-3.4 |
| 8000 | 22 | 2.7-3.3 |
| 9000 | 21 | 2.6-3.2 |
| 10,000 | 20 | 2.5-3.1 |

### *PRESSURE SENSOR VOLTAGE OUTPUT (ON-VEHICLE - Cont.)*

| Altitude (Feet) | Vacuum (In. Hg) | [1] [2] Output (Volts) |
|---|---|---|
| **Swift (SOHC)** | | |
| 0 | 30 | 3.5-4.1 |
| 1000 | 29 | 3.4-4.0 |
| 2000 | 28 | 3.2-3.8 |
| 3000 | 27 | 3.1-3.7 |
| 4000 | 26 | 3.0-3.6 |
| 5000 | 25 | 2.9-3.5 |
| 6000 | 24 | 2.8-3.3 |
| 7000 | 23 | 2.7-3.2 |
| 8000 | 22 | 2.6-3.1 |
| 9000 | 21 | 2.5-3.0 |
| 10,000 | 20 | 2.4-2.9 |

[1] - Pressure sensor output voltage is tested at ECM connector. ECM is located near glove box on Samurai or upper left corner of instrument panel on Sidekick and Swift (SOHC). Before testing pressure sensor output voltage, ensure ECM supply voltage is 4.75-5.52 volts at terminal A23 (Gray/Red wire on Samurai and Sidekick) or terminal A5 (Light Green wire on Swift SOHC) of ECM connector.

[2] - Output voltage is checked at terminal A22 (Gray/Green wire on Samurai and Sidekick) or terminal A5 Light (Green/Red wire on Swift SOHC) of ECM connector.

### *PRESSURE SENSOR VOLTAGE OUTPUT (OFF-VEHICLE)*

| Altitude (Feet) | Vacuum (In. Hg) | [1] [2] Output (Volts) |
|---|---|---|
| **Samurai & Sidekick** | | |
| 0 | 30 | 3.4-3.8 |
| 1000 | 29 | 3.3-3.7 |
| 2000 | 28 | 3.1-3.6 |
| 3000 | 27 | 3.0-3.5 |
| 4000 | 26 | 2.9-3.3 |
| 5000 | 25 | 2.8-3.2 |
| 6000 | 24 | 2.7-3.1 |
| 7000 | 23 | 2.6-3.0 |
| 8000 | 22 | 2.5-2.9 |
| 9000 | 21 | 2.4-2.8 |
| 10,000 | 20 | 2.3-2.7 |
| **Swift (SOHC)** | | |
| 0-2000 | 28-30 | 2.9-4.2 |
| 2001-5000 | 25-28 | 2.7-4.0 |
| 5001-8000 | 22-25 | 2.5-3.8 |
| 8001-10,000 | 20-22 | 2.0-3.3 |

[1] - Pressure sensor output voltage is tested with three 1.5-volt batteries connected in series. Positive lead is connected to Gray/Red wire terminal (Samurai and Sidekick) or Light Green wire terminal (Swift SOHC) and negative lead to Gray/Yellow wire terminal (Samurai and Sidekick) or Light Green/Black wire terminal (Swift SOHC).

[2] - Output voltage is checked at Gray/Green wire (Samurai and Sidekick) or Light Green/Red wire (Swift SOHC) of pressure sensor.

### *THROTTLE POSITION SENSOR (TPS) RESISTANCE*

| Application | Ohms |
|---|---|
| **Samurai** | |
| Between Terminals "C" & "D" | |
| With .008" (.20 mm) Clearance At Stop Screw | 0-550 |
| With .016" (.41 mm) Clearance At Stop Screw | Infinity |
| Between Terminals "A" & "D" | 3500-6500 |
| Between Terminals "B" & "D" | |
| At Idle [1] | 0-2000 |
| At Wide Open Throttle [2] | 2000-6500 |

# 1991 ENGINE PERFORMANCE
# Sensor Operating Range Charts (Cont.)

*THROTTLE POSITION SENSOR (TPS) RESISTANCE (Cont.)*

| Application | Ohms |
|---|---|
| **Sidekick** | |
| Between Terminals "C" & "D" | |
| At Idle [1] | 0-500 |
| At Wide Open Throttle | Infinity |
| Between Terminals "A" & "D" | 3500-6500 |
| Between terminals "B" & "D" | |
| At Idle [1] | 300-2000 |
| At Wide Open Throttle [2] | 2000-6500 |
| **Swift (DOHC)** | |
| Between Terminals "C" & "D" | |
| With .012" (.30 mm) Clearance At Stop Screw | 0-500 |
| With .035" (.89 mm) Clearance At Stop Screw | Infinity |
| Between Terminals "C" & "A" | 3500-6500 |
| Between Terminals "C" & "B" | |
| At Idle | 0-500 |
| At Wide Open Throttle | 3500-6500 |
| **Swift (SOHC)** [3] | |
| Between Terminals "A" & "B" | |
| With .012" (.30 mm) Clearance At Stop Screw | 0 |
| With .035" (.89 mm) Clearance At Stop Screw | Infinity |
| Between Terminals "A" & "D" | 4370-8130 |
| Between Terminals "A" & "C" | |
| At Idle | 240-1140 |
| At Wide Open Throttle | 3170-6600 |

[1] – To obtain idle position, apply 19 in. Hg vacuum to throttle opener.
[2] – There should be more than 2000 ohms difference between idle and wide open throttle readings.
[3] – Throttle position sensor is used only on auto. transaxle, as man. transaxle uses a throttle switch.

**Vehicle Speed Sensor** – With ohmmeter leads connected to vehicle speed sensor terminals, ohmmeter should alternate between zero and infinity 4 times per speedometer revolution.

# 1991 ENGINE PERFORMANCE
# Wiring Diagrams

## Samurai, Sidekick, Swift

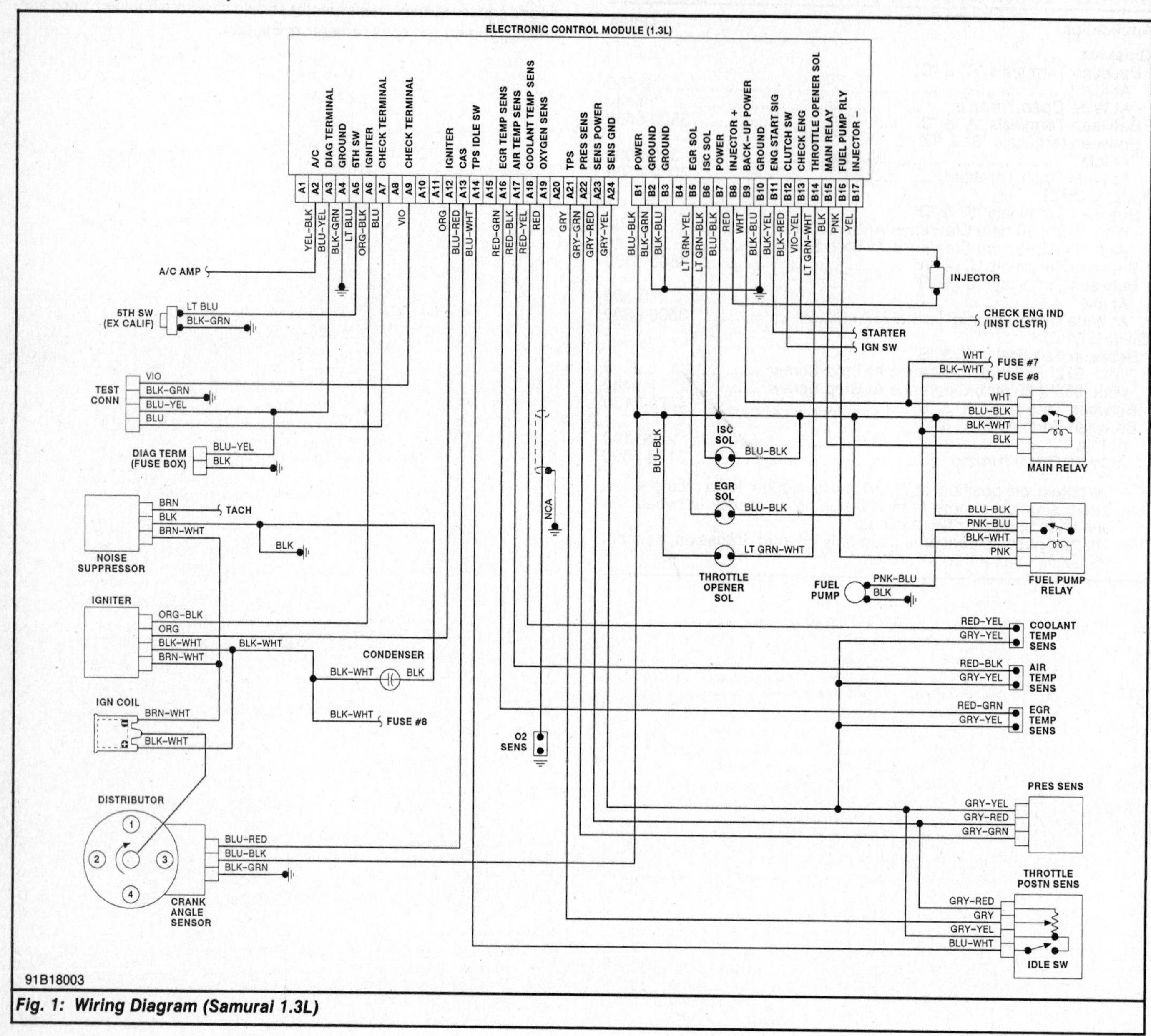


*Fig. 1: Wiring Diagram (Samurai 1.3L)*

# 1991 ENGINE PERFORMANCE
## Wiring Diagrams (Cont.)

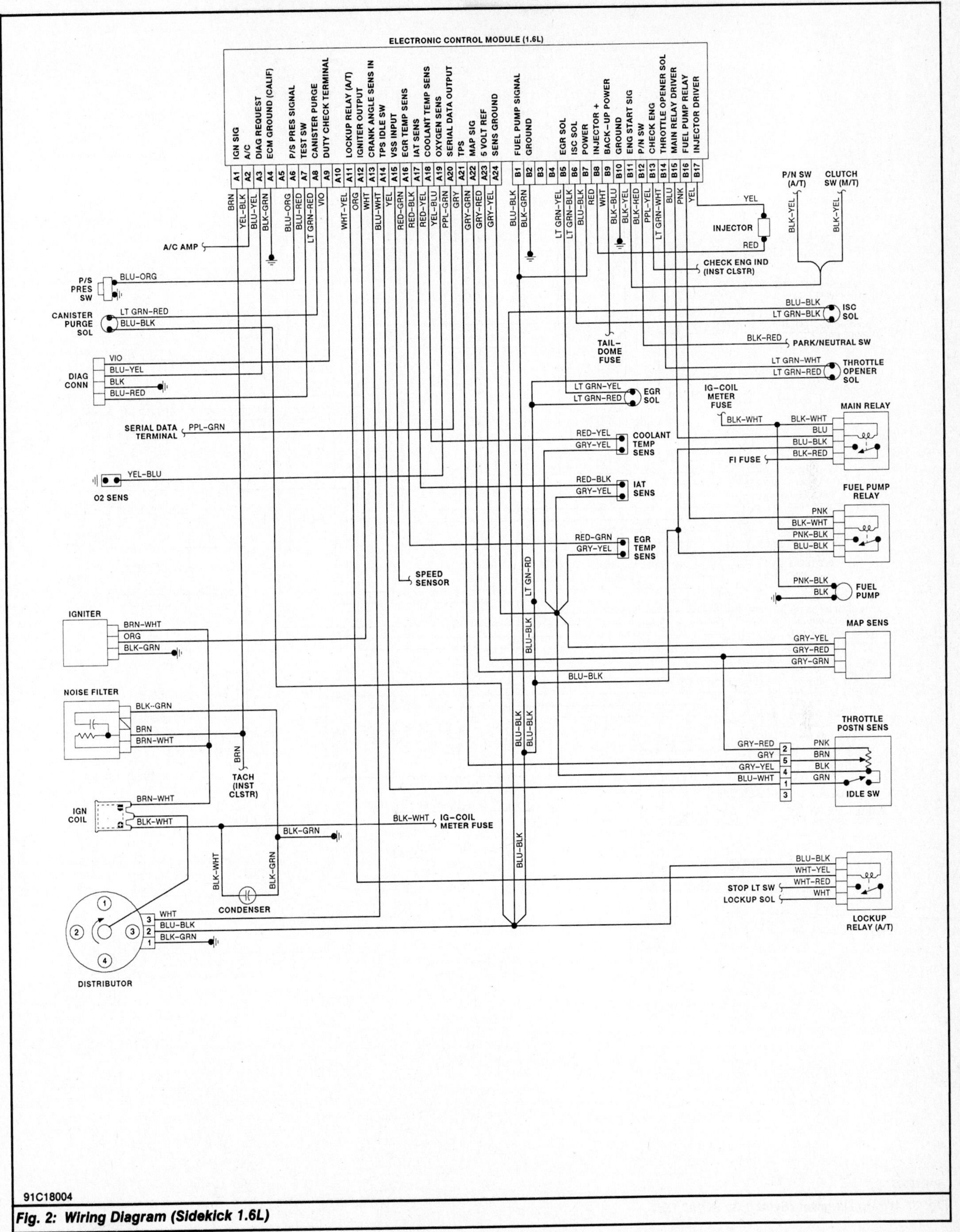


Fig. 2: Wiring Diagram (Sidekick 1.6L)

# 1991 ENGINE PERFORMANCE
## Wiring Diagrams (Cont.)

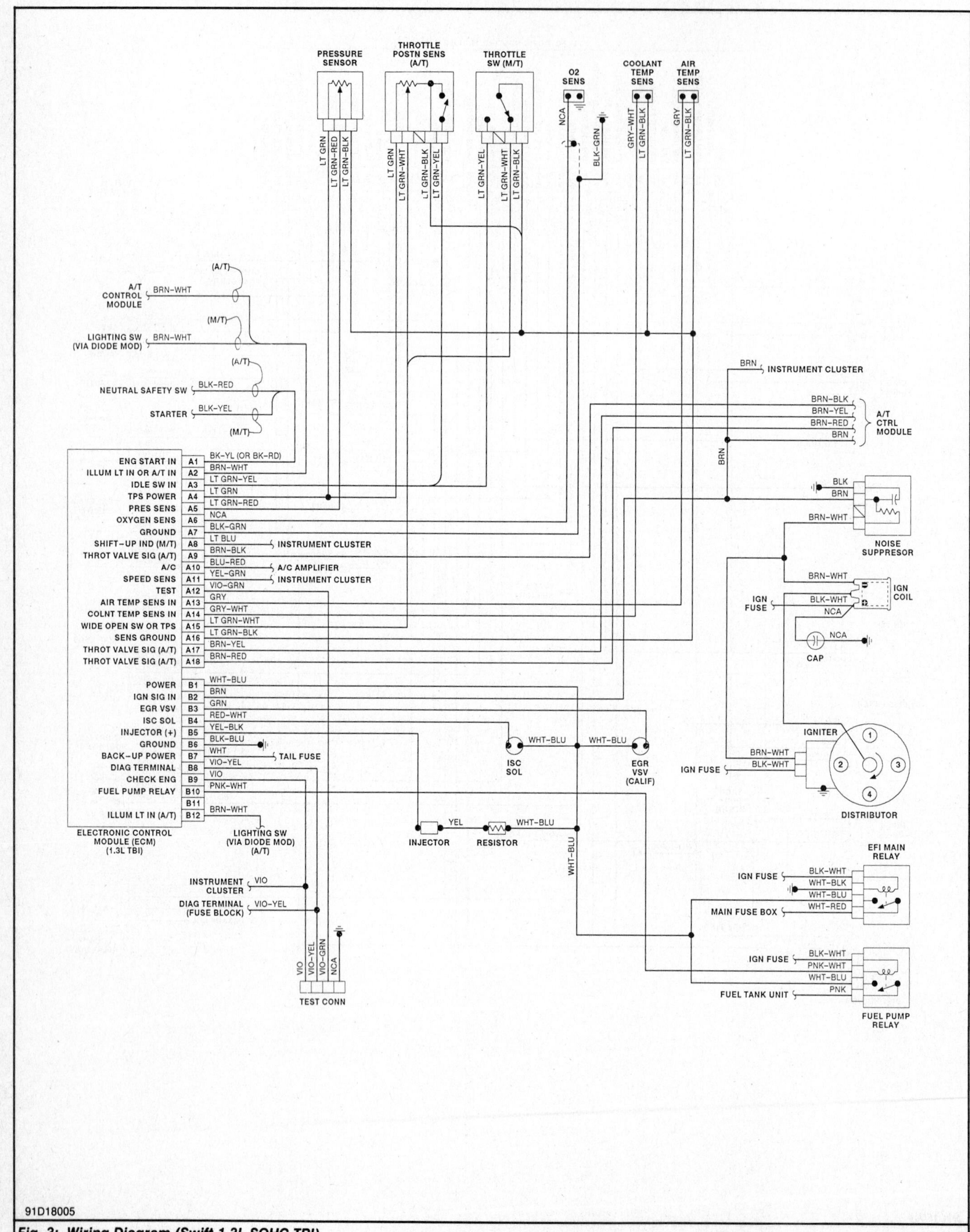


*Fig. 3: Wiring Diagram (Swift 1.3L SOHC TBI)*

# 1991 ENGINE PERFORMANCE
## Wiring Diagrams (Cont.)

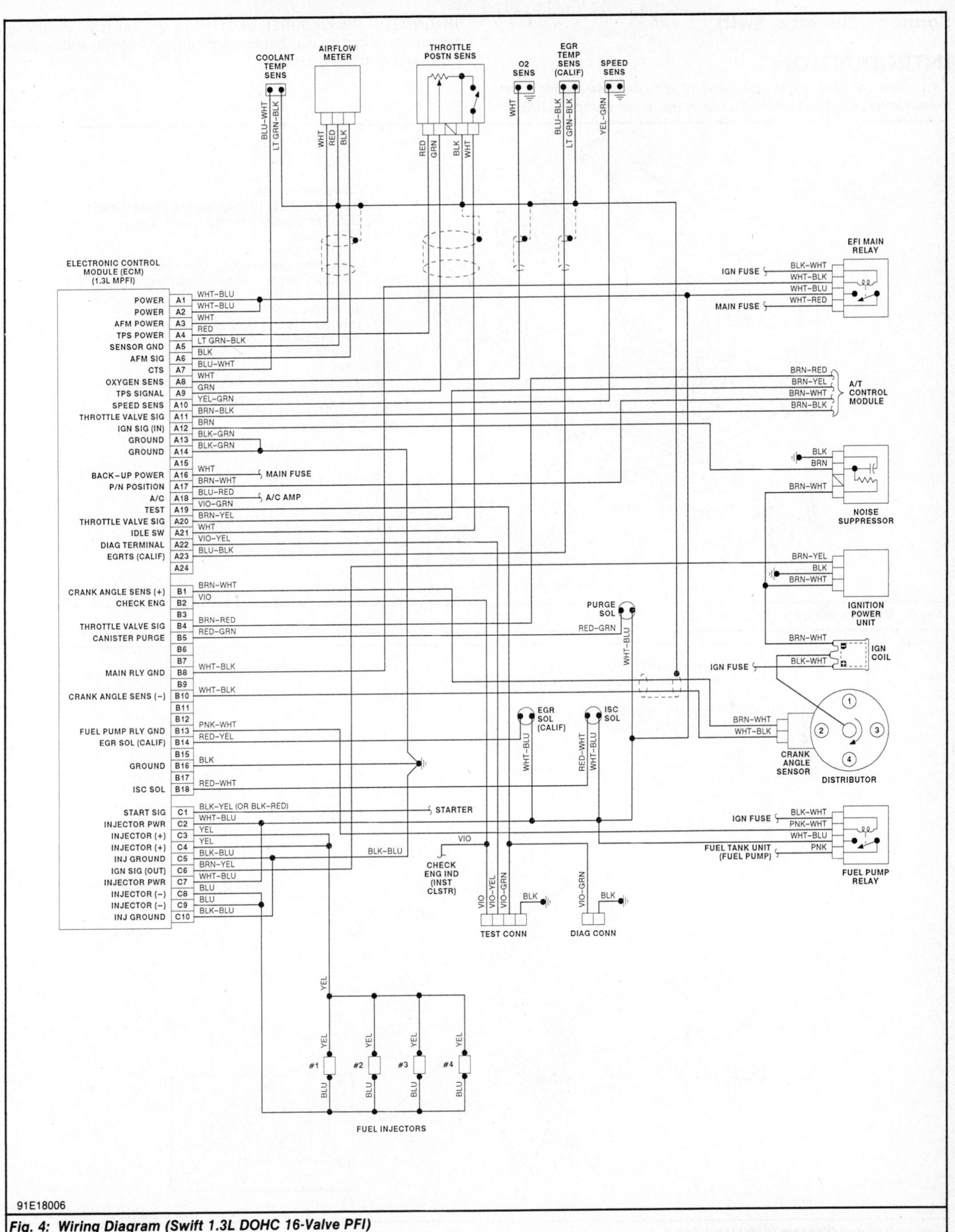


*Fig. 4: Wiring Diagram (Swift 1.3L DOHC 16-Valve PFI)*

# 1991 ENGINE PERFORMANCE
# Vacuum Diagrams

## Samurai, Sidekick, Swift

## INTRODUCTION

This article contains underhood views of vacuum hose routing. Use these vacuum diagrams during the visual inspection portion of BASIC DIAGNOSTIC PROCEDURES article. This will assist in identifying improperly routed vacuum hoses which cause driveability and/or computer-indicated malfunctions.

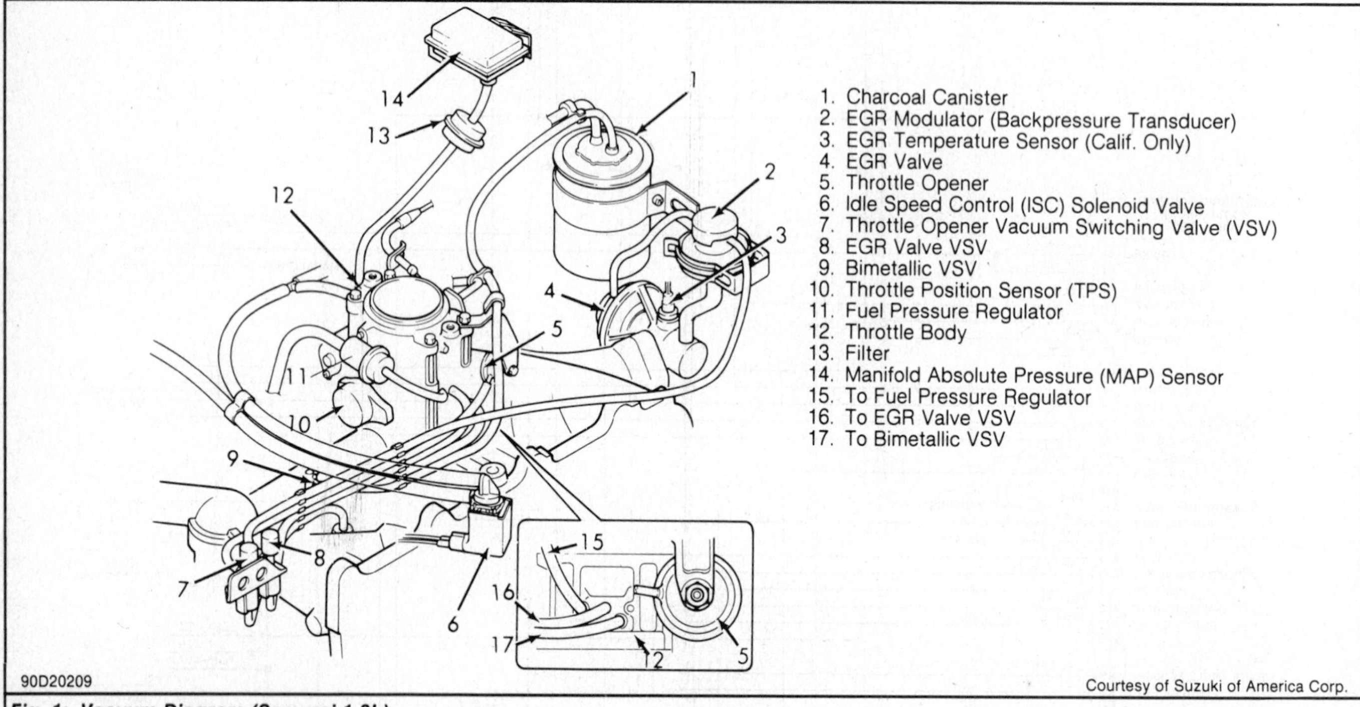


*Fig. 1: Vacuum Diagram (Samurai 1.3L)*

1. Charcoal Canister
2. Canister Purge Vacuum Switching Valve (VSV)
3. EGR Valve
4. Fuel Pressure Regulator
5. EGR Modulator (Backpressure Transducer)
6. Throttle Body
7. Filter
8. Manifold Absolute Pressure (MAP) Sensor
9. Throttle Opener
10. Intake Manifold
11. EGR Valve VSV
12. Throttle Opener VSV
13. To EGR VSV

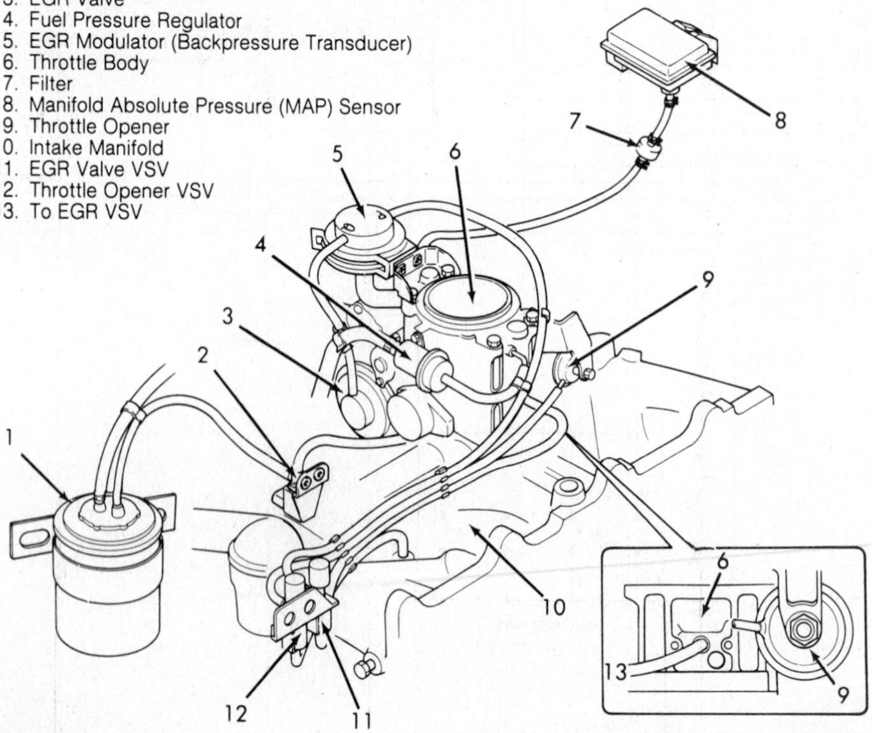

91A17863

Courtesy of Suzuki of America Corp.

*Fig. 2: Vacuum Diagram (Sidekick 1.6L)*

# 1991 ENGINE PERFORMANCE
# Vacuum Diagrams (Cont.)

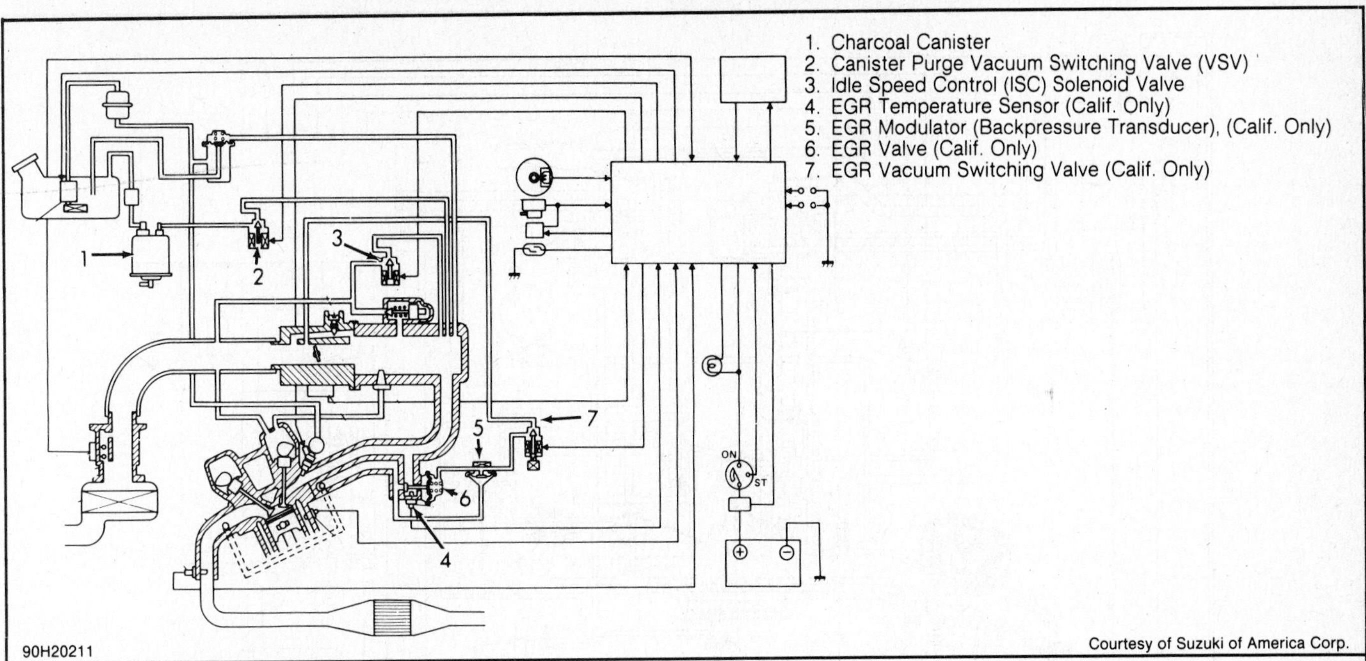


*Fig. 3: Vacuum Diagram (Swift 1.3L DOHC)*

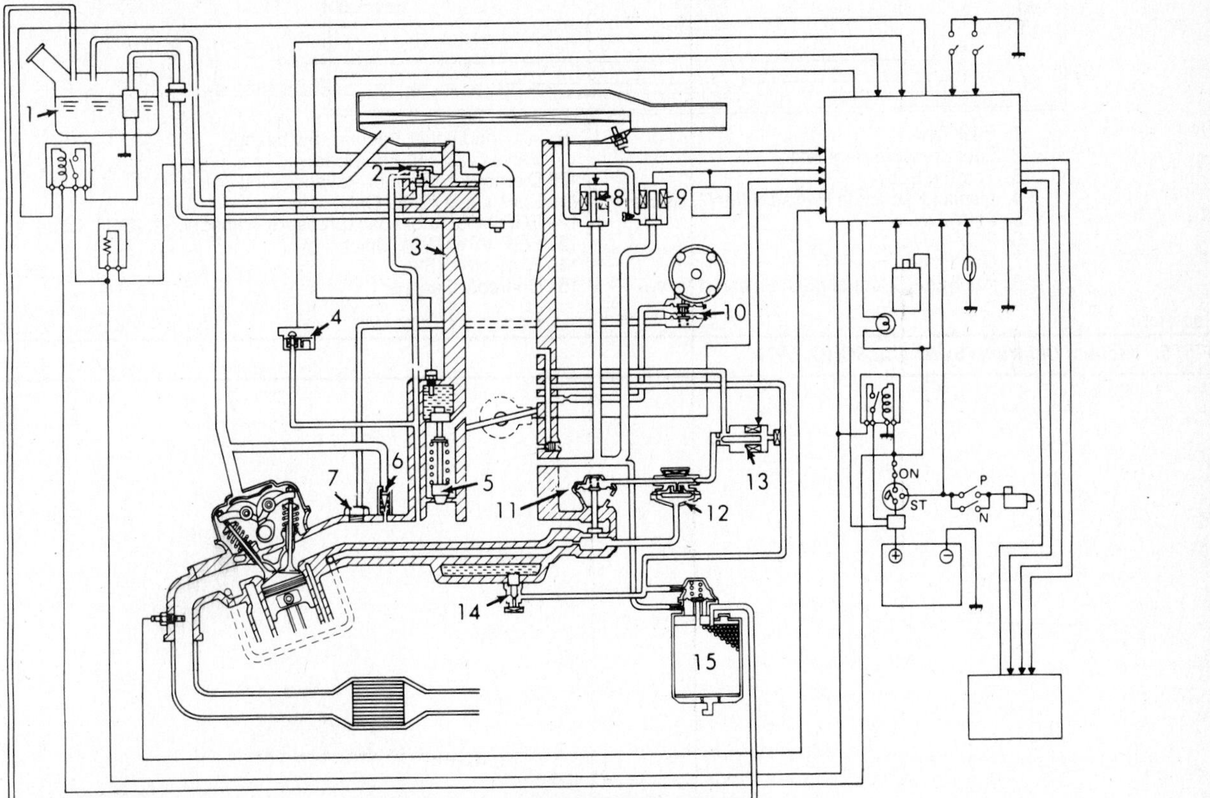

1. Fuel Tank
2. Fuel Pressure Regulator
3. Throttle Body
4. Manifold Absolute Pressure (MAP) Sensor
5. Air Valve
6. PCV Valve
7. Gas Filter
8. Idle Speed Control (ISC) Solenoid Valve
9. Air Conditioner Vacuum Switching Valve (VSV), (If Equipped)
10. Distributor Vacuum Advance Unit
11. EGR Valve (Calif. Only)
12. EGR Modulator (Backpressure Transducer), (Calif. Only)
13. EGR Valve VSV (Calif. Only)
14. Bimetallic VSV
15. Charcoal Canister

90B21049

Courtesy of Suzuki of America Corp.

*Fig. 4: Vacuum Diagram (Swift 1.3L SOHC, A/T)*

# 1991 ENGINE PERFORMANCE
## Vacuum Diagrams (Cont.)

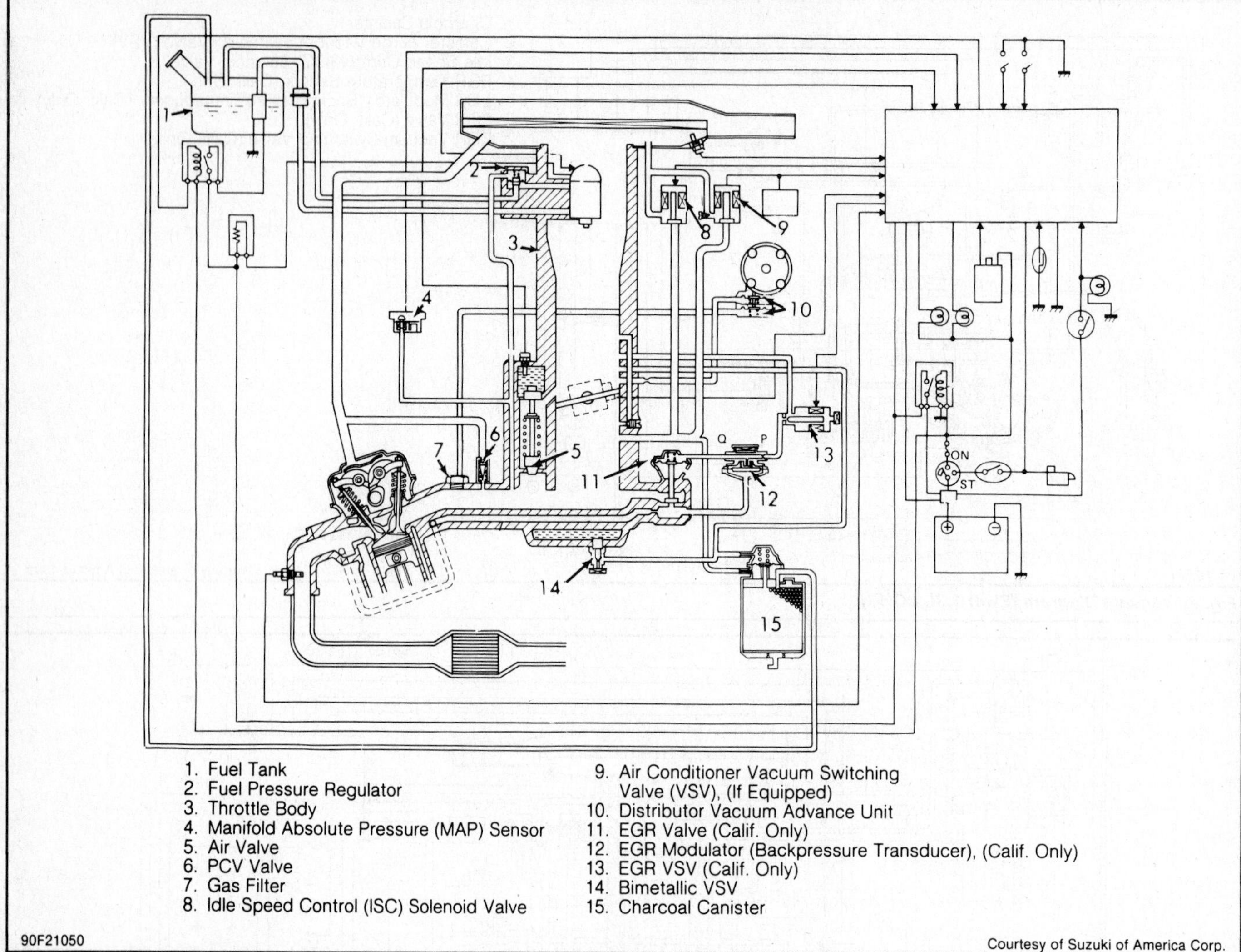


*Fig. 5: Vacuum Diagram (Swift 1.3L SOHC, M/T)*

# 1991 ENGINE PERFORMANCE
# Removal, Overhaul & Installation

## Samurai, Sidekick, Swift

## INTRODUCTION

Removal, overhaul and installation procedures (when given by manufacturer) are covered in this article. If component removal and installation is primarily an unbolt and bolt-on procedure, only a torque specification may be furnished.

## IGNITION SYSTEM

### DISTRIBUTOR

**Removal (Samurai, Sidekick & Swift)** - Remove spark plug wires and distributor cap. Disconnect distributor harness connector. Mark rotor-to-distributor housing reference for reinstallation. Remove distributor hold-down bolt and lift out distributor.

**Overhaul** - *See Figs. 1-4.*

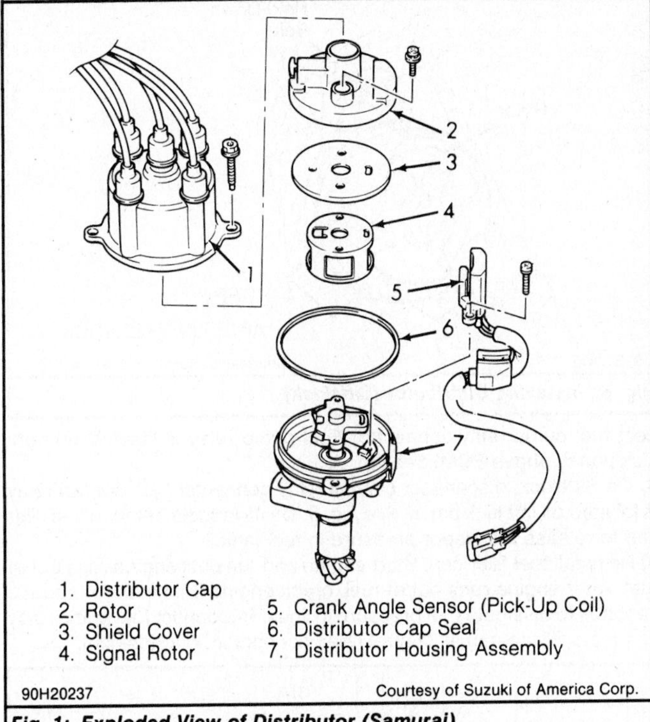


**Fig. 1: Exploded View of Distributor (Samurai)**

**Installation (Samurai & Sidekick)** - **1)** To install, reverse removal procedure. If reference mark was not made as described in removal procedure, go to next step.

**2)** Turn crankshaft (clockwise direction) until No. 1 cylinder is at TDC of compression stroke. Align rotor with center of cap bolt hole. Perform STEP 1. *See Fig. 5 or 6.*

**3)** On all models, install distributor into gearbox. On Samurai, when distributor is fully seated, rotor should point in direction shown in illustration. Perform STEP 2. *See Fig. 5.*

**4)** On Sidekick, when distributor is fully seated, rotor should point to center of hold-down bolt. Perform STEP 2. *See Fig. 6.*

**5)** On all models, ensure distributor is fully seated. Install distributor hold-down bolt. Adjust ignition timing. See ON-VEHICLE ADJUSTMENTS article.

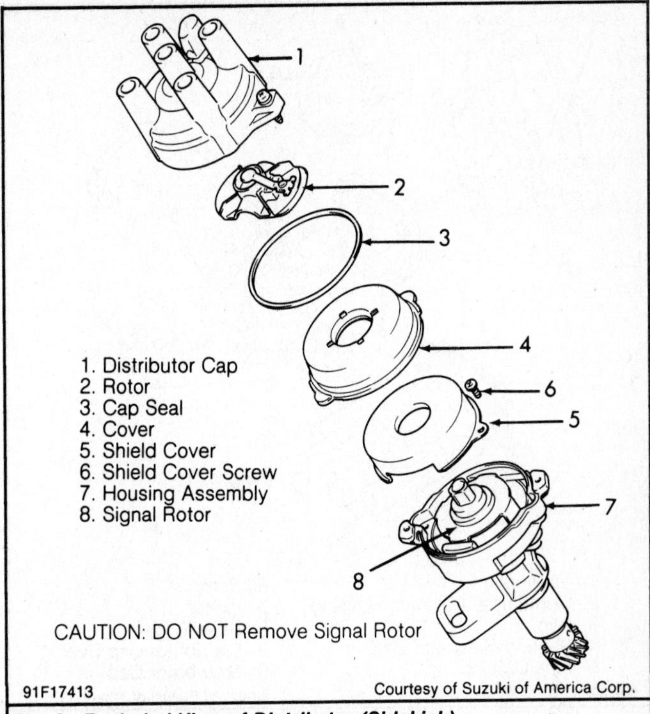


**Fig. 2: Exploded View of Distributor (Sidekick)**

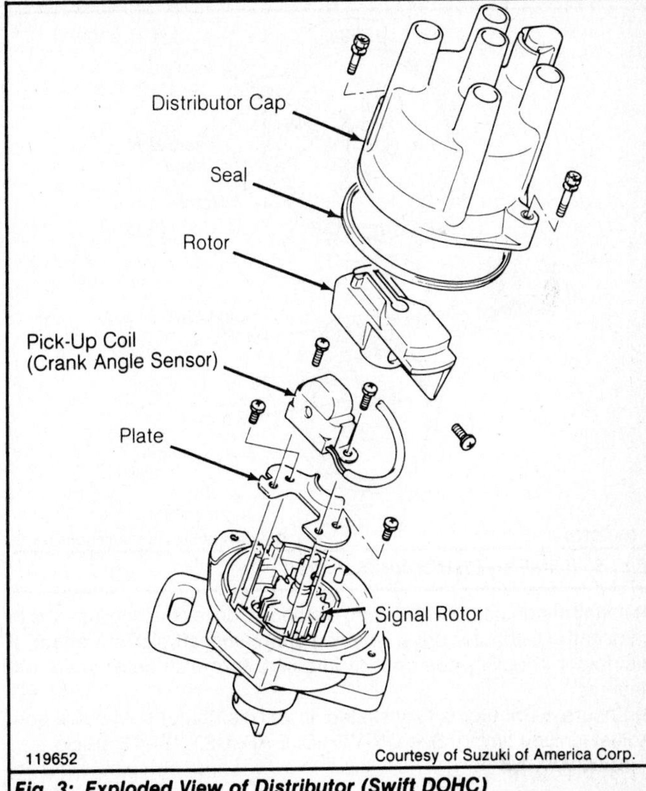


**Fig. 3: Exploded View of Distributor (Swift DOHC)**

***NOTE: On Swift, distributor drive coupling and camshaft slot are off-set. Distributor cannot be installed backward.***

**Installation (Swift)** - **1)** Before installing distributor, ensure "O" ring is in good condition. Replace as required. If new "O" ring is installed, lubricate with engine oil.

# 1991 ENGINE PERFORMANCE
## Removal, Overhaul & Installation (Cont.)

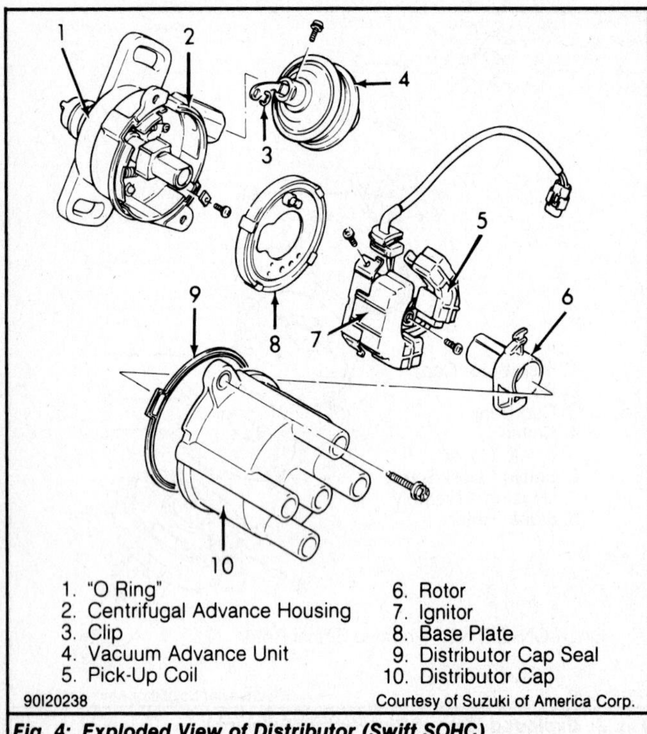


*Fig. 4: Exploded View of Distributor (Swift SOHC)*

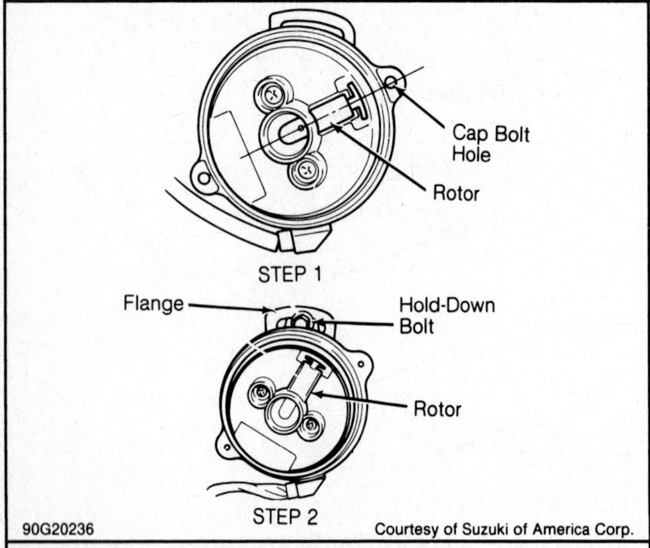


*Fig. 5: Installing Distributor (Samurai)*

**2)** Install distributor while aligning distributor drive coupling into slot of camshaft. Distributor drive coupling and camshaft slot are offset. If distributor coupling does not fit into slot, turn distributor shaft 180 degrees.

**3)** Ensure distributor is fully seated. Install distributor hold-down bolt. Adjust ignition timing. See ON-VEHICLE ADJUSTMENTS article.

## FUEL SYSTEM

***WARNING: ALWAYS relieve fuel pressure before disconnecting any fuel injection-related component. DO NOT allow fuel to contact engine or electrical components.***

### FUEL SYSTEM PRESSURE RELEASE

**Samurai & Sidekick – 1)** Place transmission in Neutral (M/T) or Park (A/T). Set parking brake and block drive wheels. On Samurai, disconnect fuel pump relay connector. Fuel pump relay is located on right kick panel, above ECM. *See Fig. 7*.

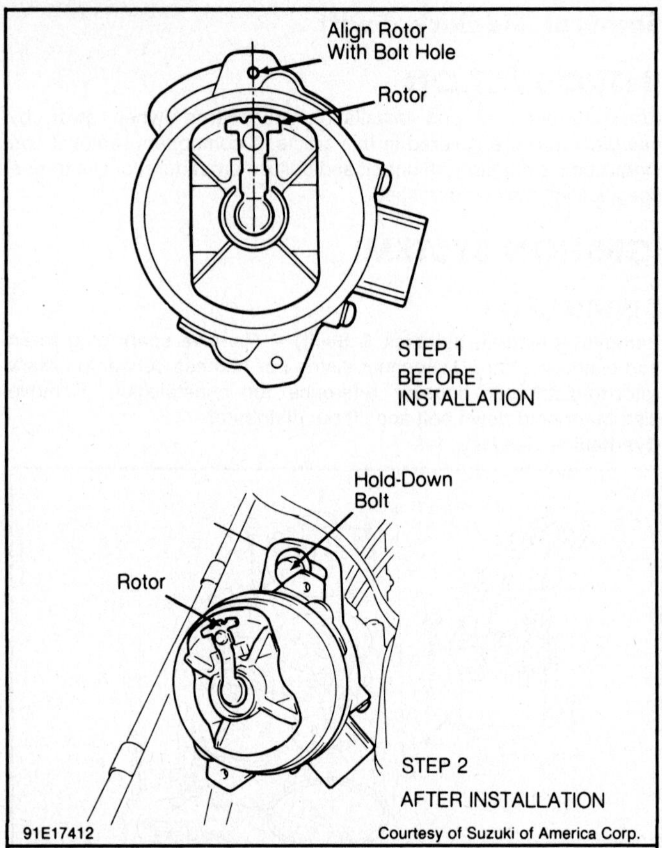


*Fig. 6: Installing Distributor (Sidekick)*

**2)** On Sidekick, disconnect control relay connector "A." Control relay is located on left kick panel. *See Fig. 8*. On all models, remove fuel filler cap to release fuel vapor pressure in fuel tank.

**3)** Reinstall fuel filler cap. Start engine and run until engine runs out of fuel. After engine runs out of fuel, crank engine 2-3 times for about 3 seconds to dissipate fuel pressure in lines. Reconnect fuel pump relay connector (Samurai) or control relay connector "A" (Sidekick).

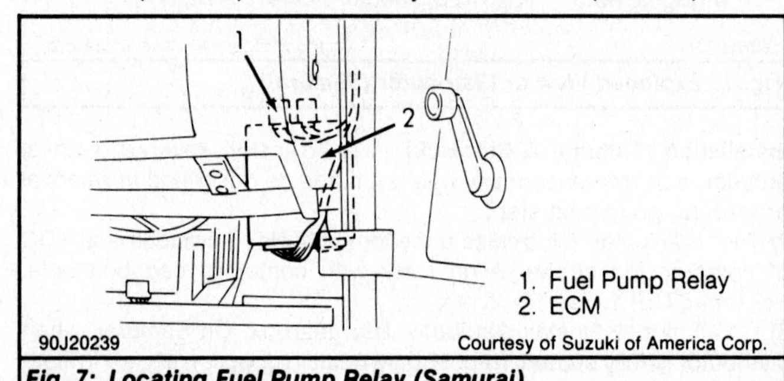


*Fig. 7: Locating Fuel Pump Relay (Samurai)*

**Swift – 1)** Place transmission in Neutral (M/T) or Park (A/T). Set parking brake and block drive wheels. Remove coolant reservoir from bracket. Remove main fuse box cover.

**2)** Main fuse box is located near battery. Disconnect main fuse box from body. Disconnect fuel pump relay connector. *See Fig. 9*. Remove fuel filler cap to release fuel vapor pressure in fuel tank. Reinstall fuel filler cap.

**3)** Start engine and run until engine runs out of fuel. Crank engine 2-3 times for about 3 seconds to dissipate fuel pressure in lines.

### FUEL RAILS & INJECTORS (PFI)

**Removal (Swift DOHC) – 1)** Relieve fuel system pressure. See FUEL SYSTEM PRESSURE RELEASE under FUEL SYSTEM. Disconnect negative battery cable. Remove idle speed control solenoid valve.

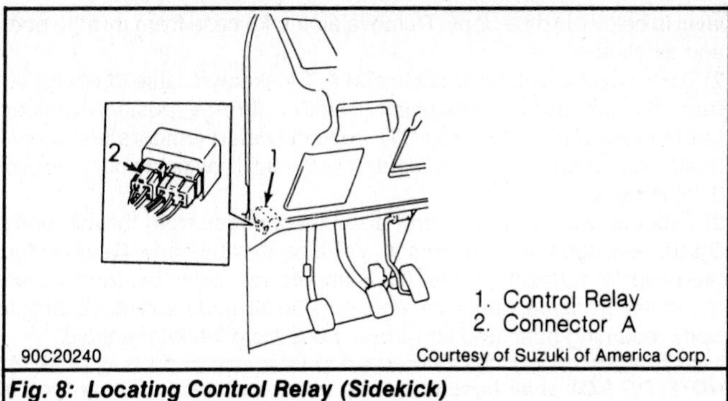


*Fig. 8: Locating Control Relay (Sidekick)*

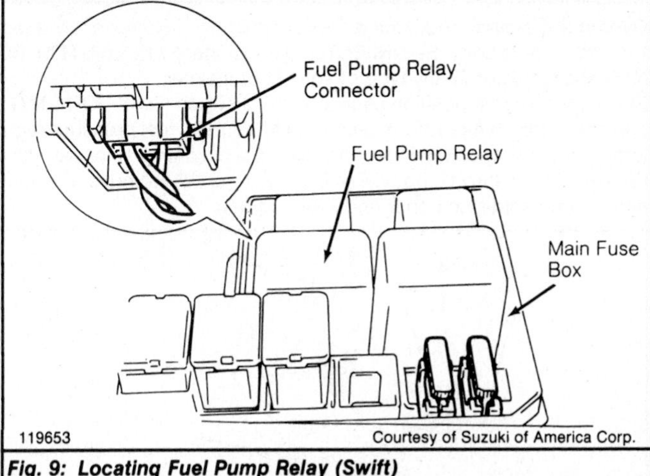


*Fig. 9: Locating Fuel Pump Relay (Swift)*

**2)** Remove EGR modulator bracket from intake manifold (if equipped). Disconnect fuel delivery and return hoses from fuel rail. Disconnect vacuum hose from fuel pressure regulator.

**3)** Unplug injector electrical connector from each injector. Remove mounting bolts and lift off fuel rail with injectors. Remove injectors from fuel rail.

**Installation – 1)** Coat new "O" rings with thin coat of fuel. Install new grommets and "O" rings on injectors. *See Fig. 10*. Install injectors on fuel rail. Ensure injectors rotate smoothly on fuel rail. If not, check for binding "O" ring.

**2)** Install insulators in cylinder head. Install fuel rail with injectors. Install and torque fuel rail mounting bolts to 14-20 ft. lbs. (19-27 N.m). To complete installation, reverse removal procedure.

**3)** Check for fuel leaks. With fuel pump relay connected, install a jumper wire between fuel pump relay Pink and White/Blue wires. Fuel pump relay is located in main fuse box, near battery. *See Fig. 9*. Turn ignition on (engine off) to activate fuel pump.

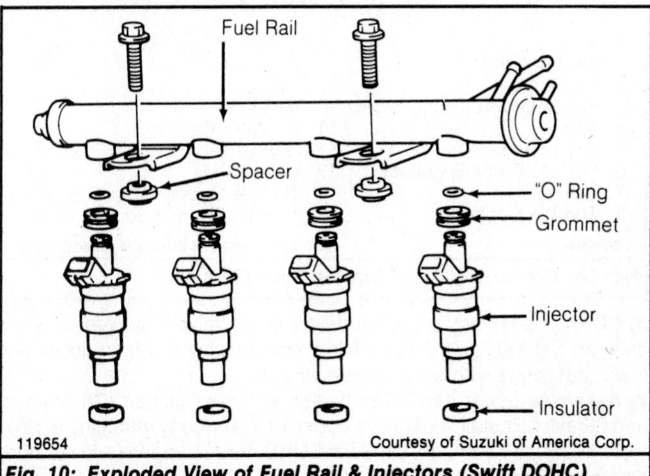


*Fig. 10: Exploded View of Fuel Rail & Injectors (Swift DOHC)*

## INJECTOR (TBI)

***CAUTION: DO NOT soak injector in any type of solvent or cleaner.***

**Removal (Samurai & Sidekick) – 1)** Relieve fuel system pressure. See FUEL SYSTEM PRESSURE RELEASE under FUEL SYSTEM. Disconnect negative battery cable.

**2)** Remove air intake from top of throttle body. Remove fuel feed pipe clamp from intake manifold. Disconnect fuel feed pipe from throttle body. Remove injector cover.

***WARNING: To prevent personal injury and damage to injector, DO NOT use more than 70 psi (4.9 kg/cm²) of air pressure to remove injector.***

**3)** Unplug injector harness connector. *See Fig. 11*. Slide injector grommet from throttle body. Place shop towel over injector. To remove injector, apply less than 70 psi (4.9 kg/cm²) compressed air into fuel inlet port of throttle body.

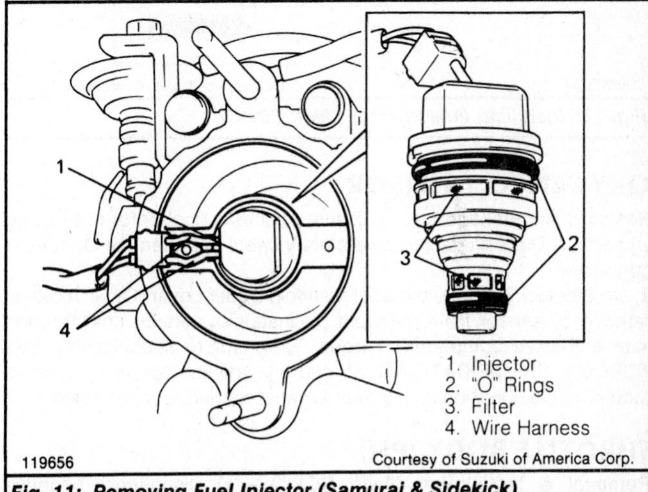


*Fig. 11: Removing Fuel Injector (Samurai & Sidekick)*

**Installation – 1)** Apply thin coat of fuel to new injector "O" rings. Install "O" rings on injector. Insert injector into throttle body. Carefully install wiring harness connector to injector.

**2)** Apply thread locking compound to injector cover mounting screws and install injector cover. Torque injector cover screws to 17 INCH lbs. (1.9 N.m). Connect fuel feed pipe with new "O" ring. Torque fuel feed pipe bolts to 71-106 INCH lbs. (8.0-11.9 N.m). Connect negative battery cable. Check for fuel leaks.

**3)** On Samurai, with fuel pump relay connected, install a jumper wire between fuel pump relay Pink/Black and Black/White wires. Fuel pump relay is located on right kick panel, above ECM. *See Fig. 7*.

**4)** On Sidekick, with control relay connected, install a jumper wire between control relay Pink/Black and Black/White wires. Control relay is located on left kick panel. *See Fig. 8*. On all models, turn ignition on (engine off) to activate fuel pump.

**Removal (Swift SOHC) – 1)** Relieve fuel system pressure. See FUEL SYSTEM PRESSURE RELEASE under FUEL SYSTEM. Disconnect negative battery cable. Remove air cleaner assembly.

**2)** Remove air cleaner mounting bracket from throttle body. Remove injector cover and upper insulator. Disconnect fuel injector connector. Remove fuel injector.

**Installation – 1)** Apply thin coat of fuel to new upper and lower fuel injector "O" rings. Install lower "O" ring to fuel injector cavity and upper "O" ring to injector. *See Fig. 12*.

**2)** Install new lower insulator to injector cavity. Install injector by pushing straight into fuel injector cavity. DO NOT turn injector while pushing. Install new upper insulator and injector cover.

**3)** Torque injector cover screws to 25-35 INCH lbs. (2.8-3.9 N.m). Reconnect fuel injector connector with lug side facing upward. Install connector cover. Connect negative battery cable. Check for fuel leaks.

**4)** With fuel pump relay connected, install a jumper wire between fuel pump relay Pink and White/Blue wires. Fuel pump relay is located in main fuse box, near battery. *See Fig. 9*. Turn ignition on (engine off) to activate fuel pump.

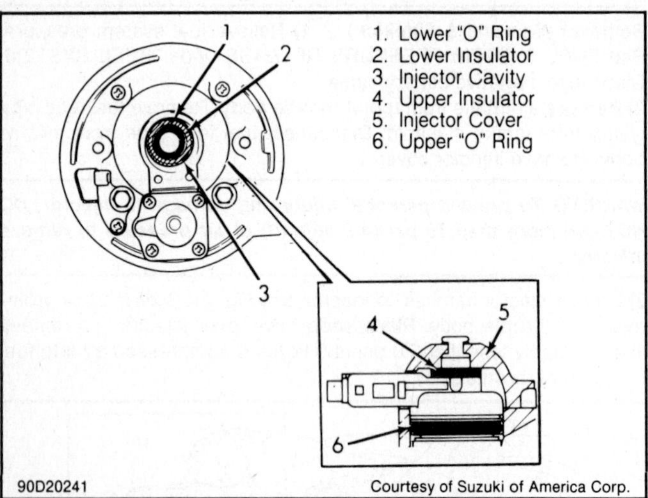


***Fig. 12: Installing Fuel Injector (Swift SOHC)***

## OXYGEN ($O_2$) SENSOR

**Removal & Installation – 1)** Ensure engine is cool before removing $O_2$ sensor. Disconnect negative battery cable and then the $O_2$ sensor connector.

**2)** On Sidekick, remove exhaust manifold upper cover. On all models, remove $O_2$ sensor from manifold. To install $O_2$ sensor, coat threads with anti-seize compound. Torque $O_2$ sensor to specification. See TORQUE SPECIFICATIONS at end of article. Connect negative battery cable. On Sidekick, install exhaust manifold upper cover.

## THROTTLE BODY (PFI)

**Removal & Installation (Swift DOHC) – 1)** Disconnect negative battery cable. Drain engine coolant so level is below throttle body. Disconnect accelerator cable from throttle lever and cable bracket.

**2)** Disconnect airflow meter outlet hose. Disconnect throttle position sensor connector. Label and disconnect all vacuum hoses from throttle body. Disconnect engine coolant hoses from throttle body. Remove throttle body from intake manifold.

**3)** To install, reverse removal procedure. Using new gasket, install throttle body on intake manifold. Torque throttle body mounting bolts and nuts to 13-20 ft. lbs. (18-27 N.m). After installing accelerator cable, ensure cable has .12-.20" (3.0-5.0 mm) play.

**4)** Hold exposed portion of cable at center and move cable up and down to measure play. *See Fig. 13*. Use lock nuts on cable bracket to adjust play. Refill cooling system.

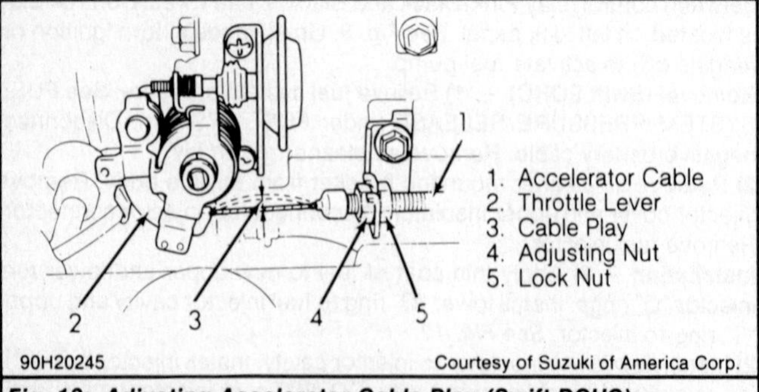


***Fig. 13: Adjusting Accelerator Cable Play (Swift DOHC)***

## THROTTLE BODY (TBI)

**Removal (Samurai, Sidekick & Swift SOHC) – 1)** Relieve fuel system pressure. See FUEL SYSTEM PRESSURE RELEASE under FUEL SYSTEM. Disconnect negative battery cable. Drain engine coolant so level is below throttle body. Remove air intake case from throttle body and air cleaner.

**2)** Disconnect accelerator cable and A/T kickdown cable (if equipped) from throttle body. Disconnect injector, throttle position sensor, throttle switch (Swift SOHC M/T), coolant (water) temperature sensor (Swift SOHC) and idle speed control solenoid (Sidekick) connectors at throttle body.

**3)** Label all vacuum hoses and disconnect hoses from throttle body. Disconnect coolant hose from air valve on throttle body. Remove fuel feed line from throttle body. On Samurai and Sidekick, remove fuel return line from fuel pressure regulator. On all models, remove throttle body mounting bolts and lift throttle body from intake manifold.

***NOTE: DO NOT soak injector or any electrical device in any type of solvent or cleaner***

**Overhaul (Samurai, Sidekick & Swift SOHC) – 1)** Remove fuel injector from throttle body. See INJECTOR (TBI) under FUEL SYSTEM. DO NOT soak injector in any type of solvent or cleaner.

**2)** Remove throttle position sensor, throttle switch (Swift SOHC M/T), coolant (water) temperature sensor (Swift SOHC), fuel pressure regulator (Samurai and Sidekick) and idle speed control solenoid valve (Sidekick) from throttle body. *See Fig. 14, 17 or 18*. Remove attaching screws and separate upper and lower bodies.

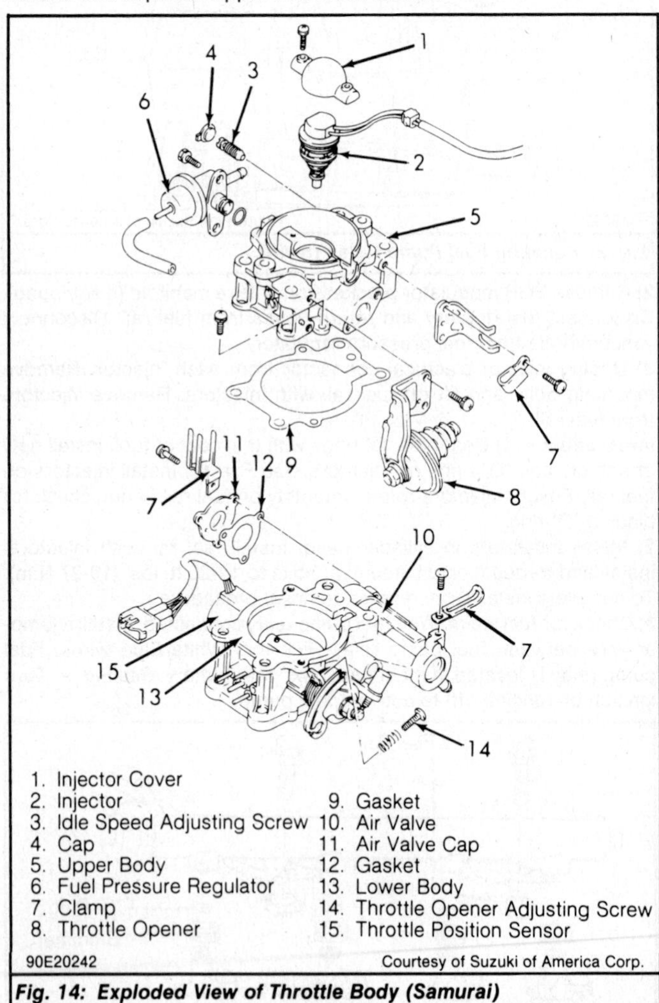


***Fig. 14: Exploded View of Throttle Body (Samurai)***

**3)** DO NOT soak any electrical device or air valve in solvent or other cleaner. DO NOT put drills or wires into passages. Clean upper and lower passages with compressed air only.

**4)** Assemble upper and lower bodies with new gasket. On Samurai and Sidekick, Install and torque upper-to-lower body attaching screws to 31 INCH lbs. (3.5 N.m). On Swift SOHC, torque upper-to-lower body attaching screws to 25-35 INCH lbs. (2.8-3.9 N.m).

# 1991 ENGINE PERFORMANCE
# Removal, Overhaul & Installation (Cont.)

**5)** On Samurai and Sidekick, install fuel pressure regulator with new "O" ring. Torque fuel pressure regulator mounting screws to 31 INCH lbs. (3.5 N.m).
**6)** On Sidekick, install idle speed control solenoid valve with new gasket. Torque idle speed control solenoid mounting valve screws to 31 INCH lbs. (3.5 N.m).
**7)** On Swift SOHC, install coolant (water) temperature sensor. Torque sensor to 15-22 ft. lbs (20-30 N.m). On all models, install fuel injector. See INJECTOR (TBI). Apply thread locking compound to injector cover mounting screws and install cover.
**8)** On all models except Swift SOHC, torque injector cover screws to 17 INCH lbs. (1.9 N.m). On Swift SOHC, torque injector cover screws to 25-35 INCH lbs. (2.8-3.9 N.m).
**9)** On Samurai, Sidekick and Swift (SOHC A/T), install throttle position sensor so adjusting holes slightly cover mounting bolt holes. *See Fig. 15*. Turn sensor so mounting holes align.

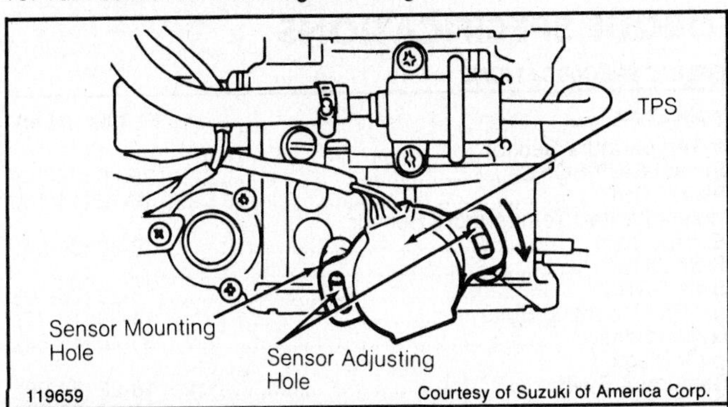


***Fig. 15: Aligning Throttle Position Sensor (Samurai, Sidekick & Swift SOHC A/T)***

**10)** On Swift SOHC M/T, install throttle switch to throttle shaft by aligning flat part of throttle switch rotor with cut part of throttle shaft. *See Fig. 16*. Push throttle switch in until it makes full contact with throttle body.

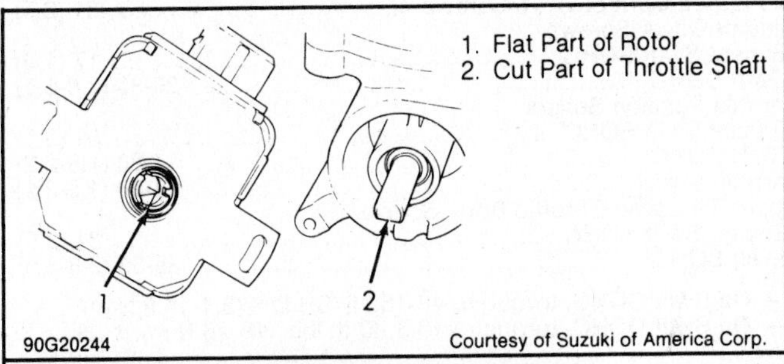


***Fig. 16: Aligning Throttle Switch (Swift SOHC M/T)***

**11)** On all models, install sensor mounting bolts (finger tighten only). Clamp wiring harness securely to side of throttle body.

**Installation (Samurai, Sidekick & Swift SOHC) – 1)** On all models, install new throttle body base gasket on intake manifold. Install throttle body. Torque throttle body mounting bolts to 13-20 ft. lbs. (18-27 N.m).
**2)** Connect fuel feed pipe with new "O" ring. Torque fuel feed pipe bolts to 71-106 INCH lbs. (8.0-11.9 N.m). Connect fuel return line to fuel pressure regulator (Samurai and Sidekick).
**3)** To complete installation, reverse removal procedure. Refill cooling system. Connect negative battery cable. Check for fuel leaks. On Samurai and Sidekick, with fuel pump relay connected, install a jumper wire between fuel pump relay Pink/Black and Black/White wires. Fuel pump relay is located on right kick panel, above ECM. *See Fig. 7*.
**4)** On Sidekick, with control relay connected, install a jumper wire between control relay Pink/Black and Black/White wires. Control relay is located on left kick panel. *See Fig. 8*.
**5)** On Swift SOHC, with fuel pump relay connected, install a jumper wire between fuel pump relay Pink and White/Blue wires. Fuel pump relay is located in main fuse box, near battery. *See Fig. 9*.

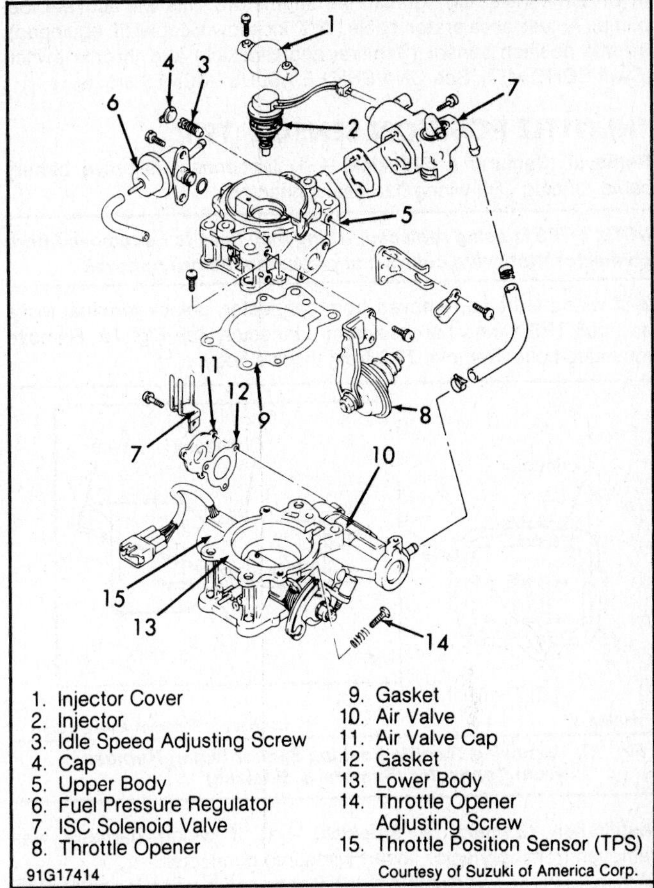


***Fig. 17: Exploded View of Throttle Body (Sidekick)***

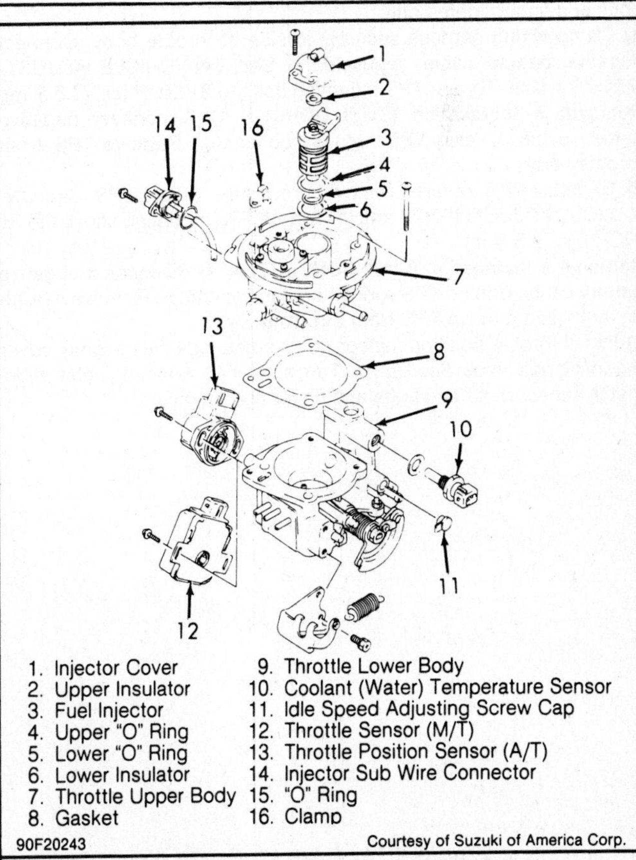


***Fig. 18: Exploded View of Throttle Body (Swift SOHC)***

# 1991 ENGINE PERFORMANCE
# Removal, Overhaul & Installation (Cont.)

**6)** On all models, turn ignition on, engine off. This will activate fuel pump. Adjust accelerator cable, A/T kickdown cable (if equipped), throttle position sensor (Samurai and Sidekick) and throttle switch (Swift SOHC M/T). See ON-VEHICLE ADJUSTMENTS article.

## THROTTLE POSITION SENSOR (TPS)

**Removal (Samurai & Sidekick) - 1)** Disconnect negative battery cable. Unplug TPS wiring harness connector.

***NOTE: If TPS is being replaced, wiring may have to be removed from connector. Note wire colors and placement before removal.***

**2)** If wiring is being removed from connector, unlock terminal locks and pull TPS wiring harness from connector. *See Fig. 19.* Remove mounting bolts. Remove TPS from throttle body.

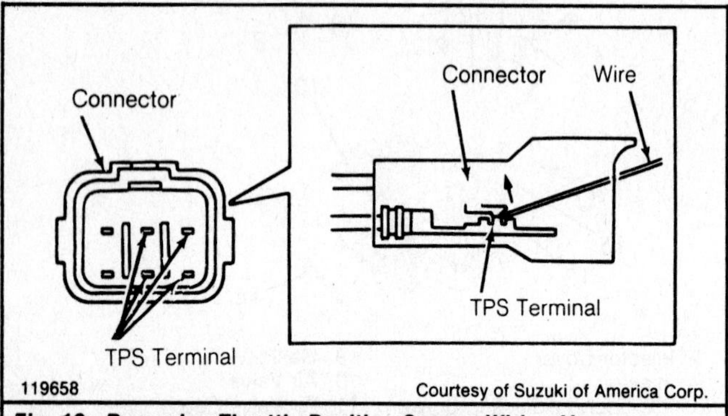


***Fig. 19: Removing Throttle Position Sensor Wiring Harness From Connector (Samurai & Sidekick)***

**Installation (Samurai & Sidekick) - 1)** If wiring harness was removed from connector, insert wires into connector.
**2)** Install TPS so its adjusting holes slightly cover mounting bolt holes. *See Fig. 15.* Turn TPS so mounting holes align. Install TPS mounting bolts and finger tighten only.
**3)** Clamp wiring harness securely to side of throttle body. Connect negative battery cable. Adjust TPS. See ON-VEHICLE ADJUSTMENTS article. Torque TPS mounting bolts to 31 INCH lbs. (3.5 N.m).
**Removal & Installation (Swift DOHC) - 1)** Disconnect negative battery cable. Unplug TPS harness connector. Remove TPS from throttle body.
**2)** To install TPS, reverse removal procedure. Adjust TPS. See ON-VEHICLE ADJUSTMENTS article. Torque TPS mounting screws to 31 INCH lbs. (3.5 N.m).
**Removal & Installation (Swift SOHC A/T) - 1)** Disconnect negative battery cable. Unplug TPS wiring harness connector. Remove mounting bolts and remove TPS from throttle body.
**2)** Install throttle position sensor so its adjusting holes slightly cover mounting bolt holes. *See Fig. 15.* Turn sensor so mounting holes align. Install sensor mounting bolts and finger tighten only.
**3)** Clamp wiring harness securely to side of throttle body. Connect negative battery cable. Adjust TPS. See ON-VEHICLE ADJUSTMENTS article. Torque TPS mounting bolts to 14-20 INCH lbs. (1.5-2.2 N.m).

## THROTTLE SWITCH

**Removal & Installation (Swift SOHC M/T) - 1)** Disconnect negative battery cable. Unplug throttle switch harness connector. Remove throttle switch from throttle body.
**2)** Install throttle switch to throttle shaft by aligning flat part of throttle switch rotor with cut part of throttle shaft. *See Fig. 16.* Push throttle switch in until it is making full contact with throttle body.
**3)** Install sensor mounting bolts and finger tighten only. Adjust throttle switch. See ON-VEHICLE ADJUSTMENTS article. Torque throttle switch mounting bolts to 14-20 INCH lbs. (1.5-2.2 N.m).

## TORQUE SPECIFICATIONS

***TORQUE SPECIFICATIONS***

| Application | Ft. Lbs. (N.m) |
|---|---|
| Air Temperature Sensor | |
| Except Swift SOHC | 26-40 (35-54) |
| Swift SOHC | 10-12 (14-16) |
| Coolant (Water) Temperature Sensor | |
| Except Swift | 26-40 (35-54) |
| Swift DOHC | [1] |
| Swift SOHC | 15-22 (20-30) |
| Fuel Rail Mounting Bolts | 14-20 (19-27) |
| Oxygen Sensor | 33-40 (45-54) |
| Spark Plugs | |
| Samurai & Swift | 18-22 (24-30) |
| Sidekick | 15-22 (20-30) |
| Throttle Body Mounting Bolts & Nuts | 13-20 (18-27) |
| | **INCH Lbs. (N.m)** |
| EGR Temperature Sensor | 72-168 (8.1-18.9) |
| Fuel Feed Pipe Bolts | |
| Except Swift DOHC | 71-106 (8.0-11.9) |
| Swift DOHC | [2] |
| Fuel Pressure Regulator Screws | 31 (3.5) |
| Idle Speed Control Valve Screws | 31 (3.5) |
| Injector Cover Screws | |
| Except Swift SOHC | 17 (1.9) |
| Swift SOHC | 25-35 (2.8-3.9) |
| Throttle Position Sensor | |
| Except Swift SOHC | 31 (3.5) |
| Swift SOHC | 14-20 (1.5-2.2) |
| Throttle Switch | 14-20 (1.5-2.2) |
| Upper-To-Lower Throttle Body Screws | |
| Except Swift SOHC | 31 (3.5) |
| Swift SOHC | 25-35 (2.8-3.9) |

[1] – On Swift DOHC, torque to 48-132 INCH lbs. (5.4-14.9 N.m).
[2] – On Swift DOHC, torque to 13.5-20 ft. lbs. (18-28 N.m).

# 1991 ELECTRICAL
# Alternators & Regulators

## Samurai, Sidekick, Swift

## DESCRIPTION

Alternators are conventional 3-phase alternators utilizing 3 positive and 3 negative diodes to rectify current. Internal Integrated Circuit (IC) voltage regulator controls charging system voltage. *See Fig. 1.*

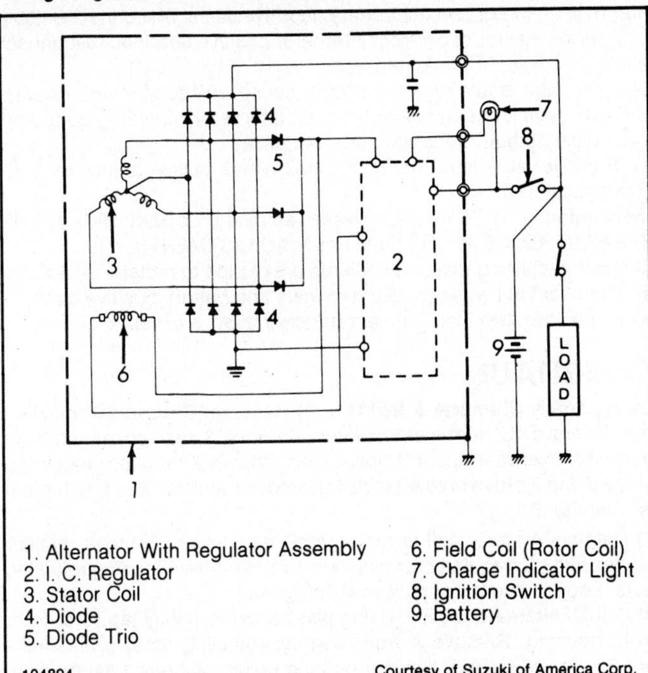


***Fig. 1: Alternator Circuit Diagram (Typical)***

## ADJUSTMENTS

### BELT TENSION

***BELT ADJUSTMENT (NEW BELT)***

| Application | [1] Deflection - In. (mm) |
|---|---|
| **Samurai** | |
| Water Pump Belt | .24-.35 (6.1-8.9) |
| **Sidekick** | |
| A/C Belt | .20-.25 (5.1-6.4) |
| Power Steering Belt | .24-.35 (6.1-8.9) |
| Water Pump Belt | .24-.32 (6.1-8.1) |
| **Swift (DOHC & SOHC)** | |
| A/C Belt | .20-.25 (5.1-6.4) |
| Water Pump Belt | .24-.32 (6.1-8.1) |

[1] - Deflection is checked with 22 lbs. (10 kg) pressure applied midway on longest belt run.

## TROUBLE SHOOTING

***NOTE: See TROUBLE SHOOTING article in GENERAL INFORMATION.***

## ON-VEHICLE TESTING

**Preliminary Inspection** - Check alternator wiring harness connections and drive belt tension. Battery must be fully charged. Connect a voltmeter to battery and start engine. Voltmeter reading should be 13.4-15.6 volts depending on regulator case temperature. If voltage reading is not within specification, disassemble alternator and test individual components

## BENCH TESTING

**Condenser** - Using an ohmmeter set to read capacitance, check capacity of condenser in regulator. *See Fig. 2.* Condenser capacitance should be .5 microfarads. If not, replace the regulator.

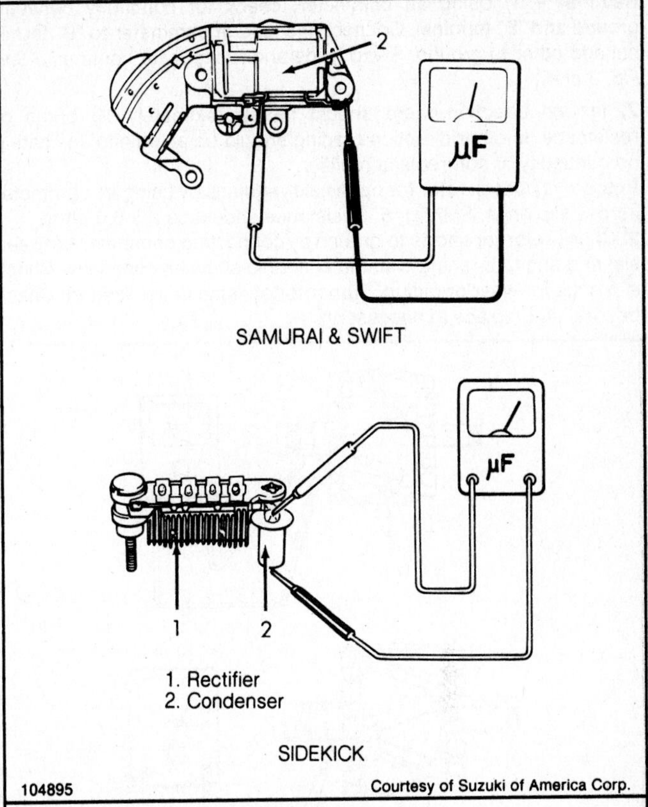


***Fig. 2: Testing Condenser Capacitance***

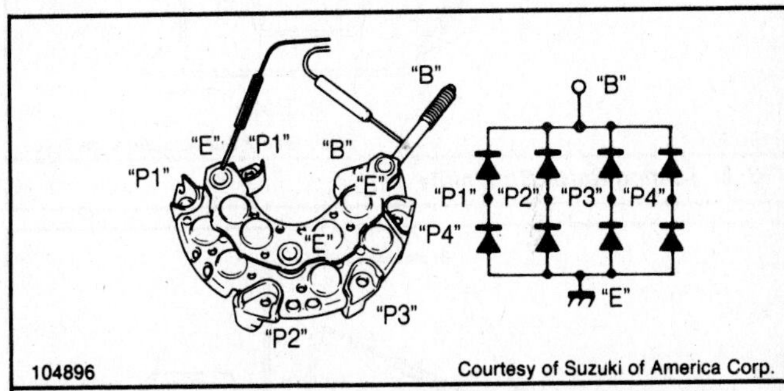


***Fig. 3: Testing Rectifier Diode Continuity (Samurai & Swift)***

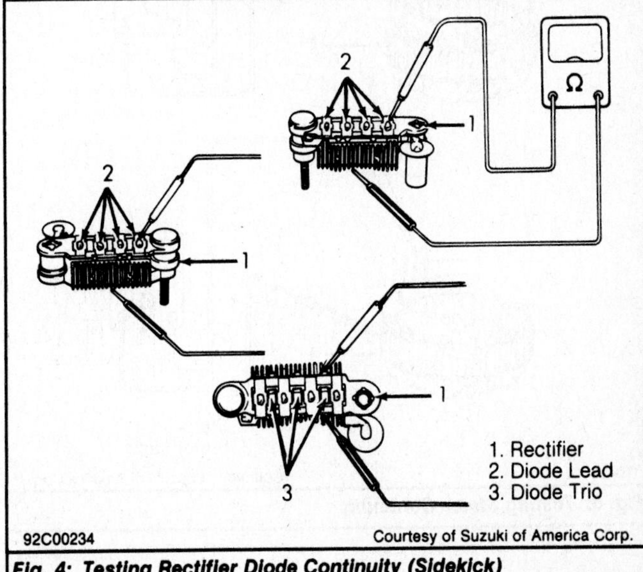


***Fig. 4: Testing Rectifier Diode Continuity (Sidekick)***

# 1991 ELECTRICAL
# Alternators & Regulators (Cont.)

**Rectifier – 1)** Using an ohmmeter, check for continuity between ground and "B" terminal. Connect one lead of ohmmeter to "B" terminal and other to ground. Swap leads and recheck for continuity. *See Fig. 3 or 4.*

**2)** In one direction there should be approximately 10 ohms of resistance. In other direction reading should be an infinite, indicating no continuity. If not, replace rectifier.

**Rotor – 1)** Check rotor for open field windings by using an ohmmeter across slip rings. *See Fig. 5.* Resistance should be 2.8-3.0 ohms.

**2)** Check rotor for shorts to ground by connecting ohmmeter between slip ring and rotor shaft. Ohmmeter should show no continuity. Check slip rings for wear or pitting. Turn rotor on lathe (if necessary). Check bearing and replace (if necessary).

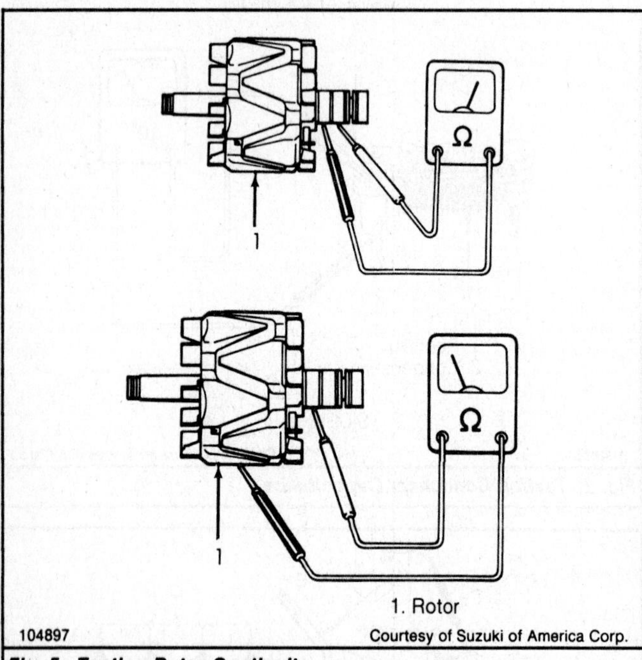


***Fig. 5: Testing Rotor Continuity***

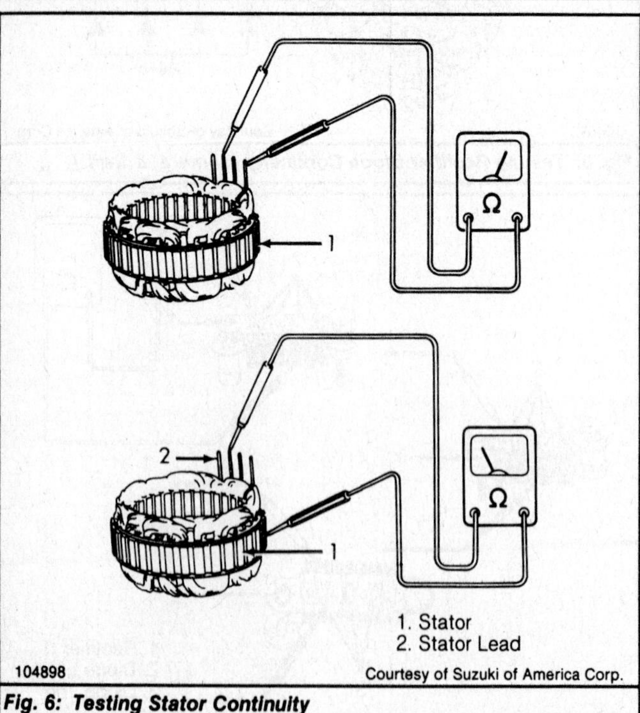


***Fig. 6: Testing Stator Continuity***

**Stator** – Connect ohmmeter between 2 stator leads. *See Fig 6.* Ensure continuity exists between all stator leads. Connect ohmmeter between each stator lead and metal core. Ohmmeter should show no continuity. If continuity is indicated, replace stator.

## REMOVAL & INSTALLATION

**Removal – 1)** Disconnect battery negative cable. Disconnect battery positive connector cable from alternator positive terminal. Disconnect White wire from "F" (field) terminal.

**2)** Disengage brake pipe from pipe clamp on radiator undercover. Remove radiator undercover. Loosen alternator mounting bolts and belt adjusting bolt. Separate belt from pulley.

**3)** Remove alternator mounting bolts and pulley adjusting bolt. Remove alternator.

**Installation – 1)** To install, reverse removal procedure. Adjust belt. See BELT ADJUSTMENT table under ADJUSTMENTS.

**2)** Install radiator undercover. Clamp brake pipe to radiator undercover. Connect field wires to field terminals and battery positive connector to positive terminal. Connect battery negative cable.

## OVERHAUL

**Disassembly (Samurai & Swift) – 1)** Remove "B" terminal retaining nut. Remove "B" terminal insulator. Remove 3 rear cover retaining nuts. Remove rear cover. Loosen and remove 2 regulator mounting screws and 3 brush holder screws. Remove regulator and brush holder. *See Fig. 8.*

**2)** Remove 4 stator coil terminal retaining screws. Remove rectifier holder with I.C. regulator. Loosen and remove 4 rear housing retaining nuts. Loosen alternator pulley retaining nut.

**3)** Pull off alternator pulley. Using plastic mallet, lightly tap rotor from front housing. Remove 4 front bearing retaining screws and front bearing (if necessary). Using a bearing puller, pull rear bearing from rotor (if necessary).

**Inspection – 1)** Check brushes for cracks. Using a vernier caliper, measure brush length. Standard measurement is .43" (11.0 mm). Minimum length is .18" (4.5 mm). Ensure brushes slide smoothly in holders.

**2)** If damaged or worn, replace brushes and brush holder. Install NEW springs when replacing brushes.

**Reassembly – 1)** To reassemble, reverse disassembly procedure. To install new bearings on either rotor or front housing, use a hydraulic press.

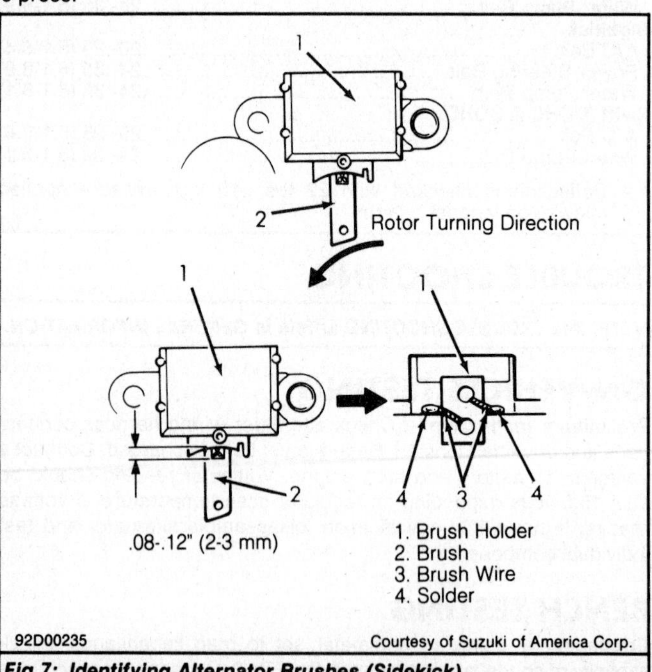


***Fig 7: Identifying Alternator Brushes (Sidekick)***

# 1991 ELECTRICAL
# Alternators & Regulators (Cont.)

**2)** Ensure that stator terminal insulation is properly installed. Install alternator pulley. Tighten pulley nut to 69-94 ft. lbs. (95-130 N.m).

**Disassembly (Sidekick) – 1)** Scribe mark on front and rear housing for reassembly reference. Remove housing bolts. Using a 200-watt soldering iron, heat rear bearing to 120-140° F (50-60° C). Insert lever between stator core and front housing and separate alternator halves.

**2)** Mount alternator rotor in a soft-jawed vise. Remove pulley nut and pulley. Remove rotor from front housing. *See Fig. 9*. Remove 4 retaining screws, front bearing retainer plate and front bearing from front housing (if required).

**3)** If rear bearing requires replacement, mount rotor in bearing separator plate and remove bearing using a hydraulic press. Remove 4 stator retaining screws, battery terminal nut and stator from alternator rear housing. If brushes require replacement, remove wire cover from brush holder and remove brush wires from regulator using a soldering iron.

**Inspection – 1)** Check brushes for cracks. Using a vernier caliper, measure brush length. Standard measurement is .63" (16.0 mm). Minimum length is .08" (2.0 mm). Ensure brushes slide smoothly in holders.

**2)** If damaged or worn, replace brushes and brush holder. Install NEW springs when replacing brushes.

**Reassembly – 1)** Install new bearings on either rotor or front drive housing (if required) using a hydraulic press. Install alternator pulley. Tighten pulley nut to 44-51 ft. lbs. (60-70 N.m).

**2)** Solder brushes to regulator in proper direction. *See Fig. 7.* Install new brush springs. Install brushes into brush holder and slide appropriate sized piece of wire through holes in brush holder to retain brushes. Install brush holder so that wire protrudes through rear of alternator case.

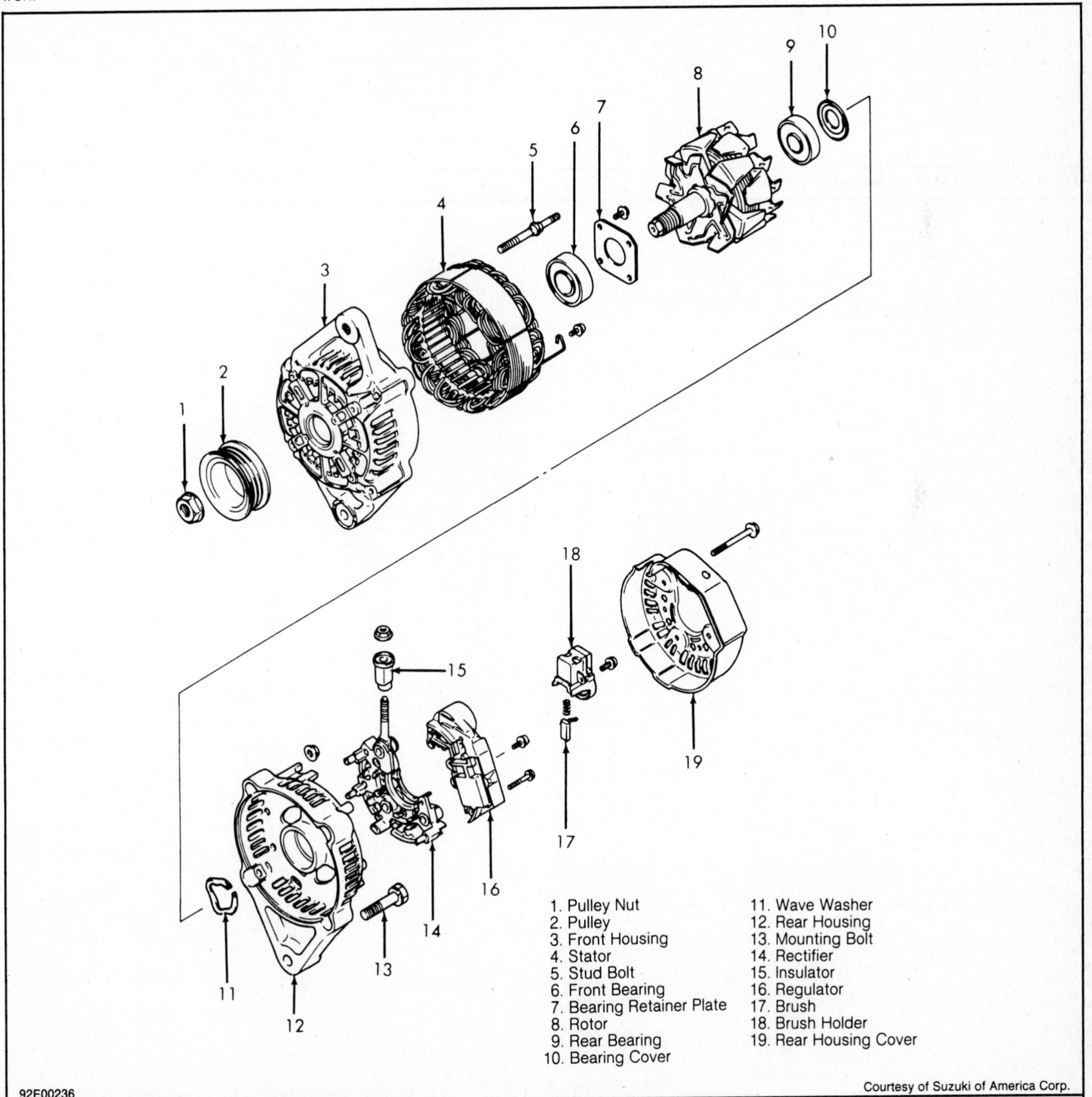


***Fig. 8: Exploded View of Alternator (Samurai & Swift)***

# 1991 ELECTRICAL
# Alternators & Regulators (Cont.)

**3)** Ensure that stator terminal insulation is properly installed and install stator. Heat rear bearing as in step **1)** and assemble alternator halves, making sure to align scribe marks.

***CAUTION: Ensure wire that retains brushes is removed before reconnecting negative battery cable.***

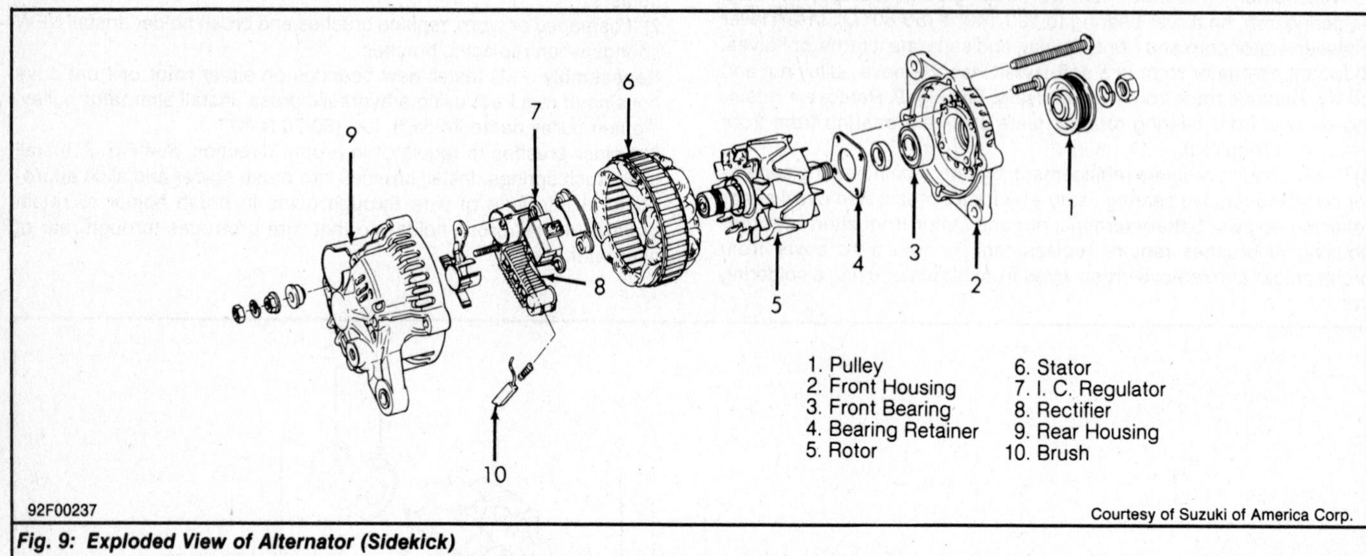


***Fig. 9: Exploded View of Alternator (Sidekick)***

## Samurai, Sidekick, Swift

# DESCRIPTION

Two types of starter motors are used, conventional and reduction. Both types of starters consist of a starter motor assembly and separate plunger-style solenoid (magnetic switch). Solenoid is activated when the ignition switch is turned to the START position, causing a yoke to engage the starter pinion with the flywheel. *See Fig. 1.* In addition, the reduction type starter has a reduction gear assembly with a shock absorber mechanism.

# TROUBLE SHOOTING

***NOTE: See TROUBLE SHOOTING article in GENERAL INFORMATION.***

# BENCH TESTING

## COMMUTATOR

**Ground Test** – Check for continuity between commutator and armature coil core. *See Fig. 2.* If there is NO continuity, armature is good, proceed to OPEN CIRCUIT TEST. If there is continuity, armature is grounded and must be replaced.

**Open Circuit Test** – Check for continuity between individual segments of the brush end of the armature. *See Fig. 3.* If there is continuity between all the segments, armature is good. If there is no continuity, there is an open circuit and armature must be replaced.

## FIELD COIL

Using a volt/ohmmeter, check for continuity between brush and bare surface. *See Fig. 4.* If there is no continuity, field coil is good. If there is continuity, field coil is bad and must be replaced.

## BRUSH HOLDER & SPRING

**1)** Check for smooth movement of brush in brush holder. If movement is sluggish, inspect holder for distortion and/or contamination. Clean, repair or replace as necessary.

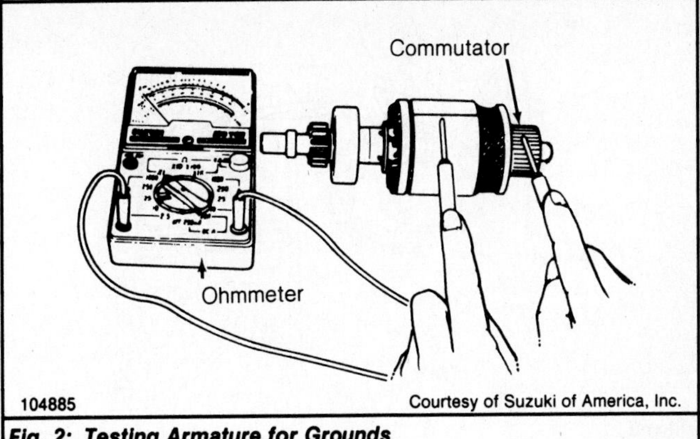


***Fig. 2: Testing Armature for Grounds***

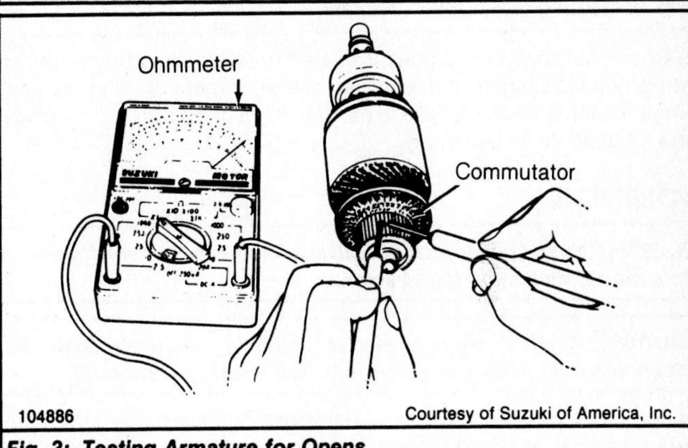


***Fig. 3: Testing Armature for Opens***

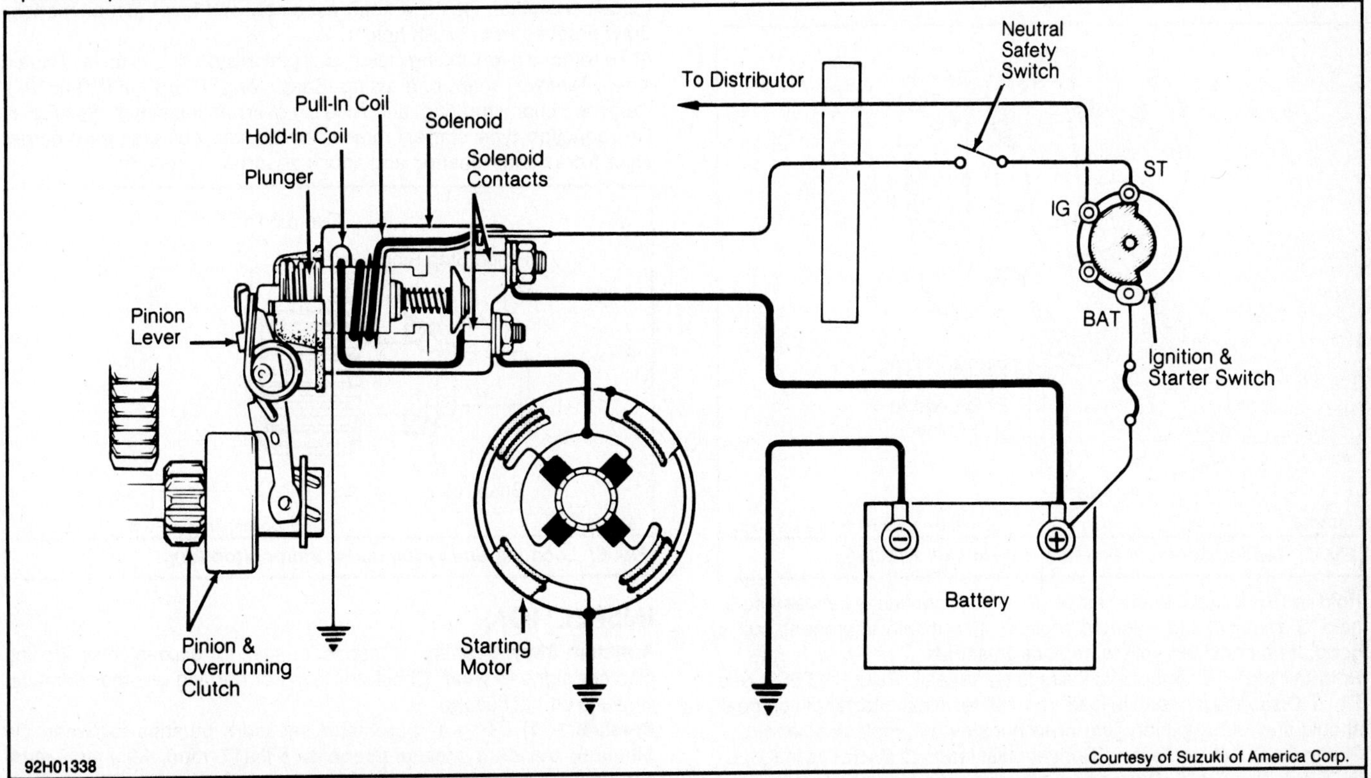

92H01338 Courtesy of Suzuki of America Corp.

***Fig. 1: Wiring Schematic of Starter Cranking Circuit (Typical)***

# 1991 ELECTRICAL
# Starters (Cont.)

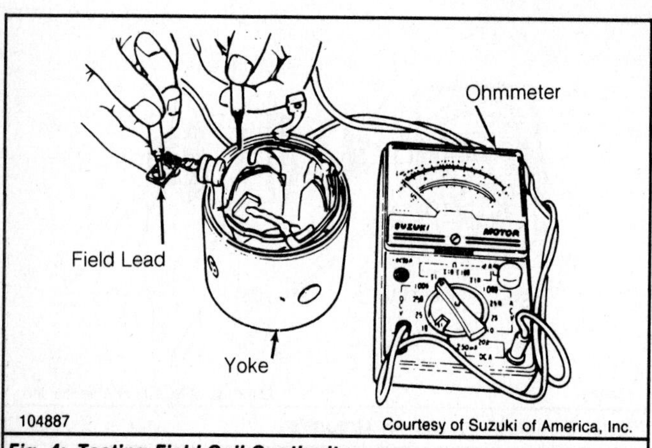


104887 Courtesy of Suzuki of America, Inc.

***Fig. 4: Testing Field Coil Continuity***

**2)** Check for continuity across insulated (positive side) brush holder and grounded (negative side) brush holder. If there is no continuity, brush holder is good. If there is continuity, insulation is bad. Replace brush holder as an assembly.

## SOLENOID

***NOTE: Tests must be performed with starter assembled and field lead from starter disconnected at solenoid.***

***CAUTION: DO NOT engage starter solenoid for more than 3-5 seconds during testing or damage to coil winding may result.***

**Pull-In Coil Open Circuit Test** – Using an ohmmeter, check for continuity between solenoid "S" and "M" terminals. If continuity is present, coil is good. If no continuity exists, replace solenoid.

**Pull-In Test** – Connect test leads to starter. *See Fig. 5.* Connect battery negative leads to starter housing and "M" terminal. Connect battery positive lead to "S" terminal. If starter pinion gear does not move out, replace solenoid.

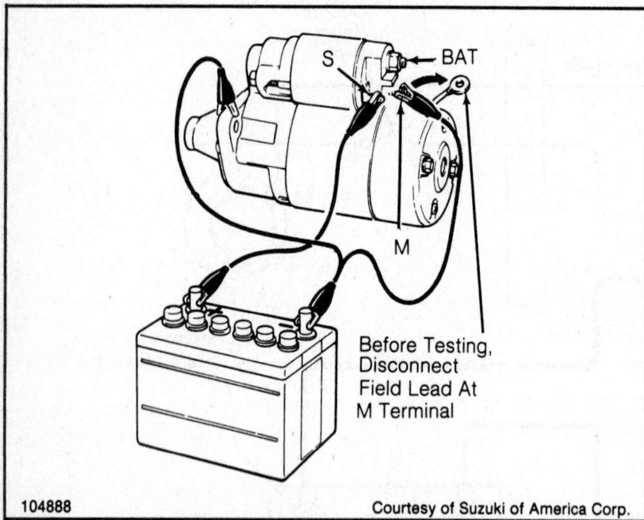


104888 Courtesy of Suzuki of America Corp.

***Fig. 5: Testing Solenoid Pull-In & Hold-In Coil Windings***

**Hold-In Open Coil Circuit Test** – Check for continuity between solenoid "S" terminal and solenoid housing. If continuity is present, coil is good. If no continuity exists, replace solenoid.

**Hold-In Test** – Connect test leads to starter as in PULL-IN TEST. *See Fig. 5.* Disconnect negative lead from "M" terminal. Starter pinion gear should stay out. If pinion gear does not stay out, replace solenoid.

**Pinion Gear Return Test** – Connect test leads to starter as in PULL-IN TEST. *See Fig. 5.* Disconnect negative lead from starter housing. Starter pinion should retract.

**No-Load Performance Test** – **1)** Using a jumper wire, connect battery negative terminal to starter housing. Connect battery positive to ammeter. Connect other side of ammeter to starter "S" and BAT terminals. Ensure starter rotates smoothly.

**2)** On Samurai, starter current draw should be less than 60 amps at 11.5 volts. On Sidekick and Swift GT (A/T), starter current draw should be less than 90 amps at 11 volts. On Swift GT (M/T), starter current draw should be less than 90 amps at 11.5 volts.

**3)** On all Swift models using conventional type starter, starter current draw should be less than 50 amps at 11 volts. On Swift models using reduction type starter, starter current draw should be less than 90 amps at 11.5 volts.

## REMOVAL & INSTALLATION

**Removal** – Disconnect negative battery cable from battery. Disconnect solenoid lead and battery cable from solenoid terminals. Remove 2 starter motor retaining bolts. Remove starter motor.

**Installation** – Install starter motor. Install and tighten 2 starter motor retaining bolts. Connect solenoid lead and battery cable to solenoid. Connect battery negative cable to battery.

## OVERHAUL

### DISASSEMBLY

**1)** Scribe mating surfaces of starter housing and solenoid housing and starter housing and yoke for reassembly reference. Remove starter housing field coil lead from solenoid terminal. Remove 2 screws holding solenoid to starter housing. Remove solenoid.

***NOTE: On conventional type starter, remove solenoid from starter housing by lifting up and out to release hook from pinion lever.***

**2)** Loosen and remove 2 bolts and 2 screws holding commutator cover to starter housing. On conventional type starter, remove armature plate and brake spring. Remove commutator cover from yoke. Separate brush holder, armature and yoke from starter housing.

**3)** On reduction type starter, remove gasket and gears. Remove seal rubber and plate. Remove shaft assembly and lever. On all models, draw brushes from brush holder.

**4)** To remove overrunning clutch, pull pinion stop ring in toward clutch side. Remove snap ring using Snap Ring Pliers (09900-06107). Remove pinion stop ring, and slide off overrunning clutch. *See Fig. 6.* On reduction type starter, remove circlip and pull planetary carrier shaft from center bearing and shock absorber assembly.

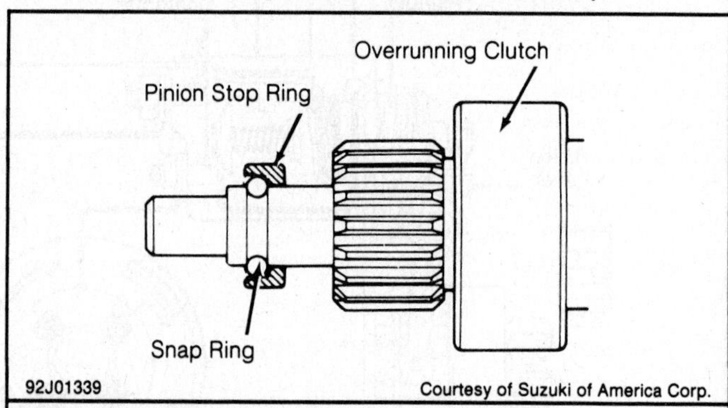


92J01339 Courtesy of Suzuki of America Corp.

***Fig. 6: Locating Snap Ring under Pinion Stop Ring***

### INSPECTION

**Armature Shaft Bushing** – Inspect bushes for excessive scratching or other signs of wear. Check for signs of burning or other damage. Replace as necessary.

**Brushes** – **1)** Using a micrometer, measure brushes for wear. On Samurai, standard measurement is .67" (17 mm). Minimum measurement is .45" (11.5 mm). On Sidekick and Swift GT (A/T), standard measurement is .69" (17.5 mm). Minimum measurement is .47" (12 mm).

**2)** On Swift GT (M/T) and all other Swift models with reduction type starters, minimum measurement is .35" (9. mm). On Swift models with conventional type starters, minimum measurement is .42" (10.7 mm). If less than minimum, replace brushes.

**Brush Holder & Spring - 1)** Check for smooth movement of brush in brush holder. If movement is sluggish, inspect holder for distortion and/or contamination. Clean, repair or replace as necessary.

**2)** Inspect brush spring for wear, damage or other abnormal conditions. Using a spring tension gauge, check tension of brush spring. On Samurai, standard tension is 3.53 lbs. (1.6 kg). Minimum tension is 2.2 lbs. (1.0 kg). On Sidekick and Swift GT (A/T), standard tension is 4.19 lbs. (1.96 kg). Minimum tension is 1.54 lbs. (0.7 kg). If less than minimum, replace brush spring.

***NOTE: On all Swift models except GT (A/T), replace brush holder and spring as an assembly.***

**Commutator - 1)** Inspect commutator for dirt or signs of burning. If dirt or burning is present, sand lightly with No. 300-400 sand paper or lathe as necessary to clean surface.

**2)** Using a dial indicator, check commutator for runout. Standard runout is .0019" (.05 mm). Maximum runout is .015" (.4 mm). If runout exceeds maximum limit, replace commutator.

**3)** Using a micrometer, measure diameter of brush end of commutator. On Samurai, standard measurement is 1.26" (32 mm). Minimum measurement is 1.22" (31 mm). On Sidekick and Swift GT (A/T), standard measurement is 1.16" (29 mm). Minimum measurement is 1.13" (29 mm). On all Swift models except GT (A/T), minimum measurement is 1.06" (27 mm). If measurement is less than minimum, replace commutator.

**4)** Measure depth of grooves between commutator segments and insulators. *See Fig. 7.* On Samurai, standard depth is .015-.023" (.4-.6 mm). Minimum depth is .0078" (.2 mm). On Sidekick and Swift GT (A/T), standard depth is .020-.031" (.5-.8 mm). Minimum depth is .0078" (.2 mm). On all Swift models except GT (A/T), minimum depth is .0078" (.2 mm). If measurement is less than minimum depth, replace commutator.

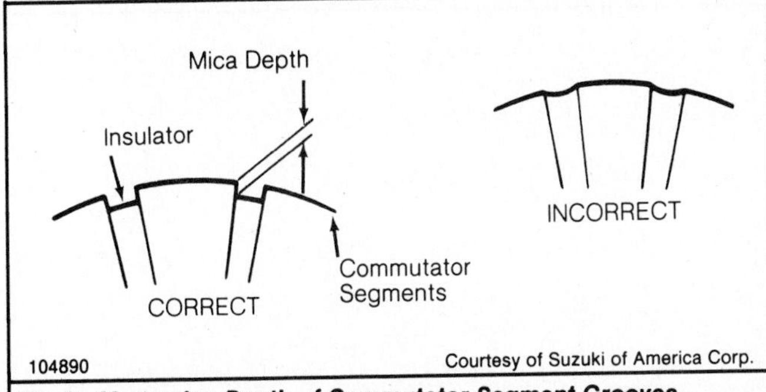


***Fig. 7: Measuring Depth of Commutator Segment Grooves***

**Drive Lever Yoke -** Inspect all pivot points for excessive wear. If any pivot or engagement points show excessive signs of wear, replace drive lever.

**Pinion - 1)** Inspect pinion for wear or damage. Ensure that clutch locks-up when turned in direction of drive and rotates easily and smoothly in reverse direction. Replace as necessary.

**2)** Check teeth for wear or damage. Check pinion for smooth movement. Replace as necessary.

## REASSEMBLY

**1)** Lubricate all friction surfaces. On reduction type starter, install center bearing and shock absorber assembly onto planetary carrier shaft, and install circlip. *See Fig. 8.* On all models, install overrunning clutch, pinion stop ring and snap ring (if removed). Install brushes into brush holder.

**2)** On reduction type starter, install shaft assembly and lever. Install seal rubber and plate. Install gasket and gears. On all models, install armature, yoke and brush holder into starter housing, matching reference marks scribed during disassembly. Place commutator cover over starter housing.

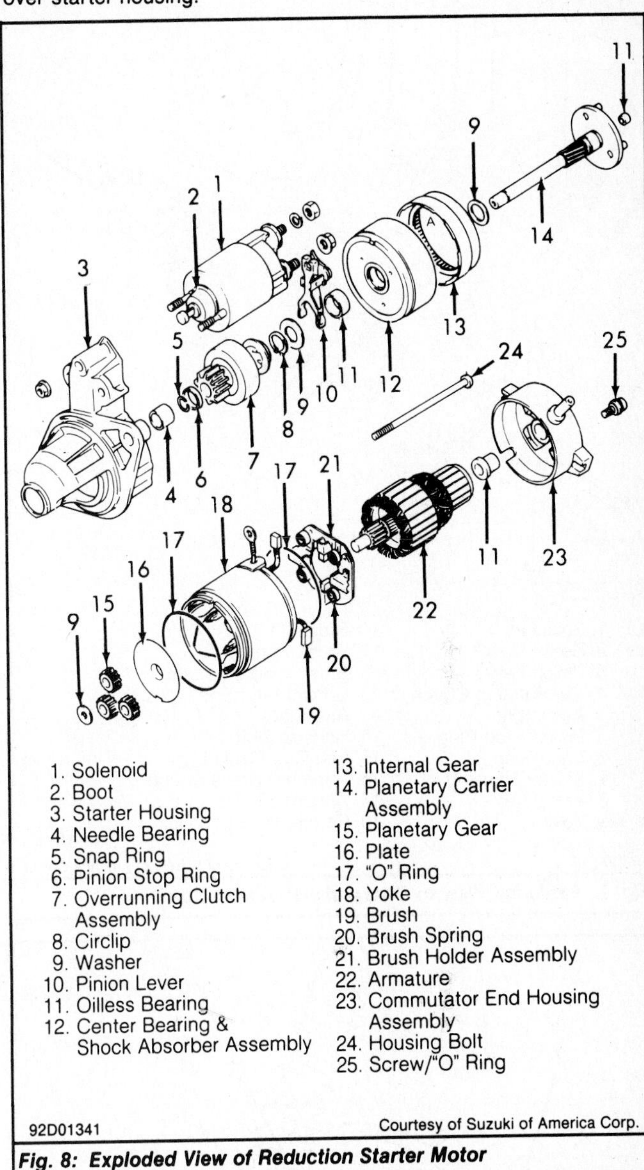


***Fig. 8: Exploded View of Reduction Starter Motor***

**3)** On conventional type starter, install armature plate and brake spring. *See Fig. 9.* On all models, install 2 bolts and 2 screws holding commutator cover to starter housing. Align solenoid with scribe marks and install to starter housing.

**4)** Install and tighten 2 solenoid-to-starter housing screws. Install starter housing field coil lead-to-solenoid terminal and tighten retaining nut.

# ADJUSTMENTS

## NEUTRAL SAFETY SWITCH

**Automatic Transmission -** Adjust shift lever neutral safety switch by moving switch in direction of arrow. *See Fig. 10.* Stop and secure switch when click is heard or felt.

**Manual Transmission -** Adjust clutch neutral safety switch so clearance between switch threaded end and clutch pedal is .02-.04" (.05-1.0 mm). *See Fig. 11.*

# 1991 ELECTRICAL
## Starters (Cont.)

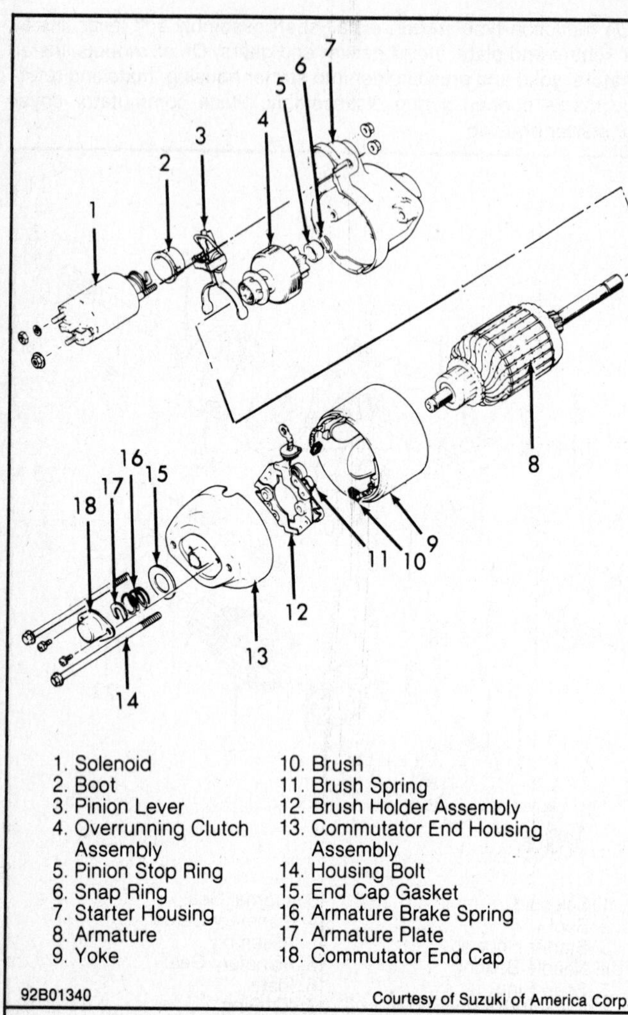


1. Solenoid
2. Boot
3. Pinion Lever
4. Overrunning Clutch Assembly
5. Pinion Stop Ring
6. Snap Ring
7. Starter Housing
8. Armature
9. Yoke
10. Brush
11. Brush Spring
12. Brush Holder Assembly
13. Commutator End Housing Assembly
14. Housing Bolt
15. End Cap Gasket
16. Armature Brake Spring
17. Armature Plate
18. Commutator End Cap

92B01340 Courtesy of Suzuki of America Corp.

**Fig. 9: Exploded View of Conventional Starter Motor**

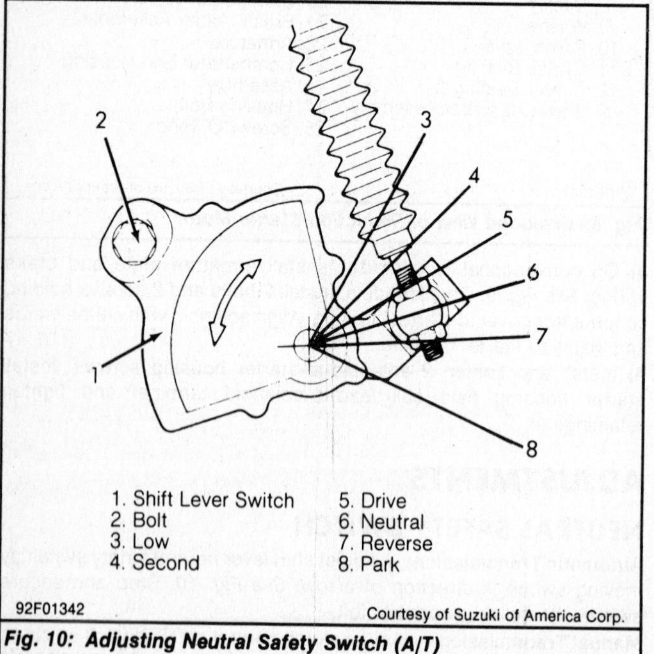


1. Shift Lever Switch
2. Bolt
3. Low
4. Second
5. Drive
6. Neutral
7. Reverse
8. Park

92F01342 Courtesy of Suzuki of America Corp.

**Fig. 10: Adjusting Neutral Safety Switch (A/T)**

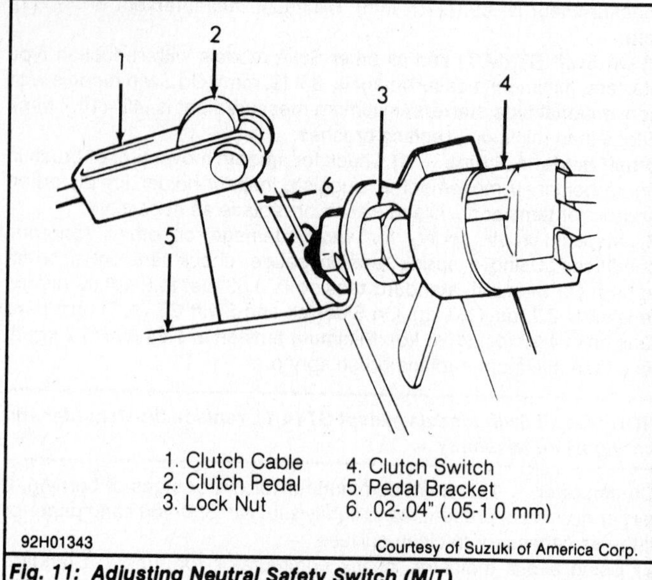


1. Clutch Cable
2. Clutch Pedal
3. Lock Nut
4. Clutch Switch
5. Pedal Bracket
6. .02-.04" (.05-1.0 mm)

92H01343 Courtesy of Suzuki of America Corp.

**Fig. 11: Adjusting Neutral Safety Switch (M/T)**

# TORQUE SPECIFICATIONS

***TORQUE SPECIFICATIONS***

| Application | INCH Lbs. (N.m) |
|---|---|
| Clutch Switch Lock Nut | 89-133 (10-15) |
| Field Lead Wire Nut | |
| Swift GT (M/T) | 71-106 (8-12) |
| All Others | 1 |
| Shift Lever Switch Bolt | 115-204 (13-23) |
| Solenoid Nuts | |
| Swift GT (M/T) | 53-97 (6-11) |
| All Others | 1 |
| Starter Housing Bolts | |
| Swift GT (M/T) | 44-62 (5-7) |
| All Others | 159-248 (18-28) |

1 – Specification is not available from manufacturer.

# 1991 WIRING DIAGRAMS
## Samurai

COMPONENT LOCATOR:

| Component | Location |
|---|---|
| A/C COUPLER | A 4 |
| ALTERNATOR | C 3 |
| BACK-UP LT SW | C 11 |
| BATTERY | A 2 |
| CHECK RELAY | B 3 |
| CLUTCH SW | B 3 |
| COMBINATION SW | D-E 12-14 |
| DEFOG SW | B 10 |
| DOME LT | B 8 |
| DOOR WARN BUZZER | B 8 |
| ELECTRONIC CONTROL MODULE | A-E 4-7 |
| FUSE BLOCK | D-E 8-11 |
| HEATER FAN SW | A 8 |
| HORN RELAY | E 3 |
| IGNITER | B-C 4 |
| IGNITION SW | E 11 |
| ILLUM LTS RHEOSTAT | A-B 10-11 |
| INSTRUMENT CLUSTER | A-C 12-14 |
| MAIN RELAY | B 7 |
| NOISE SUPPRESSOR | B-C 4 |
| STARTER | A 3 |
| STOP LT SW | D 8 |
| TEST CONN | B 4 |
| WASHER MOTOR | E 12 |
| WIPER MOTOR | E 12 |

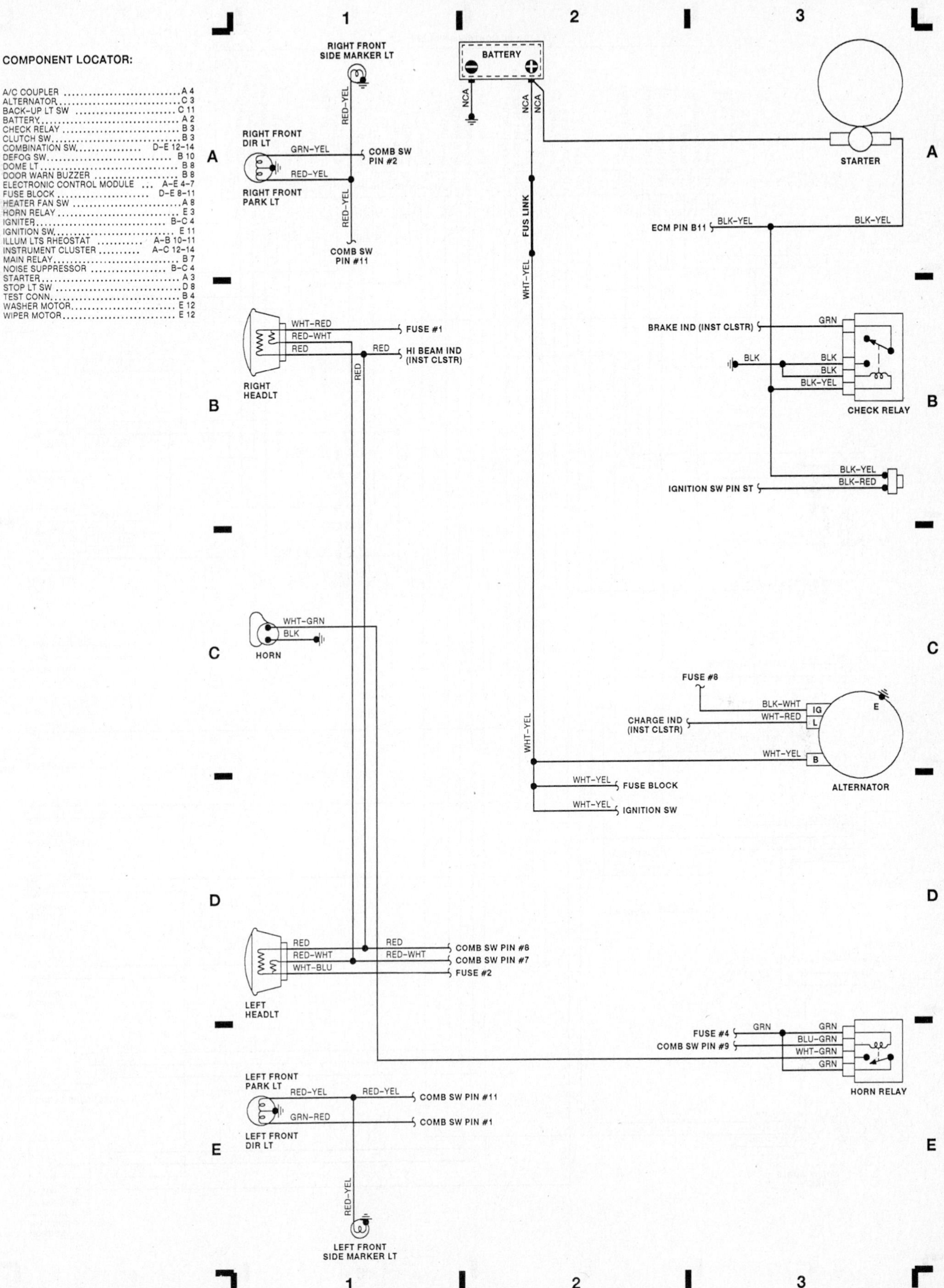

# 1991 WIRING DIAGRAMS
## Samurai (Cont.)

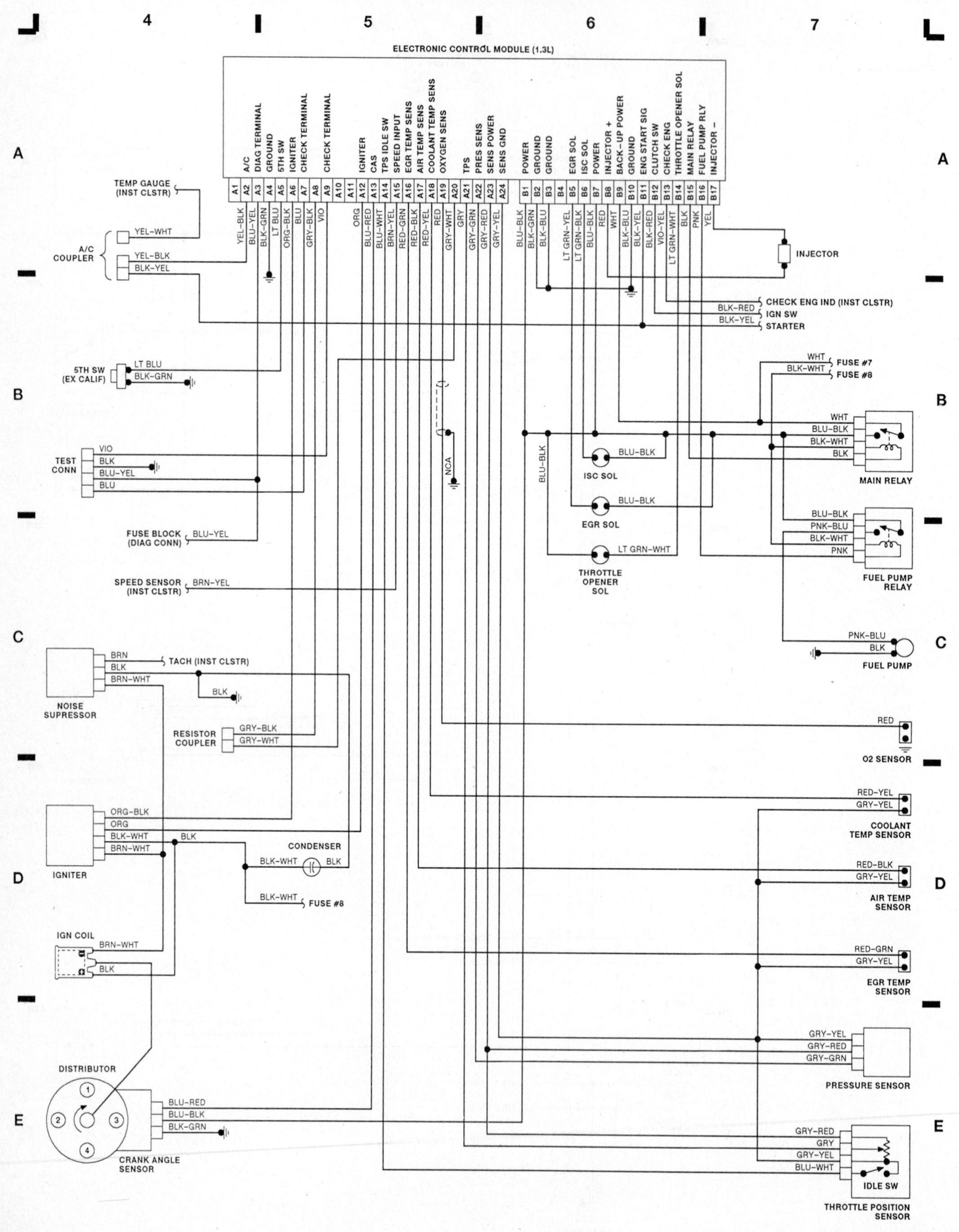

# 1991 WIRING DIAGRAMS
## Samurai (Cont.)

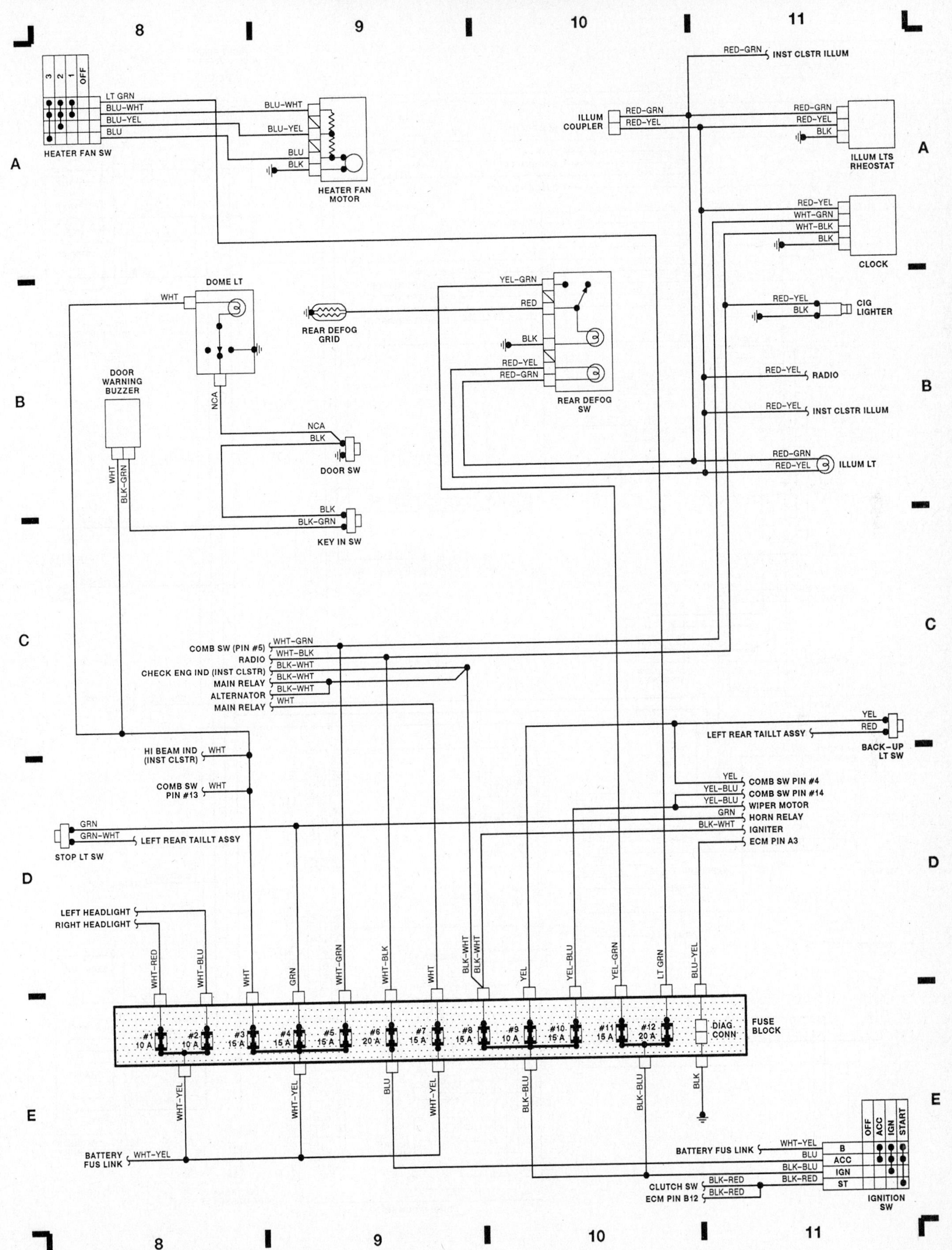

# 1991 WIRING DIAGRAMS
## Samurai (Cont.)

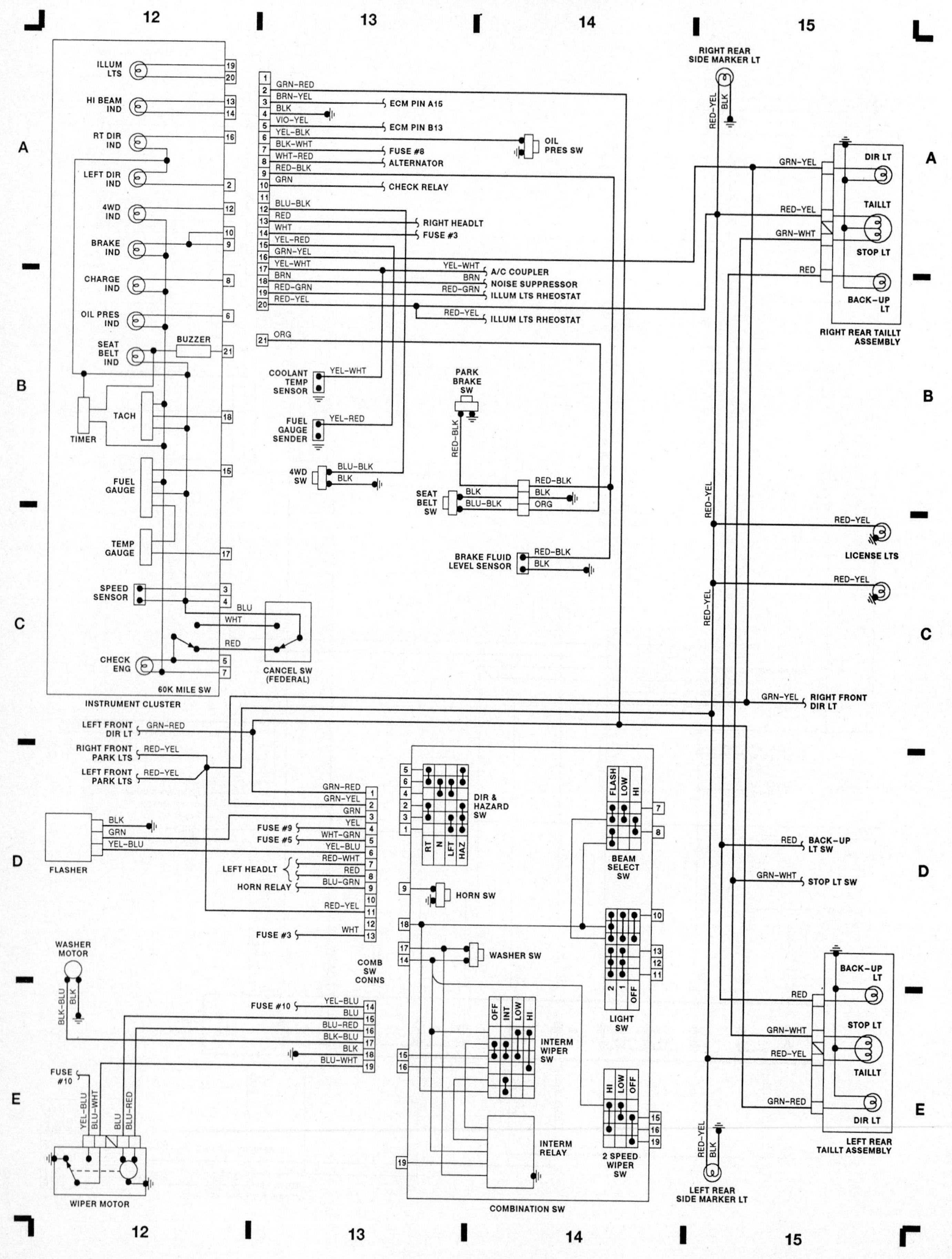

# 1991 WIRING DIAGRAMS
## Sidekick

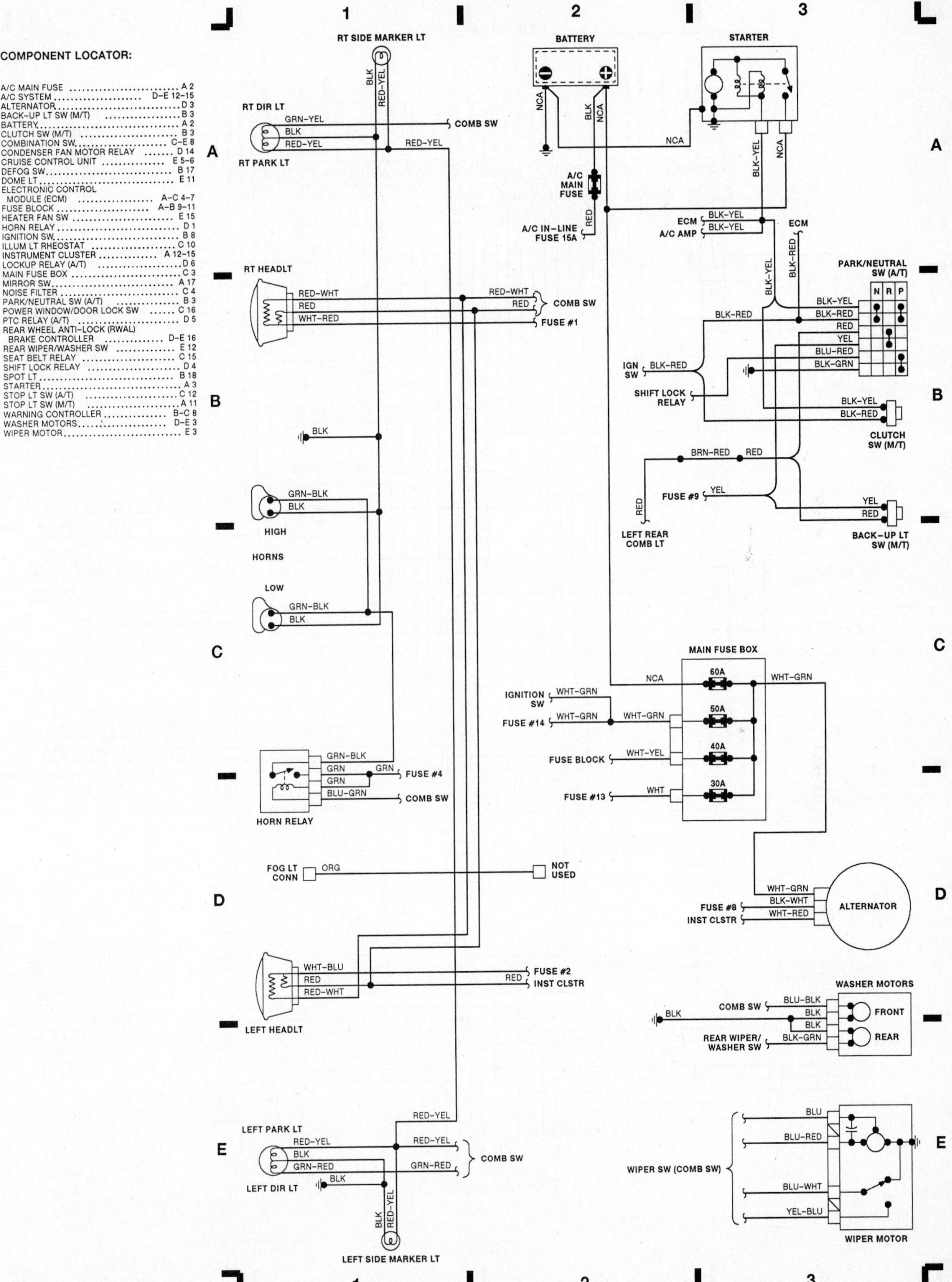
COMPONENT LOCATOR:
A/C MAIN FUSE ........ A 2
A/C SYSTEM ........ D-E 12-15
ALTERNATOR ........ D 3
BACK-UP LT SW (M/T) ........ B 3
BATTERY ........ A 2
CLUTCH SW (M/T) ........ B 3
COMBINATION SW ........ C-E 8
CONDENSER FAN MOTOR RELAY ........ D 14
CRUISE CONTROL UNIT ........ E 5-6
DEFOG SW ........ B 17
DOME LT ........ E 11
ELECTRONIC CONTROL MODULE (ECM) ........ A-C 4-7
FUSE BLOCK ........ A-B 9-11
HEATER FAN SW ........ E 15
HORN RELAY ........ D 1
IGNITION SW ........ B 8
ILLUM LT RHEOSTAT ........ C 10
INSTRUMENT CLUSTER ........ A 12-15
LOCKUP RELAY (A/T) ........ D 6
MAIN FUSE BOX ........ C 3
MIRROR SW ........ A 17
NOISE FILTER ........ C 4
PARK/NEUTRAL SW (A/T) ........ B 3
POWER WINDOW/DOOR LOCK SW ........ C 16
PTC RELAY (A/T) ........ D 5
REAR WHEEL ANTI-LOCK (RWAL) BRAKE CONTROLLER ........ D-E 16
REAR WIPER/WASHER SW ........ E 12
SEAT BELT RELAY ........ C 15
SHIFT LOCK RELAY ........ D 4
SPOT LT ........ B 18
STARTER ........ A 3
STOP LT SW (A/T) ........ C 12
STOP LT SW (M/T) ........ A 11
WARNING CONTROLLER ........ B-C 8
WASHER MOTORS ........ D-E 3
WIPER MOTOR ........ E 3
RT SIDE MARKER LT
RT DIR LT
RT PARK LT
COMB SW
BATTERY
STARTER
A/C MAIN FUSE
A/C IN-LINE FUSE 15A
ECM
A/C AMP
PARK/NEUTRAL SW (A/T)
RT HEADLT
FUSE #1
IGN SW
SHIFT LOCK RELAY
CLUTCH SW (M/T)
FUSE #9
LEFT REAR COMB LT
BACK-UP LT SW (M/T)
HIGH
HORNS
LOW
MAIN FUSE BOX
60A
50A
40A
30A
IGNITION SW
FUSE #14
FUSE BLOCK
FUSE #13
FUSE #4
HORN RELAY
FOG LT CONN
NOT USED
ALTERNATOR
FUSE #8
INST CLSTR
FUSE #2
LEFT HEADLT
WASHER MOTORS
FRONT
REAR
REAR WIPER/WASHER SW
LEFT PARK LT
LEFT DIR LT
LEFT SIDE MARKER LT
WIPER SW (COMB SW)
WIPER MOTOR

# 1991 WIRING DIAGRAMS
## Sidekick (Cont.)

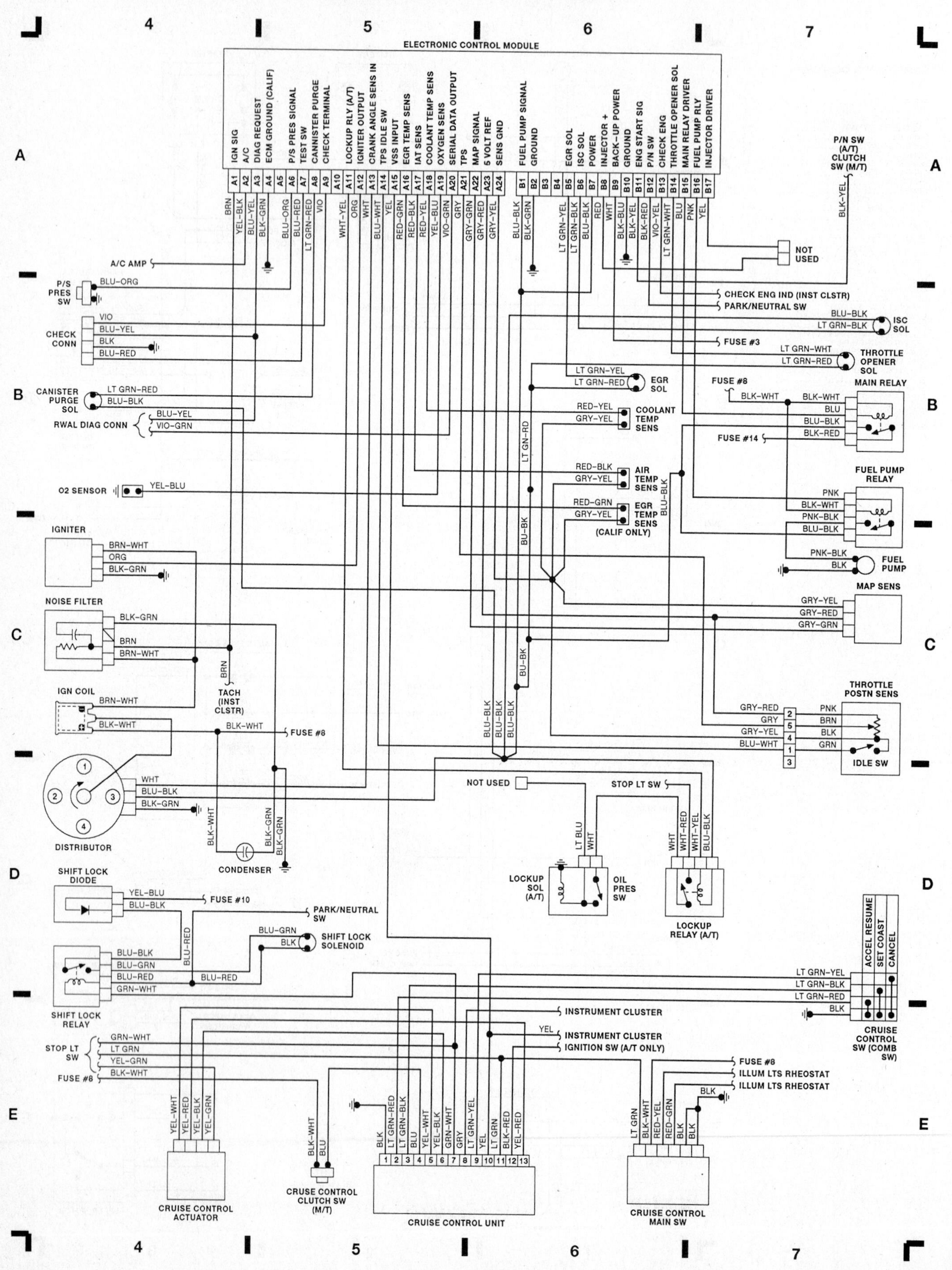

# 1991 WIRING DIAGRAMS
## Sidekick (Cont.)

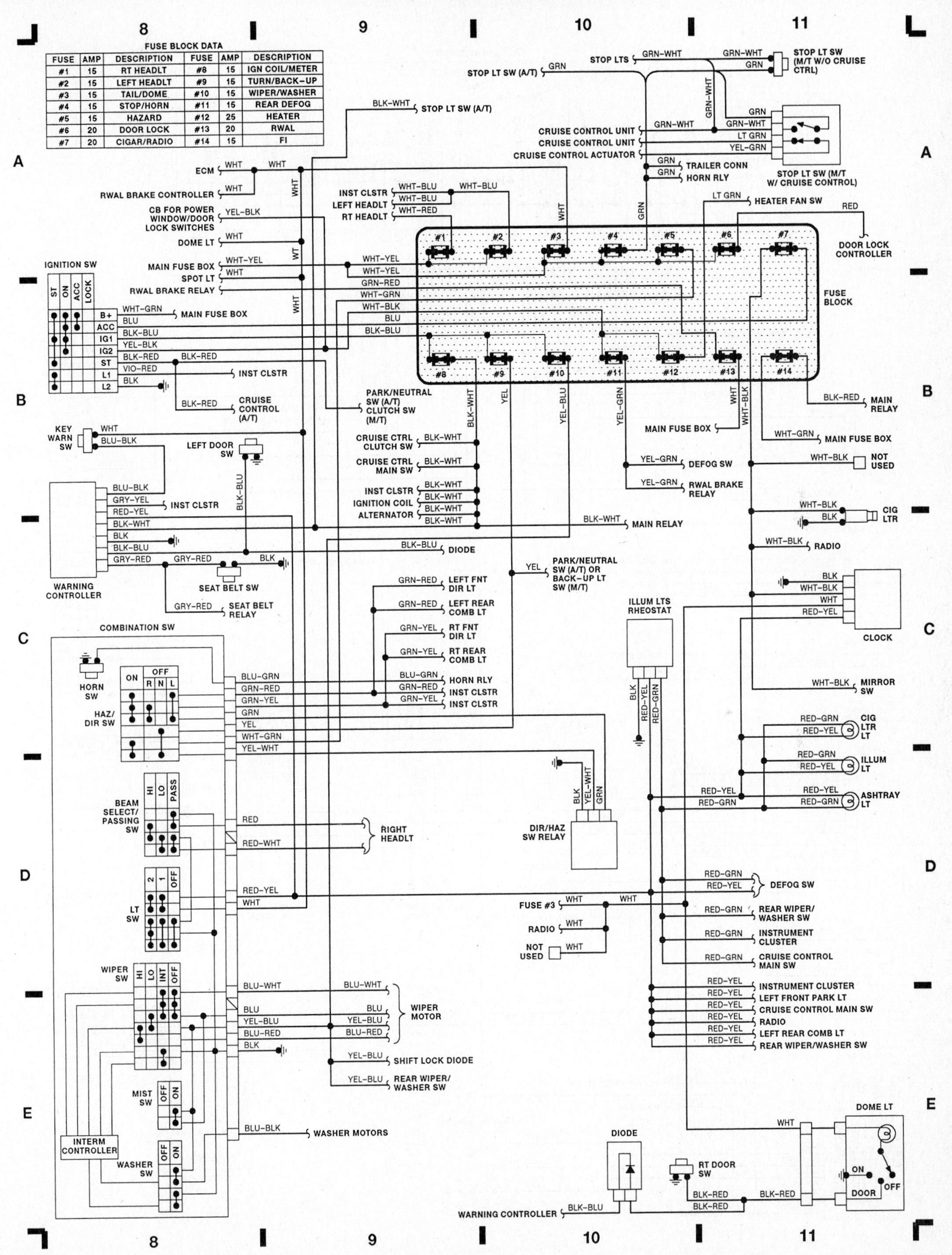


FUSE BLOCK DATA

| FUSE | AMP | DESCRIPTION | FUSE | AMP | DESCRIPTION |
|---|---|---|---|---|---|
| #1 | 15 | RT HEADLT | #8 | 15 | IGN COIL/METER |
| #2 | 15 | LEFT HEADLT | #9 | 15 | TURN/BACK-UP |
| #3 | 15 | TAIL/DOME | #10 | 15 | WIPER/WASHER |
| #4 | 15 | STOP/HORN | #11 | 15 | REAR DEFOG |
| #5 | 15 | HAZARD | #12 | 25 | HEATER |
| #6 | 20 | DOOR LOCK | #13 | 20 | RWAL |
| #7 | 20 | CIGAR/RADIO | #14 | 15 | FI |

# 1991 WIRING DIAGRAMS
## Sidekick (Cont.)

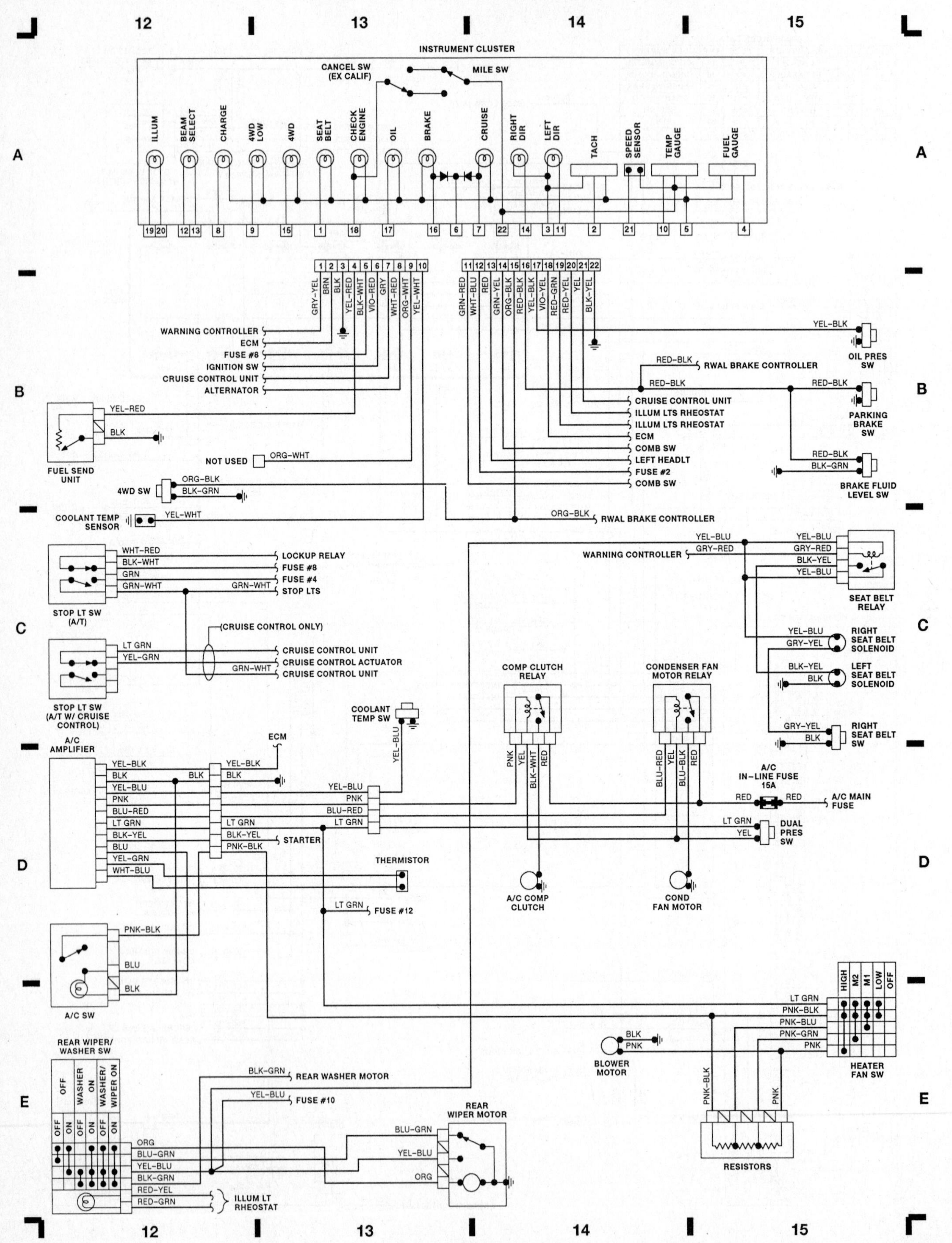

# 1991 WIRING DIAGRAMS
## Sidekick (Cont.)

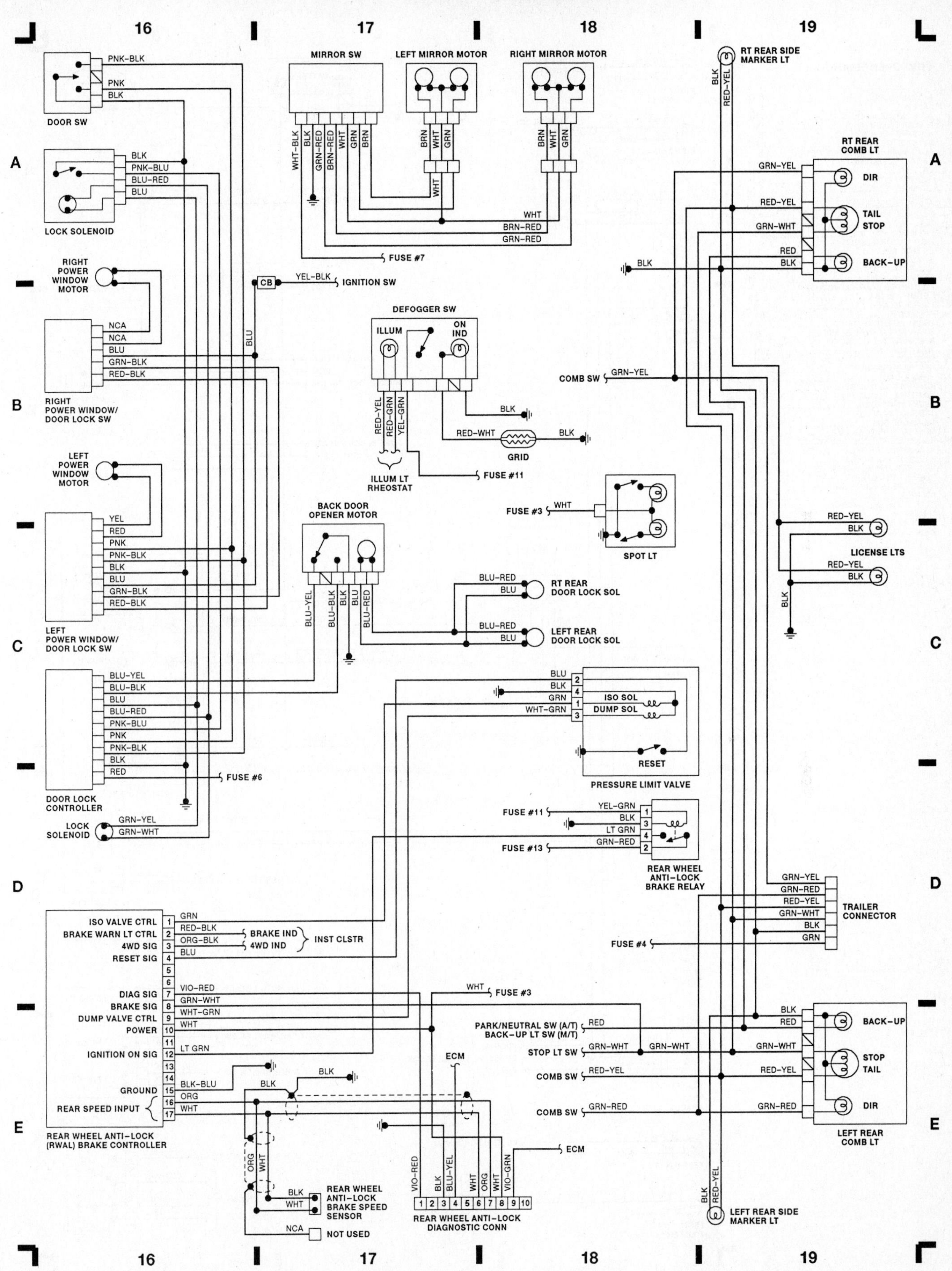

# 1991 WIRING DIAGRAMS
## Swift

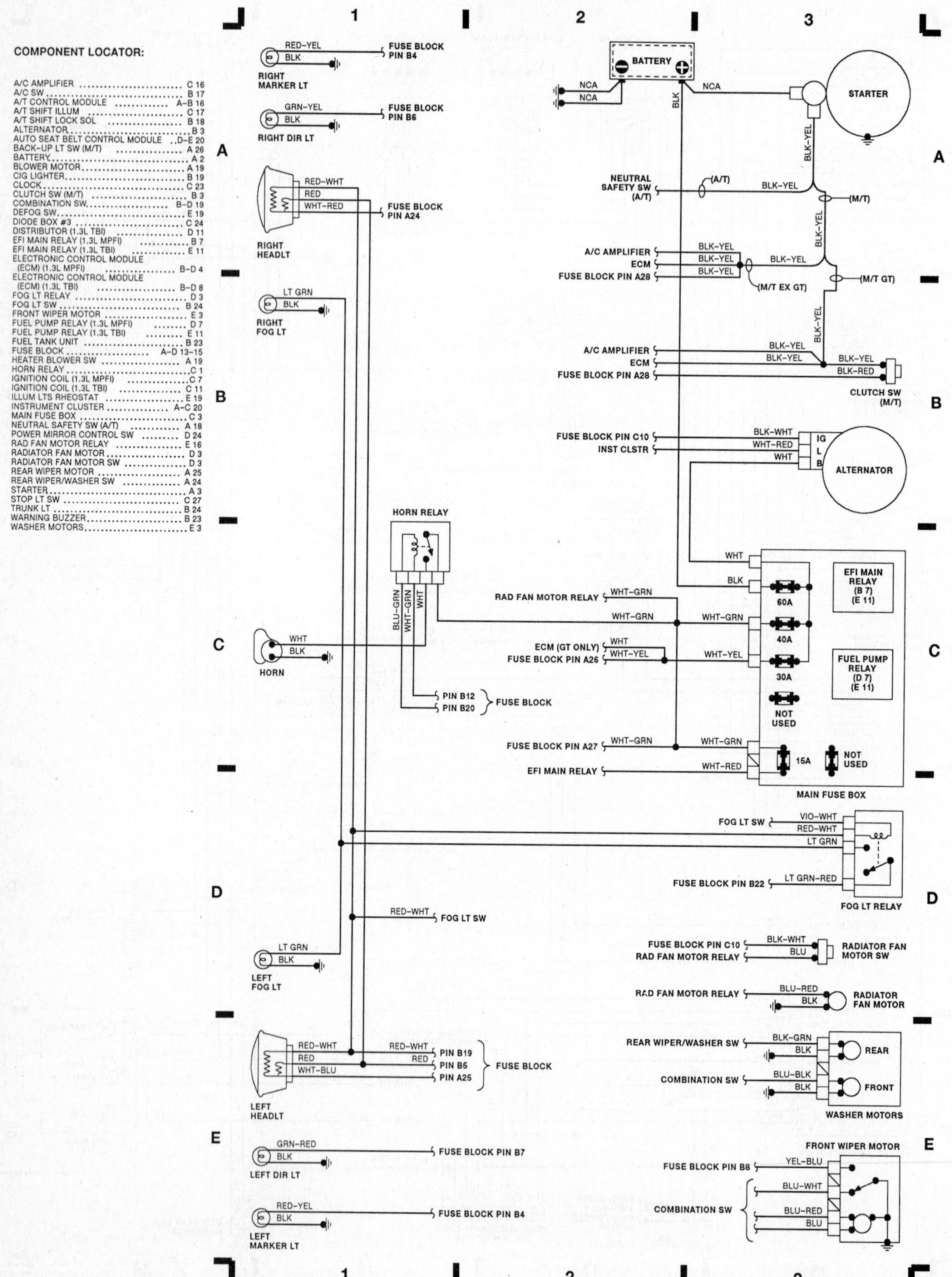

# 1991 WIRING DIAGRAMS
## Swift (Cont.)

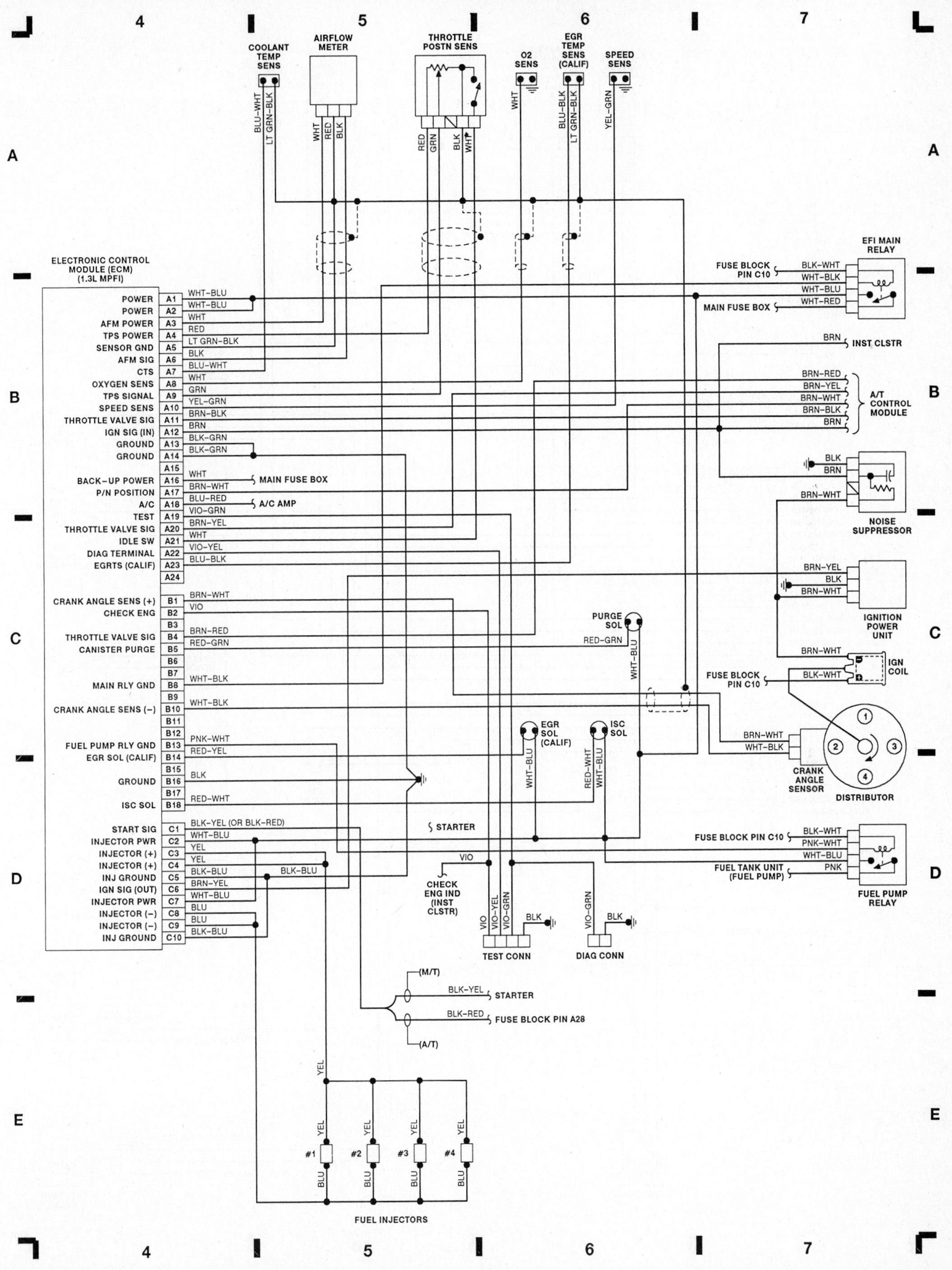

# 1991 WIRING DIAGRAMS
## Swift (Cont.)

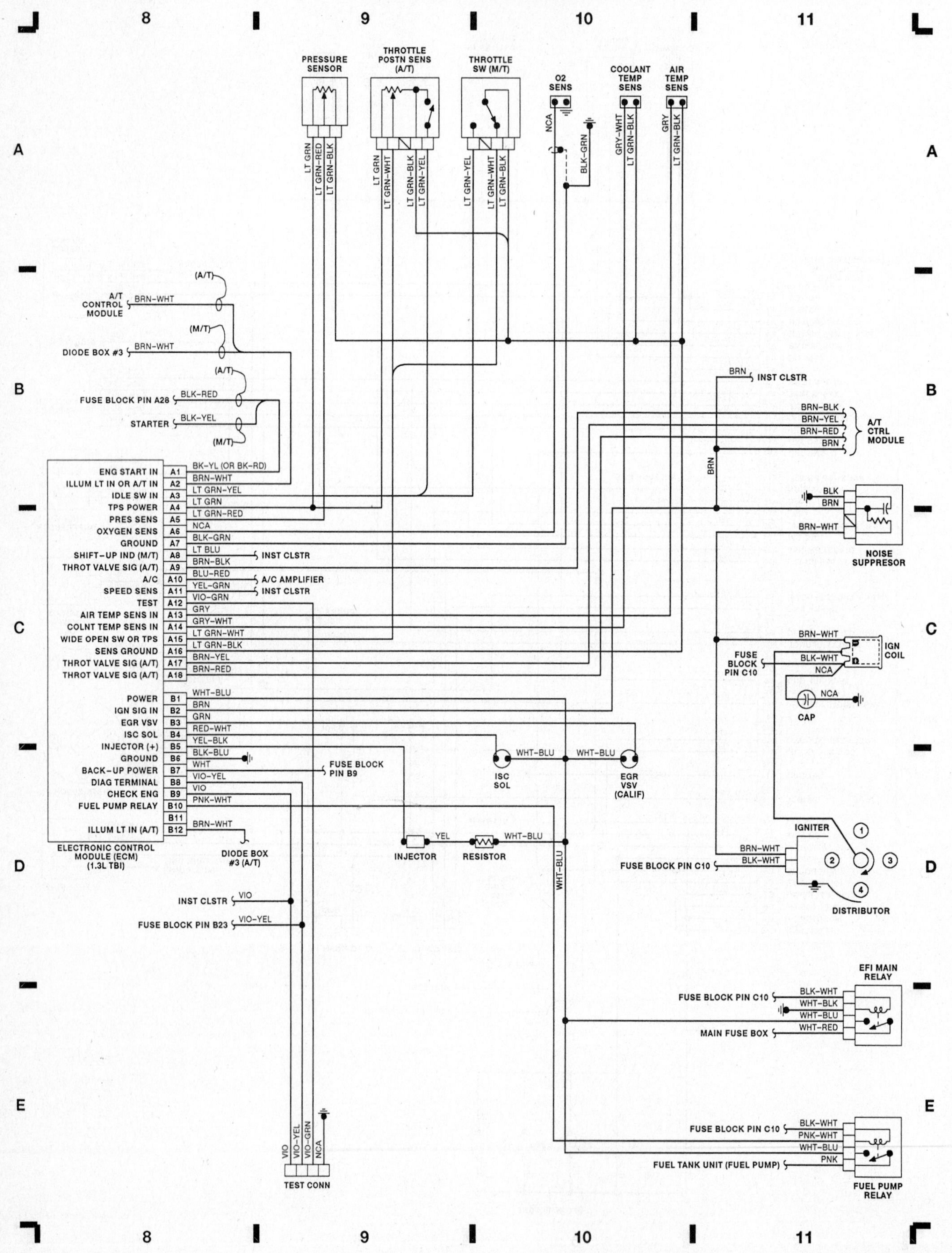

# 1991 WIRING DIAGRAMS
## Swift (Cont.)

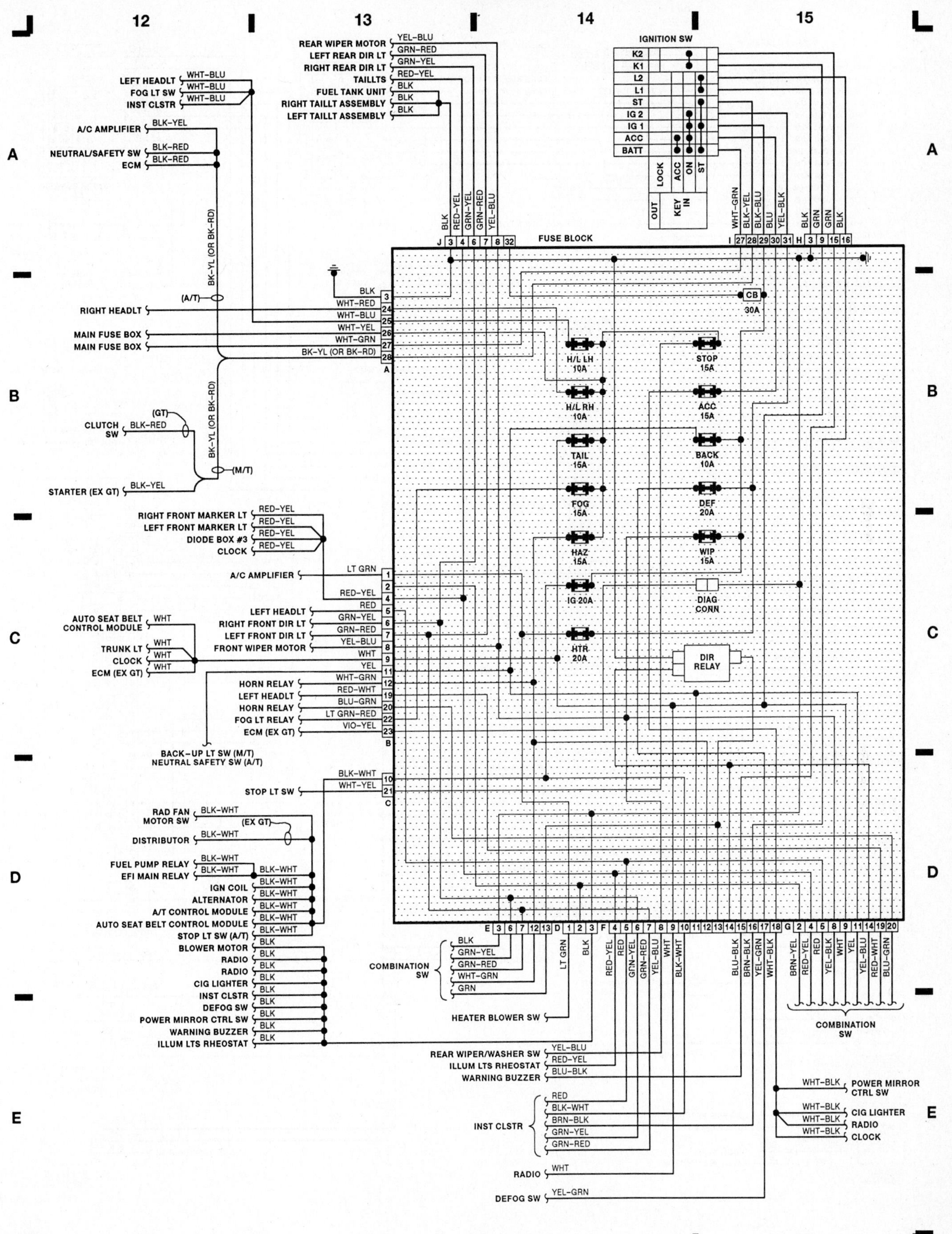

# 1991 WIRING DIAGRAMS
## Swift (Cont.)

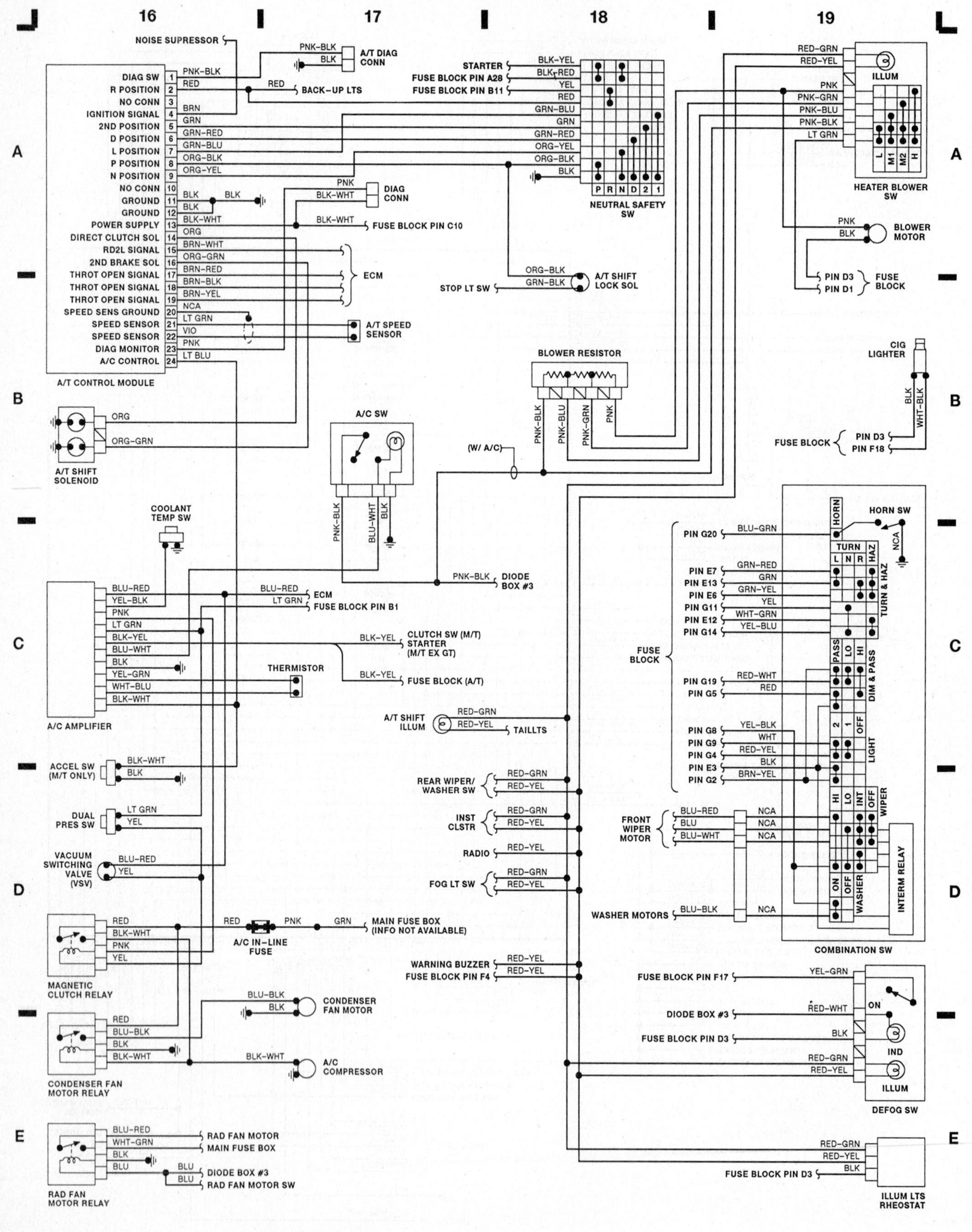

# 1991 WIRING DIAGRAMS
## Swift (Cont.)

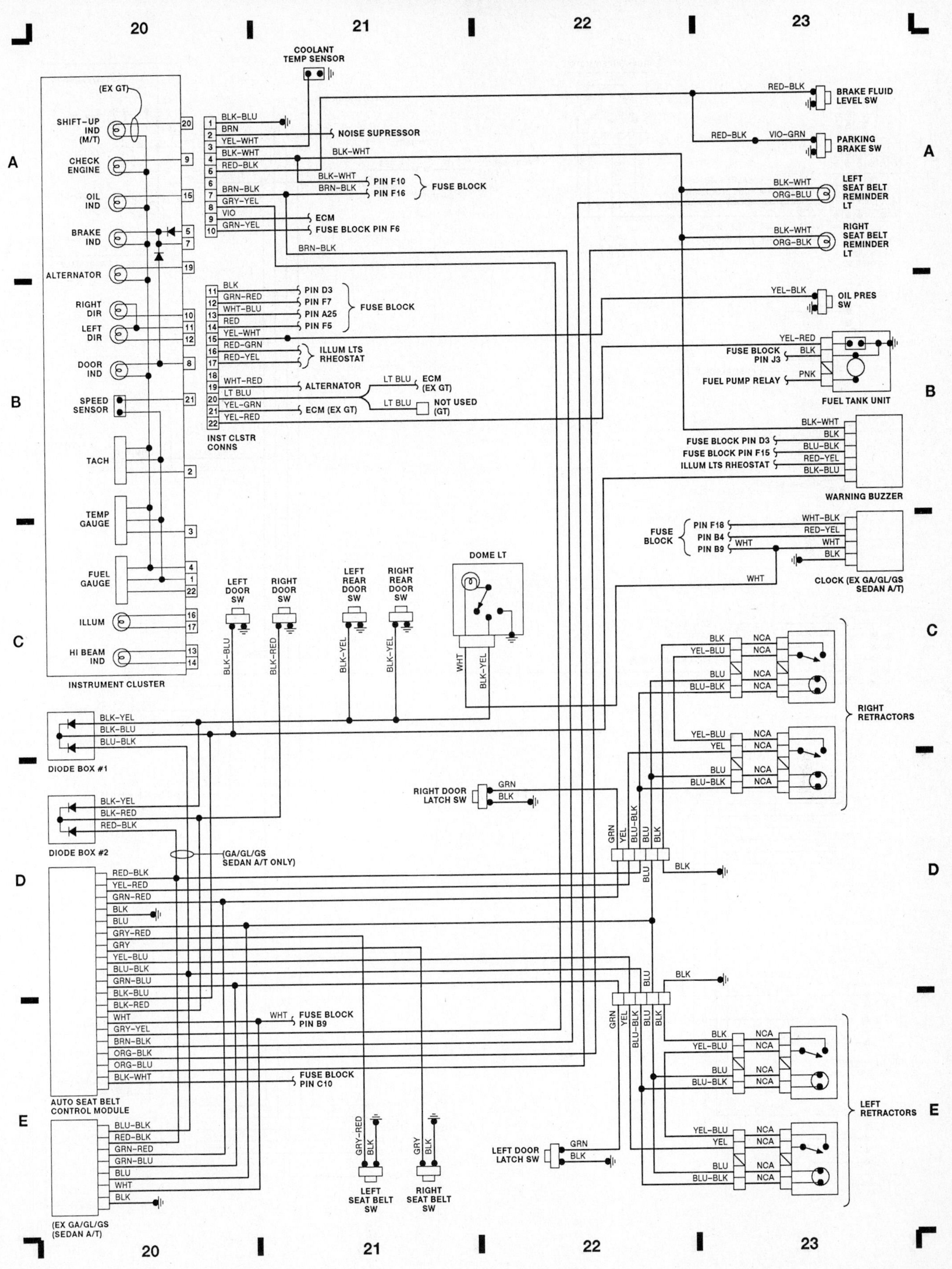

# 1991 WIRING DIAGRAMS
## Swift (Cont.)

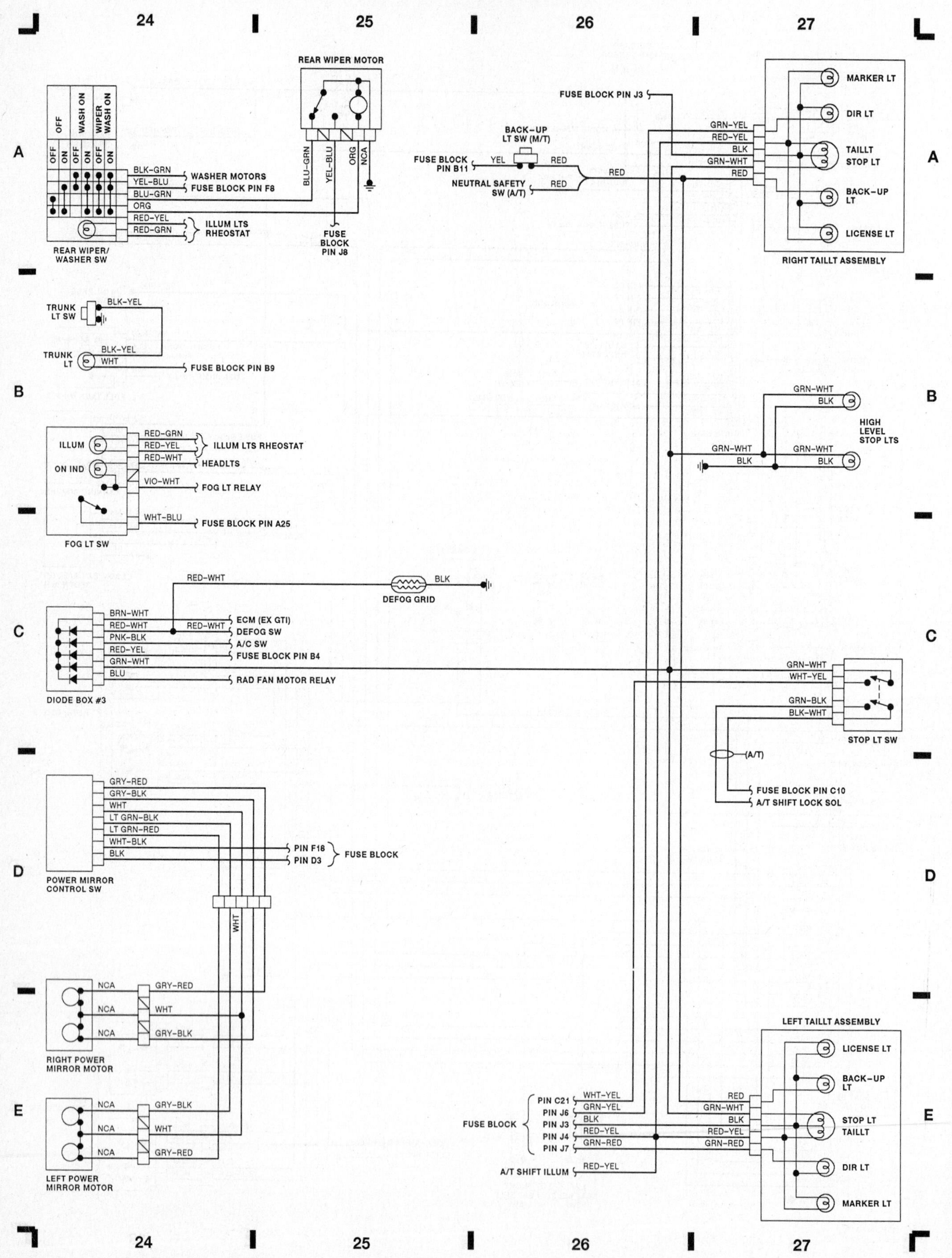

# 1991 SAFETY EQUIPMENT
# Instrument Panels

## Samurai, Sidekick, Swift

## DESCRIPTION

Standard instrument cluster includes speedometer, coolant temperature and fuel gauges. Oil pressure, brake and seat belt warnings are indicated by lights.

## TESTING

### FUEL GAUGE

Disconnect Yellow/Red wire connector at fuel tank sending unit. Connect a 12-volt, 3.4-watt bulb to harness side of connector, between power terminal and ground. Turn ignition on. Ensure light flashes on and off and fuel gauge needle deflects. If not, replace fuel gauge.

### FUEL GAUGE SENDING UNIT

Remove fuel gauge sending unit from vehicle. Connect an ohmmeter between sending unit connector terminals. With float in full (up) position, resistance should be 1-5 ohms. With float in empty (down) position, resistance should be 113-127 ohms. With float in 1/2 (middle) position, resistance should be 28.5-36.5 ohms. If resistance is not as specified, replace sending unit. *See Fig. 1.*

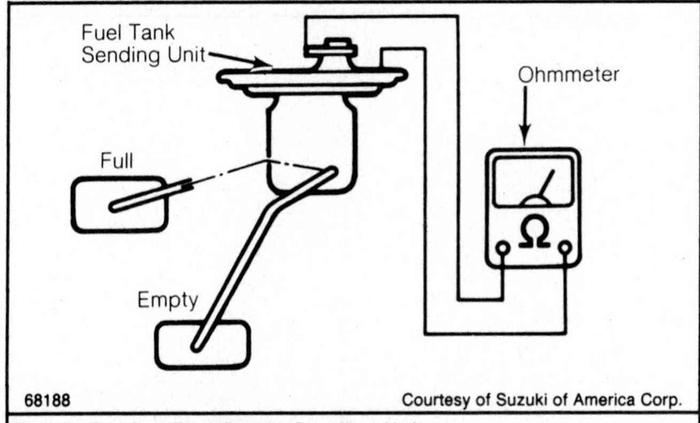


***Fig. 1: Testing Fuel Gauge Sending Unit***

### COOLANT TEMPERATURE GAUGE

Disconnect Yellow/White wire connector at temperature sending unit. Connect a 12-volt, 3.4-watt bulb to harness side of connector, between power terminal and ground. Turn ignition on. Ensure test light flashes and temperature gauge needle deflects. If not, replace temperature gauge. *See Fig. 2.*

### COOLANT TEMPERATURE SENDING UNIT

Warm sending unit in water. *See Fig. 2.* Using an ohmmeter check sending unit resistance. Sending unit resistance should be 134-179 ohms at 122° F (50° C), 48-57 ohms at 176° F (80° C) and 26-29 ohms at 212° F (100° C).

### OIL PRESSURE SWITCH

Disconnect wire to switch. Using an ohmmeter, measure resistance between switch terminal and body ground. There should be continuity with engine stopped; no continuity when engine is running. Replace switch as necessary.

### BRAKE WARNING INDICATOR

BRAKE warning indicator on instrument panel will illuminate when ignition switch is turned on. Light will go out when engine is started. If light does not go out, check brake fluid level switch and parking brake switch for a short in wiring harness.

**Brake Fluid Level Switch** – Using ohmmeter, measure resistance of brake fluid level switch at master cylinder. With float in up position, there should be no continuity. With float in down position, there should be continuity.

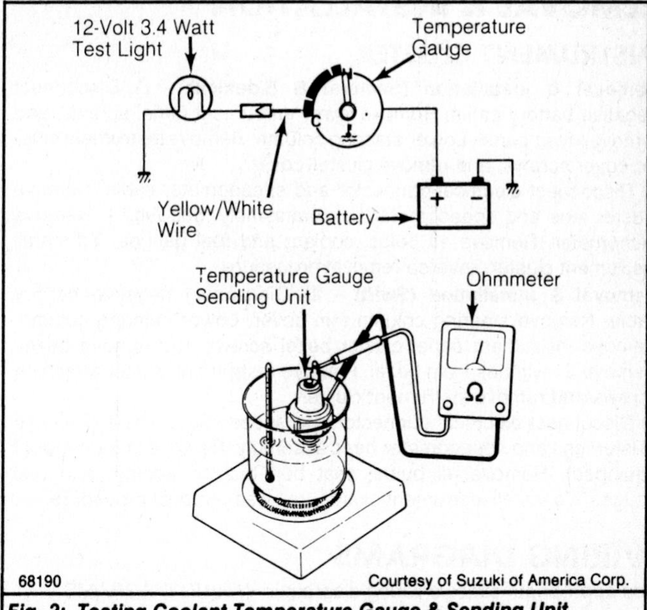


***Fig. 2: Testing Coolant Temperature Gauge & Sending Unit***

**Parking Brake Switch** – Using an ohmmeter, measure continuity between lead wire and ground, continuity should be present with parking brake applied. With parking brake off (switch deactivated), continuity should be infinite.

### SEAT BELT WARNING

Connect negative battery terminal to terminals No. 1 and 7 of controller. *See Fig. 3.* Connect positive battery terminal to terminals No. 4 and 5 of controller. Buzzer should sound for 4-8 seconds. Replace buzzer if it does not sound.

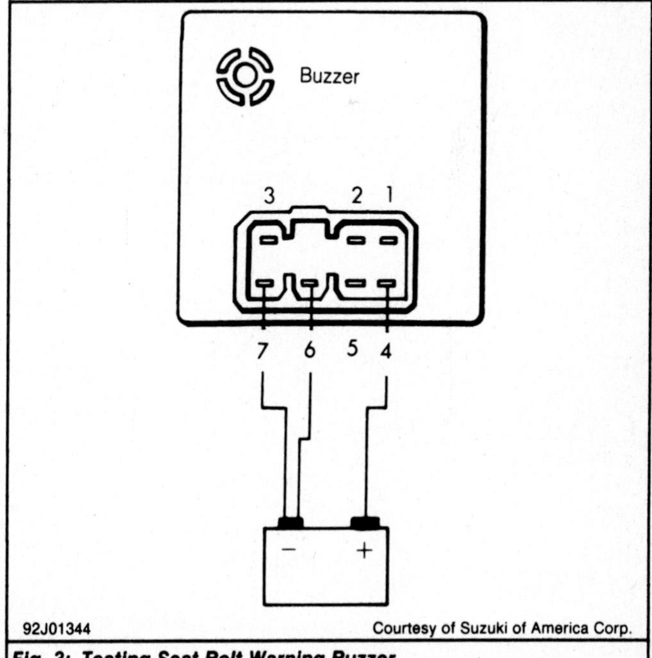


***Fig. 3: Testing Seat Belt Warning Buzzer***

# 1991 SAFETY EQUIPMENT
# Instrument Panels (Cont.)

## REMOVAL & INSTALLATION

### INSTRUMENT CLUSTER

**Removal & Installation (Samurai & Sidekick) – 1)** Disconnect negative battery cable. Remove lower instrument panel screws, and remove lower panel. Lower steering column. Remove instrument cluster cover screws, and remove cluster cover.

**2)** Disconnect electrical connector and speedometer cable. Remove cluster lens and speedometer head assembly. *See Fig. 4.* Remove tachometer. Remove all bulbs, coolant and fuel gauges. To install instrument cluster, reverse removal procedure.

**Removal & Installation (Swift) – 1)** Disconnect negative battery cable. Remove steering column trim cover. Lower steering column. Remove instrument panel cluster bezel screws and remove bezel. Remove 2 switches from bezel. Remove instrument cluster attaching screws and remove instrument cluster.

**2)** Disconnect electrical connector and speedometer cable. Remove cluster lens and speedometer head assembly. Remove tachometer (if equipped). Remove all bulbs, seat belt buzzer, coolant and fuel gauges. To install instrument cluster, reverse removal procedure.

## WIRING DIAGRAMS

See appropriate chassis wiring diagram in WIRING DIAGRAMS.

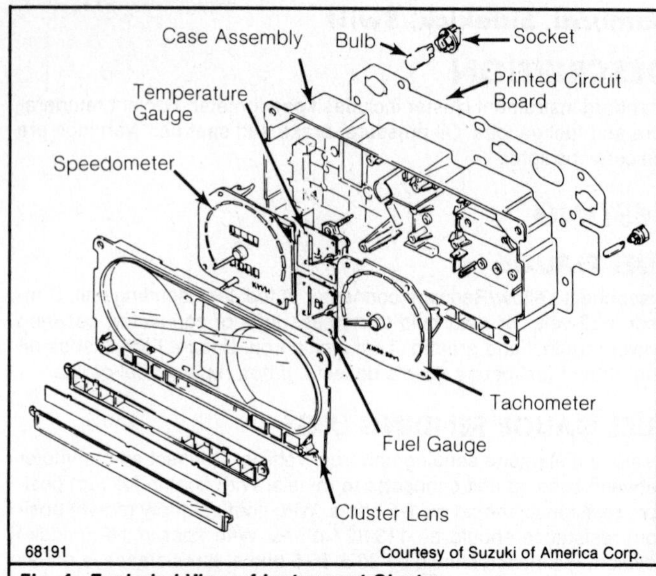


**Fig. 4: Exploded View of Instrument Cluster (Samurai Shown; Sidekick Is Similar)**

# 1991 SAFETY EQUIPMENT
# Rear Window Defogger

## Samurai, Sidekick, Swift

## TROUBLE SHOOTING

**Defogger Inoperative** – Check fuse, defogger switch and defogger wiring.
**Indicator Light Inoperative** – Check switch and wiring.

## TESTING

### DEFOGGER SWITCH TEST

Disconnect defogger switch connectors. Using an ohmmeter, check continuity across switch terminals. See DEFOGGER SWITCH CONTINUITY table.

***DEFOGGER SWITCH CONTINUITY***

| Switch Position | Terminal-To-Terminal (Wire Color) |
|---|---|
| Samurai | |
| Off | RED-BLK, RED/YEL-RED/GRN |
| On | YEL/GRN-RED-BLK, RED/YEL-RED/GRN |
| Sidekick & Swift | |
| Off | RED/WHT-BLK, [1] BLK-RED/YEL |
| On | YEL/GRN-RED/WHT-BLK, [1] BLK-RED/YEL |

[1] – Black wire has Red/Green tracer.

### GRID FILAMENT TEST

**1)** With ignition switch in ACC position and defogger switch activated, test filaments with voltmeter. Wrap negative probe of voltmeter with foil and press against filament. *See Fig. 1.*

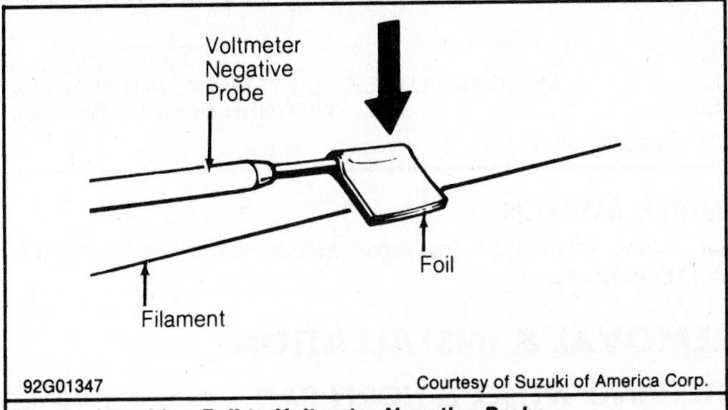


***Fig. 1: Attaching Foil to Voltmeter Negative Probe***

**2)** Attach positive probe of voltmeter to heat filament positive terminal. Slowly slide negative probe along filament from positive heat wire terminal to negative heat wire terminal. *See Fig. 2.*

**3)** If voltage read 4-6 volts, wire is good. If voltage reads 0 volts, wire is damaged between wire center and ground. If voltage reads 10 volts, wire is damaged between wire center and positive end.

**4)** If filament is good, voltage will read 12 volts at positive end and decrease as probe is moved towards negative end. If voltmeter needle fluctuates, damaged area of filament has been located.

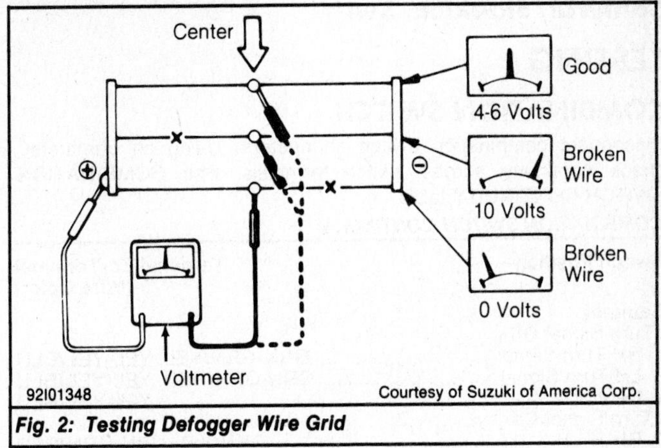


***Fig. 2: Testing Defogger Wire Grid***

## ON-VEHICLE SERVICE

### GRID FILAMENT REPAIR

**1)** If necessary, use razor blade or equivalent to remove small amount of silicone covering from damaged area, to expose grid line. Clean exposed broken grid line area with alcohol. Place masking tape along both sides of grid line area to be repaired. *See Fig. 3.*

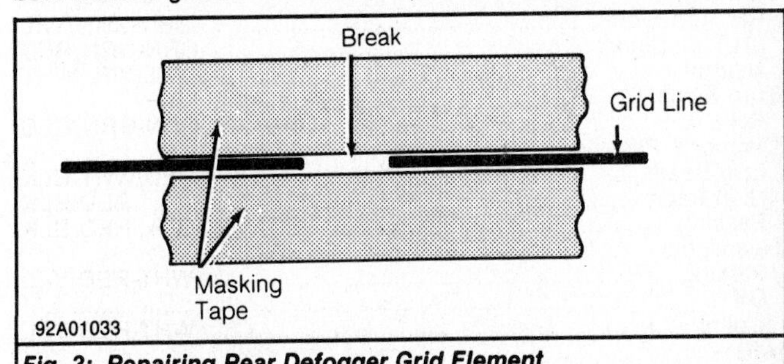


***Fig. 3: Repairing Rear Defogger Grid Element***

**2)** Thoroughly mix small amount of repair agent and apply to grid line break area, overlapping both lines. After a couple of minutes, carefully remove tape from line edges. DO NOT touch repaired area or operate defogger for 24 hours.

## REMOVAL & INSTALLATION

### DEFOGGER SWITCH

Disconnect negative battery cable. Remove defogger switch from instrument panel and disconnect electrical connectors. To install, reverse removal procedure.

## WIRING DIAGRAMS

See appropriate chassis wiring diagram in WIRING DIAGRAMS.

# 1991 SAFETY EQUIPMENT
# Steering Column Switches

**Samurai, Sidekick, Swift**

## TESTING

### COMBINATION SWITCH

Disconnect combination switch connectors. Using an ohmmeter, check continuity across switch terminals. See COMBINATION SWITCH CONTINUITY table.

***COMBINATION SWITCH CONTINUITY***

| Switch Position | Terminal-To-Terminal (Wire Color) |
|---|---|
| **Samurai** | |
| Turn Signal Off | |
| RH Turn Signal | GRN-GRN/YEL, YEL-YEL/BLU |
| LH Turn Signal | GRN-GRN/RED, YEL-YEL/BLU |
| Neutral | YEL-YEL/BLU |
| Turn Signal On | |
| RH-N-LH | GRN/YEL-GRN-GRN/RED |
| Dimmer & Passing | |
| Low Beam | RED/WHT-BLK |
| High Beam | RED-BLK |
| Passing | RED-BLK |
| Headlights | |
| Parking | WHT/YEL-RED/BLK |
| Off | [1] |
| Lights | WHT/YEL-RED/BLK |
| **Sidekick** | |
| Turn Signal Off | |
| RH Turn Signal | GRN-GRN/YEL |
| LH Turn Signal | GRN-GRN/RED |
| Neutral | YEL-YEL/WHT |
| Turn Signal On | |
| RH-N-LH | GRN/YEL-GRN-GRN/RED |
| Dimmer & Passing | |
| Low Beam | RED/WHT-BLK |
| High Beam | RED-BLK |
| Passing | RED/WHT-BLK, RED-BLK |
| Headlights | |
| Parking | WHT-RED/YEL |
| Off | [1] |
| Lights | WHT-RED/YEL |
| **Swift** | |
| Turn Signal Off | |
| RH Turn Signal | GRN-GRN/YEL |
| LH Turn Signal | GRN-GRN/RED |
| Neutral | YEL-YEL/BLU |
| Turn Signal On | |
| RH-N-LH | GRN/YEL-GRN-GRN/RED |
| Dimmer & Passing | |
| Low Beam | BRN/YEL-RED/WHT |
| High Beam | BRN/YEL-RED |
| Passing | BRN/YEL-RED/WHT, RED-BLK |
| Headlights | |
| Parking | WHT-RED/YEL |
| Off | [1] |
| Lights | WHT-RED/YEL, BLK-BRN/YEL |

[1] - No continuity.

### DAYTIME RUNNING LIGHT SWITCH

Disconnect daytime running light switch connector. Using an ohmmeter, check continuity across switch terminals. See DAYTIME RUNNING LIGHT SWITCH CONTINUITY table.

***DAYTIME RUNNING LIGHT SWITCH CONTINUITY***

| Switch Position | Terminal-To-Terminal (Wire Color) |
|---|---|
| Off | [1] |
| Parking | [1] |
| Lights | BRN/YEL-BLK |
| High Beam | BRN/YEL-RED |
| Low Beam | RED/GRN-BRN/YEL |
| Passing | RED/GRN-BRN/YEL, BRN-RED |

[1] - No continuity.

### HAZARD WARNING SWITCH

Disconnect hazard waring switch connectors. Using an ohmmeter, check continuity across switch terminals. See HAZARD WARNING SWITCH CONTINUITY table.

***HAZARD WARNING SWITCH CONTINUITY***

| Switch Position | Terminal-To-Terminal (Wire Color) |
|---|---|
| Samurai & Swift | |
| Off | [1] |
| Hazard | WHT/GRN-YEL/BLU |
| Sidekick | |
| Hazard | WHT/GRN-YEL/WHT |

[1] - No continuity.

### HORN SWITCH

Horn switch has a Blue/Green wire and produces no continuity.

### IGNITION SWITCH

Disconnect ignition switch connectors. Using an ohmmeter, check continuity across switch terminals. See IGNITION SWITCH CONTINUITY table.

***IGNITION SWITCH CONTINUITY***

| Switch Position | Terminal-To-Terminal (Wire Color) |
|---|---|
| **Samurai** | |
| Off | BLK/GRN-BLK |
| ACC | WHT/YEL-BLU |
| On | WHT/YEL-BLU-BLK/BLU |
| Start | WHT/YEL-BLK/BLU-BLK/RED |
| **Sidekick** | |
| Off | [1] |
| ACC | WHT/GRN-BLU |
| On | WHT/GRN-BLU-BLK/BLU-YEL/BLK, WHT-BLU/BLK |
| Start | WHT/GRN-BLK/BLU-BLK/RED, VIO/RED-BLK |
| **Swift** | |
| Off | [1] |
| ACC | WHT/GRN-BLU |
| On | WHT/GRN-BLU-BLK/BLU-YEL/BLK, WHT-BLU/BLK |
| Start | WHT/GRN-BLK/BLU-BLK/YEL |

[1] - No continuity.

### WIPER SWITCH

For testing information for wiper switch, see WIPER/WASHER SYSTEMS article.

## REMOVAL & INSTALLATION

### STEERING WHEEL & HORN PAD

**Removal (Samurai & Sidekick)** - Disconnect negative battery cable. Pry horn pad from steering wheel. Remove steering wheel nut. Make reference marks on steering wheel and steering shaft for installation. *See Fig. 2.* Use Puller (09944-36010) to remove steering wheel from steering shaft. *See Fig. 1.*

**Installation** - To install, reverse removal procedure. Ensure reference marks align. Tighten steering wheel nut to 18-30 ft. lbs. (24-41 N.m).

**Removal (Swift)** - Disconnect negative battery cable. Remove horn pad by pulling upward. *See Fig. 9.* Remove steering wheel nut. Remove steering wheel upper cover and disconnect horn connector. *See Fig. 9.* Make reference marks on steering wheel and steering shaft for later installation. *See Fig. 2.* Use Puller (09944-36010) to remove steering wheel from steering shaft. *See Fig. 1.*

**Installation** - To install, reverse removal procedure. Ensure reference marks align. Tighten steering wheel nut to 18-30 ft. lbs. (24-41 N.m).

### COMBINATION SWITCH

**Removal & Installation (Samurai & Sidekick)** - Remove steering wheel. See STEERING WHEEL & HORN PAD. Remove screws and

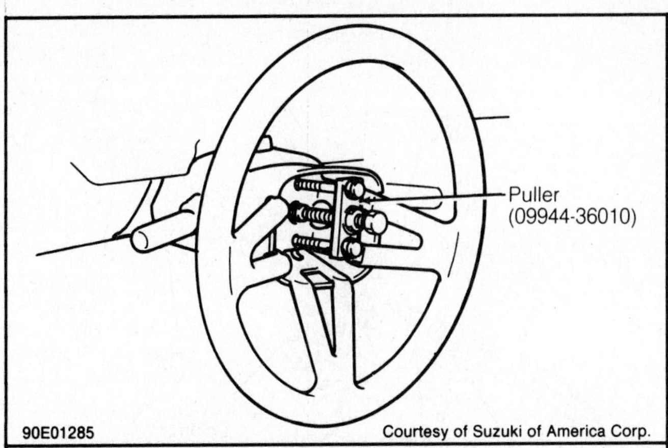


*Fig. 1: Using Puller to Remove Steering Wheel*

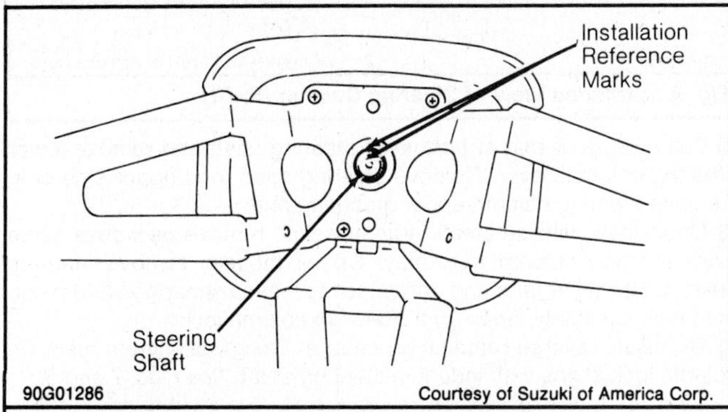


*Fig. 2: Making Steering Wheel-To-Steering Shaft Alignment Marks*

steering column covers. Disconnect combination switch connectors. Remove bottom screws and combination switch. *See Fig. 3 or 4.* To install, reverse removal procedure.

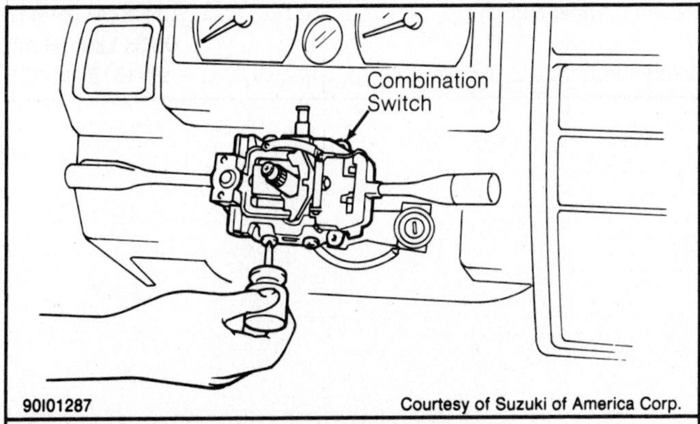


*Fig. 3: Removing Combination Switch (Samurai)*

**Removal & Installation (Swift)** – Remove steering wheel. See STEERING WHEEL & HORN PAD. Remove screws and steering column covers. Disconnect lead wire from combination switch at coupler. Loosen wire bands. Remove 3 mounting screws and combination switch. To install, reverse removal procedure. Ensure lead wire is not pinched between column covers during installation.

## IGNITION SWITCH & COLUMN LOCK

***NOTE: Manufacturer recommends removing steering column before removing steering column lock.***

**Removal (Samurai & Sidekick)** – **1)** Ensure front wheels are pointed straight-ahead. Disconnect negative battery cable. Remove steering

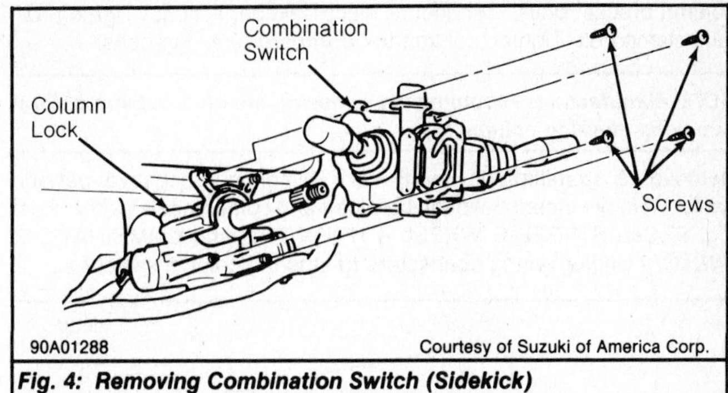


*Fig. 4: Removing Combination Switch (Sidekick)*

wheel, horn pad and combination switch. See STEERING WHEEL & HORN PAD and COMBINATION SWITCH.

**2)** Disconnect ignition switch connectors. Remove screw and ignition switch. *See Fig. 5.* To remove steering column lock, complete steps **3)** and **4)**.

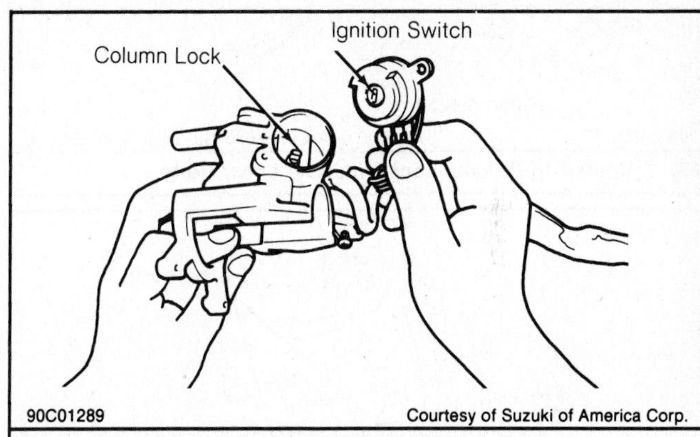


*Fig. 5: Removing Ignition Switch from Column Lock*

**3)** Remove lower instrument panel cover. Remove "U" joint clamp bolt. Separate steering shafts at "U" joint. Remove steering column floorboard bracket bolts. Remove steering column upper bracket bolts. On vehicles with automatic transmission, remove backdrive cable from steering column assembly. Pull steering column from floorboard.

**4)** Use a hammer and drift punch to loosen shear bolts from column lock assembly. *See Fig. 6.* Remove shear bolts and column lock.

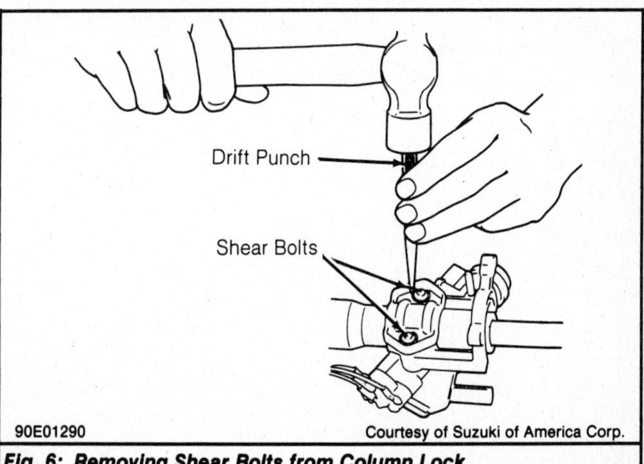


*Fig. 6: Removing Shear Bolts from Column Lock*

**Installation** – **1)** Install column lock on steering column with NEW shear bolts. Ensure alignment mark on column lock aligns with indent in steering shaft. *See Figs. 7 and 8.*

**2)** Insert column through floorboard into "U" joint. Install upper bracket retaining bolts. Install column-to-floorboard retaining bolts. Tighten

# 1991 SAFETY EQUIPMENT
# Steering Column Switches (Cont.)

column bracket bolts. Connect all electrical connections. Tighten "U" joint clamp bolt. Tighten column-to-floorboard retaining bolts.

***NOTE: Manufacturer recommends removing steering column before removing steering column lock.***

**Removal & Installation (Swift) – 1)** Disconnect negative battery cable. Remove steering wheel, horn pad and combination switch. See *Fig. 9.* See STEERING WHEEL & HORN PAD and COMBINATION SWITCH. Unplug wiring connectors to steering column switches.

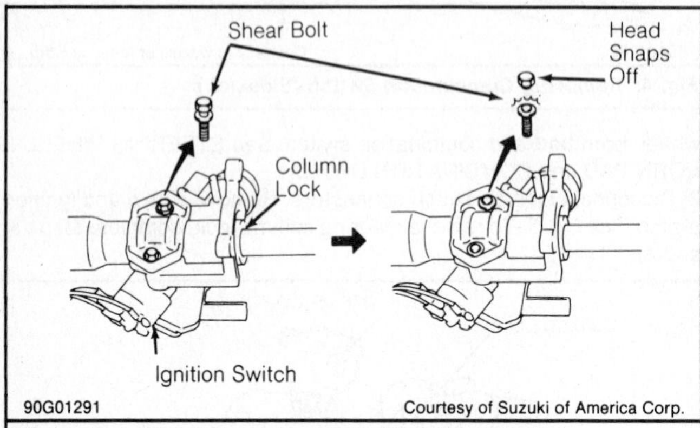


***Fig. 7: Installing Column Lock with New Shear Bolts***

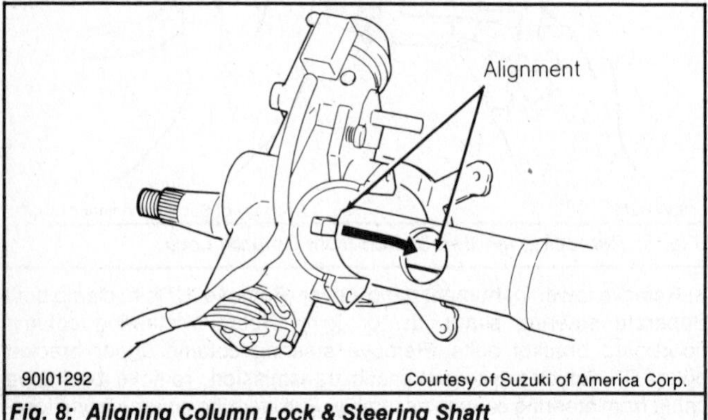


***Fig. 8: Aligning Column Lock & Steering Shaft***

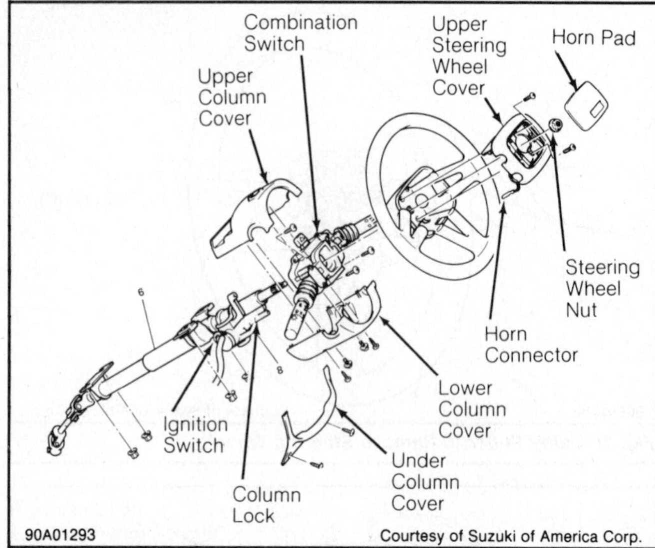


***Fig. 9: Exploded View of Steering Column (Swift)***

**2)** Pull back floor mat at bottom of steering shaft and remove lower steering column cover. Remove steering shaft joint upper side bolt. Remove steering column upper mounting nuts.

**3)** On models with automatic transmission, remove backdrive cable from steering column assembly. On all models, remove steering column. Use a hammer and drift punch to loosen shear bolts from column lock assembly. *See Fig. 6.* Remove column lock.

**4)** To install, reverse removal procedure. Ensure alignment mark on column lock aligns with indent in steering shaft. *See Figs. 7 and 8.*

## TORQUE SPECIFICATIONS

***TORQUE SPECIFICATIONS***

| Application | Ft. Lbs. (N.m) |
|---|---|
| Flexible Joint Bolt/Nut | 11-18 (15-25) |
| Steering Shaft Joint Bolt | 15-22 (20-30) |
| Steering Wheel Nut | 18-30 (24-41) |
| | **INCH Lbs. (N.m)** |
| Column Floorboard Bracket Bolt | 97-1512 (11-17) |

# 1991 SAFETY EQUIPMENT
# Wiper/Washer Systems

## Samurai, Sidekick, Swift

## DESCRIPTION

A 2-speed wiper motor is standard on all models. An intermittent or 3-speed motor is optional. Washer system uses an electric pump mounted under fluid reservoir. A one-speed rear wiper/washer is available on Swift and Sidekick. Sidekick is also equipped with a mist wiper. When the mist wiper is activated, the wipers run at low speed with no washer fluid and will continue to run until deactivated.

## TESTING

### FRONT WIPER MOTOR

**Motor Test - 1)** Disconnect wiper motor connector. Connect a jumper wire from battery voltage to Blue wire terminal of wiper motor connector. Ground wiper motor. Low-speed revolutions should be 45-55 RPM. Connect battery voltage to Blue/Red wire terminal of connector. High-speed revolutions should be 68-78 RPM.

**2)** If wiper motor does not operate, operates at only one speed or less than specified RPM, check for open in wiring or faulty switch. If wiring and switch are okay, replace motor.

**Automatic Stop Test - 1)** Connect a jumper between battery voltage and Yellow/Blue wire on Sidekick, Yellow/Black wire on Swift or Yellow wire on Samurai. Connect a second jumper wire between negative battery terminal and wiper motor ground.

**2)** Use a paper clip jumper to short Orange and Blue/Green wire terminals. *See Fig. 1.* Motor should stop at park position. Remove paper clip and short same wires again. Motor should stop at same point. If motor does not stop at same point, replace motor.

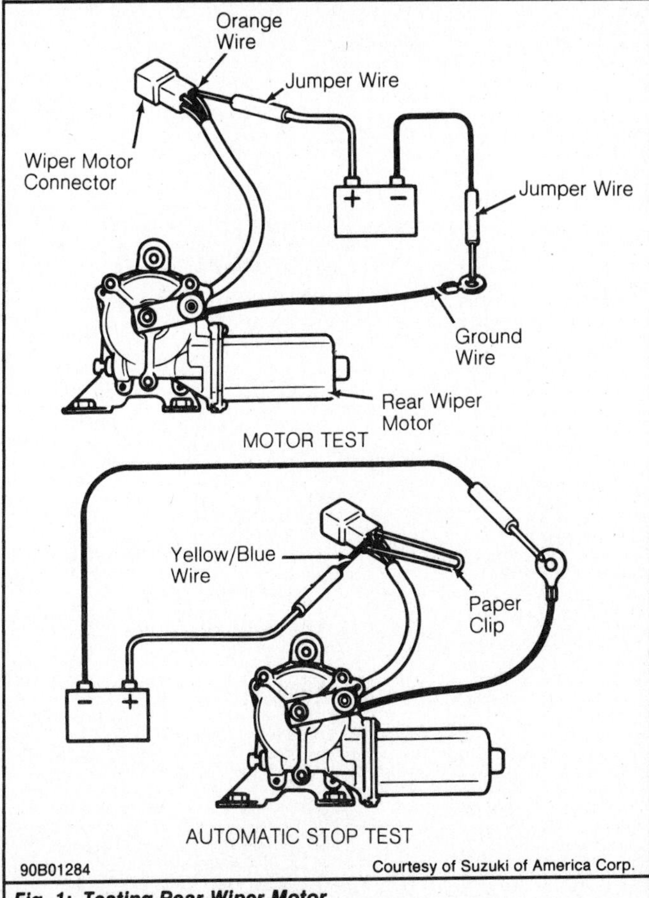


*Fig. 1: Testing Rear Wiper Motor (Swift & Sidekick; Front Wiper Test Is Similar)*

### REAR WIPER MOTOR

**Motor Test (Swift & Sidekick) -** Disconnect rear wiper motor connector. Connect a jumper between battery voltage and Orange wire. *See Fig. 1.* Connect a second jumper wire between negative battery terminal and wiper motor ground. Motor should rotate at 38-46 RPM. If motor RPM is not within specification, replace motor.

**Automatic Stop Test (Swift & Sidekick) - 1)** Connect a jumper between battery voltage and Yellow/Blue wire. Connect a second jumper wire between negative battery terminal and wiper motor ground.

**2)** Use a paper clip jumper to short Orange and Blue/Green wire terminals together. *See Fig. 1.* Motor should stop at park position. Remove paper clip and short same wires again. Motor should stop at same point. If motor does not stop at same point, replace motor.

### WIPER RELAY

Disconnect wiper/washer switch connector. Turn wiper switch to INTERMITTENT position. Connect a jumper from battery voltage to Yellow/Blue wire on Sidekick, Yellow/Black wire on Swift and Yellow/White wire on Samurai. Ground Black terminal of switch connector. If relay clicks, relay is operating properly.

### WIPER/WASHER SWITCH

Disconnect wiper/washer switch. Using an ohmmeter, check continuity across switch terminals. *See Figs. 2-5.*

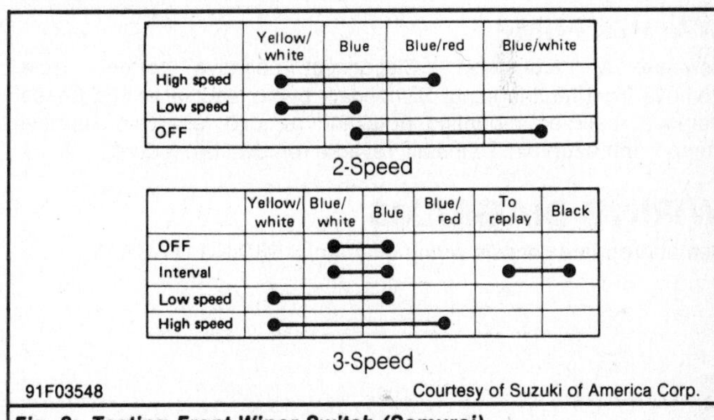

| | Yellow/white | Blue | Blue/red | Blue/white |
|---|---|---|---|---|
| High speed | ● | — | ● | |
| Low speed | ● | ● | | |
| OFF | | ● | — | ● |

2-Speed

| | Yellow/white | Blue/white | Blue | Blue/red | To replay | Black |
|---|---|---|---|---|---|---|
| OFF | | ● | ● | | | |
| Interval | | ● | ● | | ● | ● |
| Low speed | ● | — | ● | | | |
| High speed | ● | — | — | ● | | |

3-Speed

91F03548 Courtesy of Suzuki of America Corp.

*Fig. 2: Testing Front Wiper Switch (Samurai)*

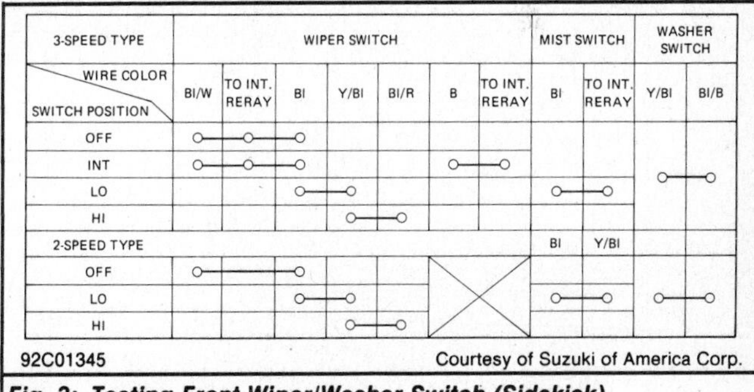

| 3-SPEED TYPE | WIPER SWITCH | | | | | | | MIST SWITCH | | WASHER SWITCH | |
|---|---|---|---|---|---|---|---|---|---|---|---|
| WIRE COLOR / SWITCH POSITION | BI/W | TO INT. RERAY | BI | Y/BI | BI/R | B | TO INT. RERAY | BI | TO INT. RERAY | Y/BI | BI/B |
| OFF | ○ | ○ | ○ | | | | | | | | |
| INT | ○ | ○ | ○ | | | ○ | ○ | | | | |
| LO | | | ○ | ○ | | | | ○ | ○ | ○ | ○ |
| HI | | | | ○ | ○ | | | | | | |
| 2-SPEED TYPE | | | | | | | | BI | Y/BI | | |
| OFF | ○ | — | ○ | | | X | X | | | | |
| LO | | | ○ | ○ | | X | X | ○ | ○ | ○ | ○ |
| HI | | | | ○ | ○ | X | X | | | | |

92C01345 Courtesy of Suzuki of America Corp.

*Fig. 3: Testing Front Wiper/Washer Switch (Sidekick)*

### BRUSH & COMMUTATOR

**Sidekick & Swift -** Check Orange wire on Sidekick and Blue wire on Swift to Black lead wire for continuity. If continuity is poor, check brush to commutator contact surface. Wipe clean with gasoline or smooth surface with sandpaper.

## REMOVAL & INSTALLATION

### WIPER MOTOR

**Removal & Installation -** Remove pivot shaft mounting nut and wiper arm. Open hood and unplug wiring connector. Remove wiper

# 1991 SAFETY EQUIPMENT
# Wiper/Washer Systems (Cont.)

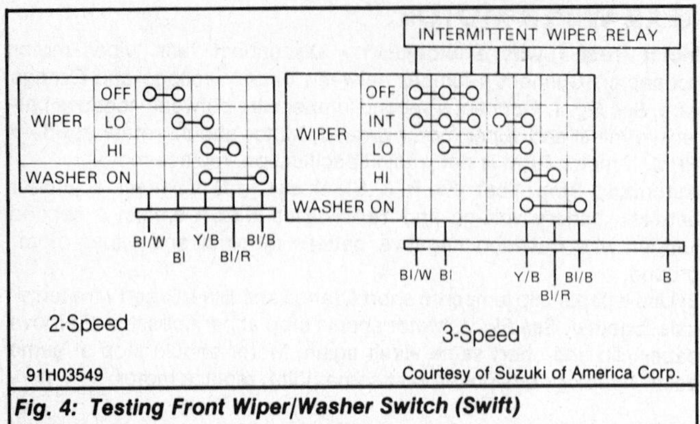


91H03549 Courtesy of Suzuki of America Corp.

***Fig. 4: Testing Front Wiper/Washer Switch (Swift)***

linkage assembly. Remove wiper motor mounting bolts. Remove motor with bracket. To install, reverse removal procedure.

## FRONT WIPER SWITCH

**Removal & Installation** – Remove horn pad and unplug horn cable connector. Remove steering wheel and steering column cover. Unplug combination switch connectors. Remove combination switch by lifting off toward end of steering shaft. To install, reverse removal procedure.

## WASHER PUMP

**Removal & Installation** – Disconnect negative battery cable. Remove front fender lining. Disconnect pump lead wires and hoses. Remove reservoir mounting nuts and remove reservoir. Remove pump from reservoir. To install, reverse removal procedure.

## WIRING DIAGRAMS

See appropriate chassis wiring diagram in WIRING DIAGRAMS.

| CONTINUITY BETWEEN TERMINALS | | |
|---|---|---|
| Switch Position | | Terminal-to-Terminal Continuity |
| Washer & Wiper | Wiper | |
| OFF | OFF | Bl/G – O |
| | ON | Y/Bl – O |
| WASHER ON | OFF | B/G – Y/Bl |
| | ON | B/G – Y/Bl – O |
| WASHER & WIPER ON | OFF | B/G – Y/Bl – O |
| | ON | B/G – Y/Bl – O |
| R/G, an illumination light lead wire of lighting switch, produces constant R/G – R/Y continuity. | | |

92E01346 Courtesy of Suzuki of America Corp.

***Fig. 5: Testing Rear Wiper/Washer Switch (Swift & Sidekick)***

# 1991 ENGINES
# 1.3L & 1.6L 4-Cylinder

## Samurai, Sidekick, Swift

***NOTE: For repair procedures not covered in this article, see ENGINE OVERHAUL PROCEDURES article in GENERAL INFORMATION.***

## ENGINE IDENTIFICATION

Engine code is stamped on rear portion of cylinder block at bellhousing (horizontal to oil filter). The Vehicle Identification Number (VIN) is stamped on a metal tag. On Samurai and Sidekick, tag is attached to left side of instrument panel near pillar. On Swift, tag is attached to top of instrument panel on driver's side. The sixth character of the VIN identifies engine model.

***ENGINE IDENTIFICATION CODE***

| Application | VIN |
|---|---|
| Samurai 1.3L | 3 |
| Sidekick 1.6L | 0 |
| Swift 1.3L (DOHC & SOHC) | 3 |

## ADJUSTMENTS

### VALVE CLEARANCE ADJUSTMENT

***NOTE: Swift DOHC engines have automatic valve lash adjusters. No adjustment is required.***

**1)** Ensure engine has reached normal operating temperature. Place No. 1 piston at TDC position. Remove distributor cap. Ensure rotor is pointing toward No. 1 distributor terminal.
**2)** If rotor is not correctly positioned, rotate crankshaft clockwise 360 degrees until No. 1 piston is at TDC of compression stroke. Remove rocker arm cover.
**3)** Check valve lash of cylinders No. 1, No. 2, No. 5 and No. 7. If valve lash is not as specified, loosen adjustment screw lock nut and turn adjustment screw until desired specification is obtained. See VALVE CLEARANCE SPECIFICATIONS table. Hold adjustment screw stationary and tighten lock nut. Rotate crankshaft 360 degrees clockwise.
**4)** Check valve lash of cylinders No. 3, No. 4, No. 6 and No. 8. Adjust valve lash as needed. Tighten adjusting screw lock nuts. Install rocker arm cover.

***VALVE CLEARANCE SPECIFICATIONS***

| Valve | Hot In. (mm) | Cold In. (mm) |
|---|---|---|
| Exhaust | .010-.012 (.25-.30) | .006-.008 (.15-.21) |
| Intake | .009-.011 (.23-27) | .005-.006 (.13-.17) |

## REMOVAL & INSTALLATION

***NOTE: For reassembly reference, label all electrical connectors, vacuum hoses and fuel lines before removal. Also place mating marks on engine hood and other major assemblies before removal.***

### FUEL PRESSURE RELEASE

**1)** Before beginning any work on fuel injection system or disconnecting any fuel lines, relieve fuel pressure. Place gear shift lever in Neutral or Park. Set parking brake.
**2)** On Swift, remove engine cooling reservoir from bracket and remove main fuse box cover. Remove main fuse box from body to access fuel pump relay connector. On all models, disconnect wire connector from fuel pump relay. *See Fig. 1, 2 or 3.*
**3)** Remove fuel cap from gas tank to allow pressure to equalize. Reinstall cap. Start engine and idle until engine dies. Crank engine 2 or 3 times to ensure lines are empty. Reconnect fuel pump relay connector.

### ENGINE

***NOTE: On Samurai, remove engine and transmission as an assembly.***

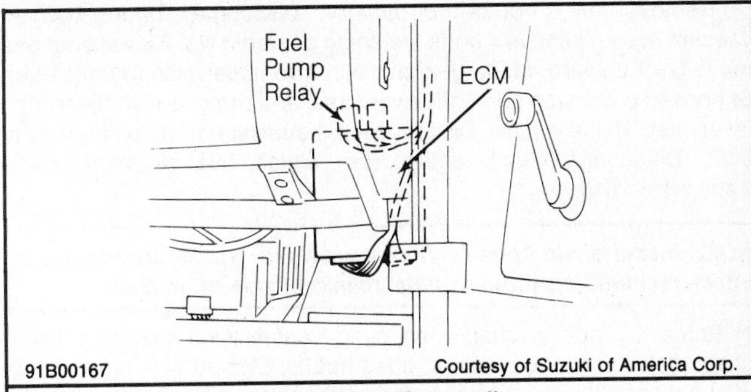


***Fig. 1: Locating Fuel Pump Relay (Samurai)***

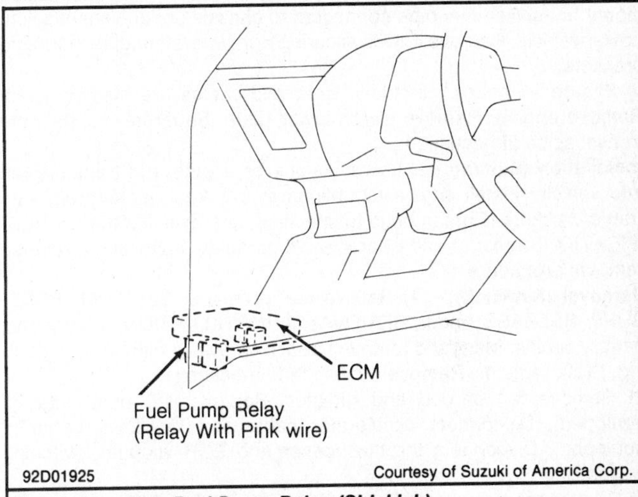


***Fig. 2: Locating Fuel Pump Relay (Sidekick)***

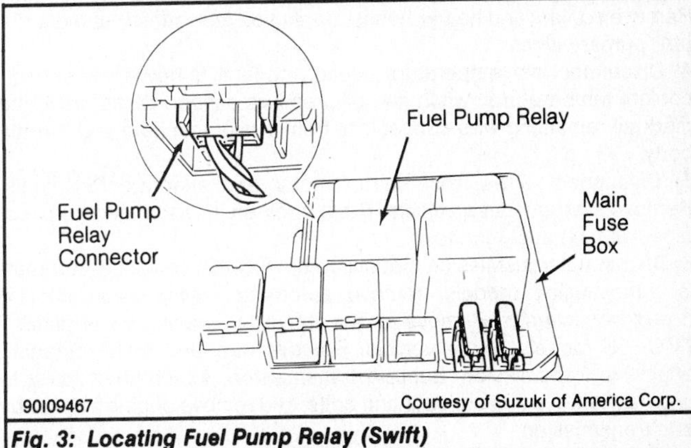


***Fig. 3: Locating Fuel Pump Relay (Swift)***

**Removal (Samurai) – 1)** Release fuel pressure. See FUEL PRESSURE RELEASE under REMOVAL & INSTALLATION. Disconnect battery cables. Mark and remove hood. Remove warm air hose. Disconnect breather hose from air cleaner case. Remove air cleaner case from throttle body and air inlet hose.
**2)** Mark and disconnect all remaining connectors from throttle body and intake manifold. Disconnect accelerator cable from throttle body. Disconnect and mark wires from starter motor and alternator terminals.
**3)** Disconnect fuel supply line and return hoses from throttle body. Disconnect wire connector from oil pressure sending unit and oxygen sensor. Disconnect wire connector from back-up light switch and 5th gear switch.
**4)** Disconnect distributor primary lead wires at distributor. Remove high tension wire from ignition coil. Drain radiator. Disconnect hoses from thermostat cap and inlet pipe. Remove cooling fan and clutch.

# 1991 ENGINES
# 1.3L & 1.6L 4-Cylinder (Cont.)

**5)** Remove fan shroud and radiator. Disconnect brake booster vacuum hose. Remove 4 bolts fastening gearshift No. 2 lever boot and move boot upward. Move gearshift No. 1 to upper side of shift lever.
**6)** Loosen 3 bolts on gearshift lever case, and remove shift lever from lever case. Raise vehicle. Disconnect exhaust pipe from exhaust manifold. Disengage clutch cable from clutch release lever. Drain transmission oil.

***NOTE: Install chain hoist on hooks provided. Hooks are located on intake manifold side and exhaust manifold side of engine.***

**7)** Remove propeller shaft connecting transmission case to transfer case. Install chain hoist on provided hooks. One hook is mounted on intake manifold side and another on exhaust manifold side of engine.
**8)** Remove exhaust center pipe mounting bracket and 4 transmission mount bolts. Remove pipe connected to chassis under transmission. Lower vehicle. Remove 4 bolts securing right and left engine mounting brackets.
**9)** Ensure all hoses, electrical wires and cables are disconnected. Remove engine. Remove clutch lower plate. Separate engine from transmission (if necessary).
**Installation (Samurai)** – Lower engine or engine and transmission into vehicle. Install engine mountings to brackets. Install bolts into frame brackets. Tighten bolts to specifications. See TORQUE SPECIFICATIONS table at end of article. To complete installation, reverse removal procedure.
**Removal (Sidekick)** – **1)** Relieve fuel pressure. See FUEL PRESSURE RELEASE under REMOVAL & INSTALLATION. Disconnect battery cables. Mark and remove hood. Remove air cleaner and ducting. Drain radiator. Remove cooling fan and clutch.
**2)** Remove fan shroud and radiator. Remove A/C condenser (if equipped). Disconnect accelerator cable and kickdown cable (if equipped). Disconnect throttle opener and EGR vacuum switching valves.
**3)** Disconnect connectors from fuel injector, TPS and idle speed control solenoid. Mark and remove fuel and vacuum hoses from engine. Remove coolant and heater hoses. Unplug oxygen sensor and distributor primary wires.
**4)** Disconnect air temperature sensor, coolant temperature sensor, coolant temperature switch and oil pressure sensor. Disconnect and mark all remaining wire connectors from intake manifold and throttle body.
**5)** Disconnect wires from starter motor and alternator terminals. Remove starter. Raise vehicle. Drain engine oil. Disconnect exhaust pipe from exhaust manifold.
**6)** On manual transmission models, remove clutch cable. On automatic transmission models, remove automatic transmission cooling hoses from clamps. Remove torque converter housing lower plate.
**7)** On all models, lower vehicle. Remove nuts and bolts fastening engine to transmission. Support transmission. Attach chain hoist to engine. Remove engine mounting bolts, and remove engine from body and transmission.
**Installation (Sidekick)** – Lower engine or engine and transmission into vehicle. Install engine mountings to brackets. Install bolts into frame brackets. Tighten bolts to specifications. See TORQUE SPECIFICATIONS table at end of article. To complete installation, reverse removal procedure.

***NOTE: On Swift, remove engine and transmission as an assembly.***

**Removal (Swift)** – **1)** Release fuel pressure. See FUEL PRESSURE RELEASE under REMOVAL & INSTALLATION. Disconnect battery cables. Remove battery, battery tray and hood. Drain coolant and remove radiator hoses.
**2)** Disconnect cooling fan wires. Remove air cleaner assembly. Remove radiator and cooling fan as an assembly. Disconnect fuel lines and heater hoses. Identify, mark and remove vacuum lines and hoses at engine.
**3)** Disconnect accelerator cable at throttle body. Remove fresh air duct. Disconnect speedometer and clutch cable with bracket at transmission. Label and disconnect all engine and transmission wiring.
**4)** Loosen A/C compressor adjusting bolt. Remove drive belt splash shield. Raise vehicle and disconnect exhaust pipe at manifold. Loosen A/C compressor pivot bolt. Remove A/C drive belt and compressor mounting bracket (if equipped).
**5)** On automatic transmission, disconnect gearshift control shaft and gearshift extension rod at transaxle. Remove engine torque rod bracket. On manual transmission, disconnect clutch control cable.
**6)** On all models, drain transmission and engine oil. Remove charcoal canister. Disconnect ball joints, and remove drive axles. See FWD AXLE SHAFTS article in DRIVE AXLES.
**7)** Lower vehicle. Attach chain hoist to engine. Disconnect rear and side engine mounts with brackets. Remove engine and transmission as an assembly.
**Installation (Swift)** – Lower engine or engine and transmission into vehicle. Install engine mountings to brackets. Install bolts into frame brackets. Tighten bolts to specifications. See TORQUE SPECIFICATIONS table at end of article. To complete installation, reverse removal procedure.

## INTAKE MANIFOLD

**Removal** – **1)** Release fuel pressure. See FUEL PRESSURE RELEASE under REMOVAL & INSTALLATION. Disconnect negative battery cable. Drain cooling system. Remove air intake hoses and air breather hoses.
**2)** Remove air cleaner assembly. Disconnect all electrical connections from intake manifold, injectors and throttle body. Disconnect vacuum hoses from intake manifold.
**3)** Disconnect coolant hoses from manifold and remove upper radiator hose. Remove fuel supply and return lines from delivery pipe. On Sidekick, remove throttle body. On Swift GT, remove injector connectors. On all models, disconnect all control cables.
**4)** Remove intake manifold-to-cylinder head bolts. Remove intake manifold and gasket. Remaining components can be removed from intake manifold as required.
**Installation** – To install, reverse removal procedure using new gaskets. Tighten bolts to specification. See TORQUE SPECIFICATIONS table at end of article. Adjust all control cables and fill cooling system.

## EXHAUST MANIFOLD

**Removal** – **1)** Disconnect negative battery cable. Remove air cleaner assembly (if necessary). Disconnect oxygen sensor wire connector.
**2)** Disconnect exhaust pipe from exhaust manifold. Remove exhaust manifold cover. Remove exhaust manifold-to-cylinder head bolts. Remove exhaust manifold and gasket.
**Installation** – To install, reverse removal procedure using new exhaust manifold gasket. Tighten bolts to specification. See TORQUE SPECIFICATIONS table at end of article.

## CYLINDER HEAD

**Removal (Samurai)** – **1)** Release fuel pressure. See FUEL PRESSURE RELEASE under REMOVAL & INSTALLATION. Remove intake and exhaust manifolds. See INTAKE MANIFOLD and EXHAUST MANIFOLD under REMOVAL & INSTALLATION.
**2)** Remove timing belt. See TIMING BELT under REMOVAL & INSTALLATION. Loosen cylinder head bolts in reverse order of tightening sequence. *See Fig. 4*. Loosen head bolts in 2 or 3 steps to prevent cylinder head warpage. Remove bolts and cylinder head.
**Removal (Sidekick & Swift)** – **1)** Release fuel pressure. See FUEL PRESSURE RELEASE under REMOVAL & INSTALLATION. Label and remove hoses, lines and electrical connectors for intake and exhaust manifold removal. Disconnect exhaust pipe from manifold.
**2)** It is not necessary to remove exhaust and intake manifolds at this time. Remove timing belt. See TIMING BELT under REMOVAL & INSTALLATION. Discharge A/C system. Remove compressor suction hose from suction pipe (if equipped).
**3)** Loosen cylinder head bolts in reverse order of tightening sequence. *See Fig. 4*. Loosen head bolts in 2 or 3 steps to prevent cylinder head

warpage. Remove bolts and cylinder head with intake and exhaust manifolds.

**Inspection (All Models) - 1)** Check cylinder head for evidence of water leakage or damage. Remove carbon from combustion chambers. Check cylinder head for cracks in intake and exhaust ports, combustion chambers and head surface.

**2)** Check head warpage at 6 locations. If warpage exceeds specification, cylinder head should be machined or replaced. See CYLINDER HEAD table under ENGINE SPECIFICATIONS at end of article.

**3)** Check intake and exhaust manifold seating faces on cylinder head for warpage. Warpage limit for manifold seating faces is .004" (.10 mm). If warpage exceeds specification, cylinder head should be machined or replaced.

**Installation (All Models) -** To install cylinder head, reverse removal procedure. Use NEW head and manifold gaskets. Tighten cylinder head in sequence, using 3 steps, to specifications. *See Fig. 4.* See TORQUE SPECIFICATIONS table at end of article. Adjust timing belt.

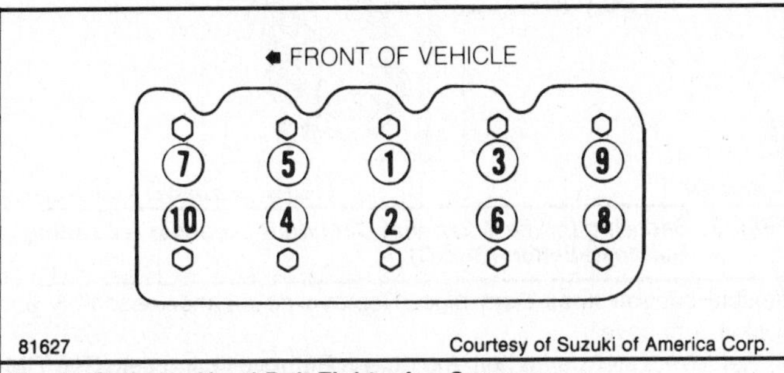


***Fig. 4: Cylinder Head Bolt Tightening Sequence***

## FRONT COVER OIL SEAL

**Removal - 1)** Remove water pump, crankshaft pulley and alternator. Remove timing belt cover and timing belt. See TIMING BELT under REMOVAL & INSTALLATION.

**2)** Drain engine oil. Remove oil dipstick and oil pan. Remove oil pump pick-up screen. Remove oil pump assembly. Remove oil pump rotor plate.

**3)** Mark outer gear with felt pen for reassembly reference. Remove inner and outer oil pump gears. Remove plug, relief spring and relief valve. Drive out oil seal.

**Installation - 1)** Drive in new oil seal. Ensure gears are assembled in same direction as originally installed. Apply thin coat of engine oil to lip portion of oil seal and inside surfaces of oil pump case and plate. Install inner and outer rotors.

**2)** Install gear plate. Tighten 5 screws. Install 2 oil pump pins, new dip stick "O" ring, new seal for oil pick-up tube and new oil pump gasket. Use Oil Seal Guide (09926-18210) to prevent damage to oil seal during installation of oil pump. *See Fig. 5.*

**3)** Apply engine oil to guide and install oil pump. Install dipstick guide with new seal. Install oil pan using silicone-type sealant. To complete installation, reverse removal procedure. Tighten bolts to specification. See TORQUE SPECIFICATIONS table at end of article.

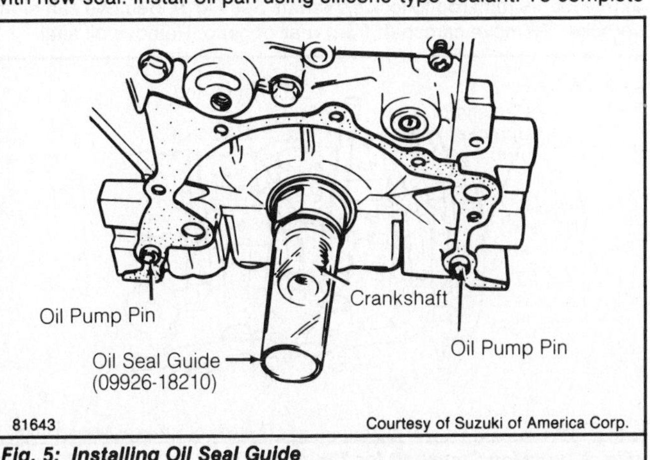


***Fig. 5: Installing Oil Seal Guide***

## TIMING BELT

**Removal (1.3L & 1.6L SOHC) - 1)** On Sidekick and Samurai, remove cooling fan and clutch. Remove fan shroud. Discharge A/C system and disconnect compressor flexible suction hose from suction pipe (if equipped). Remove A/C compressor belt (if equipped).

**2)** On Swift, raise vehicle and remove fender apron extension by pushing center pin into clip. DO NOT push in too far, as pin may fall into fender. On all models, loosen alternator and remove water pump pulley and belt.

**3)** Remove crankshaft pulley. On Swift, it will be necessary to remove center bolt to remove crankshaft pulley if engine is in vehicle. Remove timing belt cover. Move up and secure timing belt tensioner.

**4)** Mark belt with an arrow indicating direction of rotation for installation reference, and remove timing belt. Remove timing belt from camshaft and crankshaft sprocket.

**Installation - 1)** Loosen all valve adjusting screws fully before installing timing belt. Camshaft must be permitted to rotate freely during belt tension adjustment. Align timing mark on camshaft sprocket with "V" mark on timing belt inner cover. *See Fig. 6.*

**2)** Turn crankshaft clockwise until punch mark on crankshaft sprocket is aligned with arrow mark on oil pump. With timing marks aligned, install timing belt. Ensure drive side of belt is free of slack.

**3)** Move tensioner plate up with finger pressure, and loosely secure tensioner bolt. Turn crankshaft 2 revolutions clockwise to remove all slack from belt. Tighten tensioner nut and then tensioner bolt. See TORQUE SPECIFICATIONS table at end of article.

**4)** Ensure timing marks are aligned. Install timing belt outer cover and tighten to specification. See TORQUE SPECIFICATIONS table at end of article. Reverse removal procedure to complete installation. Adjust valve clearance. See VALVE CLEARANCE ADJUSTMENT under ADJUSTMENTS.

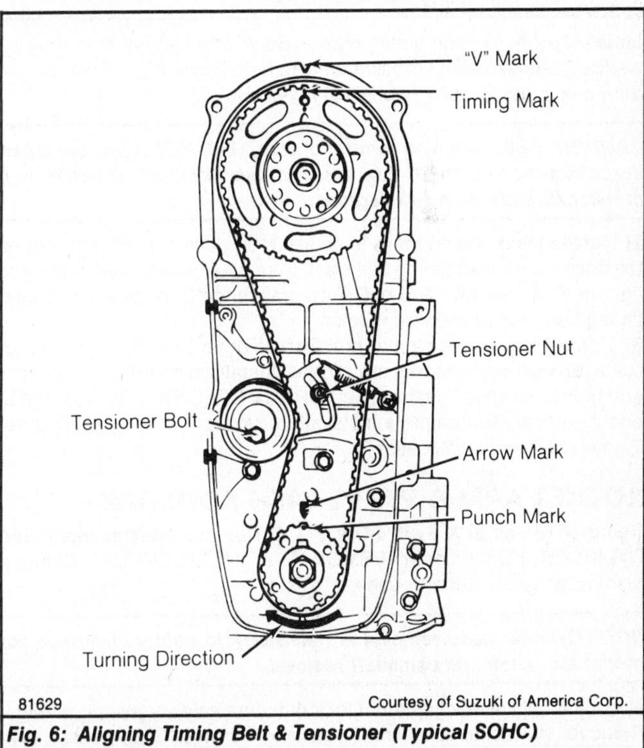


***Fig. 6: Aligning Timing Belt & Tensioner (Typical SOHC)***

**Removal (1.3L DOHC) - 1)** Remove negative battery cable. Remove air cleaner and airflow meter assembly. Raise vehicle and remove right fender apron extension by pushing center pin into clip. DO NOT push in too far, as pin may fall into fender. Remove water pump pulley and belt.

# 1991 ENGINES
# 1.3L & 1.6L 4-Cylinder (Cont.)

2) Remove crankshaft pulley 5-mm hexagon bolts. If engine is in vehicle, remove crankshaft pulley center bolt. Remove crankshaft pulley. Loosen right engine mount bolt, and push air cleaner bracket away from work area. Remove timing belt covers.
3) Align all sprocket timing marks with timing marks on engine. *See Fig. 7.* Move timing belt tensioner up and secure. Mark timing belt for direction of rotation if belt is to be reused. Remove timing belt from sprockets.

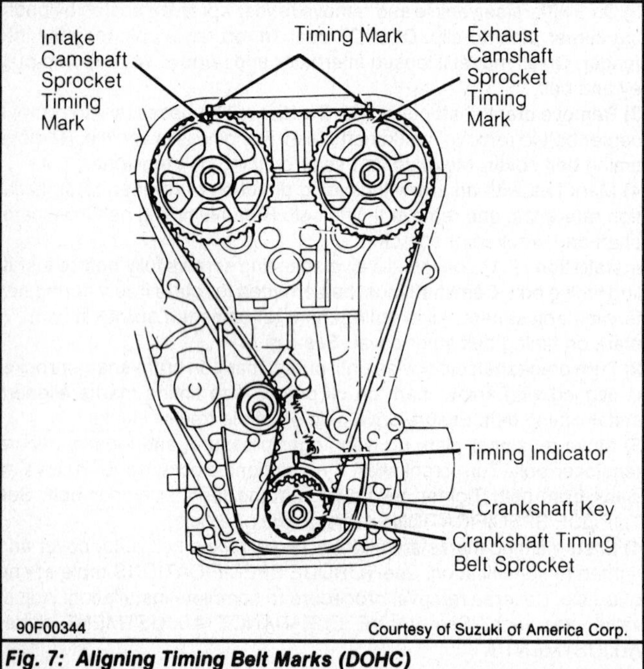


*Fig. 7: Aligning Timing Belt Marks (DOHC)*

**Installation - 1)** Align timing marks. Bolts with flanged nuts may be wedged between cam sprocket teeth to hold camshaft on timing mark during belt installation (if necessary). *See Fig. 8.*

***CAUTION: While aligning timing marks, DO NOT turn camshaft sprockets more than 20 degrees in either direction. DO NOT turn crankshaft more than 180 degrees.***

2) Install timing belt so there is no slack on drive side of belt. Adjust tensioner to remove timing belt slack from other side of belt, and hand tighten tensioner bolt and nut. Turn crankshaft 2 revolutions to seat timing belt, and readjust tensioner.
3) Tighten tensioner bolt and nut. Ensure drive side of belt is free of slack. Ensure timing marks are aligned. Install timing belt outer covers and tighten to specification. See TORQUE SPECIFICATIONS table at end of article. To complete installation, reverse removal procedure. Tighten bolts to specification.

## ROCKER ARM & VALVE LASH ADJUSTER

**Removal (Samurai & Swift SOHC) - 1)** Remove cylinder head. See CYLINDER HEAD under REMOVAL & INSTALLATION. Remove distributor and distributor case.

***NOTE: Cylinder head removal is necessary to obtain clearance for rocker arm shaft and camshaft removal.***

2) Loosen all valve adjustment lock nuts and valve adjusting screws. Remove 10 rocker arm shaft retaining screws. Slide rocker arm shaft(s) out of rear side of head assembly. Remove rocker arms and springs.
**Removal (Sidekick) - 1)** Disconnect negative battery cable. Remove hood, hood lock and hood lock support member. Remove front grille. Push center pin of clips to release grille clips.
2) Drain cooling system. Remove radiator, cooling fan and shroud. If vehicle has A/C, discharge refrigerant and disconnect compressor

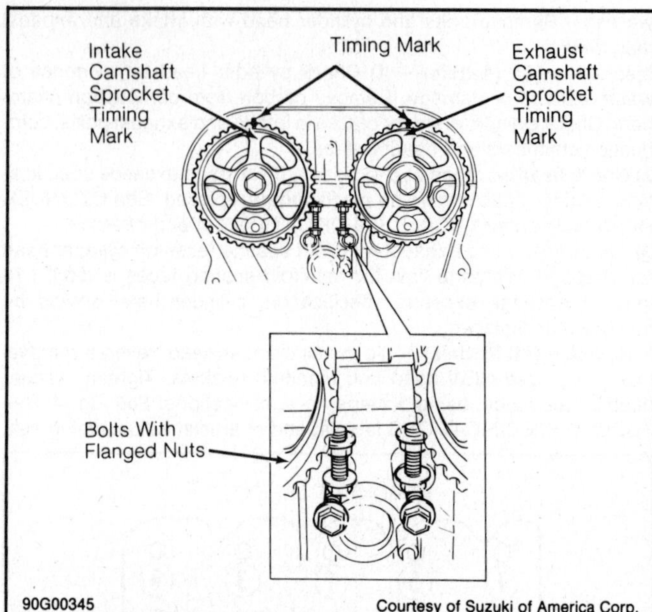


*Fig. 8: Securing Intake & Exhaust Camshaft Sprocket for Timing Belt Installation (DOHC)*

flexible suction hose from pipe. Remove air cleaner assembly and rocker arm cover.
3) Remove water pump belt and pulley. Remove timing belt. See TIMING BELT under REMOVAL & INSTALLATION. Insert .35" (9 mm) rod into hole on front part of camshaft to lock camshaft, and remove camshaft sprocket bolt and sprocket.
4) Loosen all valve adjustment lock nuts and valve adjusting screws. Remove rocker arm shaft retaining screws. Slide rocker arm shaft(s) out of front side of head assembly. Remove rocker arms and springs.
**Installation (All Models) -** To install, reverse removal procedure. Intake rocker shaft has a .55" (14 mm) stepped end. Exhaust rocker shaft has a .59" (15 mm) stepped end. Ensure intake rocker shaft stepped end faces front of engine and exhaust rocker shaft stepped end faces rear of engine. Adjust valve clearance. See VALVE CLEARANCE ADJUSTMENT under ADJUSTMENTS.

## CAMSHAFT

***NOTE: On SOHC models, cylinder head removal is necessary to obtain enough clearance for camshaft removal.***

**Removal (SOHC) - 1)** Remove cylinder head. See CYLINDER HEAD under REMOVAL & INSTALLATION. Remove rocker arms and shafts. See ROCKER ARM & VALVE LASH ADJUSTER under REMOVAL & INSTALLATION.
2) Use .35" (9 mm) rod to lock camshaft. *See Fig. 9.* Remove camshaft sprocket. Remove camshaft from rear of head. Remove oil seal.

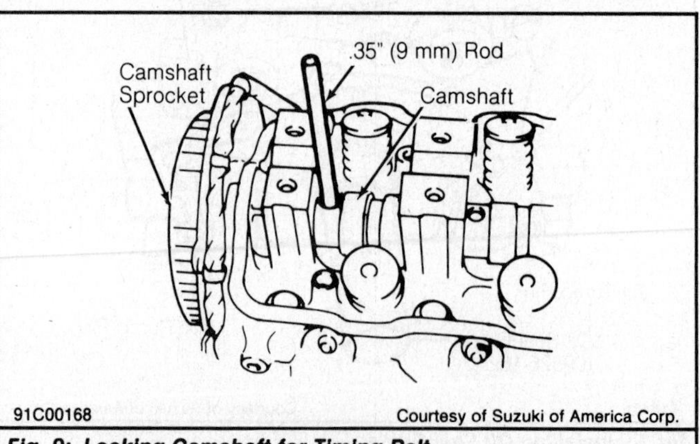


*Fig. 9: Locking Camshaft for Timing Belt Sprocket Removal (SOHC)*

**Removal (DOHC) - 1)** Remove negative battery cable. Remove timing belt. See TIMING BELT under REMOVAL & INSTALLATION. Turn crankshaft timing belt sprocket key to horizontal position, 180 degrees away from dipstick guide tube. *See Fig. 10.*
**2)** Remove cylinder head cover. Remove distributor. Remove camshaft sprockets. Install a brass rod in under camshaft in groove between lobes to lock camshaft into position. Remove camshaft sprocket bolts. Remove camshaft sprockets.
**3)** Remove camshaft bearing cap bolts in reverse order of tightening sequence. *See Fig. 11.* Loosen bolts in 2 or 3 steps to prevent warpage. Remove camshaft and oil seals. Valve lash adjusters can be lifted out of cylinder head (if necessary).

***CAUTION: Hydraulic valve lash adjusters cannot be disassembled or repaired. DO NOT apply force to adjuster body. If removed, keep immersed in container of clean engine oil.***

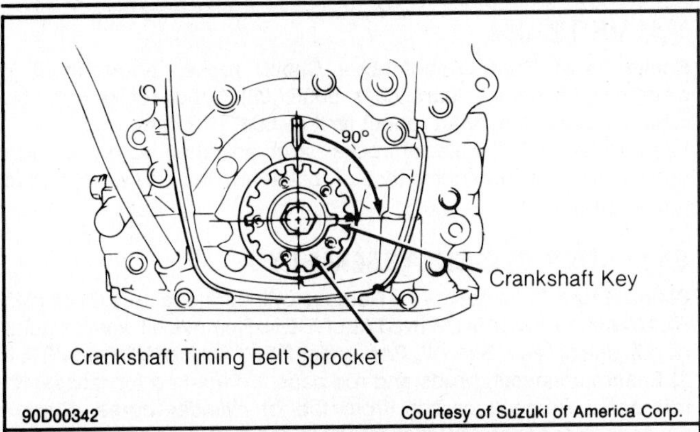


***Fig. 10: Positioning Crankshaft Timing Belt Sprocket for Camshaft Removal (DOHC)***

**Inspection (All Models) - 1)** Check cam lobes and journals for wear and damage. Use Plastigage to check bearing clearance. If wear exceeds specification, repair or replace as necessary. See CAMSHAFT table under ENGINE SPECIFICATIONS at end of article.
**2)** Use dial indicator and "V" blocks to measure camshaft runout at center of shaft. If wear exceeds specifications, repair or replace as necessary. See CAMSHAFT table.
**Installation (All Models) - 1)** Lubricate camshaft lobes and camshaft bearing journals. Install camshaft and new oil seal in cylinder head. On DOHC model, install oil seal flush with bearing cap surface. Install camshaft bearing caps and tighten in sequence. *See Fig. 11.*
**2)** On all models, install camshaft sprocket. Ensure camshaft sprocket marks align with timing marks on cylinder head. *See Figs. 6 and 7.* To complete installation, reverse removal procedure.

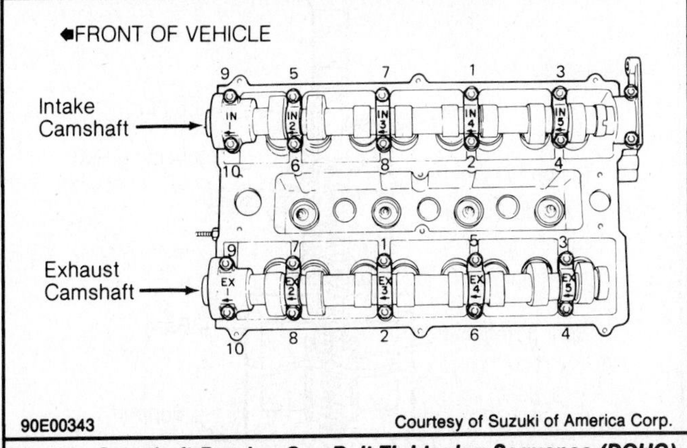


***Fig. 11: Camshaft Bearing Cap Bolt Tightening Sequence (DOHC)***

## REAR CRANKSHAFT OIL SEAL

**Removal -** Remove engine or engine and transmission. See ENGINE under REMOVAL & INSTALLATION. Separate transmission from engine. Remove flywheel. Remove oil seal housing. Remove seal. Inspect oil seal housing for wear or damage. Repair or replace as necessary. *See Fig. 12.*
**Installation -** Install oil seal in housing. Apply oil to seal lip. Install oil seal housing and new gasket. Tighten housing bolts to specification. See TORQUE SPECIFICATIONS table at end of article. Oil seal housing gasket will bulge after mounting bolts have been tightened. Trim excess gasket material even with oil pan gasket surface.

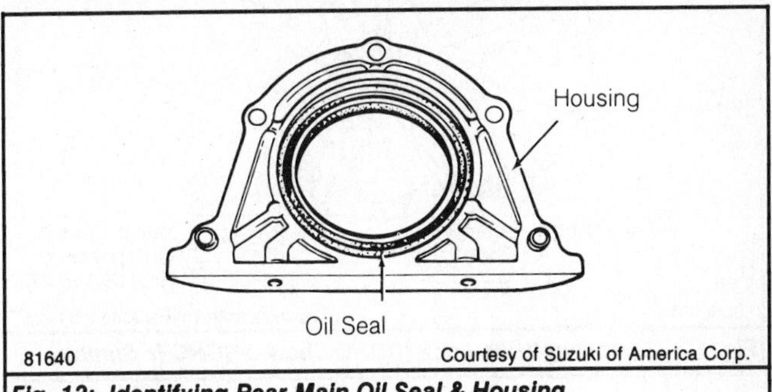


***Fig. 12: Identifying Rear Main Oil Seal & Housing***

## WATER PUMP

**Removal - 1)** Drain cooling system. Disconnect negative battery cable. Remove drive belts. Discharge A/C system and disconnect compressor flexible suction hose from suction pipe (if equipped). On Samurai and Sidekick, remove cooling fan, fan shroud and fan clutch.
**2)** On all models, remove pump pulley. Ensure No. 1 piston is at TDC of compression stroke. Remove crankshaft pulley bolts and crankshaft pulley. Remove timing belt cover. See TIMING BELT under REMOVAL & INSTALLATION. Remove dipstick and tube. Remove alternator mounting bracket. Remove water pump.
**Installation -** To install, reverse removal procedure. Ensure all mating surfaces are clean. Use new gasket.

***NOTE: For further information on cooling systems, see SPECIFICATIONS & ELECTRIC COOLING FANS article in ENGINE COOLING.***

## OIL PAN

**Removal - 1)** Raise vehicle. On Samurai and Sidekick 4WD, remove front differential assembly. See appropriate article in DRIVE AXLES. On all models, drain engine oil.
**2)** Remove clutch housing lower plate or torque convertor housing lower plate. Remove oil pan nuts and bolts. Remove oil pan.
**Installation -** To install, reverse removal procedure. Install oil pan using silicone-type sealant. Tighten bolts to specification. See TORQUE SPECIFICATIONS table at end of article.

# OVERHAUL

## CYLINDER HEAD

**Cylinder Head Disassembly (1.3L SOHC & 1.6L) - 1)** Remove cylinder head. See CYLINDER HEAD under REMOVAL & INSTALLATION. Remove manifolds and distributor assembly. Remove rocker arms and shafts. Remove camshaft. See CAMSHAFT under REMOVAL & INSTALLATION.
**2)** Use a Valve Spring Compressor (09916-14510) and Valve Lifter Attachment (09916-48210) to remove retainer locks. Remove retainers, springs, spring seats and valves. Keep all components in order for reassembly reference.
**Cylinder Head Disassembly (1.3L DOHC) - 1)** Remove cylinder head. See CYLINDER HEAD under REMOVAL & INSTALLATION. Remove manifolds with throttle body, distributor assembly and delivery pipe with injectors. Remove camshaft. See CAMSHAFT under REMOVAL & INSTALLATION.

# 1991 ENGINES
# 1.3L & 1.6L 4-Cylinder (Cont.)

**2)** Use Valve Spring Compressor (09916-14510) and Valve Spring Retainer Remover (09916-84510) to remove retainer locks. *See Fig. 13.* Remove retainers, springs, spring seats and valves. Keep all components in order for reassembly reference.

**Cylinder Head Reassembly (All Models)** - To assemble, reverse disassembly procedure. Ensure valve springs are installed with close coiled (small pitch) end down, toward cylinder head.

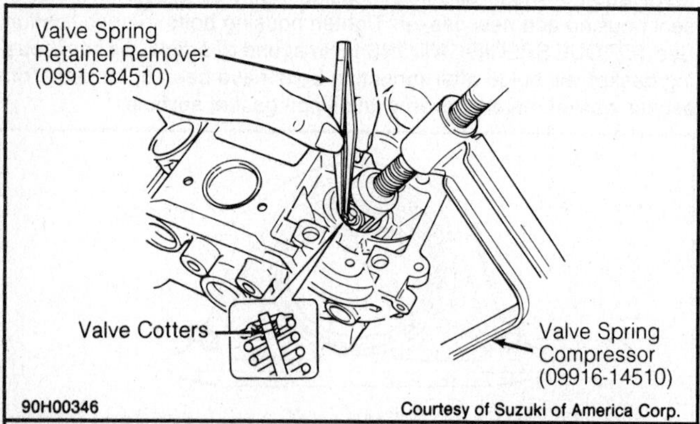


***Fig. 13: Removing Valve Lock (DOHC Shown; SOHC Is Similar)***

**Valve Springs** - Check valve springs for damage. Use a square and flat surface plate to check spring squareness. Maximum out-of-square is .079" (2.00 mm). Using valve spring tester, check valve spring preload pressure. See VALVES & VALVE SPRINGS table under ENGINE SPECIFICATIONS at end of article. Replace any weak springs.

**Valve Stem Oil Seals** - Place lubricated stem seal on valve guide. Use Valve Stem Seal Installer (09917-98220 on DOHC or 09917-98210 on SOHC). Press seal on valve guide using hand pressure only. When installer bottoms on head, seal is positioned properly. DO NOT reuse old seals. Avoid twisting seals during installation.

**Valve Guides** - **1)** Check valve stem-to-guide clearance. If clearance exceeds specification, replace with oversize valve guide. See CYLINDER HEAD table under ENGINE SPECIFICATIONS at end of article.

**2)** On Sidekick and Swift SOHC, use Valve Guide Remover (09916-46010). On Swift DOHC, use Valve Guide Remover (09916-44910). On Samurai, use Valve Guide Remover (09916-44511). Drive old guide out.

**3)** Ream guide bore in cylinder head with 12-mm Reamer (09916-37310) for SOHC engines and 11-mm Reamer (09916-38210) for DOHC engines. Heat cylinder head to 176-212°F (80-100°C).

**4)** Using Valve Guide Installer (09917-88210 for SOHC or 09916-56020 for DOHC), drive in new oversized valve guide until valve guide installer contacts cylinder head.

**5)** Valve guide protrusion is .55" (14.0 mm) for SOHC engines and .91" (23.0 mm) for DOHC engines. Ream valve guide with 7-mm Reamer (09916-34520) for SOHC engines or 5.5-mm Reamer (09916-34550) for DOHC engines.

**6)** Clean valve guide bore after reaming. Install valve and ensure valve stem oil clearance is correct. See CYLINDER HEAD table under ENGINE SPECIFICATIONS at end of article.

**Valve Seat (SOHC)** - **1)** Inspect valve seats for damage or wear. If exhaust valve seat rework is necessary, use 3 cutters to obtain required angles. The second cut should be 75 degrees for Samurai and Swift or 60 degrees for Sidekick. The third cut should be 45 degrees to obtain correct seat angle.

**2)** For intake valves, the procedure is the same except the second cut should be 60 degrees for all models. After cutting valve seats to correct angles, valve seat should be lapped in 2 steps. Use a course compound in the first step and a fine compound in the second step.

**Valve Seat (DOHC)** - **1)** Inspect valve seats for damage or wear. If valve seat rework is necessary, use 2 cutters to obtain required angles. On intake and exhaust valves, the first cut should be 15 degrees. The second cut should be 45 degrees to obtain correct seat angle.

**2)** After cutting valve seats to correct angles, valve seat should be lapped in 2 steps. Use a course compound in the first step and a fine compound in the second step.

**Valves** - **1)** Remove carbon deposits. Inspect for wear, burns or distortion at face and stem. Replace as necessary. Measure valve head margin. Check valve stem end for pitting or wear.

**2)** Measure valve length. Valve stem end may be resurfaced if no more than .14" (3.6 mm) is removed from valve length. See VALVES & VALVE SPRINGS table under ENGINE SPECIFICATIONS at end of article. Using "V" block and dial gauge, check valve head radial runout. Maximum limit is .003 (.08 mm). If runout exceeds limit, replace valve.

**Seat Correction Angles** - On SOHC exhaust valves, use 15 degrees and 75 degrees to narrow seat and 45 degrees to widen seat. On SOHC intake valves, use 15 degrees and 60 degrees to narrow seat and 45 degrees to widen seat. On DOHC intake and exhaust valves, use 15 degrees to narrow seat and 45 degrees to widen seat.

## VALVE TRAIN

**Rocker Arm Shaft Assembly** - Check rocker arm-to-shaft oil clearance. Maximum clearance is .0035 (.09). Check rocker arm shaft runout. Rocker arm shaft runout limit is .004" (.10 mm).

**Lash Adjusters** - If tip of rocker arm adjusting screw is worn, replace screw. If cam riding face of rocker arm is badly worn, replace rocker arm.

## CYLINDER BLOCK ASSEMBLY

**Piston & Rod Assembly** - **1)** Remove cylinder head. See CYLINDER HEAD under REMOVAL & INSTALLATION. Remove oil dipstick guide, oil pan and screen. See OIL PAN under REMOVAL & INSTALLATION.

**2)** Ensure connecting rods and rod caps are marked for reassembly reference. Remove carbon from top of cylinder bores. Remove connecting rod caps. Install protective hose over connecting rod bolts.

**3)** Remove connecting rod and piston assembly through top of cylinder block. Mark cylinder number on piston crown. Remove piston rings.

**4)** Use Piston Pin Remover/Installer (09910-38211) on 1.3L SOHC engines. On 1.3L DOHC and 1.6L engines, remove circlips, and push piston pin out by hand.

**5)** Check piston pin-to-bore fit. Pin should press in piston smoothly by hand at room temperature. When assembling, apply engine oil to outside of pin and to piston pin bore.

**6)** Position piston upward. Align piston, pin and rod with Piston Pin Remover/Installer (09910-38211) for 1.3L SOHC. Press pin into piston

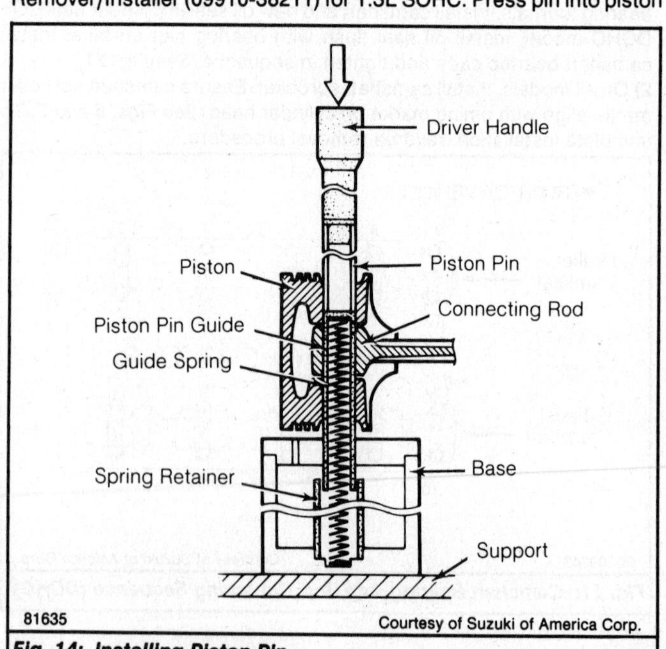


***Fig. 14: Installing Piston Pin***

# 1991 ENGINES
# 1.3L & 1.6L 4-Cylinder (Cont.)

and rod using a hydraulic press. *See Fig. 14.* On 1.3L DOHC and 1.6L engines, install circlips and piston pin.

**Fitting Pistons – 1)** Check cylinder bore for damage, wear and taper. See CYLINDER BLOCK under CYLINDER BLOCK ASSEMBLY under OVERHAUL. See CYLINDER BLOCK table under ENGINE SPECIFICATIONS at end of article to determine if block must be rebored.

**2)** Pistons are available in .010" (.25 mm) and .020" (.50 mm) oversizes. Check outside diameter of piston. On 1.6L engine, measure at a point .63" (16.0 mm) from bottom of skirt and at 90 degrees to pin bore. On 1.3L engine, measure at a point .59" (15.0 mm) from bottom of skirt and at 90 degrees to pin bore.

**3)** On all models, standard pistons are available in 2 sizes to ensure correct piston-to-cylinder clearance. Each standard piston has a number "1" or number "2" stamped on piston crown. *See Fig. 15.*

**4)** The cylinder block is stamped with 4 numbers, either number "1" or number "2". The first number stamped on cylinder block indicates bore size of No. 1 cylinder. Second number indicates bore size of No. 2 cylinder. Third number indicates bore size of No. 3 cylinder. Fourth number indicates bore size of No. 4 cylinder.

**5)** Install piston stamped number "1" into cylinder stamped number "1". Use a piston stamped number "2" in a cylinder stamped number "2".

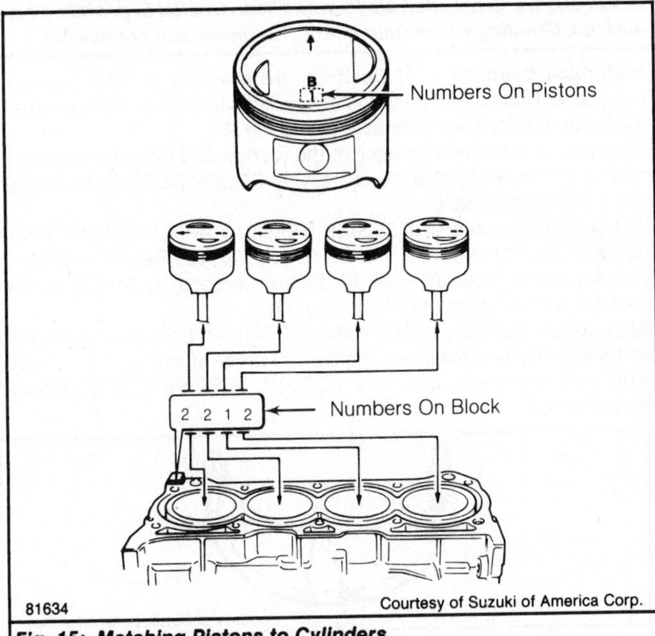


*Fig. 15: Matching Pistons to Cylinders*

**Piston Rings – 1)** Install rings with "R", "RN" or "T" mark facing upward. Some Samurai top rings are unmarked and can be installed either side upward. Position piston ring gaps. *See Fig. 16.* Lubricate all internal surfaces with engine oil before installation.

**2)** Ensure arrow on piston head faces front of engine. Ensure oil hole in connecting rod faces intake side of engine. Install cylinder head, oil pick-up screen and oil pan. To complete installation, reverse removal procedure.

***CAUTION: Install spacer gap more than 45 degrees from side rail gaps. Rails should turn smoothly when installed.***

**Rod Bearings – 1)** Inspect journals for wear, taper and out-of-round. If specifications are exceeded, grind journals to undersize or replace crankshaft. See CRANKSHAFT, MAIN & CONNECTING ROD BEARINGS table under ENGINE SPECIFICATIONS at end of article.

**2)** Inspect bearing shells for signs of fusion, pitting, burning or flaking. Observe contact pattern. Standard bearings are unmarked. Undersized bearings are stamped US025 on the back of the bearing to indicate .010" (.25 mm) undersize.

**3)** Check bearing clearance using Plastigage measuring method. See CRANKSHAFT, MAIN & CONNECTING ROD BEARINGS table. Connecting rod side clearance limit is .0137" (.35 mm).

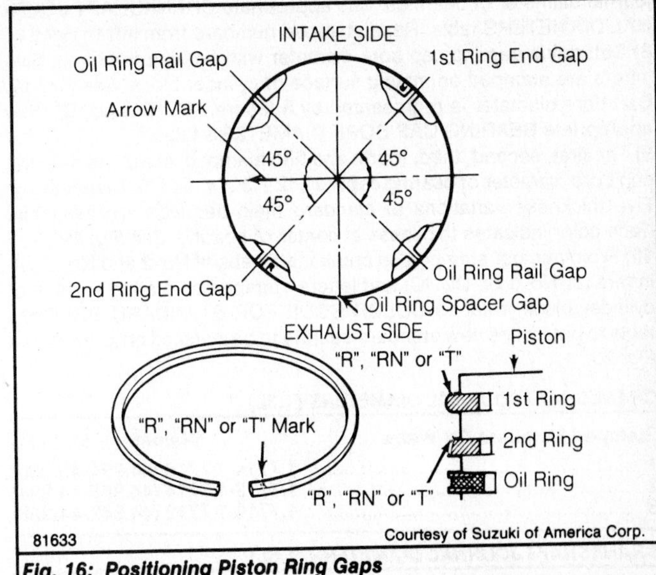


*Fig. 16: Positioning Piston Ring Gaps*

**4)** To install, reverse removal procedure. Tighten connecting rod nuts to specification. See TORQUE SPECIFICATIONS table at end of article.

**Crankshaft & Main Bearings – 1)** Remove engine or engine and transmission. See ENGINE under REMOVAL & INSTALLATION. Separate transmission from engine. Remove timing belt, sprockets, pulley and tensioner. See TIMING BELT under REMOVAL & INSTALLATION.

**2)** Remove flywheel and oil pan. Remove rear main oil seal housing. Remove connecting rod caps. Remove main bearing caps. Remove crankshaft.

**3)** Inspect journals for wear, taper and out-of-round condition. If specifications are exceeded, grind journals to undersize or replace crankshaft. See CRANKSHAFT, MAIN & CONNECTING ROD BEARINGS table under ENGINE SPECIFICATIONS at end of article.

**4)** Standard main bearings are coded with a color patch and are available in 5 thickness variations. *See Fig. 19.* Upper half of bearing has an oil groove. An arrow mark and number are embossed on each main bearing cap.

**5)** Ensure arrow mark on main bearing cap faces toward crankshaft pulley. Bearing No. 1 is at crankshaft pulley end of engine. Bearing No. 5 is at flywheel end of engine.

**6)** On SOHC engines, crankshaft webs of No. 2 and No. 3 cylinders have 5 stamped numbers. *See Fig. 17.* On DOHC engines, crankshaft web of No. 1 cylinder has 5 stamped numbers.

**7)** Journal diameter is represented by the numbers, "1", "2" or "3". The first, second, third, fourth and fifth stamped numbers on web indicate

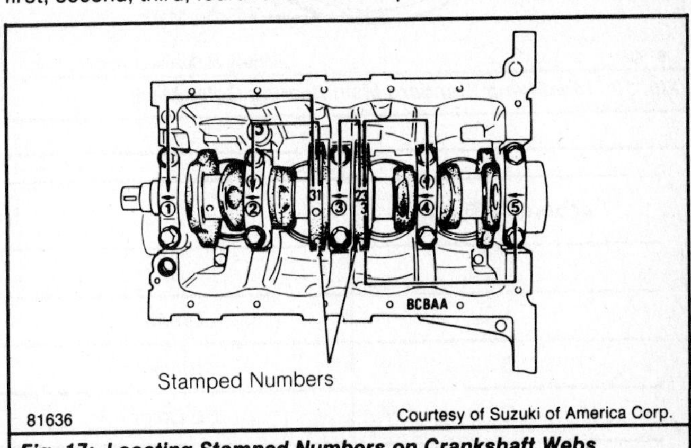


*Fig. 17: Locating Stamped Numbers on Crankshaft Webs of No. 2 & No. 3 Cylinders (SOHC)*

# 1991 ENGINES
# 1.3L & 1.6L 4-Cylinder (Cont.)

journal diameter of bearings. See appropriate CRANKSHAFT JOURNAL DIAMETERS table. Read stamped numbers from left to right.

**8)** Determine bearing cap bore diameter with bearing removed. Five letters are stamped on mating surface of cylinder block. *See Fig. 18.* Cap bore diameter is represented by 3 letters, "A", "B" and "C". See appropriate BEARING CAP BORE DIAMETERS table.

**9)** The first, second, third, fourth and fifth stamped letters indicate the cap bore diameter of bearing caps "1", "2", "3", "4" and "5" respectively. Five thickness variations of standard main bearings are available. Each color indicates thickness at center of bearing. *See Fig. 19.*

**10)** From number stamped on crankshaft webs of No. 2 and No. 3 cylinders (or No. 1 on DOHC) and letters stamped on mating surface of cylinder block, refer to COLOR CODE FOR STANDARD BEARING table to determine new standard bearing to be installed on journal. *See Fig. 20.*

***CRANKSHAFT JOURNAL DIAMETERS (1.3L)***

| Stamped Numbers On Webs | Diameter - In. (mm) |
|---|---|
| 1 | 1.7714-1.7716 (44.994-45.000) |
| 2 | 1.7712-1.7714 (44.988-44.994) |
| 3 | 1.7710-1.7712 (44.982-44.988) |

***CRANKSHAFT JOURNAL DIAMETERS (1.6L)***

| Stamped Numbers On Webs | Diameter - In. (mm) |
|---|---|
| 1 | 2.0470-2.0472 (51.994-52.000) |
| 2 | 2.0468-2.0470 (51.988-51.994) |
| 3 | 2.0465-2.0468 (51.982-51.988) |

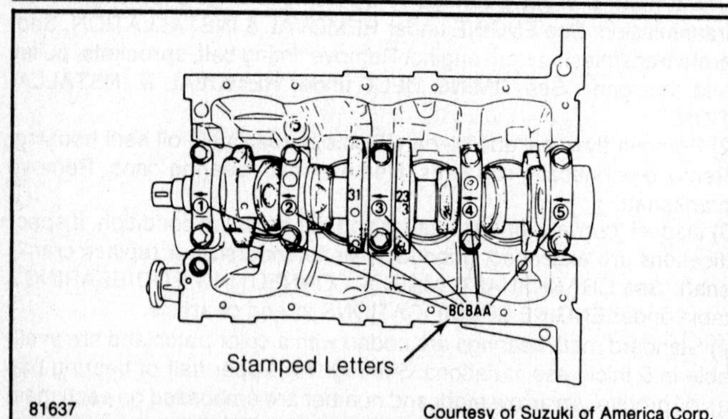


***Fig. 18: Locating Stamped Letters on Cylinder Block***

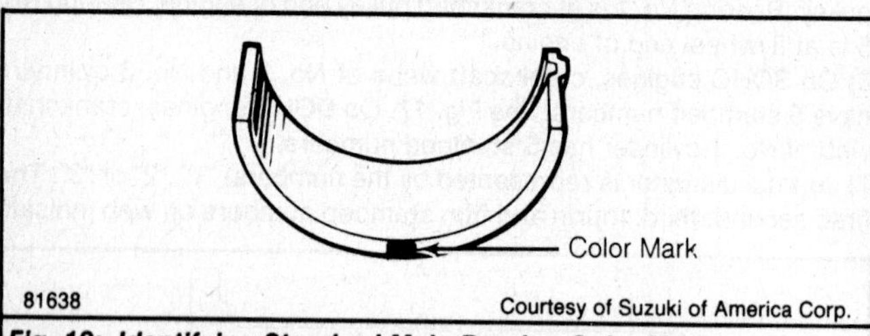


***Fig. 19: Identifying Standard Main Bearing Color Mark***

***BEARING CAP BORE DIAMETERS (SAMURAI & SWIFT)***

| Stamped Letters On Block | Diameter - In. (mm) |
|---|---|
| A | 1.9292-1.9294 (49.000-49.006) |
| B | 1.9294-1.9296 (49.006-49.012) |
| C | 1.9296-1.9298 (49.012-49.018) |

***BEARING CAP BORE DIAMETERS (SIDEKICK)***

| Stamped Letters On Block | Diameter - In. (mm) |
|---|---|
| A | 2.2047-2.2050 (56.000-56.006) |
| B | 2.2050-2.2052 (56.006-56.012) |
| C | 2.2052-2.2054 (56.012-56.018) |

***COLOR CODE FOR STANDARD BEARINGS***

| Color Painted | Bearing Thickness - In. (mm) |
|---|---|
| Black | .0787-.0788 (2.000-2.003) |
| Blue | .0790-.0791 (2.009-2.012) |
| Green | .0786-.0787 (1.996-2.000) |
| No Paint | .0788-.0789 (2.002-2.006) |
| Yellow | .0789-.0790 (2.006-2.009) |

***NOTE: Manufacturer does not recommend grinding crankshaft on DOHC engine. Crankshaft surface has been treated to provide a hard surface. Grinding will reduce journal hardness and service life.***

**Undersize Bearings - 1)** Bearings are available in .010" (.25 mm) undersize. Undersized bearings are coded with 2 color marks and are available in 5 thickness variations. *See Fig. 21.*

**2)** Using the finished diameter of the journal and letters stamped on mating surface of cylinder block, refer to COLOR CODE FOR UNDERSIZE BEARINGS table.

**3)** For Sidekick, see UNDERSIZE BEARING APPLICATION CHART (SIDEKICK). For Samurai and Swift, *see Fig. 22.* Select undersized bearing to be installed. Use Plastigage method to ensure correct clearance of installed undersize bearing.

**4)** Lubricate bearings before installing. Tighten bolts to specification in 3 steps. Tighten main bearing caps in order of center, No. 2, No. 4, front and rear main caps. See TORQUE SPECIFICATIONS table at end of article.

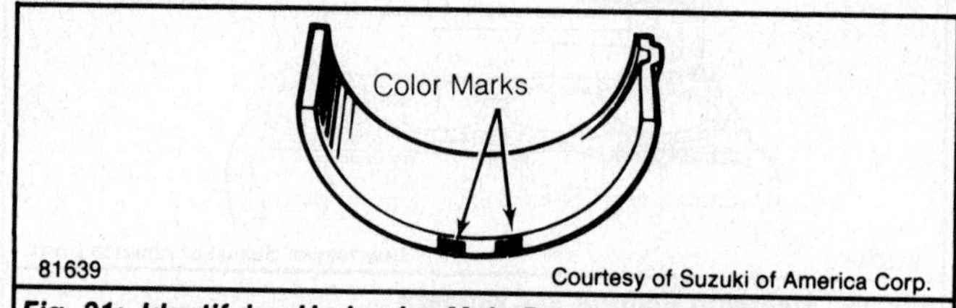


***Fig. 21: Identifying Undersize Main Bearing Color Marks***

***COLOR CODE FOR UNDERSIZE BEARINGS***

| Color Painted | Bearing Thickness - In. (mm) |
|---|---|
| Black & Red | .0836-.0837 (2.124-2.128) |
| Blue & Red | .0839-.0840 (2.134-2.137) |
| Green & Red | .0835-.0836 (2.121-2.124) |
| Red Only | .0837-.0838 (2.128-2.131) |
| Yellow & Red | .0838-.0839 (2.131-2.134) |

| Letters On Block | Numbers Stamped On Crankshaft Webs | | |
|---|---|---|---|
| | 1 | 2 | 3 |
| A | Green | Black | No Color |
| B | Black | No Color | Yellow |
| C | No Color | Yellow | Blue |

90I00347 — Courtesy of Suzuki of America Corp.

***Fig. 20: Standard Bearing Application Chart***

# 1991 ENGINES
# 1.3L & 1.6L 4-Cylinder (Cont.)

| Letters On Block | Measured Journal Diameter In. (mm) | | |
|---|---|---|---|
| | 1.7616-1.7618 (44.744-44.750) | 1.7614-1.7616 (44.738-44.744) | 1.7612-1.7614 (44.732-44.738) |
| A | Green & Red | Black & Red | Red Only |
| B | Black & Red | Red Only | Yellow & Red |
| C | Red Only | Yellow & Red | Blue & Red |

Courtesy of Suzuki of America Corp.

90J00348

*Fig. 22: Undersize Bearing Application Chart (Samurai & Swift SOHC)*

***UNDERSIZE BEARING APPLICATION CHART (SIDEKICK)***

| Letter on Block | Measured Journal Diam. - In. (mm) 2.0371-2.0373 (51.744-51.750) | 2.0369-2.0371 (51.738-51.744) | 2.0367-2.0369 (51.732-51.738) |
|---|---|---|---|
| A | Green & Red | Black & Red | Red Only |
| B | Black & Red | Red Only | Yellow & Red |
| C | Red Only | Yellow & Red | Blue & Red |

**Thrust Bearing - 1)** With crankshaft bearing caps installed, check thrust clearance (end play) using dial gauge to read displacement in axial thrust direction of crankshaft.

**2)** Standard thickness of thrust bearing is .0984" (2.50 mm). Oversize thrust bearings are available in increments of .0049" (.125 mm). If clearance exceeds specification, replace thrust bearing. See CRANKSHAFT, MAIN & CONNECTING ROD table under ENGINE SPECIFICATIONS at end of article.

**Cylinder Block - 1)** Inspect block for distortion of deck surface. Warpage limit is .002" (.05 mm). Inspect block for cracks, scratches and other defects. Measure bores at 3 levels for wear, taper and out-of-round condition.

**2)** If bore wear, taper or out-of-round exceed specification, rebore cylinders. See CYLINDER BLOCK table under ENGINE SPECIFICATIONS at end of article.

## ENGINE OILING

### ENGINE LUBRICATION SYSTEM

A force-feed type lubrication system is used. The oil pump is a trochoid-type pump mounted on the forward portion of the crankshaft. *See Fig. 23.*

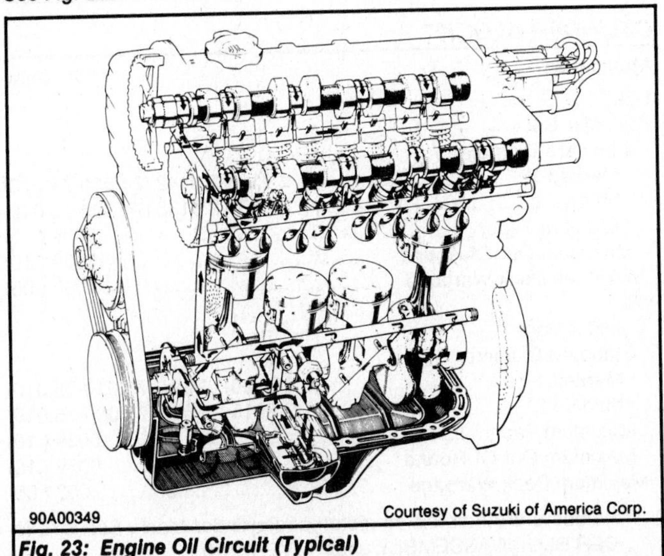

90A00349 Courtesy of Suzuki of America Corp.

*Fig. 23: Engine Oil Circuit (Typical)*

**Crankcase Capacity -** Samurai crankcase capacity, with filter, is 3.7 qts. (3.5L). Sidekick crankcase capacity, with filter, is 4.5 qts. (4.2L). Swift crankcase capacity, with filter, is 3.5 qts. (3.3L). Check dipstick to verify oil level is correct.

**Oil Pressure -** On Samurai and Swift (SOHC), normal oil pressure is 42.7-59.7 psi (3.0-4.2 kg/cm²) at 3000 RPM. On Sidekick and Swift (DOHC), normal oil pressure is 51.2-62.2 psi (3.6-4.4 kg/cm²) at 3000 RPM.

### OIL PUMP

**Removal & Disassembly - 1)** Position No. 1 piston at TDC of compression stroke. Remove water pump, crankshaft pulley and alternator. Remove timing belt cover and timing belt. See TIMING BELT under REMOVAL & INSTALLATION.

**2)** Drain engine oil. Remove oil dipstick and oil pan. Remove oil pump pick-up screen. Remove oil pump assembly. Remove oil pump rotor plate.

**3)** Mark outer gear with felt pen for reassembly reference. Remove inner and outer oil pump gears. Remove plug, relief spring and relief valve.

**Inspection - 1)** Inspect oil pump housing for cracks or damage. Inspect oil screen for clogging or damage. Inspect oil screen "O" ring. Ensure relief valve slides smoothly in bore. Inspect pressure relief spring for damaged coils.

**2)** Inspect oil pump gears for wear or damage. Using a feeler gauge, measure radial and side clearance. *See Figs. 24 and 25.* If clearance exceeds specification, replace outer rotor or case. See OIL PUMP SPECIFICATIONS table.

***OIL PUMP SPECIFICATIONS***

| Application | Radial Clearance In. (mm) | Side Clearance In. (mm) |
|---|---|---|
| All Models | .0122 (.309) | .0059 (.150) |

**Reassembly & Installation - 1)** Ensure gears are assembled in same direction as originally installed. Apply thin coat of engine oil to inner

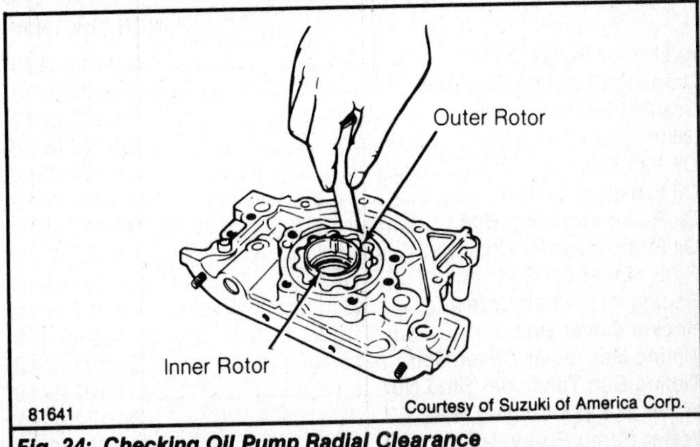


81641 Courtesy of Suzuki of America Corp.

*Fig. 24: Checking Oil Pump Radial Clearance*

# 1991 ENGINES
# 1.3L & 1.6L 4-Cylinder (Cont.)

and outer rotors, lip portion of oil seal and inside surfaces of oil pump case and plate. Install inner and outer rotors.

2) Install gear plate. Ensure gears turn freely by hand after gear plate is installed. Install oil pump pins, new dipstick "O" ring, new seal for oil pick-up tube and new oil pump gasket. Use Oil Seal Guide (09926-18210) to prevent damage to oil seal during installation of oil pump.

3) Apply engine oil to guide, and install pump. Install dipstick guide with new seal. Install oil pan using silicone-type sealant. Tighten bolts to specification. See TORQUE SPECIFICATIONS table.

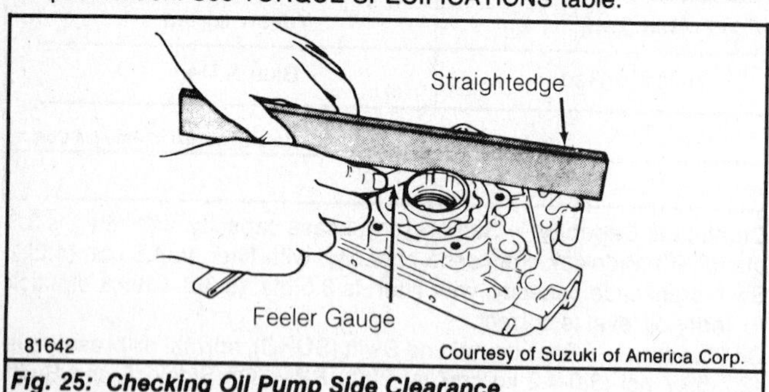


*Fig. 25: Checking Oil Pump Side Clearance*

## TORQUE SPECIFICATIONS

### TORQUE SPECIFICATIONS

| Application | Ft. Lbs. (N.m) |
|---|---|
| Camshaft Sprocket Bolt | 41-46 (56-64) |
| Connecting Rod Cap Nut | 24-27 (33-37) |
| Crankshaft Sprocket Bolt | 76-83 (105-115) |
| Cylinder Head Bolt | |
| DOHC | [1] 48-51 (65-70) |
| SOHC | [1] 51-54 (70-75) |
| Drive Plate-To-Torque Converter Bolt | |
| Sidekick | 36-43 (50-60) |
| Swift | 14 (19) |
| Engine-To-Transmission Bolt | |
| Samurai | 16-25 (22-35) |
| Sidekick | |
| Auto. Trans. | 62 (85) |
| Man. Trans. | 51-72 (70-100) |
| Swift | 29-43 (40-60) |
| Exhaust Manifold Bolt | 13-20 (18-28) |
| Flywheel Bolt (Drive Plate For A/T) | |
| Samurai | 42-47 (57-65) |
| Sidekick | 55-57 (75-80) |
| Swift | 50-52 (62-72) |
| Intake Manifold Bolt | 13-20 (18-28) |
| Main Bearing Cap Bolt | 37-41 (50-56) |
| Oil Pan Drain Plug | 22-29 (30-40) |
| Rocker Arm Adjustment Lock Nut | 11-14 (15-19) |
| Timing Belt Tensioner Bolt | 18-22 (24-30) |
| | INCH Lbs. (N.m) |
| Alternator Pulley Bolt | 90-108 (10-13) |
| Camshaft Bearing Cap Bolt | 84-102 (9-12) |
| Crankshaft Pulley Bolt | 84-102 (9-12) |
| Distributor Case Bolt | 72-102 (8-12) |
| Oil Pan Bolt | 84-102 (9-12) |
| Oil Pressure Switch | 102-126 (12-15) |
| Oil Pump Mounting Bolt | 84-102 (9-12) |
| Oil Pump Strainer Bolt | 84-102 (9-12) |
| Rear Main Seal Bolt | 90-108 (10-13) |
| Rocker Arm Shaft Screw | 72-102 (8-12) |
| Rocker Cover Bolt | 36-42 (4-5) |
| Timing Belt Outer Cover Bolt | 84-102 (9-12) |
| Timing Belt Tensioner Stud Nut | 84-102 (9-12) |
| Water Pump Mounting Bolt | 84-102 (9-12) |
| Water Pump Pulley Bolt | 90-108 (10-13) |

[1] - Tighten in sequence. *See Fig. 4.*

## ENGINE SPECIFICATIONS

### GENERAL SPECIFICATIONS

| Application | Specification |
|---|---|
| 1.3L | |
| Displacement | 79.2 Cu. In. (1.3L) |
| Bore | 2.91" (74.0 mm) |
| Stroke | 2.97" (75.5 mm) |
| Compression Ratio | |
| DOHC | 10:1 |
| SOHC | 9.2:1 |
| Fuel System | |
| DOHC | PFI |
| SOHC | TBI |
| HP @ RPM | |
| Samurai | 66 @ 6000 |
| Swift | |
| DOHC | 100 @ 6500 |
| SOHC | 70 @ 6000 |
| Torque | Ft. Lbs. @ RPM |
| Samurai | 76 @ 3500 |
| Swift | |
| DOHC | 83 @ 5000 |
| SOHC | 74 @ 3500 |
| 1.6L | |
| Displacement | 97.0 Cu. In. (1.6L) |
| Bore | 2.95" (75.0 mm) |
| Stroke | 3.54" (90.0 mm) |
| Compression Ratio | 8.9:1 |
| Fuel System | TBI |
| HP @ RPM | 80 @ 5400 |
| Torque | Ft. Lbs. @ RPM |
| Sidekick | 94 @ 3000 |

### CONNECTING RODS

| Application | In. (mm) |
|---|---|
| 1.3L & 1.6L | |
| Bore Diameter | |
| Pin Bore | |
| DOHC | .748 (19.00) |
| SOHC | [1] |
| Maximum Bend | .002 (.05) |
| Maximum Twist | .004 (.10) |
| Side Play | .004-.008 (.10-.20) |

[1] - Information is not available from manufacturer.

### CYLINDER BLOCK

| Application | In. (mm) |
|---|---|
| 1.3L | |
| Cylinder Bore | |
| Standard Diameter [1] | |
| Marked 1 | 2.9138-2.9142 (74.010-74.020) |
| Marked 2 | 2.9134-2.9138 (74.000-74.010) |
| Maximum Taper | .0039 (.10) |
| Maximum Out-Of-Round | .0039 (.10) |
| Maximum Deck Warpage | .002 (.05) |
| 1.6L | |
| Cylinder Bore | |
| Standard Diameter [1] | |
| Marked 1 | 2.9520-2.9524 (75.010-75.020) |
| Marked 2 | 2.9516-2.9520 (75.000-75.010) |
| Maximum Taper | .0039 (.10) |
| Maximum Out-Of-Round | .0039 (.10) |
| Maximum Deck Warpage | .002 (.05) |

[1] - Numbers are marked on piston and cylinder block. See CYLINDER BLOCK ASSEMBLY under OVERHAUL.

# 1991 ENGINES
# 1.3L & 1.6L 4-Cylinder (Cont.)

## CRANKSHAFT, MAIN & CONNECTING ROD BEARINGS

| Application | In. (mm) |
|---|---|
| 1.3L | |
| Crankshaft | |
| End Play | .004-.012 (.11-.31) |
| Runout | .002 (.06) |
| Main Bearings | |
| Journal Diameter [1] | |
| Marked 1 | 1.7714-1.7716 (44.994-45.000) |
| Marked 2 | 1.7712-1.7714 (44.988-44.994) |
| Marked 3 | 1.7710-1.7712 (44.982-44.988) |
| Journal Out-Of-Round | .0004 (.010) |
| Journal Taper | .0004 (.010) |
| Oil Clearance | .0012 (.030) |
| Connecting Rod Bearings | |
| Journal Diameter | 1.6529-1.6535 (41.982-42.000) |
| Journal Out-Of-Round | .0004 (.010) |
| Journal Taper | .0004 (.010) |
| Oil Clearance | .001-.003 (.03-.08) |
| 1.6L | |
| Crankshaft | |
| End Play | .004-.012 (.11-.31) |
| Runout | .002 (.06) |
| Main Bearings | |
| Journal Diameter [1] | |
| Marked 1 | 2.0470-2.0472 (51.994-52.000) |
| Marked 2 | 2.0468-2.0470 (51.988-51.994) |
| Marked 3 | 2.0465-2.0468 (51.982-51.988) |
| Journal Out-Of-Round | .0004 (.010) |
| Journal Taper | .0004 (.010) |
| Oil Clearance | .0012 (.030) |
| Connecting Rod Bearings | |
| Journal Diameter | 1.7316-1.7323 (43.982-44.000) |
| Journal Out-Of-Round | .0004 (.010) |
| Journal Taper | .0004 (.010) |
| Oil Clearance | .001-.003 (.03-.08) |

[1] – Numbers are marked on crankshaft web.

## CYLINDER HEAD

| Application | Specification |
|---|---|
| 1.3L & 1.6L | |
| Maximum Warpage | .002" (.05 mm) |
| Valve Seats | |
| Intake & Exhaust Valves | |
| Seat Angle | 45° |
| Seat Width | .05-.06" (1.3-1.5 mm) |
| Valve Guides | |
| Intake Valve | |
| Valve Guide I.D. | |
| DOHC | .2165-.170" (5.50-5.51 mm) |
| SOHC | .2756-.2761" (7.00-7.02 mm) |
| Valve Guide Installed Height | |
| DOHC | .91" (23.0 mm) |
| SOHC | .55" (14.0 mm) |
| Valve Stem-To-Guide Oil Clearance | |
| DOHC | .0008-.0018" (.020-.047 mm) |
| SOHC | .0008-.0019" (.020-.050 mm) |
| Exhaust Valve | |
| Valve Guide I.D. | |
| DOHC | .2165-.2170" (5.50-5.51 mm) |
| SOHC | .2756-.2761" (7.00-7.02 mm) |
| Valve Guide Installed Height | |
| DOHC | .91" (23.0 mm) |
| SOHC | .55" (14.0 mm) |
| Valve Stem-To-Guide Oil Clearance | |
| DOHC | .0014-.0024" (.035-.062 mm) |
| SOHC | .0014-.0025" (.035-.065 mm) |

## PISTONS, PINS & RINGS

| Application | In. (mm) |
|---|---|
| 1.3L | |
| Pistons | |
| Clearance | .0008-.0015 (.02-.04) |
| Diameter [1] | |
| Marked 1 | 2.9126-2.9130 (73.980-73.990) |
| Marked 2 | 2.9122-2.9126 (73.970-73.980) |
| Pins | |
| Diameter | |
| DOHC | .7478-.7480 (18.995-19.000) |
| SOHC | [2] |
| Piston Fit | Slip |
| Rod Fit | |
| DOHC | .0001-.0006 (.003-.016) |
| SOHC | Press |
| Rings | |
| No. 1 | |
| End Gap | .0079-.0118 (.20-.30) |
| Side Clearance | .0012-.0027 (.030-.070) |
| No. 2 | |
| End Gap | .0079-.0118 (.20-.30) |
| Side Clearance | .0008-.0023 (.02-.06) |
| No. 3 (Oil) | |
| End Gap | .0079-.0275 (.20-.70) |
| 1.6L | |
| Pistons | |
| Clearance | .0008-.0015 (.02-.04) |
| Diameter [1] | |
| Marked 1 | 2.9520-2.9524 (74.980-74.990) |
| Marked 2 | 2.9516-2.9520 (74.970-74.980) |
| Pins | |
| Piston Fit | Slip |
| Rod Fit | Press |
| Rings | |
| No. 1 | |
| End Gap | .0079-.0137 (.20-.35) |
| Side Clearance | .0012-.0027 (.030-.070) |
| No. 2 | |
| End Gap | .0079-.0137 (.20-.35) |
| Side Clearance | .0008-.0023 (.02-.06) |
| No. 3 (Oil) | |
| End Gap | .0079-.0275 (.20-.70) |

[1] – Numbers are marked on piston and cylinder block.
[2] – Information is not available from manufacturer.

# 1991 ENGINES
# 1.3L & 1.6L 4-Cylinder (Cont.)

## VALVES & VALVE SPRINGS

| Application | Specification |
|---|---|
| 1.3L | |
| Intake Valves | |
| Face Angle | 45° |
| Minimum Margin | .023" (.6 mm) |
| Stem Diameter | |
| DOHC | .2152-.2157" (5.465-5.480 mm) |
| SOHC | .2742-.2748" (6.965-6.980 mm) |
| Valve Tip Maximum Refinish | .019" (.5 mm) |
| Exhaust Valves | |
| Face Angle | 45° |
| Minimum Margin | .027" (.7 mm) |
| Stem Diameter | |
| DOHC | .2146-.2151" (5.450-5.465 mm) |
| SOHC | .2737-.2742" (6.950-6.964 mm) |
| Valve Tip Maximum Refinish | .019" (.5 mm) |
| Valve Springs | |
| Free Length | |
| DOHC | 2.008" (51.00 mm) |
| SOHC | 1.941" (49.30 mm) |
| Out-Of-Square | .079" (2.00 mm) |
| | **Lbs. @ In. (Kg @ mm)** |
| Pressure | |
| DOHC | 61-74 @ 1.67 (27.5-33.5 @ 42.5 mm) |
| SOHC | 55-64 @ 1.63 (24.8-29.2 @ 41.4 mm) |
| 1.6L | **Specification** |
| Intake Valves | |
| Face Angle | 45° |
| Minimum Margin | .023" (.6 mm) |
| Stem Diameter | .2742-.2748" (6.965-6.980 mm) |
| Valve Tip Maximum Refinish | .019" (.5 mm) |
| Exhaust Valves | |
| Face Angle | 45° |
| Minimum Margin | .027" (.7 mm) |
| Stem Diameter | .2737-.2742" (6.950-6.965 mm) |
| Valve Tip Maximum Refinish | .019" (.5 mm) |
| Valve Springs | |
| Free Length | 1.987" (50.46 mm) |
| Out-Of-Square | .079" (2.00 mm) |
| | **Lbs. @ In. (Kg @ mm)** |
| Pressure | |
| Valve Closed | 55-64 @ 1.63 (24.8-29.2 @ 41.5) |

## CAMSHAFT

| Application | In. (mm) |
|---|---|
| 1.3L & 1.6L | |
| Bore Diameter | |
| DOHC | 1.1024-1.1032 (28.000-28.021) |
| SOHC [1] | |
| No. 1 | 1.7402-1.7407 (44.200-44.216) |
| No. 2 | 1.7480-1.7486 (44.400-44.416) |
| No. 3 | 1.7560-1.7565 (44.600-44.616) |
| No. 4 | 1.7638-1.7644 (44.800-44.816) |
| No. 5 | 1.7716-1.7723 (45.000-45.016) |
| Journal Diameter | |
| DOHC | 1.1007-1.1015 (27.959-27.980) |
| SOHC [1] | |
| No. 1 | 1.7372-1.7381 (44.125-44.150) |
| No. 2 | 1.7451-1.7460 (44.325-44.350) |
| No. 3 | 1.7530-1.7539 (44.525-44.550) |
| No. 4 | 1.7609-1.7618 (44.725-44.750) |
| No. 5 | 1.7687-1.7697 (44.925-44.950) |
| Journal Runout | .0039 (.10) |
| Lobe Height | |
| Samurai | 1.5019 (38.148) |
| Sidekick | 1.4763 (37.500) |
| Swift | |
| DOHC | |
| Exhaust | 1.5917-1.5979 (40.429-40.589) |
| Intake | 1.5920-1.5983 (40.436-40.596) |
| SOHC | 1.5014 (38.136) |
| Oil Clearance | |
| DOHC | .0008-.0024 (.020-.062 ) |
| SOHC | .0020-.0036 (.050-.091 ) |

[1] – Journals are numbered from front of engine.

## VALVE LIFTERS

| Application | In. (mm) |
|---|---|
| 1.3L (DOHC) | |
| Bore Diameter | 1.2205-1.2214 (31.000-31.025) |
| Lifter Diameter | 1.2188-1.2194 (30.959-30.975) |
| Oil Clearance | .0010-.0025 (.025-.066) |

# 1991 ENGINE COOLING
# Specifications & Electric Cooling Fans

## Samurai, Sidekick, Swift

## SPECIFICATIONS

### BELT ADJUSTMENT

*BELT ADJUSTMENT SPECIFICATIONS*

| Application | [1] Belt Deflection - In. (mm) |
|---|---|
| **Samurai** | |
| Water Pump Belt | .24-.35 (6.1-8.9) |
| **Sidekick** | |
| A/C Belt | .20-.25 (5.1-6.4) |
| P/S Belt | .24-.35 (6.1-8.9) |
| Water Pump Belt | .20-.32 (5.1-8.1) |
| **Swift** | |
| A/C Belt | .20-.25 (5.1-6.4) |
| Water Pump Belt | .25-.32 (6.4-8.1) |

[1] - With 22 lbs. (10 kg) pressure applied midway on longest belt run.

### COOLING SYSTEM

*COOLING SYSTEM SPECIFICATIONS*

| Application | Specification |
|---|---|
| **Cooling System Capacity** [1] | |
| Samurai | 5.0 Qts. (4.8L) |
| Sidekick | |
| A/T | 5.5 Qts. (5.2L) |
| M/T | 5.6 Qts. (5.3L) |
| Swift | 4.2 Qts. (4.0L) |
| **Pressure Cap** | |
| Samurai & Sidekick | 13 psi (.91 kg/cm²) |
| Swift | 12.8 psi (.88 kg/cm²) |
| **Thermostat** | |
| Samurai & Swift [2] | |
| "A" Thermostat | 190°F (88°C) |
| "B" Thermostat | 197°F (92°C) |
| Sidekick | 176-183°F (80-84°C) |

[1] - Includes heater core.
[2] - Either "A" or "B" thermostat is used by manufacturer. Ensure replacement thermostat has same temperature specification as original.

## ELECTRIC COOLING FAN (SWIFT)

### TROUBLE SHOOTING & TESTING

**System Testing - 1)** Start engine. Ensure coolant temperature is less than 199°F (93°C). If cooling fan operates, go to next step. If cooling fan does not operate, go to step **3)**.

**2)** Disconnect cooling fan thermoswitch, located near distributor. *See Fig. 1*. If cooling fan continues to operate after cooling fan thermoswitch is disconnected, check for short in Blue wire between cooling fan thermoswitch and cooling fan motor. If cooling fan stops running, replace cooling fan thermoswitch.

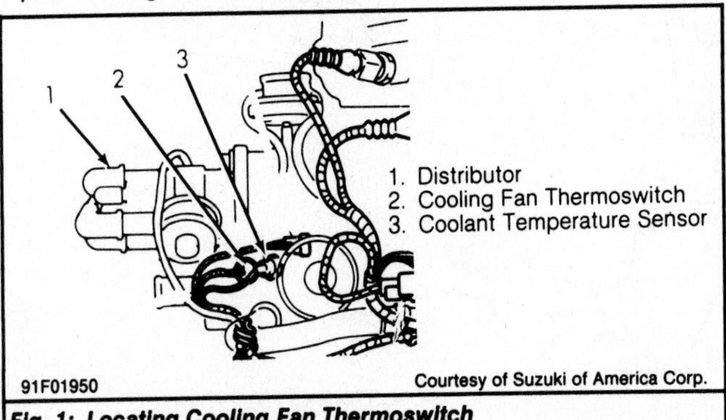


*Fig. 1: Locating Cooling Fan Thermoswitch*

**3)** If cooling fan does not operate with coolant temperature less than 199°F (93°C), run engine until engine coolant temperature is greater than 208°F (98°C). If cooling fan operates, system is okay. If cooling fan does not operate, go to next step.

**4)** With cooling fan thermoswitch connector disconnected, connect a fused jumper wire between thermoswitch connector terminals (Black/White and Blue wires). If cooling fan operates, replace cooling fan thermoswitch. If cooling fan does not operate, go to next step.

**5)** Turn ignition off. Check for continuity between Black (ground) wire of fan motor connector and ground. If no continuity is present, go to next step. If continuity is present, repair open or bad ground connection at Black (ground) wire. Ground connection is located on left front inner fender. *See Fig. 2*.

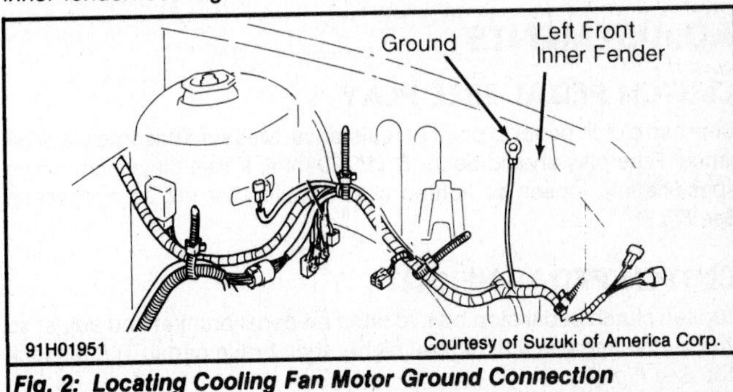


*Fig. 2: Locating Cooling Fan Motor Ground Connection*

**6)** Using a test light, backprobe cooling fan motor connector Blue wire. If test light lights, replace cooling fan motor. If test light does not light, go to next step.

**7)** Using test light, backprobe cooling fan thermoswitch connector Black/White wire. If test light does not light, repair open in Black/White wire between cooling fan thermoswitch and junction block connector. Junction block is located behind left side of instrument panel. *See Fig. 3*. If test light lights, repair open in Blue wire between cooling fan thermoswitch and cooling fan motor.

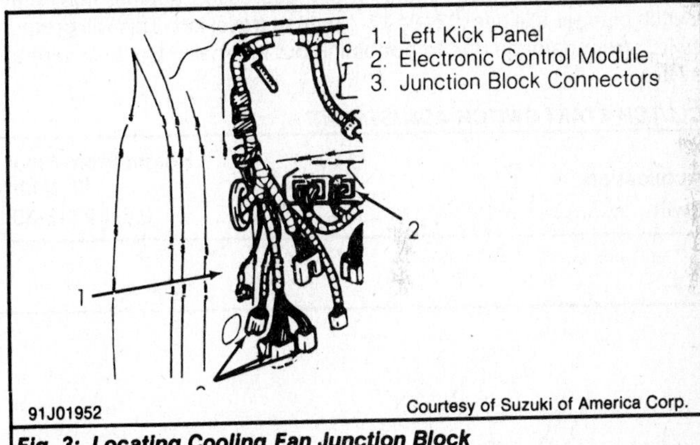


*Fig. 3: Locating Cooling Fan Junction Block*

### COMPONENT TESTING

**Cooling Fan Thermoswitch -** Remove thermoswitch from vehicle. Using ohmmeter, ensure continuity is correct across thermoswitch terminals. Thermoswitch may be gradually heated in water for testing. See COOLING FAN THERMOSWITCH table.

*COOLING FAN THERMOSWITCH* [1]

| Application | Continuity °F (°C) | No Continuity °F (°C) |
|---|---|---|
| Thermostat "A" | Above 208 (98) | Below 199 (93) |
| Thermostat "B" | Above 215 (102) | Below 206 (97) |

[1] - Before testing cooling fan thermoswitch, determine if vehicle has an "A" or "B" thermostat. "A" thermostat opens at 190°F (88°C). "B" thermostat opens at 197°F (92°C).

## WIRING DIAGRAMS

See appropriate chassis wiring diagram in WIRING DIAGRAMS.

# 1991 CLUTCHES
# FWD

## Swift

## DESCRIPTION

Clutch is a single disc type using a diaphragm spring to engage the pressure plate. Clutch is mechanically controlled by clutch pedal, clutch cable, return spring, release fork and prelubricated release bearing. System incorporates a clutch switch that disables ignition and starter circuits unless clutch pedal is fully depressed.

## ADJUSTMENTS

### CLUTCH PEDAL FREE PLAY

Depress clutch pedal to point of resistance. Measure this free play distance. Free play should be .6-.8" (15-20 mm). If free play is not within specification, loosen or tighten clutch cable joint nut as necessary. *See Fig. 1.*

### CLUTCH PEDAL HEIGHT

Loosen clutch pedal stop bolt, located on pedal bracket and adjust so that clutch pedal is 0.3" (8 mm) higher than brake pedal. Tighten lock nut. *See Fig. 1.*

### CLUTCH START SWITCH

**1)** Apply parking brake firmly. Place gearshift lever in Neutral. Disconnect wire at switch. Loosen lock nut and turn switch outward. Depress clutch pedal to floor. Release clutch pedal to its adjustment height position. See CLUTCH START SWITCH ADJUSTMENT table.

**2)** Connect ohmmeter to clutch start switch terminals. Slowly screw switch in until it is on. Hold switch at this position and tighten lock nut to specification. See TORQUE SPECIFICATIONS table at end of article. Ensure when clutch pedal is fully depressed against floor that switch plunger still has .02-.04 (.5-1 mm) of travel left. This will protect switch from damage due to bottoming out internally. Connect wire to switch.

***CLUTCH START SWITCH ADJUSTMENT***

| Application | Height From Floor In. (mm) |
|---|---|
| Swift | 0.6-1.2 (15-30) |

## REMOVAL & INSTALLATION

### CLUTCH ASSEMBLY

**Removal & Installation – 1)** Disconnect battery ground cable. Remove battery and tray. Disconnect clutch cable and bracket from transaxle. Disconnect wiring harness clamps and connectors. Disconnect speedometer cable from transaxle. Remove transaxle-to-engine mounting bolts. Remove starter and mounting plate.

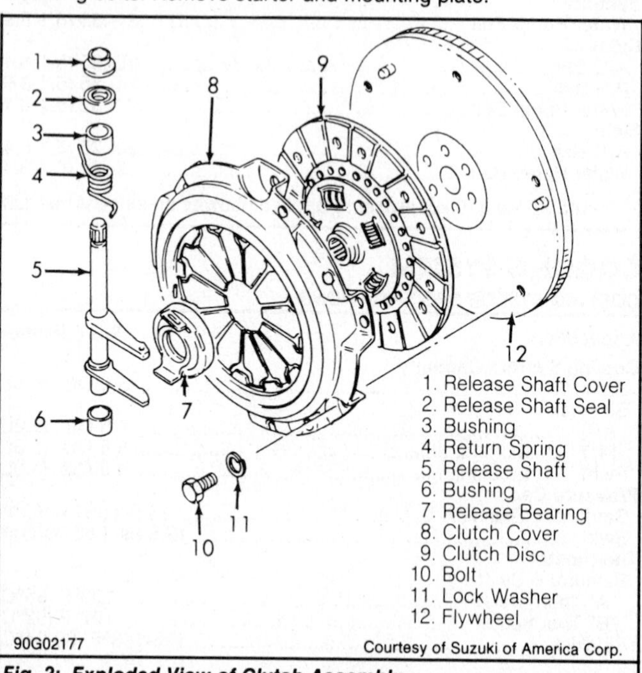


***Fig. 2: Exploded View of Clutch Assembly***

**2)** Raise and support vehicle on lift. Drain transaxle fluid. Remove left side inner fender panel. Remove front section of exhaust pipe. Disconnect shift rod, bushings, and control shaft from transaxle. Remove lower plate/dust shield from clutch housing.

**3)** Disconnect lower ball studs and suspension control arms. Disconnect left side drive axle from transaxle, using a screwdriver to pry drive axle from differential. Remove drive axle center support bearing

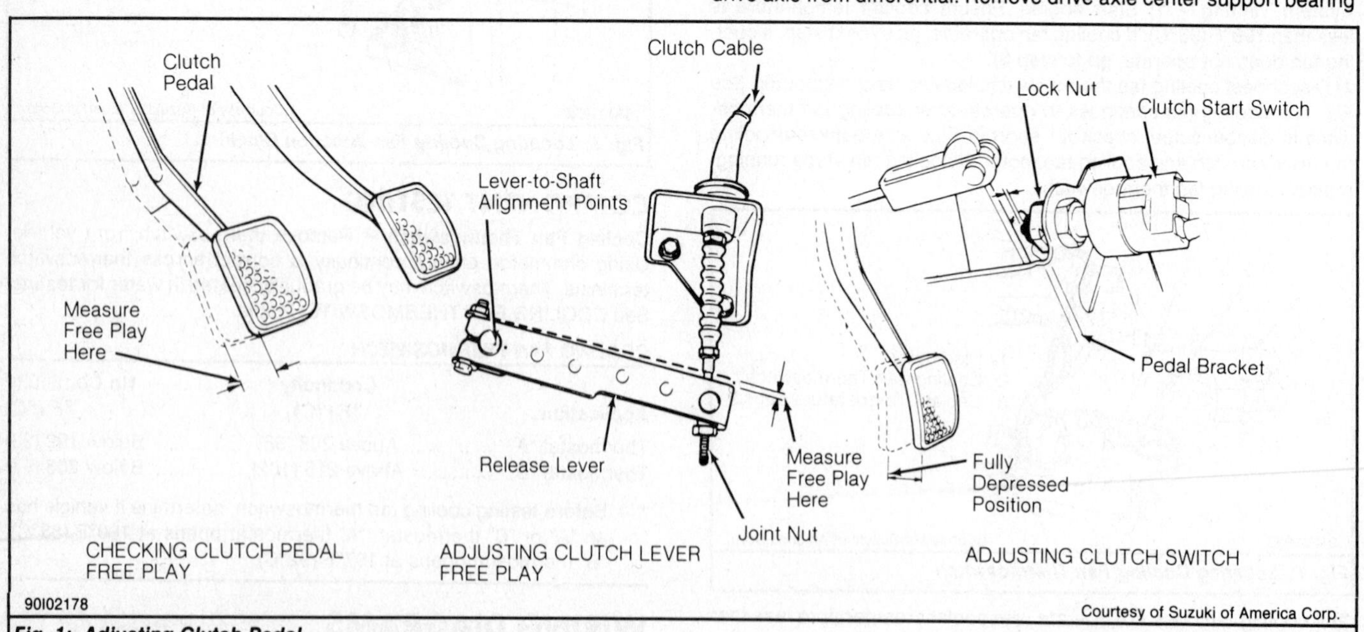


***Fig. 1: Adjusting Clutch Pedal***

# 1991 ENGINE COOLING
# Specifications & Electric Cooling Fans

## Samurai, Sidekick, Swift

## SPECIFICATIONS

### BELT ADJUSTMENT

*BELT ADJUSTMENT SPECIFICATIONS*

| Application | [1] Belt Deflection - In. (mm) |
|---|---|
| **Samurai** | |
| Water Pump Belt | .24-.35 (6.1-8.9) |
| **Sidekick** | |
| A/C Belt | .20-.25 (5.1-6.4) |
| P/S Belt | .24-.35 (6.1-8.9) |
| Water Pump Belt | .20-.32 (5.1-8.1) |
| **Swift** | |
| A/C Belt | .20-.25 (5.1-6.4) |
| Water Pump Belt | .25-.32 (6.4-8.1) |

[1] - With 22 lbs. (10 kg) pressure applied midway on longest belt run.

### COOLING SYSTEM

*COOLING SYSTEM SPECIFICATIONS*

| Application | Specification |
|---|---|
| **Cooling System Capacity** [1] | |
| Samurai | 5.0 Qts. (4.8L) |
| Sidekick | |
| A/T | 5.5 Qts. (5.2L) |
| M/T | 5.6 Qts. (5.3L) |
| Swift | 4.2 Qts. (4.0L) |
| **Pressure Cap** | |
| Samurai & Sidekick | 13 psi (.91 kg/cm²) |
| Swift | 12.8 psi (.88 kg/cm²) |
| **Thermostat** | |
| Samurai & Swift [2] | |
| "A" Thermostat | 190°F (88°C) |
| "B" Thermostat | 197°F (92°C) |
| Sidekick | 176-183°F (80-84°C) |

[1] - Includes heater core.
[2] - Either "A" or "B" thermostat is used by manufacturer. Ensure replacement thermostat has same temperature specification as original.

## ELECTRIC COOLING FAN (SWIFT)

### TROUBLE SHOOTING & TESTING

**System Testing - 1)** Start engine. Ensure coolant temperature is less than 199°F (93°C). If cooling fan operates, go to next step. If cooling fan does not operate, go to step **3)**.

**2)** Disconnect cooling fan thermoswitch, located near distributor. *See Fig. 1.* If cooling fan continues to operate after cooling fan thermoswitch is disconnected, check for short in Blue wire between cooling fan thermoswitch and cooling fan motor. If cooling fan stops running, replace cooling fan thermoswitch.

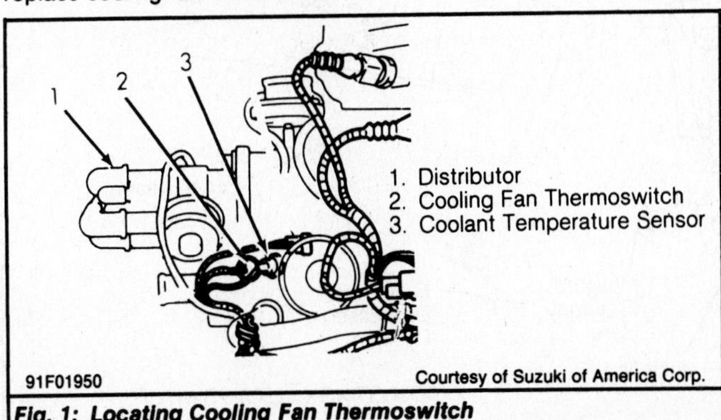


*Fig. 1: Locating Cooling Fan Thermoswitch*

**3)** If cooling fan does not operate with coolant temperature less than 199°F (93°C), run engine until engine coolant temperature is greater than 208°F (98°C). If cooling fan operates, system is okay. If cooling fan does not operate, go to next step.

**4)** With cooling fan thermoswitch connector disconnected, connect a fused jumper wire between thermoswitch connector terminals (Black/White and Blue wires). If cooling fan operates, replace cooling fan thermoswitch. If cooling fan does not operate, go to next step.

**5)** Turn ignition off. Check for continuity between Black (ground) wire of fan motor connector and ground. If no continuity is present, go to next step. If continuity is present, repair open or bad ground connection at Black (ground) wire. Ground connection is located on left front inner fender. *See Fig. 2.*

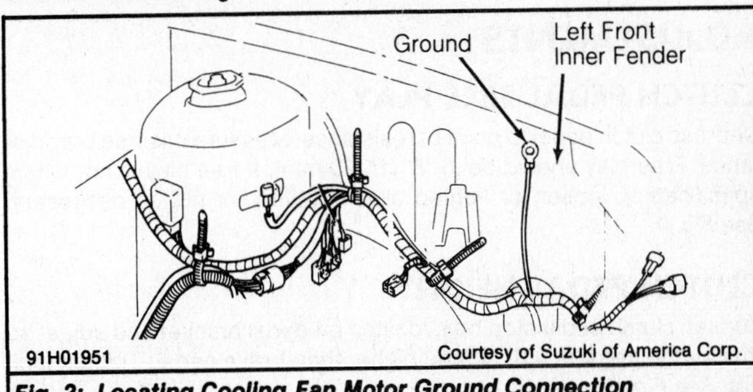


*Fig. 2: Locating Cooling Fan Motor Ground Connection*

**6)** Using a test light, backprobe cooling fan motor connector Blue wire. If test light lights, replace cooling fan motor. If test light does not light, go to next step.

**7)** Using test light, backprobe cooling fan thermoswitch connector Black/White wire. If test light does not light, repair open in Black/White wire between cooling fan thermoswitch and junction block connector. Junction block is located behind left side of instrument panel. *See Fig. 3.* If test light lights, repair open in Blue wire between cooling fan thermoswitch and cooling fan motor.

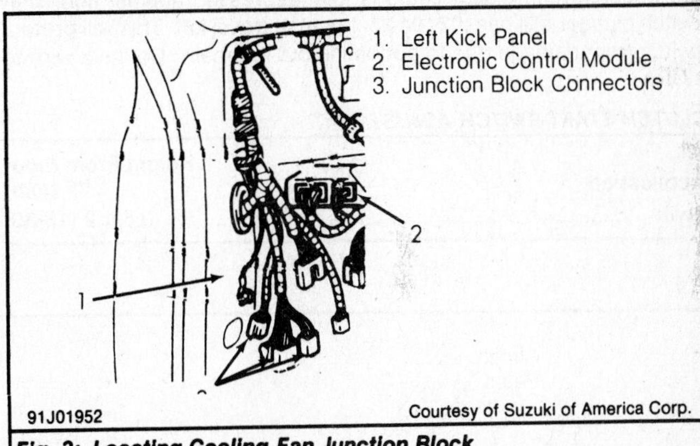


*Fig. 3: Locating Cooling Fan Junction Block*

### COMPONENT TESTING

**Cooling Fan Thermoswitch** - Remove thermoswitch from vehicle. Using ohmmeter, ensure continuity is correct across thermoswitch terminals. Thermoswitch may be gradually heated in water for testing. See COOLING FAN THERMOSWITCH table.

*COOLING FAN THERMOSWITCH* [1]

| Application | Continuity °F (°C) | No Continuity °F (°C) |
|---|---|---|
| Thermostat "A" | Above 208 (98) | Below 199 (93) |
| Thermostat "B" | Above 215 (102) | Below 206 (97) |

[1] - Before testing cooling fan thermoswitch, determine if vehicle has an "A" or "B" thermostat. "A" thermostat opens at 190°F (88°C). "B" thermostat opens at 197°F (92°C).

## WIRING DIAGRAMS

See appropriate chassis wiring diagram in WIRING DIAGRAMS.

# 1991 CLUTCHES
# FWD

Swift

## DESCRIPTION

Clutch is a single disc type using a diaphragm spring to engage the pressure plate. Clutch is mechanically controlled by clutch pedal, clutch cable, return spring, release fork and prelubricated release bearing. System incorporates a clutch switch that disables ignition and starter circuits unless clutch pedal is fully depressed.

## ADJUSTMENTS

### CLUTCH PEDAL FREE PLAY

Depress clutch pedal to point of resistance. Measure this free play distance. Free play should be .6-.8" (15-20 mm). If free play is not within specification, loosen or tighten clutch cable joint nut as necessary. *See Fig. 1.*

### CLUTCH PEDAL HEIGHT

Loosen clutch pedal stop bolt, located on pedal bracket and adjust so that clutch pedal is 0.3" (8 mm) higher than brake pedal. Tighten lock nut. *See Fig. 1.*

### CLUTCH START SWITCH

**1)** Apply parking brake firmly. Place gearshift lever in Neutral. Disconnect wire at switch. Loosen lock nut and turn switch outward. Depress clutch pedal to floor. Release clutch pedal to its adjustment height position. See CLUTCH START SWITCH ADJUSTMENT table.
**2)** Connect ohmmeter to clutch start switch terminals. Slowly screw switch in until it is on. Hold switch at this position and tighten lock nut to specification. See TORQUE SPECIFICATIONS table at end of article. Ensure when clutch pedal is fully depressed against floor that switch plunger still has .02-.04 (.5-1 mm) of travel left. This will protect switch from damage due to bottoming out internally. Connect wire to switch.

***CLUTCH START SWITCH ADJUSTMENT***

| Application | Height From Floor In. (mm) |
|---|---|
| Swift | 0.6-1.2 (15-30) |

## REMOVAL & INSTALLATION

### CLUTCH ASSEMBLY

**Removal & Installation – 1)** Disconnect battery ground cable. Remove battery and tray. Disconnect clutch cable and bracket from transaxle. Disconnect wiring harness clamps and connectors. Disconnect speedometer cable from transaxle. Remove transaxle-to-engine mounting bolts. Remove starter and mounting plate.

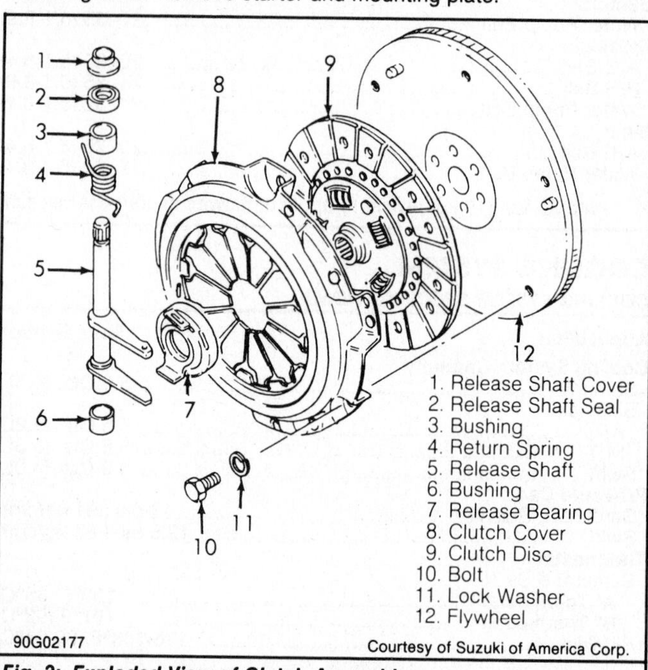


***Fig. 2: Exploded View of Clutch Assembly***

**2)** Raise and support vehicle on lift. Drain transaxle fluid. Remove left side inner fender panel. Remove front section of exhaust pipe. Disconnect shift rod, bushings, and control shaft from transaxle. Remove lower plate/dust shield from clutch housing.
**3)** Disconnect lower ball studs and suspension control arms. Disconnect left side drive axle from transaxle, using a screwdriver to pry drive axle from differential. Remove drive axle center support bearing

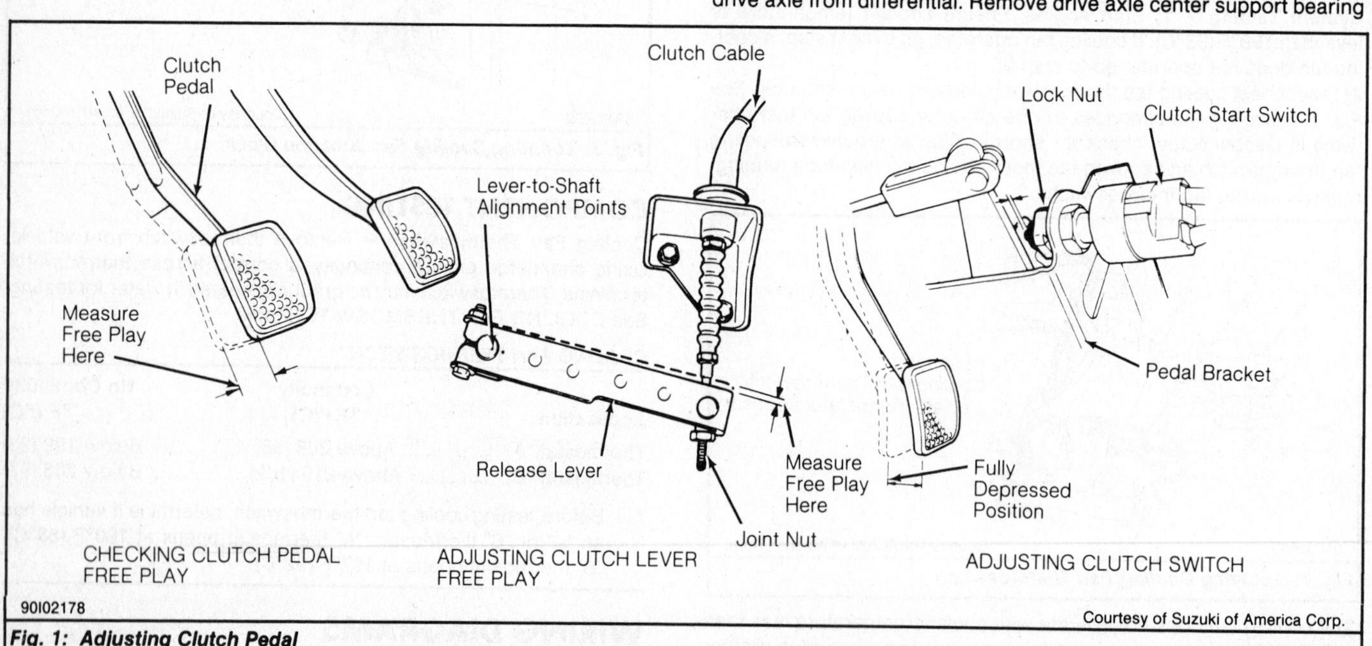


***Fig. 1: Adjusting Clutch Pedal***

# 1991 CLUTCHES
# FWD (Cont.)

and pull center shaft assembly from differential. Remove transaxle brace. Remove remaining engine-to-transaxle mounting bolts. Remove rear engine mount bolts.

**4)** Lower vehicle, and support engine using hoist. Support transaxle using a jack. Remove left engine mount and brace. Remove any remaining components attached to transaxle assembly. Remove transmission from vehicle.

**5)** Mark pressure plate and flywheel for reassembly reference. *See Fig. 2.* Loosen pressure plate attaching bolts alternately until pressure plate is released. Remove clutch disc and pressure plate. To install components, reverse removal procedures.

**Inspection – 1)** Check wear on clutch disc facings by measuring depth of each rivet head. Minimum depth at any rivet is .02" (.5 mm). Replace clutch disc if not within specification.

**2)** Check diaphragm spring and pressure plate for wear or damage. Replace pressure plate assembly if excessively worn or damaged. Check pilot bearing rotation. Replace bearing if roughness is felt. Inspect flywheel runout.

**3)** Clean flywheel and pressure plate of all oil, grease, and metal deposits. Inspect for damage, cracks or warpage. Slight surface scoring can be removed with sandpaper. Replace or repair as necessary.

## RELEASE BEARING

**Removal & Installation – 1)** Disconnect return spring from shaft fork. Remove clutch release bearing. Inspect release bearing for rough rotation, wear or damage. If necessary, replace bearing.

**2)** Lightly lubricate release bearing with grease. Install clutch release bearing on transaxle retainer. Ensure bearing pads are located on fork ends (pads must be indexed) and both spring ends are in fork holes with spring completely seated in bearing groove.

## PILOT BEARING

**Removal & Installation –** Remove transaxle from vehicle. Remove clutch cover and clutch disc. Remove pilot bearing from flywheel. Inspect pilot bearing for rough rotation, wear or damage. Replace bearing if necessary. Install clutch disc and pressure plate. Install transaxle.

## CLUTCH START SWITCH

**Removal & Installation –** Disconnect negative battery cable. Disconnect wire at switch. Remove switch mounting screw at clutch pedal stop bracket. Disconnect switch from clutch pedal bracket. To install, reverse removal procedure. Adjust switch. See CLUTCH START SWITCH under ADJUSTMENTS.

## CLUTCH CABLE

**Removal & Inspection –** Remove clutch cable joint nut. Disconnect inner cable from release arm. Remove clutch cable bracket retaining bolts from dash panel. Reaching through firewall, use a screwdriver to unhook cable end from top of pedal. Remove cable. Check cable for fraying, friction, bends or kinks, torn boots, and wear.

**Installation – 1)** Apply grease to hook and pin of clutch cable before installing. Hook cable end to clutch pedal using a screwdriver or long nose pliers. Install clutch cable bracket on cable.

**2)** Connect inner cable to release arm. Seal cable housing mounting surface at firewall and install 2 mounting bolts. Tighten mounting bolts to specification. See TORQUE SPECIFICATIONS table at end of article. Adjust free play. See CLUTCH PEDAL FREE PLAY under ADJUSTMENTS. Ensure clutch functions correctly with engine running.

## TORQUE SPECIFICATIONS

***TORQUE SPECIFICATIONS***

| Application | Ft. Lbs. (N.m) |
|---|---|
| Engine Mount Nuts | 30-44 (40-60) |
| Flywheel Mounting Bolts | 42-48 (57-65) |
| Gear Shift Control Shaft | 11-15 (15-20) |
| Gear Shift Extension Rod Nut | 18-30 (25-40) |
| Pressure Plate-To-Flywheel Bolts | 13-21 (18-28) |
| Starter Mount Bolts | 16-23 (22-31) |
| Transaxle-To-Engine Bolts | 30-44 (40-60) |
| | **INCH Lbs. (N.m)** |
| Clutch Cable Mounting Bolts | 35-62 (4-7) |
| Clutch Start Switch Lock Nut | 89-133 (10-15) |

# 1991 CLUTCHES
# RWD

## Samurai, Sidekick

## DESCRIPTION

The clutch is a diaphragm spring, single disc type. Clutch operation is mechanically controlled by clutch cable, release lever, release shaft and release bearing.

## ADJUSTMENTS

### CLUTCH PEDAL FREE PLAY

**Samurai** - If clutch pedal free play is not between .8-1.2" (20-30 mm), adjust clutch cable end nuts on transmission until correct specification is obtained.
**Sidekick** - Measure amount of free play at clutch pedal. Clutch pedal play should be .6-1.1" (15-28 mm). If play is out of specification, loosen or tighten clutch cable joint nut at release arm as required.

### CLUTCH PEDAL HEIGHT

**Samurai** - Loosen clutch pedal stop bolt and adjust so clutch pedal is level with brake pedal. Tighten lock nut after adjusting.
**Sidekick** - Loosen clutch pedal stop bolt and adjust so clutch pedal is .2" (5 mm) higher than brake pedal. Tighten lock nut after adjusting.

### CLUTCH START SWITCH

**1)** - Apply parking brake firmly. Place gearshift lever in Neutral. Disconnect wires at clutch start switch. Loosen lock nut and turn switch outward. Depress clutch pedal to floor. Return clutch pedal along its travel from floor. See CLUTCH START SWITCH ADJUSTMENT table.
**2)** - Connect ohmmeter to switch. Slowly screw switch in until it is on. Hold switch at this position and tighten lock nut. Connect wire.

***CLUTCH START SWITCH ADJUSTMENT***

| Application | Height From Floor In. (mm) |
|---|---|
| Samurai [1] | |
| Sidekick | 2.0-2.7 (50-70) |

[1] Adjustment specification is not available from manufacturer.

## REMOVAL & INSTALLATION

### CLUTCH ASSEMBLY

**Removal & Installation (Samurai) - 1)** Remove shift lever boot. Remove shift lever case cover bolts and remove shift lever. Disconnect negative battery cable. Disconnect back-up light and 5th gear switch. Disconnect starter motor wiring and remove stater. Remove clamps attaching fuel hoses to transmission case. Drain transmission oil.
**2)** Disconnect clutch cable from clutch release lever. Remove both drive shafts. Remove clutch inspection plate. Remove engine-to-transmission bolts and nuts. Remove crossmember and center exhaust pipe. Remove transmission rear mounting bracket.
**3)** Lower transmission from vehicle. Install flywheel holder. Mark pressure plate and flywheel for reassembly reference. Remove 6 pressure plate-to-flywheel bolts. Remove pressure plate and clutch disc. Remove clutch release bearing. *See Fig. 1.*
**4)** Check flywheel and pressure plate contact surface for damage. Replace clutch disc if rivet head depression is .02" (.5 mm) or less. Mount clutch disc on transmission input shaft. Turn disc back and forth to check backlash.
**5)** Replace disc assembly if backlash exceeds .03" (.8 mm). Inspect pressure plate assembly for loose diaphragm spring rivets. Check diaphragm fingers for wear. Replace parts as necessary.
**6)** Install clutch alignment tool. Position clutch disc to pressure plate and align index marks. Tighten pressure plate-to-flywheel bolts to specification in a diagonal pattern. See TORQUE SPECIFICATIONS table at end of article. Complete installation by reversing removal procedure.

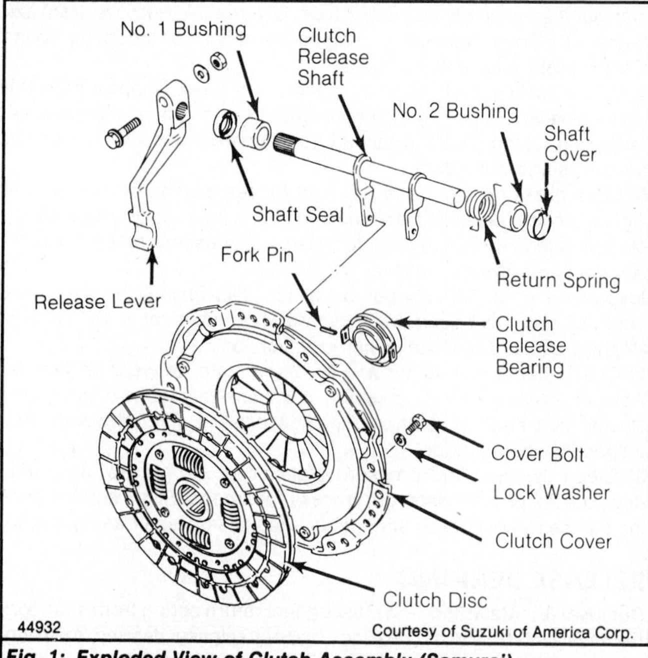

***Fig. 1: Exploded View of Clutch Assembly (Samurai)***

**Removal & Installation (Sidekick) - 1)** Disconnect negative battery cable. Remove transmission and transfer case shift levers. Remove breather hose from clamp at rear of cylinder head. Release clamp at rear of intake manifold to free wiring harness. Disconnect harness connector. Remove starter motor. Remove transmission mounting bolts.
**2)** Raise vehicle and drain fluid from transfer case. Remove front and rear drive shafts. Disconnect clutch cable. Remove clutch housing lower plate. Remove center exhaust pipe. Remove engine-to-transmission mounting nuts. Disconnect speedometer cable.
**3)** Support transmission/transfer case assembly with floor jack. Remove rear engine mount crossmember. Move transmission/transfer case assembly to rear and lower. Remove wiring harness and breather hose.
**4)** Mark pressure plate and flywheel for reassembly reference. Alternately loosen pressure plate attaching bolts until pressure plate is released. Remove clutch disc and pressure plate.
**5)** Check wear on facings of clutch disc by measuring depth of each rivet head. Minimum depth at any rivet is .02" (.5 mm). Replace clutch disc if not within specification.
**6)** Check diaphragm spring and pressure plate for wear or damage. If assembly is excessively worn or damaged, replace pressure plate. Check pilot bearing rotation. If roughness is felt, replace bearing. Inspect flywheel runout.
**7)** Clean flywheel and pressure plate of all oil, grease, and metal deposits. Inspect for damage, cracks or warpage. Remove slight surface scoring with sandpaper. Replace or repair as necessary.
**8)** Install clutch alignment tool. Position clutch disc to pressure plate and align index marks. Tighten pressure plate-to-flywheel bolts to specification in a diagonal pattern. See TORQUE SPECIFICATIONS table at end of article. Complete installation by reversing removal procedure.

### CLUTCH RELEASE BEARING

**Removal & Installation (Samurai)** - Remove clutch assembly. Remove clutch release fork pin and remove bearing from transmission input shaft bearing retainer. Before installing release bearing, apply grease to inner surface. Reverse removal procedures to complete installation.

***NOTE: Replace release bearing if it binds or makes abnormal noise when rotated.***

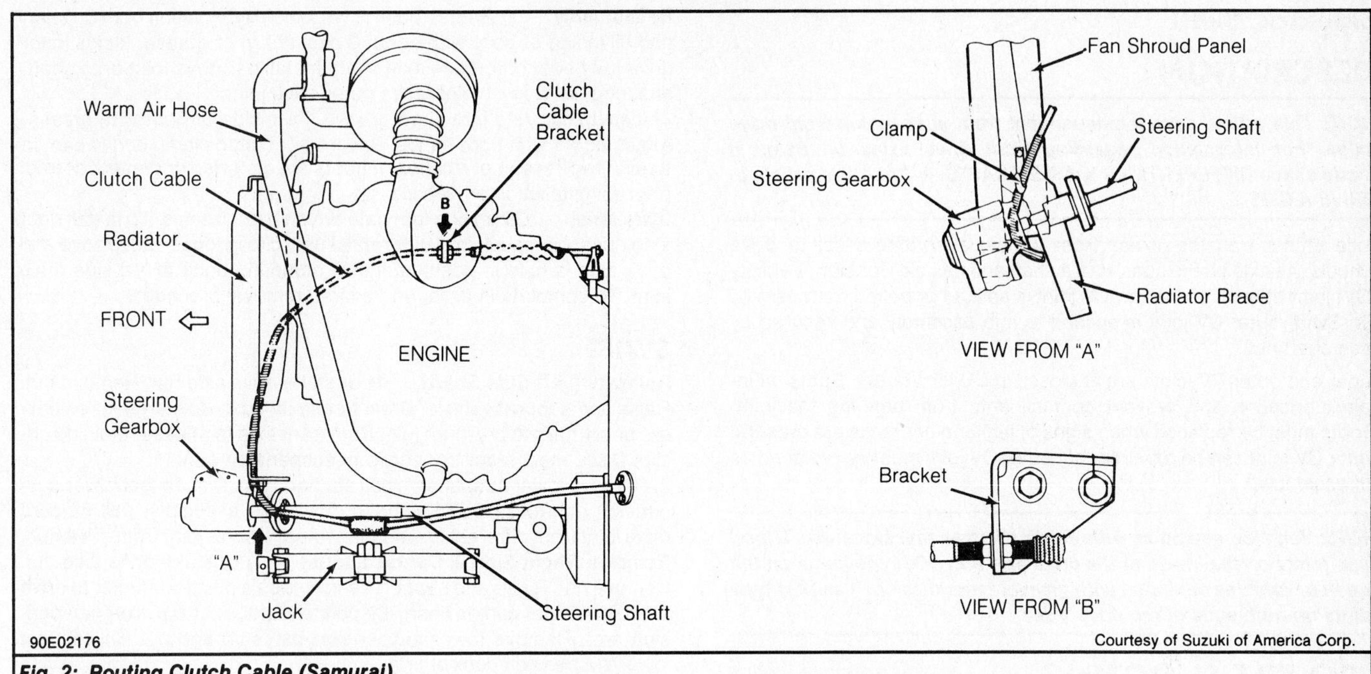


*Fig. 2: Routing Clutch Cable (Samurai)*

**Removal & Installation (Sidekick) - 1)** Disconnect return spring from shaft fork. Remove clutch release bearing. Inspect release bearing for rough rotation, wear or damage. If necessary, replace bearing.
**2)** Lightly lubricate release bearing with grease. Install clutch release bearing on transaxle retainer. Make sure bearing pads are located on fork ends (pads must be indexed) and both spring ends are in fork holes with spring completely seated in bearing groove.

## CLUTCH RELEASE SHAFT

**Removal & Installation (Samurai) - 1)** Remove clutch release bearing. Remove release lever. Remove return spring from clutch release shaft. Check shaft for wear or damage.
**2)** Position Clutch Release Bushing Remover (09925-48210) against No. 2 bushing and lightly tap out bushing and cap. Repeat procedure and remove No. 1 bushing with seal. *See Fig. 1.*
**3)** Install release shaft. Apply grease to release fork contact surfaces. Apply grease to both ends of clutch cable. To complete installation, reverse removal procedures. Clutch release arm bolt and nut should be tightened to 90-138 INCH lbs. (10-16 N.m).

## PILOT BEARING

***NOTE: Install NEW pilot bearing if removed.***

**Removal & Installation (Samurai)** - Remove clutch assembly. Rotate pilot bearing by hand while installed in crankshaft. If pilot bearing sticks or has excessive wear, remove and replace. Remove pilot bearing using Bearing Remover (09917-58010). Install pilot bearing to flywheel using bearing driver.
**Removal & Installation (Sidekick)** - Remove transaxle or transmission. Remove clutch cover and clutch disc. Rotate pilot bearing by hand while still installed in flywheel. If pilot bearing sticks or has excessive wear, remove from flywheel and replace.

## CLUTCH CABLE

***NOTE: Clutch cable removal and installation procedures are not available for Samurai. See Fig. 2.***

**Removal & Installation (Sidekick) - 1)** Disconnect negative battery cable. Remove clutch cable joint nut. Loosen outer cable nuts and disconnect cable from release arm. Untie cable clamps. Remove clutch cable outer bolts at firewall. Unhook cable at clutch pedal shaft and remove cable
**2)** Apply grease to hook and pin of clutch cable before installing. Connect cable to clutch pedal and install retaining bolts. Connect clutch cable to release lever and install joint nut on cable. Adjust clutch pedal free play. See CLUTCH PEDAL FREE PLAY under ADJUSTMENTS. Connect negative battery cable.

## TORQUE SPECIFICATIONS

***TORQUE SPECIFICATIONS***

| Application | Ft. Lbs. (N.m) |
|---|---|
| **Samurai** | |
| Flywheel Mounting Bolts | 41-47 (57-65) |
| Pressure Plate-To-Flywheel Bolts | 13-20 (18-28) |
| Starter Mount Bolts | 16-23 (22-31) |
| Transmission-To-Engine Bolts | 32-39 (43-53) |
| **Sidekick** | |
| Flywheel Mounting Bolts | 41-47 (57-65) |
| Pressure Plate-To-Flywheel Bolts | 13-20 (18-28) |
| Rear Engine Mounts | 21-32 (29-43) |
| Starter Mount Bolts | 16-23 (22-31) |
| Transmission Filler Plugs | 13-21 (18-28) |
| Transmission-To-Engine Bolts | 52-74 (70-100) |
| "U" Joint Companion Flange | 27-32 (37-43) |

# 1991 DRIVE AXLES
# FWD Axle Shafts

## Sidekick, Swift

## DESCRIPTION

***NOTE: This article covers independent front suspension front drive axles. For information regarding front drive axles on Samurai models, see DIFFERENTIALS & AXLE SHAFTS - SAMURAI article in DRIVE AXLES.***

Axle shafts transfer power from transaxle or differential to drive wheels. All axle shafts consist of a shaft and flexible Constant Velocity (CV) joint at each end. Inner CV joint is splined or bolted to transaxle. On Swift, outer CV joint is splined to hub assembly and secured by axle shaft nut.

Inner and outer CV joints are enclosed in CV joint boots. Boots maintain lubrication and prevent contaminants from entering the joint. Boots must be replaced when signs of leakage or cracks are present. Inner CV joint can be repaired, but outer CV joint must be replaced as an assembly.

***NOTE: Vehicles equipped with automatic transmissions use Tripod type joints on the inside of the drive axle and DOJ type joints on the outside. Vehicles equipped with manual transmissions use DOJ type joints on both ends of the drive axles.***

## TROUBLE SHOOTING

***NOTE: See TROUBLE SHOOTING article in GENERAL INFORMATION.***

## REMOVAL, DISASSEMBLY, REASSEMBLY & INSTALLATION

***NOTE: When removing or overhauling FWD axle shafts, refer to illustrations. See Figs. 1-3.***

### SIDEKICK

**Removal - 1)** Raise vehicle and remove drive wheel. Drain transaxle fluid. Remove locking hub. Remove circlip from drive axle. Remove stabilizer ball joint nut. Remove castle nut from tie rod end. Remove mounting bolts from brake caliper. Remove caliper from steering knuckle and suspend with wire. Remove stud nut from steering knuckle.

**2)** Support lower suspension arm with a jack. Remove lower strut bracket bolts. Lower jack and disconnect knuckle from lower suspension control arm. Pull outer drive axles from drive hubs. To remove right side inner joint, use large screwdrivers or pry bars to pry inner joint from transaxle to release retaining circlip. To remove left side inner joint, remove mounting bolts from inner drive joint.

**Disassembly -** Remove boot band from differential side drive joint. Remove circlip from drive joint housing. Remove drive joint from housing. Remove circlip from drive axle. Remove ball drive joint from shaft. Remove inner and outer boots from drive axle shaft.

***NOTE: DO NOT disassemble outer CV drive joint. If joint is faulty, replace as an assembly. DO NOT disassemble differential side joint assembly.***

**Inspection & Cleaning -** Check boots for breakage or deterioration. Replace as necessary. Check circlip, snap ring and boot bands, and replace as necessary. Clean disassembled parts (except boots), in degreaser. Dry components with compressed air. Clean boots with cloth. DO NOT wash boots in degreaser.

**Reassembly - 1)** Grease outer drive joint fully. Position boot on shaft and fill inside of boot with about 3 ozs. (90 g) of grease. Install inner drive joint boot onto drive axle shaft. Install ball drive joint onto shaft, ensuring flat side of joint faces outer drive joint.

**2)** Install snap ring into shaft groove. Fill inside of boot with grease. Attach boots with boot bands. Ensure boot band clamp end is bent in a reverse direction of rotation. If boots are distorted or dented, correct prior to installation on vehicle.

**Installation -** Clean and lubricate drive shaft oil seals. To install right side drive joint, push into differential until circlip locks into groove and drive axle is held in position. Install mounting bolts to left side drive joint. To complete installation, reverse removal procedure.

### SWIFT

**Removal (Left Side Shaft) - 1)** Unstake drive axle nut. Remove nut. Raise and support vehicle. Drain transaxle fluid. Use large screwdrivers or pry bars to pry inner joint from transaxle to release retaining circlip. Disconnect stabilizer bar from suspension arm.

**2)** Remove lower suspension ball stud and nut. Disconnect lower suspension control arm. To remove drive axle assembly, pull inboard drive joint from differential, and then remove outer joint from drive hub.

**Removal (Right Side & Center Shafts) - 1)** Unstake drive axle nut. Remove nut. Raise and support vehicle. Use a plastic hammer to drive shaft joint from center shaft. Disconnect stabilizer bar from suspension arm. Remove lower suspension ball stud and nut. Disconnect lower suspension control arm.

**2)** To remove drive axle assembly, pull inboard drive joint from differential, and then remove outer joint from drive hub. To remove center shaft, drain transaxle fluid. Remove center bearing support bolts and remove center shaft from differential gear.

***NOTE: DO NOT disassemble outer CV drive joint. If joint is faulty, replace as an assembly. DO NOT disassemble differential side joint assembly.***

**Disassembly - 1)** Remove boot band from differential side drive joint. Remove circlip. Remove drive joint housing. Remove circlip from drive axle. Remove ball joint from shaft. Remove inner and outer boots from drive axle shaft.

**2)** To disassemble center shaft and bearing, remove right side oil seal and circlip. Pull center shaft from center bearing. Remove left side oil seal and circlip. Remove center bearing from support.

**Inspection & Cleaning -** Check boots for breakage or deterioration. Replace as necessary. Check circlip, snap ring and boot bands, replace as necessary. Clean disassembled parts (except boots), in degreaser. Dry components with compressed air. Clean boots with cloth. DO NOT wash boots in degreaser.

**Reassembly - 1)** Grease outer drive joint fully. Position boot on shaft and fill inside of boot with about 3 ozs. (90 g) of grease. Install inner drive joint boot onto drive axle shaft. Install ball drive joint onto shaft, ensuring flat side of joint faces outer drive joint.

**2)** Install snap ring into shaft groove. Fill inside of boot with grease. Attach boots with boot bands. Ensure boot band clamp end is bent in a reverse direction of rotation. If boots are distorted or dented, correct prior to installation on vehicle.

**3)** To install center bearing and shaft, reverse removal procedure. Install circlip securely into groove of bearing support. Apply grease to oil seals.

**Installation -** Clean and lubricate drive shaft oil seals. To install right side drive joint, push into differential until circlip locks into groove and drive axle is held in position. To complete installation, reverse removal procedures.

# 1991 DRIVE AXLES
# FWD Axle Shafts (Cont.)

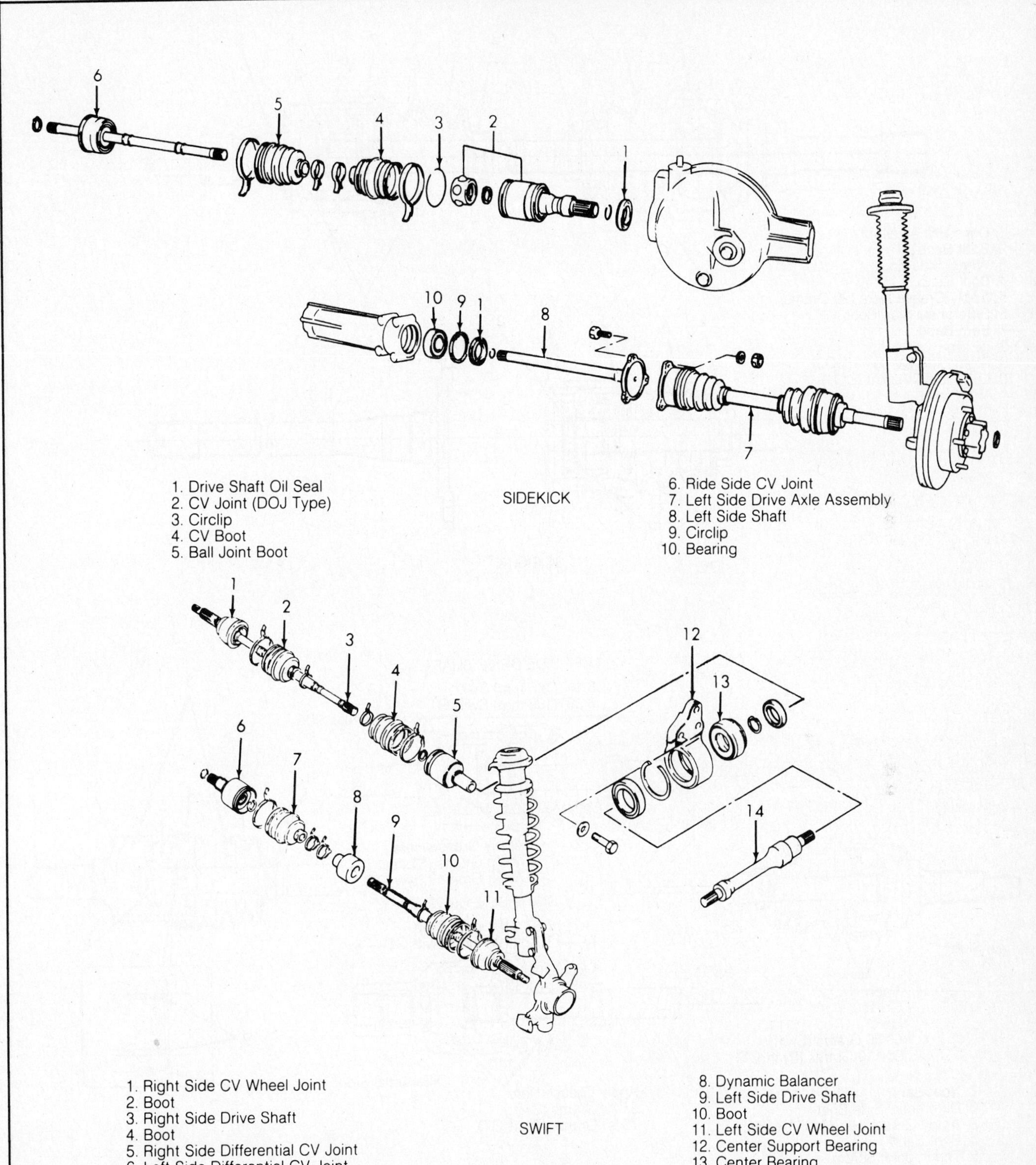


*Fig. 1: Identifying FWD Axle Components*

# 1991 DRIVE AXLES
## FWD Axle Shafts (Cont.)

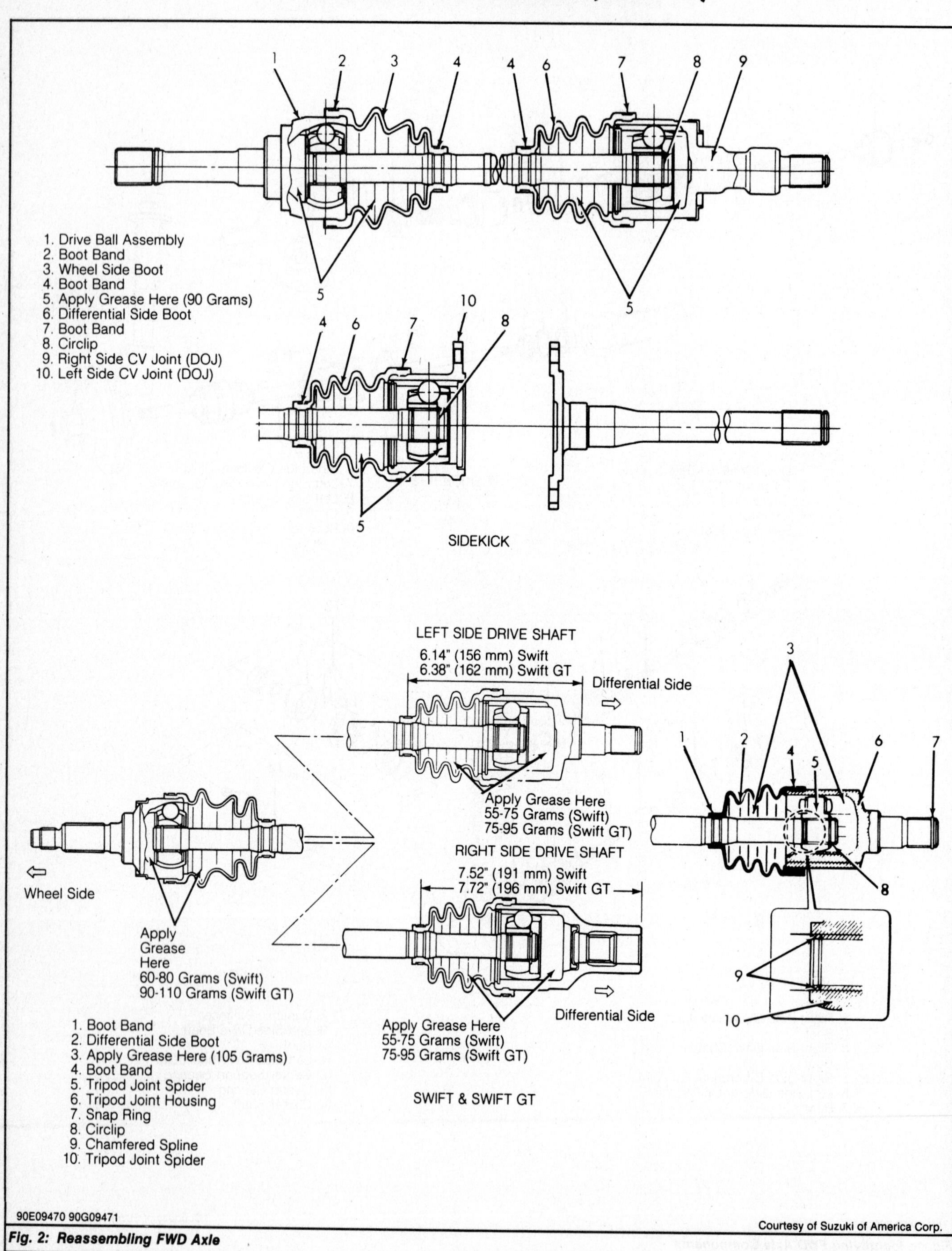


Courtesy of Suzuki of America Corp.

**Fig. 2: Reassembling FWD Axle**

# 1991 DRIVE AXLES
# FWD Axle Shafts (Cont.)

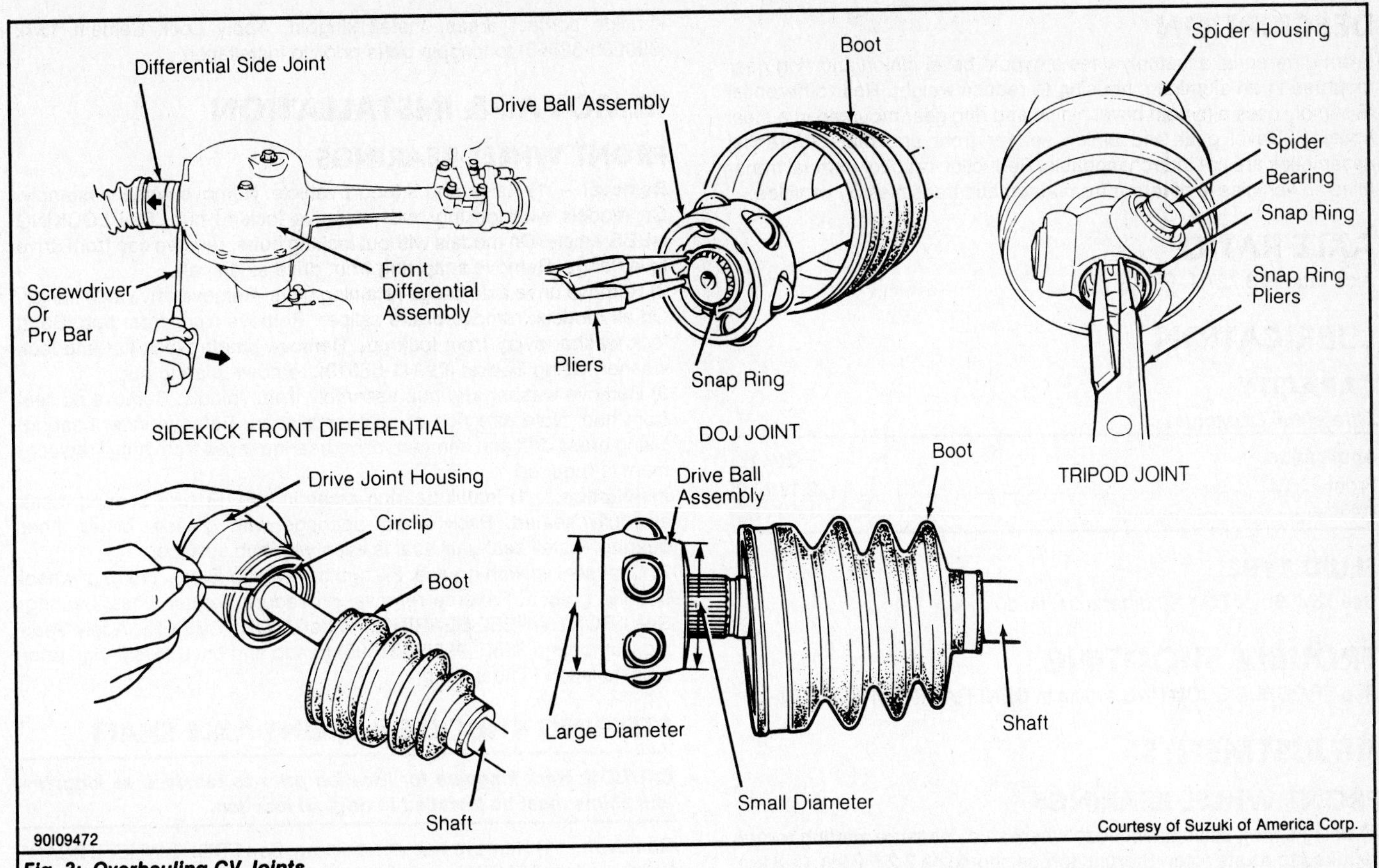


*Fig. 3: Overhauling CV Joints*

## TORQUE SPECIFICATIONS

*TORQUE SPECIFICATIONS*

| Application | Ft. lbs. (N.m) |
|---|---|
| Sidekick | |
| Ball Joint Nut | 16-26 (22-35) |
| Ball Joint Stud Castle Nut | 33-52 (45-70) |
| Caliper Mounting Bolts | 52-74 (70-100) |
| Left Side Inner CV Bolts | 30-44 (40-60) |
| Lower Strut Bracket Bolts | 59-74 (80-100) |
| Oil Drain Plug | 26-37 (35-50) |
| Tie Rod End Castle Nut | 22-41 (30-55) |
| Wheel Nuts | 59-81 (80-110) |
| Swift | |
| Center Bearing Support Bolts | 30-44 (40-60) |
| Drive Axle Outer Nut | 111-148 (150-200) |
| Lower Ball Joint Stud | 37-52 (50-70) |
| Oil Drain Plug | |
| Automatic Transmission | 13-17 (18-23) |
| Manual Transmission | 18-22 (25-30) |
| Oil Filler & Level Plug | 27-40 (36-54) |
| Stabilizer Joint Nut | 13-21 (18-28) |

# 1991 DRIVE AXLES
# Differentials & Axle Shafts – Samurai

## DESCRIPTION

Front differential assembly uses a hypoid bevel pinion and ring gear mounted in an aluminum housing to reduce weight. Rear differential assembly uses a hypoid bevel pinion and ring gear mounted in a steel housing. Bevel gear and pinion set for front and rear differential assemblies are not interchangeable. Reduction ratio for manual transmission vehicles is different from automatic transmission vehicles.

## AXLE RATIO

Axle ratio is 3.727:1

## LUBRICATION

### CAPACITY

***Differential Capacities***

| Application | Qts. (L) |
|---|---|
| Front | 2.11 (2.0) |
| Rear | 1.58 (1.5) |

### FLUID TYPE

Use 75W-90 or 80W-90 differential fluid.

## TROUBLE SHOOTING

See TROUBLE SHOOTING article in GENERAL INFORMATION.

## ADJUSTMENTS

### FRONT WHEEL BEARINGS

**1)** Using spring scale attached to wheel stud, measure starting torque required to rotate rotor. Starting torque should be 2.2-6.6 lbs. (1-3 kg). If adjustment is required, bend lock washer away from lock nut. Remove bearing lock nut and lock washer.

**2)** Using Socket (09941-58010) and foot-pound torque wrench, tighten bearing nut to 58 ft. lbs. (79 N.m) while spinning hub assembly. Loosen bearing nut. Using inch-pound torque wrench, tighten bearing nut to 84-120 INCH lbs. (9-13 N.m). Install lock washer and lock nut. Tighten lock nut to 44-65 ft. lbs. (60-90 N.m). Bend tab on lock washer against lock nut.

**3)** Using spring scale, recheck starting torque. Starting torque should be 2.2-6.6 lbs. (1-3 kg). Reverse removal procedures. Apply Sealing Compound 366E (99000-31090) to hub and drive axle flange prior to installation (if equipped).

### KINGPIN

**1)** Raise and support vehicle. Remove wheel assembly. Remove tie rod nut at steering knuckle. Using tie rod separator, separate tie rod from steering knuckle. Disconnect tie rod from steering knuckle. Remove steering knuckle oil seal. See STEERING KNUCKLE OIL SEAL under REMOVAL & INSTALLATION.

***CAUTION: Before checking starting torque, remove steering knuckle oil seal and tighten kingpin retaining bolts to specification.***

**2)** Ensure kingpin retaining bolts are tightened to specification prior to measuring starting torque. Attach a spring scale to tie rod area of steering knuckle. Measure starting torque required to move steering knuckle. Starting torque should be 2.20-3.96 lbs. (1.0-1.8 kg).

**3)** If starting torque is not within specification, adjust kingpin preload. Remove kingpin retaining bolts. Install a large amount of kingpin shims. Install kingpin and tighten bolts to specification. See TORQUE SPECIFICATIONS table at end of article.

**4)** Recheck kingpin starting torque. Gradually decrease shim thickness until starting torque is obtained. If correct starting torque cannot be obtained when no shims are used, inspect kingpins or bearings for damage.

**5)** Once correct starting torque is obtained, remove kingpin. Apply Sealing Compound 366E (99000-31090) to kingpin-to-steering knuckle contact areas. Install kingpin. Apply Lock Cement 1342 (990000-32050) to kingpin bolts prior to installation.

## REMOVAL & INSTALLATION

### FRONT WHEEL BEARINGS

**Removal – 1)** Raise and support vehicle. Remove wheel assembly. On models with locking hubs, remove locking hub. See LOCKING HUBS article. On models without locking hubs, remove cap from drive axle flange. Remove snap ring from drive axle shaft.

**2)** Remove drive axle flange retaining bolts. Remove drive axle flange. On all models, remove brake caliper. Remove rotor from hub. Bend lock washer away from lock nut. Remove bearing lock nut and lock washer. Using Socket (09941-58010), remove bearing nut.

**3)** Remove washer and hub assembly from spindle. Remove oil seal from hub. Note direction of seal installation. Remove inner bearing. Using brass drift and hammer, drive bearing races from hub if replacement is required.

**Installation – 1)** Install bearing races in hub. Ensure bearing races are fully seated. Pack wheel bearings with grease. Install inner bearing. Install seal until seal is even with hub surface.

**2)** Coat seal lip with grease. Fill hub cavity with .5 ozs. (15 g) of wheel bearing grease. Reverse removal procedure. Adjust wheel bearing. See FRONT WHEEL BEARINGS under ADJUSTMENTS. Apply Sealing Compound 366E (99000-31090) to hub and drive axle flange prior to installation (if equipped).

### STEERING KNUCKLE & FRONT AXLE SHAFT

***CAUTION: Mark kingpins for location prior to removal, as kingpins and shims must be installed in original location.***

**Removal – 1)** Remove hub and bearing. See FRONT WHEEL BEARINGS under REMOVAL & INSTALLATION. Loosen but DO NOT remove upper and lower kingpin retaining bolts. Remove dust cover, caliper holder and wheel spindle from axle housing.

**2)** Separate tie rod from steering knuckle. Remove 8 bolts retaining oil seal cover. Remove felt pad, oil seal and seal retainer from steering knuckle. Remove steering knuckle oil seal. Mark kingpins for location. Remove kingpins from steering knuckle.

**3)** Note location of shims. Install shims and kingpins in original location. Drain differential fluid. Slowly remove axle shaft and spindle assembly from both sides of vehicle. Remove steering knuckle and kingpin bearings. DO NOT allow lower kingpin bearing to drop during steering knuckle removal.

**Installation – 1)** To install, reverse removal procedures. Pack kingpin bearings and spindle bushing with Grease (99000-25010) prior to installation. Apply approximately 5 ozs. (150 g) of Grease (99000-25120) to the inside of steering knuckle prior to installation.

**2)** Install kingpins and shims in original location. Check kingpin adjustment. See KINGPIN under ADJUSTMENTS. Apply Sealing Compound 366E (99000-31090) on dust cover-to-steering knuckle contact areas, spindle-to-brake caliper holder and spindle-to-steering knuckle areas prior to installation.

**3)** Install hub assembly. Adjust wheel bearings. See FRONT WHEEL BEARINGS under ADJUSTMENTS.

### STEERING KNUCKLE OIL SEAL

***NOTE: Steering knuckle oil seal controls steering damping. Replace oil seal if it fails, causing oil leakage or wheel shimmy.***

**Removal & Installation – 1)** Remove oil seal cover retaining bolts. Move oil seal cover and pad toward inside of vehicle. Remove oil seal from oil seal retainer. Note direction of seal installation.

**2)** Using scissors, cut and remove oil seal. Cut replacement seal, and install in oil seal retainer approximately 30 degrees from top side of seal retainer area.

**3)** Apply Grease (99000-25120) to inside of oil seal. Apply Sealing Compound 366E (99000-31090) around entire mating surface of seal

# 1991 DRIVE AXLES
# Differentials & Axle Shafts - Samurai (Cont.)

retainer to prevent water from entering seal area. Reverse removal procedures for seal installation.

## FRONT DIFFERENTIAL ASSEMBLY

**Removal & Installation** - Mark front drive shaft position for installation reference. Disconnect drive shaft from differential assembly. Remove front differential assembly. To install, reverse removal procedure.

## REAR AXLE & BEARING

**Removal & Installation** - **1)** Raise and support vehicle. Using slide hammer and adapter, remove brake drums. Disconnect rear brake lines. Plug all line openings. Remove backing plate retaining bolts.

**2)** Using Rear Axle Remover (09922-66010) and a slide hammer, remove axle shaft and backing plate as an assembly. Grind retainer ring down until it is thin enough to be cut with a chisel. Cut retainer. Using a puller, remove bearing from axle shaft. Remove backing plate. To install, reverse removal procedure.

## REAR CARRIER ASSEMBLY

**Removal & Installation** - Raise and support vehicle. Remove axle shaft. See REAR AXLE & BEARING. Mark drive shaft position. Disconnect drive shaft from differential. Remove rear differential assembly. To install, reverse removal procedure.

# OVERHAUL

## CARRIER ASSEMBLY

**Disassembly** - **1)** Remove flange nut. Mark side bearing caps for reassembly reference and remove. Remove carrier assembly from differential housing. *See Fig. 1*. Remove ring gear.

**2)** Mark differential case halves for reassembly reference. Remove right case half from left case half. Remove side gears, pinions and thrust washers from differential halves. Remove side bearings from case. Remove pinion assembly from housing. Using a hydraulic press, remove pinion bearing from shaft.

***NOTE: Replace pinion and ring gear as a set if worn or damaged.***

**Reassembly** - **1)** Press side bearings onto differential case halves. To reassemble differential case, reverse disassembly procedure and see DIFFERENTIAL under OVERHAUL . Ensure reference marks on halves align. Position ring gear on differential case halves. Apply Locking Cement 133B (99000-32020) on ring gear retaining bolt threads.

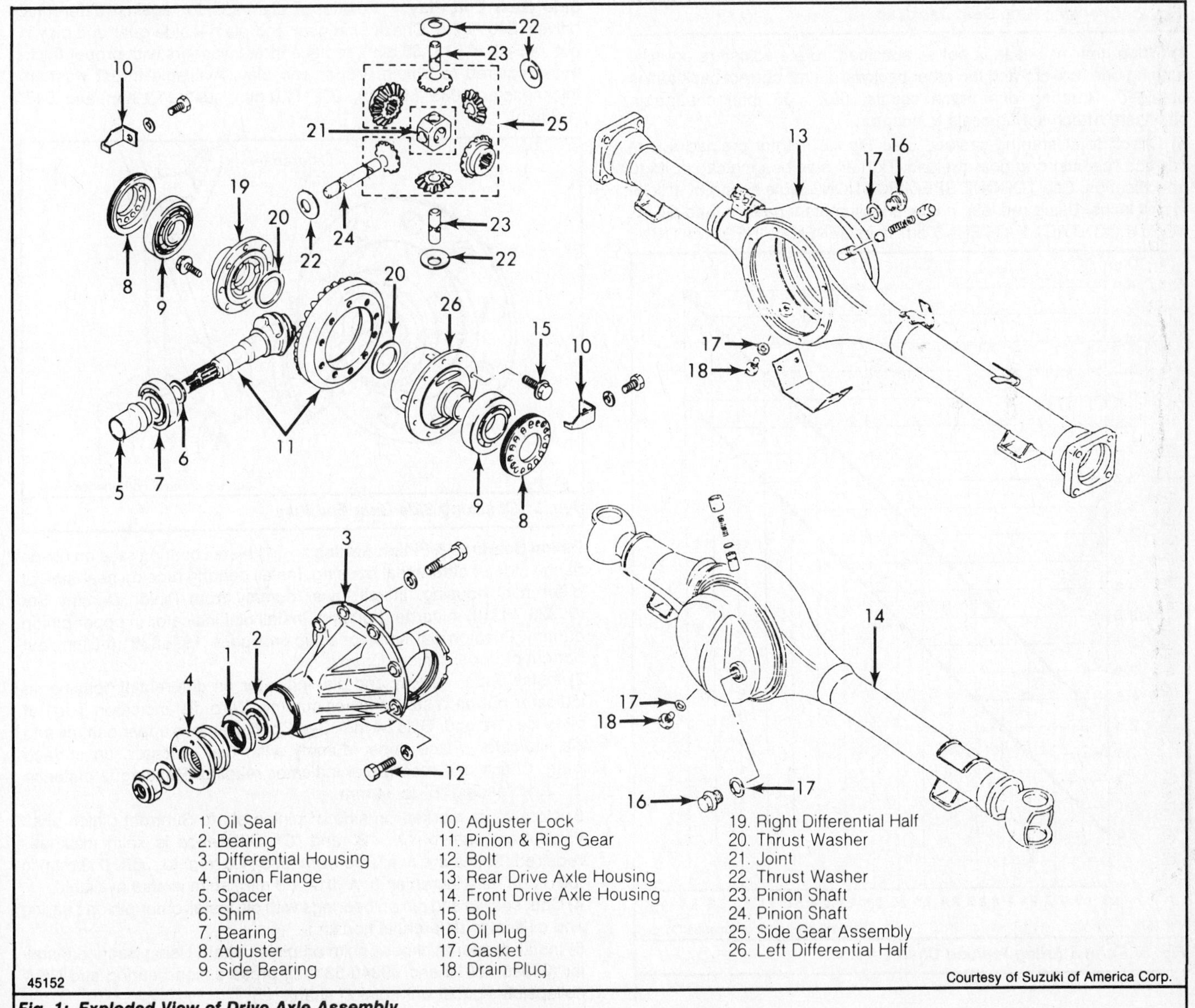


***Fig. 1: Exploded View of Drive Axle Assembly***

# 1991 DRIVE AXLES
# Differentials & Axle Shafts – Samurai (Cont.)

**2)** Place carrier assembly in differential housing. Position side bearing caps and adjusters in housing. Ensure marks made on side bearing caps during disassembly are aligned.
**3)** Tighten side bearing caps bolts to 90-168 INCH lbs. (10-19 N.m). Rotate adjusters until they contact side bearing races. Position a dial indicator against ring gear. *See Fig. 2.* Check ring gear backlash. Backlash should be .004-.006" (.10-.15 mm).

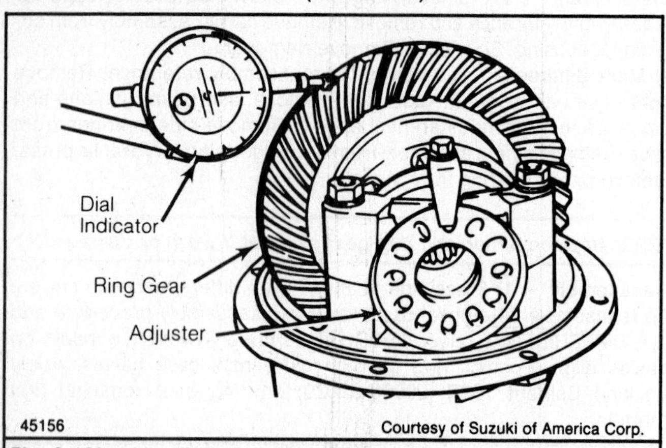


***Fig. 2: Checking Ring Gear Backlash***

**4)** If ring gear backlash is not as specified, rotate adjusters equally, running one forward and the other backward, until correct backlash is obtained. Rotating one notch equals .002" (.05 mm) change in backlash. Attach spring scale to adapter.
**5)** Check total starting preload. *See Fig. 3.* If total preload is not correct, readjust ring gear preload. Tighten side bearing cap bolts to specification. See TORQUE SPECIFICATIONS table at end of article. Install locks. Using red lead paste, check contact pattern. See GEAR TOOTH CONTACT PATTERNS article in GENERAL INFORMATION.

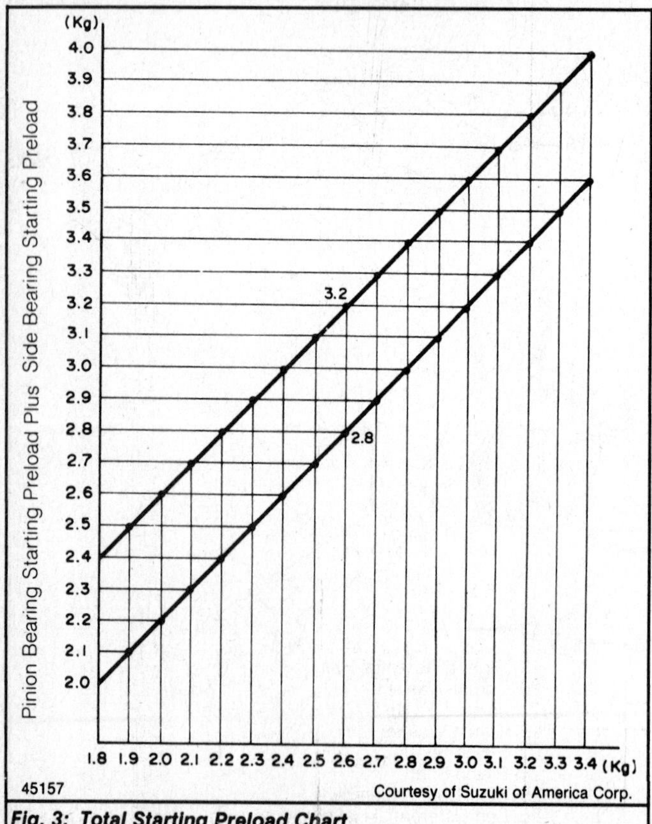


***Fig. 3: Total Starting Preload Chart***

## DIFFERENTIAL

**Assembly** – Position side gears, thrust washers and pinions in left differential half. Ensure shafts for pinions are installed properly. *See Fig. 4.* Place right differential half on left half. Install 8 bolts securing differential halves together.

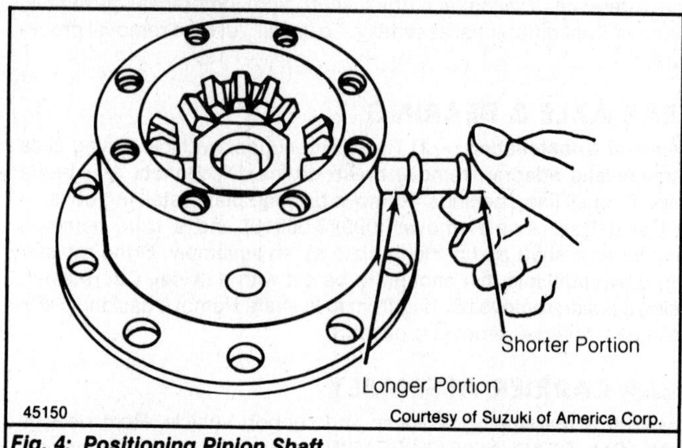


***Fig. 4: Positioning Pinion Shaft***

**Side Gear End Play** – Position a dial indicator against differential halves. *See Fig. 5.* Check side gear end play. If side gear end play is not .005-.014" (.13-.36 mm), replace thrust washers with proper thickness required to obtain proper end play. Available thrust washers thickness are .035" (.9 mm), .039" (1.0 mm), .043" (1.1 mm) and .047" (1.2 mm).

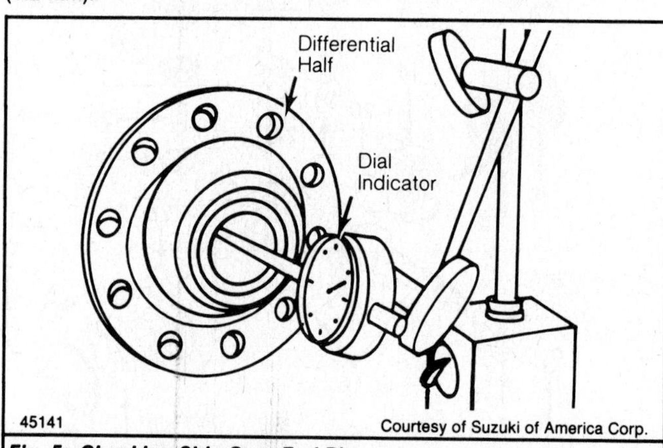


***Fig. 5: Checking Side Gear End Play***

**Pinion Bearings & Pinion Settings** – **1)** Install bearing race on pinion flange side of differential housing. Install bearing race on gear side of differential housing. Install lower dummy from Pinion Dummy Set (09926-78310) in carrier housing. Install dial indicator in upper pinion dummy. Position dial indicator so tip protrudes .197-.236" (5-6 mm) out bottom of upper pinion dummy.
**2)** Install upper dummy and dial indicator on differential housing so indicator button rests on lower dummy. Zero dial indicator. Total of distances "A" and "C" is 94 mm. *See Fig. 6.* Remove upper dummy and dial indicator. Place upper dummy, with dial indicator, on surface plate. Check and record dial indicator reading. Reading is distance "B". Add reading "B" to 94 mm.
**3)** Note value marked on side of pinion shaft. Subtract pinion shaft value from sum of "A", "B" and "C". Difference is shim thickness required. Shims are available from .039 (1.0 mm) to .050" (1.3 mm) in .001" (.03 mm) increments. A .012" (.3 mm) shim is also available.
**4)** Coat seal lip and pinion bearings with oil. Install outer pinion bearing and oil seal in differential housing.
**5)** Install proper thickness shim on pinion shaft. Using Bearing Installer (09925-18010 and 09940-53111), press pinion bearing and NEW collapsible spacer onto pinion shaft.

# 1991 DRIVE AXLES
# Differentials & Axle Shafts – Samurai (Cont.)

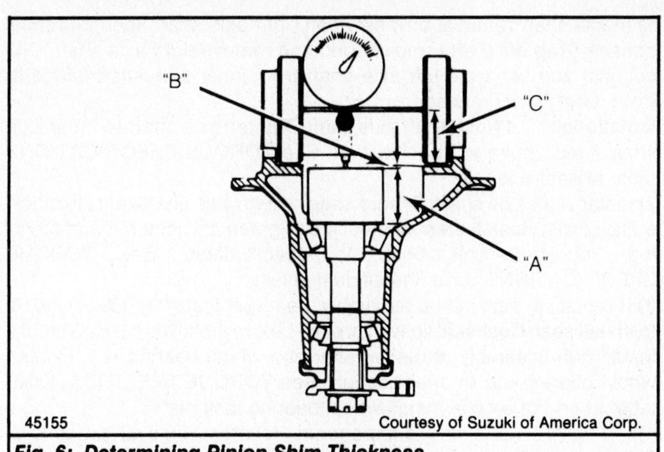


*Fig. 6: Determining Pinion Shim Thickness*

**Bearing Preload – 1)** Place pinion shaft in differential housing. Install flange, washer and retaining nut. Install Preload Adjuster (09922-75221) on pinion flange. *See Fig. 7.*

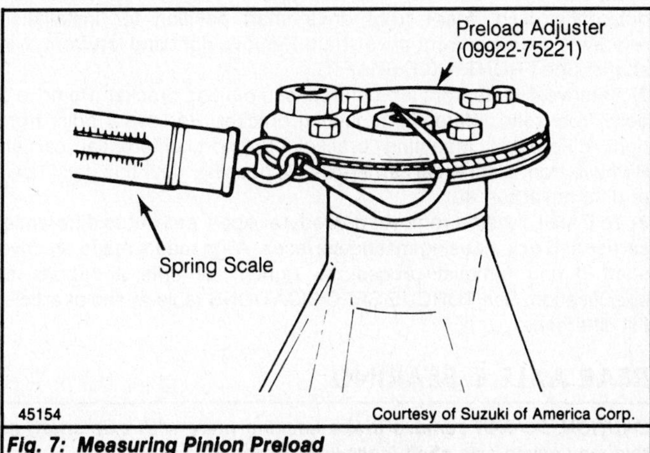


*Fig. 7: Measuring Pinion Preload*

**2)** Using a spring scale, check starting preload, not rotating preload. Tighten pinion nut until specified starting preload is obtained. See PINION BEARING PRELOAD SPECIFICATIONS table.

*PINION BEARING PRELOAD SPECIFICATIONS*

| Application | Lbs. (kg) |
|---|---|
| Starting Preload | 4.0-7.5 (1.8-3.4) |
| Rotating Preload | [1] |

[1] – Preload is 7.8-14.7 INCH lbs. (.9-1.7 N.m) when not using preload adjuster.

**3)** Install pinion flange on pinion shaft. Hand tighten pinion nut. Install Preload Adjuster (09922-75221) on pinion flange. Rotate pinion flange several times to seat bearings. Attach spring scale to preload adjuster. Check starting preload.

**4)** Tighten pinion nut until specified starting preload is obtained. See PINION BEARING PRELOAD SPECIFICATIONS table. If starting preload is exceeded, replace collapsible spacer and recheck. DO NOT loosen pinion nut to obtain correct starting preload. Stake pinion nut.

## TORQUE SPECIFICATIONS

*TORQUE SPECIFICATIONS*

| Application | Ft. Lbs. (N.m) |
|---|---|
| Backing Plate Bolt | 14-20 (19-27) |
| Caliper Guide Pin | 19-22 (26-30) |
| Caliper Holder Bolt | 29-43 (39-58) |
| Carrier Half Bolt | 14-20 (19-27) |
| Differential Housing Bolt | 27-33 (37-45) |
| Drain Plug | 14-18 (19-24) |
| Drive Axle Flange Bolt | 15-22 (20-30) |
| Fill Plug | 26-36 (35-49) |
| Kingpin Bolt | 15-22 (20-30) |
| Leaf Spring Nut | 44-63 (60-85) |
| Locking Hub Body-To-Hub Bolt | 15-22 (20-30) |
| Ring Gear Bolts | 58-66 (80-90) |
| Shackle Pin Nut | 22-40 (30-54) |
| Shock Absorber | |
| Front | |
| Lower Nut | 26-40 (35-54) |
| Upper Nut | 16-25 (22-34) |
| Rear | 26-40 (35-54) |
| Side Bearing Cap Bolts | 52-74 (70-100) |
| Stabilizer Bar Mount Bracket Bolt | 13-20 (18-27) |
| Stabilizer Bar Mount-To-Crossmember Bolt | 16-25 (22-34) |
| Stabilizer Bar-To-Spring Seat Bolt | 51-65 (69-88) |
| "U" Bolt Nut | 44-58 (60-79) |
| Wheel Bearing Lock Nut | 44-66 (60-90) |
| | INCH Lbs. (N.m) |
| Locking Hub Cover Bolt | 71-106 (8-12) |
| Side Bearing Adjuster Lock Bolt | 80-124 (9-14) |
| Steering Knuckle Seal Retainer Bolt | 71-106 (8-12) |

# 1991 DRIVE AXLES
# Differentials & Axle Shafts – Sidekick

## DESCRIPTION

Front differential assembly uses a hypoid bevel pinion and ring gear mounted in an aluminum housing to reduce weight. Rear differential assembly uses a hypoid bevel pinion and ring gear mounted in a steel housing. Bevel gear and pinion set for front and rear differential assemblies are not interchangeable. Reduction ratio for manual transmission vehicles is different than ratio for automatic transmission vehicles.

## AXLE RATIO

***AXLE RATIO SPECIFICATIONS***

| Application | Ratio |
|---|---|
| 2-Door | |
| A/T | 4.625:1 |
| M/T | 5.125:1 |
| 4-Door | |
| A/T | 4.625:1 |
| M/T | 5.375:1 |

## LUBRICATION

### CAPACITY

***Differential Capacities***

| Application | Qts. (L) |
|---|---|
| Front | 1.05 (1.0) |
| Rear | 2.33 (2.2) |

### FLUID TYPE

Use 75W-90 or 80W-90 differential fluid.

## TROUBLE SHOOTING

See TROUBLE SHOOTING article in GENERAL INFORMATION.

## REMOVAL & INSTALLATION

### FRONT WHEEL BEARINGS

**Removal – 1)** Raise and support vehicle. Remove wheel assembly. On models with locking hubs, remove locking hub. See LOCKING HUBS article in DRIVE AXLES. On models without locking hubs, remove cap from hub.

**2)** On all models, remove 4 bearing lock plate screws. Remove brake caliper. Using Socket (09951-16050), remove bearing lock nut and lock washer. Remove hub assembly. Remove oil seal from hub. Remove bearing circlip. Using brass drift and hammer, drive bearing race from hub (if replacement is required).

**Installation –** Install bearing race in hub. Ensure bearing race is fully seated. Pack wheel bearings with grease. Install seal until seal is even with hub surface. Coat seal lip with grease. To complete installation, reverse removal procedure.

### FRONT AXLE SHAFTS

**Removal – 1)** Raise and support vehicle. Remove front wheels. Remove locking hub retaining bolts, locking hubs and "O" rings. Remove snap rings and washers from end of axle shafts.

**2)** Disconnect stabilizer bar from control arms. Remove stabilizer bar mount bolts and stabilizer bar. Remove cotter pins and nuts from tie rods at steering knuckles. Separate tie rods from steering knuckles. Remove brake caliper retaining bolts. Remove brake calipers and wire aside. DO NOT disconnect lines from brake calipers.

**3)** Remove brake rotor. Remove lock plate for wheel bearing. Using Wheel Bearing Socket (09951-16050), remove wheel bearing nut and thrust washer. Remove hub assembly with bearings and oil seal.

**4)** Remove dust shield from steering knuckle. Support front suspension with floor jack. Remove steering knuckle-to-strut retaining bolts. Remove nut and separate steering knuckle from ball joint. Remove steering knuckle.

**5)** Install shaft removal fork between right axle shaft and differential housing. Tap on shaft removal fork, and remove right axle shaft. Disconnect and separate left axle shaft from inner axle shaft flange at front differential housing.

**Installation – 1)** Install left axle shaft. Tighten axle shaft-to-inner axle shaft flange bolts to specification. See TORQUE SPECIFICATIONS table at end of article.

**2)** Install right axle shaft. Ensure snap ring on axle shaft seats in differential carrier. Install steering knuckle. Tighten ball joint nut and steering knuckle-to-strut bolts to specification. See TORQUE SPECIFICATIONS table. Install dust shield.

**3)** If replacing seal in hub assembly, use Seal Installer (09944-66010) to install seal. Coat seal lip with grease before installing hub assembly. Install hub assembly, thrust washer and wheel bearing nut. Tighten wheel bearing nut to specification. See TORQUE SPECIFICATIONS table at end of article. Install wheel bearing lock plate.

**4)** To install remaining components, reverse removal procedure. Tighten bolts to specification. See TORQUE SPECIFICATIONS table at end of article. When installing locking hub, use NEW "O" ring.

### FRONT CARRIER ASSEMBLY

**Removal & Installation – 1)** Raise and support vehicle. Drain differential fluid. Mark front drive shaft position for installation reference. Remove front drive shaft. Remove right and left front axle shafts. See FRONT AXLE SHAFTS.

**2)** Remove 4 bolts from left differential mounting bracket. Remove 2 bolts from rear differential mounting bracket. Remove 3 bolts from right differential mounting bracket. Support differential carrier. Remove front differential carrier-to-axle housing mounting nuts. Lower differential carrier.

**3)** To install, reverse removal procedure. Apply sealant to differential carrier and axle housing mating surfaces. Align marks made on drive shaft during removal procedure. Tighten all nuts and bolts to specification. See TORQUE SPECIFICATIONS table at end of article. Fill differential.

### REAR AXLE & BEARING

***CAUTION: DO NOT remove brake backing plate with axle shaft, as this may cause axle shaft inner seal damage.***

**Removal & Installation – 1)** Raise and support vehicle. Remove wheels. Remove rear brake drums. Drain differential fluid. Remove rear wheel bearing retaining nuts from axle housing. Remove brake shoe return spring. Ensure there is clearance between bearing retainer and parking brake shoe lever. Using axle shaft Puller (09922-66010) with Slide Hammer (09942-15510), remove axle shaft.

**2)** Using a grinder, flatten 2 sides of bearing retainer ring. Remove bearing retainer ring from axle shaft using a metal chisel and hammer. Using a press, remove wheel bearing from axle shaft. Remove axle shaft inner oil seal from differential axle housing.

**3)** To install, reverse removal procedure. Using Seal Installer (99000-25010), install NEW inner oil seal. Apply wheel bearing grease to inner oil seal lip. Apply sealant to mating surface of wheel bearing retainer and brake backing plate. Tighten wheel bearing retaining nuts to specification. See TORQUE SPECIFICATIONS table at end of article. Fill differential.

### REAR AXLE HOUSING

**Removal & Installation – 1)** Raise and support vehicle. Drain differential fluid. Remove wheels and brake drums. Disconnect brake lines from wheel cylinders. Remove rear axle shafts. See REAR AXLE & BEARING.

**2)** Disconnect metal brake line from flexible hose and "E" clip. Remove brake lines from axle housing. Remove breather hose from axle housing. Remove rear drive shaft.

**3)** Support center of rear axle housing. Remove ball joint bracket from differential carrier. Disconnect wheel speed sensor (if equipped). Remove differential carrier assembly. See REAR CARRIER ASSEMBLY. Remove rear mount nuts of trailing rods. DO NOT remove bolts.

4) Remove shock absorber lower mount bolts. Lower differential housing until suspension coil spring tension is relieved. Remove trailing rod mount bolts. Remove coil springs. Lower rear axle housing. To install, reverse removal procedure.

### REAR CARRIER ASSEMBLY

**Removal & Installation – 1)** Raise and support vehicle. Drain differential fluid. Mark rear drive shaft position for installation reference. Remove rear drive shaft.

**2)** Remove right and left rear axle shafts. See REAR AXLE & BEARING. Remove rear wheel speed sensor cover from differential carrier. Disconnect wheel speed sensor electrical harness.

**3)** Remove 4 bolts from upper rear suspension arm. Support differential carrier. Remove rear differential carrier-to-axle housing mounting nuts. Lower differential carrier.

**4)** To install, reverse removal procedure. Apply sealant to differential carrier and axle housing mating surfaces. Align marks made on drive shaft during removal procedure. Tighten all nuts and bolts to specification. See TORQUE SPECIFICATIONS table at end of article. Fill differential.

## OVERHAUL

### FRONT & REAR DIFFERENTIAL ASSEMBLIES

**Disassembly – 1)** Mount differential carrier in Holding Fixture (09944-76010) and vise. Mark differential side bearing caps for installation reference. *See Fig. 8 or 10.*

**2)** Remove side bearing lock plates and caps. Remove side bearing adjusters and outer bearing races. On rear differentials, remove rear wheel speed sensor. On front and rear differentials, remove ring gear assembly.

**3)** On rear differentials, separate differential left case with rear wheel anti-lock exciter ring from right case. Using a copper hammer, remove exciter ring from left case. Tap evenly along outer edge of exciter ring.

**4)** On front and rear differentials, turn differential carrier in fixture 90 degrees. Using pinion Flange Holder (09922-66020), remove universal joint flange nut. Remove universal joint flange. Remove pinion shaft. Using Oil Seal Remover (09951-18210) and slide hammer, remove pinion oil seal.

**5)** Remove outer pinion bearing from differential carrier. Remove outer and inner pinion bearing races. Using side bearing Puller (09913-61510) and Differential Side Bearing Remover (09913-85230), remove differential side bearings.

**6)** Mount differential case in vise. Using arbor punch and hammer, remove spring pin. *See Fig. 1.* Remove differential side gears, selective shims, pinion gears, thrust washers and shafts. Remove collapsible spacer and inner pinion bearing. Discard collapsible spacer.

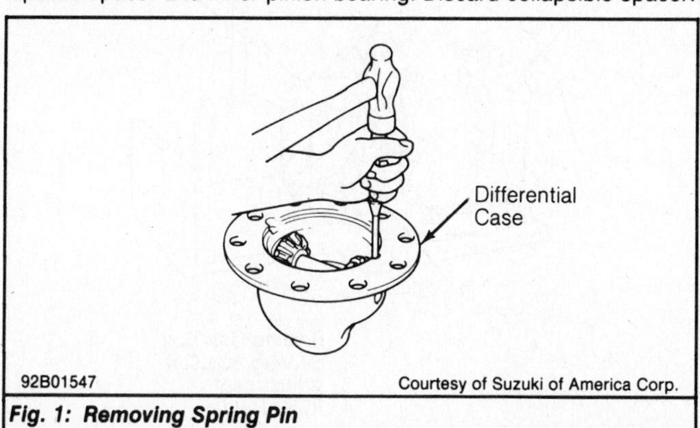


***Fig. 1: Removing Spring Pin***

***NOTE: Replace ring gear, pinion and taper roller bearings and races as a set.***

**Reassembly & Adjustments – 1)** On rear differentials, install rear wheel anti-lock brake exciter ring to differential left case, using Exciter Ring Installer (09928-26010), Differential Side Bearing Remover (09913-85230) and press. Pressure exerted on exciter ring should not exceed 1102 lbs. (500 kg).

**2)** Ensure press fit is applied evenly around perimeter of exciter ring. Install wheel speed sensor. On front and rear differentials, install differential pinion gears, thrust washers and left side gear with selective shim in differential case. *See Fig. 2.*

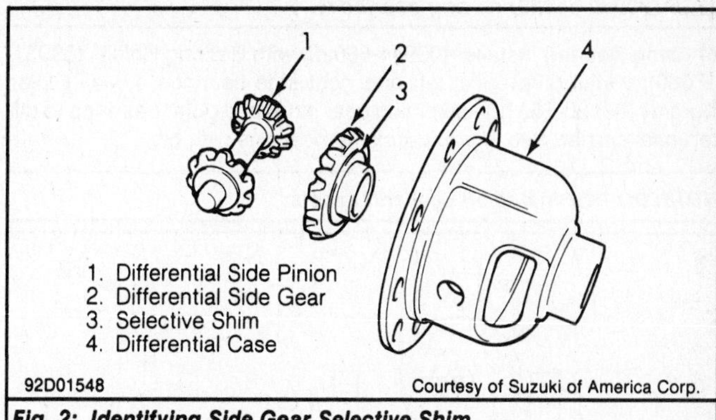


***Fig. 2: Identifying Side Gear Selective Shim***

**3)** Using dial indicator, measure differential side gear end play. *See Fig. 3.* If end play is not .005-.014" (13-36 mm), select another shim to obtain end play.

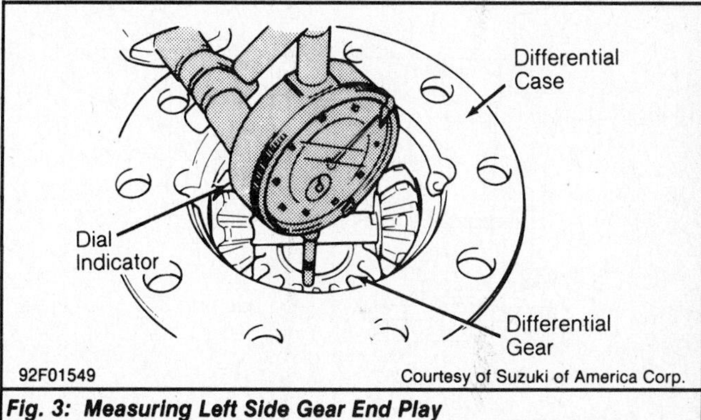


***Fig. 3: Measuring Left Side Gear End Play***

**4)** Install spring pin into differential case until flush with differential case surface. Install right differential side gear, selective shim and ring gear to differential case.

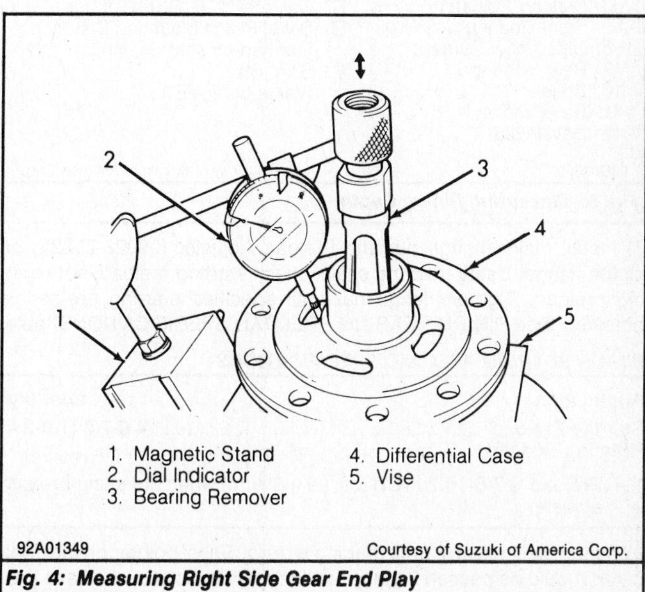


***Fig. 4: Measuring Right Side Gear End Play***

**5)** Tighten ring gear bolts to specification. See TORQUE SPECIFICATIONS table at end of article. Using dial indicator and Magnetic Stand (09900-20701), measure differential side gear end play. *See Fig. 4.* If end play is not .005-.014" (13-36 mm), select another shim to obtain end play.

***NOTE: After proper end play is obtained, install Thread Lock Cement 133B (99000-66020) on ring gear bolts.***

**6)** Using Bearing Installer (09944-66020) with Bearing Holder (09951-16060), install differential left and right side bearings. Install Pinion Dummy (09926-78310) and pinion gear inner and outer bearings to differential carrier. *See Fig. 5.* Lubricate bearings with oil.

***NOTE: DO NOT install oil seal and spacer.***

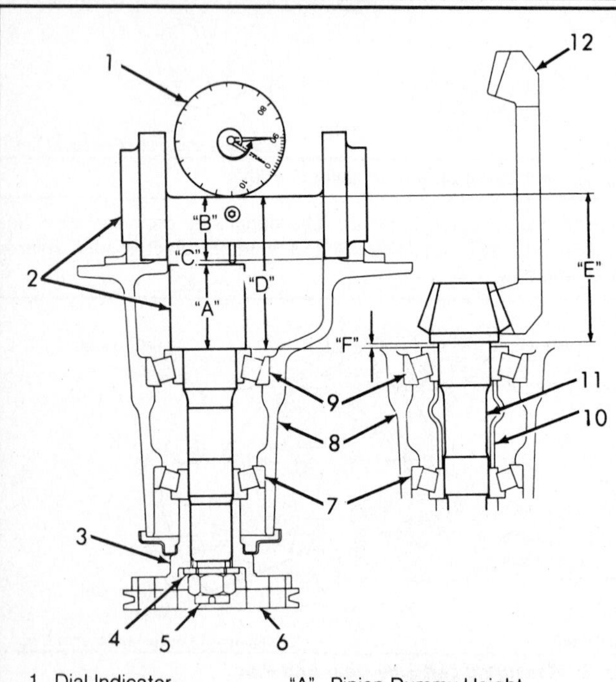


1. Dial Indicator
2. Pinion Dummy
3. Universal Joint Flange
4. Washer
5. Nut
6. Preload Adjuster
7. Front Bearing
8. Differential Carrier
9. Rear Bearing
10. Spacer
11. Bevel Pinion
12. Bevel Gear

"A". Pinion Dummy Height
"B". Axle Dummy Radius
"A"+"B". Front is 94 mm.
Rear is 97 mm.
"C". Measured Dimension
"D". Value of "A"+"B"+"C"
"E". Bevel Pinion Mounting Distance (Marked on shaft in mm.)
"F". Shim Size (Value of "D"-"E")

92C01350 Courtesy of Suzuki of America Corp.

***Fig. 5: Measuring Pinion Depth***

**7)** Install pinion flange nut and Preload Adjuster (09922-75222) on pinion flange. Using a spring scale, check starting preload, not rotating preload. Tighten flange nut until specified starting preload is obtained. See PINION BEARING PRELOAD SPECIFICATIONS table.

***PINION BEARING PRELOAD SPECIFICATIONS***

| Application | Lbs. (kg) |
|---|---|
| Starting Preload | 4.0-7.5 (1.8-3.4) |
| Rotating Preload | [1] |

[1] – Preload is 7.8-14.7 INCH lbs. (.9-1.7 N.m) when not using preload adjuster.

**8)** Adjust dial indicator until reading is zero. Short pointer on dial indicator should be passed 2 mm when long pointer is at zero. Place pre-adjusted dial indicator and dummy on pinion dummy. Note reading of indicator between zero position with measuring tip extended.

**9)** Measure distance "A" and "B". *See Fig. 5.* On front differential, the sum of "A" and "B" is 94 mm. On rear differential, the sum of "A" and "B" is 97 mm. Record reading of measurement "C". *See Fig. 5.* Record value marked on side of pinion shaft ("E").

**10)** Add the recorded value of measurement "C" to the sum of "A" and "B" (94 mm for front, 97 mm for rear). Subtract value "E", recorded form side of pinion shaft, from the sum of "A", "B" and "C". Select adjusting shim size closest to calculated value.

**11)** Shims are available from .039 (1.0 mm) to .050" (1.3 mm) in .001" (.03 mm) increments. A .012" (.3 mm) shim is also available. Install pinion selective shim on pinion gear shaft. Install pinion gear shaft. Install NEW collapsible spacer on pinion gear shaft.

**12)** Install outer pinion bearing in differential carrier. Using Oil Seal Installer (09951-18210), install pinion oil seal. Apply lubricant to oil seal lip. Install pinion flange, washer and flange nut using Pinion Flange Holder (09922-66020).

***CAUTION: Tightening flange nut will preload pinion bearings. Exceeding preload specification will compress collapsible spacer too far and will require installation of a new spacer.***

**13)** Adjust bearing preload starting torque to 4.0-7.5 ft. lbs. (1.8-3.4 N.m.). Measure pinion bearing preload again after rotating pinion several times to ensure bearings are seated.

**14)** If preload is reduced, reset bearing preload. Install side bearing races on differential side bearings. Install ring gear. Install differential case on differential carrier.

**15)** Install side bearing adjusters and bearing caps. Align caps with differential carrier match marks made during disassembly procedure. Tighten differential side bearing cap bolts to specification. See TORQUE SPECIFICATIONS table at end of article.

***NOTE: For identification purposes, right bearing adjuster nut is on ring gear side of carrier. Left bearing adjuster nut is on pinion gear side of carrier.***

**16)** Using spanner wrench, loosen left adjuster nut until it does not contact side bearing race. Tighten right adjuster nut until ring gear is fully engaged into pinion gear with zero backlash.

**17)** Check left adjuster nut to ensure it still does not contact side bearing race. Rotate pinion gear to ensure no binding is present. To adjust bearing preload, install dial indicator to differential case. *See Fig. 6.*

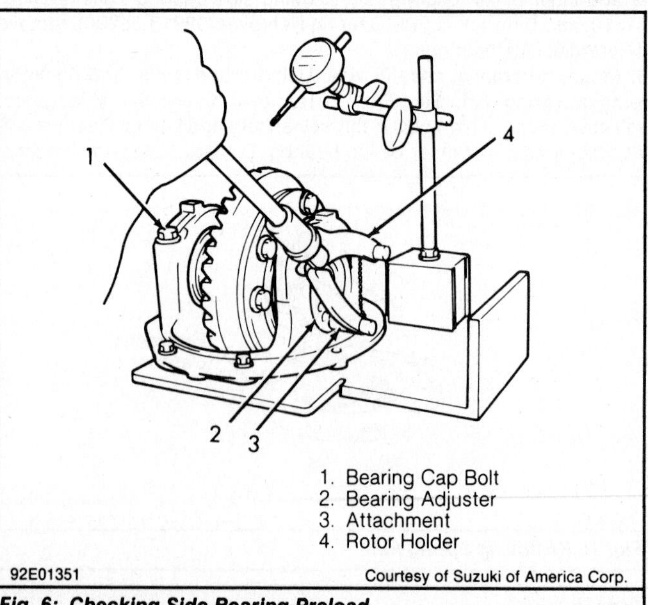


1. Bearing Cap Bolt
2. Bearing Adjuster
3. Attachment
4. Rotor Holder

92E01351 Courtesy of Suzuki of America Corp.

***Fig. 6: Checking Side Bearing Preload***

**18)** Using spanner wrench, tighten left adjuster nut until it contacts side bearing. Set dial indicator to zero against side bearing cap. Adjust side bearing preload by tightening right adjuster nut with spanner wrench until preload is obtained. *See Fig. 7.* Rotate pinion gear to ensure side bearings seat.

# 1991 DRIVE AXLES
## Differentials & Axle Shafts – Sidekick (Cont.)

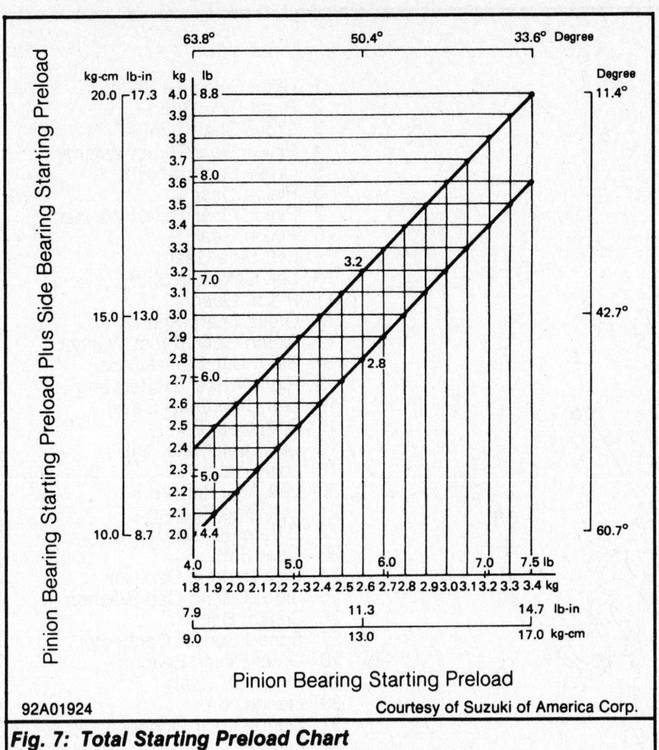


*Fig. 7: Total Starting Preload Chart*

**19)** Tighten differential side bearing caps to specification. See TORQUE SPECIFICATIONS table. To check gear backlash, install dial indicator to differential case. *See Fig. 9.*

**20)** If backlash is not .005-.007" (.13-.18 mm), use spanner wrench to loosen one adjuster and tighten opposite nut an equal amount. This will move ring gear away from (or toward) pinion gear and maintain side bearing preload.

***NOTE: Tightening right adjuster nut moves ring gear into pinion gear to decrease backlash. Tightening left adjuster nut moves ring gear away from pinion gear to increase backlash. When moving adjuster nuts, make final movement in tightening direction to ensure correct side bearing preload.***

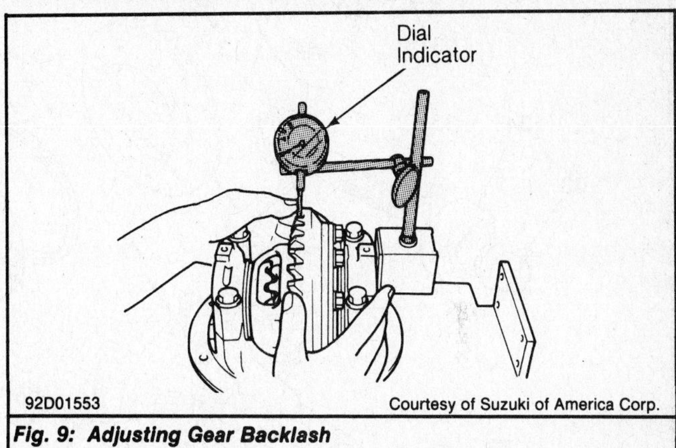


*Fig. 9: Adjusting Gear Backlash*

FRONT OF VEHICLE

1. Shaft Nut
2. Lock Washer
3. Shaft Bolt
4. Selective Shim
5. Differential Gear
6. Axle Shaft Snap Ring
7. Front Axle Shaft
8. Differential Pinion Gear
9. Pinion Thrust Washer
10. Differential Pinion Shaft
11. Shaft Pin
12. Bearing Lock Plate Bolt
13. Bearing Lock Plate
14. Axle Shaft Oil Seal
15. Bearing Snap Ring
16. Axle Shaft Bearing
17. Bearing Adjuster Nut
18. Differential Side Bearing
19. Left Differential Case
20. Collapsible Spacer
21. Pinion Inner Bearing
22. Pinion Selective Shim
23. Bevel Pinion Gear Set
24. Right Differential Case
25. Bevel Gear Bolt
26. Side Bearing Cap Bolt
27. Front Differential Carrier Case
28. Carrier Nut
29. Lock Washer
30. Carrier Unit
31. Pinion Outer Bearing
32. Pinion Oil Seal
33. Universal Joint Flange
34. Flange Washer
35. Flange Nut

92F01554

Courtesy of Suzuki of America Corp.

*Fig. 8: Exploded View of Front Differential Assembly*

# 1991 DRIVE AXLES
## Differentials & Axle Shafts – Sidekick (Cont.)

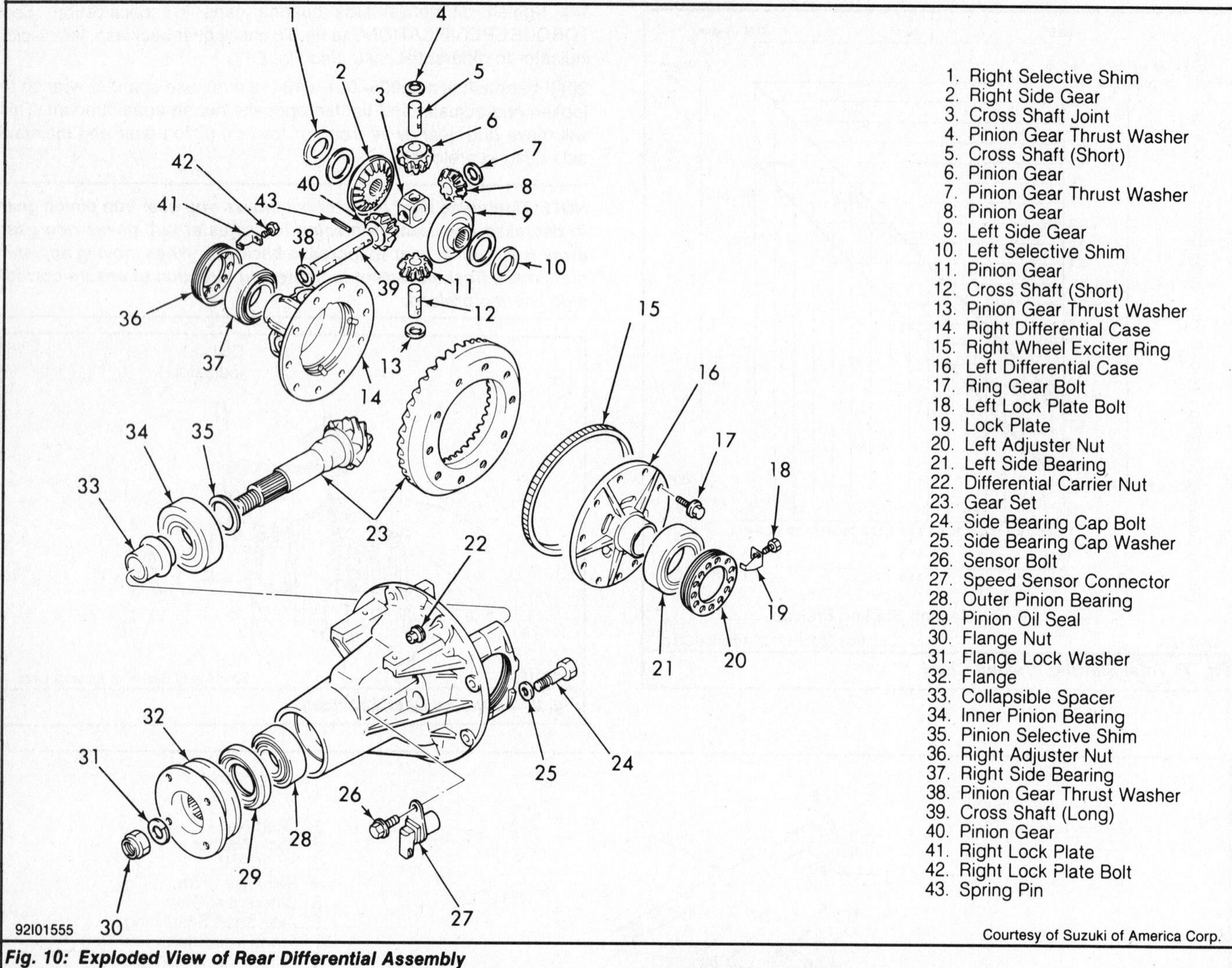


*Fig. 10: Exploded View of Rear Differential Assembly*

**21)** Install bearing lock plates and tighten bolts to specification. See TORQUE SPECIFICATIONS table at end of article. Using marking compound, check gear tooth contact pattern. See GEAR TOOTH CONTACT PATTERNS article in GENERAL INFORMATION. Stake pinion flange nut.

## TORQUE SPECIFICATIONS

*TORQUE SPECIFICATIONS*

| Application | Ft. Lbs. (N.m) |
|---|---|
| Differential Drain Plug | 17 (23) |
| Drive Shaft Bolt & Nut | 37 (50) |
| Front Brake Caliper Bolt | 65 (88) |
| Front Differential | |
| Carrier Nut | 17 (23) |
| Mount Bolt | 37 (50) |
| Ring Gear Bolt | 70 (95) |
| Side Bearing Cap Bolt | 44 (60) |
| Side Bearing Lock Plate Bolt | 25 (34) |
| Front Locking Hub Bolt | 18 (24) |
| Front Stabilizer Bar Mount Bolt | 37 (50) |
| Front Stabilizer Bar-To-Control Arm Bolt | 21 (28) |
| Front Wheel Bearing Nut | 155 (210) |
| Left Front Axle Shaft-To-Inner Flange Bolt | 37 (50) |
| Oil Filler/Level Plug | 30 (41) |
| Rear Ball Joint Bracket Bolt | 37 (50) |
| Rear Differential | |
| Carrier Nut | 17 (23) |
| Ring Gear Bolt | 63 (85) |
| Side Bearing Cap Bolt | 63 (85) |
| Side Bearing Lock Plate Bolt | 25 (34) |
| Upper Rear Suspension Arm Bolt | 41 (56) |
| Rear Shock Absorber Nut | 66 (89) |
| Rear Trailing Rod Nut | 66 (89) |
| Rear Wheel Bearing Retaining Nut | 17 (23) |
| Steering Knuckle-To-Ball Joint Nut | 40 (54) |
| Steering Knuckle-To-Strut Bolt | 66 (89) |
| Tie Rod-To-Steering Knuckle Nut | 30 (41) |
| Wheel Lug Nut | 48 (65) |

# 1991 DRIVE AXLES
# Locking Hubs

## Samurai, Sidekick

## DESCRIPTION & OPERATION

Manual locking hubs engage and disengage front wheels from axle shafts on 4WD vehicles. These hubs are an option on Samurai and Sidekick models. When hubs are engaged in LOCK position, wheels and axle shafts rotate together. When hubs are disengaged or unlocked in the FREE position, front wheels free wheel on hub bearings.

Engagement is accomplished through action of a gear clutch and spring within hub. When hub is locked, hub clutch engages inner hub, which is always connected to axle shaft by inner splines of hub. Hub clutch is always connected by outer splines to hub body. Control knob applies or releases spring tension to control hub clutch position.

Sidekick models have automatic locking hubs as standard equipment. Automatic hubs are engaged by rotational force of axle shaft when 4WD is selected at transfer case. Automatic hubs disengage when 2WD is selected and vehicle is driven in reverse. Cams, brakes and

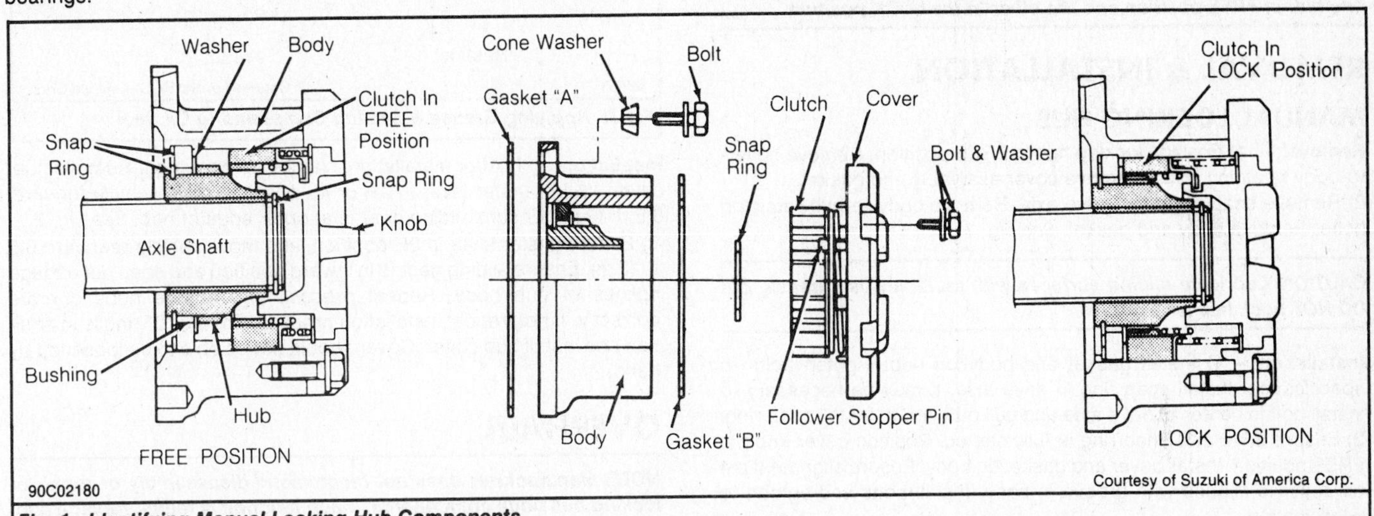


*Fig. 1: Identifying Manual Locking Hub Components*

90E02181

Courtesy of Suzuki of America Corp.

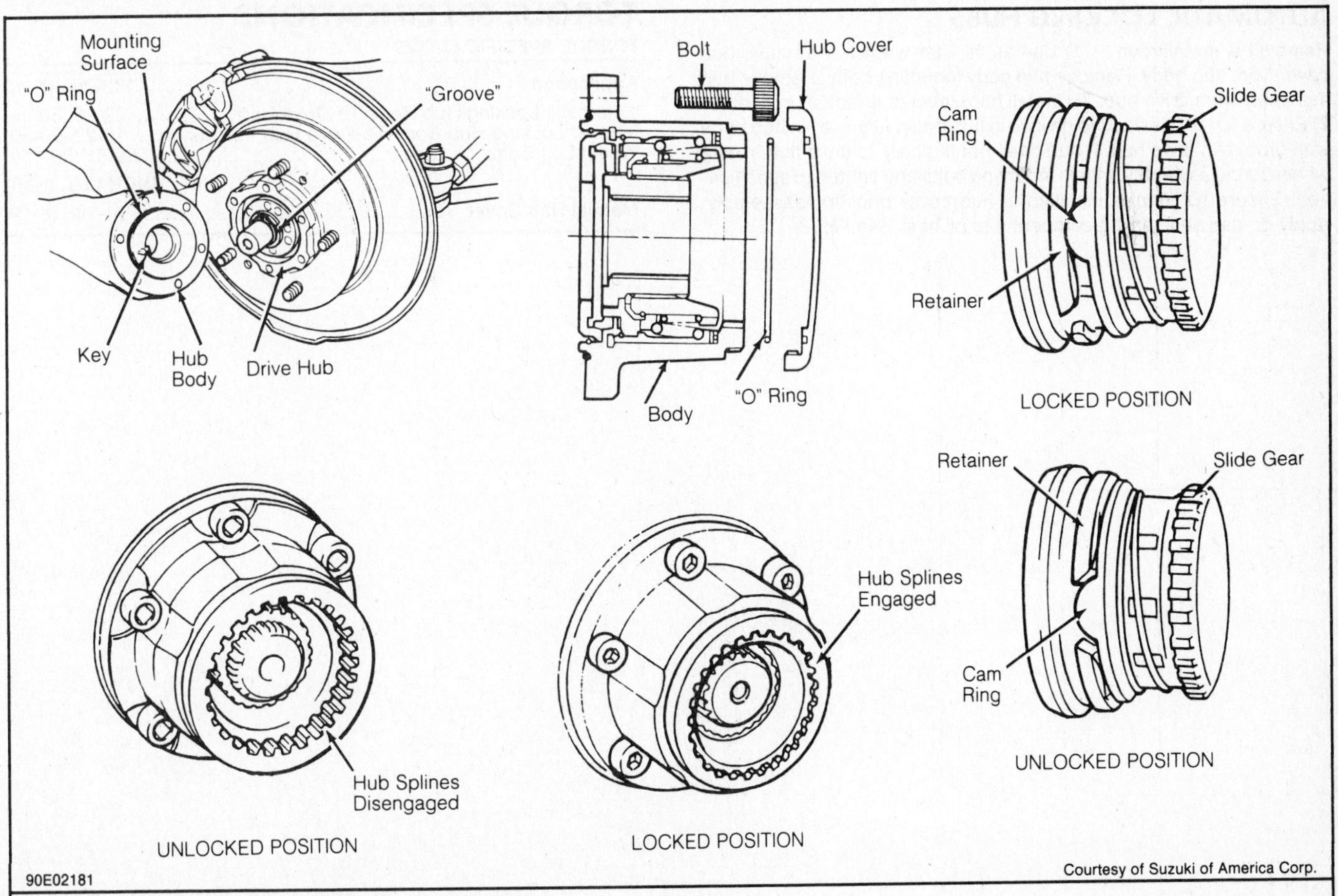

*Fig. 2: Identifying Automatic Locking Hub Components*

# 1991 DRIVE AXLES
# Locking Hubs (Cont.)

springs are used to lock or unlock automatic hubs. Automatic locking function will take place within 6.5 ft. (2 m) of vehicle travel.

Manual hubs have control knob marked with LOCK and FREE rotation direction. Outer edge of hub cover on manual hubs is marked with LOCK and FREE positions. Automatic hubs do not have an engagement knob on hub cover.

***CAUTION: When operating vehicle with manual locking hubs, both hubs must be set in the same position. Never operate vehicle with one hub in FREE position and the other in the LOCK position.***

## REMOVAL & INSTALLATION

### MANUAL LOCKING HUB

**Removal - 1)** Position locking hub in FREE position. Remove cover-to-body retaining bolts. Remove cover assembly and gasket.
**2)** Remove snap ring from drive axle. Remove body-to-hub retaining bolts. Remove body and gasket. *See Fig. 1.*

***CAUTION: Lubricate sliding surfaces with multipurpose grease, but DO NOT pack hub with grease.***

**Installation - 1)** Install gasket and body on hub. Tighten bolts to specification. Install snap ring in drive axle. It may be necessary to install bolt in center of drive axle and pull outward to install snap ring.
**2)** Ensure drive axle snap ring is fully seated. Position cover knob in FREE position. Install cover and gasket on body. Ensure alignment pin on cover is aligned with groove in body. Install bolts and tighten to specification.

### AUTOMATIC LOCKING HUBS

**Removal & Installation - 1)** Use an oil filter wrench to remove hub cover from hub body. Remove hub body mounting bolts. Remove hub assembly from drive hub. To install hub, reverse removal procedure.
**2)** Ensure "O" ring is fitted to groove in hub body. Align key in hub body with groove in drive hub. If hub does not fit easily to drive hub, rotate wheel during assembly. Install mounting bolts and tighten to specification. Ensure "O" ring is installed in hub cover prior to reassembly. Apply grease and sealing compound to oil seal. *See Fig. 3.*

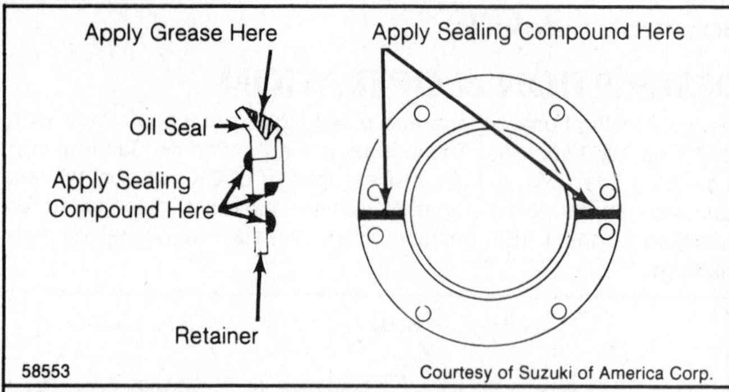


***Fig 3: Applying Grease & Sealing Compound to Oil Seal***

**Inspection - 1)** After installation, check hub operation. Remove hub cover. With transfer lever in 4H or 4L position, drive vehicle forward 6.5 ft. (2 m). Ensure sliding gear is at outer edge of hub. *See Fig. 2.*
**2)** Place transfer lever in 2H position, and move vehicle rearward 6.5 ft. (2 m). Ensure sliding gear is in inward position and does not engage splines of hub body. Repeat process and ensure hubs operate correctly. If not, repeat installation process. Ensure "O" ring is in position and install hub cover. Cover should not be able to be loosened by hand.

## OVERHAUL

***NOTE: Manufacturer does not recommend disassembly or repair of locking hub body components. If hub function is faulty, replace hub.***

## TORQUE SPECIFICATIONS

***TORQUE SPECIFICATIONS***

| Application | Ft. Lbs. (N.m) |
|---|---|
| Automatic Locking Hub Body-To-Drive Hub | 22-26 (30-35) |
| Manual Locking Hub Body-To-Drive Hub | 15-22 (20-30) |
| Wheel Lug Bolts | 59-81 (80-110) |
| | **INCH Lbs. (N.m)** |
| Manual Hub Cover | 71-106 (8-12) |

# 1991 BRAKES
# Disc & Drum

## Samurai, Sidekick, Swift

## DESCRIPTION

The hydraulically operated brake system uses a tandem master cylinder, with a vacuum assisted power brake booster and single piston, sliding caliper disc brakes. Swift GT has 4-wheel power disc brakes. Samurai, Sidekick and other Swift models have self-adjusting rear drum brakes. All models have cable actuated rear parking brakes.

## BLEEDING BRAKE SYSTEM

***CAUTION: DO NOT allow brake fluid to contact paint.***

Raise and support vehicle. Fill master cylinder reservoir to maximum mark. Bleed brakes in sequence. See BRAKE LINE BLEEDING SEQUENCE table. After bleeding brakes, depress brake pedal with a force equal to an abrupt stop. If sponginess exists, repeat bleeding procedure.

***BRAKE LINE BLEEDING SEQUENCE***

| Application | Sequence |
|---|---|
| Samurai | LF, RF, Proportioning Valve, RR |
| Sidekick | LR, Proportioning Valve, LF, RF |
| Swift | RR, LR, RF, LF |
| Swift GT | RR, LF,LR, RF |

## ADJUSTMENTS

### PARKING BRAKE

***NOTE: Before adjusting parking brake, ensure pedal height is correct and that brake shoes are not worn beyond limit.***

Loosen lock nut on end of parking brake cable. Hold cable nut to prevent cable from twisting and tighten adjusting nut. Pull parking brake handle slowly with 44-55 lbs. (20-25 kg) and count clicks. There should be 3-8 clicks on Samurai, 7-9 clicks on Sidekick and 4-9 clicks on Swift.

### FRONT WHEEL BEARINGS

**Samurai - 1)** Using spring scale attached to wheel stud, measure starting torque required to rotate rotor. Starting torque should be 2.2-6.6 lbs. (1-3 kg). If adjustment is required, bend lock washer away from lock nut. Remove bearing lock nut and lock washer.

**2)** Using Socket (09941-58010) and ft. lb. torque wrench, tighten bearing nut to 59 ft. lbs. (80 N.m) while spinning hub assembly. Loosen bearing nut. Using INCH-pound torque wrench, tighten bearing nut to 84-115 INCH lbs. (9-13 N.m). Install lock washer and lock nut. Tighten lock nut to specification. See TORQUE SPECIFICATIONS table at end of article. Bend tab on lock washer against lock nut.

**3)** Using spring scale, recheck starting torque. Reverse removal procedures. Apply Sealing Compound 366E (99000-31090) to hub and drive axle flange prior to installation (if equipped).

***NOTE: Sidekick and Swift have nonadjustable, sealed wheel bearings.***

### PEDAL HEIGHT & FREE PLAY

**1)** Start engine. Depress brake pedal several times. Depress brake pedal with approximately 66 lbs. (30 kg) of load and measure from top of pedal pad to floorboard. Clearance must not be less than 2.95" (75 mm) on Samurai, 5.12" (130 mm) on Sidekick and 2.36" (60 mm) on Swift.

**2)** If clearance is less than specified, check for worn rear brake shoes, air in brake lines, malfunction of rear brake shoe adjuster or booster push rod length out of adjustment.

**3)** On all models, pedal free play should be .04-.31" (1-8 mm). If not, check stoplight switch for proper installation position and adjust (if necessary).

### BRAKE BOOSTER PUSH ROD

Length of brake booster push rod is adjusted to provide zero clearance between piston rod end and master cylinder piston. Push piston rod several times to ensure reaction disc is in place. Set Booster Piston Rod Gauge (09950-98210 or 09950-96010) on master cylinder, and push pin on gauge until it contacts piston. Turn tool upside down and place it on booster. Adjust clearance by turning adjusting bolt of booster piston rod.

### STOPLIGHT SWITCH

Loosen switch lock nut. Pull brake pedal up. Adjust switch position so clearance between end of switch thread and brake pedal contact is .02-.04" (0.5-1 mm). Tighten lock nut.

## REMOVAL & INSTALLATION

### FRONT DISC BRAKE PADS

**Removal & Installation (Samurai) - 1)** Raise and support vehicle. Remove front wheel. Remove caliper anti-rattle spring. Remove caliper guide pin caps. Remove caliper guide pins with 6-mm hex wrench. Remove pad protectors.

**2)** Pull caliper assembly up and suspend with wire. Remove brake pads. To depress piston, open bleeder screw and press piston back into caliper bore. To install, reverse removal procedure. Bleed brake system (if necessary).

**Removal & Installation (Sidekick & Swift) -** Raise and support vehicle. Remove caliper pin bolts. Remove caliper from caliper carrier and suspend with wire. Remove brake pads and anti-rattle clips. To install, reverse removal procedure. Bleed brake system (if necessary).

### FRONT DISC BRAKE CALIPER

**Removal & Installation (Samurai) - 1)** Raise and support vehicle. Remove front wheel. Remove caliper anti-rattle spring. Remove pad protectors. Remove caliper guide pin caps. Remove caliper guide pins.

**2)** Pull caliper assembly up and disconnect brake line. Plug all line openings. To install, reverse removal procedure and bleed system.

**Removal & Installation (Sidekick & Swift) -** Raise and support vehicle. Remove front wheel. Remove caliper pin bolts. Remove caliper from caliper carrier. Disconnect brake flexhose. Plug all line openings. To install, reverse removal procedure.

### FRONT ROTOR

**Removal & Installation - 1)** Raise and support vehicle. Remove front wheel. Remove caliper and suspend with wire. Mount dial indicator and check rotor runout before removal. Maximum runout is .006" (.15 mm).

**2)** Remove caliper carrier. Install two 8-mm bolts into rotor holes between wheel studs. On Swift, remove screws before installing 8-mm bolts. Alternately tighten bolts and pull rotor from hub. To install, place rotor on hub and reverse removal procedure.

### REAR DISC BRAKE PADS

**Removal & Installation (Swift GT) - 1)** Raise and support vehicle. Remove rear wheels. Ensure parking brake is fully released. Remove caliper pin bolts.

**2)** Remove parking brake cable-to-caliper clip. Disconnect parking brake cable from caliper. Remove caliper and support with wire. Remove brake pads.

**3)** Using Piston Installer (09945-16030), rotate piston clockwise until fully seated in caliper. Install new brake pads. Reverse removal procedure to complete installation.

### REAR DISC BRAKE CALIPER

**Removal & Installation (Swift GT) - 1)** Raise and support vehicle. Remove rear wheels. Remove brake flexhose and drain fluid into a container. Release parking brake lever and remove caliper pin bolts.

# 1991 BRAKES
# Disc & Drum (Cont.)

**2)** Remove parking brake cable-to-caliper clip. Disconnect parking brake cable from caliper lever.
**3)** To install, reverse removal procedure. Turn caliper piston counterclockwise to achieve correct brake pad-to-rotor clearance. Fill and bleed system.

## REAR DISC BRAKE ROTOR & HUB

**Removal & Installation (Swift GT) – 1)** Raise and support vehicle. Remove rear wheels. Remove brake caliper. Remove caliper carrier. Remove rotor screws.
**2)** Install two 8-mm bolts into rotor holes between wheel studs. Alternately tighten bolts and pull rotor from hub. Remove spindle dust cap. Unstake hub nut. Remove hub nut and washer. Discard hub nut. Use a slide hammer to remove hub.
**3)** To install, reverse removal procedure. Tighten NEW hub nut to specification. See TORQUE SPECIFICATIONS table at end of article.

## REAR DRUM

**Removal & Installation (Samurai & Sidekick) – 1)** Remove wheel center cap. Loosen, but do not remove, brake drum nuts and rear wheel lug nuts. Raise rear of vehicle. Remove lug nuts and rear wheel. Ensure parking brake lever is fully released.
**2)** To increase clearance between brake shoe and drum, remove parking brake shoe lever return spring. Disconnect parking brake cable joint from parking brake shoe lever. Remove parking brake shoe lever stopper plate. Remove brake drum nuts. Remove brake drum. If drum sticks, use Slide Hammer (09942-15510) and Adapter (09943-17911).
**3)** Install brake drum, ensuring grease or oil does not contaminate brake drum or brake shoes friction surface. Install brake drum. Install parking brake shoe lever stopper plate. *See Fig. 1.* Reverse remainder of removal procedure. Apply brake several times to set self-adjusting mechanism.

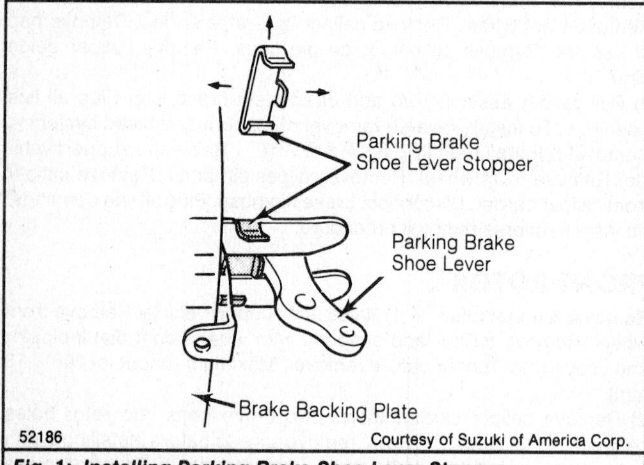


***Fig. 1: Installing Parking Brake Shoe Lever Stopper (Samurai & Sidekick)***

**Removal & Installation (Swift, Except GT) – 1)** Raise and support vehicle. Remove wheel and spindle cap. Remove spindle nut. Ensure parking brake is fully released. Loosen adjustment nut on parking brake cable.
**2)** To increase drum-to-shoe clearance, remove plug from back side of backing plate. Insert screwdriver into hole until it contacts shoe hold-down spring. Push screwdriver toward front of vehicle depressing hold-down spring and releasing tension on parking brake lever.
**3)** Remove brake drum. If drum sticks, use Slide Hammer (09942-15510) and Adapter (09943-17911).
**4)** Install brake drum using NEW spindle nut. Tighten spindle nut to specification. See TORQUE SPECIFICATIONS table at end of article. Install backing plate plug. Adjust parking brake. See PARKING BRAKE under ADJUSTMENTS.

## REAR BRAKE SHOES

**Removal & Installation (Samurai & Swift, Except GT) –** Remove brake drum. Remove shoe hold-down springs. Remove brake shoes. Remove brake shoe strut and return springs. Check springs and brake shoe strut ratchet for wear or damage. To install, reverse removal procedure. Pump brake pedal several times to set automatic adjuster.
**Removal (Sidekick) –** Raise and support vehicle. Remove tire and wheel. Remove 4 brake drum-to-axle nuts. Remove brake drum using Slide Hammer (J 2619-01) and Remover (J 37781). Pull drum from axle flange. It may be necessary to loosen brake adjustment before removing drum.
**Installation –** Maximize shoe-to-drum clearance by placing screwdriver between rod and ratchet and pushing down on ratchet. Install brake drums and 4 brake drum-to-axle nuts. Before moving vehicle, apply brakes firmly 3-5 times to obtain proper brake shoe-to-drum clearance.

## REAR WHEEL CYLINDER

**Removal & Installation –** With brake drum and shoes removed, disconnect hydraulic line from wheel cylinder. Remove mounting bolts and remove wheel cylinder. To install, reverse removal procedure.

## MASTER CYLINDER

***NOTE: DO NOT permit brake fluid to contact painted surfaces.***

**Removal & Installation –** Disconnect connector at fluid level sensor (if equipped). Loosen brake lines on master cylinder. Remove 2 nuts and washers attaching master cylinder to brake booster. Disconnect brake lines from master cylinder and plug outlet holes. Remove master cylinder. To install, reverse removal procedure. Bench bleed new master cylinder and bleed system.

## POWER BRAKE BOOSTER

**Removal & Installation – 1)** Remove master cylinder. Disconnect vacuum hose from booster. Disconnect push rod clevis from brake pedal arm. Remove 4 nuts attaching booster to firewall. Remove booster.
**2)** To install, reverse removal procedure. Bleed hydraulic system. Check and adjust push rod clevis measurement from booster firewall mounting base to brake pedal clevis pin hole. *See Fig. 2.*

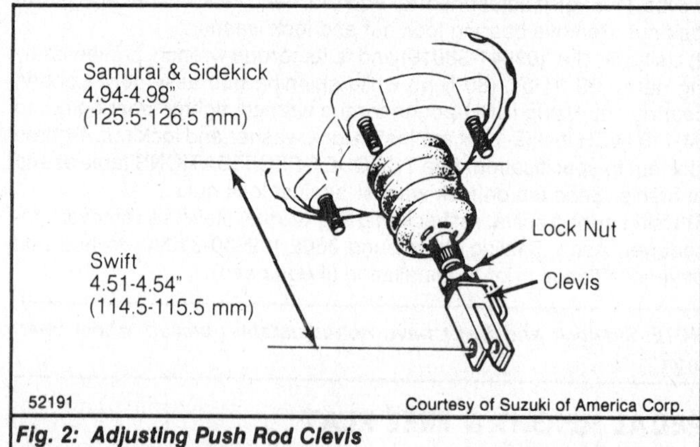


***Fig. 2: Adjusting Push Rod Clevis***

## REAR AXLE & OIL SEAL

**Removal & Installation (Samurai & Sidekick) – 1)** Raise and support vehicle. Remove rear wheels. Remove rear brake drum. Disconnect brake line from wheel cylinder. Plug line openings. Remove 4 backing plate-to-rear axle bolts.
**2)** Using Adapter (09922-66010) and Slide Hammer (09942-15510), remove rear axle and backing plate as an assembly. Remove oil seal from axle housing. To install, reverse removal procedure.

## OVERHAUL

### FRONT CALIPER

**Disassembly** – Insert shop towel between caliper piston and pad retainer arms. Apply low-pressure compressed air through brake line inlet port to remove piston. Remove piston dust seal. Remove piston seal using a thin blade. Remove bleeder screw.

**Cleaning & Inspection** – Clean all parts in clean brake fluid. Inspect bores and pistons for excessive wear or damage. Replace defective parts. *See Fig. 3.*

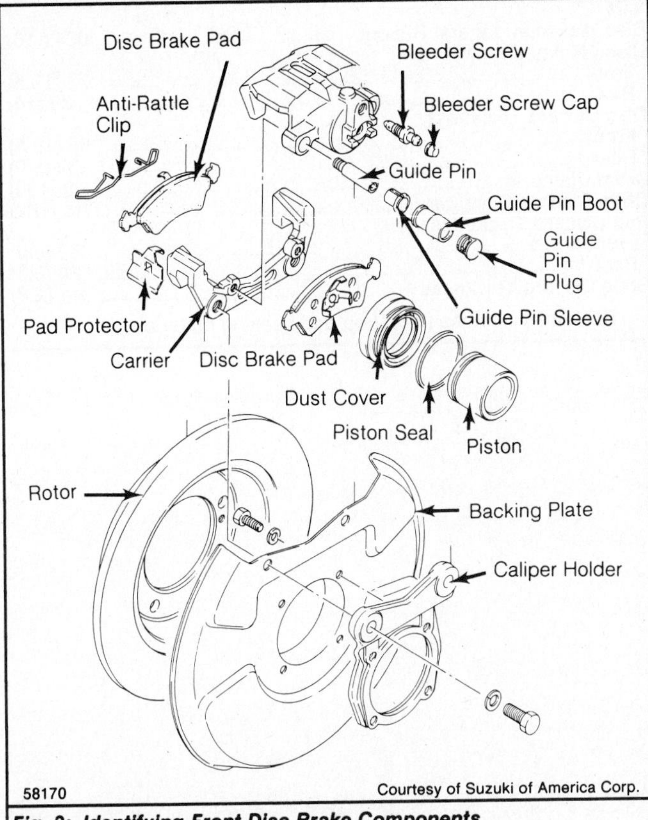


*Fig. 3: Identifying Front Disc Brake Components*

**Reassembly** – Lubricate NEW piston seal with brake fluid. Insert seal into piston cylinder seal groove. Carefully insert piston into cylinder using finger pressure. Apply brake fluid to piston and install NEW dust cover. Install bleeder screw.

### REAR CALIPER

**Disassembly (Swift GT)** – **1)** Using Piston Installer (09945-16030), rotate piston and boot counterclockwise to remove. Remove piston seal using a thin blade.

**2)** Remove snap ring, outer spring seat, spring and inner spring seat. Remove screw rod and key plate. Remove return spring, camshaft lever, camshaft and camshaft boot.

**Cleaning & Inspection** – Clean all parts in clean brake fluid. Inspect components for excessive wear or damage. Replace defective parts. Replace all seals and boots.

**Reassembly** – **1)** Lubricate all parts with clean brake fluid. Install boot in camshaft bore. Install camshaft.

**2)** Install screw rod and key plate in piston bore. Ensure screw pin is inserted in camshaft recess.

**3)** Install piston seal in caliper bore. Using Piston Installer (09945-16030), slowly rotate piston clockwise on screw rod until piston is fully installed in caliper bore. Install camshaft lever and camshaft return spring. *See Fig. 4.*

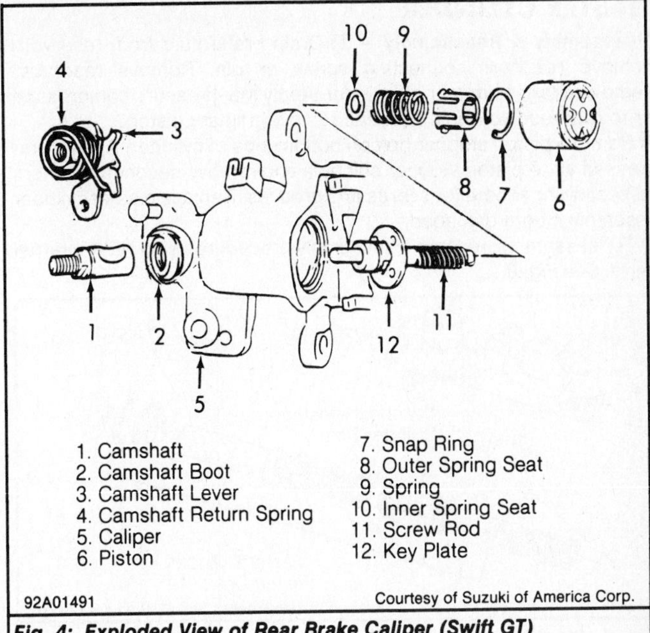


*Fig. 4: Exploded View of Rear Brake Caliper (Swift GT)*

### WHEEL CYLINDER

**Disassembly** – Remove rubber dust boots. Remove piston assembly and expander spring. Note installed direction for each cup. Remove cups from piston. Discard boots and cups.

**Inspection** – Wash all parts in clean brake fluid. Inspect cylinder bore and pistons for damage. Replace defective parts.

**Reassembly** – Lubricate bore with brake fluid. Install spring expander. Place new piston cups on piston with flare facing center of cylinder. Install piston assemblies into cylinder. *See Fig. 5.* Press new boots onto cylinder.

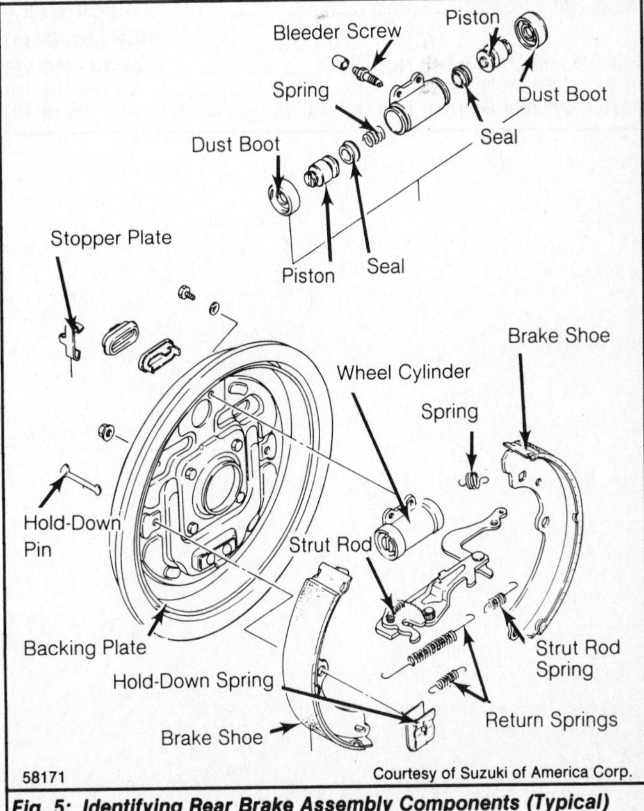


*Fig. 5: Identifying Rear Brake Assembly Components (Typical)*

# 1991 BRAKES
# Disc & Drum (Cont.)

## MASTER CYLINDER

**Disassembly & Reassembly** – **1)** Drain brake fluid from reservoir. Remove reservoir connecting screw or pin. Remove reservoir. Remove circlip from rear of cylinder. Apply low-pressure compressed air to rear reservoir fluid inlet and remove primary piston.

**2)** Remove piston stopper bolt on bottom side of cylinder. Apply compressed air to piston stopper bolt hole and remove secondary piston. Inspect cylinder bore for scores and grooves. Replace master cylinder assembly if bore damaged.

**3)** To reassemble, reverse disassembly procedure using NEW internal parts. *See Fig. 6.*

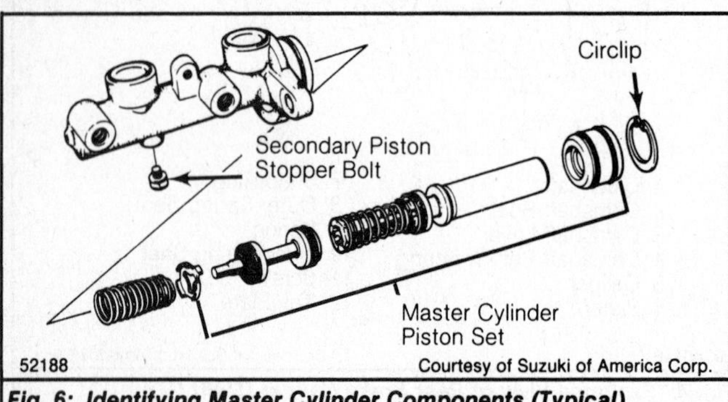


*Fig. 6: Identifying Master Cylinder Components (Typical)*

## TORQUE SPECIFICATIONS

*TORQUE SPECIFICATIONS*

| Application | Ft. Lbs. (N.m) |
|---|---|
| Backing Plate Nut | 14-20 (19-27) |
| Brake Hose Bolt | 15-18 (20-24) |
| Brake Line Flare Nut | 10-13 (14-18) |
| Caliper Carrier Bolt | 51-72 (69-98) |
| Caliper Guide Pin | 19-22 (26-30) |
| Hub Nut (Swift) | 111-148 (150-200) |
| Rear Spindle Nut (Swift) | 59-89 (80-120) |
| Wheel Bearing Lock Nut | 65 (88) |
| Wheel Nut | 37-59 (50-80) |
| | **INCH Lbs. (N.m)** |
| Brake Booster Mounting Nut | 89-142 (10-16) |
| Master Cylinder Nut | 89-142 (10-16) |
| Master Cylinder Stopper Bolt | 71-106 (8-12) |

## DISC & DRUM BRAKE SPECIFICATIONS

*DISC & DRUM BRAKE SPECIFICATIONS*

| Application | In. (mm) |
|---|---|
| **Samurai & Sidekick** | |
| Disc Maximum Lateral Runout | .006 (.15) |
| Disc Thickness | .394 (10) |
| Disc Discard Thickness | .334 (8.5) |
| Drum Diameter | 8.66 (220) |
| Drum Discard Diameter | 8.74 (222) |
| Pad Discard Thickness [1] | .24 (6.0) |
| Shoe Discard Thickness [1] | .12 (3.0) |
| **Swift** | |
| Disc Maximum Lateral Runout | .004 (.10) |
| Disc Thickness | |
| Front | .73 (18.5) |
| Rear | .39 (10) |
| Disc Discard Thickness | |
| Front | .65 (16.5) |
| Rear | .32 (8.0) |
| Drum Diameter | 7.09 (180) |
| Drum Discard Diameter | 7.16 (182) |
| Pad Discard Thickness | |
| Front [1] | .32 (8.0) |
| Rear [1] | .24 (6.0) |
| Shoe Discard Thickness [1] | .11 (2.8) |

[1] – Thickness includes pad/shoe and backing material.

# 1991 BRAKES
# Rear Anti-Lock

## Sidekick

## DESCRIPTION

The Rear Wheel Anti-Lock (RWAL) brake system is designed to control braking force of rear wheels. This serves to eliminate wheel lock and maintain directional stability during hard brake application. System consists of a wheel speed sensor (mounted in rear differential), pressure limit valve, RWAL Electronic Control Module (ECM) and connecting wiring harness.

Power is supplied to the RWAL ECM through the RWAL power relay. System also use a self-diagnostic function, which enables technician to quickly trouble shoot system by monitoring stored RWAL trouble codes through flashes of the BRAKE warning light.

***NOTE: RWAL ECM may also be referred to as the RWAL Brake Controller.***

***NOTE: For more information on brake system, see DISC & DRUM article in BRAKES.***

## OPERATION

The RWAL ECM continuously monitors various input signals to determine control of the pressure limit valve and BRAKE warning light. Available input signals include wheel speed sensor, stoplight switch, pressure differential switch (located on proportioning/differential valve), monitor coupler signal (diagnostic test), parking brake switch and 4WD switch (if equipped).

### PRESSURE LIMIT VALVE

Based upon wheel speed input signals, RWAL ECM controls hydraulic brake pressure to both rear wheels. Under normal conditions, RWAL system functions like a conventional brake system.

Normal wheel speed-to-acceleration/deceleration braking is programmed into RWAL ECM memory. If the difference between optimum braking rear wheel speed and actual braking rear wheel speed exceeds programmed limits, RWAL system will enter anti-lock mode.

During anti-lock mode, pressure in the rear wheel hydraulic circuit is modulated by the ECM through the pressure limit valve. This prevents rear wheel lock, while providing maximum stopping and directional stability. Pressure limit valve is located under the master cylinder and actually consists of 2 valves: a dump valve that releases pressure into an accumulator and an isolation valve that maintains rear wheel hydraulic pressure.

During anti-lock operation, a series of rapid pulsations (caused by the fluctuating position of the pressure limit valve) will be felt at the brake pedal. These pulsations, in conjunction with possible tire "chirping" (on dry pavement), are considered normal during anti-lock operation and will cease when normal braking is resumed or vehicle comes to a complete stop.

### WHEEL SPEED SENSOR

The 2-wire rear wheel speed sensor is mounted in the rear differential carrier. Sensor transmits wheel speed information to the RWAL ECM. This low AC voltage signal is generated through magnetic induction when a toothed exciter ring inside the differential passes the stationary magnetic coil of the sensor. This voltage signal increases in both frequency and amplitude as rear wheel speed increases.

### BRAKE WARNING LIGHT

As a bulb check, the BRAKE warning light will turn on when the ignition switch is turned to the BULB CHECK position. Light should go out when ignition switch is turned to the ON position. BRAKE light will also illuminate if parking brake lever is not fully released or if brake fluid level is low.

Should the RWAL system malfunction, RWAL ECM will turn on the BRAKE warning light and disable the anti-lock function. BRAKE warning light is used to retrieve stored malfunction codes from RWAL system by jumpering appropriate terminals of diagnostic connector. See RETRIEVING CODES under DIAGNOSIS & TESTING.

***CAUTION: See ANTI-LOCK BRAKE SAFETY PRECAUTIONS article in GENERAL INFORMATION.***

## BLEEDING BRAKE SYSTEM

### BLEEDING PROCEDURES

***NOTE: See HYDRAULIC BRAKE BLEEDING article in GENERAL INFORMATION.***

When bleeding hydraulic system, follow normal manual or pressure bleeding procedures. Bleed longest line first.

## ADJUSTMENTS

### PEDAL HEIGHT

Remove power brake unit. Measure distance between power brake unit mounting surface with gasket installed and center of brake push rod clevis pin. Correct distance is 4.96-5.00" (126-127 mm).

### PEDAL TRAVEL

**1)** With engine off, pump brake pedal until all vacuum is exhausted from power brake unit. Push brake pedal with a force of approximately 66 lbs. (30 kg). Measure distance between brake pedal face and floor.
**2)** Distance must not be less than 5.1" (130 mm). If measured distance is less than specified, check for air in hydraulic system, worn rear brake shoes, defective rear brake self-adjusters and improper brake pedal push rod adjustment.

### PEDAL FREE PLAY

**1)** With engine off, depress brake pedal several times to exhaust vacuum from power brake unit. Depress brake pedal, and measure brake pedal travel until initial resistance is felt.
**2)** Brake pedal free play should be .04-.32" (1.0-8.0 mm). If brake pedal free play is not within specification, check stoplight switch for proper adjustment. See STOPLIGHT SWITCH under ADJUSTMENTS.
**3)** If stoplight adjustment is okay, check brake pedal push rod and master cylinder pin for looseness. If brake pedal push rod and master cylinder pin are okay, check brake pedal height. See PEDAL HEIGHT under ADJUSTMENTS.

### STOPLIGHT SWITCH

Pull up and hold brake pedal. Measure distance between face of brake pedal arm and stoplight switch. Adjust stoplight switch if distance is not .02-.04" (.5-1.0 mm). Tighten stoplight switch lock nut to 10 ft. lbs. (14 N.m).

### PARKING BRAKE

***NOTE: Ensure rear brakes are correctly adjusted before adjusting parking brake.***

**1)** Using pulling force of 44-55 lbs. (20-25 kg), apply parking brake lever, and count number of notches lever travels. Adjustment is okay if lever clicks 7-9 notches.
**2)** If parking brake cable adjustment is required, remove parking brake lever assembly trim cover. Loosen parking brake cable lock nut. Turn cable adjusting nut as required to obtain correct number of clicks at parking brake lever. After adjustment, check for brake drag with parking brake off.

## TROUBLE SHOOTING

To trouble shoot electronic portion of RWAL system, perform RWAL SYSTEM CHECK. *See Fig. 1.*

# 1991 BRAKES
# Rear Anti-Lock (Cont.)

## DIAGNOSIS & TESTING

### RETRIEVING CODES

To retrieve stored RWAL trouble codes, perform RWAL SYSTEM CHECK. *See Fig. 1.* The 10-pin diagnostic connector is located under dash, behind RWAL ECM. *See Fig. 2.* Stored trouble codes are flashed by BRAKE warning light. If more than one fault is present, lowest number code will flash repeatedly until it is repaired and cleared from memory. Last flash of indicated code will last longer than others, indicating code is about to repeat. See RWAL TROUBLE CODES table. See TROUBLE CODES under DIAGNOSIS & TESTING.

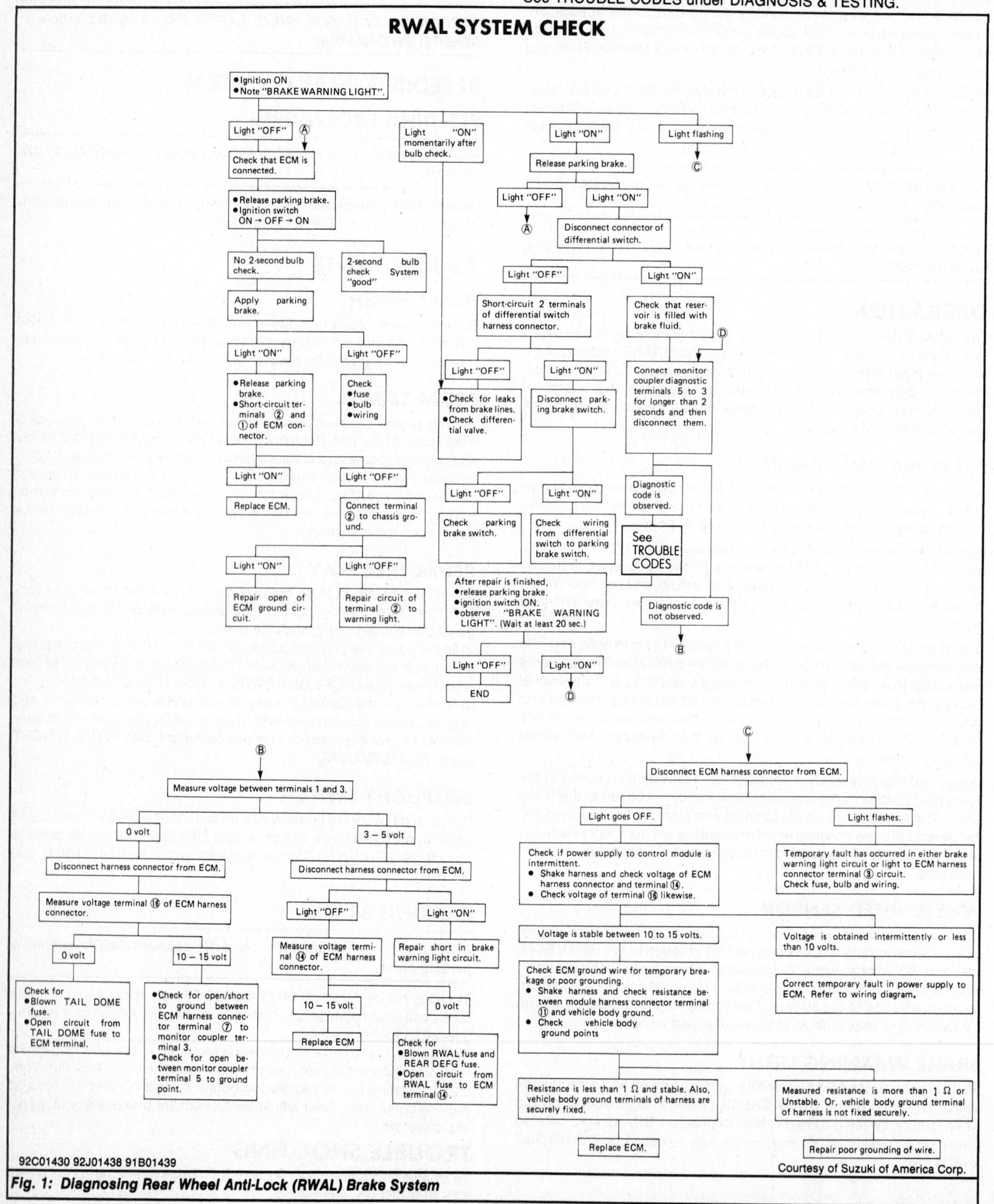


*Fig. 1: Diagnosing Rear Wheel Anti-Lock (RWAL) Brake System*

# 1991 BRAKES
# Rear Anti-Lock (Cont.)

**RWAL TROUBLE CODES**

| Code | Condition/Circuit |
|---|---|
| 2 | Open Isolation Solenoid Circuit |
| 3 | Open Dump Solenoid Circuit |
| 4 | Limit Valve Reset Switch Closed |
| 5 | Excessive Dump Valve Action |
| 6 | Wheel Speed Sensor Signal Changed Rapidly |
| 7 | Shorted Isolation Solenoid Circuit |
| 8 | Shorted Dump Solenoid Circuit |
| 9 | Open Wheel Speed Sensor Circuit |
| 10 | Stoplight Switch On Constantly |
| 11 | Shorted Wheel Speed Sensor |
| 13 | RWAL ECM Malfunction |

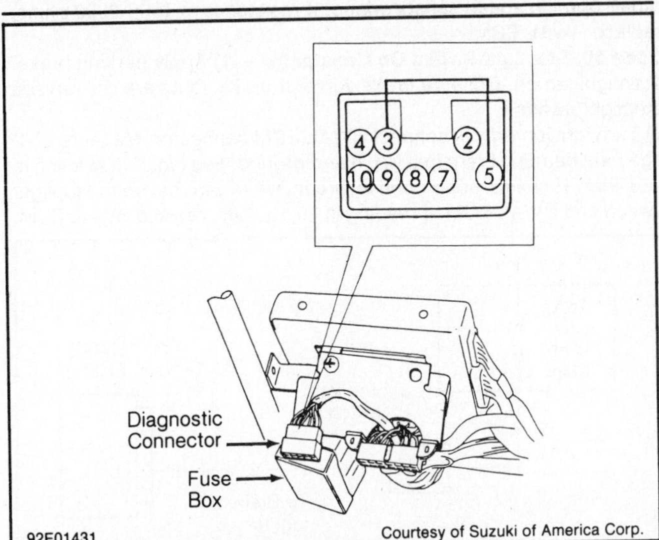


*Fig. 2: Identifying Diagnostic Connector Location & Terminals*

## CLEARING TROUBLE CODES

Only Codes 4 and 5 will store as "hard" codes. All other codes will clear as soon as fault ceases to exist. To clear Code 4 or 5, disconnect negative battery cable for at least 5 seconds.

## TROUBLE CODES

***NOTE: Prior to performing diagnostic procedures covered in TROUBLE CODES, perform RWAL SYSTEM CHECK. See Fig. 1.***

**Code 2, Open Isolation Solenoid Circuit – 1)** Turn ignition off. Disconnect RWAL ECM connector. Measure resistance between ECM harness connector terminal No. 1 and ground. *See Fig. 3.*

**2)** If resistance reading is 3-6 ohms, check RWAL ECM connections. If connections are okay, replace RWAL ECM.

**3)** If resistance reading is greater than 6 ohms, disconnect pressure limit valve connector. Measure resistance between limit valve isolation solenoid terminal No. 2 and ground terminal No. 4. *See Fig. 4.*

**4)** If resistance is now 3-6 ohms, repair open in harness Green or Black wire. If resistance is greater than 6 ohms, isolation solenoid winding is open. Replace pressure limit valve.

**Code 3, Open Dump Solenoid Circuit – 1)** Turn ignition off. Disconnect RWAL ECM connector. Measure resistance between RWAL ECM terminal No. 17 and ground. *See Fig. 3.*

**2)** If resistance reading is 1-3 ohms, check RWAL ECM connections. If connections are okay, replace RWAL ECM.

**3)** If resistance reading is greater than 3 ohms, disconnect pressure limit valve. Measure resistance between limit valve terminal No. 1 and ground terminal No. 4. *See Fig. 4.*

**4)** If resistance is now 1-3 ohms, repair open in harness White/Green or Black wire. If resistance is greater than 3 ohms, dump solenoid winding is open. Replace pressure limit valve.

**Code 4, Limit Valve Reset Switch Closed – 1)** Turn ignition off. Disconnect RWAL ECM connector. Measure resistance between ECM harness connector terminal No. 4 and ground. *See Fig. 3.*

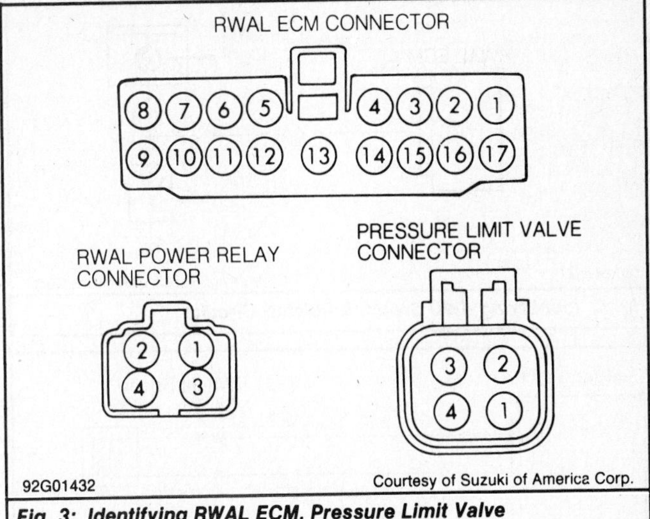


*Fig. 3: Identifying RWAL ECM, Pressure Limit Valve & Power Relay Connector Terminals*

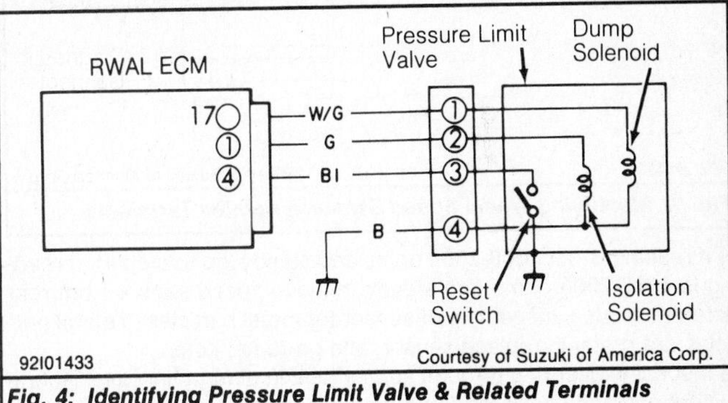


*Fig. 4: Identifying Pressure Limit Valve & Related Terminals*

**2)** If resistance reading is greater than 10 k/ohms, check RWAL ECM connections. If connections are okay, replace RWAL ECM. If resistance reading is less than 10 k/ohms, disconnect pressure limit valve connector.

**3)** Measure resistance between limit valve reset switch connector terminal No. 3 and ground terminal No. 4. *See Fig. 4.* If resistance is less than 10 k/ohms, replace pressure limit valve.

**4)** If resistance is greater than 10 k/ohms, measure resistance between valve connector terminal No. 3 and ground. If resistance is less than 100 k/ohms, repair short to ground in Blue wire of harness.

**5)** If resistance is greater than 100 k/ohms, firmly press brake pedal. Measure resistance between limit valve terminal No. 3 and ground terminal No. 4. If resistance is less than 10 k/ohms, replace pressure limit valve. If resistance is greater than 10 k/ohms, replace RWAL ECM.

**6)** Clear Code 4 by disconnecting negative battery cable for at least 5 seconds.

**Code 5, Excessive Dump Valve Action – 1)** Ensure rear brakes are not dragging. If rear brakes are dragging, repair mechanical problem before proceeding with electronic testing.

**2)** If rear brakes are not dragging on 2WD models, go to step **4)**. On 4WD models, turn ignition off, and disconnect RWAL ECM connector. Shift into 4WD. Turn ignition on.

**3)** Check voltage on RWAL ECM harness connector terminal No. 3. If reading is less than one volt, go to next step. If reading is greater than one volt, repair 4WD switch or open in its wiring. *See Fig. 5.*

**4)** Replace pressure limit valve. Clear Code 5 by disconnecting negative battery cable for at least 5 seconds. Drive vehicle in 2WD setting. In a safe area, firmly apply brakes and ensure rear wheels do not lock.

**Code 6, Wheel Speed Sensor Signal Changes Rapidly – 1)** Turn ignition off. Disconnect RWAL ECM connector. Check resistance between ECM terminals No. 9 and 10 while wiggling harness between sensor and ECM. *See Fig. 6.*

# 1991 BRAKES
# Rear Anti-Lock (Cont.)

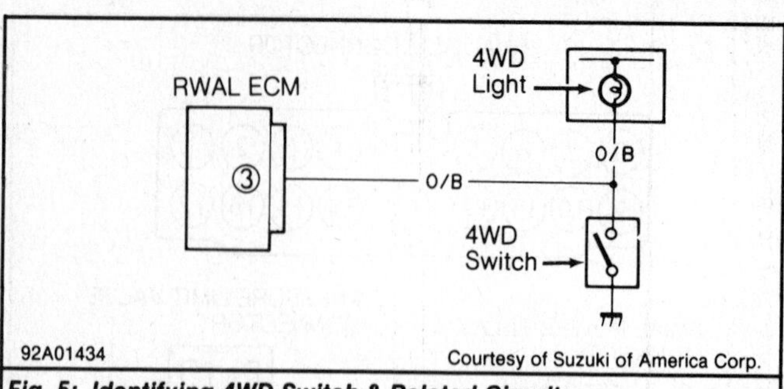


*Fig. 5: Identifying 4WD Switch & Related Circuits*

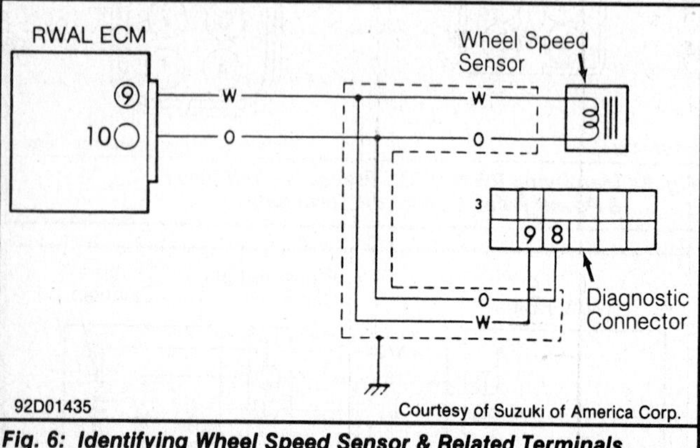


*Fig. 6: Identifying Wheel Speed Sensor & Related Terminals*

**2)** If reading is not 1000-2000 ohms and steady, go to step **4)**. If reading is 1000-2000 ohms and steady, remove speed sensor from rear differential case. Inspect tip of sensor for metal particles. If metal particles are present, replace sensor, and go to next step.

**3)** Inspect exciter ring through sensor hole in differential case. Rotate exciter ring and check for damaged teeth and lateral runout. If exciter ring is damaged or lateral runout is present, replace exciter ring. If no faults are found, go to step **6)**.

**4)** If resistance between terminals No. 9 and 10 of RWAL ECM connector is not 1000-2000 ohms and steady, disconnect speed sensor connector. Measure resistance across sensor connector terminals. If resistance is 1000-2000 ohms, repair open or short in White or Orange wire between RWAL ECM and speed sensor.

**5)** If resistance is greater than 2000 ohms or less than 1000 ohms, replace wheel speed sensor. After replacing sensor, verify speed sensor signal by using procedure described in steps **6)** and **7)**.

**6)** Reinstall speed sensor, and reconnect connector. Reconnect RWAL ECM connector. Raise vehicle, and support with rear wheels off of floor. Start engine, and drive vehicle faster than 20 MPH. Backprobe RWAL ECM terminals No. 9 and 10 using a 10-megohm DVOM on AC-volts scale.

**7)** If voltage reading is greater than 650 mV and steady, replace RWAL ECM. If voltage reading is less than 650 mV or is erratic, replace wheel speed sensor.

**Code 7, Shorted Isolation Solenoid Circuit – 1)** Turn ignition off. Disconnect pressure limit valve connector. Measure resistance between limit valve terminals No. 2 and 4. *See Fig. 4.*

**2)** If resistance is less than 3 ohms, replace pressure limit valve. If resistance is 3-6 ohms, disconnect RWAL ECM connector. Measure resistance between ECM harness connector terminal No. 1 and ground.

**3)** If resistance is greater than 20 k/ohms, replace RWAL ECM. If resistance is less than 20 k/ohms, repair short to ground in Green wire of harness.

**Code 8, Shorted Dump Solenoid Circuit – 1)** Turn ignition off. Disconnect pressure limit valve connector. Measure resistance between limit valve terminals No. 1 and 4. *See Fig. 4.*

**2)** If resistance is less than one ohm, replace pressure limit valve. If resistance is 1-3 ohms, disconnect RWAL ECM connector. Measure resistance between ECM harness connector terminal No. 17 and ground.

**3)** If resistance is greater than 20 k/ohms, replace RWAL ECM. If resistance is less than 20 k/ohms, repair short to ground in White/Green wire of harness.

**Code 9, Open Wheel Speed Sensor Circuit – 1)** Turn ignition off. Disconnect speed sensor connector. Measure resistance across sensor terminals. *See Fig. 6.* If resistance is greater than 2000 ohms, replace speed sensor.

**2)** If resistance is 1000-2000 ohms, disconnect RWAL ECM connector. Reconnect speed sensor connector. Measure resistance between ECM terminals No. 9 and 10. If resistance is greater than 2000 ohms, repair open in speed sensor wiring. If resistance is 1000-2000 ohms, replace RWAL ECM.

**Code 10, Stoplight Switch On Constantly – 1)** Apply parking brake. Turn ignition on. Observe brake lights. If brake lights are on, replace stoplight switch.

**2)** Turn ignition off. Disconnect RWAL ECM connector. Measure voltage between ECM terminal No. 8 and ground. *See Fig. 7.* If reading is less than 10 volts, repair open in Green/White wire between stoplight switch and RWAL ECM. If reading is 10-15 volts, replace RWAL ECM.

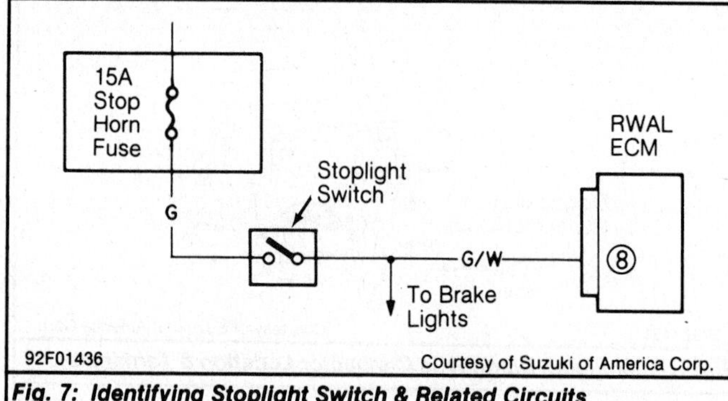


*Fig. 7: Identifying Stoplight Switch & Related Circuits*

**Code 11, Shorted Wheel Speed Sensor – 1)** Turn ignition off. Disconnect speed sensor connector, and measure resistance across sensor terminals. If resistance is less than 1000 ohms, replace speed sensor.

**2)** If resistance is 1000-2000 ohms, disconnect RWAL ECM connector. Leave speed sensor disconnected. Measure resistance between ECM terminal No. 10 and ground. *See Fig. 6.* Repair short to ground in Orange wire if resistance is less than 20 k/ohms.

**3)** If resistance is greater than 20 k/ohms, measure resistance between RWAL ECM terminals No. 9 and 10. If resistance is greater than 20 k/ohms, replace RWAL ECM. Repair short between Orange and White wires in speed sensor harness if resistance is less than 20 k/ohms.

**Code 13, RWAL ECM Malfunction** – Replace RWAL ECM.

## COMPONENT TESTING

### WHEEL SPEED SENSOR

Remove wheel speed sensor from differential. Using an ohmmeter, check resistance across sensor terminals and between terminals and sensor body. Resistance between terminals at 77°F (25°C) should be 1282-1568 ohms. Resistance between sensor terminals and sensor body should be greater than 100 k/ohms. Ensure tip of sensor is free of metal particles.

### STOPLIGHT SWITCH

Disconnect stoplight switch connector. Connect ohmmeter across switch terminals. With brake pedal depressed, continuity should exist between switch terminals. With brake pedal released, continuity should not exist.

### RWAL POWER RELAY

**1)** Disconnect negative battery cable. Remove radio speaker (if equipped) from lower left side of dash. Remove engine ECM with cover, bracket and fuse box from steering column holder.

# 1991 BRAKES
# Rear Anti-Lock (Cont.)

**2)** Disconnect Yellow connector from RWAL power relay. Remove relay. Check continuity across relay terminals No. 1 and 3. *See Fig. 3.* Resistance should be 90-110 ohms.
**3)** Check resistance across relay terminals No. 2 and 4. Reading should be infinite. Continuity should exist between terminals No. 2 and 4 with battery voltage and ground applied to terminals No. 1 and 3. If relay does not test as indicated, replace relay.

## PRESSURE LIMIT VALVE

**1)** Disconnect pressure limit valve connector. Check resistance of isolation valve solenoid winding between terminals No. 2 and 4 of pressure limit valve. *See Fig. 3.* Resistance should be 3-6 ohms.
**2)** Check resistance of dump valve solenoid winding between pressure limit valve terminals No. 1 and 4. Resistance should be 1-3 ohms.
**3)** Check resistance of reset switch across terminals No. 3 and 4 of pressure limit valve. Resistance reading should be infinite. If any resistance value is not within specification, replace pressure limit valve as an assembly.

## RWAL SYSTEM ELECTRICAL CIRCUIT CHECK

**1)** Remove RWAL ECM from under dash so rear of harness connector can be accessed with a DVOM. See RWAL ELECTRONIC CONTROL MODULE under REMOVAL & INSTALLATION.
**2)** Check voltage at each terminal of connector under conditions described in RWAL ECM PIN VOLTAGES table. *See Fig. 3.*

# REMOVAL & INSTALLATION

***NOTE: After replacing any component, perform RWAL SYSTEM CHECK. See Fig. 1.***

## RWAL ELECTRONIC CONTROL MODULE

**Removal** – Disconnect negative battery cable. Remove radio speaker (if equipped) from lower left side of dash. Remove engine ECM with cover, bracket and fuse box from steering column holder. Disconnect RWAL connector. Remove RWAL ECM from dash panel.

**Installation** – Install RWAL ECM to dash panel. Tighten nuts to 35 INCH lbs. (4 N.m). If specified torque cannot be obtained, replace nuts with new ones. DO NOT overtighten nuts.

## WHEEL SPEED SENSOR

**Removal** – Turn ignition off. Raise and support vehicle. Remove sensor cover on rear differential. Unplug sensor connector. Remove sensor retaining bolt. Remove sensor.
**Installation** – To install, reverse removal procedure. Replace "O" ring if damaged. Ensure tip of sensor is free of metal particles. Coat "O" ring with differential lubricant. Tighten sensor retaining bolt to specification. See TORQUE SPECIFICATIONS table at end of article.

## PRESSURE LIMIT & PRESSURE/DIFFERENTIAL VALVES

**Removal** – **1)** Remove air cleaner. Disconnect master cylinder fluid level sensor connector. Clean outside of brake fluid reservoir. Using a syringe, remove as much fluid from reservoir as possible. Unplug pressure/differential valve electrical connector. Unplug pressure limit valve electrical connector.
**2)** Disconnect brake hydraulic lines leading from master cylinder to wheels. Remove heat protector bolt from master cylinder bracket. Remove 2 master cylinder attaching bolts. Remove master cylinder, pressure/differential valve and pressure limit valve assembly from vehicle. Remove pressure limit valve. Remove pressure/differential valve.
**Installation** – To install valves, reverse removal procedure. Tighten nuts and hydraulic flare fittings to specifications. See TORQUE SPECIFICATIONS table at end of article.

# TORQUE SPECIFICATIONS

*TORQUE SPECIFICATIONS*

| Application | Ft. Lbs. (N.m) |
|---|---|
| Tubing Flare Nuts | 11-13 (14-18) |
| Wheel Speed Sensor Bolt | 13-21 (18-28) |
| | **INCH Lbs. (N.m)** |
| Master Cylinder Nuts | 89-142 (10-16) |
| RWAL ECM Nuts | 35 (4) |

*RWAL ECM PIN VOLTAGES*

| Terminal No. | Circuit | Normal Voltage | Condition |
|---|---|---|---|
| 1 | Isolation Solenoid | 0 | During Normal Driving |
| | | 10-15 | During Hard Braking |
| 2 | Brake Warning Light | 10-15 | When Brake Light Is Off |
| | | 0-3 | When Brake Light Is On |
| 3 | 4WD Signal | 10-15 | In 2WD |
| | | 0-0.5 | In 4WD |
| 4 | Valve Reset Switch | 4-5 | During Normal Driving |
| | | 0-0.5 | During Hard Braking |
| 5 | Not Used | ..... | ..... |
| 6 | Not Used | ..... | ..... |
| 7 | Diagnostic Test | 3-5 | When Terminal Is Open |
| | | 0-0.5 | When Terminal Is Grounded |
| 8 | Stoplight Switch | 0-0.5 | With Pedal Released |
| | | 10-15 | With Pedal Depressed |
| 9 & 10 | Wheel Speed Sensor | [1] 3.5 | At About 20 MPH |
| 11 | ECM Ground | 0 | Normal Condition |
| 12 & 13 | Not Used | ..... | ..... |
| 14 | Power Supply (Ignition) | 10-15 | With Ignition On |
| 15 | Not Used | ..... | ..... |
| 16 | Power Supply (Battery) | 10-15 | At All Times |
| 17 | Dump Solenoid | 0 | Normal Driving |

[1] – Approximate AC voltage.

# 1991 BRAKES
## Rear Anti-Lock (Cont.)

## WIRING DIAGRAM

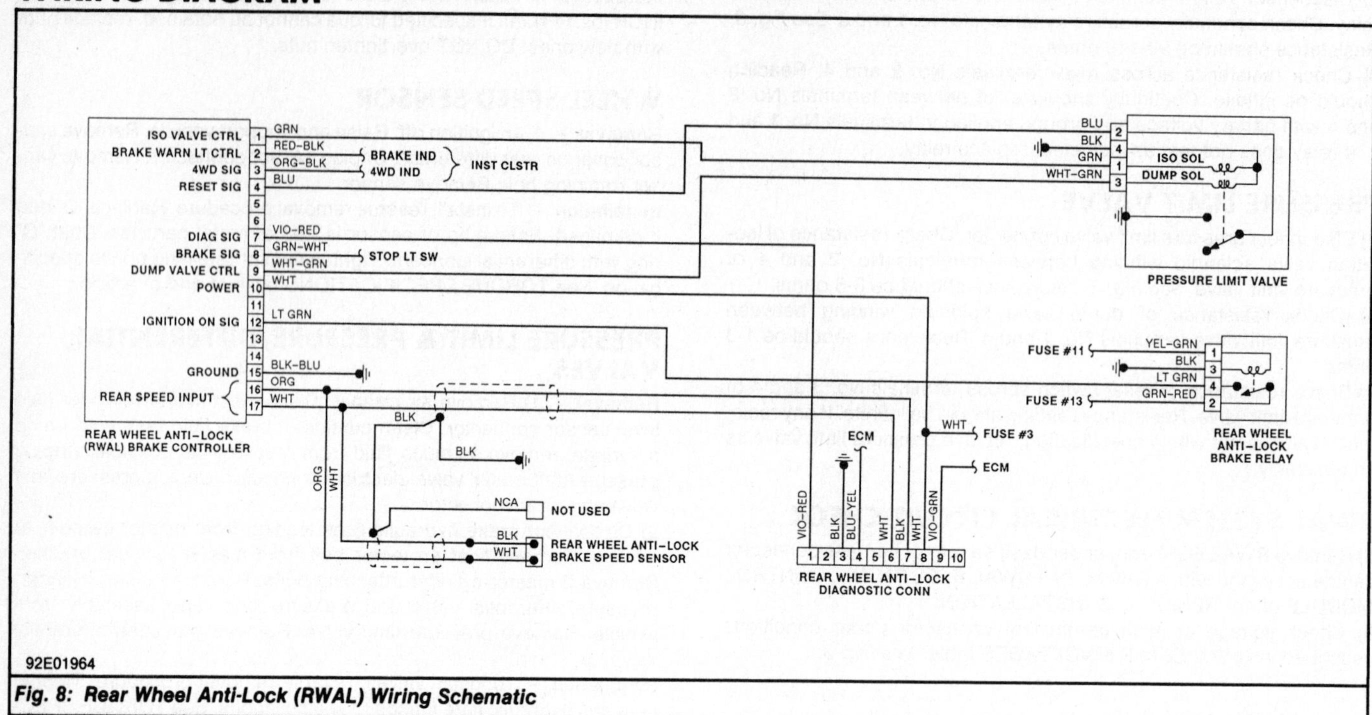


*Fig. 8: Rear Wheel Anti-Lock (RWAL) Wiring Schematic*

# 1991 WHEEL ALIGNMENT Specifications & Procedures

## Samurai, Sidekick, Swift

***NOTE:* *Prior to performing wheel alignment, perform preliminary visual and mechanical inspection of wheels, tires and suspension components. See PRE-ALIGNMENT INSTRUCTIONS in WHEEL ALIGNMENT THEORY & OPERATION article in GENERAL INFORMATION.***

## RIDING HEIGHT ADJUSTMENT

Before adjusting alignment, check riding height. Riding height must be checked with vehicle on level floor and tires properly inflated. Bounce vehicle several times and allow suspension to settle.

Visually inspect vehicle for signs of abnormal height from front to rear or side to side. Check passenger and luggage compartments for extra heavy items and remove if present. On Swift, riding height between right and left sides should vary less than .6" (15 mm). On all other models, riding height between left and right side of vehicle should vary less than 1" (25.4 mm).

## WHEEL ALIGNMENT SPECIFICATIONS

*WHEEL ALIGNMENT SPECIFICATIONS*

| Application | Preferred | Range |
|---|---|---|
| **Samurai** | | |
| Camber [1] | | |
| Front | 1 | 1/4 To 1 3/4 |
| Caster [1] | 3 1/2 | 2 1/2 To 4 1/2 |
| Toe-In [2] | | |
| Front | 3/16 (4.5) | 3/32 To 9/32 (2.5 To 7) |
| Toe-In [1] | | |
| Front | 3/8 | 3/16 To 9/16 |
| Toe-Out On Turns [1] | | |
| Inner | 29 | .... |
| Outer | 26 | .... |
| **Sidekick** | | |
| Camber [1] | | |
| Front | 1/2 | -1 To 1 1/2 |
| Rear | 0 | -1 To 1 |
| Caster [1] | 1 1/2 | 1/2 To 2 1/2 |
| Toe-In [2] | | |
| Front | 5/32 (4) | 3/32 To 7/32 (2 To 6) |
| Rear | 0 (0) | -3/32 To 3/32 (-2 To 2) |
| Toe-In [1] | | |
| Front | 5/16 | 3/16 To 7/16 |
| Rear | 0 | -3/16 To 3/16 |
| Toe-Out On Turns [1] | | |
| Inner | 32 1/2 | .... |
| Outer | 30 1/2 | .... |
| **Swift** | | |
| Camber [1] | | |
| Front | 0 | -1 To 1 |
| Rear | 0 | -1 To 1 |
| Caster [1] | 3 | 1 To 5 |
| Toe-In [2] | | |
| Front | 0 (0) | -3/32 To 3/32 (-2 To 2) |
| Rear | 3/32 (2) | 0 To 5/32 (0 To 4) |
| Toe-In [1] | | |
| Front | 0 | -3/16 To 3/16 |
| Rear | 3/16 | 0 To 5/16 |
| Toe-Out On Turns [1] | | |
| Inner | 12 15/16 | .... |
| Outer | .... | .... |

[1] – Measurement in degrees.
[2] – Measurement in inches (mm).

# 1991 SUSPENSION
# Front – Sidekick

## DESCRIPTION

Independent suspension is a MacPherson strut type. Top of strut is anchored to vehicle body by strut support. Lower end of strut is bolted to steering knuckle, which is attached to ball joint. Ball joint is attached to suspension control arm. As steering knuckle moves, strut also rotates by means of upper strut bearing and lower ball joint.

## ADJUSTMENTS & INSPECTION

### WHEEL ALIGNMENT SPECIFICATIONS & PROCEDURES

***NOTE: See SPECIFICATIONS & PROCEDURES article in WHEEL ALIGNMENT.***

### WHEEL BEARINGS

**1)** To achieve correct front wheel bearing preload, tighten wheel bearing to 155 ft. lbs. (210 N.m). No further adjustment is required.
**2)** To check wheel bearing(s) for excessive wear, raise and support vehicle, remove wheel. On 2WD models, remove hub center cap. On 4WD models, remove free-wheeling hub. See FREE-WHEELING HUB (4WD) under REMOVAL & INSTALLATION.
**3)** Mount a dial indicator to rotor and to hub center shaft. Push in and pull out on rotor. Note indicator reading. If movement exceeds .016" (.41 mm), replace bearing.

## REMOVAL & INSTALLATION

### COIL SPRING

**Removal – 1)** Raise and support vehicle. Remove front wheel(s). On 2WD models, remove hub center cover. On 4WD models, remove free-wheeling hub. See FREE-WHEELING HUB (4WD) under REMOVAL & INSTALLATION. On 4WD models, remove axle shaft snap ring. On all models, disconnect brake line from strut. Remove caliper from steering knuckle and wire aside. Remove tie rod end from steering knuckle using Tie Rod Remover (09913-65210). Remove stabilizer ball joint.
**2)** Remove brake disc. If disc cannot be remove by hand, install (2) 8 mm bolts into threaded holes. Alternately tighten bolts to remove rotor from hub. Support control arm with jack. Remove strut-to-steering knuckle bolts. Disconnect ball joint from steering knuckle. Remove steering knuckle from vehicle. Slowly lower jack supporting control arm and remove coil spring from stubber.
**Installation –** Position largest diameter end of coil spring to bottom spring seat stop on lower control arm. To complete installation, reverse removal procedure. Tighten all nuts and bolts to specification. See TORQUE SPECIFICATIONS table at end of article. Check wheel alignment. See SPECIFICATIONS & PROCEDURES article in WHEEL ALIGNMENT.

### FREE-WHEELING HUB (4WD)

**Removal –** Remove free-wheeling hub cover mounting bolts. Remove free-wheeling hub body as an assembly by sliding off axle shaft and away from hub. *See Fig. 1.*
**Installation –** Place NEW "O" ring on free-wheeling hub body. *See Fig. 1.* Position free-wheeling hub body to wheel hub flange, aligning bolt holes. Install free-wheeling hub body bolts and tighten to 18 ft. lbs. (25 N.m) using a "star" pattern tightening sequence. Place new gasket on free-wheeling hub cover. Install free-wheeling hub cover and tighten bolts to 106 INCH Lbs. (12 N.m) using a "star" pattern tightening sequence.

### LOWER CONTROL ARM & BALL JOINT

**Removal –** Remove coil spring. See COIL SPRING under REMOVAL & INSTALLATION. Remove lower control arm-to-crossmember bolts. Remove lower control arm. Remove 3 ball joint attaching nuts. Remove ball joint.
**Installation –** Connect lower control arm to crossmember, and partially tighten bolts. Reverse removal procedure to complete installation. Lower vehicle. Bounce vehicle to settle suspension. Tighten lower control arm-to-crossmember bolts to specification. See TORQUE SPECIFICATIONS table at end of article. Check wheel alignment. See SPECIFICATIONS & PROCEDURES article in WHEEL ALIGNMENT.

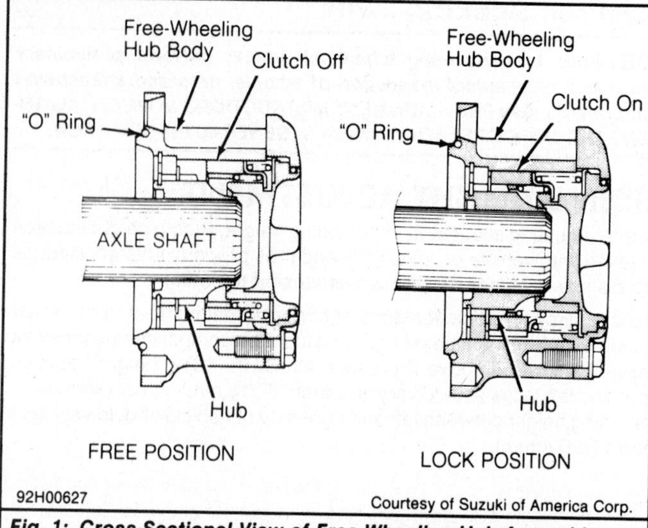


***Fig. 1: Cross-Sectional View of Free-Wheeling Hub Assembly (Manual Hub Is Shown; Automatic Hub Is Similar)***

### LOWER CONTROL ARM BUSHINGS

**Removal – 1)** Remove lower control arm. SEE LOWER CONTROL ARM & BALL JOINT. To remove front bushing, first cut off .20" (5 mm) of bushing flange with hacksaw. *See Fig. 2.*

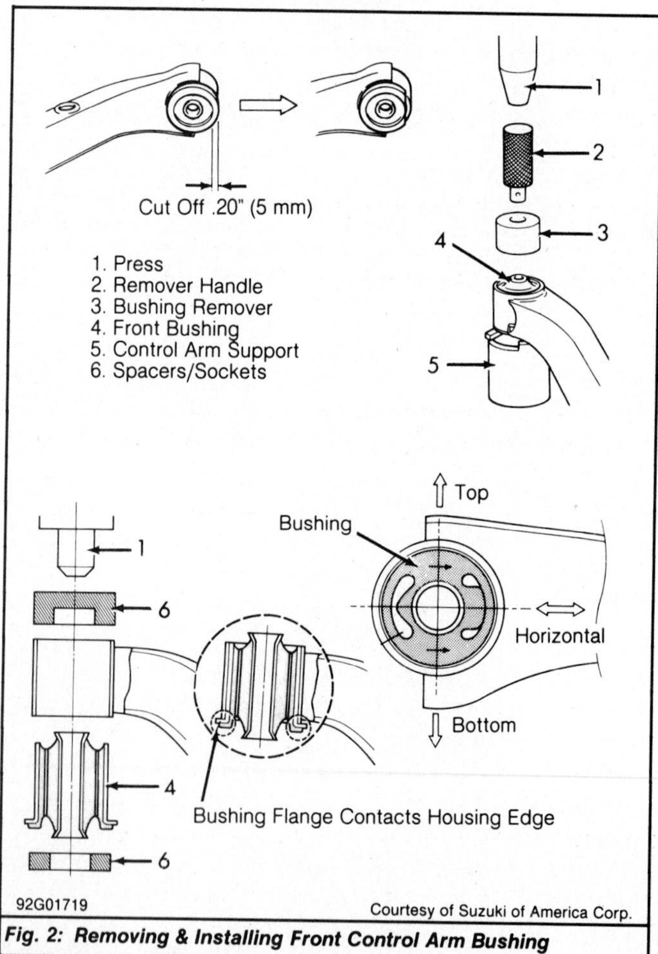


***Fig. 2: Removing & Installing Front Control Arm Bushing***

**2)** Using a press, Control Arm Support (09951-46020), Bush Remover (09951-16060), Handle (09924-74510), press out front bushing. Position Control Arm Support (09951-46020) on cut off area of bushing. *See Fig. 2.* Remove rear bushing by cutting off rubber flange and pressing out bushing using Bushing Remover/Installer Set (09951-16040). *See Fig. 3.*

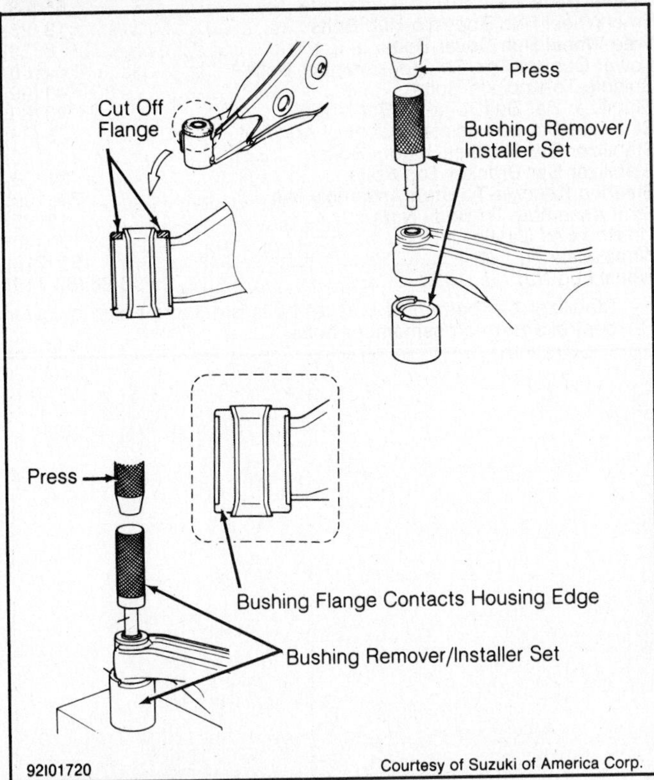


***Fig. 3: Removing & Installing Rear Control Arm Bushing***

**Installation – 1)** Lightly lube bushings before pressing. Ensure front bushing is installed correctly. *See Fig. 2.* Using press and spacers/sockets, install front bushing until bushing flange contacts control arm housing edge. *See Fig. 2.*

**2)** Using press and Bushing Remover/Installer Set (09951-16040), install rear bushing until both rubber bushing flanges are on outside of control arm. *See Fig. 3.* Install lower control arm. SEE LOWER CONTROL ARM & BALL JOINT.

## STABILIZER BAR

**Removal & Installation – 1)** Raise and support vehicle. Remove splash shield. Remove wheels. Disconnect left and right control arm stabilizer links from stabilizer bar.

**2)** Disconnect right and left stabilizer brackets from body mountings. Remove stabilizer bar from vehicle. To install, reverse removal procedure. Ensure paint marks on stabilizer bar align with bushing mounts to ensure bar is centered. *See Fig. 4.*

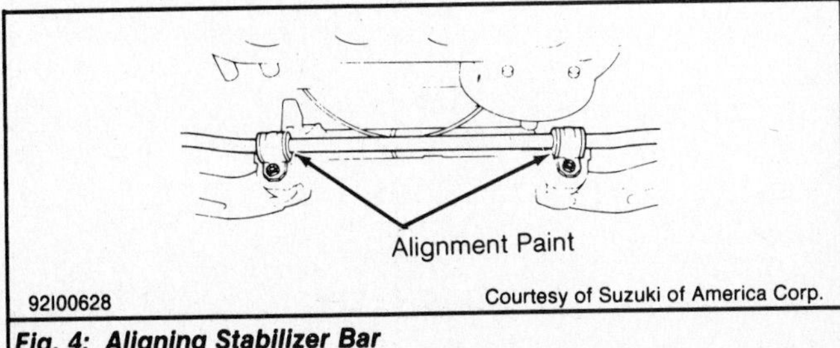


***Fig. 4: Aligning Stabilizer Bar***

## STEERING KNUCKLE

**Removal – 1)** Raise and support vehicle. Remove front wheel(s). On 2WD models, remove hub center cover. On 4WD models, remove free-wheeling hub. See FREE-WHEELING HUB (4WD) under REMOVAL & INSTALLATION. On 4WD models, remove axle shaft snap ring. On all models, disconnect brake line from strut. Remove caliper from steering knuckle and wire aside. Remove brake disc. If disc cannot be remove by hand, install (2) 8-mm bolts into threaded holes of disc. Alternately tighten bolts to remove rotor from hub.

**2)** Remove tie rod end from steering knuckle using Tie Rod Remover (09913-65210). Remove axle shaft snap ring. Remove hub. See WHEEL BEARING & HUB under REMOVAL & INSTALLATION. Remove backing plate. Support lower control arm with jack. Remove strut-to-steering knuckle bolts.

**3)** Disconnect ball joint from steering knuckle. Remove steering knuckle from vehicle. On 2WD models, separate spindle from knuckle.

**Installation – 1)** To install, reverse removal procedure. Tighten all nuts and bolts to specification. See TORQUE SPECIFICATIONS table at end of article. On 2WD models, coat spindle and knuckle mating surfaces with sealant. Tighten spindle bolts to 29-43 ft. lbs. (40-60 N.m).

**2)** To complete hub-to-spindle shaft installation, see WHEEL BEARING & HUB under REMOVAL & INSTALLATION. Tighten lock nut to specification. See WHEEL BEARINGS under ADJUSTMENTS & INSPECTION.

**3)** On 4WD models, install free-wheeling hub. See FREE-WHEELING HUB (4WD) under REMOVAL & INSTALLATION. Check wheel alignment. See SPECIFICATIONS & PROCEDURES article in WHEEL ALIGNMENT.

## STRUT ASSEMBLY

**Removal – 1)** Raise and support vehicle. Allow suspension to hang freely. Remove wheels. Disconnect disc brake caliper hose from strut. Remove caliper from steering knuckle and wire aside.

**2)** Scribe mating marks on strut and steering knuckle for installation reference. Remove lower strut-to-steering knuckle bolts. Remove upper strut-to-body mounting nuts at strut tower. Compress and remove strut assembly from vehicle.

**Installation –** To install, reverse removal procedure. Align strut and steering knuckle mating marks made during removal (if re-installing original strut). Tighten all nuts and bolts to specification. See TORQUE SPECIFICATIONS table at end of article. Check wheel alignment. See SPECIFICATIONS & PROCEDURES article in WHEEL ALIGNMENT.

## WHEEL BEARING & HUB

**Removal – 1)** Raise and support vehicle. Remove front wheel(s). On 2WD models, remove hub center cover. On 4WD models, remove free-wheeling hub. See FREE-WHEELING HUB (4WD) under REMOVAL & INSTALLATION. On all models, remove caliper from steering knuckle and wire aside.

**2)** Remove brake disc. If disc cannot be remove by hand, install (2) 8-mm bolts into threaded holes of disc. Alternately tighten bolts to remove rotor from hub. Remove wheel bearing lock plate locking screws. Remove lock nut using Socket (09951-16050). Remove lock washer.

**3)** Remove wheel hub, bearing and seals as an assembly. If wheel hub cannot be removed by hand, use slide hammer and Hub Remover Adapter (09930-30102). Remove hub seal and snap ring from hub. Using Hub Bearing Installer/Remover (09944-68210), press bearing assembly from hub.

***NOTE: DO NOT reuse bearing assembly once it has been pressed out of hub. Replace with NEW one-piece bearing assembly***

**Installation – 1)** Ensure NEW bearing assembly is packed with high-temperature multipurpose disc brake bearing grease. (Most NEW bearing assemblies are of a "sealed" one-piece design). Using Hub

# 1991 SUSPENSION
# Front – Sidekick (Cont.)

Bearing Installer/Remover (09944-68210), press bearing assembly into hub.

**2)** Install snap ring. Install NEW inner grease seal into hub using Hub Seal Installer (09944-66010) and Installer Handle (09924-74510). Lightly coat seal lip with multipurpose grease. Install outer dust seal to hub, DO NOT grease this seal.

**3)** To complete hub-to-spindle shaft installation, reverse removal procedure. Tighten lock nut to specification. See WHEEL BEARINGS under ADJUSTMENTS & INSPECTION. On 4WD models, install free-wheeling hub. See FREE-WHEELING HUB (4WD) under REMOVAL & INSTALLATION.

## TORQUE SPECIFICATIONS

*TORQUE SPECIFICATIONS*

| Application | Ft. Lbs. (N.m) |
|---|---|
| Ball Joint Stud Castle Nut | 50 (70) |
| Ball Joint-To-Control Arm Nut | 63 (85) |
| Caliper Bolts | 65 (88) |
| Free-Wheel Hub Body-To-Hub Bolts | 18 (25) |
| Free-Wheel Hub Cover Bolts | 8 (12) |
| Lower Control Arm-To-Crossmember Bolts [1] | 74 (100) |
| Spindle-To-Knuckle Bolts | 43 (60) |
| Stabilizer Bar Ball Joint-To-Bar Nut | 43 (60) |
| Stabilizer Bar Ball Joint-To-Control Arm Nut | 23 (35) |
| Stabilizer Bar Bracket Bottom Bolts [1] | 74 (100) |
| Stabilizer Bar Bracket Top Bolts | 21 (28) |
| Steering Knuckle-To-Strut Assembly Nut | 74 (100) |
| Strut Assembly-To-Body Nuts | 18 (25) |
| Tie Rod End Castle Nut | 30 (40) |
| Wheel Bearing Nut | 155 (210) |
| Wheel Lug Nut | 58-80 (80-110) |

[1] – Stabilizer bar bottom of bracket bolts are same bolts as lower control arm-to-crossmember bolts.

# 1991 SUSPENSION
# Front – Swift

## DESCRIPTION & OPERATION

MacPherson strut independent front suspension is used. Strut and strut support are isolated by rubber mounts. Lower end of strut is connected to steering knuckle. Lower end of steering knuckle is attached by ball joint to lower control arm. *See Fig. 1.*

Steering wheel movement is transmitted to tie rod end and steering knuckle, causing wheel to turn. With steering knuckle movement, strut also rotates by means of top strut bearing and lower ball joint pivot.

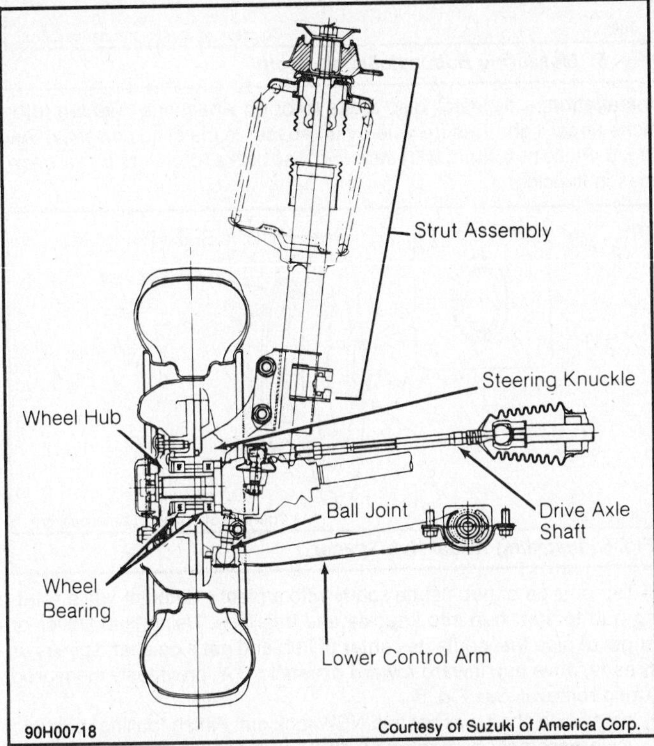


***Fig. 1: Cross-Sectional View of Front Suspension Assembly***

## ADJUSTMENTS & INSPECTION

### WHEEL ALIGNMENT SPECIFICATIONS & PROCEDURES

***NOTE: See SPECIFICATIONS & PROCEDURES article in WHEEL ALIGNMENT.***

### BALL JOINT CHECKING

Raise and support vehicle, allowing front suspension to hang freely. Hold tire at top and bottom. Move top of tire in and out. No horizontal or vertical movement should exist at ball joint. Disconnect ball joint from steering knuckle. If there is looseness in joint, or ball stud can be turned by hand, replace ball joint.

### WHEEL BEARINGS

Wheel bearings are not adjustable. To check wheel bearing(s) for excessive wear, raise and support vehicle, remove wheel. Remove hub center cap and mount a dial indicator to rotor and to center hub shaft. Grasp rotor and apply pull/push force in and out. Note indicator reading. Replace bearing if movement exceeds .016" (.41 mm).

## REMOVAL & INSTALLATION

### STRUT ASSEMBLY

***WARNING: Use care when working with strut coil springs. Springs are under extreme tension when compressed.***

**Removal & Disassembly – 1)** Raise and support vehicle on safety stands. Allow front suspension to hang freely. Remove front wheels. Remove brake hose "E" clip and brake hose from bracket. Remove strut-to-steering knuckle bolts and nuts. While holding strut by hand, remove strut upper mounting nuts. Remove strut.

**2)** Install strut assembly in spring compressor. Compress strut spring until piston rod nut extends approximately 1/2" (13 mm) above stopper. NEVER bottom out spring. Remove piston rod nut. Disassemble strut assembly, noting position of assembled parts for reassembly. *See Fig. 2.*

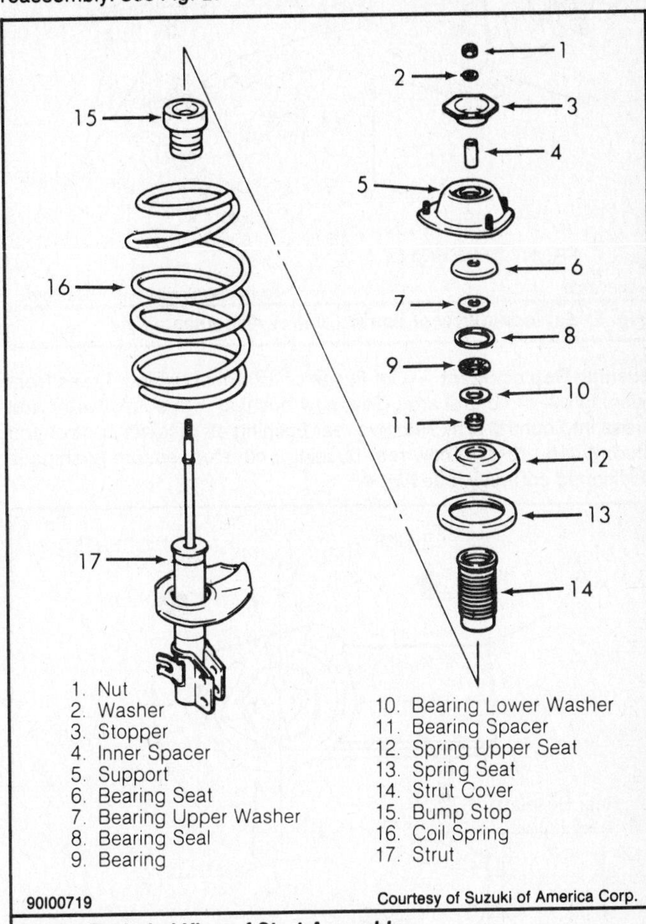


***Fig. 2: Exploded View of Strut Assembly***

**Inspection –** Check for deterioration or damage. Check for even resistance as strut is moved through full travel. Replace as necessary.

**Reassembly & Installation –** Ensure spring seats and spring are properly positioned. Ensure arrow on upper spring seat points OUTWARD when strut is installed in vehicle. To complete reassembly and installation, reverse disassembly and removal procedure.

## LOWER CONTROL ARM & BALL JOINT

**Removal –** Raise and support vehicle on safety stands, allowing suspension to hang freely. Remove ball joint pinch bolt. Separate ball joint from steering knuckle. Remove suspension arm bracket bolts. *See Fig. 3.* Remove lower control arm assembly.

***NOTE: If ball joint is worn or damaged, replace lower control arm and ball joint as an assembly.***

**Inspection –** Check parts for deterioration, cracks, or damage. Check ball joint for smoothness of rotation. Replace worn or damaged bushings.

# 1991 SUSPENSION
# Front – Swift (Cont.)

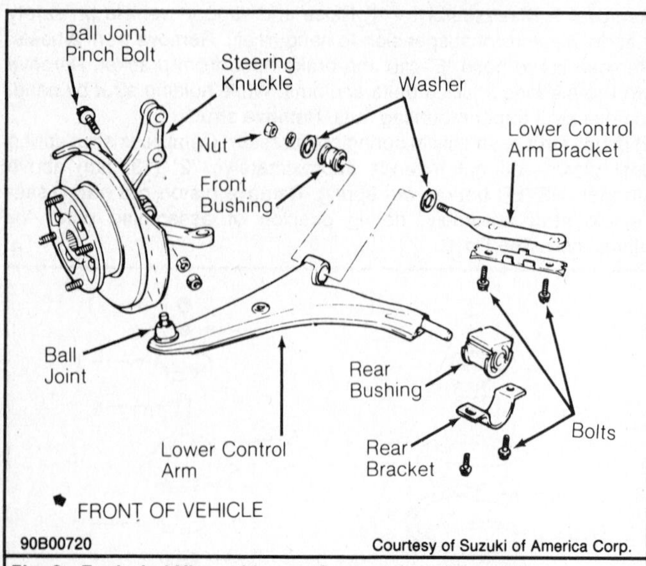


***Fig. 3: Exploded View of Lower Control Arm Assembly***

**Bushing Replacement** – Cut flange off of front bushing. Press front bushing out of control arm. Coat new bushing with soapy water and press into control arm. Remove rear bushing off of lower control arm stud. When pressing new rear bushing onto stud, ensure bushing is positioned correctly. *See Fig. 4*.

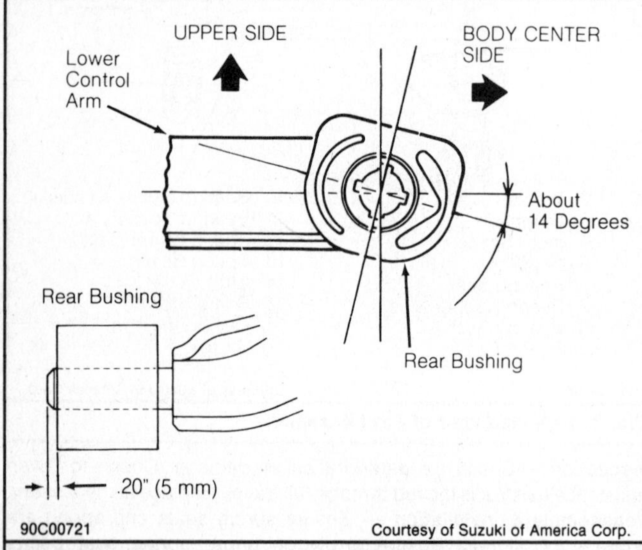


***Fig. 4: Installing Lower Control Arm Rear Bushing***

**Installation – 1)** Install suspension arm on body and finger tighten nuts and bolts. Install ball joint into steering knuckle clamp. Install ball joint pinch bolt so that bolt head is toward front of vehicle.

**2)** Tighten ball joint and both control arm bushings to specification. See TORQUE SPECIFICATIONS table at end of article. Install wheels and lower vehicle. Check and adjust toe setting. See SPECIFICATIONS & PROCEDURES article in WHEEL ALIGNMENT.

## WHEEL HUB & DISC BRAKE ROTOR

**Removal (Except GT) – 1)** Raise and support vehicle on safety stands with suspension hanging freely. Remove wheel. Measure hub installation depth "A" for use in reassembly. *See Fig. 5*.

**2)** Straighten "staked" part of drive axle lock nut. Depress brake pedal. Remove and discard drive axle lock nut. Loosen, but do not remove disc brake rotor bolts.

**3)** Remove caliper bolts. Remove caliper and hang aside. Remove hub and disc brake rotor with slide hammer and Adapter (09943-17911). Separate wheel hub and disc brake rotor.

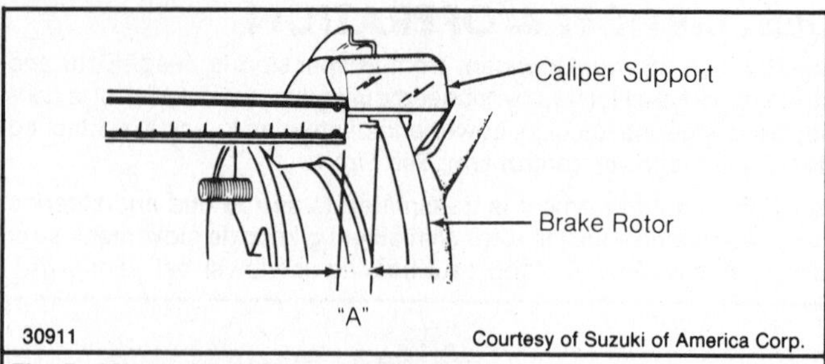


***Fig. 5: Measuring Hub Installation Depth***

**Installation – 1)** Install disc brake rotor on wheel hub. Tighten rotor bolts finger tight. Ensure wheel hub spacer is installed correctly. *See Fig. 6*. Place hub shaft, with attached disc brake rotor, into wheel bearings in knuckle.

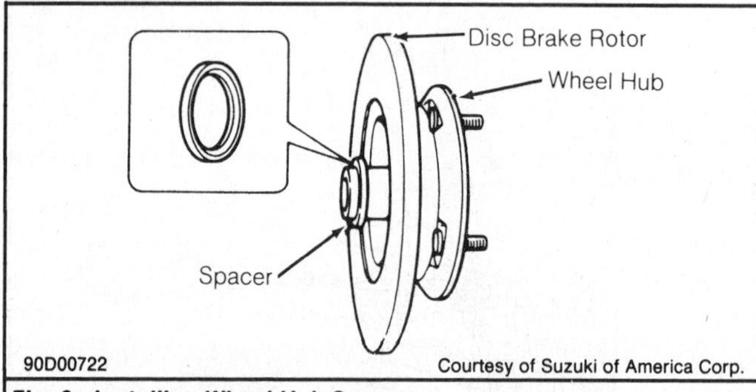


***Fig. 6: Installing Wheel Hub Spacer***

**2)** Tap outside of hub flange lightly with a plastic hammer while rotating hub to start hub into knuckle and bearings. Using Hub Driver or length of pipe that contacts center of hub and not axle shaft splines or threads, drive hub inward toward dimension "A" previously measured during removal. *See Fig. 5*

**3)** Install axle shaft washer and NEW lock nut. Finish "pulling" hub into knuckle assembly by tightening NEW axle shaft lock nut. To install remaining components, reverse removal procedure. Depress brake pedal and tighten axle shaft lock nut to specification. See TORQUE SPECIFICATIONS table at end of article. Stake NEW axle shaft lock nut.

**Removal (GT) – 1)** Raise and support vehicle on safety stands, allowing suspension to hang freely. Remove wheel. Straighten "staked" part of drive axle lock nut. Depress brake pedal. Remove and discard drive axle lock nut.

**2)** Remove caliper mounting bolts. Remove caliper and hang aside. Remove disc brake rotor. Remove hub with slide hammer and Adapter (09943-17911). Remove outer bearing inner race from hub shaft using Bearing Puller (09913-61110).

**Installation – 1)** Install outer bearing inner race onto wheel hub shaft using Bearing Installer (099944-98010). Apply grease to inner race and hub shaft. Install wheel hub to knuckle and axle shaft, and install axle shaft washer and NEW lock nut. DO NOT tap or hammer on hub flange. Pull hub into knuckle assembly by tightening NEW axle shaft lock nut.

**2)** Install disc rotor to hub. Install caliper to rotor and knuckle. Tighten caliper bolts to specification. See TORQUE SPECIFICATIONS table at end of article. Depress brake pedal and tighten axle shaft lock nut to specification. See TORQUE SPECIFICATIONS table at end of article. Stake NEW axle shaft lock nut.

## STEERING KNUCKLE

**Removal – 1)** Raise and support vehicle on safety stands, allowing suspension to hang freely. Remove wheel. Remove wheel hub and disc brake rotor. See WHEEL HUB & DISC BRAKE ROTOR under REMOVAL & INSTALLATION.

# 1991 SUSPENSION
# Front – Swift (Cont.)

**2)** Remove tie rod end cotter pin and castle nut. Separate tie rod end from steering knuckle using Tie Rod Remover (09913-65210). Remove strut-to-knuckle assembly bolts and nuts. Remove ball joint pinch bolt and nut. Remove steering knuckle from ball joint.

**Installation – 1)** Install steering knuckle clamp onto ball joint. Install ball joint pinch bolt so that bolt head is toward front of vehicle. Install strut to knuckle assembly. Install tie rod to steering knuckle.

**2)** Tighten all fasteners to specification. See TORQUE SPECIFICATIONS table at end of article. Install wheel hub and disc rotor. See WHEEL HUB & DISC BRAKE ROTOR under REMOVAL & INSTALLATION. Install wheels and lower vehicle. Check and adjust toe setting. See SPECIFICATIONS & PROCEDURES article in WHEEL ALIGNMENT.

## WHEEL BEARINGS

**Removal (Except GT) –** Remove steering knuckle. See STEERING KNUCKLE. Remove outer seal and snap ring, and inner seal and inner bearing. Remove bearing races using press and Bearing Remover/Installer (09913-75520), or by using a brass drift and hammer to tap inner and outer wheel bearing races out of steering knuckle bore.

**Installation – 1)** Apply special grease to bearings and races. Press inner bearing into knuckle bore using Bearing Remover/Installer (09913-75520). Press outer bearing into knuckle bore using Bearing Installer Support (09944-78210), Bearing Installer (09944-68210), and Bearing Installer Handle (09924-74510).

**2)** Install inner seal flush with knuckle surface. *See Fig. 7.* Install outer snap ring. Install outer seal to knuckle bore and bottom it against snap ring using Bearing Installer (09944-68210). To complete installation, reverse steering knuckle removal procedure. See WHEEL HUB & DISC BRAKE ROTOR under REMOVAL & INSTALLATION.

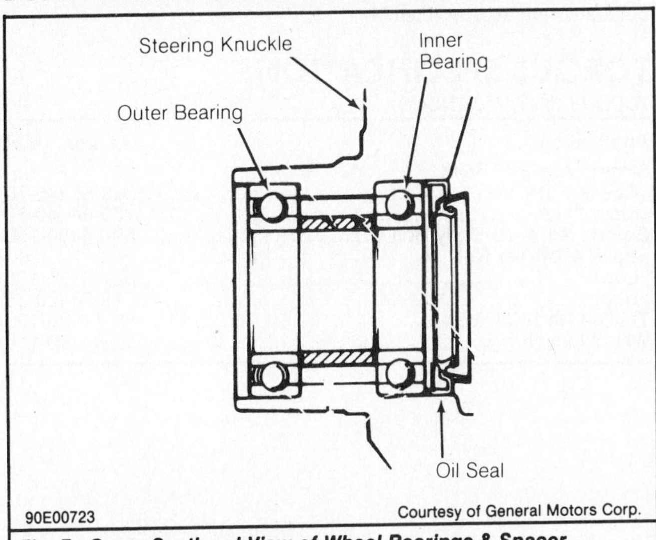


***Fig. 7: Cross-Sectional View of Wheel Bearings & Spacer (Except GT)***

**Removal (GT) –** Remove steering knuckle. See STEERING KNUCKLE under REMOVAL & INSTALLATION. Remove outer seal, snap ring and inner seal. *See Fig. 8.* Remove bearing assembly using press, Bearing Remover/Installer (09924-74510) and Attachment (09944-68510). Press bearing outward from inner seal side.

***NOTE: On GT, always replace inner and outer wheel bearings as an assembly.***

**Installation – 1)** Apply special grease to bearings and races. Press bearing assembly into knuckle bore from outer side using Bearing & Seal Remover/Installer (09951-16090), Bearing Installer Handle (09924-74510) and Bearing Installer Support (09944-78210).

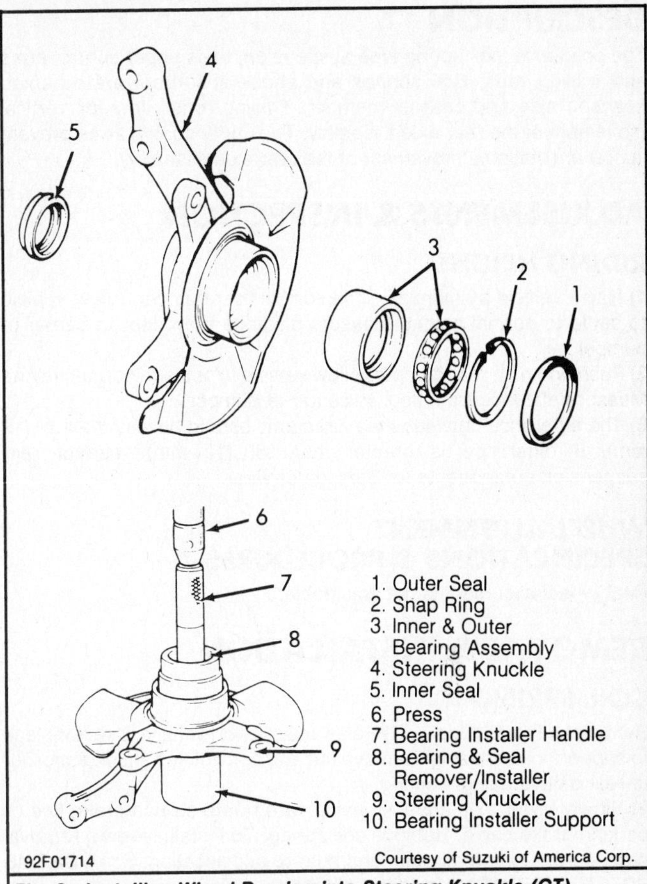


***Fig. 8: Installing Wheel Bearing into Steering Knuckle (GT)***

**2)** Install outer snap ring. Install outer seal using Bearing/Seal Installer (09944-66010) until seal is bottomed against snap ring. Using Bearing Installer Support (09944-78210), press inner seal into knuckle until seal is flush with knuckle surface. To complete installation, reverse steering knuckle removal procedure. See WHEEL HUB & DISC BRAKE ROTOR under REMOVAL & INSTALLATION.

## TORQUE SPECIFICATIONS

***TORQUE SPECIFICATIONS***

| Application | Ft. Lbs. (N.m) |
|---|---|
| Ball Joint Pinch Bolt | 44 (60) |
| Brake Disc Caliper Bolts | 22 (30) |
| Brake Disc Rotor-To-Hub Bolts | 37 (50) |
| Control Arm Pivot Bolts | 37-52 (50-70) |
| Drive Axle Shaft Lock Nut | 129 (175) |
| Lower Control Arm | |
| Bracket Bolts | 59 (80) |
| Front Bushing Nut | 74 (100) |
| Rear Bracket Bolts | 32 (43) |
| Strut Assembly-To-Body Nuts | 20 (27) |
| Strut Assembly-To-Knuckle | 51-66 (70-90) |
| Strut Piston Nut | 37 (50) |
| Tie Rod-To-Steering Knuckle Nut | 32 (43) |
| Wheel Lug Nuts | 44 (60) |

# 1991 SUSPENSION
# Rear – Sidekick

## DESCRIPTION

The solid axle, coil spring type suspension, uses upper control arms and trailing rods. Coil springs and shock absorbers are mounted between axle and chassis member. Trailing rods allow for vertical movement of the rear axle assembly. The upper control arms prevent lateral or rotational movement of the rear axle assembly.

## ADJUSTMENTS & INSPECTION

### RIDING HEIGHT

**1)** Raise vehicle by manually lifting up on rear bumper. Allow vehicle to settle to normal height. Measure distance from floor to center of bumper.

**2)** Push down on rear bumper. Allow vehicle to settle to normal height. Measure distance from floor to center of bumper.

**3)** The difference between measurements should be less than .5" (12 mm). If difference is greater than .5" (12 mm), inspect rear suspension components for damage or wear.

### WHEEL ALIGNMENT SPECIFICATIONS & PROCEDURES

Rear wheel alignment is not adjustable.

## REMOVAL & INSTALLATION

### COIL SPRING

**Removal & Installation – 1)** Raise and support vehicle. Use floor jack to support axle housing. Remove nut and bolt holding shock absorber to rear axle housing. *See Fig. 1.*

**2)** Slowly lower axle housing, using care not to stretch brake line or parking brake cable. Remove coil spring. To install, reverse removal procedure. Tighten all bolts and nuts to specification. See TORQUE SPECIFICATIONS table at end of article.

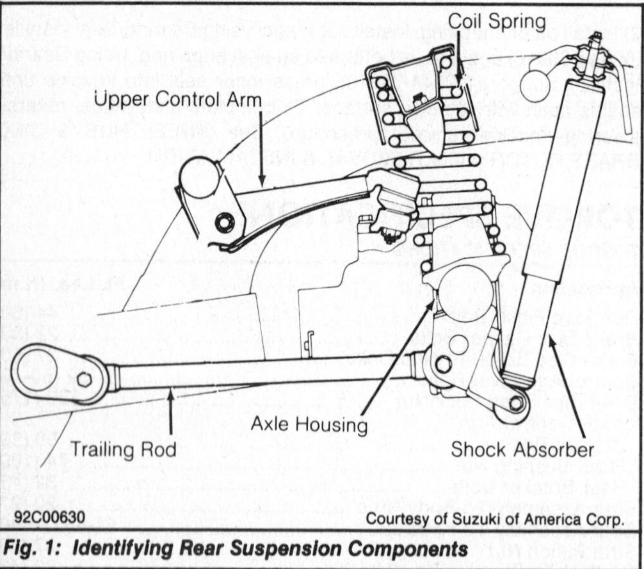


***Fig. 1: Identifying Rear Suspension Components***

### SHOCK ABSORBER

**Removal & Installation –** Raise and support vehicle. Remove nut retaining shock absorber to rear axle housing. Remove nut holding shock absorber to body and remove shock absorber. To install, reverse removal procedure. Tighten all bolts to specification. See TORQUE SPECIFICATIONS table at end of article.

### TRAILING ROD

**Removal & Installation – 1)** Raise and support vehicle. Remove wheels. Disconnect parking brake hanger from trailing rod. Use floor jack to support axle housing. Remove nuts attaching trailing rod to body and axle housing. *See Fig. 1.* Remove trailing rod.

**2)** To install, reverse removal procedure. DO NOT tighten fasteners. Lower vehicle. Bounce vehicle to stabilize suspension. Raise axle housing, and tighten trailing rod nuts to specification. See TORQUE SPECIFICATIONS table at end of article.

### UPPER CONTROL ARMS

**Removal – 1)** Raise and support vehicle. Remove wheels. Use jack to support axle assembly.

**2)** Disconnect ball joint mount from axle assembly. Remove bolt and nut holding upper control arm to body. Remove upper control arm. *See Fig. 1.*

**Installation – 1)** To install, reverse removal procedure. DO NOT tighten fasteners. Lower vehicle to ground and bounce vehicle to stabilize suspension. Raise and support vehicle with jack stands. Raise axle housing with jack until body is free from jack stands.

**2)** Tighten bolts and nuts retaining control arms to body. Tighten bolts and nuts retaining control arm to axle housing. Tighten all remaining bolts and nuts to specification.

## TORQUE SPECIFICATIONS

***TORQUE SPECIFICATIONS***

| Application | Ft. Lbs. (N.m) |
|---|---|
| Control Arm Ball Joint | |
| Castle Nut | 33-52 (45-70) |
| Mount Nut | 30-44 (40-60) |
| Control Arms-To-Body Bolt | 59-74 (80-100) |
| Shock Absorber Nut | |
| Lower | 52-74 (70-100) |
| Upper | 16-26 (22-35) |
| Trailing Rod Nut | 59-74 (80-100) |
| Wheel Lug Nut | 59-81 (80-110) |

# 1991 SUSPENSION
# Rear – Swift

## DESCRIPTION

Rear suspension is strut-type with independent coil spring and lower control arm. Control rods connect rear knuckle and body, to control lateral movement. GT models have a rear stabilizer bar.

## ADJUSTMENTS & INSPECTION

### WHEEL ALIGNMENT SPECIFICATIONS & PROCEDURES

*NOTE: See SPECIFICATIONS & PROCEDURES article in WHEEL ALIGNMENT.*

### WHEEL BEARINGS

Wheel bearings are not adjustable. To check wheel bearing(s) for excessive wear, raise and support vehicle, remove wheel. Remove spindle/hub cap and mount a dial indicator to rotor/drum and to center of spindle shaft. Push in and pull out on rotor/drum. Note indicator reading. If movement exceeds .012" (.30 mm), replace bearing(s).

## REMOVAL & INSTALLATION

### CONTROL RODS

**Removal – 1)** Raise and support vehicle, allowing suspension to hang freely. Disconnect brake flexhose from bracket on control rod by removing "E" clip. *See Fig. 1.* Scribe location marks on mounting bracket and toe-in adjustment cam for installation reference.

**2)** Remove outer control rod nut from knuckle. Remove toe-in adjustment cam bolt. *See Fig. 1.* Lift off control rod. Check control rod bushings for wear.

**Installation – 1)** Install control rod with adjustment cam facing down, and brake flexhose bracket facing direction shown in illustration. *See Fig. 1.* Align toe-in cam with location marks made during removal.

**2)** DO NOT "final" tighten control rod toe-in cam bolt or outer control rod nut with vehicle on hoist. Lower vehicle until suspension is at normal riding height, and then tighten fasteners to specification. See TORQUE SPECIFICATIONS table at end of article. Check toe-in. See SPECIFICATIONS & PROCEDURES article in WHEEL ALIGNMENT.

### COIL SPRING & LOWER CONTROL ARM

**Removal – 1)** Raise and support vehicle on safety stands, allowing rear suspension to hang freely. Remove rear wheel. Scribe location marks on mounting bracket and toe-in adjustment cam for installation reference.

**2)** Remove control rod from knuckle rear stud. Loosen, but DO NOT remove, control arm pivot bolts at body side of lower control arm. *See Fig. 1.*

**3)** Loosen, but DO NOT remove, control arm-to-knuckle bolt. Place floor jack under lower control arm. Lift control arm enough to remove control arm-to-knuckle bolt.

**4)** Pull outward on brake drum/backing plate assembly to separate knuckle from control arm. Slowly lower jack and remove coil spring. *See Fig. 2.* On GT models, remove stabilizer link from control arm. Remove control arm front bushing bracket bolts and rear control arm bolt. Remove control arm.

**Installation – 1)** Install control arm to body and tighten front bushing bracket bolts. DO NOT tighten front and rear control arm pivot bolts and nut yet. Install coil spring in control arm.

**2)** Match bottom of spring with stepped part of control arm. Raise control arm with jack. Install control arm-to-knuckle bolt and tighten to specification. See TORQUE SPECIFICATIONS table at end of article. Remove jack. On GT models, install stabilizer link to control arm.

**3)** Install control rod, but DO NOT "final" tighten knuckle stud nut and toe-in cam bolt yet. Install wheel. Lower hoist so vehicle weight rests on ground. Tighten control rod-to-knuckle stud nut and toe-in adjustment cam to specification. Tighten control arm pivot bolts and nut to specification. See TORQUE SPECIFICATIONS table at end of article.

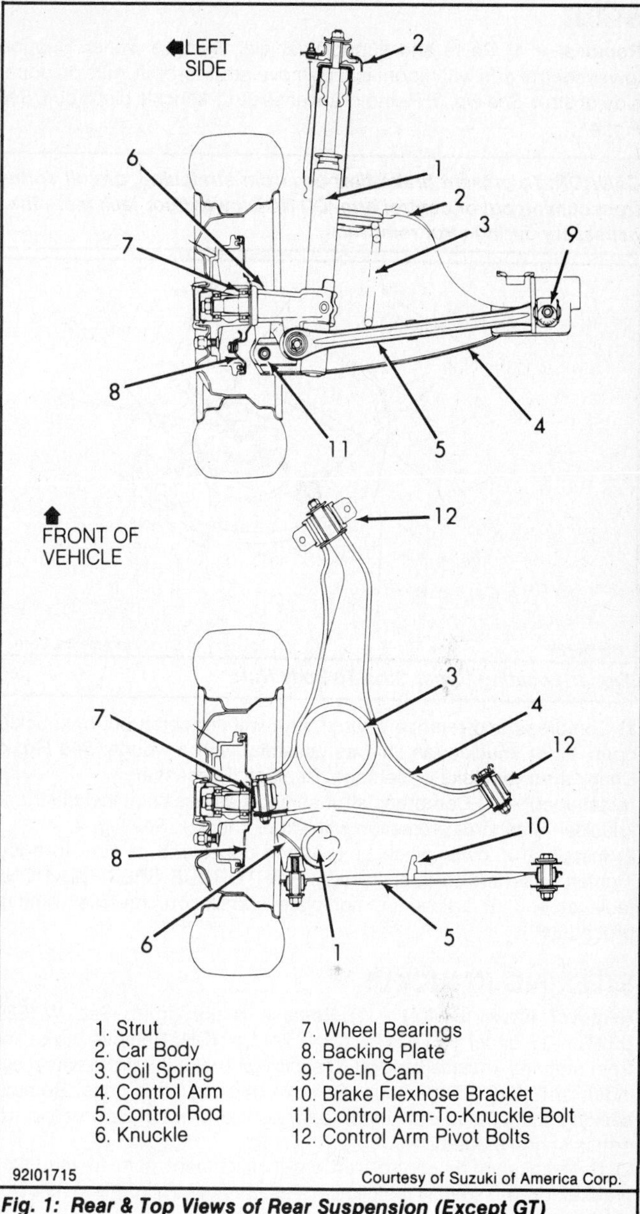


***Fig. 1: Rear & Top Views of Rear Suspension (Except GT)***

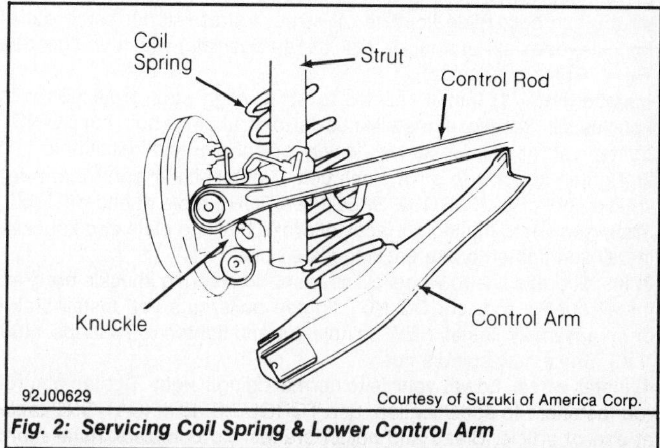


***Fig. 2: Servicing Coil Spring & Lower Control Arm***

**4)** When tightening front control arm pivot nut, ensure bushing washer (behind nut) has flat section facing down and round section facing up. To complete installation, check rear toe-in. See SPECIFICATIONS & PROCEDURES article in WHEEL ALIGNMENT.

# 1991 SUSPENSION
# Rear – Swift (Cont.)

## STRUT

**Removal – 1)** Raise and support vehicle. Remove wheel. Support lower control arm with floor jack. Remove strut-to-body nuts on upper side of strut. *See Fig. 3.* Remove lower strut-to-knuckle pinch bolt. *See Fig. 4.*

***CAUTION: To prevent brake flexhose from stretching, or coil spring from coming out of control arm, DO NOT lower floor jack more than necessary during strut removal.***

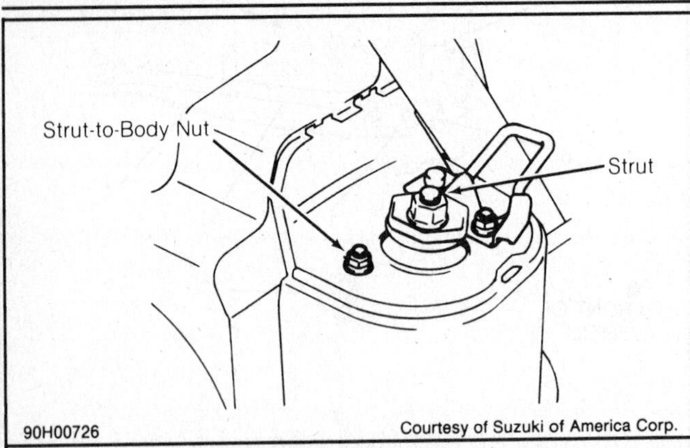


***Fig. 3: Locating Upper Strut-To-Body Nuts***

**2)** Compress and remove strut. If strut will not come out of knuckle, open slit of knuckle (as little as possible) with a wedge. *See Fig. 4.* Check strut for leaks or damage. Replace if necessary.

**Installation – 1)** Compress strut as short as possible. Install strut in knuckle. Align strut projection with slit in knuckle. *See Fig. 4.*

**2)** Install strut lower pinch bolt. Attach upper end of strut to body. Tighten fasteners to specification. See TORQUE SPECIFICATIONS table at end of article. To complete installation, reverse removal procedure.

## STEERING KNUCKLE

**Removal (Drum Brake) – 1)** Remove brake drum. See WHEEL BEARINGS under REMOVAL & INSTALLATION. Remove brake line from steering knuckle bracket. Disconnect brake line from wheel cylinder, and plug all openings. Remove backing plate bolts. Remove backing plate. Place jack under lower control arm for support (control arm is spring loaded).

**2)** Reference mark control rod toe-in alignment cam to mounting bracket for reassembly installation. Remove control rod from knuckle stud and inboard mounting bracket.

**3)** Remove lower control arm-to-knuckle bolt. Remove knuckle-to-strut pinch bolt. Slide knuckle off strut. If strut will not come out of knuckle, open slit of knuckle (as little as possible) with a wedge. *See Fig. 4.* Remove knuckle.

**Installation – 1)** Install knuckle to strut. Align strut projection with knuckle slit. *See Fig. 4.* Install knuckle-to-strut pinch bolt, but DO NOT tighten yet. Align knuckle with lower control arm and install bolt.

**2)** Tighten knuckle-to-strut pinch bolt. Tighten lower control arm-to-knuckle bolt. See TORQUE SPECIFICATIONS table at end of article. Apply sealant to mating surfaces of brake backing plate and knuckle. Install and tighten brake backing plate bolts.

**3)** Install brake line to wheel cylinder and to steering knuckle bracket. Install control rod, but DO NOT tighten bolts/nuts yet. Install brake drum assembly. Install NEW spindle nut and tighten to 74 ft. lbs. (100 N.m). Stake new spindle nut.

**4)** Install wheel. Lower vehicle to normal riding height. Tighten control rod fasteners to specification. See TORQUE SPECIFICATIONS table at end of article. Bleed and adjust brakes. To complete installation, check rear toe-in. See SPECIFICATIONS & PROCEDURES article in WHEEL ALIGNMENT.

**Removal (Disc Brake) – 1)** Raise and support vehicle, allowing suspension to hang freely. Remove wheel. Remove caliper pin bolts. Release parking brake lever. Disconnect brake line bracket from

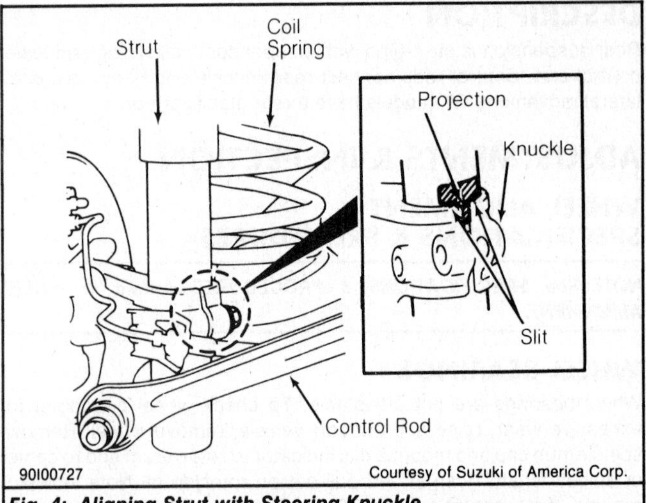


***Fig. 4: Aligning Strut with Steering Knuckle***

knuckle. Remove caliper from support bracket and wire aside. Remove caliper support bracket from knuckle. If reusing brake pads, mark pads for inner and outer identification for reassembly reference.

**2)** Remove rotor. See WHEEL BEARINGS under REMOVAL & INSTALLATION. Remove backing plate. Place jack under lower control arm for support (control arm is spring loaded).

**3)** Reference mark control rod toe-in alignment cam to mounting bracket for reassembly installation. Remove control rod from knuckle stud and inboard mounting bracket.

**4)** Remove lower control arm-to-knuckle bolt. Remove knuckle-to-strut pinch bolt. Slide knuckle off strut. If strut will not come out of knuckle, open slit of knuckle (as little as possible) with a wedge. *See Fig. 4.* Remove knuckle.

**Installation – 1)** Install knuckle to strut. Align strut projection with knuckle slit. *See Fig. 4.* Install knuckle-to-strut pinch bolt, but DO NOT tighten yet. Align knuckle with lower control arm and install bolt.

**2)** Tighten knuckle-to-strut pinch bolt. Tighten lower control arm-to-knuckle bolt. See TORQUE SPECIFICATIONS table at end of article. Apply sealant to mating surfaces of brake backing plate and knuckle. Install and tighten brake backing plate bolts.

**3)** Install control rod, but DO NOT tighten bolts/nuts yet. Install rotor assembly. See WHEEL BEARINGS under REMOVAL & INSTALLATION. Install new spindle nut, and tighten to 74 ft. lbs. (100 N.m). Stake spindle nut. Install caliper support bracket. Install inner and outer disc pads.

**4)** Install caliper to support bracket and brake line bracket to knuckle. Tighten fasteners to specification. See TORQUE SPECIFICATIONS table at end of article. Install wheel. Lower vehicle to normal riding height. Tighten control rod fasteners to specification. See TORQUE SPECIFICATIONS table at end of article.

**5)** Bleed and adjust brakes, if required. Pump brake pedal a few times before driving to set disc pads clearance to rotor. To complete installation, check rear toe-in. See SPECIFICATIONS & PROCEDURES article in WHEEL ALIGNMENT.

## WHEEL BEARINGS

**Removal (Drum Brake) – 1)** Raise and support vehicle, allowing suspension to hang freely. Remove wheel. Remove spindle/hub cap. Straighten staked portion of spindle nut. Remove and discard spindle nut. Remove washer.

**2)** Pull brake drum/hub assembly from spindle using slide hammer and Adapter (09943-17911) attached to wheel lug nuts. Remove bearings ONLY if NEW bearing assembly is available. Remove bearings using either a press, or a brass drift and hammer. Press or tap wheel bearings and oil seal out of brake drum hub.

***NOTE: Always use NEW spindle nut on installation.***

**Installation – 1)** Apply grease to bearing cavity, inside wheel bearings and lightly to seal lips. Using Bearing Installer (09913-76010),

# 1991 SUSPENSION
# Rear – Swift (Cont.)

install bearings with seal side facing outward (away from inner spacer). Spacer MUST be installed with largest opening toward spindle base. *See Fig. 5*.

**2)** Install brake drum assembly. Install NEW spindle nut and tighten to 74 ft. lbs. (100 N.m). Stake new spindle nut. To complete installation, reverse removal procedure.

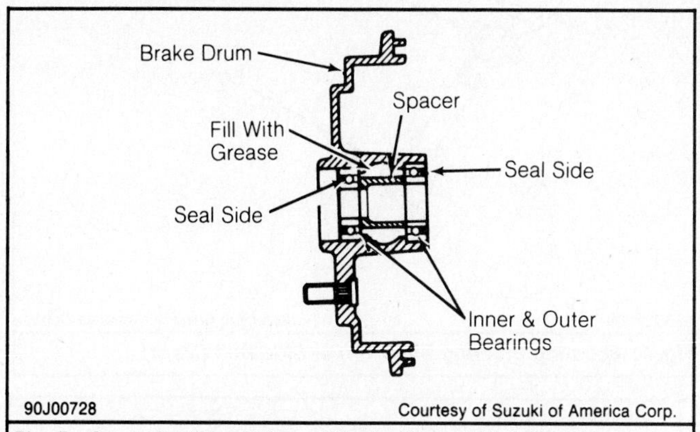


***Fig. 5: Cross-Sectional View of Brake Drum & Hub Bearings***

**Removal (Disc Brake) – 1)** Raise and support vehicle, allowing suspension to hang freely. Remove wheel. Remove caliper pin bolts. Release parking brake lever. Disconnect brake line bracket from knuckle. Remove caliper from support bracket and wire aside.

**2)** Remove caliper support bracket from knuckle. If reusing brake pads, mark pads for inner and outer identification for reassembly reference. Remove spindle/hub cap. Straighten staked portion of spindle nut. Remove and discard spindle nut. Remove washer.

**3)** Pull hub assembly from spindle using slide hammer and Adapter (09943-17911) attached to wheel lug nuts. On disc brake and GT models, bearing assembly and hub are to be replaced as one unit.

***NOTE: Always use NEW spindle nut on installation.***

**Installation** – Install NEW hub/bearing assembly. Install NEW spindle nut and tighten to 74 ft. lbs. (100 N.m). Stake new spindle nut. To complete installation, reverse removal procedure.

## TORQUE SPECIFICATIONS

***TORQUE SPECIFICATIONS***

| Application | Ft. Lbs. (N.m) |
|---|---|
| Brake Backing Plate Bolts | 29-43 (40-60) |
| Caliper-To-Support Bolts | 16-23 (22-32) |
| Caliper Support-To-Knuckle Bolts | 29-43 (40-60) |
| Control Rod | |
| Toe-In Cam Bolt | 59 (80) |
| Knuckle Stud Nut | 59 (80) |
| Lower Control Arm | |
| Front Bushing Bracket Bolts | 33 (45) |
| Front Pivot Bolt Nut | 44 (60) |
| Rear Pivot Bolt Nut | 37 (50) |
| Spindle Nut | |
| Disc | 108.5-144.5 (150-200) |
| Drum | 74 (100) |
| Stabilizer Bar Link-To-Control Arm Nut | 13.5-20 (18-28) |
| Stabilizer Bar-To-Link Ball Joint Nut | 29-43 (40-60) |
| Stabilizer Bar Bracket Bolts | 13.5-20 (18-28) |
| Steering Knuckle Lower Mount Bolt | 44 (60) |
| Steering Knuckle-To-Strut Pinch Bolts | 44 (60) |
| Strut-To-Body Nut | 22 (30) |
| Wheel Lug Nut | 44 (60) |

# 1991 STEERING
# Steering Columns

## Samurai, Sidekick, Swift

## DESCRIPTION

Collapsible steering columns are used on all models. Upper and lower column sections are joined by a "U" joint. The upper column sliding section compresses on impact. The column lower end connects to the steering gear pinion flange with a flexible coupling.

## REMOVAL & INSTALLATION

### STEERING WHEEL & HORN PAD

**Removal & Installation (Samurai & Sidekick) - 1)** Disconnect negative battery cable. Pry horn pad from steering wheel. Remove steering wheel nut.

**2)** Mark steering wheel and steering shaft for installation reference. Use Puller (09944-36010) to remove steering wheel from steering shaft.To install, reverse removal procedure. Tighten steering wheel nut to specification. See TORQUE SPECIFICATIONS table at end of article.

**Removal & Installation (Swift) - 1)** Disconnect negative battery cable. Remove horn pad by pulling upward. Remove steering wheel nut. Remove steering wheel upper cover and disconnect horn connectors.

**2)** Mark steering wheel and steering shaft for installation reference. Use Puller (09944-36010) to remove steering wheel from steering shaft. To install, reverse removal procedure. Tighten steering wheel nut to specification. See TORQUE SPECIFICATIONS table at end of article.

### COMBINATION SWITCH

**Removal & Installation -** Remove steering wheel. See STEERING WHEEL & HORN PAD. Remove screws and steering column covers. Disconnect combination switch connectors. Remove combination switch. To install, reverse removal procedure.

### STEERING COLUMN

***CAUTION: Applying excessive pressure, or causing impact to steering shaft during service, may cause column to collapse.***

**Removal (Samurai & Sidekick) - 1)** Disconnect negative battery cable. Remove steering wheel, horn pad and combination switch. See STEERING WHEEL & HORN PAD and COMBINATION SWITCH.

**2)** Remove lower instrument panel cover. Remove "U" joint pinch bolt. Separate steering shafts at "U" joint. Unplug wiring connectors to steering column switches. Remove steering column floorboard bracket bolts. Remove steering column upper bracket nuts. Pull steering column from floorboard.

**Installation - 1)** Insert column through floorboard into "U" joint. Install upper bracket retaining bolts. Install steering column floorboard bracket bolts.

**2)** Tighten column bracket nuts to specification. Tighten "U" joint pinch bolt. Tighten column floorboard bracket bolts to specification. See TORQUE SPECIFICATIONS table at end of article. Connect all electrical connectors.

**Removal & Installation (Swift) - 1)** Disconnect negative battery cable. Remove steering wheel, horn pad and combination switch. See STEERING WHEEL & HORN PAD and COMBINATION SWITCH. Unplug wiring connectors to steering column switches.

**2)** Pull back floor mat at bottom of steering shaft and remove lower steering column cover. Remove steering shaft joint upper side bolt. *See Fig. 1.*

**3)** Remove steering column upper bracket nuts. *See Fig. 2.* On A/T vehicles, remove backdrive cable from steering column assembly. Remove steering column. To install, reverse removal procedure.

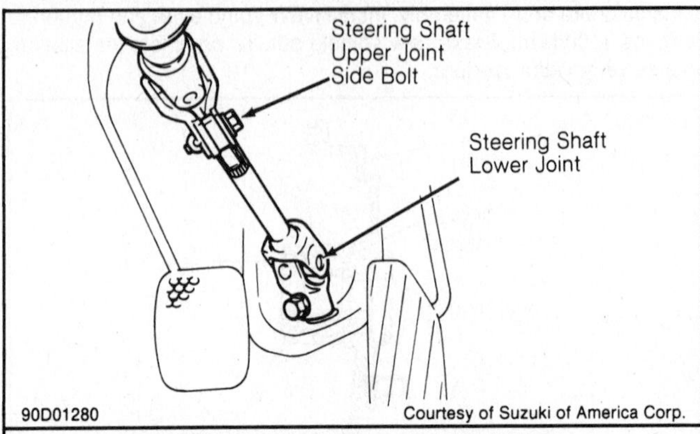


***Fig. 1: Locating Steering Shaft Upper Side Bolt (Swift)***

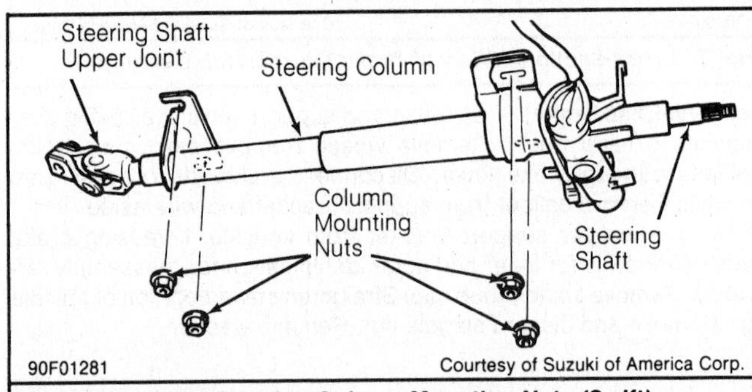


***Fig. 2: Removing Steering Column Mounting Nuts (Swift)***

## OVERHAUL

### STEERING COLUMN

**Disassembly & Reassembly -** It is not recommended to separate steering column and shaft. If steering column is defective, replace as an assembly.

**Inspection -** *See Fig. 3 or 4* for column damage measurements. If measurements are not within specification, replace steering column.

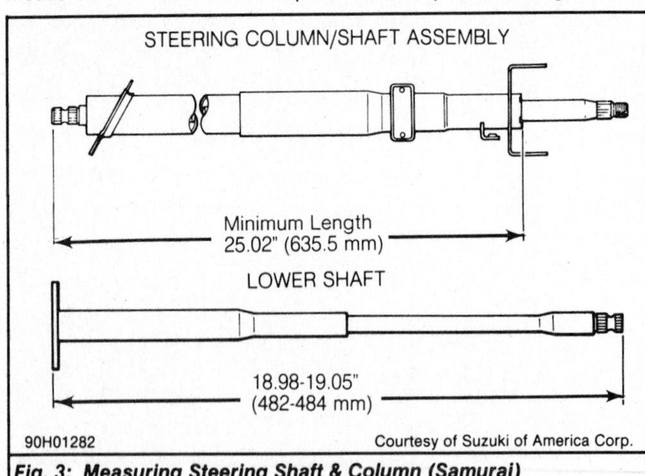


***Fig. 3: Measuring Steering Shaft & Column (Samurai)***

# 1991 STEERING
# Steering Columns (Cont.)

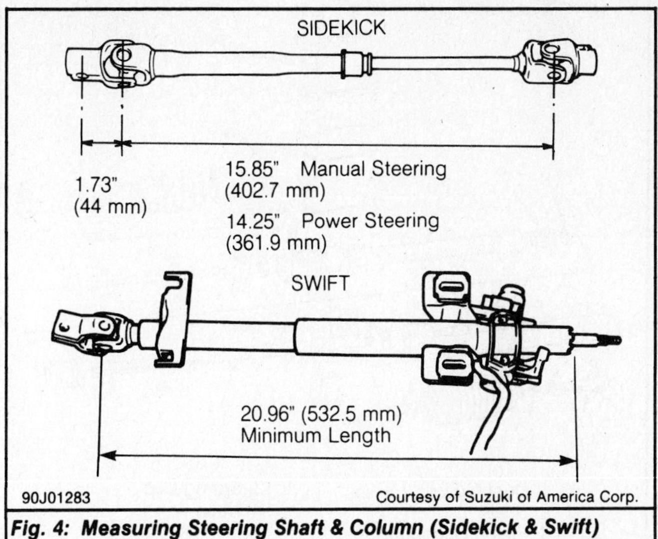


*Fig. 4: Measuring Steering Shaft & Column (Sidekick & Swift)*

## TORQUE SPECIFICATIONS

*TORQUE SPECIFICATIONS*

| Application | Ft. Lbs. (N.m) |
|---|---|
| Column Upper Bracket Nuts | 10 (14) |
| Flexible Joint Bolt/Nut | 11-18 (15-25) |
| Steering Shaft Joint Bolt | 15-22 (20-30) |
| Steering Wheel Nut | 18-30 (25-40) |
| | **INCH lbs. (N.m)** |
| Column Floorboard Bracket Bolts | |
| Samurai & Sidekick | 97-151 (11-17) |

# 1991 STEERING
# Manual Rack & Pinion

## Swift

## DESCRIPTION

Steering gear is a rack and pinion type. Rotating steering wheel turns pinion against rack, causing movement of rack. Rack movement is transferred to steering knuckles by tie rods.

## LUBRICATION

### FLUID TYPE

Use Suzuki Super Grease "E" (99000-25050).

## ADJUSTMENTS

Adjustments are made during reassembly procedure. See OVERHAUL.

## REMOVAL & INSTALLATION

### STEERING GEAR

**Removal - 1)** Remove steering shaft cover from inside vehicle. Loosen but DO NOT remove bolt at steering shaft joint assembly, located at bottom of steering column (not steering gear).

**2)** Remove bolt from steering shaft joint assembly at steering gear. Slide shaft assembly upward away from steering gear. Raise and support vehicle. Remove front wheels.

**3)** Remove tie rod-to-steering knuckle retaining nuts. Using Puller (09913-65210), separate tie rod ends from steering knuckles. Remove steering gear mounting bolts and brackets. Remove steering gear assembly.

**Installation -** To install, reverse removal procedure. Tighten all fasteners to specification. See TORQUE SPECIFICATIONS table at end of article.

## OVERHAUL

### STEERING GEAR

**Disassembly - 1)** Place steering gear in a soft-jawed vise. Place reference marks on tie rod ends and inner tie rods for reassembly reference. Loosen lock nuts and remove tie rod ends.

**2)** Remove spring clip, boot clamp and boot. Bend up lock washer tab. Unscrew inner tie rod from rack. Remove cap, rack adjusting screw, spring and rack plunger. *See Fig. 1.*

**3)** Remove dust cover. Using Socket (09944-28210), remove pinion bearing plug and case seal. To remove pinion, use soft-faced hammer and tap on housing while holding pinion. Remove rack from housing.

**Inspection - 1)** Check all components for damage or deterioration. Check for play in tie rod end ball joints. Check pinion teeth surfaces for wear or damage.

**2)** Check rack for runout and excessive tooth wear. Runout must not exceed .016" (.41 mm). Inspect needle bearing and rack bushing for wear.

**3)** If needle bearing requires replacement, use Bearing Remover (09921-20200) to remove needle bearing from housing.

**4)** If rack bushing requires replacement, remove rack bushing retaining snap ring. Using Bushing Remover (09944-48210), remove rack bushing from housing.

***CAUTION: DO NOT pull rack bushing from housing while clamping housing in a vise. Use bushing remover to prevent separating tube from rest of housing.***

***NOTE: Before reassembly, coat all components with light coat of grease.***

**Reassembly - 1)** If rack bushing was removed, use Bushing Installer (09943-78210) to install NEW rack bushing. Bushing must be positioned .04-.08" (1.0-2.0 mm) below surface of housing.

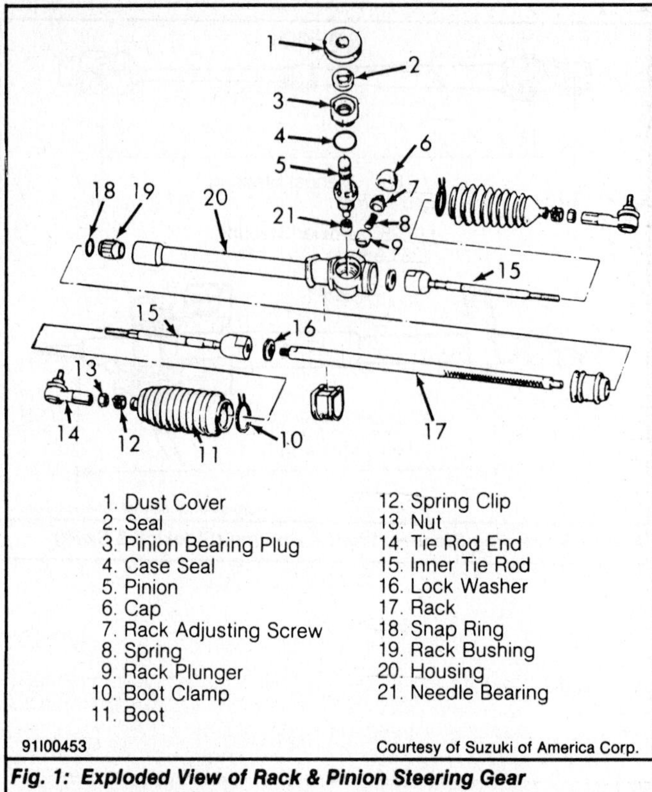


***Fig. 1: Exploded View of Rack & Pinion Steering Gear***

***CAUTION: Inside diameter of rack bushing is coated with special coating. DO NOT damage coating when installing bushing.***

**2)** Install rack bushing retaining snap ring. If needle bearing was removed, use Bearing Installer (09943-88211] to install needle bearing.

**3)** Install rack in the housing. Use care not to damage coating on rack bushing during installation. Install pinion in housing.

**4)** Install case seal and pinion bearing plug. Using Socket (09944-28210), tighten pinion bearing plug to specification. See TORQUE SPECIFICATIONS table at end of article. Install dust cover.

**5)** Install rack plunger, spring and rack adjusting screw. Tighten rack adjusting screw until snug. Back off adjusting screw 90 degrees. Install INCH lb. torque wrench and Socket (09944-18211) on pinion.

**6)** Rotate pinion and note rotating torque. Adjust rack adjusting screw until rotating torque is 9 INCH lbs. (1.2 N.m). Ensure rack moves smoothly. Once adjustment is correct, install cap on rack adjusting screw.

**7)** Install lock washer and inner tie rods on rack. Tighten inner tie rod nut to specification. See TORQUE SPECIFICATIONS table at end of article. Bend lock washer over on flat area of inner tie rod.

**8)** Apply grease on boot-to-inner tie rod areas. Install boot clamp and boot. Boot clamp wire must be wrapped around boot twice and ends twisted together. Ensure boot seats in grooves on housing and is not twisted. Install spring clip.

**9)** Install nut and tie rod end. Ensure reference marks on tie rod end and inner tie rod are aligned. Tighten nut to specification. See TORQUE SPECIFICATIONS table.

## TORQUE SPECIFICATIONS

***TORQUE SPECIFICATIONS***

| Application | Ft. Lbs. (N.m) |
|---|---|
| Inner Tie Rod-To-Rack | 63 (85) |
| Pinion Bearing Plug | 70 (95) |
| Steering Gear Mounting Bolt | 18 (24) |
| Steering Shaft Joint Assembly | 18 (24) |
| Tie Rod-To-Inner Tie Rod Nut | 33 (45) |
| Tie Rod-To-Steering Knuckle Nut | 32 (43) |
| Wheel Lug Nut | 44 (60) |

# 1991 STEERING
# Manual Recirculating Ball

## Samurai, Sidekick

## DESCRIPTION

Steering system uses steel balls in a recirculating pattern to transfer rotary motion of steering shaft into a linear motion in the rack gear. Rack gear, in turn, moves the sector gear. The pitman arm is solidly attached to sector gear and, through the tie rods, allows the vehicle to turn.

## LUBRICATION

### FLUID TYPE

Steering gear uses SAE 90W gear oil.

## ADJUSTMENTS

***NOTE: Pinion shaft starting torque and operating torque adjustments are made with steering gear removed from vehicle.***

### PINION SHAFT STARTING TORQUE

**Samurai** - **1)** Ensure oil is at proper level. Oil level should be approximately 1.4" (36 mm) from bottom of oil fill plug. Adjustment of pinion shaft starting torque is made with adjusting bolt.

**2)** Remove steering gear from vehicle. See REMOVAL & INSTALLATION. Align pitman arm so it is parallel with pinion shaft. *See Fig. 1.*

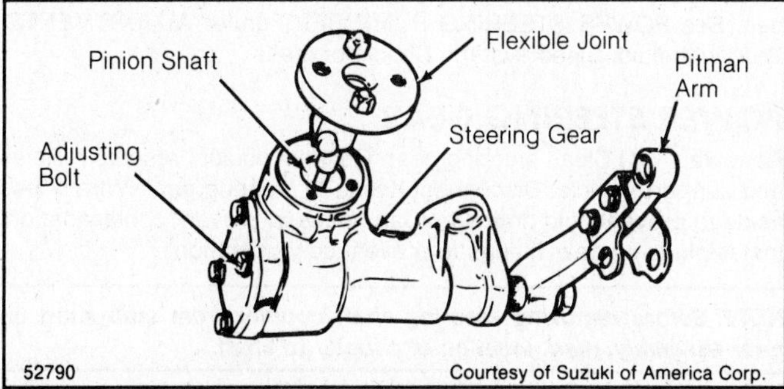


***Fig. 1: Locating Torque Adjusting Bolt***

**3)** Attach spring scale to bolt on outermost edge of flexible joint with a string. *See Fig. 2.* Pull spring scale and note starting torque measurement. Starting torque should be 11 lbs. (5 kg).

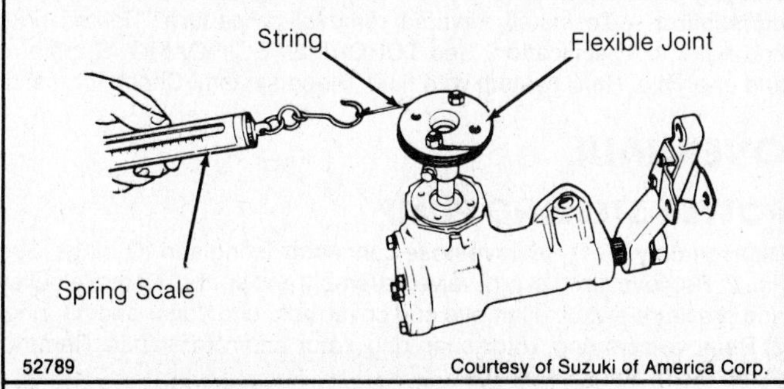


***Fig. 2: Measuring Pinion Shaft Starting Torque***

**4)** If starting torque is not within specification, loosen or tighten adjusting bolt accordingly and recheck measurement.

**Sidekick** - **1)** Ensure pinion shaft thrust play is not excessive. Position pitman arm parallel with pinion shaft. This will simulate front wheels being straight with steering gear installed.

**2)** Connect Torque Check Socket (09944-18211) and INCH-lb. torque wrench to pinion shaft. Shaft should start to move with 4.8-8.4 INCH lbs. (.5-1 N.m) of torque applied. If starting torque is not within specification, loosen or tighten adjusting screw and recheck.

### PINION SHAFT OPERATING TORQUE

**Samurai** - **1)** Repeat steps **1)** through **3)** of PINION SHAFT STARTING TORQUE procedure. Pull on the spring scale to turn flexible joint through one complete turning cycle.

**2)** Note the operating torque measurement. Operating torque should be less than 6.94 lbs. (3.15 kg). Loosen or tighten adjusting bolt as necessary to achieve proper torque.

**3)** If pinion shaft starting torque and operating torque tests have been performed and adjustment is not possible, replace steering gear.

**Sidekick** - **1)** Connect Torque Check Socket (09944-18211) and INCH-lb. torque wrench to pinion shaft. Move pinion shaft through its entire operating range to right and left. Operating torque should be approximately 10 INCH lbs. (1.2 N.m).

**2)** If operating torque is not within specification, recheck PINION SHAFT STARTING TORQUE. Recheck operating torque. If starting torque is correct and operating torque is not within specification, replace steering gear assembly.

## REMOVAL & INSTALLATION

### IDLER ARM & BUSHING

**Removal & Installation** - **1)** Raise and support vehicle. Remove idler arm cotter pin and castle nut from center link. Remove idler arm from center link with Puller (09913-65210). Remover idler arm bushing nut. Remove idler arm and washers.

**2)** Remove bushing from idler arm with press and Adapter (09943-88211). Install new bushing with press and Adapters (09943-88211 and 09940-53111). To install, reverse removal procedure. Tighten bolts and nuts to specification. See TORQUE SPECIFICATIONS table at end of article.

### STEERING GEAR

**Removal** - **1)** Raise and support vehicle. Remove radiator lower cover. Remove tie rod ends cotter pins and castle nuts. Using Puller (09913-65210), remove tie rods from steering knuckles.

**2)** Remove steering damper-to-center link attaching bolts. Remove cotter pins and castle nuts connecting center link to idler arm and pitman arm.

**3)** Remove center link from pitman arm and idler arm with Puller (09913-65210). Remove flexible coupling pinch bolt from pinion shaft. Remove steering gear attaching bolts and nuts. Remove steering gear.

**Inspection** - **1)** Check pinion shaft starting torque and operating torque. Refer to PINION SHAFT STARTING TORQUE and PINION SHAFT OPERATING TORQUE under ADJUSTMENTS. Inspect steering gear case for cracks and abnormalities.

**2)** Check pinion shaft for excessive play. Check oil seals for leaking or cracking. Disassembly of steering gear is not recommended by manufacturer. If abnormalities are found, replace steering gear assembly.

**Installation** - To install, reverse removal procedure. Install steering gear attaching bolts from inside engine compartment. Tighten bolts to specification. See TORQUE SPECIFICATIONS table. Always use NEW cotter pins.

## TORQUE SPECIFICATIONS

***TORQUE SPECIFICATIONS***

| Application | Ft. Lbs. (N.m) |
|---|---|
| Center Link Castle Nut | 22-52 (30-70) |
| Flexible Coupling Pinch Bolt | 11-18 (15-25) |
| Idler Arm Bushing Nut | 52-74 (70-100) |
| Steering Damper Attaching Nut | 26-39 (35-53) |
| Steering Damper Pin Nut | 16-26 (22-35) |
| Steering Damper Stay Nut | 13-21 (18-28) |
| Steering Gear Attaching Bolt | 52-66 (70-90) |
| Tie Rod Castle Nut | 22-41 (30-55) |
| Tie Rod End Lock Nut | 52-74 (70-100) |
| Wheel Nuts | 37-59 (50-80) |

# 1991 STEERING
# Power Recirculating Ball

## Sidekick

## DESCRIPTION & OPERATION

Power steering gear is an integral type, consisting of conventional ball/screw type steering gear. The gear combines with a rotary and torsion bar type control valve and power cylinder. Belt-driven oil pump is a constant delivery vane type.

## LUBRICATION

### CAPACITY

Fill with fluid to MAX level indicated on reservoir.

### FLUID TYPE

Use Suzuki ATF or Dexron-II ATF.

### HYDRAULIC SYSTEM BLEEDING

**1)** Raise and support front of vehicle. Fill reservoir. Wait 2 or 3 minutes, and refill reservoir. With engine off, turn steering wheel lock-to-lock several times. Check fluid level. Refill as necessary.
**2)** With engine at idle, turn steering wheel lock-to-lock 3-4 times. Turn off engine. Recheck fluid level. Add fluid (if necessary). Lower vehicle. Turn steering wheel lock-to-lock with engine at idle.

***CAUTION: DO NOT hold steering wheel at full lock position longer than 5 seconds.***

**3)** With wheels in straight-ahead position and engine off, check fluid level. If fluid rises, air is trapped in system. Repeat bleeding procedure.

## ADJUSTMENTS

### POWER STEERING PUMP BELT

Belt deflection is 1/4-3/8" measured between pump and idler pulley with 22 lbs. (10 kg) of force applied to belt.

## TESTING

### HYDRAULIC SYSTEM PRESSURE TEST

**1)** With engine off, disconnect pressure hose from pump. Install Power Steering Tester (J-5176-D) between power steering pump and steering unit. *See Fig. 1.*

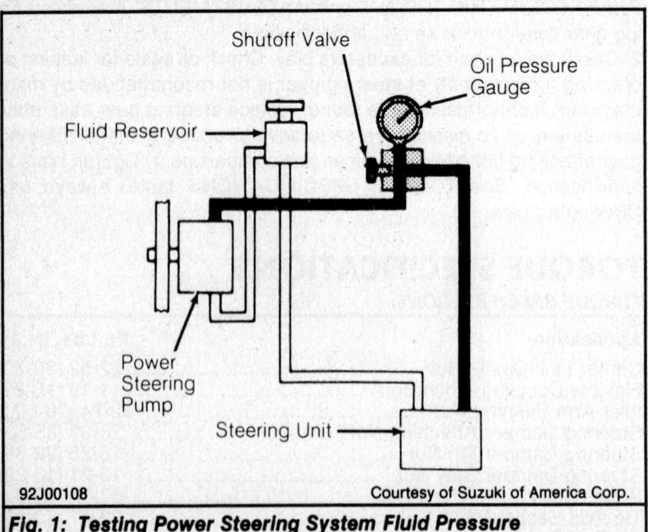


***Fig. 1: Testing Power Steering System Fluid Pressure***

**2)** Bleed system by holding gauge beneath fluid reservoir with shutoff valve open. With engine idling, check fluid level in reservoir. Refill reservoir if necessary.

**3)** If steering system still malfunctions, start engine. Turn steering wheel lock-to-lock several times until fluid temperature is 122-140° F (50-60° C).
**4)** With steering wheel straight ahead, check pressure gauge. If gauge reads more than 142 psi (10.0 kg/cm²), check flow control valve, pressure hoses and pipes for restrictions.
**5)** Slowly close pressure gauge valve while watching gauge. If fluid pressure is more than 1137 psi (80 kg/cm²) or less than 853 psi (60 kg/cm²), inspect relief pressure valve, pressure hose and pipes for restrictions. Open pressure gauge valve.

***CAUTION: DO NOT leave shutoff valve closed longer than 15 seconds or pump may be damaged.***

**6)** Hold engine speed at 1500 RPM and check pressure gauge reading. If pressure reading is less than 853 psi (60 kg/cm²), inspect spool valve for restrictions.

## REMOVAL & INSTALLATION

### POWER STEERING PUMP

**Removal – 1)** Disconnect hoses at pump. Secure hoses using wire to prevent drainage of oil. Cap hoses to prevent contamination.
**2)** Cap pump fittings to prevent contamination. Loosen bracket-to-pump mounting bolts. Remove pump belts. Remove brackets from pump. Remove pump.
**Installation –** To install pump, reverse removal procedure. Adjust belt. See POWER STEERING PUMP BELT under ADJUSTMENTS. Refill with fluid. Bleed system. Check for leaks.

### POWER STEERING GEAR

**Removal – 1)** Clean steering gear. Remove coolant reservoir. Raise and support vehicle. Disconnect hoses at steering gear. Wire hoses aside to prevent fluid drainage. Cap hoses to prevent contamination. Install plugs on gear fittings to prevent contamination.

***NOTE: Before removing steering shaft coupler from stub shaft on gear assembly, mark location of coupler to shaft.***

**2)** Remove steering shaft coupler pinch bolt. Remove steering column-to-instrument panel bolts. Disconnect coupler from stub shaft by pulling column and shaft about 2" in toward cab.
**3)** Remove pitman arm nut and washer. Using Puller (J-29107), separate pitman arm from shaft. Remove engine splash shield. Remove steering gear-to-frame bolts. Remove steering gear from vehicle.
**Installation –** To install, reverse removal procedure. Tighten nuts and bolts to specification. See TORQUE SPECIFICATIONS table at end of article. Refill system with fluid. Bleed system. Check for leaks.

## OVERHAUL

### POWER STEERING PUMP

**Disassembly – 1)** Remove hose connector fitting and "O" rings. *See Fig. 2*. Remove flow control valve assembly and spring. Remove pulley and pressure switch. Remove end cover bolt, end cover and "O" ring.
**2)** Remove cam ring, rotor snap ring, rotor and rotor vanes. Remove pump shaft. Remove oil seal.

# 1991 STEERING
# Power Recirculating Ball (Cont.)

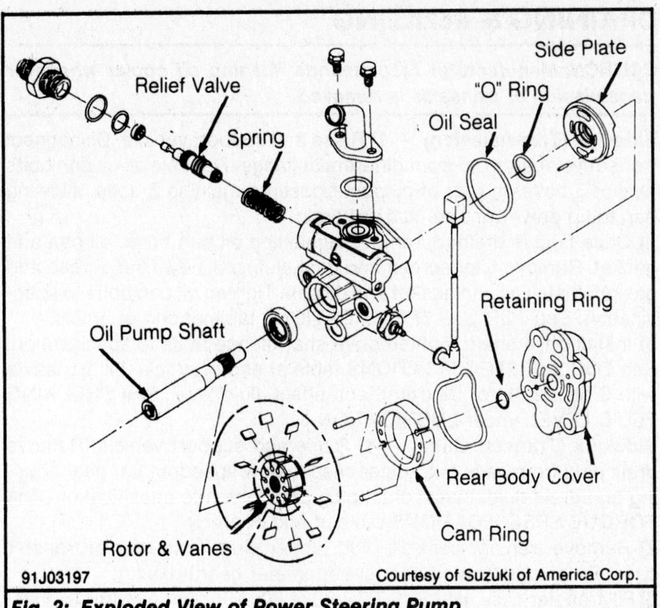


*Fig. 2: Exploded View of Power Steering Pump*

**Inspection** – Check pump housing for cracks. Check valve sliding face for burrs and damage. Parts with minor scores may be reused after polishing using very fine emery cloth.

**Reassembly** – To assemble, reverse disassembly procedure. Install rotor, cam ring and vane in order. Ensure round end of vane matches cam ring inner surface. Tighten pump body bolts and hose connector fitting to specification. See TORQUE SPECIFICATIONS table at end of article.

## POWER STEERING GEAR

*NOTE: No overhaul procedures are available from manufacturer.*

## TORQUE SPECIFICATIONS

*TORQUE SPECIFICATIONS*

| Application | Ft. Lbs. (N.m) |
|---|---|
| Pitman Arm-To-Center Link Attaching Nut | 41 (55) |
| Pitman Arm-To-Steering Gear Attaching Nut | 96 (130) |
| Pressure Switch | 22 (30) |
| Pulley Retaining Nut | 32 (43) |
| Pump Body Bolts | 16 (22) |
| Pump Hose Connector Fitting | 44 (60) |
| Steering Gear Mounting Bolts | 74 (100) |
| Steering Shaft Coupler Pinch Bolt | 29 (39) |

# 1991 TRANSMISSION SERVICING
# Automatic Transmission

## Sidekick, Swift

## IDENTIFICATION

*AUTOMATIC TRANSMISSION APPLICATIONS*

| Model | Transaxle/Transmission |
|---|---|
| Sidekick | [1] General Motors 3L30 |
| Swift | Suzuki 3-Speed Transaxle |

[1] - This is also known as Turbo Hydra-Matic 180C.

## LUBRICATION

### SERVICE INTERVALS

**Sidekick - 1)** Manufacturer recommends replacing transmission oil cooler hoses at 45,000 mile intervals. Under normal driving conditions, replace transmission fluid every 100,000 miles. Replace transfer case fluid at 7500 miles, 30,000 miles and thereafter at 30,000 mile intervals.

**2)** Under severe driving conditions, replace transmission fluid every 15,000 miles or 15 months. Replace transfer case fluid at 7500 miles and then every 15,000 miles or 15 months. Severe driving conditions is when vehicle is operated under one of the following conditions:

- Most driving is in stop-and-go traffic.
- Delivery service.
- Trailer towing.
- Most trips are less than 4 miles.
- Most trips are less than 10 miles, and outside temperature remains below freezing.
- Driving in dusty areas.

**Swift -** Manufacturer recommends replacing transaxle oil cooler hoses at 45,000 mile intervals. Replace transaxle fluid every 100,000 miles under normal driving conditions. Change fluid every 15,000 miles or 15 months under severe driving conditions. Severe conditions are same as listed under SIDEKICK.

### CHECKING FLUID LEVEL

***CAUTION: Check differential fluid level on Swift and transfer case level on Sidekick.***

**Transaxle & Transmission - 1)** Engine must be at normal operating temperature. Park vehicle on level surface and apply parking brake. Place selector lever in Park.

**2)** Start engine and allow engine to idle. Apply brakes, shift through all gears and return selector lever to Park.

**3)** Remove dipstick. Fluid level should be in HOT or FULL HOT range. Add fluid (if necessary) and recheck. DO NOT overfill.

**Transfer Case (Sidekick) -** Remove transfer case fill plug (upper plug) from rear of transfer case. Fill plug is located near speedometer gear housing. Fluid level must be at bottom of fill plug hole. Install fill plug and tighten to specification. See TORQUE SPECIFICATIONS table at end of article.

### RECOMMENDED FLUID

**Transaxle & Transmission -** All models use Dexron-II ATF.
**Transfer Case (Sidekick) -** Use SAE 75W-90 or 80W-90 gear oil with GL-4 rating.

### FLUID CAPACITIES

*TRANSMISSION/TRANSAXLE REFILL CAPACITIES*

| Application | Refill Qts. (L) | Dry Fill Qts. (L) |
|---|---|---|
| Sidekick | 3.0 (2.8) | 4.9 (4.6) |
| Swift | 1.6 (1.5) | 5.2 (4.9) |

*TRANSFER CASE REFILL CAPACITIES*

| Application | Pts. (L) |
|---|---|
| Sidekick | 3.6 (1.7) |

## DRAINING & REFILLING

***CAUTION: Manufacturer recommends flushing oil cooler whenever transmission or transaxle is removed.***

**Sidekick (Transmission) - 1)** Raise and support vehicle. Disconnect front drive shaft from front differential flange. Remove all oil pan bolts except 3 bolts on rear of oil pan. Loosen remaining 3 bolts, allowing pan to tip downward so fluid will drain.

**2)** Once fluid is drained, remove remaining oil pan bolts, oil pan and gasket. Remove filter screen and gasket. Install new filter screen and gasket. Install oil pan gasket and oil pan. Tighten oil pan bolts to specification. See TORQUE SPECIFICATIONS table at end of article.

**3)** Install drive shaft. Tighten drive shaft flange bolts to specification. See TORQUE SPECIFICATIONS table at end of article. Fill transaxle with 3 qts. (2.8L) of Dexron-II and check fluid level. See CHECKING FLUID LEVEL under LUBRICATION.

**Sidekick (Transfer Case) - 1)** Raise and support vehicle. Remove drain plug from back of transfer case, below speedometer gear housing and drain fluid. Install drain plug and tighten to specification. See TORQUE SPECIFICATIONS table at end of article.

**2)** Remove transfer case fill plug (upper plug) from rear of transfer case. Fill plug is located near speedometer gear housing.

**3)** Fill transfer case with SAE 75W-90 or 80W-90 gear oil with GL-4 rating until fluid level is at bottom of fill plug hole. Install fill plug and tighten to specification. See TORQUE SPECIFICATIONS table at end of article.

**Swift - 1)** Remove drain plug from bottom of oil pan and drain fluid. If removing filter screen, note position of cross-grooved oil pan bolts. *See Fig. 1.* Remove oil pan bolts, oil pan, gasket, filter screen bolts and filter screen.

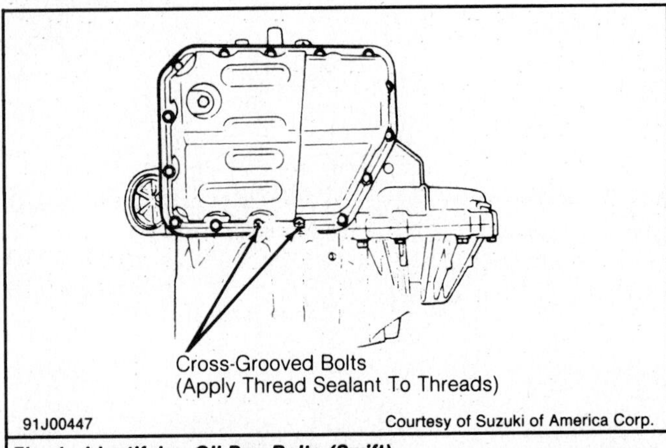


***Fig. 1: Identifying Oil Pan Bolts (Swift)***

**2)** Install filter screen. Install oil pan with new gasket. Apply thread sealant to threads of cross-grooved bolts. Tighten oil pan bolts to specification. Tighten drain plug to specification. See TORQUE SPECIFICATIONS table at end of article.

**3)** Add 1.6 qts. (1.5L) of Dexron-II through dipstick tube. Check fluid level. See CHECKING FLUID LEVEL under LUBRICATION.

## ADJUSTMENTS

### BACKDRIVE CABLE (PARK LOCK CABLE)

***NOTE: Backdrive system will not allow gearshift to move from Park unless ignition is turned on. It also prevents ignition key removal unless gearshift is in Park.***

**Sidekick - 1)** Remove console covers. Backdrive cable is adjusted at bracket, located near the gearshift. Place ignition in ACC position.

**2)** Loosen backdrive cable lock nut. *See Fig. 2.* Lift cable from bracket, but not from backdrive cam.

# 1991 TRANSMISSION SERVICING
## Automatic Transmission (Cont.)

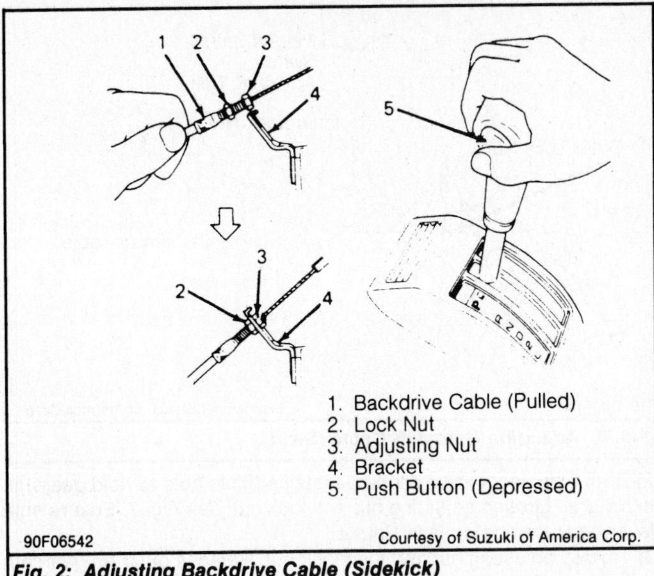


*Fig. 2: Adjusting Backdrive Cable (Sidekick)*

**3)** Place gearshift in Park with release button on gearshift fully depressed. Align adjusting nut with bracket with backdrive cable pulled tight. Rotate adjusting nut one revolution inward, away from backdrive cam. Tighten lock nut. Install console covers.

**Swift - 1)** Remove center console cover. Place gearshift in Park. Loosen inner and outer lock nuts. Pull backdrive cable sheath forward until all slack is removed from inner wire. *See Fig. 3.*

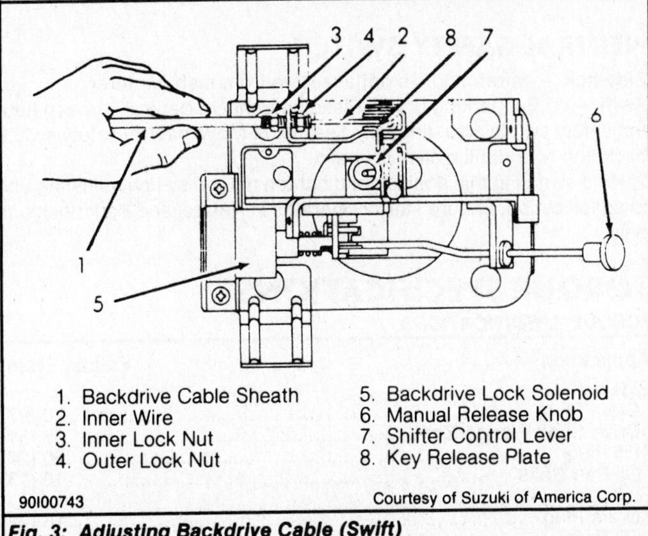


*Fig. 3: Adjusting Backdrive Cable (Swift)*

**2)** While holding backdrive cable sheath forward, hand tighten outer lock nut. Tighten inner lock nut and tighten outer lock nut.

**3)** Ensure ignition key operates from ACC to LOCK position and ignition key can be removed when gearshift is in Park.

**4)** Move transaxle gearshift lever to any other position. Ensure ignition key cannot be turned from ACC to LOCK position. If ignition key will turn, readjust backdrive cable.

## BACKDRIVE SOLENOID

**Sidekick -** Backdrive solenoid is nonadjustable.

**Swift - 1)** Remove center console. Solenoid should be adjusted so when ignition is in OFF position, solenoid is inoperative. With ignition on and brake pedal depressed, solenoid should be engaged and lock plate will be in correct position. *See Fig. 4.*

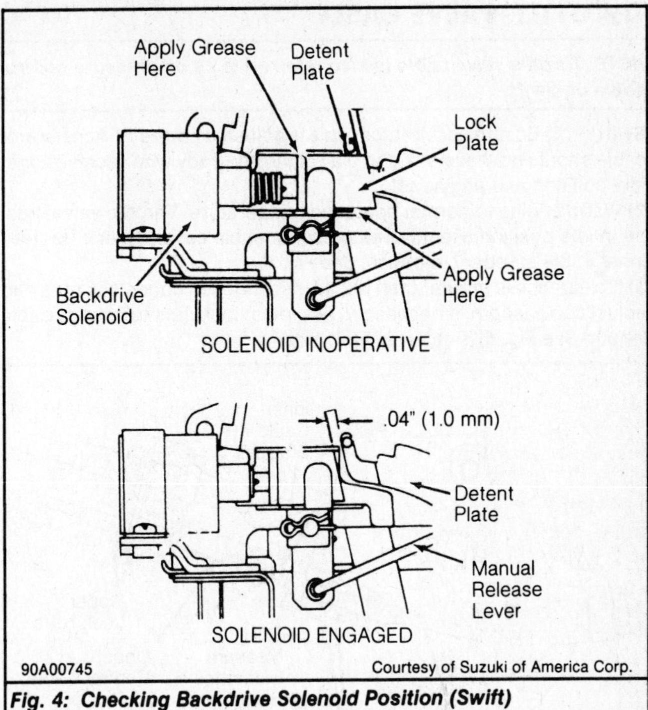


*Fig. 4: Checking Backdrive Solenoid Position (Swift)*

**2)** Clearance between lock plate and detent plate should be more than .04" (1.0 mm). If clearance requires adjustment, loosen solenoid mounting screws and reposition solenoid.

**3)** With ignition off, gearshift should not shift from Park. If manual release lever is pulled with ignition off, gearshift should move from Park to other gear positions.

## KICKDOWN CABLE

**Sidekick - 1)** Ensure accelerator cable is adjusted correctly. Loosen kickdown cable lock nut and adjusting nut. *See Fig. 5.* Fully depress and hold accelerator pedal.

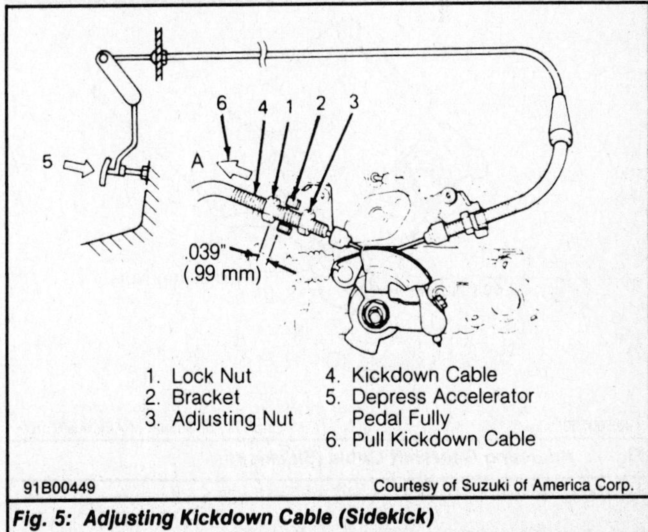


*Fig. 5: Adjusting Kickdown Cable (Sidekick)*

**2)** Pull kickdown cable in direction "A". *See Fig. 5.* Rotate lock nut to obtain a .039" (.99 mm) lock nut-to-bracket clearance. When adjusting clearance, ensure adjusting nut DOES NOT contact bracket.

**3)** Release accelerator pedal. Maintain lock nut-to-bracket clearance at .039" (.99 mm). Rotate adjusting nut until it engages bracket. With adjusting nut even with bracket surface, tighten lock nut securely.

# 1991 TRANSMISSION SERVICING
## Automatic Transmission (Cont.)

### THROTTLE VALVE CABLE

***NOTE: Throttle valve cable is also referred to as oil pressure control cable on Swift.***

**Swift - 1)** Ensure accelerator cable is adjusted correctly. Accelerator cable should not have any end play at throttle body with accelerator at idle position and engine off.
**2)** Warm engine to normal operating temperature. Throttle valve must be in idle position. Remove oil pressure cable cover. Check boot-to-inner cable stopper clearance. *See Fig. 6.*
**3)** If clearance is greater than .02" (.5 mm), loosen upper lock nuts and adjust cable length. If necessary, use lower lock nuts to change cable length. *See Fig. 6.* Tighten all lock nuts.

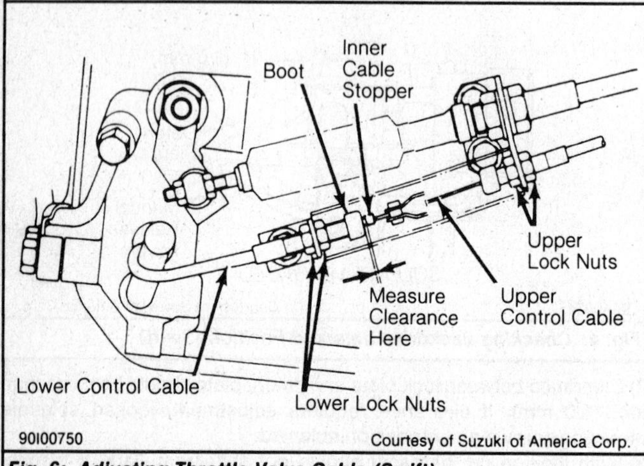

***Fig. 6: Adjusting Throttle Valve Cable (Swift)***

### GEARSHIFT CABLE

**Sidekick - 1)** Remove center console covers. Place gearshift in Neutral. Looking at gearshift assembly from passenger side, note 2 holes on rear of lever detent bracket, below level of console cover.

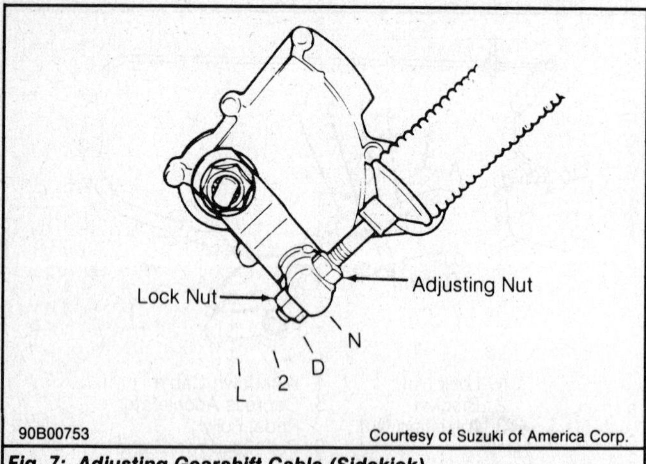

***Fig. 7: Adjusting Gearshift Cable (Sidekick)***

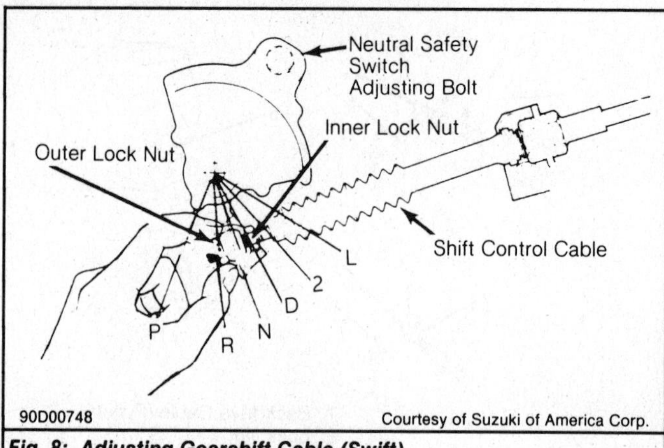

***Fig. 8: Adjusting Gearshift Cable (Swift)***

**2)** Both holes should be aligned. Install a pin in hole to hold gearshift in Neutral. Loosen adjusting nut and lock nut. *See Fig. 7.* Ensure shift lever on transmission is in Neutral.
**3)** Tighten adjusting nut and then lock nut. Remove pin from gearshift assembly. Ensure gearshift operates properly in all gear ranges. Install console covers.

**Swift - 1)** Set parking brake. Move gearshift lever to Neutral. Loosen inner and outer lock nuts. *See Fig. 8.* Ensure transaxle control lever is in Neutral. Tighten outer lock nut by hand until it contacts control lever.
**2)** Using wrench, tighten inner lock nut. Ensure transaxle operates in all gear positions. Shift transaxle gearshift lever to Park and ensure vehicle will not move.

### NEUTRAL SAFETY SWITCH

**Sidekick -** Information is not available from manufacturer.
**Swift - 1)** Set parking brake. Place gearshift in Neutral. Loosen neutral safety switch adjusting bolt. *See Fig. 8.* Move neutral safety switch back and forth until a click is heard.
**2)** Hold switch at this position and tighten neutral switch adjusting bolt to specification. Ensure starter operates in Neutral and Park positions only.

### TORQUE SPECIFICATIONS

***TORQUE SPECIFICATIONS***

| Application | Ft. Lbs. (N.m) |
|---|---|
| Sidekick | |
| Drain Plug | 20 (27) |
| Drive Shaft Flange Bolts | 38 (51) |
| Fill Plug | 20 (27) |
| Oil Pan Bolts | 10 (13) |
| Swift | |
| Drain Plug | 16 (22) |
| Fill Plug | 20 (27) |
| Oil Pan Bolts | [1] |
| Neutral Switch Adjusting Bolt | 17 (23) |

[1] - Tighten to 44 INCH Lbs. (5 N.m).

# 1991 TRANSMISSION SERVICING
# Manual Transmission

### Samurai, Sidekick, Swift

## IDENTIFICATION

*SUZUKI MANUAL TRANSMISSION/TRANSAXLE APPLICATION*

| Model | Transmission/Transaxle |
|---|---|
| Samurai & Sidekick | 5-Speed Transmission |
| Swift | 5-Speed Transaxle |

## LUBRICATION

### SERVICE INTERVALS

**Samurai & Sidekick** - Replace transmission and transfer case fluid at first 7500 miles. Replace fluid every 100,000 miles under normal driving conditions. Under severe service driving conditions, replace fluids every 15,000 miles.
**Swift** - Replace transaxle fluid every 15,000 miles.

### CHECKING FLUID LEVEL

***NOTE: Apply RTV sealant to threads of drain and filler plugs before installation.***

**Samurai & Sidekick (Transmission & Transfer Case)** - **1)** Transmission and transfer case have separate drain and filler plugs. Park vehicle on level surface with engine off. Remove transmission filler plug on right side of case. DO NOT remove reverse idler gear bolt (hex head bolt) near right rear of case. Fluid level should be level with bottom of filler plug hole. Fill, if necessary.
**2)** On transfer case, remove filler plug on rear side of transfer case. Fluid level should be to level of filler plug hole. Fill, if necessary
**Swift** - Park vehicle on level surface. Remove filler plug from side of transaxle case. Fluid level should be level with bottom of filler plug hole. Fill if necessary. Install filler plug and tighten to specification. See TORQUE SPECIFICATIONS table at end of article.

### CHANGING FLUID

Transmission and transfer case have separate drain plugs. Place appropriate receptacle under drain hole. Remove drain plug. Clean magnetic drain plug before installation. Inspect oil for excessive grit or metal particles. Install drain plug and tighten to specification. See TORQUE SPECIFICATIONS table at end of article. Fill to proper fluid level. See CHECKING FLUID LEVEL.

### RECOMMENDED FLUID

**Samurai & Sidekick** - For transmission and transfer case, use API GL-4 gear lubricant, SAE 75W-90.
**Swift** - For transaxle, use hypoid oil SAE 75W or 80W-90 (API GL-5).

### FLUID CAPACITIES

*TRANSMISSION REFILL CAPACITIES*

| Application | Pts. (L) |
|---|---|
| Samurai & Sidekick | 3.2 (1.5) |
| Swift | 5.1 (2.4) |

*TRANSFER CASE REFILL CAPACITIES*

| Application | Pts. (L) |
|---|---|
| Samurai & Sidekick | 3.6 (1.7) |

## ADJUSTMENTS

### LINKAGE

No external adjustments are necessary.

## TORQUE SPECIFICATIONS

*TORQUE SPECIFICATIONS*

| Application | Ft. Lbs. (N.m) |
|---|---|
| Oil Drain Plug | 13-21 (18-28) |
| Oil Filler Plug | 10-16 (14-22) |

# 1991 TRANSMISSION SERVICING
# Transmission Removal & Installation

**Sidekick, Swift**

## MANUAL

***NOTE: For manual transmission/transaxle replacement procedures, see appropriate article in CLUTCHES.***

## AUTOMATIC

### SIDEKICK

**Removal - 1)** Disconnect negative battery cable. Remove transfer case shift lever knob. Remove console box. Remove retaining screws, shift lever boot and bracket.

**2)** Remove clamp and small boot located on top of transfer case at shift lever opening. Push downward on case cover (center area around shift lever) and rotate counterclockwise. Remove transfer case shift lever.

**3)** Disconnect kickdown cable at throttle body. Remove fan shroud, transmission dipstick and distributor cap. Using Engine Support Fixture (J-28467-A), support engine.

**4)** Disconnect electrical connections, breather hose and control cables from transmission. Disconnect speedometer cable from transfer case. Disconnect and plug oil cooler lines from transmission. Remove gearshift assembly, if necessary.

**5)** Raise and support vehicle. Remove transfer case skid plate. Mark drive shaft flange and yokes for reassembly reference. Remove front and rear drive shafts.

**6)** Remove drive plate cover. Remove torque converter-to-drive plate bolts. Remove exhaust pipe bracket at catalytic converter and transmission. Support transmission with jack.

**7)** Remove crossmember located below transmission and transfer case. Remove remaining transmission-to-engine bolts. Move transmission and transfer case away from engine, and remove from vehicle.

**Installation -** To install, reverse removal procedure. Tighten all fasteners to specification. See TORQUE SPECIFICATIONS table at end of article. Ensure reference marks are aligned on drive shaft flanges and yokes. Adjust all control cables. See ADJUSTMENTS in AUTOMATIC TRANSMISSION article in TRANSMISSION SERVICING. Fill and check fluid levels.

### SWIFT

**Removal - 1)** Disconnect air intake tubing from air cleaner. Disconnect battery cables. Remove battery and tray. Disconnect ground cable at transaxle. Disconnect electrical connections, speedometer cable and control cables from transaxle.

**2)** Remove starter. Raise and support vehicle. Drain transaxle fluid. Disconnect and plug oil cooler lines from transaxle. Disconnect exhaust pipe from exhaust manifold. Remove lower cover from torque converter housing.

**3)** Remove drive plate-to-torque converter bolts. Drive plate can be held by engaging a screwdriver into drive plate gear through notch provided at underside of transaxle case.

**4)** Remove left axle shaft and disengage right axle shaft from differential. Remove left wheel. Remove staked area from left axle shaft nut at hub assembly. Remove nut and washer from left axle shaft.

**5)** Remove left ball joint-to-steering knuckle bolt. Separate ball joint from steering knuckle. Using 2 screwdrivers, pry axle shafts from transaxle case. Remove left axle shaft. Disconnect engine torque rod and bracket from transaxle.

**6)** Support transaxle with a jack. Disconnect transaxle mounts. Remove transaxle-to-engine bolts. Remove transaxle assembly.

**Installation - 1)** To install transaxle, apply grease around cup at center of torque converter and reverse removal procedure.

**2)** Ensure torque converter is correctly installed. Distance from torque converter drive lugs to engine mating surface of transaxle housing should be at least .84" (21.4 mm).

**3)** When installing transaxle, guide right axle into differential side gear as transaxle is being raised. After inserting inner CV joints of right and left axles into differential side gears, push inner joints into side gears until snap rings on axle shafts engage with side gears.

**4)** Tighten all fasteners to specification. See TORQUE SPECIFICATIONS table at end of article. Adjust all cables. See ADJUSTMENTS in AUTOMATIC TRANSMISSION article in TRANSMISSION SERVICING. Fill and check fluid levels.

## TORQUE SPECIFICATIONS

***TORQUE SPECIFICATIONS***

| Application | Ft. Lbs. (N.m) |
|---|---|
| **Sidekick** | |
| Crossmember Bolt | 62 (84) |
| Drive Shaft Flange Bolt | 38 (51) |
| Torque Converter Bolt | 41 (55) |
| Transfer Case Skid Plate | 41 (55) |
| Transmission-To-Engine Bolt | 62 (84) |
| **Swift** | |
| Axle Shaft Nut | 129 (175) |
| Ball Joint Bolt | 44 (60) |
| Torque Converter Bolt | 14 (19) |
| Transaxle-To-Engine Bolt | 40 (54) |
| Wheel Lug Nut | 44 (60) |

# TOYOTA

# 1991 TOYOTA CONTENTS

## GENERAL INFORMATION [1]

### ALL MODELS



[1] - For all GENERAL INFORMATION, see front of Volume 1.

## ENGINE PERFORMANCE

### INTRODUCTION



### EMISSION APPLICATIONS



### SERVICE & ADJUSTMENT SPECIFICATIONS



## ENGINE PERFORMANCE (Cont.)

### ON-VEHICLE ADJUSTMENTS



### THEORY & OPERATION



### BASIC DIAGNOSTIC PROCEDURES



### SELF-DIAGNOSTICS

# 1991 TOYOTA CONTENTS (Cont.)

## ENGINE PERFORMANCE (Cont.)

### SELF-DIAGNOSTICS (Cont.)



### TROUBLE SHOOTING - NO CODES



### SYSTEM & COMPONENT TESTING



### PIN VOLTAGE CHARTS



## ENGINE PERFORMANCE (Cont.)

### SENSOR OPERATING RANGE CHARTS



### WIRING DIAGRAMS



### VACUUM DIAGRAMS

# 1991 TOYOTA CONTENTS (Cont.)

## ENGINE PERFORMANCE (Cont.)

### VACUUM DIAGRAMS (Cont.)



### REMOVAL, OVERHAUL & INSTALLATION



## ELECTRICAL

### ALTERNATORS & REGULATORS



### STARTERS



## WIRING DIAGRAMS

### CHASSIS WIRING DIAGRAMS



## SAFETY EQUIPMENT

### AIR BAG RESTRAINT SYSTEM



### INSTRUMENT PANELS



### POWER MIRRORS



### REAR WINDOW DEFOGGER

# 1991 TOYOTA CONTENTS (Cont.)

## SAFETY EQUIPMENT (Cont.)



## ENGINES



## ENGINES (Cont.)

# 1991 TOYOTA CONTENTS (Cont.)

## ENGINES (Cont.)

### 3.0L & 3.0L TURBO 6-CYLINDER



### 4.0L 6-CYLINDER



## ENGINE COOLING

### SPECIFICATIONS & ELECTRIC COOLING FANS



## CLUTCHES

### FWD



### RWD



## DRIVE AXLES

### FWD AXLE SHAFTS



### 4WD FRONT AXLE SHAFTS



### RWD AXLE SHAFTS



### DIFFERENTIALS & AXLE SHAFTS – INTEGRAL HOUSING



### DIFFERENTIALS & AXLE SHAFTS – SEPARATE CARRIER



### LOCKING HUBS

# 1991 TOYOTA CONTENTS (Cont.)

## BRAKES

### DISC & DRUM – FWD CARS



### DISC & DRUM – RWD CARS



### DISC & DRUM – LIGHT TRUCKS & VANS



### ANTI-LOCK



## BRAKES (Cont.)

### ANTI-LOCK (Cont.)

# 1991 TOYOTA CONTENTS (Cont.)

## WHEEL ALIGNMENT



## SUSPENSION



## SUSPENSION (Cont.)



## STEERING

# 1991 TOYOTA CONTENTS (Cont.)

## STEERING (Cont.)



## STEERING (Cont.)



## TRANSMISSION SERVICING

# 1991 ENGINE PERFORMANCE
## Toyota Introduction

### 1991 MODEL COVERAGE

| MODEL | BODY CODE | [1] ENGINE | ENGINE ID | [2] FUEL SYSTEM | IGNITION SYSTEM |
|---|---|---|---|---|---|
| Camry | SV | 2.0L 4-Cyl. (3S-FE) | S | PFI | Magnetic |
| | VZV | 2.5L V6 (2VZ-FE) | V | PFI | Magnetic |
| Celica | AT | 1.6L 4-Cyl. (4A-FE) | A | PFI | Magnetic |
| | ST (4WD) | 2.0L 4-Cyl. (3S-GTE) | S | PFI Turbo | Magnetic |
| | ST | 2.2L 4-Cyl. (5S-FE) | S | PFI | Magnetic |
| Corolla | AE | 1.6L 4-Cyl. (4A-FE) | A | PFI | Magnetic |
| | AE | 1.6L 4-Cyl. (4A-GE) | A | PFI | Magnetic |
| Cressida | MX | 3.0L 6-Cyl. (7M-GE) | M | PFI | Magnetic |
| Land Cruiser | FJ | 4.0L 6-Cyl. (3F-E) | F | PFI | Magnetic |
| MR2 | SW | 2.0L 4-Cyl. (3S-GTE) | S | PFI Turbo | Magnetic |
| | SW | 2.2L 4-Cyl. (5S-FE) | S | PFI | Magnetic |
| Pickup | RN | 2.4L 4-Cyl. (22R-E) | R | PFI | Magnetic |
| | VZN | 3.0L V6 (3VZ-E) | V | PFI | Magnetic |
| Previa | TCR | 2.4L 4-Cyl. (2TZ-FE) | T | PFI | Magnetic |
| Supra | MA | 3.0L 6-Cyl. (7M-GE) | M | PFI | Magnetic |
| | MA | 3.0L 6-Cyl. (7M-GTE) | M | PFI Turbo | [3] DIS |
| Tercel | EL | 1.5L 4-Cyl. (3E-E) | E | PFI | Magnetic |
| 4Runner | RN | 2.4L 4-Cyl. (22R-E) | R | PFI | Magnetic |
| | VZN | 3.0L V6 (3VZ-E) | V | PFI | Magnetic |

[1] – Engine can be identified by the Vehicle Identification Number (VIN) or number stamped on engine block. *See Figs. 1 and 2.* VIN is located on stamped plate on left side of instrument panel. VIN is also found in other locations.
[2] – Port Fuel Injection (PFI).
[3] – Distributorless Ignition System (DIS).

### VIN DEFINITION

**JT2AE92E6M3165709**
① ② ③ ④ ⑤ ⑥ ⑦ ⑧ ⑨ ⑩ ⑪ ⑫ ⑬ ⑭ ⑮ ⑯ ⑰

① Indicates Nation of Origin.
② Indicates Manufacturer.
③ Indicates Vehicle Type.
④ **Indicates Engine Type and Make.**
⑤ Indicates Vehicle Line.
⑥ Indicates Model Change Code (Car).
⑥ Indicates Drive Train (Truck).
⑦ Indicates Series Type (Car).
⑦ Indicates Model (Truck).
⑧ Indicates Body Type/Restraint System (Car).
⑧ Indicates Series (Truck).
⑨ Indicates Check Digit.
⑩ **Indicates Model Year.**
⑪ Indicates Assembly Plant.
⑫⑬⑭⑮⑯⑰ Indicates Plant Sequential Number.

121973

### *MODEL YEAR VIN CODE APPLICATION*

| VIN Code | Model Year |
|---|---|
| 1990 | L |
| 1991 | M |

### ENGINE CODE EXPLANATION

**7M-GTE**

C – U.S. specifications. (Engines without "C" may also meet U.S. specifications).
E – Fuel Injection
F – Twin Camshafts
G – Twin Camshafts
L – Transverse Engine
T – Turbocharged

Engine Generation Code

Engine Model Code & VIN VDS Code

121974

# 1991 ENGINE PERFORMANCE
## Toyota Introduction (Cont.)

A
B
C
TYPICAL PASSENGER CAR
PREVIA
PICKUP & 4RUNNER
A & B - VEHICLE IDENTIFICATION NUMBER (VIN) PLATES
C - CERTIFICATION LABEL

118442 91F17314 119525

Courtesy of Toyota Motor Sales, U.S.A., Inc.

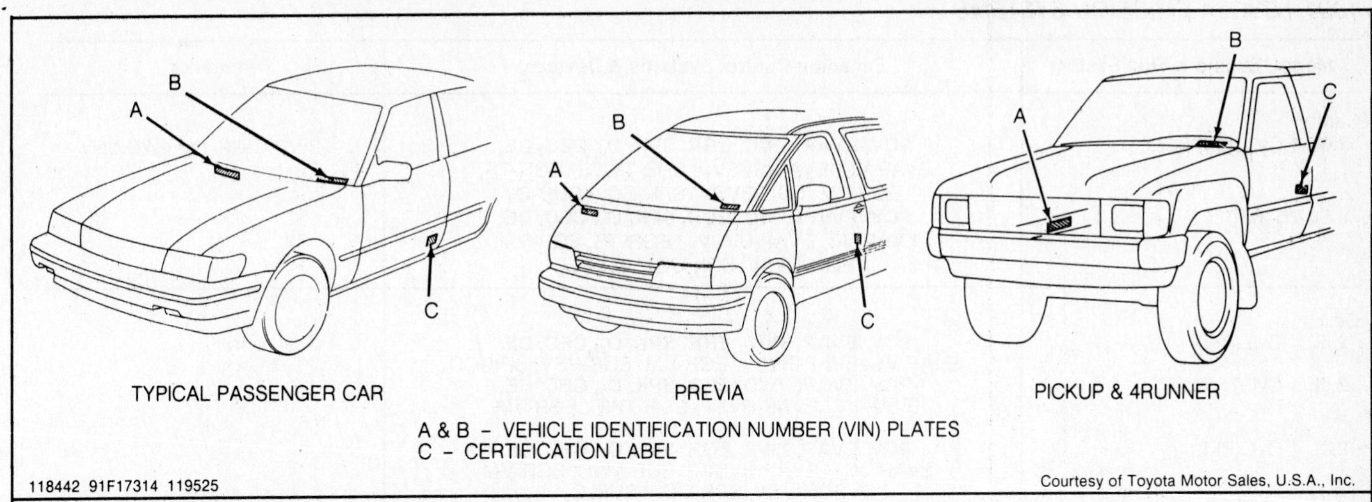

***Fig. 1: Locating Vehicle Identification Number (VIN)***

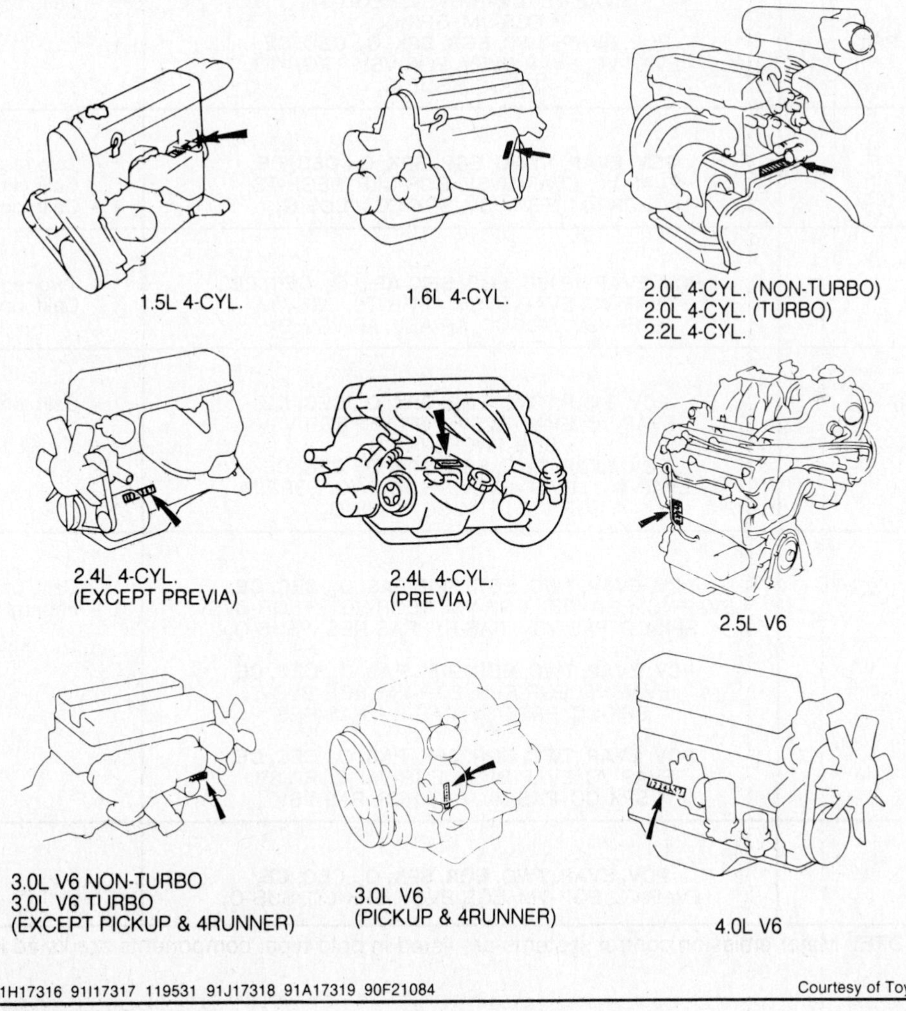

1.5L 4-CYL.
1.6L 4-CYL.
2.0L 4-CYL. (NON-TURBO)
2.0L 4-CYL. (TURBO)
2.2L 4-CYL.
2.4L 4-CYL.
(EXCEPT PREVIA)
2.4L 4-CYL.
(PREVIA)
2.5L V6
3.0L V6 NON-TURBO
3.0L V6 TURBO
(EXCEPT PICKUP & 4RUNNER)
3.0L V6
(PICKUP & 4RUNNER)
4.0L V6

118443 119527 91G17315 91H17316 91I17317 119531 91J17318 91A17319 90F21084

Courtesy of Toyota Motor Sales, U.S.A., Inc.

***Fig. 2: Locating Engine Identification Codes***

# 1991 ENGINE PERFORMANCE
## Emission Applications

*1991 TOYOTA EMISSION SYSTEMS*

| Model, Engine & Fuel System | Emission Control Systems & Devices | Remarks |
|---|---|---|
| Camry<br>2.0L 4-Cyl. (PFI) | **PCV, EVAP, TWC, EGR, SPK, $O_2$, CEC, CE,** EVAP-VC, EVAP-BVSV, [1] SUB-TWC, [2] EGR-TS, EGR-VM, EGR-BVSV, SPK-CC, [2] SUB-$O_2$ | [1] – 2WD Calif. and 4WD only.<br>[2] – Calif. only. |
| 2.5L V6 (PFI) | **PCV, EVAP, TWC, EGR, SPK, $O_2$, CEC, CE,** EVAP-VC, EVAP-BVSV, [2] EGR-TS, EGR-VM, EGR-BVSV, SPK-CC, [2] SUB-$O_2$ | |
| Celica<br>1.6L 4-Cyl. (PFI) | **PCV, EVAP, TWC, EGR, SPK, $O_2$, CEC, CE,** EVAP-VC, EVAP-BVSV, EGR-VM, EGR-VSV, SPK-CC | [1] – Calif. only. |
| 2.0L 4-Cyl. Turbo (PFI) | **PCV, EVAP, TWC, EGR, SPK, $O_2$, CEC, CE,** EVAP-VC, EVAP-BVSV, SUB-TWC, EGR-VM, EGR-VSV, SPK-CC | |
| 2.2L 4-Cyl. (PFI) | **PCV, EVAP, TWC, EGR, SPK, $O_2$, CEC, CE,** EVAP-VC, [1] EVAP-BVSV, [1] SUB-TWC, EGR-VM, EGR-VSV, SPK-CC, [1] SUB-$O_2$ | |
| Corolla<br>1.6L 4-Cyl. (4A-FE – PFI) | **PCV, EVAP, TWC, [1] EGR, SPK, $O_2$, CEC, CE,** EVAP-VC, EVAP-BVSV, [2] EGR-TS, [1] EGR-VM, SPK-CC | [1] – 2WD Calif. and 4WD only.<br>[2] – Calif. only. |
| 1.6L 4-Cyl. (4A-GE – PFI) | **PCV, EVAP, TWC, EGR, SPK, $O_2$, CEC, CE,** EVAP-VC, EVAP-BVSV, EGR-VSV, [2] EGR-TS, SPK-CC, [2] SUB-$O_2$ | |
| Cressida<br>3.0L 6-Cyl. (PFI) | **PCV, EVAP, [1] TWC, EGR, SPK, $O_2$, CEC, CE,** EVAP-VC, EVAP-BVSV, EGR-CLR, [2] EGR-TS, EGR-VM, EGR-VSV, SPK-CC, [2] SUB-$O_2$ | [1] – Two required on Calif. models.<br>[2] – Calif. only. |
| Land Cruiser<br>4.0L 6-Cyl. (PFI) | **PCV, EVAP, [1] TWC, EGR, SPK, AP, [1] $O_2$, CEC, CE,** EVAP-VC, EVAP-BVSV, [2] EGR-TS, EGR-VM, EGR-VSV, SPK-CC, AP-ASV, AP-VSV, DP | [1] – Two required.<br>[2] – Calif. only. |
| MR2<br>2.0L 4-Cyl. Turbo (PFI) | **PCV, EVAP, TWC, EGR, SPK, $O_2$, CEC, CE,** EVAP-VC, EVAP-BVSV, EGR-VM, EGR-VSV, SUB-TWC, SPK-CC | [1] – Calif. only. |
| 2.2L 4-Cyl. (PFI) | **PCV, EVAP, TWC, EGR, SPK, $O_2$, CEC, CE,** EVAP-VC, [1] EVAP-BVSV, [1] SUB-TWC, EGR-VM, EGR-VSV, SPK-CC, [1] SUB-$O_2$ | |
| Pickup<br>2.4L 4-Cyl. (PFI) | **PCV, EVAP, TWC, EGR, SPK, PAS, $O_2$, CEC, CE,** EVAP-VC, EGR-CLR, EGR-VM, [1] EGR-VSV, [2] EGR-BVSV, SPK-CC, PAS-VSV, PAS-RV, PAS-RES, [1] SUB-$O_2$ | [1] – Calif. only.<br>[2] – Federal and Canada only. |
| 4Runner<br>2.4L 4-Cyl. (PFI) | **PCV, EVAP, TWC, EGR, SPK, PAS, $O_2$, CEC, CE,** EVAP-VC, EGR-CLR, EGR-VM, EGR-BVSV, SPK-CC, PAS-VSV, PAS-RV, PAS-RES | |
| Pickup & 4Runner<br>3.0L V6 (PFI) | **PCV, EVAP, TWC, EGR, SPK, PAS, $O_2$, CEC, CE,** EVAP-VC, EVAP-BVSV, EGR-VM, EGR-VSV, SPK-CC, PAS-RV, PAS-RES, PAS-VSV | |
| Previa<br>2.4L 4-Cyl. (PFI) | **PCV, EVAP, TWC, EGR, SPK, $O_2$, CEC, CE,** EVAP-VC, EGR-VM, EGR-BVSV, SPK-CC, SUB-$O_2$ | |

**NOTE:** Major emission control systems are listed in bold type; components are listed in light type.

# 1991 ENGINE PERFORMANCE
# Emission Applications (Cont.)

### *1991 TOYOTA EMISSION SYSTEMS (Cont.)*

| Model, Engine & Fuel System | Emission Control Systems & Devices | Remarks |
|---|---|---|
| Supra | | |
| 3.0L 6-Cyl. Non Turbo (PFI) | **PCV, EVAP, [1] TWC, EGR, SPK, $O_2$, CEC, CE,** EVAP-VC, EVAP-BVSV, EGR-CLR, EGR-VM, [2] EGR-TS, EGR-VSV, SPK-CC, [2] SUB-$O_2$ | [1] - Two required on Calif. models. [2] - Calif. only. |
| 3.0L 6-Cyl. Turbo (PFI) | **PCV, EVAP, [1] TWC, EGR, SPK, $O_2$, CEC, CE,** EVAP-VC, EVAP-BVSV, EGR-CLR, EGR-VM, [2] EGR-TS, EGR-VSV, SPK-CC | |
| Tercel | | |
| 1.5L 4-Cyl. (PFI) | **PCV, EVAP, TWC, [1] EGR, SPK, $O_2$, CEC, CE,** EVAP-VC, EVAP-BVSV, [1] EGR-VM, [1] EGR-VSV, [1] EGR-TS, SPK-CC | [1] - Calif. only. |

**NOTE:** Major emission control systems are listed in bold type; components are listed in light type.

**AP** - Air Pump
**AP-ASV** - AP Air Switching Valve
**AP-VSV** - AP Vacuum Switching Valve
**CE** - Check Engine Light
**CEC** - Computerized Engine Controls
**DP** - Dash Pot
**EGR** - Exhaust Gas Recirculation
**EGR-BVSV** - EGR Bimetallic Vacuum Switching Valve
**EGR-CLR** - EGR Cooler
**EGR-TS** - EGR Temperature Sensor
**EGR-VM** - EGR Vacuum Modulator
**EVAP** - Fuel Evaporative System
**EVAP-BVSV** - EVAP Bimetallic Vacuum Switching Valve
**EVAP-VC** - EVAP Vapor Canister
**EVAP-VSV** - EVAP Vacuum Switching Valve
**$O_2$** - Oxygen Sensor
**PAS** - Pulse Air System
**PAS-RES** - PAS Resonator
**PAS-RV** - PAS Reed Valve
**PAS-VSV** - PAS Vacuum Switching Valve
**PCV** - Positive Crankcase Ventilation
**PFI** - Port Fuel Injection
**SPK** - Spark Control
**SPK-CC** - SPK Computer Controlled
**SUB-$O_2$** - Sub Oxygen Sensor
**SUB-TWC** - Sub Three-Way Catalyst
**TWC** - Three-Way Catalyst

# 1991 ENGINE PERFORMANCE
# Service & Adjustment Specifications

**Camry, Celica, Corolla, Cressida, Land Cruiser, MR2, Pickup, Previa, Supra, Tercel, 4Runner**

## INTRODUCTION

Use this article to quickly find specifications related to servicing and on-vehicle adjustments. This is a quick-reference article for when you are familiar with an adjustment procedure and only need a specification.

## CAPACITIES

### *BATTERY SPECIFICATIONS*

| Application | Amp Hr. Rating |
|---|---|
| **Camry** | |
| 2.0L | 50 |
| 2.5L | 60 |
| **Celica & MR2** | 60 |
| **Corolla** | 50 |
| **Cressida & Supra** | 70 |
| **Land Cruiser** | 56 |
| **Pickup** | |
| Standard | |
| 2.4L | 54 |
| 3.0L | 66 |
| With All Weather Guard | 66 |
| 2.4L | 66 |
| 3.0L | 90 |
| **Previa** | 50 |
| **Tercel** | 40 |
| **4Runner** | |
| Standard | 60 |
| With All Weather Guard | 90 |

### *CAMRY FLUID CAPACITIES*

| Application | Quantity |
|---|---|
| **Automatic Transaxle** [1] | |
| Transaxle | |
| 2WD (Dexron-II) | 2.6 Qts. (2.5L) |
| All-Trac (Type "T") [2] | 3.5 Qts. (3.3L) |
| Differential | |
| 2WD | |
| 2.0L (Dexron-II) | 1.7 Qts. (1.6L) |
| 2.5L (Dexron-II) | 1.1 Qts. (1.0L) |
| All-Trac | |
| Front (SAE 75W-90 With GL-5 Rating) | .74 Qts. (.70L) |
| Rear (SAE 90 With GL-5 Rating) | 1.2 Qts. (1.1L) |
| **Cooling System (Includes Heater)** | |
| 2.0L | |
| Man. Trans | 6.8 Qts. (6.4L) |
| 2WD Auto. Trans. | 6.7 Qts. (6.3L) |
| 4WD Auto. Trans. | 7.2 Qts. (6.8L) |
| 2.5L | 10.0 Qts. (9.5L) |
| **Crankcase (Includes Filter)** | |
| 2.0L | 4.3 Qts. (4.1L) |
| 2.5L | 4.1 Qts. (3.9L) |
| **Manual Transaxle** | |
| Transaxle | |
| 2WD | |
| 2.0L (Dexron-II) | 2.7 Qts. (2.6L) |
| 2.5L (SAE 90 With GL-5 Rating) | 4.4 Qts. (4.2L) |
| All-Trac (SAE 75W-90 With GL-5 Rating) | 5.2 Qts. (5.0L) |
| Differential | |
| All-Trac (Rear) | 1.2 Qts. (1.1L) |

1 – Drain and refill capacity.
2 – Toyota A/T fluid.

### *CELICA FLUID CAPACITIES*

| Application | Quantity |
|---|---|
| **Automatic Transaxle** [1] | |
| Transaxle | |
| 1.6L & 2.2L (Dexron-II) | 2.6 Qts. (2.5L) |
| **Cooling System (Includes Heater)** | |
| 1.6L | |
| Auto. Trans. | 5.9 Qts. (5.6L) |
| Man. Trans. | 5.5 Qts. (5.2L) |
| 2.0L (All-Trac) | 6.8 Qts. (6.4L) |
| 2.2L | |
| Auto. Trans. | 6.4 Qts. (6.1L) |
| Man. Trans. | 6.6 Qts. (6.2L) |
| **Crankcase (Includes Filter)** | |
| 1.6L | 3.4 Qts. (3.2L) |
| 2.0L | 3.8 Qts. (3.6L) |
| 2.2L | [2] 4.2 Qts. (4.1L) |
| **Manual Transaxle** | |
| Transaxle | |
| 1.6L (SAE 75W-90 With GL-5 Rating) | 2.7 Qts. (2.6L) |
| 2WD | |
| 2.2L (Dexron-II) | 2.7 Qts. (2.6L) |
| All-Trac (SAE 75W-90 With GL-5 Rating) | 5.5 Qts. (5.2L) |
| Differential | |
| All-Trac (SAE 90 With GL-5 Rating) | 1.2 Qts. (1.1L) |

1 – Drain and refill capacity.
2 – Specification listed is without oil cooler. With oil cooler, 4.5 qts. (4.2L).

### *COROLLA FLUID CAPACITIES*

| Application | Quantity |
|---|---|
| **Automatic Transaxle** | |
| Transaxle | |
| 2WD (Dexron-II) | |
| 3-Speed | 2.6 Qts. (2.5L) |
| 4-Speed | 3.3 Qts. (3.1L) |
| All-Trac (Type "T") [1] | 3.3 Qts. (3.1L) |
| Differential | |
| 2WD 3-Speed (Dexron-II) | 1.5 Qts. (1.4L) |
| All-Trac | |
| Rear Differential (SAE 90 With GL-5 Rating) | 1.2 Qts. (1.1L) |
| Transfer Case | |
| All-Trac (SAE 75W-90 With GL-5 Rating) | .74 Qts. (.70L) |
| **Cooling System (Includes Heater)** | |
| 4A-FE | |
| Auto. Trans. | 6.4 Qts. (6.1L) |
| Man. Trans. | 5.9 Qts. (5.6L) |
| 4A-GE | 6.3 Qts. (6.0L) |
| **Crankcase (Includes Filter)** | |
| 4A-FE | 3.3 Qts. (3.2L) |
| 4A-GE | 3.9 Qts. (3.7L) |
| **Manual Transaxle** | |
| Transaxle (SAE 75W-90 With GL-5 Rating) | |
| 2WD | 2.7 Qts. (2.6L) |
| All-Trac | 5.3 Qts. (5.0L) |
| Differential | |
| All-Trac | |
| Rear Differential (SAE 90 With GL-5 Rating) | 1.2 Qts. (1.1L) |

1 – Toyota A/T fluid.

# 1991 ENGINE PERFORMANCE
# Service & Adjustment Specifications (Cont.)

### CRESSIDA, LAND CRUISER & SUPRA FLUID CAPACITIES

| Application | Quantity |
|---|---|
| **Automatic Transmission (Dexron-II)** [1] | |
| Cressida & Supra | 1.7 Qts. (1.6L) |
| Land Cruiser | 6.3 Qts. (6.0L) |
| **Cooling System (Includes Heater)** | |
| Cressida | 8.8 Qts. (8.3L) |
| Land Cruiser | |
| With Front Heater | 18.5 Qts. (17.5L) |
| With Rear Heater | 20.6 Qts. (19.5L) |
| Supra | 8.6 Qts. (8.1L) |
| **Crankcase (Includes Filter)** | |
| Cressida & Supra | 4.7 Qts. (4.4L) |
| Land Cruiser | 8.2 Qts. (7.8L) |
| **Differential (SAE 90 With GL-5 Rating)** | |
| Cressida & Supra | 1.4 Qts. (1.3L) |
| Land Cruiser | |
| Front | 3.2 Qts. (3.0L) |
| Rear | 2.6 Qts. (2.5L) |
| **Manual Transmission (SAE 75W-90 With GL-5 Rating)** | |
| Supra Non-Turbo | 2.5 Qts. (2.4L) |
| Supra Turbo | 3.2 Qts. (3.0L) |
| **Transfer Case (SAE 90 With GL-5 Rating)** | |
| Land Cruiser | 2.2 Qts. (2.1L) |

[1] - Drain and refill capacity.

### MR2 FLUID CAPACITIES

| Application | Quantity |
|---|---|
| **Automatic Transaxle (Dexron-II)** [1] | 3.6 Qts. (3.3L) |
| **Cooling System (Includes Heater)** | |
| 2.0L | 14.4 Qts. (13.6L) |
| 2.2L | 13.7 Qts. (13.0L) |
| **Crankcase (Includes Filter)** | |
| 2.0L | 4.1 Qts. (3.9L) |
| 2.2L | 4.4 Qts. (4.2L) |
| **Manual Transaxle** | |
| 2.0L (SAE 75W–90) | 4.4 Qts. (4.2L) |
| 2.2L (Dexron-II) | 2.7 Qts. (2.6L) |

[1] - Drain and refill capacity.

### PREVIA FLUID CAPACITIES

| Application | Quantity |
|---|---|
| Automatic Transmission (Dexron-II) [1] | 2.5 Qts. (2.4L) |
| Cooling System (Includes Heater) | 12.3 Qts. (11.6L) |
| Crankcase (Includes Filter) | 6.1 Qts. (5.8L) |
| Differential (SAE 90 With GL-5 Rating) | |
| Front | 1.1 Qts. (1.0L) |
| Rear | 1.5 Qts. (1.6L) |
| Manual Transmission (GL-4 or GL-5 Rating) | |
| 2WD | 2.3 Qts. (2.2L) |
| 4WD | 2.7 Qts. (3.0L) |
| Transfer Case (SAE 75W–90) | 1.5 Qts. (1.4L) |

[1] - Drain and refill capacity.

### PICKUP & 4RUNNER FLUID CAPACITIES

| Application | Quantity |
|---|---|
| **Automatic Transmission (Dexron-II)** [1] | |
| 2WD | |
| A43D & A44D Trans. | 2.5 Qts. (2.4L) |
| A340E, A340F & A340H Trans. (3.0L) | 1.7 Qts. (1.6L) |
| 4WD [2] | 4.8 Qts. (4.5L) |
| **Cooling System (Includes Heater)** | |
| 2.4L | |
| 4WD Auto. Trans. | 9.6 Qts. (9.1L) |
| All Others | 8.9 Qts. (8.4L) |
| 3.0L | 11.0 Qts. (10.4L) |
| **Crankcase (Includes Filter)** | |
| 2.4L | 4.5 Qts. (4.3L) |
| 3.0L | 4.8 Qts. (4.5L) |
| **Differential (SAE 90 With GL-5 Rating)** | |
| Front | 1.7 Qts. (1.6L) |
| Rear | 2.3 Qts. (2.2L) |
| **Manual Transmission (SAE 75W-90 With GL-5 Rating)** | |
| 2.4L | |
| 2WD | 2.5 Qts. (2.4L) |
| 4WD Pickup & 4Runner | [2] 3.2 Qts. (3.0L) |
| 3.0L | 3.2 Qts. (3.0L) |
| **Transfer Case** | |
| Auto. Trans. (Dexron-II) [3] | .85 Qts. (.80L) |
| Man. Trans. (SAE 90) | 1.7 Qts. (1.6L) |

[1] - Drain and refill capacity.
[2] - Use 4.1 qts. (3.9L) for 5-speed with 4Wheel Demand.
[3] - A340H auto. trans. used on 4WD has separate drain plug for transfer case section.

### TERCEL FLUID CAPACITIES

| Application | Quantity |
|---|---|
| Automatic Transaxle (Dexron-II) | |
| Differential | 1.5 Qts. (1.4L) |
| Transaxle [1] | 2.6 Qts. (2.5L) |
| Cooling System (Includes Heater) | 5.9 Qts. (5.6L) |
| Crankcase (Includes Filter) | 3.4 Qts. (3.2L) |
| Manual Transaxle (SAE 75W-90 With GL-5 Rating) | |
| 4 & 5-Speed | 2.5 Qts. (2.4L) |

[1] - Drain and refill capacity.

## QUICK-SERVICE

## SERVICE INTERVALS & SPECIFICATIONS

### REPLACEMENT INTERVALS

| Component | Months | Miles |
|---|---|---|
| Air Filter | 36 | 30,000 |
| Coolant | 36 | [1] 45,000 |
| Fuel Filter | .... | 60,000 |
| Oil & Filter [2] | | |
| MR2 2.0L | 6 | 5000 |
| All Others | 12 | 7500 |
| Oxygen Sensor | .... | [3] 80,000 |
| Spark Plugs | 36 | 30,000 |
| Timing Belt | .... | 60,000 |

[1] - After first coolant change, replace coolant every 30,000 miles or 24 months.
[2] - For severe service, replace every 3500 miles or 6 months. Severe service is taxi, trailer towing or local delivery service.
[3] - Except Calif.

### VALVE ADJUSTMENT INTERVALS

| Application | Months | Miles |
|---|---|---|
| Land Cruiser | 15 | 15,000 |
| Pickup & 4Runner 2.4L | 36 | 30,000 |
| Pickup & 4Runner 3.0L | 72 | 60,000 |
| Tercel | 36 | 30,000 |
| All Others | 72 | 60,000 |

# 1991 ENGINE PERFORMANCE
# Service & Adjustment Specifications (Cont.)

***4-CYLINDER BELT ADJUSTMENT***
***Tension in Lbs. (kg) Using Burroughs Tension Gauge***

| Application | New Belt | Used Belt |
|---|---|---|
| **Camry & Celica** | | |
| A/C | 160 (73) | 100 (45) |
| Alternator | | |
| With A/C | 175 (79) | 130 (59) |
| Without A/C | 125 (57) | 95 (43) |
| Power Steering | 125 (57) | 80 (36) |
| **Corolla** | | |
| A/C | 160 (73) | 100 (45) |
| Alternator | 160 (73) | 125 (57) |
| Power Steering | 125 (57) | 80 (36) |
| **MR2** | | |
| A/C | 160 (73) | 100 (45) |
| Alternator | 120 (55) | 104 (47) |
| **Pickup & 4Runner** | | |
| "V" Ribbed | | |
| A/C | 160 (73) | 100 (45) |
| Non-A/C | 105 (48) | 85 (39) |
| Conventional | 125 (57) | 80 (36) |
| **Previa** | | |
| Alternator & Power Steering | 170 (77) | 125 (57) |
| A/C | 140 (64) | 120 (55) |
| **Tercel** | | |
| Alternator | 160 (73) | 100 (45) |
| A/C | 165 (75) | 110 (50) |
| Power Steering | 175 (79) | 115 (52) |

***6-CYLINDER BELT ADJUSTMENT***
***Tension in Lbs. (kg) Using Burroughs Tension Gauge***

| Application | New Belt | Used Belt |
|---|---|---|
| **Cressida** | | |
| Alternator | 175 (79) | 115 (52) |
| A/C | 160 (73) | 105 (48) |
| Power Steering | 160 (73) | 100 (45) |
| **Land Cruiser** | | |
| A/C | 125 (57) | 80 (36) |
| All Others | 145 (66) | 100 (45) |
| **Supra** | | |
| Alternator | 175 (79) | 115 (52) |
| A/C & Power Steering | 160 (73) | 105 (48) |

***V6 BELT ADJUSTMENT***
***Tension in Lbs. (kg) Using Burroughs Tension Gauge***

| Application | New Belt | Used Belt |
|---|---|---|
| **Camry** | | |
| Alternator | 175 (79) | 115 (52) |
| Power Steering | 125 (57) | 80 (36) |
| **Pickup & 4Runner** | | |
| Alternator | 160 (73) | 100 (45) |
| All Others | 125 (57) | 80 (36) |

## MECHANICAL CHECKS

### ENGINE COMPRESSION

***4-CYLINDER COMPRESSION SPECIFICATIONS***

| Application | Specification |
|---|---|
| **Compression Ratio** | |
| Camry & Celica | |
| 1.6L | 9.5:1 |
| 2.0L (Camry) | 9.3:1 |
| 2.0L (Celica) | 8.8:1 |
| 2.2L | 9.5:1 |
| Corolla | |
| 4A-FE | 9.5:1 |
| 4A-GE | 10.3:1 |
| MR2 | |
| 2.0L | 8.8:1 |
| 2.2L | 9.5:1 |
| Previa | NA |
| Pickup & 4Runner | |
| 2.4L | 9.3:1 |
| Tercel | 9.3:1 |
| **Normal Compression Pressure** | |
| Celica Turbo | 164 psi (11.5 kg/cm²) |
| Corolla | |
| 4A-FE & 4A-GE | 191 psi (13.4 kg/cm²) |
| MR2 | |
| 2.0L | 164 psi (11.5 kg/cm²) |
| 2.2L | 178 psi (12.5 kg/cm²) |
| Pickup & 4Runner | 171 psi (12.0 kg/cm²) |
| Previa | 178 psi (12.5 kg/cm²) |
| Tercel | 185 psi (13.0 kg/cm²) |
| All Others | 178 psi (12.5 kg/cm²) |
| **Minimum Compression Pressure** | |
| Celica Turbo | 164 psi (11.5 kg/cm²) |
| MR2 2.0L & Previa | 128 psi (9.0 kg/cm²) |
| All Others | 142 psi (10.0 kg/cm²) |
| **Maximum Variation Between Cylinders** | 14 psi (1.0 kg/cm²) |

***6-CYLINDER COMPRESSION SPECIFICATIONS***

| Application | Specification |
|---|---|
| **Compression Ratio** | |
| Cressida | 9.2:1 |
| Land Cruiser | 8.1:1 |
| Supra | |
| Non-Turbo | 9.2:1 |
| Turbo | 8.4:1 |
| **Normal Compression Pressure** | |
| Cressida | 156 psi (10.9 kg/cm²) |
| Land Cruiser | 149 psi (10.5 kg/cm²) |
| Supra | |
| Non-Turbo | 156 psi (10.9 kg/cm²) |
| Turbo | 142 psi (10.0 kg/cm²) |
| **Minimum Compression Pressure** | |
| Cressida & Supra | 128 psi (9.0 kg/cm²) |
| Land Cruiser | 114 psi (8.0 kg/cm²) |
| **Maximum Variation Between Cylinders** | |
| Cressida & Supra | 14 psi (1.0 kg/cm²) |
| Land Cruiser | 7 psi (.5 kg/cm²) |

***V6 COMPRESSION SPECIFICATIONS***

| Application | Specification |
|---|---|
| **Compression Ratio** | 9.0:1 |
| **Normal Compression Pressure** | |
| Camry | 178 psi (12.5 kg/cm²) |
| Pickup & 4Runner | 171 psi (12.0 kg/cm²) |
| **Minimum Compression Pressure** | 142 psi (10.0 kg/cm²) |
| **Max. Variation Between Cylinders** | 14 psi (1.0 kg/cm²) |

# 1991 ENGINE PERFORMANCE
# Service & Adjustment Specifications (Cont.)

## VALVE CLEARANCE

*4-CYLINDER VALVE CLEARANCE SPECIFICATIONS*

| Application [1] | In. (mm) |
|---|---|
| **Camry** | |
| Exhaust | .011-.015 (.28-.38) |
| Intake | .007-.011 (.18-.28) |
| **Celica** | |
| 1.6L & 2.2L | |
| Exhaust | .008-.012 (.20-.30) |
| Intake | .006-.010 (.15-.25) |
| 2.2L | |
| Exhaust | .011-.015 (.28-.38) |
| Intake | .007-.011 (.18-.28) |
| **Corolla** | |
| Exhaust | .008-.012 (.20-.30) |
| Intake | .006-.010 (.15-.25) |
| **MR2** | |
| 2.0L | |
| Exhaust | .008-.012 (.20-.30) |
| Intake | .006-.010 (.15-.25) |
| 2.2L | |
| Exhaust | .011-.015 (.28-.38) |
| Intake | .007-.011 (.18-.28) |
| **Pickup & 4Runner** | |
| Exhaust | .012 (.30) |
| Intake | .008 (.20) |
| **Previa** | |
| Exhaust | .010-.014 (.25-.35) |
| Intake | .006-.010 (.15-.25) |
| **Tercel** | .008 (.20) |

[1] – On Pickup, Tercel and 4Runner models, adjust valves at normal operating temperature. On all other models, adjust valves with engine cold.

*6-CYLINDER VALVE CLEARANCE SPECIFICATIONS*

| Application | In. (mm) |
|---|---|
| **Cressida** [1] | |
| Exhaust | .008-.012 (.20-.30) |
| Intake | .006-.010 (.15-.25) |
| **Land Cruiser** [2] | |
| Exhaust | .014 (.36) |
| Intake | .008 (.20) |
| **Supra** [1] | |
| Exhaust | .008-.012 (.20-.30) |
| Intake | .006-.010 (.15-.25) |

[1] – Adjust valve clearance with engine cold.
[2] – Adjust valve clearance with engine hot.

*V6 VALVE CLEARANCE SPECIFICATIONS*

| Application [1] | In. (mm) |
|---|---|
| **Camry** | |
| Exhaust | .011-.015 (.28-.38) |
| Intake | .005-.009 (.13-.23) |
| **Pickup & 4Runner** | |
| Exhaust | .009-.013 (.23-.33) |
| Intake | .007-.011 (.18-.28) |

[1] – Adjust valves with engine cold.

## IGNITION SYSTEM

### DISTRIBUTOR

*DISTRIBUTOR PICK-UP COIL AIR GAP* [1]

| Application | In. (mm) |
|---|---|
| All Models | .008-.016 (.20-.40) |

[1] – Air gap also applies to Supra Turbo cam position sensor gap.

*DISTRIBUTOR PICK-UP COIL RESISTANCE*

| Application | Pick-Up Coil | Ohms |
|---|---|---|
| Celica 2.0L, Cressida, MR2 2.0L, Previa & Supra Non-Turbo | G1 | 125-190 |
| | G2 | 125-190 |
| | NE | 155-240 |
| Celica 2.2L & MR2 2.2L | .... | 150-230 |
| Tercel | | |
| Gray | .... | 265-420 |
| Green | .... | 370-530 |
| All Others | | |
| Gray | .... | 130-210 |
| Green | .... | 185-265 |

## IGNITION COIL

*4-CYLINDER IGNITION COIL RESISTANCE – Ohms @ 68°F (20°C)*

| Application | Primary | Secondary |
|---|---|---|
| **Camry 2.0L** | .4-.5 | 7700-10,400 |
| **Celica** | | |
| 1.6L | 1.3-1.6 | 10,400-14,000 |
| 2.0L & 2.2L | .4-.5 | 10,200-13,800 |
| **Corolla** | | |
| 4A-FE | 1.3-1.6 | 10,400-14,000 |
| 4A-GE | .4-.5 | 10,200-13,800 |
| **MR2 2.0L & 2.2L** | .4-.5 | 10,000-14,000 |
| **Pickup & 4Runner 2.4L** | .5-.7 | 11,400-15,600 |
| **Previa** | .4-.5 | 10,000-14,000 |
| **Tercel** | .4-.5 | 10,200-13,800 |

*6-CYLINDER IGNITION COIL RESISTANCE – Ohms @ 68°F (20°C)*

| Application | Primary | Secondary |
|---|---|---|
| Cressida | .24-.30 | 9200-12,400 |
| Supra | | |
| Non-Turbo | .24-.30 | 9200-12,400 |
| Turbo | .30-.50 | [1] |
| Land Cruiser | .52-.64 | 11,500-15,500 |

[1] – Secondary ignition coil resistance cannot be measured.

*V6 IGNITION COIL RESISTANCE – Ohms @ 68°F (20°C)*

| Application | Primary | Secondary |
|---|---|---|
| All Models | .4-.5 | 10,200-13,800 |

## HIGH TENSION WIRE RESISTANCE

*HIGH TENSION WIRE RESISTANCE*

| Application | Maximum Ohms |
|---|---|
| All Models | 25,000 |

# 1991 ENGINE PERFORMANCE
# Service & Adjustment Specifications (Cont.)

## SPARK PLUGS

### 4-CYLINDER SPARK PLUG TYPE

| Application | NGK | Nippondenso |
|---|---|---|
| **Camry 2.0L** | BCPR5EY11 | Q16R-U11 |
| **Celica** | | |
| 1.6L | BCPR5EY | Q16R-U |
| 2.0L | BKR6EP8 | PK20R8 |
| 2.2L | BKR5EYA11 | K16R-U11 |
| **Corolla** | | |
| 4A-FE | BCPR5EY | Q16R-U |
| 4A-GE | BKR6EP8 | PK20R8 |
| **MR2** | | |
| 2.0L | BKR6EP8 | PK20R8 |
| 2.2L | BKR5EYA11 | K16R-U11 |
| **Pickup & 4Runner** | BPR5EY | W16EXR-U |
| **Previa** | BKR5EP11 | PK16R11 |
| **Tercel** | BPR5EY11 | W16EXR-U11 |

### 4-CYLINDER SPARK PLUG SPECIFICATIONS

| Application | Gap In. (mm) | Torque Ft. Lbs. (N.m) |
|---|---|---|
| Celica 1.6L & 2.0L & Corolla | .031 (.80) | 13 (18) |
| Pickup & 4Runner | .031 (.80) | 13 (18) |
| All Others | .043 (1.10) | 13 (18) |

### 6-CYLINDER SPARK PLUG TYPE

| Application | NGK | Nippondenso |
|---|---|---|
| Cressida | BCPR5EP11 | PQ16R |
| Land Cruiser | BPR5EY | W16EXR-U |
| Supra | | |
| Non-Turbo | BCPR5EP11 | PQ16R |
| Turbo | BCPR6EP-N8 | PQ20R-P8 |

### 6-CYLINDER SPARK PLUG SPECIFICATIONS

| Application | Gap In. (mm) | Torque Ft. Lbs. (N.m) |
|---|---|---|
| Cressida | .043 (1.10) | 13 (18) |
| Land Cruiser | .031 (.80) | 13 (18) |
| Supra | | |
| Non-Turbo | .043 (1.10) | 13 (18) |
| Turbo | .031 (.80) | 13 (18) |

### V6 SPARK PLUG TYPE

| Application | NGK | Nippondenso |
|---|---|---|
| Camry | BCPR6EP11 | PQ20R |
| Pickup & 4Runner | BCPR5EY | Q16R-U |

### V6 SPARK PLUG SPECIFICATIONS

| Application | Gap In. (mm) | Torque Ft. Lbs. (N.m) |
|---|---|---|
| Camry | .043 (1.10) | 13 (18) |
| Pickup & 4Runner | .031 (.80) | 13 (18) |

## IGNITION TIMING

### 4-CYLINDER IGNITION TIMING – Degrees BTDC @ RPM

| Application | Base Timing [1] | Advance Timing |
|---|---|---|
| **Camry & Celica** | | |
| 1.6L | 10 @ Idle | 5-15 @ Idle |
| 2.0L | 10 @ 750 | 14-19 @ Idle |
| 2.2L | 10 @ 700 | 13-22 @ Idle |
| **Corolla** | | |
| 4A-FE | 10 @ 800 | 5-15 @ Idle |
| 4A-GE | 10 @ 800 | 16 @ Idle |
| **MR2** | | |
| 2.0L | 10 @ Idle | 12-21 @ Idle |
| 2.2L | 10 @ Idle | 13-22 @ Idle |
| **Pickup & 4Runner** | 5 @ Idle | 10-14 @ Idle |
| **Previa** | 5 @ Idle | 12 @ Idle |
| **Tercel** | 10 @ Idle | 7-17 @ Idle |

1 – With check connector terminals TE1 and E1 jumpered.

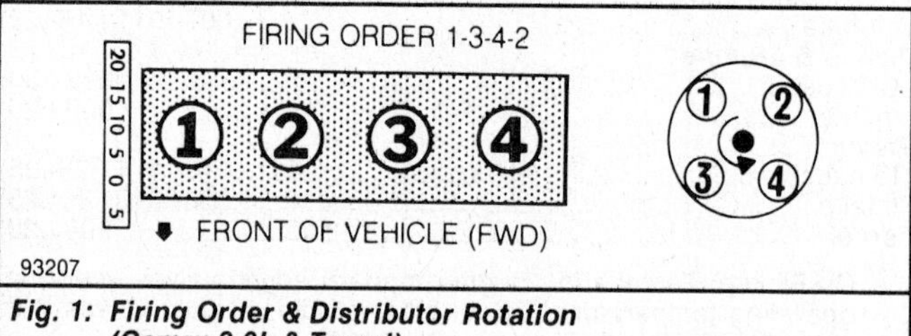


Fig. 1: Firing Order & Distributor Rotation (Camry 2.0L & Tercel)

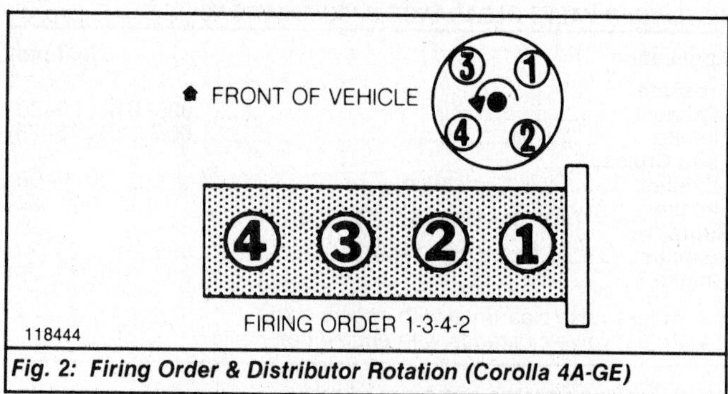


Fig. 2: Firing Order & Distributor Rotation (Corolla 4A-GE)

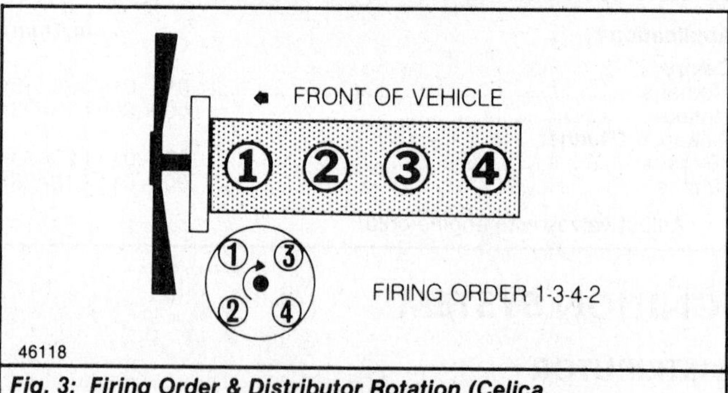


Fig. 3: Firing Order & Distributor Rotation (Celica, Corolla 4A-FE, MR2, Pickup 2.4L, Previa & 4Runner 2.4L)

### 6-CYLINDER IGNITION TIMING (Degrees BTDC @ RPM)

| Application | Base Timing | Advance Timing |
|---|---|---|
| Cressida | 10 @ 700 | 9-11 @ Idle |
| Land Cruiser | 7 @ 650 | 12 @ Idle |
| Supra | | |
| Non-Turbo | 10 @ 700 | 9-10 @ Idle |
| Turbo | 10 @ 650 | More than 12 @ Idle |

# 1991 ENGINE PERFORMANCE
# Service & Adjustment Specifications (Cont.)

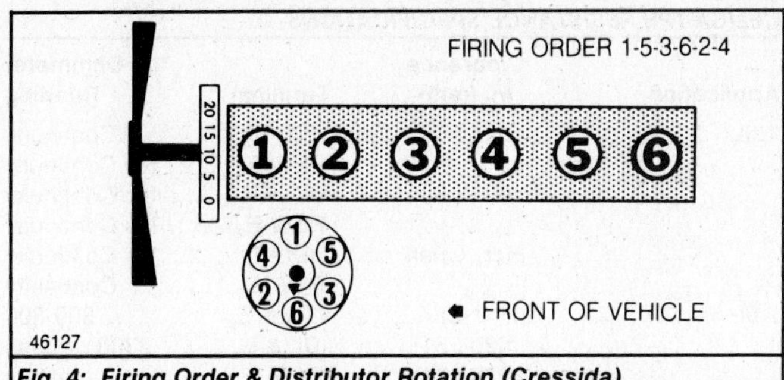


*Fig. 4: Firing Order & Distributor Rotation (Cressida)*

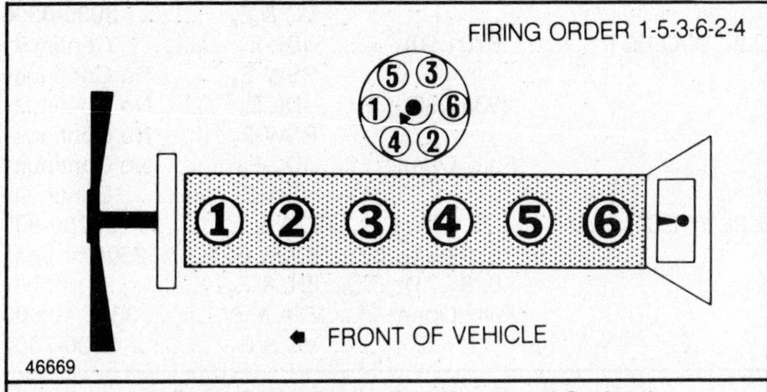


*Fig. 5: Firing Order & Distributor Rotation (Land Cruiser)*

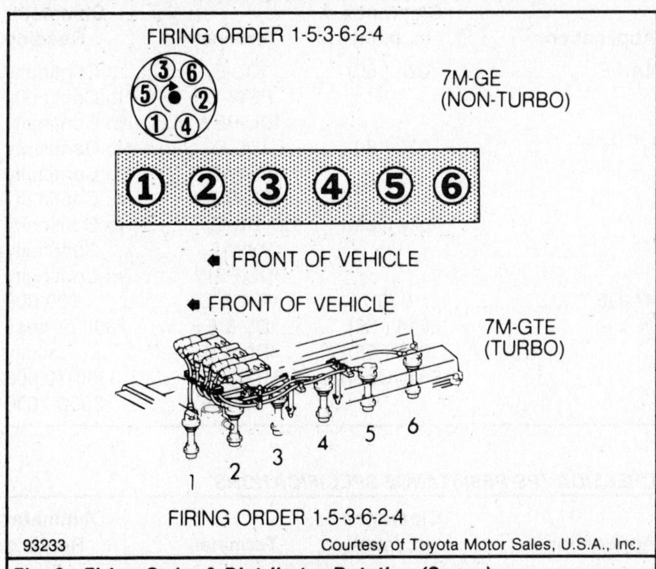


*Fig. 6: Firing Order & Distributor Rotation (Supra)*

***V6 IGNITION TIMING (Degrees BTDC @ RPM)***

| Application | Base Timing | Advance Timing |
|---|---|---|
| Camry | 10 @ 700 | 13-27 @ Idle |
| Pickup & 4Runner | 10 @ 800 | 8 @ Idle |

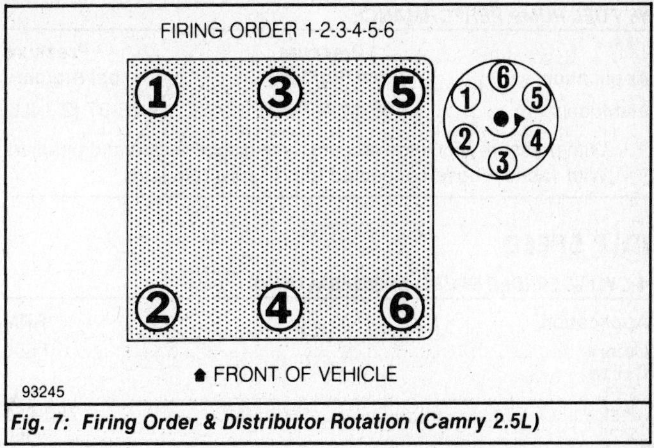


*Fig. 7: Firing Order & Distributor Rotation (Camry 2.5L)*

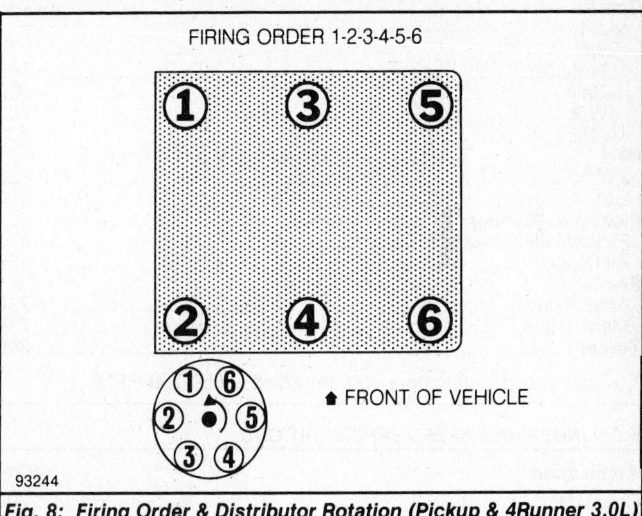


*Fig. 8: Firing Order & Distributor Rotation (Pickup & 4Runner 3.0L)*

## FUEL SYSTEM

### FUEL PUMP

***4-CYLINDER FUEL PUMP PERFORMANCE***

| Application | [1] Pressure psi (kg/cm²) | [2] Pressure psi (kg/cm²) |
|---|---|---|
| **Camry 2.0L** | 38-44 (2.7-3.1) | 33-37 (2.3-2.6) |
| **Celica** | | |
| 1.6L & 2.2L | 38-44 (2.7-3.1) | 33-37 (2.3-2.6) |
| 2.0L | 33-38 (2.3-2.7) | 27-31 (1.9-2.2) |
| **Corolla & Previa** | 38-44 (2.7-3.1) | 30-37 (2.1-2.6) |
| **MR2** | 33-38 (2.3-2.7) | 27-31 (1.9-2.2) |
| **Pickup, Tercel & 4Runner** | 38-44 (2.7-3.1) | 33-37 (2.3-2.6) |

[1] – With pressure regulator vacuum hose disconnected and plugged.
[2] – With vacuum hose connected to pressure regulator.

***6-CYLINDER FUEL PUMP PERFORMANCE***

| Application | [1] Pressure psi (kg/cm²) | [2] Pressure psi (kg/cm²) |
|---|---|---|
| Cressida | 38-44 (2.7-3.1) | 33-37 (2.3-2.6) |
| Land Cruiser | 37-46 (2.6-3.2) | 33-37 (2.3-2.6) |
| Supra | | |
| Non-Turbo | 38-44 (2.7-3.1) | 33-37 (2.3-2.6) |
| Turbo | 33-40 (2.3-2.8) | 23-30 (1.6-2.1) |

[1] – With pressure regulator vacuum hose disconnected and plugged.
[2] – With vacuum hose connected to pressure regulator.

# 1991 ENGINE PERFORMANCE
# Service & Adjustment Specifications (Cont.)

### V6 FUEL PUMP PERFORMANCE

| Application | [1] Pressure psi ($kg/cm^2$) | [2] Pressure psi ($kg/cm^2$) |
|---|---|---|
| All Models | 38-44 (2.7-3.1) | 33-37 (2.3-2.6) |

[1] – With pressure regulator vacuum hose disconnected and plugged.
[2] – With vacuum hose connected to pressure regulator.

## IDLE SPEED

### 4-CYLINDER IDLE SPEED SPECIFICATIONS

| Application | RPM |
|---|---|
| **Camry** | [1] 650 |
| **Celica** | |
| 1.6L | 800 |
| 2.0L | 750-850 |
| 2.2L | [1] 650 |
| **Corolla** | |
| 4A-FE | |
| 2WD | |
| Federal | 700 |
| Calif. | 800 |
| 4WD | 800 |
| 4A-GE | 800 |
| **MR2** | |
| 2.0L | 750-850 |
| 2.2L | 650 |
| **Pickup & 4Runner** | |
| Pickup W/4WD & A/T | 850 |
| All Others | 750 |
| **Previa** | |
| Auto. Trans. | 750 |
| Man. Trans. | 750 |
| **Tercel** | 800 |

[1] – Idle speed with jumper wire removed is 650-750 RPM.

### 6-CYLINDER IDLE SPEED SPECIFICATIONS

| Application | RPM |
|---|---|
| Cressida | 700 |
| Land Cruiser | 650 |
| Supra | |
| Non-Turbo | 700 |
| Turbo | 650 |

### V6 IDLE SPEED SPECIFICATIONS

| Application | RPM |
|---|---|
| Camry | 700 |
| Pickup & 4Runner | 800 |

## THROTTLE POSITION SENSOR (TPS)

### CAMRY TPS RESISTANCE SPECIFICATIONS

| Application | Clearance In. (mm) | Terminal | Ohmmeter Reading |
|---|---|---|---|
| 2.0L W/O ECT | .020 (.51) | IDL & $E_1$ | Continuity |
| | | PSW & $E_1$ | No Continuity |
| | .035 (.90) | IDL & $E_1$ | No Continuity |
| | | PSW & $E_1$ | No Continuity |
| | Fully Open | IDL & $E_1$ | No Continuity |
| | | PSW & $E_1$ | Continuity |
| 2.0L W/ ECT | 0 (0) | VTA & $E_2$ | 200-800 |
| | .020 (.51) | IDL & $E_2$ | 2300 or Less |
| | .028 (.70) | IDL & $E_2$ | Infinity |
| | Fully Open | VAT & $E_2$ | 3300-10,000 |
| | | VC & $E_2$ | 3000-7000 |
| 2.5L | 0 (0) | VTA & $E_2$ | 300-6300 |
| | .012 (.30) | IDL & $E_2$ | 2300 or Less |
| | .028 (.71) | IDL & $E_2$ | Infinity |
| | Fully Open | VTA & $E_2$ | 3500-10,300 |
| | | VC & $E_2$ | 4250-8250 |

### CELICA TPS RESISTANCE SPECIFICATIONS

| Application | Clearance In. (mm) | Terminal | Ohmmeter Reading |
|---|---|---|---|
| 1.6L | .024 (.60) | IDL-$E_2$ | Continuity |
| | | PSW-$E_2$ | No Continuity |
| | .031 (.80) | IDL-$E_2$ | No Continuity |
| | | PSW-$E_2$ | No Continuity |
| | Fully Open | IDL-$E_2$ | No Continuity |
| | | PSW-$E_2$ | Continuity |
| 2.0L | 0 (0) | VTA & $E_2$ | 200-800 |
| | .020 (.51) | IDL & $E_2$ | 2300 or Less |
| | .028 (.71) | IDL & $E_2$ | Infinity |
| | Fully Open | VTA & $E_2$ | 3300-10,300 |
| | | VC & $E_2$ | 3000-8300 |
| 2.2L W/O ECT | .020 (.50) | IDL-$E_2$ | Continuity |
| | | PSW-$E_2$ | No Continuity |
| | .035 (.90) | IDL-$E_2$ | No Continuity |
| | | PSW-$E_2$ | No Continuity |
| | Fully Open | IDL-$E_2$ | No Continuity |
| | | PSW-$E_2$ | Continuity |
| 2.2L W/ECT | 0 (0) | VTA & $E_2$ | 200-800 |
| | .020 (.51) | IDL & $E_2$ | 2300 or Less |
| | .028 (.71) | IDL & $E_2$ | Infinity |
| | Fully Open | VTA & $E_2$ | 3300-10,000 |
| | | VC & $E_2$ | 3000-7000 |

### COROLLA TPS RESISTANCE SPECIFICATIONS

| Application | Clearance In. (mm) | Terminal | Ohmmeter Reading |
|---|---|---|---|
| 4A-FE | .024 (.60) | IDL-$E_2$ | Continuity |
| | | PSW-$E_2$ | No Continuity |
| | | IDL-PSW | No Continuity |
| | .032 (.80) | IDL-$E_2$ | No Continuity |
| | | PSW-$E_2$ | No Continuity |
| | | IDL-PSW | No Continuity |
| | Fully Open | IDL-$E_2$ | No Continuity |
| | | PSW-$E_2$ | Continuity |
| | | IDL-PSW | No Continuity |
| 4A-GE | 0 (0) | VTA & $E_2$ | 200-800 |
| | .014 (.36) | IDL & $E_2$ | 2300 or Less |
| | .023 (.58) | IDL & $E_2$ | Infinity |
| | Fully Open | VTA & $E_2$ | 3300-10,000 |
| | | VCC & $E_2$ | 3000-7000 |

### CRESSIDA TPS RESISTANCE SPECIFICATIONS

| Application | Clearance In. (mm) | Terminal | Ohmmeter Reading |
|---|---|---|---|
| 3.0L | 0 (0) | VTA & $E_2$ | 300-6300 |
| | .020 (.51) | IDL & $E_2$ | 2300 or Less |
| | .035 (.89) | IDL & $E_2$ | Infinity |
| | Fully Open | VTA & $E_2$ | 3500-10,300 |
| | | VC & $E_2$ | 4250-8250 |

### LAND CRUISER TPS RESISTANCE SPECIFICATIONS

| Application | Clearance In. (mm) | Terminal | Ohmmeter Reading |
|---|---|---|---|
| 4.0L | 0 (0) | VTA & $E_2$ | 300-6300 |
| | .030 (.76) | IDL & $E_2$ | 2300 or Less |
| | .043 (1.09) | IDL & $E_2$ | Infinity |
| | Fully Open | VTA & $E_2$ | 3500-10,300 |
| | | VC & $E_2$ | 4250-8250 |

# 1991 ENGINE PERFORMANCE
# Service & Adjustment Specifications (Cont.)

### *MR2 TPS RESISTANCE SPECIFICATIONS*

| Application | Clearance In. (mm) | Terminal | Ohmmeter Reading |
|---|---|---|---|
| 2.0L & 2.2L (A/T) | 0 (0) | VTA & $E_2$ | 200-800 |
| | .020 (.51) | IDL & $E_2$ | 2300 or Less |
| | .028 (.71) | IDL & $E_2$ | Infinity |
| | Fully Open | VTA & $E_2$ | 3300-10,300 |
| | | VC & $E_2$ | 3000-8300 |
| 2.2L (M/T) | .020 (.50) | IDL-$E_1$ | Continuity |
| | | PSW-$E_1$ | No Continuity |
| | .035 (.90) | IDL-$E_1$ | No Continuity |
| | | PSW-$E_1$ | No Continuity |
| | Fully Open | IDL-$E_1$ | No Continuity |
| | | PSW-$E_1$ | Continuity |

### *PICKUP & 4RUNNER TPS RESISTANCE SPECIFICATIONS*

| Application | Clearance In. (mm) | Terminal | Ohmmeter Reading |
|---|---|---|---|
| 2.4L | 0 (0) | VTA & $E_2$ | 200-800 |
| | .022 (.56) | IDL & $E_2$ | 2300 or Less |
| | .034 (.86) | IDL & $E_2$ | Infinity |
| | Fully Open | VTA & $E_2$ | 3300-10,000 |
| | | VCC & $E_2$ | 4000-9000 |
| 3.0L | 0 (0) | VTA & $E_2$ | 200-800 |
| | .020 (.51) | IDL & $E_2$ | 2300 or Less |
| | .030 (.76) | IDL & $E_2$ | Infinity |
| | Fully Open | VTA & $E_2$ | 3300-10,000 |
| | | VCC & $E_2$ | 4000-9000 |

### *PREVIA TPS RESISTANCE SPECIFICATIONS*

| Application | Clearance In. (mm) | Terminal | Ohmmeter Reading |
|---|---|---|---|
| 2.4L | 0 (0) | VTA & $E_2$ | 300-6300 |
| | .014 (.36) | IDL & $E_2$ | 2300 or Less |
| | .023 (.58) | IDL & $E_2$ | Infinity |
| | Fully Open | VTA & $E_2$ | 3500-10,3000 |
| | | VCC & $E_2$ | 425-825 |

### *SUPRA TPS RESISTANCE SPECIFICATIONS*

| Application | Clearance In. (mm) | Terminal | Ohmmeter Reading |
|---|---|---|---|
| Non-Turbo | 0 (0) | VTA & $E_2$ | 200-1200 |
| | .016 (.41) | IDL & $E_2$ | 2300 or Less |
| | .030 (.76) | IDL & $E_2$ | Infinity |
| | Fully Open | VTA & $E_2$ | 3500-10,300 |
| | | VC & $E_2$ | 4250-8250 |
| Turbo | 0 (0) | VTA & $E_2$ | 200-1200 |
| | .020 (.51) | IDL & $E_2$ | 2300 or Less |
| | .035 (.89) | IDL & $E_2$ | Infinity |
| | Fully Open | VTA & $E_2$ | 3500-10,300 |
| | | VC & $E_2$ | 4250-8250 |

### *TERCEL TPS RESISTANCE SPECIFICATIONS*

| Application | Clearance In. (mm) | Terminal | Ohmmeter Reading |
|---|---|---|---|
| 1.5L | .024 (.60) | IDL & $E_2$ | Continuity |
| | .024 (.60) | PSW & $E_2$ | No Continuity |
| | .024 (.60) | PSW & IDL | No Continuity |
| | .032 (.80) | IDL & $E_2$ | No Continuity |
| | .032 (.80) | PSW & $E_2$ | No Continuity |
| | .032 (.80) | PSW & IDL | No Continuity |
| | Fully Open | IDL & $E_2$ | No Continuity |
| | | PSW & $E_2$ | Continuity |
| | | PSW & IDL | No Continuity |

# 1991 ENGINE PERFORMANCE
# On-Vehicle Adjustments

## Camry, Celica, Corolla, Cressida, Land Cruiser, MR2, Pickup, Previa, Supra, Tercel, 4Runner

## ENGINE MECHANICAL

Before performing any on-vehicle adjustments to fuel or ignition systems, ensure engine mechanical condition is okay.

## VALVE CLEARANCE

### 4-CYLINDER

**Camry, Celica, Corolla, MR2 & Previa - 1)** Check and adjust valves with engine cold. On Previa, remove 3 screws and right front seat scuff plate. Remove bolt and disconnect right seat belt from floor panel.

**2)** Remove 4 bolts and right front seat. Remove 2 bolts and right front seat leg. Remove 2 bolts and jack holder. Remove 9 bolts and right engine service hole cover.

**3)** On all models, remove valve covers. Rotate crankshaft so No. 1 cylinder is at TDC of compression stroke. Ensure timing mark on crankshaft pulley aligns with "0" mark on timing chain cover. Ensure valves on No. 1 cylinder are closed.

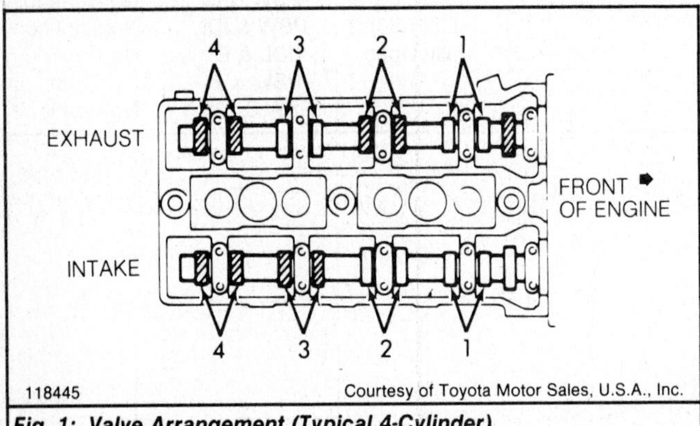


*Fig. 1: Valve Arrangement (Typical 4-Cylinder)*

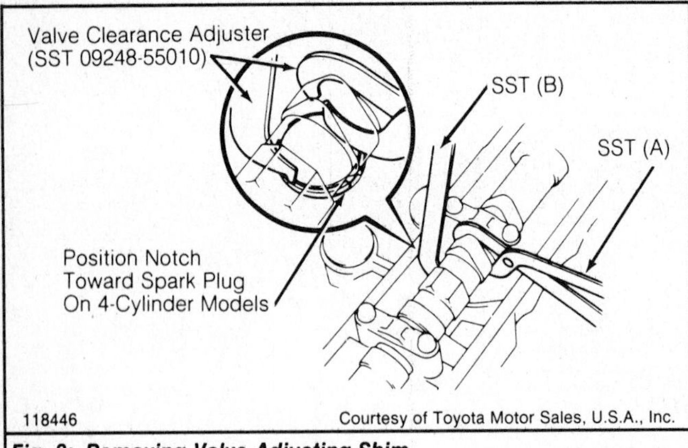


*Fig. 2: Removing Valve Adjusting Shim*

**4)** With No. 1 cylinder at TDC, check clearance on specified valves. See VALVE CLEARANCE ADJUSTMENT SEQUENCE (CAMRY, CELICA, COROLLA, MR2 & PREVIA) table. *See Fig. 1.* Using feeler gauge, measure and record clearance between valve lifter and camshaft. Ensure clearance is within specification. See VALVE CLEARANCE SPECIFICATIONS (4-CYLINDER) table.

**5)** To check remaining valves, rotate crankshaft 360 degrees (one full turn) until No. 4 piston is at TDC of compression stroke. Measure valve clearance on specified valves. See VALVE CLEARANCE ADJUSTMENT SEQUENCE (CAMRY, CELICA, COROLLA, MR2 & PREVIA) table. If valves require adjustment, rotate crankshaft so camshaft lobe on valve to be adjusted is facing upward, away from valve lifter.

**6)** Rotate valve lifter so notch on valve lifter is toward spark plug. Press valve lifter downward using Valve Clearance Adjuster (SST 09248-55010) and SST (A). *See Fig. 2.* Install SST (B) between camshaft and valve lifter. Remove SST (A).

**7)** Using small screwdriver and magnet, remove adjusting shim. Measure thickness of shim removed. Determine correct thickness of adjusting shim to be used. *See Figs. 3-11.* Install shim and recheck valve clearance. Install valve cover.

***VALVE CLEARANCE ADJUSTMENT SEQUENCE (CAMRY, CELICA, COROLLA, MR2 & PREVIA)***

| Piston No. On TDC | Adjust Intake Valves | Adjust Exhaust Valves |
|---|---|---|
| 1 | 1 & 2 | 1 & 3 |
| 4 | 3 & 4 | 2 & 4 |

***VALVE CLEARANCE SPECIFICATIONS (4-CYLINDER)***

| Application [1] | In. (mm) |
|---|---|
| Camry | |
| Exhaust | .011-.015 (.28-.38) |
| Intake | .007-.011 (.18-.28) |
| Celica | |
| 1.6L & 2.0L Turbo | |
| Exhaust | .008-.012 (.20-.30) |
| Intake | .006-.010 (.15-.25) |
| 2.2L | |
| Exhaust | .011-.015 (.28-.38) |
| Intake | .007-.011 (.18-.28) |
| Corolla | |
| Exhaust | .008-.012 (.20-.30) |
| Intake | .006-.010 (.15-.25) |
| MR2 | |
| 2.0L | |
| Exhaust | .008-.012 (.20-.30) |
| Intake | .006-.010 (.15-.25) |
| 2.2L | |
| Exhaust | .011-.015 (.28-.38) |
| Intake | .007-.011 (.18-.28) |
| Previa | |
| Exhaust | .010-.014 (.25-.35) |
| Intake | .006-.010 (.15-.25) |
| Pickup & 4Runner | |
| Exhaust | .012 (.30) |
| Intake | .008 (.20) |
| Tercel | |
| Exhaust & Intake | .008 (.20) |

[1] - On Pickup, Tercel and 4Runner, adjust valves at normal operating temperature. On all other models, adjust valves with engine cold.

# 1991 ENGINE PERFORMANCE
## On-Vehicle Adjustments (Cont.)

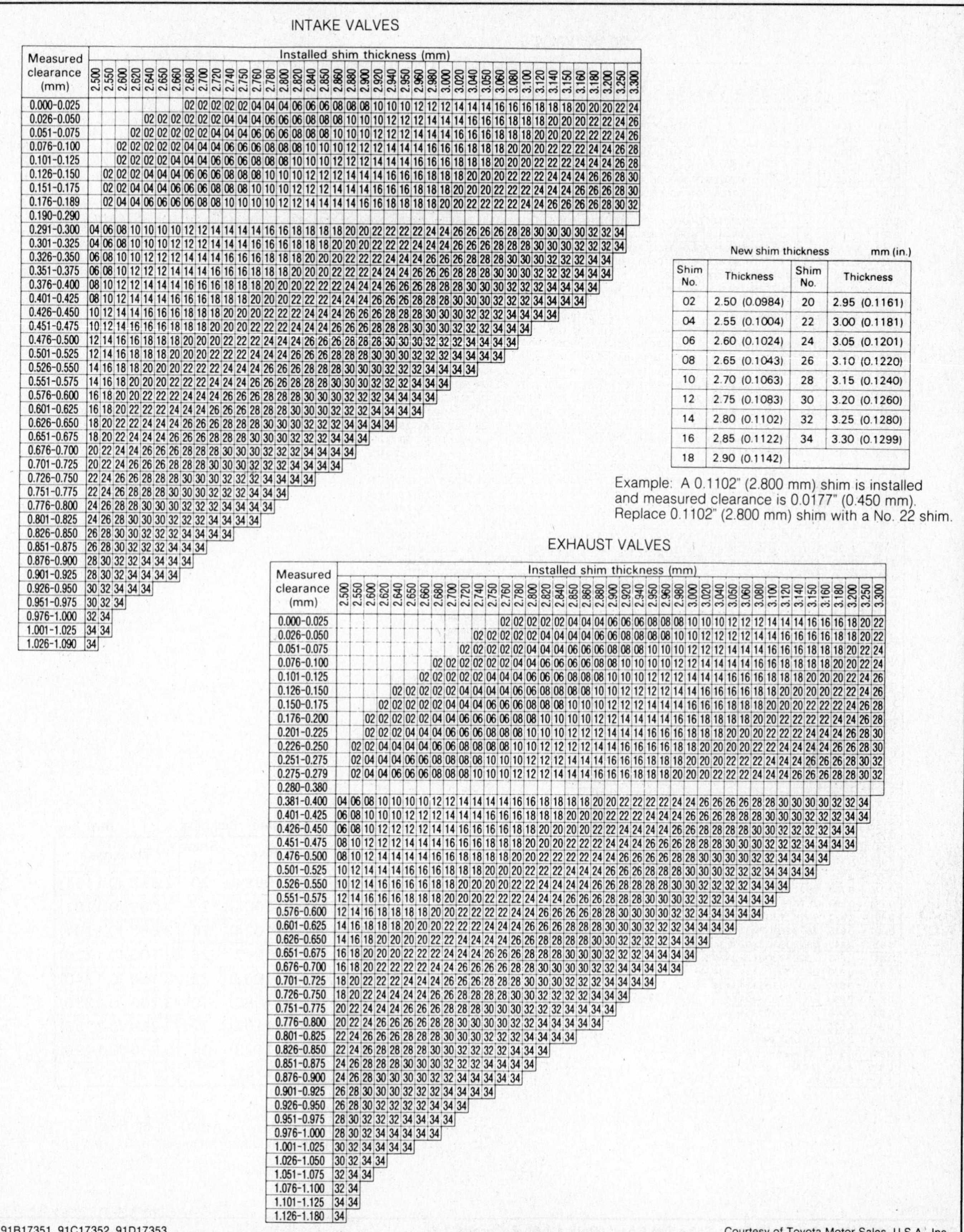

INTAKE VALVES

| Measured clearance (mm) | Installed shim thickness (mm) | | | | | | | | | | | | | | | | | | | | | | | | | | | | | | | | | | | | | | | |
|---|---|---|---|---|---|---|---|---|---|---|---|---|---|---|---|---|---|---|---|---|---|---|---|---|---|---|---|---|---|---|---|---|---|---|---|---|---|---|---|---|
| | 2.500 | 2.550 | 2.600 | 2.620 | 2.640 | 2.650 | 2.660 | 2.680 | 2.700 | 2.720 | 2.740 | 2.750 | 2.760 | 2.780 | 2.800 | 2.820 | 2.840 | 2.850 | 2.860 | 2.880 | 2.900 | 2.920 | 2.940 | 2.950 | 2.960 | 2.980 | 3.000 | 3.020 | 3.040 | 3.050 | 3.060 | 3.080 | 3.100 | 3.120 | 3.140 | 3.150 | 3.160 | 3.180 | 3.200 | 3.250 | 3.300 |
| 0.000-0.025 | | | | | | | | 02 | 02 | 02 | 02 | 02 | 04 | 04 | 04 | 06 | 06 | 06 | 08 | 08 | 08 | 10 | 10 | 10 | 12 | 12 | 12 | 14 | 14 | 14 | 16 | 16 | 16 | 18 | 18 | 18 | 20 | 20 | 20 | 22 | 24 |
| 0.026-0.050 | | | | | 02 | 02 | 02 | 02 | 02 | 02 | 04 | 04 | 04 | 06 | 06 | 06 | 08 | 08 | 08 | 10 | 10 | 10 | 12 | 12 | 12 | 14 | 14 | 14 | 16 | 16 | 16 | 18 | 18 | 18 | 20 | 20 | 20 | 22 | 22 | 24 | 26 |
| 0.051-0.075 | | | | 02 | 02 | 02 | 02 | 02 | 02 | 04 | 04 | 04 | 06 | 06 | 06 | 08 | 08 | 08 | 10 | 10 | 10 | 12 | 12 | 12 | 14 | 14 | 14 | 16 | 16 | 16 | 18 | 18 | 18 | 20 | 20 | 20 | 22 | 22 | 22 | 24 | 26 |
| 0.076-0.100 | | | 02 | 02 | 02 | 02 | 02 | 04 | 04 | 04 | 06 | 06 | 06 | 08 | 08 | 08 | 10 | 10 | 10 | 12 | 12 | 12 | 14 | 14 | 14 | 16 | 16 | 16 | 18 | 18 | 18 | 20 | 20 | 20 | 22 | 22 | 22 | 24 | 24 | 26 | 28 |
| 0.101-0.125 | | | 02 | 02 | 02 | 02 | 04 | 04 | 04 | 06 | 06 | 06 | 08 | 08 | 08 | 10 | 10 | 10 | 12 | 12 | 12 | 14 | 14 | 14 | 16 | 16 | 16 | 18 | 18 | 18 | 20 | 20 | 20 | 22 | 22 | 22 | 24 | 24 | 24 | 26 | 28 |
| 0.126-0.150 | | 02 | 02 | 02 | 04 | 04 | 04 | 06 | 06 | 06 | 08 | 08 | 08 | 10 | 10 | 10 | 12 | 12 | 12 | 14 | 14 | 14 | 16 | 16 | 16 | 18 | 18 | 18 | 20 | 20 | 20 | 22 | 22 | 22 | 24 | 24 | 24 | 26 | 26 | 28 | 30 |
| 0.151-0.175 | | 02 | 02 | 04 | 04 | 04 | 06 | 06 | 06 | 08 | 08 | 08 | 10 | 10 | 10 | 12 | 12 | 12 | 14 | 14 | 14 | 16 | 16 | 16 | 18 | 18 | 18 | 20 | 20 | 20 | 22 | 22 | 22 | 24 | 24 | 24 | 26 | 26 | 26 | 28 | 30 |
| 0.176-0.189 | | 02 | 04 | 04 | 06 | 06 | 06 | 06 | 08 | 08 | 10 | 10 | 10 | 10 | 12 | 12 | 14 | 14 | 14 | 14 | 16 | 16 | 18 | 18 | 18 | 18 | 20 | 20 | 22 | 22 | 22 | 22 | 24 | 24 | 26 | 26 | 26 | 26 | 28 | 30 | 32 |
| 0.190-0.290 | | | | | | | | | | | | | | | | | | | | | | | | | | | | | | | | | | | | | | | | | |
| 0.291-0.300 | 04 | 06 | 08 | 10 | 10 | 10 | 10 | 12 | 12 | 14 | 14 | 14 | 14 | 16 | 16 | 18 | 18 | 18 | 18 | 20 | 20 | 22 | 22 | 22 | 22 | 24 | 24 | 26 | 26 | 26 | 26 | 28 | 28 | 30 | 30 | 30 | 30 | 32 | 32 | 34 | |
| 0.301-0.325 | 04 | 06 | 08 | 10 | 10 | 10 | 12 | 12 | 12 | 14 | 14 | 14 | 16 | 16 | 16 | 18 | 18 | 18 | 20 | 20 | 20 | 22 | 22 | 22 | 24 | 24 | 24 | 26 | 26 | 26 | 28 | 28 | 28 | 30 | 30 | 30 | 32 | 32 | 32 | 34 | |
| 0.326-0.350 | 06 | 08 | 10 | 10 | 12 | 12 | 12 | 14 | 14 | 14 | 16 | 16 | 16 | 18 | 18 | 18 | 20 | 20 | 20 | 22 | 22 | 22 | 24 | 24 | 24 | 26 | 26 | 26 | 28 | 28 | 28 | 30 | 30 | 30 | 32 | 32 | 32 | 34 | 34 | | |
| 0.351-0.375 | 06 | 08 | 10 | 12 | 12 | 12 | 14 | 14 | 14 | 16 | 16 | 16 | 18 | 18 | 18 | 20 | 20 | 20 | 22 | 22 | 22 | 24 | 24 | 24 | 26 | 26 | 26 | 28 | 28 | 28 | 30 | 30 | 30 | 32 | 32 | 32 | 34 | 34 | 34 | | |
| 0.376-0.400 | 08 | 10 | 12 | 12 | 14 | 14 | 14 | 16 | 16 | 16 | 18 | 18 | 18 | 20 | 20 | 20 | 22 | 22 | 22 | 24 | 24 | 24 | 26 | 26 | 26 | 28 | 28 | 28 | 30 | 30 | 30 | 32 | 32 | 32 | 34 | 34 | 34 | 34 | | | |
| 0.401-0.425 | 08 | 10 | 12 | 14 | 14 | 14 | 16 | 16 | 16 | 18 | 18 | 18 | 20 | 20 | 20 | 22 | 22 | 22 | 24 | 24 | 24 | 26 | 26 | 26 | 28 | 28 | 28 | 30 | 30 | 30 | 32 | 32 | 32 | 34 | 34 | 34 | 34 | | | | |
| 0.426-0.450 | 10 | 12 | 14 | 14 | 16 | 16 | 16 | 18 | 18 | 18 | 20 | 20 | 20 | 22 | 22 | 22 | 24 | 24 | 24 | 26 | 26 | 26 | 28 | 28 | 28 | 30 | 30 | 30 | 32 | 32 | 32 | 34 | 34 | 34 | 34 | | | | | | |
| 0.451-0.475 | 10 | 12 | 14 | 16 | 16 | 16 | 18 | 18 | 18 | 20 | 20 | 20 | 22 | 22 | 22 | 24 | 24 | 24 | 26 | 26 | 26 | 28 | 28 | 28 | 30 | 30 | 30 | 32 | 32 | 32 | 34 | 34 | 34 | | | | | | | | |
| 0.476-0.500 | 12 | 14 | 16 | 16 | 18 | 18 | 18 | 20 | 20 | 20 | 22 | 22 | 22 | 24 | 24 | 24 | 26 | 26 | 26 | 28 | 28 | 28 | 30 | 30 | 30 | 32 | 32 | 32 | 34 | 34 | 34 | 34 | | | | | | | | | |
| 0.501-0.525 | 12 | 14 | 16 | 18 | 18 | 18 | 20 | 20 | 20 | 22 | 22 | 22 | 24 | 24 | 24 | 26 | 26 | 26 | 28 | 28 | 28 | 30 | 30 | 30 | 32 | 32 | 32 | 34 | 34 | 34 | 34 | | | | | | | | | | |
| 0.526-0.550 | 14 | 16 | 18 | 18 | 20 | 20 | 20 | 22 | 22 | 22 | 24 | 24 | 24 | 26 | 26 | 26 | 28 | 28 | 28 | 30 | 30 | 30 | 32 | 32 | 32 | 34 | 34 | 34 | 34 | | | | | | | | | | | | |
| 0.551-0.575 | 14 | 16 | 18 | 20 | 20 | 20 | 22 | 22 | 22 | 24 | 24 | 24 | 26 | 26 | 26 | 28 | 28 | 28 | 30 | 30 | 30 | 32 | 32 | 32 | 34 | 34 | 34 | | | | | | | | | | | | | | |
| 0.576-0.600 | 16 | 18 | 20 | 20 | 22 | 22 | 22 | 24 | 24 | 24 | 26 | 26 | 26 | 28 | 28 | 28 | 30 | 30 | 30 | 32 | 32 | 32 | 34 | 34 | 34 | 34 | | | | | | | | | | | | | | | |
| 0.601-0.625 | 16 | 18 | 20 | 22 | 22 | 22 | 24 | 24 | 24 | 26 | 26 | 26 | 28 | 28 | 28 | 30 | 30 | 30 | 32 | 32 | 32 | 34 | 34 | 34 | 34 | | | | | | | | | | | | | | | | |
| 0.626-0.650 | 18 | 20 | 22 | 22 | 24 | 24 | 24 | 26 | 26 | 26 | 28 | 28 | 28 | 30 | 30 | 30 | 32 | 32 | 32 | 34 | 34 | 34 | 34 | | | | | | | | | | | | | | | | | | |
| 0.651-0.675 | 18 | 20 | 22 | 24 | 24 | 24 | 26 | 26 | 26 | 28 | 28 | 28 | 30 | 30 | 30 | 32 | 32 | 32 | 34 | 34 | 34 | | | | | | | | | | | | | | | | | | | | |
| 0.676-0.700 | 20 | 22 | 24 | 24 | 26 | 26 | 26 | 28 | 28 | 28 | 30 | 30 | 30 | 32 | 32 | 32 | 34 | 34 | 34 | 34 | | | | | | | | | | | | | | | | | | | | | |
| 0.701-0.725 | 20 | 22 | 24 | 26 | 26 | 26 | 28 | 28 | 28 | 30 | 30 | 30 | 32 | 32 | 32 | 34 | 34 | 34 | 34 | | | | | | | | | | | | | | | | | | | | | | |
| 0.726-0.750 | 22 | 24 | 26 | 26 | 28 | 28 | 28 | 30 | 30 | 30 | 32 | 32 | 32 | 34 | 34 | 34 | 34 | | | | | | | | | | | | | | | | | | | | | | | | |
| 0.751-0.775 | 22 | 24 | 26 | 28 | 28 | 28 | 30 | 30 | 30 | 32 | 32 | 32 | 34 | 34 | 34 | | | | | | | | | | | | | | | | | | | | | | | | | | |
| 0.776-0.800 | 24 | 26 | 28 | 28 | 30 | 30 | 30 | 32 | 32 | 32 | 34 | 34 | 34 | 34 | | | | | | | | | | | | | | | | | | | | | | | | | | | |
| 0.801-0.825 | 24 | 26 | 28 | 30 | 30 | 30 | 32 | 32 | 32 | 34 | 34 | 34 | 34 | | | | | | | | | | | | | | | | | | | | | | | | | | | | |
| 0.826-0.850 | 26 | 28 | 30 | 30 | 32 | 32 | 32 | 34 | 34 | 34 | 34 | | | | | | | | | | | | | | | | | | | | | | | | | | | | | | |
| 0.851-0.875 | 26 | 28 | 30 | 32 | 32 | 32 | 34 | 34 | 34 | | | | | | | | | | | | | | | | | | | | | | | | | | | | | | | | |
| 0.876-0.900 | 28 | 30 | 32 | 32 | 34 | 34 | 34 | 34 | | | | | | | | | | | | | | | | | | | | | | | | | | | | | | | | | |
| 0.901-0.925 | 28 | 30 | 32 | 34 | 34 | 34 | 34 | | | | | | | | | | | | | | | | | | | | | | | | | | | | | | | | | | |
| 0.926-0.950 | 30 | 32 | 34 | 34 | 34 | | | | | | | | | | | | | | | | | | | | | | | | | | | | | | | | | | | | |
| 0.951-0.975 | 30 | 32 | 34 | | | | | | | | | | | | | | | | | | | | | | | | | | | | | | | | | | | | | | |
| 0.976-1.000 | 32 | 34 | | | | | | | | | | | | | | | | | | | | | | | | | | | | | | | | | | | | | | | |
| 1.001-1.025 | 34 | 34 | | | | | | | | | | | | | | | | | | | | | | | | | | | | | | | | | | | | | | | |
| 1.026-1.090 | 34 | | | | | | | | | | | | | | | | | | | | | | | | | | | | | | | | | | | | | | | | |

New shim thickness mm (in.)

| Shim No. | Thickness | Shim No. | Thickness |
|---|---|---|---|
| 02 | 2.50 (0.0984) | 20 | 2.95 (0.1161) |
| 04 | 2.55 (0.1004) | 22 | 3.00 (0.1181) |
| 06 | 2.60 (0.1024) | 24 | 3.05 (0.1201) |
| 08 | 2.65 (0.1043) | 26 | 3.10 (0.1220) |
| 10 | 2.70 (0.1063) | 28 | 3.15 (0.1240) |
| 12 | 2.75 (0.1083) | 30 | 3.20 (0.1260) |
| 14 | 2.80 (0.1102) | 32 | 3.25 (0.1280) |
| 16 | 2.85 (0.1122) | 34 | 3.30 (0.1299) |
| 18 | 2.90 (0.1142) | | |

Example: A 0.1102" (2.800 mm) shim is installed and measured clearance is 0.0177" (0.450 mm). Replace 0.1102" (2.800 mm) shim with a No. 22 shim.

EXHAUST VALVES

| Measured clearance (mm) | Installed shim thickness (mm) | | | | | | | | | | | | | | | | | | | | | | | | | | | | | | | | | | | | | | | |
|---|---|---|---|---|---|---|---|---|---|---|---|---|---|---|---|---|---|---|---|---|---|---|---|---|---|---|---|---|---|---|---|---|---|---|---|---|---|---|---|---|
| | 2.500 | 2.550 | 2.600 | 2.620 | 2.640 | 2.650 | 2.660 | 2.680 | 2.700 | 2.720 | 2.740 | 2.750 | 2.760 | 2.780 | 2.800 | 2.820 | 2.840 | 2.850 | 2.860 | 2.880 | 2.900 | 2.920 | 2.940 | 2.950 | 2.960 | 2.980 | 3.000 | 3.020 | 3.040 | 3.050 | 3.060 | 3.080 | 3.100 | 3.120 | 3.140 | 3.150 | 3.160 | 3.180 | 3.200 | 3.250 | 3.300 |
| 0.000-0.025 | | | | | | | | | | | | | 02 | 02 | 02 | 02 | 02 | 04 | 04 | 04 | 06 | 06 | 06 | 08 | 08 | 08 | 10 | 10 | 10 | 12 | 12 | 12 | 14 | 14 | 14 | 16 | 16 | 16 | 18 | 20 | 22 |
| 0.026-0.050 | | | | | | | | | | | 02 | 02 | 02 | 02 | 02 | 04 | 04 | 04 | 04 | 06 | 06 | 08 | 08 | 08 | 08 | 10 | 10 | 12 | 12 | 12 | 12 | 14 | 14 | 16 | 16 | 16 | 16 | 18 | 18 | 20 | 22 |
| 0.051-0.075 | | | | | | | | | | 02 | 02 | 02 | 02 | 02 | 04 | 04 | 04 | 06 | 06 | 06 | 08 | 08 | 08 | 10 | 10 | 10 | 12 | 12 | 12 | 14 | 14 | 14 | 16 | 16 | 16 | 18 | 18 | 18 | 20 | 22 | 24 |
| 0.076-0.100 | | | | | | | | 02 | 02 | 02 | 02 | 02 | 02 | 04 | 04 | 06 | 06 | 06 | 06 | 08 | 08 | 10 | 10 | 10 | 10 | 12 | 12 | 14 | 14 | 14 | 14 | 16 | 16 | 18 | 18 | 18 | 18 | 20 | 20 | 22 | 24 |
| 0.101-0.125 | | | | | | | 02 | 02 | 02 | 02 | 02 | 04 | 04 | 04 | 06 | 06 | 06 | 08 | 08 | 08 | 10 | 10 | 10 | 12 | 12 | 12 | 14 | 14 | 14 | 16 | 16 | 16 | 18 | 18 | 18 | 20 | 20 | 20 | 22 | 24 | 26 |
| 0.126-0.150 | | | | | 02 | 02 | 02 | 02 | 02 | 04 | 04 | 04 | 04 | 06 | 06 | 08 | 08 | 08 | 08 | 10 | 10 | 12 | 12 | 12 | 12 | 14 | 14 | 16 | 16 | 16 | 16 | 18 | 18 | 20 | 20 | 20 | 20 | 22 | 22 | 24 | 26 |
| 0.150-0.175 | | | | 02 | 02 | 02 | 02 | 02 | 04 | 04 | 04 | 06 | 06 | 06 | 08 | 08 | 08 | 10 | 10 | 10 | 12 | 12 | 12 | 14 | 14 | 14 | 16 | 16 | 16 | 18 | 18 | 18 | 20 | 20 | 20 | 22 | 22 | 22 | 24 | 26 | 28 |
| 0.176-0.200 | | | 02 | 02 | 02 | 02 | 02 | 04 | 04 | 06 | 06 | 06 | 06 | 08 | 08 | 10 | 10 | 10 | 10 | 12 | 12 | 14 | 14 | 14 | 14 | 16 | 16 | 18 | 18 | 18 | 18 | 20 | 20 | 22 | 22 | 22 | 22 | 24 | 24 | 26 | 28 |
| 0.201-0.225 | | | 02 | 02 | 02 | 04 | 04 | 04 | 06 | 06 | 06 | 08 | 08 | 08 | 10 | 10 | 10 | 12 | 12 | 12 | 14 | 14 | 14 | 16 | 16 | 16 | 18 | 18 | 18 | 20 | 20 | 20 | 22 | 22 | 22 | 24 | 24 | 24 | 26 | 28 | 30 |
| 0.226-0.250 | | 02 | 02 | 04 | 04 | 04 | 04 | 06 | 06 | 08 | 08 | 08 | 08 | 10 | 10 | 12 | 12 | 12 | 12 | 14 | 14 | 16 | 16 | 16 | 16 | 18 | 18 | 20 | 20 | 20 | 20 | 22 | 22 | 24 | 24 | 24 | 24 | 26 | 26 | 28 | 30 |
| 0.251-0.275 | | 02 | 04 | 04 | 04 | 06 | 06 | 08 | 08 | 08 | 08 | 10 | 10 | 10 | 12 | 12 | 12 | 14 | 14 | 14 | 16 | 16 | 16 | 18 | 18 | 18 | 20 | 20 | 20 | 22 | 22 | 22 | 24 | 24 | 24 | 26 | 26 | 26 | 28 | 30 | 32 |
| 0.275-0.279 | | 02 | 04 | 04 | 06 | 06 | 06 | 08 | 08 | 08 | 10 | 10 | 10 | 12 | 12 | 12 | 14 | 14 | 14 | 16 | 16 | 16 | 18 | 18 | 18 | 20 | 20 | 20 | 22 | 22 | 22 | 24 | 24 | 24 | 26 | 26 | 26 | 28 | 28 | 30 | 32 |
| 0.280-0.380 | | | | | | | | | | | | | | | | | | | | | | | | | | | | | | | | | | | | | | | | | |
| 0.381-0.400 | 04 | 06 | 08 | 10 | 10 | 10 | 10 | 12 | 12 | 14 | 14 | 14 | 14 | 16 | 16 | 18 | 18 | 18 | 18 | 20 | 20 | 22 | 22 | 22 | 22 | 24 | 24 | 26 | 26 | 26 | 26 | 28 | 28 | 30 | 30 | 30 | 30 | 32 | 32 | 34 | |
| 0.401-0.425 | 06 | 08 | 10 | 10 | 10 | 12 | 12 | 12 | 14 | 14 | 14 | 16 | 16 | 16 | 18 | 18 | 18 | 20 | 20 | 20 | 22 | 22 | 22 | 24 | 24 | 24 | 26 | 26 | 26 | 28 | 28 | 28 | 30 | 30 | 30 | 32 | 32 | 32 | 34 | 34 | |
| 0.426-0.450 | 06 | 08 | 10 | 12 | 12 | 12 | 12 | 14 | 14 | 16 | 16 | 16 | 16 | 18 | 18 | 20 | 20 | 20 | 20 | 22 | 22 | 24 | 24 | 24 | 24 | 26 | 26 | 28 | 28 | 28 | 28 | 30 | 30 | 32 | 32 | 32 | 32 | 34 | 34 | | |
| 0.451-0.475 | 08 | 10 | 12 | 12 | 12 | 14 | 14 | 14 | 16 | 16 | 16 | 18 | 18 | 18 | 20 | 20 | 20 | 22 | 22 | 22 | 24 | 24 | 24 | 26 | 26 | 26 | 28 | 28 | 28 | 30 | 30 | 30 | 32 | 32 | 32 | 34 | 34 | 34 | 34 | | |
| 0.476-0.500 | 08 | 10 | 12 | 14 | 14 | 14 | 14 | 16 | 16 | 18 | 18 | 18 | 18 | 20 | 20 | 22 | 22 | 22 | 22 | 24 | 24 | 26 | 26 | 26 | 26 | 28 | 28 | 30 | 30 | 30 | 30 | 32 | 32 | 34 | 34 | 34 | 34 | | | | |
| 0.501-0.525 | 10 | 12 | 14 | 14 | 14 | 16 | 16 | 16 | 18 | 18 | 18 | 20 | 20 | 20 | 22 | 22 | 22 | 24 | 24 | 24 | 26 | 26 | 26 | 28 | 28 | 28 | 30 | 30 | 30 | 32 | 32 | 32 | 34 | 34 | 34 | 34 | | | | | |
| 0.526-0.550 | 10 | 12 | 14 | 16 | 16 | 16 | 16 | 18 | 18 | 20 | 20 | 20 | 20 | 22 | 22 | 24 | 24 | 24 | 24 | 26 | 26 | 28 | 28 | 28 | 28 | 30 | 30 | 32 | 32 | 32 | 32 | 34 | 34 | 34 | | | | | | | |
| 0.551-0.575 | 12 | 14 | 16 | 16 | 16 | 18 | 18 | 18 | 20 | 20 | 20 | 22 | 22 | 22 | 24 | 24 | 24 | 26 | 26 | 26 | 28 | 28 | 28 | 30 | 30 | 30 | 32 | 32 | 32 | 34 | 34 | 34 | 34 | | | | | | | | |
| 0.576-0.600 | 12 | 14 | 16 | 18 | 18 | 18 | 18 | 20 | 20 | 22 | 22 | 22 | 22 | 24 | 24 | 26 | 26 | 26 | 26 | 28 | 28 | 30 | 30 | 30 | 30 | 32 | 32 | 34 | 34 | 34 | 34 | 34 | | | | | | | | | |
| 0.601-0.625 | 14 | 16 | 18 | 18 | 18 | 20 | 20 | 20 | 22 | 22 | 22 | 24 | 24 | 24 | 26 | 26 | 26 | 28 | 28 | 28 | 30 | 30 | 30 | 32 | 32 | 32 | 34 | 34 | 34 | 34 | | | | | | | | | | | |
| 0.626-0.650 | 14 | 16 | 18 | 20 | 20 | 20 | 20 | 22 | 22 | 24 | 24 | 24 | 24 | 26 | 26 | 28 | 28 | 28 | 28 | 30 | 30 | 32 | 32 | 32 | 32 | 34 | 34 | 34 | | | | | | | | | | | | | |
| 0.651-0.675 | 16 | 18 | 20 | 20 | 20 | 22 | 22 | 22 | 24 | 24 | 24 | 26 | 26 | 26 | 28 | 28 | 28 | 30 | 30 | 30 | 32 | 32 | 32 | 34 | 34 | 34 | 34 | | | | | | | | | | | | | | |
| 0.676-0.700 | 16 | 18 | 20 | 22 | 22 | 22 | 22 | 24 | 24 | 26 | 26 | 26 | 26 | 28 | 28 | 30 | 30 | 30 | 30 | 32 | 32 | 34 | 34 | 34 | 34 | 34 | | | | | | | | | | | | | | | |
| 0.701-0.725 | 18 | 20 | 22 | 22 | 22 | 24 | 24 | 24 | 26 | 26 | 26 | 28 | 28 | 28 | 30 | 30 | 30 | 32 | 32 | 32 | 34 | 34 | 34 | 34 | | | | | | | | | | | | | | | | | |
| 0.726-0.750 | 18 | 20 | 22 | 24 | 24 | 24 | 24 | 26 | 26 | 28 | 28 | 28 | 28 | 30 | 30 | 32 | 32 | 32 | 32 | 34 | 34 | 34 | | | | | | | | | | | | | | | | | | | |
| 0.751-0.775 | 20 | 22 | 24 | 24 | 24 | 26 | 26 | 26 | 28 | 28 | 28 | 30 | 30 | 30 | 32 | 32 | 32 | 34 | 34 | 34 | 34 | | | | | | | | | | | | | | | | | | | | |
| 0.776-0.800 | 20 | 22 | 24 | 26 | 26 | 26 | 26 | 28 | 28 | 30 | 30 | 30 | 30 | 32 | 32 | 34 | 34 | 34 | 34 | 34 | | | | | | | | | | | | | | | | | | | | | |
| 0.801-0.825 | 22 | 24 | 26 | 26 | 26 | 28 | 28 | 28 | 30 | 30 | 30 | 32 | 32 | 32 | 34 | 34 | 34 | 34 | | | | | | | | | | | | | | | | | | | | | | | |
| 0.826-0.850 | 22 | 24 | 26 | 28 | 28 | 28 | 28 | 30 | 30 | 32 | 32 | 32 | 32 | 34 | 34 | 34 | | | | | | | | | | | | | | | | | | | | | | | | | |
| 0.851-0.875 | 24 | 26 | 28 | 28 | 28 | 30 | 30 | 30 | 32 | 32 | 32 | 34 | 34 | 34 | 34 | | | | | | | | | | | | | | | | | | | | | | | | | | |
| 0.876-0.900 | 24 | 26 | 28 | 30 | 30 | 30 | 30 | 32 | 32 | 34 | 34 | 34 | 34 | 34 | | | | | | | | | | | | | | | | | | | | | | | | | | | |
| 0.901-0.925 | 26 | 28 | 30 | 30 | 30 | 32 | 32 | 32 | 34 | 34 | 34 | 34 | | | | | | | | | | | | | | | | | | | | | | | | | | | | | |
| 0.926-0.950 | 26 | 28 | 30 | 32 | 32 | 32 | 32 | 34 | 34 | 34 | | | | | | | | | | | | | | | | | | | | | | | | | | | | | | | |
| 0.951-0.975 | 28 | 30 | 32 | 32 | 32 | 34 | 34 | 34 | 34 | | | | | | | | | | | | | | | | | | | | | | | | | | | | | | | | |
| 0.976-1.000 | 28 | 30 | 32 | 34 | 34 | 34 | 34 | 34 | | | | | | | | | | | | | | | | | | | | | | | | | | | | | | | | | |
| 1.001-1.025 | 30 | 32 | 34 | 34 | 34 | 34 | | | | | | | | | | | | | | | | | | | | | | | | | | | | | | | | | | | |
| 1.026-1.050 | 30 | 32 | 34 | 34 | | | | | | | | | | | | | | | | | | | | | | | | | | | | | | | | | | | | | |
| 1.051-1.075 | 32 | 34 | 34 | | | | | | | | | | | | | | | | | | | | | | | | | | | | | | | | | | | | | | |
| 1.076-1.100 | 32 | 34 | | | | | | | | | | | | | | | | | | | | | | | | | | | | | | | | | | | | | | | |
| 1.101-1.125 | 34 | 34 | | | | | | | | | | | | | | | | | | | | | | | | | | | | | | | | | | | | | | | |
| 1.126-1.180 | 34 | | | | | | | | | | | | | | | | | | | | | | | | | | | | | | | | | | | | | | | | |

91B17351 91C17352 91D17353

Courtesy of Toyota Motor Sales, U.S.A., Inc.

*Fig. 3: Intake & Exhaust Valve Adjusting Shim Selection Charts (Camry 1.6L, Celica 2.2L & MR2 2.2L)*

# 1991 ENGINE PERFORMANCE
## On-Vehicle Adjustments (Cont.)

INTAKE VALVES

| Measured Clearance (mm) | Installed Shim Thickness (mm) | | | | | | | | | | | | | | | | | | | | | | | | | | | | | | | | | | | | | | | | | | | | |
|---|---|---|---|---|---|---|---|---|---|---|---|---|---|---|---|---|---|---|---|---|---|---|---|---|---|---|---|---|---|---|---|---|---|---|---|---|---|---|---|---|---|---|---|---|---|
| | 2.500 | 2.525 | 2.550 | 2.575 | 2.600 | 2.620 | 2.640 | 2.650 | 2.660 | 2.680 | 2.700 | 2.720 | 2.740 | 2.750 | 2.760 | 2.780 | 2.800 | 2.820 | 2.840 | 2.850 | 2.860 | 2.880 | 2.900 | 2.920 | 2.940 | 2.950 | 2.960 | 2.980 | 3.000 | 3.020 | 3.040 | 3.050 | 3.060 | 3.080 | 3.100 | 3.120 | 3.140 | 3.150 | 3.160 | 3.180 | 3.200 | 3.225 | 3.250 | 3.275 | 3.300 |
| 0.000 — 0.009 | | | | | | | | | | 02 | 02 | 04 | 04 | 04 | 04 | 06 | 06 | 08 | 08 | 08 | 08 | 10 | 10 | 12 | 12 | 12 | 12 | 14 | 14 | 16 | 16 | 16 | 16 | 18 | 18 | 20 | 20 | 20 | 20 | 22 | 22 | 24 | 24 | 26 | 26 |
| 0.010 — 0.025 | | | | | | | | | 02 | 02 | 02 | 04 | 04 | 04 | 06 | 06 | 06 | 08 | 08 | 08 | 10 | 10 | 10 | 12 | 12 | 12 | 14 | 14 | 14 | 16 | 16 | 16 | 18 | 18 | 18 | 20 | 20 | 20 | 22 | 22 | 22 | 24 | 24 | 26 | 26 |
| 0.026 — 0.029 | | | | | | | | 02 | 02 | 02 | 04 | 04 | 04 | 06 | 06 | 06 | 08 | 08 | 08 | 10 | 10 | 10 | 12 | 12 | 12 | 14 | 14 | 14 | 16 | 16 | 16 | 18 | 18 | 18 | 20 | 20 | 20 | 22 | 22 | 22 | 24 | 24 | 26 | 26 | 28 |
| 0.030 — 0.040 | | | | | | | 02 | 02 | 02 | 02 | 04 | 04 | 04 | 06 | 06 | 06 | 08 | 08 | 08 | 10 | 10 | 10 | 12 | 12 | 12 | 14 | 14 | 14 | 16 | 16 | 16 | 18 | 18 | 18 | 20 | 20 | 20 | 22 | 22 | 22 | 24 | 24 | 26 | 26 | 28 |
| 0.041 — 0.050 | | | | | | | 02 | 02 | 02 | 02 | 04 | 04 | 06 | 06 | 06 | 06 | 08 | 08 | 10 | 10 | 10 | 10 | 12 | 12 | 14 | 14 | 14 | 14 | 16 | 16 | 18 | 18 | 18 | 18 | 20 | 20 | 22 | 22 | 22 | 22 | 24 | 24 | 26 | 26 | 28 |
| 0.051 — 0.070 | | | | | | 02 | 02 | 02 | 02 | 04 | 04 | 06 | 06 | 06 | 06 | 08 | 08 | 10 | 10 | 10 | 10 | 12 | 12 | 14 | 14 | 14 | 14 | 16 | 16 | 18 | 18 | 18 | 18 | 20 | 20 | 22 | 22 | 22 | 22 | 24 | 24 | 26 | 26 | 28 | 28 |
| 0.071 — 0.075 | | | | | 02 | 02 | 02 | 02 | 04 | 04 | 04 | 06 | 06 | 06 | 08 | 08 | 08 | 10 | 10 | 10 | 12 | 12 | 12 | 14 | 14 | 14 | 16 | 16 | 16 | 18 | 18 | 18 | 20 | 20 | 20 | 22 | 22 | 22 | 24 | 24 | 24 | 26 | 26 | 28 | 28 |
| 0.076 — 0.090 | | | | | 02 | 02 | 02 | 04 | 04 | 04 | 06 | 06 | 06 | 08 | 08 | 08 | 10 | 10 | 10 | 12 | 12 | 12 | 14 | 14 | 14 | 16 | 16 | 16 | 18 | 18 | 18 | 20 | 20 | 20 | 22 | 22 | 22 | 24 | 24 | 24 | 26 | 26 | 28 | 28 | 30 |
| 0.091 — 0.100 | | | | | 02 | 02 | 04 | 04 | 04 | 04 | 06 | 06 | 08 | 08 | 08 | 08 | 10 | 10 | 12 | 12 | 12 | 12 | 14 | 14 | 16 | 16 | 16 | 16 | 18 | 18 | 20 | 20 | 20 | 20 | 22 | 22 | 24 | 24 | 24 | 24 | 26 | 26 | 28 | 28 | 30 |
| 0.101 — 0.120 | | | | 02 | 02 | 02 | 04 | 04 | 04 | 06 | 06 | 06 | 08 | 08 | 08 | 10 | 10 | 10 | 12 | 12 | 12 | 14 | 14 | 14 | 16 | 16 | 16 | 18 | 18 | 18 | 20 | 20 | 20 | 22 | 22 | 22 | 24 | 24 | 24 | 26 | 26 | 28 | 28 | 30 | 30 |
| 0.121 — 0.125 | | | 02 | 02 | 02 | 04 | 04 | 04 | 06 | 06 | 06 | 08 | 08 | 08 | 10 | 10 | 10 | 12 | 12 | 12 | 14 | 14 | 14 | 16 | 16 | 16 | 18 | 18 | 18 | 20 | 20 | 20 | 22 | 22 | 22 | 24 | 24 | 24 | 26 | 26 | 26 | 28 | 28 | 30 | 30 |
| 0.126 — 0.140 | | | 02 | 02 | 04 | 04 | 04 | 06 | 06 | 06 | 08 | 08 | 08 | 10 | 10 | 10 | 12 | 12 | 12 | 14 | 14 | 14 | 16 | 16 | 16 | 18 | 18 | 18 | 20 | 20 | 20 | 22 | 22 | 22 | 24 | 24 | 24 | 26 | 26 | 26 | 28 | 28 | 30 | 30 | 32 |
| 0.141 — 0.149 | | | 02 | 02 | 04 | 04 | 06 | 06 | 06 | 06 | 08 | 08 | 10 | 10 | 10 | 10 | 12 | 12 | 14 | 14 | 14 | 14 | 16 | 16 | 18 | 18 | 18 | 18 | 20 | 20 | 22 | 22 | 22 | 22 | 24 | 24 | 26 | 26 | 26 | 26 | 28 | 28 | 30 | 30 | 32 |
| 0.150 — 0.250 | | | | | | | | | | | | | | | | | | | | | | | | | | | | | | | | | | | | | | | | | | | | | |
| 0.251 — 0.270 | 04 | 06 | 06 | 08 | 08 | 10 | 10 | 10 | 10 | 12 | 12 | 14 | 14 | 14 | 14 | 16 | 16 | 18 | 18 | 18 | 18 | 20 | 20 | 22 | 22 | 22 | 22 | 24 | 24 | 26 | 26 | 26 | 26 | 28 | 28 | 30 | 30 | 30 | 30 | 32 | 32 | 34 | 34 | | |
| 0.271 — 0.275 | 04 | 06 | 06 | 08 | 08 | 10 | 10 | 10 | 12 | 12 | 12 | 14 | 14 | 14 | 16 | 16 | 16 | 18 | 18 | 18 | 20 | 20 | 20 | 22 | 22 | 22 | 24 | 24 | 24 | 26 | 26 | 26 | 28 | 28 | 28 | 30 | 30 | 30 | 32 | 32 | 32 | 34 | 34 | | |
| 0.276 — 0.290 | 06 | 06 | 08 | 08 | 10 | 10 | 10 | 12 | 12 | 12 | 14 | 14 | 14 | 16 | 16 | 16 | 18 | 18 | 18 | 20 | 20 | 20 | 22 | 22 | 22 | 24 | 24 | 24 | 26 | 26 | 26 | 28 | 28 | 28 | 30 | 30 | 30 | 32 | 32 | 32 | 34 | 34 | | | |
| 0.291 — 0.300 | 06 | 06 | 08 | 08 | 10 | 10 | 12 | 12 | 12 | 12 | 14 | 14 | 16 | 16 | 16 | 16 | 18 | 18 | 20 | 20 | 20 | 20 | 22 | 22 | 24 | 24 | 24 | 24 | 26 | 26 | 28 | 28 | 28 | 28 | 30 | 30 | 32 | 32 | 32 | 32 | 34 | 34 | | | |
| 0.301 — 0.320 | 06 | 08 | 08 | 10 | 10 | 12 | 12 | 12 | 12 | 14 | 14 | 16 | 16 | 16 | 16 | 18 | 18 | 20 | 20 | 20 | 20 | 22 | 22 | 24 | 24 | 24 | 24 | 26 | 26 | 28 | 28 | 28 | 28 | 30 | 30 | 32 | 32 | 32 | 32 | 34 | 34 | | | | |
| 0.321 — 0.325 | 06 | 08 | 08 | 10 | 10 | 12 | 12 | 12 | 14 | 14 | 24 | 16 | 16 | 16 | 18 | 18 | 18 | 20 | 20 | 20 | 22 | 22 | 22 | 24 | 24 | 24 | 26 | 26 | 26 | 28 | 28 | 28 | 30 | 30 | 30 | 32 | 32 | 32 | 34 | 34 | 34 | | | | |
| 0.326 — 0.340 | 08 | 08 | 10 | 10 | 12 | 12 | 12 | 14 | 14 | 24 | 16 | 16 | 16 | 18 | 18 | 18 | 20 | 20 | 20 | 22 | 22 | 22 | 24 | 24 | 24 | 26 | 26 | 26 | 28 | 28 | 28 | 30 | 30 | 30 | 32 | 32 | 32 | 34 | 34 | 34 | | | | | |
| 0.341 — 0.350 | 08 | 08 | 10 | 10 | 12 | 12 | 14 | 14 | 14 | 14 | 16 | 16 | 18 | 18 | 18 | 18 | 20 | 20 | 22 | 22 | 22 | 22 | 24 | 24 | 26 | 26 | 26 | 26 | 28 | 28 | 30 | 30 | 30 | 30 | 32 | 32 | 34 | 34 | 34 | | | | | | |
| 0.351 — 0.370 | 08 | 10 | 10 | 12 | 12 | 14 | 14 | 14 | 14 | 16 | 16 | 18 | 18 | 18 | 18 | 20 | 20 | 22 | 22 | 22 | 22 | 24 | 24 | 26 | 26 | 26 | 26 | 28 | 28 | 30 | 30 | 30 | 30 | 32 | 32 | 34 | 34 | 34 | 34 | | | | | | |
| 0.371 — 0.375 | 08 | 10 | 10 | 12 | 12 | 14 | 14 | 14 | 16 | 16 | 16 | 18 | 18 | 18 | 20 | 20 | 20 | 22 | 22 | 22 | 24 | 24 | 24 | 26 | 26 | 26 | 28 | 28 | 28 | 30 | 30 | 30 | 32 | 32 | 32 | 34 | 34 | 34 | | | | | | | |
| 0.376 — 0.390 | 10 | 10 | 12 | 12 | 14 | 14 | 14 | 16 | 16 | 16 | 18 | 18 | 18 | 20 | 20 | 20 | 22 | 22 | 22 | 24 | 24 | 24 | 26 | 26 | 26 | 28 | 28 | 28 | 30 | 30 | 30 | 32 | 32 | 32 | 34 | 34 | 34 | | | | | | | | |
| 0.391 — 0.400 | 10 | 10 | 12 | 12 | 14 | 14 | 16 | 16 | 16 | 16 | 18 | 18 | 20 | 20 | 20 | 20 | 22 | 22 | 24 | 24 | 24 | 24 | 26 | 26 | 28 | 28 | 28 | 28 | 30 | 30 | 32 | 32 | 32 | 32 | 34 | 34 | | | | | | | | | |
| 0.401 — 0.420 | 10 | 12 | 12 | 14 | 14 | 16 | 16 | 16 | 16 | 18 | 18 | 20 | 20 | 20 | 20 | 22 | 22 | 24 | 24 | 24 | 24 | 26 | 26 | 28 | 28 | 28 | 28 | 30 | 30 | 32 | 32 | 32 | 32 | 34 | 34 | | | | | | | | | | |
| 0.421 — 0.425 | 10 | 12 | 12 | 14 | 14 | 16 | 16 | 16 | 18 | 18 | 18 | 20 | 20 | 20 | 22 | 22 | 22 | 24 | 24 | 24 | 26 | 26 | 26 | 28 | 28 | 28 | 30 | 30 | 30 | 32 | 32 | 32 | 34 | 34 | 34 | | | | | | | | | | |
| 0.426 — 0.440 | 12 | 12 | 14 | 14 | 16 | 16 | 16 | 18 | 18 | 18 | 20 | 20 | 20 | 22 | 22 | 22 | 24 | 24 | 24 | 26 | 26 | 26 | 28 | 28 | 28 | 30 | 30 | 30 | 32 | 32 | 32 | 34 | 34 | 34 | | | | | | | | | | | |
| 0.441 — 0.450 | 12 | 12 | 14 | 14 | 16 | 16 | 18 | 18 | 18 | 18 | 20 | 20 | 22 | 22 | 22 | 22 | 24 | 24 | 26 | 26 | 26 | 26 | 28 | 28 | 30 | 30 | 30 | 30 | 32 | 32 | 34 | 34 | 34 | 34 | | | | | | | | | | | |
| 0.451 — 0.470 | 12 | 14 | 14 | 16 | 16 | 18 | 18 | 18 | 18 | 20 | 20 | 22 | 22 | 22 | 22 | 24 | 24 | 26 | 26 | 26 | 26 | 28 | 28 | 30 | 30 | 30 | 30 | 32 | 32 | 34 | 34 | 34 | 34 | | | | | | | | | | | | |
| 0.471 — 0.475 | 12 | 14 | 14 | 16 | 16 | 18 | 18 | 18 | 20 | 20 | 20 | 22 | 22 | 22 | 24 | 24 | 24 | 26 | 26 | 26 | 28 | 28 | 28 | 30 | 30 | 30 | 32 | 32 | 32 | 34 | 34 | 34 | | | | | | | | | | | | | |
| 0.476 — 0.490 | 14 | 14 | 16 | 16 | 18 | 18 | 18 | 20 | 20 | 20 | 22 | 22 | 22 | 24 | 24 | 24 | 26 | 26 | 26 | 28 | 28 | 28 | 30 | 30 | 30 | 32 | 32 | 32 | 34 | 34 | 34 | | | | | | | | | | | | | | |
| 0.491 — 0.500 | 14 | 14 | 16 | 16 | 18 | 18 | 20 | 20 | 20 | 20 | 22 | 22 | 24 | 24 | 24 | 24 | 26 | 26 | 28 | 28 | 28 | 28 | 30 | 30 | 32 | 32 | 32 | 32 | 34 | 34 | | | | | | | | | | | | | | | |
| 0.501 — 0.520 | 14 | 16 | 16 | 18 | 18 | 20 | 20 | 20 | 20 | 22 | 22 | 24 | 24 | 24 | 24 | 26 | 26 | 28 | 28 | 28 | 28 | 30 | 30 | 32 | 32 | 32 | 32 | 34 | 34 | | | | | | | | | | | | | | | | |
| 0.521 — 0.525 | 14 | 16 | 16 | 18 | 18 | 20 | 20 | 20 | 22 | 22 | 22 | 24 | 24 | 24 | 26 | 26 | 26 | 28 | 28 | 28 | 30 | 30 | 30 | 32 | 32 | 32 | 34 | 34 | 34 | | | | | | | | | | | | | | | | |
| 0.526 — 0.540 | 16 | 16 | 18 | 18 | 20 | 20 | 20 | 22 | 22 | 22 | 24 | 24 | 24 | 26 | 26 | 26 | 28 | 28 | 28 | 30 | 30 | 30 | 32 | 32 | 32 | 34 | 34 | 34 | | | | | | | | | | | | | | | | | |
| 0.541 — 0.550 | 16 | 16 | 18 | 18 | 20 | 20 | 22 | 22 | 22 | 22 | 24 | 24 | 26 | 26 | 26 | 26 | 28 | 28 | 30 | 30 | 30 | 30 | 32 | 32 | 34 | 34 | 34 | 34 | | | | | | | | | | | | | | | | | |
| 0.551 — 0.570 | 16 | 18 | 18 | 20 | 20 | 22 | 22 | 22 | 22 | 24 | 24 | 26 | 26 | 26 | 26 | 28 | 28 | 30 | 30 | 30 | 30 | 32 | 32 | 34 | 34 | 34 | 34 | | | | | | | | | | | | | | | | | | |
| 0.571 — 0.575 | 16 | 18 | 18 | 20 | 20 | 22 | 22 | 22 | 24 | 24 | 24 | 26 | 26 | 26 | 28 | 28 | 28 | 30 | 30 | 30 | 32 | 32 | 32 | 34 | 34 | 34 | | | | | | | | | | | | | | | | | | | |
| 0.575 — 0.590 | 18 | 18 | 20 | 20 | 22 | 22 | 22 | 24 | 24 | 24 | 26 | 26 | 26 | 28 | 28 | 28 | 30 | 30 | 30 | 32 | 32 | 32 | 34 | 34 | 34 | | | | | | | | | | | | | | | | | | | | |
| 0.591 — 0.600 | 18 | 18 | 20 | 20 | 22 | 22 | 24 | 24 | 24 | 24 | 26 | 26 | 28 | 28 | 28 | 28 | 30 | 30 | 32 | 32 | 32 | 32 | 34 | 34 | | | | | | | | | | | | | | | | | | | | | |
| 0.601 — 0.620 | 18 | 20 | 20 | 22 | 22 | 24 | 24 | 24 | 24 | 26 | 26 | 28 | 28 | 28 | 28 | 30 | 30 | 32 | 32 | 32 | 32 | 34 | 34 | | | | | | | | | | | | | | | | | | | | | | |
| 0.621 — 0.625 | 18 | 20 | 20 | 22 | 22 | 24 | 24 | 24 | 26 | 26 | 26 | 28 | 28 | 28 | 30 | 30 | 30 | 32 | 32 | 32 | 34 | 34 | 34 | | | | | | | | | | | | | | | | | | | | | | |
| 0.626 — 0.640 | 20 | 20 | 22 | 22 | 24 | 24 | 24 | 26 | 26 | 26 | 28 | 28 | 28 | 30 | 30 | 30 | 32 | 32 | 32 | 34 | 34 | 34 | | | | | | | | | | | | | | | | | | | | | | | |
| 0.641 — 0.650 | 20 | 20 | 22 | 22 | 24 | 24 | 26 | 26 | 26 | 26 | 28 | 28 | 30 | 30 | 30 | 30 | 32 | 32 | 34 | 34 | 34 | 34 | | | | | | | | | | | | | | | | | | | | | | | |
| 0.651 — 0.670 | 20 | 22 | 22 | 24 | 24 | 26 | 26 | 26 | 26 | 28 | 28 | 30 | 30 | 30 | 30 | 32 | 32 | 34 | 34 | 34 | 34 | | | | | | | | | | | | | | | | | | | | | | | | |
| 0.671 — 0.675 | 20 | 22 | 22 | 24 | 24 | 26 | 26 | 26 | 28 | 28 | 28 | 30 | 30 | 30 | 32 | 32 | 32 | 34 | 34 | 34 | | | | | | | | | | | | | | | | | | | | | | | | | |
| 0.676 — 0.690 | 22 | 22 | 24 | 24 | 26 | 26 | 26 | 28 | 28 | 28 | 30 | 30 | 30 | 32 | 32 | 32 | 34 | 34 | 34 | | | | | | | | | | | | | | | | | | | | | | | | | | |
| 0.691 — 0.700 | 22 | 22 | 24 | 24 | 26 | 26 | 28 | 28 | 28 | 28 | 30 | 30 | 32 | 32 | 32 | 32 | 34 | 34 | | | | | | | | | | | | | | | | | | | | | | | | | | | |
| 0.701 — 0.720 | 22 | 24 | 24 | 26 | 26 | 28 | 28 | 28 | 28 | 30 | 30 | 32 | 32 | 32 | 32 | 34 | 34 | | | | | | | | | | | | | | | | | | | | | | | | | | | | |
| 0.721 — 0.725 | 22 | 24 | 24 | 26 | 26 | 28 | 28 | 28 | 30 | 30 | 30 | 32 | 32 | 32 | 34 | 34 | 34 | | | | | | | | | | | | | | | | | | | | | | | | | | | | |
| 0.726 — 0.740 | 24 | 24 | 26 | 26 | 28 | 28 | 28 | 30 | 30 | 30 | 32 | 32 | 32 | 34 | 34 | 34 | | | | | | | | | | | | | | | | | | | | | | | | | | | | | |
| 0.741 — 0.750 | 24 | 24 | 26 | 26 | 28 | 28 | 30 | 30 | 30 | 30 | 32 | 32 | 34 | 34 | 34 | | | | | | | | | | | | | | | | | | | | | | | | | | | | | | |
| 0.751 — 0.770 | 24 | 26 | 26 | 28 | 28 | 30 | 30 | 30 | 30 | 32 | 32 | 34 | 34 | 34 | 34 | | | | | | | | | | | | | | | | | | | | | | | | | | | | | | |
| 0.771 — 0.775 | 24 | 26 | 26 | 28 | 28 | 30 | 30 | 30 | 32 | 32 | 32 | 34 | 34 | 34 | | | | | | | | | | | | | | | | | | | | | | | | | | | | | | | |
| 0.776 — 0.790 | 26 | 26 | 28 | 28 | 30 | 30 | 30 | 32 | 32 | 32 | 34 | 34 | 34 | | | | | | | | | | | | | | | | | | | | | | | | | | | | | | | | |
| 0.791 — 0.800 | 26 | 26 | 28 | 28 | 30 | 30 | 32 | 32 | 32 | 32 | 34 | 34 | | | | | | | | | | | | | | | | | | | | | | | | | | | | | | | | | |
| 0.801 — 0.820 | 26 | 28 | 28 | 30 | 30 | 32 | 32 | 32 | 32 | 34 | 34 | | | | | | | | | | | | | | | | | | | | | | | | | | | | | | | | | | |
| 0.821 — 0.825 | 26 | 28 | 28 | 30 | 30 | 32 | 32 | 32 | 34 | 34 | 34 | | | | | | | | | | | | | | | | | | | | | | | | | | | | | | | | | | |
| 0.826 — 0.840 | 28 | 28 | 30 | 30 | 32 | 32 | 32 | 34 | 34 | 34 | | | | | | | | | | | | | | | | | | | | | | | | | | | | | | | | | | | |
| 0.841 — 0.850 | 28 | 28 | 30 | 30 | 32 | 32 | 34 | 34 | 34 | 34 | | | | | | | | | | | | | | | | | | | | | | | | | | | | | | | | | | | |
| 0.851 — 0.870 | 28 | 30 | 30 | 32 | 32 | 34 | 34 | 34 | 34 | | | | | | | | | | | | | | | | | | | | | | | | | | | | | | | | | | | | |
| 0.871 — 0.875 | 28 | 30 | 30 | 32 | 32 | 34 | 34 | 34 | | | | | | | | | | | | | | | | | | | | | | | | | | | | | | | | | | | | | |
| 0.876 — 0.890 | 30 | 30 | 32 | 32 | 34 | 34 | 34 | | | | | | | | | | | | | | | | | | | | | | | | | | | | | | | | | | | | | | |
| 0.891 — 0.900 | 30 | 30 | 32 | 32 | 34 | 34 | | | | | | | | | | | | | | | | | | | | | | | | | | | | | | | | | | | | | | | |
| 0.901 — 0.925 | 30 | 32 | 32 | 34 | 34 | | | | | | | | | | | | | | | | | | | | | | | | | | | | | | | | | | | | | | | | |
| 0.926 — 0.950 | 32 | 32 | 34 | 34 | | | | | | | | | | | | | | | | | | | | | | | | | | | | | | | | | | | | | | | | | |
| 0.951 — 0.975 | 32 | 34 | 34 | | | | | | | | | | | | | | | | | | | | | | | | | | | | | | | | | | | | | | | | | | |
| 0.976 — 1.000 | 34 | 34 | | | | | | | | | | | | | | | | | | | | | | | | | | | | | | | | | | | | | | | | | | | |
| 1.001 — 1.025 | 34 | | | | | | | | | | | | | | | | | | | | | | | | | | | | | | | | | | | | | | | | | | | | |

New shim thickness mm (in.)

| Shim No. | Thickness | Shim No. | Thickness |
|---|---|---|---|
| 02 | 2.500 (0.0984) | 20 | 2.950 (0.1161) |
| 04 | 2.550 (0.1004) | 22 | 3.000 (0.1181) |
| 06 | 2.600 (0.1024) | 24 | 3.050 (0.1201) |
| 08 | 2.650 (0.1043) | 26 | 3.100 (0.1220) |
| 10 | 2.700 (0.1063) | 28 | 3.150 (0.1240) |
| 12 | 2.750 (0.1083) | 30 | 3.200 (0.1260) |
| 14 | 2.800 (0.1102) | 32 | 3.250 (0.1280) |
| 16 | 2.850 (0.1122) | 34 | 3.300 (0.1299) |
| 18 | 2.900 (0.1142) | | |

Example: A 0.1102" (2.800 mm) shim is installed and measured clearance is 0.0177" (0.450 mm). Replace 0.1102" (2.800 mm) shim with a No. 24 shim.

91E17354

Courtesy of Toyota Motor Sales, U.S.A., Inc.

***Fig. 4: Intake Valve Adjusting Shim Selection Chart (Celica 1.6L & Corolla 1.6L)***

EXHAUST VALVES

| Measured Clearance (mm) | Installed Shim Thickness (mm) | | | | | | | | | | | | | | | | | | | | | | | | | | | | | | | | | | | | | | | | | | | | |
|---|---|---|---|---|---|---|---|---|---|---|---|---|---|---|---|---|---|---|---|---|---|---|---|---|---|---|---|---|---|---|---|---|---|---|---|---|---|---|---|---|---|---|---|---|---|
| | 2.500 | 2.525 | 2.550 | 2.575 | 2.600 | 2.620 | 2.640 | 2.650 | 2.660 | 2.680 | 2.700 | 2.720 | 2.740 | 2.750 | 2.760 | 2.780 | 2.800 | 2.820 | 2.840 | 2.850 | 2.860 | 2.880 | 2.900 | 2.920 | 2.940 | 2.950 | 2.960 | 2.980 | 3.000 | 3.020 | 3.040 | 3.050 | 3.060 | 3.080 | 3.100 | 3.120 | 3.140 | 3.150 | 3.160 | 3.180 | 3.200 | 3.225 | 3.250 | 3.275 | 3.300 |
| 0.000 — 0.009 | | | | | | | | | | | | 02 | 02 | 02 | 02 | 04 | 04 | 06 | 06 | 06 | 06 | 08 | 08 | 10 | 10 | 10 | 10 | 12 | 12 | 14 | 14 | 14 | 14 | 16 | 16 | 18 | 18 | 18 | 18 | 20 | 20 | 22 | 22 | 24 | 24 |
| 0.010 — 0.025 | | | | | | | | | | | | 02 | 02 | 02 | 04 | 04 | 06 | 06 | 06 | 06 | 08 | 08 | 10 | 10 | 10 | 10 | 12 | 12 | 14 | 14 | 14 | 14 | 16 | 16 | 18 | 18 | 18 | 18 | 20 | 20 | 22 | 22 | 22 | 24 | 26 |
| 0.026 — 0.040 | | | | | | | | | | | 02 | 02 | 02 | 04 | 04 | 04 | 06 | 06 | 06 | 08 | 08 | 08 | 10 | 10 | 10 | 12 | 12 | 12 | 14 | 14 | 14 | 16 | 16 | 16 | 18 | 18 | 18 | 20 | 20 | 20 | 22 | 22 | 24 | 24 | 26 |
| 0.041 — 0.050 | | | | | | | | | | 02 | 02 | 02 | 04 | 04 | 04 | 06 | 06 | 06 | 08 | 08 | 08 | 10 | 10 | 10 | 12 | 12 | 12 | 14 | 14 | 14 | 16 | 16 | 16 | 18 | 18 | 18 | 20 | 20 | 20 | 22 | 22 | 22 | 24 | 24 | 26 |
| 0.051 — 0.070 | | | | | | | | | | 02 | 02 | 04 | 04 | 04 | 04 | 06 | 06 | 08 | 08 | 08 | 08 | 10 | 10 | 12 | 12 | 12 | 12 | 14 | 14 | 16 | 16 | 16 | 16 | 18 | 18 | 20 | 20 | 20 | 20 | 22 | 22 | 24 | 24 | 26 | 26 |
| 0.071 — 0.090 | | | | | | | | 02 | 02 | 02 | 04 | 04 | 04 | 06 | 06 | 06 | 08 | 08 | 08 | 10 | 10 | 10 | 12 | 12 | 12 | 14 | 14 | 14 | 16 | 16 | 16 | 18 | 18 | 18 | 20 | 20 | 20 | 22 | 22 | 22 | 24 | 24 | 26 | 26 | 28 |
| 0.091 — 0.100 | | | | | | | 02 | 02 | 02 | 04 | 04 | 04 | 06 | 06 | 06 | 08 | 08 | 08 | 10 | 10 | 10 | 12 | 12 | 12 | 14 | 14 | 14 | 16 | 16 | 16 | 18 | 18 | 18 | 20 | 20 | 20 | 22 | 22 | 22 | 24 | 24 | 24 | 26 | 26 | 28 |
| 0.101 — 0.120 | | | | | | 02 | 02 | 02 | 02 | 04 | 04 | 06 | 06 | 06 | 06 | 08 | 08 | 10 | 10 | 10 | 10 | 12 | 12 | 14 | 14 | 14 | 14 | 16 | 16 | 18 | 18 | 18 | 18 | 20 | 20 | 22 | 22 | 22 | 22 | 24 | 24 | 26 | 26 | 28 | 28 |
| 0.121 — 0.140 | | | | | 02 | 02 | 02 | 04 | 04 | 04 | 06 | 06 | 06 | 08 | 08 | 08 | 10 | 10 | 10 | 12 | 12 | 12 | 14 | 14 | 14 | 16 | 16 | 16 | 18 | 18 | 18 | 20 | 20 | 20 | 22 | 22 | 22 | 24 | 24 | 24 | 26 | 26 | 28 | 28 | 30 |
| 0.141 — 0.150 | | | | | 02 | 02 | 04 | 04 | 04 | 06 | 06 | 06 | 08 | 08 | 08 | 10 | 10 | 10 | 12 | 12 | 12 | 14 | 14 | 14 | 16 | 16 | 16 | 18 | 18 | 18 | 20 | 20 | 20 | 22 | 22 | 22 | 24 | 24 | 24 | 26 | 26 | 26 | 28 | 28 | 30 |
| 0.151 — 0.170 | | | | | 02 | 02 | 04 | 04 | 04 | 06 | 06 | 06 | 08 | 08 | 08 | 10 | 10 | 10 | 12 | 12 | 12 | 14 | 14 | 14 | 16 | 16 | 16 | 18 | 18 | 18 | 20 | 20 | 20 | 22 | 22 | 22 | 24 | 24 | 24 | 26 | 26 | 26 | 28 | 28 | 30 |
| 0.171 — 0.190 | | | 02 | 02 | 04 | 04 | 04 | 06 | 06 | 06 | 08 | 08 | 08 | 10 | 10 | 10 | 12 | 12 | 12 | 14 | 14 | 14 | 16 | 16 | 16 | 18 | 18 | 18 | 20 | 20 | 20 | 22 | 22 | 22 | 24 | 24 | 24 | 26 | 26 | 26 | 28 | 28 | 30 | 30 | 32 |
| 0.191 — 0.199 | | | 02 | 02 | 04 | 04 | 06 | 06 | 06 | 08 | 08 | 08 | 10 | 10 | 10 | 12 | 12 | 12 | 14 | 14 | 14 | 16 | 16 | 16 | 18 | 18 | 18 | 20 | 20 | 20 | 22 | 22 | 22 | 24 | 24 | 24 | 26 | 26 | 26 | 28 | 28 | 28 | 30 | 30 | 32 |
| 0.200 — 0.300 | | | | | | | | | | | | | | | | | | | | | | | | | | | | | | | | | | | | | | | | | | | | | |
| 0.301 — 0.320 | 04 | 06 | 06 | 08 | 08 | 10 | 10 | 10 | 10 | 12 | 12 | 14 | 14 | 14 | 14 | 16 | 16 | 18 | 18 | 18 | 18 | 20 | 20 | 22 | 22 | 22 | 22 | 24 | 24 | 26 | 26 | 26 | 26 | 28 | 28 | 30 | 30 | 30 | 30 | 32 | 32 | 34 | 34 | | |
| 0.321 — 0.325 | 04 | 06 | 06 | 08 | 08 | 10 | 10 | 10 | 12 | 12 | 12 | 14 | 14 | 14 | 16 | 16 | 16 | 18 | 18 | 18 | 20 | 20 | 20 | 22 | 22 | 22 | 24 | 24 | 24 | 26 | 26 | 26 | 28 | 28 | 28 | 30 | 30 | 30 | 32 | 32 | 32 | 34 | 34 | | |
| 0.326 — 0.340 | 06 | 06 | 08 | 08 | 10 | 10 | 10 | 12 | 12 | 12 | 14 | 14 | 14 | 16 | 16 | 16 | 18 | 18 | 18 | 20 | 20 | 20 | 22 | 22 | 22 | 24 | 24 | 24 | 26 | 26 | 26 | 28 | 28 | 28 | 30 | 30 | 30 | 32 | 32 | 32 | 34 | 34 | | | |
| 0.341 — 0.350 | 06 | 06 | 08 | 08 | 10 | 10 | 12 | 12 | 12 | 12 | 14 | 14 | 16 | 16 | 16 | 16 | 18 | 18 | 20 | 20 | 20 | 20 | 22 | 22 | 24 | 24 | 24 | 24 | 26 | 26 | 28 | 28 | 28 | 28 | 30 | 30 | 32 | 32 | 32 | 32 | 34 | 34 | | | |
| 0.351 — 0.370 | 06 | 08 | 08 | 10 | 10 | 12 | 12 | 12 | 12 | 14 | 14 | 16 | 16 | 16 | 16 | 18 | 18 | 20 | 20 | 20 | 20 | 22 | 22 | 24 | 24 | 24 | 24 | 26 | 26 | 28 | 28 | 28 | 28 | 30 | 30 | 32 | 32 | 32 | 32 | 34 | 34 | | | | |
| 0.371 — 0.375 | 06 | 08 | 08 | 10 | 10 | 12 | 12 | 12 | 14 | 14 | 14 | 16 | 16 | 16 | 18 | 18 | 18 | 20 | 20 | 20 | 22 | 22 | 22 | 24 | 24 | 24 | 26 | 26 | 26 | 28 | 28 | 28 | 30 | 30 | 30 | 32 | 32 | 32 | 34 | 34 | 34 | | | | |
| 0.376 — 0.390 | 08 | 08 | 10 | 10 | 12 | 12 | 12 | 14 | 14 | 14 | 16 | 16 | 16 | 18 | 18 | 18 | 20 | 20 | 20 | 22 | 22 | 22 | 24 | 24 | 24 | 26 | 26 | 26 | 28 | 28 | 28 | 30 | 30 | 30 | 32 | 32 | 32 | 34 | 34 | 34 | | | | | |
| 0.391 — 0.400 | 08 | 08 | 10 | 10 | 12 | 12 | 14 | 14 | 14 | 14 | 16 | 16 | 18 | 18 | 18 | 18 | 20 | 20 | 22 | 22 | 22 | 22 | 24 | 24 | 26 | 26 | 26 | 26 | 28 | 28 | 30 | 30 | 30 | 30 | 32 | 32 | 34 | 34 | 34 | 34 | | | | | |
| 0.401 — 0.420 | 08 | 10 | 10 | 12 | 12 | 14 | 14 | 14 | 14 | 16 | 16 | 18 | 18 | 18 | 18 | 20 | 20 | 22 | 22 | 22 | 22 | 24 | 24 | 26 | 26 | 26 | 26 | 28 | 28 | 30 | 30 | 30 | 30 | 32 | 32 | 34 | 34 | 34 | 34 | | | | | | |
| 0.421 — 0.425 | 08 | 10 | 10 | 12 | 12 | 14 | 14 | 14 | 16 | 16 | 16 | 18 | 18 | 18 | 20 | 20 | 20 | 22 | 22 | 22 | 24 | 24 | 24 | 26 | 26 | 26 | 28 | 28 | 28 | 30 | 30 | 30 | 32 | 32 | 32 | 34 | 34 | 34 | | | | | | | |
| 0.426 — 0.440 | 10 | 10 | 12 | 12 | 14 | 14 | 14 | 16 | 16 | 16 | 18 | 18 | 18 | 20 | 20 | 20 | 22 | 22 | 22 | 24 | 24 | 24 | 26 | 26 | 26 | 28 | 28 | 28 | 30 | 30 | 30 | 32 | 32 | 32 | 34 | 34 | 34 | | | | | | | | |
| 0.441 — 0.450 | 10 | 10 | 12 | 12 | 14 | 14 | 16 | 16 | 16 | 16 | 18 | 18 | 20 | 20 | 20 | 20 | 22 | 22 | 24 | 24 | 24 | 24 | 26 | 26 | 28 | 28 | 28 | 28 | 30 | 30 | 32 | 32 | 32 | 32 | 34 | 34 | | | | | | | | | |
| 0.451 — 0.470 | 10 | 12 | 12 | 14 | 14 | 16 | 16 | 16 | 16 | 18 | 18 | 20 | 20 | 20 | 20 | 22 | 22 | 24 | 24 | 24 | 24 | 26 | 26 | 28 | 28 | 28 | 28 | 30 | 30 | 30 | 32 | 32 | 32 | 34 | 34 | | | | | | | | | | |
| 0.471 — 0.475 | 10 | 12 | 12 | 14 | 14 | 16 | 16 | 16 | 18 | 18 | 18 | 20 | 20 | 20 | 22 | 22 | 22 | 24 | 24 | 24 | 26 | 26 | 26 | 28 | 28 | 28 | 30 | 30 | 30 | 32 | 32 | 32 | 34 | 34 | 34 | | | | | | | | | | |
| 0.476 — 0.490 | 12 | 12 | 14 | 14 | 16 | 16 | 16 | 18 | 18 | 18 | 20 | 20 | 20 | 22 | 22 | 22 | 24 | 24 | 24 | 26 | 26 | 26 | 28 | 28 | 28 | 30 | 30 | 30 | 32 | 32 | 32 | 34 | 34 | 34 | | | | | | | | | | | |
| 0.491 — 0.500 | 12 | 12 | 14 | 14 | 16 | 16 | 18 | 18 | 18 | 18 | 20 | 20 | 22 | 22 | 22 | 22 | 24 | 24 | 26 | 26 | 26 | 26 | 28 | 28 | 30 | 30 | 30 | 30 | 32 | 32 | 34 | 34 | 34 | 34 | | | | | | | | | | | |
| 0.501 — 0.520 | 12 | 14 | 14 | 16 | 16 | 18 | 18 | 18 | 18 | 20 | 20 | 22 | 22 | 22 | 22 | 24 | 24 | 26 | 26 | 26 | 26 | 28 | 28 | 30 | 30 | 30 | 30 | 32 | 32 | 34 | 34 | 34 | 34 | | | | | | | | | | | | |
| 0.521 — 0.525 | 12 | 14 | 14 | 16 | 16 | 18 | 18 | 18 | 20 | 20 | 20 | 22 | 22 | 22 | 24 | 24 | 24 | 26 | 26 | 26 | 28 | 28 | 28 | 30 | 30 | 30 | 32 | 32 | 32 | 34 | 34 | 34 | | | | | | | | | | | | | |
| 0.526 — 0.540 | 14 | 14 | 16 | 16 | 18 | 18 | 18 | 20 | 20 | 20 | 22 | 22 | 22 | 24 | 24 | 24 | 26 | 26 | 26 | 28 | 28 | 28 | 30 | 30 | 30 | 32 | 32 | 32 | 34 | 34 | 34 | | | | | | | | | | | | | | |
| 0.541 — 0.550 | 14 | 14 | 16 | 16 | 18 | 18 | 20 | 20 | 20 | 20 | 22 | 22 | 24 | 24 | 24 | 24 | 26 | 26 | 28 | 28 | 28 | 28 | 30 | 30 | 32 | 32 | 32 | 32 | 34 | 34 | | | | | | | | | | | | | | | |
| 0.551 — 0.570 | 14 | 16 | 16 | 18 | 18 | 20 | 20 | 20 | 20 | 22 | 22 | 24 | 24 | 24 | 24 | 26 | 26 | 28 | 28 | 28 | 28 | 30 | 30 | 32 | 32 | 32 | 32 | 34 | 34 | | | | | | | | | | | | | | | | |
| 0.571 — 0.575 | 14 | 16 | 16 | 18 | 18 | 20 | 20 | 20 | 22 | 22 | 22 | 24 | 24 | 24 | 26 | 26 | 26 | 28 | 28 | 28 | 30 | 30 | 30 | 32 | 32 | 32 | 34 | 34 | 34 | | | | | | | | | | | | | | | | |
| 0.576 — 0.590 | 16 | 16 | 18 | 18 | 20 | 20 | 20 | 22 | 22 | 22 | 24 | 24 | 24 | 26 | 26 | 26 | 28 | 28 | 28 | 30 | 30 | 30 | 32 | 32 | 32 | 34 | 34 | 34 | | | | | | | | | | | | | | | | | |
| 0.591 — 0.600 | 16 | 16 | 18 | 18 | 20 | 20 | 22 | 22 | 22 | 22 | 24 | 24 | 26 | 26 | 26 | 26 | 28 | 28 | 30 | 30 | 30 | 30 | 32 | 32 | 34 | 34 | 34 | 34 | | | | | | | | | | | | | | | | | |
| 0.601 — 0.620 | 16 | 18 | 18 | 20 | 20 | 22 | 22 | 22 | 22 | 24 | 24 | 26 | 26 | 26 | 26 | 28 | 28 | 30 | 30 | 30 | 30 | 32 | 32 | 34 | 34 | 34 | 34 | | | | | | | | | | | | | | | | | | |
| 0.621 — 0.625 | 16 | 18 | 18 | 20 | 20 | 22 | 22 | 22 | 24 | 24 | 24 | 26 | 26 | 26 | 28 | 28 | 28 | 30 | 30 | 30 | 32 | 32 | 32 | 34 | 34 | 34 | | | | | | | | | | | | | | | | | | | |
| 0.626 — 0.640 | 18 | 18 | 20 | 20 | 22 | 22 | 22 | 24 | 24 | 24 | 26 | 26 | 26 | 28 | 28 | 28 | 30 | 30 | 30 | 32 | 32 | 32 | 34 | 34 | 34 | | | | | | | | | | | | | | | | | | | | |
| 0.641 — 0.650 | 18 | 18 | 20 | 20 | 22 | 22 | 24 | 24 | 24 | 24 | 26 | 26 | 28 | 28 | 28 | 28 | 30 | 30 | 32 | 32 | 32 | 32 | 34 | 34 | | | | | | | | | | | | | | | | | | | | | |
| 0.651 — 0.670 | 18 | 20 | 20 | 22 | 22 | 24 | 24 | 24 | 24 | 26 | 26 | 28 | 28 | 28 | 28 | 30 | 30 | 32 | 32 | 32 | 32 | 34 | 34 | | | | | | | | | | | | | | | | | | | | | | |
| 0.671 — 0.675 | 18 | 20 | 20 | 22 | 22 | 24 | 24 | 24 | 26 | 26 | 26 | 28 | 28 | 28 | 30 | 30 | 30 | 32 | 32 | 32 | 34 | 34 | 34 | | | | | | | | | | | | | | | | | | | | | | |
| 0.676 — 0.690 | 20 | 20 | 22 | 22 | 24 | 24 | 24 | 26 | 26 | 26 | 28 | 28 | 28 | 30 | 30 | 30 | 32 | 32 | 32 | 34 | 34 | 34 | | | | | | | | | | | | | | | | | | | | | | | |
| 0.691 — 0.700 | 20 | 20 | 22 | 22 | 24 | 24 | 26 | 26 | 26 | 26 | 28 | 28 | 30 | 30 | 30 | 30 | 32 | 32 | 34 | 34 | 34 | 34 | | | | | | | | | | | | | | | | | | | | | | | |
| 0.701 — 0.720 | 20 | 22 | 22 | 24 | 24 | 26 | 26 | 26 | 26 | 28 | 28 | 30 | 30 | 30 | 30 | 32 | 32 | 34 | 34 | 34 | 34 | | | | | | | | | | | | | | | | | | | | | | | | |
| 0.721 — 0.725 | 20 | 22 | 22 | 24 | 24 | 26 | 26 | 26 | 28 | 28 | 28 | 30 | 30 | 30 | 32 | 32 | 32 | 34 | 34 | 34 | | | | | | | | | | | | | | | | | | | | | | | | | |
| 0.726 — 0.740 | 22 | 22 | 24 | 24 | 26 | 26 | 26 | 28 | 28 | 28 | 30 | 30 | 30 | 32 | 32 | 32 | 34 | 34 | 34 | | | | | | | | | | | | | | | | | | | | | | | | | | |
| 0.741 — 0.750 | 22 | 22 | 24 | 24 | 26 | 26 | 28 | 28 | 28 | 28 | 30 | 30 | 32 | 32 | 32 | 32 | 34 | 34 | | | | | | | | | | | | | | | | | | | | | | | | | | | |
| 0.751 — 0.770 | 22 | 24 | 24 | 26 | 26 | 28 | 28 | 28 | 28 | 30 | 30 | 32 | 32 | 32 | 32 | 34 | 34 | | | | | | | | | | | | | | | | | | | | | | | | | | | | |
| 0.771 — 0.775 | 22 | 24 | 24 | 26 | 26 | 28 | 28 | 28 | 30 | 30 | 30 | 32 | 32 | 32 | 34 | 34 | 34 | | | | | | | | | | | | | | | | | | | | | | | | | | | | |
| 0.776 — 0.790 | 24 | 24 | 26 | 26 | 28 | 28 | 28 | 30 | 30 | 30 | 32 | 32 | 32 | 34 | 34 | 34 | | | | | | | | | | | | | | | | | | | | | | | | | | | | | |
| 0.791 — 0.800 | 24 | 24 | 26 | 26 | 28 | 28 | 30 | 30 | 30 | 30 | 32 | 32 | 34 | 34 | 34 | 34 | | | | | | | | | | | | | | | | | | | | | | | | | | | | | |
| 0.801 — 0.820 | 24 | 26 | 26 | 28 | 28 | 30 | 30 | 30 | 30 | 32 | 32 | 34 | 34 | 34 | 34 | | | | | | | | | | | | | | | | | | | | | | | | | | | | | | |
| 0.821 — 0.825 | 24 | 26 | 26 | 28 | 28 | 30 | 30 | 30 | 32 | 32 | 32 | 34 | 34 | 34 | | | | | | | | | | | | | | | | | | | | | | | | | | | | | | | |
| 0.826 — 0.840 | 26 | 26 | 28 | 28 | 30 | 30 | 30 | 32 | 32 | 32 | 34 | 34 | 34 | | | | | | | | | | | | | | | | | | | | | | | | | | | | | | | | |
| 0.841 — 0.850 | 26 | 26 | 28 | 28 | 30 | 30 | 32 | 32 | 32 | 32 | 34 | 34 | | | | | | | | | | | | | | | | | | | | | | | | | | | | | | | | | |
| 0.851 — 0.870 | 26 | 28 | 28 | 30 | 30 | 32 | 32 | 32 | 32 | 34 | 34 | | | | | | | | | | | | | | | | | | | | | | | | | | | | | | | | | | |
| 0.871 — 0.875 | 26 | 28 | 28 | 30 | 30 | 32 | 32 | 32 | 34 | 34 | 34 | | | | | | | | | | | | | | | | | | | | | | | | | | | | | | | | | | |
| 0.876 — 0.890 | 28 | 28 | 30 | 30 | 32 | 32 | 32 | 34 | 34 | 34 | | | | | | | | | | | | | | | | | | | | | | | | | | | | | | | | | | | |
| 0.891 — 0.900 | 28 | 28 | 30 | 30 | 32 | 32 | 34 | 34 | 34 | 34 | | | | | | | | | | | | | | | | | | | | | | | | | | | | | | | | | | | |
| 0.901 — 0.925 | 28 | 30 | 30 | 32 | 32 | 34 | 34 | 34 | | | | | | | | | | | | | | | | | | | | | | | | | | | | | | | | | | | | | |
| 0.926 — 0.950 | 30 | 30 | 32 | 32 | 34 | 34 | | | | | | | | | | | | | | | | | | | | | | | | | | | | | | | | | | | | | | | |
| 0.951 — 0.975 | 30 | 32 | 32 | 34 | 34 | | | | | | | | | | | | | | | | | | | | | | | | | | | | | | | | | | | | | | | | |
| 0.976 — 1.000 | 32 | 32 | 34 | 34 | | | | | | | | | | | | | | | | | | | | | | | | | | | | | | | | | | | | | | | | | |
| 1.001 — 1.025 | 32 | 34 | 34 | | | | | | | | | | | | | | | | | | | | | | | | | | | | | | | | | | | | | | | | | | |
| 1.026 — 1.050 | 34 | 34 | | | | | | | | | | | | | | | | | | | | | | | | | | | | | | | | | | | | | | | | | | | |
| 1.051 — 1.075 | 34 | | | | | | | | | | | | | | | | | | | | | | | | | | | | | | | | | | | | | | | | | | | | |

New shim thickness mm (in.)

| Shim No. | Thickness | Shim No. | Thickness |
|---|---|---|---|
| 02 | 2.500 (0.0984) | 20 | 2.950 (0.1161) |
| 04 | 2.550 (0.1004) | 22 | 3.000 (0.1181) |
| 06 | 2.600 (0.1024) | 24 | 3.050 (0.1201) |
| 08 | 2.650 (0.1043) | 26 | 3.100 (0.1220) |
| 10 | 2.700 (0.1063) | 28 | 3.150 (0.1240) |
| 12 | 2.750 (0.1083) | 30 | 3.200 (0.1260) |
| 14 | 2.800 (0.1102) | 32 | 3.250 (0.1280) |
| 16 | 2.850 (0.1122) | 34 | 3.300 (0.1299) |
| 18 | 2.900 (0.1142) | | |

Example: A 0.1102" (2.800 mm) shim is installed and measured clearance is 0.0177" (0.450 mm). Replace 0.1102" (2.800 mm) shim with a No. 22 shim.

91F17355

Courtesy of Toyota Motor Sales, U.S.A., Inc.

***Fig. 5: Exhaust Valve Adjusting Shim Selection Chart (Celica 1.6L & Corolla 1.6L)***

# 1991 ENGINE PERFORMANCE
# On-Vehicle Adjustments (Cont.)

INTAKE VALVES

| Measured clearance (mm) | Installed shim thickness (mm) | | | | | | | | | | | | | | | | | | | | | | | | | | | | | | | | | | | | | | | | | | | | | | | | | | | | |
|---|---|---|---|---|---|---|---|---|---|---|---|---|---|---|---|---|---|---|---|---|---|---|---|---|---|---|---|---|---|---|---|---|---|---|---|---|---|---|---|---|---|---|---|---|---|---|---|---|---|---|---|---|---|
| | 2.000 | 2.025 | 2.050 | 2.075 | 2.100 | 2.125 | 2.150 | 2.175 | 2.200 | 2.225 | 2.250 | 2.275 | 2.300 | 2.325 | 2.350 | 2.375 | 2.400 | 2.425 | 2.450 | 2.475 | 2.500 | 2.525 | 2.550 | 2.575 | 2.600 | 2.625 | 2.650 | 2.675 | 2.700 | 2.725 | 2.750 | 2.775 | 2.800 | 2.825 | 2.850 | 2.875 | 2.900 | 2.925 | 2.950 | 2.975 | 3.000 | 3.025 | 3.050 | 3.075 | 3.100 | 3.125 | 3.150 | 3.175 | 3.200 | 3.225 | 3.250 | 3.275 | 3.300 |
| 0.000 – 0.025 | | | | | | | 02 | 02 | 02 | 04 | 04 | 06 | 06 | 08 | 08 | 10 | 10 | 12 | 12 | 14 | 14 | 16 | 16 | 18 | 18 | 20 | 20 | 22 | 22 | 24 | 24 | 26 | 26 | 28 | 28 | 30 | 30 | 32 | 32 | 34 | 34 | 36 | 36 | 38 | 38 | 40 | 40 | 42 | 42 | 44 | 44 | 46 | 46 |
| 0.026 – 0.050 | | | | | | 02 | 02 | 02 | 04 | 04 | 06 | 06 | 08 | 08 | 10 | 10 | 12 | 12 | 14 | 14 | 16 | 16 | 18 | 18 | 20 | 20 | 22 | 22 | 24 | 24 | 26 | 26 | 28 | 28 | 30 | 30 | 32 | 32 | 34 | 34 | 36 | 36 | 38 | 38 | 40 | 40 | 42 | 42 | 44 | 44 | 46 | 46 | 48 |
| 0.051 – 0.075 | | | | | 02 | 02 | 02 | 04 | 04 | 06 | 06 | 08 | 08 | 10 | 10 | 12 | 12 | 14 | 14 | 16 | 16 | 18 | 18 | 20 | 20 | 22 | 22 | 24 | 24 | 26 | 26 | 28 | 28 | 30 | 30 | 32 | 32 | 34 | 34 | 36 | 36 | 38 | 38 | 40 | 40 | 42 | 42 | 44 | 44 | 46 | 46 | 48 | 48 |
| 0.076 – 0.100 | | | | 02 | 02 | 02 | 04 | 04 | 06 | 06 | 08 | 08 | 10 | 10 | 12 | 12 | 14 | 14 | 16 | 16 | 18 | 18 | 20 | 20 | 22 | 22 | 24 | 24 | 26 | 26 | 28 | 28 | 30 | 30 | 32 | 32 | 34 | 34 | 36 | 36 | 38 | 38 | 40 | 40 | 42 | 42 | 44 | 44 | 46 | 46 | 48 | 48 | 50 |
| 0.101 – 0.125 | | | 02 | 02 | 02 | 04 | 04 | 06 | 06 | 08 | 08 | 10 | 10 | 12 | 12 | 14 | 14 | 16 | 16 | 18 | 18 | 20 | 20 | 22 | 22 | 24 | 24 | 26 | 26 | 28 | 28 | 30 | 30 | 32 | 32 | 34 | 34 | 36 | 36 | 38 | 38 | 40 | 40 | 42 | 42 | 44 | 44 | 46 | 46 | 48 | 48 | 50 | 50 |
| 0.126 – 0.149 | | 02 | 02 | 02 | 04 | 04 | 06 | 06 | 08 | 08 | 10 | 10 | 12 | 12 | 14 | 14 | 16 | 16 | 18 | 18 | 20 | 20 | 22 | 22 | 24 | 24 | 26 | 26 | 28 | 28 | 30 | 30 | 32 | 32 | 34 | 34 | 36 | 36 | 38 | 38 | 40 | 40 | 42 | 42 | 44 | 44 | 46 | 46 | 48 | 48 | 50 | 50 | 52 |
| 0.150 – 0.250 | | | | | | | | | | | | | | | | | | | | | | | | | | | | | | | | | | | | | | | | | | | | | | | | | | | | | |
| 0.251 – 0.275 | 04 | 06 | 06 | 08 | 08 | 10 | 10 | 12 | 12 | 14 | 14 | 16 | 16 | 18 | 18 | 20 | 20 | 22 | 22 | 24 | 24 | 26 | 26 | 28 | 28 | 30 | 30 | 32 | 32 | 34 | 34 | 36 | 36 | 38 | 38 | 40 | 40 | 42 | 42 | 44 | 44 | 46 | 46 | 48 | 48 | 50 | 50 | 52 | 52 | 54 | 54 | 54 | |
| 0.276 – 0.300 | 06 | 06 | 08 | 08 | 10 | 10 | 12 | 12 | 14 | 14 | 16 | 16 | 18 | 18 | 20 | 20 | 22 | 22 | 24 | 24 | 26 | 26 | 28 | 28 | 30 | 30 | 32 | 32 | 34 | 34 | 36 | 36 | 38 | 38 | 40 | 40 | 42 | 42 | 44 | 44 | 46 | 46 | 48 | 48 | 50 | 50 | 52 | 52 | 54 | 54 | 54 | | |
| 0.301 – 0.325 | 06 | 08 | 08 | 10 | 10 | 12 | 12 | 14 | 14 | 16 | 16 | 18 | 18 | 20 | 20 | 22 | 22 | 24 | 24 | 26 | 26 | 28 | 28 | 30 | 30 | 32 | 32 | 34 | 34 | 36 | 36 | 38 | 38 | 40 | 40 | 42 | 42 | 44 | 44 | 46 | 46 | 48 | 48 | 50 | 50 | 52 | 52 | 54 | 54 | 54 | | | |
| 0.326 – 0.350 | 08 | 08 | 10 | 10 | 12 | 12 | 14 | 14 | 16 | 16 | 18 | 18 | 20 | 20 | 22 | 22 | 24 | 24 | 26 | 26 | 28 | 28 | 30 | 30 | 32 | 32 | 34 | 34 | 36 | 36 | 38 | 38 | 40 | 40 | 42 | 42 | 44 | 44 | 46 | 46 | 48 | 48 | 50 | 50 | 52 | 52 | 54 | 54 | 54 | | | | |
| 0.351 – 0.375 | 08 | 10 | 10 | 12 | 12 | 14 | 14 | 16 | 16 | 18 | 18 | 20 | 20 | 22 | 22 | 24 | 24 | 26 | 26 | 28 | 28 | 30 | 30 | 32 | 32 | 34 | 34 | 36 | 36 | 38 | 38 | 40 | 40 | 42 | 42 | 44 | 44 | 46 | 46 | 48 | 48 | 50 | 50 | 52 | 52 | 54 | 54 | 54 | | | | | |
| 0.376 – 0.400 | 10 | 10 | 12 | 12 | 14 | 14 | 16 | 16 | 18 | 18 | 20 | 20 | 22 | 22 | 24 | 24 | 26 | 26 | 28 | 28 | 30 | 30 | 32 | 32 | 34 | 34 | 36 | 36 | 38 | 38 | 40 | 40 | 42 | 42 | 44 | 44 | 46 | 46 | 48 | 48 | 50 | 50 | 52 | 52 | 54 | 54 | 54 | | | | | | |
| 0.401 – 0.425 | 10 | 12 | 12 | 14 | 14 | 16 | 16 | 18 | 18 | 20 | 20 | 22 | 22 | 24 | 24 | 26 | 26 | 28 | 28 | 30 | 30 | 32 | 32 | 34 | 34 | 36 | 36 | 38 | 38 | 40 | 40 | 42 | 42 | 44 | 44 | 46 | 46 | 48 | 48 | 50 | 50 | 52 | 52 | 54 | 54 | 54 | | | | | | | |
| 0.426 – 0.450 | 12 | 12 | 14 | 14 | 16 | 16 | 18 | 18 | 20 | 20 | 22 | 22 | 24 | 24 | 26 | 26 | 28 | 28 | 30 | 30 | 32 | 32 | 34 | 34 | 36 | 36 | 38 | 38 | 40 | 40 | 42 | 42 | 44 | 44 | 46 | 46 | 48 | 48 | 50 | 50 | 52 | 52 | 54 | 54 | 54 | | | | | | | | |
| 0.451 – 0.475 | 12 | 14 | 14 | 16 | 16 | 18 | 18 | 20 | 20 | 22 | 22 | 24 | 24 | 26 | 26 | 28 | 28 | 30 | 30 | 32 | 32 | 34 | 34 | 36 | 36 | 38 | 38 | 40 | 40 | 42 | 42 | 44 | 44 | 46 | 46 | 48 | 48 | 50 | 50 | 52 | 52 | 54 | 54 | 54 | | | | | | | | | |
| 0.476 – 0.500 | 14 | 14 | 16 | 16 | 18 | 18 | 20 | 20 | 22 | 22 | 24 | 24 | 26 | 26 | 28 | 28 | 30 | 30 | 32 | 32 | 34 | 34 | 36 | 36 | 38 | 38 | 40 | 40 | 42 | 42 | 44 | 44 | 46 | 46 | 48 | 48 | 50 | 50 | 52 | 52 | 54 | 54 | 54 | | | | | | | | | | |
| 0.501 – 0.525 | 14 | 16 | 16 | 18 | 18 | 20 | 20 | 22 | 22 | 24 | 24 | 26 | 26 | 28 | 28 | 30 | 30 | 32 | 32 | 34 | 34 | 36 | 36 | 38 | 38 | 40 | 40 | 42 | 42 | 44 | 44 | 46 | 46 | 48 | 48 | 50 | 50 | 52 | 52 | 54 | 54 | 54 | | | | | | | | | | | |
| 0.526 – 0.550 | 16 | 16 | 18 | 18 | 20 | 20 | 22 | 22 | 24 | 24 | 26 | 26 | 28 | 28 | 30 | 30 | 32 | 32 | 34 | 34 | 36 | 36 | 38 | 38 | 40 | 40 | 42 | 42 | 44 | 44 | 46 | 46 | 48 | 48 | 50 | 50 | 52 | 52 | 54 | 54 | 54 | | | | | | | | | | | | |
| 0.551 – 0.575 | 16 | 18 | 18 | 20 | 20 | 22 | 22 | 24 | 24 | 26 | 26 | 28 | 28 | 30 | 30 | 32 | 32 | 34 | 34 | 36 | 36 | 38 | 38 | 40 | 40 | 42 | 42 | 44 | 44 | 46 | 46 | 48 | 48 | 50 | 50 | 52 | 52 | 54 | 54 | 54 | | | | | | | | | | | | | |
| 0.576 – 0.600 | 18 | 18 | 20 | 20 | 22 | 22 | 24 | 24 | 26 | 26 | 28 | 28 | 30 | 30 | 32 | 32 | 34 | 34 | 36 | 36 | 38 | 38 | 40 | 40 | 42 | 42 | 44 | 44 | 46 | 46 | 48 | 48 | 50 | 50 | 52 | 52 | 54 | 54 | 54 | | | | | | | | | | | | | | |
| 0.601 – 0.625 | 18 | 20 | 20 | 22 | 22 | 24 | 24 | 26 | 26 | 28 | 28 | 30 | 30 | 32 | 32 | 34 | 34 | 36 | 36 | 38 | 38 | 40 | 40 | 42 | 42 | 44 | 44 | 46 | 46 | 48 | 48 | 50 | 50 | 52 | 52 | 54 | 54 | 54 | | | | | | | | | | | | | | | |
| 0.626 – 0.650 | 20 | 20 | 22 | 22 | 24 | 24 | 26 | 26 | 28 | 28 | 30 | 30 | 32 | 32 | 34 | 34 | 36 | 36 | 38 | 38 | 40 | 40 | 42 | 42 | 44 | 44 | 46 | 46 | 48 | 48 | 50 | 50 | 52 | 52 | 54 | 54 | 54 | | | | | | | | | | | | | | | | |
| 0.651 – 0.675 | 20 | 22 | 22 | 24 | 24 | 26 | 26 | 28 | 28 | 30 | 30 | 32 | 32 | 34 | 34 | 36 | 36 | 38 | 38 | 40 | 40 | 42 | 42 | 44 | 44 | 46 | 46 | 48 | 48 | 50 | 50 | 52 | 52 | 54 | 54 | 54 | | | | | | | | | | | | | | | | | |
| 0.676 – 0.700 | 22 | 22 | 24 | 24 | 26 | 26 | 28 | 28 | 30 | 30 | 32 | 32 | 34 | 34 | 36 | 36 | 38 | 38 | 40 | 40 | 42 | 42 | 44 | 44 | 46 | 46 | 48 | 48 | 50 | 50 | 52 | 52 | 54 | 54 | 54 | | | | | | | | | | | | | | | | | | |
| 0.701 – 0.725 | 22 | 24 | 24 | 26 | 26 | 28 | 28 | 30 | 30 | 32 | 32 | 34 | 34 | 36 | 36 | 38 | 38 | 40 | 40 | 42 | 42 | 44 | 44 | 46 | 46 | 48 | 48 | 50 | 50 | 52 | 52 | 54 | 54 | 54 | | | | | | | | | | | | | | | | | | | |
| 0.726 – 0.750 | 24 | 24 | 26 | 26 | 28 | 28 | 30 | 30 | 32 | 32 | 34 | 34 | 36 | 36 | 38 | 38 | 40 | 40 | 42 | 42 | 44 | 44 | 46 | 46 | 48 | 48 | 50 | 50 | 52 | 52 | 54 | 54 | 54 | | | | | | | | | | | | | | | | | | | | |
| 0.751 – 0.775 | 24 | 26 | 26 | 28 | 28 | 30 | 30 | 32 | 32 | 34 | 34 | 36 | 36 | 38 | 38 | 40 | 40 | 42 | 42 | 44 | 44 | 46 | 46 | 48 | 48 | 50 | 50 | 52 | 52 | 54 | 54 | 54 | | | | | | | | | | | | | | | | | | | | | |
| 0.776 – 0.800 | 26 | 26 | 28 | 28 | 30 | 30 | 32 | 32 | 34 | 34 | 36 | 36 | 38 | 38 | 40 | 40 | 42 | 42 | 44 | 44 | 46 | 46 | 48 | 48 | 50 | 50 | 52 | 52 | 54 | 54 | 54 | | | | | | | | | | | | | | | | | | | | | | |
| 0.801 – 0.825 | 26 | 28 | 28 | 30 | 30 | 32 | 32 | 34 | 34 | 36 | 36 | 38 | 38 | 40 | 40 | 42 | 42 | 44 | 44 | 46 | 46 | 48 | 48 | 50 | 50 | 52 | 52 | 54 | 54 | 54 | | | | | | | | | | | | | | | | | | | | | | | |
| 0.826 – 0.850 | 28 | 28 | 30 | 30 | 32 | 32 | 34 | 34 | 36 | 36 | 38 | 38 | 40 | 40 | 42 | 42 | 44 | 44 | 46 | 46 | 48 | 48 | 50 | 50 | 52 | 52 | 54 | 54 | 54 | | | | | | | | | | | | | | | | | | | | | | | | |
| 0.851 – 0.875 | 28 | 30 | 30 | 32 | 32 | 34 | 34 | 36 | 36 | 38 | 38 | 40 | 40 | 42 | 42 | 44 | 44 | 46 | 46 | 48 | 48 | 50 | 50 | 52 | 52 | 54 | 54 | 54 | | | | | | | | | | | | | | | | | | | | | | | | | |
| 0.876 – 0.900 | 30 | 30 | 32 | 32 | 34 | 34 | 36 | 36 | 38 | 38 | 40 | 40 | 42 | 42 | 44 | 44 | 46 | 46 | 48 | 48 | 50 | 50 | 52 | 52 | 54 | 54 | 54 | | | | | | | | | | | | | | | | | | | | | | | | | | |
| 0.901 – 0.925 | 30 | 32 | 32 | 34 | 34 | 36 | 36 | 38 | 38 | 40 | 40 | 42 | 42 | 44 | 44 | 46 | 46 | 48 | 48 | 50 | 50 | 52 | 52 | 54 | 54 | 54 | | | | | | | | | | | | | | | | | | | | | | | | | | | |
| 0.926 – 0.950 | 32 | 32 | 34 | 34 | 36 | 36 | 38 | 38 | 40 | 40 | 42 | 42 | 44 | 44 | 46 | 46 | 48 | 48 | 50 | 50 | 52 | 52 | 54 | 54 | 54 | | | | | | | | | | | | | | | | | | | | | | | | | | | | |
| 0.951 – 0.975 | 32 | 34 | 34 | 36 | 36 | 38 | 38 | 40 | 40 | 42 | 42 | 44 | 44 | 46 | 46 | 48 | 48 | 50 | 50 | 52 | 52 | 54 | 54 | 54 | | | | | | | | | | | | | | | | | | | | | | | | | | | | | |
| 0.976 – 1.000 | 34 | 34 | 36 | 36 | 38 | 38 | 40 | 40 | 42 | 42 | 44 | 44 | 46 | 46 | 48 | 48 | 50 | 50 | 52 | 52 | 54 | 54 | 54 | | | | | | | | | | | | | | | | | | | | | | | | | | | | | | |
| 1.001 – 1.025 | 34 | 36 | 36 | 38 | 38 | 40 | 40 | 42 | 42 | 44 | 44 | 46 | 46 | 48 | 48 | 50 | 50 | 52 | 52 | 54 | 54 | 54 | | | | | | | | | | | | | | | | | | | | | | | | | | | | | | | |
| 1.026 – 1.050 | 36 | 36 | 38 | 38 | 40 | 40 | 42 | 42 | 44 | 44 | 46 | 46 | 48 | 48 | 50 | 50 | 52 | 52 | 54 | 54 | 54 | | | | | | | | | | | | | | | | | | | | | | | | | | | | | | | | |
| 1.051 – 1.075 | 36 | 38 | 38 | 40 | 40 | 42 | 42 | 44 | 44 | 46 | 46 | 48 | 48 | 50 | 50 | 52 | 52 | 54 | 54 | 54 | | | | | | | | | | | | | | | | | | | | | | | | | | | | | | | | | |
| 1.076 – 1.100 | 38 | 38 | 40 | 40 | 42 | 42 | 44 | 44 | 46 | 46 | 48 | 48 | 50 | 50 | 52 | 52 | 54 | 54 | 54 | | | | | | | | | | | | | | | | | | | | | | | | | | | | | | | | | | |
| 1.101 – 1.125 | 38 | 40 | 40 | 42 | 42 | 44 | 44 | 46 | 46 | 48 | 48 | 50 | 50 | 52 | 52 | 54 | 54 | 54 | | | | | | | | | | | | | | | | | | | | | | | | | | | | | | | | | | | |
| 1.126 – 1.150 | 40 | 40 | 42 | 42 | 44 | 44 | 46 | 46 | 48 | 48 | 50 | 50 | 52 | 52 | 54 | 54 | 54 | | | | | | | | | | | | | | | | | | | | | | | | | | | | | | | | | | | | |
| 1.151 – 1.175 | 40 | 42 | 42 | 44 | 44 | 46 | 46 | 48 | 48 | 50 | 50 | 52 | 52 | 54 | 54 | 54 | | | | | | | | | | | | | | | | | | | | | | | | | | | | | | | | | | | | | |
| 1.176 – 1.200 | 42 | 42 | 44 | 44 | 46 | 46 | 48 | 48 | 50 | 50 | 52 | 52 | 54 | 54 | 54 | | | | | | | | | | | | | | | | | | | | | | | | | | | | | | | | | | | | | | |
| 1.201 – 1.225 | 42 | 44 | 44 | 46 | 46 | 48 | 48 | 50 | 50 | 52 | 52 | 54 | 54 | 54 | | | | | | | | | | | | | | | | | | | | | | | | | | | | | | | | | | | | | | | |
| 1.226 – 1.250 | 44 | 44 | 46 | 46 | 48 | 48 | 50 | 50 | 52 | 52 | 54 | 54 | 54 | | | | | | | | | | | | | | | | | | | | | | | | | | | | | | | | | | | | | | | | |
| 1.251 – 1.275 | 44 | 46 | 46 | 48 | 48 | 50 | 50 | 52 | 52 | 54 | 54 | 54 | | | | | | | | | | | | | | | | | | | | | | | | | | | | | | | | | | | | | | | | | |
| 1.276 – 1.300 | 46 | 46 | 48 | 48 | 50 | 50 | 52 | 52 | 54 | 54 | 54 | | | | | | | | | | | | | | | | | | | | | | | | | | | | | | | | | | | | | | | | | | |
| 1.301 – 1.325 | 46 | 48 | 48 | 50 | 50 | 52 | 52 | 54 | 54 | 54 | | | | | | | | | | | | | | | | | | | | | | | | | | | | | | | | | | | | | | | | | | | |
| 1.326 – 1.350 | 48 | 48 | 50 | 50 | 52 | 52 | 54 | 54 | 54 | | | | | | | | | | | | | | | | | | | | | | | | | | | | | | | | | | | | | | | | | | | | |
| 1.351 – 1.375 | 48 | 50 | 50 | 52 | 52 | 54 | 54 | 54 | | | | | | | | | | | | | | | | | | | | | | | | | | | | | | | | | | | | | | | | | | | | | |
| 1.376 – 1.400 | 50 | 50 | 52 | 52 | 54 | 54 | 54 | | | | | | | | | | | | | | | | | | | | | | | | | | | | | | | | | | | | | | | | | | | | | | |
| 1.401 – 1.425 | 50 | 52 | 52 | 54 | 54 | 54 | | | | | | | | | | | | | | | | | | | | | | | | | | | | | | | | | | | | | | | | | | | | | | | |
| 1.426 – 1.450 | 52 | 52 | 54 | 54 | 54 | | | | | | | | | | | | | | | | | | | | | | | | | | | | | | | | | | | | | | | | | | | | | | | | |
| 1.451 – 1.475 | 52 | 54 | 54 | 54 | | | | | | | | | | | | | | | | | | | | | | | | | | | | | | | | | | | | | | | | | | | | | | | | | |
| 1.476 – 1.500 | 54 | 54 | 54 | | | | | | | | | | | | | | | | | | | | | | | | | | | | | | | | | | | | | | | | | | | | | | | | | | |
| 1.501 – 1.525 | 54 | 54 | | | | | | | | | | | | | | | | | | | | | | | | | | | | | | | | | | | | | | | | | | | | | | | | | | | |
| 1.526 – 1.550 | 54 | | | | | | | | | | | | | | | | | | | | | | | | | | | | | | | | | | | | | | | | | | | | | | | | | | | | |

New shim thickness mm (in.)

| Shim No. | Thickness | Shim No. | Thickness |
|---|---|---|---|
| 02 | 2.00 (0.0787) | 30 | 2.70 (0.1063) |
| 04 | 2.05 (0.0807) | 32 | 2.75 (0.1083) |
| 06 | 2.10 (0.0827) | 34 | 2.80 (0.1102) |
| 08 | 2.15 (0.0846) | 36 | 2.85 (0.1122) |
| 10 | 2.20 (0.0866) | 38 | 2.90 (0.1142) |
| 12 | 2.25 (0.0886) | 40 | 2.95 (0.1161) |
| 14 | 2.30 (0.0906) | 42 | 3.00 (0.1181) |
| 16 | 2.35 (0.0925) | 44 | 3.05 (0.1201) |
| 18 | 2.40 (0.0945) | 46 | 3.10 (0.1220) |
| 20 | 2.45 (0.0965) | 48 | 3.15 (0.1240) |
| 22 | 2.50 (0.0984) | 50 | 3.20 (0.1260) |
| 24 | 2.55 (0.1004) | 52 | 3.25 (0.1280) |
| 26 | 2.60 (0.1024) | 54 | 3.30 (0.1299) |
| 28 | 2.65 (0.1043) | | |

Example: A 0.1102" (2.800 mm) shim is installed and measured clearance is 0.0177" (0.450 mm). Replace 0.1102" (2.800 mm) shim with a No. 44 shim.

91G17356

Courtesy of Toyota Motor Sales, U.S.A., Inc.

*Fig. 6: Intake Valve Adjusting Shim Selection Chart (Celica 2.0L Turbo & MR2 2.0L Turbo)*

# 1991 ENGINE PERFORMANCE
## On-Vehicle Adjustments (Cont.)

EXHAUST VALVES

| Measured clearance (mm) | Installed shim thickness (mm) | | | | | | | | | | | | | | | | | | | | | | | | | | | | | | | | | | | | | | | | | | | | | | | | | | | |
|---|---|---|---|---|---|---|---|---|---|---|---|---|---|---|---|---|---|---|---|---|---|---|---|---|---|---|---|---|---|---|---|---|---|---|---|---|---|---|---|---|---|---|---|---|---|---|---|---|---|---|---|---|
| | 2.000 | 2.025 | 2.050 | 2.075 | 2.100 | 2.125 | 2.150 | 2.175 | 2.200 | 2.225 | 2.250 | 2.275 | 2.300 | 2.325 | 2.350 | 2.375 | 2.400 | 2.425 | 2.450 | 2.475 | 2.500 | 2.525 | 2.550 | 2.575 | 2.600 | 2.625 | 2.650 | 2.675 | 2.700 | 2.725 | 2.750 | 2.775 | 2.800 | 2.825 | 2.850 | 2.875 | 2.900 | 2.925 | 2.950 | 2.975 | 3.000 | 3.025 | 3.050 | 3.075 | 3.100 | 3.125 | 3.150 | 3.175 | 3.200 | 3.225 | 3.250 | 3.275 | 3.300 |
| 0.000 – 0.025 | | | | | | | | | 02 | 02 | 02 | 04 | 04 | 06 | 06 | 08 | 08 | 10 | 10 | 12 | 12 | 14 | 14 | 16 | 16 | 18 | 18 | 20 | 20 | 22 | 22 | 24 | 24 | 26 | 26 | 28 | 28 | 30 | 30 | 32 | 32 | 34 | 34 | 36 | 36 | 38 | 38 | 40 | 40 | 42 | 42 | 44 | 44 |
| 0.026 – 0.050 | | | | | | | | 02 | 02 | 02 | 04 | 04 | 06 | 06 | 08 | 08 | 10 | 10 | 12 | 12 | 14 | 14 | 16 | 16 | 18 | 18 | 20 | 20 | 22 | 22 | 24 | 24 | 26 | 26 | 28 | 28 | 30 | 30 | 32 | 32 | 34 | 34 | 36 | 36 | 38 | 38 | 40 | 40 | 42 | 42 | 44 | 44 | 46 |
| 0.051 – 0.075 | | | | | | | 02 | 02 | 02 | 04 | 04 | 06 | 06 | 08 | 08 | 10 | 10 | 12 | 12 | 14 | 14 | 16 | 16 | 18 | 18 | 20 | 20 | 22 | 22 | 24 | 24 | 26 | 26 | 28 | 28 | 30 | 30 | 32 | 32 | 34 | 34 | 36 | 36 | 38 | 38 | 40 | 40 | 42 | 42 | 44 | 44 | 46 | 46 |
| 0.076 – 0.100 | | | | | | 02 | 02 | 02 | 04 | 04 | 06 | 06 | 08 | 08 | 10 | 10 | 12 | 12 | 14 | 14 | 16 | 16 | 18 | 18 | 20 | 20 | 22 | 22 | 24 | 24 | 26 | 26 | 28 | 28 | 30 | 30 | 32 | 32 | 34 | 34 | 36 | 36 | 38 | 38 | 40 | 40 | 42 | 42 | 44 | 44 | 46 | 46 | 48 |
| 0.101 – 0.125 | | | | | 02 | 02 | 02 | 04 | 04 | 06 | 06 | 08 | 08 | 10 | 10 | 12 | 12 | 14 | 14 | 16 | 16 | 18 | 18 | 20 | 20 | 22 | 22 | 24 | 24 | 26 | 26 | 28 | 28 | 30 | 30 | 32 | 32 | 34 | 34 | 36 | 36 | 38 | 38 | 40 | 40 | 42 | 42 | 44 | 44 | 46 | 46 | 48 | 48 |
| 0.126 – 0.150 | | | | 02 | 02 | 02 | 04 | 04 | 06 | 06 | 08 | 08 | 10 | 10 | 12 | 12 | 14 | 14 | 16 | 16 | 18 | 18 | 20 | 20 | 22 | 22 | 24 | 24 | 26 | 26 | 28 | 28 | 30 | 30 | 32 | 32 | 34 | 34 | 36 | 36 | 38 | 38 | 40 | 40 | 42 | 42 | 44 | 44 | 46 | 46 | 48 | 48 | 50 |
| 0.151 – 0.175 | | | 02 | 02 | 02 | 04 | 04 | 06 | 06 | 08 | 08 | 10 | 10 | 12 | 12 | 14 | 14 | 16 | 16 | 18 | 18 | 20 | 20 | 22 | 22 | 24 | 24 | 26 | 26 | 28 | 28 | 30 | 30 | 32 | 32 | 34 | 34 | 36 | 36 | 38 | 38 | 40 | 40 | 42 | 42 | 44 | 44 | 46 | 46 | 48 | 48 | 50 | 50 |
| 0.176 – 0.199 | | 02 | 02 | 02 | 04 | 04 | 06 | 06 | 08 | 08 | 10 | 10 | 12 | 12 | 14 | 14 | 16 | 16 | 18 | 18 | 20 | 20 | 22 | 22 | 24 | 24 | 26 | 26 | 28 | 28 | 30 | 30 | 32 | 32 | 34 | 34 | 36 | 36 | 38 | 38 | 40 | 40 | 42 | 42 | 44 | 44 | 46 | 46 | 48 | 48 | 50 | 50 | 52 |
| 0.200 – 0.300 | | | | | | | | | | | | | | | | | | | | | | | | | | | | | | | | | | | | | | | | | | | | | | | | | | | | | |
| 0.301 – 0.325 | 04 | 06 | 06 | 08 | 08 | 10 | 10 | 12 | 12 | 14 | 14 | 16 | 16 | 18 | 18 | 20 | 20 | 22 | 22 | 24 | 24 | 26 | 26 | 28 | 28 | 30 | 30 | 32 | 32 | 34 | 34 | 36 | 36 | 38 | 38 | 40 | 40 | 42 | 42 | 44 | 44 | 46 | 46 | 48 | 48 | 50 | 50 | 52 | 52 | 54 | 54 | 54 | |
| 0.326 – 0.350 | 06 | 06 | 08 | 08 | 10 | 10 | 12 | 12 | 14 | 14 | 16 | 16 | 18 | 18 | 20 | 20 | 22 | 22 | 24 | 24 | 26 | 26 | 28 | 28 | 30 | 30 | 32 | 32 | 34 | 34 | 36 | 36 | 38 | 38 | 40 | 40 | 42 | 42 | 44 | 44 | 46 | 46 | 48 | 48 | 50 | 50 | 52 | 52 | 54 | 54 | 54 | | |
| 0.351 – 0.375 | 06 | 08 | 08 | 10 | 10 | 12 | 12 | 14 | 14 | 16 | 16 | 18 | 18 | 20 | 20 | 22 | 22 | 24 | 24 | 26 | 26 | 28 | 28 | 30 | 30 | 32 | 32 | 34 | 34 | 36 | 36 | 38 | 38 | 40 | 40 | 42 | 42 | 44 | 44 | 46 | 46 | 48 | 48 | 50 | 50 | 52 | 52 | 54 | 54 | 54 | | | |
| 0.376 – 0.400 | 08 | 08 | 10 | 10 | 12 | 12 | 14 | 14 | 16 | 16 | 18 | 18 | 20 | 20 | 22 | 22 | 24 | 24 | 26 | 26 | 28 | 28 | 30 | 30 | 32 | 32 | 34 | 34 | 36 | 36 | 38 | 38 | 40 | 40 | 42 | 42 | 44 | 44 | 46 | 46 | 48 | 48 | 50 | 50 | 52 | 52 | 54 | 54 | 54 | | | | |
| 0.401 – 0.425 | 08 | 10 | 10 | 12 | 12 | 14 | 14 | 16 | 16 | 18 | 18 | 20 | 20 | 22 | 22 | 24 | 24 | 26 | 26 | 28 | 28 | 30 | 30 | 32 | 32 | 34 | 34 | 36 | 36 | 38 | 38 | 40 | 40 | 42 | 42 | 44 | 44 | 46 | 46 | 48 | 48 | 50 | 50 | 52 | 52 | 54 | 54 | 54 | | | | | |
| 0.426 – 0.450 | 10 | 10 | 12 | 12 | 14 | 14 | 16 | 16 | 18 | 18 | 20 | 20 | 22 | 22 | 24 | 24 | 26 | 26 | 28 | 28 | 30 | 30 | 32 | 32 | 34 | 34 | 36 | 36 | 38 | 38 | 40 | 40 | 42 | 42 | 44 | 44 | 46 | 46 | 48 | 48 | 50 | 50 | 52 | 52 | 54 | 54 | 54 | | | | | | |
| 0.451 – 0.475 | 10 | 12 | 12 | 14 | 14 | 16 | 16 | 18 | 18 | 20 | 20 | 22 | 22 | 24 | 24 | 26 | 26 | 28 | 28 | 30 | 30 | 32 | 32 | 34 | 34 | 36 | 36 | 38 | 38 | 40 | 40 | 42 | 42 | 44 | 44 | 46 | 46 | 48 | 48 | 50 | 50 | 52 | 52 | 54 | 54 | 54 | | | | | | | |
| 0.476 – 0.500 | 12 | 12 | 14 | 14 | 16 | 16 | 18 | 18 | 20 | 20 | 22 | 22 | 24 | 24 | 26 | 26 | 28 | 28 | 30 | 30 | 32 | 32 | 34 | 34 | 36 | 36 | 38 | 38 | 40 | 40 | 42 | 42 | 44 | 44 | 46 | 46 | 48 | 48 | 50 | 50 | 52 | 52 | 54 | 54 | 54 | | | | | | | | |
| 0.501 – 0.525 | 12 | 14 | 14 | 16 | 16 | 18 | 18 | 20 | 20 | 22 | 22 | 24 | 24 | 26 | 26 | 28 | 28 | 30 | 30 | 32 | 32 | 34 | 34 | 36 | 36 | 38 | 38 | 40 | 40 | 42 | 42 | 44 | 44 | 46 | 46 | 48 | 48 | 50 | 50 | 52 | 52 | 54 | 54 | 54 | | | | | | | | | |
| 0.526 – 0.550 | 14 | 14 | 16 | 16 | 18 | 18 | 20 | 20 | 22 | 22 | 24 | 24 | 26 | 26 | 28 | 28 | 30 | 30 | 32 | 32 | 34 | 34 | 36 | 36 | 38 | 38 | 40 | 40 | 42 | 42 | 44 | 44 | 46 | 46 | 48 | 48 | 50 | 50 | 52 | 52 | 54 | 54 | 54 | | | | | | | | | | |
| 0.551 – 0.575 | 14 | 16 | 16 | 18 | 18 | 20 | 20 | 22 | 22 | 24 | 24 | 26 | 26 | 28 | 28 | 30 | 30 | 32 | 32 | 34 | 34 | 36 | 36 | 38 | 38 | 40 | 40 | 42 | 42 | 44 | 44 | 46 | 46 | 48 | 48 | 50 | 50 | 52 | 52 | 54 | 54 | 54 | | | | | | | | | | | |
| 0.576 – 0.600 | 16 | 16 | 18 | 18 | 20 | 20 | 22 | 22 | 24 | 24 | 26 | 26 | 28 | 28 | 30 | 30 | 32 | 32 | 34 | 34 | 36 | 36 | 38 | 38 | 40 | 40 | 42 | 42 | 44 | 44 | 46 | 46 | 48 | 48 | 50 | 50 | 52 | 52 | 54 | 54 | 54 | | | | | | | | | | | | |
| 0.601 – 0.625 | 16 | 18 | 18 | 20 | 20 | 22 | 22 | 24 | 24 | 26 | 26 | 28 | 28 | 30 | 30 | 32 | 32 | 34 | 34 | 36 | 36 | 38 | 38 | 40 | 40 | 42 | 42 | 44 | 44 | 46 | 46 | 48 | 48 | 50 | 50 | 52 | 52 | 54 | 54 | 54 | | | | | | | | | | | | | |
| 0.626 – 0.650 | 18 | 18 | 20 | 20 | 22 | 22 | 24 | 24 | 26 | 26 | 28 | 28 | 30 | 30 | 32 | 32 | 34 | 34 | 36 | 36 | 38 | 38 | 40 | 40 | 42 | 42 | 44 | 44 | 46 | 46 | 48 | 48 | 50 | 50 | 52 | 52 | 54 | 54 | 54 | | | | | | | | | | | | | | |
| 0.651 – 0.675 | 18 | 20 | 20 | 22 | 22 | 24 | 24 | 26 | 26 | 28 | 28 | 30 | 30 | 32 | 32 | 34 | 34 | 36 | 36 | 38 | 38 | 40 | 40 | 42 | 42 | 44 | 44 | 46 | 46 | 48 | 48 | 50 | 50 | 52 | 52 | 54 | 54 | 54 | | | | | | | | | | | | | | | |
| 0.676 – 0.700 | 20 | 20 | 22 | 22 | 24 | 24 | 26 | 26 | 28 | 28 | 30 | 30 | 32 | 32 | 34 | 34 | 36 | 36 | 38 | 38 | 40 | 40 | 42 | 42 | 44 | 44 | 46 | 46 | 48 | 48 | 50 | 50 | 52 | 52 | 54 | 54 | 54 | | | | | | | | | | | | | | | | |
| 0.701 – 0.725 | 20 | 22 | 22 | 24 | 24 | 26 | 26 | 28 | 28 | 30 | 30 | 32 | 32 | 34 | 34 | 36 | 36 | 38 | 38 | 40 | 40 | 42 | 42 | 44 | 44 | 46 | 46 | 48 | 48 | 50 | 50 | 52 | 52 | 54 | 54 | 54 | | | | | | | | | | | | | | | | | |
| 0.726 – 0.750 | 22 | 22 | 24 | 24 | 26 | 26 | 28 | 28 | 30 | 30 | 32 | 32 | 34 | 34 | 36 | 36 | 38 | 38 | 40 | 40 | 42 | 42 | 44 | 44 | 46 | 46 | 48 | 48 | 50 | 50 | 52 | 52 | 54 | 54 | 54 | | | | | | | | | | | | | | | | | | |
| 0.751 – 0.775 | 22 | 24 | 24 | 26 | 26 | 28 | 28 | 30 | 30 | 32 | 32 | 34 | 34 | 36 | 36 | 38 | 38 | 40 | 40 | 42 | 42 | 44 | 44 | 46 | 46 | 48 | 48 | 50 | 50 | 52 | 52 | 54 | 54 | 54 | | | | | | | | | | | | | | | | | | | |
| 0.776 – 0.800 | 24 | 24 | 26 | 26 | 28 | 28 | 30 | 30 | 32 | 32 | 34 | 34 | 36 | 36 | 38 | 38 | 40 | 40 | 42 | 42 | 44 | 44 | 46 | 46 | 48 | 48 | 50 | 50 | 52 | 52 | 54 | 54 | 54 | | | | | | | | | | | | | | | | | | | | |
| 0.801 – 0.825 | 24 | 26 | 26 | 28 | 28 | 30 | 30 | 32 | 32 | 34 | 34 | 36 | 36 | 38 | 38 | 40 | 40 | 42 | 42 | 44 | 44 | 46 | 46 | 48 | 48 | 50 | 50 | 52 | 52 | 54 | 54 | 54 | | | | | | | | | | | | | | | | | | | | | |
| 0.826 – 0.850 | 26 | 26 | 28 | 28 | 30 | 30 | 32 | 32 | 34 | 34 | 36 | 36 | 38 | 38 | 40 | 40 | 42 | 42 | 44 | 44 | 46 | 46 | 48 | 48 | 50 | 50 | 52 | 52 | 54 | 54 | 54 | | | | | | | | | | | | | | | | | | | | | | |
| 0.851 – 0.875 | 26 | 28 | 28 | 30 | 30 | 32 | 32 | 34 | 34 | 36 | 36 | 38 | 38 | 40 | 40 | 42 | 42 | 44 | 44 | 46 | 46 | 48 | 48 | 50 | 50 | 52 | 52 | 54 | 54 | 54 | | | | | | | | | | | | | | | | | | | | | | | |
| 0.876 – 0.900 | 28 | 28 | 30 | 30 | 32 | 32 | 34 | 34 | 36 | 36 | 38 | 38 | 40 | 40 | 42 | 42 | 44 | 44 | 46 | 46 | 48 | 48 | 50 | 50 | 52 | 52 | 54 | 54 | 54 | | | | | | | | | | | | | | | | | | | | | | | | |
| 0.901 – 0.925 | 28 | 30 | 30 | 32 | 32 | 34 | 34 | 36 | 36 | 38 | 38 | 40 | 40 | 42 | 42 | 44 | 44 | 46 | 46 | 48 | 48 | 50 | 50 | 52 | 52 | 54 | 54 | 54 | | | | | | | | | | | | | | | | | | | | | | | | | |
| 0.926 – 0.950 | 30 | 30 | 32 | 32 | 34 | 34 | 36 | 36 | 38 | 38 | 40 | 40 | 42 | 42 | 44 | 44 | 46 | 46 | 48 | 48 | 50 | 50 | 52 | 52 | 54 | 54 | 54 | | | | | | | | | | | | | | | | | | | | | | | | | | |
| 0.951 – 0.975 | 30 | 32 | 32 | 34 | 34 | 36 | 36 | 38 | 38 | 40 | 40 | 42 | 42 | 44 | 44 | 46 | 46 | 48 | 48 | 50 | 50 | 52 | 52 | 54 | 54 | 54 | | | | | | | | | | | | | | | | | | | | | | | | | | | |
| 0.976 – 1.000 | 32 | 32 | 34 | 34 | 36 | 36 | 38 | 38 | 40 | 40 | 42 | 42 | 44 | 44 | 46 | 46 | 48 | 48 | 50 | 50 | 52 | 52 | 54 | 54 | 54 | | | | | | | | | | | | | | | | | | | | | | | | | | | | |
| 1.001 – 1.025 | 32 | 34 | 34 | 36 | 36 | 38 | 38 | 40 | 40 | 42 | 42 | 44 | 44 | 46 | 46 | 48 | 48 | 50 | 50 | 52 | 52 | 54 | 54 | 54 | | | | | | | | | | | | | | | | | | | | | | | | | | | | | |
| 1.026 – 1.050 | 34 | 34 | 36 | 36 | 38 | 38 | 40 | 40 | 42 | 42 | 44 | 44 | 46 | 46 | 48 | 48 | 50 | 50 | 52 | 52 | 54 | 54 | 54 | | | | | | | | | | | | | | | | | | | | | | | | | | | | | | |
| 1.051 – 1.075 | 34 | 36 | 36 | 38 | 38 | 40 | 40 | 42 | 42 | 44 | 44 | 46 | 46 | 48 | 48 | 50 | 50 | 52 | 52 | 54 | 54 | 54 | | | | | | | | | | | | | | | | | | | | | | | | | | | | | | | |
| 1.076 – 1.100 | 36 | 36 | 38 | 38 | 40 | 40 | 42 | 42 | 44 | 44 | 46 | 46 | 48 | 48 | 50 | 50 | 52 | 52 | 54 | 54 | 54 | | | | | | | | | | | | | | | | | | | | | | | | | | | | | | | | |
| 1.101 – 1.125 | 36 | 38 | 38 | 40 | 40 | 42 | 42 | 44 | 44 | 46 | 46 | 48 | 48 | 50 | 50 | 52 | 52 | 54 | 54 | 54 | | | | | | | | | | | | | | | | | | | | | | | | | | | | | | | | | |
| 1.126 – 1.150 | 38 | 38 | 40 | 40 | 42 | 42 | 44 | 44 | 46 | 46 | 48 | 48 | 50 | 50 | 52 | 52 | 54 | 54 | 54 | | | | | | | | | | | | | | | | | | | | | | | | | | | | | | | | | | |
| 1.151 – 1.175 | 38 | 40 | 40 | 42 | 42 | 44 | 44 | 46 | 46 | 48 | 48 | 50 | 50 | 52 | 52 | 54 | 54 | 54 | | | | | | | | | | | | | | | | | | | | | | | | | | | | | | | | | | | |
| 1.176 – 1.200 | 40 | 40 | 42 | 42 | 44 | 44 | 46 | 46 | 48 | 48 | 50 | 50 | 52 | 52 | 54 | 54 | 54 | | | | | | | | | | | | | | | | | | | | | | | | | | | | | | | | | | | | |
| 1.201 – 1.225 | 40 | 42 | 42 | 44 | 44 | 46 | 46 | 48 | 48 | 50 | 50 | 52 | 52 | 54 | 54 | 54 | | | | | | | | | | | | | | | | | | | | | | | | | | | | | | | | | | | | | |
| 1.226 – 1.250 | 42 | 42 | 44 | 44 | 46 | 46 | 48 | 48 | 50 | 50 | 52 | 52 | 54 | 54 | 54 | | | | | | | | | | | | | | | | | | | | | | | | | | | | | | | | | | | | | | |
| 1.251 – 1.275 | 42 | 44 | 44 | 46 | 46 | 48 | 48 | 50 | 50 | 52 | 52 | 54 | 54 | 54 | | | | | | | | | | | | | | | | | | | | | | | | | | | | | | | | | | | | | | | |
| 1.276 – 1.300 | 44 | 44 | 46 | 46 | 48 | 48 | 50 | 50 | 52 | 52 | 54 | 54 | 54 | | | | | | | | | | | | | | | | | | | | | | | | | | | | | | | | | | | | | | | | |
| 1.301 – 1.325 | 44 | 46 | 46 | 48 | 48 | 50 | 50 | 52 | 52 | 54 | 54 | 54 | | | | | | | | | | | | | | | | | | | | | | | | | | | | | | | | | | | | | | | | | |
| 1.326 – 1.350 | 46 | 46 | 48 | 48 | 50 | 50 | 52 | 52 | 54 | 54 | 54 | | | | | | | | | | | | | | | | | | | | | | | | | | | | | | | | | | | | | | | | | | |
| 1.351 – 1.375 | 46 | 48 | 48 | 50 | 50 | 52 | 52 | 54 | 54 | 54 | | | | | | | | | | | | | | | | | | | | | | | | | | | | | | | | | | | | | | | | | | | |
| 1.376 – 1.400 | 48 | 48 | 50 | 50 | 52 | 52 | 54 | 54 | 54 | | | | | | | | | | | | | | | | | | | | | | | | | | | | | | | | | | | | | | | | | | | | |
| 1.401 – 1.425 | 48 | 50 | 50 | 52 | 52 | 54 | 54 | 54 | | | | | | | | | | | | | | | | | | | | | | | | | | | | | | | | | | | | | | | | | | | | | |
| 1.426 – 1.450 | 50 | 50 | 52 | 52 | 54 | 54 | 54 | | | | | | | | | | | | | | | | | | | | | | | | | | | | | | | | | | | | | | | | | | | | | | |
| 1.451 – 1.475 | 50 | 52 | 52 | 54 | 54 | 54 | | | | | | | | | | | | | | | | | | | | | | | | | | | | | | | | | | | | | | | | | | | | | | | |
| 1.476 – 1.500 | 52 | 52 | 54 | 54 | 54 | | | | | | | | | | | | | | | | | | | | | | | | | | | | | | | | | | | | | | | | | | | | | | | | |
| 1.501 – 1.525 | 52 | 54 | 54 | 54 | | | | | | | | | | | | | | | | | | | | | | | | | | | | | | | | | | | | | | | | | | | | | | | | | |
| 1.526 – 1.550 | 54 | 54 | 54 | | | | | | | | | | | | | | | | | | | | | | | | | | | | | | | | | | | | | | | | | | | | | | | | | | |
| 1.551 – 1.575 | 54 | 54 | | | | | | | | | | | | | | | | | | | | | | | | | | | | | | | | | | | | | | | | | | | | | | | | | | | |
| 1.576 – 1.600 | 54 | | | | | | | | | | | | | | | | | | | | | | | | | | | | | | | | | | | | | | | | | | | | | | | | | | | | |

New shim thickness mm (in.)

| Shim No. | Thickness | Shim No. | Thickness |
|---|---|---|---|
| 02 | 2.00 (0.0787) | 30 | 2.70 (0.1063) |
| 04 | 2.05 (0.0807) | 32 | 2.75 (0.1083) |
| 06 | 2.10 (0.0827) | 34 | 2.80 (0.1102) |
| 08 | 2.15 (0.0846) | 36 | 2.85 (0.1122) |
| 10 | 2.20 (0.0866) | 38 | 2.90 (0.1142) |
| 12 | 2.25 (0.0886) | 40 | 2.95 (0.1161) |
| 14 | 2.30 (0.0906) | 42 | 3.00 (0.1181) |
| 16 | 2.35 (0.0925) | 44 | 3.05 (0.1201) |
| 18 | 2.40 (0.0945) | 46 | 3.10 (0.1220) |
| 20 | 2.45 (0.0965) | 48 | 3.15 (0.1240) |
| 22 | 2.50 (0.0984) | 50 | 3.20 (0.1260) |
| 24 | 2.55 (0.1004) | 52 | 3.25 (0.1280) |
| 26 | 2.60 (0.1024) | 54 | 3.30 (0.1299) |
| 28 | 2.65 (0.1043) | | |

EXAMPLE: A 0.1102" (2.800 mm) shim is installed and measured clearance is 0.0177" (0.450 mm). Replace 0.1102" (2.800 mm) shim with a No. 42 shim.

91H17357

Courtesy of Toyota Motor Sales, U.S.A., Inc.

*Fig. 7: Exhaust Valve Adjusting Shim Selection Chart (Celica 2.0L Turbo & MR2 2.0L Turbo)*

# 1991 ENGINE PERFORMANCE
## On-Vehicle Adjustments (Cont.)

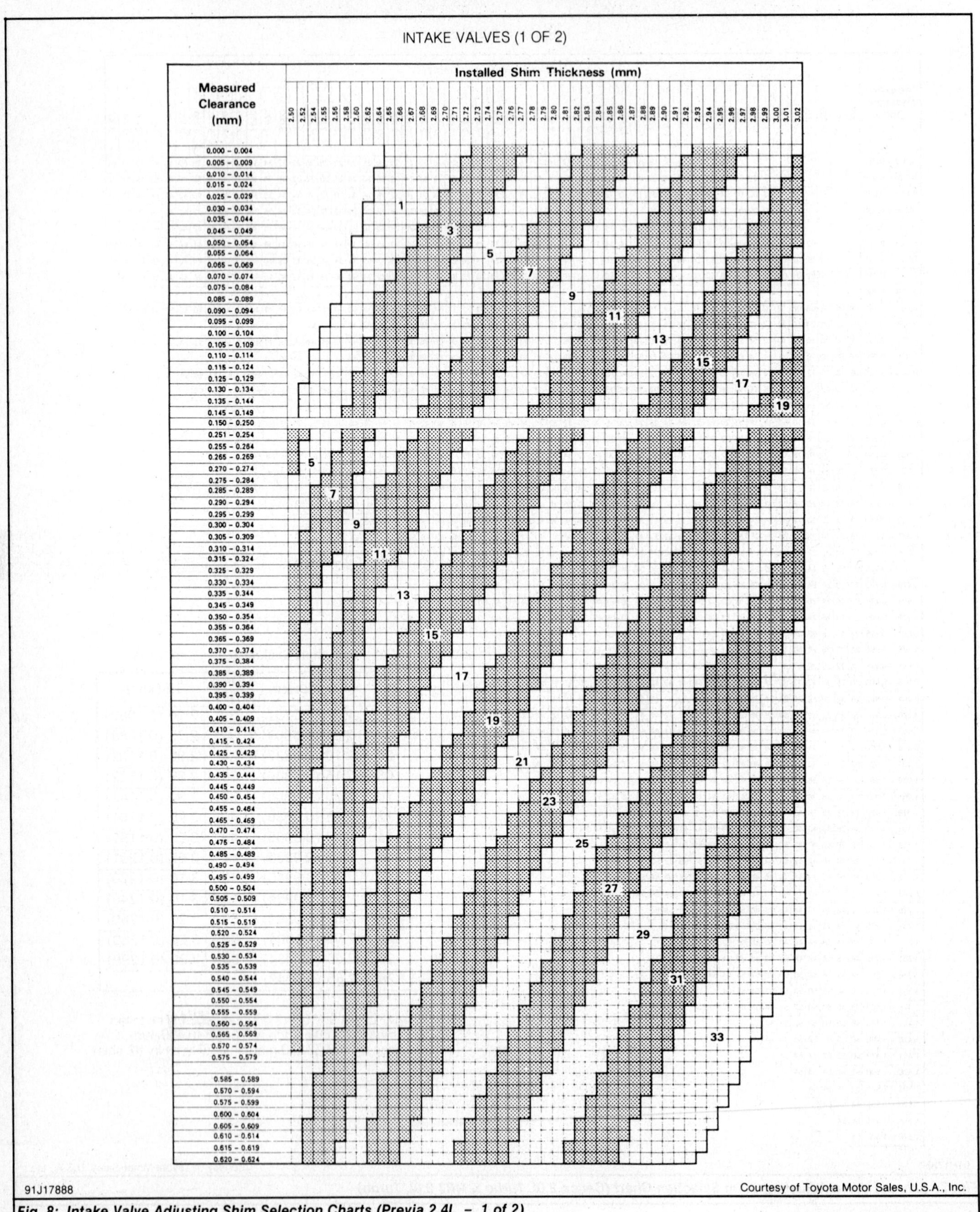


*Fig. 8: Intake Valve Adjusting Shim Selection Charts (Previa 2.4L – 1 of 2)*

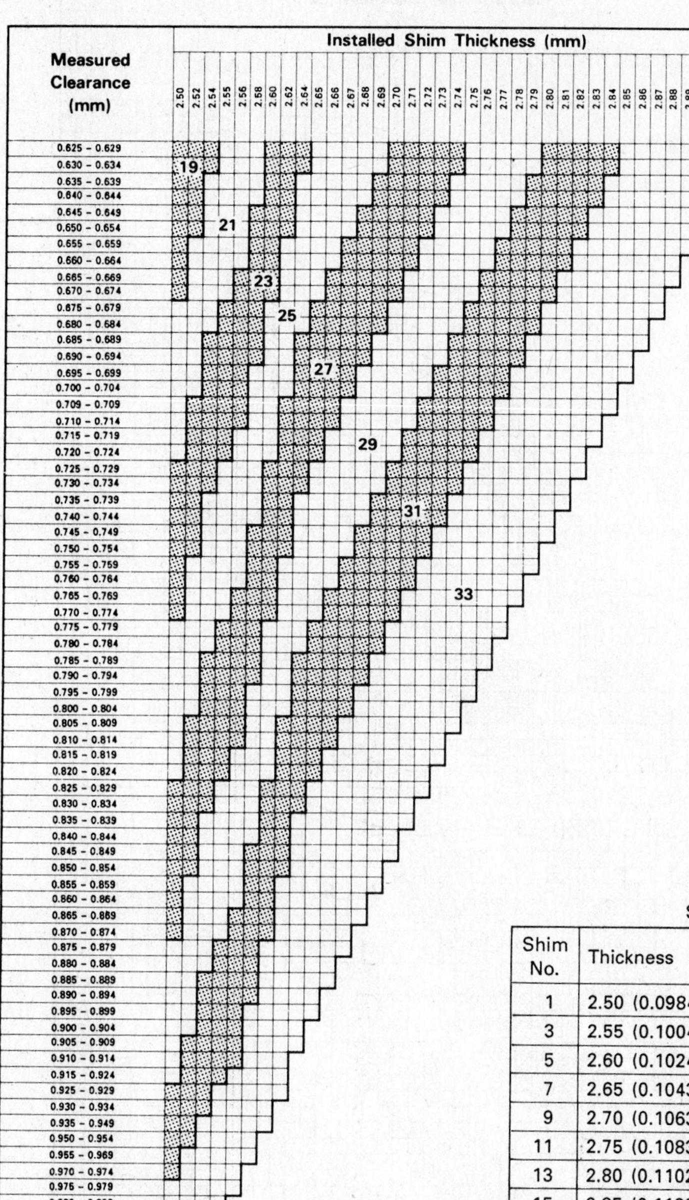


Shim Thickness

| Shim No. | Thickness mm (in.) | Shim No. | Thickness mm (in.) |
|---|---|---|---|
| 1 | 2.50 (0.0984) | 19 | 2.95 (0.1161) |
| 3 | 2.55 (0.1004) | 21 | 3.00 (0.1181) |
| 5 | 2.60 (0.1024) | 23 | 3.05 (0.1201) |
| 7 | 2.65 (0.1043) | 25 | 3.10 (0.1220) |
| 9 | 2.70 (0.1063) | 27 | 3.15 (0.1240) |
| 11 | 2.75 (0.1083) | 29 | 3.20 (0.1260) |
| 13 | 2.80 (0.1102) | 31 | 3.25 (0.1280) |
| 15 | 2.85 (0.1122) | 33 | 3.30 (0.1299) |
| 17 | 2.90 (0.1142) | | |

EXAMPLE: A 0.0992" (2.52 mm) shim is installed and measured clearance is 0.0246" (0.625 mm). Replace 0.0992" (2.52 mm) shim with a No. 19 shim.

91A17889 91D17890



***Fig. 9: Intake Valve Adjusting Shim Selection Charts (Previa 2.4L - 2 of 2)***

# 1991 ENGINE PERFORMANCE
## On-Vehicle Adjustments (Cont.)

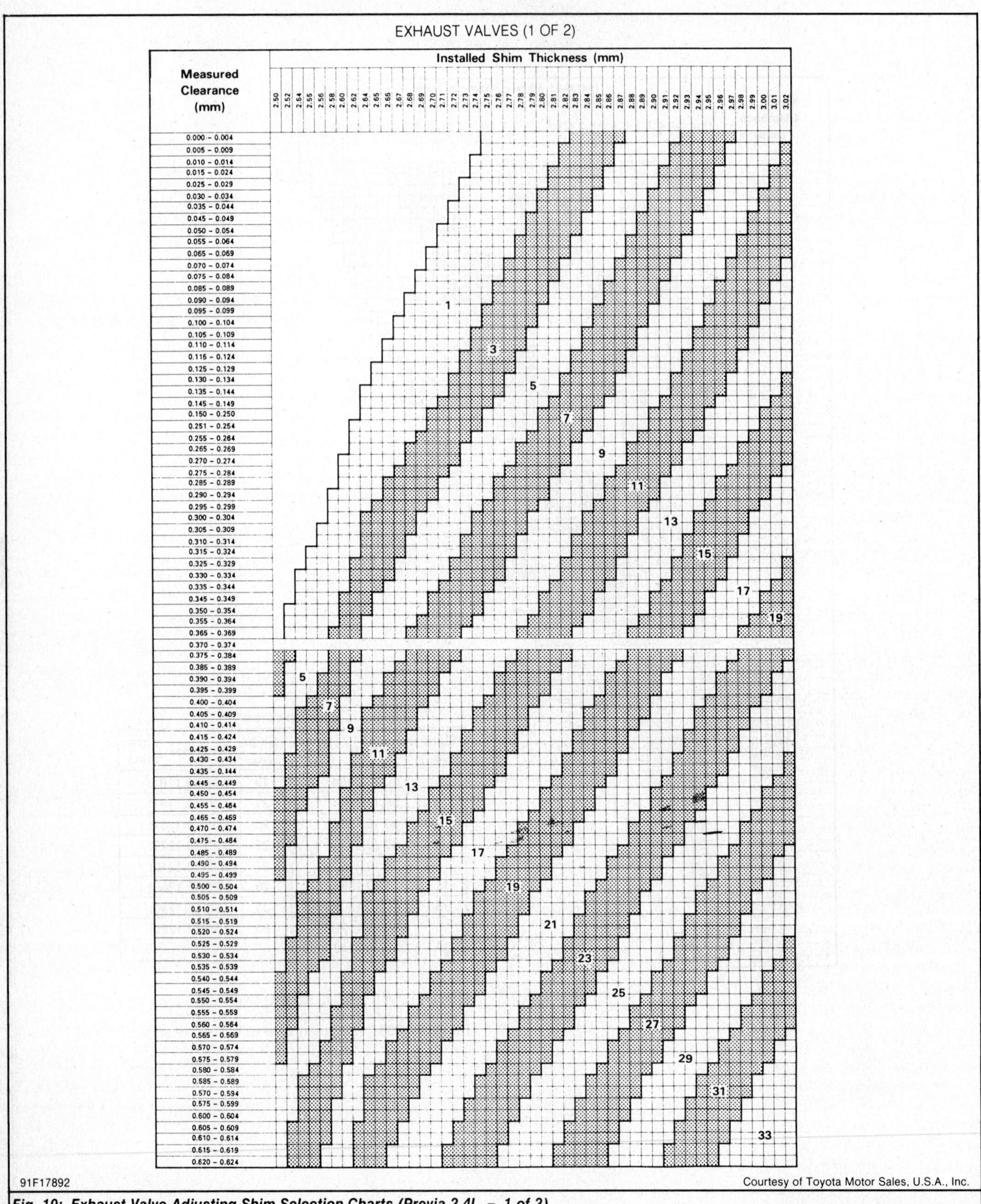


Courtesy of Toyota Motor Sales, U.S.A., Inc.

*Fig. 10: Exhaust Valve Adjusting Shim Selection Charts (Previa 2.4L – 1 of 2)*

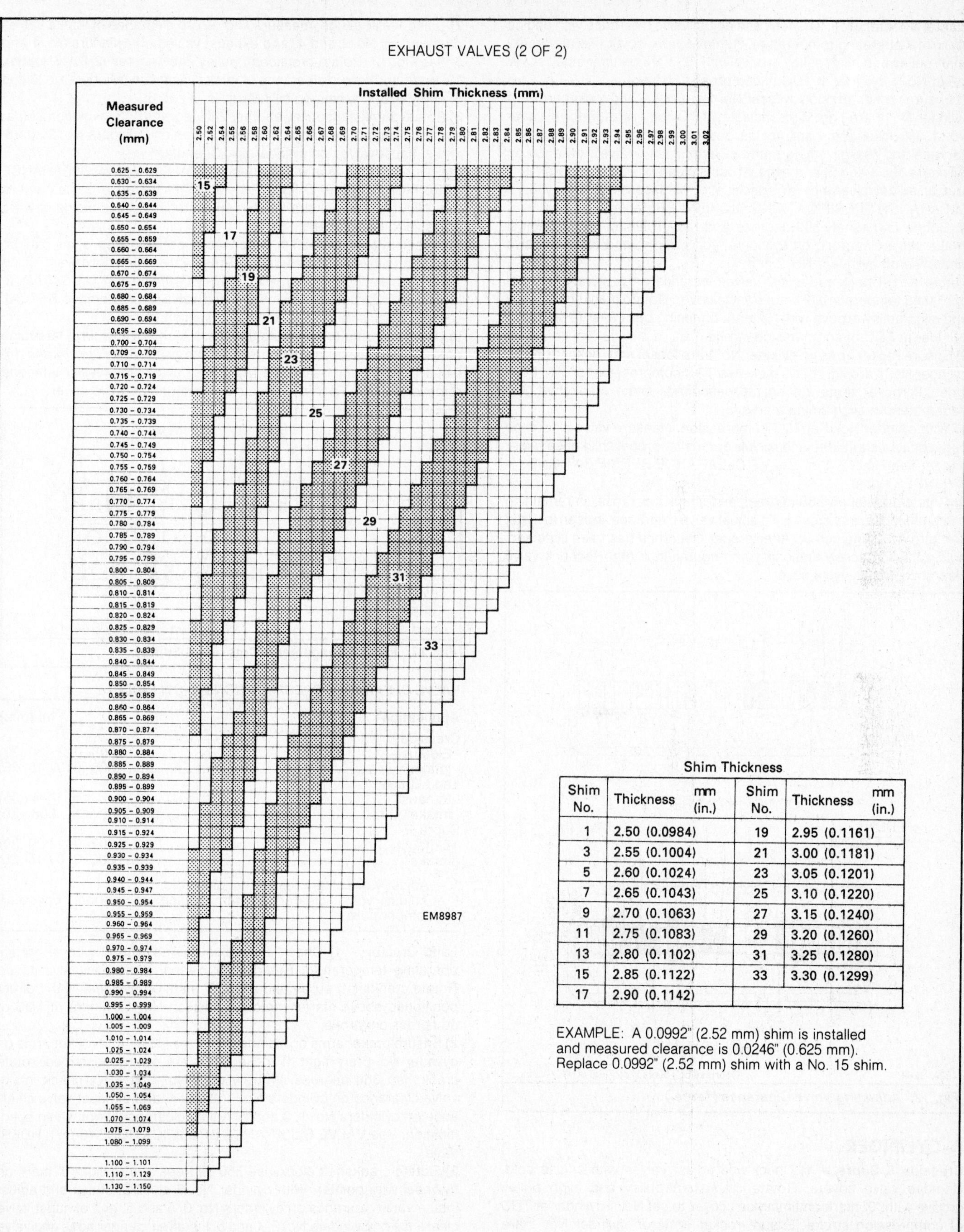


Shim Thickness

| Shim No. | Thickness mm (in.) | Shim No. | Thickness mm (in.) |
|---|---|---|---|
| 1 | 2.50 (0.0984) | 19 | 2.95 (0.1161) |
| 3 | 2.55 (0.1004) | 21 | 3.00 (0.1181) |
| 5 | 2.60 (0.1024) | 23 | 3.05 (0.1201) |
| 7 | 2.65 (0.1043) | 25 | 3.10 (0.1220) |
| 9 | 2.70 (0.1063) | 27 | 3.15 (0.1240) |
| 11 | 2.75 (0.1083) | 29 | 3.20 (0.1260) |
| 13 | 2.80 (0.1102) | 31 | 3.25 (0.1280) |
| 15 | 2.85 (0.1122) | 33 | 3.30 (0.1299) |
| 17 | 2.90 (0.1142) | | |

EXAMPLE: A 0.0992" (2.52 mm) shim is installed and measured clearance is 0.0246" (0.625 mm). Replace 0.0992" (2.52 mm) shim with a No. 15 shim.

91G17893 91H17894

Courtesy of Toyota Motor Sales, U.S.A., Inc.

*Fig. 11: Exhaust Valve Adjusting Shim Selection Charts (Previa 2.4L - 2 of 2)*

# 1991 ENGINE PERFORMANCE
# On-Vehicle Adjustments (Cont.)

**Pickup & 4Runner** – **1)** Check and adjust valve clearance with engine at normal operating temperature. Remove valve cover. Rotate crankshaft pulley and align pulley groove with "0" mark on timing belt cover to set No. 1 cylinder at TDC of compression stroke.
**2)** Ensure rocker arms on cylinder No. 1 are loose, and rocker arms on cylinder No. 4 are tight. This indicates TDC compression for cylinder No. 1. If rocker arms are not as described, rotate crankshaft 360 degrees and realign timing marks. Check intake valve clearance on cylinders No. 1 and 2, and exhaust valve clearance on cylinders No. 1 and 3; adjust clearance to specification if necessary. See VALVE CLEARANCE SPECIFICATIONS (4-CYLINDER) table.
**3)** Rotate crankshaft 360 degrees and realign timing marks. Adjust intake valve clearance on cylinders No. 3 and 4, and exhaust valve clearance on cylinders No. 2 and 4.
**Tercel** – **1)** Check and adjust valve clearance with engine at normal operating temperature. Remove valve cover. Rotate crankshaft pulley and align pulley groove with "0" mark on timing belt cover to set No. 1 cylinder at TDC of compression stroke.
**2)** Ensure rocker arms on cylinder No. 1 are loose, and rocker arms on cylinder No. 4 are tight. This indicates TDC compression for No. 1 cylinder. If rocker arms are not as described, rotate crankshaft 360 degrees and realign timing marks.
**3)** With cylinder No. 1 at TDC compression, measure valve clearance between camshaft lobe and rocker arm using proper thickness feeler gauge. *See Fig. 12.* See VALVE CLEARANCE SPECIFICATIONS (4-CYLINDER) table.
**4)** Rotate crankshaft 360 degrees and check clearance on remaining camshaft lobes. *See Fig. 12.* To adjust valve clearance, loosen lock nut and turn adjusting screw. After proper clearance has been obtained, hold adjusting screw stationary and tighten lock nut. Recheck valve clearance. Install valve cover.

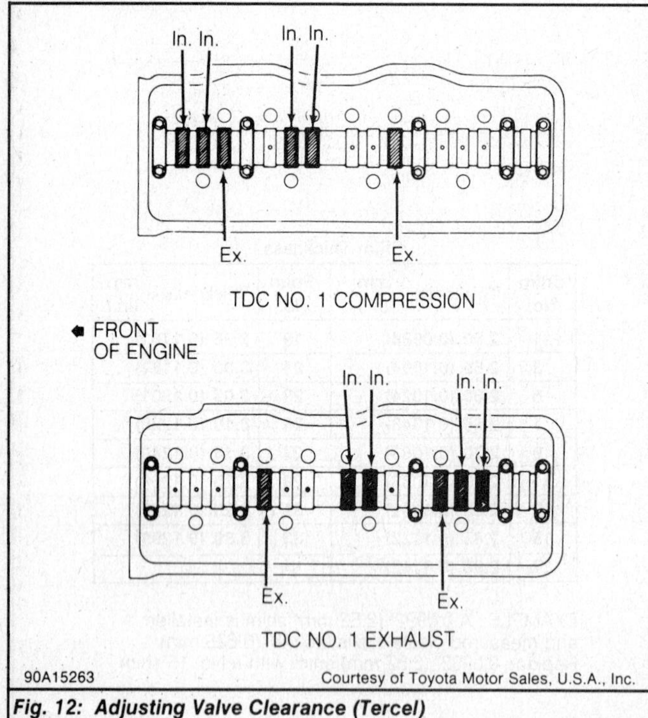


*Fig. 12: Adjusting Valve Clearance (Tercel)*

## 6-CYLINDER

**Cressida & Supra** – **1)** Check and adjust valves with engine cold. Remove valve covers. Rotate crankshaft pulley and align pulley groove with "0" mark on timing belt cover to set No. 1 cylinder at TDC of compression stroke. Ensure rocker arms on cylinder No. 1 are loose, and rocker arms on cylinder No. 6 are tight. If rocker arms are not as described, rotate crankshaft 360 degrees and realign timing marks.
**2)** Using feeler gauge, measure and record clearance of intake valves on cylinders No. 1 and 4, and exhaust valves on cylinders No. 1 and 5. *See Fig. 13.* Rotate crankshaft pulley 240 degrees (2/3 revolution). Measure and record clearance of intake valves on cylinders No. 3 and 5, and exhaust valves on cylinders No. 3 and 6.
**3)** Rotate crankshaft pulley another 240 degrees (2/3 revolution). Measure and record clearance of intake valves on cylinders No. 2 and 6, and exhaust valves on cylinders No. 2 and 4.
**4)** Ensure clearance is within specification. See VALVE CLEARANCE SPECIFICATIONS (6-CYLINDER) table. If clearance adjustment is required, rotate crankshaft pulley so camshaft lobe is facing upward on valve to be adjusted.
**5)** Position adjusting shim notch area so adjusting shim can be removed with small screwdriver. Press valve lifter downward using Valve Clearance Adjuster (SST 09248-55010) and SST (A). *See Fig. 2.* Install SST (B) between camshaft and valve lifter. Remove SST (A). Using a small screwdriver, remove adjusting shim.
**6)** Using micrometer, measure thickness of removed shim. Determine correct thickness of adjusting shim to be used. *See Figs. 14 and 15.* Install proper shim. Using SST (A), press downward on valve lifter and remove SST (B). Recheck valve clearance. Install valve cover.

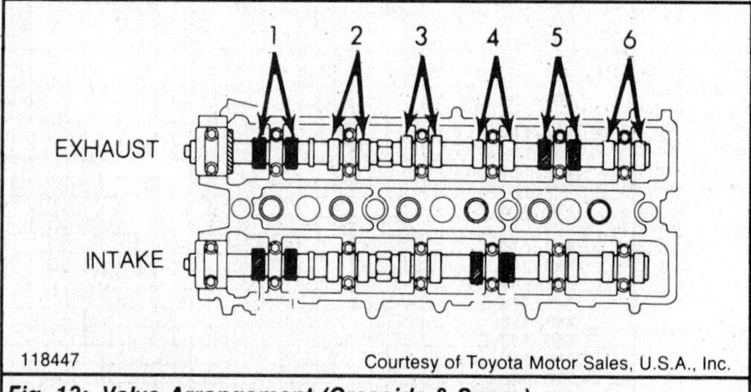


*Fig. 13: Valve Arrangement (Cressida & Supra)*

***VALVE CLEARANCE SPECIFICATIONS (6-CYLINDER)***

| Application | In. (mm) |
|---|---|
| Cressida [1] | |
| Exhaust | .008-.012 (.20-.30) |
| Intake | .006-.010 (.15-.25) |
| Land Cruiser [2] | |
| Exhaust | .014 (.36) |
| Intake | .008 (.20) |
| Supra [1] | |
| Exhaust | .008-.012 (.20-.30) |
| Intake | .006-.010 (.15-.25) |

[1] – Adjust valve clearance with engine cold.
[2] – Adjust valve clearance with engine at normal operating temperature.

**Land Cruiser** – **1)** Check and adjust valves with engine at normal operating temperature. Remove air cleaner hose and valve cover. Rotate crankshaft pulley and align "0" mark on flywheel, with pointer positioned above starter motor to position No. 1 cylinder at TDC of compression stroke.
**2)** Ensure rocker arms on cylinder No. 1 are loose, and rocker arms on cylinder No. 6 are tight. If rocker arms are not as described, rotate crankshaft 360 degrees. With cylinder No. 1 at TDC, check intake valve clearance on cylinders No. 1, 2 and 4, and exhaust valve clearance on cylinders No. 1, 3 and 5. Adjust clearance if not within specification. See VALVE CLEARANCE SPECIFICATIONS (6-CYLINDER) table.
**3)** Rotate crankshaft clockwise 360 degrees and realign "0" mark on flywheel with pointer. With cylinder No. 6 at TDC, check and adjust intake valve clearance on cylinders No. 3, 5 and 6, and exhaust valve clearance on cylinders No. 2, 4 and 6. Install air cleaner hose and valve cover.

# 1991 ENGINE PERFORMANCE
## On-Vehicle Adjustments (Cont.)

INTAKE VALVES

| Measured Clearance (mm) | Installed Shim Thickness (mm) | | | | | | | | | | | | | | | | | | | | | | | | | | | | | | | | | | | | | | | | | | | | | | | | | | | | | | | |
|---|---|---|---|---|---|---|---|---|---|---|---|---|---|---|---|---|---|---|---|---|---|---|---|---|---|---|---|---|---|---|---|---|---|---|---|---|---|---|---|---|---|---|---|---|---|---|---|---|---|---|---|---|---|---|---|---|
| | 2.500 | 2.525 | 2.550 | 2.575 | 2.600 | 2.620 | 2.625 | 2.640 | 2.650 | 2.660 | 2.675 | 2.680 | 2.700 | 2.720 | 2.725 | 2.740 | 2.750 | 2.760 | 2.775 | 2.780 | 2.800 | 2.820 | 2.825 | 2.840 | 2.850 | 2.860 | 2.875 | 2.880 | 2.900 | 2.920 | 2.925 | 2.940 | 2.950 | 2.960 | 2.975 | 2.980 | 3.000 | 3.020 | 3.025 | 3.040 | 3.050 | 3.060 | 3.075 | 3.080 | 3.100 | 3.120 | 3.125 | 3.140 | 3.150 | 3.160 | 3.175 | 3.180 | 3.200 | 3.225 | 3.250 | 3.275 | 3.300 |
| 0.000–0.009 | | | | | | | | | | | 02 | 02 | 02 | 04 | 04 | 04 | 04 | 04 | 06 | 06 | 06 | 08 | 08 | 08 | 08 | 08 | 10 | 10 | 10 | 12 | 12 | 12 | 12 | 12 | 14 | 14 | 14 | 16 | 16 | 16 | 16 | 16 | 18 | 18 | 18 | 20 | 20 | 20 | 20 | 20 | 22 | 22 | 22 | 24 | 24 | 26 | 26 |
| 0.010–0.025 | | | | | | | | | | 02 | 02 | 02 | 02 | 04 | 04 | 04 | 04 | 06 | 06 | 06 | 06 | 08 | 08 | 08 | 08 | 10 | 10 | 10 | 10 | 12 | 12 | 12 | 12 | 14 | 14 | 14 | 14 | 16 | 16 | 16 | 16 | 18 | 18 | 18 | 18 | 20 | 20 | 20 | 20 | 22 | 22 | 22 | 22 | 24 | 24 | 26 | 26 |
| 0.026–0.029 | | | | | | | | | 02 | 02 | 02 | 02 | 04 | 04 | 04 | 04 | 06 | 06 | 06 | 06 | 08 | 08 | 08 | 08 | 10 | 10 | 10 | 10 | 12 | 12 | 12 | 12 | 14 | 14 | 14 | 14 | 16 | 16 | 16 | 16 | 18 | 18 | 18 | 18 | 20 | 20 | 20 | 20 | 22 | 22 | 22 | 22 | 24 | 24 | 26 | 26 | 28 |
| 0.030–0.040 | | | | | | | | 02 | 02 | 02 | 02 | 02 | 04 | 04 | 04 | 04 | 06 | 06 | 06 | 06 | 08 | 08 | 08 | 08 | 10 | 10 | 10 | 10 | 12 | 12 | 12 | 12 | 14 | 14 | 14 | 14 | 16 | 16 | 16 | 16 | 18 | 18 | 18 | 18 | 20 | 20 | 20 | 20 | 22 | 22 | 22 | 22 | 24 | 24 | 26 | 26 | 28 |
| 0.041–0.050 | | | | | | | | 02 | 02 | 02 | 02 | 02 | 04 | 04 | 04 | 06 | 06 | 06 | 06 | 06 | 08 | 08 | 08 | 10 | 10 | 10 | 10 | 10 | 12 | 12 | 12 | 14 | 14 | 14 | 14 | 14 | 16 | 16 | 16 | 18 | 18 | 18 | 18 | 18 | 20 | 20 | 20 | 22 | 22 | 22 | 22 | 22 | 24 | 24 | 26 | 26 | 28 |
| 0.051–0.070 | | | | | | 02 | 02 | 02 | 02 | 02 | 04 | 04 | 04 | 06 | 06 | 06 | 06 | 06 | 08 | 08 | 08 | 10 | 10 | 10 | 10 | 10 | 12 | 12 | 12 | 14 | 14 | 14 | 14 | 14 | 16 | 16 | 16 | 18 | 18 | 18 | 18 | 18 | 20 | 20 | 20 | 22 | 22 | 22 | 22 | 22 | 24 | 24 | 24 | 26 | 26 | 28 | 28 |
| 0.071–0.075 | | | | | 02 | 02 | 02 | 02 | 02 | 04 | 04 | 04 | 04 | 06 | 06 | 06 | 06 | 08 | 08 | 08 | 08 | 10 | 10 | 10 | 10 | 12 | 12 | 12 | 12 | 14 | 14 | 14 | 14 | 16 | 16 | 16 | 16 | 18 | 18 | 18 | 18 | 20 | 20 | 20 | 20 | 22 | 22 | 22 | 22 | 24 | 24 | 24 | 24 | 26 | 26 | 28 | 28 |
| 0.076–0.090 | | | | | 02 | 02 | 02 | 02 | 04 | 04 | 04 | 04 | 06 | 06 | 06 | 06 | 08 | 08 | 08 | 08 | 10 | 10 | 10 | 10 | 12 | 12 | 12 | 12 | 14 | 14 | 14 | 14 | 16 | 16 | 16 | 16 | 18 | 18 | 18 | 18 | 20 | 20 | 20 | 20 | 22 | 22 | 22 | 22 | 24 | 24 | 24 | 24 | 26 | 26 | 28 | 28 | 30 |
| 0.091–0.100 | | | | | 02 | 02 | 02 | 04 | 04 | 04 | 04 | 04 | 06 | 06 | 06 | 08 | 08 | 08 | 08 | 08 | 10 | 10 | 10 | 12 | 12 | 12 | 12 | 12 | 14 | 14 | 14 | 16 | 16 | 16 | 16 | 16 | 18 | 18 | 18 | 20 | 20 | 20 | 20 | 20 | 22 | 22 | 22 | 24 | 24 | 24 | 24 | 24 | 26 | 26 | 28 | 28 | 30 |
| 0.101–0.120 | | | | 02 | 02 | 04 | 04 | 04 | 04 | 04 | 06 | 06 | 06 | 08 | 08 | 08 | 08 | 08 | 10 | 10 | 10 | 12 | 12 | 12 | 12 | 12 | 14 | 14 | 14 | 16 | 16 | 16 | 16 | 16 | 18 | 18 | 18 | 20 | 20 | 20 | 20 | 20 | 22 | 22 | 22 | 24 | 24 | 24 | 24 | 24 | 26 | 26 | 26 | 28 | 28 | 30 | 30 |
| 0.121–0.125 | | | 02 | 02 | 02 | 04 | 04 | 04 | 04 | 06 | 06 | 06 | 06 | 08 | 08 | 08 | 08 | 10 | 10 | 10 | 10 | 12 | 12 | 12 | 12 | 14 | 14 | 14 | 14 | 16 | 16 | 16 | 16 | 18 | 18 | 18 | 18 | 20 | 20 | 20 | 20 | 22 | 22 | 22 | 22 | 24 | 24 | 24 | 24 | 26 | 26 | 26 | 26 | 28 | 28 | 30 | 30 |
| 0.126–0.140 | | | 02 | 02 | 04 | 04 | 04 | 04 | 06 | 06 | 06 | 06 | 08 | 08 | 08 | 08 | 10 | 10 | 10 | 10 | 12 | 12 | 12 | 12 | 14 | 14 | 14 | 14 | 16 | 16 | 16 | 16 | 18 | 18 | 18 | 18 | 20 | 20 | 20 | 20 | 22 | 22 | 22 | 22 | 24 | 24 | 24 | 24 | 26 | 26 | 26 | 26 | 28 | 28 | 30 | 30 | 32 |
| 0.141–0.149 | | | 02 | 02 | 04 | 04 | 04 | 06 | 06 | 06 | 06 | 06 | 08 | 08 | 08 | 10 | 10 | 10 | 10 | 10 | 12 | 12 | 12 | 14 | 14 | 14 | 14 | 14 | 16 | 16 | 16 | 18 | 18 | 18 | 18 | 18 | 20 | 20 | 20 | 22 | 22 | 22 | 22 | 22 | 24 | 24 | 24 | 26 | 26 | 26 | 26 | 26 | 28 | 28 | 30 | 30 | 32 |
| 0.150–0.250 | | | | | | | | | | | | | | | | | | | | | | | | | | | | | | | | | | | | | | | | | | | | | | | | | | | | | | | | | |
| 0.251–0.270 | 04 | 06 | 06 | 08 | 08 | 10 | 10 | 10 | 10 | 10 | 12 | 12 | 12 | 14 | 14 | 14 | 14 | 14 | 16 | 16 | 16 | 18 | 18 | 18 | 18 | 18 | 20 | 20 | 20 | 22 | 22 | 22 | 22 | 22 | 24 | 24 | 24 | 26 | 26 | 26 | 26 | 26 | 28 | 28 | 28 | 30 | 30 | 30 | 30 | 30 | 32 | 32 | 32 | 34 | 34 | | |
| 0.271–0.275 | 04 | 06 | 06 | 08 | 08 | 10 | 10 | 10 | 10 | 12 | 12 | 12 | 12 | 14 | 14 | 14 | 14 | 16 | 16 | 16 | 16 | 18 | 18 | 18 | 18 | 20 | 20 | 20 | 20 | 22 | 22 | 22 | 22 | 24 | 24 | 24 | 24 | 26 | 26 | 26 | 26 | 28 | 28 | 28 | 28 | 30 | 30 | 30 | 30 | 32 | 32 | 32 | 32 | 34 | 34 | | |
| 0.276–0.290 | 06 | 06 | 08 | 08 | 10 | 10 | 10 | 10 | 12 | 12 | 12 | 12 | 14 | 14 | 14 | 14 | 16 | 16 | 16 | 16 | 18 | 18 | 18 | 18 | 20 | 20 | 20 | 20 | 22 | 22 | 22 | 22 | 24 | 24 | 24 | 24 | 26 | 26 | 26 | 26 | 28 | 28 | 28 | 28 | 30 | 30 | 30 | 30 | 32 | 32 | 32 | 32 | 34 | 34 | | | |
| 0.291–0.300 | 06 | 06 | 08 | 08 | 10 | 10 | 10 | 12 | 12 | 12 | 12 | 12 | 14 | 14 | 14 | 16 | 16 | 16 | 16 | 16 | 18 | 18 | 18 | 20 | 20 | 20 | 20 | 20 | 22 | 22 | 22 | 24 | 24 | 24 | 24 | 24 | 26 | 26 | 26 | 28 | 28 | 28 | 28 | 28 | 30 | 30 | 30 | 32 | 32 | 32 | 32 | 32 | 34 | 34 | | | |
| 0.301–0.320 | 06 | 08 | 08 | 10 | 10 | 12 | 12 | 12 | 12 | 12 | 14 | 14 | 14 | 16 | 16 | 16 | 16 | 16 | 18 | 18 | 18 | 20 | 20 | 20 | 20 | 20 | 22 | 22 | 22 | 24 | 24 | 24 | 24 | 24 | 26 | 26 | 26 | 28 | 28 | 28 | 28 | 28 | 30 | 30 | 30 | 32 | 32 | 32 | 32 | 32 | 34 | 34 | 34 | | | | |
| 0.321–0.325 | 06 | 08 | 08 | 10 | 10 | 12 | 12 | 12 | 12 | 14 | 14 | 14 | 14 | 16 | 16 | 16 | 16 | 18 | 18 | 18 | 18 | 20 | 20 | 20 | 20 | 22 | 22 | 22 | 22 | 24 | 24 | 24 | 24 | 26 | 26 | 26 | 26 | 28 | 28 | 28 | 28 | 30 | 30 | 30 | 30 | 32 | 32 | 32 | 32 | 34 | 34 | 34 | 34 | | | | |
| 0.326–0.340 | 08 | 08 | 10 | 10 | 12 | 12 | 12 | 12 | 14 | 14 | 14 | 14 | 16 | 16 | 16 | 16 | 18 | 18 | 18 | 18 | 20 | 20 | 20 | 20 | 22 | 22 | 22 | 22 | 24 | 24 | 24 | 24 | 26 | 26 | 26 | 26 | 28 | 28 | 28 | 28 | 30 | 30 | 30 | 30 | 32 | 32 | 32 | 32 | 34 | 34 | 34 | 34 | | | | | |
| 0.341–0.350 | 08 | 08 | 10 | 10 | 12 | 12 | 12 | 14 | 14 | 14 | 14 | 14 | 16 | 16 | 16 | 18 | 18 | 18 | 18 | 18 | 20 | 20 | 20 | 22 | 22 | 22 | 22 | 22 | 24 | 24 | 24 | 26 | 26 | 26 | 26 | 26 | 28 | 28 | 28 | 30 | 30 | 30 | 30 | 30 | 32 | 32 | 32 | 34 | 34 | 34 | 34 | | | | | | |
| 0.351–0.370 | 08 | 10 | 10 | 12 | 12 | 14 | 14 | 14 | 14 | 14 | 16 | 16 | 16 | 18 | 18 | 18 | 18 | 18 | 20 | 20 | 20 | 22 | 22 | 22 | 22 | 22 | 24 | 24 | 24 | 26 | 26 | 26 | 26 | 26 | 28 | 28 | 28 | 30 | 30 | 30 | 30 | 30 | 32 | 32 | 32 | 34 | 34 | 34 | 34 | 34 | | | | | | | |
| 0.371–0.375 | 08 | 10 | 10 | 12 | 12 | 14 | 14 | 14 | 14 | 16 | 16 | 16 | 16 | 18 | 18 | 18 | 18 | 20 | 20 | 20 | 20 | 22 | 22 | 22 | 22 | 24 | 24 | 24 | 24 | 26 | 26 | 26 | 26 | 28 | 28 | 28 | 28 | 30 | 30 | 30 | 30 | 32 | 32 | 32 | 32 | 34 | 34 | 34 | 34 | | | | | | | | |
| 0.376–0.390 | 10 | 10 | 12 | 12 | 14 | 14 | 14 | 14 | 16 | 16 | 16 | 16 | 18 | 18 | 18 | 18 | 20 | 20 | 20 | 20 | 22 | 22 | 22 | 22 | 24 | 24 | 24 | 24 | 26 | 26 | 26 | 26 | 28 | 28 | 28 | 28 | 30 | 30 | 30 | 30 | 32 | 32 | 32 | 32 | 34 | 34 | 34 | 34 | | | | | | | | | |
| 0.391–0.400 | 10 | 10 | 12 | 12 | 14 | 14 | 14 | 16 | 16 | 16 | 16 | 16 | 18 | 18 | 18 | 20 | 20 | 20 | 20 | 20 | 22 | 22 | 22 | 24 | 24 | 24 | 24 | 24 | 26 | 26 | 26 | 28 | 28 | 28 | 28 | 28 | 30 | 30 | 30 | 32 | 32 | 32 | 32 | 32 | 34 | 34 | 34 | | | | | | | | | | |
| 0.401–0.420 | 10 | 12 | 12 | 14 | 14 | 16 | 16 | 16 | 16 | 16 | 18 | 18 | 18 | 20 | 20 | 20 | 20 | 20 | 22 | 22 | 22 | 24 | 24 | 24 | 24 | 24 | 26 | 26 | 26 | 28 | 28 | 28 | 28 | 28 | 30 | 30 | 30 | 32 | 32 | 32 | 32 | 32 | 34 | 34 | 34 | | | | | | | | | | | | |
| 0.421–0.425 | 10 | 12 | 12 | 14 | 14 | 16 | 16 | 16 | 16 | 18 | 18 | 18 | 18 | 20 | 20 | 20 | 20 | 22 | 22 | 22 | 22 | 24 | 24 | 24 | 24 | 26 | 26 | 26 | 26 | 28 | 28 | 28 | 28 | 30 | 30 | 30 | 30 | 32 | 32 | 32 | 32 | 34 | 34 | 34 | 34 | | | | | | | | | | | | |
| 0.426–0.440 | 12 | 12 | 14 | 14 | 16 | 16 | 16 | 16 | 18 | 18 | 18 | 18 | 20 | 20 | 20 | 20 | 22 | 22 | 22 | 22 | 24 | 24 | 24 | 24 | 26 | 26 | 26 | 26 | 28 | 28 | 28 | 28 | 30 | 30 | 30 | 30 | 32 | 32 | 32 | 32 | 34 | 34 | 34 | 34 | | | | | | | | | | | | | |
| 0.441–0.450 | 12 | 12 | 14 | 14 | 16 | 16 | 16 | 18 | 18 | 18 | 18 | 18 | 20 | 20 | 20 | 22 | 22 | 22 | 22 | 22 | 24 | 24 | 24 | 26 | 26 | 26 | 26 | 26 | 28 | 28 | 28 | 30 | 30 | 30 | 30 | 30 | 32 | 32 | 32 | 34 | 34 | 34 | 34 | 34 | | | | | | | | | | | | | |
| 0.451–0.470 | 12 | 14 | 14 | 16 | 16 | 18 | 18 | 18 | 18 | 18 | 20 | 20 | 20 | 22 | 22 | 22 | 22 | 22 | 24 | 24 | 24 | 26 | 26 | 26 | 26 | 26 | 28 | 28 | 28 | 30 | 30 | 30 | 30 | 30 | 32 | 32 | 32 | 34 | 34 | 34 | 34 | 34 | | | | | | | | | | | | | | | |
| 0.471–0.475 | 12 | 14 | 14 | 16 | 16 | 18 | 18 | 18 | 18 | 20 | 20 | 20 | 20 | 22 | 22 | 22 | 22 | 24 | 24 | 24 | 24 | 26 | 26 | 26 | 26 | 28 | 28 | 28 | 28 | 30 | 30 | 30 | 30 | 32 | 32 | 32 | 32 | 34 | 34 | 34 | 34 | | | | | | | | | | | | | | | | |
| 0.476–0.490 | 14 | 14 | 16 | 16 | 18 | 18 | 18 | 18 | 20 | 20 | 20 | 20 | 22 | 22 | 22 | 22 | 24 | 24 | 24 | 24 | 26 | 26 | 26 | 26 | 28 | 28 | 28 | 28 | 30 | 30 | 30 | 30 | 32 | 32 | 32 | 32 | 34 | 34 | 34 | 34 | | | | | | | | | | | | | | | | | |
| 0.491–0.500 | 14 | 14 | 16 | 16 | 18 | 18 | 18 | 20 | 20 | 20 | 20 | 20 | 22 | 22 | 22 | 24 | 24 | 24 | 24 | 24 | 26 | 26 | 26 | 28 | 28 | 28 | 28 | 28 | 30 | 30 | 30 | 32 | 32 | 32 | 32 | 32 | 34 | 34 | 34 | | | | | | | | | | | | | | | | | | |
| 0.501–0.520 | 14 | 16 | 16 | 18 | 18 | 20 | 20 | 20 | 20 | 20 | 22 | 22 | 22 | 24 | 24 | 24 | 24 | 24 | 26 | 26 | 26 | 28 | 28 | 28 | 28 | 28 | 30 | 30 | 30 | 32 | 32 | 32 | 32 | 32 | 34 | 34 | 34 | | | | | | | | | | | | | | | | | | | | |
| 0.521–0.525 | 14 | 16 | 16 | 18 | 18 | 20 | 20 | 20 | 20 | 22 | 22 | 22 | 22 | 24 | 24 | 24 | 24 | 26 | 26 | 26 | 26 | 28 | 28 | 28 | 28 | 30 | 30 | 30 | 30 | 32 | 32 | 32 | 32 | 34 | 34 | 34 | 34 | | | | | | | | | | | | | | | | | | | | |
| 0.526–0.540 | 16 | 16 | 18 | 18 | 20 | 20 | 20 | 20 | 22 | 22 | 22 | 22 | 24 | 24 | 24 | 24 | 26 | 26 | 26 | 26 | 28 | 28 | 28 | 28 | 30 | 30 | 30 | 30 | 32 | 32 | 32 | 32 | 34 | 34 | 34 | 34 | | | | | | | | | | | | | | | | | | | | | |
| 0.541–0.550 | 16 | 16 | 18 | 18 | 20 | 20 | 20 | 22 | 22 | 22 | 22 | 22 | 24 | 24 | 24 | 26 | 26 | 26 | 26 | 26 | 28 | 28 | 28 | 30 | 30 | 30 | 30 | 30 | 32 | 32 | 32 | 34 | 34 | 34 | 34 | 34 | | | | | | | | | | | | | | | | | | | | | |
| 0.551–0.570 | 16 | 18 | 18 | 20 | 20 | 22 | 22 | 22 | 22 | 22 | 24 | 24 | 24 | 26 | 26 | 26 | 26 | 26 | 28 | 28 | 28 | 30 | 30 | 30 | 30 | 30 | 32 | 32 | 32 | 34 | 34 | 34 | 34 | 34 | | | | | | | | | | | | | | | | | | | | | | | |
| 0.571–0.575 | 16 | 18 | 18 | 20 | 20 | 22 | 22 | 22 | 22 | 24 | 24 | 24 | 24 | 26 | 26 | 26 | 26 | 28 | 28 | 28 | 28 | 30 | 30 | 30 | 30 | 32 | 32 | 32 | 32 | 34 | 34 | 34 | 34 | | | | | | | | | | | | | | | | | | | | | | | | |
| 0.576–0.590 | 18 | 18 | 20 | 20 | 22 | 22 | 22 | 22 | 24 | 24 | 24 | 24 | 26 | 26 | 26 | 26 | 28 | 28 | 28 | 28 | 30 | 30 | 30 | 30 | 32 | 32 | 32 | 32 | 34 | 34 | 34 | 34 | | | | | | | | | | | | | | | | | | | | | | | | | |
| 0.591–0.600 | 18 | 18 | 20 | 20 | 22 | 22 | 22 | 24 | 24 | 24 | 24 | 24 | 26 | 26 | 26 | 28 | 28 | 28 | 28 | 28 | 30 | 30 | 30 | 32 | 32 | 32 | 32 | 32 | 34 | 34 | 34 | | | | | | | | | | | | | | | | | | | | | | | | | | |
| 0.601–0.620 | 18 | 20 | 20 | 22 | 22 | 24 | 24 | 24 | 24 | 24 | 26 | 26 | 26 | 28 | 28 | 28 | 28 | 28 | 30 | 30 | 30 | 32 | 32 | 32 | 32 | 32 | 34 | 34 | 34 | | | | | | | | | | | | | | | | | | | | | | | | | | | | |
| 0.621–0.625 | 18 | 20 | 20 | 22 | 22 | 24 | 24 | 24 | 24 | 26 | 26 | 26 | 26 | 28 | 28 | 28 | 28 | 30 | 30 | 30 | 30 | 32 | 32 | 32 | 32 | 34 | 34 | 34 | 34 | | | | | | | | | | | | | | | | | | | | | | | | | | | | |
| 0.626–0.640 | 20 | 20 | 22 | 22 | 24 | 24 | 24 | 24 | 26 | 26 | 26 | 26 | 28 | 28 | 28 | 28 | 30 | 30 | 30 | 30 | 32 | 32 | 32 | 32 | 34 | 34 | 34 | 34 | | | | | | | | | | | | | | | | | | | | | | | | | | | | | |
| 0.641–0.650 | 20 | 20 | 22 | 22 | 24 | 24 | 24 | 26 | 26 | 26 | 26 | 26 | 28 | 28 | 28 | 30 | 30 | 30 | 30 | 30 | 32 | 32 | 32 | 34 | 34 | 34 | 34 | 34 | | | | | | | | | | | | | | | | | | | | | | | | | | | | | |
| 0.651–0.670 | 20 | 22 | 22 | 24 | 24 | 26 | 26 | 26 | 26 | 26 | 28 | 28 | 28 | 30 | 30 | 30 | 30 | 30 | 32 | 32 | 32 | 34 | 34 | 34 | 34 | 34 | | | | | | | | | | | | | | | | | | | | | | | | | | | | | | | |
| 0.671–0.675 | 20 | 22 | 22 | 24 | 24 | 26 | 26 | 26 | 26 | 28 | 28 | 28 | 28 | 30 | 30 | 30 | 30 | 32 | 32 | 32 | 32 | 34 | 34 | 34 | 34 | | | | | | | | | | | | | | | | | | | | | | | | | | | | | | | | |
| 0.676–0.690 | 22 | 22 | 24 | 24 | 26 | 26 | 26 | 26 | 28 | 28 | 28 | 28 | 30 | 30 | 30 | 30 | 32 | 32 | 32 | 32 | 34 | 34 | 34 | 34 | | | | | | | | | | | | | | | | | | | | | | | | | | | | | | | | | |
| 0.691–0.700 | 22 | 22 | 24 | 24 | 26 | 26 | 26 | 28 | 28 | 28 | 28 | 28 | 30 | 30 | 30 | 32 | 32 | 32 | 32 | 32 | 34 | 34 | 34 | | | | | | | | | | | | | | | | | | | | | | | | | | | | | | | | | | |
| 0.701–0.720 | 22 | 24 | 24 | 26 | 26 | 28 | 28 | 28 | 28 | 28 | 30 | 30 | 30 | 32 | 32 | 32 | 32 | 32 | 34 | 34 | 34 | | | | | | | | | | | | | | | | | | | | | | | | | | | | | | | | | | | | |
| 0.721–0.725 | 22 | 24 | 24 | 26 | 26 | 28 | 28 | 28 | 28 | 30 | 30 | 30 | 30 | 32 | 32 | 32 | 32 | 34 | 34 | 34 | 34 | | | | | | | | | | | | | | | | | | | | | | | | | | | | | | | | | | | | |
| 0.726–0.740 | 24 | 24 | 26 | 26 | 28 | 28 | 28 | 28 | 30 | 30 | 30 | 30 | 32 | 32 | 32 | 32 | 34 | 34 | 34 | 34 | | | | | | | | | | | | | | | | | | | | | | | | | | | | | | | | | | | | | |
| 0.741–0.750 | 24 | 24 | 26 | 26 | 28 | 28 | 28 | 30 | 30 | 30 | 30 | 30 | 32 | 32 | 32 | 34 | 34 | 34 | 34 | | | | | | | | | | | | | | | | | | | | | | | | | | | | | | | | | | | | | | |
| 0.751–0.770 | 24 | 26 | 26 | 28 | 28 | 30 | 30 | 30 | 30 | 30 | 32 | 32 | 32 | 34 | 34 | 34 | 34 | 34 | | | | | | | | | | | | | | | | | | | | | | | | | | | | | | | | | | | | | | | |
| 0.771–0.775 | 24 | 26 | 26 | 28 | 28 | 30 | 30 | 30 | 30 | 32 | 32 | 32 | 32 | 34 | 34 | 34 | 34 | | | | | | | | | | | | | | | | | | | | | | | | | | | | | | | | | | | | | | | | |
| 0.776–0.790 | 26 | 26 | 28 | 28 | 30 | 30 | 30 | 30 | 32 | 32 | 32 | 32 | 34 | 34 | 34 | 34 | | | | | | | | | | | | | | | | | | | | | | | | | | | | | | | | | | | | | | | | |
| 0.791–0.800 | 26 | 26 | 28 | 28 | 30 | 30 | 30 | 32 | 32 | 32 | 32 | 32 | 34 | 34 | 34 | | | | | | | | | | | | | | | | | | | | | | | | | | | | | | | | | | | | | | | | | | |
| 0.801–0.820 | 26 | 28 | 28 | 30 | 30 | 32 | 32 | 32 | 32 | 32 | 34 | 34 | 34 | | | | | | | | | | | | | | | | | | | | | | | | | | | | | | | | | | | | | | | | | | | | |
| 0.821–0.825 | 26 | 28 | 28 | 30 | 30 | 32 | 32 | 32 | 32 | 34 | 34 | 34 | 34 | | | | | | | | | | | | | | | | | | | | | | | | | | | | | | | | | | | | | | | | | | | | |
| 0.826–0.840 | 28 | 28 | 30 | 30 | 32 | 32 | 32 | 32 | 34 | 34 | 34 | 34 | | | | | | | | | | | | | | | | | | | | | | | | | | | | | | | | | | | | | | | | | | | | | |
| 0.841–0.850 | 28 | 28 | 30 | 30 | 32 | 32 | 32 | 34 | 34 | 34 | 34 | 34 | | | | | | | | | | | | | | | | | | | | | | | | | | | | | | | | | | | | | | | | | | | | | |
| 0.851–0.870 | 28 | 30 | 30 | 32 | 32 | 34 | 34 | 34 | 34 | 34 | | | | | | | | | | | | | | | | | | | | | | | | | | | | | | | | | | | | | | | | | | | | | | | |
| 0.871–0.875 | 28 | 30 | 30 | 32 | 32 | 34 | 34 | 34 | 34 | | | | | | | | | | | | | | | | | | | | | | | | | | | | | | | | | | | | | | | | | | | | | | | | |
| 0.876–0.890 | 30 | 30 | 32 | 32 | 34 | 34 | 34 | 34 | | | | | | | | | | | | | | | | | | | | | | | | | | | | | | | | | | | | | | | | | | | | | | | | | |
| 0.891–0.900 | 30 | 30 | 32 | 32 | 34 | 34 | 34 | | | | | | | | | | | | | | | | | | | | | | | | | | | | | | | | | | | | | | | | | | | | | | | | | | |
| 0.901–0.925 | 30 | 32 | 32 | 34 | 34 | | | | | | | | | | | | | | | | | | | | | | | | | | | | | | | | | | | | | | | | | | | | | | | | | | | | |
| 0.926–0.950 | 32 | 32 | 34 | 34 | | | | | | | | | | | | | | | | | | | | | | | | | | | | | | | | | | | | | | | | | | | | | | | | | | | | | |
| 0.951–0.975 | 32 | 34 | 34 | | | | | | | | | | | | | | | | | | | | | | | | | | | | | | | | | | | | | | | | | | | | | | | | | | | | | |
| 0.976–1.000 | 34 | 34 | | | | | | | | | | | | | | | | | | | | | | | | | | | | | | | | | | | | | | | | | | | | | | | | | | | | | | | |
| 1.001–1.025 | 34 | | | | | | | | | | | | | | | | | | | | | | | | | | | | | | | | | | | | | | | | | | | | | | | | | | | | | | | | |

Shim thickness mm (in.)

| Shim No. | Thickness | Shim No. | Thickness |
|---|---|---|---|
| 02 | 2.500 (0.0984) | 20 | 2.950 (0.1161) |
| 04 | 2.550 (0.1004) | 22 | 3.000 (0.1181) |
| 06 | 2.600 (0.1024) | 24 | 3.050 (0.1201) |
| 08 | 2.650 (0.1043) | 26 | 3.100 (0.1220) |
| 10 | 2.700 (0.1063) | 28 | 3.150 (0.1240) |
| 12 | 2.750 (0.1083) | 30 | 3.200 (0.1260) |
| 14 | 2.800 (0.1102) | 32 | 3.250 (0.1280) |
| 16 | 2.850 (0.1122) | 34 | 3.300 (0.1299) |
| 18 | 2.900 (0.1142) | | |

EXAMPLE: A 0.1102" (2.800 mm) shim is installed and measured clearance is 0.0177" (0.450 mm). Replace 0.1102" (2.800 mm) shim with a No. 24 shim.

91J17896

Courtesy of Toyota Motor Sales, U.S.A., Inc.

*Fig. 14: Intake Valve Adjusting Shim Selection Chart (Cressida 3.0L & Supra 3.0L)*

# 1991 ENGINE PERFORMANCE
## On-Vehicle Adjustments (Cont.)

EXHAUST VALVES

| Measured Clearance (mm) | Installed Shim Thickness (mm) | | | | | | | | | | | | | | | | | | | | | | | | | | | | | | | | | | | | | | | | | | | | | | | | | | | | | | | | |
|---|---|---|---|---|---|---|---|---|---|---|---|---|---|---|---|---|---|---|---|---|---|---|---|---|---|---|---|---|---|---|---|---|---|---|---|---|---|---|---|---|---|---|---|---|---|---|---|---|---|---|---|---|---|---|---|---|---|
| | 2.500 | 2.525 | 2.550 | 2.575 | 2.600 | 2.620 | 2.625 | 2.640 | 2.650 | 2.660 | 2.675 | 2.680 | 2.700 | 2.720 | 2.725 | 2.740 | 2.750 | 2.760 | 2.775 | 2.780 | 2.800 | 2.820 | 2.825 | 2.840 | 2.850 | 2.860 | 2.875 | 2.880 | 2.900 | 2.920 | 2.925 | 2.940 | 2.950 | 2.960 | 2.975 | 2.980 | 3.000 | 3.020 | 3.025 | 3.040 | 3.050 | 3.060 | 3.075 | 3.080 | 3.100 | 3.120 | 3.125 | 3.140 | 3.150 | 3.160 | 3.175 | 3.180 | 3.200 | 3.225 | 3.250 | 3.275 | 3.300 |
| 0.000 – 0.009 | | | | | | | | | | | | | | 02 | 02 | 02 | 02 | 02 | 04 | 04 | 04 | 06 | 06 | 06 | 06 | 06 | 08 | 08 | 08 | 10 | 10 | 10 | 10 | 10 | 12 | 12 | 12 | 14 | 14 | 14 | 14 | 14 | 16 | 16 | 16 | 18 | 18 | 18 | 18 | 18 | 20 | 20 | 20 | 22 | 22 | 24 | 24 |
| 0.010 – 0.025 | | | | | | | | | | | | | | 02 | 02 | 02 | 02 | 04 | 04 | 04 | 06 | 06 | 06 | 06 | 06 | 08 | 08 | 08 | 10 | 10 | 10 | 10 | 10 | 12 | 12 | 12 | 14 | 14 | 14 | 14 | 14 | 16 | 16 | 16 | 18 | 18 | 18 | 18 | 18 | 20 | 20 | 20 | 22 | 22 | 22 | 24 | 26 |
| 0.026 – 0.040 | | | | | | | | | | | | | 02 | 02 | 02 | 02 | 04 | 04 | 04 | 04 | 06 | 06 | 06 | 06 | 08 | 08 | 08 | 08 | 10 | 10 | 10 | 10 | 12 | 12 | 12 | 12 | 14 | 14 | 14 | 14 | 16 | 16 | 16 | 16 | 18 | 18 | 18 | 18 | 20 | 20 | 20 | 20 | 22 | 22 | 24 | 24 | 26 |
| 0.041 – 0.050 | | | | | | | | | | | | 02 | 02 | 02 | 02 | 04 | 04 | 04 | 04 | 06 | 06 | 06 | 06 | 08 | 08 | 08 | 08 | 10 | 10 | 10 | 10 | 12 | 12 | 12 | 12 | 14 | 14 | 14 | 14 | 16 | 16 | 16 | 16 | 18 | 18 | 18 | 18 | 20 | 20 | 20 | 20 | 22 | 22 | 22 | 24 | 24 | 26 |
| 0.051 – 0.070 | | | | | | | | | | | 02 | 02 | 02 | 04 | 04 | 04 | 04 | 04 | 06 | 06 | 06 | 08 | 08 | 08 | 08 | 08 | 10 | 10 | 10 | 12 | 12 | 12 | 12 | 12 | 14 | 14 | 14 | 16 | 16 | 16 | 16 | 16 | 18 | 18 | 18 | 20 | 20 | 20 | 20 | 20 | 22 | 22 | 22 | 24 | 24 | 26 | 26 |
| 0.071 – 0.090 | | | | | | | | | 02 | 02 | 02 | 02 | 04 | 04 | 04 | 04 | 06 | 06 | 06 | 06 | 08 | 08 | 08 | 08 | 10 | 10 | 10 | 10 | 12 | 12 | 12 | 12 | 14 | 14 | 14 | 14 | 16 | 16 | 16 | 16 | 18 | 18 | 18 | 18 | 20 | 20 | 20 | 20 | 22 | 22 | 22 | 22 | 24 | 24 | 26 | 26 | 28 |
| 0.091 – 0.100 | | | | | | | | 02 | 02 | 02 | 02 | 04 | 04 | 04 | 04 | 06 | 06 | 06 | 06 | 08 | 08 | 08 | 08 | 10 | 10 | 10 | 10 | 12 | 12 | 12 | 12 | 14 | 14 | 14 | 14 | 16 | 16 | 16 | 16 | 18 | 18 | 18 | 18 | 20 | 20 | 20 | 20 | 22 | 22 | 22 | 22 | 24 | 24 | 24 | 26 | 26 | 28 |
| 0.101 – 0.120 | | | | | | 02 | 02 | 02 | 02 | 02 | 04 | 04 | 04 | 06 | 06 | 06 | 06 | 06 | 08 | 08 | 08 | 10 | 10 | 10 | 10 | 10 | 12 | 12 | 12 | 14 | 14 | 14 | 14 | 14 | 16 | 16 | 16 | 18 | 18 | 18 | 18 | 18 | 20 | 20 | 20 | 22 | 22 | 22 | 22 | 22 | 24 | 24 | 24 | 26 | 26 | 28 | 28 |
| 0.121 – 0.140 | | | | | 02 | 02 | 02 | 02 | 04 | 04 | 04 | 04 | 06 | 06 | 06 | 06 | 08 | 08 | 08 | 08 | 10 | 10 | 10 | 10 | 12 | 12 | 12 | 12 | 14 | 14 | 14 | 14 | 16 | 16 | 16 | 16 | 18 | 18 | 18 | 18 | 20 | 20 | 20 | 20 | 22 | 22 | 22 | 22 | 24 | 24 | 24 | 24 | 26 | 26 | 28 | 28 | 30 |
| 0.141 – 0.150 | | | | | 02 | 02 | 02 | 04 | 04 | 04 | 04 | 06 | 06 | 06 | 06 | 08 | 08 | 08 | 08 | 10 | 10 | 10 | 10 | 12 | 12 | 12 | 12 | 14 | 14 | 14 | 14 | 16 | 16 | 16 | 16 | 18 | 18 | 18 | 18 | 20 | 20 | 20 | 20 | 22 | 22 | 22 | 22 | 24 | 24 | 24 | 24 | 26 | 26 | 26 | 28 | 28 | 30 |
| 0.151 – 0.170 | | | | 02 | 02 | 04 | 04 | 04 | 04 | 04 | 06 | 06 | 06 | 08 | 08 | 08 | 08 | 08 | 10 | 10 | 10 | 12 | 12 | 12 | 12 | 12 | 14 | 14 | 14 | 16 | 16 | 16 | 16 | 16 | 18 | 18 | 18 | 20 | 20 | 20 | 20 | 20 | 22 | 22 | 22 | 24 | 24 | 24 | 24 | 24 | 26 | 26 | 26 | 28 | 28 | 30 | 30 |
| 0.171 – 0.190 | | | 02 | 02 | 04 | 04 | 04 | 04 | 06 | 06 | 06 | 06 | 08 | 08 | 08 | 08 | 10 | 10 | 10 | 10 | 12 | 12 | 12 | 12 | 14 | 14 | 14 | 14 | 16 | 16 | 16 | 16 | 18 | 18 | 18 | 18 | 20 | 20 | 20 | 20 | 22 | 22 | 22 | 22 | 24 | 24 | 24 | 24 | 26 | 26 | 26 | 26 | 28 | 28 | 30 | 30 | 32 |
| 0.191 – 0.199 | | | 02 | 02 | 04 | 04 | 04 | 06 | 06 | 06 | 06 | 08 | 08 | 08 | 08 | 10 | 10 | 10 | 10 | 12 | 12 | 12 | 12 | 14 | 14 | 14 | 14 | 16 | 16 | 16 | 16 | 18 | 18 | 18 | 18 | 20 | 20 | 20 | 20 | 22 | 22 | 22 | 22 | 24 | 24 | 24 | 24 | 26 | 26 | 26 | 26 | 28 | 28 | 28 | 30 | 30 | 32 |
| 0.200 – 0.300 |
| 0.301 – 0.320 | 04 | 06 | 06 | 08 | 08 | 10 | 10 | 10 | 10 | 10 | 12 | 12 | 12 | 14 | 14 | 14 | 14 | 14 | 16 | 16 | 16 | 18 | 18 | 18 | 18 | 18 | 20 | 20 | 20 | 22 | 22 | 22 | 22 | 22 | 24 | 24 | 24 | 26 | 26 | 26 | 26 | 26 | 28 | 28 | 28 | 30 | 30 | 30 | 30 | 30 | 32 | 32 | 32 | 34 | 34 |
| 0.321 – 0.325 | 04 | 06 | 06 | 08 | 08 | 10 | 10 | 10 | 10 | 12 | 12 | 12 | 12 | 14 | 14 | 14 | 14 | 16 | 16 | 16 | 16 | 18 | 18 | 18 | 18 | 20 | 20 | 20 | 20 | 22 | 22 | 22 | 22 | 24 | 24 | 24 | 24 | 26 | 26 | 26 | 26 | 28 | 28 | 28 | 28 | 30 | 30 | 30 | 30 | 32 | 32 | 32 | 32 | 34 | 34 |
| 0.326 – 0.340 | 06 | 06 | 08 | 08 | 10 | 10 | 10 | 10 | 12 | 12 | 12 | 12 | 14 | 14 | 14 | 14 | 16 | 16 | 16 | 16 | 18 | 18 | 18 | 18 | 20 | 20 | 20 | 20 | 22 | 22 | 22 | 22 | 24 | 24 | 24 | 24 | 26 | 26 | 26 | 26 | 28 | 28 | 28 | 28 | 30 | 30 | 30 | 30 | 32 | 32 | 32 | 32 | 34 | 34 |
| 0.341 – 0.350 | 06 | 06 | 08 | 08 | 10 | 10 | 10 | 12 | 12 | 12 | 12 | 12 | 14 | 14 | 14 | 16 | 16 | 16 | 16 | 16 | 18 | 18 | 18 | 20 | 20 | 20 | 20 | 20 | 22 | 22 | 22 | 24 | 24 | 24 | 24 | 24 | 26 | 26 | 26 | 28 | 28 | 28 | 28 | 28 | 30 | 30 | 30 | 32 | 32 | 32 | 32 | 32 | 34 | 34 |
| 0.351 – 0.370 | 06 | 08 | 08 | 10 | 10 | 12 | 12 | 12 | 12 | 12 | 14 | 14 | 14 | 16 | 16 | 16 | 16 | 16 | 18 | 18 | 18 | 20 | 20 | 20 | 20 | 20 | 22 | 22 | 22 | 24 | 24 | 24 | 24 | 24 | 26 | 26 | 26 | 28 | 28 | 28 | 28 | 28 | 30 | 30 | 30 | 32 | 32 | 32 | 32 | 32 | 34 | 34 | 34 |
| 0.371 – 0.375 | 06 | 08 | 08 | 10 | 10 | 12 | 12 | 12 | 12 | 14 | 14 | 14 | 14 | 16 | 16 | 16 | 16 | 18 | 18 | 18 | 18 | 20 | 20 | 20 | 20 | 22 | 22 | 22 | 22 | 24 | 24 | 24 | 24 | 26 | 26 | 26 | 26 | 28 | 28 | 28 | 28 | 30 | 30 | 30 | 30 | 32 | 32 | 32 | 32 | 34 | 34 | 34 | 34 |
| 0.376 – 0.390 | 08 | 08 | 10 | 10 | 12 | 12 | 12 | 12 | 14 | 14 | 14 | 14 | 16 | 16 | 16 | 16 | 18 | 18 | 18 | 18 | 20 | 20 | 20 | 20 | 22 | 22 | 22 | 22 | 24 | 24 | 24 | 24 | 26 | 26 | 26 | 26 | 28 | 28 | 28 | 28 | 30 | 30 | 30 | 30 | 32 | 32 | 32 | 32 | 34 | 34 | 34 | 34 |
| 0.391 – 0.400 | 08 | 08 | 10 | 10 | 12 | 12 | 12 | 14 | 14 | 14 | 14 | 14 | 16 | 16 | 16 | 18 | 18 | 18 | 18 | 18 | 20 | 20 | 20 | 22 | 22 | 22 | 22 | 22 | 24 | 24 | 24 | 26 | 26 | 26 | 26 | 26 | 28 | 28 | 28 | 30 | 30 | 30 | 30 | 30 | 32 | 32 | 32 | 34 | 34 | 34 | 34 | 34 |
| 0.401 – 0.420 | 08 | 10 | 10 | 12 | 12 | 14 | 14 | 14 | 14 | 14 | 16 | 16 | 16 | 18 | 18 | 18 | 18 | 18 | 20 | 20 | 20 | 22 | 22 | 22 | 22 | 22 | 24 | 24 | 24 | 26 | 26 | 26 | 26 | 26 | 28 | 28 | 28 | 30 | 30 | 30 | 30 | 30 | 32 | 32 | 32 | 34 | 34 | 34 | 34 | 34 |
| 0.421 – 0.425 | 08 | 10 | 10 | 12 | 12 | 14 | 14 | 14 | 14 | 16 | 16 | 16 | 16 | 18 | 18 | 18 | 18 | 20 | 20 | 20 | 20 | 22 | 22 | 22 | 22 | 24 | 24 | 24 | 24 | 26 | 26 | 26 | 26 | 28 | 28 | 28 | 28 | 30 | 30 | 30 | 30 | 32 | 32 | 32 | 32 | 34 | 34 | 34 | 34 |
| 0.426 – 0.440 | 10 | 10 | 12 | 12 | 14 | 14 | 14 | 14 | 16 | 16 | 16 | 16 | 18 | 18 | 18 | 18 | 20 | 20 | 20 | 20 | 22 | 22 | 22 | 22 | 24 | 24 | 24 | 24 | 26 | 26 | 26 | 26 | 28 | 28 | 28 | 28 | 30 | 30 | 30 | 30 | 32 | 32 | 32 | 32 | 34 | 34 | 34 | 34 |
| 0.441 – 0.450 | 10 | 10 | 12 | 12 | 14 | 14 | 14 | 16 | 16 | 16 | 16 | 16 | 18 | 18 | 18 | 20 | 20 | 20 | 20 | 20 | 22 | 22 | 22 | 24 | 24 | 24 | 24 | 24 | 26 | 26 | 26 | 28 | 28 | 28 | 28 | 28 | 30 | 30 | 30 | 32 | 32 | 32 | 32 | 32 | 34 | 34 | 34 |
| 0.451 – 0.470 | 10 | 12 | 12 | 14 | 14 | 16 | 16 | 16 | 16 | 16 | 18 | 18 | 18 | 20 | 20 | 20 | 20 | 20 | 22 | 22 | 22 | 24 | 24 | 24 | 24 | 24 | 26 | 26 | 26 | 28 | 28 | 28 | 28 | 28 | 30 | 30 | 30 | 32 | 32 | 32 | 32 | 32 | 34 | 34 | 34 |
| 0.471 – 0.475 | 10 | 12 | 12 | 14 | 14 | 16 | 16 | 16 | 16 | 18 | 18 | 18 | 18 | 20 | 20 | 20 | 20 | 22 | 22 | 22 | 22 | 24 | 24 | 24 | 24 | 26 | 26 | 26 | 26 | 28 | 28 | 28 | 28 | 30 | 30 | 30 | 30 | 32 | 32 | 32 | 32 | 34 | 34 | 34 | 34 |
| 0.476 – 0.490 | 12 | 12 | 14 | 14 | 16 | 16 | 16 | 16 | 18 | 18 | 18 | 18 | 20 | 20 | 20 | 20 | 22 | 22 | 22 | 22 | 24 | 24 | 24 | 24 | 26 | 26 | 26 | 26 | 28 | 28 | 28 | 28 | 30 | 30 | 30 | 30 | 32 | 32 | 32 | 32 | 34 | 34 | 34 | 34 |
| 0.491 – 0.500 | 12 | 12 | 14 | 14 | 16 | 16 | 16 | 18 | 18 | 18 | 18 | 18 | 20 | 20 | 20 | 22 | 22 | 22 | 22 | 22 | 24 | 24 | 24 | 26 | 26 | 26 | 26 | 26 | 28 | 28 | 28 | 30 | 30 | 30 | 30 | 30 | 32 | 32 | 32 | 34 | 34 | 34 | 34 | 34 |
| 0.501 – 0.520 | 12 | 14 | 14 | 16 | 16 | 18 | 18 | 18 | 18 | 18 | 20 | 20 | 20 | 22 | 22 | 22 | 22 | 22 | 24 | 24 | 24 | 26 | 26 | 26 | 26 | 26 | 28 | 28 | 28 | 30 | 30 | 30 | 30 | 30 | 32 | 32 | 32 | 34 | 34 | 34 | 34 | 34 |
| 0.521 – 0.525 | 12 | 14 | 14 | 16 | 16 | 18 | 18 | 18 | 18 | 20 | 20 | 20 | 20 | 22 | 22 | 22 | 22 | 24 | 24 | 24 | 24 | 26 | 26 | 26 | 26 | 28 | 28 | 28 | 28 | 30 | 30 | 30 | 30 | 32 | 32 | 32 | 32 | 34 | 34 | 34 | 34 |
| 0.526 – 0.540 | 14 | 14 | 16 | 16 | 18 | 18 | 18 | 18 | 20 | 20 | 20 | 20 | 22 | 22 | 22 | 22 | 24 | 24 | 24 | 24 | 26 | 26 | 26 | 26 | 28 | 28 | 28 | 28 | 30 | 30 | 30 | 30 | 32 | 32 | 32 | 32 | 34 | 34 | 34 | 34 |
| 0.541 – 0.550 | 14 | 14 | 16 | 16 | 18 | 18 | 18 | 20 | 20 | 20 | 20 | 20 | 22 | 22 | 22 | 24 | 24 | 24 | 24 | 24 | 26 | 26 | 26 | 28 | 28 | 28 | 28 | 28 | 30 | 30 | 30 | 32 | 32 | 32 | 32 | 32 | 34 | 34 | 34 |
| 0.551 – 0.570 | 14 | 16 | 16 | 18 | 18 | 20 | 20 | 20 | 20 | 20 | 22 | 22 | 22 | 24 | 24 | 24 | 24 | 24 | 26 | 26 | 26 | 28 | 28 | 28 | 28 | 28 | 30 | 30 | 30 | 32 | 32 | 32 | 32 | 32 | 34 | 34 | 34 |
| 0.571 – 0.575 | 14 | 16 | 16 | 18 | 18 | 20 | 20 | 20 | 20 | 22 | 22 | 22 | 22 | 24 | 24 | 24 | 24 | 26 | 26 | 26 | 26 | 28 | 28 | 28 | 28 | 30 | 30 | 30 | 30 | 32 | 32 | 32 | 32 | 34 | 34 | 34 | 34 |
| 0.576 – 0.590 | 16 | 16 | 18 | 18 | 20 | 20 | 20 | 20 | 22 | 22 | 22 | 22 | 24 | 24 | 24 | 24 | 26 | 26 | 26 | 26 | 28 | 28 | 28 | 28 | 30 | 30 | 30 | 30 | 32 | 32 | 32 | 32 | 34 | 34 | 34 | 34 |
| 0.591 – 0.600 | 16 | 16 | 18 | 18 | 20 | 20 | 20 | 22 | 22 | 22 | 22 | 22 | 24 | 24 | 24 | 26 | 26 | 26 | 26 | 26 | 28 | 28 | 28 | 30 | 30 | 30 | 30 | 30 | 32 | 32 | 32 | 34 | 34 | 34 | 34 | 34 |
| 0.601 – 0.620 | 16 | 18 | 18 | 20 | 20 | 22 | 22 | 22 | 22 | 22 | 24 | 24 | 24 | 26 | 26 | 26 | 26 | 26 | 28 | 28 | 28 | 30 | 30 | 30 | 30 | 30 | 32 | 32 | 32 | 34 | 34 | 34 | 34 | 34 |
| 0.621 – 0.625 | 16 | 18 | 18 | 20 | 20 | 22 | 22 | 22 | 22 | 24 | 24 | 24 | 24 | 26 | 26 | 26 | 26 | 28 | 28 | 28 | 28 | 30 | 30 | 30 | 30 | 32 | 32 | 32 | 32 | 34 | 34 | 34 | 34 |
| 0.626 – 0.640 | 18 | 18 | 20 | 20 | 22 | 22 | 22 | 22 | 24 | 24 | 24 | 24 | 26 | 26 | 26 | 26 | 28 | 28 | 28 | 28 | 30 | 30 | 30 | 30 | 32 | 32 | 32 | 32 | 34 | 34 | 34 | 34 |
| 0.641 – 0.650 | 18 | 18 | 20 | 20 | 22 | 22 | 22 | 24 | 24 | 24 | 24 | 24 | 26 | 26 | 26 | 28 | 28 | 28 | 28 | 28 | 30 | 30 | 30 | 32 | 32 | 32 | 32 | 32 | 34 | 34 | 34 |
| 0.651 – 0.670 | 18 | 20 | 20 | 22 | 22 | 24 | 24 | 24 | 24 | 24 | 26 | 26 | 26 | 28 | 28 | 28 | 28 | 28 | 30 | 30 | 30 | 32 | 32 | 32 | 32 | 32 | 34 | 34 | 34 |
| 0.671 – 0.675 | 18 | 20 | 20 | 22 | 22 | 24 | 24 | 24 | 24 | 26 | 26 | 26 | 26 | 28 | 28 | 28 | 28 | 30 | 30 | 30 | 30 | 32 | 32 | 32 | 32 | 34 | 34 | 34 | 34 |
| 0.676 – 0.690 | 20 | 20 | 22 | 22 | 24 | 24 | 24 | 24 | 26 | 26 | 26 | 26 | 28 | 28 | 28 | 28 | 30 | 30 | 30 | 30 | 32 | 32 | 32 | 32 | 34 | 34 | 34 | 34 |
| 0.691 – 0.700 | 20 | 20 | 22 | 22 | 24 | 24 | 24 | 26 | 26 | 26 | 26 | 26 | 28 | 28 | 28 | 30 | 30 | 30 | 30 | 30 | 32 | 32 | 32 | 34 | 34 | 34 | 34 | 34 |
| 0.701 – 0.720 | 20 | 22 | 22 | 24 | 24 | 26 | 26 | 26 | 26 | 26 | 28 | 28 | 28 | 30 | 30 | 30 | 30 | 30 | 32 | 32 | 32 | 34 | 34 | 34 | 34 | 34 |
| 0.721 – 0.725 | 20 | 22 | 22 | 24 | 24 | 26 | 26 | 26 | 26 | 28 | 28 | 28 | 28 | 30 | 30 | 30 | 30 | 32 | 32 | 32 | 32 | 34 | 34 | 34 | 34 |
| 0.726 – 0.740 | 22 | 22 | 24 | 24 | 26 | 26 | 26 | 26 | 28 | 28 | 28 | 28 | 30 | 30 | 30 | 30 | 32 | 32 | 32 | 32 | 34 | 34 | 34 | 34 |
| 0.741 – 0.750 | 22 | 22 | 24 | 24 | 26 | 26 | 26 | 28 | 28 | 28 | 28 | 28 | 30 | 30 | 30 | 32 | 32 | 32 | 32 | 32 | 34 | 34 | 34 |
| 0.751 – 0.770 | 22 | 24 | 24 | 26 | 26 | 28 | 28 | 28 | 28 | 28 | 30 | 30 | 30 | 32 | 32 | 32 | 32 | 32 | 34 | 34 | 34 |
| 0.771 – 0.775 | 22 | 24 | 24 | 26 | 26 | 28 | 28 | 28 | 28 | 30 | 30 | 30 | 30 | 32 | 32 | 32 | 32 | 34 | 34 | 34 | 34 |
| 0.776 – 0.790 | 24 | 24 | 26 | 26 | 28 | 28 | 28 | 28 | 30 | 30 | 30 | 30 | 32 | 32 | 32 | 32 | 34 | 34 | 34 | 34 |
| 0.791 – 0.800 | 24 | 24 | 26 | 26 | 28 | 28 | 28 | 30 | 30 | 30 | 30 | 30 | 32 | 32 | 32 | 34 | 34 | 34 | 34 | 34 |
| 0.801 – 0.820 | 24 | 26 | 26 | 28 | 28 | 30 | 30 | 30 | 30 | 30 | 32 | 32 | 32 | 34 | 34 | 34 | 34 | 34 |
| 0.821 – 0.825 | 24 | 26 | 26 | 28 | 28 | 30 | 30 | 30 | 30 | 32 | 32 | 32 | 32 | 34 | 34 | 34 | 34 |
| 0.826 – 0.840 | 26 | 26 | 28 | 28 | 30 | 30 | 30 | 30 | 32 | 32 | 32 | 32 | 34 | 34 | 34 | 34 |
| 0.841 – 0.850 | 26 | 26 | 28 | 28 | 30 | 30 | 30 | 32 | 32 | 32 | 32 | 32 | 34 | 34 | 34 |
| 0.851 – 0.870 | 26 | 28 | 28 | 30 | 30 | 32 | 32 | 32 | 32 | 32 | 34 | 34 | 34 |
| 0.871 – 0.875 | 26 | 28 | 28 | 30 | 30 | 32 | 32 | 32 | 32 | 34 | 34 | 34 | 34 |
| 0.876 – 0.890 | 28 | 28 | 30 | 30 | 32 | 32 | 32 | 32 | 34 | 34 | 34 | 34 |
| 0.891 – 0.900 | 28 | 28 | 30 | 30 | 32 | 32 | 32 | 34 | 34 | 34 | 34 | 34 |
| 0.901 – 0.925 | 28 | 30 | 30 | 32 | 32 | 34 | 34 | 34 | 34 |
| 0.926 – 0.950 | 30 | 30 | 32 | 32 | 34 | 34 | 34 |
| 0.951 – 0.975 | 30 | 32 | 32 | 34 | 34 |
| 0.976 – 1.000 | 32 | 32 | 34 | 34 |
| 1.001 – 1.025 | 32 | 34 | 34 |
| 1.026 – 1.050 | 34 | 34 |
| 1.051 – 1.075 | 34 |

Shim thickness mm (in.)

| Shim No. | Thickness | Shim No. | Thickness |
|---|---|---|---|
| 02 | 2.500 (0.0984) | 20 | 2.950 (0.1161) |
| 04 | 2.550 (0.1004) | 22 | 3.000 (0.1181) |
| 06 | 2.600 (0.1024) | 24 | 3.050 (0.1201) |
| 08 | 2.650 (0.1043) | 26 | 3.100 (0.1220) |
| 10 | 2.700 (0.1063) | 28 | 3.150 (0.1240) |
| 12 | 2.750 (0.1083) | 30 | 3.200 (0.1260) |
| 14 | 2.800 (0.1102) | 32 | 3.250 (0.1280) |
| 16 | 2.850 (0.1122) | 34 | 3.300 (0.1299) |
| 18 | 2.900 (0.1142) | | |

EXAMPLE: A 0.1102" (2.800 mm) shim is installed and measured clearance is 0.0177" (0.450 mm). Replace 0.1102" (2.800 mm) shim with a No. 22 shim.

91A17897

Courtesy of Toyota Motor Sales, U.S.A., Inc.

*Fig. 15: Exhaust Valve Adjusting Shim Selection Chart (Cressida 3.0L & Supra 3.0L)*

## V6

**Camry - 1)** Check and adjust valves with engine cold. Remove valve covers. Rotate crankshaft pulley and align pulley groove with "0" mark on timing belt cover to position No. 1 cylinder at TDC of compression stroke. Ensure cylinder No. 1 intake valve lifters are loose and exhaust valve lifters are tight. If valve lifters are not as described, rotate crankshaft 360 degrees and realign timing marks.

**2)** Measure and record clearance of intake valves on cylinders No. 1 and 6, and exhaust valves on cylinders No. 2 and 3. *See Fig. 16.* Rotate crankshaft pulley 240 degrees (2/3 of a revolution). Measure and record clearance of intake valves on cylinders No. 2 and 3, and exhaust valves on cylinders No. 4 and 5.

**3)** Rotate crankshaft pulley another 240 degrees (2/3 of a revolution). Measure and record clearance of intake valves on cylinders No. 4 and 5, and exhaust valves on cylinders No. 1 and 6.

**4)** Ensure clearance is within specification. See VALVE CLEARANCE SPECIFICATIONS (V6) table. If clearance adjustment is required, rotate crankshaft pulley so camshaft lobe is facing upward on valve to be adjusted.

**5)** Position adjusting shim notch toward spark plug. Use Valve Clearance Adjuster (SST 09248-55010) and SST (A) to press valve lifter downward. *See Fig. 2.* Install SST (B) between camshaft and valve lifter. Remove SST (A). Using a small screwdriver and magnet, remove adjusting shim.

**6)** Using micrometer, measure thickness of shim removed. Determine correct thickness of replacement shim to be used. *See Figs. 17 and 18.* Install proper shim. Using SST (A), press downward on valve lifter and remove SST (B). Recheck valve clearance. Install valve cover.

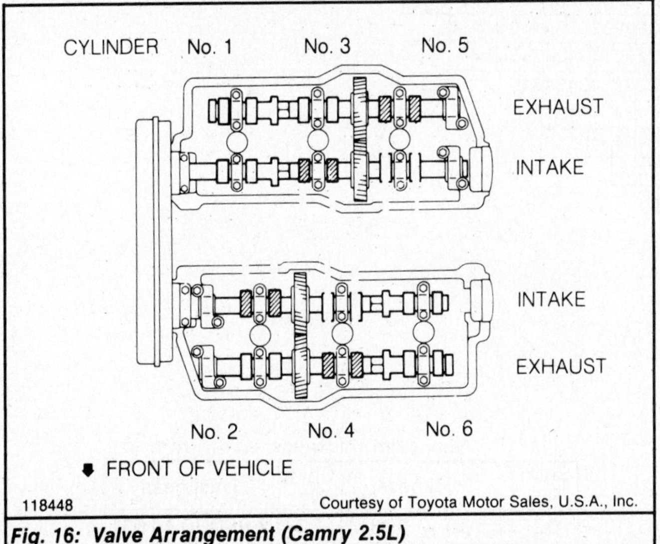


***Fig. 16: Valve Arrangement (Camry 2.5L)***

***VALVE CLEARANCE SPECIFICATIONS (V6)***

| Application [1] | In. (mm) |
|---|---|
| Camry | |
| Exhaust | .011-.015 (.28-.38) |
| Intake | .005-.009 (.13-.23) |
| Pickup & 4Runner | |
| Exhaust | .009-.013 (.23-.33) |
| Intake | .007-.011 (.18-.28) |

[1] - Adjust valves with engine cold.

**Pickup & 4Runner - 1)** Check and adjust valves with engine cold. Remove valve covers. Rotate crankshaft pulley and align pulley groove with "0" mark on timing belt cover to set cylinder No. 1 at TDC of compression stroke.

**2)** Ensure cylinder No. 1 valve lifters are loose and cylinder No. 4 valve lifters are tight. If valve lifters are not as described, rotate crankshaft 360 degrees and realign timing marks.

**3)** Measure and record clearance of exhaust valve on cylinder No. 2, and intake valve on cylinder No. 6. *See Fig. 19.* Rotate crankshaft pulley 120 degrees (1/3 of a revolution). Measure and record clearance of intake valve on cylinder No. 1, and exhaust valve on cylinder No. 3.

**4)** Rotate crankshaft pulley 120 degrees (1/3 of a revolution). Measure and record clearance of intake valve on cylinder No. 2, and exhaust valve on cylinder No. 4.

**5)** Rotate crankshaft pulley 120 degrees (1/3 of a revolution). Measure and record clearance of intake valve on cylinder No. 3, and exhaust valve on cylinder No. 5. Rotate crankshaft pulley another 120 degrees (1/3 of a revolution). Measure and record clearance of intake valve on cylinder No. 4, and exhaust valve on cylinder No. 6.

**6)** Rotate crankshaft pulley 120 degrees (1/3 of a revolution). Measure and record clearance of intake valve on cylinder No. 5, and exhaust valve on cylinder No. 1.

**7)** Ensure clearance is within specification. See VALVE CLEARANCE SPECIFICATIONS (V6) table. If clearance adjustment is required, rotate crankshaft pulley so camshaft lobe is facing upward on the valve to be adjusted.

**8)** Position adjusting shim notch area in the direction in which the shim will be removed. Use Valve Clearance Adjuster (SST 09248-55010) and SST (A) to press valve lifter downward. *See Fig. 2.* Install SST (B) between camshaft and valve lifter. Remove SST (A). Using a small screwdriver and magnet, remove adjusting shim.

**9)** Using micrometer, measure thickness of shim removed. Determine correct thickness of replacement shim to be used. *See Figs. 20-25.* Install proper shim. Using SST (A), press downward on valve lifter and remove SST (B). Recheck valve clearance. Install valve cover.

# 1991 ENGINE PERFORMANCE
## On-Vehicle Adjustments (Cont.)

INTAKE VALVES

| Measured clearance (mm) | Installed shim thickness (mm) | | | | | | | | | | | | | | | | | | | | | | | | | | | | | | | | | | | | | | | | | | | | |
|---|---|---|---|---|---|---|---|---|---|---|---|---|---|---|---|---|---|---|---|---|---|---|---|---|---|---|---|---|---|---|---|---|---|---|---|---|---|---|---|---|---|---|---|---|---|
| | 2.500 | 2.525 | 2.550 | 2.575 | 2.600 | 2.620 | 2.640 | 2.650 | 2.660 | 2.680 | 2.700 | 2.720 | 2.740 | 2.750 | 2.760 | 2.780 | 2.800 | 2.820 | 2.840 | 2.850 | 2.860 | 2.880 | 2.900 | 2.920 | 2.940 | 2.950 | 2.960 | 2.980 | 3.000 | 3.020 | 3.040 | 3.050 | 3.060 | 3.080 | 3.100 | 3.120 | 3.140 | 3.150 | 3.160 | 3.180 | 3.200 | 3.225 | 3.250 | 3.275 | 3.300 |
| 0.000 - 0.025 | | | | | | 02 | 02 | 02 | 02 | 02 | 04 | 04 | 04 | 06 | 06 | 06 | 08 | 08 | 08 | 10 | 10 | 10 | 12 | 12 | 12 | 14 | 14 | 14 | 16 | 16 | 16 | 18 | 18 | 18 | 20 | 20 | 20 | 22 | 22 | 22 | 24 | 24 | 26 | 26 | 28 |
| 0.026 - 0.050 | | | | | 02 | 02 | 02 | 02 | 02 | 04 | 04 | 06 | 06 | 06 | 06 | 08 | 08 | 10 | 10 | 10 | 10 | 12 | 12 | 14 | 14 | 14 | 14 | 16 | 16 | 18 | 18 | 18 | 18 | 20 | 20 | 22 | 22 | 22 | 22 | 24 | 24 | 26 | 26 | 28 | 28 |
| 0.051 - 0.075 | | | | 02 | 02 | 02 | 02 | 04 | 04 | 04 | 06 | 06 | 06 | 08 | 08 | 08 | 10 | 10 | 10 | 12 | 12 | 12 | 14 | 14 | 14 | 16 | 16 | 16 | 18 | 18 | 18 | 20 | 20 | 20 | 22 | 22 | 22 | 24 | 24 | 24 | 26 | 26 | 28 | 28 | 30 |
| 0.076 - 0.100 | | | 02 | 02 | 02 | 04 | 04 | 04 | 04 | 06 | 06 | 08 | 08 | 08 | 08 | 10 | 10 | 12 | 12 | 12 | 12 | 14 | 14 | 16 | 16 | 16 | 16 | 18 | 18 | 20 | 20 | 20 | 20 | 22 | 22 | 24 | 24 | 24 | 24 | 26 | 26 | 28 | 28 | 30 | 30 |
| 0.101 - 0.125 | | 02 | 02 | 02 | 04 | 04 | 04 | 06 | 06 | 06 | 08 | 08 | 08 | 10 | 10 | 10 | 12 | 12 | 12 | 14 | 14 | 14 | 16 | 16 | 16 | 18 | 18 | 18 | 20 | 20 | 20 | 22 | 22 | 22 | 24 | 24 | 24 | 26 | 26 | 26 | 28 | 28 | 30 | 30 | 32 |
| 0.126 - 0.129 | | 02 | 02 | 04 | 04 | 04 | 06 | 06 | 06 | 08 | 08 | 08 | 10 | 10 | 10 | 12 | 12 | 12 | 14 | 14 | 14 | 16 | 16 | 16 | 18 | 18 | 18 | 20 | 20 | 20 | 22 | 22 | 22 | 24 | 24 | 24 | 26 | 26 | 26 | 28 | 28 | 28 | 30 | 30 | 32 |
| 0.130 - 0.230 | | | | | | | | | | | | | | | | | | | | | | | | | | | | | | | | | | | | | | | | | | | | | |
| 0.231 - 0.250 | 04 | 06 | 06 | 08 | 08 | 10 | 10 | 10 | 10 | 12 | 12 | 14 | 14 | 14 | 14 | 16 | 16 | 18 | 18 | 18 | 18 | 20 | 20 | 22 | 22 | 22 | 22 | 24 | 24 | 26 | 26 | 26 | 26 | 28 | 28 | 30 | 30 | 30 | 30 | 32 | 32 | 34 | 34 | 34 | |
| 0.251 - 0.275 | 06 | 06 | 08 | 08 | 10 | 10 | 10 | 12 | 12 | 12 | 14 | 14 | 14 | 16 | 16 | 16 | 18 | 18 | 18 | 20 | 20 | 20 | 22 | 22 | 22 | 24 | 24 | 24 | 26 | 26 | 26 | 28 | 28 | 28 | 30 | 30 | 30 | 32 | 32 | 32 | 34 | 34 | 34 | 34 | |
| 0.276 - 0.300 | 06 | 08 | 08 | 10 | 10 | 12 | 12 | 12 | 12 | 14 | 14 | 16 | 16 | 16 | 16 | 18 | 18 | 20 | 20 | 20 | 20 | 22 | 22 | 24 | 24 | 24 | 24 | 26 | 26 | 28 | 28 | 28 | 28 | 30 | 30 | 32 | 32 | 32 | 32 | 34 | 34 | 34 | 34 | | |
| 0.301 - 0.325 | 08 | 08 | 10 | 10 | 12 | 12 | 12 | 14 | 14 | 14 | 16 | 16 | 16 | 18 | 18 | 18 | 20 | 20 | 20 | 22 | 22 | 22 | 24 | 24 | 24 | 26 | 26 | 26 | 28 | 28 | 28 | 30 | 30 | 30 | 32 | 32 | 32 | 34 | 34 | 34 | 34 | 34 | | | |
| 0.326 - 0.350 | 08 | 10 | 10 | 12 | 12 | 14 | 14 | 14 | 14 | 16 | 16 | 18 | 18 | 18 | 18 | 20 | 20 | 22 | 22 | 22 | 22 | 24 | 24 | 26 | 26 | 26 | 26 | 28 | 28 | 30 | 30 | 30 | 30 | 32 | 32 | 34 | 34 | 34 | 34 | 34 | 34 | | | | |
| 0.351 - 0.375 | 10 | 10 | 12 | 12 | 14 | 14 | 14 | 16 | 16 | 16 | 18 | 18 | 18 | 20 | 20 | 20 | 22 | 22 | 22 | 24 | 24 | 24 | 26 | 26 | 26 | 28 | 28 | 28 | 30 | 30 | 30 | 32 | 32 | 32 | 34 | 34 | 34 | 34 | 34 | | | | | | |
| 0.376 - 0.400 | 10 | 12 | 12 | 14 | 14 | 16 | 16 | 16 | 16 | 18 | 18 | 20 | 20 | 20 | 20 | 22 | 22 | 24 | 24 | 24 | 24 | 26 | 26 | 28 | 28 | 28 | 28 | 30 | 30 | 32 | 32 | 32 | 32 | 34 | 34 | 34 | 34 | 34 | | | | | | | |
| 0.401 - 0.425 | 12 | 12 | 14 | 14 | 16 | 16 | 16 | 18 | 18 | 18 | 20 | 20 | 20 | 22 | 22 | 22 | 24 | 24 | 24 | 26 | 26 | 26 | 28 | 28 | 28 | 30 | 30 | 30 | 32 | 32 | 32 | 34 | 34 | 34 | 34 | 34 | | | | | | | | | |
| 0.426 - 0.450 | 12 | 14 | 14 | 16 | 16 | 18 | 18 | 18 | 18 | 20 | 20 | 22 | 22 | 22 | 22 | 24 | 24 | 26 | 26 | 26 | 26 | 28 | 28 | 30 | 30 | 30 | 30 | 32 | 32 | 34 | 34 | 34 | 34 | 34 | 34 | | | | | | | | | | |
| 0.451 - 0.475 | 14 | 14 | 16 | 16 | 18 | 18 | 18 | 20 | 20 | 20 | 22 | 22 | 22 | 24 | 24 | 24 | 26 | 26 | 26 | 28 | 28 | 28 | 30 | 30 | 30 | 32 | 32 | 32 | 34 | 34 | 34 | 34 | 34 | | | | | | | | | | | | |
| 0.476 - 0.500 | 14 | 16 | 16 | 18 | 18 | 20 | 20 | 20 | 20 | 22 | 22 | 24 | 24 | 24 | 24 | 26 | 26 | 28 | 28 | 28 | 28 | 30 | 30 | 32 | 32 | 32 | 32 | 34 | 34 | 34 | 34 | 34 | | | | | | | | | | | | | |
| 0.501 - 0.525 | 16 | 16 | 18 | 18 | 20 | 20 | 20 | 22 | 22 | 22 | 24 | 24 | 24 | 26 | 26 | 26 | 28 | 28 | 28 | 30 | 30 | 30 | 32 | 32 | 32 | 34 | 34 | 34 | 34 | 34 | | | | | | | | | | | | | | | |
| 0.526 - 0.550 | 16 | 18 | 18 | 20 | 20 | 22 | 22 | 22 | 22 | 24 | 24 | 26 | 26 | 26 | 26 | 28 | 28 | 30 | 30 | 30 | 30 | 32 | 32 | 34 | 34 | 34 | 34 | 34 | 34 | | | | | | | | | | | | | | | | |
| 0.551 - 0.575 | 18 | 18 | 20 | 20 | 22 | 22 | 22 | 24 | 24 | 24 | 26 | 26 | 26 | 28 | 28 | 28 | 30 | 30 | 30 | 32 | 32 | 32 | 34 | 34 | 34 | 34 | 34 | | | | | | | | | | | | | | | | | | |
| 0.576 - 0.600 | 18 | 20 | 20 | 22 | 22 | 24 | 24 | 24 | 24 | 26 | 26 | 28 | 28 | 28 | 28 | 30 | 30 | 32 | 32 | 32 | 32 | 34 | 34 | 34 | 34 | 34 | | | | | | | | | | | | | | | | | | | |
| 0.601 - 0.625 | 20 | 20 | 22 | 22 | 24 | 24 | 24 | 26 | 26 | 26 | 28 | 28 | 28 | 30 | 30 | 30 | 32 | 32 | 32 | 34 | 34 | 34 | 34 | 34 | | | | | | | | | | | | | | | | | | | | | |
| 0.626 - 0.650 | 20 | 22 | 22 | 24 | 24 | 26 | 26 | 26 | 26 | 28 | 28 | 30 | 30 | 30 | 30 | 32 | 32 | 34 | 34 | 34 | 34 | 34 | 34 | | | | | | | | | | | | | | | | | | | | | | |
| 0.651 - 0.675 | 22 | 22 | 24 | 24 | 26 | 26 | 26 | 28 | 28 | 28 | 30 | 30 | 30 | 32 | 32 | 32 | 34 | 34 | 34 | 34 | 34 | | | | | | | | | | | | | | | | | | | | | | | | |
| 0,676 - 0.700 | 22 | 24 | 24 | 26 | 26 | 28 | 28 | 28 | 28 | 30 | 30 | 32 | 32 | 32 | 32 | 34 | 34 | 34 | 34 | 34 | | | | | | | | | | | | | | | | | | | | | | | | | |
| 0.701 - 0.725 | 24 | 24 | 26 | 26 | 28 | 28 | 28 | 30 | 30 | 30 | 32 | 32 | 32 | 34 | 34 | 34 | 34 | 34 | | | | | | | | | | | | | | | | | | | | | | | | | | | |
| 0.726 - 0.750 | 24 | 26 | 26 | 28 | 28 | 30 | 30 | 30 | 30 | 32 | 32 | 34 | 34 | 34 | 34 | 34 | | | | | | | | | | | | | | | | | | | | | | | | | | | | | |
| 0.751 - 0.775 | 26 | 26 | 28 | 28 | 30 | 30 | 30 | 32 | 32 | 32 | 34 | 34 | 34 | 34 | 34 | | | | | | | | | | | | | | | | | | | | | | | | | | | | | | |
| 0.776 - 0.800 | 26 | 28 | 28 | 30 | 30 | 32 | 32 | 32 | 32 | 34 | 34 | 34 | 34 | 34 | | | | | | | | | | | | | | | | | | | | | | | | | | | | | | | |
| 0.801 - 0.825 | 28 | 28 | 30 | 30 | 32 | 32 | 32 | 34 | 34 | 34 | 34 | 34 | | | | | | | | | | | | | | | | | | | | | | | | | | | | | | | | | |
| 0.826 - 0.850 | 28 | 30 | 30 | 32 | 32 | 32 | 34 | 34 | 34 | 34 | 34 | | | | | | | | | | | | | | | | | | | | | | | | | | | | | | | | | | |
| 0.851 - 0.875 | 30 | 30 | 32 | 32 | 34 | 34 | 34 | 34 | 34 | | | | | | | | | | | | | | | | | | | | | | | | | | | | | | | | | | | | |
| 0.876 - 0.900 | 30 | 32 | 32 | 34 | 34 | 34 | 34 | 34 | | | | | | | | | | | | | | | | | | | | | | | | | | | | | | | | | | | | | |
| 0.901 - 0.925 | 32 | 32 | 34 | 34 | 34 | 34 | | | | | | | | | | | | | | | | | | | | | | | | | | | | | | | | | | | | | | | |
| 0.926 - 0.950 | 32 | 34 | 34 | 34 | 34 | | | | | | | | | | | | | | | | | | | | | | | | | | | | | | | | | | | | | | | | |
| 0.951 - 0.975 | 34 | 34 | 34 | 34 | | | | | | | | | | | | | | | | | | | | | | | | | | | | | | | | | | | | | | | | | |
| 0.976 - 1.000 | 34 | 34 | 34 | | | | | | | | | | | | | | | | | | | | | | | | | | | | | | | | | | | | | | | | | | |
| 1.001 - 1.025 | 34 | 34 | | | | | | | | | | | | | | | | | | | | | | | | | | | | | | | | | | | | | | | | | | | |
| 1.026 - 1.030 | 34 | | | | | | | | | | | | | | | | | | | | | | | | | | | | | | | | | | | | | | | | | | | | |

New shim thickness mm (in.)

| Shim No. | Thickness | Shim No. | Thickness |
|---|---|---|---|
| 02 | 2.500 (0.0984) | 20 | 2.950 (0.1161) |
| 04 | 2.550 (0.1004) | 22 | 3.000 (0.1181) |
| 06 | 2.600 (0.1024) | 24 | 3.050 (0.1201) |
| 08 | 2.650 (0.1043) | 26 | 3.100 (0.1220) |
| 10 | 2.700 (0.1063) | 28 | 3.150 (0.1240) |
| 12 | 2.750 (0.1083) | 30 | 3.200 (0.1260) |
| 14 | 2.800 (0.1102) | 32 | 3.250 (0.1280) |
| 16 | 2.850 (0.1122) | 34 | 3.300 (0.1299) |
| 18 | 2.900 (0.1142) | | |

EXAMPLE: A 0.1102" (2.800 mm) shim is installed and measured clearance is 0.0177" (0.450 mm). Replace 0.1102" (2.800 mm) shim with a No. 24 shim.

91B17898

Courtesy of Toyota Motor Sales, U.S.A., Inc.

*Fig. 17: Intake Valve Adjusting Shim Selection Chart (Camry 2.5L)*

EXHAUST VALVES

| Measured clearance (mm) | Installed shim thickness (mm) | | | | | | | | | | | | | | | | | | | | | | | | | | | | | | | | | | | | | | | | | | | | |
|---|---|---|---|---|---|---|---|---|---|---|---|---|---|---|---|---|---|---|---|---|---|---|---|---|---|---|---|---|---|---|---|---|---|---|---|---|---|---|---|---|---|---|---|---|---|
| | 2.500 | 2.525 | 2.550 | 2.575 | 2.600 | 2.620 | 2.640 | 2.650 | 2.660 | 2.680 | 2.700 | 2.720 | 2.740 | 2.750 | 2.760 | 2.780 | 2.800 | 2.820 | 2.840 | 2.850 | 2.860 | 2.880 | 2.900 | 2.920 | 2.940 | 2.950 | 2.960 | 2.980 | 3.000 | 3.020 | 3.040 | 3.050 | 3.060 | 3.080 | 3.100 | 3.120 | 3.140 | 3.150 | 3.160 | 3.180 | 3.200 | 3.225 | 3.250 | 3.275 | 3.300 |
| 0.000 – 0.025 | | | | | | | | | | | | | | 02 | 02 | 02 | 02 | 02 | 04 | 04 | 04 | 04 | 06 | 06 | 08 | 08 | 08 | 08 | 10 | 10 | 12 | 12 | 12 | 12 | 14 | 14 | 16 | 16 | 16 | 16 | 18 | 18 | 20 | 20 | 22 |
| 0.026 – 0.050 | | | | | | | | | | | | 02 | 02 | 02 | 02 | 02 | 02 | 04 | 04 | 04 | 06 | 06 | 06 | 08 | 08 | 08 | 10 | 10 | 10 | 12 | 12 | 12 | 14 | 14 | 14 | 16 | 16 | 16 | 18 | 18 | 18 | 20 | 20 | 22 | 22 |
| 0.051 – 0.075 | | | | | | | | | | | 02 | 02 | 02 | 02 | 02 | 02 | 04 | 04 | 06 | 06 | 06 | 06 | 08 | 08 | 10 | 10 | 10 | 10 | 12 | 12 | 14 | 14 | 14 | 14 | 16 | 16 | 18 | 18 | 18 | 18 | 20 | 20 | 22 | 22 | 24 |
| 0.076 – 0.100 | | | | | | | | | | 02 | 02 | 02 | 02 | 02 | 04 | 04 | 04 | 06 | 06 | 06 | 08 | 08 | 08 | 10 | 10 | 10 | 12 | 12 | 12 | 14 | 14 | 14 | 16 | 16 | 16 | 18 | 18 | 18 | 20 | 20 | 20 | 22 | 22 | 24 | 24 |
| 0.101 – 0.125 | | | | | | | | 02 | 02 | 02 | 02 | 02 | 04 | 04 | 04 | 04 | 06 | 06 | 08 | 08 | 08 | 08 | 10 | 10 | 12 | 12 | 12 | 12 | 14 | 14 | 16 | 16 | 16 | 16 | 18 | 18 | 20 | 20 | 20 | 20 | 22 | 22 | 24 | 24 | 26 |
| 0.126 – 0.150 | | | | | | 02 | 02 | 02 | 02 | 02 | 02 | 04 | 04 | 04 | 06 | 06 | 06 | 08 | 08 | 08 | 10 | 10 | 10 | 12 | 12 | 12 | 14 | 14 | 14 | 16 | 16 | 16 | 18 | 18 | 18 | 20 | 20 | 20 | 22 | 22 | 22 | 24 | 24 | 26 | 26 |
| 0.151 – 0.175 | | | | | 02 | 02 | 02 | 02 | 02 | 02 | 04 | 04 | 06 | 06 | 06 | 06 | 08 | 08 | 10 | 10 | 10 | 10 | 12 | 12 | 14 | 14 | 14 | 14 | 16 | 16 | 18 | 18 | 18 | 18 | 20 | 20 | 22 | 22 | 22 | 22 | 24 | 24 | 26 | 26 | 28 |
| 0.176 – 0.200 | | | | 02 | 02 | 02 | 02 | 02 | 04 | 04 | 04 | 06 | 06 | 06 | 08 | 08 | 08 | 10 | 10 | 10 | 12 | 12 | 12 | 14 | 14 | 14 | 16 | 16 | 16 | 18 | 18 | 18 | 20 | 20 | 20 | 22 | 22 | 22 | 24 | 24 | 24 | 26 | 26 | 28 | 28 |
| 0.201 – 0.225 | | | 02 | 02 | 02 | 02 | 04 | 04 | 04 | 04 | 06 | 06 | 08 | 08 | 08 | 08 | 10 | 10 | 12 | 12 | 12 | 12 | 14 | 14 | 16 | 16 | 16 | 16 | 18 | 18 | 20 | 20 | 20 | 20 | 22 | 22 | 24 | 24 | 24 | 24 | 26 | 26 | 28 | 28 | 30 |
| 0.226 – 0.250 | | 02 | 02 | 02 | 02 | 04 | 04 | 04 | 06 | 06 | 06 | 08 | 08 | 08 | 10 | 10 | 10 | 12 | 12 | 12 | 14 | 14 | 14 | 16 | 16 | 16 | 18 | 18 | 18 | 20 | 20 | 20 | 22 | 22 | 22 | 24 | 24 | 24 | 26 | 26 | 26 | 28 | 28 | 30 | 30 |
| 0.251 – 0.269 | | 02 | 02 | 02 | 04 | 04 | 06 | 06 | 06 | 06 | 08 | 08 | 10 | 10 | 10 | 10 | 12 | 12 | 14 | 14 | 14 | 14 | 16 | 16 | 18 | 18 | 18 | 18 | 20 | 20 | 22 | 22 | 22 | 22 | 24 | 24 | 26 | 26 | 26 | 26 | 28 | 28 | 30 | 30 | 32 |
| 0.270 – 0.370 | | | | | | | | | | | | | | | | | | | | | | | | | | | | | | | | | | | | | | | | | | | | | |
| 0.371 – 0.375 | 04 | 06 | 06 | 08 | 08 | 08 | 10 | 10 | 10 | 12 | 12 | 12 | 14 | 14 | 14 | 16 | 16 | 16 | 18 | 18 | 18 | 20 | 20 | 20 | 22 | 22 | 22 | 24 | 24 | 24 | 26 | 26 | 26 | 28 | 28 | 28 | 30 | 30 | 30 | 32 | 32 | 34 | 34 | 34 | |
| 0.376 – 0.400 | 04 | 06 | 06 | 08 | 08 | 10 | 10 | 10 | 12 | 12 | 12 | 14 | 14 | 14 | 16 | 16 | 16 | 18 | 18 | 18 | 20 | 20 | 20 | 22 | 22 | 22 | 24 | 24 | 24 | 26 | 26 | 26 | 28 | 28 | 28 | 30 | 30 | 30 | 32 | 32 | 32 | 34 | 34 | 34 | |
| 0.401 – 0.425 | 06 | 06 | 08 | 08 | 10 | 10 | 12 | 12 | 12 | 12 | 14 | 14 | 16 | 16 | 16 | 16 | 18 | 18 | 20 | 20 | 20 | 20 | 22 | 22 | 24 | 24 | 24 | 24 | 26 | 26 | 28 | 28 | 28 | 28 | 30 | 30 | 32 | 32 | 32 | 32 | 34 | 34 | 34 | | |
| 0.426 – 0.450 | 06 | 08 | 08 | 10 | 10 | 12 | 12 | 12 | 14 | 14 | 14 | 16 | 16 | 16 | 18 | 18 | 18 | 20 | 20 | 20 | 22 | 22 | 22 | 24 | 24 | 24 | 26 | 26 | 26 | 28 | 28 | 28 | 30 | 30 | 30 | 32 | 32 | 32 | 34 | 34 | 34 | 34 | | | |
| 0.451 – 0.475 | 08 | 08 | 10 | 10 | 12 | 12 | 14 | 14 | 14 | 14 | 16 | 16 | 18 | 18 | 18 | 18 | 20 | 20 | 22 | 22 | 22 | 22 | 24 | 24 | 26 | 26 | 26 | 26 | 28 | 28 | 30 | 30 | 30 | 30 | 32 | 32 | 34 | 34 | 34 | 34 | 34 | | | | |
| 0.476 – 0.500 | 08 | 10 | 10 | 12 | 12 | 14 | 14 | 14 | 16 | 16 | 16 | 18 | 18 | 18 | 20 | 20 | 20 | 22 | 22 | 22 | 24 | 24 | 24 | 26 | 26 | 26 | 28 | 28 | 28 | 30 | 30 | 30 | 32 | 32 | 32 | 34 | 34 | 34 | 34 | 34 | | | | | |
| 0.501 – 0.525 | 10 | 10 | 12 | 12 | 14 | 14 | 16 | 16 | 16 | 16 | 18 | 18 | 20 | 20 | 20 | 20 | 22 | 22 | 24 | 24 | 24 | 24 | 26 | 26 | 28 | 28 | 28 | 28 | 30 | 30 | 32 | 32 | 32 | 32 | 34 | 34 | 34 | 34 | 34 | | | | | | |
| 0.526 – 0.550 | 10 | 12 | 12 | 14 | 14 | 16 | 16 | 16 | 18 | 18 | 18 | 20 | 20 | 20 | 22 | 22 | 22 | 24 | 24 | 24 | 26 | 26 | 26 | 28 | 28 | 28 | 30 | 30 | 30 | 32 | 32 | 32 | 34 | 34 | 34 | 34 | 34 | | | | | | | | |
| 0.551 – 0.575 | 12 | 12 | 14 | 14 | 16 | 16 | 18 | 18 | 18 | 18 | 20 | 20 | 22 | 22 | 22 | 22 | 24 | 24 | 26 | 26 | 26 | 26 | 28 | 28 | 30 | 30 | 30 | 30 | 32 | 32 | 34 | 34 | 34 | 34 | 34 | | | | | | | | | | |
| 0.576 – 0.600 | 12 | 14 | 14 | 16 | 16 | 18 | 18 | 18 | 20 | 20 | 20 | 22 | 22 | 22 | 24 | 24 | 24 | 26 | 26 | 26 | 28 | 28 | 28 | 30 | 30 | 30 | 32 | 32 | 32 | 34 | 34 | 34 | 34 | 34 | | | | | | | | | | | |
| 0.601 – 0.625 | 14 | 14 | 16 | 16 | 18 | 18 | 20 | 20 | 20 | 20 | 22 | 22 | 24 | 24 | 24 | 24 | 26 | 26 | 28 | 28 | 28 | 28 | 30 | 30 | 32 | 32 | 32 | 32 | 34 | 34 | 34 | 34 | 34 | | | | | | | | | | | | |
| 0.626 – 0.650 | 14 | 16 | 16 | 18 | 18 | 20 | 20 | 20 | 22 | 22 | 22 | 24 | 24 | 24 | 26 | 26 | 26 | 28 | 28 | 28 | 30 | 30 | 30 | 32 | 32 | 32 | 34 | 34 | 34 | 34 | 34 | | | | | | | | | | | | | | |
| 0.651 – 0.675 | 16 | 16 | 18 | 18 | 20 | 20 | 22 | 22 | 22 | 22 | 24 | 24 | 26 | 26 | 26 | 26 | 28 | 28 | 30 | 30 | 30 | 30 | 32 | 32 | 34 | 34 | 34 | 34 | 34 | | | | | | | | | | | | | | | | |
| 0.676 – 0.700 | 16 | 18 | 18 | 20 | 20 | 22 | 22 | 22 | 24 | 24 | 24 | 26 | 26 | 26 | 28 | 28 | 28 | 30 | 30 | 30 | 32 | 32 | 32 | 34 | 34 | 34 | 34 | 34 | | | | | | | | | | | | | | | | | |
| 0.701 – 0.725 | 18 | 18 | 20 | 20 | 22 | 22 | 24 | 24 | 24 | 24 | 26 | 26 | 28 | 28 | 28 | 28 | 30 | 30 | 32 | 32 | 32 | 32 | 34 | 34 | 34 | 34 | 34 | | | | | | | | | | | | | | | | | | |
| 0.726 – 0.750 | 18 | 20 | 20 | 22 | 22 | 24 | 24 | 24 | 26 | 26 | 26 | 28 | 28 | 28 | 30 | 30 | 30 | 32 | 32 | 32 | 34 | 34 | 34 | 34 | 34 | | | | | | | | | | | | | | | | | | | | |
| 0.751 – 0.775 | 20 | 20 | 22 | 22 | 24 | 24 | 26 | 26 | 26 | 28 | 28 | 30 | 30 | 30 | 30 | 32 | 32 | 34 | 34 | 34 | 34 | 34 | 34 | | | | | | | | | | | | | | | | | | | | | | |
| 0.776 – 0.800 | 20 | 22 | 22 | 24 | 24 | 26 | 26 | 26 | 28 | 28 | 28 | 30 | 30 | 30 | 32 | 32 | 32 | 34 | 34 | 34 | 34 | 34 | | | | | | | | | | | | | | | | | | | | | | | |
| 0.801 – 0.825 | 22 | 22 | 24 | 24 | 26 | 26 | 28 | 28 | 28 | 28 | 30 | 30 | 32 | 32 | 32 | 32 | 34 | 34 | 34 | 34 | 34 | | | | | | | | | | | | | | | | | | | | | | | | |
| 0.826 – 0.850 | 22 | 24 | 24 | 26 | 26 | 28 | 28 | 28 | 30 | 30 | 30 | 32 | 32 | 32 | 34 | 34 | 34 | 34 | 34 | | | | | | | | | | | | | | | | | | | | | | | | | | |
| 0.851 – 0.875 | 24 | 24 | 26 | 26 | 28 | 28 | 30 | 30 | 30 | 30 | 32 | 32 | 34 | 34 | 34 | 34 | 34 | | | | | | | | | | | | | | | | | | | | | | | | | | | | |
| 0.876 – 0.900 | 24 | 26 | 26 | 28 | 28 | 30 | 30 | 30 | 32 | 32 | 32 | 34 | 34 | 34 | 34 | 34 | | | | | | | | | | | | | | | | | | | | | | | | | | | | | |
| 0.901 – 0.925 | 26 | 26 | 28 | 28 | 30 | 30 | 32 | 32 | 32 | 32 | 34 | 34 | 34 | 34 | 34 | | | | | | | | | | | | | | | | | | | | | | | | | | | | | | |
| 0.926 – 0.950 | 26 | 28 | 28 | 30 | 30 | 32 | 32 | 32 | 34 | 34 | 34 | 34 | 34 | | | | | | | | | | | | | | | | | | | | | | | | | | | | | | | | |
| 0.951 – 0.975 | 28 | 28 | 30 | 30 | 32 | 32 | 34 | 34 | 34 | 34 | 34 | | | | | | | | | | | | | | | | | | | | | | | | | | | | | | | | | | |
| 0.976 – 1.000 | 28 | 30 | 30 | 32 | 32 | 34 | 34 | 34 | 34 | 34 | | | | | | | | | | | | | | | | | | | | | | | | | | | | | | | | | | | |
| 1.001 – 1.025 | 30 | 30 | 32 | 32 | 34 | 34 | 34 | 34 | 34 | | | | | | | | | | | | | | | | | | | | | | | | | | | | | | | | | | | | |
| 1.026 – 1.050 | 30 | 32 | 32 | 34 | 34 | 34 | 34 | | | | | | | | | | | | | | | | | | | | | | | | | | | | | | | | | | | | | | |
| 1.051 – 1.075 | 32 | 32 | 34 | 34 | 34 | | | | | | | | | | | | | | | | | | | | | | | | | | | | | | | | | | | | | | | | |
| 1.076 – 1.100 | 32 | 34 | 34 | 34 | | | | | | | | | | | | | | | | | | | | | | | | | | | | | | | | | | | | | | | | | |
| 1.101 – 1.125 | 34 | 34 | 34 | | | | | | | | | | | | | | | | | | | | | | | | | | | | | | | | | | | | | | | | | | |
| 1.126 – 1.150 | 34 | 34 | | | | | | | | | | | | | | | | | | | | | | | | | | | | | | | | | | | | | | | | | | | |
| 1.151 – 1.170 | 34 | | | | | | | | | | | | | | | | | | | | | | | | | | | | | | | | | | | | | | | | | | | | |

New shim thickness mm (in.)

| Shim No. | Thickness | Shim No. | Thickness |
|---|---|---|---|
| 02 | 2.500 (0.0984) | 20 | 2.950 (0.1161) |
| 04 | 2.550 (0.1004) | 22 | 3.000 (0.1181) |
| 06 | 2.600 (0.1024) | 24 | 3.050 (0.1201) |
| 08 | 2.650 (0.1043) | 26 | 3.100 (0.1220) |
| 10 | 2.700 (0.1063) | 28 | 3.150 (0.1240) |
| 12 | 2.750 (0.1083) | 30 | 3.200 (0.1260) |
| 14 | 2.800 (0.1102) | 32 | 3.250 (0.1280) |
| 16 | 2.850 (0.1122) | 34 | 3.300 (0.1299) |
| 18 | 2.900 (0.1142) | | |

EXAMPLE: A 0.1102" (2.800 mm) shim is installed and measured clearance is 0.0177" (0.450 mm). Replace 0.1102" (2.800 mm) shim with a No. 18 shim.

91C17899

Courtesy of Toyota Motor Sales, U.S.A., Inc.

***Fig. 18: Exhaust Valve Adjusting Shim Selection Chart (Camry 2.5L)***

# 1991 ENGINE PERFORMANCE
# On-Vehicle Adjustments (Cont.)

## IGNITION TIMING

***CAUTION: Some tachometers may not be compatible with ignition system. Consult tachometer manufacturer before connecting tachometer to system. To avoid possible damage to ignitor and/or coil, DO NOT allow tachometer terminal to become grounded.***

**1)** Ensure engine is at normal operating temperature. Connect timing light to engine. Connect tachometer to proper location. *See Fig. 26.*

**2)** Install jumper wire between proper terminals of engine check connector. *See Figs. 27 and 28.* Ensure idle speed is within specification. See appropriate IDLE SPEED SPECIFICATIONS table under IDLE SPEED & MIXTURE. Ensure base timing is within specification. See IGNITION TIMING - DEGREES BTDC @ RPM table.

**3)** On Supra turbo with Distributorless Ignition System (DIS), adjust timing by turning cam position sensor. On all other models, adjust timing by turning distributor.

**4)** Remove jumper wire from engine check connector and ensure advance timing is within specification. See IGNITION TIMING - DEGREES BTDC @ RPM table. Tighten distributor hold-down bolt or cam position sensor bolt (Supra turbo). See TORQUE SPECIFICATIONS table at end of article.

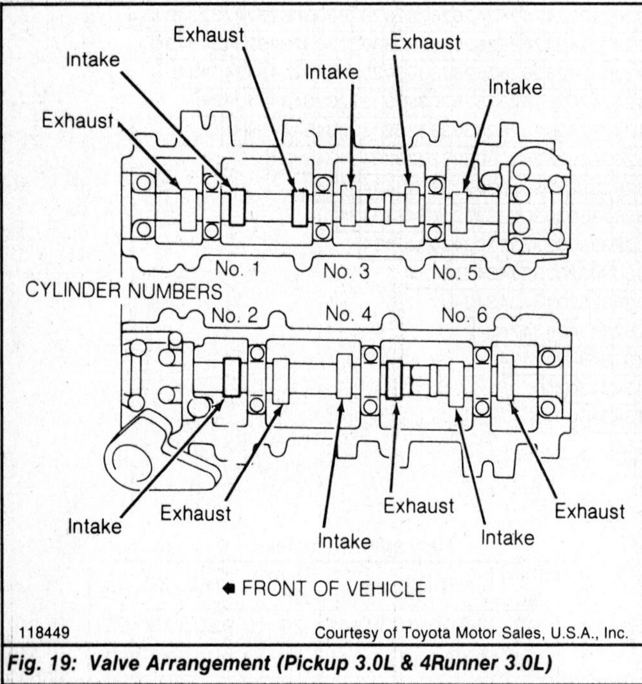


***Fig. 19: Valve Arrangement (Pickup 3.0L & 4Runner 3.0L)***

*IGNITION TIMING - Degrees BTDC @ RPM*

| Application | [1] Base Timing | [2] Advance Timing |
|---|---|---|
| 4-Cylinder | | |
| Camry | 10 @ Idle | 13-22 @ Idle |
| Celica | | |
| 1.6L | 10 @ Idle | 0-20 @ Idle |
| 2.0L | 10 @ Idle | 12-21 @ Idle |
| 2.2L | 10 @ Idle | 13-22 @ Idle |
| Corolla | | |
| 1.6L (4A-FE) | 10 @ Idle | 0-20 @ Idle |
| 1.6L (4A-GE) | 10 @ Idle | 9-19 @ Idle |
| MR2 | | |
| 2.0L | 10 @ Idle | 12-21 @ Idle |
| 2.2L | 10 @ Idle | 13-22 @ Idle |
| Pickup & 4Runner | 5 @ Idle | 10-14 @ Idle |
| Previa | 5 @ Idle | 12 @ Idle |
| Tercel | 10 @ Idle | 7-17 @ Idle |
| 6-Cylinder | | |
| Cressida | 10 @ Idle | 9-11 @ Idle |
| Land Cruiser | 7 @ Idle | 12 @ Idle |
| Supra | | |
| Non-Turbo | 10 @ Idle | 9-10 @ Idle |
| Turbo | 10 @ Idle | [3] |
| V6 | | |
| Camry | 10 @ Idle | 13-27 @ Idle |
| Pickup & 4Runner | 10 @ Idle | 8 @ Idle |

[1] - Check ignition timing with transmission in Neutral, and jumper wire connected between proper terminals of check connector.

[2] - Check ignition timing with transmission in Neutral, and jumper wire removed from check connector terminals.

[3] - More than 12 degrees at idle.

# 1991 ENGINE PERFORMANCE
## On-Vehicle Adjustments (Cont.)

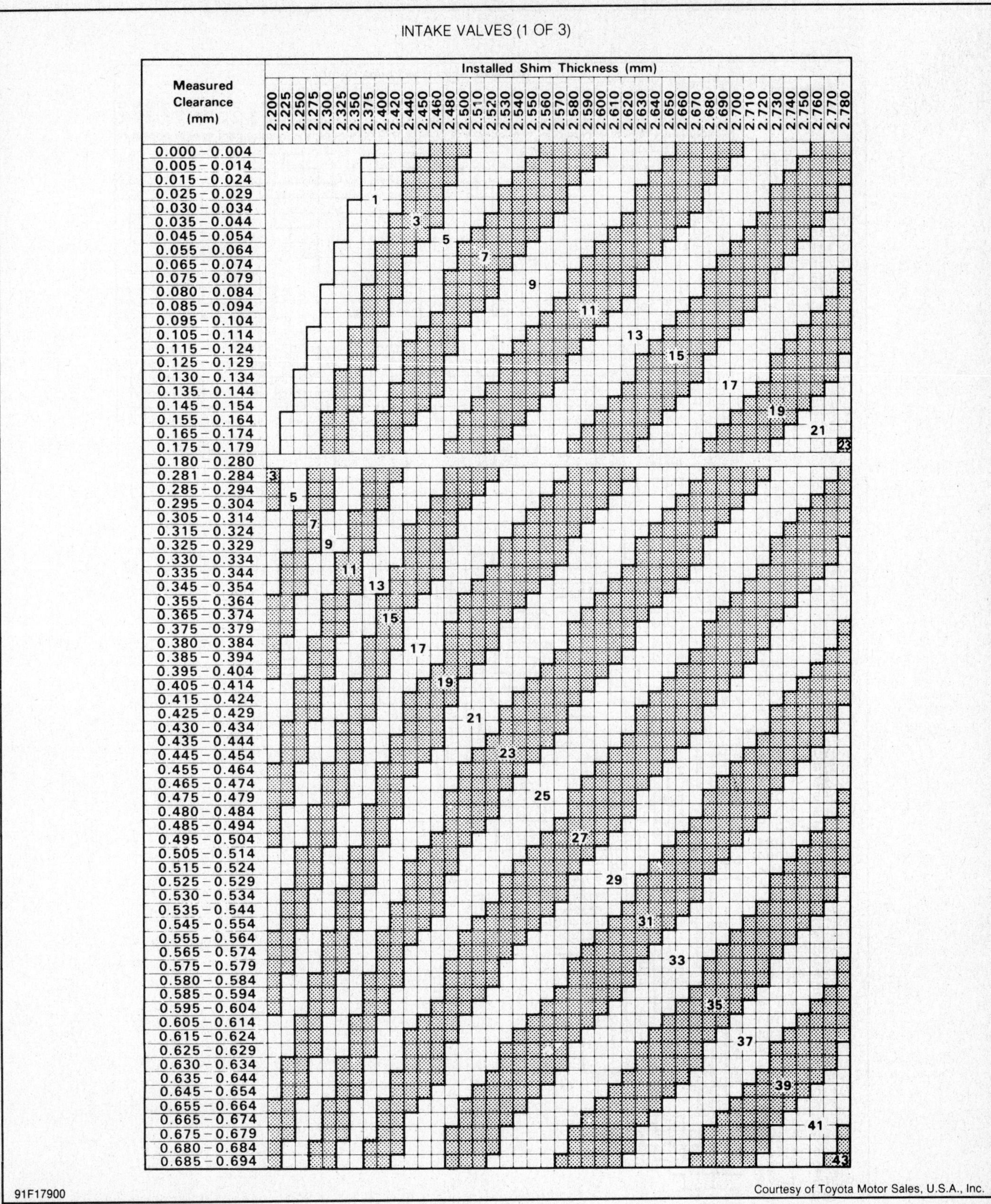


*Fig. 20: Intake Valve Adjusting Shim Selection Charts (Pickup 3.0L & 4Runner 3.0L – 1 of 3)*

# 1991 ENGINE PERFORMANCE
## On-Vehicle Adjustments (Cont.)

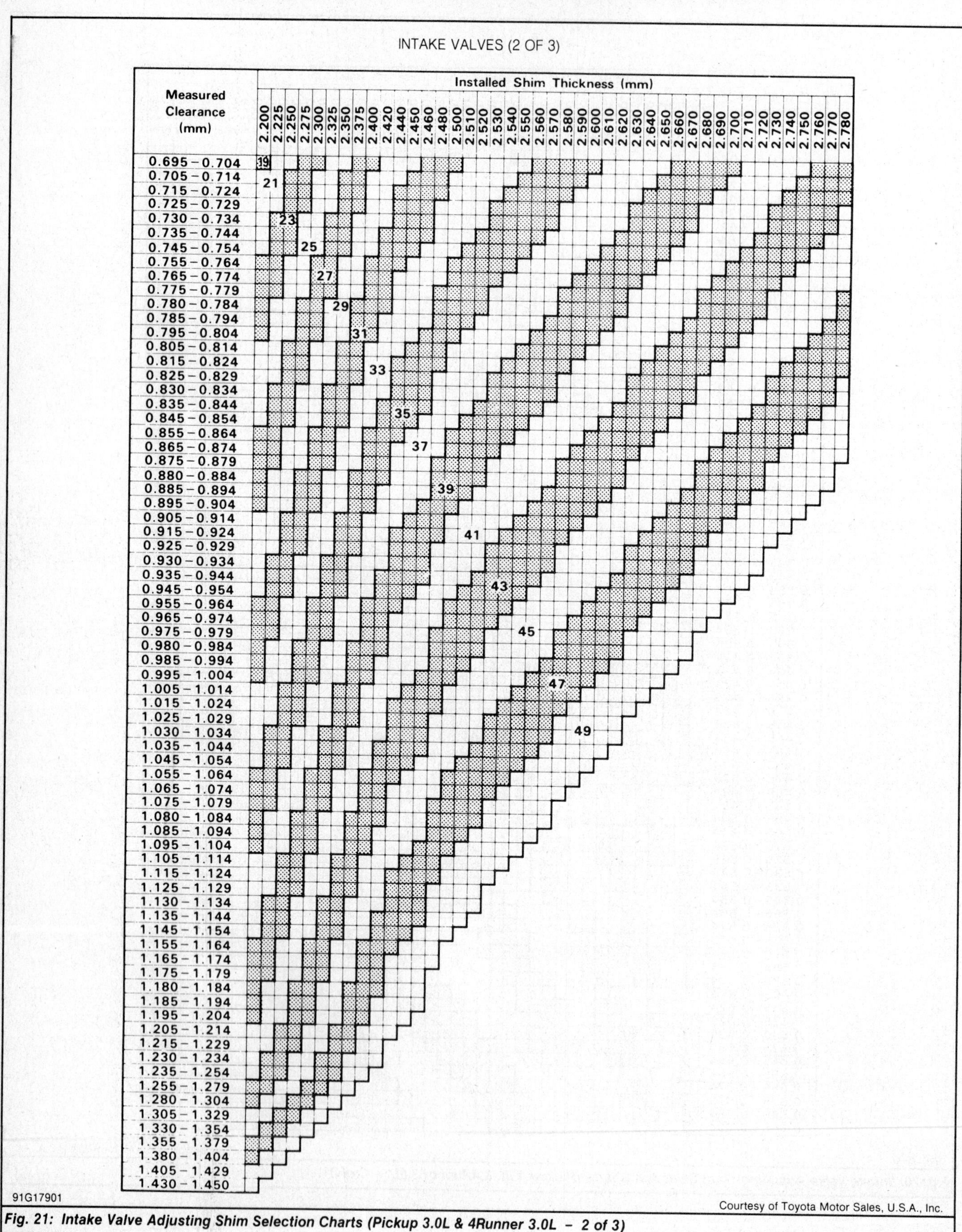


*Fig. 21: Intake Valve Adjusting Shim Selection Charts (Pickup 3.0L & 4Runner 3.0L - 2 of 3)*

# 1991 ENGINE PERFORMANCE
## On-Vehicle Adjustments (Cont.)

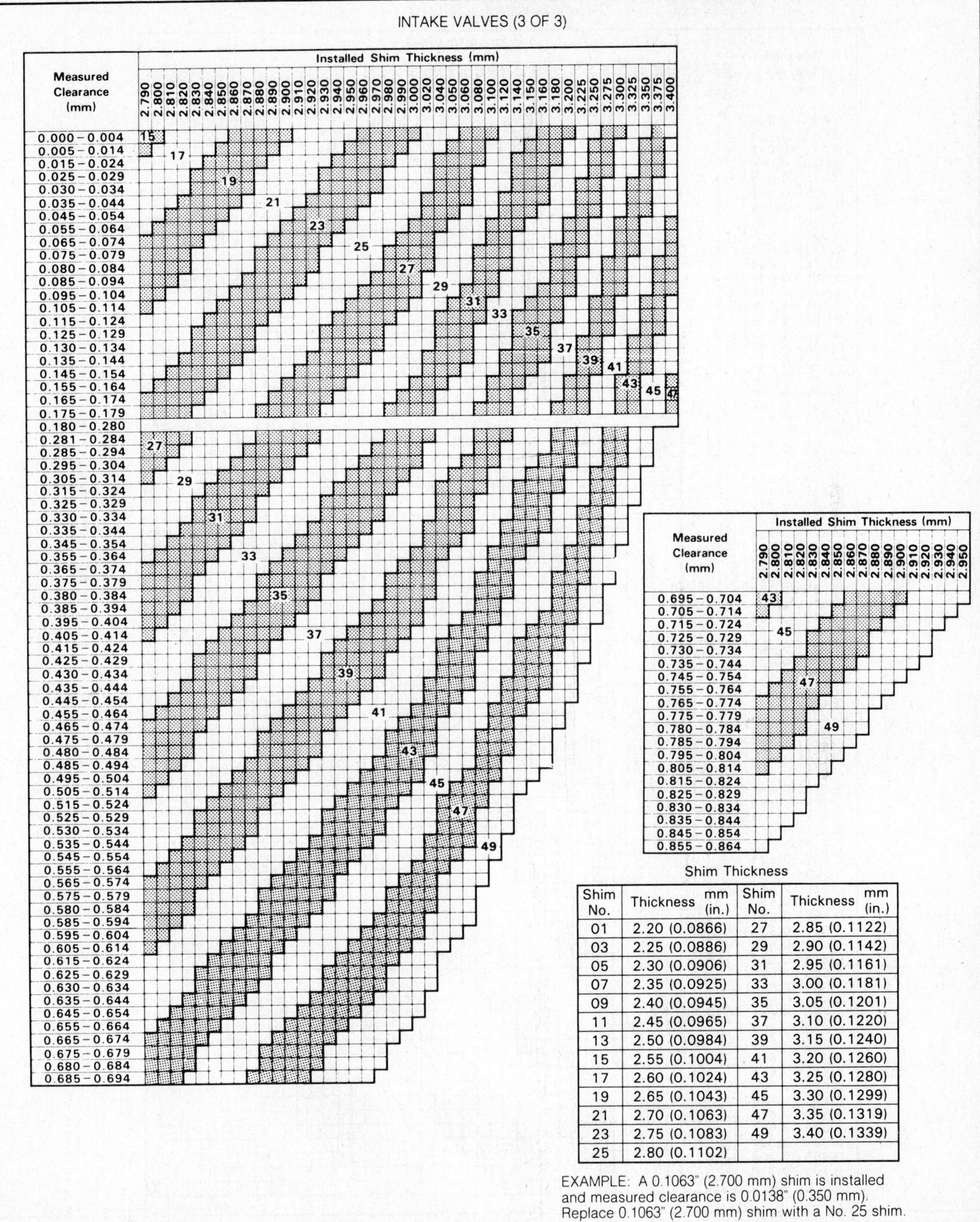


Shim Thickness

| Shim No. | Thickness mm (in.) | Shim No. | Thickness mm (in.) |
|---|---|---|---|
| 01 | 2.20 (0.0866) | 27 | 2.85 (0.1122) |
| 03 | 2.25 (0.0886) | 29 | 2.90 (0.1142) |
| 05 | 2.30 (0.0906) | 31 | 2.95 (0.1161) |
| 07 | 2.35 (0.0925) | 33 | 3.00 (0.1181) |
| 09 | 2.40 (0.0945) | 35 | 3.05 (0.1201) |
| 11 | 2.45 (0.0965) | 37 | 3.10 (0.1220) |
| 13 | 2.50 (0.0984) | 39 | 3.15 (0.1240) |
| 15 | 2.55 (0.1004) | 41 | 3.20 (0.1260) |
| 17 | 2.60 (0.1024) | 43 | 3.25 (0.1280) |
| 19 | 2.65 (0.1043) | 45 | 3.30 (0.1299) |
| 21 | 2.70 (0.1063) | 47 | 3.35 (0.1319) |
| 23 | 2.75 (0.1083) | 49 | 3.40 (0.1339) |
| 25 | 2.80 (0.1102) | | |

EXAMPLE: A 0.1063" (2.700 mm) shim is installed and measured clearance is 0.0138" (0.350 mm). Replace 0.1063" (2.700 mm) shim with a No. 25 shim.

91H17902 91I17903 91I17895

Courtesy of Toyota Motor Sales, U.S.A., Inc.

*Fig. 22: Intake Valve Adjusting Shim Selection Charts (Pickup 3.0L & 4Runner 3.0L - 3 of 3)*

# 1991 ENGINE PERFORMANCE
## On-Vehicle Adjustments (Cont.)

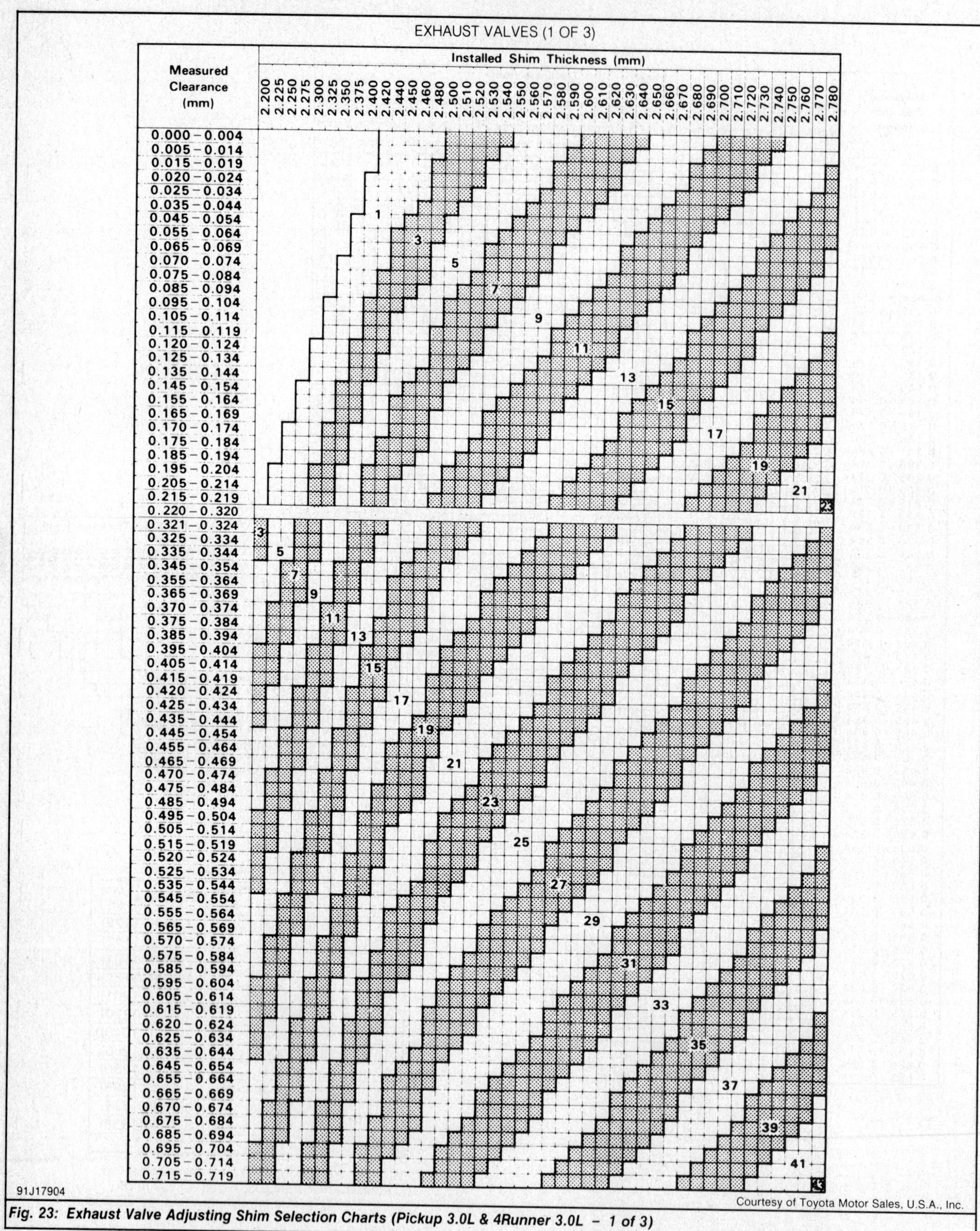


Courtesy of Toyota Motor Sales, U.S.A., Inc.

*Fig. 23: Exhaust Valve Adjusting Shim Selection Charts (Pickup 3.0L & 4Runner 3.0L – 1 of 3)*

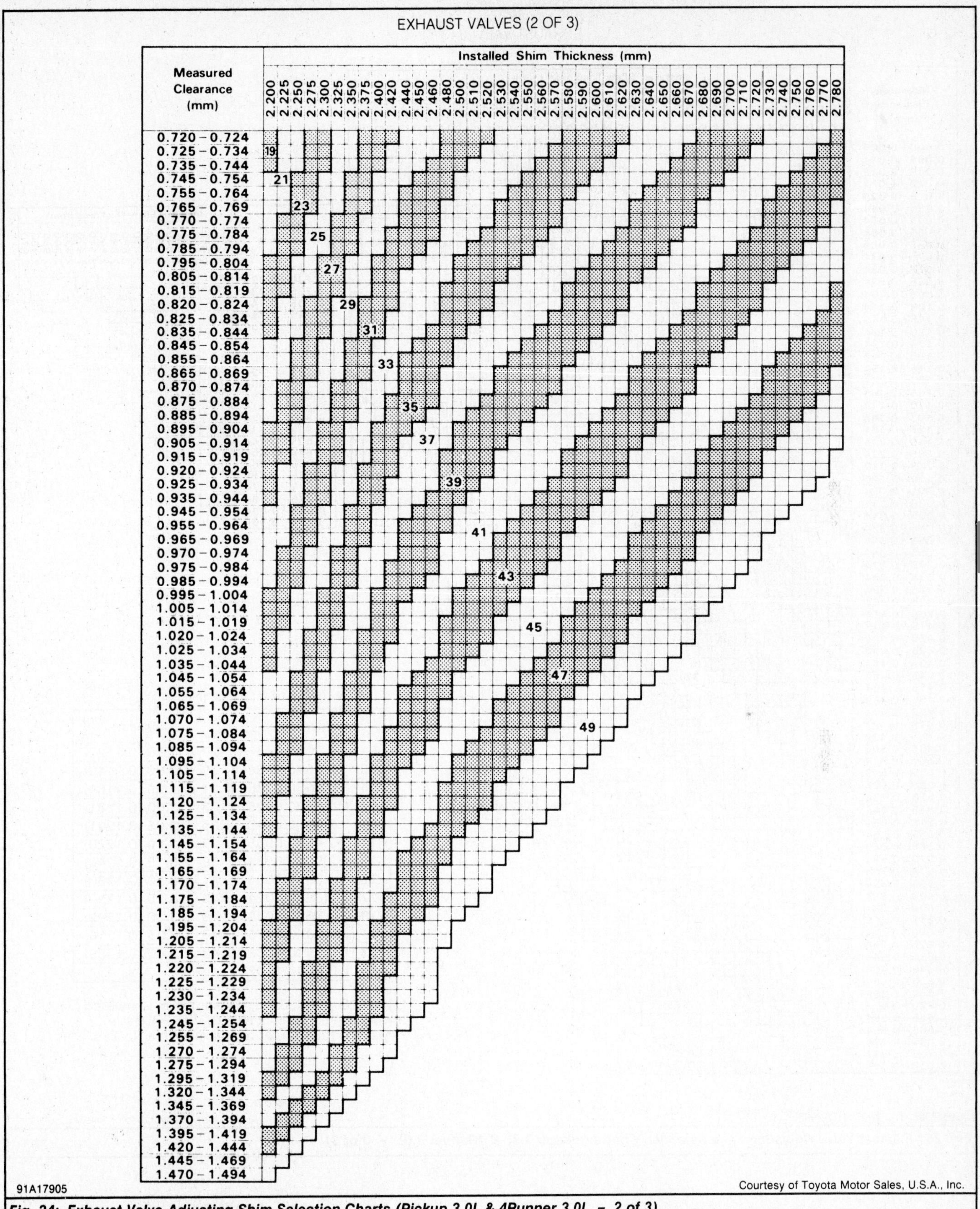


*Fig. 24: Exhaust Valve Adjusting Shim Selection Charts (Pickup 3.0L & 4Runner 3.0L - 2 of 3)*

# 1991 ENGINE PERFORMANCE
## On-Vehicle Adjustments (Cont.)

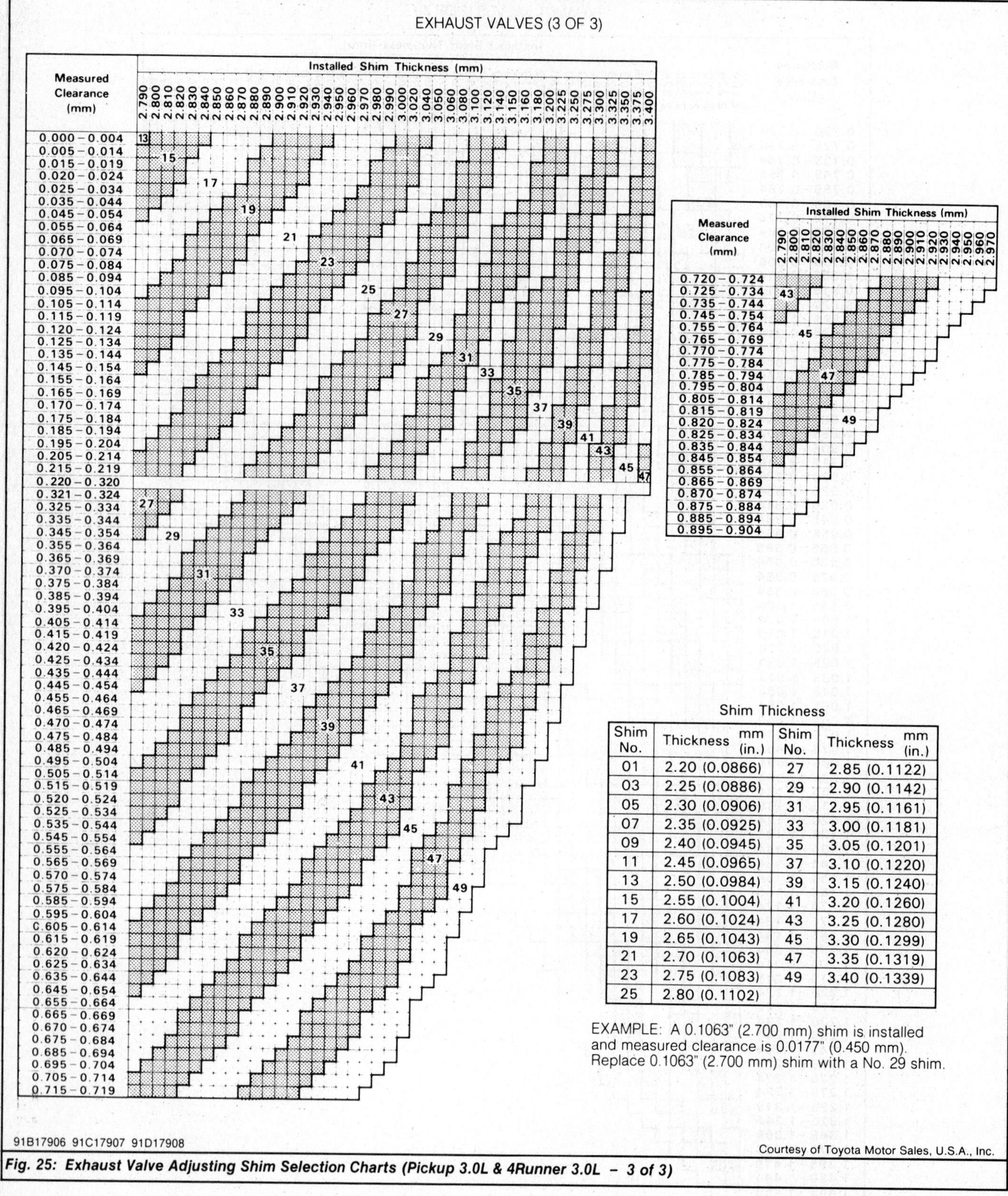


Shim Thickness

| Shim No. | Thickness mm (in.) | Shim No. | Thickness mm (in.) |
|---|---|---|---|
| 01 | 2.20 (0.0866) | 27 | 2.85 (0.1122) |
| 03 | 2.25 (0.0886) | 29 | 2.90 (0.1142) |
| 05 | 2.30 (0.0906) | 31 | 2.95 (0.1161) |
| 07 | 2.35 (0.0925) | 33 | 3.00 (0.1181) |
| 09 | 2.40 (0.0945) | 35 | 3.05 (0.1201) |
| 11 | 2.45 (0.0965) | 37 | 3.10 (0.1220) |
| 13 | 2.50 (0.0984) | 39 | 3.15 (0.1240) |
| 15 | 2.55 (0.1004) | 41 | 3.20 (0.1260) |
| 17 | 2.60 (0.1024) | 43 | 3.25 (0.1280) |
| 19 | 2.65 (0.1043) | 45 | 3.30 (0.1299) |
| 21 | 2.70 (0.1063) | 47 | 3.35 (0.1319) |
| 23 | 2.75 (0.1083) | 49 | 3.40 (0.1339) |
| 25 | 2.80 (0.1102) | | |

EXAMPLE: A 0.1063" (2.700 mm) shim is installed and measured clearance is 0.0177" (0.450 mm). Replace 0.1063" (2.700 mm) shim with a No. 29 shim.

*Fig. 25: Exhaust Valve Adjusting Shim Selection Charts (Pickup 3.0L & 4Runner 3.0L - 3 of 3)*

# 1991 ENGINE PERFORMANCE
# On-Vehicle Adjustments (Cont.)

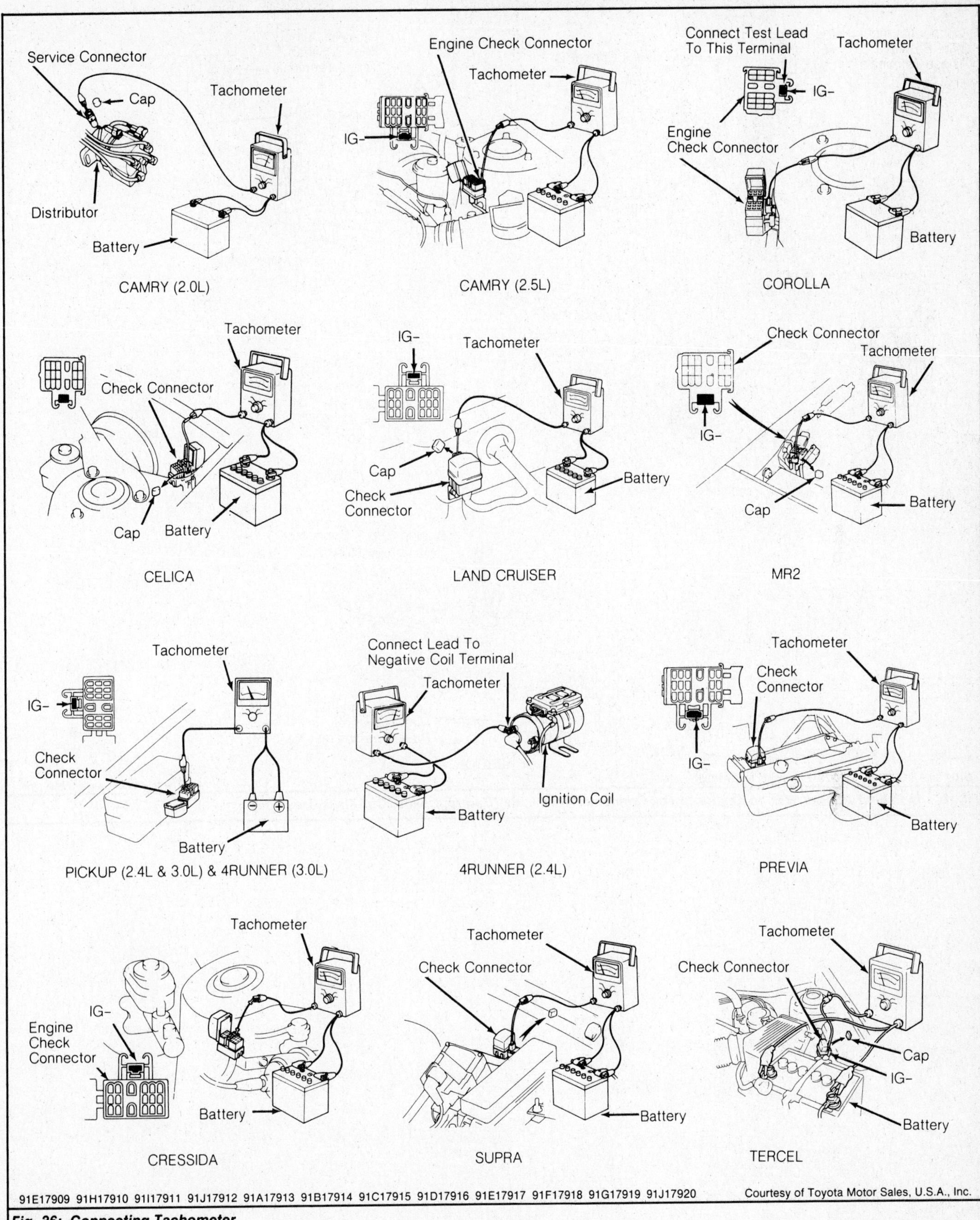


*Fig. 26: Connecting Tachometer*

# 1991 ENGINE PERFORMANCE
## On-Vehicle Adjustments (Cont.)

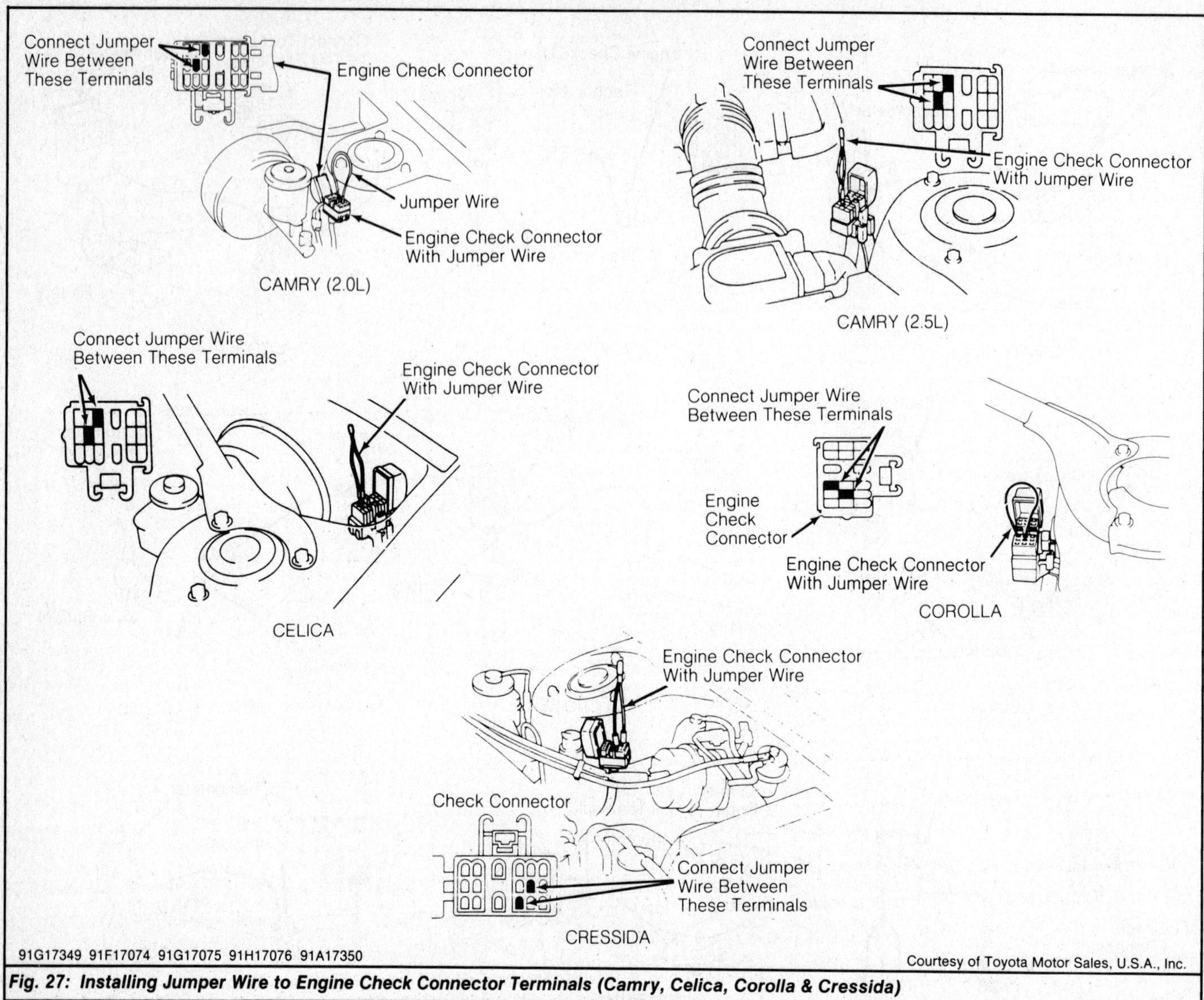


*Fig. 27: Installing Jumper Wire to Engine Check Connector Terminals (Camry, Celica, Corolla & Cressida)*

# 1991 ENGINE PERFORMANCE
# On-Vehicle Adjustments (Cont.)

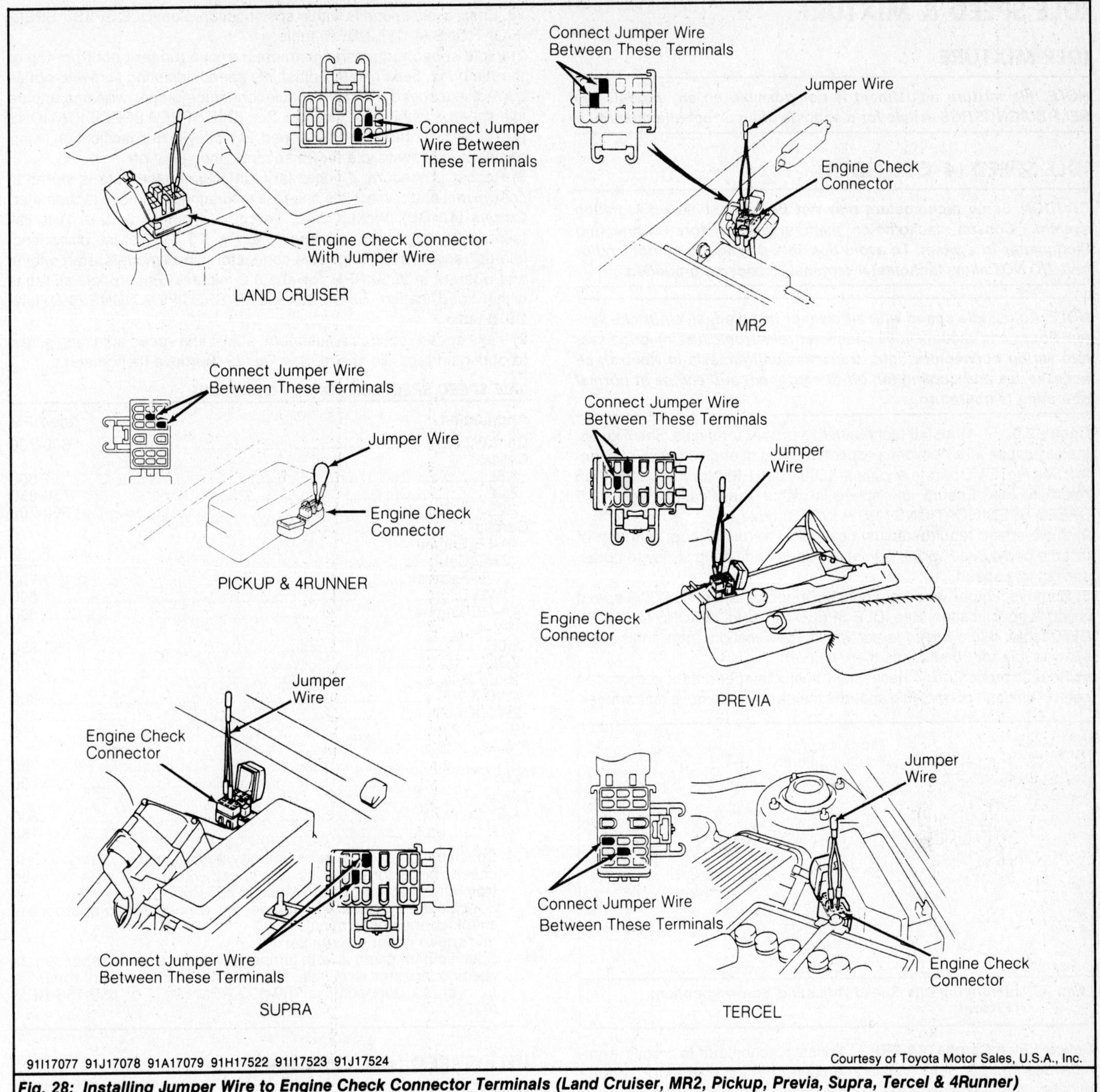


**Fig. 28: Installing Jumper Wire to Engine Check Connector Terminals (Land Cruiser, MR2, Pickup, Previa, Supra, Tercel & 4Runner)**

# 1991 ENGINE PERFORMANCE
# On-Vehicle Adjustments (Cont.)

## IDLE SPEED & MIXTURE

### IDLE MIXTURE

***NOTE: Idle mixture adjustment is not possible on any model. See SELF-DIAGNOSTICS article for diagnosis of incorrect idle mixture.***

### IDLE SPEED (4-CYLINDER)

***CAUTION: Some tachometers may not be compatible with ignition system. Consult tachometer manufacturer before connecting tachometer to system. To avoid possible damage to ignitor and/or coil, DO NOT allow tachometer terminal to become grounded.***

***NOTE: Adjust idle speed with air cleaner installed, all air intake system hoses and vacuum lines connected, electronic fuel injection system wiring connectors tight, transmission/transaxle in Neutral, all accessories and cooling fan off (if equipped) and engine at normal operating temperature.***

**Camry 2.0L - 1)** Install tachometer to proper terminals. *See Fig. 26.* Install jumper wire between proper terminals of engine check connector. *See Fig. 27.* Operate engine at 1000-1300 RPM for 5 seconds then return to idle. Ensure idle speed is within specification. See IDLE SPEED SPECIFICATIONS (4-CYLINDER) table.
**2)** If idle speed requires adjustment, remove rubber boot from top of throttle body. *See Fig. 29.* Adjust idle speed adjusting screw to obtain correct idle speed.
**3)** Remove jumper wire from check connector and ensure idle speed is within specification. See IDLE SPEED SPECIFICATIONS (4-CYLINDER) table. If idle speed is not within specification, start engine and allow to idle for 30 seconds then shut off.
**4)** Repeat procedure, if necessary, until idle speed data is stored in control unit and correct idle speed is maintained. Remove tachometer.

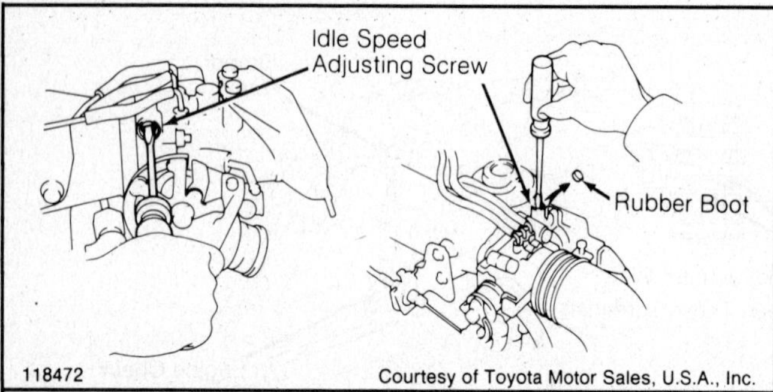


***Fig. 29: Identifying Idle Speed Adjusting Screw Locations (Typical)***

**Celica 1.6L & Corolla (4A-FE) - 1)** Install tachometer to proper terminals. *See Fig. 26.* Start engine and operate at 2500 RPM for about 2 minutes. Allow engine to idle. Install jumper wire between proper terminals of engine check connector. *See Fig. 27.* Ensure idle speed is within specification. See IDLE SPEED SPECIFICATIONS (4-CYLINDER) table.
**2)** If idle speed requires adjustment, remove rubber boot from top of throttle body. *See Fig. 29.* Adjust idle speed adjusting screw to obtain correct idle speed. Remove tachometer.
**Celica 2.0L, MR2 2.0L & Previa - 1)** Install tachometer to proper terminals. *See Fig. 26.* Start engine and check if idle speed is within specification. See IDLE SPEED SPECIFICATIONS (4-CYLINDER) table.
**2)** If idle speed is not within specification, check Idle Speed Control (ISC) valve, wiring and ECU. See IDLE CONTROL SYSTEMS in SYSTEM & COMPONENT TESTING article.
**Celica 2.2L & MR2 2.2L - 1)** Install tachometer to proper terminals. *See Fig. 26.* Start engine and operate at 1000-3000 RPM for about 5 seconds. Allow engine to idle. Install check connector jumper wire between proper terminals of engine check connector. *See Figs. 27 and 28.* Ensure idle speed is within specification. See IDLE SPEED SPECIFICATIONS (4-CYLINDER) table.
**2)** If idle speed requires adjustment, remove rubber boot from top of throttle body. *See Fig. 29.* Adjust idle speed adjusting screw to obtain correct idle speed. Remove check connector jumper wire and ensure idle speed is within specification. See IDLE SPEED SPECIFICATIONS (4-CYLINDER) table. If idle speed is not within specification, start engine and allow to idle for 30 seconds then shut off.
**3)** Repeat procedure, if necessary, until idle speed data is stored in control unit and correct idle speed is maintained. Remove tachometer.
**Corolla (4A-GE), Pickup 2.4L, Tercel & 4Runner 2.4L - 1)** Install tachometer to proper terminals. *See Fig. 26.* On Tercel, disconnect idle-up vacuum switching valve connector. On all models, start engine and operate at 2500 RPM for about 2 minutes. Ensure idle speed is within specification. See IDLE SPEED SPECIFICATIONS (4-CYLINDER) table.
**2)** If idle speed requires adjustment, adjust idle speed adjusting screw to obtain correct idle speed. *See Fig. 29.* Remove tachometer.

***IDLE SPEED SPECIFICATIONS (4-CYLINDER)***

| Application | Idle RPM |
|---|---|
| Camry 2.0L | [1] 600-700 |
| Celica | |
| 1.6L | [2] 800 |
| 2.0L | [3] 750-850 |
| 2.2L | [1] 600-700 |
| Corolla | |
| 4A-FE Engine | |
| 2WD Calif. | [2] 800 |
| 2WD Federal | [2] 700 |
| 4WD | [2] 800 |
| 4A-GE Engine | 800 |
| MR2 | |
| 2.0L | [3] 750-850 |
| 2.2L | [4] 650 |
| Pickup 2.4L | |
| 4WD & A/T | 850 |
| 2WD & M/T | 750 |
| 4Runner 2.4L | 750 |
| Previa | |
| A/T | [3] 750 |
| M/T | [3] 700 |
| Tercel | |
| A/T | 800 |
| M/T | 750 |

[1] - Specification given is with jumper wire connected to appropriate check connector terminals. Idle speed with jumper wire removed from check connector terminals is 650-750 RPM.
[2] - Specification given is with jumper wire connected to appropriate check connector terminals.
[3] - Idle speed is not adjustable.
[4] - Specification given is with jumper wire connected to appropriate check connector terminals. Idle speed with jumper wire removed from check connector is 700-800 RPM (M/T) or 650-750 RPM (A/T).

### IDLE SPEED (6-CYLINDER)

***CAUTION: Some tachometers may not be compatible with ignition system. Consult tachometer manufacturer before connecting tachometer to system. To avoid possible damage to ignitor and/or coil, DO NOT allow tachometer terminal to become grounded.***

***NOTE: Idle speed is controlled by the computer and idle speed control system.***

**Cressida, Land Cruiser & Supra - 1)** Install tachometer to proper terminals. *See Fig. 26.* Start engine and check if idle speed is within specification. See IDLE SPEED SPECIFICATIONS (6-CYLINDER) table.
**2)** If idle speed is not within specification, check Idle Speed Control (ISC) valve, wiring and ECU. See IDLE CONTROL SYSTEMS in SYSTEM & COMPONENT TESTING article.

# 1991 ENGINE PERFORMANCE
# On-Vehicle Adjustments (Cont.)

*IDLE SPEED SPECIFICATIONS (6-CYLINDER)*

| Application | [1] Idle RPM |
|---|---|
| Cressida | 700 |
| Land Cruiser | 650 |
| Supra | |
| Non-Turbo | 700 |
| Turbo | 650 |

[1] – Idle speed is not adjustable.

## IDLE SPEED (V6)

***CAUTION: Some tachometers may not be compatible with ignition system. Consult tachometer manufacturer before connecting tachometer to system. To avoid possible damage to ignitor and/or coil, DO NOT allow tachometer terminal to become grounded.***

***NOTE: Idle speed on Camry 2.5L is controlled by the computer and idle speed control system.***

**Camry 2.5L – 1)** Install tachometer to proper terminals. *See Fig. 26.* Start engine and check if idle speed is within specification. See IDLE SPEED SPECIFICATIONS (V6) table.
**2)** If idle speed is not within specification, check the Idle Speed Control (ISC) valve, wiring and ECU. See IDLE CONTROL SYSTEMS in SYSTEM & COMPONENT TESTING article.
**Pickup 3.0L & 4Runner 3.0L – 1)** Install tachometer to proper terminals. *See Fig. 26.* Start engine and operate at 2500 RPM for about 2 minutes. Check if idle speed is within specification. See IDLE SPEED SPECIFICATIONS (V6) table.
**2)** If idle speed requires adjustment, adjust idle speed adjusting screw to obtain correct idle speed. *See Fig. 29.* Remove tachometer.

*IDLE SPEED SPECIFICATIONS (V6)*

| Application | Idle RPM |
|---|---|
| Camry 2.5L | [1] 650-750 |
| Pickup 3.0L & 4Runner 3.0L | 800 |

[1] – Idle speed on Camry 2.5L is not adjustable.

## THROTTLE POSITION SENSOR (TPS)

***NOTE: Vehicles with Electronically Controlled Transaxle (ECT) use signals sent from TPS to Electronic Control Unit (ECU) to calculate gear shift and lock-up timing.***

**1)** Loosen mounting screws. Unplug TPS connector. Connect ohmmeter between terminals IDL and E2 (terminals IDL and E1 on Camry 2.0L without ECT). *See Fig. 30.*
**2)** To set initial clearance, insert proper thickness feeler gauge between throttle stop screw and throttle lever. See appropriate THROTTLE POSITION SENSOR ADJUSTMENT table.
**3)** With ohmmeter showing infinity, rotate TPS clockwise until continuity exists. Tighten mounting screws. Using specified feeler gauge, recheck adjusted clearance. Disconnect ohmmeter and reconnect TPS after adjustment.

*THROTTLE POSITION SENSOR ADJUSTMENT (4-CYLINDER)*

| Application | Initial Clearance In. (mm) | Adjusted Clearance In. (mm) | Ohmmeter Reading |
|---|---|---|---|
| Camry 2.0L | | | |
| w/ ECT | .024 (.60) | .020 (.50) | Continuity |
| | | .028 (.70) | Infinity |
| w/o ECT | .028 (.70) | .020 (.50) | Continuity |
| | | .035 (.90) | Infinity |
| Celica | | | |
| 1.6L | .028 (.70) | .024 (.60) | Continuity |
| | | .031 (.79) | Infinity |
| 2.0L | .024 (.60) | .020 (.50) | Continuity |
| | | .028 (.70) | Infinity |
| 2.2L | | | |
| w/ ECT | .024 (.60) | .020 (.50) | Continuity |
| | | .028 (.70) | Infinity |
| w/o ECT | .028 (.70) | .020 (.50) | Continuity |
| | | .035 (.90) | Infinity |
| Corolla | | | |
| 4A-FE | .028 (.70) | .024 (.60) | Continuity |
| | | .032 (.81) | Infinity |
| 4A-GE | .019 (.48) | .014 (.36) | Continuity |
| | | .023 (.58) | Infinity |
| MR2 | | | |
| 2.0L | .024 (.60) | .020 (.50) | Continuity |
| | | .028 (.70) | Infinity |
| 2.2L | | | |
| A/T | .024 (.60) | .020 (.50) | Continuity |
| | | .028 (.70) | Infinity |
| M/T | .028 (.70) | .020 (.50) | Continuity |
| | | .035 (.90) | Infinity |
| Pickup 2.4L & 4Runner 2.4L | .028 (.70) | .022 (.56) | Continuity |
| | | .034 (.86) | Infinity |
| Previa | .033 (.84) | .033 (.84) | Continuity |
| Tercel | .024 (.60) | .020 (.50) | Continuity |
| | | .028 (.70) | Infinity |

*THROTTLE POSITION SENSOR ADJUSTMENT (6-CYLINDER)*

| Application | Initial Clearance | Adjusted Clearance | Ohmmeter Reading |
|---|---|---|---|
| Cressida | .028 (.70) | .020 (.50) | Continuity |
| | | .035 (.90) | Infinity |
| Land Cruiser | .037 (.94) | .030 (.76) | Continuity |
| | | .043 (1.09) | Infinity |
| Supra | | | |
| Non-Turbo | .023 (.58) | .016 (.41) | Continuity |
| | | .029 (.74) | Infinity |
| Turbo | .028 (.70) | .020 (.50) | Continuity |
| | | .035 (.90) | Infinity |

*THROTTLE POSITION SENSOR ADJUSTMENT (V6)*

| Application | Initial Clearance | Adjusted Clearance | Ohmmeter Reading |
|---|---|---|---|
| Camry 2.5L | .020 (.50) | .012 (.30) | Continuity |
| | | .028 (.70) | Infinity |
| Pickup 3.0L & 4Runner 3.0L | .023 (.58) | .020 (.50) | Continuity |
| | | .030 (.76) | Infinity |

# 1991 ENGINE PERFORMANCE
# On-Vehicle Adjustments (Cont.)

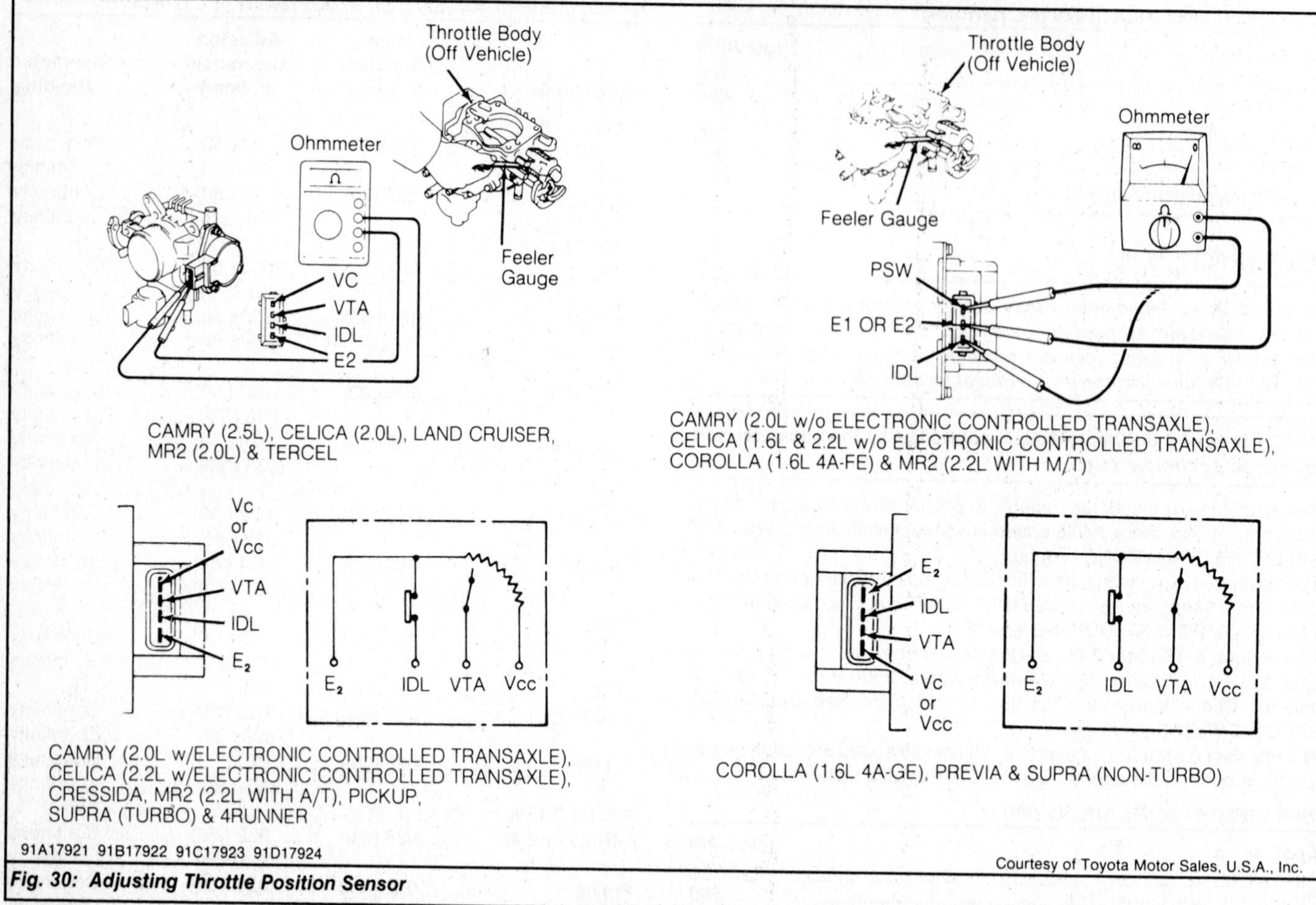


*Fig. 30: Adjusting Throttle Position Sensor*

## DASHPOT CONTROL SYSTEM

For testing and adjustment procedures, see THROTTLE CONTROLS under EMISSION SYSTEMS & SUB-SYSTEMS in SYSTEM & COMPONENT TESTING article.

## TORQUE SPECIFICATIONS

*TORQUE SPECIFICATIONS*

| Application | Ft. lbs. (N.m) |
|---|---|
| Cam Position Sensor Bolt | |
| Supra Turbo | 10 (14) |
| Distributor Hold-Down Bolt | |
| Camry 2.0L | 9 (13) |
| Camry 2.5L | 13 (18) |
| Celica | |
| 1.6L | 14 (20) |
| 2.0L | 29 (39) |
| 2.2L | 9 (13) |
| Corolla, Pickup 2.4L & 4Runner 2.4L | 14 (20) |
| Cressida & Supra | 10 (14) |
| Land Cruiser | 13 (18) |
| MR2 | |
| 2.0L | 29 (39) |
| 2.2L | 9 (13) |
| Previa | [1] |
| Pickup 3.0L & 4Runner 3.0L | 13 (18) |
| Tercel | 13 (18) |

[1] – Information is not available from manufacturer.

# 1991 ENGINE PERFORMANCE
# Theory & Operation

**Camry, Celica, Corolla, Cressida, Land Cruiser, MR2, Pickup, Previa, Supra, Tercel, 4Runner**

## INTRODUCTION

This article covers basic description and operation of engine performance-related systems and components. Read this article before diagnosing vehicles or systems with which you are not completely familiar.

## AIR INDUCTION SYSTEM

### INTAKE AIR CONTROL SYSTEM

**Supra (7M-GE)** – ECU uses inputs from engine RPM and throttle position sensor to change amount of airflow into manifold runner. This is done to increase power in low speed range. ECU opens an air control valve through a vacuum switching valve.

### VARIABLE INDUCTION SYSTEM

**Celica Turbo & MR2 Turbo** – Each cylinder runner in the intake manifold is divided into 2 parts. An intake air control valve is installed in one passage on each cylinder runner. The opening and closing of this valve gives the best airflow possible, preventing low-speed performance loss and improved fuel economy. The intake control valves are vacuum actuated. The vacuum signal is controlled by the ECU through a vacuum switching valve.

### TURBOCHARGERS

**Celica Turbo, MR2 Turbo & Supra Turbo** – All systems are equipped with an air-cooled intercooler and use a wastegate system to control maximum boost pressure. On Celica and MR2, maximum boost pressure is controlled by a dual control wastegate actuator. One pressure signal is direct from downstream of the impeller wheel and one pressure signal is ECU controlled, through a vacuum switching valve, from upstream of the impeller wheel.

On Supra, wastegate valve is actuated by pressure signal from intake manifold. Celica and MR2 use a vane-type airflow meter and turbocharging pressure sensor to signal the ECU. On Supra, there is not a separate pressure sensor for the ECU. The Karman-Vortex mass airflow meter senses boost pressure for the ECU.

## COMPUTERIZED ENGINE CONTROLS

### TOYOTA COMPUTER CONTROL SYSTEM (TCCS)

Toyota Computer Control System (TCCS) is a computerized emission, ignition and fuel injection control system. TCCS lowers exhaust emissions while maintaining good fuel economy and driveability.

An Electronic Control Unit (ECU) governs TCCS based on input signals received from various input devices. ECU contains preprogrammed data to maintain optimum engine performance under all operating conditions.

ECU is also equipped with a self-diagnostic function. Trouble codes are set by the malfunction of engine sensors or circuits and stored in the ECU memory. A CHECK ENGINE light on the instrument panel will come on if a trouble code is stored.

### CONTROL UNIT

Electronic Control Unit (ECU) is a microprocessor which controls all functions of TCCS. ECU receives signals from sensors, switches, and ignition and starting systems. ECU has constant source of battery power at BATT terminal. EFI main relay provides battery voltage to terminals +B and $+B_1$ of ECU. EFI main relay is activated by turning on ignition switch.

Signals are processed by the ECU for controlling various functions. See OUTPUT SIGNALS in this article.

**Fail-Safe System** – The ECU contains a fail-safe function that is used in case of sensor or switch failure. The fail-safe function uses preprogrammed engine values to provide a limp-in mode so the vehicle may be driven. If malfunction is serious enough, ECU may shut down engine.

***ECU LOCATIONS***

| Model | Location |
|---|---|
| Camry, Celica, Corolla & Tercel | Bottom Center Of Dash, In Front Of Console |
| Cressida, Land Cruiser & Supra | Above Glove Box |
| MR2 | Left Rear Of Engine Compartment |
| Pickup & 4Runner | Behind Right Kick Panel |
| Previa | Under Driver's Seat |

### POWER SUPPLY

**EFI Main Relay** – EFI main relay provides battery voltage to terminals +B and $+B_1$ of ECU. It also supplies current to circuit opening relay, engine check connector and, depending on model application, idle speed control valve and oxygen sensor heater. EFI fuse supplies constant battery voltage to EFI main relay.

**Circuit Opening Relay** – Circuit opening relay controls fuel pump circuit. ECU receives input signal at STA terminal when engine is cranking. This same starter signal is also applied to terminal STA of circuit opening relay. Starter signal energizes circuit opening relay during cranking, which in turn, activates fuel pump. On Camry, Corolla (4A-GE), Cressida, Land Cruiser, Pickup, Previa, Supra (7M-GE) and 4Runner, circuit opening relay is grounded through airflow meter when it senses airflow to engine. On Celica, Corolla (4A-FE), MR2, Supra (7M-GTE) and Tercel, circuit opening relay is grounded by ECU through FC terminal.

***NOTE: Components are grouped into 2 categories. The first category covers INPUT DEVICES, which control or produce voltage signals monitored by the control unit. The second category covers OUTPUT SIGNALS, which are components controlled by the control unit.***

### INPUT DEVICES

Vehicles are equipped with different combinations of input devices. Not all devices are used on all models. To determine the input usage on a specific model, see appropriate wiring diagram in WIRING DIAGRAMS article. The available input signals include the following:

**A/C Switch** – When the air conditioner is turned on, the ECU monitors the signal that turns on the compressor clutch. ECU uses this signal for controlling idle speed during A/C operation.

**Airflow Sensor** – On all models except Supra Turbo, the airflow sensor in the airflow meter measures airflow volume. Airflow meter converts intake air readings into a voltage signal by means of a variable resistor (potentiometer). Signal is sent to ECU for controlling fuel injection duration and spark advance system. On Supra Turbo, the airflow volume is measured by a Karman-Vortex airflow meter. This input signal is sent to the ECU.

**Air Temperature Sensor** – Sensor is mounted in either airflow meter or air filter housing. Sensor measures incoming air temperature. Signal is sent to ECU for controlling fuel injection duration.

**Battery Signal** – Battery voltage is always present at BATT terminal of ECU. When ignition switch is turned to ON position, voltage for ECU operation is applied through the EFI main relay to terminals +B and $+B_1$.

**Brake Light Signal** – The brake light switch is used to detect when the vehicle is braking. This signal is sent to terminal STP of the ECU.

**Camshaft Position Sensor (Supra Turbo)** – This sensor sends crankshaft position and engine RPM signal to the ECU.

**Coolant Temperature Sensor (CTS)** – Monitors coolant temperature. CTS has a built-in thermistor whose resistance varies according to engine temperature. CTS signal is input to ECU at terminal THW. ECU uses sensor signal for controlling fuel injection duration, overdrive operation on electronically controlled transmissions, spark advance system, idle speed control system and EGR system.

# 1991 ENGINE PERFORMANCE
# Theory & Operation (Cont.)

**Coolant Temperature Switch (Land Cruiser)** – Switch turns on when coolant exceeds a specified temperature. Signal is used for fuel pressure control by the ECU. ECU receives signal from terminal TWS.

**Cranking Signal** – While the engine is cranking, the voltage applied the starter is also input to terminal STA of the ECU.

**EGR Gas Temperature Sensor (Calif.)** – Sensor determines EGR gas temperature and sends signal to ECU.

**Knock Sensor** – Sensor monitors ignition knock conditions and sends a signal to the ECU. ECU will in turn retard engine timing until knocking stops.

**Neutral/Start Switch** – Switch is installed on A/T models to inform ECU of gear selection. Information is used by the ECU to allow starter operation and control engine idle.

**Oil Pressure Switch Signal (Supra Turbo)** – Engine oil pressure is monitored by the ECU at the OIL terminal.

**Oxygen ($O_2$) Sensor (Zirconia Type – Calif.)** – This oxygen sensor is installed in the exhaust system and monitors oxygen content of exhaust gases. Signal is sent to the ECU and is used for determining fuel injection duration. Some models are equipped with a second, sub-oxygen sensor downstream from the main oxygen sensor.

The oxygen sensor can be monitored at the engine check connector at terminal VF or VF1. The ECU sends out a special 5-volt signal on this wire so the number of cross-counts the ECU sees from the $O_2$ sensor can be read with an analog voltmeter.

**Oxygen ($O_2$) Sensor (Titania Type – Federal)** – This oxygen sensor is installed in the exhaust system and monitors oxygen content of exhaust gases. Signal is sent to the ECU and is used for determining fuel injection duration.

The oxygen sensor is supplied a potential one volt by the ECU on terminal Ox+. The signal returns to the ECU at terminal Ox. Through a comparator resistor, the ECU compares voltage drop at terminal Ox and a predetermined reference voltage. If the Ox voltage is greater than the reference voltage, the ECU judges the air/fuel ratio rich. If the Ox voltage is lower than the reference voltage, the ECU judges the air/fuel ratio lean.

**RPM Signal** – On all models except Supra Turbo, crankshaft position and engine RPM are detected by pick-up coils in the distributor. On all models except 4-cylinder Pickup and 4Runner, and Tercel, crankshaft position is read by ECU at $G_1$ terminal (and $G_2$ on some models), and engine RPM is input to ECU terminal Ne.

On Pickup/4Runner (22R-E) and Tercel, a single pick-up coil is used in the distributor. ECU monitors pick-up coil signal at terminal Ne.

On Supra Turbo models, crankshaft position and engine RPM are detected by the camshaft position sensor. Crankshaft position is input to ECU terminals $G_1$ and $G_2$, and engine RPM is input to terminal Ne.

**Sub-Oxygen Sensor (Calif.)** – Sensor is used in conjunction with $O_2$ sensor. Sensor monitors oxygen content of exhaust gases and sends signal to the ECU.

**Throttle Position Sensor (TPS)** – Throttle Position Sensor (TPS) is mounted on throttle body. Sensor determines changes in throttle valve position and sends signals to the ECU. Signals are used for controlling fuel injection duration and idle speed control system.

**Turbo Pressure Sensor (Celica Turbo)** – Sensor monitors turbo pressure and sends signal to ECU.

**Vacuum Sensor (Celica Non-Turbo, Corolla 4A-FE, MR2 5S-FE & Tercel)** – Sensor is also known as Manifold Absolute Pressure (MAP) sensor. This sensor monitors engine vacuum for the ECU. ECU uses this signal to help control fuel injection pulse width.

**Vehicle Speed Sensor (VSS)** – Sensor is used to monitor vehicle speed. Vehicle speed information is used by the ECU for fuel injection, air injection (Land Cruiser only), cruise control and electronic control of automatic transmission.

**4WD Switch (Land Cruiser, Pickup & 4Runner)** – Switch indicates 4WD operation and sends signal to ECU.

## OUTPUT SIGNALS

***NOTE: Vehicles are equipped with different combinations of computer-controlled components. Not all components listed below are used on every vehicle. For theory and operation on each output component, refer to the system indicated after component.***

The ECU receives input from data sensors and, depending on model application, controls the following components and subsystems:

**A/C Cut Control System** – See IDLE SPEED.
**Air Injection Solenoid** – See EMISSION SYSTEMS.
**Air Suction Control Solenoid** – See EMISSION SYSTEMS.
**Circuit Opening Relay** – See FUEL DELIVERY.
**Dashpot System** – See DASHPOT SYSTEM.
**Electronic Fuel Injection** – See FUEL CONTROL.
**Electronic Spark Advance** – See IGNITION SYSTEM.
**EGR Control Solenoid** – See EMISSION SYSTEMS.
**Electronic Controlled Transmission (ECT)** – See MISCELLANEOUS CONTROLS.
**Fuel Pressure Vacuum Switching Valve** – See FUEL DELIVERY.
**Fuel Pump** – See FUEL DELIVERY.
**Idle Speed Control** – See IDLE SPEED.
**Idle-Up System** – See IDLE SPEED.
**Intake Air Control System** – See AIR INDUCTION SYSTEM.
**$O_2$ Sensor Heater** – See FUEL CONTROL.
**Self-Diagnostic System** – See SELF-DIAGNOSTIC SYSTEM.
**Turbocharger Vacuum Switching Valve (VSV)** – See AIR INDUCTION SYSTEM.
**Variable Induction Vacuum Switching Valve (VSV)** – See AIR INDUCTION SYSTEM.

# FUEL SYSTEM

## FUEL DELIVERY

**Circuit Opening Relay** – The ECU receives an input signal at terminal STA when the engine is cranking. This same starter signal is also applied to terminal STA of the circuit opening relay.

The starter signal energizes the relay during cranking, turning on the fuel pump. On Camry, Corolla (4A-GE), Cressida, Land Cruiser, Pickup, Previa, Supra (7M-GE) and 4Runner, when the airflow meter senses airflow to the engine, the fuel pump switch in the airflow meter provides an alternate ground for the relay. On Celica, Corolla (4A-FE), Supra Turbo and Tercel, the ECU keeps the relay energized through ECU terminal FC while engine is running.

**Fuel Pump** – All models use an electric fuel pump. Fuel pump is turned on by signal from the circuit opening relay, which in turn is controlled by the EFI main relay. Some models use a fuel pump relay. The fuel pump can be run with the engine off by turning on the ignition key and placing a jumper wire across terminals +B and FP of the engine check connector.

On Celica (3S-GTE), Cressida, MR2 (3S-GTE) and Supra models, fuel pump volume can be varied. Based on intake volume and engine RPM signal, the ECU signals the fuel pump relay to change fuel pump speed. If engine requires a large volume of fuel, fuel pump turns at high speed; when a small volume of fuel is required, pump turns at a slower speed.

**Fuel Pressure Regulator** – Mounted on the fuel rail, the pressure regulator maintains constant fuel pressure to the injectors. The pressure regulator is vacuum operated. As the throttle is depressed and manifold vacuum drops, the pressure regulator increases fuel pressure to maintain a constant flow to the injectors.

**Fuel Pressure-Up System (Camry 3S-FE, Corolla 4A-GE, Land Cruiser, MR2 5S-FE, Pickup, Previa, Supra Turbo, Tercel & 4Runner)** – The fuel pressure-up system increases fuel pressure slightly on hot restarts for improved starting and idle stability. The pressure rise is accomplished by cutting off the vacuum signal to the fuel pressure regulator. The ECU controls the vacuum signal through the Vacuum Switching Valve (VSV). Pressure rise lasts for about 90-180 seconds after hot restart.

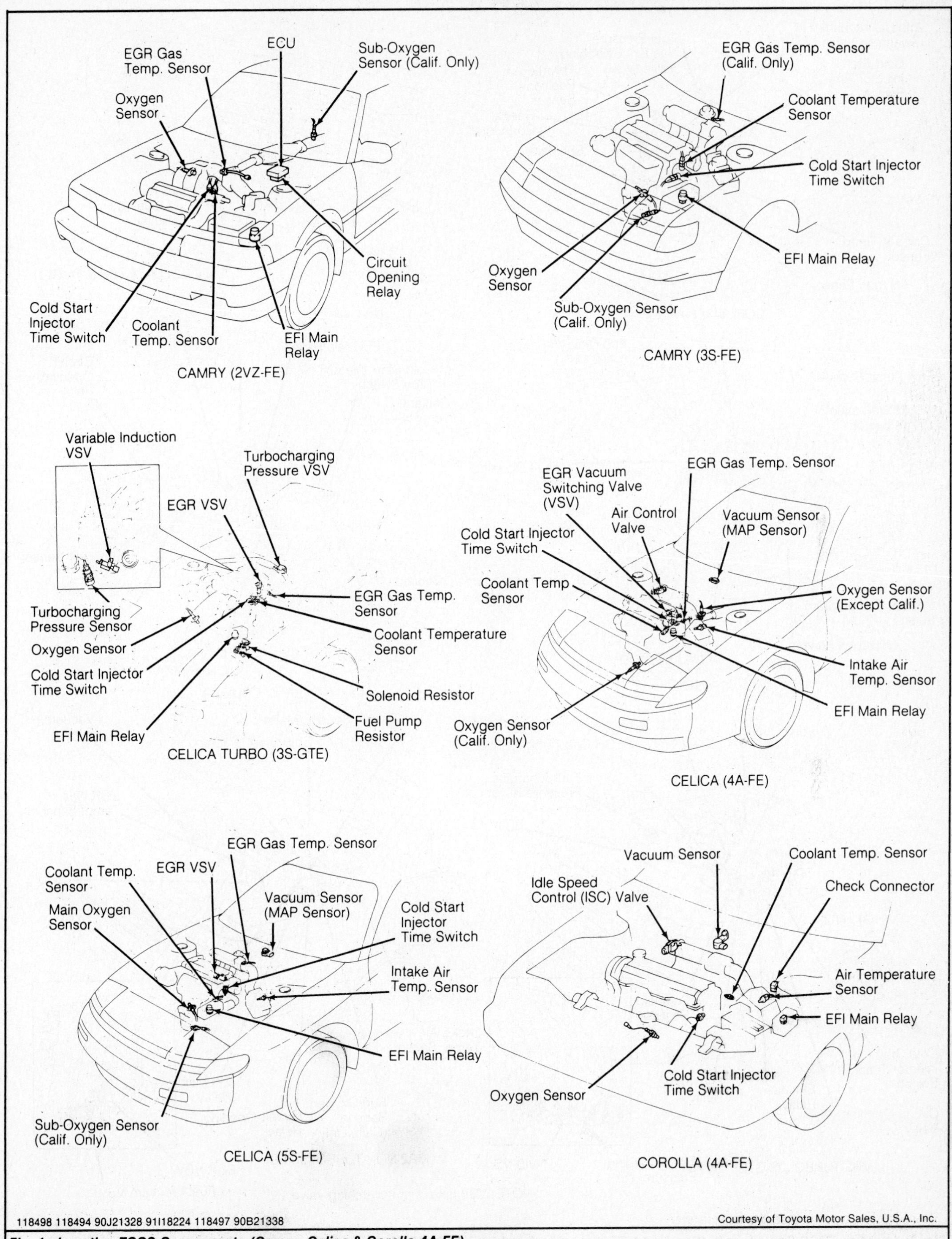


***Fig. 1: Locating TCCS Components (Camry, Celica & Corolla 4A-FE)***

# 1991 ENGINE PERFORMANCE
# Theory & Operation (Cont.)

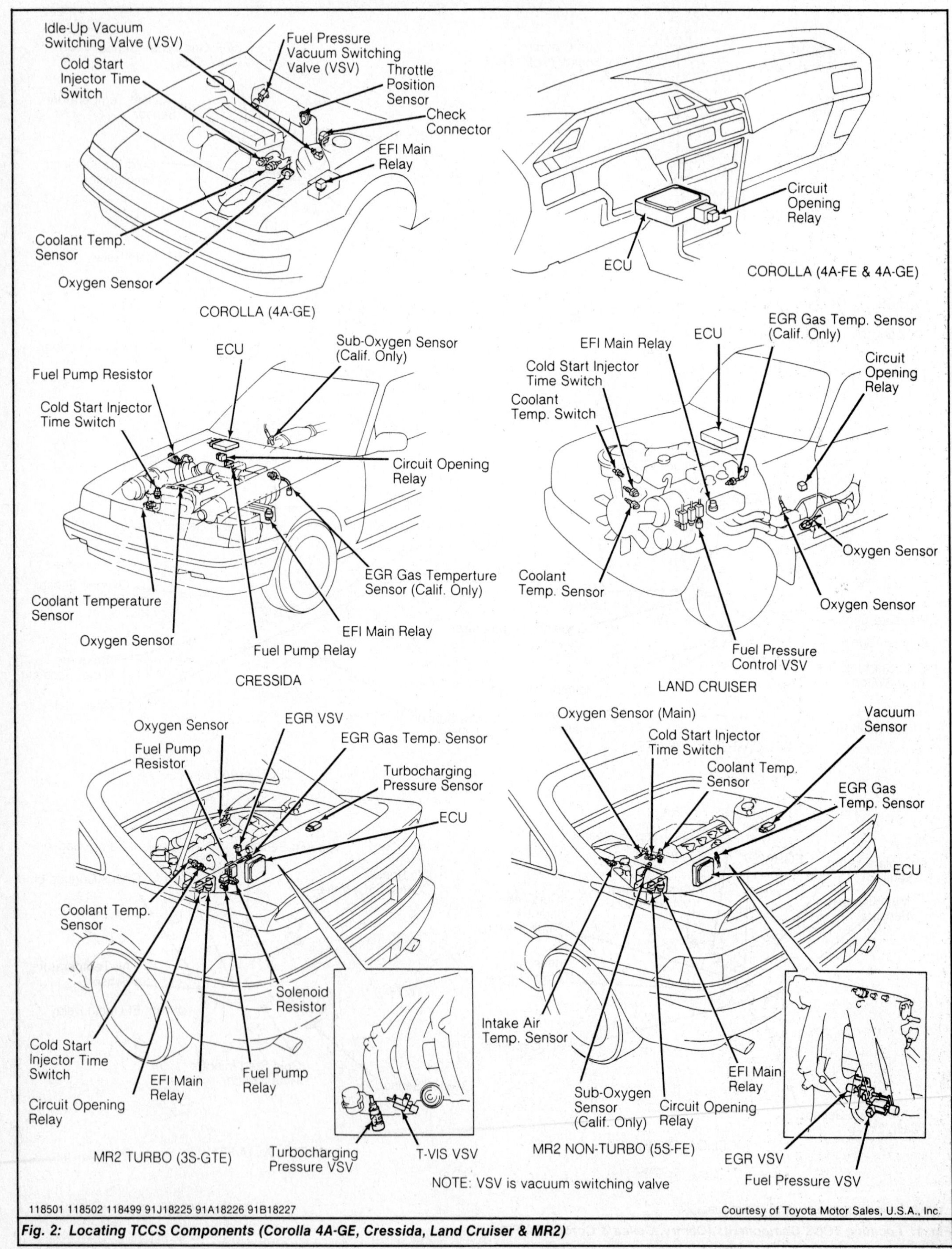


*Fig. 2: Locating TCCS Components (Corolla 4A-GE, Cressida, Land Cruiser & MR2)*

# 1991 ENGINE PERFORMANCE
# Theory & Operation (Cont.)

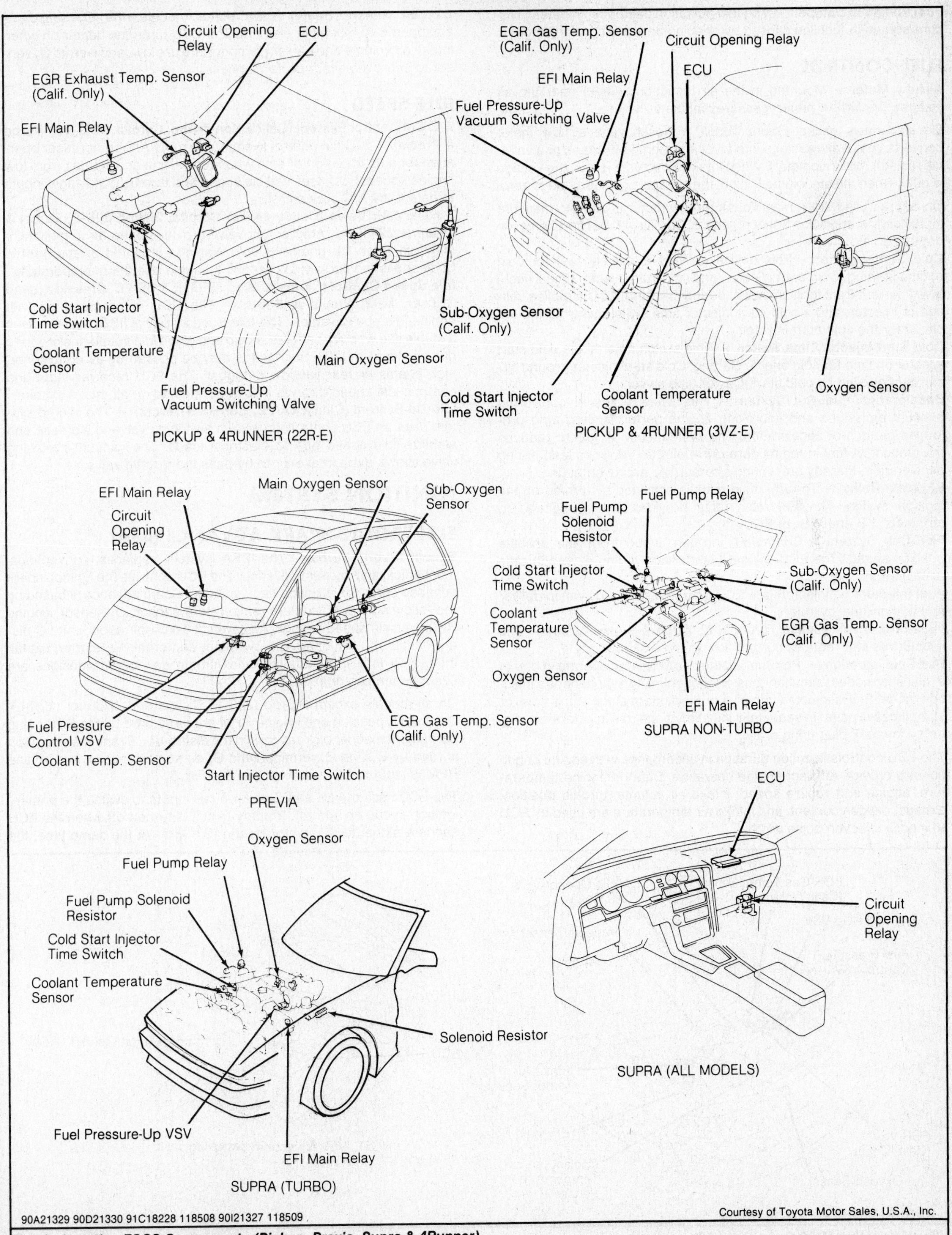


*Fig. 3: Locating TCCS Components (Pickup, Previa, Supra & 4Runner)*

# 1991 ENGINE PERFORMANCE
# Theory & Operation (Cont.)

**Fuel Pulsation Damper** – The fuel pulsation damper eliminates pressure surges in fuel line caused by opening and closing of injectors.

## FUEL CONTROL

**Airflow Meter** – Mounted in the air induction system near the air cleaner, the airflow meter measures intake air volume.

On all models except Supra Turbo, a Bosch vane airflow meter converts intake air readings into a voltage signal by means of a variable resistor (potentiometer). When intake air volume is low, the voltage is high; when the air volume is high, the voltage signal is close to zero.

On Supra Turbo, a Karman-Vortex airflow meter is used to measure intake airflow and turbo boost pressure. Corolla (4A-FE) and Tercel do not use an airflow meter.

**Cold Start Injector** – This device delivers additional fuel for cold engine starting. Cold start injector (and cold start injector time switch) is fed current from ignition switch during cranking. ECU supplies voltage to injector, and a cold start injector time switch controls ground circuit for the cold start injector.

**Cold Start Injector Time Switch** – This switch determines cold start injector on time for cold engine starting. Cold start injector ground circuit is controlled by cold start injector time switch.

**Deceleration Fuel-Cut System** – This system aids in controlling exhaust emissions and improving engine performance during prolonged periods of deceleration. The system cuts off fuel or reduces the amount of fuel in the mixture. Air/fuel ratio becomes lean during deceleration, thereby preventing afterburning and overheating.

**EFI Main Relay** – The EFI main relay is activated by turning on the ignition switch. The EFI main relay provides battery voltage to terminals +B and $+B_1$ of ECU.

**Fuel-Cut System** – Controlled through input from the throttle position sensor, the ECU will cut fuel delivery during closed throttle deceleration.

**Fuel Injectors** – Injectors are ECU actuated solenoids which deliver fuel to individual cylinders.

**Injector Resistor (Celica Turbo, MR2 Turbo & Supra Turbo)** – The injector resistor reduces current flow to the fuel injectors.

**Port Fuel Injection** – Port fuel injected vehicles can operate in one of 2 injection modes, simultaneous or sequential. In simultaneous injection mode, fuel is injected into all 4 or 6 cylinders at the same time, or sometimes in pairs. In sequential injection mode, the injectors are triggered in spark plug firing order.

The ECU controls injection duration in accordance with engine conditions to provide efficient engine operation. Data on engine temperature, engine and vehicle speed, intake air volume, throttle position, exhaust oxygen content, and intake air temperature are used by ECU to modify injection pulse width.

**Oxygen Sensor Heater** – On some models, the $O_2$ sensor is equipped with a heating element. The ECU turns the heater on when intake air volume and coolant temperature are low, and warms $O_2$ sensor to improve sensor performance.

## IDLE SPEED

**A/C Cut Control System (Celica Non-Turbo, Corolla, MR2 Non-Turbo & Previa)** – A/C cut control system interrupts A/C compressor operation for a fixed period of time when the vehicle accelerates from low engine speed. ECU uses vehicle speed and throttle plate angle inputs to determine A/C cut control.

**Auxiliary Air Valve (Celica 4A-FE, Corolla, Pickup 22R-E, Tercel & 4Runner 22R-E)** – Auxiliary air valve provides extra air to the intake manifold when the engine is cold. Valve is mounted on the throttle body and is fed coolant to determine engine operating temperature.

**Idle Speed Control (Camry, Celica 3S-GTE & 5S-FE, Cressida, Land Cruiser, MR2, Previa & Supra)** – The ECU is programmed with engine idle speed values. The Idle Speed Control (ISC) system gives a stable idle when the engine is cold and when idle speed has dropped due to electrical load. Such loads may be caused by air conditioner, high beams or rear window defogger. The ECU receives input and controls idle speed through ISC valve, located on air intake system.

**Idle-Up System (Celica 4A-FE, Corolla & Tercel)** – The idle-up system uses an ECU controlled vacuum switching valve to increase and stabilize idle speed due to electrical loads. The vacuum switching valve allows extra intake air to by-pass the throttle valve.

# IGNITION SYSTEM

## ELECTRONIC SPARK ADVANCE (ESA)

**Except Supra Turbo** – The ESA system replaces conventional mechanical and vacuum advance. The ECU controls the ignition spark advance curve for every driving condition. Spark advance is based on the following inputs: coolant temperature sensor, $O_2$ sensor, engine RPM, vehicle speed sensor, A/C switch, 4WD operation (Land Cruiser, Pickup and 4Runner), airflow meter and cranking (starter) signal. Integrated (coil in distributor) and remote coil ignition designs are used, depending on model.

On all models except Pickup (22R-E), Tercel and 4Runner (22R-E), crankshaft position and engine RPM are monitored by the ECU using permanent magnet pick-up coils in the distributor. Crankshaft position is read by ECU at $G_1$ terminal (and $G_2$ on some models), and engine RPM is input to ECU terminal Ne. *See Fig. 5.*

The ECU uses the Ne and G pick-up coil inputs to switch the primary ignition circuit on and off. Primary circuit is turned off when the ECU sends a signal to the ignitor on the IGT wire. At the same time, the

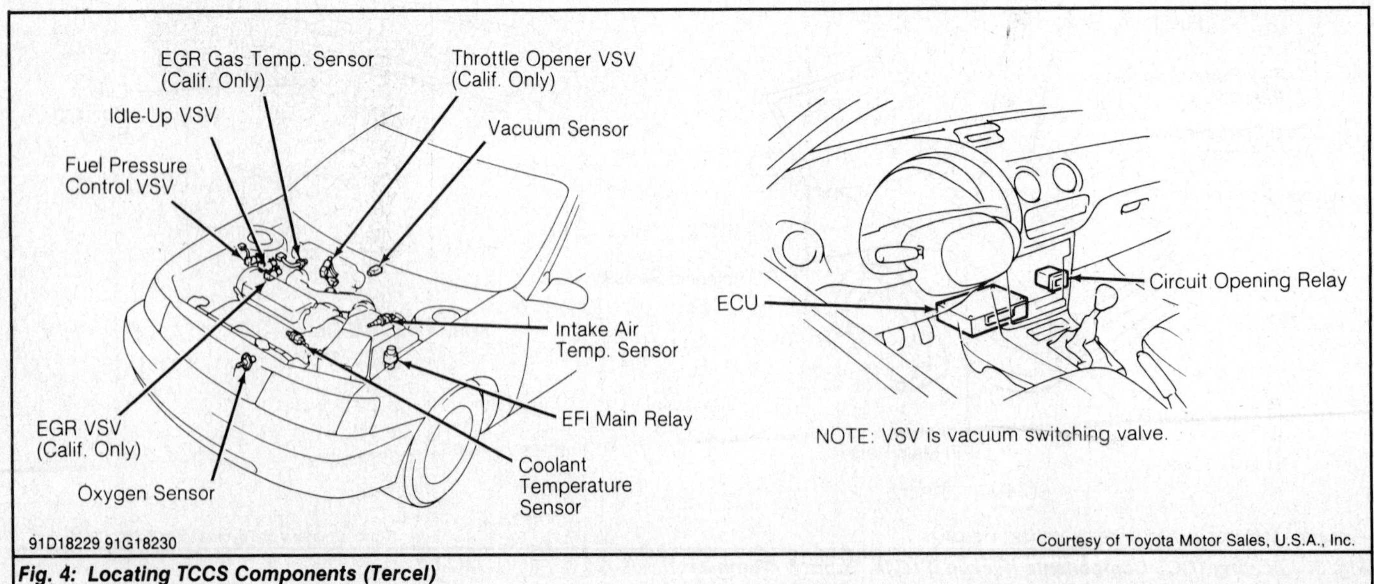


*Fig. 4: Locating TCCS Components (Tercel)*

ignitor sends an IGF signal to the ECU. The ECU feeds voltage to the IGF circuit. The ground for this voltage is momentarily cut when the primary circuit is turned off.

The ECU watches the IGF signal and can tell if the primary was switched on and off. After sending a command to turn off the primary circuit on the IGT wire, the ECU monitors the IGF circuit to ensure primary switching occurred. Normal cranking or running IGT voltage is 0.60-1.70 volts.

***NOTE: The TCCS system uses the input signal on the IGF line to fire the injectors. If this line is open or shorted to ground, the injectors will not fire.***

On Pickup (22R-E), Tercel and 4Runner (22R-E), a single pick-up coil is used in the distributor. Ignition system operation is similar to other models except there are no G signals. The ECU monitors the pick-up coil signal at Ne terminal.

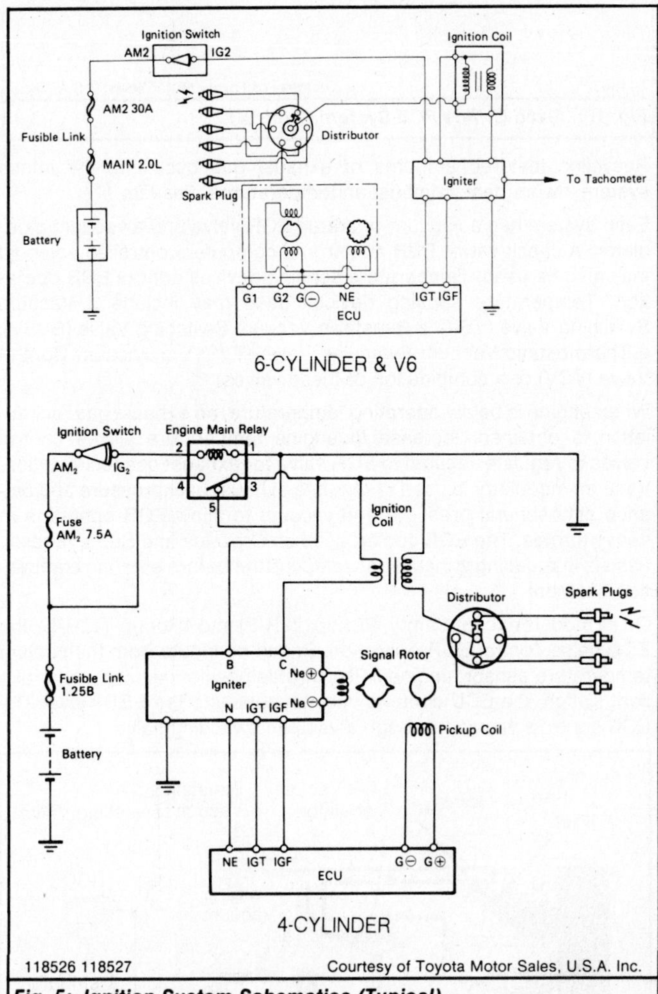


***Fig. 5: Ignition System Schematics (Typical)***

**Supra Turbo** – Supra Turbo models are equipped with a distributorless ignition system. Companion cylinders No. 1 and 6, 2 and 5, and 3 and 4 are fired together. One cylinder in each pair is on compression stroke while the other is on the exhaust stroke. Since the spark for one cylinder in each pair is fired on exhaust stroke, this is commonly known as the waste-spark method of ignition distribution.

The conventional distributor and pick-up coil have been replaced by a camshaft position sensor. *See Fig. 6*. Crankshaft position and engine RPM are detected by 3 pick-up coils in the camshaft position sensor. The ECU uses the crankshaft ($G_1$ and $G_2$ coils) and RPM (Ne coil) signals to control the 3 coils. Toyota refers to the 3 ignition primary control signals for the 3 coils as IGT, IGDA and IGDB signals.

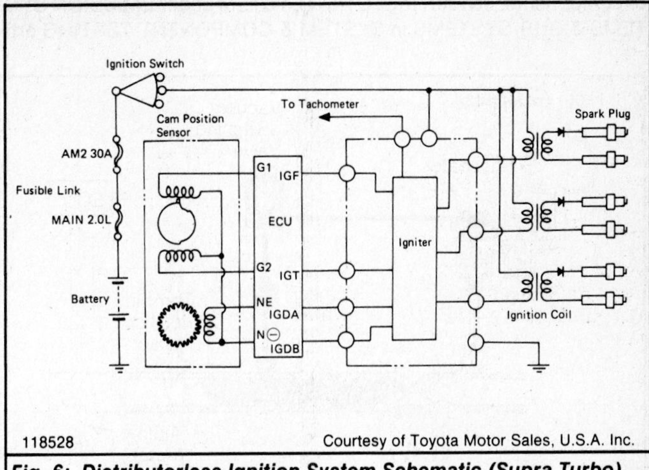


***Fig. 6: Distributorless Ignition System Schematic (Supra Turbo)***

## EMISSION SYSTEMS

### AIR INJECTION

**Air Pump System (Land Cruiser)** – This model is equipped with an Air Injection System (AIS). The AIS is designed to reduce hydrocarbons (HC) and carbon monoxide (CO) emissions by injecting air into the exhaust manifold. *See Fig. 7*.

Fresh air is drawn from the air cleaner and compressed by the air pump. Using a solenoid and air suction valve, this compressed air is injected into the exhaust manifold or exhausted into the atmosphere as determined by the Electronic Control Unit (ECU). The ECU receives various valve signals, depending on engine operating conditions, to determine compressed airflow. AIS components and operating parameters vary between models. For specific system operating parameters and testing of system or components, see AIR INJECTION SYSTEM under EMISSION SYSTEMS & SUB-SYSTEMS in SYSTEM & COMPONENT TESTING article.

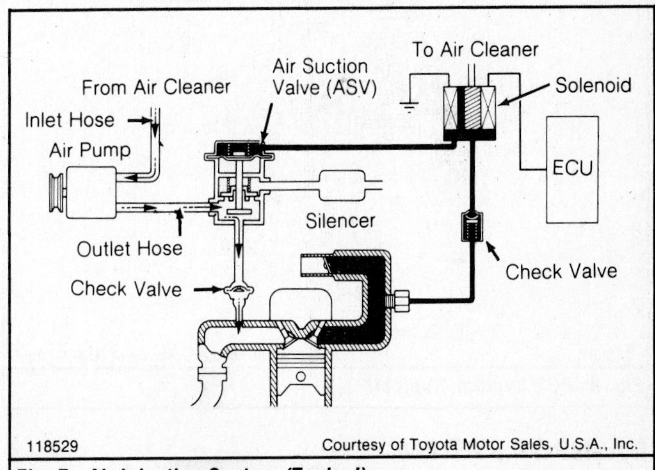


***Fig. 7: Air Injection System (Typical)***

**Air Suction (AS) System (Pickup & 4Runner)** – The AS system uses exhaust gas pulses to draw air into the exhaust manifold or catalytic converter to reduce hydrocarbons (HC) and carbon monoxide (CO) emissions. The AS system works by drawing air through the air filter and reed valve into the exhaust manifold or catalytic converter. *See Fig. 8*. Based on coolant temperature, engine RPM, throttle valve position, and vehicle speed sensor inputs, fresh air flow into the exhaust manifold can be turned on or off by the ECU through Air Suction Valve (ASV) and Vacuum Switching Valve (VSV).

AS system components and operating parameters vary between models. For specific system operating parameters and testing of system

# 1991 ENGINE PERFORMANCE
# Theory & Operation (Cont.)

or components, see AIR INJECTION SYSTEM under EMISSION SYSTEMS & SUB-SYSTEMS in SYSTEM & COMPONENT TESTING article.

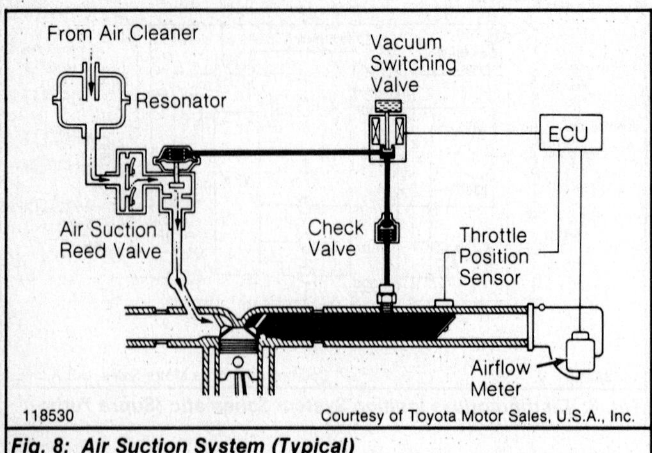


*Fig. 8: Air Suction System (Typical)*

## CRANKCASE VENTILATION

The Positive Crankcase Ventilation (PCV) system is designed to prevent contaminating hydrocarbons (HC), created in the crankcase, from escaping into the atmosphere.

Crankcase vapors are routed from the crankcase through a vacuum controlled fixed orifice or PCV valve, into the intake manifold. When vapors reach the intake manifold, they are mixed with air/fuel and burned in the combustion process. *See Figs. 9 and 10.*

The PCV system provides primary control by metering the flow of blow-by vapors, according to manifold vacuum. When manifold vacuum is high (at idle) the PCV restricts the flow to maintain a smooth idle condition.

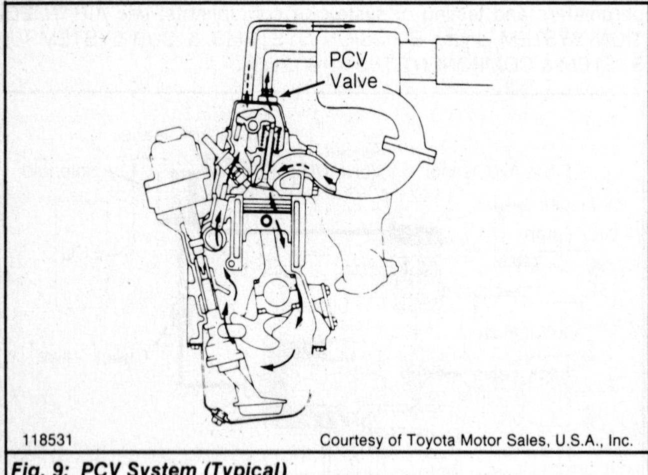


*Fig. 9: PCV System (Typical)*

## DASHPOT SYSTEM

This system controls exhaust emissions during deceleration by holding throttle plate at an above-idle position during deceleration. This aids in complete burning of the air/fuel mixture.

On most EFI models, the system consists of the ECU and throttle position sensor. The ECU adjusts the fuel injection duration depending on engine RPM. On Camry (2VZ-FE), Celica (4A-FE), Corolla (4A-FE) and Land Cruiser, throttle plate is held above idle on deceleration by a vacuum actuated dashpot.

## EGR SYSTEM

The Exhaust Gas Recirculation (EGR) system is used to reduce oxides of nitrogen (NOx) emissions by lowering combustion temperatures.

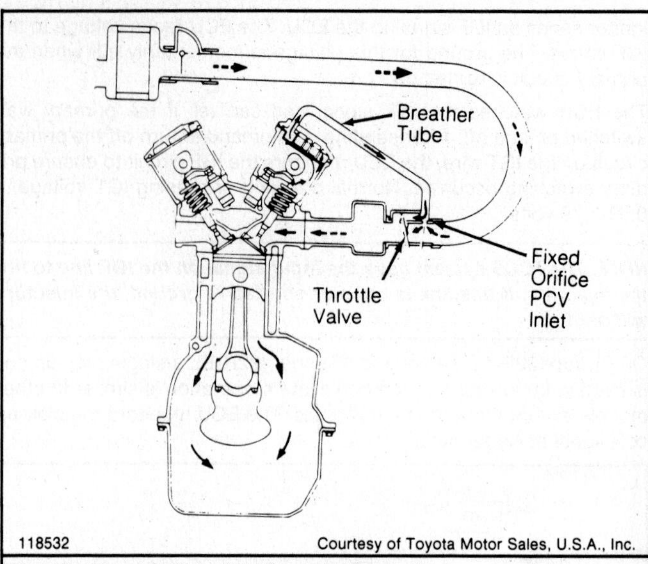


*Fig. 10: Fixed Orifice PCV System (Typical)*

Recycling metered amounts of exhaust gas back into the intake system lowers peak combustion temperatures. *See Fig. 11.*

Each system has a vacuum-operated EGR valve and a vacuum modulator. A check valve, EGR cooler and computer controlled solenoid may also be used. Temperature sensing devices control EGR operation. Temperature sensing devices used may include a Vacuum Switching Valve (VSV), a Bimetallic Vacuum Switching Valve (BVSV), a Thermostatic Vacuum Switching Valve (TVSV), a Vacuum Control Valve (VCV) or a combination of these valves.

When engine is below operating temperature, no exhaust gas recirculation is obtained. Increase in engine temperature allows control valves to regulate vacuum to EGR valve for exhaust gas recirculation. Vacuum modulator is used to regulate exhaust backpressure and balance atmospheric pressure and vacuum to allow EGR operation at heavy throttle. The EGR cooler, used on Cressida and Supra models, assists in reducing exhaust gas temperature before entering combustion chamber.

On all models except Camry, Pickup (22R-E) and 4Runner (22R-E), the ECU helps control EGR operation. Based on inputs from the coolant temperature sensor, engine RPM, throttle position sensor, and brake light switch, the ECU controls vacuum supply to the EGR valve. The ECU controls vacuum through a vacuum switching valve.

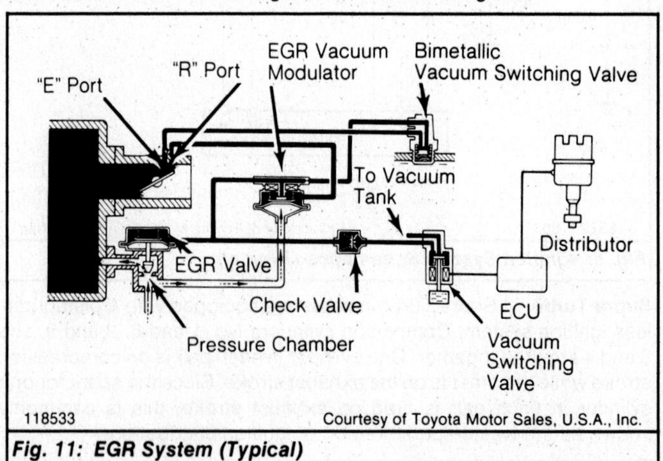


*Fig. 11: EGR System (Typical)*

## EVAPORATIVE EMISSION SYSTEM (EVAP)

Purpose of EVAP system is to prevent the escape of gasoline vapors (hydrocarbons) from the fuel tank into the atmosphere. To reduce

# 1991 ENGINE PERFORMANCE
## Basic Diagnostic Procedures (Cont.)

***NOTE: All models use in-tank fuel pump. Fuel pump contains internal relief valve and check valve.***

**5)** If fuel pump ran after battery source was connected to FP terminal in step **3)**, check EFI main relay and related wiring. Also check EFI and IGN fuses. See FUEL PUMP CONTROL CIRCUIT. For more information on wiring, see appropriate wiring diagram in WIRING DIAGRAMS article.

***ENGINE CHECK CONNECTOR LOCATION***

| Model | [1] Location |
|---|---|
| Camry, Corolla & Cressida | On Left Shock Tower |
| Celica & Tercel | Behind Left Shock Tower |
| Land Cruiser | On Firewall, Under Wiper Motor |
| MR2 | Left Rear Engine Compartment |
| Pickup & 4Runner | On Right Fenderwell |
| Previa | Under Center Console |
| Supra | In Front of Left Shock Tower |

[1] - Check connector cover has check connector pin identification. All FP and +B pins will be in same location.

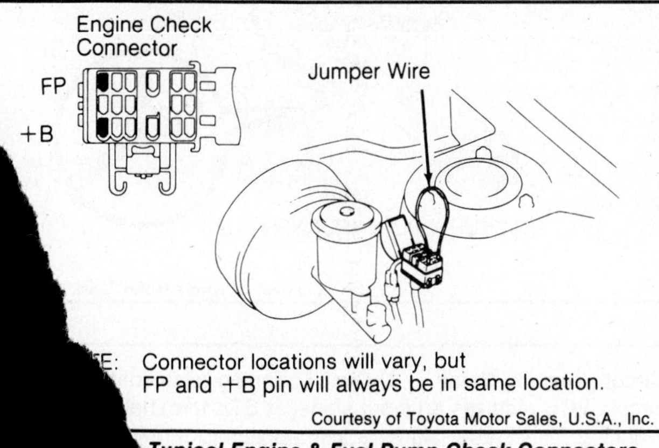
Engine Check
Connector
FP
+B
Jumper Wire
E: Connector locations will vary, but
FP and +B pin will always be in same location.

Courtesy of Toyota Motor Sales, U.S.A., Inc.

*Typical Engine & Fuel Pump Check Connectors*

### PRESSURE TEST

***g fuel pressure, check all fuel delivery and return***

nsure battery is fully charged. Turn ignition off. attery cable. On Previa, remove right (engine) ll models, place container or shop towel under

ry pipe union bolt to relieve fuel pressure. gaskets. Install fuel pressure gauge between ry pipe. *See Fig. 2*. Wipe off excess fuel. ween engine check connector FP and +B NE CHECK CONNECTOR LOCATION table. able. Turn ignition on, with engine off. Mea-

be same as unregulated pressure. See P PERFORMANCE table. If fuel pressure is ure regulator. If fuel pressure is low, check ctions, fuel pump, fuel filter and fuel pressure

wire installed in step **3)**. Start engine. Disconnect sensing hose from fuel pressure regulator, and plug hose end. Fuel pressure regulator is mounted on fuel rail. Measure unregulated fuel pressure at idle speed. See 4-CYLINDER FUEL PUMP PERFORMANCE table.

**6)** With engine idling, connect fuel pressure regulator vacuum hose. Measure regulated pressure at idle. If regulated pressure is not as specified, check vacuum sensing hose to fuel pressure regulator.

**7)** Stop engine. Note fuel pressure. Leave fuel pressure gauge attached to engine for at least 5 minutes. Residual fuel pressure after 5 minutes should be at least 21 psi (1.5 kg/cm²). If pressure is not as specified, check for leaking injectors, faulty fuel pressure regulator or bad check valve in fuel pump.

**8)** Relieve fuel system pressure. Remove fuel pressure gauge. Install fuel supply line to delivery pipe. Run engine and check for fuel leaks.

**Except MR2 & Previa - 1)** Ensure battery is fully charged. Turn ignition off. Disconnect negative battery cable. On Pickup (3.0L) and 4Runner (3.0L), place container or shop towel under No. 3 fuel supply pipe. On Tercel, place container or shop towel under fuel filter.

**2)** On all other models, place container or shop towel under cold start injector. Disconnect cold start injector (if equipped). Slowly loosen cold start injector or No. 3 fuel supply pipe union bolt to relieve fuel pressure.

**3)** Remove union bolt and gaskets. Install fuel pressure gauge to cold start injector delivery pipe. *See Fig. 2*. Wipe off excess fuel. On Pickup (3.0L) and 4Runner (3.0L), attach gauge to No. 3 fuel pipe using same method. *See Fig. 2*.

**4)** Install jumper wire between engine check connector FP and +B pins. *See Fig. 1*. See ENGINE CHECK CONNECTOR LOCATION table. Reconnect negative battery cable, and turn ignition on, with engine off. Measure fuel pressure. Fuel pressure should be same as unregulated pressure. See appropriate FUEL PUMP PERFORMANCE table.

**5)** If fuel pressure is high, replace fuel pressure regulator. If fuel pressure is low, check fuel hoses and connections, fuel pump, fuel filter, and fuel pressure regulator

**6)** Remove jumper wire installed in step **3)**. Start engine. Disconnect vacuum sensing hose from fuel pressure regulator, and plug hose end. Fuel pressure regulator is mounted on fuel rail.

**7)** Measure unregulated fuel pressure at idle speed. See appropriate FUEL PUMP PERFORMANCE table. With engine still idling, reconnect fuel pressure regulator vacuum hose.

**8)** Measure regulated pressure at idle. If regulated pressure is not as specified, check vacuum sensing hose to fuel pressure regulator. On models so equipped, check fuel pressure-up system. See SYSTEM & COMPONENT TESTING article.

**9)** Stop engine. Note fuel pressure. Leave fuel pressure gauge attached to engine for at least 5 minutes. Residual fuel pressure after 5 minutes should be at least 21 psi (1.5 kg/cm²).

**10)** If pressure is not as specified, check for leaking injectors, faulty fuel pressure regulator or bad check valve in fuel pump. Relieve fuel system pressure. Remove fuel pressure gauge. Install cold start injector. Run engine and check for fuel leaks.

***NOTE: For more information on checking fuel injectors and other fuel sub-systems, see SYSTEM & COMPONENT TESTING article.***

***4-CYLINDER FUEL PUMP PERFORMANCE***

| Application | [1] Unregulated Pressure psi (kg/cm²) | [2] Regulated Pressure psi (kg/cm²) |
|---|---|---|
| Camry, Pickup, | | |
| Tercel & 4Runner | 38-44 (2.7-3.1) | 33-37 (2.3-2.6) |
| Celica | | |
| Non-Turbo | 38-44 (2.7-3.1) | 33-37 (2.3-2.6) |
| Turbo | 33-38 (2.3-2.7) | 27-31 (1.9-2.2) |
| Corolla | 38-44 (2.7-3.1) | 30-37 (2.1-2.6) |
| MR2 | 33-38 (2.3-2.7) | 27-31 (1.9-2.2) |
| Previa | 38-44 (2.7-3.1) | 30-36 (2.1-2.5) |

[1] - With pressure regulator vacuum hose disconnected and plugged.
[2] - With vacuum hose connected to pressure regulator.

# 1991 ENGINE PERFORMANCE
## Basic Diagnostic Procedures (Cont.)

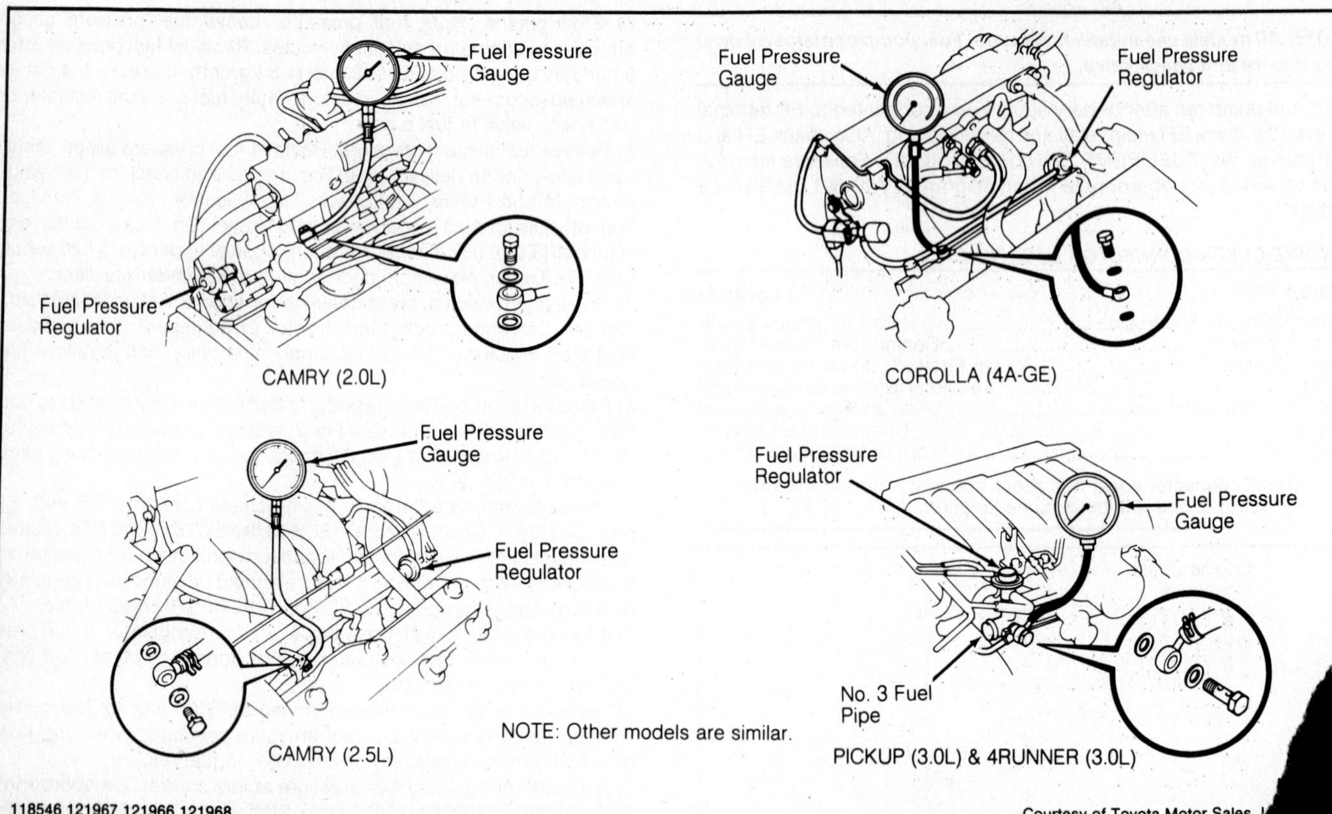


*Fig. 2: Locating Fuel Pressure Gauge Connections*

**6-CYLINDER FUEL PUMP PERFORMANCE**

| Application | [1] Unregulated Pressure psi (kg/cm²) | [2] Regulated Pressure psi (kg/cm²) |
|---|---|---|
| Cressida | 38-44 (2.7-3.1) | 33-37 (2.3-2.6) |
| Land Cruiser | 37-46 (2.6-3.2) | 33-37 (2.3-2.6) |
| Supra | | |
| Non-Turbo | 38-44 (2.7-3.1) | 30-37 (2.1-2.6) |
| Turbo | 33-40 (2.3-2.8) | 23-30 (1.6-2.1) |

[1] - With pressure regulator vacuum hose disconnected and plugged.
[2] - With vacuum hose connected to pressure regulator.

**V6 FUEL PUMP PERFORMANCE**

| Application | [1] Unregulated Pressure psi (kg/cm²) | [2] Regulated Pressure psi (kg/cm²) |
|---|---|---|
| All Models | 38-44 (2.7-3.1) | 33-37 (2.3-2.6) |

[1] - With pressure regulator vacuum hose disconnected and plugged.
[2] - With vacuum hose connected to pressure regulator.

## FUEL PUMP CONTROL CIRCUIT

**EFI Main Relay - 1)** EFI fuse supplies constant battery voltage to EFI main relay. EFI main relay provides battery voltage to +B terminal of circuit opening relay and engine check connector.

**2)** If fuel pump does not turn on when +B and FP pins are jumpered with ignition on, check EFI main relay. *See Fig. 3*. Also check EFI main relay circuit. Depending on model, relay may either be turned on directly by ignition switch or by M-REL terminal of ECU. For more information on wiring, see WIRING DIAGRAMS article in ENGINE PERFORMANCE.

**Circuit Opening Relay - 1)** Circuit opening relay con
circuit. ECU receives an input signal at STA terminal
cranking. This starter signal is also applied to termi
opening relay.

**2)** Starter signal energizes circuit opening relay dur
in turn activates fuel pump. On all models except
FE), Supra (Turbo) and Tercel, fuel pump switch
vides relay ground. On Celica, Corolla (4A-FE), Su
cel, circuit opening relay is grounded by ECU th

**Fuel Pump Relay & Fuel Pump Resistor (Celic Supra) -** These models use a separate fuel p
between circuit opening relay and fuel pump.

*NOTE: For more information on testing r components, see SYSTEM & COMPONENT T*

## IGNITION CHECKS (EXCEPT SUPRA TURBO)

### DIAGNOSTIC CODES

*NOTE: ECU is programmed to detect ignitio trouble codes can speed up diagnosis. If EC diagnostic code will be set in memory. For self-diagnostic capabilities and how to retrie DIAGNOSTICS article.*

**Code 12 (No RPM Signal) -** ECU will store Code 12 in memory if it does not receive signal from either NE pick-up coil (RPM) or "G" pick-up coil (crank position) terminal within 2 seconds of engine cranking.

**Code 13 (No RPM Signal) -** ECU will store Code 13 in memory if it does not receive signal from NE pick-up coil (RPM) terminal when engine speed is above 1000 RPM.

**Code 14 (Ignition Signal Problem) -** ECU will store Code 14 in memory if it does not receive IGF (ignition detection) signal a specified number of times. See CODE 14 SET SPECIFICATIONS table.

# 1991 ENGINE PERFORMANCE
# Basic Diagnostic Procedures (Cont.)

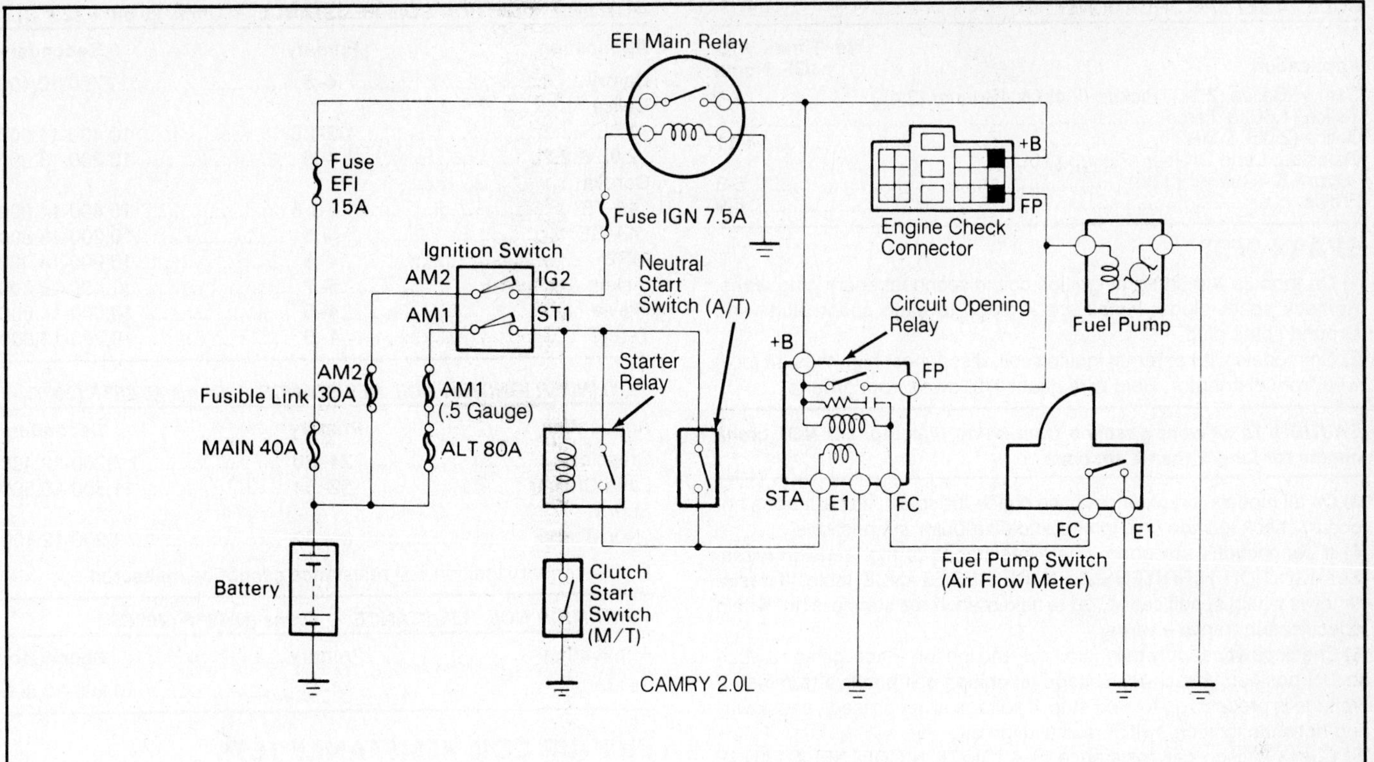


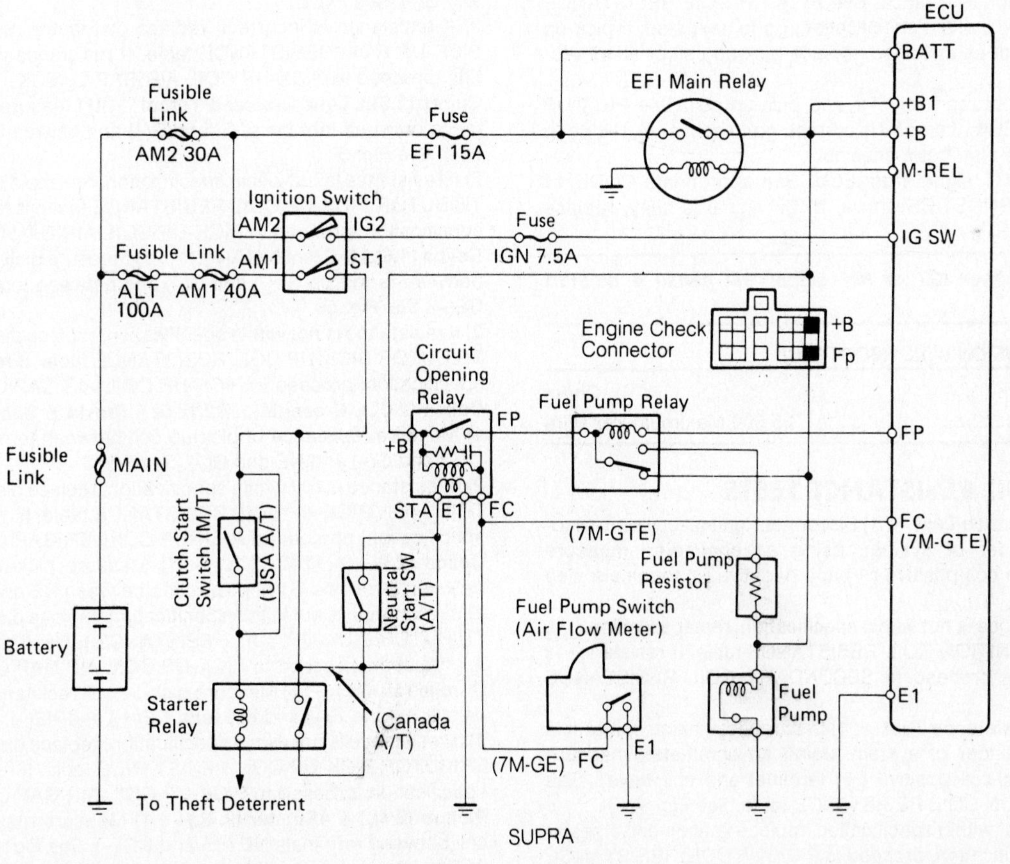


118547 118548

Courtesy of Toyota Motor Sales, U.S.A., Inc.

*Fig. 3: Fuel Pump Wiring Schematics (Camry 2.0L & Supra Shown; Others Similar)*

# 1991 ENGINE PERFORMANCE
# Basic Diagnostic Procedures (Cont.)

*CODE 14 SET SPECIFICATIONS*

| Application | No. Times W/O IGF Signal |
|---|---|
| Camry, Celica (2.2L), Pickup (2.4L) & 4Runner (2.4L) | 4-5 |
| Celica (1.6L) & Tercel | 4 |
| Celica (2.0L) & MR2 | 8-11 |
| Cressida, Land Cruiser, Pickup (3.0L), Supra & 4Runner (3.0L) | 6-8 |
| Previa | 8-9 |

## SPARK TEST

**1)** On models with integral ignition coil, disconnect spark plug wires. Remove spark plugs. Install spark plugs to each spark plug wire. Ground spark plug.

**2)** On models with external ignition coil, disconnect high tension (coil) wire from distributor. Hold wire about 1/2" away from ground.

***CAUTION: To prevent gasoline from being injected, DO NOT crank engine for longer than 2 seconds.***

**3)** On all models, crank engine and check for spark. If spark does not occur, check ignition coil, ignitor and distributor connections.

**4)** If connections are good, check resistance of high tension wires. See IGNITION HIGH-TENSION WIRE RESISTANCE table. If resistance is within specification, go to next step. If resistance is not within specification, replace wires.

**5)** Check power supply to ignition coil and ignitor. Place ignition switch in ON position. Check for voltage at ignition coil positive terminal. If voltage is present, go to next step. If voltage is not present, check wiring between ignition switch, coil and ignitor.

**6)** Check ignition coil resistance. See IGNITION COIL RESISTANCE TESTS. If ignition coil resistance is not as specified, replace coil. If coil resistance is within specification, go to next step.

**7)** Check pick-up coil resistance. See PICK-UP COIL RESISTANCE TEST. If resistance is within specification, go to next step. If pick-up coil resistance is not as specified, replace pick-up coil or distributor assembly.

**8)** Check air gap between reluctor and pick-up coil. See PICK-UP COIL AIR GAP CHECK. If air gap is correct, go to next step. If air gap is incorrect, replace distributor assembly.

**9)** Check ignition IGT signal from ECU. See appropriate CODE 14 chart in SELF-DIAGNOSTICS article. If IGT signal is okay, replace ignitor.

***NOTE: A loss of either IGT or IGF signal will cause a no-start condition.***

*IGNITION HIGH-TENSION WIRE RESISTANCE*

| Application | Ohms |
|---|---|
| All Models | 25,000 Maximum Per Wire |

## IGNITION COIL RESISTANCE TESTS

**Primary Coil Resistance Test – 1)** Disconnect ignition coil so it is isolated from remainder of system. Using an ohmmeter, measure resistance between coil positive (+) and negative (-) terminals. *See Fig. 4.*

**2)** If primary resistance is not within specification, replace ignition coil. See appropriate IGNITION COIL RESISTANCE table. If resistance is within specification, proceed to SECONDARY COIL RESISTANCE TEST.

**Secondary Coil Resistance Test – 1)** Disconnect ignition coil so it is isolated from remainder of system. Using an ohmmeter, measure resistance between coil positive (+) terminal and coil tower. See appropriate IGNITION COIL RESISTANCE table. *See Fig. 4.*

**2)** If resistance is not within specification, replace ignition coil. If resistance is within specification, proceed to PICK-UP COIL RESISTANCE TEST.

*4-CYLINDER IGNITION COIL RESISTANCE – Ohms @ 68°F (20°C)*

| Application | Primary | Secondary |
|---|---|---|
| Camry | .4-.5 | 7700-10,400 |
| Celica | | |
| 1.6L | 1.3-1.6 | 10,400-14,000 |
| 2.0L & 2.2L | .4-.5 | 10,200-13,800 |
| Corolla | | |
| 4A-FE | 1.3-1.6 | 10,400-14,000 |
| 4A-GE | .4-.5 | 10,200-13,800 |
| MR2 | .4-.5 | 10,000-14,000 |
| Pickup & 4Runner | .5-.7 | 11,400-15,600 |
| Previa | .4-.5 | 10,000-14,000 |
| Tercel | .4-.5 | 10,200-13,800 |

*6-CYLINDER IGNITION COIL RESISTANCE – Ohms @ 68°F (20°C)*

| Application | Primary | Secondary |
|---|---|---|
| Cressida | .24-.30 | 9200-12,400 |
| Land Cruiser | .52-.64 | 11,500-15,500 |
| Supra | | |
| Non-Turbo | .24-.30 | 9200-12,400 |

[1] – Secondary ignition coil resistance cannot be measured.

*V6 IGNITION COIL RESISTANCE – Ohms @ 68°F (20°C)*

| Application | Primary | Secondary |
|---|---|---|
| All Models | .4-.5 | 10,200-13,800 |

## PICK-UP COIL RESISTANCE TEST

**Camry (2.5L), Pickup (3.0L) & 4Runner (3.0L) – 1)** Measure pick-up coil resistance between terminals G1 and G(-), G2 and G(-) and NE and G(-). *See Fig. 5.*

**2)** If resistance is incorrect, replace distributor. See DISTRIBUTOR PICK-UP COIL RESISTANCE table. If resistance is within specification, proceed to PICK-UP COIL AIR GAP CHECK.

**Camry (2.0L), Land Cruiser & Tercel – 1)** Measure pick-up coil resistance between terminals "G" and G(-) and between terminals NE and G(-). *See Fig. 5.*

**2)** If resistance is not within specification, replace distributor. See DISTRIBUTOR PICK-UP COIL RESISTANCE table. If resistance is within specification, proceed to PICK-UP COIL AIR GAP CHECK.

**Celica (1.6L) & Corolla (4A-FE) – 1)** Measure pick-up coil resistance between terminals G(+) and G(-) and between terminals NE(+) and GE(-). *See Fig. 5.*

**2)** If resistance is not within specification, replace distributor. See DISTRIBUTOR PICK-UP COIL RESISTANCE table. If resistance is within specification, proceed to PICK-UP COIL AIR GAP CHECK.

**Celica (2.0L), Cressida, MR2 (2.0L), Previa & Supra (Non-Turbo) – 1)** Measure resistance of pick-up coil between terminals G1 and G(-), G2 and G(-) and NE and G(-). *See Fig. 5.*

**2)** If resistance is not within specification, replace distributor. See DISTRIBUTOR PICK-UP COIL RESISTANCE table. If resistance is within specification, proceed to PICK-UP COIL AIR GAP CHECK.

**Celica (2.2L) & MR2 (2.2L) – 1)** Measure pick-up coil resistance between terminals G1 and G(-) and between NE and G(-). *See Fig. 5.*

**2)** If resistance is not within specification, replace distributor. See DISTRIBUTOR PICK-UP COIL RESISTANCE table. If resistance is within specification, proceed to PICK-UP COIL AIR GAP CHECK.

**Corolla (4A-GE) – 1)** Measure pick-up coil resistance between terminals G(+) and G(-) and between NE(+) and NE(-). *See Fig. 5.*

**2)** If resistance is not within specification, replace distributor. See DISTRIBUTOR PICK-UP COIL RESISTANCE table. If resistance is within specification, proceed to PICK-UP COIL AIR GAP CHECK.

**Pickup (2.4L) & 4Runner (2.4L) – 1)** Measure resistance of pick-up coil between terminals NE (+) and NE (-). *See Fig. 5.*

**2)** If resistance is not within specification, replace distributor. See DISTRIBUTOR PICK-UP COIL RESISTANCE table. If resistance is within specification, proceed to PICK-UP COIL AIR GAP CHECK.

# 1991 ENGINE PERFORMANCE
## Basic Diagnostic Procedures (Cont.)

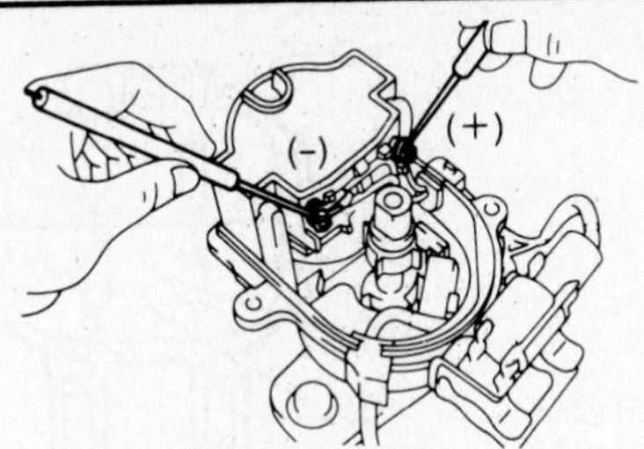


PRIMARY RESISTANCE
Camry (2.0L), Celica (1.6L & 2.2L), MR2 (2.2L) & Corolla (4A-FE)

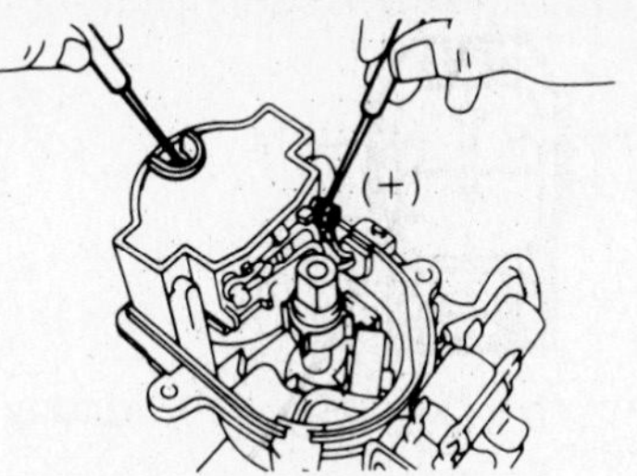


SECONDARY RESISTANCE
Camry (2.0L), Celica (1.6L & 2.2L), MR2 (2.2L) & Corolla (4A-FE)

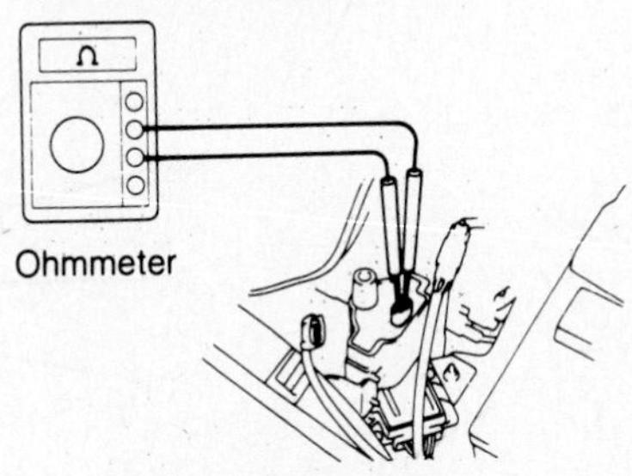


PRIMARY RESISTANCE
Camry (2.5L)

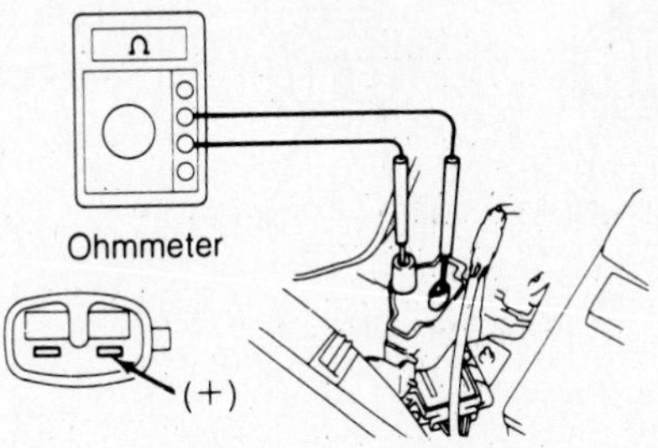


SECONDARY RESISTANCE
Camry (2.5L)

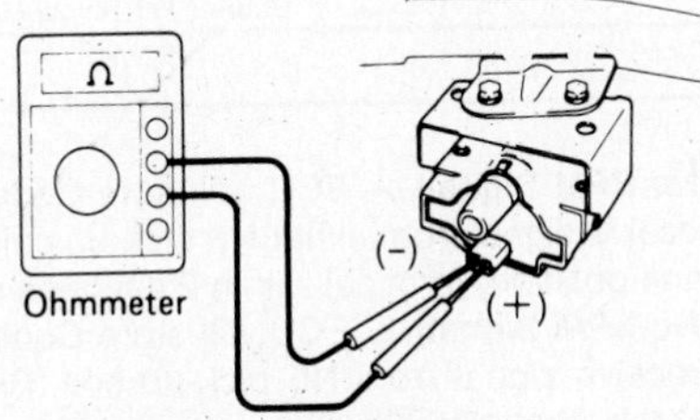


PRIMARY RESISTANCE
Celica (2.0L), Corolla (4A-GE), MR2 (2.0L), Previa & Pickup (3.0L)

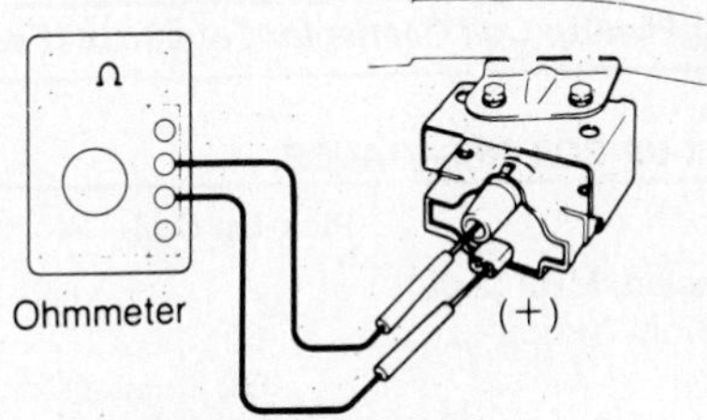


SECONDARY RESISTANCE
Celica (2.0L), Corolla (4A-GE), MR2 (2.0L), Previa & Pickup (3.0L)

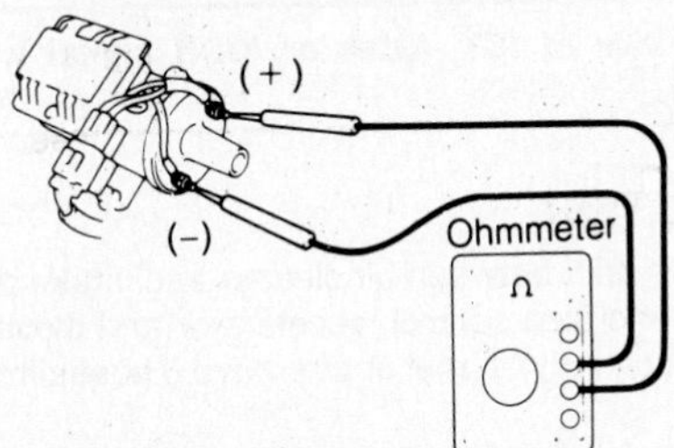


PRIMARY RESISTANCE
Land Cruiser, Pickup (2.4L) & 4Runner

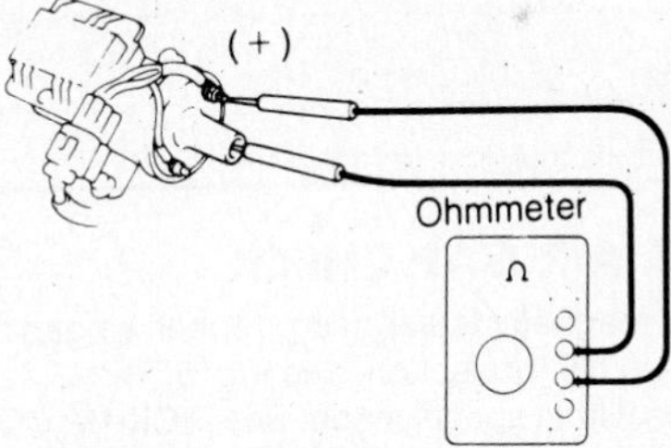


SECONDARY RESISTANCE
Land Cruiser, Pickup (2.4L) & 4Runner

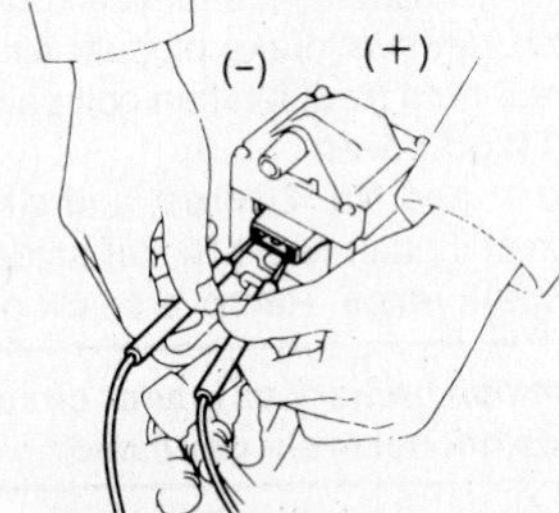


PRIMARY RESISTANCE
Cressida & Supra (Non-Turbo)

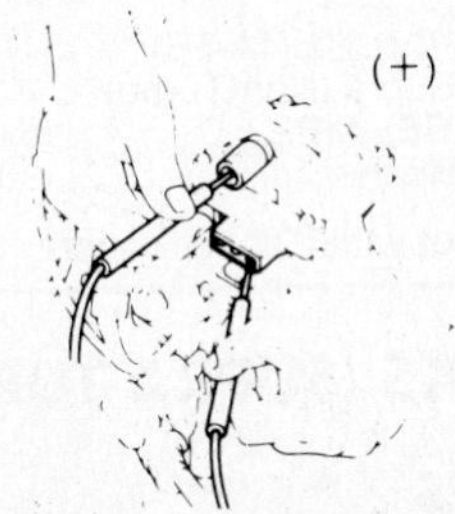


SECONDARY RESISTANCE
Cressida & Supra (Non-Turbo)

118550 118551 118552 118553 118554 118555 118556 118557 118558 118559

Courtesy of Toyota Motor Sales, U.S.A., Inc.

***Fig. 4: Testing Ignition Coil Resistance (Except Supra Turbo)***

# 1991 ENGINE PERFORMANCE
## Basic Diagnostic Procedures (Cont.)

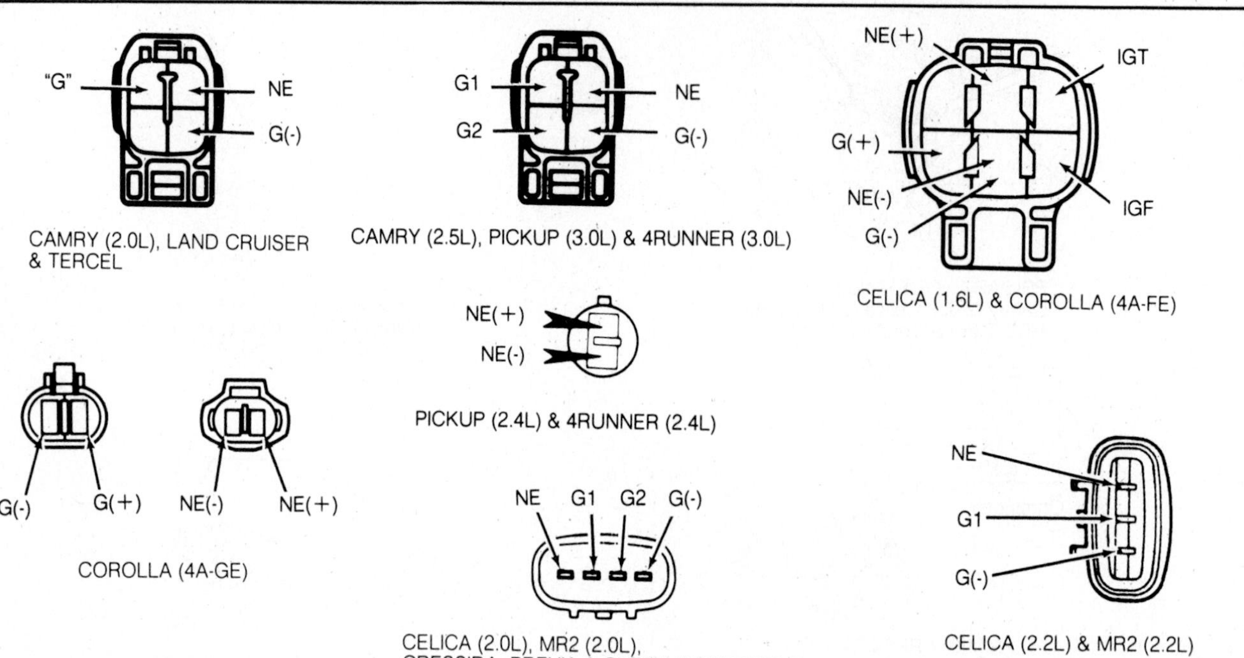


***Fig. 5: Identifying Pick-Up Coil Connector Terminals (Except Supra Turbo)***

***DISTRIBUTOR PICK-UP COIL RESISTANCE***

| Application | Pick-Up Coil | Ohms |
|---|---|---|
| Celica (2.0L), Cressida, MR2 (2.0L), Previa & Supra (Non-Turbo) | G1 | 125-190 |
| | G2 | 125-190 |
| | NE | 155-240 |
| Celica (2.2L) & MR2 (2.2L) | | 150-230 |
| Tercel | | |
| Gray | | 265-420 |
| Green | | 370-530 |
| All Others | | |
| Gray | | 130-210 |
| Green | | 185-265 |

## PICK-UP COIL AIR GAP CHECK

**1)** Using a flat, non-magnetic feeler gauge, check air gap between signal rotor and pick-up coil projection. *See Fig. 6.*

**2)** Air gap should be within specification. See PICK-UP COIL ADJUSTMENT table. If air gap is not within specification, replace distributor.

***PICK-UP COIL ADJUSTMENT***

| Application | In. (mm) |
|---|---|
| Camry, Celica (Non-Turbo), Corolla (4A-FE), Cressida, Land Cruiser & Supra (Non-Turbo) | [1] At least .008 (.20) |
| Celica (Turbo), Corolla (4A-GE), MR2, Pickup, Previa, Tercel & 4Runner | [1] .008-.016 (.20-.40) |

[1] – Replace distributor if not within specification.

# IGNITION CHECKS (SUPRA TURBO)

## DIAGNOSTIC CODES

***NOTE: ECU is programmed to detect ignition problems. Checking for trouble codes can speed up diagnosis. If ECU detects a problem, a diagnostic code will be set in memory. For information on system self-diagnostic capabilities and how to retrieve codes, see SELF-DIAGNOSTICS article.***

**Code 12 (No RPM Signal)** – ECU will store Code 12 in memory if it does not receive signal from either NE pick-up coil (RPM) or "G" pick-up coil (crank position) terminal within 2 seconds of engine cranking.

**Code 13 (No RPM Signal)** – ECU will store Code 13 in memory if it does not receive signal from NE pick-up coil (RPM) terminal when engine speed is above 1000 RPM.

**Code 14 (Ignition Signal Problem)** – ECU will store Code 14 in memory if it does not receive IGF (ignition detection) signal 3 times in succession.

***NOTE: A loss of IGT, IGDA or IGDB signal will cause a no-start condition.***

## SPARK TEST

**1)** Remove duct between air cleaner and intake plenum air connector. Disconnect cruise control, accelerator and throttle cables (automatic transmission only). Label and remove 6 hoses from idle speed control pipe.

**2)** Remove 2 bolts and idle speed control pipe from intake plenum air connector. Remove oxygen sensor wire from clamps. Disconnect hose from PCV pipe. Remove PCV pipe from cylinder head covers and throttle body.

**3)** Disconnect hose from intake plenum air connector. Remove 2 bolts, loosen clamps and remove intake plenum air connector. Remove oil filler cap. Remove 5 nuts from ignition coil pack cover labeled TOYOTA TURBO, and lift off cover.

**4)** Disconnect No. 1 and No. 2 wires, and clamp away from ignition coil. Move ignition coil pack with bracket aside, and remove all spark plug wires from spark plugs. Remove spark plugs.

***CAUTION: Ignition coil primary or ignitor circuit damage can result if each spark plug is not securely grounded.***

**5)** Install oil filter cap. Install spark plug wires onto original 6 spark plugs. Ground each spark plug securely. Disconnect solenoid resistor block and cold start injector connector.

**6)** Cold start injector is on bottom of air intake chamber. Solenoid resistor block is on top of right shock tower (4-wire connector). Crank engine and check for consistent Blue spark across plug gaps.

# 1991 ENGINE PERFORMANCE
## Basic Diagnostic Procedures (Cont.)

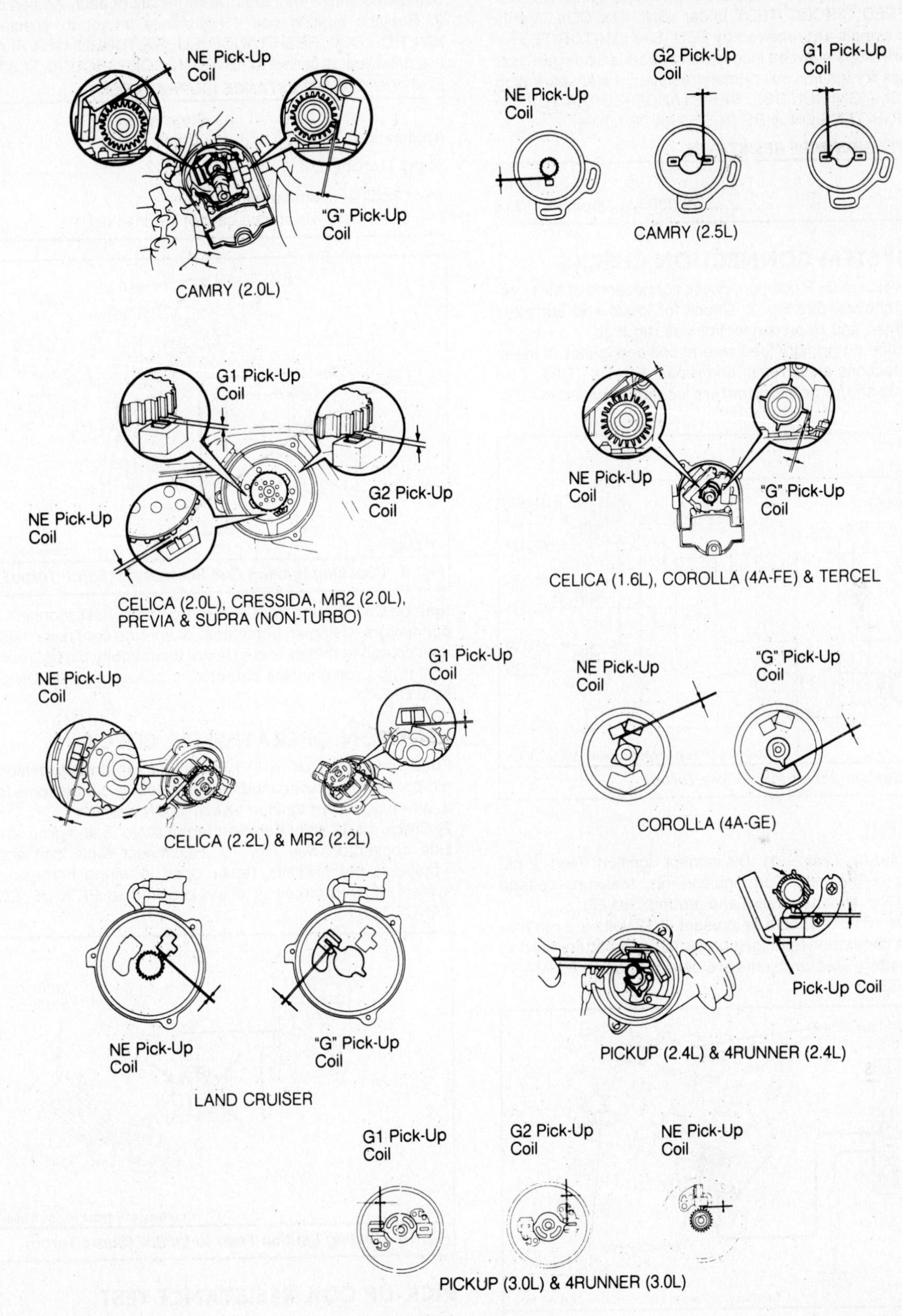


118569 118570 118573 118571 90F18387 118572 118574 118575 118576

Courtesy of Toyota Motor Sales, U.S.A., Inc.

***Fig. 6: Checking Pick-Up Coil Air Gap (Except Supra Turbo)***

# 1991 ENGINE PERFORMANCE
# Basic Diagnostic Procedures (Cont.)

**7)** If all spark plugs do not fire, verify camshaft sensor moves when engine is cranked. Check ignition feed to coil pack and ignitor circuits. See IGNITION FEED CIRCUIT TEST under IGNITION COIL. Verify camshaft sensor signals are received by ECU. See IGNITOR TEST.

**8)** If one or 2 spark plugs show an inconsistent spark across gap, test particular coil pack for ignition coil primary resistance and spark plug wire resistance. See IGNITION COIL RESISTANCE (SUPRA TURBO) and IGNITION HIGH-TENSION WIRE RESISTANCE tables.

***IGNITION HIGH-TENSION WIRE RESISTANCE***

| Application | Ohms |
|---|---|
| Supra (Turbo) | 25,000 Maximum Per Wire |

## IGNITION SYSTEM CONNECTION CHECKS

**1)** With ignition switch in OFF position, check connections of all 3 ignition coil primary circuits. *See Fig. 7.* Check for loose and corroded connections. Tighten and clean connections as required.

**2)** Check connection on primary feed wire to coil and ignitor. If loose or corroded connections exist, repair and repeat SPARK TEST. If no spark output exists and/or no problems are located, proceed to IGNITION COIL.

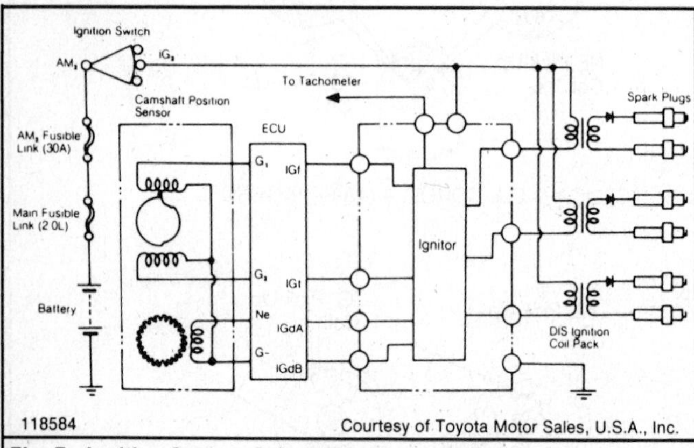


***Fig. 7: Ignition System Schematic (Supra Turbo)***

## IGNITION COIL

**Ignition Feed Circuit Test – 1)** Disconnect ignition feed 2-pin connectors from coil packs. Turn ignition on. Measure voltage between terminal No. 1 (battery feed) and ground. *See Fig. 8.*

**2)** With ignition on, 12 volts should be present. If 12 volts are not present, repair open circuit between ignition switch and battery feed to coil pack. If no battery feed problems are detected, go to PRIMARY COIL RESISTANCE.

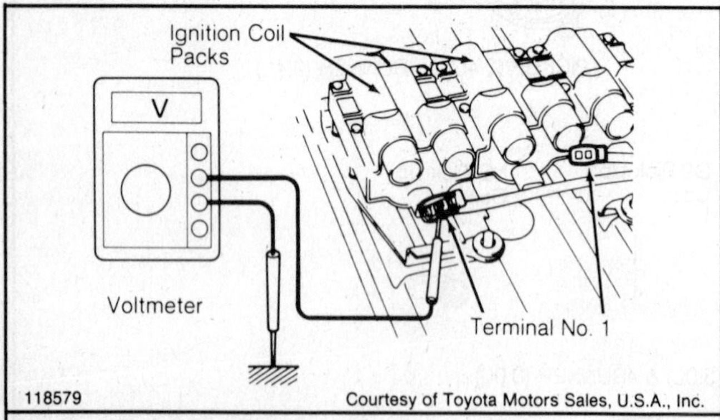


***Fig. 8: Checking Ignition Feed Circuit at Coil Packs (Supra Turbo)***

**Primary Coil Resistance –** Using an ohmmeter, measure resistance between positive and negative terminals of each ignition coil. *See Fig. 9.* Replace ignition coil if resistance is not to specification. See IGNITION COIL RESISTANCE (SUPRA TURBO) table. If no problems are detected, proceed to IGNITION COIL GROUND TEST.

***IGNITION COIL RESISTANCE (SUPRA TURBO)***

| Application | Primary Ohms | Secondary Ohms |
|---|---|---|
| Supra (Turbo) | [1] .34-.42 | [2] |

[1] – Check at room temperature.
[2] – Secondary resistance cannot be checked.

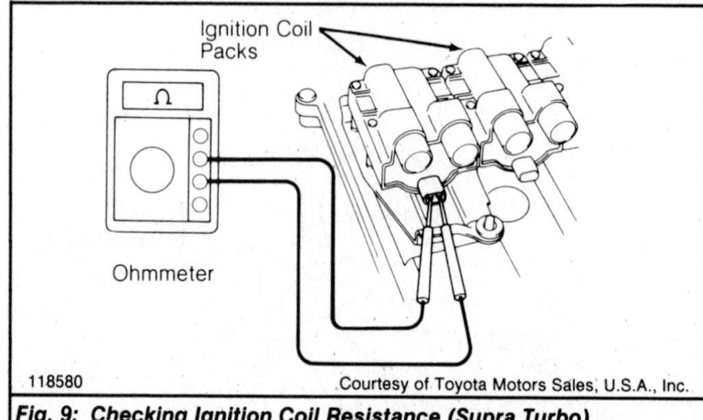


***Fig. 9: Checking Ignition Coil Resistance (Supra Turbo)***

**Ignition Coil Ground Test –** Turn ignition off. Disconnect ignition coil connectors. Using an ohmmeter, ensure no continuity exists between ignition coil terminals and ground. If continuity exists, replace ignition coil. If no problems are detected, proceed to IGNITION OPERATIONAL CHECK.

## IGNITION OPERATIONAL CHECK

**Feed To Ignitor Test – 1)** Turn ignition off. Unplug ignition module 6-pin connector. Ignition module 6-pin module connector is located next to alternator. Turn ignition switch to ON position.

**2)** Check for 12 volts between terminal No. 3 and ground on harness side connector. *See Fig. 10.* Reconnect 6-pin connector. If feed voltage is not present, repair open in wiring harness, and retest system. If feed circuit is okay, proceed to PICK-UP COIL RESISTANCE TEST.

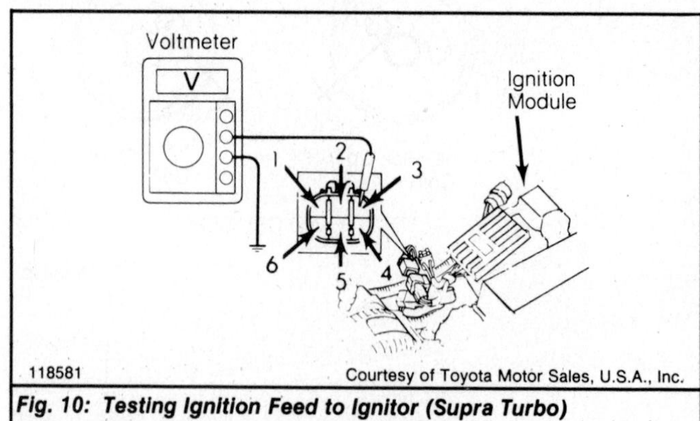


***Fig. 10: Testing Ignition Feed to Ignitor (Supra Turbo)***

## PICK-UP COIL RESISTANCE TEST

**1)** Disconnect negative battery cable. Disconnect camshaft position sensor 4-pin connector. Measure resistance from terminal G(-) to terminals G1, G2 and NE. *See Fig. 11.*

**2)** Resistance of each pick-up coil should be 185-265 ohms. If resistance is not as specified, replace camshaft position sensor assembly. If pick-up coil resistance is within specification, proceed to PICK-UP COIL AIR GAP CHECK.

# 1991 ENGINE PERFORMANCE
# Basic Diagnostic Procedures (Cont.)

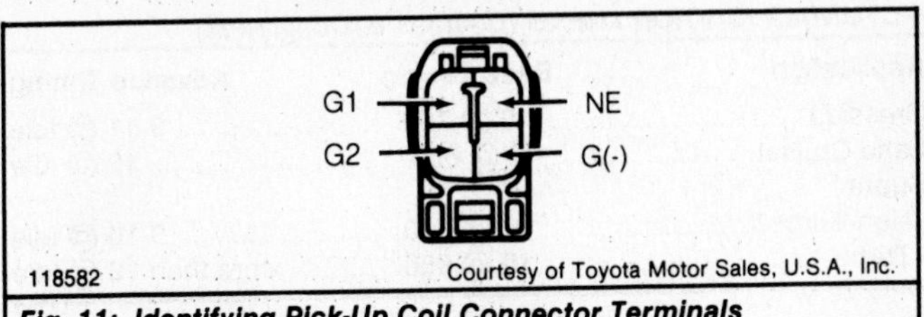


***Fig. 11: Identifying Pick-Up Coil Connector Terminals (Supra Turbo)***

## PICK-UP COIL AIR GAP CHECK

**1)** Using flat, non-magnetic feeler gauge, check air gap between signal rotor and pick-up coil projection. *See Fig. 12.* Air gap should be .008-.016" (.20-.40 mm).
**2)** If air gap is incorrect, replace camshaft position sensor assembly. If air gap clearance is within specification, proceed to IGNITOR TEST.

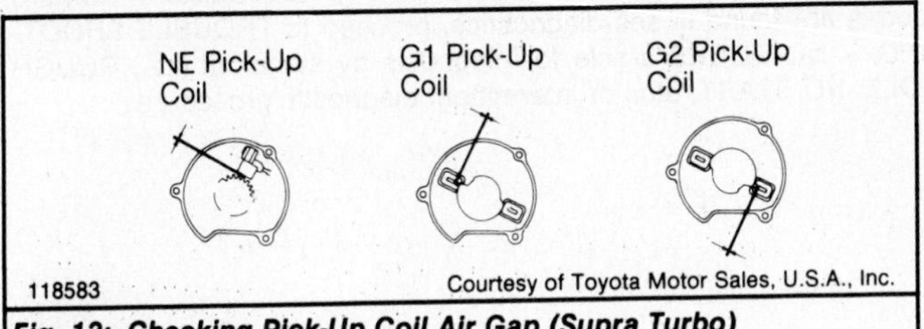


***Fig. 12: Checking Pick-Up Coil Air Gap (Supra Turbo)***

## IGNITOR TEST

**Ignitor Power Transistor Check – 1)** Turn ignition off. Unplug ignition module 4-pin connector. Disconnect each ignition coil pack 2-pin connector. Turn ignition on. Connect ohmmeter between terminal No. 2 of third ignition coil and ground. *See Fig. 13.*
**2)** Using a 3-volt dry cell battery, apply 3 volts to terminal No. 2 of 4-pin connector. With 3 volts applied, ensure ohmmeter indicates momentary continuity. Connect ohmmeter between terminal No. 2 of first ignition coil and ground.
**3)** Apply 3 volts to terminal No. 4 of 4-pin connector. With 3 volts still applied to terminal No. 4, also apply 3 volts to terminal No. 2. Ensure ohmmeter indicates momentary continuity. *See Fig. 13.* Connect ohmmeter between terminal No. 2 of second ignition coil and ground.
**4)** Apply 3 volts to terminal No. 3 of 4-pin connector. With 3 volts still applied to terminal No. 3, also apply 3 volts to terminal No. 2. Ensure ohmmeter indicates momentary continuity. *See Fig. 13.* Replace ignitor if tests are not as specified.

## IDLE SPEED & IGNITION TIMING

Ensure idle speed and ignition timing are set to specification. For adjustment procedures, see ON-VEHICLE ADJUSTMENTS article.

### IDLE SPEED

***4-CYLINDER IDLE SPEED SPECIFICATIONS***

| Application | RPM |
|---|---|
| Camry | [1] 650 |
| Celica | |
| 1.6L | 800 |
| 2.0L | 750-850 |
| 2.2L | [1] 650 |
| Corolla | |
| 4A-FE | |
| 2WD | |
| Federal | 700 |
| California | 800 |
| 4WD | 800 |
| 4A-GE | 800 |
| MR2 | |
| 2.0L | 750-850 |
| 2.2L | 650 |
| Pickup | |
| 4WD & A/T | 850 |
| All Others | 750 |
| 4Runner | 750 |
| Previa | 750 |
| Tercel | 800 |

[1] – Idle speed with jumper wire removed is 650-750 RPM.

***6-CYLINDER IDLE SPEED SPECIFICATIONS***

| Application | RPM |
|---|---|
| Cressida | 700 |
| Land Cruiser | 650 |
| Supra | |
| Non-Turbo | 700 |
| Turbo | 650 |

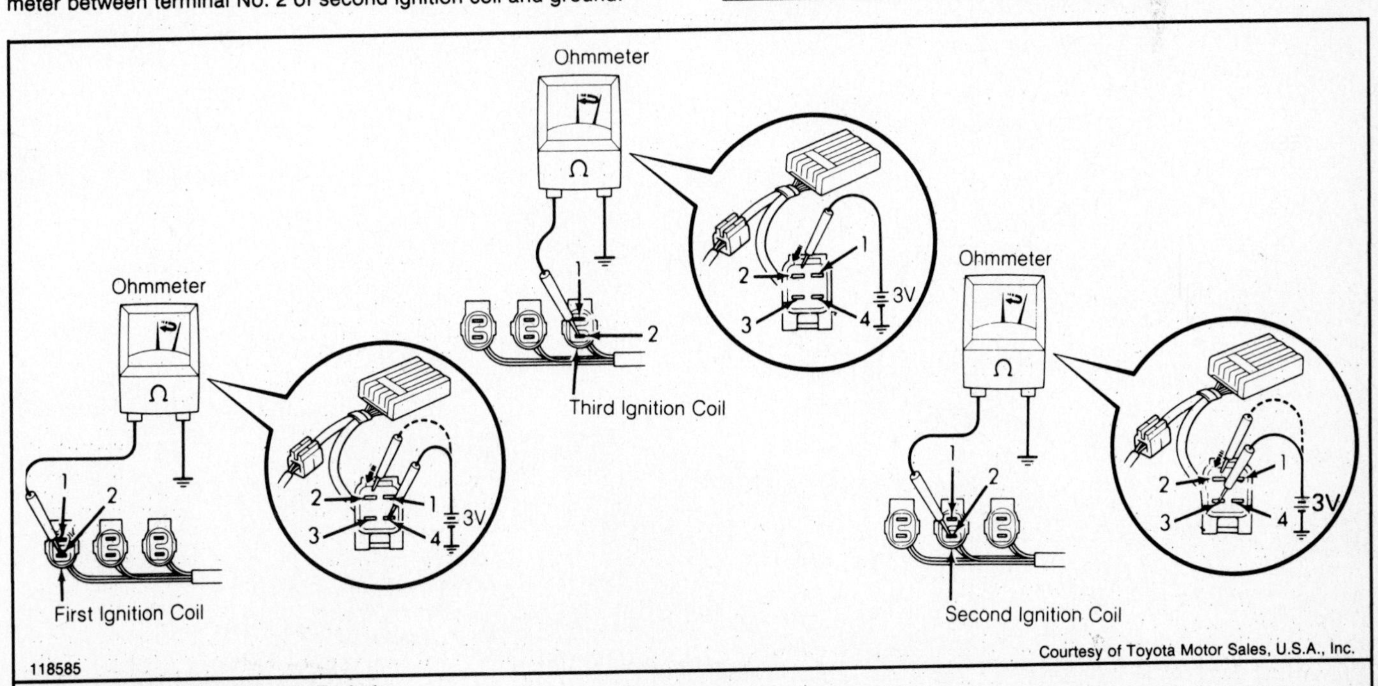


***Fig. 13: Testing Ignitor (Supra Turbo)***

# 1991 ENGINE PERFORMANCE
# Basic Diagnostic Procedures (Cont.)

***V6 IDLE SPEED SPECIFICATIONS***

| Application | RPM |
|---|---|
| Camry | 700 |
| Pickup & 4Runner | 800 |

## IGNITION TIMING

***4-CYLINDER IGNITION TIMING – Degrees BTDC @ RPM***

| Application | Base Timing [1] | Advance Timing |
|---|---|---|
| Camry & Celica | | |
| 1.6L | 10 @ Idle | 5-15 @ Idle |
| 2.0L | 10 @ 750 | 14-19 @ Idle |
| 2.2L | 10 @ 700 | 13-22 @ Idle |
| Corolla | | |
| 4A-FE | 10 @ 800 | 5-15 @ Idle |
| 4A-GE | 10 @ 800 | 16 @ Idle |
| MR2 | | |
| 2.0L | 10 @ Idle | 12-21 @ Idle |
| 2.2L | 10 @ Idle | 13-22 @ Idle |
| Pickup & 4Runner | 5 @ Idle | 10-14 @ Idle |
| Previa | 5 @ Idle | 12 @ Idle |
| Tercel | 10 @ Idle | 7-17 @ Idle |

[1] – With check connector terminals TE1 and E1 jumpered.

***6-CYLINDER IGNITION TIMING (Degrees BTDC @ RPM)***

| Application | Base Timing | Advance Timing |
|---|---|---|
| Cressida | 10 @ 700 | 9-11 @ Idle |
| Land Cruiser | 7 @ 650 | 12 @ Idle |
| Supra | | |
| Non-Turbo | 10 @ 700 | 9-10 @ Idle |
| Turbo | 10 @ 650 | More than 12 @ Idle |

***V6 IGNITION TIMING (Degrees BTDC @ RPM)***

| Application | Base Timing | Advance Timing |
|---|---|---|
| Camry | 10 @ 700 | 13-27 @ Idle |
| Pickup & 4Runner | 10 @ 800 | 8 @ Idle |

## SUMMARY

If no faults were found while performing BASIC DIAGNOSTIC PROCEDURES, proceed to SELF-DIAGNOSTICS article. If no hard codes are found in self-diagnostics, proceed to TROUBLE SHOOTING – NO CODES article for diagnosis by symptom (i.e., ROUGH IDLE, NO START, etc.) or intermittent diagnostic procedures.

# 1991 ENGINE PERFORMANCE
# Self-Diagnostics

## Camry, Celica, Corolla, Cressida, Land Cruiser, MR2, Pickup, Previa, Supra, Tercel, 4Runner

## INTRODUCTION

If no faults were found while performing BASIC DIAGNOSTIC PROCEDURES, proceed with self-diagnostics. If no fault codes or only pass codes are present after entering self-diagnostics, proceed to TROUBLE SHOOTING – NO CODES article for diagnosis by symptom (i.e., ROUGH IDLE, NO START, etc.).

## SELF-DIAGNOSTIC SYSTEM

**Hard Failures** – Hard failures cause malfunction light to illuminate and remain on until problem is repaired. If light comes on and remains on (light may flash) during vehicle operation, cause of malfunction must be determined using diagnostic (code) charts. If a sensor fails, control unit will use a substitute value in its calculations to continue engine operation. In this condition, commonly known as limp-in mode, the vehicle runs but driveability will not be optimum.

**Intermittent Failures** – Intermittent failures may cause CHECK ENGINE light to flicker or illuminate and go out after the intermittent fault goes away. However, the corresponding trouble code will be retained in ECU memory. If related fault does not reoccur within a certain time frame, related trouble code will be erased from ECU memory. Intermittent failures may be caused by a sensor, connector or wiring related problems. See INTERMITTENTS in TROUBLE SHOOTING – NO CODES article.

### RETRIEVING CODES

**All Except Cressida – 1)** Before retrieving codes, verify CHECK ENGINE light comes on with ignition on and engine off. The CHECK ENGINE light should go off when engine is started. If CHECK ENGINE light does not come on, see appropriate DIAGNOSTIC CIRCUIT CHECK under CODE CHARTS. If light remains on, system has detected a malfunction or abnormality.

**2)** Ensure battery voltage is greater than 11 volts and charging system is okay. Engine should be at normal operating temperature.

**3)** Apply parking brake. Shift transaxle to Neutral (M/T) or Park (A/T). Turn A/C and all accessories off. Close throttle valve.

**4)** Turn ignition on with engine off. Install jumper wire between terminals TE1 (or T) and E1 in engine check connector. *See Figs. 1 and 2.*

**5)** Count number of flashes from CHECK ENGINE light. If system is operating properly (with no codes), CHECK ENGINE light will flash continuously and evenly. *See Fig. 3.*

***NOTE: If CHECK ENGINE light will not flash diagnostic codes, see appropriate DIAGNOSTIC CIRCUIT CHECK under CODE CHARTS.***

**6)** If code exists, digits of each code will flash at 1/2-second intervals, with a 1 1/2-second pause between first and second digits. *See Fig. 3.*

**7)** If more than one code is stored, a 2 1/2-second pause will occur before next code is flashed. Once all codes are displayed, a 4 1/2-second pause will occur then code(s) will be repeated.

**8)** Codes are displayed from the smallest to largest code. After codes are retrieved, remove jumper wire to exit diagnostic mode.

***NOTE: Cressida has a normal and test mode for retrieving codes. To prevent damage to ECU, connect only specified terminals.***

**Cressida (Normal Mode) – 1)** Before retrieving codes, verify CHECK ENGINE light comes on with ignition on and engine off. CHECK ENGINE light should go off when engine is started. If CHECK ENGINE light does not come on, see CRESSIDA DIAGNOSTIC CIRCUIT CHECK under CODE CHARTS. If light remains on, system has detected a malfunction or abnormality.

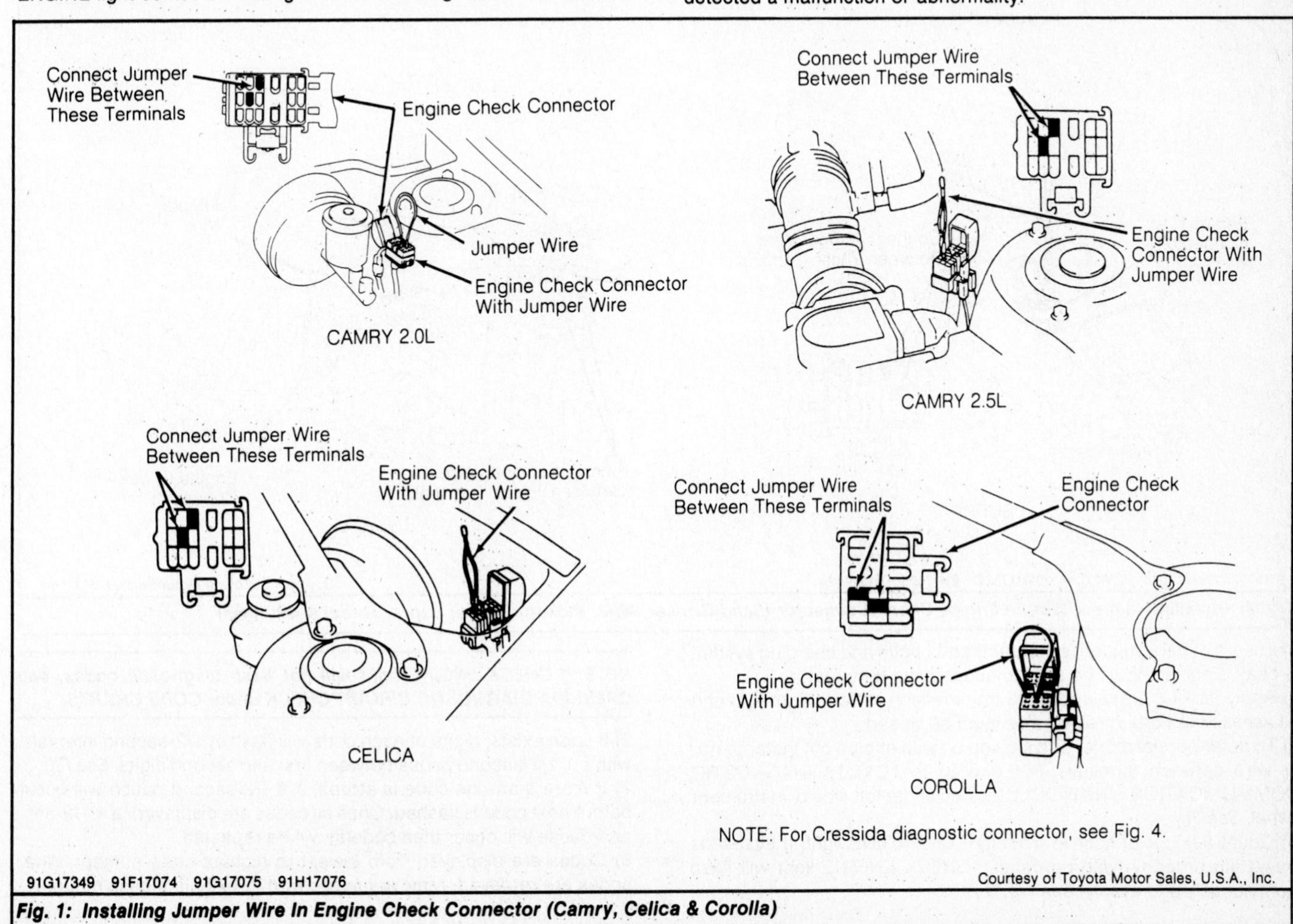


***Fig. 1: Installing Jumper Wire In Engine Check Connector (Camry, Celica & Corolla)***

# 1991 ENGINE PERFORMANCE
## Self-Diagnostics (Cont.)

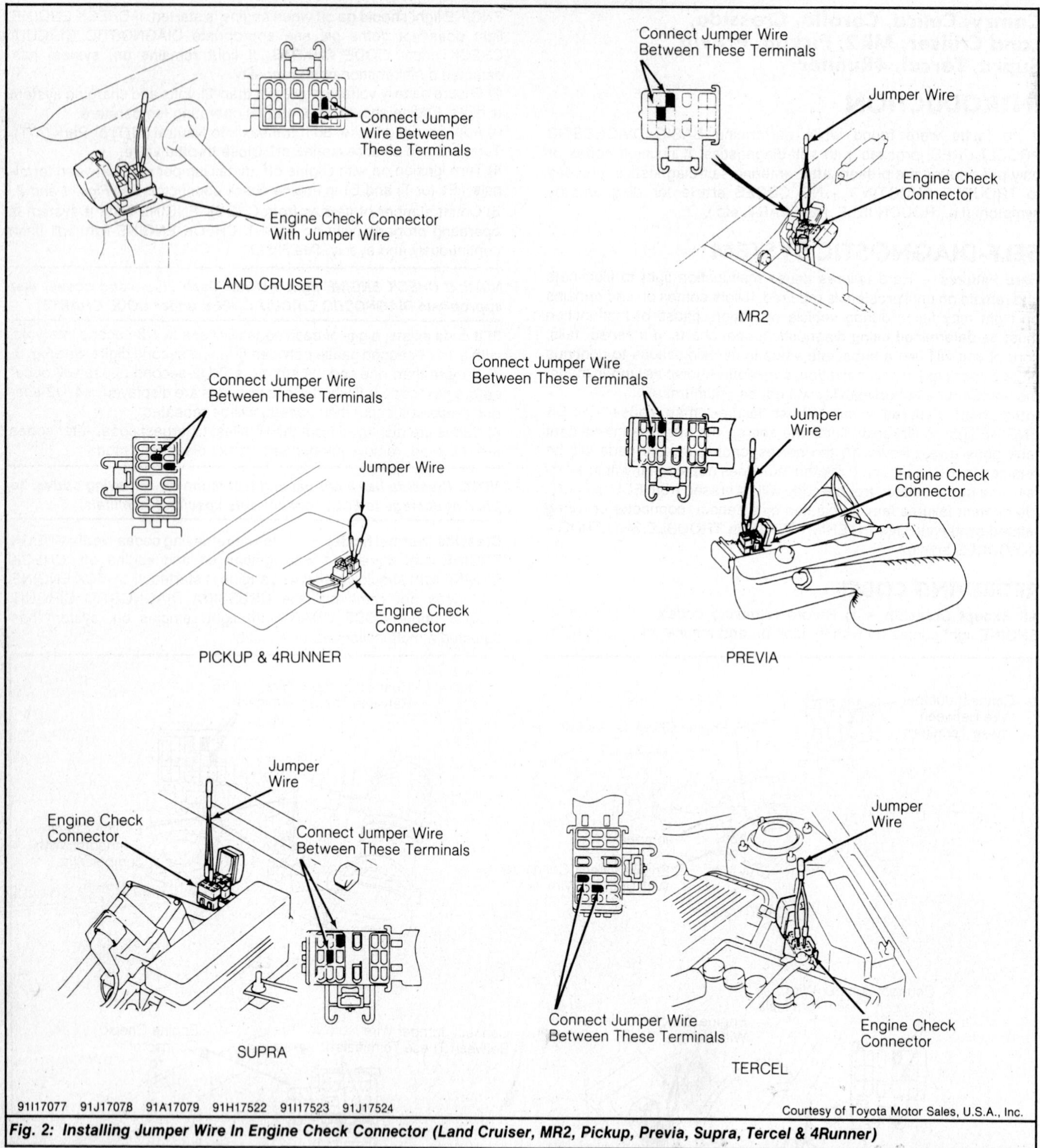


*Fig. 2: Installing Jumper Wire In Engine Check Connector (Land Cruiser, MR2, Pickup, Previa, Supra, Tercel & 4Runner)*

**2)** Ensure battery voltage is greater than 11 volts and charging system is okay. Engine should be at normal operating temperature.

**3)** Apply parking brake and place transmission in Park. Turn A/C and all accessories off. Throttle valve must be closed.

**4)** To enter normal mode, turn ignition on with engine off. Install jumper wire between terminals TE1 and E1 in TOYOTA DIAGNOSTIC COMMUNICATION LINK (TDCL), located under left side of instrument panel. *See Fig. 4*.

**5)** Count number of flashes from CHECK ENGINE light. If system is operating properly (with no codes), CHECK ENGINE light will flash continuously and evenly. *See Fig. 3*.

***NOTE: If CHECK ENGINE light will not flash diagnostic codes, see CRESSIDA DIAGNOSTIC CIRCUIT CHECK under CODE CHARTS.***

**6)** If code exists, digits of each code will flash at 1/2-second intervals, with a 1 1/2-second pause between first and second digits. *See Fig. 3*.

**7)** If more than one code is stored, a 2 1/2-second pause will occur before next code is flashed. Once all codes are displayed, a 4 1/2-second pause will occur then code(s) will be repeated.

**8)** Codes are displayed from lowest to highest code number. After codes are retrieved, remove jumper wire to exit diagnostic mode.

# 1991 ENGINE PERFORMANCE
# Self-Diagnostics (Cont.)

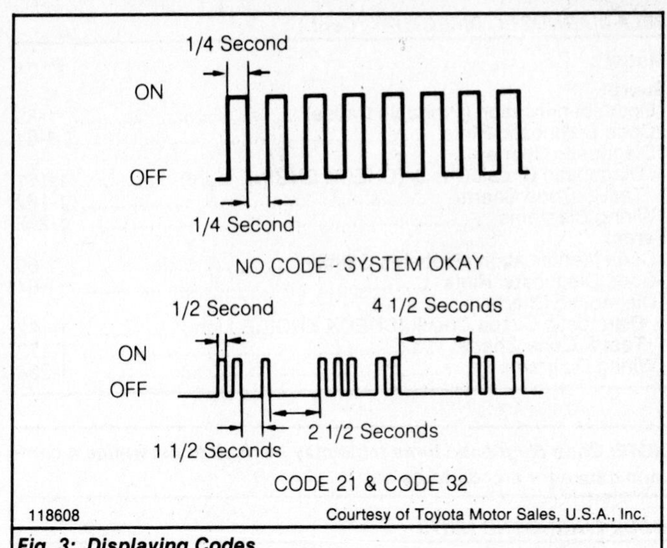


*Fig. 3: Displaying Codes*

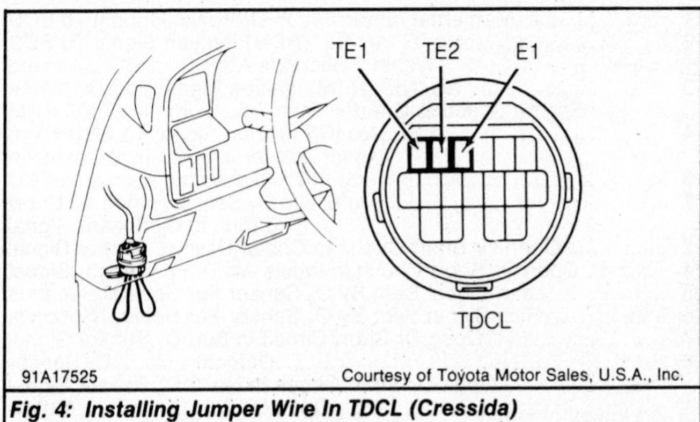


*Fig. 4: Installing Jumper Wire In TDCL (Cressida)*

***NOTE: Test mode can be used to check for codes when operating vehicle. This will simulate conditions in which codes were set.***

**Cressida (Test Mode) – 1)** Before retrieving codes, verify CHECK ENGINE light comes on with ignition on and engine off. CHECK ENGINE light should go off when engine is started. If CHECK ENGINE light does not come on, see CRESSIDA DIAGNOSTIC CIRCUIT CHECK under CODE CHARTS. If light remains on, system has detected a malfunction or abnormality.

**2)** Ensure battery voltage is greater than 11 volts and charging system is okay. Engine should be at normal operating temperature.

**3)** Apply parking brake and place transmission in Park. Turn air conditioner and all accessories off. Throttle valve must be closed.

**4)** To enter test mode, install jumper wire between terminals TE2 and E1 terminals in TOYOTA DIAGNOSTIC COMMUNICATION LINK (TDCL), located under left side of instrument panel. *See Fig. 4*.

**5)** Turn ignition on. Test mode is operational if CHECK ENGINE light flashes with key on and engine off.

**6)** Start engine. Drive vehicle at a speed greater than 10 MPH. The ECU will set a Code 42 and 43 if vehicle is not driven. Try to simulate the driveability complaint. Stop vehicle, but DO NOT turn engine off.

**7)** Using jumper wire, connect terminals TE1 and E1 of TDCL. *See Fig. 4*. Count number of flashes from CHECK ENGINE light. If system is operating properly (with no codes), CHECK ENGINE light will flash continuously and evenly. *See Fig. 3*.

**8)** If codes exist, digits of each code will flash at 1/2-second intervals, with a 1 1/2-second pause between first and second digits. *See Fig. 3*.

**9)** If more than one code is stored, a 2 1/2-second pause will occur before next code is flashed. Once all codes are displayed, a 4 1/2-second pause will occur then code(s) will be repeated.

**10)** Codes are displayed from the smallest to largest code. After codes are retrieved, remove jumper wire to exit diagnostic mode.

## NOTES ON CODES

**1)** No other code will appear with Code 11.

**2)** On all models except Land Cruiser, MR2 and Previa, when Codes 21 (Camry V6 and Tercel), 25, 26, 27 and 71 initially happen, they will be temporarily stored in ECU memory, but CHECK ENGINE light will not come on. The second time code is detected, CHECK ENGINE light will then come on. This is referred to as the 2 trip detection logic.

**3)** On all models except Cressida, after malfunction is repaired, CHECK ENGINE light will go off, but codes (except 51 and 53) will remain in ECU memory until code is cleared.

**4)** On Cressida models, when in normal mode, once malfunction is repaired, CHECK ENGINE light will go off, but code will remain in ECU memory except for Codes 16, 43, 51 and 53 until codes are cleared.

**5)** When in test mode, codes will remain in ECU memory as long as ignition remains on, even if malfunction is repaired (except for codes 43, 51 and 53). Once ignition is turned off, codes will be erased from ECU memory. During test mode, if vehicle is not driven at a speed greater than 10 MPH, ECU will set a Code 42 and 43.

## CLEARING CODES

**1)** After repairs are performed, clear ECU memory of all stored codes. To clear memory, turn ignition off. Remove fuse from main fuse block below left side of instrument panel (Corolla), near center of instrument panel (Previa) or in engine compartment fuse/relay box (all others) for approximately 30 seconds or more. See CLEARING CODES table for appropriate fuse.

**2)** Depending on ambient temperature, fuse may need to be removed for more than 30 seconds. Replace fuse and exit diagnostic mode. Codes can also be cleared by disconnecting vehicle battery. However, other memory functions (clock, radio, etc.) will need to be reset.

***CLEARING CODES***

| Application | Fuse (Amperage) |
|---|---|
| Corolla | STOP (15) |
| Cressida | EFI (20) |
| All Others | EFI (15) |

## ECU LOCATION

***ECU LOCATION***

| Model | Location |
|---|---|
| Camry, Celica, Corolla & Tercel | Bottom Center Of Dash, In Front Of Console |
| Cressida | Above Glove Box |
| Land Cruiser | Above Glove Box |
| MR2 | Center Of Panel Behind Engine, Toward Rear Of Vehicle |
| Pickup & 4Runner | Behind Right Kick Panel |
| Previa | Below Driver's Seat |
| Supra | Above Glove Box |

## SUMMARY

If no hard fault codes (or only pass codes) are present, driveability symptoms exist or intermittent codes exist, proceed to TROUBLE SHOOTING – NO CODES article for diagnosis by symptom (i.e., ROUGH IDLE, NO START, etc.) or intermittent diagnostic procedures.

# 1991 ENGINE PERFORMANCE
# Self-Diagnostics (Cont.)

## SELF-DIAGNOSTICS DIRECTORY

*SELF-DIAGNOSTIC DIRECTORY*



*SELF-DIAGNOSTIC DIRECTORY (Cont.)*



***NOTE: Code diagnostic hints table may be used to determine a common cause for a code to be set.***

*CODE DIAGNOSTIC HINTS*

| Code | Diagnostic Hints |
|---|---|
| 11 | Momentary Interruption Of Power Supply To ECU |
| 12 | No "G" or "NE" (RPM) Ignition Signal To ECU Within 2 Seconds After Engine Is Cranked |
| 13 | No "NE" (RPM) Ignition Signal To ECU When Engine Speed Is Greater Than Approximately 1000 RPM |
| 14 | No IGF Ignition Signal To ECU From Ignitor Several Times In Succession |
| 16 | Fault In Transmission/Transaxle ECU |
| 21 | Defective $O_2$ Sensor, Open Or Short Circuit In $O_2$ Sensor Signal |
| 22 | Open Or Short Circuit In Coolant Temp. Sensor Signal |
| 24 | Open Or Short Circuit In Intake Air Temp. Sensor Signal |
| 25 | Lean Signal Sent By $O_2$ Sensor For Several Seconds |
| 26 | Rich Signal Sent By $O_2$ Sensor For Several Seconds |
| 27 | Open Or Short Circuit In Sub-$O_2$ Sensor Signal |
| 28 | Defective No. 2 $O_2$ Sensor Open Or Short Circuit In No. 2 $O_2$ Sensor Signal |
| 31 | Open Or Short Circuit In Airflow Meter Or Vacuum Sensor Signal |
| 32 | Open Or Short Circuit Between Airflow Meter Terminals |
| 34 | Turbocharger Pressure Is Abnormal |
| 35 | Open Or Short Circuit In Turbocharger Pressure Sensor Or High Altitude Compensator Signal |
| 41 | Open Or Short Circuit In Throttle Position Sensor Signal |
| 42 | No SPD Signal From Vehicle Speed Sensor For Several Seconds With Engine Speed Approximately 2500-5500 RPM |
| 43 | No STA Signal To ECU Until Engine Reaches 800 RPM With Vehicle Not Moving |
| 51 | [1] Problem In One Of 3 Circuits Monitored By ECU |
| 52 | Open Or Short Circuit In Knock Sensor Signal |
| 53 | Knock Control In ECU Is Faulty |
| 71 | EGR Gas Below Predetermined Level During EGR Control |

[1] – The throttle position sensor, neutral safety switch and A/C Signal circuits are monitored.

# 1991 ENGINE PERFORMANCE
# Self-Diagnostics (Cont.)

## CODE CHARTS

*CAMRY CODE IDENTIFICATION*

| Code No. | System Affected | Probable Cause |
|---|---|---|
| 12 & 13 | RPM Signal | Distributor Or Circuit, Starter Circuit, ECU |
| 14 | Ignition Signal | Ignitor Or Circuit To ECU, ECU |
| 16 | Electronic Controlled Transaxle Signal | Transaxle ECU Or Wiring Circuit |
| 21 | Oxygen Sensor Signal | Oxygen Sensor Or Circuit, [1] Oxygen Sensor Heater, ECU |
| 22 | Coolant Temp. Sensor Signal | Coolant Temp. Sensor Or Circuit, ECU |
| 24 [2] | Intake Air Temperature Sensor Signal | Intake Air Temperature Sensor Or Circuit, ECU |
| 25 | Lean Air/Fuel Mixture | Injector Or Circuit, Oxygen Sensor Or Circuit, Fuel Pressure, Ignition System, Coolant Temp. Sensor, Airflow Meter, ECU |
| 26 | Rich Air/Fuel Mixture | Airflow Meter, ECU, Injector Or Circuit, Oxygen Sensor Or Circuit, Fuel Pressure, Cold Start Injector Or Circuit, Coolant Temp. Sensor |
| 27 [3] | Sub-Oxygen Sensor Signal | Sub-Oxygen Sensor Or Circuit, ECU |
| 31 & 32 | Airflow Meter Signal | Airflow Meter Or Circuit, ECU |
| 41 [2] | Throttle Position Sensor Signal | Throttle Position Sensor Or Circuit, ECU |
| 42 [4] | Vehicle Speed Sensor Signal | Vehicle Speed Sensor Or Circuit, ECU |
| 43 [4] | Starter Signal | Starter Signal Circuit, Ignition Switch Or Circuit, ECU |
| 51 [4] | Switch Condition Signal | A/C Switch Circuit, ECU, Neutral/Start Switch Or Circuit, TPS Or Circuit |
| 52 [1] | Knock Sensor Signal | Knock Sensor Or Circuit, ECU |
| 53 [1] | Knock Sensor Control (ECU) | ECU |
| 71 [3] | EGR System Malfunction | EGR System, EGR Temp. Sensor Or Circuit, ECU, [1] EGR BVSV |

[1] – Used on V6 models only.
[2] – CHECK ENGINE light comes on code sets on (Calif. only).
[3] – Used on Calif. only.
[4] – CHECK ENGINE light will not come on when code is set.

*CELICA CODE IDENTIFICATION*

| Code No. | System Affected | Probable Cause |
|---|---|---|
| 12 & 13 | RPM Signal | Distributor Or Circuit, Starter Circuit, ECU |
| 14 | Ignition Signal | Ignitor Or Circuit To ECU, ECU |
| 21 | Oxygen Sensor Signal | Oxygen Sensor Or Circuit, [1] Oxygen Sensor Heater, ECU |
| 22 | Coolant Temp. Sensor Signal | Coolant Temp. Sensor Or Circuit, ECU |
| 24 [2] | Intake Air Temp. Sensor Signal | Intake Air Temp. Sensor Or Circuit, ECU |
| 25 | Lean Air/Fuel Mixture | ECU, Injector Or Circuit, Oxygen Sensor Or Circuit, Fuel Pressure, Ignition System, Coolant Temp. Sensor, [3] Airflow Meter/Vacuum Sensor |
| 26 | Rich Air/Fuel Mixture | Fuel Pressure, [3] Airflow Meter/Vacuum Sensor, ECU, Injector Or Circuit, Oxygen Sensor Or Circuit, Cold Start Injector Or Circuit, Coolant Temp. Sensor |
| 27 [4] [5] | Sub-Oxygen Sensor Signal | Sub-Oxygen Sensor Or Circuit, ECU |
| 31 | [3] Airflow Meter/Vacuum Sensor Signal | Airflow Meter/Vacuum Sensor Or Circuit, ECU |
| 32 [6] | Airflow Meter Signal | Airflow Meter Or Circuit, ECU |
| 34 [6] | Turbocharger Pressure Sensor | Turbocharger Pressure Sensor Or Circuit, ECU |
| 35 [6] [7] | Turbocharger Pressure Sensor | Turbocharger Pressure Sensor Or Circuit, ECU |
| 41 [2] | Throttle Position Sensor Signal | Throttle Position Sensor Or Circuit, ECU |
| 42 [7] | Vehicle Speed Sensor Signal | Vehicle Speed Sensor Or Circuit, ECU |
| 43 [7] | Starter Signal | Starter Signal Circuit, Ignition Switch Or Circuit, Main Relay, ECU |
| 51 [7] | Switch Condition Signal | A/C Switch Circuit, ECU, Neutral/Start Switch Or Circuit, TPS Or Circuit |
| 52 [6] | Knock Sensor Signal | Knock Sensor Or Circuit, ECU |
| 53 [6] | Knock Sensor Control (ECU) | ECU |
| 71 [8] | EGR System Malfunction | EGR System, EGR Temp. Sensor Or Circuit, ECU, EGR VSV |

[1] – Used on 3S-GTE and 4A-FE only.
[2] – CHECK ENGINE light comes on when code sets (Calif. only).
[3] – Airflow meter used on 3S-GTE and vacuum sensor on all others.
[4] – Used on 5S-FE only.
[5] – Used on Calif. only.
[6] – Used on 3S-GTE only.
[7] – CHECK ENGINE light will not come on when code is set.
[8] – Used on 3S-GTE and Calif. only on 4A-FE and 5S-FE.

# 1991 ENGINE PERFORMANCE
## Self-Diagnostics (Cont.)

### *COROLLA CODE IDENTIFICATION*

| Code No. | System Affected | Probable Cause |
|---|---|---|
| 12 & 13 | RPM Signal | Distributor/Integrated Ignition Assembly Or Circuit, Starter Circuit, ECU |
| 14 | Ignition Signal | Ignitor Or Circuit To ECU, ECU |
| 21 | Oxygen Sensor Signal | Oxygen Sensor Or Circuit, [1] Oxygen Sensor Heater, ECU |
| 22 | Coolant Temp. Sensor Signal | Coolant Temp. Sensor Or Circuit, ECU |
| 24 [2] | Intake Air Temp. Sensor Signal | Intake Air Temp. Sensor Or Circuit, ECU |
| 25 | Lean Air/Fuel Mixture | ECU, Injector Or Circuit, Oxygen Sensor Or Circuit, Fuel Pressure, Ignition System, Coolant Temp. Sensor, [3] Airflow Meter/Vacuum Sensor |
| 26 | Rich Air/Fuel Mixture | Fuel Pressure, [3] Airflow Meter/Vacuum Sensor, ECU, Injector Or Circuit, Oxygen Sensor Or Circuit, Cold Start Injector Or Circuit, Coolant Temp. Sensor |
| 27 [4] | Sub-Oxygen Sensor Signal | Sub-Oxygen Sensor Or Circuit, ECU |
| 31 | [3] Airflow Meter/Vacuum Sensor Signal | Airflow Meter/Vacuum Sensor Or Circuit, ECU |
| 41 [2] | Throttle Position Sensor Signal | Throttle Position Sensor Or Circuit, ECU |
| 42 [5] | Vehicle Speed Sensor Signal | Vehicle Speed Sensor Or Circuit, ECU |
| 43 [5] | Starter Signal | Starter Signal Circuit, Ignition Switch Or Circuit, ECU |
| 51 [5] | Switch Condition Signal | A/C Switch Circuit, ECU, Neutral/Start Switch Or Circuit, TPS Or Circuit |
| 52 [1] | Knock Sensor Signal | Knock Sensor Or Circuit, ECU |
| 53 [1] | Knock Sensor Control (ECU) | ECU |
| 71 [6] | EGR System Malfunction | EGR System, EGR Temp. Sensor Or Circuit, ECU, EGR VSV |

[1] – Used on 4A-GE only.
[2] – CHECK ENGINE light comes on when code sets (Calif. only).
[3] – Airflow meter used on 4A-GE and vacuum sensor on 4A-FE.
[4] – Used on 4A-GE (Calif. only).
[5] – CHECK ENGINE light will not come on when code is set.
[6] – Used on Calif. only.

### *CRESSIDA CODE IDENTIFICATION*

| Code No. | System Affected | Probable Cause |
|---|---|---|
| 11 [1] | ECU Power Supply | Ignition Switch Or Circuit, Main Relay Or Circuit, ECU |
| 12 & 13 | RPM Signal | Distributor Or Circuit, Starter Circuit, ECU |
| 14 | Ignition Signal | Ignitor Or Circuit To ECU, ECU |
| 16 | Electronic Controlled Transaxle Signal | Transaxle ECU Or Wiring Circuit |
| 21 | Oxygen Sensor Signal | Oxygen Sensor Or Circuit, ECU |
| 22 | Coolant Temp. Sensor Signal | Coolant Temp. Sensor Or Circuit, ECU |
| 24 [2] | Intake Air Temp. Sensor Signal | Intake Air Temp. Sensor Or Circuit, ECU |
| 25 | Lean Air/Fuel Mixture | ECU, Injector Or Circuit, Oxygen Sensor Or Circuit, Fuel Pressure, Ignition System, Coolant Temp. Sensor, Airflow Meter |
| 26 | Rich Air/Fuel Mixture | Fuel Pressure, Airflow Meter, ECU, Injector Or Circuit, Oxygen Sensor Or Circuit, Cold Start Injector Or Circuit, Coolant Temp. Sensor |
| 27 [3] | Sub-Oxygen Sensor Signal | Sub-Oxygen Sensor Or Circuit, ECU |
| 31 & 32 | Airflow Meter Signal | Airflow Meter Or Circuit, ECU |
| 41 [2] | Throttle Position Sensor Signal | Throttle Position Sensor Or Circuit, ECU |
| 42 [1] | Vehicle Speed Sensor Signal | Vehicle Speed Sensor Or Circuit, ECU |
| 43 [1] | Starter Signal | Starter Signal Circuit, Ignition Switch Or Circuit, Main Relay Or Circuit, ECU |
| 51 [1] | Switch Condition Signal | A/C Switch Circuit, ECU, Neutral/Start Switch Or Circuit, TPS Or Circuit |
| 52 | Knock Sensor Signal | Knock Sensor Or Circuit, ECU |
| 53 | Knock Sensor Control (ECU) | ECU |
| 71 [3] | EGR System Malfunction | EGR System, EGR Temp. Sensor Or Circuit, ECU, EGR VSV |

[1] – CHECK ENGINE light will not come on when code is set.
[2] – CHECK ENGINE light comes on when code sets (Calif. only).
[3] – Used on Calif. only.

# 1991 ENGINE PERFORMANCE
# Self-Diagnostics (Cont.)

**LAND CRUISER CODE IDENTIFICATION**

| Code No. | System Affected | Probable Cause |
|---|---|---|
| 12 & 13 | RPM Signal | Distributor Or Circuit, Starter Circuit, ECU |
| 14 | Ignition Signal | Ignitor And Ignition Coil Or Circuit To ECU, ECU |
| 21 | [1] Oxygen Sensor Signal | Oxygen Sensor Or Circuit, Oxygen Sensor Heater, ECU |
| 22 | Coolant Temp. Sensor Signal | Coolant Temp. Sensor Or Circuit, ECU |
| 24 | Intake Air Temp. Sensor Signal | Intake Air Temp. Sensor Or Circuit, ECU |
| 25 | Lean Air/Fuel Mixture | ECU, Injector Or Circuit, Oxygen Sensor Or Circuit, Fuel Pressure, Ignition System, Coolant Temp. Sensor, Airflow Meter |
| 26 | Rich Air/Fuel Mixture | Fuel Pressure, Airflow Meter, ECU, Injector Or Circuit, Oxygen Sensor Or Circuit, Cold Start Injector Or Circuit, Coolant Temp. Sensor |
| 28 | [2] Oxygen Sensor Signal | Oxygen Sensor Or Circuit, Oxygen Sensor Heater, ECU |
| 31 & 32 | Airflow Meter Signal | Airflow Meter Or Circuit, ECU |
| 35 | High Altitude Compensator Signal | ECU |
| 41 | Throttle Position Sensor Signal | Throttle Position Sensor Or Circuit, ECU |
| 42 | Vehicle Speed Sensor Signal | Vehicle Speed Sensor Or Circuit, ECU |
| 43 | Starter Signal | Starter Signal Circuit, Ignition Switch Or Circuit, ECU |
| 51 | Switch Condition Signal | A/C Switch Circuit, ECU, Neutral/Start Switch Or Circuit, TPS Or Circuit |
| 71 [3] | EGR System Malfunction | EGR System, EGR Temp. Sensor Or Circuit, ECU, EGR VSV |

[1] – This is the No. 1 oxygen sensor.
[2] – This is the No. 2 oxygen sensor.
[3] – Used on Calif. only.

**MR2 CODE IDENTIFICATION**

| Code No. | System Affected | Probable Cause |
|---|---|---|
| 12 & 13 | RPM Signal | Distributor Or Circuit, Starter Circuit, ECU |
| 14 | Ignition Signal | Distributor Or Circuit To ECU, ECU |
| 21 | Oxygen Sensor Signal | Oxygen Sensor Or Circuit, [1] Oxygen Sensor Heater, ECU |
| 22 | Coolant Temp. Sensor Signal | Coolant Temp. Sensor Or Circuit, ECU |
| 24 | Intake Air Temp. Sensor Signal | Intake Air Temp. Sensor Or Circuit, ECU |
| 25 | Lean Air/Fuel Mixture | ECU, Injector Or Circuit, Oxygen Sensor Or Circuit, Fuel Pressure, Ignition System, Coolant Temp. Sensor, [2] Airflow Meter/Vacuum Sensor |
| 26 | Rich Air/Fuel Mixture | Fuel Pressure, [2] Airflow Meter/Vacuum Sensor, ECU, Injector Or Circuit, Oxygen Sensor Or Circuit, Cold Start Injector Or Circuit, Coolant Temp. Sensor |
| 27 [3] | Sub-Oxygen Sensor Signal | Sub-Oxygen Sensor Or Circuit, ECU |
| 31 | [2] Airflow Meter/Vacuum Sensor Signal | Airflow Meter/Vacuum Sensor Or Circuit, ECU |
| 32 [1] | Airflow Meter Signal | Airflow Meter Or Circuit, ECU |
| 34 & 35 [1] | Turbocharger Pressure Sensor | Turbocharger Pressure Sensor Or Circuit, ECU |
| 41 | Throttle Position Sensor Signal | Throttle Position Sensor Or Circuit, ECU |
| 42 | Vehicle Speed Sensor Signal | Vehicle Speed Sensor Or Circuit, ECU |
| 43 | Starter Signal | Starter Signal Circuit, Ignition Switch Or Circuit, ECU |
| 51 | Switch Condition Signal | A/C Switch/Amplifier Circuit, ECU, Neutral/Start Switch Or Circuit, TPS Or Circuit |
| 52 [1] | Knock Sensor Signal | Knock Sensor Or Circuit, ECU |
| 53 [1] | Knock Sensor Control (ECU) | ECU |
| 71 [4] | EGR System Malfunction | EGR System, EGR Temp. Sensor Or Circuit, ECU, EGR VSV Or BVSV |

[1] – Used on 3S-GTE only.
[2] – Airflow meter used on 3S-GTE and vacuum sensor on 5S-FE.
[3] – Used on Calif. 5S-FE only.
[4] – Used on Calif. 3S-GTE and all 5S-FE.

# 1991 ENGINE PERFORMANCE
## Self-Diagnostics (Cont.)

### PICKUP & 4RUNNER CODE IDENTIFICATION

| Code No. | System Affected | Probable Cause |
|---|---|---|
| 12 & 13 | RPM Signal | Distributor Or Circuit, Starter Circuit, ECU |
| 14 | Ignition Signal | Ignitor Or Circuit To ECU, ECU |
| 21 | Oxygen Sensor Signal | Oxygen Sensor Or Circuit, Oxygen Sensor Heater, ECU |
| 22 | Coolant Temp. Sensor Signal | Coolant Temp. Sensor Or Circuit, ECU |
| 24 [1] | Intake Air Temperature Sensor Signal | Intake Air Temperature Sensor Or Circuit, ECU |
| 25 | Lean Air/Fuel Mixture | Injector Or Circuit, Oxygen Sensor Or Circuit, Fuel Pressure, Ignition System, Coolant Temp. Sensor, Airflow Meter, ECU |
| 26 | Rich Air/Fuel Mixture | Airflow Meter, ECU, Injector Or Circuit, Oxygen Sensor Or Circuit, Fuel Pressure, Cold Start Injector Or Circuit, Coolant Temp. Sensor |
| 27 [2] | Sub-Oxygen Sensor Signal | Sub-Oxygen Sensor Or Circuit, ECU |
| 31 | Airflow Meter Signal | Airflow Meter Or Circuit, ECU |
| 32 [3] | Airflow Meter Signal | Airflow Meter Or Circuit, ECU |
| 35 [4] | High Altitude Compensator | ECU |
| 41 [1] | Throttle Position Sensor Signal | Throttle Position Sensor Or Circuit, ECU |
| 42 [5] | Vehicle Speed Sensor Signal | Vehicle Speed Sensor Or Circuit, ECU |
| 43 [5] | Starter Signal | Starter Signal Circuit, Ignition Switch Or Circuit, Main Relay, ECU |
| 51 [5] | Switch Condition Signal | A/C Switch Circuit, ECU, Neutral/Start Switch Or Circuit, TPS Or Circuit |
| 52 | Knock Sensor Signal | Knock Sensor Or Circuit, ECU |
| 53 | Knock Sensor Control (ECU) | ECU |
| 71 [6] | EGR System Malfunction | EGR System, EGR Temp. Sensor Or Circuit, ECU, EGR VSV |

[1] – CHECK ENGINE light comes on when code is set on Calif. only.
[2] – Used on Pickup 22R-E (4-cylinder) Calif. only.
[3] – Used on V6 models only.
[4] – Used on V6 Pickup cab and chassis models only.
[5] – CHECK ENGINE light will not come on when code is set.
[6] – Used on Calif. only.

### PREVIA CODE IDENTIFICATION

| Code No. | System Affected | Probable Cause |
|---|---|---|
| 12 & 13 | RPM Signal | Distributor/Ignitor Or Circuit, Starter Circuit, ECU |
| 14 | Ignition Signal | Ignitor Or Circuit To ECU, ECU |
| 21 | Oxygen Sensor Signal | Oxygen Sensor Or Circuit, Oxygen Sensor Heater, ECU |
| 22 | Coolant Temp. Sensor Signal | Coolant Temp. Sensor Or Circuit, ECU |
| 24 | Intake Air Temperature Sensor Signal | Intake Air Temperature Sensor Or Circuit, ECU |
| 25 | Lean Air/Fuel Mixture | Injector Or Circuit, Oxygen Sensor Or Circuit, Fuel Pressure, Ignition System, Coolant Temp. Sensor, Airflow Meter, ECU |
| 26 | Rich Air/Fuel Mixture | Airflow Meter, ECU, Injector Or Circuit, Oxygen Sensor Or Circuit, Fuel Pressure, Cold Start Injector Or Circuit, Coolant Temp. Sensor |
| 27 | Sub-Oxygen Sensor Signal | Sub-Oxygen Sensor Or Circuit, ECU |
| 31 & 32 | Airflow Meter Signal | Airflow Meter Or Circuit, ECU |
| 41 | Throttle Position Sensor Signal | Throttle Position Sensor Or Circuit, ECU |
| 42 | Vehicle Speed Sensor Signal | Vehicle Speed Sensor Or Circuit, ECU |
| 43 | Starter Signal | Starter Signal Circuit, Ignition Switch Or Circuit, ECU |
| 51 | Switch Condition Signal | A/C Switch/Amplifier Circuit, ECU, Neutral/Start Switch Or Circuit, TPS Or Circuit |
| 52 | Knock Sensor Signal | Knock Sensor Or Circuit, ECU |
| 53 | Knock Sensor Control (ECU) | ECU |
| 71 [1] | EGR System Malfunction | EGR System, EGR Temp. Sensor Or Circuit, ECU |

[1] – Used on Calif. only.

# 1991 ENGINE PERFORMANCE
# Self-Diagnostics (Cont.)

***SUPRA CODE IDENTIFICATION***

| Code No. | System Affected | Probable Cause |
|---|---|---|
| 12 & 13 | RPM Signal | Distributor Or Circuit, Starter Circuit, ECU |
| 14 | Ignition Signal | Ignitor Or Circuit To ECU, ECU |
| 21 | Oxygen Sensor Signal | Oxygen Sensor Or Circuit, [1] Oxygen Sensor Heater, ECU |
| 22 | Coolant Temp. Sensor Signal | Coolant Temp. Sensor Or Circuit, ECU |
| 24 [2] | Intake Air Temperature Sensor Signal | Intake Air Temperature Sensor Or Circuit, ECU |
| 25 | Lean Air/Fuel Mixture | Injector Or Circuit, Oxygen Sensor Or Circuit, Fuel Pressure, Ignition System, Coolant Temp. Sensor, Airflow Meter, ECU |
| 26 | Rich Air/Fuel Mixture | Airflow Meter, ECU, Injector Or Circuit, Oxygen Sensor Or Circuit, Fuel Pressure, Cold Start Injector Or Circuit, Coolant Temp. Sensor |
| 27 [3] [4] | Sub-Oxygen Sensor Signal | Sub-Oxygen Sensor Or Circuit, ECU |
| 31 | Airflow Meter Signal | Airflow Meter Or Circuit, ECU |
| 32 [4] | Airflow Meter Signal | Airflow Meter Or Circuit, ECU |
| 34 [1] | Turbocharger Pressure Sensor | Turbocharger Pressure Sensor Or Circuit, Turbocharger, ECU |
| 35 [1] | High Altitude Compensator Sensor | ECU |
| 41 [2] | Throttle Position Sensor Signal | Throttle Position Sensor Or Circuit, ECU |
| 42 [5] | Vehicle Speed Sensor Signal | Vehicle Speed Sensor Or Circuit, ECU |
| 43 [5] | Starter Signal | Starter Signal Circuit, Ignition Switch Or Circuit, Main Relay, ECU |
| 51 [5] | Switch Condition Signal | A/C Switch Circuit, ECU, Neutral/Start Switch Or Circuit, TPS Or Circuit |
| 52 | Knock Sensor Signal | Knock Sensor Or Circuit, ECU |
| 53 | Knock Sensor Control (ECU) | ECU |
| 71 [3] | EGR System Malfunction | EGR System, EGR Temp. Sensor Or Circuit, ECU, EGR VSV |

[1] - Used on 7M-GTE only.
[2] - CHECK ENGINE light comes on when code sets on Calif. models only.
[3] - Used on Calif. only.
[4] - Used on 7M-GE only.
[5] - CHECK ENGINE light will not come on when code is set.

***TERCEL CODE IDENTIFICATION***

| Code No. | System Affected | Probable Cause |
|---|---|---|
| 12 & 13 | RPM Signal | Distributor Or Circuit, Starter Circuit, ECU |
| 14 | Ignition Signal | Ignitor Or Circuit To ECU, ECU |
| 21 | Oxygen Sensor Signal | Oxygen Sensor Or Circuit, ECU |
| 22 | Coolant Temp. Sensor Signal | Coolant Temp. Sensor Or Circuit, ECU |
| 24 [1] | Intake Air Temperature Sensor Signal | Intake Air Temperature Sensor Or Circuit, ECU |
| 25 | Lean Air/Fuel Mixture | Injector Or Circuit, Oxygen Sensor Or Circuit, Fuel Pressure, Ignition System, Coolant Temp. Sensor, Vacuum Sensor, ECU |
| 26 [2] | Rich Air/Fuel Mixture | Vacuum Sensor, ECU, Injector Or Circuit, Oxygen Sensor Or Circuit, Fuel Pressure, Cold Start Injector Or Circuit, Coolant Temp. Sensor |
| 31 | Vacuum Sensor | Vacuum Sensor Or Circuit, ECU |
| 41 [1] | Throttle Position Sensor Signal | Throttle Position Sensor Or Circuit, ECU |
| 42 [3] | Vehicle Speed Sensor Signal | Vehicle Speed Sensor Or Circuit, ECU |
| 43 [3] | Starter Signal | Starter Signal Circuit, Ignition Switch Or Circuit, Main Relay, ECU |
| 51 [3] | Switch Condition Signal | A/C Switch Circuit, ECU, Neutral/Start Switch Or Circuit, TPS Or Circuit |
| 71 [2] | EGR System Malfunction | EGR System, EGR Temp. Sensor Or Circuit, ECU, EGR VSV |

[1] - CHECK ENGINE light comes on when code sets on Calif. models only.
[2] - Used on Calif. only.
[3] - CHECK ENGINE light will not come on when code is set.

# 1991 ENGINE PERFORMANCE
# Self-Diagnostics (Cont.)

## CAMRY DIAGNOSTIC CIRCUIT CHECK

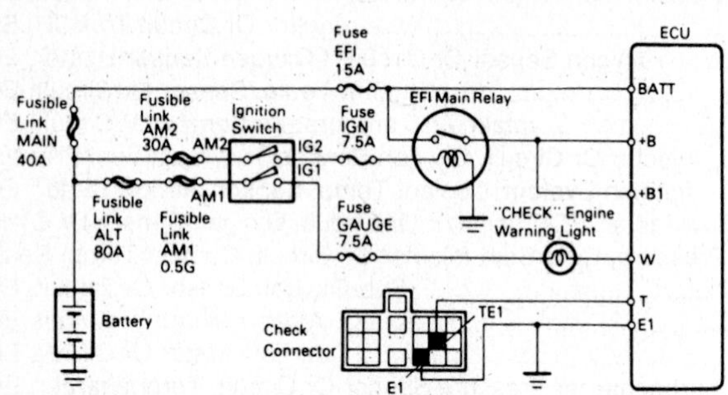


**4-CYLINDER**

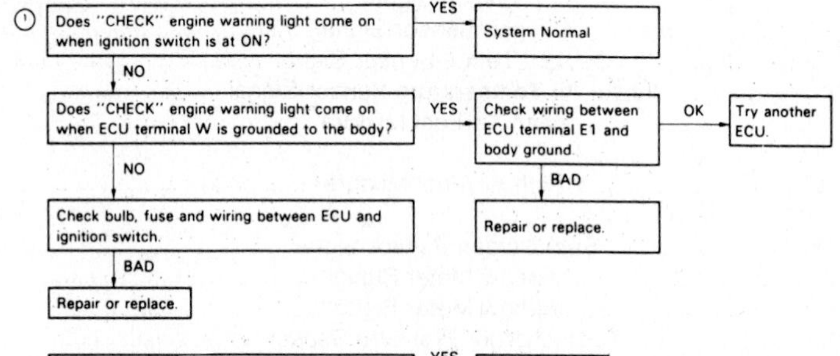

① Does "CHECK" engine warning light come on when ignition switch is at ON?
YES
System Normal
NO
Does "CHECK" engine warning light come on when ECU terminal W is grounded to the body?
YES
Check wiring between ECU terminal E1 and body ground.
OK
Try another ECU.
BAD
Repair or replace.
NO
Check bulb, fuse and wiring between ECU and ignition switch.
BAD
Repair or replace.


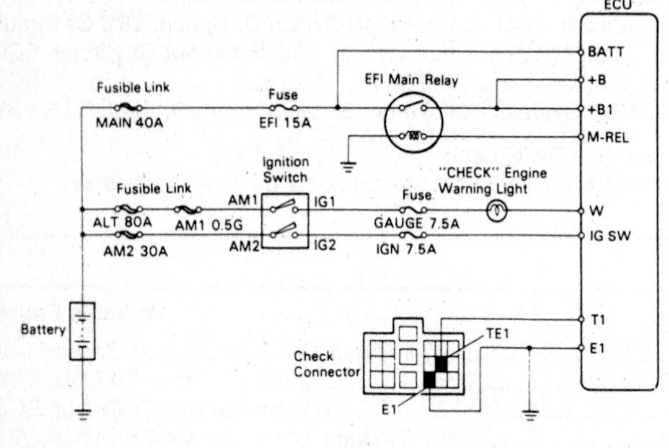


**V6**

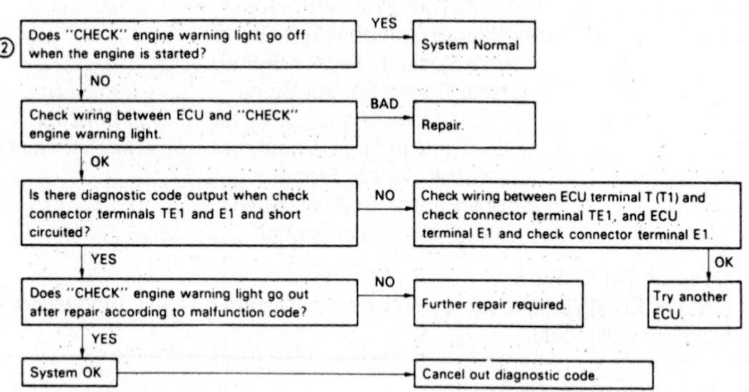


CAUTION: Perform all voltage measurements with ECU harness connector installed. Use a high-impedance DVOM (10,000-ohm minimum). Verify battery voltage is greater than 11 volts.

## ECU TERMINAL IDENTIFICATION

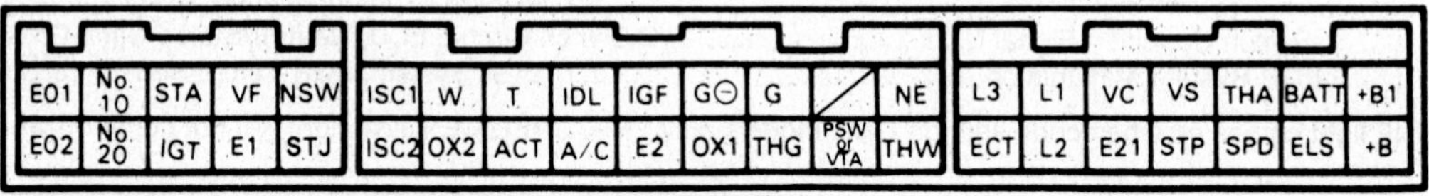


**4-CYLINDER**

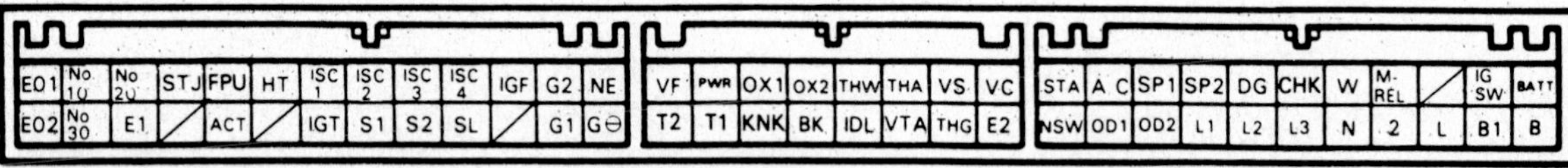


**V6**

91B17526 91C17527 91D17528 91E17529 91H17530

Courtesy of Toyota Motor Sales, U.S.A., Inc.

## CAMRY TEST NO. 1
### ECU POWER SOURCE

| Terminals | Trouble | Condition | STD voltage |
|---|---|---|---|
| BATT – E1 | No voltage | – | 10 – 14 V |

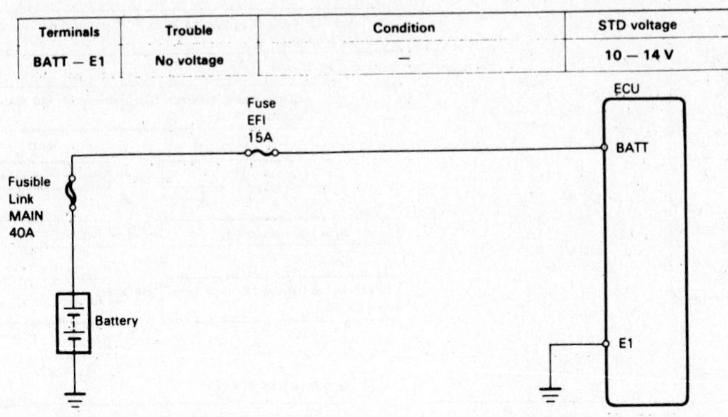
ECU
Fuse
EFI
15A
BATT
Fusible
Link
MAIN
40A
Battery
E1

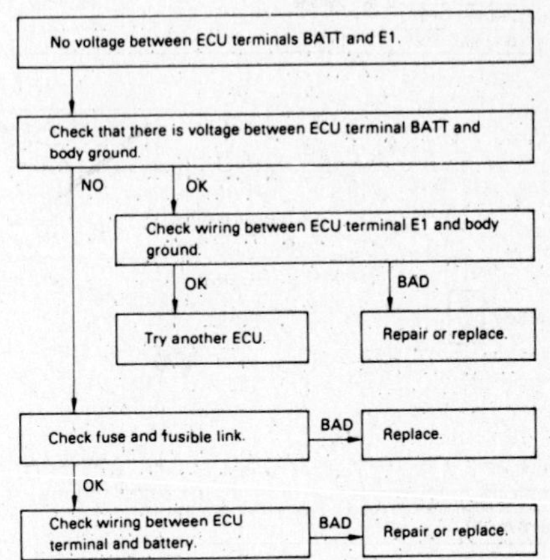
No voltage between ECU terminals BATT and E1.
Check that there is voltage between ECU terminal BATT and body ground.
NO
OK
Check wiring between ECU terminal E1 and body ground.
OK
BAD
Try another ECU.
Repair or replace.
Check fuse and fusible link.
BAD
Replace.
OK
Check wiring between ECU terminal and battery.
BAD
Repair or replace.

## CAMRY TEST NO. 2
### ECU (+B) CIRCUIT

| Terminals | Trouble | Condition | STD voltage |
|---|---|---|---|
| +B<br>+B1 – E1 | No voltage | Ignition SW ON | 10 – 14 V |

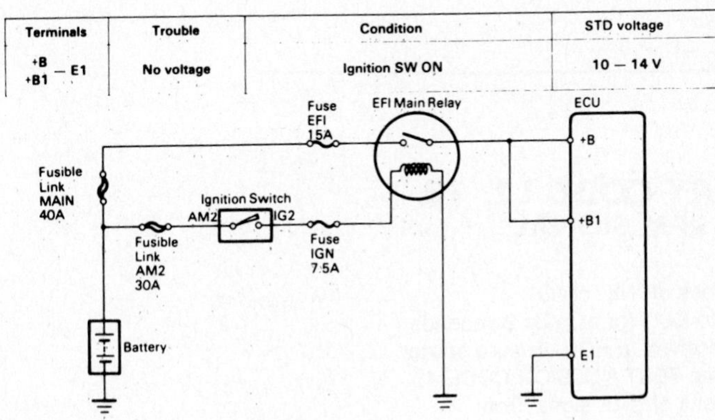
Fuse
EFI
15A
EFI Main Relay
ECU
+B
Fusible
Link
MAIN
40A
Ignition Switch
AM2
IG2
+B1
Fusible
Link
AM2
30A
Fuse
IGN
7.5A
Battery
E1

**4-CYLINDER**

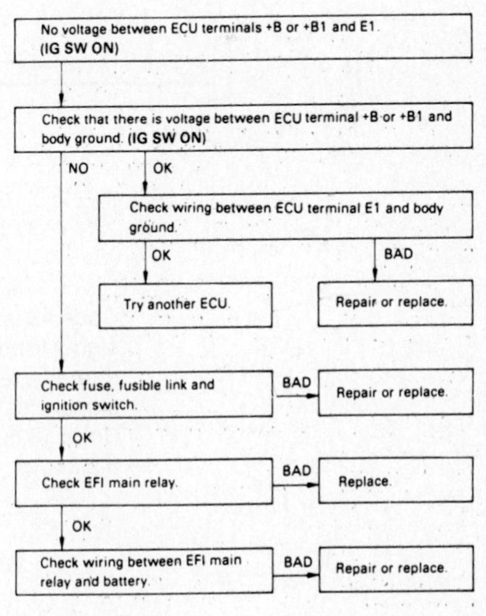
No voltage between ECU terminals +B or +B1 and E1.
(IG SW ON)
Check that there is voltage between ECU terminal +B or +B1 and body ground. (IG SW ON)
NO
OK
Check wiring between ECU terminal E1 and body ground.
OK
BAD
Try another ECU.
Repair or replace.
Check fuse, fusible link and ignition switch.
BAD
Repair or replace.
OK
Check EFI main relay.
BAD
Replace.
OK
Check wiring between EFI main relay and battery.
BAD
Repair or replace.

**Continued On Next Page**

91I17531 91J17532 91A17533 91B17534

# 1991 ENGINE PERFORMANCE
# Self-Diagnostics (Cont.)

## CAMRY TEST NO. 2
### ECU (+B) CIRCUIT (Cont.)

| Terminals | Trouble | Condition | STD voltage |
|---|---|---|---|
| BATT – E1 | No voltage | IG SW ON | 10 – 14 V |
| IG SW – E1 | | | |
| M-REL – E1 | | | |
| +B (+B1) – E1 | | | |

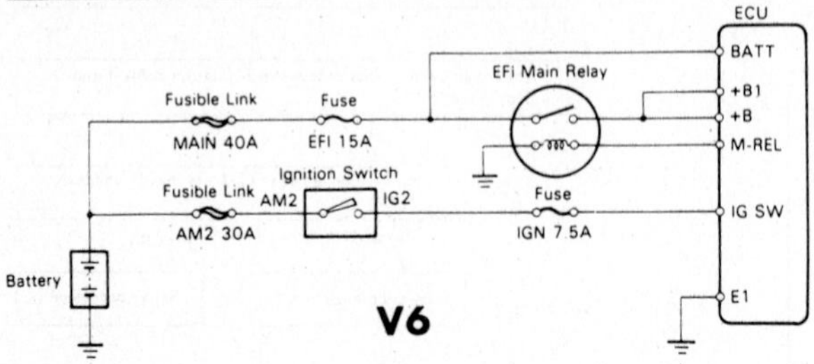

ECU
BATT
+B1
+B
M-REL
IG SW
E1
EFi Main Relay
Fusible Link
MAIN 40A
Fuse
EFI 15A
Ignition Switch
Fusible Link
AM2
IG2
AM2 30A
Fuse
IGN 7.5A
Battery
V6

① • BATT – E1

- There is no voltage between ECU terminals BATT and E1.
- Check that there is voltage between ECU terminal BATT and body ground.
  - OK: Check wiring between ECU terminal E1 and body ground.
    - OK: Try another ECU.
    - BAD: Repair or replace.
  - NO: Check fuse and fusible link.
    - BAD: Replace.
    - OK: Check wiring between ECU terminal and battery.
      - BAD: Repair or replace.

② • IG SW – E1

- There is no voltage between ECU terminals IG SW and E1. **(IG SW ON)**
- Check taht there is voltage between ECU terminal IG SW and body ground. **(IG SW ON)**
  - OK: Check wiring between ECU terminal E1 and body ground.
    - OK: Try another ECU.
    - BAD: Repair or replace.
  - NO: Check fuse, fusible link and ignition switch.
    - BAD: Repair or replace.

③ • M-REL – E1

- There is no voltage between ECU terminals M-REL and E1. **(IG SW ON)**
- Check that there is voltage between ECU terminal M-REL and body ground. **(IG SW ON)**
  - OK: Check wiring between ECU terminal E1 and body ground.
    - OK: Try another ECU.
    - BAD: Repair or replace.
  - NO: Check EFI main relay and wiring harness.
    - BAD: Replace.
    - OK: Try another ECU.

④ • +B (+B1) – E1

- There is no voltage between ECU terminals +B (+B1) and E1. **(IG SW ON)**
- Check that there is voltage between ECU terminal +B (+B1) and body ground. **(IG SW ON)**
  - OK: Check wiring between ECU terminal E1 and body ground.
    - OK: Try another ECU.
    - BAD: Repair or replace.
  - NO: Check fuse, fusible link and wiring harness.
    - BAD: Repair or replace.
    - OK: Check EFI main relay.
      - BAD: Replace.
      - OK: Refer to M-REL – E1

---

## CAMRY CODE 12, 13
### RPM SIGNAL

Code 12 is caused by loss of "NE" or "G" signal from distributor to ECU for at least 2 seconds after starter signal is received at ECU. Ensure starter signal exists at ECU. See TEST NO. 9 OR CODE 43. Code 13 is caused by loss of "NE" signal from distributor to ECU when engine RPM exceeds 1000 RPM.

**NOTE – Diagnostic chart not available from manufacturer.**

91C17535 91D17536 91E17537 91F17538 91G17539

Courtesy of Toyota Motor Sales, U.S.A., Inc.

## CAMRY TEST NO. 3 OR CODE 14
### IGNITION SIGNAL

| Terminals | Trouble | Condition | STD voltage |
|---|---|---|---|
| IGT – E1 | No voltage | Idling | 0.7 – 1.0 V |

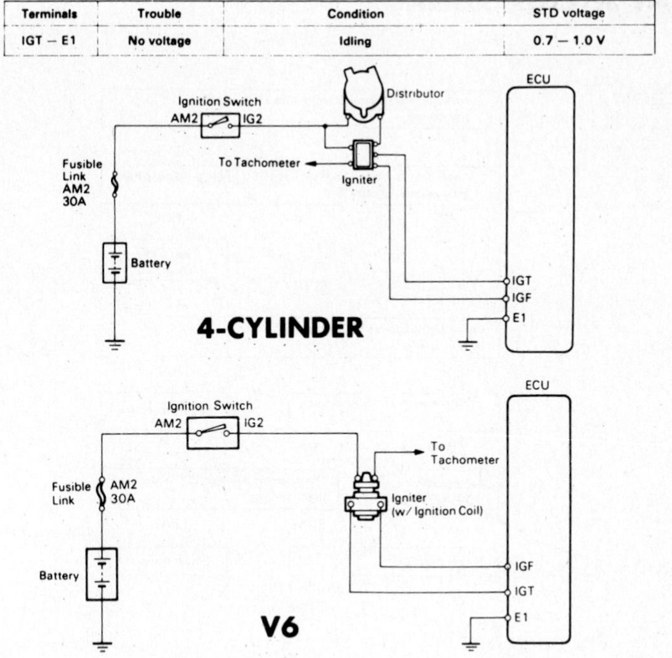


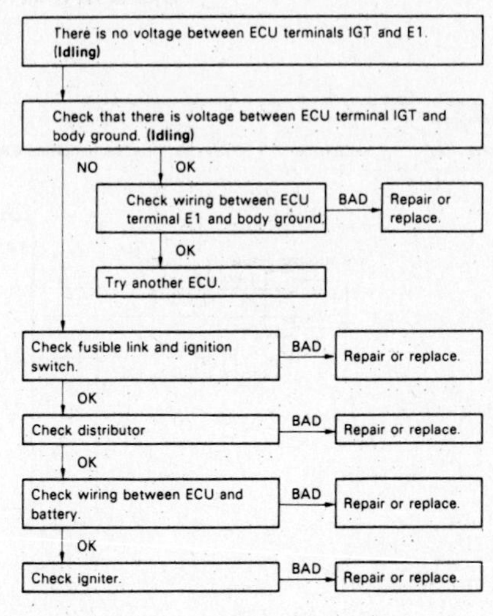


NOTE: To check ignition system components, see SYSTEM & COMPONENT TESTING article.

## CAMRY TEST NO. 4 OR CODE 21, 27
### OXYGEN SENSOR SIGNAL

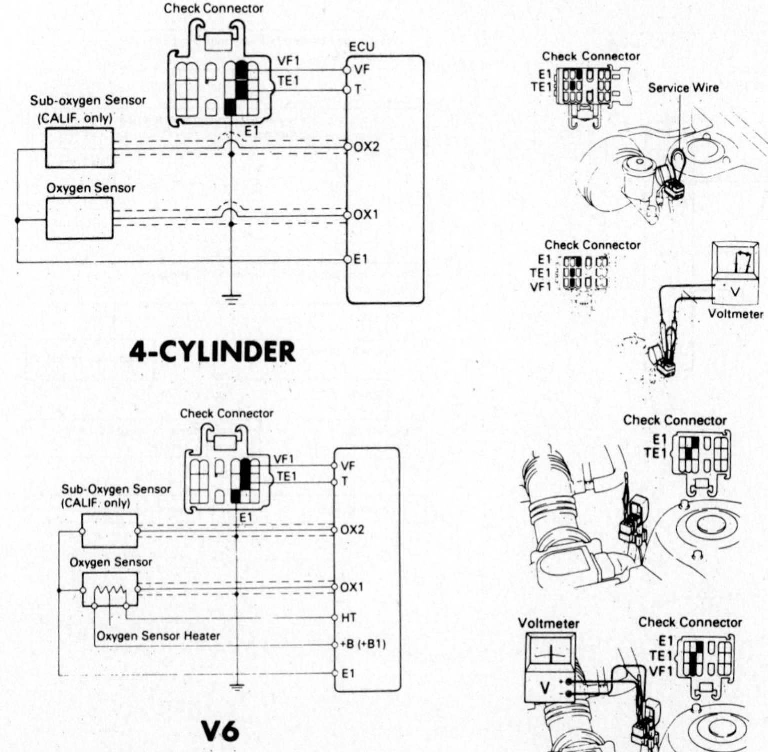


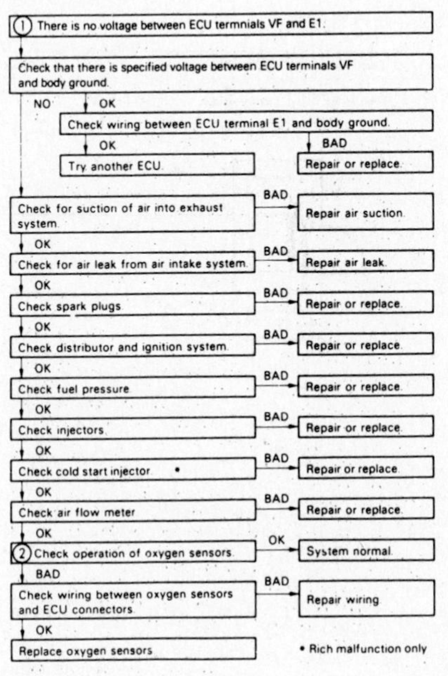


91B17542 91C17543 91D17544 91E17545 91F17546 91G17547 91F17678 91G17679

Courtesy of Toyota Motor Sales, U.S.A., Inc.

# 1991 ENGINE PERFORMANCE
# Self-Diagnostics (Cont.)

## CAMRY TEST NO. 5 OR CODE 22
### COOLANT TEMPERATURE SENSOR SIGNAL

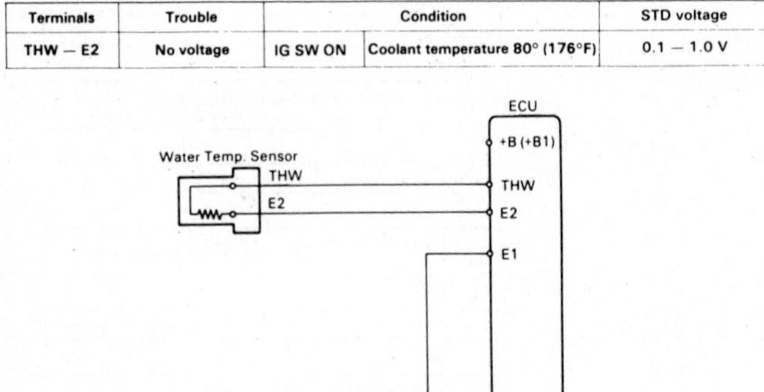

| Terminals | Trouble | Condition | | STD voltage |
|---|---|---|---|---|
| THW – E2 | No voltage | IG SW ON | Coolant temperature 80° (176°F) | 0.1 – 1.0 V |

ECU
+B (+B1)
Water Temp. Sensor
THW
E2
THW
E2
E1



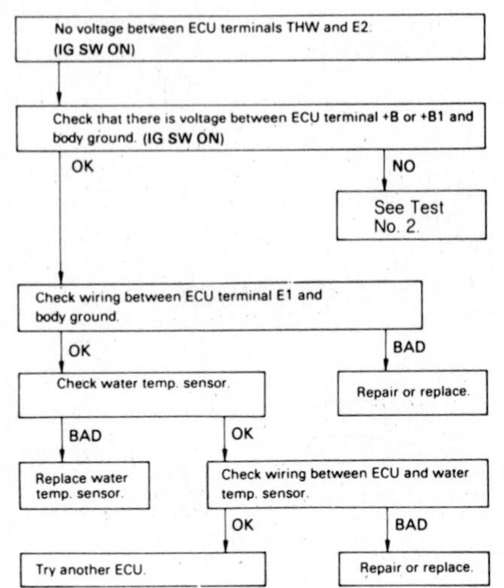

No voltage between ECU terminals THW and E2. (IG SW ON)
Check that there is voltage between ECU terminal +B or +B1 and body ground. (IG SW ON)
OK
NO
See Test No. 2.
Check wiring between ECU terminal E1 and body ground.
OK
BAD
Check water temp. sensor.
Repair or replace.
BAD
OK
Replace water temp. sensor.
Check wiring between ECU and water temp. sensor.
OK
BAD
Try another ECU.
Repair or replace.


NOTE: Water temperature sensor is also referred to as coolant temperature sensor.

## CAMRY TEST NO. 6 OR CODE 24
### INTAKE AIR TEMPERATURE SENSOR SIGNAL

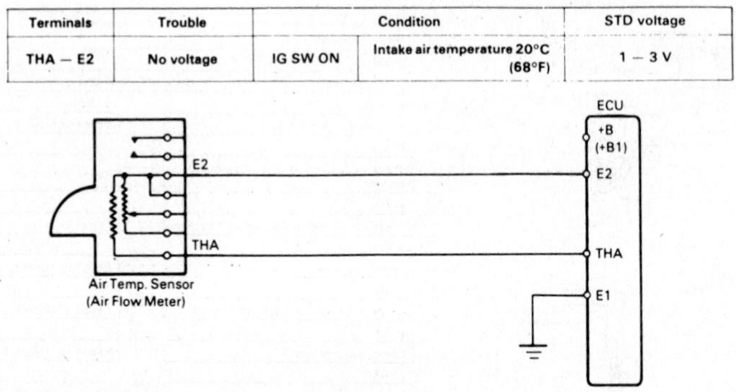

| Terminals | Trouble | Condition | | STD voltage |
|---|---|---|---|---|
| THA – E2 | No voltage | IG SW ON | Intake air temperature 20°C (68°F) | 1 – 3 V |

ECU
+B
(+B1)
E2
THA
E1
E2
THA
Air Temp. Sensor
(Air Flow Meter)



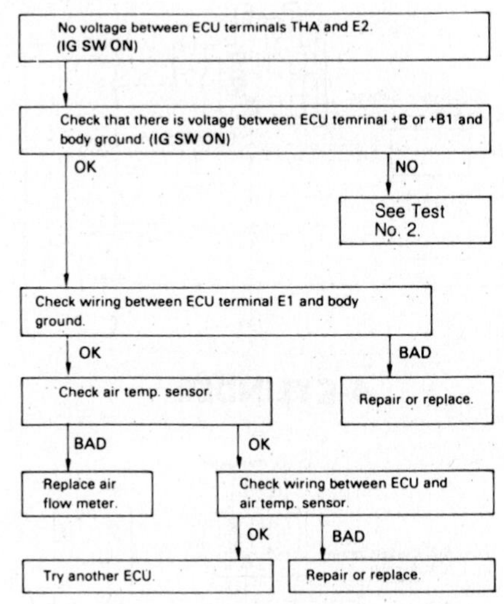

No voltage between ECU terminals THA and E2. (IG SW ON)
Check that there is voltage between ECU temrinal +B or +B1 and body ground. (IG SW ON)
OK
NO
See Test No. 2.
Check wiring between ECU terminal E1 and body ground.
OK
BAD
Check air temp. sensor.
Repair or replace.
BAD
OK
Replace air flow meter.
Check wiring between ECU and air temp. sensor.
OK
BAD
Try another ECU.
Repair or replace.


91J17680 91A17681 91B17682 91C17683

Courtesy of Toyota Motor Sales, U.S.A., Inc.

## CAMRY CODE 25
### LEAN AIR/FUEL MIXTURE

**Probable Causes**
- Airflow Meter
- Air Intake System
- Coolant Temperature Sensor
- Fuel Pressure
- Ignition System
- Injector Circuit or Injector
- Oxygen Sensor or Sensor Circuit
- ECU

**NOTE – Diagnostic chart not available from manufacturer.**

## CAMRY CODE 26
### RICH AIR/FUEL MIXTURE

**Probable Causes**
- Airflow Meter
- Cold Start Injector
- Coolant Temperature Sensor
- ECU
- Fuel Pressure
- Injector Circuit or Injector
- Oxygen Sensor or Sensor Circuit

**NOTE – Diagnostic chart not available from manufacturer.**

## CAMRY TEST NO. 7 OR CODE 31, 32
### AIRFLOW METER SIGNAL

| Terminals | Trouble | Condition | | STD voltage |
|---|---|---|---|---|
| VC – E2 | No voltage | IG SW ON | — | 4 – 6 V |
| VS – E2 | | | Measuring plate fully closed | 3.7 – 4.3 V |
| VS – E2 | | | Measuring plate fully open | 0.2 – 0.5 V |
| VS – E2 | | Idling | | 1.6 – 4.1 V |
| VS – E2 | | 3,000 rpm | | 1.0 – 2.0 V |

**4-CYLINDER**

| Terminals | Trouble | Condition | | STD voltage |
|---|---|---|---|---|
| VC – E2 | No voltage | IG SW ON | – | 4 – 6 V |
| VS – E2 | | | Measuring plate fully closed | 4.0 – 5.5 V |
| | | | Measuring plate fully open | 0 – 1 V |
| | | Idling | | 2.0 – 4.0 V |
| | | 3,000 rpm | | 1.0 – 2.0 V |

**V6**

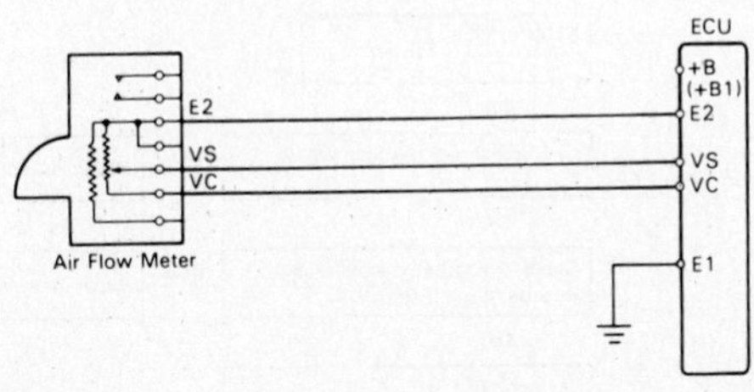
ECU
+B
(+B1)
E2
VS
VC
E1
E2
VS
VC
Air Flow Meter

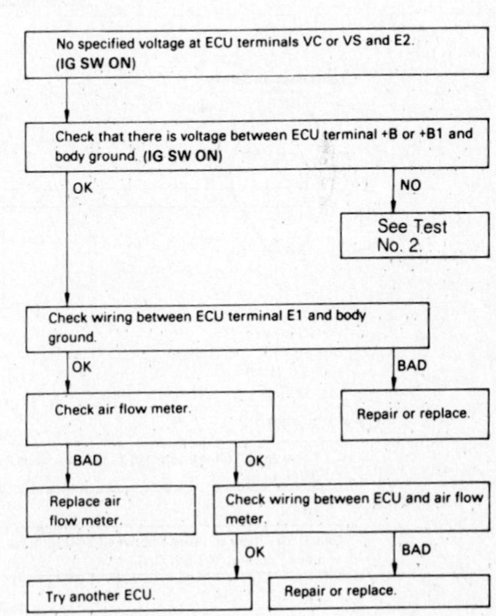
No specified voltage at ECU terminals VC or VS and E2. (IG SW ON)
Check that there is voltage between ECU terminal +B or +B1 and body ground. (IG SW ON)
OK
NO
See Test No. 2.
Check wiring between ECU terminal E1 and body ground.
OK
BAD
Check air flow meter.
Repair or replace.
BAD
OK
Replace air flow meter.
Check wiring between ECU and air flow meter.
OK
BAD
Try another ECU.
Repair or replace.

91D17684 91E17685

Courtesy of Toyota Motor Sales, U.S.A., Inc.

# 1991 ENGINE PERFORMANCE
# Self-Diagnostics (Cont.)

## CAMRY TEST NO. 8 OR CODE 41
### THROTTLE POSITION SENSOR SIGNAL

### 4-CYLINDER WITHOUT ELECTRONIC CONTROLLED TRANSAXLE

| Terminals | Trouble | Condition | | STD voltage |
|---|---|---|---|---|
| IDL — E1 | No voltage | IG SW ON | Throttle valve open | 8 — 14 V |
| PSW — E1 | | | Throttle valve fully closed | 4 — 6 V |

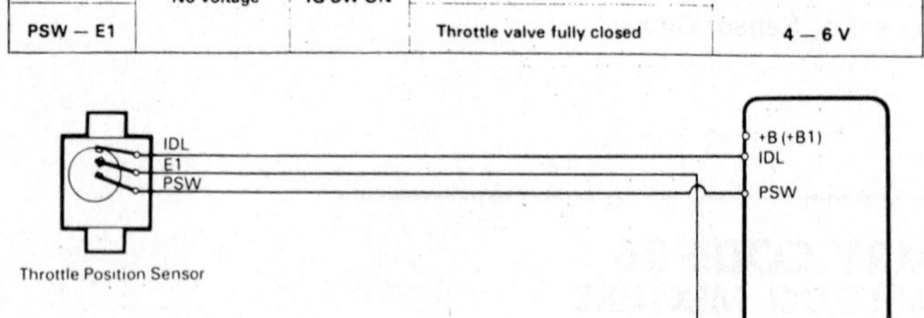
IDL
E1
PSW
Throttle Position Sensor
+B (+B1)
IDL
PSW
E1

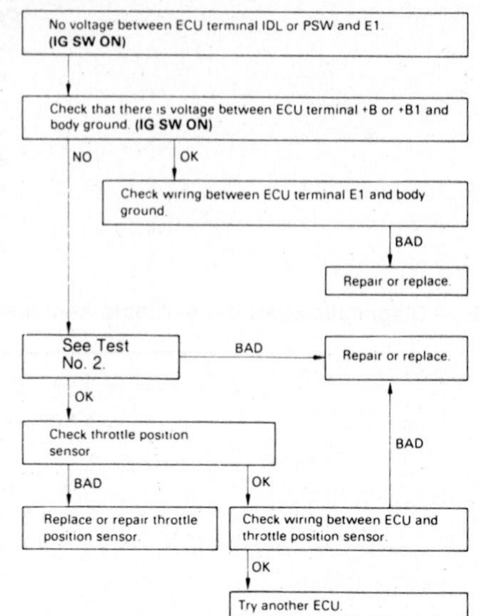
No voltage between ECU terminal IDL or PSW and E1. (IG SW ON)
Check that there is voltage between ECU terminal +B or +B1 and body ground. (IG SW ON)
NO
OK
Check wiring between ECU terminal E1 and body ground.
BAD
Repair or replace.
See Test No. 2.
BAD
Repair or replace.
OK
Check throttle position sensor.
BAD
OK
BAD
Replace or repair throttle position sensor.
Check wiring between ECU and throttle position sensor.
OK
Try another ECU.

### 4-CYLINDER WITH ELECTRONIC CONTROLLED TRANSAXLE

| Terminals | Trouble | Condition | | STD voltage |
|---|---|---|---|---|
| IDL — E2 | No voltage | IG SW ON | Throttle valve open | 8 — 14V |
| VC — E2 | | | — | 4 — 6 V |
| VTA — E2 | | | Throttle valve fully closed | 0.1 — 1.0 V |
| | | | Throttle valve fully open | 4 — 6 |

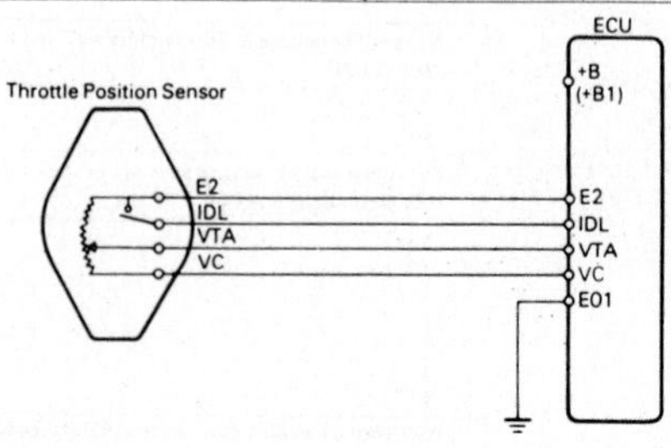
Throttle Position Sensor
ECU
+B (+B1)
E2
IDL
VTA
VC
E01

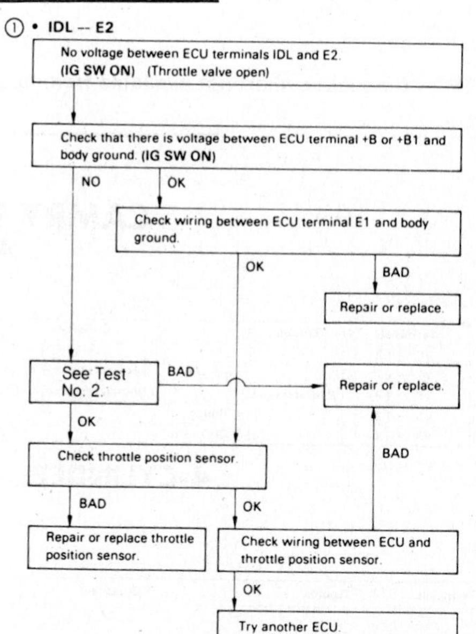
① • IDL — E2
No voltage between ECU terminals IDL and E2. (IG SW ON) (Throttle valve open)
Check that there is voltage between ECU terminal +B or +B1 and body ground. (IG SW ON)
NO
OK
Check wiring between ECU terminal E1 and body ground.
OK
BAD
Repair or replace.
See Test No. 2.
BAD
Repair or replace.
OK
Check throttle position sensor.
BAD
BAD
OK
Repair or replace throttle position sensor.
Check wiring between ECU and throttle position sensor.
OK
Try another ECU.

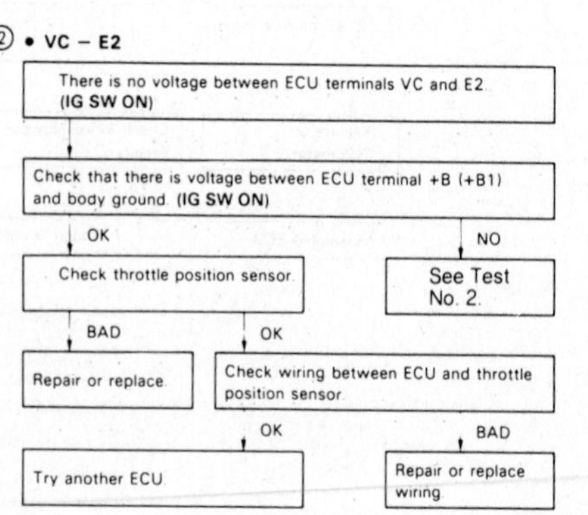
② • VC — E2
There is no voltage between ECU terminals VC and E2. (IG SW ON)
Check that there is voltage between ECU terminal +B (+B1) and body ground. (IG SW ON)
OK
NO
Check throttle position sensor.
See Test No. 2.
BAD
OK
Repair or replace.
Check wiring between ECU and throttle position sensor.
OK
BAD
Try another ECU.
Repair or replace wiring.

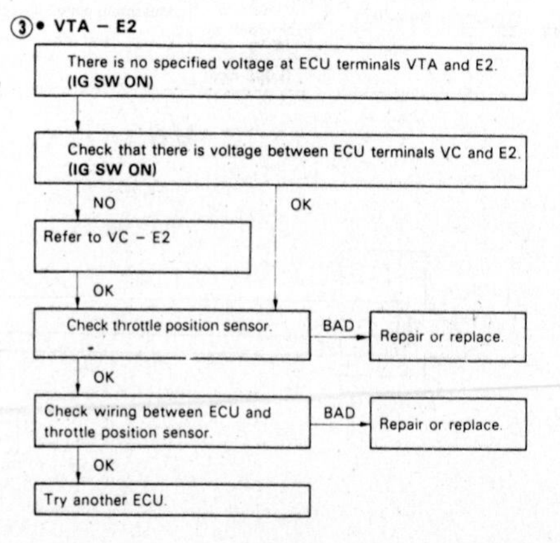
③ • VTA — E2
There is no specified voltage at ECU terminals VTA and E2. (IG SW ON)
Check that there is voltage between ECU terminals VC and E2. (IG SW ON)
NO
OK
Refer to VC — E2
OK
Check throttle position sensor.
BAD
Repair or replace.
OK
Check wiring between ECU and throttle position sensor.
BAD
Repair or replace.
OK
Try another ECU.

Continued on Next Page

91F17686 91G17687 91H17688 91I17689 91B17690 91C17691

Courtesy of Toyota Motor Sales, U.S.A., Inc.

# CAMRY TEST NO. 8 OR CODE 41
## THROTTLE POSITION SENSOR SIGNAL (Cont.)

### V6

| Terminals | Trouble | Condition | | STD voltage |
|---|---|---|---|---|
| IDL – E2 | No voltage | IG SW ON | Throttle valve open | 4 – 6 V |
| VC – E2 | | | — | 4 – 6 V |
| VTA – E2 | | | Throttle valve fully closed | 0.1 – 1.0 V |
| | | | Throttle valve fully open | 3.2 – 4.2 V |

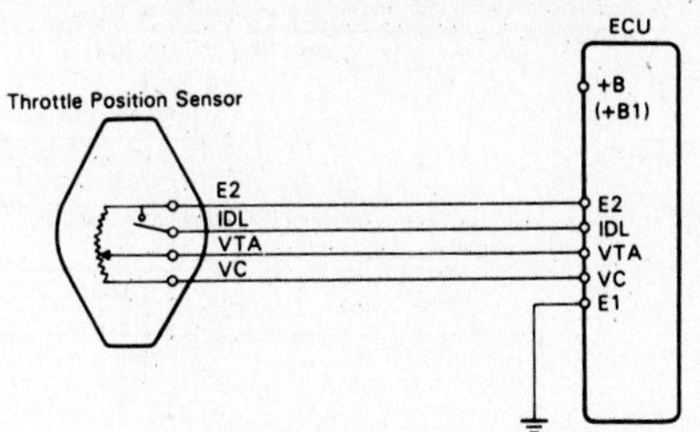
ECU
Throttle Position Sensor
+B
(+B1)
E2
IDL
VTA
VC
E2
IDL
VTA
VC
E1

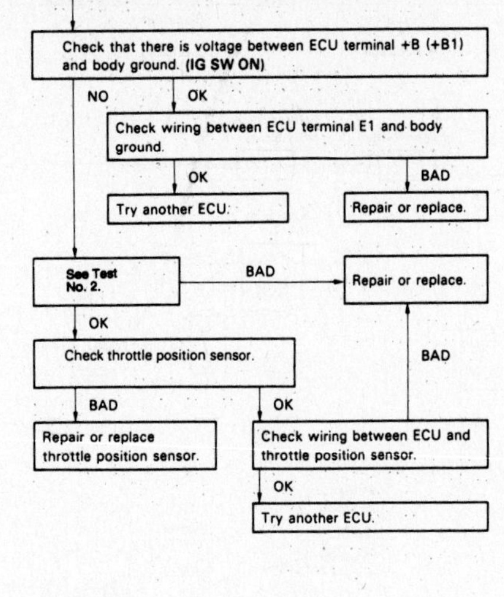
① • IDL – E2
There is no voltage between ECU terminals IDL and E2. (IG SW ON) (Throttle valve open)
Check that there is voltage between ECU terminal +B (+B1) and body ground. (IG SW ON)
NO
OK
Check wiring between ECU terminal E1 and body ground.
OK
BAD
Try another ECU.
Repair or replace.
See Test No. 2.
BAD
Repair or replace.
OK
Check throttle position sensor.
BAD
BAD
OK
Repair or replace throttle position sensor.
Check wiring between ECU and throttle position sensor.
OK
Try another ECU.

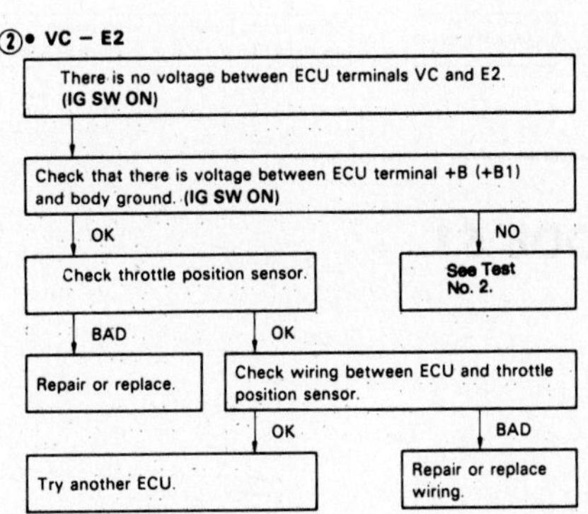
② • VC – E2
There is no voltage between ECU terminals VC and E2. (IG SW ON)
Check that there is voltage between ECU terminal +B (+B1) and body ground. (IG SW ON)
OK
NO
Check throttle position sensor.
See Test No. 2.
BAD
OK
Repair or replace.
Check wiring between ECU and throttle position sensor.
OK
BAD
Try another ECU.
Repair or replace wiring.

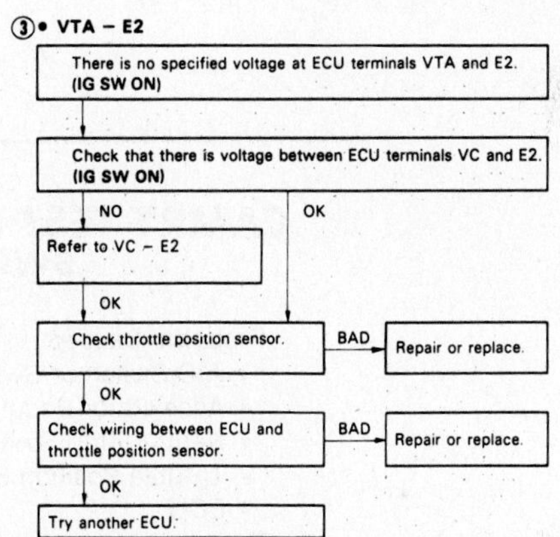
③ • VTA – E2
There is no specified voltage at ECU terminals VTA and E2. (IG SW ON)
Check that there is voltage between ECU terminals VC and E2. (IG SW ON)
NO
OK
Refer to VC – E2
OK
Check throttle position sensor.
BAD
Repair or replace.
OK
Check wiring between ECU and throttle position sensor.
BAD
Repair or replace.
OK
Try another ECU.

# CAMRY CODE 42
## VEHICLE SPEED SENSOR SIGNAL

**Probable Causes**
- Vehicle Speed Sensor or Sensor Circuit
- ECU

**NOTE – Diagnostic chart not available from manufacturer.**

91H17688 91I17689 91B17690 91C17691

Courtesy of Toyota Motor Sales, U.S.A., Inc.

# 1991 ENGINE PERFORMANCE
# Self-Diagnostics (Cont.)

## CAMRY TEST NO. 9 OR CODE 43
### STARTER SIGNAL

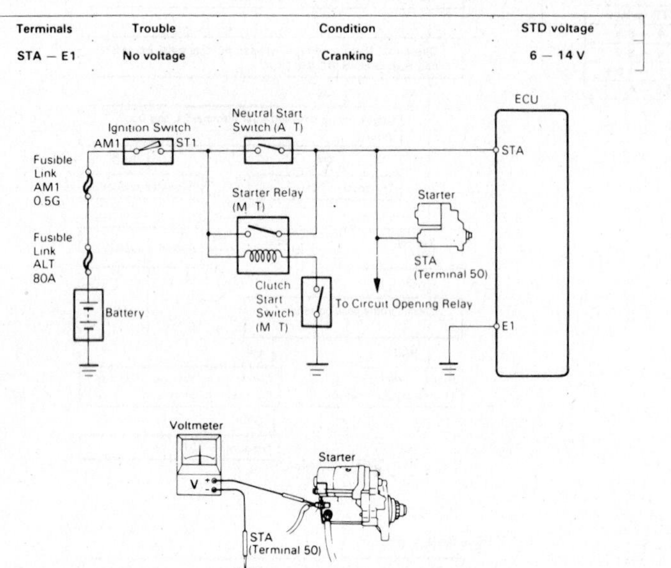

| Terminals | Trouble | Condition | STD voltage |
|---|---|---|---|
| STA – E1 | No voltage | Cranking | 6 – 14 V |

ECU
Ignition Switch
AM1
ST1
Neutral Start
Switch (A T)
STA
Fusible
Link
AM1
0.5G
Starter Relay
(M T)
Starter
Fusible
Link
ALT
80A
STA
(Terminal 50)
Clutch
Start
Switch
(M T)
To Circuit Opening Relay
Battery
E1
Voltmeter
Starter
V
STA
(Terminal 50)

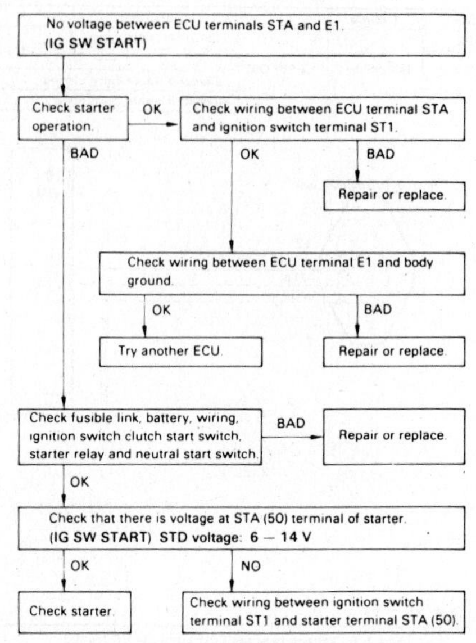

No voltage between ECU terminals STA and E1.
(IG SW START)
Check starter operation.
OK
Check wiring between ECU terminal STA and ignition switch terminal ST1.
BAD
OK
BAD
Repair or replace.
Check wiring between ECU terminal E1 and body ground.
OK
BAD
Try another ECU.
Repair or replace.
Check fusible link, battery, wiring, ignition switch clutch start switch, starter relay and neutral start switch.
BAD
Repair or replace.
OK
Check that there is voltage at STA (50) terminal of starter.
(IG SW START) STD voltage: 6 – 14 V
OK
NO
Check starter.
Check wiring between ignition switch terminal ST1 and starter terminal STA (50).

## CAMRY TEST NO. 10 OR CODE 51
### SWITCH SIGNAL

**Probable Causes**

- A/C Switch or Switch Circuit
- Accelerator Pedal or Cable
- Neutral/Start Switch or Switch Circuit
- Throttle Position Sensor IDL Circuit
- ECU

To check A/C switch signal, use the following procedure.

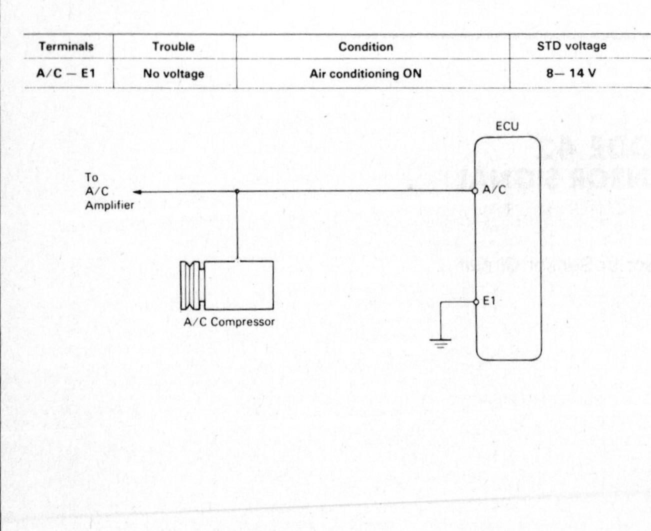

| Terminals | Trouble | Condition | STD voltage |
|---|---|---|---|
| A/C – E1 | No voltage | Air conditioning ON | 8– 14 V |

ECU
To
A/C
Amplifier
A/C
A/C Compressor
E1

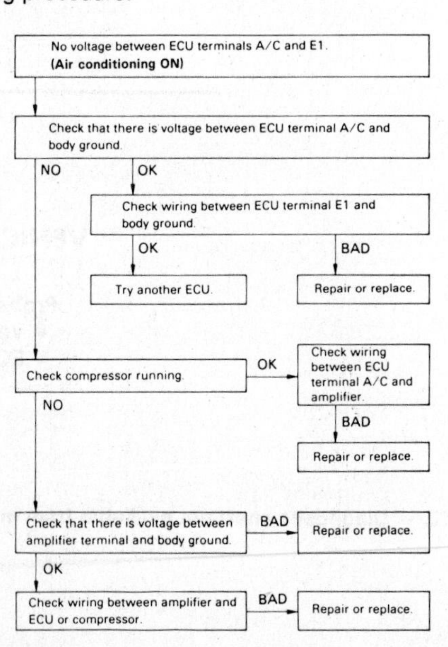

No voltage between ECU terminals A/C and E1.
(Air conditioning ON)
Check that there is voltage between ECU terminal A/C and body ground.
NO
OK
Check wiring between ECU terminal E1 and body ground.
OK
BAD
Try another ECU.
Repair or replace.
Check compressor running.
OK
Check wiring between ECU terminal A/C and amplifier.
NO
BAD
Repair or replace.
Check that there is voltage between amplifier terminal and body ground.
BAD
Repair or replace.
OK
Check wiring between amplifier and ECU or compressor.
BAD
Repair or replace.

91D17692 91E17693 91F17694 91G17695 91H17696

Courtesy of Toyota Motor Sales, U.S.A., Inc.

## CAMRY CODE 52 (V6)
### KNOCK SENSOR SIGNAL

**Probable Causes**
- Knock Sensor
- Knock Sensor Circuit
- ECU

**NOTE – Diagnostic chart not available from manufacturer.**

---

## CAMRY CODE 53 (V6)
### KNOCK CONTROL SIGNAL

**Probable Causes**
- ECU

**NOTE – Diagnostic chart not available from manufacturer.**

---

## CAMRY TEST NO. 11 OR CODE 71
### EGR SYSTEM MALFUNCTION

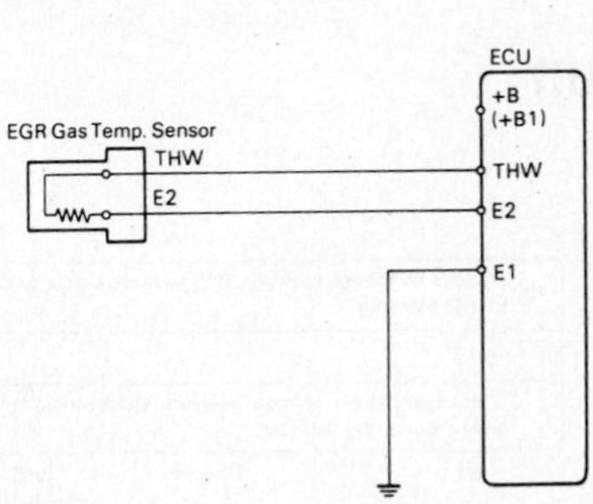
ECU
+B
(+B1)
EGR Gas Temp. Sensor
THW
THW
E2
E2
E1

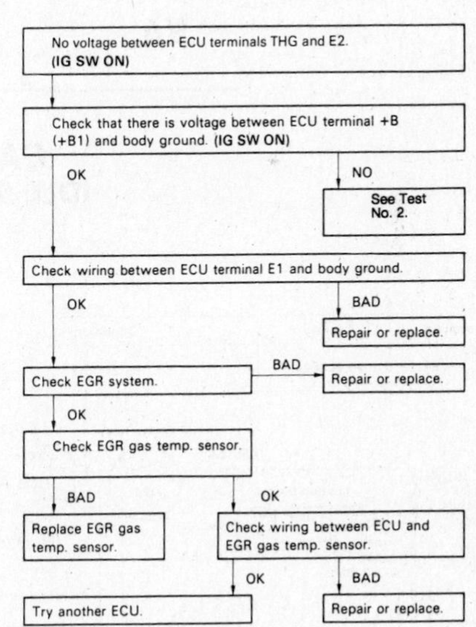
No voltage between ECU terminals THG and E2.
(IG SW ON)
Check that there is voltage between ECU terminal +B (+B1) and body ground. (IG SW ON)
OK
NO
See Test No. 2.
Check wiring between ECU terminal E1 and body ground.
OK
BAD
Repair or replace.
Check EGR system.
BAD
Repair or replace.
OK
Check EGR gas temp. sensor.
BAD
OK
Replace EGR gas temp. sensor.
Check wiring between ECU and EGR gas temp. sensor.
OK
BAD
Try another ECU.
Repair or replace.

91I17697 91J17698

# 1991 ENGINE PERFORMANCE
# Self-Diagnostics (Cont.)

## CAMRY TEST NO. 12
### INJECTOR CIRCUIT

| Terminals | Trouble | Condition | STD voltage |
|---|---|---|---|
| No. 10 – E01<br>No. 20 – E02 | No voltage | IG SW ON | 10 – 14 V |

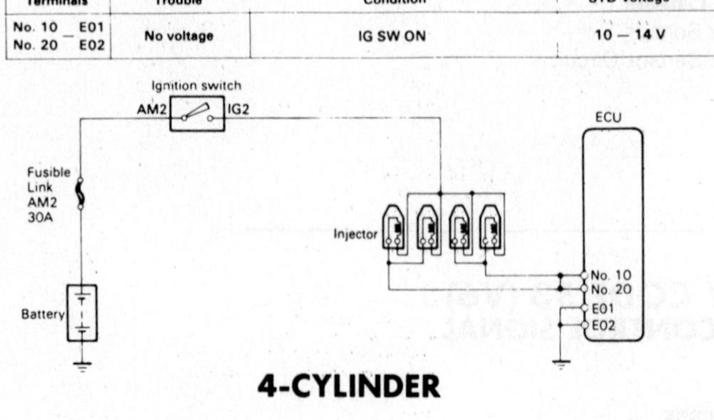
Ignition switch
AM2
IG2
ECU
Fusible Link AM2 30A
Injector
No. 10
No. 20
E01
E02
Battery

**4-CYLINDER**

| Terminals | Trouble | Condition | STD voltage |
|---|---|---|---|
| No. 10 E01<br>No. 20 –<br>No. 30 E02 | No voltage | IG SW ON | 10 – 14 V |

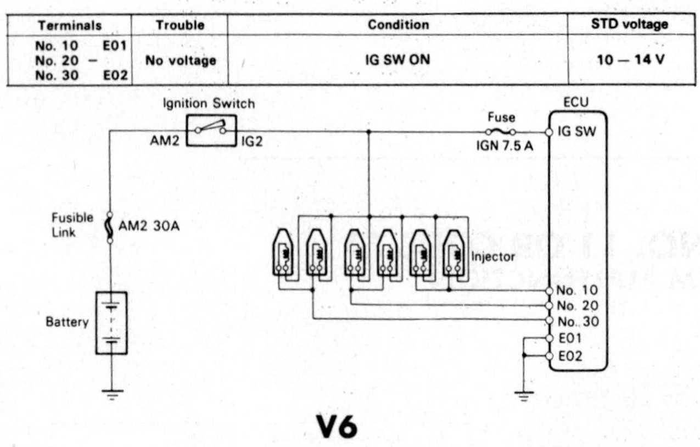
Ignition Switch
AM2
IG2
Fuse
IGN 7.5 A
ECU
IG SW
Fusible Link
AM2 30A
Injector
No. 10
No. 20
No. 30
E01
E02
Battery

**V6**

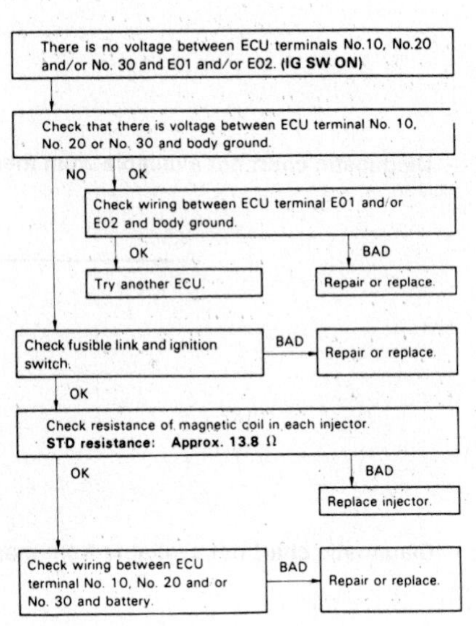
There is no voltage between ECU terminals No.10, No.20 and/or No. 30 and E01 and/or E02. (IG SW ON)
Check that there is voltage between ECU terminal No. 10, No. 20 or No. 30 and body ground.
NO
OK
Check wiring between ECU terminal E01 and/or E02 and body ground.
OK
BAD
Try another ECU.
Repair or replace.
Check fusible link and ignition switch.
BAD
Repair or replace.
OK
Check resistance of magnetic coil in each injector.
STD resistance: Approx. 13.8 Ω
OK
BAD
Replace injector.
Check wiring between ECU terminal No. 10, No. 20 and or No. 30 and battery.
BAD
Repair or replace.

## CAMRY TEST NO. 13
### IDLE SPEED CONTROL CIRCUIT

| Terminals | Trouble | Condition | STD voltage |
|---|---|---|---|
| ISC1<br>ISC2 – E1 | No voltage | IG SW ON | 9 – 14 V |

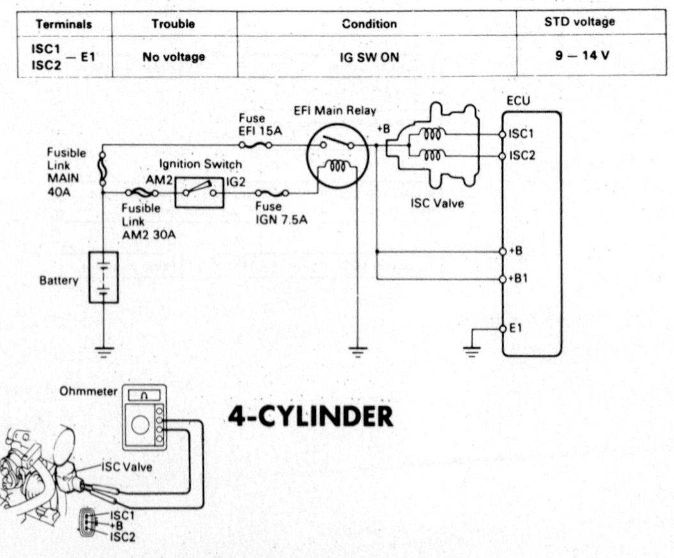
Fuse
EFI 15A
EFI Main Relay
+B
ECU
ISC1
ISC2
Fusible Link MAIN 40A
Ignition Switch
AM2
IG2
Fusible Link AM2 30A
Fuse
IGN 7.5A
ISC Valve
+B
+B1
E1
Battery
Ohmmeter
ISC Valve
ISC1
+B
ISC2

**4-CYLINDER**

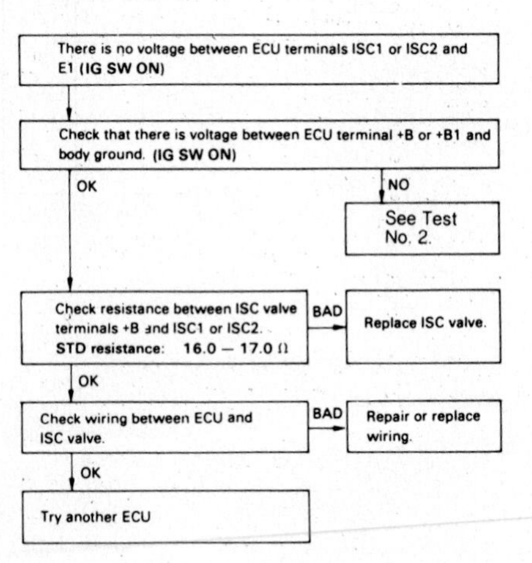
There is no voltage between ECU terminals ISC1 or ISC2 and E1 (IG SW ON)
Check that there is voltage between ECU terminal +B or +B1 and body ground. (IG SW ON)
OK
NO
See Test No. 2.
Check resistance between ISC valve terminals +B and ISC1 or ISC2.
STD resistance: 16.0 – 17.0 Ω
BAD
Replace ISC valve.
OK
Check wiring between ECU and ISC valve.
BAD
Repair or replace wiring.
OK
Try another ECU

**Continued On Next Page**

91A17699 91D17700 91E17701 91F17702 91G17703 91B18102

Courtesy of Toyota Motor Sales, U.S.A., Inc.

## CAMRY TEST NO. 13
### IDLE SPEED CONTROL CIRCUIT (Cont.)

| Terminals | Trouble | Condition | STD voltage |
|---|---|---|---|
| ISC1 ~ ISC4 – E1 | No voltage | IG SW ON | 9 – 14 V |

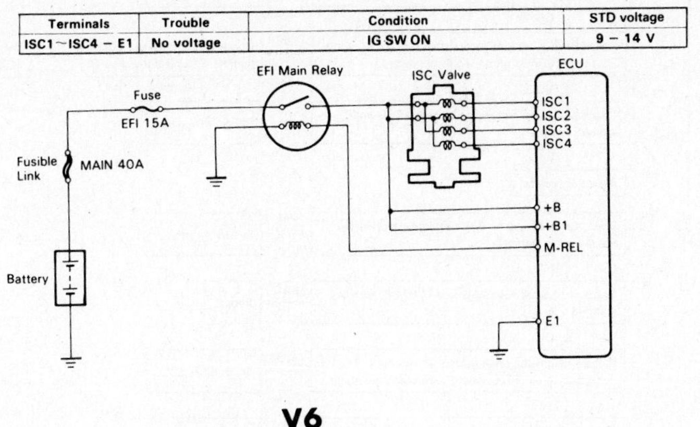

EFI Main Relay
ISC Valve
ECU
Fuse
EFI 15A
Fusible Link
MAIN 40A
Battery
ISC1
ISC2
ISC3
ISC4
+B
+B1
M-REL
E1

**V6**

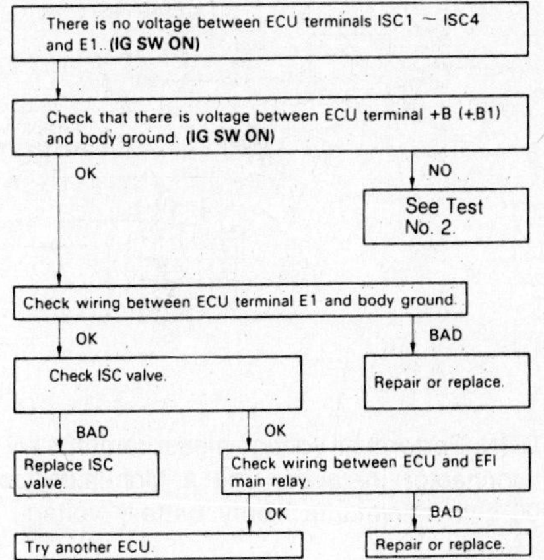

There is no voltage between ECU terminals ISC1 ~ ISC4 and E1. (IG SW ON)
Check that there is voltage between ECU terminal +B (+B1) and body ground. (IG SW ON)
OK
NO
See Test No. 2.
Check wiring between ECU terminal E1 and body ground.
OK
BAD
Check ISC valve.
Repair or replace.
BAD
OK
Replace ISC valve.
Check wiring between ECU and EFI main relay.
OK
BAD
Try another ECU.
Repair or replace.

## CAMRY TEST NO. 14
### CHECK ENGINE LIGHT CIRCUIT

| Terminals | Trouble | Condition | STD voltage |
|---|---|---|---|
| W – E1 | No voltage | No trouble ("CHECK" engine warning light off) and engine running | 10 – 14 V |

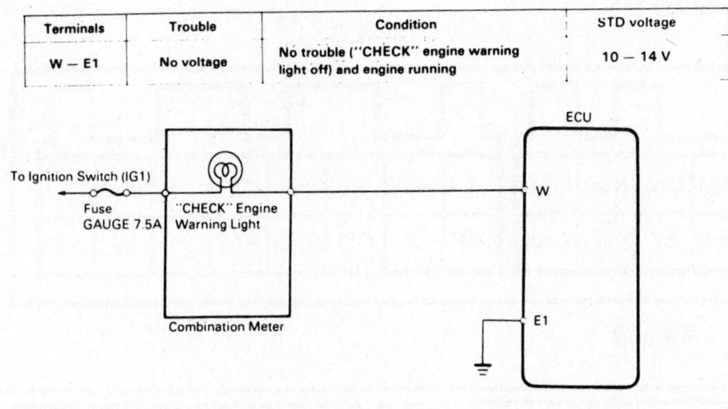

ECU
To Ignition Switch (IG1)
Fuse
GAUGE 7.5A
"CHECK" Engine Warning Light
Combination Meter
W
E1

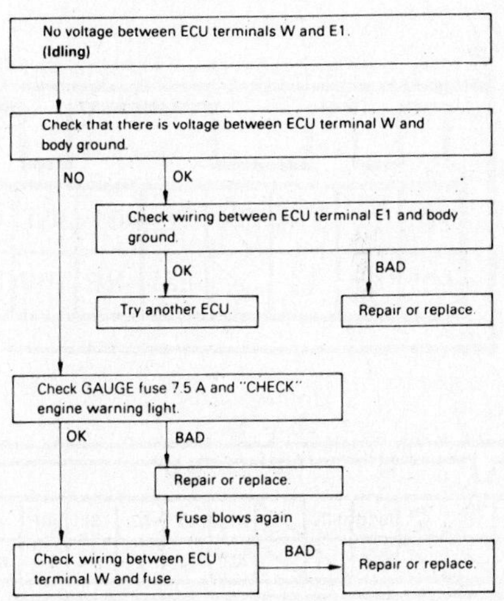

No voltage between ECU terminals W and E1. (Idling)
Check that there is voltage between ECU terminal W and body ground.
NO
OK
Check wiring between ECU terminal E1 and body ground.
OK
BAD
Try another ECU.
Repair or replace.
Check GAUGE fuse 7.5 A and "CHECK" engine warning light.
OK
BAD
Repair or replace.
Fuse blows again
Check wiring between ECU terminal W and fuse.
BAD
Repair or replace.

# 1991 ENGINE PERFORMANCE
# Self-Diagnostics (Cont.)

## CELICA DIAGNOSTIC CIRCUIT CHECK

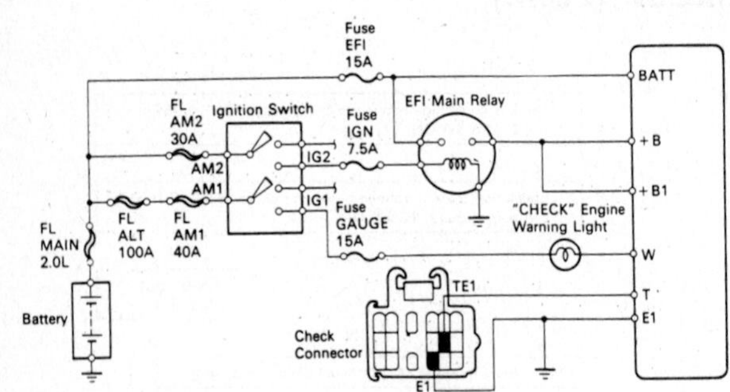
Fuse
EFI
15A
BATT
FL
AM2
30A
Ignition Switch
EFI Main Relay
Fuse
IGN
7.5A
IG2
AM2
AM1
+B
+B1
IG1
FL
MAIN
2.0L
FL
ALT
100A
FL
AM1
40A
Fuse
GAUGE
15A
"CHECK" Engine
Warning Light
W
TE1
T
E1
Battery
Check
Connector
E1

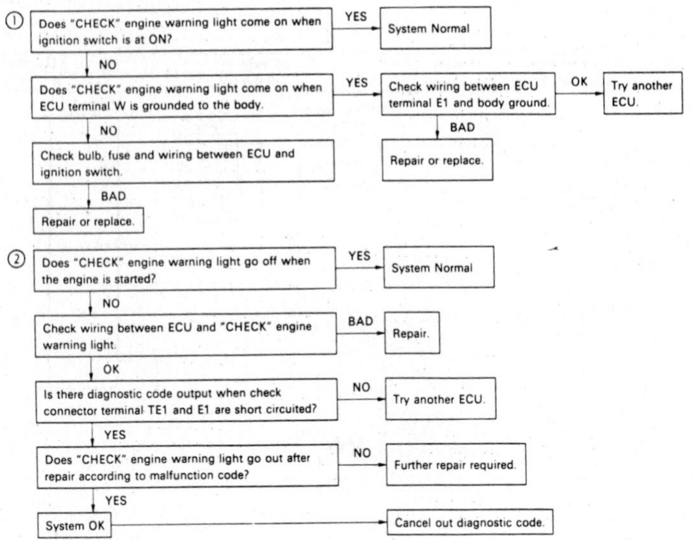
①
Does "CHECK" engine warning light come on when ignition switch is at ON?
YES
System Normal
NO
Does "CHECK" engine warning light come on when ECU terminal W is grounded to the body.
YES
Check wiring between ECU terminal E1 and body ground.
OK
Try another ECU.
BAD
Repair or replace.
NO
Check bulb, fuse and wiring between ECU and ignition switch.
BAD
Repair or replace.
②
Does "CHECK" engine warning light go off when the engine is started?
YES
System Normal
NO
Check wiring between ECU and "CHECK" engine warning light.
BAD
Repair.
OK
Is there diagnostic code output when check connector terminal TE1 and E1 are short circuited?
NO
Try another ECU.
YES
Does "CHECK" engine warning light go out after repair according to malfunction code?
NO
Further repair required.
YES
System OK
Cancel out diagnostic code.

CAUTION: Perform all voltage measurements with ECU harness connector installed. Use a high-impedance DVOM (10,000-ohm minimum). Verify battery voltage is greater than 11 volts.

## ECU TERMINAL IDENTIFICATION

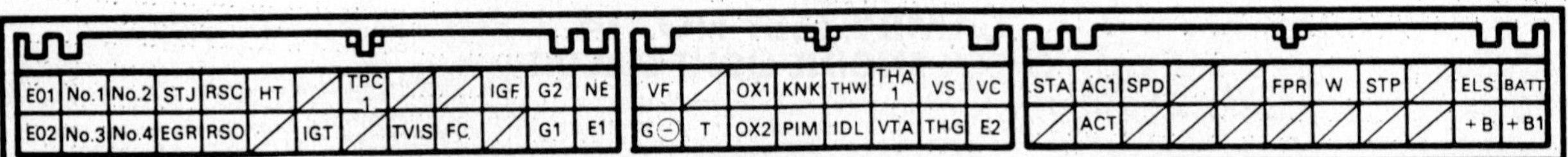
E01 No.1 No.2 STJ RSC HT TPC 1 IGF G2 NE
E02 No.3 No.4 EGR RSO IGT TVIS FC G1 E1
VF OX1 KNK THW THA 1 VS VC
G⊖ T OX2 PIM IDL VTA THG E2
STA AC1 SPD FPR W STP ELS BATT
ACT +B +B1

3S-GTE

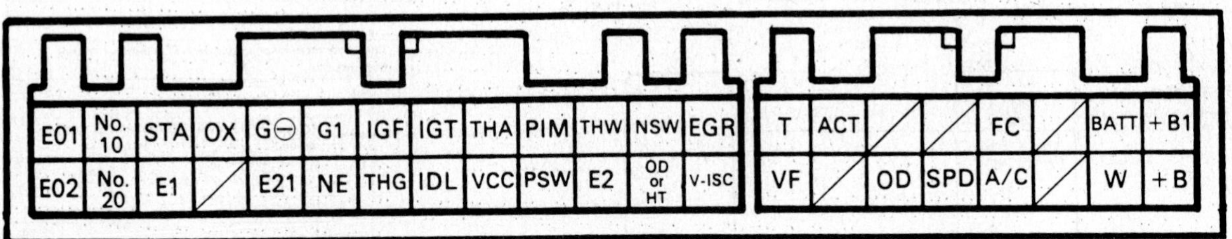
E01 No. 10 STA OX G⊖ G1 IGF IGT THA PIM THW NSW EGR
E02 No. 20 E1 E21 NE THG IDL VCC PSW E2 OD or HT V-ISC
T ACT FC BATT +B1
VF OD SPD A/C W +B

4A-FE

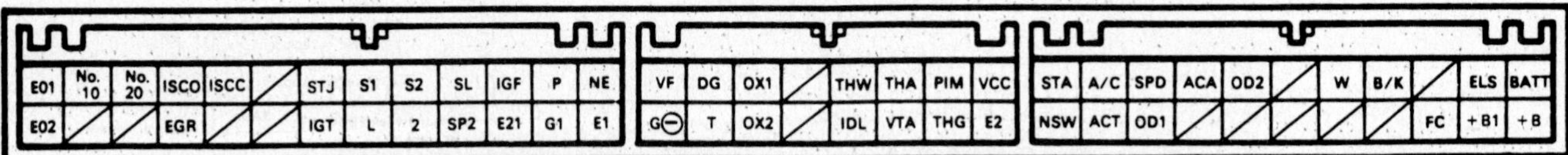
E01 No. 10 No. 20 ISCO ISCC STJ S1 S2 SL IGF P NE
E02 EGR IGT L 2 SP2 E21 G1 E1
VF DG OX1 THW THA PIM VCC
G⊖ T OX2 IDL VTA THG E2
STA A/C SPD ACA OD2 W B/K ELS BATT
NSW ACT OD1 FC +B1 +B

5S-FE (WITH ELECTRONICALLY CONTROLLED TRANSAXLE)

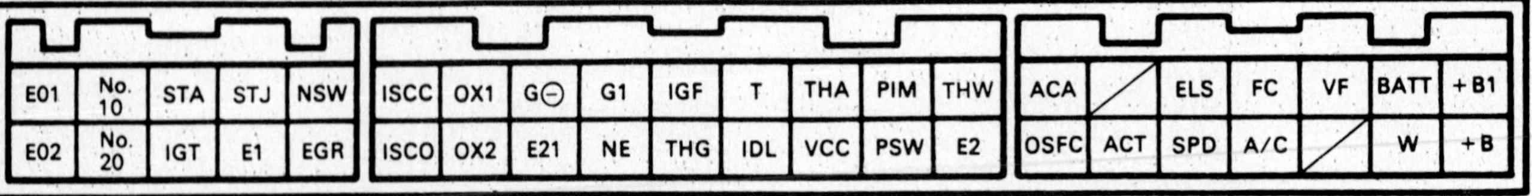
E01 No. 10 STA STJ NSW
E02 No. 20 IGT E1 EGR
ISCC OX1 G⊖ G1 IGF T THA PIM THW
ISCO OX2 E21 NE THG IDL VCC PSW E2
ACA ELS FC VF BATT +B1
OSFC ACT SPD A/C W +B

5S-FE (WITHOUT ELECTRONICALLY CONTROLLED TRANSAXLE)

91B17708 91C17709 91F17710 91G17711 91H17712 91I17713

Courtesy of Toyota Motor Sales, U.S.A., Inc.

## CELICA TEST NO. 1
### ECU POWER SOURCE

| Terminals | Trouble | Condition | STD voltage |
|---|---|---|---|
| BATT- E1 | No Voltage | – | 10 – 14 V |

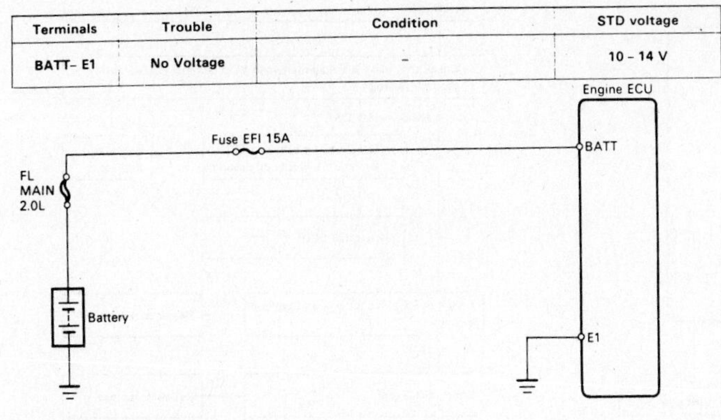

Engine ECU
Fuse EFI 15A
BATT
FL
MAIN
2.0L
Battery
E1

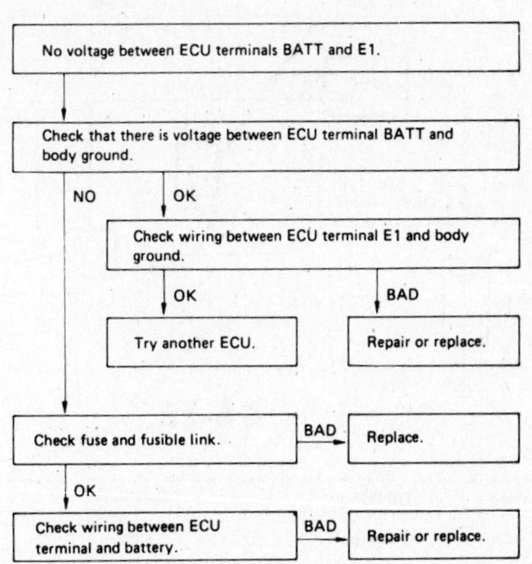

No voltage between ECU terminals BATT and E1.
Check that there is voltage between ECU terminal BATT and body ground.
NO
OK
Check wiring between ECU terminal E1 and body ground.
OK
BAD
Try another ECU.
Repair or replace.
Check fuse and fusible link.
BAD
Replace.
OK
Check wiring between ECU terminal and battery.
BAD
Repair or replace.

## CELICA TEST NO. 2
### ECU (+B) CIRCUIT

| Terminals | Trouble | Condition | STD voltage |
|---|---|---|---|
| +B<br>+B1 - E1 | No voltage | IG SW ON | 10 – 14 V |

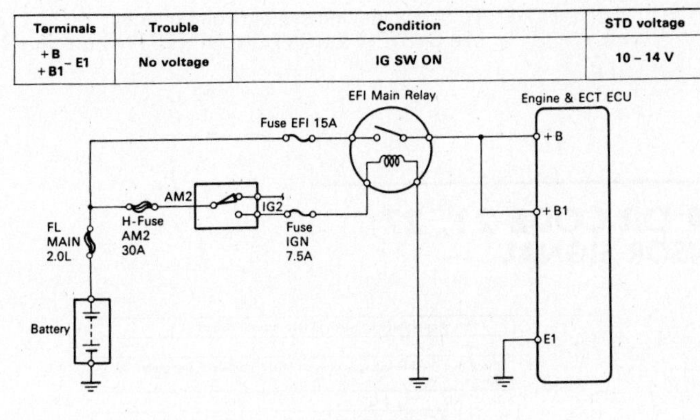

EFI Main Relay
Engine & ECT ECU
Fuse EFI 15A
+B
AM2
IG2
+B1
FL
MAIN
2.0L
H-Fuse
AM2
30A
Fuse
IGN
7.5A
Battery
E1

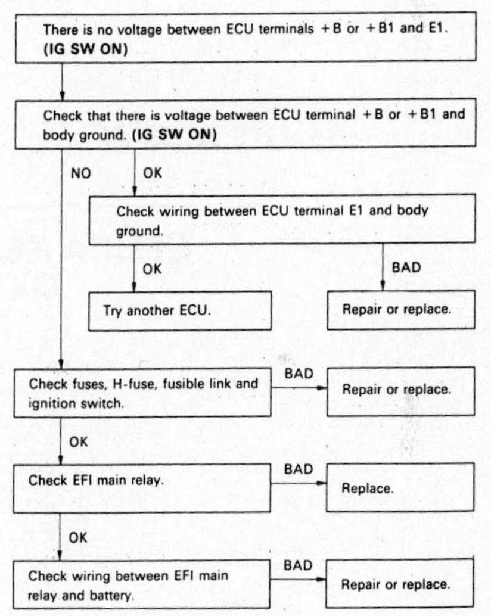

There is no voltage between ECU terminals +B or +B1 and E1. (IG SW ON)
Check that there is voltage between ECU terminal +B or +B1 and body ground. (IG SW ON)
NO
OK
Check wiring between ECU terminal E1 and body ground.
OK
BAD
Try another ECU.
Repair or replace.
Check fuses, H-fuse, fusible link and ignition switch.
BAD
Repair or replace.
OK
Check EFI main relay.
BAD
Replace.
OK
Check wiring between EFI main relay and battery.
BAD
Repair or replace.

## CELICA CODE 12, 13
### RPM SIGNAL

Code 12 is caused by loss of signal "G2", "G1", or "NE" (3S-GTE) or "G" or "NE" (all others) from distributor to ECU for at least 2 seconds after starter signal is received at ECU. Ensure starter signal exists at ECU. See TEST NO. 10 OR CODE 43.
Code 13 is caused by loss of "NE" signal from distributor to ECU when engine RPM exceeds 1000 RPM.

**NOTE - Diagnostic chart not available from manufacturer.**

91J17714 91A17715 91B17716 91C17717

# 1991 ENGINE PERFORMANCE
# Self-Diagnostics (Cont.)

## CELICA TEST NO. 3 OR CODE 14
### IGNITION SIGNAL

| Terminals | Trouble | Condition | STD voltage |
|---|---|---|---|
| IGT – E1 | No voltage | Idling | 0.8 – 1.2 V |

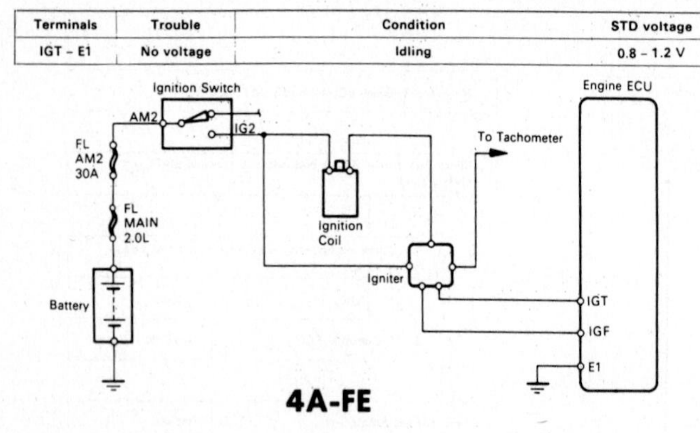
Ignition Switch
Engine ECU
AM2
IG2
To Tachometer
FL
AM2
30A
FL
MAIN
2.0L
Ignition
Coil
Igniter
Battery
IGT
IGF
E1
4A-FE

| Terminals | Trouble | Condition | STD voltage |
|---|---|---|---|
| IGT – E1 | No voltage | Idling | 0.7 – 1.0 V |

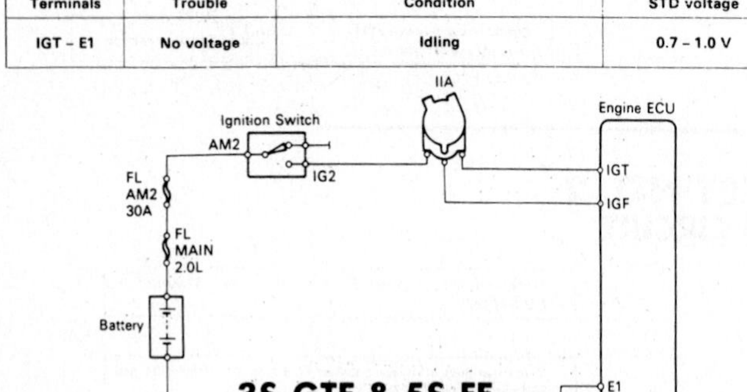
IIA
Ignition Switch
Engine ECU
AM2
IG2
FL
AM2
30A
FL
MAIN
2.0L
Battery
IGT
IGF
E1
3S-GTE & 5S-FE

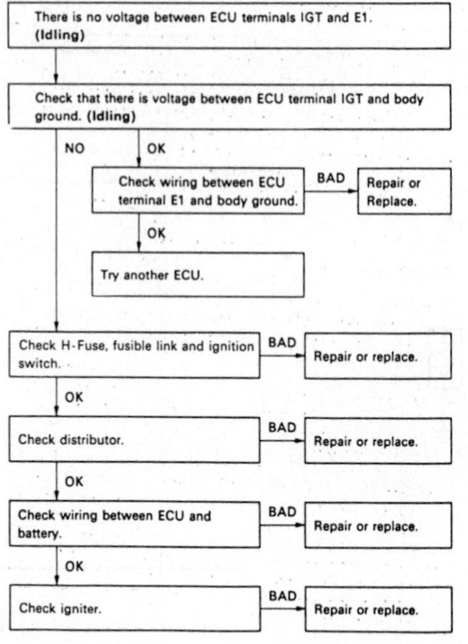
There is no voltage between ECU terminals IGT and E1. (Idling)
Check that there is voltage between ECU terminal IGT and body ground. (Idling)
NO
OK
Check wiring between ECU terminal E1 and body ground.
BAD
Repair or Replace.
OK
Try another ECU.
Check H-Fuse, fusible link and ignition switch.
BAD
Repair or replace.
OK
Check distributor.
BAD
Repair or replace.
OK
Check wiring between ECU and battery.
BAD
Repair or replace.
OK
Check igniter.
BAD
Repair or replace.

NOTE: To check ignition system components, see SYSTEM & COMPONENT TESTING article.

## CELICA TEST NO. 4 OR CODE 21, 27
### OXYGEN SENSOR SIGNAL

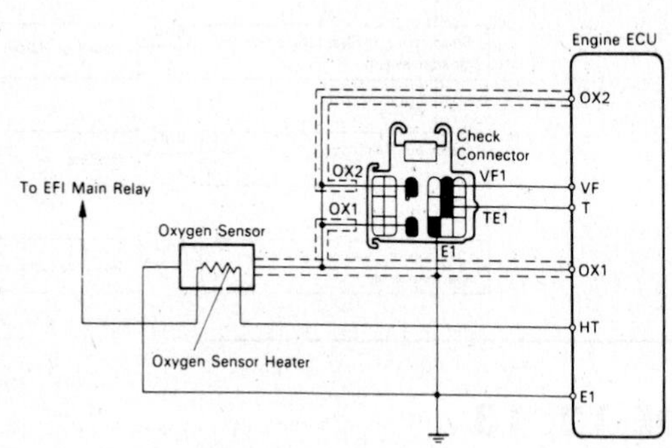
Engine ECU
OX2
Check
Connector
To EFI Main Relay
OX2
VF1
VF
T
OX1
TE1
E1
Oxygen Sensor
OX1
HT
Oxygen Sensor Heater
E1

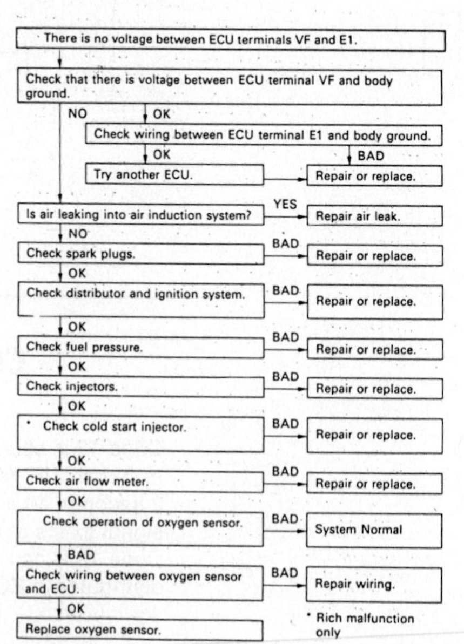
There is no voltage between ECU terminals VF and E1.
Check that there is voltage between ECU terminal VF and body ground.
NO
OK
Check wiring between ECU terminal E1 and body ground.
OK
BAD
Try another ECU.
Repair or replace.
Is air leaking into air induction system?
YES
Repair air leak.
NO
Check spark plugs.
BAD
Repair or replace.
OK
Check distributor and ignition system.
BAD
Repair or replace.
OK
Check fuel pressure.
BAD
Repair or replace.
OK
Check injectors.
BAD
Repair or replace.
OK
* Check cold start injector.
BAD
Repair or replace.
OK
Check air flow meter.
BAD
Repair or replace.
OK
Check operation of oxygen sensor.
BAD
System Normal
BAD
Check wiring between oxygen sensor and ECU.
BAD
Repair wiring.
OK
Replace oxygen sensor.
* Rich malfunction only

3S-GTE

Code 27 applies to 5S-FE only.

Continued On Next Page

91D17718 91E17719 91H17720 91I17721 91J17722

## CELICA TEST NO. 4 OR CODE 21, 27
### OXYGEN SENSOR SIGNAL (Cont.)

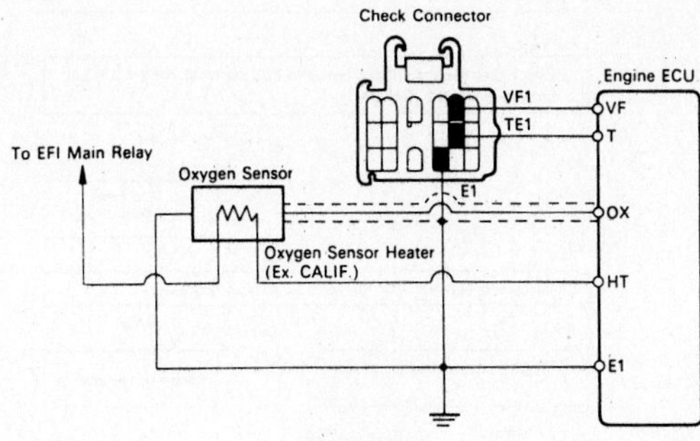


**4A-FE**

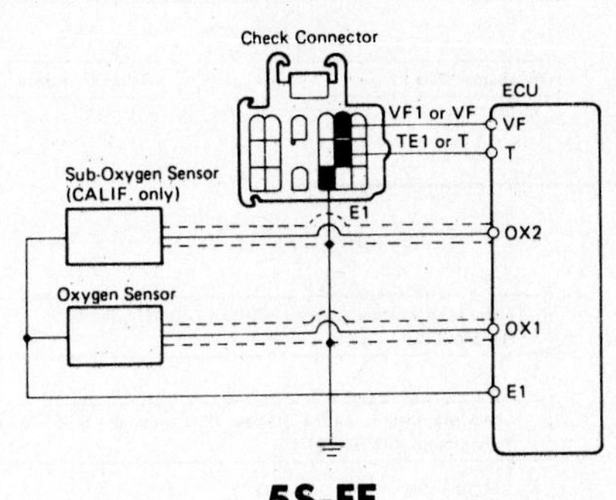


**5S-FE**

There is no voltage between ECU terminals VF and E1.

↓

Check that there is voltage between ECU terminal VF and body ground.

- NO → Is air leaking into air induction system?
- OK → Check wiring between ECU terminal E1 and body ground.
  - BAD → Repair or replace.
  - OK → Try another ECU.
    - BAD → Repair or replace.

Is air leaking into air induction system? — BAD → Repair or replace.
↓ OK
Check spark plugs. — BAD → Repair or replace.
↓ OK
Check distributor and Ignition system. — BAD → Repair or replace.
↓ OK
Check fuel pressure. — BAD → Repair or replace.
↓ OK
Check injectorts. — BAD → Repair or replace.
↓ OK
* Check cold start injector. — BAD → Repair or replace.
↓ OK
Check vacuum sensor — BAD → Repair or replace.
↓ OK
Check operation of oxygen sensors. — OK → System normal.
↓ BAD
Check wiring between oxygen sensor and ECU. — BAD → Repair wiring.
↓ OK
Replace oxygen sensors.

* Rich malfunction only

**4A-FE & 5S-FE**

Code 27 applies to 5S-FE only.

---

## CELICA TEST NO. 5 OR CODE 22
### COOLANT TEMPERATURE SENSOR SIGNAL

| Terminals | Trouble | Condition | | STD voltage |
|---|---|---|---|---|
| THW - E2 | No voltage | IG SW ON | Coolant temperature 80°C (176°F) | 0.1 - 1.1 V |

**3S-GTE & 5S-FE**

| Terminals | Trouble | Condition | | STD voltage |
|---|---|---|---|---|
| THW- E2 | No Voltage | IG SW ON | Coolant temperature 80°C (176°F) | 0.1 - 1.0 V |

**4A-FE**

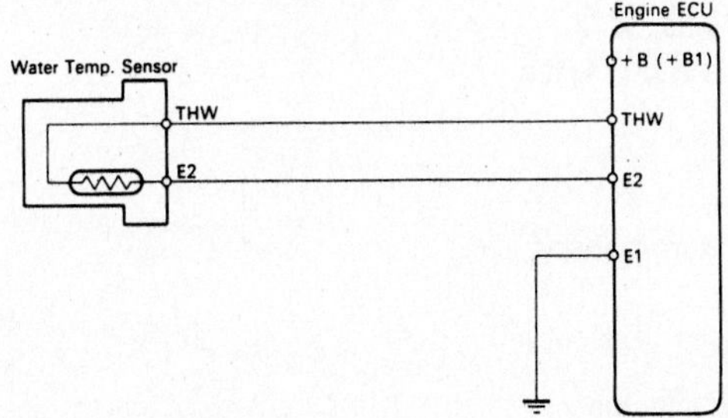


There is no voltage between ECU terminals THW and E2. (IG SW ON)

↓

Check that there is voltage between ECU terminal +B or +B1 and body ground. (IS SW ON)

- NO → See Test No. 2.
- OK → Check wiring between ECU terminal E1 and body ground.
  - BAD → Repair or replace.
  - OK → Check water temp. sensor.
    - BAD → Replace water temp. sensor.
    - OK → Check wiring between ECU and water temp. sensor.
      - OK → Try another ECU.
      - BAD → Repair or replace.

NOTE: Water temperature sensor is also referred to as coolant temperature sensor.

91A17723 91B17724 91C17725 91J17680 91D17726

Courtesy of Toyota Motor Sales, U.S.A., Inc.

# 1991 ENGINE PERFORMANCE
# Self-Diagnostics (Cont.)

## CELICA TEST NO. 6 OR CODE 24
### INTAKE AIR TEMPERATURE SENSOR SIGNAL

| Terminals | Trouble | Condition | | STD voltage |
|---|---|---|---|---|
| THA1 – E2 | No voltage | IG SW ON | Intake air temperature 20°C (68°F) | 1 – 3 V |

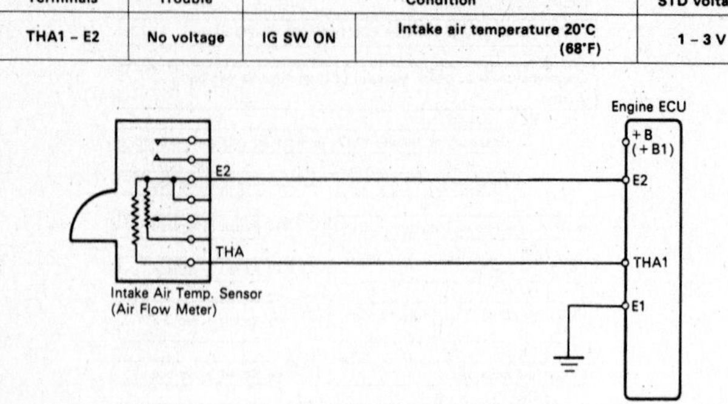
Engine ECU
+B
(+B1)
E2
E2
THA
THA1
E1
Intake Air Temp. Sensor
(Air Flow Meter)

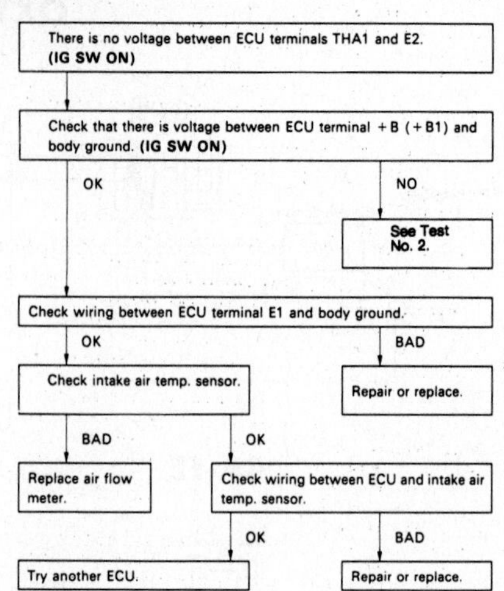
There is no voltage between ECU terminals THA1 and E2. (IG SW ON)
Check that there is voltage between ECU terminal +B (+B1) and body ground. (IG SW ON)
OK
NO
See Test No. 2.
Check wiring between ECU terminal E1 and body ground.
OK
BAD
Check intake air temp. sensor.
Repair or replace.
BAD
OK
Replace air flow meter.
Check wiring between ECU and intake air temp. sensor.
OK
BAD
Try another ECU.
Repair or replace.

**3S-GTE**

---

| Terminals | Trouble | Condition | | STD voltage |
|---|---|---|---|---|
| THA – E2 | No voltage | IG SW ON | Intake air temperature 20°C (68°F) | 1 – 3 V |

**4A-FE**

| Terminals | Trouble | Condition | | STD voltage |
|---|---|---|---|---|
| THA – E2 | No voltage | IG SW ON | Intake air temperature 20°C (68°F) | 1.9 – 2.9 V |

**5S-FE**

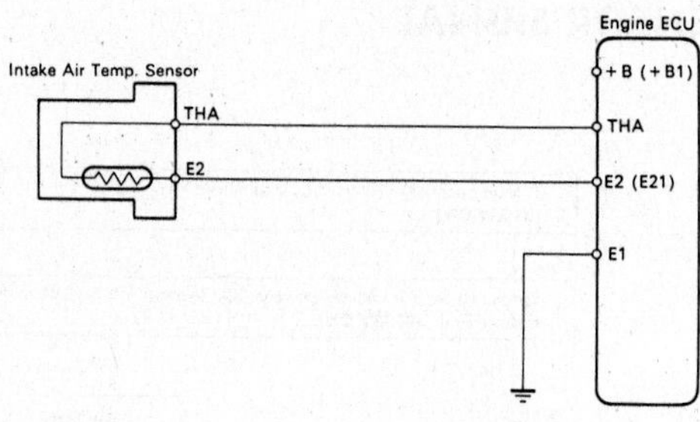
Engine ECU
Intake Air Temp. Sensor
+B (+B1)
THA
THA
E2
E2 (E21)
E1

There is no voltage between ECU terminals THA and E2. (IG SW ON)

Check that there is voltage between ECU terminal +B or +B1 and body ground. (IG SW ON)

OK — NO → See Test No. 2.

Check wiring between ECU terminal E1 and body ground.

OK → Check intake air temp. sensor. — BAD → Repair or replace.

BAD → Replace air temp. sensor. — OK → Check wiring between ECU and air temp. sensor.

OK → Try another ECU. — BAD → Repair or replace.

**4A-FE & 5S-FE**

---

## CELICA CODE 25
### LEAN AIR/FUEL MIXTURE

**Probable Causes**

- Airflow Meter
- Air Intake System
- Coolant Temperature Sensor
- ECU
- Fuel Pressure
- Ignition System
- Injector Circuit or Injector
- Oxygen Sensor or Sensor Circuit
- Vacuum Sensor

**NOTE – Diagnostic chart not available from manufacturer.**

91E17727 91F17728 91G17729 91J17730

Courtesy of Toyota Motor Sales, U.S.A., Inc.

# CELICA CODE 26
## RICH AIR/FUEL MIXTURE

**Probable Causes**
- Airflow Meter
- Cold Start Injector
- Coolant Temperature Sensor
- ECU
- Fuel Pressure
- Injector Circuit or Injector
- Oxygen Sensor or Sensor Circuit
- Vacuum Sensor Circuit

**NOTE - Diagnostic chart not available from manufacturer.**

---

# CELICA TEST NO. 7 OR CODE 31
## VACUUM SENSOR SIGNAL (4A-FE & 5S-FE)

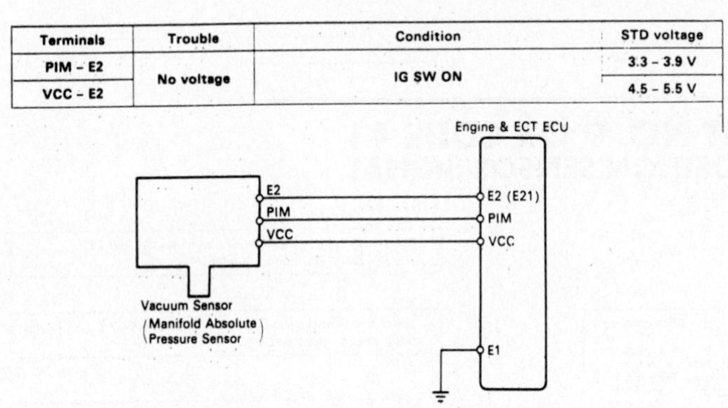

| Terminals | Trouble | Condition | STD voltage |
|---|---|---|---|
| PIM - E2 | No voltage | IG SW ON | 3.3 - 3.9 V |
| VCC - E2 | | | 4.5 - 5.5 V |

Engine & ECT ECU
E2
PIM
VCC
E2 (E21)
PIM
VCC
E1
Vacuum Sensor
(Manifold Absolute Pressure Sensor)

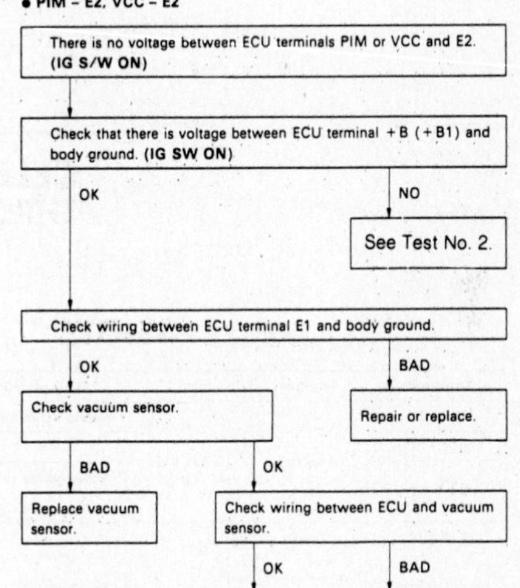
• PIM - E2, VCC - E2
There is no voltage between ECU terminals PIM or VCC and E2. (IG S/W ON)
Check that there is voltage between ECU terminal + B (+ B1) and body ground. (IG SW ON)
OK
NO
See Test No. 2.
Check wiring between ECU terminal E1 and body ground.
OK
BAD
Check vacuum sensor.
Repair or replace.
BAD
OK
Replace vacuum sensor.
Check wiring between ECU and vacuum sensor.
OK
BAD
Try another ECU.
Repair or replace.

---

# CELICA TEST NO. 7 OR CODE 31, 32
## AIRFLOW METER SIGNAL (3S-GTE)

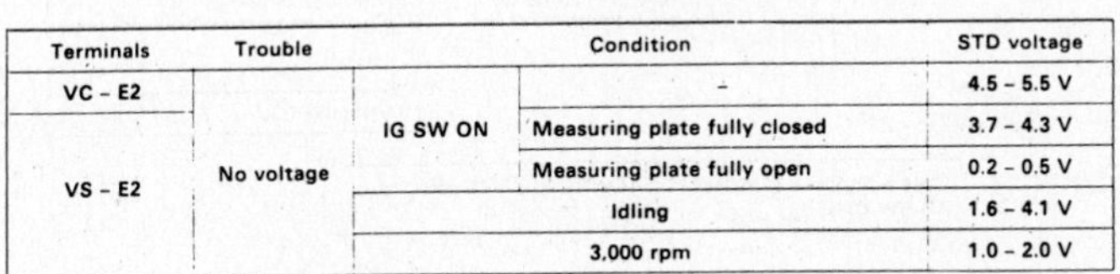

| Terminals | Trouble | Condition | | STD voltage |
|---|---|---|---|---|
| VC - E2 | No voltage | IG SW ON | - | 4.5 - 5.5 V |
| VS - E2 | | | Measuring plate fully closed | 3.7 - 4.3 V |
| | | | Measuring plate fully open | 0.2 - 0.5 V |
| | | Idling | | 1.6 - 4.1 V |
| | | 3,000 rpm | | 1.0 - 2.0 V |

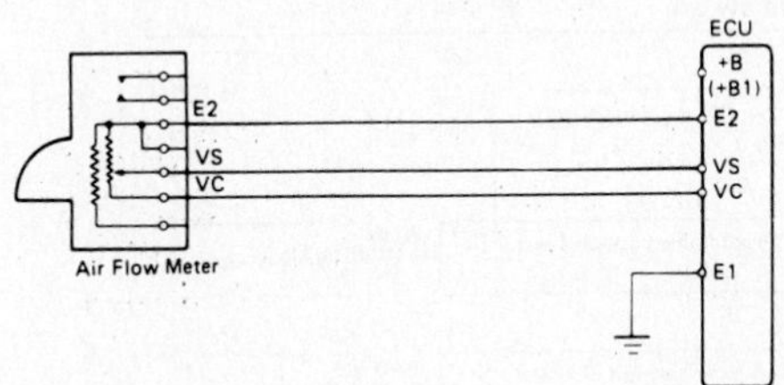
ECU
+B (+B1)
E2
VS
VC
E1
E2
VS
VC
Air Flow Meter

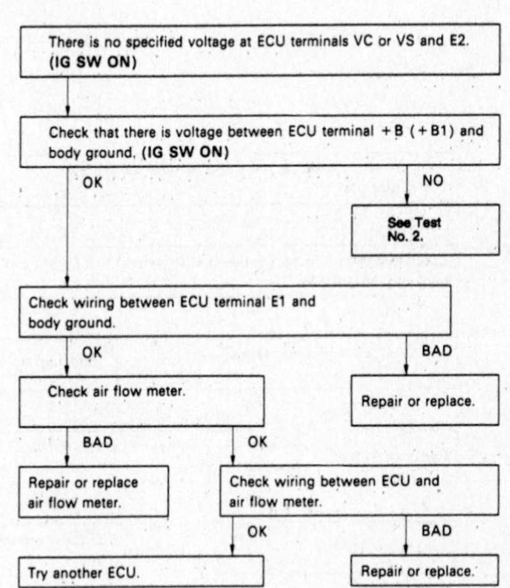
There is no specified voltage at ECU terminals VC or VS and E2. (IG SW ON)
Check that there is voltage between ECU terminal + B (+ B1) and body ground. (IG SW ON)
OK
NO
See Test No. 2.
Check wiring between ECU terminal E1 and body ground.
OK
BAD
Check air flow meter.
Repair or replace.
BAD
OK
Repair or replace air flow meter.
Check wiring between ECU and air flow meter.
OK
BAD
Try another ECU.
Repair or replace.

91A17731 91B17732 91D17684 91E17685

Courtesy of Toyota Motor Sales, U.S.A., Inc.

# 1991 ENGINE PERFORMANCE
# Self-Diagnostics (Cont.)

## CELICA TEST NO. 8 OR CODE 34, 35 (3S-GTE)
### TURBOCHARGER PRESSURE

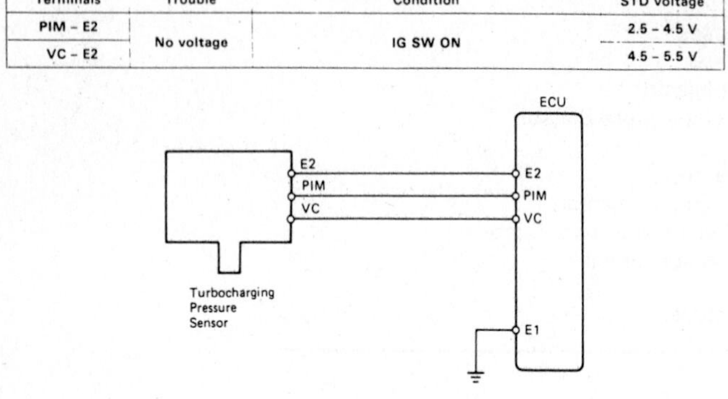

| Terminals | Trouble | Condition | STD voltage |
|---|---|---|---|
| PIM – E2 | No voltage | IG SW ON | 2.5 – 4.5 V |
| VC – E2 | | | 4.5 – 5.5 V |

ECU
E2
PIM
VC
E2
PIM
VC
E1
Turbocharging
Pressure
Sensor

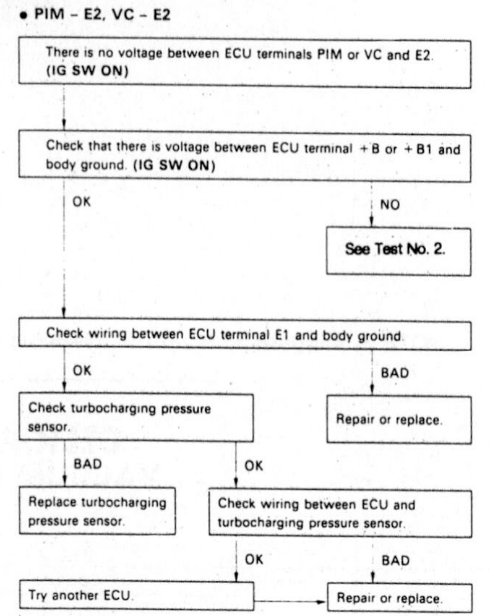
• PIM – E2, VC – E2
There is no voltage between ECU terminals PIM or VC and E2. (IG SW ON)
Check that there is voltage between ECU terminal +B or +B1 and body ground. (IG SW ON)
OK
NO
See Test No. 2.
Check wiring between ECU terminal E1 and body ground.
OK
BAD
Check turbocharging pressure sensor.
Repair or replace.
BAD
OK
Replace turbocharging pressure sensor.
Check wiring between ECU and turbocharging pressure sensor.
OK
BAD
Try another ECU.
Repair or replace.

## CELICA TEST NO. 9 OR CODE 41
### THROTTLE POSITION SENSOR SIGNAL

### 3S-GTE

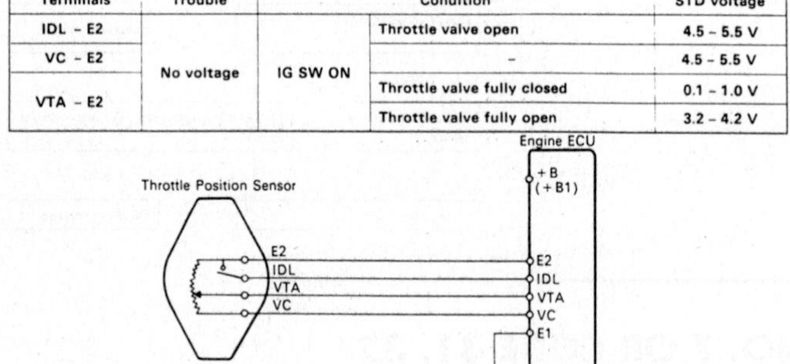

| Terminals | Trouble | | Condition | STD voltage |
|---|---|---|---|---|
| IDL – E2 | No voltage | IG SW ON | Throttle valve open | 4.5 – 5.5 V |
| VC – E2 | | | – | 4.5 – 5.5 V |
| VTA – E2 | | | Throttle valve fully closed | 0.1 – 1.0 V |
| | | | Throttle valve fully open | 3.2 – 4.2 V |

Engine ECU
+B
(+B1)
Throttle Position Sensor
E2
IDL
VTA
VC
E2
IDL
VTA
VC
E1

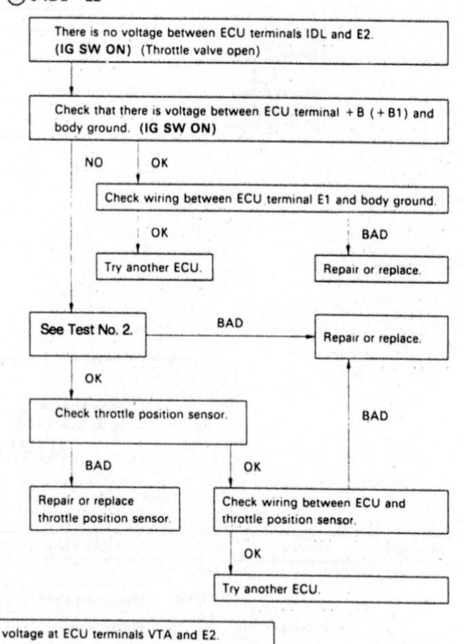
① • IDL – E2
There is no voltage between ECU terminals IDL and E2. (IG SW ON) (Throttle valve open)
Check that there is voltage between ECU terminal +B (+B1) and body ground. (IG SW ON)
NO
OK
Check wiring between ECU terminal E1 and body ground.
OK
BAD
Try another ECU.
Repair or replace.
See Test No. 2.
BAD
Repair or replace.
OK
Check throttle position sensor.
BAD
BAD
OK
Repair or replace throttle position sensor.
Check wiring between ECU and throttle position sensor.
OK
Try another ECU.

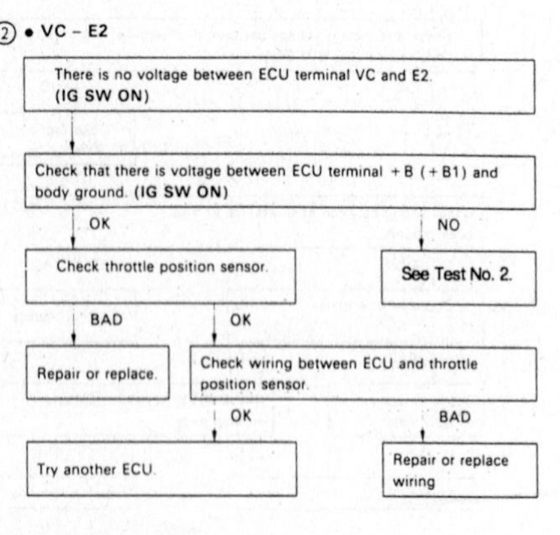
② • VC – E2
There is no voltage between ECU terminal VC and E2. (IG SW ON)
Check that there is voltage between ECU terminal +B (+B1) and body ground. (IG SW ON)
OK
NO
Check throttle position sensor.
See Test No. 2.
BAD
OK
Repair or replace.
Check wiring between ECU and throttle position sensor.
OK
BAD
Try another ECU.
Repair or replace wiring.

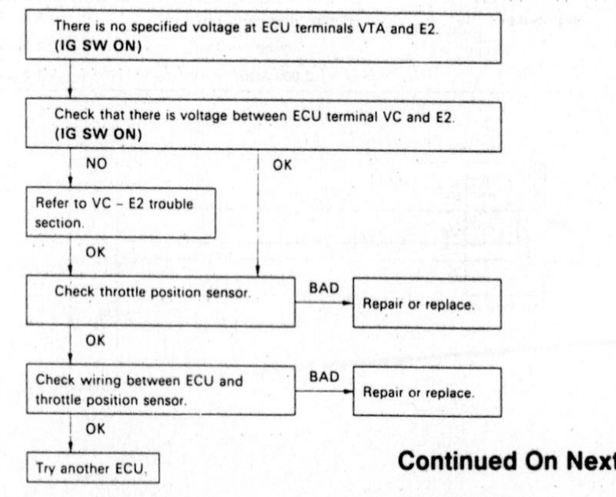
③ • VTA – E2
There is no specified voltage at ECU terminals VTA and E2. (IG SW ON)
Check that there is voltage between ECU terminal VC and E2. (IG SW ON)
NO
OK
Refer to VC – E2 trouble section.
OK
Check throttle position sensor.
BAD
Repair or replace.
OK
Check wiring between ECU and throttle position sensor.
BAD
Repair or replace.
OK
Try another ECU.

**Continued On Next Page**

91C17733 91D17734 91H17688 91I17689 91B17690 91C17691

## CELICA TEST NO. 9 OR CODE 41
### THROTTLE POSITION SENSOR SIGNAL (Cont.)

### 4A-FE

| Terminals | Trouble | Condition | | STD voltage |
|---|---|---|---|---|
| IDL – E2 | No voltage | IG SW ON | Throttle valve open | 10 – 14 V |
| PSW – E2 | | | Throttle valve fully closed | 10 – 14 V |

Engine ECU
+B
IDL
E2 (E21)
PSW
E1
IDL
E2
PSW
Throttle Position Sensor

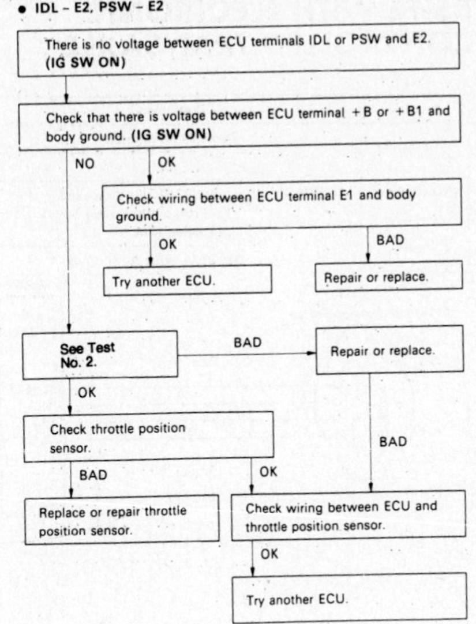

• IDL – E2, PSW – E2
There is no voltage between ECU terminals IDL or PSW and E2. (IG SW ON)
Check that there is voltage between ECU terminal +B or +B1 and body ground. (IG SW ON)
NO
OK
Check wiring between ECU terminal E1 and body ground.
OK
BAD
Try another ECU.
Repair or replace.
See Test No. 2.
BAD
Repair or replace.
OK
Check throttle position sensor.
BAD
BAD
OK
Replace or repair throttle position sensor.
Check wiring between ECU and throttle position sensor.
OK
Try another ECU.

### 5S-FE WITHOUT ELECTRONIC CONTROLLED TRANSAXLE

| Terminals | Trouble | Condition | | STD voltage |
|---|---|---|---|---|
| IDL – E1 | No voltage | IG SW ON | Throttle valve open | 8 – 14 V |
| PSW – E1 | | | Throttle valve fully closed (Throttle opener must be cancelled first) | 4.5 – 5.5 V |

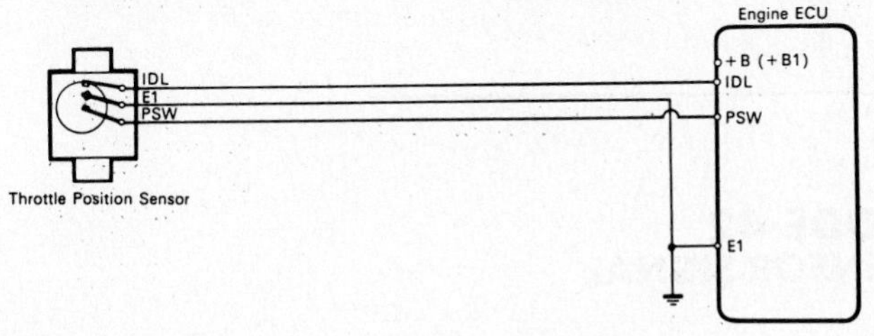

Engine ECU
+B (+B1)
IDL
PSW
E1
IDL
E1
PSW
Throttle Position Sensor

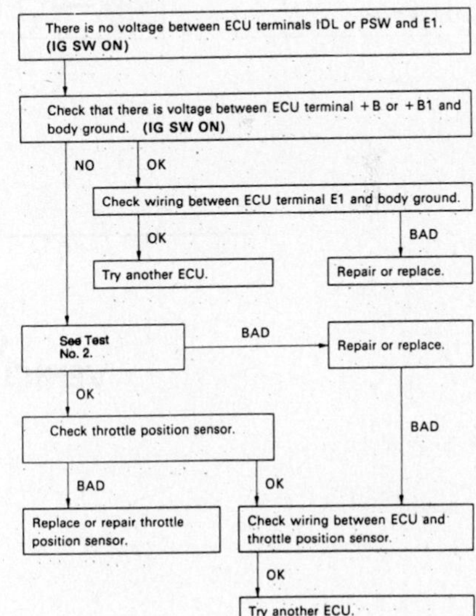

• IDL – E1, PSW – E1
There is no voltage between ECU terminals IDL or PSW and E1. (IG SW ON)
Check that there is voltage between ECU terminal +B or +B1 and body ground. (IG SW ON)
NO
OK
Check wiring between ECU terminal E1 and body ground.
OK
BAD
Try another ECU.
Repair or replace.
See Test No. 2.
BAD
Repair or replace.
OK
Check throttle position sensor.
BAD
BAD
OK
Replace or repair throttle position sensor.
Check wiring between ECU and throttle position sensor.
OK
Try another ECU.

Continued On Next Page

91F17736 91G17737 91H17738 91I17739

# CELICA TEST NO. 9 OR CODE 41
## THROTTLE POSITION SENSOR SIGNAL (Cont.)

### 5S-FE WITH ELECTRONIC CONTROLLED TRANSAXLE

| Terminals | Trouble | | Condition | STD voltage |
|---|---|---|---|---|
| IDL – E2 | No voltage | IG SW ON | Throttle valve open | 8 – 14 V |
| VCC – E2 | | | – | 4.5 – 5.5 V |
| VTA – E2 | | | Throttle valve fully closed (Throttle opener must be cancelled first) | 0.8 – 1.2 V |
| | | | Throttle valve fully open | 3.2 – 4.2 V |

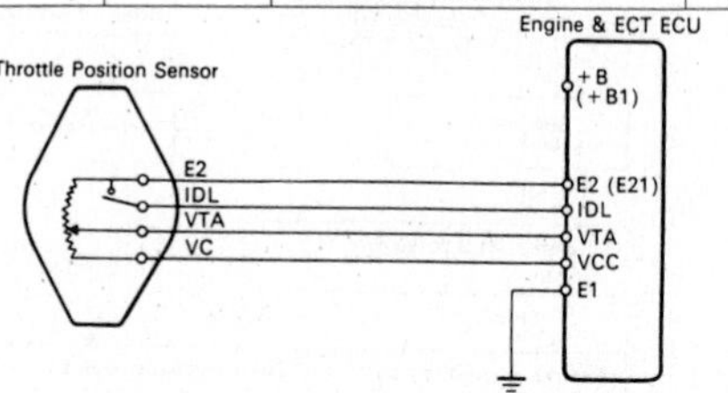
Engine & ECT ECU
Throttle Position Sensor
E2
IDL
VTA
VC
+B
(+B1)
E2 (E21)
IDL
VTA
VCC
E1

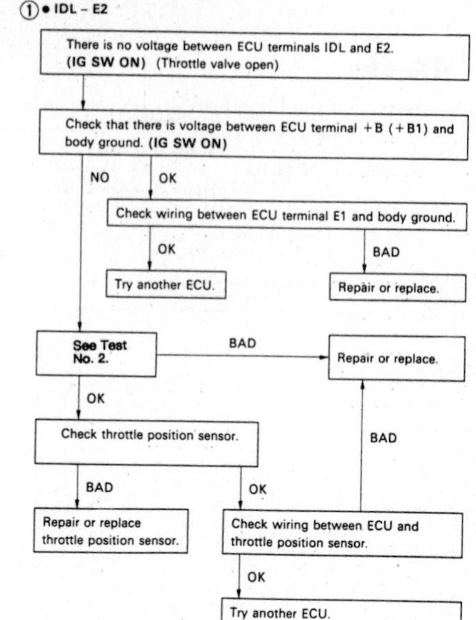
① • IDL – E2
There is no voltage between ECU terminals IDL and E2. (IG SW ON) (Throttle valve open)
Check that there is voltage between ECU terminal +B (+B1) and body ground. (IG SW ON)
NO
OK
Check wiring between ECU terminal E1 and body ground.
OK
BAD
Try another ECU.
Repair or replace.
See Test No. 2.
BAD
Repair or replace.
OK
Check throttle position sensor.
BAD
BAD
OK
Repair or replace throttle position sensor.
Check wiring between ECU and throttle position sensor.
OK
Try another ECU.

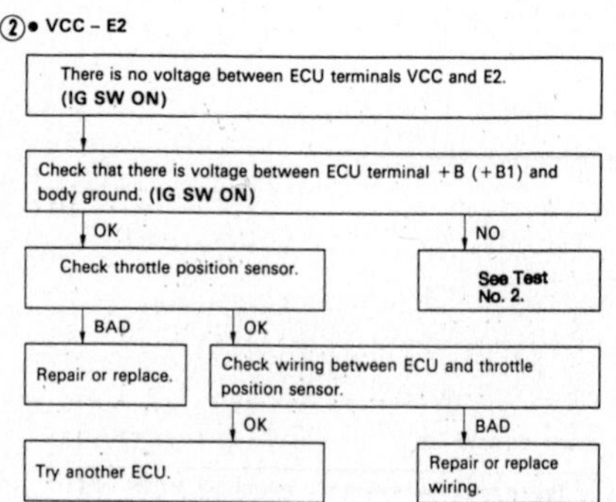
② • VCC – E2
There is no voltage between ECU terminals VCC and E2. (IG SW ON)
Check that there is voltage between ECU terminal +B (+B1) and body ground. (IG SW ON)
OK
NO
Check throttle position sensor.
See Test No. 2.
BAD
OK
Repair or replace.
Check wiring between ECU and throttle position sensor.
OK
BAD
Try another ECU.
Repair or replace wiring.

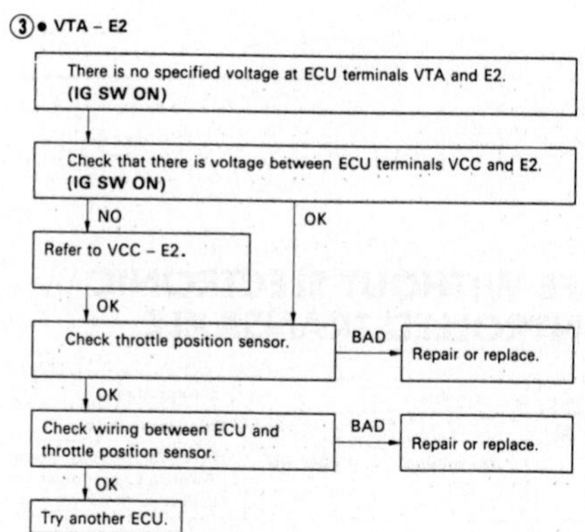
③ • VTA – E2
There is no specified voltage at ECU terminals VTA and E2. (IG SW ON)
Check that there is voltage between ECU terminals VCC and E2. (IG SW ON)
NO
OK
Refer to VCC – E2.
OK
Check throttle position sensor.
BAD
Repair or replace.
OK
Check wiring between ECU and throttle position sensor.
BAD
Repair or replace.
OK
Try another ECU.

---

# CELICA CODE 42
## VEHICLE SPEED SENSOR SIGNAL

**Probable Causes**

- Vehicle Speed Sensor or Sensor Circuit
- ECU

**NOTE** – **Diagnostic chart not available from manufacturer.**

91B17740 91I17689 91C17741 91D17742

# 1991 ENGINE PERFORMANCE
# Self-Diagnostics (Cont.)

## CELICA TEST NO. 10 OR CODE 43
### STARTER SIGNAL

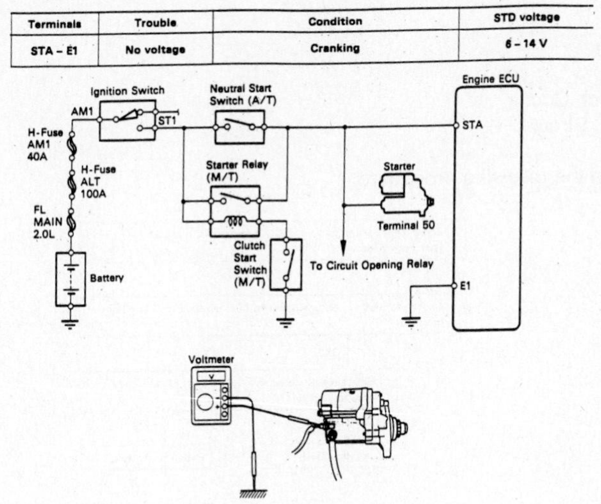

| Terminals | Trouble | Condition | STD voltage |
|---|---|---|---|
| STA – E1 | No voltage | Cranking | 6 – 14 V |

Ignition Switch
AM1
ST1
Neutral Start Switch (A/T)
Engine ECU
STA
H-Fuse AM1 40A
H-Fuse ALT 100A
FL MAIN 2.0L
Starter Relay (M/T)
Starter
Terminal 50
Clutch Start Switch (M/T)
To Circuit Opening Relay
E1
Battery
Voltmeter

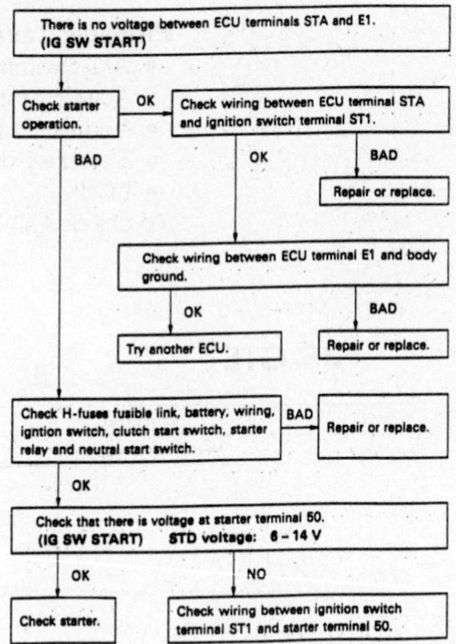
There is no voltage between ECU terminals STA and E1. (IG SW START)
Check starter operation.
OK
Check wiring between ECU terminal STA and ignition switch terminal ST1.
BAD
OK
BAD
Repair or replace.
Check wiring between ECU terminal E1 and body ground.
OK
BAD
Try another ECU.
Repair or replace.
Check H-fuses fusible link, battery, wiring, igntion switch, clutch start switch, starter relay and neutral start switch.
BAD
Repair or replace.
OK
Check that there is voltage at starter terminal 50. (IG SW START) STD voltage: 6 – 14 V
OK
NO
Check starter.
Check wiring between ignition switch terminal ST1 and starter terminal 50.

## CELICA TEST NO. 11 OR CODE 51
### SWITCH SIGNAL

**Probable Causes**

- A/C Switch or Switch Circuit
- Accelerator Pedal or Cable
- Neutral/Start Switch or Switch Circuit
- Throttle Position Sensor IDL Circuit
- ECU

To check A/C switch signal, use the following procedure.

### 4A-FE & 5S-FE

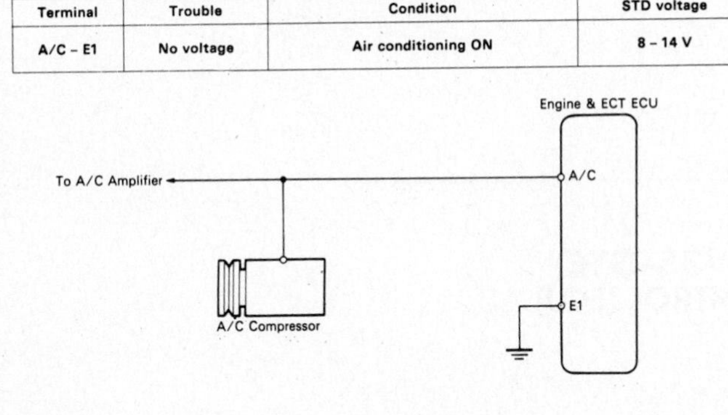

| Terminal | Trouble | Condition | STD voltage |
|---|---|---|---|
| A/C – E1 | No voltage | Air conditioning ON | 8 – 14 V |

Engine & ECT ECU
To A/C Amplifier
A/C
E1
A/C Compressor

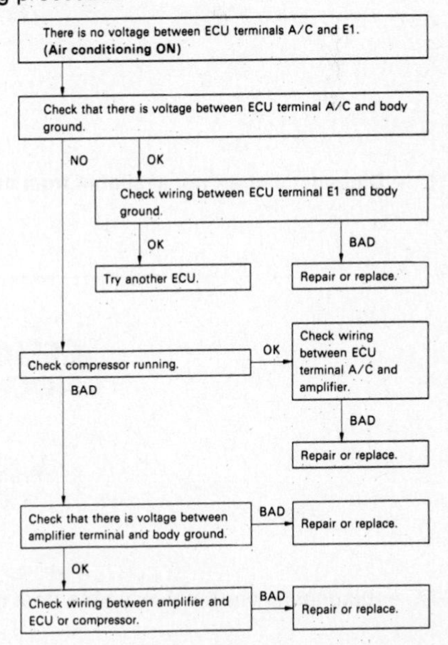
There is no voltage between ECU terminals A/C and E1. (Air conditioning ON)
Check that there is voltage between ECU terminal A/C and body ground.
NO
OK
Check wiring between ECU terminal E1 and body ground.
OK
BAD
Try another ECU.
Repair or replace.
Check compressor running.
OK
Check wiring between ECU terminal A/C and amplifier.
BAD
BAD
Repair or replace.
Check that there is voltage between amplifier terminal and body ground.
BAD
Repair or replace.
OK
Check wiring between amplifier and ECU or compressor.
BAD
Repair or replace.

**Continued On Next Page**

91E17743 91F17744 91F17694 91G17695 91G17745

# 1991 ENGINE PERFORMANCE
# Self-Diagnostics (Cont.)

## CELICA TEST NO. 11 OR CODE 51
### SWITCH SIGNAL (Cont.)

**Probable Causes**
- A/C Switch or Switch Circuit
- Accelerator Pedal or Cable
- Neutral/Start Switch or Switch Circuit
- Throttle Position Sensor IDL Circuit
- ECU

To check A/C switch signal, use the following procedure.

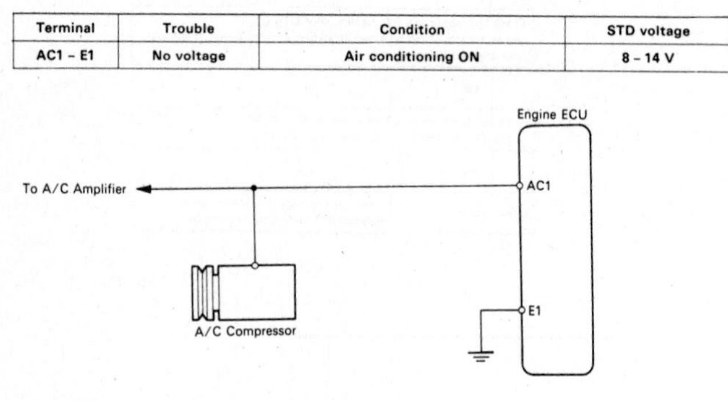
3S-GTE
Terminal
Trouble
Condition
STD voltage
AC1 - E1
No voltage
Air conditioning ON
8 - 14 V
Engine ECU
To A/C Amplifier
AC1
E1
A/C Compressor

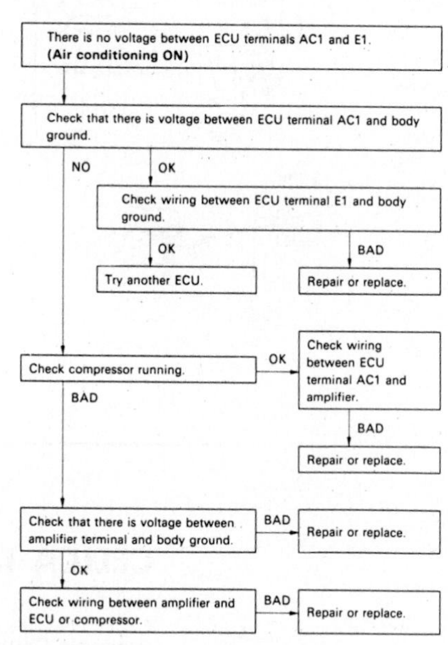
There is no voltage between ECU terminals AC1 and E1.
(Air conditioning ON)
Check that there is voltage between ECU terminal AC1 and body ground.
NO
OK
Check wiring between ECU terminal E1 and body ground.
OK
BAD
Try another ECU.
Repair or replace.
Check compressor running.
OK
Check wiring between ECU terminal AC1 and amplifier.
BAD
Repair or replace.
BAD
Check that there is voltage between amplifier terminal and body ground.
BAD
Repair or replace.
OK
Check wiring between amplifier and ECU or compressor.
BAD
Repair or replace.

## CELICA CODE 52 (3S-GTE)
### KNOCK SENSOR SIGNAL

**Probable Causes**
- Knock Sensor or Sensor Circuit
- ECU

**NOTE - Diagnostic chart not available from manufacturer.**

## CELICA CODE 53 (3S-GTE)
### KNOCK SENSOR CONTROL (ECU)

**Probable Causes**
- ECU

**NOTE - Diagnostic chart not available from manufacturer.**

91H17746 91I17747

Courtesy of Toyota Motor Sales, U.S.A., Inc.

## CELICA TEST NO. 12 OR CODE 71
### EGR SYSTEM MALFUNCTION

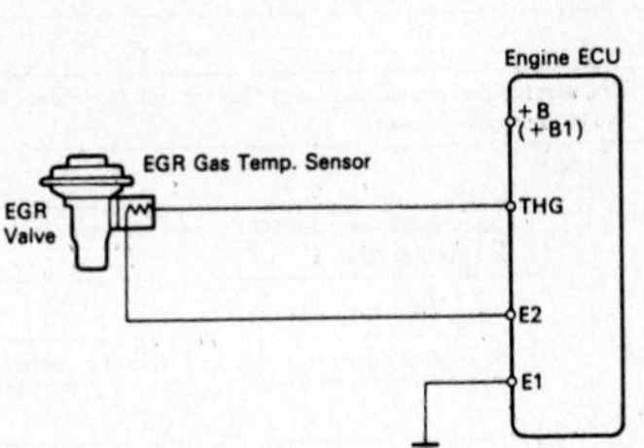
Engine ECU
+B
(+B1)
EGR Gas Temp. Sensor
EGR Valve
THG
E2
E1

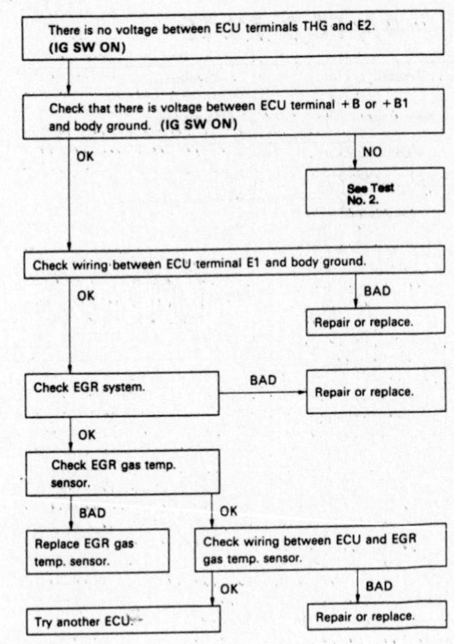
There is no voltage between ECU terminals THG and E2. (IG SW ON)
Check that there is voltage between ECU terminal +B or +B1 and body ground. (IG SW ON)
OK
NO
See Test No. 2.
Check wiring between ECU terminal E1 and body ground.
OK
BAD
Repair or replace.
Check EGR system.
BAD
Repair or replace.
OK
Check EGR gas temp. sensor.
BAD
OK
Replace EGR gas temp. sensor.
Check wiring between ECU and EGR gas temp. sensor.
OK
BAD
Try another ECU.
Repair or replace.

## CELICA TEST NO. 13
### INJECTOR CIRCUIT

### 3S-GTE

| No. | Terminals | Trouble | Condition | STD voltage |
|---|---|---|---|---|
| 5 | No. 1<br>No. 2 – E01<br>No. 3 – E02<br>No. 4 | No voltage | IG SW ON | 10 – 14 V |

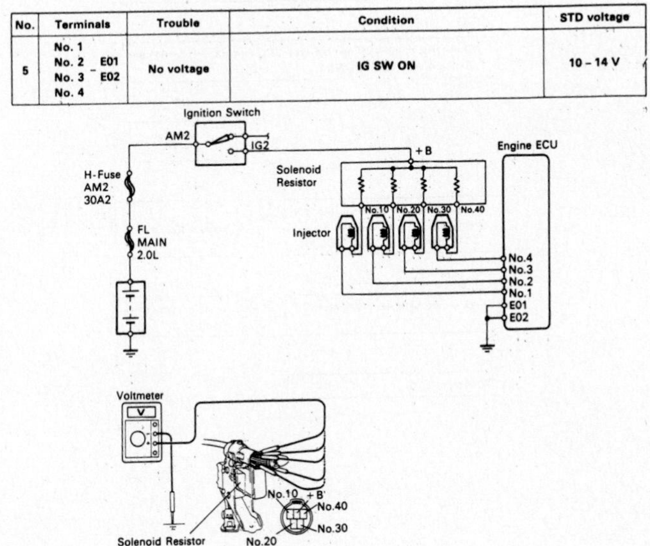
Ignition Switch
AM2
IG2
+B
Engine ECU
H-Fuse AM2 30A2
Solenoid Resistor
No.10
No.20
No.30
No.40
Injector
FL MAIN 2.0L
No.4
No.3
No.2
No.1
E01
E02
Voltmeter
V
No.10
+B
No.40
No.30
Solenoid Resistor
No.20

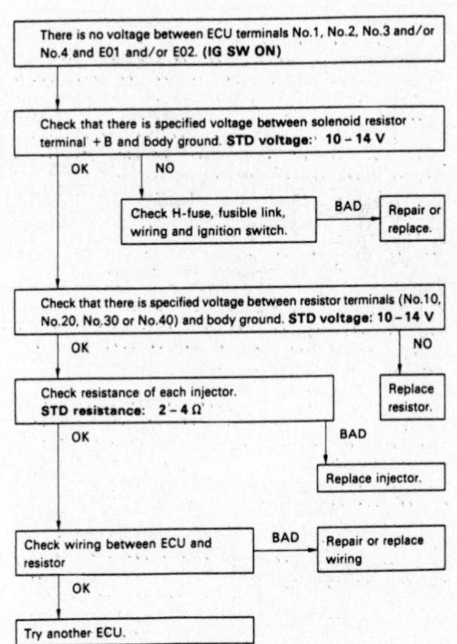
There is no voltage between ECU terminals No.1, No.2, No.3 and/or No.4 and E01 and/or E02. (IG SW ON)
Check that there is specified voltage between solenoid resistor terminal +B and body ground. STD voltage: 10 – 14 V
OK
NO
Check H-fuse, fusible link, wiring and ignition switch.
BAD
Repair or replace.
Check that there is specified voltage between resistor terminals (No.10, No.20, No.30 or No.40) and body ground. STD voltage: 10 – 14 V
OK
NO
Check resistance of each injector. STD resistance: 2 – 4 Ω
Replace resistor.
OK
BAD
Replace injector.
Check wiring between ECU and resistor
BAD
Repair or replace wiring
OK
Try another ECU.

Continued On Next Page

Courtesy of Toyota Motor Sales, U.S.A., Inc.

91H17787 91J17748 91A17749 91E17750 91F17751

# 1991 ENGINE PERFORMANCE
# Self-Diagnostics (Cont.)

## CELICA TEST NO. 13
### INJECTOR CIRCUIT (Cont.)

### 4A-FE & 5S-FE

| No. | Terminals | Trouble | Condition | STD voltage |
|---|---|---|---|---|
| 5 | No.10 – E01<br>No.20 – E02 | No voltage | IG SW ON | 10 – 14 V |

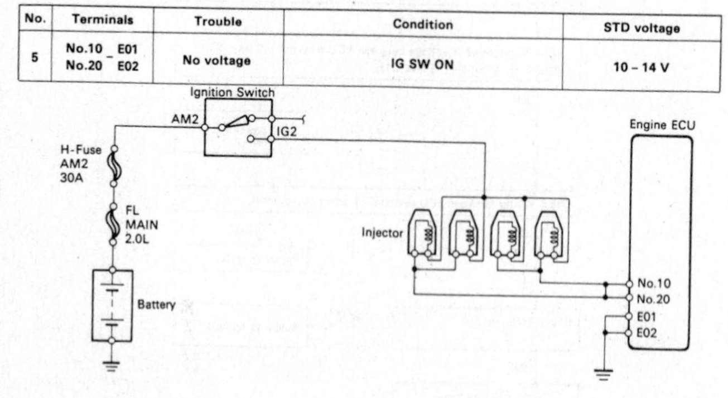
Ignition Switch
AM2
IG2
H-Fuse
AM2
30A
FL
MAIN
2.0L
Battery
Injector
Engine ECU
No.10
No.20
E01
E02

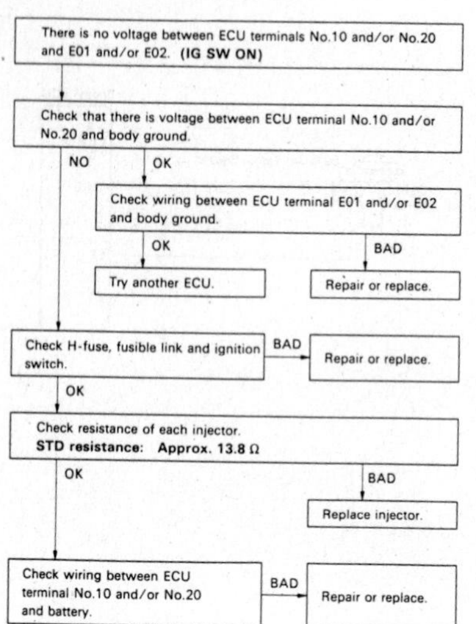
There is no voltage between ECU terminals No.10 and/or No.20 and E01 and/or E02. (IG SW ON)
Check that there is voltage between ECU terminal No.10 and/or No.20 and body ground.
NO
OK
Check wiring between ECU terminal E01 and/or E02 and body ground.
OK
BAD
Try another ECU.
Repair or replace.
Check H-fuse, fusible link and ignition switch.
BAD
Repair or replace.
OK
Check resistance of each injector.
STD resistance: Approx. 13.8 Ω
OK
BAD
Replace injector.
Check wiring between ECU terminal No.10 and/or No.20 and battery.
BAD
Repair or replace.

---

## CELICA TEST NO. 14
### IDLE SPEED CONTROL CIRCUIT

### 3S-GTE

| No. | Terminals | Trouble | Condition | STD voltage |
|---|---|---|---|---|
| 10 | RSC<br>RSO – E1 | No voltage | IG SW ON | 8 – 14 V |

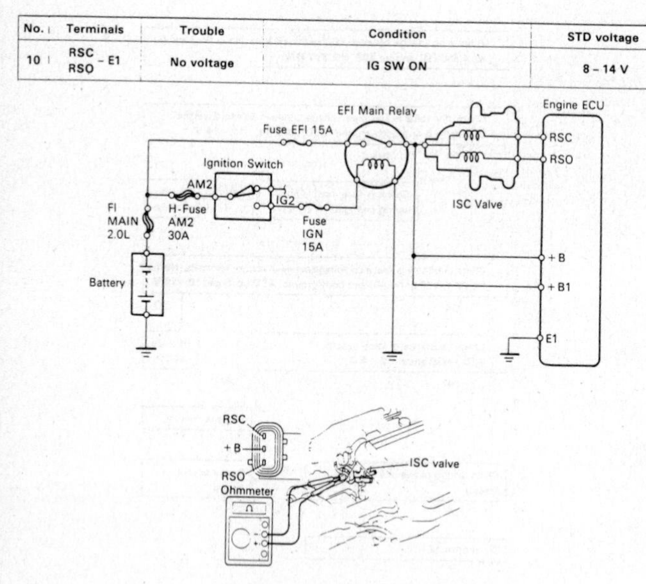
EFI Main Relay
Engine ECU
Fuse EFI 15A
RSC
RSO
Ignition Switch
AM2
IG2
ISC Valve
FI
MAIN
2.0L
H-Fuse
AM2
30A
Fuse
IGN
15A
Battery
+B
+B1
E1
RSC
+B
RSO
Ohmmeter
ISC valve

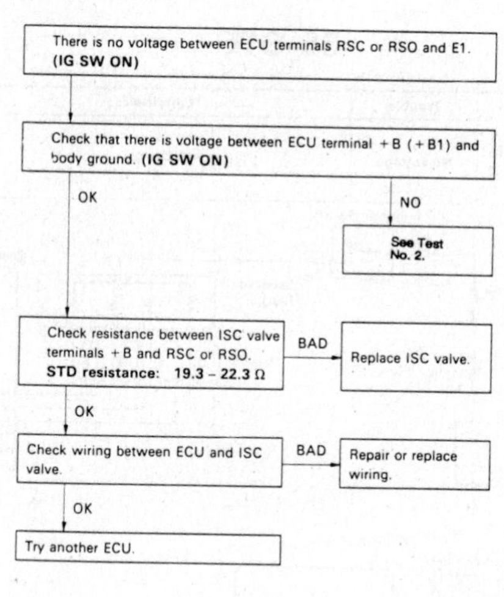
There is no voltage between ECU terminals RSC or RSO and E1. (IG SW ON)
Check that there is voltage between ECU terminal +B (+B1) and body ground. (IG SW ON)
OK
NO
See Test No. 2.
Check resistance between ISC valve terminals +B and RSC or RSO.
STD resistance: 19.3 – 22.3 Ω
BAD
Replace ISC valve.
OK
Check wiring between ECU and ISC valve.
BAD
Repair or replace wiring.
OK
Try another ECU.

**Continued On Next Page**

91G17752 91H17753 91I17754 91J17755 91I18091

# CELICA TEST NO. 14
## IDLE SPEED CONTROL CIRCUIT (Cont.)

### 5S-FE

| No. | Terminals | Trouble | Condition | STD voltage |
|---|---|---|---|---|
| 10 | ISCC – E1<br>ISCO | No voltage | IG SW ON | 8 – 14 V |

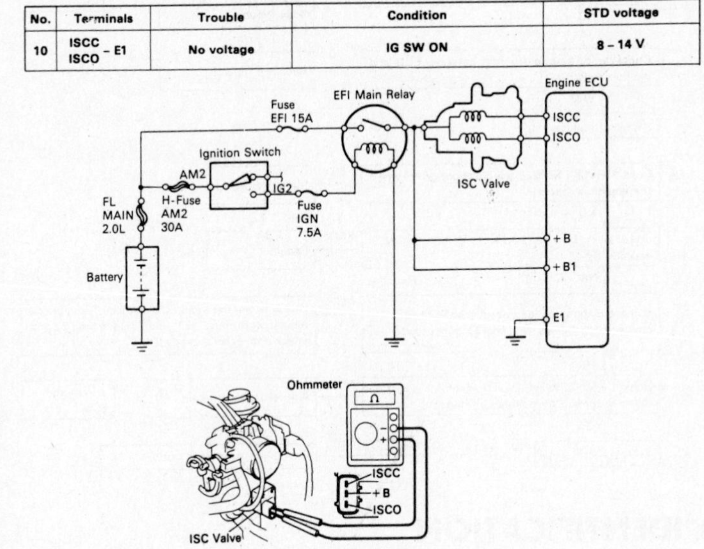
Fuse
EFI 15A
EFI Main Relay
Engine ECU
ISCC
ISCO
Ignition Switch
AM2
IG2
ISC Valve
FL
MAIN
2.0L
H-Fuse
AM2
30A
Fuse
IGN
7.5A
+B
+B1
Battery
E1
Ohmmeter
ISCC
+B
ISCO
ISC Valve

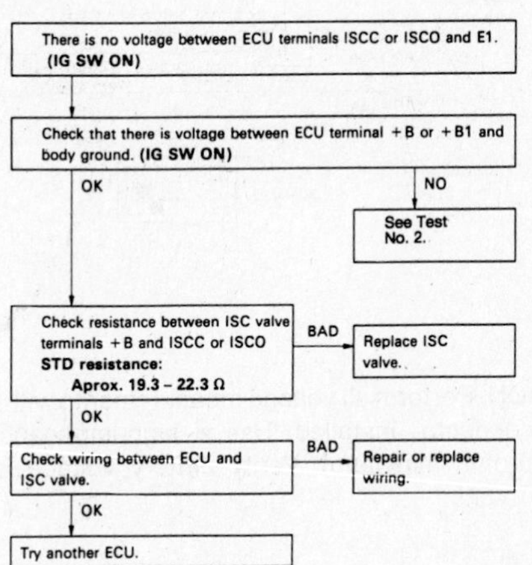
There is no voltage between ECU terminals ISCC or ISCO and E1. (IG SW ON)
Check that there is voltage between ECU terminal +B or +B1 and body ground. (IG SW ON)
OK
NO
See Test No. 2.
Check resistance between ISC valve terminals +B and ISCC or ISCO
STD resistance:
Aprox. 19.3 – 22.3 Ω
BAD
Replace ISC valve.
OK
Check wiring between ECU and ISC valve.
BAD
Repair or replace wiring.
OK
Try another ECU.

# CELICA TEST NO. 15
## CHECK ENGINE LIGHT CIRCUIT

| No. | Terminals | Trouble | Condition | STD voltage |
|---|---|---|---|---|
| 11 | W – E1 | No voltage | No trouble ("CHECK" warning light off) and engine running | 10 – 14 V |

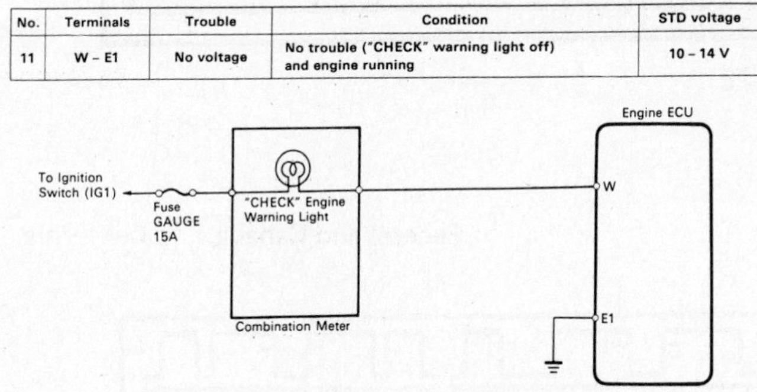
Engine ECU
To Ignition
Switch (IG1)
Fuse
GAUGE
15A
"CHECK" Engine
Warning Light
W
E1
Combination Meter

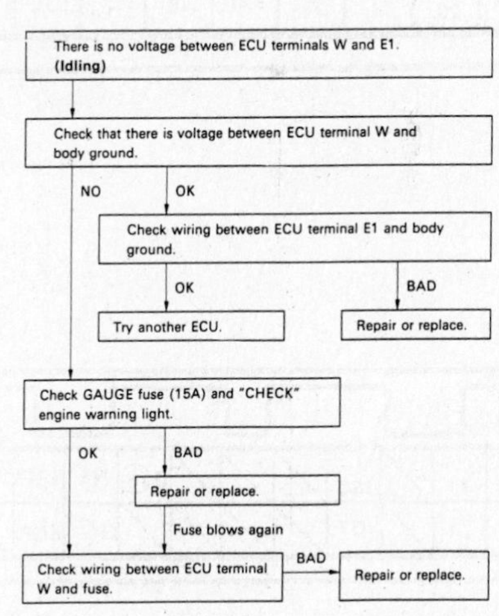
There is no voltage between ECU terminals W and E1. (Idling)
Check that there is voltage between ECU terminal W and body ground.
NO
OK
Check wiring between ECU terminal E1 and body ground.
OK
BAD
Try another ECU.
Repair or replace.
Check GAUGE fuse (15A) and "CHECK" engine warning light.
OK
BAD
Repair or replace.
Fuse blows again
Check wiring between ECU terminal W and fuse.
BAD
Repair or replace.

91A17756 91B17757 91C17758 91J17706 91D17759

Courtesy of Toyota Motor Sales, U.S.A., Inc.

# 1991 ENGINE PERFORMANCE
# Self-Diagnostics (Cont.)

## COROLLA DIAGNOSTIC CIRCUIT CHECK

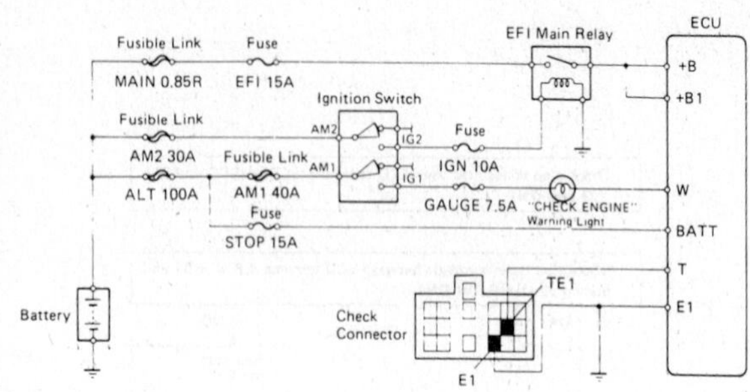
Fusible Link
Fuse
EFI Main Relay
ECU
MAIN 0.85R
EFI 15A
+B
+B1
Ignition Switch
Fusible Link
AM2
IG2
Fuse
AM2 30A
Fusible Link
AM1
IGN 10A
IG1
ALT 100A
AM1 40A
GAUGE 7.5A
"CHECK ENGINE" Warning Light
W
Fuse
STOP 15A
BATT
TE1
T
Battery
Check Connector
E1
E1

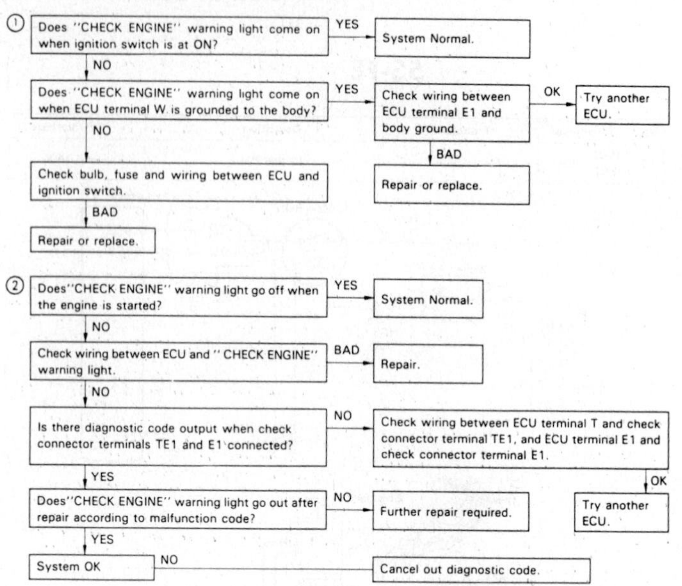
1
Does "CHECK ENGINE" warning light come on when ignition switch is at ON?
YES
System Normal.
NO
Does "CHECK ENGINE" warning light come on when ECU terminal W is grounded to the body?
YES
Check wiring between ECU terminal E1 and body ground.
OK
Try another ECU.
BAD
Repair or replace.
NO
Check bulb, fuse and wiring between ECU and ignition switch.
BAD
Repair or replace.
2
Does "CHECK ENGINE" warning light go off when the engine is started?
YES
System Normal.
NO
Check wiring between ECU and "CHECK ENGINE" warning light.
BAD
Repair.
NO
Is there diagnostic code output when check connector terminals TE1 and E1 connected?
NO
Check wiring between ECU terminal T and check connector terminal TE1, and ECU terminal E1 and check connector terminal E1.
OK
Try another ECU.
YES
Does "CHECK ENGINE" warning light go out after repair according to malfunction code?
NO
Further repair required.
YES
System OK
NO
Cancel out diagnostic code.

CAUTION: Perform all voltage measurements with ECU harness connector installed. Use a high-impedance DVOM (10,000-ohm minimum). Verify battery voltage is greater than 11 volts.

## ECU TERMINAL IDENTIFICATION

*1: 2WD M/T, *2: A/T, *3: 4A/T, *4: Calif., *5: Calif. and 4WD, *6: 2WD

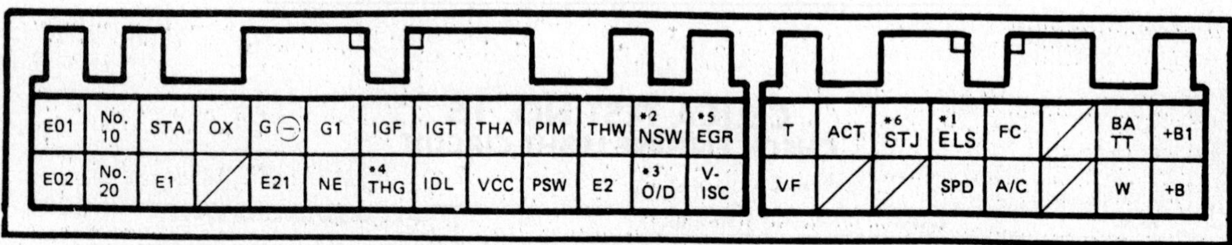
E01
No. 10
STA
OX
G⊖
G1
IGF
IGT
THA
PIM
THW
*2 NSW
*5 EGR
T
ACT
*6 STJ
*1 ELS
FC
BA TT
+B1
E02
No. 20
E1
E21
NE
*4 THG
IDL
VCC
PSW
E2
*3 O/D
V-ISC
VF
SPD
A/C
W
+B

4A-FE

*1: Federal and Canada, *2: California

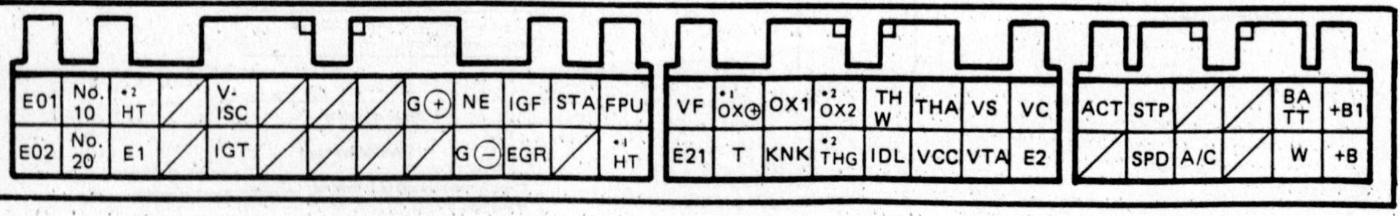
E01
No. 10
*2 HT
V-ISC
G⊕
NE
IGF
STA
FPU
VF
*1 OX⊕
OX1
*2 OX2
TH W
THA
VS
VC
ACT
STP
BA TT
+B1
E02
No. 20
E1
IGT
G⊖
EGR
*1 HT
E21
T
KNK
*2 THG
IDL
VCC
VTA
E2
SPD
A/C
W
+B

4A-GE

91G17760 91H17761 91I17762 91J17763

Courtesy of Toyota Motor Sales, U.S.A., Inc.

# COROLLA TEST NO. 1
## ECU POWER SOURCE

| Terminal | Trouble | Condition | STD voltage |
|---|---|---|---|
| BATT – E1 | No voltage | – | 10 – 14 V |

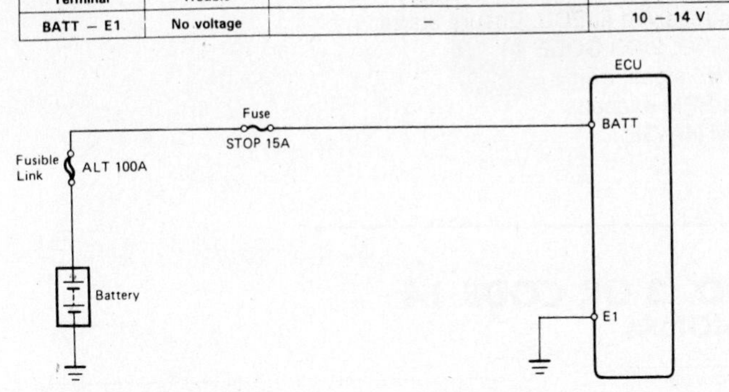
ECU
Fuse
STOP 15A
BATT
Fusible Link
ALT 100A
Battery
E1

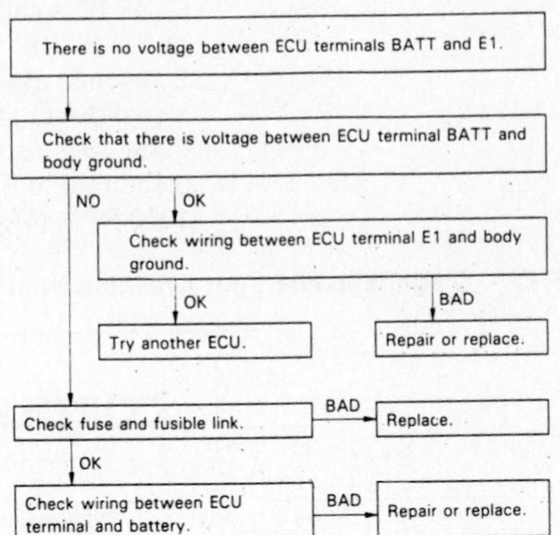
There is no voltage between ECU terminals BATT and E1.
Check that there is voltage between ECU terminal BATT and body ground.
NO
OK
Check wiring between ECU terminal E1 and body ground.
OK
BAD
Try another ECU.
Repair or replace.
Check fuse and fusible link.
BAD
Replace.
OK
Check wiring between ECU terminal and battery.
BAD
Repair or replace.

# COROLLA TEST NO. 2
## ECU (+B) CIRCUIT

| Terminal | Trouble | Condition | STD voltage |
|---|---|---|---|
| +B<br>+B1 – E1 | No voltage | IG SW ON | 10 – 14 V |

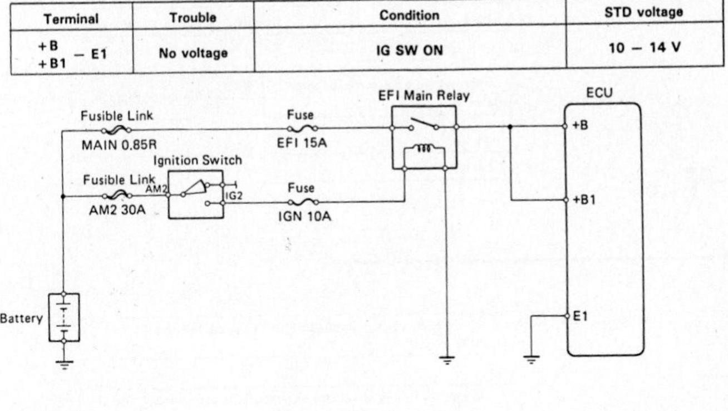
Fusible Link
MAIN 0.85R
Fuse
EFI 15A
EFI Main Relay
ECU
+B
Ignition Switch
Fusible Link
AM2
IG2
AM2 30A
Fuse
IGN 10A
+B1
Battery
E1

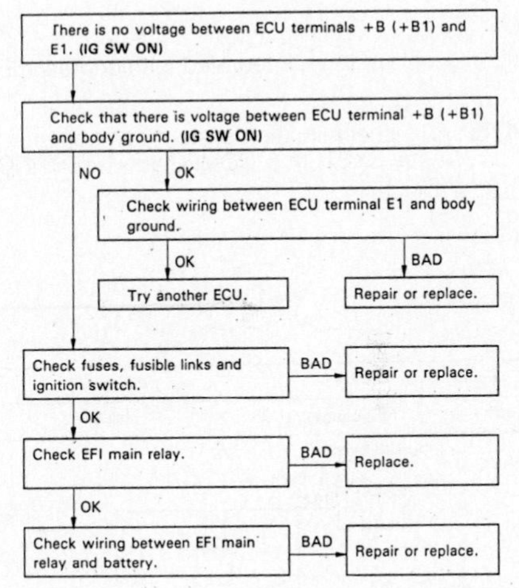
There is no voltage between ECU terminals +B (+B1) and E1. (IG SW ON)
Check that there is voltage between ECU terminal +B (+B1) and body ground. (IG SW ON)
NO
OK
Check wiring between ECU terminal E1 and body ground.
OK
BAD
Try another ECU.
Repair or replace.
Check fuses, fusible links and ignition switch.
BAD
Repair or replace.
OK
Check EFI main relay.
BAD
Replace.
OK
Check wiring between EFI main relay and battery.
BAD
Repair or replace.

91A17764 91A17715 91B17765 91C17717

Courtesy of Toyota Motor Sales, U.S.A., Inc.

## COROLLA CODE 12, 13
### RPM SIGNAL

Code 12 is caused by loss of signal "G2", "G1", or "NE" (3S-GTE) or "G" or "NE" (all others) from distributor to ECU for at least 2 seconds after starter signal is received at ECU. Ensure starter signal exists at ECU. See TEST NO. 9 OR CODE 43.
Code 13 is caused by loss of "NE" signal from distributor to ECU when engine RPM exceeds 1000 RPM (4A-FE) or 1500 RPM (4A-GE).

**NOTE – Diagnostic chart not available from manufacturer.**

---

## COROLLA TEST NO. 3 OR CODE 14
### RPM SIGNAL

| Terminal | Trouble | Condition | STD voltage |
|---|---|---|---|
| IGT – E1 | No voltage | Idling | 0.7 – 1.0 V |

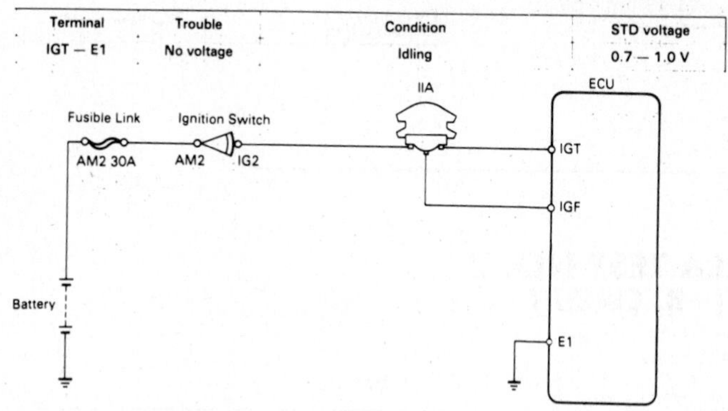
IIA
ECU
Fusible Link
Ignition Switch
AM2 30A
AM2
IG2
IGT
IGF
Battery
E1

IIA – Integrated Ignition Assembly

NOTE: To check ignition system components, see SYSTEM & COMPONENT TESTING article.

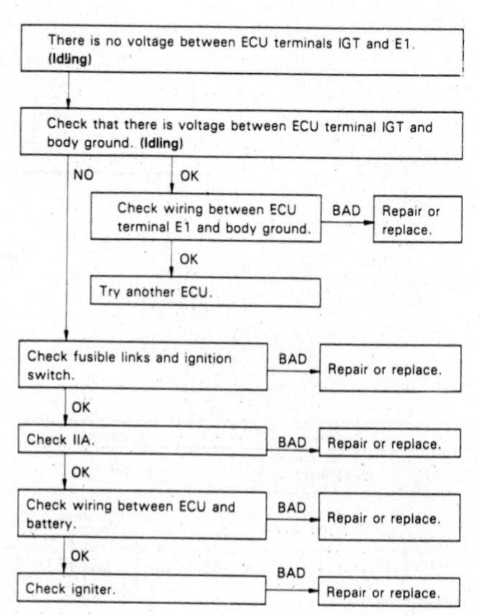
There is no voltage between ECU terminals IGT and E1. (Idling)
Check that there is voltage between ECU terminal IGT and body ground. (Idling)
NO
OK
Check wiring between ECU terminal E1 and body ground.
BAD
Repair or replace.
OK
Try another ECU.
Check fusible links and ignition switch.
BAD
Repair or replace.
OK
Check IIA.
BAD
Repair or replace.
OK
Check wiring between ECU and battery.
BAD
Repair or replace.
OK
Check igniter.
BAD
Repair or replace.

**4A-FE**

---

| No. | Terminal | Trouble | Condition | STD voltage |
|---|---|---|---|---|
| 10 | IGT – E1 | No voltage | Idling | 0.7 – 1.0 V |

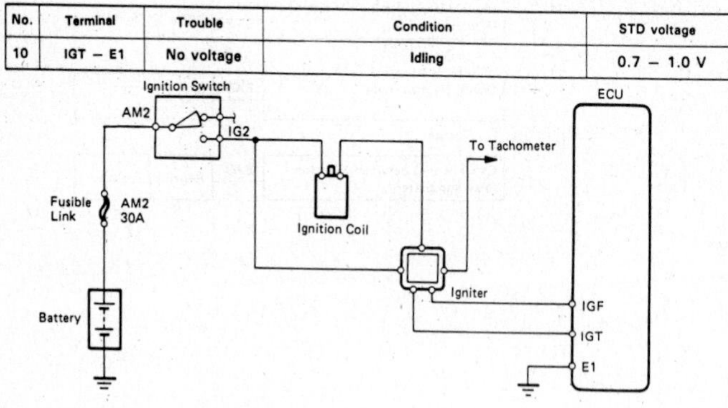
Ignition Switch
AM2
IG2
ECU
To Tachometer
Fusible Link
AM2 30A
Ignition Coil
Igniter
Battery
IGF
IGT
E1

NOTE: To check ignition system components, see SYSTEM & COMPONENT TESTING article.

There is no voltage between ECU terminals IGT and E1. (Idling)

Check that there is voltage between ECU terminal IGT and body ground. (Idling)

OK

Check wiring between ECU terminal E1 and body ground.

BAD

See Test No. 2.

BAD

Repair or replace.

OK

Check wiring between ECU and distributor.

BAD

Repair or replace.

OK

Check distributor.

BAD

Replace.

OK

Check wiring between ECU and igniter.

BAD

Repair or replace.

OK

Check igniter.

BAD

Repair or replace.

OK

Try another ECU.

**4A-GE**

91C17766 91D17767 91E17768 91F17769

## COROLLA TEST NO. 4 OR CODE 21, 27
### $O_2$ SENSOR SIGNAL

NOTE: Code 27 applies to 4A-GE only.

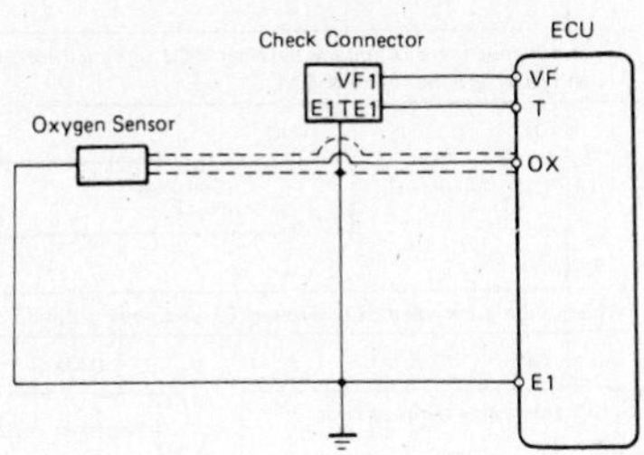
Check Connector
ECU
VF1
E1TE1
VF
T
Oxygen Sensor
OX
E1

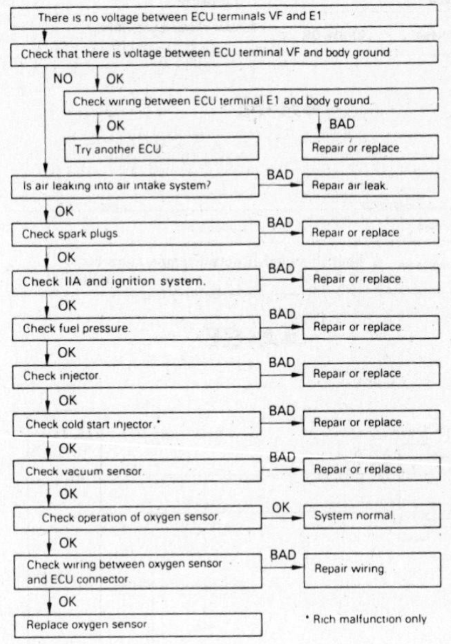
There is no voltage between ECU terminals VF and E1
Check that there is voltage between ECU terminal VF and body ground
NO
OK
Check wiring between ECU terminal E1 and body ground
OK
BAD
Try another ECU
Repair or replace
Is air leaking into air intake system?
BAD
Repair air leak
OK
Check spark plugs
BAD
Repair or replace
OK
Check IIA and ignition system
BAD
Repair or replace
OK
Check fuel pressure
BAD
Repair or replace
OK
Check injector
BAD
Repair or replace
OK
Check cold start injector *
BAD
Repair or replace
OK
Check vacuum sensor
BAD
Repair or replace
OK
Check operation of oxygen sensor
OK
System normal
OK
Check wiring between oxygen sensor and ECU connector
BAD
Repair wiring
OK
Replace oxygen sensor
* Rich malfunction only

4A-FE

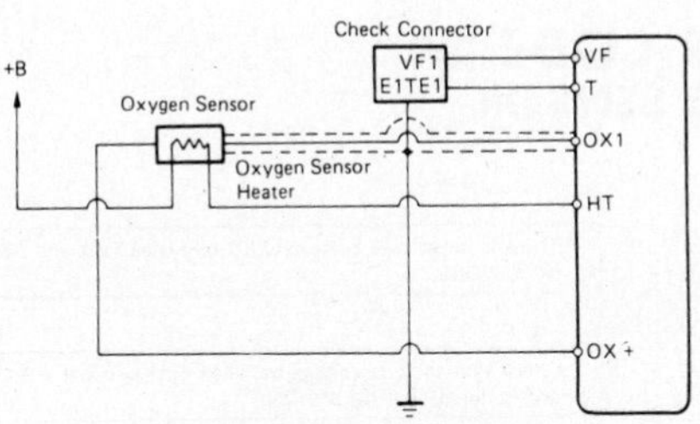
Check Connector
+B
VF1
E1TE1
VF
T
Oxygen Sensor
OX1
Oxygen Sensor Heater
HT
OX+

CALIFORNIA

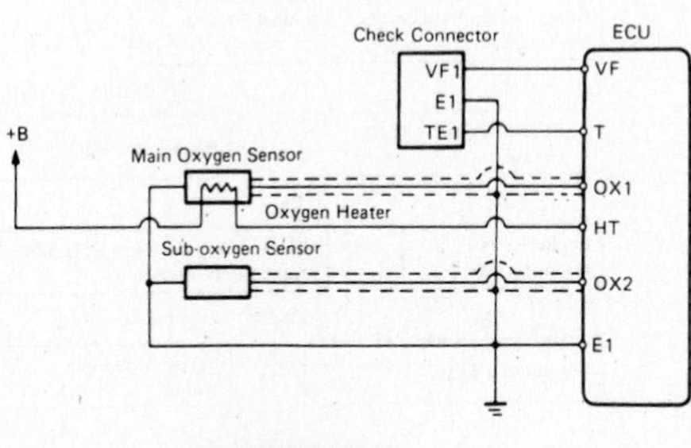
Check Connector
ECU
VF1
E1
TE1
VF
T
+B
Main Oxygen Sensor
OX1
Oxygen Heater
HT
Sub-oxygen Sensor
OX2
E1

FEDERAL

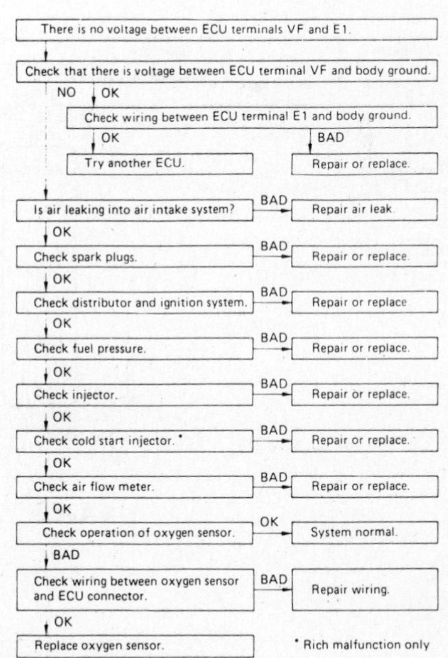
There is no voltage between ECU terminals VF and E1.
Check that there is voltage between ECU terminal VF and body ground.
NO
OK
Check wiring between ECU terminal E1 and body ground.
OK
BAD
Try another ECU.
Repair or replace.
Is air leaking into air intake system?
BAD
Repair air leak.
OK
Check spark plugs.
BAD
Repair or replace.
OK
Check distributor and ignition system.
BAD
Repair or replace
OK
Check fuel pressure.
BAD
Repair or replace.
OK
Check injector.
BAD
Repair or replace.
OK
Check cold start injector. *
BAD
Repair or replace.
OK
Check air flow meter.
BAD
Repair or replace.
OK
Check operation of oxygen sensor.
OK
System normal.
BAD
Check wiring between oxygen sensor and ECU connector.
BAD
Repair wiring.
OK
Replace oxygen sensor.
* Rich malfunction only

4A-GE

91I17770 91J17771 91A17772 91J17722 91B17773

Courtesy of Toyota Motor Sales, U.S.A., Inc.

# 1991 ENGINE PERFORMANCE
# Self-Diagnostics (Cont.)

## COROLLA TEST NO. 5 OR CODE 22
### COOLANT TEMPERATURE SENSOR SIGNAL

| Terminal | Trouble | Condition | | STD voltage |
|---|---|---|---|---|
| THW – E2 | No voltage | IG SW ON | Coolant temperature 80°C (176°F) | 0.4 – 0.7 V |

**4A-FE**

| Terminals | Trouble | Condition | | STD voltage |
|---|---|---|---|---|
| THW – E2 | No voltage | Ignition switch ON | Coolant temperature 80°C (176°F) | 0.1 – 1.0 V |

**4A-GE**

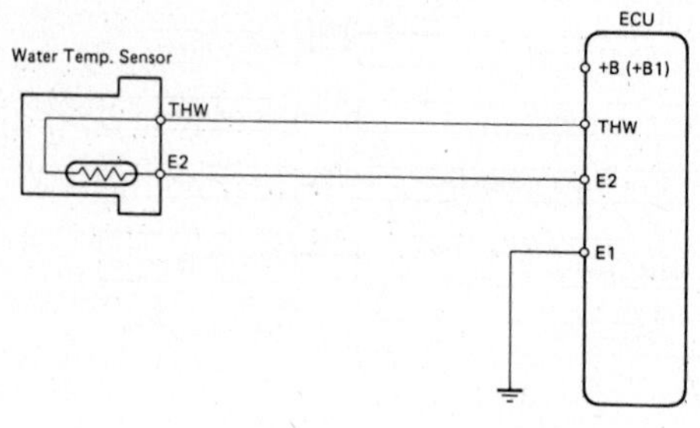
ECU
Water Temp. Sensor
+B (+B1)
THW
THW
E2
E2
E1

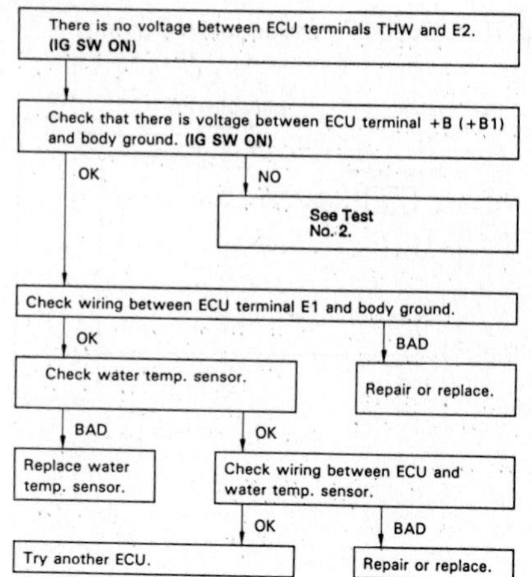
There is no voltage between ECU terminals THW and E2. (IG SW ON)
Check that there is voltage between ECU terminal +B (+B1) and body ground. (IG SW ON)
OK
NO
See Test No. 2.
Check wiring between ECU terminal E1 and body ground.
OK
BAD
Check water temp. sensor.
Repair or replace.
BAD
OK
Replace water temp. sensor.
Check wiring between ECU and water temp. sensor.
OK
BAD
Try another ECU.
Repair or replace.

NOTE: Water temperature sensor is also referred to as coolant temperature sensor.

---

## COROLLA TEST NO. 6 OR CODE 24
### INTAKE AIR TEMPERATURE SENSOR

| Terminal | Trouble | Condition | | STD voltage |
|---|---|---|---|---|
| THA – E2 | No voltage | IG SW ON | Intake air temperature 20°C (68°F) | 2.0 – 2.5 V |

ECU
Intake Air Temp. Sensor
+B (+B1)
THA
THA
E2
E2
E1

**4A-FE**

There is no voltage between ECU terminals THA and E2. (IG SW ON)

Check that there is voltage between ECU terminal +B (+B1) and body ground. (IG SW ON)

OK / NO

See Test No. 2.

Check wiring between ECU terminal E1 and body ground.

OK / BAD

Check intake air temp. sensor.

Repair or replace.

BAD / OK

Replace intake air temp. sensor.

Check wiring between ECU and intake temp. sensor.

OK / BAD

Try another ECU.

Repair or replace wiring.

**Continued On Next Page**

91J17680 91D17726 91G17729 91J17730

Courtesy of Toyota Motor Sales, U.S.A., Inc.

# 1991 ENGINE PERFORMANCE
# Self-Diagnostics (Cont.)

## COROLLA TEST NO. 6 OR CODE 24
### INTAKE AIR TEMPERATURE SENSOR (Cont.)

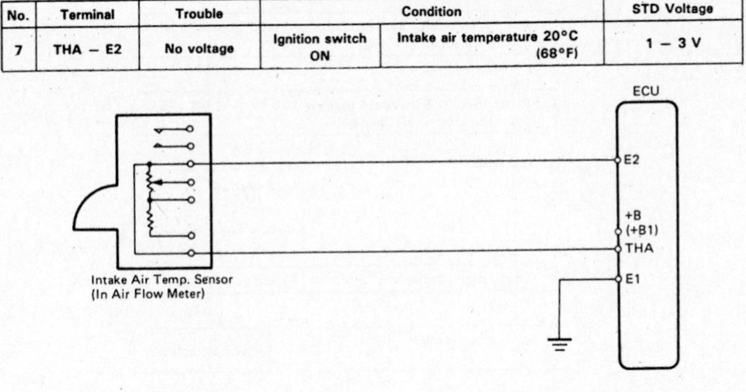

| No. | Terminal | Trouble | Condition | | STD Voltage |
|---|---|---|---|---|---|
| 7 | THA – E2 | No voltage | Ignition switch ON | Intake air temperature 20°C (68°F) | 1 – 3 V |

ECU
E2
+B
(+B1)
THA
E1
Intake Air Temp. Sensor
(In Air Flow Meter)

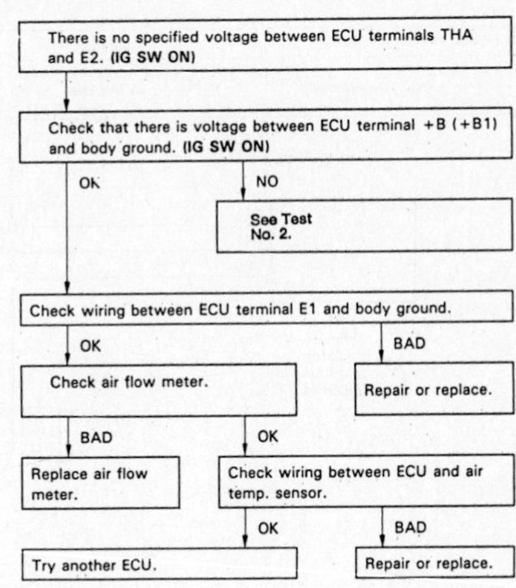
There is no specified voltage between ECU terminals THA and E2. (IG SW ON)
Check that there is voltage between ECU terminal +B (+B1) and body ground. (IG SW ON)
OK
NO
See Test No. 2.
Check wiring between ECU terminal E1 and body ground.
OK
BAD
Check air flow meter.
Repair or replace.
BAD
OK
Replace air flow meter.
Check wiring between ECU and air temp. sensor.
OK
BAD
Try another ECU.
Repair or replace.

**4A-GE**

---

## COROLLA CODE 25
### LEAN AIR/FUEL MIXTURE

**Probable Causes**

- Airflow Meter
- Air Intake System
- Coolant Temperature Sensor
- Fuel Pressure
- Ignition System
- Injector Circuit or Injector
- Oxygen Sensor or Sensor Circuit
- ECU
- Vacuum Sensor

**NOTE – Diagnostic chart not available from manufacturer.**

---

## COROLLA CODE 26
### RICH AIR/FUEL MIXTURE

**Probable Causes**

- Airflow Meter
- Cold Start Injector
- Coolant Temperature Sensor
- ECU
- Fuel Pressure
- Injector Circuit or Injector
- Oxygen Sensor or Sensor Circuit
- Vacuum Sensor

**NOTE – Diagnostic chart not available from manufacturer.**

91C17774 91D17775

# 1991 ENGINE PERFORMANCE
# Self-Diagnostics (Cont.)

## COROLLA TEST NO. 7 OR CODE 31
### VACUUM SENSOR SIGNAL (4A-FE)

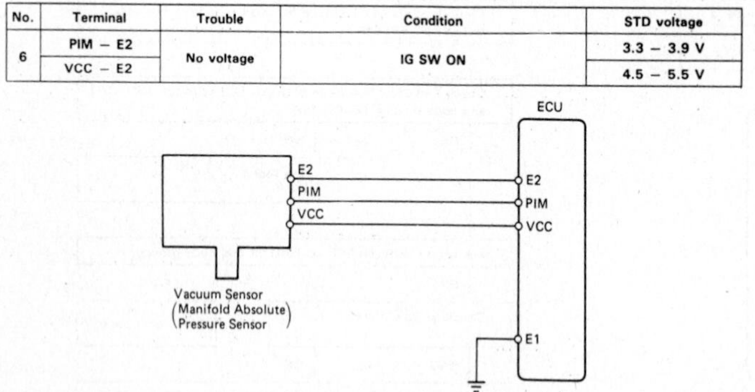

| No. | Terminal | Trouble | Condition | STD voltage |
|---|---|---|---|---|
| 6 | PIM – E2 | No voltage | IG SW ON | 3.3 – 3.9 V |
| | VCC – E2 | | | 4.5 – 5.5 V |

ECU
E2
PIM
VCC
E2
PIM
VCC
E1
Vacuum Sensor
(Manifold Absolute Pressure Sensor)

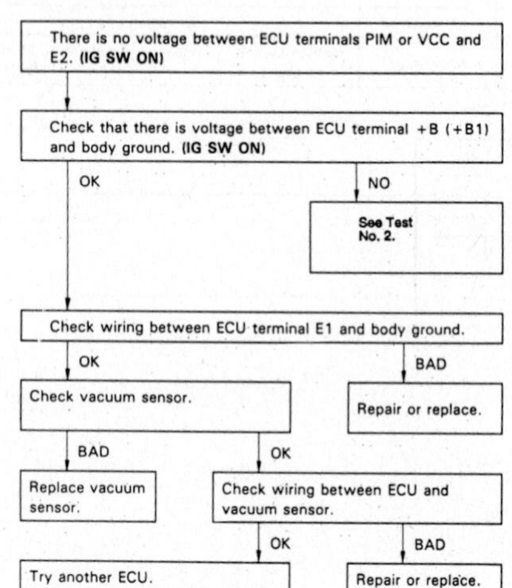
There is no voltage between ECU terminals PIM or VCC and E2. (IG SW ON)
Check that there is voltage between ECU terminal +B (+B1) and body ground. (IG SW ON)
OK
NO
See Test No. 2.
Check wiring between ECU terminal E1 and body ground.
OK
BAD
Check vacuum sensor.
Repair or replace.
BAD
OK
Replace vacuum sensor.
Check wiring between ECU and vacuum sensor.
OK
BAD
Try another ECU.
Repair or replace.

## COROLLA TEST NO. 7 OR CODE 31
### AIRFLOW METER SIGNAL (4A-GE)

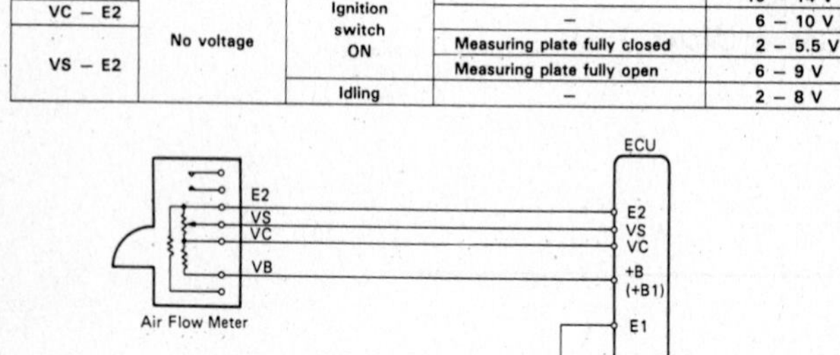

| Terminal | Trouble | Condition | | STD Voltage |
|---|---|---|---|---|
| +B1 – E2 | No voltage | Ignition switch ON | – | 10 – 14 V |
| VC – E2 | | | – | 6 – 10 V |
| VS – E2 | | | Measuring plate fully closed | 2 – 5.5 V |
| | | | Measuring plate fully open | 6 – 9 V |
| | | Idling | – | 2 – 8 V |

ECU
E2
VS
VC
VB
E2
VS
VC
+B
(+B1)
E1
Air Flow Meter

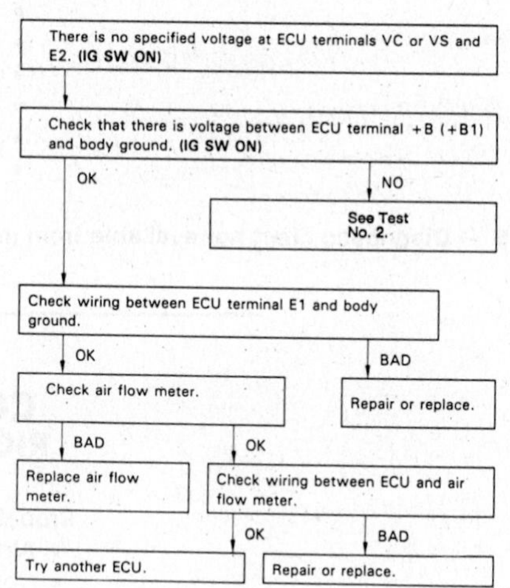
There is no specified voltage at ECU terminals VC or VS and E2. (IG SW ON)
Check that there is voltage between ECU terminal +B (+B1) and body ground. (IG SW ON)
OK
NO
See Test No. 2.
Check wiring between ECU terminal E1 and body ground.
OK
BAD
Check air flow meter.
Repair or replace.
BAD
OK
Replace air flow meter.
Check wiring between ECU and air flow meter.
OK
BAD
Try another ECU.
Repair or replace.

# COROLLA TEST NO. 8 OR CODE 41
## THROTTLE POSITION SENSOR SIGNAL

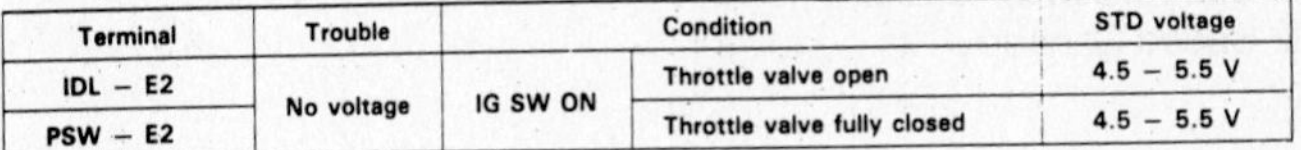

| Terminal | Trouble | Condition | | STD voltage |
|---|---|---|---|---|
| IDL – E2 | No voltage | IG SW ON | Throttle valve open | 4.5 – 5.5 V |
| PSW – E2 | | | Throttle valve fully closed | 4.5 – 5.5 V |

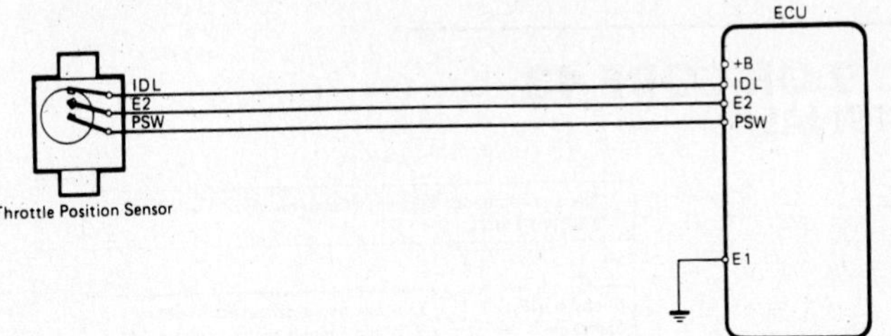
ECU
+B
IDL
E2
PSW
E1
IDL
E2
PSW
Throttle Position Sensor

There is no voltage between ECU terminals IDL and E2 (IG SW ON) (Throttle valve open)

Check that there is voltage between ECU terminal +B (+B1) and body ground. (IG SW ON)

- NO: See Test No. 2.
  - BAD: Repair or replace.
  - OK: Check throttle position sensor.
    - BAD: Replace or repair throttle position sensor.
    - OK: Check wiring between ECU and throttle position sensor.
      - BAD: Repair or replace.
      - OK: Try another ECU.
- OK: Check wiring between ECU terminal E1 and body ground.
  - OK: Try another ECU.
  - BAD: Repair or replace.

**4A-FE**

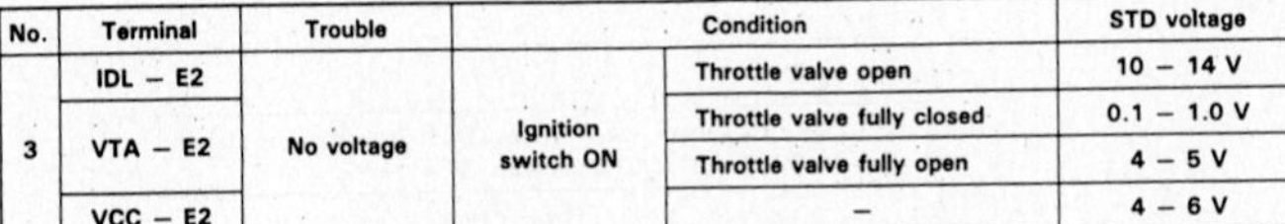

| No. | Terminal | Trouble | Condition | | STD voltage |
|---|---|---|---|---|---|
| 3 | IDL – E2 | No voltage | Ignition switch ON | Throttle valve open | 10 – 14 V |
| | VTA – E2 | | | Throttle valve fully closed | 0.1 – 1.0 V |
| | | | | Throttle valve fully open | 4 – 5 V |
| | VCC – E2 | | | – | 4 – 6 V |

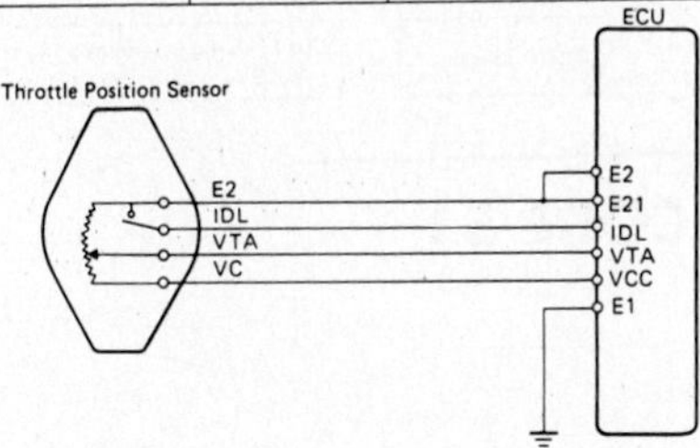
ECU
Throttle Position Sensor
E2
IDL
VTA
VC
E2
E21
IDL
VTA
VCC
E1

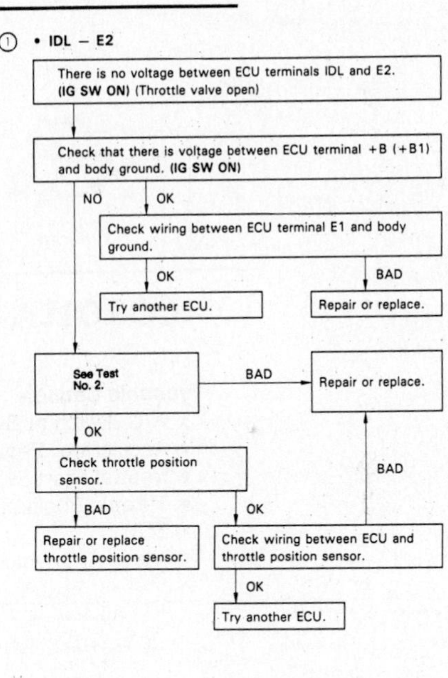
① • IDL – E2
There is no voltage between ECU terminals IDL and E2. (IG SW ON) (Throttle valve open)
Check that there is voltage between ECU terminal +B (+B1) and body ground. (IG SW ON)
NO
OK
Check wiring between ECU terminal E1 and body ground.
OK
BAD
Try another ECU.
Repair or replace.
See Test No. 2.
BAD
Repair or replace.
OK
Check throttle position sensor.
BAD
BAD
OK
Repair or replace throttle position sensor.
Check wiring between ECU and throttle position sensor.
OK
Try another ECU.

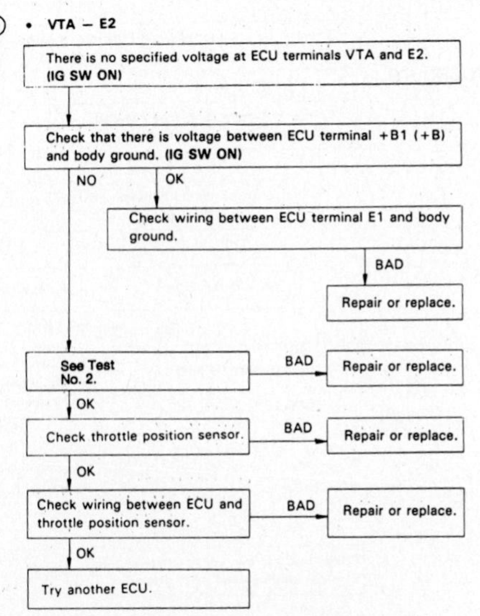
② • VTA – E2
There is no specified voltage at ECU terminals VTA and E2. (IG SW ON)
Check that there is voltage between ECU terminal +B1 (+B) and body ground. (IG SW ON)
NO
OK
Check wiring between ECU terminal E1 and body ground.
BAD
Repair or replace.
See Test No. 2.
BAD
Repair or replace.
OK
Check throttle position sensor.
BAD
Repair or replace.
OK
Check wiring between ECU and throttle position sensor.
BAD
Repair or replace.
OK
Try another ECU.

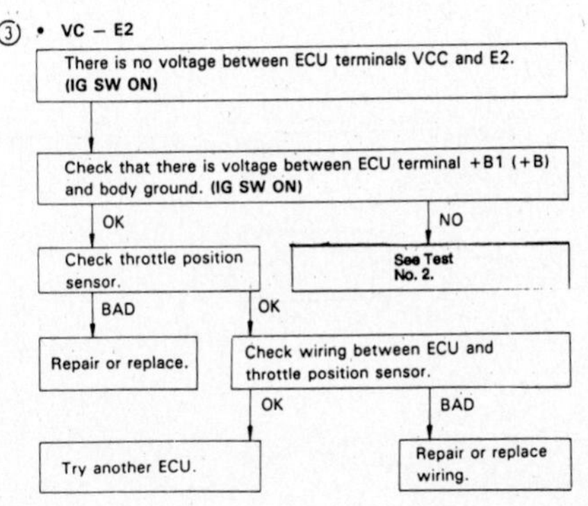
③ • VC – E2
There is no voltage between ECU terminals VCC and E2. (IG SW ON)
Check that there is voltage between ECU terminal +B1 (+B) and body ground. (IG SW ON)
OK
NO
Check throttle position sensor.
See Test No. 2.
BAD
OK
Repair or replace.
Check wiring between ECU and throttle position sensor.
OK
BAD
Try another ECU.
Repair or replace wiring.

**4A-GE**

91H17779 91A17780 91B17781 91C17782 91D17783 91E17784

# 1991 ENGINE PERFORMANCE
# Self-Diagnostics (Cont.)

## COROLLA CODE 42
### VEHICLE SPEED SENSOR SIGNAL

**Probable Cause**

- Vehicle Speed Sensor Circuit
- Vehicle Speed Sensor
- ECU

**NOTE - Diagnostic chart not available from manufacturer.**

## COROLLA TEST NO. 9 OR CODE 43
### STARTER SIGNAL

| Terminal | Trouble | Condition | STD voltage |
|---|---|---|---|
| STA – E1 | No voltage | Cranking | 6 – 14 V |

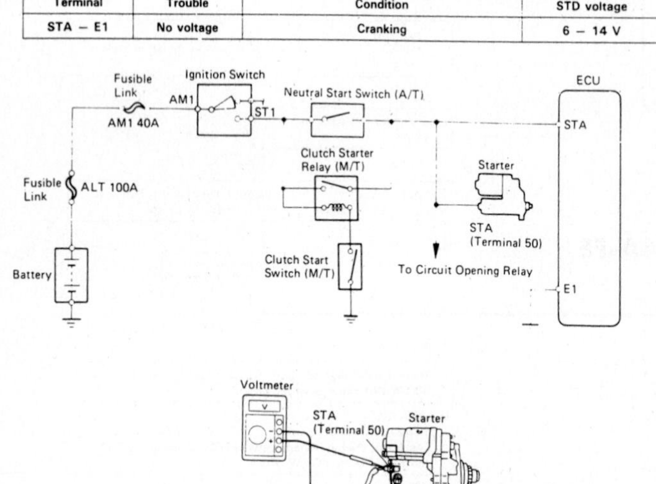
Fusible Link
Ignition Switch
AM1
AM1 40A
ST1
Neutral Start Switch (A/T)
ECU
STA
Clutch Starter Relay (M/T)
Starter
Fusible Link
ALT 100A
STA (Terminal 50)
Battery
Clutch Start Switch (M/T)
To Circuit Opening Relay
E1
Voltmeter
STA (Terminal 50)
Starter

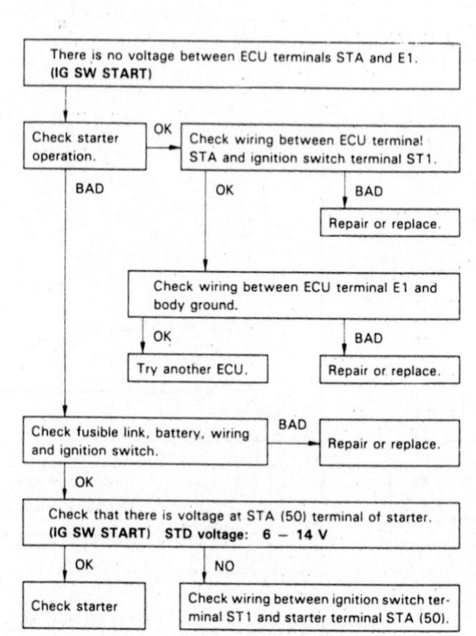
There is no voltage between ECU terminals STA and E1. (IG SW START)
Check starter operation.
OK
Check wiring between ECU terminal STA and ignition switch terminal ST1.
BAD
OK
BAD
Repair or replace.
Check wiring between ECU terminal E1 and body ground.
OK
BAD
Try another ECU.
Repair or replace.
Check fusible link, battery, wiring and ignition switch.
BAD
Repair or replace.
OK
Check that there is voltage at STA (50) terminal of starter. (IG SW START) STD voltage: 6 – 14 V
OK
NO
Check starter
Check wiring between ignition switch terminal ST1 and starter terminal STA (50).

## COROLLA TEST NO. 10 OR CODE 51
### SWITCH SIGNAL

**Probable Causes**

- A/C Switch or Switch Circuit
- Accelerator Pedal or Cable
- Neutral/Start Switch or Switch Circuit
- Throttle Position Sensor IDL Circuit
- ECU

To check A/C switch signal, use the following procedure.

| Terminals | Trouble | Condition | STD Voltage |
|---|---|---|---|
| A/C – E1 | No voltage | Air conditioning ON | 5 – 14 V |

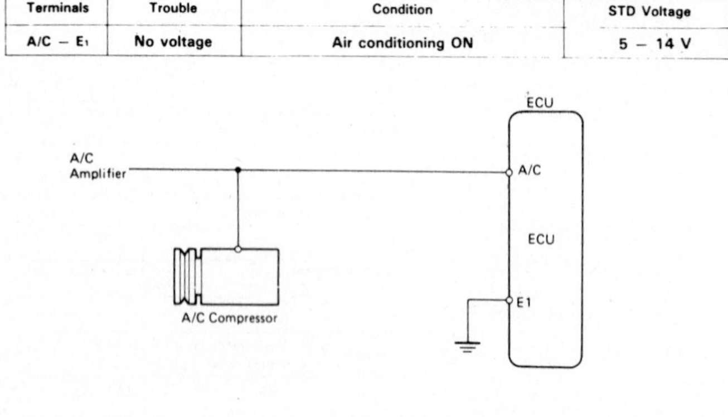
ECU
A/C Amplifier
A/C
ECU
E1
A/C Compressor

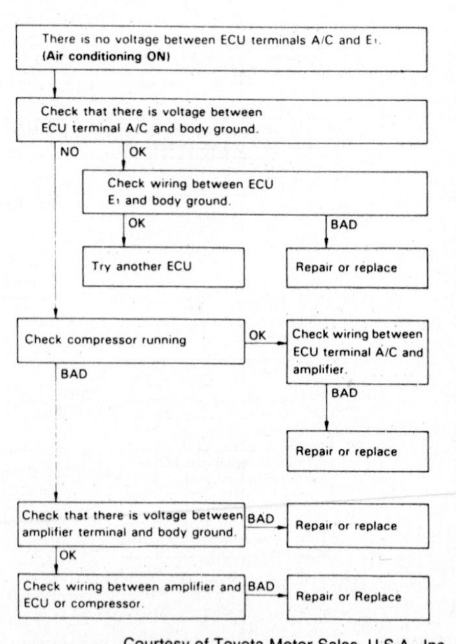
There is no voltage between ECU terminals A/C and E1. (Air conditioning ON)
Check that there is voltage between ECU terminal A/C and body ground.
NO
OK
Check wiring between ECU E1 and body ground.
OK
BAD
Try another ECU
Repair or replace
Check compressor running
OK
Check wiring between ECU terminal A/C and amplifier.
BAD
BAD
Repair or replace
Check that there is voltage between amplifier terminal and body ground.
BAD
Repair or replace
OK
Check wiring between amplifier and ECU or compressor.
BAD
Repair or Replace

91F17785 91G17786 91F17694 91G17695 91G17745

## COROLLA CODE 52 (4A-GE)
### KNOCK SENSOR SIGNAL

**Probable Causes**
- Knock Sensor or Sensor Circuit
- ECU

**NOTE - Diagnostic chart not available from manufacturer.**

---

## COROLLA CODE 53 (4A-GE)
### KNOCK SENSOR CONTROL (ECU)

**Probable Causes**
- ECU

**NOTE - Diagnostic chart not available from manufacturer.**

---

## COROLLA TEST NO. 11 OR CODE 71
### EGR SYSTEM MALFUNCTION

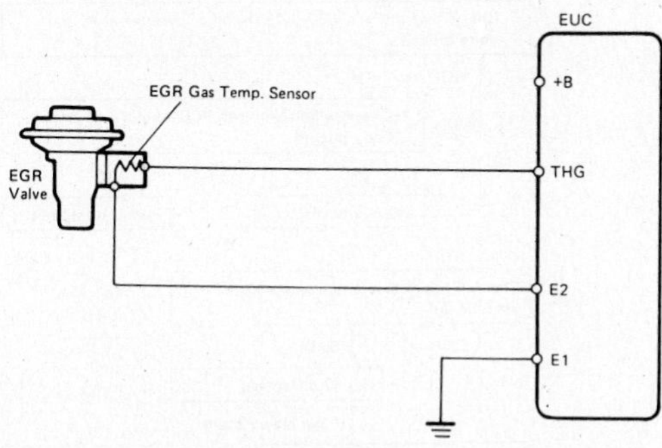
EUC
+B
EGR Gas Temp. Sensor
EGR
Valve
THG
E2
E1

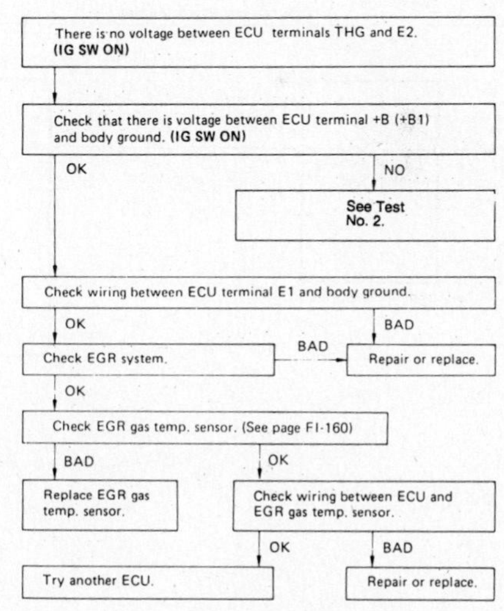
There is no voltage between ECU terminals THG and E2. (IG SW ON)
Check that there is voltage between ECU terminal +B (+B1) and body ground. (IG SW ON)
OK
NO
See Test No. 2.
Check wiring between ECU terminal E1 and body ground.
OK
BAD
Check EGR system.
BAD
Repair or replace.
OK
Check EGR gas temp. sensor. (See page FI-160)
BAD
OK
Replace EGR gas temp. sensor.
Check wiring between ECU and EGR gas temp. sensor.
OK
BAD
Try another ECU.
Repair or replace.

# 1991 ENGINE PERFORMANCE
## Self-Diagnostics (Cont.)

### COROLLA TEST NO. 12
#### INJECTOR CIRCUIT

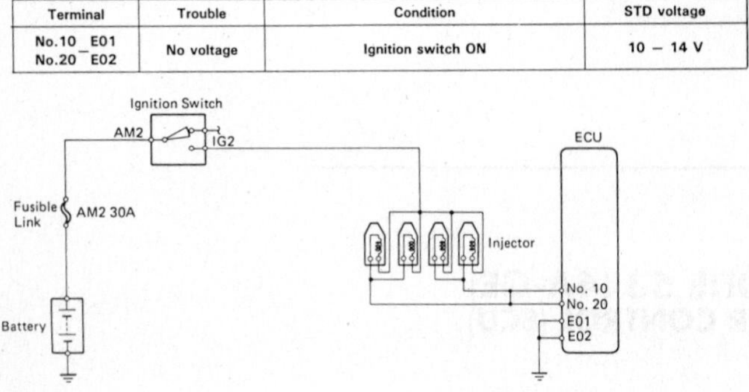

| Terminal | Trouble | Condition | STD voltage |
|---|---|---|---|
| No.10 – E01<br>No.20 – E02 | No voltage | Ignition switch ON | 10 – 14 V |

Ignition Switch
AM2
IG2
Fusible Link
AM2 30A
Battery
ECU
Injector
No. 10
No. 20
E01
E02



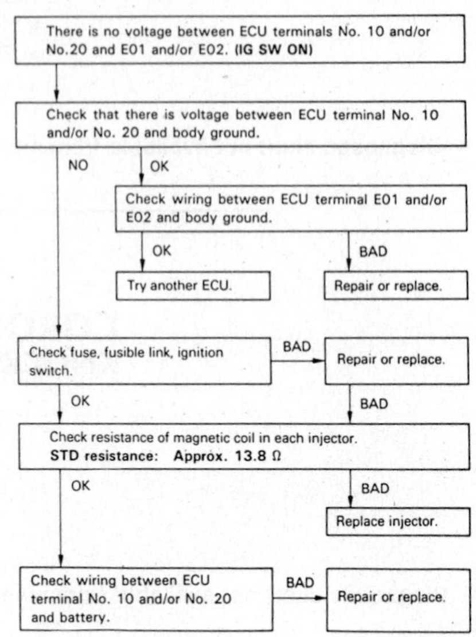

There is no voltage between ECU terminals No. 10 and/or No.20 and E01 and/or E02. (IG SW ON)
Check that there is voltage between ECU terminal No. 10 and/or No. 20 and body ground.
NO
OK
Check wiring between ECU terminal E01 and/or E02 and body ground.
OK
BAD
Try another ECU.
Repair or replace.
Check fuse, fusible link, ignition switch.
BAD
Repair or replace.
OK
BAD
Check resistance of magnetic coil in each injector.
STD resistance: Approx. 13.8 Ω
OK
BAD
Replace injector.
Check wiring between ECU terminal No. 10 and/or No. 20 and battery.
BAD
Repair or replace.


### COROLLA TEST NO. 13
#### CHECK ENGINE CIRCUIT

| Terminal | Trouble | Condition | STD voltage |
|---|---|---|---|
| W – E1 | No voltage | No trouble ("CHECK ENGINE" warning light off) and engine running. | 10 – 14 V |

ECU
From IG SW (IG1)
Fuse
GAUGE 7.5A
"CHECK ENGINE" Warning Light
Combination Meter
W
E1

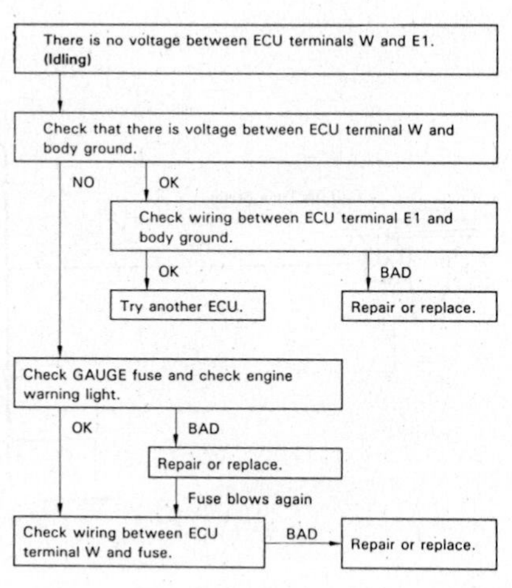


91I17788 91J17789 91C17790 91D17791

Courtesy of Toyota Motor Sales, U.S.A., Inc.

## CRESSIDA DIAGNOSTIC CIRCUIT CHECK

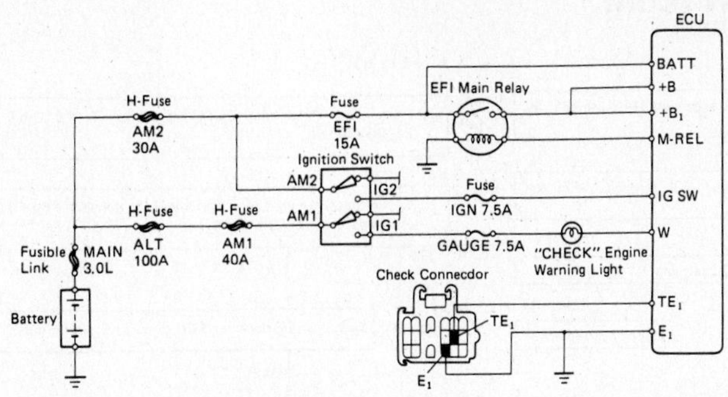
ECU
BATT
+B
+B1
M-REL
IG SW
W
TE1
E1
EFI Main Relay
H-Fuse
AM2
30A
Fuse
EFI
15A
Ignition Switch
AM2
IG2
H-Fuse
ALT
100A
H-Fuse
AM1
40A
AM1
IG1
Fuse
IGN 7.5A
GAUGE 7.5A
"CHECK" Engine
Warning Light
Fusible Link
MAIN
3.0L
Check Connecdor
TE1
E1
Battery

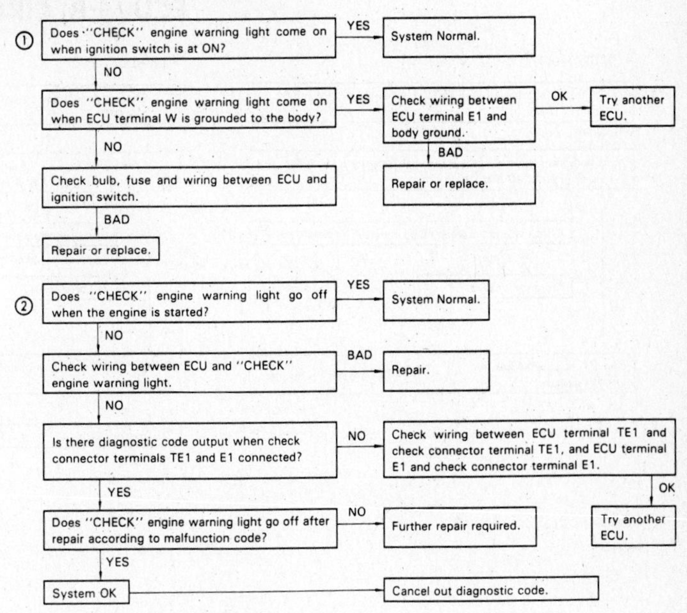
①
Does "CHECK" engine warning light come on when ignition switch is at ON?
YES
System Normal.
NO
Does "CHECK" engine warning light come on when ECU terminal W is grounded to the body?
YES
Check wiring between ECU terminal E1 and body ground.
OK
Try another ECU.
BAD
Repair or replace.
NO
Check bulb, fuse and wiring between ECU and ignition switch.
BAD
Repair or replace.
②
Does "CHECK" engine warning light go off when the engine is started?
YES
System Normal.
NO
Check wiring between ECU and "CHECK" engine warning light.
BAD
Repair.
NO
Is there diagnostic code output when check connector terminals TE1 and E1 connected?
NO
Check wiring between ECU terminal TE1 and check connector terminal TE1, and ECU terminal E1 and check connector terminal E1.
OK
Try another ECU.
YES
Does "CHECK" engine warning light go off after repair according to malfunction code?
NO
Further repair required.
YES
System OK
Cancel out diagnostic code.

CAUTION: Perform all voltage measurements with ECU harness connector installed. Use a high-impedance DVOM (10,000-ohm minimum). Verify battery voltage is greater than 11 volts.

## ECU TERMINAL IDENTIFICATION

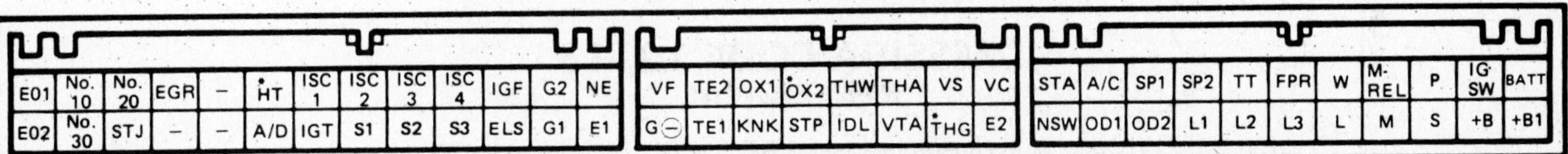
E01
No. 10
No. 20
EGR
–
*HT
ISC 1
ISC 2
ISC 3
ISC 4
IGF
G2
NE
E02
No. 30
STJ
–
–
A/D
IGT
S1
S2
S3
ELS
G1
E1
VF
TE2
OX1
*OX2
THW
THA
VS
VC
G⊖
TE1
KNK
STP
IDL
VTA
*THG
E2
STA
A/C
SP1
SP2
TT
FPR
W
M-REL
P
IG SW
BATT
NSW
OD1
OD2
L1
L2
L3
L
M
S
+B
+B1

* California models only.

## CRESSIDA TEST NO. 1 OR CODE 11
### ECU (+B) CIRCUIT

| No. | Terminals | Trouble | Condition | STD Voltage |
|---|---|---|---|---|
| 1 | BATT – E1 | No voltage | – | 10 – 14 V |
| | IG SW – E1 | No voltage | Ignition switch ON | 10 – 14 V |
| | M-REL – E1 | No voltage | Ignition switch ON | 10 – 14 V |
| | +B (+B1) – E1 | No voltage | Ignition switch ON | 10 – 14 V |

ECU
BATT
+B1
+B
M-REL
IG SW
E1
EFI Main Relay
H-Fuse
AM2
30A
Fuse
EFI
15A
Ignition Switch
IG2
AM2
Fuse
IGN
7.5A
Fusible Link
MAIN
2.0L
Battery

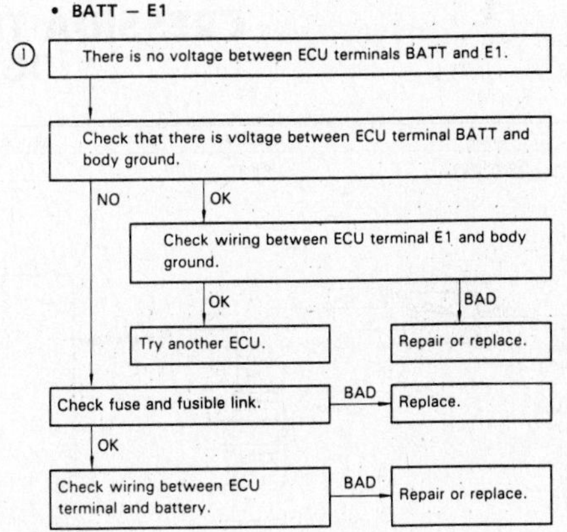
• BATT – E1
①
There is no voltage between ECU terminals BATT and E1.
Check that there is voltage between ECU terminal BATT and body ground.
NO
OK
Check wiring between ECU terminal E1 and body ground.
OK
BAD
Try another ECU.
Repair or replace.
Check fuse and fusible link.
BAD
Replace.
OK
Check wiring between ECU terminal and battery.
BAD
Repair or replace.

Continued On Next Page

# 1991 ENGINE PERFORMANCE
## Self-Diagnostics (Cont.)

## CRESSIDA TEST NO. 1 OR CODE 11
### ECU (+B) CIRCUIT (Cont.)

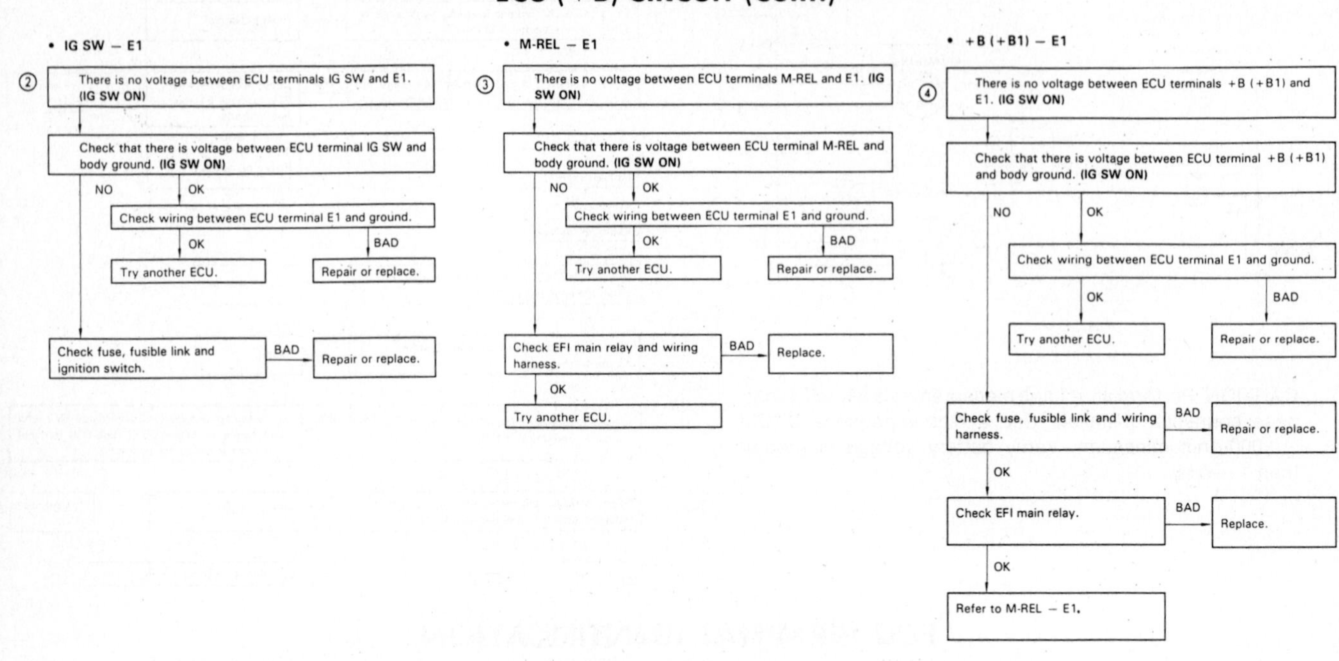
• IG SW – E1
②
There is no voltage between ECU terminals IG SW and E1. (IG SW ON)
Check that there is voltage between ECU terminal IG SW and body ground. (IG SW ON)
NO
OK
Check wiring between ECU terminal E1 and ground.
OK
BAD
Try another ECU.
Repair or replace.
Check fuse, fusible link and ignition switch.
BAD
Repair or replace.
• M-REL – E1
③
There is no voltage between ECU terminals M-REL and E1. (IG SW ON)
Check that there is voltage between ECU terminal M-REL and body ground. (IG SW ON)
NO
OK
Check wiring between ECU terminal E1 and ground.
OK
BAD
Try another ECU.
Repair or replace.
Check EFI main relay and wiring harness.
BAD
Replace.
OK
Try another ECU.
• +B (+B1) – E1
④
There is no voltage between ECU terminals +B (+B1) and E1. (IG SW ON)
Check that there is voltage between ECU terminal +B (+B1) and body ground. (IG SW ON)
NO
OK
Check wiring between ECU terminal E1 and ground.
OK
BAD
Try another ECU.
Repair or replace.
Check fuse, fusible link and wiring harness.
BAD
Repair or replace.
OK
Check EFI main relay.
BAD
Replace.
OK
Refer to M-REL – E1.

## CRESSIDA CODE 12, 13
### RPM SIGNAL

Code 12 is caused by loss of "NE" or "G" signal from distributor to ECU for at least 2 seconds after starter signal is received at ECU. Ensure starter signal exists at ECU. See TEST NO. 8 OR CODE 43. Code 13 is caused by loss of "NE" signal from distributor to ECU when engine RPM exceeds 1000 RPM.

**NOTE – Diagnostic chart not available from manufacturer.**

## CRESSIDA TEST NO. 2 OR CODE 14
### IGNITION SIGNAL

| No. | Terminals | Trouble | Condition | STD Voltage |
|---|---|---|---|---|
| 8 | IGT – E1 | No voltage | Idling | 0.7 – 1.0 V |

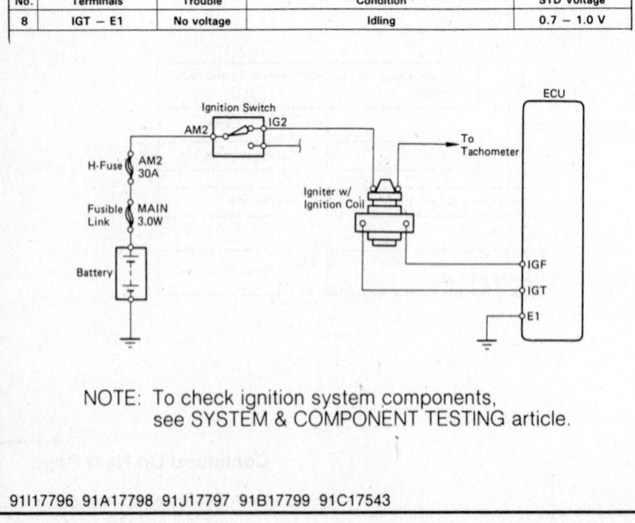
Ignition Switch
AM2
IG2
H-Fuse
AM2 30A
Fusible Link
MAIN 3.0W
Battery
To Tachometer
Igniter w/ Ignition Coil
ECU
IGF
IGT
E1

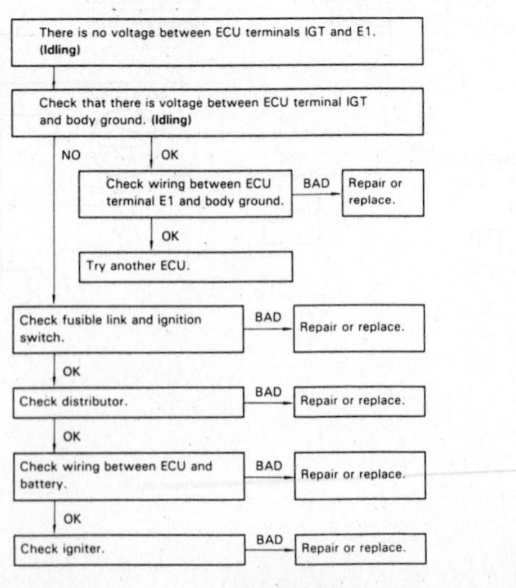
There is no voltage between ECU terminals IGT and E1. (Idling)
Check that there is voltage between ECU terminal IGT and body ground. (Idling)
NO
OK
Check wiring between ECU terminal E1 and body ground.
BAD
Repair or replace.
OK
Try another ECU.
Check fusible link and ignition switch.
BAD
Repair or replace.
OK
Check distributor.
BAD
Repair or replace.
OK
Check wiring between ECU and battery.
BAD
Repair or replace.
OK
Check igniter.
BAD
Repair or replace.

NOTE: To check ignition system components, see SYSTEM & COMPONENT TESTING article.

91I17796 91A17798 91J17797 91B17799 91C17543

Courtesy of Toyota Motor Sales, U.S.A., Inc.

## CRESSIDA CODE 16
### ECT SIGNAL

**Probable Causes**
- ECT Program Faulty

**NOTE – Diagnostic chart not available from manufacturer.**

---

## CRESSIDA TEST NO. 3 OR CODE 21, 27
### OXYGEN SENSOR CIRCUIT

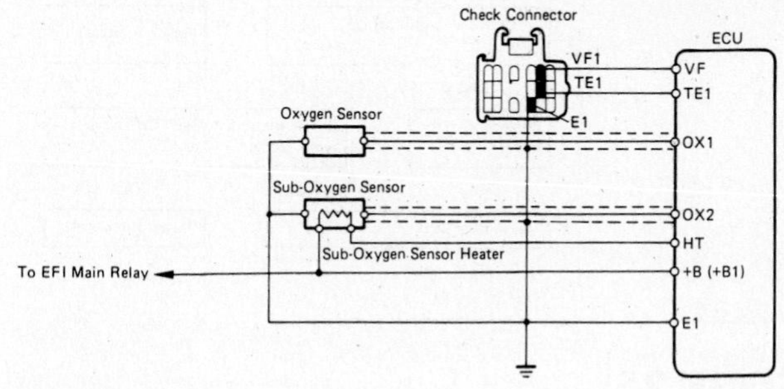

Check Connector
ECU
VF1
TE1
E1
VF
TE1
Oxygen Sensor
OX1
Sub-Oxygen Sensor
OX2
HT
Sub-Oxygen Sensor Heater
To EFI Main Relay
+B (+B1)
E1

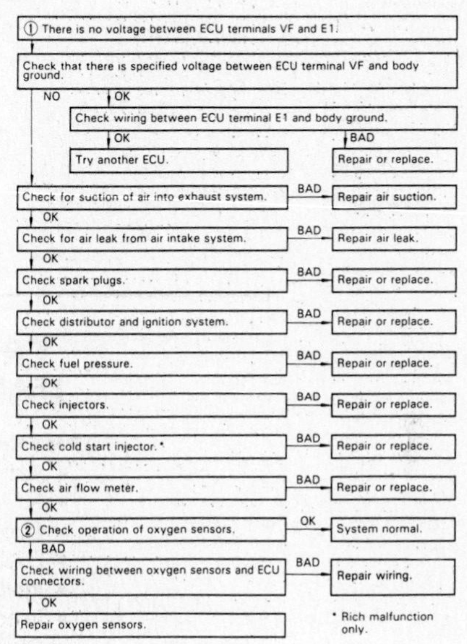

① There is no voltage between ECU terminals VF and E1.
Check that there is specified voltage between ECU terminal VF and body ground.
NO
OK
Check wiring between ECU terminal E1 and body ground.
OK
BAD
Try another ECU.
Repair or replace.
Check for suction of air into exhaust system.
BAD
Repair air suction.
OK
Check for air leak from air intake system.
BAD
Repair air leak.
OK
Check spark plugs.
BAD
Repair or replace.
OK
Check distributor and ignition system.
BAD
Repair or replace.
OK
Check fuel pressure.
BAD
Repair or replace.
OK
Check injectors.
BAD
Repair or replace.
OK
Check cold start injector.*
BAD
Repair or replace.
OK
Check air flow meter.
BAD
Repair or replace.
OK
② Check operation of oxygen sensors.
OK
System normal.
BAD
Check wiring between oxygen sensors and ECU connectors.
BAD
Repair wiring.
OK
Repair oxygen sensors.
* Rich malfunction only.

---

## CRESSIDA TEST NO. 4 OR CODE 22
### COOLANT TEMPERATURE SENSOR SIGNAL

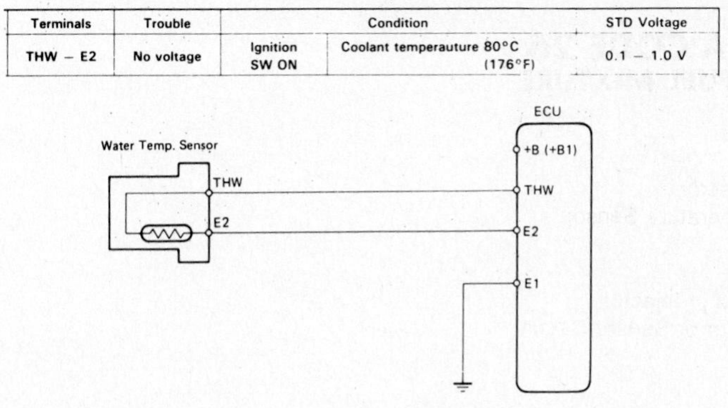

| Terminals | Trouble | Condition | | STD Voltage |
|---|---|---|---|---|
| THW – E2 | No voltage | Ignition SW ON | Coolant temperauture 80°C (176°F) | 0.1 – 1.0 V |

ECU
Water Temp. Sensor
+B (+B1)
THW
THW
E2
E2
E1

NOTE: Water temperature sensor is also referred to as coolant temperature sensor.

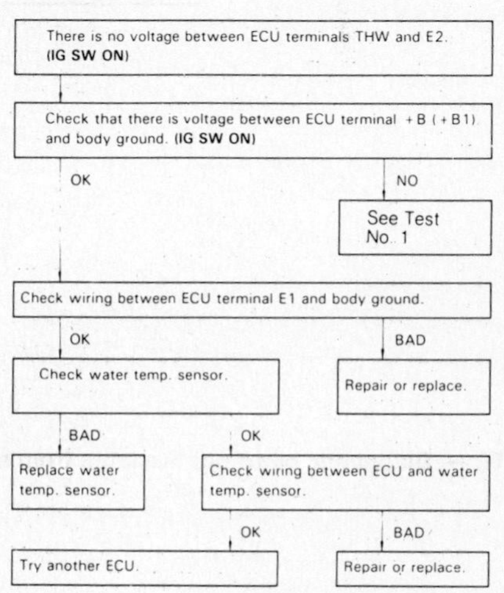

There is no voltage between ECU terminals THW and E2. (IG SW ON)
Check that there is voltage between ECU terminal +B (+B1) and body ground. (IG SW ON)
OK
NO
See Test No. 1
Check wiring between ECU terminal E1 and body ground.
OK
BAD
Check water temp. sensor.
Repair or replace.
BAD
OK
Replace water temp. sensor.
Check wiring between ECU and water temp. sensor.
OK
BAD
Try another ECU.
Repair or replace.

# 1991 ENGINE PERFORMANCE
# Self-Diagnostics (Cont.)

## CRESSIDA TEST NO. 5 OR CODE 24
### INTAKE AIR TEMPERATURE SENSOR SIGNAL

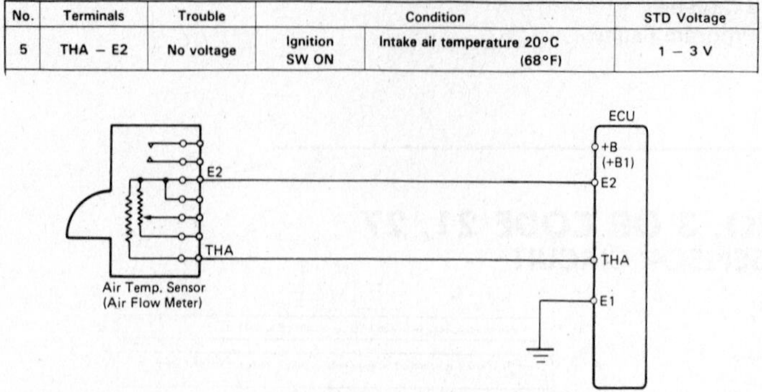

| No. | Terminals | Trouble | Condition | | STD Voltage |
|---|---|---|---|---|---|
| 5 | THA – E2 | No voltage | Ignition SW ON | Intake air temperature 20°C (68°F) | 1 – 3 V |

ECU
+B
(+B1)
E2
THA
E1
E2
THA
Air Temp. Sensor
(Air Flow Meter)

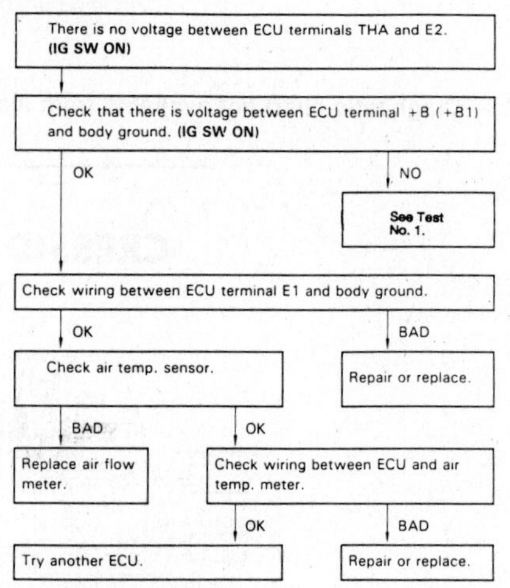
There is no voltage between ECU terminals THA and E2. (IG SW ON)
Check that there is voltage between ECU terminal +B (+B1) and body ground. (IG SW ON)
OK
NO
See Test No. 1.
Check wiring between ECU terminal E1 and body ground.
OK
BAD
Check air temp. sensor.
Repair or replace.
BAD
OK
Replace air flow meter.
Check wiring between ECU and air temp. meter.
OK
BAD
Try another ECU.
Repair or replace.

## CRESSIDA CODE 25
### LEAN AIR/FUEL MIXTURE

**Probable Causes**

- Airflow Meter
- Air Intake System
- Coolant Temperature Sensor
- Fuel Pressure
- Ignition System
- Injector Circuit or Injector
- Oxygen Sensor or Sensor Circuit
- ECU

**NOTE – Diagnostic chart not available from manufacturer.**

## CRESSIDA CODE 26
### RICH AIR/FUEL MIXTURE

**Probable Causes**

- Airflow Meter
- Cold Start Injector
- Coolant Temperature Sensor
- ECU
- Fuel Pressure
- Injector Circuit or Injector
- Oxygen Sensor or Sensor Circuit

**NOTE – Diagnostic chart not available from manufacturer.**

91B17682 91G17802

Courtesy of Toyota Motor Sales, U.S.A., Inc.

# CRESSIDA TEST NO. 6 OR CODE 31, 32
## AIRFLOW METER SIGNAL

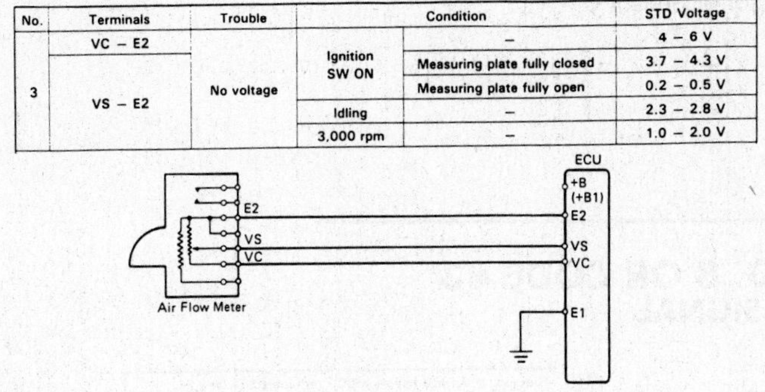

| No. | Terminals | Trouble | Condition | | STD Voltage |
|---|---|---|---|---|---|
| 3 | VC – E2 | No voltage | Ignition SW ON | – | 4 – 6 V |
| | VS – E2 | | Ignition SW ON | Measuring plate fully closed | 3.7 – 4.3 V |
| | | | | Measuring plate fully open | 0.2 – 0.5 V |
| | | | Idling | – | 2.3 – 2.8 V |
| | | | 3,000 rpm | – | 1.0 – 2.0 V |

ECU
+B
(+B1)
E2
VS
VC
E1
E2
VS
VC
Air Flow Meter

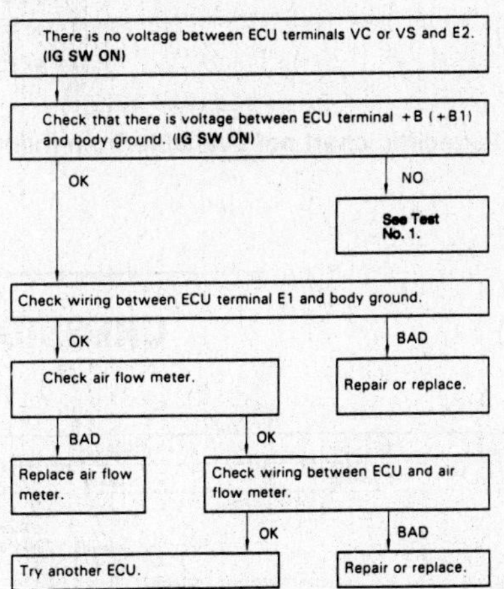
There is no voltage between ECU terminals VC or VS and E2. (IG SW ON)
Check that there is voltage between ECU terminal +B (+B1) and body ground. (IG SW ON)
OK
NO
See Test No. 1.
Check wiring between ECU terminal E1 and body ground.
OK
BAD
Check air flow meter.
Repair or replace.
BAD
OK
Replace air flow meter.
Check wiring between ECU and air flow meter.
OK
BAD
Try another ECU.
Repair or replace.

# CRESSIDA TEST NO. 7 OR CODE 41
## THROTTLE POSITION SENSOR SIGNAL

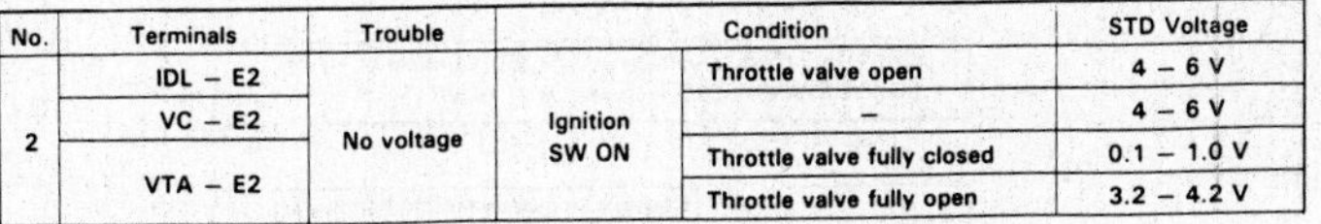

| No. | Terminals | Trouble | Condition | | STD Voltage |
|---|---|---|---|---|---|
| 2 | IDL – E2 | No voltage | Ignition SW ON | Throttle valve open | 4 – 6 V |
| | VC – E2 | | | – | 4 – 6 V |
| | VTA – E2 | | | Throttle valve fully closed | 0.1 – 1.0 V |
| | | | | Throttle valve fully open | 3.2 – 4.2 V |

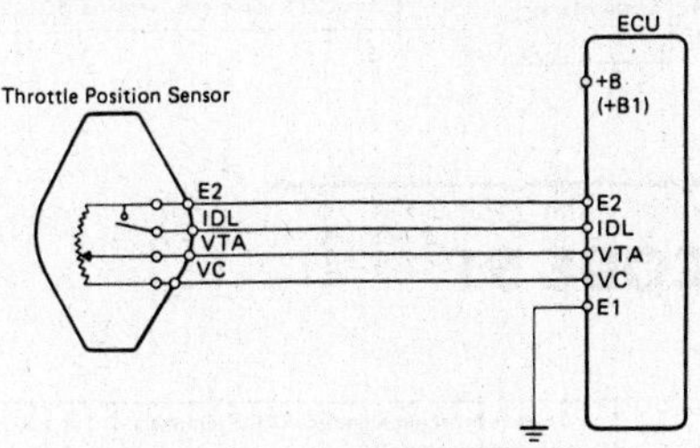
ECU
Throttle Position Sensor
+B
(+B1)
E2
IDL
VTA
VC
E2
IDL
VTA
VC
E1

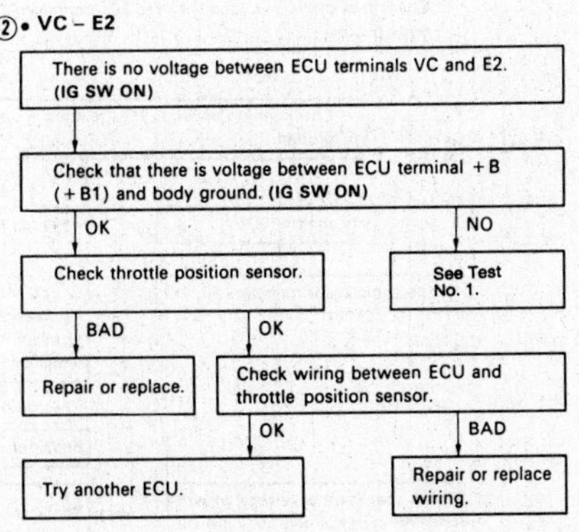
② • VC – E2
There is no voltage between ECU terminals VC and E2. (IG SW ON)
Check that there is voltage between ECU terminal +B (+B1) and body ground. (IG SW ON)
OK
NO
Check throttle position sensor.
See Test No. 1.
BAD
OK
Repair or replace.
Check wiring between ECU and throttle position sensor.
OK
BAD
Try another ECU.
Repair or replace wiring.

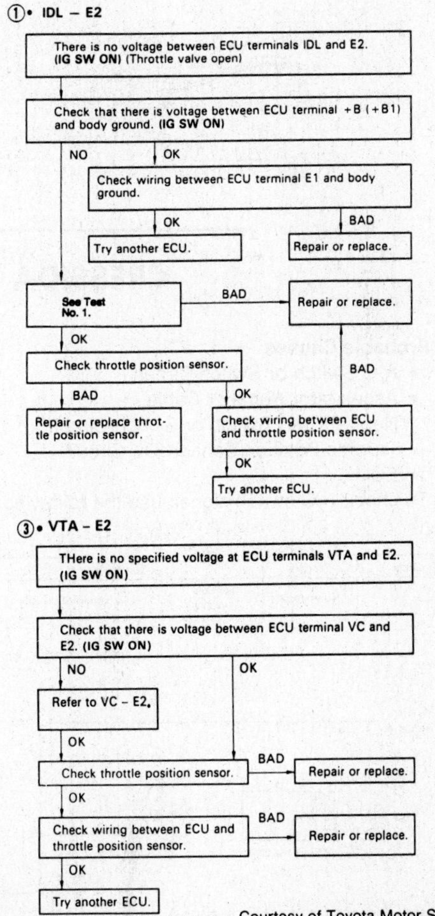
① • IDL – E2
There is no voltage between ECU terminals IDL and E2. (IG SW ON) (Throttle valve open)
Check that there is voltage between ECU terminal +B (+B1) and body ground. (IG SW ON)
NO
OK
Check wiring between ECU terminal E1 and body ground.
OK
BAD
Try another ECU.
Repair or replace.
See Test No. 1.
BAD
Repair or replace.
OK
Check throttle position sensor.
BAD
BAD
OK
Repair or replace throttle position sensor.
Check wiring between ECU and throttle position sensor.
OK
Try another ECU.
③ • VTA – E2
THere is no specified voltage at ECU terminals VTA and E2. (IG SW ON)
Check that there is voltage between ECU terminal VC and E2. (IG SW ON)
NO
OK
Refer to VC – E2.
OK
Check throttle position sensor.
BAD
Repair or replace.
OK
Check wiring between ECU and throttle position sensor.
BAD
Repair or replace.
OK
Try another ECU.

91D17684 91H17803 91H17688 91I17804 91J17805 91A17806

Courtesy of Toyota Motor Sales, U.S.A., Inc.

# 1991 ENGINE PERFORMANCE
# Self-Diagnostics (Cont.)

## CRESSIDA CODE 42
### VEHICLE SPEED SENSOR SIGNAL

**Probable Causes**
- Vehicle Speed Sensor or Sensor Circuit
- ECU

**NOTE – Diagnostic chart not available from manufacturer.**

## CRESSIDA TEST NO. 8 OR CODE 43
### STARTER SIGNAL

| No. | Terminals | Trouble | Condition | STD Voltage |
|---|---|---|---|---|
| 7 | STA – E1 | No voltage | Cranking | 6 – 14 V |

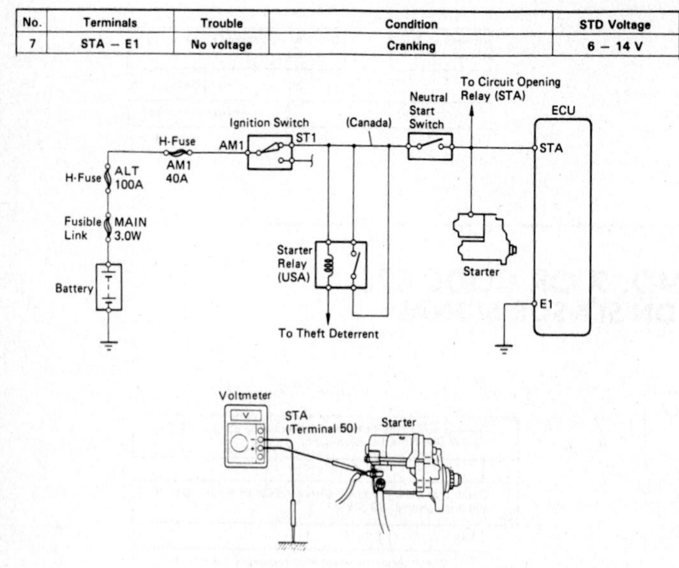
To Circuit Opening Relay (STA)
Neutral Start Switch
Ignition Switch
(Canada)
ECU
H-Fuse
AM1
ST1
STA
H-Fuse
ALT 100A
AM1 40A
Fusible Link
MAIN 3.0W
Battery
Starter Relay (USA)
Starter
E1
To Theft Deterrent
Voltmeter
STA (Terminal 50)
Starter

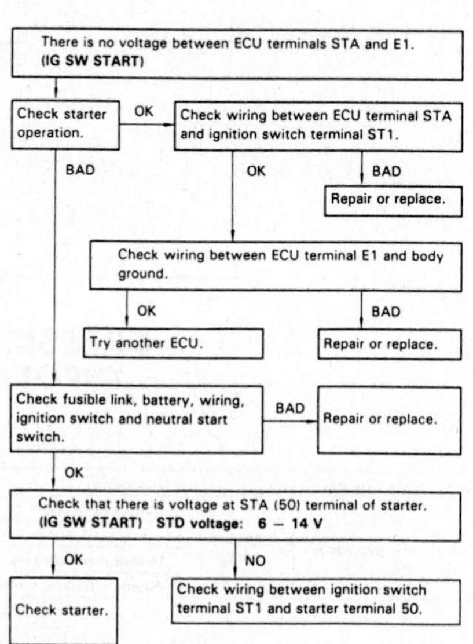
There is no voltage between ECU terminals STA and E1. (IG SW START)
Check starter operation.
OK
Check wiring between ECU terminal STA and ignition switch terminal ST1.
BAD
OK
BAD
Repair or replace.
Check wiring between ECU terminal E1 and body ground.
OK
BAD
Try another ECU.
Repair or replace.
Check fusible link, battery, wiring, ignition switch and neutral start switch.
BAD
Repair or replace.
OK
Check that there is voltage at STA (50) terminal of starter. (IG SW START) STD voltage: 6 – 14 V
OK
NO
Check starter.
Check wiring between ignition switch terminal ST1 and starter terminal 50.

## CRESSIDA TEST NO. 9 OR CODE 51
### SWITCH SIGNAL

**Probable Causes**
- A/C Switch or Switch Circuit
- Accelerator Pedal or Cable
- Neutral/Start Switch or Switch Circuit
- Throttle Position Sensor IDL Circuit
- ECU

To check A/C switch signal, use the following procedure.

| No. | Terminals | Trouble | Condition | | STD Voltage |
|---|---|---|---|---|---|
| 11 | A/C – E1 | No voltage | Ignition SW ON | Air conditioning ON | 10 – 14 V |

ECU
To A/C Amplifier
A/C
E1
A/C Compressor

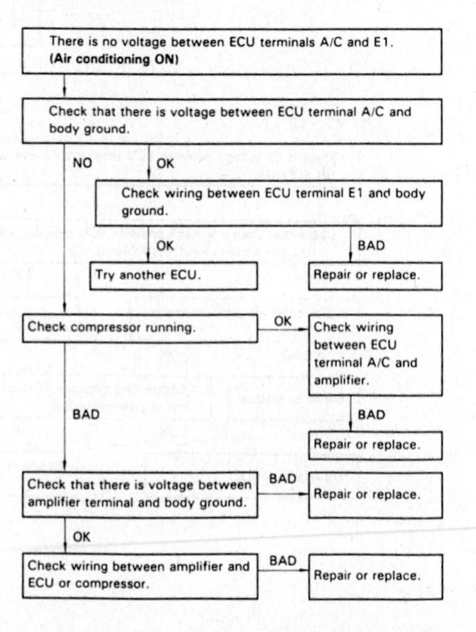
There is no voltage between ECU terminals A/C and E1. (Air conditioning ON)
Check that there is voltage between ECU terminal A/C and body ground.
NO
OK
Check wiring between ECU terminal E1 and body ground.
OK
BAD
Try another ECU.
Repair or replace.
Check compressor running.
OK
Check wiring between ECU terminal A/C and amplifier.
BAD
BAD
Repair or replace.
Check that there is voltage between amplifier terminal and body ground.
BAD
Repair or replace.
OK
Check wiring between amplifier and ECU or compressor.
BAD
Repair or replace.

91B17807 91C17808 91F17694 91G17695 91G17745

Courtesy of Toyota Motor Sales, U.S.A., Inc.

# 1991 ENGINE PERFORMANCE
# Self-Diagnostics (Cont.)

## CRESSIDA CODE 52
### KNOCK SENSOR SIGNAL

**Probable Causes**
- Knock Sensor or Sensor Circuit
- ECU

**NOTE – Diagnostic chart not available from manufacturer.**

## CRESSIDA CODE 53
### KNOCK SENSOR CONTROL (ECU)

**Probable Causes**
- ECU

**NOTE – Diagnostic chart not available from manufacturer.**

## CRESSIDA TEST NO. 10 OR CODE 71
### EGR SYSTEM MALFUNCTION

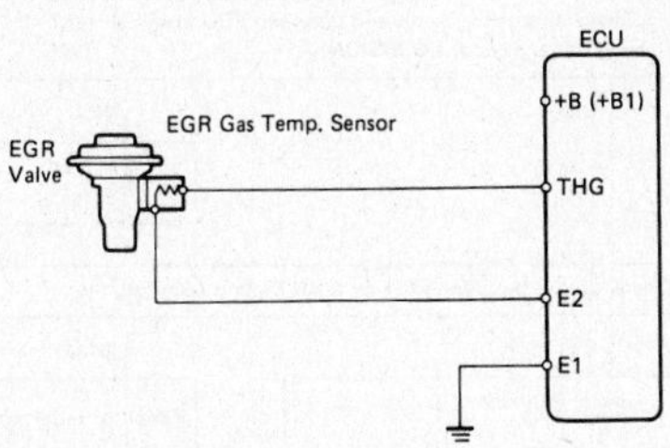
ECU
+B (+B1)
EGR Gas Temp. Sensor
EGR Valve
THG
E2
E1

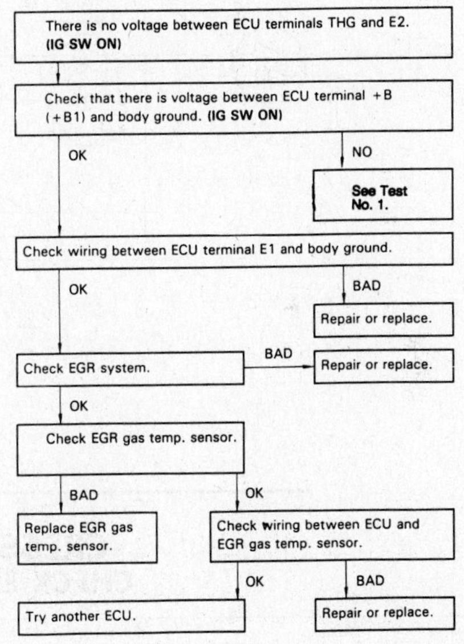
There is no voltage between ECU terminals THG and E2. (IG SW ON)
Check that there is voltage between ECU terminal +B (+B1) and body ground. (IG SW ON)
OK
NO
See Test No. 1.
Check wiring between ECU terminal E1 and body ground.
OK
BAD
Repair or replace.
Check EGR system.
BAD
Repair or replace.
OK
Check EGR gas temp. sensor.
BAD
OK
Replace EGR gas temp. sensor.
Check wiring between ECU and EGR gas temp. sensor.
OK
BAD
Try another ECU.
Repair or replace.

91H17787 91D17809

Courtesy of Toyota Motor Sales, U.S.A., Inc.

# 1991 ENGINE PERFORMANCE
# Self-Diagnostics (Cont.)

## CRESSIDA TEST NO. 11
## INJECTOR CIRCUIT

| Terminals | Trouble | Condition | STD Voltage |
|---|---|---|---|
| No.10 / No.20 / No.30 – E01 / E02 | No voltage | Ignition SW ON | 10 – 14 V |

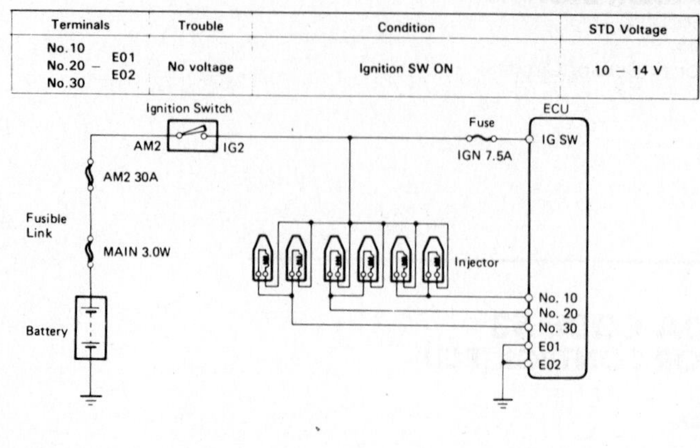
Ignition Switch
AM2
IG2
AM2 30A
Fusible Link
MAIN 3.0W
Battery
Fuse
IGN 7.5A
ECU
IG SW
Injector
No. 10
No. 20
No. 30
E01
E02

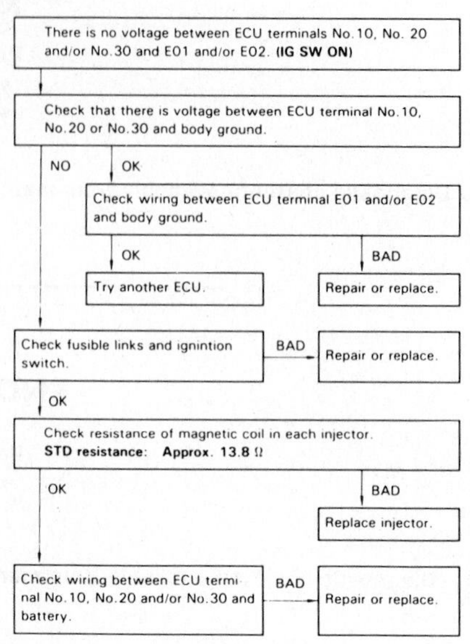
There is no voltage between ECU terminals No.10, No. 20 and/or No.30 and E01 and/or E02. (IG SW ON)
Check that there is voltage between ECU terminal No.10, No.20 or No.30 and body ground.
NO
OK
Check wiring between ECU terminal E01 and/or E02 and body ground.
OK
BAD
Try another ECU.
Repair or replace.
Check fusible links and ignintion switch.
BAD
Repair or replace.
OK
Check resistance of magnetic coil in each injector.
STD resistance: Approx. 13.8 Ω
OK
BAD
Replace injector.
Check wiring between ECU terminal No.10, No.20 and/or No.30 and battery.
BAD
Repair or replace.

## CRESSIDA TEST NO. 12
## IDLE SPEED CONTROL CIRCUIT

| No. | Terminals | Trouble | Condition | STD Voltage |
|---|---|---|---|---|
| 9 | ISC1 ~ ISC4 – E1 | No voltage | Ignition SW ON | 9 – 14 V |

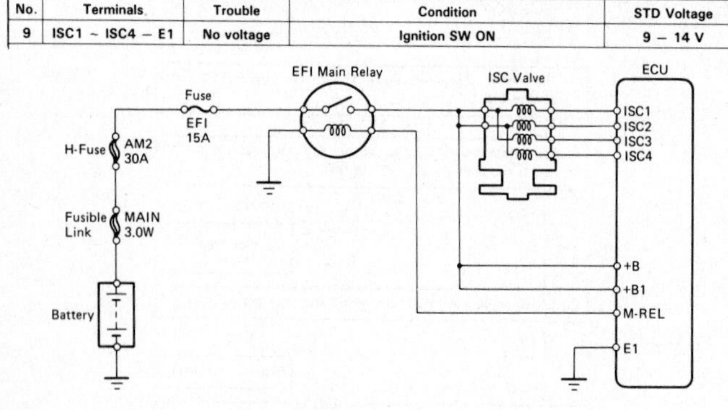
EFI Main Relay
ISC Valve
ECU
Fuse
EFI 15A
H-Fuse
AM2 30A
Fusible Link
MAIN 3.0W
Battery
ISC1
ISC2
ISC3
ISC4
+B
+B1
M-REL
E1

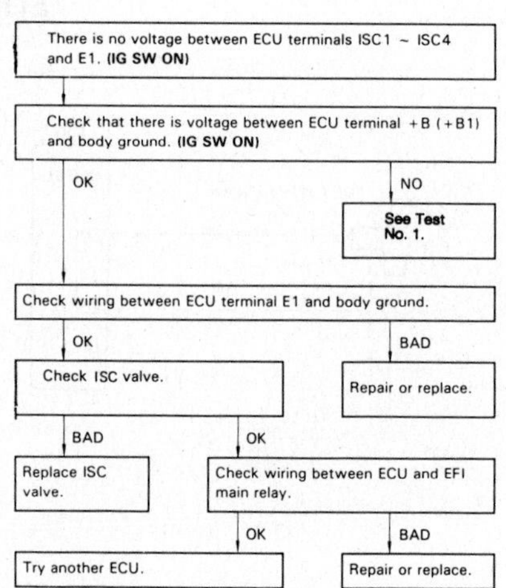
There is no voltage between ECU terminals ISC1 ~ ISC4 and E1. (IG SW ON)
Check that there is voltage between ECU terminal +B (+B1) and body ground. (IG SW ON)
OK
NO
See Test No. 1.
Check wiring between ECU terminal E1 and body ground.
OK
BAD
Check ISC valve.
Repair or replace.
BAD
OK
Replace ISC valve.
Check wiring between ECU and EFI main relay.
OK
BAD
Try another ECU.
Repair or replace.

## CRESSIDA TEST NO. 13
## CHECK ENGINE LIGHT CIRCUIT

| Terminals | Trouble | Condition | STD Voltage |
|---|---|---|---|
| W – E1 | No voltage | No trouble ("CHECK" engine warning light off) and engine running | 8 – 14 V |

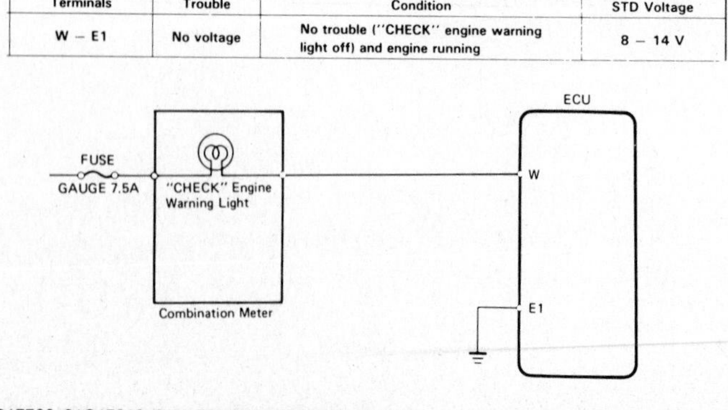
ECU
FUSE
GAUGE 7.5A
"CHECK" Engine Warning Light
Combination Meter
W
E1

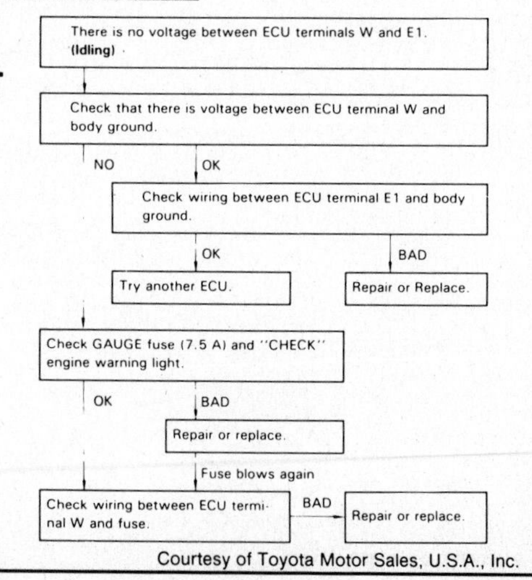
There is no voltage between ECU terminals W and E1. (Idling)
Check that there is voltage between ECU terminal W and body ground.
NO
OK
Check wiring between ECU terminal E1 and body ground.
OK
BAD
Try another ECU.
Repair or Replace.
Check GAUGE fuse (7.5 A) and "CHECK" engine warning light.
OK
BAD
Repair or replace.
Fuse blows again
Check wiring between ECU terminal W and fuse.
BAD
Repair or replace.

91J18118 91D17700 91G17810 91H17811 91C17790 91D17791

# 1991 ENGINE PERFORMANCE
## Self-Diagnostics (Cont.)

## LAND CRUISER DIAGNOSTIC CIRCUIT CHECK

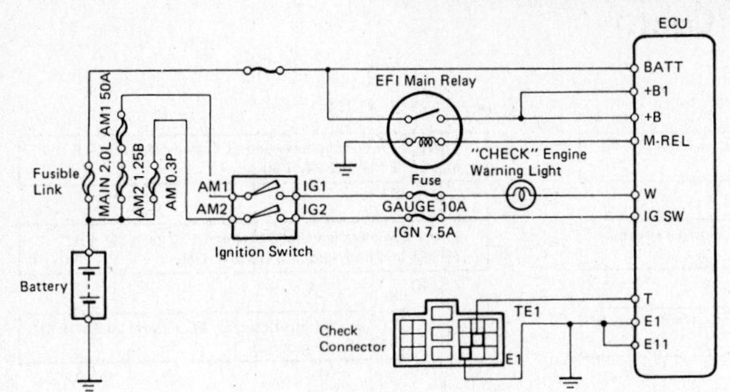
ECU
BATT
+B1
+B
M-REL
W
IG SW
T
E1
E11
EFI Main Relay
"CHECK" Engine Warning Light
Fuse
GAUGE 10A
IGN 7.5A
Fusible Link
MAIN 2.0L
AM1 50A
AM2 1.25B
AM 0.3P
AM1
AM2
IG1
IG2
Ignition Switch
Battery
Check Connector
TE1
E1

CAUTION: Perform all voltage measurements with ECU harness connector installed. Use a high-impedance DVOM (10,000-ohm minimum). Verify battery voltage is greater than 11 volts.

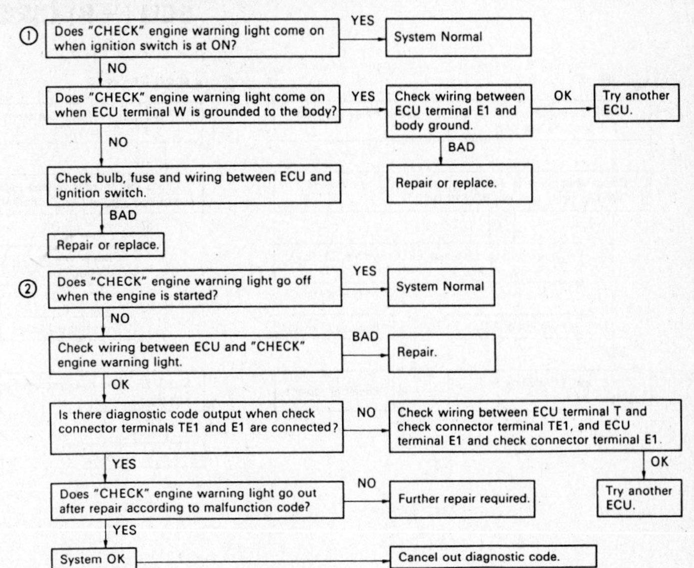
① Does "CHECK" engine warning light come on when ignition switch is at ON?
YES
System Normal
NO
Does "CHECK" engine warning light come on when ECU terminal W is grounded to the body?
YES
Check wiring between ECU terminal E1 and body ground.
OK
Try another ECU.
BAD
Repair or replace.
NO
Check bulb, fuse and wiring between ECU and ignition switch.
BAD
Repair or replace.
② Does "CHECK" engine warning light go off when the engine is started?
YES
System Normal
NO
Check wiring between ECU and "CHECK" engine warning light.
BAD
Repair.
OK
Is there diagnostic code output when check connector terminals TE1 and E1 are connected?
NO
Check wiring between ECU terminal T and check connector terminal TE1, and ECU terminal E1 and check connector terminal E1.
OK
Try another ECU.
YES
Does "CHECK" engine warning light go out after repair according to malfunction code?
NO
Further repair required.
YES
System OK
Cancel out diagnostic code.

## ECU TERMINAL IDENTIFICATION

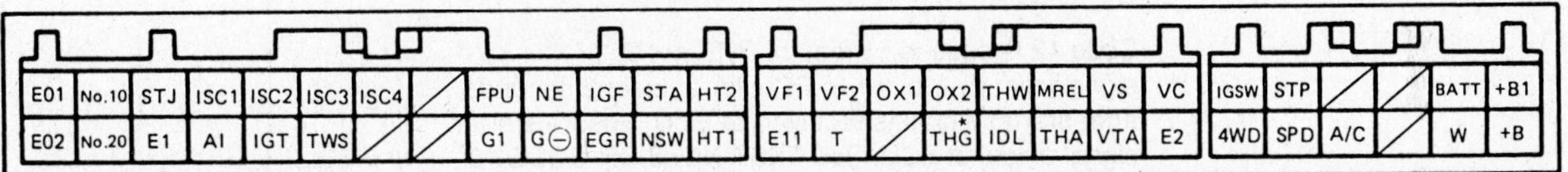
E01
No.10
STJ
ISC1
ISC2
ISC3
ISC4
FPU
NE
IGF
STA
HT2
E02
No.20
E1
AI
IGT
TWS
G1
G⊖
EGR
NSW
HT1
VF1
VF2
OX1
OX2
THW
MREL
VS
VC
E11
T
THG*
IDL
THA
VTA
E2
IGSW
STP
BATT
+B1
4WD
SPD
A/C
W
+B

* California vehicles only

## LAND CRUISER TEST NO. 1
### ECU (+B) CIRCUIT

| No. | Terminals | Trouble | Condition | STD Voltage |
|---|---|---|---|---|
| 1 | BATT–E1 (E11) | No voltage | — | 10 – 14 V |
| | IG SW–E1 (E11) | No voltage | Ignition switch ON | 10 – 14 V |
| | M-REL–E1 (E11) | No voltage | Ignition switch ON | 10 – 14 V |
| | +B (+B1) –E1 (E11) | No voltage | Ignition switch ON | 10 – 14 V |

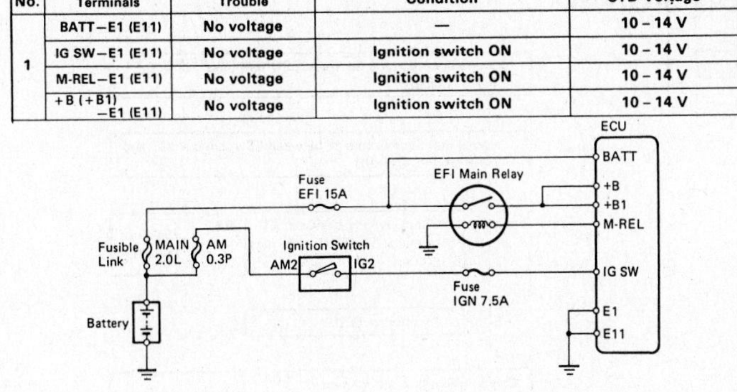
ECU
BATT
+B
+B1
M-REL
IG SW
E1
E11
Fuse
EFI 15A
EFI Main Relay
Fusible Link
MAIN 2.0L
AM 0.3P
Ignition Switch
AM2
IG2
Fuse
IGN 7.5A
Battery

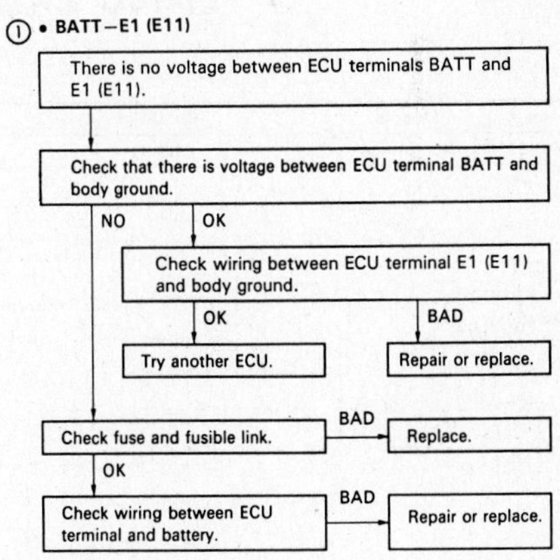
① • BATT–E1 (E11)
There is no voltage between ECU terminals BATT and E1 (E11).
Check that there is voltage between ECU terminal BATT and body ground.
NO
OK
Check wiring between ECU terminal E1 (E11) and body ground.
OK
Try another ECU.
BAD
Repair or replace.
Check fuse and fusible link.
BAD
Replace.
OK
Check wiring between ECU terminal and battery.
BAD
Repair or replace.

Continued On Next Page

# 1991 ENGINE PERFORMANCE
# Self-Diagnostics (Cont.)

## LAND CRUISER TEST NO. 1
### ECU (+B) CIRCUIT (Cont.)

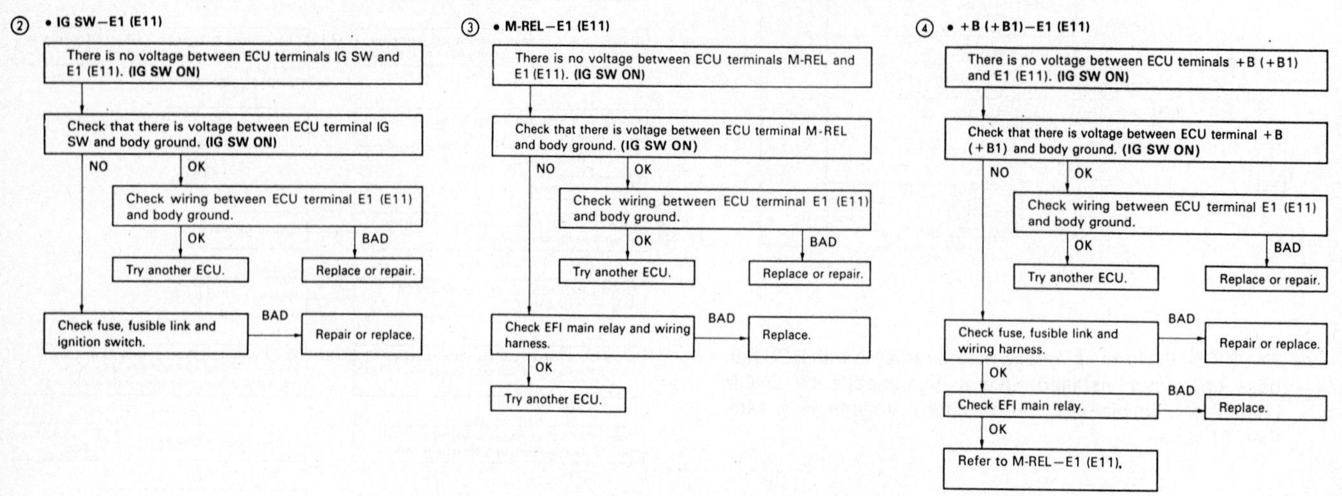
② • IG SW—E1 (E11)
There is no voltage between ECU terminals IG SW and E1 (E11). (IG SW ON)
Check that there is voltage between ECU terminal IG SW and body ground. (IG SW ON)
NO
OK
Check wiring between ECU terminal E1 (E11) and body ground.
OK
BAD
Try another ECU.
Replace or repair.
Check fuse, fusible link and ignition switch.
BAD
Repair or replace.
③ • M-REL—E1 (E11)
There is no voltage between ECU terminals M-REL and E1 (E11). (IG SW ON)
Check that there is voltage between ECU terminal M-REL and body ground. (IG SW ON)
NO
OK
Check wiring between ECU terminal E1 (E11) and body ground.
OK
BAD
Try another ECU.
Replace or repair.
Check EFI main relay and wiring harness.
BAD
Replace.
OK
Try another ECU.
④ • +B (+B1)—E1 (E11)
There is no voltage between ECU teminals +B (+B1) and E1 (E11). (IG SW ON)
Check that there is voltage between ECU terminal +B (+B1) and body ground. (IG SW ON)
NO
OK
Check wiring between ECU terminal E1 (E11) and body ground.
OK
BAD
Try another ECU.
Replace or repair.
Check fuse, fusible link and wiring harness.
BAD
Repair or replace.
OK
Check EFI main relay.
BAD
Replace.
OK
Refer to M-REL—E1 (E11).

## LAND CRUISER CODE 12, 13
### RPM SIGNAL

Code 12 is caused by loss of "NE" or "G" signal from distributor to ECU for at least 2 seconds after starter signal is received at ECU. Ensure starter signal exists at ECU. See TEST NO. 8 OR CODE 43. Code 13 is caused by loss of "NE" signal from distributor to ECU when engine RPM exceeds 1000 RPM.

**NOTE - Diagnostic chart not available from manufacturer.**

## LAND CRUISER TEST NO. 2 OR CODE 14
### IGNITION SIGNAL

| No. | Terminals | Trouble | Condition | STD Voltage |
|---|---|---|---|---|
| 9 | IGT—E1 (E11) | No voltage | Idling | 0.7 – 1.0 V |

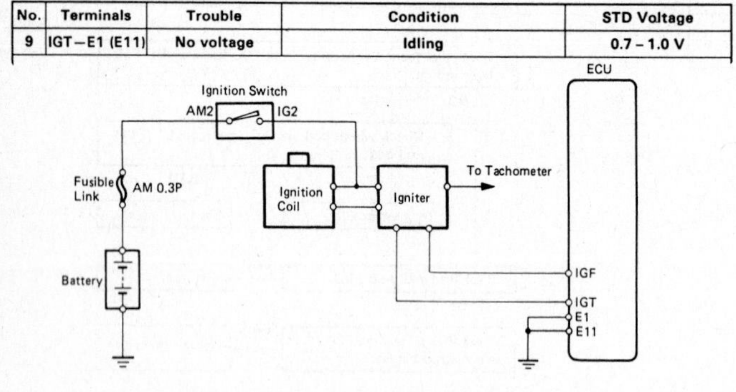
ECU
Ignition Switch
AM2
IG2
Fusible Link
AM 0.3P
Ignition Coil
Igniter
To Tachometer
Battery
IGF
IGT
E1
E11

NOTE: To check ignition system components, see SYSTEM & COMPONENT TESTING article.

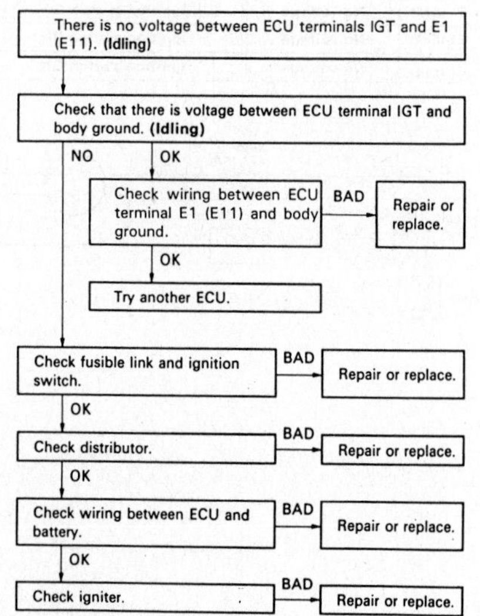
There is no voltage between ECU terminals IGT and E1 (E11). (Idling)
Check that there is voltage between ECU terminal IGT and body ground. (Idling)
NO
OK
Check wiring between ECU terminal E1 (E11) and body ground.
BAD
Repair or replace.
OK
Try another ECU.
Check fusible link and ignition switch.
BAD
Repair or replace.
OK
Check distributor.
BAD
Repair or replace.
OK
Check wiring between ECU and battery.
BAD
Repair or replace.
OK
Check igniter.
BAD
Repair or replace.

91C17816 91D17817 91E17818 91F17819 91I17820

## LAND CRUISER TEST NO. 3 OR CODE 21, 28
### OXYGEN SENSOR SIGNAL

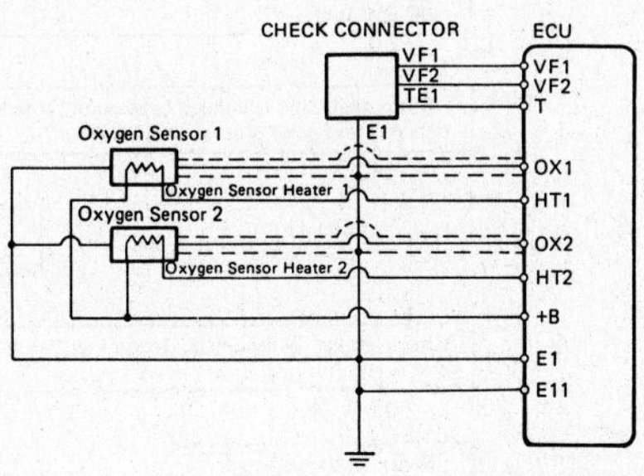

CHECK CONNECTOR
ECU
VF1
VF2
TE1
VF1
VF2
T
E1
Oxygen Sensor 1
Oxygen Sensor Heater 1
Oxygen Sensor 2
Oxygen Sensor Heater 2
OX1
HT1
OX2
HT2
+B
E1
E11

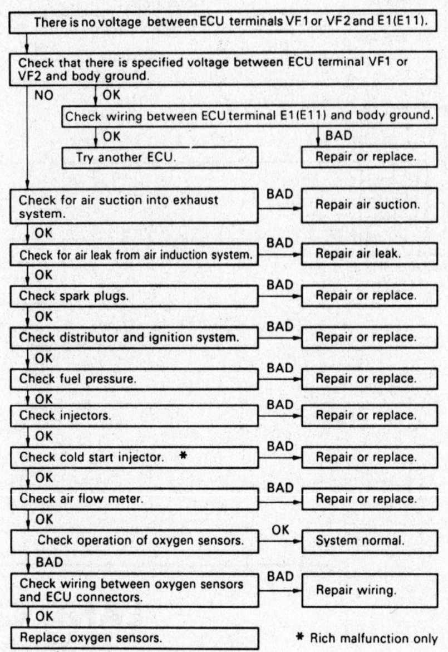

There is no voltage between ECU terminals VF1 or VF2 and E1(E11).
Check that there is specified voltage between ECU terminal VF1 or VF2 and body ground.
NO
OK
Check wiring between ECU terminal E1(E11) and body ground.
OK
BAD
Try another ECU.
Repair or replace.
Check for air suction into exhaust system.
BAD
Repair air suction.
OK
Check for air leak from air induction system.
BAD
Repair air leak.
OK
Check spark plugs.
BAD
Repair or replace.
OK
Check distributor and ignition system.
BAD
Repair or replace.
OK
Check fuel pressure.
BAD
Repair or replace.
OK
Check injectors.
BAD
Repair or replace.
OK
Check cold start injector. *
BAD
Repair or replace.
OK
Check air flow meter.
BAD
Repair or replace.
OK
Check operation of oxygen sensors.
OK
System normal.
BAD
Check wiring between oxygen sensors and ECU connectors.
BAD
Repair wiring.
OK
Replace oxygen sensors.
* Rich malfunction only

## LAND CRUISER TEST NO. 4 OR CODE 22
### COOLANT TEMPERATURE SENSOR SIGNAL

| No. | Terminals | Trouble | Condition | | STD Voltage |
|---|---|---|---|---|---|
| 5 | THW - E2 | No voltage | Ignition switch ON | Coolant temperature 80°C (176°F) | 0.1 - 1.0 V |

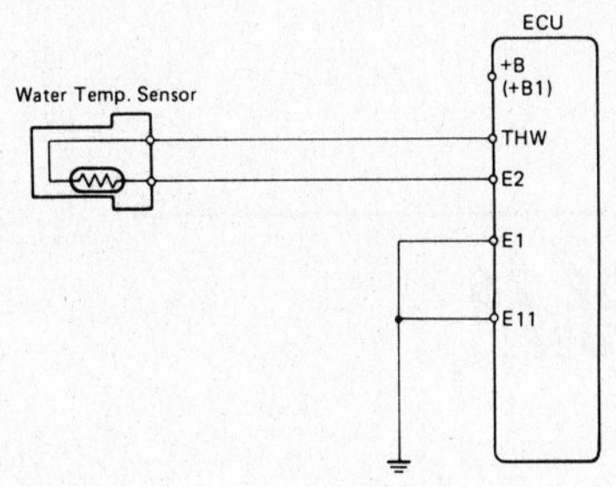

ECU
Water Temp. Sensor
+B
(+B1)
THW
E2
E1
E11

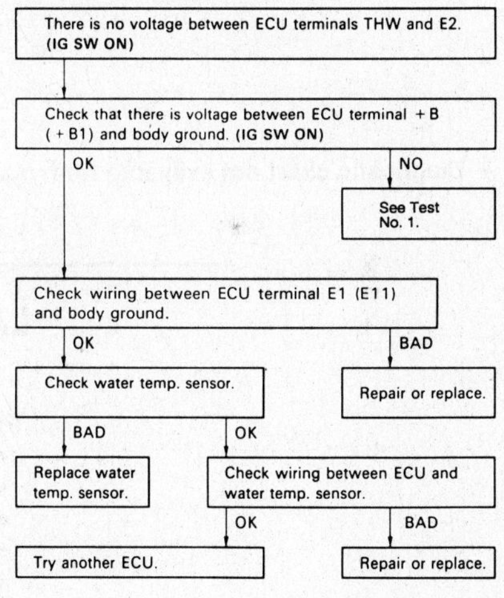

There is no voltage between ECU terminals THW and E2. (IG SW ON)
Check that there is voltage between ECU terminal +B (+B1) and body ground. (IG SW ON)
OK
NO
See Test No. 1.
Check wiring between ECU terminal E1 (E11) and body ground.
OK
BAD
Check water temp. sensor.
Repair or replace.
BAD
OK
Replace water temp. sensor.
Check wiring between ECU and water temp. sensor.
OK
BAD
Try another ECU.
Repair or replace.

NOTE: Water temperature sensor is also referred to as coolant temperature sensor.

91J17821 91A17822 91B17823 91C17824

Courtesy of Toyota Motor Sales, U.S.A., Inc.b

# 1991 ENGINE PERFORMANCE
# Self-Diagnostics (Cont.)

## LAND CRUISER TEST NO. 5 OR CODE 24
### INTAKE AIR TEMPERATURE SENSOR SIGNAL

| No. | Terminals | Trouble | Condition | | STD Voltage |
|---|---|---|---|---|---|
| 4 | THA – E2 | No voltage | Ignition switch ON | Intake air temperature 20°C (68°F) | 1 – 3 V |

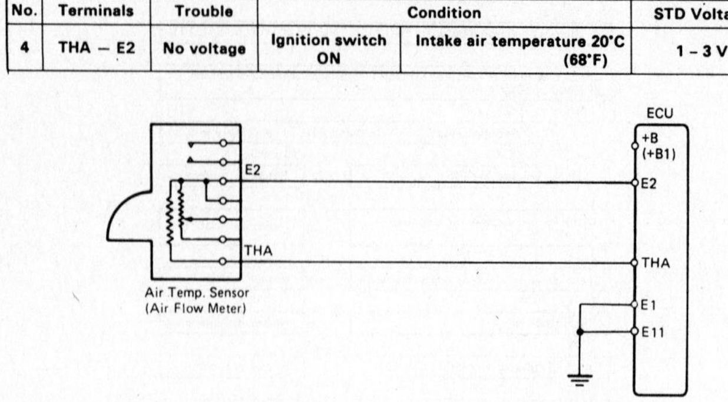
ECU
+B
(+B1)
E2
E2
THA
THA
E1
E11
Air Temp. Sensor
(Air Flow Meter)

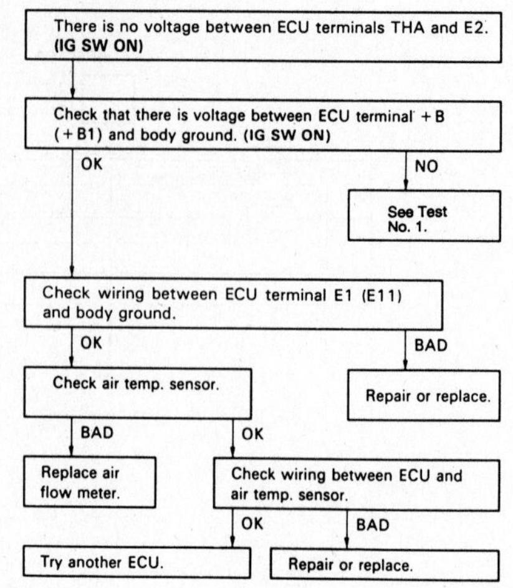
There is no voltage between ECU terminals THA and E2. (IG SW ON)
Check that there is voltage between ECU terminal +B (+B1) and body ground. (IG SW ON)
OK
NO
See Test No. 1.
Check wiring between ECU terminal E1 (E11) and body ground.
OK
BAD
Check air temp. sensor.
Repair or replace.
BAD
OK
Replace air flow meter.
Check wiring between ECU and air temp. sensor.
OK
BAD
Try another ECU.
Repair or replace.

## LAND CRUISER CODE 25
### LEAN AIR/FUEL MIXTURE

**Probable Causes**
- Airflow Meter
- Air Intake System
- Coolant Temperature Sensor
- ECU
- Fuel Pressure
- Ignition System
- Injector Circuit or Injector
- Oxygen Sensor or Sensor Circuit

**NOTE – Diagnostic chart not available from manufacturer.**

## LAND CRUISER CODE 26
### RICH AIR/FUEL MIXTURE

**Probable Causes**
- Airflow Meter
- Cold Start Injector
- Coolant Temperature Sensor
- ECU
- Fuel Pressure
- Injector Circuit or Injector
- Oxygen Sensor or Sensor Circuit

**NOTE – Diagnostic chart not available from manufacturer.**

91D17825 91E17826

# 1991 ENGINE PERFORMANCE
# Self-Diagnostics (Cont.)

## LAND CRUISER TEST NO. 6 OR CODE 31, 32
### AIRFLOW METER SIGNAL

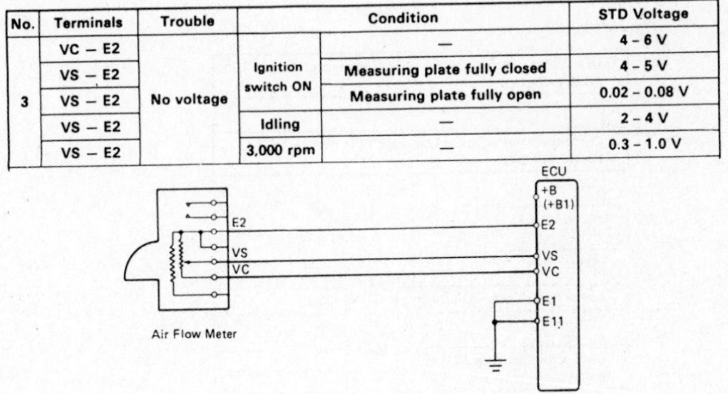

| No. | Terminals | Trouble | Condition | | STD Voltage |
|---|---|---|---|---|---|
| 3 | VC – E2 | No voltage | Ignition switch ON | — | 4 – 6 V |
| | VS – E2 | | | Measuring plate fully closed | 4 – 5 V |
| | VS – E2 | | | Measuring plate fully open | 0.02 – 0.08 V |
| | VS – E2 | | Idling | — | 2 – 4 V |
| | VS – E2 | | 3,000 rpm | — | 0.3 – 1.0 V |

ECU
+B
(+B1)
E2
VS
VC
E1
E11
E2
VS
VC
Air Flow Meter

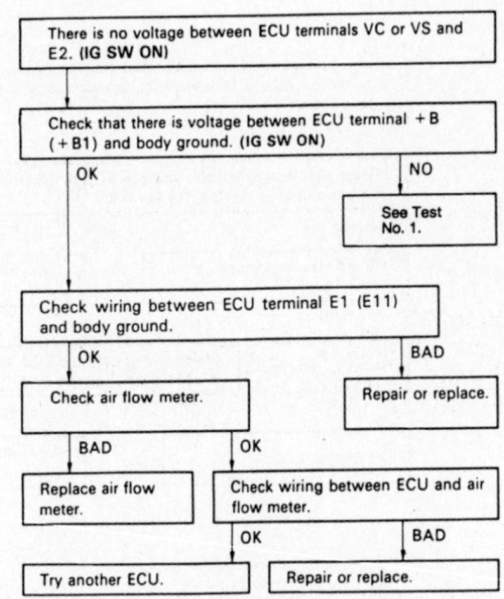
There is no voltage between ECU terminals VC or VS and E2. (IG SW ON)
Check that there is voltage between ECU terminal +B (+B1) and body ground. (IG SW ON)
OK
NO
See Test No. 1.
Check wiring between ECU terminal E1 (E11) and body ground.
OK
BAD
Check air flow meter.
Repair or replace.
BAD
OK
Replace air flow meter.
Check wiring between ECU and air flow meter.
OK
BAD
Try another ECU.
Repair or replace.

## LAND CRUISER CODE 35
### HIGH ALTITUDE COMPENSATOR (HAC) SIGNAL

**Probable Causes**

- HAC Sensor or Sensor Circuit
- ECU

**NOTE – Diagnostic chart not available from manufacturer.**

## LAND CRUISER TEST NO. 7 OR CODE 41
### THROTTLE POSITION SENSOR SIGNAL

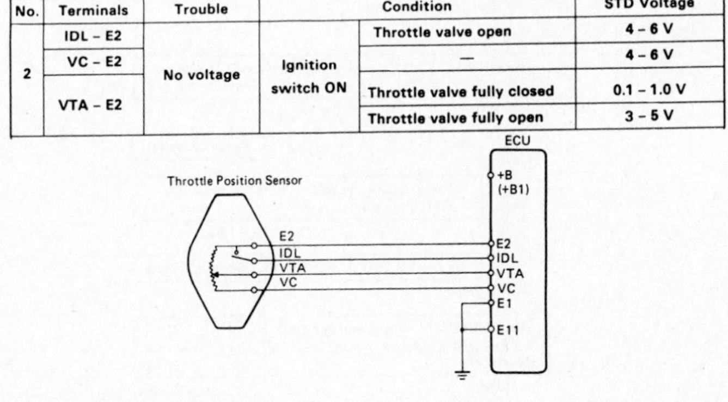

| No. | Terminals | Trouble | Condition | | STD Voltage |
|---|---|---|---|---|---|
| 2 | IDL – E2 | No voltage | Ignition switch ON | Throttle valve open | 4 – 6 V |
| | VC – E2 | | | — | 4 – 6 V |
| | VTA – E2 | | | Throttle valve fully closed | 0.1 – 1.0 V |
| | | | | Throttle valve fully open | 3 – 5 V |

ECU
+B
(+B1)
Throttle Position Sensor
E2
IDL
VTA
VC
E2
IDL
VTA
VC
E1
E11

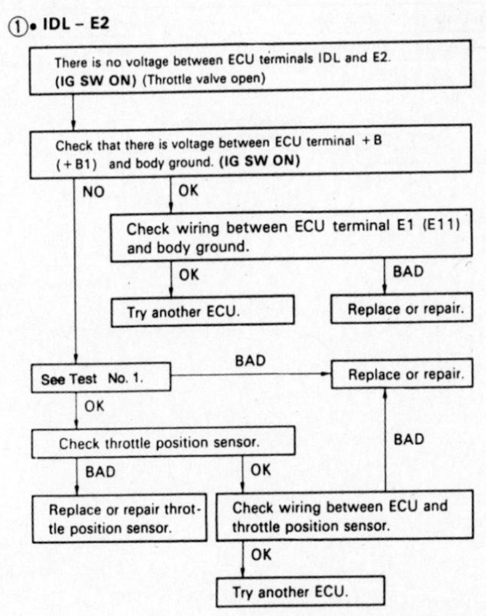
① • IDL – E2
There is no voltage between ECU terminals IDL and E2. (IG SW ON) (Throttle valve open)
Check that there is voltage between ECU terminal +B (+B1) and body ground. (IG SW ON)
NO
OK
Check wiring between ECU terminal E1 (E11) and body ground.
OK
BAD
Try another ECU.
Replace or repair.
See Test No. 1.
BAD
Replace or repair.
OK
Check throttle position sensor.
BAD
BAD
OK
Replace or repair throttle position sensor.
Check wiring between ECU and throttle position sensor.
OK
Try another ECU.

Continued On Next Page

Courtesy of Toyota Motor Sales, U.S.A., Inc.

91F17827 91G17828 91H17829 91A17830

# 1991 ENGINE PERFORMANCE
# Self-Diagnostics (Cont.)

## LAND CRUISER TEST NO. 7 OR CODE 41
### THROTTLE POSITION SENSOR SIGNAL (Cont.)

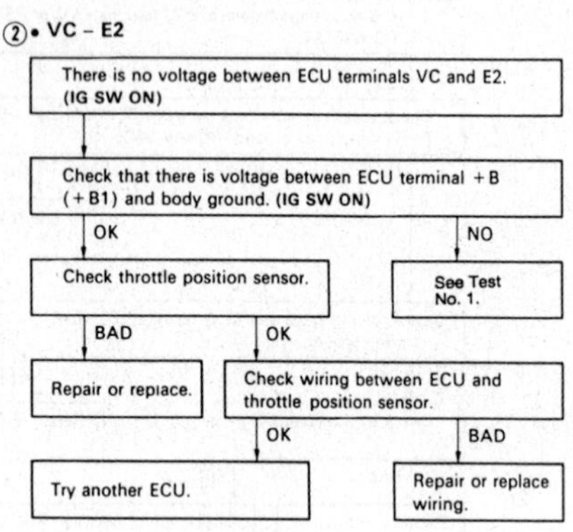
② • VC – E2
There is no voltage between ECU terminals VC and E2. (IG SW ON)
Check that there is voltage between ECU terminal +B (+B1) and body ground. (IG SW ON)
OK
NO
Check throttle position sensor.
See Test No. 1.
BAD
OK
Repair or replace.
Check wiring between ECU and throttle position sensor.
OK
BAD
Try another ECU.
Repair or replace wiring.

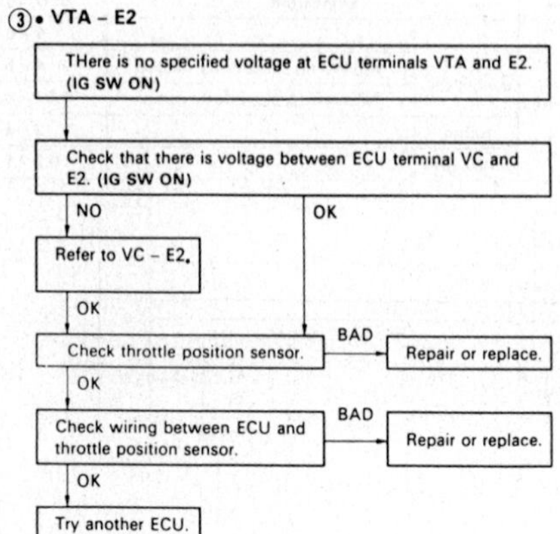
③ • VTA – E2
THere is no specified voltage at ECU terminals VTA and E2. (IG SW ON)
Check that there is voltage between ECU terminal VC and E2. (IG SW ON)
NO
OK
Refer to VC – E2.
OK
Check throttle position sensor.
BAD
Repair or replace.
OK
Check wiring between ECU and throttle position sensor.
BAD
Repair or replace.
OK
Try another ECU.

## LAND CRUISER CODE 42
### VEHICLE SPEED SENSOR SIGNAL

**Probable Causes**

- Vehicle Speed Sensor or Sensor Circuit
- ECU

**NOTE – Diagnostic chart not available from manufacturer.**

## LAND CRUISER TEST NO. 8 OR CODE 43
### STARTER SIGNAL

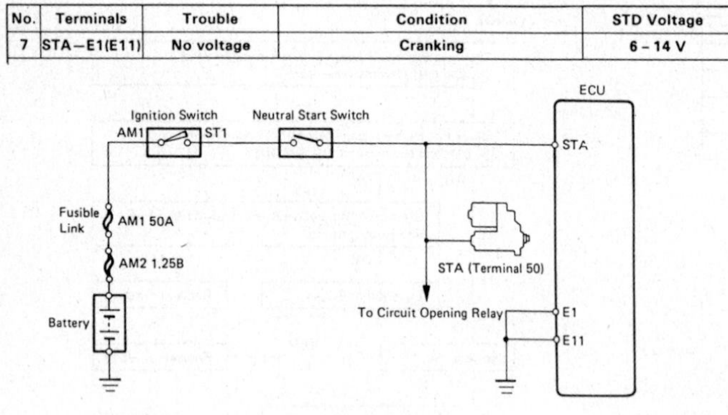

| No. | Terminals | Trouble | Condition | STD Voltage |
|---|---|---|---|---|
| 7 | STA–E1(E11) | No voltage | Cranking | 6 – 14 V |

Ignition Switch
Neutral Start Switch
AM1
ST1
ECU
STA
Fusible Link
AM1 50A
AM2 1.25B
Battery
STA (Terminal 50)
To Circuit Opening Relay
E1
E11

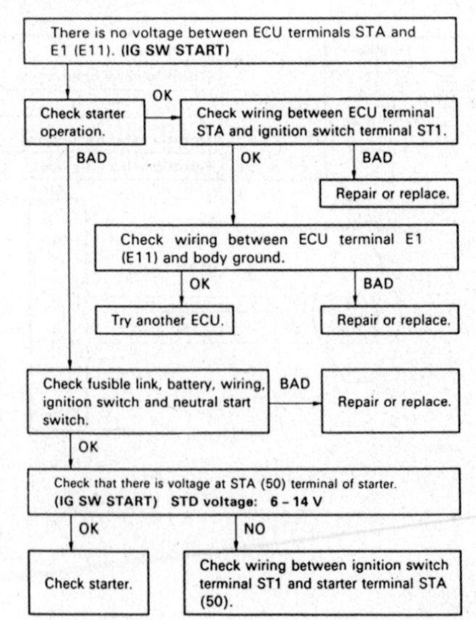
There is no voltage between ECU terminals STA and E1 (E11). (IG SW START)
OK
Check starter operation.
Check wiring between ECU terminal STA and ignition switch terminal ST1.
BAD
OK
BAD
Repair or replace.
Check wiring between ECU terminal E1 (E11) and body ground.
OK
BAD
Try another ECU.
Repair or replace.
Check fusible link, battery, wiring, ignition switch and neutral start switch.
BAD
Repair or replace.
OK
Check that there is voltage at STA (50) terminal of starter. (IG SW START) STD voltage: 6 – 14 V
OK
NO
Check starter.
Check wiring between ignition switch terminal ST1 and starter terminal STA (50).

91J17805 91A17806 91B17831 91C17832 91F17694

Courtesy of Toyota Motor Sales, U.S.A., Inc.

## LAND CRUISER TEST NO. 9 OR CODE 51
### SWITCH SIGNAL

**Probable Causes**

- A/C Switch or Switch Circuit
- A/C Amplifier
- Accelerator Pedal or Cable
- ECU
- Neutral/Start Switch or Switch Circuit
- Throttle Position Sensor or Sensor Circuit

To check A/C switch signal, use the following procedure.

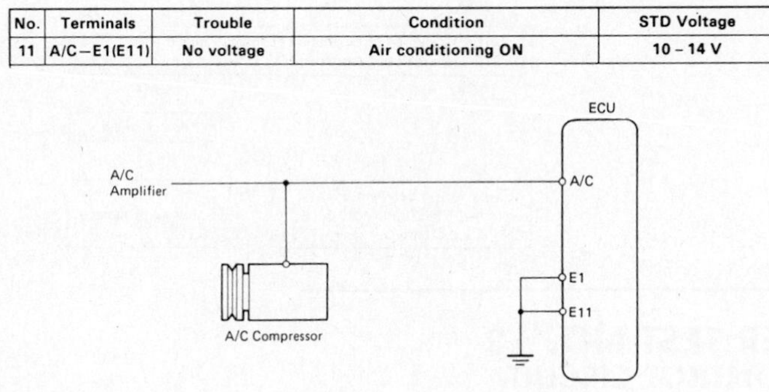

| No. | Terminals | Trouble | Condition | STD Voltage |
|---|---|---|---|---|
| 11 | A/C – E1(E11) | No voltage | Air conditioning ON | 10 – 14 V |

ECU
A/C Amplifier
A/C
E1
E11
A/C Compressor

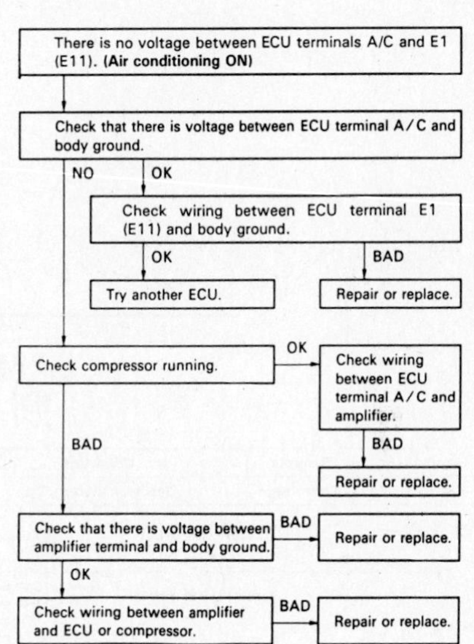

There is no voltage between ECU terminals A/C and E1 (E11). (Air conditioning ON)
Check that there is voltage between ECU terminal A/C and body ground.
NO
OK
Check wiring between ECU terminal E1 (E11) and body ground.
OK
BAD
Try another ECU.
Repair or replace.
Check compressor running.
OK
Check wiring between ECU terminal A/C and amplifier.
BAD
BAD
Repair or replace.
Check that there is voltage between amplifier terminal and body ground.
BAD
Repair or replace.
OK
Check wiring between amplifier and ECU or compressor.
BAD
Repair or replace.

## LAND CRUISER TEST NO. 10 OR CODE 71
### EGR SYSTEM MALFUNCTION

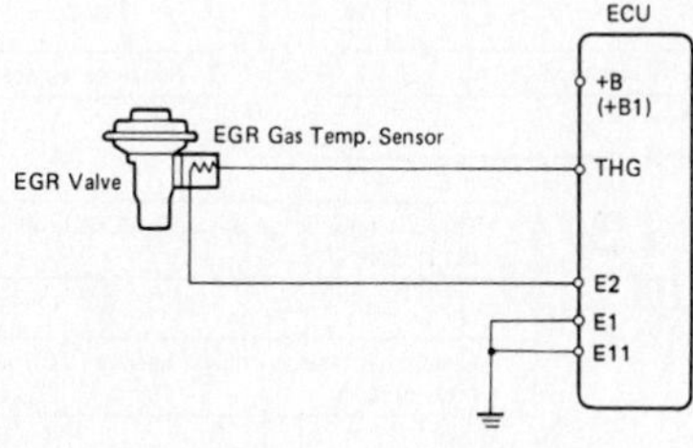

ECU
+B (+B1)
EGR Gas Temp. Sensor
EGR Valve
THG
E2
E1
E11

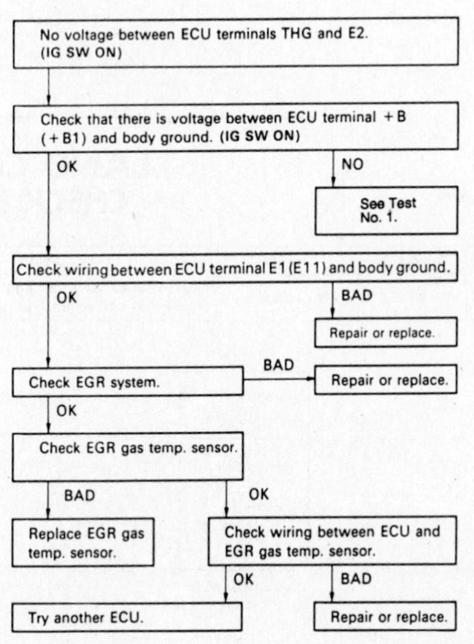

No voltage between ECU terminals THG and E2. (IG SW ON)
Check that there is voltage between ECU terminal +B (+B1) and body ground. (IG SW ON)
OK
NO
See Test No. 1.
Check wiring between ECU terminal E1 (E11) and body ground.
OK
BAD
Repair or replace.
Check EGR system.
BAD
Repair or replace.
OK
Check EGR gas temp. sensor.
BAD
OK
Replace EGR gas temp. sensor.
Check wiring between ECU and EGR gas temp. sensor.
OK
BAD
Try another ECU.
Repair or replace.

91D17833 91G18016 91H18017 91I18018

Courtesy of Toyota Motor Sales, U.S.A., Inc.

# 1991 ENGINE PERFORMANCE
# Self-Diagnostics (Cont.)

## LAND CRUISER TEST NO. 11
### INJECTOR CIRCUIT

| Terminals | Trouble | Condition | STD Voltage |
|---|---|---|---|
| No. 10 - E01<br>No. 20 - E02 | No voltage | Ignition switch ON | 10 - 14 V |

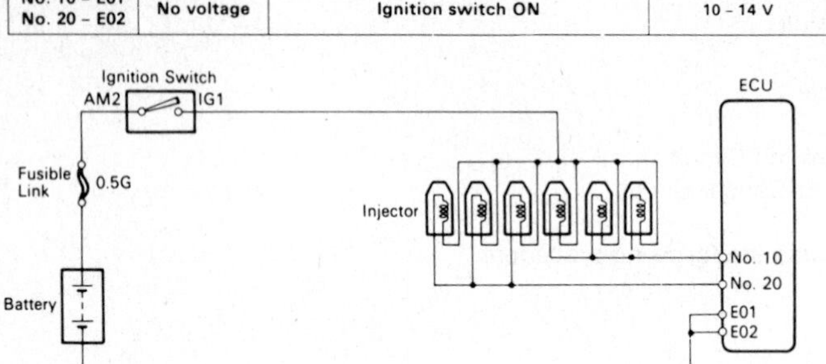
Ignition Switch
AM2
IG1
Fusible Link
0.5G
Battery
Injector
ECU
No. 10
No. 20
E01
E02

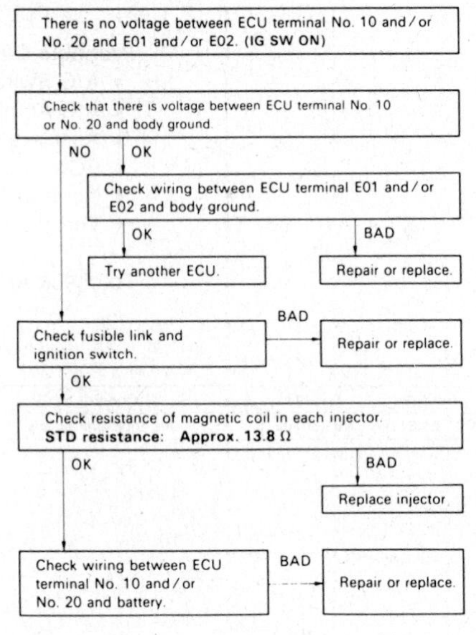
There is no voltage between ECU terminal No. 10 and/or No. 20 and E01 and/or E02. (IG SW ON)
Check that there is voltage between ECU terminal No. 10 or No. 20 and body ground.
NO
OK
Check wiring between ECU terminal E01 and/or E02 and body ground.
OK
BAD
Try another ECU.
Repair or replace.
Check fusible link and ignition switch.
BAD
Repair or replace.
OK
Check resistance of magnetic coil in each injector.
STD resistance: Approx. 13.8 Ω
OK
BAD
Replace injector.
Check wiring between ECU terminal No. 10 and/or No. 20 and battery.
BAD
Repair or replace.

## LAND CRUISER TEST NO. 12
### IDLE SPEED CONTROL CIRCUIT

| No. | Terminals | Trouble | Condition | STD Voltage |
|---|---|---|---|---|
| 8 | ISC1 ~ ISC4 – E1(E11) | No voltage | Ignition switch ON | 10 – 14 V |

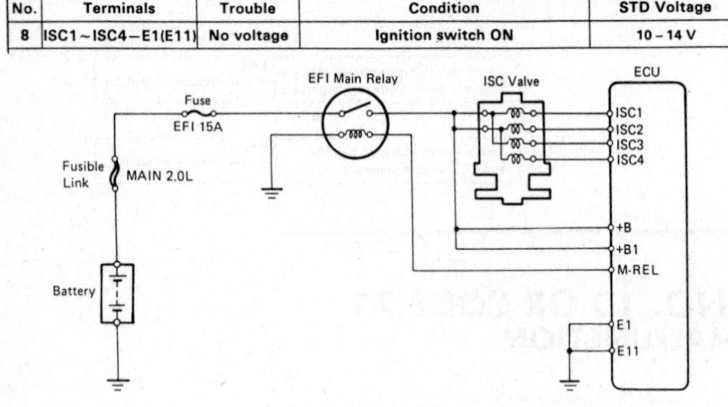
EFI Main Relay
ISC Valve
ECU
Fuse
EFI 15A
Fusible Link
MAIN 2.0L
Battery
ISC1
ISC2
ISC3
ISC4
+B
+B1
M-REL
E1
E11

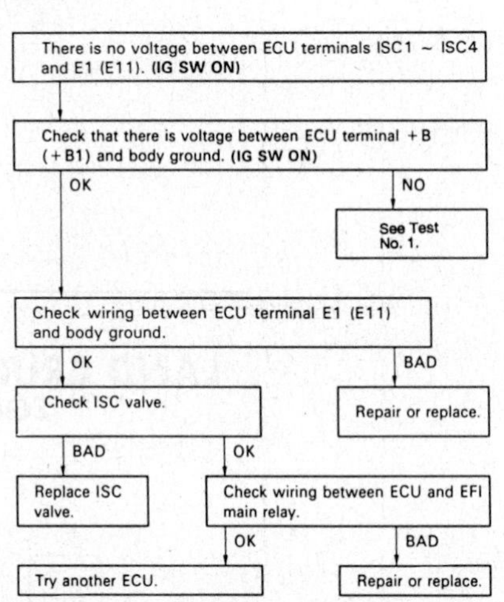
There is no voltage between ECU terminals ISC1 ~ ISC4 and E1 (E11). (IG SW ON)
Check that there is voltage between ECU terminal +B (+B1) and body ground. (IG SW ON)
OK
NO
See Test No. 1.
Check wiring between ECU terminal E1 (E11) and body ground.
OK
BAD
Check ISC valve.
Repair or replace.
BAD
OK
Replace ISC valve.
Check wiring between ECU and EFI main relay.
OK
BAD
Try another ECU.
Repair or replace.

## LAND CRUISER TEST NO. 13
### CHECK ENGINE LIGHT CIRCUIT

| No. | Terminals | Trouble | Condition | STD Voltage |
|---|---|---|---|---|
| 10 | W – E1 (E11) | No voltage | No trouble ("CHECK" engine warning light off) and engine running | 10 – 14 V |

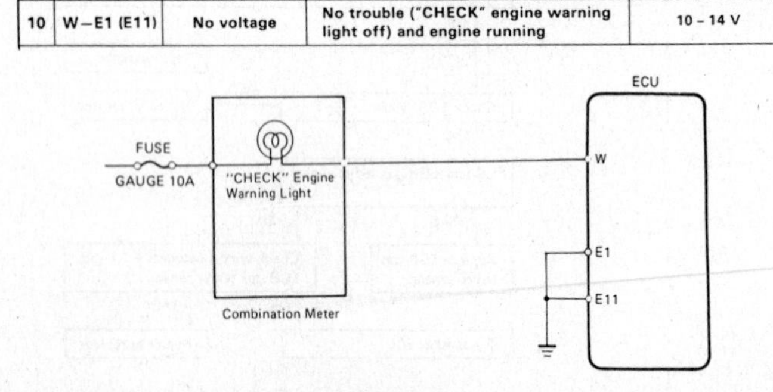
ECU
FUSE
GAUGE 10A
"CHECK" Engine Warning Light
W
E1
E11
Combination Meter

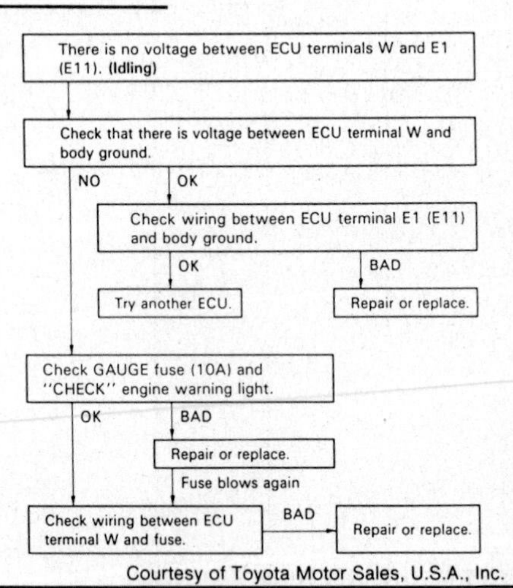
There is no voltage between ECU terminals W and E1 (E11). (Idling)
Check that there is voltage between ECU terminal W and body ground.
NO
OK
Check wiring between ECU terminal E1 (E11) and body ground.
OK
BAD
Try another ECU.
Repair or replace.
Check GAUGE fuse (10A) and "CHECK" engine warning light.
OK
BAD
Repair or replace.
Fuse blows again
Check wiring between ECU terminal W and fuse.
BAD
Repair or replace.

91J18019 91J17789 91C18020 91D18021 91E18022 91F18023

# 1991 ENGINE PERFORMANCE
## Self-Diagnostics (Cont.)

## MR2 DIAGNOSTIC CIRCUIT CHECK

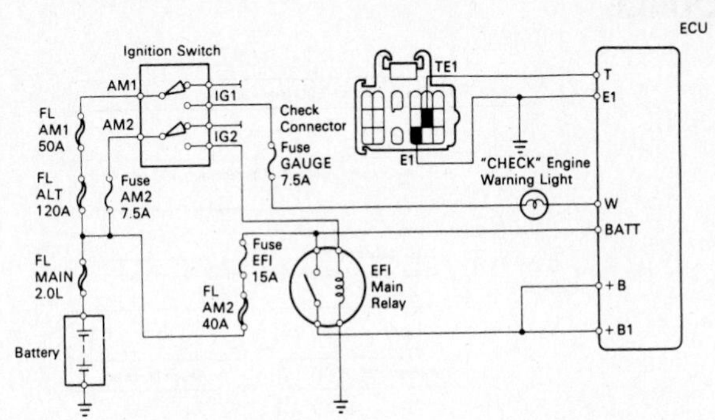
Ignition Switch
AM1
IG1
AM2
IG2
FL AM1 50A
FL ALT 120A
FL MAIN 2.0L
Battery
Fuse AM2 7.5A
Check Connector
Fuse GAUGE 7.5A
TE1
E1
"CHECK" Engine Warning Light
Fuse EFI 15A
FL AM2 40A
EFI Main Relay
ECU
T
E1
W
BATT
+B
+B1

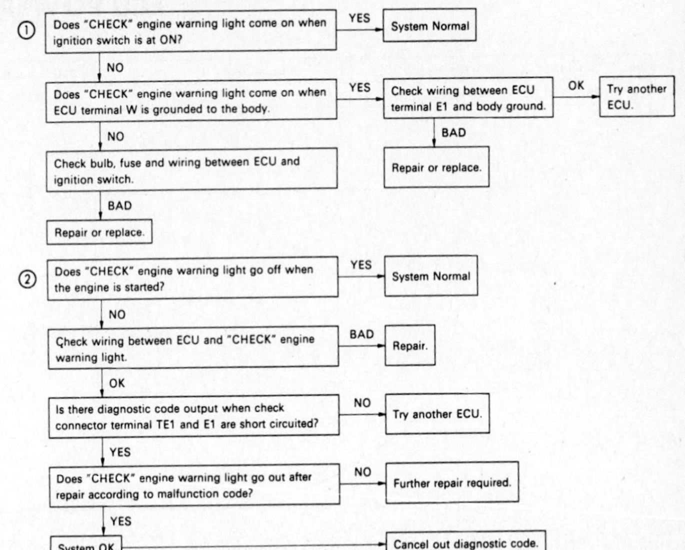
①
Does "CHECK" engine warning light come on when ignition switch is at ON?
YES
System Normal
NO
Does "CHECK" engine warning light come on when ECU terminal W is grounded to the body.
YES
Check wiring between ECU terminal E1 and body ground.
OK
Try another ECU.
BAD
Repair or replace.
NO
Check bulb, fuse and wiring between ECU and ignition switch.
BAD
Repair or replace.
②
Does "CHECK" engine warning light go off when the engine is started?
YES
System Normal
NO
Check wiring between ECU and "CHECK" engine warning light.
BAD
Repair.
OK
Is there diagnostic code output when check connector terminal TE1 and E1 are short circuited?
NO
Try another ECU.
YES
Does "CHECK" engine warning light go out after repair according to malfunction code?
NO
Further repair required.
YES
System OK
Cancel out diagnostic code.

CAUTION: Perform all voltage measurements with ECU harness connector installed. Use a high-impedance DVOM (10,000-ohm minimum). Verify battery voltage is greater than 11 volts.

## ECU TERMINAL IDENTIFICATION

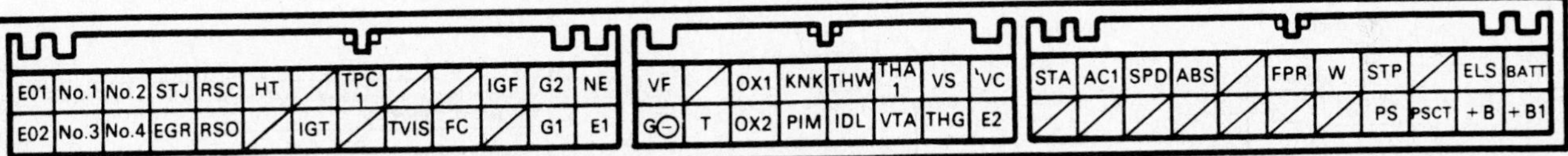
E01 No.1 No.2 STJ RSC HT / TPC 1 / / IGF G2 NE
E02 No.3 No.4 EGR RSO / IGT / TVIS FC / G1 E1
VF / OX1 KNK THW THA 1 VS VC
G⊖ T OX2 PIM IDL VTA THG E2
STA AC1 SPD ABS / FPR W STP / ELS BATT
/ / / / / / / PS PSCT +B +B1

3S-GTE

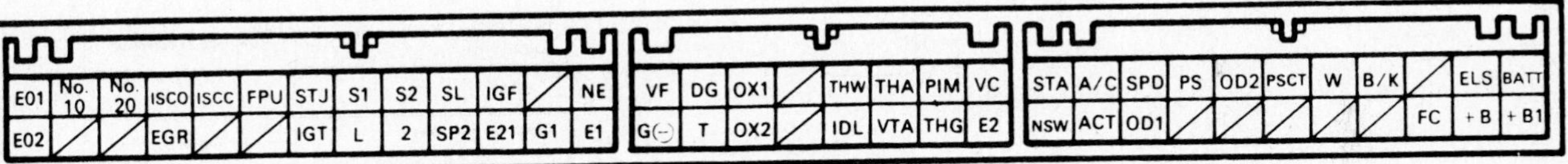
E01 No. 10 No. 20 ISCO ISCC FPU STJ S1 S2 SL IGF / NE
E02 / / EGR / / IGT L 2 SP2 E21 G1 E1
VF DG OX1 / THW THA PIM VC
G⊖ T OX2 / IDL VTA THG E2
STA A/C SPD PS OD2 PSCT W B/K / ELS BATT
NSW ACT OD1 / / / / / FC +B +B1

5S-FE WITH A/T

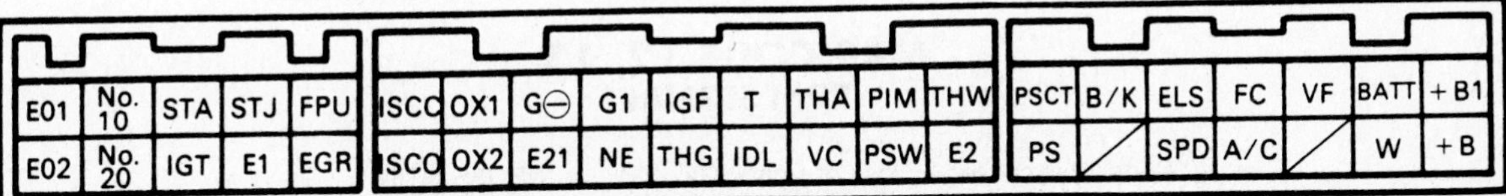
E01 No. 10 STA STJ FPU
E02 No. 20 IGT E1 EGR
ISCC OX1 G⊖ G1 IGF T THA PIM THW
ISCO OX2 E21 NE THG IDL VC PSW E2
PSCT B/K ELS FC VF BATT +B1
PS / SPD A/C / W +B

5S-FE WITH M/T

91G18024 91C17709 91H18025 91I18026 91J18027

Courtesy of Toyota Motor Sales, U.S.A., Inc.

# 1991 ENGINE PERFORMANCE
## Self-Diagnostics (Cont.)

### MR2 TEST NO. 1
#### ECU POWER SOURCE

| No. | Terminals | Trouble | Condition | STD voltage |
|---|---|---|---|---|
| 2 | BATT – E1 | No voltage | – | 10 – 14 V |

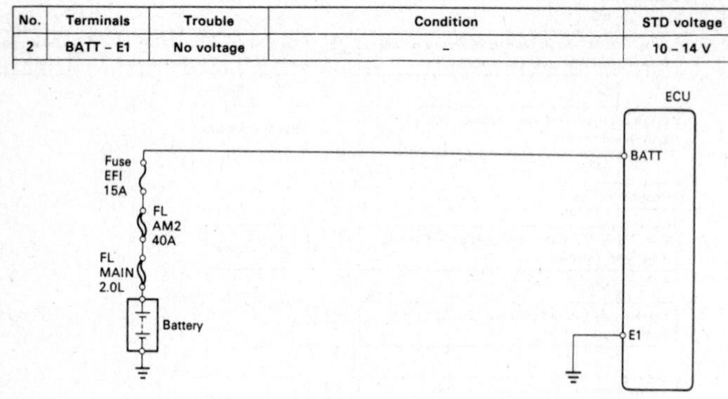
ECU
BATT
Fuse
EFI
15A
FL
AM2
40A
FL
MAIN
2.0L
Battery
E1

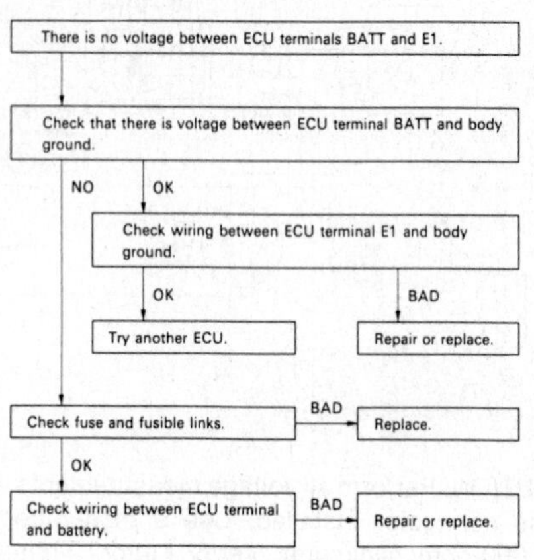
There is no voltage between ECU terminals BATT and E1.
Check that there is voltage between ECU terminal BATT and body ground.
NO
OK
Check wiring between ECU terminal E1 and body ground.
OK
BAD
Try another ECU.
Repair or replace.
Check fuse and fusible links.
BAD
Replace.
OK
Check wiring between ECU terminal and battery.
BAD
Repair or replace.

### MR2 TEST NO. 2
#### ECU (+B) CIRCUIT

| No. | Terminals | Trouble | Condition | STD voltage |
|---|---|---|---|---|
| 1 | +B<br>+B1 – E1 | No voltage | IG SW ON | 10 – 14 V |

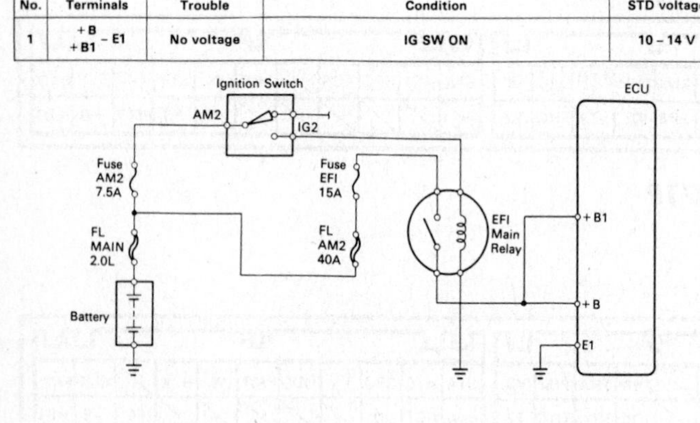
Ignition Switch
AM2
IG2
ECU
Fuse
AM2
7.5A
Fuse
EFI
15A
EFI
Main
Relay
+B1
FL
MAIN
2.0L
FL
AM2
40A
+B
Battery
E1

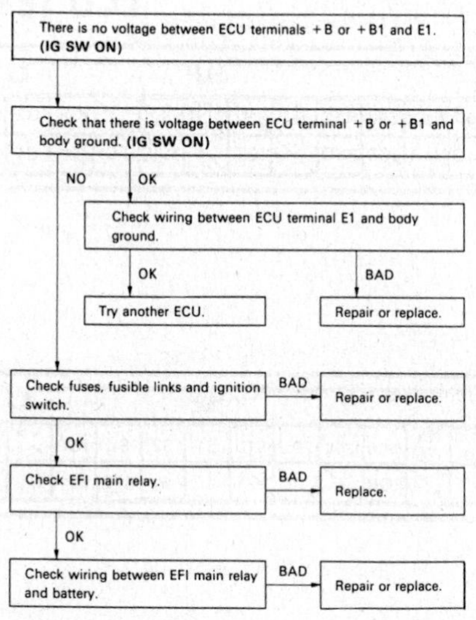
There is no voltage between ECU terminals +B or +B1 and E1. (IG SW ON)
Check that there is voltage between ECU terminal +B or +B1 and body ground. (IG SW ON)
NO
OK
Check wiring between ECU terminal E1 and body ground.
OK
BAD
Try another ECU.
Repair or replace.
Check fuses, fusible links and ignition switch.
BAD
Repair or replace.
OK
Check EFI main relay.
BAD
Replace.
OK
Check wiring between EFI main relay and battery.
BAD
Repair or replace.

### MR2 CODE 12, 13
#### RPM SIGNAL

Code 12 is caused by loss of signal "G2", "G1", or "NE" (3S-GTE) or "G" or "NE" (all others) from distributor to ECU for at least 2 seconds after starter signal is received at ECU. Ensure starter signal exists at ECU. See TEST NO. 10 OR CODE 43.
Code 13 is caused by loss of "NE" signal from distributor to ECU when engine RPM exceeds 1000 RPM.

**NOTE – Diagnostic chart not available from manufacturer.**

91A18028 91A17715 91B18029 91C17717

# 1991 ENGINE PERFORMANCE
# Self-Diagnostics (Cont.)

## MR2 TEST NO. 3 OR CODE 14
### IGNITION SIGNAL

| No. | Terminals | Trouble | Condition | STD voltage |
|---|---|---|---|---|
| 9 | IGT - E1 | No voltage | Idling | 0.8 - 1.2 V |

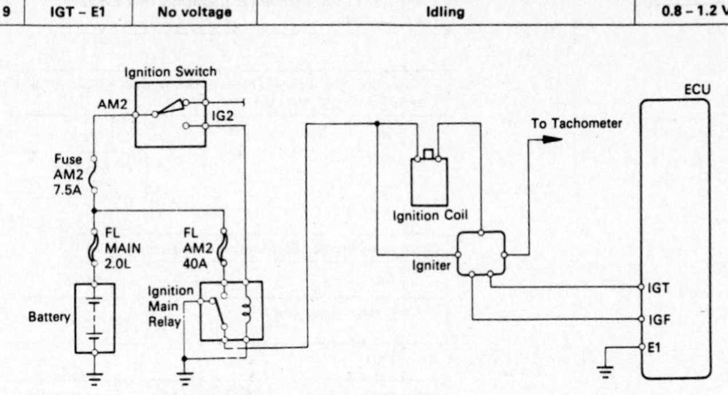

Ignition Switch
AM2
IG2
Fuse
AM2
7.5A
FL
MAIN
2.0L
FL
AM2
40A
Battery
Ignition
Main
Relay
Ignition Coil
Igniter
To Tachometer
ECU
IGT
IGF
E1

NOTE: To check ignition system components, see SYSTEM & COMPONENT TESTING article.

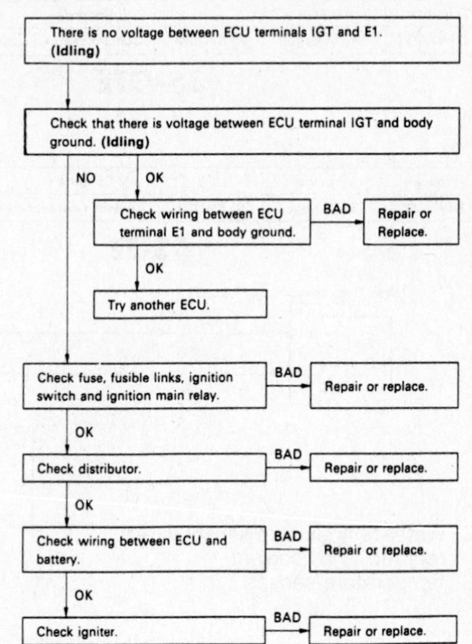

There is no voltage between ECU terminals IGT and E1. (Idling)
Check that there is voltage between ECU terminal IGT and body ground. (Idling)
NO
OK
Check wiring between ECU terminal E1 and body ground.
BAD
Repair or Replace.
OK
Try another ECU.
Check fuse, fusible links, ignition switch and ignition main relay.
BAD
Repair or replace.
OK
Check distributor.
BAD
Repair or replace.
OK
Check wiring between ECU and battery.
BAD
Repair or replace.
OK
Check igniter.
BAD
Repair or replace.

## MR2 TEST NO. 4 OR CODE 21, 27
### OXYGEN SENSOR SIGNAL

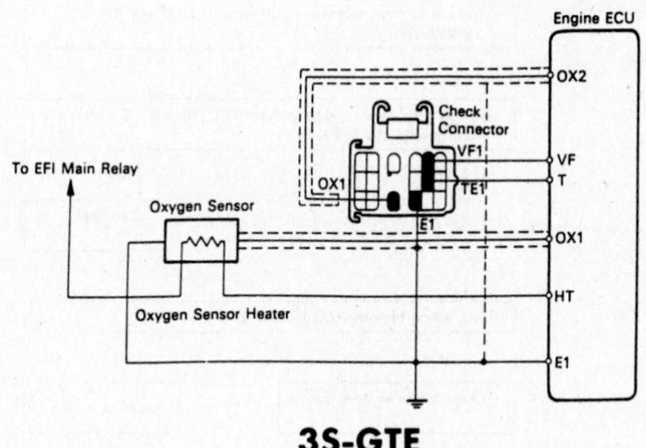

Engine ECU
OX2
Check Connector
VF1
VF
T
TE1
OX1
To EFI Main Relay
Oxygen Sensor
E1
OX1
HT
Oxygen Sensor Heater
E1

**3S-GTE**

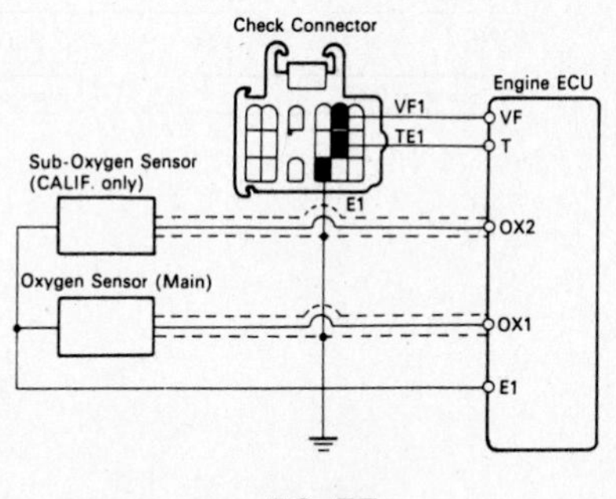

Check Connector
Engine ECU
VF1
VF
TE1
T
Sub-Oxygen Sensor
(CALIF. only)
E1
OX2
Oxygen Sensor (Main)
OX1
E1

**5S-FE**

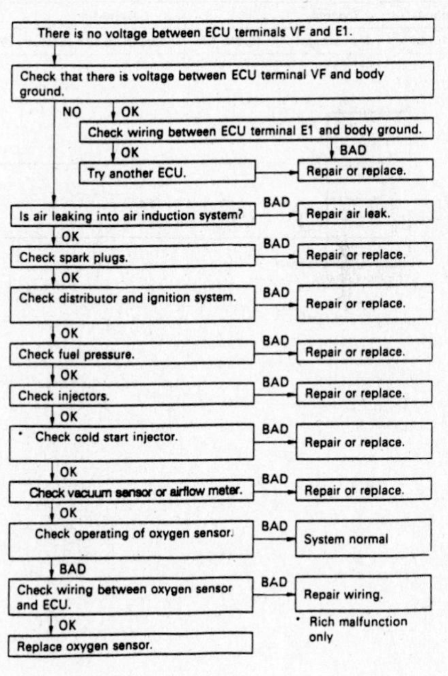

There is no voltage between ECU terminals VF and E1.
Check that there is voltage between ECU terminal VF and body ground.
NO
OK
Check wiring between ECU terminal E1 and body ground.
OK
BAD
Try another ECU.
Repair or replace.
Is air leaking into air induction system?
BAD
Repair air leak.
OK
Check spark plugs.
BAD
Repair or replace.
OK
Check distributor and ignition system.
BAD
Repair or replace.
OK
Check fuel pressure.
BAD
Repair or replace.
OK
Check injectors.
BAD
Repair or replace.
OK
* Check cold start injector.
BAD
Repair or replace.
OK
Check vacuum sensor or airflow meter.
BAD
Repair or replace.
OK
Check operating of oxygen sensor.
BAD
System normal
BAD
Check wiring between oxygen sensor and ECU.
BAD
Repair wiring.
OK
Replace oxygen sensor.
* Rich malfunction only

Code 27 applies to 5S-FE only.

# 1991 ENGINE PERFORMANCE
## Self-Diagnostics (Cont.)

### MR2 TEST NO. 5 OR CODE 22
### COOLANT TEMPERATURE SENSOR SIGNAL

| No. | Terminals | Trouble | Condition | | STD voltage |
|---|---|---|---|---|---|
| 7 | THW – E2 | No voltage | IG SW ON | Coolant temperature 80°C (176°C) | 0.1 – 1.1 V |

**3S-GTE**

| No. | Terminals | Trouble | Condition | | STD voltage |
|---|---|---|---|---|---|
| 7 | THW – E2 | No voltage | IG SW ON | Coolant temperature 80°C (176°F) | 0.3 – 0.8 V |

**5S-FE**

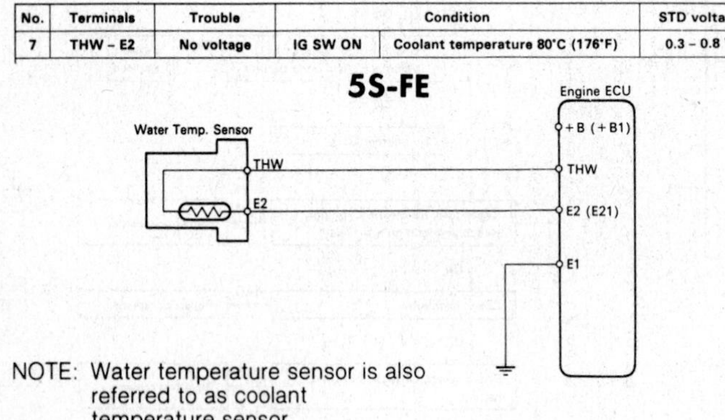
Engine ECU
Water Temp. Sensor
+B (+B1)
THW
THW
E2
E2 (E21)
E1

NOTE: Water temperature sensor is also referred to as coolant temperature sensor.

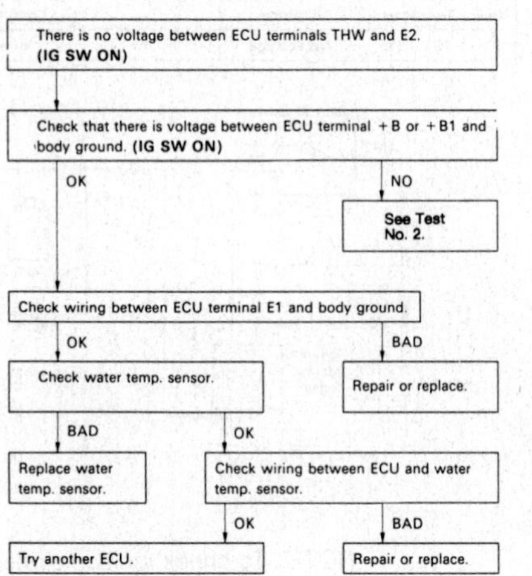
There is no voltage between ECU terminals THW and E2. (IG SW ON)
Check that there is voltage between ECU terminal +B or +B1 and body ground. (IG SW ON)
OK
NO
See Test No. 2.
Check wiring between ECU terminal E1 and body ground.
OK
BAD
Check water temp. sensor.
Repair or replace.
BAD
OK
Replace water temp. sensor.
Check wiring between ECU and water temp. sensor.
OK
BAD
Try another ECU.
Repair or replace.

### MR2 TEST NO. 6 OR CODE 24
### INTAKE AIR TEMPERATURE SENSOR SIGNAL

| No. | Terminals | Trouble | Condition | | STD voltage |
|---|---|---|---|---|---|
| 6 | THA1 – E2 | No voltage | IG SW ON | Intake air temperature 20°C (68°F) | 1 – 3 V |

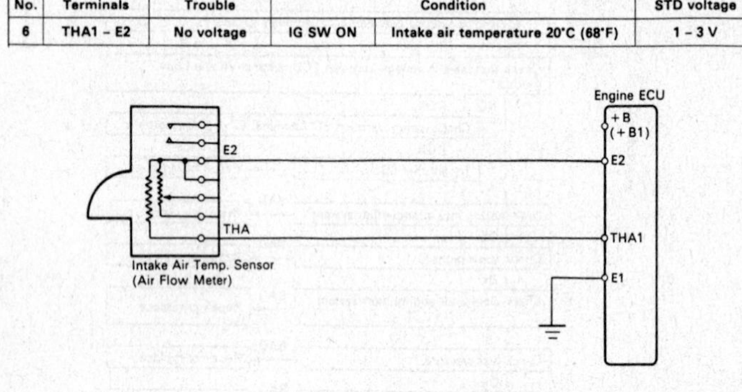
Engine ECU
+B (+B1)
E2
E2
THA
THA1
E1
Intake Air Temp. Sensor (Air Flow Meter)

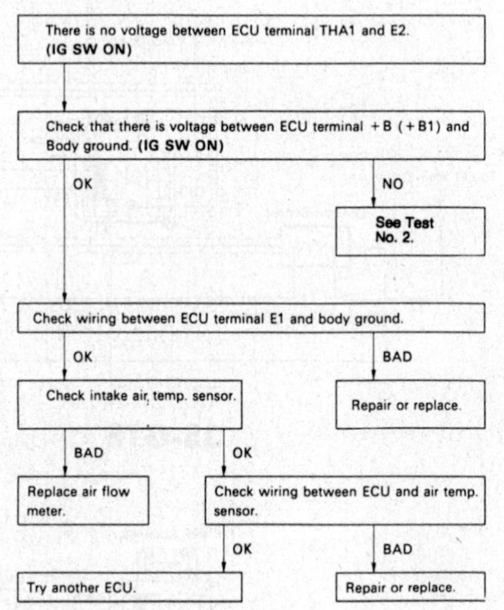
There is no voltage between ECU terminal THA1 and E2. (IG SW ON)
Check that there is voltage between ECU terminal +B (+B1) and Body ground. (IG SW ON)
OK
NO
See Test No. 2.
Check wiring between ECU terminal E1 and body ground.
OK
BAD
Check intake air temp. sensor.
Repair or replace.
BAD
OK
Replace air flow meter.
Check wiring between ECU and air temp. sensor.
OK
BAD
Try another ECU.
Repair or replace.

**3S-GTE**

Continued On Next Page

91J17680 91D17726 91E17727 91F17728

Courtesy of Toyota Motor Sales, U.S.A., Inc.

## MR2 TEST NO. 6 OR CODE 24
### INTAKE AIR TEMPERATURE SENSOR SIGNAL (Cont.)

| No. | Terminals | Trouble | Condition | | STD voltage |
|---|---|---|---|---|---|
| 6 | THA – E2 | No voltage | IG SW ON | Intake air temperature 20°C (68°F) | 1.7 – 3.1 V |

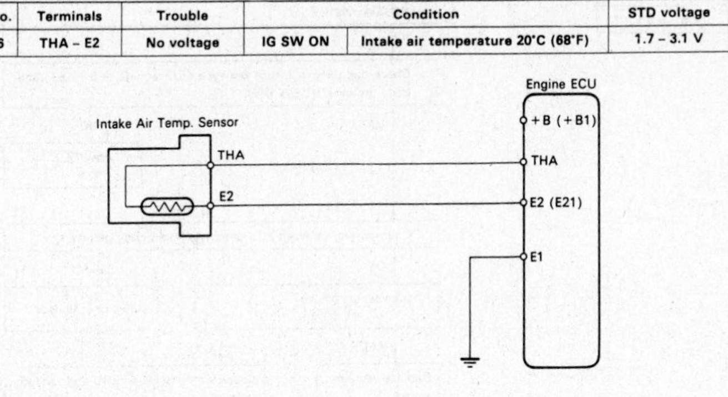
Engine ECU
Intake Air Temp. Sensor
+B (+B1)
THA
THA
E2
E2 (E21)
E1

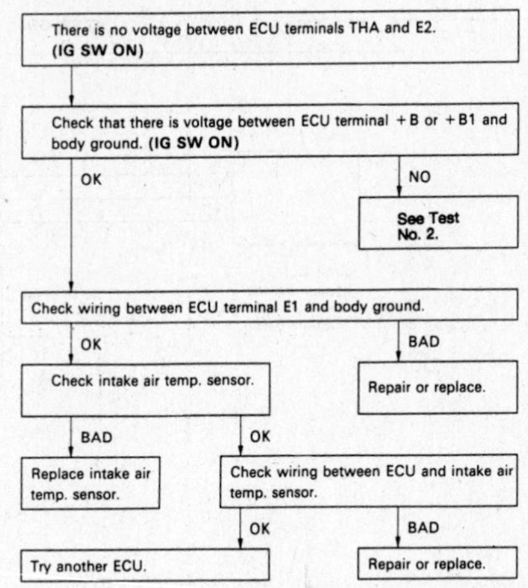
There is no voltage between ECU terminals THA and E2. (IG SW ON)
Check that there is voltage between ECU terminal +B or +B1 and body ground. (IG SW ON)
OK
NO
See Test No. 2.
Check wiring between ECU terminal E1 and body ground.
OK
BAD
Check intake air temp. sensor.
Repair or replace.
BAD
OK
Replace intake air temp. sensor.
Check wiring between ECU and intake air temp. sensor.
OK
BAD
Try another ECU.
Repair or replace.

## 5S-FE

---

## MR2 CODE 25
### LEAN AIR/FUEL MIXTURE

**Probable Causes**

- Airflow Meter
- Air Intake System
- Coolant Temperature Sensor
- ECU
- Fuel Pressure
- Ignition System
- Injector Circuit or Injector
- Oxygen Sensor or Sensor Circuit
- Vacuum Sensor

**NOTE – Diagnostic chart not available from manufacturer.**

---

## MR2 CODE 26
### RICH AIR/FUEL MIXTURE

**Probable Causes**

- Airflow Meter
- Cold Start Injector
- Coolant Temperature Sensor
- ECU
- Fuel Pressure
- Injector Circuit or Injector
- Oxygen Sensor or Sensor Circuit
- Vacuum Sensor Circuit

**NOTE – Diagnostic chart not available from manufacturer.**

91G17729 91J17730

# 1991 ENGINE PERFORMANCE
# Self-Diagnostics (Cont.)

## MR2 TEST NO. 7 OR CODE 31
### VACUUM SENSOR SIGNAL (5S-FE)

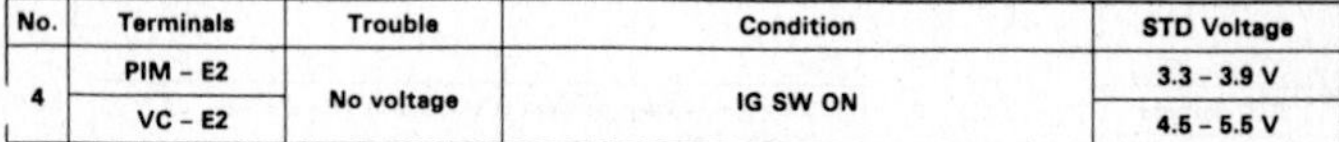

| No. | Terminals | Trouble | Condition | STD Voltage |
|---|---|---|---|---|
| 4 | PIM – E2 | No voltage | IG SW ON | 3.3 – 3.9 V |
| | VC – E2 | | | 4.5 – 5.5 V |

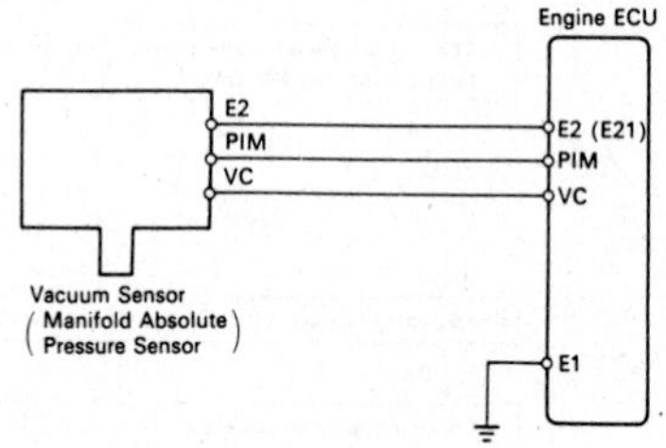
Engine ECU
E2
PIM
VC
E2 (E21)
PIM
VC
E1
Vacuum Sensor
(Manifold Absolute Pressure Sensor)

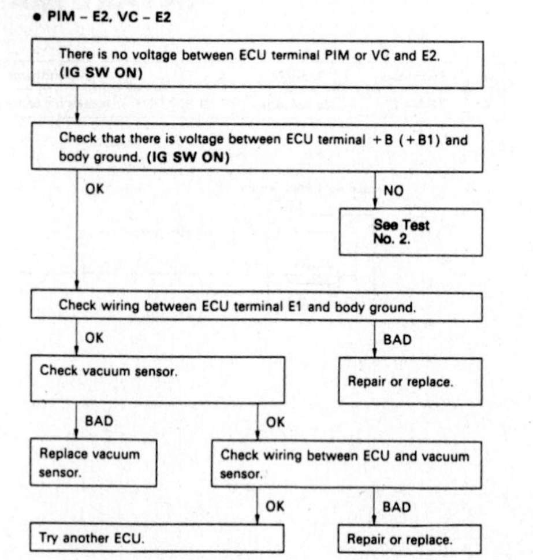
• PIM – E2, VC – E2
There is no voltage between ECU terminal PIM or VC and E2. (IG SW ON)
Check that there is voltage between ECU terminal +B (+B1) and body ground. (IG SW ON)
OK
NO
See Test No. 2.
Check wiring between ECU terminal E1 and body ground.
OK
BAD
Check vacuum sensor.
Repair or replace.
BAD
OK
Replace vacuum sensor.
Check wiring between ECU and vacuum sensor.
OK
BAD
Try another ECU.
Repair or replace.

## MR2 TEST NO. 7 OR CODE 31, 32
### AIRFLOW METER SIGNAL (3S-GTE)

| No. | Terminals | Trouble | Condition | | STD voltage |
|---|---|---|---|---|---|
| 4 | VC – E2 | No voltage | IG SW ON | – | 4 – 6 V |
| | VS – E2 | | | Measuring plate fully closed | 3.7 – 4.3 V |
| | | | | Measuring plate fully open | 0.2 – 0.5 V |
| | | | Idling (No load) | | 2.6 – 3.6 V |
| | | | 3,000 rpm (No load) | | 1.0 – 2.0 V |

Engine ECU
+B (+B1)
E2
VS
VC
E1
Air Flow Meter

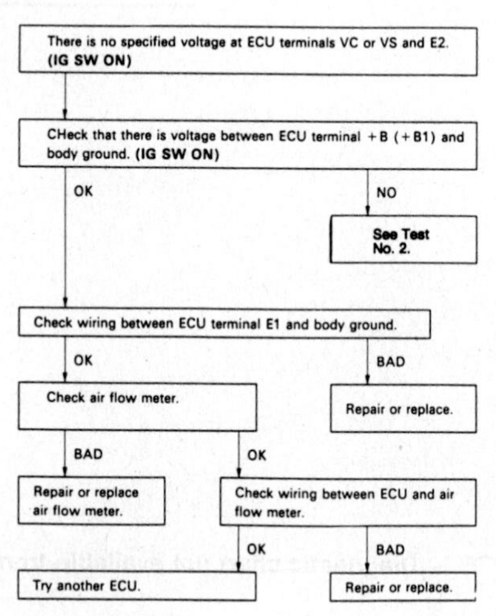
There is no specified voltage at ECU terminals VC or VS and E2. (IG SW ON)
CHeck that there is voltage between ECU terminal +B (+B1) and body ground. (IG SW ON)
OK
NO
See Test No. 2.
Check wiring between ECU terminal E1 and body ground.
OK
BAD
Check air flow meter.
Repair or replace.
BAD
OK
Repair or replace air flow meter.
Check wiring between ECU and air flow meter.
OK
BAD
Try another ECU.
Repair or replace.

## MR2 TEST NO. 8 OR CODE 34, 35 (3S-GTE)
### TURBOCHARGER PRESSURE

| No. | Terminals | Trouble | Condition | STD voltage |
|---|---|---|---|---|
| 12 | PIM – E2 | No voltage | IG SW ON | 2.5 – 4.5 V |
| | VC – E2 | | | 4 – 6 V |

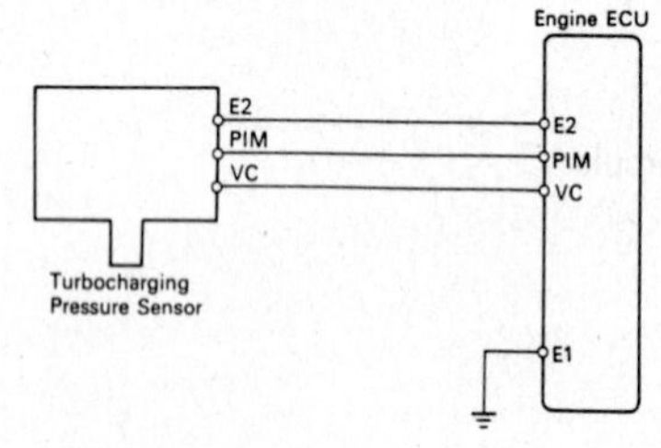
Engine ECU
E2
PIM
VC
E2
PIM
VC
E1
Turbocharging Pressure Sensor

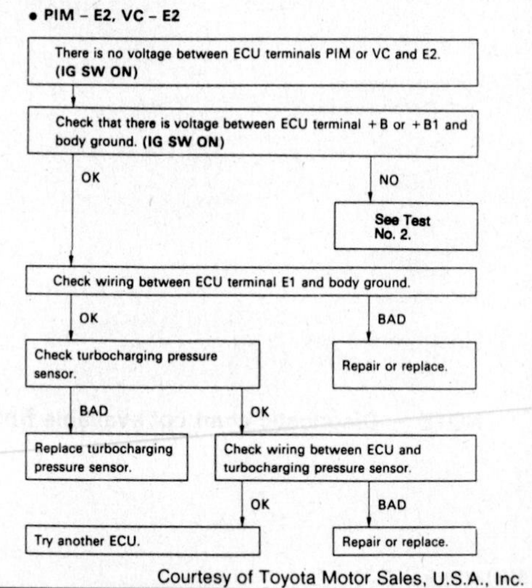
• PIM – E2, VC – E2
There is no voltage between ECU terminals PIM or VC and E2. (IG SW ON)
Check that there is voltage between ECU terminal +B or +B1 and body ground. (IG SW ON)
OK
NO
See Test No. 2.
Check wiring between ECU terminal E1 and body ground.
OK
BAD
Check turbocharging pressure sensor.
Repair or replace.
BAD
OK
Replace turbocharging pressure sensor.
Check wiring between ECU and turbocharging pressure sensor.
OK
BAD
Try another ECU.
Repair or replace.

91H18033 91I18034 91D17684 91E17685 91C17733 91D17734

# MR2 TEST NO. 9 OR CODE 41
## THROTTLE POSITION SENSOR SIGNAL

| No. | Terminals | Trouble | | Condition | STD Voltage |
|---|---|---|---|---|---|
| 3 | IDL – E2 | No voltage | IG SW ON | Throttle valve open | 8 – 14 V |
| | VC – E2 | | | – | 4.5 – 5.5 V |
| | VTA – E2 | | | Throttle valve fully closed (Throttle opener must be cancelled first) | 0.8 – 1.2 V |
| | | | | Throttle valve fully open | 3.2 – 4.2 V |

**5S-FE WITH A/T**

| No. | Terminals | Trouble | | Condition | STD voltage |
|---|---|---|---|---|---|
| 3 | IDL – E2 | No voltage | IG SW ON | Throttle valve open | 8 – 14 V |
| | VC – E2 | | | – | 4 – 6 V |
| | VTA – E2 | | | Throttle valve fully closed | 0.7 – 1.0 V |
| | | | | Throttle valve fully open | 3.2 – 4.2 V |

**3S-GTE**

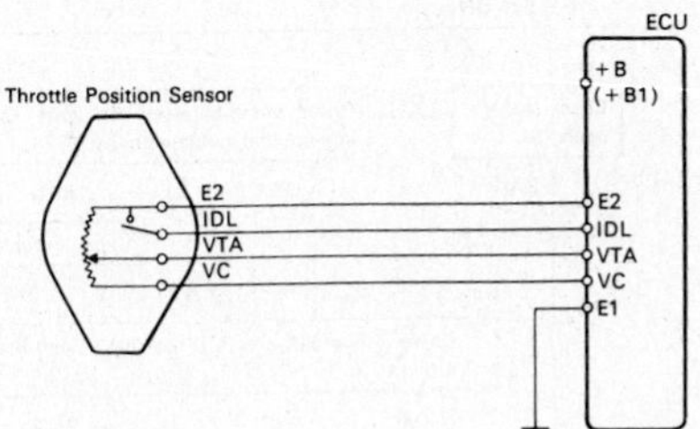
ECU
+B
(+B1)
Throttle Position Sensor
E2
IDL
VTA
VC
E2
IDL
VTA
VC
E1

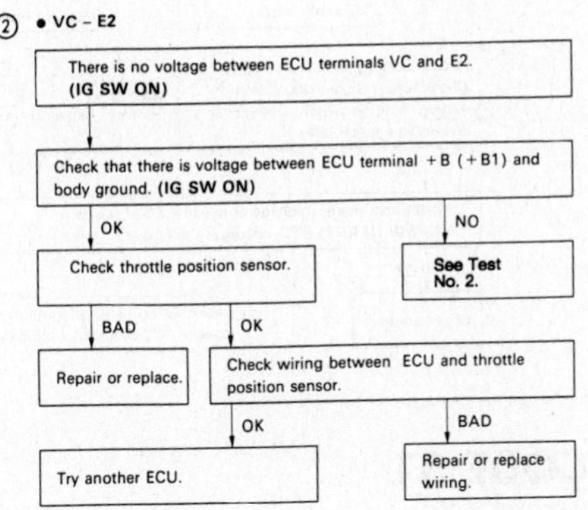
② • VC – E2
There is no voltage between ECU terminals VC and E2. (IG SW ON)
Check that there is voltage between ECU terminal +B (+B1) and body ground. (IG SW ON)
OK
NO
Check throttle position sensor.
See Test No. 2.
BAD
OK
Repair or replace.
Check wiring between ECU and throttle position sensor.
OK
BAD
Try another ECU.
Repair or replace wiring.

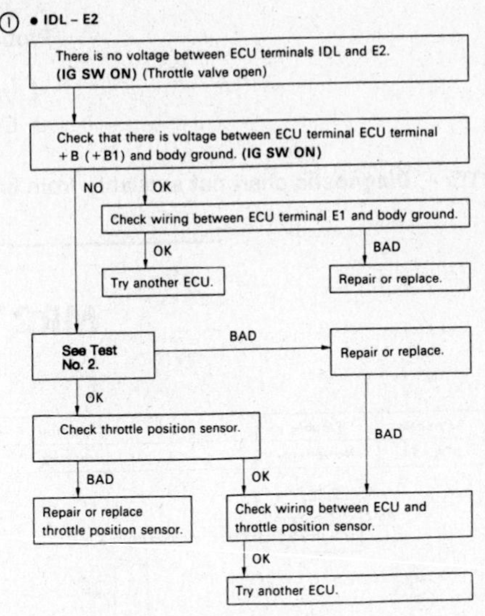
① • IDL – E2
There is no voltage between ECU terminals IDL and E2. (IG SW ON) (Throttle valve open)
Check that there is voltage between ECU terminal ECU terminal +B (+B1) and body ground. (IG SW ON)
NO
OK
Check wiring between ECU terminal E1 and body ground.
OK
BAD
Try another ECU.
Repair or replace.
See Test No. 2.
BAD
Repair or replace.
OK
Check throttle position sensor.
BAD
BAD
OK
Repair or replace throttle position sensor.
Check wiring between ECU and throttle position sensor.
OK
Try another ECU.

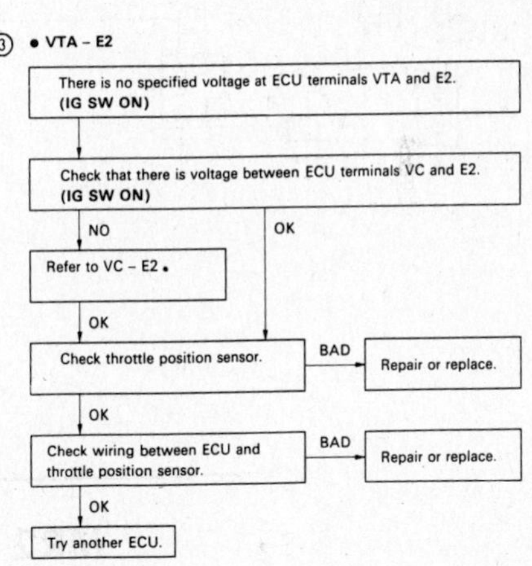
③ • VTA – E2
There is no specified voltage at ECU terminals VTA and E2. (IG SW ON)
Check that there is voltage between ECU terminals VC and E2. (IG SW ON)
NO
OK
Refer to VC – E2 •
OK
Check throttle position sensor.
BAD
Repair or replace.
OK
Check wiring between ECU and throttle position sensor.
BAD
Repair or replace.
OK
Try another ECU.

**3S-GTE & 5S-FE WITH A/T**

| No. | Terminals | Trouble | | Condition | STD Voltage |
|---|---|---|---|---|---|
| 3 | IDL – E1 | No voltage | IG SW ON | Throttle valve open | 8 – 14 V |
| | PSW – E1 | | | Throttle valve fully closed (Throttle opener must be cancelled first) | 4 – 6 V |

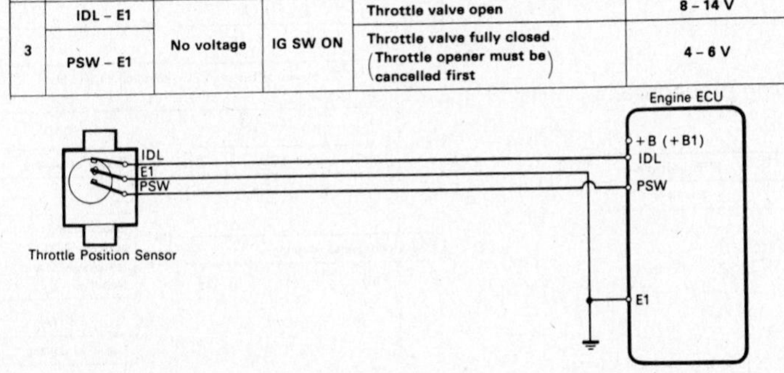
Engine ECU
IDL
E1
PSW
+B (+B1)
IDL
PSW
E1
Throttle Position Sensor

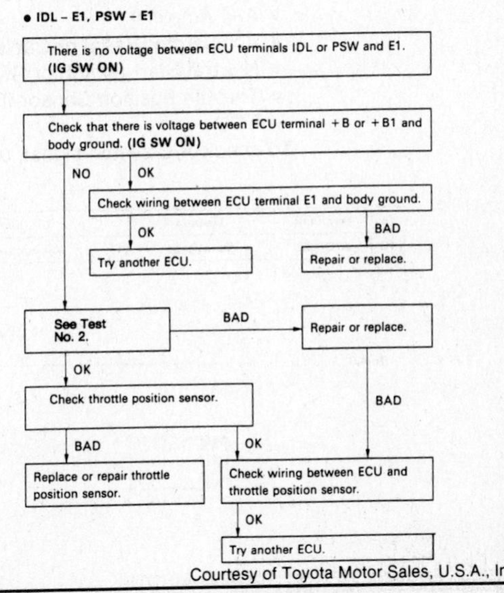
• IDL – E1, PSW – E1
There is no voltage between ECU terminals IDL or PSW and E1. (IG SW ON)
Check that there is voltage between ECU terminal +B or +B1 and body ground. (IG SW ON)
NO
OK
Check wiring between ECU terminal E1 and body ground.
OK
BAD
Try another ECU.
Repair or replace.
See Test No. 2.
BAD
Repair or replace.
OK
Check throttle position sensor.
BAD
BAD
OK
Replace or repair throttle position sensor.
Check wiring between ECU and throttle position sensor.
OK
Try another ECU.

**5S-FE WITH M/T**

91H17688 91I17689 91B17690 91C17691 91F17686 91G17687

## MR2 CODE 42
### VEHICLE SPEED SENSOR SIGNAL

**Probable Causes**

- Vehicle Speed Sensor or Sensor Circuit
- ECU

**NOTE – Diagnostic chart not available from manufacturer.**

---

## MR2 TEST NO. 10 OR CODE 43
### STARTER SIGNAL

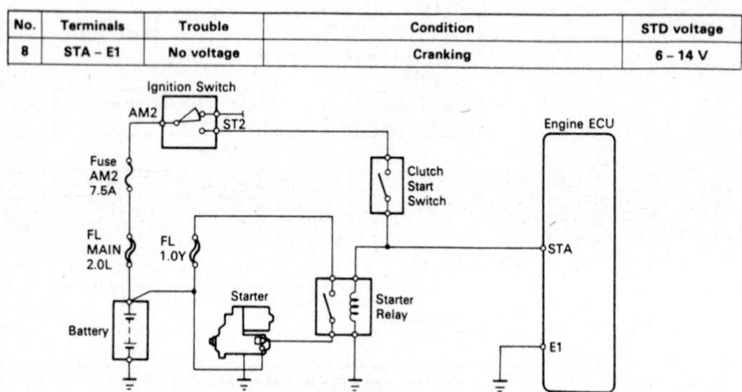

| No. | Terminals | Trouble | Condition | STD voltage |
|---|---|---|---|---|
| 8 | STA – E1 | No voltage | Cranking | 6 – 14 V |

Ignition Switch
AM2
ST2
Engine ECU
Fuse
AM2
7.5A
Clutch
Start
Switch
FL
MAIN
2.0L
FL
1.0Y
STA
Starter
Starter
Relay
Battery
E1

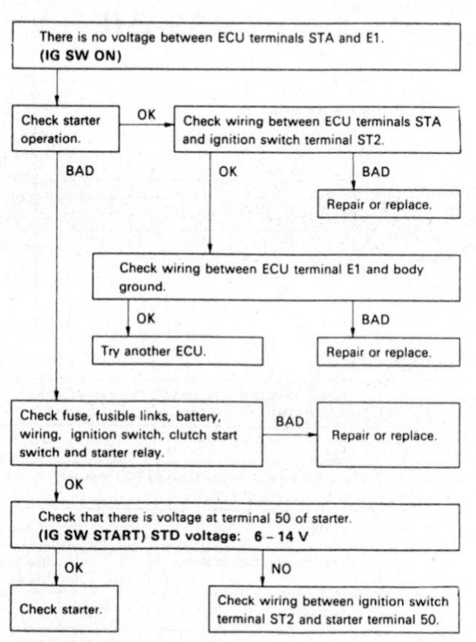
There is no voltage between ECU terminals STA and E1.
(IG SW ON)
Check starter operation.
OK
Check wiring between ECU terminals STA and ignition switch terminal ST2.
BAD
OK
BAD
Repair or replace.
Check wiring between ECU terminal E1 and body ground.
OK
BAD
Try another ECU.
Repair or replace.
Check fuse, fusible links, battery, wiring, ignition switch, clutch start switch and starter relay.
BAD
Repair or replace.
OK
Check that there is voltage at terminal 50 of starter.
(IG SW START) STD voltage: 6 – 14 V
OK
NO
Check starter.
Check wiring between ignition switch terminal ST2 and starter terminal 50.

---

## MR2 TEST NO. 11 OR CODE 51
### SWITCH SIGNAL

**Probable Causes**

- A/C Switch or Switch Circuit
- A/C Amplifier
- Accelerator Pedal or Cable
- Neutral/Start Switch or Switch Circuit
- Throttle Position Sensor IDL Circuit
- ECU

To check A/C switch signal, use the following procedure.

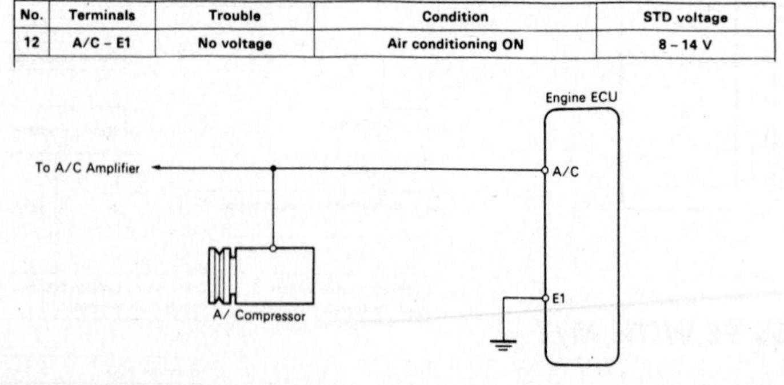

| No. | Terminals | Trouble | Condition | STD voltage |
|---|---|---|---|---|
| 12 | A/C – E1 | No voltage | Air conditioning ON | 8 – 14 V |

Engine ECU
To A/C Amplifier
A/C
E1
A/ Compressor

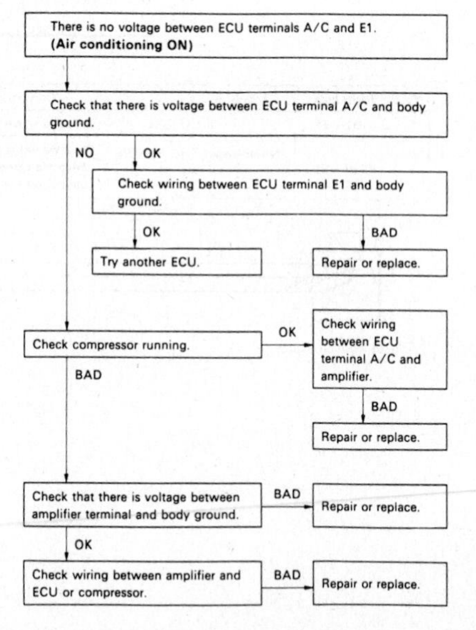
There is no voltage between ECU terminals A/C and E1.
(Air conditioning ON)
Check that there is voltage between ECU terminal A/C and body ground.
NO
OK
Check wiring between ECU terminal E1 and body ground.
OK
BAD
Try another ECU.
Repair or replace.
Check compressor running.
OK
Check wiring between ECU terminal A/C and amplifier.
BAD
BAD
Repair or replace.
Check that there is voltage between amplifier terminal and body ground.
BAD
Repair or replace.
OK
Check wiring between amplifier and ECU or compressor.
BAD
Repair or replace.

91J18035 91A18036 91F17694 91G17695 91H17696

## MR2 CODE 52 (3S-GTE)
### KNOCK SENSOR SIGNAL

**Probable Causes**
- Knock Sensor or Sensor Circuit
- ECU

**NOTE – Diagnostic chart not available from manufacturer.**

---

## MR2 CODE 53 (3S-GTE)
### KNOCK SENSOR CONTROL (ECU)

**Probable Causes**
- ECU

**NOTE – Diagnostic chart not available from manufacturer.**

---

## MR2 TEST NO. 12 OR CODE 71
### EGR SYSTEM MALFUNCTION

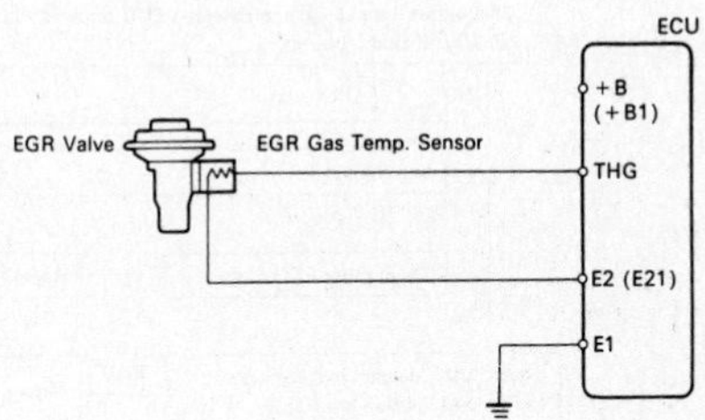
ECU
+B
(+B1)
EGR Valve
EGR Gas Temp. Sensor
THG
E2 (E21)
E1

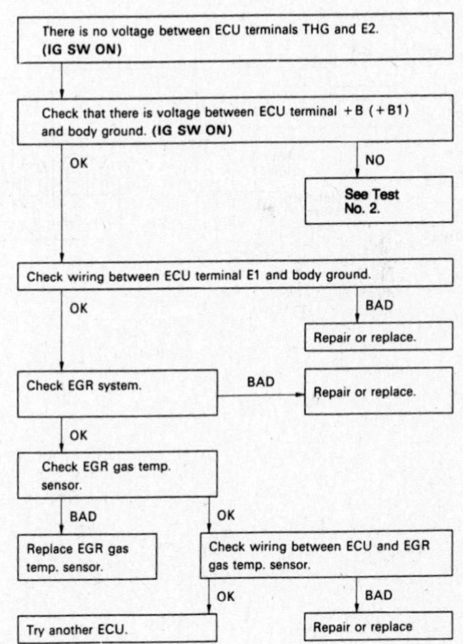
There is no voltage between ECU terminals THG and E2.
(IG SW ON)
Check that there is voltage between ECU terminal +B (+B1) and body ground. (IG SW ON)
OK
NO
See Test No. 2.
Check wiring between ECU terminal E1 and body ground.
OK
BAD
Repair or replace.
Check EGR system.
BAD
Repair or replace.
OK
Check EGR gas temp. sensor.
BAD
OK
Replace EGR gas temp. sensor.
Check wiring between ECU and EGR gas temp. sensor.
OK
BAD
Try another ECU.
Repair or replace

91H17787 91J17748

Courtesy of Toyota Motor Sales, U.S.A., Inc.

# 1991 ENGINE PERFORMANCE
# Self-Diagnostics (Cont.)

## MR2 TEST NO. 13
## INJECTOR CIRCUIT

| No. | Terminals | Trouble | Condition | STD voltage |
|---|---|---|---|---|
| 5 | No. 1<br>No. 2 – E01<br>No. 3 – E02<br>No. 4 | No voltage | IG SW ON | 10 – 14 V |

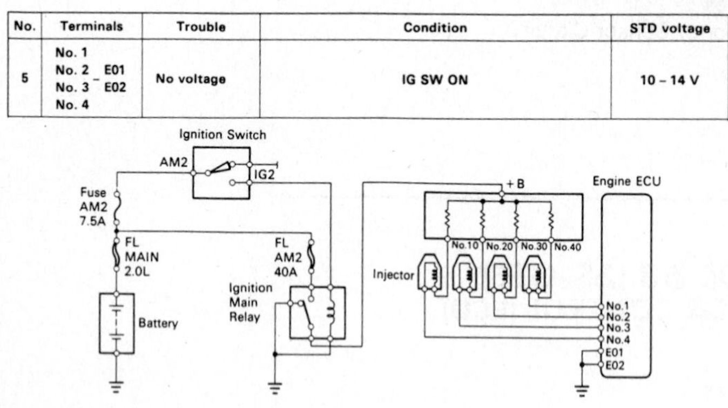
Ignition Switch
AM2
IG2
Fuse
AM2
7.5A
FL
MAIN
2.0L
Battery
FL
AM2
40A
Ignition
Main
Relay
+B
Engine ECU
No.10
No.20
No.30
No.40
Injector
No.1
No.2
No.3
No.4
E01
E02

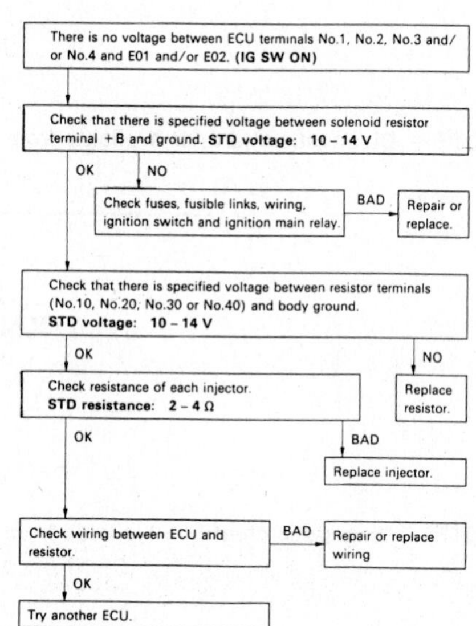
There is no voltage between ECU terminals No.1, No.2, No.3 and/or No.4 and E01 and/or E02. (IG SW ON)
Check that there is specified voltage between solenoid resistor terminal +B and ground. STD voltage: 10 – 14 V
OK
NO
Check fuses, fusible links, wiring, ignition switch and ignition main relay.
BAD
Repair or replace.
Check that there is specified voltage between resistor terminals (No.10, No.20, No.30 or No.40) and body ground. STD voltage: 10 – 14 V
OK
NO
Replace resistor.
Check resistance of each injector. STD resistance: 2 – 4 Ω
OK
BAD
Replace injector.
Check wiring between ECU and resistor.
BAD
Repair or replace wiring
OK
Try another ECU.

### 3S-GTE

---

| No. | Terminals | Trouble | Condition | STD voltage |
|---|---|---|---|---|
| 5 | No.10 – E01<br>No.20 – E02 | No voltage | IG SW ON | 10 – 14 V |

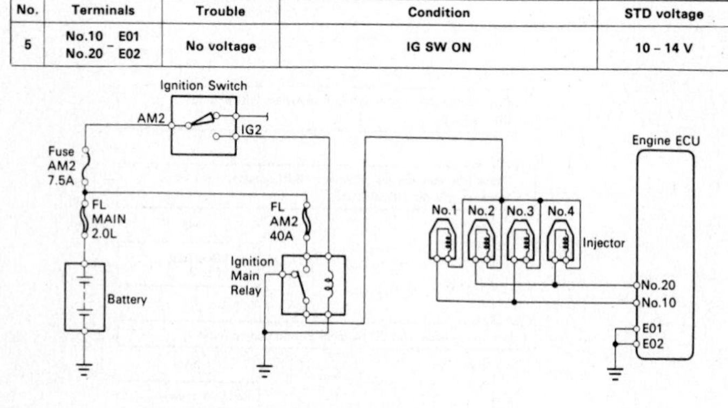
Ignition Switch
AM2
IG2
Fuse
AM2
7.5A
FL
MAIN
2.0L
Battery
FL
AM2
40A
Ignition
Main
Relay
Engine ECU
No.1
No.2
No.3
No.4
Injector
No.20
No.10
E01
E02

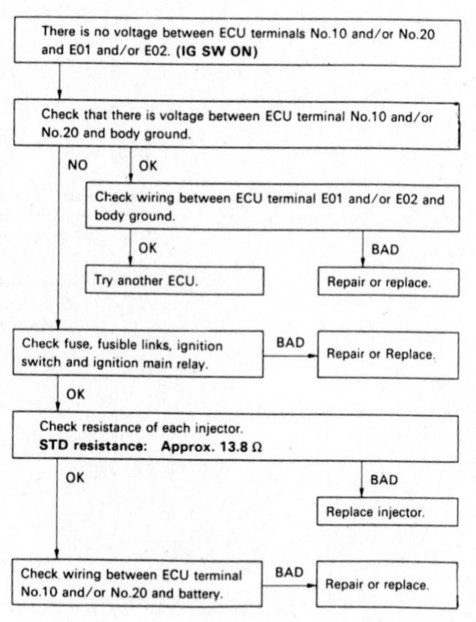
There is no voltage between ECU terminals No.10 and/or No.20 and E01 and/or E02. (IG SW ON)
Check that there is voltage between ECU terminal No.10 and/or No.20 and body ground.
NO
OK
Check wiring between ECU terminal E01 and/or E02 and body ground.
OK
BAD
Try another ECU.
Repair or replace.
Check fuse, fusible links, ignition switch and ignition main relay.
BAD
Repair or Replace.
OK
Check resistance of each injector. STD resistance: Approx. 13.8 Ω
OK
BAD
Replace injector.
Check wiring between ECU terminal No.10 and/or No.20 and battery.
BAD
Repair or replace.

### 5S-FE

## MR2 TEST NO. 14
### IDLE SPEED CONTROL CIRCUIT

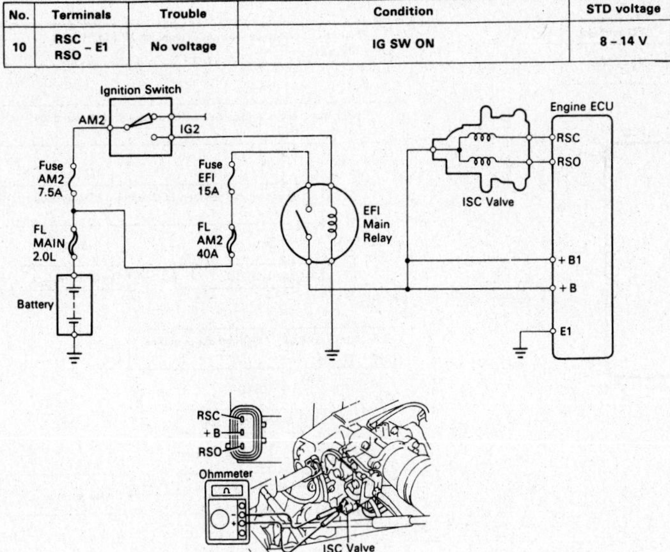

| No. | Terminals | Trouble | Condition | STD voltage |
|---|---|---|---|---|
| 10 | RSC RSO - E1 | No voltage | IG SW ON | 8 - 14 V |

Ignition Switch
AM2
IG2
Fuse AM2 7.5A
Fuse EFI 15A
FL MAIN 2.0L
FL AM2 40A
Battery
EFI Main Relay
ISC Valve
Engine ECU
RSC
RSO
+B1
+B
E1
RSC
+B
RSO
Ohmmeter
ISC Valve

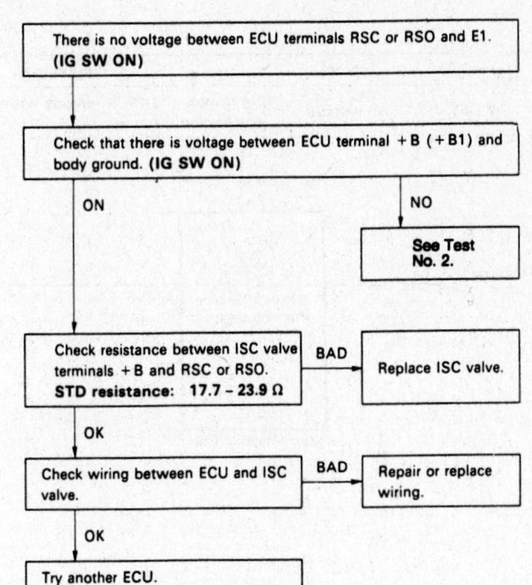

There is no voltage between ECU terminals RSC or RSO and E1. (IG SW ON)
Check that there is voltage between ECU terminal +B (+B1) and body ground. (IG SW ON)
ON
NO
See Test No. 2.
Check resistance between ISC valve terminals +B and RSC or RSO. STD resistance: 17.7 - 23.9 Ω
BAD
Replace ISC valve.
OK
Check wiring between ECU and ISC valve.
BAD
Repair or replace wiring.
OK
Try another ECU.

**3S-GTE**

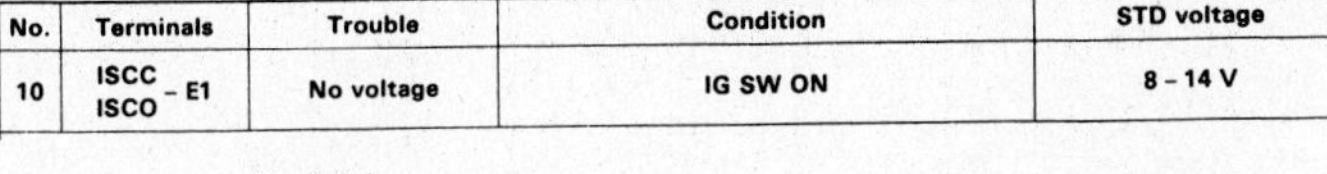

| No. | Terminals | Trouble | Condition | STD voltage |
|---|---|---|---|---|
| 10 | ISCC ISCO - E1 | No voltage | IG SW ON | 8 - 14 V |

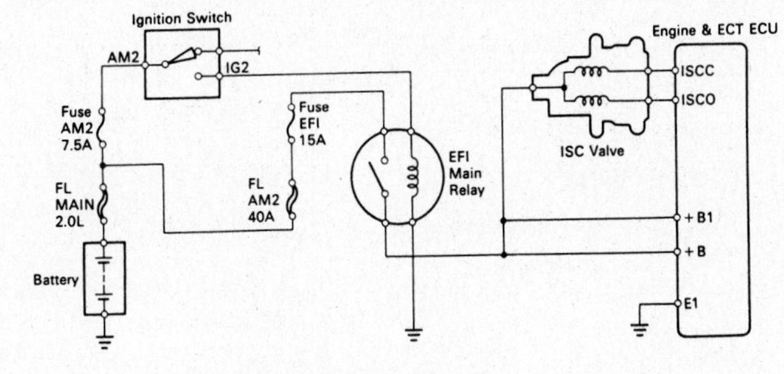

Ignition Switch
AM2
IG2
Fuse AM2 7.5A
Fuse EFI 15A
FL MAIN 2.0L
FL AM2 40A
Battery
EFI Main Relay
ISC Valve
Engine & ECT ECU
ISCC
ISCO
+B1
+B
E1

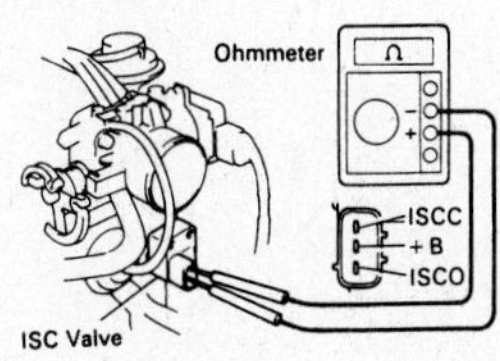

Ohmmeter
ISCC
+B
ISCO
ISC Valve

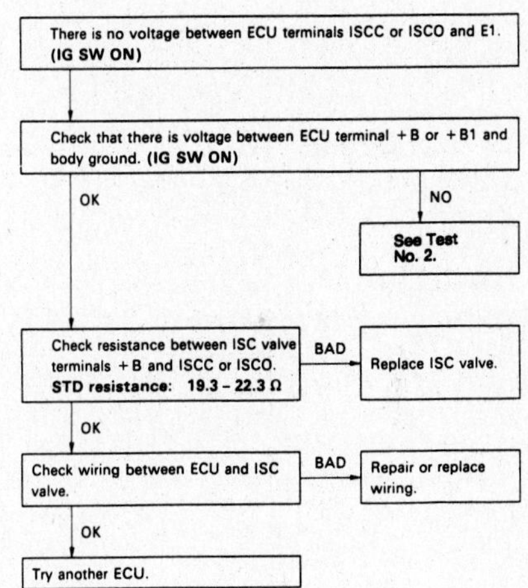

There is no voltage between ECU terminals ISCC or ISCO and E1. (IG SW ON)
Check that there is voltage between ECU terminal +B or +B1 and body ground. (IG SW ON)
OK
NO
See Test No. 2.
Check resistance between ISC valve terminals +B and ISCC or ISCO. STD resistance: 19.3 - 22.3 Ω
BAD
Replace ISC valve.
OK
Check wiring between ECU and ISC valve.
BAD
Repair or replace wiring.
OK
Try another ECU.

**5S-FE**

91I18042 91J18043 91A18044 91B18045 91C18046 91D18047

# 1991 ENGINE PERFORMANCE
# Self-Diagnostics (Cont.)

## MR2 TEST NO. 15
### CHECK ENGINE LIGHT CIRCUIT

| No. | Terminals | Trouble | Condition | STD voltage |
|---|---|---|---|---|
| 11 | W - E1 | No voltage | No trouble ("CHECK" engine warning light off) and engine running. | 10 - 14 V |

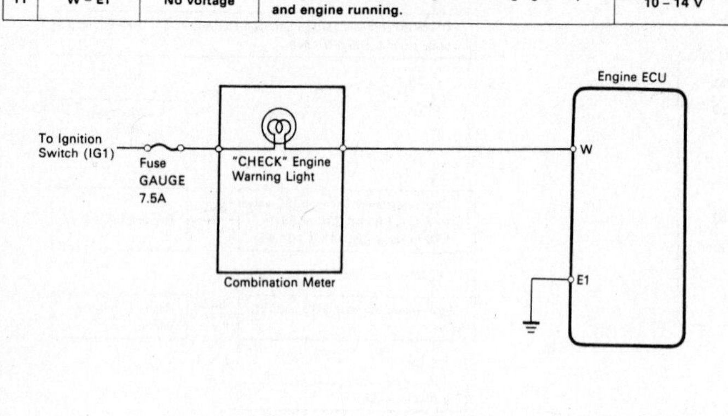
Engine ECU
To Ignition Switch (IG1)
Fuse GAUGE 7.5A
"CHECK" Engine Warning Light
Combination Meter
W
E1

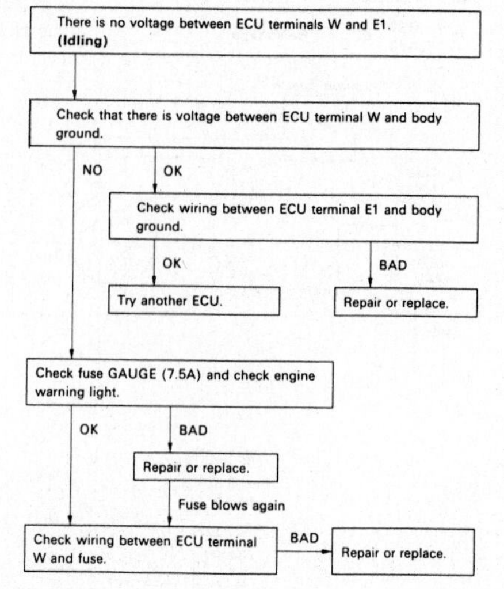
There is no voltage between ECU terminals W and E1. (Idling)
Check that there is voltage between ECU terminal W and body ground.
NO
OK
Check wiring between ECU terminal E1 and body ground.
OK
BAD
Try another ECU.
Repair or replace.
Check fuse GAUGE (7.5A) and check engine warning light.
OK
BAD
Repair or replace.
Fuse blows again
Check wiring between ECU terminal W and fuse.
BAD
Repair or replace.

91C17790 91D17791

Courtesy of Toyota Motor Sales, U.S.A., Inc.

## PICKUP & 4RUNNER (22R-E) DIAGNOSTIC CIRCUIT CHECK

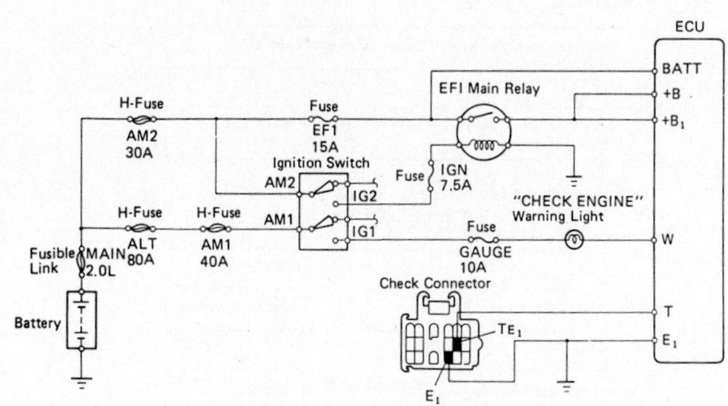


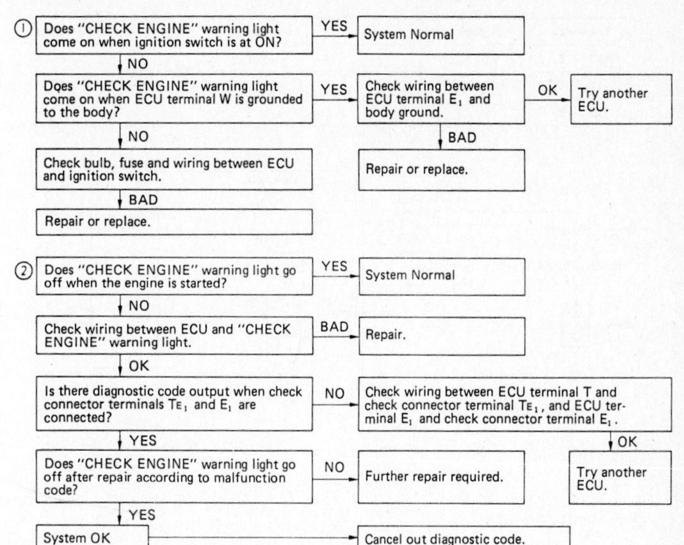

① Does "CHECK ENGINE" warning light come on when ignition switch is at ON?
YES
System Normal
NO
Does "CHECK ENGINE" warning light come on when ECU terminal W is grounded to the body?
YES
Check wiring between ECU terminal $E_1$ and body ground.
OK
Try another ECU.
NO
BAD
Check bulb, fuse and wiring between ECU and ignition switch.
Repair or replace.
BAD
Repair or replace.
② Does "CHECK ENGINE" warning light go off when the engine is started?
YES
System Normal
NO
Check wiring between ECU and "CHECK ENGINE" warning light.
BAD
Repair.
OK
Is there diagnostic code output when check connector terminals $TE_1$ and $E_1$ are connected?
NO
Check wiring between ECU terminal T and check connector terminal $TE_1$, and ECU terminal $E_1$ and check connector terminal $E_1$.
OK
Try another ECU.
YES
Does "CHECK ENGINE" warning light go off after repair according to malfunction code?
NO
Further repair required.
YES
System OK
Cancel out diagnostic code.


CAUTION: Perform all voltage measurements with ECU harness connector installed. Use a high-impedance DVOM (10,000-ohm minimum). Verify battery voltage is greater than 11 volts.

## ECU TERMINAL IDENTIFICATION

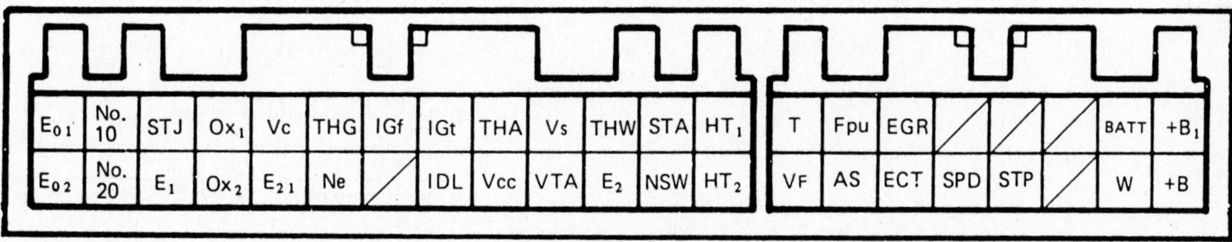


PICKUP 2WD

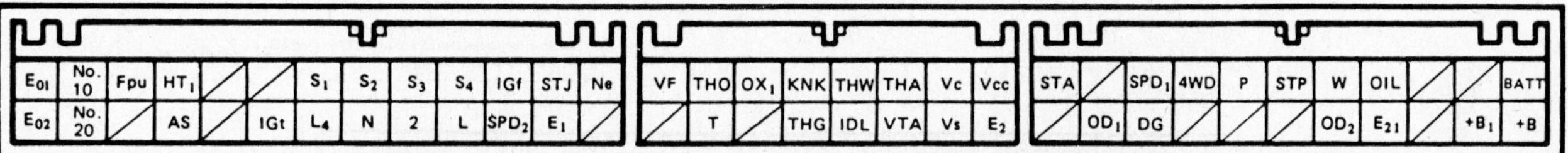


PICKUP 4WD W/AUTOMATIC TRANSMISSION

| $E_{01}$ | No. 10 | STA | STJ | NSW | Fpu | W | T | IDL | IGf | $Ox_2$ | THG | KNK | Ne | $HT_2$ | / | Vc | Vs | THA | BATT | $+B_1$ |
|---|---|---|---|---|---|---|---|---|---|---|---|---|---|---|---|---|---|---|---|---|
| $E_{02}$ | No. 20 | IGt | $E_1$ | VF | / | AS | EGR | $HT_1$ | $E_2$ | $Ox_1$ | Vcc | VTA | THW | / | / | $E_{21}$ | 4WD | SPD | STP | +B |

PICKUP 4WD W/MANUAL TRANSMISSION

| $E_{01}$ | No.10 | STA | STJ | NSW | Fpu | W | T | IDL | IGf | / | THG | KNK | Ne | / | / | Vc | Vs | THA | BATT | $+B_1$ |
|---|---|---|---|---|---|---|---|---|---|---|---|---|---|---|---|---|---|---|---|---|
| $E_{02}$ | No.20 | IGt | $E_1$ | VF | / | AS | / | HT1 | $E_2$ | $Ox_1$ | Vcc | VTA | THW | ECT | / | $E_{21}$ | 4WD | SPD | STP | +B |

4RUNNER 2WD & 4WD W/MANUAL TRANSMISSION

| $E_{01}$ | No. 10 | Epu | $HT_1$ | $HT_2$ | / | $S_1$ | $S_2$ | $S_3$ | / | IGf | STJ | Ne | VF | THO | $OX_1$ | KNK | THW | THA | Vc | Vcc | STA | / | $SPD_1$ | 4WD | P | STP | W | OIL | / | / | BATT |
|---|---|---|---|---|---|---|---|---|---|---|---|---|---|---|---|---|---|---|---|---|---|---|---|---|---|---|---|---|---|---|---|
| $E_{02}$ | No. 20 | / | As | EGR | IGt | $L_4$ | N | 2 | L | $SPD_2$ | $E_1$ | / | / | T | $OX_2$ | THG | IDL | VTA | Vs | $E_2$ | / | $OD_1$ | DG | / | / | / | $OD_2$ | $E_{21}$ | / | $+B_1$ | +B |

4RUNNER 4WD W/AUTOMATIC TRANSMISSION

91E18048 91G18081 91F18049 91J18050 91A18051 91B18052 91C18053

Courtesy of Toyota Motor Sales, U.S.A., Inc.

# 1991 ENGINE PERFORMANCE
# Self-Diagnostics (Cont.)

## PICKUP & 4RUNNER (22R-E) TEST NO. 1
### ECU (+B) CIRCUIT

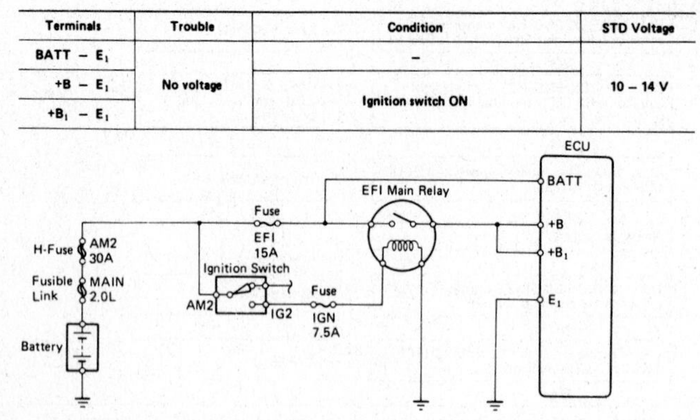

| Terminals | Trouble | Condition | STD Voltage |
|---|---|---|---|
| BATT – $E_1$ | No voltage | – | 10 – 14 V |
| +B – $E_1$ | | Ignition switch ON | |
| $+B_1$ – $E_1$ | | | |

ECU
BATT
EFI Main Relay
Fuse
EFI
15A
+B
$+B_1$
H-Fuse
AM2
30A
Ignition Switch
Fusible Link
MAIN
2.0L
AM2
IG2
Fuse
IGN
7.5A
$E_1$
Battery

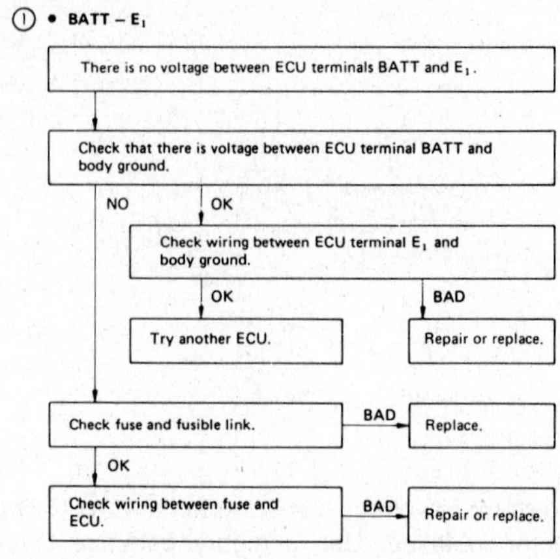

① • BATT – $E_1$
There is no voltage between ECU terminals BATT and $E_1$.
Check that there is voltage between ECU terminal BATT and body ground.
NO
OK
Check wiring between ECU terminal $E_1$ and body ground.
OK
BAD
Try another ECU.
Repair or replace.
Check fuse and fusible link.
BAD
Replace.
OK
Check wiring between fuse and ECU.
BAD
Repair or replace.

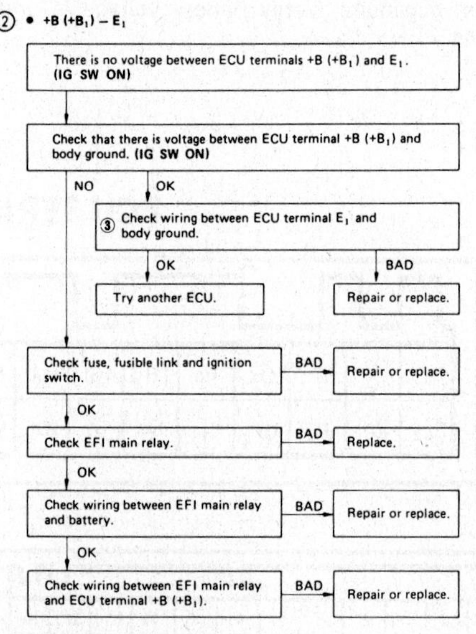

② • +B ($+B_1$) – $E_1$
There is no voltage between ECU terminals +B ($+B_1$) and $E_1$. (IG SW ON)
Check that there is voltage between ECU terminal +B ($+B_1$) and body ground. (IG SW ON)
NO
OK
③ Check wiring between ECU terminal $E_1$ and body ground.
OK
BAD
Try another ECU.
Repair or replace.
Check fuse, fusible link and ignition switch.
BAD
Repair or replace.
OK
Check EFI main relay.
BAD
Replace.
OK
Check wiring between EFI main relay and battery.
BAD
Repair or replace.
OK
Check wiring between EFI main relay and ECU terminal +B ($+B_1$).
BAD
Repair or replace.

## PICKUP & 4RUNNER (22R-E) CODE 12, 13
### RPM SIGNAL

Code 12 is caused by loss of "NE" signal from distributor to ECU for at least 2 seconds after starter signal is received at ECU. Ensure starter signal exists at ECU. See TEST NO. 7 OR CODE 43. Code 13 is caused by loss of "NE" signal from distributor to ECU when engine RPM exceeds 1500 RPM.

**NOTE – Diagnostic chart not available from manufacturer.**

91D18054 91H17795 91E18055

## PICKUP & 4RUNNER (22R-E) TEST NO. 2 OR CODE 14
### IGNITION SIGNAL

| Terminals | Trouble | Condition | STD Voltage |
|---|---|---|---|
| IGt – $E_1$ | No voltage | Idling | 0.7 – 1.0 V |

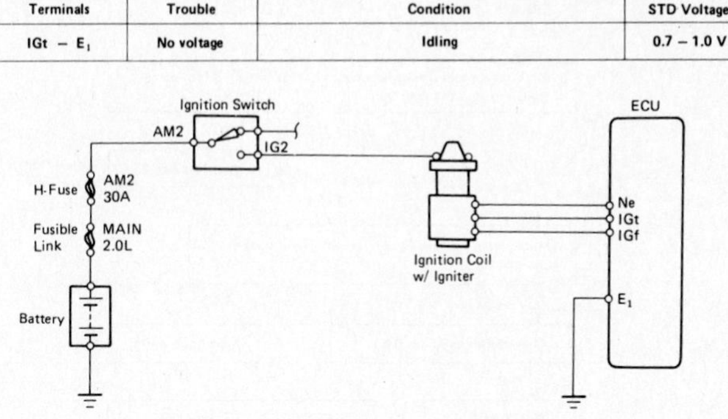
Ignition Switch
AM2
IG2
ECU
H-Fuse
AM2
30A
Fusible Link
MAIN
2.0L
Battery
Ne
IGt
IGf
Ignition Coil
w/ Igniter
E1

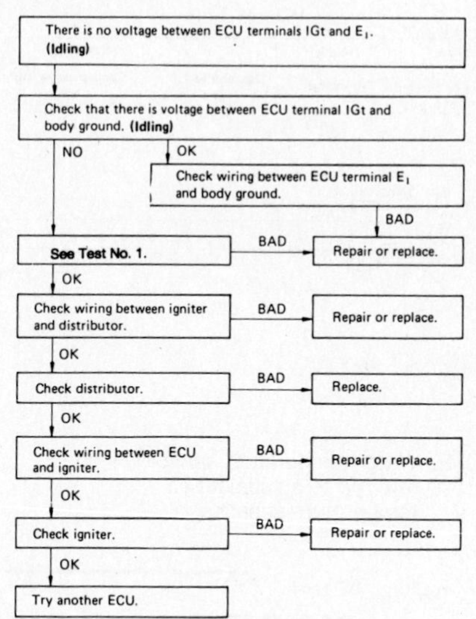
There is no voltage between ECU terminals IGt and E1. (Idling)
Check that there is voltage between ECU terminal IGt and body ground. (Idling)
NO
OK
Check wiring between ECU terminal E1 and body ground.
BAD
See Test No. 1.
BAD
Repair or replace.
OK
Check wiring between igniter and distributor.
BAD
Repair or replace.
OK
Check distributor.
BAD
Replace.
OK
Check wiring between ECU and igniter.
BAD
Repair or replace.
OK
Check igniter.
BAD
Repair or replace.
OK
Try another ECU.

NOTE: To check ignition system components, see SYSTEM & COMPONENT TESTING article.

## PICKUP & 4RUNNER (22R-E) TEST NO. 3 OR CODE 21, 27
### OXYGEN SENSOR SIGNAL

Code 27 applies to Pickup only.

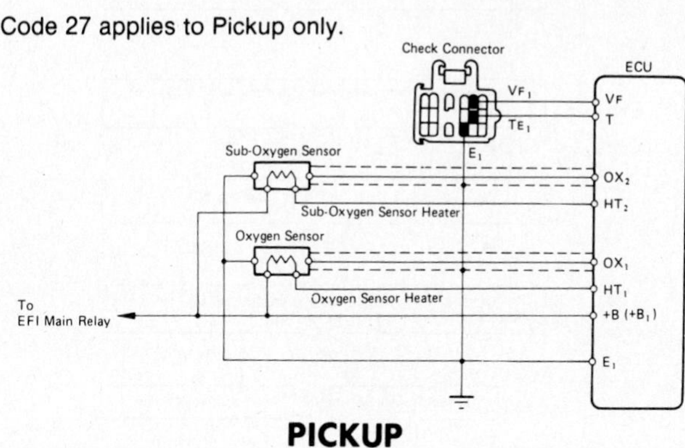
Check Connector
ECU
VF1
TE1
VF
T
E1
Sub-Oxygen Sensor
OX2
HT2
Sub-Oxygen Sensor Heater
Oxygen Sensor
OX1
HT1
Oxygen Sensor Heater
To EFI Main Relay
+B (+B1)
E1

**PICKUP**

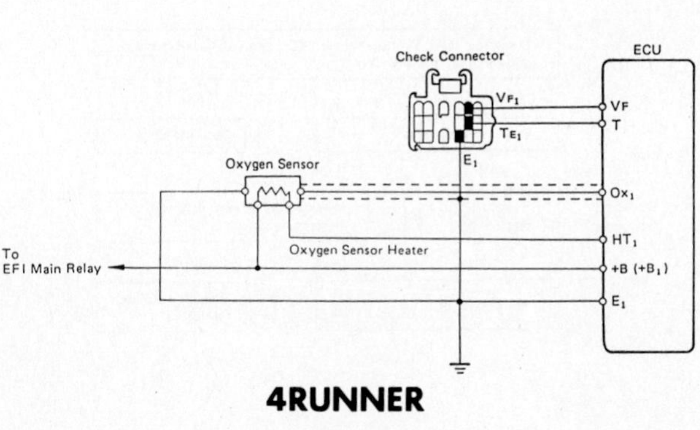
Check Connector
ECU
VF1
TE1
VF
T
E1
Oxygen Sensor
Ox1
Oxygen Sensor Heater
HT1
To EFI Main Relay
+B (+B1)
E1

**4RUNNER**

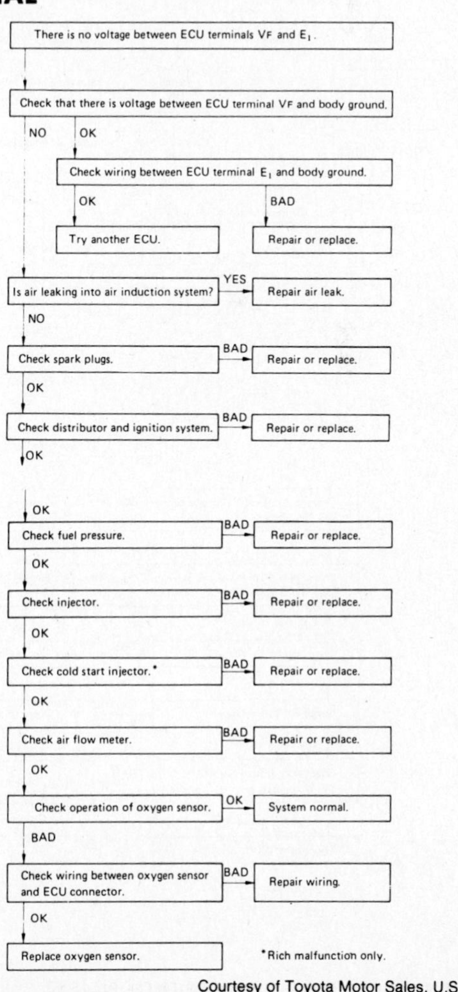
There is no voltage between ECU terminals VF and E1.
Check that there is voltage between ECU terminal VF and body ground.
NO
OK
Check wiring between ECU terminal E1 and body ground.
OK
BAD
Try another ECU.
Repair or replace.
Is air leaking into air induction system?
YES
Repair air leak.
NO
Check spark plugs.
BAD
Repair or replace.
OK
Check distributor and ignition system.
BAD
Repair or replace.
OK
OK
Check fuel pressure.
BAD
Repair or replace.
OK
Check injector.
BAD
Repair or replace.
OK
Check cold start injector.*
BAD
Repair or replace.
OK
Check air flow meter.
BAD
Repair or replace.
OK
Check operation of oxygen sensor.
OK
System normal.
BAD
Check wiring between oxygen sensor and ECU connector.
BAD
Repair wiring.
OK
Replace oxygen sensor.
*Rich malfunction only.

91F18056 91G18057 91H18058 91J17722 91I18059

Courtesy of Toyota Motor Sales, U.S.A., Inc.

# 1991 ENGINE PERFORMANCE
# Self-Diagnostics (Cont.)

## PICKUP & 4RUNNER (22R-E) TEST NO. 4 OR CODE 22
### COOLANT TEMPERATURE SENSOR SIGNAL

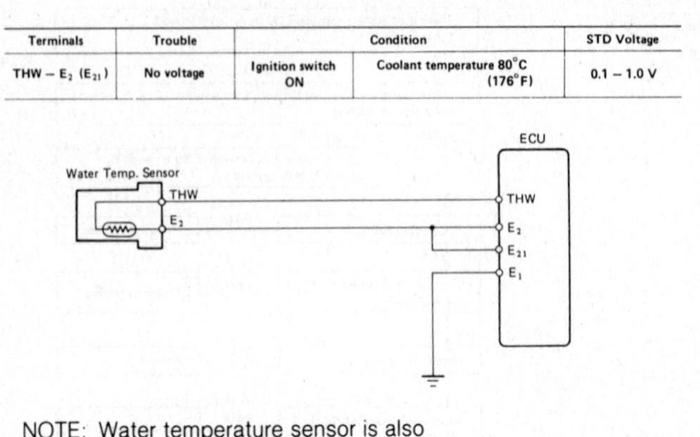

| Terminals | Trouble | Condition | | STD Voltage |
|---|---|---|---|---|
| THW – $E_2$ ($E_{21}$) | No voltage | Ignition switch ON | Coolant temperature 80°C (176°F) | 0.1 – 1.0 V |



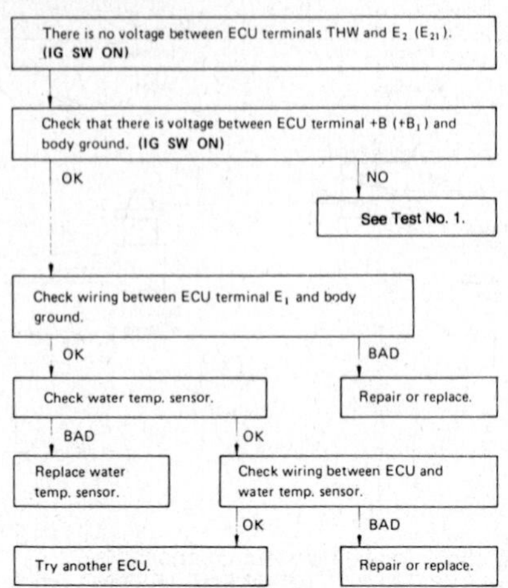


NOTE: Water temperature sensor is also referred to as coolant temperature sensor.

## PICKUP & 4RUNNER (22R-E) TEST NO. 5 OR CODE 24, 31
### INTAKE AIR TEMPERATURE SENSOR & AIRFLOW METER SIGNAL

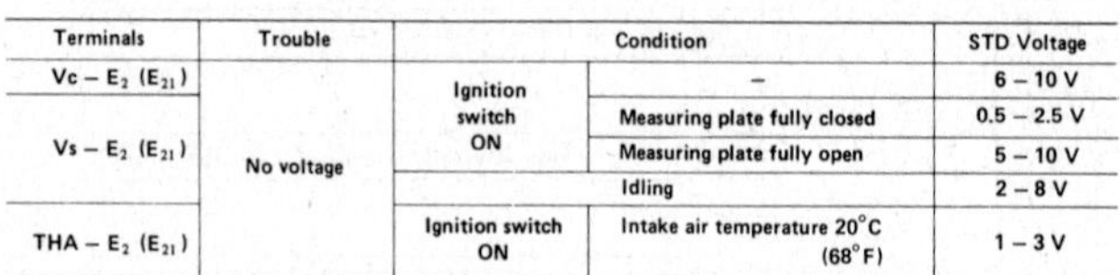

| Terminals | Trouble | Condition | | STD Voltage |
|---|---|---|---|---|
| Vc – $E_2$ ($E_{21}$) | No voltage | Ignition switch ON | – | 6 – 10 V |
| Vs – $E_2$ ($E_{21}$) | | Ignition switch ON | Measuring plate fully closed | 0.5 – 2.5 V |
| | | Ignition switch ON | Measuring plate fully open | 5 – 10 V |
| | | | Idling | 2 – 8 V |
| THA – $E_2$ ($E_{21}$) | | Ignition switch ON | Intake air temperature 20°C (68°F) | 1 – 3 V |

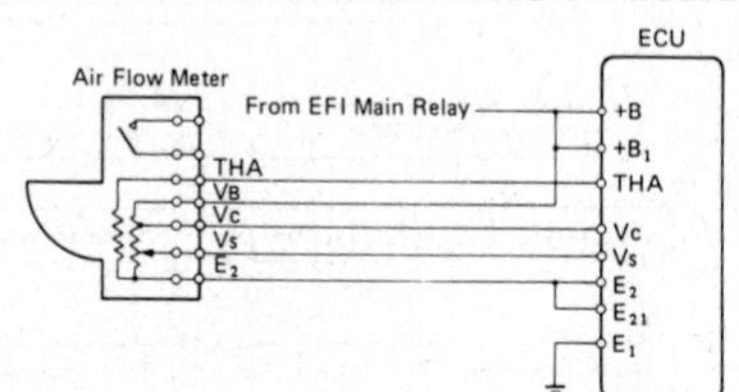


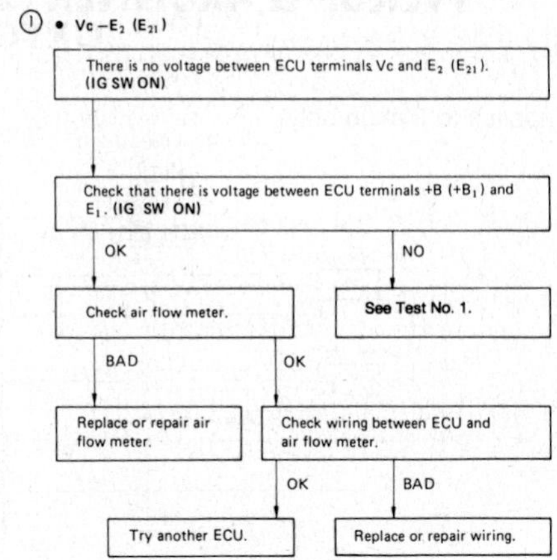


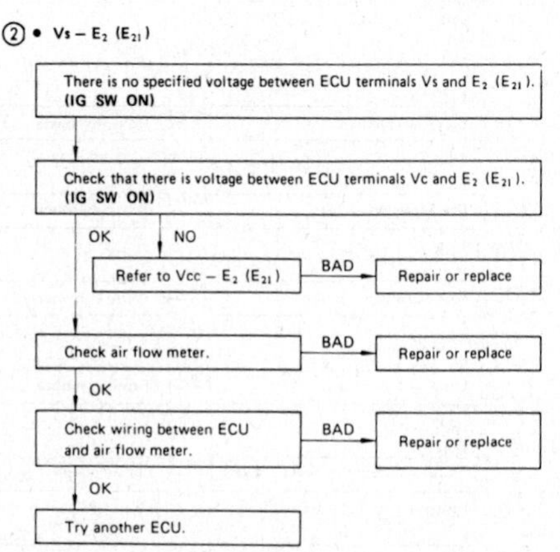


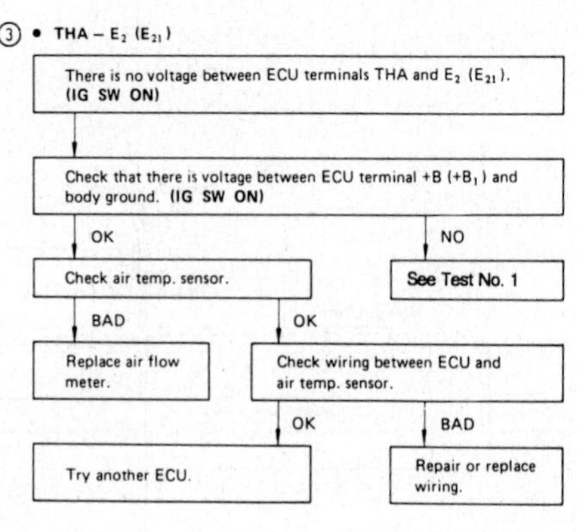

③ • THA – $E_2$ ($E_{21}$)
There is no voltage between ECU terminals THA and $E_2$ ($E_{21}$). (IG SW ON)
Check that there is voltage between ECU terminal +B (+$B_1$) and body ground. (IG SW ON)
OK
NO
Check air temp. sensor.
See Test No. 1
BAD
OK
Replace air flow meter.
Check wiring between ECU and air temp. sensor.
OK
BAD
Try another ECU.
Repair or replace wiring.


91B18060 91C18061 91D18062 91E18063 91F18064 91G18065

## PICKUP & 4RUNNER (22R-E) CODE 25
### LEAN AIR/FUEL MIXTURE

**Probable Causes**

- Airflow Meter
- Air Intake System
- Coolant Temperature Sensor
- Fuel Pressure
- Ignition System
- Injector Circuit or Injector
- Oxygen Sensor or Sensor Circuit
- ECU

**NOTE – Diagnostic chart not available from manufacturer.**

---

## PICKUP & 4RUNNER (22R-E) CODE 26
### RICH AIR/FUEL MIXTURE

**Probable Causes**

- Airflow Meter
- Cold Start Injector
- Coolant Temperature Sensor
- ECU
- Fuel Pressure
- Injector Circuit or Injector
- Oxygen Sensor or Sensor Circuit

**NOTE – Diagnostic chart not available from manufacturer.**

---

## PICKUP & 4RUNNER (22R-E) TEST NO. 6 OR CODE 41
### THROTTLE POSITION SENSOR SIGNAL

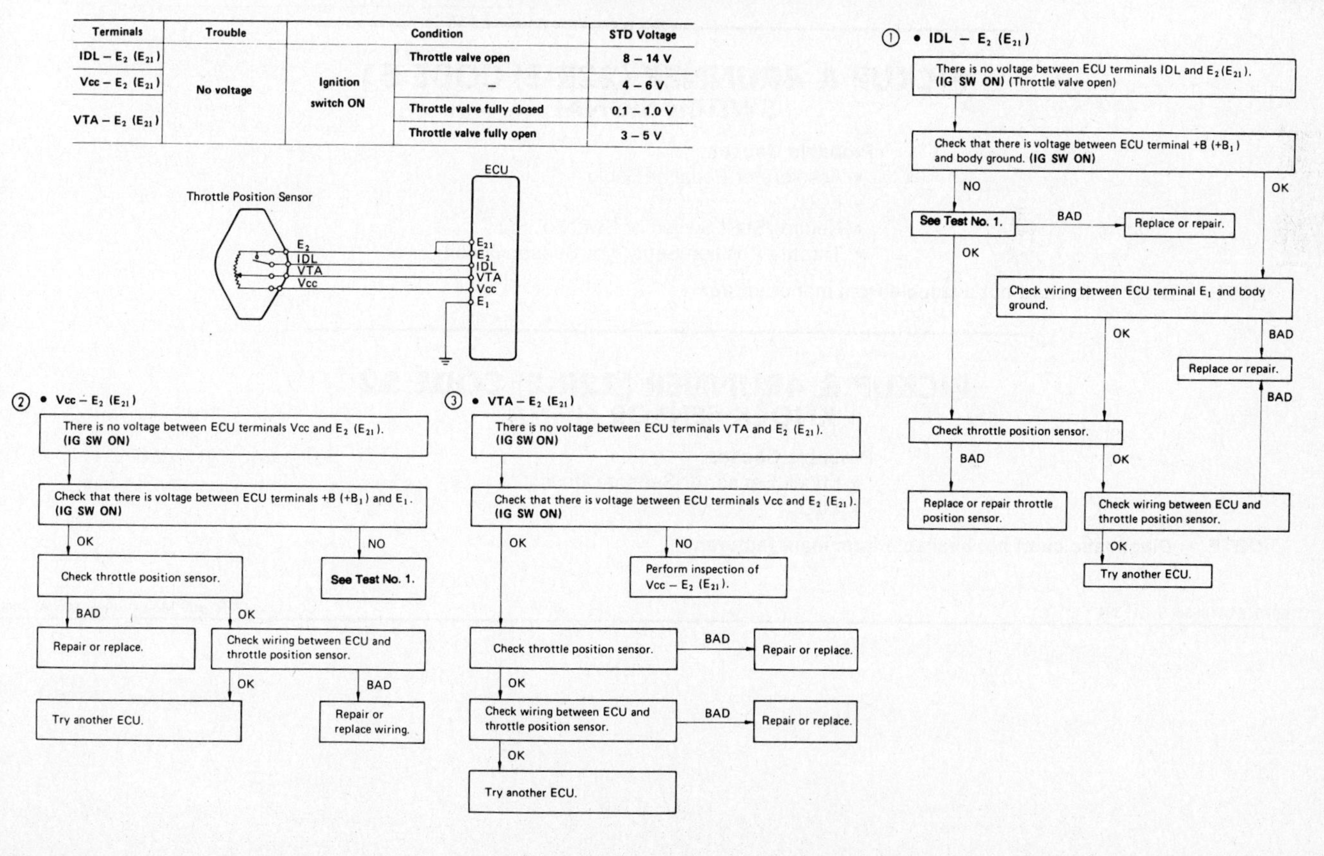

| Terminals | Trouble | | Condition | STD Voltage |
|---|---|---|---|---|
| IDL – $E_2$ ($E_{21}$) | No voltage | Ignition switch ON | Throttle valve open | 8 – 14 V |
| Vcc – $E_2$ ($E_{21}$) | | | – | 4 – 6 V |
| VTA – $E_2$ ($E_{21}$) | | | Throttle valve fully closed | 0.1 – 1.0 V |
| | | | Throttle valve fully open | 3 – 5 V |

Throttle Position Sensor
ECU
E2
IDL
VTA
Vcc
E21
E2
IDL
VTA
Vcc
E1
① • IDL – E2 (E21)
There is no voltage between ECU terminals IDL and E2 (E21). (IG SW ON) (Throttle valve open)
Check that there is voltage between ECU terminal +B (+B1) and body ground. (IG SW ON)
NO
OK
See Test No. 1.
BAD
Replace or repair.
OK
Check wiring between ECU terminal E1 and body ground.
OK
BAD
Replace or repair.
BAD
Check throttle position sensor.
BAD
OK
Replace or repair throttle position sensor.
Check wiring between ECU and throttle position sensor.
OK
Try another ECU.
② • Vcc – E2 (E21)
There is no voltage between ECU terminals Vcc and E2 (E21). (IG SW ON)
Check that there is voltage between ECU terminals +B (+B1) and E1. (IG SW ON)
OK
NO
Check throttle position sensor.
See Test No. 1.
BAD
OK
Repair or replace.
Check wiring between ECU and throttle position sensor.
OK
BAD
Try another ECU.
Repair or replace wiring.
③ • VTA – E2 (E21)
There is no voltage between ECU terminals VTA and E2 (E21). (IG SW ON)
Check that there is voltage between ECU terminals Vcc and E2 (E21). (IG SW ON)
OK
NO
Perform inspection of Vcc – E2 (E21).
Check throttle position sensor.
BAD
Repair or replace.
OK
Check wiring between ECU and throttle position sensor.
BAD
Repair or replace.
OK
Try another ECU.

91H18066 91I18067 91J18068 91A18069

Courtesy of Toyota Motor Sales, U.S.A., Inc.

# 1991 ENGINE PERFORMANCE
# Self-Diagnostics (Cont.)

## PICKUP & 4RUNNER (22R-E) CODE 42
### VEHICLE SPEED SENSOR SIGNAL

**Probable Causes**

- Vehicle Speed Sensor or Sensor Circuit
- ECU

**NOTE – Diagnostic chart not available from manufacturer.**

---

## PICKUP & 4RUNNER (22R-E) TEST NO. 7 OR CODE 43
### STARTER SIGNAL

| Terminals | Trouble | Condition | STD Voltage |
|---|---|---|---|
| STA – $E_1$ | No voltage | Ignition switch START position | 6 – 12 V |

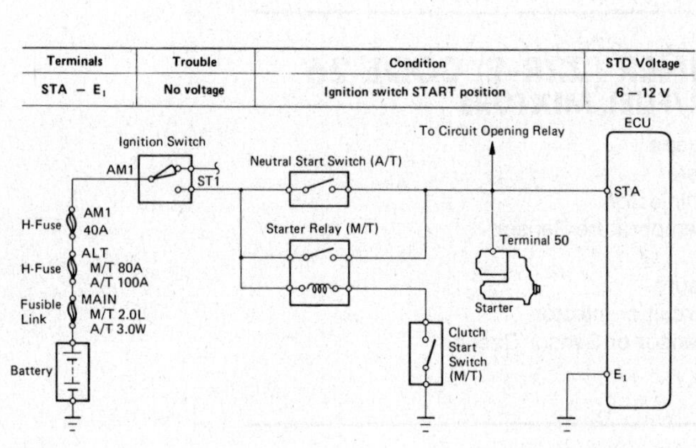


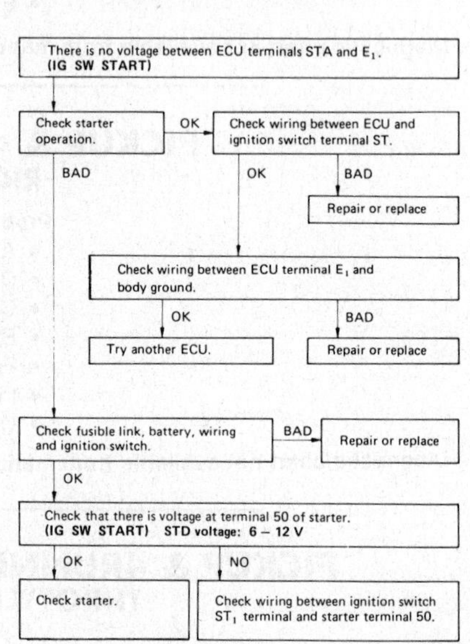


---

## PICKUP & 4RUNNER (22R-E) CODE 51
### SWITCH SIGNAL

**Probable Causes**

- Accelerator Pedal or Cable
- ECU
- Neutral/Start Switch or Switch Circuit
- Throttle Position Sensor or Sensor Circuit

**NOTE – Diagnostic chart not available from manufacturer.**

---

## PICKUP & 4RUNNER (22R-E) CODE 52
### KNOCK SENSOR SIGNAL

**Probable Causes**

- Knock Sensor or Sensor Circuit
- ECU

**NOTE – Diagnostic chart not available from manufacturer.**

91D18070 91A18036 91F17694

## PICKUP & 4RUNNER (22R-E) CODE 53
### KNOCK SENSOR CONTROL (ECU)

**Probable Causes**

- ECU

**NOTE – Diagnostic chart not available from manufacturer.**

## PICKUP & 4RUNNER (22R-E) TEST NO. 8 OR CODE 71
### EGR SYSTEM MALFUNCTION

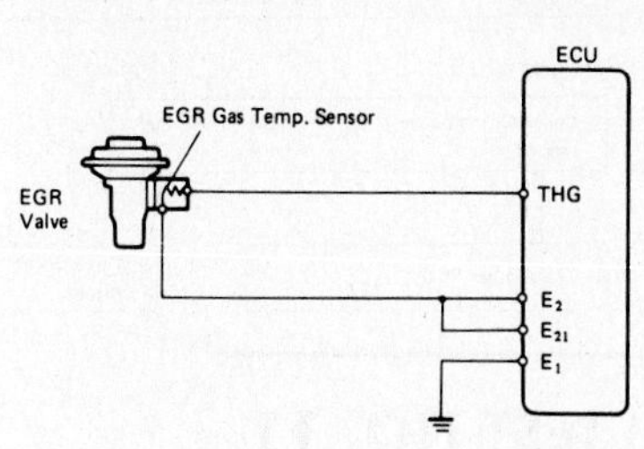
ECU
EGR Gas Temp. Sensor
EGR Valve
THG
$E_2$
$E_{21}$
$E_1$

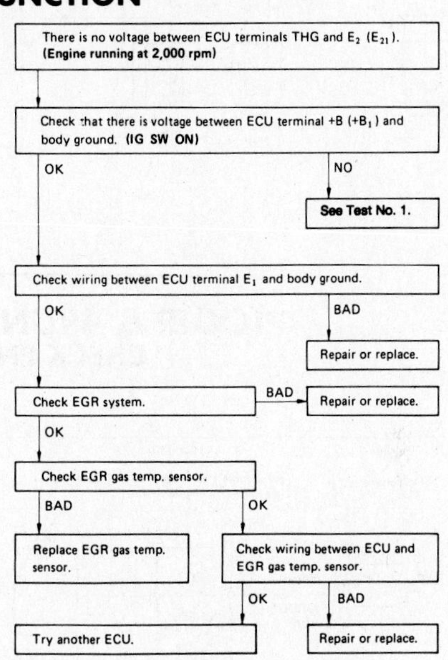
There is no voltage between ECU terminals THG and $E_2$ ($E_{21}$). (Engine running at 2,000 rpm)
Check that there is voltage between ECU terminal +B (+$B_1$) and body ground. (IG SW ON)
OK
NO
See Test No. 1.
Check wiring between ECU terminal $E_1$ and body ground.
OK
BAD
Repair or replace.
Check EGR system.
BAD
Repair or replace.
OK
Check EGR gas temp. sensor.
BAD
OK
Replace EGR gas temp. sensor.
Check wiring between ECU and EGR gas temp. sensor.
OK
BAD
Try another ECU.
Repair or replace.

## PICKUP & 4RUNNER (22R-E) TEST NO. 9
### INJECTOR CIRCUIT

| Terminals | Trouble | Condition | STD Voltage |
|---|---|---|---|
| No. 10 – $E_{01}$<br>No. 20 – $E_{02}$ | No voltage | Ignition switch ON | 10 – 14 V |

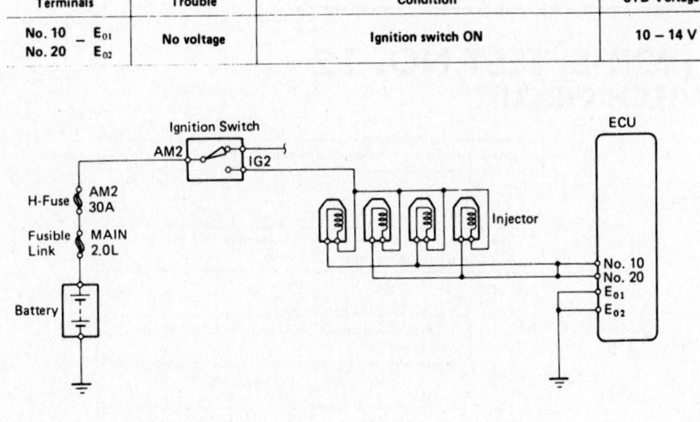
Ignition Switch
AM2
IG2
H-Fuse
AM2 30A
Fusible Link
MAIN 2.0L
Battery
Injector
ECU
No. 10
No. 20
$E_{01}$
$E_{02}$

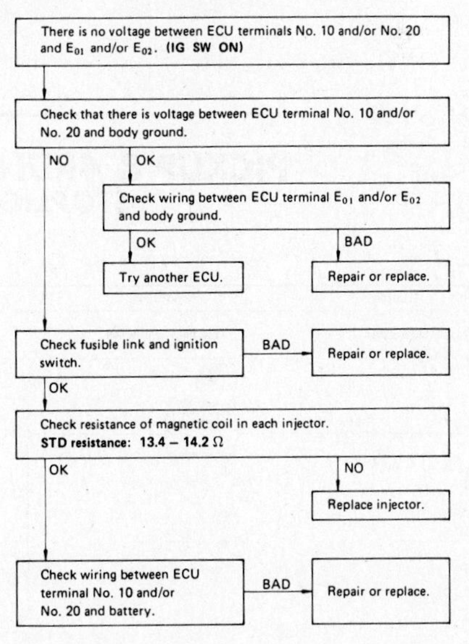
There is no voltage between ECU terminals No. 10 and/or No. 20 and $E_{01}$ and/or $E_{02}$. (IG SW ON)
Check that there is voltage between ECU terminal No. 10 and/or No. 20 and body ground.
NO
OK
Check wiring between ECU terminal $E_{01}$ and/or $E_{02}$ and body ground.
OK
BAD
Try another ECU.
Repair or replace.
Check fusible link and ignition switch.
BAD
Repair or replace.
OK
Check resistance of magnetic coil in each injector.
STD resistance: 13.4 – 14.2 Ω
OK
NO
Replace injector.
Check wiring between ECU terminal No. 10 and/or No. 20 and battery.
BAD
Repair or replace.

91E18071 91F18072 91G17752 91G18073

Courtesy of Toyota Motor Sales, U.S.A., Inc.

# 1991 ENGINE PERFORMANCE
# Self-Diagnostics (Cont.)

## PICKUP & 4RUNNER (22R-E) TEST NO. 10
### COLD START INJECTOR CIRCUIT

| Terminal | Trouble | Condition | | STD Voltage |
|---|---|---|---|---|
| STJ – $E_1$ | No voltage | Ignition switch START position | Coolant temperature 80°C (176°F) | 6 – 12 V |

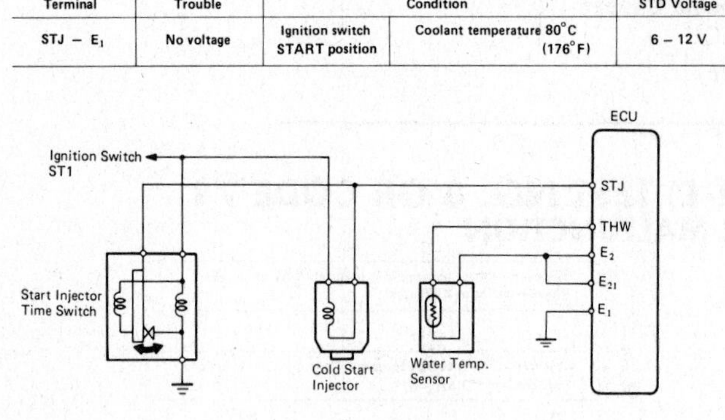
ECU
Ignition Switch
ST1
STJ
THW
$E_2$
$E_{21}$
$E_1$
Start Injector
Time Switch
Cold Start
Injector
Water Temp.
Sensor

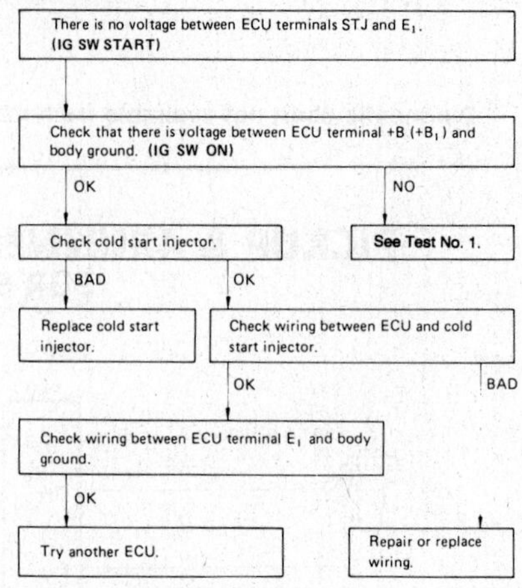
There is no voltage between ECU terminals STJ and $E_1$.
(IG SW START)
Check that there is voltage between ECU terminal +B (+$B_1$) and body ground. (IG SW ON)
OK
NO
Check cold start injector.
See Test No. 1.
BAD
OK
Replace cold start injector.
Check wiring between ECU and cold start injector.
OK
BAD
Check wiring between ECU terminal $E_1$ and body ground.
OK
Try another ECU.
Repair or replace wiring.

## PICKUP & 4RUNNER (22R-E) TEST NO. 11
### CHECK ENGINE LIGHT CIRCUIT

| Terminals | Trouble | Condition | STD Voltage |
|---|---|---|---|
| W – $E_1$ | No voltage | No trouble ("CHECK ENGINE" warning light off) and engine running | 10 – 14 V |

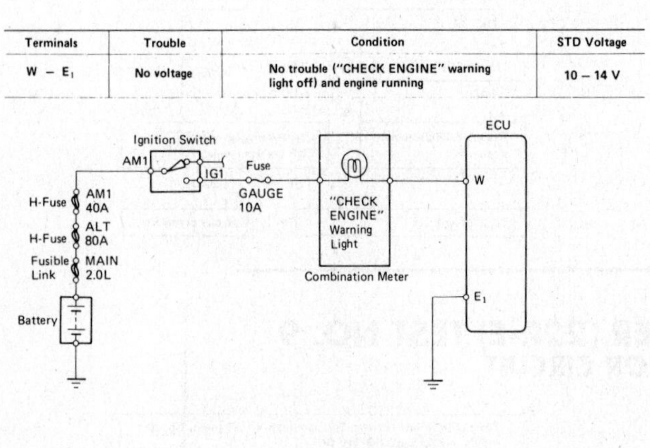
Ignition Switch
AM1
IG1
Fuse
GAUGE
10A
"CHECK
ENGINE"
Warning
Light
Combination Meter
ECU
W
$E_1$
H-Fuse
AM1
40A
H-Fuse
ALT
80A
Fusible
Link
MAIN
2.0L
Battery

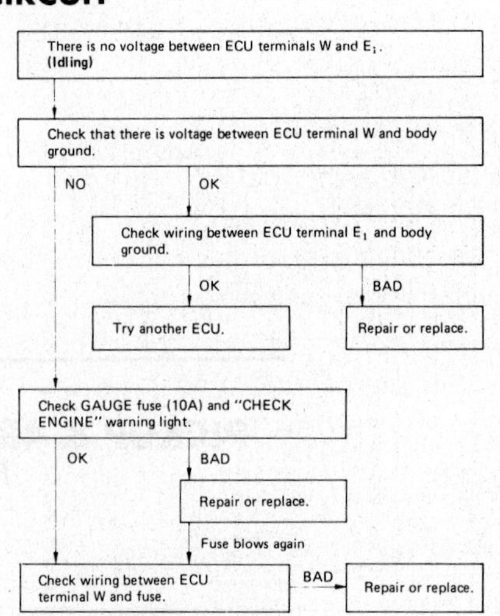
There is no voltage between ECU terminals W and $E_1$.
(Idling)
Check that there is voltage between ECU terminal W and body ground.
NO
OK
Check wiring between ECU terminal $E_1$ and body ground.
OK
BAD
Try another ECU.
Repair or replace.
Check GAUGE fuse (10A) and "CHECK ENGINE" warning light.
OK
BAD
Repair or replace.
Fuse blows again
Check wiring between ECU terminal W and fuse.
BAD
Repair or replace.

## PICKUP & 4RUNNER (22R-E) TEST NO. 12
### STOPLIGHT SWITCH CIRCUIT

| Terminals | Trouble | Condition | STD Voltage |
|---|---|---|---|
| STP – $E_1$ | No voltage | Stop light switch ON | 8 – 14 V |

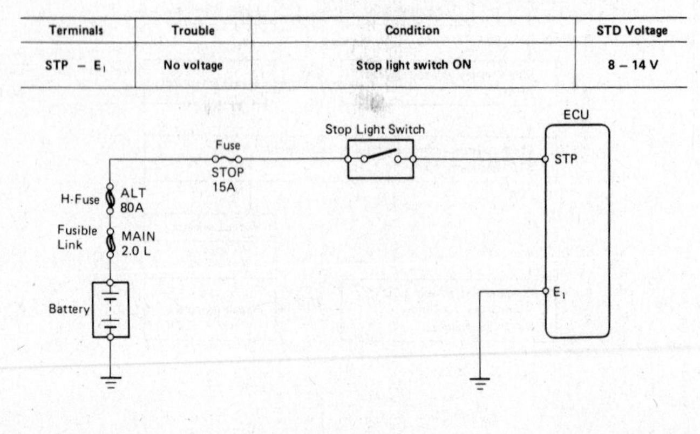
Fuse
STOP
15A
Stop Light Switch
ECU
STP
$E_1$
H-Fuse
ALT
80A
Fusible
Link
MAIN
2.0 L
Battery

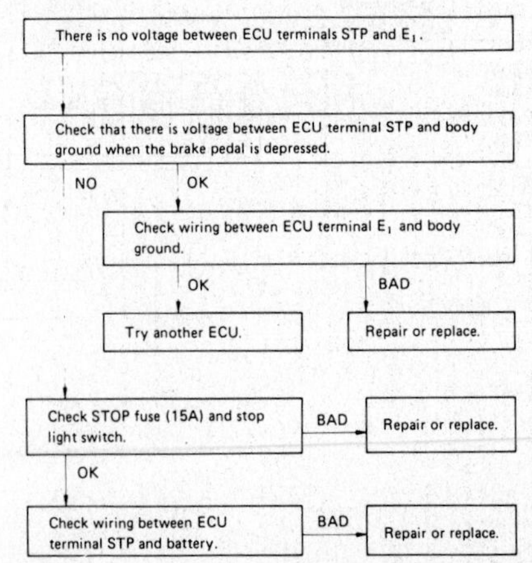
There is no voltage between ECU terminals STP and $E_1$.
Check that there is voltage between ECU terminal STP and body ground when the brake pedal is depressed.
NO
OK
Check wiring between ECU terminal $E_1$ and body ground.
OK
BAD
Try another ECU.
Repair or replace.
Check STOP fuse (15A) and stop light switch.
BAD
Repair or replace.
OK
Check wiring between ECU terminal STP and battery.
BAD
Repair or replace.

91H18074 91I18075 91J18076 91D17791 91A18077 91B18078

## PICKUP & 4RUNNER (3VZ-E) DIAGNOSTIC CIRCUIT CHECK

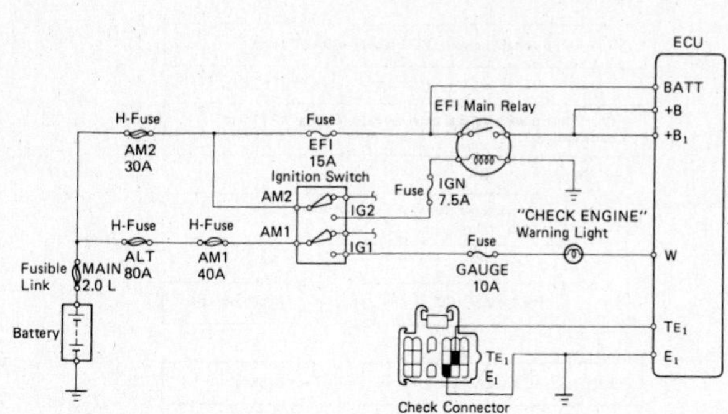
ECU
BATT
+B
+B1
EFI Main Relay
H-Fuse
AM2
30A
Fuse
EFI
15A
Ignition Switch
AM2
IG2
Fuse
IGN
7.5A
"CHECK ENGINE"
Warning Light
H-Fuse
ALT
80A
H-Fuse
AM1
40A
AM1
IG1
Fuse
GAUGE
10A
W
Fusible Link
MAIN
2.0 L
Battery
TE1
E1
Check Connector

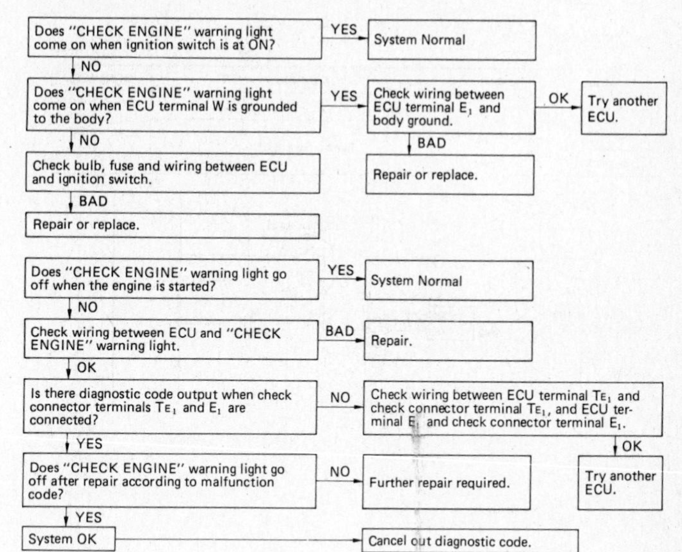
Does "CHECK ENGINE" warning light come on when ignition switch is at ON?
YES
System Normal
NO
Does "CHECK ENGINE" warning light come on when ECU terminal W is grounded to the body?
YES
Check wiring between ECU terminal E1 and body ground.
OK
Try another ECU.
BAD
Repair or replace.
NO
Check bulb, fuse and wiring between ECU and ignition switch.
BAD
Repair or replace.
Does "CHECK ENGINE" warning light go off when the engine is started?
YES
System Normal
NO
Check wiring between ECU and "CHECK ENGINE" warning light.
BAD
Repair.
OK
Is there diagnostic code output when check connector terminals TE1 and E1 are connected?
NO
Check wiring between ECU terminal TE1 and check connector terminal TE1, and ECU terminal E1 and check connector terminal E1.
OK
Try another ECU.
YES
Does "CHECK ENGINE" warning light go off after repair according to malfunction code?
NO
Further repair required.
YES
System OK
Cancel out diagnostic code.

CAUTION: Perform all voltage measurements with ECU harness connector installed. Use a high-impedance DVOM (10,000-ohm minimum). Verify battery voltage is greater than 11 volts.

## ECU TERMINAL IDENTIFICATION

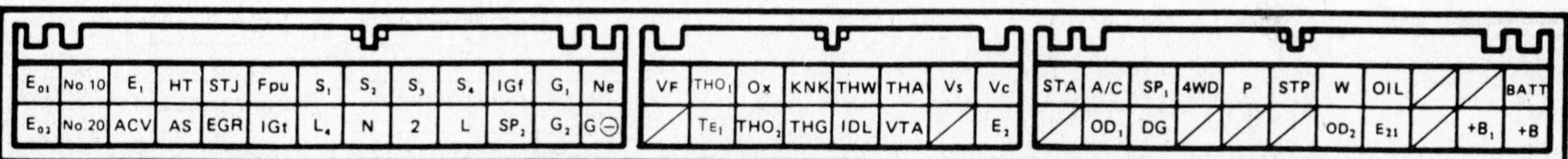
E01 No.10 E1 HT STJ Fpu S1 S2 S3 S4 IGf G1 Ne
E02 No.20 ACV AS EGR IGt L4 N 2 L SP2 G2 G⊖
VF THO1 Ox KNK THW THA Vs Vc
TE1 THO2 THG IDL VTA E2
STA A/C SP1 4WD P STP W OIL BATT
OD1 DG OD2 E21 +B1 +B

PICKUP

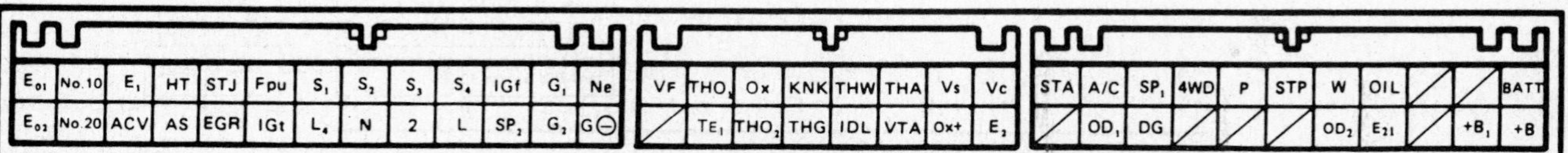
E01 No.10 E1 HT STJ Fpu S1 S2 S3 S4 IGf G1 Ne
E02 No.20 ACV AS EGR IGt L4 N 2 L SP2 G2 G⊖
VF THO1 Ox KNK THW THA Vs Vc
TE1 THO2 THG IDL VTA Ox+ E2
STA A/C SP1 4WD P STP W OIL BATT
OD1 DG OD2 E21 +B1 +B

4RUNNER

91E18048 91G18081 91C18079 91F18080

Courtesy of Toyota Motor Sales, U.S.A., Inc.

# 1991 ENGINE PERFORMANCE
# Self-Diagnostics (Cont.)

## PICKUP & 4RUNNER (3VZ-E) TEST NO. 1
### ECU (+B) CIRCUIT

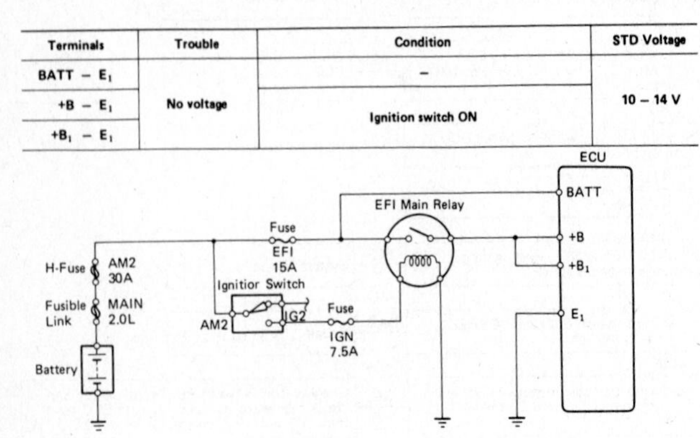

| Terminals | Trouble | Condition | STD Voltage |
|---|---|---|---|
| BATT − $E_1$ | No voltage | − | 10 − 14 V |
| +B − $E_1$ | | Ignition switch ON | |
| $+B_1$ − $E_1$ | | | |

ECU
BATT
+B
+B1
E1
EFI Main Relay
Fuse
EFI
15A
H-Fuse
AM2
30A
Ignition Switch
Fusible Link
MAIN
2.0L
AM2
IG2
Fuse
IGN
7.5A
Battery

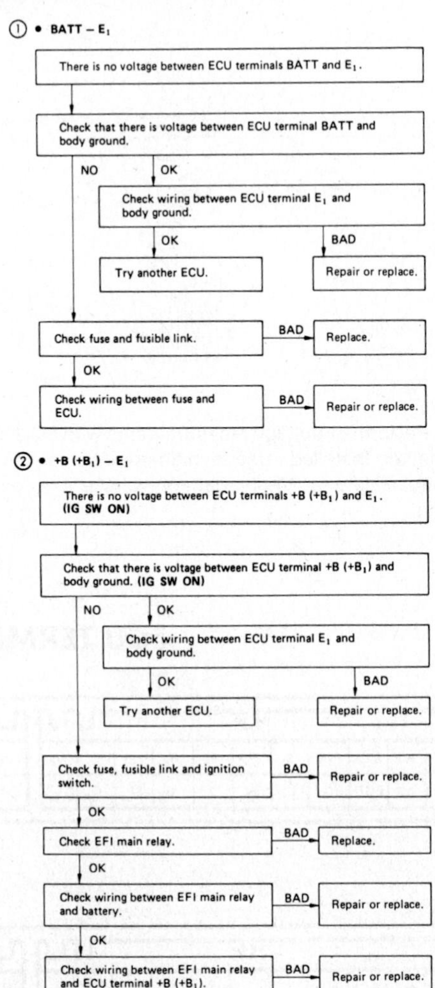

① • BATT − E1
There is no voltage between ECU terminals BATT and E1.
Check that there is voltage between ECU terminal BATT and body ground.
NO
OK
Check wiring between ECU terminal E1 and body ground.
OK
BAD
Try another ECU.
Repair or replace.
Check fuse and fusible link.
BAD
Replace.
OK
Check wiring between fuse and ECU.
BAD
Repair or replace.
② • +B (+B1) − E1
There is no voltage between ECU terminals +B (+B1) and E1. (IG SW ON)
Check that there is voltage between ECU terminal +B (+B1) and body ground. (IG SW ON)
NO
OK
Check wiring between ECU terminal E1 and body ground.
OK
BAD
Try another ECU.
Repair or replace.
Check fuse, fusible link and ignition switch.
BAD
Repair or replace.
OK
Check EFI main relay.
BAD
Replace.
OK
Check wiring between EFI main relay and battery.
BAD
Repair or replace.
OK
Check wiring between EFI main relay and ECU terminal +B (+B1).
BAD
Repair or replace.

## PICKUP & 4RUNNER (3VZ-E) CODE 12, 13
### RPM SIGNAL

Code 12 is caused by loss of "NE" or "G" signal from distributor to ECU for at least 2 seconds after starter signal is received at ECU. Ensure starter signal exists at ECU. See TEST NO. 7 OR CODE 43. Code 13 is caused by loss of "NE" signal from distributor to ECU when engine RPM exceeds 1000 RPM.

**NOTE – Diagnostic chart not available from manufacturer.**

91D18054 91H17795 91E18055

# 1991 ENGINE PERFORMANCE
# Self-Diagnostics (Cont.)

## PICKUP & 4RUNNER (3VZ-E) TEST NO. 2 OR CODE 14
### IGNITION SIGNAL

| Terminals | Trouble | Condition | STD Voltage |
|---|---|---|---|
| IGt – $E_1$ | No voltage | Cranking or Idling | 0.7 – 1.0 V |

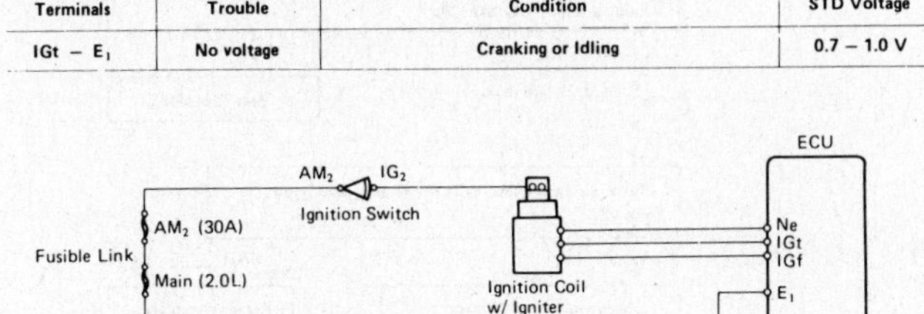
AM₂
IG₂
Ignition Switch
AM₂ (30A)
Fusible Link
Main (2.0L)
Battery
Ignition Coil
w/ Igniter
ECU
Ne
IGt
IGf
E₁

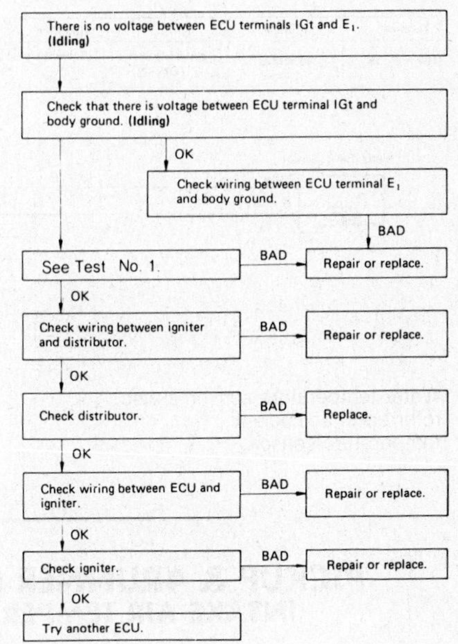
There is no voltage between ECU terminals IGt and E₁. (Idling)
Check that there is voltage between ECU terminal IGt and body ground. (Idling)
OK
Check wiring between ECU terminal E₁ and body ground.
BAD
See Test No. 1.
BAD
Repair or replace.
OK
Check wiring between igniter and distributor.
BAD
Repair or replace.
OK
Check distributor.
BAD
Replace.
OK
Check wiring between ECU and igniter.
BAD
Repair or replace.
OK
Check igniter.
BAD
Repair or replace.
OK
Try another ECU.

NOTE: To check ignition system components, see SYSTEM & COMPONENT TESTING article.

## PICKUP & 4RUNNER (3VZ-E) TEST NO. 3 OR CODE 21
### OXYGEN SENSOR SIGNAL

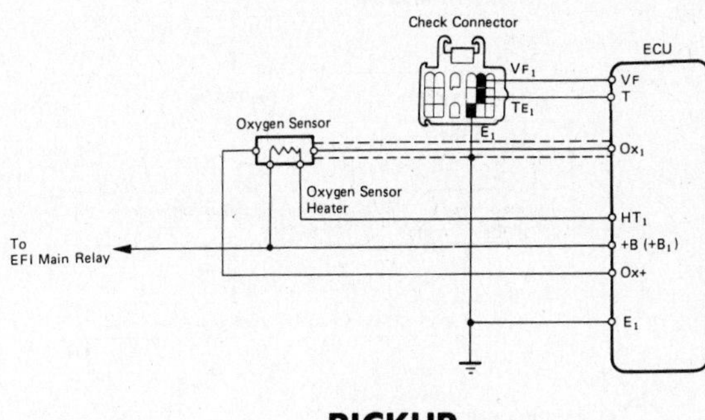
Check Connector
ECU
VF₁
TE₁
E₁
VF
T
Oxygen Sensor
Ox₁
Oxygen Sensor
Heater
HT₁
To
EFI Main Relay
+B (+B₁)
Ox+
E₁

PICKUP

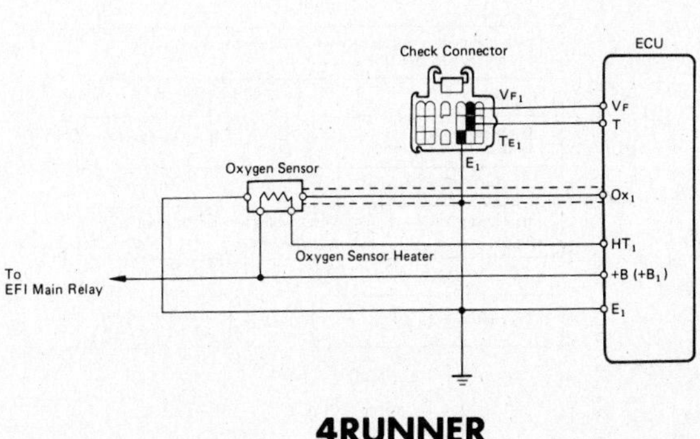
Check Connector
ECU
VF₁
TE₁
E₁
VF
T
Oxygen Sensor
Ox₁
Oxygen Sensor Heater
HT₁
To
EFI Main Relay
+B (+B₁)
E₁

4RUNNER

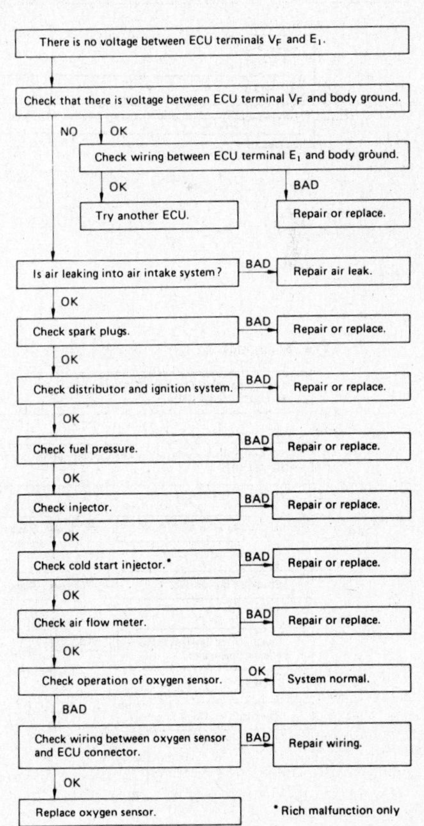
There is no voltage between ECU terminals V_F and E₁.
Check that there is voltage between ECU terminal V_F and body ground.
NO
OK
Check wiring between ECU terminal E₁ and body ground.
OK
BAD
Try another ECU.
Repair or replace.
Is air leaking into air intake system?
BAD
Repair air leak.
OK
Check spark plugs.
BAD
Repair or replace.
OK
Check distributor and ignition system.
BAD
Repair or replace.
OK
Check fuel pressure.
BAD
Repair or replace.
OK
Check injector.
BAD
Repair or replace.
OK
Check cold start injector.*
BAD
Repair or replace.
OK
Check air flow meter.
BAD
Repair or replace.
OK
Check operation of oxygen sensor.
OK
System normal.
BAD
Check wiring between oxygen sensor and ECU connector.
BAD
Repair wiring.
OK
Replace oxygen sensor.
* Rich malfunction only

Courtesy of Toyota Motor Sales, U.S.A., Inc.

# 1991 ENGINE PERFORMANCE
# Self-Diagnostics (Cont.)

## PICKUP & 4RUNNER (3VZ-E) TEST NO. 4 OR CODE 22
### COOLANT TEMPERATURE SENSOR SIGNAL

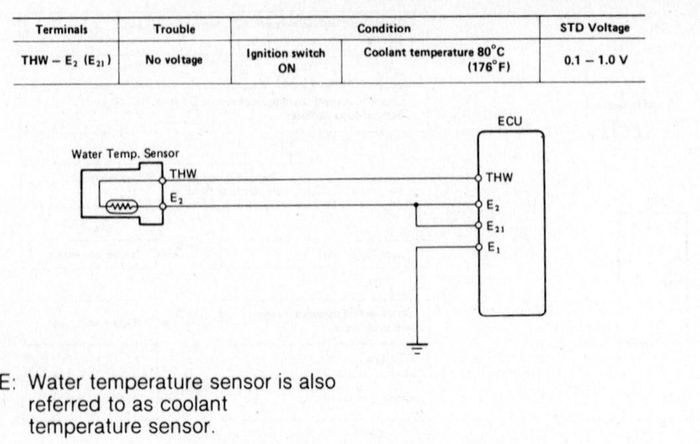

| Terminals | Trouble | Condition | | STD Voltage |
|---|---|---|---|---|
| THW – $E_2$ ($E_{21}$) | No voltage | Ignition switch ON | Coolant temperature 80°C (176°F) | 0.1 – 1.0 V |

ECU
Water Temp. Sensor
THW
$E_2$
THW
$E_2$
$E_{21}$
$E_1$

NOTE: Water temperature sensor is also referred to as coolant temperature sensor.

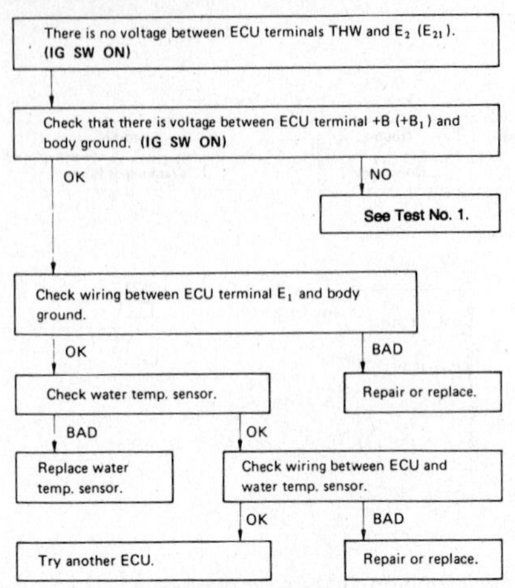
There is no voltage between ECU terminals THW and $E_2$ ($E_{21}$). (IG SW ON)
Check that there is voltage between ECU terminal +B (+$B_1$) and body ground. (IG SW ON)
OK
NO
See Test No. 1.
Check wiring between ECU terminal $E_1$ and body ground.
OK
BAD
Check water temp. sensor.
Repair or replace.
BAD
OK
Replace water temp. sensor.
Check wiring between ECU and water temp. sensor.
OK
BAD
Try another ECU.
Repair or replace.

## PICKUP & 4RUNNER (3VZ-E) TEST NO. 5 OR CODE 24, 31, 32
### INTAKE AIR TEMPERATURE SENSOR & AIRFLOW METER SIGNAL

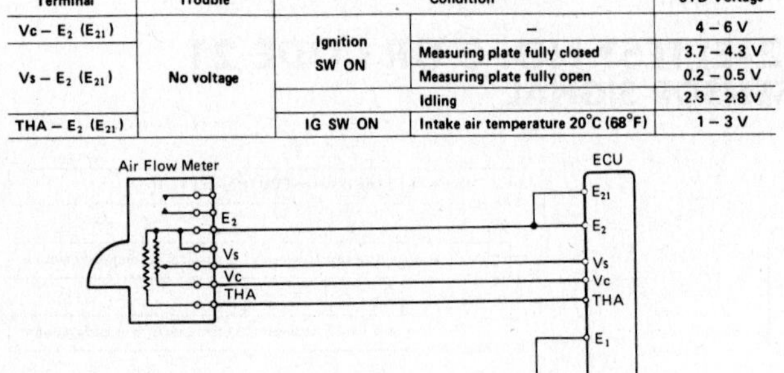

| Terminal | Trouble | Condition | | STD Voltage |
|---|---|---|---|---|
| Vc – $E_2$ ($E_{21}$) | No voltage | Ignition SW ON | – | 4 – 6 V |
| Vs – $E_2$ ($E_{21}$) | | | Measuring plate fully closed | 3.7 – 4.3 V |
| | | | Measuring plate fully open | 0.2 – 0.5 V |
| | | | Idling | 2.3 – 2.8 V |
| THA – $E_2$ ($E_{21}$) | | IG SW ON | Intake air temperature 20°C (68°F) | 1 – 3 V |

Air Flow Meter
ECU
$E_2$
Vs
Vc
THA
$E_{21}$
$E_2$
Vs
Vc
THA
$E_1$

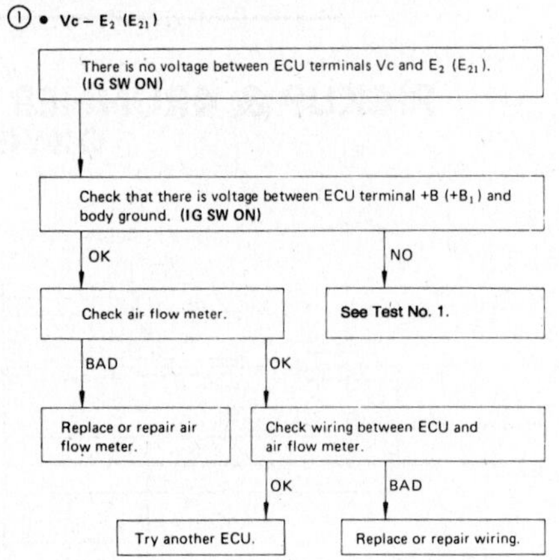
① • Vc – $E_2$ ($E_{21}$)
There is no voltage between ECU terminals Vc and $E_2$ ($E_{21}$). (IG SW ON)
Check that there is voltage between ECU terminal +B (+$B_1$) and body ground. (IG SW ON)
OK
NO
Check air flow meter.
See Test No. 1.
BAD
OK
Replace or repair air flow meter.
Check wiring between ECU and air flow meter.
OK
BAD
Try another ECU.
Replace or repair wiring.

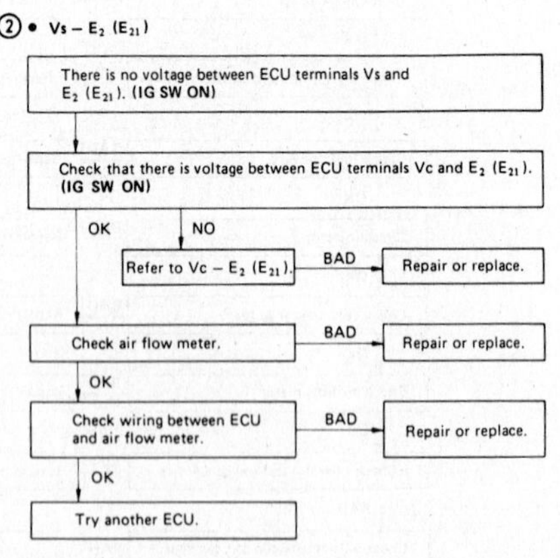
② • Vs – $E_2$ ($E_{21}$)
There is no voltage between ECU terminals Vs and $E_2$ ($E_{21}$). (IG SW ON)
Check that there is voltage between ECU terminals Vc and $E_2$ ($E_{21}$). (IG SW ON)
OK
NO
Refer to Vc – $E_2$ ($E_{21}$).
BAD
Repair or replace.
Check air flow meter.
BAD
Repair or replace.
OK
Check wiring between ECU and air flow meter.
BAD
Repair or replace.
OK
Try another ECU.

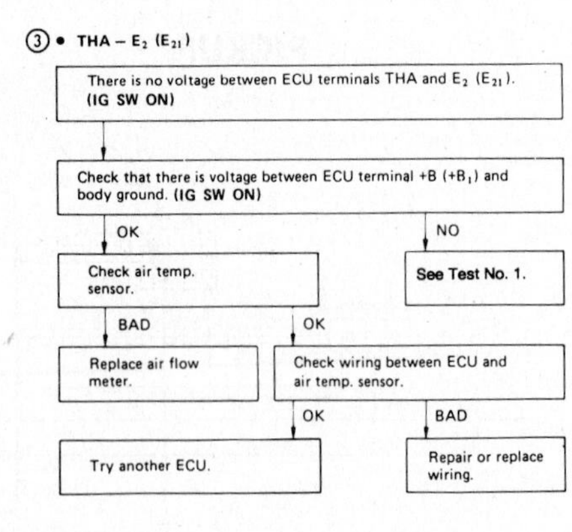
③ • THA – $E_2$ ($E_{21}$)
There is no voltage between ECU terminals THA and $E_2$ ($E_{21}$). (IG SW ON)
Check that there is voltage between ECU terminal +B (+$B_1$) and body ground. (IG SW ON)
OK
NO
Check air temp. sensor.
See Test No. 1.
BAD
OK
Replace air flow meter.
Check wiring between ECU and air temp. sensor.
OK
BAD
Try another ECU.
Repair or replace wiring.

91B18060 91C18061 91A18085 91E18063 91F18064 91G18065

# 1991 ENGINE PERFORMANCE
# Self-Diagnostics (Cont.)

## PICKUP & 4RUNNER (3VZ-E) CODE 25
### LEAN AIR/FUEL MIXTURE

**Probable Causes**
- Airflow Meter
- Air Intake System
- Coolant Temperature Sensor
- ECU
- Fuel Pressure
- Ignition System
- Injector Circuit or Injector
- Oxygen Sensor or Sensor Circuit

**NOTE – Diagnostic chart not available from manufacturer.**

## PICKUP & 4RUNNER (3VZ-E) CODE 26
### RICH AIR/FUEL MIXTURE

**Probable Causes**
- Airflow Meter
- Cold Start Injector
- Coolant Temperature Sensor
- ECU
- Fuel Pressure
- Injector Circuit or Injector
- Oxygen Sensor or Sensor Circuit

**NOTE – Diagnostic chart not available from manufacturer.**

## PICKUP (3VZ-E) CODE 35 (CAB & CHASSIS ONLY)
### HIGH ALTITUDE COMPENSATOR (HAC) SENSOR SIGNAL

**Probable Causes**
- ECU

**NOTE – Diagnostic chart not available from manufacturer.**

Courtesy of Toyota Motor Sales, U.S.A., Inc.

# 1991 ENGINE PERFORMANCE
# Self-Diagnostics (Cont.)

## PICKUP & 4RUNNER (3VZ-E) TEST NO. 6 OR CODE 41
### THROTTLE POSITION SENSOR SIGNAL

| Terminals | Trouble | Condition | | STD Voltage |
|---|---|---|---|---|
| IDL – $E_2$ ($E_{21}$) | No voltage | Ignition switch ON | Throttle valve open | 8 – 14 V |
| Vc – $E_2$ ($E_{21}$) | | | – | 4 – 6 V |
| VTA – $E_2$ ($E_{21}$) | | | Throttle valve fully closed | 0.1 – 1.0 V |
| | | | Throttle valve fully open | 3 – 5 V |

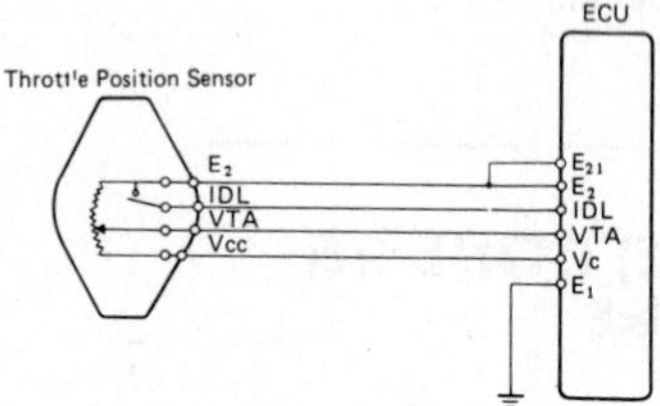


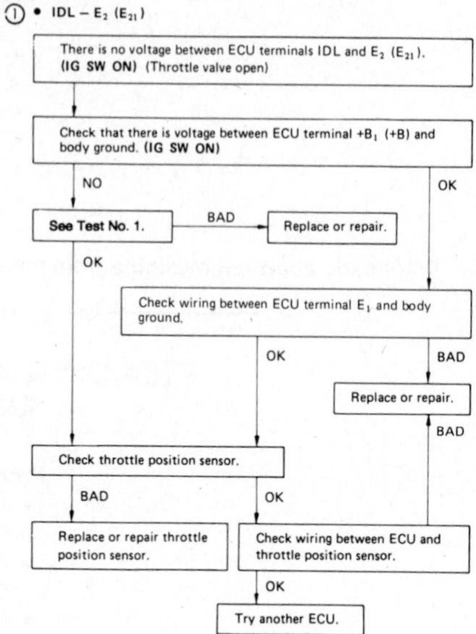

① • IDL – $E_2$ ($E_{21}$)
There is no voltage between ECU terminals IDL and $E_2$ ($E_{21}$). (IG SW ON) (Throttle valve open)
Check that there is voltage between ECU terminal $+B_1$ (+B) and body ground. (IG SW ON)
NO
OK
See Test No. 1.
BAD
Replace or repair.
OK
Check wiring between ECU terminal $E_1$ and body ground.
OK
BAD
Replace or repair.
BAD
Check throttle position sensor.
BAD
OK
Replace or repair throttle position sensor.
Check wiring between ECU and throttle position sensor.
OK
Try another ECU.


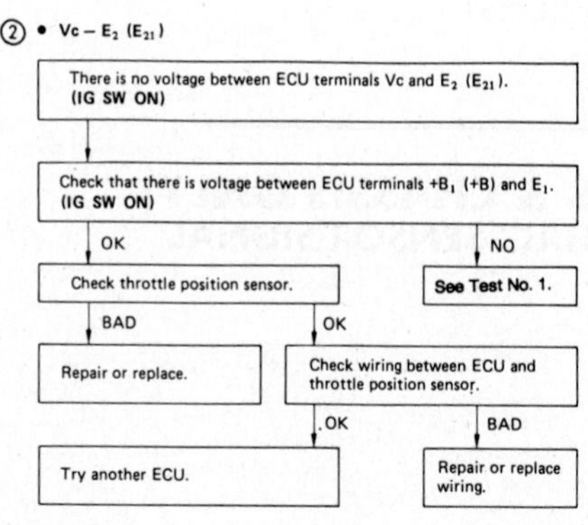


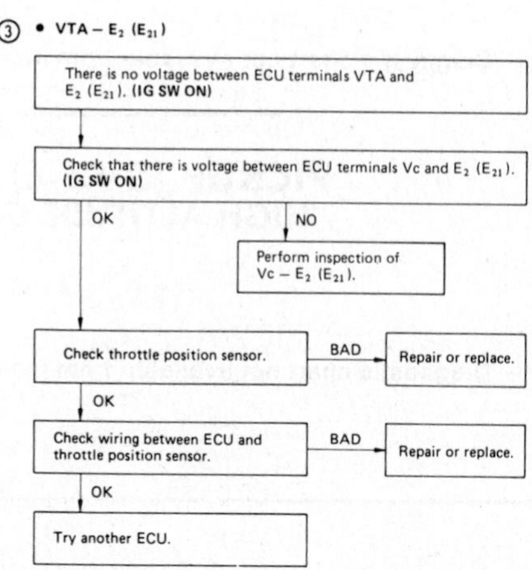


## PICKUP & 4RUNNER (3VZ-E) CODE 42
### VEHICLE SPEED SENSOR SIGNAL

**Probable Causes**

- Vehicle Speed Sensor or Sensor Circuit
- ECU

**NOTE – Diagnostic chart not available from manufacturer.**

91B18086 91I18067 91C18087 91D18088

## PICKUP & 4RUNNER (3VZ-E) TEST NO. 7 OR CODE 43
### STARTER SIGNAL

| Terminals | Trouble | Condition | STD Voltage |
|---|---|---|---|
| STA – $E_1$ | No voltage | Ignition switch START position | 6 – 12 V |

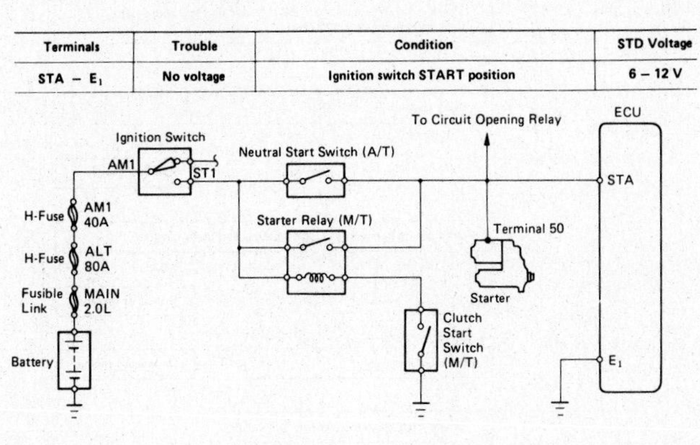


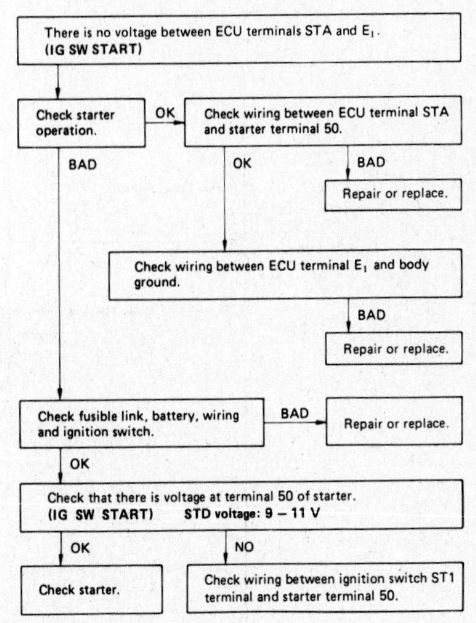

There is no voltage between ECU terminals STA and E1.
(IG SW START)
Check starter operation.
OK
Check wiring between ECU terminal STA and starter terminal 50.
BAD
OK
BAD
Repair or replace.
Check wiring between ECU terminal E1 and body ground.
BAD
Repair or replace.
Check fusible link, battery, wiring and ignition switch.
BAD
Repair or replace.
OK
Check that there is voltage at terminal 50 of starter.
(IG SW START) STD voltage: 9 – 11 V
OK
NO
Check starter.
Check wiring between ignition switch ST1 terminal and starter terminal 50.


## PICKUP & 4RUNNER (3VZ-E) CODE 51
### SWITCH SIGNAL

**Probable Causes**

- A/C Switch or Switch Circuit
- Accelerator Pedal or Cable
- ECU
- Neutral/Start Switch or Switch Circuit
- Throttle Position Sensor or Sensor Circuit

**NOTE – Diagnostic chart not available from manufacturer.**

## PICKUP & 4RUNNER (3VZ-E) CODE 52
### KNOCK SENSOR SIGNAL

**Probable Causes**

- Knock Sensor or Sensor Circuit
- ECU

**NOTE – Diagnostic chart not available from manufacturer.**

## PICKUP & 4RUNNER (3VZ-E) CODE 53
### KNOCK SENSOR CONTROL (ECU)

**Probable Causes**

- ECU

**NOTE – Diagnostic chart not available from manufacturer.**

91D18070 91E18089 91F17694

# 1991 ENGINE PERFORMANCE
# Self-Diagnostics (Cont.)

## PICKUP & 4RUNNER (3VZ-E) TEST NO. 8 OR CODE 71
### EGR SYSTEM MALFUNCTION

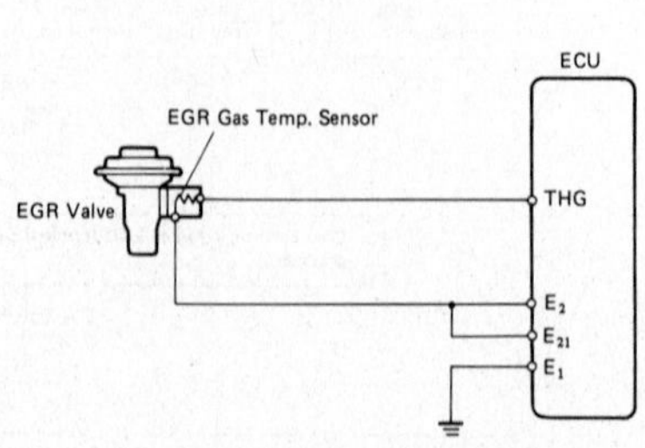


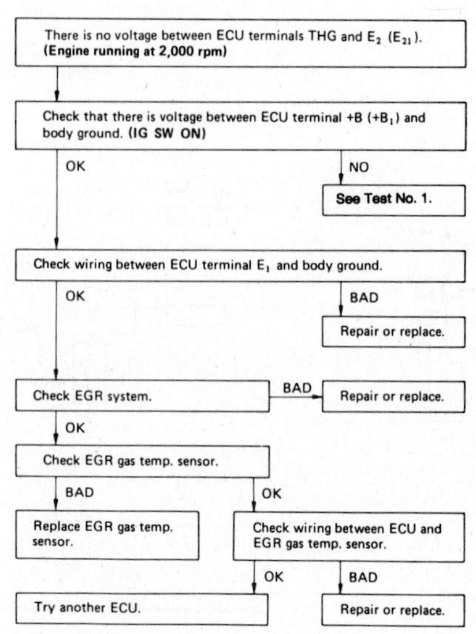

There is no voltage between ECU terminals THG and $E_2$ ($E_{21}$).
(Engine running at 2,000 rpm)
Check that there is voltage between ECU terminal +B (+$B_1$) and body ground. (IG SW ON)
OK
NO
See Test No. 1.
Check wiring between ECU terminal $E_1$ and body ground.
OK
BAD
Repair or replace.
Check EGR system.
BAD
Repair or replace.
OK
Check EGR gas temp. sensor.
BAD
OK
Replace EGR gas temp. sensor.
Check wiring between ECU and EGR gas temp. sensor.
OK
BAD
Try another ECU.
Repair or replace.


## PICKUP & 4RUNNER (3VZ-E) TEST NO. 9
### INJECTOR CIRCUIT

| Terminals | Trouble | Condition | STD Voltage |
|---|---|---|---|
| No. 10 – $E_{01}$<br>No. 20 – $E_{02}$ | No voltage | Ignition switch ON | 10 – 14 V |

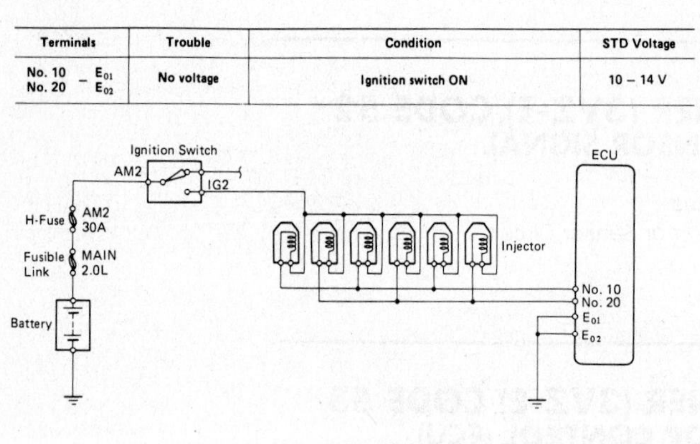


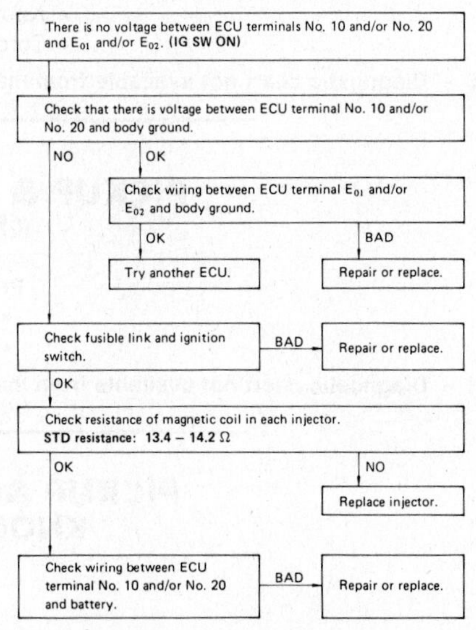

There is no voltage between ECU terminals No. 10 and/or No. 20 and $E_{01}$ and/or $E_{02}$. (IG SW ON)
Check that there is voltage between ECU terminal No. 10 and/or No. 20 and body ground.
NO
OK
Check wiring between ECU terminal $E_{01}$ and/or $E_{02}$ and body ground.
OK
BAD
Try another ECU.
Repair or replace.
Check fusible link and ignition switch.
BAD
Repair or replace.
OK
Check resistance of magnetic coil in each injector.
STD resistance: 13.4 – 14.2 Ω
OK
NO
Replace injector.
Check wiring between ECU terminal No. 10 and/or No. 20 and battery.
BAD
Repair or replace.


91E18071 91F18072 91H18090 91G18073

## PICKUP & 4RUNNER (3VZ-E) TEST NO. 10
### COLD START INJECTOR CIRCUIT

| Terminals | Trouble | Condition | | STD Voltage |
|---|---|---|---|---|
| STJ – $E_1$ | No voltage | Ignition switch START position | Coolant temperature 80°C (176°F) | 6 – 12 V |

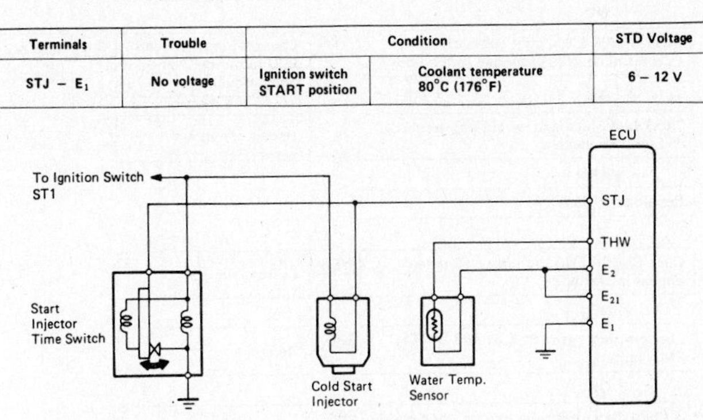
ECU
To Ignition Switch
ST1
STJ
THW
E2
E21
E1
Start
Injector
Time Switch
Cold Start
Injector
Water Temp.
Sensor

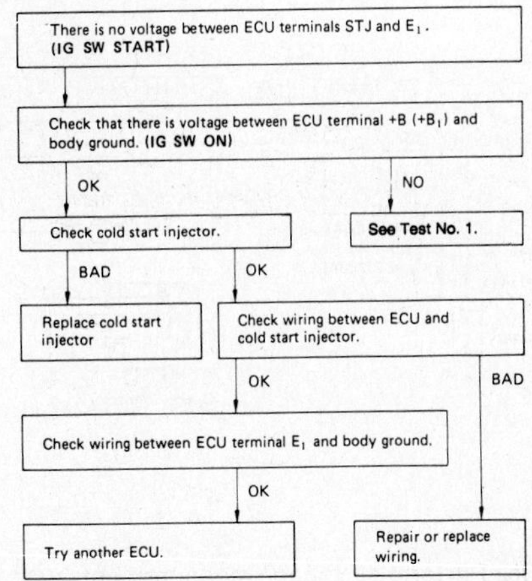
There is no voltage between ECU terminals STJ and E1.
(IG SW START)
Check that there is voltage between ECU terminal +B (+B1) and body ground. (IG SW ON)
OK
NO
Check cold start injector.
See Test No. 1.
BAD
OK
Replace cold start injector
Check wiring between ECU and cold start injector.
OK
BAD
Check wiring between ECU terminal E1 and body ground.
OK
Try another ECU.
Repair or replace wiring.

## PICKUP & 4RUNNER (3VZ-E) TEST NO. 11
### CHECK ENGINE LIGHT CIRCUIT

| Terminals | Trouble | Condition | STD Voltage |
|---|---|---|---|
| W – $E_1$ | No voltage | No trouble ("CHECK ENGINE" warning light off) and engine running | 10 – 14 V |

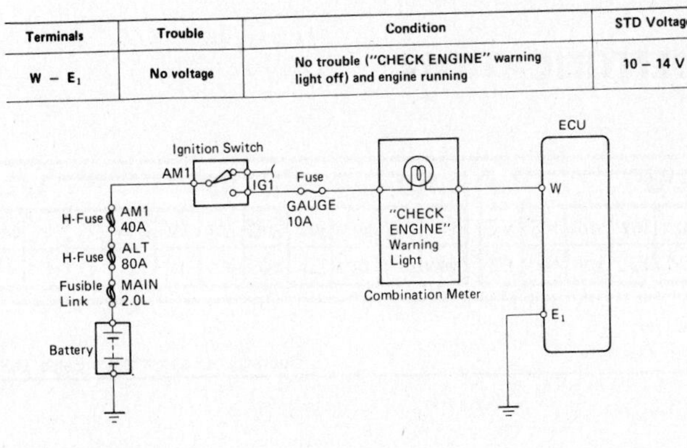
Ignition Switch
AM1
IG1
Fuse
GAUGE
10A
ECU
W
E1
H-Fuse
AM1
40A
H-Fuse
ALT
80A
Fusible
Link
MAIN
2.0L
Battery
"CHECK
ENGINE"
Warning
Light
Combination Meter

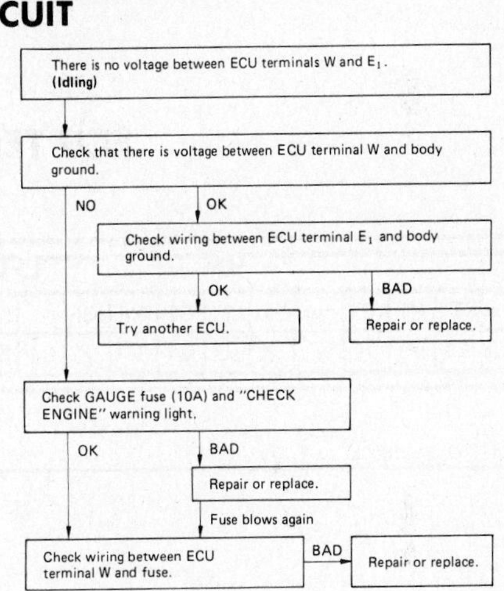
There is no voltage between ECU terminals W and E1.
(Idling)
Check that there is voltage between ECU terminal W and body ground.
NO
OK
Check wiring between ECU terminal E1 and body ground.
OK
BAD
Try another ECU.
Repair or replace.
Check GAUGE fuse (10A) and "CHECK ENGINE" warning light.
OK
BAD
Repair or replace.
Fuse blows again
Check wiring between ECU terminal W and fuse.
BAD
Repair or replace.

## PICKUP & 4RUNNER (3VZ-E) TEST NO. 12
### STOPLIGHT SWITCH CIRCUIT

| Terminals | Trouble | Condition | STD Voltage |
|---|---|---|---|
| STP – $E_1$ | No voltage | Stop light switch ON | 8 – 14 V |

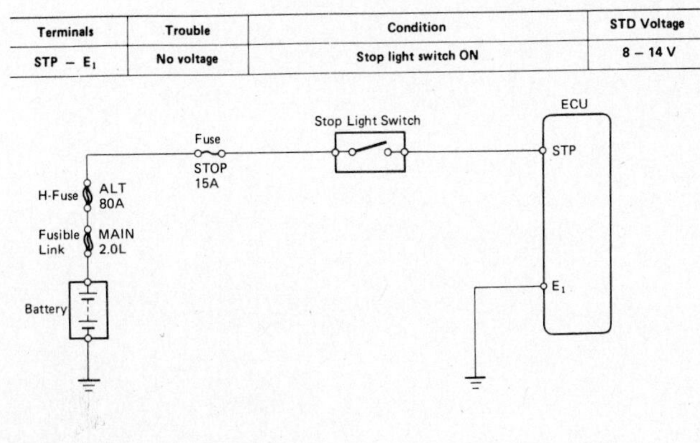
Fuse
STOP
15A
Stop Light Switch
ECU
STP
E1
H-Fuse
ALT
80A
Fusible
Link
MAIN
2.0L
Battery

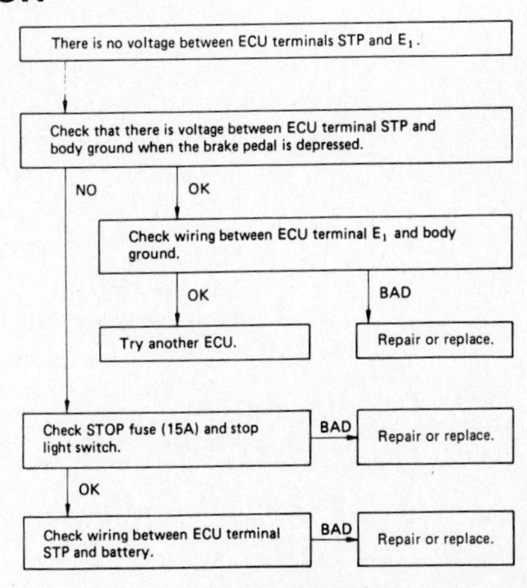
There is no voltage between ECU terminals STP and E1.
Check that there is voltage between ECU terminal STP and body ground when the brake pedal is depressed.
NO
OK
Check wiring between ECU terminal E1 and body ground.
OK
BAD
Try another ECU.
Repair or replace.
Check STOP fuse (15A) and stop light switch.
BAD
Repair or replace.
OK
Check wiring between ECU terminal STP and battery.
BAD
Repair or replace.

91H18074 91I18075 91J18076 91D17791 91A18077 91B18078

# 1991 ENGINE PERFORMANCE
## Self-Diagnostics (Cont.)

### PREVIA DIAGNOSTIC CIRCUIT CHECK

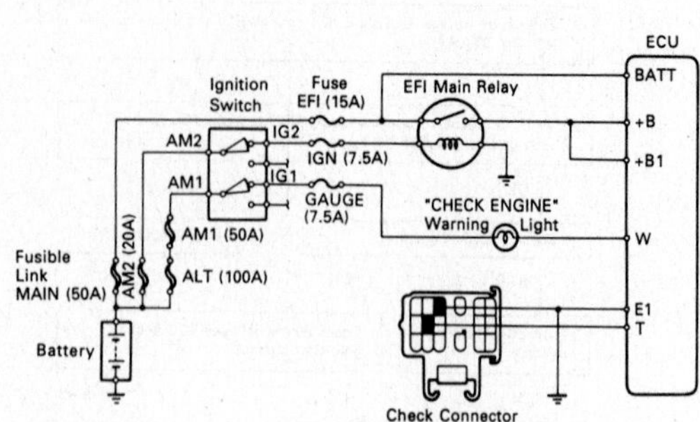
ECU
Ignition Switch
Fuse EFI (15A)
EFI Main Relay
BATT
+B
+B1
AM2
IG2
IGN (7.5A)
AM1
IG1
GAUGE (7.5A)
"CHECK ENGINE" Warning Light
W
AM1 (50A)
AM2 (20A)
Fusible Link MAIN (50A)
ALT (100A)
Battery
E1
T
Check Connector

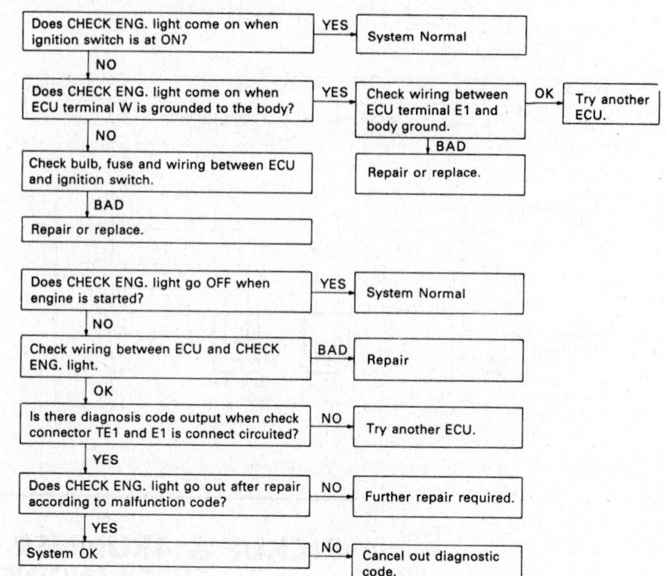
Does CHECK ENG. light come on when ignition switch is at ON?
YES
System Normal
NO
Does CHECK ENG. light come on when ECU terminal W is grounded to the body?
YES
Check wiring between ECU terminal E1 and body ground.
OK
Try another ECU.
BAD
Repair or replace.
NO
Check bulb, fuse and wiring between ECU and ignition switch.
BAD
Repair or replace.
Does CHECK ENG. light go OFF when engine is started?
YES
System Normal
NO
Check wiring between ECU and CHECK ENG. light.
BAD
Repair
OK
Is there diagnosis code output when check connector TE1 and E1 is connect circuited?
NO
Try another ECU.
YES
Does CHECK ENG. light go out after repair according to malfunction code?
NO
Further repair required.
YES
System OK
NO
Cancel out diagnostic code.

CAUTION: Perform all voltage measurements with ECU harness connector installed. Use a high-impedance DVOM (10,000-ohm minimum). Verify battery voltage is greater than 11 volts.

### ECU TERMINAL IDENTIFICATION

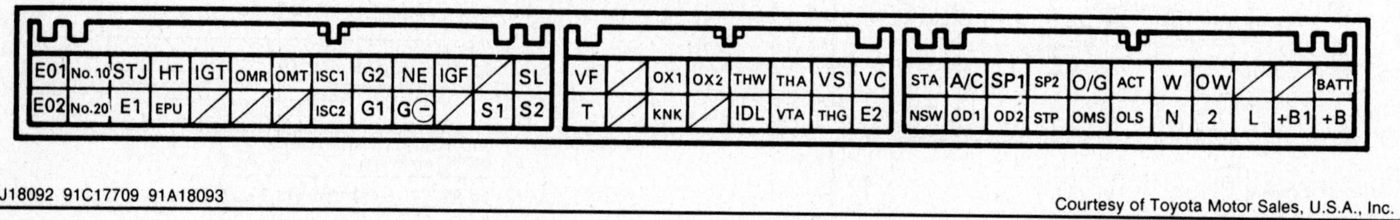
E01 No.10 STJ HT IGT OMR OMT ISC1 G2 NE IGF SL
E02 No.20 E1 EPU ISC2 G1 G⊖ S1 S2
VF OX1 OX2 THW THA VS VC
T KNK IDL VTA THG E2
STA A/C SP1 SP2 O/G ACT W OW BATT
NSW OD1 OD2 STP OMS OLS N 2 L +B1 +B

91J18092 91C17709 91A18093

Courtesy of Toyota Motor Sales, U.S.A., Inc.

## PREVIA TEST NO. 1
### ECU (+B) CIRCUIT

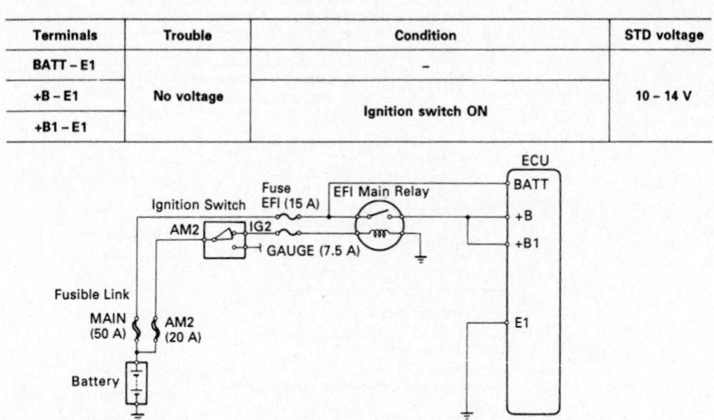

| Terminals | Trouble | Condition | STD voltage |
|---|---|---|---|
| BATT – E1 | No voltage | – | 10 – 14 V |
| +B – E1 | | Ignition switch ON | |
| +B1 – E1 | | | |

ECU
Fuse
EFI (15 A)
EFI Main Relay
BATT
Ignition Switch
+B
AM2
IG2
+B1
GAUGE (7.5 A)
Fusible Link
MAIN
(50 A)
AM2
(20 A)
E1
Battery

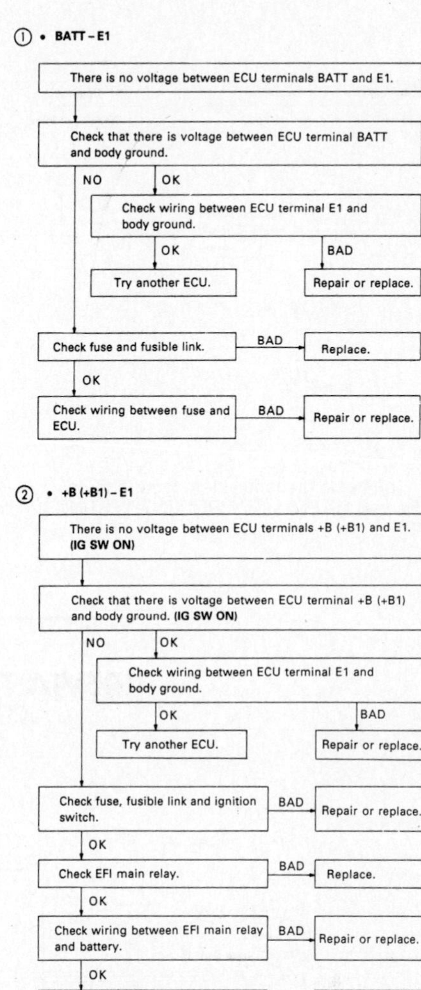

① • BATT – E1
There is no voltage between ECU terminals BATT and E1.
Check that there is voltage between ECU terminal BATT and body ground.
NO
OK
Check wiring between ECU terminal E1 and body ground.
OK
BAD
Try another ECU.
Repair or replace.
Check fuse and fusible link.
BAD
Replace.
OK
Check wiring between fuse and ECU.
BAD
Repair or replace.
② • +B (+B1) – E1
There is no voltage between ECU terminals +B (+B1) and E1. (IG SW ON)
Check that there is voltage between ECU terminal +B (+B1) and body ground. (IG SW ON)
NO
OK
Check wiring between ECU terminal E1 and body ground.
OK
BAD
Try another ECU.
Repair or replace.
Check fuse, fusible link and ignition switch.
BAD
Repair or replace.
OK
Check EFI main relay.
BAD
Replace.
OK
Check wiring between EFI main relay and battery.
BAD
Repair or replace.
OK
Check wiring between EFI main relay and ECU terminal +B (+B1).
BAD
Repair or replace.

## PREVIA CODE 12, 13
### RPM SIGNAL

Code 12 is caused by loss of "NE" signal or "G" signal from distributor to ECU for at least 2 seconds after starter signal is received at ECU. Ensure starter signal exists at ECU. See TEST NO. 8 OR CODE 43. Code 13 is caused by loss of "NE" signal from distributor to ECU when engine RPM exceeds 1000 RPM.

**NOTE – Diagnostic chart not available from manufacturer.**

91B18094 91H17795 91E18055

# 1991 ENGINE PERFORMANCE
# Self-Diagnostics (Cont.)

## PREVIA TEST NO. 2 OR CODE 14
### IGNITION SIGNAL

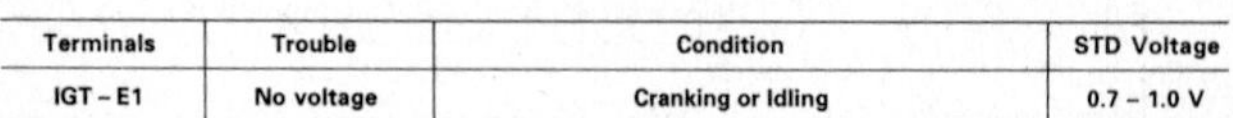

| Terminals | Trouble | Condition | STD Voltage |
|---|---|---|---|
| IGT – E1 | No voltage | Cranking or Idling | 0.7 – 1.0 V |

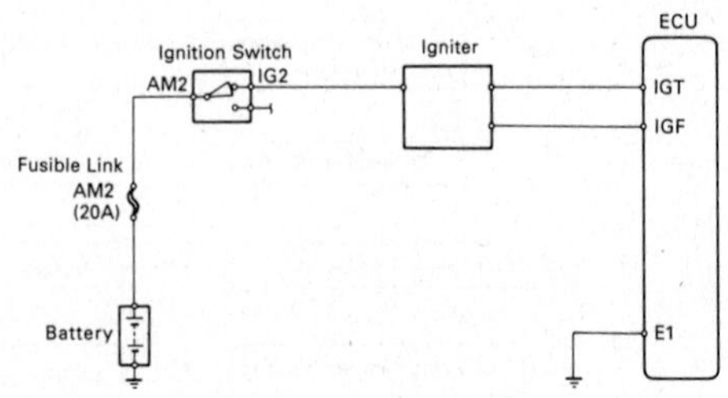
ECU
Ignition Switch
Igniter
AM2
IG2
IGT
IGF
Fusible Link
AM2
(20A)
Battery
E1

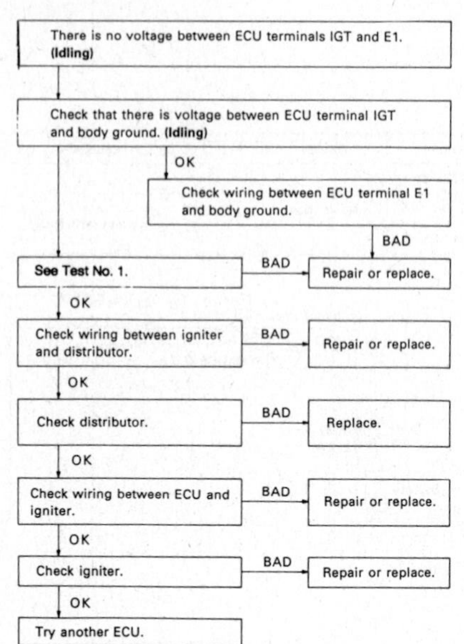
There is no voltage between ECU terminals IGT and E1. (Idling)
Check that there is voltage between ECU terminal IGT and body ground. (Idling)
OK
Check wiring between ECU terminal E1 and body ground.
BAD
See Test No. 1.
BAD
Repair or replace.
OK
Check wiring between igniter and distributor.
BAD
Repair or replace.
OK
Check distributor.
BAD
Replace.
OK
Check wiring between ECU and igniter.
BAD
Repair or replace.
OK
Check igniter.
BAD
Repair or replace.
OK
Try another ECU.

NOTE: To check ignition system components, see SYSTEM & COMPONENT TESTING article.

## PREVIA TEST NO. 3 OR CODE 21, 27
### OXYGEN SENSOR SIGNAL

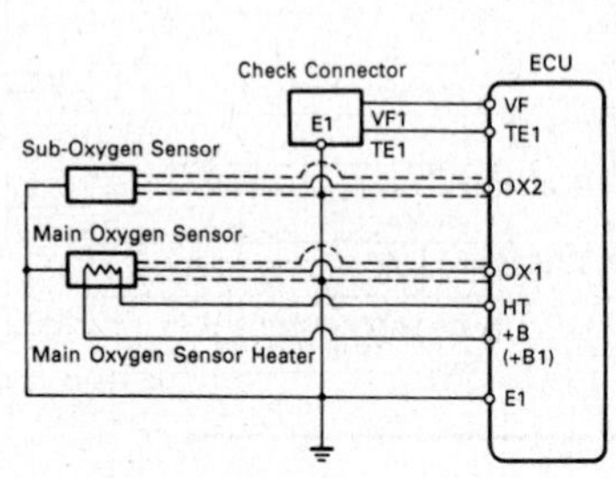
Check Connector
ECU
E1
VF1
TE1
VF
TE1
Sub-Oxygen Sensor
OX2
Main Oxygen Sensor
OX1
HT
+B
(+B1)
Main Oxygen Sensor Heater
E1

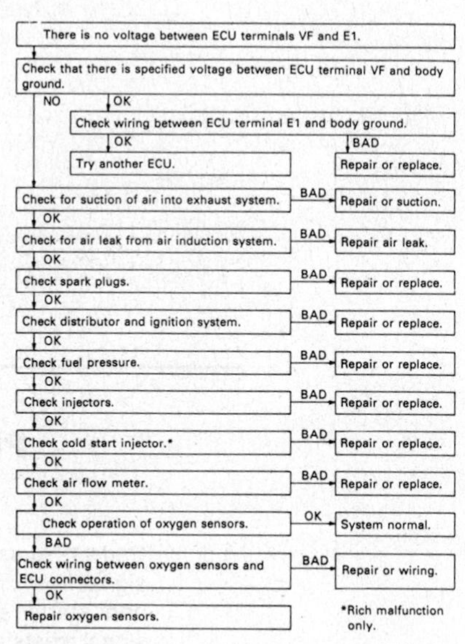
There is no voltage between ECU terminals VF and E1.
Check that there is specified voltage between ECU terminal VF and body ground.
NO
OK
Check wiring between ECU terminal E1 and body ground.
OK
BAD
Try another ECU.
Repair or replace.
Check for suction of air into exhaust system.
BAD
Repair or suction.
OK
Check for air leak from air induction system.
BAD
Repair air leak.
OK
Check spark plugs.
BAD
Repair or replace.
OK
Check distributor and ignition system.
BAD
Repair or replace.
OK
Check fuel pressure.
BAD
Repair or replace.
OK
Check injectors.
BAD
Repair or replace.
OK
Check cold start injector.*
BAD
Repair or replace.
OK
Check air flow meter.
BAD
Repair or replace.
OK
Check operation of oxygen sensors.
OK
System normal.
BAD
Check wiring between oxygen sensors and ECU connectors.
BAD
Repair or wiring.
OK
Repair oxygen sensors.
*Rich malfunction only.

91C18095 91G18057 91D18096 91G17547

Courtesy of Toyota Motor Sales, U.S.A., Inc.

## PREVIA TEST NO. 4 OR CODE 22
### COOLANT TEMPERATURE SENSOR SIGNAL

| Terminals | Trouble | Condition | | STD Voltage |
|---|---|---|---|---|
| THW – E2 | No voltage | Ignition SW ON | Coolant temperature 80°C (176°F) | 0.1 – 1.0 V |

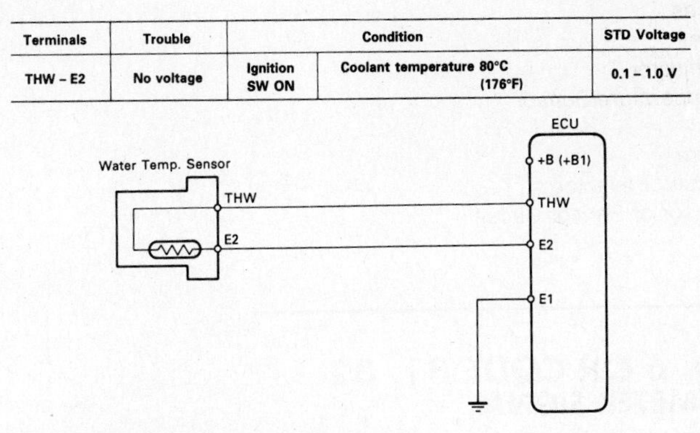
ECU
Water Temp. Sensor
THW
E2
+B (+B1)
THW
E2
E1

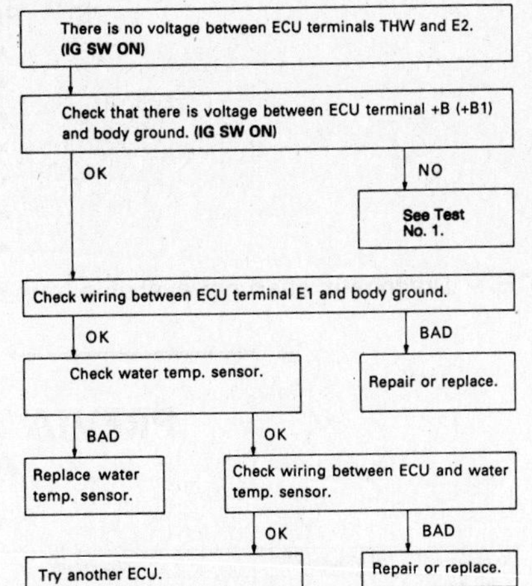
There is no voltage between ECU terminals THW and E2. (IG SW ON)
Check that there is voltage between ECU terminal +B (+B1) and body ground. (IG SW ON)
OK
NO
See Test No. 1.
Check wiring between ECU terminal E1 and body ground.
OK
BAD
Check water temp. sensor.
Repair or replace.
BAD
OK
Replace water temp. sensor.
Check wiring between ECU and water temp. sensor.
OK
BAD
Try another ECU.
Repair or replace.

NOTE: Water temperature sensor is also referred to as coolant temperature sensor.

## PREVIA TEST NO. 5 OR CODE 24
### INTAKE AIR TEMPERATURE SENSOR SIGNAL

| Terminals | Trouble | Condition | | STD Voltage |
|---|---|---|---|---|
| THA – E2 | No voltage | Ignition SW ON | Intake air temperature 20°C (68°F) | 1 – 3 V |

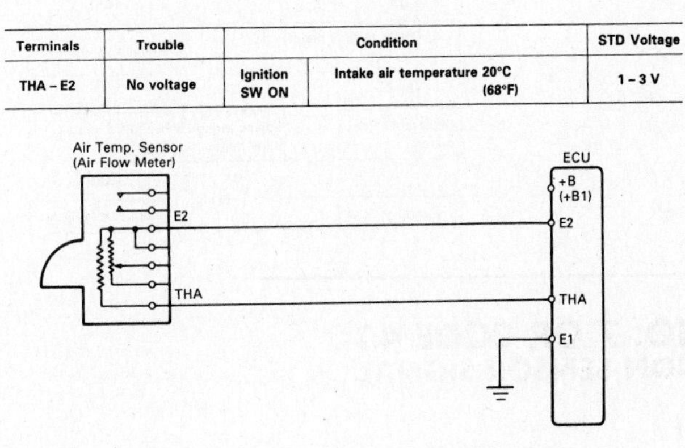
Air Temp. Sensor
(Air Flow Meter)
E2
THA
ECU
+B
(+B1)
E2
THA
E1

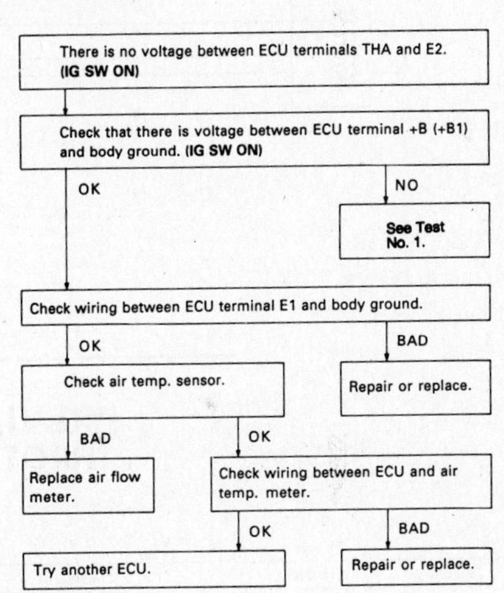
There is no voltage between ECU terminals THA and E2. (IG SW ON)
Check that there is voltage between ECU terminal +B (+B1) and body ground. (IG SW ON)
OK
NO
See Test No. 1.
Check wiring between ECU terminal E1 and body ground.
OK
BAD
Check air temp. sensor.
Repair or replace.
BAD
OK
Replace air flow meter.
Check wiring between ECU and air temp. meter.
OK
BAD
Try another ECU.
Repair or replace.

## PREVIA CODE 25
### LEAN AIR/FUEL MIXTURE

**Probable Causes**

- Airflow Meter
- Air Intake System
- Coolant Temperature Sensor
- ECU
- Fuel Pressure
- Ignition System
- Injector Circuit or Injector
- Oxygen Sensor or Sensor Circuit

**NOTE – Diagnostic chart not available from manufacturer.**

91J17680 91F17801 91B17682 91G17802

# 1991 ENGINE PERFORMANCE
## Self-Diagnostics (Cont.)

## PREVIA CODE 26
### RICH AIR/FUEL MIXTURE

**Probable Causes**
- Airflow Meter
- Cold Start Injector
- Coolant Temperature Sensor
- ECU
- Fuel Pressure
- Injector Circuit or Injector
- Oxygen Sensor or Sensor Circuit

**NOTE – Diagnostic chart not available from manufacturer.**

## PREVIA TEST NO. 6 OR CODE 31, 32
### AIRFLOW METER SIGNAL

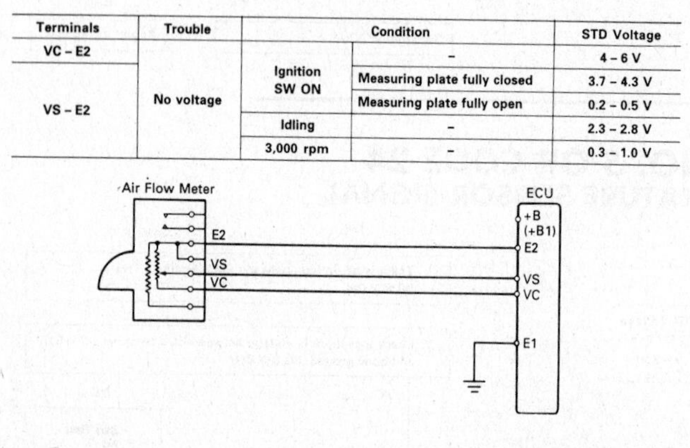

| Terminals | Trouble | Condition | | STD Voltage |
|---|---|---|---|---|
| VC – E2 | No voltage | Ignition SW ON | – | 4 – 6 V |
| VS – E2 | | | Measuring plate fully closed | 3.7 – 4.3 V |
| | | | Measuring plate fully open | 0.2 – 0.5 V |
| | | Idling | – | 2.3 – 2.8 V |
| | | 3,000 rpm | – | 0.3 – 1.0 V |

Air Flow Meter
E2
VS
VC
ECU
+B
(+B1)
E2
VS
VC
E1

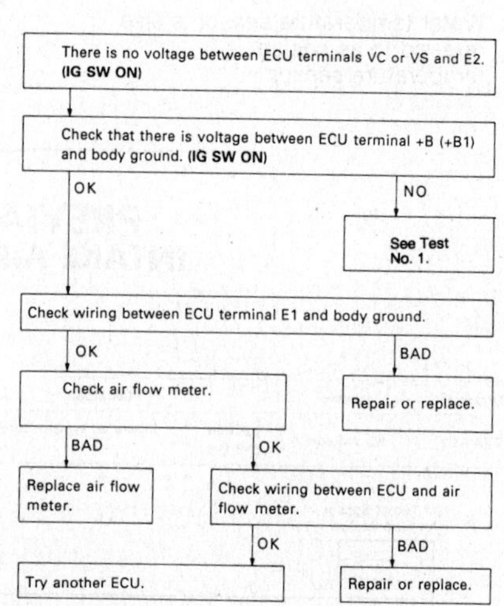
There is no voltage between ECU terminals VC or VS and E2. (IG SW ON)
Check that there is voltage between ECU terminal +B (+B1) and body ground. (IG SW ON)
OK
NO
See Test No. 1.
Check wiring between ECU terminal E1 and body ground.
OK
BAD
Check air flow meter.
Repair or replace.
BAD
OK
Replace air flow meter.
Check wiring between ECU and air flow meter.
OK
BAD
Try another ECU.
Repair or replace.

## PREVIA TEST NO. 7 OR CODE 41
### THROTTLE POSITION SENSOR SIGNAL

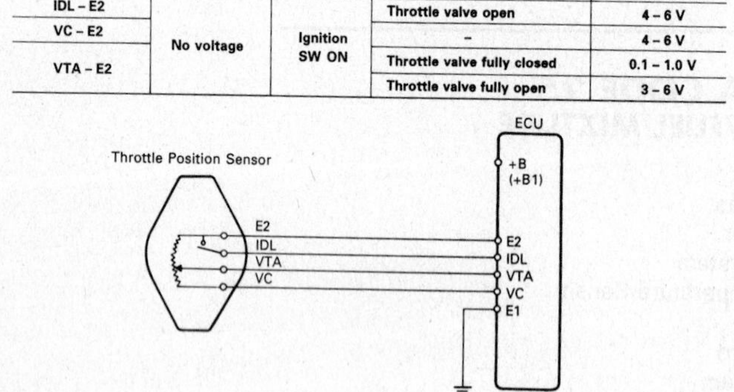

| Terminals | Trouble | Condition | | STD Voltage |
|---|---|---|---|---|
| IDL – E2 | No voltage | Ignition SW ON | Throttle valve open | 4 – 6 V |
| VC – E2 | | | – | 4 – 6 V |
| VTA – E2 | | | Throttle valve fully closed | 0.1 – 1.0 V |
| | | | Throttle valve fully open | 3 – 6 V |

Throttle Position Sensor
E2
IDL
VTA
VC
ECU
+B
(+B1)
E2
IDL
VTA
VC
E1

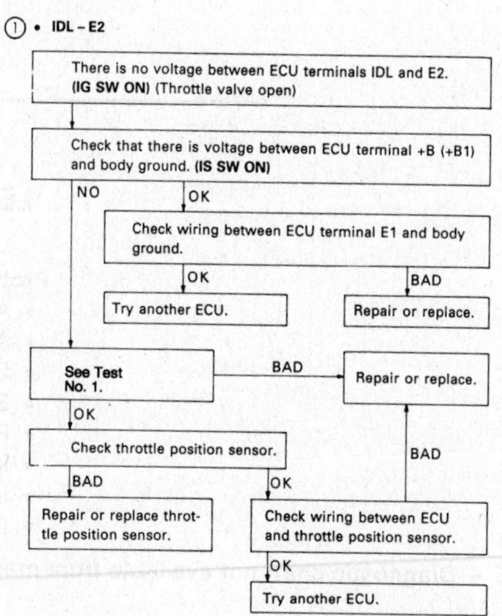
① • IDL – E2
There is no voltage between ECU terminals IDL and E2. (IG SW ON) (Throttle valve open)
Check that there is voltage between ECU terminal +B (+B1) and body ground. (IS SW ON)
NO
OK
Check wiring between ECU terminal E1 and body ground.
OK
BAD
Try another ECU.
Repair or replace.
See Test No. 1.
BAD
Repair or replace.
OK
Check throttle position sensor.
BAD
BAD
OK
Repair or replace throttle position sensor.
Check wiring between ECU and throttle position sensor.
OK
Try another ECU.

**Continued On Next Page**

91D17684 91H17803 91H17688 91I17805

Courtesy of Toyota Motor Sales, U.S.A., Inc.

# PREVIA TEST NO. 7 OR CODE 41
## THROTTLE POSITION SENSOR SIGNAL (Cont.)

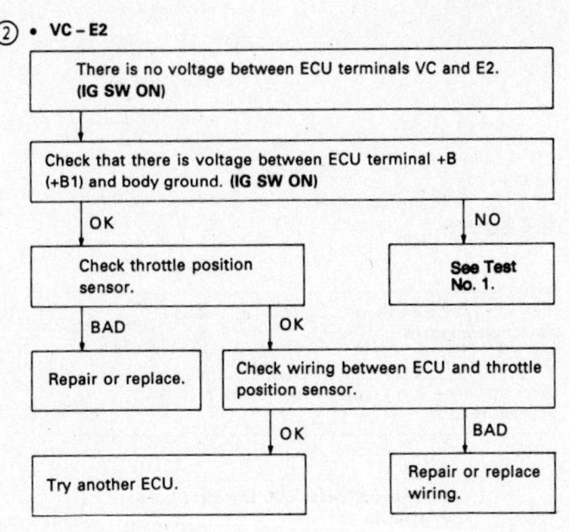
② • VC – E2
There is no voltage between ECU terminals VC and E2. (IG SW ON)
Check that there is voltage between ECU terminal +B (+B1) and body ground. (IG SW ON)
OK
NO
Check throttle position sensor.
See Test No. 1.
BAD
OK
Repair or replace.
Check wiring between ECU and throttle position sensor.
OK
BAD
Try another ECU.
Repair or replace wiring.

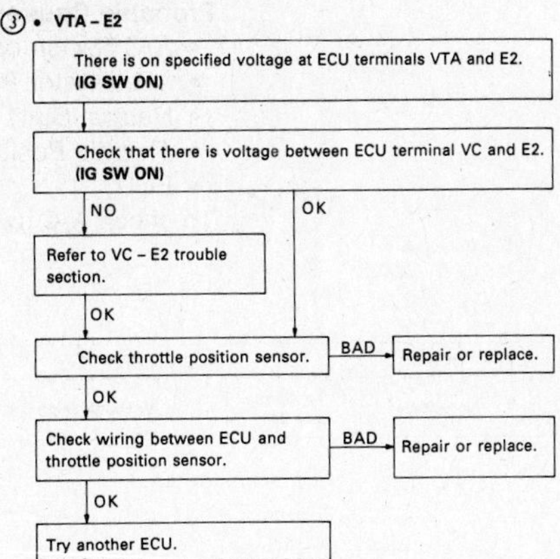
③ • VTA – E2
There is on specified voltage at ECU terminals VTA and E2. (IG SW ON)
Check that there is voltage between ECU terminal VC and E2. (IG SW ON)
NO
OK
Refer to VC – E2 trouble section.
OK
Check throttle position sensor.
BAD
Repair or replace.
OK
Check wiring between ECU and throttle position sensor.
BAD
Repair or replace.
OK
Try another ECU.

# PREVIA CODE 42
## VEHICLE SPEED SENSOR SIGNAL

**Probable Causes**

- Vehicle Speed Sensor or Sensor Circuit
- ECU

**NOTE - Diagnostic chart not available from manufacturer.**

# PREVIA TEST NO. 8 OR CODE 43
## STARTER SIGNAL

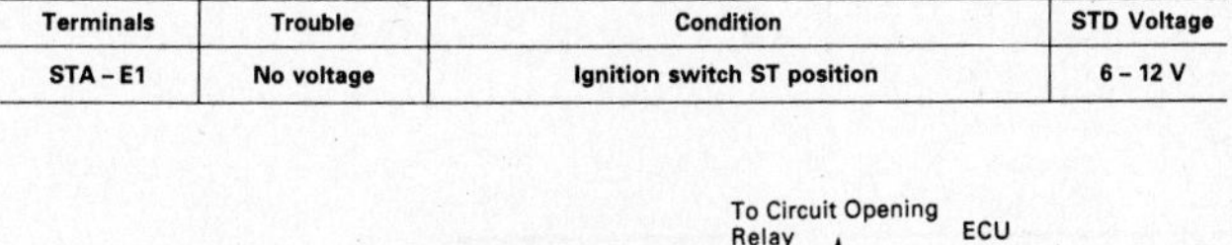

| Terminals | Trouble | Condition | STD Voltage |
|---|---|---|---|
| STA – E1 | No voltage | Ignition switch ST position | 6 – 12 V |

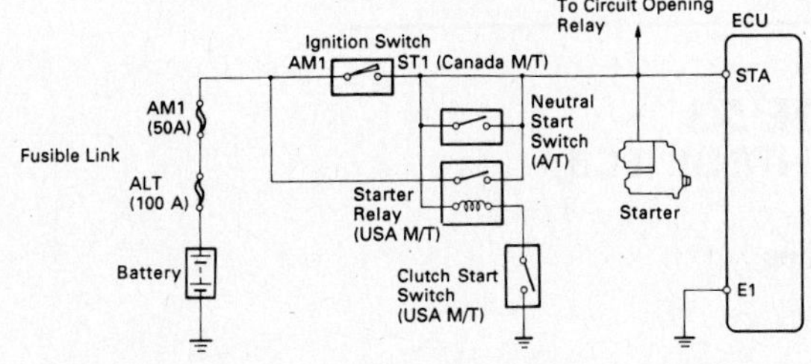
To Circuit Opening Relay
ECU
Ignition Switch
AM1
ST1 (Canada M/T)
STA
AM1 (50A)
Neutral Start Switch (A/T)
Fusible Link
ALT (100 A)
Starter Relay (USA M/T)
Starter
Battery
Clutch Start Switch (USA M/T)
E1

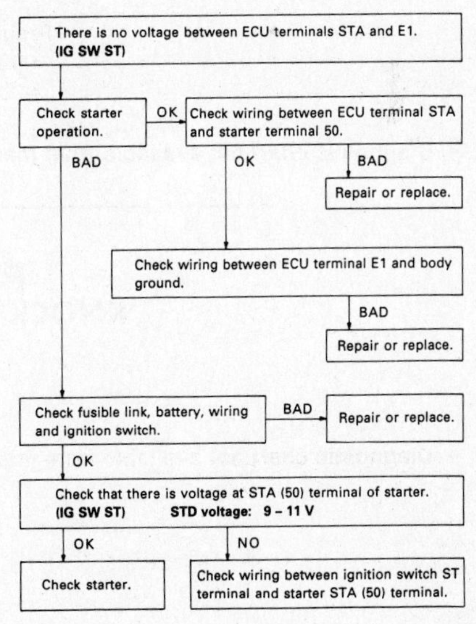
There is no voltage between ECU terminals STA and E1. (IG SW ST)
Check starter operation.
OK
Check wiring between ECU terminal STA and starter terminal 50.
BAD
OK
BAD
Repair or replace.
Check wiring between ECU terminal E1 and body ground.
BAD
Repair or replace.
Check fusible link, battery, wiring and ignition switch.
BAD
Repair or replace.
OK
Check that there is voltage at STA (50) terminal of starter. (IG SW ST) STD voltage: 9 – 11 V
OK
NO
Check starter.
Check wiring between ignition switch ST terminal and starter STA (50) terminal.

91J17805 91A17806 91E18097 91E18089 91F17694

Courtesy of Toyota Motor Sales, U.S.A., Inc.

# 1991 ENGINE PERFORMANCE
## Self-Diagnostics (Cont.)

### PREVIA TEST NO. 9 OR CODE 51
#### SWITCH SIGNAL

**Probable Causes**
- A/C Switch or Switch Circuit
- Accelerator Pedal or Cable
- Neutral/Start Switch or Switch Circuit
- Throttle Position Sensor IDL Circuit
- ECU

To check A/C switch signal, use the following procedure.

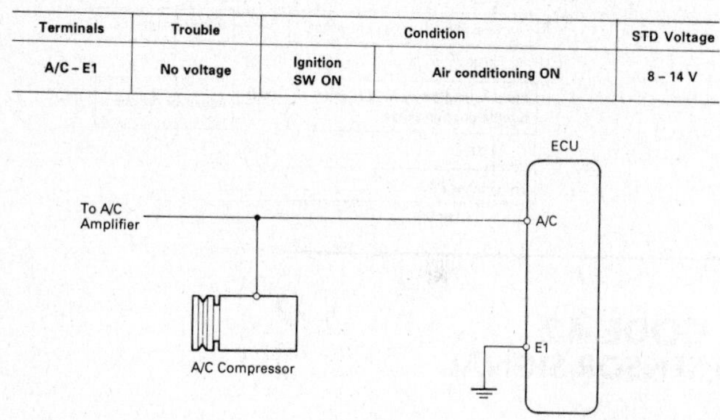

| Terminals | Trouble | Condition | | STD Voltage |
|---|---|---|---|---|
| A/C – E1 | No voltage | Ignition SW ON | Air conditioning ON | 8 – 14 V |

ECU
To A/C
Amplifier
A/C
E1
A/C Compressor



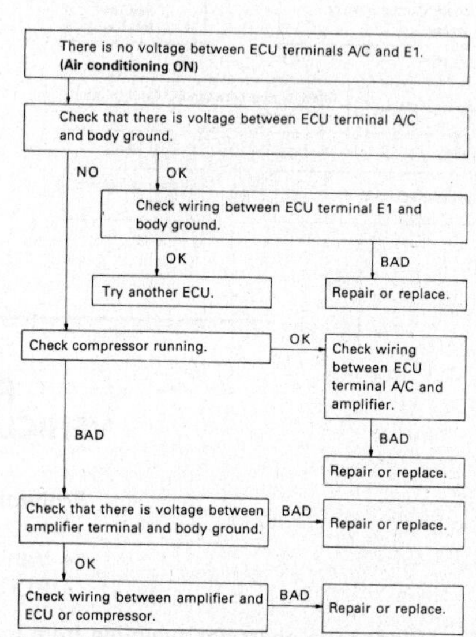

There is no voltage between ECU terminals A/C and E1. (Air conditioning ON)
Check that there is voltage between ECU terminal A/C and body ground.
NO
OK
Check wiring between ECU terminal E1 and body ground.
OK
BAD
Try another ECU.
Repair or replace.
Check compressor running.
OK
Check wiring between ECU terminal A/C and amplifier.
BAD
Repair or replace.
BAD
Check that there is voltage between amplifier terminal and body ground.
BAD
Repair or replace.
OK
Check wiring between amplifier and ECU or compressor.
BAD
Repair or replace.


### PREVIA CODE 52
#### KNOCK SENSOR SIGNAL

**Probable Causes**
- Knock Sensor or Sensor Circuit
- ECU

**NOTE – Diagnostic chart not available from manufacturer.**

### PREVIA CODE 53
#### KNOCK SENSOR CONTROL (ECU)

**Probable Causes**
- ECU

**NOTE – Diagnostic chart not available from manufacturer.**

91G17695 91H17696

Courtesy of Toyota Motor Sales, U.S.A., Inc.

## PREVIA TEST NO. 10 OR CODE 71
### EGR SYSTEM MALFUNCTION

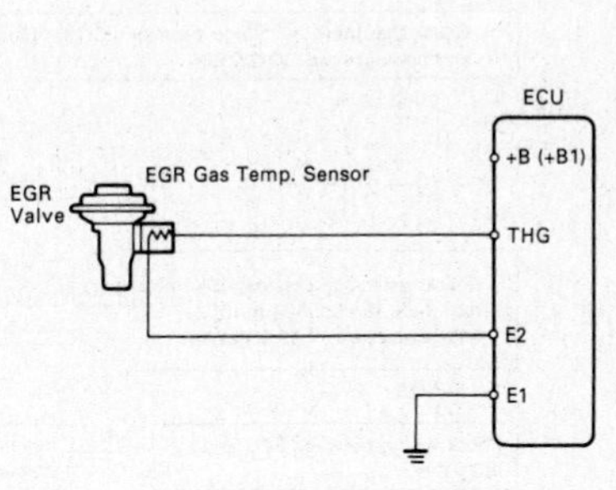
ECU
+B (+B1)
EGR Gas Temp. Sensor
EGR Valve
THG
E2
E1

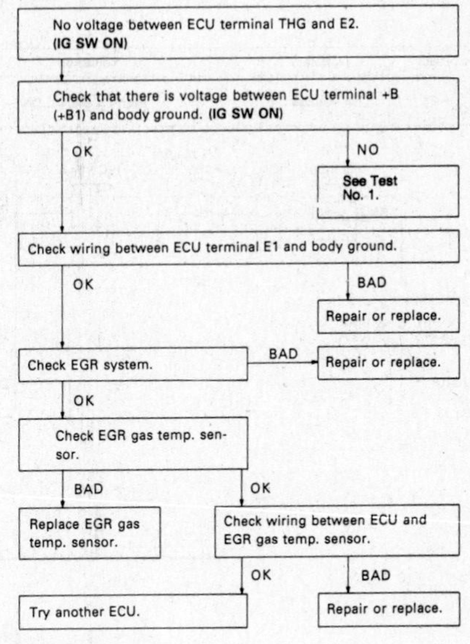
No voltage between ECU terminal THG and E2. (IG SW ON)
Check that there is voltage between ECU terminal +B (+B1) and body ground. (IG SW ON)
OK
NO
See Test No. 1.
Check wiring between ECU terminal E1 and body ground.
OK
BAD
Repair or replace.
Check EGR system.
BAD
Repair or replace.
OK
Check EGR gas temp. sensor.
BAD
OK
Replace EGR gas temp. sensor.
Check wiring between ECU and EGR gas temp. sensor.
OK
BAD
Try another ECU.
Repair or replace.

## PREVIA TEST NO. 11
### INJECTOR CIRCUIT

| Terminals | Trouble | Condition | STD Voltage |
|---|---|---|---|
| No. 10 – E01<br>No. 20 – E02 | No voltage | Ignition switch ON | 10 – 14 V |

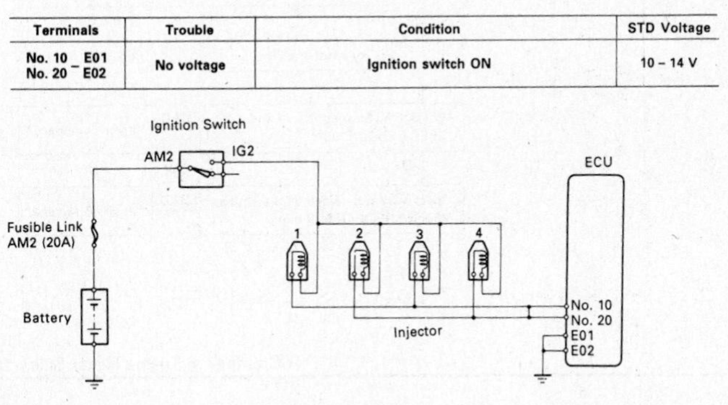
Ignition Switch
AM2
IG2
Fusible Link AM2 (20A)
Battery
1
2
3
4
Injector
ECU
No. 10
No. 20
E01
E02

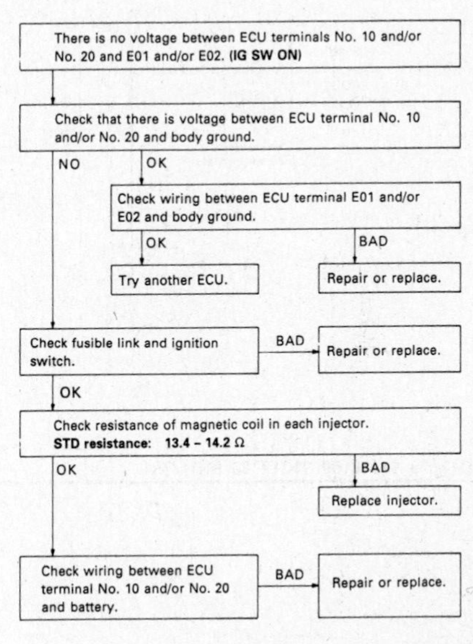
There is no voltage between ECU terminals No. 10 and/or No. 20 and E01 and/or E02. (IG SW ON)
Check that there is voltage between ECU terminal No. 10 and/or No. 20 and body ground.
NO
OK
Check wiring between ECU terminal E01 and/or E02 and body ground.
OK
BAD
Try another ECU.
Repair or replace.
Check fusible link and ignition switch.
BAD
Repair or replace.
OK
Check resistance of magnetic coil in each injector.
STD resistance: 13.4 – 14.2 Ω
OK
BAD
Replace injector.
Check wiring between ECU terminal No. 10 and/or No. 20 and battery.
BAD
Repair or replace.

91H17787 91D17809 91I17788 91G18073

Courtesy of Toyota Motor Sales, U.S.A., Inc.

# 1991 ENGINE PERFORMANCE
# Self-Diagnostics (Cont.)

## PREVIA TEST NO. 12
### IDLE SPEED CONTROL CIRCUIT

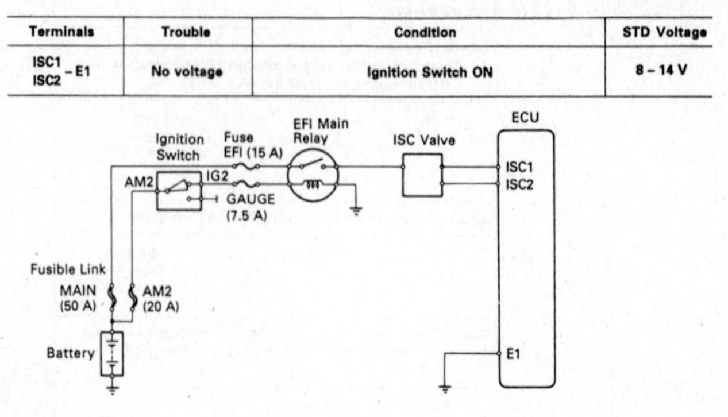

| Terminals | Trouble | Condition | STD Voltage |
|---|---|---|---|
| ISC1 - E1<br>ISC2 | No voltage | Ignition Switch ON | 8 - 14 V |

ECU
EFI Main Relay
Ignition Switch
Fuse EFI (15 A)
ISC Valve
AM2
IG2
GAUGE (7.5 A)
ISC1
ISC2
Fusible Link
MAIN (50 A)
AM2 (20 A)
Battery
E1

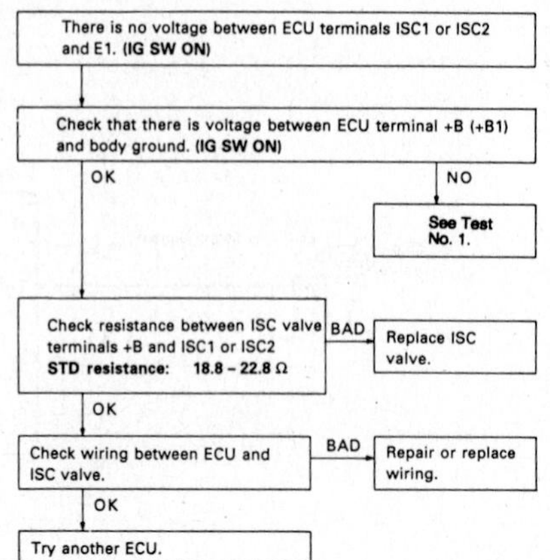
There is no voltage between ECU terminals ISC1 or ISC2 and E1. (IG SW ON)
Check that there is voltage between ECU terminal +B (+B1) and body ground. (IG SW ON)
OK
NO
See Test No. 1.
Check resistance between ISC valve terminals +B and ISC1 or ISC2
STD resistance: 18.8 - 22.8 Ω
BAD
Replace ISC valve.
OK
Check wiring between ECU and ISC valve.
BAD
Repair or replace wiring.
OK
Try another ECU.

## PREVIA TEST NO. 13
### CHECK ENGINE LIGHT CIRCUIT

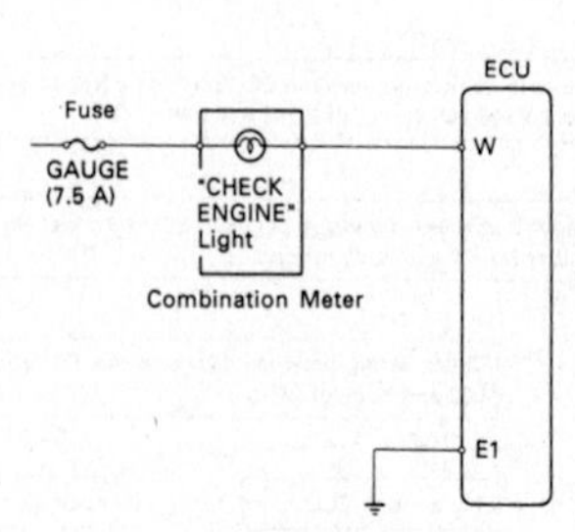
ECU
Fuse
GAUGE (7.5 A)
"CHECK ENGINE" Light
Combination Meter
W
E1

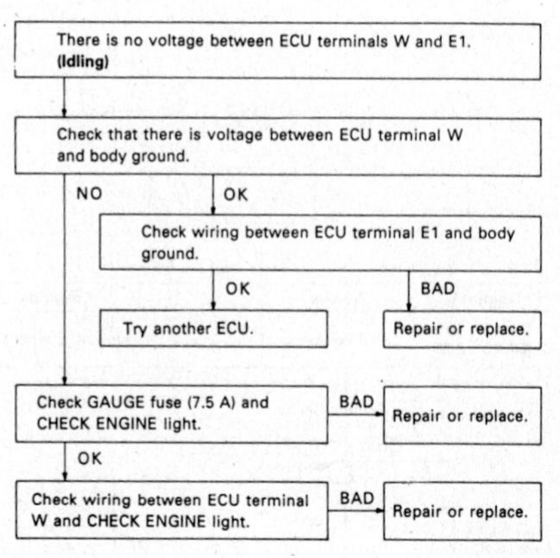
There is no voltage between ECU terminals W and E1. (Idling)
Check that there is voltage between ECU terminal W and body ground.
NO
OK
Check wiring between ECU terminal E1 and body ground.
OK
BAD
Try another ECU.
Repair or replace.
Check GAUGE fuse (7.5 A) and CHECK ENGINE light.
BAD
Repair or replace.
OK
Check wiring between ECU terminal W and CHECK ENGINE light.
BAD
Repair or replace.

91F18098 91G18099 91J18100 91C17790 91D17791

Courtesy of Toyota Motor Sales, U.S.A., Inc.

# 1991 ENGINE PERFORMANCE
# Self-Diagnostics (Cont.)

## SUPRA DIAGNOSTIC CIRCUIT CHECK

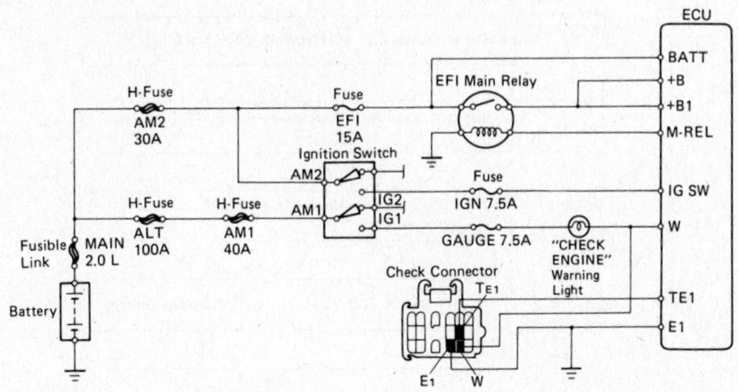
ECU
BATT
+B
+B1
M-REL
IG SW
W
TE1
E1
EFI Main Relay
H-Fuse
AM2
30A
Fuse
EFI
15A
Ignition Switch
AM2
AM1
IG2
IG1
Fuse
IGN 7.5A
GAUGE 7.5A
H-Fuse
ALT
100A
H-Fuse
AM1
40A
Fusible Link
MAIN
2.0 L
Battery
"CHECK ENGINE" Warning Light
Check Connector
TE1
E1
W

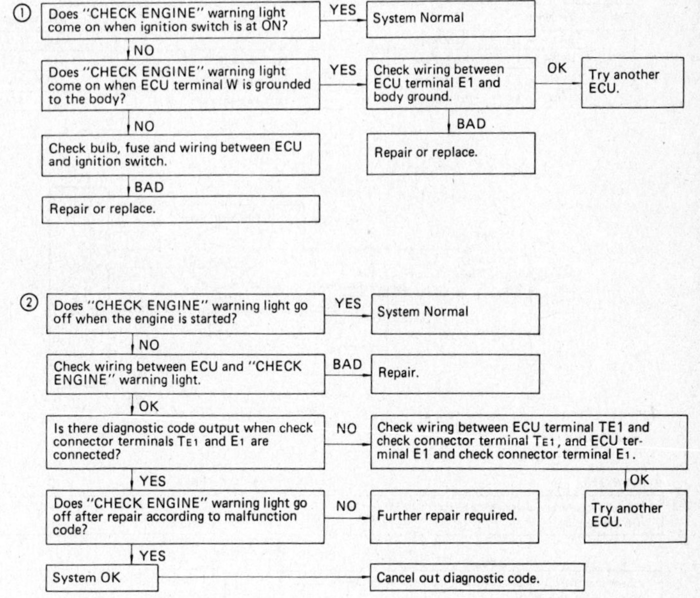
① Does "CHECK ENGINE" warning light come on when ignition switch is at ON?
YES
System Normal
NO
Does "CHECK ENGINE" warning light come on when ECU terminal W is grounded to the body?
YES
Check wiring between ECU terminal E1 and body ground.
OK
Try another ECU.
BAD
Repair or replace.
NO
Check bulb, fuse and wiring between ECU and ignition switch.
BAD
Repair or replace.
② Does "CHECK ENGINE" warning light go off when the engine is started?
YES
System Normal
NO
Check wiring between ECU and "CHECK ENGINE" warning light.
BAD
Repair.
OK
Is there diagnostic code output when check connector terminals TE1 and E1 are connected?
NO
Check wiring between ECU terminal TE1 and check connector terminal TE1, and ECU terminal E1 and check connector terminal E1.
OK
Try another ECU.
YES
Does "CHECK ENGINE" warning light go off after repair according to malfunction code?
NO
Further repair required.
YES
System OK
Cancel out diagnostic code.

CAUTION: Perform all voltage measurements with ECU harness connector installed. Use a high-impedance DVOM (10,000-ohm minimum). Verify battery voltage is greater than 11 volts.

## ECU TERMINAL IDENTIFICATION

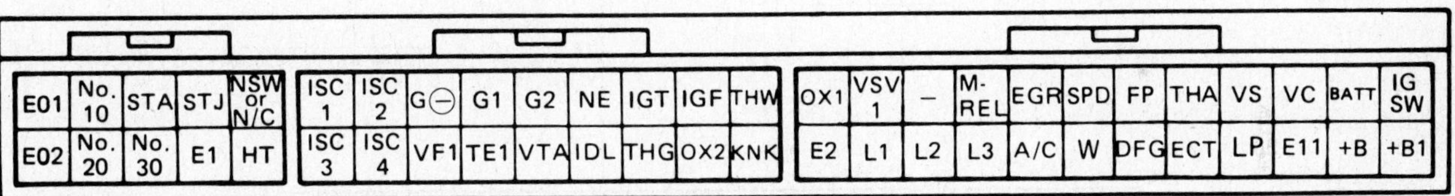
E01 | No. 10 | STA | STJ | NSW or N/C
E02 | No. 20 | No. 30 | E1 | HT
ISC 1 | ISC 2 | G⊖ | G1 | G2 | NE | IGT | IGF | THW
ISC 3 | ISC 4 | VF1 | TE1 | VTA | IDL | THG | OX2 | KNK
OX1 | VSV 1 | – | M-REL | EGR | SPD | FP | THA | VS | VC | BATT | IG SW
E2 | L1 | L2 | L3 | A/C | W | DFG | ECT | LP | E11 | +B | +B1

NON-TURBO

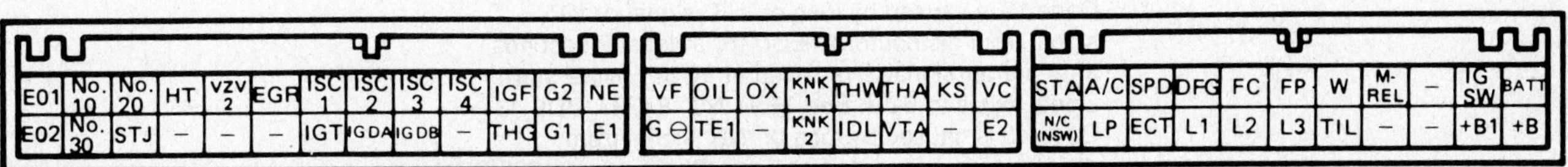
E01 | No. 10 | No. 20 | HT | VZV 2 | EGR | ISC 1 | ISC 2 | ISC 3 | ISC 4 | IGF | G2 | NE
E02 | No. 30 | STJ | – | – | – | IGT | IGDA | IGDB | – | THG | G1 | E1
VF | OIL | OX | KNK 1 | THW | THA | KS | VC
G⊖ | TE1 | – | KNK 2 | IDL | VTA | – | E2
STA | A/C | SPD | DFG | FC | FP | W | M-REL | – | IG SW | BATT
N/C (NSW) | LP | ECT | L1 | L2 | L3 | TIL | – | – | +B1 | +B

TURBO

91E17792 91G18081 91C18103 91D18104

Courtesy of Toyota Motor Sales, U.S.A., Inc.

# 1991 ENGINE PERFORMANCE
## Self-Diagnostics (Cont.)

## SUPRA TEST NO. 1
### ECU (+B) CIRCUIT

| No. | Terminals | Trouble | Condition | STD Voltage |
|---|---|---|---|---|
| 1 | BATT – E1 | No voltage | — | 10 – 14 V |
| | IG SW – E1 | No voltage | Ignition switch ON | 10 – 14 V |
| | M-REL – E1 | No voltage | Ignition switch ON | 10 – 14 V |
| | +B (+B1) – E1 | No voltage | Ignition switch ON | 10 – 14 V |

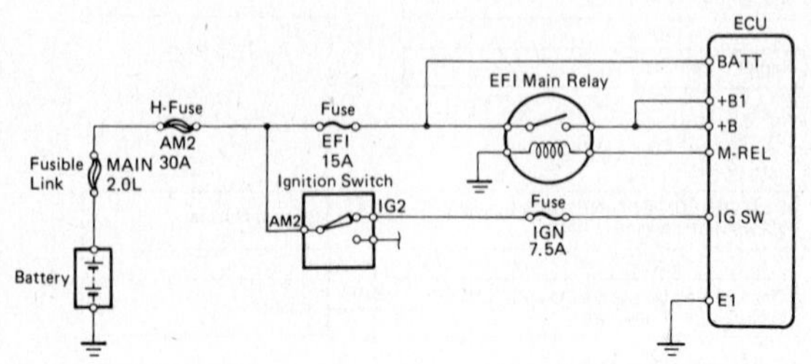
ECU
BATT
EFI Main Relay
+B1
+B
M-REL
IG SW
E1
H-Fuse
AM2
30A
Fuse
EFI
15A
Fusible Link
MAIN
2.0L
Ignition Switch
AM2
IG2
Fuse
IGN
7.5A
Battery

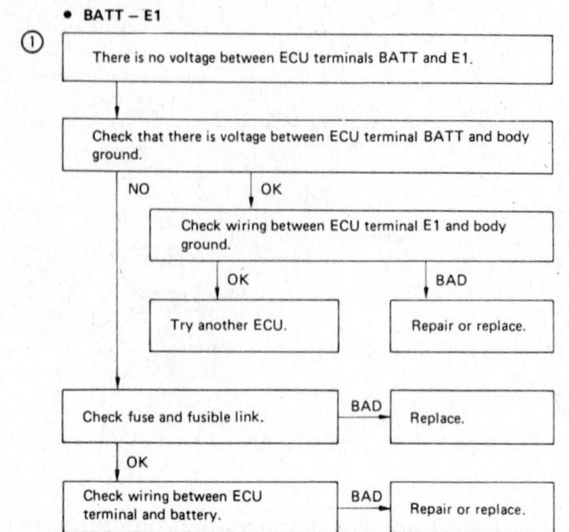
• BATT – E1
① There is no voltage between ECU terminals BATT and E1.
Check that there is voltage between ECU terminal BATT and body ground.
NO
OK
Check wiring between ECU terminal E1 and body ground.
OK
BAD
Try another ECU.
Repair or replace.
Check fuse and fusible link.
BAD
Replace.
OK
Check wiring between ECU terminal and battery.
BAD
Repair or replace.

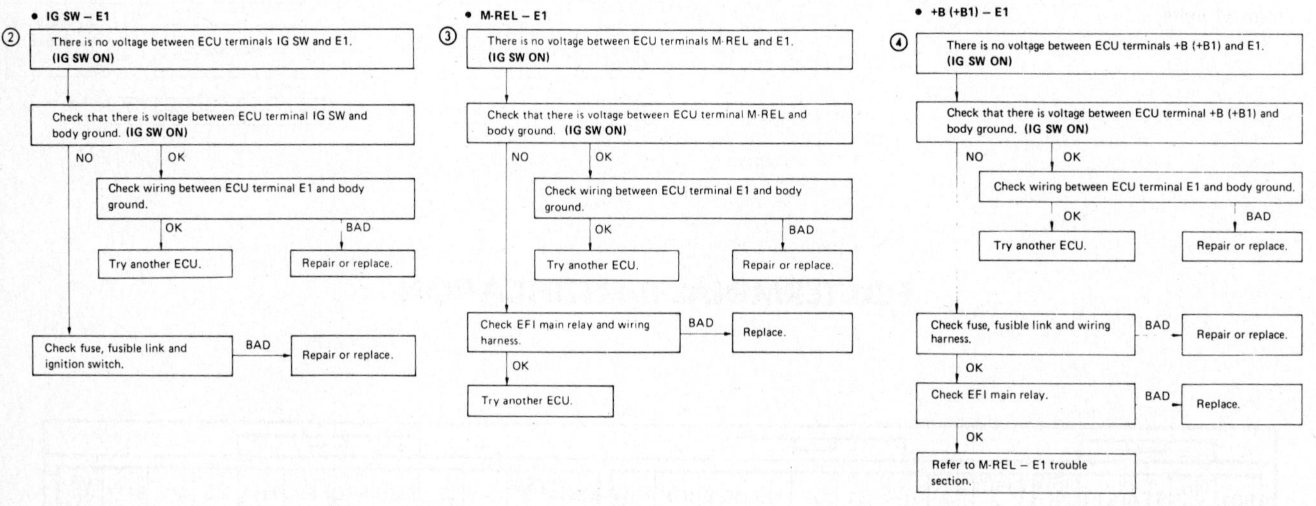
• IG SW – E1
② There is no voltage between ECU terminals IG SW and E1. (IG SW ON)
Check that there is voltage between ECU terminal IG SW and body ground. (IG SW ON)
NO
OK
Check wiring between ECU terminal E1 and body ground.
OK
BAD
Try another ECU.
Repair or replace.
Check fuse, fusible link and ignition switch.
BAD
Repair or replace.
• M-REL – E1
③ There is no voltage between ECU terminals M-REL and E1. (IG SW ON)
Check that there is voltage between ECU terminal M-REL and body ground. (IG SW ON)
NO
OK
Check wiring between ECU terminal E1 and body ground.
OK
BAD
Try another ECU.
Repair or replace.
Check EFI main relay and wiring harness.
BAD
Replace.
OK
Try another ECU.
• +B (+B1) – E1
④ There is no voltage between ECU terminals +B (+B1) and E1. (IG SW ON)
Check that there is voltage between ECU terminal +B (+B1) and body ground. (IG SW ON)
NO
OK
Check wiring between ECU terminal E1 and body ground.
OK
BAD
Try another ECU.
Repair or replace.
Check fuse, fusible link and wiring harness.
BAD
Repair or replace.
OK
Check EFI main relay.
BAD
Replace.
OK
Refer to M-REL – E1 trouble section.

## SUPRA CODE 12, 13
### RPM SIGNAL

Code 12 is caused by loss of "NE" signal or "G" signal from distributor to ECU for at least 2 seconds after starter signal is received at ECU. Ensure starter signal exists at ECU. See TEST NO. 8 OR CODE 43. Code 13 is caused by loss of "NE" signal from distributor to ECU when engine RPM exceeds 1000 RPM.

**NOTE – Diagnostic chart not available from manufacturer.**

91G17794 91H17795 91I17796 91A17798 91J17797

# 1991 ENGINE PERFORMANCE
# Self-Diagnostics (Cont.)

## SUPRA TEST NO. 2 OR CODE 14
### IGNITION SIGNAL

| Terminals | Trouble | Condition | STD Voltage |
|---|---|---|---|
| IGT – E1 | No voltage | Idling | 0.7 – 1.0 V |

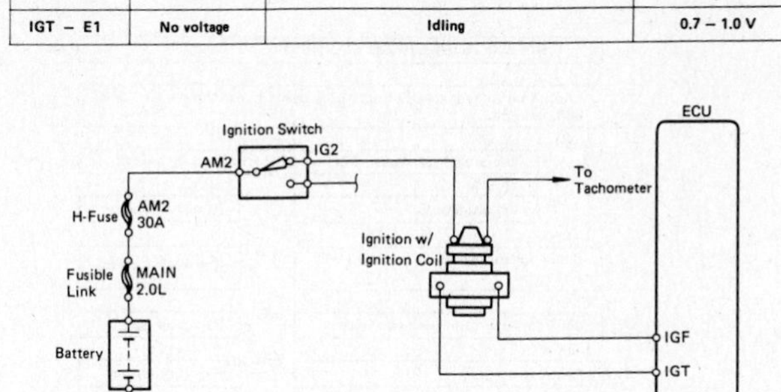
Ignition Switch
AM2
IG2
AM2
30A
H-Fuse
To
Tachometer
ECU
Ignition w/
Ignition Coil
Fusible
Link
MAIN
2.0L
Battery
IGF
IGT
E1

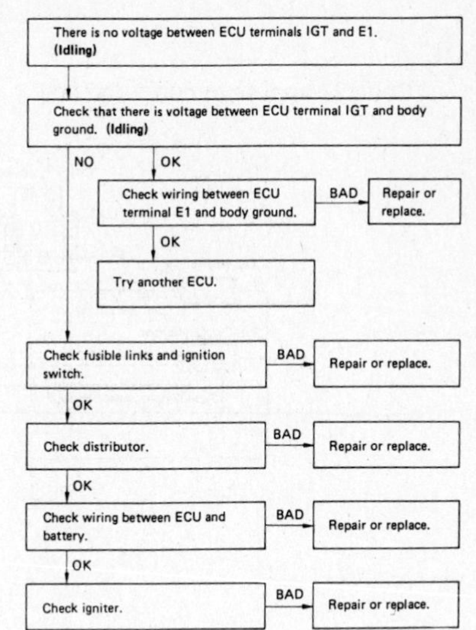
There is no voltage between ECU terminals IGT and E1. (Idling)
Check that there is voltage between ECU terminal IGT and body ground. (Idling)
NO
OK
Check wiring between ECU terminal E1 and body ground.
BAD
Repair or replace.
OK
Try another ECU.
Check fusible links and ignition switch.
BAD
Repair or replace.
OK
Check distributor.
BAD
Repair or replace.
OK
Check wiring between ECU and battery.
BAD
Repair or replace.
OK
Check igniter.
BAD
Repair or replace.

NOTE: To check ignition system components, see SYSTEM & COMPONENT TESTING article.

**NON-TURBO**

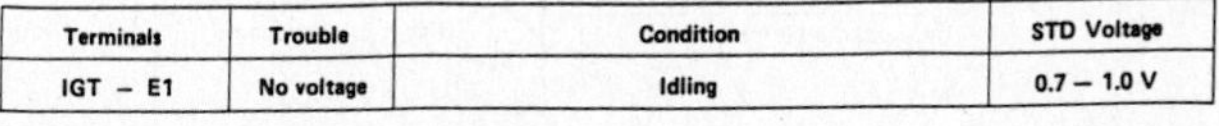

| Terminals | Trouble | Condition | STD Voltage |
|---|---|---|---|
| IGT – E1 | No voltage | Idling | 0.7 – 1.0 V |

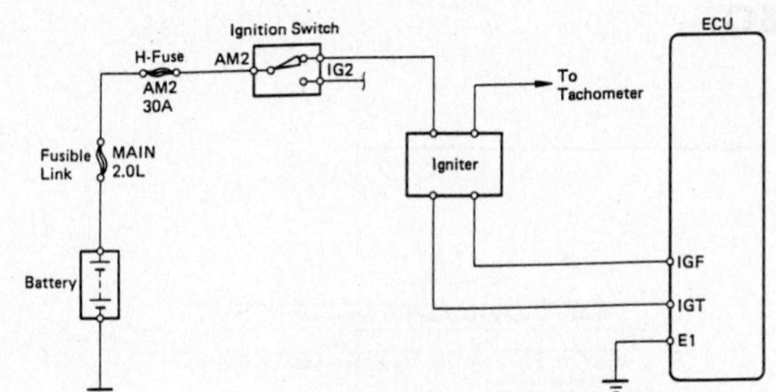
Ignition Switch
H-Fuse
AM2
AM2
30A
IG2
To
Tachometer
ECU
Fusible
Link
MAIN
2.0L
Igniter
Battery
IGF
IGT
E1

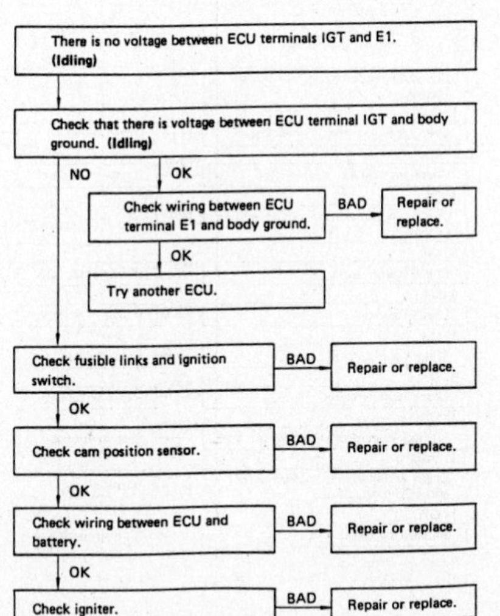
There is no voltage between ECU terminals IGT and E1. (Idling)
Check that there is voltage between ECU terminal IGT and body ground. (Idling)
NO
OK
Check wiring between ECU terminal E1 and body ground.
BAD
Repair or replace.
OK
Try another ECU.
Check fusible links and ignition switch.
BAD
Repair or replace.
OK
Check cam position sensor.
BAD
Repair or replace.
OK
Check wiring between ECU and battery.
BAD
Repair or replace.
OK
Check igniter.
BAD
Repair or replace.

| Terminals | Trouble | Condition | STD Voltage |
|---|---|---|---|
| IGDA IGDB – E1 | No voltage | Idling | 1 – 3 V |

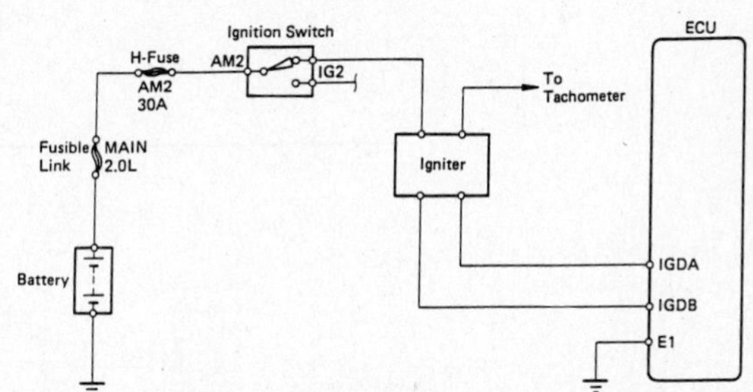
Ignition Switch
H-Fuse
AM2
AM2
30A
IG2
To
Tachometer
ECU
Fusible
Link
MAIN
2.0L
Igniter
Battery
IGDA
IGDB
E1

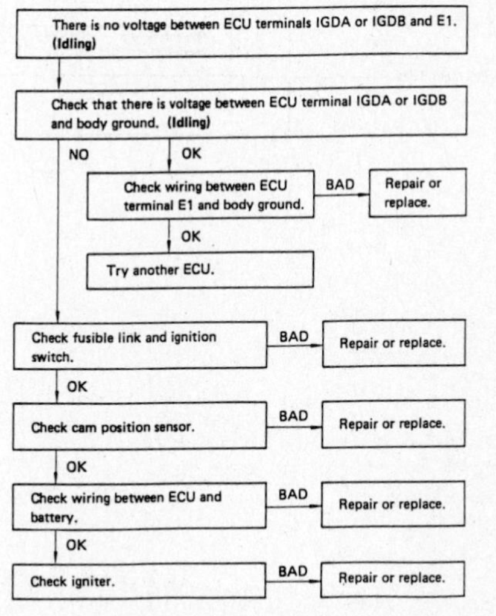
There is no voltage between ECU terminals IGDA or IGDB and E1. (Idling)
Check that there is voltage between ECU terminal IGDA or IGDB and body ground. (Idling)
NO
OK
Check wiring between ECU terminal E1 and body ground.
BAD
Repair or replace.
OK
Try another ECU.
Check fusible link and ignition switch.
BAD
Repair or replace.
OK
Check cam position sensor.
BAD
Repair or replace.
OK
Check wiring between ECU and battery.
BAD
Repair or replace.
OK
Check igniter.
BAD
Repair or replace.

NOTE: To check ignition system components, see SYSTEM & COMPONENT TESTING article.

**TURBO**

91B17799 91C17543 91E18105 91F18106 91G18107 91H18108

Courtesy of Toyota Motor Sales, U.S.A., Inc.

## SUPRA TEST NO. 3 OR CODE 21, 27
### OXYGEN SENSOR SIGNAL

Code 27 applies to non-turbo only.

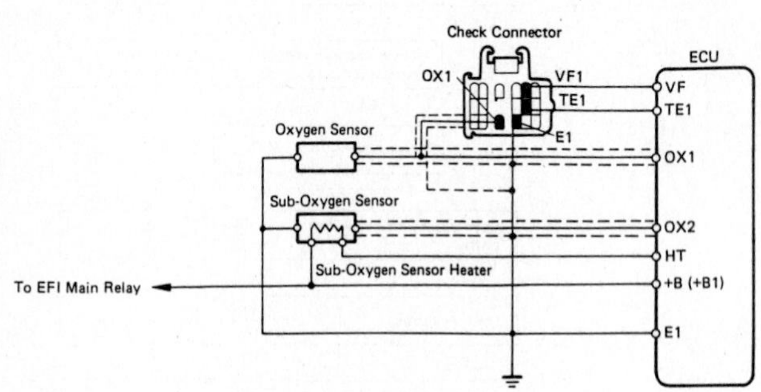
Check Connector
ECU
OX1
VF1
TE1
E1
VF
TE1
Oxygen Sensor
OX1
Sub-Oxygen Sensor
OX2
HT
Sub-Oxygen Sensor Heater
To EFI Main Relay
+B (+B1)
E1

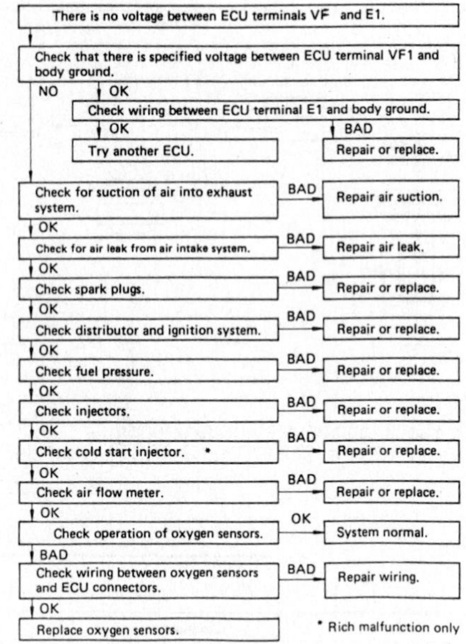
There is no voltage between ECU terminals VF and E1.
Check that there is specified voltage between ECU terminal VF1 and body ground.
NO
OK
Check wiring between ECU terminal E1 and body ground.
OK
BAD
Try another ECU.
Repair or replace.
Check for suction of air into exhaust system.
BAD
Repair air suction.
OK
Check for air leak from air intake system.
BAD
Repair air leak.
OK
Check spark plugs.
BAD
Repair or replace.
OK
Check distributor and ignition system.
BAD
Repair or replace.
OK
Check fuel pressure.
BAD
Repair or replace.
OK
Check injectors.
BAD
Repair or replace.
OK
Check cold start injector. •
BAD
Repair or replace.
OK
Check air flow meter.
BAD
Repair or replace.
OK
Check operation of oxygen sensors.
OK
System normal.
BAD
Check wiring between oxygen sensors and ECU connectors.
BAD
Repair wiring.
OK
Replace oxygen sensors.
• Rich malfunction only

**NON-TURBO**

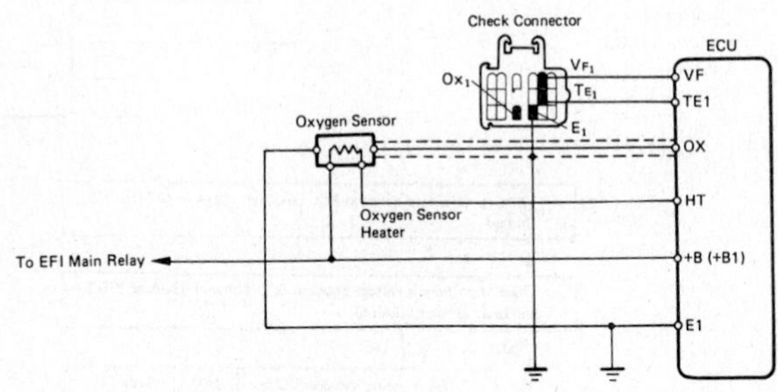
Check Connector
ECU
Ox1
VF1
TE1
E1
VF
TE1
Oxygen Sensor
OX
HT
Oxygen Sensor Heater
To EFI Main Relay
+B (+B1)
E1

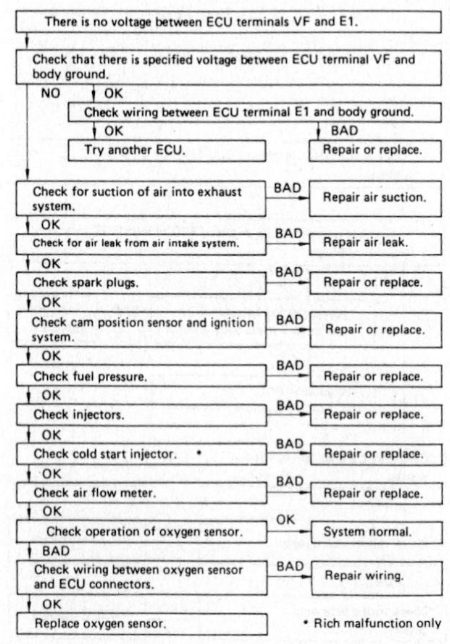
There is no voltage between ECU terminals VF and E1.
Check that there is specified voltage between ECU terminal VF and body ground.
NO
OK
Check wiring between ECU terminal E1 and body ground.
OK
BAD
Try another ECU.
Repair or replace.
Check for suction of air into exhaust system.
BAD
Repair air suction.
OK
Check for air leak from air intake system.
BAD
Repair air leak.
OK
Check spark plugs.
BAD
Repair or replace.
OK
Check cam position sensor and ignition system.
BAD
Repair or replace.
OK
Check fuel pressure.
BAD
Repair or replace.
OK
Check injectors.
BAD
Repair or replace.
OK
Check cold start injector. •
BAD
Repair or replace.
OK
Check air flow meter.
BAD
Repair or replace.
OK
Check operation of oxygen sensor.
OK
System normal.
BAD
Check wiring between oxygen sensor and ECU connectors.
BAD
Repair wiring.
OK
Replace oxygen sensor.
• Rich malfunction only

**TURBO**

91I18109 91G17547 91B18110 91C18111

# 1991 ENGINE PERFORMANCE
# Self-Diagnostics (Cont.)

## SUPRA TEST NO. 4 OR CODE 22
### COOLANT TEMPERATURE SENSOR SIGNAL

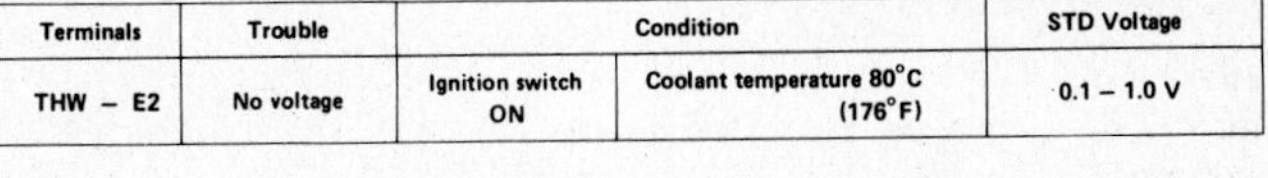

| Terminals | Trouble | Condition | | STD Voltage |
|---|---|---|---|---|
| THW – E2 | No voltage | Ignition switch ON | Coolant temperature 80°C (176°F) | 0.1 – 1.0 V |

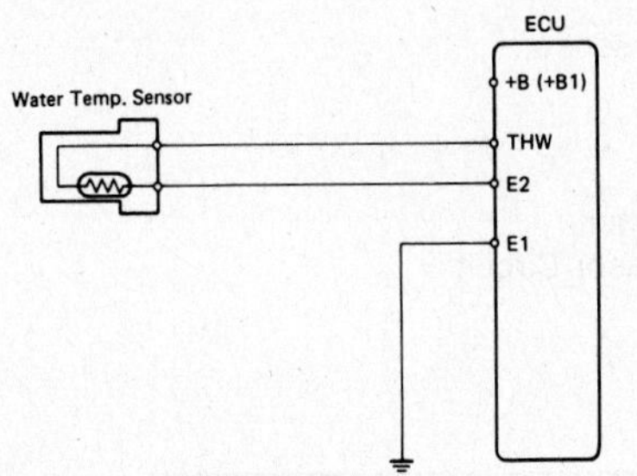

ECU
Water Temp. Sensor
+B (+B1)
THW
E2
E1

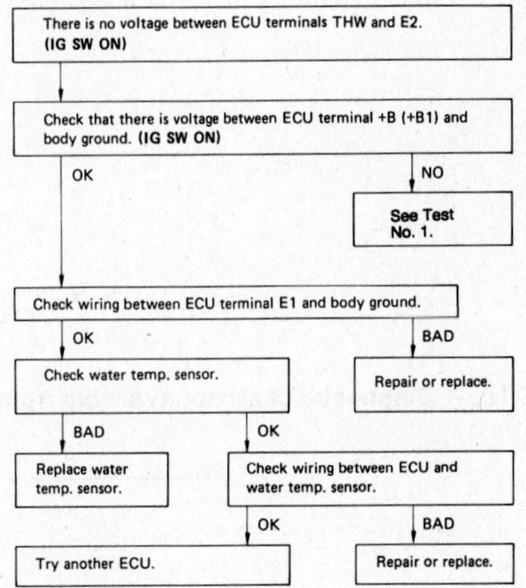

There is no voltage between ECU terminals THW and E2. (IG SW ON)
Check that there is voltage between ECU terminal +B (+B1) and body ground. (IG SW ON)
OK
NO
See Test No. 1.
Check wiring between ECU terminal E1 and body ground.
OK
BAD
Check water temp. sensor.
Repair or replace.
BAD
OK
Replace water temp. sensor.
Check wiring between ECU and water temp. sensor.
OK
BAD
Try another ECU.
Repair or replace.

NOTE: Water temperature sensor is also referred to as coolant temperature sensor.

## SUPRA TEST NO. 5 OR CODE 24
### INTAKE AIR TEMPERATURE SENSOR SIGNAL

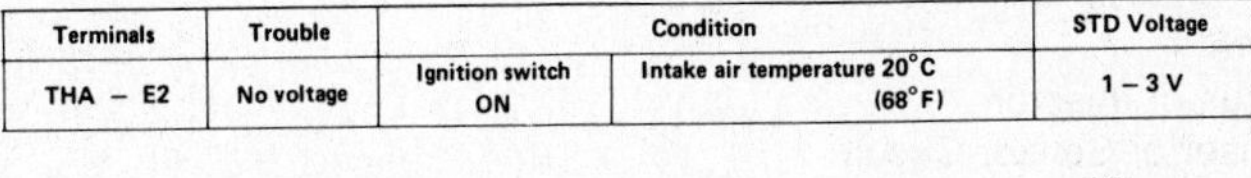

| Terminals | Trouble | Condition | | STD Voltage |
|---|---|---|---|---|
| THA – E2 | No voltage | Ignition switch ON | Intake air temperature 20°C (68°F) | 1 – 3 V |

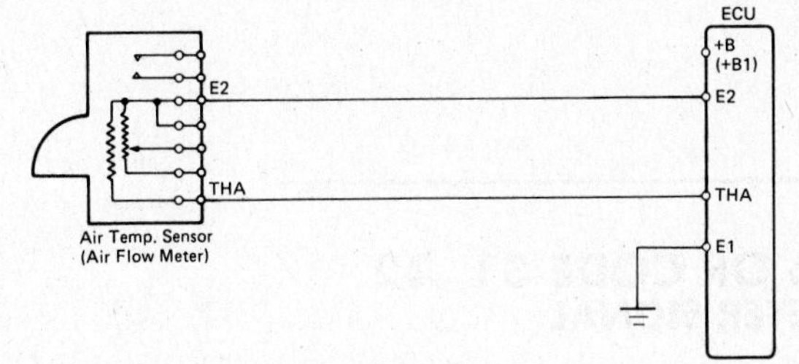

ECU
+B (+B1)
E2
THA
E1
Air Temp. Sensor (Air Flow Meter)

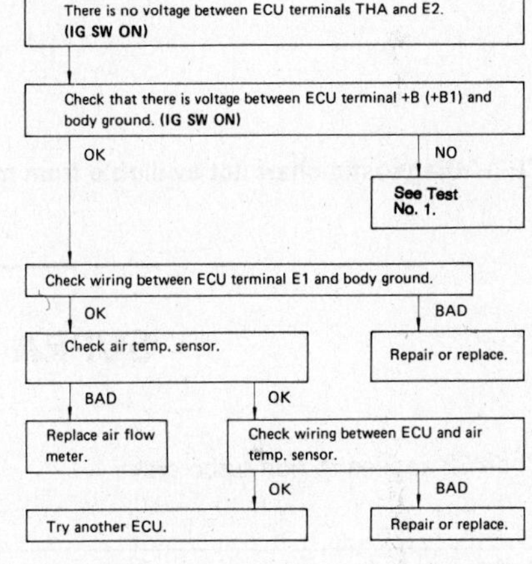

There is no voltage between ECU terminals THA and E2. (IG SW ON)
Check that there is voltage between ECU terminal +B (+B1) and body ground. (IG SW ON)
OK
NO
See Test No. 1.
Check wiring between ECU terminal E1 and body ground.
OK
BAD
Check air temp. sensor.
Repair or replace.
BAD
OK
Replace air flow meter.
Check wiring between ECU and air temp. sensor.
OK
BAD
Try another ECU.
Repair or replace.

**NON-TURBO**

| Terminals | Trouble | Condition | | STD Voltage |
|---|---|---|---|---|
| THA – E2 | No voltage | Ignition switch ON | Intake air temperature 20°C (68°F) | 1 – 3 V |

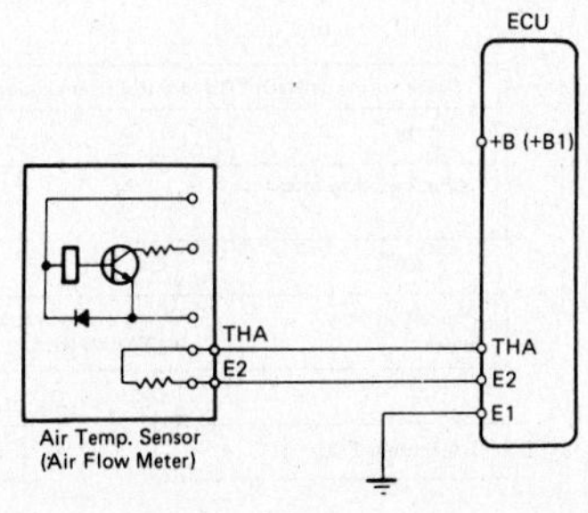

ECU
+B (+B1)
THA
E2
E1
Air Temp. Sensor (Air Flow Meter)

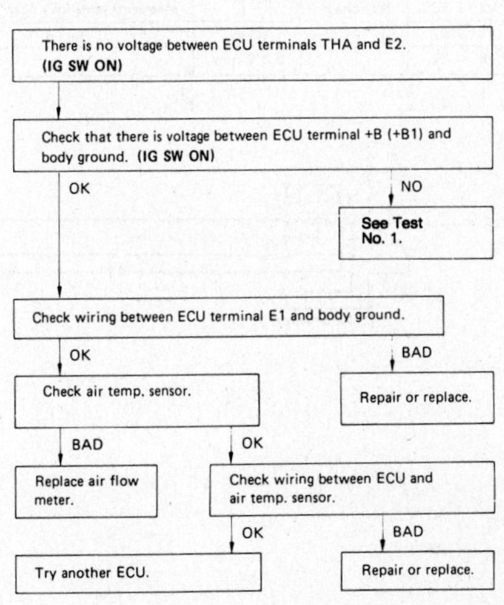

There is no voltage between ECU terminals THA and E2. (IG SW ON)
Check that there is voltage between ECU terminal +B (+B1) and body ground. (IG SW ON)
OK
NO
See Test No. 1.
Check wiring between ECU terminal E1 and body ground.
OK
BAD
Check air temp. sensor.
Repair or replace.
BAD
OK
Replace air flow meter.
Check wiring between ECU and air temp. sensor.
OK
BAD
Try another ECU.
Repair or replace.

**TURBO**

91J17680 91F17801 91B17682 91G17802 91D18112 91G17802

Courtesy of Toyota Motor Sales, U.S.A., Inc.

# 1991 ENGINE PERFORMANCE
# Self-Diagnostics (Cont.)

## SUPRA CODE 25
### LEAN AIR/FUEL MIXTURE

**Probable Causes**
- Airflow Meter
- Air Intake System
- Coolant Temperature Sensor
- ECU
- Fuel Pressure
- Ignition System
- Injector Circuit or Injector
- Oxygen Sensor or Sensor Circuit

**NOTE – Diagnostic chart not available from manufacturer.**

## SUPRA CODE 26
### RICH AIR/FUEL MIXTURE

**Probable Causes**
- Airflow Meter
- Cold Start Injector
- Coolant Temperature Sensor
- ECU
- Fuel Pressure
- Injector Circuit or Injector
- Oxygen Sensor or Sensor Circuit

**NOTE – Diagnostic chart not available from manufacturer.**

## SUPRA TEST NO. 6 OR CODE 31, 32
### AIRFLOW METER SIGNAL

Code 32 applies to non-turbo only.

| Terminals | Trouble | Condition | | STD Voltage |
|---|---|---|---|---|
| VC – E2 | No voltage | Ignition SW ON | – | 4 – 6 V |
| VS – E2 | | | Measuring plate fully closed | 3.7 – 4.3 V |
| VS – E2 | | | Measuring plate fully open | 0.2 – 0.5 V |
| VS – E2 | | Idling | – | 2.3 – 2.8 V |
| VS – E2 | | 3,000 rpm | – | 1.0 – 2.0 V |

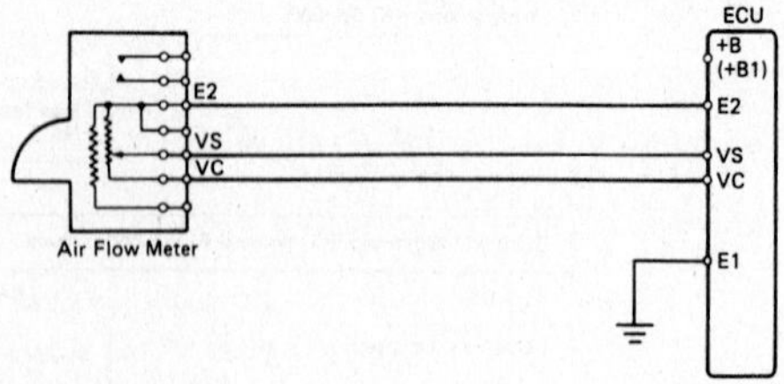
ECU
+B
(+B1)
E2
VS
VC
E1
E2
VS
VC
Air Flow Meter

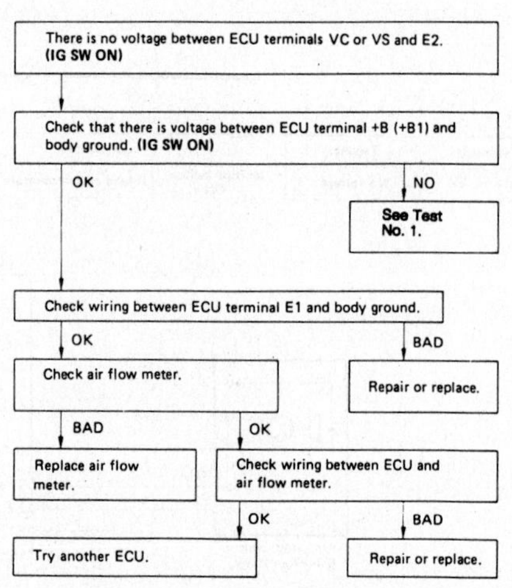
There is no voltage between ECU terminals VC or VS and E2. (IG SW ON)
Check that there is voltage between ECU terminal +B (+B1) and body ground. (IG SW ON)
OK
NO
See Test No. 1.
Check wiring between ECU terminal E1 and body ground.
OK
BAD
Check air flow meter.
Repair or replace.
BAD
OK
Replace air flow meter.
Check wiring between ECU and air flow meter.
OK
BAD
Try another ECU.
Repair or replace.

NON-TURBO

Continued on Next Page

91D17684 91H17803

## SUPRA TEST NO. 6 OR CODE 31, 32
### AIRFLOW METER SIGNAL (Cont.)

Code 32 applies to non-turbo only.

| Terminals | Trouble | Condition | STD Voltage |
|---|---|---|---|
| KS – Body ground | No voltage | Ignition SW ON | 4 – 6 V |
| | | Cranking or running | 2 – 4 V |
| VC – Body ground | | Ignition SW ON | 4 – 6 V |

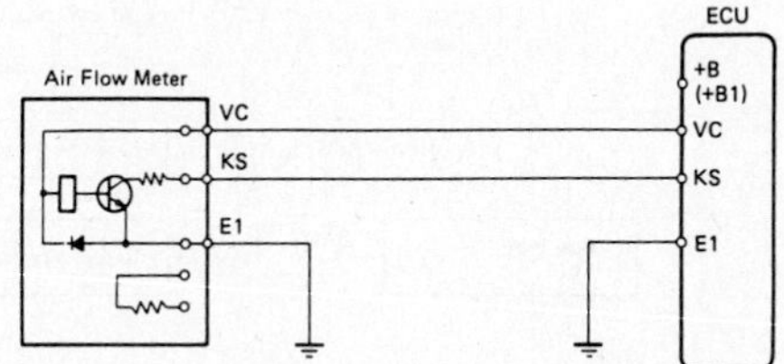


• KS – Body ground

① There is no voltage between ECU terminal KS and body ground. (IG SW ON)

Check that there is voltage between ECU terminal +B (+B1) and body ground. (IG SW ON)
- NO: See Test No. 1.
- OK: Check wiring between ECU terminal E1 and body ground.
  - BAD: Repair or replace.
  - OK: Check wiring between ECU and air flow meter.
    - BAD: Repair or replace.
    - OK: Try another ECU.

• VC – Body ground

② There is no voltage between ECU terminal VC and body ground. (IG SW ON)

Check that there is voltage between ECU terminal +B (+B1) and body ground. (IG SW ON)
- NO: See Test No. 1.
- OK: Check wiring between ECU terminal E1 and body ground.
  - BAD: Repair or replace.
  - OK: Check wiring between ECU and air flow meter.
    - BAD: Repair or replace.
    - OK: Try another ECU.

**TURBO**

---

## SUPRA CODE 34
### TURBOCHARGER PRESSURE

Code 34 applies to turbo only.

**Probable Causes**
- Pressure Sensor or Sensor Circuit
- Turbocharger
- ECU

**NOTE – Diagnostic chart not available from manufacturer.**

---

## SUPRA CODE 35
### HIGH ALTITUDE COMPENSATOR (HAC) SENSOR SIGNAL

Code 35 applies to turbo only.

**Probable Causes**
- ECU

**NOTE – Diagnostic chart not available from manufacturer.**

91E18113 91F18114 91G18115

# 1991 ENGINE PERFORMANCE
# Self-Diagnostics (Cont.)

## SUPRA TEST NO. 7 OR CODE 41
### THROTTLE POSITION SENSOR SIGNAL

| Terminals | Trouble | Condition | | STD voltage |
|---|---|---|---|---|
| IDL – E2 | No voltage | Ignition switch ON | Throttle valve open | 10 – 14 V |
| VC – E2 | | | – | 4 – 6 V |
| VTA – E2 | | | Throttle valve fully closed | 0.1 – 1.0 V |
| | | | Throttle valve fully open | 4 – 5 V |

**NON-TURBO**

| Terminals | Trouble | Condition | | STD voltage |
|---|---|---|---|---|
| IDL – E2 | No voltage | Ignition switch ON | Throttle valve open | 4 – 6 V |
| VC – E2 | | | – | 4 – 6 V |
| | | | Throttle valve fully closed | 0.1 – 1.0 V |
| VTA – E2 | | | Throttle valve fully open | 3.2 – 4.2 V |

**TURBO**

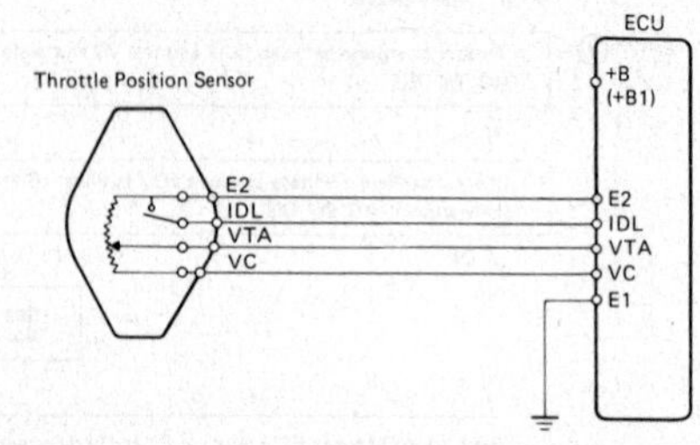
ECU
Throttle Position Sensor
+B
(+B1)
E2
IDL
VTA
VC
E2
IDL
VTA
VC
E1

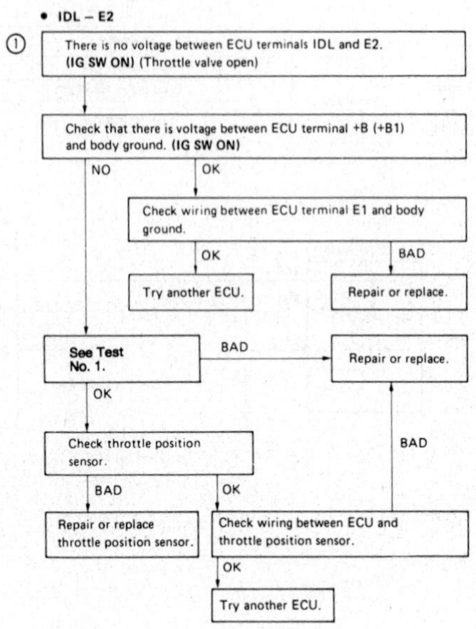
• IDL – E2
①
There is no voltage between ECU terminals IDL and E2. (IG SW ON) (Throttle valve open)
Check that there is voltage between ECU terminal +B (+B1) and body ground. (IG SW ON)
NO
OK
Check wiring between ECU terminal E1 and body ground.
OK
BAD
Try another ECU.
Repair or replace.
See Test No. 1.
BAD
Repair or replace.
OK
Check throttle position sensor.
BAD
BAD
OK
Repair or replace throttle position sensor.
Check wiring between ECU and throttle position sensor.
OK
Try another ECU.

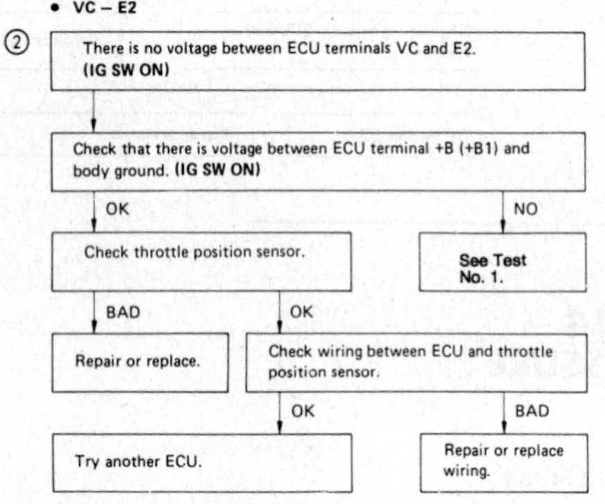
• VC – E2
②
There is no voltage between ECU terminals VC and E2. (IG SW ON)
Check that there is voltage between ECU terminal +B (+B1) and body ground. (IG SW ON)
OK
NO
Check throttle position sensor.
See Test No. 1.
BAD
OK
Repair or replace.
Check wiring between ECU and throttle position sensor.
OK
BAD
Try another ECU.
Repair or replace wiring.

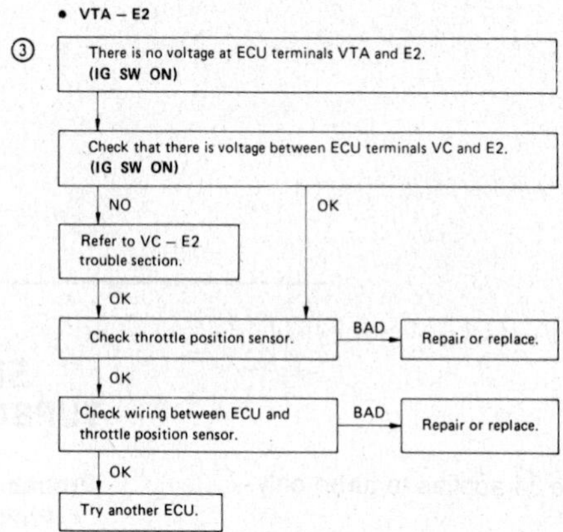
• VTA – E2
③
There is no voltage at ECU terminals VTA and E2. (IG SW ON)
Check that there is voltage between ECU terminals VC and E2. (IG SW ON)
NO
OK
Refer to VC – E2 trouble section.
OK
Check throttle position sensor.
BAD
Repair or replace.
OK
Check wiring between ECU and throttle position sensor.
BAD
Repair or replace.
OK
Try another ECU.

## SUPRA CODE 42
### VEHICLE SPEED SENSOR SIGNAL

**Probable Causes**

- Vehicle Speed Sensor or Sensor Circuit
- ECU

**NOTE – Diagnostic chart not available from manufacturer.**

91H17688 91I17804 91J17805 91A17806

## SUPRA TEST NO. 8 OR CODE 43
### STARTER SIGNAL

| Terminals | Trouble | Condition | STD Voltage |
|---|---|---|---|
| STA – E1 | No voltage | Cranking | 6 – 14 V |

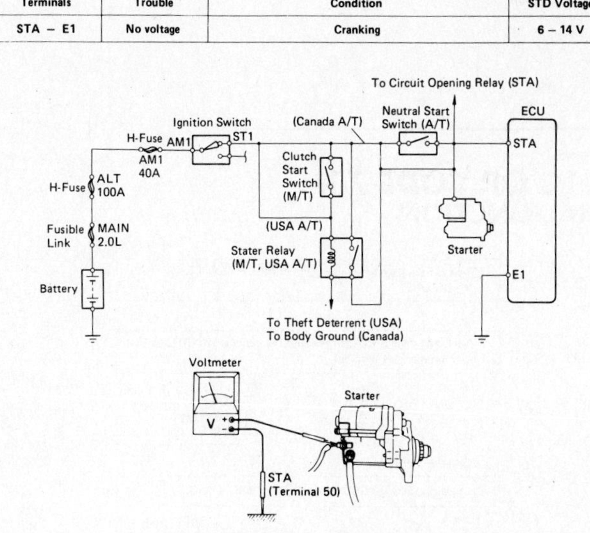

To Circuit Opening Relay (STA)
Neutral Start Switch (A/T)
ECU
Ignition Switch
(Canada A/T)
H-Fuse
AM1
ST1
STA
AM1 40A
Clutch Start Switch (M/T)
H-Fuse
ALT 100A
Fusible Link
MAIN 2.0L
(USA A/T)
Stater Relay (M/T, USA A/T)
Starter
E1
Battery
To Theft Deterrent (USA)
To Body Ground (Canada)
Voltmeter
Starter
V
STA (Terminal 50)

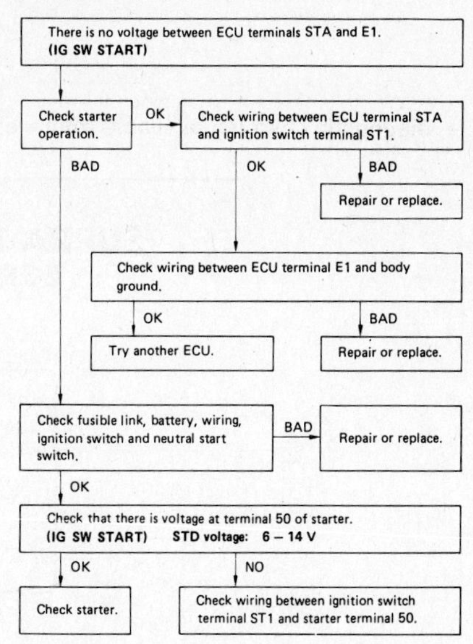

There is no voltage between ECU terminals STA and E1. (IG SW START)
Check starter operation.
OK
Check wiring between ECU terminal STA and ignition switch terminal ST1.
BAD
OK
BAD
Repair or replace.
Check wiring between ECU terminal E1 and body ground.
OK
BAD
Try another ECU.
Repair or replace.
Check fusible link, battery, wiring, ignition switch and neutral start switch.
BAD
Repair or replace.
OK
Check that there is voltage at terminal 50 of starter. (IG SW START) STD voltage: 6 – 14 V
OK
NO
Check starter.
Check wiring between ignition switch terminal ST1 and starter terminal 50.

## SUPRA TEST NO. 9 OR CODE 51
### SWITCH SIGNAL

**Probable Causes**

- A/C Switch or Switch Circuit
- Accelerator Pedal or Cable
- Neutral/Start Switch or Switch Circuit
- Throttle Position Sensor IDL Circuit
- ECU

To check A/C switch signal, use the following procedure.

| Terminals | Trouble | Condition | STD Voltage |
|---|---|---|---|
| A/C – E1 | No voltage | Air conditioning ON | 10 – 14 V |

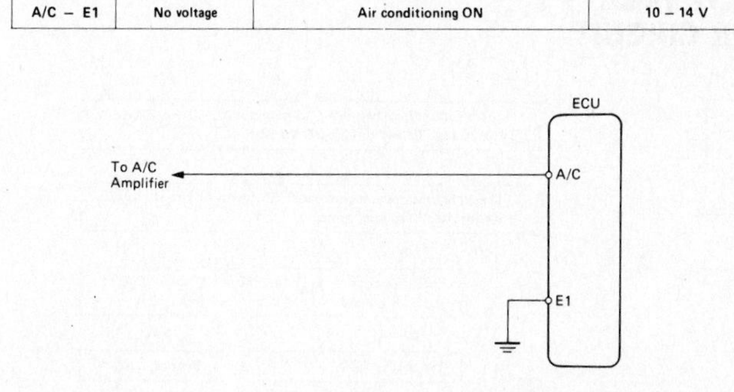

ECU
To A/C Amplifier
A/C
E1

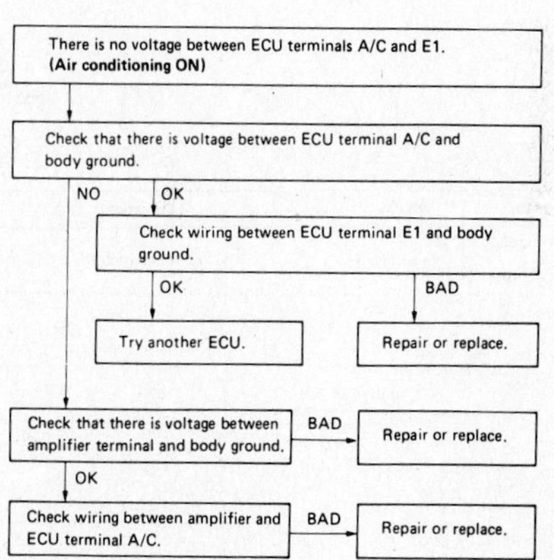

There is no voltage between ECU terminals A/C and E1. (Air conditioning ON)
Check that there is voltage between ECU terminal A/C and body ground.
NO
OK
Check wiring between ECU terminal E1 and body ground.
OK
BAD
Try another ECU.
Repair or replace.
Check that there is voltage between amplifier terminal and body ground.
BAD
Repair or replace.
OK
Check wiring between amplifier and ECU terminal A/C.
BAD
Repair or replace.

## SUPRA CODE 52
### KNOCK SENSOR SIGNAL

**Probable Causes**

- ECU
- Knock Sensor or Sensor Circuit

**NOTE – Diagnostic chart not available from manufacturer.**

# 1991 ENGINE PERFORMANCE
# Self-Diagnostics (Cont.)

## SUPRA CODE 53
### KNOCK SENSOR CONTROL (ECU)

**Probable Causes**

- ECU

**NOTE - Diagnostic chart not available from manufacturer.**

---

## SUPRA TEST NO. 10 OR CODE 71
### EGR SYSTEM MALFUNCTION

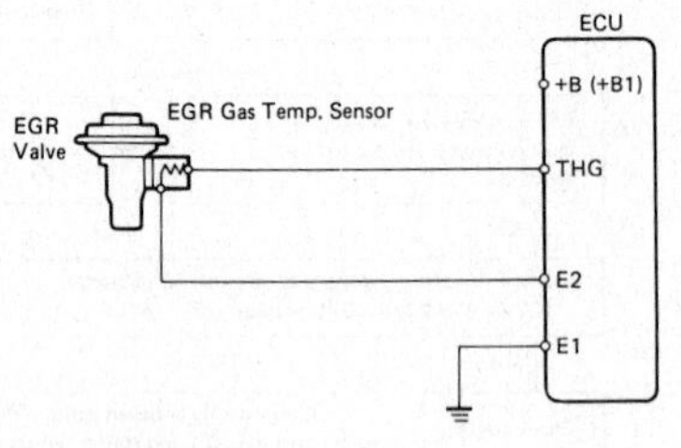
ECU
+B (+B1)
EGR Valve
EGR Gas Temp. Sensor
THG
E2
E1

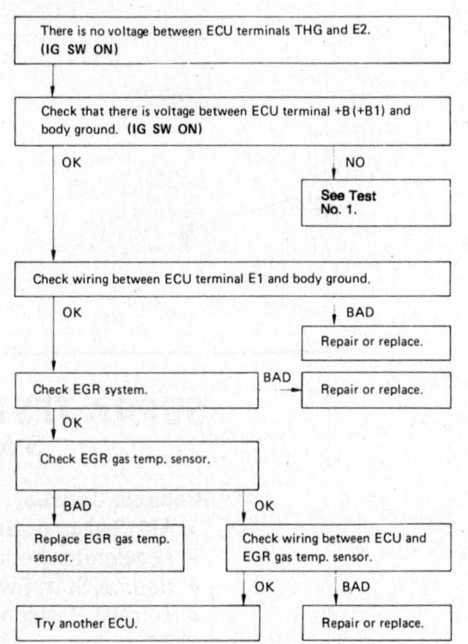
There is no voltage between ECU terminals THG and E2. (IG SW ON)
Check that there is voltage between ECU terminal +B (+B1) and body ground. (IG SW ON)
OK
NO
See Test No. 1.
Check wiring between ECU terminal E1 and body ground.
OK
BAD
Repair or replace.
Check EGR system.
BAD
Repair or replace.
OK
Check EGR gas temp. sensor.
BAD
OK
Replace EGR gas temp. sensor.
Check wiring between ECU and EGR gas temp. sensor.
OK
BAD
Try another ECU.
Repair or replace.

---

## SUPRA TEST NO. 11
### INJECTOR CIRCUIT

| Terminals | Trouble | Condition | STD Voltage |
|---|---|---|---|
| No. 10 E01<br>No. 20 –<br>No. 30 E02 | No voltage | Ignition switch ON | 10 – 14 V |

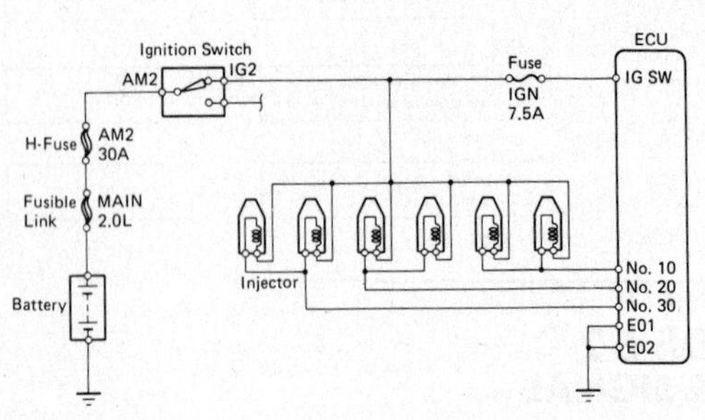
Ignition Switch
AM2
IG2
Fuse
IGN
7.5A
ECU
IG SW
H-Fuse
AM2
30A
Fusible Link
MAIN
2.0L
Battery
Injector
No. 10
No. 20
No. 30
E01
E02

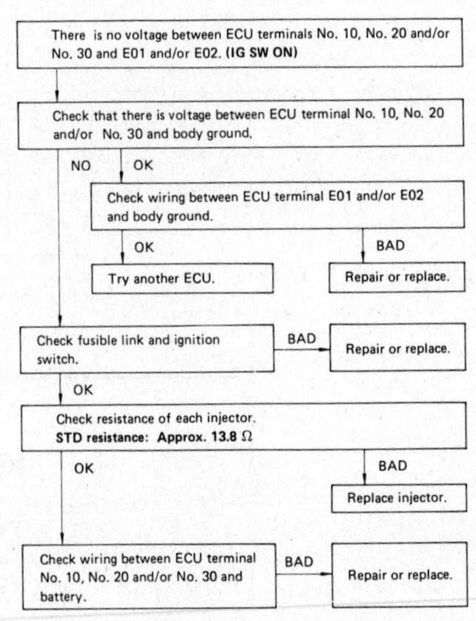
There is no voltage between ECU terminals No. 10, No. 20 and/or No. 30 and E01 and/or E02. (IG SW ON)
Check that there is voltage between ECU terminal No. 10, No. 20 and/or No. 30 and body ground.
NO
OK
Check wiring between ECU terminal E01 and/or E02 and body ground.
OK
BAD
Try another ECU.
Repair or replace.
Check fusible link and ignition switch.
BAD
Repair or replace.
OK
Check resistance of each injector.
STD resistance: Approx. 13.8 Ω
OK
BAD
Replace injector.
Check wiring between ECU terminal No. 10, No. 20 and/or No. 30 and battery.
BAD
Repair or replace.

**NON-TURBO**

**Continued On Next Page**

91H17787 91J17748 91J18118 91D17700

## SUPRA TEST NO. 11
### INJECTOR CIRCUIT (Cont.)

| Terminals | Trouble | Condition | STD Voltage |
|---|---|---|---|
| No. 10<br>No. 20 – E01<br>No. 30 E02 | No voltage | Ignition switch ON | 10 – 14 V |

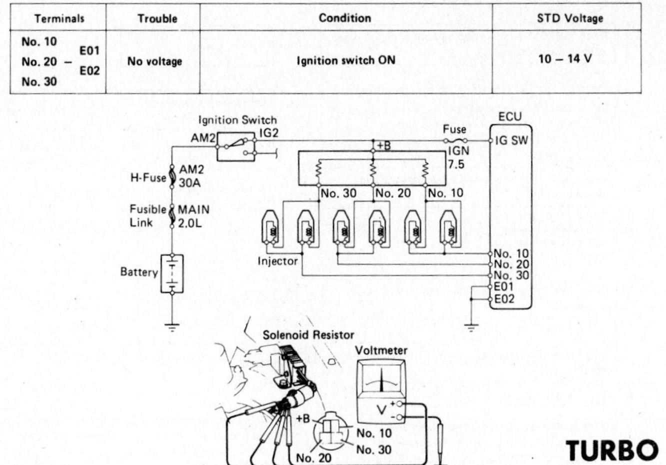

Ignition Switch
AM2
IG2
Fuse
IGN
7.5
+B
ECU
IG SW
H-Fuse
AM2
30A
Fusible Link
MAIN
2.0L
No. 30
No. 20
No. 10
Battery
Injector
No. 10
No. 20
No. 30
E01
E02
Solenoid Resistor
Voltmeter
V
+B
No. 10
No. 30
No. 20
TURBO

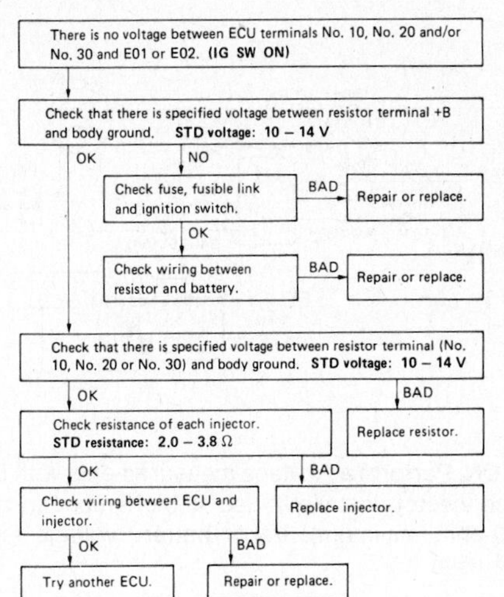

There is no voltage between ECU terminals No. 10, No. 20 and/or No. 30 and E01 or E02. (IG SW ON)
Check that there is specified voltage between resistor terminal +B and body ground. STD voltage: 10 – 14 V
OK
NO
Check fuse, fusible link and ignition switch.
BAD
Repair or replace.
OK
Check wiring between resistor and battery.
BAD
Repair or replace.
Check that there is specified voltage between resistor terminal (No. 10, No. 20 or No. 30) and body ground. STD voltage: 10 – 14 V
OK
BAD
Check resistance of each injector. STD resistance: 2.0 – 3.8 Ω
Replace resistor.
OK
BAD
Check wiring between ECU and injector.
Replace injector.
OK
BAD
Try another ECU.
Repair or replace.

## SUPRA TEST NO. 12
### IDLE SPEED CONTROL CIRCUIT

| Terminals | Trouble | Condition | STD Voltage |
|---|---|---|---|
| ISC1~ISC4–E1 | No voltage | Ignition switch ON | 9 – 14 V |

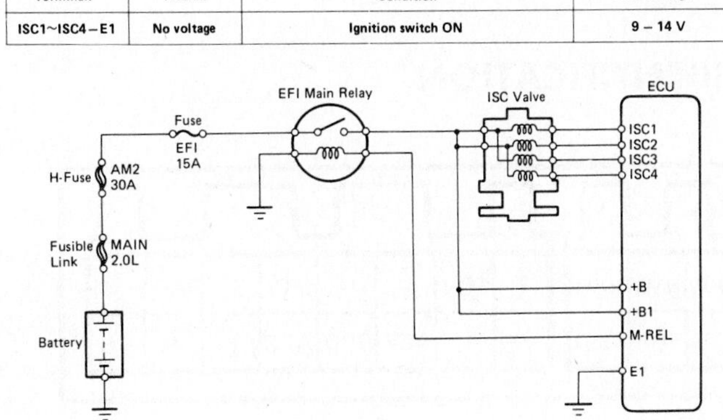

EFI Main Relay
ISC Valve
ECU
Fuse
EFI
15A
H-Fuse
AM2
30A
Fusible Link
MAIN
2.0L
Battery
ISC1
ISC2
ISC3
ISC4
+B
+B1
M-REL
E1

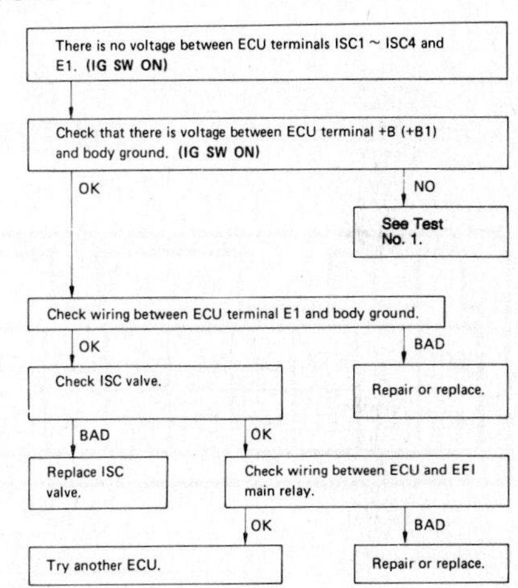

There is no voltage between ECU terminals ISC1 ~ ISC4 and E1. (IG SW ON)
Check that there is voltage between ECU terminal +B (+B1) and body ground. (IG SW ON)
OK
NO
See Test No. 1.
Check wiring between ECU terminal E1 and body ground.
OK
BAD
Check ISC valve.
Repair or replace.
BAD
OK
Replace ISC valve.
Check wiring between ECU and EFI main relay.
OK
BAD
Try another ECU.
Repair or replace.

## SUPRA TEST NO. 13
### CHECK ENGINE LIGHT CIRCUIT

| Terminals | Trouble | Condition | STD Voltage |
|---|---|---|---|
| W – E1 | No voltage | No trouble ("CHECK ENGINE" warning light off) and engine running | 8 – 14 V |

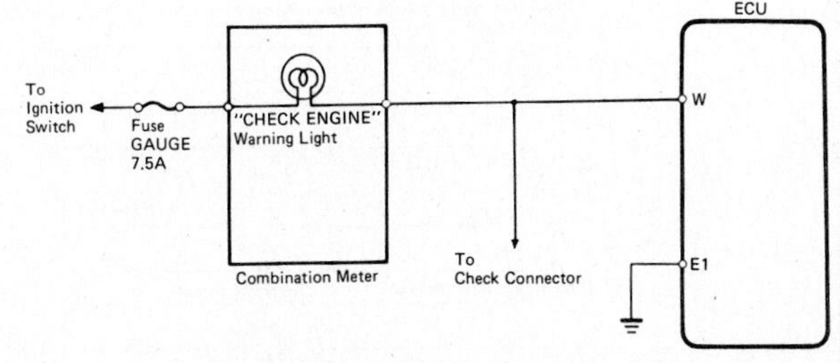

ECU
To Ignition Switch
Fuse
GAUGE
7.5A
"CHECK ENGINE" Warning Light
Combination Meter
To Check Connector
W
E1

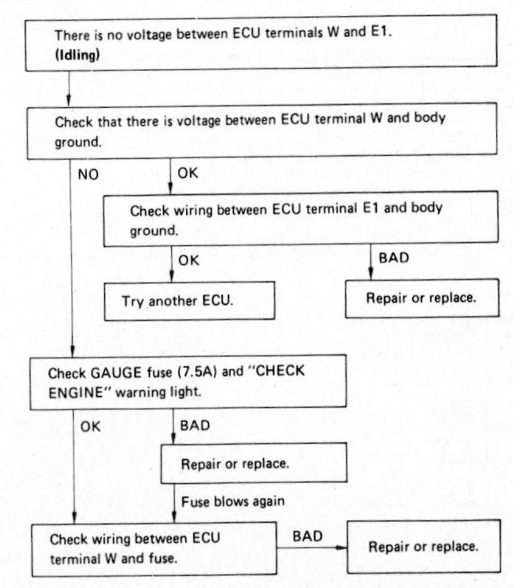

There is no voltage between ECU terminals W and E1. (Idling)
Check that there is voltage between ECU terminal W and body ground.
NO
OK
Check wiring between ECU terminal E1 and body ground.
OK
BAD
Try another ECU.
Repair or replace.
Check GAUGE fuse (7.5A) and "CHECK ENGINE" warning light.
OK
BAD
Repair or replace.
Fuse blows again
Check wiring between ECU terminal W and fuse.
BAD
Repair or replace.

91A18119 91D18146 91E18147 91G17810 91H17811 91C17790 91D17791

# 1991 ENGINE PERFORMANCE
## Self-Diagnostics (Cont.)

### TERCEL DIAGNOSTIC CIRCUIT CHECK

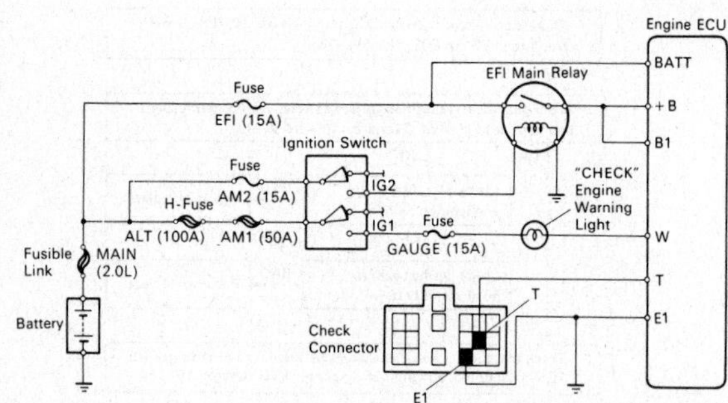
Engine ECU
BATT
EFI Main Relay
Fuse
EFI (15A)
+B
B1
Ignition Switch
Fuse
AM2 (15A)
IG2
H-Fuse
"CHECK" Engine Warning Light
IG1
Fuse
ALT (100A)
AM1 (50A)
GAUGE (15A)
W
Fusible Link
MAIN (2.0L)
T
Battery
Check Connector
E1
T
E1

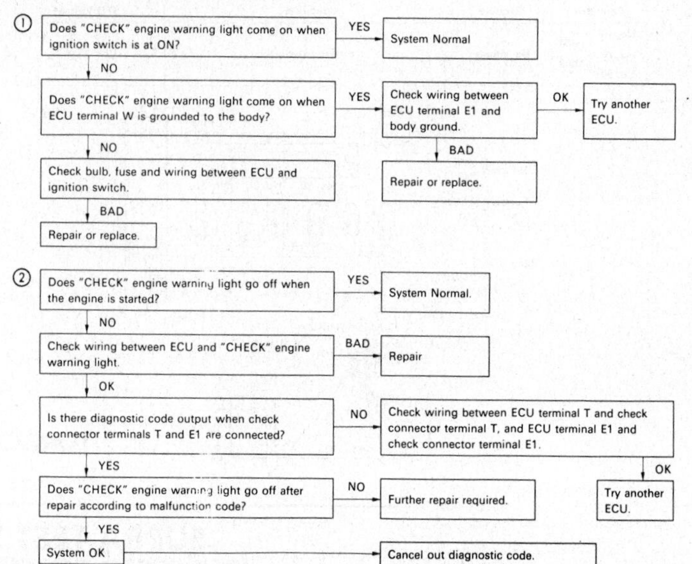
①
Does "CHECK" engine warning light come on when ignition switch is at ON?
YES
System Normal
NO
Does "CHECK" engine warning light come on when ECU terminal W is grounded to the body?
YES
Check wiring between ECU terminal E1 and body ground.
OK
Try another ECU.
BAD
NO
Check bulb, fuse and wiring between ECU and ignition switch.
Repair or replace.
BAD
Repair or replace.
②
Does "CHECK" engine warning light go off when the engine is started?
YES
System Normal.
NO
Check wiring between ECU and "CHECK" engine warning light.
BAD
Repair
OK
Is there diagnostic code output when check connector terminals T and E1 are connected?
NO
Check wiring between ECU terminal T and check connector terminal T, and ECU terminal E1 and check connector terminal E1.
OK
YES
Does "CHECK" engine warning light go off after repair according to malfunction code?
NO
Further repair required.
Try another ECU.
YES
System OK
Cancel out diagnostic code.

CAUTION: Perform all voltage measurements with ECU harness connector installed. Use a high-impedance DVOM (10,000-ohm minimum). Verify battery voltage is greater than 11 volts.

### ECU TERMINAL IDENTIFICATION

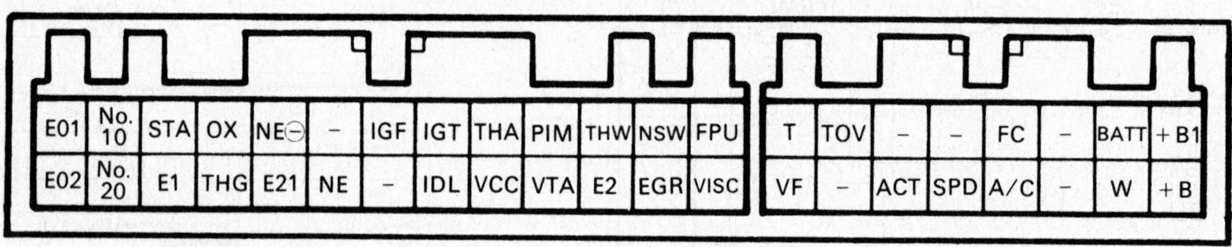
E01
No. 10
STA
OX
NE⊖
–
IGF
IGT
THA
PIM
THW
NSW
FPU
T
TOV
–
–
FC
–
BATT
+B1
E02
No. 20
E1
THG
E21
NE
–
IDL
VCC
VTA
E2
EGR
VISC
VF
–
ACT
SPD
A/C
–
W
+B

### TERCEL TEST NO. 1
### ECU POWER SOURCE

| Terminals | Trouble | Condition | STD voltage |
|---|---|---|---|
| BATT – E1 | No voltage | – | 10 – 14 V |

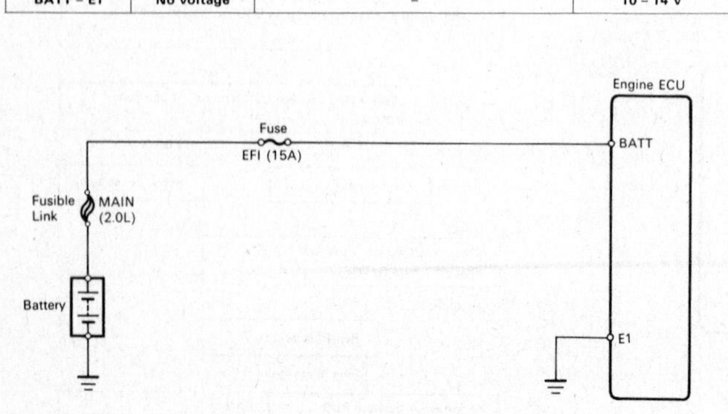
Engine ECU
Fuse
EFI (15A)
BATT
Fusible Link
MAIN (2.0L)
Battery
E1

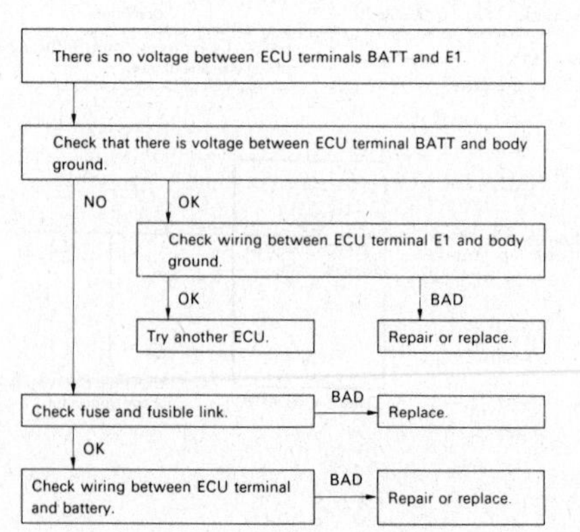
There is no voltage between ECU terminals BATT and E1
Check that there is voltage between ECU terminal BATT and body ground.
NO
OK
Check wiring between ECU terminal E1 and body ground.
OK
BAD
Try another ECU.
Repair or replace.
Check fuse and fusible link.
BAD
Replace.
OK
Check wiring between ECU terminal and battery.
BAD
Repair or replace.

## TERCEL TEST NO. 2
### ECU (+B) CIRCUIT

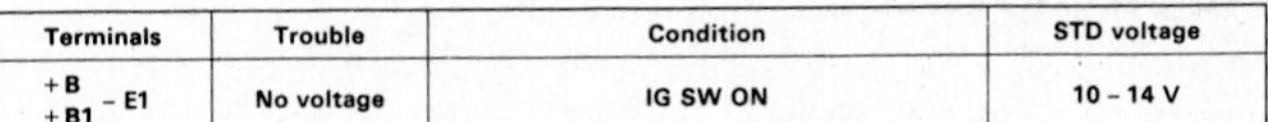

| Terminals | Trouble | Condition | STD voltage |
|---|---|---|---|
| +B<br>+B1 - E1 | No voltage | IG SW ON | 10 - 14 V |

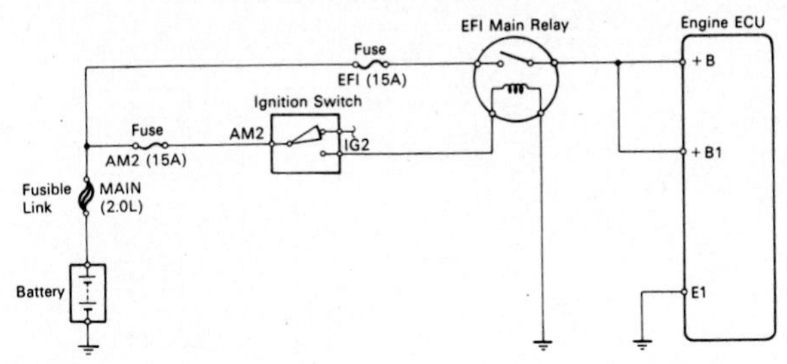

EFI Main Relay
Engine ECU
Fuse
EFI (15A)
Ignition Switch
Fuse
AM2
AM2 (15A)
IG2
+B
+B1
Fusible Link
MAIN (2.0L)
Battery
E1

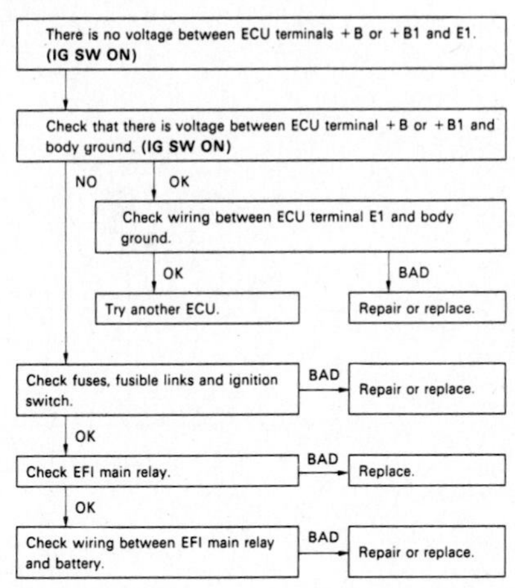

There is no voltage between ECU terminals +B or +B1 and E1. (IG SW ON)
Check that there is voltage between ECU terminal +B or +B1 and body ground. (IG SW ON)
NO
OK
Check wiring between ECU terminal E1 and body ground.
OK
BAD
Try another ECU.
Repair or replace.
Check fuses, fusible links and ignition switch.
BAD
Repair or replace.
OK
Check EFI main relay.
BAD
Replace.
OK
Check wiring between EFI main relay and battery.
BAD
Repair or replace.

## TERCEL CODE 12, 13
### RPM SIGNAL

Code 12 is caused by loss of "NE" signal signal from distributor to ECU for at least 2 seconds after starter signal is received at ECU. Ensure starter signal exists at ECU. See TEST NO. 9 OR CODE 43. Code 13 is caused by loss of "NE" signal from distributor to ECU when engine RPM exceeds 1500 RPM.

**NOTE - Diagnostic chart not available from manufacturer.**

## TERCEL TEST NO. 3 OR CODE 14
### IGNITION SIGNAL

| Terminals | trouble | Condition | STD voltage |
|---|---|---|---|
| IGT - E1 | No voltage | Idling | 0.7 - 1.0 V |

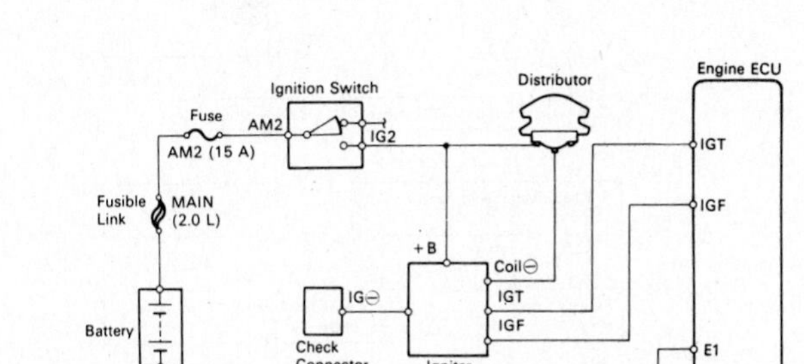

Ignition Switch
Distributor
Engine ECU
Fuse
AM2
AM2 (15 A)
IG2
IGT
IGF
Fusible Link
MAIN (2.0 L)
+B
Coil⊖
IG⊖
IGT
IGF
Battery
Check Connector
Igniter
E1

NOTE: To check ignition system components, see SYSTEM & COMPONENT TESTING article.

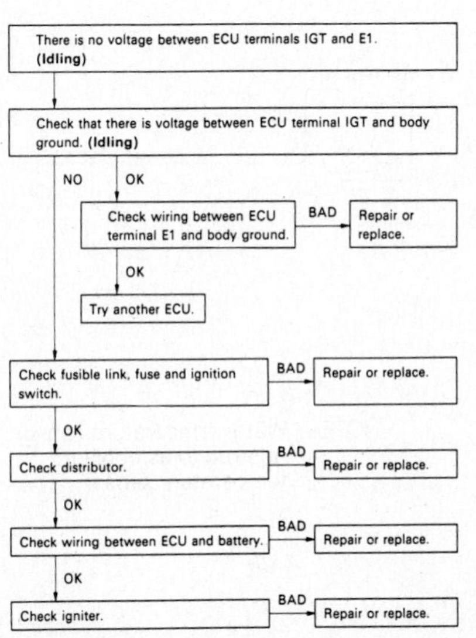

There is no voltage between ECU terminals IGT and E1. (Idling)
Check that there is voltage between ECU terminal IGT and body ground. (Idling)
NO
OK
Check wiring between ECU terminal E1 and body ground.
BAD
Repair or replace.
OK
Try another ECU.
Check fusible link, fuse and ignition switch.
BAD
Repair or replace.
OK
Check distributor.
BAD
Repair or replace.
OK
Check wiring between ECU and battery.
BAD
Repair or replace.
OK
Check igniter.
BAD
Repair or replace.

91C18152 91C17717 91D18153 91C17543

Courtesy of Toyota Motor Sales, U.S.A., Inc.

# 1991 ENGINE PERFORMANCE
## Self-Diagnostics (Cont.)

## TERCEL TEST NO. 4 OR CODE 21
### OXYGEN SENSOR SIGNAL

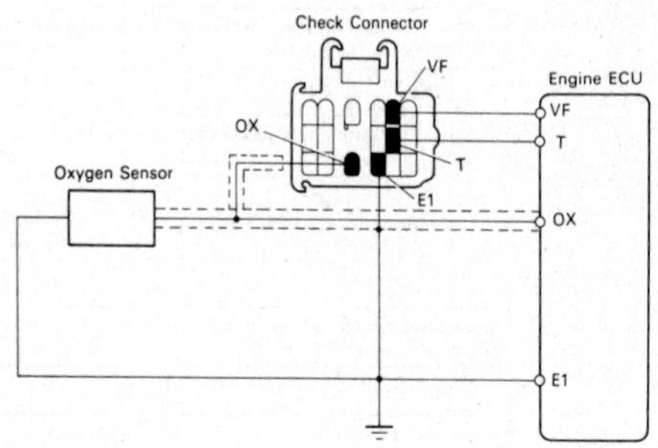
Check Connector
VF
OX
T
E1
Oxygen Sensor
Engine ECU
VF
T
OX
E1

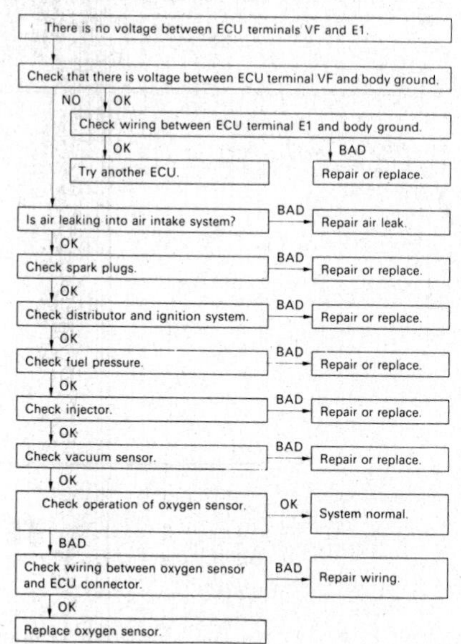
There is no voltage between ECU terminals VF and E1.
Check that there is voltage between ECU terminal VF and body ground.
NO
OK
Check wiring between ECU terminal E1 and body ground.
OK
BAD
Try another ECU.
Repair or replace.
Is air leaking into air intake system?
BAD
Repair air leak.
OK
Check spark plugs.
BAD
Repair or replace.
OK
Check distributor and ignition system.
BAD
Repair or replace.
OK
Check fuel pressure.
BAD
Repair or replace.
OK
Check injector.
BAD
Repair or replace.
OK
Check vacuum sensor.
BAD
Repair or replace.
OK
Check operation of oxygen sensor.
OK
System normal.
BAD
Check wiring between oxygen sensor and ECU connector.
BAD
Repair wiring.
OK
Replace oxygen sensor.

## TERCEL TEST NO. 5 OR CODE 22
### COOLANT TEMPERATURE SENSOR SIGNAL

| Terminals | Trouble | Condition | | STD voltage |
|---|---|---|---|---|
| THW – E2 | No voltage | IG SW ON | Coolant temperature 80°C (176°F) | 0.4 – 0.7 V |

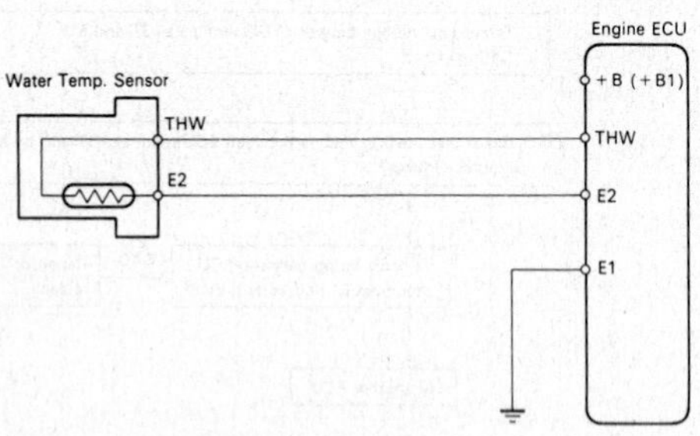
Engine ECU
Water Temp. Sensor
THW
E2
+B (+B1)
THW
E2
E1

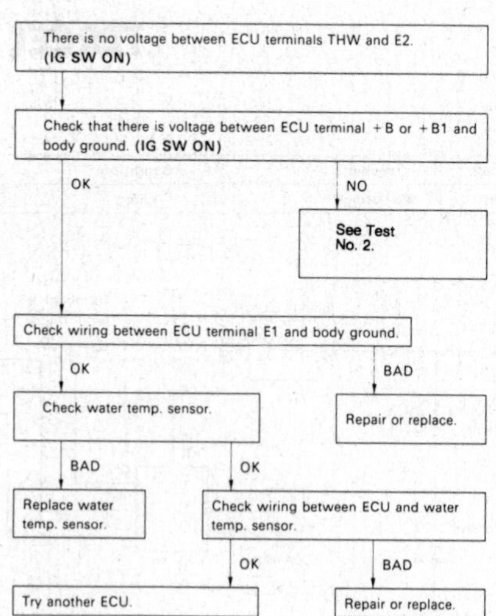
There is no voltage between ECU terminals THW and E2. (IG SW ON)
Check that there is voltage between ECU terminal +B or +B1 and body ground. (IG SW ON)
OK
NO
See Test No. 2.
Check wiring between ECU terminal E1 and body ground.
OK
BAD
Check water temp. sensor.
Repair or replace.
BAD
OK
Replace water temp. sensor.
Check wiring between ECU and water temp. sensor.
OK
BAD
Try another ECU.
Repair or replace.

NOTE: Water temperature sensor is also referred to as coolant temperature sensor.

91E18154 91F18155 91J17680 91D17726

# TERCEL TEST NO. 6 OR CODE 24
## INTAKE AIR TEMPERATURE

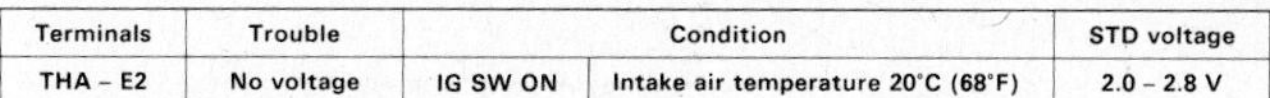

| Terminals | Trouble | Condition | | STD voltage |
|---|---|---|---|---|
| THA – E2 | No voltage | IG SW ON | Intake air temperature 20°C (68°F) | 2.0 – 2.8 V |

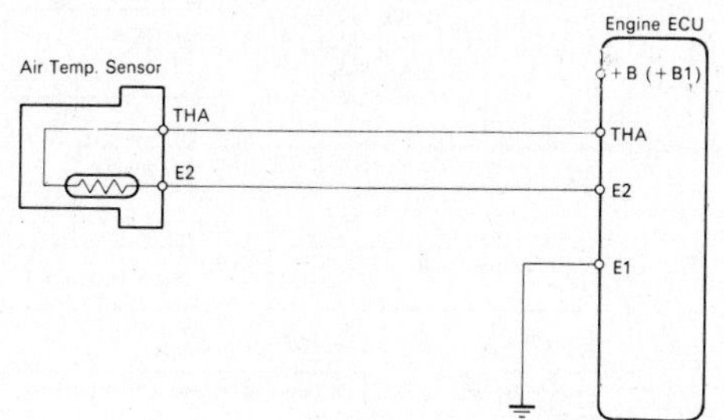
Engine ECU
Air Temp. Sensor
+B (+B1)
THA
THA
E2
E2
E1

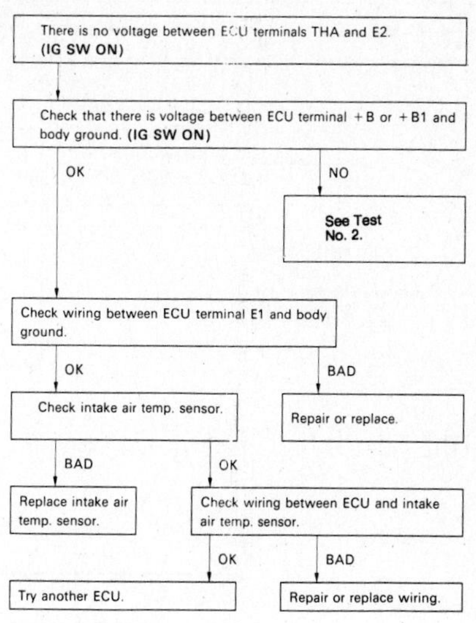
There is no voltage between ECU terminals THA and E2. (IG SW ON)
Check that there is voltage between ECU terminal +B or +B1 and body ground. (IG SW ON)
OK
NO
See Test No. 2.
Check wiring between ECU terminal E1 and body ground.
OK
BAD
Check intake air temp. sensor.
Repair or replace.
BAD
OK
Replace intake air temp. sensor.
Check wiring between ECU and intake air temp. sensor.
OK
BAD
Try another ECU.
Repair or replace wiring.

# TERCEL CODE 25
## LEAN AIR/FUEL MIXTURE

**Probable Causes**
- Vacuum Sensor
- Air Intake System
- Coolant Temperature Sensor
- ECU
- Fuel Pressure
- Ignition System
- Injector Circuit or Injector
- Oxygen Sensor or Sensor Circuit
- EGR System

**NOTE – Diagnostic chart not available from manufacturer.**

# TERCEL CODE 26
## RICH AIR/FUEL MIXTURE

**Probable Causes**
- Vacuum Sensor
- Cold Start Injector
- Coolant Temperature Sensor
- ECU
- Fuel Pressure
- Injector Circuit or Injector
- Oxygen Sensor or Sensor Circuit

**NOTE – Diagnostic chart not available from manufacturer.**

91G17729 91J17730

Courtesy of Toyota Motor Sales, U.S.A., Inc.

# 1991 ENGINE PERFORMANCE
## Self-Diagnostics (Cont.)

## TERCEL TEST NO. 7 OR CODE 31
### VACUUM SENSOR SIGNAL

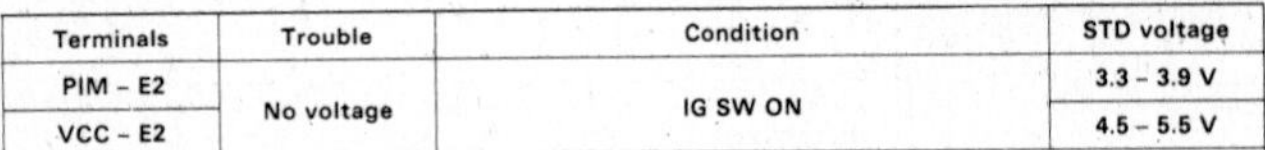

| Terminals | Trouble | Condition | STD voltage |
|---|---|---|---|
| PIM – E2 | No voltage | IG SW ON | 3.3 – 3.9 V |
| VCC – E2 | | | 4.5 – 5.5 V |

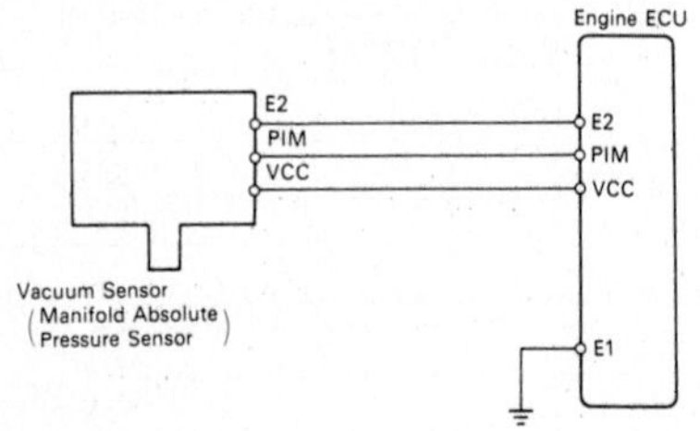
Engine ECU
E2
PIM
VCC
E2
PIM
VCC
E1
Vacuum Sensor
(Manifold Absolute Pressure Sensor)

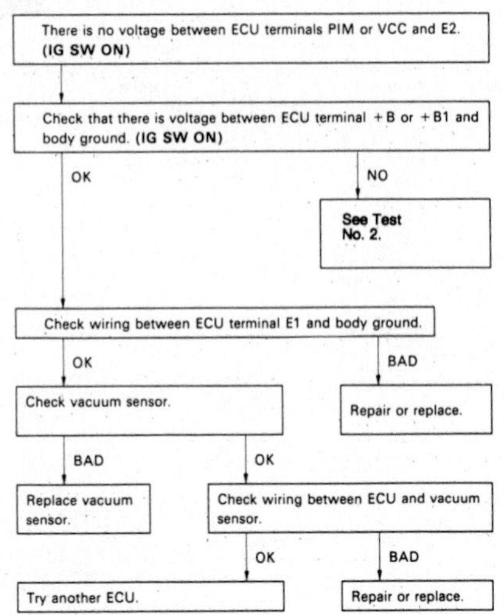
There is no voltage between ECU terminals PIM or VCC and E2. (IG SW ON)
Check that there is voltage between ECU terminal +B or +B1 and body ground. (IG SW ON)
OK
NO
See Test No. 2.
Check wiring between ECU terminal E1 and body ground.
OK
BAD
Check vacuum sensor.
Repair or replace.
BAD
OK
Replace vacuum sensor.
Check wiring between ECU and vacuum sensor.
OK
BAD
Try another ECU.
Repair or replace.

## TERCEL TEST NO. 8 OR CODE 41
### THROTTLE POSITION SENSOR SIGNAL

| Terminals | Trouble | Condition | | STD voltage |
|---|---|---|---|---|
| IDL – E2 | No voltage | IG SW ON | Throttle valve open | 4.5 – 5.5 V |
| VCC – E2 | | | – | 4.5 – 5.5 V |
| VTA – E2 | | | Throttle valve fully closed | 0.8 – 1.2 V |
| | | | Throttle valve fully open | 3.2 – 4.2 V |

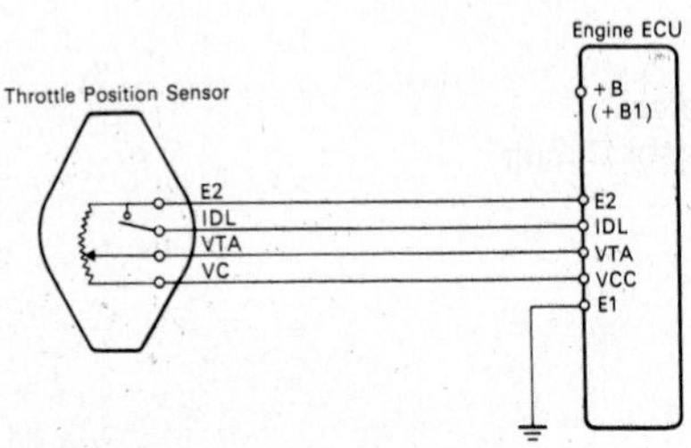
Engine ECU
Throttle Position Sensor
+B
(+B1)
E2
IDL
VTA
VC
E2
IDL
VTA
VCC
E1

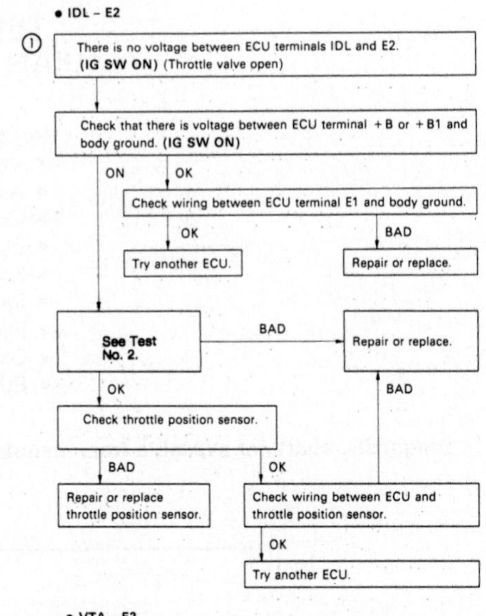
• IDL – E2
①
There is no voltage between ECU terminals IDL and E2. (IG SW ON) (Throttle valve open)
Check that there is voltage between ECU terminal +B or +B1 and body ground. (IG SW ON)
ON
OK
Check wiring between ECU terminal E1 and body ground.
OK
BAD
Try another ECU.
Repair or replace.
See Test No. 2.
BAD
Repair or replace.
OK
BAD
Check throttle position sensor.
BAD
OK
Repair or replace throttle position sensor.
Check wiring between ECU and throttle position sensor.
OK
Try another ECU.

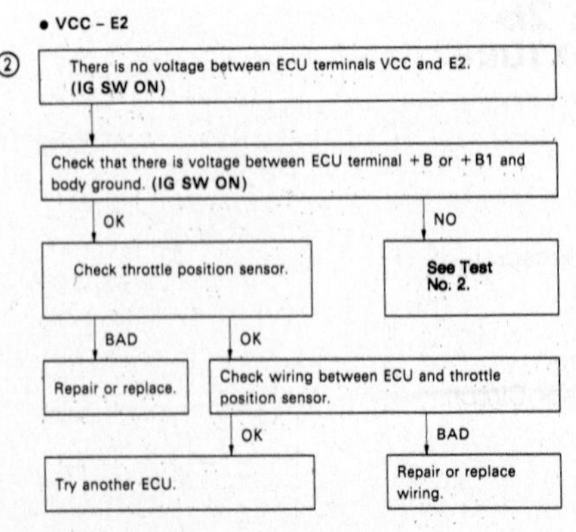
• VCC – E2
②
There is no voltage between ECU terminals VCC and E2. (IG SW ON)
Check that there is voltage between ECU terminal +B or +B1 and body ground. (IG SW ON)
OK
NO
Check throttle position sensor.
See Test No. 2.
BAD
OK
Repair or replace.
Check wiring between ECU and throttle position sensor.
OK
BAD
Try another ECU.
Repair or replace wiring.

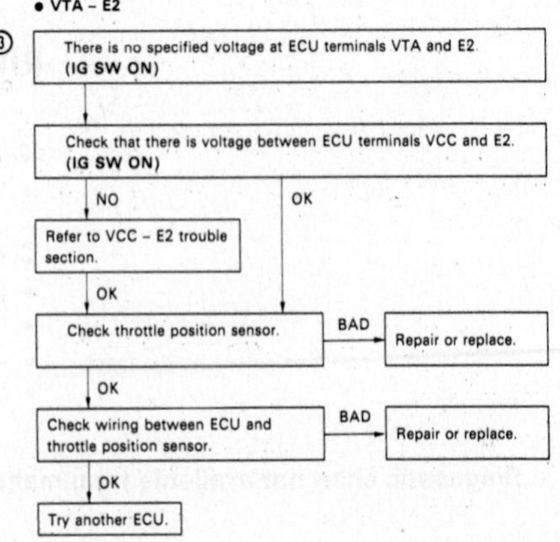
• VTA – E2
③
There is no specified voltage at ECU terminals VTA and E2. (IG SW ON)
Check that there is voltage between ECU terminals VCC and E2. (IG SW ON)
NO
OK
Refer to VCC – E2 trouble section.
OK
Check throttle position sensor.
BAD
Repair or replace.
OK
Check wiring between ECU and throttle position sensor.
BAD
Repair or replace.
OK
Try another ECU.

91A17731 91B17732 91G18156 91H17688 91H18157 91I18158

## TERCEL CODE 42
### VEHICLE SPEED SENSOR SIGNAL

**Probable Causes**

- Vehicle Speed Sensor Circuit
- Vehicle Speed Sensor
- ECU

**NOTE - Diagnostic chart not available from manufacturer.**

---

## TERCEL TEST NO. 9 OR CODE 43
### STARTER SIGNAL

| Terminals | Trouble | Condition | STD voltage |
|---|---|---|---|
| STA - E1 | No voltage | Cranking | 6 - 14 V |

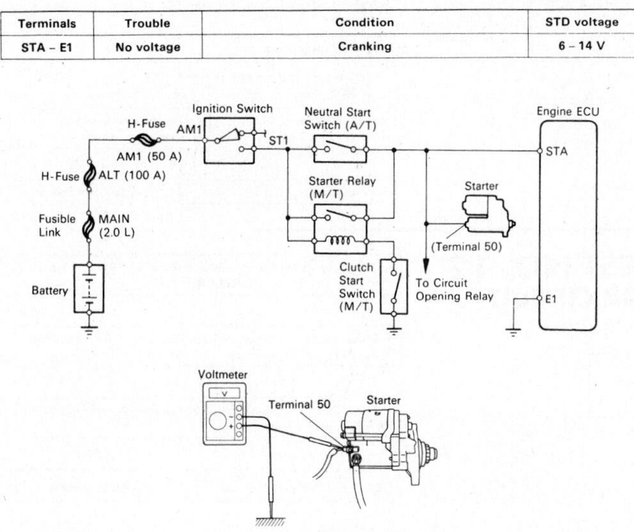

Ignition Switch
H-Fuse
AM1
ST1
AM1 (50 A)
H-Fuse
ALT (100 A)
Fusible Link
MAIN (2.0 L)
Battery
Neutral Start Switch (A/T)
Starter Relay (M/T)
Clutch Start Switch (M/T)
Starter
(Terminal 50)
To Circuit Opening Relay
Engine ECU
STA
E1
Voltmeter
Terminal 50
Starter

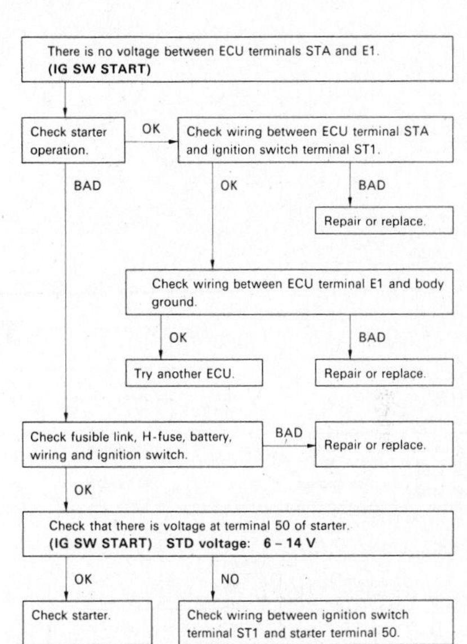

There is no voltage between ECU terminals STA and E1. (IG SW START)
Check starter operation.
OK
Check wiring between ECU terminal STA and ignition switch terminal ST1.
BAD
OK
BAD
Repair or replace.
Check wiring between ECU terminal E1 and body ground.
OK
BAD
Try another ECU.
Repair or replace.
Check fusible link, H-fuse, battery, wiring and ignition switch.
BAD
Repair or replace.
OK
Check that there is voltage at terminal 50 of starter. (IG SW START) STD voltage: 6 - 14 V
OK
NO
Check starter.
Check wiring between ignition switch terminal ST1 and starter terminal 50.

---

## TERCEL TEST NO. 10 OR CODE 51
### SWITCH SIGNAL

**Probable Causes**

- A/C Switch or Switch Circuit
- Accelerator Pedal or Cable
- Neutral/Start Switch or Switch Circuit
- Throttle Position Sensor IDL Circuit
- ECU

To check A/C switch signal, use the following procedure.

| Terminals | trouble | Condition | STD voltage |
|---|---|---|---|
| A/C - E1 | No voltage | Air conditioning ON | 8 - 14 V |

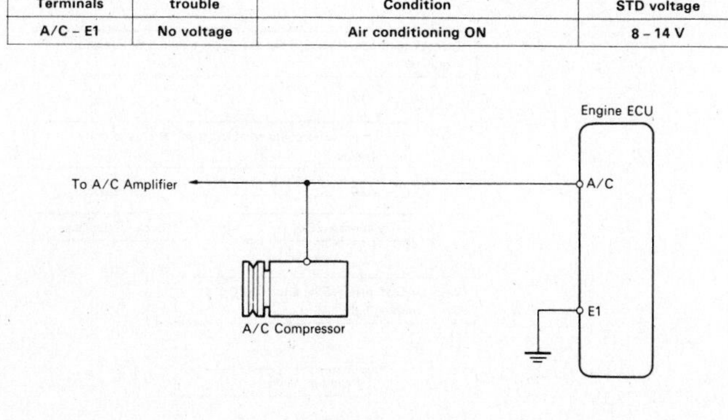

Engine ECU
To A/C Amplifier
A/C
E1
A/C Compressor

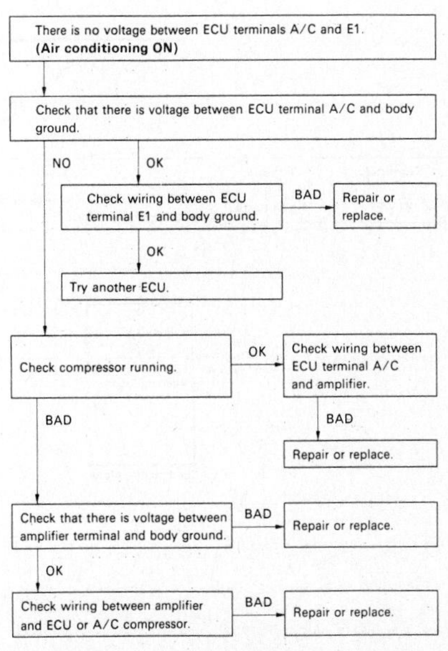

There is no voltage between ECU terminals A/C and E1. (Air conditioning ON)
Check that there is voltage between ECU terminal A/C and body ground.
NO
OK
Check wiring between ECU terminal E1 and body ground.
BAD
Repair or replace.
OK
Try another ECU.
Check compressor running.
OK
Check wiring between ECU terminal A/C and amplifier.
BAD
BAD
Repair or replace.
Check that there is voltage between amplifier terminal and body ground.
BAD
Repair or replace.
OK
Check wiring between amplifier and ECU or A/C compressor.
BAD
Repair or replace.

91J18159 91C18160 91F17694 91G17695 91G17745

Courtesy of Toyota Motor Sales, U.S.A., Inc.

# 1991 ENGINE PERFORMANCE
## Self-Diagnostics (Cont.)

## TERCEL TEST NO. 11 OR CODE 71
### EGR SYSTEM MALFUNCTION

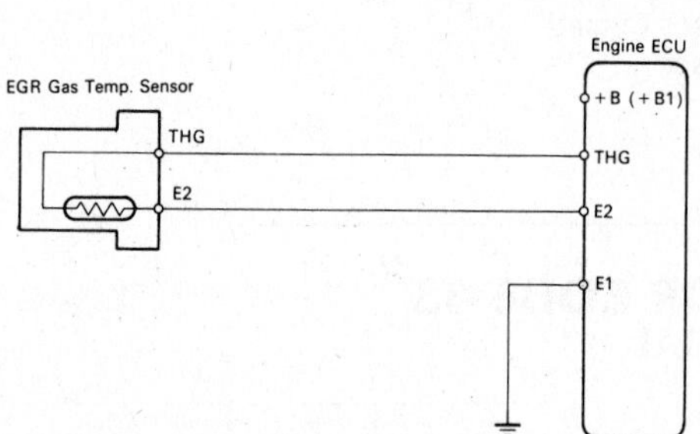
Engine ECU
EGR Gas Temp. Sensor
THG
E2
+B (+B1)
THG
E2
E1

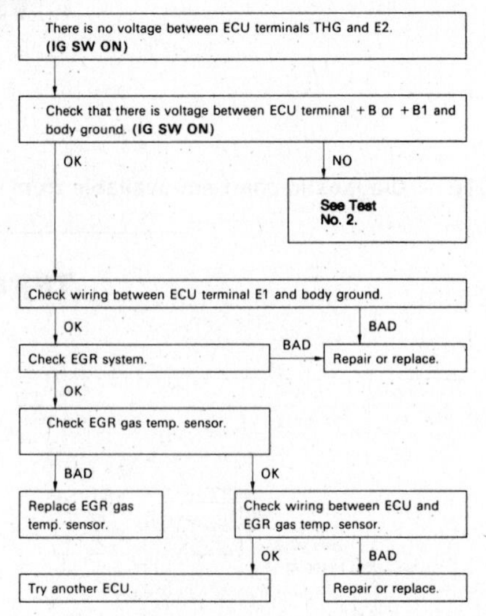
There is no voltage between ECU terminals THG and E2. (IG SW ON)
Check that there is voltage between ECU terminal +B or +B1 and body ground. (IG SW ON)
OK
NO
See Test No. 2.
Check wiring between ECU terminal E1 and body ground.
OK
BAD
Check EGR system.
BAD
Repair or replace.
OK
Check EGR gas temp. sensor.
BAD
OK
Replace EGR gas temp. sensor.
Check wiring between ECU and EGR gas temp. sensor.
OK
BAD
Try another ECU.
Repair or replace.

## TERCEL TEST NO. 12
### INJECTOR CIRCUIT

| Terminals | Trouble | Condition | STD voltage |
|---|---|---|---|
| No. 10 – E01<br>No. 20 – E02 | No voltage | IG SW ON | 10 – 14 V |

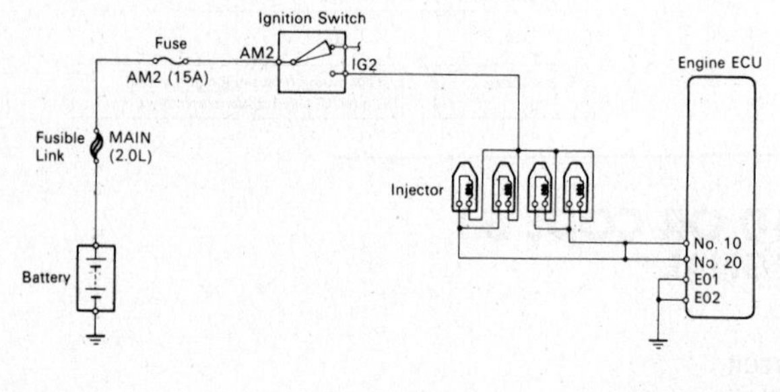
Ignition Switch
Fuse
AM2
AM2 (15A)
IG2
Engine ECU
Fusible Link
MAIN (2.0L)
Injector
Battery
No. 10
No. 20
E01
E02

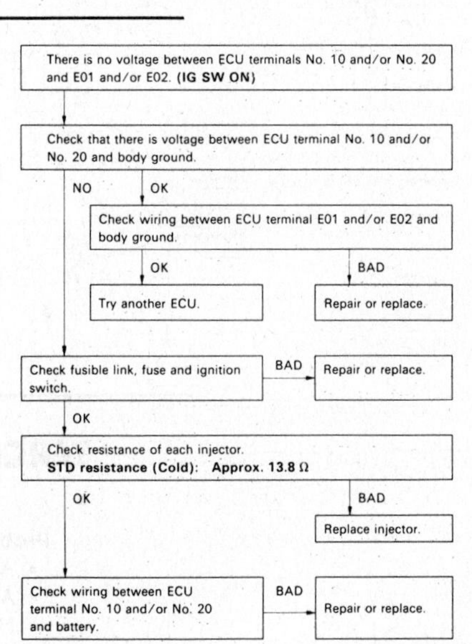
There is no voltage between ECU terminals No. 10 and/or No. 20 and E01 and/or E02. (IG SW ON)
Check that there is voltage between ECU terminal No. 10 and/or No. 20 and body ground.
NO
OK
Check wiring between ECU terminal E01 and/or E02 and body ground.
OK
BAD
Try another ECU.
Repair or replace.
Check fusible link, fuse and ignition switch.
BAD
Repair or replace.
OK
Check resistance of each injector.
STD resistance (Cold): Approx. 13.8 Ω
OK
BAD
Replace injector.
Check wiring between ECU terminal No. 10 and/or No. 20 and battery.
BAD
Repair or replace.

## TERCEL TEST NO. 13
### CHECK ENGINE LIGHT CIRCUIT

| Terminals | Trouble | Condition | STD voltage |
|---|---|---|---|
| W – E1 | No voltage | No trouble ("CHECK" engine warning light off) and engine running. | 10 – 14 V |

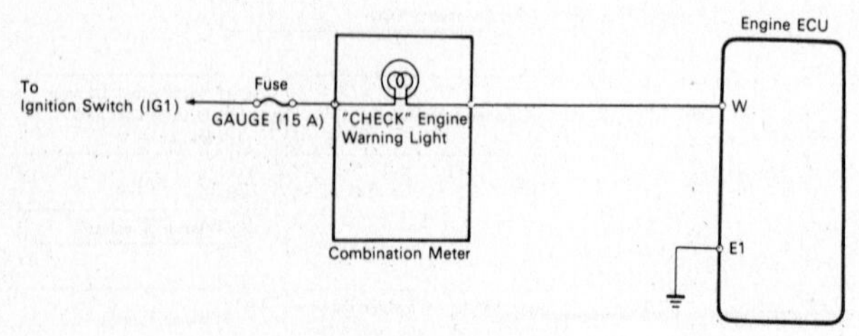
Engine ECU
To Ignition Switch (IG1)
Fuse
GAUGE (15 A)
"CHECK" Engine Warning Light
Combination Meter
W
E1

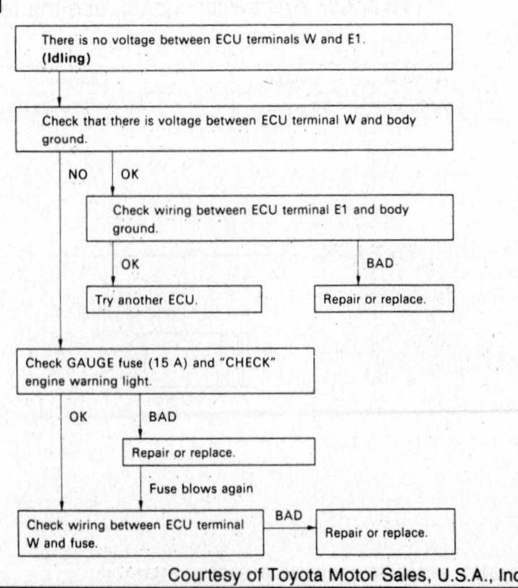
There is no voltage between ECU terminals W and E1. (Idling)
Check that there is voltage between ECU terminal W and body ground.
NO
OK
Check wiring between ECU terminal E1 and body ground.
OK
BAD
Try another ECU.
Repair or replace.
Check GAUGE fuse (15 A) and "CHECK" engine warning light.
OK
BAD
Repair or replace.
Fuse blows again
Check wiring between ECU terminal W and fuse.
BAD
Repair or replace.

91I17697 91J17698 91D18161 91J17789 91C17790 91D17791

Courtesy of Toyota Motor Sales, U.S.A., Inc.

# 1991 ENGINE PERFORMANCE
# Trouble Shooting – No Codes

**Camry, Celica, Corolla, Cressida, Land Cruiser, MR2, Pickup, Previa, Supra, Tercel, 4Runner**

## INTRODUCTION

Before diagnosing symptoms or intermittent faults, perform steps in BASIC DIAGNOSTIC PROCEDURES and SELF-DIAGNOSTICS articles. Use this article to diagnose driveability problems existing when a hard fault code is not present.

***NOTE: Some driveability problems may have been corrected by manufacturer with a revised computer calibration chip or computer control unit. Check with manufacturer for latest chip or computer application.***

Symptom checks can direct the technician to malfunctioning component(s) for further diagnosis. A symptom should lead to a specific component, a system test or an adjustment.

Use intermittent test procedures to locate driveability problems that DO NOT occur when the vehicle is being tested. These test procedures should also be used if a soft (intermittent) trouble code was present, but no problem was found during self-diagnostic testing.

This article covers 2 trouble shooting areas:

- Symptom Diagnosis
- Intermittents

***NOTE: For specific testing procedures, see SYSTEM & COMPONENT TESTING article. For specifications, see ON-VEHICLE ADJUSTMENTS or SERVICE & ADJUSTMENT SPECIFICATIONS article.***

## SYMPTOMS

### SYMPTOM DIAGNOSIS

Symptom checks cannot be used properly unless the problem occurs while the vehicle is being tested. To reduce diagnostic time, ensure steps in BASIC DIAGNOSTIC PROCEDURES and SELF-DIAGNOSTICS articles were performed before diagnosing a symptom. Symptoms available for diagnosis include:

- Difficult To Start/No Start (Engine Will Not Crank Or Cranks Slowly)
- Difficult To Start/No Start (Cranks Okay)
- Engine Stalls Often
- Engine Stalls Sometimes
- Rough Idle/Missing
- High Idle Speed (No Drop)
- Engine Backfires (Lean Fuel Mixture)
- Muffler Explosion (Rich Fuel Mixture)
- Engine Hesitates/Poor Acceleration

### DIFFICULT TO START/NO START (ENGINE WILL NOT CRANK OR CRANKS SLOWLY)

- Check battery and cables, charging system and fusible links.
- Check ignition switch.
- Check starter relay.
- Check clutch start switch (M/T) or neutral start switch (A/T).
- Check starter and wiring connections.

### DIFFICULT TO START/NO START (CRANKS OKAY)

- Check for vacuum leaks (oil filler cap, oil dipstick, hose connections, PCV valve and hose).
- Verify secondary ignition system performance.
- Check cam position sensor (if equipped).
- Ensure ignition timing is correct.
- Check auxiliary air valve (if equipped).
- Ensure fuel system (pump, lines, filter and pressure regulator) performs properly.
- Verify proper compression and valve clearance.
- Check circuit opening relay.
- If engine starts with accelerator pedal depressed, check idle speed control valve (if equipped) and wiring connection.
- Check fuel pump switch in airflow meter.
- Check wiring connection to ECU.
- Check power to ECU via fusible links, fuses and EFI main relay.
- Check airflow meter, coolant temperature sensor and air temperature sensor.
- Check injection signal circuit.

### ENGINE STALLS OFTEN

- Check for vacuum leaks (oil filler cap, oil dipstick, hose connections, PCV valve and hose).
- Ensure fuel system (pump, lines, filter and pressure regulator) performs properly.
- Check air filter.
- Check idle speed and ensure ignition timing is correct.
- Verify secondary ignition system performance.
- Verify proper compression and valve clearance.
- Check cold start injector and cold start injector time switch.
- Check auxiliary air valve (if equipped) or idle speed control valve (if equipped).
- Check circuit opening relay.
- Check fuel injectors.
- Check power to ECU via fusible links, fuses and EFI main relay.
- Check airflow meter, coolant temperature sensor and air temperature sensor.
- Check injection signal circuit.

### ENGINE STALLS SOMETIMES

- Check airflow meter and connectors.
- Check EFI main relay, circuit opening relay and connectors. Check for slight change in engine idle when connector or relay are slightly tapped or wiggled.

### ROUGH IDLE/MISSING

- Check for vacuum leaks (oil filler cap, oil dipstick, hose connections, PCV valve and hose).
- Check air filter.
- Check idle speed and ensure ignition timing is correct.
- Verify secondary ignition system performance.
- Verify proper compression and valve clearance.
- Check variable induction system (if equipped).
- Check cold start injector and cold start injector time switch.
- Ensure fuel system (pump, lines, filter and pressure regulator) performs properly.
- Check fuel injectors.
- Check power to ECU via fusible links, fuses and EFI main relay.
- Check airflow meter, coolant temperature sensor and air temperature sensor.
- Check injection signal circuit.
- Check $O_2$ sensor(s).

### HIGH IDLE SPEED (NO DROP)

- Check accelerator linkage.
- Check power steering idle-up circuit (if equipped).
- Check A/C idle-up circuit (if equipped).
- Check idle speed control valve (if equipped) or auxiliary air valve (if equipped) and wiring.
- Check variable induction system (if equipped).
- Ensure ignition timing is correct.
- Check throttle position sensor.
- Check for high fuel pressure.
- Check for leakage at cold start injector or fuel injectors.
- Check power to ECU via fusible links, fuses and EFI main relay.

# 1991 ENGINE PERFORMANCE
# Trouble Shooting – No Codes (Cont.)

- Check airflow meter, coolant temperature sensor and air temperature sensor.
- Check injection signal circuit.

## ENGINE BACKFIRES (LEAN FUEL MIXTURE)

- Check for vacuum leaks (oil filler cap, oil dipstick, hose connections, PCV valve and hose).
- Check idle speed and ensure ignition timing is correct.
- Check cold start injector and cold start injector time switch.
- Ensure fuel system (pump, lines, filter and pressure regulator) performs properly.
- Check for clogged fuel injectors.
- Check power to ECU via fusible links, fuses and EFI main relay.
- Check airflow meter, coolant temperature sensor, throttle position sensor and air temperature sensor.
- Check injection signal circuit.
- Check $O_2$ sensor(s).

## MUFFLER EXPLOSION (RICH FUEL MIXTURE)

- Check idle speed and ensure ignition timing is correct.
- Check cold start injector and cold start injector time switch.
- Ensure fuel system (pump, lines, filter and pressure regulator) performs properly.
- Check for fuel injector leakage.
- Verify secondary ignition system performance.
- Verify proper compression and valve clearance.
- Check throttle position sensor, injection signal circuit and $O_2$ sensor(s).
- Check for exhaust system leaks.

## ENGINE HESITATES/POOR ACCELERATION

- Check for clutch slipping or brakes dragging.
- Check for vacuum leaks (oil filler cap, oil dipstick, hose connections, PCV valve and hose).
- Check air filter.
- Check for leakage or clogging between air filter and turbocharger inlet and between turbocharger outlet and cylinder head (if equipped).
- Verify secondary ignition system performance and timing.
- Verify proper compression and valve clearance.
- Ensure fuel system (pump, lines, filter and pressure regulator) performs properly.
- Check for clogged fuel injectors.
- Check variable induction system (if equipped).
- Check power to ECU via fusible links, fuses and EFI main relay.
- Check airflow meter, coolant temperature sensor, air temperature sensor and throttle position sensor.
- Check injection signal circuit.

# INTERMITTENTS

## INTERMITTENT PROBLEM DIAGNOSIS

Intermittent fault testing requires duplicating circuit or component failure to identify the problem. These procedures may lead to the computer setting a fault code, which may help in diagnosis.

If problem vehicle does not produce fault codes, monitor voltage or resistance values using a DVOM while attempting to reproduce conditions causing intermittent fault. A status change on DVOM indicates a fault has been located.

Use a DVOM to pinpoint faults. When monitoring voltage, ensure ignition switch is in ON position or engine is running. Ensure ignition switch is in OFF position or negative battery cable is disconnected when monitoring circuit resistance. Status changes on DVOM during test procedures indicate area of fault.

## TEST PROCEDURES

**Intermittent Simulation** – To reproduce the conditions creating an intermittent fault, use the following methods:

- Lightly vibrate component. See VIBRATION METHOD.
- Heat component. See HEAT METHOD.
- Wiggle or bend wiring harness. See VIBRATION METHOD.
- Spray component with light water mist or radiator with water. See HUMIDITY METHOD.
- Remove/apply vacuum source.

Monitor circuit/component voltage or resistance while simulating intermittent. If engine is running, monitor for self-diagnostic codes. Use test results to identify a faulty component or circuit.

## VIBRATION METHOD

**Wiring Harness Testing** – If vibration is suspected as cause of an intermittent, lightly shake wiring harness vertically and horizontally while monitoring suspected circuit or component with a DVOM. Look for a voltage fluctuation during this test procedure. Inspect connector joint, fulcrum of the vibration and body through-portion. *See Fig. 1.*

**Component & Sensor Testing** – Lightly vibrate suspect component, relay or sensor, while monitoring suspected circuit or component with a DVOM. Look for a voltage fluctuation during this test procedure. *See Fig. 1.*

**Electrical Connector Testing** – Lightly shake connector vertically and horizontally, while monitoring suspected circuit or component with a DVOM. Look for a voltage fluctuation during this test procedure. Visually inspect connector and repair as required.

## HEAT METHOD

Apply heat to a suspected component with a hair dryer or similar device and monitor suspected circuit or component with a DVOM.

***CAUTION: DO NOT heat any component to more than 140°F (60°C). DO NOT apply heat directly to any part of the ECU.***

## HUMIDITY METHOD

***CAUTION: Never apply water directly onto suspected component. Indirectly change the temperature and humidity by spraying water on front of radiator.***

If humidity or moisture are suspected of causing an intermittent failure, spray water on the radiator to increase humidity in the engine compartment. Check if a malfunction occurs by monitoring the suspected circuit or component with a DVOM.

If a vehicle is subject to water leakage, the admitted water may contaminate the ECU. When testing a vehicle where water leakage has occurred, carefully inspect the ECU terminals for corrosion. Repair or replace the ECU connectors as required.

## ELECTRICAL LOAD METHOD

To check if an intermittent occurs under electrical load, turn on all electrical loads (heater blower, headlights, rear window defogger, wipers, etc.). Check if the malfunction occurs by monitoring the suspected circuit or component with a DVOM.

# 1991 ENGINE PERFORMANCE
# Trouble Shooting – No Codes (Cont.)

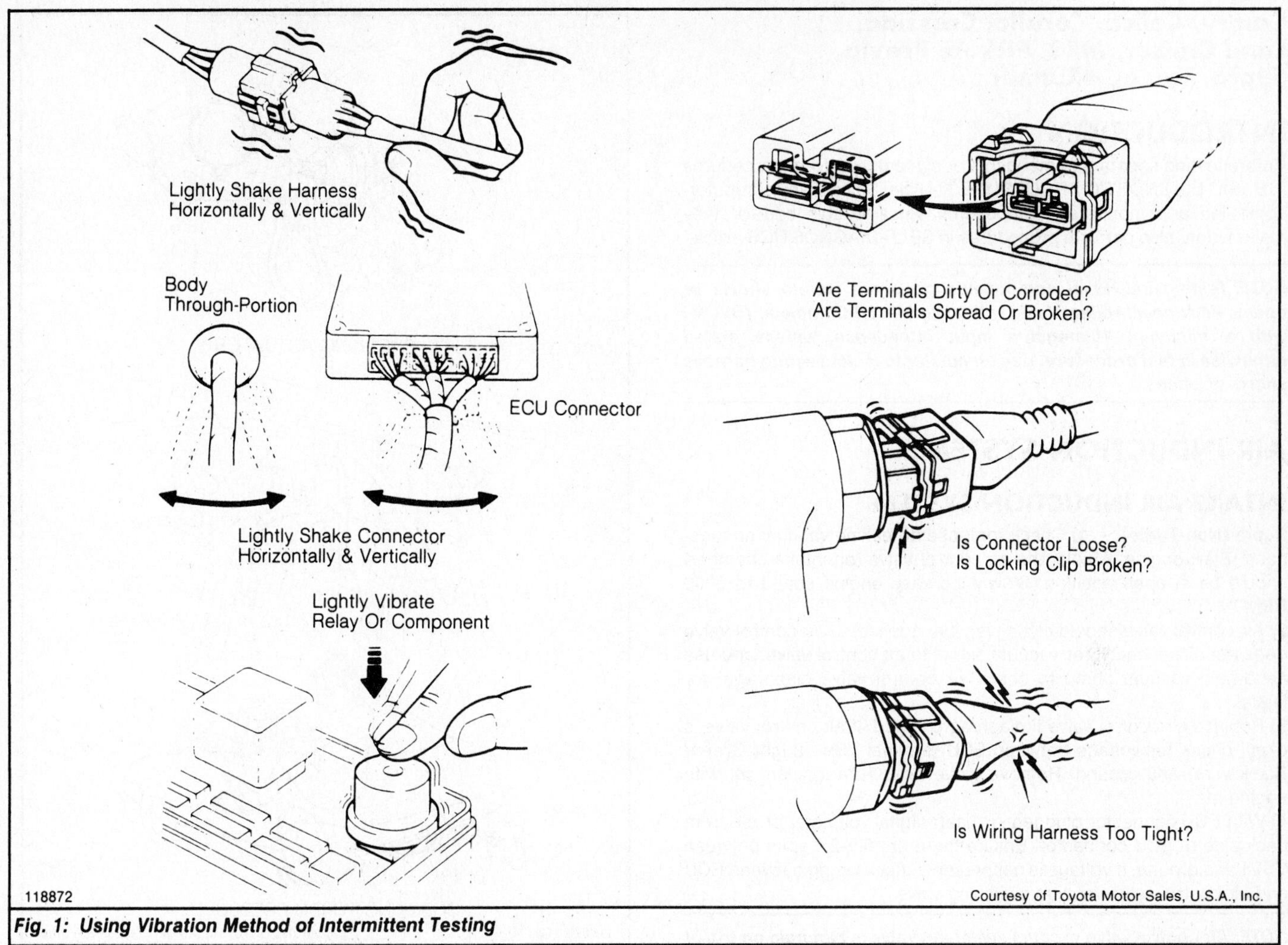
Lightly Shake Harness
Horizontally & Vertically
Are Terminals Dirty Or Corroded?
Are Terminals Spread Or Broken?
Body
Through-Portion
ECU Connector
Lightly Shake Connector
Horizontally & Vertically
Is Connector Loose?
Is Locking Clip Broken?
Lightly Vibrate
Relay Or Component
Is Wiring Harness Too Tight?
118872
Courtesy of Toyota Motor Sales, U.S.A., Inc.

***Fig. 1: Using Vibration Method of Intermittent Testing***

# 1991 ENGINE PERFORMANCE
# System & Component Testing

**Camry, Celica, Corolla, Cressida, Land Cruiser, MR2, Pickup, Previa, Supra, Tercel, 4Runner**

## INTRODUCTION

Before testing separate components or systems, perform procedures in BASIC DIAGNOSTIC PROCEDURES article. Since many computer-controlled and monitored components set a trouble code if they malfunction, also perform procedures in SELF-DIAGNOSTICS article.

***NOTE: Testing individual components does not isolate shorts or opens. Perform all voltage tests with a Digital Volt-Ohmmeter (DVOM) with a minimum 10-megohm input impedance, unless stated otherwise in test procedure. Use ohmmeter to isolate wiring harness shorts or opens.***

## AIR INDUCTION SYSTEMS

### INTAKE AIR INDUCTION SYSTEM

**Supra (Non-Turbo) - 1)** Check for loose or leaking vacuum connections. Start engine. At idle, the air control valve (on intake chamber) should be in open position. Slowly increase engine speed to 5000 RPM.

**2)** Air control valve should close (vacuum applied). If air control valve does not close, check for vacuum signal to air control valve, and use hand-held vacuum pump to check air control valve diaphragm for leaks.

**3)** Replace air control valve if diaphragm is bad. If air control valve is okay, check for voltage between ECU terminal VSV1 (Light Green/Black wire) and ground. Remove glove box. Turn ignition on, with engine off.

**4)** With ECU connector plugged in, insert digital voltmeter probe from back side of ECU connector. Ensure there are 0.5-2.0 volts between VSV1 and ground. If voltage is not present, check wiring between ECU and air control valve vacuum switching valve.

***NOTE: Air control valve vacuum switching valve is mounted on top of vacuum reservoir (Light Green/Black and Black/Red wires), in left side of engine compartment.***

**5)** Ensure there are 0.5-2.0 volts between ECU terminals VSV1 and E1 (Brown wire). If voltage is not present, check voltage between ECU and body ground. If power circuit is okay, unplug vacuum switching valve connector.

**6)** Ground one terminal and apply 12 volts to other terminal. Air should flow through valve ports. Remove 12-volt source. Air should flow from one port to air filter. Replace valve if defective.

### TURBOCHARGERS

**Initial Checks - 1)** Check air intake system for cracks or restrictions. Inspect exhaust system for leaks or restrictions. Check for leaks or clogging between cylinder head and turbocharger inlet.

**2)** Check air intake system and exhaust system for signs of oil leaks from turbocharger. Excessive carbon deposits on the turbine wheel may indicate leaking oil seals in the turbocharger. Replace turbocharger if oil seals are leaking.

**Actuator & Wastegate -** Disconnect all air intake hoses from turbocharger and set aside. Disconnect actuator hose. Using a pressure gauge and pump, apply 9.4 psi (.66 kg/cm²) of pressure to actuator hose. *See Fig. 1.* Ensure rod moves .0098" (.25 mm) or more. If rod does not move as indicate, replace turbocharger assembly.

***CAUTION: DO NOT exceed 11.4 psi (.8 kg/cm²) pressure to actuator.***

**Impeller Wheel Rotation -** Disconnect air cleaner hose. Turn impeller wheel to verify smooth rotation. If impeller wheel does not turn or drags, replace turbocharger assembly.

**Turbine Shaft End Play & Radial Play -** Disconnect intake and exhaust hoses from turbocharger. Use a dial indicator to measure turbine shaft end play and radial play. End play is measured through the oil outlet hole. Replace turbocharger if specifications are out of range. See TURBINE SHAFT END & RADIAL PLAY table.

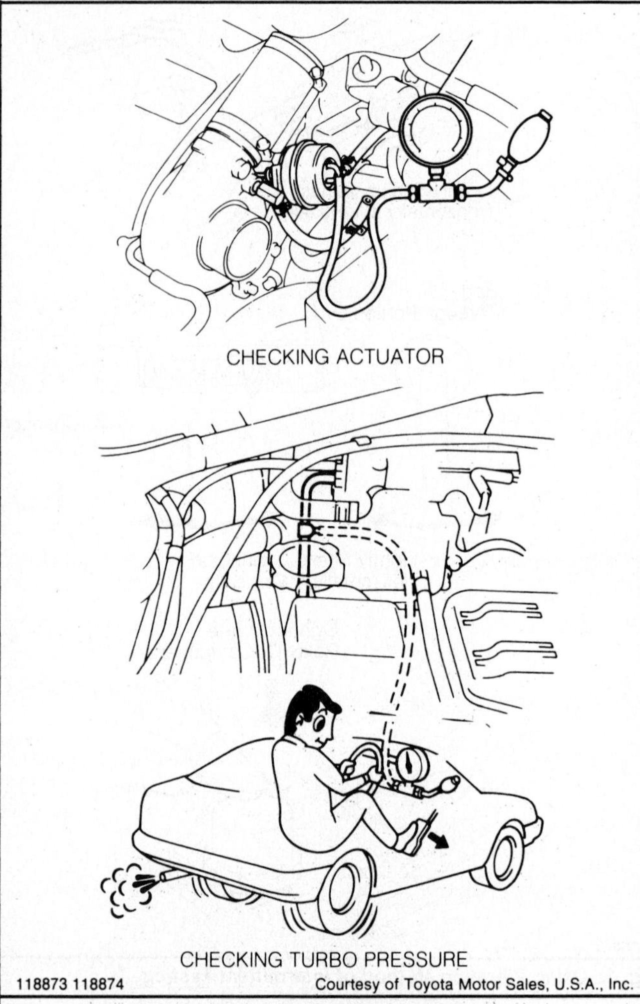


***Fig. 1: Checking Turbocharger Actuator & Pressure (Celica Shown; MR2 & Supra Are Similar)***

***TURBINE SHAFT END & RADIAL PLAY***

| Measurement | In. (mm) |
|---|---|
| End Play | .005 (.13) |
| Radial Play | .007 (.18) |

**Pressure Check - 1)** Ensure all intake air hoses are connected. Place pressure hose and "T" fitting in actuator hose leading to intake manifold. *See Fig. 1.* Start engine.

**2)** On Celica, drive vehicle with engine running at 2800 RPM or more with throttle fully open and transaxle in second gear. Check pressure. See TURBOCHARGER PRESSURE table.

**3)** On Supra with manual transmission, accelerate vehicle with throttle valve fully open. Measure pressure when engine RPM is greater than 2500 RPM. See TURBOCHARGER PRESSURE table. On Supra with automatic transmission, drive vehicle from standing start with transmission in L with throttle valve fully open. Measure pressure with engine speed greater than 3500 RPM. See TURBOCHARGER PRESSURE table.

**4)** If pressure is less than specification, check intake air and exhaust systems for leaks. If there are no leaks, replace turbocharger. If pressure is greater than specification, check actuator hose for leaks or cracks. If no leaks or cracks are present, replace turbocharger.

***NOTE: To check turbocharger pressure sensor and vacuum switching valve, see ENGINE SENSORS & SWITCHES in this article.***

# 1991 ENGINE PERFORMANCE
# System & Component Testing (Cont.)

***TURBOCHARGER PRESSURE***

| Application | psi (kg/cm²) |
|---|---|
| Celica & MR2 | 7.1-11.8 (.50-.86) |
| Supra | |
| Automatic Transmission | 4.8-6.0 (.33-.44) |
| Manual Transmission | 5.5-7.5 (.40-.55) |

## VARIABLE INDUCTION SYSTEM

**Celica (2.0L) - 1)** Using a vacuum "T", connect a vacuum gauge into vacuum line between vacuum switching valve and Toyota Variable Induction System (T-VIS) diaphragm. *See Fig. 2*. Connect tachometer to engine. See ON-VEHICLE ADJUSTMENTS article for correct tachometer attachment.

**2)** Start engine and warm to normal operating temperature. Vacuum gauge should show high vacuum at idle (internal throttle valve closed). Increase engine speed to greater than 4000 RPM.

**3)** Vacuum gauge should indicate zero. If gauge does not indicate zero, use hand held vacuum pump to verify T-VIS diaphragm holds vacuum. If T-VIS diaphragm holds vacuum, go to next step.

**4)** Check T-VIS vacuum switching valve by removing top of intake manifold. Ensure resistance across vacuum switching valve connector terminals is 33-39 ohms. Ensure there is no continuity between wiring terminals and valve body. Check airflow through valve. *See Fig. 3.*

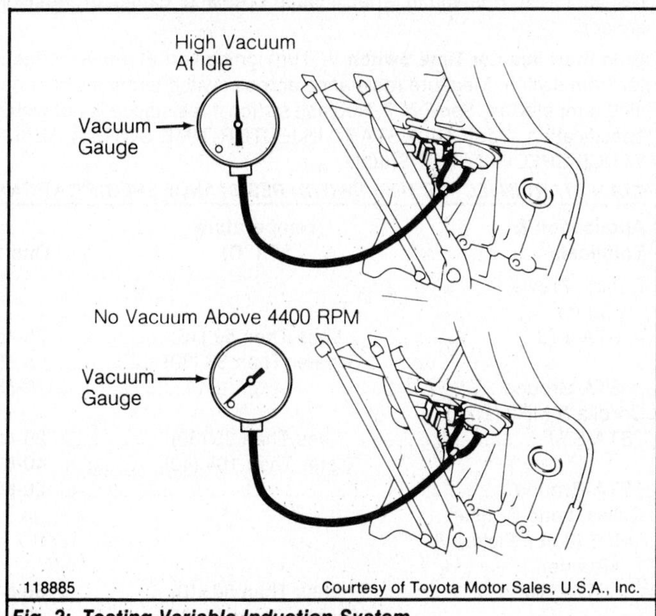


***Fig. 2: Testing Variable Induction System***

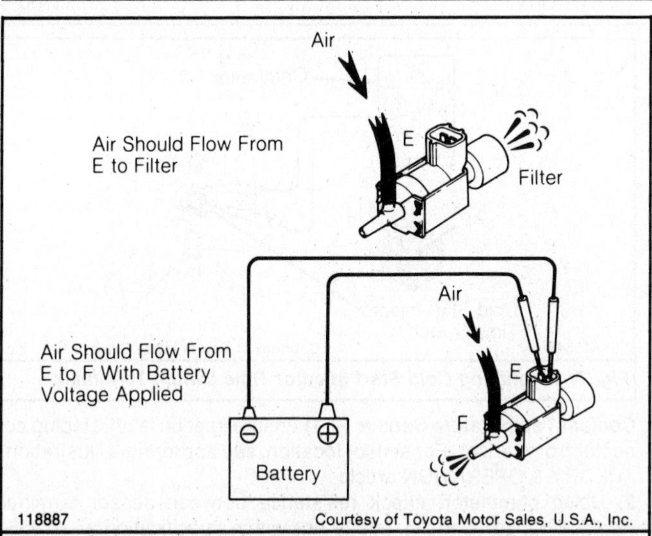


***Fig. 3: Testing Variable Induction System Vacuum Switching Valve***

## ENGINE SENSORS & SWITCHES

**Airflow Meter** - Turn ignition off. Unplug wiring connector from airflow meter. Note terminal identification. *See Fig. 5.* Use ohmmeter to measure resistance between specified terminals. On Supra Turbo models, use only an analog ohmmeter. See AIRFLOW METER RESISTANCE SPECIFICATIONS table. Replace airflow meter if not within specification.

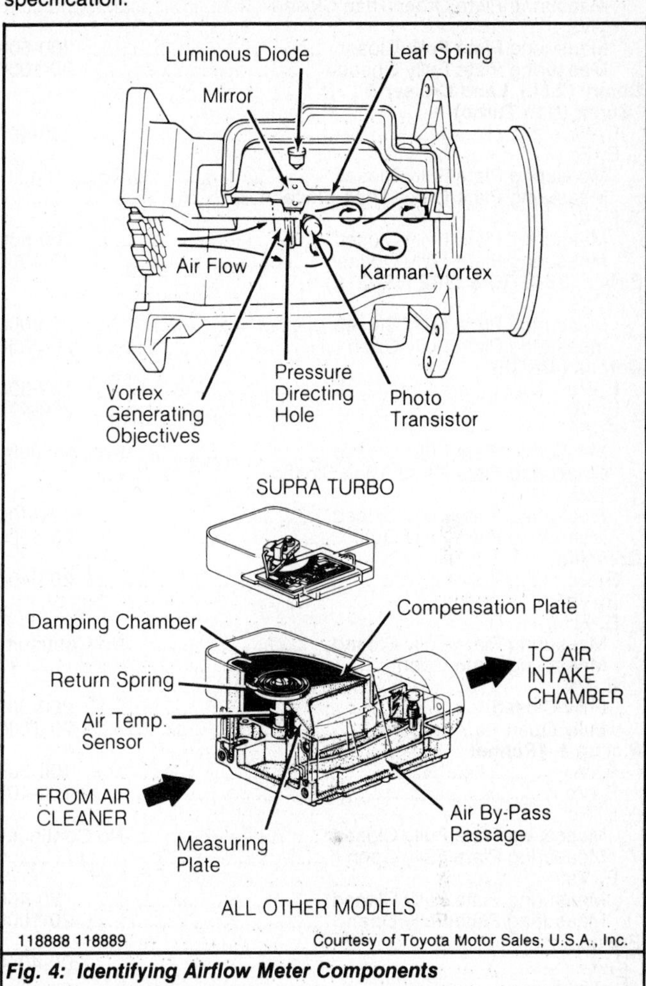


***Fig. 4: Identifying Airflow Meter Components***

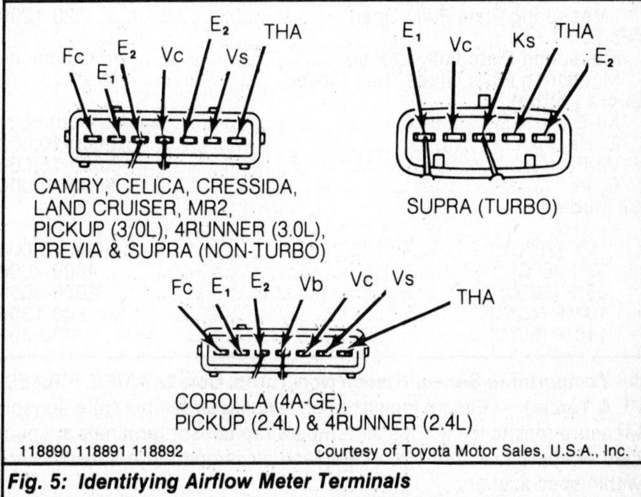


***Fig. 5: Identifying Airflow Meter Terminals***

# 1991 ENGINE PERFORMANCE
## System & Component Testing (Cont.)

***AIRFLOW METER RESISTANCE SPECIFICATIONS***

| Application & Terminals | Ohms |
|---|---|
| **Camry (2.0L)** | |
| $E_2$-Vc | 3000-7000 |
| $E_1$-Fc | |
| Measuring Plate Fully Closed | No Continuity |
| Measuring Plate Other Than Closed | 0 |
| $E_2$-Vs | |
| Measuring Plate Fully Closed | 200-600 |
| Measuring Plate Fully Opened | 20-1000 |
| **Camry (2.5L), Land Cruiser & Supra (Non Turbo)** | |
| $E_2$-Vc | 200-400 |
| $E_1$-Fc | |
| Measuring Plate Fully Closed | No Continuity |
| Measuring Plate Other Than Closed | 0 |
| $E_2$-Vs | |
| Measuring Plate Fully Closed | 200-600 |
| Measuring Plate Fully Opened | 20-1000 |
| **Celica (3S-GTE) & MR2 (3S-GTE)** | |
| $E_2$-Vs | |
| Measuring Plate Fully Closed | 200-600 |
| Measuring Plate Fully Open | 20-1200 |
| **Corolla (4A-GE)** | |
| $E_2$-Vc | 100-300 |
| $E_2$-Vb | 200-400 |
| $E_1$-Fc | |
| Measuring Plate Fully Closed | No Continuity |
| Measuring Plate Other Than Closed | 0 |
| $E_2$-Vs | |
| Measuring Plate Fully Closed | 20-400 |
| Measuring Plate Fully Open | 20-3000 |
| **Cressida** | |
| $E_2$-Vc | 200-400 |
| $E_2$-Vb | |
| $E_1$-Fc | |
| Measuring Plate Fully Closed | No Continuity |
| Measuring Plate Open | 0 |
| $E_2$-Vs | |
| Fully Closed | 200-600 |
| Fully Open | 20-1200 |
| **Pickup & 4Runner** | |
| $E_2$-Vc | 100-300 |
| $E_2$-Vb | 200-400 |
| $E_1$-Fc | |
| Measuring Plate Fully Closed | No Continuity |
| Measuring Plate Fully Open | 0 |
| $E_2$-Vs | |
| Measuring Plate Fully Closed | 20-400 |
| Measuring Plate Fully Open | 20-1000 |
| **Previa** | |
| $E_2$-Vc | 200-4600 |
| $E_2$-Vs | |
| Measuring Plate Fully Closed | 200-600 |
| Measuring Plate Fully Open | 20-1200 |
| Fc-$E_1$ | |
| Measuring Plate Fully Closed | No Continuity |
| Measuring Plate Other Than Closed | 0 |
| **Supra (Turbo)** | |
| Ks-$E_1$ | No Continuity |
| $E_1$-Ks | 5000-10,000 |
| Vc-$E_1$ | 10,000-15,000 |
| $E_1$-Vc | 5000-10,000 |
| **All Models** | |
| $E_2$-THA | |
| -4°F (20°C) | 10,000-20,000 |
| 32°F (0°C) | 4000-7000 |
| 68°F (20°C) | 2000-3000 |
| 104°F (40°C) | 900-1300 |
| 140°F (60°C) | 400-700 |

**Air Temperature Sensor (Celica Non-Turbo, Corolla 4A-FE, MR2 5S-FE & Tercel)** - Ensure ignition is off. Unplug air temperature sensor. Measure resistance across air temperature sensor terminals at specified temperature. *See Fig. 6.* Replace air temperature sensor if not within specification.

**Camshaft Position Sensor (Supra Turbo)** - For camshaft position sensor, see PICK-UP COIL AIR GAP CHECK and PICK-UP COIL RESISTANCE TEST under IGNITION CHECKS (SUPRA TURBO) in BASIC DIAGNOSTIC PROCEDURES article. If pick-up coil air gap or resistance is not within specification, replace camshaft position sensor.

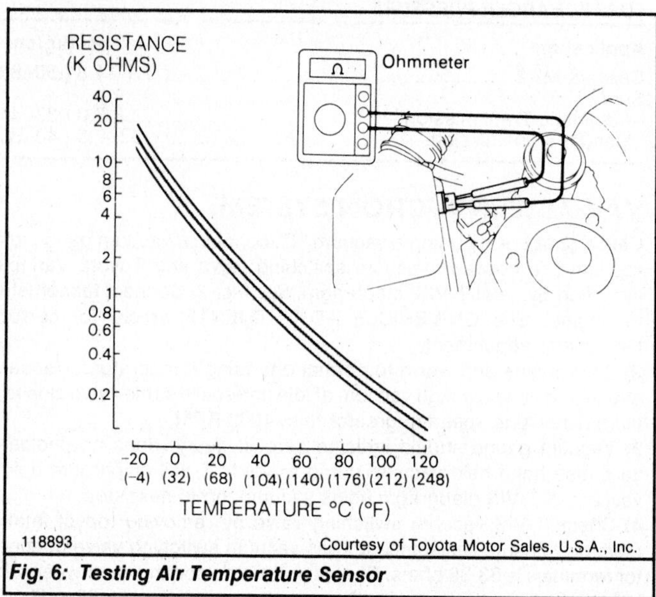


***Fig. 6: Testing Air Temperature Sensor***

**Cold Start Injector Time Switch** - Turn ignition off. Remove connector from switch. Measure resistance across switch terminals at specified temperature. *See Fig. 7.* Replace switch if resistance is not within specification. See COLD START INJECTOR TIME SWITCH RESISTANCE SPECIFICATIONS table.

***COLD START INJECTOR TIME SWITCH RESISTANCE SPECIFICATIONS***

| Application & Terminals | Temperature °F (°C) | Ohms |
|---|---|---|
| Camry, Previa & Supra | | |
| STA-STJ | Less Than 59 (15) | 25-45 |
| | Greater Than 86 (30) | 65-85 |
| STA-Ground | | 25-85 |
| Corolla & MR2 (2.2L) | | |
| STA-STJ | Less Than 86 (30) | 20-40 |
| | Grater Than 104 (40) | 40-60 |
| STA-Ground | | 20-80 |
| Celica, Land Cruiser, MR2 (2.0L), Pickup & 4Runner | | |
| STA-STJ | Less Than 50 (10) | 30-50 |
| | Greater Than 77 (25) | 70-90 |
| STA-Ground | | 30-90 |

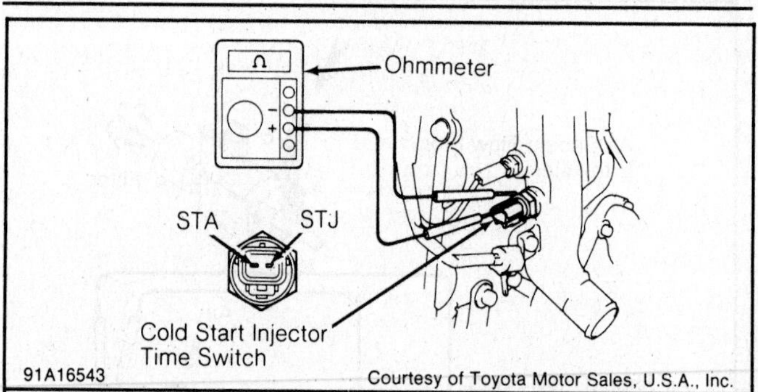


***Fig. 7: Identifying Cold Start Injector Time Switch Terminals***

**Coolant Temperature Sensor** - **1)** Ensure ignition is off. Unplug connector from sensor. For sensor location, see appropriate illustration in THEORY & OPERATION article.

**2)** Using ohmmeter, check resistance between sensor terminals. Replace sensor if resistance is not within specification at specified temperature. *See Fig. 8.*

# 1991 ENGINE PERFORMANCE
# System & Component Testing (Cont.)

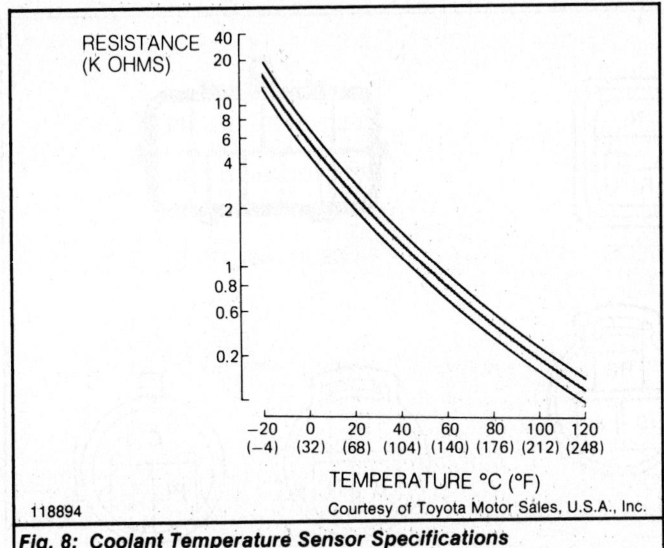


***Fig. 8: Coolant Temperature Sensor Specifications***

**EGR Gas Temperature Sensor – 1)** Remove sensor from side of EGR valve. Place threaded end of sensor and thermometer in container of oil. *See Fig. 9*.

**2)** Attach ohmmeter to sensor terminals. Heat oil and note resistance at specified temperature. See EGR TEMPERATURE SENSOR SPECIFICATIONS table. Replace sensor if not within specification.

***EGR TEMPERATURE SENSOR SPECIFICATIONS***

| Temperature °F (°C) | Ohms |
|---|---|
| 122 (50) | 69-89 |
| 212 (100) | 12-14 |
| 302 (150) | 3-4 |

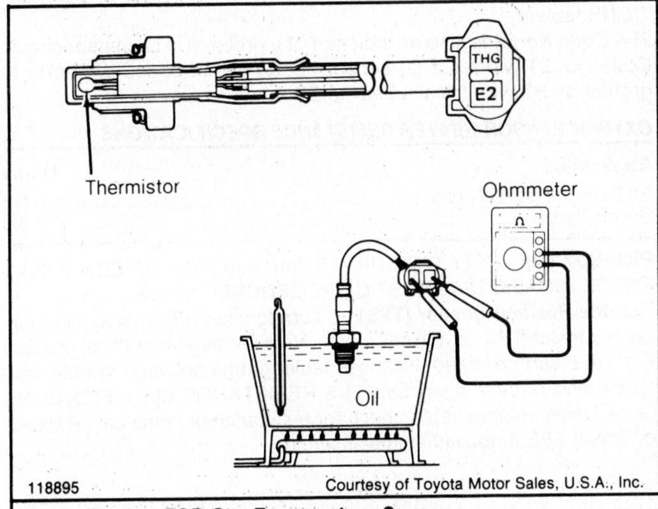


***Fig. 9: Testing EGR Gas Temperature Sensor***

**Knock Sensor –** On models equipped with knock sensor, use diagnosis in Code 52 and 53 charts. For code charts, see SELF-DIAGNOSTICS article.

**Manifold Absolute Pressure (MAP) Sensor –** See VACUUM SENSOR under ENGINE SENSORS & SWITCHES in this article.

**Neutral/Start Switch –** Unplug switch connector at transmission or transaxle. Note terminal identification. *See Fig. 10.* Using ohmmeter, check for continuity at specified terminals with gearshift in correct range. See NEUTRAL/START SWITCH SPECIFICATIONS table.

***NOTE: Information for MR2 and Previa neutral/start switch is not available from manufacturer.***

***NEUTRAL/START SWITCH SPECIFICATIONS***

| Application & Gearshift Position | Terminal Continuity |
|---|---|
| **Camry** | |
| 2.5L Engine | |
| P | B & N, RB & PL |
| R | RL & RB |
| N | B & N, RB & NL |
| 2 | 2L & RB |
| L | LL & RB |
| 2.0L Engine | |
| N | NL & C |
| 2 | 2L & C |
| L | LL & C |
| **Celica** | |
| P | B & N, PL & C |
| R | C & RL |
| N | B & N, NL & C |
| D | C & DL |
| 2 | C & 2L |
| L | C & LL |
| **Corolla** | |
| P | 3 & 4 |
| R | 1 & 2 |
| N | 3 & 4 |
| **Cressida, Pickup/4Runner (2.4L) & Supra** | |
| P | B & N, C & PB |
| R | C & RB |
| N | B & N, C & NB |
| D | C & DB |
| 2 | C & 2B |
| L | C & LB |
| **Land Cruiser** | |
| P | C & PL, N & B |
| R | C & RL |
| N | B & N |
| **Pickup (3.0L Engine W/A340E A/T)** | |
| P | B & N, C & PL |
| R | C & RL |
| N | B & N, C & NL |
| D | C & DL |
| 2 | C & 2L |
| L | C & LL |

**Oxygen ($O_2$) Sensor Feedback Voltage Test – 1)** Warm engine to normal operating temperature. Connect analog-type voltmeter to engine check connector VF1 (or VF) and E1 terminals. *See Fig. 11.* Perform procedures listed in *Fig. 12*.

**2)** Depending on model application, some vehicles may be equipped with a main $O_2$ sensor, sub-oxygen sensor and an $O_2$ sensor heater. See OXYGEN SENSOR USAGE table.

***NOTE: Codes No. 21, 25, 26 and 27 are $O_2$ sensor circuit codes. Also check for coolant temperature sensor Code No. 22. Faulty coolant temperature sensor could cause faulty $O_2$ sensor readings.***

***OXYGEN SENSOR USAGE***

| Application | Main | Sub | Heater |
|---|---|---|---|
| Camry | X | [1] X | [2] X |
| Celica & MR2 | | | |
| 1.6L | X | ..... | [3] X |
| 2.0L | X | ..... | X |
| 2.2L | X | [1] X | ..... |
| Corolla | | | |
| 4A-FE | X | ..... | ..... |
| 4A-GE | X | [1] X | X |
| Cressida | X | [1] X | X |
| Land Cruiser | X | ..... | X |
| Pickup/4Runner | X | ..... | X |
| Previa | X | X | X |
| Supra | X | [4] X | X |

[1] – Calif. only.
[2] – 2VZ-E engine only.
[3] – Except Calif.
[4] – Non Turbo, Calif. only.

# 1991 ENGINE PERFORMANCE
## System & Component Testing (Cont.)

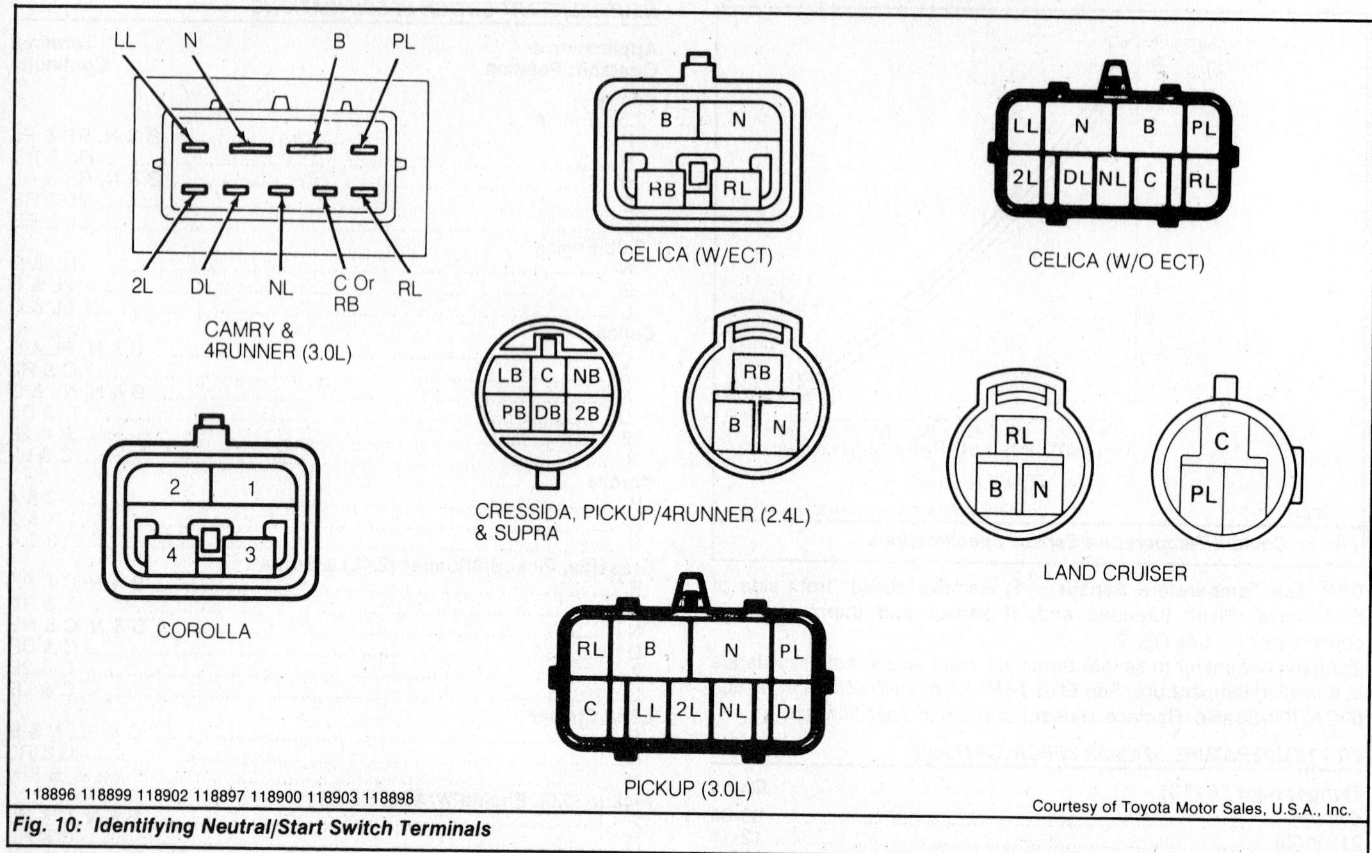


*Fig. 10: Identifying Neutral/Start Switch Terminals*

**Sub-Oxygen Sensor – 1)** Warm engine to normal operating temperature. Check ECU for stored fault code(s). If sub-oxygen sensor or circuit fails, a Code 27 fault code will set in ECU memory. Clear codes if present. See CLEARING TROUBLE CODES in SELF-DIAGNOSTICS article.

***NOTE: DO NOT drive vehicle more than 62 MPH or code will cancel.***

**2)** On all except Supra, drive vehicle between 50 and 61 MPH for at least 5 minutes in 4th or 5th gear (M/T) or Drive (A/T). On Supra, drive vehicle at 50 MPH or less for at least 5 minutes in 4th or 5th gear (M/T) or Drive (A/T).

**3)** On all models, fully depress accelerator pedal for at least 10 seconds with engine RPM at least 3000 RPM. Stop engine and turn ignition off.

**4)** Repeat previous steps and note if Code 27 exists again. If Code 27 exists again, check sub-oxygen sensor circuit for continuity, shorts or grounds. Replace sub-oxygen sensor if circuit is okay.

**Oxygen ($O_2$) Sensor Heater – 1)** Unplug $O_2$ sensor connector. Using ohmmeter, measure resistance between sensor terminals. +B and HT. *See Fig. 13.* Replace sensor if resistance is not within specification. See OXYGEN SENSOR HEATER RESISTANCE SPECIFICATIONS table.

**2)** A Code No. 21 is also an indicator of a problem in $O_2$ sensor circuit. Code No. 21 will set if $O_2$ sensor heater circuit opens or shorts to ground on HT wire from sensor to ECU.

***OXYGEN SENSOR HEATER RESISTANCE SPECIFICATIONS***

| Application | Ohms |
|---|---|
| All Except Supra Turbo | 5.1-6.3 |
| Supra Turbo | 3.0-3.6 |

**Pick-Up Coils –** See PICK-UP AIR GAP and PICK-UP COIL RESISTANCE in BASIC DIAGNOSTIC PROCEDURES article.

**Throttle Position Sensor (TPS) –** Turn ignition off. Unplug electrical connector at TPS on throttle body. Note terminal identification. *See Fig. 14.* Insert specified thickness feeler gauge between throttle stop screw and throttle lever. See TPS RESISTANCE SPECIFICATIONS table. Using an ohmmeter, check for resistance or continuity. Replace or adjust TPS if not within specification.

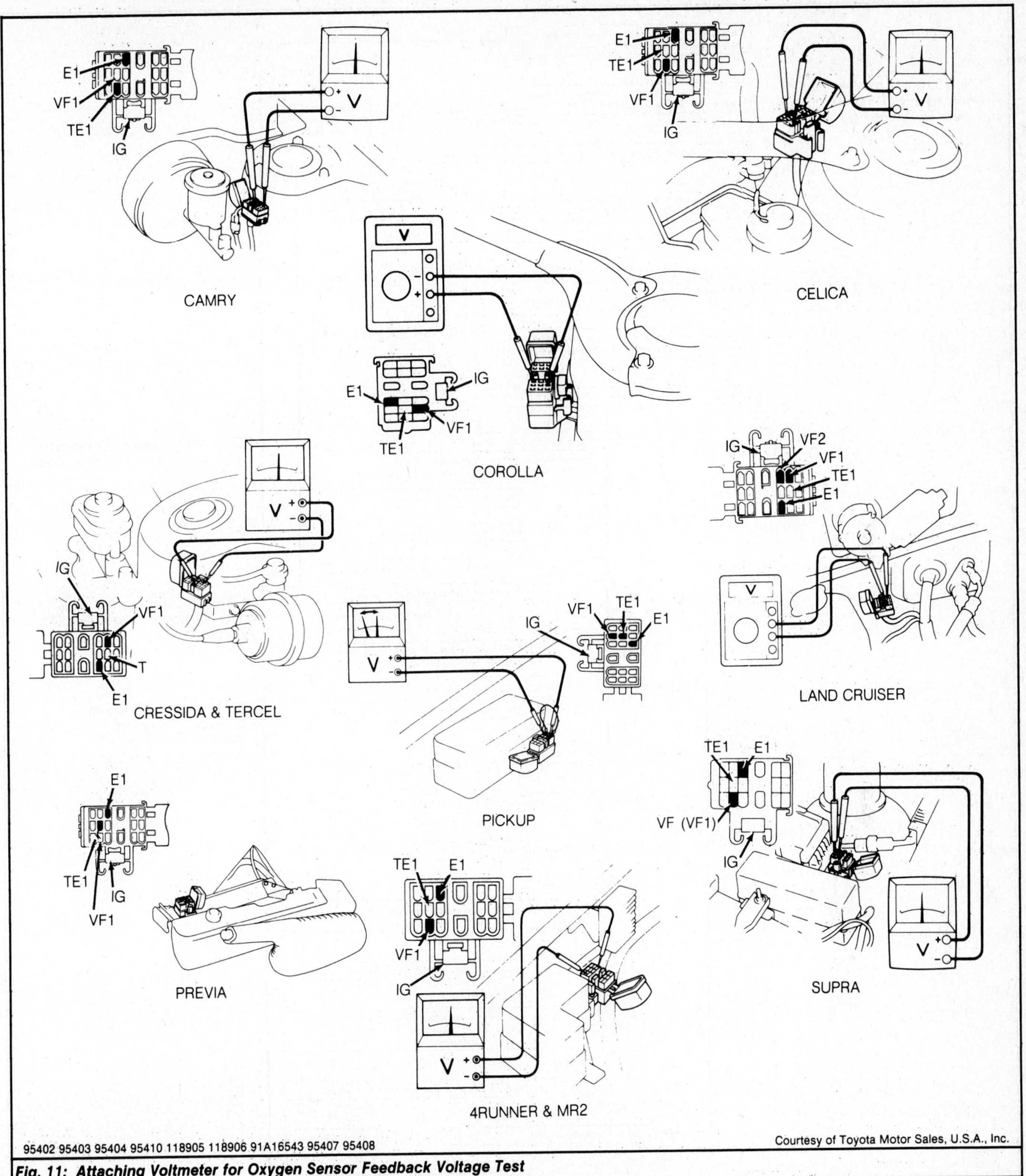


*Fig. 11: Attaching Voltmeter for Oxygen Sensor Feedback Voltage Test*

# 1991 ENGINE PERFORMANCE
## System & Component Testing (Cont.)

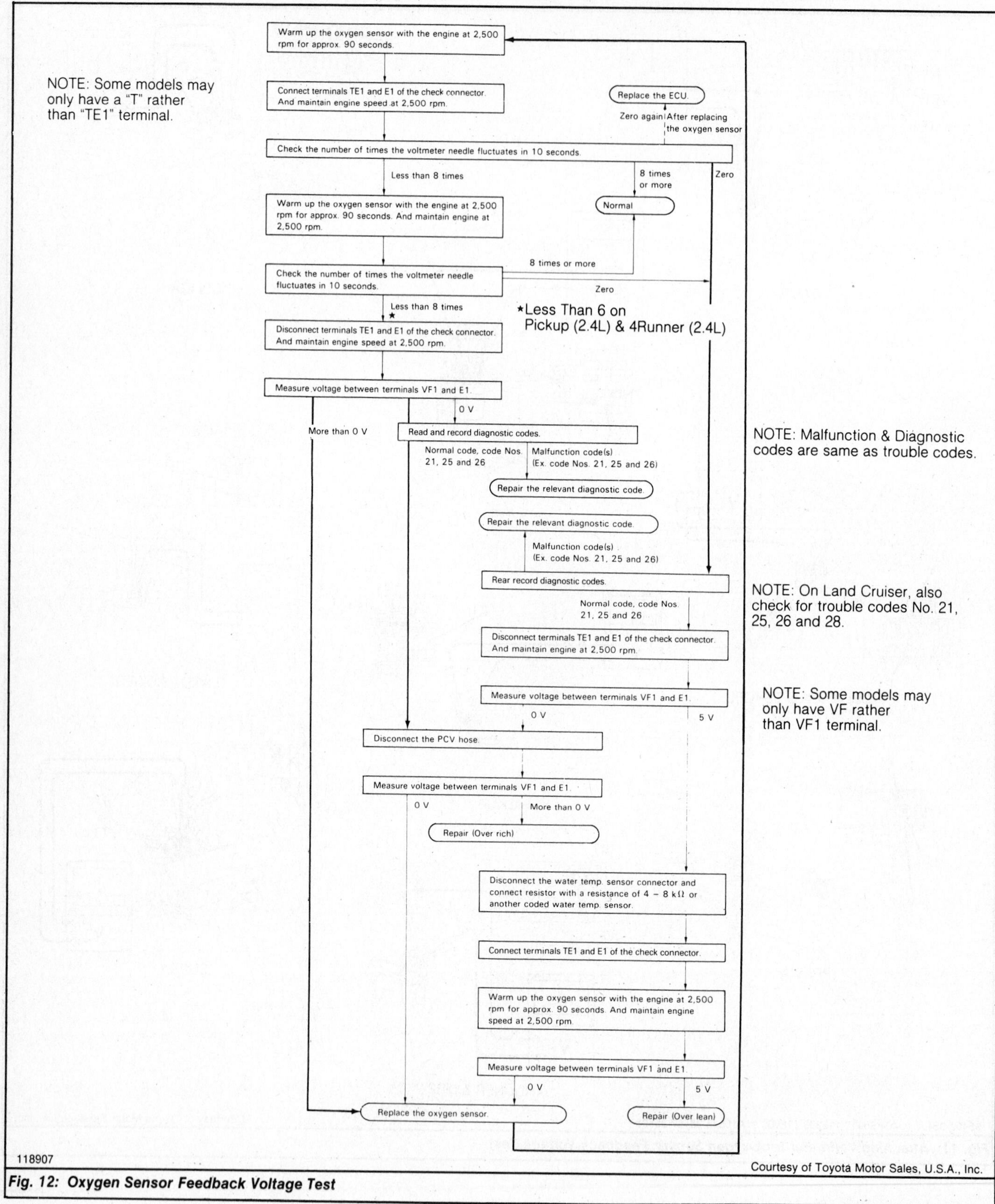


**Fig. 12: Oxygen Sensor Feedback Voltage Test**

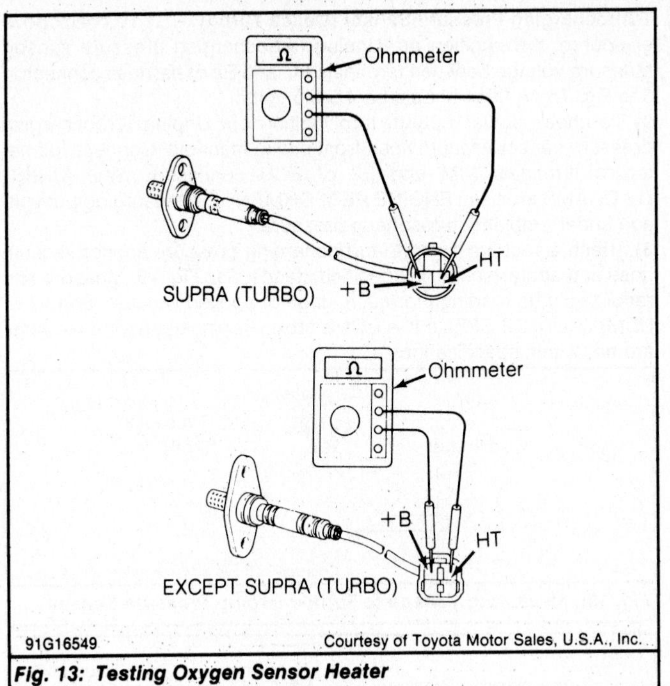

*Fig. 13: Testing Oxygen Sensor Heater*

***TPS RESISTANCE SPECIFICATIONS***

| Application | Clearance In. (mm) | Terminal | Ohmmeter Reading |
|---|---|---|---|
| **Camry** | | | |
| 2.0L | | | |
| (W/O ECT) | .020 (.51) | IDL & $E_1$ | Continuity |
| | | PSW & $E_1$ | No Continuity |
| | .035 (.90) | IDL & $E_1$ | No Continuity |
| | | PSW & $E_1$ | No Continuity |
| | Fully Open | IDL & $E_1$ | No Continuity |
| | | PSW & $E_1$ | Continuity |
| 2.0L | | | |
| (W/ ECT) | 0 (0) | VTA & $E_2$ | 200-800 |
| | .020 (.51) | IDL & $E_2$ | 2300 or Less |
| | .028 (.70) | IDL & $E_2$ | No Continuity |
| | Fully Open | VAT & $E_2$ | 3300-10,000 |
| | | VC & $E_2$ | 3000-7000 |
| 2.5L | 0 (0) | VTA & $E_2$ | 300-6300 |
| | .012 (.30) | IDL & $E_2$ | 2300 or Less |
| | .028 (.71) | IDL & $E_2$ | No Continuity |
| | Fully Open | VTA & $E_2$ | 3500-10,300 |
| | | VC & $E_2$ | 4250-8250 |
| **Celica** | | | |
| 1.6L | .024 (.60) | IDL-$E_2$ | Continuity |
| | | PSW-$E_2$ | No Continuity |
| | .031 (.80) | IDL-$E_2$ | No Continuity |
| | | PSW-$E_2$ | No Continuity |
| | Fully Open | IDL-$E_2$ | No Continuity |
| | | PSW-$E_2$ | Continuity |
| 2.2L W/O ECT | .020 (.50) | IDL-$E_2$ | Continuity |
| | | PSW-$E_2$ | No Continuity |
| | .035 (.90) | IDL-$E_2$ | No Continuity |
| | | PSW-$E_2$ | No Continuity |
| | Fully Open | IDL-$E_2$ | No Continuity |
| | | PSW-$E_2$ | Continuity |
| 2.0L | 0 (0) | VTA & $E_2$ | 200-800 |
| | .020 (.51) | IDL & $E_2$ | 2300 or Less |
| | .028 (.71) | IDL & $E_2$ | No Continuity |
| | Fully Open | VTA & $E_2$ | 3300-10,300 |
| | | VC & $E_2$ | 3000-8300 |

***TPS RESISTANCE SPECIFICATIONS (Cont.)***

| Application | Clearance In. (mm) | Terminal | Ohmmeter Reading |
|---|---|---|---|
| **Celica Cont.** | | | |
| 2.0L | .020 (.51) | IDL & $E_1$ | Continuity |
| | .020 (.51) | PSW & $E_1$ | No Continuity |
| | .035 (.89) | IDL & $E_1$ | No Continuity |
| | .035 (.89) | PSW & $E_1$ | No Continuity |
| | Fully Open | VTA & $E_2$ | 3300-10,300 |
| | | VC & $E_2$ | 3000-8300 |
| 2.0L | .020 (.51) | IDL & $E_1$ | Continuity |
| | .020 (.51) | PSW & $E_1$ | No Continuity |
| | .035 (.89) | IDL & $E_1$ | No Continuity |
| | .035 (.89) | PSW & $E_1$ | No Continuity |
| | Fully Open | IDL & $E_1$ | No Continuity |
| | | PSW & $E_1$ | Continuity |
| 5S-GTE | 0 (0) | VTA & $E_2$ | 200-800 |
| | .020 (.51) | IDL & $E_2$ | 2300 or Less |
| | .028 (.71) | IDL & $E_2$ | No Continuity |
| | Fully Open | VTA & $E_2$ | 3300-10,000 |
| | | VC & $E_2$ | 3000-7000 |
| **Corolla** | | | |
| 4A-FE | .024 (.60) | IDL-$E_2$ | Continuity |
| | | PSW-$E_2$ | No Continuity |
| | | IDL-PSW | No Continuity |
| | .032 (.80) | IDL-$E_2$ | No Continuity |
| | | PSW-$E_2$ | No Continuity |
| | | IDL-PSW | No Continuity |
| | Fully Open | IDL-$E_2$ | No Continuity |
| | | PSW-$E_2$ | Continuity |
| | | IDL-PSW | No Continuity |
| 4A-GE | 0 (0) | VTA & $E_2$ | 200-800 |
| | .014 (.36) | IDL & $E_2$ | 2300 or Less |
| | .023 (.58) | IDL & $E_2$ | No Continuity |
| | Fully Open | VTA & $E_2$ | 3300-10,000 |
| | | VCC & $E_2$ | 3000-7000 |
| **Cressida** | 0 (0) | VTA & $E_2$ | 300-6300 |
| | .020 (.51) | IDL & $E_2$ | 2300 or Less |
| | .035 (.89) | IDL & $E_2$ | No Continuity |
| | Fully Open | VTA & $E_2$ | 3500-10,300 |
| | | VC & $E_2$ | 4250-8250 |
| **Land Cruiser** | 0 (0) | VTA & $E_2$ | 300-6300 |
| | .030 (.76) | IDL & $E_2$ | 2300 or Less |
| | .043 (1.09) | IDL & $E_2$ | No Continuity |
| | Fully Open | VTA & $E_2$ | 3500-10,300 |
| | | VC & $E_2$ | 4250-8250 |
| **MR2** | | | |
| 2.0L & 2.2L (A/T) | | | |
| | 0 (0) | VTA & $E_2$ | 200-800 |
| | .020 (.51) | IDL & $E_2$ | 2300 or Less |
| | .028 (.71) | IDL & $E_2$ | No Continuity |
| | Fully Open | VTA & $E_2$ | 3300-10,300 |
| | | VC & $E_2$ | 3000-8300 |
| 2.2L (M/T) | .020 (.50) | IDL-$E_1$ | Continuity |
| | | PSW-$E_1$ | No Continuity |
| | .035 (.90) | IDL-$E_1$ | No Continuity |
| | | PSW-$E_1$ | No Continuity |
| | Fully Open | IDL-$E_1$ | No Continuity |
| | | PSW-$E_1$ | Continuity |

# 1991 ENGINE PERFORMANCE
## System & Component Testing (Cont.)

**TPS RESISTANCE SPECIFICATIONS (Cont.)**

| Application | Clearance In. (mm) | Terminal | Ohmmeter Reading |
|---|---|---|---|
| **Pickup & 4Runner** | | | |
| 2.4L | 0 (0) | VTA & $E_2$ | 200-800 |
| | .022 (.56) | IDL & $E_2$ | 2300 or Less |
| | .034 (.86) | IDL & $E_2$ | No Continuity |
| | Fully Open | VTA & $E_2$ | 3300-10,000 |
| | | VCC & $E_2$ | 4000-9000 |
| 3.0L | 0 (0) | VTA & $E_2$ | 200-800 |
| | .020 (.51) | IDL & $E_2$ | 2300 or Less |
| | .030 (.76) | IDL & $E_2$ | No Continuity |
| | Fully Open | VTA & $E_2$ | 3300-10,000 |
| | | VCC & $E_2$ | 4000-9000 |
| **Previa** | 0 (0) | VTA & $E_2$ | 300-6300 |
| | .014 (.36) | IDL & $E_2$ | 2300 or Less |
| | .023 (.58) | IDL & $E_2$ | No Continuity |
| | Fully Open | VTA & $E_2$ | 3500-10,3000 |
| | | VCC & $E_2$ | 425-825 |
| **Supra** | | | |
| Non-Turbo | 0 (0) | VTA & $E_2$ | 200-1200 |
| | .016 (.41) | IDL & $E_2$ | 2300 or Less |
| | .030 (.76) | IDL & $E_2$ | No Continuity |
| | Fully Open | VTA & $E_2$ | 3500-10,300 |
| | | VC & $E_2$ | 4250-8250 |
| Turbo | 0 (0) | VTA & $E_2$ | 200-1200 |
| | .020 (.51) | IDL & $E_2$ | 2300 or Less |
| | .035 (.89) | IDL & $E_2$ | No Continuity |
| | Fully Open | VTA & $E_2$ | 3500-10,300 |
| | | VC & $E_2$ | 4250-8250 |
| **Tercel** | .024 (.60) | IDL & $E_2$ | Continuity |
| | .024 (.60) | PSW & $E_2$ | No Continuity |
| | .024 (.60) | PSW & IDL | No Continuity |
| | .032 (.80) | IDL & $E_2$ | No Continuity |
| | .032 (.80) | PSW & $E_2$ | No Continuity |
| | .032 (.80) | PSW & IDL | No Continuity |
| | Fully Open | IDL & $E_2$ | No Continuity |
| | | PSW & $E_2$ | Continuity |
| | | PSW & IDL | No Continuity |

**Turbocharging Pressure Sensor (Celica Turbo) – 1)** To check power source, turn ignition on. Unplug turbocharging pressure sensor. Measure voltage between terminals VC and E2 of harness connector. *See Fig. 15.* Voltage should be 4.5-5.5 volts.

**2)** To check power output, turn ignition on. Unplug turbocharging pressure sensor vacuum hose from intake manifold. Connect voltmeter to terminals PIM and E2 of ECU connector. See WIRING DIAGRAMS article in ENGINE PERFORMANCE. Measure output voltage under ambient atmospheric pressure.

**3)** Attach a vacuum pump to turbocharging pressure sensor vacuum hose and apply vacuum in specified stages. *See Fig. 16.* Measure and record voltage readings for each stage of applied vacuum. See VACUUM/VOLTAGE SPECIFICATIONS table. Replace sensor if readings are not within specifications.

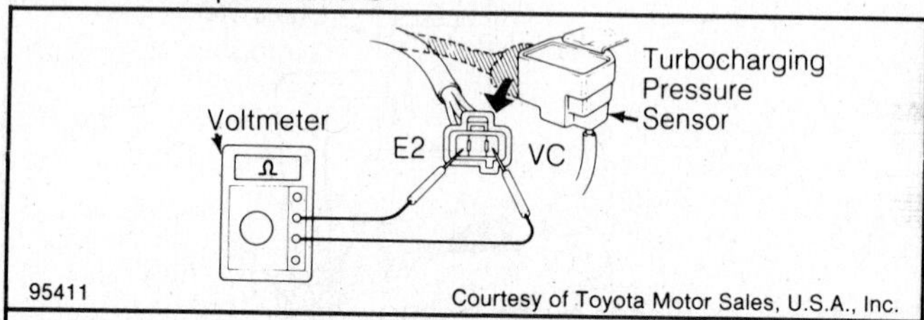


**Fig. 15: Measuring Voltage to Turbocharging Pressure Sensor**

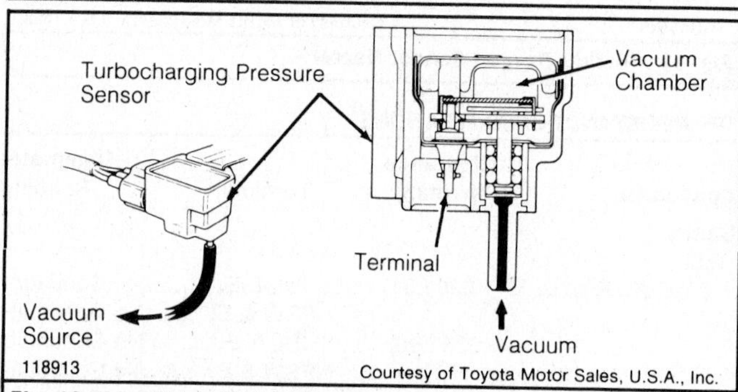


**Fig. 16: Identifying Turbocharging Pressure Sensor**

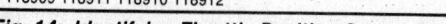

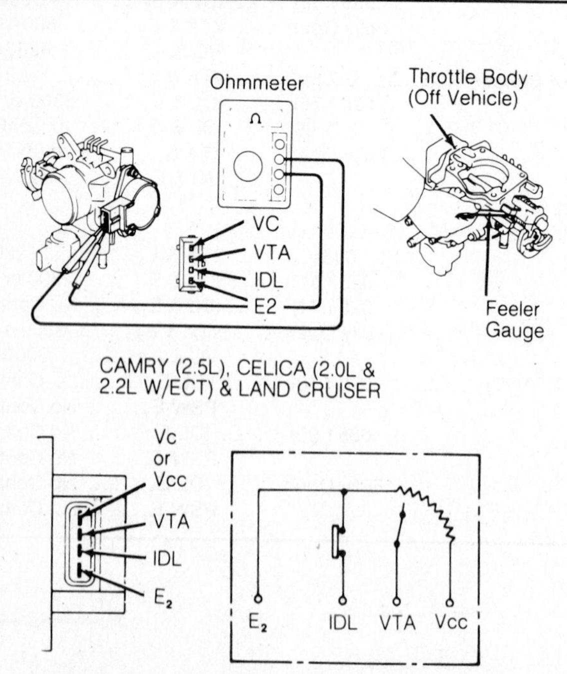


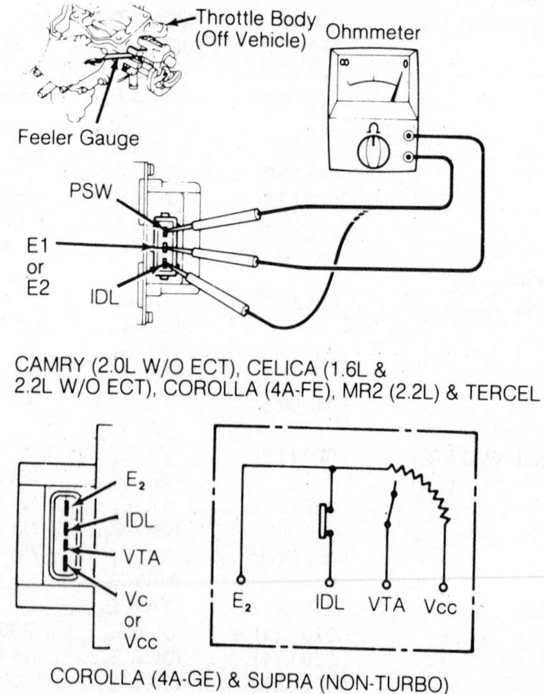


**Fig. 14: Identifying Throttle Position Sensor Terminals**

# 1991 ENGINE PERFORMANCE
# System & Component Testing (Cont.)

***VACUUM/VOLTAGE SPECIFICATIONS***

| Applied Vacuum In. Hg | Volts |
|---|---|
| 3.94 | .15-.35 |
| 7.87 | .40-.60 |
| 11.81 | .65-.85 |
| 15.75 | .90-1.10 |
| 19.69 | 1.15-1.35 |

**Turbo Pressure Sensor (Supra Turbo)** – Check ECU for stored fault code(s). If turbo pressure sensor or circuit fails, a Code 34 will set in ECU memory. Use diagnosis in Code 34 chart. See SELF-DIAGNOSTICS article.

**Turbocharger Vacuum Switching Valve (VSV)** – **1)** Using ohmmeter, check continuity between turbocharger VSV connector terminals. *See Fig. 17.* Resistance should be 24-30 ohms. Ensure no continuity exists between VSV case (body) and each terminal. If continuity is not as specified, replace VSV.

**2)** Ensure air blown into pipe "E" does not flow from pipe "F". *See Fig. 17.* If air does not pass out pipe "F", apply battery voltage and ground to VSV terminals. Air should now flow from pipe "E" to pipe "F". If air does not flow as indicated, replace VSV.

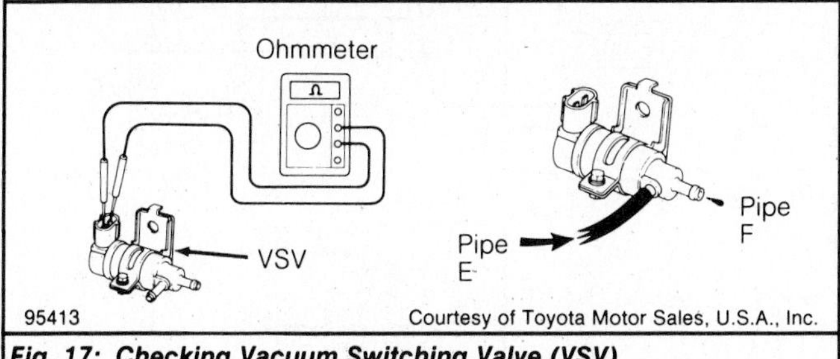


***Fig. 17: Checking Vacuum Switching Valve (VSV)***

**Vacuum Sensor (Celica, Corolla 4A-FE & Tercel)** – **1)** Ensure ignition switch is off. Locate sensor on center of firewall. Unplug vacuum sensor electrical connector. Turn ignition on, with engine off.

***NOTE: Vacuum sensor on Celica, Corolla (4A-FE) and Tercel is also known as Manifold Absolute Pressure (MAP) sensor.***

**2)** Measure voltage between both terminals of sensor harness. *See Fig. 18.* Voltage should be 4.0-6.0 volts (4.5-5.5 volts for Celica). This is reference voltage from ECU. If voltage is not present or low, check wiring and ECU.

**3)** Turn ignition off. Plug in vacuum sensor electrical connector. Disconnect vacuum sensor hose from intake chamber. Turn ignition on with engine off. With ECU connectors in place, connect DVOM to back side of terminals E2 and PIM. *See Fig. 18.*

**4)** Connect hand-held vacuum pump/gauge to sensor vacuum hose. Measure voltage drop at specified vacuum reading. See VACUUM SENSOR SPECIFICATIONS table. Replace sensor if defective.

***VACUUM SENSOR SPECIFICATIONS***

| In. Hg | Voltage Drop |
|---|---|
| 3.94 | .3-.5 |
| 7.9 | .7-.9 |
| 11.8 | 1.1-1.3 |
| 15.7 | 1.5-1.7 |
| 19.7 | 1.9-2.1 |

**Vehicle Speed Sensor (Celica, Land Cruiser & MR2)** – **1)** Apply positive battery voltage to terminal No. 1 of speed sensor. *See Fig. 19.* Connect terminal No. 3 to ground. Connect ohmmeter between terminal No. 2 and negative terminal of battery

**2)** Ohmmeter should show continuity as meter shaft is rotated (4 times per revolution). If ohmmeter does not deflect as specified, replace speed sensor.

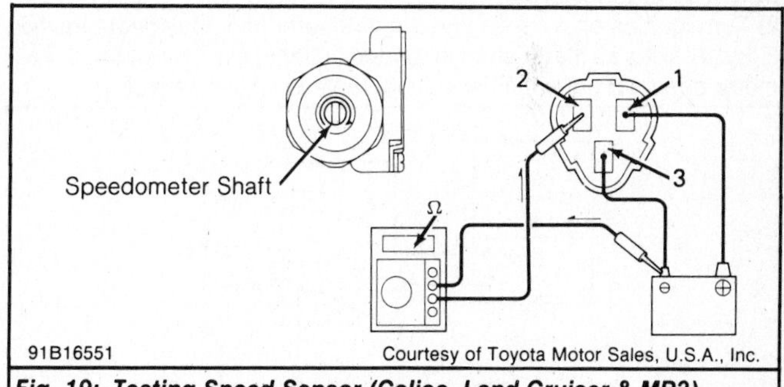


***Fig. 19: Testing Speed Sensor (Celica, Land Cruiser & MR2)***

CELICA (1.6L) & COROLLA (4A-FE)

CELICA (1.6L) & COROLLA (4A-F3)

CELICA (2.2L W/O ECT) & TERCEL

CELICA (2.2L W/ECT)

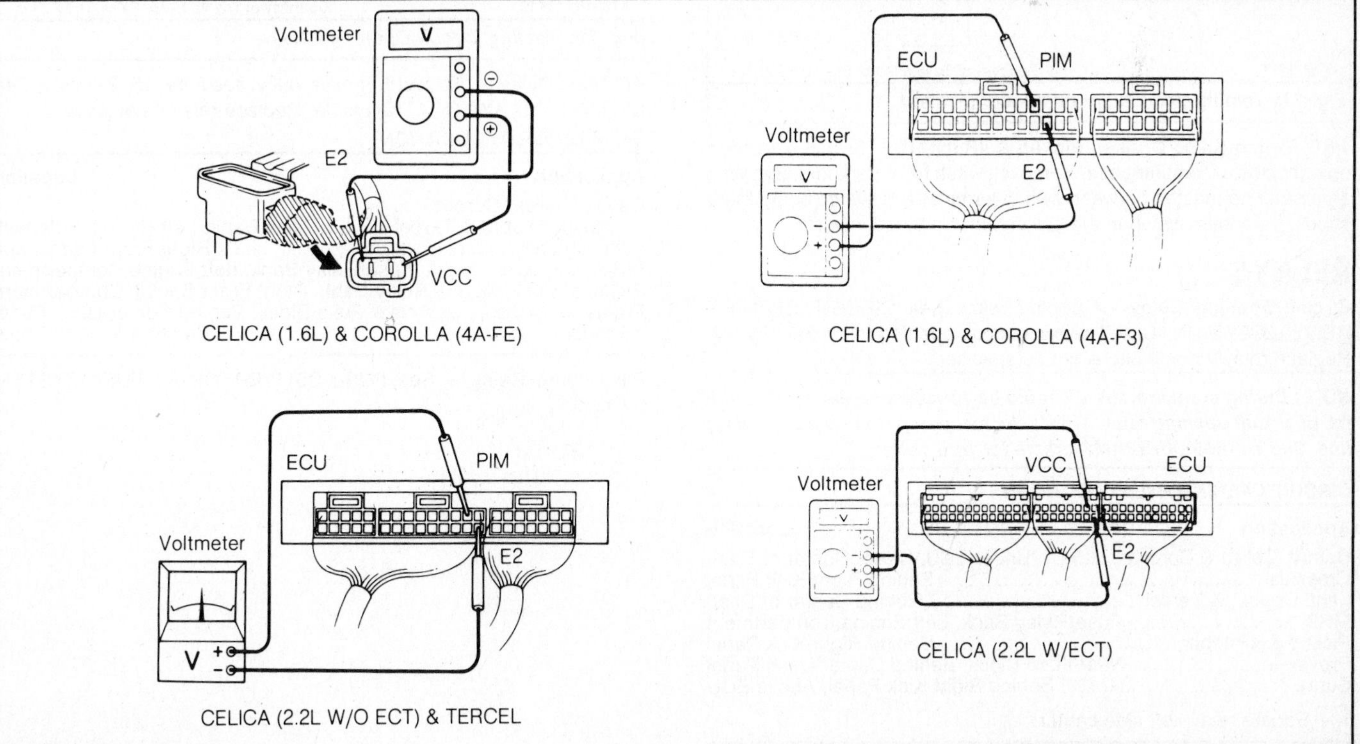

118915 90A22152 90B22153

Courtesy of Toyota Motor Sales, U.S.A., Inc.

***Fig. 18: Testing Vacuum Sensor***

# 1991 ENGINE PERFORMANCE
# System & Component Testing (Cont.)

**Vehicle Speed Sensor (Camry, Corolla, Pickup, Supra & 4Runner) –**
**1)** Remove combination meter from instrument cluster. Connect ohmmeter between terminals "A" and "B". *See Fig. 20.*
**2)** Rotate meter shaft and note reading. Ohmmeter should deflect from continuity to no continuity 4 times per revolution as shaft is rotated. If ohmmeter does not deflect as specified, replace speed sensor.

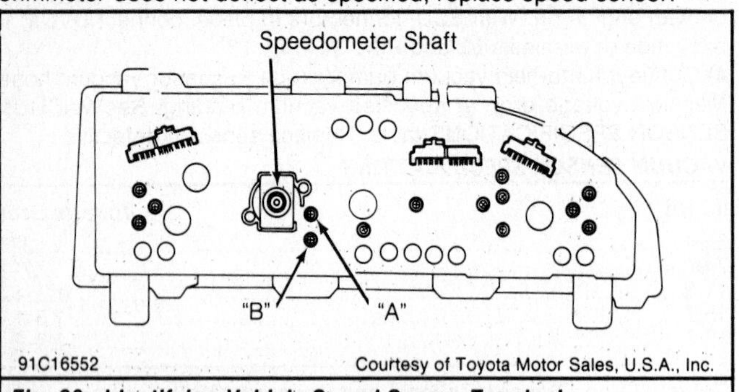


***Fig. 20: Identifying Vehicle Speed Sensor Terminals (Camry, Corolla, Pickup, Supra & 4Runner)***

**Vehicle Speed Sensor (Previa) – 1)** Apply positive battery voltage to terminal No. 3 of speed sensor. *See Fig. 21.* Connect terminal No. 2 to ground. Connect positive lead of voltmeter to terminal No. 3 and negative lead to terminal No. 1.
**2)** Turn ignition on, with engine off. Voltmeter should deflect between 2 and 12 volts as meter shaft is rotated (4 times per revolution). If voltmeter does not deflect as specified, replace speed sensor.

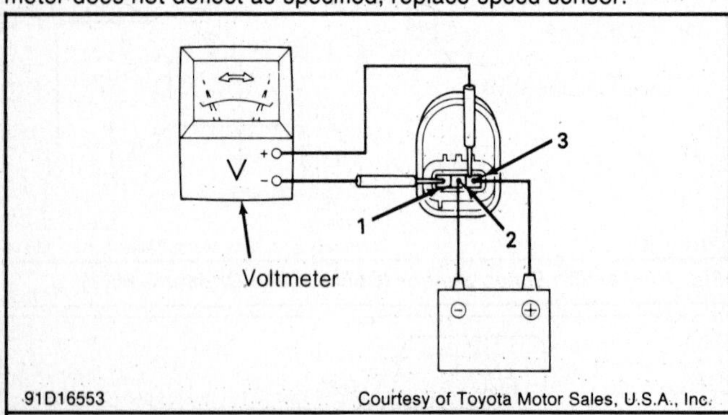


***Fig. 21: Testing Vehicle Speed Sensor (Previa)***

**4WD Switch (Land Cruiser, Pickup & 4Runner) –** Switch is located on right side of transfer case. Remove switch from transfer case. With ohmmeter connected between switch terminal and switch body, there should be continuity when the switch pin is pushed inward.

## RELAYS

**Circuit Opening Relay –** Locate relay. See CIRCUIT OPENING RELAY LOCATION table. To check circuit opening relay, *See Fig. 22.* Replace relay if continuity is not as specified.

***NOTE: During cranking, there should be 12 volts present at FP terminal of circuit opening relay. This is the fuel pump (or fuel pump relay) line. See WIRING DIAGRAMS article for wire color.***

***CIRCUIT OPENING RELAY LOCATION***

| Application | Location |
|---|---|
| Camry, Celica & Corolla | Under ECU, Under Center of Dash |
| Cressida | Behind Right Kick Panel |
| Land Cruiser & Tercel | Behind Center of Dash |
| MR2 | Fuse/Relay Bank, Left Engine Compartment |
| Pickup & 4Runner | Behind Right Kick Panel |
| Previa | Near Fuse Block, Behind Center Dash Panel |
| Supra | [1] Behind Right Kick Panel, Above ECU |

[1] – Square relay, left side center.

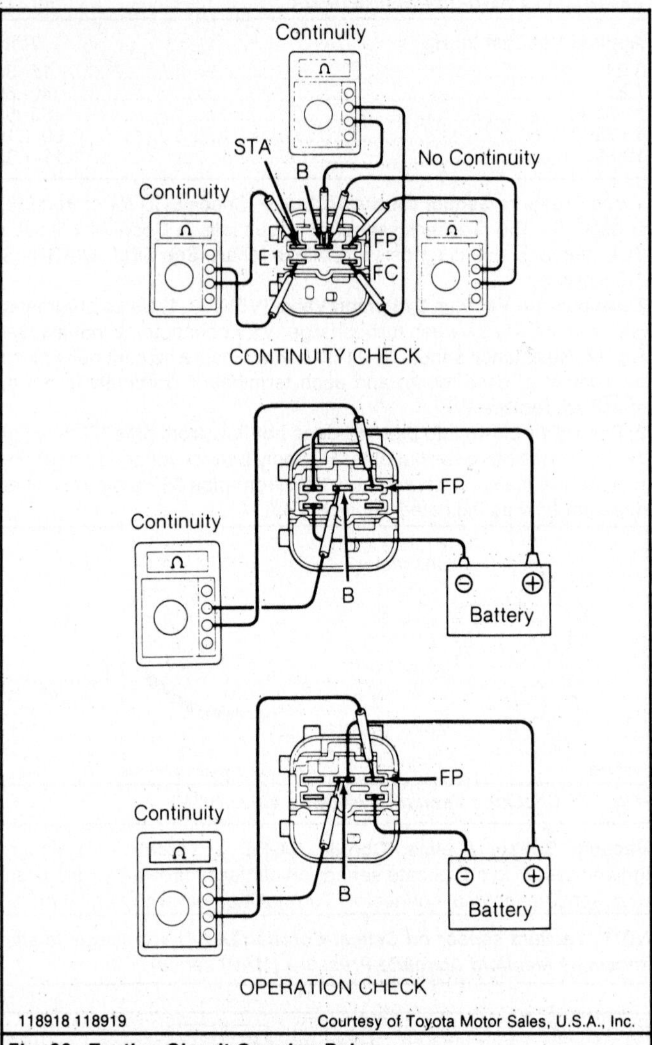


***Fig. 22: Testing Circuit Opening Relay***

**EFI Main Relay –** To test EFI main relay, *see Figs. 23, 24 or 25.* See EFI MAIN RELAY LOCATION table. Replace relay if defective.

***EFI MAIN RELAY LOCATION***

| Application | Location |
|---|---|
| Camry, Celica, Corolla, Cressida, Supra & Tercel | Relay Bank, Left Front Fenderwell |
| Land Cruiser | Right Front Fenderwell |
| MR2 | Fuse/Relay Bank, Left Engine Compartment |
| Pickup | Relay Bank, Right Front Engine Compartment |
| Previa | Near Fuse Block, Behind Center Dash Panel |
| 4Runner | Behind Left Kick Panel |

**Fuel Pump Relay –** See FUEL DELIVERY under FUEL SYSTEM for testing.

# 1991 ENGINE PERFORMANCE
# System & Component Testing (Cont.)

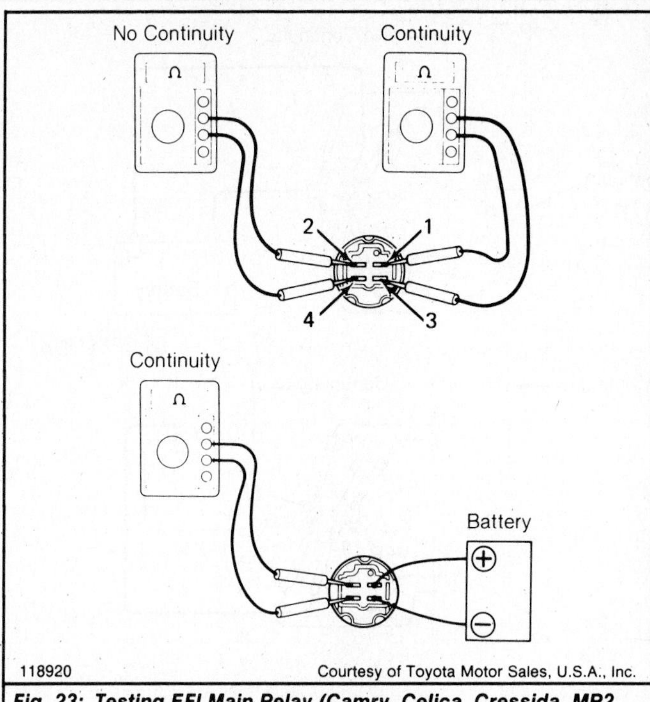

*Fig. 23: Testing EFI Main Relay (Camry, Celica, Cressida, MR2, Pickup, Supra, Tercel & 4Runner)*

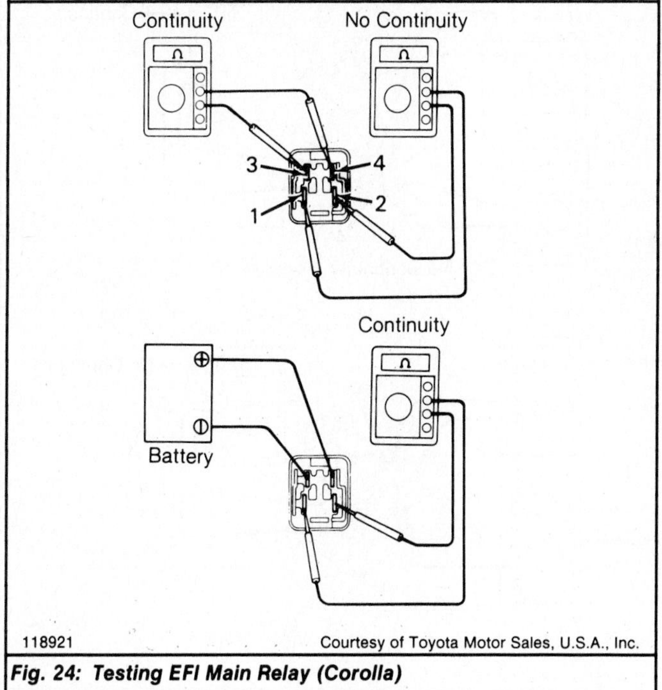


*Fig. 24: Testing EFI Main Relay (Corolla)*

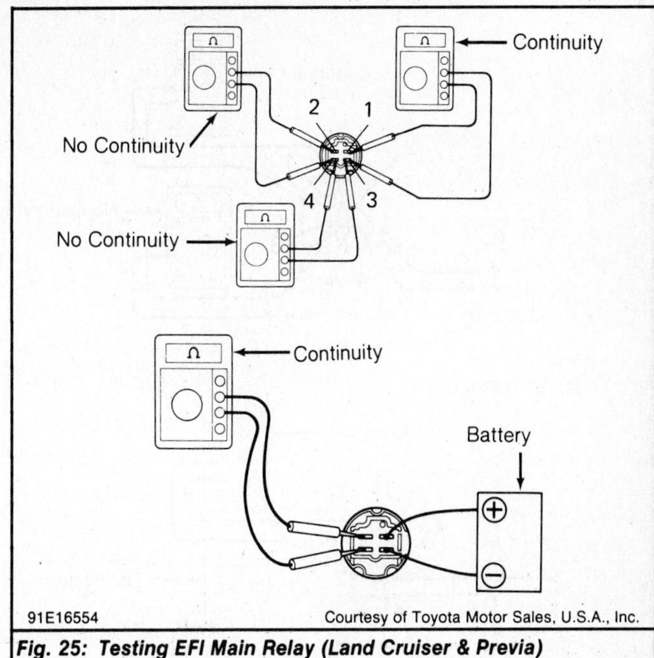


*Fig. 25: Testing EFI Main Relay (Land Cruiser & Previa)*

## FUEL SYSTEM

***WARNING: High fuel pressure may be present in fuel lines and component parts. Relieve pressure before opening system for testing or component replacement. DO NOT allow fuel to flow onto engine or electrical parts.***

### FUEL PRESSURE

**Fuel Pressure Release** – Disconnect negative battery terminal. Place container under fitting to be loosened. Use a rag to cover fuel line/component. Slowly loosen fitting, allowing pressurized fuel to spill into container. After fuel system has depressurized, disconnect and plug fitting.

### FUEL DELIVERY

For fuel pump pressure and fuel pressure regulator testing, see BASIC DIAGNOSTIC PROCEDURES article.

**Fuel Pump Relay & Resistor (Celica Turbo, Cressida & Supra)** – To test relay and resistor, *See Fig. 26*. See FUEL PUMP RELAY LOCATION table. Replace relay or resistor if defective.

***FUEL PUMP RELAY LOCATION***

| Application | Location |
|---|---|
| Celica Turbo | Center of Firewall |
| Cressida | Behind Right Kick Panel |
| Supra | Right Side Fenderwell |

# 1991 ENGINE PERFORMANCE
## System & Component Testing (Cont.)

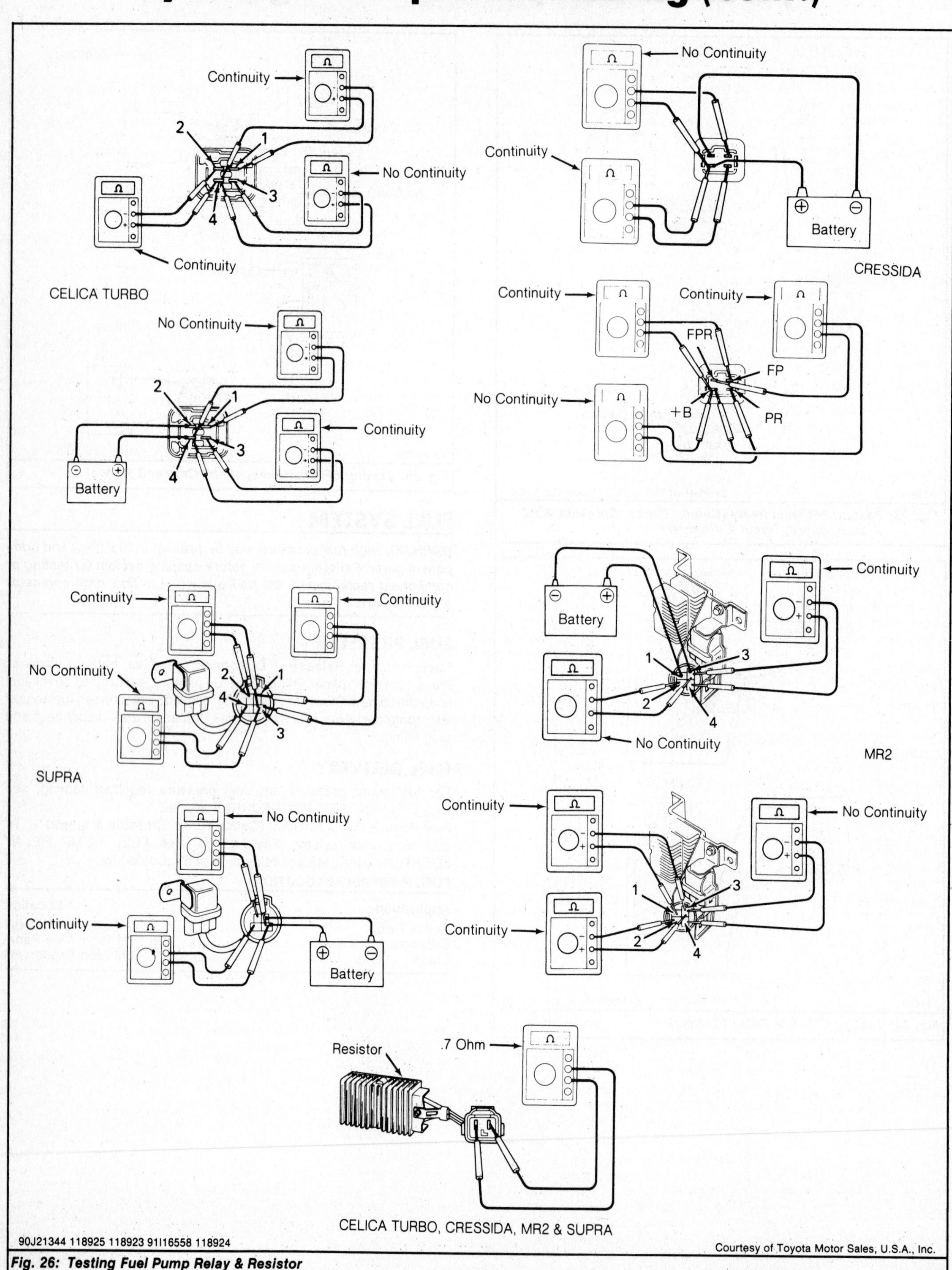


Courtesy of Toyota Motor Sales, U.S.A., Inc.

*Fig. 26: Testing Fuel Pump Relay & Resistor*

## FUEL CONTROL

**Fuel Injector Solenoid Resistor (Celica Turbo & Supra Turbo) - 1)** Turn ignition off. Unplug injector solenoid resistor. See FUEL INJECTOR SOLENOID RESISTOR LOCATION table. Check resistance between terminal B+ and other terminals. *See Fig. 27.* See FUEL INJECTOR SOLENOID RESISTOR SPECIFICATIONS table.

**2)** If resistance is not as specified, replace solenoid resistor. If resistance is as specified, check power feed to fuel injector resistor.

***FUEL INJECTOR SOLENOID RESISTOR LOCATION***

| Application | Location |
|---|---|
| Celica Turbo | By Relay, Bank Left Fenderwell |
| Supra Turbo | Left Shock Tower |

***FUEL INJECTOR SOLENOID RESISTOR SPECIFICATIONS***

| Application | Ohms |
|---|---|
| Celica Turbo | 4-6 |
| Supra Turbo | 3 |

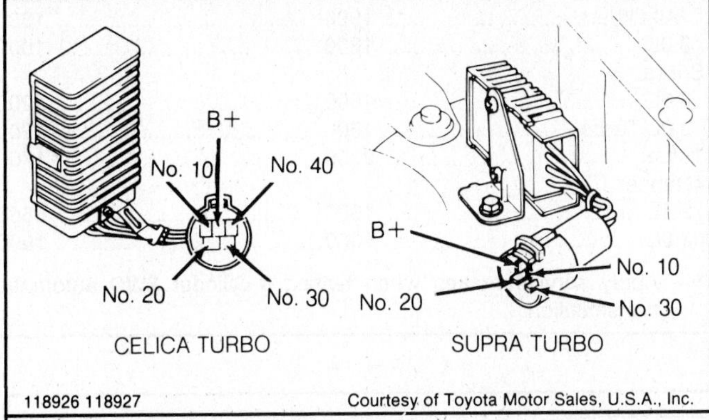


***Fig. 27: Identifying Fuel Injector Solenoid Resistor Connectors***

**Fuel Injectors - 1)** Turn ignition off. Unplug each injector connector. Measure resistance across both terminals. See FUEL INJECTOR RESISTANCE SPECIFICATIONS table. If resistance is not as specified, replace fuel injector.

***FUEL INJECTOR RESISTANCE SPECIFICATIONS***

| Application | [1] Ohms |
|---|---|
| Celica Turbo & Supra Turbo | 2.0-3.8 |
| Except Celica Turbo & Supra Turbo | 13.8 |

[1] - Measured at 68°F (20°C).

**2)** To check injector spray pattern and volume, relieve fuel system pressure. Remove injectors from engine. Disconnect fuel hose from fuel filter outlet. Use Fuel Pressure Gauge (09268-41045) to "T" fuel injector between fuel filter and fuel pressure regulator. *See Fig. 28.*

**3)** Place injector into clean container. Place tube on end of injector to prevent fuel from spilling. Connect Fuel Injector Tester (09842-30070) or trigger box with appropriate resistor to fuel injector. Turn ignition on, with engine off.

**4)** Connect jumper wire to engine check connector terminals FP and +B to pressurize fuel system. For engine check connector locations, *see Fig. 11.* Connector terminals are marked on inside of check connector cover.

**5)** Trigger injector for 15 seconds. Measure volume and check spray pattern. Test each injector 2-3 times. Replace injector if volume is not as specified. See FUEL INJECTOR VOLUME SPECIFICATIONS table.

**6)** Disconnect injector trigger. Fuel leakage from end of injector should be one drop or less in one minute. Replace injector if leakage is more than specified.

***FUEL INJECTOR VOLUME SPECIFICATIONS***

| Application | Cu. In. (cc) |
|---|---|
| Camry | 2.7-3.4 (45-55) |
| Celica | |
| 1.6L | 2.4-3.1 (40-50) |
| 2.0L | 5.8-7.3 (95-120) |
| 2.2L | 2.7-3.4 (45-55) |
| Corolla | |
| 4A-FE | 2.4-3.1 (40-50) |
| 4A-GE | 2.7-3.4 (45-55) |
| Cressida | 4.2-5.2 (69-85) |
| Land Cruiser & Previa | 2.9-3.6 (47-59) |
| MR2 | |
| 2.0L | 5.8-7.3 (95-120) |
| 2.2L | 2.7-3.4 (45-55) |
| Pickup & 4Runner | 2.7-3.4 (45-55) |
| Previa | 4.0-4.6 (65-75) |
| Supra | |
| 3.0L | 4.2-5.2 (69-85) |
| 3.0L Turbo | 6.2-7.0 (101-114) |
| Tercel | 2.1-2.7 (34-45) |
| Maximum Difference Between Each Injector | |
| All Models | .3 (5) |

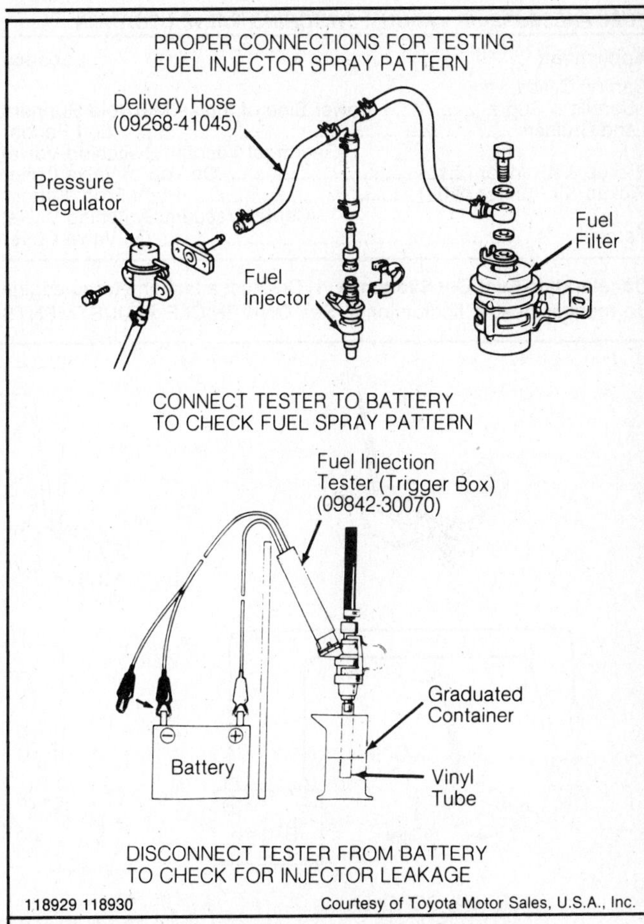


***Fig. 28: Testing Fuel Injector Spray Pattern & Volume***

**Fuel Pressure-Up System - 1)** On all models except Land Cruiser, ensure coolant temperature sensor, air temperature sensor (in airflow meter) and circuits are operating correctly. See ENGINE SENSORS & SWITCHES.

**2)** On Land Cruiser, ensure coolant temperature switch is operating correctly. Switch is in side of engine block and has a Pink wire attached. There should be no continuity between switch terminal and body when coolant temperature is less than 208°F (98°C). There should be continuity between switch terminal and body when coolant temperature is more than 220°F (105°C).

# 1991 ENGINE PERFORMANCE
## System & Component Testing (Cont.)

***NOTE: On Land Cruiser, the ECU uses signal from coolant temperature switch to control the ground circuit for fuel pressure-up vacuum switching valve. On other models, the ECU uses signal from coolant temperature sensor to control ground circuit for fuel pressure-up vacuum switching valve.***

**3)** On all models, fuel pressure-up system is controlled by ECU through a vacuum switching valve. The vacuum switching valve is fed current through the EFI main relay when the ignition is turned on. ECU controls the ground circuit. ECU will activate vacuum switching valve for 90-180 seconds when restarting engine at normal operating temperature.

**4)** On Camry, Celica and Corolla, remove vacuum switching valve from vehicle. See FUEL PRESSURE-UP VACUUM SWITCHING VALVE LOCATION table. Check for continuity across valve wiring terminals. Resistance should be about 33-50 ohms at room temperature. There should be no continuity between each terminal and body of valve. To check operation, *see Fig. 29*.

**5)** On Land Cruiser, check operation of vacuum switching valve using *Fig. 29* as a reference.

***FUEL PRESSURE-UP VACUUM SWITCHING VALVE LOCATION***

| Application | Location |
|---|---|
| Camry, Celica, Corolla & Supra | Lower Side of Intake Manifold Runners |
| Land Cruiser | Left Fender (Rearmost Vacuum Switching Valve) |
| Pickup & 4Runner (2.4L) | On Top of Valve Cover |
| Pickup & 4Runner (3.0L) | Right Front Fender (Center Vacuum Switching Valve) |
| Tercel | On Valve Cover |

**Deceleration Fuel-Cut System – 1)** Connect a tachometer to engine (to monitor needle fluctuations). See ON-VEHICLE ADJUSTMENTS

***DECELERATION FUEL-CUT & FUEL RETURN RPM***

| Application | Fuel-Cut RPM | Fuel Return RPM |
|---|---|---|
| Camry | | |
| 4-Cyl | 1500-2100 | 1000 |
| V6 | 1800 | 1200 |
| Celica | | |
| 1.6L | 2300 | 1700 |
| 2.0L | 2000 | 1600 |
| 2.2L | 1700 | 1300 |
| Corolla | | |
| 4A-FE | 1800 | 1200 |
| 4A-GE | | |
| A/C Off | 1600 | 1200 |
| A/C On | 1900 | 1500 |
| Cressida | 1800 | 1200 |
| Land Cruiser | 1300 | 1000 |
| Pickup | | |
| 2.4L | | |
| 2WD [1] With A/T | 1300 | 1000 |
| All Others | 1900 | 1600 |
| 3.0L | 1300 | 1000 |
| Supra | | |
| 3.0L | 1800 | 1200 |
| 3.0L Turbo | 1600 | 1200 |
| Tercel | 2300 | 1700 |
| 4Runner | | |
| 2.4L | 1900 | 1600 |
| 3.0L | 1300 | 1000 |

[1] – Apply service brakes when testing 4-cylinder 2WD automatic transmission.

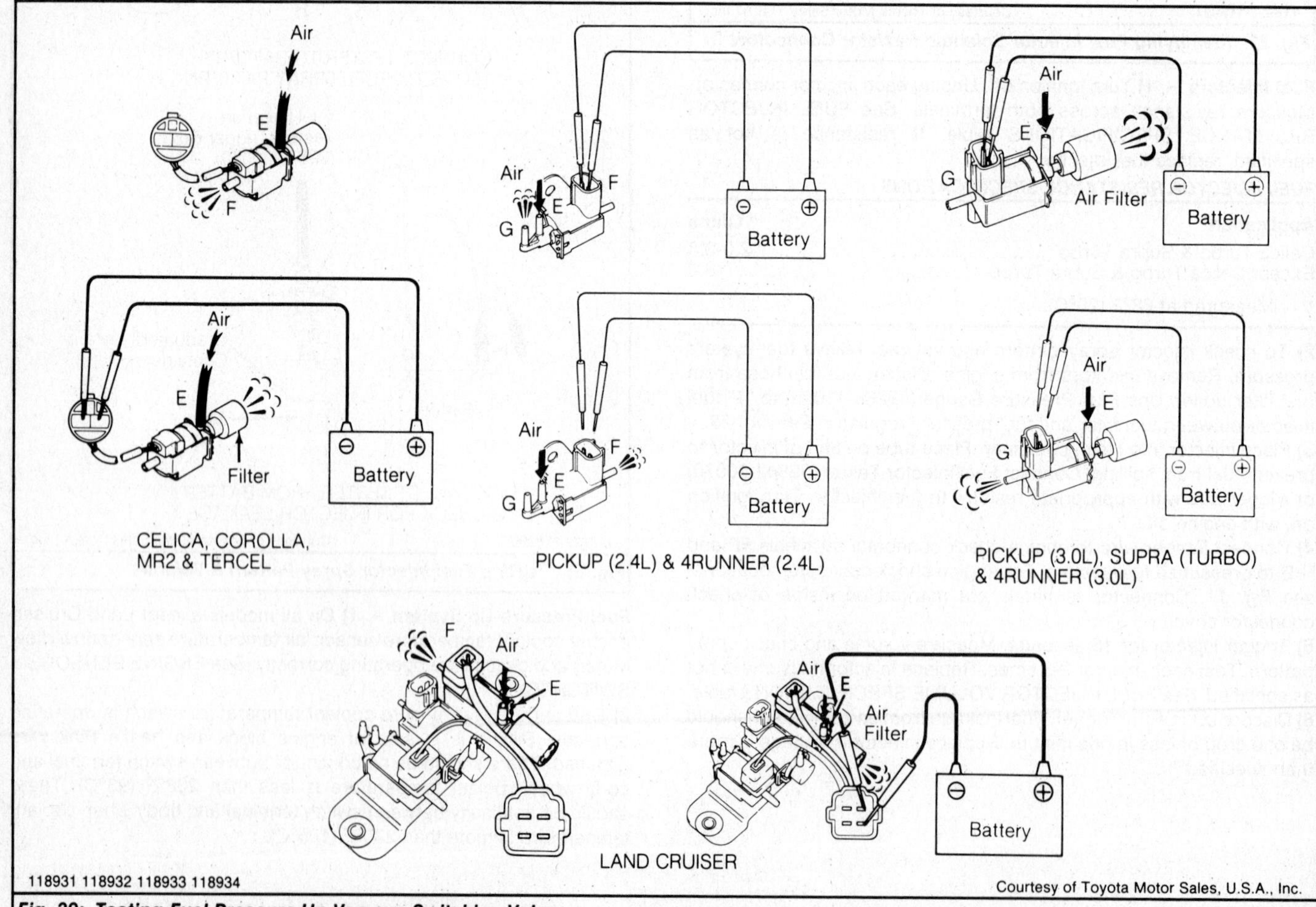


***Fig. 29: Testing Fuel Pressure-Up Vacuum Switching Valve***

# 1991 ENGINE PERFORMANCE
# System & Component Testing (Cont.)

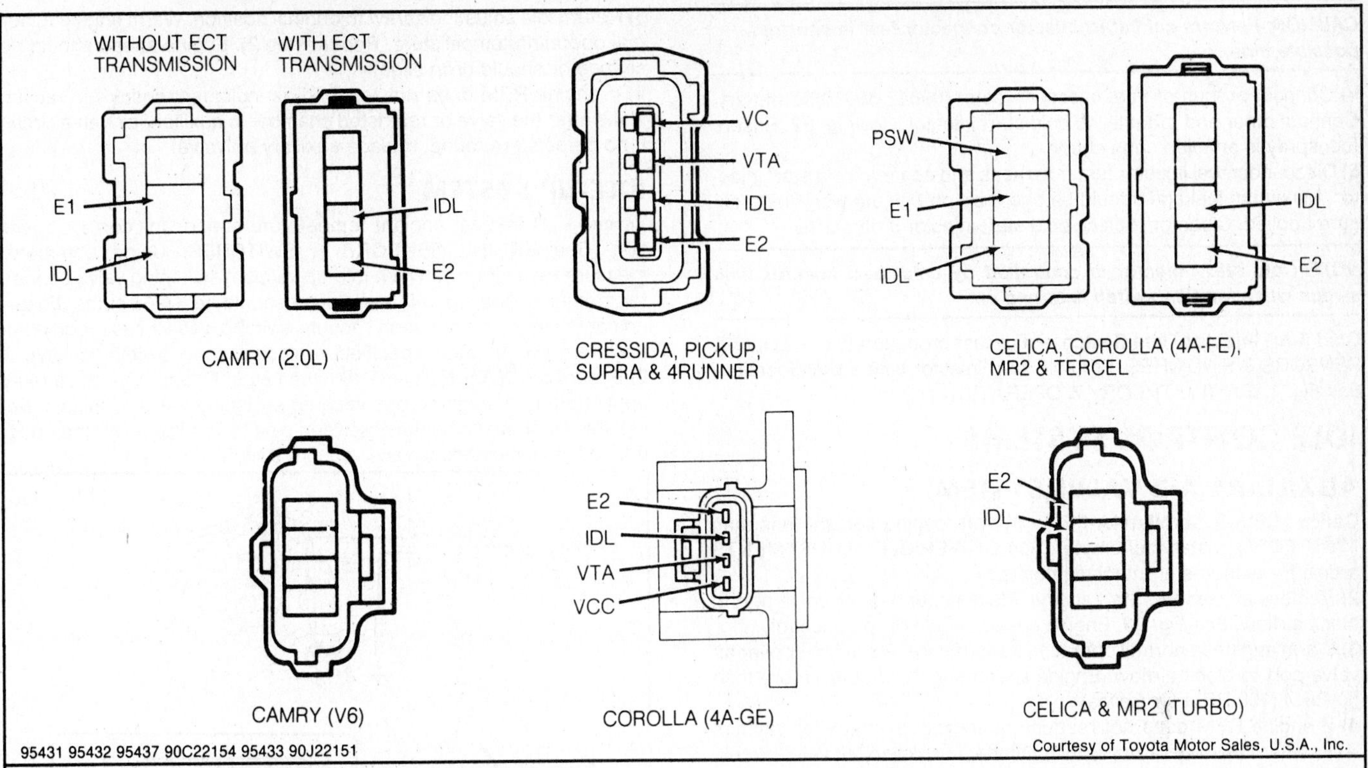


*Fig. 30: Identifying Throttle Position Sensor Connector Terminals*

article for tachometer attaching points. Start engine and warm to operating temperature. Ensure A/C and other accessories are off.

**2)** Unplug throttle position sensor connector from throttle position sensor. Short terminals IDL and $E_1$ (or $E_2$) on wire side of connector. *See Fig. 30*.

**3)** Gradually raise engine RPM. Fuel-cut operation can be checked by noting the fluctuation of tachometer needle. Fluctuation indicates fuel-cut system is being turned on and off. *See Fig. 31*. Check that fuel-cut points and fuel return points are within specifications. See DECELERATION FUEL-CUT & FUEL RETURN RPM table.

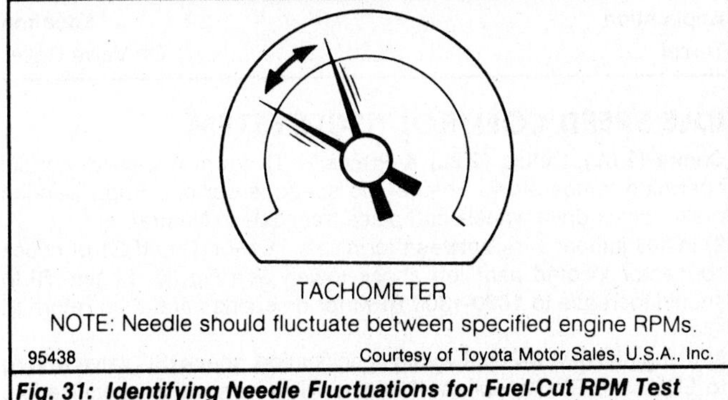


*Fig. 31: Identifying Needle Fluctuations for Fuel-Cut RPM Test*

**Cold Start Injector – 1)** Disconnect negative battery cable. Disconnect cold start injector wiring harness connector. Check resistance between terminals of injector. Replace injector if defective. See COLD START INJECTOR RESISTANCE SPECIFICATIONS table. If resistance is okay, relieve fuel system pressure.

***COLD START INJECTOR RESISTANCE SPECIFICATIONS***

| Application | Ohms |
|---|---|
| Corolla (4A-GE) | 3-5 |
| Tercel | 4.0-4.5 |
| Except Corolla (4A-GE) & Tercel | 2-4 |

**2)** Remove cold start injector from vehicle. Install fuel hose to injector. Install system Union Adapters (9268-41045) to delivery pipe and cold start injector. Connect fuel hose to union adapters. *See Fig. 32*. Connect Jumper Harness (9842-30050) to cold start injector.

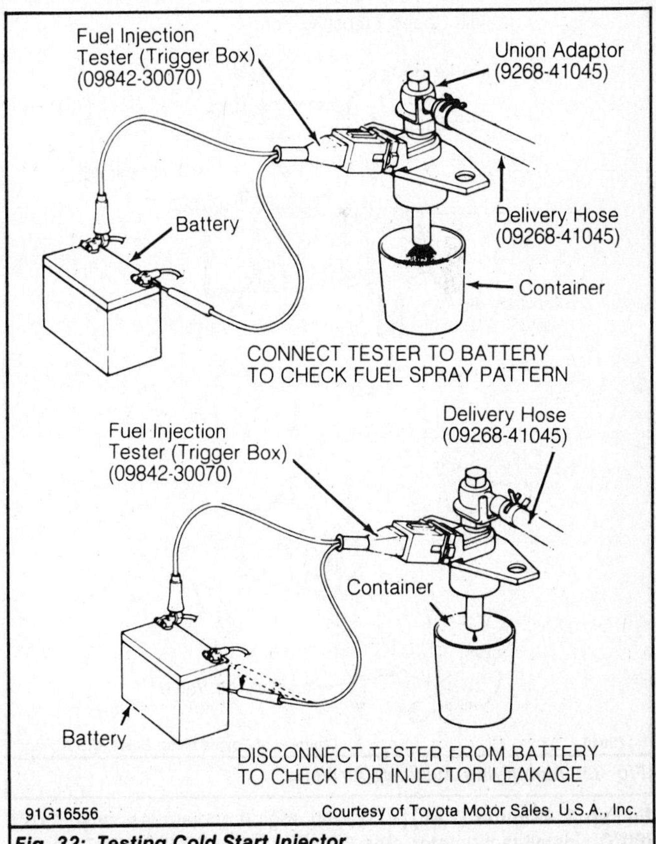


*Fig. 32: Testing Cold Start Injector*

**3)** Place container under cold start injector. Connect jumper wire to engine check connector terminals FP and B+ to pressurize fuel system. For engine check connector locations, *See Fig. 11*. Turn ignition on, with engine off.

# 1991 ENGINE PERFORMANCE
# System & Component Testing (Cont.)

***CAUTION: Perform cold start injector connector test in shortest possible time.***

**4)** Connect probes of Fuel Injection Tester (09842-30070) to battery. Connect other end of tester to cold start injector. *See Fig. 32*. Ensure fuel spray is an even cone shape.
**5)** Disconnect fuel injector tester harness and observe cold start injector. Maximum leakage should be one drop per minute with fuel pressure applied. Clean or replace cold start injector if defective.

***NOTE: Cold start injector is controlled by cold start injector time switch when ignition switch is turned on.***

**Cold Start Injector Time Switch** – For test procedures, see ENGINE SENSORS & SWITCHES. For cold start injector time switch location, *See Fig. 1, 2 or 3* in THEORY & OPERATION article.

## IDLE CONTROL SYSTEMS

### AUXILIARY AIR VALVE SYSTEM

**Celica (1.6L) & Corolla (4A-FE)** – **1)** With engine coolant less than 176°F (80°C), install tachometer. See ON-VEHICLE ADJUSTMENTS article for tachometer attaching points.
**2)** Remove air cleaner. Start engine. Place finger over air valve port to block airflow. *See Fig. 33*. Engine speed should drop noticeably.
**3)** Warm engine to normal operating temperature. Place finger over air valve port to block airflow. Engine speed should not drop more than 50 RPM (100 RPM for Celica).
**4)** If engine RPM does not respond as indicated, check for vacuum leaks after the valve or restricted chamber in auxiliary air valve circuit. If no defects are found, replace auxiliary air valve.

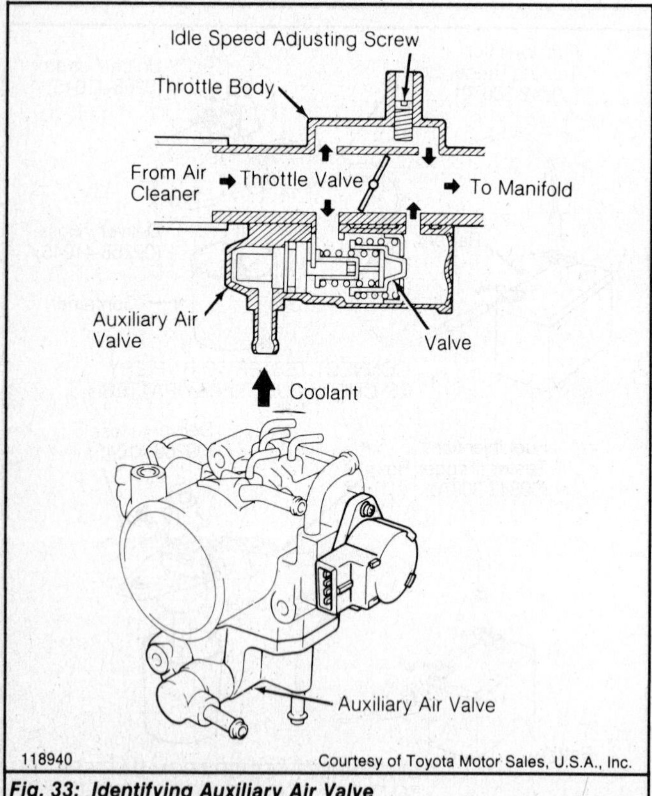


***Fig. 33: Identifying Auxiliary Air Valve***

**Pickup & 4Runner (2.4L)** – **1)** With engine coolant less than 176°F (80°C), install tachometer. See ON-VEHICLE ADJUSTMENTS article for tachometer attaching points.
**2)** Start engine. With engine idling, turn idle speed adjusting screw to bottom of bore while counting number of revolutions. Engine speed should drop noticeably.
**3)** Return idle adjusting screw to original position. Warm engine to normal operating temperature. Repeat step **2)**. Engine speed should not change or should drop slightly.
**4)** If engine RPM does not respond as indicated, check for vacuum leaks after the valve or restricted chamber in auxiliary air valve circuit. If no defects are found, replace auxiliary air valve.

### IDLE-UP SYSTEM

**Tercel** – **1)** Inspect coolant temperature sensor for correct operation. See ENGINE SENSORS & SWITCHES. Using ohmmeter, measure resistance between idle-up vacuum switching valve connector terminals. *See Fig. 34*. Resistance should be 37-44 ohms. Ensure no continuity exists between vacuum switching valve case (body) and each terminal. If not as specified, replace vacuum switching valve.
**2)** Ensure air DOES NOT flow between pipe "E" and pipe "F". If okay, apply battery voltage across vacuum switching valve terminals. *See Fig. 34*. Air should now flow between pipe "E" and pipe "F". If air does not flow as indicated, replace vacuum switching valve.

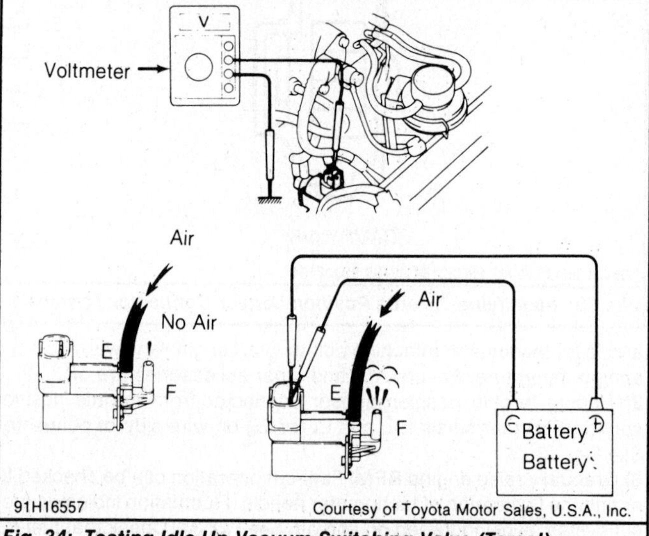


***Fig. 34: Testing Idle-Up Vacuum Switching Valve (Tercel)***

***IDLE-UP SYSTEM VACUUM SWITCHING VALVE LOCATIONS***

| Application | Location |
|---|---|
| Tercel | On Valve Cover |

### IDLE SPEED CONTROL (ISC) SYSTEM

**Camry (2.0L), Celica (2.2L) & Previa** – **1)** Warm engine to normal operating temperature. Ensure idle speed is correct. Apply parking brake, block drive wheels and place transaxle in Neutral.
**2)** Install jumper wire between terminals TE1 (or T) and E1 of check connector located near left shock tower. *See Fig 35*. Engine RPM should increase to 1000-1300 RPM for 5 seconds and then return to idle.
**3)** If engine RPM was not within specification, check ISC valve, wiring to ECU, and ECU grounds. If engine RPM was within specification, remove jumper wire. Turn ignition off.
**4)** Unplug ISC valve connector on bottom of throttle body. Using ohmmeter, measure resistance between terminals B+ and ISC1, and between ISC2 and B+. *See Fig. 35*. Replace valve if resistance is not within 16-17 ohms (Camry 2.0L), 19.3-22.3 ohms (Celica 2.2L), or 18.8-22.8 ohms (Previa).

# 1991 ENGINE PERFORMANCE
# System & Component Testing (Cont.)

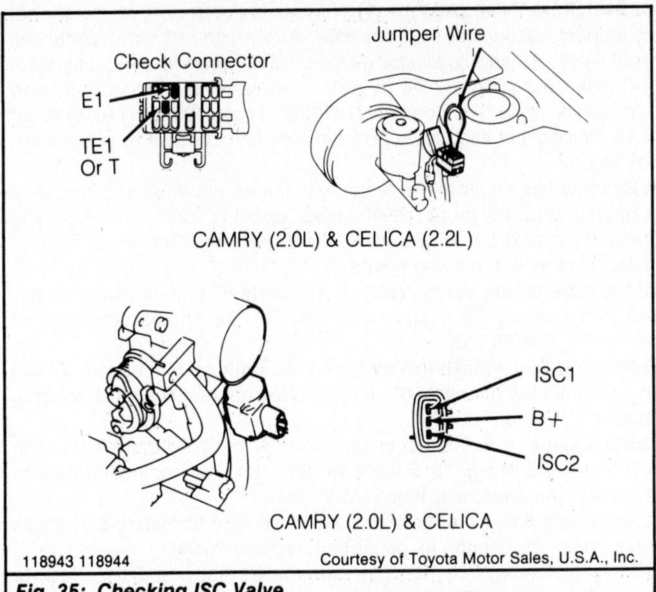


***Fig. 35: Checking ISC Valve (Camry & Celica Shown; MR2 2.0L & Previa Similar)***

**Celica (2.0L) & MR2 (2.0L) - 1)** Warm engine to normal operating temperature. Ensure idle speed is correct. Apply parking brake, block drive wheels and place transaxle in Neutral.

**2)** Unplug ISC valve connector on bottom of throttle body. Engine RPM should increase 1000 RPM or more. Plug in ISC valve connector. Engine should return to idle speed (750-850 RPM). If engine RPM does not respond as specified, check ISC valve, wiring to ECU, and ECU grounds.

**3)** To check ISC valve, turn ignition off. Unplug ISC valve connector on bottom of throttle body. Using ohmmeter, measure resistance between center terminal and each outer terminal individually. *See Fig. 35.* Replace valve if resistance is not 19.3-22.3 ohms (Celica) or 17.7-23.9 ohms (MR2).

**Camry (2.5L), Cressida, Land Cruiser & Supra - 1)** Listen for clicking sound after engine is shut off. If no sound is heard, check ISC valve and wiring.

**2)** To check wiring circuit, turn engine off. Unplug ISC valve connector. Turn ignition on with engine off. Connect voltmeter between B1 and B2 terminals of wiring harness connector. *See Fig. 36.* Battery voltage should be present. If not, check wiring between ISC valve and EFI main relay.

**3)** To check ISC valve, turn ignition off. Unplug ISC valve connector. Measure resistance between ISC valve terminals. *See Fig. 36.* See ISC VALVE RESISTANCE SPECIFICATIONS table. Replace ISC valve if resistance is not as specified.

***ISC VALVE RESISTANCE SPECIFICATIONS***

| Terminals | Ohms |
|---|---|
| $B_1$ to $S_1$ or $S_3$ | 10-30 |
| $B_2$ to $S_2$ or $S_4$ | 10-30 |

***NOTE: Before removing ISC valve, drain coolant from cooling system. Remove both coolant by-pass hoses. On Supra Turbo only, ensure check valve and seal washer are installed in air intake chamber.***

**4)** To check valve operation, remove ISC valve from vehicle. Apply battery voltage to terminal $B_1$ and terminal $B_2$. *See Fig. 36.* Repeatedly ground terminals $S_1$, $S_2$, $S_3$ and $S_4$ in sequence. Valve should close. Remove ground wires.

**5)** Apply battery voltage to terminals $B_1$ and $B_2$. Repeatedly ground terminals $S_4$, $S_3$, $S_2$ and $S_1$ in sequence. Valve should move toward open position. Replace valve if operation is not as specified.

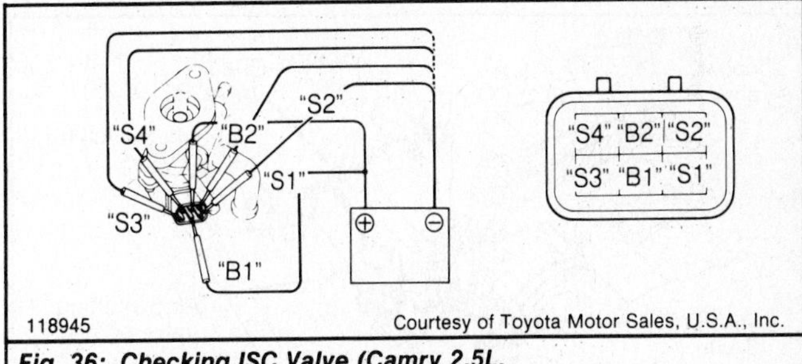


***Fig. 36: Checking ISC Valve (Camry 2.5L, Cressida, Land Cruiser & Supra)***

# 1991 ENGINE PERFORMANCE
# System & Component Testing (Cont.)

## IGNITION SYSTEM

***NOTE: For basic ignition checks, see BASIC DIAGNOSTIC PROCEDURES article.***

**Knock Sensor** - On models equipped with knock sensor, diagnosis is in Code 52 and Code 53 charts. For code charts, see SELF-DIAGNOSTICS article.

## EMISSION SYSTEMS & SUB-SYSTEMS

### AIR INJECTION SYSTEM (LAND CRUISER)

**System Test** - **1)** Inspect air pump belt. Visually check hoses and tubes for kinks, damage or loose connections. Disconnect air by-pass hose from Air Switching Valve (ASV). *See Fig. 37.*

**2)** With coolant temperatuie less than 50°F (10°C), start engine and allow to idle. Air should discharge from ASV. When coolant temperature is between 59°F (15°C) and 95°F (35°C), air should stop discharging from ASV.

**3)** When air stops discharging from ASV, increase engine speed to 3000 RPM. Air should again start discharging from ASV.

**Air Pump** - **1)** Disconnect hose at air pump outlet. Attach Air Pump Tester (09258-14010) with .217" (5.51 mm) orifice to hose. *See Fig. 37.*

**2)** Start engine and increase engine speed to 1200 RPM. Tester gauge should read in Green area. if reading is in Red area, replace air pump assembly.

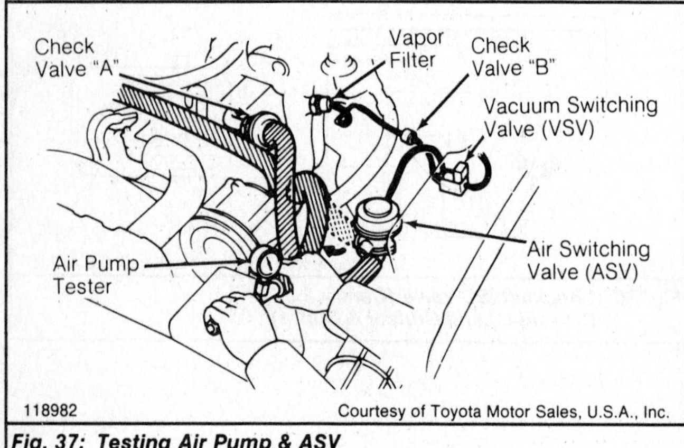


***Fig. 37: Testing Air Pump & ASV***

**Air Switching Valve (ASV)** - **1)** With engine operating at idle speed, disconnect vacuum hose from ASV. ASV is on left side fenderwell (front valve). Air should discharge from ASV. Reconnect vacuum hose.

**2)** Check opening pressure of ASV relief valve. Disconnect air hose from check valve "A". Connect Air Pump Tester (09258-14010) to air hose. Disconnect vacuum hose from ASV and connect to vapor filter. *See Fig. 37.*

**3)** Block orifice on air pump tester with finger. Increase engine speed gradually and measure relief valve opening pressure. Opening pressure should be 5.7-8.5 psi (.40-.60 kg/cm²). Remove air pump tester. Reconnect vacuum hoses.

**Vacuum Switching Valve (VSV)** - **1)** Locate VSV on left side fenderwell (front valve). Blow air into nozzle "E". Air should come out of nozzle "P". *See Fig. 38.*

**2)** Apply battery voltage to VSV terminals. Blow air into nozzle "E". Air should come out of nozzle "F". If valve does not function as described, replace VSV.

**Check Valves** - **1)** Inspect check valve "A" by blowing air from each side of valve. *See Fig. 39.* Ensure air does not flow from manifold side of valve to Air Switching Valve (ASV) side.

**2)** Air should flow from Air Switching Valve ASV to manifold. If check valve does not function as described, replace valve.

**3)** Inspect check valve "B". Ensure air does not flow from Black to Orange side of nozzle. Air should flow from Orange to Black side. If check valve does not function as described, replace valve.

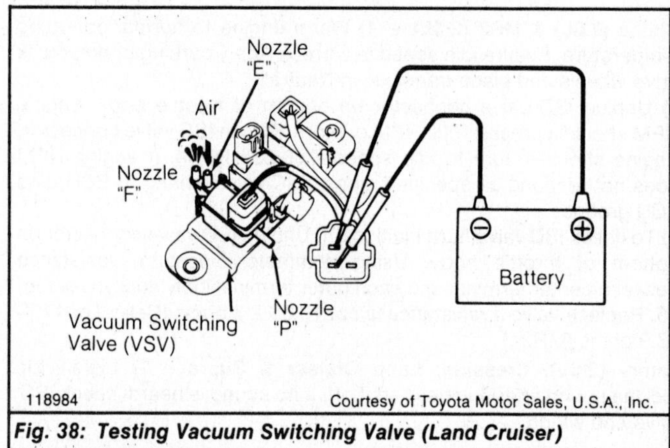


***Fig. 38: Testing Vacuum Switching Valve (Land Cruiser)***

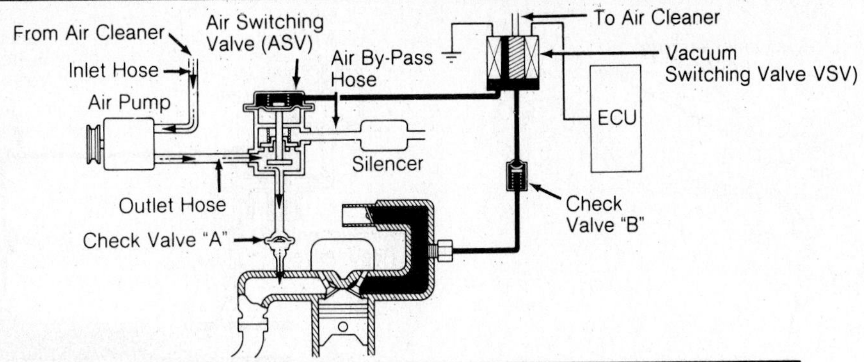

# 1991 ENGINE PERFORMANCE
# System & Component Testing (Cont.)

For reburning the unburnt HC and CO in the exhaust port, compressed air from the air pump is blown into the exhaust port.

| Coolant Temp. | Driving Condition | Engine RPM | Vehicle Speed | VSV | ASV | AI System |
|---|---|---|---|---|---|---|
| Blow 10°C (50°F) | — | — | — | OFF | CLOSED | OFF |
| Between 15 – 35°C (59 – 95°F) | — | — | — | ON | OPEN | ON |
| Above 40°C (104°F) | Ex. deceleration | — | — | OFF | CLOSED | OFF |
| | Deceleration | Above 2,000 rpm | — | OFF | CLOSED | OFF |
| | | Blow 2,000 rpm | Above 6 mph (10 km/h) | ON | OPEN | ON |

118983 Courtesy of Toyota Motor Sales, U.S.A., Inc.

***Fig. 39: Identifying Air Pump System Components & Operating Parameters (Land Cruiser)***

## PULSE AIR SYSTEM (PICKUP & 4RUNNER)

**System Test (2.4L) - 1)** Check hoses and tubes for cracks, kinks, damage, or loose connections. Check Pulse Air System (PAS) cold operating condition. *See Fig. 43*.

**2)** Ensure coolant temperature is less than 86°F (30°C). Start engine and set idle. Disconnect PAS vacuum hose from air cleaner. *See Fig. 40*. Check for air bubbling noise from PAS vacuum hose.

**3)** When engine temperature is greater than 104°F (40°C), air bubbling noise from PAS vacuum hose should not be heard. Race engine and quickly close throttle. Air bubbling noise from PAS vacuum hose should be heard and then momentarily stop.

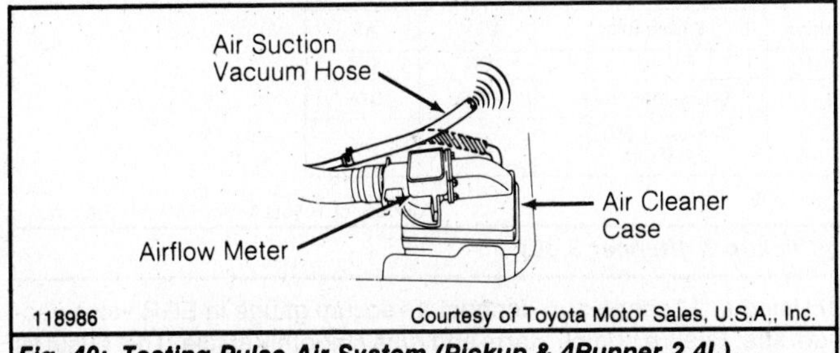


***Fig. 40: Testing Pulse Air System (Pickup & 4Runner 2.4L)***

**System Test (3.0L) - 1)** Check hoses and tubes for cracks, kinks, damage, or loose connections. Check Pulse Air (PAS) system cold operation. *See Fig. 44*.

**2)** Ensure coolant temperature is less than 77°F (25°C). Start engine and allow to idle. Disconnect pulse air hose from air pipe. *See Fig. 41*. Check for air bubbling noise from air pipe.

**3)** Check hot system operation. When engine temperature is at normal operating temperature, bubbling noise should not be heard from air pipe. Race engine to 2000 RPM. Ensure bubbling noise stops momentarily.

**Pulse Air System (Reed) Valve (3.0L) -** Apply vacuum to reed valve diaphragm. Blow air into reed valve pipe and ensure reed valve is open. Release vacuum and ensure reed valve is closed.

**Vacuum Switching Valve (VSV) - 1)** Connect battery voltage to vacuum control valve. *See Fig. 42*. Blow into port "E" and ensure air comes out of port "G". Disconnect battery voltage and blow into port "E". Air should come out of air filter. If VSV does not function as described, replace VSV.

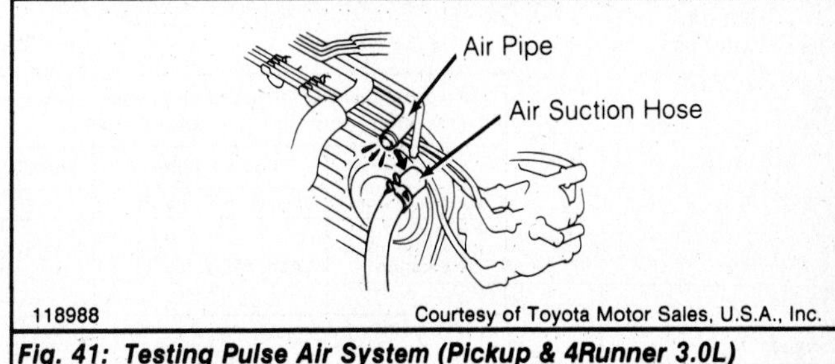


***Fig. 41: Testing Pulse Air System (Pickup & 4Runner 3.0L)***

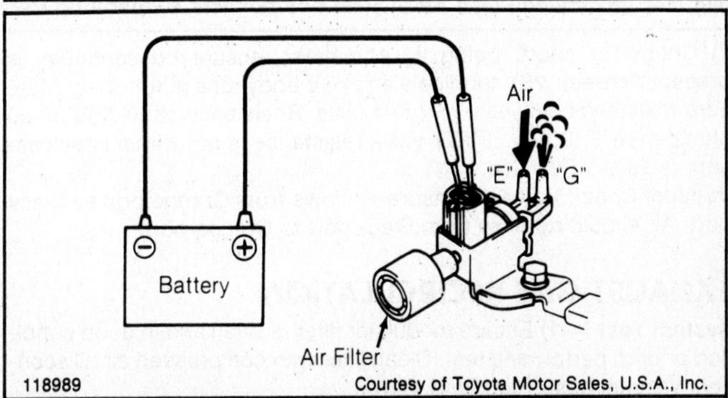


***Fig. 42: Checking Vacuum Switching Valve (Pickup & 4Runner)***

# 1991 ENGINE PERFORMANCE
## System & Component Testing (Cont.)

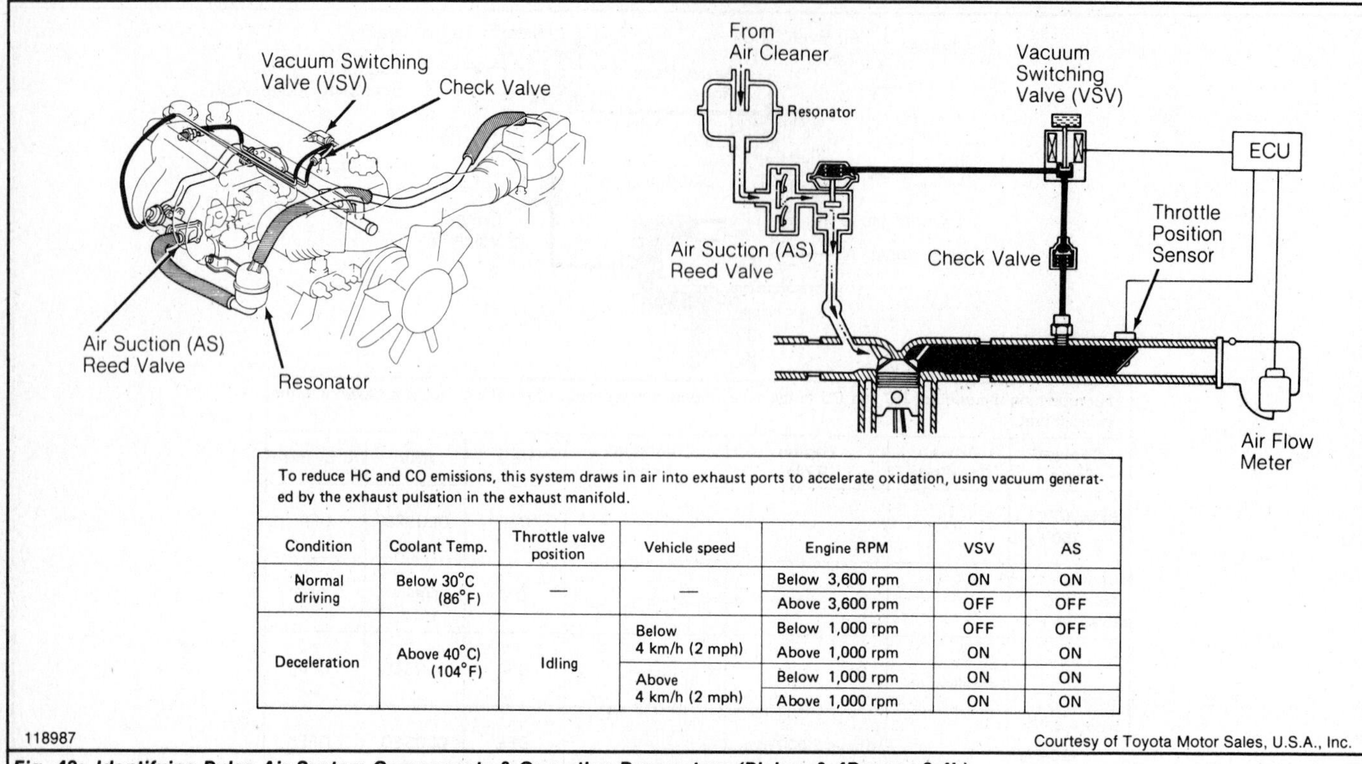


To reduce HC and CO emissions, this system draws in air into exhaust ports to accelerate oxidation, using vacuum generated by the exhaust pulsation in the exhaust manifold.

| Condition | Coolant Temp. | Throttle valve position | Vehicle speed | Engine RPM | VSV | AS |
|---|---|---|---|---|---|---|
| Normal driving | Below 30°C (86°F) | — | — | Below 3,600 rpm | ON | ON |
| | | | | Above 3,600 rpm | OFF | OFF |
| Deceleration | Above 40°C) (104°F) | Idling | Below 4 km/h (2 mph) | Below 1,000 rpm | OFF | OFF |
| | | | | Above 1,000 rpm | ON | ON |
| | | | Above 4 km/h (2 mph) | Below 1,000 rpm | ON | ON |
| | | | | Above 1,000 rpm | ON | ON |

118987

Courtesy of Toyota Motor Sales, U.S.A., Inc.

***Fig. 43: Identifying Pulse Air System Components & Operating Parameters (Pickup & 4Runner 2.4L)***

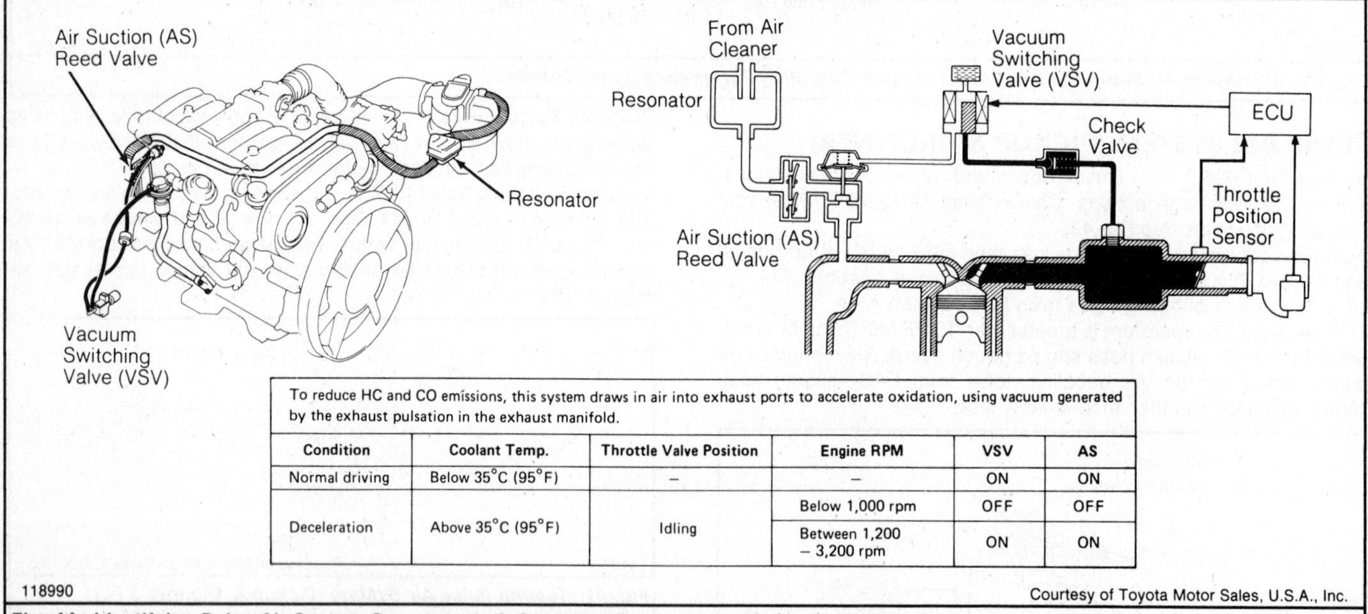


To reduce HC and CO emissions, this system draws in air into exhaust ports to accelerate oxidation, using vacuum generated by the exhaust pulsation in the exhaust manifold.

| Condition | Coolant Temp. | Throttle Valve Position | Engine RPM | VSV | AS |
|---|---|---|---|---|---|
| Normal driving | Below 35°C (95°F) | – | – | ON | ON |
| Deceleration | Above 35°C (95°F) | Idling | Below 1,000 rpm | OFF | OFF |
| | | | Between 1,200 – 3,200 rpm | ON | ON |

118990

Courtesy of Toyota Motor Sales, U.S.A., Inc.

***Fig. 44: Identifying Pulse Air System Components & Operating Parameters (Pickup & 4Runner 3.0L)***

**2)** Check for short. Using an ohmmeter, ensure no continuity is present between VSV terminals and VSV body. Check for open. Measure resistance between VSV terminals. Resistance should be 30-50 ohms at 68°F (20°C). If VSV valve resistance is not within specification, replace VSV valve.

**Vacuum Check Valve –** Ensure air flows from Orange port to Black port. Air should not flow from Black port to Orange port.

### EXHAUST GAS RECIRCULATION

**System Test – 1)** Ensure modulator filter is clean and in good condition prior to performing test. Clean filter with compressed air. Disconnect vacuum hose from EGR valve.

**2)** Using a "T" connector, connect a vacuum gauge in EGR valve vacuum line. Ensure engine starts and runs smoothly at idle. This ensures proper seating of EGR valve.

**3)** Different vacuum switching valves are used depending on model. *See Figs. 46, and 49-59*. The Bimetallic Vacuum Switching Valve (BVSV), Vacuum Switching Valve (VSV) and EGR modulator can be checked with engine coolant temperature less than minimum temperature and specified engine RPM in accordance with application. See EGR SPECIFICATIONS table.

**4)** Operate engine with engine coolant temperature less than minimum temperature and specified RPM. No vacuum reading should be obtained when operated with engine coolant temperature less than minimum temperature.

**5)** Operate engine at normal operating temperature and specified RPM. See EGR SPECIFICATIONS table. On Cressida and Supra, a vacuum reading of 2.8 in. Hg should be obtained. On all other models, a low vacuum reading should be obtained.
**6)** On all models except Celica Turbo and Supra Turbo, disconnect hose from the "R" port of EGR vacuum modulator. *See Fig. 45.*
**7)** Using additional hose, connect "R" port directly to intake manifold. High vacuum reading should be obtained at specified engine RPM. See EGR SPECIFICATIONS table.

***NOTE: Engine should misfire due to large amounts of exhaust gas being injected into intake manifold.***

**8)** To check EGR valve, apply vacuum directly to EGR valve with engine idling. Engine should run rough or stall. If system did not operate as described, each component should be tested.

***EGR SPECIFICATIONS***

| Model | Minimum Temperature | Engine RPM |
|---|---|---|
| Camry | | |
| 2.0L | 113°F (45°C) | 2500 |
| 2.5L | 104°F (40°C) | [1] 2500 |
| Celica | | |
| 2.0L | 129°F (54°C) | 2500 |
| 1.6L | 117°F (47°C) | 2500 |
| 2.2L | | |
| Calif. w/A/T | 140°F (60°C) | 2500 |
| All Others | 131°F (55°C) | 2500 |
| Corolla | | |
| 4A-FE | 117°F (47°C) | 2500 |
| 4A-GE | 129°F (54°C) | 3500 |
| Cressida | 135°F (57°C) | 2500 |
| Land Cruiser | 127°F (53°C) | 2500 |
| Pickup | | |
| 2.4L | 86°F (30°C) | [2] 3500 |
| 3.0L | 118°F (48°C) | 3500 |
| Supra | 135°F (57°C) | 2500 |
| Tercel | 117°F (47°C) | 2500 |
| 4Runner | | |
| 2.4L | 86°F (30°C) | [2] 3500 |
| 3.0L | 118°F (48°C) | 3500 |

[1] – Check at 3500 RPM with hose from EGR to manifold.
[2] – Check at 3000 RPM with hose from EGR to manifold.

**EGR Vacuum Modulator – 1)** EGR vacuum modulator may be a 2-port or 3-port type depending on application. On 2-port models, disconnect hoses from vacuum modulator. Plug one end of vacuum hose connection on EGR vacuum modulator.
**2)** Apply air pressure through remaining port. Air should pass freely through air filter side of modulator. On 3-port models, disconnect all hoses. Block ports "P" and "R". Apply air pressure to port "Q". *See Fig. 45.* Air should pass through the air filter side of modulator freely.
**3)** On all models, operate engine at specified RPM. See EGR VACUUM MODULATOR SPECIFICATIONS table. Repeat test procedures in steps **1)** and **2)**. Strong resistance of airflow should be felt. Replace EGR vacuum modulator if resistance is not felt. Reconnect vacuum hoses to proper locations

***EGR VACUUM MODULATOR SPECIFICATIONS***

| Application | Engine RPM |
|---|---|
| 2-Port Type | |
| Celica 4WD (Turbo) | 2500 |
| Supra Turbo | 2500 |
| 3-Port Type | |
| Camry | |
| 2.0L | 2500 |
| 2.5L | 3500 |
| Celica | 2500 |
| Corolla | 2500 |
| Cressida | 2500 |
| Land Cruiser | 2500 |
| Pickup/4Runner | 3500 |
| Supra (Non-Turbo) | 2500 |
| Tercel | 2500 |

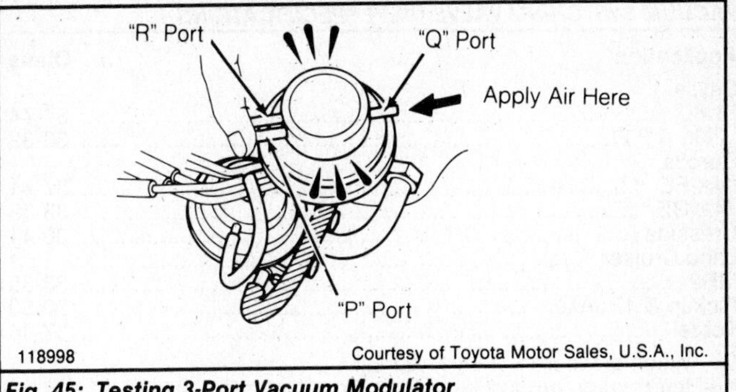


***Fig. 45: Testing 3-Port Vacuum Modulator***

**Bimetallic Vacuum Switching Valve (BVSV) (Camry 2.0L, Pickup & 4Runner 2.4L) – 1)** Drain cooling system and remove BVSV. *See Figs. 47 and 55.* Cool BVSV to minimum temperature according to application using cool water. See BVSV SPECIFICATIONS table.
**2)** Apply air to the lower port. Air should pass through air filter located on top of valve assembly. Heat BVSV valve to maximum temperature according to application. See BVSV SPECIFICATIONS table.
**3)** Apply air to the lower port. Air should pass through from the upper port but not through the air filter. Replace assembly if defective.
**Bimetallic Vacuum Switching Valve (BVSV) (Camry 2.5L) – 1)** Drain cooling system and remove BVSV. *See Fig. 48.* Using cool water, cool BVSV to less than minimum temperature according to application. See BVSV SPECIFICATIONS table.
**2)** Apply air through top port of valve. Air should NOT pass through bottom port. Heat BVSV valve to greater than maximum temperature according to application. See BVSV SPECIFICATIONS table. Apply air in top port. Air should pass through lower port. Replace assembly if defective. If BVSV does not function as described, replace valve.

***BVSV SPECIFICATIONS***

| Application | Minimum Temperature | Maximum Temperature |
|---|---|---|
| Camry | | |
| 2.0L | 113°F (45°C) | 151°F (66°C) |
| 2.5L | 104°F (40°C) | 129°F (54°C) |
| Pickup & 4Runner 2.4L | 86°F (30°C) | 111°F (44°C) |

**Vacuum Switching Valve (VSV) (Celica 1.6 & Corolla 4A-FE) – 1)** Unplug VSV connector. Apply air to port "E". Air should pass through air filter. Apply battery voltage to VSV terminals. *See Fig. 46.* Apply air pressure to port "E". Air should not pass through air filter. Disconnect battery terminals.
**2)** Using ohmmeter, measure resistance between both terminals of valve assembly. Replace valve if resistance is not within specification. See VACUUM SWITCHING VALVE (VSV) SPECIFICATIONS table.
**Vacuum Switching Valve (VSV) (Corolla 4A-GE) – 1)** Unplug VSV connector. Connect battery to VSV terminals. *See Fig. 46.* Apply air pressure to port "E". Air should pass through port "F". Disconnect battery terminals.
**2)** Apply air pressure to port "E". Air should now pass through air filter. Using ohmmeter, check for continuity between terminals and VSV body. Replace unit if incorrect airflow or continuity exists.
**3)** Using ohmmeter, measure resistance between both terminals of valve assembly. Replace valve if resistance is not within specification. See VACUUM SWITCHING VALVE (VSV) SPECIFICATIONS table.

# 1991 ENGINE PERFORMANCE
## System & Component Testing (Cont.)

*VACUUM SWITCHING VALVE (VSV) SPECIFICATIONS*

| Application | [1] Ohms |
|---|---|
| Celica | |
| 1.6L | 37-44 |
| 2.0L & 2.2L | 33-39 |
| Corolla | |
| 4A-FE | 37-44 |
| 4A-GE | 33-39 |
| Cressida | 38-44 |
| Land Cruiser | [2] |
| MR2 | 33-39 |
| Pickup & 4Runner | 30-50 |
| Tercel | 37-44 |

[1] - When measured at 68°F (20°C).
[2] - Information not available from manufacturer.

**Vacuum Switching Valve (VSV) (Supra Turbo, Pickup & 4Runner 3.0L) - 1)** Unplug VSV connector. *See Figs. 56 and 58.* Connect battery to VSV terminals. *See Fig. 46.* Apply air pressure to port "E". Air should pass through air filter. Disconnect battery terminals.

**2)** Apply air pressure to port "E". Air should now pass through port "G". Using ohmmeter, check for continuity between terminals and VSV body. Replace unit if incorrect airflow or continuity exists.

**3)** Using ohmmeter, measure resistance between both terminals of valve assembly. Replace valve if resistance is not within specification. See VACUUM SWITCHING VALVE (VSV) SPECIFICATIONS table.

**Vacuum Switching Valve (VSV) (Celica, MR2 & Land Cruiser - 1)** Disconnect VSV connector. *See Figs. 49, 50, 51 and 54.* Apply air pressure to port "E". *See Fig. 46.* Air should pass through port "F".

**2)** Connect battery to VSV terminals. Apply air pressure to port "E". On Celica, air should pass through air filter. On Land Cruiser, no air should pass through port "F".

**3)** On Celica, using ohmmeter, check for continuity between terminals and VSV body. Replace unit if continuity exists. Using ohmmeter, measure resistance between both terminals of valve assembly. Replace valve if resistance is not within specification. See VACUUM SWITCHING VALVE (VSV) SPECIFICATIONS table.

**Vacuum Switching Valve (VSV) (Cressida, Pickup 2.4L, Supra Non-Turbo & Tercel) - 1)** Unplug VSV connector. *See Figs. 53, 55 and 59.* Connect battery to VSV terminals. *See Fig. 46.* Apply air pressure to port "E". Air should pass through port "F".

**2)** Disconnect battery terminals. Apply air pressure to port "E". Air should not pass through port "F". Using ohmmeter, check for continuity between terminals and VSV body. Replace unit if incorrect airflow or continuity exists.

**3)** Using ohmmeter, measure resistance between both terminals of valve assembly. Replace valve if resistance is not within specification. See VACUUM SWITCHING VALVE (VSV) SPECIFICATIONS table.

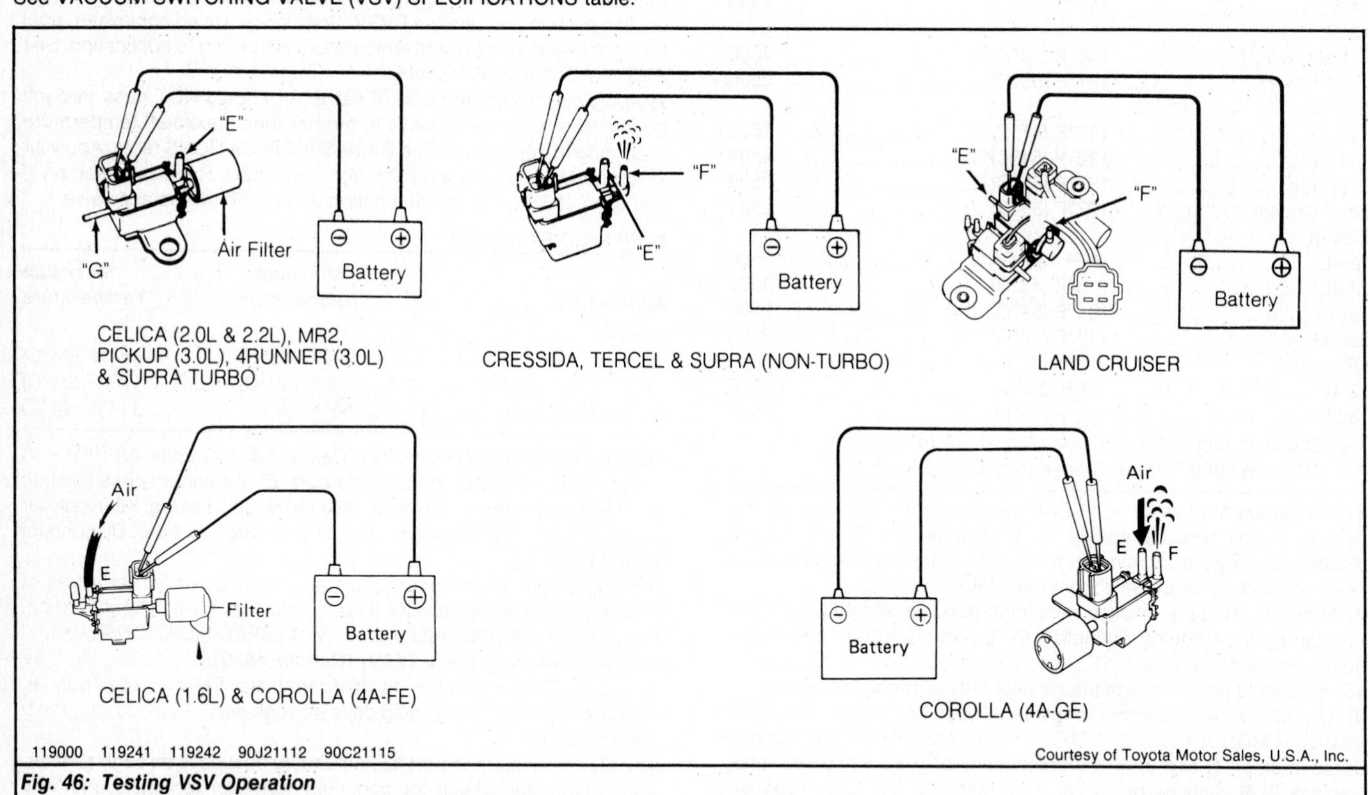


*Fig. 46: Testing VSV Operation*

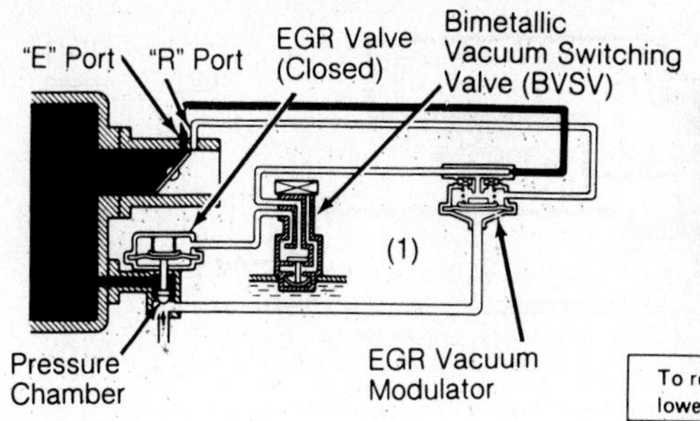

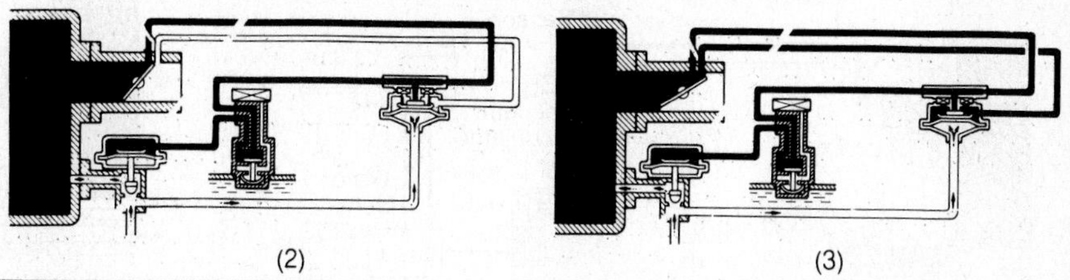

"E" Port
"R" Port
EGR Valve (Closed)
Bimetallic Vacuum Switching Valve (BVSV)
(1)
Pressure Chamber
EGR Vacuum Modulator
(2)
(3)
EGR Vacuum Modulator
EGR Valve
"E" Port
"R" Port
Bimetallic Vacuum Switching Valve (BVSV)

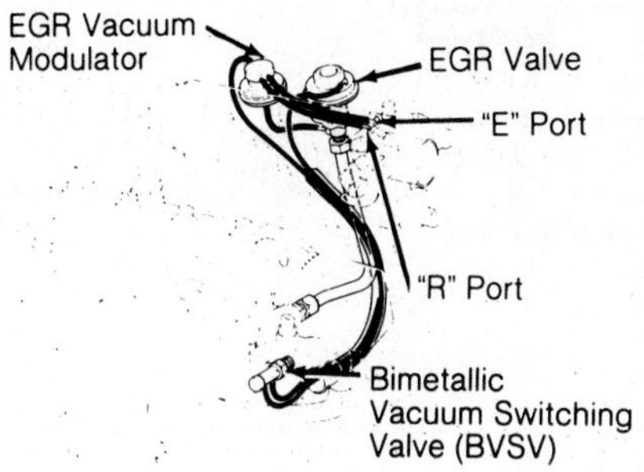

To reduce NOx emission, part of the exhaust gases are recirculated through the EGR valve to the intake manifold to lower the maximum combustion temperature.

| Coolant Temp. | BVSV | Throttle Valve Opening Angle | Pressure in the EGR Valve Pressure Chamber | | EGR Vacuum Modulator | EGR Valve | Exhaust Gas |
|---|---|---|---|---|---|---|---|
| Below 45°C (113°F) | CLOSED | – | – | | – | CLOSED | Not recirculated |
| Above 66°C (151°F) | OPEN | Positioned below E port | – | | – | CLOSED | Not recirculated |
| | | Positioned be-tween E port and R port | (1) LOW | *Pressure con-stantly alter-nating between low and high | OPENS passage to atmosphere | CLOSED | Not recirculated |
| | | | (2) HIGH | | CLOSES passage at atmosphere | OPEN | Recirculated |
| | | Positioned above R port | (3) HIGH | ** | CLOSES passage to atmosphere | OPEN | Recirculated (increase) |

Remarks: *Pressure increase → Modulator closes → EGR valve opens → Pressure drops
EGR valve closes ← Modulator opens ←
**When the throttle valve is positioned above the R port, the EGR vacuum modulator will close the atmosphere passage and open the EGR valve to increase the EGR gas, even if the exhaust pressure is insufficiently low.

90D21116

Courtesy of Toyota Motor Sales, U.S.A., Inc.

**Fig. 47: Identifying EGR System Components & Operating Parameters (Camry 2.0L)**

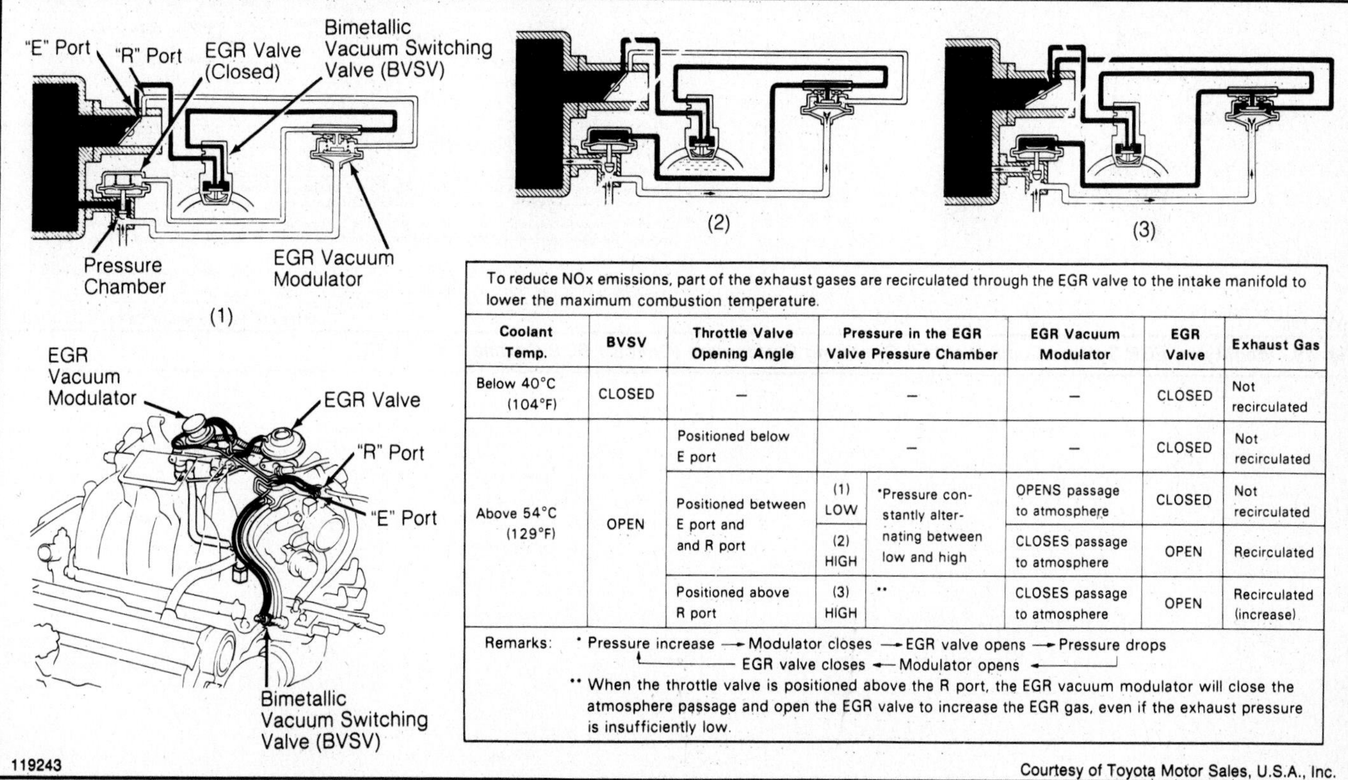


To reduce NOx emissions, part of the exhaust gases are recirculated through the EGR valve to the intake manifold to lower the maximum combustion temperature.

| Coolant Temp. | BVSV | Throttle Valve Opening Angle | Pressure in the EGR Valve Pressure Chamber | | EGR Vacuum Modulator | EGR Valve | Exhaust Gas |
|---|---|---|---|---|---|---|---|
| Below 40°C (104°F) | CLOSED | – | – | | – | CLOSED | Not recirculated |
| Above 54°C (129°F) | OPEN | Positioned below E port | – | | – | CLOSED | Not recirculated |
| | | Positioned between E port and and R port | (1) LOW | *Pressure con-stantly alter-nating between low and high | OPENS passage to atmosphere | CLOSED | Not recirculated |
| | | | (2) HIGH | | CLOSES passage to atmosphere | OPEN | Recirculated |
| | | Positioned above R port | (3) HIGH | ** | CLOSES passage to atmosphere | OPEN | Recirculated (increase) |

Remarks: * Pressure increase → Modulator closes → EGR valve opens → Pressure drops
EGR valve closes ← Modulator opens ←
** When the throttle valve is positioned above the R port, the EGR vacuum modulator will close the atmosphere passage and open the EGR valve to increase the EGR gas, even if the exhaust pressure is insufficiently low.

**Fig. 48: Identifying EGR System Components & Operating Parameters (Camry 2.5L)**

# 1991 ENGINE PERFORMANCE
## System & Component Testing (Cont.)

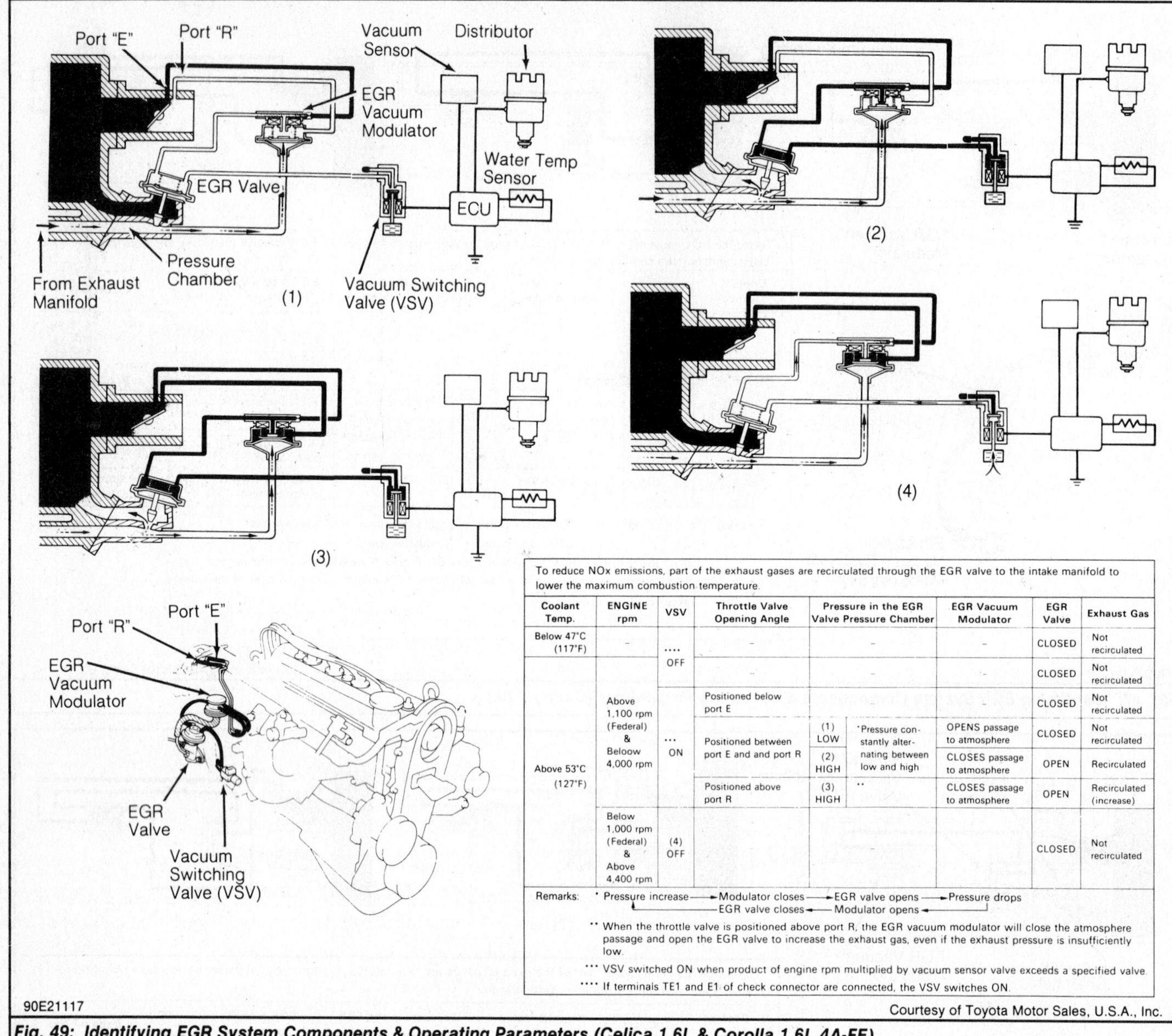


To reduce NOx emissions, part of the exhaust gases are recirculated through the EGR valve to the intake manifold to lower the maximum combustion temperature.

| Coolant Temp. | ENGINE rpm | VSV | Throttle Valve Opening Angle | Pressure in the EGR Valve Pressure Chamber | | EGR Vacuum Modulator | EGR Valve | Exhaust Gas |
|---|---|---|---|---|---|---|---|---|
| Below 47°C (117°F) | – | **** OFF | – | – | | – | CLOSED | Not recirculated |
| Above 53°C (127°F) | Above 1,100 rpm (Federal) & Beloow 4,000 rpm | | – | – | | – | CLOSED | Not recirculated |
| | | *** ON | Positioned below port E | – | | – | CLOSED | Not recirculated |
| | | | Positioned between port E and and port R | (1) LOW | *Pressure constantly alternating between low and high | OPENS passage to atmosphere | CLOSED | Not recirculated |
| | | | | (2) HIGH | | CLOSES passage to atmosphere | OPEN | Recirculated |
| | | | Positioned above port R | (3) HIGH | ** | CLOSES passage to atmosphere | OPEN | Recirculated (increase) |
| | Below 1,000 rpm (Federal) & Above 4,400 rpm | (4) OFF | | – | | | CLOSED | Not recirculated |

Remarks: * Pressure increase → Modulator closes → EGR valve opens → Pressure drops → Modulator opens → EGR valve closes → (Pressure increase)

** When the throttle valve is positioned above port R, the EGR vacuum modulator will close the atmosphere passage and open the EGR valve to increase the exhaust gas, even if the exhaust pressure is insufficiently low.

*** VSV switched ON when product of engine rpm multiplied by vacuum sensor valve exceeds a specified valve.

**** If terminals TE1 and E1 of check connector are connected, the VSV switches ON.

Courtesy of Toyota Motor Sales, U.S.A., Inc.

**Fig. 49: Identifying EGR System Components & Operating Parameters (Celica 1.6L & Corolla 1.6L 4A-FE)**

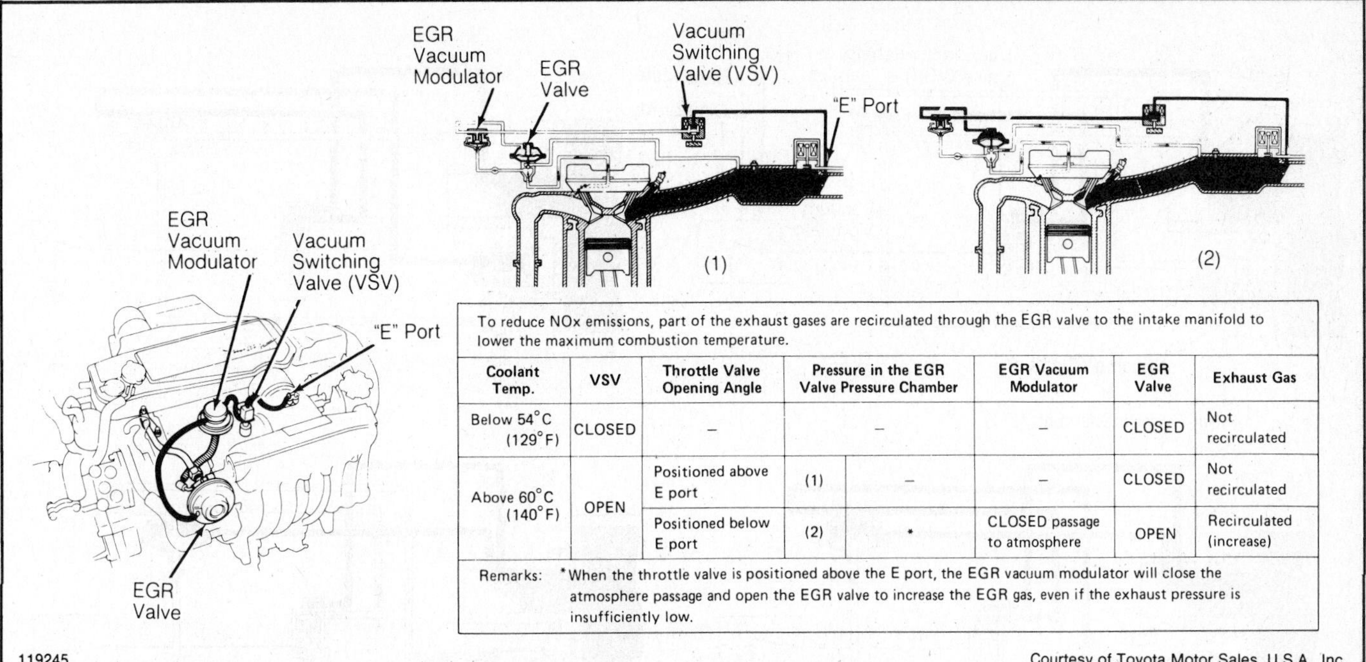


To reduce NOx emissions, part of the exhaust gases are recirculated through the EGR valve to the intake manifold to lower the maximum combustion temperature.

| Coolant Temp. | VSV | Throttle Valve Opening Angle | Pressure in the EGR Valve Pressure Chamber | | EGR Vacuum Modulator | EGR Valve | Exhaust Gas |
|---|---|---|---|---|---|---|---|
| Below 54°C (129°F) | CLOSED | – | – | | – | CLOSED | Not recirculated |
| Above 60°C (140°F) | OPEN | Positioned above E port | (1) | – | – | CLOSED | Not recirculated |
| | | Positioned below E port | (2) | * | CLOSED passage to atmosphere | OPEN | Recirculated (increase) |

Remarks: *When the throttle valve is positioned above the E port, the EGR vacuum modulator will close the atmosphere passage and open the EGR valve to increase the EGR gas, even if the exhaust pressure is insufficiently low.

Courtesy of Toyota Motor Sales, U.S.A., Inc.

***Fig. 50: Identifying EGR System Components & Operating Parameters (Celica 2.0L & MR2 2.0L)***

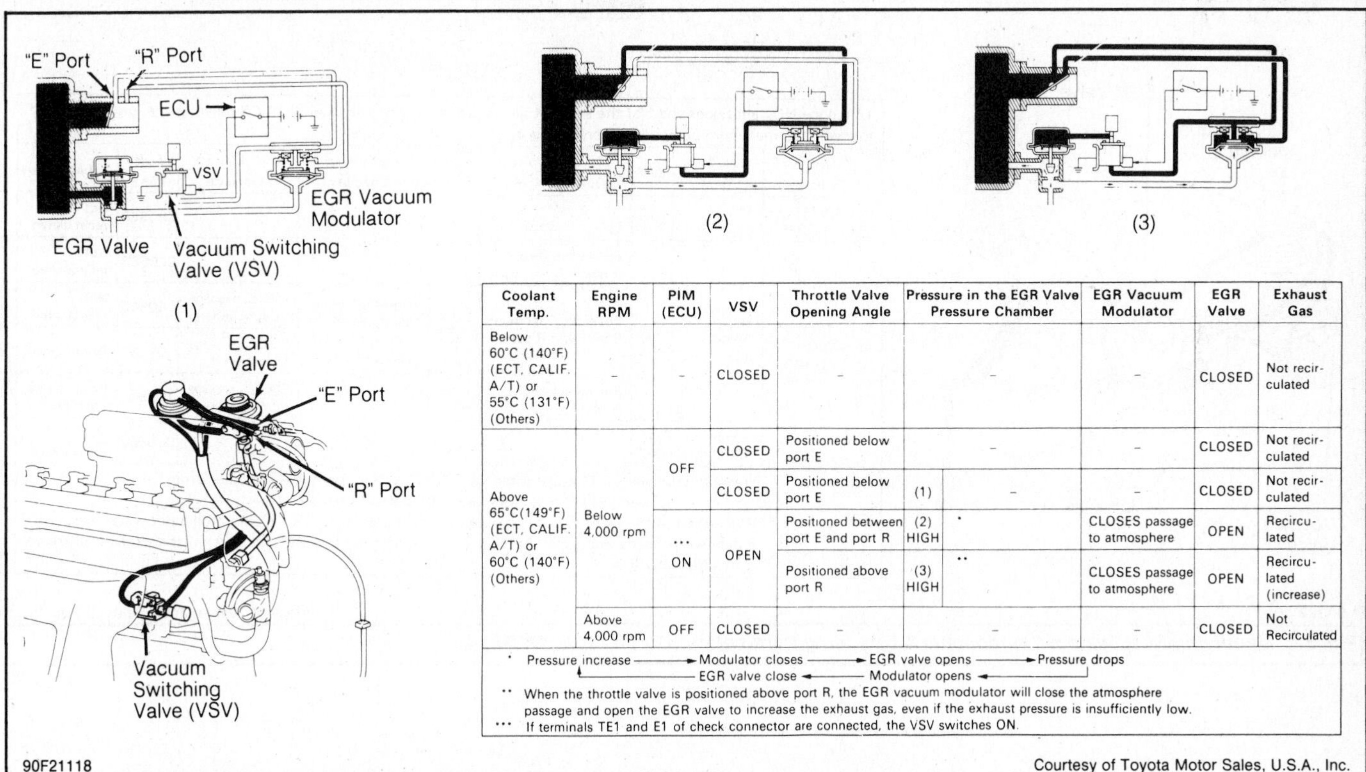


| Coolant Temp. | Engine RPM | PIM (ECU) | VSV | Throttle Valve Opening Angle | Pressure in the EGR Valve Pressure Chamber | | EGR Vacuum Modulator | EGR Valve | Exhaust Gas |
|---|---|---|---|---|---|---|---|---|---|
| Below 60°C (140°F) (ECT, CALIF. A/T) or 55°C (131°F) (Others) | – | – | CLOSED | – | – | | – | CLOSED | Not recirculated |
| Above 65°C(149°F) (ECT, CALIF. A/T) or 60°C (140°F) (Others) | Below 4,000 rpm | OFF | CLOSED | Positioned below port E | – | | – | CLOSED | Not recirculated |
| | | | CLOSED | Positioned below port E | (1) | – | – | CLOSED | Not recirculated |
| | | *** ON | OPEN | Positioned between port E and port R | (2) HIGH | * | CLOSES passage to atmosphere | OPEN | Recirculated |
| | | | | Positioned above port R | (3) HIGH | ** | CLOSES passage to atmosphere | OPEN | Recirculated (increase) |
| | Above 4,000 rpm | OFF | CLOSED | – | – | | – | CLOSED | Not Recirculated |

* Pressure increase → Modulator closes → EGR valve opens → Pressure drops → Modulator opens → EGR valve close → Pressure increase

** When the throttle valve is positioned above port R, the EGR vacuum modulator will close the atmosphere passage and open the EGR valve to increase the exhaust gas, even if the exhaust pressure is insufficiently low.

*** If terminals TE1 and E1 of check connector are connected, the VSV switches ON.

Courtesy of Toyota Motor Sales, U.S.A., Inc.

***Fig. 51: Identifying EGR System Components & Operating Parameters (Celica 2.2L & MR2 2.2L)***

# 1991 ENGINE PERFORMANCE
## System & Component Testing (Cont.)

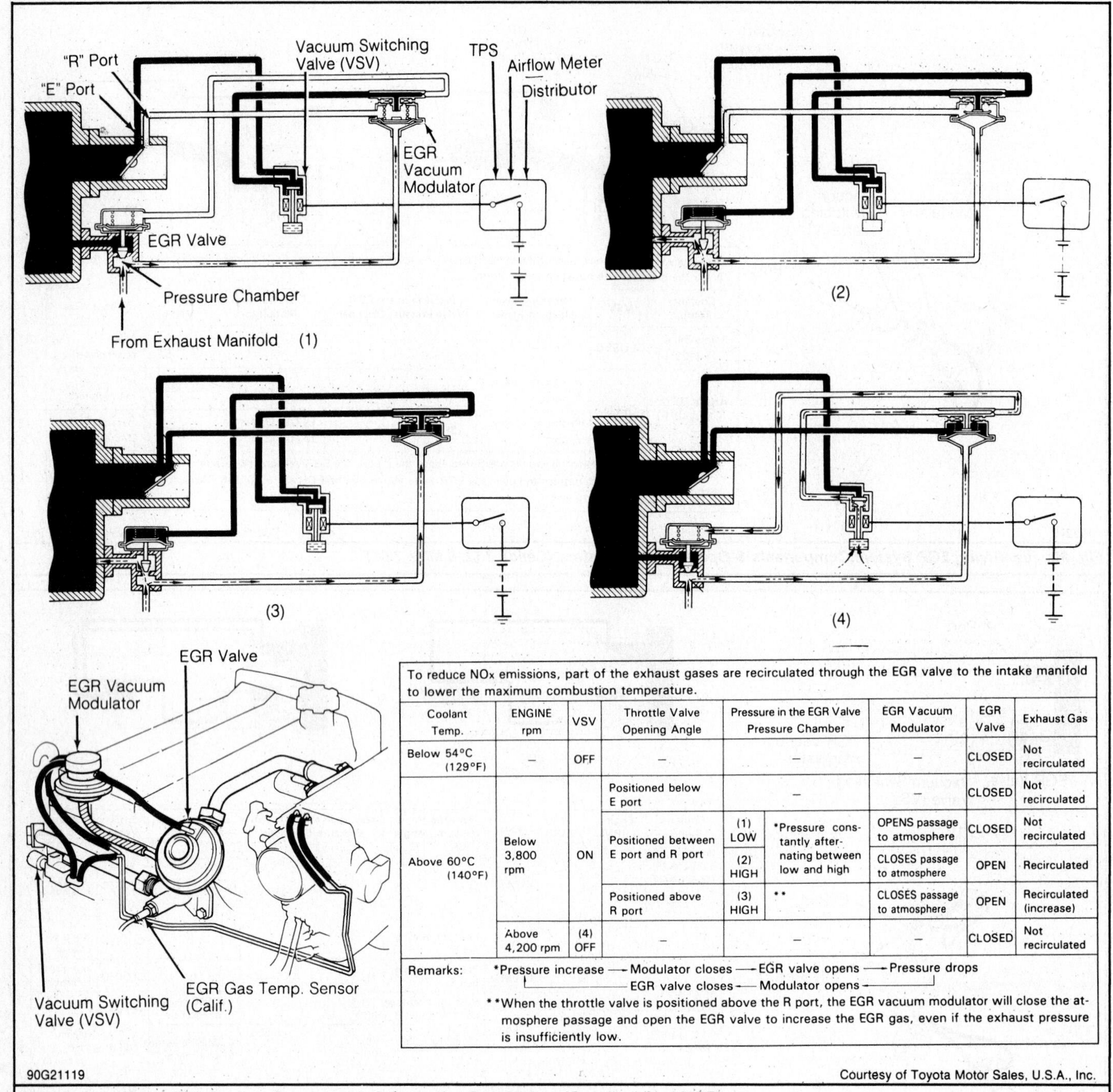


To reduce NOx emissions, part of the exhaust gases are recirculated through the EGR valve to the intake manifold to lower the maximum combustion temperature.

| Coolant Temp. | ENGINE rpm | VSV | Throttle Valve Opening Angle | Pressure in the EGR Valve Pressure Chamber | | EGR Vacuum Modulator | EGR Valve | Exhaust Gas |
|---|---|---|---|---|---|---|---|---|
| Below 54°C (129°F) | – | OFF | – | – | | – | CLOSED | Not recirculated |
| Above 60°C (140°F) | Below 3,800 rpm | ON | Positioned below E port | – | | – | CLOSED | Not recirculated |
| | | | Positioned between E port and R port | (1) LOW | *Pressure constantly alternating between low and high | OPENS passage to atmosphere | CLOSED | Not recirculated |
| | | | | (2) HIGH | | CLOSES passage to atmosphere | OPEN | Recirculated |
| | | | Positioned above R port | (3) HIGH | ** | CLOSES passage to atmosphere | OPEN | Recirculated (increase) |
| | Above 4,200 rpm | (4) OFF | – | – | | – | CLOSED | Not recirculated |

Remarks: *Pressure increase → Modulator closes → EGR valve opens → Pressure drops → EGR valve closes ← Modulator opens ←

**When the throttle valve is positioned above the R port, the EGR vacuum modulator will close the atmosphere passage and open the EGR valve to increase the EGR gas, even if the exhaust pressure is insufficiently low.

Courtesy of Toyota Motor Sales, U.S.A., Inc.

*Fig. 52: Identifying EGR System Components & Operating Parameters (Corolla 1.6L 4A-GE)*

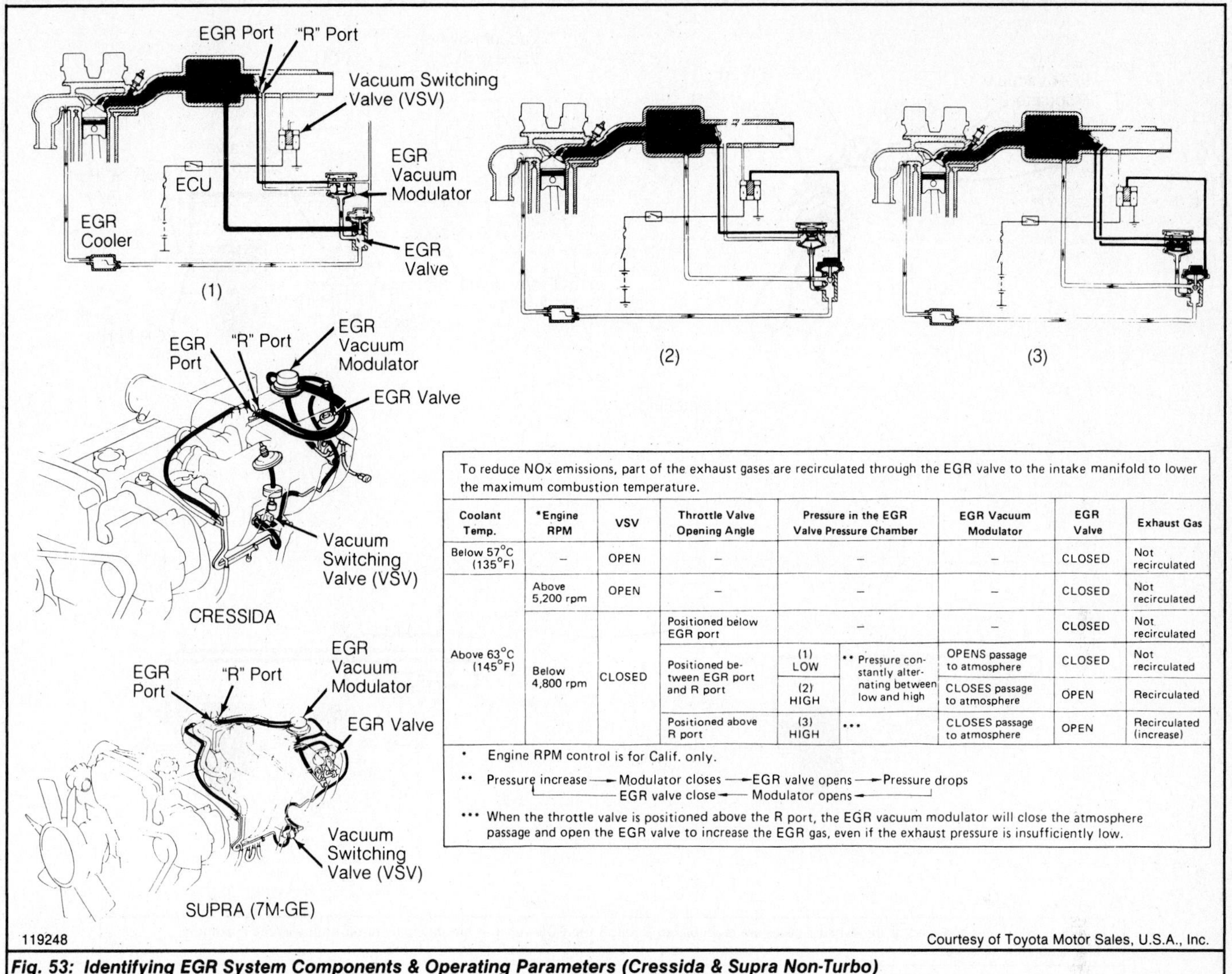


To reduce NOx emissions, part of the exhaust gases are recirculated through the EGR valve to the intake manifold to lower the maximum combustion temperature.

| Coolant Temp. | *Engine RPM | VSV | Throttle Valve Opening Angle | Pressure in the EGR Valve Pressure Chamber | | EGR Vacuum Modulator | EGR Valve | Exhaust Gas |
|---|---|---|---|---|---|---|---|---|
| Below 57°C (135°F) | – | OPEN | – | – | | – | CLOSED | Not recirculated |
| Above 63°C (145°F) | Above 5,200 rpm | OPEN | – | – | | – | CLOSED | Not recirculated |
| | Below 4,800 rpm | CLOSED | Positioned below EGR port | – | | – | CLOSED | Not recirculated |
| | | | Positioned between EGR port and R port | (1) LOW | ** Pressure constantly alternating between low and high | OPENS passage to atmosphere | CLOSED | Not recirculated |
| | | | | (2) HIGH | | CLOSES passage to atmosphere | OPEN | Recirculated |
| | | | Positioned above R port | (3) HIGH | *** | CLOSES passage to atmosphere | OPEN | Recirculated (increase) |

* Engine RPM control is for Calif. only.

** Pressure increase → Modulator closes → EGR valve opens → Pressure drops → EGR valve close → Modulator opens →

*** When the throttle valve is positioned above the R port, the EGR vacuum modulator will close the atmosphere passage and open the EGR valve to increase the EGR gas, even if the exhaust pressure is insufficiently low.

***Fig. 53: Identifying EGR System Components & Operating Parameters (Cressida & Supra Non-Turbo)***

# 1991 ENGINE PERFORMANCE
## System & Component Testing (Cont.)

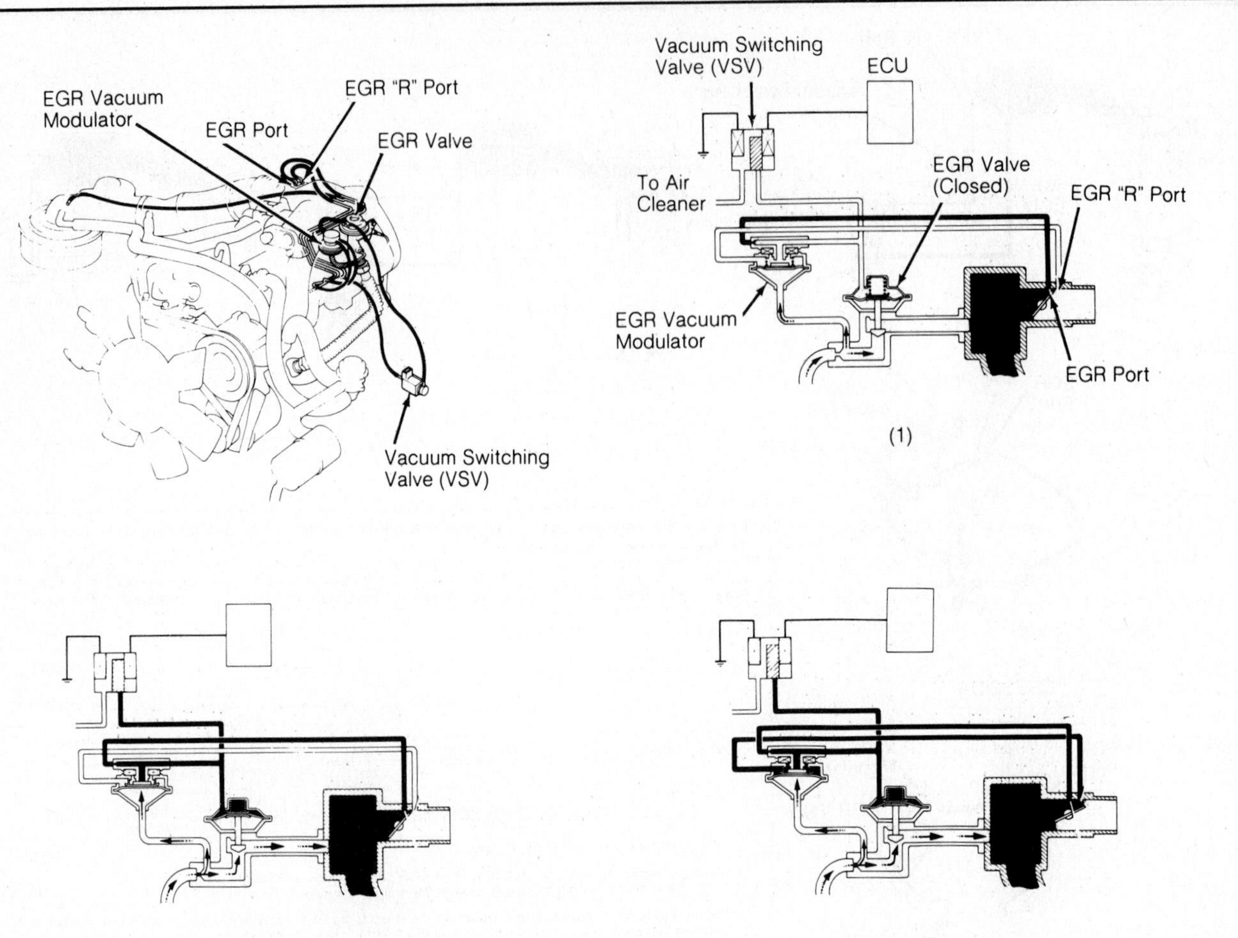


To reduce NOx emission, part of the exhaust gases are recirculated through the EGR valve to the intake manifold to lower the maximum combustion temperature.

| Coolant Temp. | Engine RPM | Driving Condition | Intake Air Volume | VSV | Throttle Valve Opening Angle | Pressure in the EGR Valve Pressure Chamber | EGR Vacuum Modulator | EGR Valve | Exhaust Gas |
|---|---|---|---|---|---|---|---|---|---|
| Below 47°C (117°F) | — | — | — | OFF | — | — | — | CLOSED | Not recirculated |
| Above 53°C (127°F) | Above 3,500 rpm | — | — | OFF | — | — | — | CLOSED | Not recirculated |
| | Blow 3,500 rpm | Deceleration | — | OFF | — | — | — | CLOSED | Not recirculated |
| | | Ex. deceleration | LOW | OFF | — | — | — | CLOSED | Not recirculated |
| | | | HIGH | OFF | — | — | — | CLOSED | Not recirculated |
| | | | | ON | Positioned below EGR port | — | — | CLOSED | Not recirculated |
| | | | | | Positioned between EGR port and EGR R port | (1) LOW — *Pressure constantly alternating between low and high | OPENS passage to atmosphere | CLOSED | Not recirculated |
| | | | | | | (2) HIGH | CLOSES passage to atmosphere | OPEN | Recirculated |
| | | | | | Positioned above EGR port | (3) HIGH — ** | CLOSES passage to atmosphere | OPEN | Recirculated (increase) |

* Pressure increase → Modulator closes → EGR valve opens → Pressure drops
↑ EGR valve closes ← Modulator opens ←

** When the throttle valve is positioned above the R port, the EGR vacuum modulator will close the atmosphere passage and open the EGR valve to increase the EGR gas, even if the exhaust pressure is insufficiently low.

119250

Courtesy of Toyota Motor Sales, U.S.A., Inc.

*Fig. 54: Identifying EGR System Components & Operating Parameters (Land Cruiser)*

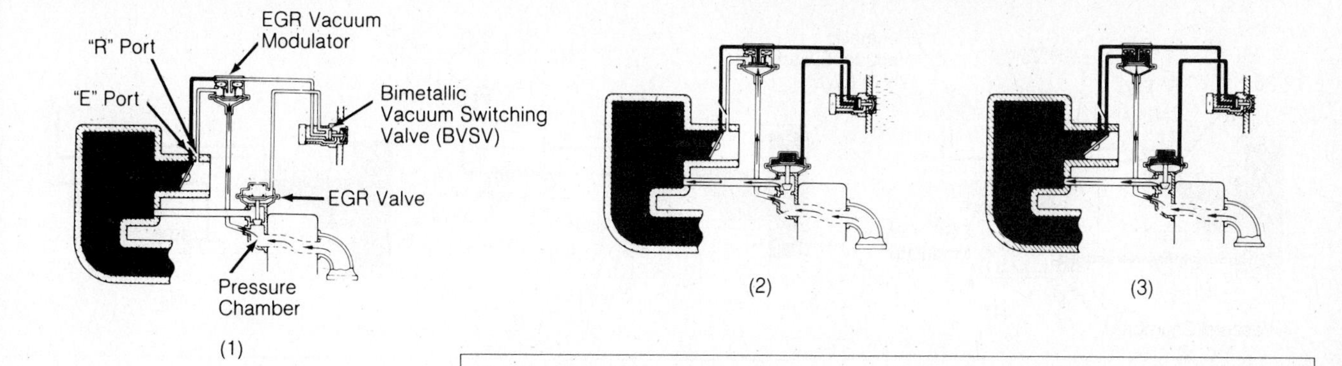

"R" Port
"E" Port
EGR Vacuum Modulator
Bimetallic Vacuum Switching Valve (BVSV)
EGR Valve
Pressure Chamber
(1)
(2)
(3)

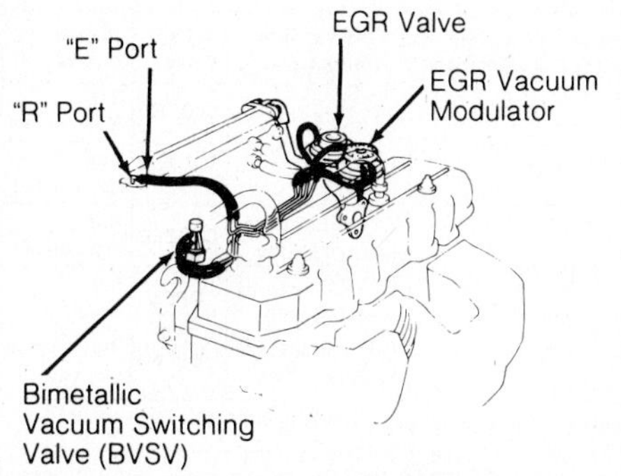

"E" Port
"R" Port
EGR Valve
EGR Vacuum Modulator
Bimetallic Vacuum Switching Valve (BVSV)

To reduce NOx emission, part of the exhaust gases are recirculated through the EGR valve to the intake manifold to lower the maximum combustion temperature.

| Coolant Temp. | BVSV | Throttle Valve Opening Angle | Pressure in the EGR Valve Pressure Chamber | | EGR Vacuum Modulator | EGR Valve | Exhaust Gas |
|---|---|---|---|---|---|---|---|
| Below 30°C (86°F) | CLOSED | — | — | | — | CLOSED | Not recirculated |
| Above 44°C (111°F) | OPEN | Positioned below E port | — | | — | CLOSED | Not recirculated |
| | | Positioned between E port and R port | (1) LOW | *Pressure constantly alternating between low and high | OPENS passage to atmosphere | CLOSED | Not recirculated |
| | | | (2) HIGH | | CLOSES passage to atmosphere | OPEN | Recirculated |
| | | Positioned above R port | (3) HIGH | ** | CLOSES passage to atmosphere | OPEN | Recirculated (increase) |

Remarks: *Pressure increase → Modulator closes → EGR valve opens → Pressure drops
EGR valve closes ← Modulator opens ←
**When the throttle valve is positioned above the R port, the EGR vacuum modulator will close the atmosphere passage and open the EGR valve to increase the EGR gas, even if the exhaust pressure is insufficiently low.

119253

Courtesy of Toyota Motor Sales, U.S.A., Inc.

*Fig. 55: Identifying EGR System Components & Operating Parameters (Pickup 2.4L & 4Runner 2.4L)*

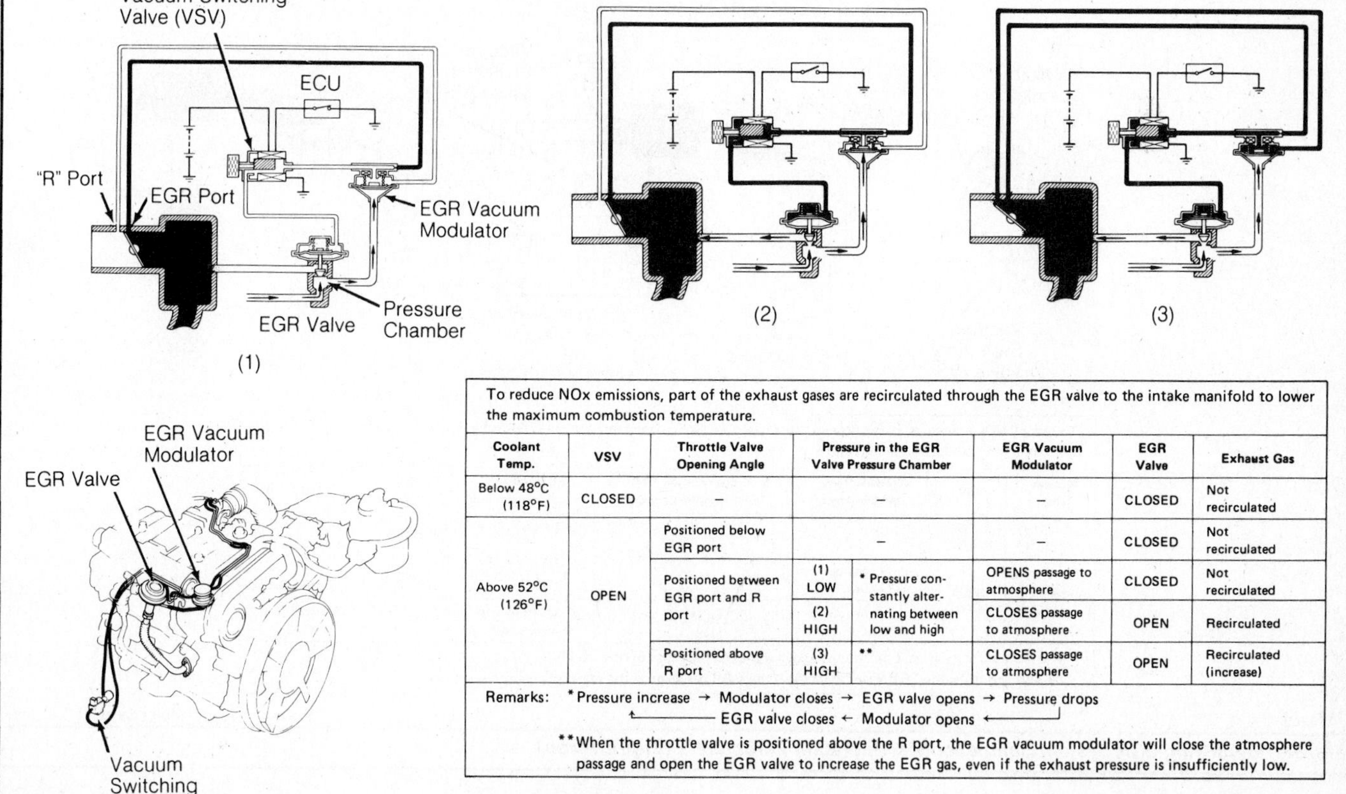


To reduce NOx emissions, part of the exhaust gases are recirculated through the EGR valve to the intake manifold to lower the maximum combustion temperature.

| Coolant Temp. | VSV | Throttle Valve Opening Angle | Pressure in the EGR Valve Pressure Chamber | | EGR Vacuum Modulator | EGR Valve | Exhaust Gas |
|---|---|---|---|---|---|---|---|
| Below 48°C (118°F) | CLOSED | – | – | | – | CLOSED | Not recirculated |
| Above 52°C (126°F) | OPEN | Positioned below EGR port | – | | – | CLOSED | Not recirculated |
| | | Positioned between EGR port and R port | (1) LOW | * Pressure constantly alternating between low and high | OPENS passage to atmosphere | CLOSED | Not recirculated |
| | | | (2) HIGH | | CLOSES passage to atmosphere | OPEN | Recirculated |
| | | Positioned above R port | (3) HIGH | ** | CLOSES passage to atmosphere | OPEN | Recirculated (increase) |

Remarks: * Pressure increase → Modulator closes → EGR valve opens → Pressure drops
EGR valve closes ← Modulator opens ←
**When the throttle valve is positioned above the R port, the EGR vacuum modulator will close the atmosphere passage and open the EGR valve to increase the EGR gas, even if the exhaust pressure is insufficiently low.

Courtesy of Toyota Motor Sales, U.S.A., Inc.

*Fig. 56: Identifying EGR System Components & Operating Parameters (Pickup 3.0L & 4Runner 3.0L)*

# 1991 ENGINE PERFORMANCE
## System & Component Testing (Cont.)

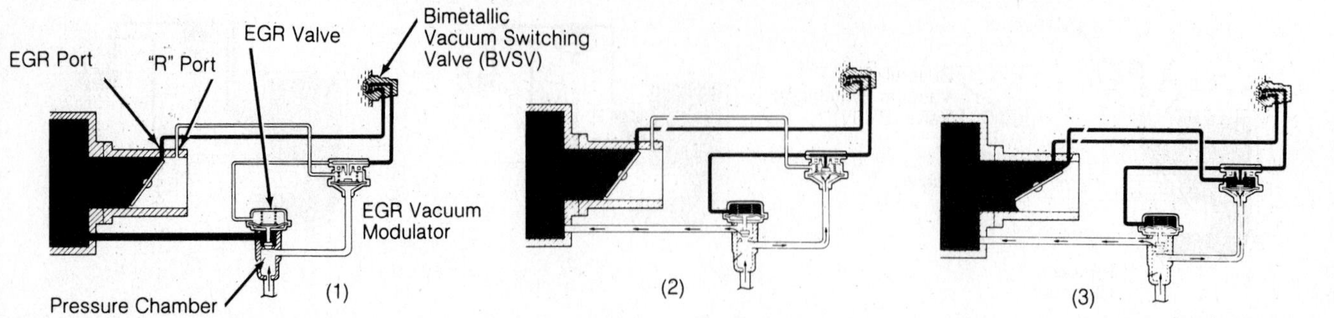

EGR Port
"R" Port
EGR Valve
Bimetallic Vacuum Switching Valve (BVSV)
EGR Vacuum Modulator
Pressure Chamber
(1)
(2)
(3)

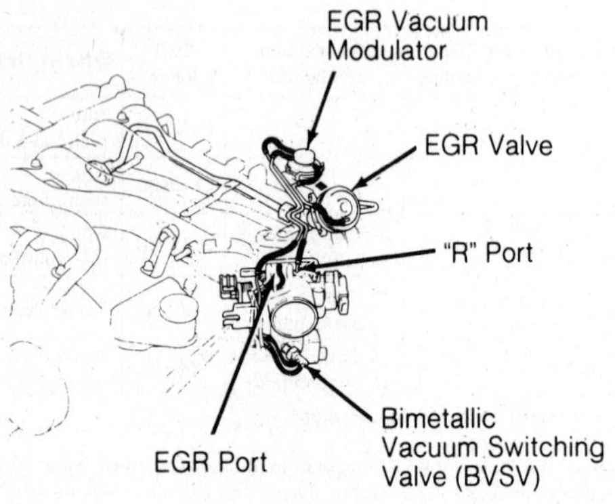

EGR Vacuum Modulator
EGR Valve
"R" Port
EGR Port
Bimetallic Vacuum Switching Valve (BVSV)

To reduce NOx emission, part of the exhaust gases are recirculated through the EGR valve to the intake manifold to lower the maximum combustion temperature.

| Coolant Temp. | BVSV | Throttle Valve Opening Angle | Pressure in the EGR Valve Pressure Chamber | | EGR Vacuum Modulator | EGR Valve | Exhaust Gas |
|---|---|---|---|---|---|---|---|
| Below 37°C (99°F) | CLOSED | — | — | | — | CLOSED | Not recirculated |
| Above 56°C (133°F) | OPEN | Positioned below EGR port | — | | — | CLOSED | Not recirculated |
| | | Positioned between EGR port and R port | (1) LOW | *Pressure constantly alternating between low and high | OPENS passage to atmosphere | CLOSED | Not recirculated |
| | | | (2) HIGH | | CLOSES passage to atmosphere | OPEN | Re-circulated |
| | | Positioned above R port | (3) HIGH | ** | CLOSES passage to atmosphere | OPEN | Recirculated (increase) |

Remarks: *Pressure increase → Modulator closes → EGR valve opens → Pressure drops → EGR valve closes ← Modulator opens ←

**When the throttle valve is positioned above the R port, the EGR vacuum modulator will close the atmosphere passage and open the EGR valve to increase the EGR gas, even if the exhaust pressure is insufficiently low.

91J16559

Courtesy of Toyota Motor Sales, U.S.A., Inc.

*Fig. 57: Identifying EGR System Components & Operating Parameters (Previa)*

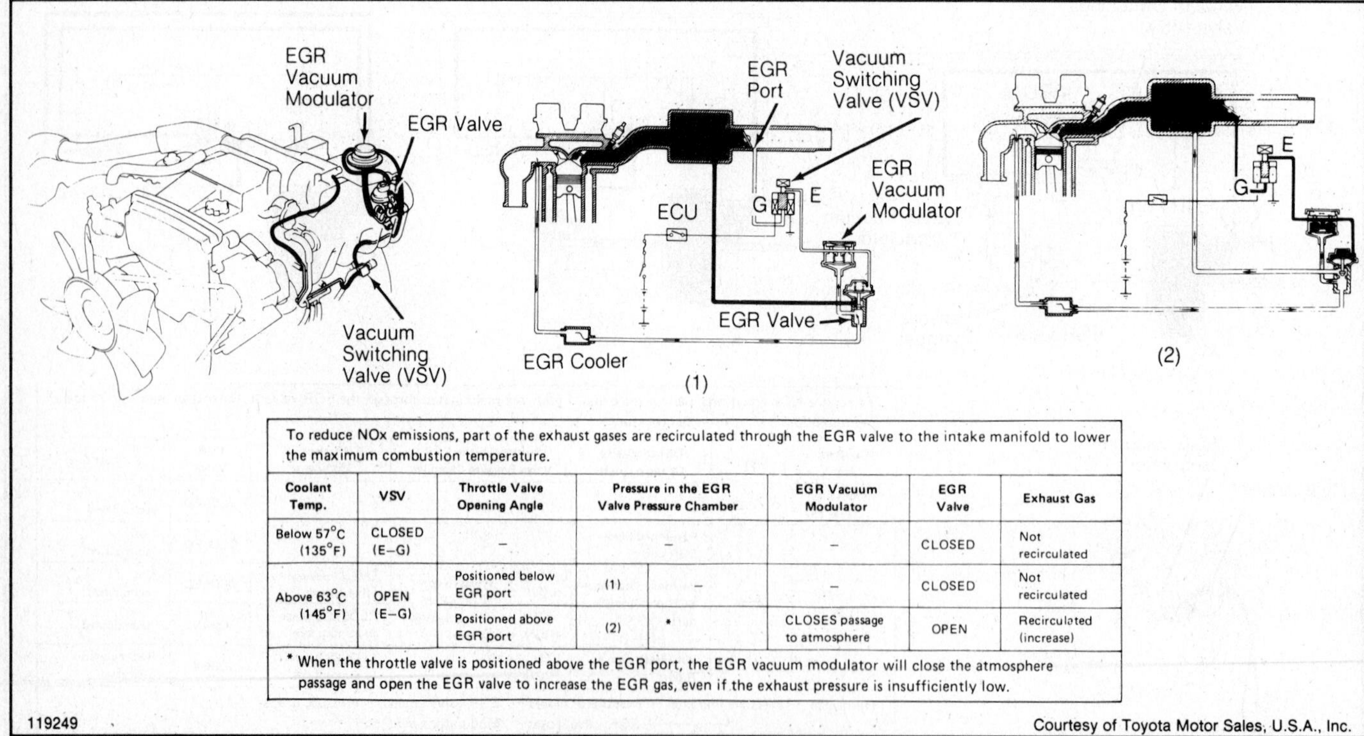


To reduce NOx emissions, part of the exhaust gases are recirculated through the EGR valve to the intake manifold to lower the maximum combustion temperature.

| Coolant Temp. | VSV | Throttle Valve Opening Angle | Pressure in the EGR Valve Pressure Chamber | | EGR Vacuum Modulator | EGR Valve | Exhaust Gas |
|---|---|---|---|---|---|---|---|
| Below 57°C (135°F) | CLOSED (E–G) | – | – | | – | CLOSED | Not recirculated |
| Above 63°C (145°F) | OPEN (E–G) | Positioned below EGR port | (1) | – | – | CLOSED | Not recirculated |
| | | Positioned above EGR port | (2) | * | CLOSES passage to atmosphere | OPEN | Recirculated (increase) |

* When the throttle valve is positioned above the EGR port, the EGR vacuum modulator will close the atmosphere passage and open the EGR valve to increase the EGR gas, even if the exhaust pressure is insufficiently low.

119249

Courtesy of Toyota Motor Sales, U.S.A., Inc.

*Fig. 58: Identifying EGR System Components & Operating Parameters (Supra Turbo)*

# 1991 ENGINE PERFORMANCE
# System & Component Testing (Cont.)

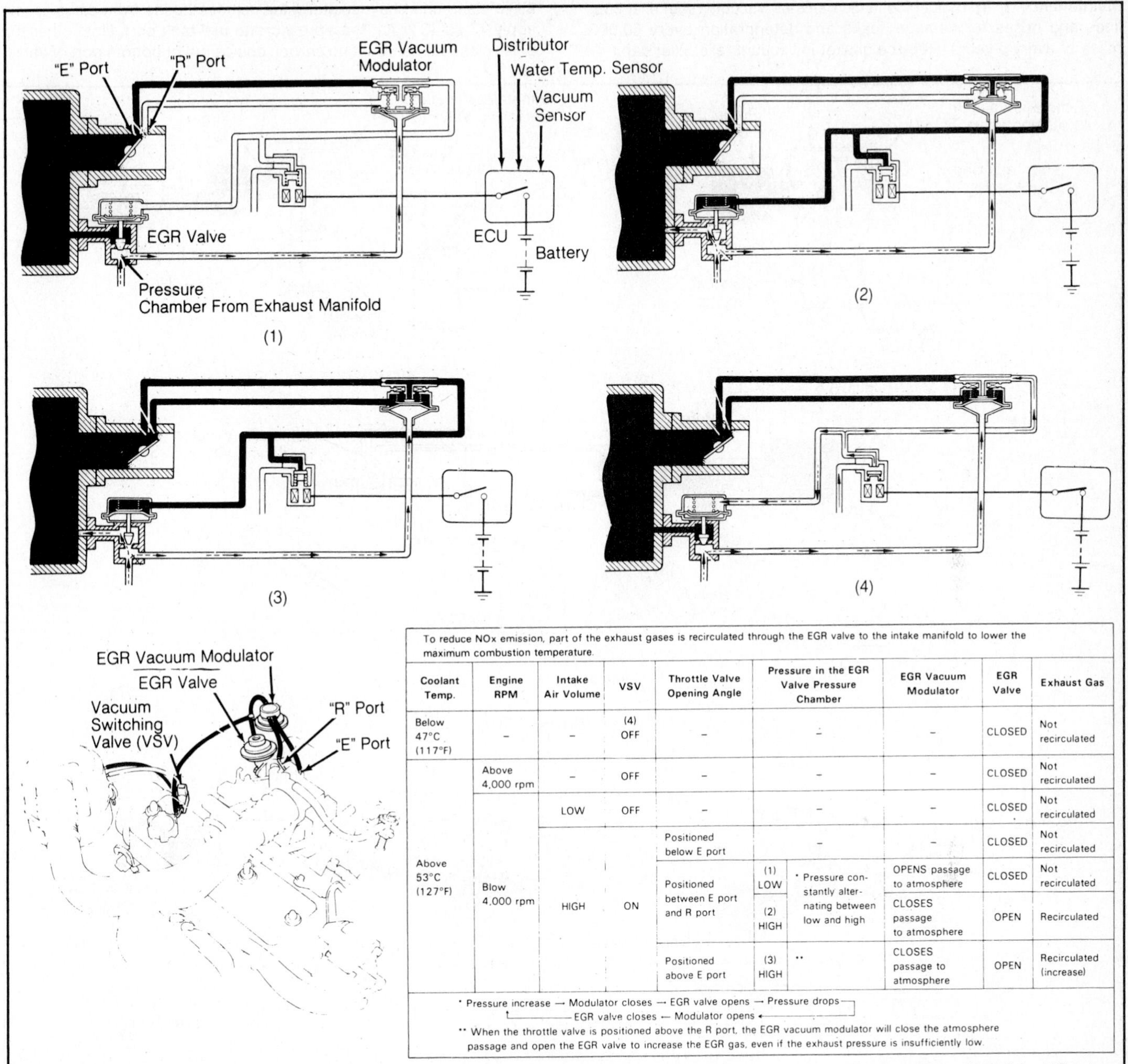


To reduce NOx emission, part of the exhaust gases is recirculated through the EGR valve to the intake manifold to lower the maximum combustion temperature.

| Coolant Temp. | Engine RPM | Intake Air Volume | VSV | Throttle Valve Opening Angle | Pressure in the EGR Valve Pressure Chamber | | EGR Vacuum Modulator | EGR Valve | Exhaust Gas |
|---|---|---|---|---|---|---|---|---|---|
| Below 47°C (117°F) | – | – | (4) OFF | – | – | | – | CLOSED | Not recirculated |
| Above 53°C (127°F) | Above 4,000 rpm | – | OFF | – | – | | – | CLOSED | Not recirculated |
| | Blow 4,000 rpm | LOW | OFF | – | – | | – | CLOSED | Not recirculated |
| | | HIGH | ON | Positioned below E port | – | | – | CLOSED | Not recirculated |
| | | | | Positioned between E port and R port | (1) LOW | * Pressure constantly alternating between low and high | OPENS passage to atmosphere | CLOSED | Not recirculated |
| | | | | | (2) HIGH | | CLOSES passage to atmosphere | OPEN | Recirculated |
| | | | | Positioned above E port | (3) HIGH | ** | CLOSES passage to atmosphere | OPEN | Recirculated (increase) |

* Pressure increase → Modulator closes → EGR valve opens → Pressure drops → Modulator opens → EGR valve closes → (Pressure increase)

** When the throttle valve is positioned above the R port, the EGR vacuum modulator will close the atmosphere passage and open the EGR valve to increase the EGR gas, even if the exhaust pressure is insufficiently low.

*Fig. 59: Identifying EGR System Components & Operating Parameters (Tercel – California)*

## FUEL EVAPORATION

***NOTE: See Figs. 60-62 to identify evaporative emission control systems and operating parameters.***

**Fuel Odor Or Gas Leaks** – Check for disconnected or cracked fuel vapor line or defective components in system. Check all lines and fittings. Check operation of system.

**Fuel Tank Or Expansion Tank Deformed** – Check for clogged canister, defective vacuum relief filler cap or restricted hoses.

**Rough Engine Operation** – Check vacuum hose between vacuum solenoid valve (if equipped) and intake manifold for damage or loose connections. Check for malfunctions in all valves. Ensure all vacuum hoses are tight and in good condition.

**Bimetallic Vacuum Switching Valve (BVSV) – 1)** Drain engine coolant. Remove BVSV. Connect hose to top port. Place valve in water that is less than 95°F (35°C). Blow air into hose. Ensure valve is closed.

**2)** Heat water to 129°F (54°C). Blow air into hose. Ensure valve is open. If valve is not open, replace valve. Apply liquid sealer to threads of valve before installing. Fill cooling system. If BVSV does not operate as described, replace valve.

***WARNING: DO NOT inhale fuel vapors when blowing into valve.***

**Charcoal Canister – 1)** On all models, check for clogged filter and/or stuck check valve by blowing low pressure compressed air into canister tank port. Ensure air flows freely out of other canister ports.

**2)** Blow air into canister purge port. Ensure air does not flow out of any other port.

**Restrictor (Camry, Celica & MR2)** – Remove hoses from restrictor and remove restrictor from vehicle. Blow air through both sides to ensure there is no blockage. Replace restrictor if airflow is blocked in either direction.

# 1991 ENGINE PERFORMANCE
## System & Component Testing (Cont.)

**Maintenance – 1)** Inspect fuel tank, canister, vacuum relief filler cap, lines and hoses for damage, leaks and deterioration every 60,000 miles or every 6 years. Replace gasket in vacuum relief filler cap.

**2)** To clean charcoal canister filter, remove hoses from canister and apply 43 psi (3 kg/cm²) air pressure to fuel tank port. Hold other top ports closed. Ensure tht no carbon comes out of bottom port of canister.

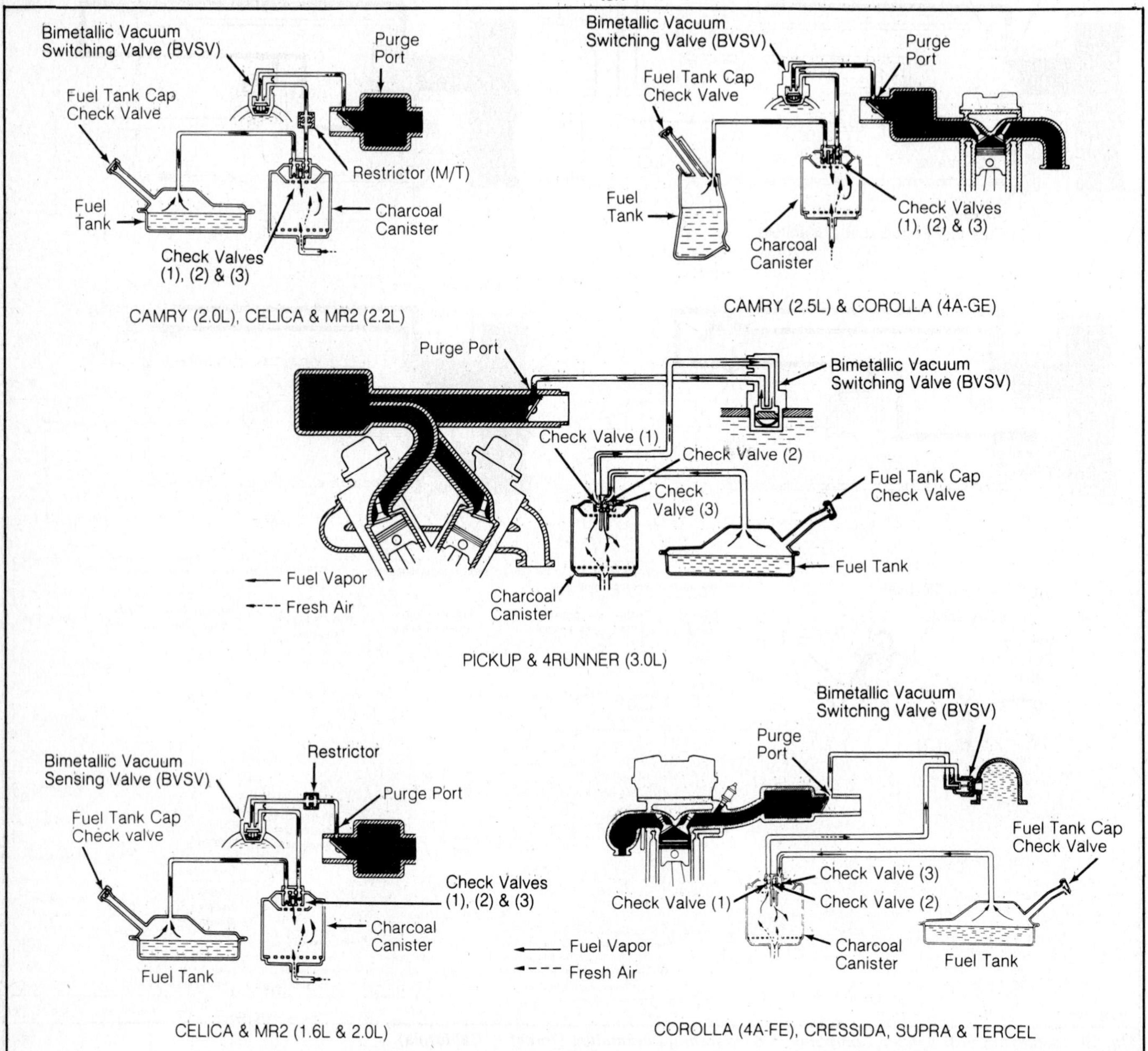

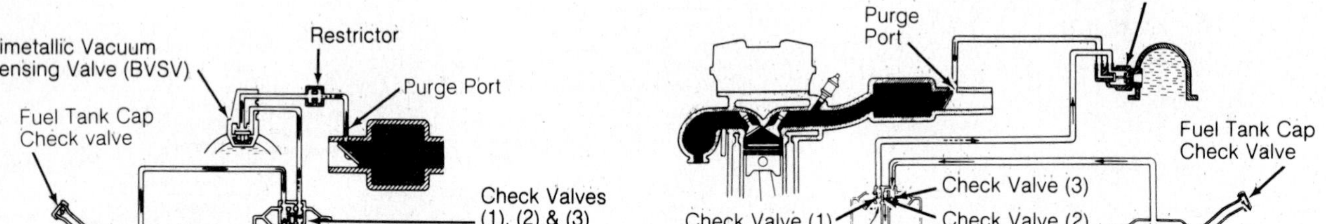


To reduce HC emission, evaporated fuel from the fuel tank is routed through the charcoal canister to the intake manifold for combustion in the cylinders.

| Coolant Temp. | BVSV | Throttle Valve Opening | Canister Check Valve (1) | Canister Check Valve (2) | Canister Check Valve (3) | Check Valve in Cap | Evaporated Fuel (HC) |
|---|---|---|---|---|---|---|---|
| Below 35°C (95°F) | CLOSED | – | – | – | – | – | HC from tank is absorbed into the canister. |
| Above * 54°C (129°F) | OPEN | Positioned below P port | CLOSED | – | – | – | |
| | | Positioned above P port | OPEN | – | – | – | HC from canister is led into air intake chamber. |
| High pressure in tank | – | – | – | OPEN | CLOSED | CLOSED | HC from tank is absorbed into the canister. |
| High vacuum in tank | – | – | – | CLOSED | OPEN | OPEN | Air is led into the fuel tank. |

NOTE: * 4WD Corolla and Cressida 122ºF (50ºC)

119255 119257 119258 119259

Courtesy of Toyota Motor Sales, U.S.A., Inc.

*Fig. 60: Identifying Evaporative Emission Control System & Operating Parameters (Camry, Celica, Corolla, Cressida, MR2, Pickup 3.0L, Supra, Tercel & 4Runner 3.0L)*

# 1991 ENGINE PERFORMANCE
# System & Component Testing (Cont.)

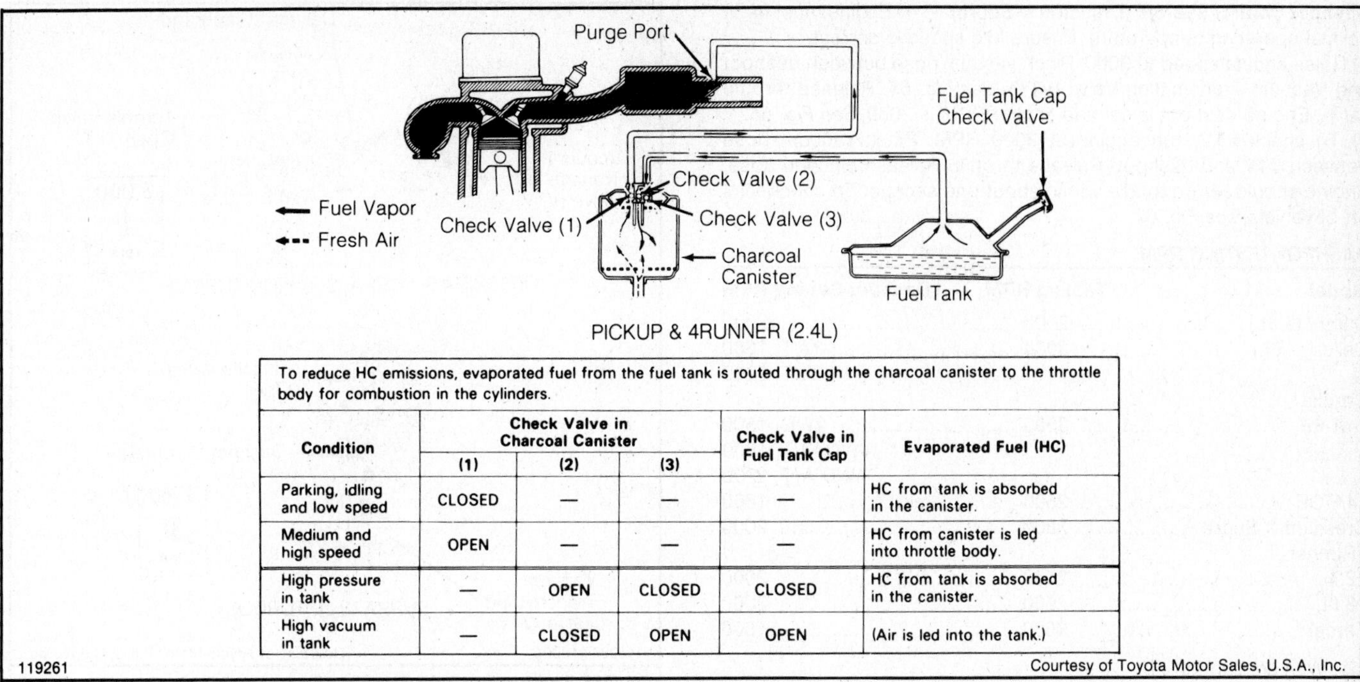


To reduce HC emissions, evaporated fuel from the fuel tank is routed through the charcoal canister to the throttle body for combustion in the cylinders.

| Condition | Check Valve in Charcoal Canister | | | Check Valve in Fuel Tank Cap | Evaporated Fuel (HC) |
|---|---|---|---|---|---|
| | (1) | (2) | (3) | | |
| Parking, idling and low speed | CLOSED | — | — | — | HC from tank is absorbed in the canister. |
| Medium and high speed | OPEN | — | — | — | HC from canister is led into throttle body. |
| High pressure in tank | — | OPEN | CLOSED | CLOSED | HC from tank is absorbed in the canister. |
| High vacuum in tank | — | CLOSED | OPEN | OPEN | (Air is led into the tank.) |

119261 Courtesy of Toyota Motor Sales, U.S.A., Inc.

***Fig. 61:** Identifying Evaporative Emission Control System & Operating Parameters (Pickup 2.4L, 4Runner 2.4L & Previa)*

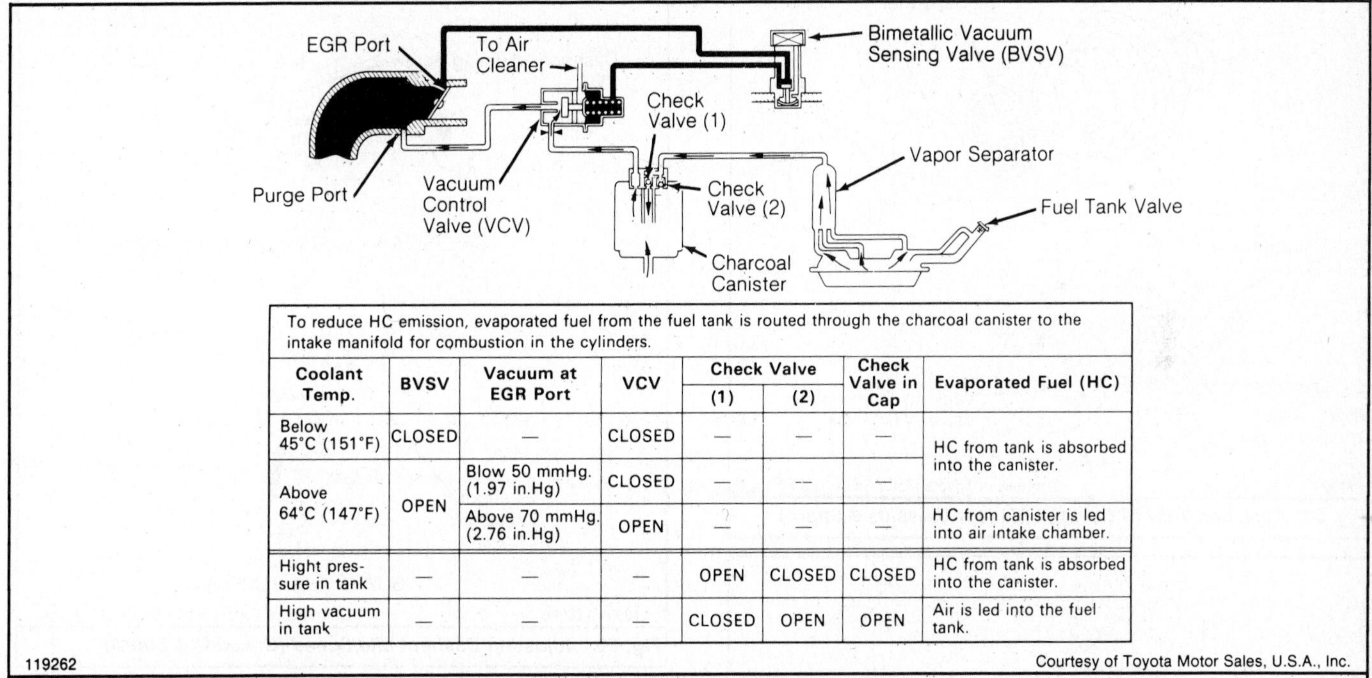


To reduce HC emission, evaporated fuel from the fuel tank is routed through the charcoal canister to the intake manifold for combustion in the cylinders.

| Coolant Temp. | BVSV | Vacuum at EGR Port | VCV | Check Valve | | Check Valve in Cap | Evaporated Fuel (HC) |
|---|---|---|---|---|---|---|---|
| | | | | (1) | (2) | | |
| Below 45°C (151°F) | CLOSED | — | CLOSED | — | — | — | HC from tank is absorbed into the canister. |
| Above 64°C (147°F) | OPEN | Blow 50 mmHg. (1.97 in.Hg) | CLOSED | — | — | — | |
| | | Above 70 mmHg. (2.76 in.Hg) | OPEN | — | — | — | HC from canister is led into air intake chamber. |
| Hight pressure in tank | — | — | — | OPEN | CLOSED | CLOSED | HC from tank is absorbed into the canister. |
| High vacuum in tank | — | — | — | CLOSED | OPEN | OPEN | Air is led into the fuel tank. |

119262 Courtesy of Toyota Motor Sales, U.S.A., Inc.

***Fig. 62:** Identifying Evaporative Emission Control System & Operating Parameters (Land Cruiser)*

## POSITIVE CRANKCASE VENTILATION (PCV)

**Fixed Orifice** – Visually inspect hose and connections for cracks, leaks or other damage. Clean deposits from orifice with solvent and blow out with compressed air

**PCV Valve** – Remove PCV valve. Attach hose to PCV valve. Blow air from cylinder head side of valve. Ensure air passes through easily. Blow air from intake manifold side. Ensure air passes through with some restriction. If PCV valve does not function as described, replace PCV valve.

## THROTTLE CONTROLS

**Dashpot Control System (All Except Cressida & Supra)** – **1)** Engine must be at normal operating temperature. Check idle speed and adjust if necessary. Remove cap, filter and separator from dashpot. *See Fig. 63.*

**2)** Start engine. Maintain engine speed at specified testing RPM. See DASHPOT TESTING RPM table. Plug Vacuum Transmitting Valve (VTV) hole with your finger. *See Fig. 63.*

**3)** Release throttle. Dashpot should be extended and dashpot setting RPM should be as specified. See DASHPOT TESTING RPM table. If idle speed is incorrect, adjust dashpot. *See Fig. 64.*

**4)** To check VTV operation, run engine at dashpot testing RPM for a few seconds. Plug the VTV hole with your finger. Release throttle. Uncover plugged hole. Engine should return to idle in about one second.

**5)** Install dashpot separator, filter and cap. Install filter with coarser surface facing outward.

# 1991 ENGINE PERFORMANCE
## System & Component Testing (Cont.)

**Dashpot Control System (Cressida & Supra) – 1)** Engine must be at normal operating temperature. Ensure idle speed is correct.
**2)** Raise engine speed to 3000. Pinch vacuum hose between dashpot and Vacuum Transmitting Valve (VTV). *See Fig. 65.* Release throttle valve. Ensure dashpot is set and engine RPM is 2000. *See Fig. 66.*
**3)** To check VTV, run engine at 3000 RPM. Pinch vacuum hose between VTV and dashpot. Release throttle. Release pinched hose. Engine should return to idle within about one second. To check VTV off of vehicle, *see Fig. 67.*

***DASHPOT TESTING RPM***

| Model | Testing RPM | [1] Dashpot Setting RPM |
|---|---|---|
| Camry (2.5L) | 2500 | 2000 |
| Celica (1.6L) | 3000 | M/T, 1800<br>A/T, 2200 |
| Corolla | | |
| 4A-FE | 3500 | 2WD, 1500<br>4WD M/T, 1800<br>4WD A/T, 2200 |
| 4A-GE | 2500 | 1800 |
| Cressida & Supra | 3000 | 2000 |
| 4Runner | | |
| 2.4L | 2500 | 2000 |
| 3.0L | 2500 | 2000 |
| Tercel | 2500 | 1500 |

[1] – With cooling fan off.

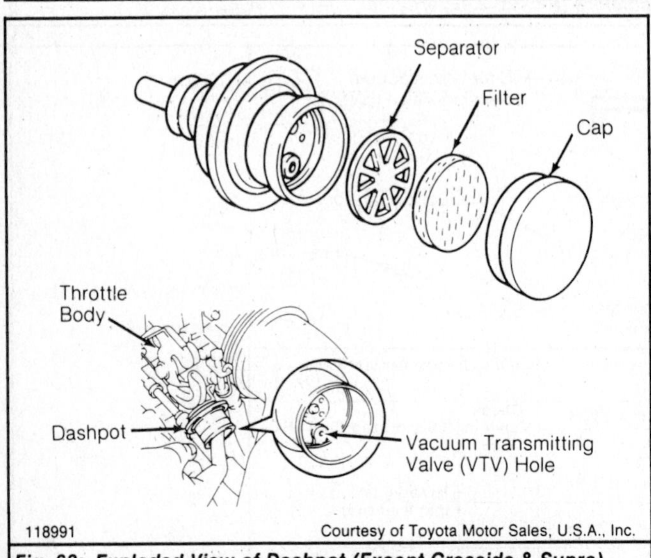


*Fig. 63: Exploded View of Dashpot (Except Cressida & Supra)*

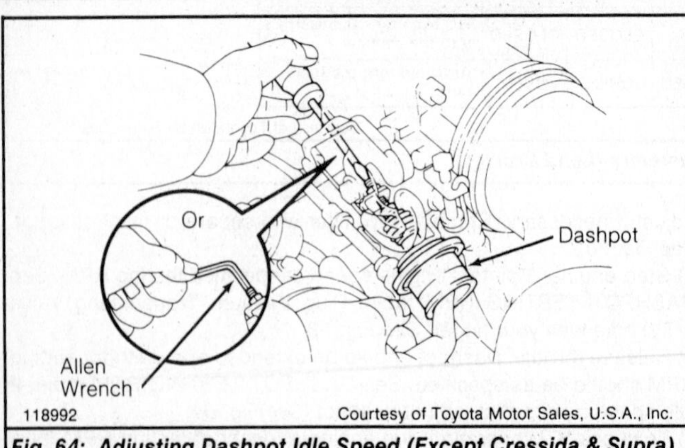


*Fig. 64: Adjusting Dashpot Idle Speed (Except Cressida & Supra)*

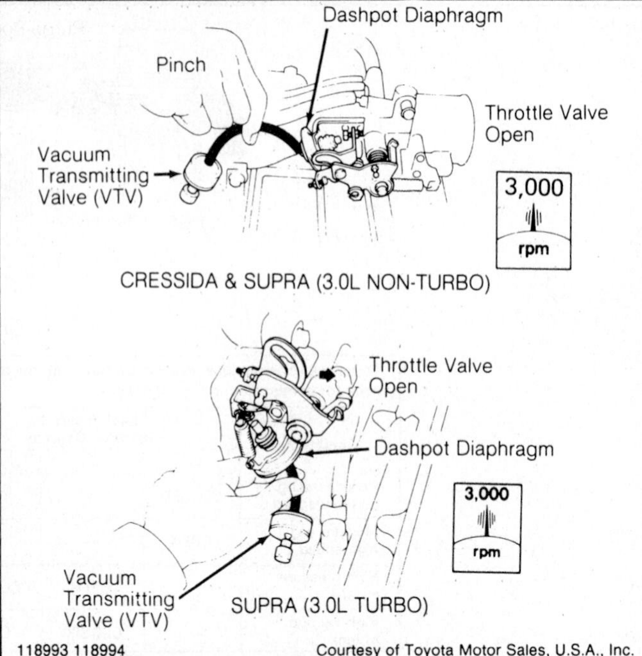


*Fig. 65: Testing Dashpot System (Cressida & Supra)*

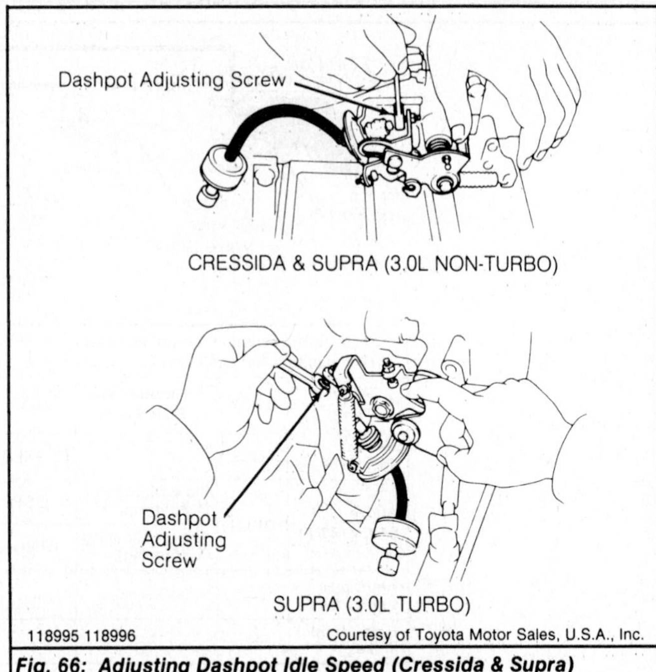


*Fig. 66: Adjusting Dashpot Idle Speed (Cressida & Supra)*

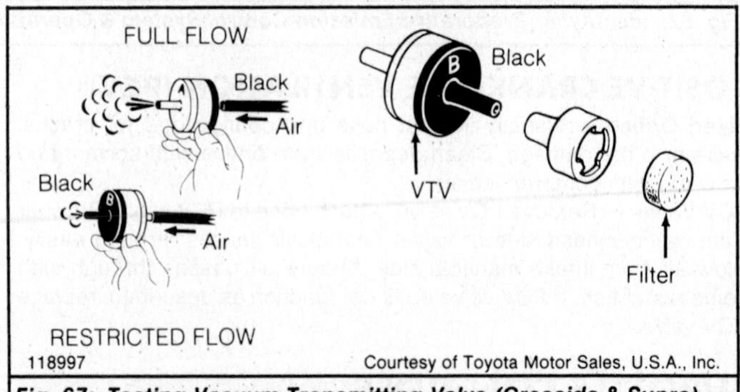


*Fig. 67: Testing Vacuum Transmitting Valve (Cressida & Supra)*

# 1991 ENGINE PERFORMANCE
# Pin Voltage Charts

**Camry, Celica, Corolla, Cressida, Land Cruiser, MR2, Pickup, Previa, Supra, Tercel, 4Runner**

## INTRODUCTION

Pin voltage charts are supplied to reduce diagnostic time. Checking pin voltages at the ECU determines whether it's receiving and transmitting proper voltage signals. Charts may also help determine if ECU harness is shorted or opened.

***NOTE: Unless stated otherwise in testing procedures, perform all voltage tests using a Digital Volt-Ohmmeter (DVOM) with a minimum 10,000 ohm input impedance. Voltage readings may vary slightly due to battery condition or charging rate.***

## ECU LOCATION

***ECU LOCATION***

| Model | Location |
|---|---|
| Camry, Celica, Corolla & Tercel | Bottom Center Of Dash, In Front Of Console |
| Cressida | Above Glove Box |
| Land Cruiser | Above Glove Box |
| MR2 | Center Of Panel Behind Engine, Toward Rear Of Vehicle |
| Pickup & 4Runner | Behind Right Kick Panel |
| Previa | Below Driver's Seat |
| Supra | Above Glove Box |

***ECU PIN CONNECTOR ABBREVIATION IDENTIFICATION***

| Abbreviation | Function |
|---|---|
| ABS | Anti-Lock Brake ECU |
| ACA | A/C Amplifier |
| ACT | A/C Amplifier |
| AC1 | A/C Magnetic Switch |
| A/D | Cruise Control Computer |
| AI | Air Injection Vacuum Switching Valve |
| AS | Air Suction Vacuum Switching Valve |
| BATT | Battery |
| BK | Brake Switch |
| +B, +B1 | EFI Main Relay |
| CHK | Sub-Oxygen Sensor |
| C1 | Distributor |
| DFG | Defogger Relay |
| DG | Check Connector |
| ECT | Electronically Controlled Transmission/Transaxle (ECT) |
| EGR | EGR Vacuum Switching Valve |
| ELS | Headlight & Defogger Relay |
| E1, E01, E02 | Engine Or Computer Ground |
| E11, E2, E21, E22 | Sensor Ground |
| FC | Circuit Opening Relay |
| FP | Fuel Pump Relay |
| FPR | Fuel Pump Relay |
| FPU | Fuel Pressure-Up Vacuum Switching Valve |
| G, G1, G2 | Cam Position Sensor Or Distributor |
| G–, G+ | Cam Position Sensor Or Distributor (Crank Angle) |
| HT | Oxygen Sensor Heater |
| HT1 | Oxygen Sensor Heater (Main) |
| HT2 | Oxygen Sensor Heater (Sub) |
| IDL | Throttle Position Sensor |
| IGDA, IGDB | Ignitor |
| IGF | Ignitor |
| IG SW | Ignition Switch |
| IGT | Ignitor (Primary Trigger) |
| ISCC, ISCO | Idle Speed Control Valve |
| ISC1, ISC2, ISC3, ISC4 | Idle Speed Control Valve Or Motor |
| KNK, KNK1, KNK2 | Knock Sensor |
| KS | Airflow Meter |
| L | Neutral Start Switch Or Shift Position Switch |

***ECU PIN CONNECTOR ABBREVIATION IDENTIFICATION (Cont.)***

| Abbreviation | Function |
|---|---|
| LP | Headlight Relay |
| L1, L2, L3 | [1] TEMS or [2] ECT |
| L4 | Transfer Position Switch |
| M | Neutral Start Switch Or Shift Position Switch |
| M-REL | EFI Main Relay |
| MS | Engine Oil Level Sensor |
| N | Neutral Start Switch Or Shift Position Switch |
| N/C | Clutch Switch (M/T) |
| NE | Cam Position Sensor Or Distributor (RPM) |
| E- | Distributor |
| NSW | Neutral/Start Switch (A/T) |
| No. 1 | Injector |
| No. 2 | Injector |
| No. 3 | Injector |
| No. 4 | Injector |
| No. 10 | Injector |
| No. 20 | Injector |
| No. 30 | Injector |
| OD | Overdrive Solenoid |
| OD1 | Cruise Control Computer |
| OD2 | Cruise Control Computer Or Overdrive Main Switch |
| O/G | Check Connector |
| OIL | Oil Pressure Switch Or A/T Oil Temperature Warning Light |
| OLS | Engine Oil Level Sensor |
| OMR | Engine Oil Feed Motor |
| OMT | Engine Oil Feed Motor Relay |
| OSFC | Overspeed Fuel Cut |
| OW | Engine Oil Warning Light |
| OX, OX1, OX+ | Oxygen Sensor |
| OX2 | Oxygen Sensor (Sub) |
| P | Shift Position Switch Or Pattern Select Switch |
| PS | Power Steering ECU |
| PSCT | Power Steering ECU |
| PSW | Throttle Position Sensor |
| PIM | Vacuum Sensor Or Turbocharger Pressure Sensor |
| PSW | Throttle Position Sensor |
| PWR | Pattern Select Switch |
| R | Neutral Start Switch Or Shift Position Switch |
| RSC | Idle Speed Control Valve |
| RSO | Idle Speed Control Valve |
| S | Neutral Start Switch Or Shift Position Switch |
| SL | [2] ECT Solenoid |
| SPD | Vehicle Speed Sensor |
| SP1 | No. 1 Vehicle Speed Sensor, [2] ECT In Instrument Cluster |
| SP2 | No. 2 Vehicle Sped Sensor, [2] ECT In Transaxle or Transmission |
| STA | Starter Signal |
| STP | Stoplight Switch |
| STJ | Cold Start Injector |
| S1, S2, S3, S4 | [2] ECT Solenoid |
| T | Check Connector |
| TE1, TE2 | Check Connector Or [3] TDCL (Cressida) |
| THA, THA1 | Air Temperature Sensor |
| THG | EGR Gas Temperature Sensor |
| THO, THO1, THO2 | Transmission Oil Temperature Sensor |
| THW | Coolant Temperature Sensor |
| TIL | Turbo Indicator Light |
| TOV | Throttle Opener Vacuum Switching Valve |
| TPC, TPC1 | Turocharger Pressure Vacuum Switching Valve |
| TT | [3] TDCL (Cressida) |

[1] – Toyota Electronic Modulated Suspension (TEMS) on Camry V6, Cressida and Supra. Used for ECT on Camry 4-cylinder.
[2] – Electronically Controlled Transmission/Transaxle (ECT).
[3] – Toyota Diagnostic Communication Link (TDCL) connector. Diagnostic connector is located under left side of dash.

# 1991 ENGINE PERFORMANCE
# Pin Voltage Charts (Cont.)

*ECU PIN CONNECTOR ABBREVIATION IDENTIFICATION (Cont.)*

| Abbreviation | Function |
|---|---|
| TVIS | Variable Induction System Vacuum Switching Valve |
| TWS | Coolant Temperature Switch |
| T2 | Check Connector |
| VC | Airflow Meter, Vacuum Sensor Or Throttle Position Sensor |
| VCC | Throttle Position Sensor Or Vacuum Sensor |
| F, VF1, VF2 | Check Connector |
| V-ISC | Auxiliary Control Valve Or Idle-Up System Vacuum Switching Valve |
| VS | Airflow Meter |
| VSV1 | Air Control Vacuum Switching Valve |
| VSV2 | Fuel Pressure-Up Vacuum Switching Valve |
| VTA | Throttle Position Sensor |
| W | Warning Light |
| 2 | Neutral Start Switch Or Shift Position Switch |
| 4WD | 4WD Indicator |

# 1991 ENGINE PERFORMANCE
# Pin Voltage Charts (Cont.)

## CAMRY (4-CYLINDER) ECU PIN VOLTAGE TEST

CAUTION
Perform all voltage measurements with ECU harness connector installed. Use high-impedance digital voltmeter (10,000 ohm minimum). Verify battery voltage is greater than 11 volts.

| No. | Terminals | Condition | | STD voltage (V) | Test No. |
|---|---|---|---|---|---|
| 1 | +B / +B1 – E1 | IG SW ON | | 10 – 14 | 2 |
| 2 | BATT – E1 | — | | 10 – 14 | 1 |
| *1 3 | IDL – E1 | IG SW ON | Throttle valve open | 8 – 14 | 8 |
| | PSW – E1 | | Throttle valve fully closed (Throttle opener must be cancelled first) | 4 – 6 | |
| *2 4 | IDL – E2 | | Throttle valve open | 8 – 14 | 8 |
| | VC – E2 | | — | 4 – 6 | |
| | VTA – E2 | | Throttle valve fully closed (Throttle opener must be cancelled first) | 0.1 – 1.0 | |
| | | | Throttle valve open | 4 – 6 | |
| 5 | VC – E2 | | — | 4 – 6 | 7 |
| | VS – E2 | | Measuring plate fully closed (Throttle opener must be cancelled first) | 4.0 – 5.5 | |
| | | | Measuring plate fully open | 0 – 1 | |
| | | Idling | | 2.0 – 4.0 | |
| | | 3,000 rpm | | 1.0 – 2.0 | |
| 6 | No. 10 / No. 20 – E01 / E02 | IG SW ON | | 10 – 14 | 12 |
| 7 | THA – E2 | IG SW ON | Intake air temp. 20°C (68°F) | 1 – 3 | 6 |
| 8 | THW – E2 | | Coolant temp. 80°C (176°F) | 0.1 – 1.0 | 5 |
| 9 | STA – E1 | Cranking | | 6 – 14 | 9 |
| 10 | IGT – E1 | Cranking or idling | | 0.7 – 1.0 | 3 |
| 11 | ISC1 / ISC2 – E1 | IG SW ON | | 9 – 14 | 13 |
| 12 | W – E1 | No trouble ("CHECK" engine warning light off) and engine running | | 10 – 14 | 14 |
| 13 | *3 A/C – E1 | IG SW ON | Air conditioning ON | 8 – 14 | 10 |

*1 w/o ECT
*2 w/ ECT
*3 w/ A/C

NOTE
If voltage value is not as specified, go to test number indicated. Tests are located in SELF-DIAGNOSTICS article with trouble code charts.

ECT – Electronic Controlled Transaxle

## CAMRY (4-CYLINDER) ECU WIRING HARNESS RESISTANCE TEST

CAUTION
When measuring resistance at ECU wiring harness, DO NOT TOUCH ECU terminals with ohmmeter. Turn ignition off and unplug ECU wiring harness connector. Tester probe should be inserted into the wiring connector from the WIRING side.

| Terminals | Condition | STD resistance (Ω) |
|---|---|---|
| *1 IDL – E1 | Throttle valve open | Infinity |
| | Throttle valve fully closed (Throttle opener must be cancelled first) | 0 |
| *1 PSW – E1 | Throttle valve fully open | 0 |
| | Throttle valve fully closed (Throttle opener must be cancelled first) | Infinity |
| *2 IDL – E2 | Throttle valve open | Infinity |
| | Throttle valve fully closed (Throttle opener must be cancelled first) | 2,300 or less |
| *2 VTA – E2 | Throttle valve fully open | 3,300 – 10,000 |
| | Throttle valve fully closed (Throttle opener must be cancelled first) | 200 – 800 |
| VC – E2 | — | 3,000 – 7,000 |
| VS – E2 | Measuring plate fully closed (Throttle opener must be cancelled first) | 200 – 600 |
| | Measuring plate fully open | 20 – 1,200 |
| THA – E2 | Intake air temp. 20°C (68°F) | 2,000 – 3,000 |
| THW – E2 | Coolant temp. 80°C (176°F) | 200 – 400 |
| G / NE – G⊖ | — | 140 – 180 |
| ISC1 / ISC2 – +B / +B1 | — | 16.0 – 17.0 |

*1 w/o ECT
*2 w/ ECT

## ECU TERMINAL IDENTIFICATION

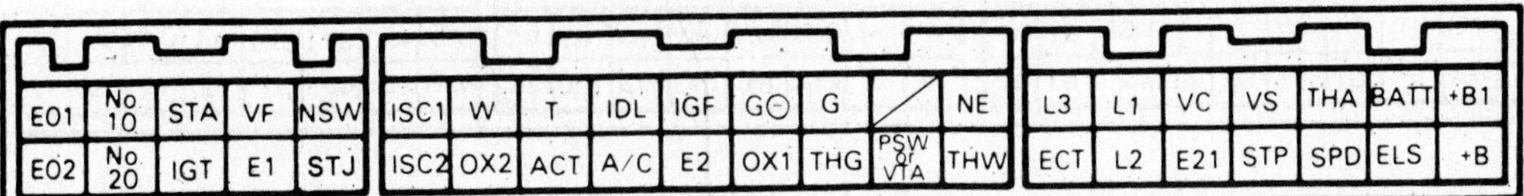


91E18162 91F18163 91E17529

Courtesy of Toyota Motor Sales, U.S.A., Inc.

# 1991 ENGINE PERFORMANCE
# Pin Voltage Charts (Cont.)

## CAMRY (V6) ECU PIN VOLTAGE TEST

CAUTION
Perform all voltage measurements with ECU harness connector installed. Use high-impedance digital voltmeter (10,000 ohm minimum). Verify battery voltage is greater than 11 volts.

NOTE
If voltage value is not as specified, proceed to test number indicated. Tests are located in SELF-DIAGNOSTICS article with trouble code charts.

| No. | Terminals | Condition | | STD voltage (V) | Test No. |
|---|---|---|---|---|---|
| 1 | BATT — E1 | — | | 10 — 14 | 2 |
| | IG SW — E1 | IG SW ON | | | |
| | M-REL — E1 | | | | |
| | +B +B1 — E1 | | | | |
| 2 | IDL — E2 | IG SW ON | Throttle valve open | 4 — 6 | 8 |
| | VC — E2 | | — | 4 — 6 | |
| | VTA — E2 | | Throttle valve fully closed | 0.1 — 1.0 | |
| | | | Throttle valve open | 3.2 — 4.2 | |
| 3 | VC — E2 | | — | 4 — 6 | 7 |
| | VS — E2 | | Measuring plate fully closed | 3.7 — 4.3 | |
| | | | Measuring plate fully open | 0.2 — 0.5 | |
| | | Idling | | 1.6 — 4.1 | |
| | | 3,000 rpm | | 1.0 — 2.0 | |
| 4 | No.10 No.20 No.30 — E01 E02 | IG SW ON | | 10 — 14 | 12 |
| 5 | THA — E2 | IG SW ON | Intake air temp. 20°C (68°F) | 1 — 3 | 6 |
| 6 | THW — E2 | | Coolant temp. 80°C (176°F) | 0.1 — 1.0 | 5 |
| 7 | STA — E1 | Cranking | | 6 — 14 | 9 |
| 8 | IGT — E1 | Cranking or idling | | 0.7 — 1.0 | 3 |
| 9 | ISC1 ISC2 ISC3 ISC4 — E1 | IG SW ON | | 9 — 14 | 13 |
| 10 | W — E1 | No trouble ("CHECK" engine warning light off) and engine running | | 10 — 14 | 14 |
| *11 | A/C — E1 | IG SW ON | Air conditioning ON | 8 — 14 | 10 |

* w/ A/C

## CAMRY (V6) ECU WIRING HARNESS RESISTANCE TEST

CAUTION
When measuring resistance at ECU wiring harness, DO NOT TOUCH ECU terminals with ohmmeter. Turn ignition off and unplug ECU wiring harness connector. Tester probe should be inserted into the wiring connector from the WIRING side.

| Terminals | Condition | STD resistance (Ω) |
|---|---|---|
| IDL — E2 | Throttle valve open | Infinity |
| | Throttle valve fully closed | 2,300 or less |
| VTA — E2 | Throttle valve fully open | 3,500 — 10,300 |
| | Throttle valve fully closed | 300 — 6,300 |
| VC — E2 | — | 200 — 400 |
| VS — E2 | Measuring plate fully closed | 200 — 600 |
| | Measuring plate fully open | 20 — 1,200 |
| THA — E2 | Intake air temp. 20°C (68°F) | 2,000 — 3,000 |
| THW — E2 | Coolant temp. 80°C (176°F) | 200 — 400 |
| G1 G2 NE — G⊖ | — | 140 — 180 |
| ISC1 ISC2 ISC3 ISC4 — +B +B1 | — | 10 — 30 |

## ECU TERMINAL IDENTIFICATION

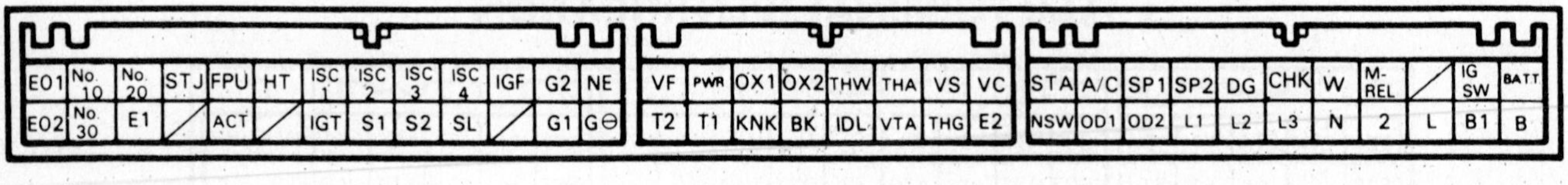

| E01 | No. 10 | No. 20 | STJ | FPU | HT | ISC 1 | ISC 2 | ISC 3 | ISC 4 | IGF | G2 | NE |
|---|---|---|---|---|---|---|---|---|---|---|---|---|
| E02 | No. 30 | E1 | | ACT | | IGT | S1 | S2 | SL | | G1 | G⊖ |

| VF | PWR | OX1 | OX2 | THW | THA | VS | VC |
|---|---|---|---|---|---|---|---|
| T2 | T1 | KNK | BK | IDL | VTA | THG | E2 |

| STA | A/C | SP1 | SP2 | DG | CHK | W | M-REL | | IG SW | BATT |
|---|---|---|---|---|---|---|---|---|---|---|
| NSW | OD1 | OD2 | L1 | L2 | L3 | N | 2 | L | B1 | B |

91G18164 91H18165 91H17530

Courtesy of Toyota Motor Sales, U.S.A., Inc.

# 1991 ENGINE PERFORMANCE
# Pin Voltage Charts (Cont.)

## CELICA (3S-GTE) ECU PIN VOLTAGE TEST

CAUTION
Perform all voltage measurements with ECU harness connector installed. Use high-impedance digital voltmeter (10,000 ohm minimum). Verify battery voltage is greater than 11 volts.

| No. | Terminals | Condition | | STD voltage (V) | Test No. |
|---|---|---|---|---|---|
| 1 | +B, +B1 – E1 | IG SW ON | | 10 – 14 | 2 |
| 2 | BATT – E1 | – | | 10 – 14 | 1 |
| 3 | IDL – E2 | IG SW ON | Throttle valve open | 4.5 – 5.5 | 9 |
| | VC – E2 | | – | 4.5 – 5.5 | |
| | VTA – E2 | | Throttle valve open | 0.1 – 1.0 | |
| | | | Throttle valve open | 3.2 – 4.2 | |
| 4 | VC – E2 | | – | 4.5 – 5.5 | 7 |
| | VS – E2 | | Measuring plate fully closed | 3.7 – 4.3 | |
| | | | Measuring plate fully open | 0.2 – 0.5 | |
| | | Idling | | 1.6 – 4.1 | |
| | | 3,000 rpm | | 1.0 – 2.0 | |
| 5 | No.1, No.2, No.3, No.4 – E01, E02 | IG SW ON | | 10 – 14 | 13 |
| 6 | THA1 – E2 | IG SW ON | Intake air temp. 20°C (68°F) | 1 – 3 | 6 |
| 7 | THW – E2 | | Coolant temp. 80°C (176°F) | 0.1 – 1.1 | 5 |
| 8 | STA – E1 | Cranking | | 6 – 14 | 10 |
| 9 | IGT – E1 | Cranking or idling | | 0.8 – 1.2 | 3 |
| 10 | RSC, RSO – E1 | IG SW ON | | 8 – 14 | 14 |
| 11 | W – E1 | No trouble ("CHECK" engine warning light off) and engine running | | 10 – 14 | 15 |
| 12 | PIM – E2 | IG SW ON | | 2.5 – 4.5 | 8 |
| | VC – E2 | | | 4.5 – 5.5 | |
| 13 | AC1 – E1 | IG SW ON | Air conditioning ON | 8 – 14 | 11 |

NOTE
If voltage value is not as specified, proceed to test number indicated. Tests are located in SELF-DIAGNOSTICS article with trouble code charts.

## CELICA (3S-GTE) ECU WIRING HARNESS RESISTANCE TEST

CAUTION
When measuring resistance at ECU wiring harness, DO NOT TOUCH ECU terminals with ohmmeter. Turn ignition off and unplug ECU wiring harness connector. Tester probe should be inserted into the wiring connector from the WIRING side.

| Terminals | Condition | STD resistance (Ω) |
|---|---|---|
| IDL – E2 | Throttle valve open | Infinity |
| | Throttle valve fully closed | 2,300 or less |
| VTA – E2 | Throttle valve fully open | 3,500 – 10,000 |
| | Throttle valve fully closed | 200 – 800 |
| VC – E2 | – | 200 – 400 |
| VS – E2 | Measuring plate fully closed | 200 – 600 |
| | Measuring plate fully open | 20 – 1,200 |
| THA1 – E2 | Intake air temp. 20°C (68°F) | 2,000 – 3,000 |
| THW – E2 | Coolant temp. 80°C (176°F) | 200 – 400 |
| G1, G2 – G⊖ | – | 140 – 180 |
| NE – G⊖ | – | 180 – 220 |
| RSC – +B, RSO – +B1 | – | 19.3 – 22.3 |

## ECU TERMINAL IDENTIFICATION

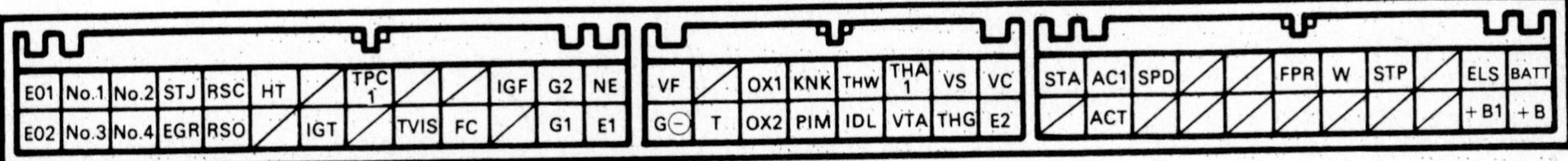


91A18168 91B18169 91F17710

Courtesy of Toyota Motor Sales, U.S.A., Inc.

# 1991 ENGINE PERFORMANCE
# Pin Voltage Charts (Cont.)

## CELICA (4A-FE) ECU PIN VOLTAGE TEST

CAUTION
Perform all voltage measurements with ECU harness connector installed. Use high-impedance digital voltmeter (10,000 ohm minimum). Verify battery voltage is greater than 11 volts.

| No. | Terminals | Condition | | STD voltage (V) | Test No. |
|---|---|---|---|---|---|
| 1 | +B<br>+B1 - E1 | IG SW ON | | 10 - 14 | 2 |
| 2 | BATT - E1 | - | | 10 - 14 | 1 |
| 3 | IDL - E2 | IG SW ON | Throttle valve open | 10 - 14 | 9 |
| | PSW - E2 | | Throttle valve fully closed | 10 - 14 | |
| 4 | PIM - E2 | IG SW ON | | 3.3 - 3.9 | 7 |
| | VCC - E2 | | | 4.5 - 5.5 | |
| 5 | No.10 - E01<br>No.20 - E02 | | | 10 - 14 | 13 |
| 6 | THA - E2 | IG SW ON | Intake air temp. 20°C (68°F) | 1 - 3 | 6 |
| 7 | THW - E2 | | Coolant temp. 80°C (176°F) | 2.0 - 2.8 | 5 |
| 8 | STA - E1 | Cranking | | 6 - 14 | 10 |
| 9 | IGT - E1 | Cranking or idling | | 0.7 - 1.0 | 3 |
| 10 | W - E1 | No trouble ("CHECK" engine warning light off) and engine running | | 10 - 14 | 15 |
| 11 | A/C - E1 | IG SW ON | Air conditioning ON | 8 - 14 | 11 |

NOTE
If voltage value is not as specified, proceed to test number indicated. Tests are located in SELF-DIAGNOSTICS article with trouble code charts.

## CELICA (4A-FE) ECU WIRING HARNESS RESISTANCE TEST

CAUTION
When measuring resistance at ECU wiring harness, DO NOT TOUCH ECU terminals with ohmmeter. Turn ignition off and unplug ECU wiring harness connector. Tester probe should be inserted into the wiring connector from the WIRING side.

| Terminals | Condition | STD resistance (Ω) |
|---|---|---|
| IDL - E2 | Throttle valve open | Infinity |
| | Throttle valve fully closed | 0 |
| PSW - E2 | Throttle valve fully open | 0 |
| | Throttle valve fully closed | Infinity |
| THA - E2 | Intake air temperature 20°C (68°F) | 2,000 - 3,000 |
| THW - E2 | Coolant temperature 80°C (176°F) | 200 - 400 |
| G1<br>NE - G⊖ | - | 140 - 180 |

## ECU TERMINAL IDENTIFICATION

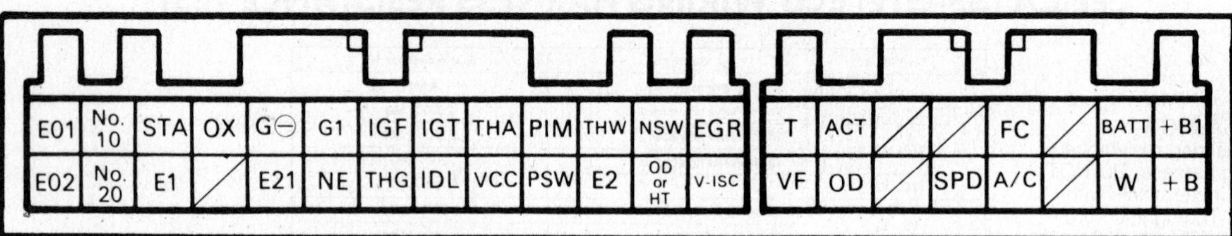


91I18166 91J18167 91G17711

Courtesy of Toyota Motor Sales, U.S.A., Inc.

# 1991 ENGINE PERFORMANCE
# Pin Voltage Charts (Cont.)

## CELICA (5S-FE WITH ECT) ECU PIN VOLTAGE TEST

ECT - Electronic Controlled Transaxle

CAUTION
Perform all voltage measurements with ECU harness connector installed. Use high-impedance digital voltmeter (10,000 ohm minimum). Verify battery voltage is greater than 11 volts.

| No. | Terminals | Condition | | STD voltage (V) | Test No. |
|---|---|---|---|---|---|
| 1 | +B / +B1 – E1 | IG SW ON | | 10 – 14 | 2 |
| 2 | BATT – E1 | — | | 10 – 14 | 1 |
| 3 | IDL – E2 | IG SW ON | Throttle valve open | 8 – 14 | 9 |
| | VC – E2 | | — | 4.5 – 5.5 | |
| | VTA – E2 | | Throttle valve fully closed (Throttle opener must be cancelled first) | 0.8 – 1.2 | |
| | | | Throttle valve open | 3.2 – 4.2 | |
| 4 | PIM – E2 | IG SW ON | | 3.3 – 3.9 | 7 |
| | VCC – E2 | | | 4.5 – 5.5 | |
| 5 | No. 10 – E01 / No. 20 – E02 | | | 10 – 14 | 13 |
| 6 | THA – E2 | IG SW ON | Intake air temp. 20°C (68°F) | 1.9 – 2.9 | 6 |
| 7 | THW – E2 | | Coolant temp. 80°C (176°F) | 0.1 – 1.1 | 5 |
| 8 | STA – E1 | Cranking | | 6 – 14 | 10 |
| 9 | IGT – E1 | Cranking or idling | | 0.8 – 1.2 | 3 |
| 10 | ISCC / ISCO – E1 | IG SW ON | | 8 – 14 | 14 |
| 11 | W – E1 | No trouble ("CHECK" engine warning light off) and engine running | | 10 – 14 | 15 |
| 12 | A/C – E1 | IG SW ON | Air conditioning ON | 8 – 14 | 11 |

NOTE
If voltage value is not as specified, proceed to test number indicated. Tests are located in SELF-DIAGNOSTICS article with trouble code charts.

## CELICA (5S-FE WITH ECT) ECU WIRING HARNESS RESISTANCE TEST

CAUTION
When measuring resistance at ECU wiring harness, DO NOT TOUCH ECU terminals with ohmmeter. Turn ignition off and unplug ECU wiring harness connector. Tester probe should be inserted into the wiring connector from the WIRING side.

| Terminals | Condition | STD resistance (Ω) |
|---|---|---|
| IDL – E2 | Throttle valve open | Infinity |
| | Throttle valve fully closed (Throttle opener must be cancelled first) | 2,300 or less |
| VTA – E2 | Throttle valve fully open | 3,300 – 10,000 |
| | Throttle valve fully closed (Throttle opener must be cancelled first) | 200 – 800 |
| VCC – E2 | – | 3,000 – 7,000 |
| THA – E2 | Intake air temp. 20°C (68°F) | 2,000 – 3,000 |
| THW – E2 | Coolant temp. 80°C (176°F) | 200 – 400 |
| G1 / NE – G⊖ | – | 170 – 210 |
| ISCC / ISCO – +B / +B1 | – | 19.3 – 22.3 |

## ECU TERMINAL IDENTIFICATION

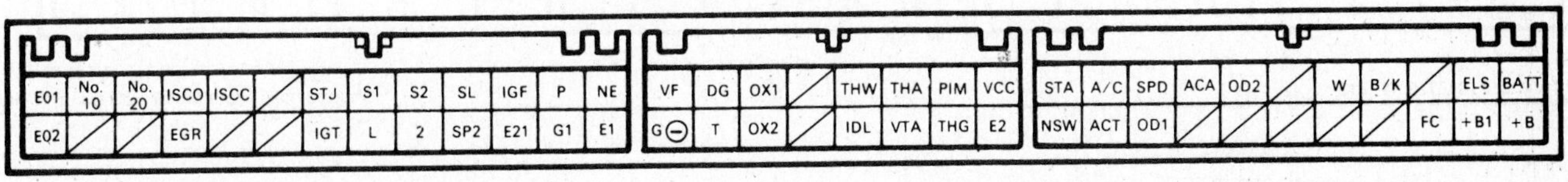

| E01 | No. 10 | No. 20 | ISCO | ISCC | | STJ | S1 | S2 | SL | IGF | P | NE |
|---|---|---|---|---|---|---|---|---|---|---|---|---|
| E02 | | | EGR | | | IGT | L | 2 | SP2 | E21 | G1 | E1 |

| VF | DG | OX1 | | THW | THA | PIM | VCC |
|---|---|---|---|---|---|---|---|
| G⊖ | T | OX2 | | IDL | VTA | THG | E2 |

| STA | A/C | SPD | ACA | OD2 | | W | B/K | | ELS | BATT |
|---|---|---|---|---|---|---|---|---|---|---|
| NSW | ACT | OD1 | | | | | | FC | +B1 | +B |

91G18172 91H18173 91H17712

Courtesy of Toyota Motor Sales, U.S.A., Inc.

# 1991 ENGINE PERFORMANCE
# Pin Voltage Charts (Cont.)

## CELICA (5S-FE WITHOUT ECT) ECU PIN VOLTAGE TEST

ECT – Electronic Controlled Transaxle

CAUTION
Perform all voltage measurements with ECU harness connector installed. Use high-impedance digital voltmeter (10,000 ohm minimum). Verify battery voltage is greater than 11 volts.

| No. | Terminals | Condition | | STD voltage (V) | Test No. |
|---|---|---|---|---|---|
| 1 | +B / +B1 – E1 | IG SW ON | | 10 – 14 | 2 |
| 2 | BATT – E1 | – | | 10 – 14 | 1 |
| 3 | IDL – E1 | IG SW ON | Throttle valve open | 8 – 14 | 9 |
| | PSW – E1 | | Throttle valve fully closed (Throttle opener must be cancelled first) | 4.5 – 5.5 | |
| 4 | PIM – E2 | IG SW ON | | 3.3 – 3.9 | 7 |
| | VCC – E2 | | | 4.5 – 5.5 | |
| 5 | No.10 / No.20 – E01 / E02 | | | 10 – 14 | 13 |
| 6 | THA – E2 | IG SW ON | Intake air temp. 20°C (68°F) | 1.9 – 2.9 | 6 |
| 7 | THW – E2 | | Coolant temp. 80°C (176°F) | 0.1 – 1.1 | 5 |
| 8 | STA – E1 | Cranking | | 6 – 14 | 10 |
| 9 | IGT – E1 | Cranking or idling | | 0.8 – 1.2 | 3 |
| 10 | ISCC / ISCO – E1 | IG SW ON | | 8 – 14 | 14 |
| 11 | W – E1 | No trouble ("CHECK" engine warning light off) and engine running | | 10 – 14 | 15 |
| 12 | A/C – E1 | IG SW ON | Air conditioning ON | 8 – 14 | 11 |

NOTE
If voltage value is not as specified, proceed to test number indicated. Tests are located in SELF-DIAGNOSTICS article with trouble code charts.

## CELICA (5S-FE WITHOUT ECT) ECU WIRING HARNESS RESISTANCE TEST

CAUTION
When measuring resistance at ECU wiring harness, DO NOT TOUCH ECU terminals with ohmmeter. Turn ignition off and unplug ECU wiring harness connector. Tester probe should be inserted into the wiring connector from the WIRING side.

| Terminals | Condition | STD resistance (Ω) |
|---|---|---|
| IDL – E1 | Throttle valve open | Infinity |
| | Throttle valve fully closed (Throttle opener must be cancelled first) | 0 |
| PSW – E1 | Throttle valve fully open | 0 |
| | Throttle valve fully closed (Throttle opener must be cancelled first) | Infinity |
| THA – E2 | Intake air temp. 20°C (68°F) | 2,000 – 3,000 |
| THW – E2 | Coolant temp. 80°C (176°F) | 200 – 400 |
| G1 / NE – G⊖ | – | 170 – 210 |
| ISCC / ISCO – +B / +B1 | – | 19.3 – 22.3 |

## ECU TERMINAL IDENTIFICATION

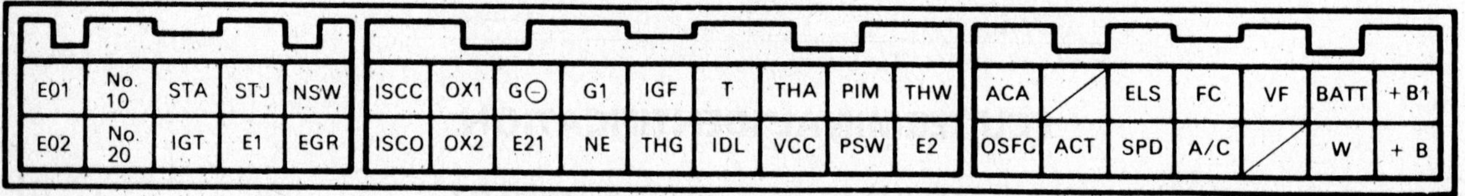


91E18170 91F18171 91I17713

Courtesy of Toyota Motor Sales, U.S.A., Inc.

# 1991 ENGINE PERFORMANCE
# Pin Voltage Charts (Cont.)

## COROLLA (4A-FE) ECU PIN VOLTAGE TEST

CAUTION
Perform all voltage measurements with ECU harness connector installed. Use high-impedance digital voltmeter (10,000 ohm minimum). Verify battery voltage is greater than 11 volts.

| No. | Terminals | STD voltage (V) | Condition | | Test No. |
|---|---|---|---|---|---|
| 1 | +B / +B1 — E1 | 10 — 14 | Ignition switch ON | | 2 |
| 2 | BATT — E1 | 10 — 14 | — | | 1 |
| 3 | IDL — E2 | 4.5 — 5.5 | Ignition switch ON | Throttle valve open | 8 |
| | PSW — E2 | | | Throttle valve fully closed | |
| 4 | No. 10 / No. 20 — E01 / E02 | 10 — 14 | Ignition switch ON | | 12 |
| 5 | W — E1 | 10 — 14 | No trouble ("CHECK ENGINE" warning light off) and engine running | | 13 |
| 6 | PIM — E2 | 3.3 — 3.9 | Ignition switch ON | | 7 |
| | VCC — E2 | 4.5 — 5.5 | | | |
| 7 | THA — E2 | 2.0 — 2.5 | Ignition switch ON | Intake air temp. 20°C (68°F) | 6 |
| 8 | THW — E2 | 0.4 — 0.7 | | Coolant temp. 80°C (176°F) | 5 |
| 9 | STA — E1 | 6 — 14 | Cranking | | 9 |
| 10 | IGT — E1 | 0.7 — 1.0 | Idling | | 3 |
| 11 | A/C — E1 | 5 — 14 | Air conditioning ON | | 10 |

NOTE
If voltage value is not as specified, proceed to test number indicated. Tests are located in SELF-DIAGNOSTICS article with trouble code charts.

## COROLLA (4A-FE) ECU WIRING HARNESS RESISTANCE TEST

CAUTION
When measuring resistance at ECU wiring harness, DO NOT TOUCH ECU terminals with ohmmeter. Turn ignition off and unplug ECU wiring harness connector. Tester probe should be inserted into the wiring connector from the WIRING side.

Resistance of ECU Wiring Connectors

| Terminals | Condition | Resistance |
|---|---|---|
| IDL — E2 | Throttle valve open | Infinity |
| | Throttle valve fully closed | 0 |
| PSW — E2 | Throttle valve fully open | 0 |
| | Throttle valve fully closed | Infinity |
| THA — E2 | Intake temperature 20°C (68°F) | 2 — 3 kΩ |
| THW — E2 | Coolant temperature 80°C (176°F) | 0.2 — 0.4 kΩ |
| G1 — G ⊖ | — | 205 — 255 Ω |
| NE — G ⊖ | — | 205 — 255 Ω |

## ECU TERMINAL IDENTIFICATION

*1: 2WD M/T, *2: A/T, *3: 4A/T, *4: Calif., *5: Calif. and 4WD, *6: 2WD

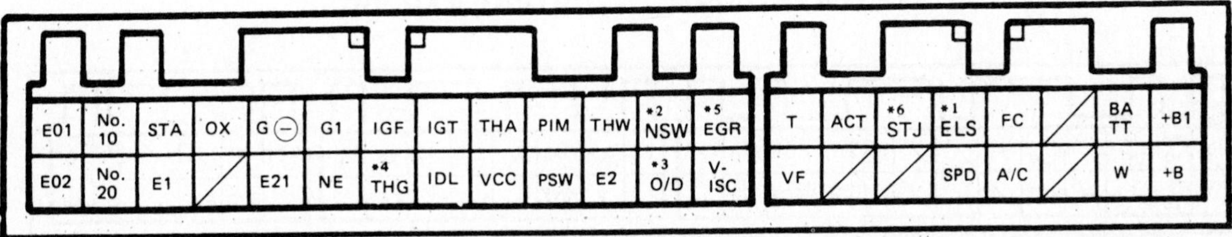


91I18174 91J18175 91I17762

Courtesy of Toyota Motor Sales, U.S.A., Inc.

# 1991 ENGINE PERFORMANCE
# Pin Voltage Charts (Cont.)

## COROLLA (4A-GE) ECU PIN VOLTAGE TEST

CAUTION
Perform all voltage measurements with ECU harness connector installed. Use high-impedance digital voltmeter (10,000 ohm minimum). Verify battery voltage is greater than 11 volts.

| No. | Terminals | STD voltage (V) | Condition | | Test No. |
|---|---|---|---|---|---|
| 1 | +B +B1 – E1 | 10 – 14 | Ignition switch ON | | 2 |
| 2 | BATT – E1 | 10 – 14 | — | | 1 |
| 3 | IDL – E2 | 10 – 14 | Ignition switch ON | Throttle valve open | 8 |
| | VTA – E2 | 0.1 – 1.0 | | Throttle valve fully closed | |
| | | 4 – 5 | | Throttle valve fully open | |
| | VCC – E2 | 4 – 6 | | — | |
| 4 | +B1 – E2 | 10 – 14 | Ignition switch ON | — | 7 |
| | VC – E2 | 6 – 10 | | — | |
| | VS – E2 | 2 – 5.5 | | Measuring plate fully closed | |
| | | 6 – 9 | | Measuring plate fully open | |
| | | 2 – 8 | Idling | — | |
| 5 | No.10 – E01<br>No.20 – E02 | 10 – 14 | Ignition switch ON | | 12 |
| 6 | W – E1 | 10 – 14 | No trouble ("CHECK ENGINE" warning light off) and engine running | | 13 |
| 7 | THA – E2 | 1 – 3 | Ignition switch ON | Intake air temperature 20°C (68°F) | 6 |
| 8 | THW – E2 | 0.1 – 1.0 | Ignition switch ON | Coolant temperature 80°C (176°F) | 5 |
| 9 | STA – E1 | 6 – 14 | Cranking | | 9 |
| 10 | IGT – E1 | 0.7 – 1.0 | Idling | | 3 |
| 11 | A/C – E1 | 5 – 14 | Air conditioning ON | | 10 |

NOTE
If voltage value is not as specified, proceed to test number indicated. Tests are located in SELF-DIAGNOSTICS article with trouble code charts.

## COROLLA (4A-GE) ECU WIRING HARNESS RESISTANCE TEST

CAUTION
When measuring resistance at ECU wiring harness, DO NOT TOUCH ECU terminals with ohmmeter. Turn ignition off and unplug ECU wiring harness connector. Tester probe should be inserted into the wiring connector from the WIRING side.

| Terminals | Condition | Resistance |
|---|---|---|
| IDL – E2 | Throttle valve open | Infinity |
| | Throttle valve fully closed | Less than 2.3 kΩ |
| VTA – E2 | Throttle valve fully open | 3.3 – 10 kΩ |
| | Throttle valve fully closed | 0.2 – 0.8 kΩ |
| VC – E2 | – | 100 – 300 Ω |
| VS – E2 | Measuring plate fully closed | 20 – 400 Ω |
| | Measuring plate fully open | 20 – 3,000 Ω |
| VCC – E2 | – | 3 – 7 kΩ |
| THA – E2 | Intake air temperature 20°C (68°F) | 2 – 3 kΩ |
| THW – E2 | Coolant temperature 80°C (176°F) | 0.2 – 0.4 kΩ |
| G ⊕ – G ⊖ | – | 205 – 255 Ω |

## ECU TERMINAL IDENTIFICATION

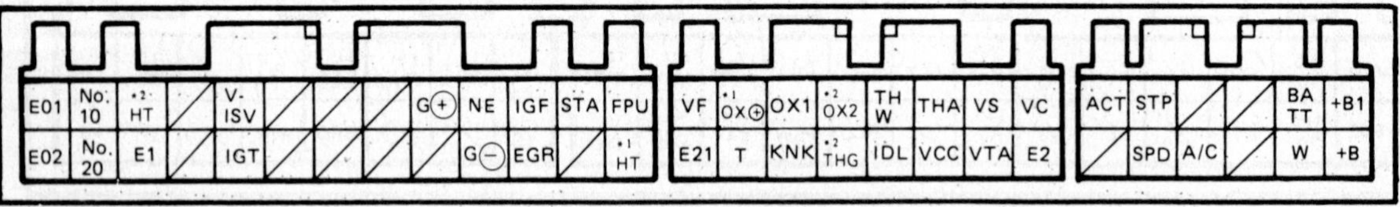


*1 – Federal and Canada
*2 – California

91A18176 91B18177 91J17763

Courtesy of Toyota Motor Sales, U.S.A., Inc.

# 1991 ENGINE PERFORMANCE
# Pin Voltage Charts (Cont.)

## CRESSIDA ECU PIN VOLTAGE TEST

CAUTION
Perform all voltage measurements with ECU harness connector installed. Use high-impedance digital voltmeter (10,000 ohm minimum). Verify battery voltage is greater than 11 volts.

| No. | Terminals | Condition | | STD Voltage | Test No. |
|---|---|---|---|---|---|
| 1 | BATT – E1 | – | | 10 – 14 | 1 |
| | IG SW – E1 | Ignition SW ON | | 10 – 14 | |
| | M-REL – E1 | | | | |
| | +B (+B1) – E1 | | | | |
| 2 | IDL – E2 | Ignition SW ON | Throttle valve open | 4 – 6 | 7 |
| | VC – E2 | | – | 4 – 6 | |
| | VTA – E2 | | Throttle valve fully closed | 0.1 – 1.0 | |
| | | | Throttle valve fully open | 3.2 – 4.2 | |
| 3 | VC – E2 | Ignition SW ON | – | 4 – 6 | 6 |
| | VS – E2 | | Measuring plate fully closed | 3.7 – 4.3 | |
| | | | Measuring plate fully open | 0.2 – 0.5 | |
| | | Idling | | 2.3 – 2.8 | |
| | | 3,000 rpm | | 1.0 – 2.0 | |
| 4 | No.10 – E01, No.20 – E02, No.10 | Ignition SW ON | | 10 – 14 | 11 |
| 5 | THA – E2 | Ignition SW ON | Intake air temperature 20°C (68°F) | 1 – 3 | 5 |
| 6 | THW – E2 | Ignition SW ON | Coolant temperature 80°C (176°F) | 0.1 – 1.0 | 4 |
| 7 | STA – E1 | Cranking | | 6 – 14 | 8 |
| 8 | IGT – E1 | Idling | | 0.7 – 1.0 | 2 |
| 9 | ISC1 – E1, ISC4 | Ignition SW ON | | 9 – 14 | 12 |
| 10 | W – E1 | No trouble ("CHECK" engine warning light off) and engine running | | 8 – 14 | 13 |
| 11 | A/C – E1 | Ignition SW ON | Air conditioning ON | 10 – 14 | 9 |

NOTE
If voltage value is not as specified, proceed to test number indicated. Tests are located in SELF-DIAGNOSTICS article with trouble code charts.

## CRESSIDA ECU WIRING HARNESS RESISTANCE TEST

CAUTION
When measuring resistance at ECU wiring harness, DO NOT TOUCH ECU terminals with ohmmeter. Turn ignition off and unplug ECU wiring harness connector. Tester probe should be inserted into the wiring connector from the WIRING side.

| Terminals | Condition | Resistance (Ω) |
|---|---|---|
| IDL – E2 | Throttle valve open | ∞ |
| | Throttle valve fully closed | 2,300 or less |
| VTA – E2 | Throttle valve open | 3,500 – 10,300 |
| | Throttle valve fully closed | 300 – 6,300 |
| VC – E2 | – | 200 – 400 |
| VS – E2 | Measuring plate fully closed | 200 – 600 |
| | Measuring plate fully open | 20 – 1,200 |
| THA – E2 | Intake air temperature 20°C (68°F) | 2,000 – 3,000 |
| THW – E2 | Coolant temperature 80°C (176°F) | 200 – 400 |
| G1, G2 – G⊖ | – | 140 – 180 |
| NE – G⊖ | – | 180 – 220 |
| ISC1, ISC2, ISC3, ISC4 – +B | – | 10 – 30 |

## ECU TERMINAL IDENTIFICATION

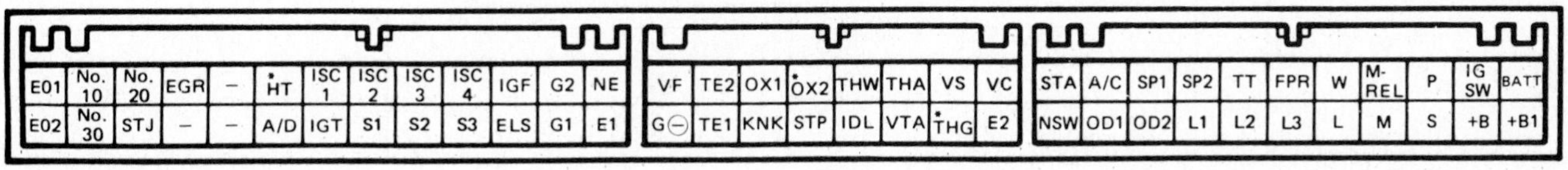

| E01 | No. 10 | No. 20 | EGR | – | *HT | ISC 1 | ISC 2 | ISC 3 | ISC 4 | IGF | G2 | NE |
|---|---|---|---|---|---|---|---|---|---|---|---|---|
| E02 | No. 30 | STJ | – | – | A/D | IGT | S1 | S2 | S3 | ELS | G1 | E1 |

| VF | TE2 | OX1 | *OX2 | THW | THA | VS | VC |
|---|---|---|---|---|---|---|---|
| G⊖ | TE1 | KNK | STP | IDL | VTA | *THG | E2 |

| STA | A/C | SP1 | SP2 | TT | FPR | W | M-REL | P | IG SW | BATT |
|---|---|---|---|---|---|---|---|---|---|---|
| NSW | OD1 | OD2 | L1 | L2 | L3 | L | M | S | +B | +B1 |

* – California Models Only

91C18178 91D18179 91F17793

Courtesy of Toyota Motor Sales, U.S.A., Inc.

# 1991 ENGINE PERFORMANCE
# Pin Voltage Charts (Cont.)

## LAND CRUISER ECU PIN VOLTAGE TEST

CAUTION
Perform all voltage measurements with ECU harness connector installed. Use high-impedance digital voltmeter (10,000 ohm minimum). Verify battery voltage is greater than 11 volts.

| No. | Terminals | Condition | | STD Voltage | Test No. |
|---|---|---|---|---|---|
| 1 | BATT – E1 (E11) | — | | 10 – 14 | 1 |
| | IG SW – E1 (E11) | Ignition switch ON | | 10 – 14 | |
| | M-REL – E1 (E11) | | | | |
| | +B (+B1) – E1 (E11) | | | | |
| 2 | IDL – E2 | Ignition switch ON | Throttle valve open | 4 – 6 | 7 |
| | VC – E2 | | — | 4 – 6 | |
| | VTA – E2 | | Throttle valve fully closed | 0.1 – 1.0 | |
| | | | Throttle valve fully open | 3 – 5 | |
| 3 | VC – E2 | Ignition switch ON | — | 4 – 6 | 6 |
| | VS – E2 | | Measuring plate fully closed | 4 – 5 | |
| | | | Measuring plate fully open | 0.02 – 0.08 | |
| | | Idling | | 2 – 4 | |
| | | 3,000 rpm | | 0.3 – 1.0 | |
| 4 | THA – E2 | Ignition switch ON | Intake air temperature 20°C (68°F) | 1 – 3 | 5 |
| 5 | THW – E2 | Ignition switch ON | Coolant temperature 80°C (176°F) | 0.1 – 1.0 | 4 |
| 6 | No.10 – E01<br>No.20 – E02 | Ignition switch ON | | 10 – 14 | 11 |
| 7 | STA – E1 (E11) | Cranking | | 6 – 14 | 8 |
| 8 | ISC1 ~ ISC4 – E1 (E11) | Ignition switch ON | | 10 – 14 | 12 |
| 9 | IGT – E1 (E11) | Idling | | 0.7 – 1.0 | 2 |
| 10 | W – E1 (E11) | No trouble ("CHECK" engine warning light off) and engine running | | 10 – 14 | 13 |
| 11 | A/C – E1 (E11) | Air conditioning ON | | 10 – 14 | 9 |

NOTE
If voltage value is not as specified, proceed to test number indicated. Tests are located in SELF-DIAGNOSTICS article with trouble code charts.

## LAND CRUISER ECU WIRING HARNESS RESISTANCE TEST

CAUTION
When measuring resistance at ECU wiring harness, DO NOT TOUCH ECU terminals with ohmmeter. Turn ignition off and unplug ECU wiring harness connector. Tester probe should be inserted into the wiring connector from the WIRING side.

| Terminals | Condition | Resistance (Ω) |
|---|---|---|
| IDL – E2 | Throttle valve open | ∞ |
| | Throttle valve fully closed | Less than 2,300 |
| VTA – E2 | Throttle valve fully open | 3,500 – 10,300 |
| | Throttle valve fully closed | 300 – 6,300 |
| VC – E2 | Air flow meter connector disconnected | 4,250 – 8,250 |
| VC – E2 | Throttle position sensor connector disconnected | 200 – 400 |
| VS – E2 | Measuring plate fully closed | 20 – 600 |
| | Measuring plate fully open | 200 – 3,000 |
| THA – E2 | Intake air temperature 20°C (68°F) | 2,000 – 1,200 |
| THW – E2 | Coolant temperature 80°C (176°F) | 200 – 400 |
| G1 – G⊖ | — | 140 – 180 |
| NE – G⊖ | — | |
| ISC1, ISC2<br>ISC3, ISC4 – +B | — | 10 – 30 |

## ECU TERMINAL IDENTIFICATION

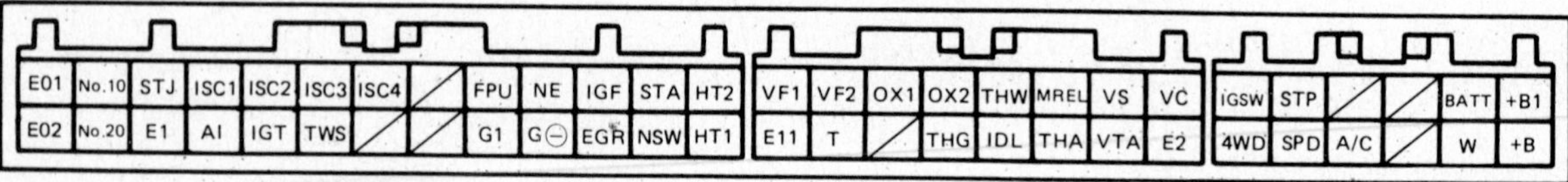


91G18180 91H18181 91J17813

Courtesy of Toyota Motor Sales, U.S.A., Inc.

# 1991 ENGINE PERFORMANCE
# Pin Voltage Charts (Cont.)

## MR2 (3S-GTE) ECU PIN VOLTAGE TEST

CAUTION
Perform all voltage measurements with ECU harness connector installed. Use high-impedance digital voltmeter (10,000 ohm minimum). Verify battery voltage is greater than 11 volts.

NOTE
If voltage value is not as specified, proceed to test number indicated. Tests are located in SELF-DIAGNOSTICS article with trouble code charts.

| No. | Terminal | Condition | | STD voltage (V) | Test No. |
|---|---|---|---|---|---|
| 1 | +B / +B1 - E1 | IG SW ON | | 10 - 14 | 2 |
| 2 | BATT - E1 | – | | 10 - 14 | 1 |
| 3 | IDL - E2 | IG SW ON | Throttle valve open | 4 - 6 | 9 |
| | VC - E2 | | – | 4 - 6 | |
| | VTA - E2 | | Throttle valve fully closed | 0.1 - 1.0 | |
| | | | Throttle valve fully open | 3.2 - 4.2 | |
| 4 | VC - E2 | | – | 4 - 6 | 7 |
| | VS - E2 | | Measuring plate fully closed | 3.7 - 4.3 | |
| | | | Measuring plate fully open | 0.2 - 0.5 | |
| | | Idling (No load) | | 2.6 - 3.6 | |
| | | 3,000 rpm (No load) | | 1.0 - 2.0 | |
| 5 | No.1 / No.2 / No.3 / No.4 - E01 / E02 | IG SW ON | | 10 - 14 | 13 |
| 6 | THA1 - E2 | IG SW ON | Intake air temp. 20°C (68°F) | 1 - 3 | 6 |
| 7 | THW - E2 | | Coolant temp. 80°C (176°F) | 0.1 - 1.1 | 5 |
| 8 | STA - E1 | Cranking | | 6 - 14 | 10 |
| 9 | IGT - E1 | Cranking or idling | | 0.8 - 1.2 | 3 |
| 10 | RSC / RSO - E1 | IG SW ON | | 8 - 14 | 14 |
| 11 | W - E1 | No trouble (check engine warning light off) and engine running | | 10 - 14 | 15 |
| 12 | PIM - E2 | IG SW ON | | 2.5 - 4.5 | 8 |
| | VC - E2 | | | 4 - 6 | |
| 13 | AC1 - E1 | IG SW ON | Air conditioning ON | 8 - 14 | 11 |

## MR2 (3S-GTE) ECU WIRING HARNESS RESISTANCE TEST

CAUTION
When measuring resistance at ECU wiring harness, DO NOT TOUCH ECU terminals with ohmmeter. Turn ignition off and unplug ECU wiring harness connector. Tester probe should be inserted into the wiring connector from the WIRING side.

| Terminals | Condition | STD resistance (Ω) |
|---|---|---|
| IDL - E2 | Throttle valve open | Infinity |
| | Throttle valve fully closed | 2,300 or less |
| VTA - E2 | Throttle valve fully open | 3,500 - 10,000 |
| | Throttle valve fully closed | 200 - 800 |
| VC - E2 | – | 200 - 400 |
| VS - E2 | Measuring plate fully closed | 200 - 600 |
| | Measuring plate fully open | 20 - 1,200 |
| THA1 - E2 | Intake air temp. 20°C (68°F) | 2,000 - 3,000 |
| THW - E2 | Coolant temp. 80°C (176°F) | 200 - 400 |
| G1 / G2 - G⊖ | – | 140 - 180 |
| NE - G⊖ | – | 180 - 220 |
| RSC / RSO - +B / +B1 | – | 17.7 - 23.9 |

## ECU TERMINAL IDENTIFICATION

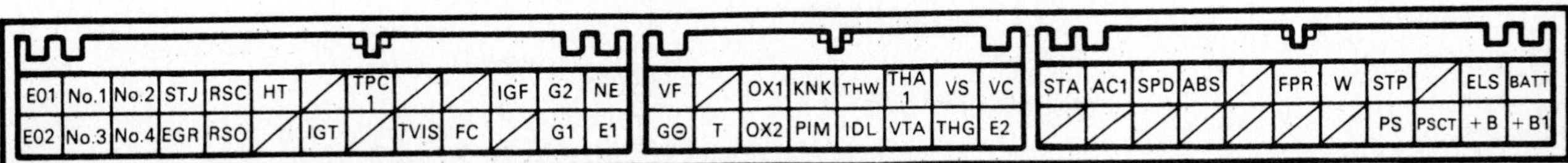


91C18186 91D18187 91H18025

Courtesy of Toyota Motor Sales, U.S.A., Inc.

# 1991 ENGINE PERFORMANCE
# Pin Voltage Charts (Cont.)

## MR2 (5S-FE WITH A/T) ECU PIN VOLTAGE TEST

CAUTION
Perform all voltage measurements with ECU harness connector installed. Use high-impedance digital voltmeter (10,000 ohm minimum). Verify battery voltage is greater than 11 volts.

| No. | Terminals | Condition | | STD voltage (V) | Test No. |
|---|---|---|---|---|---|
| 1 | + B – E1<br>+ B1 – E1 | IG SW ON | | 10 – 14 | 2 |
| 2 | BATT – E1 | — | | 10 – 14 | 1 |
| 3 | IDL – E2 | IG SW ON | Throttle valve open | 8 – 14 | 9 |
| | VC – E2 | | — | 4.5 – 5.5 | |
| | VTA – E2 | | Throttle valve fully closed (Throttle opener must be cancelled first) | 0.8 – 1.2 | |
| | | | Throttle valve fully open | 3.2 – 4.2 | |
| 4 | PIM – E2 | IG SW ON | | 3.3 – 3.9 | 7 |
| | VC – E2 | | | 4.5 – 5.5 | |
| 5 | No.10 – E01<br>No.20 – E02 | | | 10 – 14 | 13 |
| 6 | THA – E2 | IG SW ON | Intake air temp. 20°C (68°F) | 1.7 – 3.1 | 6 |
| 7 | THW – E2 | | Coolant temp. 80°C (176°F) | 0.3 – 0.8 | 5 |
| 8 | STA – E1 | Cranking | | 6 – 14 | 10 |
| 9 | IGT – E1 | Cranking or idling | | 0.8 – 1.2 | 3 |
| 10 | ISCC – E1<br>ISCO – E1 | IG SW ON | | 8 – 14 | 14 |
| 11 | W – E1 | No trouble ("CHECK" engine warning light off) and engine running | | 10 – 14 | 15 |
| 12 | A/C – E1 | IG SW ON | Air conditioning ON | 8 – 14 | 11 |

NOTE
If voltage value is not as specified, proceed to test number indicated. Tests are located in SELF-DIAGNOSTICS article with trouble code charts.

## MR2 (5S-FE WITH A/T) ECU WIRING HARNESS RESISTANCE TEST

CAUTION
When measuring resistance at ECU wiring harness, DO NOT TOUCH ECU terminals with ohmmeter. Turn ignition off and unplug ECU wiring harness connector. Tester probe should be inserted into the wiring connector from the WIRING side.

| Terminals | Condition | STD resistance (Ω) |
|---|---|---|
| IDL – E2 | Throttle valve open | Infinity |
| | Throttle valve fully closed (Throttle opener must be cancelled first) | 2,300 or less |
| VTA – E2 | Throttle valve fully open | 2,300 – 10,000 |
| | Throttle valve fully closed (Throttle opener must be cancelled first) | 200 – 800 |
| VC – E2 | – | 3,000 – 7,000 |
| THA – E2 | Intake air temp. 20°C (68°F) | 2,000 – 3,000 |
| THW – E2 | Coolant temp. 80°C (176°F) | 200 – 400 |
| G1 – G⊖<br>NE – G⊖ | – | 170 – 210 |
| ISCC – +B<br>ISCO – +B1 | – | 19.3 – 22.3 |

## ECU TERMINAL IDENTIFICATION

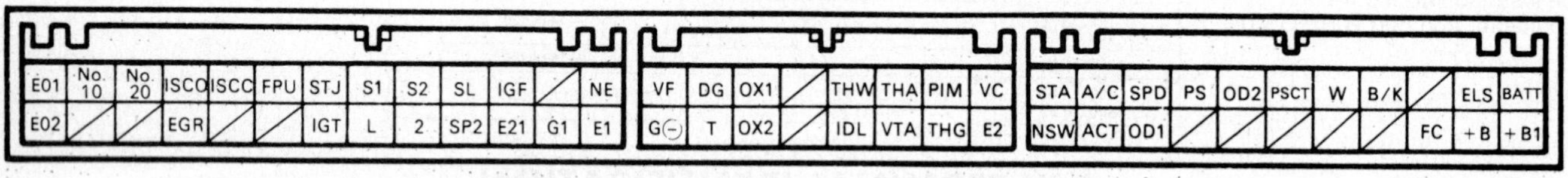
E01 No. 10 No. 20 ISCO ISCC FPU STJ S1 S2 SL IGF NE
E02 EGR IGT L 2 SP2 E21 G1 E1
VF DG OX1 THW THA PIM VC
G⊖ T OX2 IDL VTA THG E2
STA A/C SPD PS OD2 PSCT W B/K ELS BATT
NSW ACT OD1 FC +B +B1

91I18182 91J18183 91I18026

Courtesy of Toyota Motor Sales, U.S.A., Inc.

## MR2 (5S-FE WITH M/T) ECU PIN VOLTAGE TEST

CAUTION
Perform all voltage measurements with ECU harness connector installed. Use high-impedance digital voltmeter (10,000 ohm minimum). Verify battery voltage is greater than 11 volts.

| No. | Terminals | Condition | | STD voltage (V) | Test No. |
|---|---|---|---|---|---|
| 1 | +B / +B1 – E1 | IG SW ON | | 10 – 14 | 2 |
| 2 | BATT – E1 | – | | 10 – 14 | 1 |
| 3 | IDL – E1 | IG SW ON | Throttle valve open | 8 – 14 | 9 |
| | PSW – E1 | | Throttle valve fully closed (Throttle opener must be cancelled first) | 4.5 – 5.5 | |
| 4 | PIM – E2 | IG SW ON | | 3.3 – 3.9 | 7 |
| | VC – E2 | | | 4.5 – 5.5 | |
| 5 | No.10 – E01 / No.20 – E02 | | | 10 – 14 | 13 |
| 6 | THA – E2 | IG SW ON | Intake air temp. 20°C (68°F) | 1.7 – 3.1 | 6 |
| 7 | THW – E2 | | Coolant temp. 80°C (176°F) | 0.3 – 0.8 | 5 |
| 8 | STA – E1 | Cranking | | 6 – 14 | 10 |
| 9 | IGT – E1 | Cranking or idling | | 0.8 – 1.2 | 3 |
| 10 | ISCC / ISCO – E1 | IG SW ON | | 8 – 14 | 14 |
| 11 | W – E1 | No trouble ("CHECK" engine warning light off) and engine running | | 10 – 14 | 15 |
| 12 | A/C– E1 | IG SW ON | Air conditioning ON | 8 – 14 | 11 |

NOTE
If voltage value is not as specified, proceed to test number indicated. Tests are located in SELF-DIAGNOSTICS article with trouble code charts.

## MR2 (5S-FE WITH M/T) ECU WIRING HARNESS RESISTANCE TEST

CAUTION
When measuring resistance at ECU wiring harness, DO NOT TOUCH ECU terminals with ohmmeter. Turn ignition off and unplug ECU wiring harness connector. Tester probe should be inserted into the wiring connector from the WIRING side.

| Terminals | Condition | STD resistance (Ω) |
|---|---|---|
| IDL – E1 | Throttle valve open | Infinity |
| | Throttle valve fully closed (Throttle opener must be cancelled first) | 0 |
| PSW – E1 | Throttle valve fully open | 0 |
| | Throttle valve fully closed (Throttle opener must be cancelled first) | Infinity |
| THA – E2 | Intake air temp. 20°C (68°F) | 2,000 – 3,000 |
| THW – E2 | Coolant temp. 80°C (176°F) | 200 – 400 |
| G1 / NE – G⊖ | – | 170 – 210 |
| ISCC / ISCO – +B / +B1 | – | 19.3 – 22.3 |

## ECU TERMINAL IDENTIFICATION

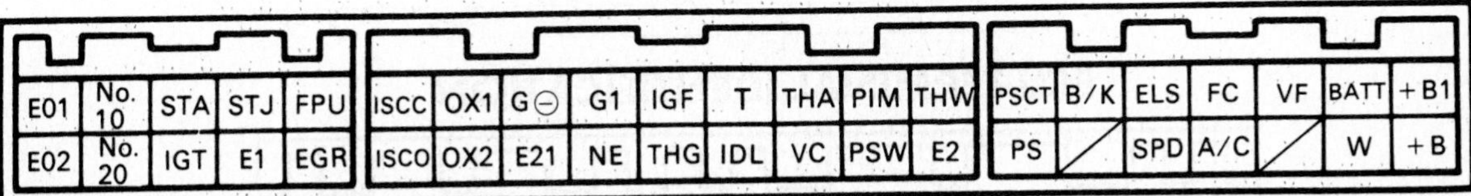


91A18184 91B18185 91J18027

Courtesy of Toyota Motor Sales, U.S.A., Inc.

# 1991 ENGINE PERFORMANCE
# Pin Voltage Charts (Cont.)

## PICKUP (22R-E) ECU PIN VOLTAGE TEST

CAUTION
Perform all voltage measurements with ECU harness connector installed. Use high-impedance digital voltmeter (10,000 ohm minimum). Verify battery voltage is greater than 11 volts.

| No. | Terminals | Condition | | STD voltage | Test No. |
|---|---|---|---|---|---|
| 1 | BATT – $E_1$ | – | | 10 – 14 | 1 |
| | +B – $E_1$ | Ignition switch ON | | | |
| | $+B_1$ – $E_1$ | | | | |
| 2 | IDL – $E_2$ ($E_{21}$) | Ignition switch ON | Throttle valve open | 8 – 14 | 6 |
| | Vcc – $E_2$ ($E_{21}$) | | – | 4 – 6 | |
| | VTA – $E_2$ ($E_{21}$) | | Throttle valve fully closed | 0.1 – 1.0 | |
| | | | Throttle valve fully open | 3 – 5 | |
| 3 | Vc – $E_2$ ($E_{21}$) | Ignition switch ON | – | 6 – 10 | 5 |
| | Vs – $E_2$ ($E_{21}$) | | Measuring plate fully closed | 0.5 – 2.5 | |
| | | | Measuring plate fully open | 5 – 10 | |
| | | Idling | | 2 – 8 | |
| | THA – $E_2$ ($E_{21}$) | Ignition switch ON | Intake air temperature 20°C (68°F) | 1 – 3 | |
| 4 | THW – $E_2$ ($E_{21}$) | Ignition switch ON | Coolant temperature 80°C (176°F) | 0.1 – 1.0 | 4 |
| 5 | STA – $E_1$ | Ignition switch START position | | 6 – 12 | 7 |
| 6 | No. 10 – $E_{01}$<br>No. 20 – $E_{02}$ | Ignition switch ON | | 10 – 14 | 9 |
| 7 | IGt – $E_1$ | Idling | | 0.7 – 1.0 | 2 |
| 8 | W – $E_1$ | No trouble ("CHECK ENGINE" warning light off) and engine running | | 10 – 14 | 11 |
| 9 | STJ – $E_1$ | Ignition switch START position | Coolant temperature 80°C (176°F) | 6 – 12 | 10 |
| 10 | STP – $E_1$ | Stop light switch ON | | 8 – 14 | 12 |

NOTE
If voltage value is not as specified, proceed to test number indicated. Tests are located in SELF-DIAGNOSTICS article with trouble code charts.

## PICKUP (22R-E) ECU WIRING HARNESS RESISTANCE TEST

CAUTION
When measuring resistance at ECU wiring harness, DO NOT TOUCH ECU terminals with ohmmeter. Turn ignition off and unplug ECU wiring harness connector. Tester probe should be inserted into the wiring connector from the WIRING side.

| Terminals | Condition | Resistance (kΩ) |
|---|---|---|
| IDL – $E_2$ ($E_{21}$) | Throttle valve open | Infinity |
| | Throttle valve fully closed | 2.3 or less |
| VTA – $E_2$ ($E_{21}$) | Throttle valve fully open | 3.3 – 10 |
| | Throttle valve fully closed | 0.2 – 0.8 |
| Vcc – $E_2$ ($E_{21}$) | – | 4 – 9 |
| THA – $E_2$ ($E_{21}$) | Intake air temperature 20°C (68°F) | 2 – 3 |
| THW – $E_2$ ($E_{21}$) | Coolant temperature 80°C (176°F) | 0.2 – 0.4 |
| +B – $E_2$ ($E_{21}$) | – | 0.2 – 0.4 |
| Vc – $E_2$ ($E_{21}$) | – | 0.1 – 0.3 |
| Vs – $E_2$ ($E_{21}$) | Measuring plate fully closed | 0.02 – 0.4 |
| | Measuring plate fully open | 0.02 – 1.00 |
| Ne – $E_1$ | – | 0.205 – 0.255 |
| STJ – $E_1$ | – | Infinity |
| FPU – $E_1$ | – | Infinity |
| $HT_1$ – $E_1$ | – | Infinity |

## ECU TERMINAL IDENTIFICATION

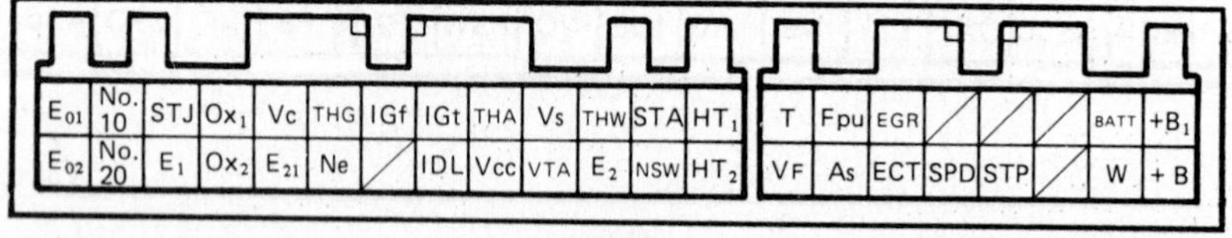


2WD

E01 No.10 STA STJ NSW | Fpu W T IDL IGf / THG KNK Ne | / / Vc Vs THA BATT +B1
E02 No.20 IGt E1 VF | / AS / HT1 E2 Ox1 Vcc VTA THW | ECT / E21 4WD SPD STP +B

4WD WITH M/T

E01 No.10 Fpu HT1 HT2 / S1 S2 S3 / IGf STJ Ne | VF THO OX1 KNK THW THA Vc Vcc | STA / SPD1 4WD P STP W OIL / / BATT
E02 No.20 / AS EGR IGt L4 N 2 L SPD2 E1 / | / T OX2 THG IDL VTA Vs E2 | / OD1 DG / / / OD2 E21 / +B1 +B

4WD WITH A/T

91E18188 91F18189 91F18049 91A18051 91J18050

# 1991 ENGINE PERFORMANCE
# Pin Voltage Charts (Cont.)

## PICKUP (3VZ-E) ECU PIN VOLTAGE TEST

CAUTION
Perform all voltage measurements with ECU harness connector installed. Use high-impedance digital voltmeter (10,000 ohm minimum). Verify battery voltage is greater than 11 volts.

| No. | Terminals | Condition | | STD voltage | Test No. |
|---|---|---|---|---|---|
| 1 | BATT – $E_1$ | – | | 10 – 14 | 1 |
| | +B – $E_1$ | Ignition SW ON | | | |
| | $+B_1$ – $E_1$ | | | | |
| 2 | IDL – $E_2$ ($E_{21}$) | Ignition SW ON | Throttle valve open | 8 – 14 | 6 |
| | Vc – $E_2$ ($E_{21}$) | | – | 4 – 6 | |
| | VTA – $E_2$ ($E_{21}$) | | Throttle valve fully closed | 0.1 – 1.0 | |
| | | | Throttle valve fully open | 3 – 5 | |
| 3 | Vc – $E_2$ ($E_{21}$) | Ignition SW ON | – | 4 – 6 | 5 |
| | Vc – $E_2$ ($E_{21}$) | | Measuring plate fully closed | 3.7 – 4.3 | |
| | | | Measuring plate fully open | 0.2 – 0.5 | |
| | | Idling | | 2.3 – 2.8 | |
| | | 3,000 rpm | | 0.3 – 1.0 | |
| | THA – $E_2$ ($E_{21}$) | IG SW ON | Intake air temperature 20°C (68°F) | 1 – 3 | |
| 4 | THW – $E_2$ ($E_{21}$) | IG SW ON | Coolant temperature 80°C (176°F) | 0.1 – 1.0 | 4 |
| 5 | STA – $E_1$ | Ignition SW START position | | 6 – 12 | 7 |
| 6 | No. 10 – $E_{01}$<br>No. 20 – $E_{02}$ | Ignition SW ON | | 10 – 14 | 9 |
| 7 | IGt – $E_1$ | Cranking or idling | | 0.7 – 1.0 | 2 |
| 8 | W – $E_1$ | No trouble ("CHECK ENGINE" warning light off) and engine running | | 10 – 14 | 11 |
| 9 | STJ – $E_1$ | Ignition SW START position | Coolant temperature 80°C (176°F) | 6 – 12 | 10 |
| 10 | STP – $E_1$ | Stop light switch ON | | 8 – 14 | 12 |

NOTE
If voltage value is not as specified, proceed to test number indicated. Tests are located in SELF-DIAGNOSTICS article with trouble code charts.

## PICKUP (3VZ-E) ECU WIRING HARNESS RESISTANCE TEST

CAUTION
When measuring resistance at ECU wiring harness, DO NOT TOUCH ECU terminals with ohmmeter. Turn ignition off and unplug ECU wiring harness connector. Tester probe should be inserted into the wiring connector from the WIRING side.

| Terminals | Condition | Resistance (kΩ) |
|---|---|---|
| IDL – $E_2$ ($E_{21}$) | Throttle valve open | Infinity |
| | Throttle valve fully closed | 2.3 or less |
| VTA – $E_2$ ($E_{21}$) | Throttle valve fully open | 3.3 – 10 |
| | Throttle valve fully closed | 0.2 – 0.8 |
| Vc – $E_2$ ($E_{21}$) | Air flow meter connector disconnected | 4 – 9 |
| THA – $E_2$ ($E_{21}$) | Intake air temperature 20°C (68°F) | 2 – 3 |
| THW – $E_2$ ($E_{21}$) | Coolant temperature 80°C (176°F) | 0.2 – 0.4 |
| +B – $E_1$ | – | 0.2 – 0.4 |
| Vc – $E_2$ ($E_{21}$) | Throttle position sensor connector disconnected | 0.1 – 0.3 |
| Vs – $E_2$ ($E_{21}$) | Measuring plate fully closed | 0.2 – 0.6 |
| | Measuring plate fully open | 0.02 – 1.20 |
| $G_1$, $G_2$ – G⊖ | – | 0.205 – 0.255 |
| Ne – G⊖ | – | 0.205 – 0.255 |
| STJ – $E_1$ | – | Infinity |
| FPU – $E_1$ | – | Infinity |
| HT – $E_1$ | – | Infinity |

## ECU TERMINAL IDENTIFICATION

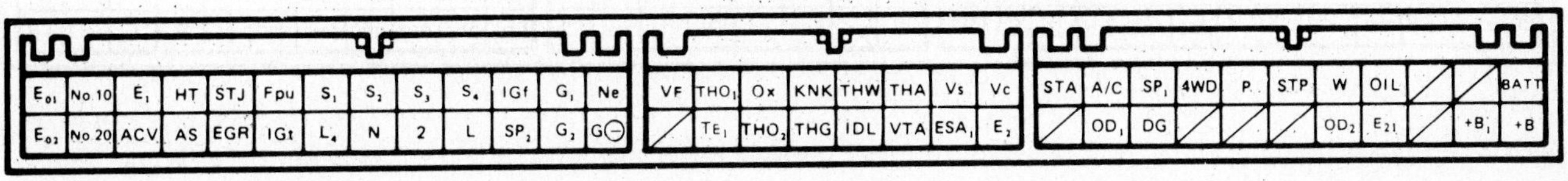

| $E_{01}$ | No 10 | $E_1$ | HT | STJ | Fpu | $S_1$ | $S_2$ | $S_3$ | $S_4$ | IGf | $G_1$ | Ne |
|---|---|---|---|---|---|---|---|---|---|---|---|---|
| $E_{02}$ | No 20 | ACV | AS | EGR | IGt | $L_4$ | N | 2 | L | $SP_2$ | $G_2$ | G⊖ |

| VF | $THO_1$ | Ox | KNK | THW | THA | Vs | Vc |
|---|---|---|---|---|---|---|---|
| / | $TE_1$ | $THO_2$ | THG | IDL | VTA | $ESA_1$ | $E_2$ |

| STA | A/C | $SP_1$ | 4WD | P | STP | W | OIL | / | / | BATT |
|---|---|---|---|---|---|---|---|---|---|---|
| / | $OD_1$ | DG | / | / | / | $OD_2$ | $E_{21}$ | / | $+B_1$ | +B |

91I18190 91J18191 91C18079

Courtesy of Toyota Motor Sales, U.S.A., Inc.

# 1991 ENGINE PERFORMANCE
# Pin Voltage Charts (Cont.)

## PREVIA ECU PIN VOLTAGE TEST

CAUTION
Perform all voltage measurements with ECU harness connector installed. Use high-impedance digital voltmeter (10,000 ohm minimum). Verify battery voltage is greater than 11 volts.

| No. | Terminals | Condition | | STD voltage | Test No. |
|---|---|---|---|---|---|
| 1 | BATT – E1 | – | | 10 – 14 | 1 |
| | +B – E1 | Ignition SW ON | | | |
| | +B1 – E1 | | | | |
| 2 | IDL – E2 | Ignition SW ON | Throttle valve open | 8 – 14 | 7 |
| | VC – E2 | | – | 4 – 6 | |
| | VTA – E2 | | Throttle valve fully closed | 0.1 – 1.0 | |
| | | | Throttle valve fully open | 3 – 6 | |
| 3 | VC – E2 | Ignition SW ON | – | 4 – 6 | 6 |
| | VS – E2 | | Measuring plate fully closed | 3.7 – 4.3 | |
| | | | Measuring plate fully open | 0.2 – 0.5 | |
| | | Idling | | 2.3 – 2.8 | |
| | | 3,000 rpm | | 0.3 – 1.0 | |
| 4 | No. 10 – E01<br>No. 20 – E02 | Ignition SW ON | | 10 – 14 | 11 |
| 5 | THA – E2 | IG SW ON | Intake air temperature 20°C (68°F) | 1 – 3 | 5 |
| 6 | THW – E2 | IG SW ON | Coolant temperature 80°C (176°F) | 0.1 – 1.0 | 4 |
| 7 | STA – E1 | Ignition SW ST position | | 6 – 12 | 8 |
| 8 | IGT – E1 | Cranking or idling | | 0.7 – 1.0 | 2 |
| 9 | W – E1 | No trouble (CHECK ENGINE light off) and engine running | | 10 – 14 | 13 |
| 10 | A/C – E1 | IG SW ON | Air conditioning ON | 8 – 14 | 9 |
| 11 | ISC1 – E1<br>ISC2 – E1 | Ignition SW ON | | 8 – 14 | 12 |

NOTE
If voltage value is not as specified, proceed to test number indicated. Tests are located in SELF-DIAGNOSTICS article with trouble code charts.

## PREVIA ECU WIRING HARNESS RESISTANCE TEST

CAUTION
When measuring resistance at ECU wiring harness, DO NOT TOUCH ECU terminals with ohmmeter. Turn ignition off and unplug ECU wiring harness connector. Tester probe should be inserted into the wiring connector from the WIRING side.

| Terminals | Condition | Resistance (kΩ) |
|---|---|---|
| IDL – E2 | Throttle valve open | Infinity |
| | Throttle valve fully closed | 0 – 0.1 |
| VTA – E2 | Throttle valve fully open | 3.3 – 10 |
| | Throttle valve fully closed | 0.2 – 0.8 |
| VC – E2 | Air flow meter connector disconnected | 4 – 9 |
| THA – E2 | Intake air temperature 20°C (68°F) | 2 – 3 |
| THW – E2 | Coolant temperature 80°C (176°F) | 0.2 – 0.4 |
| +B – E1 | – | 0.2 – 0.4 |
| VC – E2 | Throttle position sensor connector disconnected | 0.1 – 0.3 |
| VS – E2 | Measuring plate fully closed | 0.02 – 0.1 |
| | Measuring plate fully open | 0.02 – 1.00 |

## ECU TERMINAL IDENTIFICATION

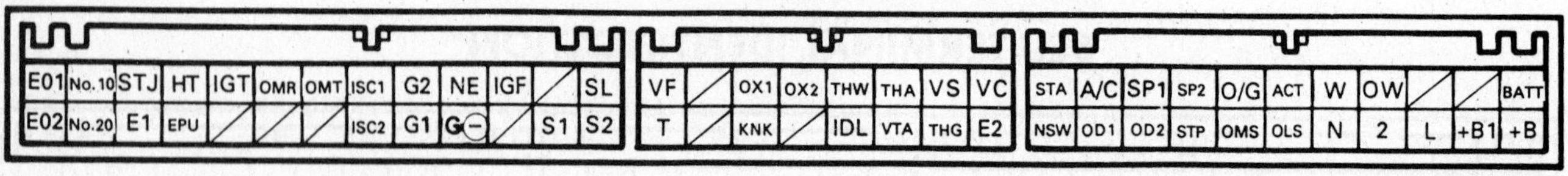

| E01 | No.10 | STJ | HT | IGT | OMR | OMT | ISC1 | G2 | NE | IGF | / | SL | VF | / | OX1 | OX2 | THW | THA | VS | VC | STA | A/C | SP1 | SP2 | O/G | ACT | W | OW | / | / | BATT |
|---|---|---|---|---|---|---|---|---|---|---|---|---|---|---|---|---|---|---|---|---|---|---|---|---|---|---|---|---|---|---|---|
| E02 | No.20 | E1 | EPU | / | / | / | ISC2 | G1 | G⊖ | / | S1 | S2 | T | / | KNK | / | IDL | VTA | THG | E2 | NSW | OD1 | OD2 | STP | OMS | OLS | N | 2 | L | +B1 | +B |

91A18192 91B18193 91A18093

Courtesy of Toyota Motor Sales, U.S.A., Inc.

# 1991 ENGINE PERFORMANCE
# Pin Voltage Charts (Cont.)

## SUPRA (NON-TURBO) ECU PIN VOLTAGE TEST

CAUTION
Perform all voltage measurements with ECU harness connector installed. Use high-impedance digital voltmeter (10,000 ohm minimum). Verify battery voltage is greater than 11 volts.

| No. | Terminals | Condition | | STD Voltage | Test No. |
|---|---|---|---|---|---|
| 1 | BATT – E1 | – | | 10 – 14 | 1 |
| | IG SW – E1 | Ignition SW ON | | 10 – 14 | |
| | M-REL – E1 | | | | |
| | +B (+B1) – E1 | | | | |
| 2 | IDL – E2 | Ignition SW ON | Throttle valve open | 10 – 14 | 7 |
| | VC – E2 | | – | 4 – 6 | |
| | VTA – E2 | | Throttle valve fully closed | 0.1 – 1.0 | |
| | | | Throttle valve fully open | 4 – 5 | |
| 3 | VC – E2 | Ignition SW ON | – | 4 – 6 | 6 |
| | VS – E2 | | Measuring plate fully closed | 3.7 – 4.3 | |
| | | | Measuring plate fully open | 0.2 – 0.5 | |
| | | Idling | | 2.3 – 2.8 | |
| | | 3,000 rpm | | 1.0 – 2.0 | |
| 4 | No. 10 E01<br>No. 20 –<br>No. 30 E02 | Ignition SW ON | | 10 – 14 | 11 |
| 5 | THA – E2 | Ignition SW ON | Intake air temperature 20°C (68°F) | 1 – 3 | 5 |
| 6 | THW – E2 | Ignition SW ON | Coolant temperature 80°C (176°F) | 0.1 – 1.0 | 4 |
| 7 | STA – E1 | Cranking | | 6 – 14 | 8 |
| 8 | IGT – E1 | Idling | | 0.7 – 1.0 | 2 |
| 9 | ISC1 ~ ISC4 – E1 | Ignition SW ON | | 9 – 14 | 12 |
| 10 | W – E1 | No trouble ("CHECK ENGINE" warning light off) and engine running | | 8 – 14 | 13 |
| 11 | A/C – E1 | Air conditioning ON | | 10 – 14 | 9 |

NOTE
If voltage value is not as specified, proceed to test number indicated. Tests are located in SELF-DIAGNOSTICS article with trouble code charts.

## SUPRA (NON-TURBO) ECU WIRING HARNESS RESISTANCE TEST

CAUTION
When measuring resistance at ECU wiring harness, DO NOT TOUCH ECU terminals with ohmmeter. Turn ignition off and unplug ECU wiring harness connector. Tester probe should be inserted into the wiring connector from the WIRING side.

| Terminals | Condition | Resistance (Ω) |
|---|---|---|
| IDL – E2 | Throttle valve open | ∞ |
| | Throttle valve fully closed | 2,300 or less |
| VTA – E2 | Throttle valve fully open | 3,500 – 10,300 |
| | Throttle valve fully closed | 200 – 1,200 |
| VC – E2 | – | 4,250 – 8,250 |
| VS – E2 | Measuring plate fully closed | 200 – 600 |
| | Measuring plate fully open | 20 – 1,200 |
| THW – E2 | Coolant temperature 80°C (176°F) | 200 – 400 |
| G1, G2 – G⊖ | – | 140 – 180 |
| NE – G⊖ | – | 180 – 220 |
| ISC1, ISC2, ISC3, ISC4 – +B (+B1) | – | 10 – 30 |

## ECU TERMINAL IDENTIFICATION

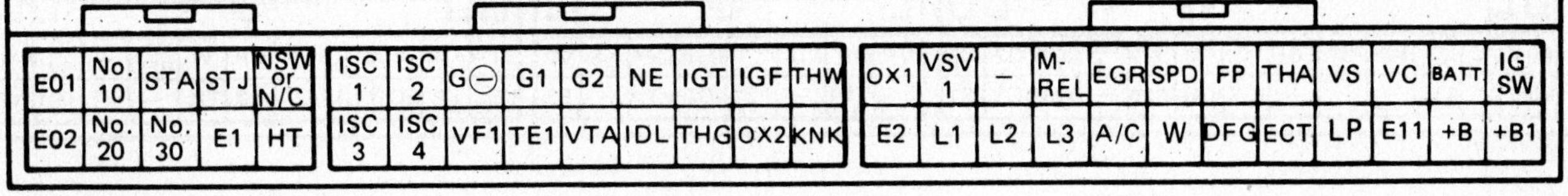

| E01 | No. 10 | STA | STJ | NSW or N/C | ISC 1 | ISC 2 | G⊖ | G1 | G2 | NE | IGT | IGF | THW | OX1 | VSV 1 | – | M-REL | EGR | SPD | FP | THA | VS | VC | BATT | IG SW |
|---|---|---|---|---|---|---|---|---|---|---|---|---|---|---|---|---|---|---|---|---|---|---|---|---|---|
| E02 | No. 20 | No. 30 | E1 | HT | ISC 3 | ISC 4 | VF1 | TE1 | VTA | IDL | THG | OX2 | KNK | E2 | L1 | L2 | L3 | A/C | W | DFG | ECT | LP | E11 | +B | +B1 |

91C18194 91D18195 91C18103

Courtesy of Toyota Motor Sales, U.S.A., Inc.

# 1991 ENGINE PERFORMANCE
# Pin Voltage Charts (Cont.)

## SUPRA (TURBO) ECU PIN VOLTAGE TEST

CAUTION
Perform all voltage measurements with ECU harness connector installed. Use high-impedance digital voltmeter (10,000 ohm minimum). Verify battery voltage is greater than 11 volts.

| No. | Terminals | Condition | | STD Voltage | Test No. |
|---|---|---|---|---|---|
| 1 | BATT – E1 | – | | 10 – 14 | 1 |
| | IG SW – E1 | Ignition SW ON | | 10 – 14 | |
| | M-REL – E1 | | | | |
| | +B (+B1) – E1 | | | | |
| 2 | IDL – E2 | Ignition SW ON | Throttle valve open | 4 – 6 | 7 |
| | VC – E2 | | – | 4 – 6 | |
| | VTA – E2 | | Throttle valve fully closed | 0.1 – 1.0 | |
| | | | Throttle valve fully open | 3.2 – 4.2 | |
| 3 | KS – Body ground | Ignition SW ON | | 4 – 6 | 6 |
| | | Cranking or running | | 2 – 4 | |
| | VC – Body ground | Ignition SW ON | | 4 – 6 | |
| 4 | No. 10 E01<br>No. 20 –<br>No. 30 E02 | Ignition SW ON | | 10 – 14 | 11 |
| 5 | THA – E2 | Ignition SW ON | Intake air temperature 20°C (68°F) | 1 – 3 | 5 |
| 6 | THW – E2 | Ignition SW ON | Coolant temperature 80°C (176°F) | 0.1 – 1.0 | 4 |
| 7 | STA – E1 | Cranking | | 6 – 14 | 8 |
| 8 | IGT – E1 | Idling | | 0.7 – 1.0 | 2 |
| 9 | IGDA<br>IGDB – E1 | Idling | | 1 – 3 | 2 |
| 10 | ISC1<br>/<br>ISC4 – E1 | Ignition SW ON | | 9 – 14 | 12 |
| 11 | W – E1 | No trouble ("CHECK ENGINE" warning light off) and engine running | | 8 – 14 | 13 |
| 12 | A/C – E1 | Air conditioning ON | | 10 – 14 | 9 |

NOTE
If voltage value is not as specified, proceed to test number indicated. Tests are located in SELF-DIAGNOSTICS article with trouble code charts.

## SUPRA (TURBO) ECU WIRING HARNESS RESISTANCE TEST

CAUTION
When measuring resistance at ECU wiring harness, DO NOT TOUCH ECU terminals with ohmmeter. Turn ignition off and unplug ECU wiring harness connector. Tester probe should be inserted into the wiring connector from the WIRING side.

| Terminals | Condition | Resistance (Ω) |
|---|---|---|
| IDL – E2 | Throttle valve open | ∞ |
| | Throttle valve fully closed | 2,300 or less |
| VTA – E2 | Throttle valve fully open | 3,600 – 10,300 |
| | Throttle valve fully closed | 200 – 1,200 |
| THW – E2 | Coolant temperature 80°C (176°F) | 200 – 400 |
| G1, G2 – G⊖ | – | 205 – 255 |
| NE – G⊖ | – | 205 – 255 |
| ISC1, ISC2<br>ISC3, ISC4 – +B (+B1) | – | 10 – 30 |

## ECU TERMINAL IDENTIFICATION

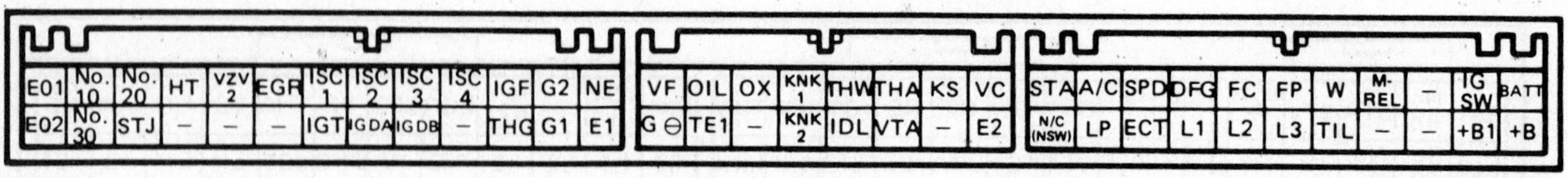

| E01 | No. 10 | No. 20 | HT | VZV 2 | EGR | ISC 1 | ISC 2 | ISC 3 | ISC 4 | IGF | G2 | NE |
|---|---|---|---|---|---|---|---|---|---|---|---|---|
| E02 | No. 30 | STJ | – | – | – | IGT | IGDA | IGDB | – | THG | G1 | E1 |

| VF | OIL | OX | KNK 1 | THW | THA | KS | VC |
|---|---|---|---|---|---|---|---|
| G⊖ | TE1 | – | KNK 2 | IDL | VTA | – | E2 |

| STA | A/C | SPD | DFG | FC | FP | W | M-REL | – | IG SW | BATT |
|---|---|---|---|---|---|---|---|---|---|---|
| N/C (NSW) | LP | ECT | L1 | L2 | L3 | TIL | – | – | +B1 | +B |

91E18196 91F18197 91D18104

## TERCEL ECU PIN VOLTAGE TEST

CAUTION
Perform all voltage measurements with ECU harness connector installed. Use high-impedance digital voltmeter (10,000 ohm minimum). Verify battery voltage is greater 11 volts.

| No. | Terminals | STD voltage (V) | Condition | | Test No. |
|---|---|---|---|---|---|
| 1 | +B – E1<br>+B1 – E1 | 10 – 14 | IG SW ON | | 2 |
| 2 | BATT – E1 | 10 – 14 | – | | 1 |
| 3 | IDL – E2 | 4.5 – 5.5 | IG SW ON | Throttle valve open | 8 |
| | VCC – E2 | 4.5 – 5.5 | | – | |
| | VTA – E2 | 0.8 – 1.2 | | Throttle valve fully closed | |
| | | 3.2 – 4.2 | | Throttle valve fully open | |
| 4 | No. 10 – E01<br>No. 20 – E02 | 10 – 14 | IG SW ON | | 12 |
| 5 | W – E1 | 10 – 14 | No trouble ("CHECK" engine warning light off) and engine running | | 13 |
| 6 | PIM – E2 | 3.3 – 3.9 | IG SW ON | | 7 |
| | VCC – E2 | 4.5 – 5.5 | | | |
| 7 | THA – E2 | 2.0 – 2.8 | IG SW ON | Intake air temperature 20°C (68°F) | 6 |
| 8 | THW – E2 | 0.4 – 0.7 | IG SW ON | Coolant temperature 80°C (176°F) | 5 |
| 9 | STA – E1 | 6 – 14 | Cranking | | 9 |
| 10 | IGT – E1 | 0.7 – 1.0 | Idling | | 3 |
| 11 | A/C – E1 | 8 – 14 | IG SW ON | Air conditioning ON | 10 |

NOTE
If voltage value is not as specified, proceed to test number indicated. Tests are located in SELF-DIAGNOSTICS article with trouble code charts.

## TERCEL ECU WIRING HARNESS RESISTANCE TEST

CAUTION
When measuring resistance at ECU wiring harness, DO NOT TOUCH ECU terminals with ohmmeter. Turn ignition off and unplug ECU wiring harness connector. Tester probe should be inserted into the wiring connector from the WIRING side.

| Terminals | Condition | Resistance |
|---|---|---|
| IDL – E2 | Throttle valve open | Infinity |
| | Throttle valve fully closed | 2.3 kΩ or less |
| VTA – E2 | Throttle valve fully open | 3.3 – 10 kΩ |
| | Throttle valve fully closed | 0.2 – 0.8 kΩ |
| VCC – E2 | – | 3 – 7 kΩ |
| THA – E2 | Intake air temperature 20°C (68°F) | 2 – 3 kΩ |
| THW – E2 | Coolant temperature 80°C (176°F) | 0.2 – 0.4 kΩ |
| NE – NE⊖ | – | 410 – 510 Ω |

## ECU TERMINAL IDENTIFICATION

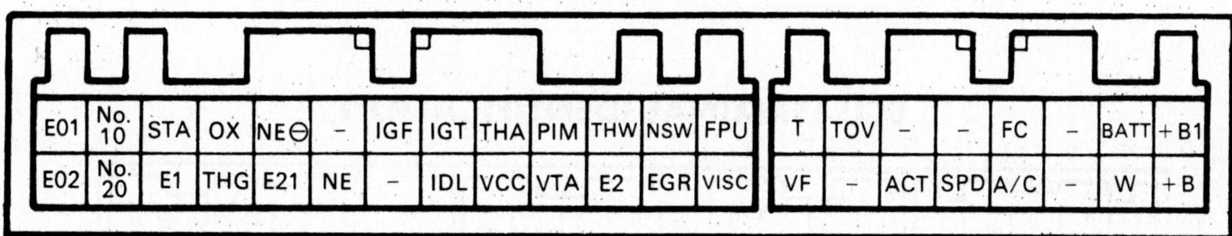

# 1991 ENGINE PERFORMANCE
# Pin Voltage Charts (Cont.)

## 4RUNNER (22R-E) ECU PIN VOLTAGE TEST

CAUTION
Perform all voltage measurements with ECU harness connector installed. Use high-impedance digital voltmeter (10,000 ohm minimum). Verify battery voltage is greater than 11 volts.

NOTE
If voltage value is not as specified, proceed to test number indicated. Tests are located in SELF-DIAGNOSTICS article with trouble code charts.

| No. | Terminals | Condition | | STD voltage | Test No. |
|---|---|---|---|---|---|
| 1 | BATT – $E_1$ | – | | 10–14 | 1 |
| | +B – $E_1$ | Ignition switch ON | | 10–14 | |
| | $+B_1$ – $E_1$ | | | 10–14 | |
| 2 | IDL – $E_2$ ($E_{21}$) | Ignition switch ON | Throttle valve open | 8–14 | 6 |
| | Vcc – $E_2$ ($E_{21}$) | | – | 4–6 | |
| | VTA – $E_2$ ($E_{21}$) | | Throttle valve fully closed | 0.1–1.0 | |
| | | | Throttle valve fully open | 3–5 | |
| 3 | Vc – $E_2$ ($E_{21}$) | Ignition switch ON | – | 6–10 | 5 |
| | Vs – $E_2$ ($E_{21}$) | | Measuring plate fully closed | 0.5–2.5 | |
| | | | Measuring plate fully open | 5–10 | |
| | | Idling | | 2–8 | |
| | THA – $E_2$ ($E_{21}$) | Ignition switch ON | Intake air temperature 20°C (68°F) | 1–3 | |
| 4 | THW – $E_2$ ($E_{21}$) | Ignition switch ON | Coolant temperature 80°C (176°F) | 0.1–1.0 | 4 |
| 5 | STA – $E_1$ | Ignition switch START position | | 6–12 | 7 |
| 6 | No. 10 – $E_{01}$<br>No. 20 – $E_{02}$ | Ignition switch ON | | 10–14 | 9 |
| 7 | IGt – $E_1$ | Idling | | 0.7–1.0 | 2 |
| 8 | W – $E_1$ | No trouble ("CHECK ENGINE" warning light off) and engine running | | 10–14 | 11 |
| 9 | STJ – $E_1$ | Ignition switch START position | Coolant temperature 80°C (176°F) | 6–12 | 10 |
| 10 | STP – $E_1$ | Stop light switch ON | | 8–14 | 12 |

## 4RUNNER (22R-E) ECU WIRING HARNESS RESISTANCE TEST

CAUTION
When measuring resistance at ECU wiring harness, DO NOT TOUCH ECU terminals with ohmmeter. Turn ignition off and unplug ECU wiring harness connector. Tester probe should be inserted into the wiring connector from the WIRING side.

| Terminals | Condition | Resistance (kΩ) |
|---|---|---|
| IDL – $E_2$ ($E_{21}$) | Throttle valve open | Infinity |
| | Throttle valve fully closed | 2.3 or less |
| VTA – $E_2$ ($E_{21}$) | Throttle valve fully open | 3.3 – 10 |
| | Throttle valve fully closed | 0.2 – 0.8 |
| Vcc – $E_2$ ($E_{21}$) | – | 4 – 9 |
| THA – $E_2$ ($E_{21}$) | Intake air temperature 20°C (68°F) | 2 – 3 |
| THW – $E_2$ ($E_{21}$) | Coolant temperature 80°C (176°F) | 0.2 – 0.4 |
| +B – $E_2$ ($E_{21}$) | – | 0.2 – 0.4 |
| Vc – $E_2$ ($E_{21}$) | – | 0.1 – 0.3 |
| Vs – $E_2$ ($E_{21}$) | Measuring plate fully closed | 0.02 – 0.4 |
| | Measuring plate fully open | 0.02 – 1.00 |
| Ne – $E_1$ | – | 0.14 – 0.18 |
| STJ – $E_1$ | – | Infinity |
| FPU – $E_1$ | – | Infinity |
| $HT_1$ – $E_1$ | – | Infinity |

## ECU TERMINAL IDENTIFICATION

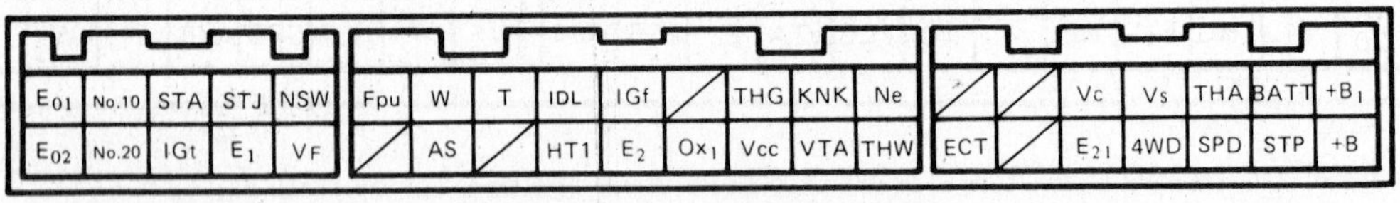

| $E_{01}$ | No.10 | STA | STJ | NSW | Fpu | W | T | IDL | IGf | | THG | KNK | Ne | | | Vc | Vs | THA | BATT | $+B_1$ |
|---|---|---|---|---|---|---|---|---|---|---|---|---|---|---|---|---|---|---|---|---|
| $E_{02}$ | No.20 | IGt | $E_1$ | VF | | AS | | HT1 | $E_2$ | $Ox_1$ | Vcc | VTA | THW | ECT | | $E_{21}$ | 4WD | SPD | STP | +B |

**2WD & 4WD WITH M/T**

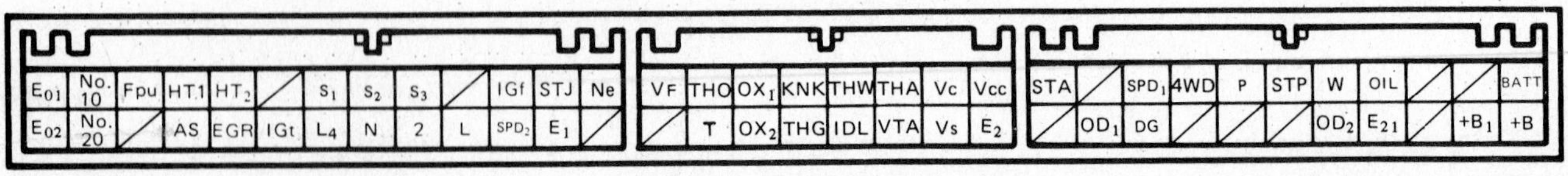

| $E_{01}$ | No. 10 | Fpu | HT1 | $HT_2$ | | $S_1$ | $S_2$ | $S_3$ | | IGf | STJ | Ne | VF | THO | $OX_1$ | KNK | THW | THA | Vc | Vcc | STA | | $SPD_1$ | 4WD | P | STP | W | OIL | | | BATT |
|---|---|---|---|---|---|---|---|---|---|---|---|---|---|---|---|---|---|---|---|---|---|---|---|---|---|---|---|---|---|---|---|
| $E_{02}$ | No. 20 | | AS | EGR | IGt | $L_4$ | N | 2 | L | $SPD_2$ | $E_1$ | | | T | $OX_2$ | THG | IDL | VTA | Vs | $E_2$ | | $OD_1$ | DG | | | | $OD_2$ | $E_{21}$ | | $+B_1$ | +B |

**4WD WITH A/T**

91D18252 91E18253 91B18052 91C18053

Courtesy of Toyota Motor Sales, U.S.A., Inc.

# 1991 ENGINE PERFORMANCE
# Pin Voltage Charts (Cont.)

## 4RUNNER (3VZ-E) ECU PIN VOLTAGE TEST

CAUTION
Perform all voltage measurements with ECU harness connector installed. Use high-impedance digital voltmeter (10,000 ohm minimum). Verify battery voltage is greater than 11 volts.

| No. | Terminals | Condition | | STD voltage | Test No. |
|---|---|---|---|---|---|
| 1 | BATT – $E_1$ | – | | 10 – 14 | 1 |
| | +B – $E_1$ | Ignition SW ON | | | |
| | $+B_1$ – $E_1$ | | | | |
| 2 | IDL – $E_2$ ($E_{21}$) | Ignition SW ON | Throttle valve open | 8 – 14 | 6 |
| | Vc – $E_2$ ($E_{21}$) | | – | 4 – 6 | |
| | VTA – $E_2$ ($E_{21}$) | | Throttle valve fully closed | 0.1 – 1.0 | |
| | | | Throttle valve fully open | 3 – 5 | |
| 3 | Vc – $E_2$ ($E_{21}$) | Ignition SW ON | – | 4 – 6 | 5 |
| | Vs – $E_2$ ($E_{21}$) | | Measuring plate fully closed | 3.7 – 4.3 | |
| | | | Measuring plate fully open | 0.2 – 0.5 | |
| | | Idling | | 2.3 – 2.8 | |
| | THA – $E_2$ ($E_{21}$) | IG SW ON | Intake air temperature 20°C (68°F) | 1 – 3 | |
| 4 | THW – $E_2$ ($E_{21}$) | IG SW ON | Coolant temperature 80°C (176°F) | 0.1 – 1.0 | 4 |
| 5 | STA – $E_1$ | Ignition SW START position | | 6 – 12 | 7 |
| 6 | No.10 – $E_{01}$<br>No.20 – $E_{02}$ | Ignition SW ON | | 10 – 14 | 9 |
| 7 | IGt – $E_1$ | Cranking or idling | | 0.7 – 1.0 | 2 |
| 8 | W – $E_1$ | No trouble ("CHECK ENGINE" warning light off) and engine running | | 10 – 14 | 11 |
| 9 | STJ – $E_1$ | Ignition SW START position | Coolant temperature 80°C (176°F) | 6 – 12 | 10 |
| 10 | STP – $E_1$ | Stop light switch ON | | 10 – 14 | 12 |

NOTE
If voltage value is not as specified, proceed to test number indicated. Tests are located in SELF-DIAGNOSTICS article with trouble code charts.

## 4RUNNER (3VZ-E) ECU WIRING HARNESS RESISTANCE TEST

CAUTION
When measuring resistance at ECU wiring harness, DO NOT TOUCH ECU terminals with ohmmeter. Turn ignition off and unplug ECU wiring harness connector. Tester probe should be inserted into the wiring connector from the WIRING side.

| Terminals | Condition | Resistance (kΩ) |
|---|---|---|
| IDL – $E_2$ ($E_{21}$) | Throttle valve open | Infinity |
| | Throttle valve fully closed | 2.3 or less |
| VTA – $E_2$ ($E_{21}$) | Throttle valve fully open | 3.3 – 10 |
| | Throttle valve fully closed | 0.2 – 0.8 |
| Vc – $E_2$ ($E_{21}$) | Air flow meter connector disconnected | 4 – 9 |
| THA – $E_2$ ($E_{21}$) | Intake air temperature 20°C (68°F) | 2 – 3 |
| THW – $E_2$ ($E_{21}$) | Coolant temperature 80°C (176°F) | 0.2 – 0.4 |
| +B – $E_1$ | – | 0.2 – 0.4 |
| Vc – $E_2$ ($E_{21}$) | Throttle position sensor connector disconnected | 0.1 – 0.3 |
| Vs – $E_2$ ($E_{21}$) | Measuring plate fully closed | 0.02 – 0.6 |
| | Measuring plate fully open | 0.02 – 1.20 |
| Ne – $E_1$ | – | 0.14 – 0.18 |
| STJ – $E_1$ | – | Infinity |
| FPU – $E_1$ | – | Infinity |
| HT – $E_1$ | – | Infinity |

## ECU TERMINAL IDENTIFICATION

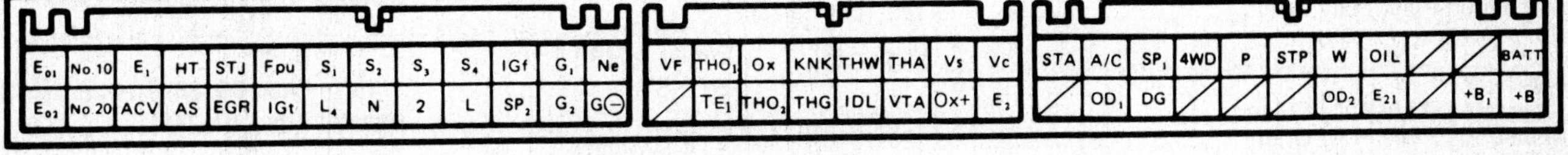

| | | | | | | | | | | | | |
|---|---|---|---|---|---|---|---|---|---|---|---|---|
| $E_{01}$ | No.10 | $E_1$ | HT | STJ | Fpu | $S_1$ | $S_2$ | $S_3$ | $S_4$ | IGf | $G_1$ | Ne |
| $E_{02}$ | No.20 | ACV | AS | EGR | IGt | $L_4$ | N | 2 | L | $SP_2$ | $G_2$ | G⊖ |

| | | | | | | | |
|---|---|---|---|---|---|---|---|
| VF | $THO_1$ | Ox | KNK | THW | THA | Vs | Vc |
| / | $TE_1$ | $THO_2$ | THG | IDL | VTA | Ox+ | $E_2$ |

| | | | | | | | | | | |
|---|---|---|---|---|---|---|---|---|---|---|
| STA | A/C | $SP_1$ | 4WD | P | STP | W | OIL | / | / | BATT |
| / | $OD_1$ | DG | / | / | / | $OD_2$ | $E_{21}$ | / | $+B_1$ | +B |

91F18254 91G18255 91F18080

Courtesy of Toyota Motor Sales, U.S.A., Inc.

# 1991 ENGINE PERFORMANCE
# Sensor Operating Range Charts

## Camry, Celica, Corolla, Cressida, Land Cruiser, MR2, Pickup, Previa, Supra, Tercel, 4Runner

## INTRODUCTION

Sensor operating range information can help determine if a sensor is out of calibration. An out-of-calibration sensor may not set a trouble code, but it may cause driveability problems.

***NOTE: Perform all voltage tests with a Digital Volt-Ohmmeter (DVOM) with a minimum 10-megohm input impedance, unless stated otherwise in test procedure.***

### *AIRFLOW METER RESISTANCE SPECIFICATIONS* [1]

| Application & Terminals | Ohms |
|---|---|
| **Camry 2.0L** | |
| $E_2$-Vc | 3000-7000 |
| $E_1$-Fc | |
| Measuring Plate Fully Closed | No Continuity |
| Measuring Plate Other Than Closed | 0 |
| $E_2$-Vs | |
| Measuring Plate Fully Closed | 200-600 |
| Measuring Plate Fully Opened | 20-1000 |
| **Camry 2.5L, Land Cruiser & Supra Non Turbo** | |
| $E_2$-Vc | 200-400 |
| $E_1$-Fc | |
| Measuring Plate Fully Closed | No Continuity |
| Measuring Plate Other Than Closed | 0 |
| $E_2$-Vs | |
| Measuring Plate Fully Closed | 200-600 |
| Measuring Plate Fully Opened | 20-1000 |
| **Celica 3S-GTE & MR2 3S-GTE** | |
| $E_2$-Vs | |
| Measuring Plate Fully Closed | 200-600 |
| Measuring Plate Fully Open | 20-1200 |
| **Corolla 4A-GE** | |
| $E_2$-Vc | 100-300 |
| $E_2$-Vb | 200-400 |
| $E_1$-Fc | |
| Measuring Plate Fully Closed | No Continuity |
| Measuring Plate Other Than Closed | 0 |
| $E_2$-Vs | |
| Measuring Plate Fully Closed | 20-400 |
| Measuring Plate Fully Open | 20-3000 |
| **Cressida** | |
| $E_2$-Vc | 200-400 |
| $E_2$-Vb | |
| $E_1$-Fc | |
| Measuring Plate Fully Closed | No Continuity |
| Measuring Plate Open | 0 |
| $E_2$-Vs | |
| Fully Closed | 200-600 |
| Fully Open | 20-1200 |
| **Pickup & 4Runner** | |
| $E_2$-Vc | 100-300 |
| $E_2$-Vb | 200-400 |
| $E_1$-Fc | |
| Measuring Plate Fully Closed | No Continuity |
| Measuring Plate Fully Open | 0 |
| $E_2$-Vs | |
| Measuring Plate Fully Closed | 20-400 |
| Measuring Plate Fully Open | 20-1000 |
| **Previa** | |
| $E_2$-Vc | 200-4600 |
| $E_2$-Vs | |
| Measuring Plate Fully Closed | 200-600 |
| Measuring Plate Fully Open | 20-1200 |
| Fc-$E_1$ | |
| Measuring Plate Fully Closed | No Continuity |
| Measuring Plate Other Than Closed | 0 |
| **Supra Turbo** | |
| Ks-$E_1$ | No Continuity |
| $E_1$-Ks | 5000-10,000 |
| Vc-$E_1$ | 10,000-15,000 |
| $E_1$-Vc | 5000-10,000 |

[1] – See Fig. 5 in SYSTEM & COMPONENT TESTING article for terminal identification.

***NOTE: On Celica Non-Turbo, Corolla 4A-FE, MR2 5S-FE and Tercel, air temperature sensor is mounted on intake air box. On all other models, air temperature sensor is an integral part of airflow meter.***

### *AIR TEMPERATURE SENSOR RESISTANCE SPECIFICATIONS* [1]

| Application & Terminals | Ohms |
|---|---|
| **Except Celica Non-Turbo, Corolla 4A-FE, MR2 5S-FE & Tercel** | |
| $E_2$-THA | |
| -4°F (-20°C) | 10,000-20,000 |
| 32°F (0°C) | 4000-7000 |
| 68°F (20°C) | 2000-3000 |
| 104°F (40°C) | 900-1300 |
| 140°F (60°C) | 400-700 |

[1] – See Fig. 5 in SYSTEM & COMPONENT TESTING article for terminal identification.

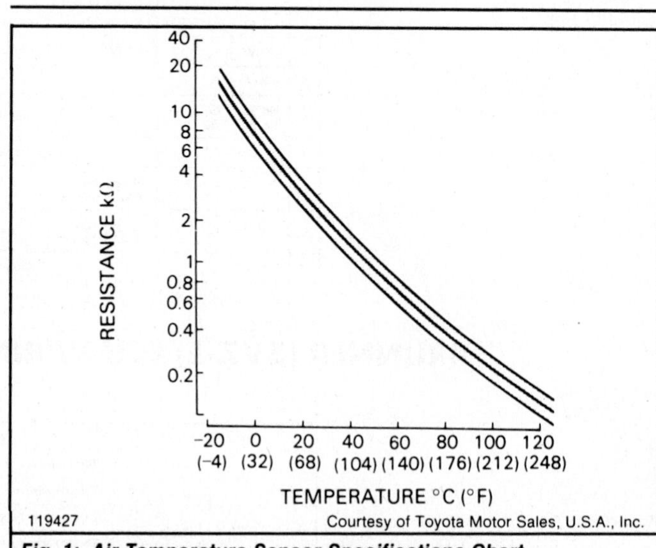


*Fig. 1: Air Temperature Sensor Specifications Chart (Celica Non-Turbo, Corolla 4A-FE, MR2 5S-FE & Tercel)*

### *COLD START INJECTOR RESISTANCE SPECIFICATIONS*

| Application | [1] Ohms |
|---|---|
| Corolla 4A-GE | 3.0-5.0 |
| Except Corolla 4A-GE | 2.0-4.0 |

[1] – Measure resistance between injector terminals.

### *COLD START INJECTOR TIME SWITCH RESISTANCE SPECIFICATIONS*

| Application & Terminals | Temperature °F (°C) | Ohms |
|---|---|---|
| **Camry, Previa & Supra** | | |
| STA-STJ | Less Than 59 (15) | 25-45 |
| | Greater Than 86 (30) | 65-85 |
| STA-Ground | | 25-85 |
| **Corolla & MR2 2.2L** | | |
| STA-STJ | Less Than 86 (30) | 20-40 |
| | Greater Than 104 (40) | 40-60 |
| STA-Ground | | 20-80 |
| **Celica, Land Cruiser, MR2 2.0L Pickup & 4Runner** | | |
| STA-STJ | Less Than 50 (10) | 30-50 |
| | Greater Than 77 (25) | 70-90 |
| STA-Ground | | 30-90 |

# 1991 ENGINE PERFORMANCE
## Sensor Operating Range Charts (Cont.)

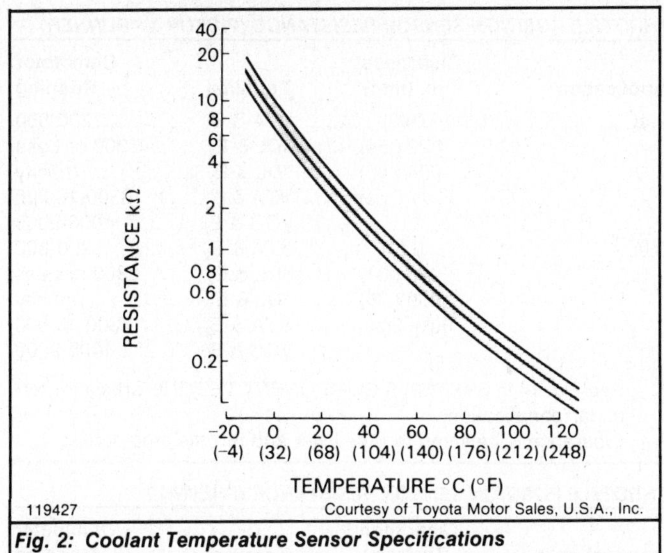


*Fig. 2: Coolant Temperature Sensor Specifications*

### *EGR GAS TEMPERATURE SENSOR SPECIFICATIONS (CALIF.)*

| Temperature °F (°C) | [1] Ohms |
|---|---|
| 122 (50) | 69-89 |
| 212 (100) | 12-14 |
| 302 (150) | 3-4 |

[1] – Measure resistance between sensor terminals.

### *FUEL INJECTOR RESISTOR SPECIFICATIONS*

| Application | [1] Ohms |
|---|---|
| Celica Turbo & MR2 Turbo | 2.0-4.0 |
| Pickup, Previa & 4Runner | 13.4-14.2 |
| Supra Turbo | 2.0-3.8 |
| All Others | 13.8 |

[1] – Measured across both terminals at 68°F (20°C).

### *ISC VALVE RESISTANCE SPECIFICATIONS*

| Application | Ohms |
|---|---|
| Camry | |
| 3S-FE [1] | 16-17 |
| 2VZ-FE [2] | 10-30 |
| Celica & MR2 | |
| 3S-GTE [3] | 18-24 |
| 5S-FE [4] | 19-22 |
| Cressida, Land Cruiser & Supra [2] | 10-30 |
| Previa [1] | 19-23 |

[1] – Measure resistance between terminals +B and ISC1, and between ISC2 and +B of ISC valve connector.
[2] – Measure resistance between terminals $B_1$ to $S_1$ or $S_3$ and terminals $B_2$ to $S_2$ or $S_4$.
[3] – Measure resistance between terminals +B to RSC or RSO.
[4] – Measure resistance between terminals +B to ISCC or ISCO.

### *MAP SENSOR VACUUM/VOLTAGE SPECIFICATIONS (Celica Non-Turbo, Corolla 4A-FE, MR2 5S-FE & Tercel)*

| Vacuum In. Hg | [1] Voltage Drop |
|---|---|
| 3.94 | .3-.5 |
| 7.87 | .7-.9 |
| 11.81 | 1.1-1.3 |
| 15.75 | 1.5-1.7 |
| 19.69 | 1.9-2.1 |

[1] – Measure voltage between back side of terminals E2 and PIM of ECU connector.

### *OXYGEN SENSOR HEATER RESISTANCE SPECIFICATIONS*

| Application | Condition | Ohms |
|---|---|---|
| Corolla 4A-GE [1] | | |
| Federal | 68°F (20°C) | 4.95-6.05 |
| California | 68°F (20°C) | 5.1-6.3 |
| Supra 7M-GTE [2] | 68°F (20°C) | 3.0-3.6 |
| All Others [1] | 68°F (20°C) | 5.1-6.3 |

[1] – Measure resistance between terminals B+ and HT.
[2] – Measure resistance between sensor terminals No. 2 and 3.

### *THROTTLE POSITION SENSOR RESISTANCE (CAMRY)* [1]

| Application | Clearance [2] In. (mm) | Terminal | Ohmmeter Reading |
|---|---|---|---|
| 2.0L W/O ECT | .020 (.51) | IDL & $E_1$ | Continuity |
| | | PSW & $E_1$ | No Continuity |
| | .035 (.90) | IDL & $E_1$ | No Continuity |
| | | PSW & $E_1$ | No Continuity |
| | Fully Open | IDL & $E_1$ | No Continuity |
| | | PSW & $E_1$ | Continuity |
| 2.0L W/ECT | 0 (0) | VTA & $E_2$ | 200-800 |
| | .020 (.51) | IDL & $E_2$ | 2300 or Less |
| | .028 (.70) | IDL & $E_2$ | Infinity |
| | Fully Open | VAT & $E_2$ | 3300-10,000 |
| | | VC & $E_2$ | 3000-7000 |
| 2.5L | 0 (0) | VTA & $E_2$ | 300-6300 |
| | .012 (.30) | IDL & $E_2$ | 2300 or Less |
| | .028 (.71) | IDL & $E_2$ | Infinity |
| | Fully Open | VTA & $E_2$ | 3500-10,300 |
| | | VC & $E_2$ | 4250-8250 |

[1] – See Fig. 14 in SYSTEM & COMPONENT TESTING article for terminal identification.
[2] – Clearance is between throttle lever and throttle stop screw.

### *THROTTLE POSITION SENSOR RESISTANCE (CELICA)* [1]

| Application | Clearance [2] In. (mm) | Terminal | Ohmmeter Reading |
|---|---|---|---|
| 1.6L | .024 (.60) | IDL-$E_2$ | Continuity |
| | | PSW-$E_2$ | No Continuity |
| | .031 (.80) | IDL-$E_2$ | No Continuity |
| | | PSW-$E_2$ | No Continuity |
| | Fully Open | IDL-$E_2$ | No Continuity |
| | | PSW-$E_2$ | Continuity |
| 2.0L | 0 (0) | VTA & $E_2$ | 200-800 |
| | .020 (.51) | IDL & $E_2$ | 2300 or Less |
| | .028 (.71) | IDL & $E_2$ | Infinity |
| | Fully Open | VTA & $E_2$ | 3300-10,300 |
| | | VC & $E_2$ | 3000-8300 |
| 2.2L W/O ECT | .020 (.50) | IDL-$E_2$ | Continuity |
| | | PSW-$E_2$ | No Continuity |
| | .035 (.90) | IDL-$E_2$ | No Continuity |
| | | PSW-$E_2$ | No Continuity |
| | Fully Open | IDL-$E_2$ | No Continuity |
| | | PSW-$E_2$ | Continuity |
| 2.2L W/ECT | 0 (0) | VTA & $E_2$ | 200-800 |
| | .020 (.51) | IDL & $E_2$ | 2300 or Less |
| | .028 (.71) | IDL & $E_2$ | Infinity |
| | Fully Open | VTA & $E_2$ | 3300-10,000 |
| | | VC & $E_2$ | 3000-7000 |

[1] – See Fig. 14 in SYSTEM & COMPONENT TESTING article for terminal identification.
[2] – Clearance is between throttle lever and throttle stop screw.

# 1991 ENGINE PERFORMANCE
## Sensor Operating Range Charts (Cont.)

### *THROTTLE POSITION SENSOR RESISTANCE (COROLLA)* [1]

| Application | Clearance [2] In. (mm) | Terminal | Ohmmeter Reading |
|---|---|---|---|
| 4A-FE | .024 (.60) | IDL-$E_2$ | Continuity |
| | | PSW-$E_2$ | No Continuity |
| | | IDL-PSW | No Continuity |
| | .032 (.80) | IDL-$E_2$ | No Continuity |
| | | PSW-$E_2$ | No Continuity |
| | | IDL-PSW | No Continuity |
| | Fully Open | IDL-$E_2$ | No Continuity |
| | | PSW-$E_2$ | Continuity |
| | | IDL-PSW | No Continuity |
| 4A-GE | 0 (0) | VTA & $E_2$ | 200-800 |
| | .014 (.36) | IDL & $E_2$ | 2300 or Less |
| | .023 (.58) | IDL & $E_2$ | Infinity |
| | Fully Open | VTA & $E_2$ | 3300-10,000 |
| | | VCC & $E_2$ | 3000-7000 |

[1] – See Fig. 14 in SYSTEM & COMPONENT TESTING article for terminal identification.
[2] – Clearance is between throttle lever and throttle stop screw.

### *THROTTLE POSITION SENSOR RESISTANCE (CRESSIDA)* [1]

| Application | Clearance [2] In. (mm) | Terminal | Ohmmeter Reading |
|---|---|---|---|
| 3.0L | 0 (0) | VTA & $E_2$ | 300-6300 |
| | .020 (.51) | IDL & $E_2$ | 2300 or Less |
| | .035 (.89) | IDL & $E_2$ | Infinity |
| | Fully Open | VTA & $E_2$ | 3500-10,300 |
| | | VC & $E_2$ | 4250-8250 |

[1] – See Fig. 14 in SYSTEM & COMPONENT TESTING article for terminal identification.
[2] – Clearance is between throttle lever and throttle stop screw.

### *THROTTLE POSITION SENSOR RESISTANCE (LAND CRUISER)* [1]

| Application | Clearance [2] In. (mm) | Terminal | Ohmmeter Reading |
|---|---|---|---|
| 4.0L | 0 (0) | VTA & $E_2$ | 300-6300 |
| | .030 (.76) | IDL & $E_2$ | 2300 or Less |
| | .043 (1.09) | IDL & $E_2$ | Infinity |
| | Fully Open | VTA & $E_2$ | 3500-10,300 |
| | | VC & $E_2$ | 4250-8250 |

[1] – See Fig. 14 in SYSTEM & COMPONENT TESTING article for terminal identification.
[2] – Clearance is between throttle lever and throttle stop screw.

### *THROTTLE POSITION SENSOR RESISTANCE (MR2)* [1]

| Application | Clearance [2] In. (mm) | Terminal | Ohmmeter Reading |
|---|---|---|---|
| 2.0L & 2.2L A/T | 0 (0) | VTA & $E_2$ | 200-800 |
| | .020 (.51) | IDL & $E_2$ | 2300 or Less |
| | .028 (.71) | IDL & $E_2$ | Infinity |
| | Fully Open | VTA & $E_2$ | 3300-10,300 |
| | | VC & $E_2$ | 3000-8300 |
| 2.2L M/T | .020 (.50) | IDL-$E_1$ | Continuity |
| | | PSW-$E_1$ | No Continuity |
| | .035 (.90) | IDL-$E_1$ | No Continuity |
| | | PSW-$E_1$ | No Continuity |
| | Fully Open | IDL-$E_1$ | No Continuity |
| | | PSW-$E_1$ | Continuity |

[1] – See Fig. 14 in SYSTEM & COMPONENT TESTING article for terminal identification.
[2] – Clearance is between throttle lever and throttle stop screw.

### *THROTTLE POSITION SENSOR RESISTANCE (PICKUP & 4RUNNER)* [1]

| Application | Clearance [2] In. (mm) | Terminal | Ohmmeter Reading |
|---|---|---|---|
| 2.4L | 0 (0) | VTA & $E_2$ | 200-800 |
| | .022 (.56) | IDL & $E_2$ | 2300 or Less |
| | .034 (.86) | IDL & $E_2$ | Infinity |
| | Fully Open | VTA & $E_2$ | 3300-10,000 |
| | | VCC & $E_2$ | 4000-9000 |
| 3.0L | 0 (0) | VTA & $E_2$ | 200-800 |
| | .020 (.51) | IDL & $E_2$ | 2300 or Less |
| | .030 (.76) | IDL & $E_2$ | Infinity |
| | Fully Open | VTA & $E_2$ | 3300-10,000 |
| | | VCC & $E_2$ | 4000-9000 |

[1] – See Fig. 14 in SYSTEM & COMPONENT TESTING article for terminal identification.
[2] – Clearance is between throttle lever and throttle stop screw.

### *THROTTLE POSITION SENSOR RESISTANCE (PREVIA)* [1]

| Application | Clearance [2] In. (mm) | Terminal | Ohmmeter Reading |
|---|---|---|---|
| 2.4L | 0 (0) | VTA & $E_2$ | 300-6300 |
| | .014 (.36) | IDL & $E_2$ | 2300 or Less |
| | .023 (.58) | IDL & $E_2$ | Infinity |
| | Fully Open | VTA & $E_2$ | 3500-10,3000 |
| | | VCC & $E_2$ | 425-825 |

[1] – See Fig. 14 in SYSTEM & COMPONENT TESTING article for terminal identification.
[2] – Clearance is between throttle lever and throttle stop screw.

### *THROTTLE POSITION SENSOR RESISTANCE (SUPRA)* [1]

| Application | Clearance [2] In. (mm) | Terminal | Ohmmeter Reading |
|---|---|---|---|
| 3.0L | | | |
| Non-Turbo | 0 (0) | VTA & $E_2$ | 200-1200 |
| | .016 (.41) | IDL & $E_2$ | 2300 or Less |
| | .030 (.76) | IDL & $E_2$ | Infinity |
| | Fully Open | VTA & $E_2$ | 3500-10,300 |
| | | VC & $E_2$ | 4250-8250 |
| Turbo | 0 (0) | VTA & $E_2$ | 200-1200 |
| | .020 (.51) | IDL & $E_2$ | 2300 or Less |
| | .035 (.89) | IDL & $E_2$ | Infinity |
| | Fully Open | VTA & $E_2$ | 3500-10,300 |
| | | VC & $E_2$ | 4250-8250 |

[1] – See Fig. 14 in SYSTEM & COMPONENT TESTING article for terminal identification.
[2] – Clearance is between throttle lever and throttle stop screw.

### *THROTTLE POSITION SENSOR RESISTANCE (TERCEL)* [1]

| Application | Clearance [2] In. (mm) | Terminal | Ohmmeter Reading |
|---|---|---|---|
| 1.5L | .024 (.60) | IDL & $E_2$ | Continuity |
| | .024 (.60) | PSW & $E_2$ | No Continuity |
| | .024 (.60) | PSW & IDL | No Continuity |
| | .032 (.80) | IDL & $E_2$ | No Continuity |
| | .032 (.80) | PSW & $E_2$ | No Continuity |
| | .032 (.80) | PSW & IDL | No Continuity |
| | Fully Open | IDL & $E_2$ | No Continuity |
| | | PSW & $E_2$ | Continuity |
| | | PSW & IDL | No Continuity |

[1] – See Fig. 14 in SYSTEM & COMPONENT TESTING article for terminal identification.
[2] – Clearance is between throttle lever and throttle stop screw.

# 1991 ENGINE PERFORMANCE
# Sensor Operating Range Charts (Cont.)

*TURBO PRESSURE SENSOR VACUUM/VOLTAGE SPECIFICATIONS*

| Applied Vacuum In. Hg | [1] Volts |
|---|---|
| 3.94 | .15-.35 |
| 7.87 | .40-.60 |
| 11.81 | .65-.85 |
| 15.75 | .90-1.10 |
| 19.69 | 1.15-1.35 |

[1] – Measure voltage between ECU connector terminals PIM and E2 (pressure sensor).

# 1991 ENGINE PERFORMANCE
## Wiring Diagrams

**Camry, Celica, Corolla, Cressida, Land Cruiser, MR2, Pickup, Previa, Supra, Tercel, 4Runner**

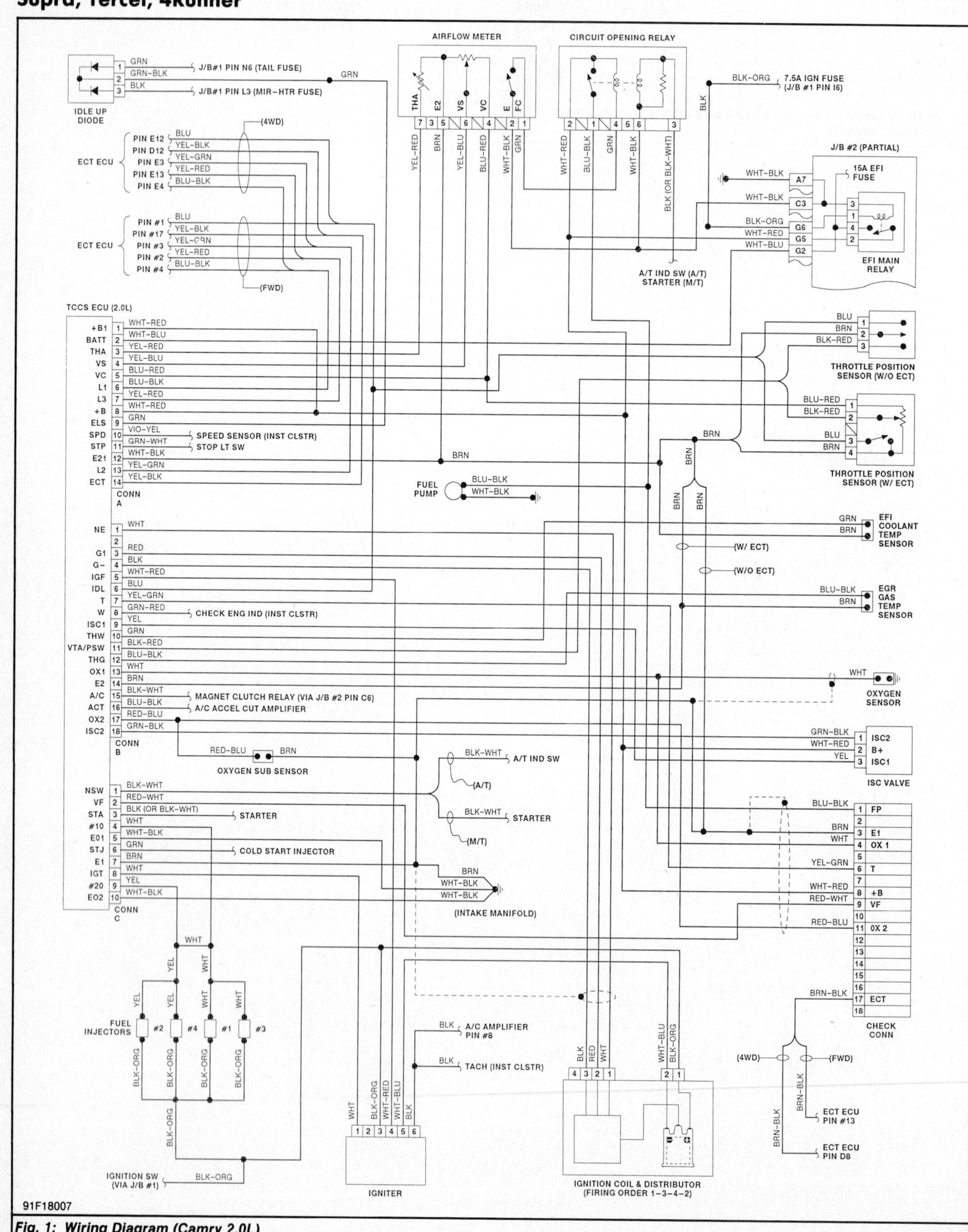


*Fig. 1: Wiring Diagram (Camry 2.0L)*

# 1991 ENGINE PERFORMANCE
## Wiring Diagrams (Cont.)

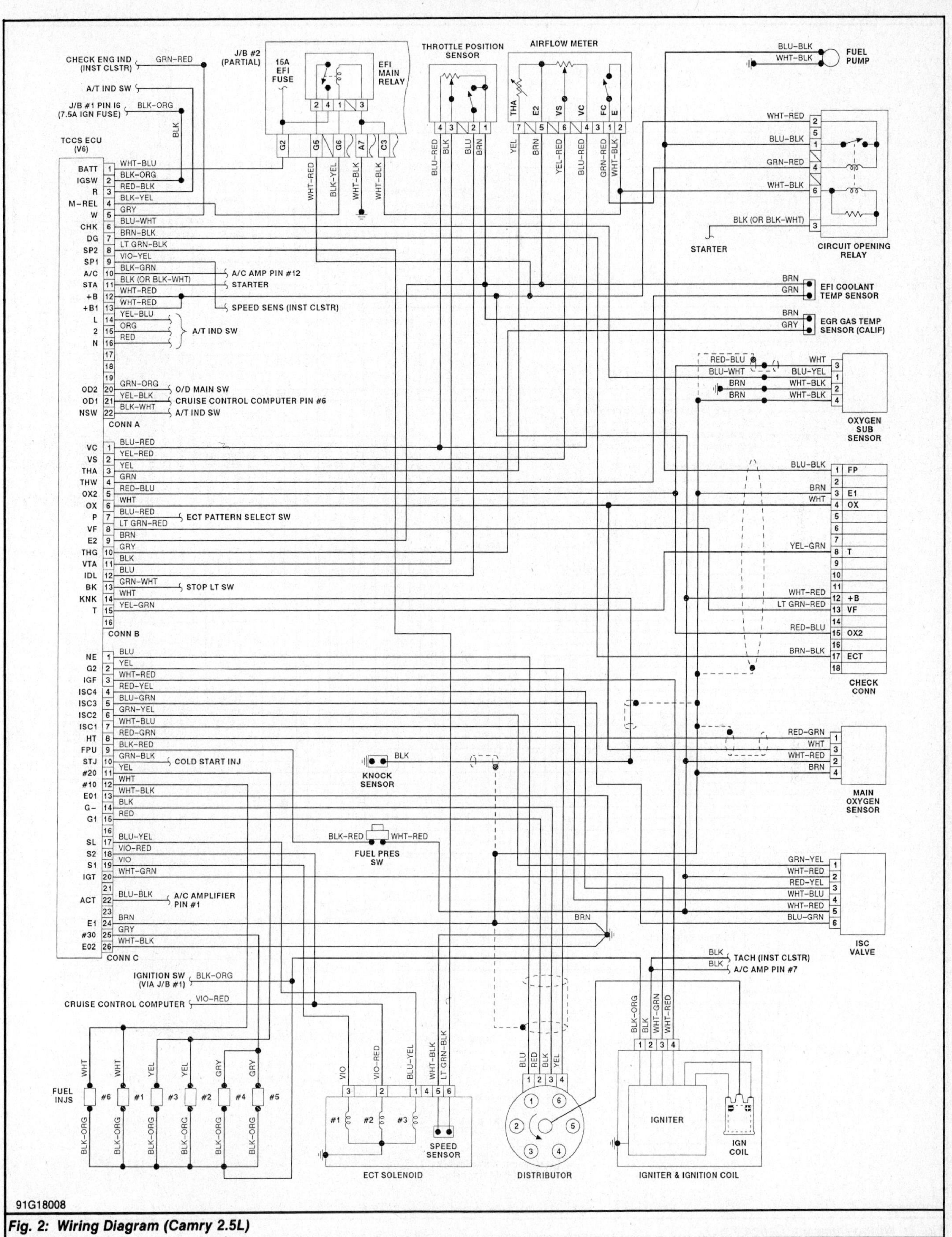


*Fig. 2: Wiring Diagram (Camry 2.5L)*

# 1991 ENGINE PERFORMANCE
## Wiring Diagrams (Cont.)

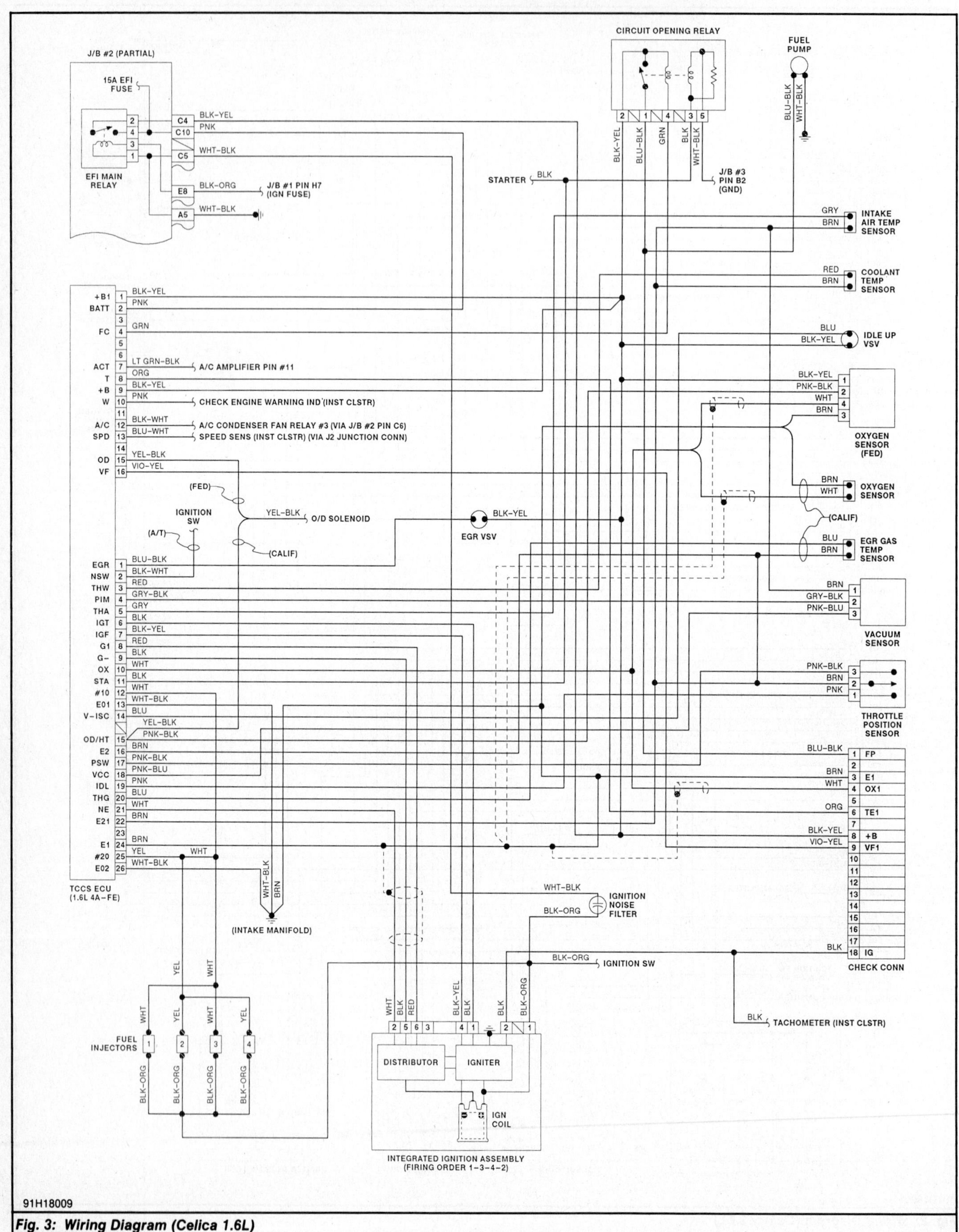


**Fig. 3: Wiring Diagram (Celica 1.6L)**

# 1991 ENGINE PERFORMANCE
## Wiring Diagrams (Cont.)

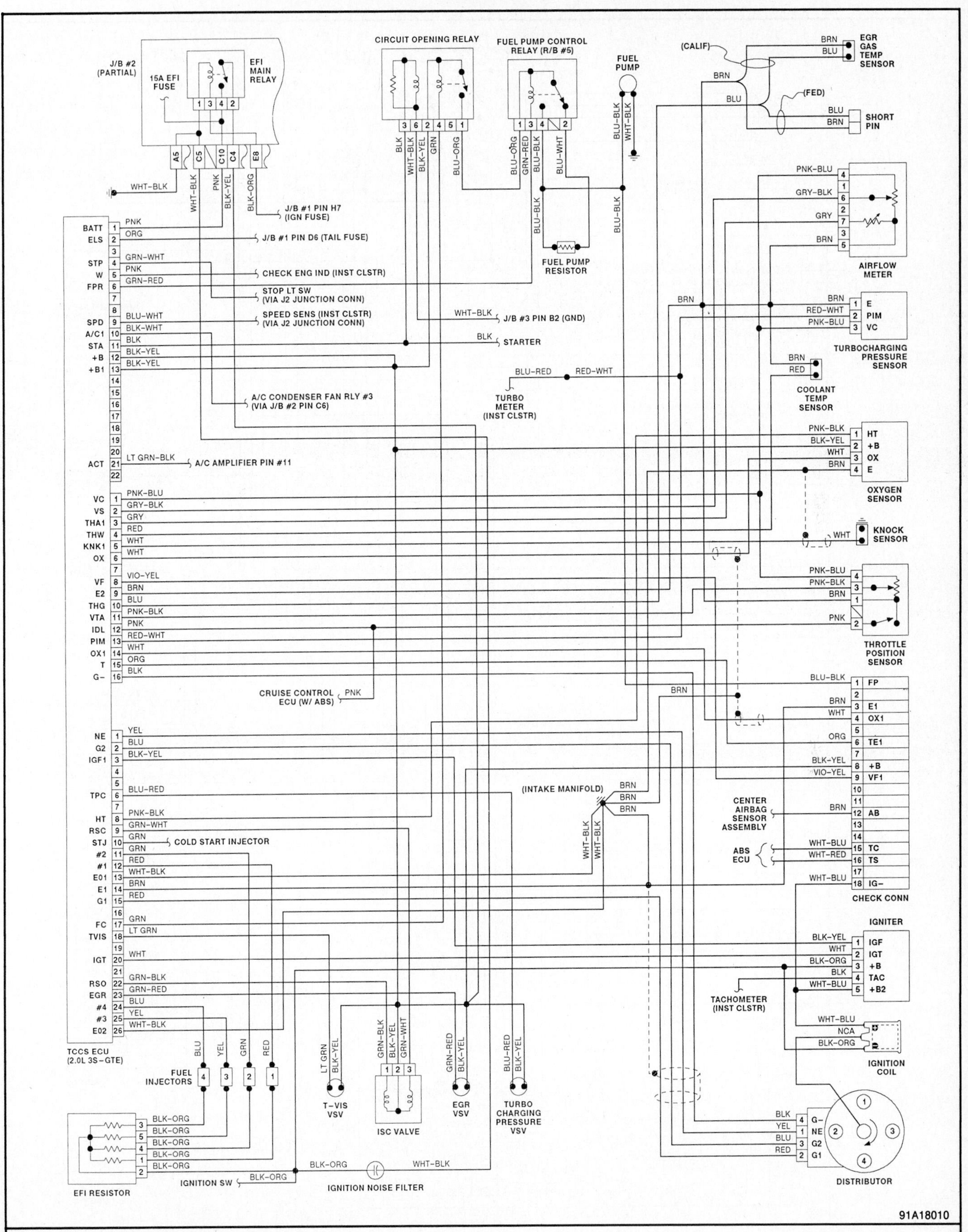


Fig. 4: Wiring Diagram (Celica 2.0L Turbo)

# 1991 ENGINE PERFORMANCE
## Wiring Diagrams (Cont.)

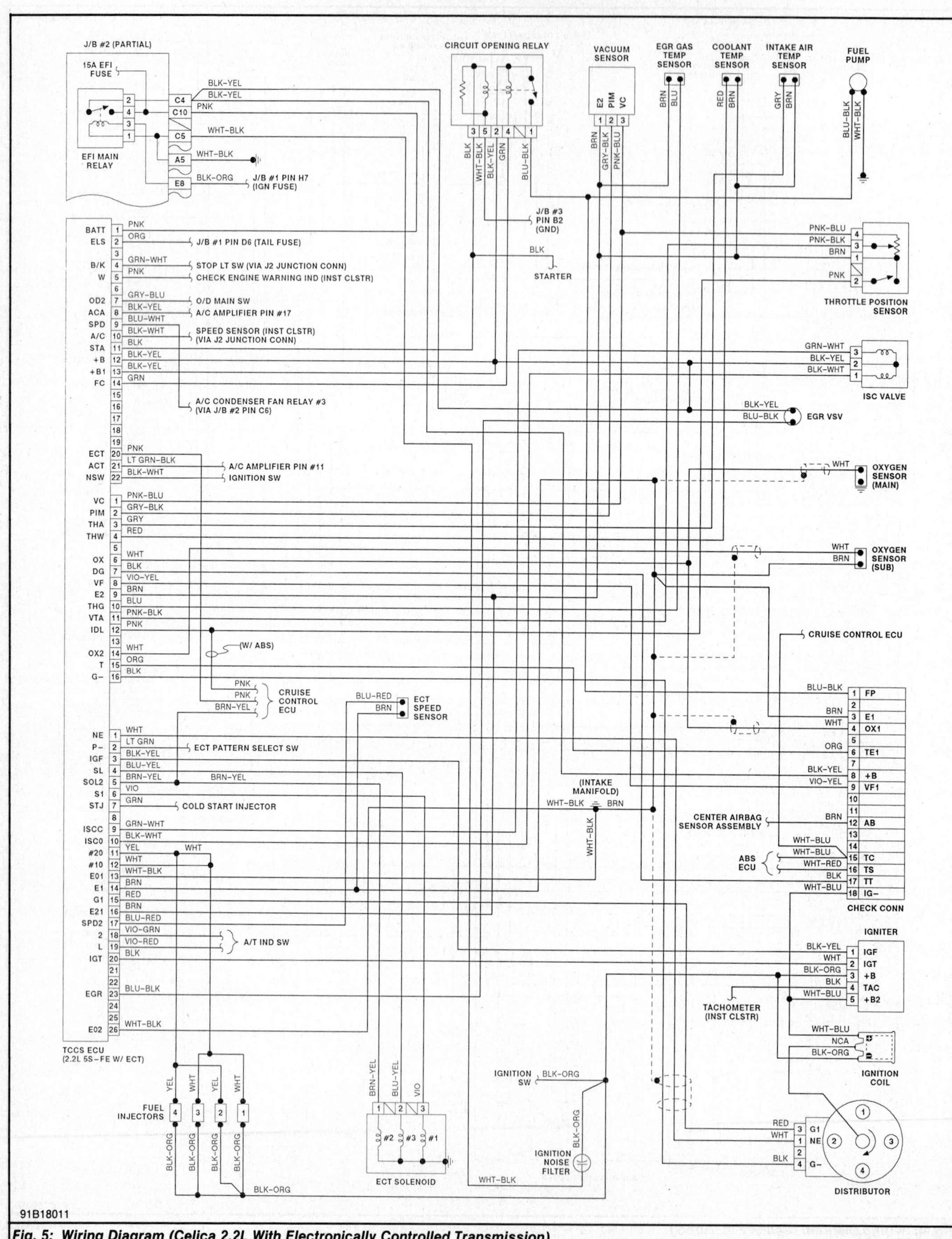


*Fig. 5: Wiring Diagram (Celica 2.2L With Electronically Controlled Transmission)*

# 1991 ENGINE PERFORMANCE
## Wiring Diagrams (Cont.)

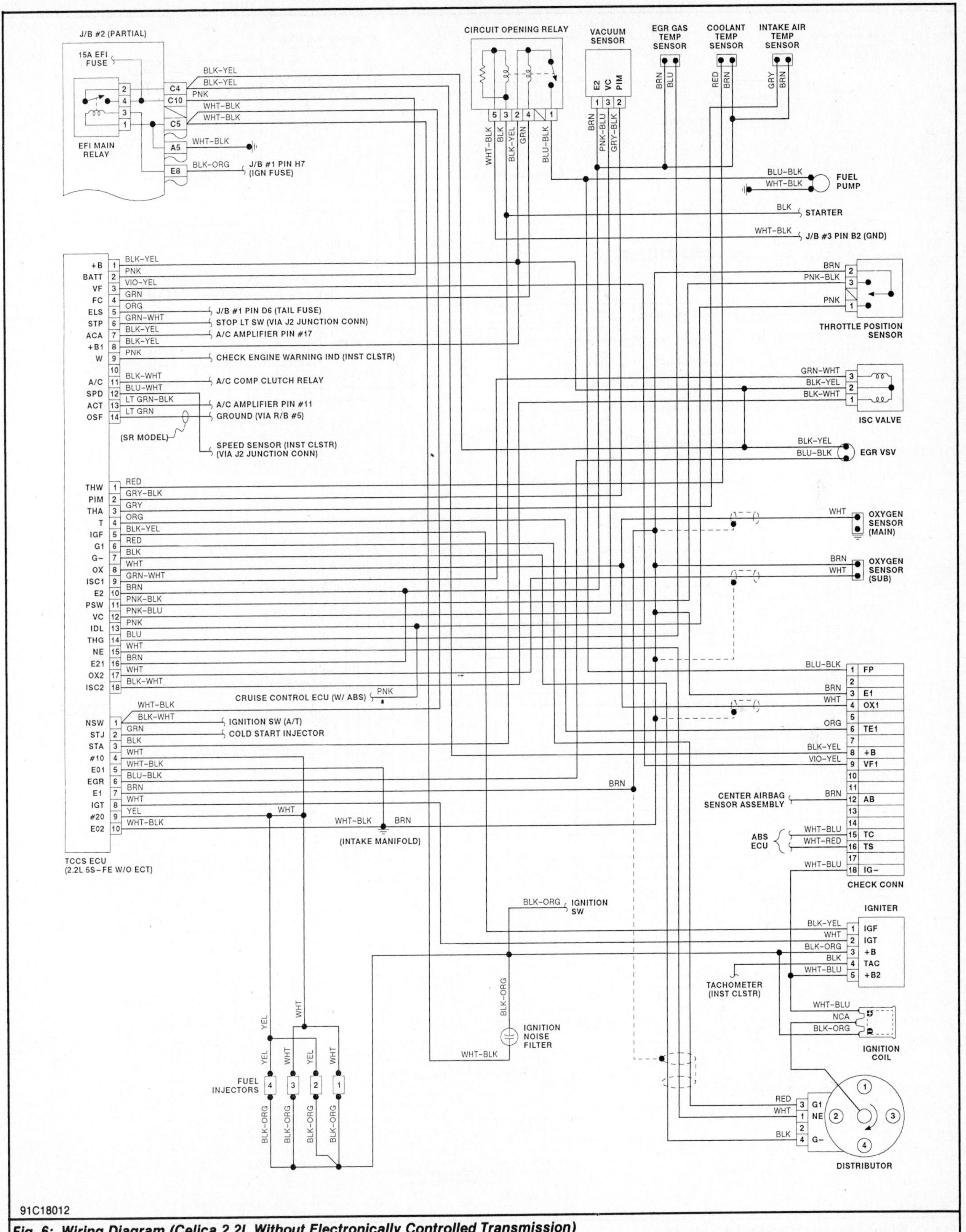


*Fig. 6: Wiring Diagram (Celica 2.2L Without Electronically Controlled Transmission)*

# 1991 ENGINE PERFORMANCE
## Wiring Diagrams (Cont.)

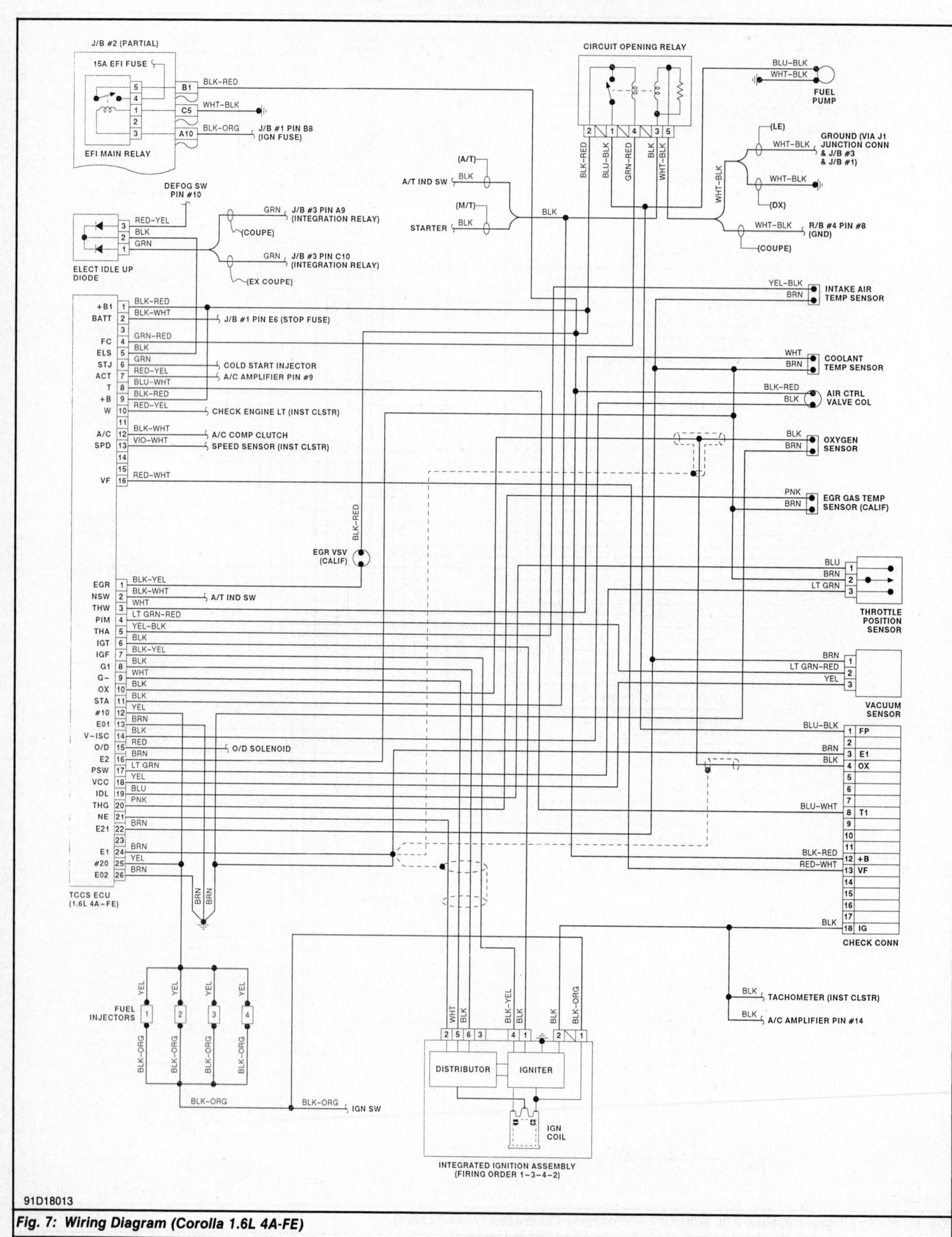


*Fig. 7: Wiring Diagram (Corolla 1.6L 4A-FE)*

# 1991 ENGINE PERFORMANCE
## Wiring Diagrams (Cont.)

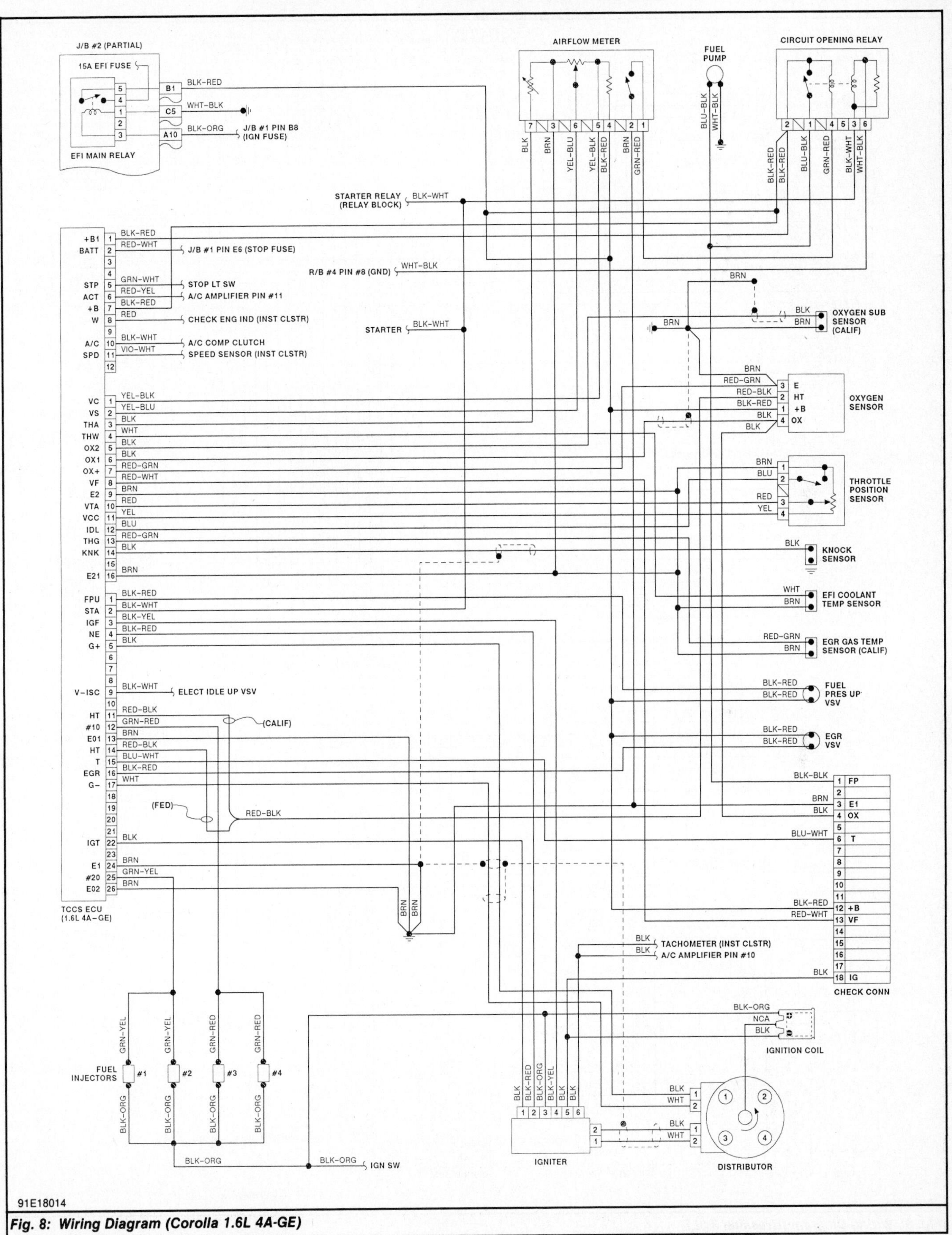


*Fig. 8: Wiring Diagram (Corolla 1.6L 4A-GE)*

# 1991 ENGINE PERFORMANCE
## Wiring Diagrams (Cont.)

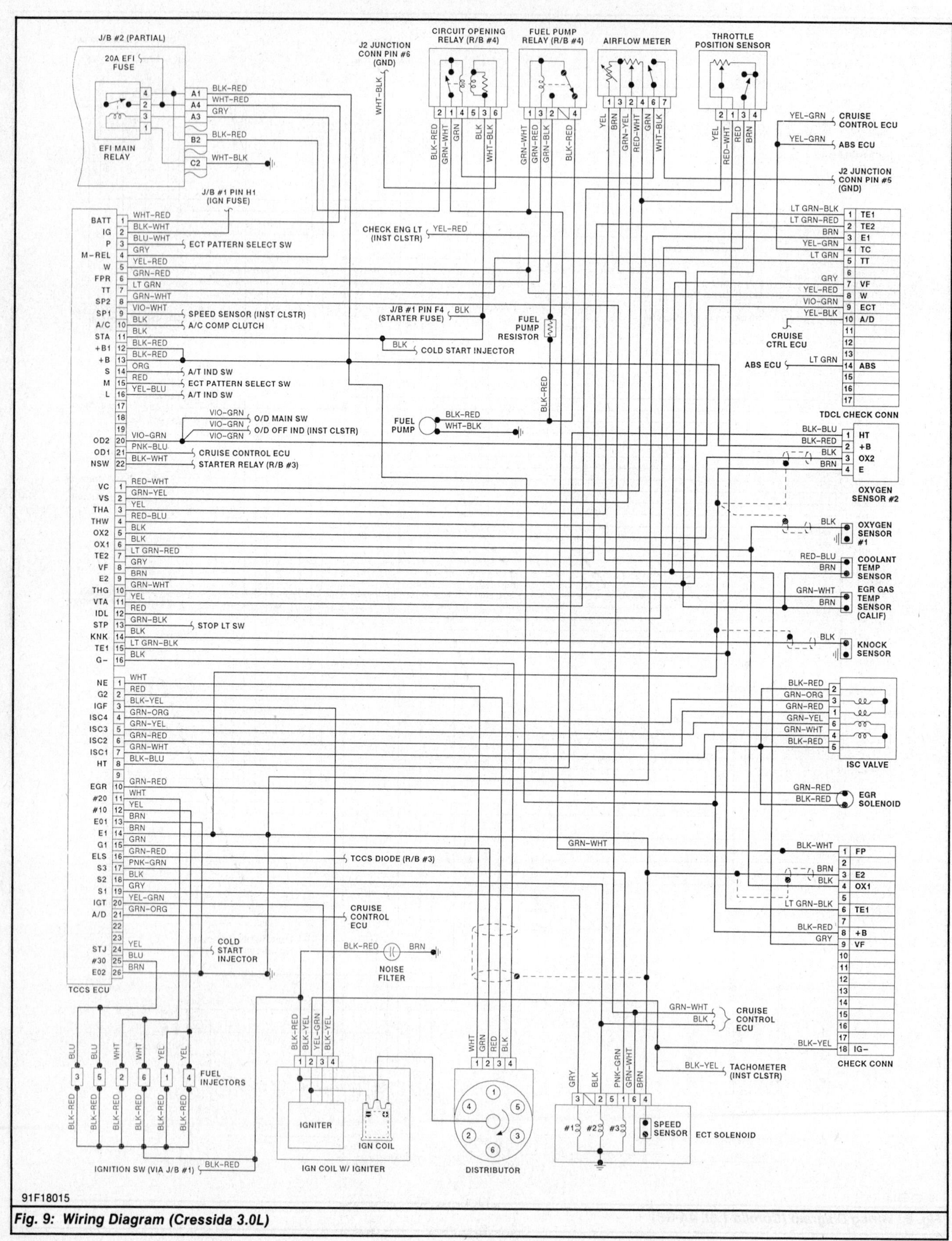

91F18015

*Fig. 9: Wiring Diagram (Cressida 3.0L)*

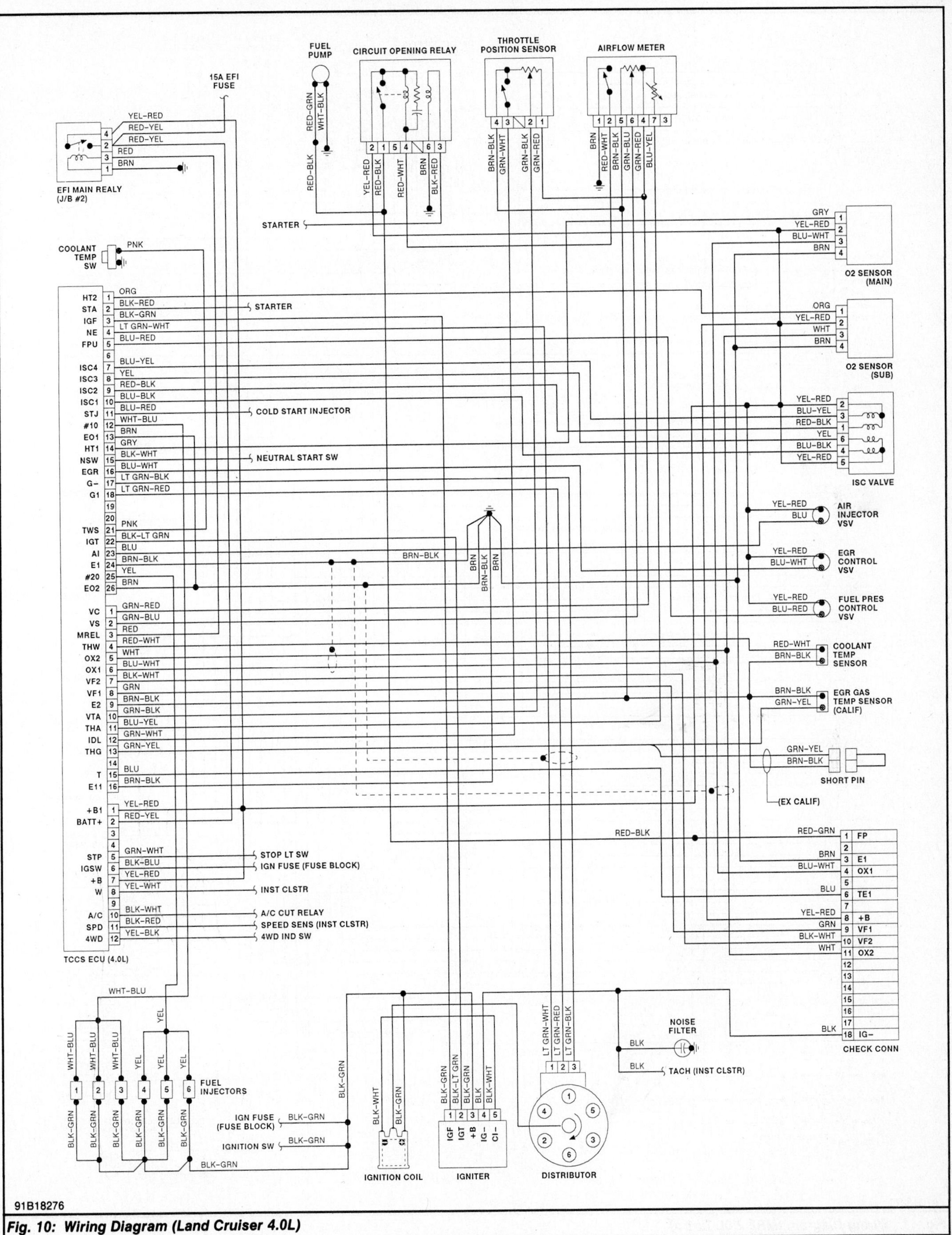


*Fig. 10: Wiring Diagram (Land Cruiser 4.0L)*

# 1991 ENGINE PERFORMANCE
## Wiring Diagrams (Cont.)

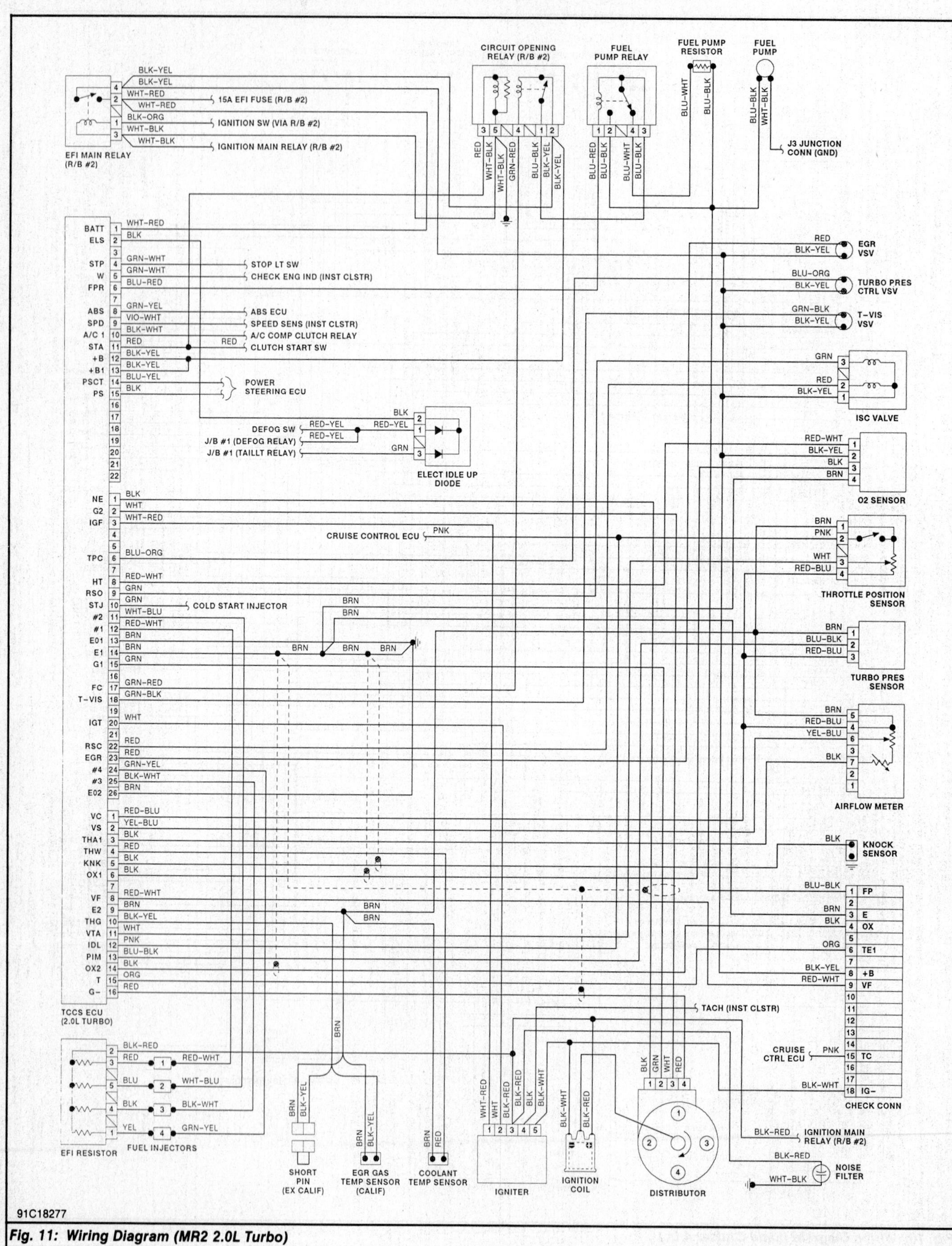


*Fig. 11: Wiring Diagram (MR2 2.0L Turbo)*

# 1991 ENGINE PERFORMANCE
## Wiring Diagrams (Cont.)

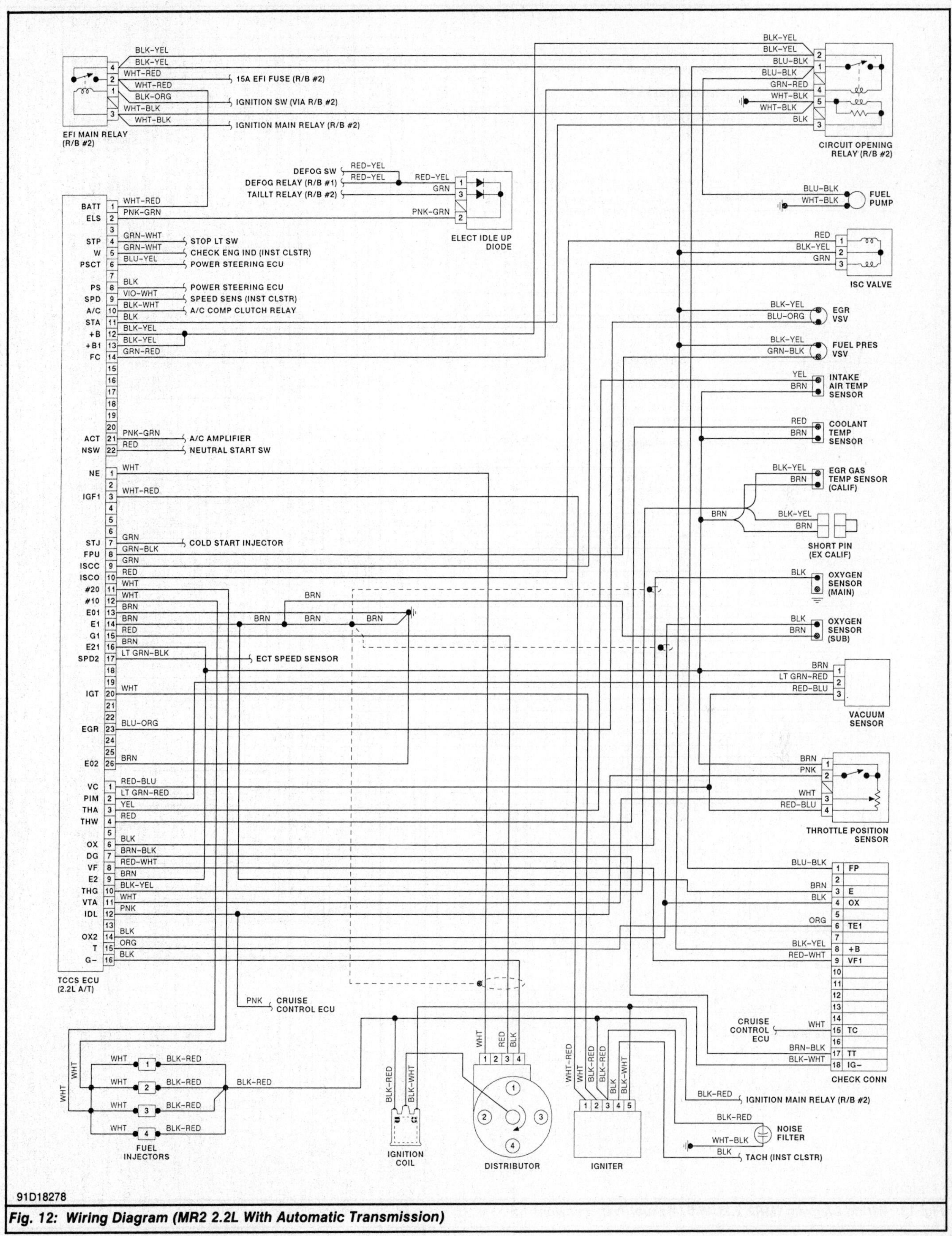


*Fig. 12: Wiring Diagram (MR2 2.2L With Automatic Transmission)*

# 1991 ENGINE PERFORMANCE
## Wiring Diagrams (Cont.)

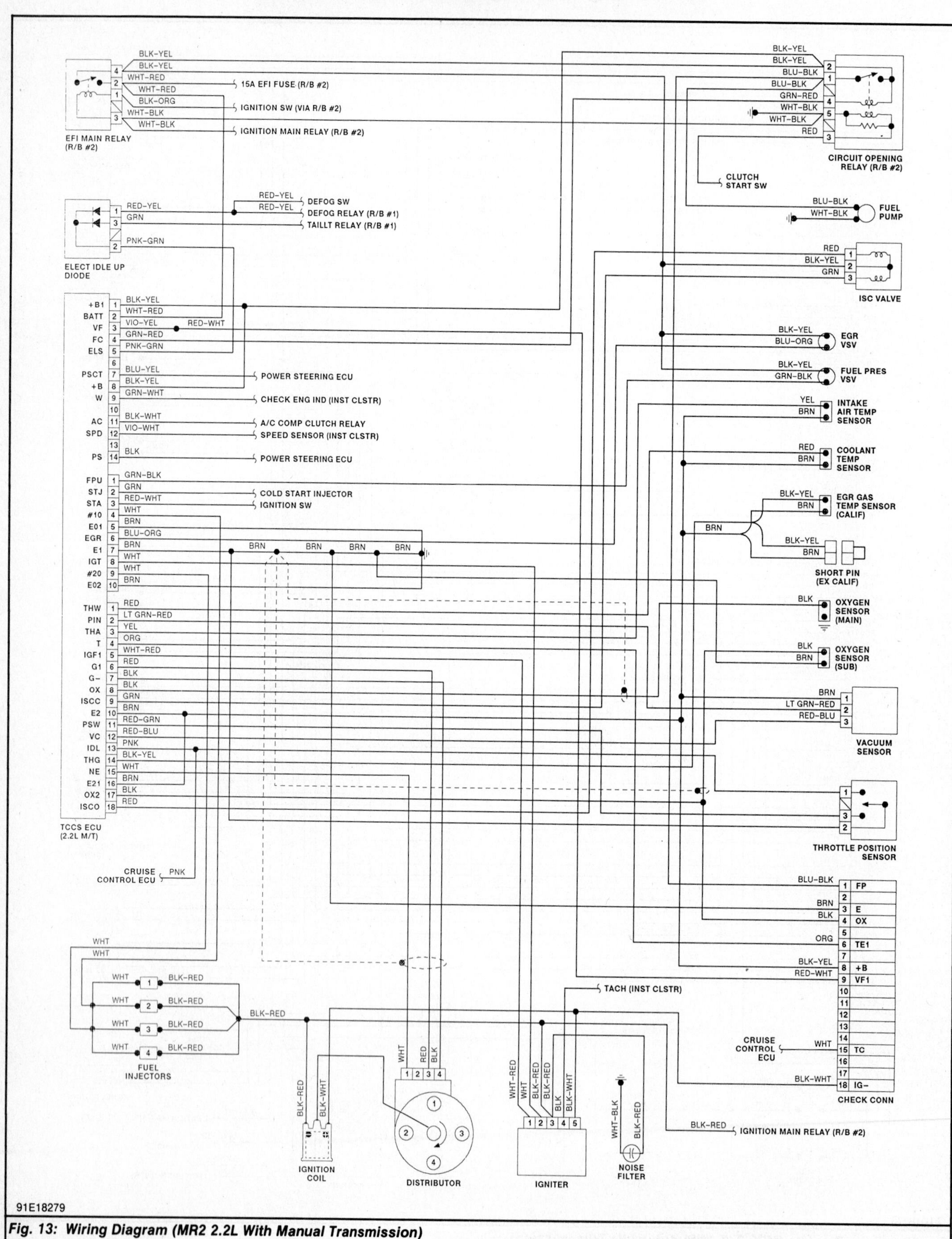


*Fig. 13: Wiring Diagram (MR2 2.2L With Manual Transmission)*

# 1991 ENGINE PERFORMANCE
# Wiring Diagrams (Cont.)

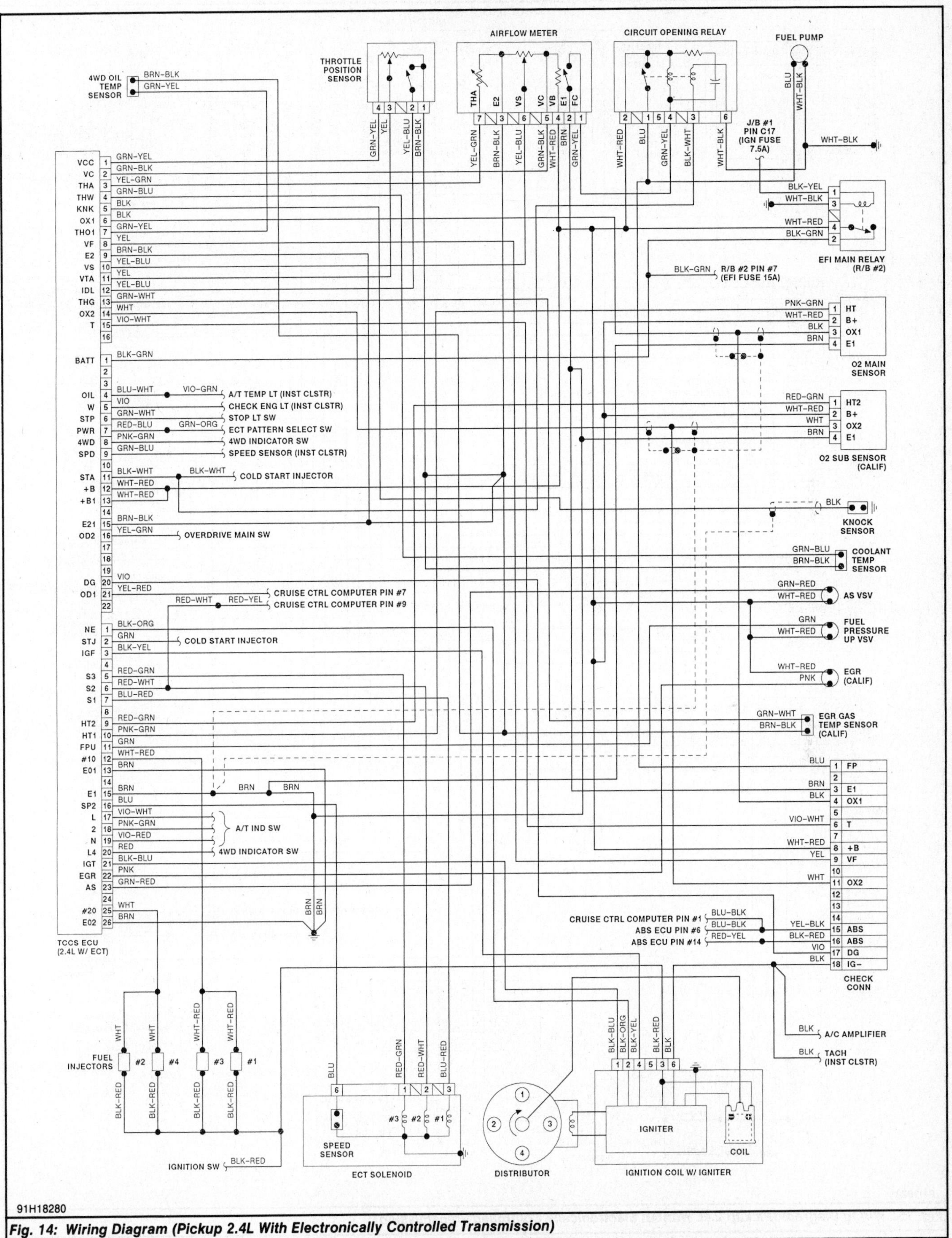


*Fig. 14: Wiring Diagram (Pickup 2.4L With Electronically Controlled Transmission)*

# 1991 ENGINE PERFORMANCE
## Wiring Diagrams (Cont.)

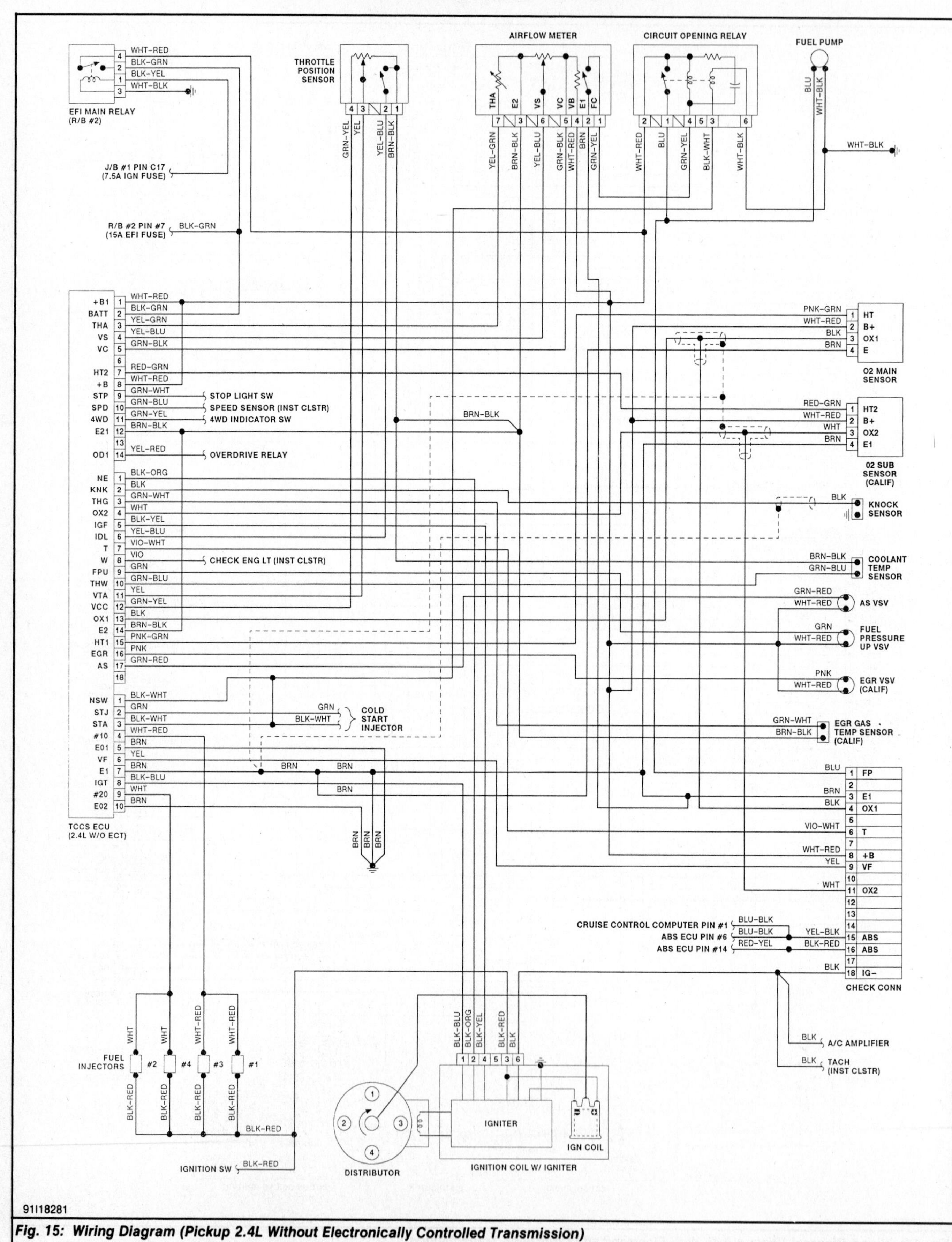


*Fig. 15: Wiring Diagram (Pickup 2.4L Without Electronically Controlled Transmission)*

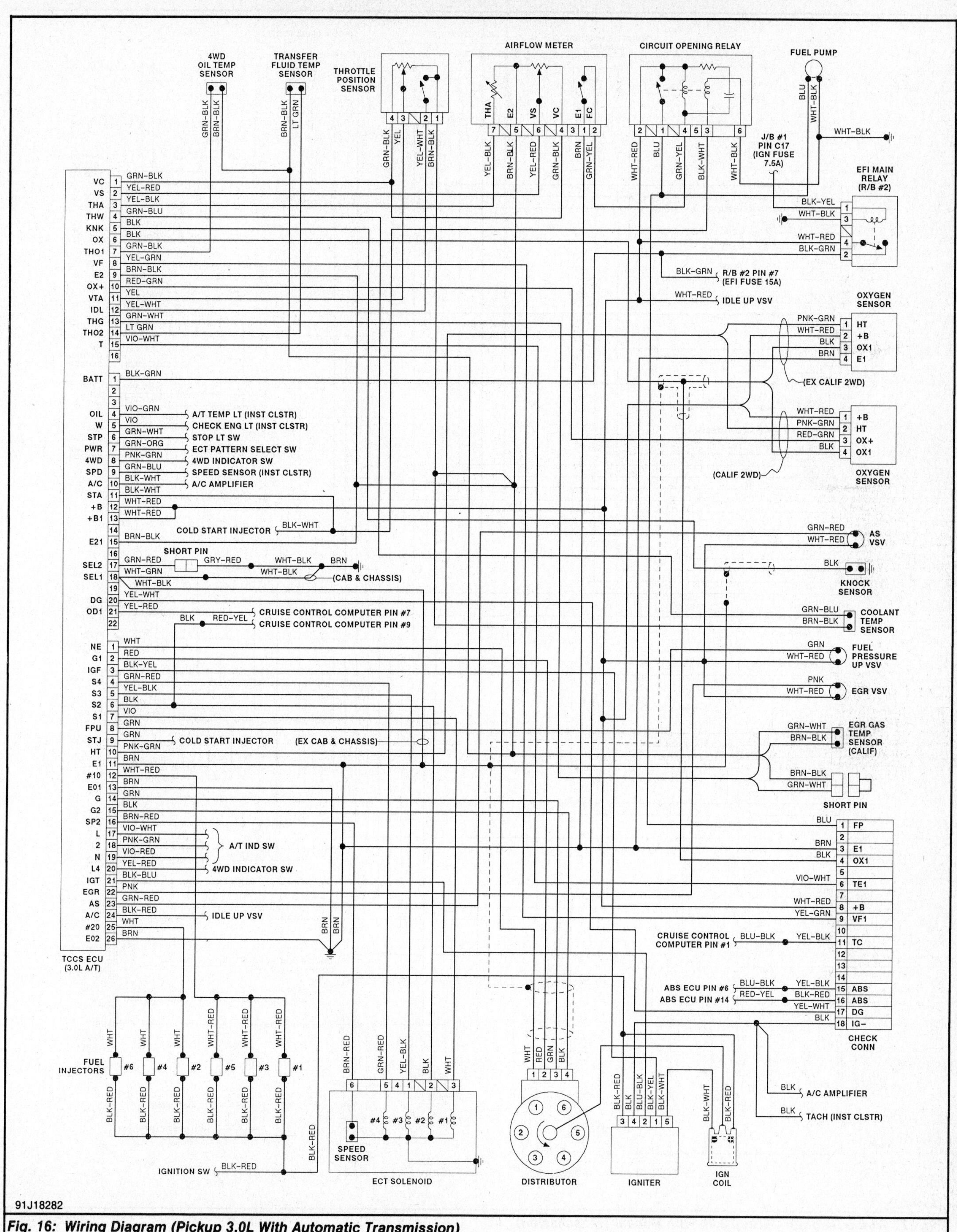


Fig. 16: Wiring Diagram (Pickup 3.0L With Automatic Transmission)

# 1991 ENGINE PERFORMANCE
## Wiring Diagrams (Cont.)

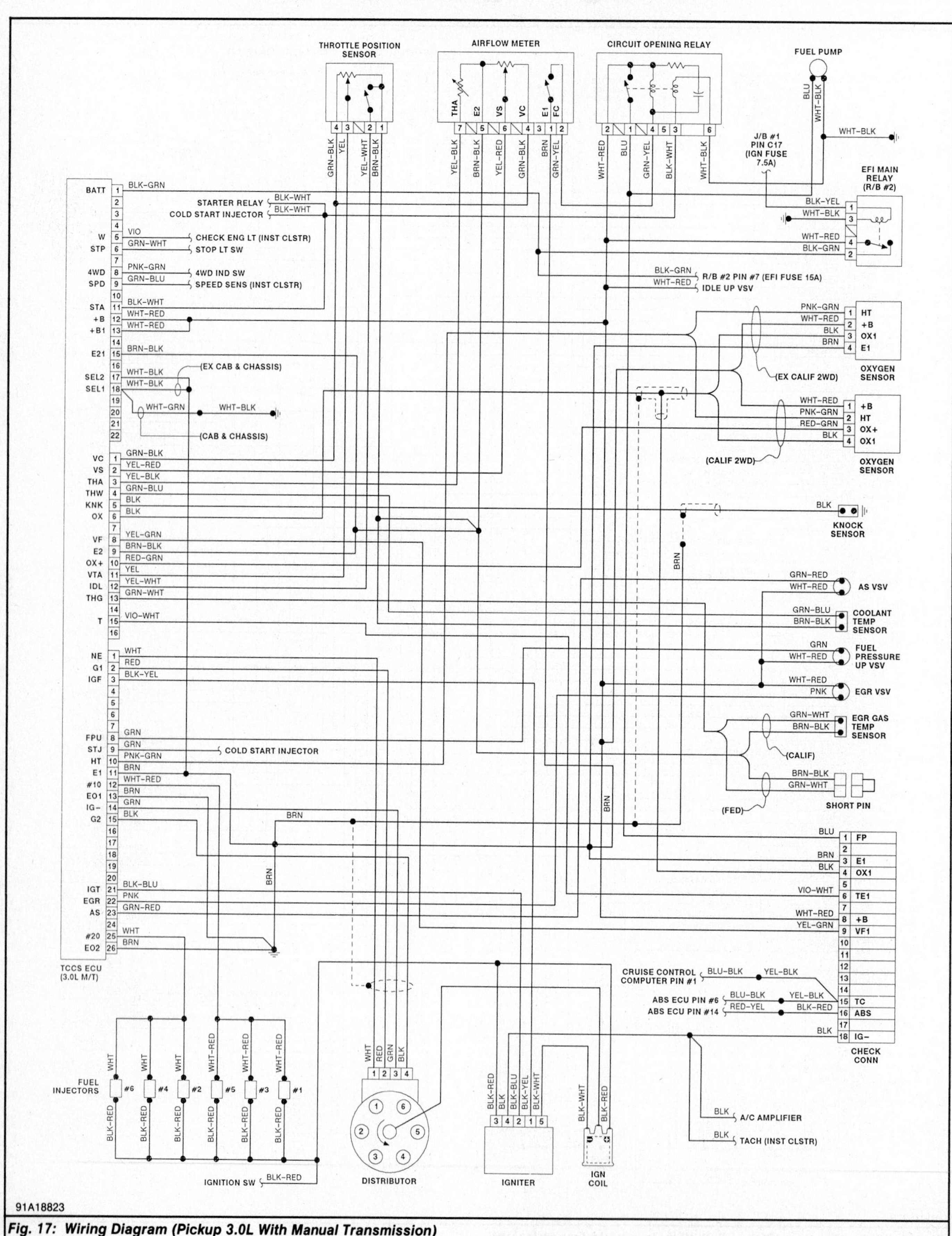

91A18823

*Fig. 17: Wiring Diagram (Pickup 3.0L With Manual Transmission)*

# 1991 ENGINE PERFORMANCE
## Wiring Diagrams (Cont.)

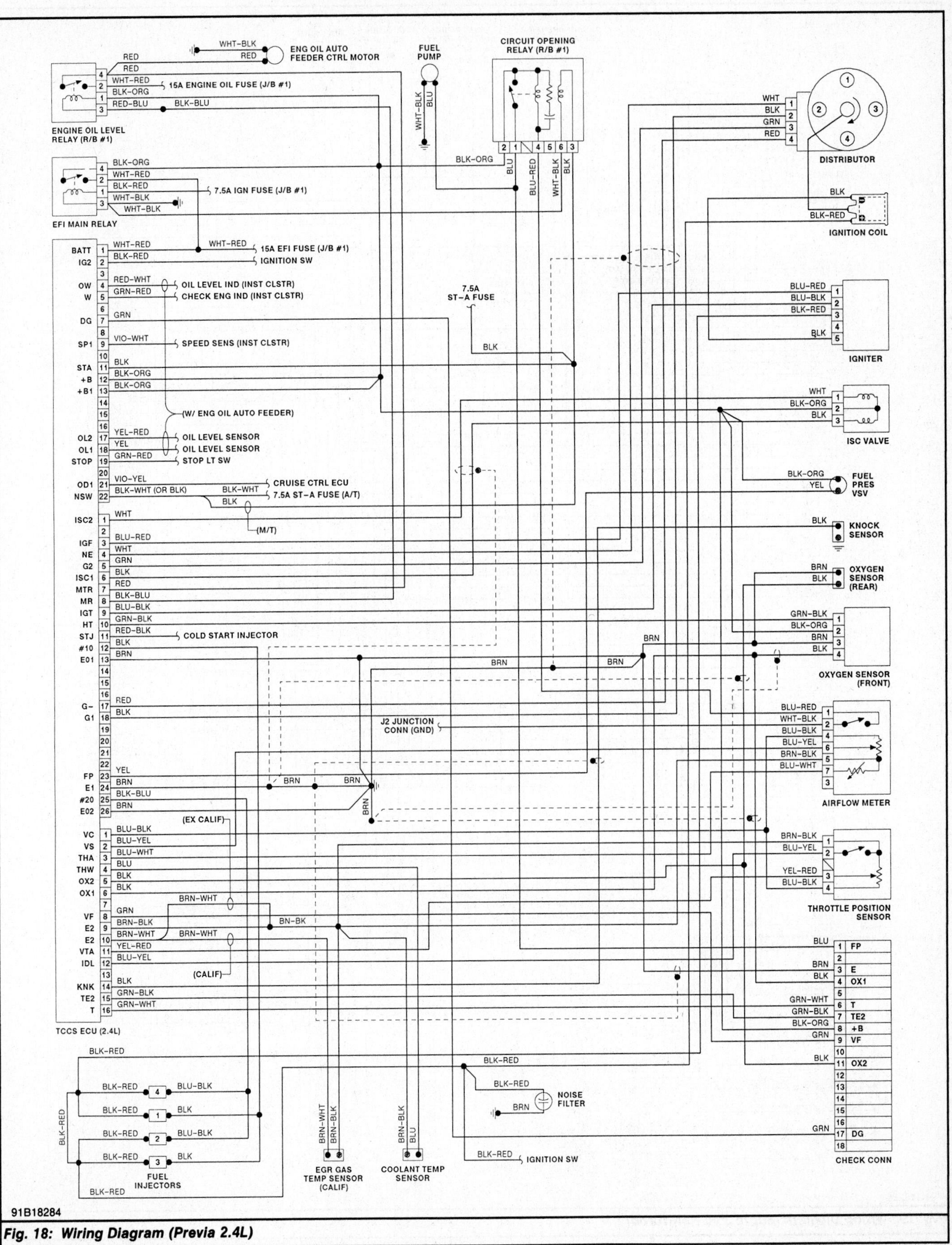


*Fig. 18: Wiring Diagram (Previa 2.4L)*

# 1991 ENGINE PERFORMANCE
## Wiring Diagrams (Cont.)

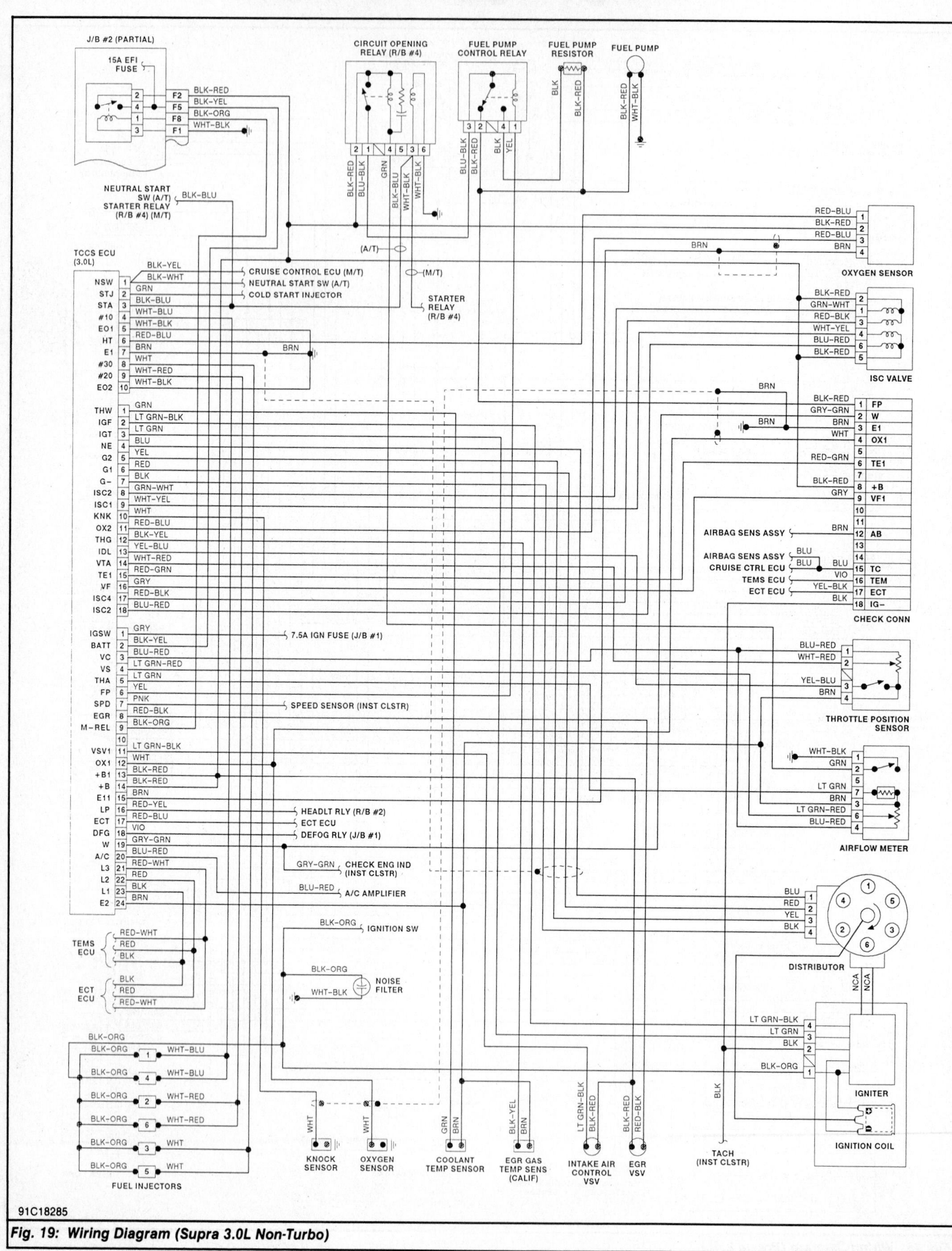

91C18285

*Fig. 19: Wiring Diagram (Supra 3.0L Non-Turbo)*

# 1991 ENGINE PERFORMANCE
## Wiring Diagrams (Cont.)

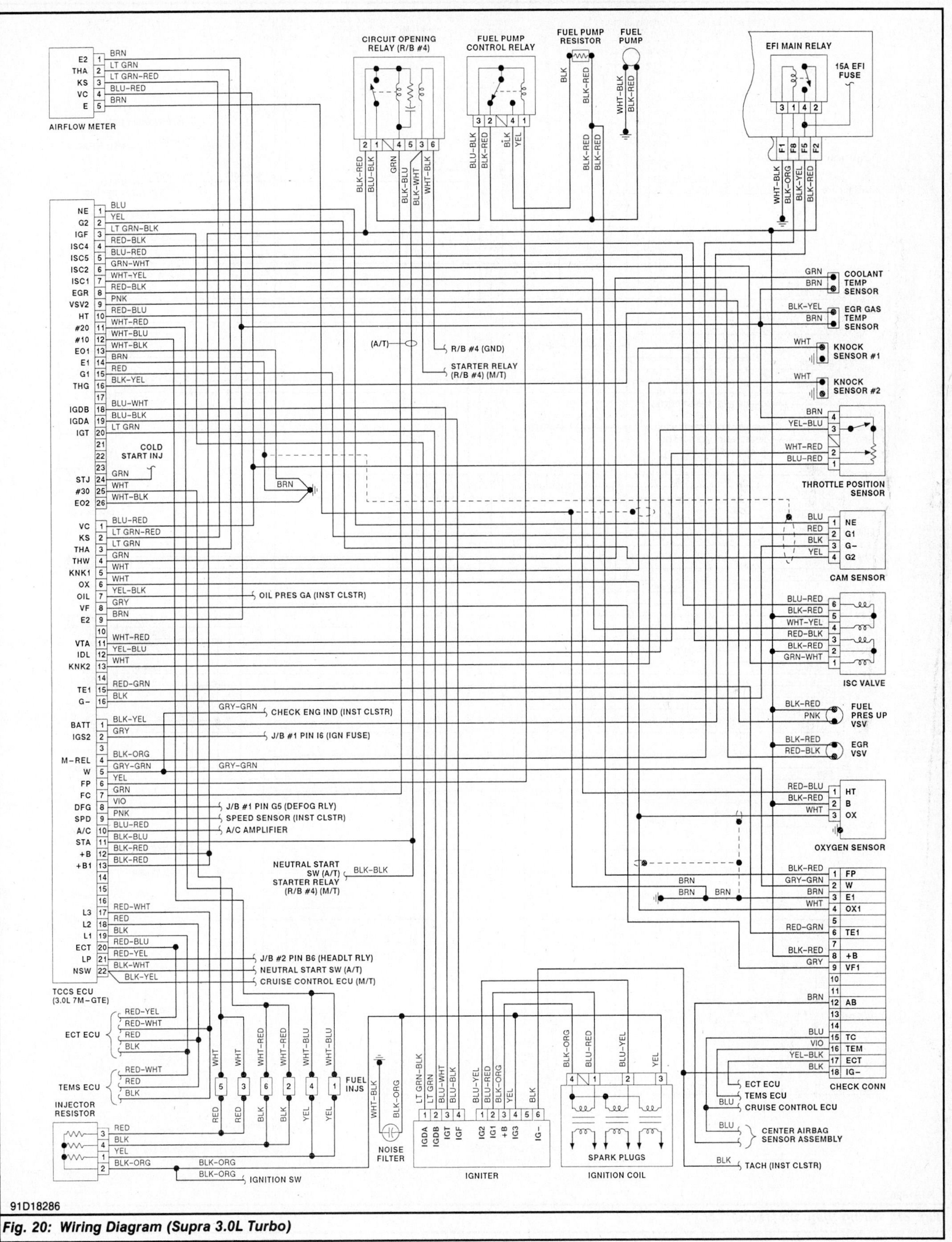


*Fig. 20: Wiring Diagram (Supra 3.0L Turbo)*

# 1991 ENGINE PERFORMANCE
## Wiring Diagrams (Cont.)

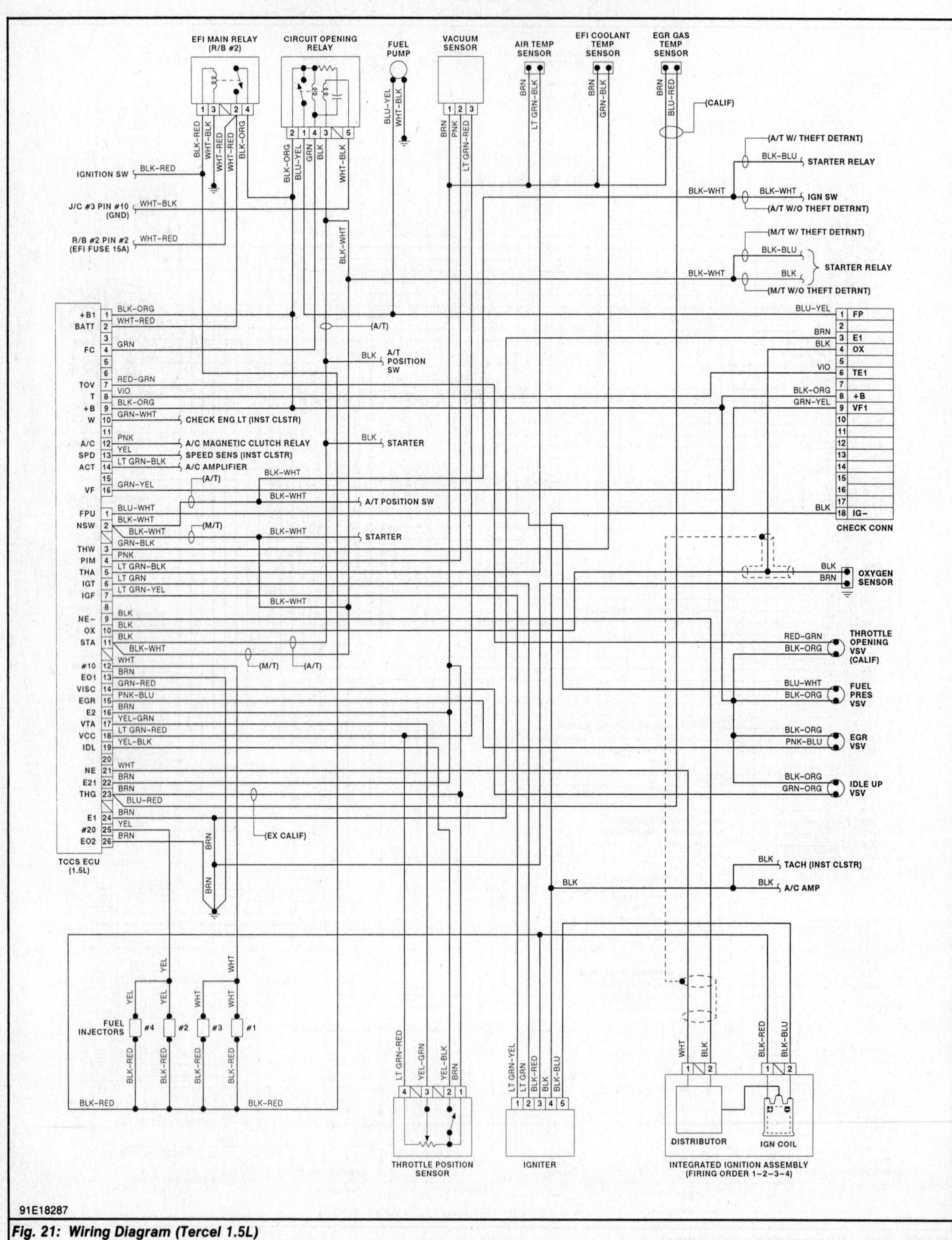


*Fig. 21: Wiring Diagram (Tercel 1.5L)*

# 1991 ENGINE PERFORMANCE
# Wiring Diagrams (Cont.)

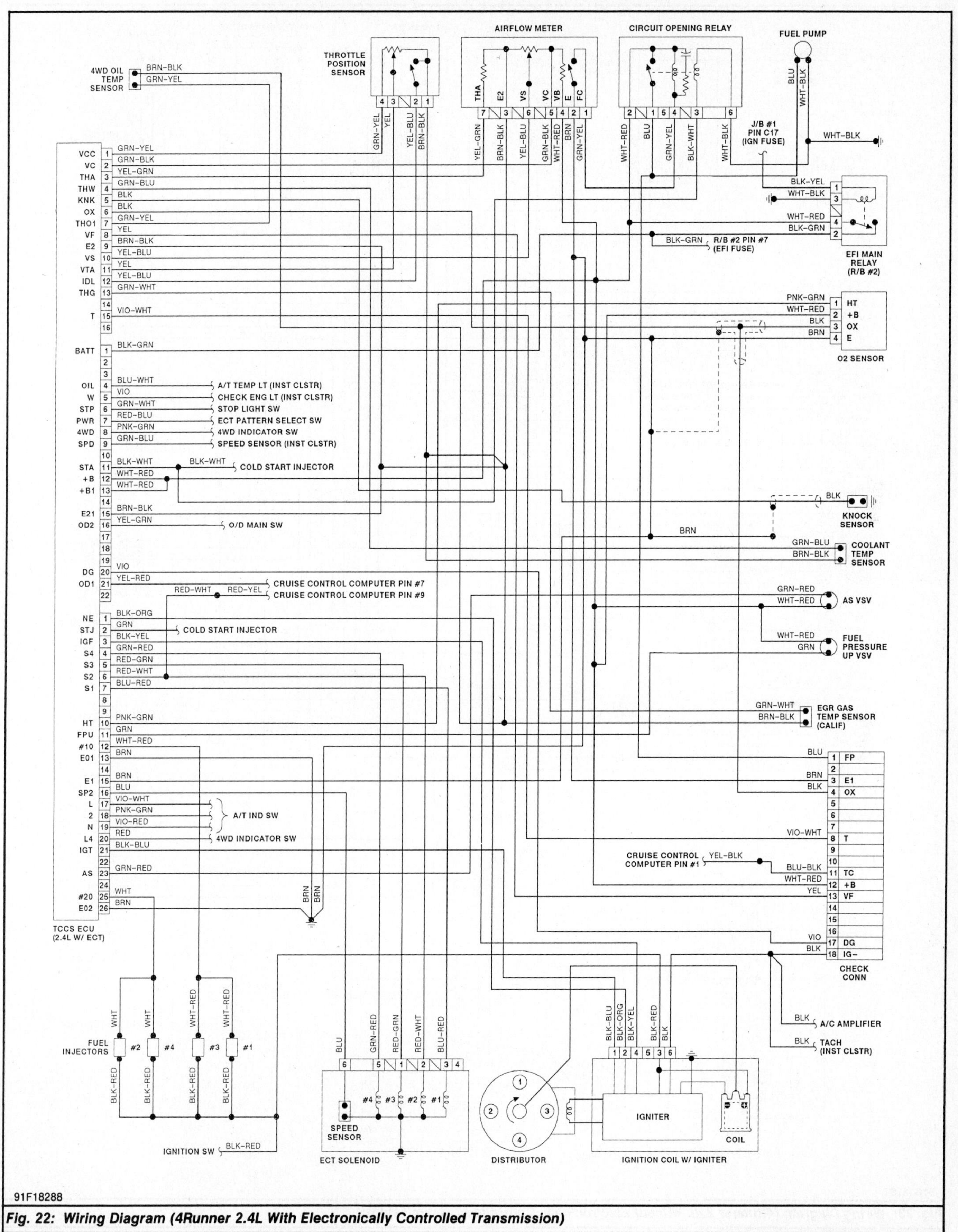


**Fig. 22: Wiring Diagram (4Runner 2.4L With Electronically Controlled Transmission)**

# 1991 ENGINE PERFORMANCE
## Wiring Diagrams (Cont.)

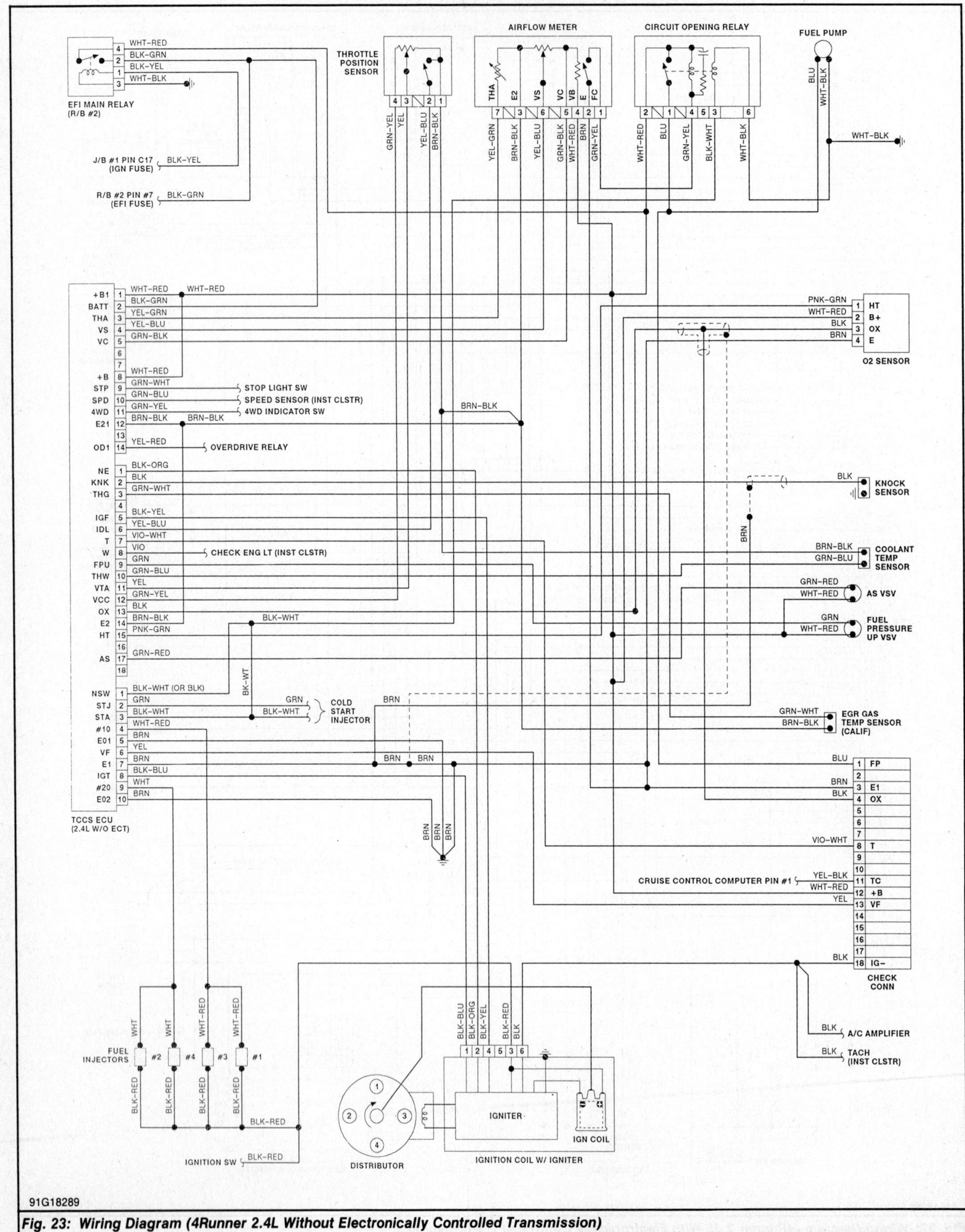


*Fig. 23: Wiring Diagram (4Runner 2.4L Without Electronically Controlled Transmission)*

# 1991 ENGINE PERFORMANCE
## Wiring Diagrams (Cont.)

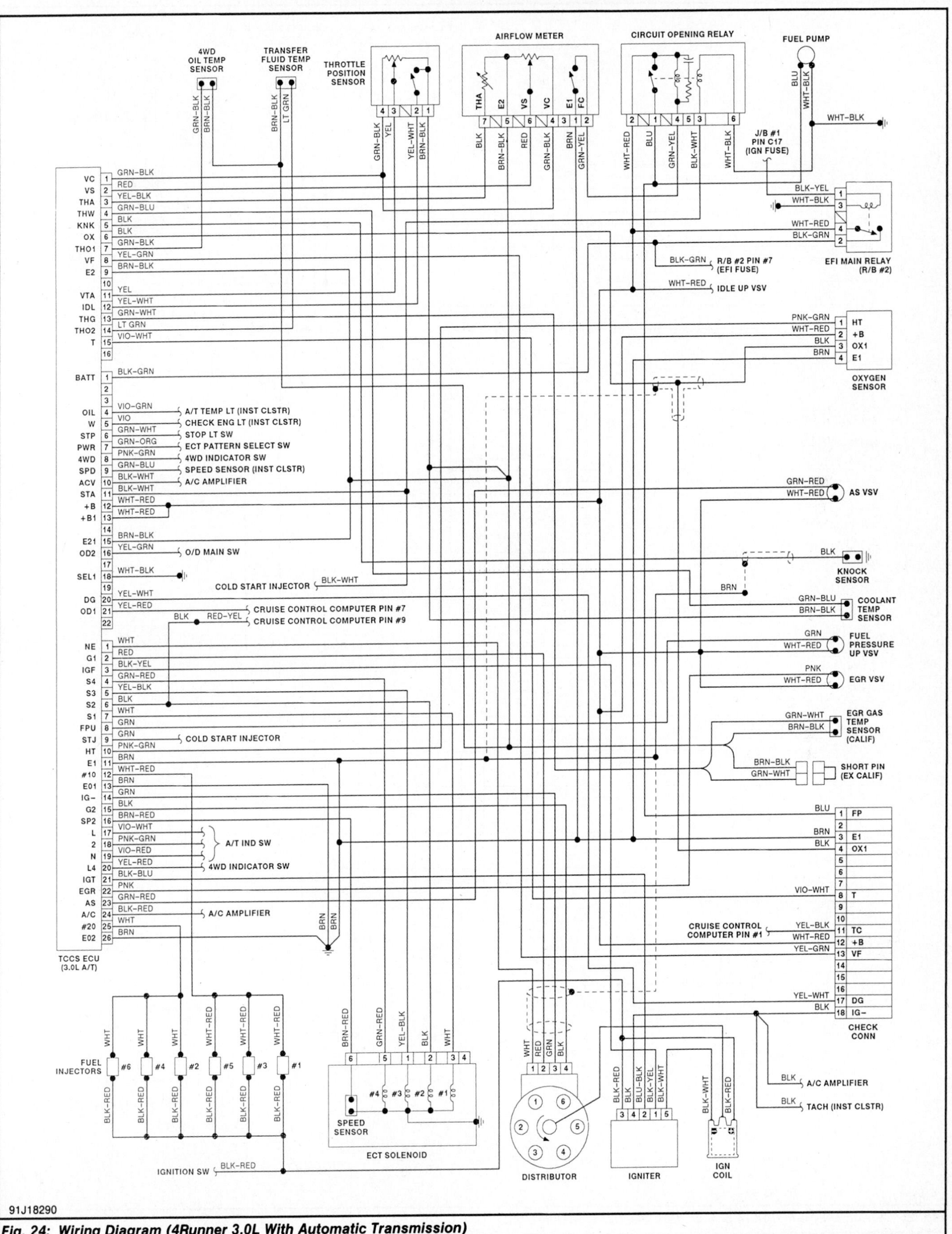


*Fig. 24: Wiring Diagram (4Runner 3.0L With Automatic Transmission)*

# 1991 ENGINE PERFORMANCE
## Wiring Diagrams (Cont.)

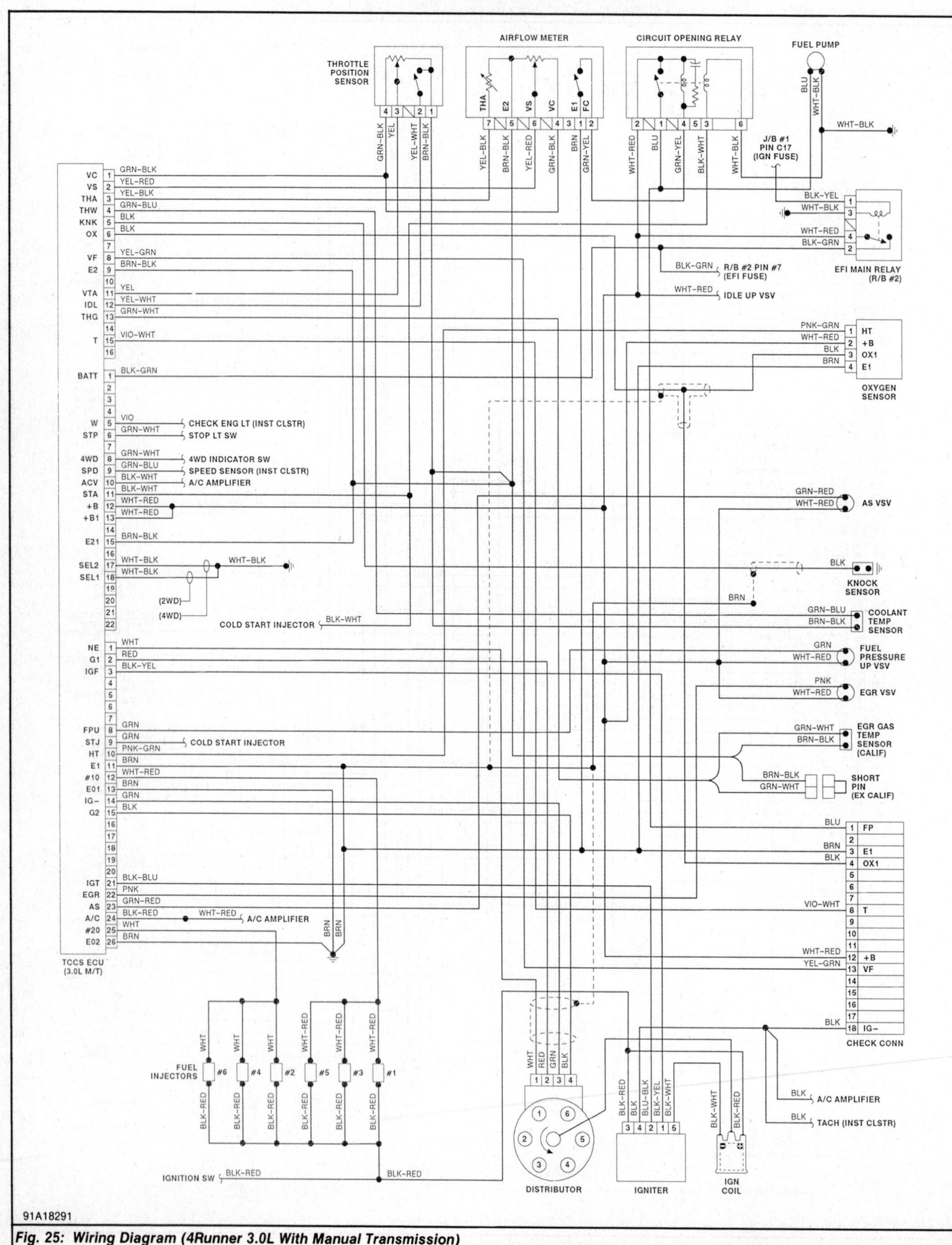


91A18291

*Fig. 25: Wiring Diagram (4Runner 3.0L With Manual Transmission)*

# 1991 ENGINE PERFORMANCE
# Vacuum Diagrams

## Camry, Celica, Corolla, Cressida, Land Cruiser, MR2, Pickup, Previa, Supra, Tercel, 4Runner

## INTRODUCTION

This article contains underhood views or schematics of vacuum hose routing. Use these vacuum diagrams during the visual inspection in BASIC DIAGNOSTIC PROCEDURES article. This will assist in identifying improperly routed vacuum hoses which cause driveability and/or computer-indicated malfunctions.

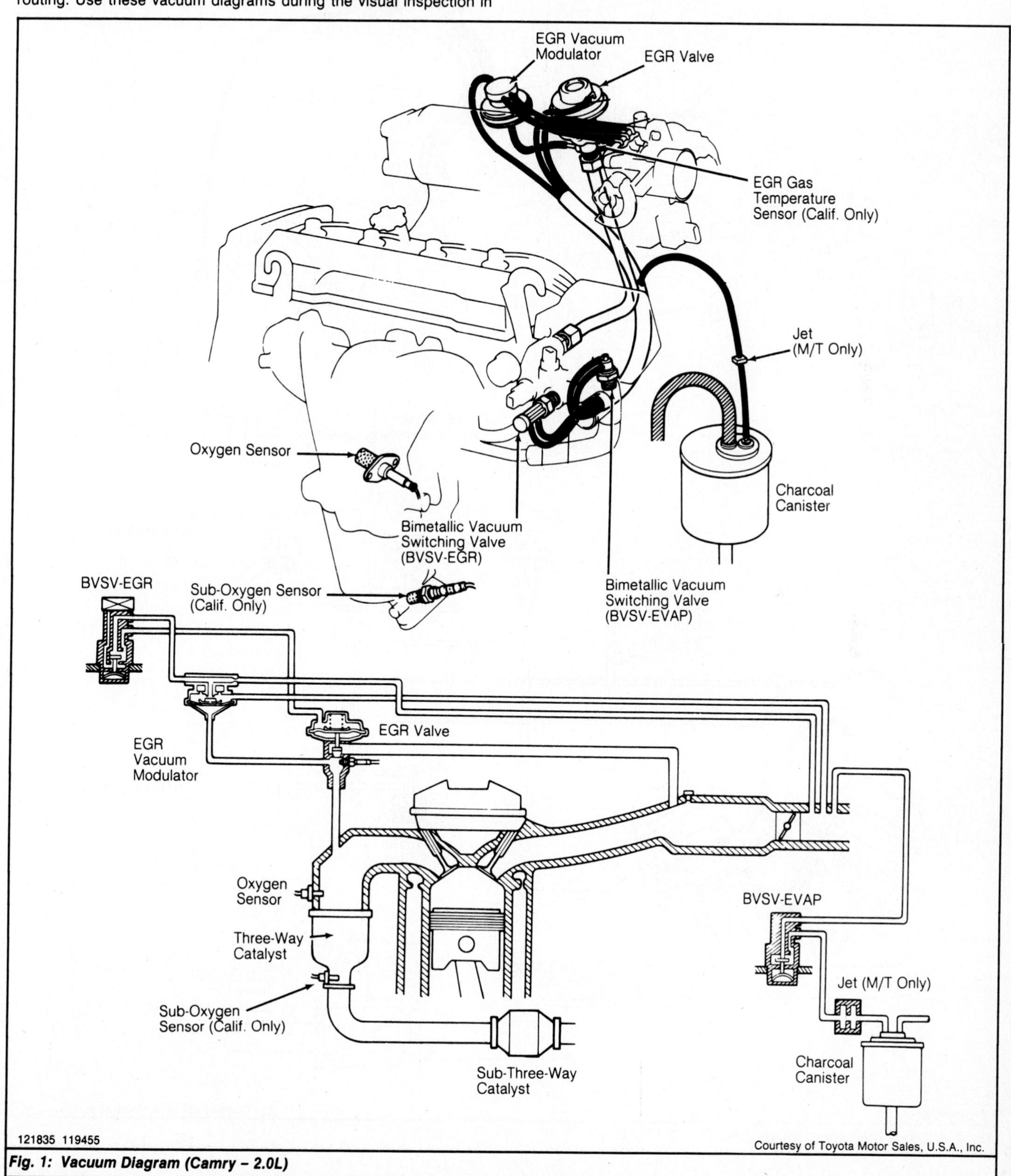


*Fig. 1: Vacuum Diagram (Camry – 2.0L)*

# 1991 ENGINE PERFORMANCE
## Vacuum Diagrams (Cont.)

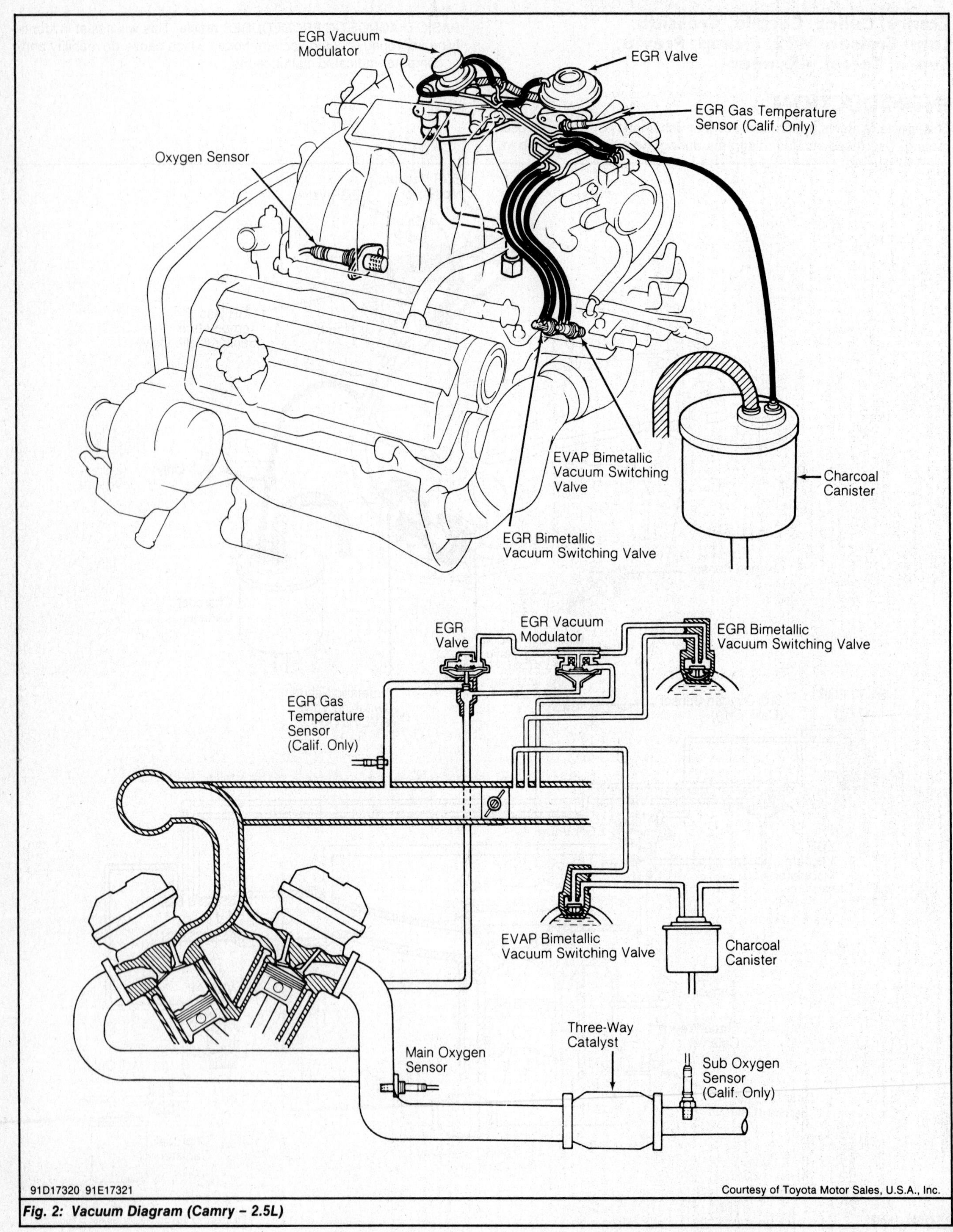


*Fig. 2: Vacuum Diagram (Camry – 2.5L)*

# 1991 ENGINE PERFORMANCE
## Vacuum Diagrams (Cont.)

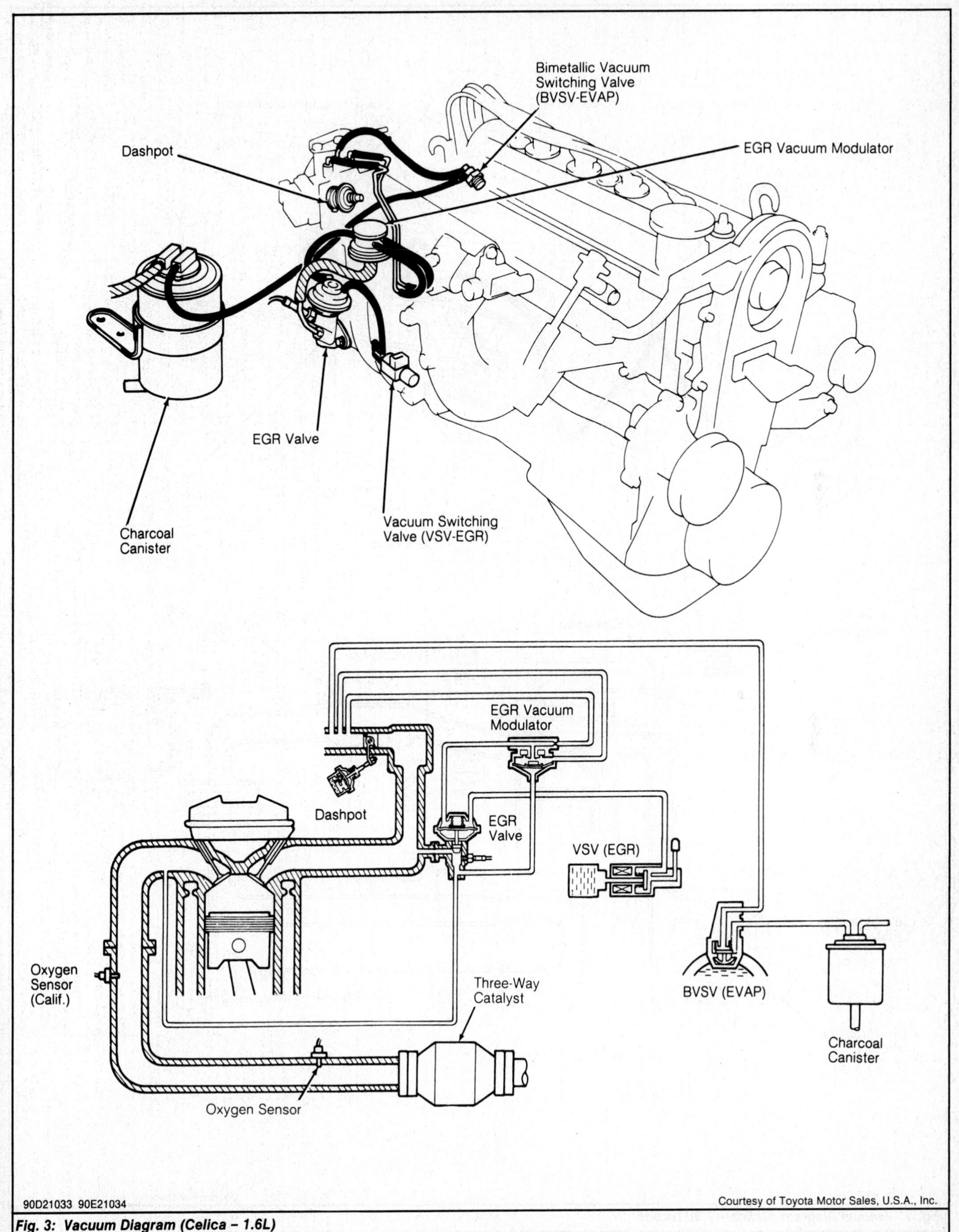


***Fig. 3: Vacuum Diagram (Celica – 1.6L)***

# 1991 ENGINE PERFORMANCE
## Vacuum Diagrams (Cont.)

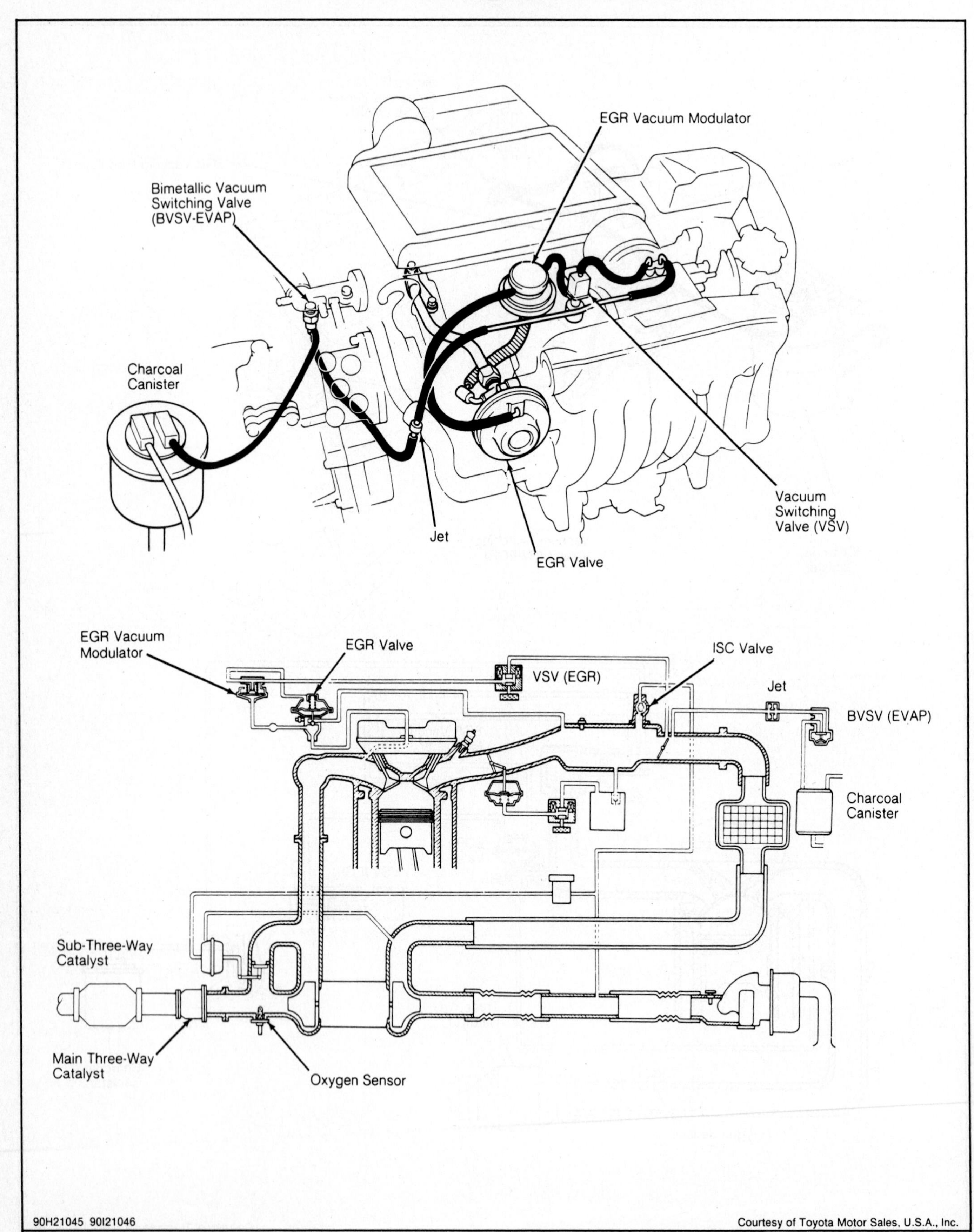


*Fig. 4: Vacuum Diagram (Celica – 2.0L Turbo)*

# 1991 ENGINE PERFORMANCE
## Vacuum Diagrams (Cont.)

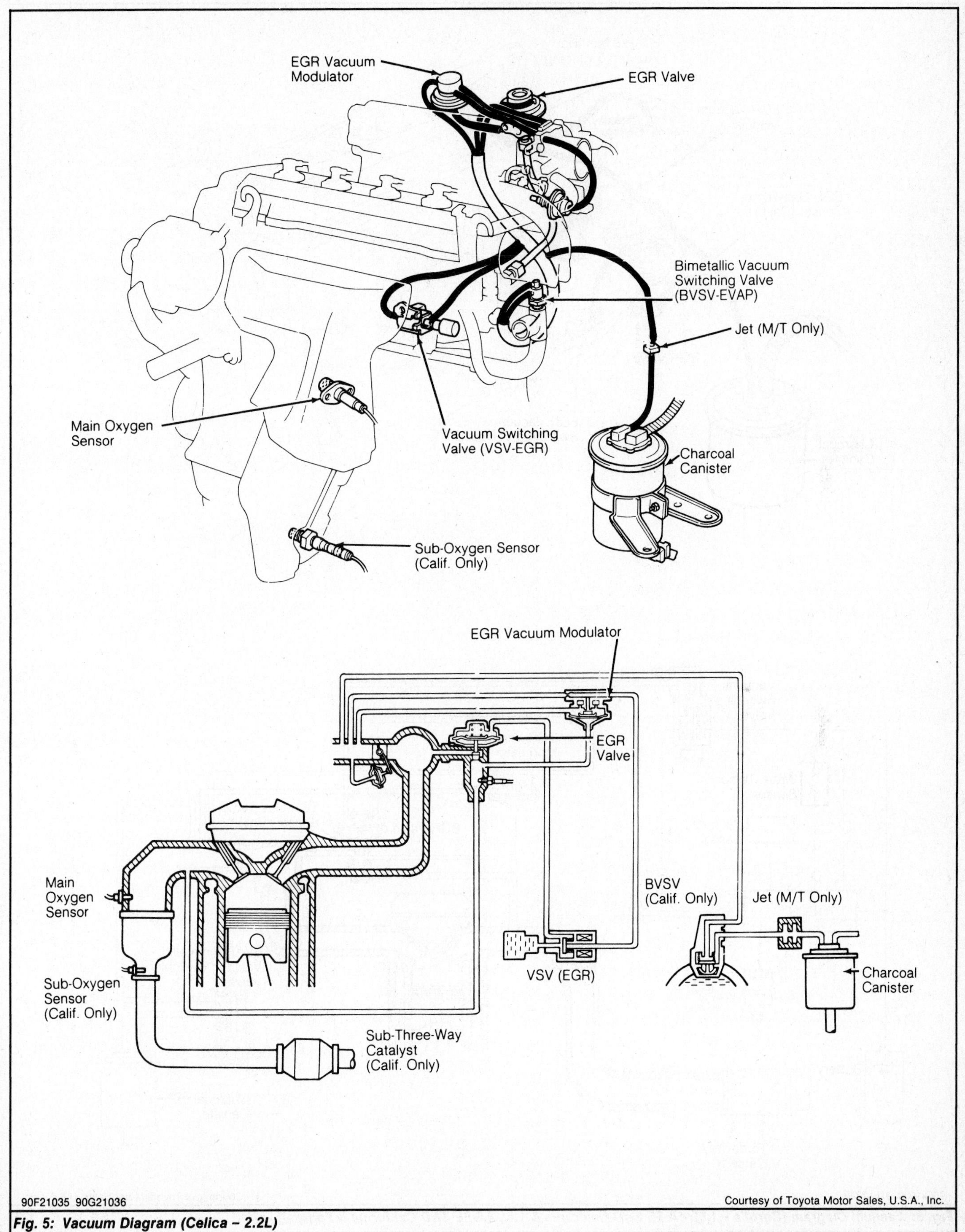


*Fig. 5: Vacuum Diagram (Celica – 2.2L)*

# 1991 ENGINE PERFORMANCE
## Vacuum Diagrams (Cont.)

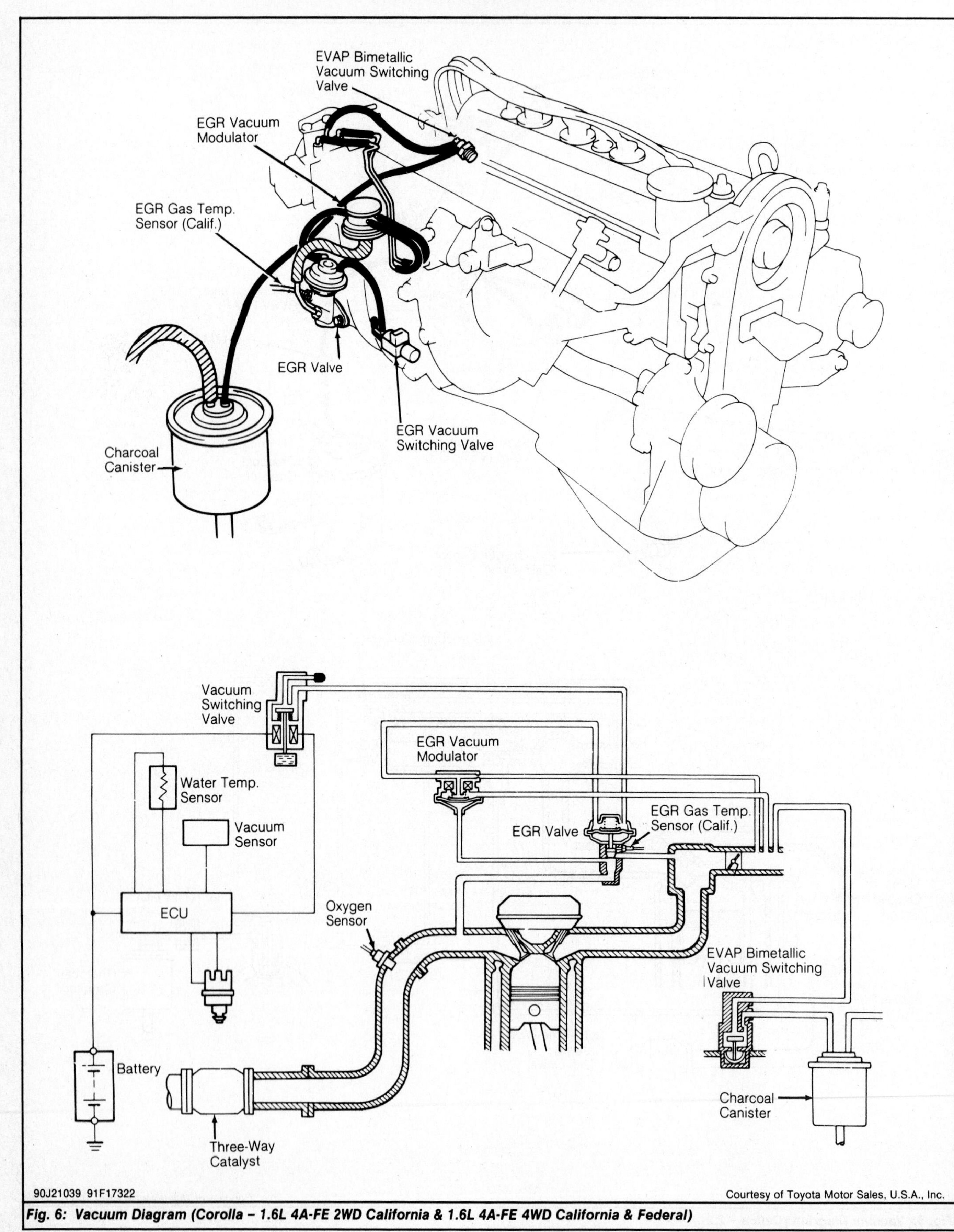


*Fig. 6: Vacuum Diagram (Corolla – 1.6L 4A-FE 2WD California & 1.6L 4A-FE 4WD California & Federal)*

# 1991 ENGINE PERFORMANCE
## Vacuum Diagrams (Cont.)

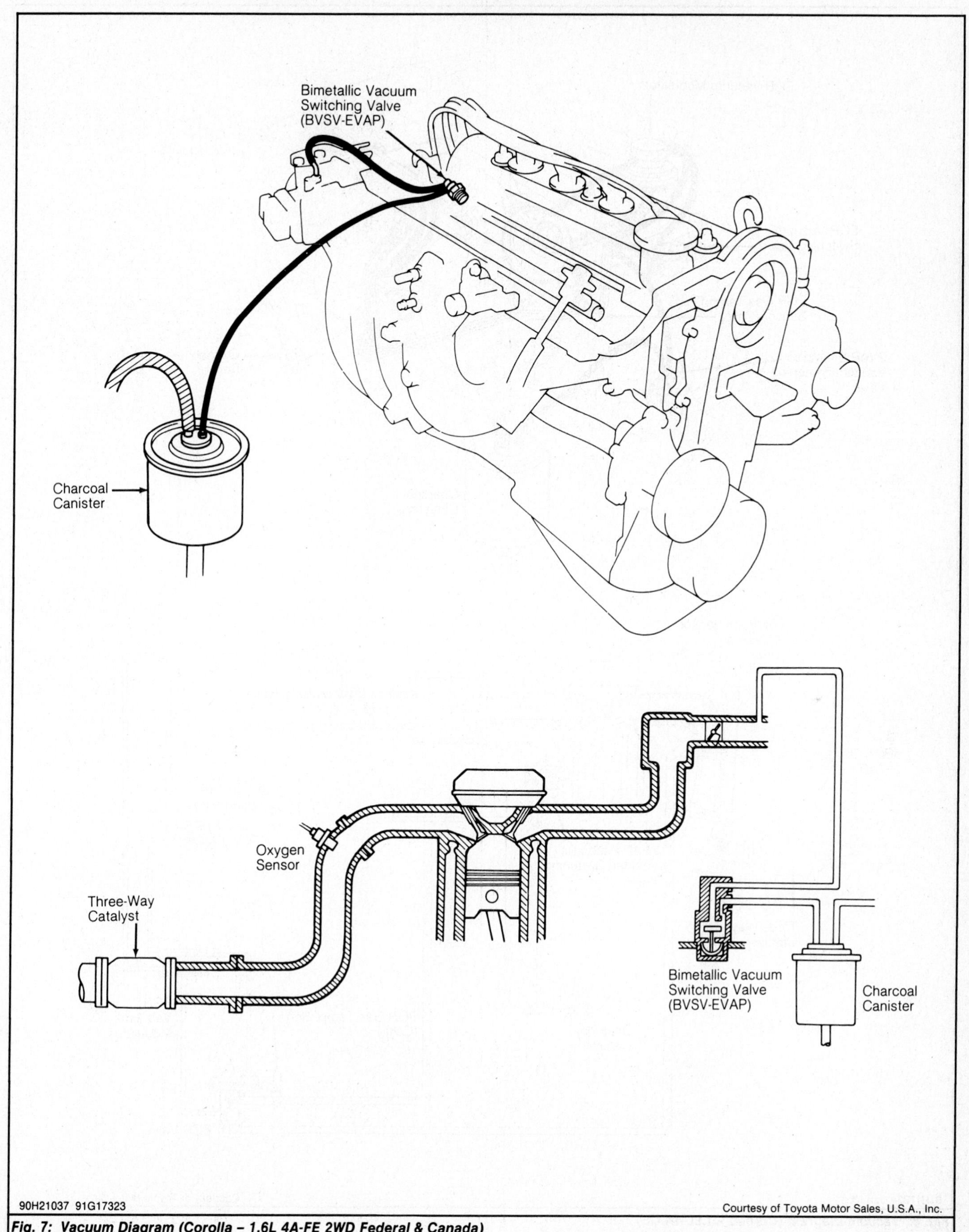


*Fig. 7: Vacuum Diagram (Corolla – 1.6L 4A-FE 2WD Federal & Canada)*

# 1991 ENGINE PERFORMANCE
## Vacuum Diagrams (Cont.)

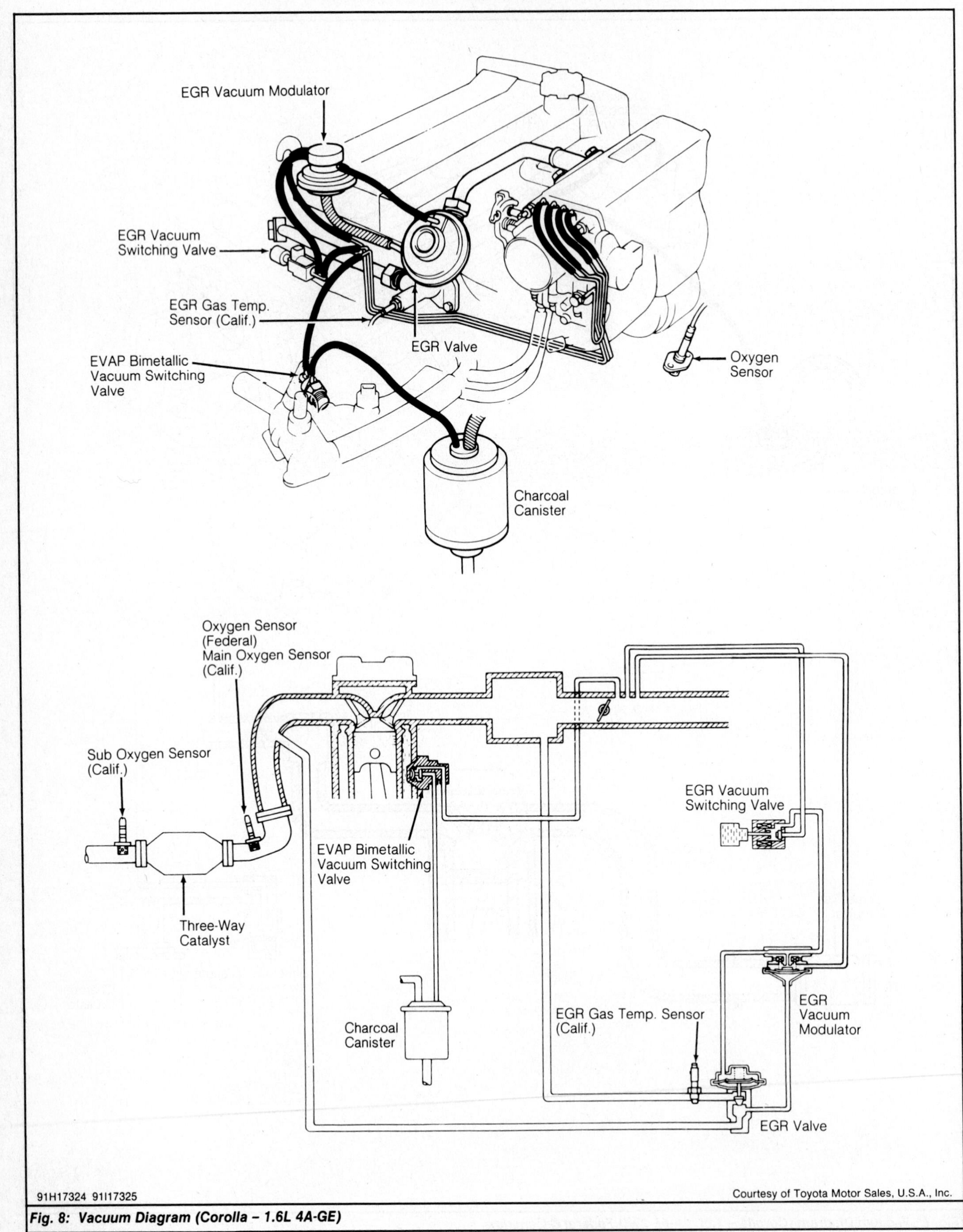


*Fig. 8: Vacuum Diagram (Corolla – 1.6L 4A-GE)*

# 1991 ENGINE PERFORMANCE
## Vacuum Diagrams (Cont.)

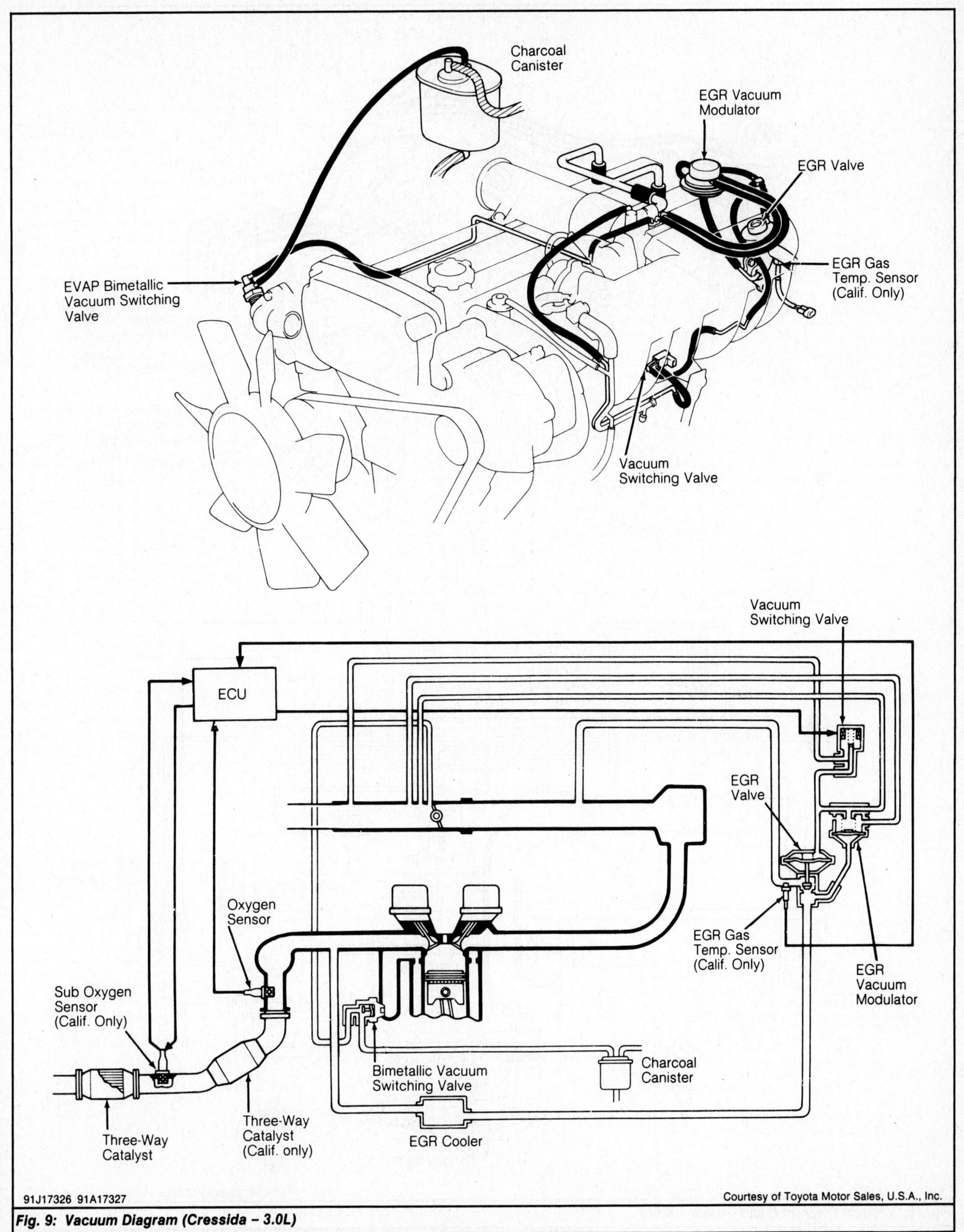


***Fig. 9: Vacuum Diagram (Cressida – 3.0L)***

# 1991 ENGINE PERFORMANCE
## Vacuum Diagrams (Cont.)

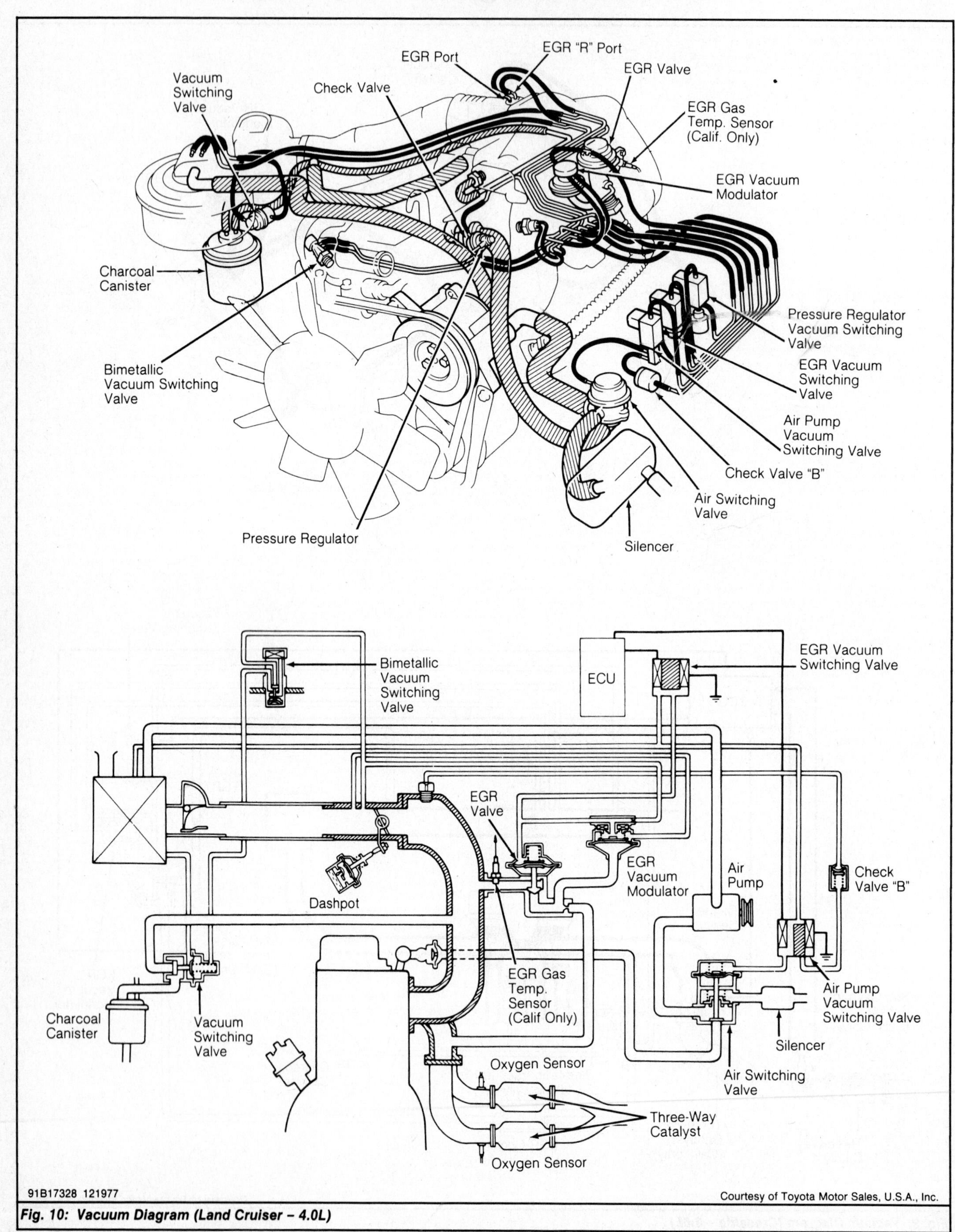


*Fig. 10: Vacuum Diagram (Land Cruiser – 4.0L)*

# 1991 ENGINE PERFORMANCE
## Vacuum Diagrams (Cont.)

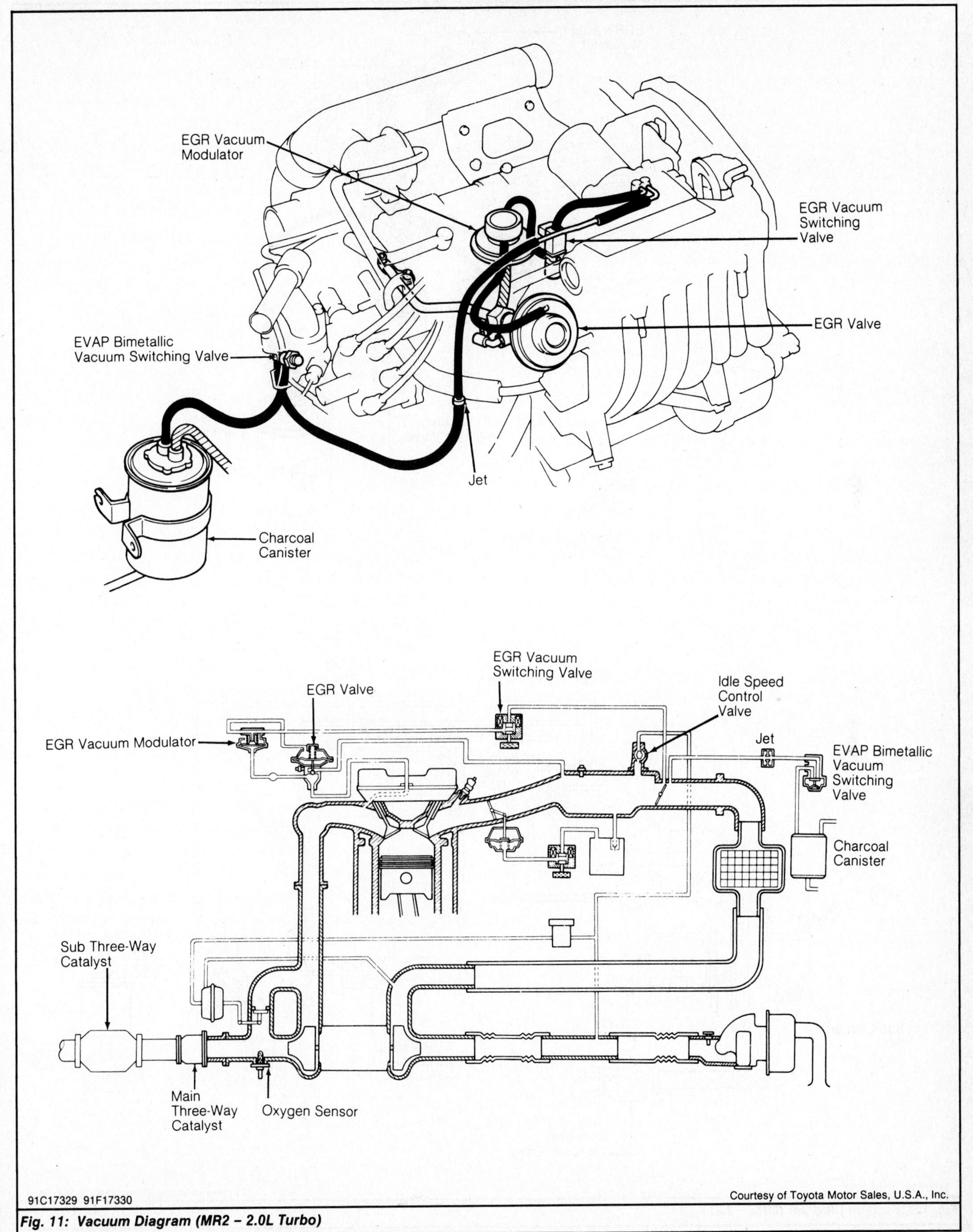


***Fig. 11: Vacuum Diagram (MR2 – 2.0L Turbo)***

# 1991 ENGINE PERFORMANCE
## Vacuum Diagrams (Cont.)

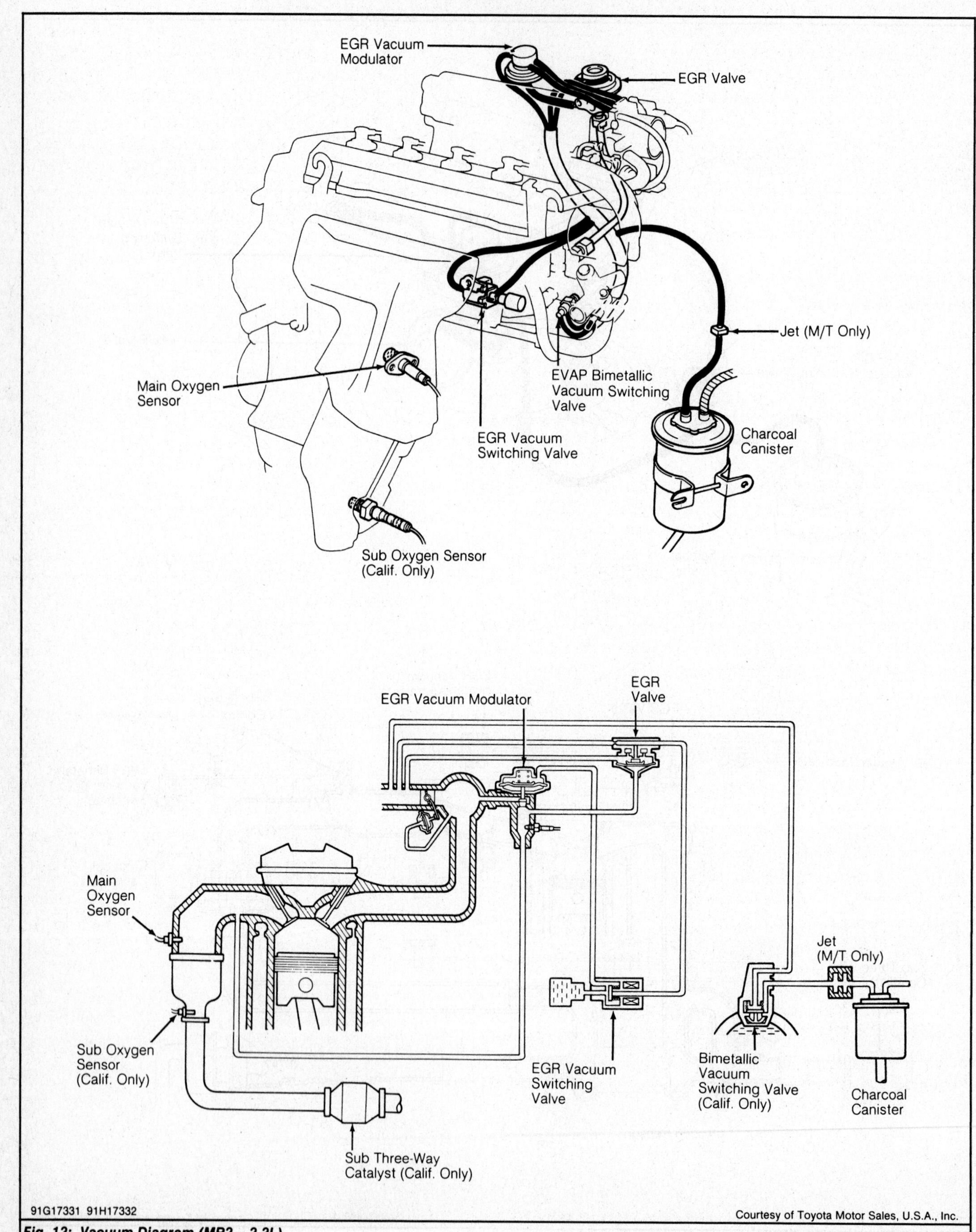


Courtesy of Toyota Motor Sales, U.S.A., Inc.

**Fig. 12: Vacuum Diagram (MR2 – 2.2L)**

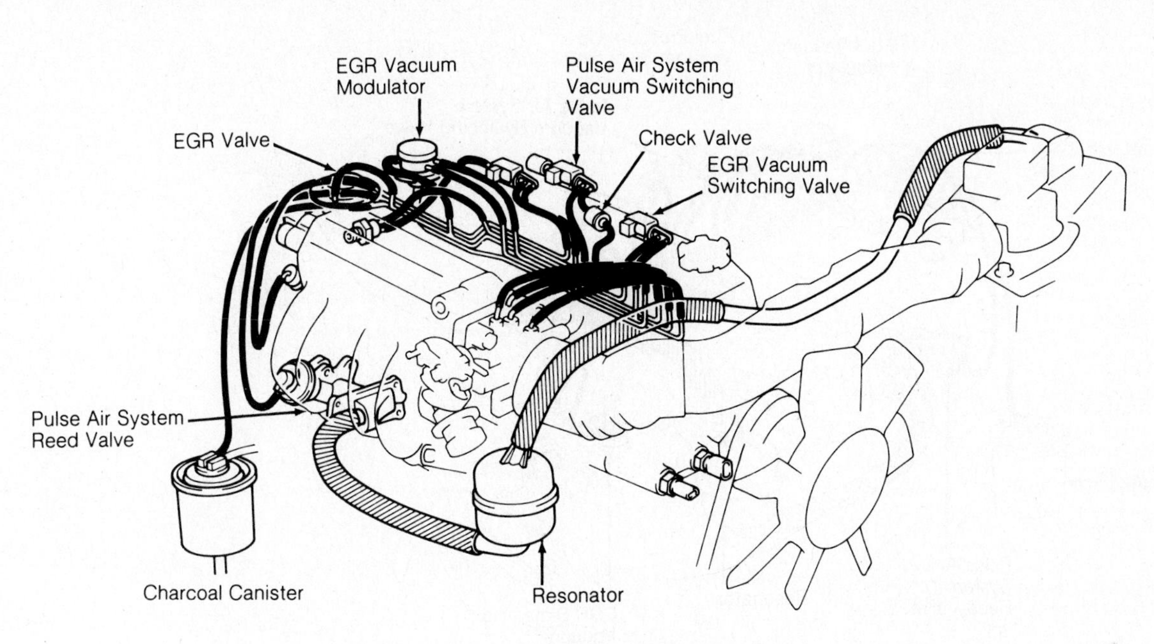


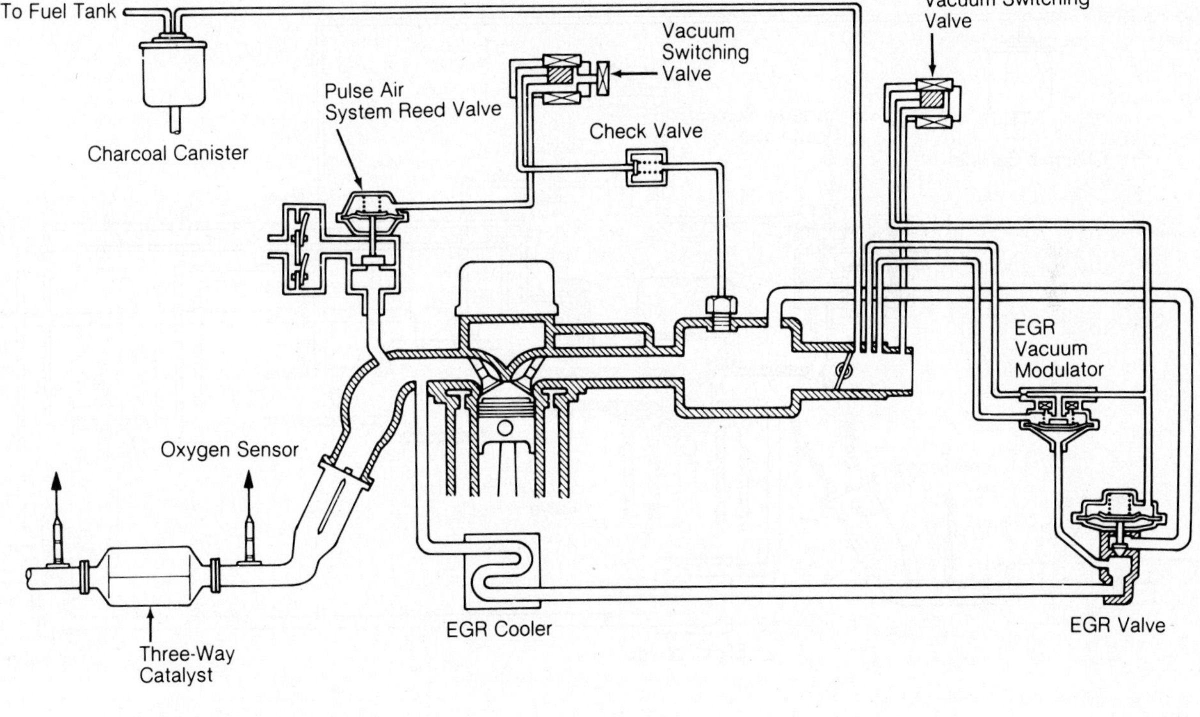


91I17333 91J17334

Courtesy of Toyota Motor Sales, U.S.A., Inc.

*Fig. 13: Vacuum Diagram (Pickup – 2.4L California)*

# 1991 ENGINE PERFORMANCE
## Vacuum Diagrams (Cont.)

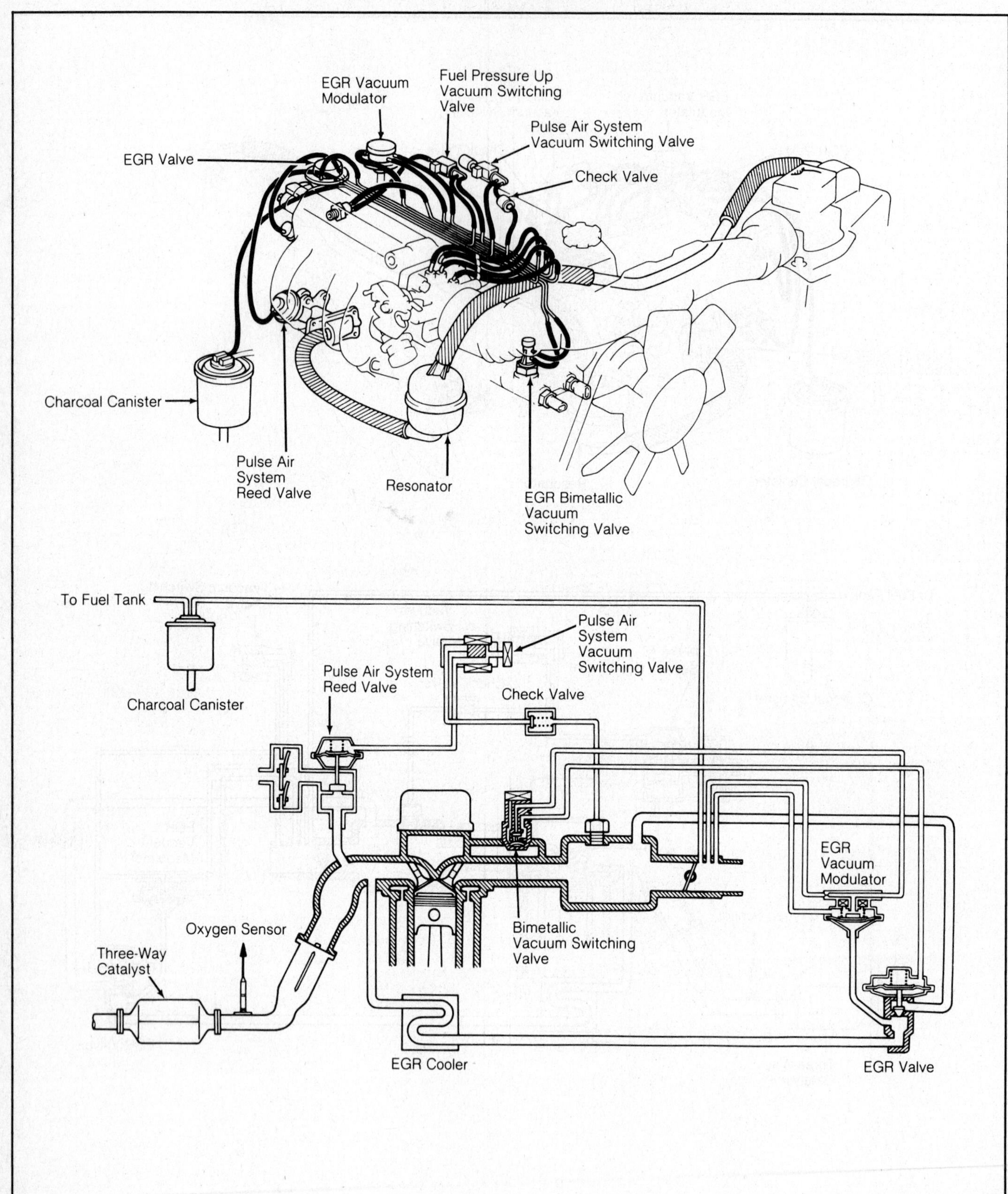


Courtesy of Toyota Motor Sales, U.S.A., Inc.

***Fig. 14: Vacuum Diagram (Pickup – 2.4L Federal & Canada; 4Runner – 2.4L California & Federal)***

# 1991 ENGINE PERFORMANCE
## Vacuum Diagrams (Cont.)

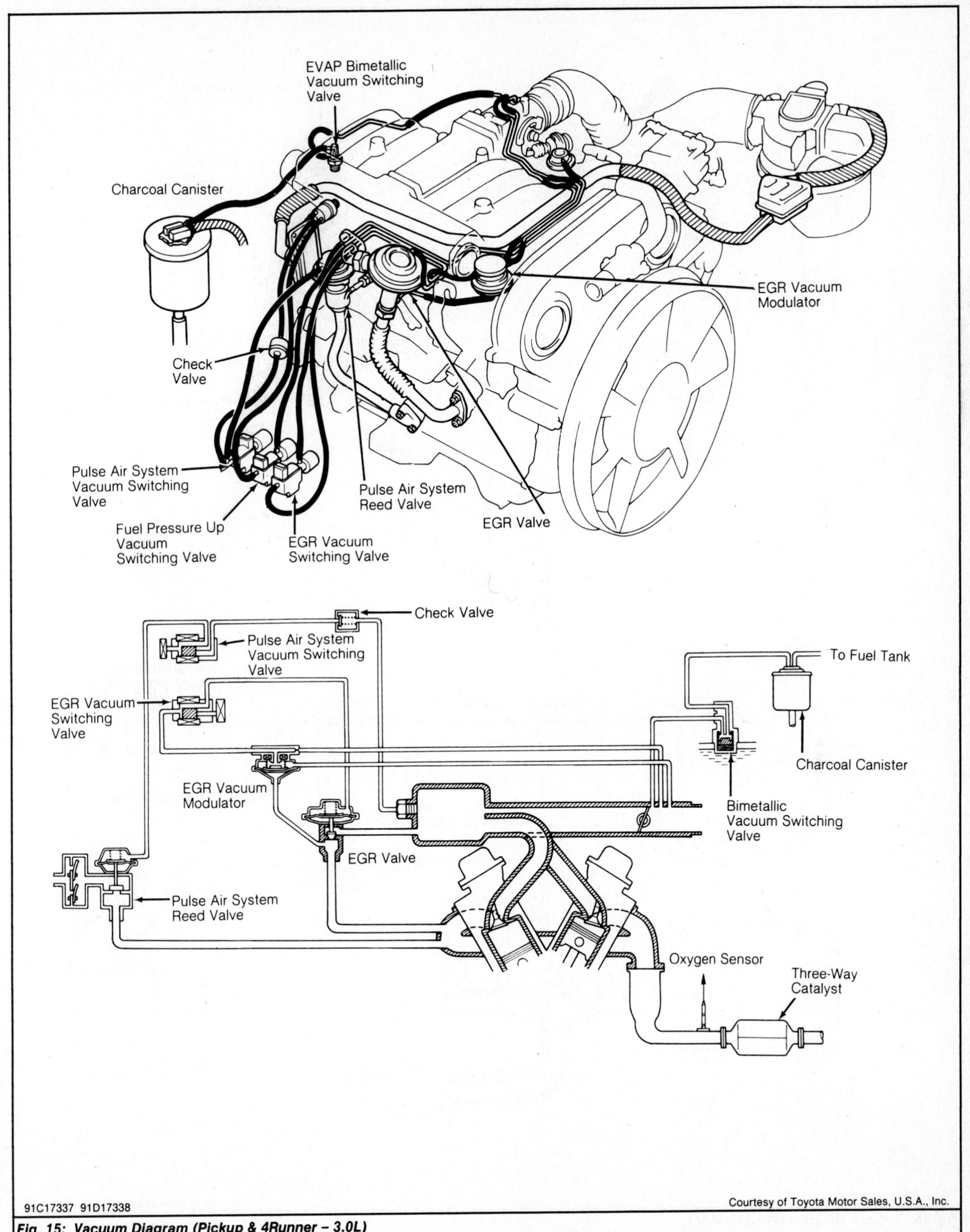


Courtesy of Toyota Motor Sales, U.S.A., Inc.

*Fig. 15: Vacuum Diagram (Pickup & 4Runner – 3.0L)*

# 1991 ENGINE PERFORMANCE
## Vacuum Diagrams (Cont.)

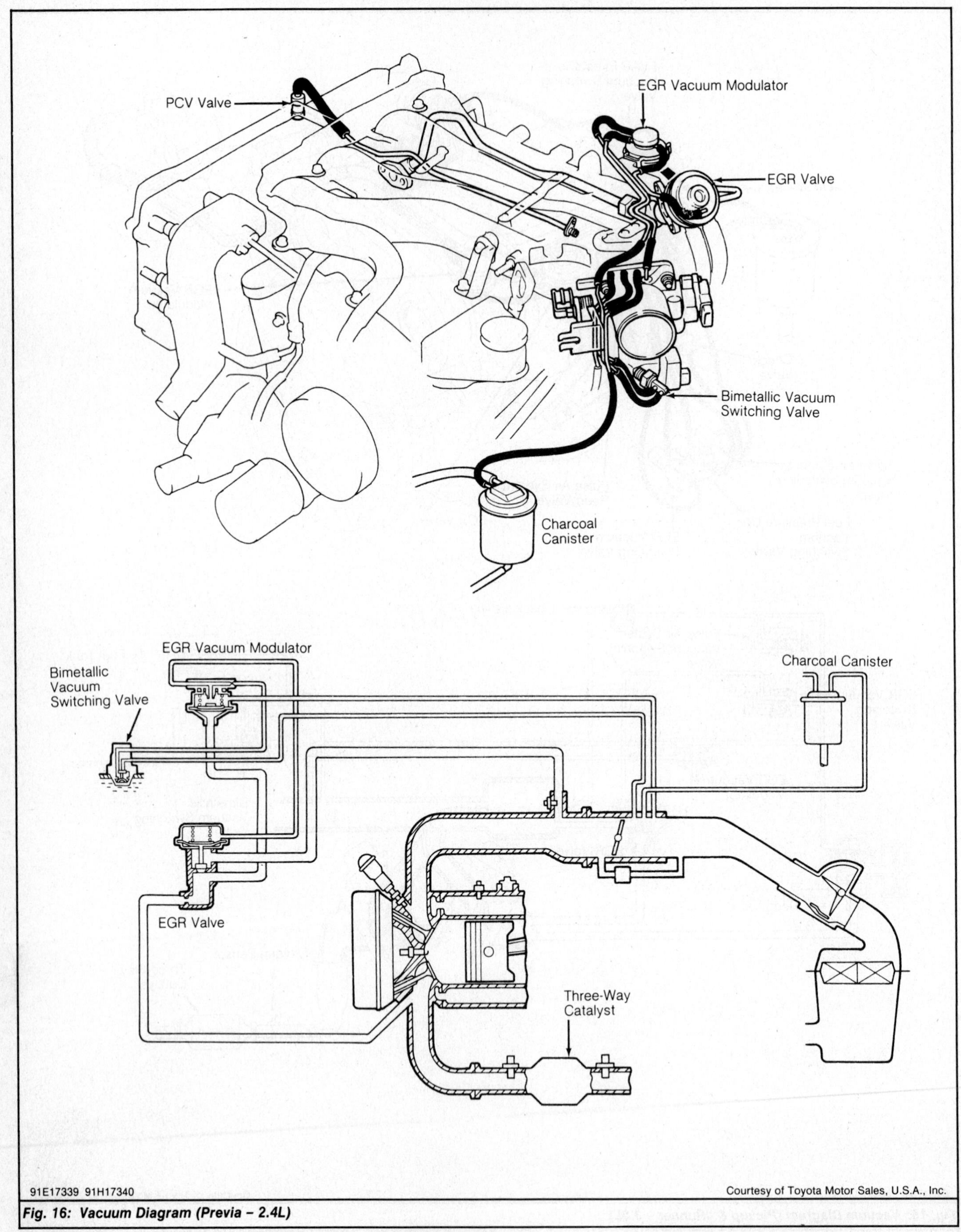


Courtesy of Toyota Motor Sales, U.S.A., Inc.

*Fig. 16: Vacuum Diagram (Previa – 2.4L)*

# 1991 ENGINE PERFORMANCE
## Vacuum Diagrams (Cont.)

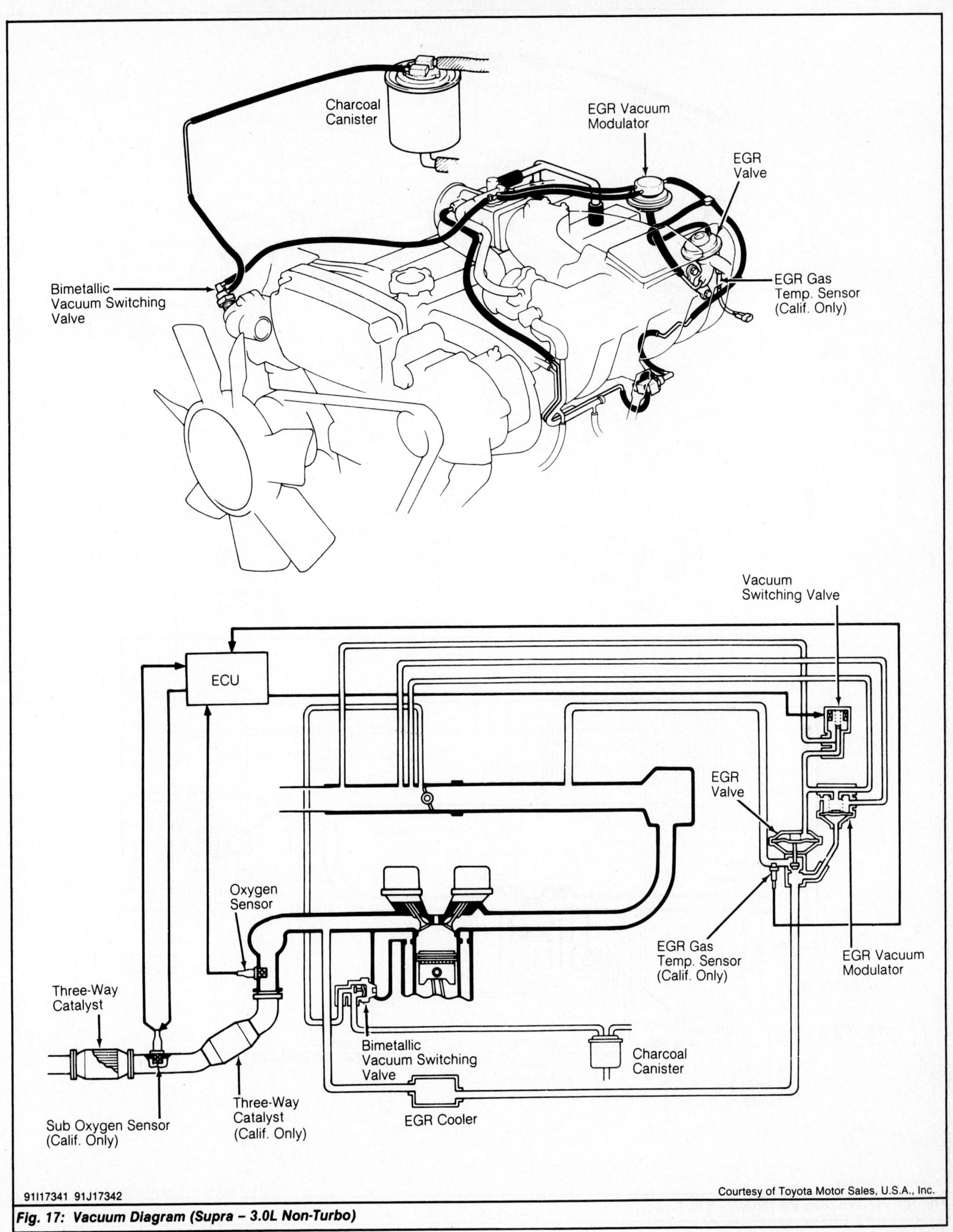


*Fig. 17: Vacuum Diagram (Supra – 3.0L Non-Turbo)*

# 1991 ENGINE PERFORMANCE
## Vacuum Diagrams (Cont.)

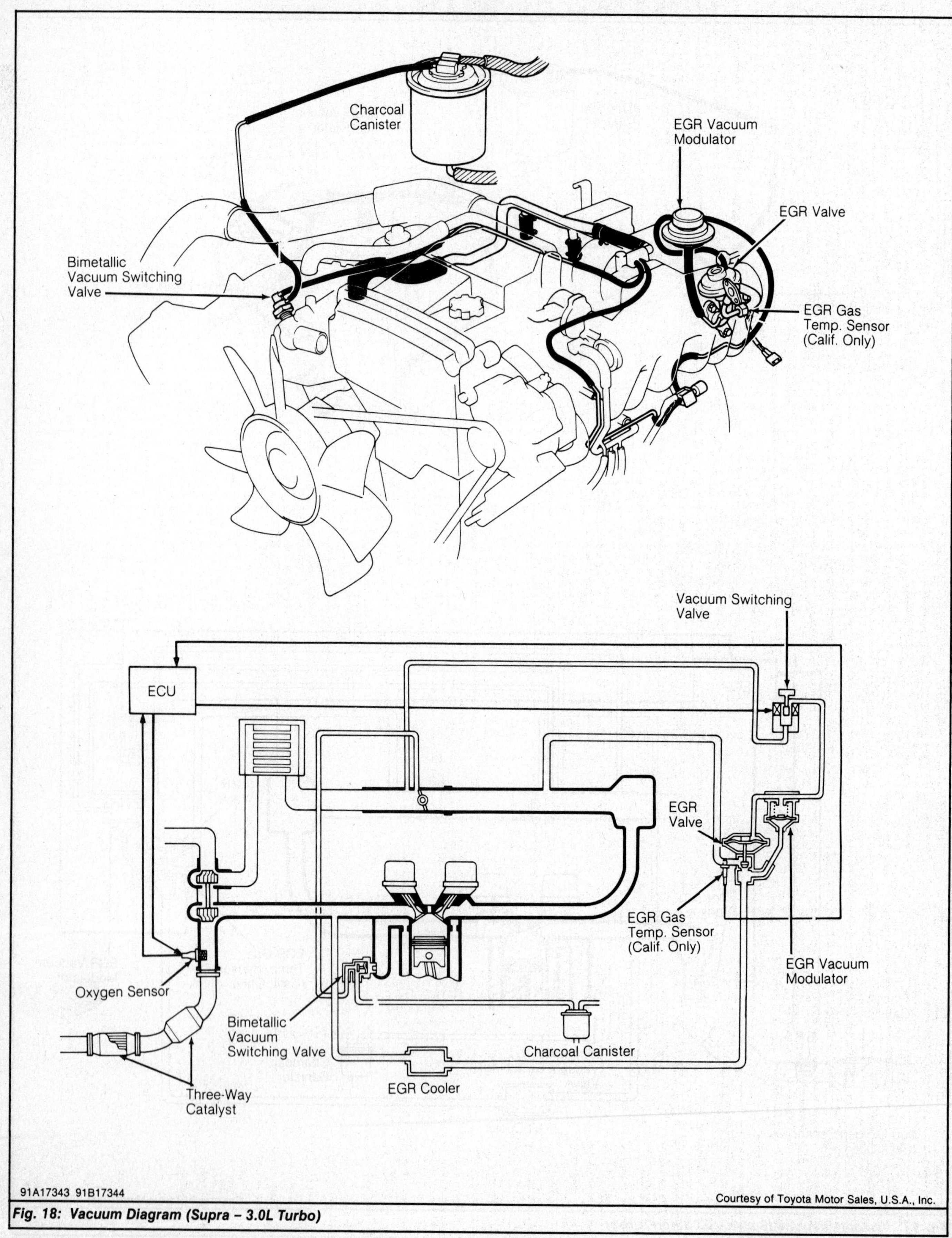


*Fig. 18: Vacuum Diagram (Supra – 3.0L Turbo)*

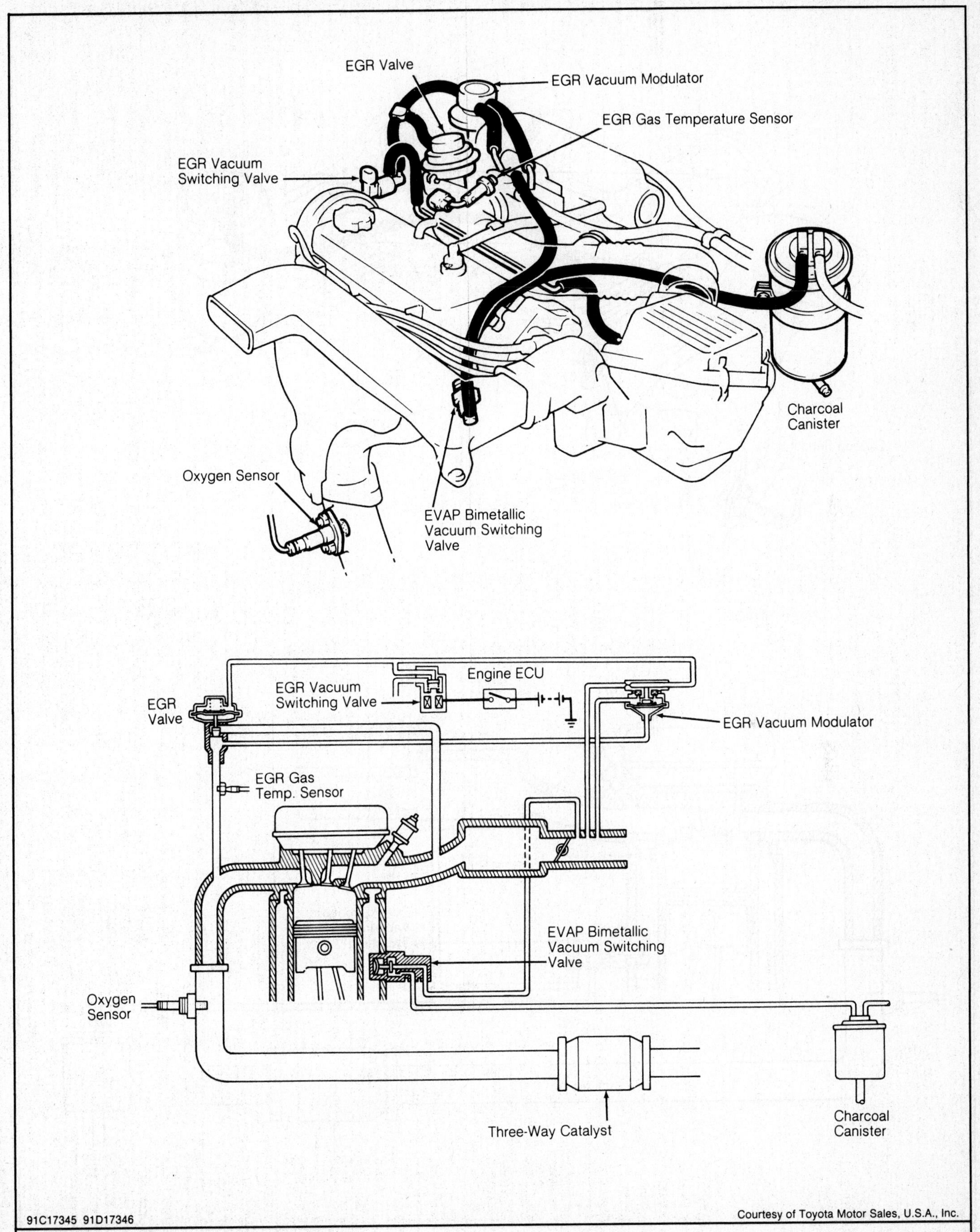
EGR Valve
EGR Vacuum Modulator
EGR Gas Temperature Sensor
EGR Vacuum Switching Valve
Charcoal Canister
Oxygen Sensor
EVAP Bimetallic Vacuum Switching Valve
Engine ECU
EGR Vacuum Switching Valve
EGR Valve
EGR Vacuum Modulator
EGR Gas Temp. Sensor
EVAP Bimetallic Vacuum Switching Valve
Oxygen Sensor
Three-Way Catalyst
Charcoal Canister
91C17345 91D17346
Courtesy of Toyota Motor Sales, U.S.A., Inc.

*Fig. 19: Vacuum Diagram (Tercel – 1.5L California)*

# 1991 ENGINE PERFORMANCE
## Vacuum Diagrams (Cont.)

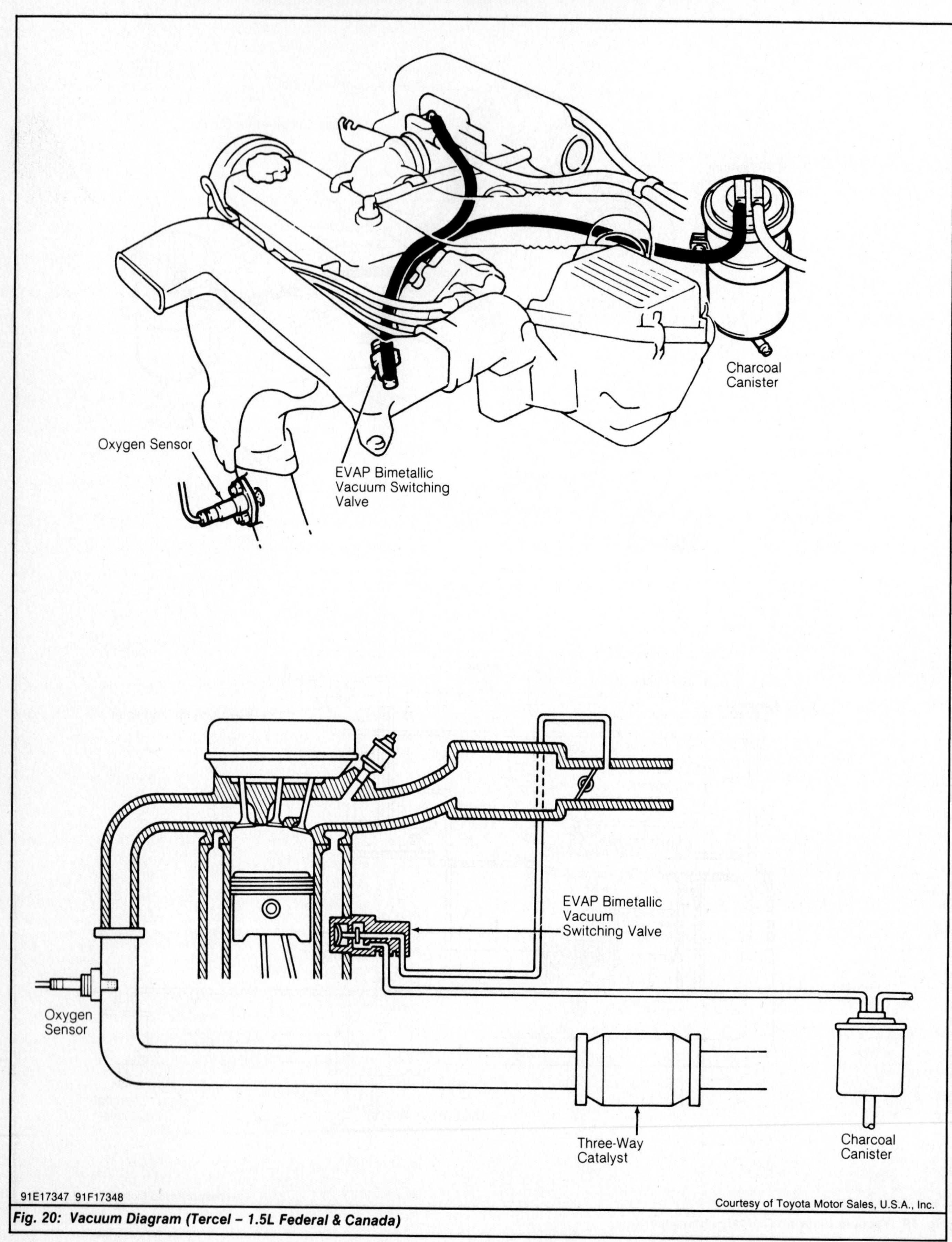


*Fig. 20: Vacuum Diagram (Tercel – 1.5L Federal & Canada)*

# 1991 ENGINE PERFORMANCE
# Removal, Overhaul & Installation

## Camry, Celica, Corolla, Cressida, Land Cruiser, MR2, Pickup, Previa, Supra, Tercel, 4Runner

## INTRODUCTION

Removal, overhaul and installation procedures are covered in this article. If component removal and installation is primarily an unbolt and bolt-on procedure, only a torque specification may be furnished.

## IGNITION SYSTEM

### DISTRIBUTOR

***NOTE: For timing specifications and procedures, see ON-VEHICLE ADJUSTMENTS article.***

**Removal (Camry 2.0L)** – Disconnect negative battery cable. Remove air cleaner hose. Disconnect spark plug wires from distributor cap. Disconnect distributor wiring connector. Remove 2 distributor hold-down bolts. Remove distributor. Remove "O" ring from distributor housing and discard.

**Installation** – **1)** Set No. 1 cylinder to TDC of compression stroke. Install new "O" ring on distributor housing. Coat "O" ring with oil. Align cutout marks of coupling with line on housing. *See Fig. 1.*

**2)** Insert distributor, aligning center of distributor flange with bolt hole on cylinder head. Connect distributor wiring connector. Install spark plug wires. Connect negative battery cable. Set ignition timing. Tighten distributor hold-down bolts. See TORQUE SPECIFICATIONS at end of article.

**Removal (Camry 2.5L)** – Disconnect negative battery cable. Remove air cleaner cap, airflow meter and air cleaner hose. Disconnect spark plug wires from distributor cap. Disconnect distributor wiring connector. Remove 2 distributor hold-down bolts. Remove distributor. Remove "O" ring from distributor housing and discard.

**Installation** – **1)** Set No. 1 cylinder to TDC of compression stroke. Install new "O" ring on distributor housing. Coat "O" ring with oil. Align cutout marks of coupling and housing. *See Fig. 1.*

**2)** Insert distributor, aligning line of housing with distributor bearing cutout. Connect distributor wiring connector. Install spark plug wires. Connect negative battery cable. Install air cleaner cap, airflow meter and air cleaner hose. Set ignition timing. Tighten distributor hold-down bolts. See TORQUE SPECIFICATIONS at end of article.

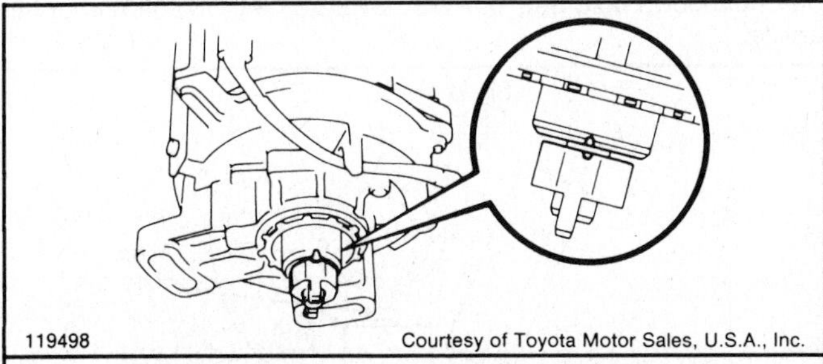
119498 Courtesy of Toyota Motor Sales, U.S.A., Inc.

***Fig. 1: Aligning Distributor Installation Marks (Camry 2.5L – Camry 2.0L, Celica, MR2 & Previa Are Similar)***

**Removal (Celica)** – **1)** Disconnect negative battery cable. On 2.0L Turbo, remove intercooler. To remove intercooler, see TURBOCHARGER under AIR INDUCTION SYSTEM.

**2)** On all engines, disconnect spark plug wires from distributor cap. Disconnect distributor wiring connector. Remove distributor hold-down bolt(s). Remove distributor. Remove "O" ring from distributor housing and discard.

**Installation** – **1)** Set No. 1 cylinder to TDC of compression stroke. Install new "O" ring on distributor housing. Coat "O" ring with oil. Align mark of coupling with groove on housing. *See Fig. 1.*

**2)** Insert distributor, aligning center of distributor flange with bolt hole on cylinder head. Connect distributor wiring connector. Install spark plug wires. Set ignition timing.

**3)** To complete installation, reverse removal procedure. Connect negative battery cable. Set ignition timing. Tighten distributor hold-down bolt(s). See TORQUE SPECIFICATIONS at end of article.

**Removal (Corolla)** – Disconnect negative battery cable. Disconnect spark plug and coil wires from distributor cap. Disconnect distributor wiring connector. Remove distributor hold-down bolts. Remove distributor. Remove "O" ring from distributor housing and discard.

**Installation** – **1)** On 1.6L (4A-FE), set No. 1 cylinder to TDC of compression stroke. Install new "O" ring into housing. Coat "O" ring with oil. Align protrusion on housing with coupling side groove. *See Fig. 2.*

**2)** Insert distributor, aligning center of distributor flange with bolt hole on cylinder head. Connect distributor wiring connector. Install spark plug wires.

**3)** Connect negative battery cable. Set ignition timing. Tighten distributor hold-down bolt. See TORQUE SPECIFICATIONS at end of article.

**4)** On 1.6L (4A-GE), set No. 1 cylinder to TDC of compression stroke. Install new "O" ring into housing. Coat "O" ring with oil. Align drilled mark on drive gear with groove in housing. *See Fig. 3.*

**5)** Insert distributor, aligning center of distributor flange with bolt hole on cylinder head. Connect distributor wiring connector. Install spark plug wires. Connect negative battery cable. Set ignition timing. Tighten distributor hold-down bolts. See TORQUE SPECIFICATIONS at end of article.

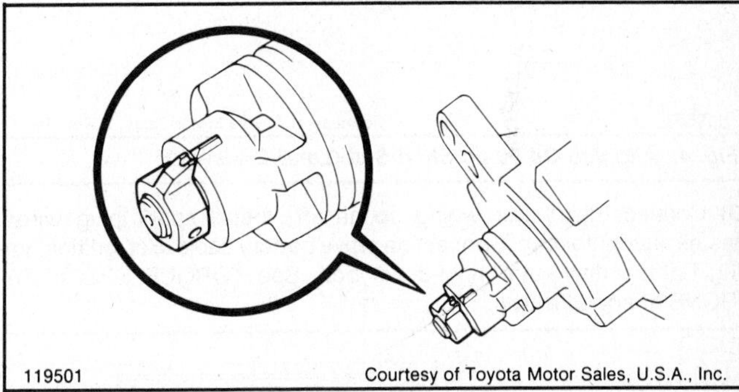
119501 Courtesy of Toyota Motor Sales, U.S.A., Inc.

***Fig. 2: Aligning Distributor Installation Marks (Corolla 1.6L 4A-FE)***

**Removal (Cressida 3.0L & Supra 3.0L Non-Turbo)** – **1)** Disconnect negative battery cable. Remove distributor waterproof cover. Disconnect spark plug wires from distributor cap. Disconnect distributor wiring connector. Remove oil filler cap. Turn crankshaft clockwise until cam lobe can be seen through oil filler hole.

**2)** Turn crankshaft counterclockwise approximately 120 degrees. Turn crankshaft clockwise 10-40 degrees until timing marks on crankshaft pulley and timing cover align. Remove distributor hold-down bolt. Remove distributor. Remove "O" ring from distributor shaft and discard.

**Installation** – **1)** Install new "O" ring into distributor housing. Coat "O" ring with oil. Align groove on distributor housing with protrusion on top of drive gear teeth. *See Fig. 3.*

**2)** Insert distributor, aligning center of distributor flange with bolt hole on cylinder head. Connect distributor wiring connector. Install spark plug wires. Connect negative battery cable. Set ignition timing. Tighten distributor hold-down bolt. See TORQUE SPECIFICATIONS at end of article.

**Removal (Land Cruiser)** – Disconnect negative battery cable. Remove air cleaner hose. Disconnect distributor wiring connector. Disconnect ventilation hoses. Disconnect spark plug wires. Remove hold-down bolt. Remove distributor. Remove "O" ring from distributor shaft and discard.

**Installation** – **1)** Remove No. 1 cylinder spark plug. Place finger over spark plug hole. Turn crankshaft clockwise until pressure is felt. This indicates No. 1 cylinder is at TDC of compression stroke. Install spark plug. Turn oil pump shaft slot. *See Fig. 4.*

**2)** Install new "O" ring into distributor housing. Coat "O" ring with oil. Install distributor with mounting flange aligned with bolt hole on cylinder head and drilled mark on drive gear facing upward. *See Fig. 5.*

# 1991 ENGINE PERFORMANCE
## Removal, Overhaul & Installation (Cont.)

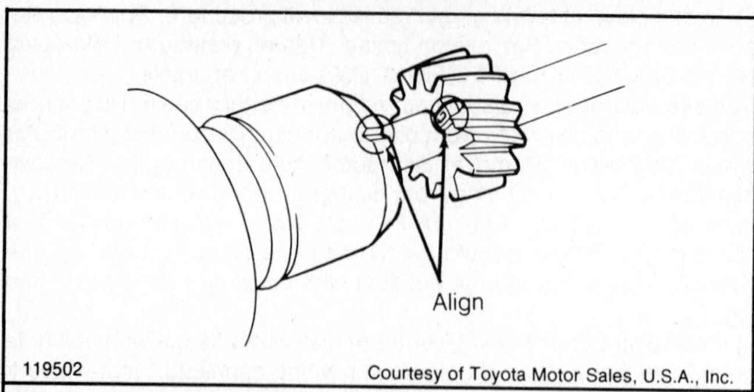


**Fig. 3: Aligning Distributor Installation Marks (Cressida 3.0L & Supra 3.0L Non-Turbo - Corolla 1.6L 4A-GE is Similar)**

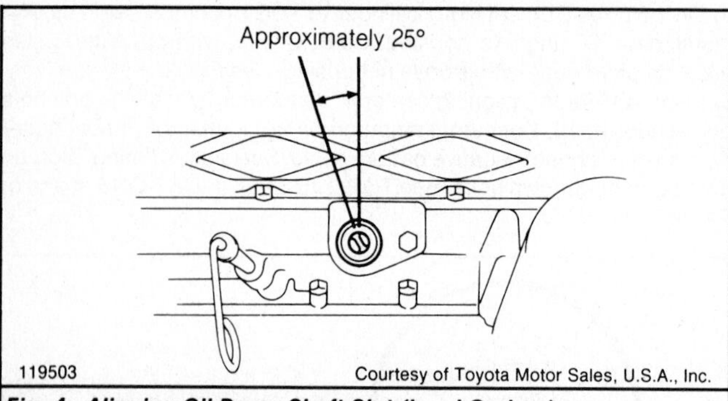


**Fig. 4: Aligning Oil Pump Shaft Slot (Land Cruiser)**

**3)** Connect distributor wiring connector. Install spark plug wires. Install distributor cap. Connect negative battery cable. Set ignition timing.Tighten distributor hold-down bolt. See TORQUE SPECIFICATIONS at end of article.

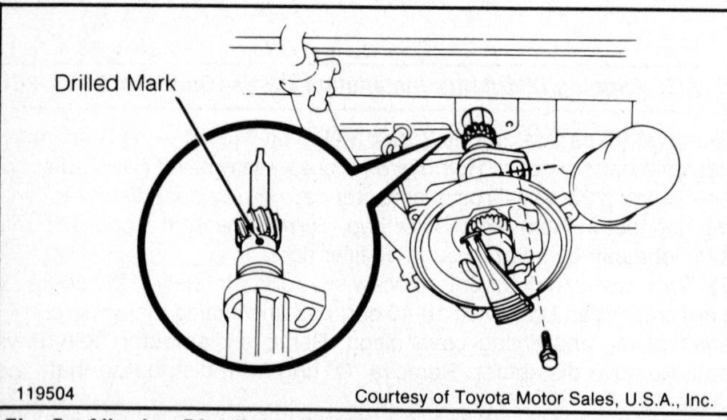


**Fig. 5: Aligning Distributor Installation Marks (Land Cruiser)**

**Removal (MR2)** - Disconnect negative battery cable. Disconnect spark plugs and coil wire from distributor cap. Disconnect distributor wiring connector. Remove distributor hold-down bolts. Remove distributor. Remove "O" ring from distributor housing and discard.

**Installation - 1)** Set No. 1 cylinder to TDC of compression stroke. Install new "O" ring on distributor housing. Coat "O" ring with oil. Turn crankshaft clockwise and position slot of intake camshaft as shown. *See Fig. 6.*

**2)** Align cutout portion of coupling with groove on distributor housing. *See Fig. 1.* Connect Distributor wiring connector. Install distributor, aligning center of flange with bolt hole on cylinder head. Connect negative battery cable.

**3)** Install spark plug wires. Set ignition timing. Tighten distributor hold-down bolts. See TORQUE SPECIFICATIONS at end of article.

**Removal (Pickup 2.4L & 4Runner 2.4L)** - Disconnect negative battery cable. Disconnect spark plug wires. Remove distributor cap. Disconnect distributor wiring connector. Remove distributor hold-down bolt. Remove distributor. Remove "O" ring from distributor housing and discard.

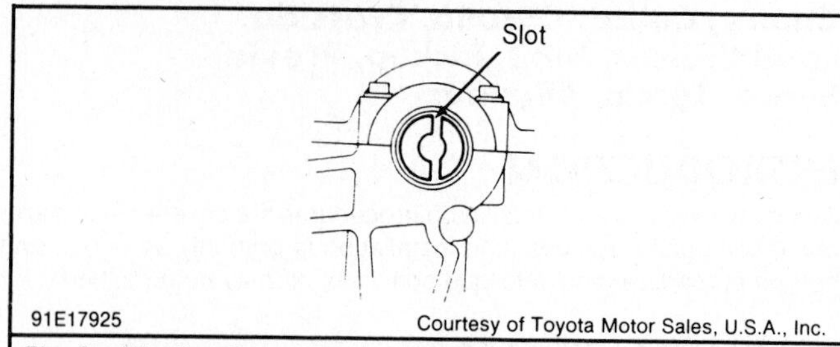


**Fig. 6: Aligning Camshaft Slot (MR2 2.0L Turbo - MR2 2.2L & Previa Are Similar)**

**Installation - 1)** Install new "O" ring into housing. Coat "O" ring with oil. Turn crankshaft until No. 1 cylinder is in compression stroke and timing mark aligns with 5°BTDC mark on timing case cover. Check that rocker arms on No. 1 cylinder are loose. If rocker arms are not loose, turn crankshaft one full turn.

**2)** Temporarily install rotor. Begin inserting distributor with rotor pointing upward and distributor mounting hole aligned with center of mounting bolt hole. When fully installed, rotor will rotate to position shown. *See Fig. 7.*

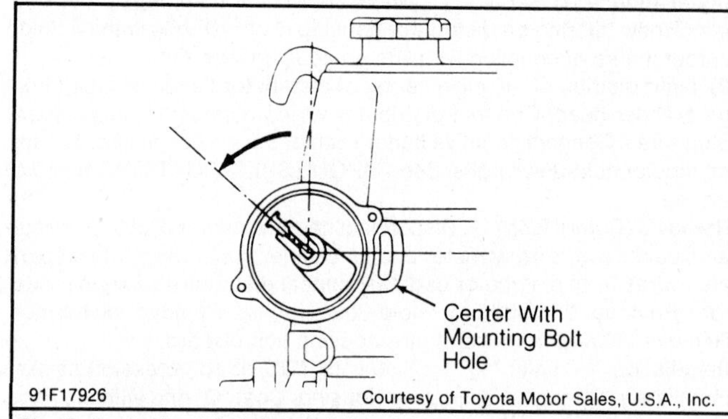


**Fig. 7: Installing Distributor (Pickup 2.4L & 4Runner 2.4L)**

**3)** Align signal rotor tooth with signal generator (pick-up coil) projection. *See Fig. 8.* Install distributor cap and spark plug wires. Connect distributor wiring connector.

**4)** Connect negative battery cable. Set ignition timing. Tighten distributor hold-down bolt. See TORQUE SPECIFICATIONS at end of this article.

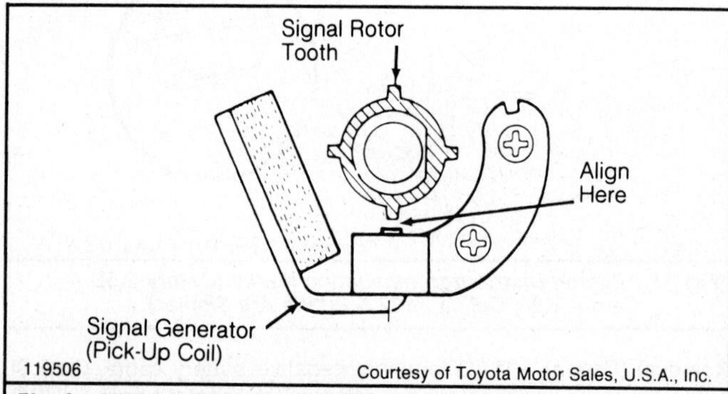


**Fig. 8: Aligning Rotor Tooth & Signal Generator (Pickup 2.4L & 4Runner 2.4L)**

**Removal (Pickup & 4Runner 3.0L) - 1)** Disconnect negative battery cable. Disconnect spark plug wires. Disconnect distributor connector. Remove distributor cap and dust-proof packing.

**2)** Set No. 1 cylinder to TDC of compression strike. Ensure distributor rotor points in direction shown. *See Fig. 9.* Remove distributor hold-down bolt. Remove distributor. Remove "O" ring from distributor housing and discard.

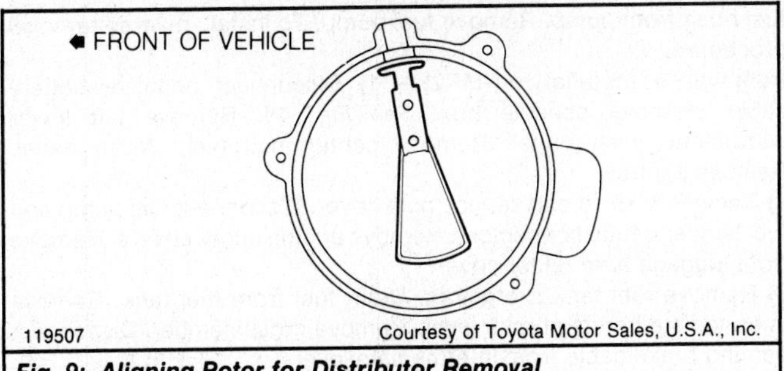


***Fig. 9: Aligning Rotor for Distributor Removal (Pickup 3.0L & 4Runner 3.0L)***

**Installation - 1)** Install new "O" ring into distributor housing. Coat "O" ring with oil. Align protrusion on top of drive gear teeth with groove on distributor housing.
**2)** Insert distributor with housing groove aligned with groove on No. 4 camshaft bearing cap. *See Fig. 10.* Install distributor hold-down bolt, distributor cap and spark plug wires.
**3)** Connect distributor wiring connector. Connect negative battery cable. Set ignition timing. Tighten distributor hold-down bolt. See TORQUE SPECIFICATIONS at end of article.

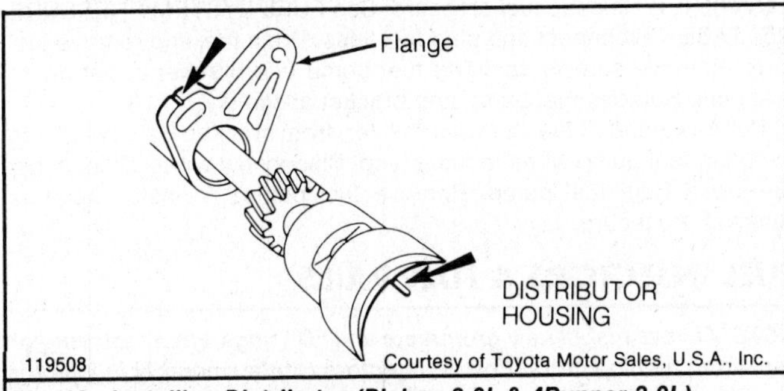


***Fig. 10: Installing Distributor (Pickup 3.0L & 4Runner 3.0L)***

**Removal (Previa) - 1)** Disconnect spark plug wires. Disconnect distributor connector. Remove distributor cap and dust-proof packing. Turn crankshaft until No. 1 cylinder is in compression stroke and timing mark aligns with TDC mark on timing case cover.
**2)** Check that distributor rotor points toward direction shown. *See Fig. 11.* If not, turn crankshaft pulley one complete revolution. Remove distributor hold-down bolts. Remove distributor. Remove "O" ring from distributor housing and discard.

**Installation - 1)** Install new "O" ring on distributor housing. Coat new "O" ring with oil. Turn crankshaft until No. 1 cylinder is in compression stroke and timing mark aligns with TDC mark on timing case cover.
**2)** Position slit of exhaust camshaft as shown. *See Fig. 6.* Align cutout marks of distributor coupling with line on distributor housing. *See Fig. 1.*
**3)** Insert distributor, aligning center of distributor flange with bolt hole on cylinder head. Install spark plug wires. Connect distributor wiring connector.
**4)** Connect negative battery cable. Set ignition timing. Tighten distributor hold-down bolts. See TORQUE SPECIFICATIONS at end of article.
**Removal (Tercel) - 1)** Disconnect negative battery cable. Disconnect spark plug wires. Disconnect distributor connector. Disconnect vacuum hoses.
**2)** Set No. 1 cylinder to TDC of compression stroke. Remove distributor hold-down bolt. Remove distributor. Remove "O" ring from distributor housing and discard.
**Installation - 1)** Install new "O" ring into housing. Coat "O" ring with oil. Align protrusion on distributor housing with groove of coupling side. *See Fig. 12.* Insert distributor with flange aligned with nut on valve cover. *See Fig. 13.*
**2)** Connect spark plug wires and vacuum hoses. Connect distributor wiring connector. Connect negative battery cable. Set ignition timing. Tighten distributor hold-down bolt. See TORQUE SPECIFICATIONS at end of article.

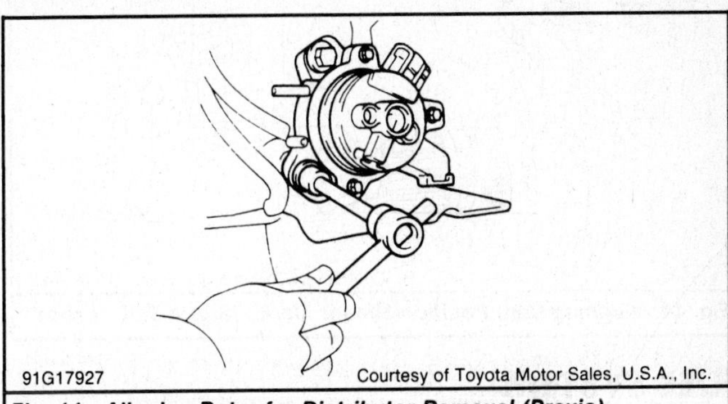


***Fig. 11: Aligning Rotor for Distributor Removal (Previa)***

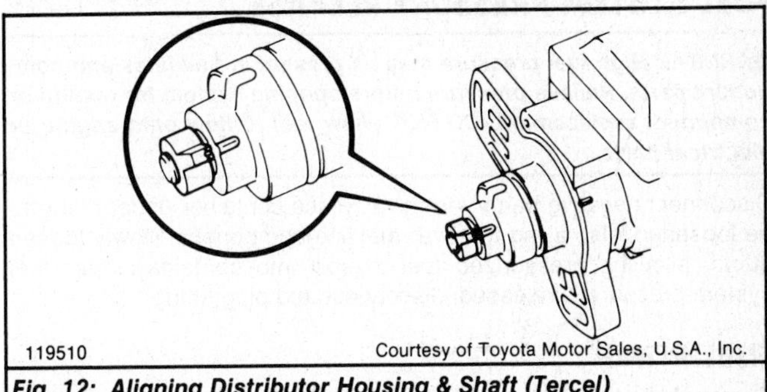


***Fig. 12: Aligning Distributor Housing & Shaft (Tercel)***

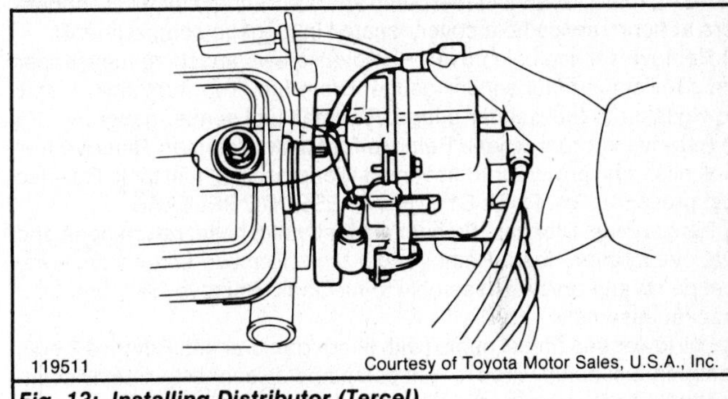


***Fig. 13: Installing Distributor (Tercel)***

## CAM POSITION SENSOR

**Removal (Supra 3.0L Turbo) - 1)** Disconnect negative battery cable. Disconnect cam position sensor connector. Set No. 1 cylinder to TDC of compression stroke. To verify TDC, remove oil filler cap and look for cam lobe facing upward.
**2)** Turn crankshaft counterclockwise approximately 120 degrees. Turn crankshaft clockwise 10-40 degrees until TDC timing marks on crankshaft pulley and timing cover align.
**3)** Remove air cleaner pipe and hoses. Remove airflow meter and air cleaner cap. Remove power steering reservoir. Remove hold-down bolt and cam position sensor. Remove "O" ring from cam position sensor housing and discard.
**Installation - 1)** Install new "O" ring into cam position sensor housing. Coat "O" ring with oil. Align groove on sensor housing with drilled mark on driven gear. *See Fig. 14.*
**2)** Insert cam position sensor with flange aligning with bolt hole on cylinder head. Lightly tighten cam position sensor hold-down bolt. Install power steering reservoir. Install air cleaner hoses, air cleaner cap and airflow meter.
**3)** Connect cam position sensor connector. Connect negative battery cable. Set ignition timing. Tighten cam position sensor hold-down bolt. See TORQUE SPECIFICATIONS at end of article.

# 1991 ENGINE PERFORMANCE
# Removal, Overhaul & Installation (Cont.)

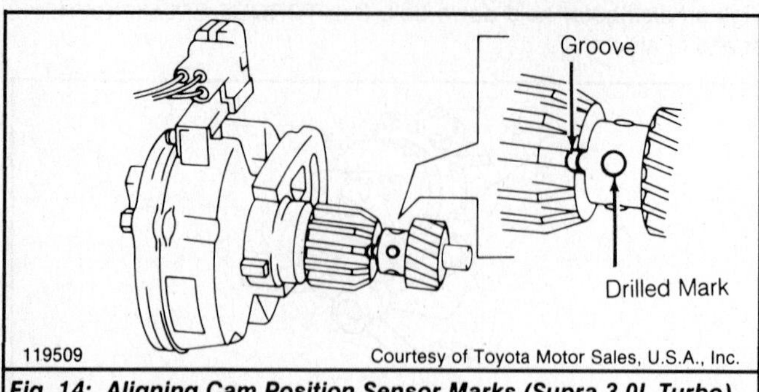


*Fig. 14: Aligning Cam Position Sensor Marks (Supra 3.0L Turbo)*

## FUEL SYSTEM

### FUEL SYSTEM PRESSURE RELEASE

***WARNING: High fuel pressure may be present in fuel lines and component parts. Relieve pressure before opening system for testing or component replacement. DO NOT allow fuel to flow onto engine or electrical parts.***

Disconnect negative battery terminal. Place container under fitting to be loosened. Use a rag to cover fuel line/component. Slowly loosen fitting, allowing pressurized fuel to spill into container. After fuel system pressure is released, disconnect and plug fitting.

### FUEL PUMP

**Removal & Installation (Celica 2.0L) - 1)** Disconnect negative battery cable. Disconnect fuel pump and fuel sender electrical connectors at floor service hole cover, located in luggage compartment.

**2)** Remove service hole cover. Remove screws attaching fuel sender gauge. Remove fuel sender gauge. Drain fuel from fuel tank. Install new gasket to fuel sender gauge. Reinstall fuel sender gauge.

**3)** Remove left rear wheel. Remove fuel tank protector. Remove fuel tank filler pipe protector. Disconnect filler pipe from fuel tank. Release fuel pressure. See FUEL SYSTEM PRESSURE RELEASE.

**4)** Remove fuel filler cap. Disconnect fuel outlet hose, return hose and fuel evaporation hose. Remove fuel tank. Remove screws securing fuel pump and bracket assembly to fuel tank. Remove fuel pump and bracket assembly.

**5)** Pull lower end of fuel pump (with filter) from bracket. Remove 2 nuts securing fuel pump wires to fuel pump and disconnect wires. Disconnect fuel hose from pump. Remove fuel pump. To install, reverse removal procedure.

**Removal & Installation (Celica 1.6L, Celica 2.2L & Tercel) - 1)** Disconnect negative battery cable. Remove gas cap. Remove rear seat cushion. Disconnect fuel pump and fuel sender electrical connector. Remove fuel pump access cover. Release fuel pressure. See FUEL SYSTEM PRESSURE RELEASE.

**2)** Disconnect fuel lines from fuel pump bracket assembly. Remove bolts securing fuel pump and bracket assembly to fuel tank. Remove fuel pump and bracket assembly.

**3)** Remove nuts and washers retaining fuel sending unit wires. Disconnect wires. Remove screws retaining sending unit and separate sending unit from fuel pump and bracket assembly.

**4)** Pull lower end of fuel pump (with filter) from bracket. Remove 2 nuts securing fuel pump wires to fuel pump. Disconnect wires. Disconnect fuel hose from fuel pump. Remove fuel pump. To install, reverse removal procedure.

**Removal & Installation (Land Cruiser) - 1)** Disconnect negative battery cable. Remove service hole cover, located in luggage compartment area. Release fuel pressure. See FUEL SYSTEM PRESSURE RELEASE. Disconnect and plug fuel lines at fuel pump. Remove screws securing fuel pump and bracket assembly to fuel tank. Remove fuel pump and bracket assembly.

**2)** Pull lower end of fuel pump (with filter) from bracket. Remove 2 nuts securing fuel pump wires to fuel pump. Disconnect wires. Disconnect fuel hose from pump. Remove fuel pump. To install, reverse removal procedure.

**Removal & Installation (MR2) - 1)** Disconnect negative battery cable. Remove console box. *See Fig. 15.* Remove left lower instrument finish panel. Remove center instrument finish panel. Remove ashtray.

**2)** Remove screws and service hole cover. Disconnect fuel pump and fuel sender gauge connectors. Remove engine under covers. Remove front luggage area under cover.

**3)** Remove fuel tank protectors. Drain fuel from fuel tank. Remove intermediate parking brake lever. Remove crossmember. Disconnect parking brake cable from intermediate lever.

**4)** Disconnect A/C hoses from body. Disconnect radiator lines from body. Remove fuel tank heat insulators. Remove fuel tank cap. Release fuel pressure. See FUEL SYSTEM PRESSURE RELEASE. Disconnect fuel and vapor hoses. Remove fuel tank.

**5)** Remove screws securing fuel pump and bracket assembly to fuel tank. Remove fuel pump and bracket assembly. Pull lower end of fuel pump (with filter) from bracket.

**6)** Remove 2 nuts securing fuel pump wires to fuel pump. Disconnect wires. Disconnect fuel hose from pump. Remove fuel pump. To install, reverse removal procedure.

**Removal & Installation (Except Celica, Land Cruiser, MR2 & Tercel) - 1)** Release fuel pressure. See FUEL SYSTEM PRESSURE RELEASE. Disconnect and plug fuel lines. Drain fuel and remove fuel tank. Remove screws securing fuel pump and bracket assembly to fuel tank. Remove fuel pump and bracket assembly.

**2)** Pull lower end of fuel pump (with filter) from bracket. Remove 2 nuts securing fuel pump wires to fuel pump. Disconnect wires. Disconnect fuel hose from fuel pump. Remove fuel pump. To install, reverse removal procedure.

### FUEL INJECTORS & FUEL RAILS

***NOTE: Always install new grommets and "O" rings when removing or replacing fuel injectors. Ensure injectors rotate smoothly in injector ports and fuel rail. If injectors DO NOT rotate smoothly, check "O" rings for proper installation.***

**Removal (Camry 2.0L) - 1)** Disconnect negative battery cable. Disconnect cold start injector connector. Release fuel pressure. See FUEL SYSTEM PRESSURE RELEASE. Slowly loosen and remove 2 union bolts, 4 gaskets and cold start injector pipe.

**2)** Disconnect vacuum sensing hose from fuel pressure regulator. Disconnect fuel injector connectors. Disconnect fuel hose from fuel return pipe. Remove fuel pressure pulsation damper and gaskets (if equipped).

**3)** Remove 2 bolts and fuel rail with 4 injectors. Remove 4 insulators and 2 spacers from intake manifold. Remove fuel injectors from fuel rail.

**Installation - 1)** Install new grommets and "O" rings on injectors. Install injectors on fuel rail. Install 4 insulators and 2 spacers in position on cylinder head.

**2)** Place injectors with fuel rail into injector ports. Ensure injectors rotate smoothly. *See Fig. 16.* If injectors do not rotate smoothly, check "O" rings for proper installation. Position injector connectors upward.

**3)** Install fuel rail bolts. Install fuel pressure pulsation damper (if equipped). To complete installation, reverse removal procedure. Tighten all nuts and bolts to specification. See TORQUE SPECIFICATIONS at end of article. Check for fuel leaks.

**Removal (Camry 2.5L) - 1)** Disconnect negative battery cable. Drain coolant. Disconnect throttle cable from throttle body and bracket (if equipped). Disconnect accelerator cable and bracket from throttle body and air intake chamber. Remove air cleaner cap, airflow meter and air cleaner hose.

**2)** Disconnect vacuum hoses as required. Disconnect wiring connectors to idle speed control, throttle position sensor and EGR gas temperature sensor (if equipped).

**3)** Remove 3 bolts and top right engine mount bracket. Disconnect cold start injector connector. Release fuel pressure. See FUEL

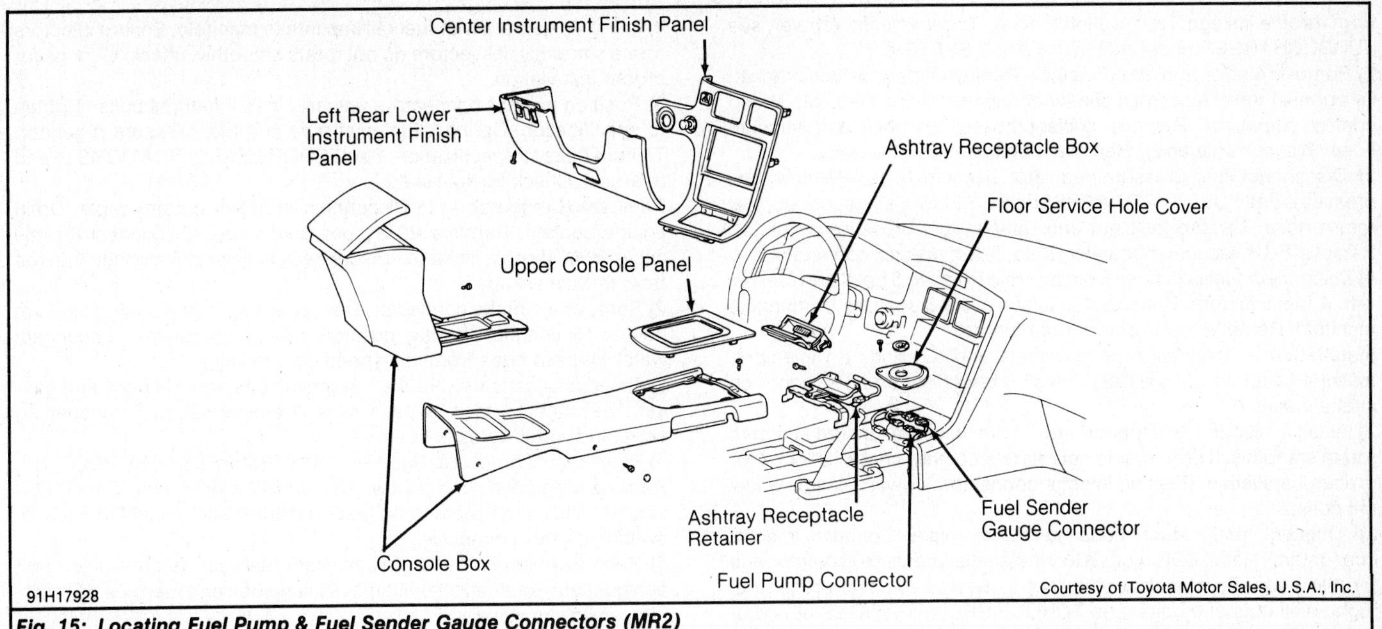


*Fig. 15: Locating Fuel Pump & Fuel Sender Gauge Connectors (MR2)*

SYSTEM PRESSURE RELEASE. Slowly loosen and remove 2 union bolts and 4 gaskets from injector pipe. Remove injector pipe.

**4)** Disconnect hoses to brake booster, power steering vacuum and cruise control. Disconnect ground strap and wiring harness clamp. Disconnect EGR pipe. Remove engine removal hook and air intake chamber bracket.

**5)** Remove 2 bolts and nuts and air intake chamber. Disconnect wiring connectors for cold start injector, coolant temperature sensor and 6 fuel injectors. Disconnect 3 wiring harness clamps from left fuel rail.

**6)** Disconnect fuel return hoses from fuel pressure regulator and No. 1 fuel pipe. Disconnect fuel inlet hose from fuel filter. Remove 2 union bolts, 4 gaskets and No. 2 fuel pipe.

**7)** Remove 2 bolts and left fuel rail with 3 injectors. Remove 3 bolts and right fuel rail with injectors. Remove 6 injectors and 4 spacers from fuel rails. Remove 6 insulators from intake manifold.

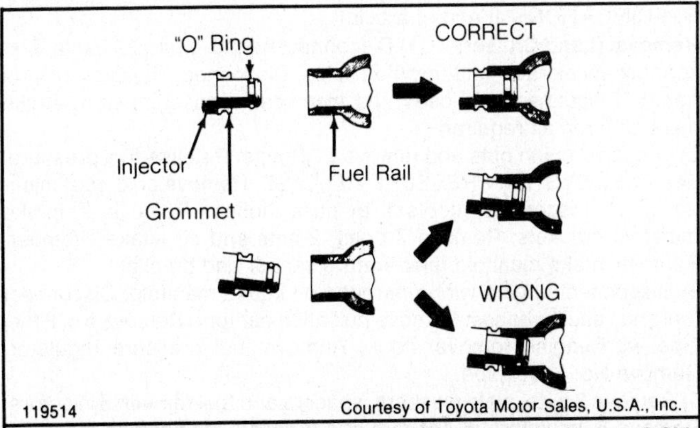


*Fig. 16: Installing Fuel Injectors into Intake Manifold (Camry 2.0L)*

**Installation - 1)** Install new grommets and "O" rings on injectors. Install injectors on fuel rail. Install 6 insulators and 4 spacers on intake manifold.

**2)** Install 3 injectors with right fuel rail into intake manifold. Ensure injectors rotate smoothly. If injectors do not rotate smoothly, check "O" rings for proper installation. Position injector connectors upward. Install 5 fuel rail bolts.

**3)** Install No. 2 fuel pipe with 4 new gaskets and union bolts. *See Fig. 17.* Connect fuel inlet and return hoses. Connect 3 wiring harness clamps to left fuel rail. Connect connectors for 6 injectors, cold start injector and coolant temperature sensor. Install air intake chamber.

**4)** Install EGR pipe. Connect wiring harness with clamp. Install engine removal hook and air intake chamber bracket. Connect hoses and connectors removed.

**5)** Connect cold start injector tube and connector. Install right top engine mount bracket. To complete installation, reverse removal procedure. Tighten all nuts and bolts to specification. See TORQUE SPECIFICATIONS at end of article. Check for fuel leaks.

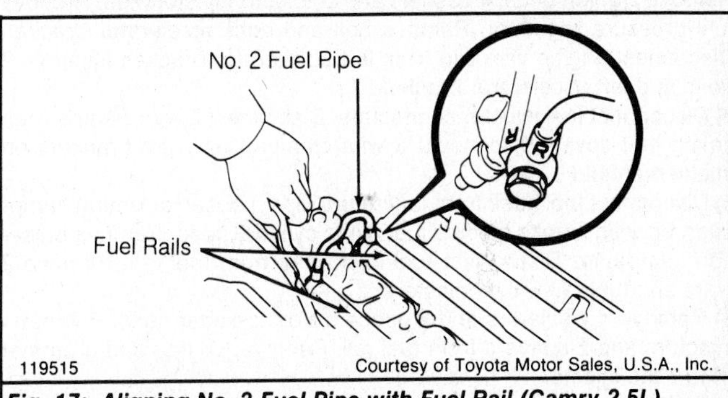


*Fig. 17: Aligning No. 2 Fuel Pipe with Fuel Rail (Camry 2.5L)*

**Removal (Celica 1.6L) - 1)** Disconnect negative battery cable. Disconnect vacuum sensing hose from fuel pressure regulator. Release fuel pressure. See FUEL SYSTEM PRESSURE RELEASE.

**2)** Disconnect fuel return hose from fuel pressure regulator. Remove union bolt, 2 gaskets and disconnect fuel inlet hose from fuel rail.

**3)** Disconnect fuel injector connectors. Remove 2 bolts and fuel rail with 4 injectors. Remove 4 insulators and 2 spacers from cylinder head. Pull out injectors from fuel rail. Remove "O" ring and grommet from each fuel injector.

**Installation - 1)** Install new grommet to each fuel injector. Apply a light coat of gasoline to new "O" ring and install on injector. Install fuel injectors to fuel rail while turning fuel injector from left to right.

**2)** Place 4 new insulators and 2 new spacers in position on cylinder head. Place 4 injectors with fuel rail and position on cylinder head. Ensure fuel injectors rotate smoothly.

**3)** Position fuel injector connector upward. Install fuel rail mounting bolts and tighten. See TORQUE SPECIFICATIONS at end of article. Connect fuel inlet hose to fuel rail.

**4)** Connect fuel injector connectors. Connect fuel return hose to fuel pressure regulator. Connect negative battery cable. Check for fuel leaks.

**Removal (Celica 2.0L) - 1)** Disconnect negative battery cable. Drain coolant from engine and intercooler. Disconnect accelerator cable

# 1991 ENGINE PERFORMANCE
# Removal, Overhaul & Installation (Cont.)

from throttle linkage. Remove intercooler. To remove intercooler, see TURBOCHARGER under AIR INDUCTION SYSTEM.
**2)** Remove 4 bolts and air connector. Remove air connector bracket. Disconnect throttle position sensor connector. Disconnect idle speed control connector. Remove coolant hoses, air hose and vacuum hoses from throttle body. Remove 4 bolts and throttle body.
**3)** Disconnect fuel pressure regulator vacuum hose. Release fuel pressure. See FUEL SYSTEM PRESSURE RELEASE. Disconnect fuel return hose. Loosen lock nut and remove fuel pressure regulator. Remove EGR vacuum modulator. Disconnect injector connectors.
**4)** Disconnect fuel inlet hose from fuel rail. Remove 3 bolts and fuel rail with 4 fuel injectors. Remove 4 insulators and 3 spacers from intake manifold. Remove fuel injectors from fuel rail.
**Installation – 1)** Install new grommets and "O" rings on injectors. Install 4 injectors on fuel rails. Install 4 insulators and 3 spacers on intake manifold.
**2)** Install 4 injectors with fuel rail into intake manifold. Ensure injectors rotate smoothly. If injectors do not rotate smoothly, check "O" rings for proper installation. Position injector connectors upward. Install 3 fuel rail bolts.
**3)** Connect fuel return hose to return pipe. Connect injector connectors. Install EGR modulator. Install fuel pressure regulator and throttle body. To complete installation, reverse removal procedure. Tighten all nuts and bolts. See TORQUE SPECIFICATIONS at end of article. Check for fuel leaks.
**Removal (Celica 2.2L) – 1)** Disconnect negative battery cable. Drain engine coolant. Disconnect throttle cable from throttle linkage (A/T). Disconnect accelerator cable from throttle linkage.
**2)** Remove air cleaner cap and air cleaner hose. Disconnect throttle position sensor connector. Disconnect water, air and vacuum hoses from throttle body as required. Remove throttle body.
**3)** Release fuel pressure. See FUEL SYSTEM PRESSURE RELEASE. Remove 2 union bolts, 4 gaskets and cold start injector pipe. Remove fuel pressure regulator. Remove bolt and right accelerator bracket. Disconnect engine wire clip from left accelerator bracket. Remove 2 bolts and left accelerator bracket.
**4)** Disconnect fuel injector connectors. Disconnect 2 wire clamps from timing belt cover. Disconnect 2 wire clamps from wire brackets on intake manifold.
**5)** Disconnect fuel hose from fuel return pipe. Loosen pulsation dampener. Loosen 2 bolts holding fuel rail to cylinder head. Remove pulsation dampener. Disconnect fuel inlet hose from fuel rail. Remove 2 bolts and fuel rail with 4 injectors.
**6)** Remove 4 insulators and 2 spacers from cylinder head. Pull out 4 injectors and 2 spacers from fuel rail. Remove "O" ring and grommet from each injector.
**Installation – 1)** Install new grommet to injectors. Apply a light coat of gasoline to new "O" ring and install to injector. Install injectors to fuel rail by turning injector from left to right.
**2)** Install 4 new insulators and 2 spacers in position on cylinder head. Place 4 injectors together with fuel rail in position on cylinder head. Temporarily install 2 bolts holding fuel rail to cylinder head. Check that injectors rotate smoothly. Position injector connectors upward.
**3)** Connect fuel inlet pipe to fuel rail with 2 new gaskets and pulsation dampener. To complete installation, reverse removal procedure. Tighten all nuts and bolts to specification. See TORQUE SPECIFICATIONS at end of article. Check for fuel leaks.
**Removal (Corolla) – 1)** Disconnect negative battery cable. Disconnect PCV hoses. Release fuel pressure. See FUEL SYSTEM PRESSURE RELEASE. Disconnect fuel pressure regulator vacuum and fuel return hoses. Disconnect injector connectors. Remove fuel pressure regulator from fuel rail. Disconnect cold start injector connector.
**2)** Remove cold start injector pipe. Remove union bolt and disconnect fuel inlet pipe. Remove bolts and fuel rail with injectors. Remove spacers and insulators from intake manifold. Remove injectors from fuel rail.
**Installation – 1)** Install new grommets and "O" rings on injectors. Apply a thin coat of gasoline to "O" rings and install injectors on fuel rail. Install insulators and spacers on intake manifold.
**2)** Install 4 injectors with fuel rail into intake manifold. Ensure injectors rotate smoothly. If injectors do not rotate smoothly, check "O" rings for proper installation.
**3)** Position injector connectors upward. Install fuel rail bolts. Tighten to specification. Connect fuel inlet pipe and fuel pressure regulator. Tighten bolts to specification. See TORQUE SPECIFICATIONS at end of article. Check for fuel leaks.
**Removal (Cressida) – 1)** Disconnect negative battery cable. Drain engine coolant. Remove PCV pipes and hoses. Disconnect throttle cable from throttle linkage. Disconnect accelerator connecting rod from throttle linkage.
**2)** Remove air intake connector. Disconnect emission control vacuum hoses. Disconnect throttle position sensor connector. Disconnect water by-pass hose from idle speed control valve.
**3)** Remove accelerator bracket. Remove bolts, throttle body and gasket. Disconnect water by-pass hose. Remove vacuum transmitting valve and water by-pass hose.
**4)** Release fuel pressure. See FUEL SYSTEM PRESSURE RELEASE. Remove idle speed control valve. Disconnect injector connectors. Disconnect cold start injector tube from fuel rail. Disconnect EGR vacuum switching valve connector.
**5)** Remove union bolt and gaskets from fuel rail. Remove union bolt and gaskets from fuel filter. Remove clamp bolt and fuel pipe with vacuum switching valve.
**6)** Disconnect vacuum sensing hose. Disconnect fuel hose from fuel pipe. Remove union bolt and gaskets from pressure regulator. Remove clamp bolts and fuel pipe.
**7)** Loosen nut and remove pressure regulator. Remove bolts and fuel rail with injectors. Pull out injectors from fuel rail. Remove insulators and spacers from cylinder head.
**Installation – 1)** Install new grommets on injectors. Apply a light coat of gasoline to new "O" rings and install on injectors. While turning injectors from left to right, install to delivery pipe.
**2)** Place injector insulators in position on cylinder head. Install Black rings on upper portion of each spacer. Install spacers on fuel rail mounting hole of cylinder head.
**3)** Place injectors together with fuel rail in position on cylinder head. Ensure injectors rotate smoothly. If not, check for incorrect installation of "O" rings.
**4)** Position injector connector upward. To complete installation, reverse removal procedure. Tighten all nuts and bolts. See TORQUE SPECIFICATIONS at end of article.
**Removal (Land Cruiser) – 1)** Disconnect negative battery cable. Disconnect accelerator and throttle cables. Disconnect emission control hoses. Disconnect all hoses and electrical connectors from intake manifold area as required.
**2)** Loosen 2 union nuts and remove EGR pipe. Release fuel pressure. See FUEL SYSTEM PRESSURE RELEASE. Remove cold start injector pipe. Disconnect coolant by-pass hoses. Remove 2 intake manifold brackets. Remove 7 bolts, 2 nuts and air intake chamber. Remove intake manifold temperature sensor and bracket.
**3)** Disconnect engine wiring harness on intake manifold. Disconnect fuel and vacuum hoses. Remove pulsation damper. Remove No. 2 fuel pipe with engine removal hook. Remove fuel pressure regulator. Remove No. 1 fuel pipe.
**4)** Remove 3 nuts, plate washers, spacers and fuel rail with 6 injectors. Remove 6 insulators, 6 spacers and 3 collars from intake manifold. Remove injectors from fuel rail.
**Installation – 1)** Install new grommets and "O" rings on injectors. Install 6 injectors on fuel rails. Install 6 insulators, 6 spacers and 3 collars on intake manifold.
**2)** Install 6 injectors with fuel rail into intake manifold. Ensure injectors rotate smoothly. If injectors do not rotate smoothly, check "O" rings for proper installation. Position injector connectors upward. Install 3 fuel rail spacers, washers and nuts.
**3)** To complete installation, reverse removal procedure. Tighten all nuts and bolts. See TORQUE SPECIFICATIONS at end of article.
**Removal (MR2) – 1)** Disconnect negative battery cable. Drain engine coolant. Disconnect accelerator cable from throttle linkage. Remove air intake connector. Remove 4 bolts and intake air connector from throttle body.

**2)** Remove air intake connector bracket and spacers. Disconnect throttle position sensor. Disconnect idle speed control valve connector. Disconnect vacuum and water hoses as required.
**3)** Remove throttle body bolts, throttle body and gasket. Remove left side engine hood side panel. Remove air cleaner. Remove charcoal canister. Remove EGR vacuum switching valve and vacuum modulator. Remove EGR valve and pipe. Release fuel pressure. See FUEL SYSTEM PRESSURE RELEASE. Remove cold start injector pipe.
**4)** Remove cold start injector. Disconnect injector connectors. Disconnect engine wiring from timing belt cover and intake manifold. Remove union bolt, gaskets and disconnect fuel inlet hose from fuel filter. Disconnect fuel return hose from fuel pressure regulator.
**5)** Remove bolt holding fuel inlet hose to water outlet. Remove bolts holding fuel rail to cylinder head. Remove fuel rail assembly. Remove insulators and spacers. Remove fuel inlet hose from fuel rail.
**6)** Disconnect vacuum sensing hose from pressure regulator. Remove screws and injector cover. Remove insulators from injectors. Apply gasoline between fuel rail and injector. Using Injector Remover (SST 09268-74010), pull out injectors from fuel rail. Remove insulator and "O" rings from each injector.
**Installation - 1)** Apply a thin coat of gasoline to new "O" rings. Install "O" rings on injectors. Push in injector and position as shown. *See Fig. 18.* Install injector cover.
**2)** Connect vacuum sensing hose to pressure regulator. Install fuel inlet hose to fuel rail. Install new insulator to each injector. Place spacers on cylinder head.
**3)** Position fuel rail on cylinder head. Install bolts and tighten. See TORQUE SPECIFICATIONS at end of article. To complete installation, reverse removal procedure. Check for fuel leaks.

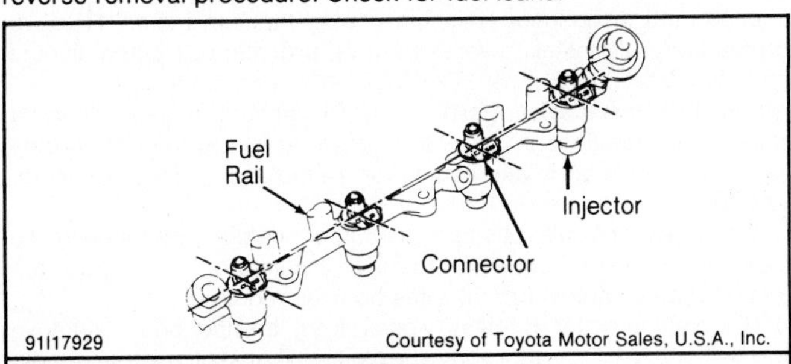


*Fig. 18: Positioning Injectors (MR2)*

**Removal (Pickup 2.4L & 4Runner 2.4L) - 1)** Disconnect negative battery cable. Drain coolant. Disconnect accelerator cable. Disconnect throttle cable (A/T). Disconnect ground strap from rear side of engine.
**2)** Disconnect all water, vacuum, and air hoses as required. Remove EGR modulator. Disconnect all electrical wiring as required. Release fuel pressure. See FUEL SYSTEM PRESSURE RELEASE. Remove union bolt holding cold start injector pipe to air intake chamber. Remove bolts holding EGR pipe to air intake chamber.
**3)** Remove bolts holding manifold bracket to air intake chamber. Remove strap and fuel hose clamp. Remove intake air chamber with throttle body, resonator and gasket. Disconnect fuel hose from fuel rail. Remove bolts and fuel rail with injectors. Pull injectors from fuel rail.
**Installation - 1)** Install grommet and new "O" ring to each injector. Apply a light coat of gasoline and install injectors to fuel rail. Ensure injectors rotate smoothly. If injectors do not rotate smoothly, check that "O" rings are properly installed.
**2)** Install insulators into injector hole of intake manifold. Position injectors with fuel rail to manifold. Install and tighten fuel rail bolts. To complete installation, reverse removal procedure. Tighten all nuts and bolts. See TORQUE SPECIFICATIONS at end of article. Check for fuel leaks.
**Removal (Pickup 3.0L & 4Runner 3.0L) - 1)** Disconnect negative battery cable. Drain coolant. Disconnect throttle position sensor connector. Disconnect canister vacuum hose from throttle body. Release fuel pressure. See FUEL SYSTEM PRESSURE RELEASE. Disconnect vacuum and fuel hoses from fuel pressure regulator. Disconnect PCV hose from union.
**2)** Disconnect water by-pass hose. Disconnect cold start injector connector and tube. Disconnect vacuum hose from gas filter. Disconnect EGR gas temperature sensor connector. Disconnect EGR vacuum hoses. Disconnect air hose from reed valve.
**3)** Remove 6 bolts, 2 nuts and air intake chamber. Disconnect electrical connectors as required. Disconnect vacuum hose from bimetallic vacuum switching valve. Remove 4 union bolts and 2 fuel pipes. Remove 4 nuts and fuel rails with injectors. Remove injectors from fuel rails.
**Installation - 1)** Install new grommets and "O" rings on injectors. Install 6 injectors on fuel rails. Install spacers and insulators. Install injectors on fuel rails.
**2)** Install injectors with fuel rail into intake manifold. Ensure injectors rotate smoothly. If injectors do not rotate smoothly, check "O" rings for proper installation. Position injector connectors upward.
**3)** Install 4 fuel rail nuts. To complete installation, reverse removal procedure. Tighten all nuts and bolts. See TORQUE SPECIFICATIONS at end of article.
**Removal (Previa) - 1)** Disconnect negative battery cable. Remove 3 screws and right front seat scuff plate. Remove bolt and disconnect right seat belt from floor panel.
**2)** Remove 4 bolts and right front seat. Remove 2 bolts and right front seat leg. Remove 2 bolts and jack holder. Remove 9 bolts and right engine service hole cover.
**3)** Remove vacuum hoses and electrical wiring as required. Release fuel pressure. See FUEL SYSTEM PRESSURE RELEASE. Remove union bolt and gaskets from fuel rail. Remove fuel rail bolts, fuel rail and spacers. Remove injector covers. Using Injector Remover (SST 09268-74010), remove injectors.
**Installation - 1)** Lightly lubricate "O" rings with gasoline. Install new "O" rings and insulator to each injector. Ensure "O" rings are not twisted or inverted.
**2)** Push injector into fuel rail by hand. Ensure injector connectors are positioned along center line of fuel rail. Install insulator to each injector. Install injector covers.
**3)** Install insulators to fuel rail. Install injectors with fuel rail to cylinder head. Tighten fuel rail bolts. See TORQUE SPECIFICATIONS at end of article. To complete installation, reverse removal procedure. Check for fuel leaks.
**Removal (Supra) - 1)** Disconnect negative battery cable. Drain coolant. Disconnect all water, air and vacuum hoses as required. Disconnect all electrical wiring as required.
**2)** Disconnect accelerator connecting rod. On 3.0L Non-Turbo, remove throttle body and air intake connector brackets. Remove bolts, nuts, intake connector and gasket.
**3)** On 3.0L Turbo, disconnect accelerator linkage with cable. Disconnect accelerator rod. Disconnect throttle cable (A/T). Remove bolts from idle speed control pipe. Disconnect air valve from intake air connector. Loosen clamps, remove bolts and intake air connector. Remove bolts, throttle body and gasket. Remove vacuum transmitting valve.
**4)** On all engines, remove idle speed control valve. Release fuel pressure. See FUEL SYSTEM PRESSURE RELEASE. Disconnect injector connectors. Loosen cold start injector tube union bolt slowly.
**5)** Remove union bolt and gaskets. Disconnect cold start injector tube. Remove union bolt (3.0L Non-Turbo) or pulsation damper (3.0L Turbo) and gaskets from fuel rail. Remove union bolt and gaskets from fuel rail support. Remove clamp bolt and fuel pipe with vacuum switching valve.
**6)** Disconnect fuel hose from fuel pipes. Remove union bolt and gaskets from fuel pressure regulator. Remove clamp bolt and fuel pipe with vacuum switching valve. Remove pressure regulator. Remove fuel rail with injectors. Remove insulators and spacers from cylinder head. Pull out injectors from fuel rail. Remove "O" ring from injectors.
**Installation - 1)** Install new grommet to each injector. Apply a thin coat of gasoline to new "O" ring and install to each injector. While turning injector from left to right, install injector to fuel rail.
**2)** Install insulators into injector hole of cylinder head. Install Black rings on upper portion of each spacer. Install spacers on fuel rail pipe mounting hole of cylinder head. Position injectors with fuel rail on cylinder head.

# 1991 ENGINE PERFORMANCE
## Removal, Overhaul & Installation (Cont.)

**3)** Check that injectors rotate smoothly. If injectors do not rotate smoothly, check for incorrect "O" ring installation on fuel injector. Install spacer, bolts and tighten fuel rail. See TORQUE SPECIFICATIONS at end of article. To complete installation, reverse removal procedure. Check for fuel leaks.

**Removal (Tercel) – 1)** Disconnect negative battery cable. Remove PCV hoses. Remove air cleaner cap and hose. Disconnect accelerator cable. Disconnect throttle cable (A/T). Disconnect vacuum sensing hose from fuel pressure regulator.

**2)** Release fuel pressure. See FUEL SYSTEM PRESSURE RELEASE. Disconnect fuel return hose from fuel return pipe. Disconnect fuel return pipe from fuel pressure regulator. Disconnect fuel inlet pipe from fuel rail. Disconnect injector connectors. Remove fuel rail with injectors.

**Installation – 1)** Install new grommets and "O" rings on injectors. Install 4 injectors on fuel rails. Install 4 insulators and 2 spacers on intake manifold.

**2)** Install 4 injectors with fuel rail into intake manifold. Ensure injectors rotate smoothly. If injectors do not rotate smoothly, check "O" rings for proper installation. Position injector connectors upward. Install 2 fuel rail bolts.

**3)** To complete installation, reverse removal procedure. Tighten all nuts and bolts to specification. See TORQUE SPECIFICATIONS at end of article.

## OXYGEN ($O_2$) & SUB-OXYGEN SENSORS

**Removal** – Disconnect sensor electrical connector. Remove 2 mounting nuts or bolts. Remove sensor. Some sub-oxygen sensors screw into exhaust manifold or header pipe.

***NOTE: When removing sensor, protect its permanent pigtail from damage. Ensure sensor is free of contaminants. Avoid using cleaning solvents of any type.***

**Installation** – Install sensor. Install nuts or bolts. Connect electrical connector. Oxygen sensor torque specification is not available from manufacturer.

## THROTTLE BODY

**Removal & Installation (Camry 2.0L) – 1)** Disconnect negative battery cable. Drain coolant. Disconnect throttle cable (A/T) and accelerator cable from throttle linkage. Disconnect air cleaner hose.

**2)** Unplug throttle position sensor connector. Disconnect idle speed control valve connector. Disconnect PCV valve hose, coolant by-pass hose and air tube hose. Disconnect emission control vacuum hoses and mark for installation. Remove throttle body.

**3)** To install, reverse removal procedure. Tighten all nuts and bolts. See TORQUE SPECIFICATIONS at end of article.

**Removal & Installation (Camry 2.5L) – 1)** Disconnect negative battery cable. Drain coolant. Disconnect throttle cable (A/T) and accelerator cable from throttle linkage. Disconnect air cleaner cap, airflow meter and air cleaner hose.

**2)** Unplug throttle position sensor. Disconnect PCV valve hose. Disconnect coolant by-pass hose. Label and disconnect emission control vacuum hoses. Disconnect throttle cable bracket. Remove mounting bolts and throttle body.

**3)** To install, reverse removal procedure. Tighten all nuts and bolts. See TORQUE SPECIFICATIONS at end of article.

**Removal & Installation (Celica 1.6L & 2.2L) – 1)** Disconnect negative battery cable. Drain coolant. Disconnect throttle cable (A/T) and accelerator cable from throttle linkage. Disconnect air cleaner cap and air cleaner hose.

**2)** Unplug throttle position sensor. Disconnect idle speed control connector (2.2L). Disconnect PCV valve hose. Disconnect coolant by-pass hoses. Label and disconnect emission control vacuum hoses. Disconnect throttle cable bracket. Remove mounting bolts and throttle body.

**3)** To install, reverse removal procedure. Tighten all nuts and bolts. See TORQUE SPECIFICATIONS at end of article.

**Removal & Installation (Celica 2.0L) – 1)** Disconnect negative battery cable. Drain coolant. Remove intercooler. Disconnect accelerator cable from throttle linkage. Remove air connector and air connector bracket.

**2)** Unplug throttle position sensor and idle speed control valve connectors. Disconnect coolant by-pass hose and air hose. Label and disconnect emission control vacuum hoses. Remove throttle body.

**3)** To install, reverse removal procedure. Tighten all nuts and bolts. See TORQUE SPECIFICATIONS at end of article.

**Removal & Installation (Corolla 1.6L 4A-FE & 4A-GE) – 1)** Disconnect negative battery cable. Drain coolant. Disconnect accelerator cable from throttle linkage. Remove cable bracket from throttle body (4A-FE).

**2)** Remove air cleaner hose. Unplug throttle position sensor. Disconnect coolant by-pass hose(s) and PCV hose. Label and disconnect emission control vacuum hoses. Remove throttle body. To install, reverse removal procedure. Tighten all nuts and bolts. See TORQUE SPECIFICATIONS at end of article.

**Removal & Installation (Cressida & Supra) – 1)** Disconnect negative battery cable. Drain coolant. Disconnect accelerator connecting rod. Remove air intake connector (Supra 3.0L Turbo). Label and disconnect emission control vacuum hoses.

**2)** Disconnect coolant by-pass hose(s). Unplug throttle position sensor. Remove air cleaner hose. Remove throttle body bracket (3.0L Non-Turbo). Remove throttle body.

**3)** To install, reverse removal procedure. Tighten all nuts and bolts. See TORQUE SPECIFICATIONS at end of article.

**Removal & Installation (Land Cruiser) – 1)** Disconnect negative battery cable. Drain coolant. Disconnect accelerator and throttle cables from throttle linkage. Disconnect air cleaner hose. Unplug throttle position sensor. Disconnect coolant by-pass hoses(s).

**2)** Label and disconnect emission control vacuum hoses. Remove throttle body. To install, reverse removal procedure. Tighten all nuts and bolts. See TORQUE SPECIFICATIONS at end of article.

**Removal & Installation (MR2) – 1)** Disconnect negative battery cable. Drain coolant. Disconnect accelerator cable from throttle linkage. Remove air intake connector. Remove air intake connector bracket.

**2)** Disconnect throttle position sensor connector. Disconnect idle speed control valve connector. Remove accelerator bracket. Disconnect all vacuum hoses from throttle body as required.

**3)** Disconnect water by-pass hoses from throttle body. Remove throttle body bolts, throttle body and gasket. To install, reverse removal procedure. Tighten all nuts and bolts. See TORQUE SPECIFICATIONS at end of article.

**Removal & Installation (Pickup 2.4L & 4Runner 2.4L) – 1)** Disconnect negative battery cable. Drain coolant. Remove intake air connector. Disconnect accelerator cable from throttle linkage. Disconnect A/C idle-up hose, PCV hose and coolant by-pass hose(s).

**2)** Label and disconnect emission control vacuum hoses. Unplug throttle position sensor. Remove throttle body. To install, reverse removal procedure. Tighten all nuts and bolts. See TORQUE SPECIFICATIONS at end of article.

**Removal & Installation (Pickup 3.0L & 4Runner 3.0L) – 1)** Disconnect negative battery cable. Drain coolant. Disconnect air cleaner hose. Unplug throttle position sensor. Label and disconnect emission control vacuum hoses.

**2)** Disconnect accelerator and throttle cables from throttle linkage. Disconnect coolant by-pass hoses. Remove throttle body. To install, reverse removal procedure. Tighten all nuts and bolts. See TORQUE SPECIFICATIONS at end of article.

**Removal & Installation (Previa) – 1)** Disconnect negative battery cable. Remove 3 screws and right front seat scuff plate. Remove bolt and disconnect right seat belt from floor panel. Remove 4 bolts and right front seat.

**2)** Remove 2 bolts and right front seat leg. Remove 2 bolts and jack holder. Remove 9 bolts and right engine service hole cover. Drain coolant. Remove air intake connector. Disconnect throttle position sensor and idle speed control valve connectors. Disconnect vacuum hoses as required.

**3)** Disconnect water by-pass hoses. Disconnect throttle cable (A/T). Disconnect accelerator cable and bracket. Remove throttle body bolts, throttle body and gasket. To install, reverse removal procedure.

# 1991 ENGINE PERFORMANCE
# Removal, Overhaul & Installation (Cont.)

Tighten all nuts and bolts to specification. See TORQUE SPECIFICATIONS at end of article.

**Removal & Installation (Tercel) - 1)** Disconnect negative battery cable. Drain coolant. Disconnect accelerator and throttle cables from throttle linkage. Disconnect air cleaner hose. Unplug throttle position sensor. Remove PCV hose.

**2)** Label and disconnect emission control and A/C vacuum hoses. Remove throttle body. To install, reverse removal procedure. Tighten all nuts and bolts. See TORQUE SPECIFICATIONS at end of article.

## AIR INDUCTION SYSTEM

### TURBOCHARGER

**Removal (Celica) - 1)** Disconnect negative battery cable. Drain coolant. Remove air cleaner. Remove lower engine covers and suspension lower crossmember for access to catalytic converter. Remove front engine mount and bracket.

**2)** Remove idler pulley bracket and A/C compressor (without disconnecting lines). Remove front exhaust pipe and catalytic converter. Remove oxygen sensor. Without disconnecting lines, remove clutch cylinder.

**3)** Remove intercooler radiator hoses, intercooler reservoir hose and intercooler coolant levels warning sensor connector. Remove intercooler and hoses. Remove alternator and bracket.

**4)** Remove dipstick. Remove turbocharger heat insulator and turbine outlet elbow. Remove turbocharger-to-block bracket. Remove oil pipe union bolt and oil pipe. Remove turbocharger.

***NOTE: Check for oil sludge in oil pipes. Replace if necessary.***

**Inspection - 1)** Ensure turbine wheel turns smoothly. If impeller wheel will not turn or drags when turned, replace turbocharger assembly.

**2)** Place dial indicator on shaft end. Axial (forward-and-backward) shaft play should be .0051" (.13 mm) or less. If not, replace turbocharger.

**3)** Insert dial indicator into oil outlet hole through hole in spacer bearing. Set dial indicator against center of turbine shaft. Radial (up-and-down) play should be .0071" (.18 mm) or less. If not, replace turbocharger.

**Installation -** To install, reverse removal procedure. Use new gaskets and "O" rings. After installing turbocharger, pour 1 fluid ounce (30 cc) of new oil into oil inlet. Turn impeller wheel by hand to circulate oil onto bearings. Fill cooling system and intercooler with coolant.

**Removal MR2 - 1)** Disconnect negative battery cable. Drain coolant. Remove engine under covers. Remove left engine hood side panel. Remove suspension upper brace.

**2)** Remove air cleaner. Remove air intake connectors. Disconnect transaxle control cables. Remove front exhaust pipe. Remove idler pulley bracket and A/C compressor.

**3)** Remove front engine mounting insulator. Remove front mounting bracket and clutch release cylinder. Remove engine cooling fan. Disconnect vacuum and air hoses as required. Disconnect electrical wiring as required. Remove air by-pass valve.

**4)** Remove turbocharger heat insulator. Remove oxygen sensor. Remove turbine outlet elbow heat insulators. Disconnect water hoses as required. Remove turbocharger bracket. Remove bolt and union bolt holding oil pipe to cylinder block. Remove union bolt gaskets. Remove 4 nuts, turbocharger and gasket.

**Inspection - 1)** Ensure turbine wheel turns smoothly. If impeller wheel will not turn or drags, replace turbocharger assembly.

**2)** Place dial indicator on shaft end. Axial (forward-and-backward) shaft play should be .0051" (.13 mm) or less. If not, replace turbocharger.

**3)** Insert dial indicator into oil outlet hole through hole in spacer bearing. Set dial indicator against center of turbine shaft. Radial (up-and-down) play should be .0071" (.18 mm) or less. If not, replace turbocharger.

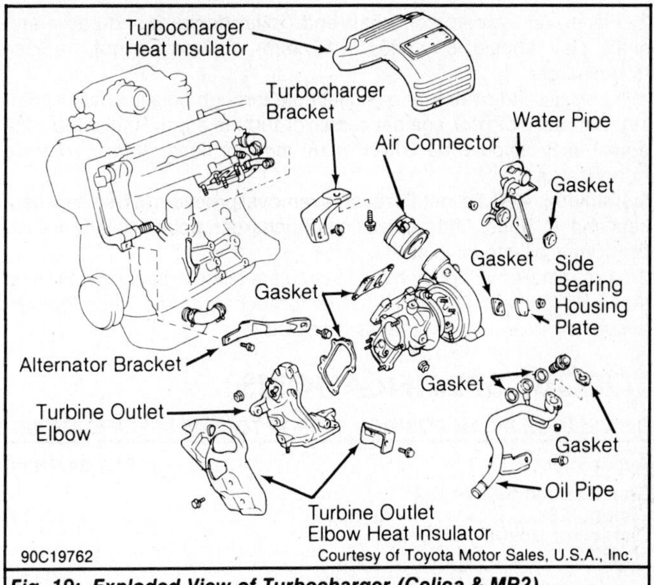


*Fig. 19: Exploded View of Turbocharger (Celica & MR2)*

**Installation -** To install, reverse removal procedure. Use new gaskets and "O" rings. After installing turbocharger, pour 1 fluid ounce (30 cc) of new oil into oil inlet. Turn impeller wheel by hand to circulate oil onto bearings. Fill cooling system and intercooler with coolant.

**Removal (Supra) - 1)** Disconnect negative battery cable. Drain cooling system. Remove hoses from air cleaner with airflow meter and air cleaner cap. Disconnect oxygen sensor. Remove turbocharger heat insulator.

**2)** Remove dipstick, dipstick guide and bolt. Remove remaining air cleaner hose clamps, air cleaner pipe mounting bolt and air cleaner pipe. Disconnect exhaust pipe from exhaust manifold. Remove gasket. Remove turbocharger oil pipe mounting nuts and union bolt.

**3)** Remove 2 turbo brackets. Disconnect turbocharger coolant hose from coolant outlet housing. Disconnect union pipe. Remove 4 mounting nuts, turbocharger and gasket.

**4)** With turbocharger on bench, remove second coolant pipe nuts, coolant pipe and gasket. Remove turbocharger oil pipe and gasket. Remove turbine outlet elbow and gasket.

**Inspection - 1)** Ensure turbine wheel turns smoothly. If impeller wheel will not turn or drags when turned, replace turbocharger assembly.

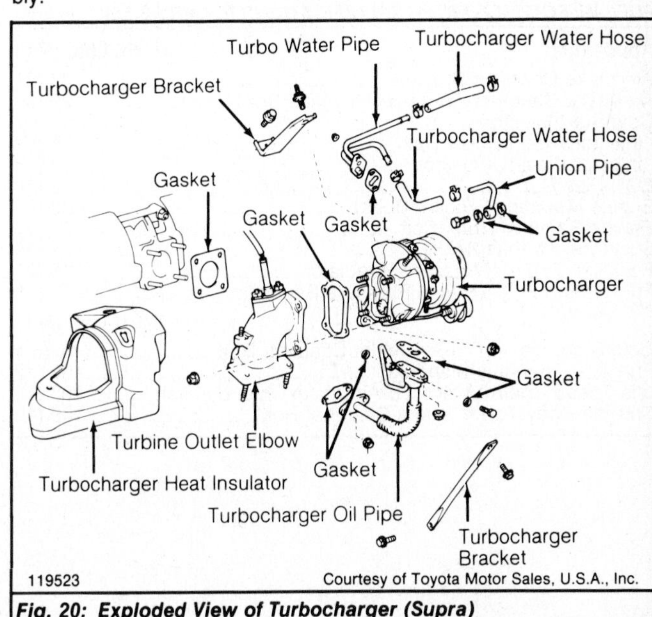


*Fig. 20: Exploded View of Turbocharger (Supra)*

# 1991 ENGINE PERFORMANCE
# Removal, Overhaul & Installation (Cont.)

2) Place dial indicator on shaft end. Axial (forward-and-backward) shaft play should be .0051" (.13 mm) or less. If not, replace turbocharger.

3) Insert dial indicator into oil outlet hole through hole in spacer bearing. Set dial indicator against center of turbine shaft. Radial (up-and-down) play should be .0071" (.18 mm) or less. If not, replace turbocharger.

**Installation - 1)** To install, reverse removal procedure. Use new gaskets and "O" rings. After replacing turbocharger, pour 1 fluid ounce (30 cc) of new oil into oil inlet.

2) Turn impeller wheel by hand to circulate oil onto bearings. Fill system with coolant. When installing turbocharger mounting gasket, ensure protrusion gasket faces rearward.

## TORQUE SPECIFICATIONS

***DISTRIBUTOR & CAM POSITION SENSOR TORQUE SPECIFICATIONS***

| Application | Ft. Lbs. (N.m) |
|---|---|
| Cam Position Sensor Bolt | |
| Supra 3.0L | 10 (14) |
| Distributor Hold-Down Bolt | |
| Camry | |
| 2.0L | 9 (12) |
| 2.5L | 13 (18) |
| Celica | |
| 1.6L | 14 (19) |
| 2.0L | 29 (39) |
| 2.2L | 9 (12) |
| Corolla, Pickup (2.4L), 4Runner (2.4L) & Previa | 14 (19) |
| Cressida & Supra | 10 (14) |
| Land Cruiser, Pickup (3.0L), Tercel & 4Runner (3.0L) | 13 (18) |
| MR2 | |
| 2.0L | 29 (39) |
| 2.2L | 9 (12) |

***FUEL INJECTION TORQUE SPECIFICATIONS (CAMRY 2.0L)***

| Application | Ft. Lbs. (N.m) |
|---|---|
| Cold Start Injector | |
| Injector Pipe-To-Fuel Rail | 13 (18) |
| Injector Pipe-To-Injector | 13 (18) |
| Fuel Return Pipe-To-Fuel Pressure Regulator | 13 (18) |
| Throttle Body-To-Air Intake Chamber Bolt | 14 (19) |
| | **INCH Lbs. (N.m)** |
| Cold Start Injector-To-Air Intake Chamber Bolt | 82 (9.3) |
| Fuel Pressure Regulator-To-Fuel Rail Bolt | 48 (5.4) |
| Fuel Rail-To-Cylinder Head Bolt | 108 (12) |

***FUEL INJECTION TORQUE SPECIFICATIONS (CAMRY 2.5L)***

| Application | Ft. Lbs. (N.m) |
|---|---|
| Air Intake Chamber Bracket | 27 (37) |
| Air Intake Chamber-To-Intake Manifold Bolt | 29 (39) |
| Cold Start Injector | |
| Injector Pipe-To-Fuel Rail | 13 (18) |
| Injector Pipe-To-Injector | 13 (18) |
| EGR Pipe Nut | 58 (78) |
| Engine Mounting Bracket Bolts | 38 (52) |
| Engine Removal Hook Bolt | 27 (37) |
| Fuel Pipe-To-Fuel Rail | 21 (29) |
| Fuel Rail-To-Fuel Pressure Regulator | 18 (25) |
| Fuel Return Pipe-To-Fuel Pressure Regulator | 13 (18) |
| | **INCH Lbs. (N.m)** |
| Cold Start Injector-To-Air Intake Chamber Bolt | 48 (5.4) |
| Fuel Rail-To-Intake Manifold | 108 (12) |
| Idle Speed Control Valve-To-Air Intake Chamber Bolt | 108 (12) |
| Throttle Body-To-Air Intake Chamber Bolt | 108 (12) |

***FUEL INJECTION TORQUE SPECIFICATIONS (CELICA 1.6L & 2.2L)***

| Application | Ft. Lbs. (N.m) |
|---|---|
| Fuel Rail-To-Cylinder Head Bolt | |
| 1.6L | 11 (15) |
| 2.2L | 9 (12) |
| Throttle Body-To-Intake Manifold | |
| 1.6L | 16 (22) |
| 2.2L | 14 (19) |
| | **INCH Lbs. (N.m)** |
| Fuel Pressure Regulator-To-Fuel Rail | |
| 1.6L | 82 (9.3) |
| 2.2L | 48 (5.4) |

***FUEL INJECTION TORQUE SPECIFICATIONS (CELICA 2.0L)***

| Application | Ft. Lbs. (N.m) |
|---|---|
| Air Connector Bracket-To-Throttle Body Bolt | 14 (19) |
| Cold Start Injector Pipe-To-Cold Start Injector Bolt | 13 (18) |
| Cold Start Injector-To-Fuel Rail Bolt | 13 (18) |
| Fuel Inlet Hose-To-Fuel Rail Bolt | 22 (29) |
| Fuel Pressure Regulator-To-Fuel Rail Nut | 22 (29) |
| Fuel Rail-To-Cylinder Head Bolt | 14 (19) |
| Throttle Body-To-Air Intake Chamber Bolt | 14 (19) |
| | **INCH Lbs. (N.m)** |
| Air Connector Bracket-To-Cylinder Head Bolt | 69 (7.8) |
| Cold Start Injector-To-Air Intake Chamber Bolt | 52 (5.9) |

***FUEL INJECTION TORQUE SPECIFICATIONS (COROLLA)***

| Application | Ft. Lbs. (N.m) |
|---|---|
| Cold Start Injector Pipe-To-Cold Start Injector Bolt | 13 (18) |
| Fuel Inlet Hose-To-Fuel Rail Bolt | 22 (29) |
| Fuel Rail-To-Cylinder Head Bolt | |
| 1.6L 4A-FE | 11 (15) |
| 1.6L 4A-GE | 13 (18) |
| | **INCH Lbs. (N.m)** |
| Cold Start Injector-To-Air Intake Chamber Bolt | 82 (9.3) |
| Fuel Pressure Regulator-To-Fuel Rail Bolt | 65 (7.4) |

***FUEL INJECTION TORQUE SPECIFICATIONS (CRESSIDA & SUPRA)***

| Application | Ft. Lbs. (N.m) |
|---|---|
| Air Intake Connector-To-Air Intake Chamber Bolt [1] | 13 (18) |
| Cold Start Injector-To-Cold Start Injector Tube Bolt | 13 (18) |
| Cold Start Injector-To-Fuel Rail Bolt | 22 (29) |
| Front Fuel Pipe-To-Cylinder Head Bolt | 18 (25) |
| Fuel Pipe-To-Fuel Rail Bolt | 29 (39) |
| Fuel Pressure Regulator-To-Fuel Rail Bolt | 18 (25) |
| Fuel Rail-To-Cylinder Head Bolt | 13 (18) |
| Rear Fuel Pipe-To-Fuel Pipe Support Bolt | 22 (29) |
| | **INCH Lbs. (N.m)** |
| Cold Start Injector-To-Air Intake Chamber Bolt | 48 (5.4) |
| Idle Speed Control Valve-To-Air Intake Chamber Bolt | 108 (12) |
| Throttle Body-To-Air Intake Chamber Bolt [2] | 108 (12) |

[1] – 3.0L Non-Turbo only.
[2] – 3.0L Turbo only.

***FUEL INJECTION TORQUE SPECIFICATIONS (LAND CRUISER)***

| Application | Ft. Lbs. (N.m) |
|---|---|
| Air Intake Chamber Bolt | 18 (25) |
| EGR Pipe Union Nuts | 58 (78) |
| Engine Removal Hook Bolt | 22 (29) |
| Fuel Pipe Bolt | 14 (19) |
| | **INCH Lbs. (N.m)** |
| Fuel Rail Nut | 108 (12) |
| Manifold Bracket Bolt | 108 (12) |
| Manifold Temp. Sensor Bracket Bolt | 108 (12) |

# 1991 ENGINE PERFORMANCE
# Removal, Overhaul & Installation (Cont.)

### FUEL INJECTION TORQUE SPECIFICATIONS (MR2)

| Application | Ft. Lbs. (N.m) |
|---|---|
| Air Intake Connector Bracket-To-Throttle Body Bolts | 14 (19) |
| Cold Start Injector Pipe-To-Cold Start Injector | 13 (18) |
| Cold Start Injector-To-Fuel Rail Bolts | 13 (18) |
| Crossmember-To-Body Bolts | 22 (29) |
| Fuel Inlet Hose-To-Fuel Filter | 22 (29) |
| | **INCH Lbs. (N.m)** |
| Air Intake Connector Bracket-To-Cylinder Head | 69 (7.8) |
| Cold Start Injector-To-Intake Manifold | 52 (5.9) |
| Injector Cover-To-Fuel Rail | 69 (7.8) |

### FUEL INJECTION TORQUE SPECIFICATIONS [1] (PICKUP 2.4L & 4RUNNER 2.4L)

| Application | Ft. Lbs. (N.m) |
|---|---|
| Fuel Pipe-To-Fuel Rail Bolt | 33 (44) |
| Fuel Rail-To-Intake Manifold Bolt | 14 (19) |
| Intake Manifold-To-Air Intake Chamber Bolt | 13 (18) |

[1] – Other fuel system torque specifications not available from manufacturer.

### FUEL INJECTION TORQUE SPECIFICATIONS (PICKUP 3.0L & 4RUNNER 3.0L)

| Application | Ft. Lbs. (N.m) |
|---|---|
| Cold Start Injector Tube Bolt | 13 (18) |
| EGR Tube-To-Exhaust Manifold Bolt | 22 (29) |
| EGR Valve-To-Air Intake Chamber Bolt | 13 (18) |
| Fuel Pipe-To-Fuel Rail Bolt | 33 (44) |
| Intake Manifold-To-Air Intake Chamber Bolt | 13 (18) |
| | **INCH Lbs. (N.m)** |
| Air Intake Chamber Bracket Bolt | 108 (12) |
| Fuel Rail-To-Manifold Bolt | 108 (12) |

### FUEL INJECTION TORQUE SPECIFICATIONS (PREVIA)

| Application | Ft. Lbs. (N.m) |
|---|---|
| Fuel Pipe-To-Cold Start Injector | 14 (19) |
| Fuel Rail-To-Cylinder Head Bolts | 14 (19) |
| Fuel Pipe-To-Fuel Rail | 22 (29) |
| | **INCH Lbs. (N.m)** |
| Cold Start Injector-To-Intake Manifold Bolts | 48 (5.4) |
| Fuel Pipe-To-Intake Manifold | 48 (5.4) |
| Injector Cover-To-Fuel Rail Bolts | 48 (5.4) |
| Pressure Regulator-To-Fuel Rail | 48 (5.4) |

### FUEL INJECTION TORQUE SPECIFICATIONS [1] (TERCEL)

| Application | Ft. Lbs. (N.m) |
|---|---|
| Cold Start Injector Union Bolt | 14 (19) |
| Fuel Rail-To-Intake Manifold Bolt | 14 (19) |
| Pulsation Damper-To-Fuel Rail | 22 (30) |
| | **INCH lbs. (N.m)** |
| Cold Start Injector Bolt | 69 (7.8) |

[1] – Other fuel system torque specifications are not available from manufacturer.

### FUEL PUMP TORQUE SPECIFICATIONS

| Application | INCH Lbs. (N.m) |
|---|---|
| Fuel Pump Bracket Retaining Bolt | |
| Previa | 48 (5.4) |
| Fuel Pump Bracket Retaining Screws | |
| Camry, Pickup, 4Runner, Celica 2.0L & Land Cruiser | 35 (3.9) |
| Celica 1.6L & 2.2L, Cressida & Previa | 26 (2.9) |
| Corolla | |
| 1.6L 4A-FE | 35 (3.9) |
| 1.6L 4A-GE | 30 (3.4) |
| Supra & Tercel | 30 (3.4) |

### THROTTLE BODY TORQUE SPECIFICATIONS

| Application | Ft. Lbs. (N.m) |
|---|---|
| **Throttle Body Bolt/Nut** | |
| Camry | |
| 2.0L | 9 (12) |
| 2.5L | 13 (18) |
| Celica | |
| 1.6L | 16 (22) |
| 2.0L | 14 (19) |
| 2.2L | 14 (19) |
| Corolla | 16 (22) |
| Cressida, Land Cruiser, Supra & Tercel | 9 (12) |
| MR2 | 14 (19) |
| Pickup & 4Runner | |
| 2.4L | 14 (19) |
| 3.0L | 13 (18) |
| Previa | 13 (18) |

### TURBOCHARGER TORQUE SPECIFICATIONS (CELICA)

| Description | Ft. Lbs. (N.m) |
|---|---|
| Alternator Bracket Bolt | |
| Others | 32 (43) |
| Turbine Outlet Side | 29 (39) |
| Catalytic Converter | |
| Mounting Bolt | 22 (29) |
| Support Bracket Bolt | 47 (64) |
| Oil Pipe-To-Turbo Nut | 13 (18) |
| Oil Pipe Union Bolt | 32 (43) |
| Turbine Outlet Elbow Nut | 47 (64) |
| Turbo Bracket Bolt | |
| Bracket-To-Block | 38 (52) |
| Bracket-To-Turbo | 59 (80) |
| Turbo-To-Manifold Nut | 47 (64) |
| | **INCH Lbs. (N.m)** |
| Air Cleaner Bracket Bolt | 108 (12) |
| Oil Pipe Nut | 108 (12) |
| Turbo Water Pipe Nut | 108 (12) |

### TURBOCHARGER TORQUE SPECIFICATIONS (MR2)

| Description | Ft. Lbs. (N.m) |
|---|---|
| Air By-Pass Valve-To-Air Tube | 14 (19) |
| Air Tube Stay-To-Air Tube | 14 (19) |
| Air Tube Stay-To-Cylinder Head | 14 (19) |
| Oil Pipe-To-Cylinder Block | |
| Bolt | 32 (43) |
| Union Bolt | 38 (51) |
| Oil Pipe-To-Turbocharger | 13 (17) |
| Turbine Outlet Elbow-To-Turbocharger Bolts | 47 (64) |
| Turbocharger Stay-To-Cylinder Block Bolts | 43 (59) |
| Turbocharger-To-Exhaust Manifold Bolts | 47 (64) |
| Turbocharger Stay-To-Turbocharger Bolts | 51 (69) |
| | **INCH Lbs. (N.m)** |
| Side Bearing Housing Plate-To-Turbocharger Bolts | 108 (12) |
| Turbo Water Pipe-To-Turbocharger Bolts | 108 (12) |

### TURBOCHARGER TORQUE SPECIFICATIONS (SUPRA)

| Description | Ft. Lbs. (N.m) |
|---|---|
| Front Exhaust Pipe Nut | 46 (62) |
| Oil Pipe Union Bolt | 25 (34) |
| Turbine Outlet Elbow Nut | 32 (43) |
| Turbo Bracket Bolt | |
| Bracket-To-Engine Mount | 43 (58) |
| Bracket-To-Turbo | 59 (80) |
| Turbo Mounting Nut | 33 (45) |
| | **INCH Lbs. (N.m)** |
| Air Cleaner Bracket Bolt | 108 (12) |
| Oil Pipe Nut | 108 (12) |
| Turbo Water Pipe Nut | 65 (7.4) |

# 1991 ELECTRICAL
# Alternators & Regulators

## Camry, Celica, Corolla, Cressida, Land Cruiser, MR2, Pickup, Previa, Supra, Tercel, 4Runner

## DESCRIPTION

Nippondenso 3-phase alternators utilize 3 positive and 3 negative diodes to rectify current. Charging system voltage is controlled by an internal Integrated Circuit (IC) voltage regulator. Some models use engine, ignition, and charging light relays.

## TROUBLE SHOOTING

*NOTE: See TROUBLE SHOOTING article in GENERAL INFORMATION.*

## ADJUSTMENTS

### BELT TENSION

*4-CYLINDER BELT TENSION SPECIFICATIONS* [1]

| Application | New Belt Lbs. (kg) | Used Belt Lbs. (kg) |
|---|---|---|
| Camry | | |
| Alternator | | |
| Without A/C | 125 (57) | 95 (43) |
| With A/C | 175 (79) | 130 (59) |
| Power Steering | 125 (57) | 80 (36) |
| Celica | | |
| "V" Ribbed | | |
| Without A/C | 150 (68) | 130 (59) |
| With A/C | 160 (72) | 130 (59) |
| Power Steering | 125 (57) | 80 (36) |
| Corolla | | |
| A/C | 160 (73) | 100 (45) |
| Alternator | 160 (73) | 130 (59) |
| Power Steering | 100 (45) | 55 (25) |
| MR2 | | |
| Alternator | 120 (56) | 105 (48) |
| A/C | 160 (73) | 100 (45) |
| Previa | | |
| Alternator & Power Steering | 170 (78) | 125 (57) |
| A/C | 140 (66) | 120 (56) |
| Pickup & 4Runner | | |
| "V" Ribbed | | |
| With A/C | 160 (73) | 100 (45) |
| Without A/C | 105 (48) | 85 (39) |
| Tercel | | |
| Alternator | 160 (73) | 100 (45) |
| A/C | 165 (75) | 110 (50) |
| Power Steering | 175 (79) | 115 (52) |

[1] – Measure tension with Burroughs tension gauge.

*6-CYLINDER BELT TENSION SPECIFICATIONS* [1]

| Application | New Belt Lbs. (kg) | Used Belt Lbs. (kg) |
|---|---|---|
| Cressida | | |
| Alternator | 175 (79) | 115 (52) |
| A/C | 160 (73) | 105 (48) |
| P/S | 160 (73) | 100 (45) |
| Land Cruiser | | |
| A/C Belt | 125 (57) | 80 (36) |
| All Others | 145 (66) | 100 (45) |
| Supra | | |
| Alternator | 175 (79) | 115 (52) |
| A/C & P/S | 160 (73) | 105 (48) |

[1] – Measure tension with Burroughs tension gauge.

*V6 BELT TENSION SPECIFICATIONS* [1]

| Application | New Belt Lbs. (kg) | Used Belt Lbs. (kg) |
|---|---|---|
| Camry | | |
| Alternator | 175 (79) | 115 (52) |
| Power Steering | 125 (57) | 80 (36) |
| Pickup & 4Runner | | |
| Alternator | 160 (73) | 100 (45) |
| All Others | 125 (57) | 80 (36) |

[1] – Measure tension with Burroughs tension gauge.

## ON-VEHICLE TESTING

### NO-LOAD TEST

1) Disconnect alternator "B" terminal wire. Using an ammeter and voltmeter, connect negative ammeter lead to disconnected alternator terminal "B" wire and positive lead to alternator "B" terminal.

2) Connect voltmeter positive lead to alternator "B" terminal and negative lead to ground. *See Fig. 2.*

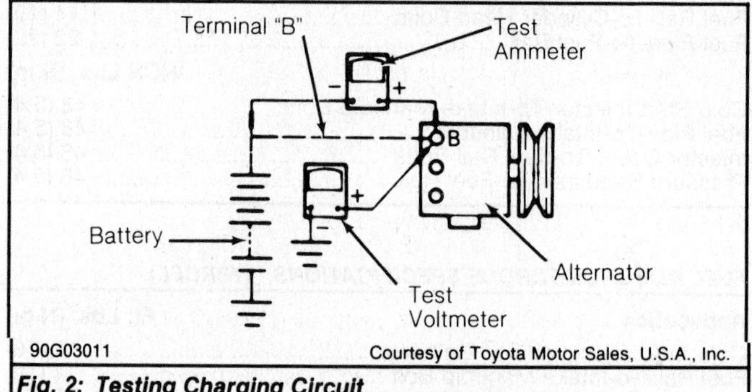


*Fig. 2: Testing Charging Circuit*

3) Start engine and increase engine speed to 2000 RPM. Both meters should read within specification. See ALTERNATOR OUTPUT SPECIFICATIONS table.

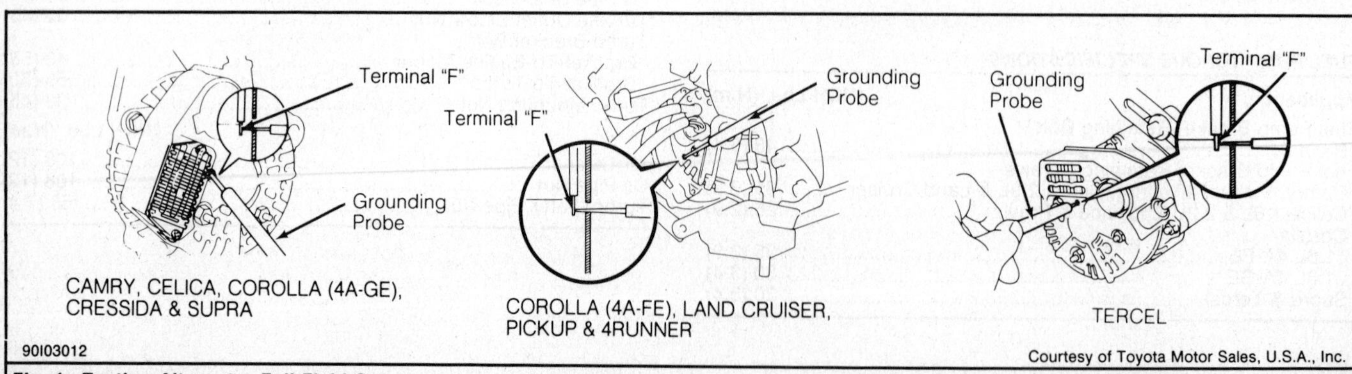


*Fig. 1: Testing Alternator Full Field Output*

# 1991 ELECTRICAL
# Alternators & Regulators (Cont.)

***ALTERNATOR OUTPUT SPECIFICATIONS @ 2000 RPM***

| Application | Amps | [1] Volts |
|---|---|---|
| Cressida | 10 | 14.0-15.0 |
| Land Cruiser | 10 | 13.8-14.4 |
| All Others | 10 | 13.9-15.1 |

[1] - With temperature at 77°F (25°C).

**4)** If voltage is more than specified, replace IC regulator. If voltage is less than specified, ground "F" (full field) terminal. *See Fig. 1*. If voltage now climbs above specified range, replace IC regulator. If voltage remains below specified range, repair or replace alternator.

## LOAD TEST

**1)** Connect an ammeter as described in NO-LOAD TEST, step **1)**. Start engine. Turn on high beam headlights and place heater control on HI Increase engine speed to 2000 RPM.

**2)** Check ammeter reading. Ammeter should read more than 30 amps. If amperage is less than specified, repair or replace alternator.

***NOTE: If battery is fully charged, disable ignition system and crank engine for about 15 seconds to partially discharge battery.***

## CONTROL RELAYS

***NOTE: Charge light relay is located above right kick panel.***

**Charge Light Relay (Land Cruiser) - 1)** Using an ohmmeter, connect positive lead to charge light relay terminal No. 4 and negative lead to terminal No. 3. See STEP 1 in *Fig. 3*.

**2)** Ohmmeter should indicate continuity. Reverse ohmmeter leads. Ohmmeter should now indicate no continuity. Connect ohmmeter between terminals No. 1 and 2. Ohmmeter should indicate no continuity. Replace relay if it does not test as indicated.

**3)** If relay does test as indicated, apply 12 volts to terminal No. 3. Connect terminal No. 4 to ground. See STEP 2 in *Fig. 3*.. Continuity should exist between relay terminals No. 1 and 2. Replace relay if it does not test as indicated.

**Engine Main Relay (Camry, Celica, Corolla & Tercel) - 1)** Using an ohmmeter, check for continuity between engine main relay terminals No. 3 and 5 and between terminals No. 1 and 2. See ENGINE MAIN RELAY LOCATION (CAMRY, CELICA, COROLLA & TERCEL) table. Ensure continuity does not exist between terminals No. 3 and 4. See STEP 1 in *Fig. 4*. Replace relay if it does not test as indicated.

**2)** If relay does test as indicated, apply 12 volts between terminals No. 1 and 2. Using an ohmmeter, check that continuity exists between terminals No. 3 and 4. Ensure continuity does not exist between terminals No. 3 and 5. See STEP 2 in *Fig. 4*. Replace relay if it does not test as indicated.

***ENGINE MAIN RELAY LOCATION (CAMRY, CELICA, COROLLA & TERCEL)***

| Application | Location |
|---|---|
| Camry (2VZ-FE) | Left Rear Fender Panel |
| All Others | Engine Compartment Relay Box |

## BENCH TESTING

***NOTE: Corolla 4A-FE (Delco) alternators are serviced as a unit and should not be disassembled.***

**Brushes -** Brushes should slide smoothly in holders. Replace brushes if damaged or worn. Check for minimum brush length of .18-.22" (4.5-5.5 mm). New brush exposed length should be .413" (10.5 mm). Minimum exposed length should be than .059" (1.5 mm). Install new springs when replacing brushes.

**Rotor - 1)** Check rotor for open field windings by using an ohmmeter across slip rings. Rotor resistance should be 2.8-3.0 ohms.

**2)** Check rotor for shorts to ground by connecting ohmmeter between slip ring and rotor shaft. Ohmmeter should indicate no continuity. Check slip rings for wear or pitting. Turn slip rings on lathe if necessary. Minimum slip ring diameter is .504" (12.8 mm).

**Stator -** Connect ohmmeter between 2 stator leads. Continuity should exist between all stator leads. Connect ohmmeter between each stator lead and metal core. Continuity should not exist. If stator does not test as indicated, replace stator.

**Diodes - 1)** With diode assembly on bench, contact diode plate with one probe and each of the 3 diode leads with other probe. Note ohmmeter reading. Reverse probes and repeat test for all diodes.

**2)** All diodes should show a low reading in one direction and NO reading in opposite direction. If any diode is defective, replace diode assembly.

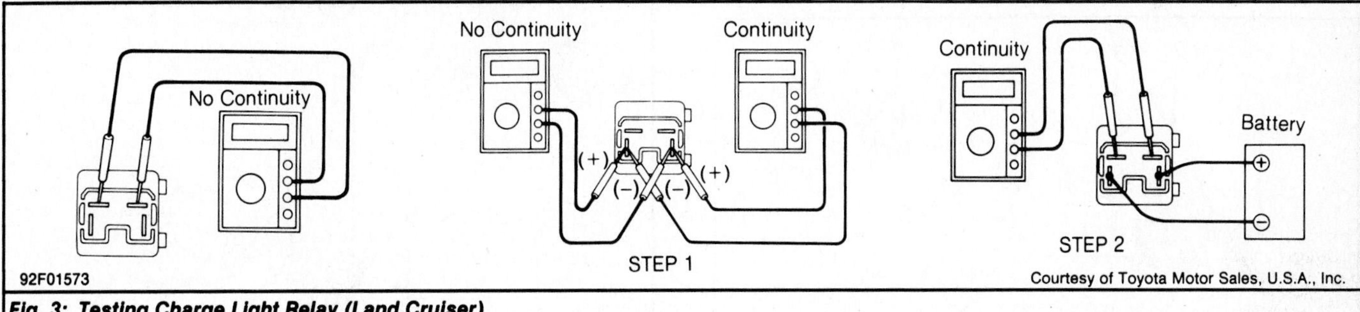


***Fig. 3: Testing Charge Light Relay (Land Cruiser)***

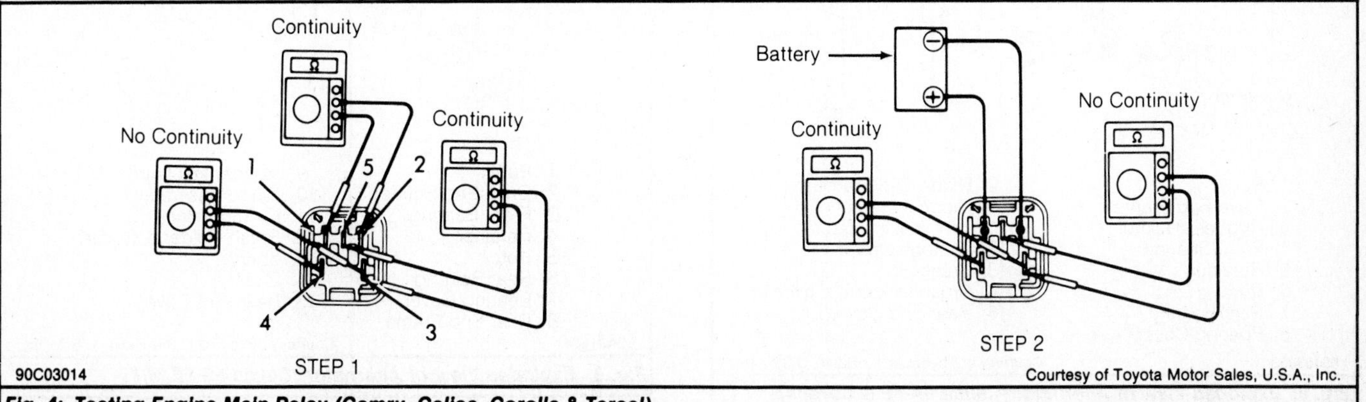


***Fig. 4: Testing Engine Main Relay (Camry, Celica, Corolla & Tercel)***

# 1991 ELECTRICAL
# Alternators & Regulators (Cont.)

## OVERHAUL

***NOTE: Overhaul procedures are not available from manufacturer. See Figs. 5-17 for exploded views of alternators.***

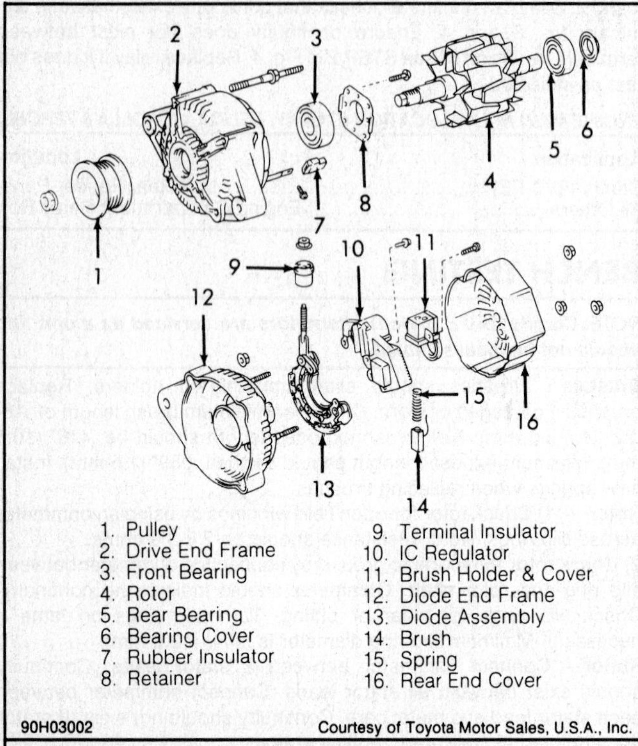

1. Pulley
2. Drive End Frame
3. Front Bearing
4. Rotor
5. Rear Bearing
6. Bearing Cover
7. Rubber Insulator
8. Retainer
9. Terminal Insulator
10. IC Regulator
11. Brush Holder & Cover
12. Diode End Frame
13. Diode Assembly
14. Brush
15. Spring
16. Rear End Cover

90H03002 Courtesy of Toyota Motor Sales, U.S.A., Inc.

***Fig. 5: Exploded View of Alternator (Camry 4A-FE M/T, Cressida & Supra 7M-GE)***

***NOTE: Corolla 4A-FE (Delco) alternators are serviced as a unit and should not be disassembled.***

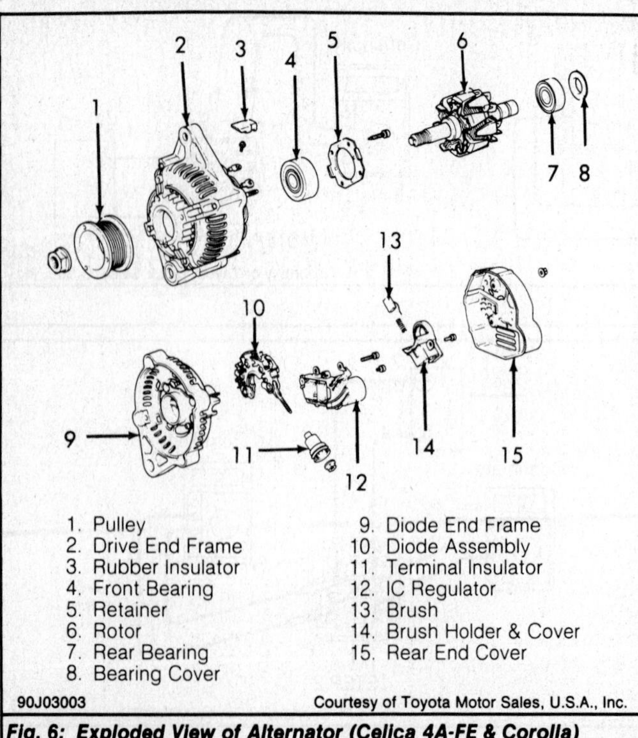

1. Pulley
2. Drive End Frame
3. Rubber Insulator
4. Front Bearing
5. Retainer
6. Rotor
7. Rear Bearing
8. Bearing Cover
9. Diode End Frame
10. Diode Assembly
11. Terminal Insulator
12. IC Regulator
13. Brush
14. Brush Holder & Cover
15. Rear End Cover

90J03003 Courtesy of Toyota Motor Sales, U.S.A., Inc.

***Fig. 6: Exploded View of Alternator (Celica 4A-FE & Corolla)***

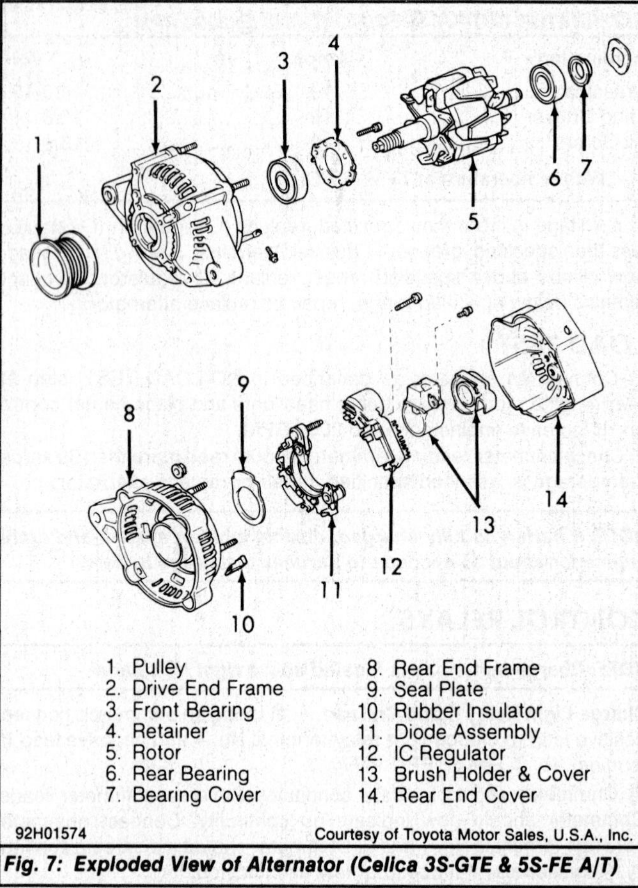

1. Pulley
2. Drive End Frame
3. Front Bearing
4. Retainer
5. Rotor
6. Rear Bearing
7. Bearing Cover
8. Rear End Frame
9. Seal Plate
10. Rubber Insulator
11. Diode Assembly
12. IC Regulator
13. Brush Holder & Cover
14. Rear End Cover

92H01574 Courtesy of Toyota Motor Sales, U.S.A., Inc.

***Fig. 7: Exploded View of Alternator (Celica 3S-GTE & 5S-FE A/T)***

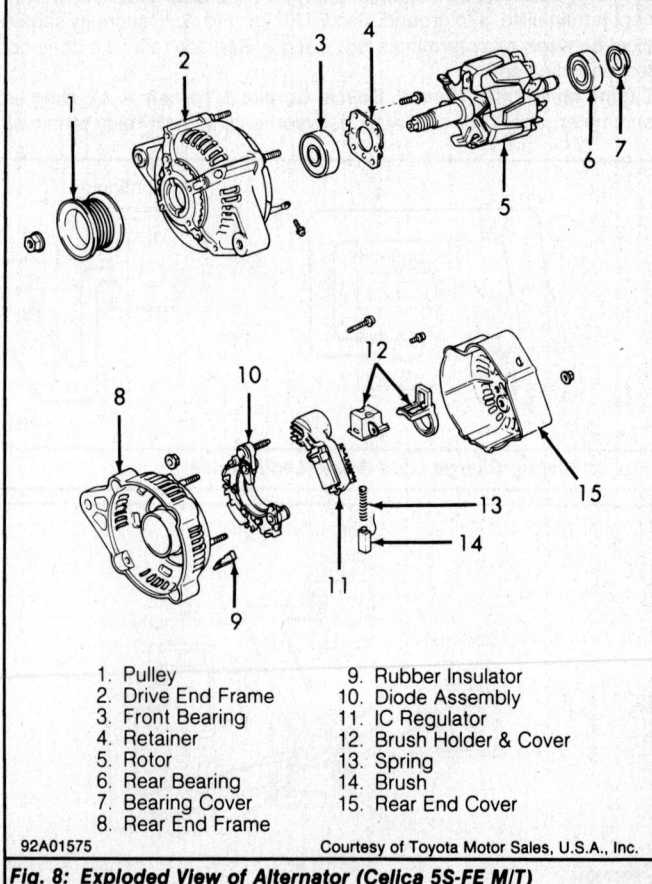

1. Pulley
2. Drive End Frame
3. Front Bearing
4. Retainer
5. Rotor
6. Rear Bearing
7. Bearing Cover
8. Rear End Frame
9. Rubber Insulator
10. Diode Assembly
11. IC Regulator
12. Brush Holder & Cover
13. Spring
14. Brush
15. Rear End Cover

92A01575 Courtesy of Toyota Motor Sales, U.S.A., Inc.

***Fig. 8: Exploded View of Alternator (Celica 5S-FE M/T)***

# 1991 ELECTRICAL
# Alternators & Regulators (Cont.)

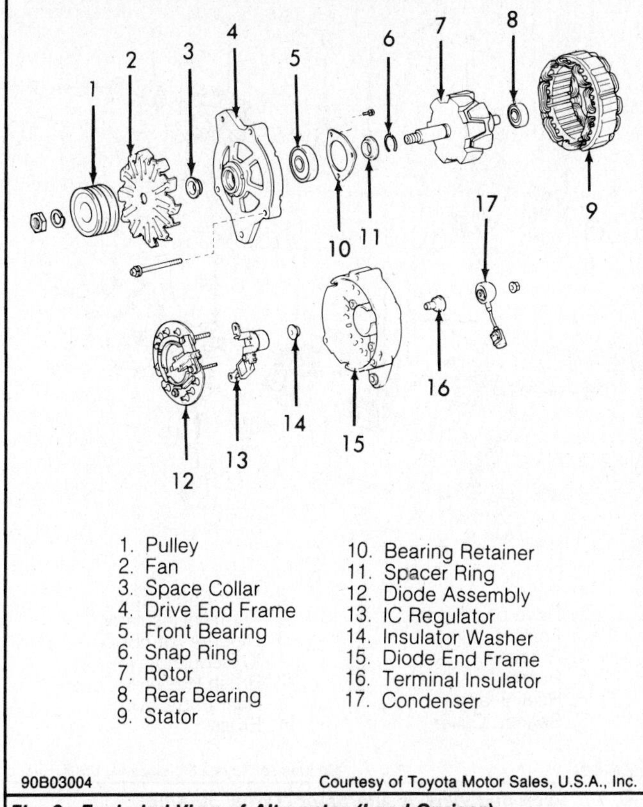


**Fig. 9: Exploded View of Alternator (Land Cruiser)**

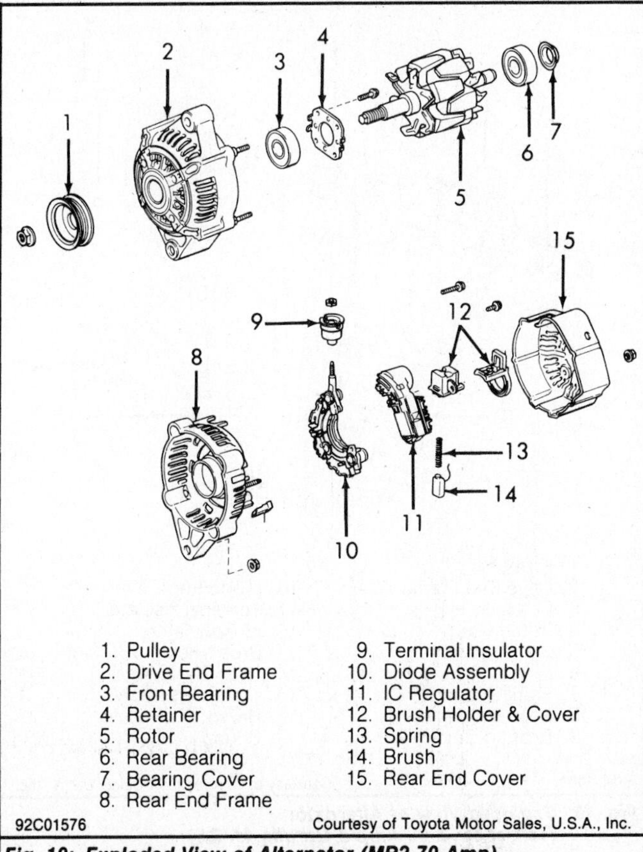


**Fig. 10: Exploded View of Alternator (MR2 70-Amp)**

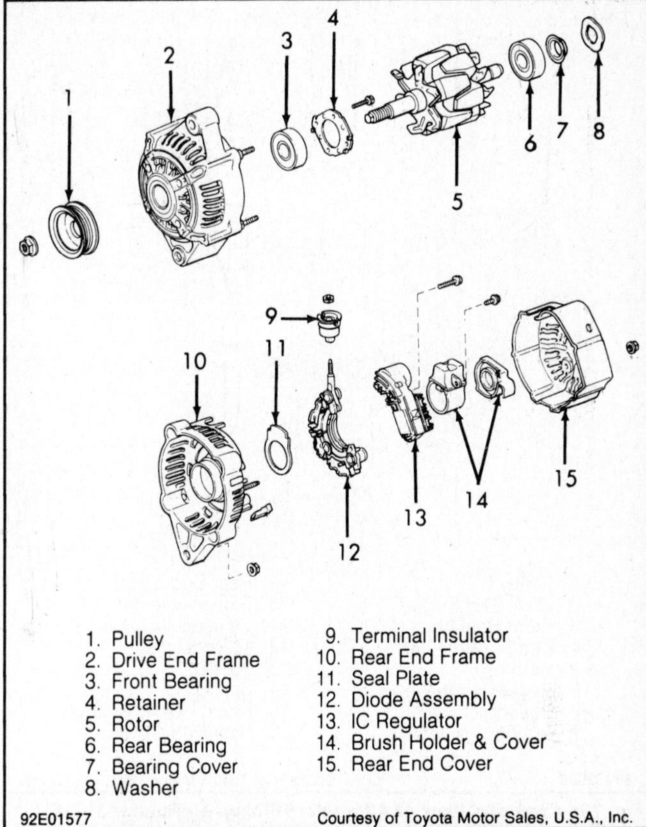


**Fig. 11: Exploded View of Alternator (MR2 80- & 100-Amp)**

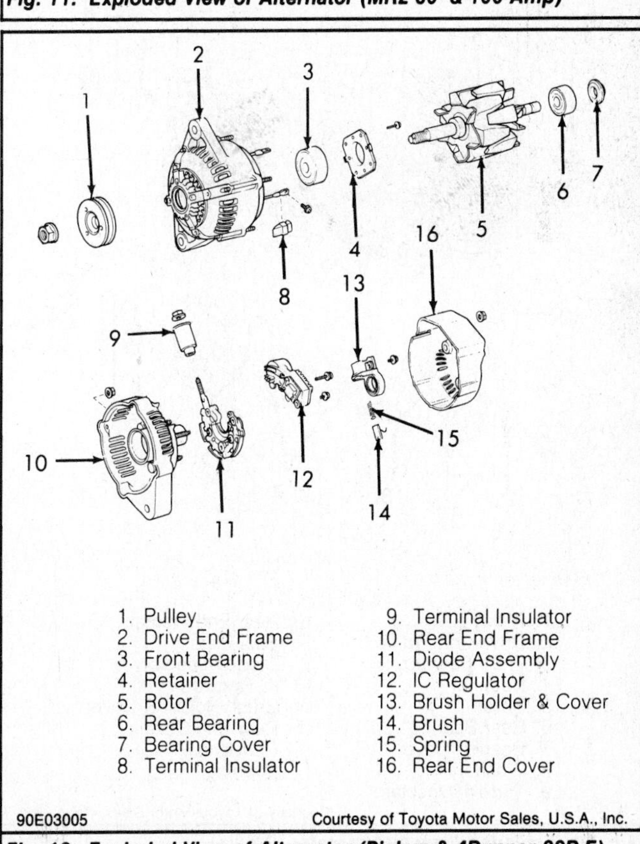


**Fig. 12: Exploded View of Alternator (Pickup & 4Runner 22R-E)**

# 1991 ELECTRICAL
# Alternators & Regulators (Cont.)

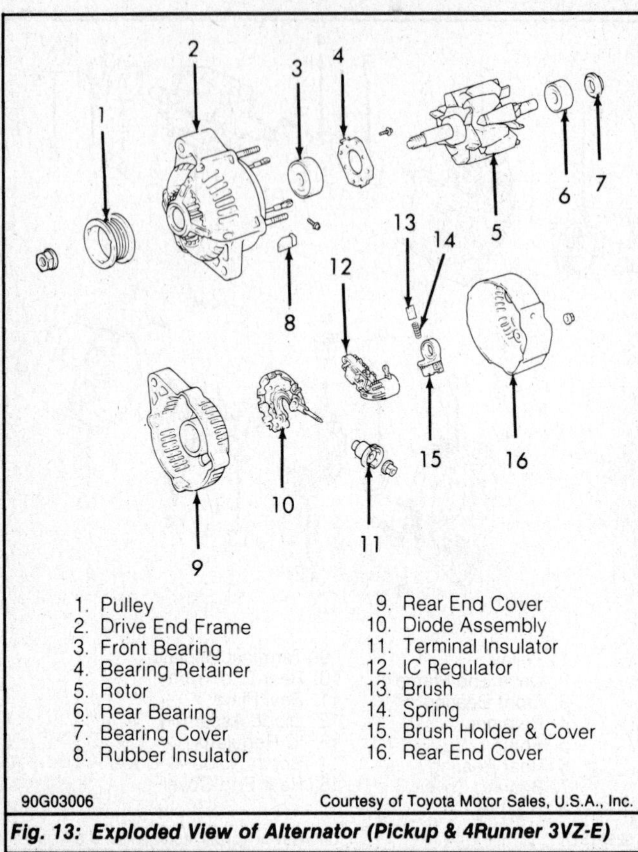

1. Pulley
2. Drive End Frame
3. Front Bearing
4. Bearing Retainer
5. Rotor
6. Rear Bearing
7. Bearing Cover
8. Rubber Insulator
9. Rear End Cover
10. Diode Assembly
11. Terminal Insulator
12. IC Regulator
13. Brush
14. Spring
15. Brush Holder & Cover
16. Rear End Cover

90G03006 Courtesy of Toyota Motor Sales, U.S.A., Inc.

***Fig. 13: Exploded View of Alternator (Pickup & 4Runner 3VZ-E)***

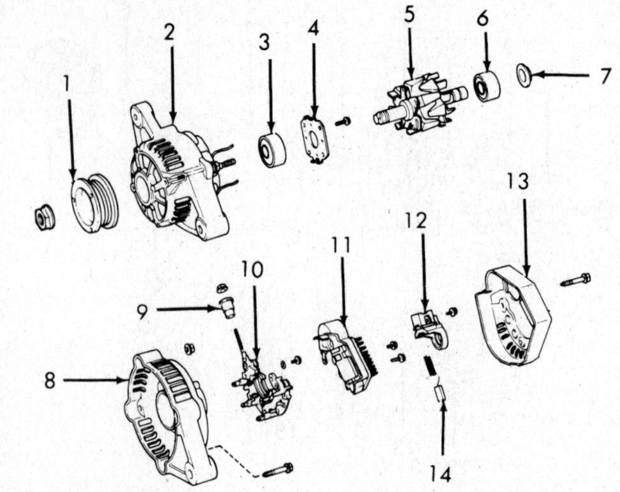

1. Pulley
2. Drive End Frame
3. Front Bearing
4. Retainer
5. Rotor
6. Rear Bearing
7. Bearing Cover
8. Washer
9. Terminal Insulator
10. Rear End Frame
11. Seal Plate
12. Diode Assembly
13. IC Regulator
14. Brush Holder & Cover
15. Rear End Cover
16. Condenser
17. Bushing

92G01578 Courtesy of Toyota Motor Sales, U.S.A., Inc.

***Fig. 14: Exploded View of Alternator (Previa)***

1. Pulley
2. Drive End Frame
3. Front Bearing
4. Retainer
5. Rotor
6. Rear Bearing
7. Bearing Cover
8. Rear End Frame
9. Terminal Insulator
10. Diode Assembly
11. IC Regulator
12. Brush Holder & Cover
13. Rear End Cover
14. Brush

90I03007 Courtesy of Toyota Motor Sales, U.S.A., Inc.

***Fig. 15: Exploded View of Alternator (Tercel 50-Amp)***

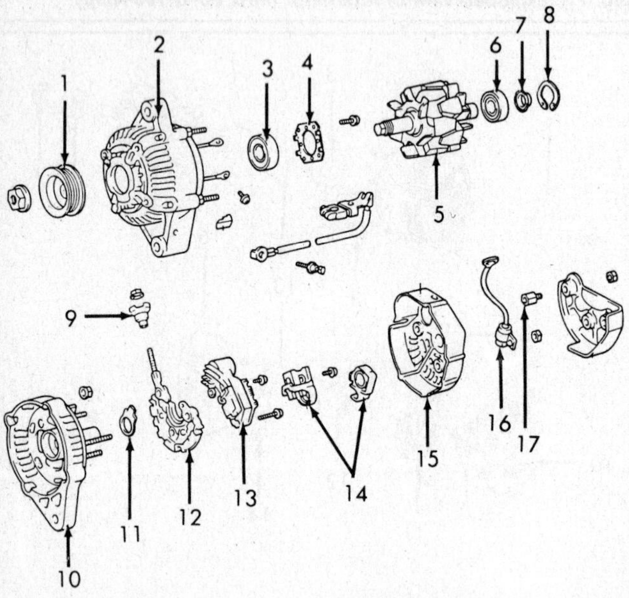

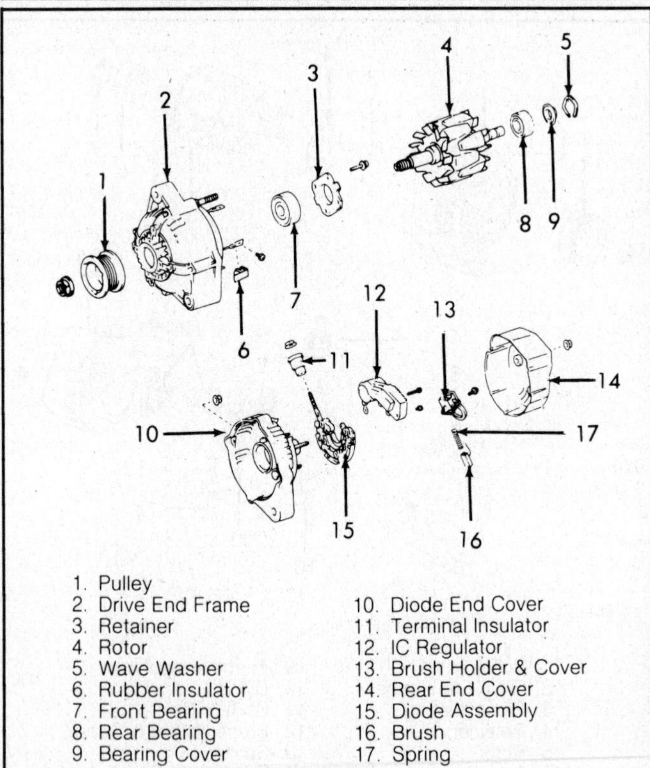

1. Pulley
2. Drive End Frame
3. Retainer
4. Rotor
5. Wave Washer
6. Rubber Insulator
7. Front Bearing
8. Rear Bearing
9. Bearing Cover
10. Diode End Cover
11. Terminal Insulator
12. IC Regulator
13. Brush Holder & Cover
14. Rear End Cover
15. Diode Assembly
16. Brush
17. Spring

90A03008 Courtesy of Toyota Motor Sales, U.S.A., Inc.

***Fig. 16: Exploded View of Alternator (Tercel 55- & 60-Amp & Corolla 4A-GE)***

# 1991 ELECTRICAL
# Alternators & Regulators (Cont.)

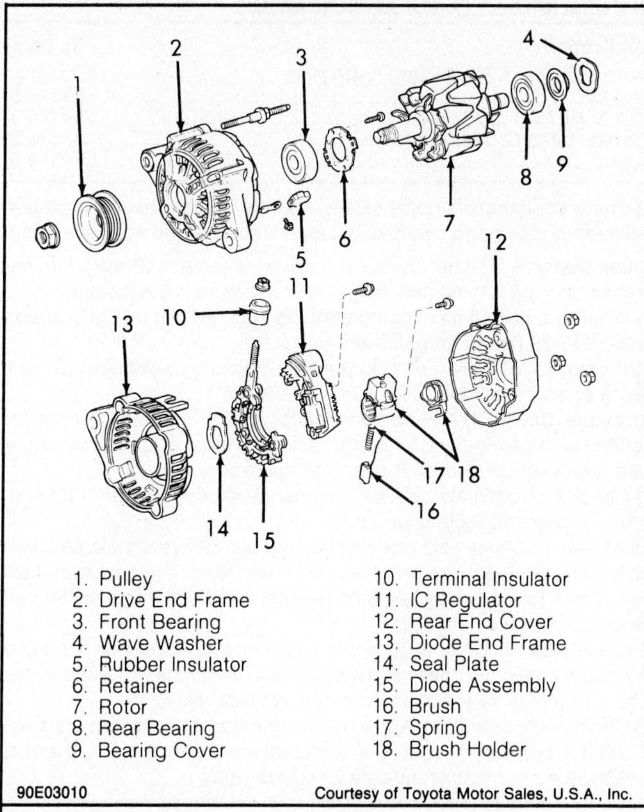


*Fig. 17: Exploded View of Alternator (Supra 7M-GTE)*

# 1991 ELECTRICAL
# Starters – Except Tercel

## Camry, Celica, Corolla, Cressida, Land Cruiser, MR2, Pickup, Previa, Supra, 4Runner

## DESCRIPTION

All models use Nippondenso 4-brush, solenoid-actuated, gear reduction-type starters, equipped with an overrunning clutch. The brush holder assembly retains brushes and springs in the starter housing.

## BENCH TESTING

***CAUTION: Do not engage starter solenoid for more than 5 seconds during testing or damage to coil winding may result.***

**Pull-In Coil Test** – Connect jumper wire from negative battery terminal to terminal "C" and starter housing. Connect positive battery terminal to terminal No. 50. *See Fig. 1.* Plunger should extend. If not, replace solenoid.

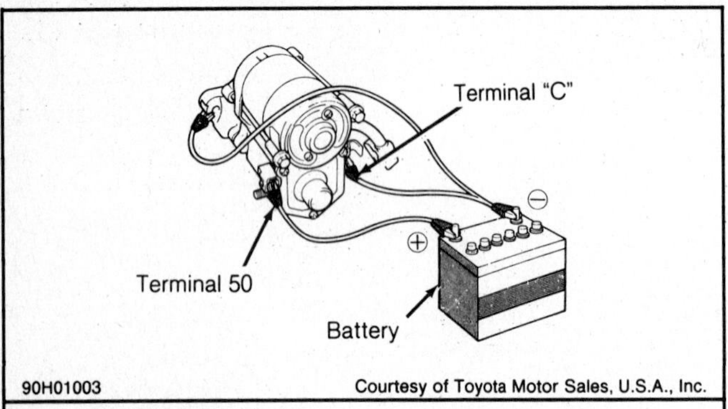


***Fig. 1: Testing Pull-In Coil***

**Hold-In & Return Test** – After pull-in testing, disconnect battery negative lead from terminal "C". *See Fig. 1.* Plunger should remain extended. If not, replace solenoid. If plunger remains extended, remove ground connection. Plunger should retract. If plunger does not retract, replace solenoid.

**No Load Test** – Connect ammeter in series with starter motor and 12-volt battery and observe readings. *See Fig. 2.* Starter should spin smoothly with the pinion out. Ensure starter draw is less than 90 amps. Battery voltage should be 11.5 volts or more. Replace starter if not within specification.

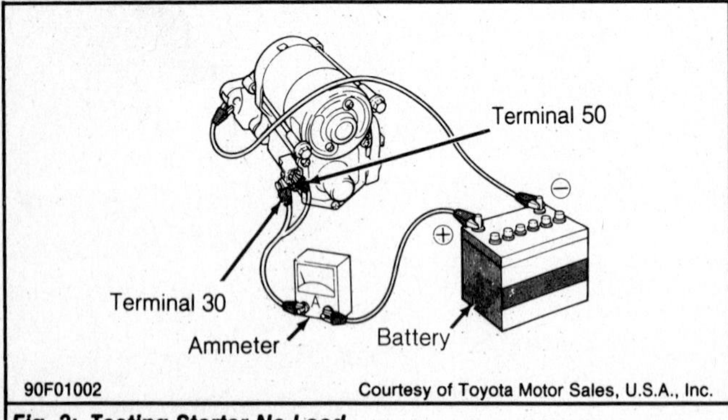


***Fig. 2: Testing Starter No Load***

## COMPONENT TESTING

**Brushes & Springs** – **1)** Check brush length. If less than specification, replace brushes. See MINIMUM BRUSH LENGTH SPECIFICATIONS table.

***MINIMUM BRUSH LENGTH SPECIFICATIONS***

| Application | In. (mm) |
|---|---|
| Camry, Celica, MR2, Pickup & 4Runner | |
| 1.0 kW | .335 (8.5) |
| 1.4 & 1.6 kW | .394 (10.0) |
| Corolla, Land Cruiser & Previa | .335 (8.5) |
| Supra | .394 (10.0) |

**2)** Check condition of brush holders, springs, spring clip and insulation between positive and negative holders. Repair or replace as needed.

**Commutator** – **1)** If out-of-round is more than .002" (.05 mm), turn the commutator on a lathe until out-of-round is within specification.
**2)** Wear or cutting limit of commutator is 1.22" (31.0 mm) for Cressida and 1.14" (29.0 mm) for all others.
**3)** If worn to less than .008" (.20 mm), undercut insulating mica to a depth of approximately .008-.024" (.20-.60 mm).

**Armature Coil** – **1)** Check commutator and armature coil core for continuity. If continuity is present, replace armature. Check armature with a growler for shorts. Replace as necessary.
**2)** Check for continuity between segments on commutator. If no continuity is present, replace armature.

**Field Coil** – Check field coil for open circuits. There should be continuity between lead wire and field coil brush lead. If not, replace field coil. Check for continuity between field coils and end frame. If continuity exists, replace field coil.

**Starter Relay** – **1)** Verify continuity between relay terminals No. 1 and 3. Ensure continuity does not exist between terminals No. 2 and 4. *See Fig. 3.* If continuity is not as indicated, replace relay.
**2)** Check relay operation. Apply battery voltage between terminals No. 1 and 3. Continuity should now exist between terminals No. 2 and 4. If relay does not test as indicated, replace relay.

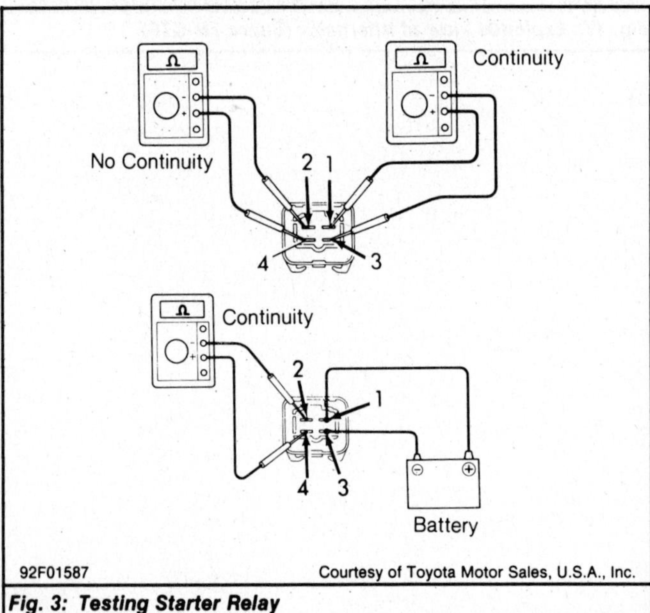


***Fig. 3: Testing Starter Relay***

***STARTER RELAY LOCATION*** [1]

| Application | Location |
|---|---|
| Camry | In left cowl |
| Celica & Supra | Behind right kick panel |
| Corolla | No. 2 fuse block in engine compartment |
| Land Cruiser | [2] |
| MR2 | Left side luggage compartment |
| Previa | Under left side instrument panel |
| Pickup & 4Runner | Driver's side fuse block |

[1] – On models with manual transmission only.
[2] – Land Cruiser models are not equipped with starter relay.

# 1991 ELECTRICAL
# Starters – Except Tercel (Cont.)

## OVERHAUL

***NOTE: Overhaul procedure is not available from manufacturer. See Figs. 4 and 5 for exploded views of starters.***

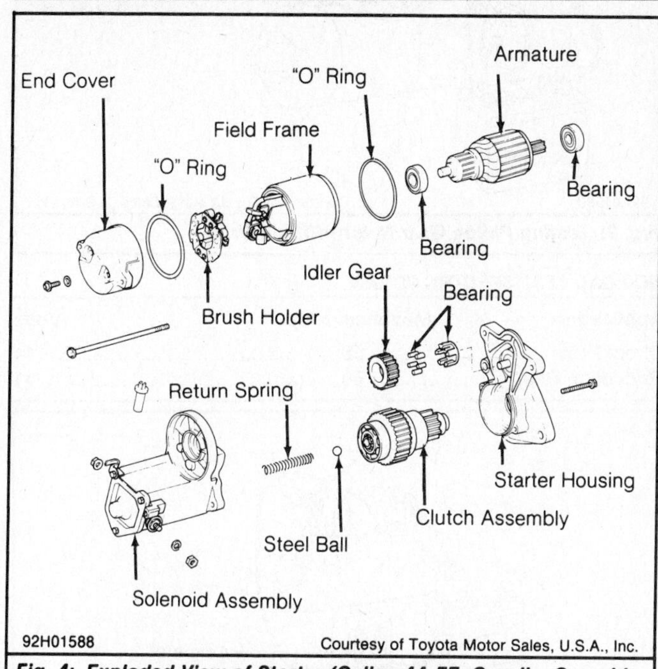


***Fig. 4: Exploded View of Starter (Celica 4A-FE, Corolla, Cressida, Land Cruiser, Pickup, Previa, Supra & 4Runner)***

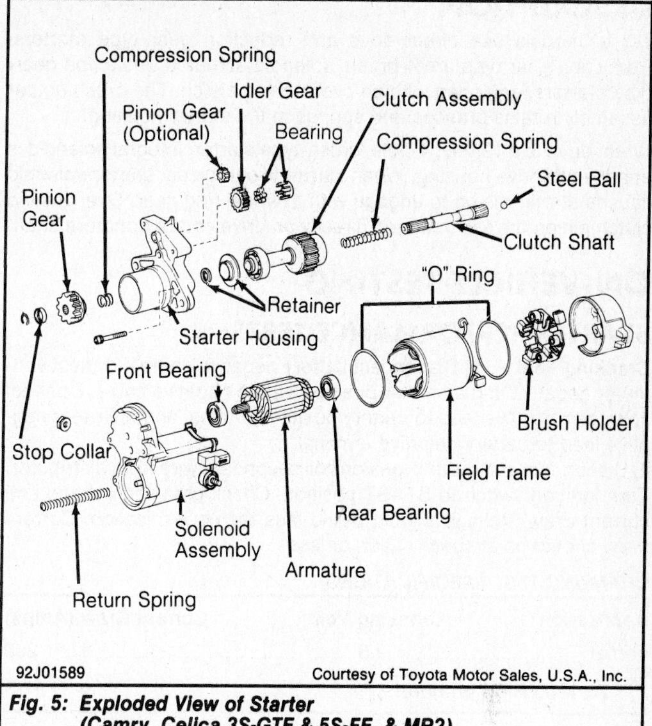


***Fig. 5: Exploded View of Starter (Camry, Celica 3S-GTE & 5S-FE, & MR2)***

# 1991 ELECTRICAL
# Starters – Tercel

## DESCRIPTION

Tercel models use direct drive and reduction gear type starters. Reduction gear type are 4-brush, solenoid-actuated, reduction gear-type starters, equipped with an overrunning clutch. The brush holder assembly retains brushes and springs in the starter housing.

Direct drive is a 12-volt, 4-pole, brush-type starter. Integral solenoid is attached to drive housing. When starter is energized, starter solenoid causes starter pinion to engage with flywheel ring gear. Overrunning clutch pinion drive is mounted directly on drive end of armature shaft.

## ON-VEHICLE TESTING

### STARTER PERFORMANCE TESTS

**Cranking Test – 1)** Disconnect battery negative cable. Connect voltmeter negative and ammeter positive lead to negative cable. Connect voltmeter positive lead to battery positive terminal and ammeter negative lead to battery negative terminal.
**2)** Disconnect and ground ignition coil secondary wire from distributor. Turn ignition switch to START position. Check cranking voltage and current draw. Voltage should be no less than specification. Current draw should be at specification or less.

***CRANKING TEST SPECIFICATIONS***

| Application | Cranking Volts | Current Draw (Amps) |
|---|---|---|
| Tercel | 9.5 | [1] 200 |

[1] – At 1200 RPM or more.

## BENCH TESTING

### DIRECT DRIVE STARTER

***CAUTION: DO NOT engage starter solenoid for more than 5 seconds during testing or damage to coil winding may result.***

**Pull-In Test** – Connect negative leads to starter housing and terminal "C". Connect battery positive lead to terminal 50. *See Fig. 1.* If starter pinion gear does not move out, replace solenoid.

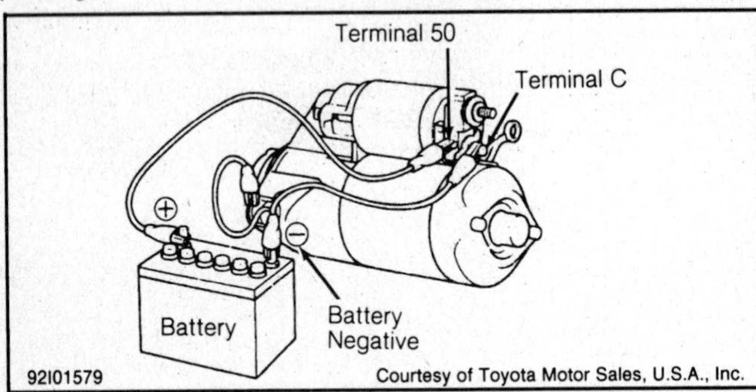


***Fig. 1: Testing Solenoid Pull-In & Hold-In (Direct Drive)***

**Hold-In Test** – Connect test leads to starter as described in PULL-IN TEST. Disconnect terminal "C". *See Fig. 2.* Starter pinion gear should stay out. If pinion gear does not stay out, replace solenoid.

**Pinion Gear Return Test** – With test leads connected as described in HOLD-IN TEST, disconnect negative lead from starter housing. *See Fig. 2.* Starter pinion should retract. If pinion gear does not retract, replace solenoid.

**No-Load Test** – Connect ammeter in series with starter motor and fully-charged 12-volt battery. *See Fig. 3.* Starter should rotate smoothly. Ensure starter draw is less than maximum specification. See NO-LOAD TEST SPECIFICATIONS table. Replace starter if not within specification.

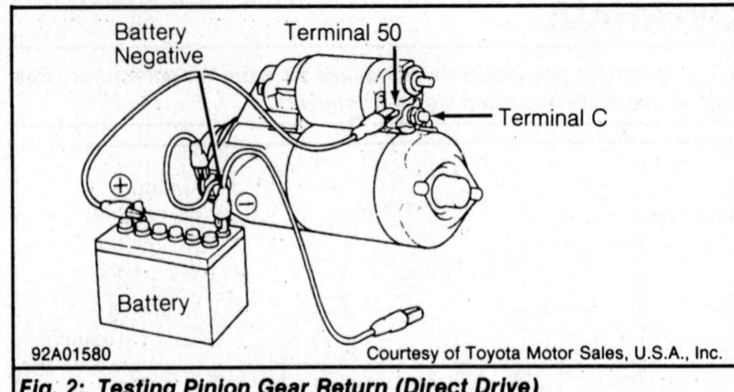


***Fig. 2: Testing Pinion Gear Return (Direct Drive)***

***NO-LOAD TEST SPECIFICATIONS***

| Application | Maximum Amps | Volts |
|---|---|---|
| Direct Drive | 50 | 11 |
| Reduction Gear | 50 | 11 |

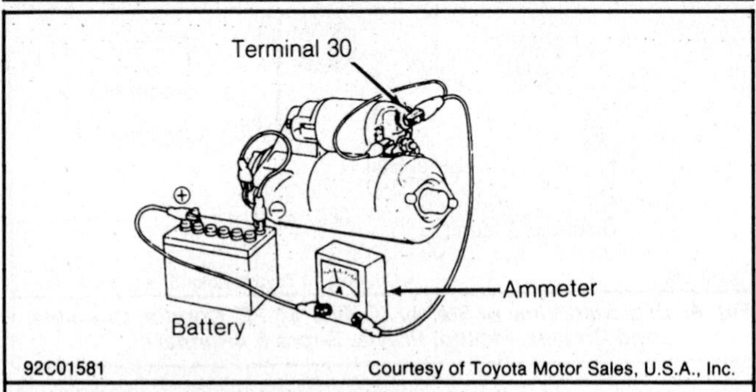


***Fig. 3: Testing Starter No-Load (Direct Drive)***

### REDUCTION GEAR STARTER

**Pull-In Coil Test** – Connect jumper wire from negative battery terminal to terminal "C" and starter housing. Connect positive battery terminal to terminal 50. *See Fig. 4.* Plunger should extend. If not, replace solenoid.

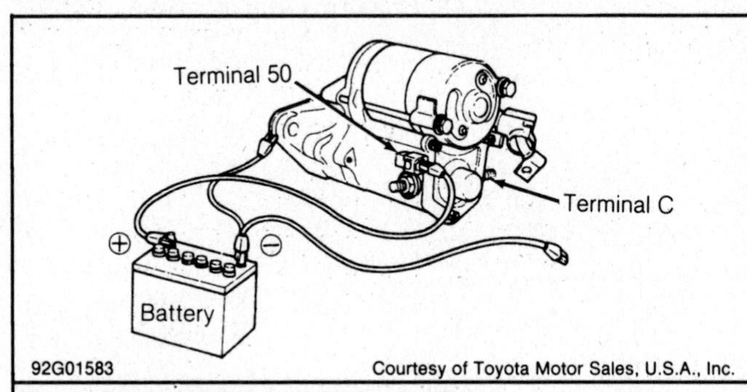


***Fig. 4: Testing Pull-In Coil (Reduction Gear)***

**Hold-In & Return Test** – After pull-in testing, disconnect battery negative lead from terminal "C". *See Fig. 4.* Plunger should remain extended. If not, replace solenoid. If plunger remains extended, remove ground connection. Plunger should retract. If plunger does not retract, replace solenoid.

**No-Load Test** – Connect ammeter in series with starter motor and 12-volt battery and observe readings. *See Fig. 5.* Starter should spin smoothly with the pinion out. Ensure starter draw is less than maximum specification. See NO-LOAD TEST SPECIFICATIONS table. Replace starter if not within specification.

# 1991 ELECTRICAL
# Starters – Tercel (Cont.)

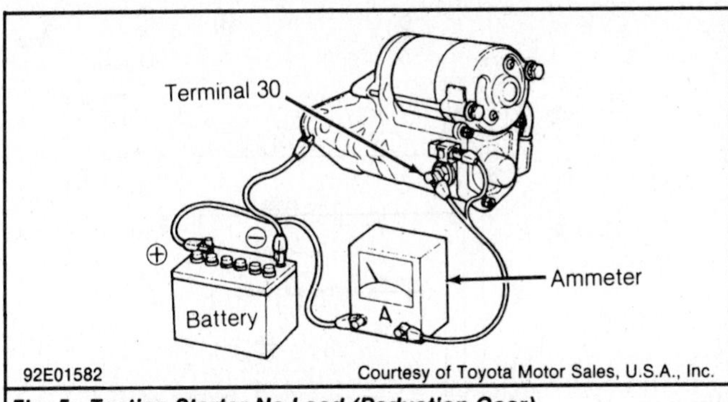


92E01582 Courtesy of Toyota Motor Sales, U.S.A., Inc.

*Fig. 5: Testing Starter No-Load (Reduction Gear)*

## COMPONENT TESTING

**Brushes & Springs – 1)** Check condition of brush holders, springs, spring clip and insulation between positive and negative holders. Repair or replace as needed.

**2)** Connect one ohmmeter lead to positive brush holder and other lead to negative brush holder. If test needle moves, brush holder assembly is shorted and must be replaced.

**3)** Check brush length. If less than specification, replace brushes. Check spring tension. Spring tension should be 37-48 ozs. (1050-1350 g). Brushes must move freely in holders.

***MINIMUM BRUSH LENGTH***

| Application | Length – In. (mm) |
|---|---|
| Direct Drive | .390 (10.0) |
| Reduction Gear Starter | .335 (8.5) |

**Commutator – 1)** Clean surface with No. 400 sandpaper if required. Check for continuity between commutator segments. If no continuity is present, replace armature.

**2)** If surface is scored, out of round or pitted, turn commutator in a lathe. Maximum commutator runout and minimum diameter of commutator must be within specification after turning.

***COMMUTATOR SPECIFICATIONS***

| Application | Maximum Runout | Minimum Thickness |
|---|---|---|
| Direct Drive | .016 (.40) | 1.06 (27.0) |
| Reduction Gear | .002 (.05) | 1.14 (29.0) |

**3)** Commutator mica undercut depth should be .024" (.60 mm). Minimum mica undercut depth is .008" (.20 mm). If not within specification, undercut with a hacksaw blade to standard depth.

**Armature Coil** – Check for continuity between commutator and armature coil. If continuity is present, replace armature. Check armature with a growler for shorts. Replace as necessary.

**Field Coil** – Check for continuity between lead wire and field coil brush lead. If continuity does not exist, replace field coil. Check for continuity between field coils and end frame. If continuity exists, replace field coil.

**Starter Relay – 1)** Using ohmmeter, ensure continuity exists between terminals No. 1 and 3. Ensure continuity does not exist between terminals No. 2 and 4. *Fig. 6.* If continuity is not as indicated, replace relay.

**2)** Check relay operation. Apply battery voltage between terminals No. 1 and 3. Continuity should now exists between terminals No. 2 and 4. If relay does not test as indicated, replace relay.

## OVERHAUL

***NOTE: Overhaul procedure is not available from manufacturer. See Figs. 7 and 8 for exploded views of starters.***

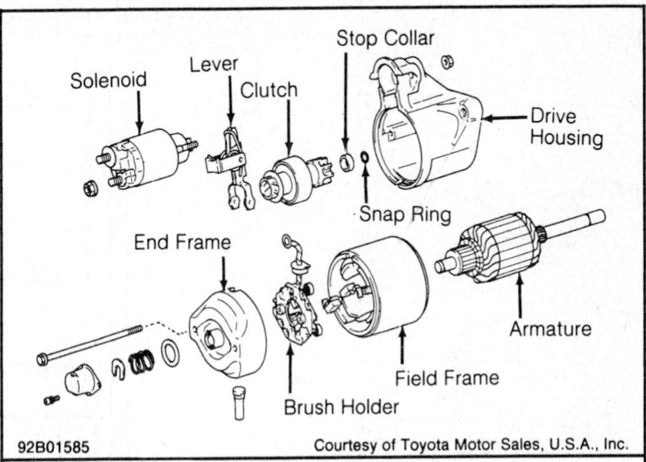


92B01585 Courtesy of Toyota Motor Sales, U.S.A., Inc.

*Fig. 7: Exploded View of Direct Drive Starter Motor*

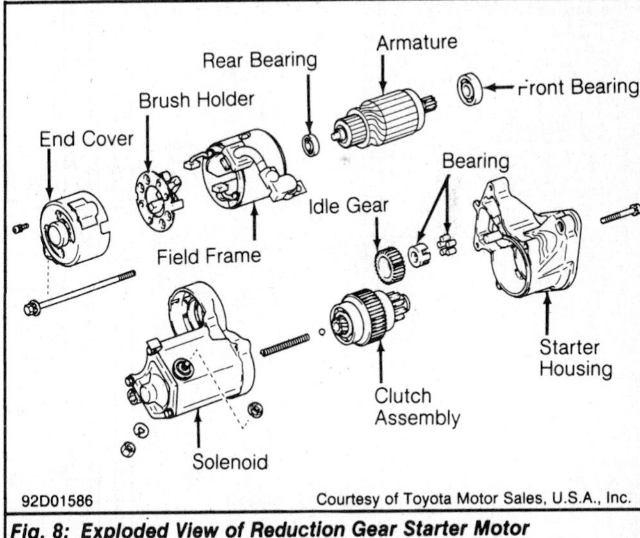


92D01586 Courtesy of Toyota Motor Sales, U.S.A., Inc.

*Fig. 8: Exploded View of Reduction Gear Starter Motor*

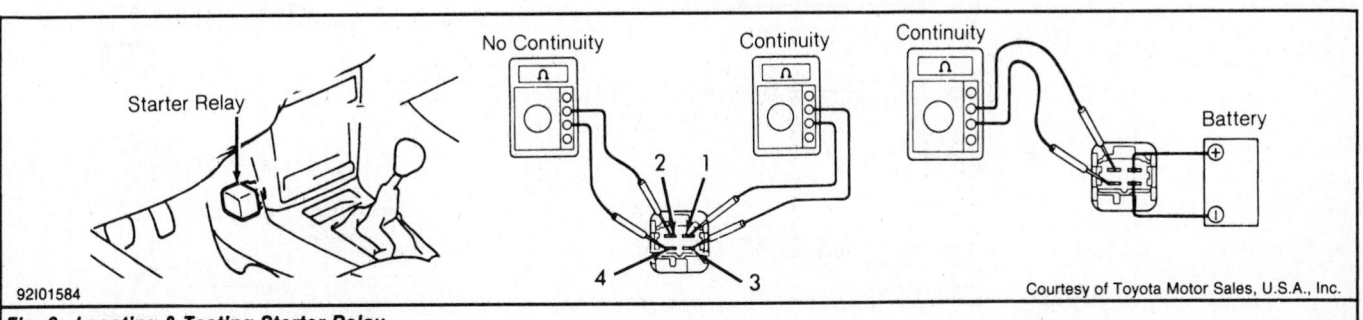

92I01584 Courtesy of Toyota Motor Sales, U.S.A., Inc.

*Fig. 6: Locating & Testing Starter Relay*

# 1991 WIRING DIAGRAMS
## Camry

**COMPONENT LOCATOR:**

| Component | Location |
|---|---|
| A/C CUT RELAY (4WD LEVER TYPE) | C 34 |
| A/C CUT RELAY (4WD PUSH TYPE) | D 35 |
| A/C SYSTEM (LEVER TYPE 4 CYL) | A–C 32–35 |
| A/C SYSTEM (LEVER TYPE V6) | A–C 36–39 |
| A/C SYSTEM (PUSH TYPE 4 CYL) | D–E 32–35 |
| A/C SYSTEM (PUSH TYPE V6) | D–E 36–39 |
| A/T INDICATOR | A 51 |
| A/T INDICATOR SW | B–C 51 |
| ABS ACTUATOR | D–E 44 |
| ABS COMPUTER | D–E 47 |
| ALTERNATOR | D 3 |
| AUTO ANTENNA | E 60 |
| AUTO SHOULDER BELT COMPUTER | A–C 52 |
| BACK DOOR LOCK SW | D 60 |
| BACK-UP LT SW (M/T) (SEDAN) | B 61 |
| BACK-UP LT SW (M/T) (WAGON) | D 61 |
| BATTERY | A 2 |
| CHECK CONN (4 CYL) | D 7 |
| CIRCUIT OPENING RELAY (4 CYL) | A 6 |
| CIRCUIT OPENING RELAY (V6) | A 10 |
| CLUTCH START SW (M/T) | B 3 |
| COLD START INJECTOR | C 3 |
| COMBINATION SW | D–E 52–55 |
| COURTESY LTS | D–E 24–27 |
| CRUISE CONTROL CLUTCH SW (M/T) | B 44 |
| CRUISE CONTROL COMPUTER | A–B 44 |
| CRUISE CONTROL MAIN SW | A 47 |
| DEFOG GRID | A 55 |
| DIFFERENTIAL LOCK CTRL SW (4WD A/T) | D 51 |
| DIFFERENTIAL LOCK CTRL SW (4WD M/T) | E 51 |
| DIFFERENTIAL LOCK IND | D 51 |
| DIFFERENTIAL LOCK SOLENOIDS | E 50 |
| DOOR LOCK CONTROL RELAY | E 58 |
| ECT ECU (4 CYL) (4WD) | C–E 40 |
| ECT ECU (4 CYL) (FWD) | A–B 40 |
| ECT PATTERN SELECT SW | C 43 |
| ECT SOLENOID (V6) | E 9 |
| FLASHER | D 52 |
| FUS LINK BOX | B–C 2 |
| GRN FUS LINK | C 1 |
| HAZARD SW | E 52 |
| HEATER CONTROL SYSTEM (PUSH TYPE) | A–E 28–31 |
| HIGH PRES SW (LEVER TYPE) | A 37 |
| HIGH PRES SW (PUSH TYPE) | D 37 |
| IDLE UP DIODE (4 CYL) | A 4 |
| IGNITER & IGNITION COIL (V6) | E 10–11 |
| IGNITER (4 CYL) | E 5 |
| IGNITION SW | E 16 |
| INSTRUMENT CLUSTER | C–E 48 |
| JUNCTION BLOCK #1 (J/B #1) | A–E 12–19 |
| JUNCTION BLOCK #2 (J/B #2) | A–C 21–22 |
| JUNCTION BLOCK #3 (J/B #3) | B 25–26 |
| JUNCTION BLOCK #4 (J/B #4) | D–E 20 |
| KEY INTERLOCK SOLENOID | E 55 |
| LT FAILURE SENSOR | C 60 |
| MOONROOF SW & MAP LT | C 56 |
| O/D DIODE | A 48 |
| O/D MAIN SW | B 48 |
| O/D SOLENOID | A 48 |
| POWER MAIN RELAY | B 56 |
| POWER MIRROR SW | D 56 |
| POWER SEAT SW | B–C 55 |
| POWER WINDOW SW | A 56–59 |
| REAR WINDOW DEFOG SW | A 55 |
| REAR WIPER ASSEMBLY | B 60 |
| REAR WIPER/WASHER SW | A 60 |
| RELAY BOX #1 (R/B #1) | D–E 23 |
| SEAT BELT WARNING RELAY | C 48 |
| SHIFT LOCK CONTROL COMPUTER | E 55 |
| SHOULDER BELT SWS | A 54 |
| STARTER | A 3 |
| STARTER RELAY | B 3 |
| STOP LT SW | C 47 |
| TCCS ECU (4 CYL) | B–D 4 |
| TCCS ECU (V6) | A–D 8 |
| UNLOCK WARNING SW | E 16 |
| WASHER MOTOR | E 3 |
| WIPER MOTOR | E 3 |
| YEL FUS LINK | C 1 |

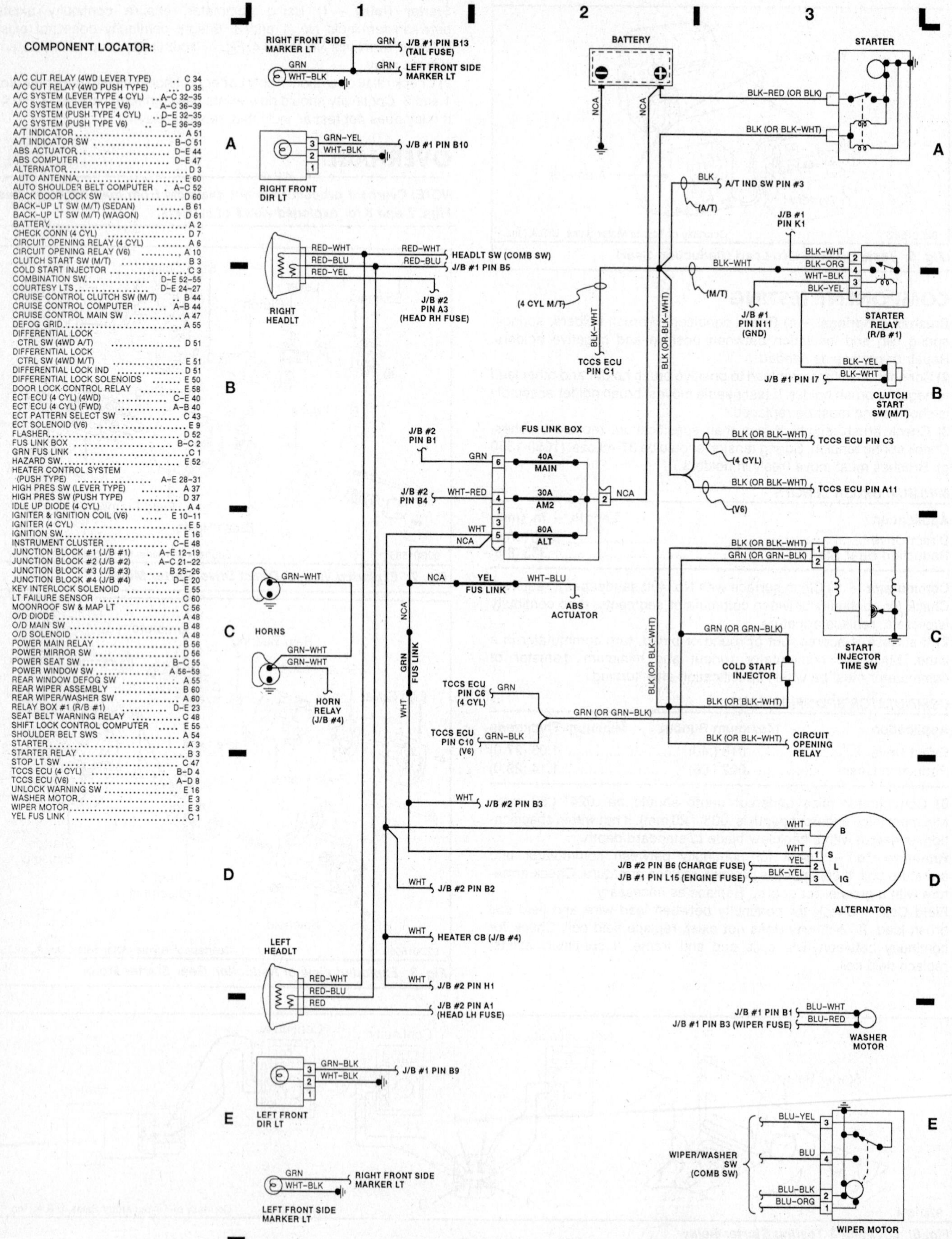

# 1991 WIRING DIAGRAMS
## Camry (Cont.)

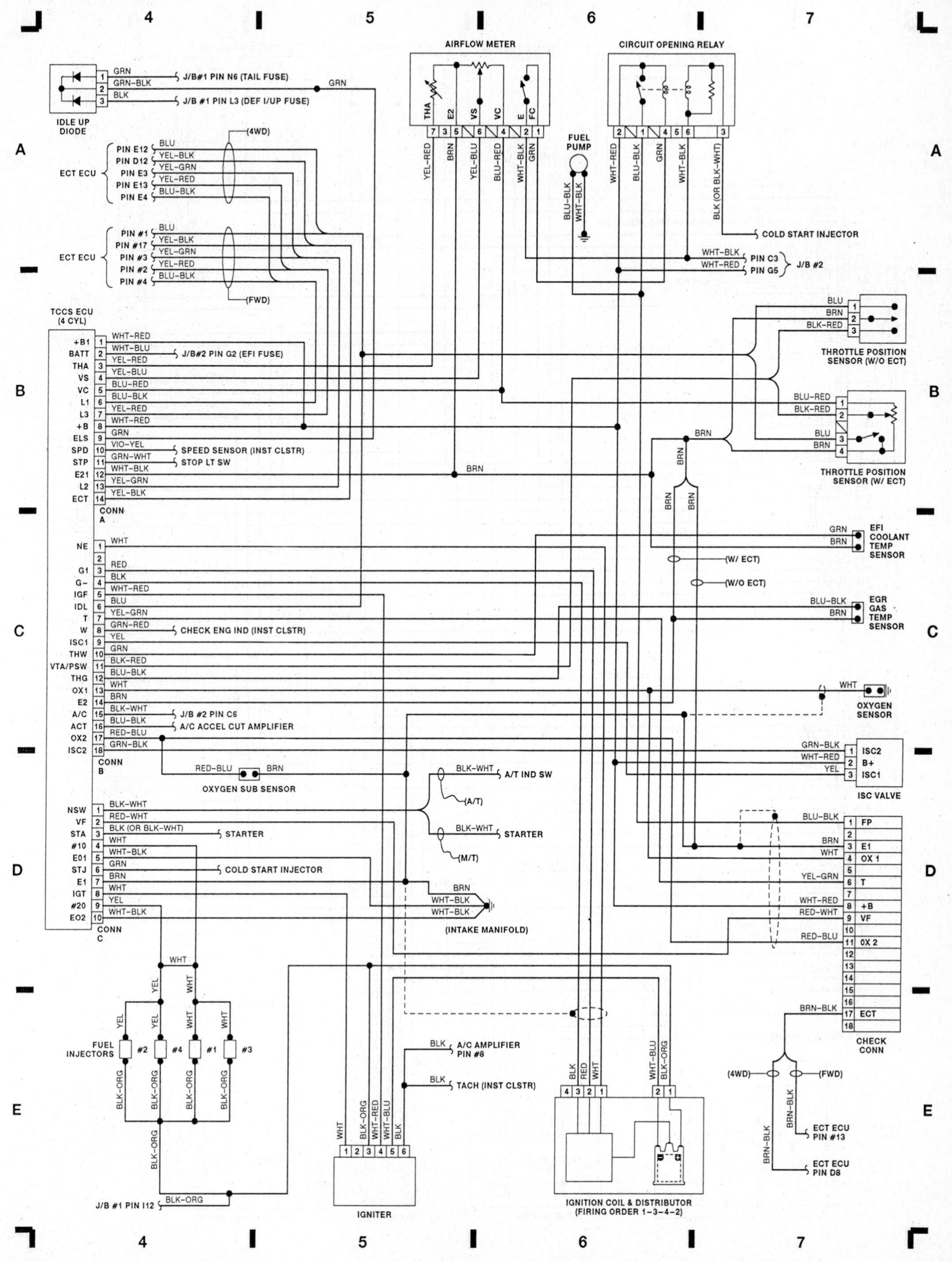

# 1991 WIRING DIAGRAMS
## Camry (Cont.)

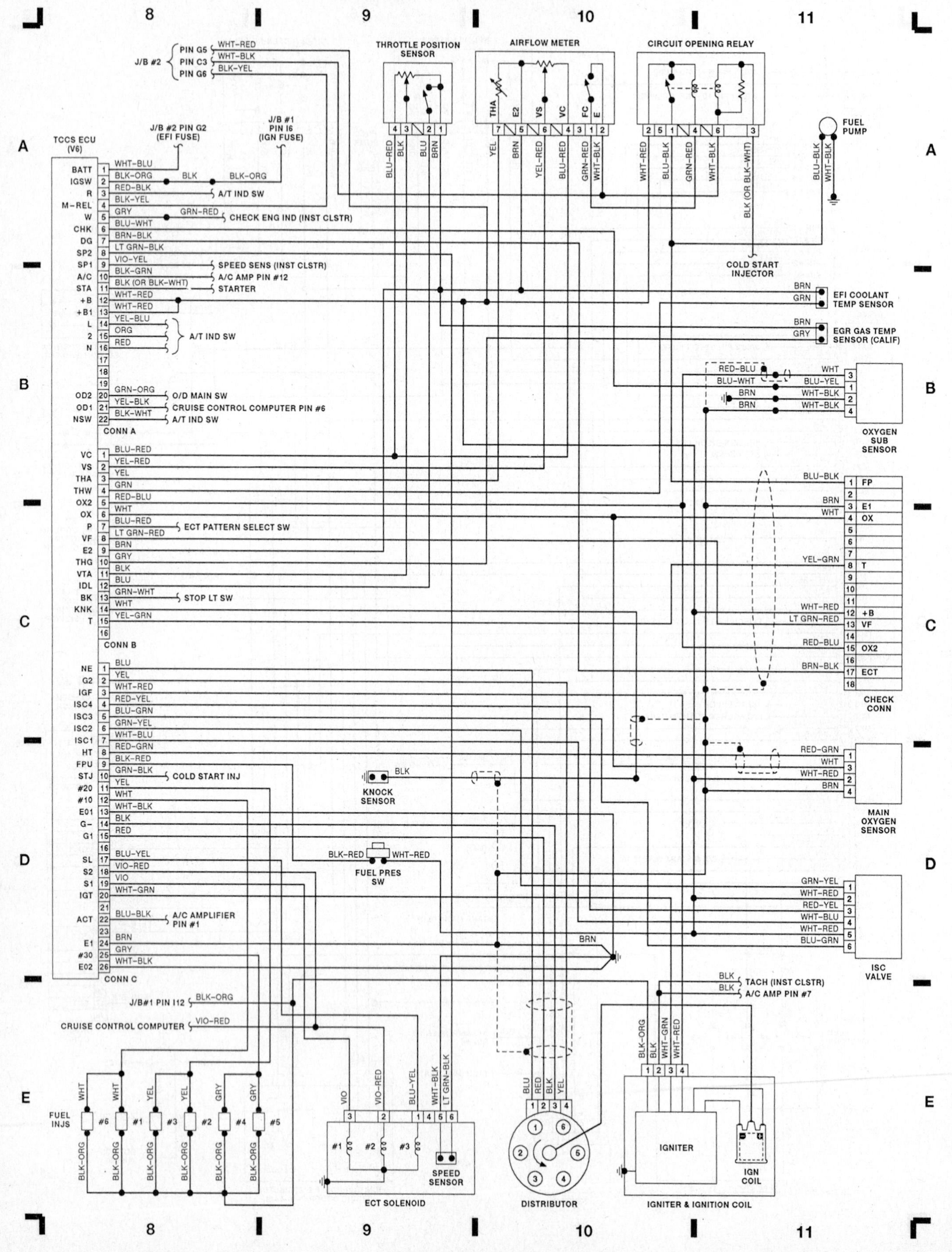

# 1991 WIRING DIAGRAMS
## Camry (Cont.)

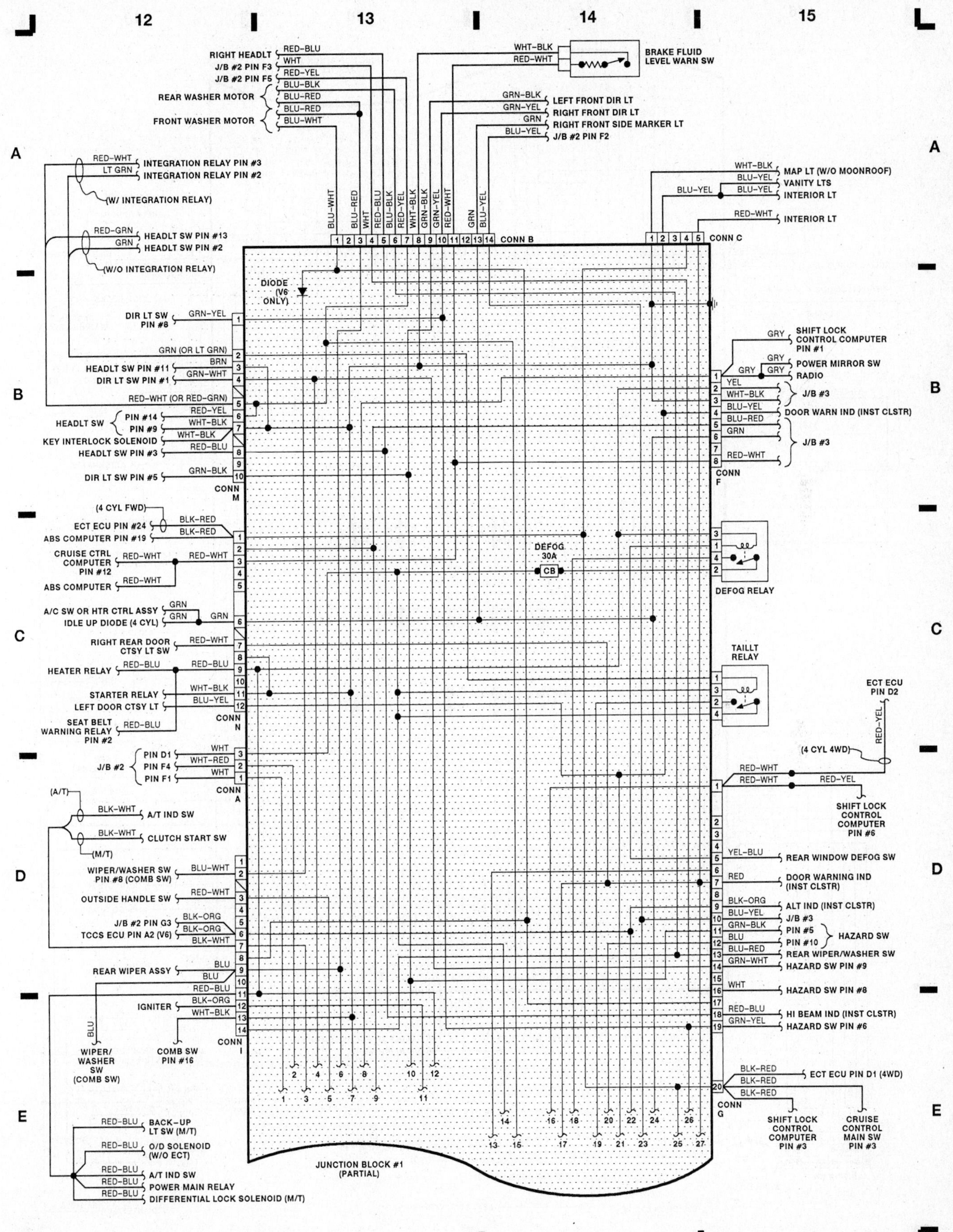

# 1991 WIRING DIAGRAMS
## Camry (Cont.)

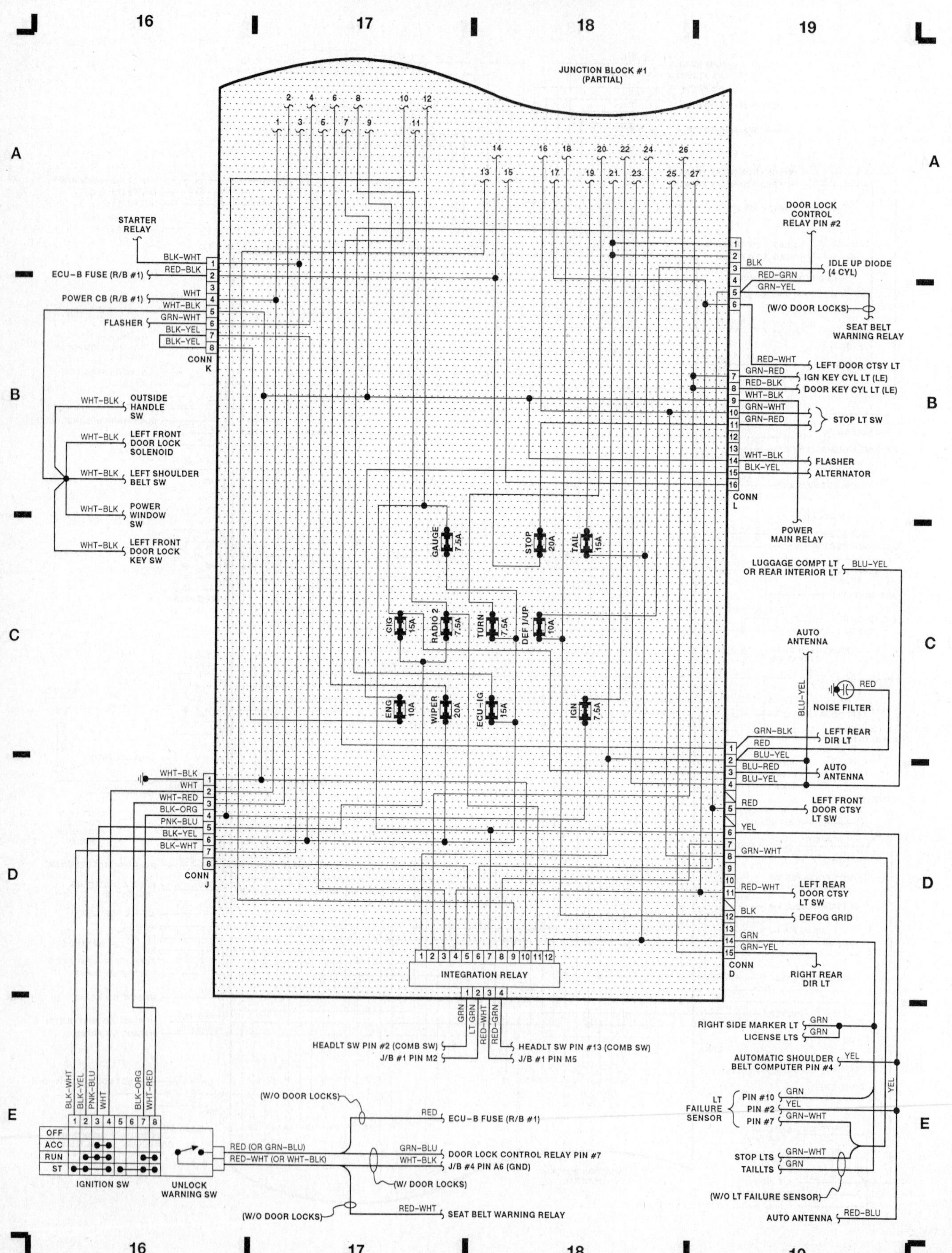

# 1991 WIRING DIAGRAMS
## Camry (Cont.)

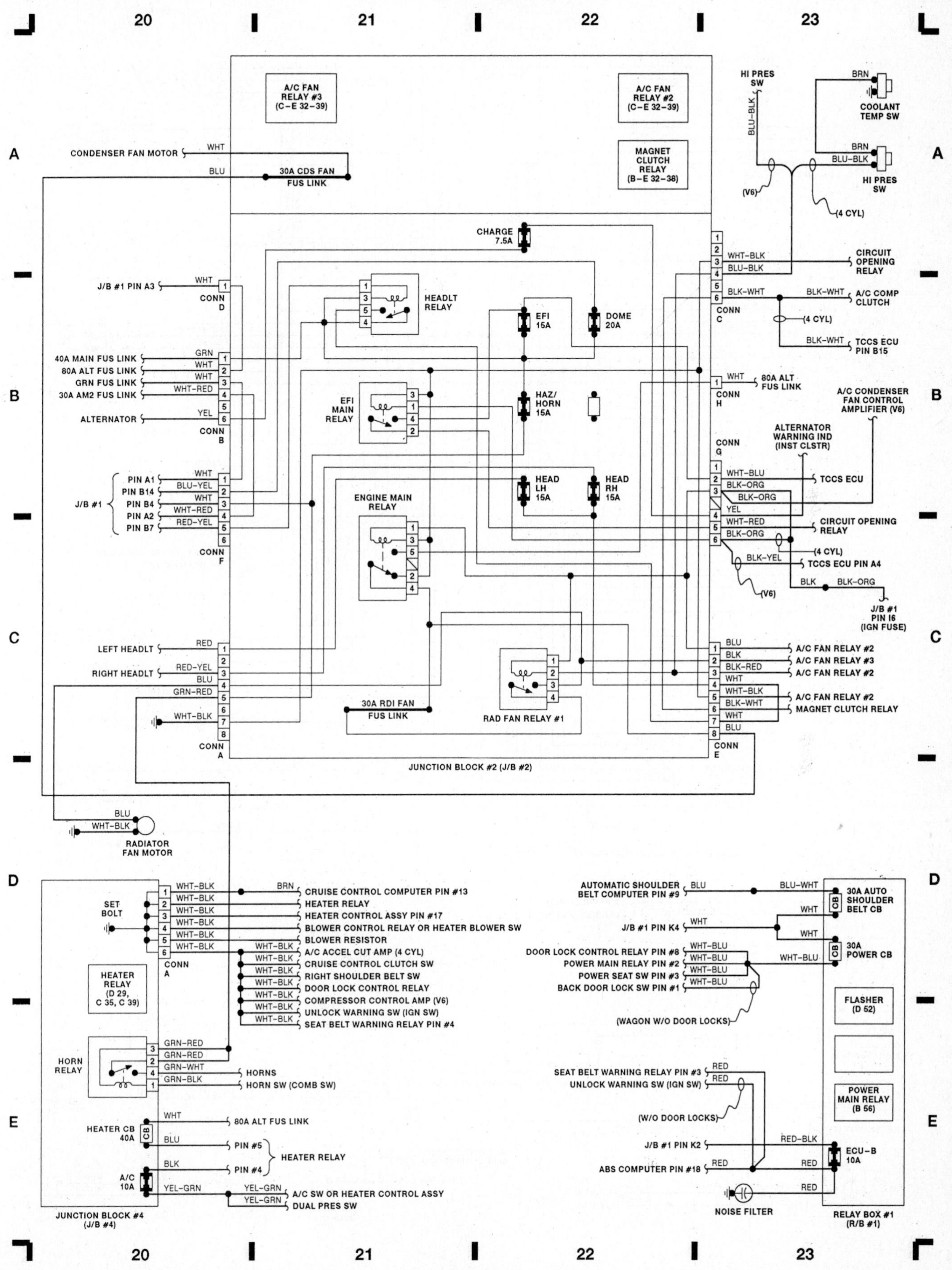

# 1991 WIRING DIAGRAMS
## Camry (Cont.)

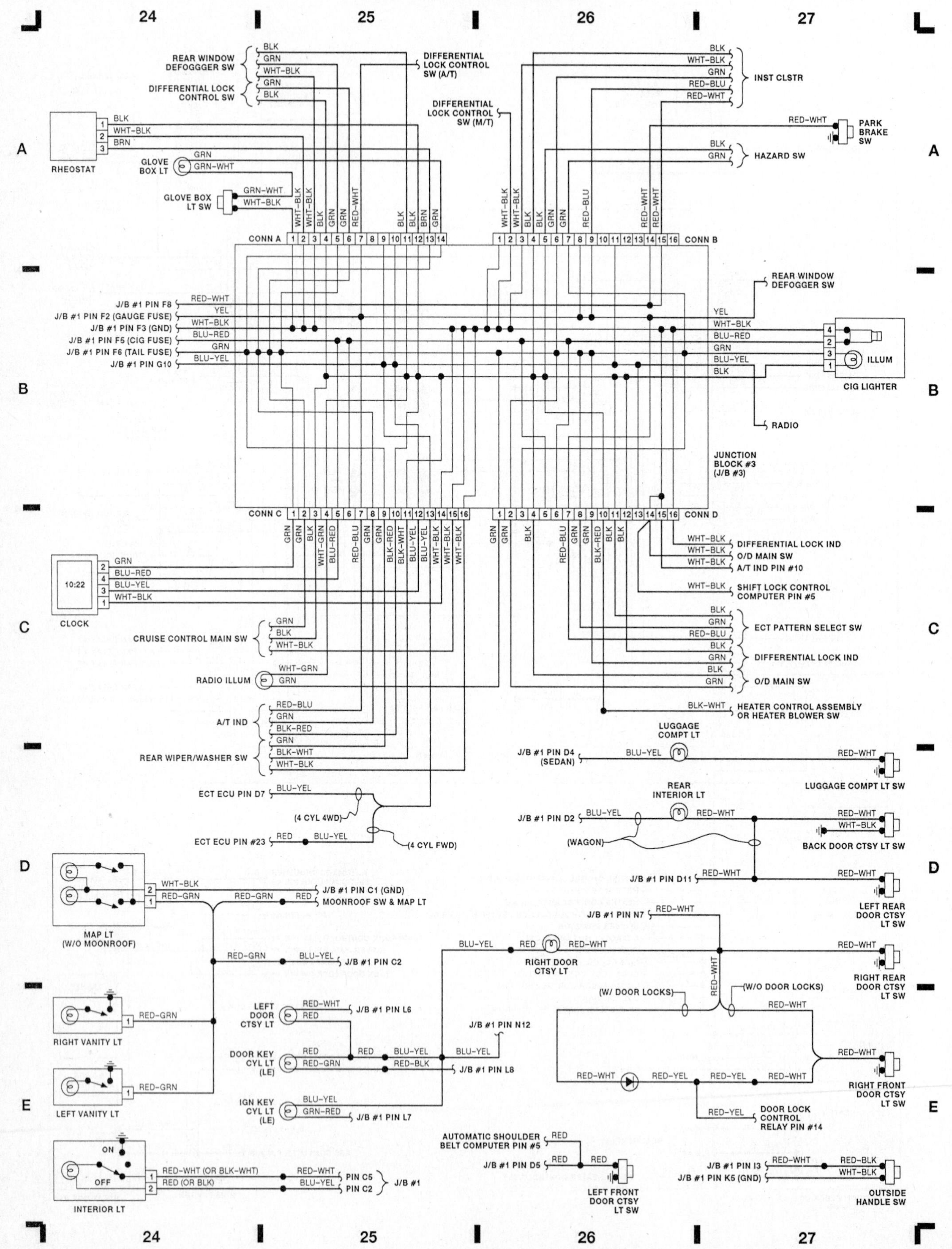

# 1991 WIRING DIAGRAMS
## Camry (Cont.)

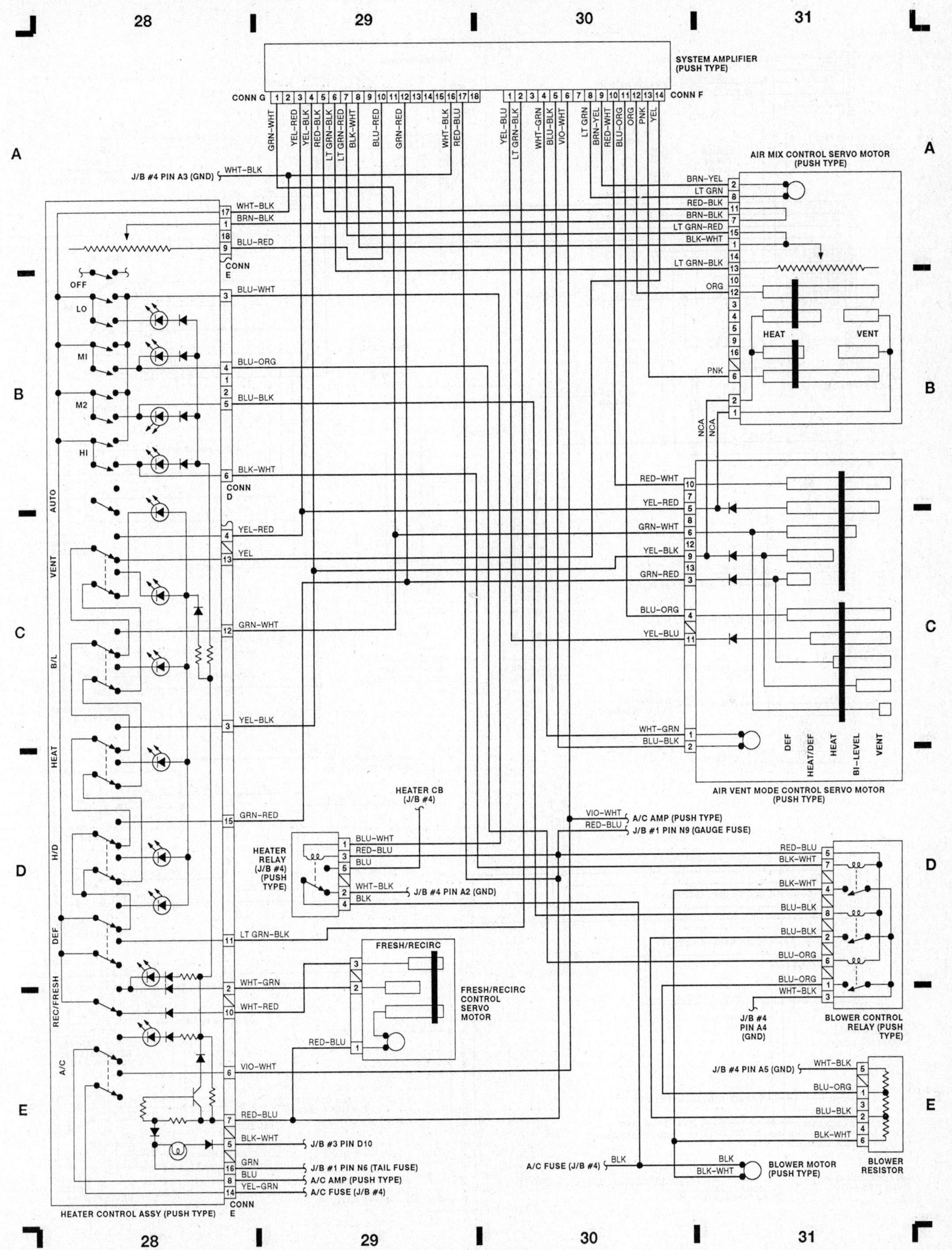

# 1991 WIRING DIAGRAMS
## Camry (Cont.)

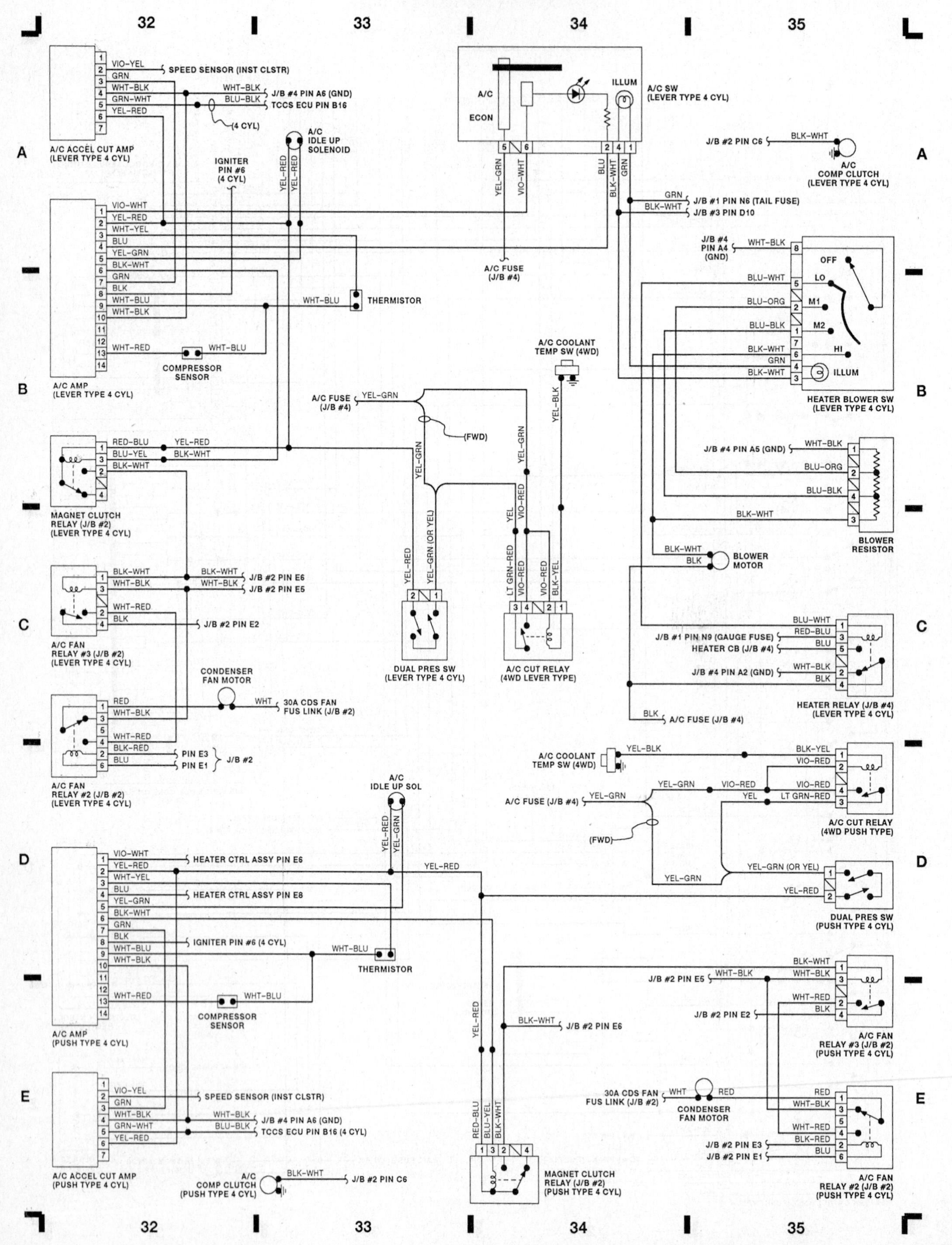

# 1991 WIRING DIAGRAMS
## Camry (Cont.)

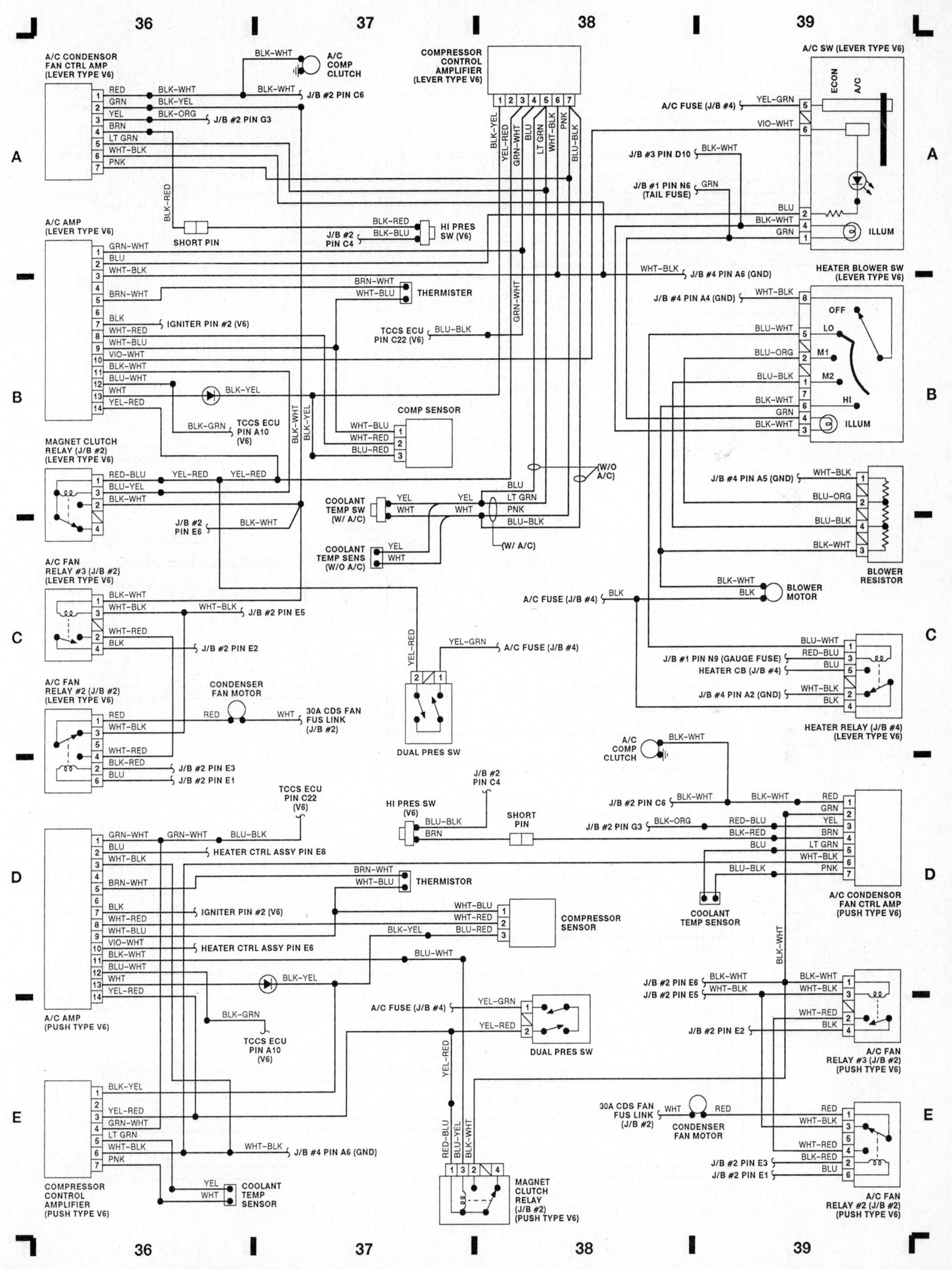

# 1991 WIRING DIAGRAMS
## Camry (Cont.)

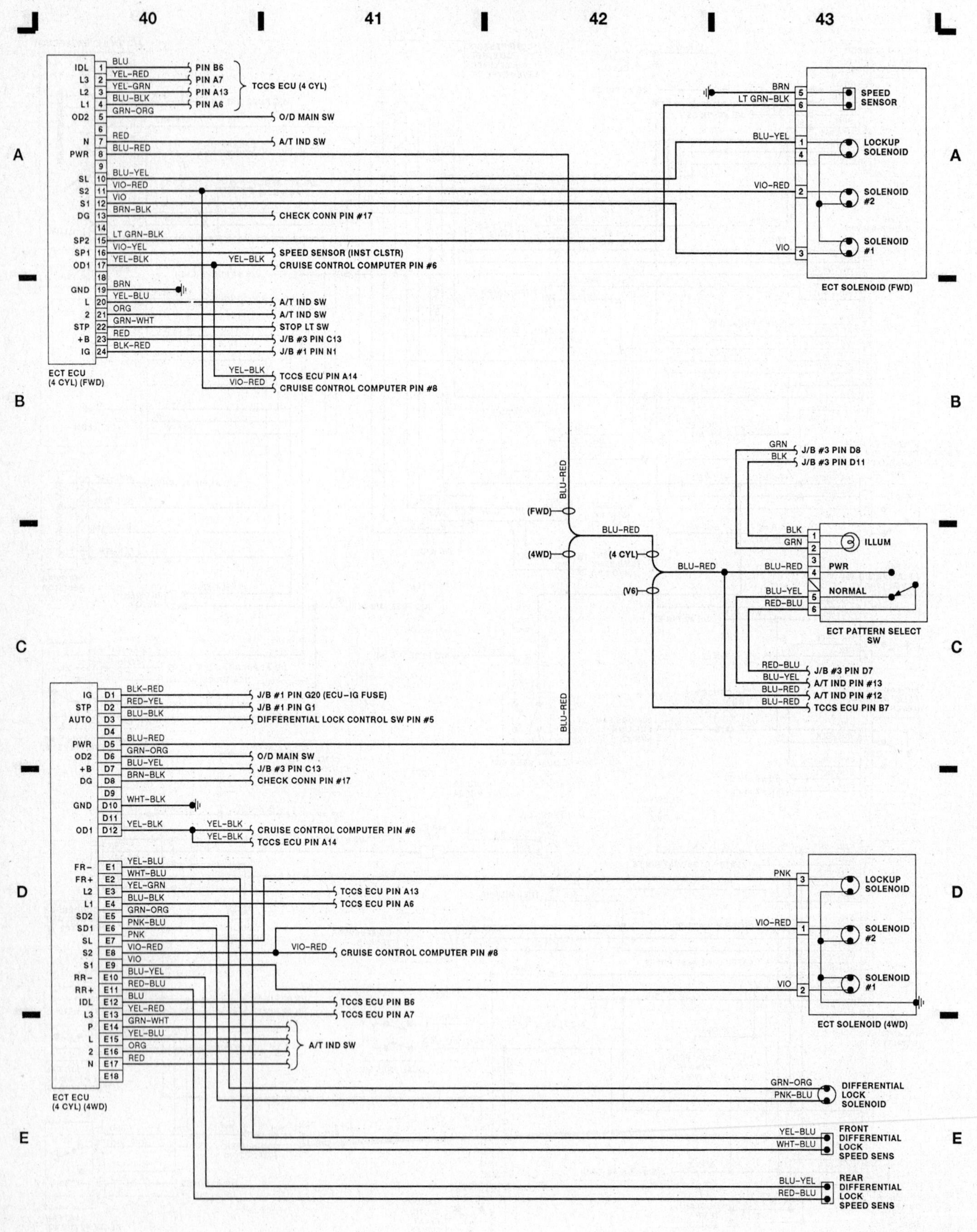

# 1991 WIRING DIAGRAMS
## Camry (Cont.)

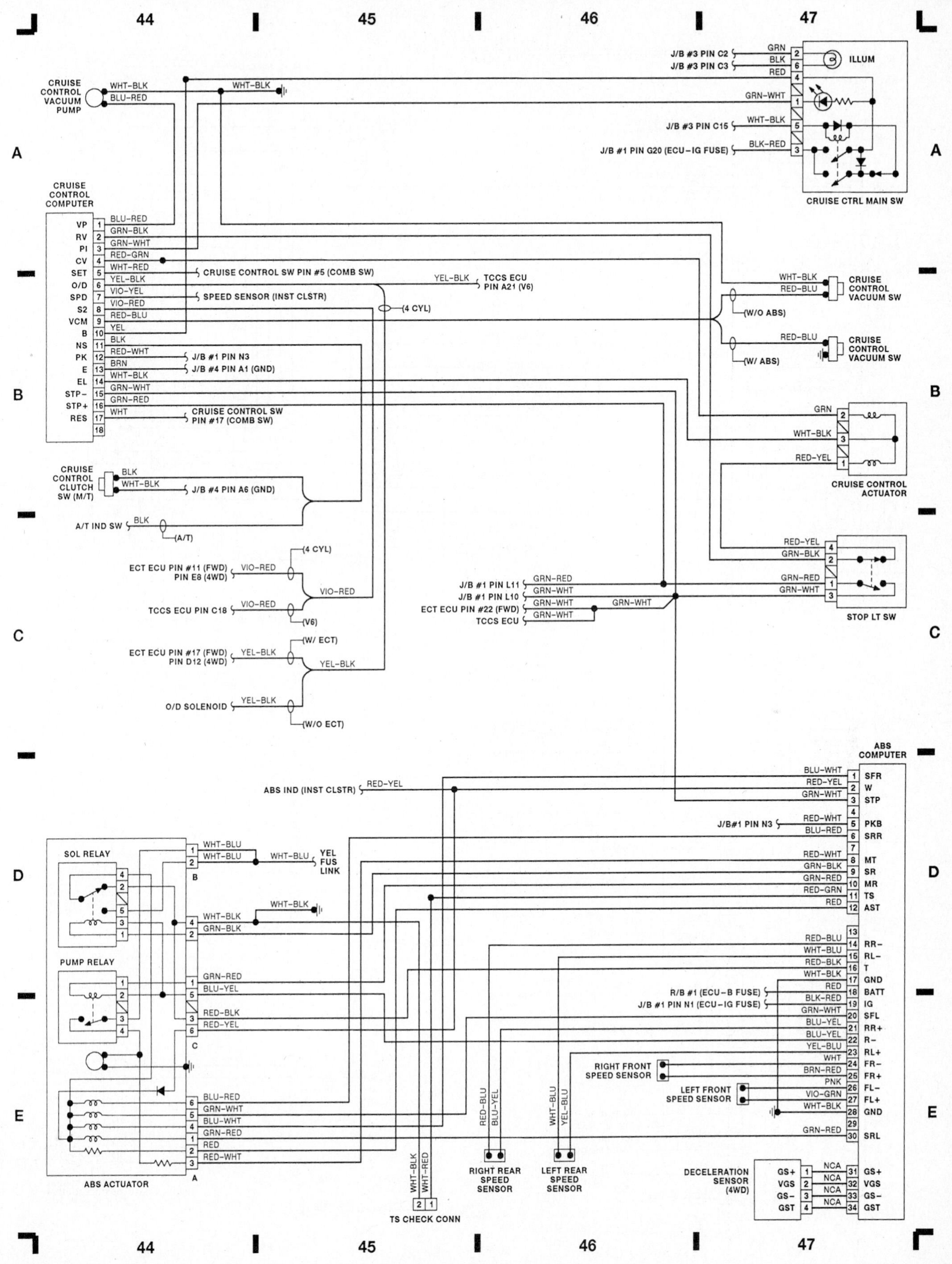

# 1991 WIRING DIAGRAMS
## Camry (Cont.)

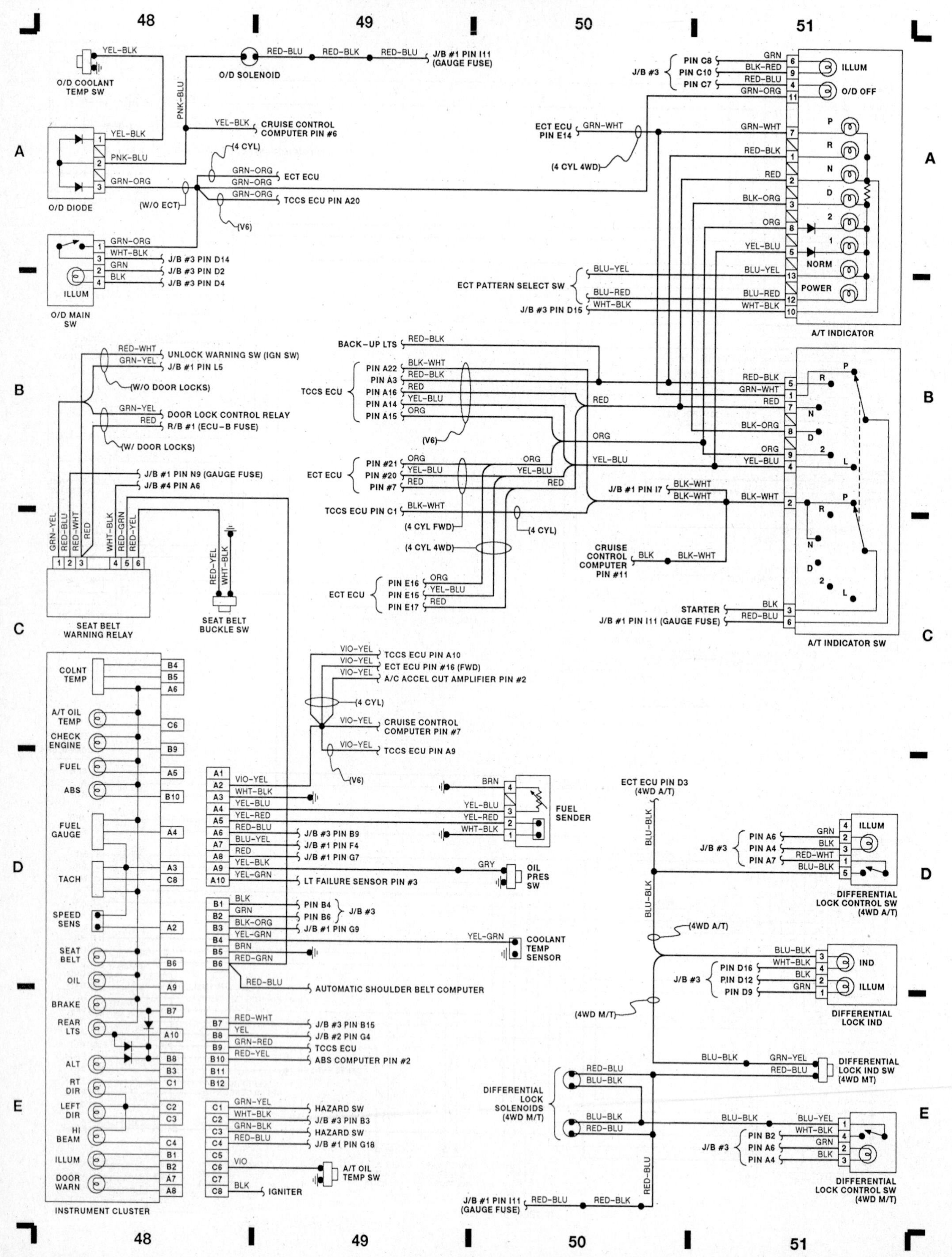

# 1991 WIRING DIAGRAMS
## Camry (Cont.)

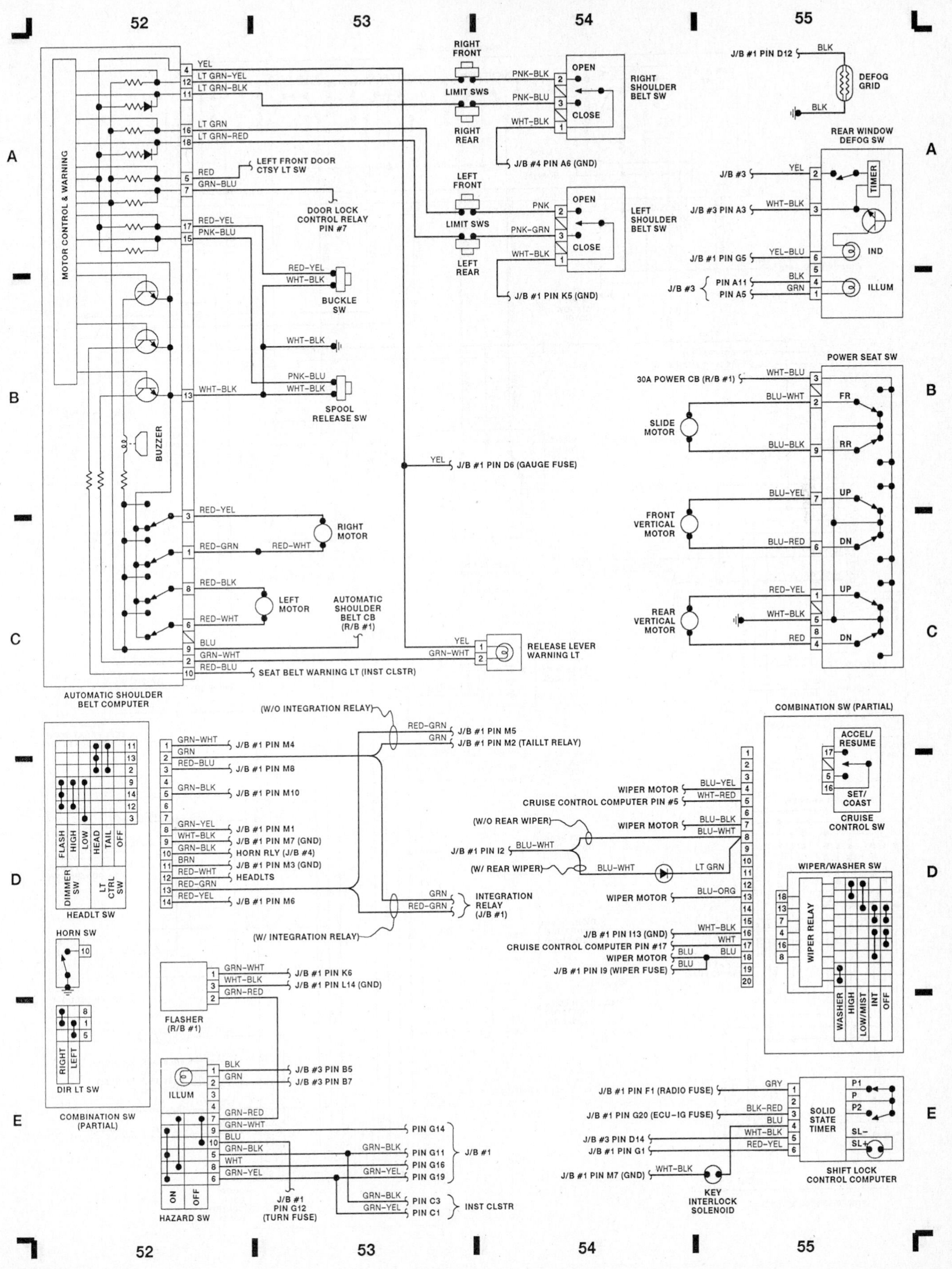

# 1991 WIRING DIAGRAMS
## Camry (Cont.)

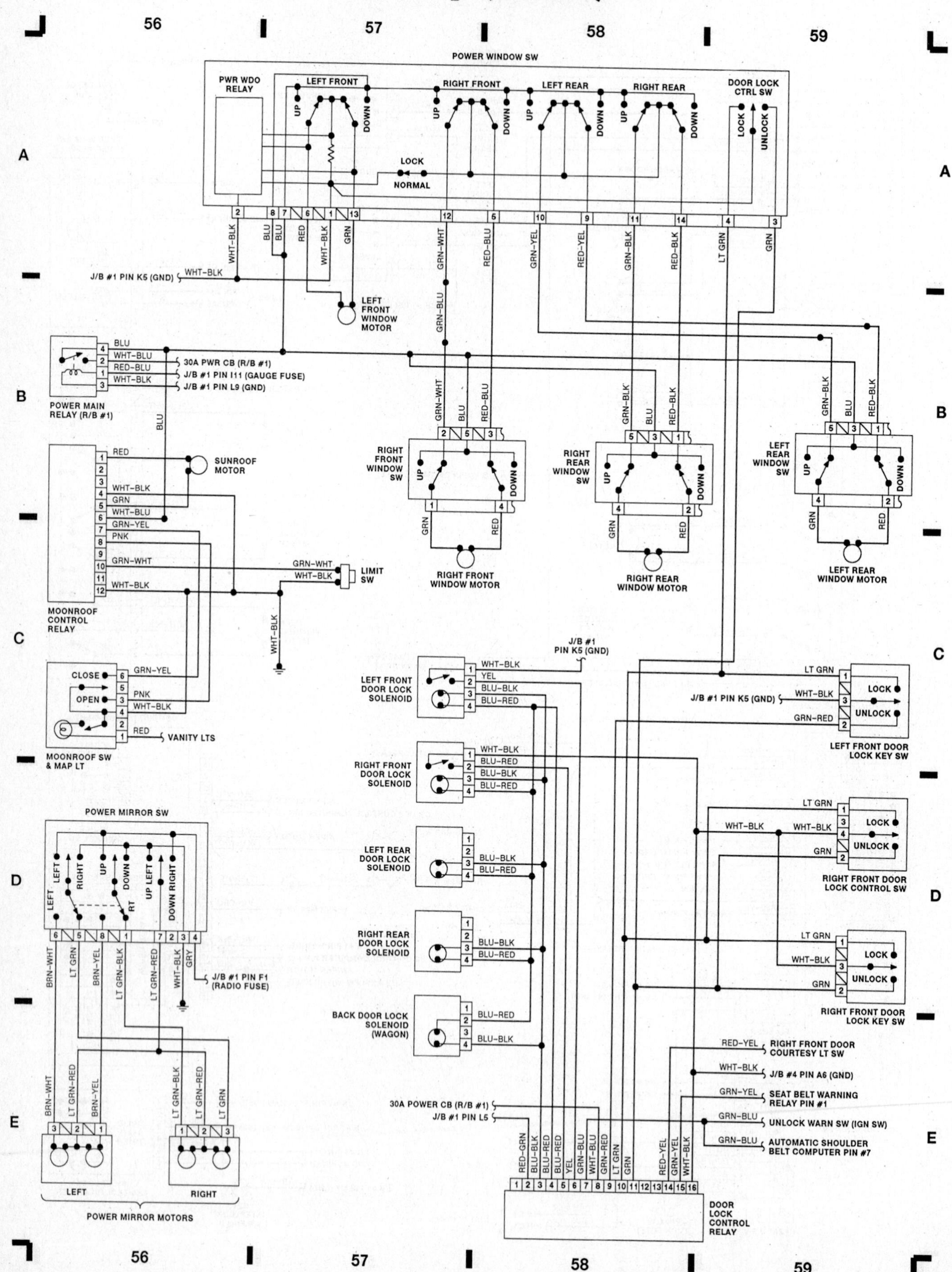

# 1991 WIRING DIAGRAMS
## Camry (Cont.)

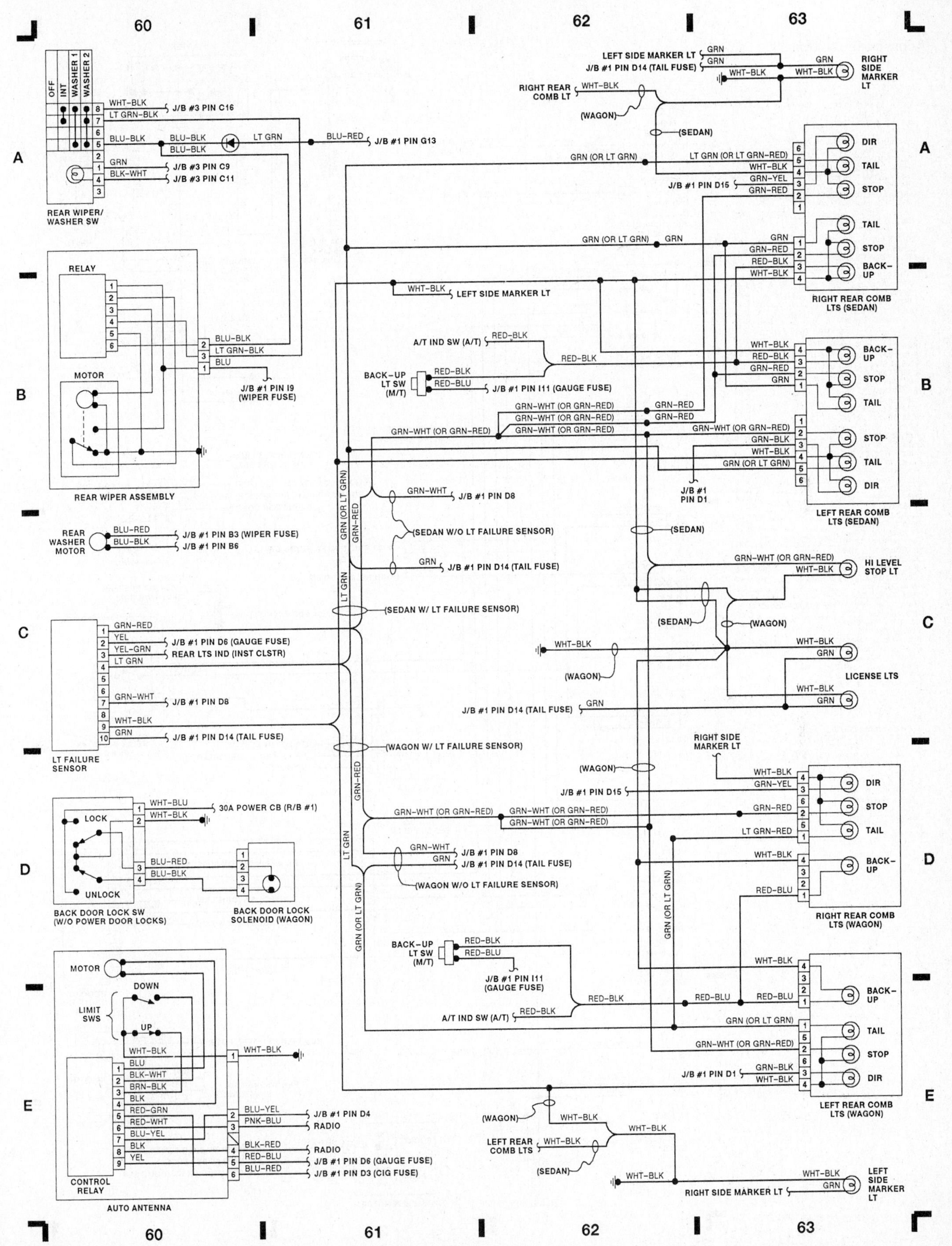

# 1991 WIRING DIAGRAMS
## Celica

**COMPONENT LOCATOR:**

| | |
|---|---|
| A/T INDICATOR SW | E 61 |
| ABS SYSTEM | A–C 56–59 |
| AUTO A/C (DIAL TYPE) | A–E 36–39/D–E 48–51 |
| AUTO A/C (PUSH TYPE) | A–E 32–35/A–C 48–51 |
| AUTO ANTENNA | D–E 63 |
| AUTO TILT AWAY ECU | E 55 |
| BATTERY | A 2 |
| CENTER AIR BAG SENSOR ASSEMBLY | E 52 |
| CHECK CONN (1.6L) | D 11 |
| CHECK CONN (2.0L) | D 15 |
| CHECK CONN (2.2L W/ ECT) | D 23 |
| CHECK CONN (2.2L W/O ECT) | D 19 |
| CIRCUIT OPENING RELAY (1.6L) | A 10 |
| CIRCUIT OPENING RELAY (2.0L) | A 13 |
| CIRCUIT OPENING RELAY (2.2L W/ ECT) | A 21 |
| CIRCUIT OPENING RELAY (2.2L W/O ECT) | A 17 |
| COLD START INJECTOR | B 3 |
| COMBINATION SW | C–E 67 |
| CRUISE CONTROL W/ ABS (MOTOR TYPE) | A–C 52–55 |
| CRUISE CONTROL W/O ABS (VACUUM TYPE) | B–D 52–55 |
| DEFOG SW | A 60 |
| DIR FLASHER | C 30 |
| DOOR COURTESY SWS | C–D 59 |
| DOOR LOCK SYSTEM | D–E 68–70 |
| ECT PATTERN SELECT SW | E 22 |
| EGR VSV (2.0L) | E 13 |
| EGR VSV (2.2L W/ ECT) | B 23 |
| EGR VSV (2.2L W/O ECT) | B 19 |
| FOG LT SW | D 2 |
| FUEL SENDER | A–B 67 |
| FUS LINK BOX | C 5–6 |
| HAZARD SW | E 64 |
| IGNITER (2.0L) | D 15 |
| IGNITER (2.2L W/ ECT) | D 23 |
| IGNITER (2.2L W/O ECT) | D 19 |
| IGNITION KEY CYLINDER LT | E 56 |
| IGNITION NOISE FILTER | E 10 |
| IGNITION NOISE FILTER (2.0L) | E 14 |
| IGNITION NOISE FILTER (2.2L W/ ECT) | E 21 |
| IGNITION NOISE FILTER (2.2L W/O ECT) | E 18 |
| IGNITION SW | A 24 |
| INST CLSTR | A–D 64 |
| INTERIOR LT | D 57 |
| J1 JUNCTION CONN | E 59 |
| J2 JUNCTION CONN | C 52 |
| J3 JUNCTION CONN | E 24 |
| J4 JUNCTION CONN | A 51,D 51 |
| J6 JUNCTION CONN | A 27 |
| JUNCTION BLOCK #1 (J/B #1) | B–E 25–30 |
| JUNCTION BLOCK #2 (J/B #2) | B–E 5–6 |
| JUNCTION BLOCK #3 (J/B #3) | B 61–62 |
| MAIN FUS LINK | A 2 |
| MANUAL A/C (DIAL TYPE) | A–E 44–47/D–E 48–51 |
| MANUAL A/C (PUSH TYPE) | A–E 40–43/A–C 48–51 |
| O/D MAIN SW | C 60 |
| POWER MIRROR SW | B 68 |
| POWER SEAT SW | A 68 |
| POWER WINDOW MASTER SW | C–D 70 |
| REAR WIPER MOTOR & RELAY | C 65 |
| RELAY BLOCK #2 (R/B #2) | A 28 |
| RELAY BLOCK #3 (R/B #3) | C 3 |
| RELAY BLOCK #4 (R/B #4) | B 30 |
| RELAY BLOCK #5 (R/B #5) | A 5–6 |
| RETRACT CONTROL RELAY | D 3 |
| SHIFT LOCK ECU | D 60 |
| START INJECTOR TIME SW | B 3 |
| STARTER | A 3 |
| STOP LT SW (W/ CRUISE) | C 55 |
| STOP LT SW (W/O CRUISE) | B 55 |
| SUNROOF CONTROL RELAY | A 69 |
| SUNROOF CONTROL SW | B 69 |
| TCCS ECU (1.6L) | B–D 8 |
| TCCS ECU (2.0L) | A–E 12 |
| TCCS ECU (2.2L W/ ECT) | A–E 20 |
| TCCS ECU (2.2L W/O ECT) | B–D 16 |
| TURBOCHARGING PRES SENS (2.0L) | B 15 |
| UNLOCK WARNING SW (IGNITION SW) | A 24 |
| WASHER MOTOR | E 2 |
| WIPER MOTOR | E 3 |

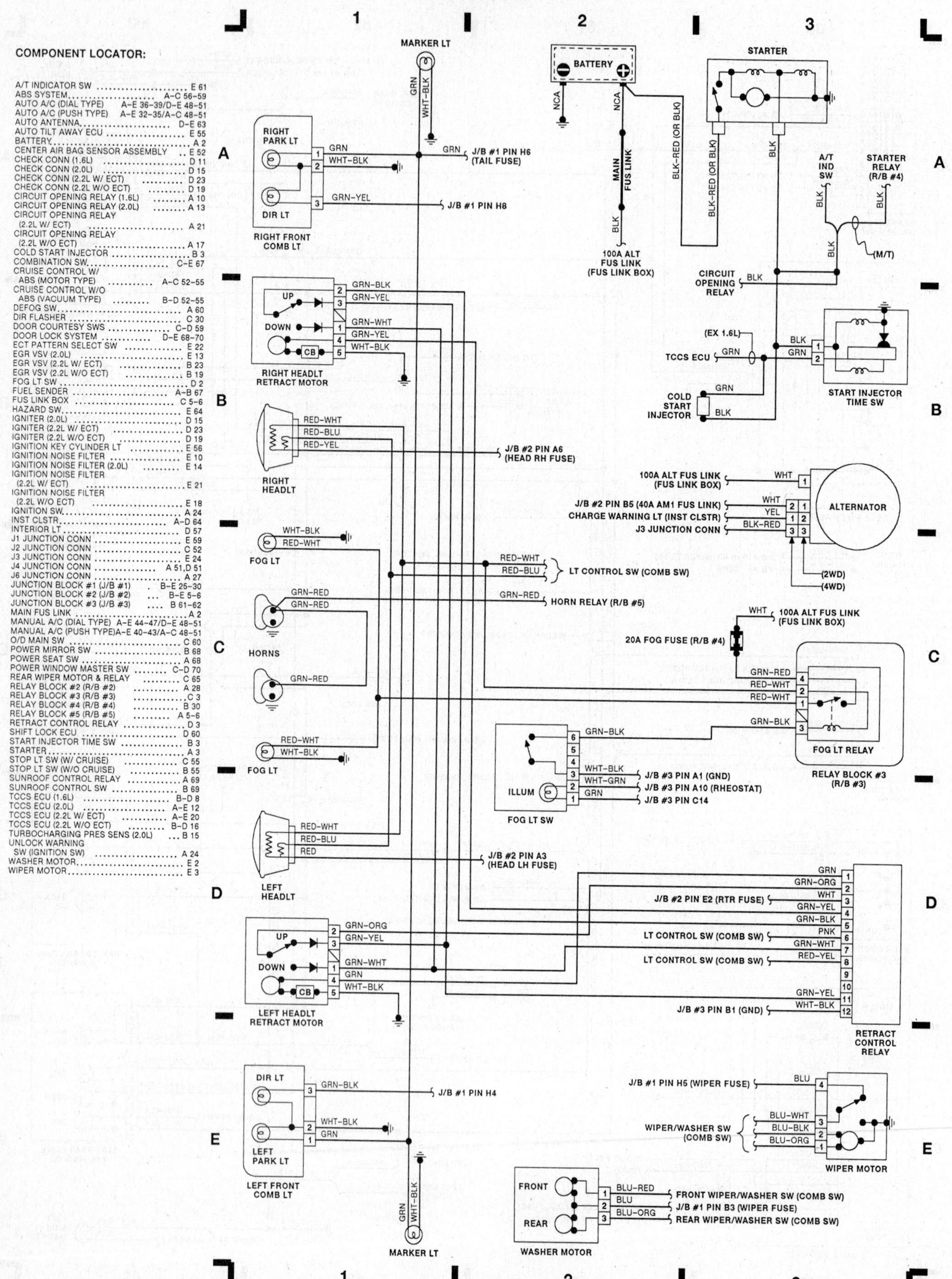

# 1991 WIRING DIAGRAMS
## Celica (Cont.)

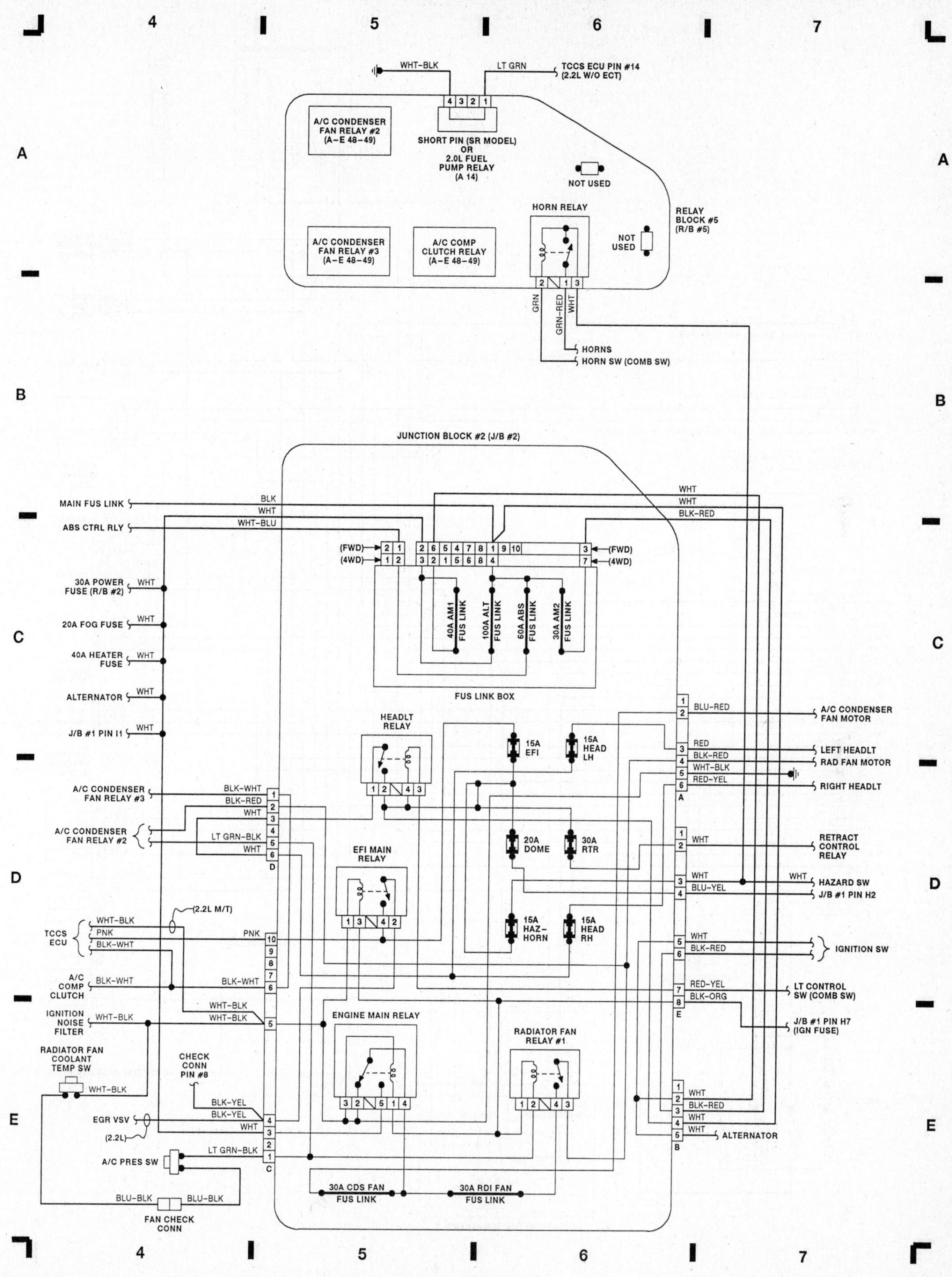

# 1991 WIRING DIAGRAMS
## Celica (Cont.)

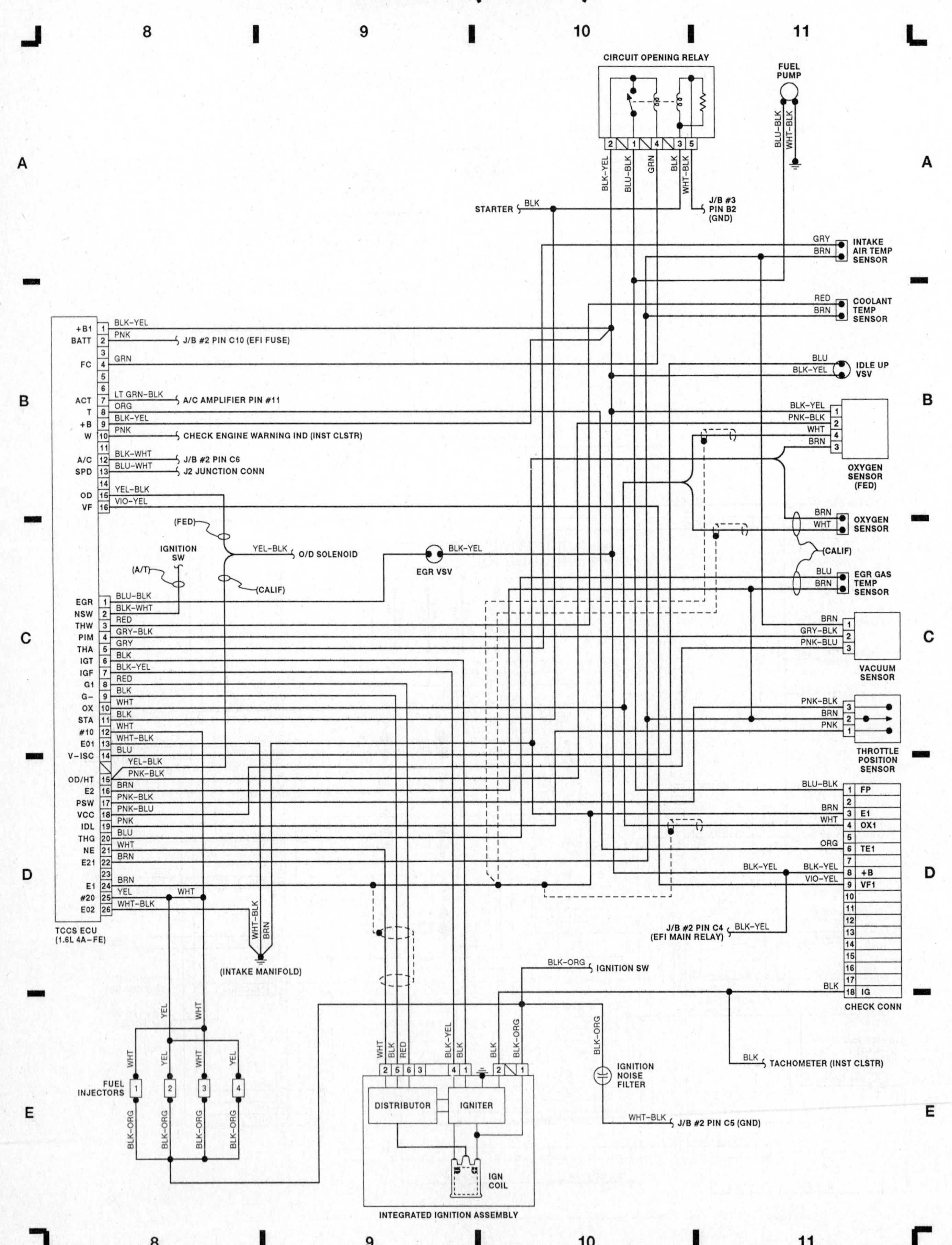

# 1991 WIRING DIAGRAMS
## Celica (Cont.)

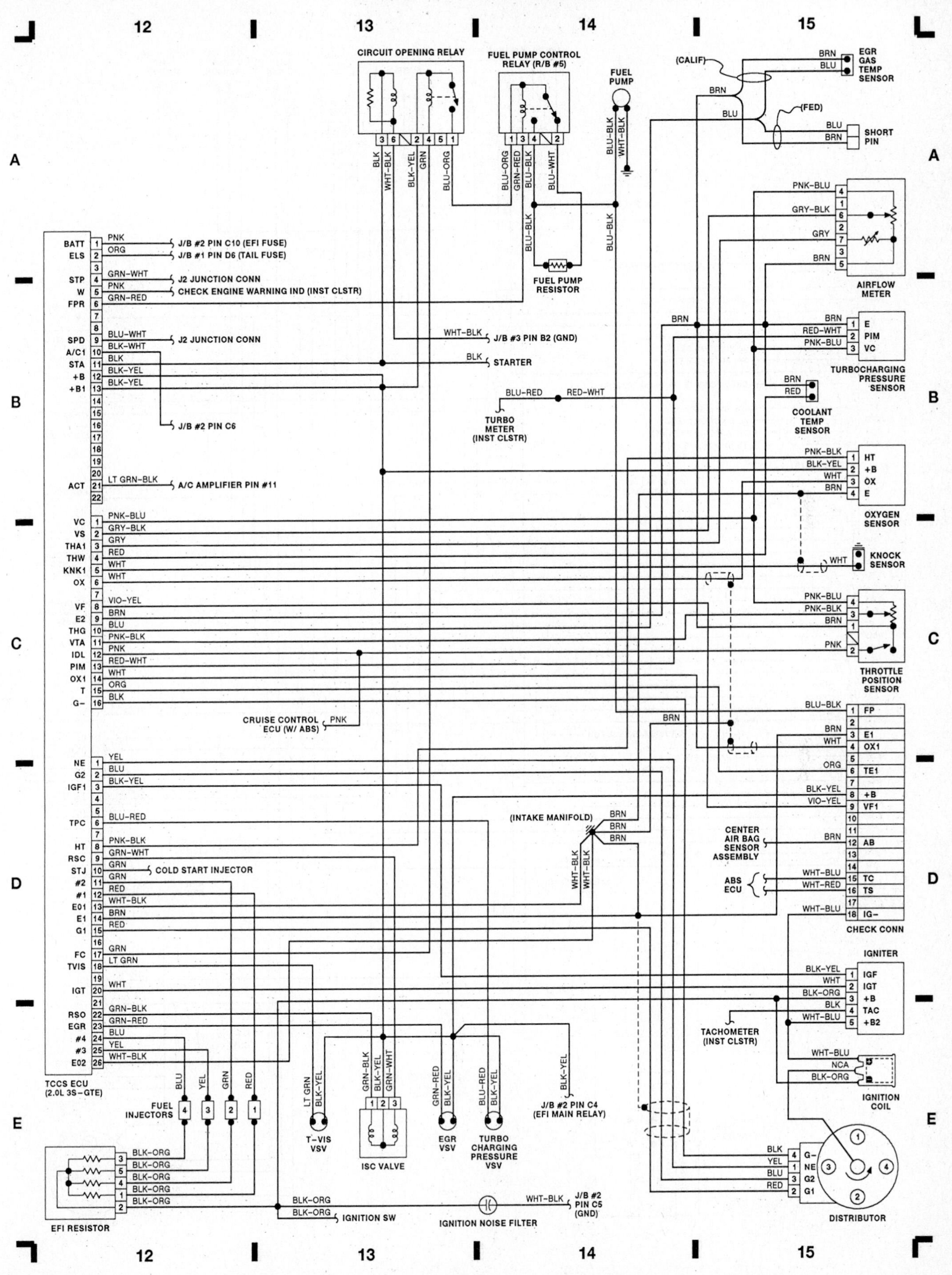

# 1991 WIRING DIAGRAMS
## Celica (Cont.)

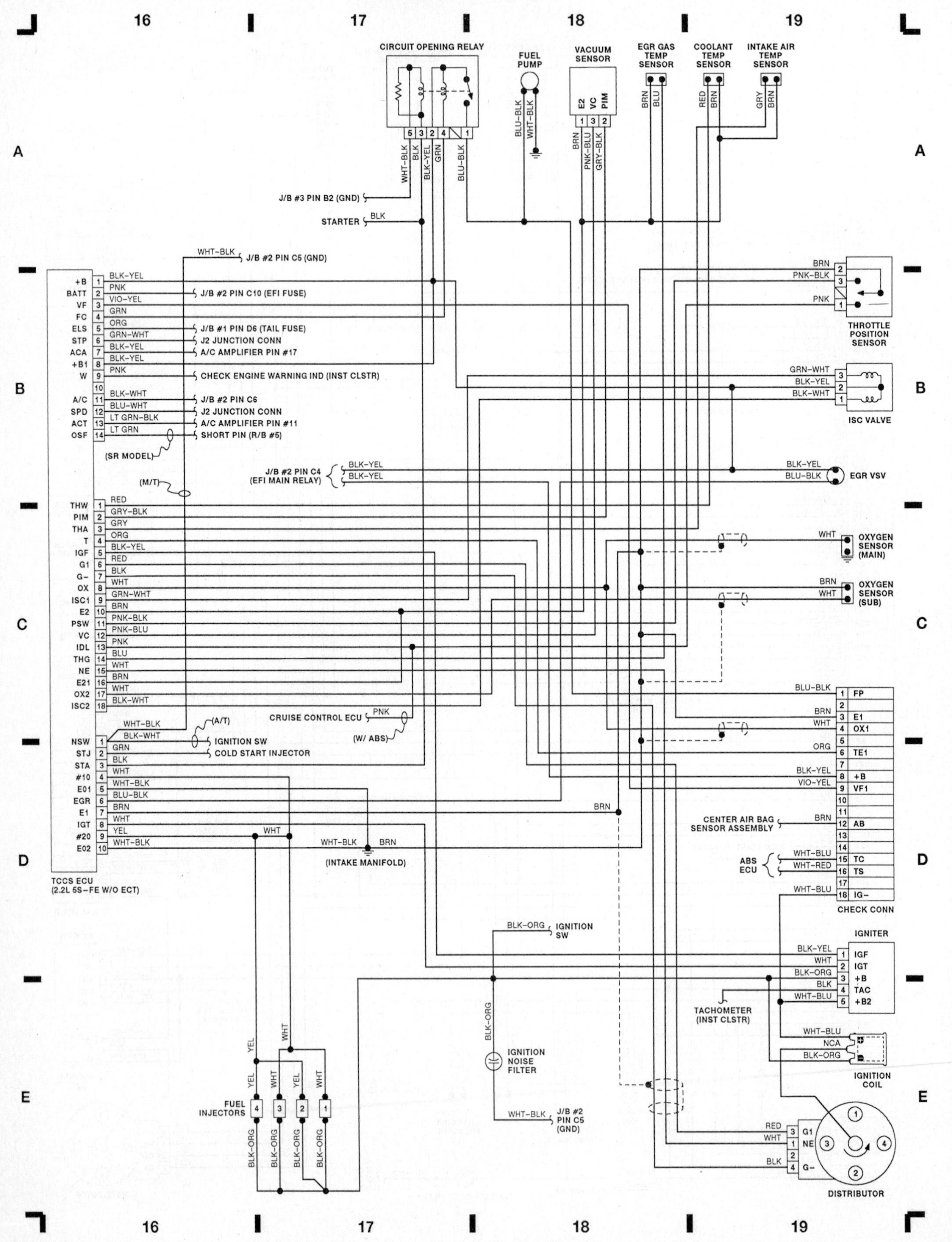

# 1991 WIRING DIAGRAMS
## Celica (Cont.)

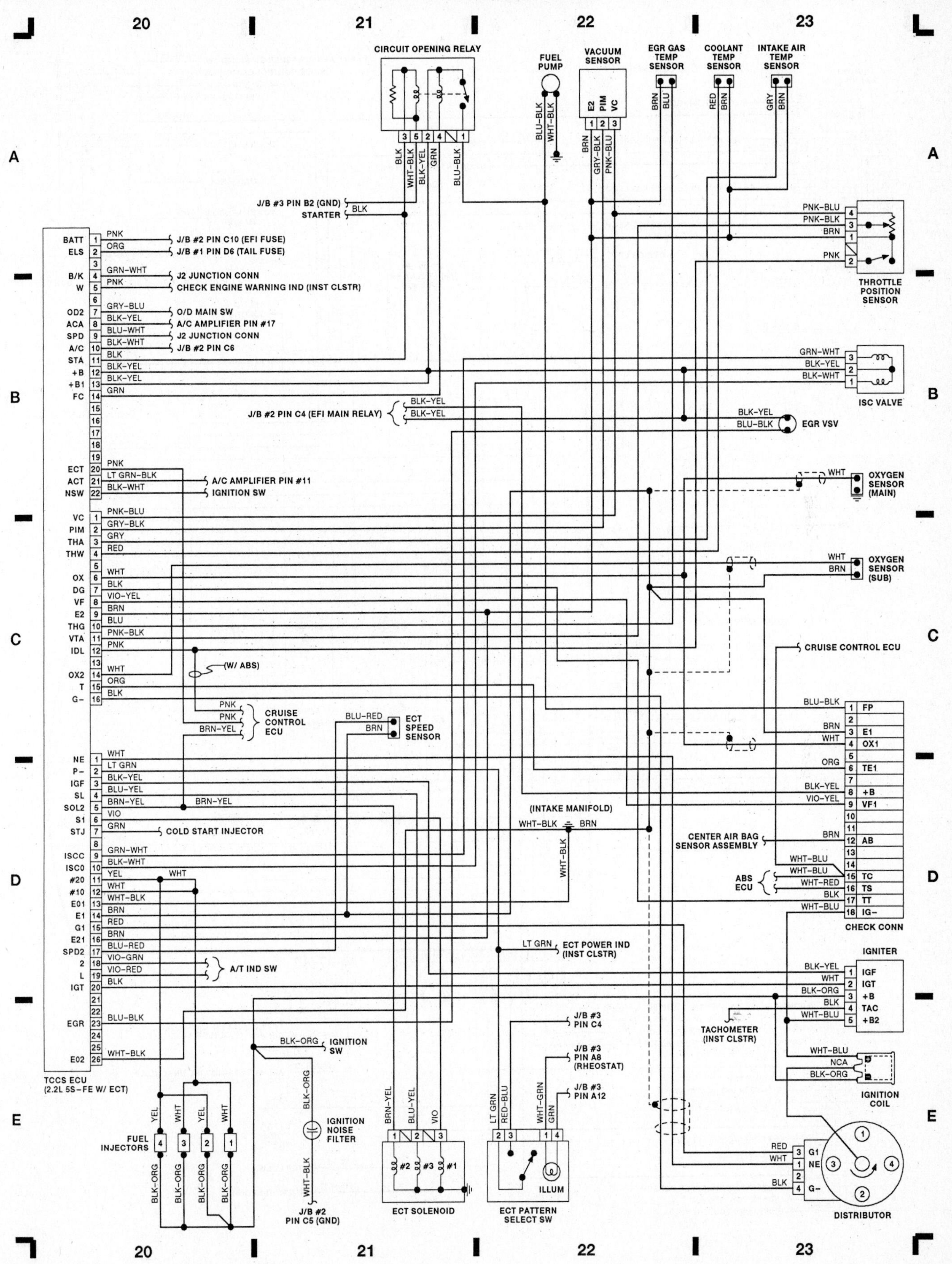

# 1991 WIRING DIAGRAMS
## Celica (Cont.)

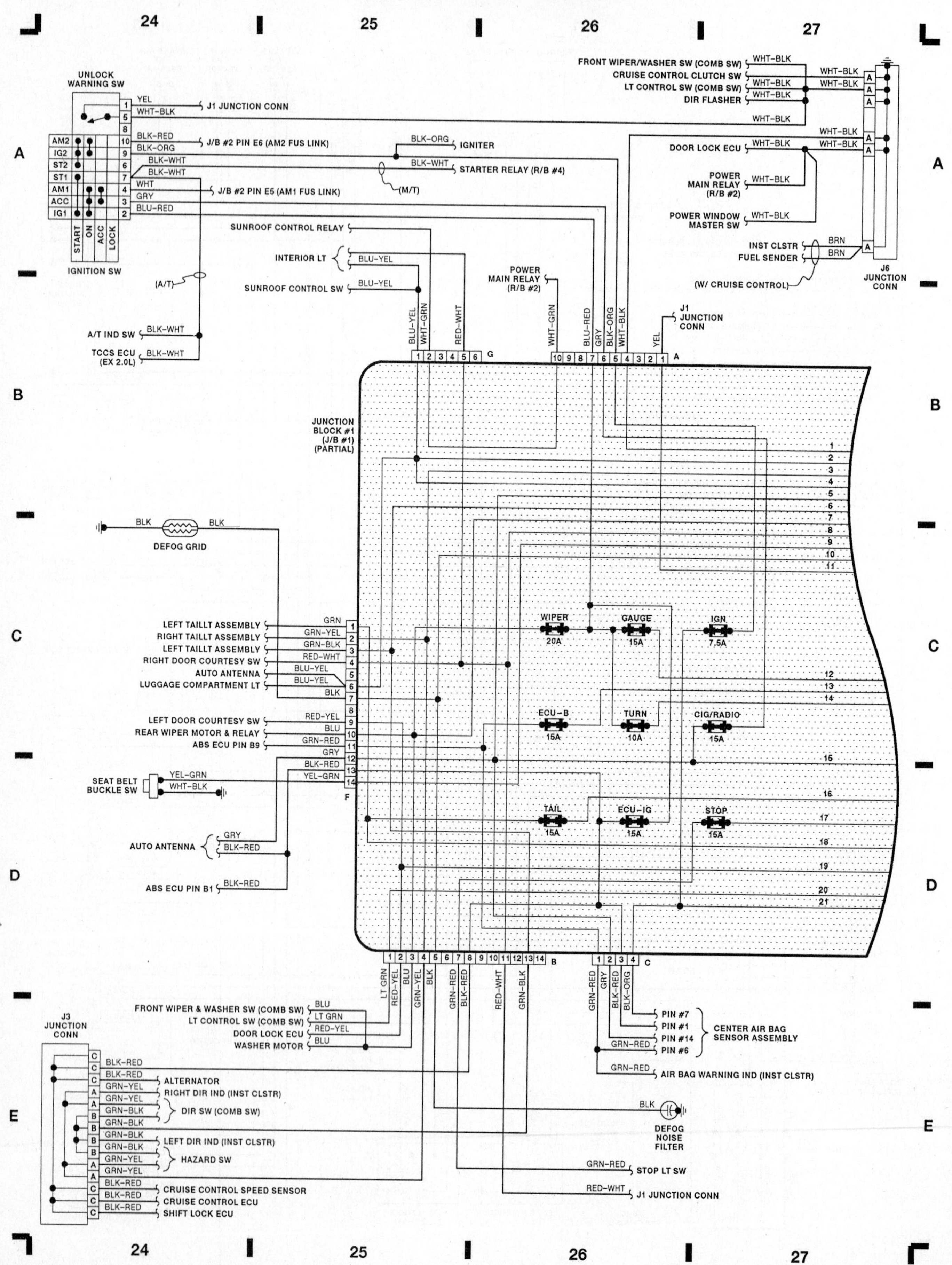

# 1991 WIRING DIAGRAMS
## Celica (Cont.)

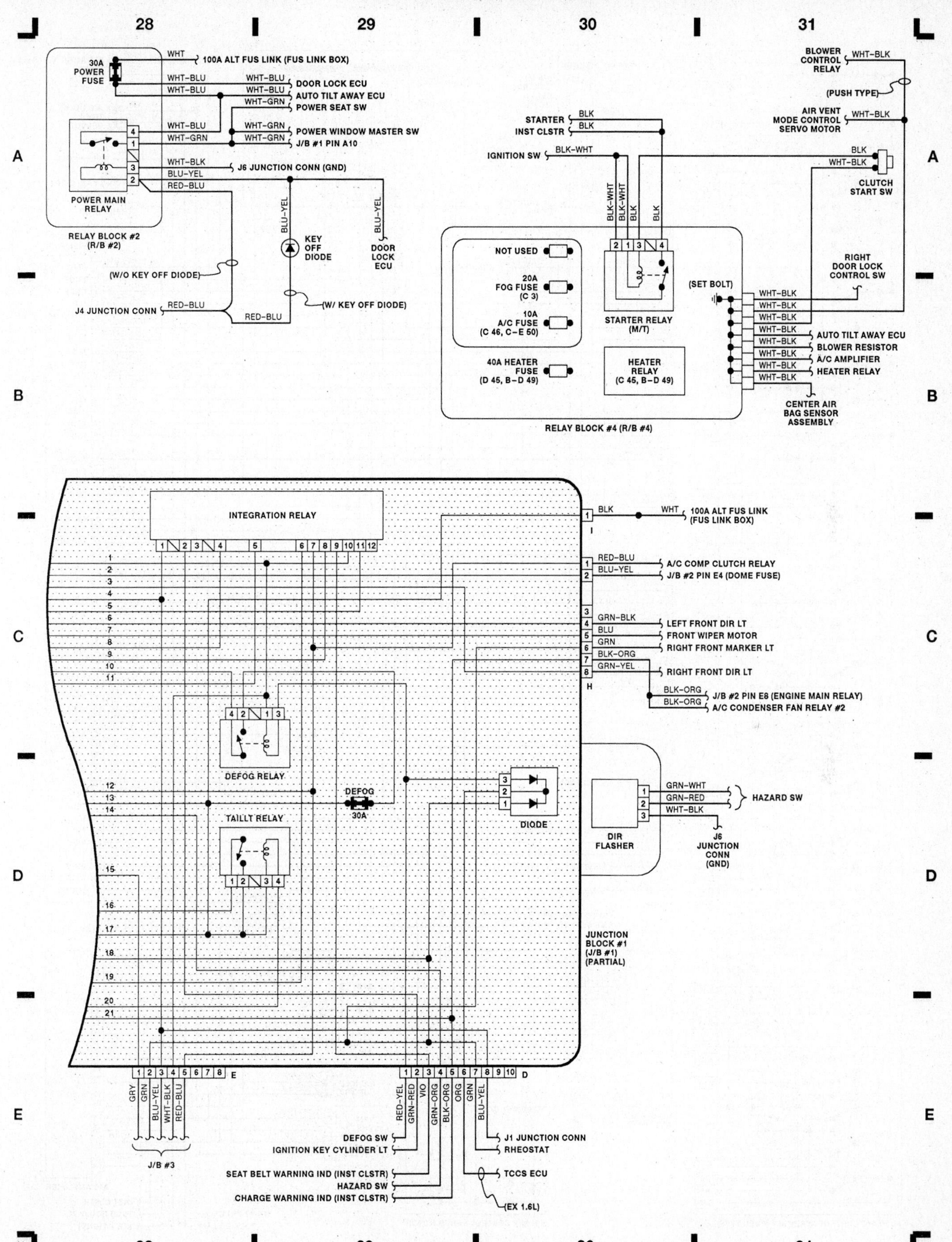

# 1991 WIRING DIAGRAMS
## Celica (Cont.)

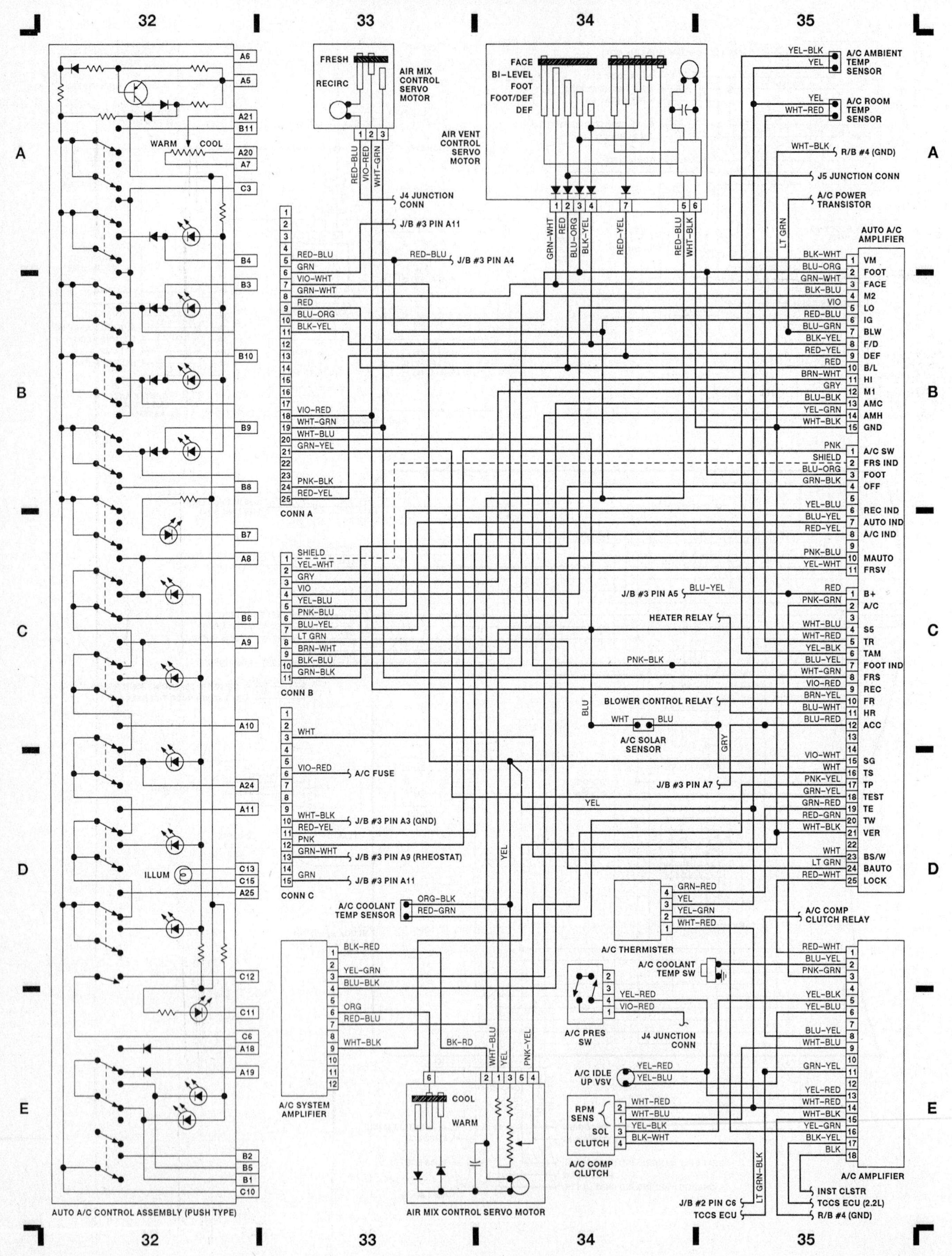

# 1991 WIRING DIAGRAMS
## Celica (Cont.)

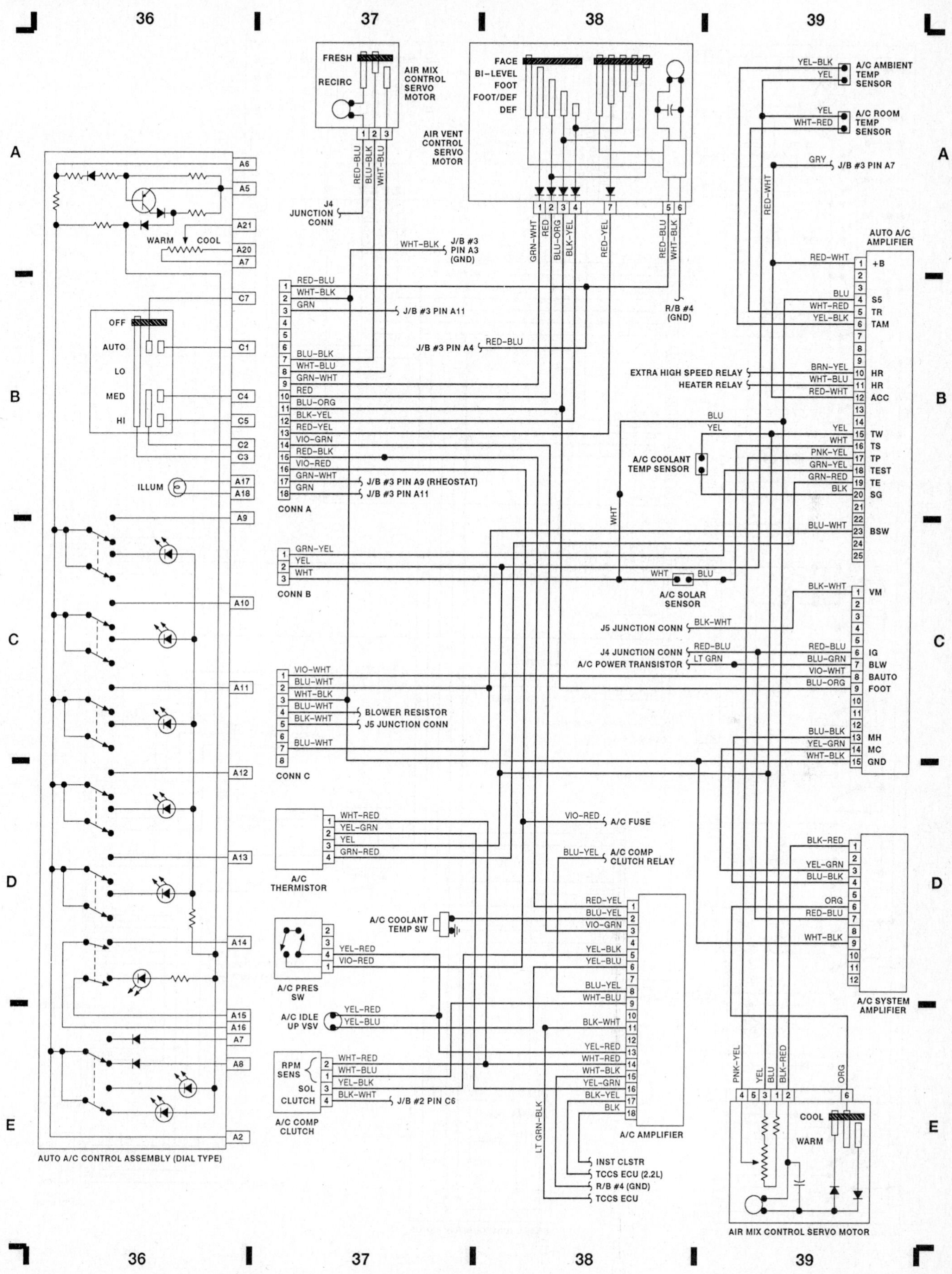

# 1991 WIRING DIAGRAMS
## Celica (Cont.)

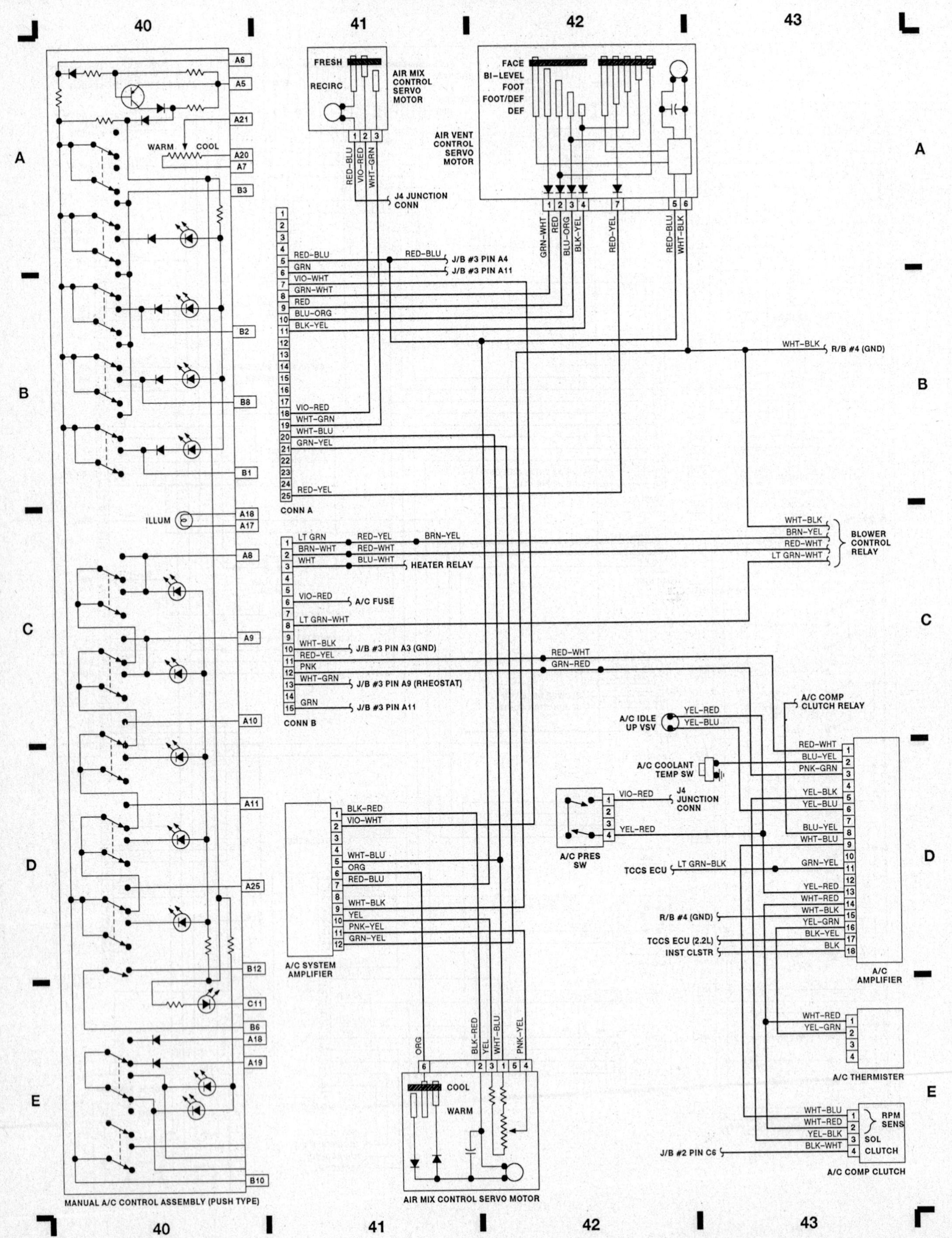

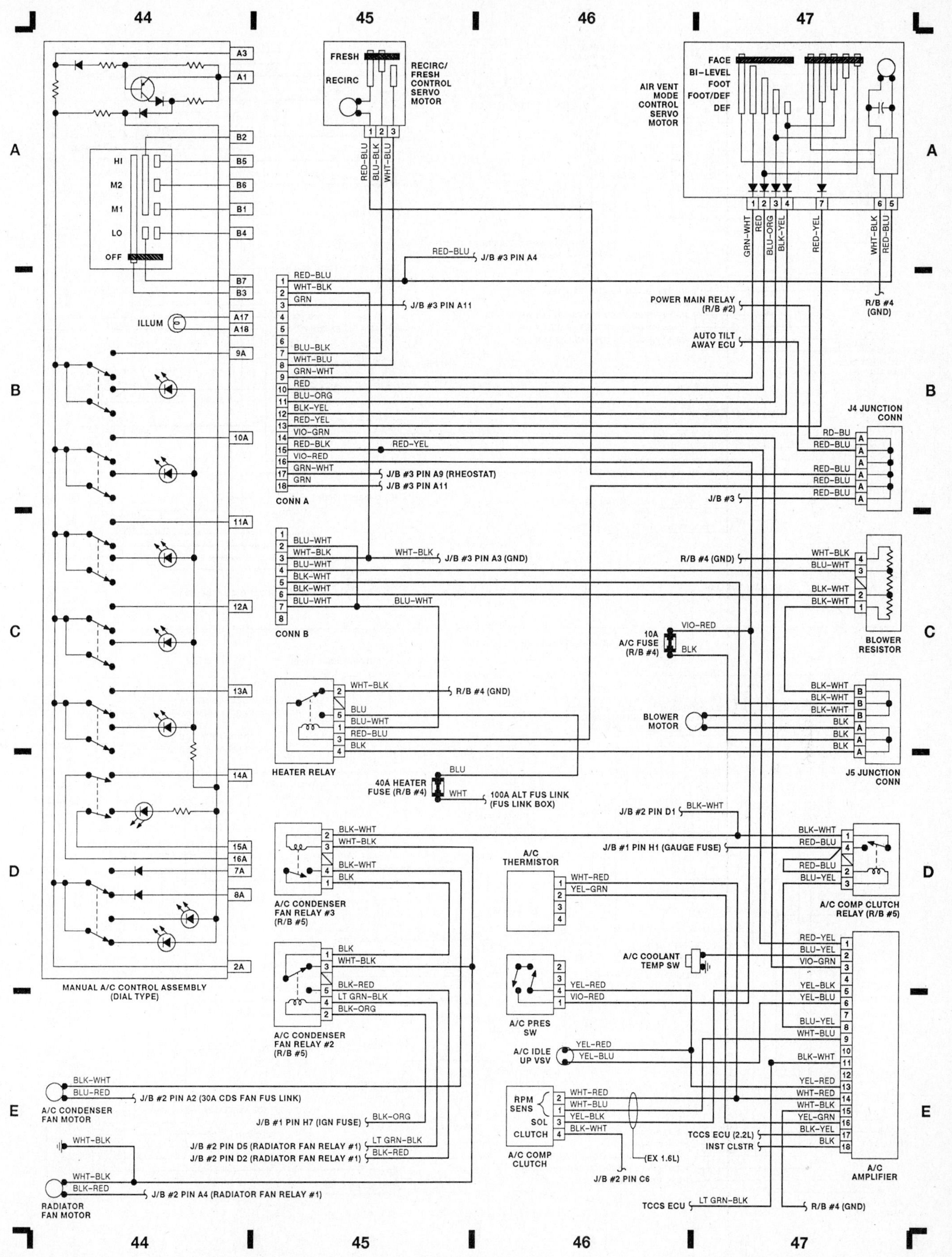
MANUAL A/C CONTROL ASSEMBLY (DIAL TYPE)
RECIRC/ FRESH CONTROL SERVO MOTOR
AIR VENT MODE CONTROL SERVO MOTOR
CONN A
CONN B
HEATER RELAY
40A HEATER FUSE (R/B #4)
100A ALT FUS LINK (FUS LINK BOX)
A/C CONDENSER FAN RELAY #3 (R/B #5)
A/C CONDENSER FAN RELAY #2 (R/B #5)
A/C CONDENSER FAN MOTOR
RADIATOR FAN MOTOR
A/C THERMISTOR
A/C COOLANT TEMP SW
A/C PRES SW
A/C IDLE UP VSV
A/C COMP CLUTCH
J4 JUNCTION CONN
BLOWER RESISTOR
BLOWER MOTOR
J5 JUNCTION CONN
10A A/C FUSE (R/B #4)
A/C COMP CLUTCH RELAY (R/B #5)
A/C AMPLIFIER
POWER MAIN RELAY (R/B #2)
AUTO TILT AWAY ECU
TCCS ECU (2.2L)
INST CLSTR
TCCS ECU
J/B #2 PIN A2 (30A CDS FAN FUS LINK)
J/B #1 PIN H7 (IGN FUSE)
J/B #2 PIN D5 (RADIATOR FAN RELAY #1)
J/B #2 PIN D2 (RADIATOR FAN RELAY #1)
J/B #2 PIN A4 (RADIATOR FAN RELAY #1)
J/B #1 PIN H1 (GAUGE FUSE)
J/B #3 PIN A9 (RHEOSTAT)

# 1991 WIRING DIAGRAMS
## Celica (Cont.)

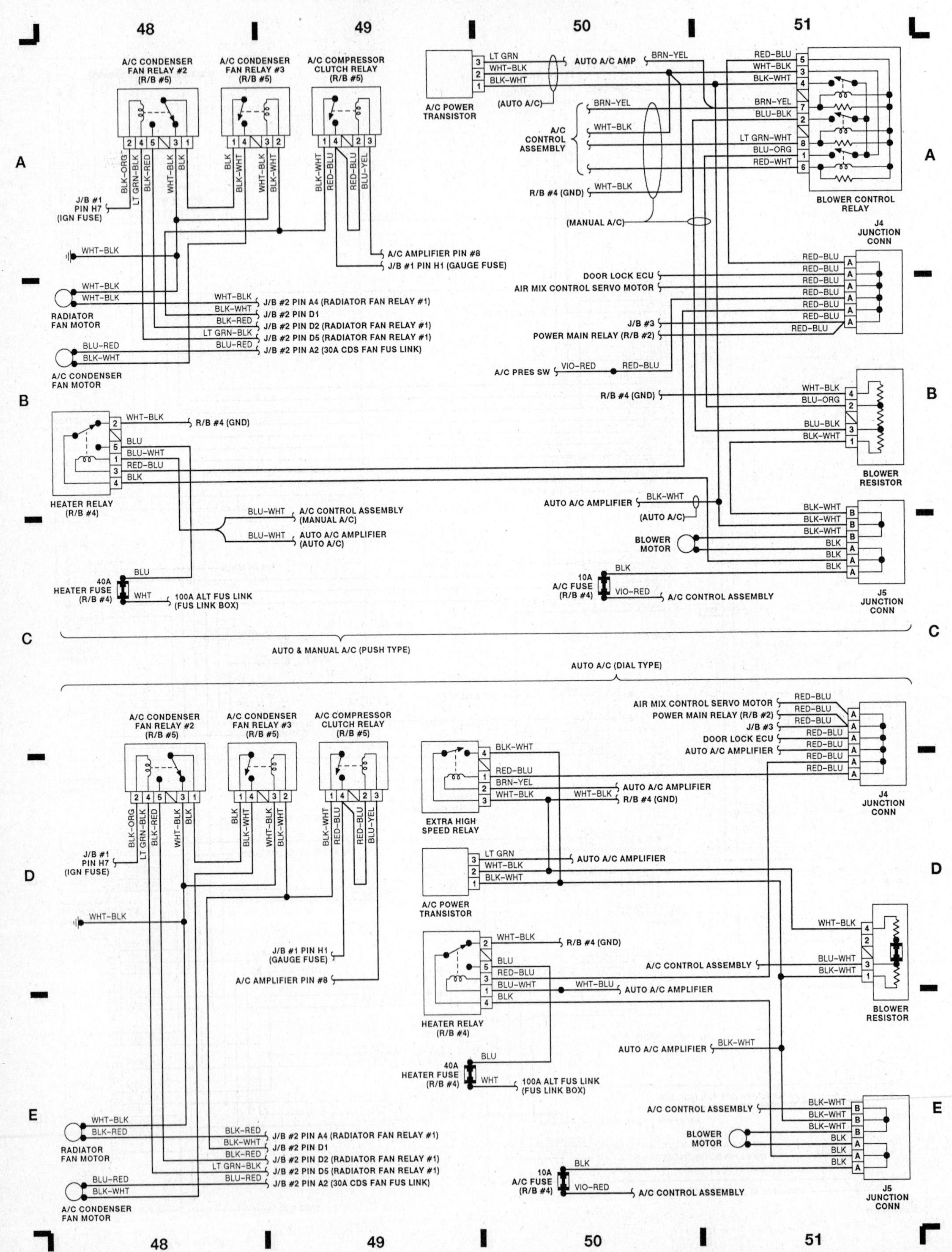

# 1991 WIRING DIAGRAMS
## Celica (Cont.)

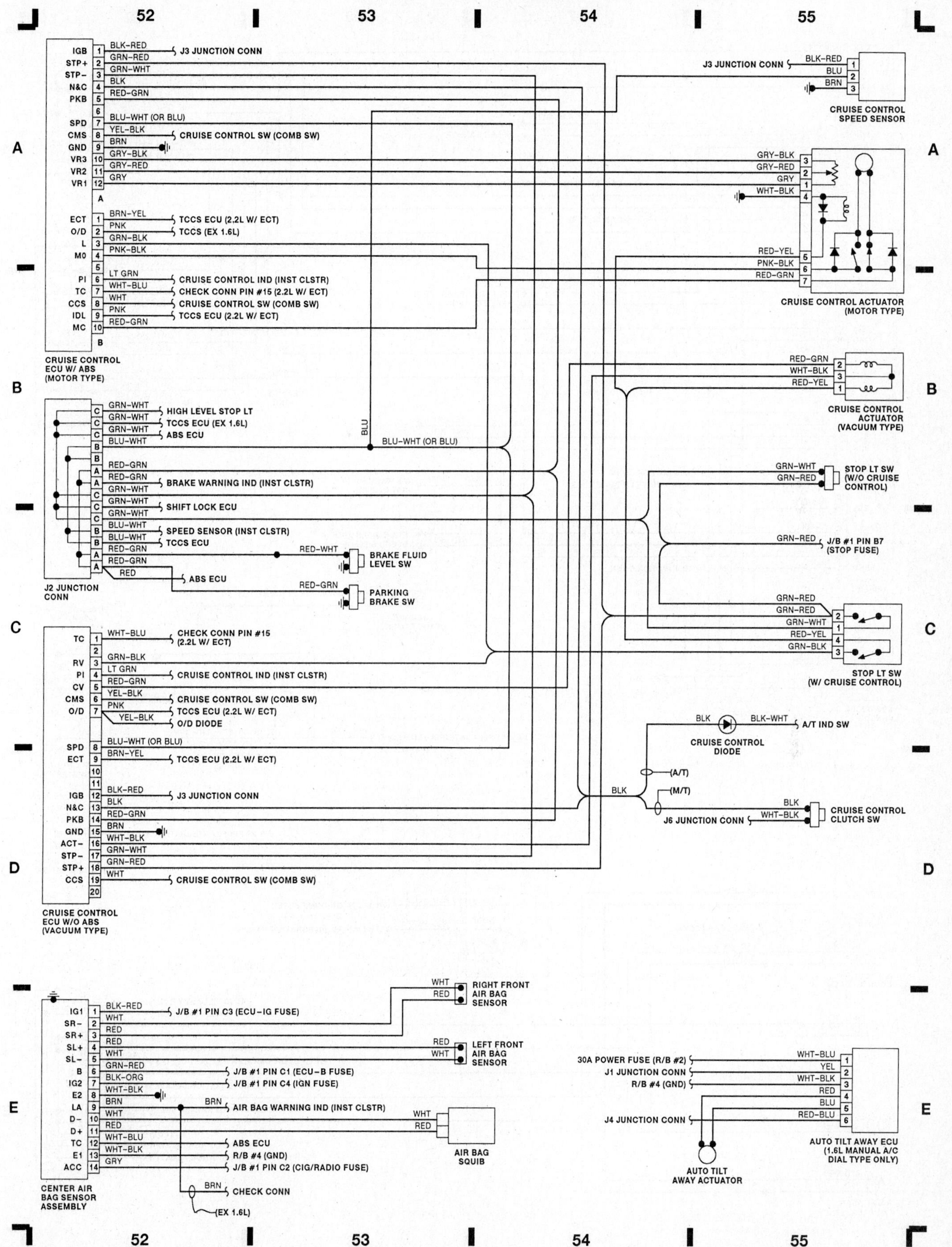

# 1991 WIRING DIAGRAMS
## Celica (Cont.)

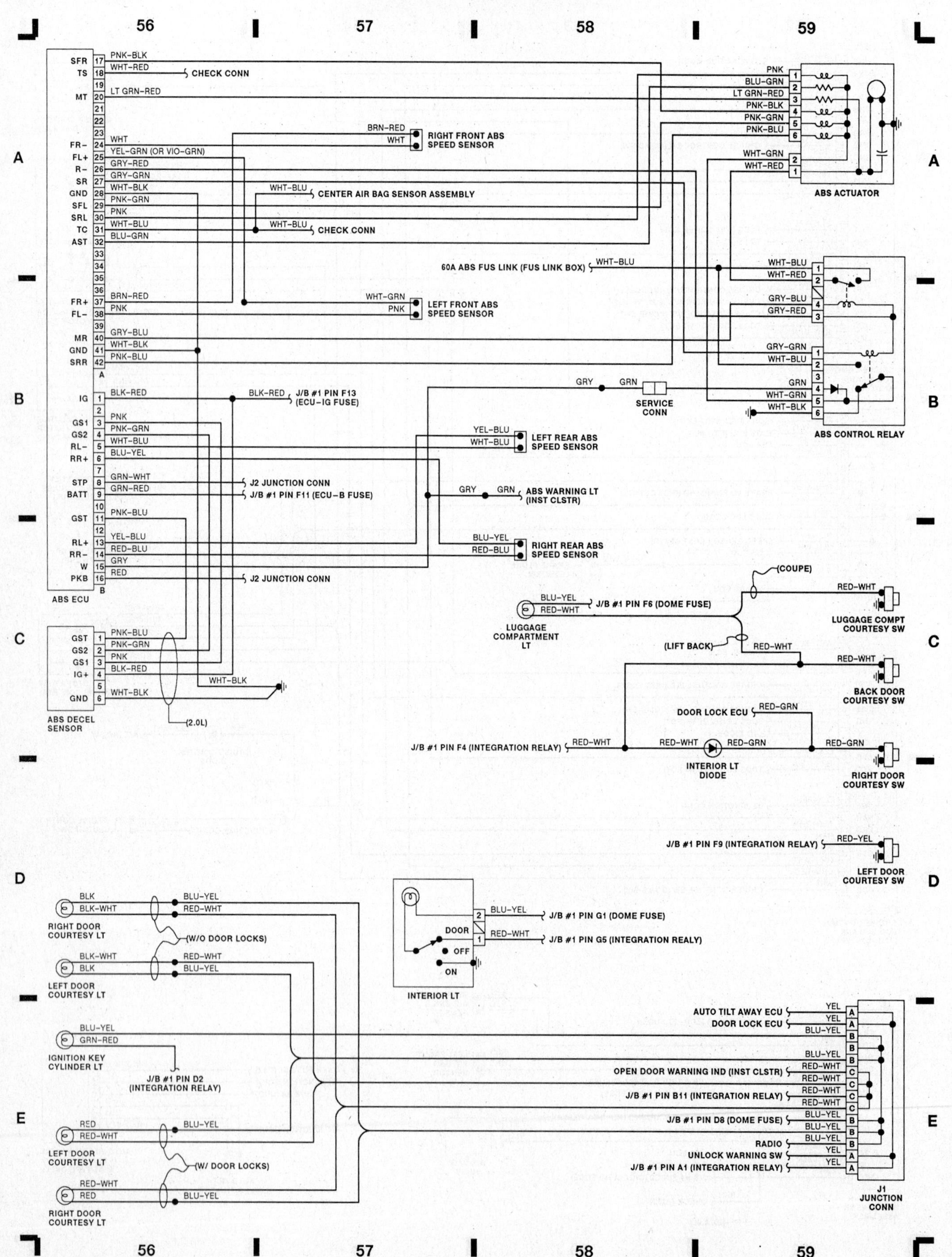

# 1991 WIRING DIAGRAMS
## Celica (Cont.)

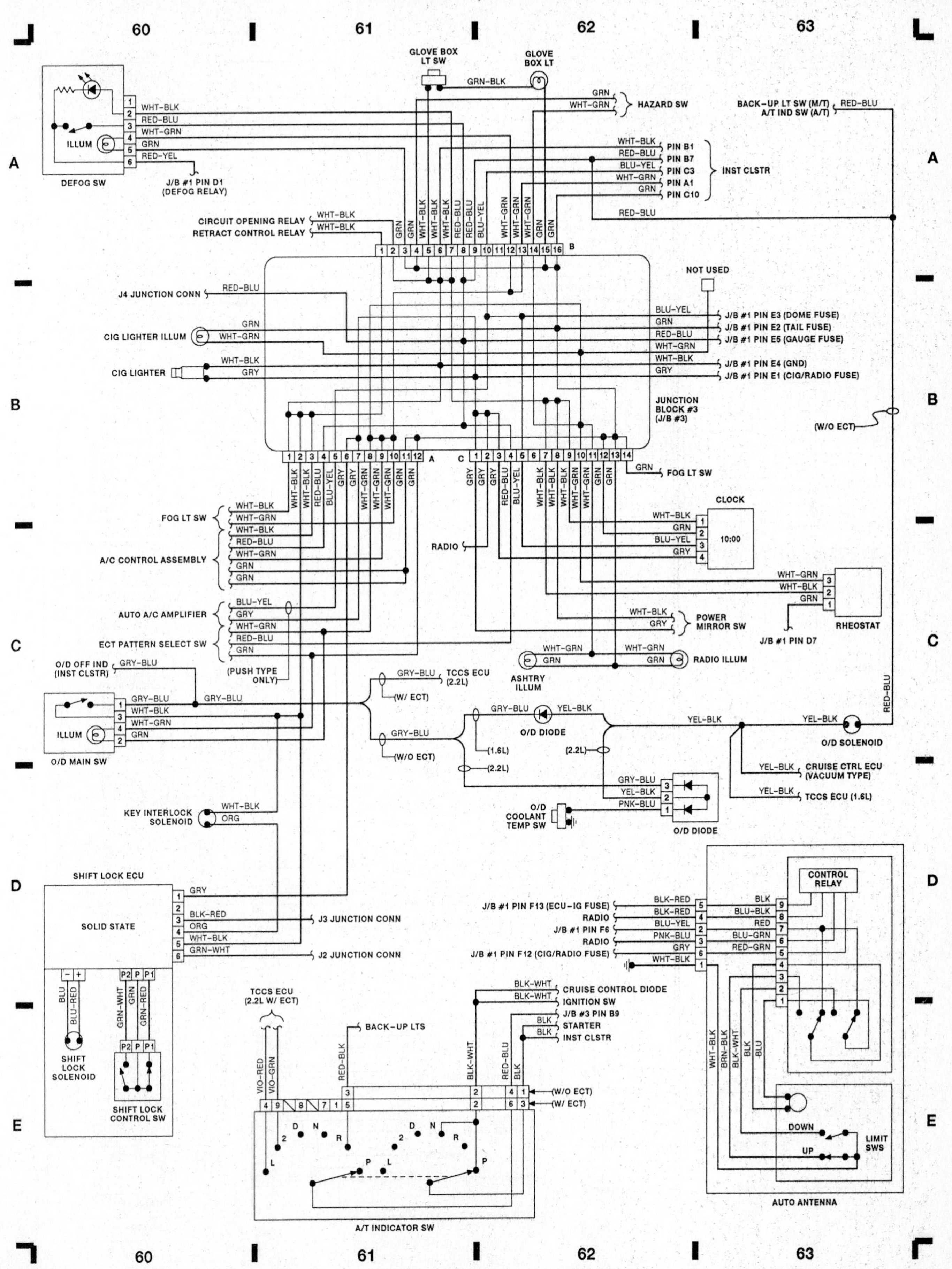

# 1991 WIRING DIAGRAMS
## Celica (Cont.)

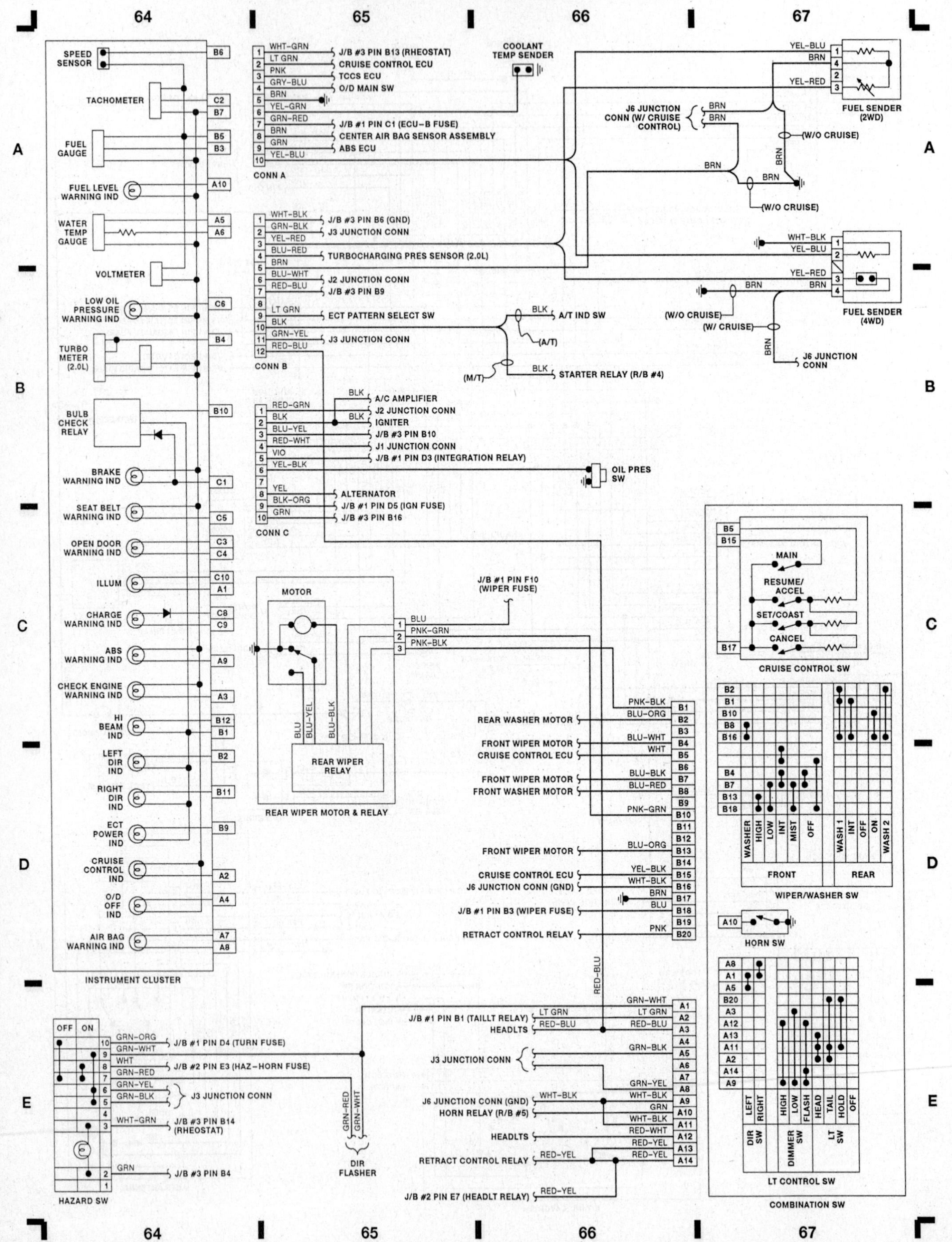

# 1991 WIRING DIAGRAMS
## Celica (Cont.)

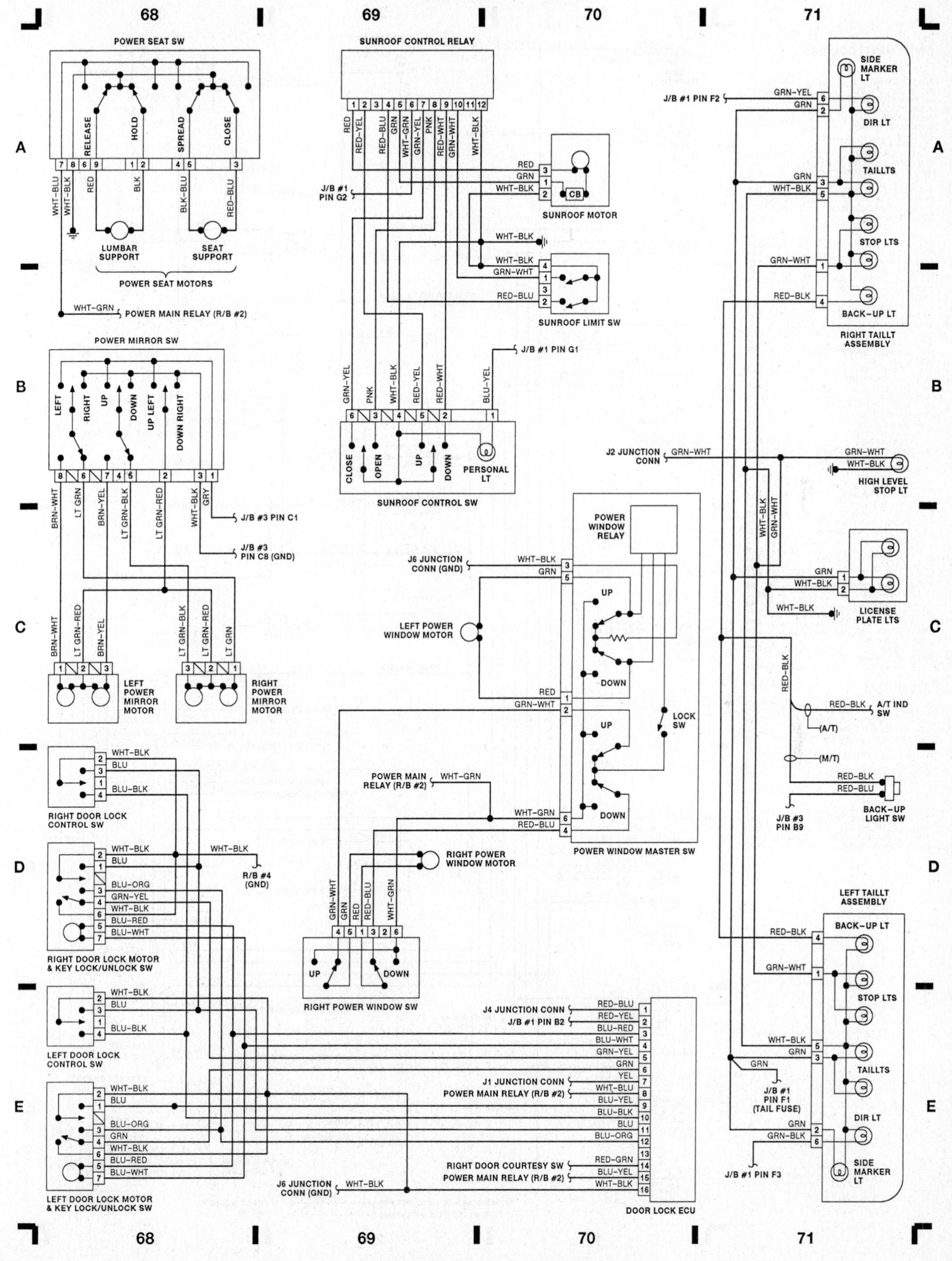

# 1991 WIRING DIAGRAMS
## Corolla

**COMPONENT LOCATOR:**

A/C SYSTEM (4A-FE) ........... A-E 20-23
A/C SYSTEM (4A-GE) ........... A-E 24-27
A/T INDICATOR SW (4A-FE) ........... E 36
A/T INDICATORS ........... D 36
ALTERNATOR ........... C 3
BACK-UP LT SW (M/T) ........... E 36
BATTERY ........... A 2
CENTER DIFFERENTIAL CONTROL SYSTEM ........... D-E 48-51
CIRCUIT OPENING RELAY (4A-FE) ........... A 6
CIRCUIT OPENING RELAY (4A-GE) ........... A 11
CLOCK ........... C 46
COLD START INJECTOR ........... A 2
COMBINATION SW ........... C-E 48
CRUISE CONTROL SYSTEM ........... A-B 28-31
DEFOG GRID ........... C 57
DEFOG SW & CRUISE CONTROL MAIN SW (EX COUPE) ........... D 31
DEFOG SW & HAZARD SW (COUPE) ........... D 28
DIR FLASHER ........... E 29
DOOR LOCK KEY SWS (W/ THEFT) ........... D 52
ECU-IG FUSE ........... A 17
ELECT IDLE UP DIODE (4A-FE) ........... A 4
FRONT WASHER MOTOR ........... E 2
FRONT WIPER MOTOR ........... E 3
FUS LINK BOX ........... C 2
HAZARD SW (EX COUPE) ........... E 28
IGNITER (4A-GE) ........... E 10
IGNITION SW ........... E 12
INST CLSTR (COUPE) ........... A-D 51
INST CLSTR (EX COUPE W/ THEFT) ........... B-E 44
INST CLSTR (EX COUPE W/O THEFT) ........... A-D 47
INTEGRATED IGNITION ASSEMBLY (4A-FE) ........... E 5-6
INTERIOR LTS ........... D-E 56-59
J1 JUNCTION CONN (COUPE) ........... D-E 39
J1 JUNCTION CONN (SEDAN & WAGON) ........... D-E 35
J1 JUNCTION CONN (STATION WAGON) ........... D-E 43
JUNCTION BLOCK #1 (J/B #1) ........... A-D 16-18
JUNCTION BLOCK #2 (J/B #2) ........... A-C 12-14
JUNCTION BLOCK #3 (J/B #3) (COUPE) ........... A-C 37-38
JUNCTION BLOCK #3 (J/B #3) (SEDAN & WAGON) ........... A-C 33-34
JUNCTION BLOCK #3 (J/B #3) (STATION WAGON) ........... A-C 41-42
LEFT FRONT DOOR LOCK SOL ........... B 55
LEFT FRONT DOOR LOCK SW ........... C 55
MAIN FUS LINK ........... C 2
O/D MAIN SW ........... C 28
O/D OFF INDICATOR (COUPE) ........... E 51
O/D SOLENOID ........... C 28
POWER CB ........... C 56
POWER DOOR LOCKS (W/O THEFT) ........... A-D 59
POWER MIRRORS ........... D-E 60
POWER WINDOWS ........... A-C 56-59
REAR WIPER RELAY ........... C 60
REAR WIPER/WASHER SW ........... A 48
RELAY BLOCK ........... E 14
RELAY BLOCK #4 (R/B #4) (4A-FE) ........... D-E 20
RELAY BLOCK #4 (R/B #4) (4A-GE) ........... D-E 24
RELAY BLOCK #5 (R/B #5) (4A-FE) ........... A 20-21
RELAY BLOCK #5 (R/B #5) (4A-GE) ........... A 24-25
RETRACT CONTROL RELAY ........... C-E 3
RIGHT FRONT DOOR LOCK SW ........... C 55
SEAT BELT BUCKLE SW ........... E 16
SECURITY INDICATOR (COUPE) ........... E 51
SHIFT LOCK ECU ........... C 31
START INJECTOR TIME SW ........... A 3
STARTER ........... A 3
STOP LT SW (W/ CRUISE) ........... B 31
STOP LT SW (W/O CRUISE) ........... C 31
SUNROOF ........... A-B 60-61
TCCS ECU (4A-FE) ........... B-D 4
TCCS ECU (4A-GE) ........... A-D 8
THEFT DETERRENT DIODE ........... D 55
THEFT DETERRENT ECU ........... B-C 52
THEFT DETERRENT HORN ........... A 52
UNLOCK WARNING SW ........... E 12

# 1991 WIRING DIAGRAMS
## Corolla (Cont.)

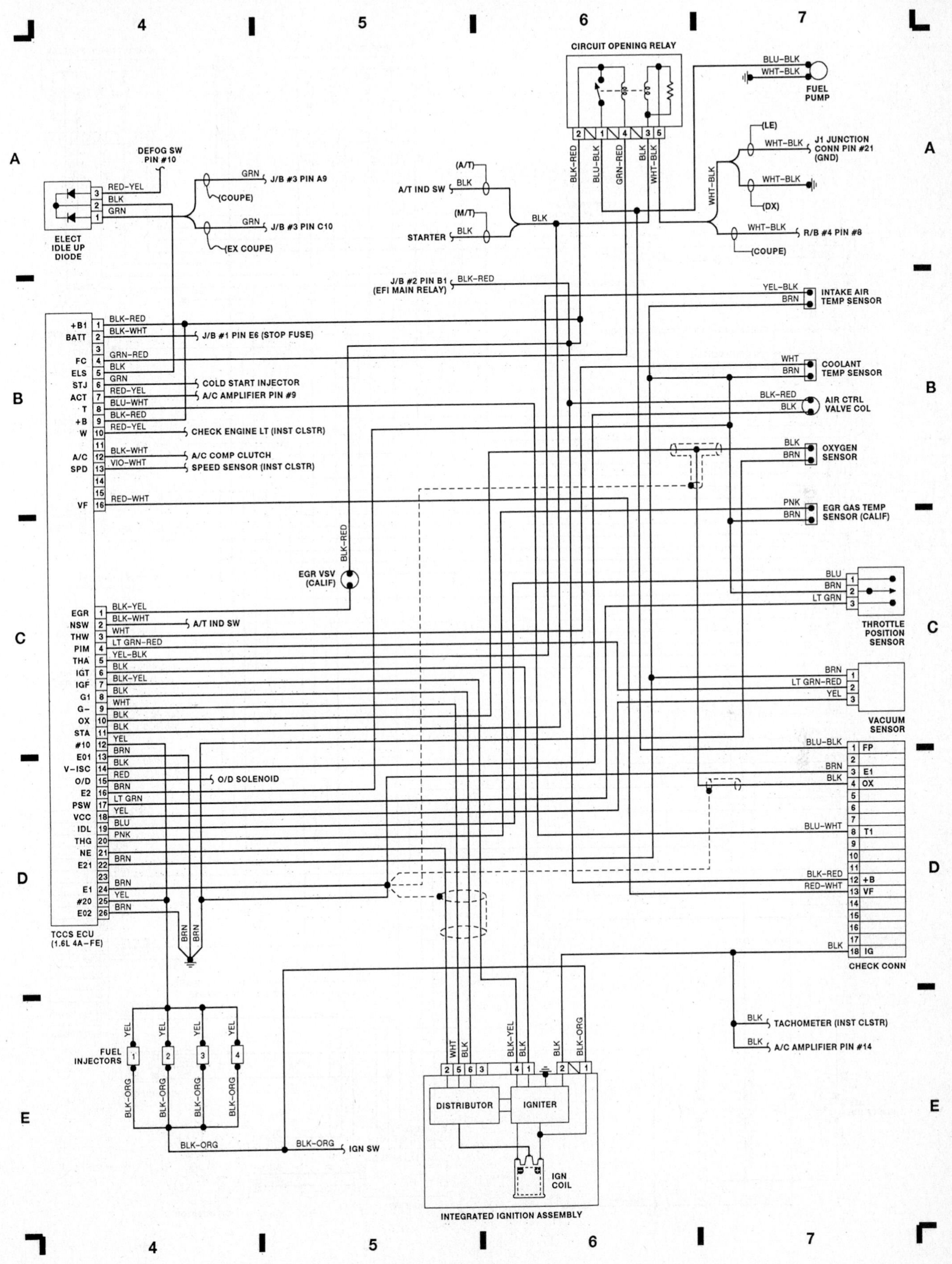

# 1991 WIRING DIAGRAMS
## Corolla (Cont.)

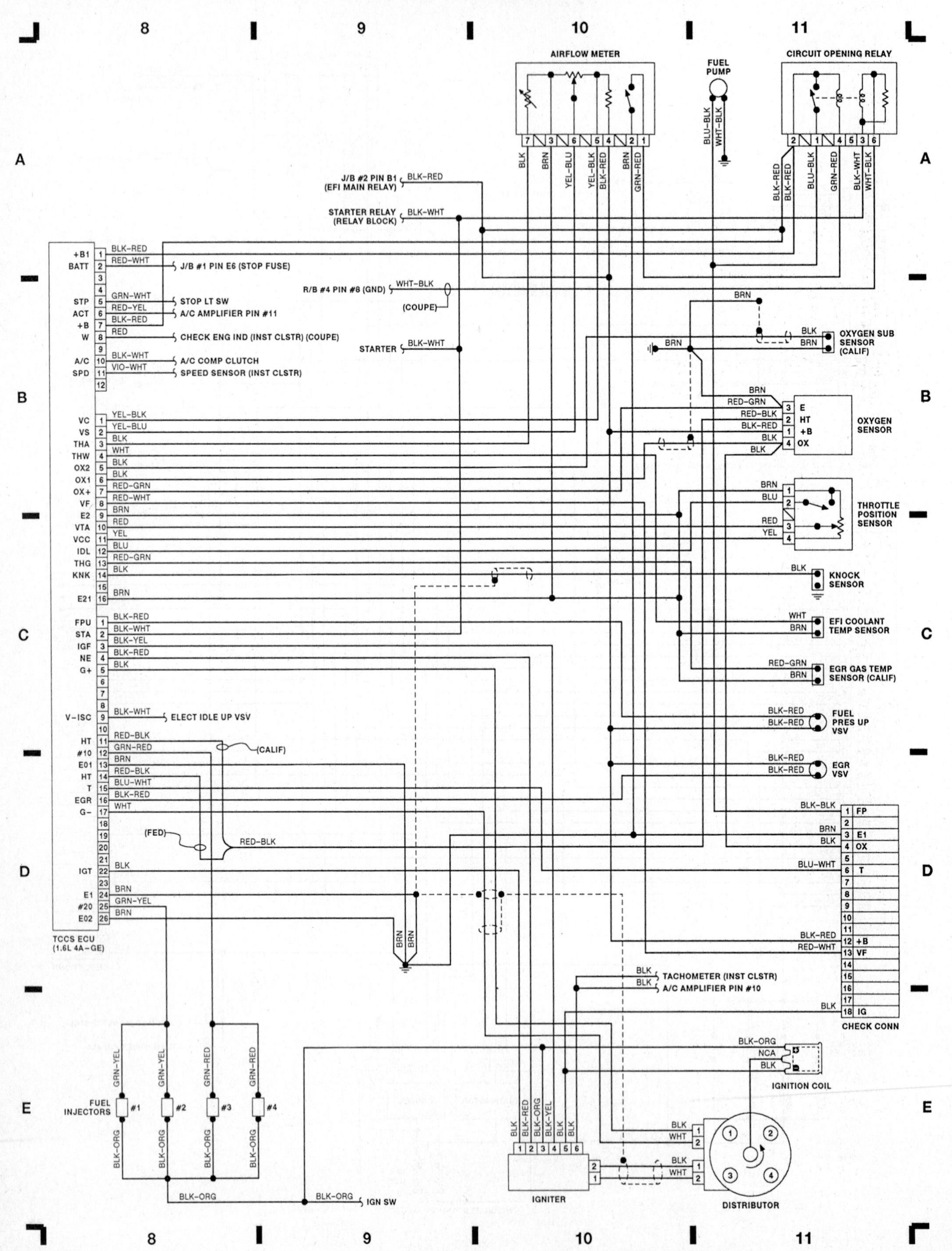

# 1991 WIRING DIAGRAMS
# Corolla (Cont.)

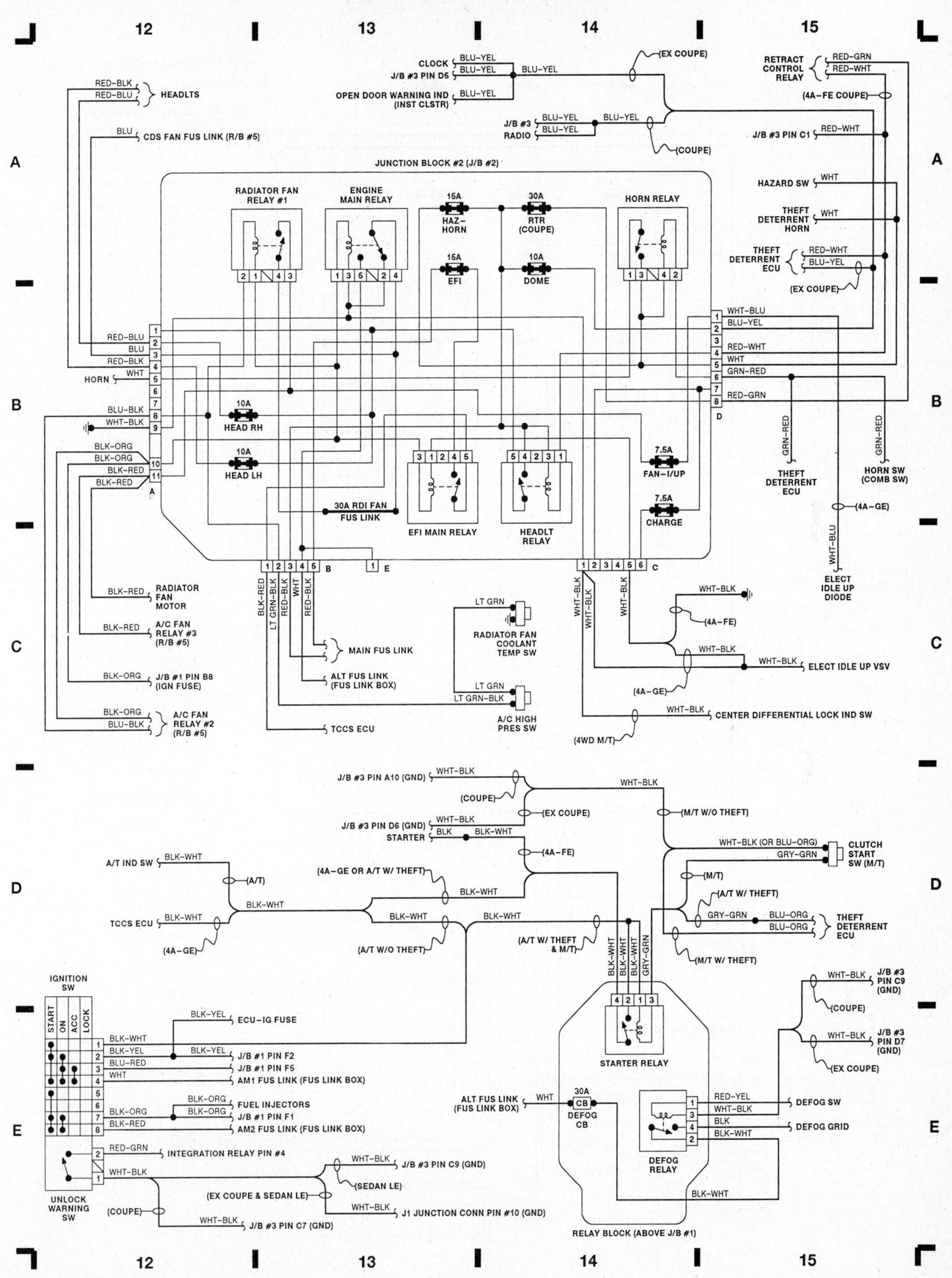

# 1991 WIRING DIAGRAMS
## Corolla (Cont.)

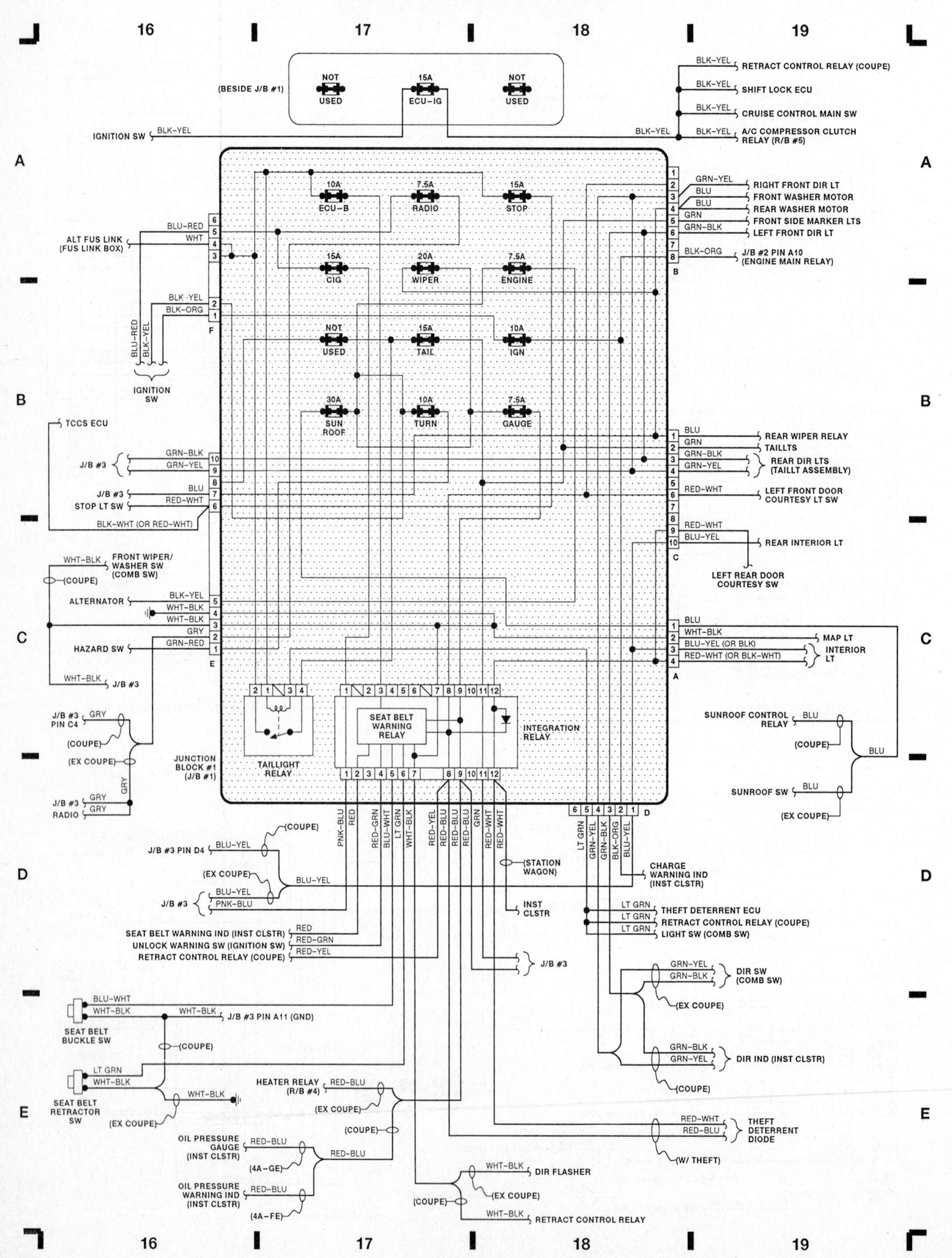

# 1991 WIRING DIAGRAMS
## Corolla (Cont.)

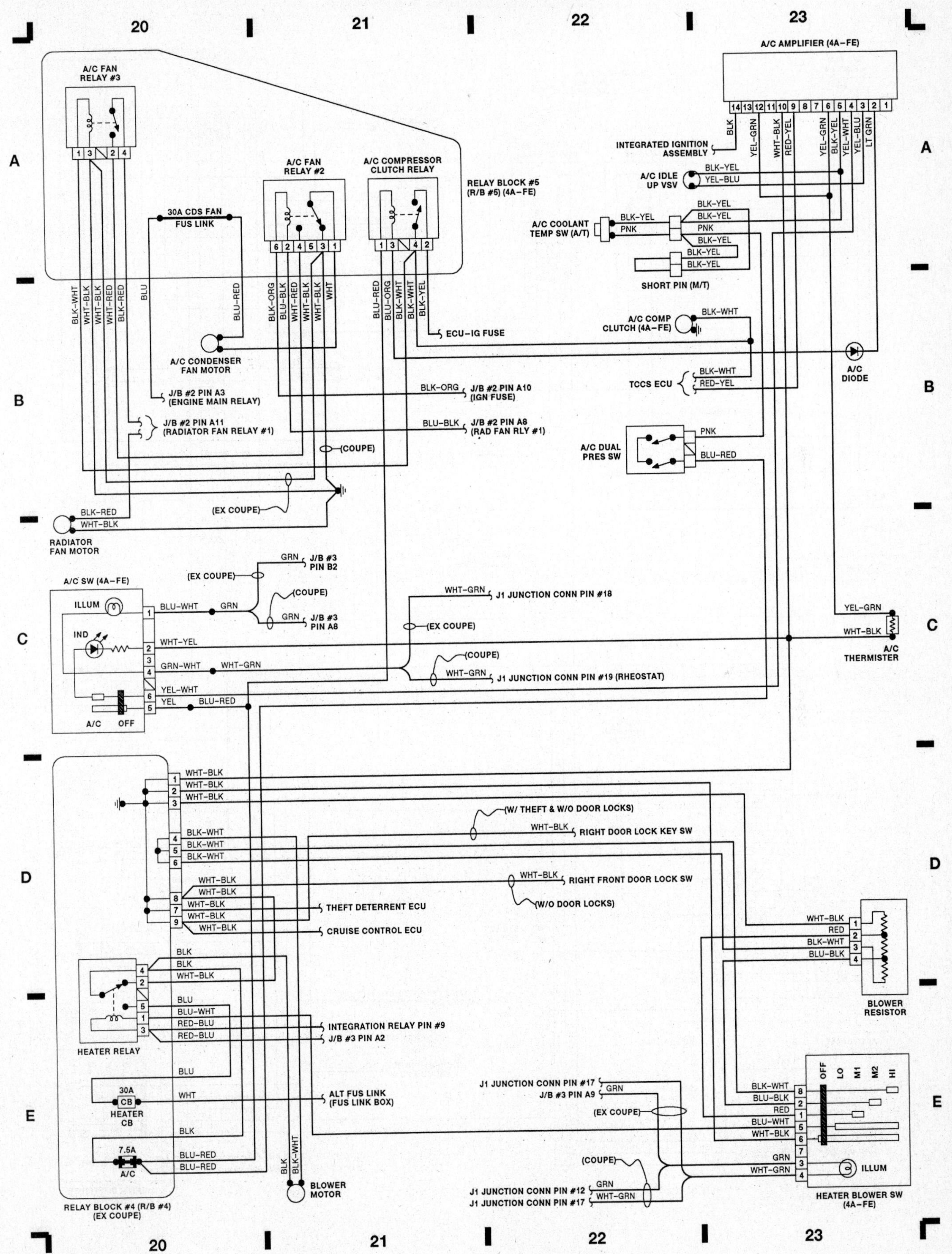

# 1991 WIRING DIAGRAMS
## Corolla (Cont.)

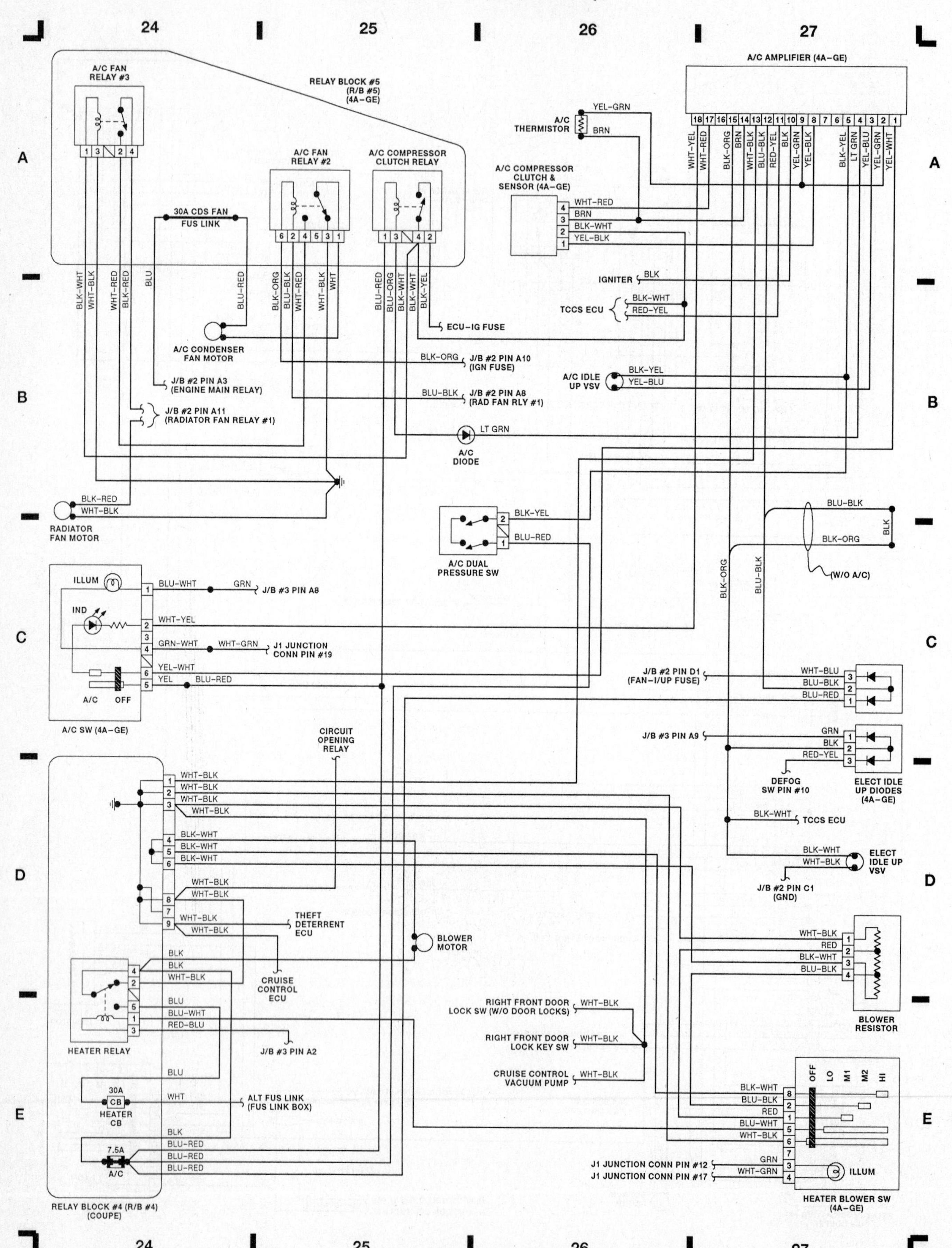

# 1991 WIRING DIAGRAMS
## Corolla (Cont.)

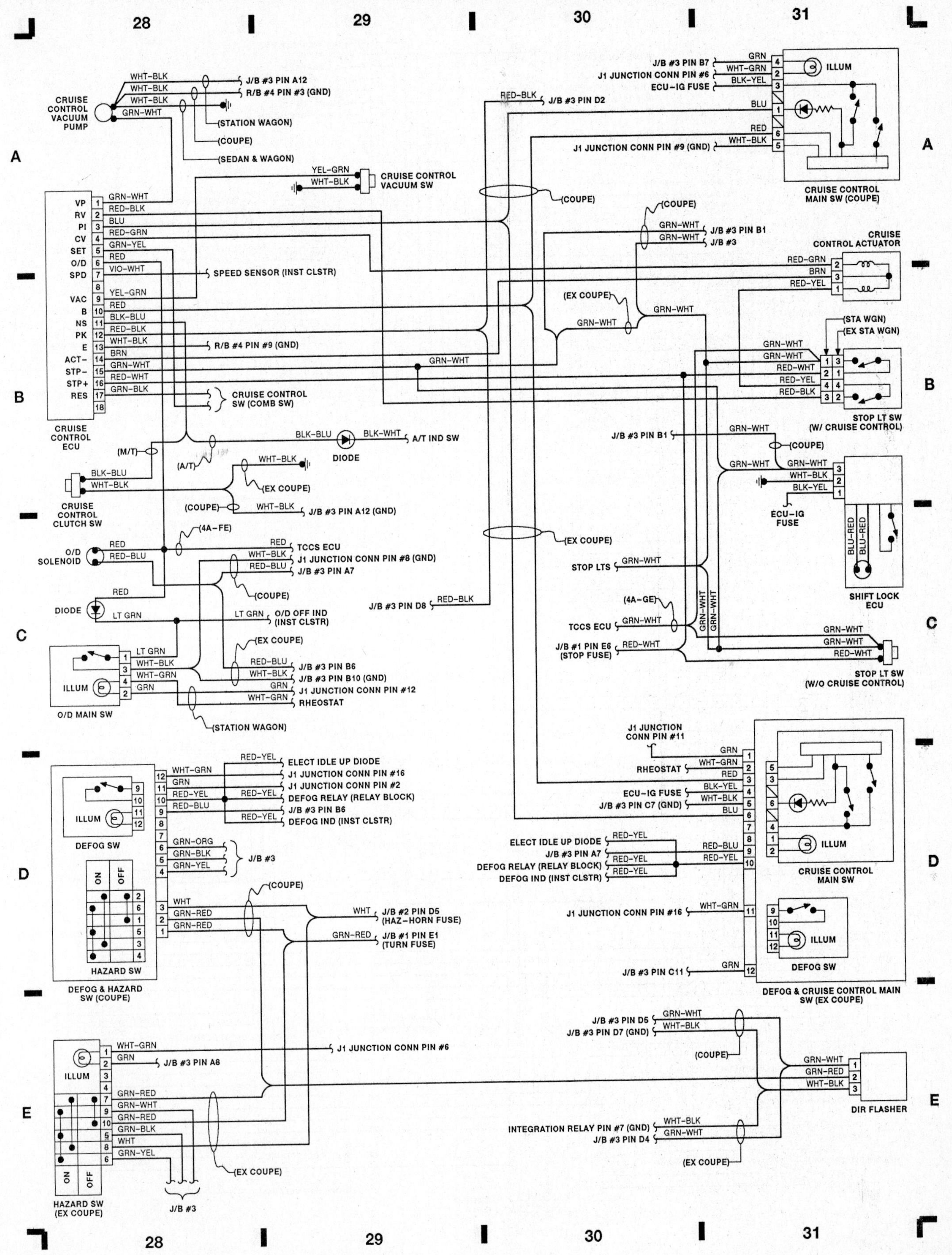

# 1991 WIRING DIAGRAMS
## Corolla (Cont.)

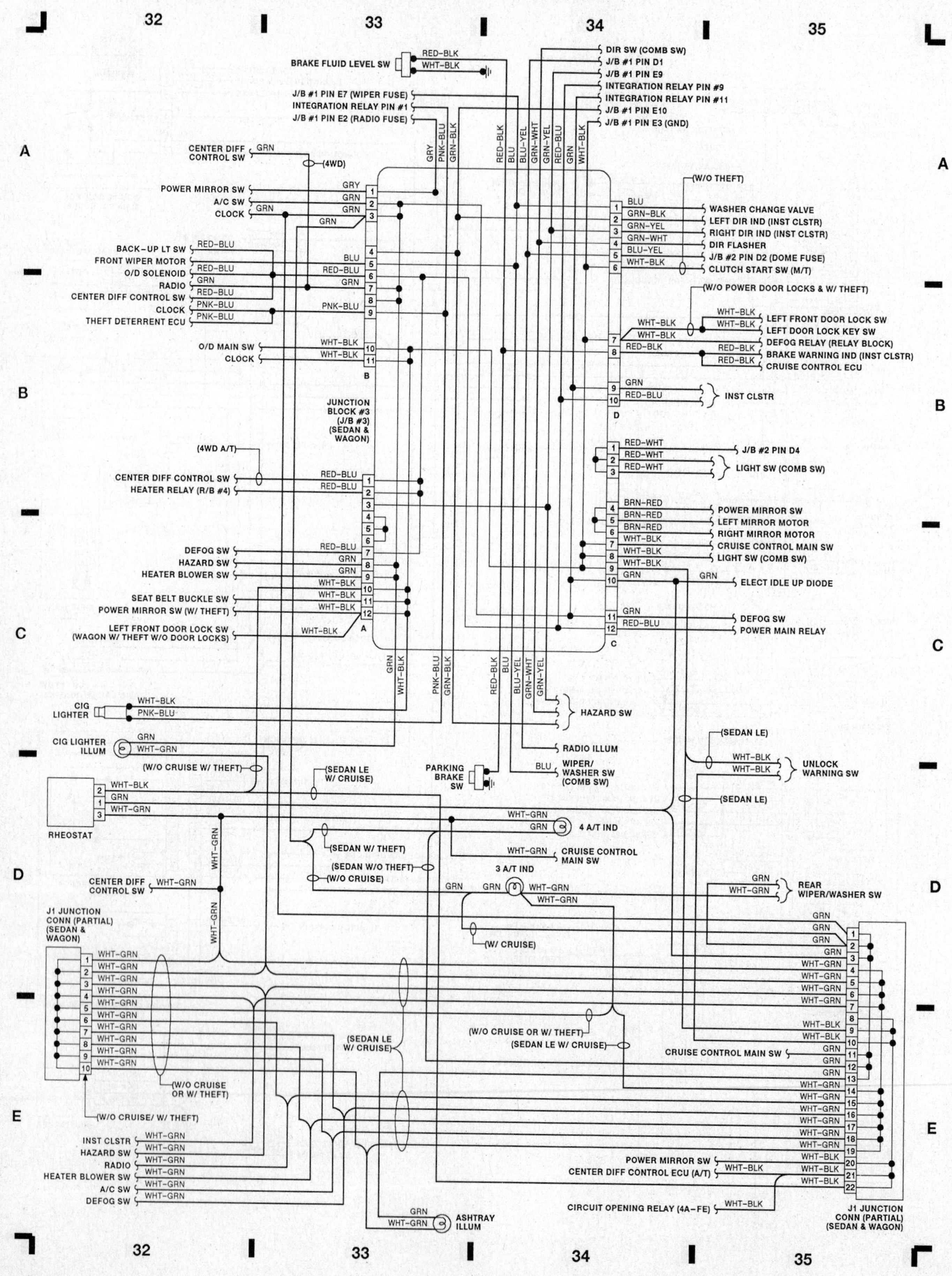

# 1991 WIRING DIAGRAMS
## Corolla (Cont.)

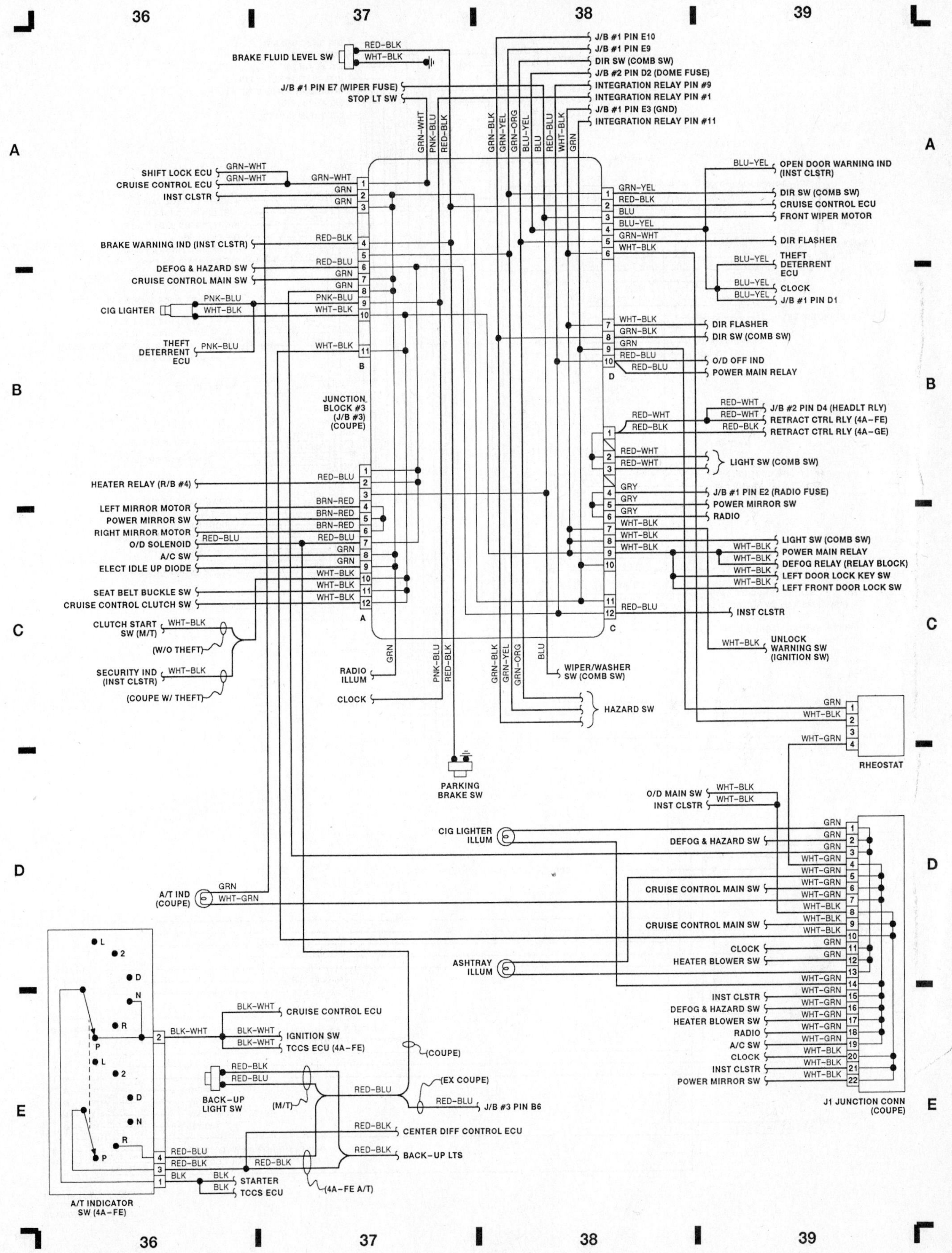

# 1991 WIRING DIAGRAMS
## Corolla (Cont.)

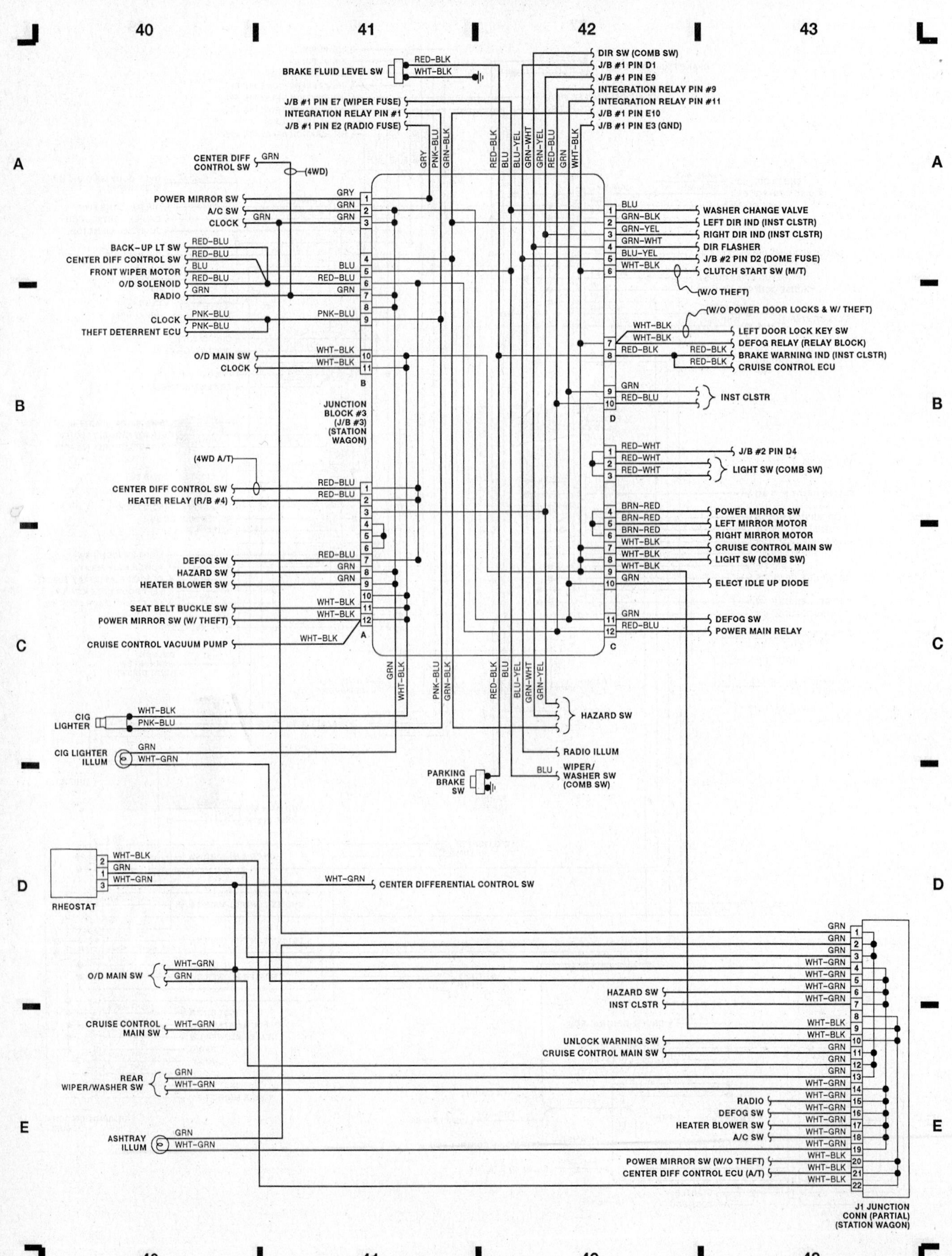

# 1991 WIRING DIAGRAMS
## Corolla (Cont.)

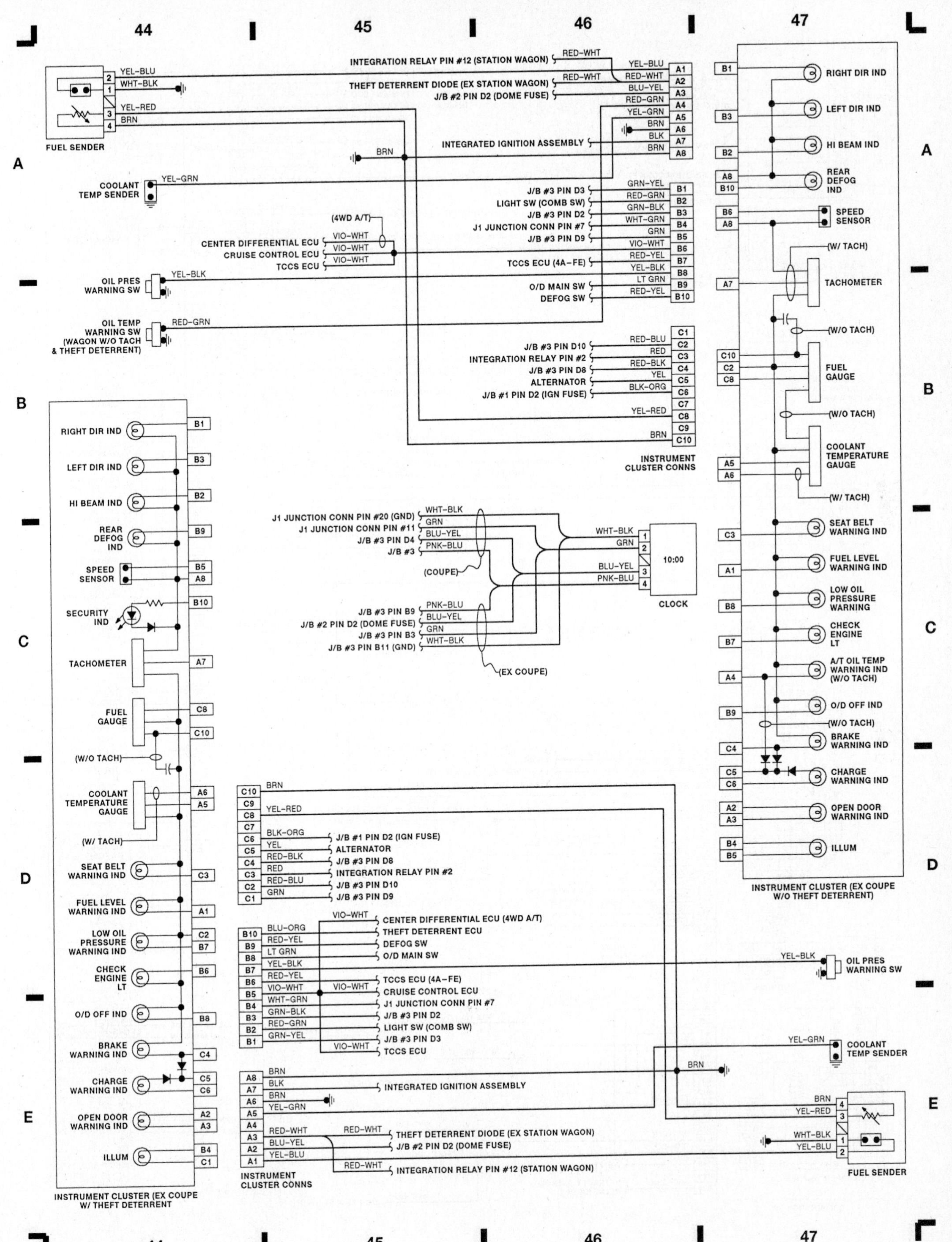

# 1991 WIRING DIAGRAMS
## Corolla (Cont.)

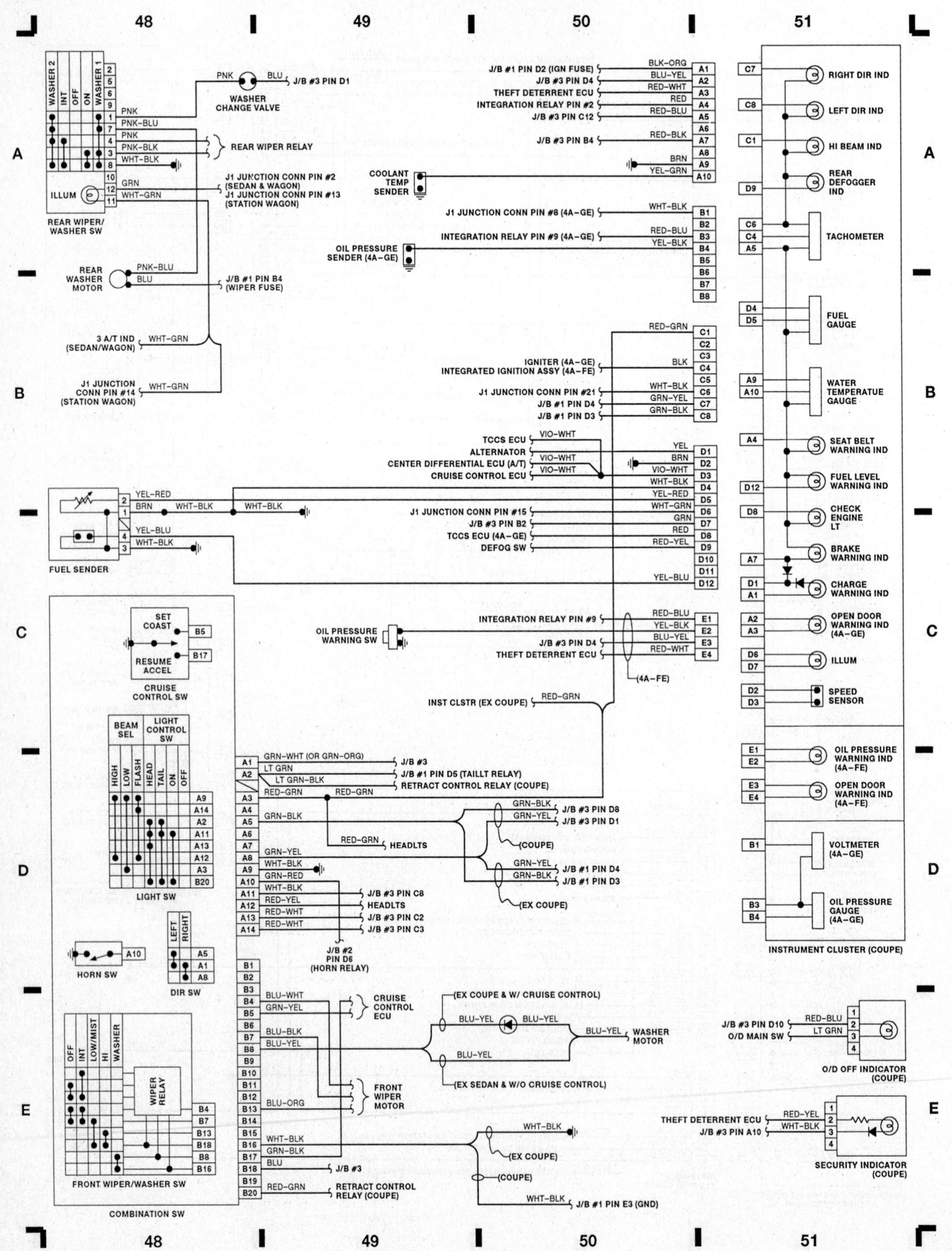

# 1991 WIRING DIAGRAMS
## Corolla (Cont.)

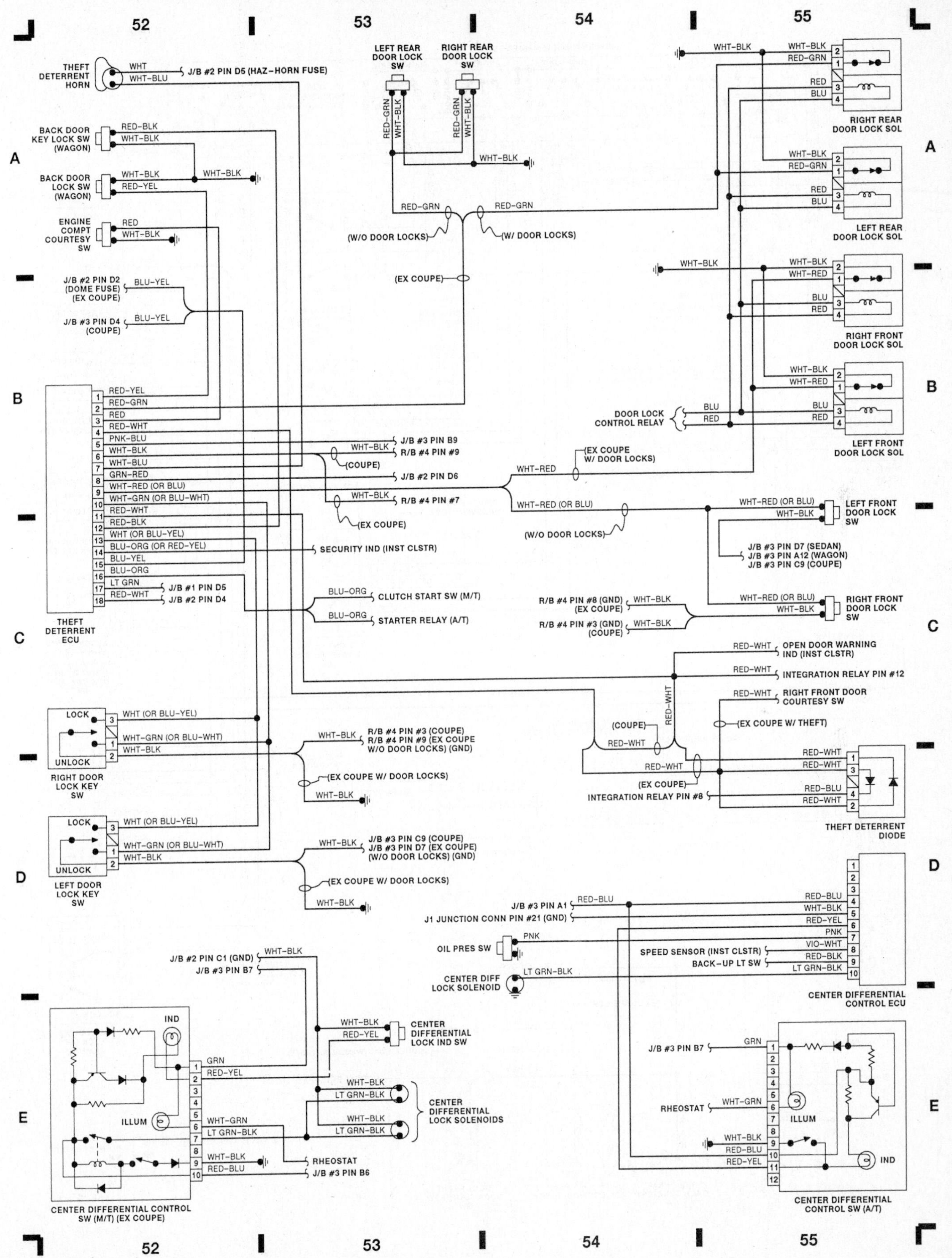

# 1991 WIRING DIAGRAMS
## Corolla (Cont.)

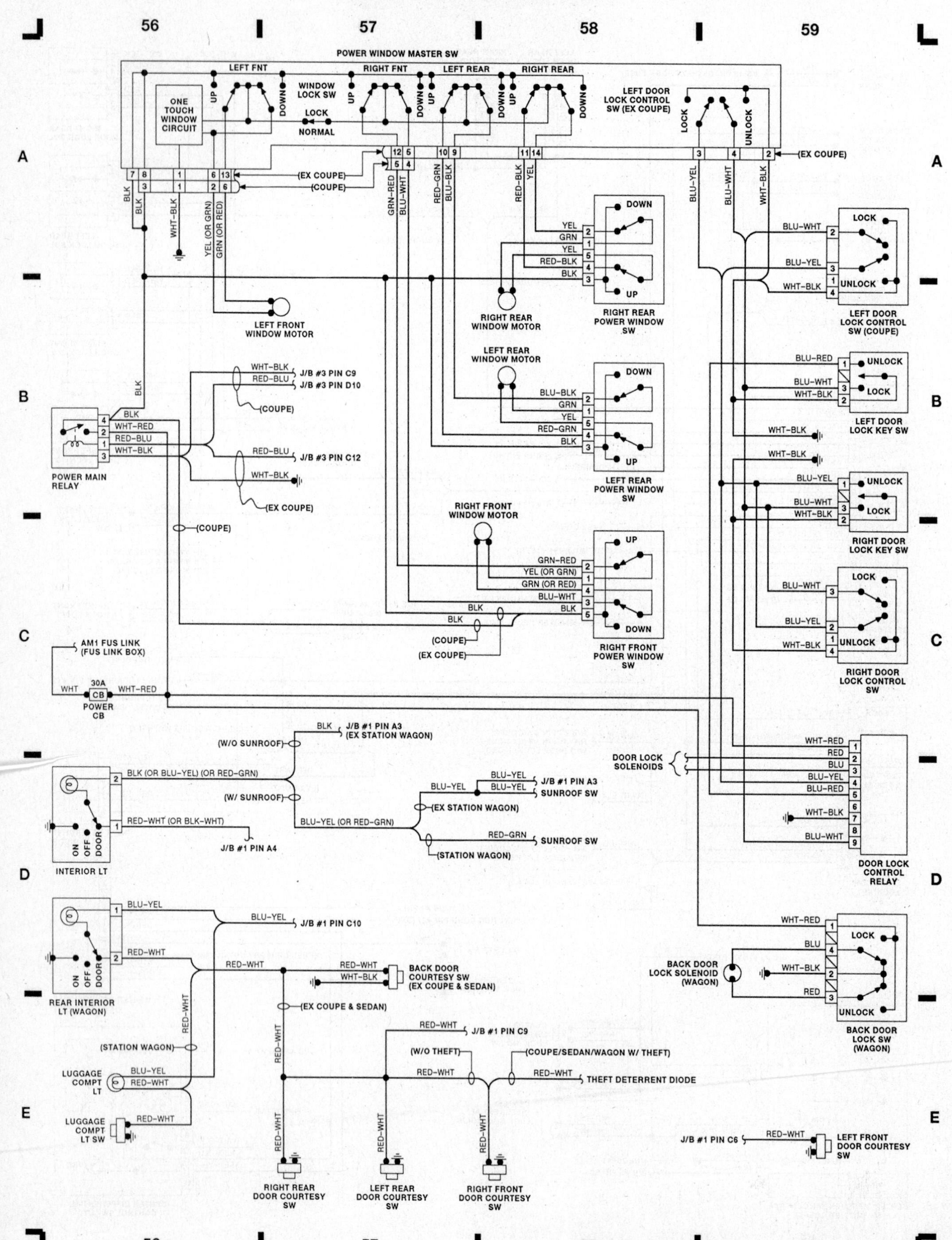

# 1991 WIRING DIAGRAMS
## Corolla (Cont.)

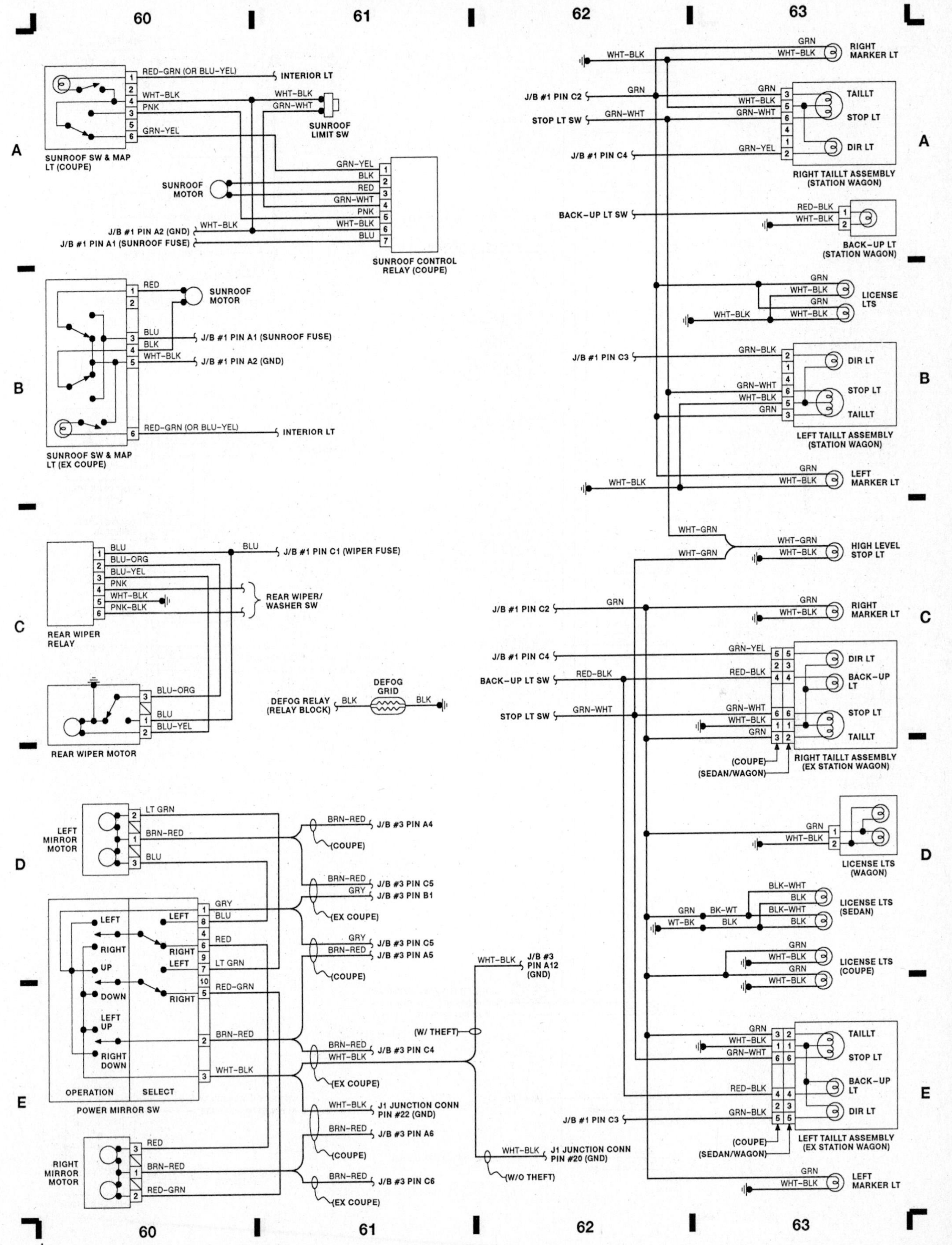

# 1991 WIRING DIAGRAMS
## Cressida

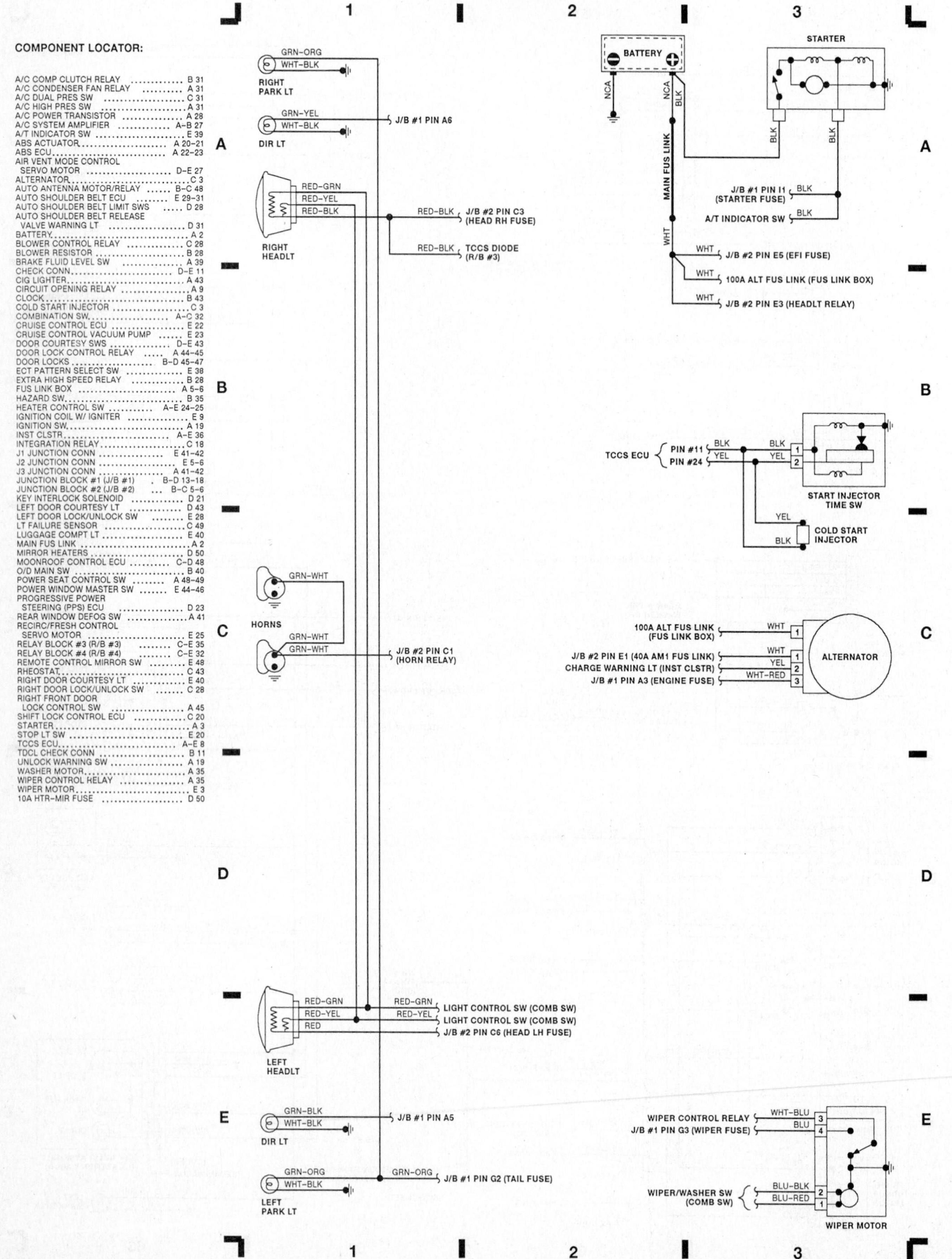
COMPONENT LOCATOR:
A/C COMP CLUTCH RELAY ..... B 31
A/C CONDENSER FAN RELAY ..... A 31
A/C DUAL PRES SW ..... C 31
A/C HIGH PRES SW ..... A 31
A/C POWER TRANSISTOR ..... A 28
A/C SYSTEM AMPLIFIER ..... A-B 27
A/T INDICATOR SW ..... E 39
ABS ACTUATOR ..... A 20-21
ABS ECU ..... A 22-23
AIR VENT MODE CONTROL SERVO MOTOR ..... D-E 27
ALTERNATOR ..... C 3
AUTO ANTENNA MOTOR/RELAY ..... B-C 48
AUTO SHOULDER BELT ECU ..... E 29-31
AUTO SHOULDER BELT LIMIT SWS ..... D 28
AUTO SHOULDER BELT RELEASE VALVE WARNING LT ..... D 31
BATTERY ..... A 2
BLOWER CONTROL RELAY ..... C 28
BLOWER RESISTOR ..... B 28
BRAKE FLUID LEVEL SW ..... A 39
CHECK CONN ..... D-E 11
CIG LIGHTER ..... A 43
CIRCUIT OPENING RELAY ..... A 9
CLOCK ..... B 43
COLD START INJECTOR ..... C 3
COMBINATION SW ..... A-C 32
CRUISE CONTROL ECU ..... E 22
CRUISE CONTROL VACUUM PUMP ..... E 23
DOOR COURTESY SWS ..... D-E 43
DOOR LOCK CONTROL RELAY ..... A 44-45
DOOR LOCKS ..... B-D 45-47
ECT PATTERN SELECT SW ..... E 38
EXTRA HIGH SPEED RELAY ..... B 28
FUS LINK BOX ..... A 5-6
HAZARD SW ..... B 35
HEATER CONTROL SW ..... A-E 24-25
IGNITION COIL W/ IGNITER ..... E 9
IGNITION SW ..... A 19
INST CLSTR ..... A-E 36
INTEGRATION RELAY ..... C 18
J1 JUNCTION CONN ..... E 41-42
J2 JUNCTION CONN ..... E 5-6
J3 JUNCTION CONN ..... A 41-42
JUNCTION BLOCK #1 (J/B #1) ..... B-D 13-18
JUNCTION BLOCK #2 (J/B #2) ..... B-C 5-6
KEY INTERLOCK SOLENOID ..... D 21
LEFT DOOR COURTESY LT ..... D 43
LEFT DOOR LOCK/UNLOCK SW ..... E 28
LT FAILURE SENSOR ..... C 49
LUGGAGE COMPT LT ..... E 40
MAIN FUS LINK ..... A 2
MIRROR HEATERS ..... D 50
MOONROOF CONTROL ECU ..... C-D 48
O/D MAIN SW ..... B 40
POWER SEAT CONTROL SW ..... A 48-49
POWER WINDOW MASTER SW ..... E 44-46
PROGRESSIVE POWER STEERING (PPS) ECU ..... D 23
REAR WINDOW DEFOG SW ..... A 41
RECIRC/FRESH CONTROL SERVO MOTOR ..... E 25
RELAY BLOCK #3 (R/B #3) ..... C-E 35
RELAY BLOCK #4 (R/B #4) ..... C-E 32
REMOTE CONTROL MIRROR SW ..... E 48
RHEOSTAT ..... C 43
RIGHT DOOR COURTESY LT ..... E 40
RIGHT DOOR LOCK/UNLOCK SW ..... C 28
RIGHT FRONT DOOR LOCK CONTROL SW ..... A 45
SHIFT LOCK CONTROL ECU ..... C 20
STARTER ..... A 3
STOP LT SW ..... E 20
TCCS ECU ..... A-E 8
TDCL CHECK CONN ..... B 11
UNLOCK WARNING SW ..... A 19
WASHER MOTOR ..... A 35
WIPER CONTROL RELAY ..... A 35
WIPER MOTOR ..... E 3
10A HTR-MIR FUSE ..... D 50
1
2
3
A
B
C
D
E
GRN-ORG
WHT-BLK
RIGHT PARK LT
GRN-YEL
WHT-BLK
J/B #1 PIN A6
DIR LT
RED-GRN
RED-YEL
RED-BLK
RED-BLK
J/B #2 PIN C3 (HEAD RH FUSE)
RIGHT HEADLT
RED-BLK
TCCS DIODE (R/B #3)
BATTERY
NCA
NCA
BLK
MAIN FUS LINK
WHT
STARTER
BLK
BLK
J/B #1 PIN I1 (STARTER FUSE)
BLK
A/T INDICATOR SW
BLK
WHT
J/B #2 PIN E5 (EFI FUSE)
WHT
100A ALT FUS LINK (FUS LINK BOX)
WHT
J/B #2 PIN E3 (HEADLT RELAY)
TCCS ECU
PIN #11
PIN #24
BLK
YEL
BLK
YEL
START INJECTOR TIME SW
YEL
BLK
COLD START INJECTOR
GRN-WHT
HORNS
GRN-WHT
GRN-WHT
J/B #2 PIN C1 (HORN RELAY)
100A ALT FUS LINK (FUS LINK BOX)
WHT
J/B #2 PIN E1 (40A AM1 FUS LINK)
WHT
CHARGE WARNING LT (INST CLSTR)
YEL
J/B #1 PIN A3 (ENGINE FUSE)
WHT-RED
ALTERNATOR
RED-GRN
RED-YEL
RED
RED-GRN
RED-YEL
LIGHT CONTROL SW (COMB SW)
LIGHT CONTROL SW (COMB SW)
J/B #2 PIN C6 (HEAD LH FUSE)
LEFT HEADLT
GRN-BLK
WHT-BLK
J/B #1 PIN A5
DIR LT
GRN-ORG
WHT-BLK
GRN-ORG
J/B #1 PIN G2 (TAIL FUSE)
LEFT PARK LT
WIPER CONTROL RELAY
WHT-BLU
J/B #1 PIN G3 (WIPER FUSE)
BLU
WIPER/WASHER SW (COMB SW)
BLU-BLK
BLU-RED
WIPER MOTOR

# 1991 WIRING DIAGRAMS
# Cressida (Cont.)

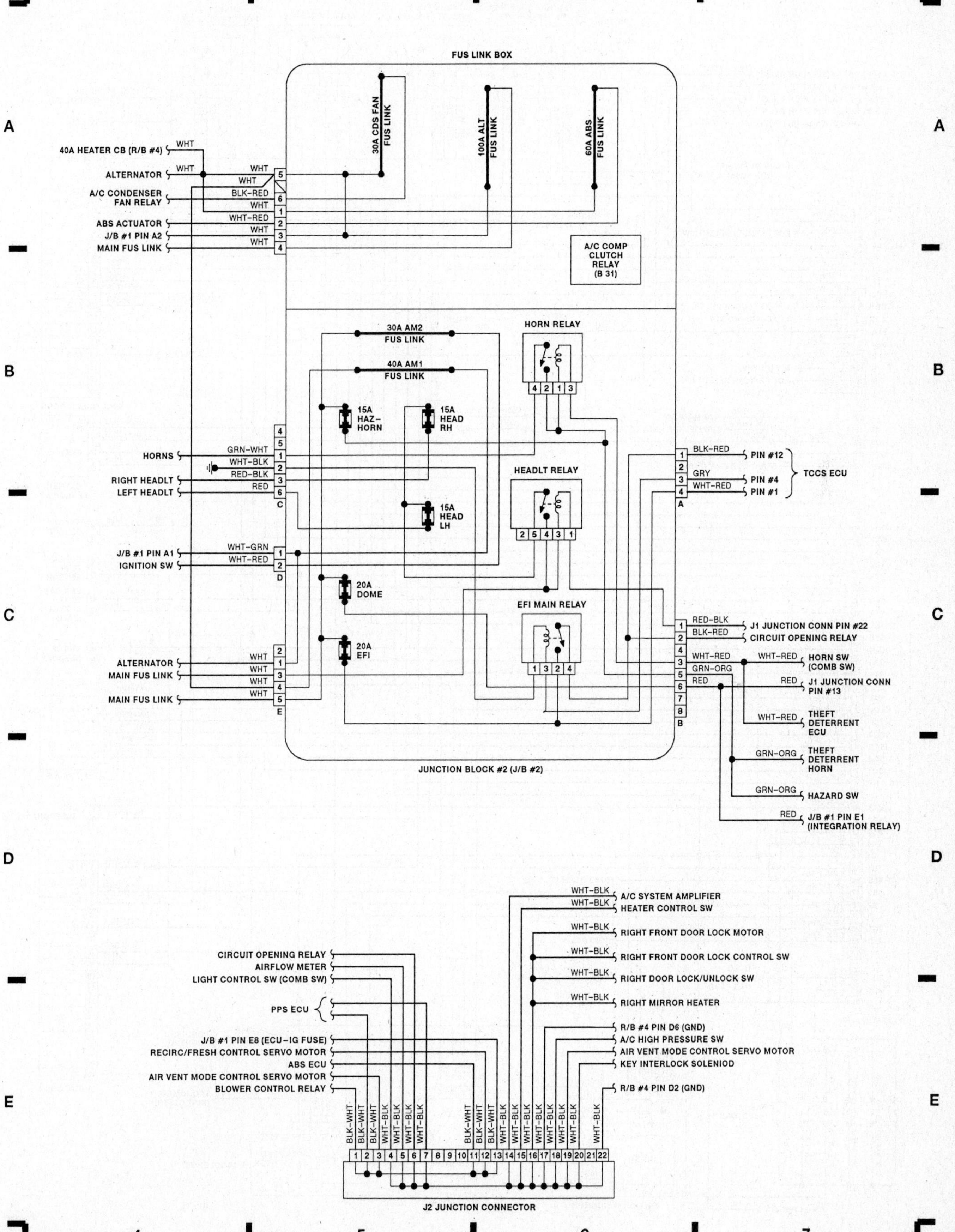

# 1991 WIRING DIAGRAMS
## Cressida (Cont.)

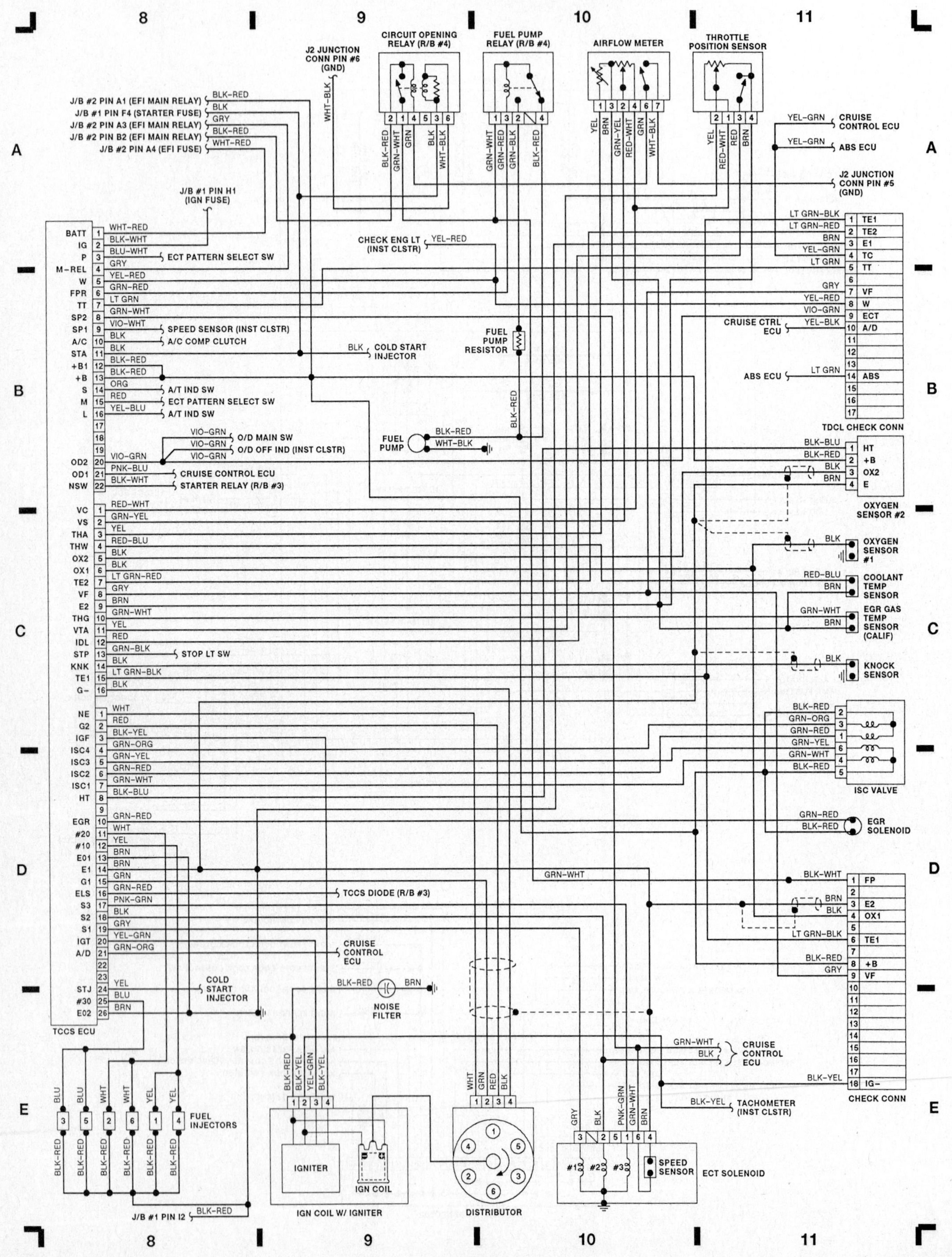

# 1991 WIRING DIAGRAMS
## Cressida (Cont.)

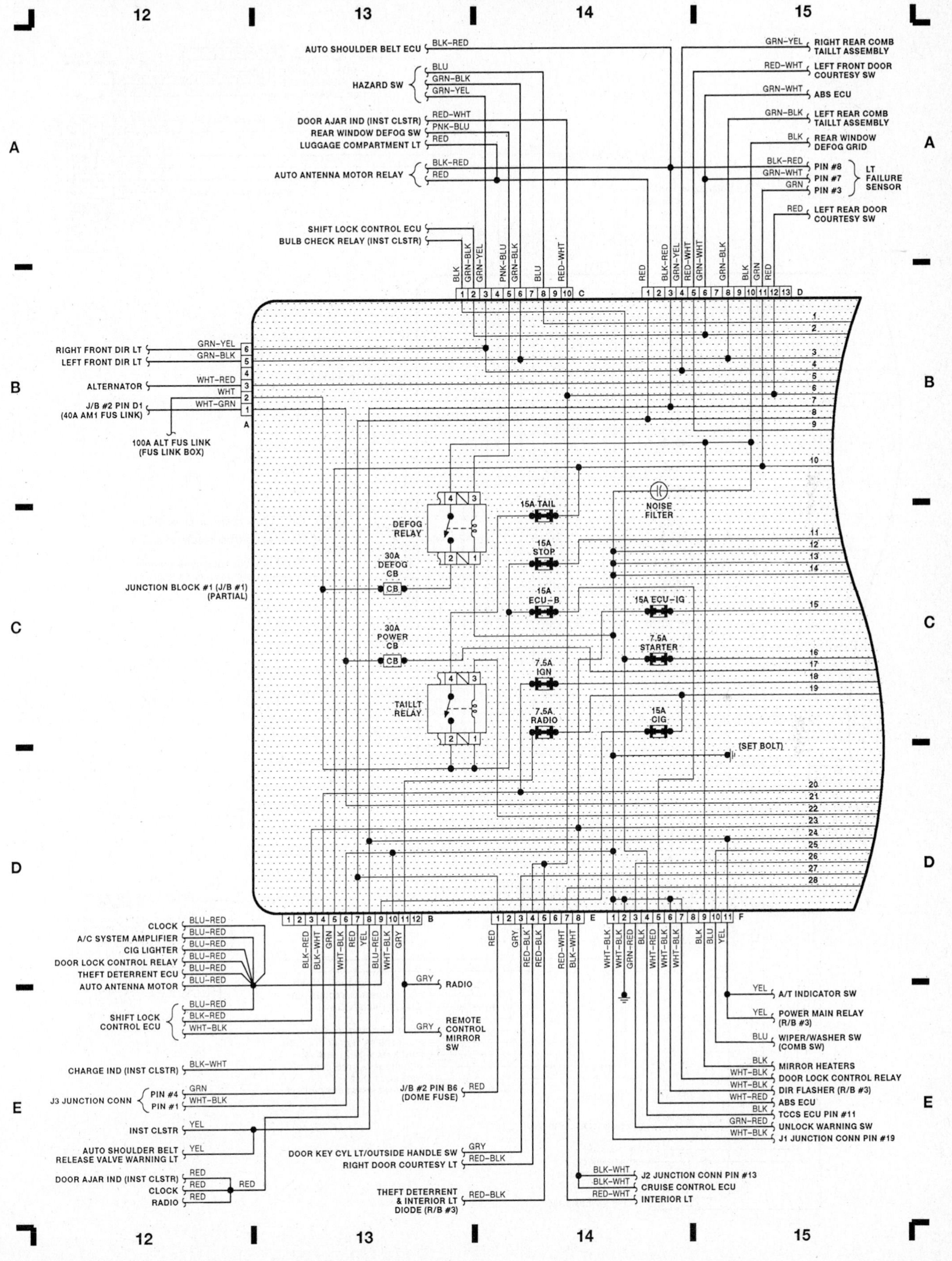

# 1991 WIRING DIAGRAMS
## Cressida (Cont.)

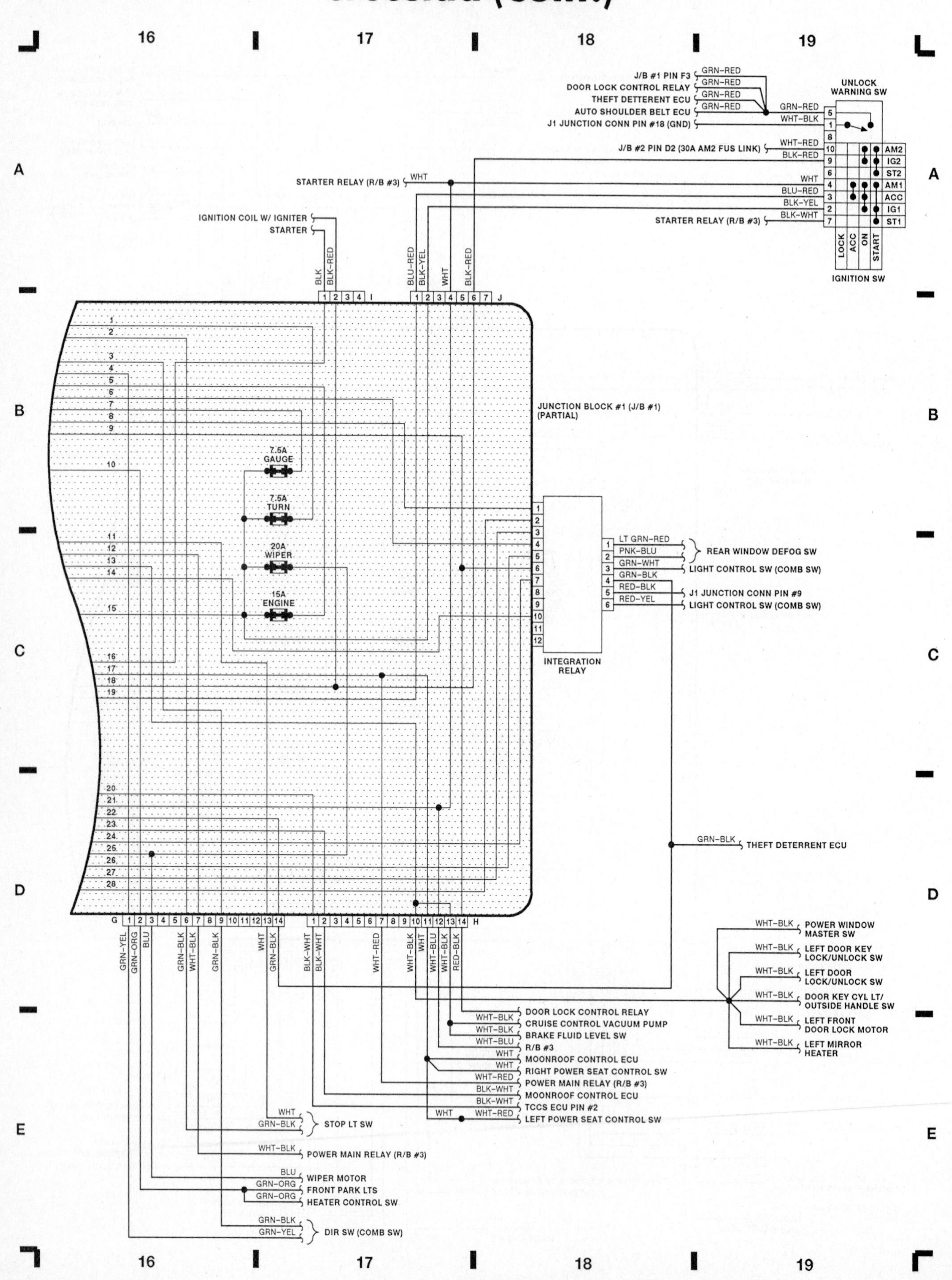

# 1991 WIRING DIAGRAMS
## Cressida (Cont.)

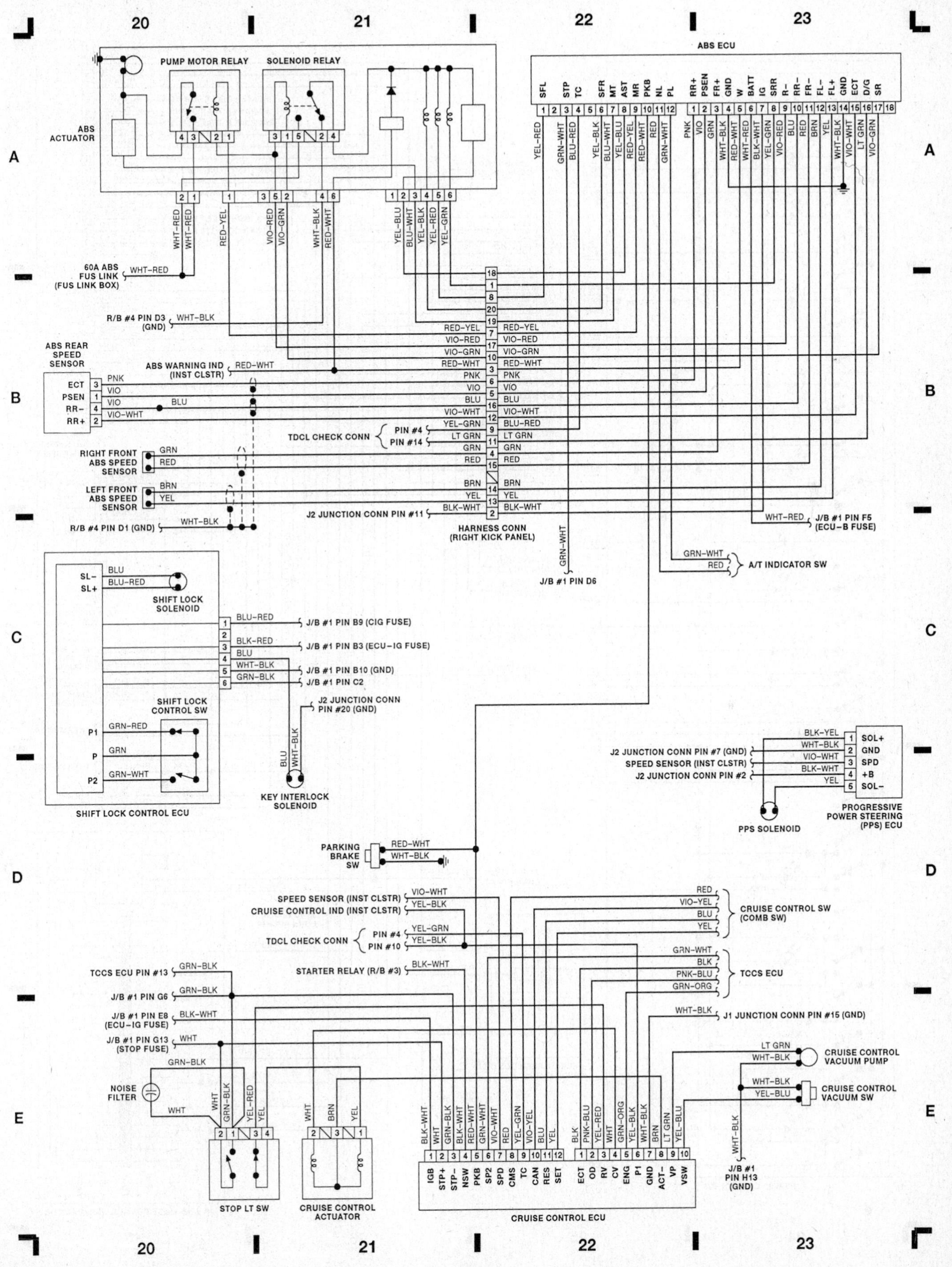

# 1991 WIRING DIAGRAMS
## Cressida (Cont.)

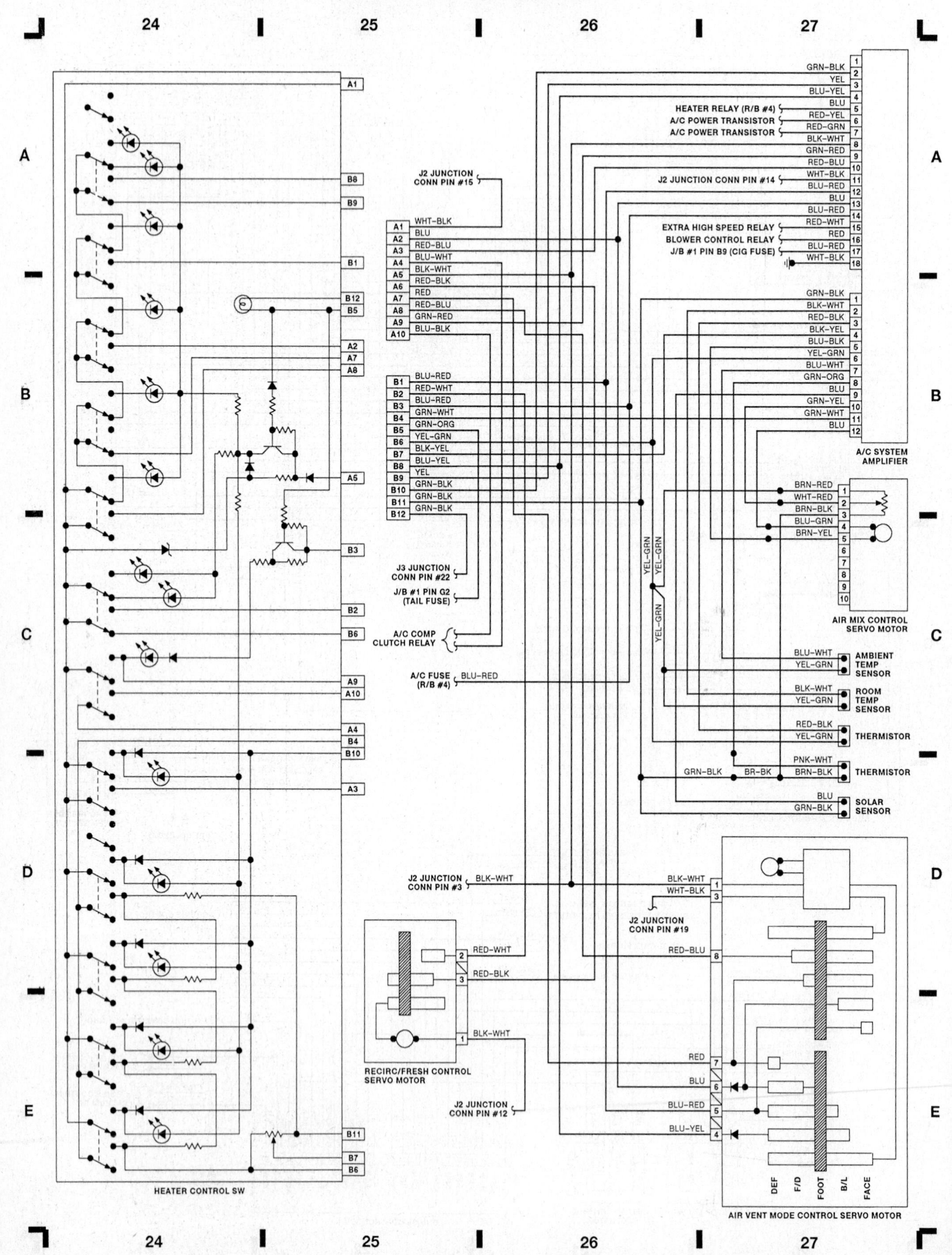
24
25
26
27
HEATER CONTROL SW
J2 JUNCTION CONN PIN #15
J3 JUNCTION CONN PIN #22
J/B #1 PIN G2 (TAIL FUSE)
A/C COMP CLUTCH RELAY
A/C FUSE (R/B #4)
J2 JUNCTION CONN PIN #3
J2 JUNCTION CONN PIN #12
J2 JUNCTION CONN PIN #19
HEATER RELAY (R/B #4)
A/C POWER TRANSISTOR
A/C POWER TRANSISTOR
J2 JUNCTION CONN PIN #14
EXTRA HIGH SPEED RELAY
BLOWER CONTROL RELAY
J/B #1 PIN B9 (CIG FUSE)
A/C SYSTEM AMPLIFIER
AIR MIX CONTROL SERVO MOTOR
AMBIENT TEMP SENSOR
ROOM TEMP SENSOR
THERMISTOR
THERMISTOR
SOLAR SENSOR
RECIRC/FRESH CONTROL SERVO MOTOR
AIR VENT MODE CONTROL SERVO MOTOR
DEF
F/D
FOOT
B/L
FACE

# 1991 WIRING DIAGRAMS
## Cressida (Cont.)

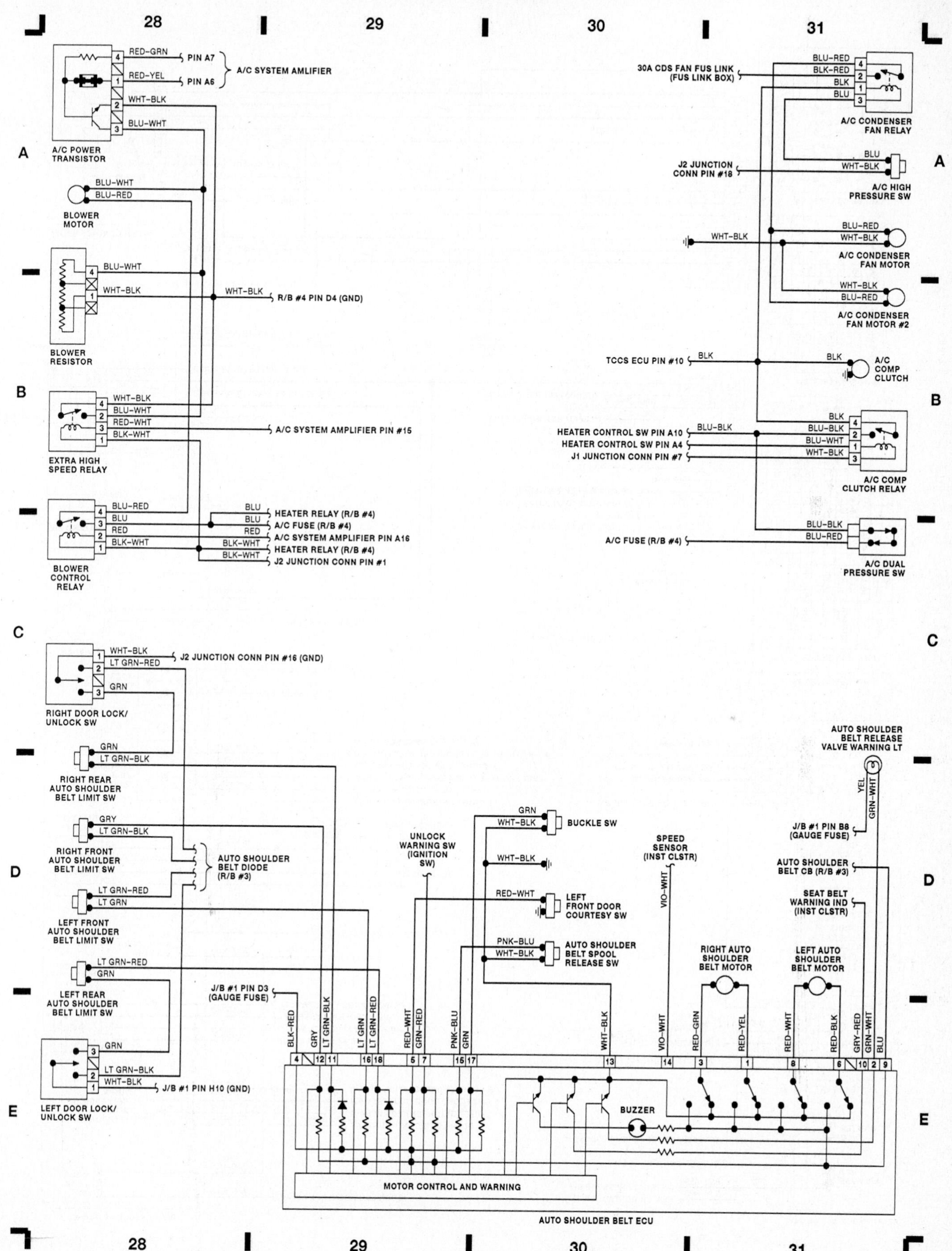

# 1991 WIRING DIAGRAMS
## Cressida (Cont.)

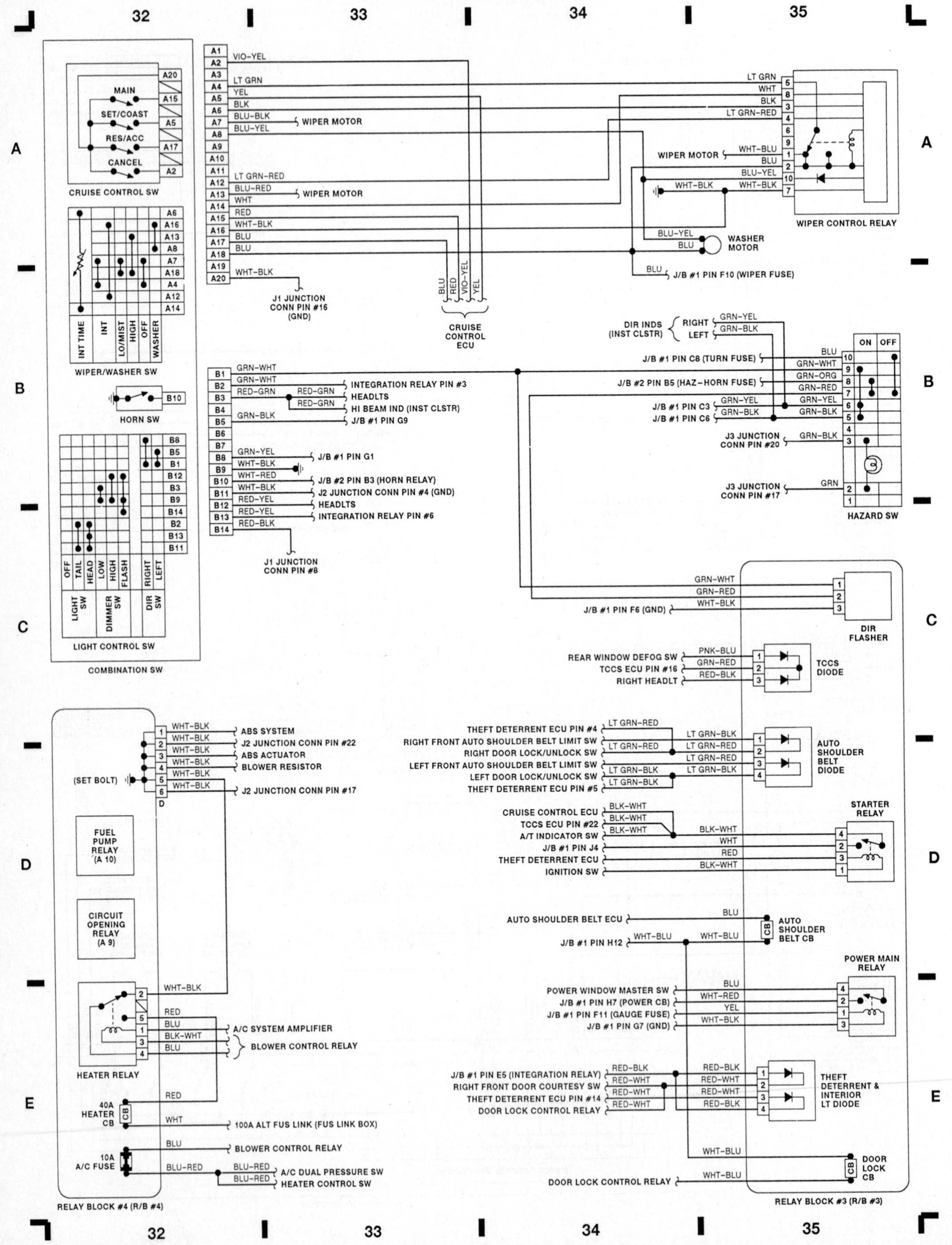

# 1991 WIRING DIAGRAMS
## Cressida (Cont.)

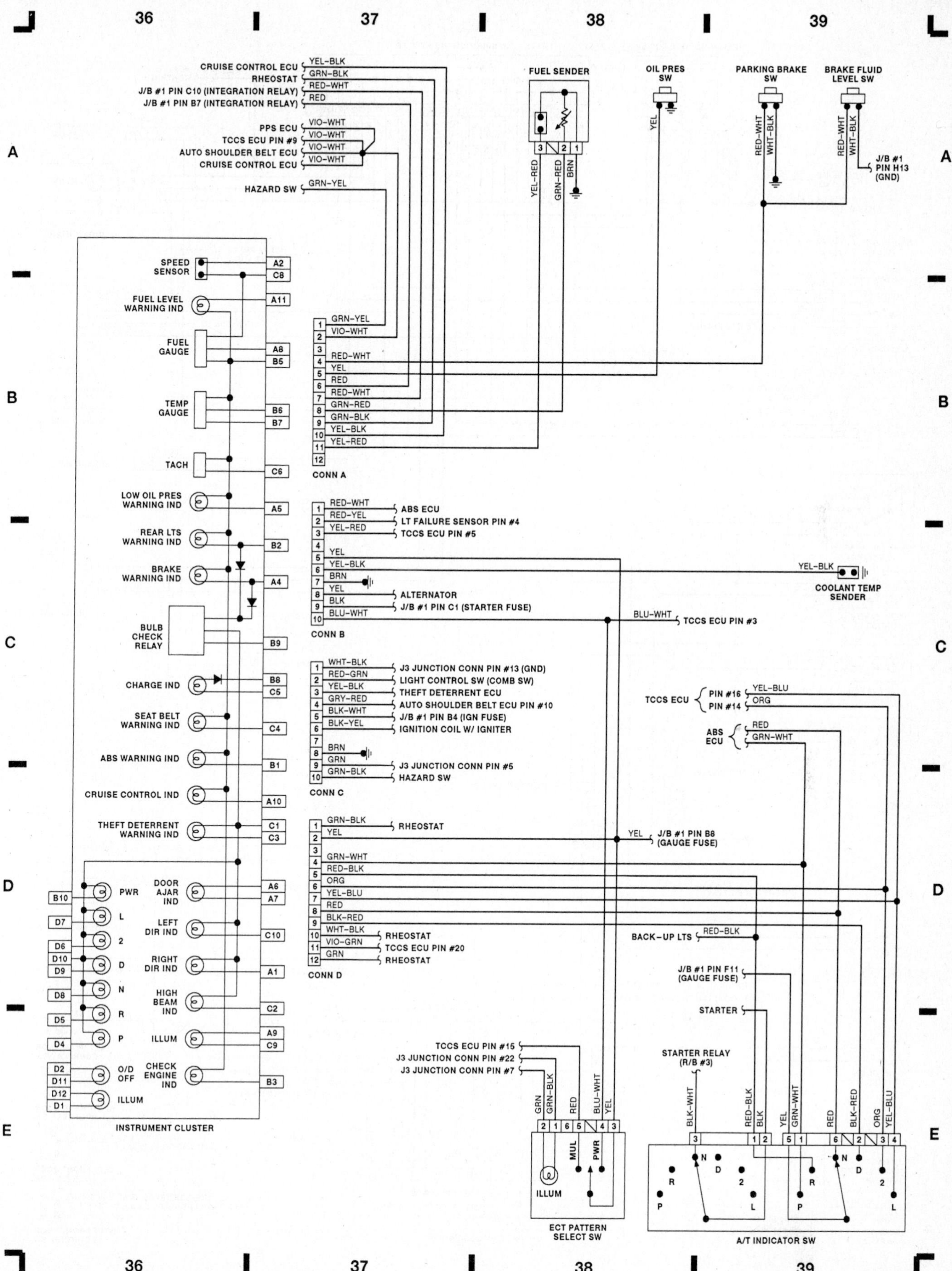

# 1991 WIRING DIAGRAMS
## Cressida (Cont.)

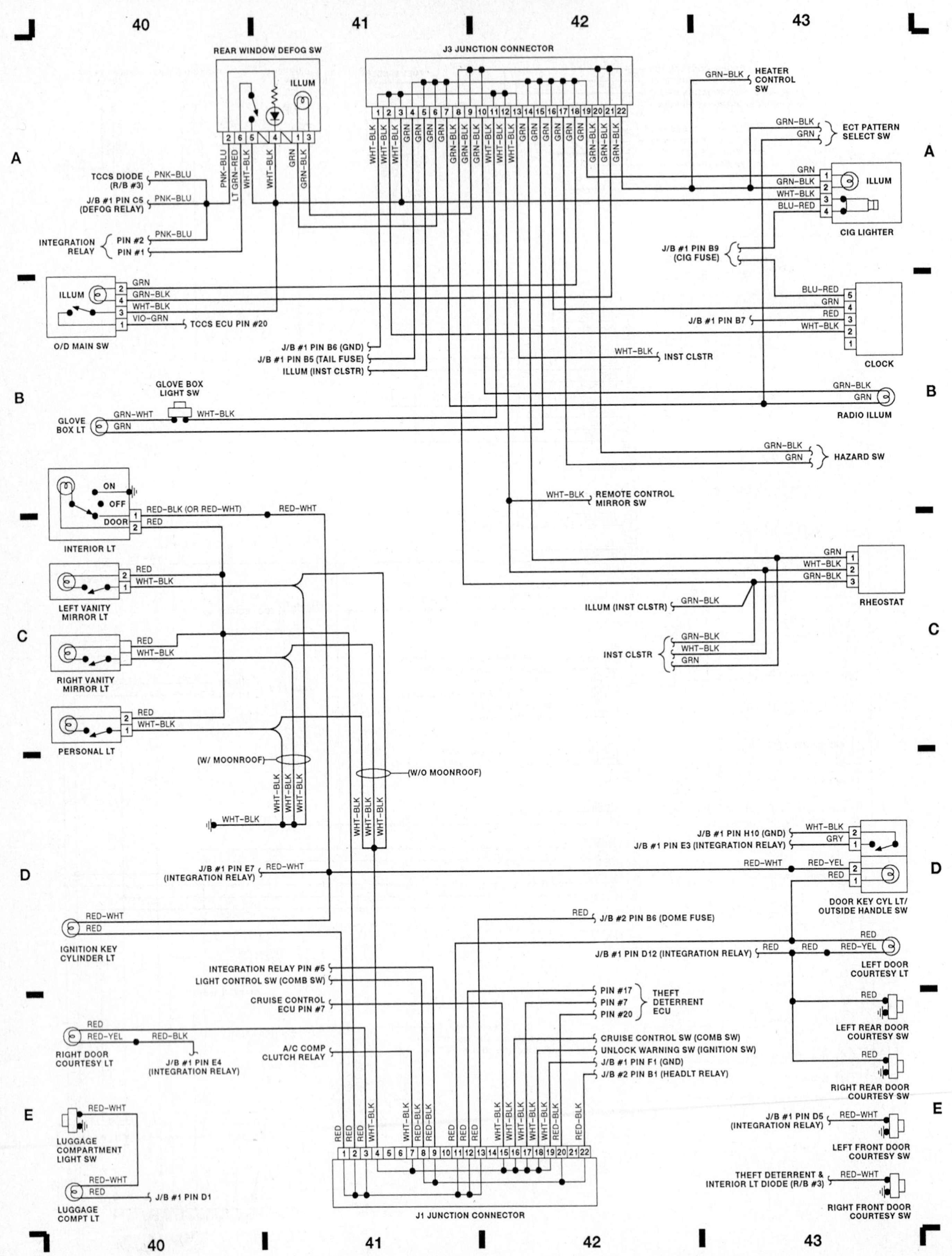

# 1991 WIRING DIAGRAMS
## Cressida (Cont.)

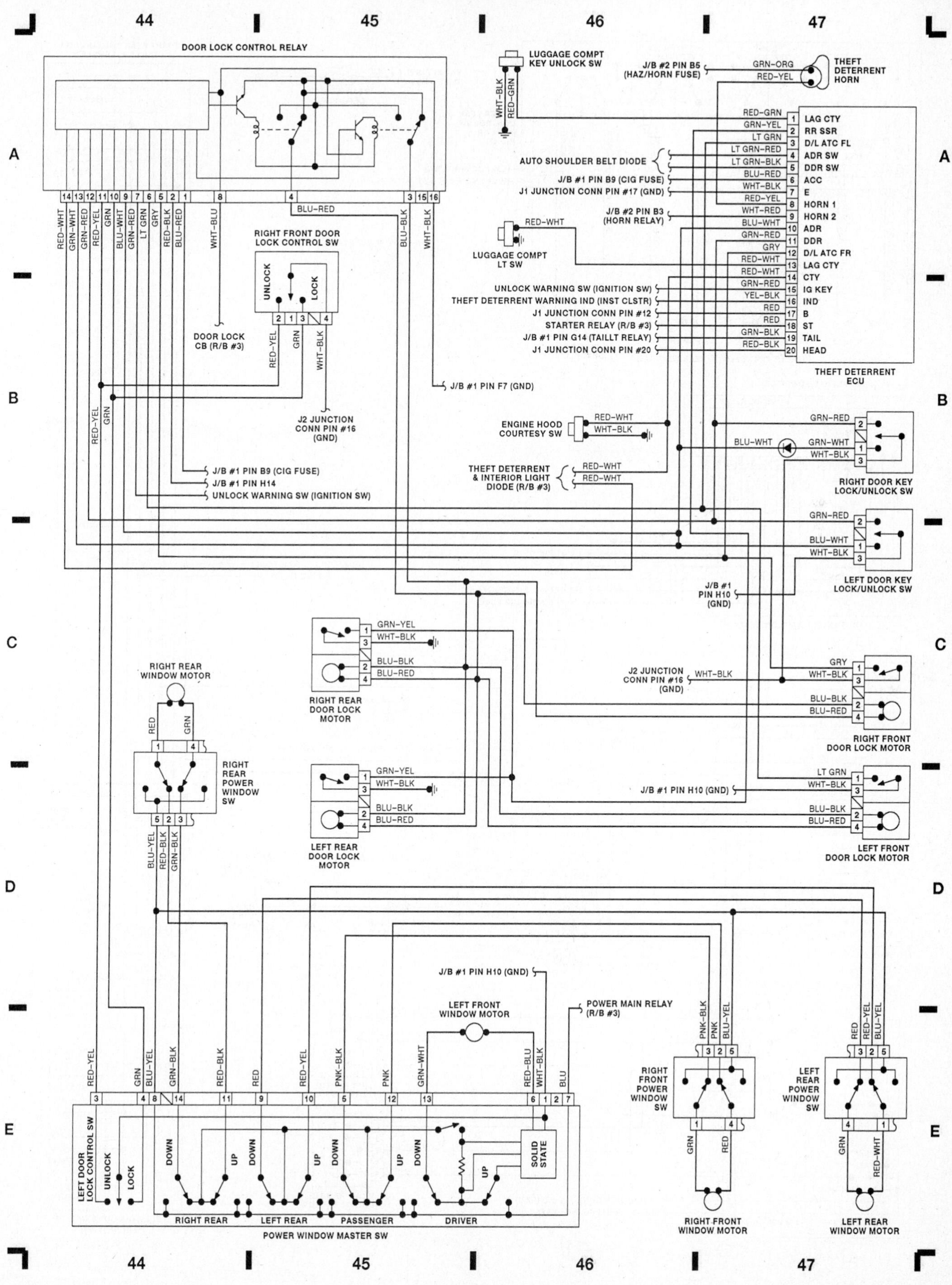

# 1991 WIRING DIAGRAMS
# Cressida (Cont.)

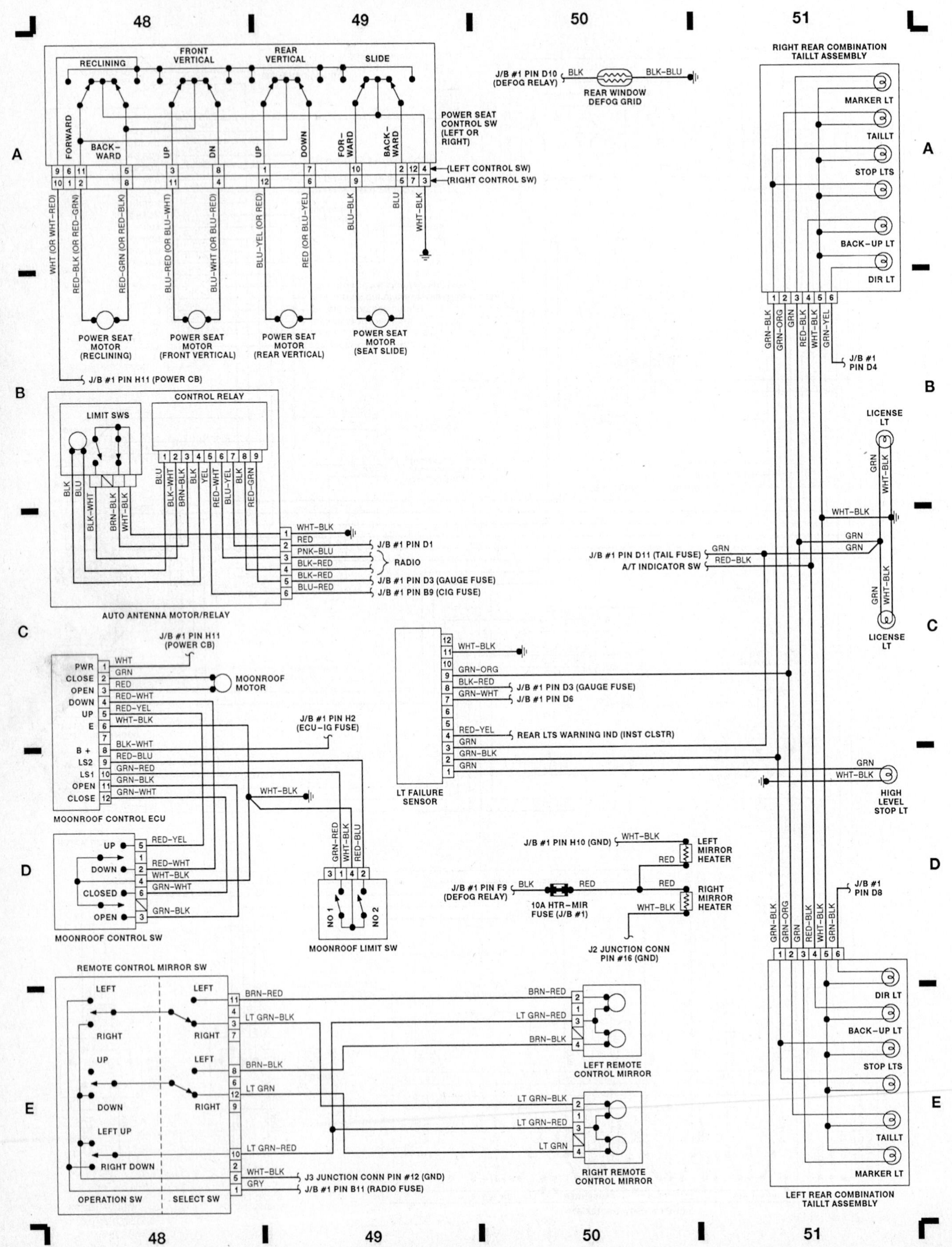

# 1991 WIRING DIAGRAMS
## Land Cruiser

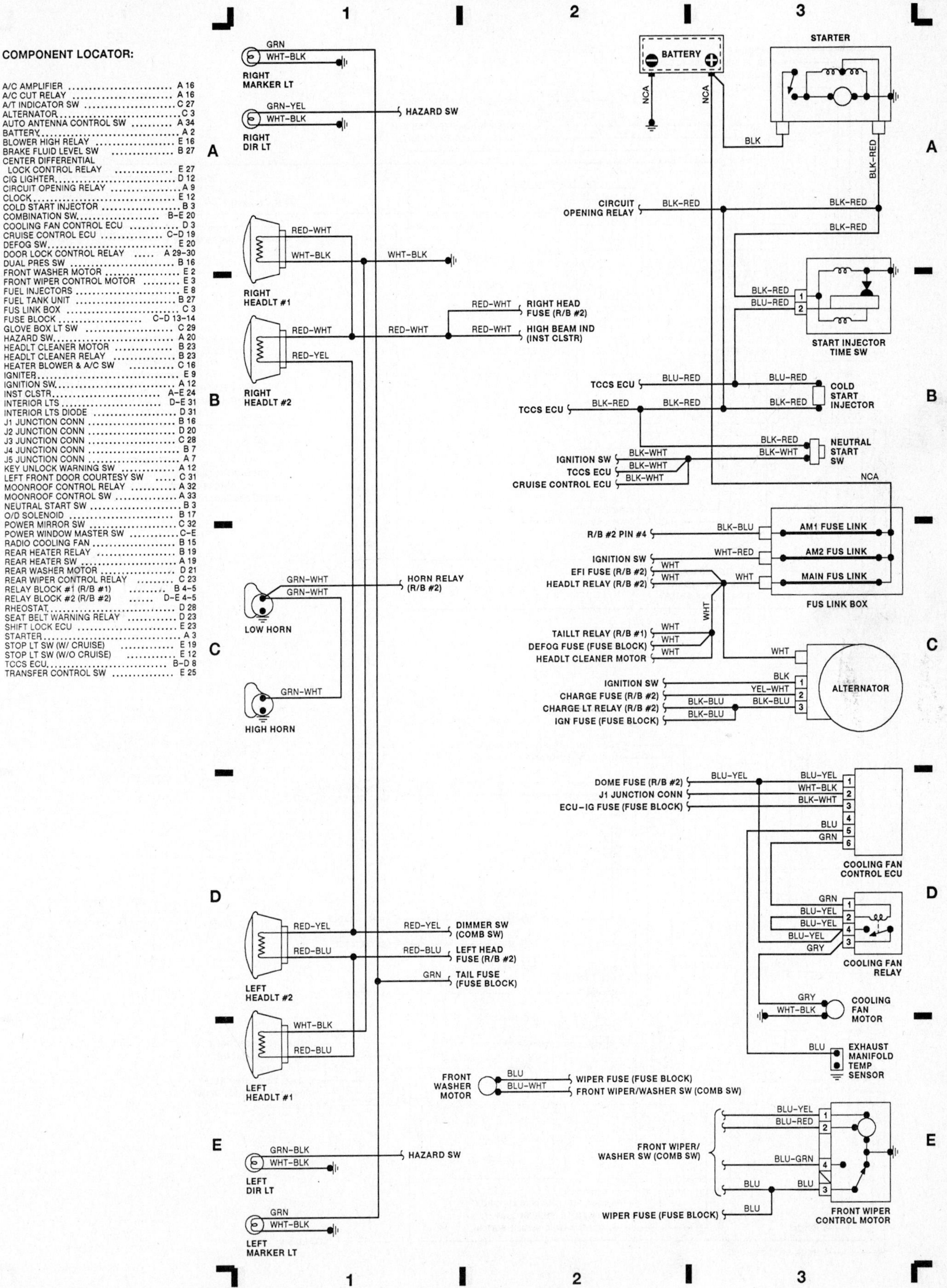
COMPONENT LOCATOR:
A/C AMPLIFIER .......... A 16
A/C CUT RELAY .......... A 16
A/T INDICATOR SW .......... C 27
ALTERNATOR .......... C 3
AUTO ANTENNA CONTROL SW .......... A 34
BATTERY .......... A 2
BLOWER HIGH RELAY .......... E 16
BRAKE FLUID LEVEL SW .......... B 27
CENTER DIFFERENTIAL
LOCK CONTROL RELAY .......... E 27
CIG LIGHTER .......... D 12
CIRCUIT OPENING RELAY .......... A 9
CLOCK .......... E 12
COLD START INJECTOR .......... B 3
COMBINATION SW .......... B-E 20
COOLING FAN CONTROL ECU .......... D 3
CRUISE CONTROL ECU .......... C-D 19
DEFOG SW .......... E 20
DOOR LOCK CONTROL RELAY .......... A 29-30
DUAL PRES SW .......... B 16
FRONT WASHER MOTOR .......... E 2
FRONT WIPER CONTROL MOTOR .......... E 3
FUEL INJECTORS .......... E 8
FUEL TANK UNIT .......... B 27
FUS LINK BOX .......... C 3
FUSE BLOCK .......... C-D 13-14
GLOVE BOX LT SW .......... C 29
HAZARD SW .......... A 20
HEADLT CLEANER MOTOR .......... B 23
HEADLT CLEANER RELAY .......... B 23
HEATER BLOWER & A/C SW .......... C 16
IGNITER .......... E 9
IGNITION SW .......... A 12
INST CLSTR .......... A-E 24
INTERIOR LTS .......... D-E 31
INTERIOR LTS DIODE .......... D 31
J1 JUNCTION CONN .......... B 16
J2 JUNCTION CONN .......... D 20
J3 JUNCTION CONN .......... C 28
J4 JUNCTION CONN .......... B 7
J5 JUNCTION CONN .......... A 7
KEY UNLOCK WARNING SW .......... A 12
LEFT FRONT DOOR COURTESY SW .......... C 31
MOONROOF CONTROL RELAY .......... A 32
MOONROOF CONTROL SW .......... A 33
NEUTRAL START SW .......... B 3
O/D SOLENOID .......... B 17
POWER MIRROR SW .......... C 32
POWER WINDOW MASTER SW .......... C-E
RADIO COOLING FAN .......... B 15
REAR HEATER RELAY .......... B 19
REAR HEATER SW .......... A 19
REAR WASHER MOTOR .......... D 21
REAR WIPER CONTROL RELAY .......... C 23
RELAY BLOCK #1 (R/B #1) .......... B 4-5
RELAY BLOCK #2 (R/B #2) .......... D-E 4-5
RHEOSTAT .......... D 28
SEAT BELT WARNING RELAY .......... D 23
SHIFT LOCK ECU .......... E 23
STARTER .......... A 3
STOP LT SW (W/ CRUISE) .......... E 19
STOP LT SW (W/O CRUISE) .......... E 12
TCCS ECU .......... B-D 8
TRANSFER CONTROL SW .......... E 25
RIGHT MARKER LT
RIGHT DIR LT
HAZARD SW
RIGHT HEADLT #1
RIGHT HEADLT #2
RIGHT HEAD FUSE (R/B #2)
HIGH BEAM IND (INST CLSTR)
LOW HORN
HIGH HORN
HORN RELAY (R/B #2)
LEFT HEADLT #2
LEFT HEADLT #1
DIMMER SW (COMB SW)
LEFT HEAD FUSE (R/B #2)
TAIL FUSE (FUSE BLOCK)
LEFT DIR LT
LEFT MARKER LT
BATTERY
STARTER
CIRCUIT OPENING RELAY
START INJECTOR TIME SW
TCCS ECU
COLD START INJECTOR
NEUTRAL START SW
IGNITION SW
CRUISE CONTROL ECU
R/B #2 PIN #4
AM1 FUSE LINK
AM2 FUS LINK
MAIN FUS LINK
FUS LINK BOX
EFI FUSE (R/B #2)
HEADLT RELAY (R/B #2)
TAILLT RELAY (R/B #1)
DEFOG FUSE (FUSE BLOCK)
HEADLT CLEANER MOTOR
ALTERNATOR
CHARGE FUSE (R/B #2)
CHARGE LT RELAY (R/B #2)
IGN FUSE (FUSE BLOCK)
DOME FUSE (R/B #2)
J1 JUNCTION CONN
ECU-IG FUSE (FUSE BLOCK)
COOLING FAN CONTROL ECU
COOLING FAN RELAY
COOLING FAN MOTOR
EXHAUST MANIFOLD TEMP SENSOR
FRONT WASHER MOTOR
WIPER FUSE (FUSE BLOCK)
FRONT WIPER/WASHER SW (COMB SW)
FRONT WIPER CONTROL MOTOR

# 1991 WIRING DIAGRAMS
## Land Cruiser (Cont.)

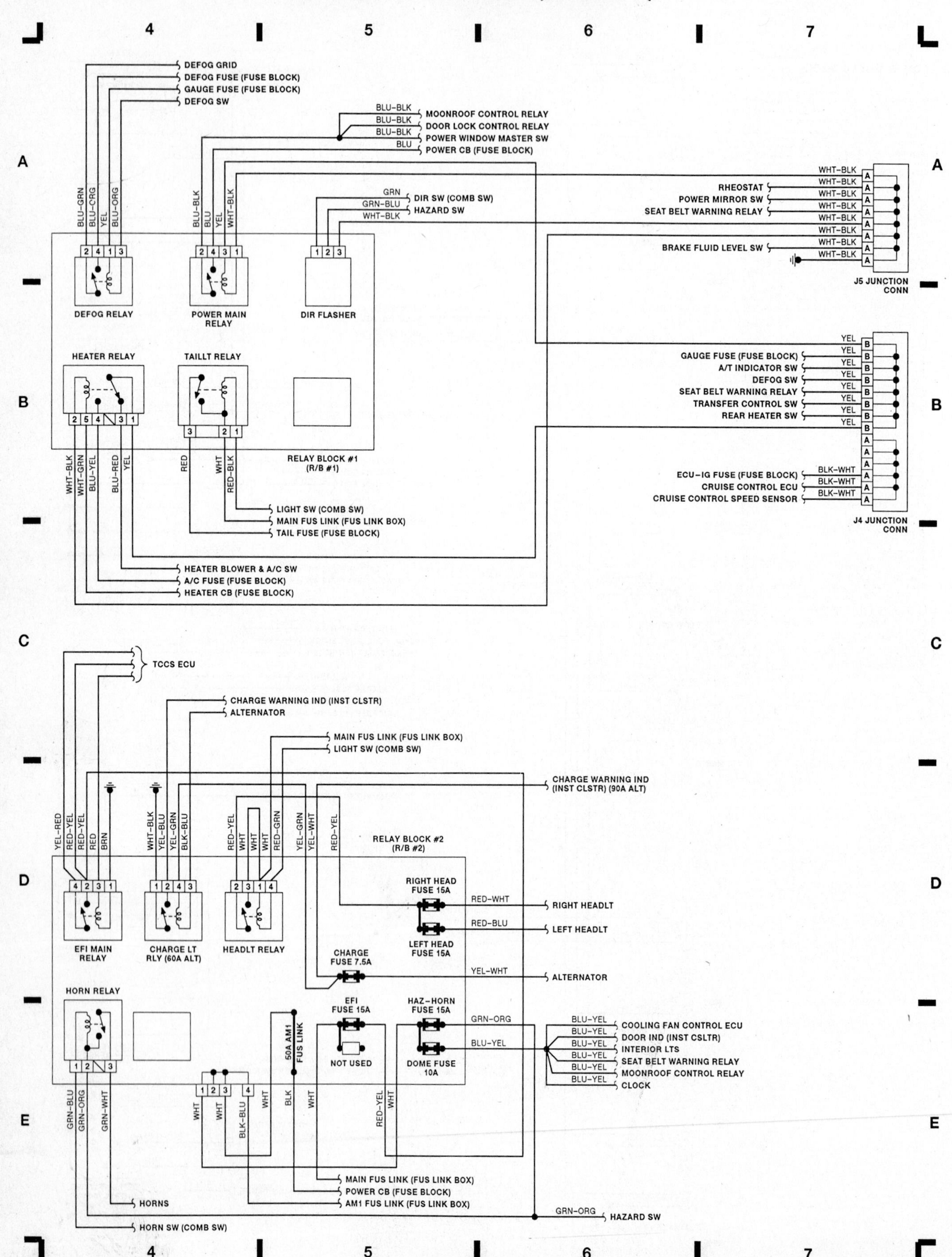

# 1991 WIRING DIAGRAMS
# Land Cruiser (Cont.)

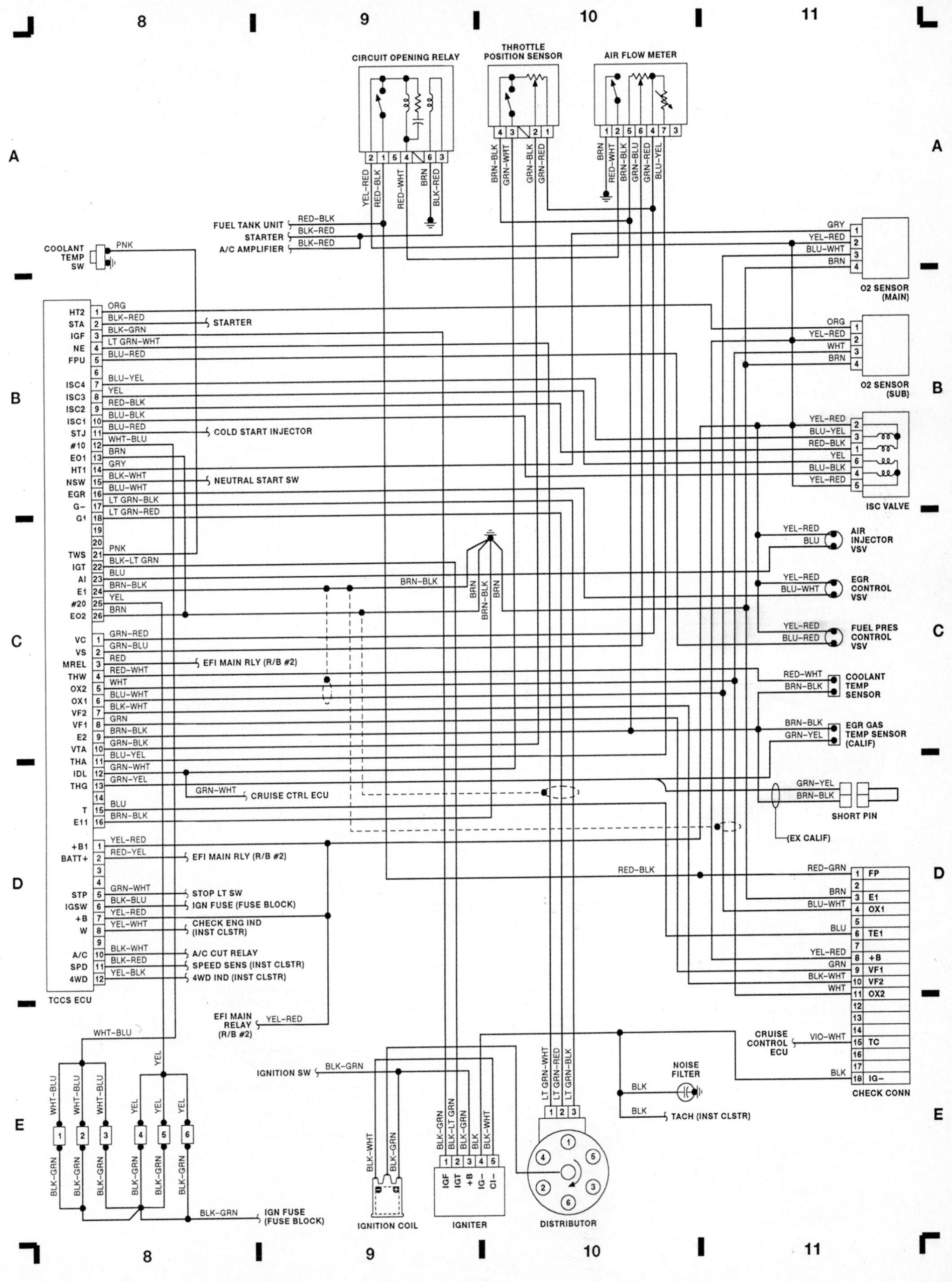

# 1991 WIRING DIAGRAMS
## Land Cruiser (Cont.)

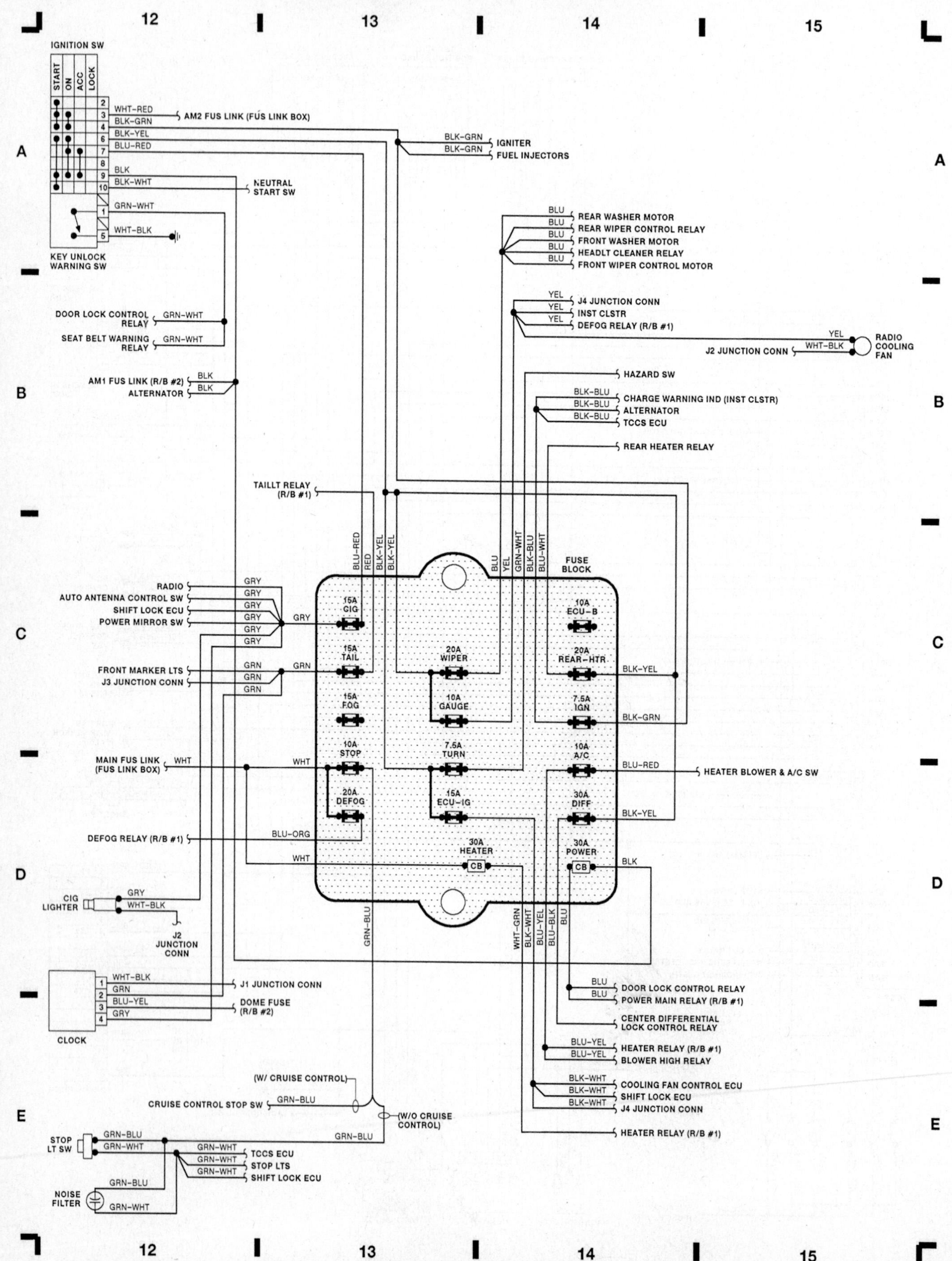

# 1991 WIRING DIAGRAMS
# Land Cruiser (Cont.)

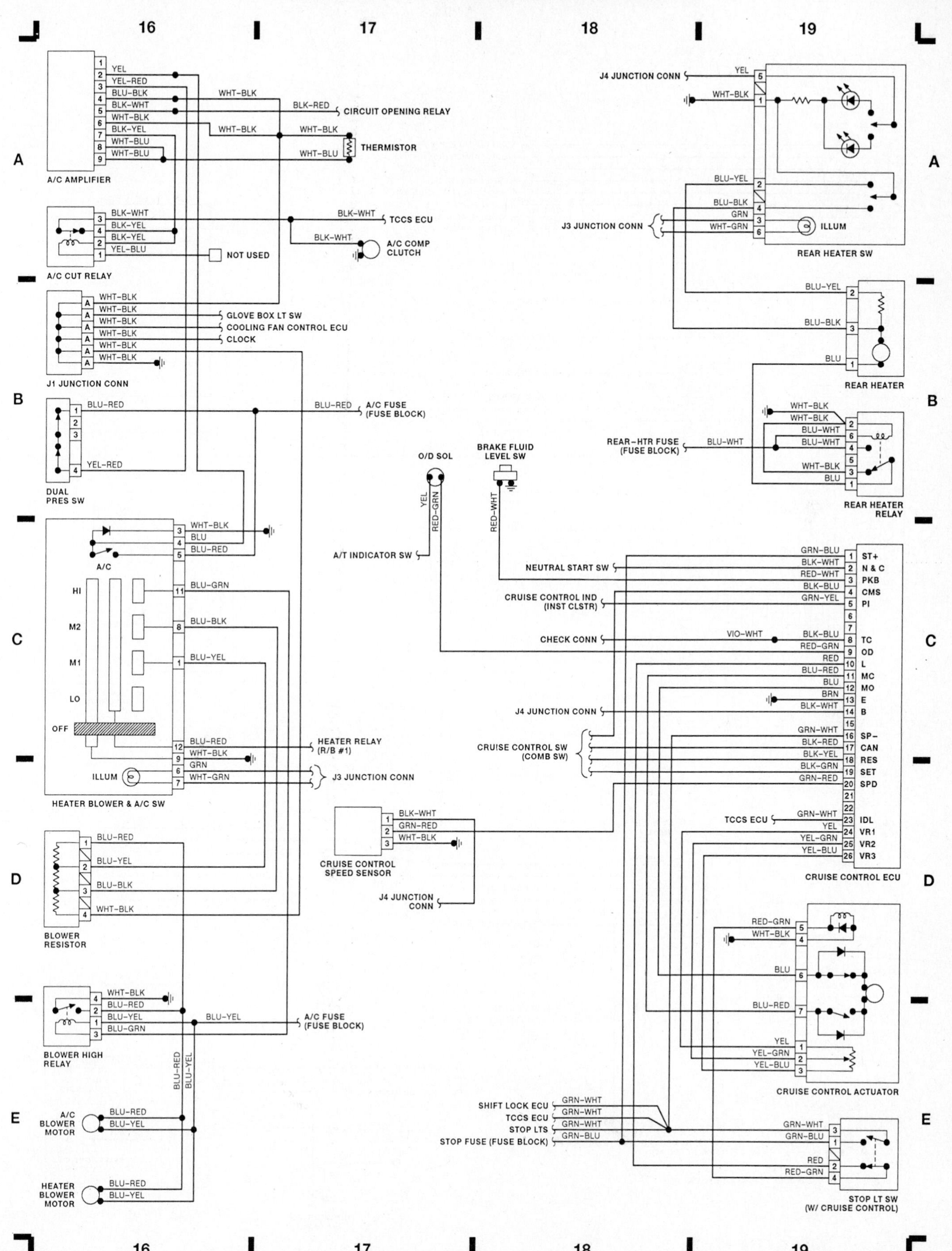

# 1991 WIRING DIAGRAMS
## Land Cruiser (Cont.)

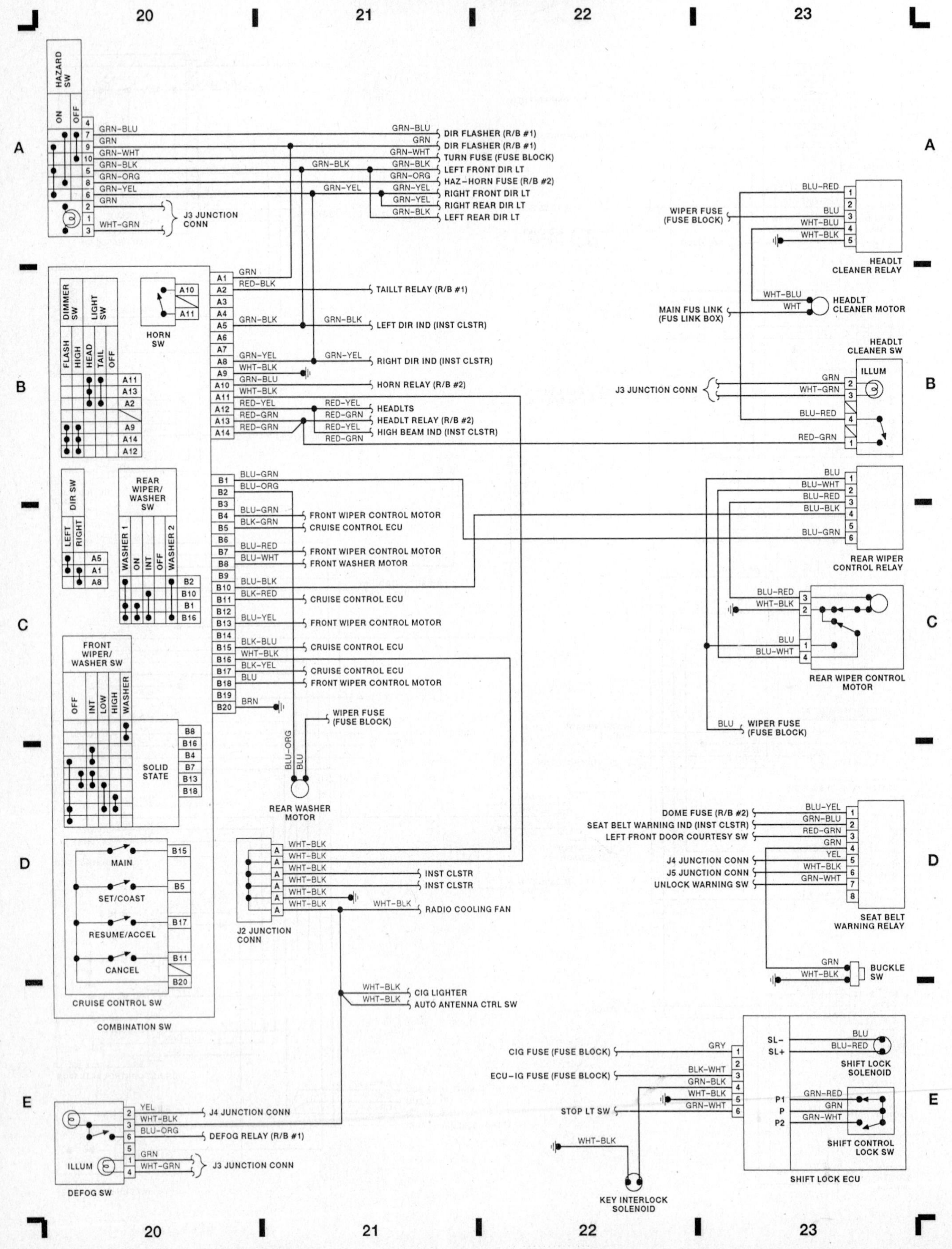

# 1991 WIRING DIAGRAMS
## Land Cruiser (Cont.)

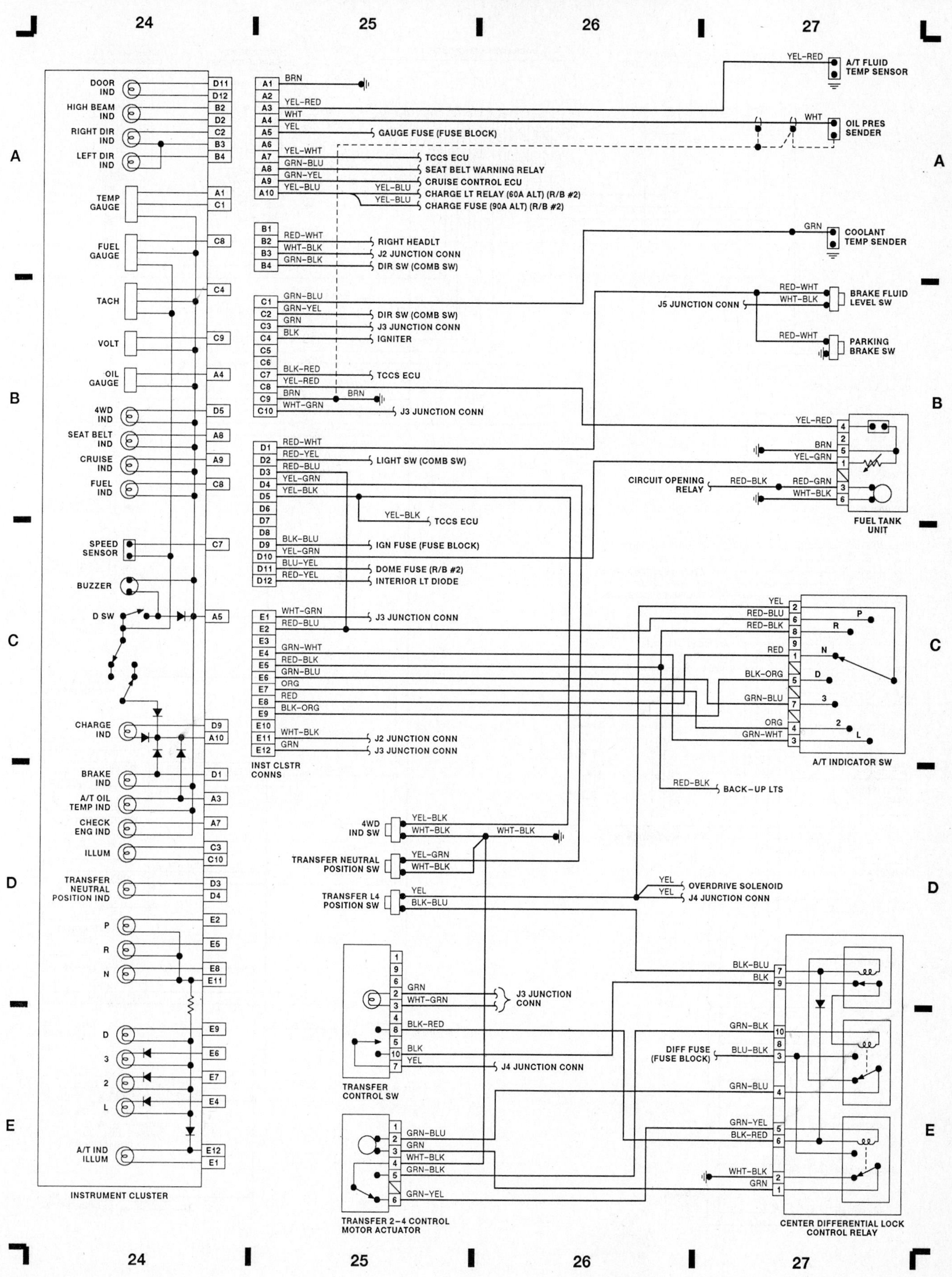

# 1991 WIRING DIAGRAMS
# Land Cruiser (Cont.)

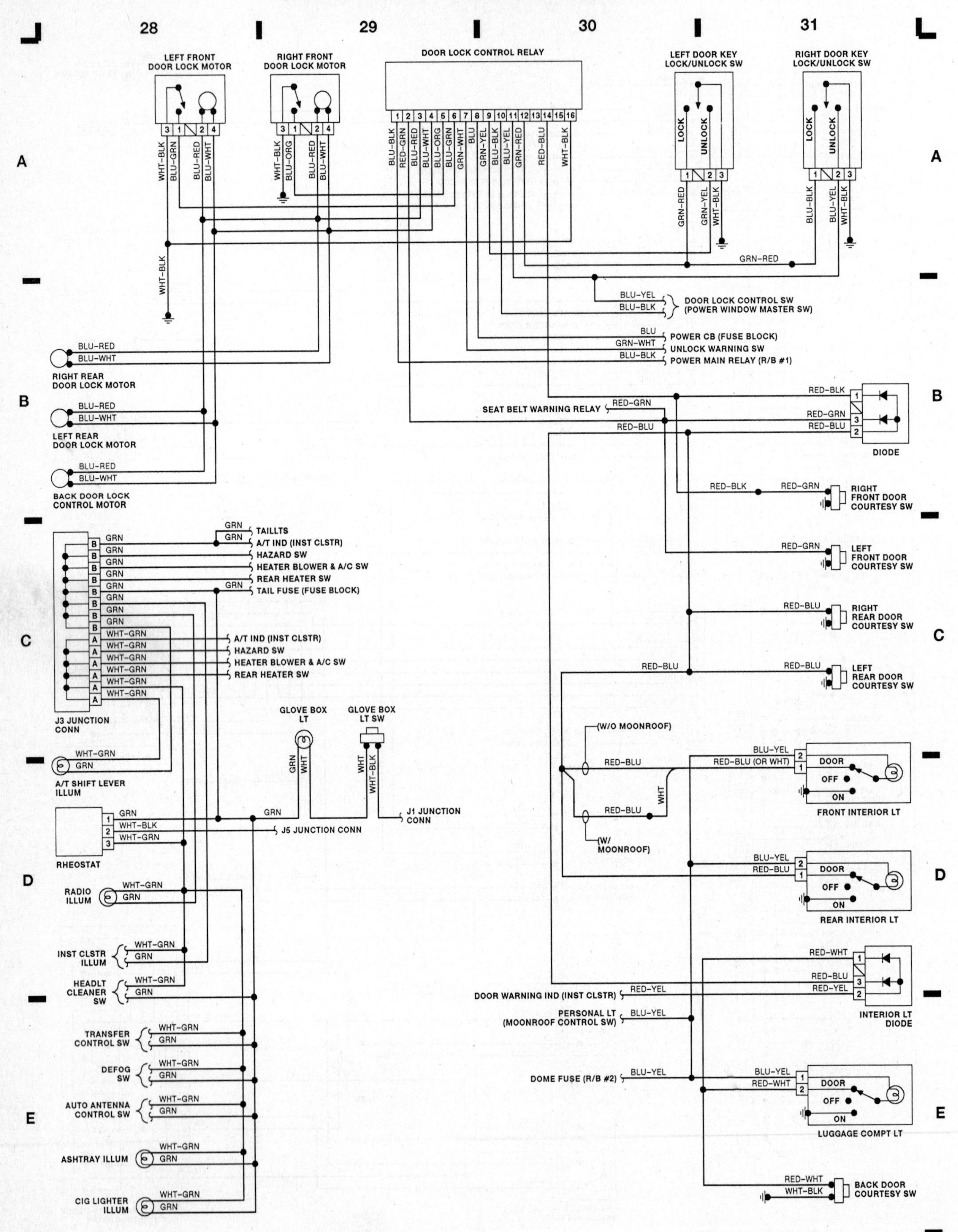

# 1991 WIRING DIAGRAMS
## Land Cruiser (Cont.)

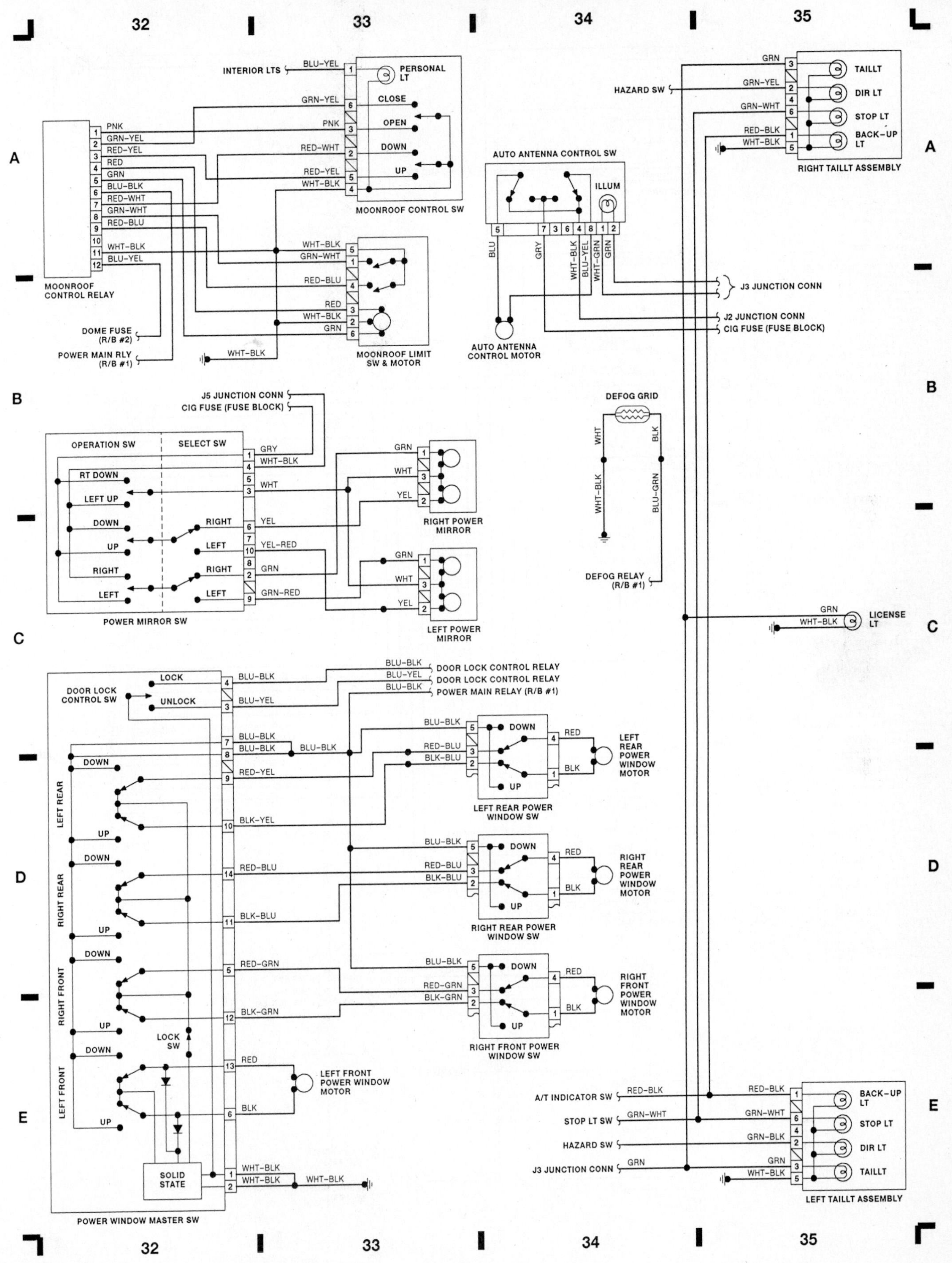

# 1991 WIRING DIAGRAMS
# MR2

## COMPONENT LOCATOR:

| | |
|---|---|
| A/C AMPLIFIER | B 23 |
| A/C COMP CLUTCH RELAY | A 27 |
| A/C COND FAN MOTOR | C 24 |
| A/C CONTROL ASSEMBLY | A–E 20 |
| A/C DIODE | A 25 |
| A/C IDLE UP VSV | A 26 |
| A/T INDICATOR SW/NEUTRAL START SW | C–D 35 |
| ABS ACTUATOR | A–C 19 |
| ABS ECU | A 16–19 |
| AIR INLET SERVO MOTOR | C 23 |
| AIR VENT MODE CONTROL SERVO MOTOR | D–E 23 |
| ALTERNATOR | C 56 |
| AUTO ANTENNA CONTROL RELAY/MOTOR | D–E 40 |
| BACK-UP LT SW (M/T) | C 59 |
| BATTERY | A 3 |
| BLOWER MOTOR | A 23 |
| BLOWER RESISTOR | A 23 |
| BUCKLE SW | D 40 |
| CENTER AIRBAG SENSOR ASSEMBLY | D 19 |
| CHECK CONN (2.2L A/T) | D–E 47 |
| CHECK CONN (2.2L M/T) | D–E 51 |
| CHECK CONN (TURBO) | D–E 55 |
| CIRCUIT OPENING RELAY (2.2L M/T) | A 51 |
| CIRCUIT OPENING RELAY (TURBO) | A 54 |
| CLOCK | A 43 |
| CLUTCH START SW (M/T) | B 57 |
| COLD START INJECTOR | B 57 |
| COMBINATION SW (COMB SW) | B–E 28 |
| COOLANT TEMP SW | B 25 |
| COOLING FAN ECU (TURBO) | D 58 |
| COURTESY LTS | D–E 33–35 |
| CRUISE CONTROL ACTUATOR | E 27 |
| CRUISE CONTROL CLUTCH SW | C 26 |
| CRUISE CONTROL ECU | C–D 27 |
| CRUISE CONTROL SPEED SENSOR | D 24 |
| CRUISE CONTROL STOP SW | C 27 |
| DOOR LOCK ECU | E 37–38 |
| DUAL PRES SW | B 27 |
| EFI MAIN RELAY (2.2L A/T) | A 44 |
| EFI MAIN RELAY (2.2L M/T) | A 48 |
| ELECT IDLE UP DIODE (2.2L A/T) | A 45 |
| ELECT IDLE UP DIODE (2.2L M/T) | A 48 |
| ELECT IDLE UP DIODE (TURBO) | B 53 |
| ENGINE OIL LEVEL ECU (TURBO) | B 35 |
| FAN RELAYS | A–C 24 |
| FOG LT SW | E 31 |
| FUEL PUMP (2.2L A/T) | A 47 |
| FUEL PUMP (2.2L M/T) | A 51 |
| FUEL PUMP (TURBO) | A 55 |
| HAZARD SW | A 28 |
| HEATER RELAY | A 27 |
| IGNITER (2.2L A/T) | E 46 |
| IGNITER (2.2L M/T) | E 50 |
| IGNITER (TURBO) | E 54 |
| IGNITION SW | A 11 |
| ILLUM LTS | D–E 16–17 |
| INST CLSTR | A–E 32 |
| INTERIOR LT CONTROL RELAY (W/ DOOR KEY CYL LT) | E 35 |
| INTERIOR LT CONTROL RELAY (W/O DOOR KEY CYL LT) | D 35 |
| J1 JUNCTION CONN | B–C 43 |
| J2 JUNCTION CONN | D 16 |
| J3 JUNCTION CONN | E 28 |
| JUNCTION BLOCK #3 (J/B #3) | C–D 12–15 |
| KEY INTERLOCK SOLENOID | E 25 |
| LEFT DOOR COURTESY SW | C 36 |
| LEFT DOOR LOCK MOTOR | D 36 |
| MAIN FUS LINK | A 3 |
| O/D MAIN SW | D 33 |
| POWER MAIN RELAY | A 40 |
| POWER STEERING ECU | E 9–10 |
| POWER STEERING RELAY | E 8 |
| POWER WINDOW MASTER SW | A–B 40 |
| REAR LUGGAGE LT | B 38 |
| RELAY BLOCK #1 (R/B #1) | A–C 8–9 |
| RELAY BLOCK #2 (R/B #2) | C–E 56 |
| RELAY BLOCK #5 (R/B #5) | A–C 4–6 |
| RETRACT CONTROL RELAY (W/ LT RETAINER) | D 3 |
| RETRACT CONTROL RELAY (W/O LT RETAINER) | B 3 |
| RHEOSTAT | C 16 |
| RIGHT DOOR LOCK MOTOR | D 39 |
| SEAT BELT WARNING RELAY | C 40 |
| SHIFT LOCK ECU | E 24 |
| START INJECTOR TIME SW | A 56 |
| STARTER | A 58 |
| STARTER RELAY | A 57 |
| STOP LT SW (W/O CRUISE) | E 57 |
| TCCS ECU (2.2L A/T) | A–E 44 |
| TCCS ECU (2.2L M/T) | B–D 48 |
| TCCS ECU (TURBO) | A–E 52 |
| THEFT DETERRENT ECU | A 37–38 |
| THEFT DETERRENT HORN | A 36 |
| UNLOCK WARNING SW | A 11 |
| WIPER MOTOR | B 31 |

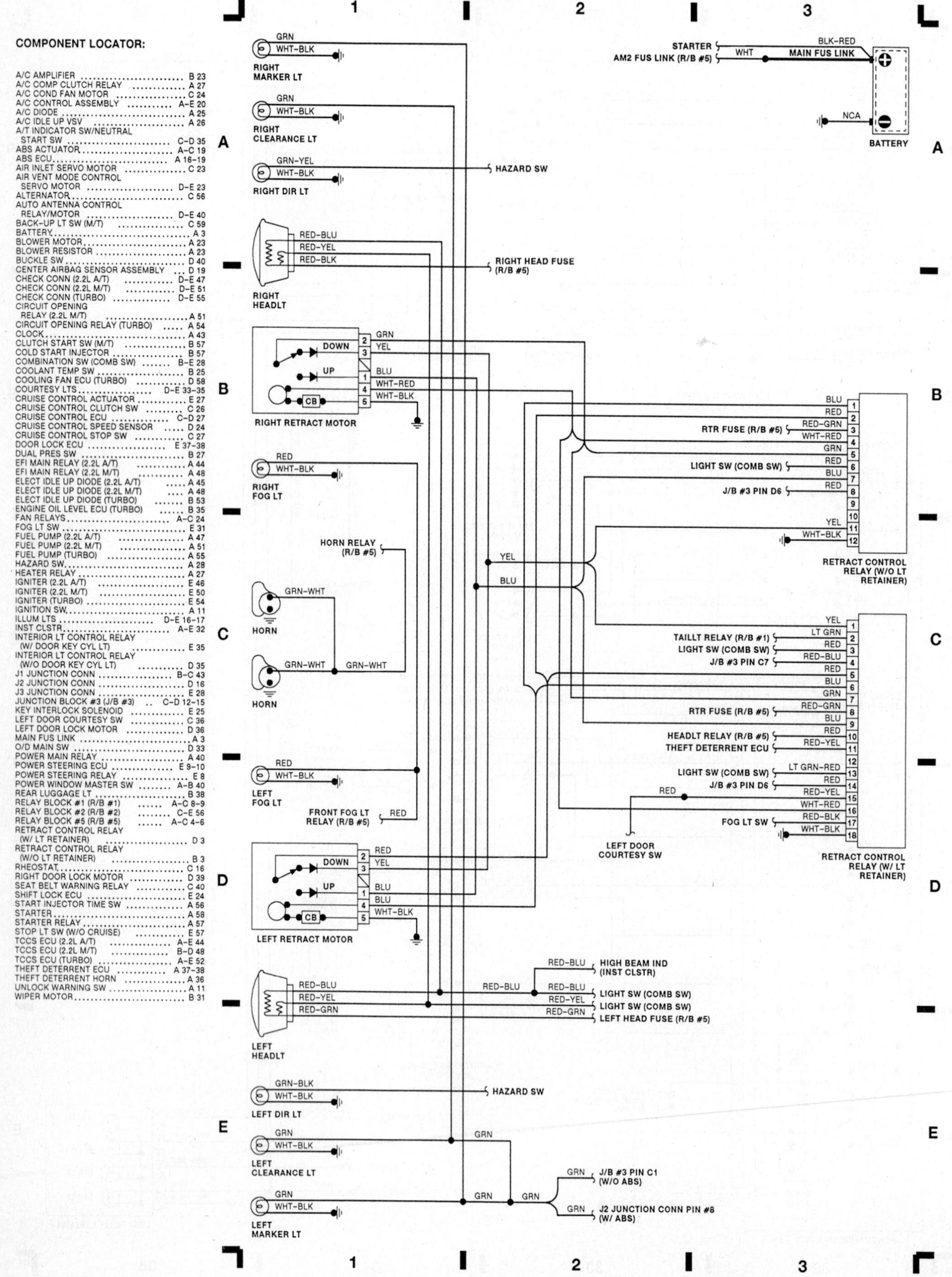

# 1991 WIRING DIAGRAMS
# MR2 (Cont.)

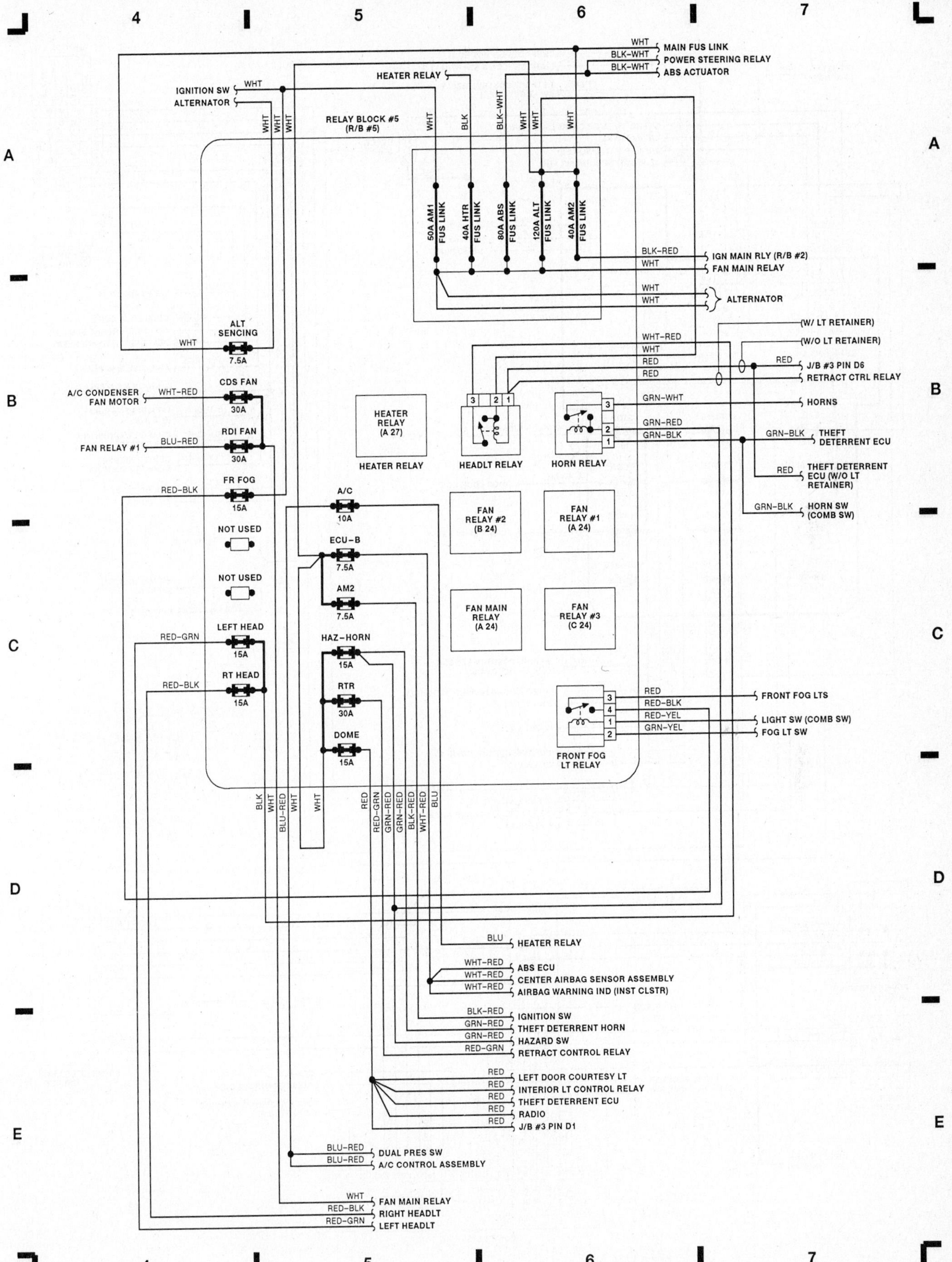

# 1991 WIRING DIAGRAMS
# MR2 (Cont.)

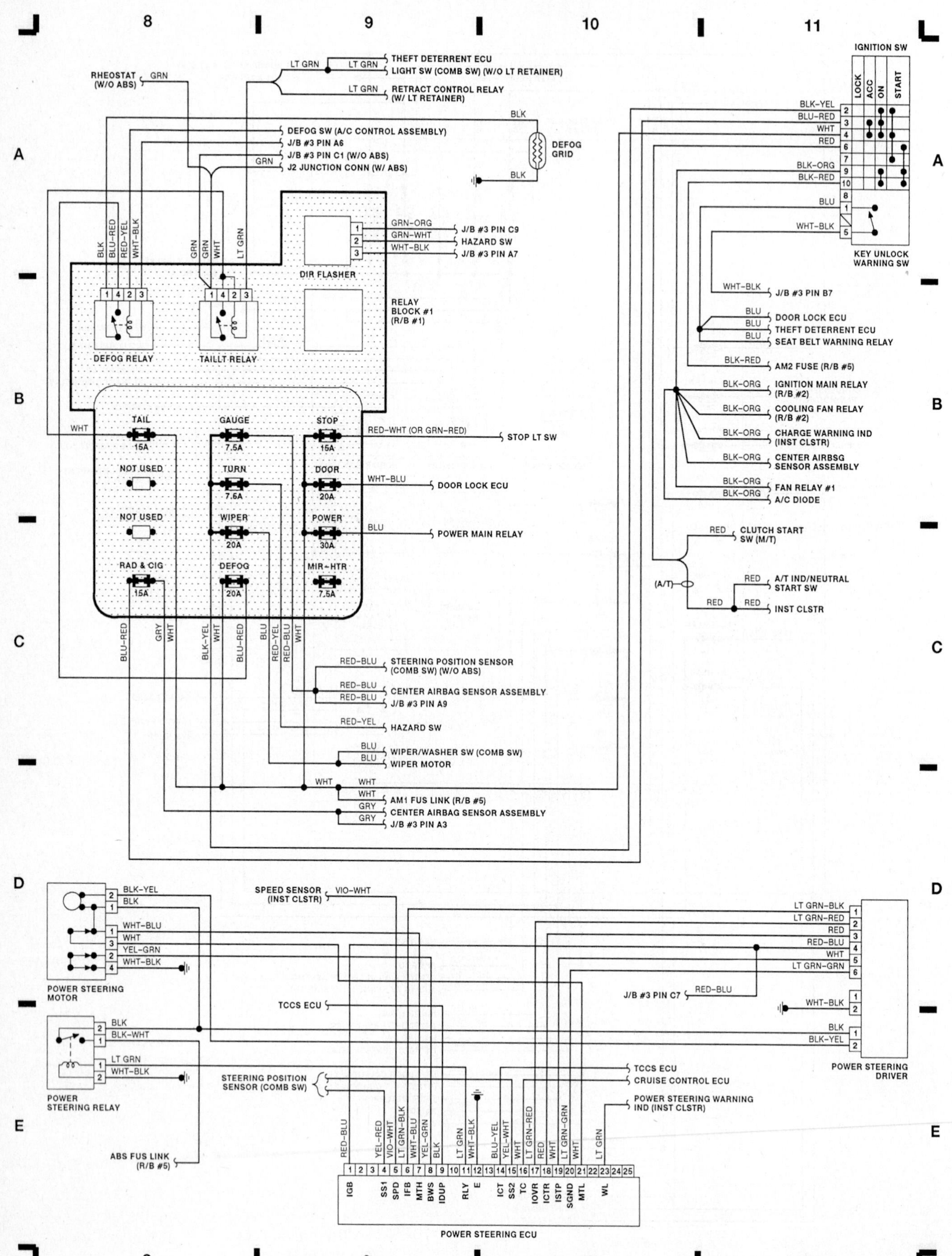

# 1991 WIRING DIAGRAMS
# MR2 (Cont.)

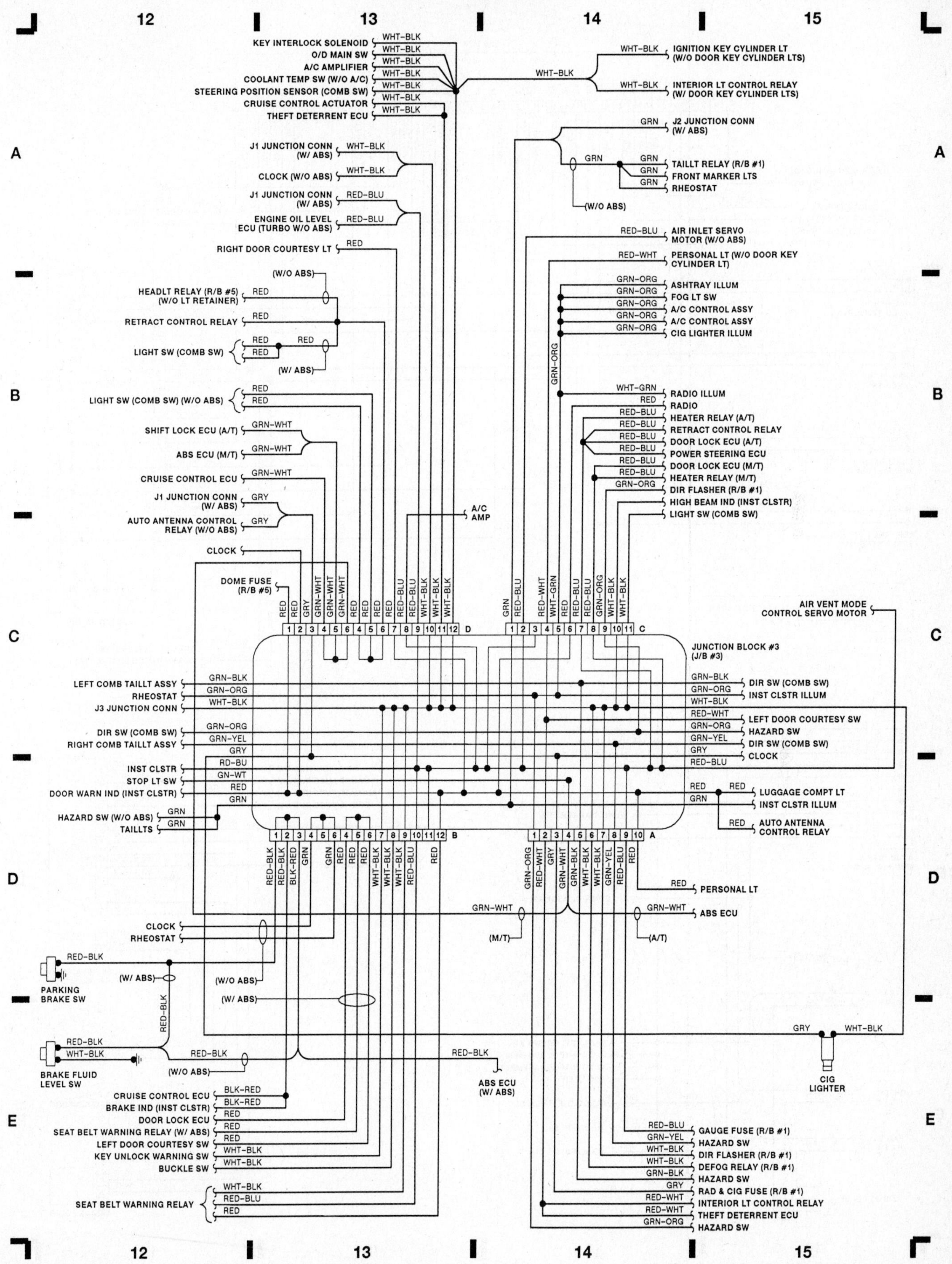

# 1991 WIRING DIAGRAMS
# MR2 (Cont.)

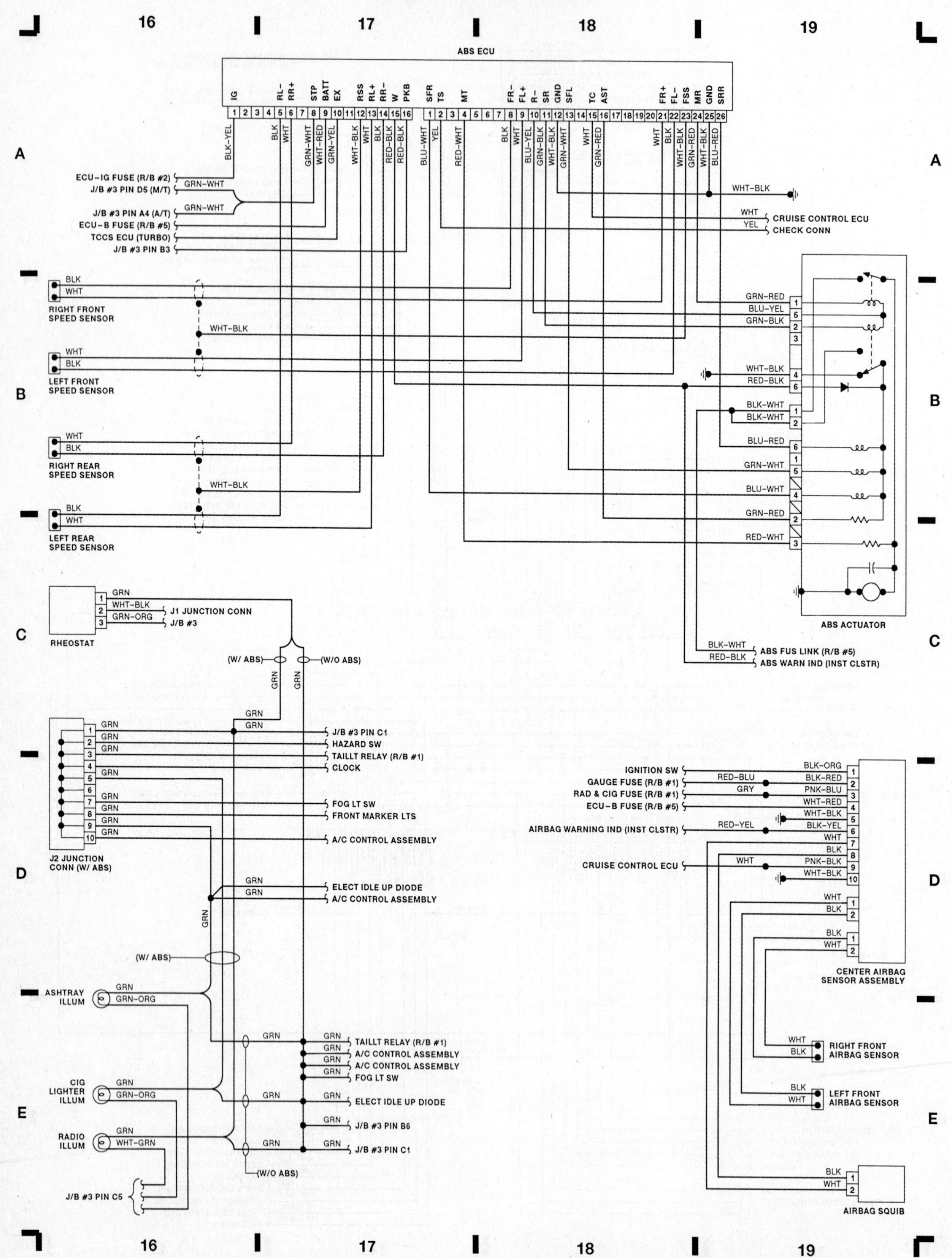

# 1991 WIRING DIAGRAMS
# MR2 (Cont.)

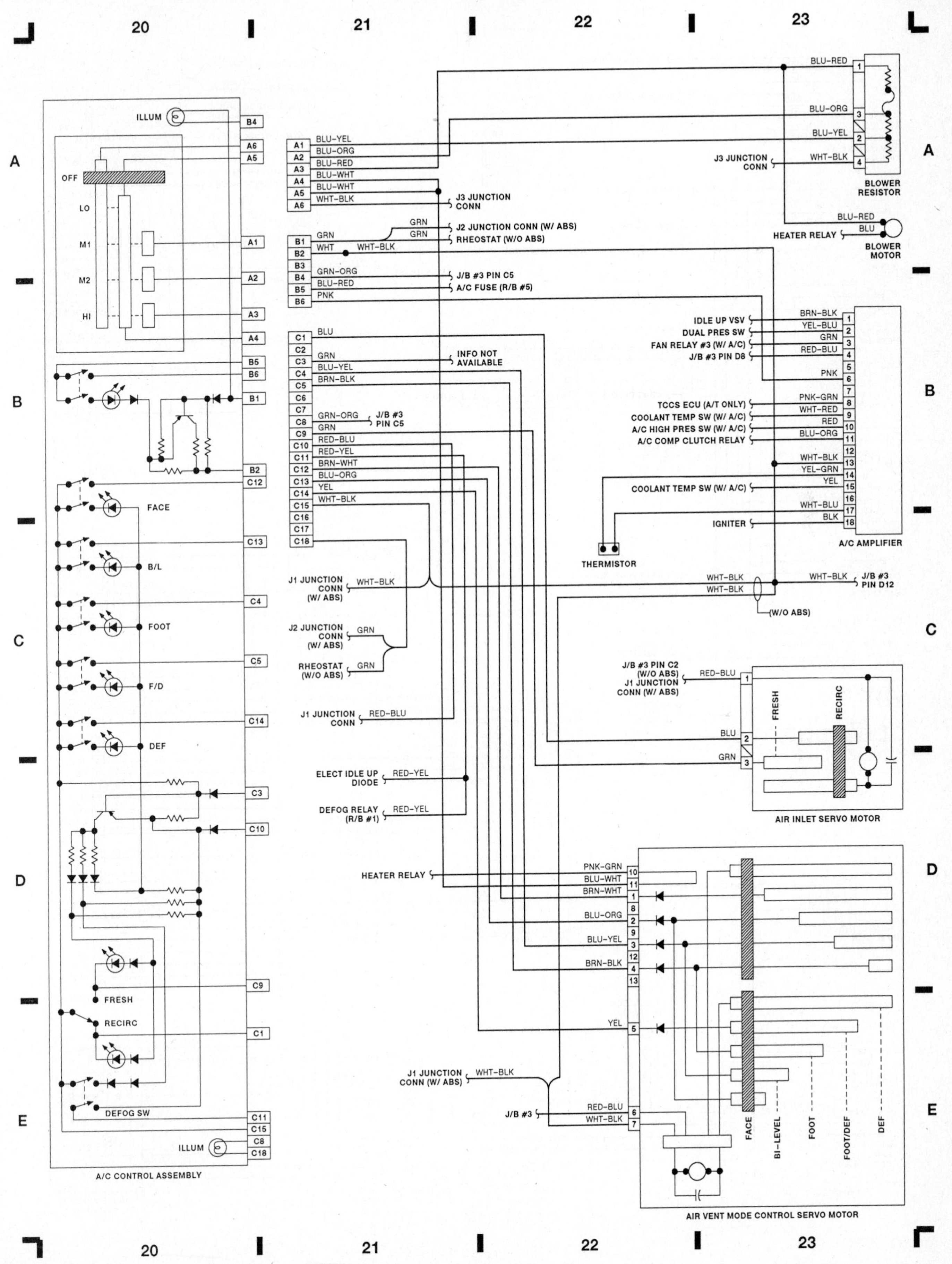

# 1991 WIRING DIAGRAMS
# MR2 (Cont.)

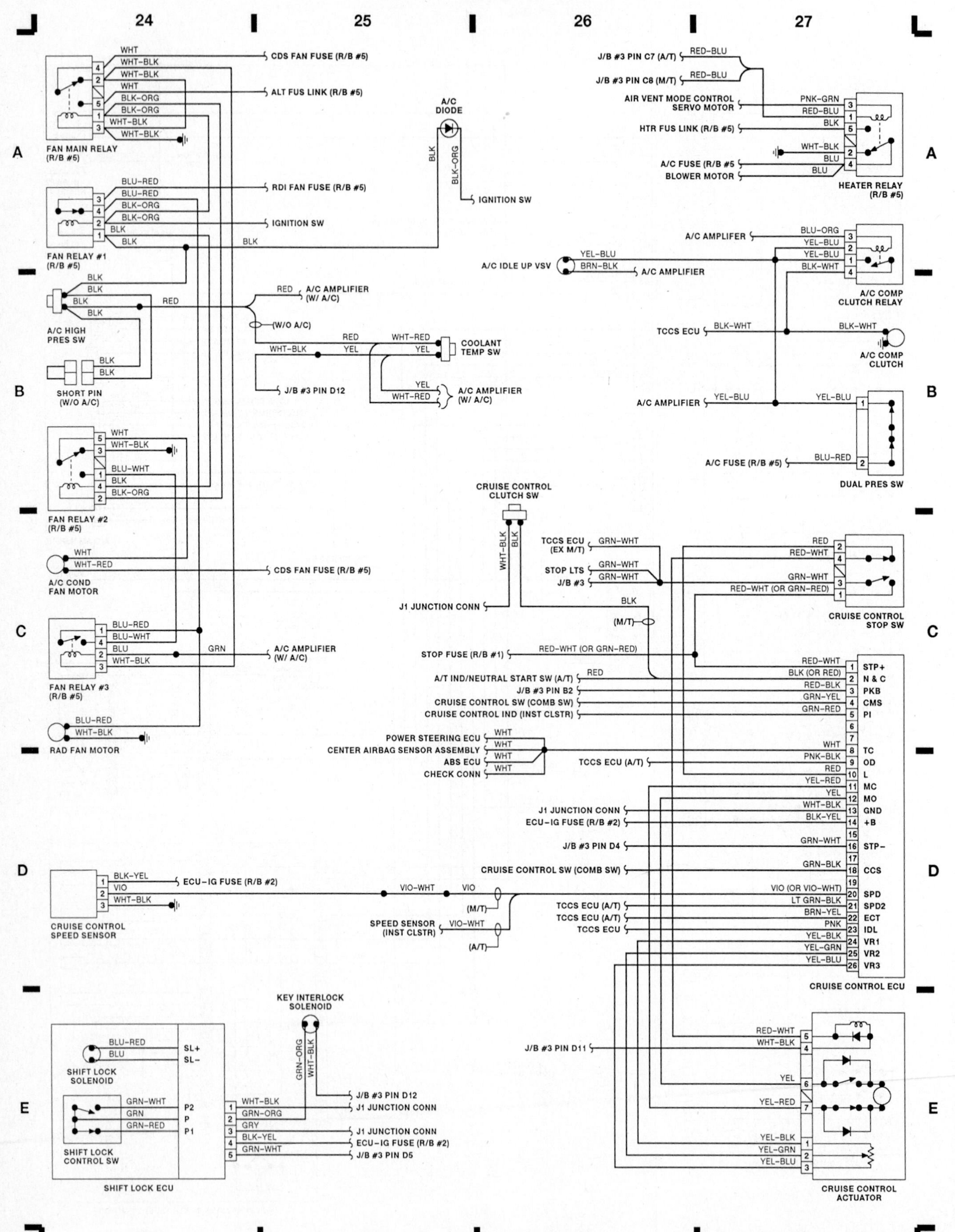

# 1991 WIRING DIAGRAMS MR2 (Cont.)

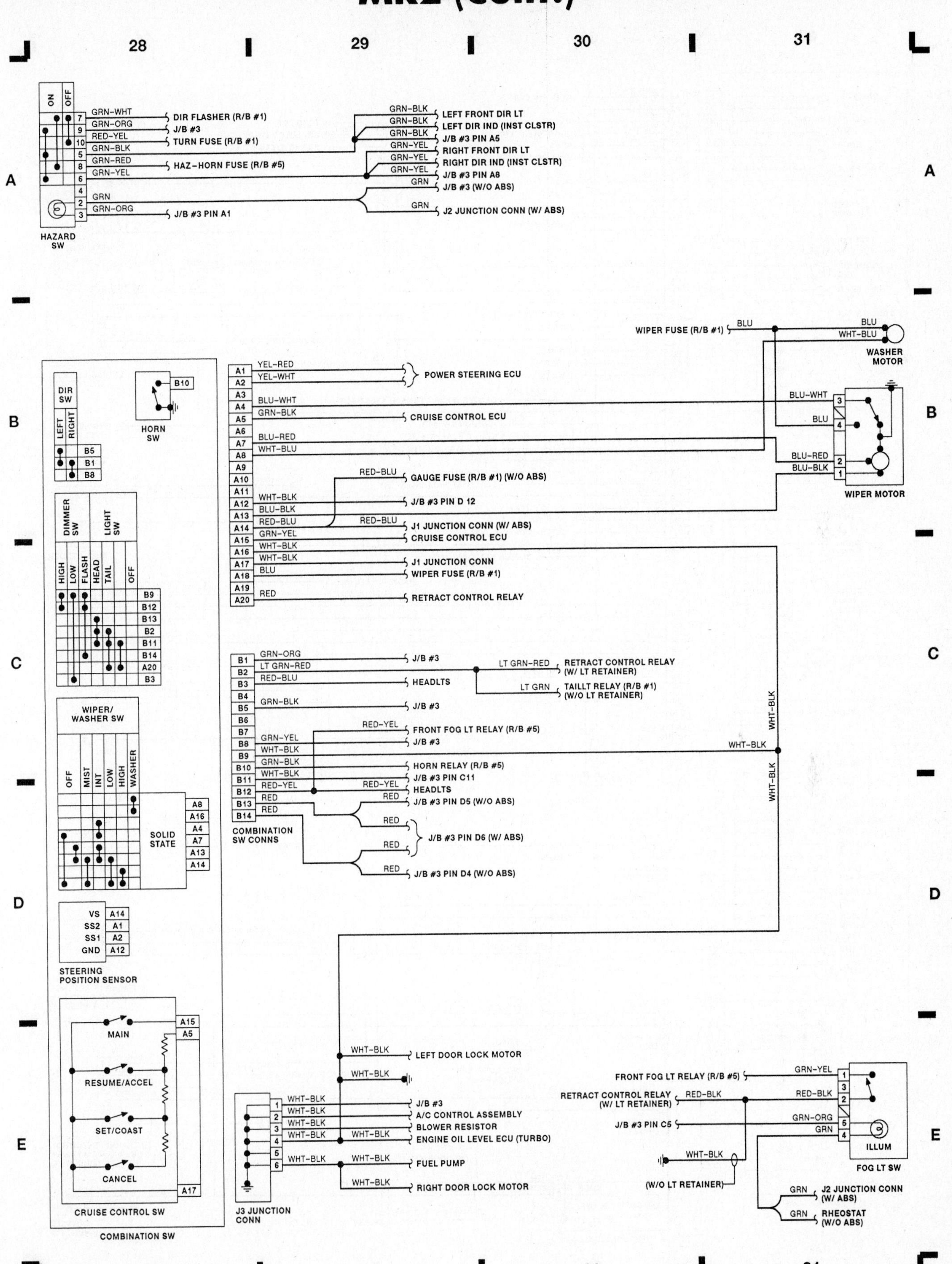

# 1991 WIRING DIAGRAMS
# MR2 (Cont.)

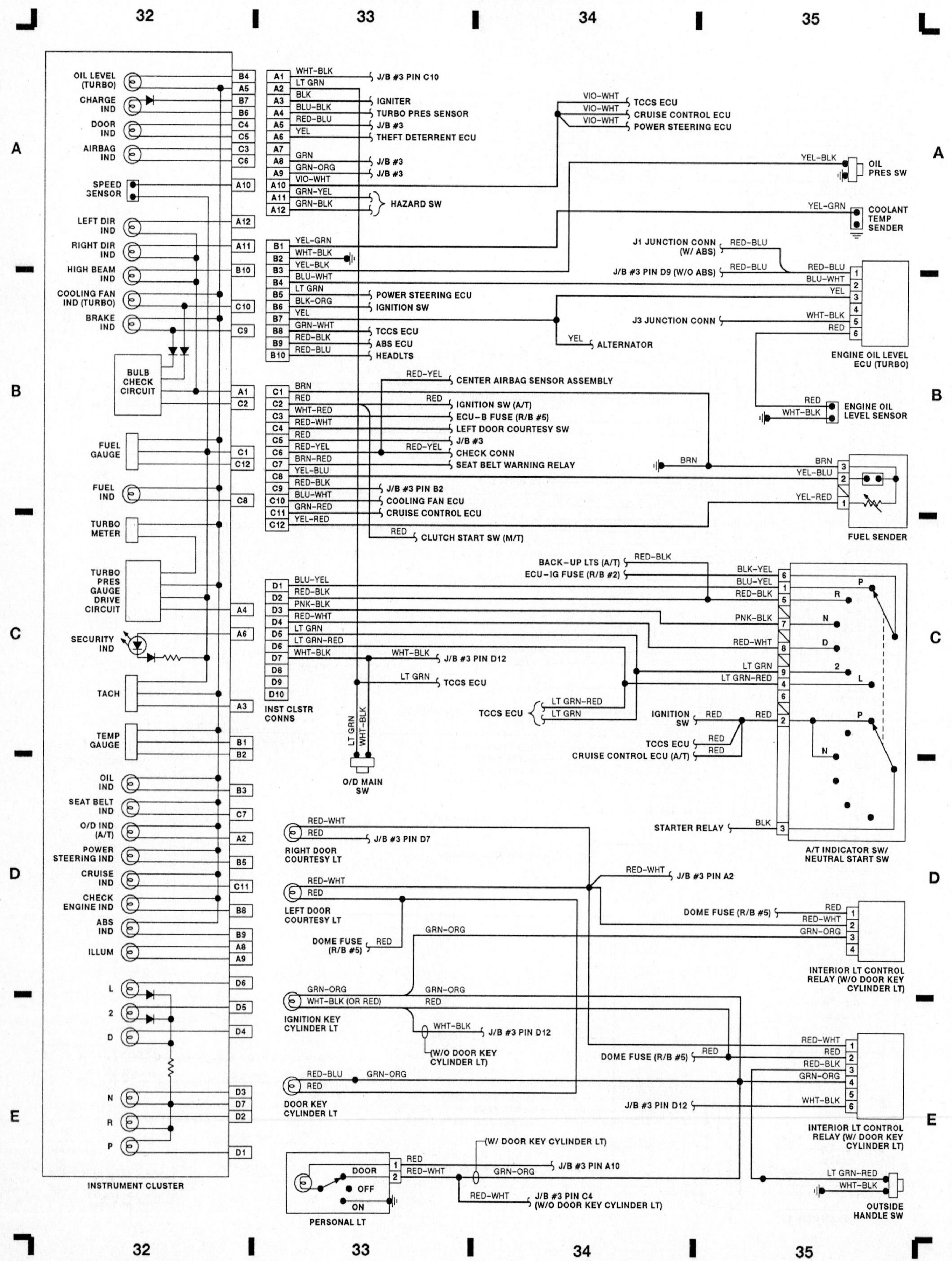

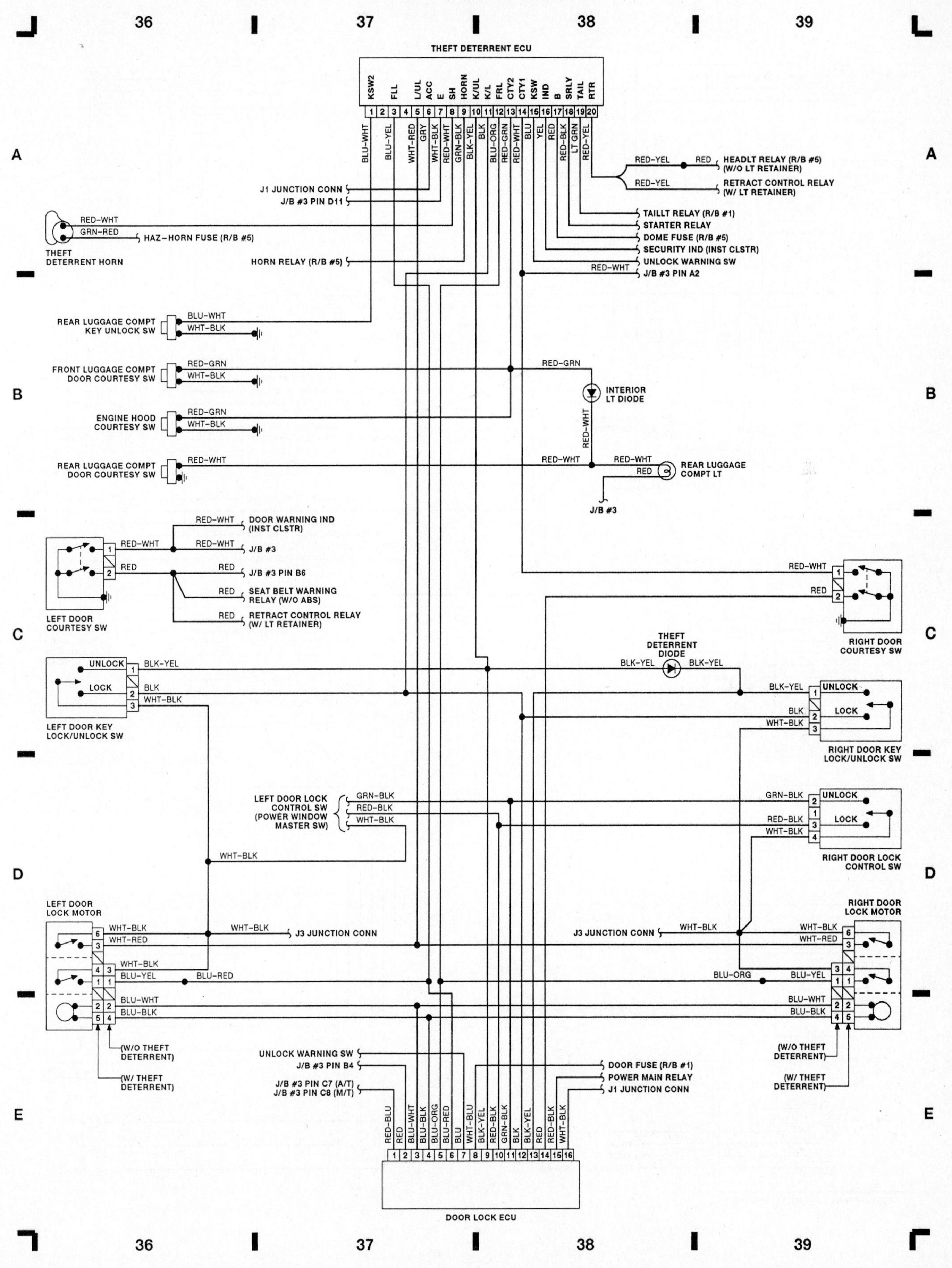
THEFT DETERRENT ECU
KSW2 FLL L/UL ACC E SH HORN K/UL K/L FRL CTY2 CTY1 KSW IND B SRLY TAIL RTR
HEADLT RELAY (R/B #5) (W/O LT RETAINER)
RETRACT CONTROL RELAY (W/ LT RETAINER)
J1 JUNCTION CONN
J/B #3 PIN D11
THEFT DETERRENT HORN
HAZ-HORN FUSE (R/B #5)
HORN RELAY (R/B #5)
TAILLT RELAY (R/B #1)
STARTER RELAY
DOME FUSE (R/B #5)
SECURITY IND (INST CLSTR)
UNLOCK WARNING SW
J/B #3 PIN A2
REAR LUGGAGE COMPT KEY UNLOCK SW
FRONT LUGGAGE COMPT DOOR COURTESY SW
INTERIOR LT DIODE
ENGINE HOOD COURTESY SW
REAR LUGGAGE COMPT DOOR COURTESY SW
REAR LUGGAGE COMPT LT
J/B #3
DOOR WARNING IND (INST CLSTR)
J/B #3
J/B #3 PIN B6
SEAT BELT WARNING RELAY (W/O ABS)
RETRACT CONTROL RELAY (W/ LT RETAINER)
LEFT DOOR COURTESY SW
RIGHT DOOR COURTESY SW
THEFT DETERRENT DIODE
UNLOCK
LOCK
LEFT DOOR KEY LOCK/UNLOCK SW
RIGHT DOOR KEY LOCK/UNLOCK SW
LEFT DOOR LOCK CONTROL SW (POWER WINDOW MASTER SW)
RIGHT DOOR LOCK CONTROL SW
LEFT DOOR LOCK MOTOR
RIGHT DOOR LOCK MOTOR
J3 JUNCTION CONN
(W/O THEFT DETERRENT)
(W/ THEFT DETERRENT)
UNLOCK WARNING SW
J/B #3 PIN B4
J/B #3 PIN C7 (A/T)
J/B #3 PIN C8 (M/T)
DOOR FUSE (R/B #1)
POWER MAIN RELAY
J1 JUNCTION CONN
DOOR LOCK ECU

# 1991 WIRING DIAGRAMS
# MR2 (Cont.)

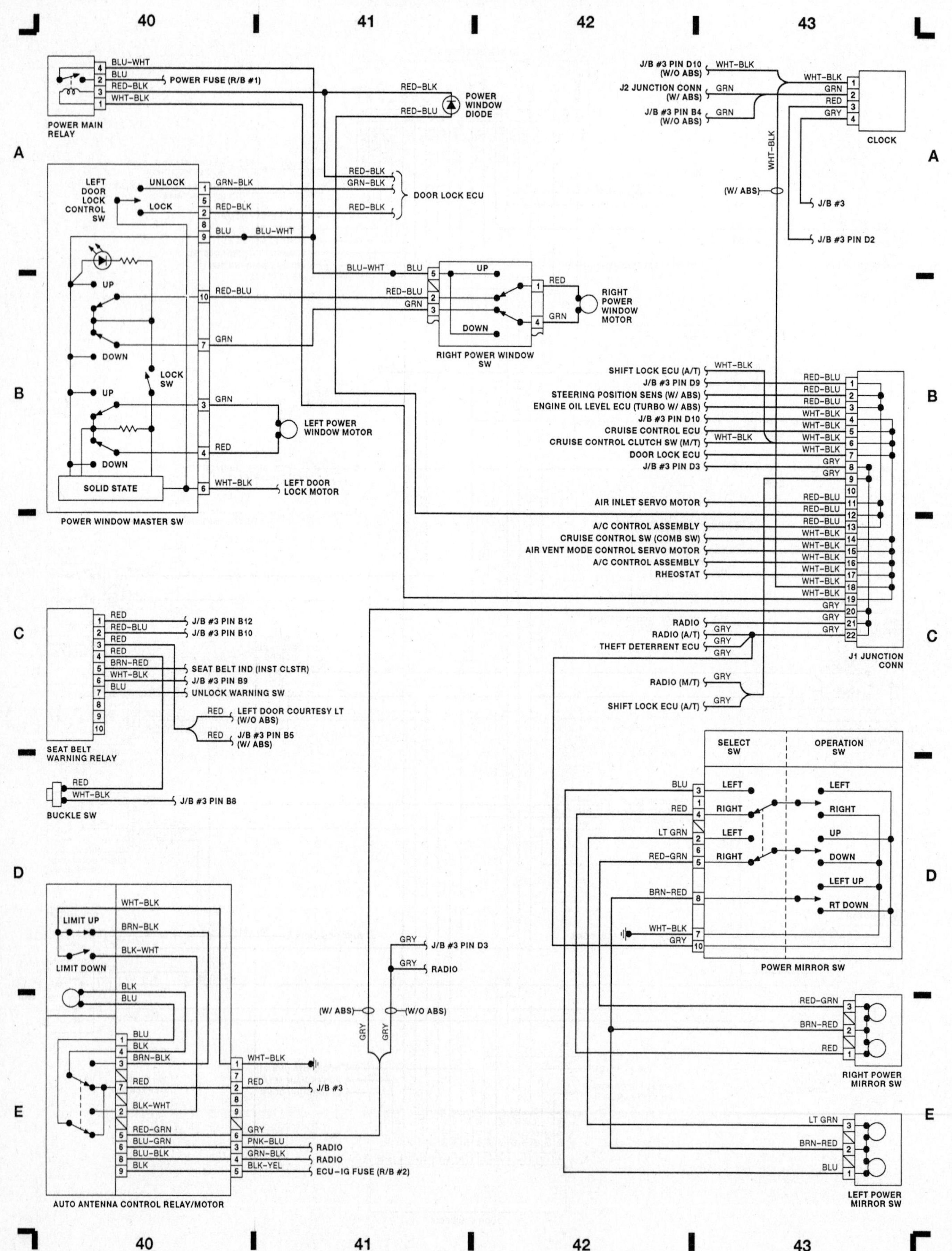

# 1991 WIRING DIAGRAMS
# MR2 (Cont.)

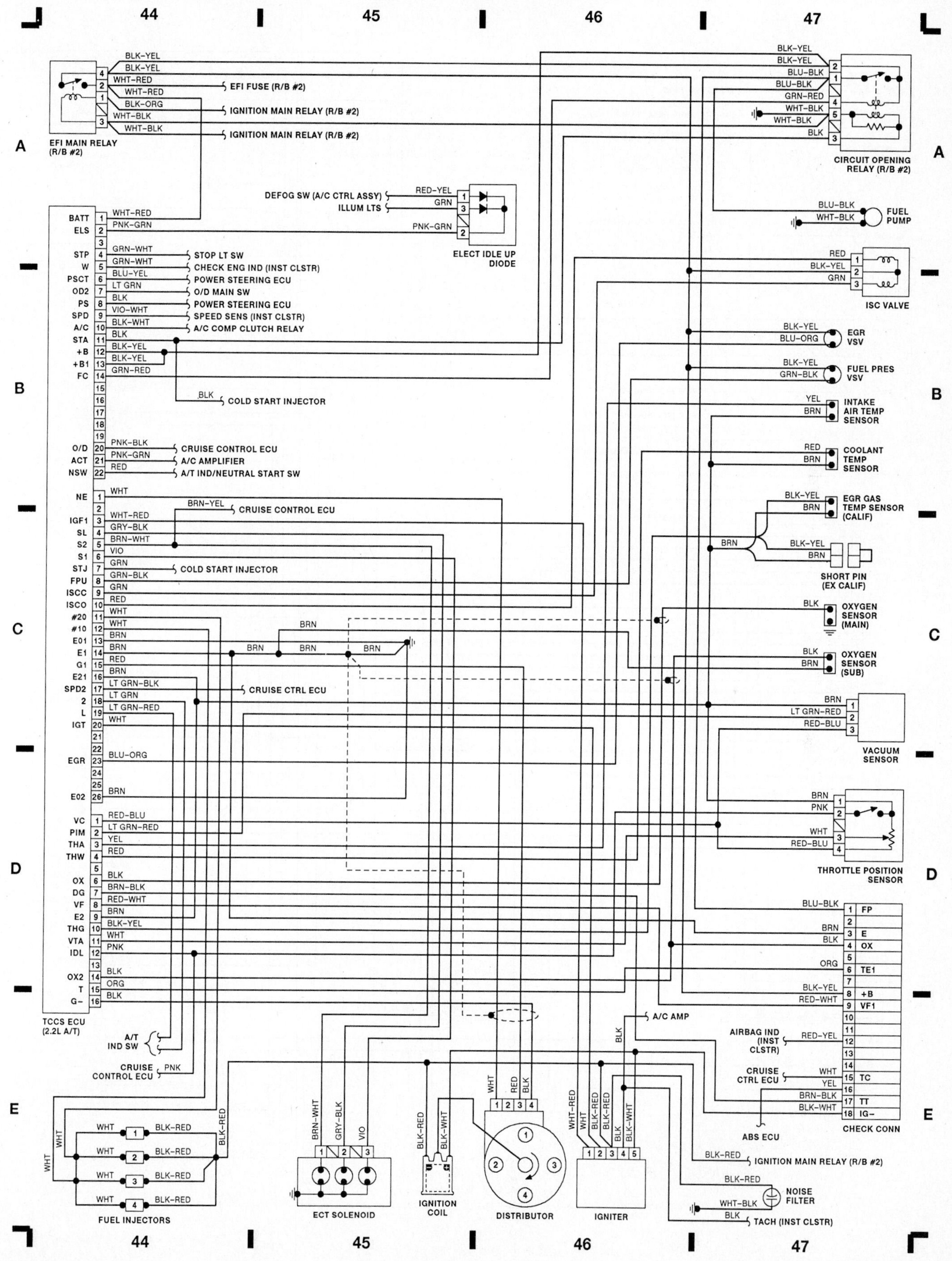

# 1991 WIRING DIAGRAMS
# MR2 (Cont.)

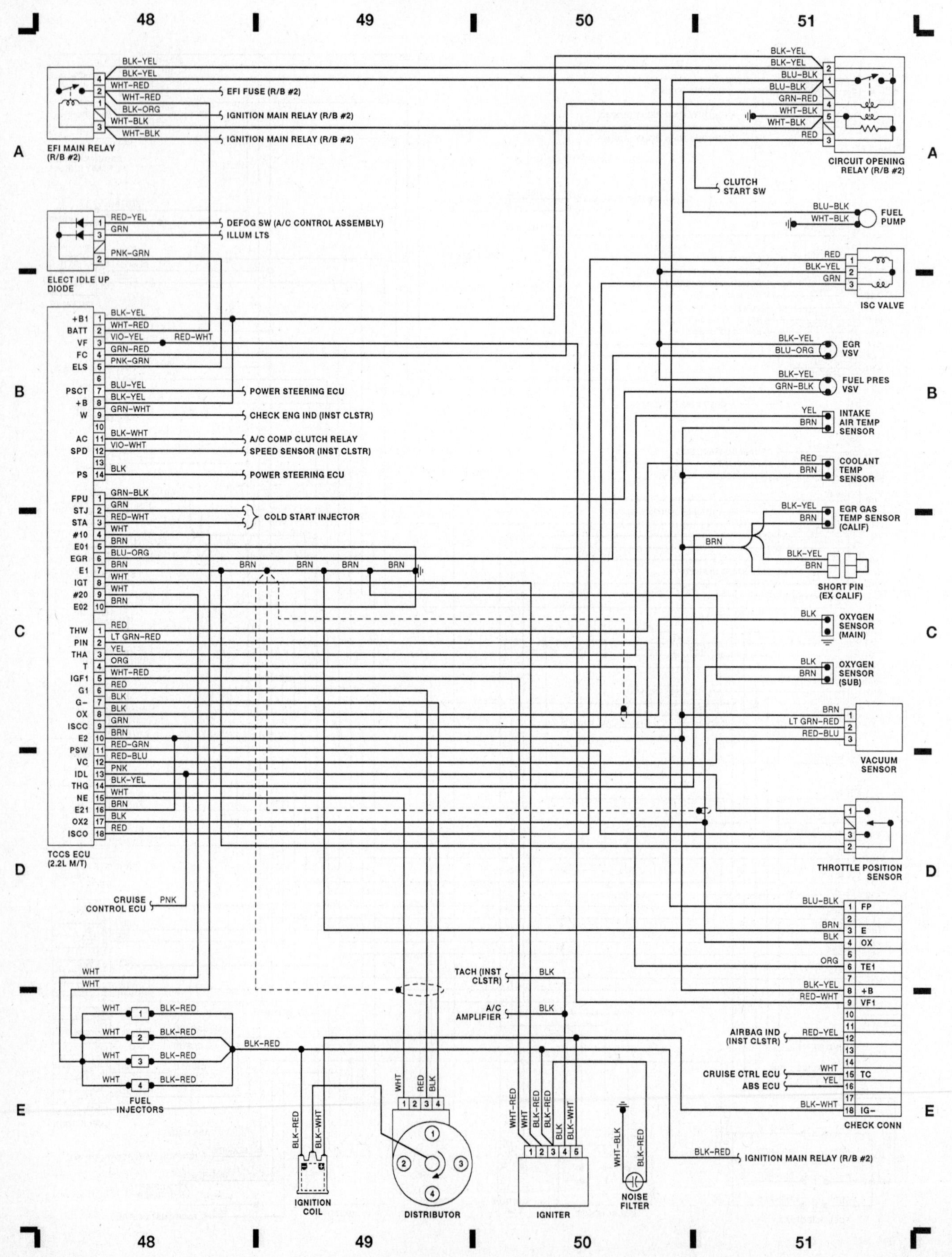

# 1991 WIRING DIAGRAMS
# MR2 (Cont.)



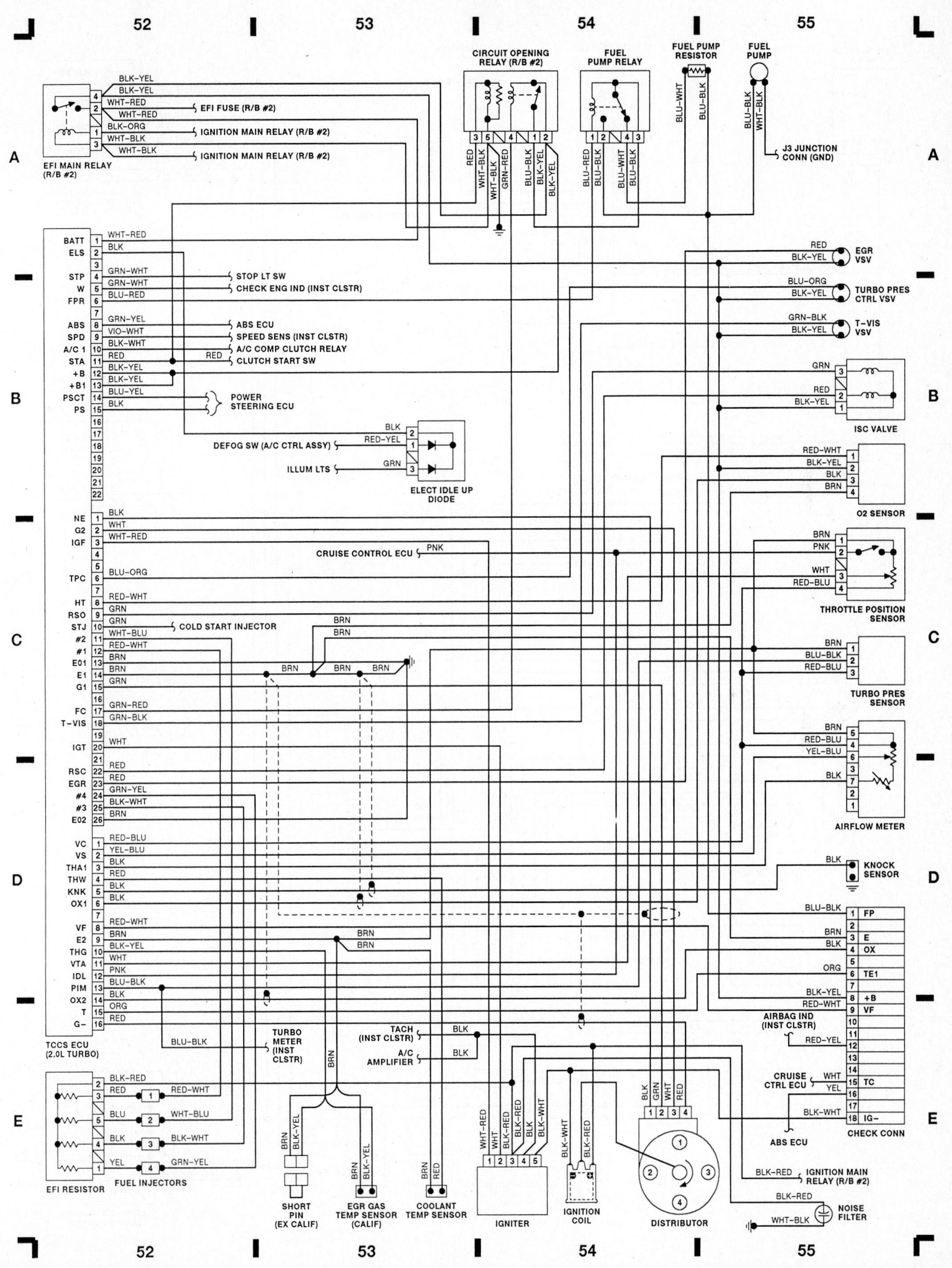

# 1991 WIRING DIAGRAMS
# MR2 (Cont.)

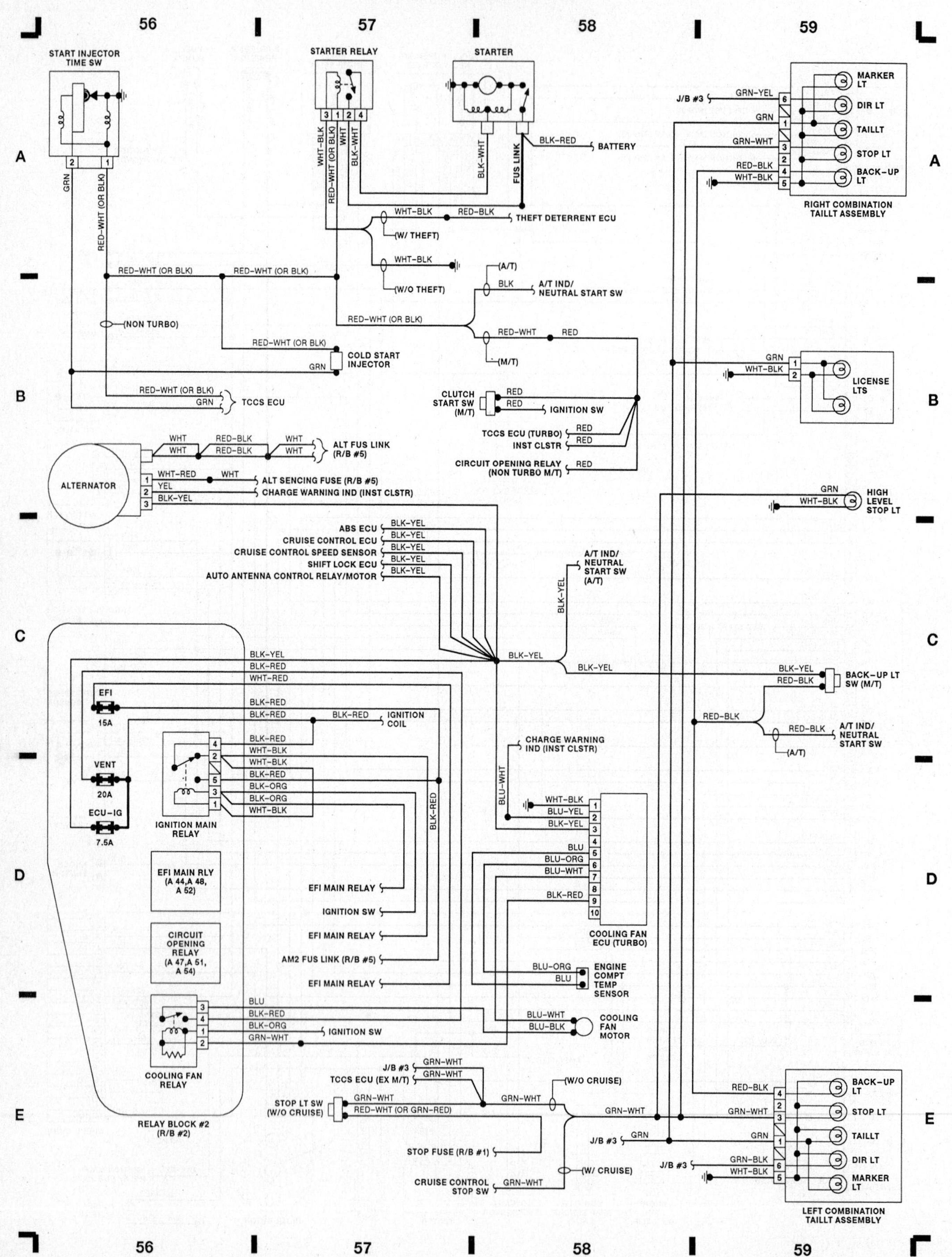

# 1991 WIRING DIAGRAMS
# Pickup

## COMPONENT LOCATOR:

| | |
|---|---|
| A/C AMPLIFIER | D–E 3 |
| A/C CUT RELAY (4WD V6 A/T) | D 2 |
| A/C SW | C–D 3 |
| A/T INDICATOR SW (W/ ECT) | D–E 34–35 |
| A/T INDICATOR SW (W/O ECT) | D–E 32–33 |
| AIRFLOW METER | A 10, A 14, A 18, A 22 |
| ALTERNATOR | C 3 |
| ANTI-LOCK BRAKE SYSTEM (ABS) | B–C 34–35 |
| AUTO ANTENNA RELAY | B 36 |
| AUTO DISCONNECT DIFFERENTIAL (ADD) (A/T) | A 32–33 |
| AUTO DISCONNECT DIFFERENTIAL (ADD) (M/T) | C 32 |
| BACK-UP LT RELAY | E 33–34 |
| BATTERY | A 2 |
| BUCKLE SW | E 24 |
| CIG LIGHTER | E 27 |
| CIRCUIT OPENING RELAY (4 CYL W/ ECT) | A 14–15 |
| CIRCUIT OPENING RELAY (4 CYL W/O ECT) | A 10–11 |
| CIRCUIT OPENING RELAY (V6 A/T) | A 22–23 |
| CIRCUIT OPENING RELAY (V6 M/T) | A 18–19 |
| CLOCK | E 27 |
| CLUTCH START CANCEL SW (M/T) | A–B 2 |
| CRUISE CONTROL ACTUATOR | A–B 31 |
| CRUISE CONTROL ECU | A–B 28–31 |
| CRUISE CONTROL MAIN RELAY | B 31 |
| DIR SW | D 31 |
| DOOR CONTROL RELAY | D 40–41 |
| ECT PATTERN SELECT SW | D 36 |
| EFI MAIN RELAY (4 CYL) | A 11, A 15 |
| EFI MAIN RELAY (V6) | A 19, A 23 |
| FUEL INJECTORS | E 8, E 12, E 16, E 20 |
| FUEL PUMP | A 11, A 15, A 19, A 23 |
| FUEL SENDER | E 36 |
| HAZARD SW | E 30–31 |
| HEADLT RELAY | C 6 |
| HEADLT SW | C–D 31 |
| HEATER BLOWER SW | A 34 |
| HORN SW | E 28 |
| IGNITION COIL (4 CYL W/ ECT) | E 14–15 |
| IGNITION COIL (4 CYL W/O ECT) | E 9–10 |
| IGNITION COIL (V6 A/T) | E 22–23 |
| IGNITION COIL (V6 M/T) | E 17–18 |
| IGNITION KEY CYL LT | E 24 |
| IGNITION SW | A 27 |
| INSTRUMENT CLUSTER | A–E 39 |
| INTERIOR LT | A 40 |
| JUNCTION BLOCK #1 (J/B #1) | B–D 24–27 |
| LEFT DOOR SW | E 24 |
| LIGHT REMINDER RELAY/BUZZER | E 25–26 |
| OVERDRIVE RELAY | B 28 |
| POWER DOOR LOCK SYSTEM | C–E 40–42 |
| POWER MIRROR SYSTEM | B 40–41 |
| POWER WINDOW SYSTEM | C 40–41 |
| PROGRESSIVE POWER STEERING (PPS) | C 28 |
| RELAY BOX #2 (R/B #2) | C–D 5–7 |
| RELAY BOX #3 (R/B #3) | A 35 |
| RHEOSTAT | A 36 |
| RIGHT DOOR SW | E 24 |
| SHIFT LOCK CONTROL | C 28 |
| SPOT LT | A 40 |
| START INJECTOR TIME SW | B 3 |
| STARTER | A 3 |
| STARTER RELAY (M/T) | A 3 |
| STOP LT SW | A 31 |
| TCCS ECU (4 CYL W/ ECT) | A–D 12 |
| TCCS ECU (4 CYL W/O ECT) | B–D 8 |
| TCCS ECU (V6 A/T) | A–D 20 |
| TCCS ECU (V6 M/T) | A–D 16 |
| WIPER/WASHER SW RELAY | D–E 28–30 |
| 4WD INDICATOR SW (4 CYL A/T) | B 32 |
| 4WD INDICATOR SW (M/T) | C 32 |
| 4WD INDICATOR SW (V6 A/T) | B 33 |

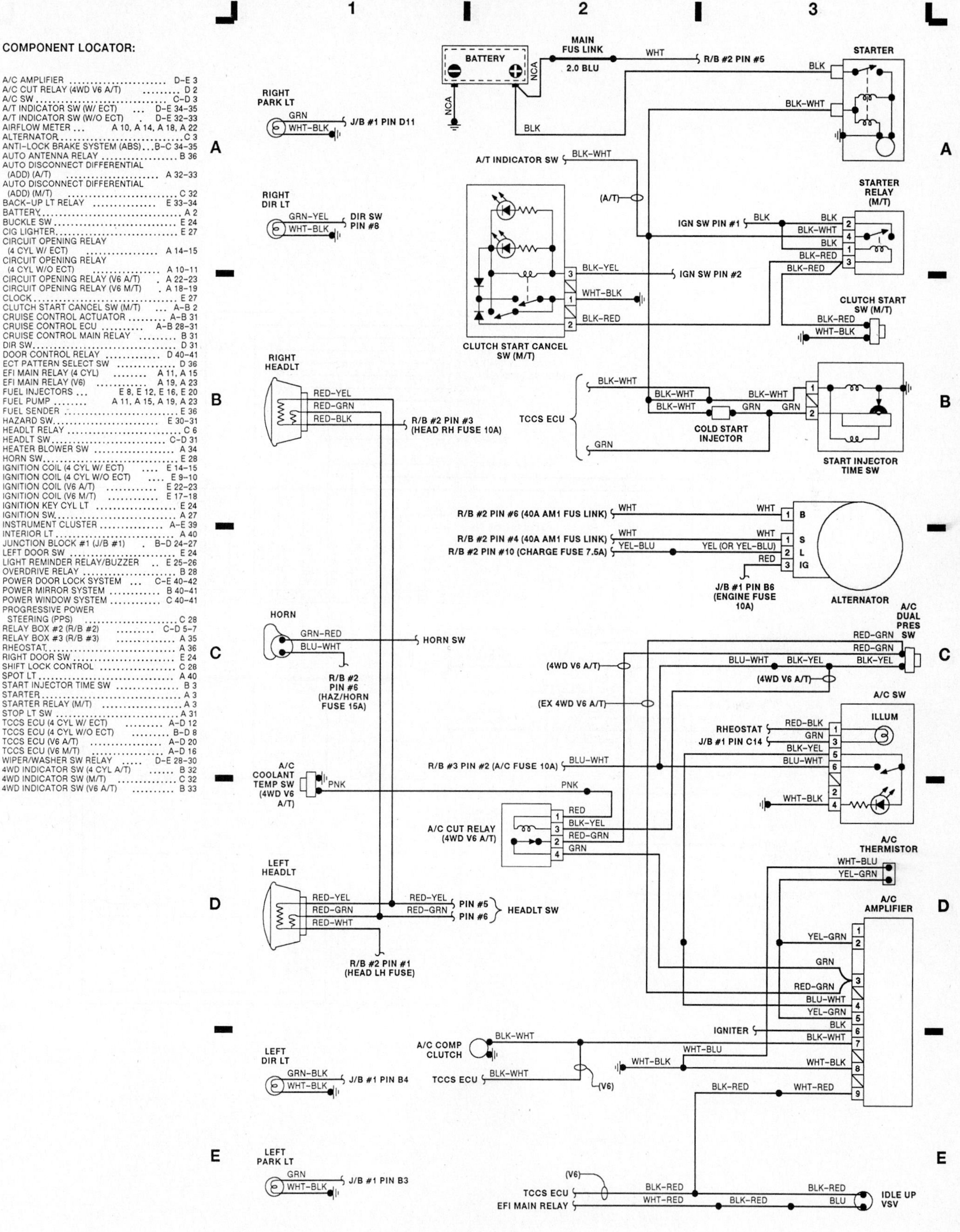

# 1991 WIRING DIAGRAMS
## Pickup (Cont.)

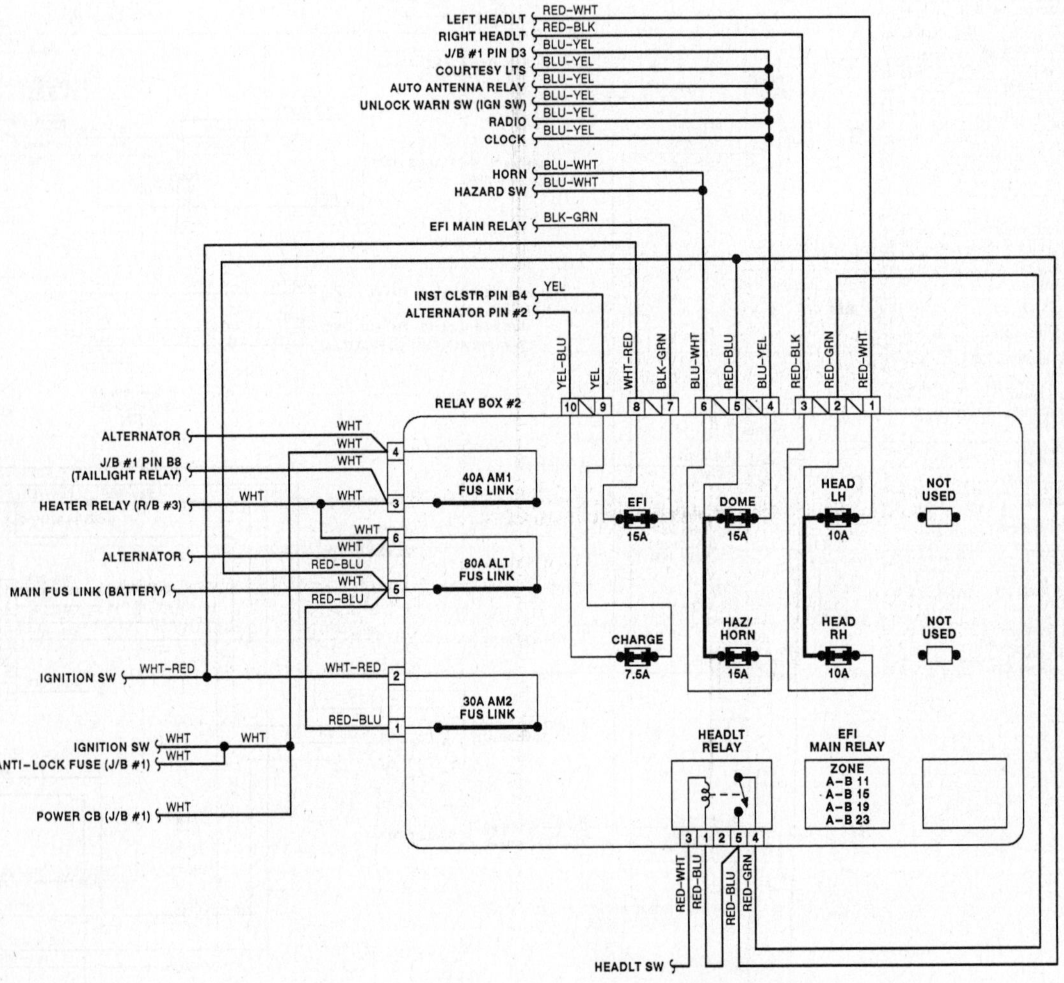

LEFT HEADLT RED-WHT
RIGHT HEADLT RED-BLK
J/B #1 PIN D3 BLU-YEL
COURTESY LTS BLU-YEL
AUTO ANTENNA RELAY BLU-YEL
UNLOCK WARN SW (IGN SW) BLU-YEL
RADIO BLU-YEL
CLOCK BLU-YEL
HORN BLU-WHT
HAZARD SW BLU-WHT
EFI MAIN RELAY BLK-GRN
INST CLSTR PIN B4 YEL
ALTERNATOR PIN #2

YEL-BLU YEL WHT-RED BLK-GRN BLU-WHT RED-BLU BLU-YEL RED-BLK RED-GRN RED-WHT

RELAY BOX #2

ALTERNATOR WHT
J/B #1 PIN B8 (TAILLIGHT RELAY) WHT
HEATER RELAY (R/B #3) WHT
ALTERNATOR RED-BLU
MAIN FUS LINK (BATTERY) WHT RED-BLU
IGNITION SW WHT-RED
IGNITION SW WHT
REAR ANTI-LOCK FUSE (J/B #1) WHT
POWER CB (J/B #1) WHT

40A AM1 FUS LINK
80A ALT FUS LINK
30A AM2 FUS LINK

EFI 15A
DOME 15A
HEAD LH 10A
NOT USED
CHARGE 7.5A
HAZ/ HORN 15A
HEAD RH 10A
NOT USED

HEADLT RELAY
EFI MAIN RELAY

ZONE
A-B 11
A-B 15
A-B 19
A-B 23

RED-WHT RED-BLU RED-BLU RED-GRN

HEADLT SW

A B C D E
4 5 6 7

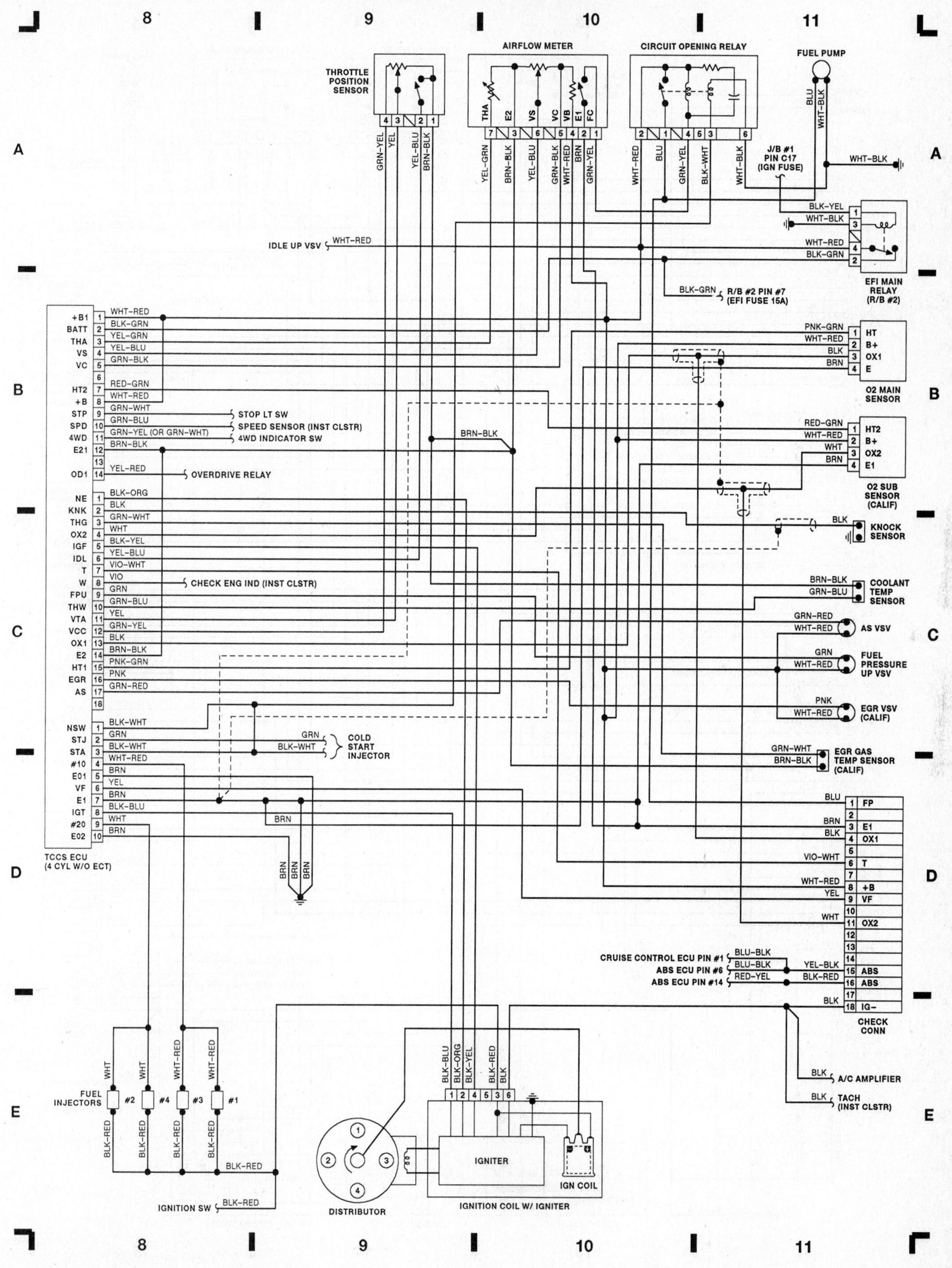

8
9
10
11
A
B
C
D
E
THROTTLE POSITION SENSOR
AIRFLOW METER
THA
E2
VS
VC
VB
E1
FC
CIRCUIT OPENING RELAY
FUEL PUMP
GRN-YEL
YEL
YEL-BLU
BRN-BLK
YEL-GRN
BRN-BLK
YEL-BLU
GRN-BLK
WHT-RED
BRN
GRN-YEL
WHT-RED
BLU
GRN-YEL
BLK-WHT
WHT-BLK
BLU
WHT-BLK
J/B #1 PIN C17 (IGN FUSE)
WHT-BLK
IDLE UP VSV
WHT-RED
BLK-YEL
WHT-BLK
WHT-RED
BLK-GRN
EFI MAIN RELAY (R/B #2)
BLK-GRN
R/B #2 PIN #7 (EFI FUSE 15A)
+B1
BATT
THA
VS
VC
HT2
+B
STP
SPD
4WD
E21
OD1
WHT-RED
BLK-GRN
YEL-GRN
YEL-BLU
GRN-BLK
RED-GRN
WHT-RED
GRN-WHT
GRN-BLU
GRN-YEL (OR GRN-WHT)
BRN-BLK
YEL-RED
STOP LT SW
SPEED SENSOR (INST CLSTR)
4WD INDICATOR SW
OVERDRIVE RELAY
PNK-GRN
WHT-RED
BLK
BRN
HT
B+
OX1
E
O2 MAIN SENSOR
BRN-BLK
RED-GRN
WHT-RED
WHT
BRN
HT2
B+
OX2
E1
O2 SUB SENSOR (CALIF)
NE
KNK
THG
OX2
IGF
IDL
T
W
FPU
THW
VTA
VCC
OX1
E2
HT1
EGR
AS
BLK-ORG
BLK
GRN-WHT
WHT
BLK-YEL
YEL-BLU
VIO-WHT
VIO
GRN
GRN-BLU
YEL
GRN-YEL
BLK
BRN-BLK
PNK-GRN
PNK
GRN-RED
CHECK ENG IND (INST CLSTR)
BLK
KNOCK SENSOR
BRN-BLK
GRN-BLU
COOLANT TEMP SENSOR
GRN-RED
WHT-RED
AS VSV
GRN
WHT-RED
FUEL PRESSURE UP VSV
PNK
WHT-RED
EGR VSV (CALIF)
NSW
STJ
STA
#10
E01
VF
E1
IGT
#20
E02
BLK-WHT
GRN
BLK-WHT
WHT-RED
BRN
YEL
BRN
BLK-BLU
WHT
BRN
GRN
BLK-WHT
COLD START INJECTOR
GRN-WHT
BRN-BLK
EGR GAS TEMP SENSOR (CALIF)
TCCS ECU (4 CYL W/O ECT)
BRN
BLU
BRN
BLK
VIO-WHT
WHT-RED
YEL
WHT
FP
E1
OX1
T
+B
VF
OX2
CRUISE CONTROL ECU PIN #1
ABS ECU PIN #6
ABS ECU PIN #14
BLU-BLK
BLU-BLK
RED-YEL
YEL-BLK
BLK-RED
BLK
ABS
ABS
IG–
CHECK CONN
BLK
A/C AMPLIFIER
BLK
TACH (INST CLSTR)
FUEL INJECTORS
#2
#4
#3
#1
WHT
WHT
WHT-RED
WHT-RED
BLK-RED
BLK-RED
IGNITION SW
BLK-BLU
BLK-ORG
BLK-YEL
BLK-RED
BLK
IGNITER
IGN COIL
DISTRIBUTOR
IGNITION COIL W/ IGNITER

# 1991 WIRING DIAGRAMS
## Pickup (Cont.)

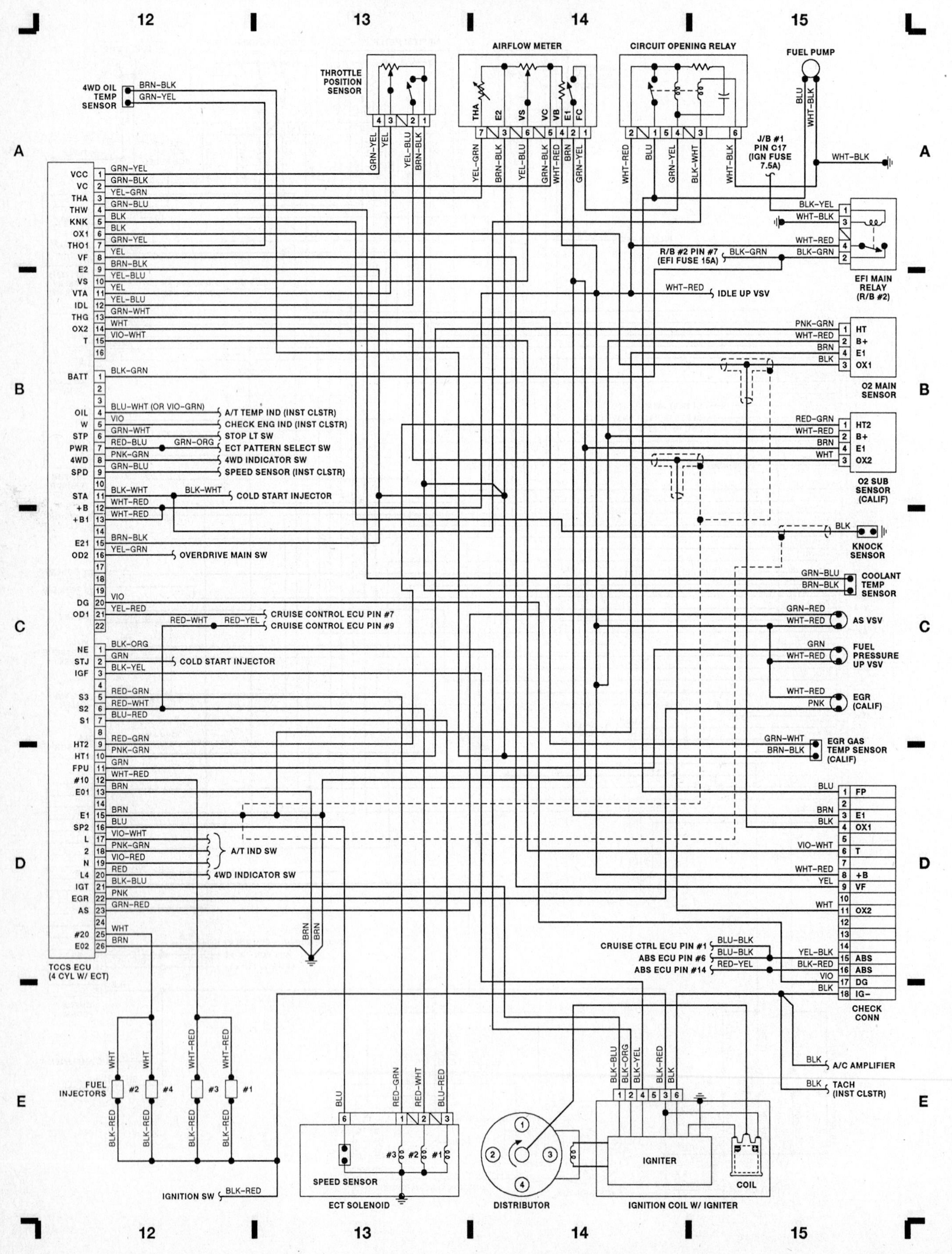

# 1991 WIRING DIAGRAMS
## Pickup (Cont.)

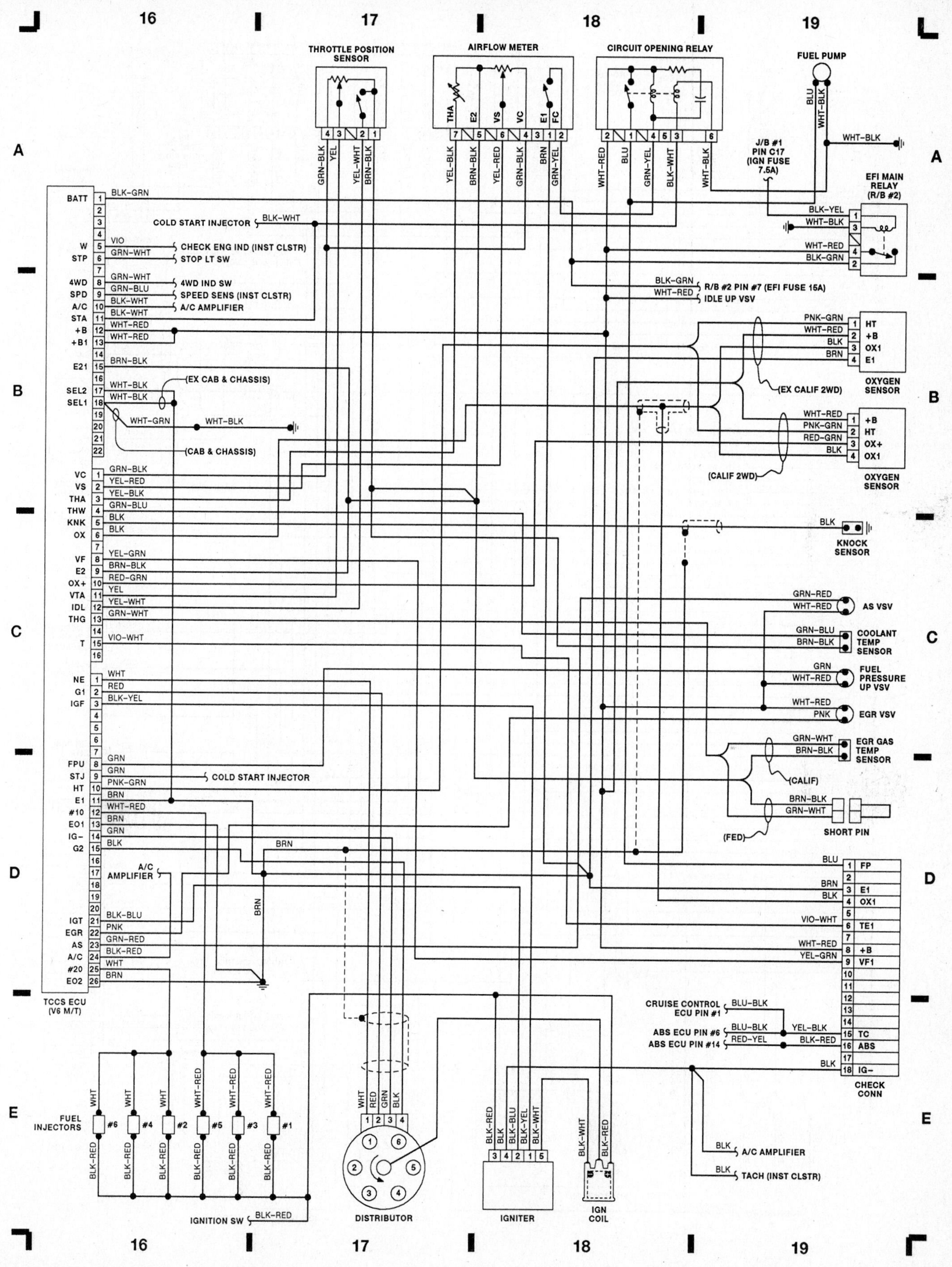

# 1991 WIRING DIAGRAMS
## Pickup (Cont.)

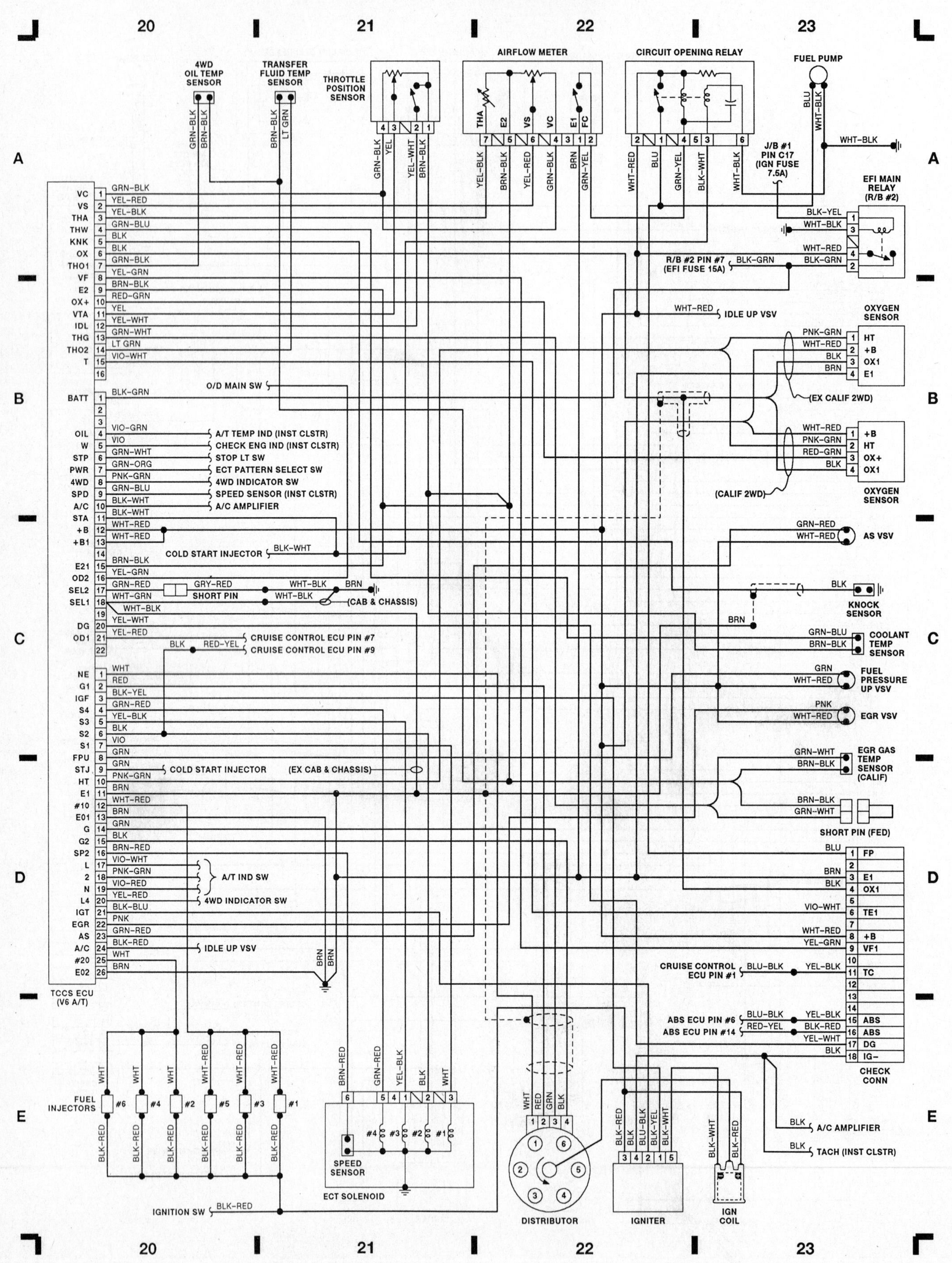

# 1991 WIRING DIAGRAMS
## Pickup (Cont.)

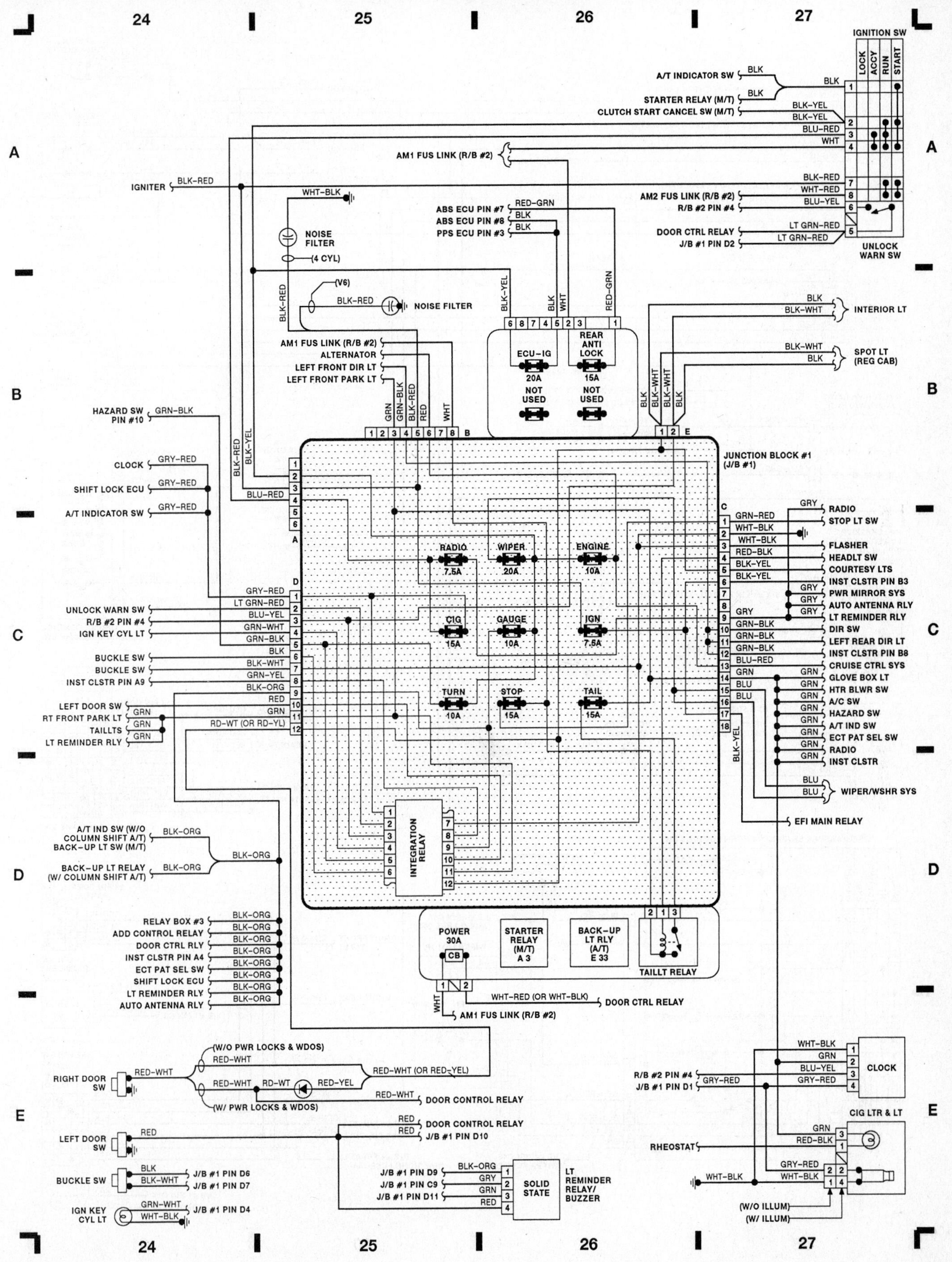

# 1991 WIRING DIAGRAMS
## Pickup (Cont.)

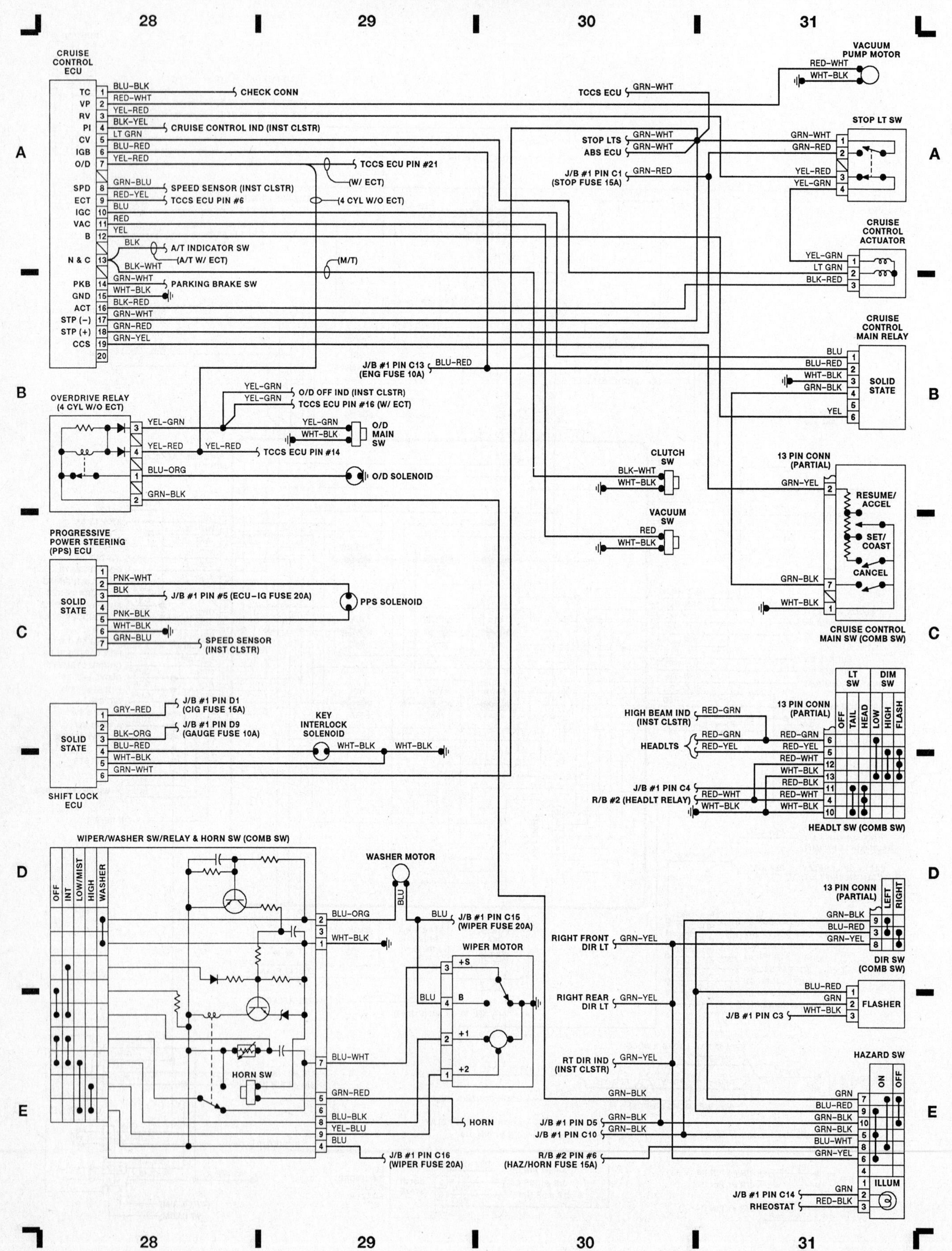

# 1991 WIRING DIAGRAMS
## Pickup (Cont.)

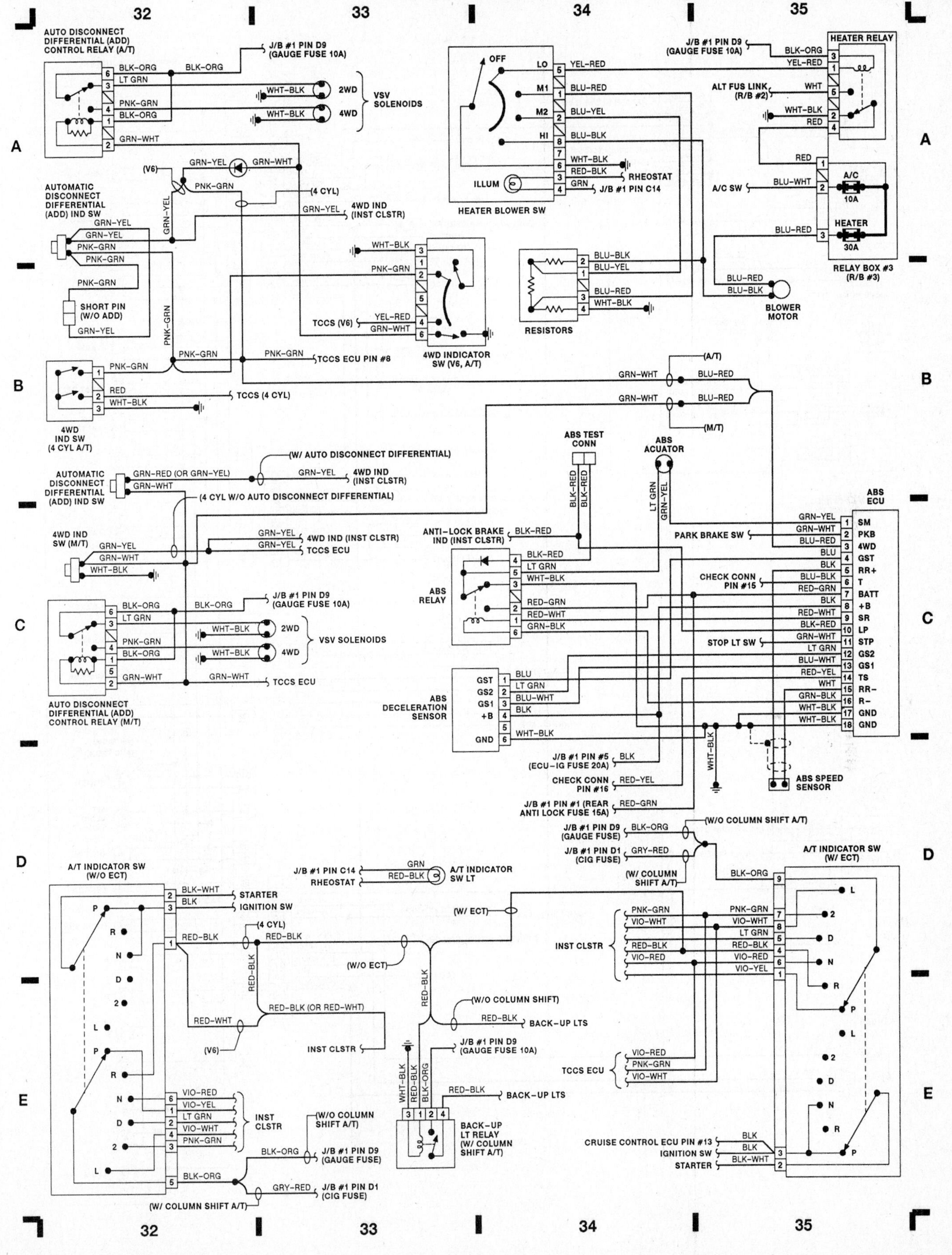

# 1991 WIRING DIAGRAMS
## Pickup (Cont.)

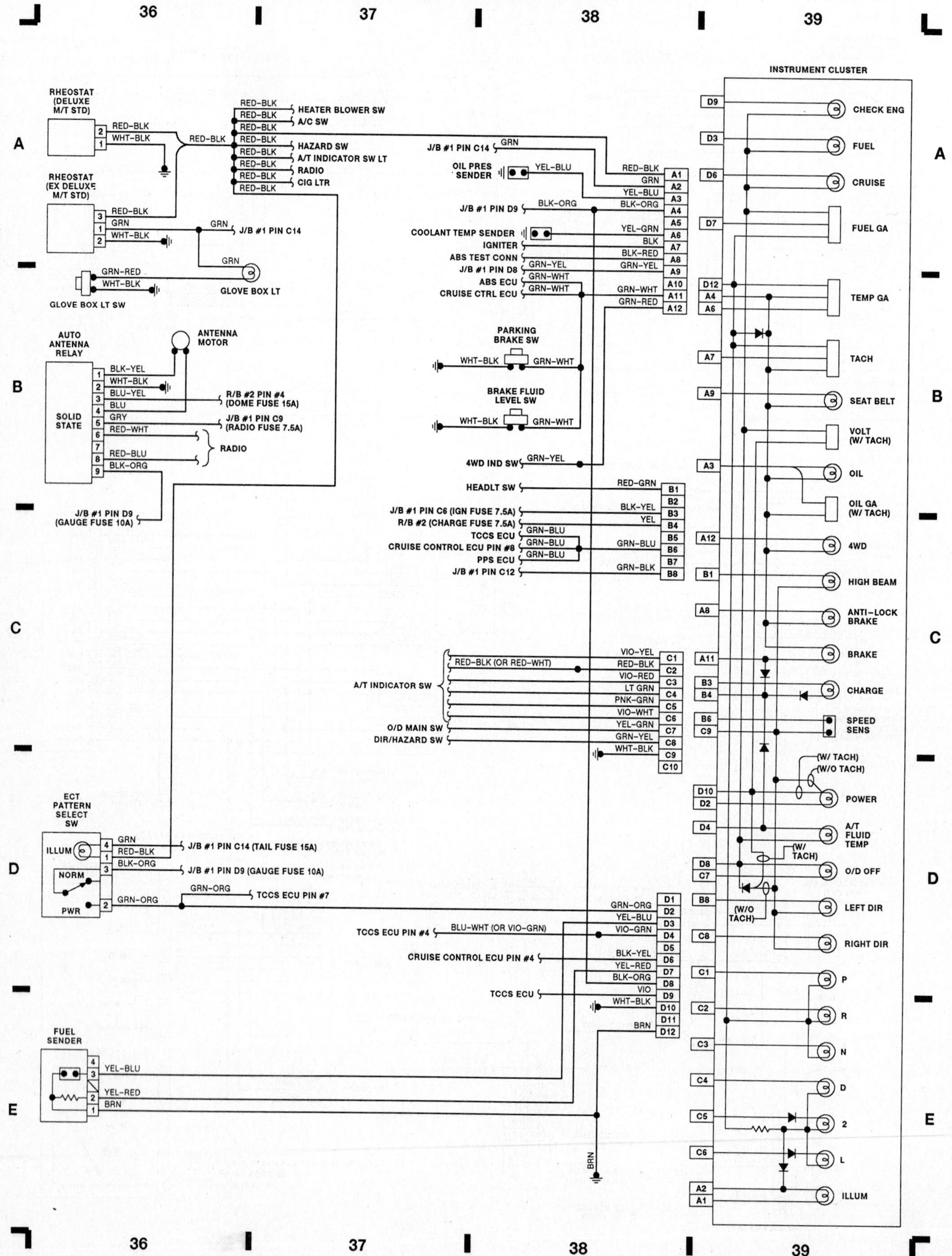

# 1991 WIRING DIAGRAMS
## Pickup (Cont.)

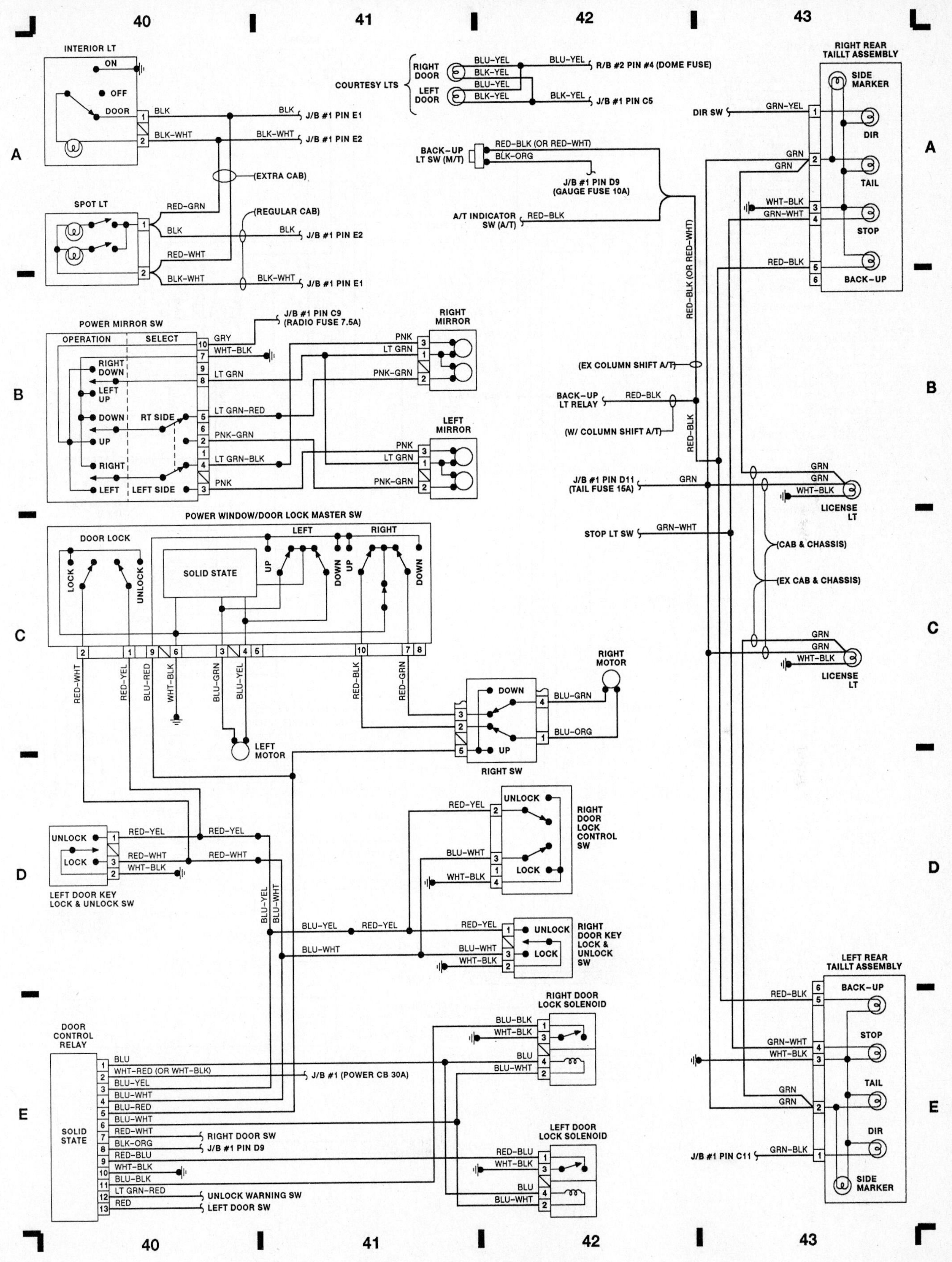

# 1991 WIRING DIAGRAMS
# Previa

**COMPONENT LOCATOR:**

A/C AMPLIFIER ........................... A 24
A/T INDICATOR SW ........................ A 19
ABS ECU.............................. A–C 20
ALTERNATOR.................................C 3
BACK–UP LT SW ........................ D 42
BATTERY.....................................A 2
CHECK CONNECTOR........................ E 7
CIG LTR.................................... B 39
CIRCUIT OPENING RELAY ...................A 6
CLUTCH START SW (M/T) ..................D 2
COMB SW............................. A–D 31
CRUISE CONTROL ECU .............. C–D 28
DECELERATION SENSOR ................ C 20
DIMMER SW (COMB SW) ................ B 31
DIR SW (COMB SW) ...................... E 23
DOOR LOCK CONTROL RELAY ....... B–C 40
ECT SOLENOID............................ A 19
FRONT WIPER MOTOR .................... B 30
FUEL SENDER ............................ C 35
FUSE BOX ............................... B 2–3
HAZARD SW.......................... D–E 23
HEATER BLOWER SW .................... C 27
HORN RELAY ............................. D 36
IGNITION SW.............................. B 11
INSTRUMENT CLUSTER (W/ TACHOMETER) ............ C–E 32–33
INSTRUMENT CLUSTER (W/O TACHOMETER) .......... A–C 32–33
INTERIOR LTS .................... D–E 20–23
JUNCTION BLOCK #1/ RELAY BLOCK #1 (J/B #1/ R/B #1) .. A–E 9–13
JUNCTION CONNECTOR #1 (J/C #1) . D–E 19
JUNCTION CONNECTOR #2 (J/C #2) .A–C 16
JUNCTION CONNECTOR #3 (J/C #3) .B–C 19
JUNCTION CONNECTOR #4 (J/C #4) . D–E 16
JUNCTION CONNECTOR #5 (J/C #5) .C–D 16
LT RETAINER RELAY ...................... A 28
MOONROOF CONTROL RELAY ............ A 36
O/D MAIN SW ................................ A 5
PARKING BRAKE SW ............ B 35, D 35
POWER WINDOW MASTER SW ....... A 40–42
REAR WIPER CONTROL RELAY ...... D–E 40
REFRIGERATOR AMPLIFIER ............... E 24
REMOTE CONTROL MIRRORS ....... A 38–39
SEAT BELT WARNING RELAY ............ B 28
SLIDE DOOR JUNCTION SW ......... B–C 36
START INJECTOR TIME SW ...................E 3
STARTER.............................. C–D 3
STOP LT SW (W/ CRUISE CONTROL) ... D 31
STOP LT SW (W/O CRUISE CONTROL) ..................A 42
TCCS ECU (2.4L) ...................... A–E 4
THEFT DETERRENT ECU ........... E 37–38

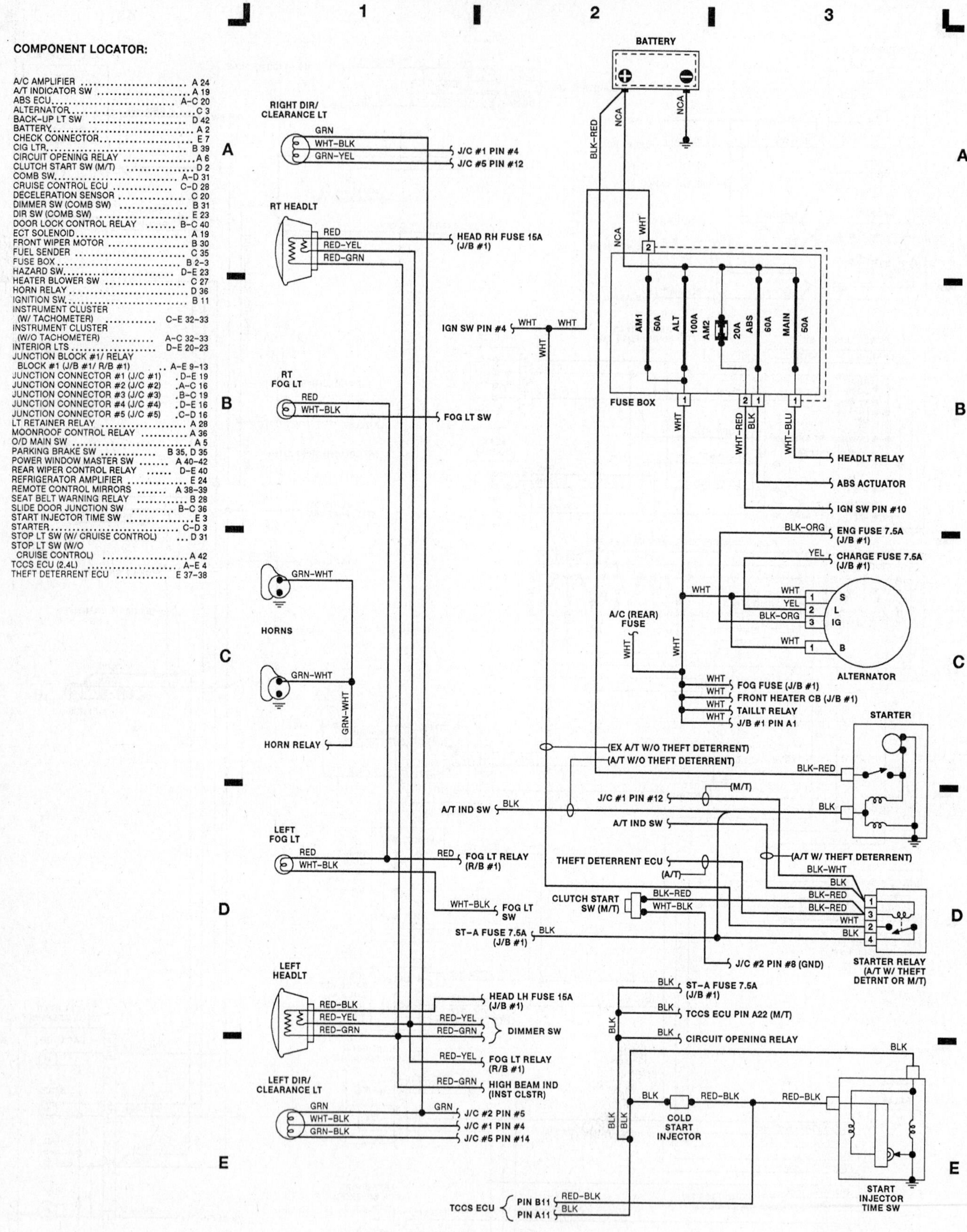

# 1991 WIRING DIAGRAMS
## Previa (Cont.)

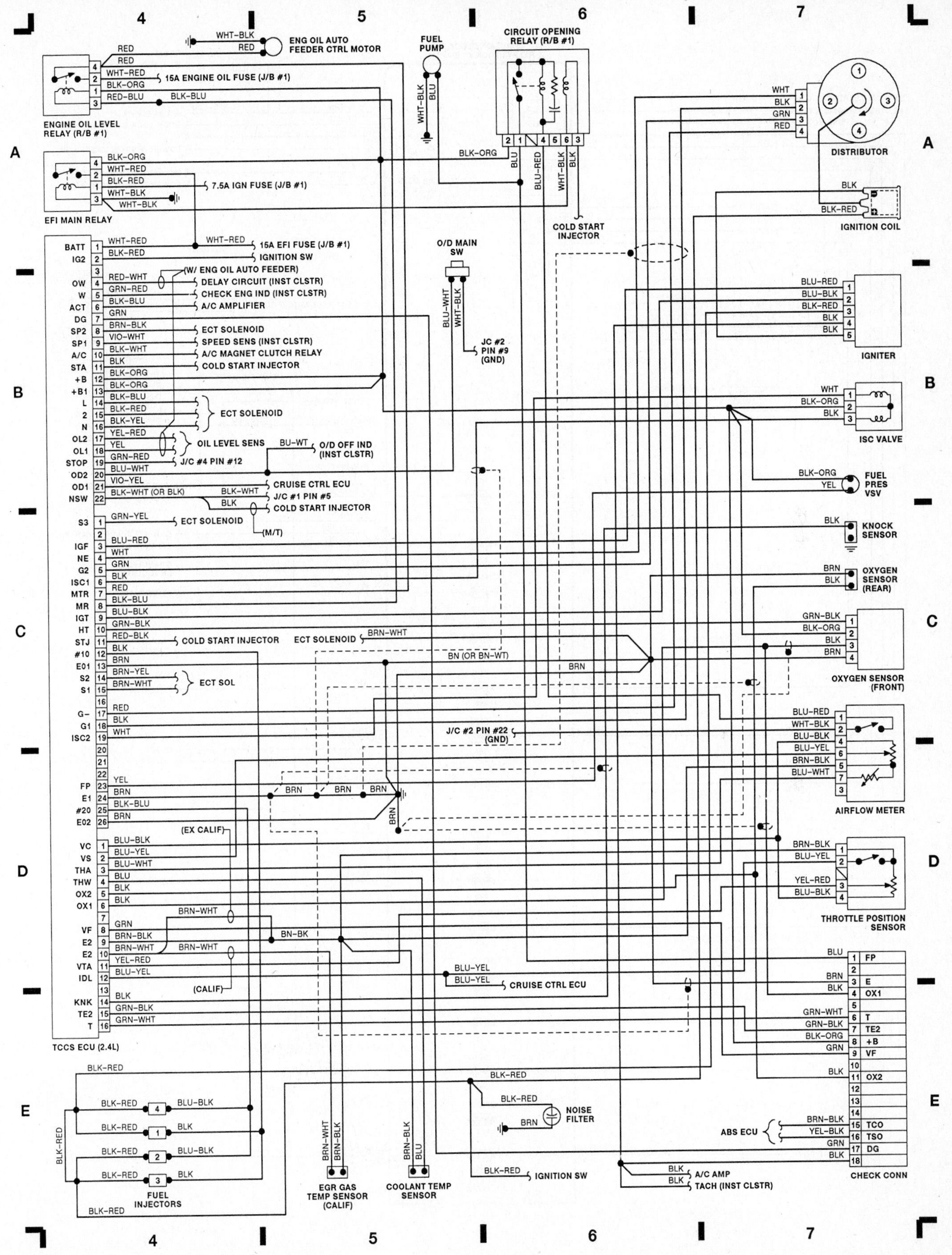

# 1991 WIRING DIAGRAMS
## Previa (Cont.)

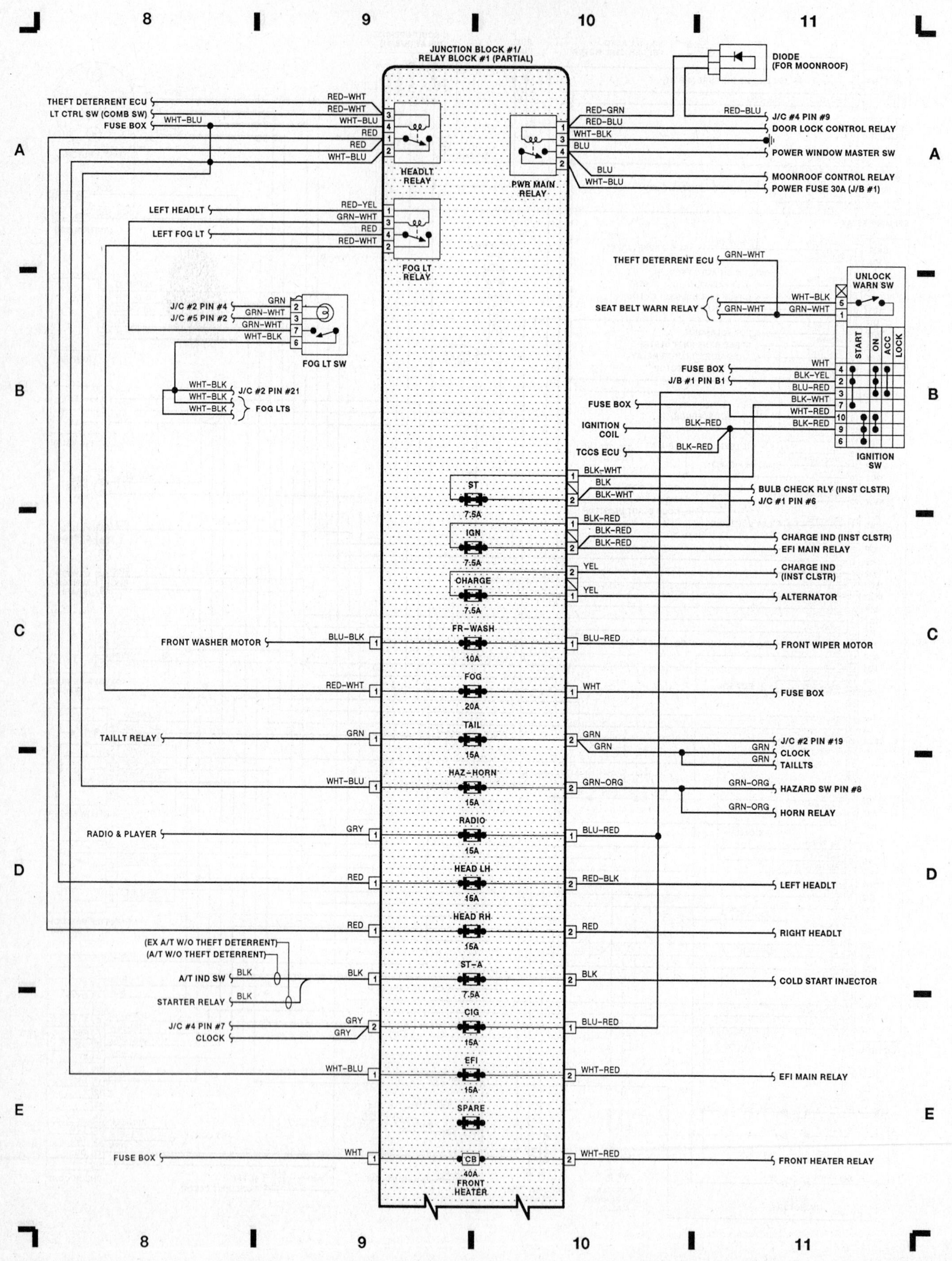

# 1991 WIRING DIAGRAMS
## Previa (Cont.)

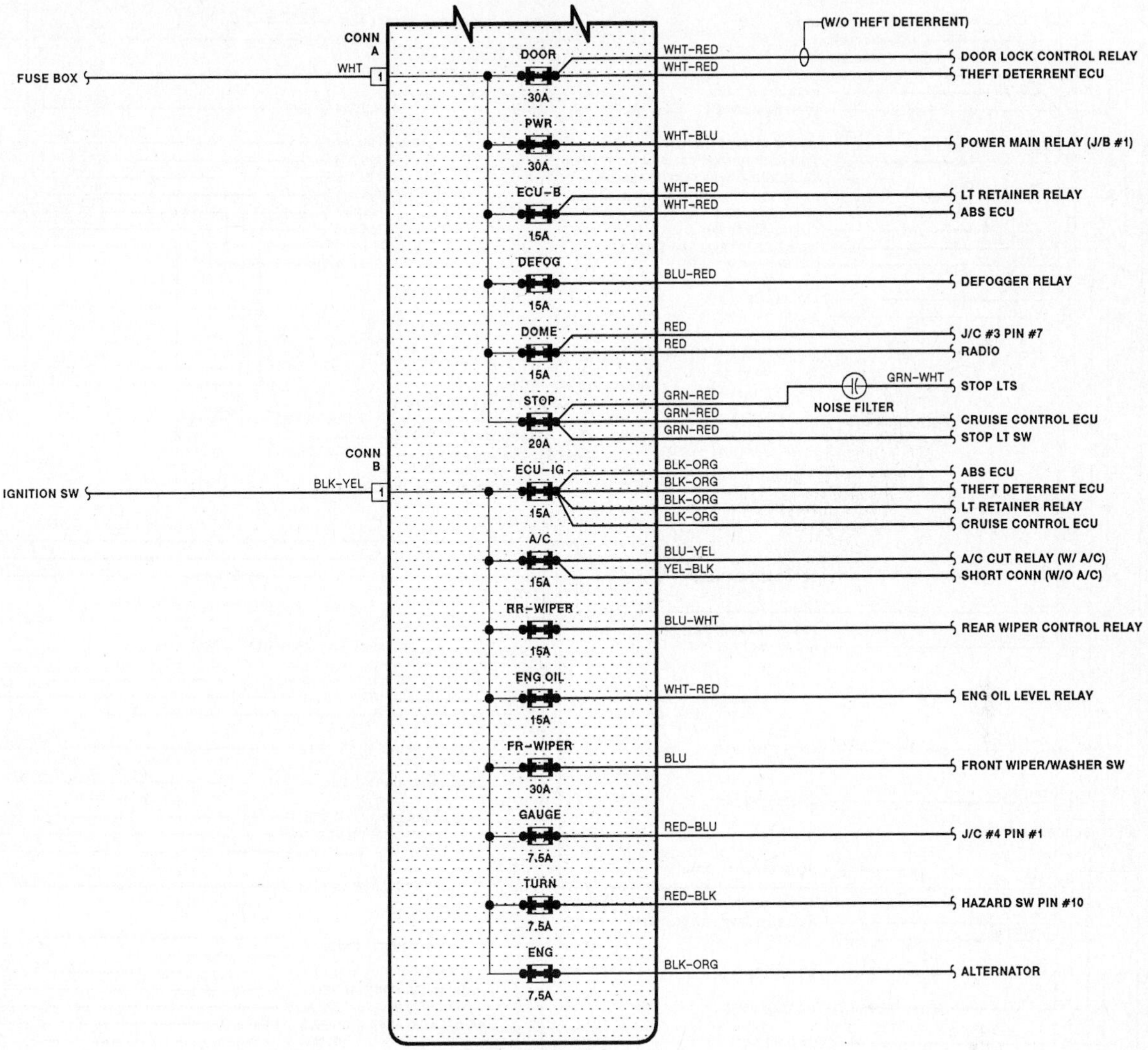

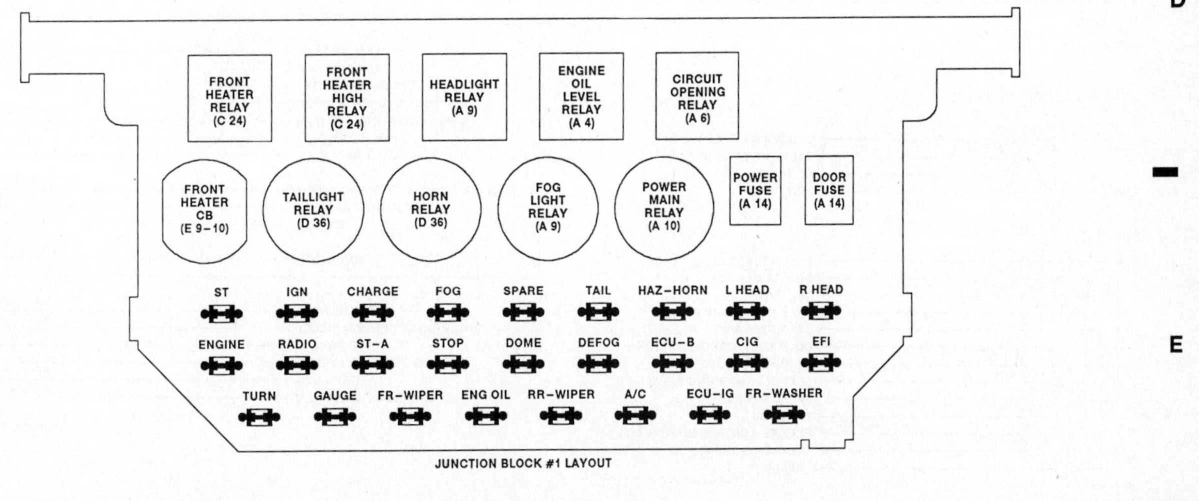

JUNCTION BLOCK #1 LAYOUT

# 1991 WIRING DIAGRAMS
## Previa (Cont.)

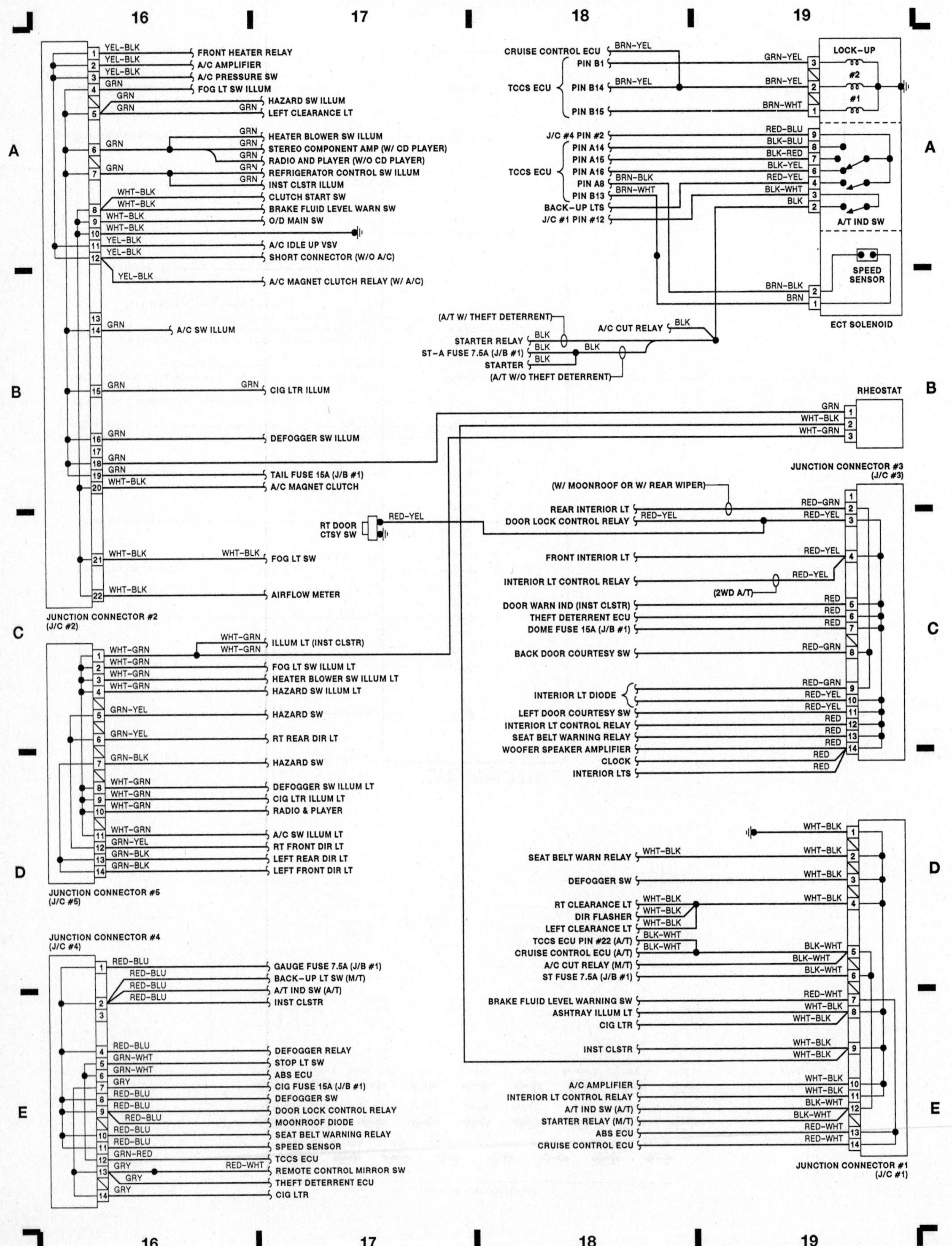

# 1991 WIRING DIAGRAMS
## Previa (Cont.)

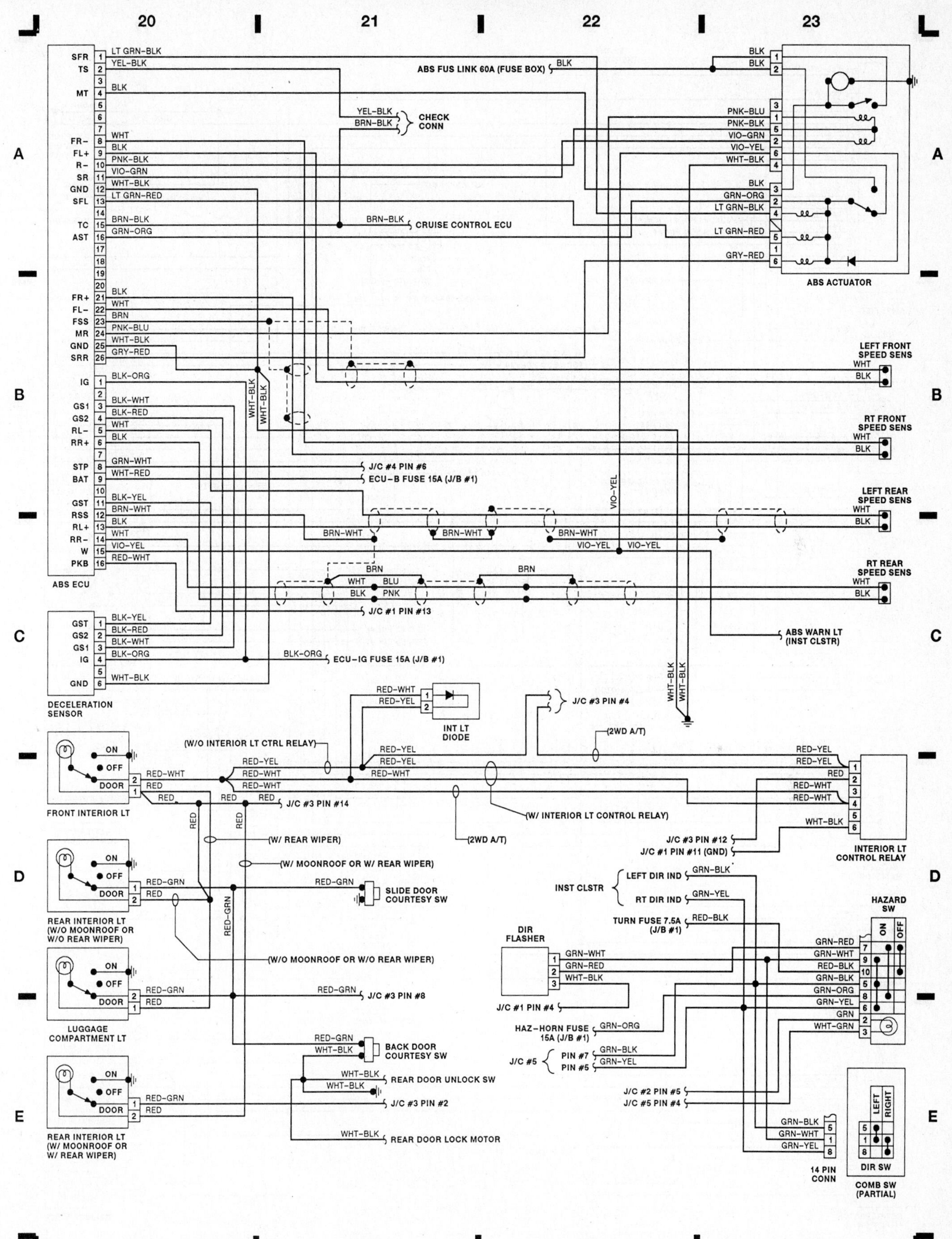

# 1991 WIRING DIAGRAMS
## Previa (Cont.)

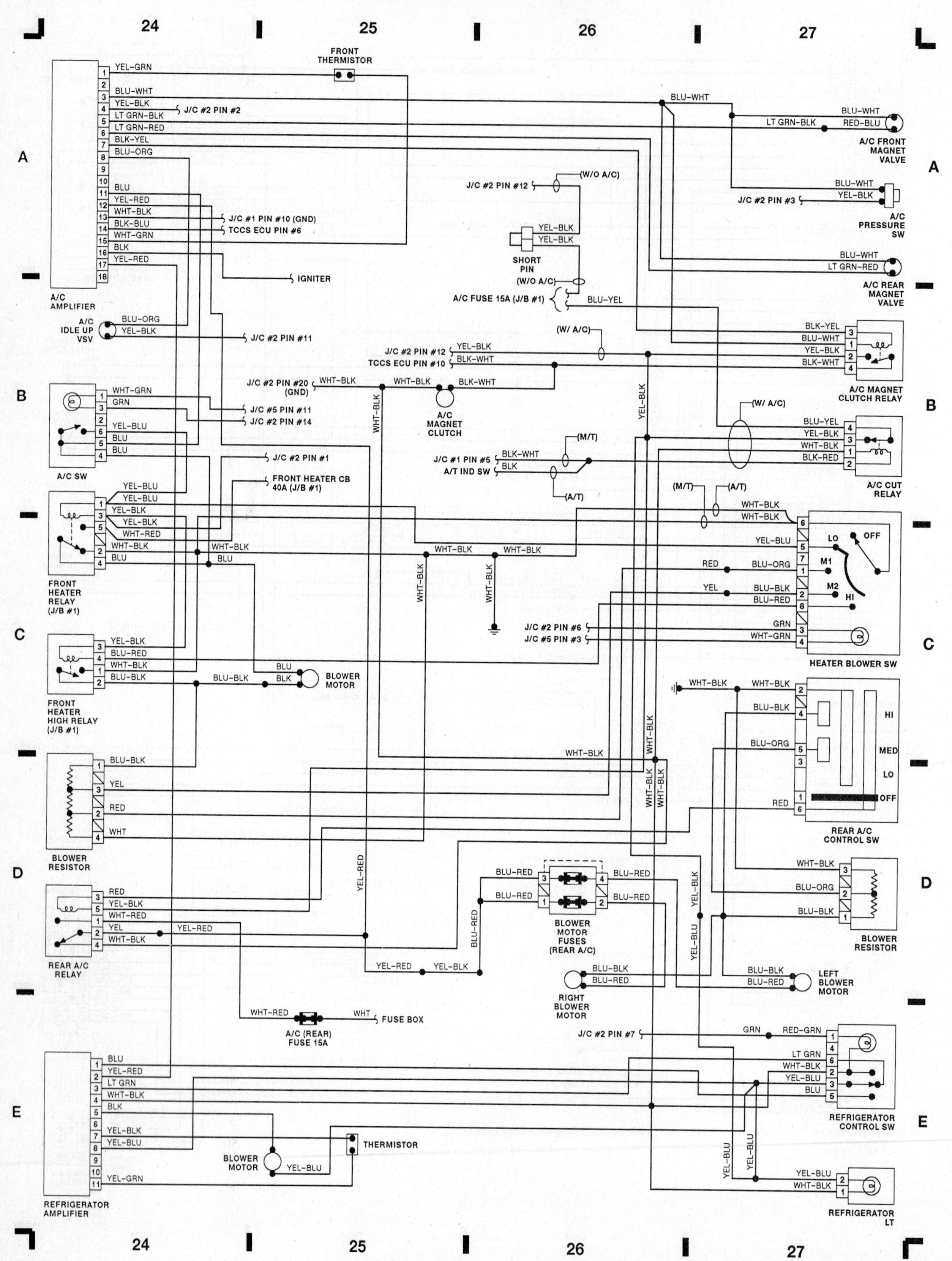

# 1991 WIRING DIAGRAMS
## Previa (Cont.)

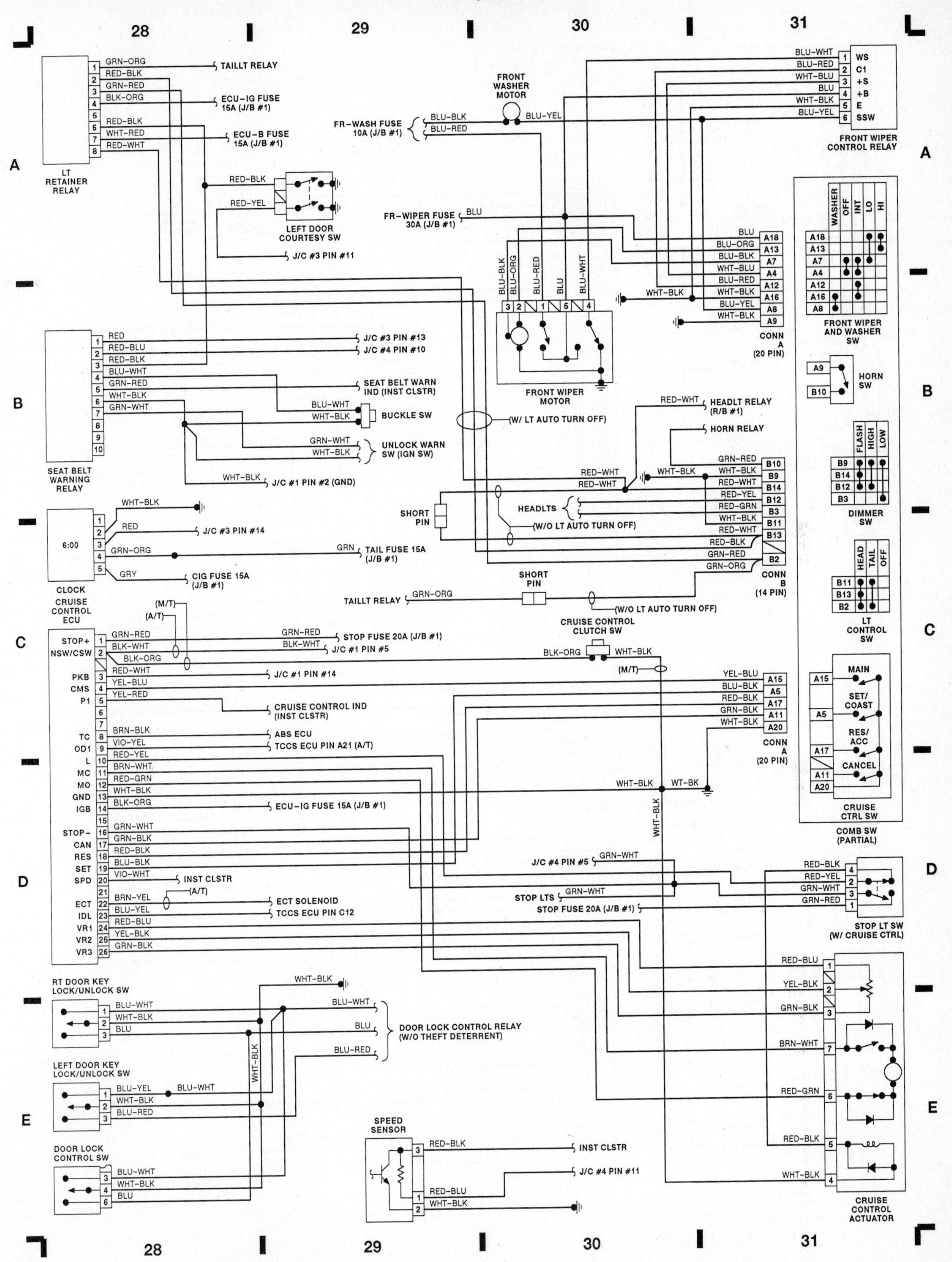

# 1991 WIRING DIAGRAMS
## Previa (Cont.)

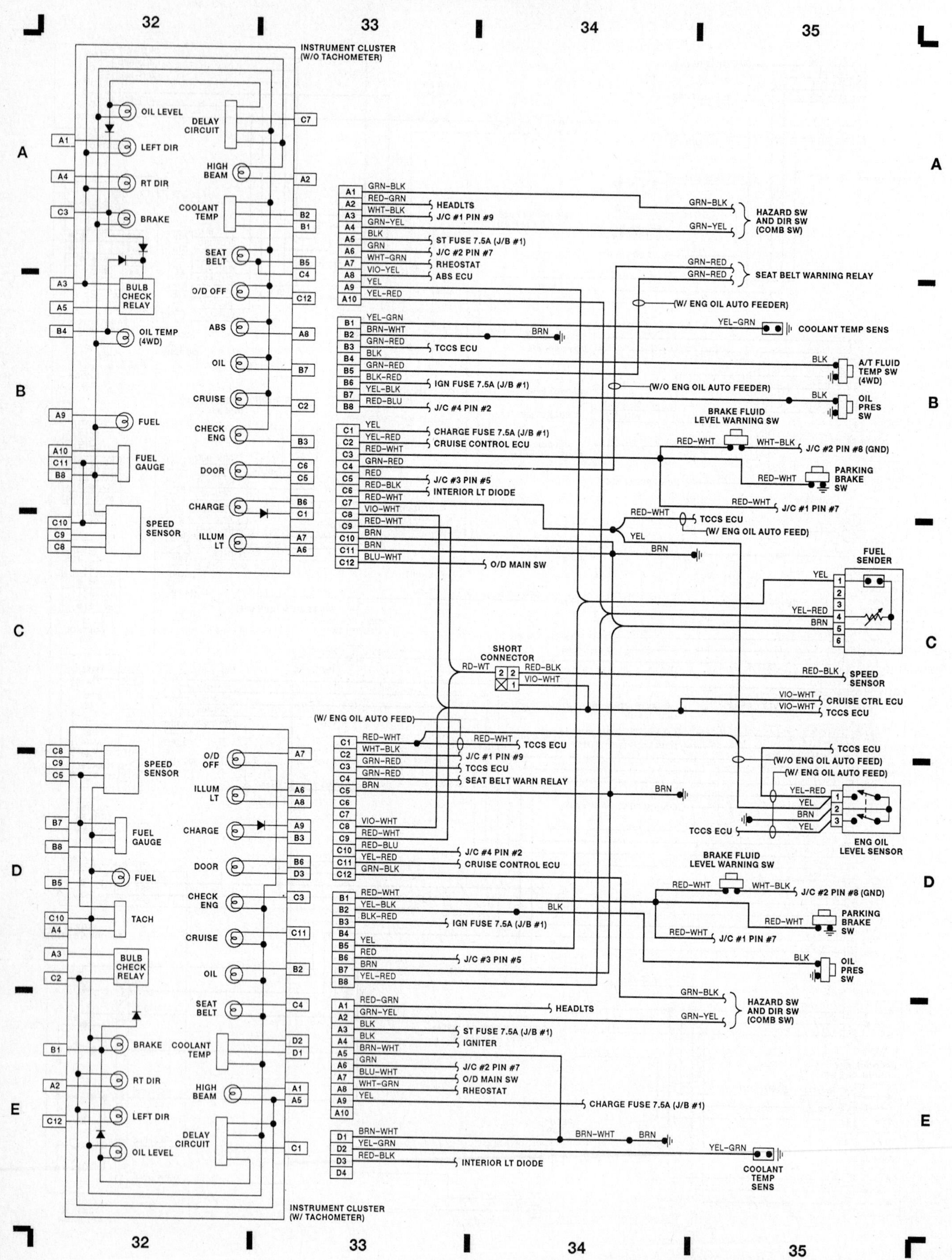

# 1991 WIRING DIAGRAMS
## Previa (Cont.)

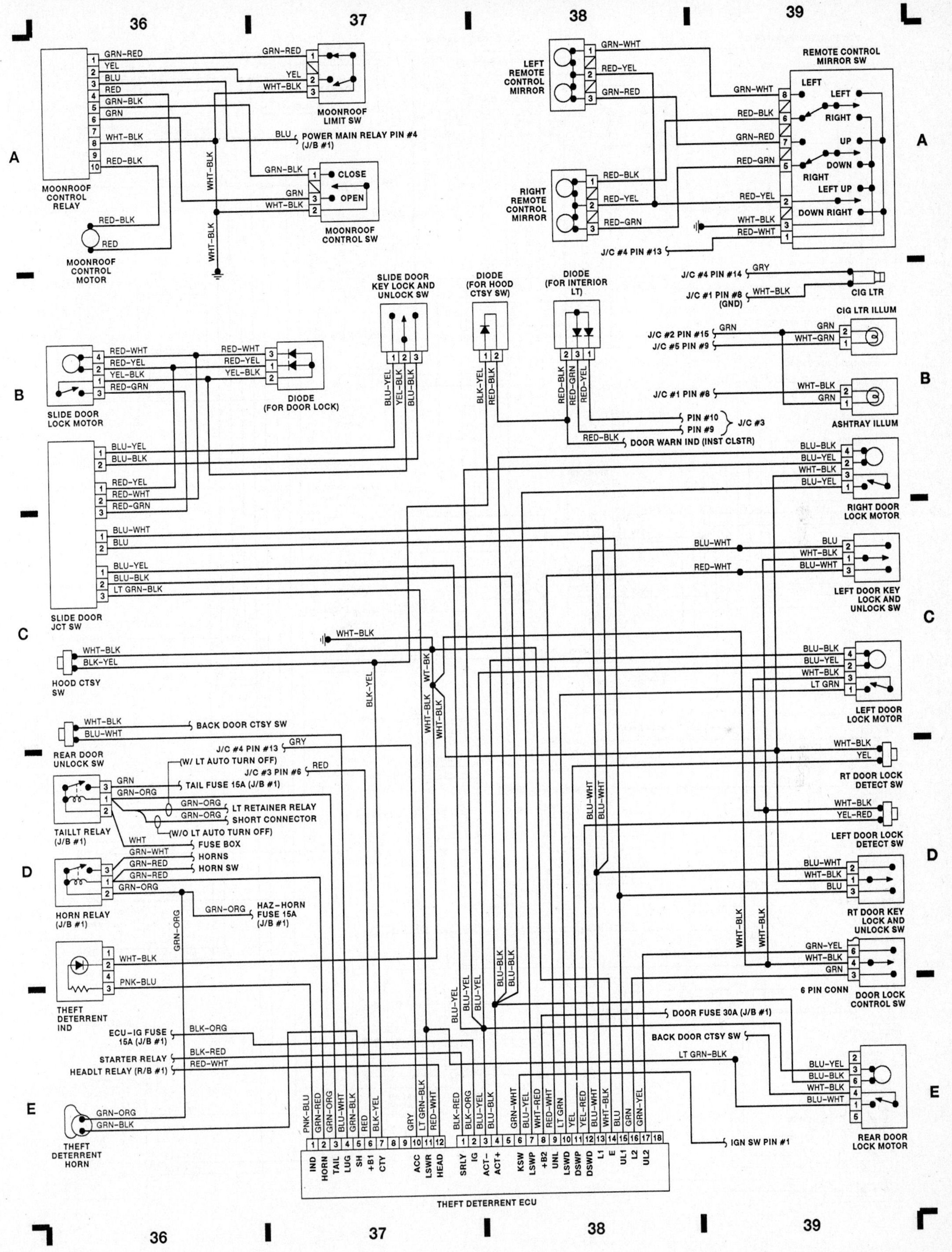

# 1991 WIRING DIAGRAMS
## Previa (Cont.)

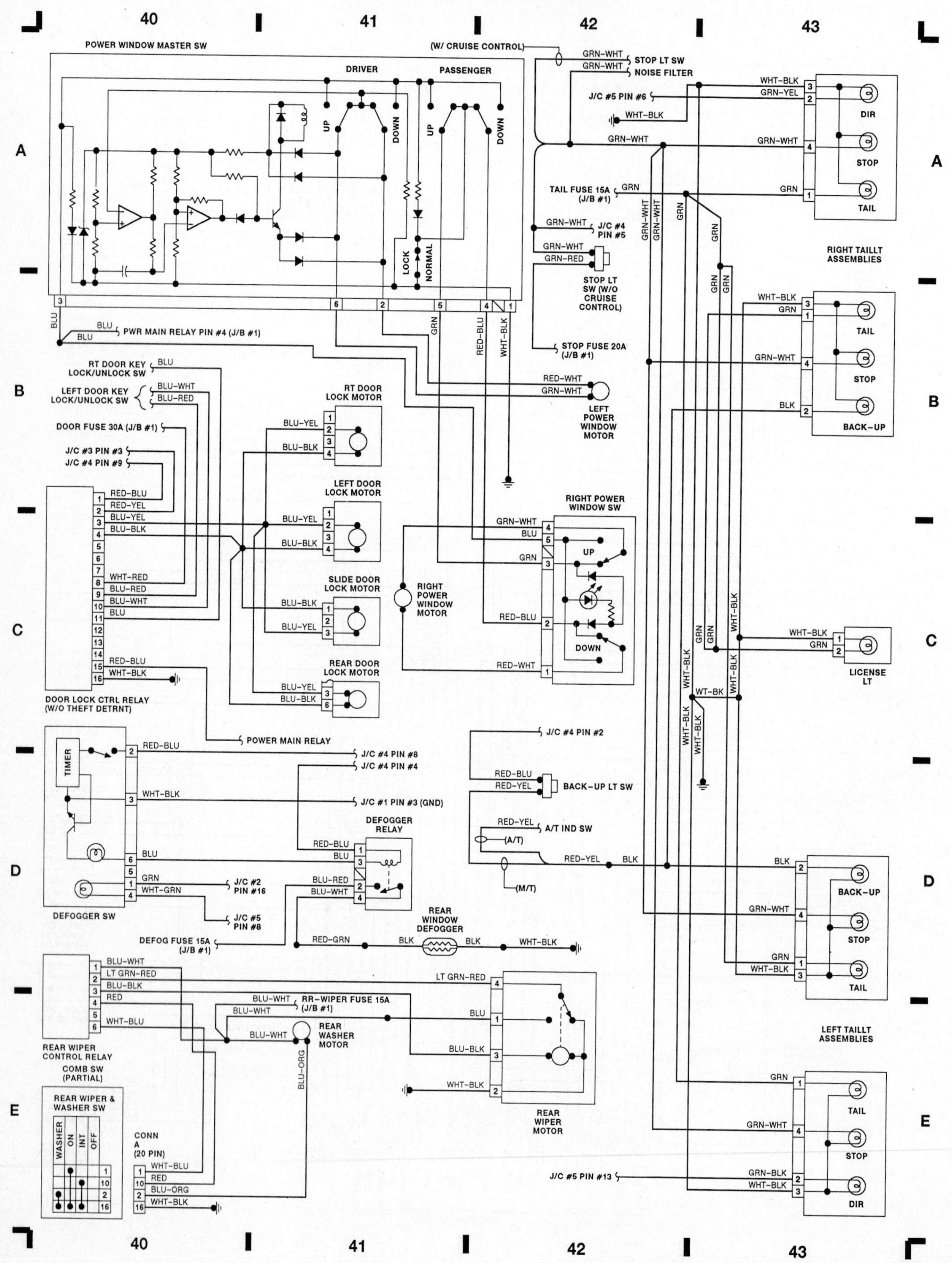

# 1991 WIRING DIAGRAMS
## Supra

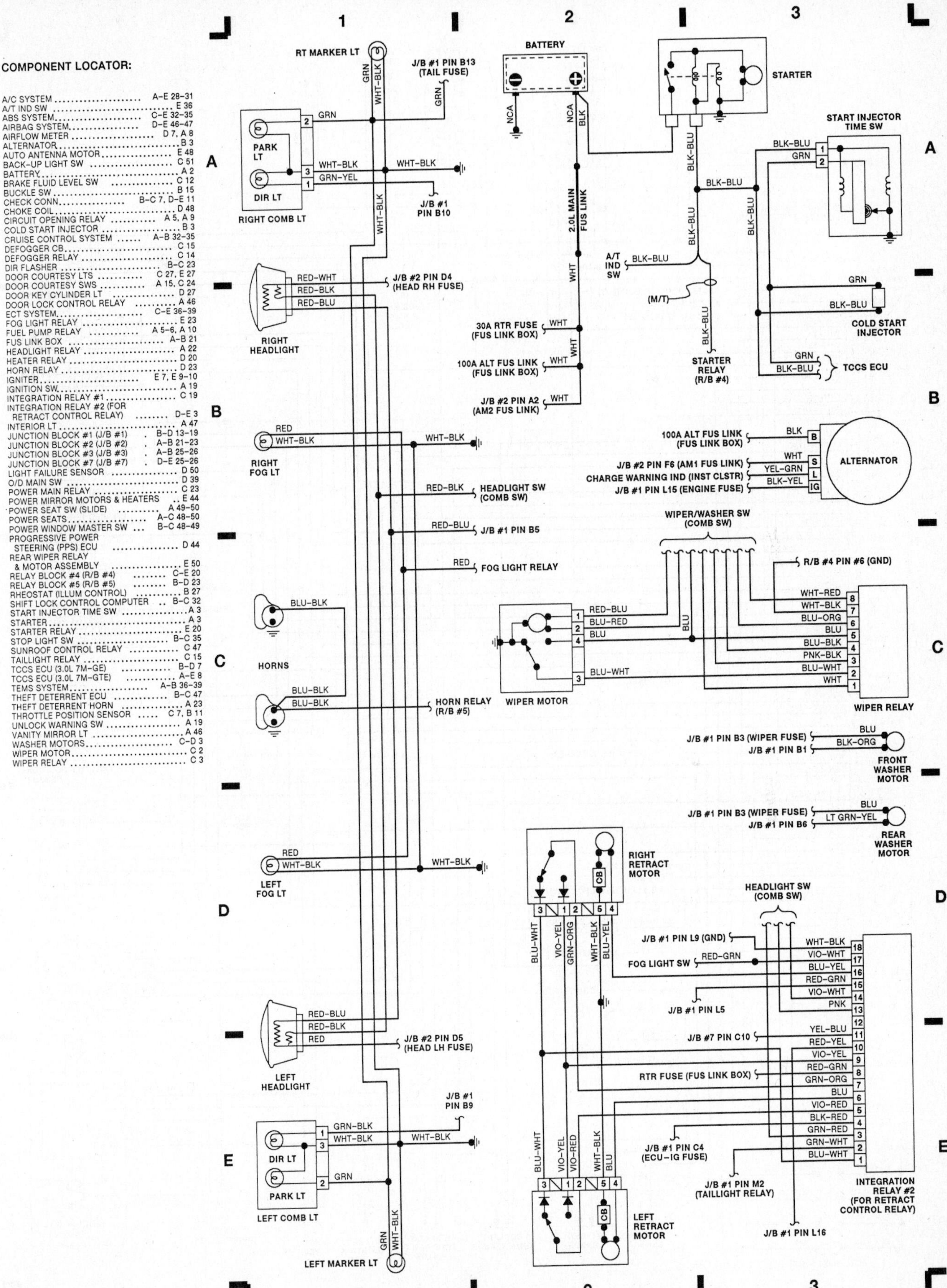

# 1991 WIRING DIAGRAMS
## Supra (Cont.)

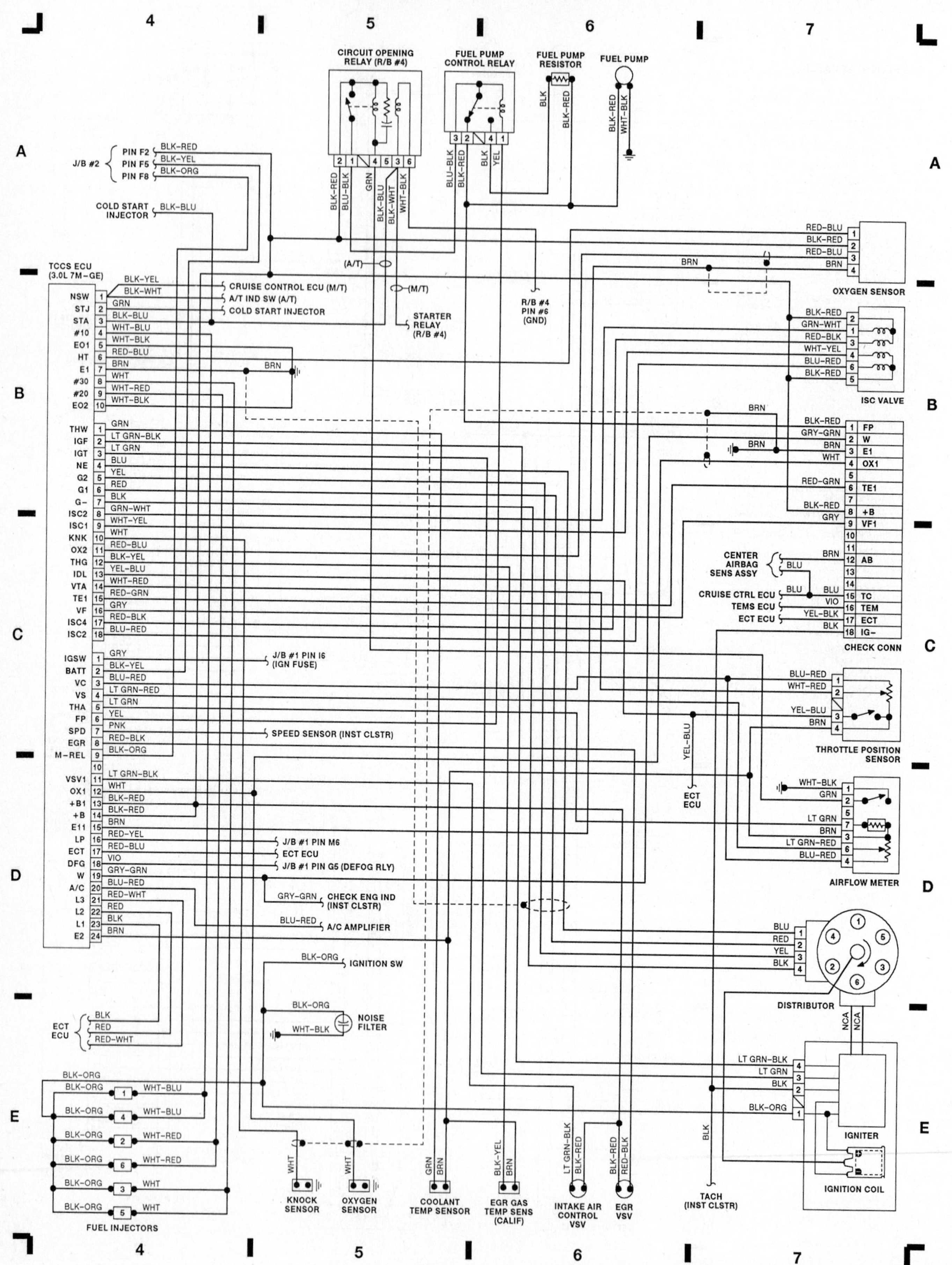

# 1991 WIRING DIAGRAMS
## Supra (Cont.)

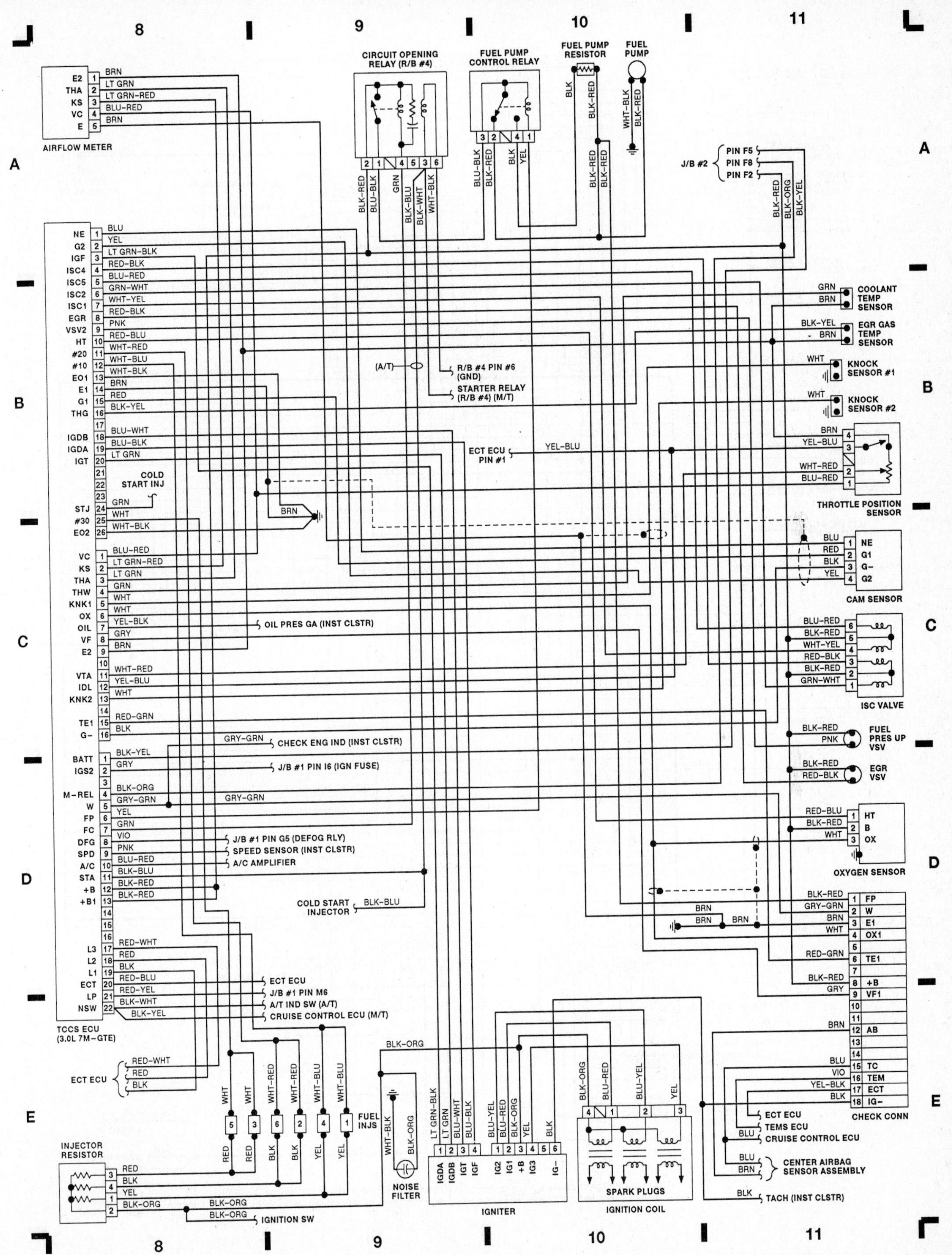

# 1991 WIRING DIAGRAMS
## Supra (Cont.)

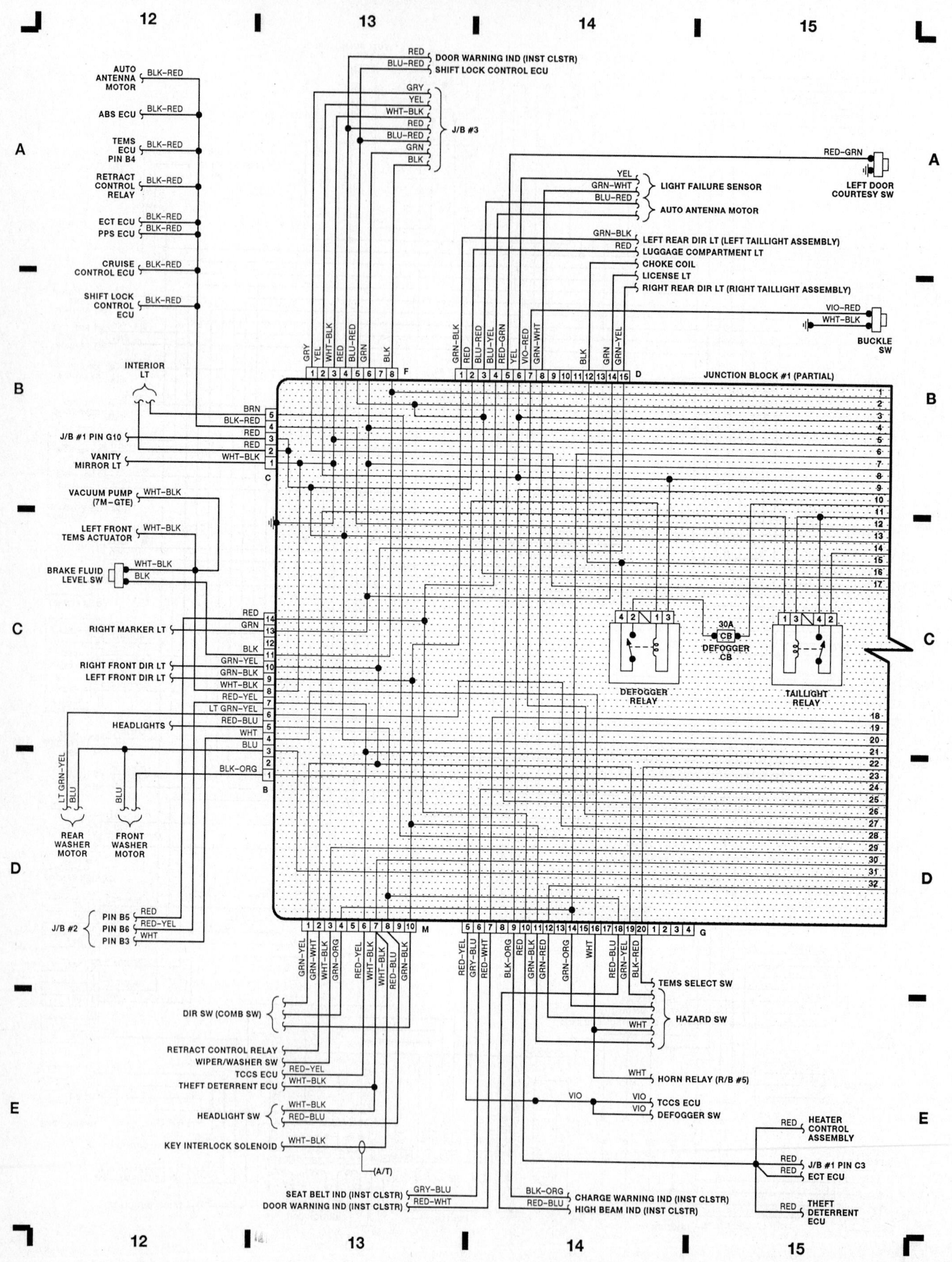

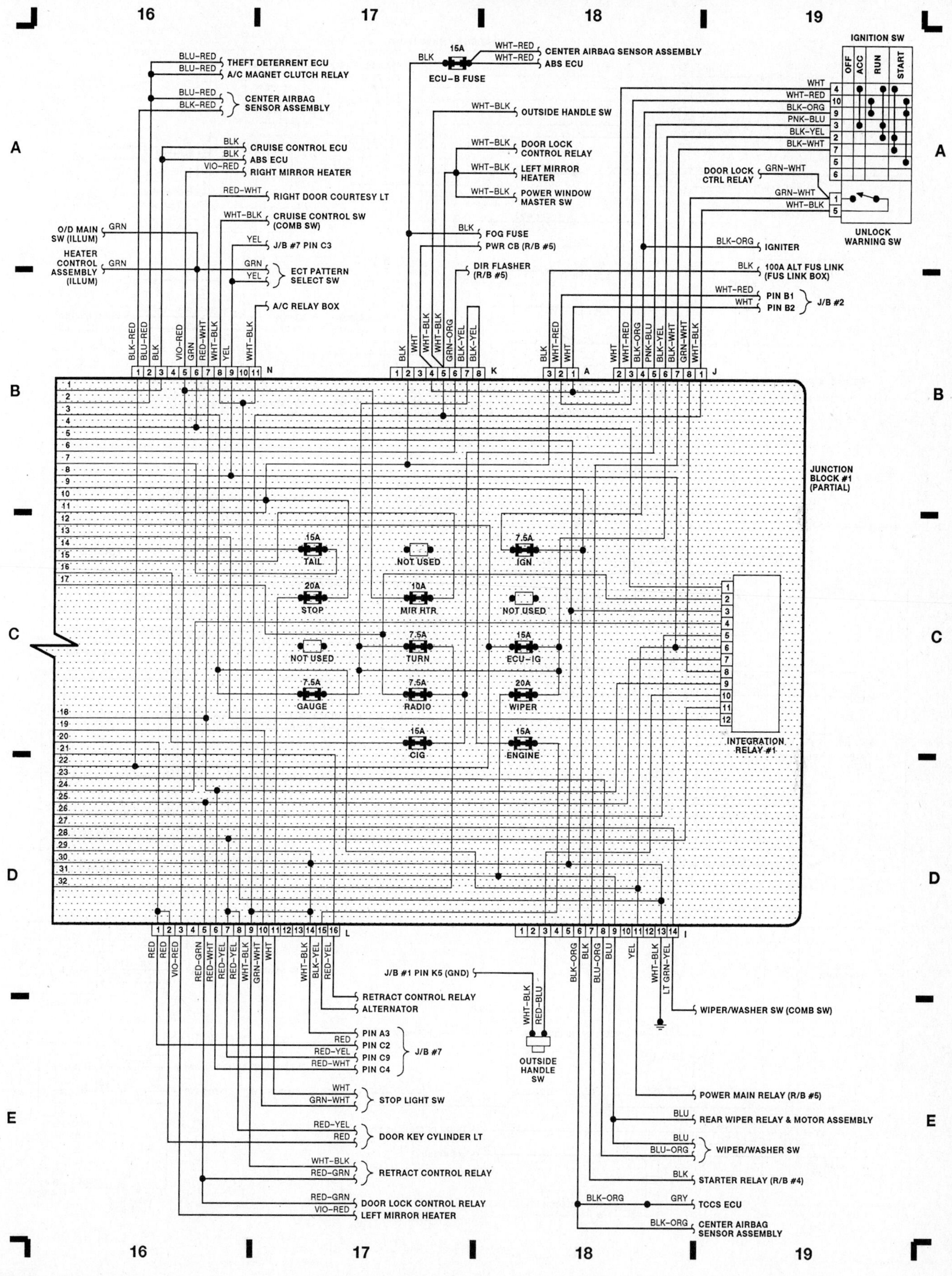
IGNITION SW
OFF
ACC
RUN
START
THEFT DETERRENT ECU
A/C MAGNET CLUTCH RELAY
CENTER AIRBAG SENSOR ASSEMBLY
CRUISE CONTROL ECU
ABS ECU
RIGHT MIRROR HEATER
RIGHT DOOR COURTESY LT
CRUISE CONTROL SW (COMB SW)
O/D MAIN SW (ILLUM)
J/B #7 PIN C3
HEATER CONTROL ASSEMBLY (ILLUM)
ECT PATTERN SELECT SW
A/C RELAY BOX
15A
ECU-B FUSE
CENTER AIRBAG SENSOR ASSEMBLY
ABS ECU
OUTSIDE HANDLE SW
DOOR LOCK CONTROL RELAY
LEFT MIRROR HEATER
POWER WINDOW MASTER SW
FOG FUSE
PWR CB (R/B #5)
DIR FLASHER (R/B #5)
DOOR LOCK CTRL RELAY
UNLOCK WARNING SW
IGNITER
100A ALT FUS LINK (FUS LINK BOX)
PIN B1
PIN B2
J/B #2
JUNCTION BLOCK #1 (PARTIAL)
15A TAIL
NOT USED
7.5A IGN
20A STOP
10A MIR HTR
NOT USED
NOT USED
7.5A TURN
15A ECU-IG
7.5A GAUGE
7.5A RADIO
20A WIPER
15A CIG
15A ENGINE
INTEGRATION RELAY #1
J/B #1 PIN K5 (GND)
RETRACT CONTROL RELAY
ALTERNATOR
PIN A3
PIN C2
PIN C9
PIN C4
J/B #7
STOP LIGHT SW
DOOR KEY CYLINDER LT
RETRACT CONTROL RELAY
DOOR LOCK CONTROL RELAY
LEFT MIRROR HEATER
OUTSIDE HANDLE SW
WIPER/WASHER SW (COMB SW)
POWER MAIN RELAY (R/B #5)
REAR WIPER RELAY & MOTOR ASSEMBLY
WIPER/WASHER SW
STARTER RELAY (R/B #4)
TCCS ECU
CENTER AIRBAG SENSOR ASSEMBLY
16
17
18
19
A
B
C
D
E

# 1991 WIRING DIAGRAMS
## Supra (Cont.)

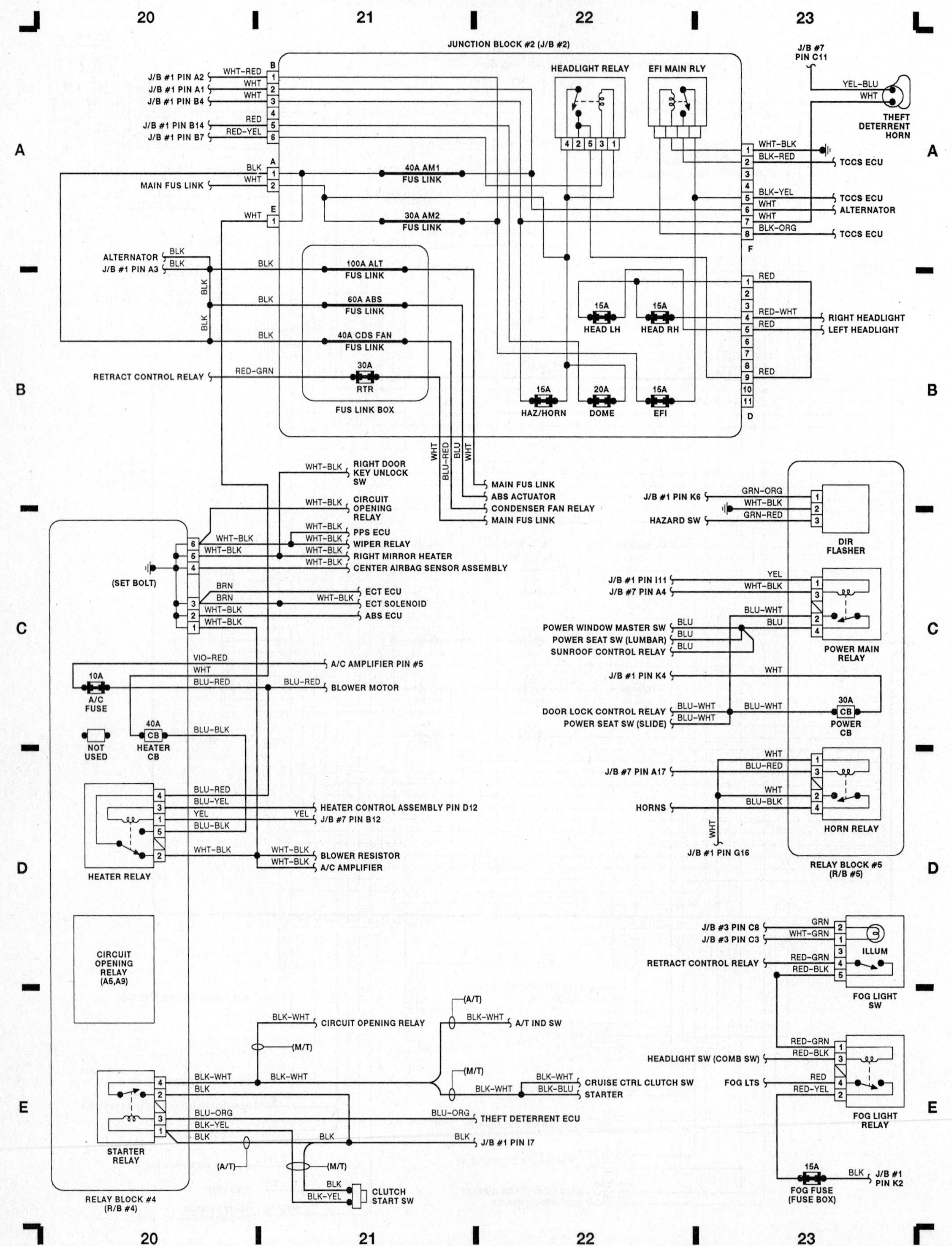

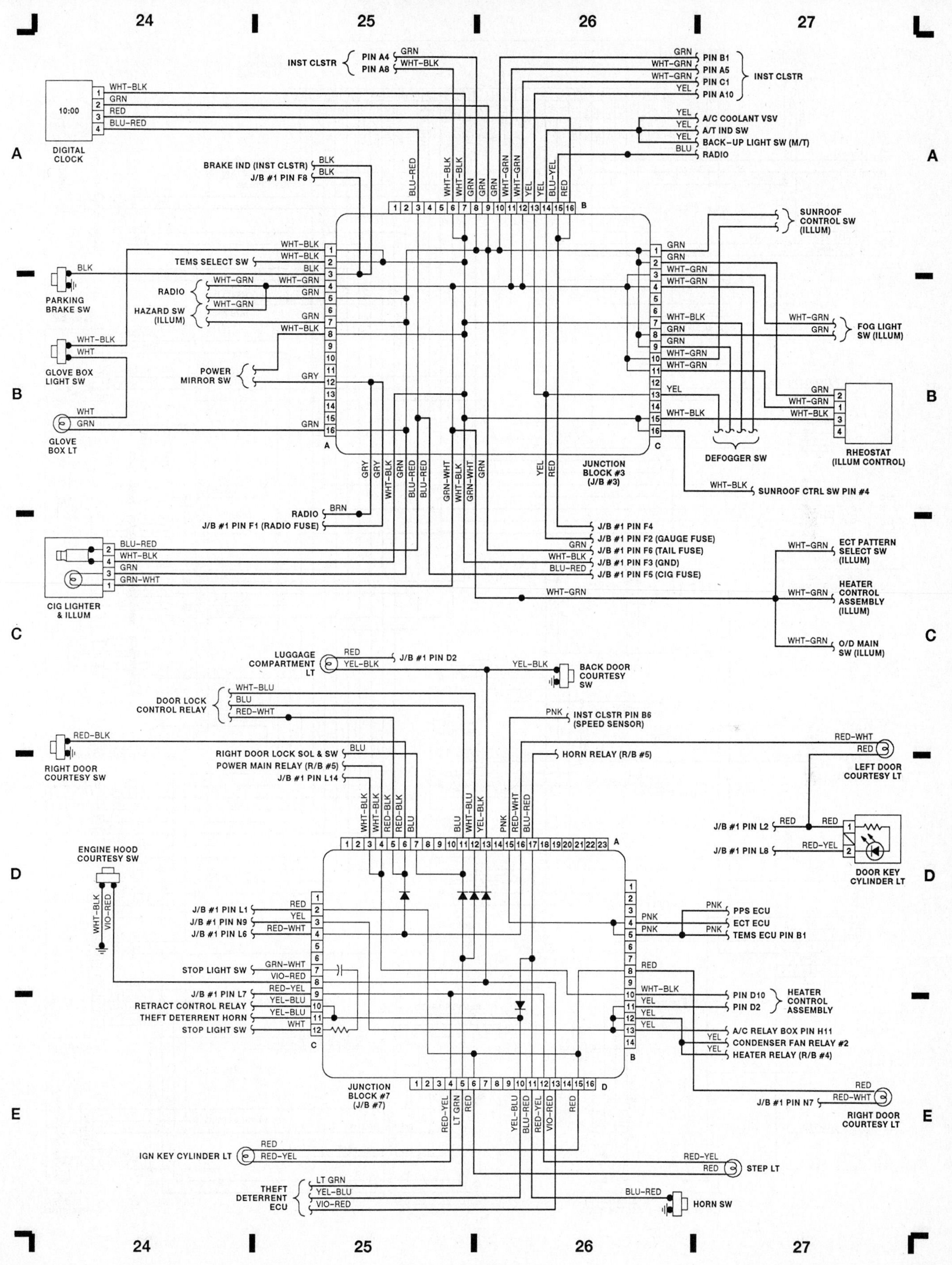
INST CLSTR
PIN A4
PIN A8
PIN B1
PIN A5
PIN C1
PIN A10
INST CLSTR
DIGITAL CLOCK
A/C COOLANT VSV
A/T IND SW
BACK-UP LIGHT SW (M/T)
RADIO
BRAKE IND (INST CLSTR)
J/B #1 PIN F8
SUNROOF CONTROL SW (ILLUM)
TEMS SELECT SW
PARKING BRAKE SW
RADIO
HAZARD SW (ILLUM)
FOG LIGHT SW (ILLUM)
GLOVE BOX LIGHT SW
POWER MIRROR SW
RHEOSTAT (ILLUM CONTROL)
GLOVE BOX LT
DEFOGGER SW
JUNCTION BLOCK #3 (J/B #3)
SUNROOF CTRL SW PIN #4
RADIO
J/B #1 PIN F1 (RADIO FUSE)
J/B #1 PIN F4
J/B #1 PIN F2 (GAUGE FUSE)
J/B #1 PIN F6 (TAIL FUSE)
J/B #1 PIN F3 (GND)
J/B #1 PIN F5 (CIG FUSE)
ECT PATTERN SELECT SW (ILLUM)
HEATER CONTROL ASSEMBLY (ILLUM)
CIG LIGHTER & ILLUM
O/D MAIN SW (ILLUM)
LUGGAGE COMPARTMENT LT
J/B #1 PIN D2
BACK DOOR COURTESY SW
DOOR LOCK CONTROL RELAY
INST CLSTR PIN B6 (SPEED SENSOR)
RIGHT DOOR COURTESY SW
RIGHT DOOR LOCK SOL & SW
POWER MAIN RELAY (R/B #5)
J/B #1 PIN L14
HORN RELAY (R/B #5)
LEFT DOOR COURTESY LT
ENGINE HOOD COURTESY SW
J/B #1 PIN L2
J/B #1 PIN L8
DOOR KEY CYLINDER LT
J/B #1 PIN L1
J/B #1 PIN N9
J/B #1 PIN L6
PPS ECU
ECT ECU
TEMS ECU PIN B1
STOP LIGHT SW
J/B #1 PIN L7
RETRACT CONTROL RELAY
THEFT DETERRENT HORN
STOP LIGHT SW
PIN D10
PIN D2
HEATER CONTROL ASSEMBLY
A/C RELAY BOX PIN H11
CONDENSER FAN RELAY #2
HEATER RELAY (R/B #4)
JUNCTION BLOCK #7 (J/B #7)
J/B #1 PIN N7
RIGHT DOOR COURTESY LT
IGN KEY CYLINDER LT
STEP LT
THEFT DETERRENT ECU
HORN SW

# 1991 WIRING DIAGRAMS
## Supra (Cont.)

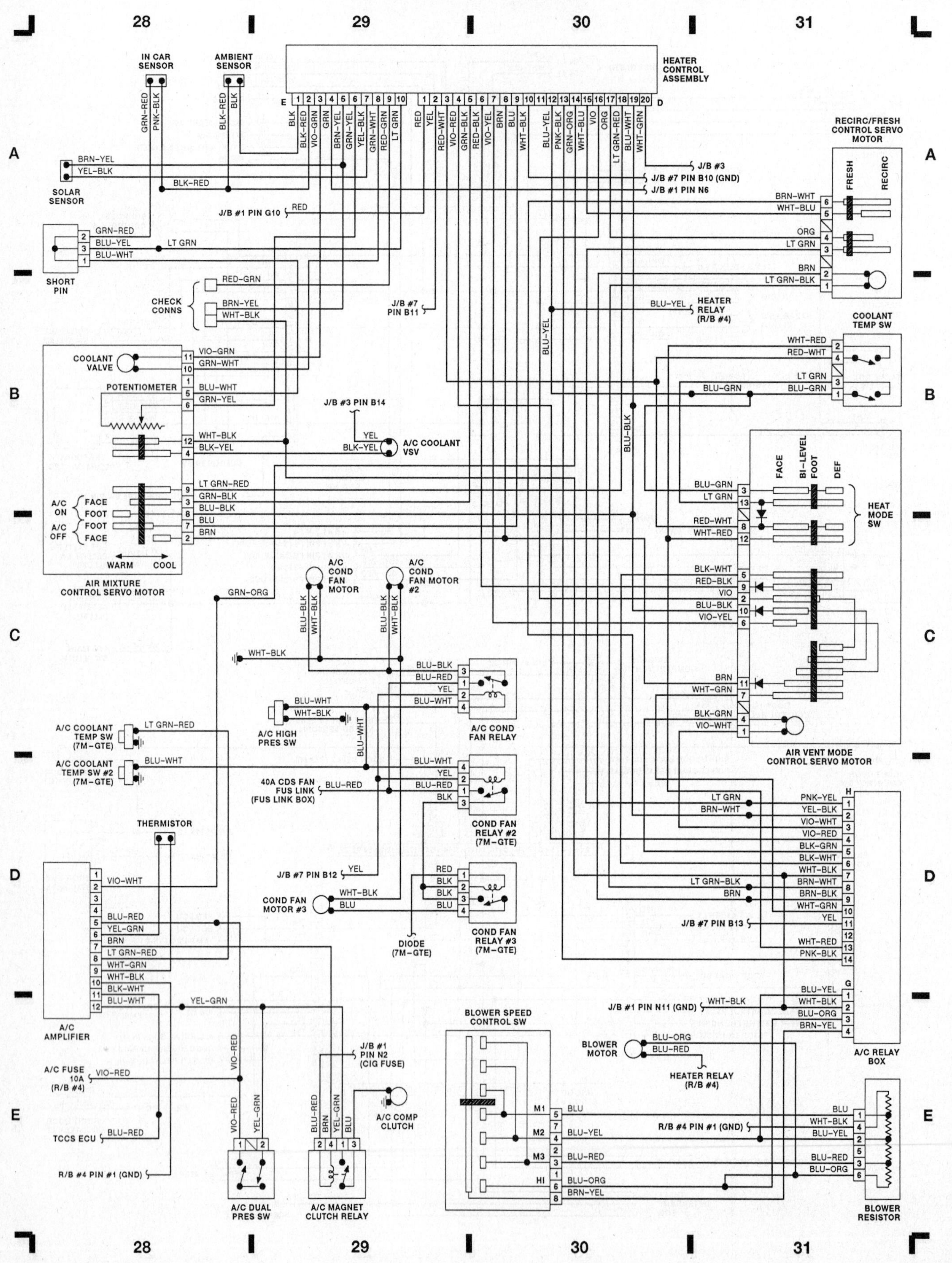

# 1991 WIRING DIAGRAMS
# Supra (Cont.)

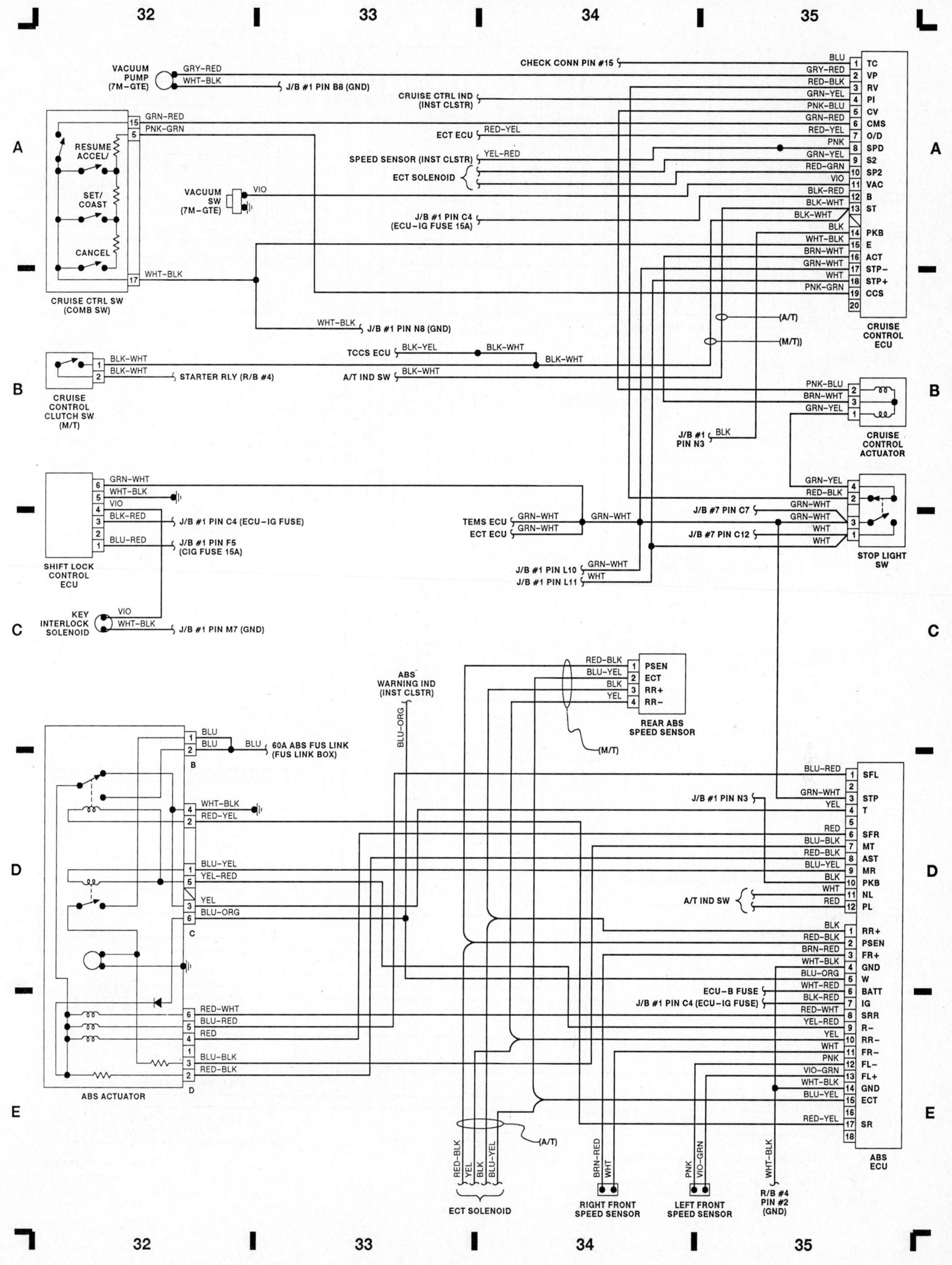

# 1991 WIRING DIAGRAMS
## Supra (Cont.)

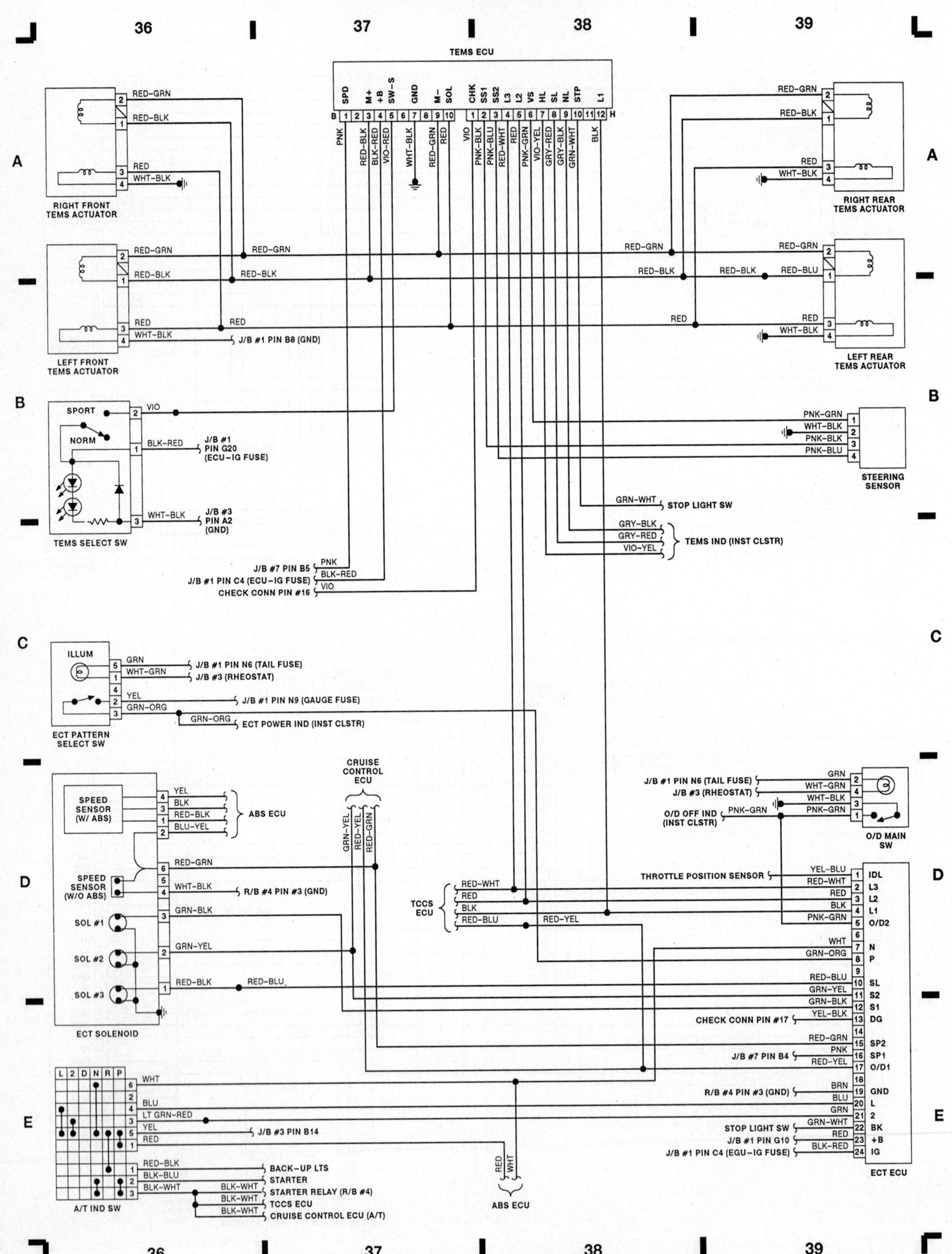

# 1991 WIRING DIAGRAMS
## Supra (Cont.)

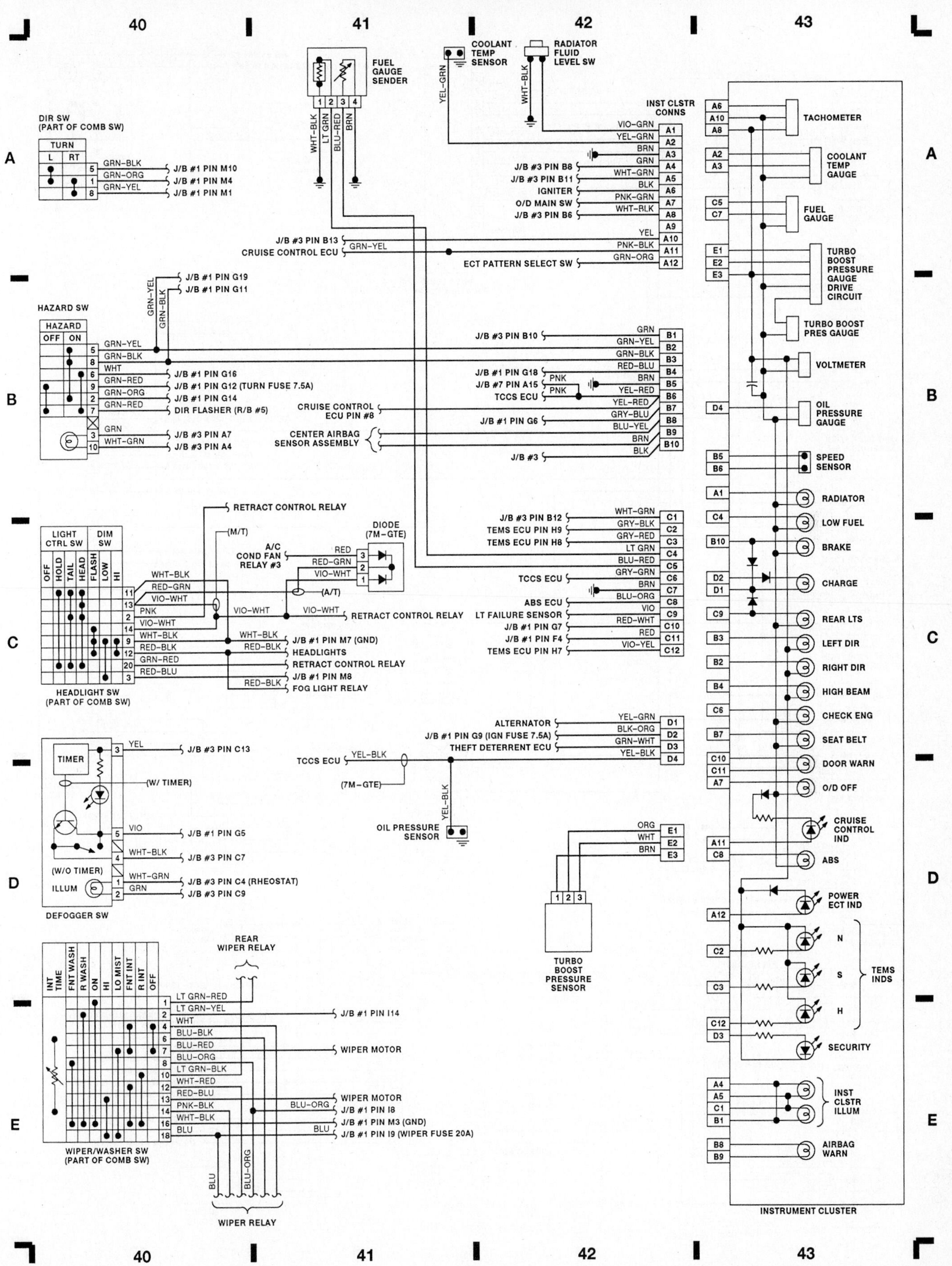

# 1991 WIRING DIAGRAMS
## Supra (Cont.)

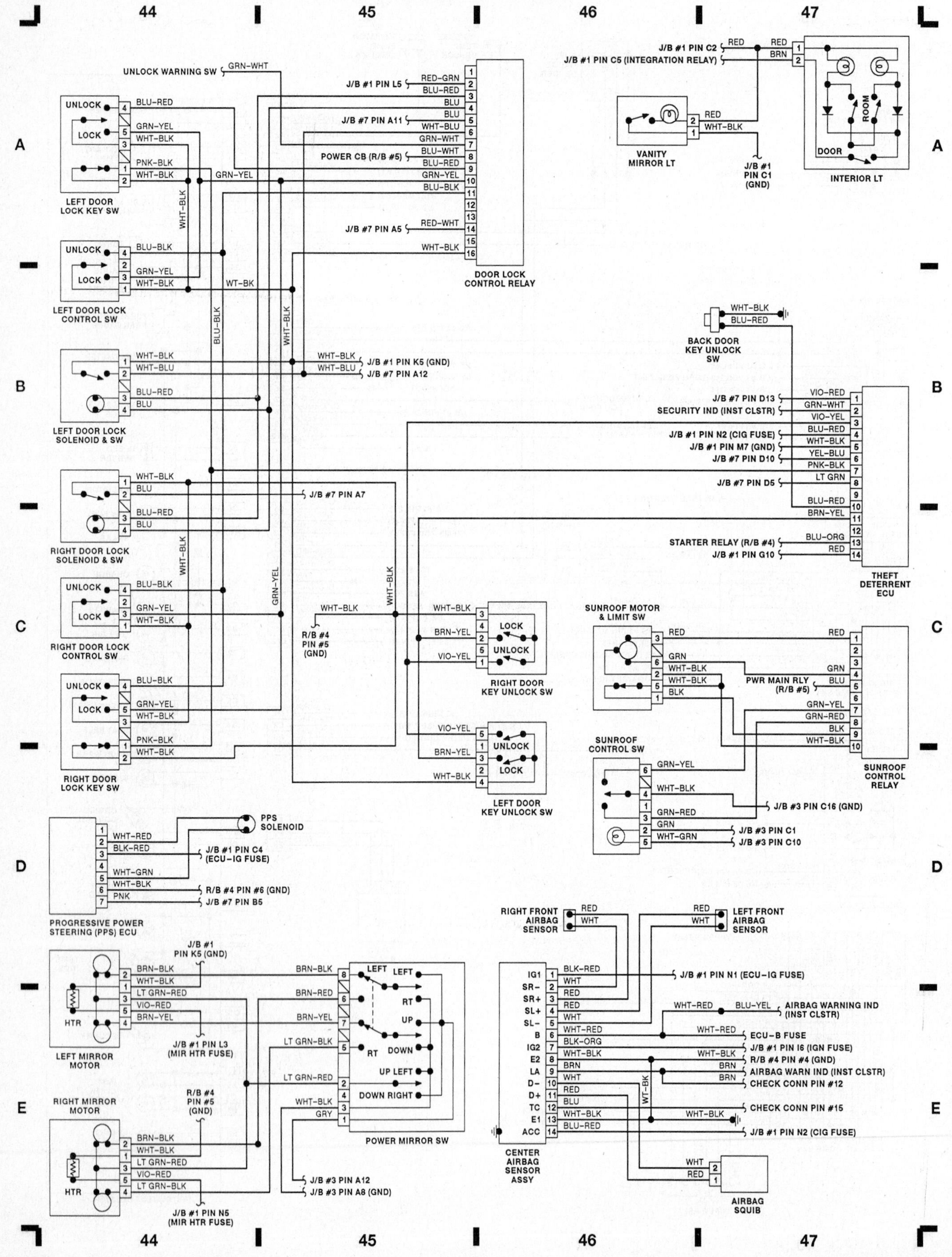

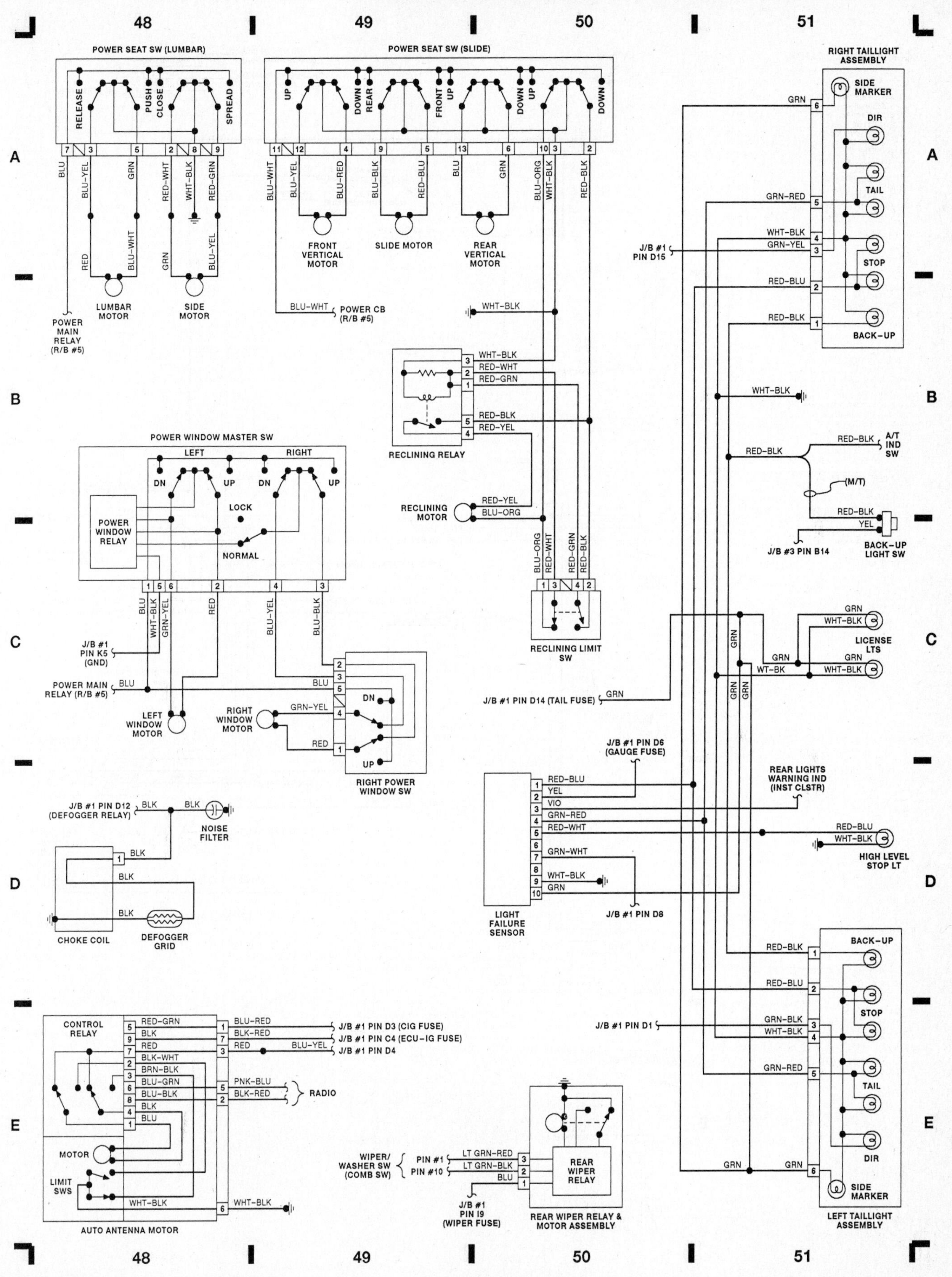

POWER SEAT SW (LUMBAR)
RELEASE
PUSH
CLOSE
SPREAD
LUMBAR MOTOR
SIDE MOTOR
POWER MAIN RELAY (R/B #5)
POWER SEAT SW (SLIDE)
FRONT VERTICAL MOTOR
SLIDE MOTOR
REAR VERTICAL MOTOR
POWER CB (R/B #5)
RECLINING RELAY
RECLINING MOTOR
RECLINING LIMIT SW
RIGHT TAILLIGHT ASSEMBLY
SIDE MARKER
DIR
TAIL
STOP
BACK-UP
J/B #1 PIN D15
A/T IND SW
(M/T)
BACK-UP LIGHT SW
J/B #3 PIN B14
POWER WINDOW MASTER SW
LEFT
RIGHT
DN
UP
LOCK
NORMAL
POWER WINDOW RELAY
J/B #1 PIN K5 (GND)
POWER MAIN RELAY (R/B #5)
LEFT WINDOW MOTOR
RIGHT WINDOW MOTOR
RIGHT POWER WINDOW SW
LICENSE LTS
J/B #1 PIN D14 (TAIL FUSE)
J/B #1 PIN D6 (GAUGE FUSE)
REAR LIGHTS WARNING IND (INST CLSTR)
LIGHT FAILURE SENSOR
HIGH LEVEL STOP LT
J/B #1 PIN D8
J/B #1 PIN D12 (DEFOGGER RELAY)
NOISE FILTER
CHOKE COIL
DEFOGGER GRID
LEFT TAILLIGHT ASSEMBLY
J/B #1 PIN D1
CONTROL RELAY
J/B #1 PIN D3 (CIG FUSE)
J/B #1 PIN C4 (ECU-IG FUSE)
J/B #1 PIN D4
RADIO
MOTOR
LIMIT SWS
AUTO ANTENNA MOTOR
WIPER/ WASHER SW (COMB SW)
PIN #1
PIN #10
J/B #1 PIN I9 (WIPER FUSE)
REAR WIPER RELAY
REAR WIPER RELAY & MOTOR ASSEMBLY

# 1991 WIRING DIAGRAMS
## Tercel

**COMPONENT LOCATOR:**

| Component | Location |
|---|---|
| A/C AMPLIFIER (W/ P/S) | C–D 16 |
| A/C AMPLIFIER (W/O P/S) | C–D 19 |
| A/C COND FAN RELAY #2 | B 19 |
| A/C COND FAN RELAY #3 | B 19 |
| A/C SWITCH (W/ P/S) | E 16 |
| A/C SWITCH (W/O P/S) | E 19 |
| A/T POSITION SW | C–D 12 |
| ALTERNATOR | A 3 |
| BATTERY | A 1 |
| CIG LTR | B 8 |
| CIRCUIT OPENING RELAY | A 5 |
| CLOCK | A 10 |
| CLUTCH START SW | D 3 |
| COMPRESSOR ASSEMBLY | B 16 |
| CONDENSER FAN MOTOR | A 19 |
| DEFOG SW (W/ TIMER) | D 20 |
| DEFOG SW (W/O TIMER) | C 20 |
| DIR SW | A 23 |
| DOOR COURTESY SW | D–E 24 |
| EFI MAIN RELAY | A 4 |
| FUEL INJECTORS | E 4 |
| FUEL TANK UNIT | A 22 |
| HAZ LT SW | B 23 |
| HEADLIGHT SW | A 23 |
| HEATER BLOWER SW | A 16 |
| HEATER RELAY | C 14 |
| HORN RELAY | A–B 13 |
| IGNITER | E 6 |
| IGNITION COIL & DISTRIBUTOR | E 7 |
| IGNITION SW | A 8 |
| INSTRUMENT CLUSTER | A–C 20 |
| INTERIOR LT | B 11 |
| JUNCTION BLOCK #1 (J/B #1) | A–E 9–10 |
| JUNCTION CONNECTOR #1 (J/C #1) | A 24 |
| JUNCTION CONNECTOR #2 (J/C #2) | B 24–25 |
| JUNCTION CONNECTOR #3 (J/C #3) | C 24–25 |
| LUGGAGE COMPARTMENT LT SW | E 25 |
| MAGNET CLUTCH RELAY | A 19 |
| RADIATOR FAN RELAY #1 | A 19 |
| RELAY BOX #2 (R/B #2) | A–B 12–15 |
| RELAY BOX #4 (R/B #4) | C 13–14 |
| RELAY BOX #6 (R/B #6) | D 20–21 |
| RHEOSTAT | C 20 |
| SEAT BELT WARN RELAY | C 23 |
| SHIFT LOCK CONTROL COMPUTER | C 15 |
| STARTER MOTOR | B 3 |
| STARTER RELAY | D–E 3 |
| STOP LT SW | B 8 |
| TCCS ECU | B–D 4 |
| THEFT DETERRENT ECU | E 13–14 |
| UNLOCK WARN SW | A 8 |
| WIPER/WASHER SW (W/ WIPER RELAY) | D–E 23 |

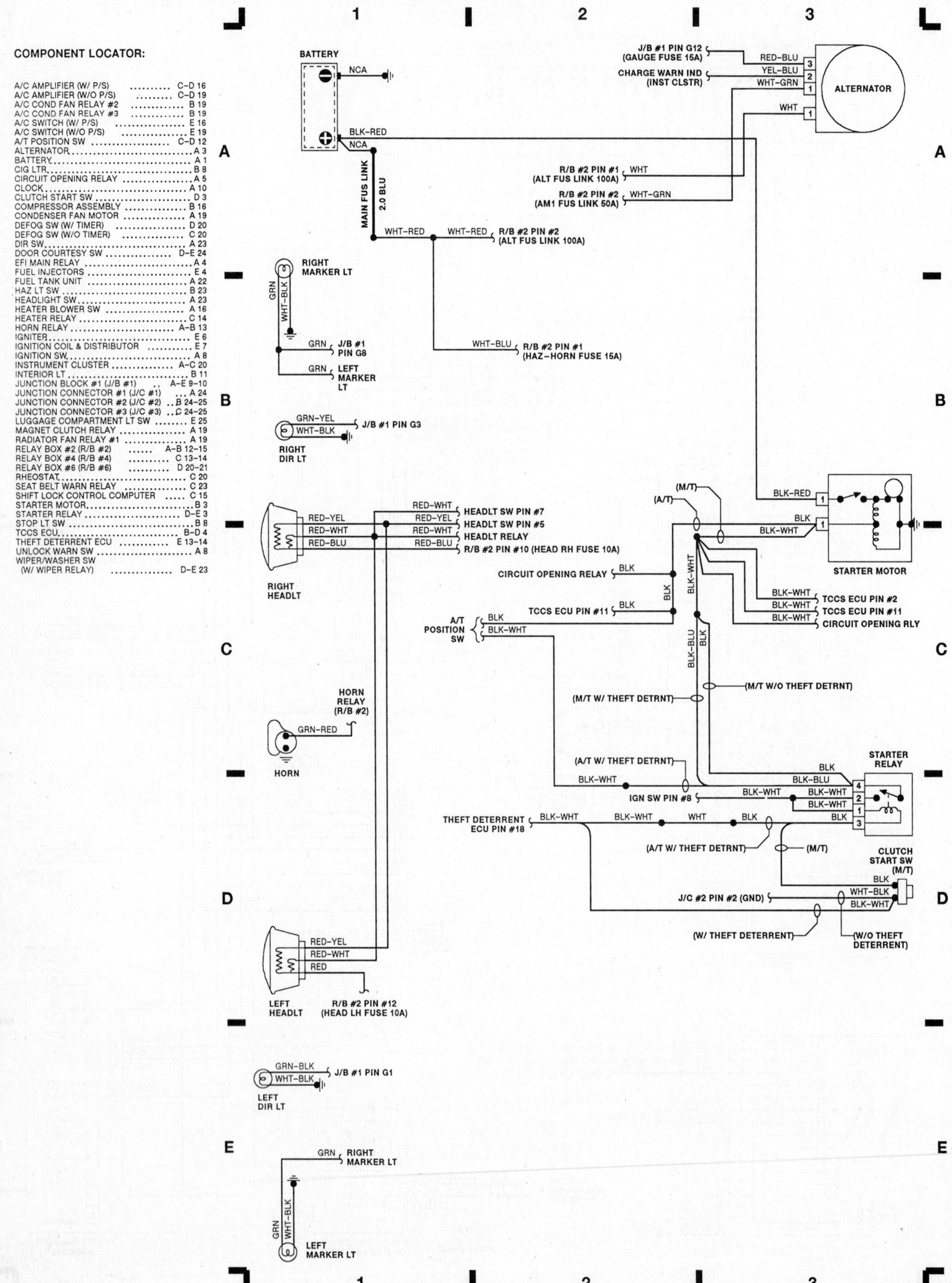

# 1991 WIRING DIAGRAMS
## Tercel (Cont.)

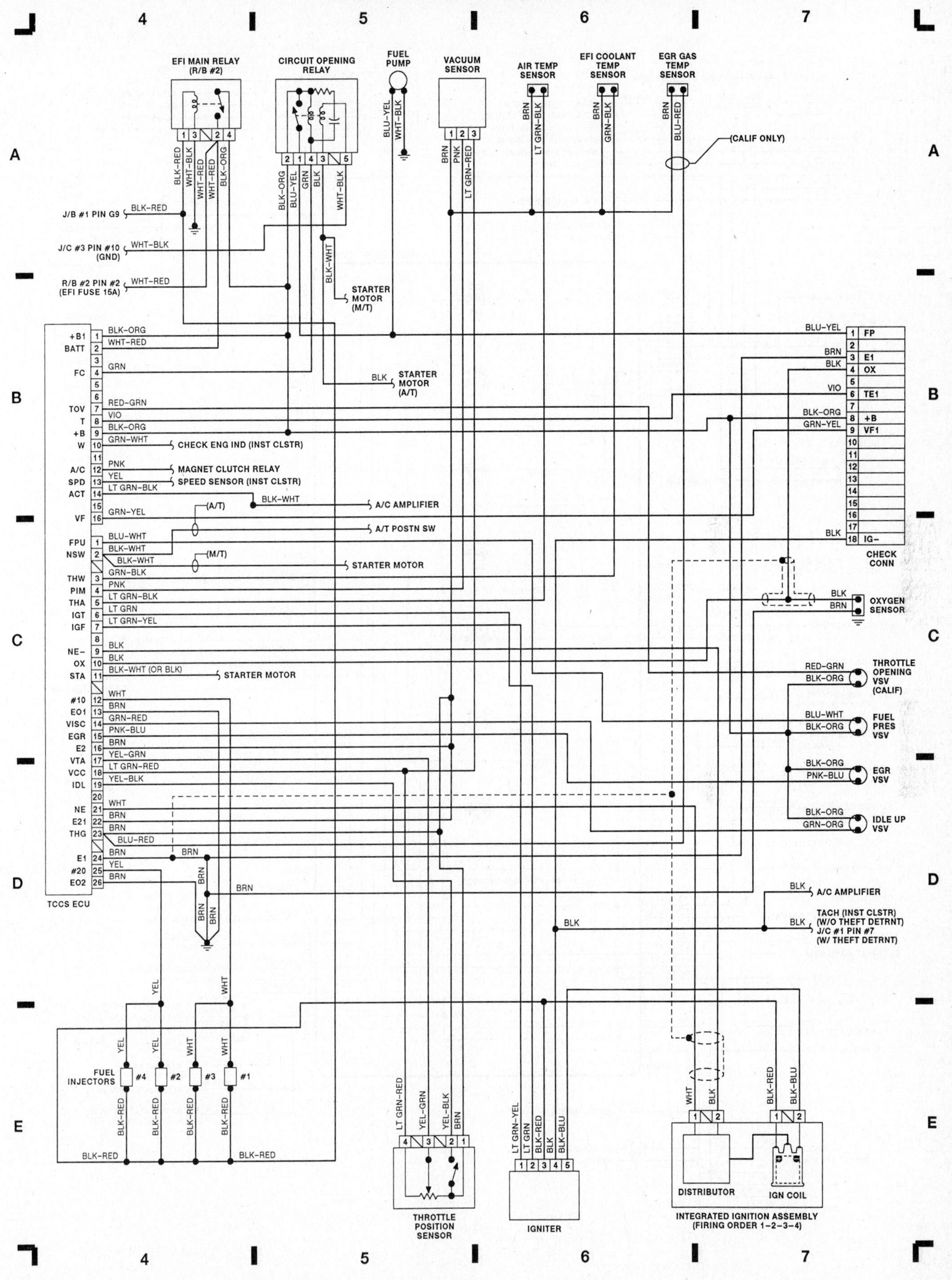

# 1991 WIRING DIAGRAMS
# Tercel (Cont.)

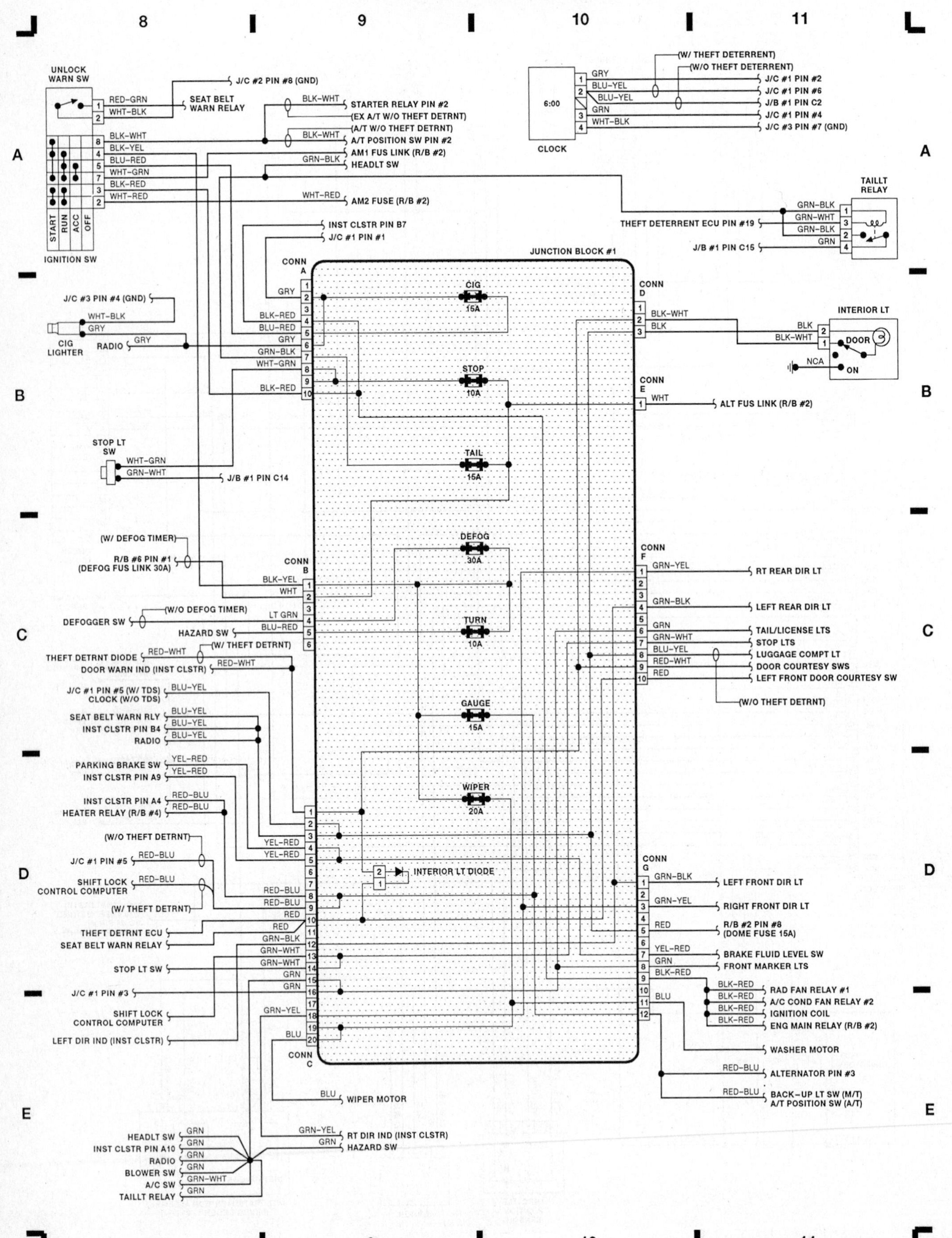

# 1991 WIRING DIAGRAMS
## Tercel (Cont.)

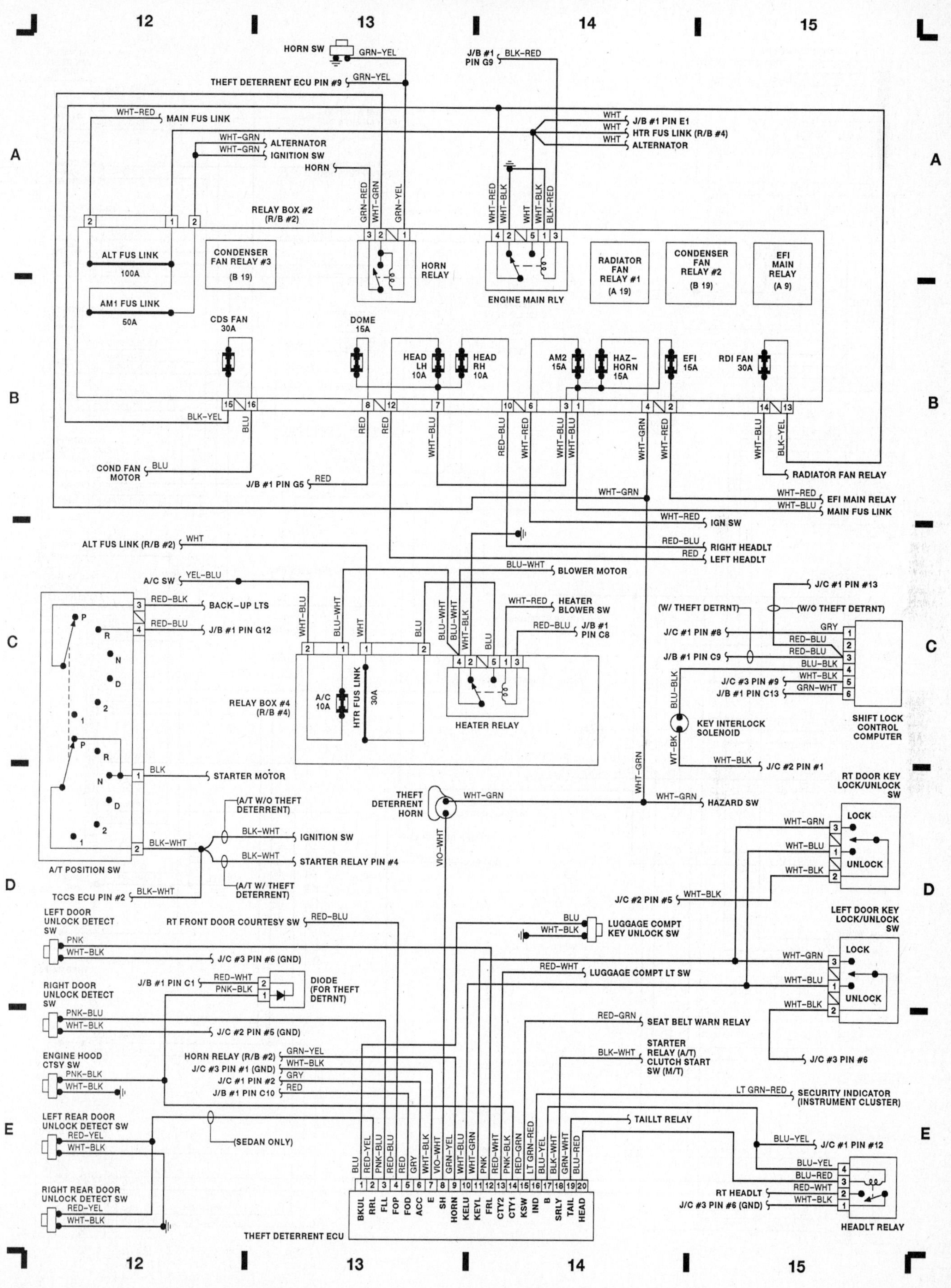

# 1991 WIRING DIAGRAMS
## Tercel (Cont.)

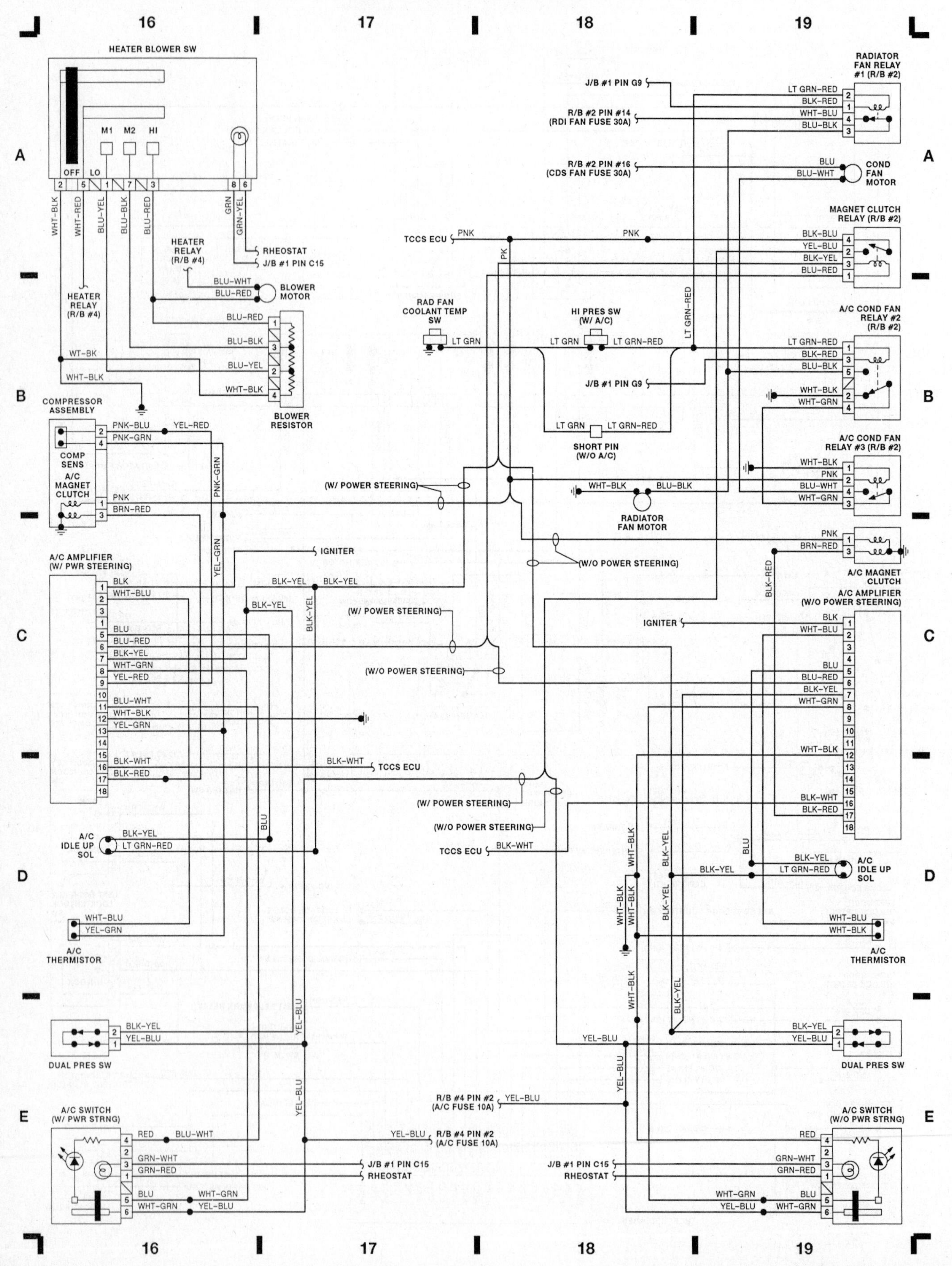

# 1991 WIRING DIAGRAMS
## Tercel (Cont.)

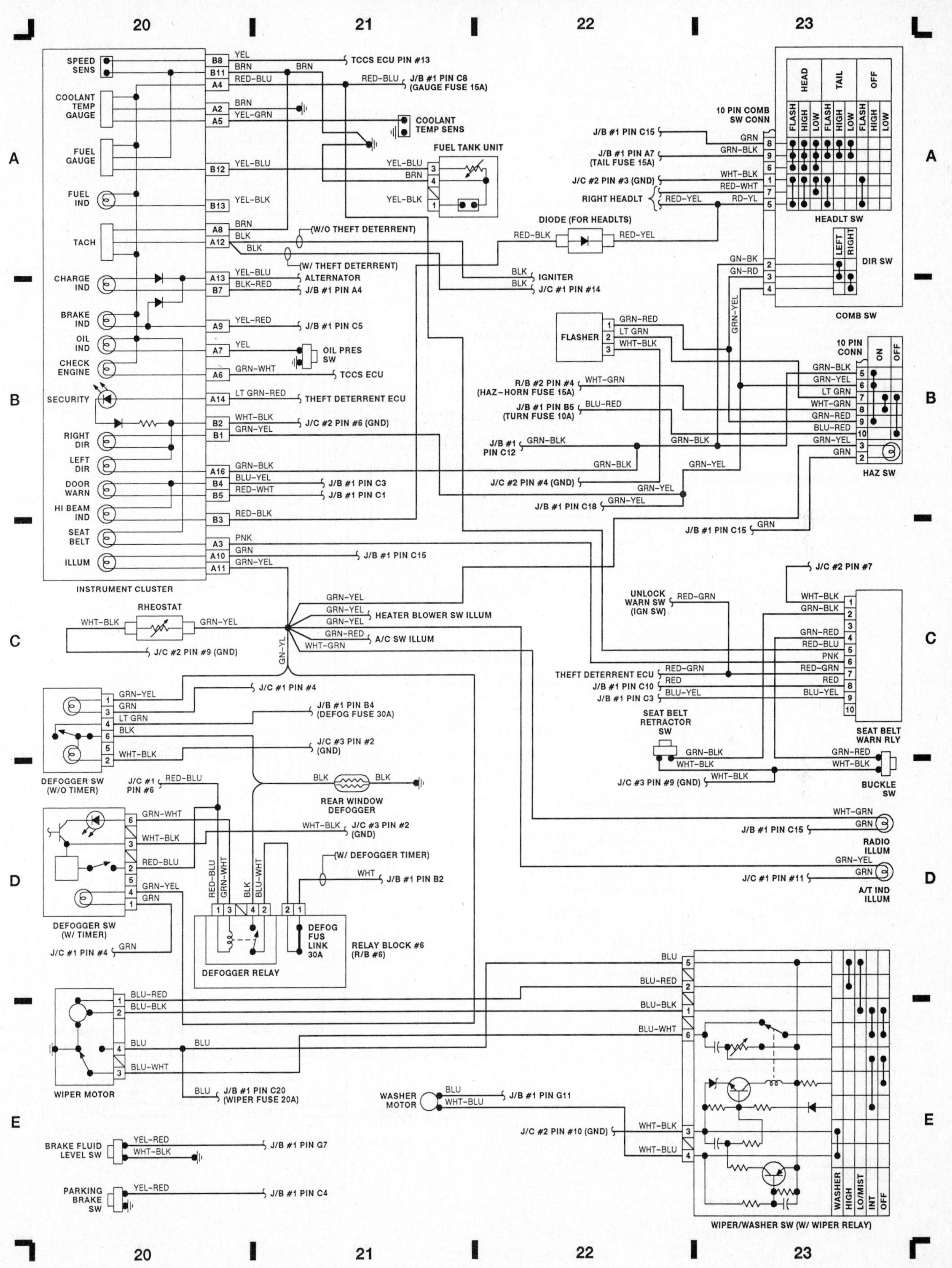

# 1991 WIRING DIAGRAMS
## Tercel (Cont.)

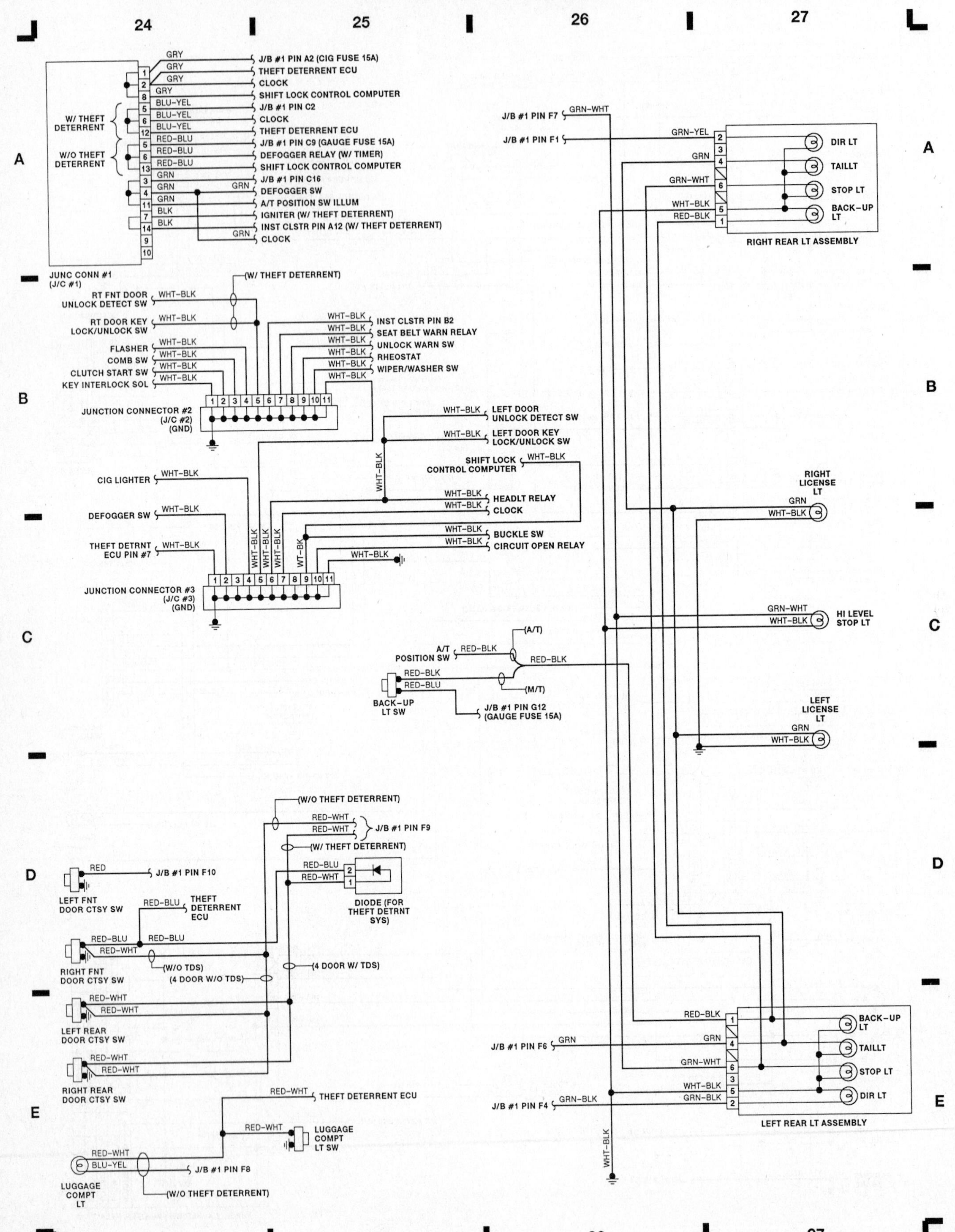

# 1991 WIRING DIAGRAMS
## 4Runner

**COMPONENT LOCATOR:**

| Component | Location |
|---|---|
| A/C AMPLIFIER | E 7 |
| A/C DUAL PRESSURE SW | C 7 |
| A/C SW | D 7 |
| A/T INDICATOR SW (W/ ECT) | D–E 34–35 |
| A/T INDICATOR SW (W/O ECT) | D–E 32–33 |
| ABS ECU | D–E 36 |
| ALTERNATOR | E 3 |
| AUTO ANTENNA RELAY | C–D 32 |
| AUTO DISCONNECT DIFFERENTIAL (ADD) CONTROL RELAY (A/T) | A 32 |
| AUTO DISCONNECT DIFFERENTIAL (ADD) CONTROL RELAY (M/T) | C 32 |
| BATTERY | A 2 |
| BUCKLE SW | E 25 |
| CHECK CONNECTOR (4 CYL W/O ECT) | D 11 |
| CHECK CONNECTOR (4CYL W/ ECT) | D 15 |
| CHECK CONNECTOR (V6 A/T) | D 23 |
| CHECK CONNECTOR (V6 M/T) | D–E 19 |
| CIGAR LTR | B 36 |
| CLOCK | B 36 |
| CLUTCH START CANCEL SW (M/T) | B–C 2 |
| COURTESY LTS | A 45–46 |
| CRUISE CONTROL COMPUTER | A–B 28–31 |
| CRUISE CONTROL MAIN RELAY | B 31 |
| DEFOGGER SW | A 43 |
| DIR SW | D 31 |
| DOOR CONTROL RELAY | C–D 42–43 |
| DOOR COURTESY SW | E 24–25 |
| ECT PATTERN SELECT SW | D 36 |
| EFI MAIN RELAY (4 CYL W/ ECT) | A 15 |
| EFI MAIN RELAY (4 CYL W/O ECT) | A–11 |
| EFI MAIN RELAY (V6 A/T) | A 23 |
| EFI MAIN RELAY (V6 M/T) | A 19 |
| FRONT INTERIOR LT | A 44 |
| GLOVE BOX LT SW | B 36 |
| HAZARD SW | E 31 |
| HEADLT SW | C–D 31 |
| HEATER BLOWER SW | B 34 |
| HORN SW | E 28 |
| IDLE UP VSV | E 7 |
| IGNITER (V6 A/T) | E 22 |
| IGNITER (V6 M/T) | E 18 |
| IGNITION COIL W/ IGNITER (4 CYL W/ ECT) | E 14–15 |
| IGNITION COIL W/ IGNITER (4 CYL W/O ECT) | E 10 |
| IGNITION SW | A 27 |
| INSTRUMENT CLUSTER | A–D 36–39 |
| INTERIOR LT (REAR) | A 46 |
| JUNCTION BLOCK #1 (J/B #1) | A–D 24–27 |
| LIGHT REMINDER RELAY | E 27 |
| OVERDRIVE RELAY | B–C 28 |
| POWER MIRROR SYSTEM | B 44–46 |
| POWER WINDOW MASTER SW | A–D 40–42 |
| REAR POWER WINDOW & REAR WIPER CONTROL RELAY | C–E 44–46 |
| REAR POWER WINDOW LOCK SW | E 45 |
| REAR POWER WINDOW SW | E 46 |
| RELAY BOX #2 (R/B #2) | A–C 4–7 |
| RELAY BOX #3 (R/B #3) | B–C 35 |
| RELAY BOX #4 (R/B #4) | D–E 4–5 |
| RHEOSTAT | A 36 |
| SHIFT LOCK CONTROL | C 28 |
| START INJECTOR TIME SW | D 3 |
| STARTER | A 3 |
| STARTER RELAY | B 3 |
| STOP LT SW | A 31 |
| SUN ROOF CONTROL SW | A 40 |
| TCCS ECU (4 CYL W/ ECT) | A–D 12–15 |
| TCCS ECU (4 CYL W/O ECT) | B–D 8–11 |
| TCCS ECU (V6 A/T) | A–D 20–23 |
| TCCS ECU (V6 M/T) | A–D 16–19 |
| UNLOCK WARN SW | A 27 |
| WIPER/WASHER SW/RELAY | D–E 28–30 |
| 4WD INDICATOR SW | B 32 |

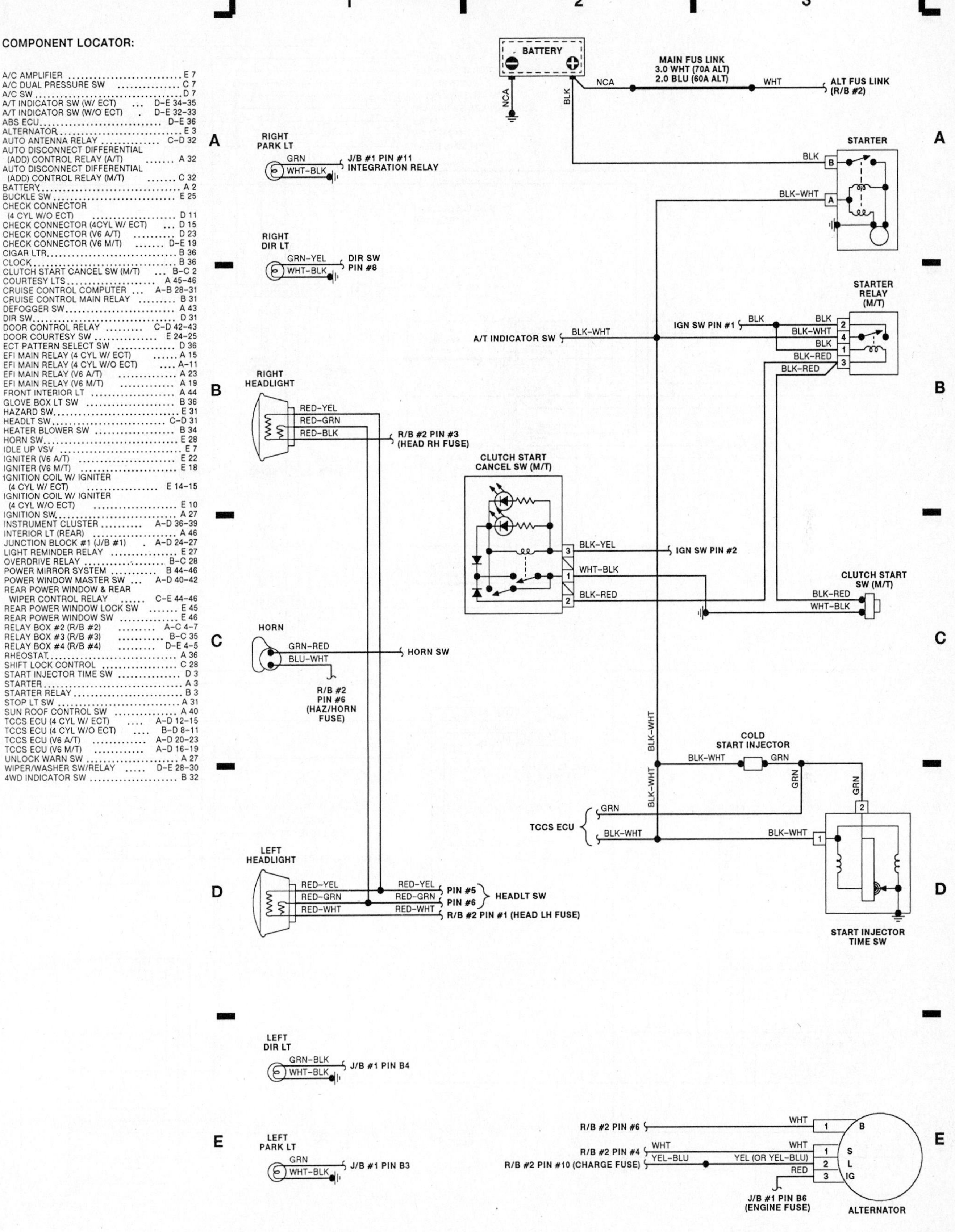

# 1991 WIRING DIAGRAMS
## 4Runner (Cont.)

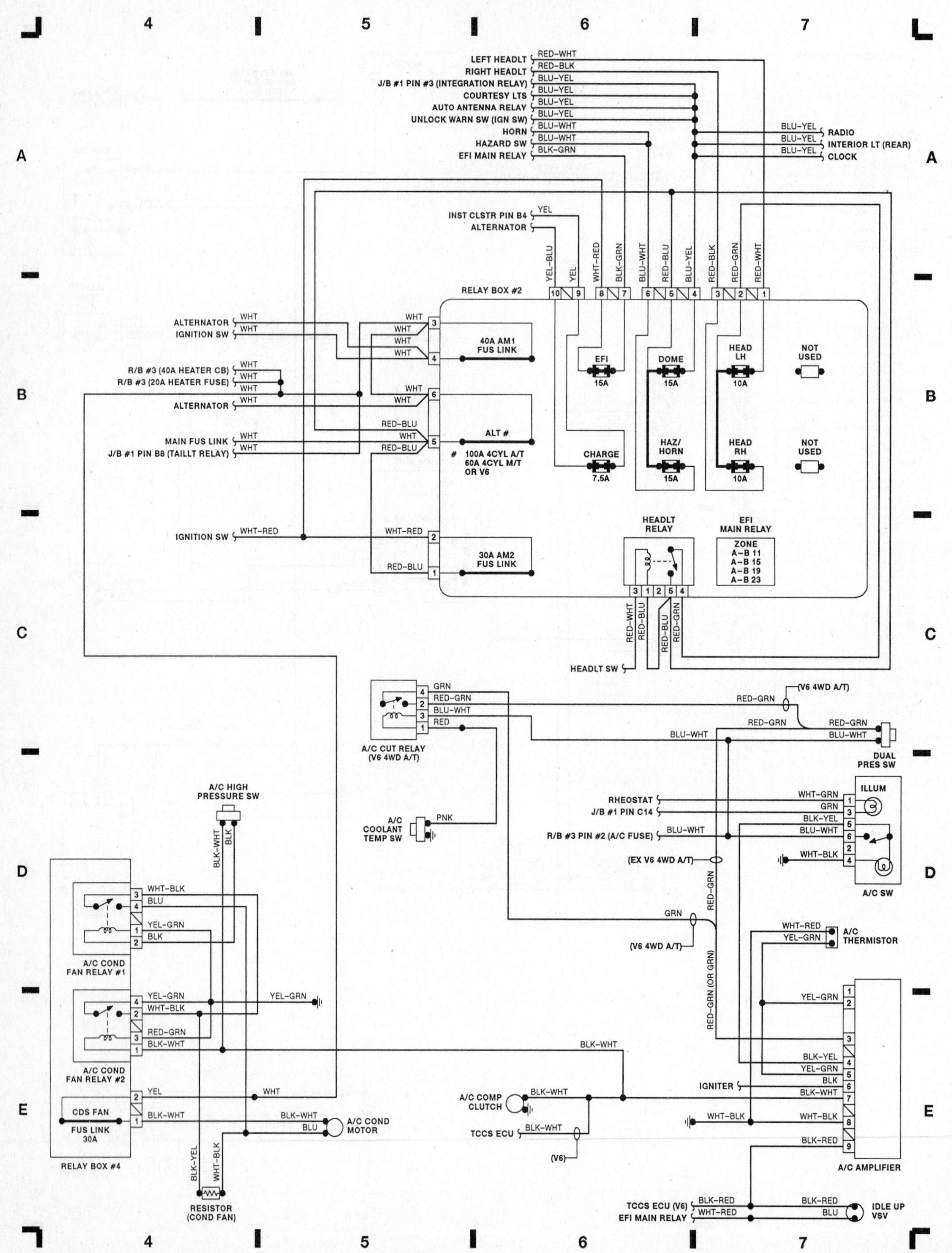

# 1991 WIRING DIAGRAMS
# 4Runner (Cont.)

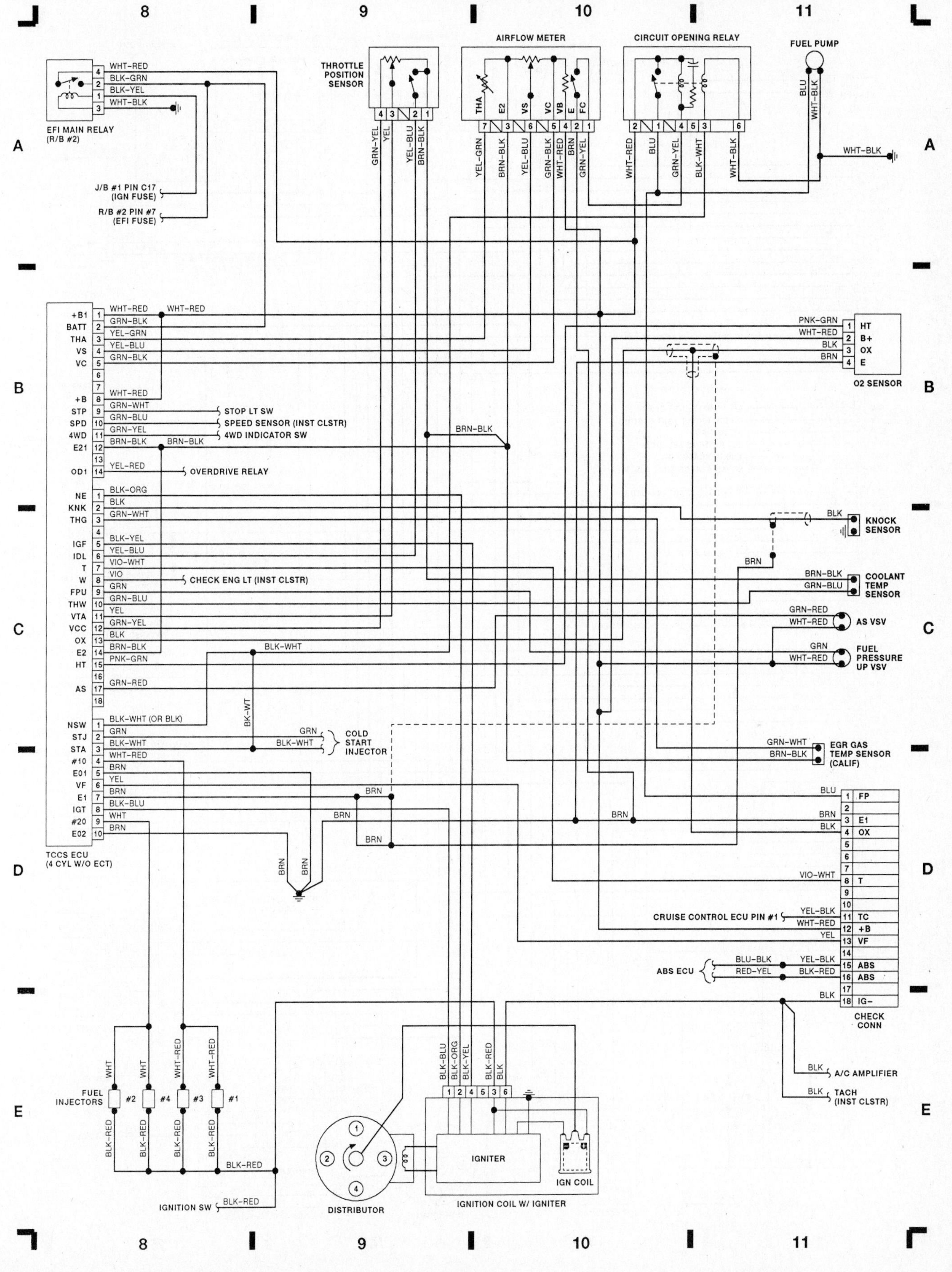

# 1991 WIRING DIAGRAMS
## 4Runner (Cont.)

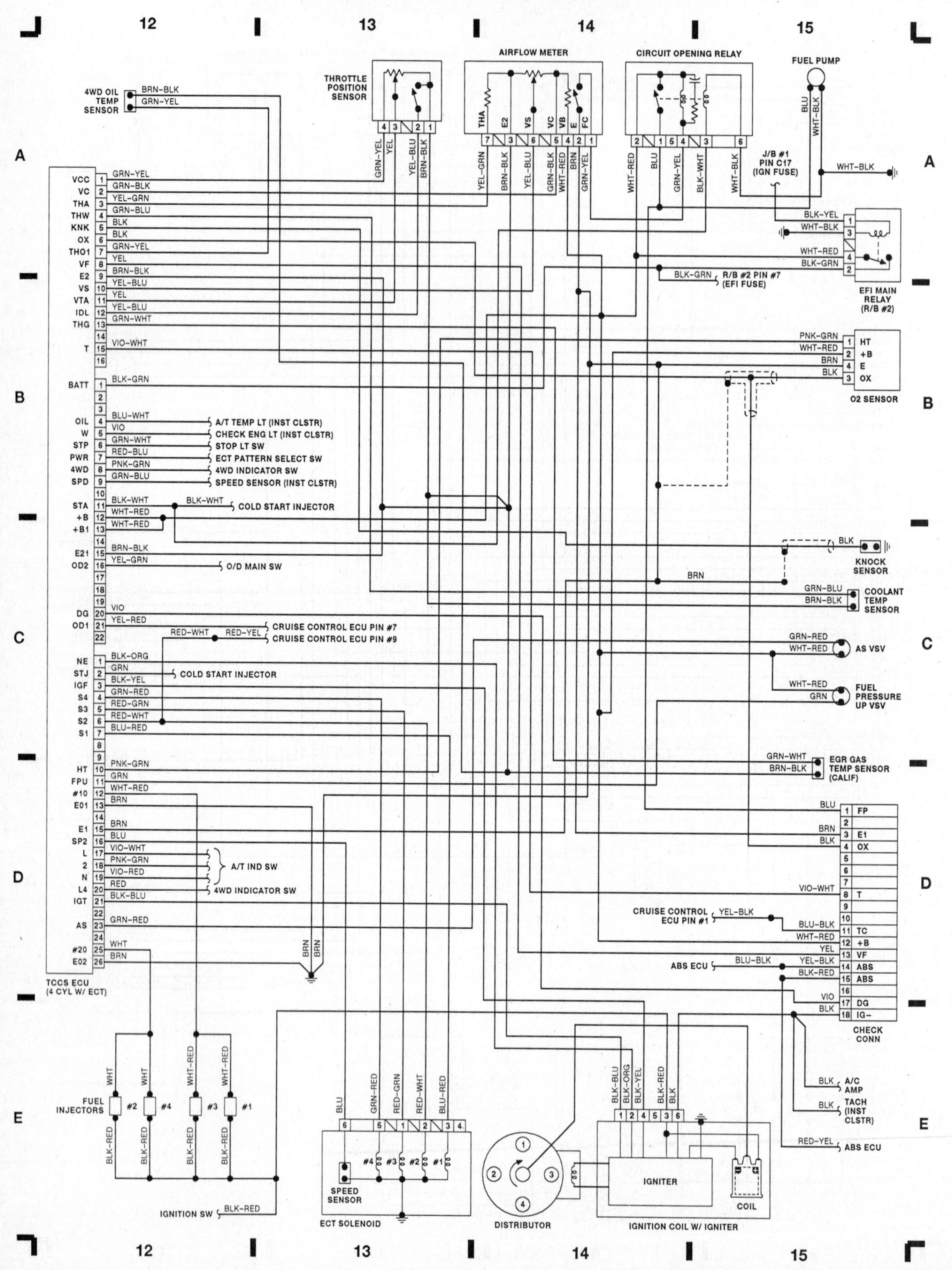

# 1991 WIRING DIAGRAMS
## 4Runner (Cont.)

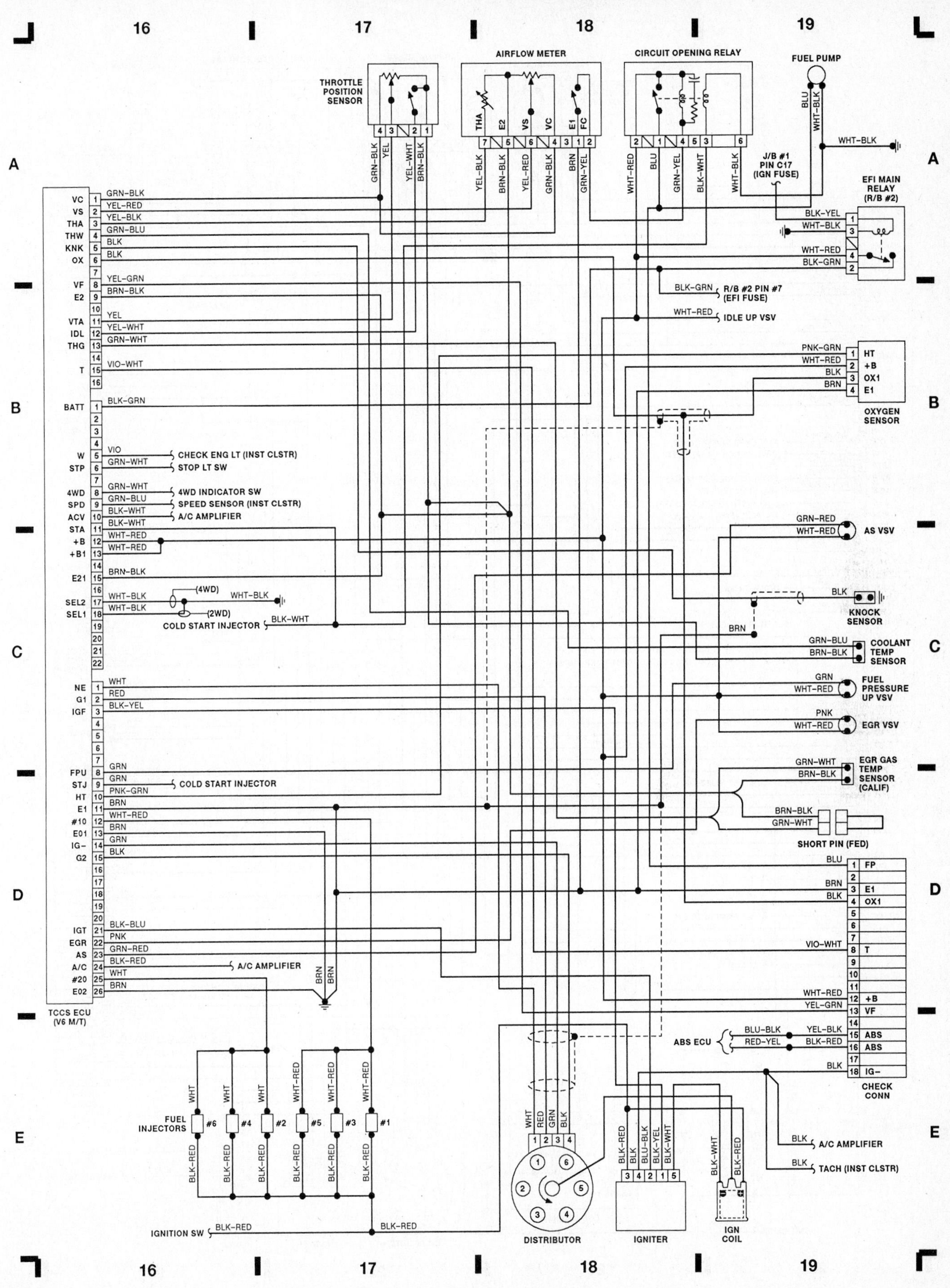

# 1991 WIRING DIAGRAMS
## 4Runner (Cont.)

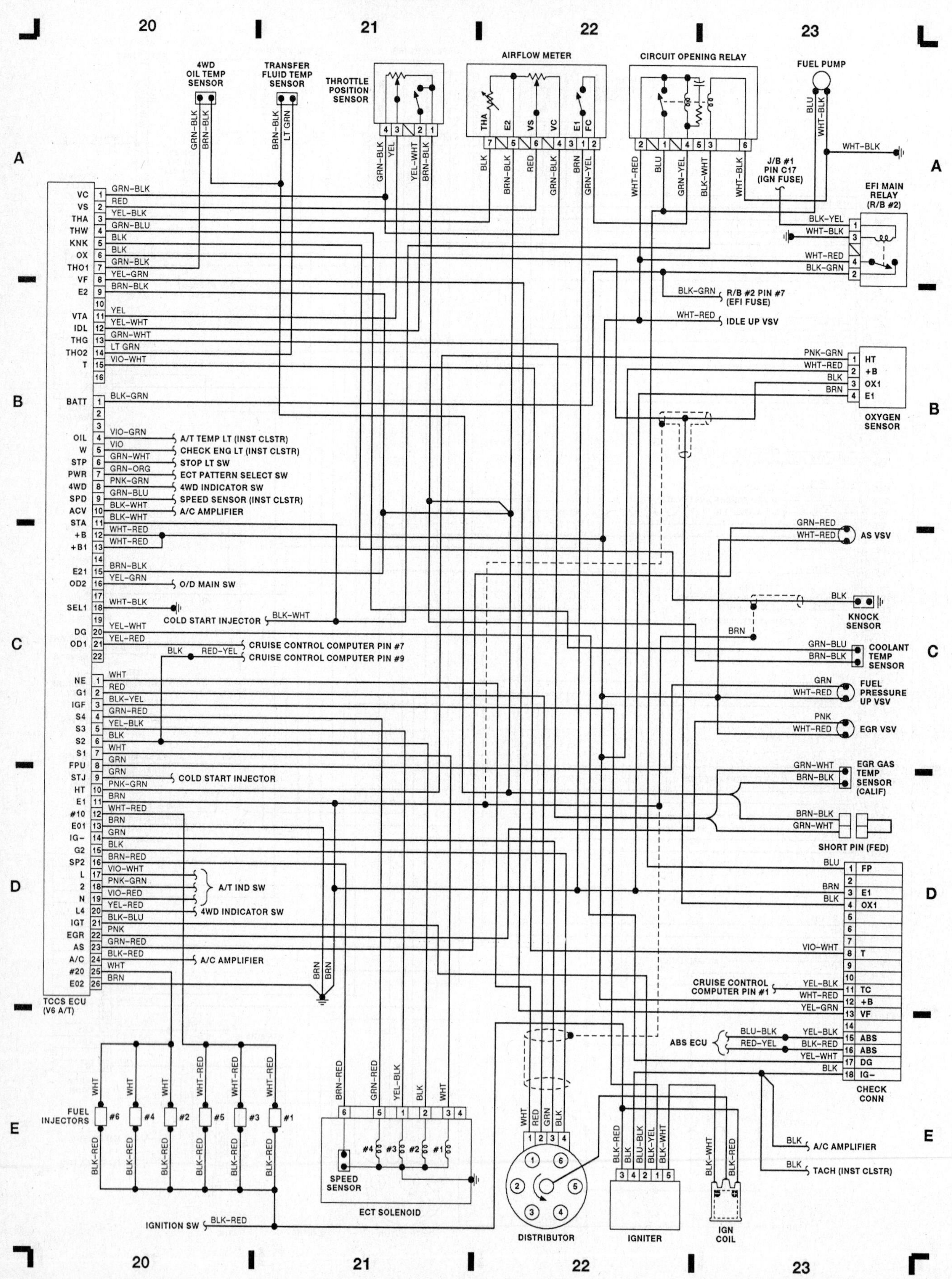

# 1991 WIRING DIAGRAMS
## 4Runner (Cont.)

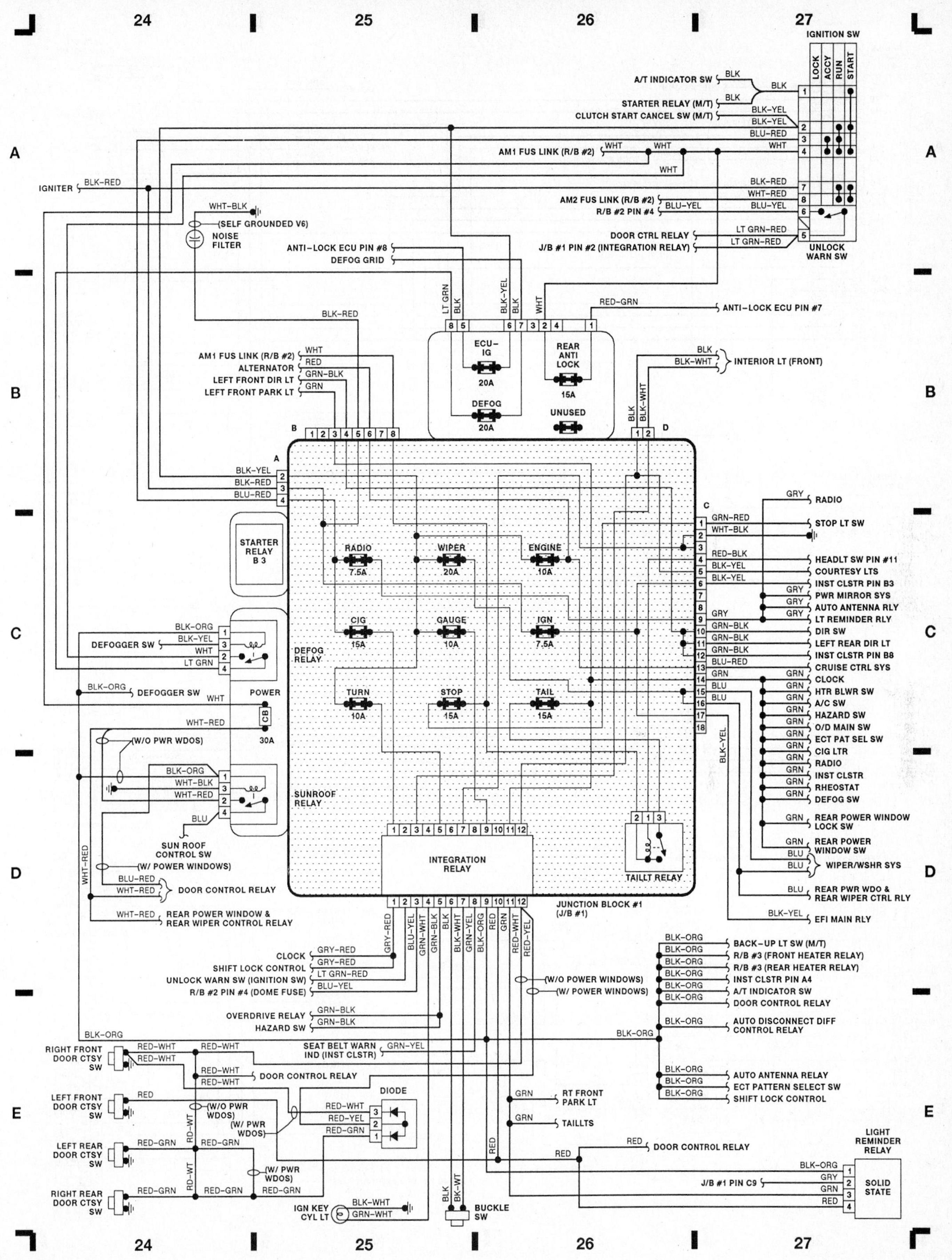

# 1991 WIRING DIAGRAMS
## 4Runner (Cont.)

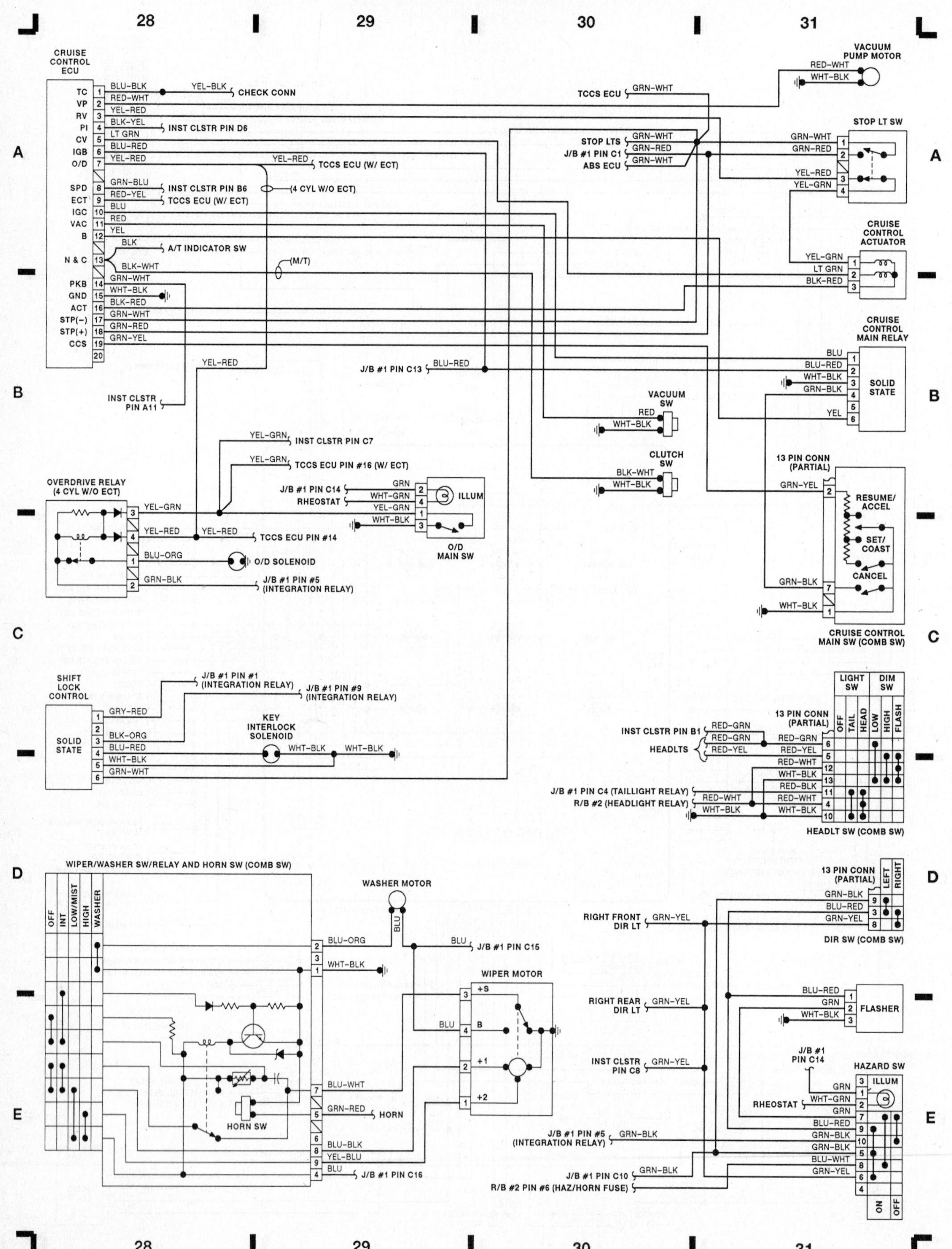

# 1991 WIRING DIAGRAMS
## 4Runner (Cont.)

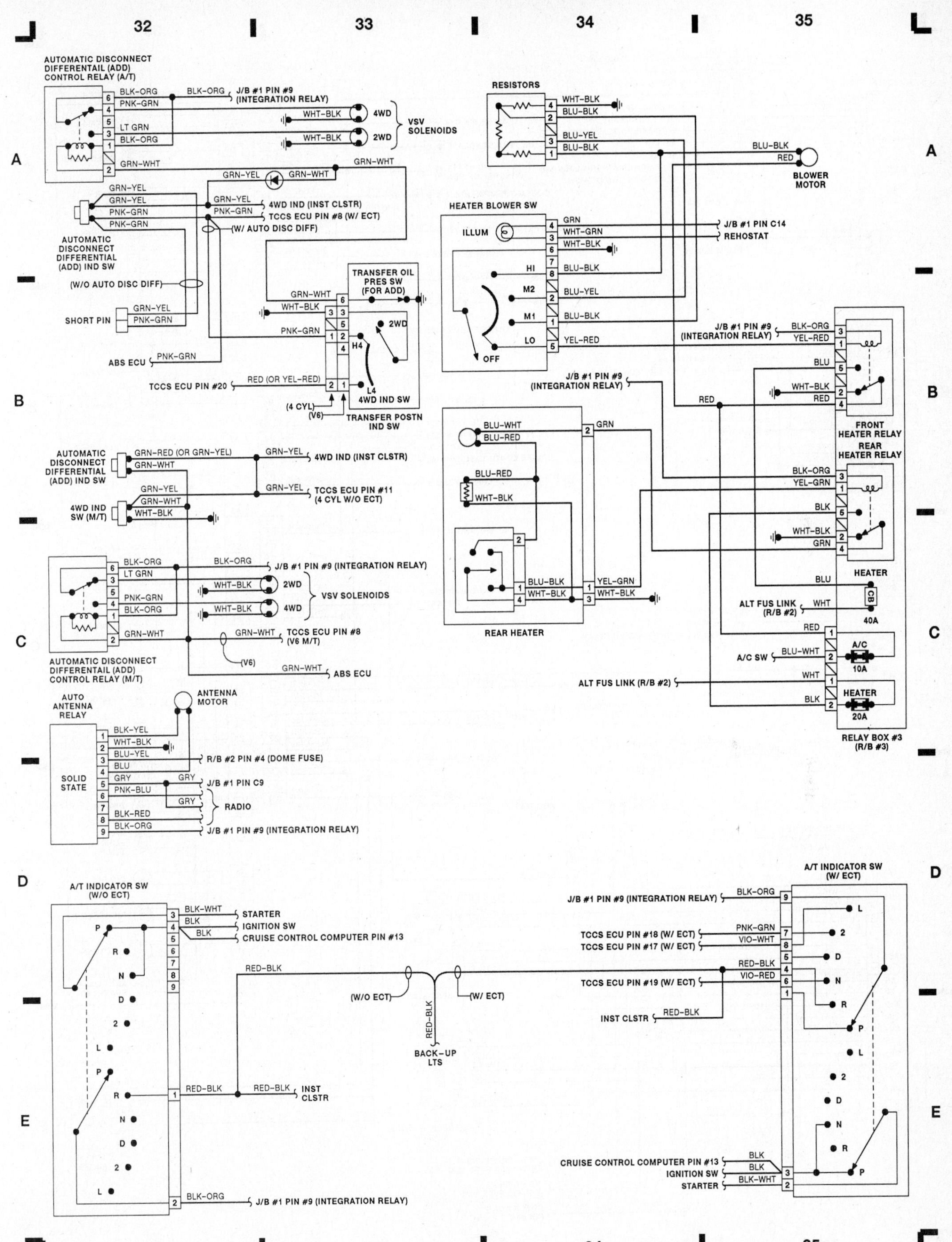

# 1991 WIRING DIAGRAMS
## 4Runner (Cont.)

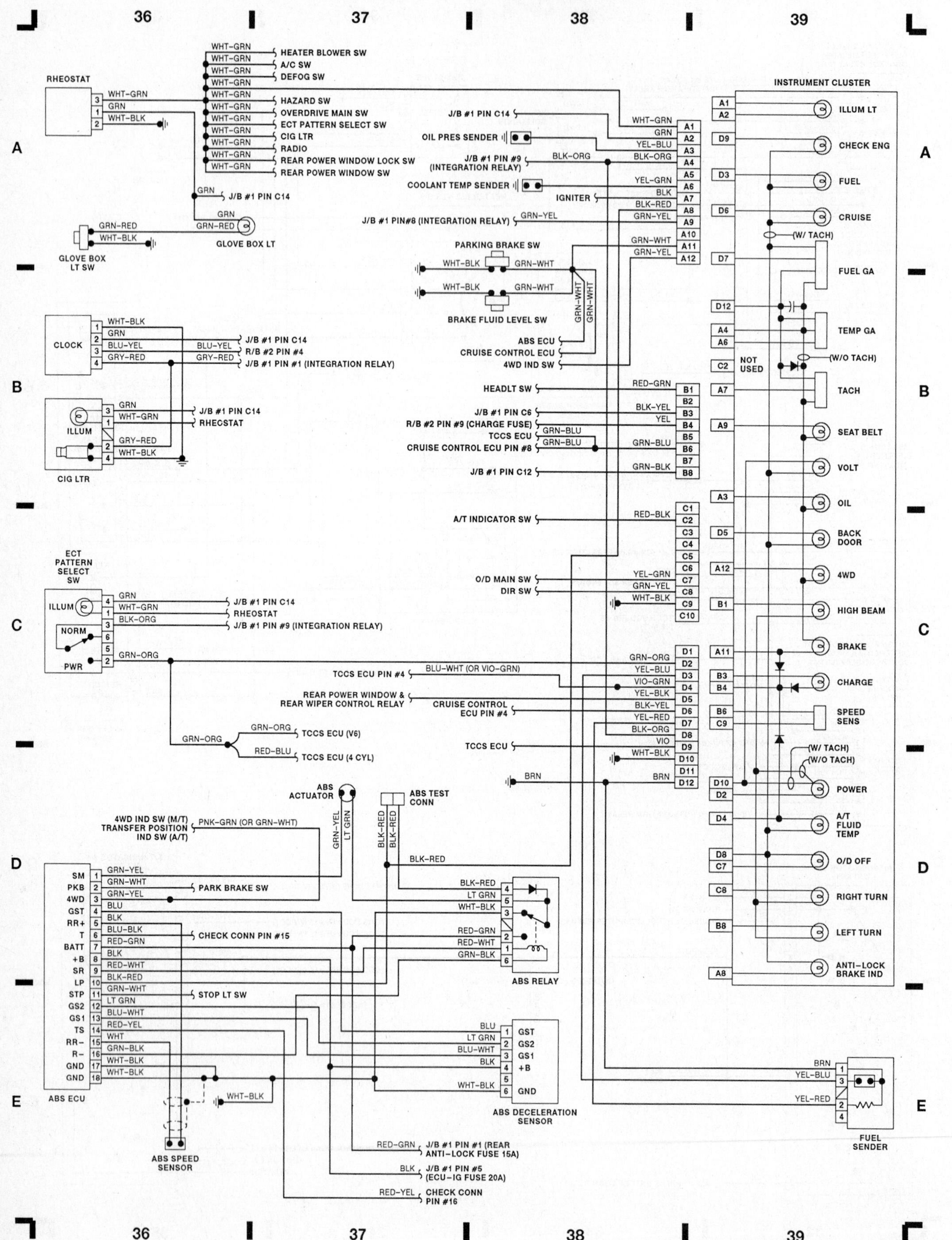

# 1991 WIRING DIAGRAMS
## 4Runner (Cont.)

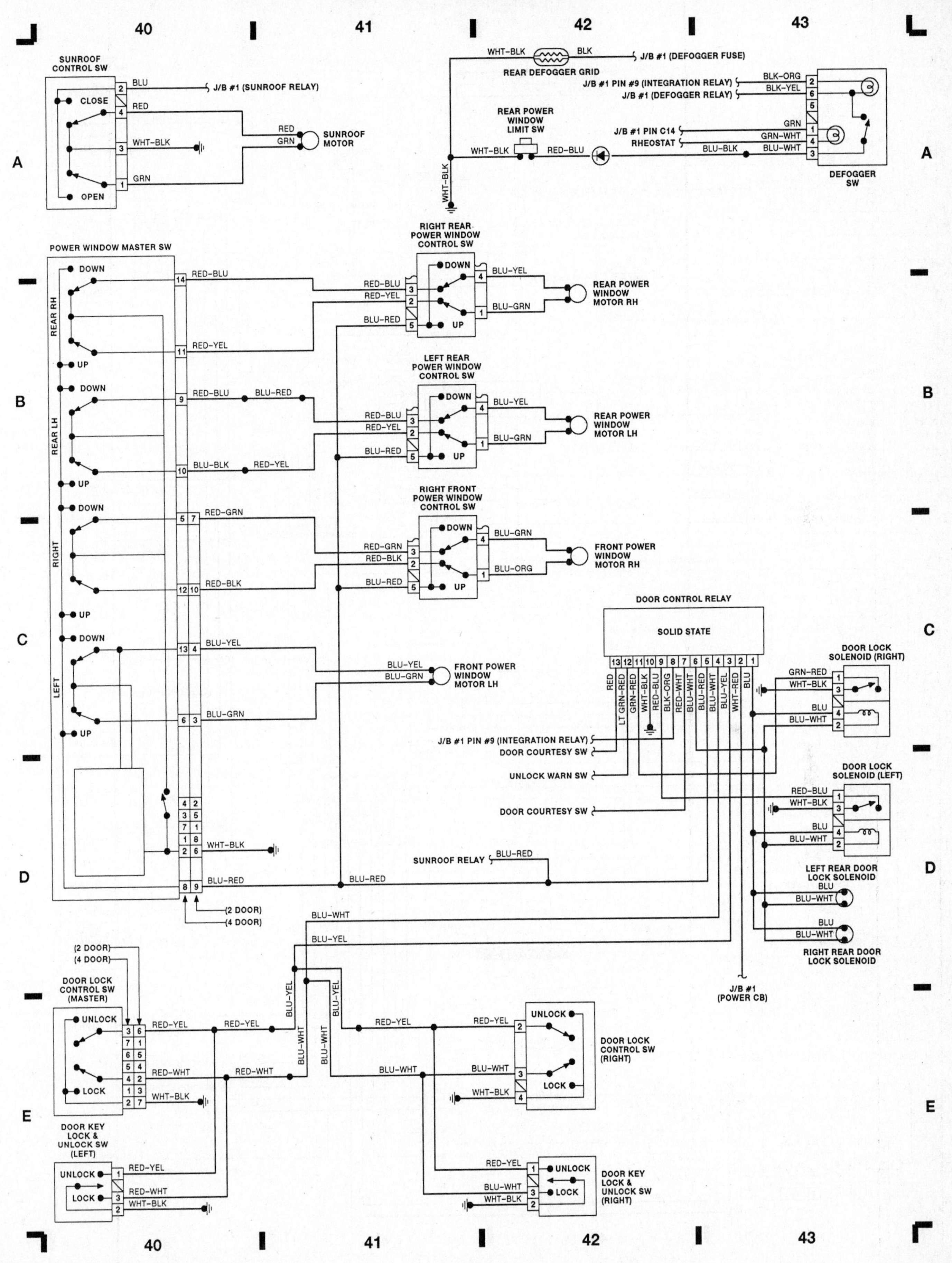

# 1991 WIRING DIAGRAMS
## 4Runner (Cont.)

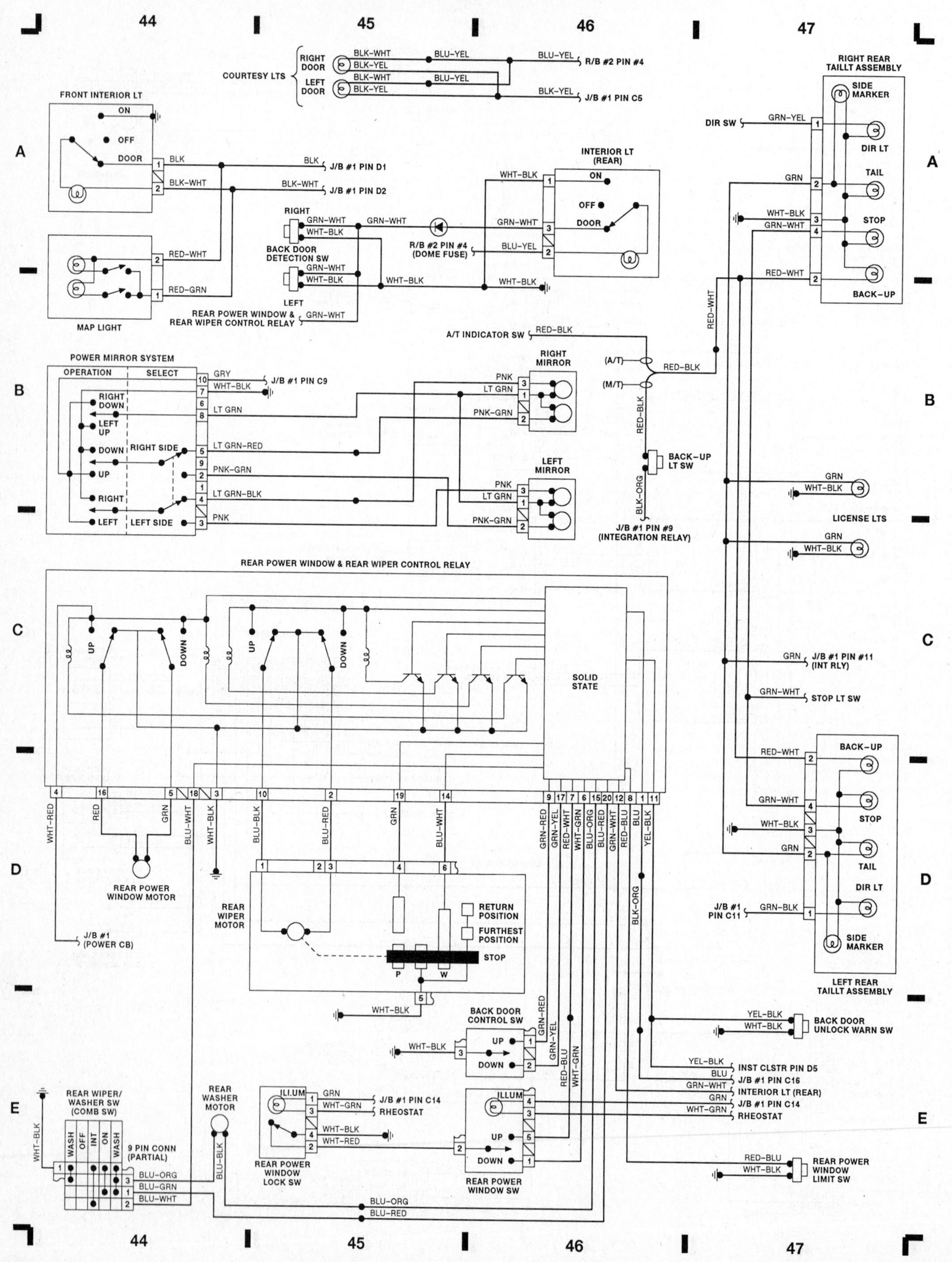

# 1991 SAFETY EQUIPMENT
# Air Bag Restraint System

## Celica, Supra, MR2

***WARNING: To avoid injury from accidental air bag deployment, read and carefully follow all WARNINGS and SERVICE PRECAUTIONS.***

***NOTE: For information on air bag DIAGNOSIS & TESTING or DISPOSAL PROCEDURES, see MITCHELL'S AIR BAG SERVICE & REPAIR MANUAL, DOMESTIC & IMPORTED MODELS.***

## DESCRIPTION & OPERATION

The Supplement Restraint System (SRS) consists of an AIR BAG warning light in the instrument cluster, left and right front impact sensors, steering wheel pad, spiral cable and center air bag sensor. Steering wheel pad contains inflater and bag assembly. Center air bag sensor contains the back-up power source circuit, safety circuit, safing sensor, memory circuit, diagnostic circuit, ignition control and drive circuits. *See Figs. 1 and 2.*

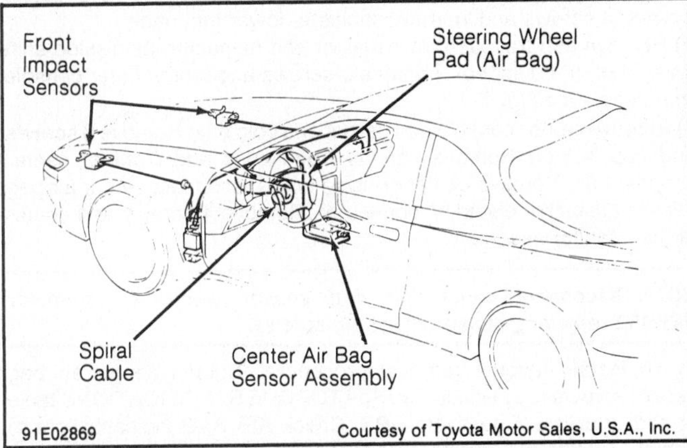


***Fig. 1: Locating SRS Components (Celica Shown; MR2 Is Similar)***

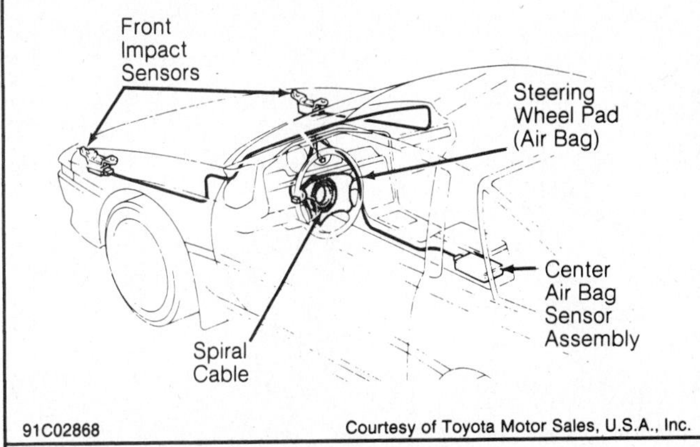


***Fig. 2: Locating SRS Components (Supra)***

The SRS is designed to deploy when the front-to-rear shock is greater than a specified value. The ignition control and drive circuits calculate signals from the center air bag sensor, deploying air bag.

## SYSTEM OPERATION CHECK

Turn ignition switch to ACC or ON position. AIR BAG warning light in instrument cluster should illuminate and go out after approximately 6 seconds. If AIR BAG warning light stays illuminated for more than 6 seconds with ignition switch in ACC or ON position, SRS system is malfunctioning and needs repair. If AIR BAG warning light illuminates with ignition off, a short circuit is likely in the AIR BAG warning light circuit.

## SERVICE PRECAUTIONS

Observe the following precautions when working with air bag systems:

- Disable SRS before servicing any SRS or steering column component. Failure to do this could result in accidental air bag deployment and possible personal injury. See DISABLING & ACTIVATING AIR BAG SYSTEM.
- When troubleshooting SRS, always check for diagnostic codes before disconnecting battery.
- Wait approximately 20 seconds or longer from time ignition switch is turned to LOCK position and negative battery cable is disconnected from battery before working on SRS. SRS is equipped with a back-up power source, so air bag may deploy within 20 seconds of disconnecting negative battery cable.
- In a minor collision in which air bag does not deploy, front air bag sensors and steering wheel pad should be inspected.
- NEVER use air bag parts from another vehicle. Replace air bag parts with new parts.
- Remove air bag sensors if shocks are likely to be applied to sensors during repairs.
- Center air bag sensor assembly contains mercury. After replacement, DO NOT destroy the old part. When scrapping vehicle or replacing center air bag sensor assembly, remove center air bag sensor assembly and dispose of as toxic waste.
- Never disassemble and repair front air bag sensors, center air bag sensor assembly or steering wheel pad.
- If front air bag sensors, center air bag sensor assembly or steering wheel pad is dropped, or if there are cracks, dents or other defects in the case, bracket or connector, replace parts with new ones.
- DO NOT expose front air bag sensors, center air bag sensor assembly or steering wheel pad directly to hot air or flame.
- Use a volt/ohmmeter with high impedance (10 k/ohm minimum) for troubleshooting electrical circuit.
- Information labels are attached to air bag components. Follow all notices on labels.
- After work on SRS is completed, check AIR BAG warning light to ensure system is functioning properly. See SYSTEM OPERATION CHECK.
- Always wear safety glasses when servicing or handling an air bag.
- When placing a live air bag on a bench or other surface, always face air bag and trim cover up, away from surface. This will reduce motion of module if accidentally deployed.
- After deployment, air bag surface may contain deposits of sodium hydroxide, which irritates skin, from the gas generant combustion. Always wear safety glasses, rubber gloves and long-sleeved shirt during clean-up, and wash hands using mild soap and water.
- When carrying a live air bag module, trim cover should be pointed away from your body to minimize injury in case of accidental deployment.
- If SRS is not fully functional for any reason, vehicle should not be driven until system is repaired and again becomes operational. DO NOT remove bulbs, modules, sensors or other components or in any way disable system from operating normally. If SRS is not functional, park vehicle until it is repaired and functions properly.

## DISABLING & ACTIVATING AIR BAG SYSTEM

***WARNING: Wait about 20 seconds after disabling SRS. Back-up power supply maintains SRS voltage for about 20 seconds after battery is disconnected. Servicing SRS before 20-second period may cause accidental air bag deployment and possible personal injury.***

To disable SRS, turn ignition switch to LOCK position and disconnect negative battery cable. Allow 20 seconds before working on system. To activate SRS, reconnect negative battery cable. Perform SYSTEM OPERATION CHECK.

# 1991 SAFETY EQUIPMENT
# Air Bag Restraint System (Cont.)

## REMOVAL & INSTALLATION

***WARNING: Failure to follow air bag service precautions may result in air bag deployment and personal injury. See SERVICE PRECAUTIONS. After component replacement, perform a system operational check to ensure proper system operation. See SYSTEM OPERATION CHECK.***

## CENTER AIR BAG SENSOR

**Removal & Installation (Celica) - 1)** Before proceeding, follow air bag service precautions. See SERVICE PRECAUTIONS. Disable SRS. See DISABLING & ACTIVATION AIR BAG SYSTEM.

**2)** Center air bag sensor is located in console. Remove center console box upper panel. Remove 4 screw covers from sides of center console box. Remove 4 center console screws and 2 bolts. Remove center console box.

**3)** Remove scuff plates. Remove 4 screws, glove box and passenger-side lower trim panel. Remove engine hood release lever. Remove screw covers, 6 screws and instrument cluster lower trim panel.

**4)** Remove 2 screws and radio trim panel. Remove 4 screws and radio. Remove screw covers and 4 screws from center console. Remove instrument panel brace. *See Fig. 3.* Disconnect center air bag sensor assembly electrical connector. Remove 4 screws and center air bag sensor assembly.

***NOTE: Disconnect center air bag sensor electrical connector BEFORE removing sensor attaching screws.***

**5)** To install, reverse removal procedure. Tighten center air bag sensor screws to specification. See TORQUE SPECIFICATIONS table at end of article. Reactivate SRS. Check AIR BAG indicator light to ensure system is functioning properly. See SYSTEM OPERATION CHECK.

**Removal & Installation (MR2) - 1)** Before proceeding, follow air bag service precautions. See SERVICE PRECAUTIONS. Disable SRS. See DISABLING & ACTIVATING AIR BAG SYSTEM.

**2)** Center air bag sensor is located in console. Remove shift lever knob and shift hole cover. Remove instrument cluster center finish panel, radio, heater control and ash tray. *See Fig. 4.* Disconnect center air bag sensor assembly electrical connectors. Remove 4 screws and center air bag sensor.

***NOTE: Disconnect center air bag sensor electrical connector BEFORE removing sensor attaching screws.***

**3)** To install, reverse removal procedure. Tighten center air bag sensor screws to specification. See TORQUE SPECIFICATIONS table at end of article. Reactivate SRS. Check AIR BAG indicator light to ensure system is functioning properly. See SYSTEM OPERATION CHECK.

**Removal & Installation (Supra) - 1)** Before proceeding, follow air bag service precautions. See SERVICE PRECAUTIONS. Disable SRS. See DISABLING & ACTIVATING AIR BAG SYSTEM.

**2)** Center air bag sensor is located in console. Remove driver's side scuff plate. Remove engine hood release lever. Remove screw covers, 4 screws and instrument cluster lower trim panel.

**3)** Remove ash tray, ash tray retainer and manual transmission shift lever knob (if equipped). Remove 3 screws and radio/center console trim panel. *See Fig. 4.*

**4)** Remove center console box carpet and coin box. Remove 8 screws and cup holder. Remove screws from sides and front of center console box. Remove center console box. Disconnect center air bag sensor assembly electrical connector. Remove 4 screws and center air bag sensor assembly.

***NOTE: Disconnect center air bag sensor electrical connector BEFORE removing sensor attaching screws.***

**5)** To install, reverse removal procedure. Tighten center air bag sensor screws to specification. See TORQUE SPECIFICATIONS table at end of article. Reactivate SRS. Check AIR BAG indicator light to ensure system is functioning properly. See SYSTEM OPERATION CHECK.

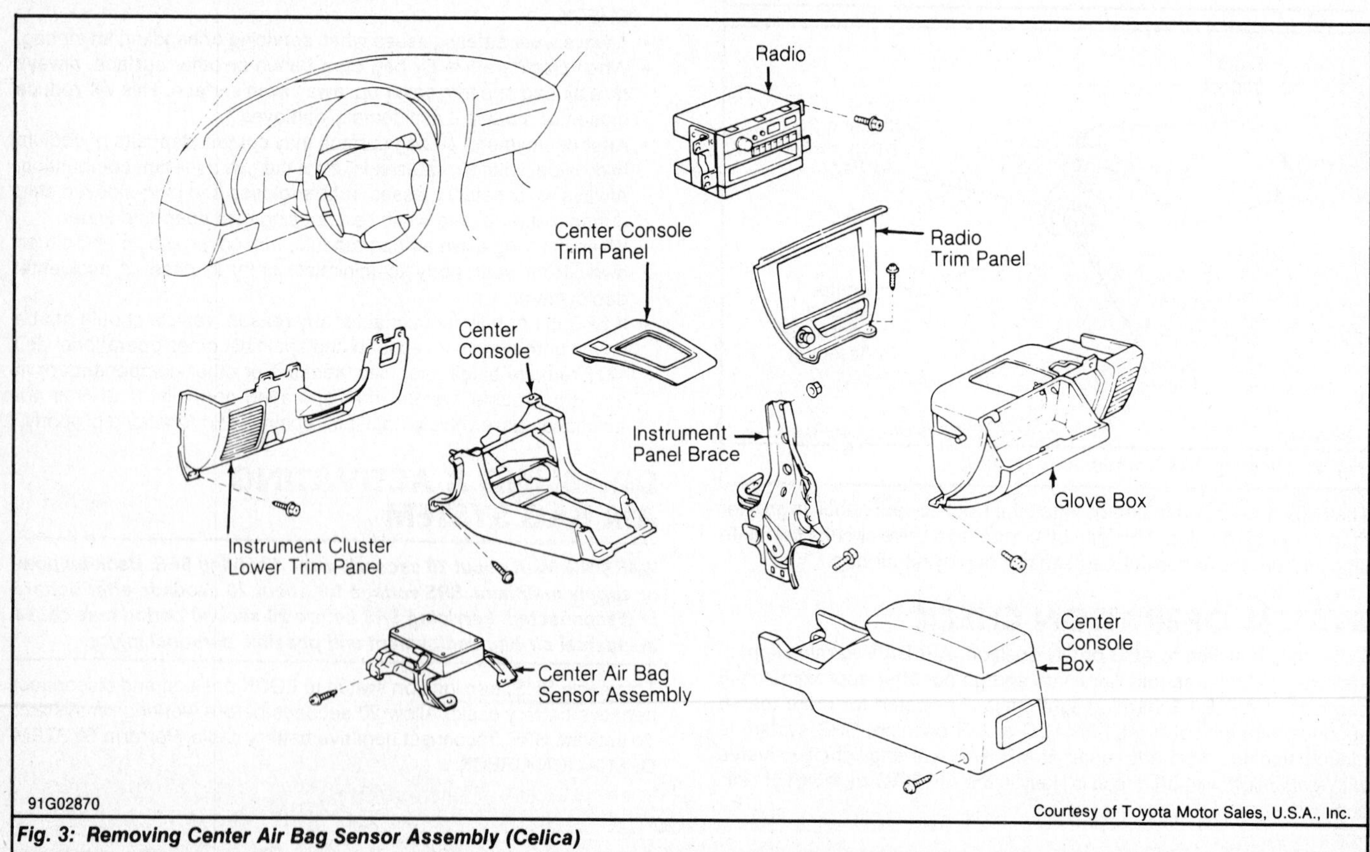


***Fig. 3: Removing Center Air Bag Sensor Assembly (Celica)***

# 1991 SAFETY EQUIPMENT
# Air Bag Restraint System (Cont.)

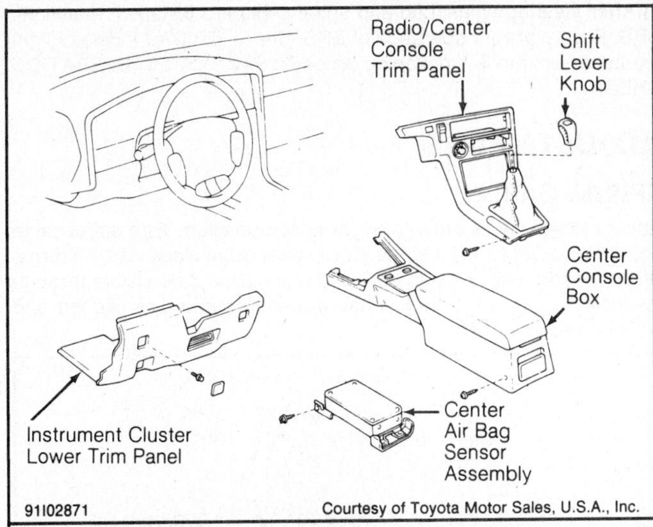


*Fig. 4: Removing Center Air Bag Sensor Assembly (Supra Shown; MR2 Is Similar)*

## FRONT AIR BAG SENSORS

**Removal & Installation - 1)** Before proceeding, follow air bag service precautions. See SERVICE PRECAUTIONS. Disable SRS. See DISABLING & ACTIVATING AIR BAG SYSTEM.

**2)** On MR2, front air bag sensors are located under hood lock protector plate, on inner side of both headlights.

**3)** On all other models, front air bag sensors are located in left and right fender area. Remove screws and clips attaching hood lock protector plate (MR2) or inner fender shield (all other models) to vehicle.

**4)** Remove hood lock protector plate or inner fender shield. Disconnect front air bag sensor electrical connector. Remove 2 bolts attaching sensor to fender. Remove front air bag sensor.

**5)** To install, reverse removal procedure. Ensure arrow marks on sensors face front of vehicle. Tighten front air bag sensor bolts to specification. See TORQUE SPECIFICATIONS table at end of article. Reactivate SRS. Check AIR BAG indicator light to ensure system is functioning properly. See SYSTEM OPERATION CHECK.

## STEERING WHEEL PAD & SPIRAL CABLE

**Removal & Installation (Celica) - 1)** Ensure front wheels are in straight-ahead position. Before proceeding, follow air bag service precautions. See SERVICE PRECAUTIONS. Disable SRS. See DISABLING & ACTIVATING AIR BAG SYSTEM. Remove driver's side scuff plate.

**2)** Remove engine hood release lever. Remove screw covers, 6 screws, and lower instrument cluster trim panel(s). Loosen 4 steering wheel pad Torx screws until groove along screw circumference catches on screw case. *See Figs. 5 and 6.*

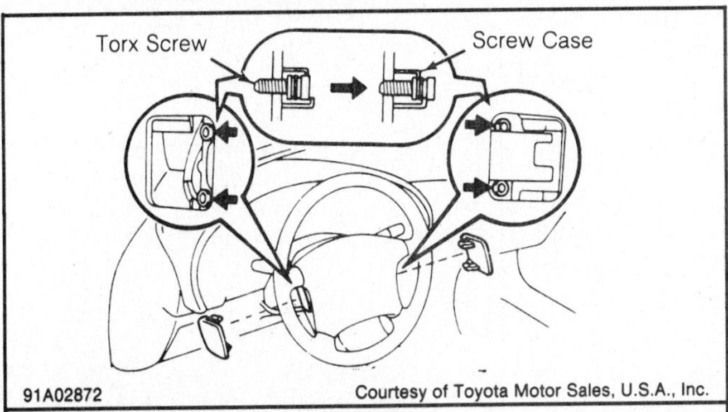


*Fig. 5: Removing Steering Wheel Pad*

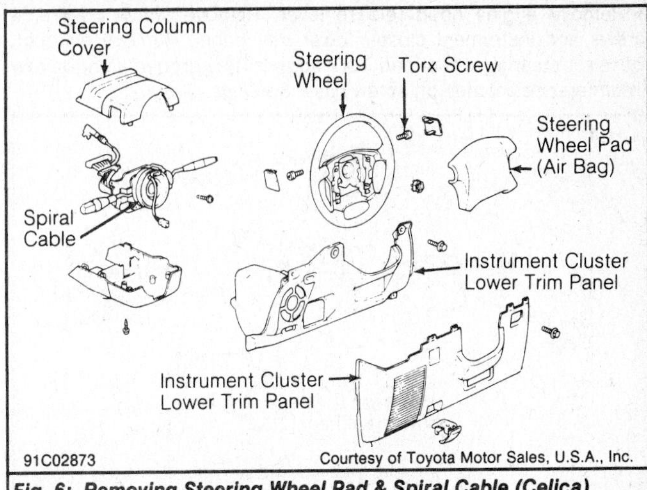


*Fig. 6: Removing Steering Wheel Pad & Spiral Cable (Celica)*

**3)** Pull steering wheel pad from steering wheel and disconnect steering wheel pad (squib) connector. Remove steering wheel pad assembly. Place steering wheel pad assembly on a flat surface with pad cover facing up.

**4)** Place a mark on steering wheel and main shaft for installation reference. Using steering wheel puller, remove steering wheel. Remove 4 screws from upper and lower steering column covers.

**5)** Remove screws attaching spiral cable to combination (headlight/ turn signal/wiper) switch. Disconnect spiral cable and remove from vehicle.

**6)** To install, reverse removal procedure. Tighten steering wheel nut and steering wheel pad screws to specification. See TORQUE SPECIFICATIONS table at end of article. Before installing spiral cable, ensure spiral cable is properly aligned. See ADJUSTMENTS.

**7)** After steering wheel pad and spiral cable are installed, reactivate SRS. Ensure proper operation of SRS. Check AIR BAG indicator light to ensure system is functioning properly. See SYSTEM OPERATION CHECK.

**Removal & Installation (MR2) - 1)** Ensure front wheels are in straight-ahead position. Before proceeding, follow air bag service precautions. See SERVICE PRECAUTIONS. Deactivate SRS. See DISABLING & ACTIVATING AIR BAG SYSTEM.

**2)** Remove lower instrument panel screw covers and screws. Remove lower instrument panel and lower instrument panel insert. Remove air duct. Loosen 4 steering wheel pad Torx screws until groove along screw circumference catches on screw case. *See Figs. 5 and 7.*

**3)** Pull steering wheel pad from steering wheel and disconnect steering wheel pad (squib) connector. Remove steering wheel pad assembly. Place steering wheel pad assembly on a flat surface with pad cover facing up.

**4)** Place a reference mark on steering wheel and main shaft. Using steering wheel puller, remove steering wheel. Remove screws from upper and lower steering column covers.

**5)** Remove screws attaching spiral cable to combination (headlight/ turn signal/wiper) switch. Disconnect spiral cable and remove from vehicle.

**6)** To install, reverse removal procedure. Tighten steering wheel nut and steering wheel pad to specification. See TORQUE SPECIFICATIONS table at end of article. Before installing spiral cable, ensure spiral cable is properly aligned. See ADJUSTMENTS.

**7)** After steering wheel pad and spiral cable are installed, reactivate SRS. Ensure proper operation of SRS. Check AIR BAG indicator light to ensure system is functioning properly. See SYSTEM OPERATION CHECK.

**Removal & Installation (Supra) - 1)** Ensure front wheels are in straight-ahead position. Before proceeding, follow air bag service precautions. See SERVICE PRECAUTIONS. Deactivate SRS. See DISABLING & ACTIVATING AIR BAG SYSTEM. Remove driver-side scuff plate.

# 1991 SAFETY EQUIPMENT
# Air Bag Restraint System (Cont.)

**2)** Remove engine hood release lever. Remove screw covers, 4 screws and instrument cluster lower trim panel. Remove air duct. Loosen 4 steering wheel pad Torx screws until groove along screw circumference catches on screw case. *See Figs. 5 and 7*.

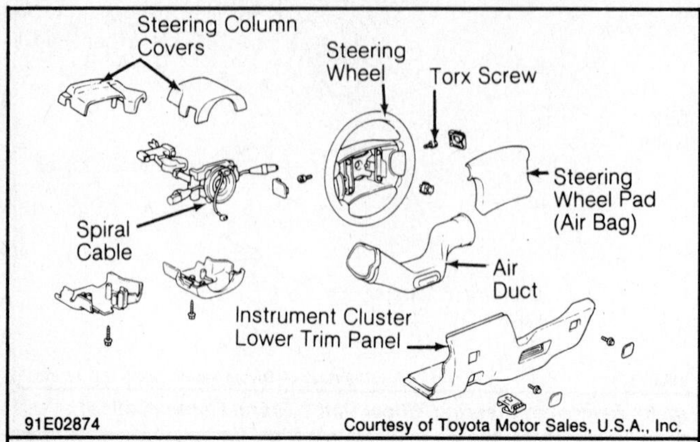


***Fig. 7: Removing Steering Wheel Pad & Spiral Cable (Supra Shown; MR2 Is Similar)***

**3)** Pull steering wheel pad from steering wheel and disconnect steering wheel pad (squib) connector. Remove steering wheel pad assembly. Place steering wheel pad assembly on a flat surface with pad cover facing up.

**4)** Place a reference mark on steering wheel and main shaft. Using steering wheel puller, remove steering wheel. Remove screws from upper and lower steering column covers.

**5)** Remove screws attaching spiral cable to combination (headlight/turn signal/wiper) switch. Disconnect spiral cable and remove from vehicle.

**6)** To install, reverse removal procedure. Tighten steering wheel nut and steering wheel pad to specification. See TORQUE SPECIFICATIONS table at end of article. Before installing spiral cable, ensure spiral cable is properly aligned. See ADJUSTMENTS.

**7)** After steering wheel pad and spiral cable are installed, reactivate SRS. Ensure proper operation of SRS. Check AIR BAG indicator light to ensure system is functioning properly. See SYSTEM OPERATION CHECK.

## ADJUSTMENTS

### SPIRAL CABLE

Ensure front wheels are in straight-ahead position. Turn spiral cable counterclockwise until it stops. Turn spiral cable clockwise 2.5 turns. Mating marks should align and Red mark should be visible through inspection hole. *See Fig. 8*. Ensure mating marks are aligned and install steering wheel.

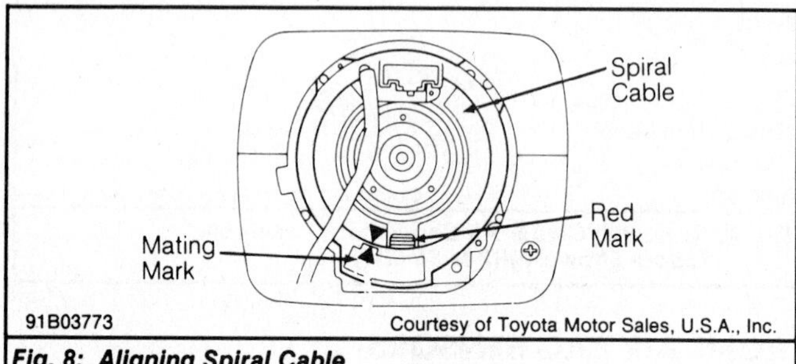


***Fig. 8: Aligning Spiral Cable***

## TORQUE SPECIFICATIONS

***TORQUE SPECIFICATIONS***

| Application | Ft. Lbs. (N.m) |
|---|---|
| Front Air Bag Sensor Bolts | 19 (26) |
| Steering Wheel Nut | 26 (35) |
| | **INCH Lbs. (N.m)** |
| Center Air Bag Sensor Screws | 108 (12) |
| Steering Wheel Pad Torx Screws | 65 (7) |

# 1991 SAFETY EQUIPMENT
# Instrument Panels

## Camry, Celica, Corolla, Cressida, Land Cruiser, MR2, Pickup, Previa, Supra, Tercel, 4Runner

## DESCRIPTION & OPERATION

### GAUGES

In addition to standard fuel and temperature gauge, some instrument panels are equipped with a tachometer, oil pressure gauge and voltmeter. Gauges may be either 2-terminal bimetallic type, or 3-terminal coil type. The 2-terminal type gauges are generally used on models without tachometers.

### SWITCHES

All models have a combination switch on steering column. For removal and installation, see STEERING COLUMN SWITCHES article.

## TESTING

### FUEL GAUGE & WARNING LIGHT

**Wiring Harness Operational Test - 1)** Unplug connector at fuel tank sending unit. Turn ignition on. Fuel gauge should be on EMPTY. If fuel gauge is not on EMPTY, repair short circuit in wiring harness.
**2)** If fuel gauge is on EMPTY, connect a 12-volt, 3.4-watt test light between appropriate terminals of harness connector. See FUEL SENDING UNIT HARNESS CONNECTOR table. *See Fig. 1.*
**3)** With ignition on, test light should flash and gauge needle should move toward FULL. If test light does not flash and needle does not move, check wiring harness for open circuit. Repair or replace as necessary.

***FUEL SENDING UNIT HARNESS CONNECTOR***

| Model | Harness Connector Test Terminal Nos. |
|---|---|
| Camry, Celica, Corolla [1], Supra & Tercel [2] | 3 & 4 |
| Cressida, Corolla [3], Land Cruiser & Pickup [4] | 1 & 2 |
| MR2 | 1 & 3 |
| 4Runner [5] | 2 & 4 |
| Previa | 2 & 3 |

[1] - Sedan and station wagon models not equipped with tachometer. When measuring sending unit resistance, connect ohmmeter between terminals No. 1 and 2.
[2] - When measuring sending unit resistance, connect ohmmeter between Red cable and Black cable.
[3] - Sedan and station wagon equipped with tachometer and all coupe models.
[4] - When measuring sending unit resistance, connect ohmmeter between terminals No. 1 and 3.
[5] - When measuring sending unit resistance, connect ohmmeter between terminals No. 1 and 2.

**Fuel Sending Unit Resistance Test - 1)** Turn ignition off. Remove fuel sending unit from tank. Connect ohmmeter to appropriate sending unit terminals. See FUEL SENDING UNIT HARNESS CONNECTOR table. Sending unit connector terminals are opposite position of harness connector terminals. *See Fig. 1* to identify harness connector terminals.
**2)** Move sender arm and ensure resistance is within specifications. See FUEL SENDING UNIT RESISTANCE SPECIFICATIONS table. After a short delay, gauge pointer should move when sender is connected and float arm is moved.

**Low Fuel Warning Light Sensor Operational Test - 1)** Remove fuel sending unit from tank. Connect battery voltage to sensor terminal. Connect a 12-volt, 3.4-watt test light between body of sending unit and ground.
**2)** With sensor dry, light should come on within 40 seconds. With sensor in gasoline or water, light should not come on. If light does not function as described, replace sensor.

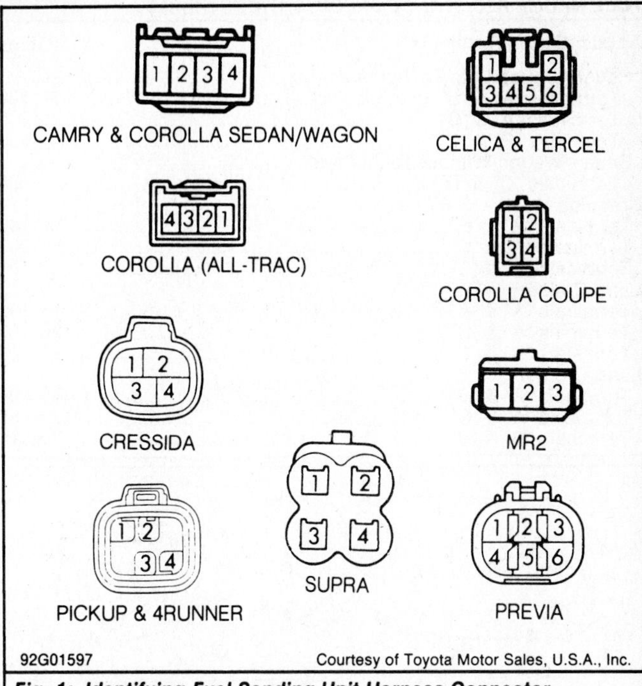


***Fig. 1: Identifying Fuel Sending Unit Harness Connector Terminals***

***FUEL SENDING UNIT RESISTANCE SPECIFICATIONS***

| Float Position | Ohms |
|---|---|
| **Full** | |
| Land Cruiser | 15-19 |
| Supra | 3-5 |
| Camry, Corolla, Cressida, Previa & 4Runner | 3 |
| All Others | 2-4 |
| **Half** | |
| 4Runner | 32-33 |
| **Empty** | |
| Land Cruiser | 113-127 |
| Camry, Corolla, Cressida, Previa & 4Runner | 110 |
| All Others | 102-118 |

**Fuel Gauge Resistance Test -** Turn ignition off. Unplug fuel gauge connector. Using an ohmmeter, check fuel gauge resistance by measuring across appropriate terminals. *See Figs. 2-11.* Replace fuel gauge if not within specifications. See FUEL GAUGE RESISTANCE SPECIFICATIONS table.

***FUEL GAUGE RESISTANCE SPECIFICATIONS***

| Application & Terminals | Ohms |
|---|---|
| **Camry** | |
| Terminals "A" & "B" | 64 |
| Terminals "A" & "C" | 233 |
| Terminals "B" & "C" | 169 |
| **Celica** | |
| 3S-GTE | |
| Terminals "A" & "B" | 83 |
| Terminals "A" & "C" | 234 |
| Terminals "B" & "C" | 151 |
| 4A-FE & 5SFE Without Voltmeter | |
| Terminals "A" & "B" | 86 |
| Terminals "A" & "C" | 274 |
| Terminals "B" & "C" | 188 |
| 5S-FE With Voltmeter | |
| Terminals "A" & "B" | 83 |
| Terminals "A" & "C" | 234 |
| Terminals "B" & "C" | 151 |
| **Corolla** | |
| Coupe | |
| Terminals "A" & "B" | 85 |
| Terminals "A" & "C" | 250 |
| Terminals "B" & "C" | 160 |

# 1991 SAFETY EQUIPMENT
## Instrument Panels (Cont.)

***FUEL GAUGE RESISTANCE SPECIFICATIONS (Cont.)***

| Application & Terminals | Ohms |
|---|---|
| Sedan/Wagon With Tachometer | |
| Terminals "A" & "B" | 100 |
| Terminals "A" & "C" | 200 |
| Terminals "B" & "C" | 100 |
| Sedan/Wagon Without Tachometer | |
| Terminals "C" & "D" | 55 |
| **Cressida** | |
| Terminals "A" & "B" | 102 |
| Terminals "A" & "C" | 203 |
| Terminals "B" & "C" | 101 |
| **Land Cruiser** | |
| Terminals "A" & "B" | 86-106 |
| Terminals "A" & "C" | 126-150 |
| Terminals "B" & "C" | 90-110 |
| **Land Cruiser** | |
| Terminals "A" & "B" | 86-106 |
| Terminals "A" & "C" | 126-150 |
| Terminals "B" & "C" | 90-110 |

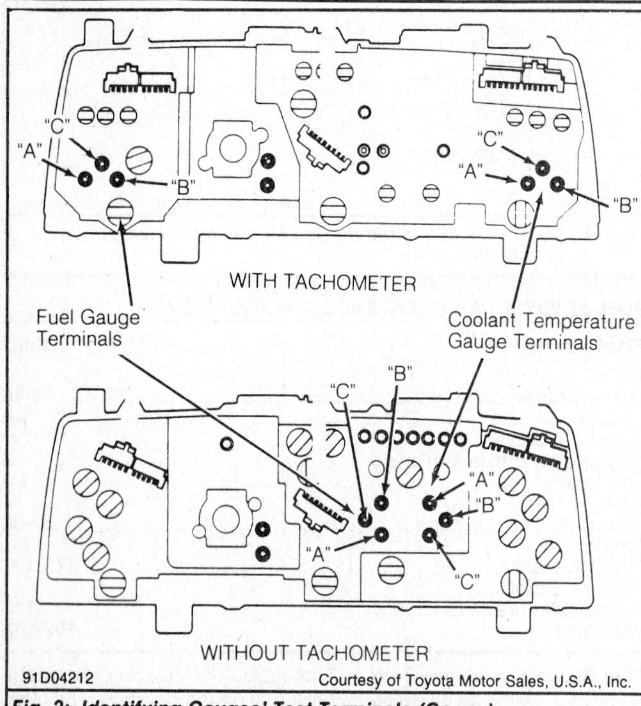


***Fig. 2: Identifying Gauges' Test Terminals (Camry)***

"B" "B" "C" "C" "A" "A"
Fuel Gauge
Terminals
WITH VOLTMETER & TURBO
Coolant Temperature
Gauge Terminals
"A" "A" "B" "B" "C" "C"
WITHOUT VOLTMETER
91F04213
Courtesy of Toyota Motor Sales, U.S.A., Inc.

***Fig. 3: Identifying Gauges' Test Terminals (Celica)***

***FUEL GAUGE RESISTANCE SPECIFICATIONS (Cont.)***

| Application & Terminals | Ohms |
|---|---|
| **Pickup & 4Runner** | |
| With Tachometer | |
| Terminals "A" & "B" | 123 |
| Terminals "A" & "C" | 260 |
| Terminals "B" & "C" | 137 |
| Without Tachometer | |
| Terminals "A" & "B" | 55 |
| **Supra** | |
| Terminals IG & "U" | 103 |
| Terminals IG & "E" | 167 |
| Terminals "U" & "E" | 65 |
| **Tercel** | |
| With Tachometer | |
| Terminals "A" & "B" | 102 |
| Terminals "A" & "C" | 203 |
| Terminals "B" & "C" | 102 |
| Without Tachometer | |
| Terminals "A" & "B" | 55 |
| Terminals "A" & "C" | 70 |
| Terminals "B" & "C" | 125 |

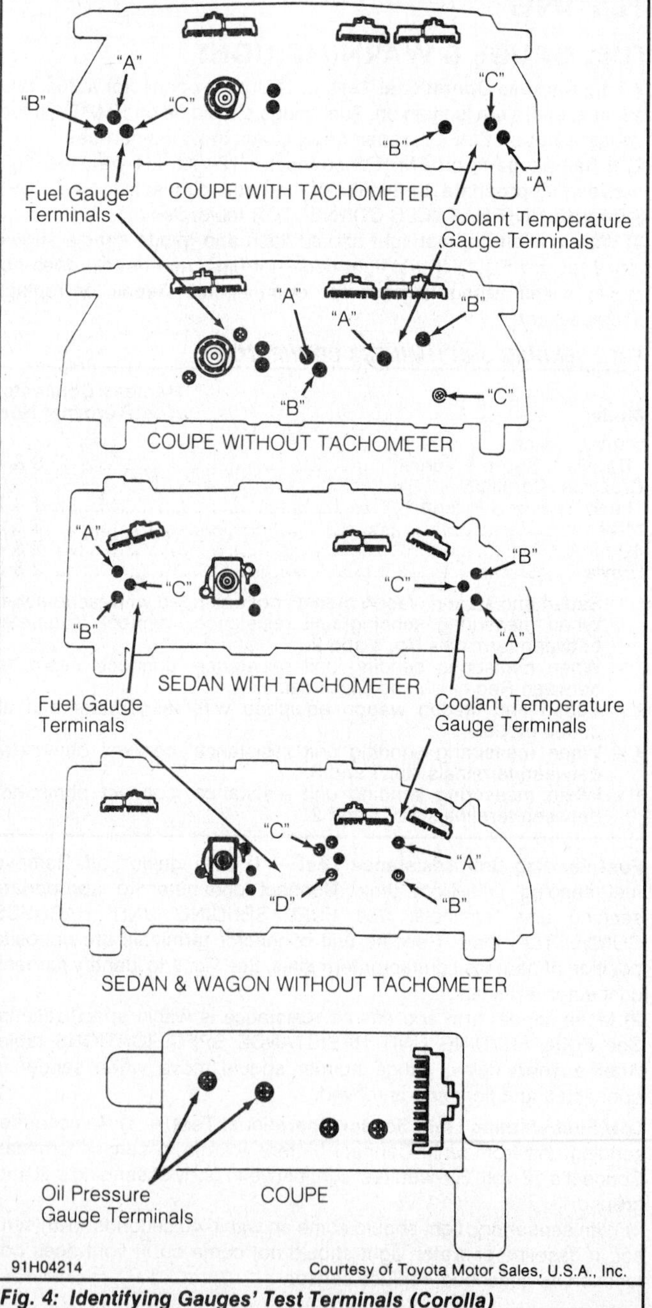


***Fig. 4: Identifying Gauges' Test Terminals (Corolla)***

# 1991 SAFETY EQUIPMENT
# Instrument Panels (Cont.)

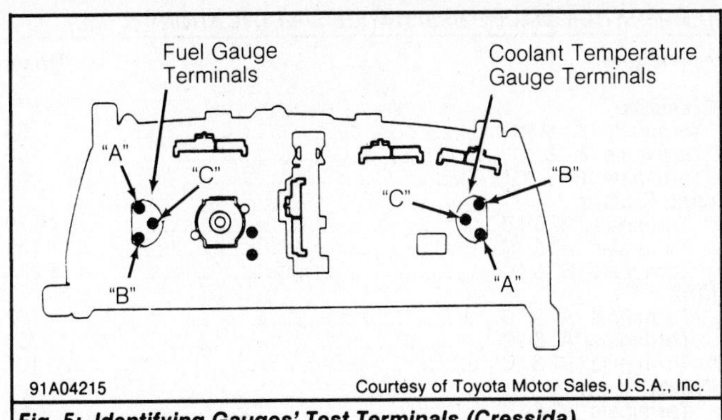


*Fig. 5: Identifying Gauges' Test Terminals (Cressida)*

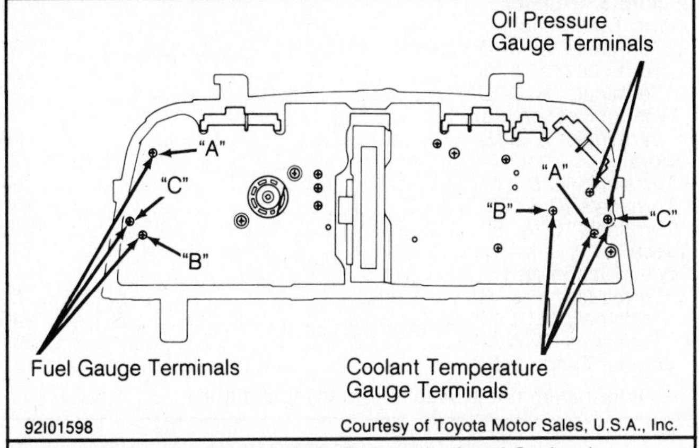


*Fig. 6: Identifying Gauges' Test Terminals (Land Cruiser)*

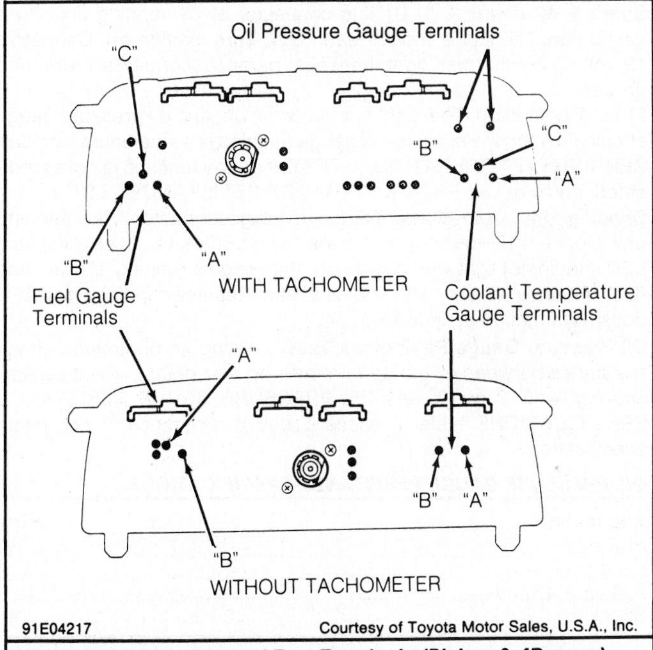


*Fig. 7: Identifying Gauges' Test Terminals (Pickup & 4Runner)*

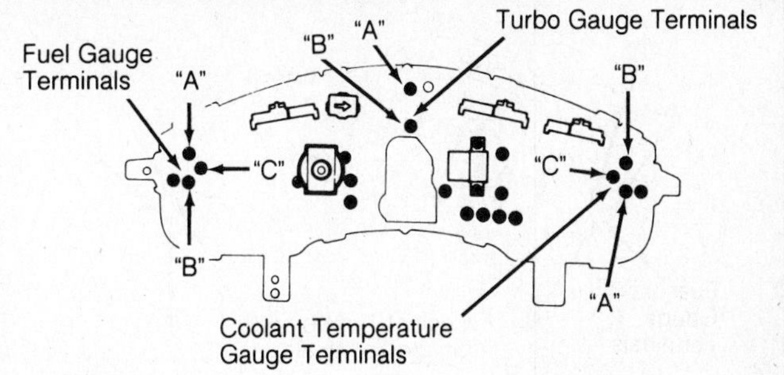

*Fig. 8: Identifying Gauges' Test Terminals (MR2)*

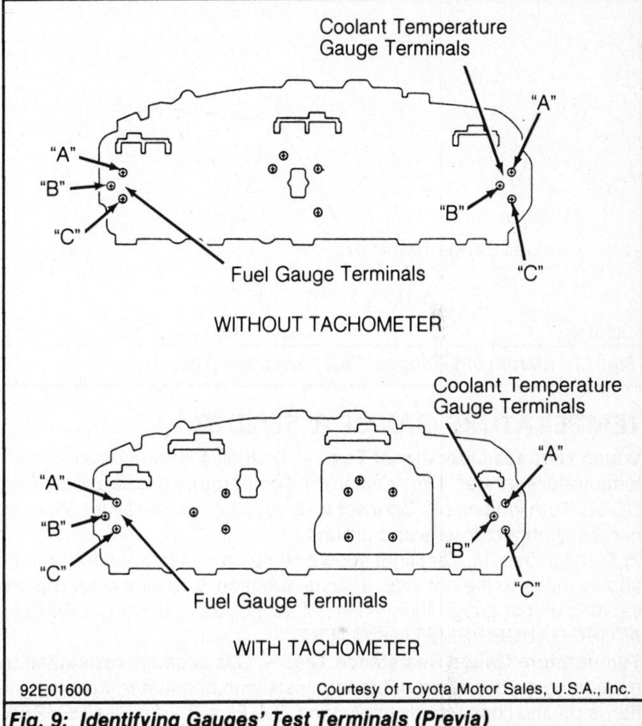


*Fig. 9: Identifying Gauges' Test Terminals (Previa)*

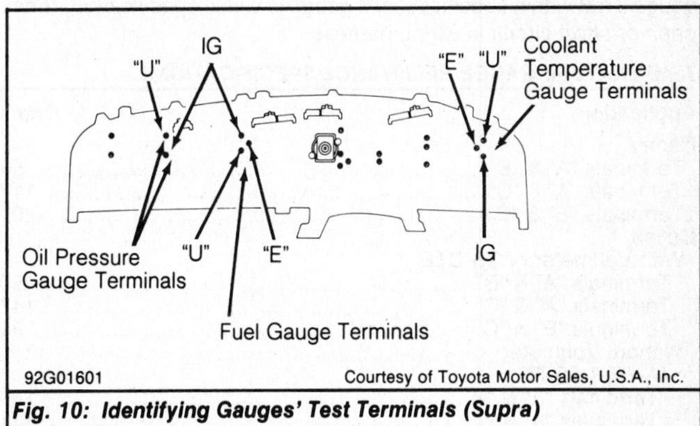


*Fig. 10: Identifying Gauges' Test Terminals (Supra)*

# 1991 SAFETY EQUIPMENT
## Instrument Panels (Cont.)

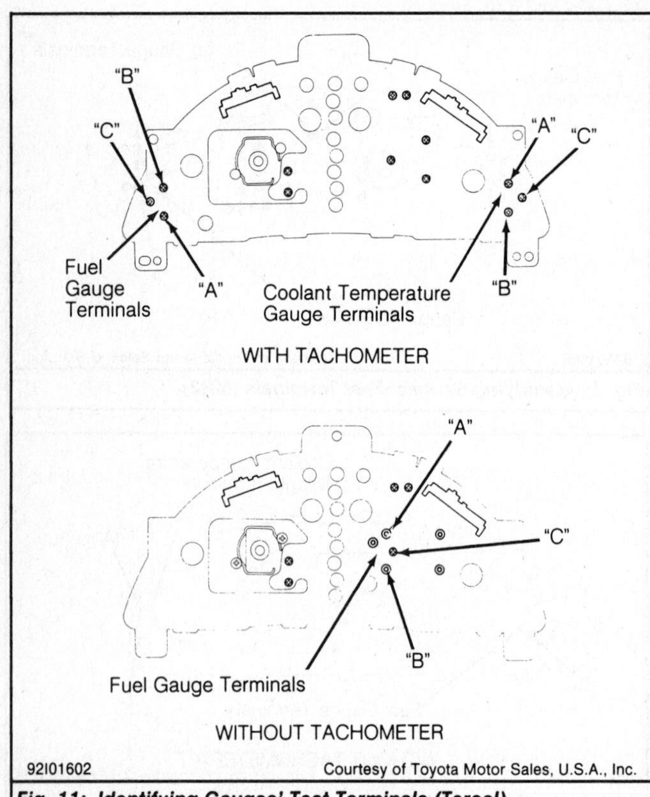


*Fig. 11: Identifying Gauges' Test Terminals (Tercel)*

## TEMPERATURE GAUGE & SENDER

**Wiring Harness Operational Test - 1)** Unplug connector at coolant temperature sender. Turn ignition on. Temperature gauge should read COOL. Turn ignition off. Connect a 12-volt, 3.4-watt test light between harness connector wire and ground.

**2)** Turn ignition on. Test light should come on and temperature gauge should move to the hot side. If gauge function is as indicated, replace sending unit. If gauge function is not as indicated, perform TEMPERATURE GAUGE RESISTANCE TEST.

**Temperature Gauge Resistance Test -** Check gauge resistance by measuring across appropriate terminals with ohmmeter. Ensure ignition is off and connector is unplugged. *See Figs. 2 - 11*. See TEMPERATURE GAUGE RESISTANCE SPECIFICATIONS table. Replace gauge if not within specification. If gauge is within specification, repair open or short circuit in wiring harness.

***TEMPERATURE GAUGE RESISTANCE SPECIFICATIONS***

| Application | Ohms |
|---|---|
| **Camry** | |
| Terminals "A" & "B" | 54 |
| Terminals "A" & "C" | 117 |
| Terminals "B" & "C" | 201 |
| **Celica** | |
| With Voltmeter or 3S-GTE | |
| Terminals "A" & "B" | 198 |
| Terminals "A" & "C" | 147 |
| Terminals "B" & "C" | 51 |
| Without Voltmeter | |
| 4A-FE & 5S-FE | |
| Terminals "A" & "B" | 182 |
| Terminals "A" & "C" | 131 |
| Terminals "B" & "C" | 51 |
| **Corolla** | |
| Coupe | |
| Terminals "A" & "B" | 55 |
| Terminals "A" & "C" | 135 |
| Terminals "B" & "C" | 210 |
| Sedan/Wagon | |
| Terminals "A" & "B" | 55 |
| Terminals "A" & "C" | 145 |
| Terminals "B" & "C" | 200 |

***TEMPERATURE GAUGE RESISTANCE SPECIFICATIONS (Cont.)***

| Application | Ohms |
|---|---|
| **Cressida** | |
| Terminals "A" & "B" | 54 |
| Terminals "A" & "C" | 146 |
| Terminals "B" & "C" | 200 |
| **Land Cruiser** | |
| Terminals "A" & "B" | 71-79 |
| Terminals "A" & "C" | 117-141 |
| Terminals "B" & "C" | 185-215 |
| **MR2** | |
| Terminals "A" & "B" | 102 |
| Terminals "A" & "C" | 204 |
| Terminals "B" & "C" | 101 |
| **Previa** | |
| Terminals "A" & "B" | 200 |
| Terminals "A" & "C" | 54 |
| Terminals "B" & "C" | 146 |
| **Pickup & 4Runner** | |
| With Tachometer | |
| Terminals "A" & "B" | 57 |
| Terminals "A" & "C" | 135 |
| Terminals "B" & "C" | 217 |
| Without Tachometer | |
| Terminals "A" & "B" | 25 |
| **Supra** | |
| Terminals IG & "U" | 54 |
| Terminals IG & "E" | 146 |
| Terminals "U" & "E" | 200 |
| **Tercel** | |
| With Tachometer | |
| Terminals "A" & "B" | 54 |
| Terminals "A" & "C" | 146 |
| Terminals "B" & "C" | 200 |
| Without Tachometer | [1] |

[1] - Information not available from manufacturer.

## OIL PRESSURE GAUGE & SENDER

**Wiring Harness Operational Test (Corolla, Land Cruiser, Pickup, Supra & 4Runner) - 1)** Unplug connector at oil sending unit. Turn ignition on. Oil gauge should read LOW. Turn ignition off. Connect a 12-volt, 3.4-watt test light between harness connector wire and ground.

**2)** Turn ignition on. Test light should come on, and oil pressure gauge should move to the high side. If gauge function is as indicated, perform SENDING UNIT OPERATIONAL TEST. If gauge function is not as indicated, perform OIL PRESSURE GAUGE RESISTANCE TEST.

**Sending Unit Operational Test -** Unplug connector from sending unit. Connect 12-volt source, in series with LED tester, to sending unit. LED should not light with engine off. With engine running, LED should flash. Flashes will vary with engine speed. Replace sending unit if LED does not function as indicated.

**Oil Pressure Gauge Resistance Test -** Using an ohmmeter, check resistance between oil gauge terminals on rear of instrument cluster. *See Fig. 4, 6, 7 or 10*. See OIL PRESSURE GAUGE RESISTANCE SPECIFICATIONS table. Replace gauge if resistance is not within specification.

***OIL PRESSURE GAUGE RESISTANCE SPECIFICATIONS***

| Application | Ohms |
|---|---|
| Corolla | 44 |
| Land Cruiser | 22-28 |
| Pickup & 4Runner | 25 |
| Supra | 42 |

## TURBO GAUGE

**Wiring Harness Operational Test - 1)** Disconnect harness from turbo pressure sensor located on right rear of firewall. Turn ignition on. Gauge needle should move to top of gauge.

**2)** Jump terminal No. 2 of harness to ground. *See Fig. 13.* Gauge needle should move to bottom of gauge. If needle functions correctly, test turbo pressure sensor and meter drive circuit. If needle does not function correctly, test turbo gauge resistance.

# 1991 SAFETY EQUIPMENT
# Instrument Panels (Cont.)

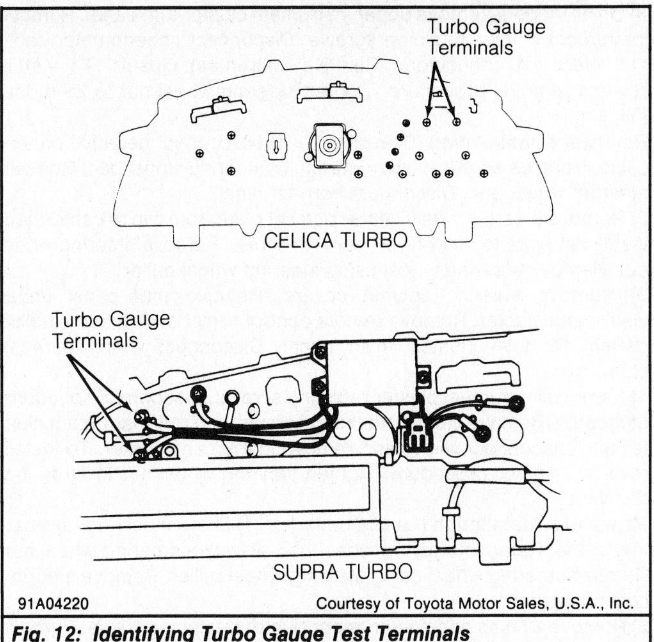


***Fig. 12: Identifying Turbo Gauge Test Terminals (Celica Turbo & Supra Turbo)***

**Turbo Gauge Resistance** – Pull instrument cluster out of dash, but leave harnesses connected. Check turbo gauge resistance. *See Fig. 8 or 12.* If resistance is not 72 ohms, replace turbo gauge. If turbo gauge tests okay, test turbo pressure sensor.

**Turbo Pressure Sensor (Voltage Test)** – **1)** Connect three 1.5-volt dry cell batteries in series. Disconnect turbo pressure sensor connector. Apply positive terminal of batteries to terminal No. 3 of pressure sensor connector. *See Fig. 13.*

**2)** Apply negative terminal of batteries to terminal No. 1. Check voltage at terminal No. 2. If voltage is not as specified, replace pressure sensor. See TURBO PRESSURE SENSOR VOLTAGE SPECIFICATIONS table. If voltage is within specification, go to step **3)**.

***TURBO PRESSURE SENSOR VOLTAGE SPECIFICATIONS***

| Application | Volts |
|---|---|
| Celica Turbo | 2.4 |
| Supra Turbo | 1.5 |

**3)** Apply 8 in. Hg to pressure sender. Ensure voltage at terminal No. 2 drops. Apply 7 psi (.5 kg/cm²) pressure to pressure sender; ensure voltage rises above previous specification. See TURBO PRESSURE SENSOR VOLTAGE SPECIFICATIONS table.

**4)** If voltage does not change as described, replace turbo pressure sensor. If components test okay, check wiring harness. Repair as necessary. For more information, see appropriate article in ENGINE PERFORMANCE.

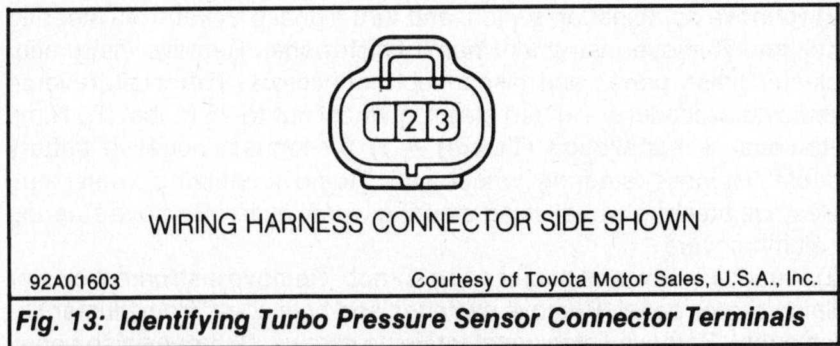


***Fig. 13: Identifying Turbo Pressure Sensor Connector Terminals***

**Turbo Meter Drive Circuit (Celica & MR2)** – Remove turbo pressure sensor connector. Remove instrument cluster. See INSTRUMENT CLUSTER under REMOVAL & INSTALLATION. Inspect wire harness connectors for damage or poor connection. Using a DVOM, check wiring harness connector terminals for correct values. *See Fig. 14.* If values are not as specified, replace meter drive circuit. See TURBO METER DRIVE CIRCUIT SPECIFICATIONS (CELICA & MR2) table.

***TURBO METER DRIVE CIRCUIT SPECIFICATIONS (CELICA & MR2)***

| Test Terminal | Ignition | Specified Value |
|---|---|---|
| **Resistance Check** | | |
| A - B | Off | Continuity |
| C - 2 [1] | Off | Continuity |
| D - Ground | Off | Continuity |
| 1 [1] - Ground | Off | Continuity |
| **Voltage Check** | | |
| E - Ground | Off | Zero Volts |
| E - Ground | On | Battery Voltage |
| 3 [1] - Ground | Off | Zero Volts |
| 3 [1] - Ground | On | Battery Voltage |

[1] - Located on turbo pressure sensor wiring harness connector. *See Fig 14.*

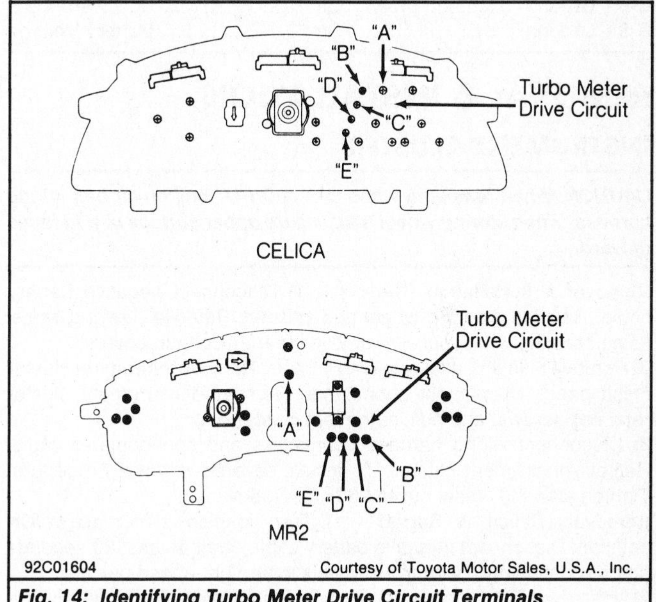


***Fig. 14: Identifying Turbo Meter Drive Circuit Terminals (Celica & MR2)***

***Fig. 15: Identifying Turbo Meter Drive Circuit Terminals (Supra)***

# 1991 SAFETY EQUIPMENT
# Instrument Panels (Cont.)

**Turbo Meter Drive Circuit (Supra) -** Remove turbo pressure sensor connector. Remove instrument cluster. See INSTRUMENT CLUSTER under REMOVAL & INSTALLATION. Inspect wire harness connectors for damage or poor connection. Using a DVOM, check wiring harness connector terminals for correct values. *See Fig. 15.* If values are not as specified, replace rheostat. See TURBO METER DRIVE CIRCUIT SPECIFICATIONS (SUPRA) table.

***TURBO METER DRIVE CIRCUIT SPECIFICATIONS (SUPRA)***

| Test Terminal | Ignition | Specified Value |
|---|---|---|
| **Resistance Check** | | |
| A-8 - Ground | Off | Continuity |
| E-1 - Ground | Off | Continuity |
| E-2 - Ground | Off | Continuity |
| E-3 - Ground | Off | Continuity |
| **Voltage Check** | | |
| C-8 - Ground | Off | Zero Volts |
| C-8 - Ground | On | Battery Voltage |

## REMOVAL & INSTALLATION

### INSTRUMENT CLUSTER

***CAUTION: When removing wheel pad, DO NOT pull on air bag wiring harness. When storing wheel pad, ensure upper surface of pad faces upward.***

**Removal & Installation (Camry) - 1)** Disconnect negative battery cable. Remove steering wheel pad and nut. Remove steering wheel using steering wheel puller. Remove steering column covers.

**2)** Remove 5 finish panel retaining screws. Remove instrument cluster finish panel. Disconnect connectors. Remove 4 instrument cluster retaining screws, and pull instrument cluster out.

**3)** Disconnect wiring harness connectors and speedometer cable. Remove instrument cluster. To install, reverse removal procedure. Tighten steering wheel nut to 26 ft. lbs. (35 N.m).

**Removal (Celica & Supra) - 1)** Turn ignition switch to LOCK position. Disconnect negative battery cable. Wait at least 20 seconds before continuing. Place front wheels in straight-ahead position.

**2)** Unscrew 4 Torx screws on side covers until groove along screw circumference catches on screw case. Pull wheel pad out from steering wheel, and disconnect air bag connector.

**3)** Disconnect wiring connector. Remove steering wheel nut. Remove steering wheel with steering wheel puller. Remove steering column covers. Remove retaining screws. Remove trim panel over instrument cluster.

**4)** Remove instrument cluster retaining screws. Pull instrument cluster out far enough to disconnect speedometer cable and harness connectors. Remove instrument cluster.

***CAUTION: When installing wheel pad, ensure air bag wiring is not pinched or interfering with other parts.***

**Installation - 1)** To install, reverse removal procedure. Before installing steering wheel, center clockspring. Ensure front wheels are straight ahead.

**2)** Turn clockspring cable counterclockwise by hand until resistance is felt. Rotate clockspring clockwise 2-3 turns and align Red marks on clockspring with outer housing.

**3)** Install steering wheel and nut. Tighten steering wheel nut to 26 ft. lbs. (35 N.m). Install remaining components in reverse order of removal procedure.

**Removal & Installation (Corolla) - 1)** Disconnect negative battery cable. Remove steering wheel pad. Remove steering wheel nut. Remove steering wheel using steering wheel puller. Remove steering column covers. On coupe model, upper column cover must be removed with lower cluster finish panel.

**2)** On sedan and wagon models, pry 2 switches out from lower cluster finish panel. Disconnect and remove switches. Remove lower cluster finish panel. Disconnect wiring harness connector.

**3)** On all models, remove upper instrument cluster trim panel. Remove instrument cluster retaining screws. Disconnect speedometer cable and electrical connectors. Remove instrument cluster. To install, reverse removal procedure. Tighten steering wheel nut to 25 ft. lbs. (35 N.m).

**Removal & Installation (Cressida) - 1)** Disconnect negative battery cable. Remove screw at lower portion of steering wheel pad. Remove steering wheel pad. Disconnect horn terminal.

**2)** Remove steering wheel center pad set plate from clip of center pad. Install set plate to steering wheel with screw. Remove steering wheel nut. Remove steering wheel using steering wheel puller.

**3)** Remove steering column covers. Remove trim panel under instrument cluster. Remove remote control mirror switch and satellite switch. Remove cluster finish panel. Disconnect wiring harness connectors.

**4)** Remove instrument cluster retaining screws. Disconnect speedometer cable. Remove cluster retaining screws, and pull instrument cluster out. Disconnect wiring and remove instrument cluster. To install, reverse removal procedure. Tighten steering wheel nut to 25 ft. lbs. (35 N.m).

**Removal & Installation (Land Cruiser) - 1)** Disconnect negative battery cable. Remove steering wheel pad. Remove steering wheel nut. Remove steering wheel using steering wheel puller. Remove steering column covers.

**2)** Remove 7 finish panel/instrument cluster retaining screws. Remove speedometer cable and disconnect wiring harness connectors. Remove finish panel/cluster as a unit. To install, reverse removal procedure. Tighten steering wheel nut to 25 ft. lbs. (35 N.m).

**Removal & Installation (MR2) - 1)** Disconnect negative battery cable. Remove steering wheel pad and nut. Remove steering wheel using steering wheel puller. Remove steering column covers. Remove finish panel from below steering column. Remove insert panel and heater duct from below steering column.

**2)** Remove combination switch, and turn signal bracket from steering column. Remove rheostat knob and nut. Remove instrument panel finish panel. Remove instrument cluster finish panel, and disconnect connectors. To install, reverse removal procedure. Tighten steering wheel nut to 25 ft. lbs. (35 N.m).

**Removal & Installation (Pickup & 4Runner) - 1)** Disconnect negative battery cable. Remove steering wheel pad. Remove steering wheel nut. Remove steering wheel using steering wheel puller. Remove steering column covers.

**2)** Remove retaining screws. Remove instrument cluster finish panel. Disconnect wiring harness connectors. Remove retaining screws and register. Remove retaining screws, and pull instrument cluster out.

**3)** Disconnect wiring harness connectors and speedometer cable. Remove instrument cluster. To install, reverse removal procedure. Tighten steering wheel nut to 25 ft. lbs. (35 N.m).

**Removal & Installation (Previa) - 1)** Disconnect negative battery cable. Remove steering wheel pad and nut. Remove steering wheel using steering wheel puller. Remove steering column covers. Remove hood release lever. Remove finish panel and knee panel from below steering column.

**2)** Remove combination switch, and turn signal bracket from steering column. Remove instrument panel finish panel. Remove instrument cluster finish panel, and disconnect connectors. To install, reverse removal procedure. Tighten steering wheel nut to 25 ft. lbs. (35 N.m).

**Removal & Installation (Tercel) - 1)** Disconnect negative battery cable. Remove steering wheel pad. Remove steering wheel nut. Remove steering wheel using steering wheel puller. Remove steering column covers.

**2)** Remove screw and heater control knob. Remove instrument cluster finish center panel. Remove switches and hole cover from cluster finish panel. Remove finish panel retaining screws. Remove finish panel.

**3)** Remove 4 instrument cluster retaining screws. Pull instrument cluster out. Disconnect speedometer and wiring harness connectors. Remove instrument cluster. To install, reverse removal procedure. Tighten steering wheel nut to 25 ft. lbs. (35 N.m).

## WIRING DIAGRAMS

See appropriate chassis wiring diagram in WIRING DIAGRAMS.

# 1991 SAFETY EQUIPMENT
# Power Mirrors

**Camry, Celica, Corolla, Cressida, Land Cruiser, Pickup, Previa, Supra, 4Runner**

## DESCRIPTION & OPERATION

Power mirrors are controlled by a dual control switch assembly located on center console or instrument panel. Left/right switch directs current to desired mirror. Horizontal/vertical switch directs current to one of 2 motors located in mirror/motor assembly. Mirror and motors must be removed and serviced as an assembly.

## TROUBLE SHOOTING

### POWER MIRROR

**Both Power Mirrors Inoperative** – Check RADIO fuse, power mirror switch, power mirror motor(s), wiring and ground. See TESTING.

**Left Or Right Power Mirror Inoperative** – Check power mirror switch, power mirror, motor(s), wiring and ground. See TESTING.

**Up/Down Or Left/Right Function Inoperative** – Check power mirror motor(s), wiring and ground. See POWER MIRROR MOTOR TEST under TESTING.

## TESTING

### POWER MIRROR SWITCH TEST

Remove power mirror switch. See POWER MIRROR SWITCH under REMOVAL & INSTALLATION. Using ohmmeter, check continuity between appropriate mirror switch terminals. *See Figs. 1-7.* See appropriate POWER MIRROR SWITCH CONTINUITY TEST table. If switch fails any test, replace switch.

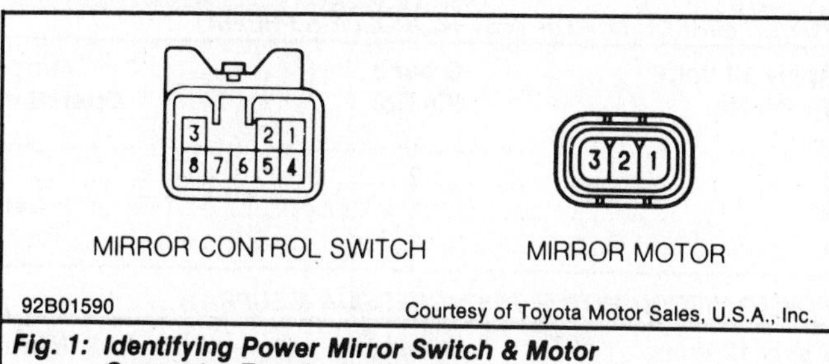


***Fig. 1: Identifying Power Mirror Switch & Motor Connector Terminals (Camry)***

***POWER MIRROR SWITCH CONTINUITY TEST (CAMRY)***

| Application | Terminals |
|---|---|
| Switch In Left Position | |
| Up | 2 & 8, 3 & 5 |
| Down | 2 & 5, 3 & 8 |
| Left | 2 & 8, 5 & 6 |
| Right | 2 & 5, 6 & 8 |
| Switch In Right Position | |
| Up | 2 & 8, 5 & 7 |
| Down | 2 & 5, 7 & 8 |
| Left | 1 & 5, 2 & 8 |
| Right | 1 & 8, 2 & 5 |

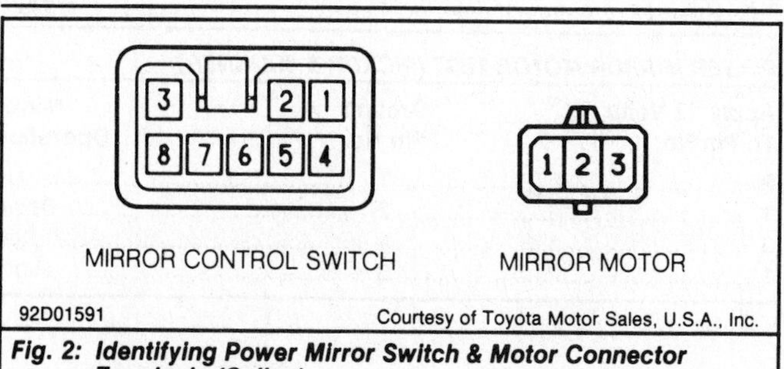


***Fig. 2: Identifying Power Mirror Switch & Motor Connector Terminals (Celica)***

***POWER MIRROR SWITCH CONTINUITY TEST (CELICA)***

| Application | Terminals |
|---|---|
| Switch In Off Position | |
| Up | 2 & 3 |
| Down | 1 & 2 |
| Left | 2 & 3 |
| Right | 1 & 2 |
| Switch In Left Position | |
| Up | 1 & 7, 2 & 3 |
| Down | 1 & 2, 3 & 7 |
| Left | 1 & 8, 2 & 3 |
| Right | 1 & 2, 3 & 8 |
| Switch In Right Position | |
| Up | 1 & 5, 2 & 3 |
| Down | 1 & 2, 3 & 5 |
| Left | 1 & 6, 2 & 3 |
| Right | 1 & 2, 3 & 6 |

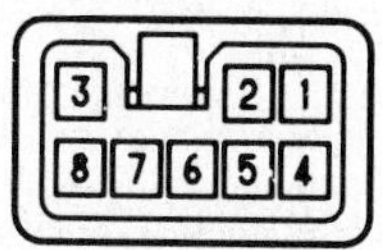

MIRROR CONTROL SWITCH MIRROR MOTOR

92F01592 Courtesy of Toyota Motor Sales, U.S.A., Inc.

***Fig. 3: Identifying Power Mirror Switch & Motor Connector Terminals (Corolla & Previa)***

***POWER MIRROR SWITCH CONTINUITY TEST (COROLLA & PREVIA)***

| Application | Terminals |
|---|---|
| Switch In Left Position | |
| Up | 1 & 7, 2 & 3 |
| Down | 1 & 2, 3 & 7 |
| Left | 1 & 8, 2 & 3 |
| Right | 1 & 2, 3 & 8 |
| Switch In Right Position | |
| Up | 1 & 5, 2 & 3 |
| Down | 1 & 2, 3 & 5 |
| Left | 1 & 6, 2 & 3 |
| Right | 1 & 2, 3 & 6 |

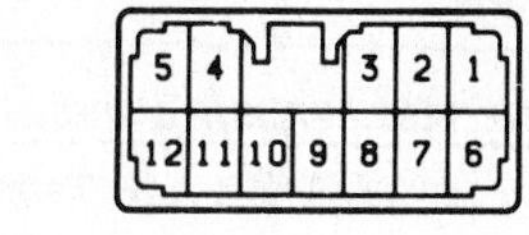

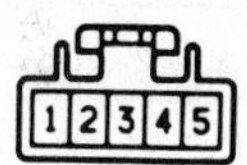


MIRROR CONTROL SWITCH MIRROR MOTOR

92H01593 Courtesy of Toyota Motor Sales, U.S.A., Inc.

***Fig. 4: Identifying Power Mirror Switch & Motor Connector Terminals (Cressida)***

***POWER MIRROR SWITCH CONTINUITY TEST (CRESSIDA)***

| Application | Terminals |
|---|---|
| Switch In Off Position | |
| Up | 5 & 10 |
| Down | 1 & 10 |
| Left | 5 & 10 |
| Right | 1 & 10 |
| Switch In Left Position | |
| Up | 1 & 8, 5 & 10 |
| Down | 1 & 10, 5 & 8 |
| Left | 1 & 11, 5 & 10 |
| Right | 1 & 10, 5 & 11 |
| Switch In Right Position | |
| Up | 1 & 12, 5 & 10 |
| Down | 1 & 10, 5 & 12 |
| Left | 1 & 3, 5 & 10 |
| Right | 1 & 10, 3 & 5 |

# 1991 SAFETY EQUIPMENT
## Power Mirrors (Cont.)

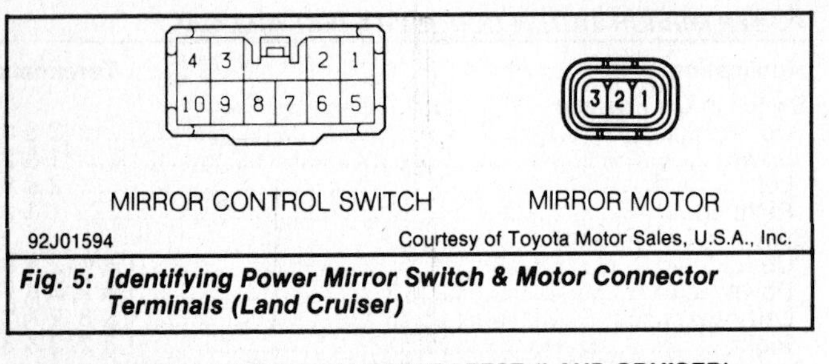


**Fig. 5: Identifying Power Mirror Switch & Motor Connector Terminals (Land Cruiser)**

### POWER MIRROR SWITCH CONTINUITY TEST (LAND CRUISER)

| Application | Terminals |
|---|---|
| Switch In Off Position | |
| Up | 3 & 4 |
| Down | 1 & 3 |
| Left | 3 & 4 |
| Right | 1 & 3 |
| Switch In Left Position | |
| Up | 1 & 10, 3 & 4 |
| Down | 1 & 3, 4 & 10 |
| Left | 1 & 9, 3 & 4 |
| Right | 1 & 3, 4 & 9 |
| Switch In Right Position | |
| Up | 1 & 6, 3 & 4 |
| Down | 1 & 3, 4 & 6 |
| Left | 1 & 2, 3 & 4 |
| Right | 1 & 3, 2 & 4 |

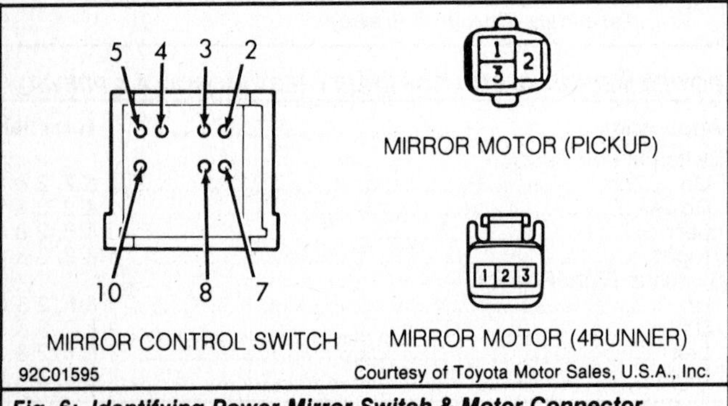


**Fig. 6: Identifying Power Mirror Switch & Motor Connector Terminals (Pickup & 4Runner)**

### POWER MIRROR SWITCH CONTINUITY TEST ( PICKUP & 4RUNNER)

| Application | Terminals |
|---|---|
| Switch In Off Position | |
| Up | 7 & 8 |
| Down | 8 & 10 |
| Left | 7 & 8 |
| Right | 8 & 10 |
| Switch In Left Position | |
| Up | 2 & 10, 7 & 8 |
| Down | 2 & 7, 8 & 10 |
| Left | 3 & 10, 7 & 8 |
| Right | 3 & 7, 8 & 10 |
| Switch In Right Position | |
| Up | 5 & 10, 7 & 8 |
| Down | 5 & 7, 8 & 10 |
| Left | 4 & 10, 7 & 8 |
| Right | 4 & 7, 8 & 10 |

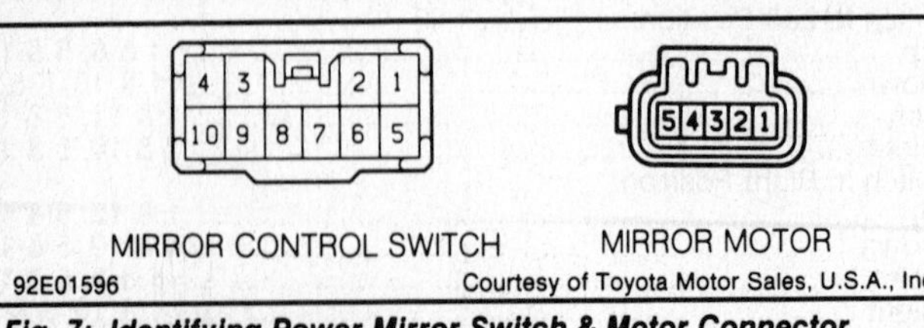


**Fig. 7: Identifying Power Mirror Switch & Motor Connector Terminals (Supra)**

### POWER MIRROR SWITCH CONTINUITY TEST (SUPRA)

| Application | Terminals |
|---|---|
| Switch In Off Position | |
| Up | 3 & 4 |
| Down | 1 & 4 |
| Left | 3 & 4 |
| Right | 1 & 4 |
| Switch In Left Position | |
| Up | 1 & 10, 3 & 4 |
| Down | 1 & 4, 3 & 10 |
| Left | 1 & 9, 3 & 4 |
| Right | 1 & 4, 3 & 9 |
| Switch In Right Position | |
| Up | 1 & 6, 3 & 4 |
| Down | 1 & 4, 3 & 6 |
| Left | 1 & 6, 3 & 4 |
| Right | 1 & 4, 2 & 3 |

## POWER MIRROR MOTOR TEST

Disconnect power mirror motor harness connector. Using 12-volt power source, connect positive and negative leads to specified pins or terminals. See appropriate POWER MIRROR MOTOR TEST table. *See Figs. 1-7.* If power mirror motor fails any test, replace power mirror assembly.

### POWER MIRROR MOTOR TEST (CAMRY & CELICA)

| Apply 12 Volts To Pin No. | Ground Pin No. | Mirror Operation |
|---|---|---|
| 3 | 2 | Up |
| 2 | 3 | Down |
| 1 | 2 | Left |
| 2 | 1 | Right |

### POWER MIRROR MOTOR TEST (COROLLA & PREVIA)

| Apply 12 Volts To Pin No. | Ground Pin No. | Mirror Operation |
|---|---|---|
| 2 | 1 | Up |
| 1 | 2 | Down |
| 3 | 1 | Left |
| 1 | 3 | Right |

### POWER MIRROR MOTOR TEST (CRESSIDA & SUPRA)

| Apply 12 Volts To Pin No. | Ground Pin No. | Mirror Operation |
|---|---|---|
| 4 | 3 | Up |
| 3 | 4 | Down |
| 2 | 3 | Left |
| 3 | 2 | Right |

### POWER MIRROR MOTOR TEST (LAND CRUISER)

| Apply 12 Volts To Pin No. | Ground Pin No. | Mirror Operation |
|---|---|---|
| 2 | 3 | Up |
| 3 | 2 | Down |
| 2 | 1 | Left |
| 1 | 2 | Right |

### POWER MIRROR MOTOR TEST (PICKUP & 4RUNNER)

| Apply 12 Volts To Pin No. | Ground Pin No. | Mirror Operation |
|---|---|---|
| 2 | 1 | Up |
| 1 | 2 | Down |
| 3 | 1 | Left |
| 1 | 3 | Right |

## REMOVAL & INSTALLATION

### POWER MIRROR SWITCH

**Removal & Installation (Celica & Supra)** – Remove console box. Push mirror switch outward from behind. Disconnect mirror switch connector and remove switch. To install switch, reverse removal procedure.

**Removal & Installation (Camry, Corolla, Cressida & Land Cruiser)** – Remove instrument panel lower trim cover. Remove left-hand lower pad. Remove power mirror switch retaining screws and pry switch out of instrument panel. Disconnect harness connector and remove switch. To install, reverse removal procedure.

**Removal & Installation (Pickup, Previa & 4Runner)** – **1)** Remove arm rest retaining screws and arm rest. Remove door trim panel. Disconnect all electrical connectors.

**2)** Remove power window master switch retaining screws and power window master switch. Push power mirror switch from reverse side of power window master switch. To install, reverse removal procedure.

### POWER MIRROR ASSEMBLY

**Removal & Installation** – Remove trim panel at base of mirror on inside of the door. Disconnect power mirror motor harness connector. Remove 3 mirror retaining screws and remove mirror. To install, reverse removal procedure.

## WIRING DIAGRAMS

See appropriate chassis wiring diagram in WIRING DIAGRAMS.

# 1991 SAFETY EQUIPMENT
# Rear Window Defogger

## Camry, Celica, Corolla, Cressida, Land Cruiser, Previa, Supra, Tercel, 4Runner

## DESCRIPTION & OPERATION

***NOTE:** Some systems use an integrated or multipurpose relay as defogger relay. Some systems use a timer between switch and heating grid, and some use only a switch and heating grid.*

Rear window defogger systems use a heating wire grid bonded to the inside of window. Heat is regulated by a control switch and a relay/timer. Most systems have an indicator light to show system is operating. Power to the control switch is through a fuse in the fuse block. Timer relay will keep power to the grid for 12-18 minutes, or until the ignition is turned off. On 4Runner, relay ground is through rear power window limit switch.

## TROUBLE SHOOTING

### DEFOGGER DOES NOT WORK

Blown fuse or poor contact. Defogger switch defective. Poor connections. Broken wire. Relay defective.

### INDICATOR LIGHT DOES NOT WORK

Bulb burned out. Open wire or poor connection.

## TESTING

### SYSTEM TESTING

**1)** Ensure all in-line fuses or circuit breakers are okay. Turn ignition and control switches to ON position. Glass should feel warm after a few minutes.
**2)** If glass is not warm, use a test light or voltmeter to check for battery voltage at grid feed wire. If voltage is not correct, check wiring harness, control switch and timer/relay.

### SWITCH TEST

**Camry, Land Cruiser, Previa & 4Runner** – Connect battery voltage to terminal No. 2, and ground terminal No. 3. *See Fig. 1*. Connect 3.4-watt test light between terminals No. 2 and 6. Turn defogger on. Ensure test light lights for 12-18 minutes and then goes out. If switch does not operate as specified, replace switch.

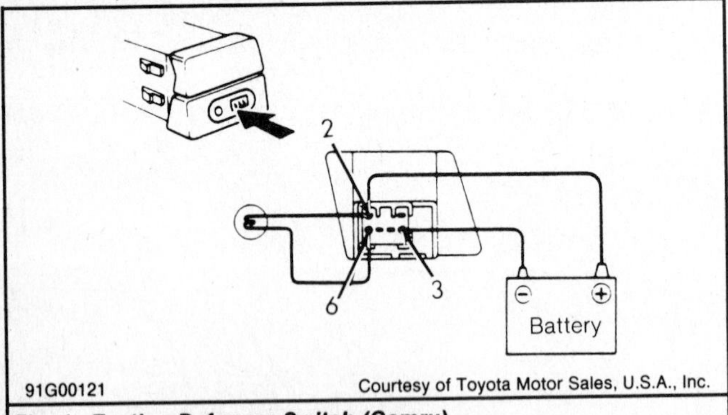


*Fig. 1: Testing Defogger Switch (Camry)*

**Celica** – **1)** To test defogger switch without timer, place switch in ON position. Ensure continuity exists between terminals No. 2, 3 and 6. Place switch in OFF position, continuity should not exist between terminals No. 2, 3 and 6. Continuity should exist at all times between terminals No. 1 and 4 (light bulb). If continuity is not as specified, replace switch. *See Fig. 2*.

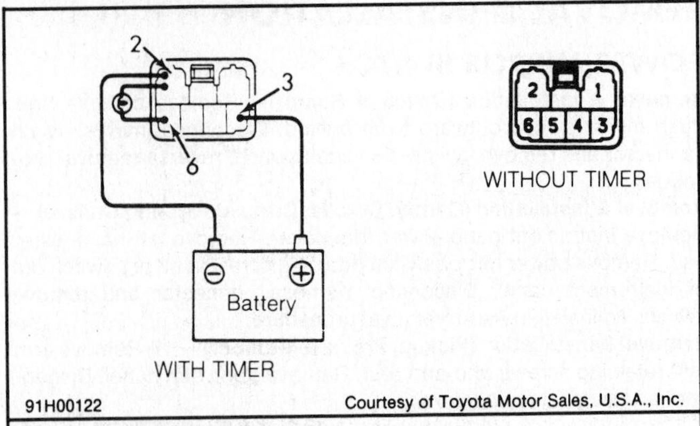


*Fig. 2: Testing Defogger Switch (Celica, Land Cruiser, Previa & 4Runner)*

**2)** To test defogger switch with timer, connect battery voltage to terminal No. 3 and ground to terminal No. 2. Connect 3.4-watt test light between terminals No. 2 and 6. Push defogger switch. Ensure test light lights for 12-18 minutes and then goes out. If switch does not operate as specified, replace switch. *See Fig. 2*.

**Corolla** – Place defogger switch in ON position. Ensure continuity exists between terminals No. 9 and 10. Place switch in OFF position, continuity should not exist between terminals No. 9 and 10. Continuity should exist at all times between terminals No. 11 and 12 (light bulb). If continuity is not as specified, replace switch. *See Fig. 3*.

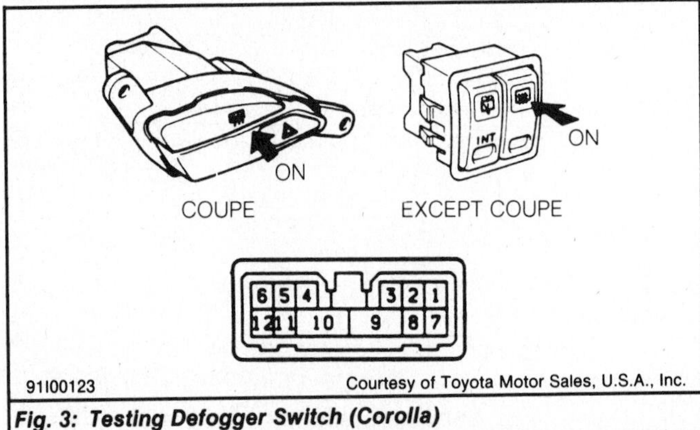


*Fig. 3: Testing Defogger Switch (Corolla)*

**Cressida** – Place defogger switch in ON position. Ensure continuity exists between terminals No. 5 and 6. Place switch in OFF position, continuity should not exist between terminals No. 5 and 6. Continuity should exist at all times between terminals No. 1 and 3 (light bulb). If continuity is not as specified, replace switch. *See Fig. 4*.

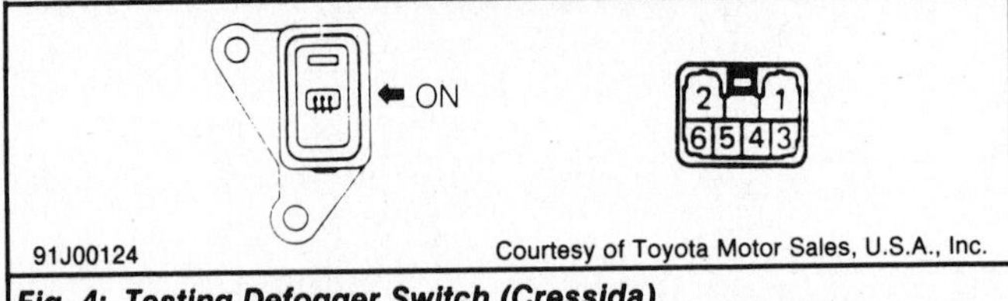


*Fig. 4: Testing Defogger Switch (Cressida)*

**Supra** – Connect battery voltage to terminal No. 3 and ground to terminal No. 4. Connect 3.4-watt test light between terminals No. 3 and 5. Turn defogger on. Ensure test light lights for 12-18 minutes and then goes out. If switch does not operate as specified, replace switch. *See Fig. 5*.

# 1991 SAFETY EQUIPMENT
# Rear Window Defogger (Cont.)

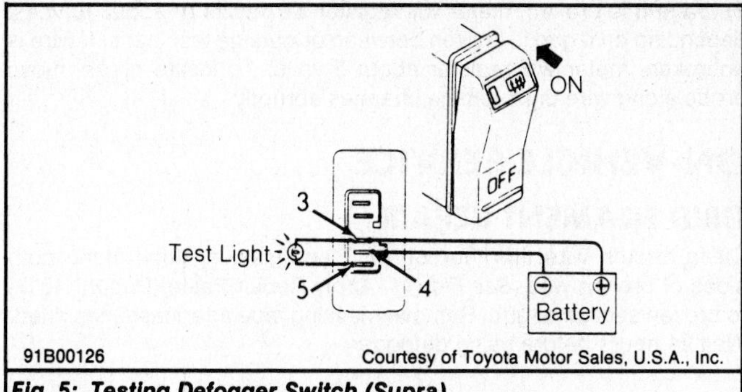


***Fig. 5: Testing Defogger Switch (Supra)***

**Tercel - 1)** To test defogger switch without timer, place switch in ON position. Ensure continuity exists between terminals No. 1, 3 and 4. Place switch in OFF position, continuity should exist between terminals No. 1 and 3. Continuity should exist at all times between terminals No. 5 and 6 (light bulb). If continuity is not as specified, replace switch. *See Fig. 6.*

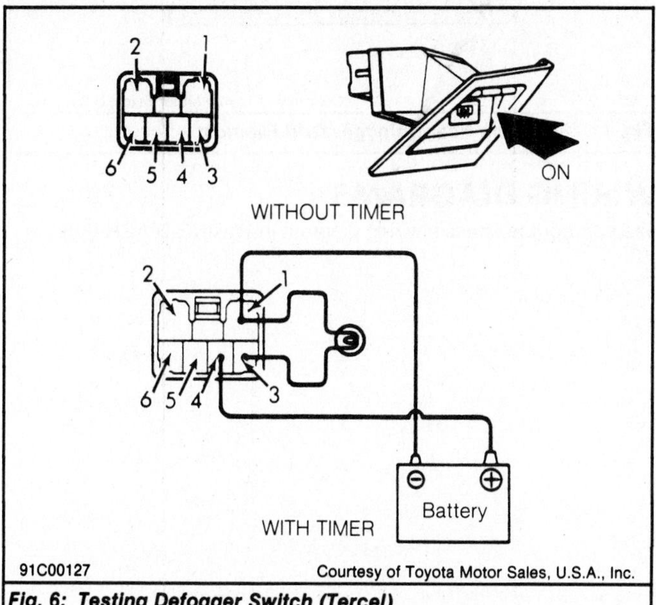


***Fig. 6: Testing Defogger Switch (Tercel)***

**2)** To test defogger switch with timer, connect battery voltage to terminal No. 4, and ground terminal No. 1. *See Fig. 6.* Connect 3.4-watt test light between terminals No. 1 and 3. Turn defogger on. Ensure test light lights for 12-18 minutes and then goes out. If switch does not operate as specified, replace switch.

## RELAY TEST

**Except Tercel - 1)** Using an ohmmeter, ensure continuity exists between terminals No. 1 and 3. Continuity should not exist between terminals No. 2 and 4 and terminals No. 3 and 4. If continuity is not as specified, replace relay.

**2)** Connect battery voltage to terminal No. 1 and ground to terminal No. 3. Continuity should exist between terminals No. 2 and 4. If operation is not as specified, replace relay. *See Fig. 7.*

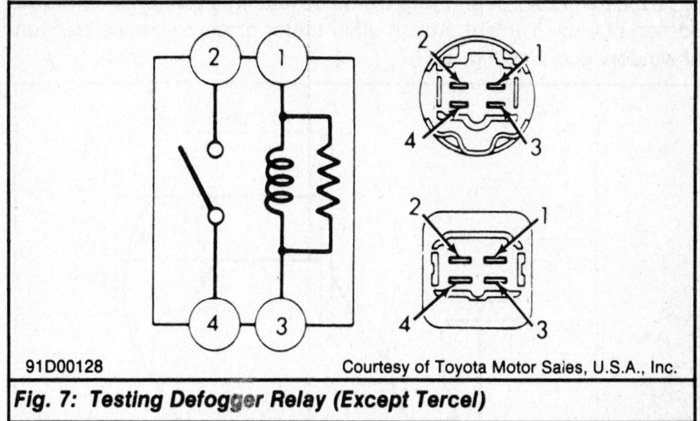


***Fig. 7: Testing Defogger Relay (Except Tercel)***

**Tercel -** Using an ohmmeter, ensure continuity exists between terminals No. 1 and 2. Continuity should not exist between terminals No. 2 and 3. If continuity is not as specified, replace relay. *See Fig. 8.*

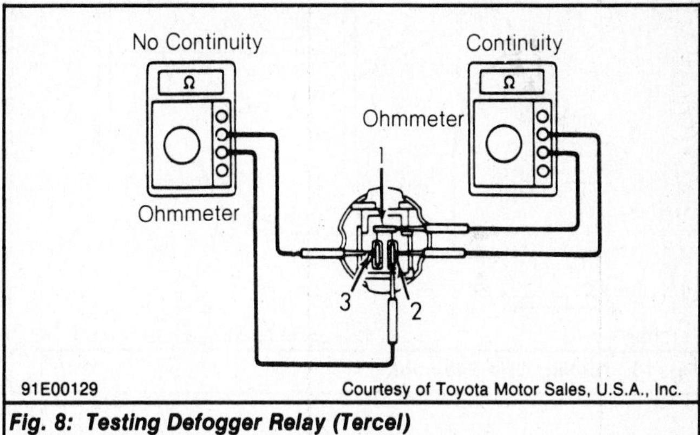


***Fig. 8: Testing Defogger Relay (Tercel)***

## POWER WINDOW LIMIT SWITCH

**4Runner -** Using an ohmmeter, ensure continuity exists between terminals No. 1 and 2 when switch is turned to ON position. Continuity should not exist between any terminals when switch is pushed to OFF position. If continuity is not as specified, replace relay. *See Fig. 9.*

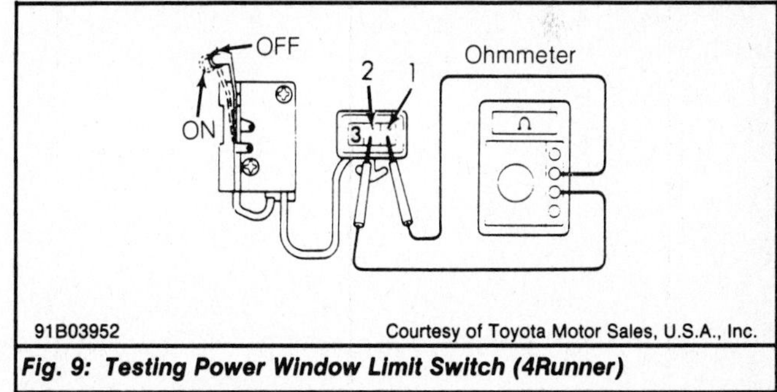


***Fig. 9: Testing Power Window Limit Switch (4Runner)***

## GRID FILAMENT TESTING

***NOTE: When testing grid wires with voltmeter, wrap aluminum foil around end of test probe, then press foil to grid wire. This will prevent probe from damaging grid wire***

# 1991 SAFETY EQUIPMENT
# Rear Window Defogger (Cont.)

**1)** To locate breaks in grid wire filaments, attach a voltmeter to middle portion of each filament. Attach other meter probe to vertical section of window grid. *See Fig. 10.*

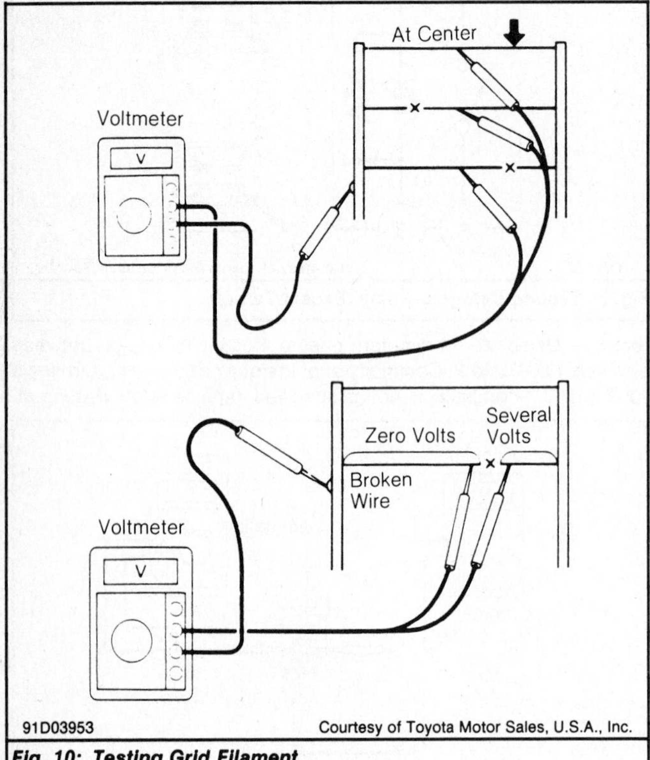


***Fig. 10: Testing Grid Filament***

**2)** If a grid is broken, meter will register zero volts or about 10 volts, depending on if grid is broken between or outside test leads. If wire is unbroken, meter will register about 5 volts. To locate break, move probe along wire until voltage changes abruptly.

## ON-VEHICLE SERVICE

### GRID FILAMENT REPAIR

Clean broken wire tips thoroughly. Place masking tape along both sides of broken wire. *See Fig. 11.* Apply Repair Paste (Dupont 4817) to broken section of grid. Remove masking tape after paste has dried. Wait 24 hours before using defogger.

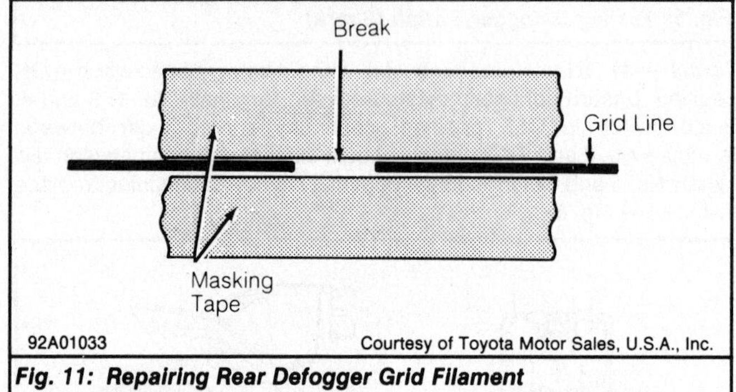


***Fig. 11: Repairing Rear Defogger Grid Filament***

## WIRING DIAGRAMS

See appropriate chassis wiring diagram in WIRING DIAGRAMS.

# 1991 SAFETY EQUIPMENT
# Steering Column Switches

## Camry, Celica, Corolla, Cressida, Land Cruiser, MR2, Pickup, Previa, Supra, Tercel, 4Runner

***WARNING:** Celica, MR2 and Supra vehicles are equipped with a driver's side air bag, use extreme caution while servicing steering column. Ensure ignition switch is in LOCK position and battery negative terminal is disconnected for at least 20 seconds before attempting any repair. DO NOT apply electrical power to any component on steering column without disconnecting air bag control unit or system may be activated. Information labels are attached to air bag components. Follow all notices on labels. Use only volt/ohmmeter with minimum of 10-k/ohm impedance to check ANY circuit.*

# TESTING

## COMBINATION SWITCH

***NOTE:** The term combination switch is used to describe headlight/ turn signal/wiper switches on column.*

Remove combination switch. See COMBINATION SWITCH under REMOVAL & INSTALLATION. Use ohmmeter to check continuity at switch terminals as switch is operated. Replace switch if continuity is not as specified. See appropriate table.

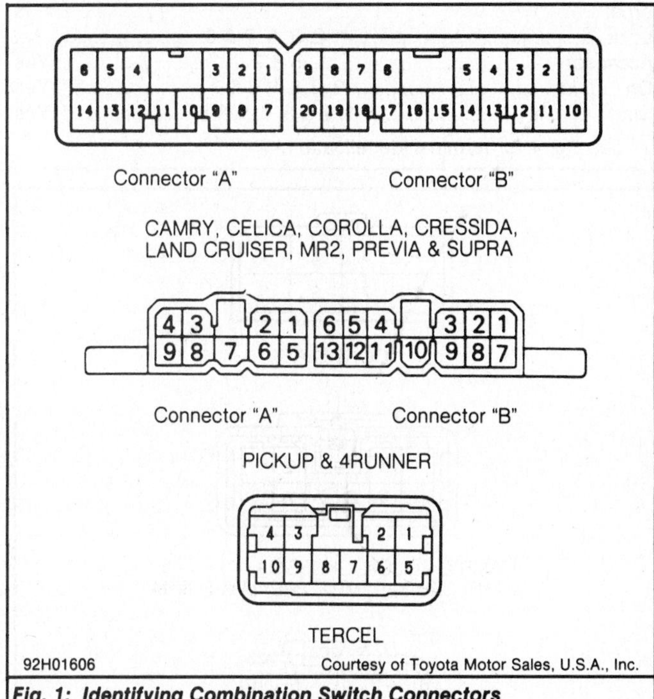


*Fig. 1: Identifying Combination Switch Connectors*

## CRUISE CONTROL SWITCH

**Corolla, Cressida & Land Cruiser –** With combination switch in specified position, ensure continuity exists between terminals listed. See CRUISE CONTROL SWITCH CONTINUITY TEST table. *See Fig. 1.* Replace switch if continuity is not as specified.

**Camry, Celica, MR2, Previa, Supra & Tercel – 1)** Use ohmmeter to check resistance between switch terminals No. 3 and 4. *See Fig. 2.* If resistance values are not as specified, replace switch. See CRUISE CONTROL SWITCH RESISTANCE SPECIFICATIONS table.

**2)** Ensure continuity exists between switch terminals No. 3 and 5 with switch in ON position. Ensure continuity does not exists between switch terminals No.3 and 5 with switch in OFF position. If continuity is not as specified, replace switch.

*CRUISE CONTROL SWITCH CONTINUITY TEST*

| Switch Position | Terminal Numbers [1] | Continuity |
|---|---|---|
| Corolla | | |
| Resume/Accel | B16 & B17 | Yes |
| Set/Coast | B5 & B16 | Yes |
| Off | B5, B16 & B17 | No |
| Cressida | | |
| Cancel | B2 & B20 | Yes |
| Main | B15 & B20 | Yes |
| Set/Coast | B5 & B20 | Yes |
| Resume/Accel | B17 & B20 | Yes |
| Off | B2, B3, B5, B15, B17 & B20 | No |
| Land Cruiser | | |
| Cancel | B11 & B20 | Yes |
| Main | B15 & B20 | Yes |
| Set/Coast | B5 & B20 | Yes |
| Resume/Accel | B17 & B20 | Yes |
| Off | B5, B11, B15, B17 & B20 | No |

[1] – *See Fig. 1* for terminal identification.

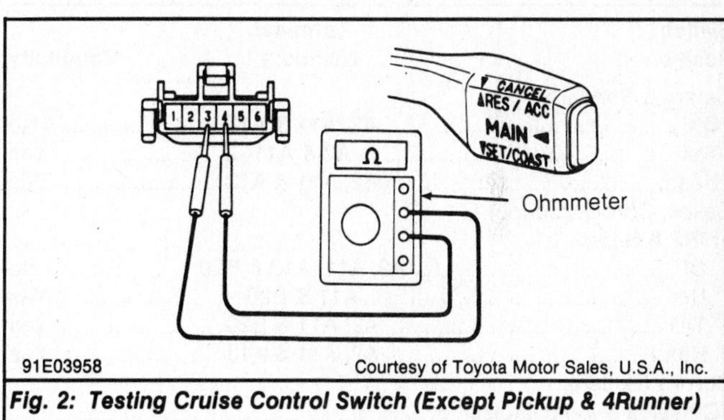


*Fig. 2: Testing Cruise Control Switch (Except Pickup & 4Runner)*

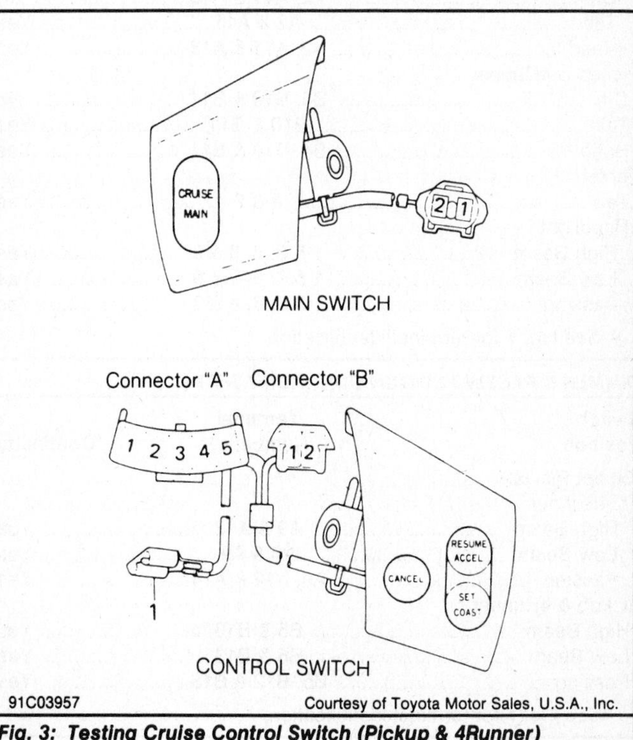


*Fig. 3: Testing Cruise Control Switch (Pickup & 4Runner)*

# 1991 SAFETY EQUIPMENT
# Steering Column Switches (Cont.)

CRUISE CONTROL SWITCH RESISTANCE SPECIFICATIONS

| Switch Position | Ohms |
|---|---|
| Resume/Accel | 68 |
| Set/Coast | 198 |
| Cancel | 418 |

**Pickup & 4Runner – 1)** Remove horn pad and disconnect cruise control switch connector(s). Check resistance between control switch terminals No. A2 and A5, A4 and A5, A2 and B2. *See Fig. 3*. If resistance values are not as specified, replace switch. See CRUISE CONTROL SWITCH RESISTANCE SPECIFICATIONS table.

**2)** Ensure continuity exists between main switch terminals No. 1 and 2 with main switch in ON position. If continuity is not as specified, replace switch.

## HEADLIGHT SWITCH

With headlight switch in specified position, ensure continuity exists between terminals listed. See LIGHTING SWITCH CONTINUITY TEST and DIMMER & PASSING SWITCH CONTINUITY TEST tables. *See Fig. 1*. Replace switch if continuity is not as specified.

LIGHTING SWITCH CONTINUITY TEST

| Switch Position | Terminal Numbers [1] | Continuity |
|---|---|---|
| Camry & Previa | | |
| Off | A2, A11 & A13 | No |
| Tail | A2 & A11 | Yes |
| Head | A2, A11 & A13 | Yes |
| Celica, Corolla (Coupe) MR2 & Supra | | |
| Off | A2, A11, A13 & B20 | No |
| Up | A11 & B20 | Yes |
| Tail | A2, A11 & B20 | Yes |
| Head | A2, A11 & A13 | Yes |
| Corolla (Sedan), Cressida & Land Cruiser | | |
| Off | A2, A11 & A13 | No |
| Tail | A2 & A11 | Yes |
| Head | A2, A11 & A13 | Yes |
| Pickup & 4Runner | | |
| Off | B4, B10 & B11 | No |
| Tail | B10 & B11 | Yes |
| Head | B4, B10 & B11 | Yes |
| Tercel | | |
| Tail | 8 & 9 | Yes |
| Headlight | | |
| High Beam | 1 & 5; 6, 8 & 9 | Yes |
| Low Beam | 1 & 7; 6, 8 & 9 | Yes |
| Passing | 1 & 5; 6, 8 & 9 | Yes |

[1] – *See Fig. 1* for terminal identification.

DIMMER & PASSING SWITCH CONTINUITY TEST

| Switch Position | Terminal Numbers [1] | Continuity |
|---|---|---|
| Except Pickup & 4Runner | | |
| High Beam | A9 & A12 | Yes |
| Low Beam | A3 & A9 | Yes |
| Passing | A9, A12 & A14 | Yes |
| Pickup & 4Runner | | |
| High Beam | B5 & B13 | Yes |
| Low Beam | B6 & B13 | Yes |
| Passing | B5, B12 & B13 | Yes |

[1] – *See Fig. 1* for terminal identification.

## IGNITION SWITCH

With ignition switch in specified position, ensure continuity exists between terminals listed. See IGNITION SWITCH CONTINUITY TEST table. *See Fig. 4*.

IGNITION SWITCH CONTINUITY TEST

| Switch Position | Terminal Numbers [1] | Continuity |
|---|---|---|
| Camry, Celica, Cressida, MR2, Previa & Supra | | |
| Lock | 2, 3, 4, 6, 7, 9 & 10 | No |
| Accessory | 3 & 4 | Yes |
| On | 2, 3 & 4; 9 & 10 | Yes |
| Start | 2, 4 & 7; 6, 9 & 10 | Yes |
| Corolla | | |
| Lock | 1, 2, 3, 4, 5, 6, 7 & 8 | No |
| Accessory | 3 & 4 | Yes |
| On | 2, 3 & 4; 7 & 8 | Yes |
| Start | 1, 2 & 4; 5, 7 & 8 | Yes |
| Land Cruiser | | |
| Lock | 2, 3, 4, 6, 7, 9 & 10 | No |
| Accessory | 7 & 9 | Yes |
| On | 3 & 4; 6, 7 & 9 | Yes |
| Start | 2, 3 & 4; 6, 9 & 10 | Yes |
| Pickup & 4Runner | | |
| Lock | 1, 2, 3, 6, 7 & 8 | No |
| Accessory | 2 & 3 | Yes |
| On | 1, 2 & 3; 7 & 8 | Yes |
| Start | 1, 3 & 6; 7 & 8 | Yes |
| Tercel | | |
| Lock | 1, 2, 3, 6, 7 & 8 | No |
| Accessory | 5 & 7 | Yes |
| On | 2, 3 & 4; 5 & 7 | Yes |
| Start | 1, 2 & 3; 4, 7 & 8 | Yes |

[1] – *See Fig. 4* for terminal identification.

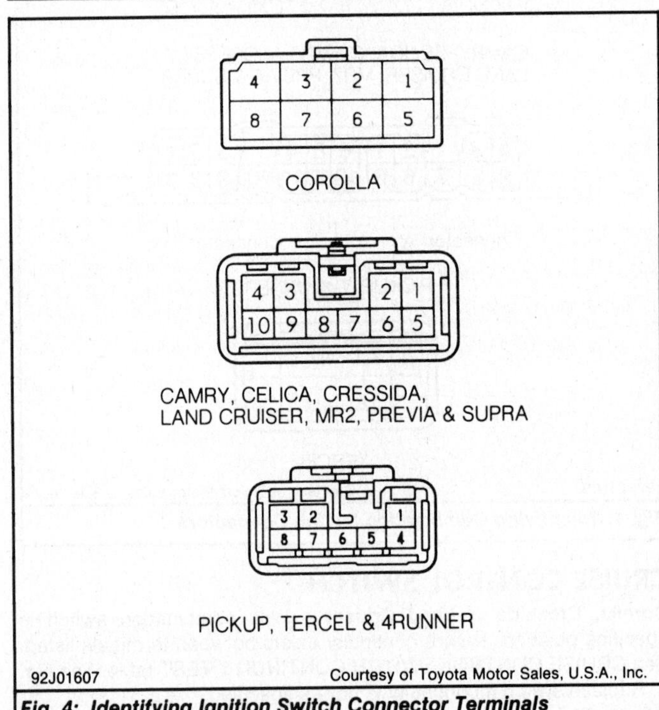


***Fig. 4: Identifying Ignition Switch Connector Terminals***

## TURN SIGNAL SWITCH

With turn signal switch in specified position, ensure continuity exists between terminals listed. See TURN SIGNAL SWITCH CONTINUITY TEST table. *See Fig. 1*. Replace switch if continuity is not as specified.

# 1991 SAFETY EQUIPMENT
# Steering Column Switches (Cont.)

**TURN SIGNAL SWITCH CONTINUITY TEST**

| Switch Position | Terminal Numbers [1] | Continuity |
|---|---|---|
| Camry [1] | | |
| Left | A1 & A5 | Yes |
| Neutral | A1, A5 & A8 | No |
| Right | A1 & A8 | Yes |
| Pickup & 4Runner [1] | | |
| Left | B3 & B9 | Yes |
| Neutral | B3, B8 & B9 | No |
| Right | B3 & B8 | Yes |
| Tercel [2] | | |
| Left | 2 & 3 | Yes |
| Neutral | 2, 3 & 4 | Yes |
| Right | 3 & 4 | Yes |
| Except Camry, Pickup Tercel & 4Runner [1] | | |
| Left | A1 & A5 | Yes |
| Neutral | A1, A5 & A8 | No |
| Right | A1 & A8 | Yes |

[1] – *See Fig. 1* for terminal identification.
[2] – *See Fig. 5* for terminal identification.

## WASHER SWITCH

With washer switch in specified position, ensure continuity exists between terminals listed. See WASHER SWITCH CONTINUITY TEST table. For all models except Tercel, *see Fig. 1*. For Tercel, *see Fig. 5*. Replace switch if continuity is not as specified.

**WASHER SWITCH CONTINUITY TEST**

| Switch Position | Terminal Numbers | Continuity |
|---|---|---|
| Pickup & 4Runner [1] | | |
| Off | A1 & A2 | No |
| On | A1 & A2 | Yes |
| Tercel [2] | | |
| Off | 1, 2, 3, 4, 5, & 6 | No |
| On | 3 & 4 | Yes |
| Except Pickup, Tercel & 4Runner [1] | | |
| Off | B8 & B16 | No |
| On | B8 & B16 | Yes |

[1] – *See Fig. 1* for terminal identification.
[2] – *See Fig. 5* for terminal identification.

## WIPER SWITCH

With wiper switch in specified position, ensure continuity exists between terminals listed. See WIPER SWITCH CONTINUITY TEST table. For all models except Tercel, *see Fig. 1*. For Tercel, *see Fig. 5*. Replace switch if continuity is not as specified.

***NOTE: For testing information for wipers, see appropriate WIPER/WASHERS article.***

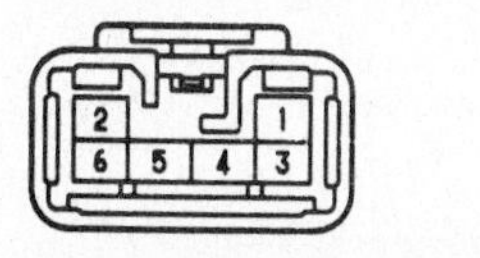


92B01608

Courtesy of Toyota Motor Sales, U.S.A., Inc.

***Fig. 5: Identifying Washer/Wiper Switch Connector Terminals (Tercel)***

**WIPER SWITCH CONTINUITY TEST**

| Switch Position | Terminal Nos. | Continuity |
|---|---|---|
| Camry, Celica & MR2 [1] | | |
| Off (Normal) | B4 & B7 | Yes |
| Off (Mist) | B7 & B18 | Yes |
| Int (Normal) | B4 & B7 | Yes |
| Int (Mist) | B7 & B18 | Yes |
| Low (Normal) | B7 & B18 | Yes |
| Low (Mist) | B7 & B18 | Yes |
| High (Normal) | B13 & B18 | Yes |
| High (Mist) | B7, B13 & B18 | Yes |
| Corolla & Previa [1] | | |
| Mist | B7 & B18 | Yes |
| Off | B4 & B7 | Yes |
| Int | B4 & B7 | Yes |
| Low | B7 & B18 | Yes |
| High | B13 & B18 | Yes |
| Cressida [1] | | |
| Off (Normal) | B4 & B7 | Yes |
| Off (Mist) | B7 & B18 | Yes |
| Int (Normal) | B4 & B7; B12 & B16 | Yes |
| Int (Mist) | B7 & B18; B12 & B16 | Yes |
| Low (Normal) | B7 & B18 | Yes |
| Low (Mist) | B7 & B18 | Yes |
| High (Normal) | B13 & B18 | Yes |
| High (Mist) | B7, B13 & B18 | Yes |
| Land Cruiser [1] | | |
| Off | B4 & B7 | Yes |
| Int | B4 & B7 | Yes |
| Low | B7 & B18 | Yes |
| High | B13 & B18 | Yes |
| Pickup & 4Runner [1] | | |
| Int | A7 & A8 | Yes |
| Mist | A4 & A8 | Yes |
| Off | A7 & A8 | Yes |
| Low | A4 & A8 | Yes |
| High | A4 & A9 | Yes |
| Supra [1] | | |
| Off | B4 & B7 | Yes |
| Int | B4 & B7; B12 & B16 | Yes |
| Low | B7 & B18 | Yes |
| High | B13 & B18 | Yes |
| Tercel [2] | | |
| Mist | 1 & 5 | Yes |
| Int | 1 & 6 | Yes |
| Off | 1 & 6 | Yes |
| Low | 1 & 5 | Yes |
| High | 2 & 5 | Yes |

[1] – *See Fig. 1* for terminal identification.
[2] – *See Fig. 5* for terminal identification.

## REMOVAL & INSTALLATION

***WARNING: Celica, MR2 and Supra vehicles are equipped with a driver's side air bag. Use extreme caution while servicing steering column. Ensure ignition switch is in LOCK position and battery negative terminal is disconnected for at least 20 seconds before starting service. DO NOT apply electrical power to any component on steering column without disconnecting air bag control unit or system may be activated. Information labels are attached to air bag components. Follow all notices on labels. Use only volt/ohmmeter with minimum of 10-k/ohm impedance to check ANY circuit.***

# 1991 SAFETY EQUIPMENT
# Steering Column Switches (Cont.)

## STEERING WHEEL & HORN PAD

**Removal (Except Celica, MR2 & Supra)** - Remove screw securing horn pad and remove horn pad. Disconnect horn electrical connector(s). Remove lock nut and washer. Make alignment mark on steering shaft and steering wheel for installation reference. Install suitable steering wheel puller and pull steering wheel from shaft.

**Installation** - Align reference marks on steering shaft and steering wheel. To complete installation, reverse removal procedure.

**Removal (Celica, MR2 & Supra)** - **1)** Ensure front wheels are in straight ahead position. Place ignition switch in LOCK position and disconnect negative battery cable. Remove screw covers from side of steering wheel. Using Torx Wrench (T30), loosen 4 screws until groove along screw circumference catches on screw case. *See Fig. 6.*

**2)** Pull steering wheel pad away from steering wheel and disconnect air bag electrical connector. DO NOT pull on electrical connector. Remove lock nut and washer from steering shaft. Make alignment mark on steering shaft and steering wheel for installation reference. Using steering wheel puller, pull steering wheel from shaft.

**Installation** - **1)** Ensure front wheels are in straight ahead position. Install spiral cable to combination switch. Turn spiral cable counterclockwise by hand until it is hard to turn. Turn spiral cable clockwise about 2 1/2 turns and align Red mark.

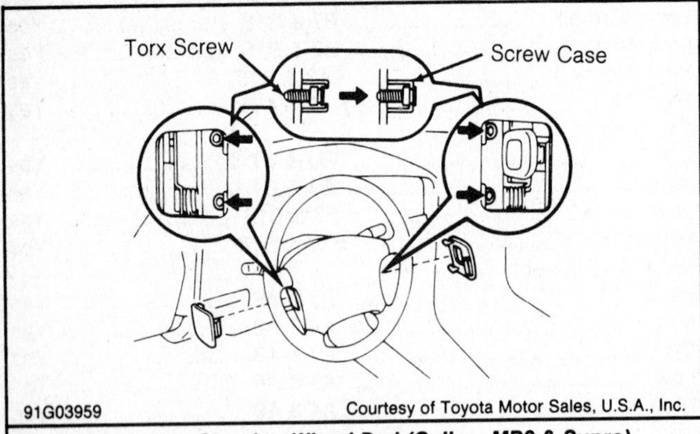


***Fig. 6: Removing Steering Wheel Pad (Celica, MR2 & Supra)***

**2)** Align reference marks on steering shaft and steering wheel and install steering wheel. Torque shaft nut to 25 ft. lbs. (34 N.m). Connect air bag connector. Ensure Torx screw groove circumference is caught on screw case. *See Fig. 6.* Install steering wheel pad and tighten Torx screws to 65 INCH lbs. (7.4 N.m).

***NOTE: Tighten steering wheel pad to specification. Ensure wiring is not pinched and does not interfere with other parts.***

## COMBINATION SWITCH

**Removal & Installation** - Remove steering wheel. See STEERING WHEEL & HORN PAD in this article. Remove instrument lower cluster finish panel. Remove upper and lower steering column covers. Disconnect combination switch electrical connector. Remove screws securing combination switch to steering column and remove combination switch. To install, reverse removal procedure.

## IGNITION SWITCH & LOCK CYLINDER

**Removal** - **1)** Remove steering wheel, upper and lower steering column covers and combination switch (if necessary). Disconnect ignition switch harness connectors.

**2)** If shear bolt studs are accessible, use a hacksaw to cut a slot into exposed studs. Using a screwdriver, remove studs.

**3)** If shear bolt studs are recessed or hard to reach with a hacksaw, center punch studs. Using a drill bit and a screw extractor, remove studs. Remove steering lock and ignition switch.

**Installation** - **1)** To install, reverse removal procedure. Install new shear bolts. Tighten shear bolts finger tight. Ensure proper operation of steering lock and ignition switch.

**2)** Tighten shear bolts until heads break off. Install combination switch, upper and lower steering column covers and steering wheel.

# 1991 SAFETY EQUIPMENT
# Wiper/Washer Systems

## Camry, Celica, Corolla, Cressida, Land Cruiser, MR2, Pickup, Previa, Supra, Tercel, 4Runner

***WARNING: Celica, MR2 and Supra are equipped with a driver's side air bag. Ensure negative battery cable is disconnected for at least 20 seconds before attempting any repair. Use extreme caution when working in steering column area.***

## DESCRIPTION & OPERATION

All models are equipped with 2-speed wiper motors. An optional intermittent wiper system is also available. Front wiper motors are protected by an internal circuit breaker.

## TESTING

### FRONT WIPER MOTOR

**Previa - 1)** Connect jumper wire from wiper motor terminal No. 1 to ground. Apply 12 volts wiper motor terminal No. 3. *See Fig. 1.* Motor should operate at low speed.

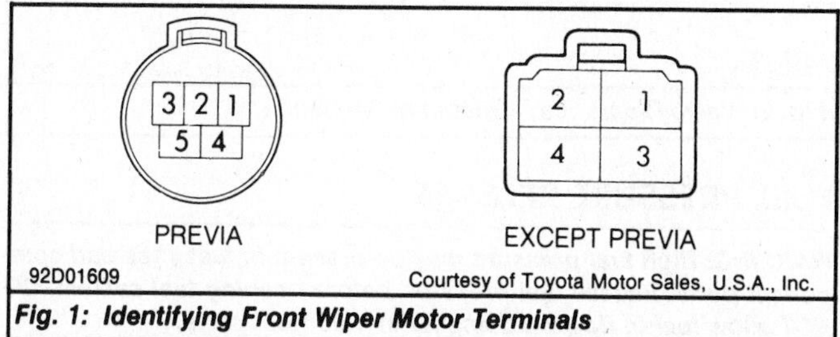


***Fig. 1: Identifying Front Wiper Motor Terminals***

**2)** Connect jumper wire from wiper motor terminal No. 1 to ground. Apply 12 volts positive battery terminal to wiper motor terminal No. 2. Motor should operate at high speed.
**3)** To check automatic park operation, run wiper motor at low speed. Stop motor at any position, except park position, by disconnecting lead from wiper motor terminal No. 3. Install jumper wire between terminals No. 3 and 4.
**4)** Apply 12 volts to terminal No. 5. Connect wiper motor terminal No. 1 to ground. Motor should start running and then stop at the park position. Replace motor if operation is not as described.
**Except Previa - 1)** Connect jumper wire between wiper motor body and ground. Using jumper wire, apply 12 volts to wiper motor terminal No. 2. *See Fig. 1.* Motor should operate at low speed.
**2)** Remove jumper wire from terminal No. 2. Apply 12 volts to wiper motor terminal No. 1. Motor should operate at high speed.
**3)** Run motor at low speed. Stop motor at any position except park position by disconnecting jumper from terminal No. 2. Install jumper wire between wiper motor terminal No. 2 and 3.
**4)** Apply 12 volts to wiper motor terminal No. 4. Jumper motor body to ground. Motor should start running and then stop at the park position. Replace motor if operation is not as described.

### REAR WIPER MOTOR

**Camry, Celica & Supra - 1)** Apply 12 volts to wiper motor terminal No. 1. *See Fig. 2.* Connect wiper motor terminal No. 3 and motor body to ground. Motor should operate.
**2)** To check automatic park operation, apply 12 volts to wiper motor terminal No. 1. Jumper terminal No. 3 and motor body to ground.
**3)** Stop motor operation anywhere except park position by disconnecting terminal No. 1. Apply 12 volts to terminal No. 1. Ensure motor operates and then stops at park position.
**Corolla - 1)** Connect wiper motor body to ground. Apply 12 volts to wiper motor terminal No. 2. *See Fig. 2.* Motor should operate.
**2)** To check automatic park operation, apply 12 volts to wiper motor terminal No. 2. Connect motor body to ground. Motor should operate.
**3)** Stop motor operation anywhere except the park position by removing power from terminal No. 2. Install a jumper wire between terminals No. 2 and 3. Apply 12 volts to wiper motor terminal No. 2. Ensure motor operates and then stops at Park position.
**Land Cruiser & Previa - 1)** Disconnect wiring connector from wiper motor. Apply 12 volts to wiper motor terminal No. 3. *See Fig. 2.* Connect wiper motor terminal No. 2 to ground. Motor should operate.
**2)** To check automatic park operation, run motor at low speed. Stop motor at any position except park position by removing power from terminal No. 3. Install jumper wire between wiper motor terminal No. 3 and 4.
**3)** Apply 12 volts to wiper motor terminal No. 1. Connect wiper motor terminal No. 2 to ground. Motor should start running and then stop at the park position. Replace motor if operation is not as described.
**4Runner -** Apply 12 volts to wiper motor terminal No. 1. *See Fig. 2.* Connect wiper motor terminal No. 1 to ground. Wiper motor should rotate clockwise. Reverse polarity to wiper motor. Wiper motor should rotate counterclockwise. Replace motor if operation is not as described.

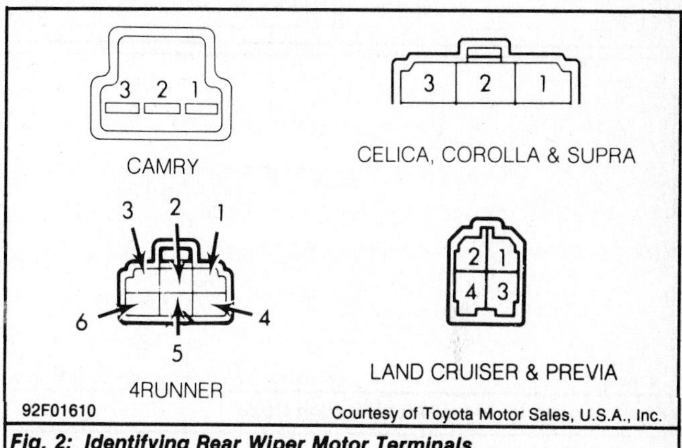


***Fig. 2: Identifying Rear Wiper Motor Terminals***

### WIPER CONTROL RELAY

**Intermittent Wipers -** If wiper motor operates when voltage is applied directly but does not operate by switch, replace relay.

## REMOVAL & INSTALLATION

### WIPER SWITCH

**Removal & Installation - 1)** Disconnect battery ground. Remove trim panel under steering column. Remove column covers. If necessary, remove horn button and steering wheel.
**2)** Note position of all wiper/washer switch wires in harness connector. Press in locking tabs on connector wires and remove wires from harness connector. Remove mounting screws and wiper/washer switch. To install, reverse removal procedure.

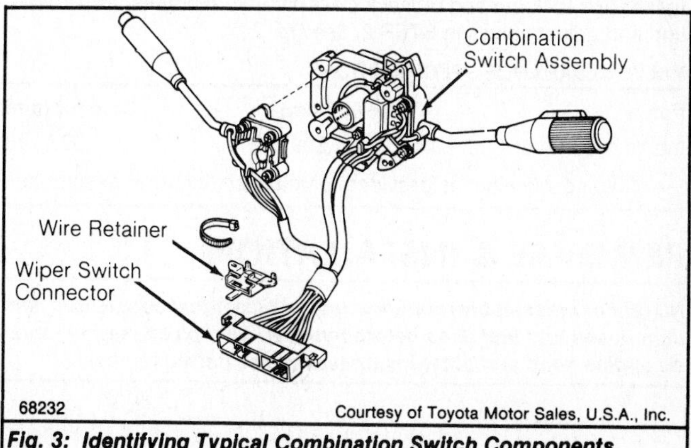


***Fig. 3: Identifying Typical Combination Switch Components***

## WIRING DIAGRAMS

See appropriate chassis wiring diagram in WIRING DIAGRAMS.

# 1991 ENGINES
# 1.5L 4-Cylinder

## Tercel

***NOTE: For repair procedures not covered in this article, see ENGINE OVERHAUL PROCEDURES article in GENERAL INFORMATION.***

## ENGINE IDENTIFICATION

Engine may be identified by using Vehicle Identification Number (VIN) stamped on a metal pad, located near lower left corner of windshield. The forth character of VIN identifies engine model. See ENGINE IDENTIFICATION CODES table.

Engine identification number, located on cylinder block below cylinder head, may be required when ordering replacement parts (if needed). *See Fig. 1.*

***ENGINE IDENTIFICATION CODES***

| Application | VIN | Engine Code |
|---|---|---|
| 1.5L PFI | E | 3E-E |

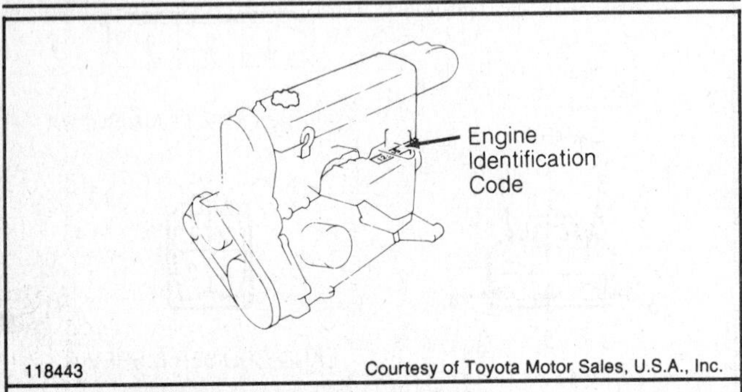


***Fig. 1: Locating Engine Identification Code***

## ADJUSTMENTS

### VALVE CLEARANCE ADJUSTMENT

***NOTE: Valves should be adjusted with engine at normal operating temperature. Cold specification is provided for initial setting after assembly.***

**1)** With engine at normal operating temperature, stop engine and remove valve cover. Turn crankshaft pulley and align timing marks on TDC.

**2)** Ensure No. 1 cylinder rocker arms are loose and No. 4 cylinder rocker arms are tight. Measure valve clearance on valves indicated in STEP 1. *See Fig. 2.*

**3)** Loosen rocker arm lock nut and turn adjusting screw to specified clearance. See VALVE CLEARANCE SPECIFICATIONS table. Tighten rocker arm lock nut and recheck clearance. Turn crankshaft 1 revolution and adjust valves in STEP 2. *See Fig. 2.*

***VALVE CLEARANCE SPECIFICATIONS***

| Valve | Hot In. (mm) | Cold In. (mm) |
|---|---|---|
| Intake & Exhaust | .008 (.20) | [1] .007 (.18) |

[1] – Cold specification is provided for initial setting after assembly.

## REMOVAL & INSTALLATION

***NOTE: For reassembly reference, label all electrical connectors, vacuum hoses and fuel lines before removal. Also place mating marks on engine hood and other major assemblies before removal.***

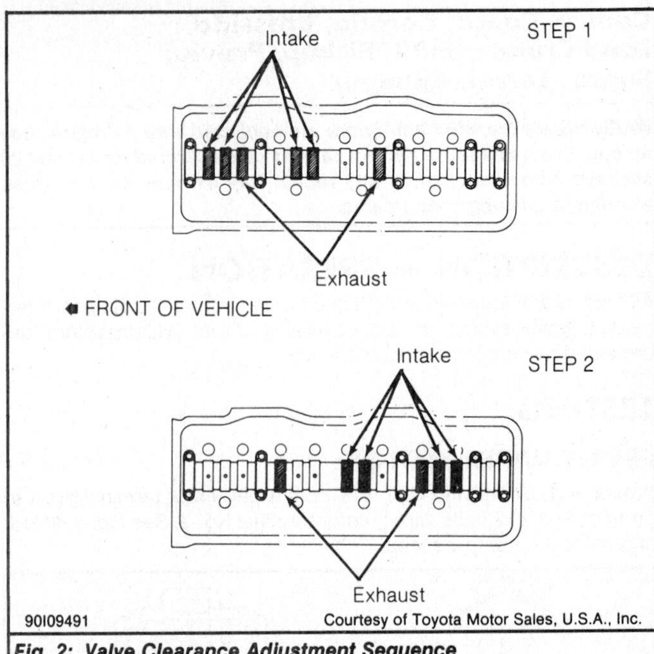


***Fig. 2: Valve Clearance Adjustment Sequence***

### FUEL PRESSURE RELEASE

***WARNING: High fuel pressure may be present in fuel lines and component parts. Relieve fuel pressure before opening fuel system. DO NOT allow fuel to flow onto engine or electrical parts.***

Disconnect negative battery cable. Place container under fitting to be loosened. Use a rag to cover fuel line/component. Slowly loosen fitting, allowing pressurized fuel to spill into container. After fuel system has depressurized, disconnect and plug fitting.

### ENGINE

***NOTE: Engine and transaxle should be removed as an assembly.***

**Removal – 1)** Drain coolant and engine oil. Remove battery. Remove radiator reservoir tank. Remove hood. Remove engine under cover (splash) shields. Remove radiator.

**2)** Disconnect accelerator cable. On A/T models, disconnect throttle cable. On all models, remove PCV hoses. Remove air cleaner assembly with air intake connector. Remove air cleaner bracket. Release fuel pressure. See FUEL PRESSURE RELEASE.

**3)** Disconnect fuel hoses. Remove charcoal canister. Disconnect all necessary electrical wiring from engine. Disconnect and mark all vacuum hoses for installation reference. Disconnect all coolant hoses.

**4)** Disconnect speedometer cable. Disconnect control cables from transaxle. On A/T models, remove control cable bracket. On M/T models, remove clutch release (slave) cylinder and wire out of way. DO NOT disconnect hydraulic line.

**5)** On all models, disconnect clamps attaching engine wire harness. Move wire harness out of way. Remove starter. Remove vacuum transmitting valves with bracket. On models with power steering, remove power steering pump and wire out of way. DO NOT disconnect power steering hoses.

**6)** On models with A/C, remove A/C compressor. DO NOT disconnect A/C hoses. Wire A/C compressor out of way. Remove A/C compressor mounting bracket. On all models, disconnect exhaust pipe.

**7)** Remove drive shafts. Attach hoist chain to engine hangers. Remove rear mount through bolt. Remove bolts and rear mount. Remove right mount through bolt. Remove bolts and right mount.

**8)** Disconnect ground strap. Remove left mount bracket. Carefully lift engine out of vehicle. Lower transaxle to clear battery carrier support.

***NOTE: Engine and transaxle should be installed as an assembly.***

**Installation** – To install, reverse removal procedures. Tighten all bolts to specification. See TORQUE SPECIFICATIONS table at end of article. Add proper amount of engine oil, transmission fluid and coolant. Start engine and check for leaks.

## CYLINDER HEAD & MANIFOLDS

**Removal & Installation – 1)** Disconnect negative battery cable. Remove right side under cover (splash) shield. Drain coolant. Disconnect exhaust pipe. Disconnect accelerator cable.

**2)** On A/T models, disconnect throttle cable. On all models, remove PCV hoses. Remove air cleaner assembly with air intake connector. Release fuel pressure. See FUEL PRESSURE RELEASE.

**3)** Disconnect fuel hoses. Disconnect all necessary electrical wiring from engine. Disconnect and mark all vacuum hoses for installation reference. Disconnect all coolant hoses.

**4)** On models with power steering, remove power steering pump. Remove power steering pump bracket. On models with A/C and without power steering, remove idler pulley bracket.

**5)** On all models, remove timing belt and camshaft timing gear. See TIMING BELT. Remove distributor. Remove water outlet housing. Remove bolts and outer exhaust manifold heat insulator. Remove 6 nuts, exhaust manifold, 2 gaskets and inner heat insulator.

**6)** Disconnect engine wiring harness from engine. Remove intake manifold bracket-to-cylinder block. Remove 5 bolts, 2 nuts and intake manifold with gasket.

**7)** Remove 2 bolts and fuel rail with fuel injectors. Use care not to drop fuel injectors. Pull out fuel injectors from fuel rail. Remove 2 spacers and 4 insulators from cylinder head.

**8)** Measure camshaft end play before removing cylinder head. End play should be within specification. See CAMSHAFT table under ENGINE SPECIFICATIONS at end of article. If clearance is greater than maximum, replace cylinder head and/or camshaft. Remove camshaft. See CAMSHAFT.

***CAUTION: Cylinder head warpage or cracking can result if cylinder head bolts are not removed in sequence.***

**9)** Remove cylinder head. Loosen cylinder head bolts in 3 stages, in reverse of tightening sequence. *See Fig. 3*. Remove cylinder head. Use care not to damage cylinder head or engine block contact surfaces.

**Installation – 1)** Ensure mating surfaces are clean and camshaft caps and rocker arm assembly are tightened. See CAMSHAFT. Apply engine oil to all moving parts. Install new cylinder head gasket and cylinder head. Apply light coat of engine oil to cylinder head bolts and cylinder block threads.

**2)** Tighten cylinder head bolts in 3 stages, in sequence. *See Fig. 3*. Tighten cylinder head bolts to specification. See TORQUE SPECIFICATIONS table at end of article.

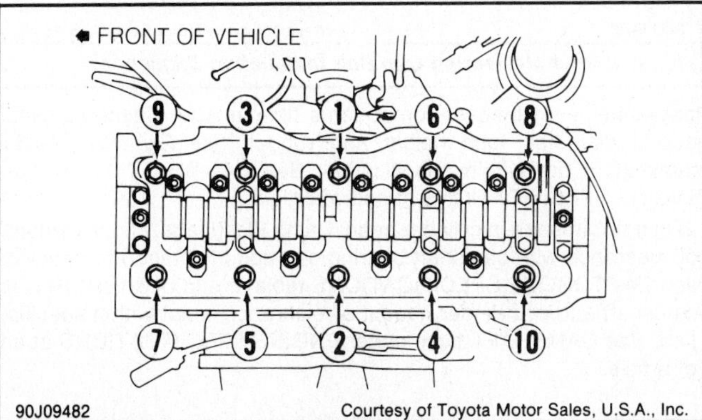


***Fig. 3: Cylinder Head Bolt Tightening Sequence***

**3)** Install timing belt, check valve timing and timing belt tension. See TIMING BELT. Install exhaust manifold gasket with "E" mark facing outward. To complete installation, reverse removal procedure.

**4)** Refill engine oil and cooling system. Set valve clearance. See VALVE CLEARANCE ADJUSTMENT under ADJUSTMENTS. When installing valve cover, apply seal packing to cylinder head. *See Fig. 5*. Tighten all bolts to specification. See TORQUE SPECIFICATIONS table at end of article. Set ignition timing and idle speed. Start engine and check for leaks.

## FRONT COVER OIL SEAL

**Removal & Installation – 1)** If oil pump is removed from cylinder block, pry out oil seal. Using Seal Installer (09309-37010), install oil seal until oil seal surface is flush with oil pump case edge. Apply multipurpose grease to oil seal lip.

**2)** If oil pump is installed to cylinder block, cut off oil seal lip. Pry out oil seal. Use care not to damage crankshaft surface. Apply multipurpose grease to new oil seal lip. Using Seal Installer (09309-37010), install oil seal until oil seal surface is flush with oil pump case edge.

## TIMING BELT

**Removal – 1)** Disconnect negative battery cable. Remove right side engine under cover (splash) shield. Remove accessory drive belts. Disconnect accelerator cable. On A/T models, disconnect throttle cable.

**2)** On all models, disconnect PCV hoses. Remove bolt, ground strap and vacuum transmitting valves with bracket from right engine mount. Slightly raise engine and remove right engine mount. Remove valve cover. Remove spark plugs.

**3)** Set No. 1 cylinder at TDC on compression stroke. Turn crankshaft pulley and align groove on crankshaft with "0" mark on timing belt cover. Ensure rocker arms on No. 1 cylinder are loose. If not, turn crankshaft pulley 1 complete revolution.

***NOTE: If reusing timing belt, mark location of belt for installation reference.***

**4)** On models with A/C and/or power steering, remove pulley. Using Holder (09213-14010), hold crankshaft pulley. Loosen crankshaft pulley bolt. Remove holder. Remove crankshaft pulley bolt. Using Puller (09330-00021), remove crankshaft pulley.

**5)** Remove timing belt covers. Remove timing belt guide from front of crankshaft. Remove tension spring from idler pulley. Loosen idler pulley bolt and push pulley to left as far as it will go and tighten bolt. Remove timing belt.

**Inspection – 1)** Check timing belt teeth for cracks or damage. If tooth damage is found, ensure camshaft, water pump and oil pump are okay. If wear or cracks on flat side of belt face are found, check for nicks on idler pulleys.

**2)** If wear or damage to only one side of belt is found, check belt guide and alignment of each pulley and sprocket. If noticeable wear is found on belt teeth, check timing cover gasket for damage or improper installation.

**3)** Ensure no foreign material is on sprocket teeth. Check idler pulley tension spring free length. Spring free length should be 1.51" (38.4 mm). If spring free length is not within specification, replace spring.

**Installation – 1)** If reusing old timing belt, align marks made during removal. If installing new timing belt, turn camshaft pulley until "3E" mark on camshaft gear is at the 12 o'clock position. Turn crankshaft and align TDC mark on oil pump body with mark on crankshaft gear. *See Fig. 4*.

**2)** Remove idler pulley tension spring if not previously removed. Loosen idler pulley bolt and push pulley to the left as far as it will go and tighten bolt. Install timing belt. Loosen idler pulley bolt and install pulley tension spring.

**3)** Turn crankshaft 2 revolutions in the clockwise direction (TDC to TDC). Ensure camshaft and crankshaft marks are in proper alignment. *See Fig. 4*. Tighten idler pulley bolt to 13 ft. lbs. (18 N.m).

**4)** To complete installation, reverse removal procedures. When installing valve cover, apply seal packing to cylinder head. *See Fig. 5*.

# 1991 ENGINE
# 1.5L 4-Cylinder (Cont.)

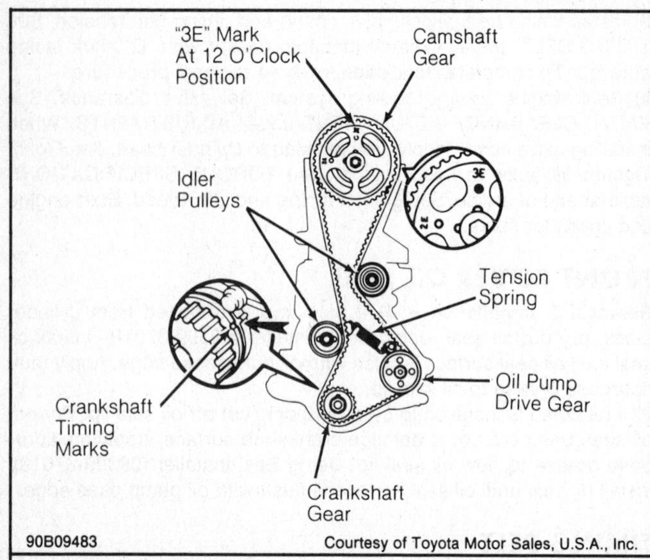

Courtesy of Toyota Motor Sales, U.S.A., Inc.

*Fig. 4: Aligning Timing Marks*

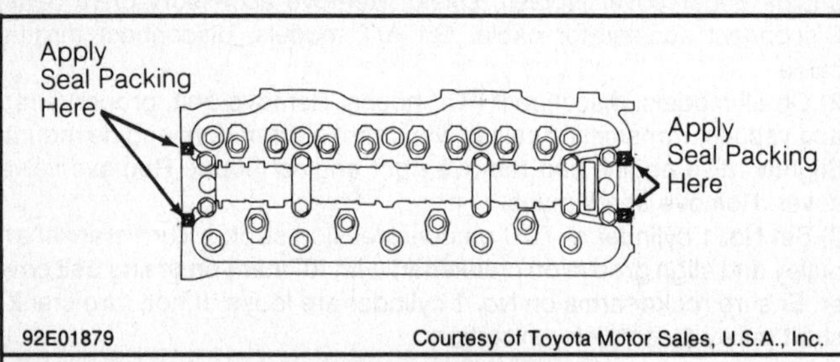

Courtesy of Toyota Motor Sales, U.S.A., Inc.

*Fig. 5: Applying Seal Packing to Cylinder Head*

## ROCKER ARM & VALVE LASH ADJUSTER

**Removal - 1)** Remove camshaft. See CAMSHAFT. Loosen rocker arm adjusting screw lock nuts. While lifting top of rocker arm spring, pry off spring. *See Fig. 6.*

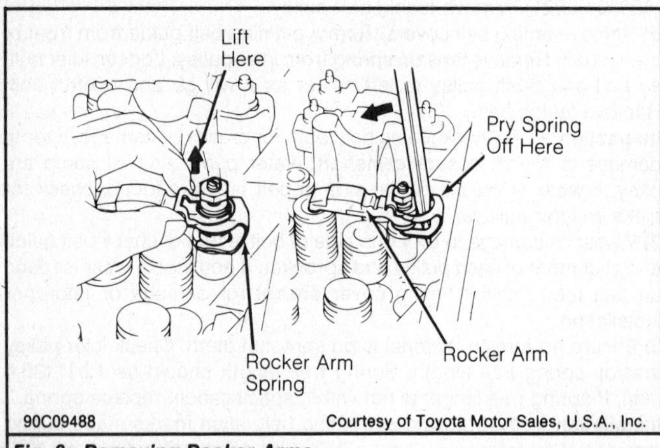

Courtesy of Toyota Motor Sales, U.S.A., Inc.

*Fig. 6: Removing Rocker Arms*

**2)** Remove rocker arms. Arrange rocker arms in order of removal for installation reference. Inspect contact surface of rocker arms, valve stem ends and camshaft lobes. If contact surfaces are excessively worn, replace as required.

**Installation - 1)** Install rocker arms with adjusting screw fully extended. *See Fig. 7.*

**2)** Install new rocker arm springs. Press bottom lip of rocker arm spring until it fits into groove on rocker arm pivot. *See Fig. 8.*

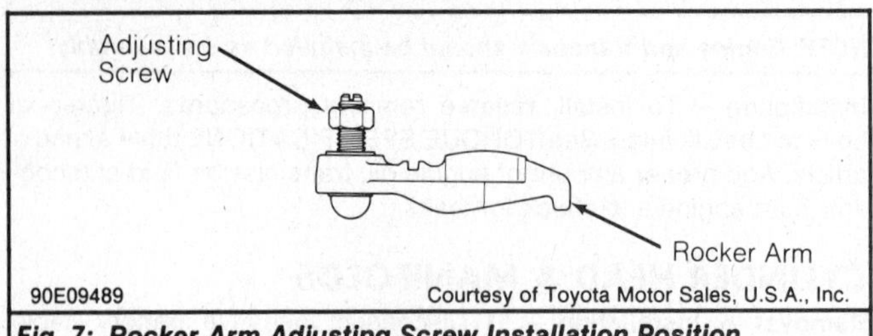

Courtesy of Toyota Motor Sales, U.S.A., Inc.

*Fig. 7: Rocker Arm Adjusting Screw Installation Position*

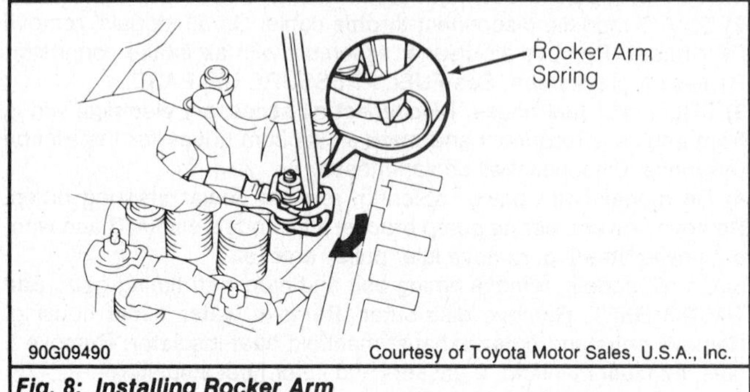

Courtesy of Toyota Motor Sales, U.S.A., Inc.

*Fig. 8: Installing Rocker Arm*

**3)** Pull rocker arm up and down. Ensure there is spring tension on rocker arm and rocker arm does not rattle. To complete installation, reverse removal procedures. Adjust valves. See VALVE CLEARANCE ADJUSTMENT under ADJUSTMENTS. When installing valve cover, apply seal packing to cylinder head. *See Fig. 5.*

## CAMSHAFT

**Removal - 1)** Mark and remove all wiring and vacuum hoses necessary for valve cover removal. Remove valve cover. Remove timing belt. See TIMING BELT.

**2)** Loosen camshaft bearing cap bolts in reverse of tightening sequence. *See Fig. 9.* Remove camshaft oil seal and camshaft bearing caps. DO NOT remove distributor bearing cap. Keep bearing caps in order for reassembly reference. Remove camshaft.

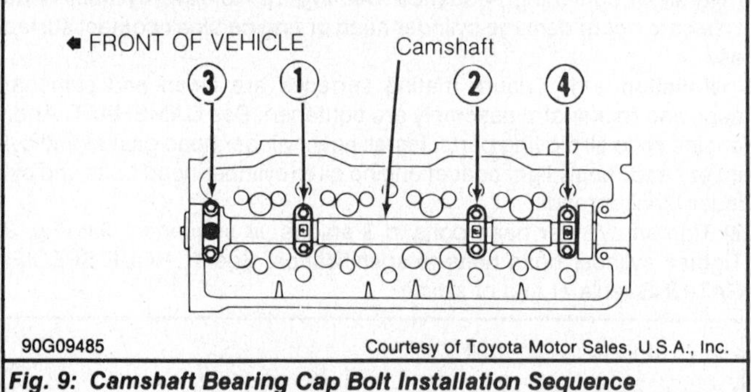

Courtesy of Toyota Motor Sales, U.S.A., Inc.

*Fig. 9: Camshaft Bearing Cap Bolt Installation Sequence*

**Inspection - 1)** Inspect components for damage. Check camshaft journal diameter, lobe height and runout. *See Fig. 10.* Replace camshaft if not within specification. See CAMSHAFT table under ENGINE SPECIFICATIONS at end of article.

**2)** Install camshaft in cylinder head. Using Plastigage, check camshaft oil clearance with camshaft bearing cap bolts tightened to specification See TORQUE SPECIFICATIONS table at end of article. Replace camshaft and/or cylinder head if oil clearance is not within specification. See CAMSHAFT table under ENGINE SPECIFICATIONS at end of article.

# 1991 ENGINES
# 1.5L 4-Cylinder (Cont.)

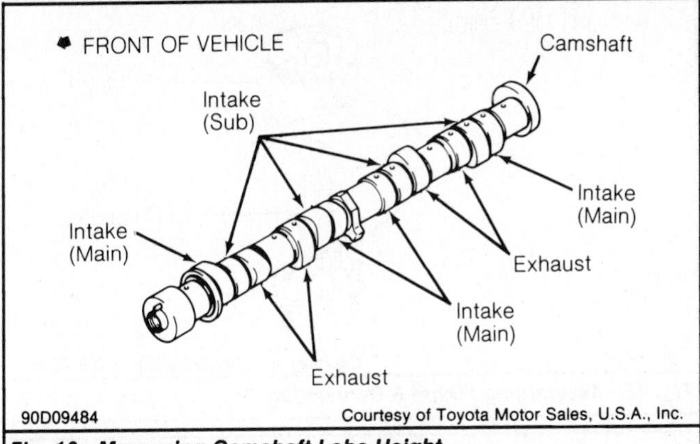


*Fig. 10: Measuring Camshaft Lobe Height*

**3)** Check camshaft end play with camshaft bearing cap bolts tightened to specification. Replace camshaft and/or cylinder head if end play is not within specification. See CAMSHAFT table under ENGINE SPECIFICATIONS at end of article.

**Installation – 1)** Set No. 1 cylinder at TDC on compression stroke. Coat all bearing journals with engine oil. Position camshaft knock pin at the 12 o'clock position. *See Fig. 11.*

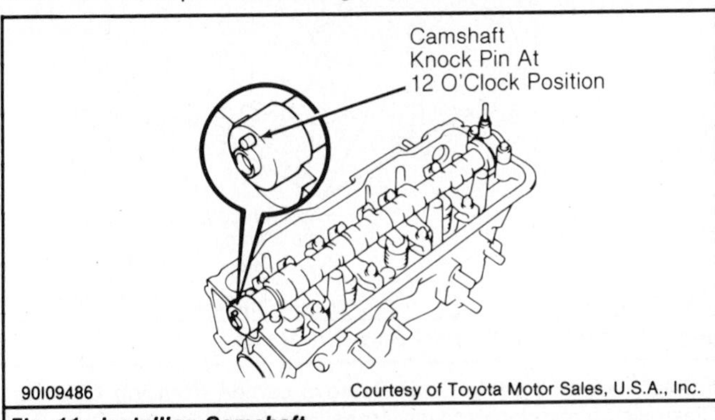


*Fig. 11: Installing Camshaft*

**2)** Place bearing caps on each journal with arrows pointing to front of engine and bearing cap numbers in numerical sequence. Apply engine oil to lip of new camshaft oil seal. Install camshaft oil seal. Apply seal packing to No. 1 camshaft bearing cap. *See Fig. 12.*

***NOTE: Install No. 1 bearing cap immediately after applying seal packing.***

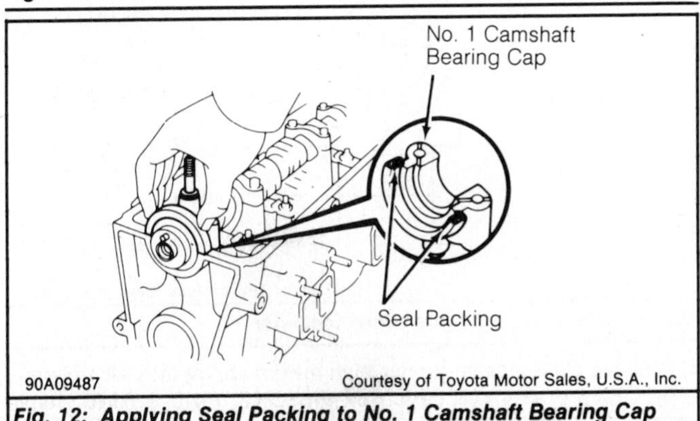


*Fig. 12: Applying Seal Packing to No. 1 Camshaft Bearing Cap*

**3)** Install No. 1 bearing cap. Tighten each bearing cap bolt in proper sequence. *See Fig. 9.* Tighten all bolts to specification. See TORQUE SPECIFICATIONS table at end of article.

**4)** To complete installation, reverse removal procedure. When installing valve cover, apply seal packing to cylinder head. *See Fig. 5.*

## REAR CRANKSHAFT OIL SEAL

***NOTE: Rear main bearing oil seal is located on rear of engine block. Transmission must be removed to replace seal. When removing oil seal, use care to avoid damage to crankshaft seal surface.***

**Removal & Installation – 1)** Remove transmission and flywheel. See REMOVAL & INSTALLATION article in TRANSMISSION SERVICING. Cut off seal lip. Use care not to damage crankshaft surface. Pry out oil seal.

**2)** Apply multipurpose grease to new seal lip. Using Seal Installer (09223-41020), install new oil seal until surface of seal is flush with rear of oil seal retainer edge. To complete installation, reverse removal procedure.

## WATER PUMP

**Removal – 1)** Disconnect negative battery cable. Drain engine coolant. Remove accessory drive belts. Remove alternator. Remove intake manifold bracket-to-cylinder block. Disconnect coolant hoses. Remove inlet water pump pipe and "O" ring.

**2)** Remove oil dipstick. Remove dipstick tube mounting bolt. Remove alternator adjusting bracket. Pull out dipstick tube. Plug dipstick tube installation hole. Remove "O" ring from dipstick tube. Remove bolt, 2 nuts and water pump.

**Inspection –** Ensure water pump bearing is not rough or noisy. Replace water pump assembly as required.

**Installation –** To install, reverse removal procedure. Install new "O" ring on water inlet pipe and oil dipstick tube. Tighten all bolts to specification. See TORQUE SPECIFICATIONS table at end of article. Refill with coolant. Start engine and check for leaks.

# OVERHAUL

## CYLINDER HEAD

**Cylinder Head –** Check for cracks, damage and coolant leakage. Remove scale, sealing compound and carbon deposits. Clean oil passages and blow compressed air through passages to ensure they are not clogged. Check EGR passage for clogging. Inspect cylinder head for warpage at deck surface. Resurface cylinder head if warpage exceeds specification. See CYLINDER HEAD table under ENGINE SPECIFICATIONS at end of article.

**Valve Springs –** Inspect valve spring free length, tension and installed height. Using a square, check squareness of each valve spring. Replace if not within specification. See VALVES & VALVE SPRINGS table under ENGINE SPECIFICATIONS at end of article. Installed spring height is measured from spring seat to valve retainer. Install all valve springs with painted area toward rocker arm.

**Valve Guides –** Measure diameter of valve stem and inside diameter of valve guide. Standard valve stem oil clearance should be within specification. See CYLINDER HEAD table under ENGINE SPECIFICATIONS at end of article. If oil clearance is greater than maximum, replace valve guide.

**Valve Guide Replacement – 1)** Using Valve Guide Remover (09201-70010), remove valve guide bushing. Measure cylinder head valve guide bore inside diameter. See CYLINDER HEAD table under ENGINE SPECIFICATIONS. at end of article. If valve guide bore is not within specification, bushing bore may be machined to .4350-.4361" (11.050-11.077 mm).

**2)** Using Valve Guide Installer (09201-70010), install new valve guide until protrusion height is .52-.56" (13.3-14.1 mm). *See Fig. 13.* Using a 6 mm reamer, ream valve guide to obtain standard specified clearance between valve guide and valve stem.

**Valve Seats –** No service procedure is given by manufacturer. Valve seats must be ground if valve guides are replaced.

**Valves –** Inspect each valve for ware, damage and distortion of head and stem. If valve stem end is pitted or worn, resurface as necessary. This correction must be limited to a minimum. Resurface valve face. If valve margin has decreased to less than service limit, replace valve.

# 1991 ENGINES
# 1.5L 4-Cylinder (Cont.)

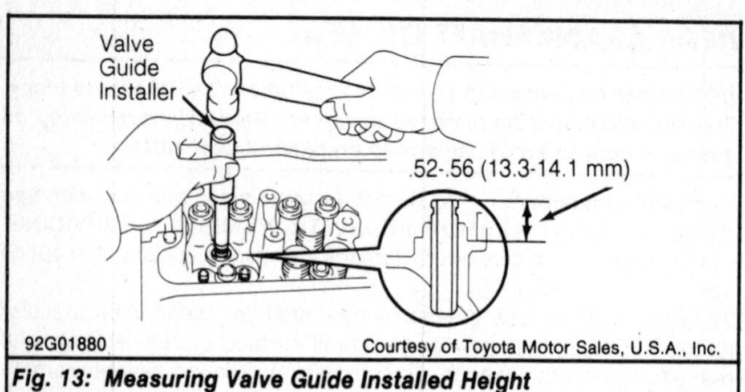


*Fig. 13: Measuring Valve Guide Installed Height*

## VALVE TRAIN

**Rocker Arm** - Check contact surfaces of rocker arm for excessive wear or damage. Replace rocker arm if grooves or pitting is present.

## CYLINDER BLOCK ASSEMBLY

**Piston & Rod Assembly** - **1)** Check connecting rod maximum bend and twist. Maximum bend and twist should be within specification. See CONNECTING RODS table under ENGINE SPECIFICATIONS at end of article.

**2)** If maximum bend and twist are not within specification, replace connecting rod. Lubricate cylinder bore and rod journals with engine oil. Cover rod bolts with short piece of hose to protect crankshaft journals from damage.

**3)** Using piston ring compressor, push correctly numbered piston and connecting rod assembly into each cylinder with front mark of piston facing forward. *See Fig. 14*.

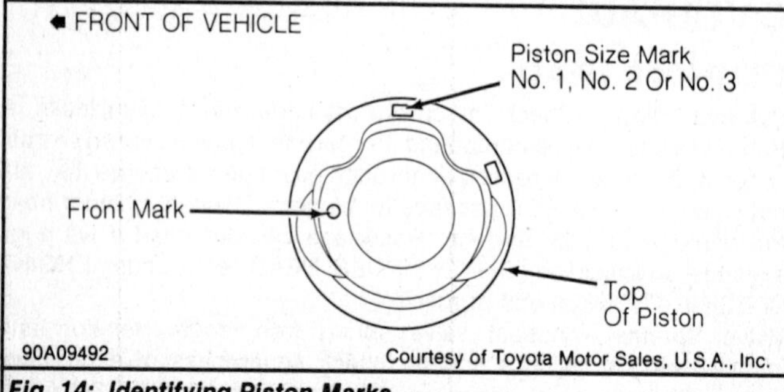


*Fig. 14: Identifying Piston Marks*

**4)** Install rod cap with front mark facing front of engine. Apply light coat of engine oil to rod bolt threads and nuts. Install and alternately tighten cap nuts in several stages to specification. See TORQUE SPECIFICATIONS table at end of article.

**5)** Ensure crankshaft turns smoothly. Check connecting rod side play. Connecting rod side play should be within specification. See CONNECTING RODS table under ENGINE SPECIFICATIONS at end of article. If clearance is greater than maximum, replace connecting rod assembly or crankshaft as required.

***NOTE: Piston and piston pin are a matched set. Keep pistons, pins, rings and rods in order for reassembly reference.***

**Piston Pin** - **1)** Check fit between piston and piston pin. If movement is felt, replace piston and pin. To remove piston pin, warm piston and rod to 68°F (20°C). Using Pin Remover/Installer (09221-25024), remove piston pin. Use care not to damage piston during removal.

**2)** Check piston pin and piston pin hole for signs of galling or excessive wear. Replace as required. To assemble, preheat piston and rod to 68°F (20°C). Align cavity on piston top with protrusion on rod.

**3)** Coat piston pin with oil. Insert pin into piston while holding parts in proper alignment. *See Fig. 15*. Using piston Pin Installer (09221-25024), install piston pin until centered in rod.

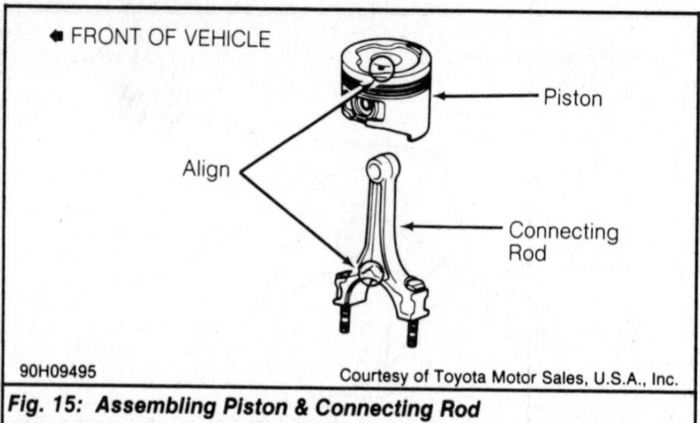


*Fig. 15: Assembling Piston & Connecting Rod*

***NOTE: There are 3 different standard piston sizes and cylinder bore diameters being used. Pistons and cylinder bores are marked No. 1, No. 2 or No. 3. Mark is stamped on top of piston and cylinder block. See Figs. 14 and 16.***

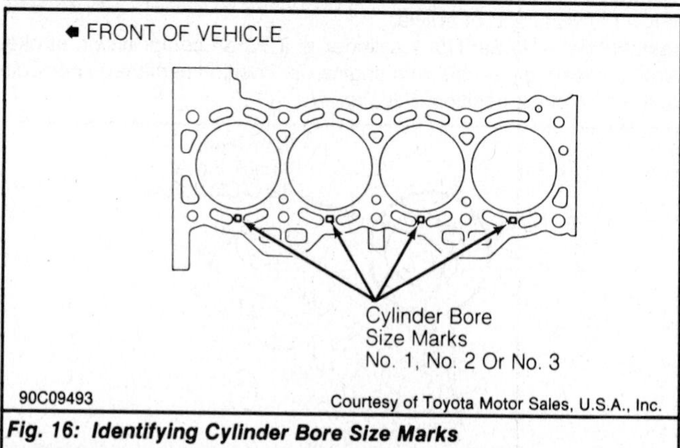


*Fig. 16: Identifying Cylinder Bore Size Marks*

**Fitting Pistons & Rings** - **1)** Remove carbon from top of piston. Clean piston and ring grooves. Measure piston clearance. Determine piston size being used. Measure piston diameter at right angles to piston pin center line. Measure .87" (22 mm) from top of piston head.

**2)** Measure cylinder bore diameter in thrust direction. *See Fig. 17*. Subtract piston diameter measurement from cylinder bore diameter measurement. Piston clearance should be within specification.

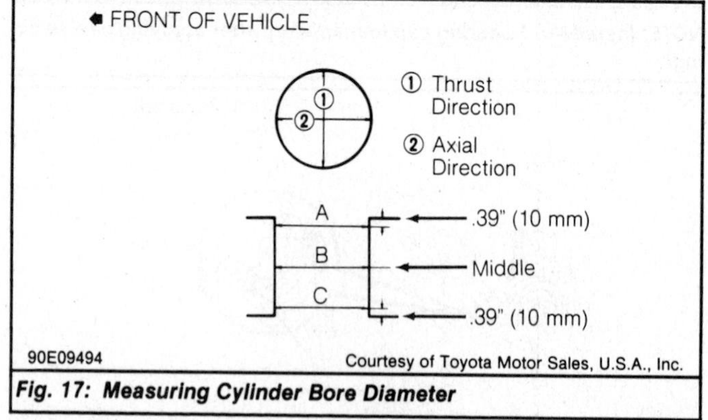


*Fig. 17: Measuring Cylinder Bore Diameter*

**3)** If piston clearance is greater than maximum, replace all 4 pistons and/or rebore all 4 cylinders. See PISTONS, PINS & RINGS table under ENGINE SPECIFICATIONS at end of article.

**Connecting Rod Bearings** - **1)** Install replacement bearing. Ensure reference marks on rod cap and connecting rod are aligned. Check bearing clearance using Plastigage method.

# 1991 ENGINES
# 1.5L 4-Cylinder (Cont.)

**2)** Lubricate all components with engine oil before reassembling. Tighten nuts to specification. See TORQUE SPECIFICATIONS table at end of article. Ensure connecting rod moves freely on crankshaft. Check connecting rod side clearance.

**Crankshaft & Main Bearings – 1)** Place crankshaft on "V" blocks. Measure main and connecting rod journal taper and runout. See ENGINE SPECIFICATIONS at end of article. Regrind or replace crankshaft as necessary.

**2)** Clean all parts to be assembled. Apply engine oil to all moving parts. Install main bearings and bearing caps in order.

***CAUTION: Ensure main bearing oil holes line up with oil hole in block.***

**3)** Install upper thrust washers on center main bearing with oil grooves facing outward. Place crankshaft in cylinder block. Install main bearing caps in proper location.

**4)** Install thrust washers on No. 3 bearing cap with oil grooves facing outward. Install bearing caps in numerical order. Apply engine oil to threads of cap bolts. Tighten cap bolts in 2 or 3 stages and in proper sequence. *See Fig. 18.*

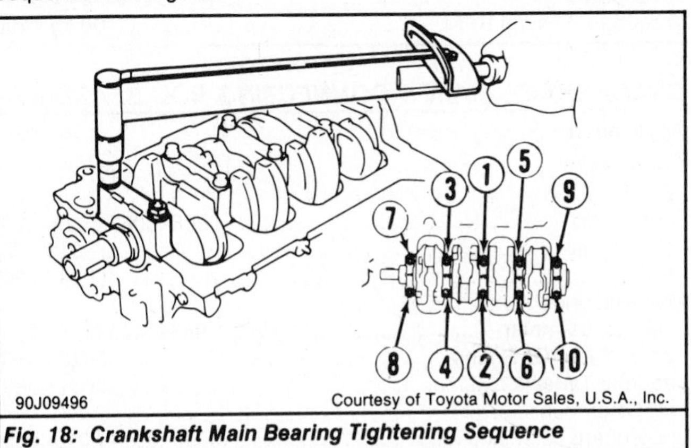


***Fig. 18: Crankshaft Main Bearing Tightening Sequence***

**5)** To complete installation, reverse removal procedure. Tighten all bolts to specification. See TORQUE SPECIFICATIONS table at end of article.

## ENGINE OILING

### ENGINE LUBRICATION SYSTEM

Oil from oil pan is pumped up by the oil pump. After it passes through oil filter, it is fed through various oil holes in crankshaft and cylinder block. After passing through cylinder block and performing its lubricating function, oil is returned by gravity to oil pan. *See Fig. 19.*

**Crankcase Capacity –** Crankcase oil capacity is 3.5 qts. (3.3L) with filter.

**Oil Pressure –** Oil pressure should be more than 4.3 psi (0.3 kg/cm²) at idle and 36-71 psi (2.5-5.0 kg/cm²) at 3000 RPM.

## OIL PUMP

***NOTE: When repairing oil pump, the oil pan and strainer should be removed and cleaned.***

**Removal & Installation – 1)** Disconnect negative battery cable. Remove engine under cover (splash) shields. Disconnect exhaust pipe. Remove timing belt. See TIMING BELT. Remove oil filler cap. Drain engine oil. Remove oil dipstick, oil pan and oil strainer. Remove oil pressure regulator assembly. *See Fig. 20.*

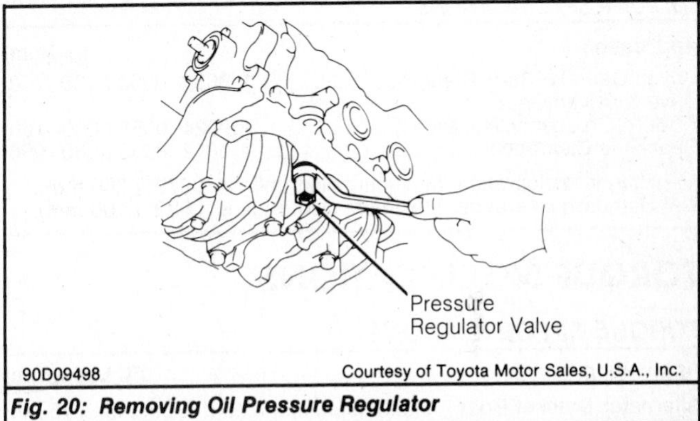


***Fig. 20: Removing Oil Pressure Regulator***

**2)** Remove pulley tension spring bracket. Remove oil pump bolts attaching oil pump body to front of engine block. Remove oil pump body and "O" ring. *See Fig. 21.* To install, reverse removal procedure. Tighten all bolts to specification. See TORQUE SPECIFICATIONS table at end of article.

**Inspection – 1)** Disassemble pressure regulator. Remove snap ring, retainer, spring and pressure regulator valve piston. Coat valve piston with engine oil and check that it falls smoothly into valve hole by its own weight. Replace pressure regulator valve if a problem exists.

**2)** Reassemble pressure regulator valve. Measure oil pump body clearance, driven gear-to-body clearance, drive and driven gear tip-to-crescent clearance and gear side clearance. See OIL PUMP SPECIFI-

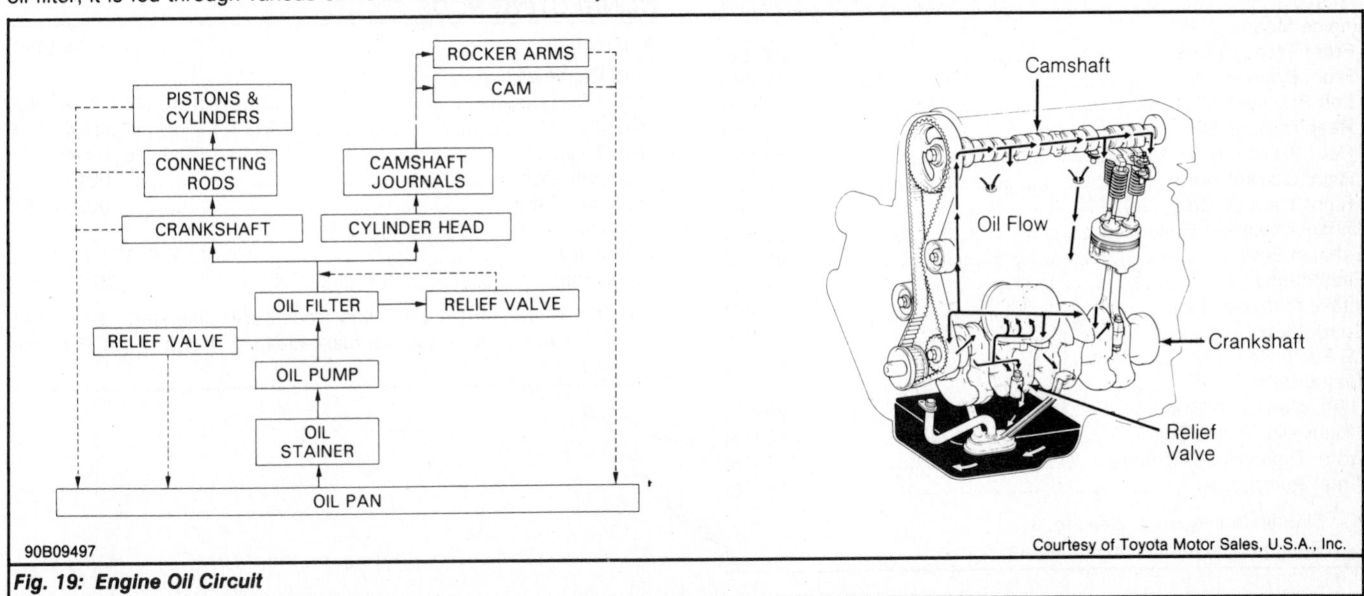


***Fig. 19: Engine Oil Circuit***

# 1991 ENGINES
# 1.5L 4-Cylinder (Cont.)

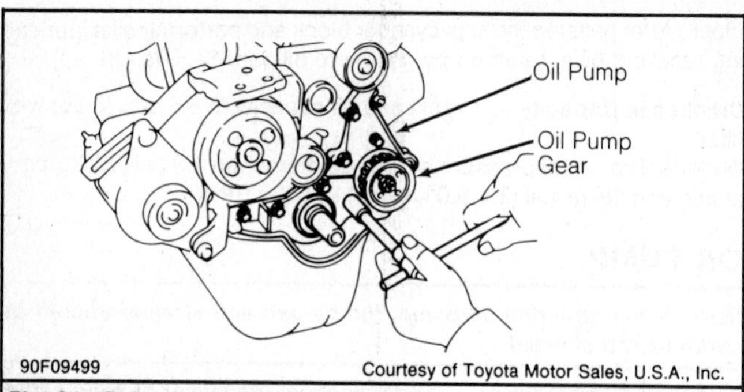


*Fig. 21: Removing Oil Pump Assembly*

CATIONS table. If oil pump is not within specification, replace oil pump rotor set and/or pump body.

### OIL PUMP SPECIFICATIONS

| Application | In. (mm) |
|---|---|
| Driven Gear-To-Body Clearance | [1] .0039-.0063 (.100-.160) |
| Drive & Driven Gear | |
| Tip-To-Crescent Clearance | [1] .0024-.0059 (.060-.150) |
| Gear Side Clearance | [2] .0012-.0035 (.030-.090) |

[1] – Standard clearance. Maximum clearance is .0079" (.200 mm).
[2] – Standard clearance. Maximum clearance is .0039" (.100 mm).

## TORQUE SPECIFICATIONS

### TORQUE SPECIFICATIONS

| Application | Ft. Lbs. (N.m) |
|---|---|
| Alternator Bracket Bolts | 13 (18) |
| Camshaft | |
| Bearing Cap Bolts | 10 (14) |
| Gear Bolt | 37 (50) |
| Timing Gear Bolt | 14 (19) |
| Connecting Rod | |
| Bearing Cap Bolts | 29 (39) |
| Crankshaft | |
| Gear Bolt | 112 (152) |
| Main Bearing Cap Bolts | 42 (57) |
| Pulley Bolts | 112 (152) |
| Cylinder Head Bolts [1] | |
| Step 1 | 22 (30) |
| Step 2 | 36 (49) |
| Step 3 | [2] |
| Engine Mount | |
| Front Through Bolt | 47 (64) |
| Front Bracket Bolts | 19 (26) |
| Left Bracket Bolts | 35 (47) |
| Rear Through Bolt | 54 (73) |
| Rear Bracket Bolts | 47 (64) |
| Right Bracket Bolts | 32 (43) |
| Right Through Bolt | 47 (64) |
| Exhaust Manifold Bolts | 35 (47) |
| Exhaust Pipe | 46 (62) |
| Fuel Pump | 9 (12) |
| Intake Manifold Bolts | 14 (19) |
| Spark Plugs | 13 (18) |
| Oil Pump Gear Bolt | 20 (27) |
| Timing Belt | |
| Left Idler Pulley Bolt | 20 (27) |
| Right Idler Pulley Bolt | 13 (18) |
| Water Outlet Housing Bolts | 13 (18) |
| Water Pump Bolts | 13 (18) |

[1] – Tighten in sequence. *See Fig. 3.*
[2] – Retighten an additional 90 degrees.

### TORQUE SPECIFICATIONS (Cont.)

| Application | INCH Lbs. (N.m) |
|---|---|
| Oil Pump Bolts | 65 (7.3) |
| Rear Oil Seal Retainer Bolts | 65 (7.3) |
| Valve Cover Bolts | 61 (6.9) |
| Intake Manifold | |
| Upper Heat Insulator Bolts | 69 (7.8) |

## ENGINE SPECIFICATIONS

### GENERAL SPECIFICATIONS

| Application | Specification |
|---|---|
| Displacement | 88.9 Cu. In. (1.5L) |
| Bore | 2.88" (73.0 mm) |
| Stroke | 3.43" (87.0 mm) |
| Compression Ratio | 9.3:1 |
| Fuel System | PFI |
| Horsepower @ RPM | 82 @ 5200 |
| Torque Ft. Lbs. @ RPM | 90 @ 4400 |

### CRANKSHAFT, MAIN & CONNECTING ROD BEARINGS

| Application | In. (mm) |
|---|---|
| Crankshaft | |
| End Play | |
| Standard | .0008-.0087 (.020-.220) |
| Maximum | .012 (.30) |
| Runout | .0024 (.060) |
| Main Bearings | |
| Journal Diameter | 1.9679-1.9685 (49.985-50.000) |
| Journal Out-Of-Round | .0028 (.070) |
| Journal Taper | .0031 (.080) |
| Oil Clearance | |
| Standard | .0006-.0014 (.016-.035) |
| Maximum | .0031 (.080) |
| Connecting Rod Bearings | |
| Journal Diameter | 1.6923-1.6929 (42.985-43.000) |
| Journal Out-Of-Round | .0028 (.070) |
| Journal Taper | .0031 (.080) |
| Oil Clearance | |
| Standard | .0006-.0019 (.016-.048) |
| Maximum | .0031 (.080) |

### CONNECTING RODS

| Application | In. (mm) |
|---|---|
| Bore Diameter [1] | |
| No. 1 | 1.8110-1.8113 (46.000-46.007) |
| No. 2 | 1.8113-1.8116 (46.007-46.014) |
| No. 3 | 1.8116-1.8118 (46.014-46.021) |
| Maximum Bend | .0012 (.030) |
| Maximum Twist | .0020 (.050) |
| Side Play | |
| Standard | .0059-.0138 (.150-.350) |
| Maximum | .0177 (.450) |

[1] – Three standard connecting rod bore diameters are used. Connecting rod bores are marked No. 1, No. 2 or No. 3 on rod cap.

# 1991 ENGINES
# 1.5L 4-Cylinder (Cont.)

## PISTONS, PINS & RINGS

| Application | In. (mm) |
|---|---|
| Pistons | |
| Clearance | |
| Standard | .0028-.0035 (.070-.090) |
| Maximum | .0079 (.200) |
| Diameter [1] | |
| No. 1 | 2.870-2.871 (72.92-72.93) |
| No. 2 | 2.871-2.872 (72.93-72.94) |
| No. 3 | 2.872-2.873 (72.94-72.95) |
| Pins | |
| Piston Fit | [2] Press Fit |
| Rod Fit | [2] Press Fit |
| Rings | |
| No. 1 | |
| End Gap | .0102-.0189 (.260-.480) |
| Side Clearance | .0016-.0031 (.040-.080) |
| No. 2 | |
| End Gap | .0118-.0224 (.300-.570) |
| Side Clearance | .0012-.0028 (.030-.070) |
| No. 3 (Oil) | |
| End Gap | .0059-.0205 (.150-.520) |

[1] - Three standard piston sizes are used. Pistons are marked No. 1, No. 2 or No. 3 on top of piston. *See Fig. 14.*

[2] - Install piston pin at temperature of 68°F (20°C).

## CYLINDER BLOCK

| Application | In. (mm) |
|---|---|
| Cylinder Bore | |
| Diameter [1] | |
| No. 1 | 2.8740-2.8744 (73.000-73.010) |
| No. 2 | 2.8744-2.8748 (73.010-73.020) |
| No. 3 | 2.8748-2.8752 (73.020-73.030) |
| Maximum Taper | .0008 (.020) |
| Maximum Out-Of-Round | .0008 (.020) |
| Maximum Deck Warpage | .002 (.05) |

[1] - Three standard cylinder bore diameters are used. Cylinder bores are marked No. 1, No. 2 or No. 3 on top of cylinder block. *See Fig. 16.*

## CAMSHAFT

| Application | In. (mm) |
|---|---|
| End Play | .0031-.0071 (.080-.180) |
| Journal Diameter | 1.0622-1.0628 (26.979-26.995) |
| Journal Runout | .0016 (.040) |
| Lobe Height | |
| Intake (Main) | 1.3917-1.3957 (35.350-35.450) |
| Intake (Sub) | 1.3744-1.3783 (34.910-35.010) |
| Exhaust | 1.4106-1.4146 (35.830-35.930) |
| Oil Clearance | .0015-.0029 (.037-.073) |

## VALVES & VALVE SPRINGS

| Application | Specification |
|---|---|
| Intake Valves | |
| Face Angle | 44.5° |
| Minimum Margin | .031" (.80 mm) |
| Minimum Refinish Length (Main) | 3.6126" (91.760 mm) |
| Minimum Refinish Length (Sub) | 3.5945" (91.300 mm) |
| Stem Diameter | .2350-.2356" (5.970-5.985 mm) |
| Exhaust Valves | |
| Face Angle | 44.5° |
| Minimum Margin | .031" (.80 mm) |
| Minimum Refinish Length | 3.6126" (91.760 mm) |
| Stem Diameter | .2348-.2354" (5.965-5.980 mm) |
| Valve Springs | |
| Free Length | 1.6346" (41.520 mm) |
| Installed Height | 1.3842" (35.160 mm) |
| Out-Of-Square | .079" (2.00 mm) |
| | **Lbs. @ In. (kg @ mm)** |
| Pressure | |
| Valve Closed | 35.1 @ 1.3842 (15.91 @ 35.16) |

## CYLINDER HEAD

| Application | Specification |
|---|---|
| Maximum Warpage | .002" (.05 mm) |
| Valve Seats | |
| Intake Valve | |
| Seat Angle | 45° |
| Seat Width | .047-.063" (1.20-1.60 mm) |
| Exhaust Valve | |
| Seat Angle | 45° |
| Seat Width | .047-.063" (1.20-1.60 mm) |
| Valve Guides | |
| Intake Valve | |
| Valve Guide Cylinder Head Bore I.D. | .4331-.4341" (11.000-11.027 mm) |
| Valve Guide I.D. | .2366-.2374" (6.010-6.030 mm) |
| Valve Guide Installed Height | .52-.55" (13.3-14.1 mm) |
| Valve Stem-To-Guide | |
| Oil Clearance | |
| Standard | .0010-.0024" (.025-.060 mm) |
| Maximum | .0031 (.080) |
| Exhaust Valve | |
| Valve Guide Cylinder Head Bore I.D. | .4331-.4341" (11.000-11.027 mm) |
| Valve Guide I.D. | .2366-.2374" (6.010-6.030 mm) |
| Valve Guide Installed Height | .52-.55" (13.3-14.1 mm) |
| Valve Stem-To-Guide | |
| Oil Clearance | |
| Standard | .0012-.0026" (.030-.065 mm) |
| Maximum | .0039 (.100) |

# 1991 ENGINES
# 1.6L 16-Valve 4-Cylinder

## Celica, Corolla

***NOTE: For repair procedures not covered in this article, see ENGINE OVERHAUL PROCEDURES article in GENERAL INFORMATION.***

## ENGINE IDENTIFICATION

Engine may be identified by using Vehicle Identification Number (VIN) stamped on a metal pad, located near lower left corner of windshield. The fourth character of VIN identifies engine model. See ENGINE IDENTIFICATION CODES table.

Engine identification number, located on cylinder block below cylinder head, may be required when ordering replacement parts (if needed). *See Fig. 1.*

***ENGINE IDENTIFICATION CODES***

| Application | VIN | Engine Code |
|---|---|---|
| 1.6L PFI | A | 4A-FE & 4A-GE |

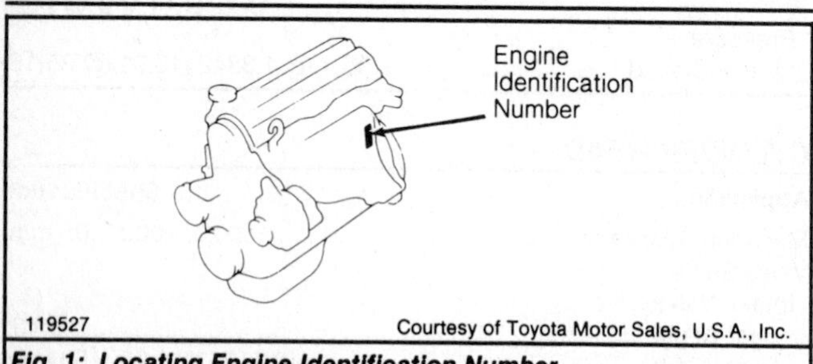


***Fig. 1: Locating Engine Identification Number***

## ADJUSTMENTS

### VALVE CLEARANCE ADJUSTMENT

***NOTE: Adjust valve clearance with engine cold.***

**1)** Remove valve covers. Rotate crankshaft so No. 1 cylinder is at TDC of compression stroke. Ensure timing mark on crankshaft pulley aligns with "0" mark on timing chain cover. Ensure valves on No. 1 cylinder are closed.

**2)** With No. 1 cylinder at TDC, check clearance on specified valves. See VALVE CLEARANCE ADJUSTMENT SEQUENCE table. *See Fig. 2.*

***VALVE CLEARANCE ADJUSTMENT SEQUENCE***

| Piston No. On TDC | Adjust Intake Valves | Adjust Exhaust Valves |
|---|---|---|
| 1 | 1 & 2 | 1 & 3 |
| 4 | 3 & 4 | 2 & 4 |

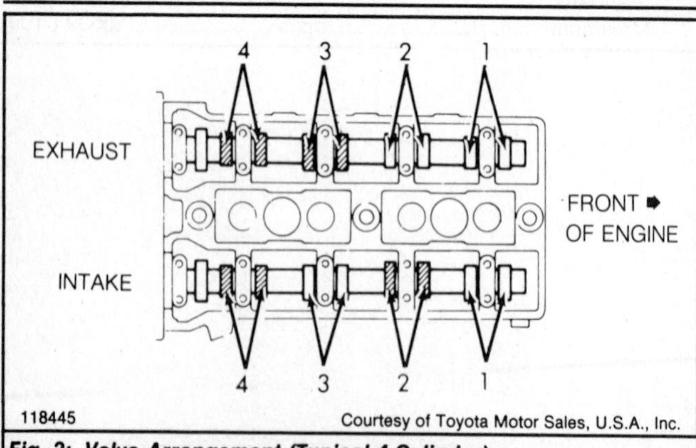


***Fig. 2: Valve Arrangement (Typical 4-Cylinder)***

**3)** Using feeler gauge, measure and record clearance between valve lifter and camshaft. Ensure clearance is within specification. See VALVE CLEARANCE table.

***VALVE CLEARANCE***

| Application [1] | In. (mm) |
|---|---|
| Intake | .006-.010 (.15-.25) |
| Exhaust | .008-.012 (.20-.30) |

[1] – Adjust valves with engine cold.

**4)** To check remaining valves, rotate crankshaft 360 degrees (one full turn) until No. 4 piston is at TDC of compression stroke. Measure valve clearance on specified valves. See VALVE CLEARANCE ADJUSTMENT SEQUENCE table.

**5)** If valves require adjustment, rotate crankshaft so camshaft lobe on valve to be adjusted is facing upward, away from valve lifter. Rotate valve lifter so notch on valve lifter is toward spark plug.

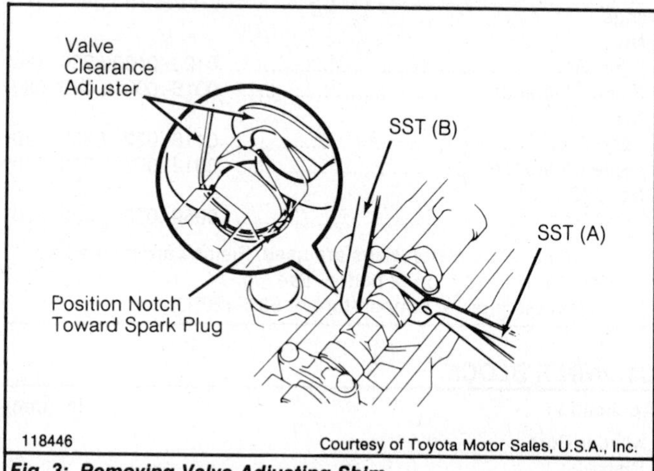


***Fig. 3: Removing Valve Adjusting Shim***

**6)** Press valve lifter downward using Valve Clearance Adjuster (09248-55010) and SST (A). *See Fig. 3.* Install SST (B) between camshaft and valve lifter. Remove SST (A).

**7)** Using small screwdriver and magnet, remove adjusting shim. Measure thickness of shim removed. Determine correct thickness of adjusting shim to be used. *See Figs. 4 and 5.* Install shim and recheck valve clearance.

## REMOVAL & INSTALLATION

***NOTE: For reassembly reference, label all electrical connectors, vacuum hoses and fuel lines before removal. Also place mating marks on engine hood and other major assemblies before removal.***

### FUEL PRESSURE RELEASE

***WARNING: High fuel pressure may be present in fuel lines and component parts. Relieve fuel pressure before opening fuel system. DO NOT allow fuel to flow onto engine or electrical parts.***

Disconnect negative battery cable. Place container under fitting to be loosened. Use a rag to cover fuel line/component. Slowly loosen fitting, allowing pressurized fuel to spill into container. After fuel system has depressurized, disconnect and plug fitting.

### ENGINE

***NOTE: Engine and transaxle should be removed as an assembly.***

**Removal – 1)** Mark and remove hood. Remove battery. Remove engine under cover (splash) shields. Drain coolant, engine oil and transaxle fluid. Mark and disconnect vacuum hoses and electrical connectors.

**2)** Remove air cleaner assembly. Disconnect coolant hoses. Mark and disconnect throttle, cruise, and kickdown cables (if equipped). Release fuel pressure. See FUEL PRESSURE RELEASE. Mark and disconnect fuel inlet and return hoses. Remove coolant reservoir tank and radiator (with cooling fan).

# 1991 ENGINES
# 1.6L 16-Valve 4-Cylinder (Cont.)

## Intake

| Measured Clearance (mm) | Installed Shim Thickness (mm) | | | | | | | | | | | | | | | | | | | | | | | | | | | | | | | | | | | | | | | | | | | | |
|---|---|---|---|---|---|---|---|---|---|---|---|---|---|---|---|---|---|---|---|---|---|---|---|---|---|---|---|---|---|---|---|---|---|---|---|---|---|---|---|---|---|---|---|---|---|
| | 2.500 | 2.525 | 2.550 | 2.575 | 2.600 | 2.620 | 2.640 | 2.650 | 2.660 | 2.680 | 2.700 | 2.720 | 2.740 | 2.750 | 2.760 | 2.780 | 2.800 | 2.820 | 2.840 | 2.850 | 2.860 | 2.880 | 2.900 | 2.920 | 2.940 | 2.950 | 2.960 | 2.980 | 3.000 | 3.020 | 3.040 | 3.050 | 3.060 | 3.080 | 3.100 | 3.120 | 3.140 | 3.150 | 3.160 | 3.180 | 3.200 | 3.225 | 3.250 | 3.275 | 3.300 |
| 0.000 — 0.009 | | | | | | | | | | 02 | 02 | 04 | 04 | 04 | 04 | 06 | 06 | 08 | 08 | 08 | 08 | 10 | 10 | 12 | 12 | 12 | 12 | 14 | 14 | 16 | 16 | 16 | 16 | 18 | 18 | 20 | 20 | 20 | 20 | 22 | 22 | 24 | 24 | 26 | 26 |
| 0.010 — 0.025 | | | | | | | | | 02 | 02 | 02 | 04 | 04 | 04 | 06 | 06 | 06 | 08 | 08 | 08 | 10 | 10 | 10 | 12 | 12 | 12 | 14 | 14 | 14 | 16 | 16 | 16 | 18 | 18 | 18 | 20 | 20 | 20 | 22 | 22 | 22 | 24 | 24 | 26 | 26 |
| 0.026 — 0.029 | | | | | | | | 02 | 02 | 02 | 04 | 04 | 04 | 06 | 06 | 06 | 08 | 08 | 08 | 10 | 10 | 10 | 12 | 12 | 12 | 14 | 14 | 14 | 16 | 16 | 16 | 18 | 18 | 18 | 20 | 20 | 20 | 22 | 22 | 22 | 24 | 24 | 26 | 26 | 28 |
| 0.030 — 0.040 | | | | | | | 02 | 02 | 02 | 02 | 04 | 04 | 04 | 06 | 06 | 06 | 08 | 08 | 08 | 10 | 10 | 10 | 12 | 12 | 12 | 14 | 14 | 14 | 16 | 16 | 16 | 18 | 18 | 18 | 20 | 20 | 20 | 22 | 22 | 22 | 24 | 24 | 26 | 26 | 28 |
| 0.041 — 0.050 | | | | | | | 02 | 02 | 02 | 02 | 04 | 04 | 06 | 06 | 06 | 06 | 08 | 08 | 10 | 10 | 10 | 10 | 12 | 12 | 14 | 14 | 14 | 14 | 16 | 16 | 18 | 18 | 18 | 18 | 20 | 20 | 22 | 22 | 22 | 22 | 24 | 24 | 26 | 26 | 28 |
| 0.051 — 0.070 | | | | | | 02 | 02 | 02 | 02 | 04 | 04 | 06 | 06 | 06 | 06 | 08 | 08 | 10 | 10 | 10 | 10 | 12 | 12 | 14 | 14 | 14 | 14 | 16 | 16 | 18 | 18 | 18 | 18 | 20 | 20 | 22 | 22 | 22 | 22 | 24 | 24 | 26 | 26 | 28 | 28 |
| 0.071 — 0.075 | | | | | 02 | 02 | 02 | 02 | 04 | 04 | 04 | 06 | 06 | 06 | 08 | 08 | 08 | 10 | 10 | 10 | 12 | 12 | 12 | 14 | 14 | 14 | 16 | 16 | 16 | 18 | 18 | 18 | 20 | 20 | 20 | 22 | 22 | 22 | 24 | 24 | 24 | 26 | 26 | 28 | 28 |
| 0.076 — 0.090 | | | | | 02 | 02 | 02 | 04 | 04 | 04 | 06 | 06 | 06 | 08 | 08 | 08 | 10 | 10 | 10 | 12 | 12 | 12 | 14 | 14 | 14 | 16 | 16 | 16 | 18 | 18 | 18 | 20 | 20 | 20 | 22 | 22 | 22 | 24 | 24 | 24 | 26 | 26 | 28 | 28 | 30 |
| 0.091 — 0.100 | | | | | 02 | 02 | 04 | 04 | 04 | 04 | 06 | 06 | 08 | 08 | 08 | 08 | 10 | 10 | 12 | 12 | 12 | 12 | 14 | 14 | 16 | 16 | 16 | 16 | 18 | 18 | 20 | 20 | 20 | 20 | 22 | 22 | 24 | 24 | 24 | 24 | 26 | 26 | 28 | 28 | 30 |
| 0.101 — 0.120 | | | | 02 | 02 | 02 | 04 | 04 | 04 | 06 | 06 | 06 | 08 | 08 | 08 | 10 | 10 | 10 | 12 | 12 | 12 | 14 | 14 | 14 | 16 | 16 | 16 | 18 | 18 | 18 | 20 | 20 | 20 | 22 | 22 | 22 | 24 | 24 | 24 | 26 | 26 | 28 | 28 | 30 | 30 |
| 0.121 — 0.125 | | | 02 | 02 | 02 | 04 | 04 | 04 | 06 | 06 | 06 | 08 | 08 | 08 | 10 | 10 | 10 | 12 | 12 | 12 | 14 | 14 | 14 | 16 | 16 | 16 | 18 | 18 | 18 | 20 | 20 | 20 | 22 | 22 | 22 | 24 | 24 | 24 | 26 | 26 | 26 | 28 | 28 | 30 | 30 |
| 0.126 — 0.140 | | | 02 | 02 | 04 | 04 | 04 | 06 | 06 | 06 | 08 | 08 | 08 | 10 | 10 | 10 | 12 | 12 | 12 | 14 | 14 | 14 | 16 | 16 | 16 | 18 | 18 | 18 | 20 | 20 | 20 | 22 | 22 | 22 | 24 | 24 | 24 | 26 | 26 | 26 | 28 | 28 | 30 | 30 | 32 |
| 0.141 — 0.149 | | | 02 | 02 | 04 | 04 | 06 | 06 | 06 | 06 | 08 | 08 | 10 | 10 | 10 | 10 | 12 | 12 | 14 | 14 | 14 | 14 | 16 | 16 | 18 | 18 | 18 | 18 | 20 | 20 | 22 | 22 | 22 | 22 | 24 | 24 | 26 | 26 | 26 | 26 | 28 | 28 | 30 | 30 | 32 |
| 0.150 — 0.250 | | | | | | | | | | | | | | | | | | | | | | | | | | | | | | | | | | | | | | | | | | | | | |
| 0.251 — 0.270 | 04 | 06 | 06 | 08 | 08 | 10 | 10 | 10 | 10 | 12 | 12 | 14 | 14 | 14 | 14 | 16 | 16 | 18 | 18 | 18 | 18 | 20 | 20 | 22 | 22 | 22 | 22 | 24 | 24 | 26 | 26 | 26 | 26 | 28 | 28 | 30 | 30 | 30 | 30 | 32 | 32 | 34 | 34 |
| 0.271 — 0.275 | 04 | 06 | 06 | 08 | 08 | 10 | 10 | 10 | 12 | 12 | 12 | 14 | 14 | 14 | 16 | 16 | 16 | 18 | 18 | 18 | 20 | 20 | 20 | 22 | 22 | 22 | 24 | 24 | 24 | 26 | 26 | 26 | 28 | 28 | 28 | 30 | 30 | 30 | 32 | 32 | 32 | 34 | 34 |
| 0.276 — 0.290 | 06 | 06 | 08 | 08 | 10 | 10 | 10 | 12 | 12 | 12 | 14 | 14 | 14 | 16 | 16 | 16 | 18 | 18 | 18 | 20 | 20 | 20 | 22 | 22 | 22 | 24 | 24 | 24 | 26 | 26 | 26 | 28 | 28 | 28 | 30 | 30 | 30 | 32 | 32 | 32 | 34 | 34 |
| 0.291 — 0.300 | 06 | 06 | 08 | 08 | 10 | 10 | 12 | 12 | 12 | 12 | 14 | 14 | 16 | 16 | 16 | 16 | 18 | 18 | 20 | 20 | 20 | 20 | 22 | 22 | 24 | 24 | 24 | 24 | 26 | 26 | 28 | 28 | 28 | 28 | 30 | 30 | 32 | 32 | 32 | 32 | 34 | 34 |
| 0.301 — 0.320 | 06 | 08 | 08 | 10 | 10 | 12 | 12 | 12 | 12 | 14 | 14 | 16 | 16 | 16 | 16 | 18 | 18 | 20 | 20 | 20 | 20 | 22 | 22 | 24 | 24 | 24 | 24 | 26 | 26 | 28 | 28 | 28 | 28 | 30 | 30 | 32 | 32 | 32 | 32 | 34 | 34 |
| 0.321 — 0.325 | 06 | 08 | 08 | 10 | 10 | 12 | 12 | 12 | 14 | 14 | 24 | 16 | 16 | 16 | 18 | 18 | 18 | 20 | 20 | 20 | 22 | 22 | 22 | 24 | 24 | 24 | 26 | 26 | 26 | 28 | 28 | 28 | 30 | 30 | 30 | 32 | 32 | 32 | 34 | 34 | 34 |
| 0.326 — 0.340 | 08 | 08 | 10 | 10 | 12 | 12 | 12 | 14 | 14 | 24 | 16 | 16 | 16 | 18 | 18 | 18 | 20 | 20 | 20 | 22 | 22 | 22 | 24 | 24 | 24 | 26 | 26 | 26 | 28 | 28 | 28 | 30 | 30 | 30 | 32 | 32 | 32 | 34 | 34 | 34 |
| 0.341 — 0.350 | 08 | 08 | 10 | 10 | 12 | 12 | 14 | 14 | 14 | 14 | 16 | 16 | 18 | 18 | 18 | 18 | 20 | 20 | 22 | 22 | 22 | 22 | 24 | 24 | 26 | 26 | 26 | 26 | 28 | 28 | 30 | 30 | 30 | 30 | 32 | 32 | 34 | 34 | 34 |
| 0.351 — 0.370 | 08 | 10 | 10 | 12 | 12 | 14 | 14 | 14 | 14 | 16 | 16 | 18 | 18 | 18 | 18 | 20 | 20 | 22 | 22 | 22 | 22 | 24 | 24 | 26 | 26 | 26 | 26 | 28 | 28 | 30 | 30 | 30 | 30 | 32 | 32 | 34 | 34 | 34 | 34 |
| 0.371 — 0.375 | 08 | 10 | 10 | 12 | 12 | 14 | 14 | 14 | 16 | 16 | 16 | 18 | 18 | 18 | 20 | 20 | 20 | 22 | 22 | 22 | 24 | 24 | 24 | 26 | 26 | 26 | 28 | 28 | 28 | 30 | 30 | 30 | 32 | 32 | 32 | 34 | 34 | 34 |
| 0.376 — 0.390 | 10 | 10 | 12 | 12 | 14 | 14 | 14 | 16 | 16 | 16 | 18 | 18 | 18 | 20 | 20 | 20 | 22 | 22 | 22 | 24 | 24 | 24 | 26 | 26 | 26 | 28 | 28 | 28 | 30 | 30 | 30 | 32 | 32 | 32 | 34 | 34 | 34 |
| 0.391 — 0.400 | 10 | 10 | 12 | 12 | 14 | 14 | 16 | 16 | 16 | 16 | 18 | 18 | 20 | 20 | 20 | 20 | 22 | 22 | 24 | 24 | 24 | 24 | 26 | 26 | 28 | 28 | 28 | 28 | 30 | 30 | 32 | 32 | 32 | 32 | 34 | 34 |
| 0.401 — 0.420 | 10 | 12 | 12 | 14 | 14 | 16 | 16 | 16 | 16 | 18 | 18 | 20 | 20 | 20 | 20 | 22 | 22 | 24 | 24 | 24 | 24 | 26 | 26 | 28 | 28 | 28 | 28 | 30 | 30 | 32 | 32 | 32 | 32 | 34 | 34 |
| 0.421 — 0.425 | 10 | 12 | 12 | 14 | 14 | 16 | 16 | 16 | 18 | 18 | 18 | 20 | 20 | 20 | 22 | 22 | 22 | 24 | 24 | 24 | 26 | 26 | 26 | 28 | 28 | 28 | 30 | 30 | 30 | 32 | 32 | 32 | 34 | 34 | 34 |
| 0.426 — 0.440 | 12 | 12 | 14 | 14 | 16 | 16 | 16 | 18 | 18 | 18 | 20 | 20 | 20 | 22 | 22 | 22 | 24 | 24 | 24 | 26 | 26 | 26 | 28 | 28 | 28 | 30 | 30 | 30 | 32 | 32 | 32 | 34 | 34 | 34 |
| 0.441 — 0.450 | 12 | 12 | 14 | 14 | 16 | 16 | 18 | 18 | 18 | 18 | 20 | 20 | 22 | 22 | 22 | 22 | 24 | 24 | 26 | 26 | 26 | 26 | 28 | 28 | 30 | 30 | 30 | 30 | 32 | 32 | 34 | 34 | 34 | 34 |
| 0.451 — 0.470 | 12 | 14 | 14 | 16 | 16 | 18 | 18 | 18 | 18 | 20 | 20 | 22 | 22 | 22 | 22 | 24 | 24 | 26 | 26 | 26 | 26 | 28 | 28 | 30 | 30 | 30 | 30 | 32 | 32 | 34 | 34 | 34 | 34 |
| 0.471 — 0.475 | 12 | 14 | 14 | 16 | 16 | 18 | 18 | 18 | 20 | 20 | 20 | 22 | 22 | 22 | 24 | 24 | 24 | 26 | 26 | 26 | 28 | 28 | 28 | 30 | 30 | 30 | 32 | 32 | 32 | 34 | 34 | 34 |
| 0.476 — 0.490 | 14 | 14 | 16 | 16 | 18 | 18 | 18 | 20 | 20 | 20 | 22 | 22 | 22 | 24 | 24 | 24 | 26 | 26 | 26 | 28 | 28 | 28 | 30 | 30 | 30 | 32 | 32 | 32 | 34 | 34 | 34 |
| 0.491 — 0.500 | 14 | 14 | 16 | 16 | 18 | 18 | 20 | 20 | 20 | 20 | 22 | 22 | 24 | 24 | 24 | 24 | 26 | 26 | 28 | 28 | 28 | 28 | 30 | 30 | 32 | 32 | 32 | 32 | 34 | 34 |
| 0.501 — 0.520 | 14 | 16 | 16 | 18 | 18 | 20 | 20 | 20 | 20 | 22 | 22 | 24 | 24 | 24 | 24 | 26 | 26 | 28 | 28 | 28 | 28 | 30 | 30 | 32 | 32 | 32 | 32 | 34 | 34 |
| 0.521 — 0.525 | 14 | 16 | 16 | 18 | 18 | 20 | 20 | 20 | 22 | 22 | 22 | 24 | 24 | 24 | 26 | 26 | 26 | 28 | 28 | 28 | 30 | 30 | 30 | 32 | 32 | 32 | 34 | 34 | 34 |
| 0.526 — 0.540 | 16 | 16 | 18 | 18 | 20 | 20 | 20 | 22 | 22 | 22 | 24 | 24 | 24 | 26 | 26 | 26 | 28 | 28 | 28 | 30 | 30 | 30 | 32 | 32 | 32 | 34 | 34 | 34 |
| 0.541 — 0.550 | 16 | 16 | 18 | 18 | 20 | 20 | 22 | 22 | 22 | 22 | 24 | 24 | 26 | 26 | 26 | 26 | 28 | 28 | 30 | 30 | 30 | 30 | 32 | 32 | 34 | 34 | 34 | 34 |
| 0.551 — 0.570 | 16 | 18 | 18 | 20 | 20 | 22 | 22 | 22 | 22 | 24 | 24 | 26 | 26 | 26 | 26 | 28 | 28 | 30 | 30 | 30 | 30 | 32 | 32 | 34 | 34 | 34 | 34 |
| 0.571 — 0.575 | 16 | 18 | 18 | 20 | 20 | 22 | 22 | 22 | 24 | 24 | 24 | 26 | 26 | 26 | 28 | 28 | 28 | 30 | 30 | 30 | 32 | 32 | 32 | 34 | 34 | 34 |
| 0,575 — 0.590 | 18 | 18 | 20 | 20 | 22 | 22 | 22 | 24 | 24 | 24 | 26 | 26 | 26 | 28 | 28 | 28 | 30 | 30 | 30 | 32 | 32 | 32 | 34 | 34 | 34 |
| 0.591 — 0.600 | 18 | 18 | 20 | 20 | 22 | 22 | 24 | 24 | 24 | 24 | 26 | 26 | 28 | 28 | 28 | 28 | 30 | 30 | 32 | 32 | 32 | 32 | 34 | 34 |
| 0.601 — 0.620 | 18 | 20 | 20 | 22 | 22 | 24 | 24 | 24 | 24 | 26 | 26 | 28 | 28 | 28 | 28 | 30 | 30 | 32 | 32 | 32 | 32 | 34 | 34 |
| 0.621 — 0.625 | 18 | 20 | 20 | 22 | 22 | 24 | 24 | 24 | 26 | 26 | 26 | 28 | 28 | 28 | 30 | 30 | 30 | 32 | 32 | 32 | 34 | 34 | 34 |
| 0.626 — 0.640 | 20 | 20 | 22 | 22 | 24 | 24 | 24 | 26 | 26 | 26 | 28 | 28 | 28 | 30 | 30 | 30 | 32 | 32 | 32 | 34 | 34 | 34 |
| 0.641 — 0.650 | 20 | 20 | 22 | 22 | 24 | 24 | 26 | 26 | 26 | 26 | 28 | 28 | 30 | 30 | 30 | 30 | 32 | 32 | 34 | 34 | 34 | 34 |
| 0.651 — 0.670 | 20 | 22 | 22 | 24 | 24 | 26 | 26 | 26 | 26 | 28 | 28 | 30 | 30 | 30 | 30 | 32 | 32 | 34 | 34 | 34 | 34 |
| 0.671 — 0.675 | 20 | 22 | 22 | 24 | 24 | 26 | 26 | 26 | 28 | 28 | 28 | 30 | 30 | 30 | 32 | 32 | 32 | 34 | 34 | 34 |
| 0.676 — 0.690 | 22 | 22 | 24 | 24 | 26 | 26 | 26 | 28 | 28 | 28 | 30 | 30 | 30 | 32 | 32 | 32 | 34 | 34 | 34 |
| 0.691 — 0.700 | 22 | 22 | 24 | 24 | 26 | 26 | 28 | 28 | 28 | 28 | 30 | 30 | 32 | 32 | 32 | 32 | 34 | 34 |
| 0.701 — 0.720 | 22 | 24 | 24 | 26 | 26 | 28 | 28 | 28 | 28 | 30 | 30 | 32 | 32 | 32 | 32 | 34 | 34 |
| 0.721 — 0.725 | 22 | 24 | 24 | 26 | 26 | 28 | 28 | 28 | 30 | 30 | 30 | 32 | 32 | 32 | 34 | 34 | 34 |
| 0.726 — 0.740 | 24 | 24 | 26 | 26 | 28 | 28 | 28 | 30 | 30 | 30 | 32 | 32 | 32 | 34 | 34 | 34 |
| 0.741 — 0.750 | 24 | 24 | 26 | 26 | 28 | 28 | 30 | 30 | 30 | 30 | 32 | 32 | 34 | 34 | 34 |
| 0.751 — 0.770 | 24 | 26 | 26 | 28 | 28 | 30 | 30 | 30 | 30 | 32 | 32 | 34 | 34 | 34 | 34 |
| 0.771 — 0.775 | 24 | 26 | 26 | 28 | 28 | 30 | 30 | 30 | 32 | 32 | 32 | 34 | 34 | 34 |
| 0.776 — 0.790 | 26 | 26 | 28 | 28 | 30 | 30 | 30 | 32 | 32 | 32 | 34 | 34 | 34 |
| 0.791 — 0.800 | 26 | 26 | 28 | 28 | 30 | 30 | 32 | 32 | 32 | 32 | 34 | 34 |
| 0.801 — 0.820 | 26 | 28 | 28 | 30 | 30 | 32 | 32 | 32 | 32 | 34 | 34 |
| 0.821 — 0.825 | 26 | 28 | 28 | 30 | 30 | 32 | 32 | 32 | 34 | 34 | 34 |
| 0.826 — 0.840 | 28 | 28 | 30 | 30 | 32 | 32 | 32 | 34 | 34 | 34 |
| 0.841 — 0.850 | 28 | 28 | 30 | 30 | 32 | 32 | 34 | 34 | 34 | 34 |
| 0.851 — 0.870 | 28 | 30 | 30 | 32 | 32 | 34 | 34 | 34 | 34 |
| 0.871 — 0.875 | 28 | 30 | 30 | 32 | 32 | 34 | 34 | 34 |
| 0.876 — 0.890 | 30 | 30 | 32 | 32 | 34 | 34 | 34 |
| 0.891 — 0.900 | 30 | 30 | 32 | 32 | 34 | 34 |
| 0.901 — 0.925 | 30 | 32 | 32 | 34 | 34 |
| 0.926 — 0.950 | 32 | 32 | 34 | 34 |
| 0.951 — 0.975 | 32 | 34 | 34 |
| 0.976 — 1.000 | 34 | 34 |
| 1.001 — 1.025 | 34 |

Shim thickness mm (in.)

| Shim No. | Thickness | Shim No. | Thickness |
|---|---|---|---|
| 02 | 2.500 (0.0984) | 20 | 2.950 (0.1161) |
| 04 | 2.550 (0.1004) | 22 | 3.000 (0.1181) |
| 06 | 2.600 (0.1024) | 24 | 3.050 (0.1201) |
| 08 | 2.650 (0.1043) | 26 | 3.100 (0.1220) |
| 10 | 2.700 (0.1063) | 28 | 3.150 (0.1240) |
| 12 | 2.750 (0.1083) | 30 | 3.200 (0.1260) |
| 14 | 2.800 (0.1102) | 32 | 3.250 (0.1280) |
| 16 | 2.850 (0.1122) | 34 | 3.300 (0.1299) |
| 18 | 2.900 (0.1142) | | |

EXAMPLE: A 0.1102" (2.800 mm) shim is installed and measured clearance is 0.0177" (0.450 mm). Replace 0.1102" (2.800 mm) shim with a No. 24 shim.

91E17354

Courtesy of Toyota Motor Sales, U.S.A., Inc.

***Fig. 4: Intake Valve Adjusting Shim Selection Chart***

# 1991 ENGINES
# 1.6L 16-Valve 4-Cylinder (Cont.)

## Exhaust

| Measured Clearance (mm) | Installed Shim Thickness (mm) 2.500 | 2.525 | 2.550 | 2.575 | 2.600 | 2.620 | 2.640 | 2.650 | 2.660 | 2.680 | 2.700 | 2.720 | 2.740 | 2.750 | 2.760 | 2.780 | 2.800 | 2.820 | 2.840 | 2.850 | 2.860 | 2.880 | 2.900 | 2.920 | 2.940 | 2.950 | 2.960 | 2.980 | 3.000 | 3.020 | 3.040 | 3.050 | 3.060 | 3.080 | 3.100 | 3.120 | 3.140 | 3.150 | 3.160 | 3.180 | 3.200 | 3.225 | 3.250 | 3.275 | 3.300 |
|---|---|---|---|---|---|---|---|---|---|---|---|---|---|---|---|---|---|---|---|---|---|---|---|---|---|---|---|---|---|---|---|---|---|---|---|---|---|---|---|---|---|---|---|---|---|
| 0.000 – 0.009 | | | | | | | | | | | | 02 | 02 | 02 | 02 | 04 | 04 | 06 | 06 | 06 | 06 | 08 | 08 | 10 | 10 | 10 | 10 | 12 | 12 | 14 | 14 | 14 | 14 | 16 | 16 | 18 | 18 | 18 | 18 | 20 | 20 | 22 | 22 | 24 | 24 |
| 0.010 – 0.025 | | | | | | | | | | | | 02 | 02 | 02 | 04 | 04 | 06 | 06 | 06 | 06 | 08 | 08 | 10 | 10 | 10 | 10 | 12 | 12 | 14 | 14 | 14 | 14 | 16 | 16 | 18 | 18 | 18 | 18 | 20 | 20 | 22 | 22 | 22 | 24 | 26 |
| 0.026 – 0.040 | | | | | | | | | | | 02 | 02 | 02 | 04 | 04 | 04 | 06 | 06 | 06 | 08 | 08 | 08 | 10 | 10 | 10 | 12 | 12 | 12 | 14 | 14 | 14 | 16 | 16 | 16 | 18 | 18 | 18 | 20 | 20 | 20 | 22 | 22 | 24 | 24 | 26 |
| 0.041 – 0.050 | | | | | | | | | | 02 | 02 | 02 | 04 | 04 | 04 | 06 | 06 | 06 | 08 | 08 | 08 | 10 | 10 | 10 | 12 | 12 | 12 | 14 | 14 | 14 | 16 | 16 | 16 | 18 | 18 | 18 | 20 | 20 | 20 | 22 | 22 | 22 | 24 | 24 | 26 |
| 0.051 – 0.070 | | | | | | | | | | 02 | 02 | 04 | 04 | 04 | 04 | 06 | 06 | 08 | 08 | 08 | 08 | 10 | 10 | 12 | 12 | 12 | 12 | 14 | 14 | 16 | 16 | 16 | 16 | 18 | 18 | 20 | 20 | 20 | 20 | 22 | 22 | 24 | 24 | 26 | 26 |
| 0.071 – 0.090 | | | | | | | | 02 | 02 | 02 | 04 | 04 | 04 | 06 | 06 | 06 | 08 | 08 | 08 | 10 | 10 | 10 | 12 | 12 | 12 | 14 | 14 | 14 | 16 | 16 | 16 | 18 | 18 | 18 | 20 | 20 | 20 | 22 | 22 | 22 | 24 | 24 | 26 | 26 | 28 |
| 0.091 – 0.100 | | | | | | | 02 | 02 | 02 | 04 | 04 | 04 | 06 | 06 | 06 | 08 | 08 | 08 | 10 | 10 | 10 | 12 | 12 | 12 | 14 | 14 | 14 | 16 | 16 | 16 | 18 | 18 | 18 | 20 | 20 | 20 | 22 | 22 | 22 | 24 | 24 | 24 | 26 | 26 | 28 |
| 0.101 – 0.120 | | | | | | 02 | 02 | 02 | 02 | 04 | 04 | 06 | 06 | 06 | 06 | 08 | 08 | 10 | 10 | 10 | 10 | 12 | 12 | 14 | 14 | 14 | 14 | 16 | 16 | 18 | 18 | 18 | 18 | 20 | 20 | 22 | 22 | 22 | 22 | 24 | 24 | 26 | 26 | 28 | 28 |
| 0.121 – 0.140 | | | | | 02 | 02 | 02 | 04 | 04 | 04 | 06 | 06 | 06 | 08 | 08 | 08 | 10 | 10 | 10 | 12 | 12 | 12 | 14 | 14 | 14 | 16 | 16 | 16 | 18 | 18 | 18 | 20 | 20 | 20 | 22 | 22 | 22 | 24 | 24 | 24 | 26 | 26 | 28 | 28 | 30 |
| 0.141 – 0.150 | | | | | 02 | 02 | 04 | 04 | 04 | 06 | 06 | 06 | 08 | 08 | 08 | 10 | 10 | 10 | 12 | 12 | 12 | 14 | 14 | 14 | 16 | 16 | 16 | 18 | 18 | 18 | 20 | 20 | 20 | 22 | 22 | 22 | 24 | 24 | 24 | 26 | 26 | 26 | 28 | 28 | 30 |
| 0.151 – 0.170 | | | | | 02 | 02 | 04 | 04 | 04 | 06 | 06 | 06 | 08 | 08 | 08 | 10 | 10 | 10 | 12 | 12 | 12 | 14 | 14 | 14 | 16 | 16 | 16 | 18 | 18 | 18 | 20 | 20 | 20 | 22 | 22 | 22 | 24 | 24 | 24 | 26 | 26 | 26 | 28 | 28 | 30 |
| 0.171 – 0.190 | | | 02 | 02 | 04 | 04 | 04 | 06 | 06 | 06 | 08 | 08 | 08 | 10 | 10 | 10 | 12 | 12 | 12 | 14 | 14 | 14 | 16 | 16 | 16 | 18 | 18 | 18 | 20 | 20 | 20 | 22 | 22 | 22 | 24 | 24 | 24 | 26 | 26 | 26 | 28 | 28 | 30 | 30 | 32 |
| 0.191 – 0.199 | | | 02 | 02 | 04 | 04 | 06 | 06 | 06 | 08 | 08 | 08 | 10 | 10 | 10 | 12 | 12 | 12 | 14 | 14 | 14 | 16 | 16 | 16 | 18 | 18 | 18 | 20 | 20 | 20 | 22 | 22 | 22 | 24 | 24 | 24 | 26 | 26 | 26 | 28 | 28 | 28 | 30 | 30 | 32 |
| 0.200 – 0.300 | | | | | | | | | | | | | | | | | | | | | | | | | | | | | | | | | | | | | | | | | | | | | |
| 0.301 – 0.320 | 04 | 06 | 06 | 08 | 08 | 10 | 10 | 10 | 10 | 12 | 12 | 14 | 14 | 14 | 14 | 16 | 16 | 18 | 18 | 18 | 18 | 20 | 20 | 22 | 22 | 22 | 22 | 24 | 24 | 26 | 26 | 26 | 26 | 28 | 28 | 30 | 30 | 30 | 30 | 32 | 32 | 34 | 34 | | |
| 0.321 – 0.325 | 04 | 06 | 06 | 08 | 08 | 10 | 10 | 10 | 12 | 12 | 12 | 14 | 14 | 14 | 16 | 16 | 16 | 18 | 18 | 18 | 20 | 20 | 20 | 22 | 22 | 22 | 24 | 24 | 24 | 26 | 26 | 26 | 28 | 28 | 28 | 30 | 30 | 30 | 32 | 32 | 32 | 34 | 34 | | |
| 0.326 – 0.340 | 06 | 06 | 08 | 08 | 10 | 10 | 10 | 12 | 12 | 12 | 14 | 14 | 14 | 16 | 16 | 16 | 18 | 18 | 18 | 20 | 20 | 20 | 22 | 22 | 22 | 24 | 24 | 24 | 26 | 26 | 26 | 28 | 28 | 28 | 30 | 30 | 30 | 32 | 32 | 32 | 34 | 34 | | | |
| 0.341 – 0.350 | 06 | 06 | 08 | 08 | 10 | 10 | 12 | 12 | 12 | 12 | 14 | 14 | 16 | 16 | 16 | 16 | 18 | 18 | 20 | 20 | 20 | 20 | 22 | 22 | 24 | 24 | 24 | 24 | 26 | 26 | 28 | 28 | 28 | 28 | 30 | 30 | 32 | 32 | 32 | 32 | 34 | 34 | | | |
| 0.351 – 0.370 | 06 | 08 | 08 | 10 | 10 | 12 | 12 | 12 | 12 | 14 | 14 | 16 | 16 | 16 | 16 | 18 | 18 | 20 | 20 | 20 | 20 | 22 | 22 | 24 | 24 | 24 | 24 | 26 | 26 | 28 | 28 | 28 | 28 | 30 | 30 | 32 | 32 | 32 | 32 | 34 | 34 | | | | |
| 0.371 – 0.375 | 06 | 08 | 08 | 10 | 10 | 12 | 12 | 12 | 14 | 14 | 14 | 16 | 16 | 16 | 18 | 18 | 18 | 20 | 20 | 20 | 22 | 22 | 22 | 24 | 24 | 24 | 26 | 26 | 26 | 28 | 28 | 28 | 30 | 30 | 30 | 32 | 32 | 32 | 34 | 34 | 34 | | | | |
| 0.376 – 0.390 | 08 | 08 | 10 | 10 | 12 | 12 | 12 | 14 | 14 | 14 | 16 | 16 | 16 | 18 | 18 | 18 | 20 | 20 | 20 | 22 | 22 | 22 | 24 | 24 | 24 | 26 | 26 | 26 | 28 | 28 | 28 | 30 | 30 | 30 | 32 | 32 | 32 | 34 | 34 | 34 | | | | | |
| 0.391 – 0.400 | 08 | 08 | 10 | 10 | 12 | 12 | 14 | 14 | 14 | 14 | 16 | 16 | 18 | 18 | 18 | 18 | 20 | 20 | 22 | 22 | 22 | 22 | 24 | 24 | 26 | 26 | 26 | 26 | 28 | 28 | 30 | 30 | 30 | 30 | 32 | 32 | 34 | 34 | 34 | 34 | | | | | |
| 0.401 – 0.420 | 08 | 10 | 10 | 12 | 12 | 14 | 14 | 14 | 14 | 16 | 16 | 18 | 18 | 18 | 18 | 20 | 20 | 22 | 22 | 22 | 22 | 24 | 24 | 26 | 26 | 26 | 26 | 28 | 28 | 30 | 30 | 30 | 30 | 32 | 32 | 34 | 34 | 34 | 34 | | | | | | |
| 0.421 – 0.425 | 08 | 10 | 10 | 12 | 12 | 14 | 14 | 14 | 16 | 16 | 16 | 18 | 18 | 18 | 20 | 20 | 20 | 22 | 22 | 22 | 24 | 24 | 24 | 26 | 26 | 26 | 28 | 28 | 28 | 30 | 30 | 30 | 32 | 32 | 32 | 34 | 34 | 34 | | | | | | | |
| 0.426 – 0.440 | 10 | 10 | 12 | 12 | 14 | 14 | 14 | 16 | 16 | 16 | 18 | 18 | 18 | 20 | 20 | 20 | 22 | 22 | 22 | 24 | 24 | 24 | 26 | 26 | 26 | 28 | 28 | 28 | 30 | 30 | 30 | 32 | 32 | 32 | 34 | 34 | 34 | | | | | | | | |
| 0.441 – 0.450 | 10 | 10 | 12 | 12 | 14 | 14 | 16 | 16 | 16 | 16 | 18 | 18 | 20 | 20 | 20 | 20 | 22 | 22 | 24 | 24 | 24 | 24 | 26 | 26 | 28 | 28 | 28 | 28 | 30 | 30 | 32 | 32 | 32 | 32 | 34 | 34 | | | | | | | | | |
| 0.451 – 0.470 | 10 | 12 | 12 | 14 | 14 | 16 | 16 | 16 | 16 | 18 | 18 | 20 | 20 | 20 | 20 | 22 | 22 | 24 | 24 | 24 | 24 | 26 | 26 | 28 | 28 | 28 | 28 | 30 | 30 | 30 | 32 | 32 | 32 | 34 | 34 | | | | | | | | | | |
| 0.471 – 0.475 | 10 | 12 | 12 | 14 | 14 | 16 | 16 | 16 | 18 | 18 | 18 | 20 | 20 | 20 | 22 | 22 | 22 | 24 | 24 | 24 | 26 | 26 | 26 | 28 | 28 | 28 | 30 | 30 | 30 | 32 | 32 | 32 | 34 | 34 | 34 | | | | | | | | | | |
| 0.476 – 0.490 | 12 | 12 | 14 | 14 | 16 | 16 | 16 | 18 | 18 | 18 | 20 | 20 | 20 | 22 | 22 | 22 | 24 | 24 | 24 | 26 | 26 | 26 | 28 | 28 | 28 | 30 | 30 | 30 | 32 | 32 | 32 | 34 | 34 | 34 | | | | | | | | | | | |
| 0.491 – 0.500 | 12 | 12 | 14 | 14 | 16 | 16 | 18 | 18 | 18 | 18 | 20 | 20 | 22 | 22 | 22 | 22 | 24 | 24 | 26 | 26 | 26 | 26 | 28 | 28 | 30 | 30 | 30 | 30 | 32 | 32 | 34 | 34 | 34 | 34 | | | | | | | | | | | |
| 0.501 – 0.520 | 12 | 14 | 14 | 16 | 16 | 18 | 18 | 18 | 18 | 20 | 20 | 22 | 22 | 22 | 22 | 24 | 24 | 26 | 26 | 26 | 26 | 28 | 28 | 30 | 30 | 30 | 30 | 32 | 32 | 34 | 34 | 34 | 34 | | | | | | | | | | | | |
| 0.521 – 0.525 | 12 | 14 | 14 | 16 | 16 | 18 | 18 | 18 | 20 | 20 | 20 | 22 | 22 | 22 | 24 | 24 | 24 | 26 | 26 | 26 | 28 | 28 | 28 | 30 | 30 | 30 | 32 | 32 | 32 | 34 | 34 | 34 | | | | | | | | | | | | | |
| 0.526 – 0.540 | 14 | 14 | 16 | 16 | 18 | 18 | 18 | 20 | 20 | 20 | 22 | 22 | 22 | 24 | 24 | 24 | 26 | 26 | 26 | 28 | 28 | 28 | 30 | 30 | 30 | 32 | 32 | 32 | 34 | 34 | 34 | | | | | | | | | | | | | | |
| 0.541 – 0.550 | 14 | 14 | 16 | 16 | 18 | 18 | 20 | 20 | 20 | 20 | 22 | 22 | 24 | 24 | 24 | 24 | 26 | 26 | 28 | 28 | 28 | 28 | 30 | 30 | 32 | 32 | 32 | 32 | 34 | 34 | | | | | | | | | | | | | | | |
| 0.551 – 0.570 | 14 | 16 | 16 | 18 | 18 | 20 | 20 | 20 | 20 | 22 | 22 | 24 | 24 | 24 | 24 | 26 | 26 | 28 | 28 | 28 | 28 | 30 | 30 | 32 | 32 | 32 | 32 | 34 | 34 | | | | | | | | | | | | | | | | |
| 0.571 – 0.575 | 14 | 16 | 16 | 18 | 18 | 20 | 20 | 20 | 22 | 22 | 22 | 24 | 24 | 24 | 26 | 26 | 26 | 28 | 28 | 28 | 30 | 30 | 30 | 32 | 32 | 32 | 34 | 34 | 34 | | | | | | | | | | | | | | | | |
| 0.576 – 0.590 | 16 | 16 | 18 | 18 | 20 | 20 | 20 | 22 | 22 | 22 | 24 | 24 | 24 | 26 | 26 | 26 | 28 | 28 | 28 | 30 | 30 | 30 | 32 | 32 | 32 | 34 | 34 | 34 | | | | | | | | | | | | | | | | | |
| 0.591 – 0.600 | 16 | 16 | 18 | 18 | 20 | 20 | 22 | 22 | 22 | 22 | 24 | 24 | 26 | 26 | 26 | 26 | 28 | 28 | 30 | 30 | 30 | 30 | 32 | 32 | 34 | 34 | 34 | 34 | | | | | | | | | | | | | | | | | |
| 0.601 – 0.620 | 16 | 18 | 18 | 20 | 20 | 22 | 22 | 22 | 22 | 24 | 24 | 26 | 26 | 26 | 26 | 28 | 28 | 30 | 30 | 30 | 30 | 32 | 32 | 34 | 34 | 34 | 34 | | | | | | | | | | | | | | | | | | |
| 0.621 – 0.625 | 16 | 18 | 18 | 20 | 20 | 22 | 22 | 22 | 24 | 24 | 24 | 26 | 26 | 26 | 28 | 28 | 28 | 30 | 30 | 30 | 32 | 32 | 32 | 34 | 34 | 34 | | | | | | | | | | | | | | | | | | | |
| 0.626 – 0.640 | 18 | 18 | 20 | 20 | 22 | 22 | 22 | 24 | 24 | 24 | 26 | 26 | 26 | 28 | 28 | 28 | 30 | 30 | 30 | 32 | 32 | 32 | 34 | 34 | 34 | | | | | | | | | | | | | | | | | | | | |
| 0.641 – 0.650 | 18 | 18 | 20 | 20 | 22 | 22 | 24 | 24 | 24 | 24 | 26 | 26 | 28 | 28 | 28 | 28 | 30 | 30 | 32 | 32 | 32 | 32 | 34 | 34 | | | | | | | | | | | | | | | | | | | | | |
| 0.651 – 0.670 | 18 | 20 | 20 | 22 | 22 | 24 | 24 | 24 | 24 | 26 | 26 | 28 | 28 | 28 | 28 | 30 | 30 | 32 | 32 | 32 | 32 | 34 | 34 | | | | | | | | | | | | | | | | | | | | | | |
| 0.671 – 0.675 | 18 | 20 | 20 | 22 | 22 | 24 | 24 | 24 | 26 | 26 | 26 | 28 | 28 | 28 | 30 | 30 | 30 | 32 | 32 | 32 | 34 | 34 | 34 | | | | | | | | | | | | | | | | | | | | | | |
| 0.676 – 0.690 | 20 | 20 | 22 | 22 | 24 | 24 | 24 | 26 | 26 | 26 | 28 | 28 | 28 | 30 | 30 | 30 | 32 | 32 | 32 | 34 | 34 | 34 | | | | | | | | | | | | | | | | | | | | | | | |
| 0.691 – 0.700 | 20 | 20 | 22 | 22 | 24 | 24 | 26 | 26 | 26 | 26 | 28 | 28 | 30 | 30 | 30 | 30 | 32 | 32 | 34 | 34 | 34 | 34 | | | | | | | | | | | | | | | | | | | | | | | |
| 0.701 – 0.720 | 20 | 22 | 22 | 24 | 24 | 26 | 26 | 26 | 26 | 28 | 28 | 30 | 30 | 30 | 30 | 32 | 32 | 34 | 34 | 34 | 34 | | | | | | | | | | | | | | | | | | | | | | | | |
| 0.721 – 0.725 | 20 | 22 | 22 | 24 | 24 | 26 | 26 | 26 | 28 | 28 | 28 | 30 | 30 | 30 | 32 | 32 | 32 | 34 | 34 | 34 | | | | | | | | | | | | | | | | | | | | | | | | | |
| 0.726 – 0.740 | 22 | 22 | 24 | 24 | 26 | 26 | 26 | 28 | 28 | 28 | 30 | 30 | 30 | 32 | 32 | 32 | 34 | 34 | 34 | | | | | | | | | | | | | | | | | | | | | | | | | | |
| 0.741 – 0.750 | 22 | 22 | 24 | 24 | 26 | 26 | 28 | 28 | 28 | 28 | 30 | 30 | 32 | 32 | 32 | 32 | 34 | 34 | | | | | | | | | | | | | | | | | | | | | | | | | | | |
| 0.751 – 0.770 | 22 | 24 | 24 | 26 | 26 | 28 | 28 | 28 | 28 | 30 | 30 | 32 | 32 | 32 | 32 | 34 | 34 | | | | | | | | | | | | | | | | | | | | | | | | | | | | |
| 0.771 – 0.775 | 22 | 24 | 24 | 26 | 26 | 28 | 28 | 28 | 30 | 30 | 30 | 32 | 32 | 32 | 34 | 34 | 34 | | | | | | | | | | | | | | | | | | | | | | | | | | | | |
| 0.776 – 0.790 | 24 | 24 | 26 | 26 | 28 | 28 | 28 | 30 | 30 | 30 | 32 | 32 | 32 | 34 | 34 | 34 | | | | | | | | | | | | | | | | | | | | | | | | | | | | | |
| 0.791 – 0.800 | 24 | 24 | 26 | 26 | 28 | 28 | 30 | 30 | 30 | 30 | 32 | 32 | 34 | 34 | 34 | 34 | | | | | | | | | | | | | | | | | | | | | | | | | | | | | |
| 0.801 – 0.820 | 24 | 26 | 26 | 28 | 28 | 30 | 30 | 30 | 30 | 32 | 32 | 34 | 34 | 34 | 34 | | | | | | | | | | | | | | | | | | | | | | | | | | | | | | |
| 0.821 – 0.825 | 24 | 26 | 26 | 28 | 28 | 30 | 30 | 30 | 32 | 32 | 32 | 34 | 34 | 34 | | | | | | | | | | | | | | | | | | | | | | | | | | | | | | | |
| 0.826 – 0.840 | 26 | 26 | 28 | 28 | 30 | 30 | 30 | 32 | 32 | 32 | 34 | 34 | 34 | | | | | | | | | | | | | | | | | | | | | | | | | | | | | | | | |
| 0.841 – 0.850 | 26 | 26 | 28 | 28 | 30 | 30 | 32 | 32 | 32 | 32 | 34 | 34 | | | | | | | | | | | | | | | | | | | | | | | | | | | | | | | | | |
| 0.851 – 0.870 | 26 | 28 | 28 | 30 | 30 | 32 | 32 | 32 | 32 | 34 | 34 | | | | | | | | | | | | | | | | | | | | | | | | | | | | | | | | | | |
| 0.871 – 0.875 | 26 | 28 | 28 | 30 | 30 | 32 | 32 | 32 | 34 | 34 | 34 | | | | | | | | | | | | | | | | | | | | | | | | | | | | | | | | | | |
| 0.876 – 0.890 | 28 | 28 | 30 | 30 | 32 | 32 | 32 | 34 | 34 | 34 | | | | | | | | | | | | | | | | | | | | | | | | | | | | | | | | | | | |
| 0.891 – 0.900 | 28 | 28 | 30 | 30 | 32 | 32 | 34 | 34 | 34 | 34 | | | | | | | | | | | | | | | | | | | | | | | | | | | | | | | | | | | |
| 0.901 – 0.925 | 28 | 30 | 30 | 32 | 32 | 34 | 34 | 34 | | | | | | | | | | | | | | | | | | | | | | | | | | | | | | | | | | | | | |
| 0.926 – 0.950 | 30 | 30 | 32 | 32 | 34 | 34 | | | | | | | | | | | | | | | | | | | | | | | | | | | | | | | | | | | | | | | |
| 0.951 – 0.975 | 30 | 32 | 32 | 34 | 34 | | | | | | | | | | | | | | | | | | | | | | | | | | | | | | | | | | | | | | | | |
| 0.976 – 1.000 | 32 | 32 | 34 | 34 | | | | | | | | | | | | | | | | | | | | | | | | | | | | | | | | | | | | | | | | | |
| 1.025 – 1.001 | 32 | 34 | 34 | | | | | | | | | | | | | | | | | | | | | | | | | | | | | | | | | | | | | | | | | | |
| 1.026 – 1.050 | 34 | 34 | | | | | | | | | | | | | | | | | | | | | | | | | | | | | | | | | | | | | | | | | | | |
| 1.051 – 1.075 | 34 | | | | | | | | | | | | | | | | | | | | | | | | | | | | | | | | | | | | | | | | | | | | |

Shim thickness mm (in.)

| Shim No. | Thickness | Shim No. | Thickness |
|---|---|---|---|
| 02 | 2.500 (0.0984) | 20 | 2.950 (0.1161) |
| 04 | 2.550 (0.1004) | 22 | 3.000 (0.1181) |
| 06 | 2.600 (0.1024) | 24 | 3.050 (0.1201) |
| 08 | 2.650 (0.1043) | 26 | 3.100 (0.1220) |
| 10 | 2.700 (0.1063) | 28 | 3.150 (0.1240) |
| 12 | 2.750 (0.1083) | 30 | 3.200 (0.1260) |
| 14 | 2.800 (0.1102) | 32 | 3.250 (0.1280) |
| 16 | 2.850 (0.1122) | 34 | 3.300 (0.1299) |
| 18 | 2.900 (0.1142) | | |

EXAMPLE: A 0.1102" (2.800 mm) shim is installed and measured clearance is 0.0177" (0.450 mm). Replace 0.1102" (2.800 mm) shim with a No. 22 shim.

91F17355

Courtesy of Toyota Motor Sales, U.S.A., Inc.

*Fig. 5: Exhaust Valve Adjusting Shim Selection Chart*

# 1991 ENGINES
# 1.6L 16-Valve 4-Cylinder (Cont.)

**3)** On 4A-FE engine, disconnect fuel injection harness from Electronic Control Unit (ECU). Remove glove box. Remove ECU. Disconnect electrical connectors and pull out ECU wire harness from cowl panel.
**4)** On 4A-GE engine (Corolla), remove ignition coil. Disconnect ECU connectors at center console and pull out wire harness from cowl.
**5)** On all engines, disconnect oil cooler hoses (if equipped). Disconnect power steering pump and A/C compressor and set aside (if equipped). Disconnect speedometer cable from transaxle. Remove clutch slave cylinder (if equipped). Mark and remove shift control cable(s).
**6)** Remove cruise control actuator assembly (if equipped). Raise vehicle and disconnect exhaust pipe from exhaust manifold. Remove axle shafts. See FWD AXLE SHAFTS article in DRIVE AXLES.
**7)** On all models, remove mounts attached to crossmember. Remove crossmember. Lower vehicle and attach engine sling to support engine. Remove engine front support bracket. Remove remaining left transaxle mount and bracket. Lift and remove engine/transaxle assembly.
**Installation** - On all models, attach engine hoist and lower engine/transaxle into position. To complete installation, reverse removal procedure. Tighten bolts and nuts to specification. See TORQUE SPECIFICATIONS table at end of article. Fill fluids to proper level.

## CYLINDER HEAD & MANIFOLDS

***WARNING: Release fuel pressure before disconnecting fuel lines. See FUEL PRESSURE RELEASE.***

***NOTE: To prevent warping or cracking, allow engine to cool before removing components.***

**Removal - 1)** Disconnect negative battery cable. Remove engine under cover (splash) shields. Drain coolant. Remove air cleaner assembly. Disconnect throttle, cruise and kickdown cables (if equipped).
**2)** Disconnect coolant hoses from cylinder head. Mark and disconnect electrical connectors and vacuum hoses for reassembly reference.
**3)** On 4A-GE engine, remove cruise control actuator assembly (if equipped). Remove ignition coil. Remove EGR valve with piping. Remove cold start injector pipe. Remove fuel supply line and fuel pressure regulator.
**4)** On 4A-FE engine, remove cruse control actuator cable (if equipped). Remove EGR valve modulator. Remove cold start injector pipe. Disconnect vacuum sensing hose from fuel pressure regulator.
**5)** On all models, remove coolant outlet housing from cylinder head. Separate inlet pipe from exhaust manifold. Remove exhaust manifold. Match mark distributor for installation reference and remove distributor assembly.
**6)** On 4A-FE engine, remove coolant inlet housing from cylinder head. Disconnect fuel return hose. Remove fuel delivery pipe with fuel injectors. Remove intake manifold.
**7)** On 4A-GE engines, remove fuel delivery pipe with fuel injectors. Remove intake manifold bracket. Remove Vacuum Switching Valve (VSV) with air tank. Remove intake manifold and air control valve with gaskets. Slightly raise engine. Remove right engine mount to gain access to timing belt cover.
**8)** On all models, remove accessory belts. Remove valve covers. Remove spark plugs. Remove water pump pulley. Remove upper and center timing belt covers. Position No. 1 cylinder at TDC on compression stroke.
**9)** Match mark timing belt-to-camshaft sprocket(s). Loosen timing belt idler pulley (tensioner) bolt. Move idler pulley away from timing belt and tighten in place. Keeping timing belt tight on crankshaft sprocket, remove timing belt from camshaft sprocket(s).
**10)** Hold camshaft and remove camshaft sprocket(s). Remove cover located behind camshaft sprocket. Measure camshaft end play. If greater than specification, replace camshaft and/or cylinder head. See CAMSHAFT table under ENGINE SPECIFICATIONS at end of article.
**11)** On 4A-GE engine, mark and remove camshaft bearing caps evenly and in reverse of tightening sequence. *See Fig. 9*. Remove camshaft oil seals and camshafts. Remove cylinder head bolts in 3 steps gradually and in reverse of tightening sequence. *See Fig. 7*. Remove cylinder head assembly.
**12)** On 4A-FE engines, thrust clearance of camshaft is small. Camshaft must be removed level. Without keeping camshaft level, portion of cylinder head receiving camshaft thrust can crack or damage.
**13)** Set intake camshaft service bolt hole in center line of camshaft. Perform STEP 1. *See Fig. 6*. This angle allows No. 1 and No. 3 intake lobes to push their lifters evenly.

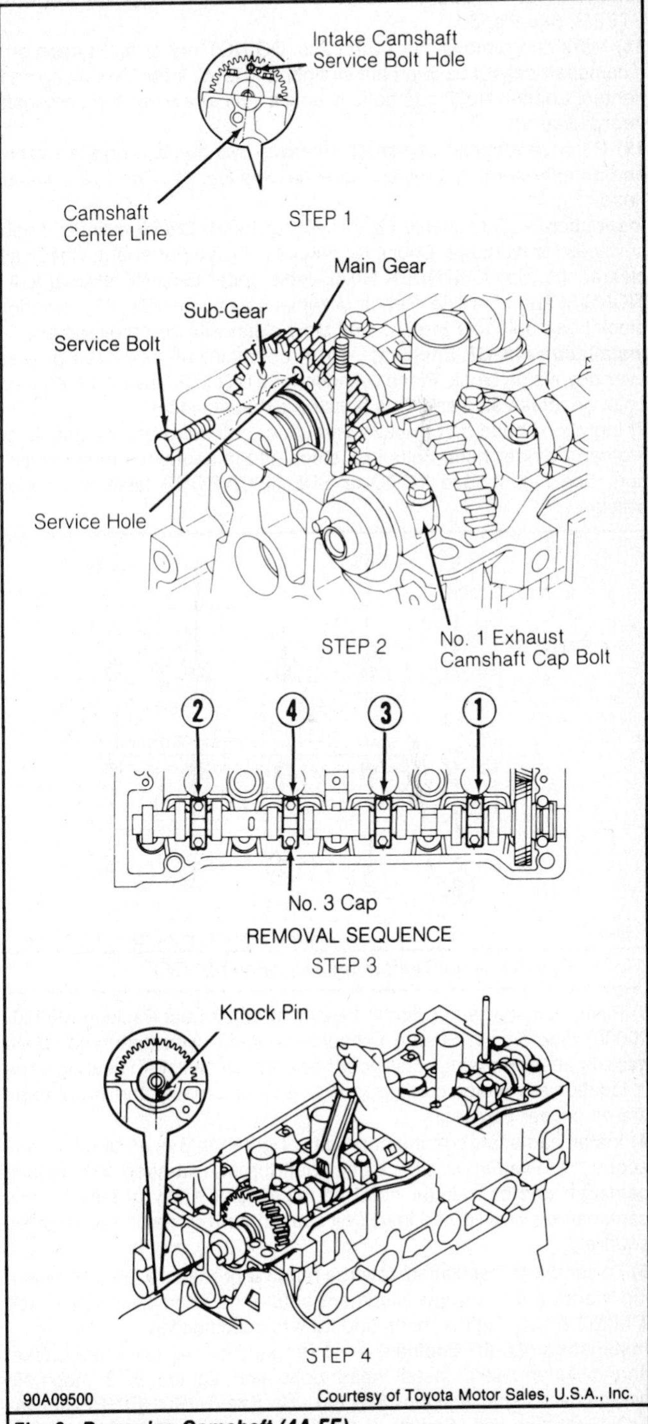


*Fig. 6: Removing Camshaft (4A-FE)*

# 1991 ENGINES
# 1.6L 16-Valve 4-Cylinder (Cont.)

**14)** Alternately loosen No. 1 intake and exhaust camshaft cap bolts a little at a time and remove caps. Secure intake camshaft sub-gear to main gear with bolt through service hole. Perform STEP 2. *See Fig. 6.* This will eliminate torsional spring force of sub-gear.
**15)** Evenly loosen each cap bolt in sequence a little at a time. Perform STEP 3. *See Fig. 6.* Mark and remove camshaft caps. DO NOT pry or force caps off. Remove camshaft.
**16)** If camshaft cannot be lifted out straight and level, install No. 3 cap and tighten. Loosen No. 3 cap bolts evenly a little at a time with camshaft gear pulled up. Remove intake camshaft. Proceed to next step.
**17)** Rotate exhaust camshaft and position knock pin. Perform STEP 4. *See Fig. 6.* This allows Nos. 1 and 3 exhaust lobes to push their lifter evenly. Loosen cap bolts evenly a little at a time, in sequence. Perform STEP 3. *See Fig. 6.*
**18)** Mark and remove camshaft caps. DO NOT pry or force caps off. If camshaft cannot be lifted out straight and level, install No. 3 cap and tighten. Loosen No. 3 cap bolts evenly a little at a time with camshaft gear pulled up.
**19)** Remove exhaust camshaft. Remove cylinder head bolts evenly and in reverse of tightening sequence. *See Fig. 10.* Remove cylinder head.
**Inspection** – Thoroughly clean cylinder head. Check cylinder head surfaces for warpage. Check for cracks with dye penetrant. Check all clearances. See CYLINDER HEAD table under ENGINE SPECIFICATIONS at end of article. Repair or replace as necessary. Tap cylinder block head bolt hole threads and blow clean with compressed air.
**Installation (4A-GE Engines)** – **1)** Properly install new head gasket over dowels on block. Place cylinder head on block. Install short head bolts on intake side and long bolts on exhaust side.
**2)** Lightly oil head bolt threads and under bolt head before installing. Tighten cylinder head bolts in 3 steps and in sequence to specification. *See Fig. 7.* See TORQUE SPECIFICATIONS table at end of article.

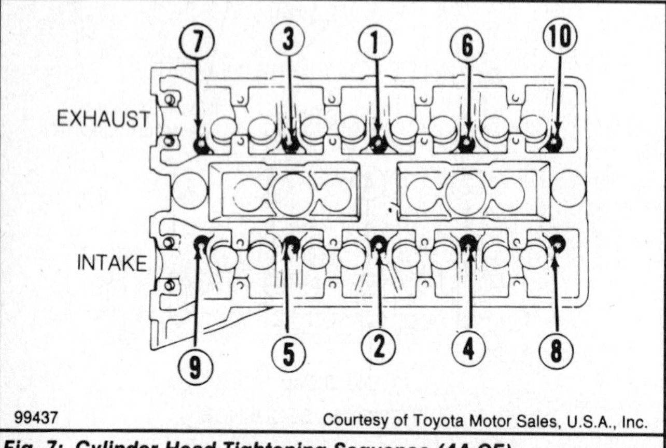


***Fig. 7: Cylinder Head Tightening Sequence (4A-GE)***

**3)** Place camshafts in cylinder head and apply Seal Packing (08826-00080). *See Fig. 8.* Ensure exhaust camshaft, with distributor drive gear, is on proper side of cylinder head. Install camshaft bearing caps to location as marked during removal. Ensure exhaust and intake caps are on proper camshaft.
**4)** Install camshaft bearing cap bolts. Tighten in 3 even steps and in sequence. *See Fig. 9.* Check camshaft thrust clearance and replace camshaft and/or cylinder head as necessary. Apply grease to new camshaft oil seal lip and install oil seal. Ensure oil seals are installed squarely.
**5)** To complete installation, reverse removal procedure. Ensure all timing marks are in proper alignment before installing timing belt. See TIMING BELT. Tighten bolts and nuts to specification.
**Installation (4A-FE Engines)** – **1)** Properly install new head gasket and cylinder head. Install head bolts and tighten in 3 steps, in sequence to specification. *See Fig. 10.* See TORQUE SPECIFICATIONS table at end of article. Place exhaust camshaft in cylinder head with knock pin as shown and apply seal packing. *See Fig. 8.*

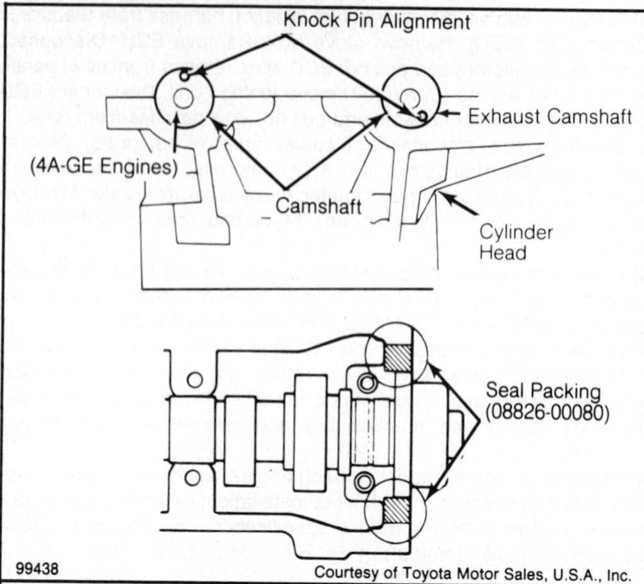


***Fig. 8: Installing Camshaft & Seal Packing***

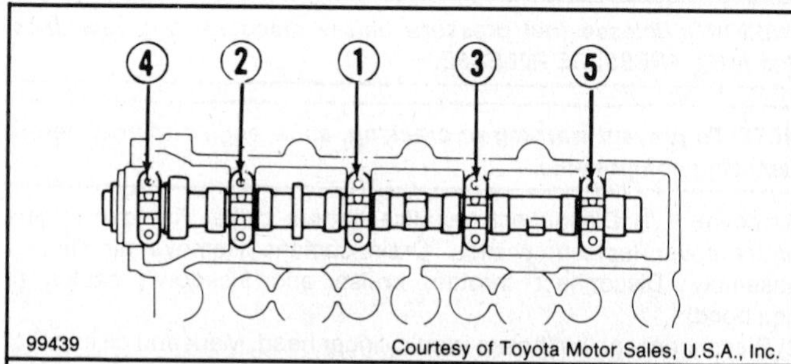


***Fig. 9: Camshaft Bearing Cap Tightening Sequence (4A-GE)***

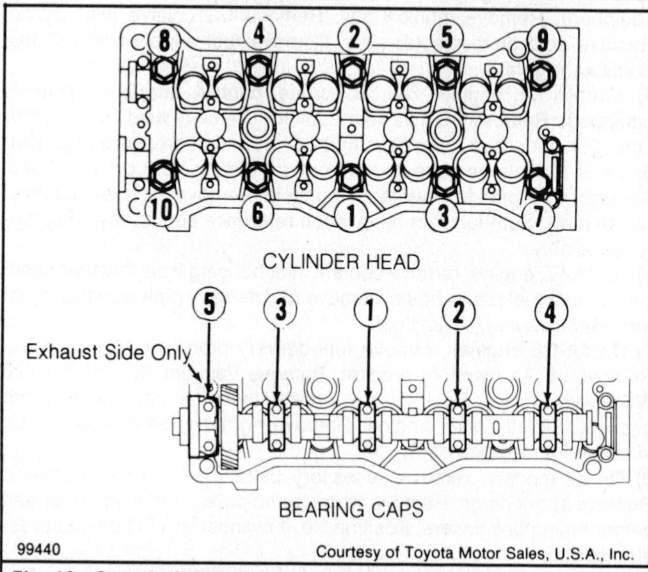


***Fig. 10: Camshaft Bearing Cap & Cylinder Head Tightening Sequence (4A-FE)***

**2)** Install camshaft bearing caps with arrow toward front and number on matching journal. Ensure exhaust and intake caps are not mixed. Gradually tighten caps in sequence to specification. *See Fig. 10.* See TORQUE SPECIFICATIONS table at end of article. Apply grease to camshaft seal and install.
**3)** Rotate exhaust camshaft until knock pin is in position shown. *See Fig. 11.* Engage intake camshaft gear to exhaust camshaft gear with

# 1991 ENGINES
# 1.6L 16-Valve 4-Cylinder (Cont.)

marks on gear aligned. See Fig. 11. Repeat step **2)** to install intake camshaft caps.

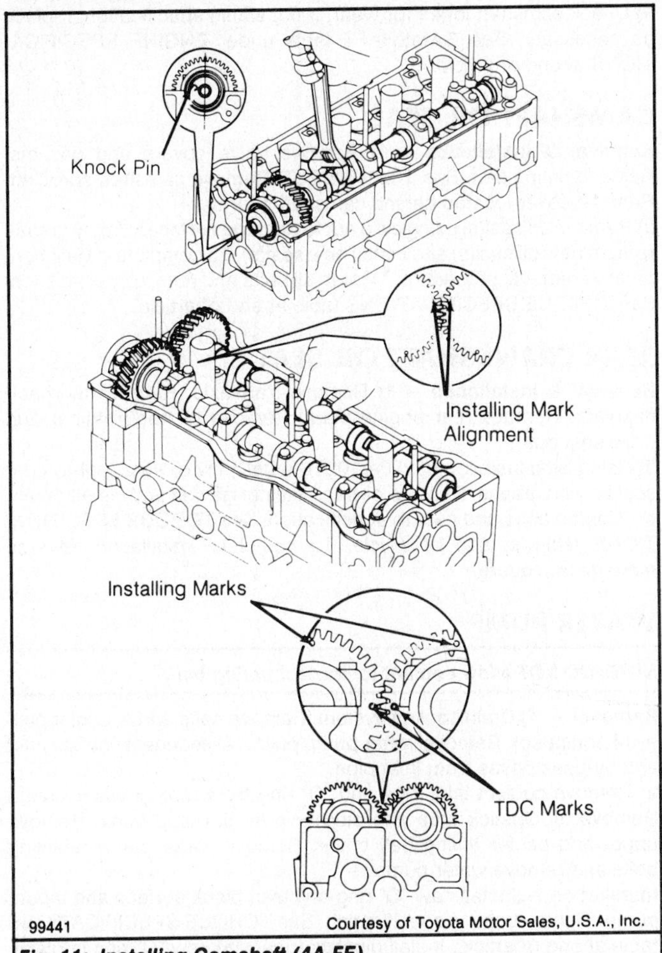


***Fig. 11: Installing Camshaft (4A-FE)***

**4)** Remove (previously installed) bolt in sub-gear. Install No. 1 bearing cap on intake camshaft. If No. 1 bearing cap does not fit properly, push camshaft gear backwards by prying apart cylinder head and camshaft gear. Evenly, a little at a time, tighten No. 1 cap to specification.

**5)** Rotate exhaust camshaft from TDC to TDC and ensure both camshaft gear marks are aligned. *See Fig. 11*. To complete installation, reverse removal procedure. Ensure timing marks are aligned properly. See TIMING BELT.

## FRONT COVER OIL SEAL

**Removal & Installation - 1)** If oil pump is removed from cylinder block, pry out oil seal. Using Seal Installer (09309-37010), install oil seal until oil seal surface is flush with oil pump case edge. Apply multipurpose grease to oil seal lip.

**2)** If oil pump is installed to cylinder block, cut off oil seal lip. Pry out oil seal. Use care not to damage crankshaft surface. Apply multipurpose grease to new oil seal lip. Using Seal Installer (09309-37010), install oil seal until oil seal surface is flush with oil pump case edge.

## TIMING BELT

**Removal (4A-GE Engine) - 1)** Remove right front tire assembly and engine under cover (splash) shields. Disconnect throttle and cruise control cable (if equipped). Remove cruise control actuator (if equipped).

**2)** On Corolla models, drain coolant. Remove water outlet hose. Remove windshield washer tank.

**3)** On all models, remove accessory belt(s) and water pump pulley. Remove spark plugs and oil filler cap. Set No. 1 cylinder at TDC on compression stroke. Check position of camshaft. *See Fig. 12*.

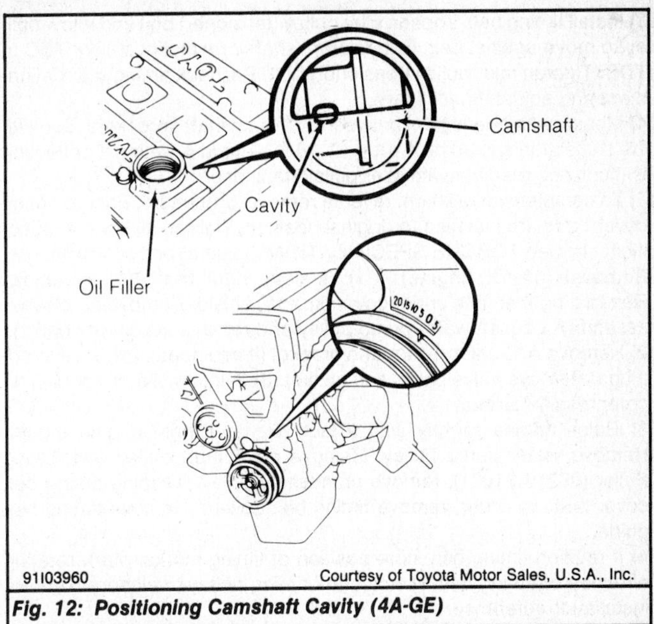


***Fig. 12: Positioning Camshaft Cavity (4A-GE)***

**4)** Slightly raise engine with a jack. Remove right engine mount. Remove crankshaft pulley bolt. Using Puller (09213-31021), remove crankshaft pulley.

**5)** Keeping bolts in order, remove timing covers. Remove timing belt guide. If reusing timing belt, note position of timing marks. Mark rotating direction of timing belt. Match mark timing belt with all sprockets for installation reference.

**6)** Loosen idler pulley (tensioner) bolt and push idler pulley to the left as far as it will go and temporarily tighten bolt. Remove timing belt.

**Inspection (4A-GE) - 1)** Check timing belt teeth for cracks or damage. If tooth damage is found, ensure camshaft and water pump are okay. If wear or cracks on flat side of belt face are found, check for nicks on idler pulleys.

**2)** If wear or damage to only one side of belt is found, check belt guide and alignment of each pulley and sprocket.

**3)** If noticeable wear is found on belt teeth, check timing cover gasket for damage or improper installation. Ensure no foreign material is on sprocket teeth.

**4)** Check idler pulley tension spring free length. Spring free length should be 1.713" (43.5 mm). If spring free length is not within specification, replace spring.

**Installation (4A-GE) - 1)** Ensure No. 1 cylinder is at TDC on compression stroke. If timing belt was not previously removed, loosen idler pulley (tensioner) bolt and push idler pulley to the left as far as it will go and temporarily tighten bolt.

**2)** If reusing old timing belt, align marks made during removal. If installing new belt, align camshaft and crankshaft sprocket timing marks. *See Fig. 13*.

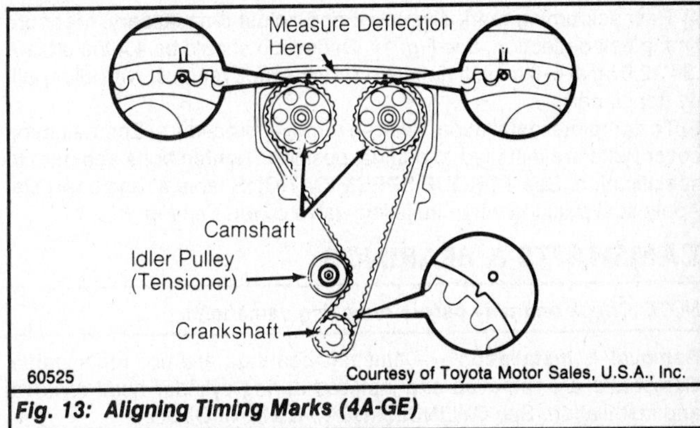


***Fig. 13: Aligning Timing Marks (4A-GE)***

# 1991 ENGINES
# 1.6L 16-Valve 4-Cylinder (Cont.)

**3)** Install timing belt. Loosen idler pulley (tensioner) bolt and allow pulley to move against belt. Rotate crankshaft 2 revolutions from TDC to TDC. Tighten idler pulley (tensioner) bolt. Recheck timing mark alignment and adjust if necessary.
**4)** Measure belt deflection between both camshaft sprockets. *See Fig. 13.* Deflection should be 4.4 lbs. at .16" (2.0 kg at 4.1 mm). If deflection is incorrect, readjust with idler pulley (tensioner).
**5)** To complete installation, reverse removal procedure. Ensure timing cover bolts are installed to original position. Tighten all bolts to specification. See TORQUE SPECIFICATIONS table at end of article.
**Removal (4A-FE Engine) - 1)** Remove right front tire assembly. Remove right engine under cover (splash) shield. Remove air cleaner assembly. Loosen water pump pulley and remove accessory belt(s).
**2)** Remove A/C compressor and bracket (if equipped). Remove spark plugs. Remove valve cover and gasket. Set No. 1 cylinder to TDC on compression stroke.
**3)** Raise engine slightly with a jack. Remove right engine mount. Remove water pump pulley. Remove crankshaft pulley bolt. Using Puller (09213-31021), remove crankshaft pulley. Keeping timing belt cover bolts in order, remove timing belt covers. Remove timing belt guide.
**4)** If reusing timing belt, note position of timing marks. Mark rotating direction of timing belt. Match mark timing belt with all sprockets for installation reference.
**5)** Loosen idler pulley (tensioner) bolt and push idler pulley to the left as far as it will go and temporarily tighten bolt. Remove timing belt.
**Inspection -** See INSPECTION (4A-FE).
**Installation (4A-FE) - 1)** Ensure No. 1 cylinder is at TDC on compression stroke. If timing belt was not previously removed, loosen idler pulley (tensioner) bolt and push idler pulley to the left as far as it will go and temporarily tighten bolt.
**2)** If reusing old timing belt, align marks made during removal. If installing new belt, align camshaft sprocket timing mark with camshaft bearing cap mark through small hole. *See Fig. 14.* Install timing belt.
**3)** Loosen idler pulley (tensioner) bolt and allow pulley to move against belt. Rotate crankshaft 2 revolutions from TDC to TDC. Tighten idler pulley (tensioner) bolt.

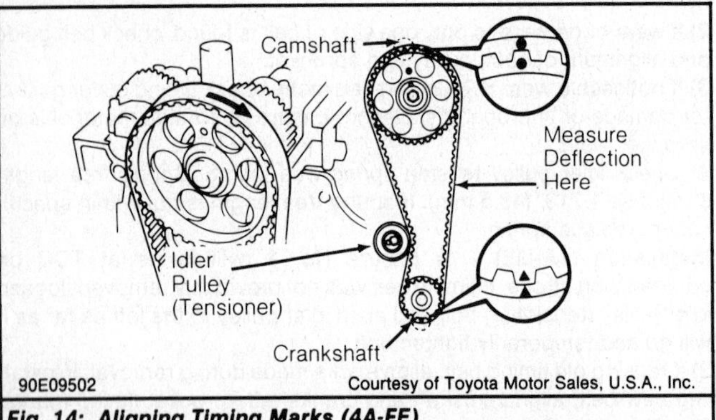


*Fig. 14: Aligning Timing Marks (4A-FE)*

**4)** Recheck timing mark alignment and adjust if necessary. Measure timing belt deflection. *See Fig. 14.* Deflection should be 4.4 lbs. at .20-.24" (2.0 kg at 5-6 mm). If deflection is incorrect, readjust with idler pulley (tensioner).
**5)** To complete installation, reverse removal procedure. Ensure timing cover bolts are installed to original position. Tighten bolts and nuts to specification. See TORQUE SPECIFICATIONS table at end of article. Apply seal packing when installing valve cover. *See Fig. 8.*

## CAMSHAFTS & BEARINGS

***NOTE: Check end play before removing camshafts.***

**Removal & Installation -** Camshaft bearings are not replaceable. Camshafts are removed and installed during cylinder head removal and installation. See CYLINDER HEAD & MANIFOLDS.
**Inspection - 1)** Measure camshaft oil clearance. If oil clearance is not within specification, replace camshaft(s) and/or cylinder head.
**2)** On 4A-FE engines, measure camshaft gear backlash without subgear installed. If greater than specification, replace camshafts.
**3)** Check camshaft lobes for wear. If not within specification, replace as necessary. See CAMSHAFT table under ENGINE SPECIFICATIONS at end of article.

## CAMSHAFT OIL SEAL

**Removal & Installation - 1)** Remove valve covers and gaskets. Remove timing belt. See TIMING BELT. Remove camshaft sprocket. Remove cover located behind camshaft gear(s).
**2)** Remove oil seal(s) using care not to damage surfaces. Apply grease to lip of new oil seal(s) and install new seal(s). To complete installation, reverse removal procedure. Tighten all bolts and nuts to specification. See TORQUE SPECIFICATIONS table at end of article.

## REAR CRANKSHAFT OIL SEAL

**Removal & Installation - 1)** Remove transaxle. Remove flywheel/flexplate. Remove rear engine plate. Remove oil seal retainer and drive seal out.
**2)** Using Seal Installer (09223-41020), install new oil seal. Lightly coat seal lip with grease. Replace oil seal retainer gasket and install retainer. Tighten bolts and nuts to specification. See TORQUE SPECIFICATIONS table at end of article. To complete installation, reverse removal procedure.

## WATER PUMP

***NOTE: DO NOT allow coolant to contact timing belt.***

**Removal - 1)** Drain cooling system. Remove belts and A/C idler pulley (if equipped). Remove water pump pulley. Disconnect coolant inlet and by-pass hoses from inlet pipe.
**2)** Remove coolant inlet pipe and "O" ring from rear of water pump. Remove oil dipstick tube and plug hole in oil pump body. Remove upper and center timing belt cover. Remove water pump retaining bolts and remove water pump.
**Installation -** Install new "O" ring on clean block surface and mount pump. Tighten bolts to specification. See TORQUE SPECIFICATIONS table at end of article. Install dipstick tube with new "O" ring in place. To complete installation, reverse removal procedure. Adjust drive belt tension, fill cooling system and check for leaks.

# OVERHAUL

## CYLINDER HEAD

**Cylinder Head -** Check for cracks, damage and coolant leakage. Remove scale, sealing compound and carbon deposits. Clean oil passages and blow compressed air through passages to ensure they are not clogged. Check EGR passage for clogging. Inspect cylinder head for warpage at deck surface. Resurface cylinder head if warpage exceeds specification. See CYLINDER HEAD table under ENGINE SPECIFICATIONS at end of article.
**Valve Springs -** Inspect valve spring free length, tension and installed height. Using a square, check squareness of each spring. Replace if not within specification. See VALVES & VALVE SPRINGS table under ENGINE SPECIFICATIONS at end of article. Installed spring height is measured from spring seat and valve retainer. Install all valve springs with painted area toward rocker arm.
**Valve Guides -** With valves removed, measure I.D. of valve guide and O.D. of valve stem. Subtract valve stem O.D. from valve guide I.D. to obtain clearance. Replace valve and/or guide if not within specification. See CYLINDER HEAD table under ENGINE SPECIFICATIONS at end of article.
**Valve Guide Replacement - 1)** On 4A-GE engines, wrap tape around an old defective valve and insert into valve guide. *See Fig. 15.* Break valve guide at snap ring. To prevent damage to lifter bore, place a shop rag in bore.

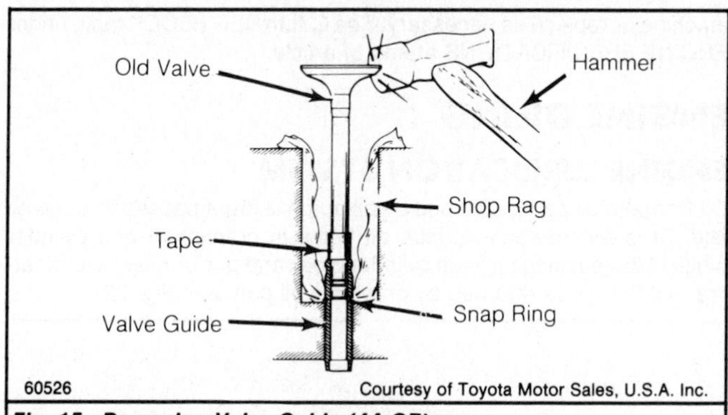


***Fig. 15: Removing Valve Guide (4A-GE)***

**2)** On all engines, gradually heat cylinder head to 176-212°F (80-100°C). Using Valve Guide Remover/Installer (09201-70010), remove valve guide(s).

**3)** To install valve guide(s), allow cylinder head to cool down. Measure valve guide bore of cylinder head. If bore exceeds .4341" (11.026 mm), machine bore to .4350-.4361" (11.049-11.077 mm) for oversize valve guide. If bore is less, use standard size guide.

**4)** Heat cylinder head to 176-212°F (80-100°C). Using remover/installer, install valve guide(s).

**5)** On 4A-GE engines, drive in guide until snap ring contact with cylinder head. On 4A-FE engines, drive guide in until protrusion height of .500-.516" (12.70-13.11 mm) is achieved. On all engines, ream valve guide to obtain proper clearance for valve being installed.

**Valve Seats -** No service procedure is given by manufacturer. Valve seats must be ground if valve guides are replaced.

**Valves -** Inspect each valve for ware, damage and distortion of head and stem. If stem end is pitted or worn, resurface as necessary. This correction must be limited to a minimum. Resurface the valve face. If valve margin has decreased to less than the service limit, replace valve. See VALVES & VALVE SPRINGS table under ENGINE SPECIFICATIONS at end of article.

## VALVE TRAIN

**Valve Lifters -** Measure O.D. of lifter and I.D. of lifter bore. Subtract lifter O.D. from bore I.D. to obtain oil clearance. Replace lifter and/or cylinder head if not within specification. See VALVE LIFTERS table under ENGINE SPECIFICATIONS at end of article.

## CYLINDER BLOCK ASSEMBLY

**Piston & Rod Assembly -** Ensure rod and rod cap are with matching cylinder number. Ensure piston and rod are installed in cylinder from which they were removed. Check piston and rod and replace if not within specification. See CONNECTING RODS and PISTONS, PINS & RINGS table under ENGINE SPECIFICATIONS at end of article.

**Piston & Pin Replacement - 1)** Piston and pin are a matched set and must be kept together. The 4A-FE engine uses a press fit pin. The 4A-GE engine uses snap rings on each end of pin.

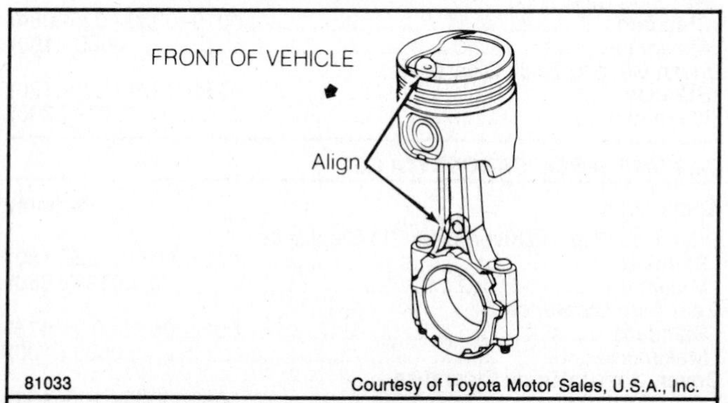


***Fig. 16: Aligning Piston & Connecting Rod***

**2)** On 4A-GE engines, gradually heat piston assembly to 158-176°F (70-80°C) to remove and install pin.

**3)** On 4A-FE and 4A-GE engines, use a press and pin kit to remove and install pin. Ensure piston is reassembled properly on rod. *See Fig. 16.*

***NOTE: Three standard piston sizes and cylinder bore diameters are used. Pistons and cylinder bores are marked No. 1, No. 2 or No. 3. Mark is stamped on top of piston and cylinder block. See Figs. 17 and 18.***

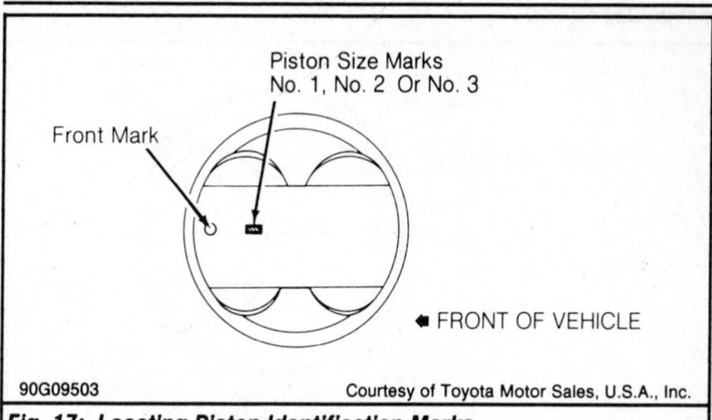


***Fig. 17: Locating Piston Identification Marks***

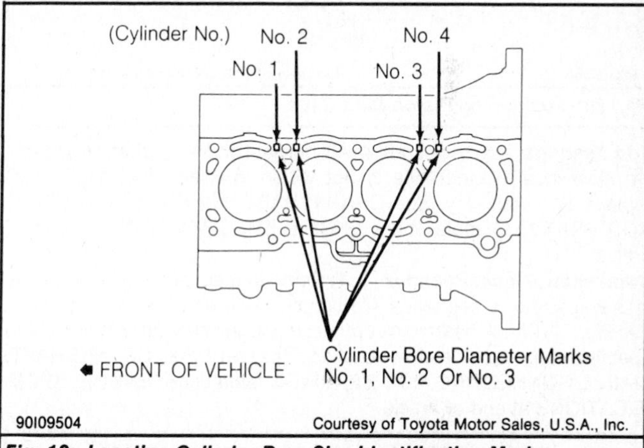


***Fig. 18: Locating Cylinder Bore Size Identification Marks***

**Fitting Pistons & Rings - 1)** Remove carbon from top of piston. Clean piston and ring grooves. Measure piston clearance. Determine piston size being used. Measure piston diameter at right angles to piston pin center line.

**2)** On 4A-FE, measure 1.58" (38.5 mm) from piston skirt bottom edge.

**3)** On 4A-GE, measure 1.65" (42.0 mm) from piston skirt bottom edge.

**4)** Measure cylinder bore diameter in thrust direction. *See Fig. 19.* Subtract piston diameter measurement from cylinder bore diameter measurement. Piston clearance should be within specification.

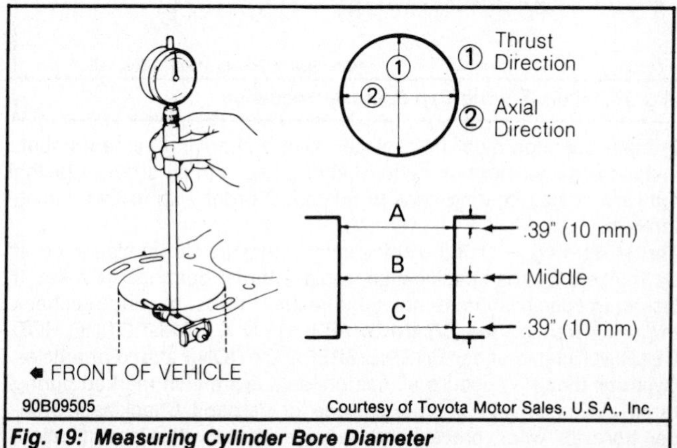


***Fig. 19: Measuring Cylinder Bore Diameter***

# 1991 ENGINES
# 1.6L 16-Valve 4-Cylinder (Cont.)

**5)** If piston clearance is greater than maximum, replace all 4 pistons and/or rebore all 4 cylinders. See PISTONS, PINS & RINGS table under ENGINE SPECIFICATIONS at end of article.
**6)** Check end gap of ring in cylinder to which it will be installed. If end gap is greater than specification, try new set of rings. If end gap is still greater than specification, rebore cylinder and use over size piston rings. See PISTONS, PINS & RINGS table under ENGINE SPECIFICATIONS at end of article.
**7)** On all engines, properly position rings on piston before installing piston. *See Fig. 20*.

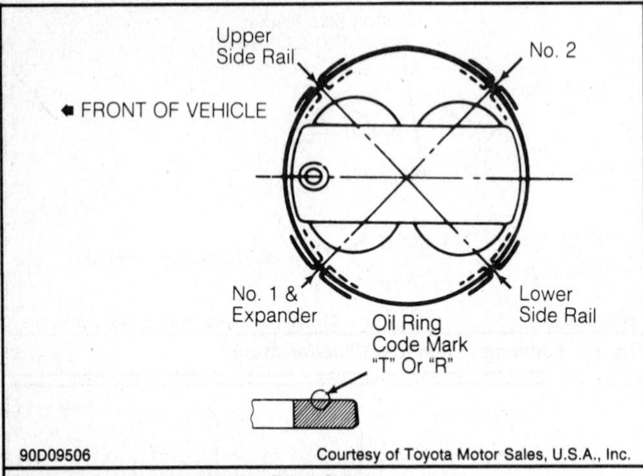


***Fig. 20: Positioning Piston Ring Gaps***

**Rod Bearings** – Check crankshaft journal condition. Check rod bearing clearance. If clearance is not within specification, machine or replace as necessary. See CRANKSHAFT, MAIN & CONNECTING ROD BEARINGS table under ENGINE SPECIFICATIONS at end of article.
**Crankshaft & Main Bearings** – **1)** Remove main bearing caps evenly in 3 steps and in sequence. To tighten, reverse removal sequence. *See Fig. 21*. Check bearing clearance. If bearing clearance is not within specification, machine or replace as necessary. See CRANKSHAFT, MAIN & CONNECTING ROD BEARINGS table under ENGINE SPECIFICATIONS at end of article.

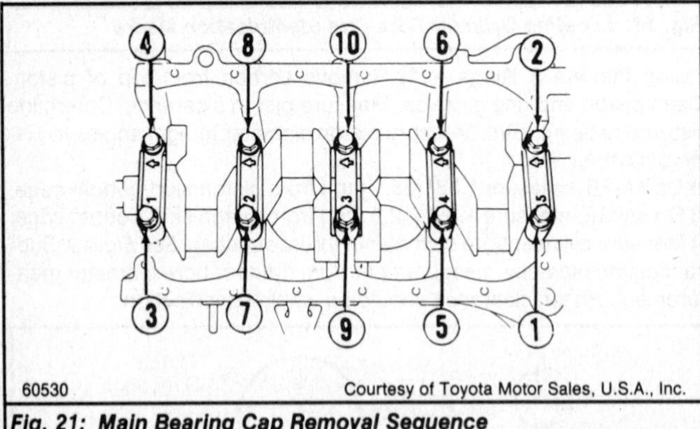


***Fig. 21: Main Bearing Cap Removal Sequence***

**2)** Main bearings must be replaced with one having same number. Install thrust washers on center bearing cap with oil grooves facing outward. Install bearing caps in numerical order with arrows facing forward.
**Thrust Bearing** – Using dial indicator, measure thrust clearance. If clearance exceeds specification, replace thrust bearings as a set. If less than specification, remove and reinstall thrust bearing. Recheck thrust clearance. See CRANKSHAFT, MAIN & CONNECTING ROD BEARINGS table under ENGINE SPECIFICATIONS at end of article.
**Cylinder Block** – Ensure all components are match marked during removal. Check cylinder block surface for warpage. Check each cylinder bore for wear, cracks and damage. If not within specification, machine or replace as necessary. See CYLINDER BLOCK table under ENGINE SPECIFICATIONS at end of article.

## ENGINE OILING

### ENGINE LUBRICATION SYSTEM

Oil from the oil pan is pumped by oil pump. After it passes through oil filter, it is fed through various oil holes in crankshaft and cylinder block. After passing through cylinder block and performing its lubricating function, oil is returned by gravity to oil pan. *See Fig. 22*.

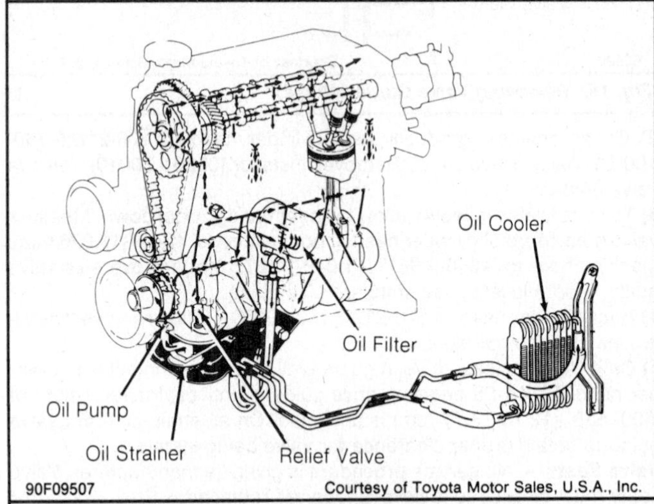


***Fig. 22: Cross-Sectional View of Engine Oil Circuit (4A-FE Shown; 4A-GE Similar)***

**Crankcase Capacity** – Crankcase oil capacity is 3.3 qts. (3.2L) with filter for Corolla 4A-FE, 3.9 qts. (3.7L) with filter for Corolla 4A-GE or 3.3 qts. (3.2L) with filter for Celica 4A-FE.
**Oil Pressure** – Normal oil pressure at idle is greater than 4.3 psi (.3 kg/cm²) and at 3000 RPM oil pressure should be 36-71 psi (2.5-5.0 kg/cm²).

## OIL PUMP

**Removal & Installation** – Remove oil pan and oil pump pick-up tube. Remove crankshaft sprocket. Remove dipstick tube from oil pump body. Remove oil pump retaining bolts. Using a plastic hammer tap oil pump assembly off block. To install, reverse removal procedure.
**Inspection** – If oil pump is not within specification, replace gear set and/or body. See appropriate OIL PUMP SPECIFICATIONS table.

***OIL PUMP SPECIFICATIONS (4A-FE)***

| Application | In. (mm) |
|---|---|
| Drive Gear Tip-to-Driven Gear Tip Clearance | |
| Standard | .0010-.0033 (.025-.084) |
| Maximum | .0138 (.350) |
| Gear Side Clearance | |
| Standard | .0010-.0033 (.025-.084) |
| Maximum | .0039 (.100) |
| Driven Gear-to-Body Clearance | |
| Standard | .0031-.0071 (.079-.180) |
| Maximum | .0079 (.200) |

***OIL PUMP SPECIFICATIONS (4A-GE)***

| Application | In. (mm) |
|---|---|
| Drive Gear Tip-to-Driven Gear Tip Clearance | |
| Standard | .0023-.0071 (.058-.180) |
| Maximum | .0138 (.350) |
| Gear Side Clearance | |
| Standard | .0010-.0030 (.025-.076) |
| Maximum | .0039 (.100) |
| Driven Gear-to-Body Clearance | |
| Standard | .0039-.0075 (.100-.191) |
| Maximum | .0079 (.200) |

# 1991 ENGINES
# 1.6L 16-Valve 4-Cylinder (Cont.)

## TORQUE SPECIFICATIONS

### TORQUE SPECIFICATIONS

| Application | Ft. Lbs. (N.m) |
|---|---|
| Camshaft Sprocket Bolt | |
| 4A-FE & 4A-GE | 43 (58) |
| Connecting Rod Nut | |
| 4A-FE | 36 (49) |
| 4A-GE | |
| Step 1 | 29 (39) |
| Step 2 | 90 Degrees Additional |
| Crankshaft Pulley Bolt | 87 (118) |
| Cylinder Head Bolt | |
| Celica 4A-FE | 47 (64) |
| Corolla 4A-FE | 44 (60) |
| Corolla 4A-GE [1] | |
| Step 1 | 22 (30) |
| Step 2 | 90 Degrees Additional |
| Step 3 | 90 Degrees Additional |
| Delivery Pipe-to-Cylinder Head | 13 (18) |
| Exhaust Manifold Bolt | 18 (24) |
| Flywheel Bolt | [2] 58 (79) |
| Flexplate | 47 (64) |
| Front Engine Mount | |
| Through Bolt | 58 (79) |
| Intake Manifold Bolt | |
| 4A-FE | 14 (19) |
| 4A-GE | 16 (22) |
| Main Bearing Cap Bolt [3] | 44 (60) |
| Oil Pump Body Mount Bolt | 13-18 (18-24) |
| Rear Engine Mount | |
| 10-mm Bolt Head | 38 (51) |
| 12-mm Bolt Head | 58 (79) |
| Right Engine Mount | |
| Nut | 38 (51) |
| Through Bolt | 64 (87) |
| Spark Plug | 13 (18) |
| Timing Belt Idler Pulley Bolt | 27 (37) |
| Timing Belt Tensioner Bolt | 27 (37) |
| Torque Converter Bolt | 20 (27) |
| Transaxle-to-Engine | |
| 10-mm Bolts | 34 (46) |
| 12-mm Bolts | 47 (64) |
| | **INCH Lbs. (N.m)** |
| Camshaft Cap Bolt [4] | 108 (12) |
| Oil Pan Bolt & Nut | 43 (5) |
| Oil Pump Cover Bolt | 72-108 (8-12) |
| Oil Pump Pick-Up Tube | 82 (9) |
| Valve Cover Bolts | |
| 4A-FE | 69 (7.8) |
| 4A-GE | 108 (12) |

[1] – Tighten in sequence. *See Fig. 7*.
[2] – Tighten evenly in a diagonal pattern.
[3] – Tighten evenly in sequence. *See Fig. 21*.
[4] – Tighten evenly in sequence. *See Fig. 9 or 10*.

## ENGINE SPECIFICATIONS

### GENERAL SPECIFICATIONS

| Application | Specification |
|---|---|
| 1.6L | |
| Displacement | 96.8 Cu. In. (1.6L) |
| Bore | 3.19" (81 mm) |
| Stroke | 3.03" (77 mm) |
| Compression Ratio | |
| 4A-FE | 9.5:1 |
| 4A-GE | 10.3:1 |
| Fuel System | PFI |
| Horsepower @ RPM | |
| 4A-FE | 102 @ 5800 |
| 4A-GE | 130 @ 6800 |
| Torque Ft. Lbs. @ RPM | |
| 4A-FE | 101 @ 4800 |
| 4A-GE | 105 @ 6000 |

### CRANKSHAFT, MAIN & CONNECTING ROD BEARINGS

| Application | In. (mm) |
|---|---|
| 1.6L | |
| Crankshaft | |
| End Play | [1] .0008-.00087 (.020-.0220) |
| Runout | .0024 (.060) |
| Main Bearings | |
| Journal Diameter | 1.8891-1.8898 (47.982-48.000) |
| Journal Out-Of-Round & Taper | .0008 (.020) |
| Oil Clearance | [2] .0006-.0013 (.015-.033) |
| Connecting Rod Bearings | |
| Journal Diameter | |
| 4A-FE | 1.5742-1.5748 (39.985-40.000) |
| 4A-GE | 1.6529-1.6142 (41.985-41.000) |
| Journal Out-Of-Round | .0008 (.020) |
| Journal Taper | .0008 (.020) |
| Oil Clearance | [3] .0008-.0020 (.020-.051) |

[1] – Standard end play is given. Maximum end play is .012" (.30 mm).
[2] – Standard main bearing oil clearance is given. Maximum oil clearance is .0039" (.100 mm).
[3] – Standard connecting rod clearance is given. Maximum connecting rod oil clearance is .0031" (.080 mm).

### CONNECTING RODS

| Application | In. (mm) |
|---|---|
| 1.6L | |
| Bore Diameter | |
| Pin Bore | |
| 4A-FE | [1] |
| 4A-GE | .7878-.7883 (20.010-20.022) |
| Maximum Bend | |
| 4A-FE | .0020 (.050) |
| 4A-GE | .0012 (.030) |
| Maximum Twist | .0020 (.050) |
| Side Play | [2] .0059-.0098 (.150-.250) |

[1] – Information not available from manufacturer.
[2] – Standard side play is given. Maximum side play is .0118" (.300 mm).

# 1991 ENGINES
# 1.6L 16-Valve 4-Cylinder (Cont.)

## PISTONS, PINS & RINGS

| Application | In. (mm) |
|---|---|
| 1.6L | |
| Pistons | |
| Clearance | |
| 4A-FE | .0024-.0031 (.060-.080) |
| 4A-GE | .0039-.0047 (.100-.120) |
| Diameter [1] | |
| 4A-FE | |
| Piston No. 1 | 3.1862-3.1866 (80.930-80.940) |
| Piston No. 2 | 3.1866-3.1870 (80.940-80.950) |
| Piston No. 3 | 3.1870-3.1874 (80.950-80.960) |
| 4A-GE | |
| Piston No. 1 | 3.1846-3.1850 (80.890-80.900) |
| Piston No. 2 | 3.1850-3.1854 (80.900-80.910) |
| Piston No. 3 | 3.1854-3.1858 (80.910-80.920) |
| Pins | |
| Diameter | |
| 4A-GE | .7876-.7880 (20.004-20.016) |
| Piston Fit | |
| 4A-FE | [2] |
| 4A-GE | [3] |
| Rings | |
| No. 1 | |
| End Gap | |
| 4A-FE | .0098-.0177 (.250-.450) |
| 4A-GE | .0098-.0185 (.250-.470) |
| Side Clearance | |
| 4A-FE | .0016-.0032 (.040-.081) |
| 4A-GE | .0012-.0031 (.030-.080) |
| No. 2 | |
| End Gap | |
| 4A-FE | .0059-.0157 (.150-.400) |
| 4A-GE | .0079-.0165 (.200-.420) |
| Side Clearance | |
| 4A-FE | .0012-.0028 (.030-.070) |
| 4A-GE | .0012-.0028 (.030-.070) |
| No. 3 (Oil) | |
| End Gap | |
| 4A-FE | .0039-.0276 (.100-.700) |
| 4A-GE | .0059-.0205 (.150-.520) |

[1] – Three piston sizes are used. Pistons are marked No. 1, No. 2, or No. 3. *See Fig. 17.*
[2] – Piston pin installation temperature is 68°F (20°C).
[3] – Piston pin installation temperature is 176°F (80°C).

## CYLINDER BLOCK

| Application | In. (mm) |
|---|---|
| 1.6L | |
| Cylinder Bore | |
| Standard Diameter [1] | |
| Cylinder Diameter No. 1. | 3.1890-3.1894 (81.000-81.010) |
| Cylinder Diameter No. 2. | 3.1894-3.1898 (81.010-81.020) |
| Cylinder Diameter No. 3. | 3.1898-3.1902 (81.020-81.030) |
| Maximum Out-Of-Round & Taper | .0008 (.020) |
| Maximum Deck Warpage | .0020 (.050) |

[1] – Three cylinder bore diameters are used. Cylinders are marked No. 1, No. 2, or No. 3. *See Fig. 18.*

## VALVES & VALVE SPRINGS

| Application | Specification |
|---|---|
| 1.6L | |
| Intake Valves | |
| Face Angle | 44.5° |
| Minimum Margin | [1] .031-.047" (.80-1.20 mm) |
| Minimum Refinish Length | |
| 4A-FE | 3.5807" (90.950 mm) |
| 4A-GE | 3.9016" (99.100 mm) |
| Stem Diameter | .2350-.2356" (5.970-5.985 mm) |
| Exhaust Valves | |
| Face Angle | 44.5° |
| Minimum Margin | [1] .031-.047" (.80-1.20 mm) |
| Minimum Refinish Length | |
| 4A-FE | 3.5984" (91.400 mm) |
| 4A-GE | 3.9075" (99.250 mm) |
| Stem Diameter | .2348-.2354" (5.965-5.980 mm) |
| Valve Springs | |
| Free Length | |
| 4A-FE | 1.724" (43.80 mm) |
| 4A-GE | 1.6177" (41.090 mm) |
| Installed Height | 1.366" (34.70 mm) |
| Out-Of-Square | |
| 4A-FE | .079" (2.00 mm) |
| 4A-GE | .071" (1.80 mm) |
| | **Lbs. @ In. (kg @ mm)** |
| Pressure | |
| Valve Closed | |
| 4A-FE | 32.2-34.8 @ 1.366 (14.6-15.8 @ 34.7 ) |
| 4A-GE | 35.9 @ 1.366 (16.3 @ 34.7) |

[1] – Standard margin is given. Minimum margin is .020" (.50 mm).

## CYLINDER HEAD

| Application | Specification |
|---|---|
| 1.6L | |
| Maximum Warpage | .0020" (.050 mm) |
| Valve Seats | |
| Intake Valve | |
| Seat Angle | 45° |
| Seat Width | |
| 4A-FE | .047-.063" (1.20-1.60 mm) |
| 4A-GE | .039-.055" (1.00-1.40 mm) |
| Exhaust Valve | |
| Seat Angle | 45° |
| Seat Width | |
| 4A-FE | .047-.063" (1.20-1.60 mm) |
| 4A-GE | .039-.055" (1.00-1.40 mm) |
| Valve Guides | |
| Intake Valve | |
| Valve Guide I.D. | |
| 4A-FE & 4A-GE | .2366-.2374" (6.010-6.030 mm) |
| Valve Guide O.D. | |
| 4A-FE | .4350-.4354" (11.048-11.059 mm) |
| 4A-GE | .4344-.4348" (11.033-11.044 mm) |
| Valve Stem-To-Guide | |
| Oil Clearance | .0010-.0024" (.025-.060 mm) |
| Exhaust Valve | |
| Valve Guide I.D. | |
| 4A-FE & 4A-GE | .2366-.2374" (6.010-6.030 mm) |
| Valve Guide O.D. | |
| 4A-FE | .4350-.4354" (11.048-11.059 mm) |
| 4A-GE | .4344-.4348" (11.033-11.044 mm) |
| Valve Stem-To-Guide | |
| Oil Clearance | .0012-.0026" (.030-.065 mm) |

# 1991 ENGINES
# 1.6L 16-Valve 4-Cylinder (Cont.)

## CAMSHAFT

| Application | In. (mm) |
|---|---|
| 1.6L | |
| End Play | |
| 4A-FE | |
| Intake | .0012-.0033 (.030-.085) |
| Exhaust | .0014-.0035 (.035-.090) |
| 4A-GE | .0008-.0087 (.020-.022) |
| Journal Diameter | |
| 4A-FE | |
| Intake | .9035-.9041 (22.949-22.965) |
| Exhaust | .9822-.9829 (24.949-24.965) |
| 4A-GE | 1.0610-1.0616 (26.949-26.965) |
| Journal Runout | .0016 (.040) |
| Lobe Height | |
| 4A-FE | |
| Intake | 1.3862-1.3902 (35.210-35.310) |
| Exhaust | 1.3744-1.3783 (34.910-35.010) |
| 4A-GE | 1.3944-1.3980 (35.419-35.510) |
| Oil Clearance | .0014-.0028 (.035-.072) |

## VALVE LIFTERS

| Application | In. (mm) |
|---|---|
| 1.6L | |
| Bore Diameter | 1.1026-1.1034 (28.005-28.026) |
| Lifter Diameter | 1.1014-1.1018 (27.975-27.985) |
| Oil Clearance | .0008-.0020 (.020-.051) |

# 1991 ENGINES
# 2.0L 4-Cylinder

## Celica All-Trac, MR2

***NOTE:* *For Camry (2.0L) repair procedures, see 2.0L & 2.2L 4-CYLINDER article in ENGINES.***

***NOTE:* *For repair procedures not covered in this article, see ENGINE OVERHAUL PROCEDURES article in GENERAL INFORMATION.***

***CAUTION:* *Before performing service procedures on vehicle, disconnect negative battery cable. After disconnecting negative battery cable, wait at least 20 seconds before proceeding to avoid accidental air bag deployment.***

## ENGINE IDENTIFICATION

Engine serial number is stamped on flywheel end of cylinder block, below cylinder head surface.

***ENGINE IDENTIFICATION CODE***

| Engine | Code |
|---|---|
| 2.0L 4-Cylinder | 3S-GTE |

## ADJUSTMENTS

### VALVE CLEARANCE ADJUSTMENT

***NOTE:* *Adjust valve clearance with engine cold.***

**1)** Disconnect negative battery cable. On MR2, remove No. 1 air intake connector from throttle body to intercooler. *See Fig. 23.*
**2)** On Celica All-Trac, remove intercooler. See INTERCOOLER under REMOVAL & INSTALLATION.
**3)** On all models, disconnect spark plug wires from spark plugs. Drain cooling system. Disconnect vacuum hoses, and remove EGR vacuum modulator assembly. Remove EGR valve and pipe. Remove intake air connector and brace from throttle body. *See Fig. 12.*
**4)** Disconnect electrical connections, control cables, vacuum hoses and coolant hoses from throttle body. Remove throttle body. Remove retaining bolts, valve cover and gaskets.
**5)** Rotate crankshaft so No. 1 cylinder is at TDC of compression stroke. Ensure timing mark on crankshaft pulley aligns with "0" mark on timing belt cover. Ensure valve lifters are loose on No. 1 cylinder and tight on No. 4 cylinder.
**6)** With No. 1 cylinder at TDC, check clearance on specified valves. See VALVE CLEARANCE ADJUSTMENT SEQUENCE table. Using feeler gauge, measure and record clearance between valve lifter and camshaft.

***VALVE CLEARANCE ADJUSTMENT SEQUENCE***

| Cylinder No. At TDC | Adjust Intake Valves | Adjust Exhaust Valves |
|---|---|---|
| 1 | 1 & 2 | 1 & 3 |
| 4 | 3 & 4 | 2 & 4 |

**7)** To check remaining valves, rotate crankshaft 360 degrees (one revolution) until No. 4 cylinder is at TDC of compression stroke. Measure and record valve clearance on specified valves. See VALVE CLEARANCE ADJUSTMENT SEQUENCE table.
**8)** Clearance should be within specification. See VALVE CLEARANCE SPECIFICATIONS table. If valves require adjustment, rotate camshaft so lobe on valve to be adjusted is upward, away from valve lifter.
**9)** Rotate valve lifter so notch on valve lifter is toward spark plug. *See Fig. 1.* Use Valve Clearance Adjuster (SST 09248-55010) to remove adjusting shim. Using SST (A) of valve clearance adjuster, push downward on valve lifter. Place SST (B) between camshaft and valve lifter. Remove SST (A).
**10)** Using small screwdriver and magnet, remove adjusting shim. Measure thickness of adjusting shim removed. Determine correct thickness of replacement adjusting shim to be used. *See Figs. 3 and 4.*

***VALVE CLEARANCE SPECIFICATIONS***

| Application | In. (mm) |
|---|---|
| Exhaust | .008-.012 (.20-.30) |
| Intake | .006-.010 (.15-.25) |

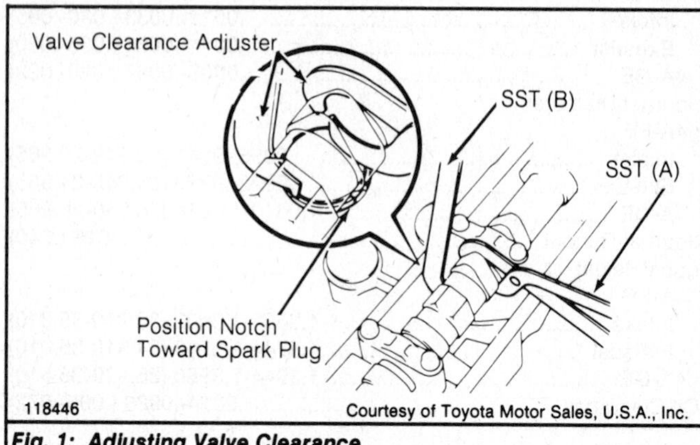


***Fig. 1:* *Adjusting Valve Clearance***

**11)** Install adjusting shim, and recheck valve clearance. Before installing valve cover and gasket, apply sealant at front and rear areas of cylinder head. *See Fig. 2.*
**12)** Install gasket and valve cover. Tighten to bolts specification. See appropriate TORQUE SPECIFICATIONS table at end article.
**13)** To install remaining components, reverse removal procedure. Install throttle body gasket with protruding area toward top of throttle body (opposite coolant line connections). Longer bolts are used in lower throttle body holes. Tighten bolts to specification. See appropriate TORQUE SPECIFICATIONS table at end of article. Fill cooling system.

***CAUTION:* *On MR2, cooling system must be bled to prevent engine damage. See COOLING SYSTEM BLEEDING under REMOVAL & INSTALLATION.***

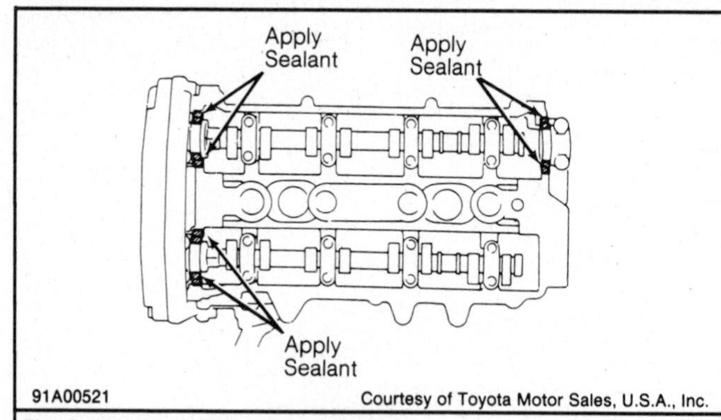


***Fig. 2:* *Applying Valve Cover Sealant***

## REMOVAL & INSTALLATION

***NOTE:* *For installation reference, label all electrical connectors, vacuum hoses and fuel lines before removal. Also place mating marks on engine hood and other major assemblies before removal.***

### FUEL PRESSURE RELEASE

With ignition off, disconnect negative battery cable. Place suitable container under fuel line. Cover fuel line connection with shop towel. Slowly loosen fuel line connection, and release fuel pressure. Once fuel pressure is released, fuel system components can be removed.

# 1991 ENGINES
# 2.0L 4-Cylinder (Cont.)

EXHAUST VALVES

Installed shim thickness (mm)

| Measured clearance (mm) | 2.000 | 2.025 | 2.050 | 2.075 | 2.100 | 2.125 | 2.150 | 2.175 | 2.200 | 2.225 | 2.250 | 2.275 | 2.300 | 2.325 | 2.350 | 2.375 | 2.400 | 2.425 | 2.450 | 2.475 | 2.500 | 2.525 | 2.550 | 2.575 | 2.600 | 2.625 | 2.650 | 2.675 | 2.700 | 2.725 | 2.750 | 2.775 | 2.800 | 2.825 | 2.850 | 2.875 | 2.900 | 2.925 | 2.950 | 2.975 | 3.000 | 3.025 | 3.050 | 3.075 | 3.100 | 3.125 | 3.150 | 3.175 | 3.200 | 3.225 | 3.250 | 3.275 | 3.300 |
|---|---|---|---|---|---|---|---|---|---|---|---|---|---|---|---|---|---|---|---|---|---|---|---|---|---|---|---|---|---|---|---|---|---|---|---|---|---|---|---|---|---|---|---|---|---|---|---|---|---|---|---|---|---|
| 0.000 – 0.025 |  |  |  |  |  |  |  |  | 02 | 02 | 02 | 04 | 04 | 06 | 06 | 08 | 08 | 10 | 10 | 12 | 12 | 14 | 14 | 16 | 16 | 18 | 18 | 20 | 20 | 22 | 22 | 24 | 24 | 26 | 26 | 28 | 28 | 30 | 30 | 32 | 32 | 34 | 34 | 36 | 36 | 38 | 38 | 40 | 40 | 42 | 42 | 44 | 44 |
| 0.026 – 0.050 |  |  |  |  |  |  |  | 02 | 02 | 02 | 04 | 04 | 06 | 06 | 08 | 08 | 10 | 10 | 12 | 12 | 14 | 14 | 16 | 16 | 18 | 18 | 20 | 20 | 22 | 22 | 24 | 24 | 26 | 26 | 28 | 28 | 30 | 30 | 32 | 32 | 34 | 34 | 36 | 36 | 38 | 38 | 40 | 40 | 42 | 42 | 44 | 44 | 46 |
| 0.051 – 0.075 |  |  |  |  |  |  | 02 | 02 | 02 | 04 | 04 | 06 | 06 | 08 | 08 | 10 | 10 | 12 | 12 | 14 | 14 | 16 | 16 | 18 | 18 | 20 | 20 | 22 | 22 | 24 | 24 | 26 | 26 | 28 | 28 | 30 | 30 | 32 | 32 | 34 | 34 | 36 | 36 | 38 | 38 | 40 | 40 | 42 | 42 | 44 | 44 | 46 | 46 |
| 0.076 – 0.100 |  |  |  |  |  | 02 | 02 | 02 | 04 | 04 | 06 | 06 | 08 | 08 | 10 | 10 | 12 | 12 | 14 | 14 | 16 | 16 | 18 | 18 | 20 | 20 | 22 | 22 | 24 | 24 | 26 | 26 | 28 | 28 | 30 | 30 | 32 | 32 | 34 | 34 | 36 | 36 | 38 | 38 | 40 | 40 | 42 | 42 | 44 | 44 | 46 | 46 | 48 |
| 0.101 – 0.125 |  |  |  |  | 02 | 02 | 02 | 04 | 04 | 06 | 06 | 08 | 08 | 10 | 10 | 12 | 12 | 14 | 14 | 16 | 16 | 18 | 18 | 20 | 20 | 22 | 22 | 24 | 24 | 26 | 26 | 28 | 28 | 30 | 30 | 32 | 32 | 34 | 34 | 36 | 36 | 38 | 38 | 40 | 40 | 42 | 42 | 44 | 44 | 46 | 46 | 48 | 48 |
| 0.126 – 0.150 |  |  |  | 02 | 02 | 02 | 04 | 04 | 06 | 06 | 08 | 08 | 10 | 10 | 12 | 12 | 14 | 14 | 16 | 16 | 18 | 18 | 20 | 20 | 22 | 22 | 24 | 24 | 26 | 26 | 28 | 28 | 30 | 30 | 32 | 32 | 34 | 34 | 36 | 36 | 38 | 38 | 40 | 40 | 42 | 42 | 44 | 44 | 46 | 46 | 48 | 48 | 50 |
| 0.151 – 0.175 |  |  | 02 | 02 | 02 | 04 | 04 | 06 | 06 | 08 | 08 | 10 | 10 | 12 | 12 | 14 | 14 | 16 | 16 | 18 | 18 | 20 | 20 | 22 | 22 | 24 | 24 | 26 | 26 | 28 | 28 | 30 | 30 | 32 | 32 | 34 | 34 | 36 | 36 | 38 | 38 | 40 | 40 | 42 | 42 | 44 | 44 | 46 | 46 | 48 | 48 | 50 | 50 |
| 0.176 – 0.199 |  | 02 | 02 | 02 | 04 | 04 | 06 | 06 | 08 | 08 | 10 | 10 | 12 | 12 | 14 | 14 | 16 | 16 | 18 | 18 | 20 | 20 | 22 | 22 | 24 | 24 | 26 | 26 | 28 | 28 | 30 | 30 | 32 | 32 | 34 | 34 | 36 | 36 | 38 | 38 | 40 | 40 | 42 | 42 | 44 | 44 | 46 | 46 | 48 | 48 | 50 | 50 | 52 |
| 0.200 – 0.300 |  |  |  |  |  |  |  |  |  |  |  |  |  |  |  |  |  |  |  |  |  |  |  |  |  |  |  |  |  |  |  |  |  |  |  |  |  |  |  |  |  |  |  |  |  |  |  |  |  |  |  |  |  |
| 0.301 – 0.325 | 04 | 06 | 06 | 08 | 08 | 10 | 10 | 12 | 12 | 14 | 14 | 16 | 16 | 18 | 18 | 20 | 20 | 22 | 22 | 24 | 24 | 26 | 26 | 28 | 28 | 30 | 30 | 32 | 32 | 34 | 34 | 36 | 36 | 38 | 38 | 40 | 40 | 42 | 42 | 44 | 44 | 46 | 46 | 48 | 48 | 50 | 50 | 52 | 52 | 54 | 54 | 54 |  |
| 0.326 – 0.350 | 06 | 06 | 08 | 08 | 10 | 10 | 12 | 12 | 14 | 14 | 16 | 16 | 18 | 18 | 20 | 20 | 22 | 22 | 24 | 24 | 26 | 26 | 28 | 28 | 30 | 30 | 32 | 32 | 34 | 34 | 36 | 36 | 38 | 38 | 40 | 40 | 42 | 42 | 44 | 44 | 46 | 46 | 48 | 48 | 50 | 50 | 52 | 52 | 54 | 54 | 54 |  |  |
| 0.351 – 0.375 | 06 | 08 | 08 | 10 | 10 | 12 | 12 | 14 | 14 | 16 | 16 | 18 | 18 | 20 | 20 | 22 | 22 | 24 | 24 | 26 | 26 | 28 | 28 | 30 | 30 | 32 | 32 | 34 | 34 | 36 | 36 | 38 | 38 | 40 | 40 | 42 | 42 | 44 | 44 | 46 | 46 | 48 | 48 | 50 | 50 | 52 | 52 | 54 | 54 | 54 |  |  |  |
| 0.376 – 0.400 | 08 | 08 | 10 | 10 | 12 | 12 | 14 | 14 | 16 | 16 | 18 | 18 | 20 | 20 | 22 | 22 | 24 | 24 | 26 | 26 | 28 | 28 | 30 | 30 | 32 | 32 | 34 | 34 | 36 | 36 | 38 | 38 | 40 | 40 | 42 | 42 | 44 | 44 | 46 | 46 | 48 | 48 | 50 | 50 | 52 | 52 | 54 | 54 | 54 |  |  |  |  |
| 0.401 – 0.425 | 08 | 10 | 10 | 12 | 12 | 14 | 14 | 16 | 16 | 18 | 18 | 20 | 20 | 22 | 22 | 24 | 24 | 26 | 26 | 28 | 28 | 30 | 30 | 32 | 32 | 34 | 34 | 36 | 36 | 38 | 38 | 40 | 40 | 42 | 42 | 44 | 44 | 46 | 46 | 48 | 48 | 50 | 50 | 52 | 52 | 54 | 54 | 54 |  |  |  |  |  |
| 0.426 – 0.450 | 10 | 10 | 12 | 12 | 14 | 14 | 16 | 16 | 18 | 18 | 20 | 20 | 22 | 22 | 24 | 24 | 26 | 26 | 28 | 28 | 30 | 30 | 32 | 32 | 34 | 34 | 36 | 36 | 38 | 38 | 40 | 40 | 42 | 42 | 44 | 44 | 46 | 46 | 48 | 48 | 50 | 50 | 52 | 52 | 54 | 54 | 54 |  |  |  |  |  |  |
| 0.451 – 0.475 | 10 | 12 | 12 | 14 | 14 | 16 | 16 | 18 | 18 | 20 | 20 | 22 | 22 | 24 | 24 | 26 | 26 | 28 | 28 | 30 | 30 | 32 | 32 | 34 | 34 | 36 | 36 | 38 | 38 | 40 | 40 | 42 | 42 | 44 | 44 | 46 | 46 | 48 | 48 | 50 | 50 | 52 | 52 | 54 | 54 | 54 |  |  |  |  |  |  |  |
| 0.476 – 0.500 | 12 | 12 | 14 | 14 | 16 | 16 | 18 | 18 | 20 | 20 | 22 | 22 | 24 | 24 | 26 | 26 | 28 | 28 | 30 | 30 | 32 | 32 | 34 | 34 | 36 | 36 | 38 | 38 | 40 | 40 | 42 | 42 | 44 | 44 | 46 | 46 | 48 | 48 | 50 | 50 | 52 | 52 | 54 | 54 | 54 |  |  |  |  |  |  |  |  |
| 0.501 – 0.525 | 12 | 14 | 14 | 16 | 16 | 18 | 18 | 20 | 20 | 22 | 22 | 24 | 24 | 26 | 26 | 28 | 28 | 30 | 30 | 32 | 32 | 34 | 34 | 36 | 36 | 38 | 38 | 40 | 40 | 42 | 42 | 44 | 44 | 46 | 46 | 48 | 48 | 50 | 50 | 52 | 52 | 54 | 54 | 54 |  |  |  |  |  |  |  |  |  |
| 0.526 – 0.550 | 14 | 14 | 16 | 16 | 18 | 18 | 20 | 20 | 22 | 22 | 24 | 24 | 26 | 26 | 28 | 28 | 30 | 30 | 32 | 32 | 34 | 34 | 36 | 36 | 38 | 38 | 40 | 40 | 42 | 42 | 44 | 44 | 46 | 46 | 48 | 48 | 50 | 50 | 52 | 52 | 54 | 54 | 54 |  |  |  |  |  |  |  |  |  |  |
| 0.551 – 0.575 | 14 | 16 | 16 | 18 | 18 | 20 | 20 | 22 | 22 | 24 | 24 | 26 | 26 | 28 | 28 | 30 | 30 | 32 | 32 | 34 | 34 | 36 | 36 | 38 | 38 | 40 | 40 | 42 | 42 | 44 | 44 | 46 | 46 | 48 | 48 | 50 | 50 | 52 | 52 | 54 | 54 | 54 |  |  |  |  |  |  |  |  |  |  |  |
| 0.576 – 0.600 | 16 | 16 | 18 | 18 | 20 | 20 | 22 | 22 | 24 | 24 | 26 | 26 | 28 | 28 | 30 | 30 | 32 | 32 | 34 | 34 | 36 | 36 | 38 | 38 | 40 | 40 | 42 | 42 | 44 | 44 | 46 | 46 | 48 | 48 | 50 | 50 | 52 | 52 | 54 | 54 | 54 |  |  |  |  |  |  |  |  |  |  |  |  |
| 0.601 – 0.625 | 16 | 18 | 18 | 20 | 20 | 22 | 22 | 24 | 24 | 26 | 26 | 28 | 28 | 30 | 30 | 32 | 32 | 34 | 34 | 36 | 36 | 38 | 38 | 40 | 40 | 42 | 42 | 44 | 44 | 46 | 46 | 48 | 48 | 50 | 50 | 52 | 54 | 54 | 54 | 54 |  |  |  |  |  |  |  |  |  |  |  |  |  |
| 0.626 – 0.650 | 18 | 18 | 20 | 20 | 22 | 22 | 24 | 24 | 26 | 26 | 28 | 28 | 30 | 30 | 32 | 32 | 34 | 34 | 36 | 36 | 38 | 38 | 40 | 40 | 42 | 42 | 44 | 44 | 46 | 46 | 48 | 48 | 50 | 50 | 52 | 52 | 54 | 54 | 54 |  |  |  |  |  |  |  |  |  |  |  |  |  |  |
| 0.651 – 0.675 | 18 | 20 | 20 | 22 | 22 | 24 | 24 | 26 | 26 | 28 | 28 | 30 | 30 | 32 | 32 | 34 | 34 | 36 | 36 | 38 | 38 | 40 | 40 | 42 | 42 | 44 | 44 | 46 | 46 | 48 | 48 | 50 | 50 | 52 | 52 | 54 | 54 | 54 |  |  |  |  |  |  |  |  |  |  |  |  |  |  |  |
| 0.676 – 0.700 | 20 | 20 | 22 | 22 | 24 | 24 | 26 | 26 | 28 | 28 | 30 | 30 | 32 | 32 | 34 | 34 | 36 | 36 | 38 | 38 | 40 | 40 | 42 | 42 | 44 | 44 | 46 | 46 | 48 | 48 | 50 | 50 | 52 | 52 | 54 | 54 | 54 |  |  |  |  |  |  |  |  |  |  |  |  |  |  |  |  |
| 0.701 – 0.725 | 20 | 22 | 22 | 24 | 24 | 26 | 26 | 28 | 28 | 30 | 30 | 32 | 32 | 34 | 34 | 36 | 36 | 38 | 38 | 40 | 40 | 42 | 42 | 44 | 44 | 46 | 46 | 48 | 48 | 50 | 50 | 52 | 52 | 54 | 54 | 54 |  |  |  |  |  |  |  |  |  |  |  |  |  |  |  |  |  |
| 0.726 – 0.750 | 22 | 22 | 24 | 24 | 26 | 26 | 28 | 28 | 30 | 30 | 32 | 32 | 34 | 34 | 36 | 36 | 38 | 38 | 40 | 40 | 42 | 42 | 44 | 44 | 46 | 46 | 48 | 48 | 50 | 50 | 52 | 52 | 54 | 54 | 54 |  |  |  |  |  |  |  |  |  |  |  |  |  |  |  |  |  |  |
| 0.751 – 0.775 | 22 | 24 | 24 | 26 | 26 | 28 | 28 | 30 | 30 | 32 | 32 | 34 | 34 | 36 | 36 | 38 | 38 | 40 | 40 | 42 | 42 | 44 | 44 | 46 | 46 | 48 | 48 | 50 | 50 | 52 | 52 | 54 | 54 | 54 |  |  |  |  |  |  |  |  |  |  |  |  |  |  |  |  |  |  |  |
| 0.776 – 0.800 | 24 | 24 | 26 | 26 | 28 | 28 | 30 | 30 | 32 | 32 | 34 | 34 | 36 | 36 | 38 | 38 | 40 | 40 | 42 | 42 | 44 | 44 | 46 | 46 | 48 | 48 | 50 | 50 | 52 | 52 | 54 | 54 | 54 |  |  |  |  |  |  |  |  |  |  |  |  |  |  |  |  |  |  |  |  |
| 0.801 – 0.825 | 24 | 26 | 26 | 28 | 28 | 30 | 30 | 32 | 32 | 34 | 34 | 36 | 36 | 38 | 38 | 40 | 40 | 42 | 42 | 44 | 44 | 46 | 46 | 48 | 48 | 50 | 50 | 52 | 52 | 54 | 54 | 54 |  |  |  |  |  |  |  |  |  |  |  |  |  |  |  |  |  |  |  |  |  |
| 0.826 – 0.850 | 26 | 26 | 28 | 28 | 30 | 30 | 32 | 32 | 34 | 34 | 36 | 36 | 38 | 38 | 40 | 40 | 42 | 42 | 44 | 44 | 46 | 46 | 48 | 48 | 50 | 50 | 52 | 52 | 54 | 54 | 54 |  |  |  |  |  |  |  |  |  |  |  |  |  |  |  |  |  |  |  |  |  |  |
| 0.851 – 0.875 | 26 | 28 | 28 | 30 | 30 | 32 | 32 | 34 | 34 | 36 | 36 | 38 | 38 | 40 | 40 | 42 | 42 | 44 | 44 | 46 | 46 | 48 | 48 | 50 | 50 | 52 | 52 | 54 | 54 | 54 |  |  |  |  |  |  |  |  |  |  |  |  |  |  |  |  |  |  |  |  |  |  |  |
| 0.876 – 0.900 | 28 | 28 | 30 | 30 | 32 | 32 | 34 | 34 | 36 | 36 | 38 | 38 | 40 | 40 | 42 | 42 | 44 | 44 | 46 | 46 | 48 | 48 | 50 | 50 | 52 | 52 | 54 | 54 | 54 |  |  |  |  |  |  |  |  |  |  |  |  |  |  |  |  |  |  |  |  |  |  |  |  |
| 0.901 – 0.925 | 28 | 30 | 30 | 32 | 32 | 34 | 34 | 36 | 36 | 38 | 38 | 40 | 40 | 42 | 42 | 44 | 44 | 46 | 46 | 48 | 48 | 50 | 50 | 52 | 52 | 54 | 54 | 54 |  |  |  |  |  |  |  |  |  |  |  |  |  |  |  |  |  |  |  |  |  |  |  |  |  |
| 0.926 – 0.950 | 30 | 30 | 32 | 32 | 34 | 34 | 36 | 36 | 38 | 38 | 40 | 40 | 42 | 42 | 44 | 44 | 46 | 46 | 48 | 48 | 50 | 50 | 52 | 52 | 54 | 54 | 54 |  |  |  |  |  |  |  |  |  |  |  |  |  |  |  |  |  |  |  |  |  |  |  |  |  |  |
| 0.951 – 0.975 | 30 | 32 | 32 | 34 | 34 | 36 | 36 | 38 | 38 | 40 | 40 | 42 | 42 | 44 | 44 | 46 | 46 | 48 | 48 | 50 | 50 | 52 | 52 | 54 | 54 | 54 |  |  |  |  |  |  |  |  |  |  |  |  |  |  |  |  |  |  |  |  |  |  |  |  |  |  |  |
| 0.976 – 1.000 | 32 | 32 | 34 | 34 | 36 | 36 | 38 | 38 | 40 | 40 | 42 | 42 | 44 | 44 | 46 | 46 | 48 | 48 | 50 | 50 | 52 | 52 | 54 | 54 | 54 |  |  |  |  |  |  |  |  |  |  |  |  |  |  |  |  |  |  |  |  |  |  |  |  |  |  |  |  |
| 1.001 – 1.025 | 32 | 34 | 34 | 36 | 36 | 38 | 38 | 40 | 40 | 42 | 42 | 44 | 44 | 46 | 46 | 48 | 48 | 50 | 50 | 52 | 52 | 54 | 54 | 54 |  |  |  |  |  |  |  |  |  |  |  |  |  |  |  |  |  |  |  |  |  |  |  |  |  |  |  |  |  |
| 1.026 – 1.050 | 34 | 34 | 36 | 36 | 38 | 38 | 40 | 40 | 42 | 42 | 44 | 44 | 46 | 46 | 48 | 48 | 50 | 50 | 52 | 52 | 54 | 54 | 54 |  |  |  |  |  |  |  |  |  |  |  |  |  |  |  |  |  |  |  |  |  |  |  |  |  |  |  |  |  |  |
| 1.051 – 1.075 | 34 | 36 | 36 | 38 | 38 | 40 | 40 | 42 | 42 | 44 | 44 | 46 | 46 | 48 | 48 | 50 | 50 | 52 | 52 | 54 | 54 | 54 |  |  |  |  |  |  |  |  |  |  |  |  |  |  |  |  |  |  |  |  |  |  |  |  |  |  |  |  |  |  |  |
| 1.076 – 1.100 | 36 | 36 | 38 | 38 | 40 | 40 | 42 | 42 | 44 | 44 | 46 | 46 | 48 | 48 | 50 | 50 | 52 | 52 | 54 | 54 | 54 |  |  |  |  |  |  |  |  |  |  |  |  |  |  |  |  |  |  |  |  |  |  |  |  |  |  |  |  |  |  |  |  |
| 1.101 – 1.125 | 36 | 38 | 38 | 40 | 40 | 42 | 42 | 44 | 44 | 46 | 46 | 48 | 48 | 50 | 50 | 52 | 52 | 54 | 54 | 54 |  |  |  |  |  |  |  |  |  |  |  |  |  |  |  |  |  |  |  |  |  |  |  |  |  |  |  |  |  |  |  |  |  |
| 1.126 – 1.150 | 38 | 38 | 40 | 40 | 42 | 42 | 44 | 44 | 46 | 46 | 48 | 48 | 50 | 50 | 52 | 52 | 54 | 54 | 54 |  |  |  |  |  |  |  |  |  |  |  |  |  |  |  |  |  |  |  |  |  |  |  |  |  |  |  |  |  |  |  |  |  |  |
| 1.151 – 1.175 | 38 | 40 | 40 | 42 | 42 | 44 | 44 | 46 | 46 | 48 | 48 | 50 | 50 | 52 | 52 | 54 | 54 | 54 |  |  |  |  |  |  |  |  |  |  |  |  |  |  |  |  |  |  |  |  |  |  |  |  |  |  |  |  |  |  |  |  |  |  |  |
| 1.176 – 1.200 | 40 | 40 | 42 | 42 | 44 | 44 | 46 | 46 | 48 | 48 | 50 | 50 | 52 | 52 | 54 | 54 | 54 |  |  |  |  |  |  |  |  |  |  |  |  |  |  |  |  |  |  |  |  |  |  |  |  |  |  |  |  |  |  |  |  |  |  |  |  |
| 1.201 – 1.225 | 40 | 42 | 42 | 44 | 44 | 46 | 46 | 48 | 48 | 50 | 50 | 52 | 52 | 54 | 54 | 54 |  |  |  |  |  |  |  |  |  |  |  |  |  |  |  |  |  |  |  |  |  |  |  |  |  |  |  |  |  |  |  |  |  |  |  |  |  |
| 1.226 – 1.250 | 42 | 42 | 44 | 44 | 46 | 46 | 48 | 48 | 50 | 50 | 52 | 52 | 54 | 54 | 54 |  |  |  |  |  |  |  |  |  |  |  |  |  |  |  |  |  |  |  |  |  |  |  |  |  |  |  |  |  |  |  |  |  |  |  |  |  |  |
| 1.251 – 1.275 | 42 | 44 | 44 | 46 | 46 | 48 | 48 | 50 | 50 | 52 | 52 | 54 | 54 | 54 |  |  |  |  |  |  |  |  |  |  |  |  |  |  |  |  |  |  |  |  |  |  |  |  |  |  |  |  |  |  |  |  |  |  |  |  |  |  |  |
| 1.276 – 1.300 | 44 | 44 | 46 | 46 | 48 | 48 | 50 | 50 | 52 | 52 | 54 | 54 | 54 |  |  |  |  |  |  |  |  |  |  |  |  |  |  |  |  |  |  |  |  |  |  |  |  |  |  |  |  |  |  |  |  |  |  |  |  |  |  |  |  |
| 1.301 – 1.325 | 44 | 46 | 46 | 48 | 48 | 50 | 50 | 52 | 52 | 54 | 54 | 54 |  |  |  |  |  |  |  |  |  |  |  |  |  |  |  |  |  |  |  |  |  |  |  |  |  |  |  |  |  |  |  |  |  |  |  |  |  |  |  |  |  |
| 1.326 – 1.350 | 46 | 46 | 48 | 48 | 50 | 50 | 52 | 52 | 54 | 54 | 54 |  |  |  |  |  |  |  |  |  |  |  |  |  |  |  |  |  |  |  |  |  |  |  |  |  |  |  |  |  |  |  |  |  |  |  |  |  |  |  |  |  |  |
| 1.351 – 1.375 | 46 | 48 | 48 | 50 | 50 | 52 | 52 | 54 | 54 | 54 |  |  |  |  |  |  |  |  |  |  |  |  |  |  |  |  |  |  |  |  |  |  |  |  |  |  |  |  |  |  |  |  |  |  |  |  |  |  |  |  |  |  |  |
| 1.376 – 1.400 | 48 | 48 | 50 | 50 | 52 | 52 | 54 | 54 | 54 |  |  |  |  |  |  |  |  |  |  |  |  |  |  |  |  |  |  |  |  |  |  |  |  |  |  |  |  |  |  |  |  |  |  |  |  |  |  |  |  |  |  |  |  |
| 1.401 – 1.425 | 48 | 50 | 50 | 52 | 52 | 54 | 54 | 54 |  |  |  |  |  |  |  |  |  |  |  |  |  |  |  |  |  |  |  |  |  |  |  |  |  |  |  |  |  |  |  |  |  |  |  |  |  |  |  |  |  |  |  |  |  |
| 1.426 – 1.450 | 50 | 50 | 52 | 52 | 54 | 54 | 54 |  |  |  |  |  |  |  |  |  |  |  |  |  |  |  |  |  |  |  |  |  |  |  |  |  |  |  |  |  |  |  |  |  |  |  |  |  |  |  |  |  |  |  |  |  |  |
| 1.451 – 1.475 | 50 | 52 | 52 | 54 | 54 | 54 |  |  |  |  |  |  |  |  |  |  |  |  |  |  |  |  |  |  |  |  |  |  |  |  |  |  |  |  |  |  |  |  |  |  |  |  |  |  |  |  |  |  |  |  |  |  |  |
| 1.476 – 1.500 | 52 | 52 | 54 | 54 | 54 |  |  |  |  |  |  |  |  |  |  |  |  |  |  |  |  |  |  |  |  |  |  |  |  |  |  |  |  |  |  |  |  |  |  |  |  |  |  |  |  |  |  |  |  |  |  |  |  |
| 1.501 – 1.525 | 52 | 54 | 54 | 54 |  |  |  |  |  |  |  |  |  |  |  |  |  |  |  |  |  |  |  |  |  |  |  |  |  |  |  |  |  |  |  |  |  |  |  |  |  |  |  |  |  |  |  |  |  |  |  |  |  |
| 1.526 – 1.550 | 54 | 54 | 54 |  |  |  |  |  |  |  |  |  |  |  |  |  |  |  |  |  |  |  |  |  |  |  |  |  |  |  |  |  |  |  |  |  |  |  |  |  |  |  |  |  |  |  |  |  |  |  |  |  |  |
| 1.551 – 1.575 | 54 | 54 |  |  |  |  |  |  |  |  |  |  |  |  |  |  |  |  |  |  |  |  |  |  |  |  |  |  |  |  |  |  |  |  |  |  |  |  |  |  |  |  |  |  |  |  |  |  |  |  |  |  |  |
| 1.576 – 1.600 | 54 |  |  |  |  |  |  |  |  |  |  |  |  |  |  |  |  |  |  |  |  |  |  |  |  |  |  |  |  |  |  |  |  |  |  |  |  |  |  |  |  |  |  |  |  |  |  |  |  |  |  |  |  |

New shim thickness mm (in.)

| Shim No. | Thickness | Shim No. | Thickness |
|---|---|---|---|
| 02 | 2.00 (0.0787) | 30 | 2.70 (0.1063) |
| 04 | 2.05 (0.0807) | 32 | 2.75 (0.1083) |
| 06 | 2.10 (0.0827) | 34 | 2.80 (0.1102) |
| 08 | 2.15 (0.0846) | 36 | 2.85 (0.1122) |
| 10 | 2.20 (0.0866) | 38 | 2.90 (0.1142) |
| 12 | 2.25 (0.0886) | 40 | 2.95 (0.1161) |
| 14 | 2.30 (0.0906) | 42 | 3.00 (0.1181) |
| 16 | 2.35 (0.0925) | 44 | 3.05 (0.1201) |
| 18 | 2.40 (0.0945) | 46 | 3.10 (0.1220) |
| 20 | 2.45 (0.0965) | 48 | 3.15 (0.1240) |
| 22 | 2.50 (0.0984) | 50 | 3.20 (0.1260) |
| 24 | 2.55 (0.1004) | 52 | 3.25 (0.1280) |
| 26 | 2.60 (0.1024) | 54 | 3.30 (0.1299) |
| 28 | 2.65 (0.1043) | | |

**Exhaust valve clearance (Cold):**
**0.20 – 0.30 mm (0.008 – 0.012 in.)**

EXAMPLE: The 2.800 mm (0.1102 in.) shim is installed, and the measured clearance is 0.450 mm (0.0177 in.). Replace the 2.800 mm (0.1102 in.) shim with a No.42 shim.

91G00519

Courtesy of Toyota Motor Sales, U.S.A., Inc.

***Fig. 3: Selecting Exhaust Valve Adjusting Shim***

# 1991 ENGINES
# 2.0L 4-Cylinder (Cont.)

INTAKE VALVES

| Measured clearance (mm) | Installed shim thickness (mm) | | | | | | | | | | | | | | | | | | | | | | | | | | | | | | | | | | | | | | | | | | | | | | | | | | | | |
|---|---|---|---|---|---|---|---|---|---|---|---|---|---|---|---|---|---|---|---|---|---|---|---|---|---|---|---|---|---|---|---|---|---|---|---|---|---|---|---|---|---|---|---|---|---|---|---|---|---|---|---|---|---|
| | 2.000 | 2.025 | 2.050 | 2.075 | 2.100 | 2.125 | 2.150 | 2.175 | 2.200 | 2.225 | 2.250 | 2.275 | 2.300 | 2.325 | 2.350 | 2.375 | 2.400 | 2.425 | 2.450 | 2.475 | 2.500 | 2.525 | 2.550 | 2.575 | 2.600 | 2.625 | 2.650 | 2.675 | 2.700 | 2.725 | 2.750 | 2.775 | 2.800 | 2.825 | 2.850 | 2.875 | 2.900 | 2.925 | 2.950 | 2.975 | 3.000 | 3.025 | 3.050 | 3.075 | 3.100 | 3.125 | 3.150 | 3.175 | 3.200 | 3.225 | 3.250 | 3.275 | 3.300 |
| 0.000 – 0.025 | | | | | | | 02 | 02 | 02 | 04 | 04 | 06 | 06 | 08 | 08 | 10 | 10 | 12 | 12 | 14 | 14 | 16 | 16 | 18 | 18 | 20 | 20 | 22 | 22 | 24 | 24 | 26 | 26 | 28 | 28 | 30 | 30 | 32 | 32 | 34 | 34 | 36 | 36 | 38 | 38 | 40 | 40 | 42 | 42 | 44 | 44 | 46 | 46 |
| 0.026 – 0.050 | | | | | | 02 | 02 | 02 | 04 | 04 | 06 | 06 | 08 | 08 | 10 | 10 | 12 | 12 | 14 | 14 | 16 | 16 | 18 | 18 | 20 | 20 | 22 | 22 | 24 | 24 | 26 | 26 | 28 | 28 | 30 | 30 | 32 | 32 | 34 | 34 | 36 | 36 | 38 | 38 | 40 | 40 | 42 | 42 | 44 | 44 | 46 | 46 | 48 |
| 0.051 – 0.075 | | | | | 02 | 02 | 02 | 04 | 04 | 06 | 06 | 08 | 08 | 10 | 10 | 12 | 12 | 14 | 14 | 16 | 16 | 18 | 18 | 20 | 20 | 22 | 22 | 24 | 24 | 26 | 26 | 28 | 28 | 30 | 30 | 32 | 32 | 34 | 34 | 36 | 36 | 38 | 38 | 40 | 40 | 42 | 42 | 44 | 44 | 46 | 46 | 48 | 48 |
| 0.076 – 0.100 | | | | 02 | 02 | 02 | 04 | 04 | 06 | 06 | 08 | 08 | 10 | 10 | 12 | 12 | 14 | 14 | 16 | 16 | 18 | 18 | 20 | 20 | 22 | 22 | 24 | 24 | 26 | 26 | 28 | 28 | 30 | 30 | 32 | 32 | 34 | 34 | 36 | 36 | 38 | 38 | 40 | 40 | 42 | 42 | 44 | 44 | 46 | 46 | 48 | 48 | 50 |
| 0.101 – 0.125 | | | 02 | 02 | 02 | 04 | 04 | 06 | 06 | 08 | 08 | 10 | 10 | 12 | 12 | 14 | 14 | 16 | 16 | 18 | 18 | 20 | 20 | 22 | 22 | 24 | 24 | 26 | 26 | 28 | 28 | 30 | 30 | 32 | 32 | 34 | 34 | 36 | 36 | 38 | 38 | 40 | 40 | 42 | 42 | 44 | 44 | 46 | 46 | 48 | 48 | 50 | 50 |
| 0.126 – 0.149 | | 02 | 02 | 02 | 04 | 04 | 06 | 06 | 08 | 08 | 10 | 10 | 12 | 12 | 14 | 14 | 16 | 16 | 18 | 18 | 20 | 20 | 22 | 22 | 24 | 24 | 26 | 26 | 28 | 28 | 30 | 30 | 32 | 32 | 34 | 34 | 36 | 36 | 38 | 38 | 40 | 40 | 42 | 42 | 44 | 44 | 46 | 46 | 48 | 48 | 50 | 50 | 52 |
| 0.150 – 0.250 | | | | | | | | | | | | | | | | | | | | | | | | | | | | | | | | | | | | | | | | | | | | | | | | | | | | | |
| 0.251 – 0.275 | 04 | 06 | 06 | 08 | 08 | 10 | 10 | 12 | 12 | 14 | 14 | 16 | 16 | 18 | 18 | 20 | 20 | 22 | 22 | 24 | 24 | 26 | 26 | 28 | 28 | 30 | 30 | 32 | 32 | 34 | 34 | 36 | 36 | 38 | 38 | 40 | 40 | 42 | 42 | 44 | 44 | 46 | 46 | 48 | 48 | 50 | 50 | 52 | 52 | 54 | 54 | 54 | |
| 0.276 – 0.300 | 06 | 06 | 08 | 08 | 10 | 10 | 12 | 12 | 14 | 14 | 16 | 16 | 18 | 18 | 20 | 20 | 22 | 22 | 24 | 24 | 26 | 26 | 28 | 28 | 30 | 30 | 32 | 32 | 34 | 34 | 36 | 36 | 38 | 38 | 40 | 40 | 42 | 42 | 44 | 44 | 46 | 46 | 48 | 48 | 50 | 50 | 52 | 52 | 54 | 54 | 54 | | |
| 0.301 – 0.325 | 06 | 08 | 08 | 10 | 10 | 12 | 12 | 14 | 14 | 16 | 16 | 18 | 18 | 20 | 20 | 22 | 22 | 24 | 24 | 26 | 26 | 28 | 28 | 30 | 30 | 32 | 32 | 34 | 34 | 36 | 36 | 38 | 38 | 40 | 40 | 42 | 42 | 44 | 44 | 46 | 46 | 48 | 48 | 50 | 50 | 52 | 52 | 54 | 54 | 54 | | | |
| 0.326 – 0.350 | 08 | 08 | 10 | 10 | 12 | 12 | 14 | 14 | 16 | 16 | 18 | 18 | 20 | 20 | 22 | 22 | 24 | 24 | 26 | 26 | 28 | 28 | 30 | 30 | 32 | 32 | 34 | 34 | 36 | 36 | 38 | 38 | 40 | 40 | 42 | 42 | 44 | 44 | 46 | 46 | 48 | 48 | 50 | 50 | 52 | 52 | 54 | 54 | 54 | | | | |
| 0.351 – 0.375 | 08 | 10 | 10 | 12 | 12 | 14 | 14 | 16 | 16 | 18 | 18 | 20 | 20 | 22 | 22 | 24 | 24 | 26 | 26 | 28 | 28 | 30 | 30 | 32 | 32 | 34 | 34 | 36 | 36 | 38 | 38 | 40 | 40 | 42 | 42 | 44 | 44 | 46 | 46 | 48 | 48 | 50 | 50 | 52 | 52 | 54 | 54 | 54 | | | | | |
| 0.376 – 0.400 | 10 | 10 | 12 | 12 | 14 | 14 | 16 | 16 | 18 | 18 | 20 | 20 | 22 | 22 | 24 | 24 | 26 | 26 | 28 | 28 | 30 | 30 | 32 | 32 | 34 | 34 | 36 | 36 | 38 | 38 | 40 | 40 | 42 | 42 | 44 | 44 | 46 | 46 | 48 | 48 | 50 | 50 | 52 | 52 | 54 | 54 | 54 | | | | | | |
| 0.401 – 0.425 | 10 | 12 | 12 | 14 | 14 | 16 | 16 | 18 | 18 | 20 | 20 | 22 | 22 | 24 | 24 | 26 | 26 | 28 | 28 | 30 | 30 | 32 | 32 | 34 | 34 | 36 | 36 | 38 | 38 | 40 | 40 | 42 | 42 | 44 | 44 | 46 | 46 | 48 | 48 | 50 | 50 | 52 | 52 | 54 | 54 | 54 | | | | | | | |
| 0.426 – 0.450 | 12 | 12 | 14 | 14 | 16 | 16 | 18 | 18 | 20 | 20 | 22 | 22 | 24 | 24 | 26 | 26 | 28 | 28 | 30 | 30 | 32 | 32 | 34 | 34 | 36 | 36 | 38 | 38 | 40 | 40 | 42 | 42 | 44 | 44 | 46 | 46 | 48 | 48 | 50 | 50 | 52 | 52 | 54 | 54 | 54 | | | | | | | | |
| 0.451 – 0.475 | 12 | 14 | 14 | 16 | 16 | 18 | 18 | 20 | 20 | 22 | 22 | 24 | 24 | 26 | 26 | 28 | 28 | 30 | 30 | 32 | 32 | 34 | 34 | 36 | 36 | 38 | 38 | 40 | 40 | 42 | 42 | 44 | 44 | 46 | 46 | 48 | 48 | 50 | 50 | 52 | 52 | 54 | 54 | 54 | | | | | | | | | |
| 0.476 – 0.500 | 14 | 14 | 16 | 16 | 18 | 18 | 20 | 20 | 22 | 22 | 24 | 24 | 26 | 26 | 28 | 28 | 30 | 30 | 32 | 32 | 34 | 34 | 36 | 36 | 38 | 38 | 40 | 40 | 42 | 42 | 44 | 44 | 46 | 46 | 48 | 48 | 50 | 50 | 52 | 52 | 54 | 54 | 54 | | | | | | | | | | |
| 0.501 – 0.525 | 14 | 16 | 16 | 18 | 18 | 20 | 20 | 22 | 22 | 24 | 24 | 26 | 26 | 28 | 28 | 30 | 30 | 32 | 32 | 34 | 34 | 36 | 36 | 38 | 38 | 40 | 40 | 42 | 42 | 44 | 44 | 46 | 46 | 48 | 48 | 50 | 50 | 52 | 52 | 54 | 54 | 54 | | | | | | | | | | | |
| 0.526 – 0.550 | 16 | 16 | 18 | 18 | 20 | 20 | 22 | 22 | 24 | 24 | 26 | 26 | 28 | 28 | 30 | 30 | 32 | 32 | 34 | 34 | 36 | 36 | 38 | 38 | 40 | 40 | 42 | 42 | 44 | 44 | 46 | 46 | 48 | 48 | 50 | 50 | 52 | 52 | 54 | 54 | 54 | | | | | | | | | | | | |
| 0.551 – 0.575 | 16 | 18 | 18 | 20 | 20 | 22 | 22 | 24 | 24 | 26 | 26 | 28 | 28 | 30 | 30 | 32 | 32 | 34 | 34 | 36 | 36 | 38 | 38 | 40 | 40 | 42 | 42 | 44 | 44 | 46 | 46 | 48 | 48 | 50 | 50 | 52 | 52 | 54 | 54 | 54 | | | | | | | | | | | | | |
| 0.576 – 0.600 | 18 | 18 | 20 | 20 | 22 | 22 | 24 | 24 | 26 | 26 | 28 | 28 | 30 | 30 | 32 | 32 | 34 | 34 | 36 | 36 | 38 | 38 | 40 | 40 | 42 | 42 | 44 | 44 | 46 | 46 | 48 | 48 | 50 | 50 | 52 | 52 | 54 | 54 | 54 | | | | | | | | | | | | | | |
| 0.601 – 0.625 | 18 | 20 | 20 | 22 | 22 | 24 | 24 | 26 | 26 | 28 | 28 | 30 | 30 | 32 | 32 | 34 | 34 | 36 | 36 | 38 | 38 | 40 | 40 | 42 | 42 | 44 | 44 | 46 | 46 | 48 | 48 | 50 | 50 | 52 | 52 | 54 | 54 | 54 | | | | | | | | | | | | | | | |
| 0.626 – 0.650 | 20 | 20 | 22 | 22 | 24 | 24 | 26 | 26 | 28 | 28 | 30 | 30 | 32 | 32 | 34 | 34 | 36 | 36 | 38 | 38 | 40 | 40 | 42 | 42 | 44 | 44 | 46 | 46 | 48 | 48 | 50 | 50 | 52 | 52 | 54 | 54 | 54 | | | | | | | | | | | | | | | | |
| 0.651 – 0.675 | 20 | 22 | 22 | 24 | 24 | 26 | 26 | 28 | 28 | 30 | 30 | 32 | 32 | 34 | 34 | 36 | 36 | 38 | 38 | 40 | 40 | 42 | 42 | 44 | 44 | 46 | 46 | 48 | 48 | 50 | 50 | 52 | 52 | 54 | 54 | 54 | | | | | | | | | | | | | | | | | |
| 0.676 – 0.700 | 22 | 22 | 24 | 24 | 26 | 26 | 28 | 28 | 30 | 30 | 32 | 32 | 34 | 34 | 36 | 36 | 38 | 38 | 40 | 40 | 42 | 42 | 44 | 44 | 46 | 46 | 48 | 48 | 50 | 50 | 52 | 52 | 54 | 54 | 54 | | | | | | | | | | | | | | | | | | |
| 0.701 – 0.725 | 22 | 24 | 24 | 26 | 26 | 28 | 28 | 30 | 30 | 32 | 32 | 34 | 34 | 36 | 36 | 38 | 38 | 40 | 40 | 42 | 42 | 44 | 44 | 46 | 46 | 48 | 48 | 50 | 50 | 52 | 52 | 54 | 54 | 54 | | | | | | | | | | | | | | | | | | | |
| 0.726 – 0.750 | 24 | 24 | 26 | 26 | 28 | 28 | 30 | 30 | 32 | 32 | 34 | 34 | 36 | 36 | 38 | 38 | 40 | 40 | 42 | 42 | 44 | 44 | 46 | 46 | 48 | 48 | 50 | 50 | 52 | 52 | 54 | 54 | 54 | | | | | | | | | | | | | | | | | | | | |
| 0.751 – 0.775 | 24 | 26 | 26 | 28 | 28 | 30 | 30 | 32 | 32 | 34 | 34 | 36 | 36 | 38 | 38 | 40 | 40 | 42 | 42 | 44 | 44 | 46 | 46 | 48 | 48 | 50 | 50 | 52 | 52 | 54 | 54 | 54 | | | | | | | | | | | | | | | | | | | | | |
| 0.776 – 0.800 | 26 | 26 | 28 | 28 | 30 | 30 | 32 | 32 | 34 | 34 | 36 | 36 | 38 | 38 | 40 | 40 | 42 | 42 | 44 | 44 | 46 | 46 | 48 | 48 | 50 | 50 | 52 | 52 | 54 | 54 | 54 | | | | | | | | | | | | | | | | | | | | | | |
| 0.801 – 0.825 | 26 | 28 | 28 | 30 | 30 | 32 | 32 | 34 | 34 | 36 | 36 | 38 | 38 | 40 | 40 | 42 | 42 | 44 | 44 | 46 | 46 | 48 | 48 | 50 | 50 | 52 | 52 | 54 | 54 | 54 | | | | | | | | | | | | | | | | | | | | | | | |
| 0.826 – 0.850 | 28 | 28 | 30 | 30 | 32 | 32 | 34 | 34 | 36 | 36 | 38 | 38 | 40 | 40 | 42 | 42 | 44 | 44 | 46 | 46 | 48 | 48 | 50 | 50 | 52 | 52 | 54 | 54 | 54 | | | | | | | | | | | | | | | | | | | | | | | | |
| 0.851 – 0.875 | 28 | 30 | 30 | 32 | 32 | 34 | 34 | 36 | 36 | 38 | 38 | 40 | 40 | 42 | 42 | 44 | 44 | 46 | 46 | 48 | 48 | 50 | 50 | 52 | 52 | 54 | 54 | 54 | | | | | | | | | | | | | | | | | | | | | | | | | |
| 0.876 – 0.900 | 30 | 30 | 32 | 32 | 34 | 34 | 36 | 36 | 38 | 38 | 40 | 40 | 42 | 42 | 44 | 44 | 46 | 46 | 48 | 48 | 50 | 50 | 52 | 52 | 54 | 54 | 54 | | | | | | | | | | | | | | | | | | | | | | | | | | |
| 0.901 – 0.925 | 30 | 32 | 32 | 34 | 34 | 36 | 36 | 38 | 38 | 40 | 40 | 42 | 42 | 44 | 44 | 46 | 46 | 48 | 48 | 50 | 50 | 52 | 52 | 54 | 54 | 54 | | | | | | | | | | | | | | | | | | | | | | | | | | | |
| 0.926 – 0.950 | 32 | 32 | 34 | 34 | 36 | 36 | 38 | 38 | 40 | 40 | 42 | 42 | 44 | 44 | 46 | 46 | 48 | 48 | 50 | 50 | 52 | 52 | 54 | 54 | 54 | | | | | | | | | | | | | | | | | | | | | | | | | | | | |
| 0.951 – 0.975 | 32 | 34 | 34 | 36 | 36 | 38 | 38 | 40 | 40 | 42 | 42 | 44 | 44 | 46 | 46 | 48 | 48 | 50 | 50 | 52 | 52 | 54 | 54 | 54 | | | | | | | | | | | | | | | | | | | | | | | | | | | | | |
| 0.976 – 1.000 | 34 | 34 | 36 | 36 | 38 | 38 | 40 | 40 | 42 | 42 | 44 | 44 | 46 | 46 | 48 | 48 | 50 | 50 | 52 | 52 | 54 | 54 | 54 | | | | | | | | | | | | | | | | | | | | | | | | | | | | | | |
| 1.001 – 1.025 | 34 | 36 | 36 | 38 | 38 | 40 | 40 | 42 | 42 | 44 | 44 | 46 | 46 | 48 | 48 | 50 | 50 | 52 | 52 | 54 | 54 | 54 | | | | | | | | | | | | | | | | | | | | | | | | | | | | | | | |
| 1.026 – 1.050 | 36 | 36 | 38 | 38 | 40 | 40 | 42 | 42 | 44 | 44 | 46 | 46 | 48 | 48 | 50 | 50 | 52 | 52 | 54 | 54 | 54 | | | | | | | | | | | | | | | | | | | | | | | | | | | | | | | | |
| 1.051 – 1.075 | 36 | 38 | 38 | 40 | 40 | 42 | 42 | 44 | 44 | 46 | 46 | 48 | 48 | 50 | 50 | 52 | 52 | 54 | 54 | 54 | | | | | | | | | | | | | | | | | | | | | | | | | | | | | | | | | |
| 1.076 – 1.100 | 38 | 38 | 40 | 40 | 42 | 42 | 44 | 44 | 46 | 46 | 48 | 48 | 50 | 50 | 52 | 52 | 54 | 54 | 54 | | | | | | | | | | | | | | | | | | | | | | | | | | | | | | | | | | |
| 1.101 – 1.125 | 38 | 40 | 40 | 42 | 42 | 44 | 44 | 46 | 46 | 48 | 48 | 50 | 50 | 52 | 52 | 54 | 54 | 54 | | | | | | | | | | | | | | | | | | | | | | | | | | | | | | | | | | | |
| 1.126 – 1.150 | 40 | 40 | 42 | 42 | 44 | 44 | 46 | 46 | 48 | 48 | 50 | 50 | 52 | 52 | 54 | 54 | 54 | | | | | | | | | | | | | | | | | | | | | | | | | | | | | | | | | | | | |
| 1.151 – 1.175 | 40 | 42 | 42 | 44 | 44 | 46 | 46 | 48 | 48 | 50 | 50 | 52 | 52 | 54 | 54 | 54 | | | | | | | | | | | | | | | | | | | | | | | | | | | | | | | | | | | | | |
| 1.176 – 1.200 | 42 | 42 | 44 | 44 | 46 | 46 | 48 | 48 | 50 | 50 | 52 | 52 | 54 | 54 | 54 | | | | | | | | | | | | | | | | | | | | | | | | | | | | | | | | | | | | | | |
| 1.201 – 1.225 | 42 | 44 | 44 | 46 | 46 | 48 | 48 | 50 | 50 | 52 | 52 | 54 | 54 | 54 | | | | | | | | | | | | | | | | | | | | | | | | | | | | | | | | | | | | | | | |
| 1.226 – 1.250 | 44 | 44 | 46 | 46 | 48 | 48 | 50 | 50 | 52 | 52 | 54 | 54 | 54 | | | | | | | | | | | | | | | | | | | | | | | | | | | | | | | | | | | | | | | | |
| 1.251 – 1.275 | 44 | 46 | 46 | 48 | 48 | 50 | 50 | 52 | 52 | 54 | 54 | 54 | | | | | | | | | | | | | | | | | | | | | | | | | | | | | | | | | | | | | | | | | |
| 1.276 – 1.300 | 46 | 46 | 48 | 48 | 50 | 50 | 52 | 52 | 54 | 54 | 54 | | | | | | | | | | | | | | | | | | | | | | | | | | | | | | | | | | | | | | | | | | |
| 1.301 – 1.325 | 46 | 48 | 48 | 50 | 50 | 52 | 52 | 54 | 54 | 54 | | | | | | | | | | | | | | | | | | | | | | | | | | | | | | | | | | | | | | | | | | | |
| 1.326 – 1.350 | 48 | 48 | 50 | 50 | 52 | 52 | 54 | 54 | 54 | | | | | | | | | | | | | | | | | | | | | | | | | | | | | | | | | | | | | | | | | | | | |
| 1.351 – 1.375 | 48 | 50 | 50 | 52 | 52 | 54 | 54 | 54 | | | | | | | | | | | | | | | | | | | | | | | | | | | | | | | | | | | | | | | | | | | | | |
| 1.376 – 1.400 | 50 | 50 | 52 | 52 | 54 | 54 | 54 | | | | | | | | | | | | | | | | | | | | | | | | | | | | | | | | | | | | | | | | | | | | | | |
| 1.401 – 1.425 | 50 | 52 | 52 | 54 | 54 | 54 | | | | | | | | | | | | | | | | | | | | | | | | | | | | | | | | | | | | | | | | | | | | | | | |
| 1.426 – 1.450 | 52 | 52 | 54 | 54 | 54 | | | | | | | | | | | | | | | | | | | | | | | | | | | | | | | | | | | | | | | | | | | | | | | | |
| 1.451 – 1.475 | 52 | 54 | 54 | 54 | | | | | | | | | | | | | | | | | | | | | | | | | | | | | | | | | | | | | | | | | | | | | | | | | |
| 1.476 – 1.500 | 54 | 54 | 54 | | | | | | | | | | | | | | | | | | | | | | | | | | | | | | | | | | | | | | | | | | | | | | | | | | |
| 1.501 – 1.525 | 54 | 54 | | | | | | | | | | | | | | | | | | | | | | | | | | | | | | | | | | | | | | | | | | | | | | | | | | | |
| 1.526 – 1.550 | 54 | | | | | | | | | | | | | | | | | | | | | | | | | | | | | | | | | | | | | | | | | | | | | | | | | | | | |

New shim thickness mm (in.)

| Shim No. | Thickness | Shim No. | Thickness |
|---|---|---|---|
| 02 | 2.00 (0.0787) | 30 | 2.70 (0.1063) |
| 04 | 2.05 (0.0807) | 32 | 2.75 (0.1083) |
| 06 | 2.10 (0.0827) | 34 | 2.80 (0.1102) |
| 08 | 2.15 (0.0846) | 36 | 2.85 (0.1122) |
| 10 | 2.20 (0.0866) | 38 | 2.90 (0.1142) |
| 12 | 2.25 (0.0886) | 40 | 2.95 (0.1161) |
| 14 | 2.30 (0.0906) | 42 | 3.00 (0.1181) |
| 16 | 2.35 (0.0925) | 44 | 3.05 (0.1201) |
| 18 | 2.40 (0.0945) | 46 | 3.10 (0.1220) |
| 20 | 2.45 (0.0965) | 48 | 3.15 (0.1240) |
| 22 | 2.50 (0.0984) | 50 | 3.20 (0.1260) |
| 24 | 2.55 (0.1004) | 52 | 3.25 (0.1280) |
| 26 | 2.60 (0.1024) | 54 | 3.30 (0.1299) |
| 28 | 2.65 (0.1043) | | |

**Intake valve clearance (Cold):**
**0.15 – 0.25 mm (0.006 – 0.010 in.)**

EXAMPLE: The 2.800 mm (0.1102 in.) shim is installed, and the measured clearance is 0.450 mm (0.0177 in.). Replace the 2.800 mm (0.1102 in.) shim with a No.44 shim.

91J00520

Courtesy of Toyota Motor Sales, U.S.A., Inc.

***Fig. 4: Selecting Intake Valve Adjusting Shim***

# 1991 ENGINES
# 2.0L 4-Cylinder (Cont.)

## COOLING SYSTEM BLEEDING

**Celica All-Trac** - No special cooling system bleeding procedure is required.

**MR2 - 1)** Remove spare tire, front luggage compartment trim and upper radiator support seal. Connect air bleed hoses to heater and radiator air drain plugs. *See Fig. 5.* Support opposite end of hoses to hood or hood support. Ensure hoses are not pinched shut.

**2)** Place heater control lever to the warmest position. Open heater and radiator air drain plugs at least 3 turns.

**3)** Slowly add coolant through coolant filler. *See Fig. 5.* Air will bleed from hoses on heater and radiator air drain plugs. Ensure coolant level in air bleed hoses is same as level in coolant filler.

**4)** If coolant level in air bleed hoses is lower, air still exists in cooling system. Check for pinched or restriction in air bleed hoses, and repeat step **3)**. When proper coolant level is obtained in air bleed hoses, close air drain plugs. Remove air bleed hoses.

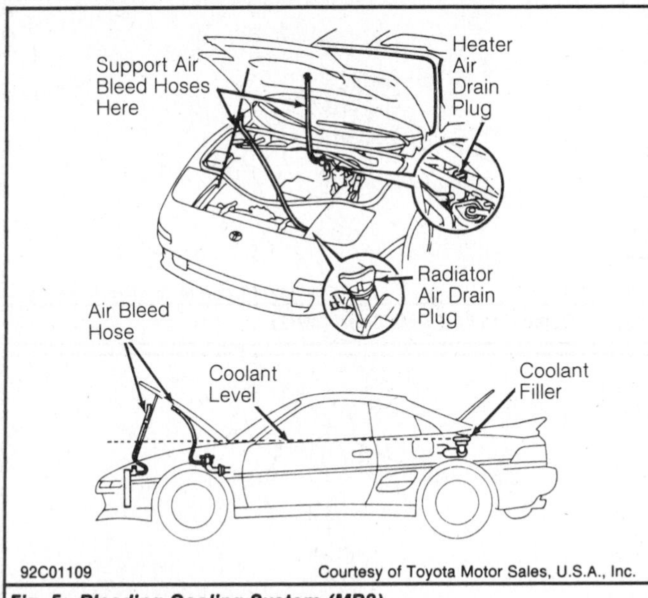


***Fig. 5: Bleeding Cooling System (MR2)***

## ENGINE

***CAUTION: To prevent accidental air bag deployment, wait at least 20 seconds after disconnecting negative battery cable before performing service procedures.***

***NOTE: Remove engine and transaxle as an assembly.***

**Removal (Celica All-Trac) - 1)** Release fuel pressure. See FUEL PRESSURE RELEASE under REMOVAL & INSTALLATION.

**2)** Drain cooling system, engine oil and transaxle oil. Remove hood and lower engine covers. Remove air cleaner assembly, air intake duct and airflow meter.

**3)** Disconnect relay box from battery. Remove lower cover from relay box. Disconnect fusible link assembly and engine wire connectors from relay box. Remove A/C relay box from bracket, located near right corner of radiator.

**4)** Remove battery. Disconnect electrical connector, and remove solenoid resistor located in front of fuse relay box, near battery. Remove radiator and radiator reservoir tank.

**5)** Remove cruise control actuator and ignition coil. Remove strut tower-to-firewall braces. Remove charcoal canister. Disconnect necessary control cables, coolant hoses, fuel lines, vacuum hoses and electrical connections.

**6)** Raise and support vehicle. Disconnect speedometer cable, oil cooler hoses and control cables at transaxle. Remove clutch release cylinder with hose attached, and secure aside.

**7)** Disconnect wiring, and remove turbo pressure sensor and A/C vacuum switching valve from firewall. Remove starter.

**8)** Disconnect electrical connectors from engine Electronic Control Unit (ECU) located left of glove box, behind center console. Disconnect remaining electrical connections so engine wiring can be pulled out through access hole in passenger's side of firewall. Remove retaining nuts, and pull engine wiring through firewall.

**9)** Remove suspension crossmember bolted to both lower suspension arm shafts. Disconnect exhaust pipe at catalytic converter (located at turbo) and center pipe. Remove exhaust pipe.

**10)** Remove front tires and wheels. Remove cotter pin, retainer, axle shaft nut and washer. Remove nut, and separate tie rod from steering knuckle.

**11)** Remove ball joint-to-steering knuckle bolts. Wrap axle shaft threads with tape. Cover axle shaft boot with shop towel. Using puller attached to hub assembly, press axle shaft from hub assembly.

**12)** To remove left axle shaft, pry between transaxle case and axle shaft until axle shaft disengages from transaxle. To remove right axle shaft, use brass drift and hammer to drive axle shaft from transaxle. *See Fig. 6.*

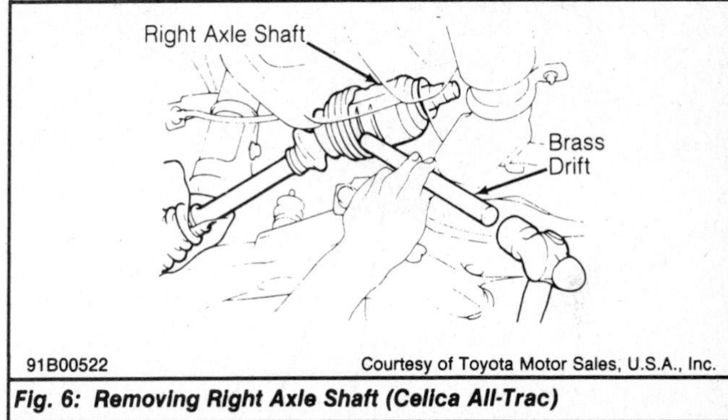


***Fig. 6: Removing Right Axle Shaft (Celica All-Trac)***

**13)** Place reference marks on front and rear drive shaft flanges at center bearing. Remove flange bolts. Remove drive shaft from transfer case. Remove seal deflector from rear of transfer case. Remove dynamic damper from transfer case. *See Fig. 7.*

**14)** Remove alternator and idler pulley bracket. Remove A/C compressor and power steering pump with hoses attached, and secure aside.

**15)** Remove engine mount crossmember located below engine. Remove catalytic converter from turbo.

**16)** Disconnect engine and transaxle mounts. Note direction of mount installation for reassembly reference. Mounts must be installed in original direction. Lift engine and transaxle from vehicle.

**Installation - 1)** To install, reverse removal procedure. Use new cushion, retainer and gasket when installing catalytic converter. Before installing axle shafts, ensure opening of snap ring on end of axle shaft faces downward.

**2)** Ensure reference marks are aligned on drive shaft flanges. Tighten fasteners to specification. See appropriate TORQUE SPECIFICATIONS table at end of article. Adjust all control cables and fluid levels.

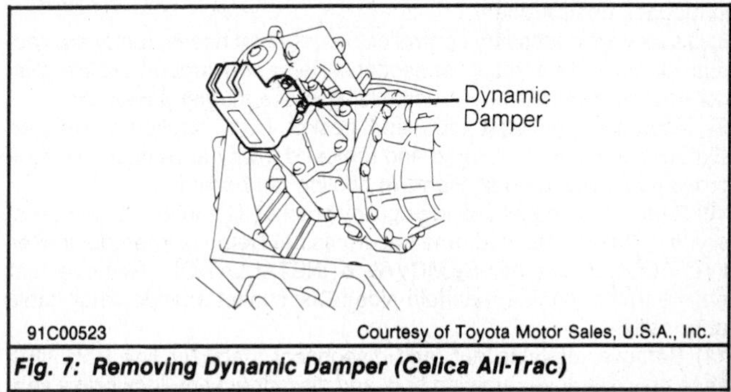


***Fig. 7: Removing Dynamic Damper (Celica All-Trac)***

***CAUTION: To prevent accidental air bag deployment, wait at least 20 seconds after disconnecting negative battery cable before performing service procedures.***

***NOTE: Remove engine and transaxle as an assembly from bottom of engine compartment.***

**Removal (MR2)** – **1)** Release fuel pressure. See FUEL PRESSURE RELEASE under REMOVAL & INSTALLATION.

**2)** Drain cooling system, engine oil and transaxle oil. Remove hood, hood side panels and lower engine covers. Remove strut tower-to-firewall braces. Remove air cleaner cap, airflow meter and air cleaner case.

**3)** Remove No. 1 and No. 2 air intake connectors. *See Fig. 23.* Remove cruise control actuator. Disconnect necessary control cables, coolant hoses, fuel lines, vacuum hoses and electrical connections.

**4)** Remove turbo pressure sensor from the body. *See Fig. 8.* Remove check connector, located near turbo pressure sensor, from the body. Disconnect electrical connectors, and remove solenoid resistor, fuel pump relay and fuel pump resistor assembly. *See Fig. 8.*

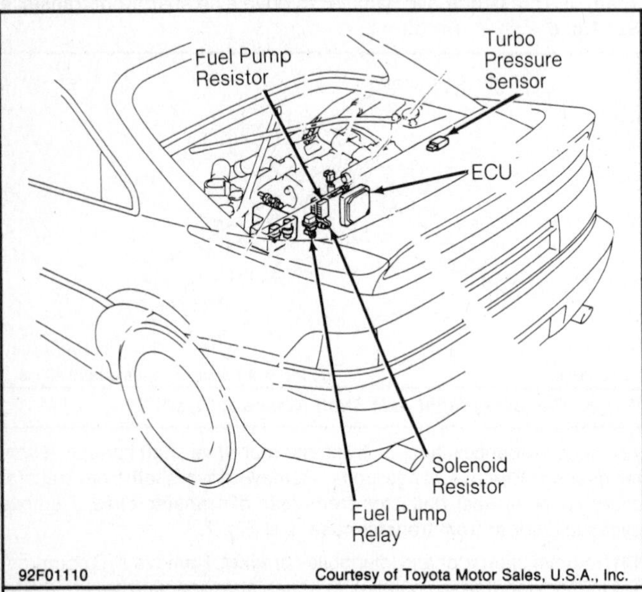


Courtesy of Toyota Motor Sales, U.S.A., Inc.

***Fig. 8: Identifying Electrical Components***

**5)** Remove radiator cap and coolant filler. *See Fig. 5.* Remove charcoal canister. Remove retaining bolts from relay box located near strut tower. Disconnect luggage compartment cable near relay box. Remove upper and lower covers from relay box.

**6)** Disconnect positive cable and electrical connections from relay box. Remove ignition coil and ignitor. Disconnect electrical connectors from Electronic Control Unit (ECU) located near luggage compartment. *See Fig. 8.*

**7)** Disconnect electrical connectors from starter relay, cooling fan relay and engine wiring connector. These electrical connectors are located near ECU. *See Fig. 8.* Pull engine wiring out through opening in luggage compartment.

**8)** Disconnect necessary control cables, coolant hoses, fuel lines, vacuum hoses and electrical connections. Raise and support vehicle. Disconnect control cables at transaxle. Remove muffler assembly.

**9)** Disconnect exhaust pipe and gasket from catalytic converter. Exhaust pipe can be rotated and removed from between suspension crossmember and body. Remove cooling fan assembly.

**10)** Remove drive belt and idler pulley bracket. Remove A/C compressor with hoses attached, and secure aside. Remove intercooler. See INTERCOOLER under REMOVAL & INSTALLATION. Remove rear engine mount (intake manifold side). Disconnect speedometer cable at transaxle.

**11)** Remove retaining nut, and disconnect stabilizer link from strut assembly. Remove retaining bolt, and disconnect anti-lock brake sensor wire from body.

**12)** Both lower control arms must be removed. Remove ball joint stud-to-lower control arm nut. Separate lower control arms from ball joints at wheel/hub assembly. Remove strut rod-to-lower control arm retaining nuts and retainers. Remove lower control arm-to-body retaining bolts. Remove lower control arms.

**13)** Remove cotter pin, retainer and axle shaft nut. Remove brake caliper, and secure aside. Place reference marks on brake rotor and hub assembly for reassembly reference. Remove brake rotor.

**14)** Remove retaining bolt, and remove anti-lock brake sensor from hub assembly carrier. Remove tie rod-to-hub assembly carrier bolt. Wrap axle shaft threads with tape. Cover axle shaft boot with shop towel.

**15)** Using puller attached to hub assembly, press axle shaft from hub assembly. To remove left axle shaft, use hammer and brass drift to drive axle shaft from transaxle. *See Fig. 9.*

**16)** To remove right axle shaft, remove snap ring and bearing retaining bolt from bearing bracket. *See Fig. 10.* Remove right axle shaft with center shaft assembly. Remove retaining bolts and bearing bracket.

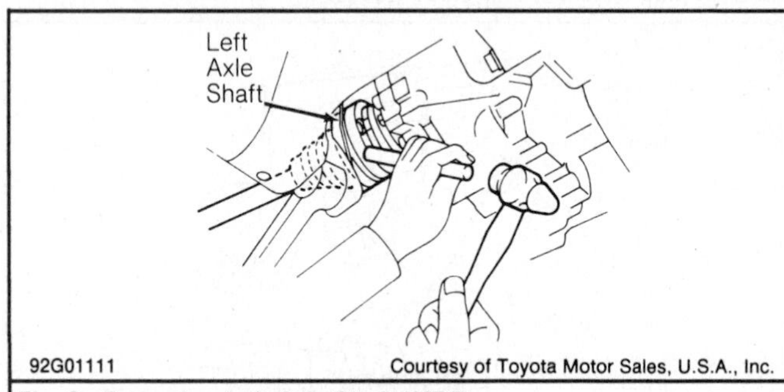


Courtesy of Toyota Motor Sales, U.S.A., Inc.

***Fig. 9: Removing Left Axle Shaft (MR2)***

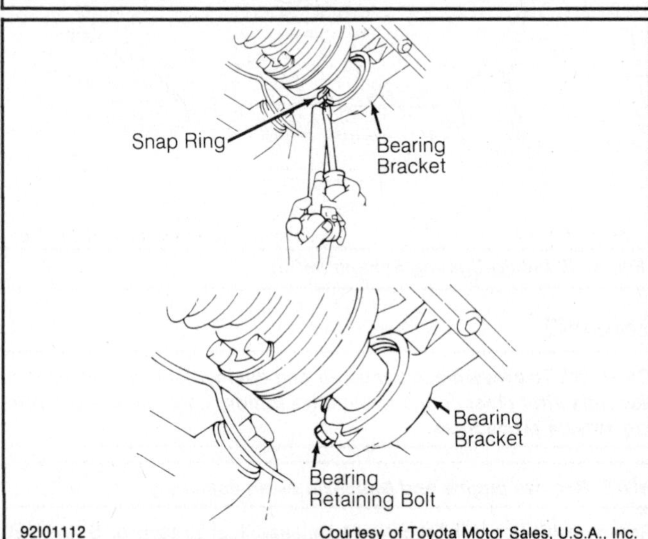


Courtesy of Toyota Motor Sales, U.S.A., Inc.

***Fig. 10: Removing Right Axle Shaft (MR2)***

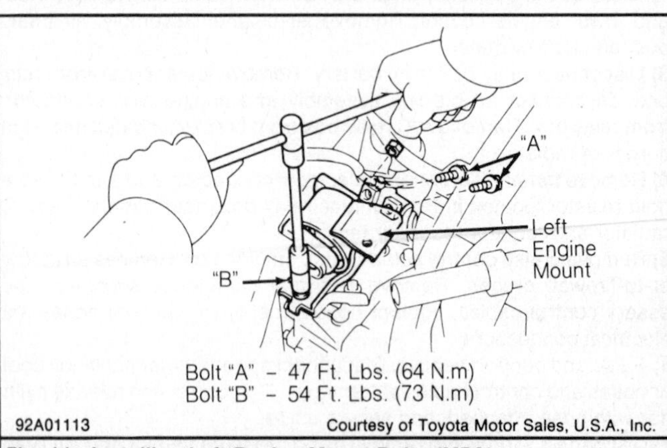


Courtesy of Toyota Motor Sales, U.S.A., Inc.

***Fig. 11: Installing Left Engine Mount Bolts (MR2)***

# 1991 ENGINES
# 2.0L 4-Cylinder (Cont.)

**17)** Support rear suspension crossmember with floor jack. Remove retaining bolts, and remove rear suspension crossmember. Remove through bolt and retaining bolts from front engine mount (exhaust manifold side). Remove clutch release cylinder from transaxle with hose attached, and secure aside.

**18)** Remove air cleaner case support bracket. Support engine with hoist. Remove remaining engine mount support brackets and through bolts. Lower engine and transaxle through bottom of engine compartment.

**Installation – 1)** Install right engine mount (timing belt side) to body with through bolt loosely installed. Secure right engine mount insulator to mounting bracket with nuts loosely installed.

**2)** Install left engine mount (flywheel side) to body with through bolt loosely installed. Install left engine mount insulator to mounting bracket, and tighten bolts to specification. *See Fig. 11.*

**3)** Install left engine mount through bolt, and tighten to specification. See appropriate TORQUE SPECIFICATIONS table at end of article. Tighten right engine mount nuts and through bolt to specification.

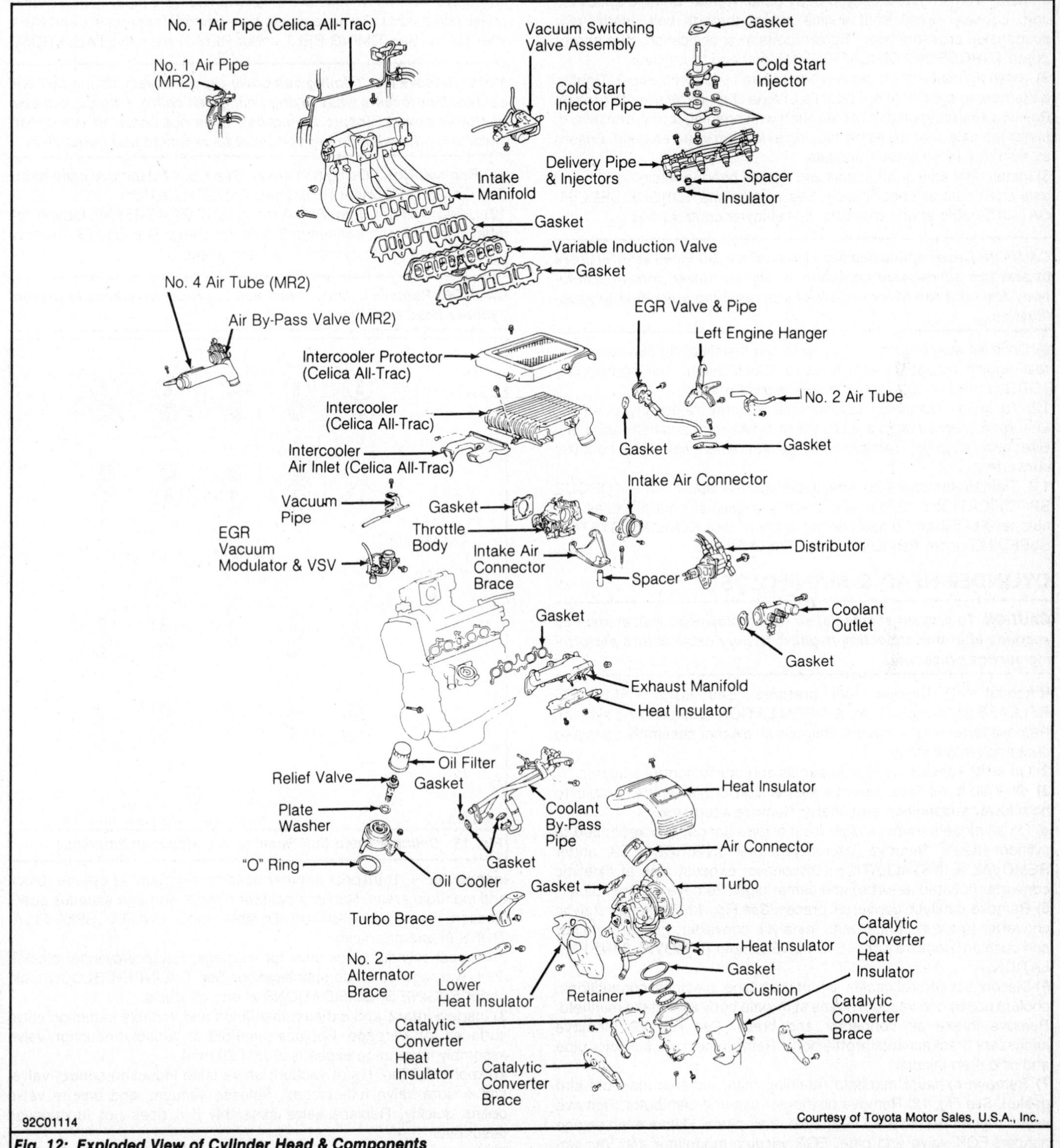


**Fig. 12: Exploded View of Cylinder Head & Components**

# 1991 ENGINES
# 2.0L 4-Cylinder (Cont.)

Install support bracket on top of right engine mount. Tighten bolts/nuts to specification.

**4)** Install air cleaner case bracket and left engine mount support bracket. Tighten bolts to specification. See appropriate TORQUE SPECIFICATIONS table at end of article.

**5)** Install clutch release cylinder with bolts loosely installed. Install front engine mount bracket (exhaust manifold side). Tighten clutch release cylinder and front engine mount bracket bolts to specification. See appropriate TORQUE SPECIFICATIONS table at end of article.

**6)** Install front engine mount-to-body bolts. Tighten bolts to specification. Loosely install front engine mount through bolt. Install rear suspension crossmember. Tighten bolts to specification. See appropriate TORQUE SPECIFICATIONS table at end of article.

**7)** Install right axle shaft bearing bracket and support bracket. Tighten bolts/nuts to specification. Coat lip of axle shaft oil seals with grease. Position snap ring on end of axle shaft with opening facing downward. Install left axle shaft by lightly tapping axle shaft into transaxle. Ensure axle shaft fully engages transaxle.

**8)** Install right axle shaft. Install and tighten bearing retaining bolt and axle shaft nuts to specification. See appropriate TORQUE SPECIFICATIONS table at end of article. Install lower control arms.

***CAUTION: Once vehicle has been lowered and bounced several times to stabilize suspension components, tighten lower control arm-to-body and strut rod-to-lower control arm retaining bolts/nuts to specification.***

**9)** Once all suspension components are installed, tighten front and rear engine mount through bolts to specification. See appropriate TORQUE SPECIFICATIONS table at end of article.

**10)** To install remaining components, reverse removal procedure. Ensure reference marks are aligned on brake rotor and hub assembly. Use new cushion, retainer and gasket when installing catalytic converter.

**11)** Tighten fasteners to specification. See appropriate TORQUE SPECIFICATIONS table at end of article. Adjust all control cables and fluid levels. Fill and bleed cooling system. See COOLING SYSTEM BLEEDING under REMOVAL & INSTALLATION.

## CYLINDER HEAD & MANIFOLDS

***CAUTION: To prevent accidental air bag deployment, wait at least 20 seconds after disconnecting negative battery cable before performing service procedures.***

**Removal – 1)** Release fuel pressure. See FUEL PRESSURE RELEASE under REMOVAL & INSTALLATION. Drain cooling system. Remove lower engine covers. Remove air cleaner assembly, air intake duct and airflow meter.

**2)** On MR2, remove hood side panels and cruise control actuator.

**3)** On Celica All-Trac, remove suspension crossmember bolted to both lower suspension arm shafts. Remove alternator.

**4)** On all models, remove right front engine hanger bracket bolted to cylinder head. Remove intercooler. See INTERCOOLER under REMOVAL & INSTALLATION. Disconnect exhaust pipe at catalytic converter (located at turbo) and center pipe. Remove exhaust pipe.

**5)** Remove catalytic converter braces. *See Fig. 12.* Remove catalytic converter-to-turbo flange bolts, catalytic converter, gasket, retainer and cushion. Remove turbo. See TURBO under REMOVAL & INSTALLATION.

**6)** Disconnect control cables, air intake tubing, electrical connections, coolant hoses and vacuum hoses at throttle body and intake manifold. Remove intake air connector and brace. *See Fig. 12.* Remove necessary brackets and throttle body. Remove cold start injector pipe and cold start injector.

**7)** Remove exhaust manifold retaining nuts, exhaust manifold and gasket. *See Fig. 12.* Remove distributor cap and distributor. Remove vacuum pipe. Remove No. 1 and No. 2 air pipes. Remove left engine hanger, EGR valve and pipe, EGR vacuum modulator and Vacuum Switching Valve (VSV).

**8)** Remove vacuum tube. Disconnect hoses, and remove coolant outlet and coolant by-pass pipe. Remove oil pressure switch. Remove VSV assembly. *See Fig. 12.* Remove oil cooler. See OIL COOLER under ENGINE OILING.

**9)** Remove intake manifold braces, intake manifold bolts/nuts, intake manifold, variable induction valve and gaskets. Remove charcoal canister. Disconnect hoses from pressure regulator and delivery pipe. Disconnect injector wiring.

**10)** Remove retaining bolts, delivery pipe, injectors, spacers and insulators. DO NOT allow injectors to fall from delivery pipe. Remove valve cover and gasket. Remove timing belt, camshaft sprockets and No. 1 idler pulley. See TIMING BELT under REMOVAL & INSTALLATION.

***NOTE: Remove No. 2 timing belt cover (upper cover), timing belt and camshaft sprockets while laying timing belt on No. 1 timing belt cover (lower cover). Ensure timing belt does not come off crankshaft sprocket, otherwise timing belt must be removed and reinstalled.***

**11)** Remove No. 3 timing belt cover. *See Fig. 17.* Remove camshafts. See CAMSHAFT under REMOVAL & INSTALLATION.

**12)** Using Cylinder Head Bolt Wrench (SST 09043-38100), loosen cylinder head bolts in sequence in several steps. *See Fig. 13.* Remove cylinder head bolts, cylinder head and gasket.

***CAUTION: Remove cylinder head bolt in proper sequence to prevent cylinder head warpage.***

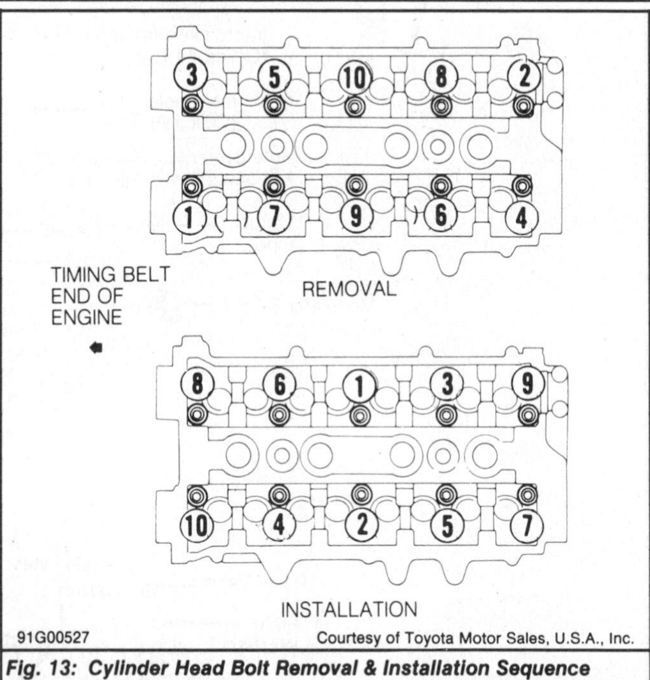


***Fig. 13: Cylinder Head Bolt Removal & Installation Sequence***

**Inspection – 1)** Inspect cylinder head for warpage at cylinder block and manifold areas. Replace cylinder head if warpage exceeds specification. See CYLINDER HEAD table under ENGINE SPECIFICATIONS at end of article.

**2)** Inspect cylinder block deck for warpage. Replace cylinder block if deck warpage exceeds specification. See CYLINDER BLOCK table under ENGINE SPECIFICATIONS at end of article.

**3)** Inspect intake and exhaust manifolds and variable induction valve surfaces for warpage. Replace manifold or variable induction valve assembly if warpage exceeds .008" (.20 mm).

**4)** Apply 15.75 in. Hg of vacuum on variable induction control valve, and ensure valve fully closes. Release vacuum, and ensure valve opens quickly. Replace valve assembly if it does not function as described.

**5)** Inspect camshaft and components. See CAMSHAFT under REMOVAL & INSTALLATION.

**Installation - 1)** To install, reverse removal procedure. Apply engine oil on cylinder head bolt threads and head bolt-to-cylinder head contact surfaces.
**2)** Install and tighten cylinder head bolts to specification in sequence. *See Fig. 13.* See appropriate TORQUE SPECIFICATIONS table at end of article.
**3)** If camshaft or cylinder head components are serviced, adjust valve clearance. See VALVE CLEARANCE ADJUSTMENT under ADJUSTMENTS.
**4)** Before installing valve cover and gasket, apply sealant at front and rear areas of cylinder head. *See Fig. 2.* Install gasket and valve cover. Tighten to bolts specification. See appropriate TORQUE SPECIFICATIONS table at end article.
**5)** Install throttle body gasket with protruding area toward top of throttle body (opposite coolant line connections). Longer bolts are used in lower throttle body holes. Tighten bolts to specification. See appropriate TORQUE SPECIFICATIONS table at end of article.
**6)** If injector was removed from delivery pipe, coat new "O" ring with gasoline. Install new insulator and "O" ring on injector.
**7)** Coat coolant by-pass pipe "O" ring with soapy water before installing. Coat distributor "O" ring with engine oil. When installing distributor, rotate crankshaft clockwise so slot area of intake camshaft is positioned vertically.
**8)** Position cutout on coupling with alignment mark on housing. *See Fig. 14.* Install distributor and retaining bolts.
**9)** Use new cushion, retainer and gasket when installing catalytic converter. To install remaining components, reverse removal procedure. Tighten all fasteners to specification. See appropriate TORQUE SPECIFICATIONS table at end of article. Adjust control cables. Fill cooling system.

***CAUTION: On MR2, cooling system must be bled to prevent engine damage. See COOLING SYSTEM BLEEDING under REMOVAL & INSTALLATION.***

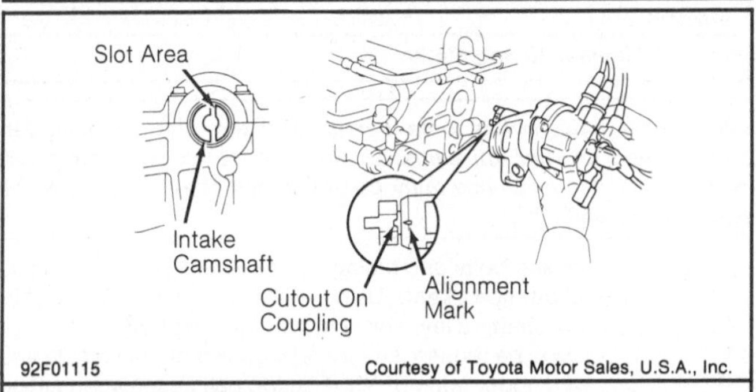


***Fig. 14: Installing Distributor***

## TURBO

**Removal (Celica All-Trac) - 1)** Disconnect negative battery cable. Remove lower engine covers. Drain cooling system. Remove air cleaner assembly, air intake duct and airflow meter.
**2)** Raise and support vehicle. Remove suspension crossmember bolted to both lower suspension arm shafts. Support engine with hoist. Remove engine mount crossmember located below engine.
**3)** Disconnect exhaust pipe at catalytic converter (located at turbo) and center pipe. Remove exhaust pipe. Remove front engine mount and bracket from cylinder block.
**4)** Remove clutch master cylinder with hose attached, and secure aside. Remove alternator. Remove idler pulley bracket. Remove A/C compressor with hoses attached, and secure aside.
**5)** Remove catalytic converter-to-turbo flange bolts, catalytic converter, gasket, retainer and cushion. *See Fig. 12.* Remove intercooler air inlet, intercooler protector and intercooler.
**6)** Remove oxygen sensor. Remove all heat insulators from turbo. *See Fig.12.* Disconnect necessary oil pipes, coolant hoses and vacuum hoses from turbo. Remove brace located below turbo. Remove turbo retaining nuts, turbo and gaskets.

**Inspection - 1)** Ensure impeller wheel rotates smoothly. Using dial indicator, check impeller shaft end play. *See Fig. 15.* Replace turbo if end play exceeds .0051" (.130 mm).
**2)** Place tip of dial indicator through oil return hole. Tip of dial indicator must be positioned through opening in bearing and on impeller wheel shaft.
**3)** Move impeller shaft toward turbo mounting flange and then toward outside of turbo, and check radial clearance. *See Fig. 15.* Replace turbo if radial clearance exceeds .0071" (.180 mm).

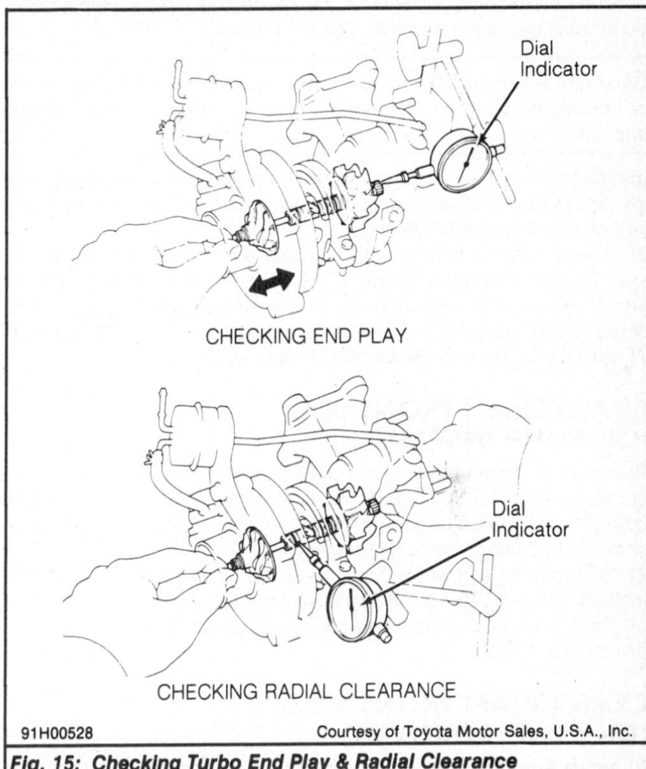


***Fig. 15: Checking Turbo End Play & Radial Clearance***

***CAUTION: When installing turbo, pour about .6 ounce (20 cc) of engine oil in oil supply pipe opening of turbo while rotating impeller shaft.***

**Installation - 1)** To install, reverse removal procedure using new gaskets. When installing turbo, loosely install all fasteners on turbo and oil pipes before tightening.
**2)** Tighten turbo retaining nuts first and then all other fasteners to specification. See appropriate TORQUE SPECIFICATIONS table at end of article. Use new cushion, retainer and gasket when installing catalytic converter. Fill cooling system.
**Removal (MR2) - 1)** Disconnect negative battery cable. Remove lower engine covers and hood side panels. Drain cooling system. Remove strut tower-to-firewall braces. Remove air cleaner assembly, air intake duct and airflow meter.
**2)** Remove No. 1 and No. 2 air intake connectors. *See Fig. 23.* Disconnect control cables at transaxle. Disconnect exhaust pipe and gasket from catalytic converter. Exhaust pipe can be rotated and removed from between suspension crossmember and body.
**3)** Remove idler pulley bracket. Remove A/C compressor with hoses attached, and secure aside. Remove front engine mount (exhaust manifold side) and bracket from cylinder block.
**4)** Remove clutch master cylinder with hose attached, and secure aside. Remove engine cooling fan.
**5)** Remove catalytic converter-to-turbo flange bolts, catalytic converter, gasket, retainer and cushion. *See Fig. 12.* Disconnect hoses, and remove air by-pass valve and No. 4 air tube.
**6)** Remove oxygen sensor. Remove all heat insulators from turbo. *See Fig. 12.* Disconnect necessary oil pipes, coolant hoses and vacuum

# 1991 ENGINES
# 2.0L 4-Cylinder (Cont.)

hoses from turbo. Remove brace located below turbo. Remove turbo retaining nuts, turbo and gaskets.

**Inspection - 1)** Ensure impeller wheel rotates smoothly. Using dial indicator, check impeller shaft end play. *See Fig. 15.* Replace turbo if end play exceeds .0051" (.130 mm).

**2)** Place tip of dial indicator through oil return hole. Tip of dial indicator must be positioned through opening in bearing and on impeller wheel shaft.

**3)** Move impeller shaft toward turbo mounting flange and then toward outside of turbo, and check radial clearance. *See Fig. 15.* Replace turbo if radial clearance exceeds .0071" (.180 mm).

***CAUTION: When installing turbo, pour approximately .6 ounces (20 cc) of engine oil in oil supply pipe opening of turbo while rotating impeller shaft.***

**Installation - 1)** To install, reverse removal procedure using new gaskets. When installing turbo, loosely install all fasteners on turbo and oil pipes before tightening.

**2)** Tighten turbo retaining nuts first and then all other fasteners to specification. See appropriate TORQUE SPECIFICATIONS table at end of article. Use new cushion, retainer and gasket when installing catalytic converter. Fill and bleed cooling system. See COOLING SYSTEM BLEEDING under REMOVAL & INSTALLATION.

## CRANKSHAFT FRONT SEAL (OIL PUMP INSTALLED)

**Removal & Installation - 1)** Remove timing belt and crankshaft sprocket. See TIMING BELT under REMOVAL & INSTALLATION. Using a knife, cut off oil seal lip. Pry seal from oil pump housing, using care not to damage sealing surfaces.

**2)** To install, apply grease to lip of new seal. Using hammer and Seal Installer (SST 09226-10010), install seal until seal surface is even with oil pump housing. To install remaining components, reverse removal procedure.

## CRANKSHAFT FRONT SEAL (OIL PUMP REMOVED)

**Removal & Installation -** Using hammer and drift, remove seal from oil pump housing. To install, using hammer and Seal Installer (09226-10010), install seal until seal surface is even with oil pump housing. Apply grease to lip of new oil seal.

## TIMING BELT

**Removal - 1)** Disconnect negative battery cable. Drain cooling system. Raise and support vehicle. Remove right front wheel.

**2)** On Celica All-Trac, remove right lower engine cover. Remove alternator.

**3)** On MR2, remove lower engine covers and right hood side panel. Remove strut tower-to-firewall braces. Remove cruise control actuator.

**4)** On all models, remove intercooler. See INTERCOOLER under REMOVAL & INSTALLATION. Remove EGR valve modulator, vacuum switching valve, EGR valve and pipe.

**5)** Disconnect control cables, electrical connections, vacuum hoses and coolant hoses from throttle body. Remove intake air connector. *See Fig. 12.* Remove accelerator cable bracket. Remove retaining bolts, throttle body and gasket.

**6)** Remove drive belts. Slightly raise engine to remove weight from mount at timing belt cover. Remove top brace on engine mount at timing belt cover.

**7)** Remove retaining bolts/nuts and engine mount assembly. Lower engine, and remove mount bracket from timing belt cover area of cylinder block. Remove valve cover and spark plugs.

**8)** Remove No. 2 timing belt cover with gasket. *See Fig. 16.* Rotate crankshaft clockwise so No. 1 cylinder is at TDC of compression stroke, with timing mark on crankshaft pulley aligned with "0" mark on No. 1 timing belt cover.

**9)** Ensure timing marks of camshaft sprockets align with timing marks on No. 3 timing belt cover. *See Fig. 17.*

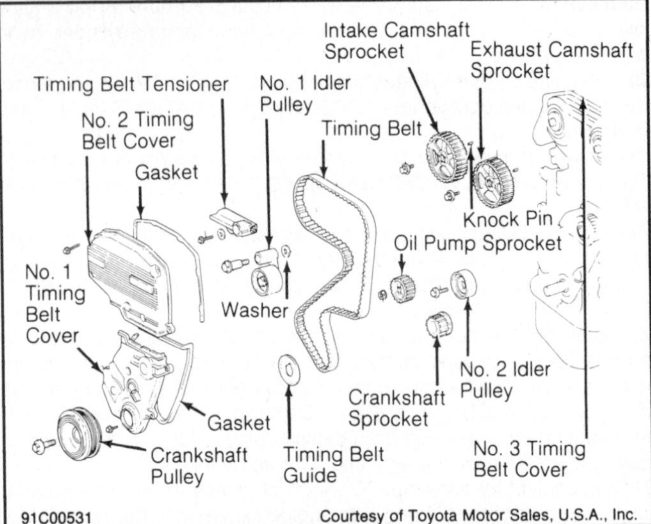


*Fig. 16: Exploded View of Timing Belt & Components*

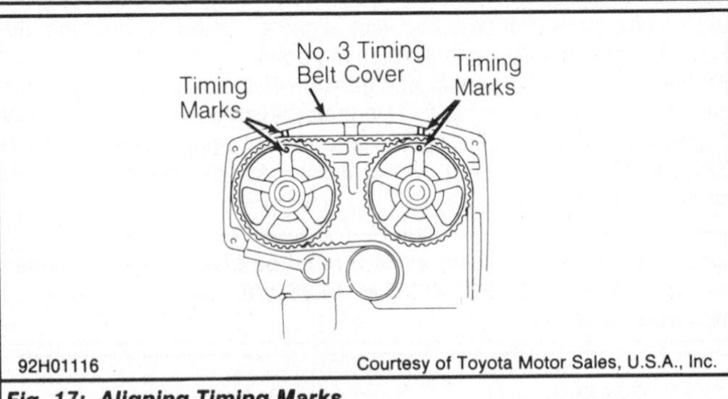


*Fig. 17: Aligning Timing Marks*

***CAUTION: If timing belt is to be reused, mark direction of timing belt rotation and location on camshaft sprocket for reassembly reference. Also place reference mark on timing belt at upper edge of the No. 1 timing belt cover.***

**10)** Remove retaining bolts and timing belt tensioner. Remove timing belt from camshaft sprockets. Using Pulley Holder (SST 09213-54015), hold crankshaft pulley, and remove retaining bolt.

**11)** If timing belt is to be reused, ensure reference mark placed on timing belt aligns with upper edge of No. 1 timing belt cover when timing mark on crankshaft pulley is aligned with "0" mark on No. 1 timing belt cover.

**12)** Using puller, remove crankshaft pulley. DO NOT allow crankshaft to rotate. Remove No. 1 timing belt cover and gasket. If timing belt is to be reused, mark direction of belt rotation, and place reference marks on timing belt and crankshaft sprocket for reassembly reference.

**13)** Note direction of timing belt guide installation for reassembly reference. Remove timing belt guide and timing belt. Remove idler pulleys (if necessary).

**14)** If removing camshaft sprockets, hold hexagonal area at front of camshaft, and remove retaining bolt, washer and camshaft sprocket.

**15)** If removing crankshaft sprocket, place shop towels against oil pump housing. Using 2 screwdrivers, pry crankshaft sprocket from crankshaft.

**16)** If removing oil pump sprocket, use Sprocket Holder (SST 09616-30011) to hold oil pump sprocket. Remove retaining nut and oil pump sprocket.

**Inspection - 1)** Inspect timing belt for damaged teeth, cracking or oil contamination. Ensure idler pulleys rotate freely. Replace damaged components.

**2)** Inspect timing belt tensioner for signs of oil leakage. Replace timing belt tensioner if oil leakage exists. Hold timing belt tensioner body, and press rod against solid surface. Replace timing belt tensioner if rod moves.

**3)** Measure timing belt tensioner rod protrusion from end of rod to edge of timing belt tensioner housing. *See Fig. 18.* Replace timing belt tensioner if distance is not .335-.374" (8.51-9.50 mm).

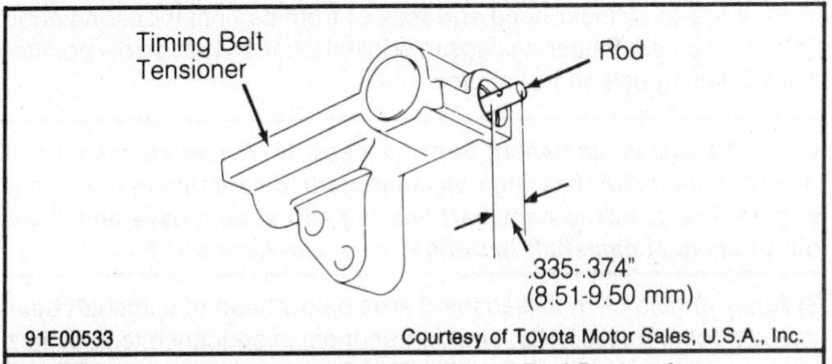


*Fig. 18: Measuring Timing Belt Tensioner Rod Protrusion*

**Installation – 1)** If oil pump sprocket is removed, align cutouts of oil pump sprocket and shaft, and install sprocket. Install and tighten nut to specification. See appropriate TORQUE SPECIFICATIONS table at end of article.

**2)** If crankshaft sprocket is removed, align crankshaft sprocket with crankshaft key, and install sprocket.

**3)** Install No. 2 idler pulley (if removed). Install and tighten retaining bolt to specification. See appropriate TORQUE SPECIFICATIONS table at end of article. Apply Loctite to No. 1 idler pulley bolt, and install idler pulley and washer. Tighten retaining bolt to specification. Ensure idler pulleys are clean and rotate smoothly.

**4)** Rotate crankshaft so keyway of crankshaft is at 12 o'clock position. Install timing belt on crankshaft sprocket, oil pump sprocket, No. 2 idler pulley, water pump sprocket and No. 1 idler pulley.

***CAUTION: If timing belt is reused, ensure reference marks are aligned on crankshaft sprocket and timing belt is installed in original direction of rotation.***

**5)** Install timing belt guide with cupped side away from crankshaft sprocket. Install No. 1 timing belt cover and gasket. Align crankshaft key with key groove of crankshaft pulley, and install pulley. Tighten retaining bolt to specification. See appropriate TORQUE SPECIFICATIONS table at end of article.

**6)** Rotate camshaft, and align grooves with drilled mark on camshaft bearing caps. *See Fig. 19.* If camshaft sprockets are removed, install camshaft sprockets on camshafts with "S" mark facing outward, toward top of cylinder head. Align knock pin holes, and install knock pin. *See Fig. 16.*

***NOTE: The "S" mark is located on camshaft sprocket, near center hub of camshaft sprocket.***

**7)** Install and tighten camshaft sprocket bolt to specification. See appropriate TORQUE SPECIFICATIONS table at end of article.

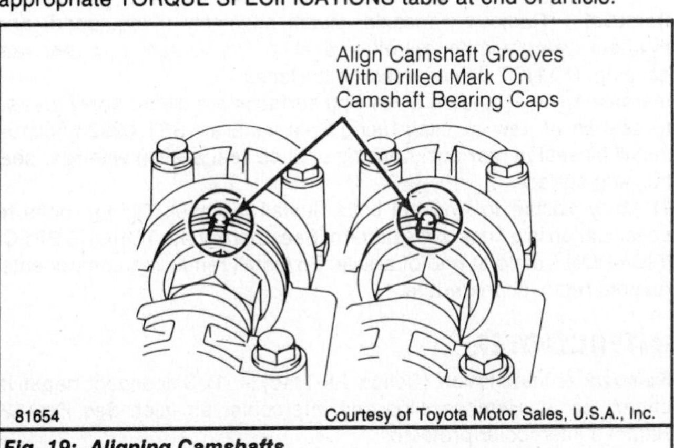


*Fig. 19: Aligning Camshafts*

**8)** Rotate crankshaft pulley so timing mark on crankshaft pulley aligns with "0" mark on No. 1 timing belt cover. Rotate camshafts so timing marks align. *See Fig. 17.*

**9)** Install timing belt on camshaft sprockets. If timing belt is reused, ensure reference marks are aligned on camshaft sprockets and upper edge of No. 1 timing belt cover.

**10)** Using press, push rod back into timing belt tensioner housing until hole in rod aligns with holes of timing belt tensioner housing. Install a .050" (1.27 mm) Allen wrench through holes of timing belt tensioner housing and rod. Remove timing belt tensioner from press.

**11)** Place torque wrench on bolt located at center of No. 1 idler pulley bolt. DO NOT use No. 1 idler pulley-to-cylinder block bolt. Rotate bolt and No. 1 idler pulley counterclockwise to obtain torque reading of 13 ft. lbs. (18 N.m). Install timing belt tensioner.

***NOTE: Torque wrench must be installed on No. 1 idler pulley bolt with handle near camshaft sprocket to obtain correct torque reading.***

**12)** Rotate crankshaft clockwise 5 to 6 revolutions, and align crankshaft pulley timing mark with 60-degree ATDC timing mark on No. 1 timing belt cover. *See Fig. 20.* DO NOT rotate crankshaft counterclockwise.

**13)** Install a .075" (1.90 mm) feeler gauge between timing belt tensioner and No. 1 idler pulley stopper. *See Fig. 21.* Place torque wrench on bolt located at center of No. 1 idler pulley. DO NOT use No. 1 idler pulley-to-cylinder block bolt.

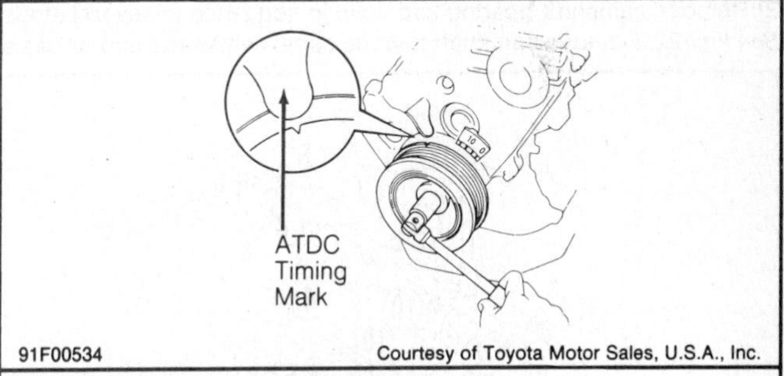


*Fig. 20: Aligning ATDC Timing Mark*

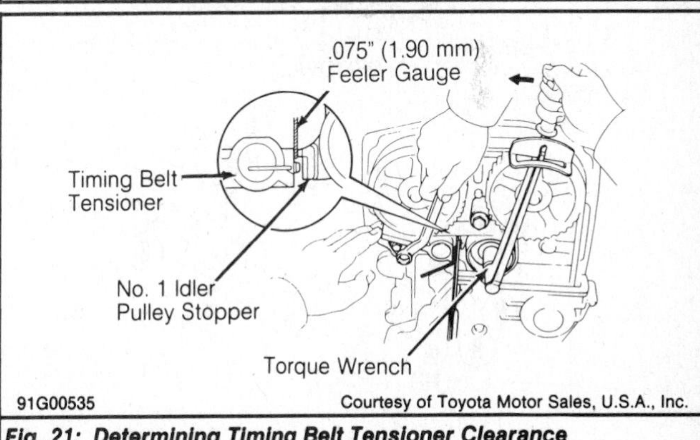


*Fig. 21: Determining Timing Belt Tensioner Clearance*

**14)** Rotate bolt and No. 1 idler pulley counterclockwise again to obtain torque reading of 13 ft. lbs. (18 N.m). With tension on timing belt tensioner, tighten belt tensioner retaining bolts to specification. See appropriate TORQUE SPECIFICATIONS table at end of article.

**15)** Remove .050" (1.27 mm) Allen wrench from timing belt tensioner. Rotate crankshaft clockwise one revolution so timing mark aligns with 60-degree ATDC mark.

**16)** Rotate bolt and No. 1 idler pulley counterclockwise again to obtain torque reading of 13 ft. lbs. (18 N.m). Recheck clearance between the No. 1 idler puller stopper and timing belt tensioner.

**17)** If clearance is not .071-.087" (1.80-2.20 mm), remove timing belt tensioner and reinstall. Rotate crankshaft clockwise 2 full revolutions from TDC to TDC.

# 1991 ENGINES
# 2.0L 4-Cylinder (Cont.)

**18)** Ensure all timing marks align. *See Fig. 17.* If timing marks do not align, remove timing belt and reinstall. To install remaining components, reverse removal procedure.
**19)** Before installing valve cover and gasket, apply sealant at front and rear areas of cylinder head. *See Fig. 2.* Install throttle body gasket with protruding area toward top of throttle body (opposite coolant line connections). Longer bolts are used in lower throttle body holes.
**20)** Tighten bolts to specification. See appropriate TORQUE SPECIFICATIONS table at end of article. Fill cooling system.

***CAUTION: On MR2, cooling system must be bled to prevent engine damage. See COOLING SYSTEM BLEEDING under REMOVAL & INSTALLATION.***

## CAMSHAFT

**Removal - 1)** Remove timing belt and camshaft sprockets. See TIMING BELT under REMOVAL & INSTALLATION. Remove No. 3 timing belt cover. *See Fig. 17.* When removing intake camshaft, remove distributor.

***NOTE: Camshaft bearing caps are numbered for location with No. 1 toward timing belt end of cylinder head. Top of camshaft bearing cap is marked with "I" for intake or "E" for exhaust. Arrow on camshaft bearing cap must point toward timing belt end of engine.***

**2)** Remove camshaft bearing cap bolts in sequence in several steps. *See Fig. 22.* Remove camshaft bearing caps, camshafts and oil seals.

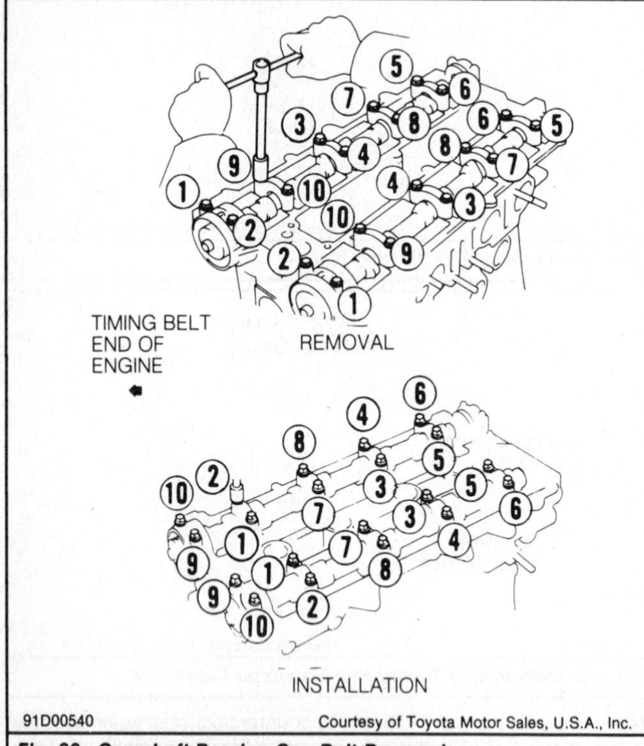


***Fig. 22: Camshaft Bearing Cap Bolt Removal & Installation Sequence***

**Inspection - 1)** Inspect components for damage. Check camshaft journal diameter, lobe height and runout. Replace camshaft if measurements are not within specification. See CAMSHAFT table under ENGINE SPECIFICATIONS at end of article.
**2)** Install camshaft in cylinder head. Using Plastigage, check camshaft oil clearance. Tighten camshaft bearing cap bolts to specification in sequence when checking oil clearance. *See Fig. 22.* See appropriate TORQUE SPECIFICATIONS table at end of article.
**3)** Replace camshaft and/or cylinder head if oil clearance is not within specification. See CAMSHAFT table.
**4)** Check camshaft end play with camshaft bearing cap bolts tightened to specification. Replace camshaft and/or cylinder head if end play is not within specification. See CAMSHAFT table.

**Installation - 1)** Install camshafts with front camshaft lobes pointing toward outside of cylinder head. Apply Seal Packing (08826-00080) on outer edge-to-cylinder head surfaces of front camshaft bearing caps.
**2)** Install camshaft bearing caps in original location with arrow pointing toward timing belt end of engine.

***CAUTION: Install camshaft bearing caps in numerical sequence. Arrow on camshaft bearing cap must point toward timing belt end of engine. Top of intake camshaft bearing cap should have an "I" and top of exhaust camshaft bearing cap should have an "E".***

**3)** Apply engine oil to threads and area below head of camshaft bearing cap bolts. Install bolts, and tighten them in sequence to specification in several steps. *See Fig. 22.* See appropriate TORQUE SPECIFICATIONS table at end of article.
**4)** Coat new camshaft oil seal with grease. Using Seal Installer (SST 09223-50010), install oil seals. To install remaining components, reverse removal procedure.

***CAUTION: If cylinder head or camshaft is serviced or replaced, check valve clearance. See VALVE CLEARANCE ADJUSTMENT under ADJUSTMENTS.***

**5)** Before installing valve cover and gasket, apply sealant at front and rear areas of cylinder head. *See Fig. 2.* Install valve cover and gasket.
**6)** When installing distributor, rotate crankshaft clockwise so slot area of intake camshaft is positioned vertically. Position cutout on coupling with alignment mark on housing. *See Fig. 14.* Install distributor and retaining bolts.
**7)** To install remaining components, reverse removal procedure. Tighten all fasteners to specification. See appropriate TORQUE SPECIFICATIONS table at end of article.

## VALVE LIFTER

**Removal -** Remove camshaft. See CAMSHAFT under REMOVAL & INSTALLATION. Note location of adjusting shims and valve lifter for reassembly reference. Remove adjusting shim and valve lifter from cylinder head.
**Inspection -** Inspect components for damage. Measure lifter diameter and bore diameter. Ensure oil clearance is within specification. Replace components if diameters are not within specification. See VALVE LIFTERS table under ENGINE SPECIFICATIONS at end of article.
**Installation -** To install, reverse removal procedure. Ensure components are installed in original location. If camshaft, adjusting shims or valve lifter are replaced, check valve clearance. See VALVE CLEARANCE ADJUSTMENT under ADJUSTMENTS.

## REAR CRANKSHAFT OIL SEAL

**Removal -** Remove transaxle, clutch assembly (if equipped) and flywheel. Using a knife, cut off oil seal lip. Pry oil seal from rear seal housing. DO NOT damage sealing surfaces.
**Installation - 1)** Ensure all sealing surfaces are clean. Apply grease to seal lip of new oil seal. Using Seal Installer (SST 09223-63010), install oil seal in rear seal housing until oil seal is even with rear seal housing surface.
**2)** Apply Loctite to flywheel bolts. Install flywheel. Tighten bolts to specification in a crisscross pattern. See appropriate TORQUE SPECIFICATIONS table at end of article. To install remaining components, reverse removal procedure.

## INTERCOOLER

**Removal & Installation (Celica All-Trac) - 1)** Disconnect negative battery cable. Remove clips and intercooler air inlet. *See Fig. 12.* Remove intercooler protector.

2) Remove bolts, and disconnect intercooler from turbo air intake air connector. Remove intercooler assembly. To install, reverse removal procedure.

**Removal & Installation (MR2) – 1)** Disconnect negative battery cable. Remove lower engine covers and right hood side panel. Remove No. 1 and No. 2 air intake connectors. *See Fig. 23.* Remove cruise control actuator and accelerator linkage.

**2)** Remove cooling fan assembly. Disconnect engine wiring from timing belt cover. Remove engine hanger from front corner of cylinder head. Disconnect parking brake cable from body.

**3)** Remove suspension brace. *See Fig. 23.* Remove drive belt and idler pulley bracket. Remove A/C compressor with hoses attached, and secure aside. Remove retaining bolts, and remove intercooler. To install, reverse removal procedure.

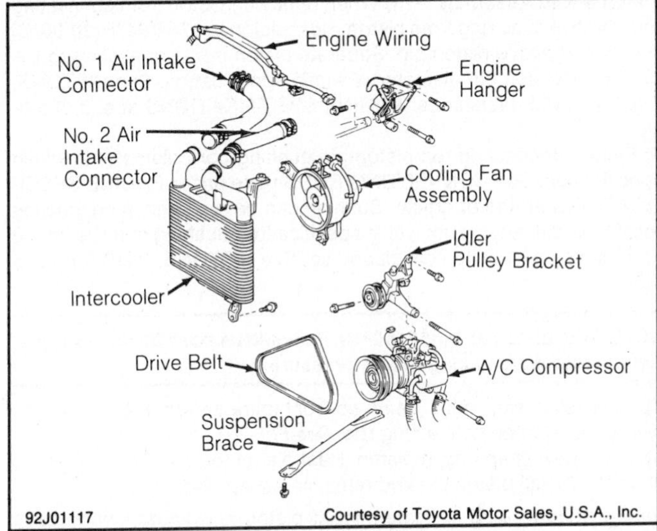


*Fig. 23: Exploded View of Intercooler (MR2)*

## WATER PUMP

**Removal (Celica All-Trac) – 1)** Disconnect negative battery cable. Drain cooling system. Remove timing belt and No. 2 idler pulley. See TIMING BELT under REMOVAL & INSTALLATION.

**2)** On models without A/C, remove drive belt and idler pulley bracket. Disconnect radiator hose at water pump. Disconnect oil cooler coolant by-pass hose. *See Fig. 24.* Remove coolant by-pass pipe-to-water pump cover retaining nuts.

**3)** Remove water pump bolts in sequence. *See Fig. 25.* Remove water, water pump cover and "O" rings. Remove retaining bolts, and separate water pump and gasket from water pump cover. *See Fig. 24.*

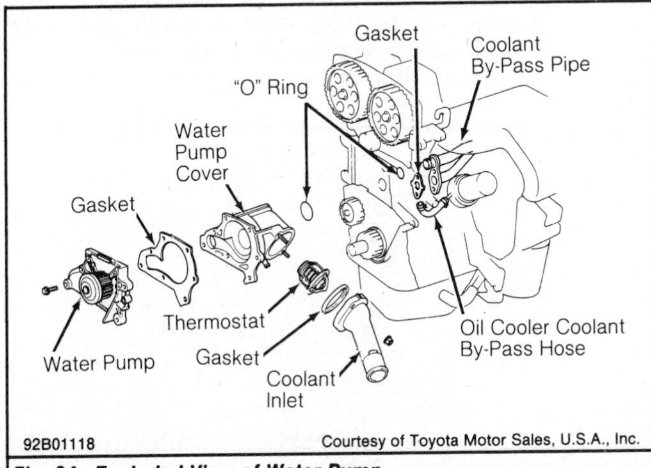


*Fig. 24: Exploded View of Water Pump*

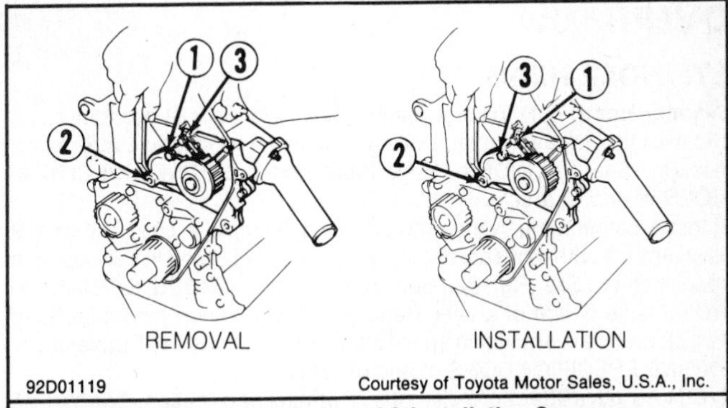


*Fig. 25: Water Pump Bolt Removal & Installation Sequence*

**Installation – 1)** To install, reverse removal procedure using new gaskets and "O" rings. Apply soapy water solution to coolant by-pass pipe "O" ring before installing water pump. DO NOT tighten coolant by-pass pipe-to-water pump cover retaining nuts until water pump bolts are tightened to specification.

**2)** Tighten water pump bolts to specification in sequence. *See Fig. 25.* See appropriate TORQUE SPECIFICATIONS table at end of article. To install remaining components, reverse removal procedure. Fill cooling system.

**Removal (MR2) – 1)** Drain cooling system. Remove timing belt and No. 2 idler pulley. See TIMING BELT under REMOVAL & INSTALLATION. Disconnect radiator hose at water pump. Remove oil cooler. See OIL COOLER under ENGINE OILING.

**2)** Remove coolant by-pass pipe-to-water pump cover retaining nuts. *See Fig. 24.* Remove water pump bolts in sequence. *See Fig. 25.* Remove water, water pump cover and "O" rings. Remove retaining bolts, and separate water pump and gasket from water pump cover. *See Fig. 24.*

**Installation – 1)** To install, reverse removal procedure using new gaskets and "O" rings. Apply soapy water solution to coolant by-pass pipe "O" ring before installing water pump. DO NOT tighten coolant by-pass pipe-to-water pump cover retaining nuts until water pump bolts are tightened to specification.

**2)** Tighten water pump bolts to specification in sequence. *See Fig. 25.* See appropriate TORQUE SPECIFICATIONS table at end of article. To install remaining components, reverse removal procedure. Fill and bleed cooling system. See COOLING SYSTEM BLEEDING under REMOVAL & INSTALLATION.

## OIL PAN

**Removal – 1)** Disconnect negative battery cable. Remove hood. Raise and support vehicle. Remove lower engine covers. Drain engine oil.

**2)** Disconnect exhaust pipe at catalytic converter (located at turbo) and center pipe. Remove exhaust pipe. Remove stiffener support brace near rear of oil pan. Remove dipstick. Disconnect turbo oil return hose at oil pan. Remove retaining bolts/nuts, and remove oil pan.

***NOTE: On Celica All-Trac, it may be necessary to remove suspension crossmember, bolted to lower suspension arm shafts and engine mount crossmember, for access to oil pan.***

**Installation – 1)** To install, ensure sealing surfaces are clean. Apply bead of sealant at center of oil pan sealing surface, between bolt/nut holes and on inside of bolt/nut holes.

**2)** Install oil pan, and tighten bolts/nuts to specification. See appropriate TORQUE SPECIFICATIONS table at end of article. To install remaining components, reverse removal procedure. Fill crankcase with oil.

# 1991 ENGINES
# 2.0L 4-Cylinder (Cont.)

## OVERHAUL

### CYLINDER HEAD

**Cylinder Head - 1)** Inspect cylinder head warpage at cylinder block and manifold areas. Replace cylinder head if warpage exceeds specification. See CYLINDER HEAD table under ENGINE SPECIFICATIONS at end of article.
**2)** Install camshaft in cylinder head. Using Plastigage, check camshaft oil clearance with camshaft bearing cap bolts tightened in sequence to specification. *See Fig. 22.* See appropriate TORQUE SPECIFICATIONS table at end of article. Replace camshaft and/or cylinder head if oil clearance is not within specification. See CAMSHAFT table under ENGINE SPECIFICATIONS at end of article.
**3)** Ensure valve lifter bore diameter is within specification. See VALVE LIFTERS table under ENGINE SPECIFICATIONS at end of article.
**Valve Springs -** Ensure valve spring free length, pressure and out-of-square are within specification. See VALVES & VALVE SPRINGS table under ENGINE SPECIFICATIONS at end of article.

***CAUTION: Ensure valve springs are installed with painted area away from cylinder head surface.***

**Valve Stem Oil Seals -** Lubricate valve stem oil seal with engine oil. Intake valve stem oil seals are Brown and exhaust valve stem oil seals are Black. Install valve stem oil seal using Oil Seal Installer (SST 09201-41020).
**Valve Guides - 1)** Check valve stem-to-valve guide clearance. Ensure valve stem diameter is within specification. Replace valve guide if clearance exceeds specification. See CYLINDER HEAD table under ENGINE SPECIFICATIONS at end of article.
**2)** To replace valve guide, wrap tape around old valve stem. Tape must be approximately .51" (12.9 mm) from end of valve stem. From top of cylinder head, install old valve in valve guide with tape area resting on valve guide.
**3)** Hit old valve with hammer to break off old valve guide. Remove snap ring. Heat cylinder head to 176-212°F (80-100°C). Using hammer and Valve Guide Remover/Installer (SST 09201-70010), drive valve guide from top of cylinder head.
**4)** Measure I.D. of cylinder head valve guide bore. If bore I.D. is .4326-.4333" (10.988-11.006 mm), use standard valve guide. If bore I.D. is .4346-.4353" (11.038-11.056 mm), use oversize valve guide.
**5)** If bore I.D. exceeds .4333" (11.006 mm), valve guide bore must be machined to .4346-.4353" (11.038-11.056 mm) for oversize valve guide. If bore I.D. exceeds .4353" (11.056 mm), replace cylinder head.
**6)** To install valve guide, heat cylinder head to 176-212°F (80-100°C). Using hammer and valve guide remover/installer, drive valve guide from top of cylinder head until snap ring contacts cylinder head surface.
**7)** Using .236" (6.00 mm) reamer, ream valve guide to obtain correct valve stem-to-guide oil clearance. See CYLINDER HEAD table under ENGINE SPECIFICATIONS at end of article.
**Valve Seat -** Ensure valve seat angle and seat width are within specification. See CYLINDER HEAD table under ENGINE SPECIFICATIONS at end of article. Valve seat replacement information is not available from manufacturer.

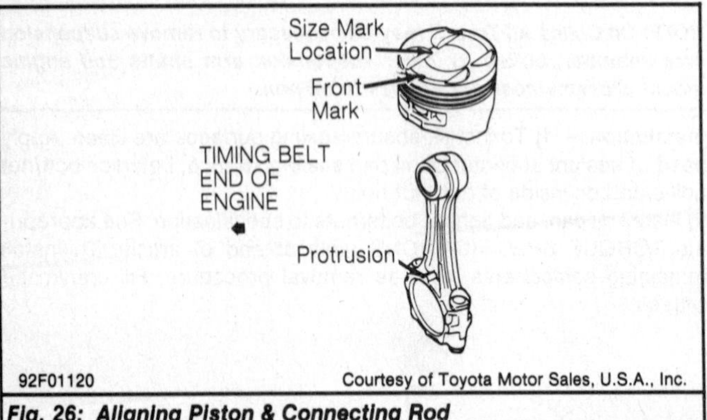

***Fig. 26: Aligning Piston & Connecting Rod***

**Valves -** Ensure minimum refinish length, stem diameter and valve margin are within specification. See VALVES & VALVE SPRINGS table under ENGINE SPECIFICATIONS at end of article.
**Seat Correction Angles -** Use 30- and 45-degree stones to lower valve seat contact area. Use 45- and 75-degree stones to raise valve seat contact area.

### VALVE TRAIN

**Valve Lifters -** Ensure valve lifter diameter, bore diameter and oil clearance are within specification. See VALVE LIFTERS table under ENGINE SPECIFICATIONS at end of article.

### CYLINDER BLOCK ASSEMBLY

**Piston & Rod Assembly - 1)** When removing piston from connecting rod, remove snap ring from piston. Heat piston to 176-194°F (80-90°C) in water. Remove piston pin. Separate piston from connecting rod.
**2)** Ensure piston pin diameter is within specification. See PISTONS, PINS & RINGS table under ENGINE SPECIFICATIONS at end of article.
**3)** Ensure connecting rod piston pin bushing bore diameter is within specification. See CONNECTING RODS table under ENGINE SPECIFICATIONS at end of article. Bushing can be replaced in connecting rod if bore diameter is not within specification. Bushing must be honed to obtain correct piston pin clearance. See PISTONS, PINS & RINGS table.

***NOTE: With piston at 140°F (60°C), it should be possible to press piston pin into piston using thumb pressure.***

**4)** To reassemble, install piston so front mark on top of piston aligns with protrusion on connecting rod. *See Fig. 26.*
**5)** Install new snap ring in piston. Heat piston to 176-194°F (80-90°C) in water. Install piston pin and remaining snap ring.
**Fitting Pistons - 1)** To determine if piston-to-cylinder clearance is within specification, measure piston skirt diameter at 1.185" (30.10 mm) from top of piston, at 90-degree angle to piston pin.
**2)** Different piston sizes are used. Piston size can be identified by size mark ("1", "2" or "3") stamped on top of piston. *See Fig. 26.*
**3)** Ensure piston diameter is within specification. See PISTONS, PINS & RINGS table under ENGINE SPECIFICATIONS at end of article.
**4)** Measure cylinder bore diameter at .39" (10 mm) from top and bottom and at middle of cylinder bore. Different cylinder bores are used and can be identified by size mark ("1", "2" or "3") stamped on cylinder block deck surface. *See Fig. 31.*
**5)** Ensure cylinder bore diameter is within specification. See CYLINDER BLOCK table under ENGINE SPECIFICATIONS at end of article. Determine piston clearance. Replace piston or cylinder block if clearance is not within specification. See PISTONS, PINS & RINGS table.
**Piston Rings -** Ensure piston ring end gap and side clearance are within specification. See PISTONS, PINS & RINGS table under ENGINE SPECIFICATIONS at end of article. Position piston ring gaps in proper areas with identification mark on ring toward top of piston. *See Fig. 27.*

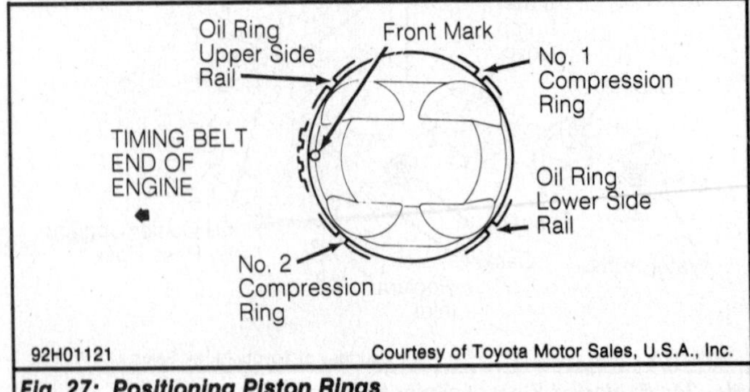

***Fig. 27: Positioning Piston Rings***

**Rod Bearings – 1)** Note direction of connecting rod and cap installation. Connecting rod must be installed so protrusion at center of connecting rod is toward timing belt end of engine. *See Fig. 26.*
**2)** Connecting rod cap and rod bearing are marked with a "1", "2" or "3" size mark. *See Fig. 28.* Size marks on connecting rod cap and rod bearing must be the same. If size mark cannot be read, measure rod bearing thickness to determine size mark. See CONNECTING ROD BEARING SPECIFICATIONS table.

***NOTE: If replacing rod bearing, ensure replacement rod bearing have the same size mark number as old rod bearing.***

**3)** Coat nuts and threads with engine oil before tightening them to specification.
**4)** Ensure bearing oil clearance and connecting rod side play are within specification. See CRANKSHAFT, MAIN & CONNECTING ROD BEARINGS and CONNECTING RODS tables under ENGINE SPECIFICATIONS at end of article.

***CONNECTING ROD BEARING SPECIFICATIONS***

| Bearing Size Mark Number | Bearing Thickness In. (mm) |
|---|---|
| 1 | .0584-.0586 (1.484-1.488) |
| 2 | .0586-.0587 (1.488-1.491) |
| 3 | .0587-.0589 (1.491-1.496) |

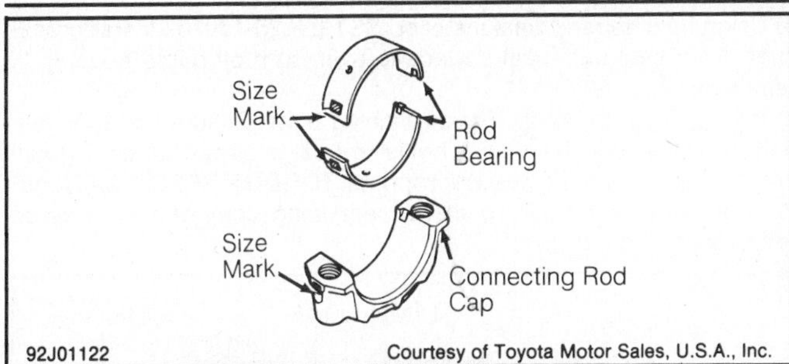

***Fig. 28: Identifying Connecting Rod Cap & Bearing Size Marks***

**Crankshaft & Main Bearings – 1)** Main bearing caps are numbered for location with No. 1 at timing belt end of engine. Arrow mark on cap must point toward timing belt end of crankshaft.
**2)** Cylinder block main bearing bore size is indicated by size mark ("1", "2" or "3") stamped on cylinder block. *See Fig. 29.* Front size mark indicates No. 1 main bearing bore, and rear size mark indicates No. 5 main bearing bore.
**3)** Crankshaft main bearing journal size is determined by size mark ("0", "1" or "2") located on crankshaft counterweight. *See Fig. 29.* Ensure main bearing journal diameter, taper, runout and out-of-round are with within specification. See CRANKSHAFT, MAIN & CONNECTING ROD BEARINGS table under ENGINE SPECIFICATIONS at end of article.
**4)** Main bearings size mark is located on side of main bearing. *See Fig. 29.* If replacing main bearing, replacement bearing must have same size mark number.

***MAIN BEARING SPECIFICATIONS***

| Bearing Size Mark Number | Bearing Thickness In. (mm) |
|---|---|
| No. 3 Main Bearing | |
| 1 | .0784-.0785 (1.991-1.994) |
| 2 | .0785-.0787 (1.994-1.999) |
| 3 | .0787-.0788 (1.999-2.002) |
| 4 | .0788-.0789 (2.002-2.004) |
| 5 | .0789-.0790 (2.004-2.007) |
| All Others | |
| 1 | .0786-.0787 (1.996-1.999) |
| 2 | .0787-.0789 (1.999-2.004) |
| 3 | .0789-.0790 (2.004-2.007) |
| 4 | .0790-.0791 (2.007-2.009) |
| 5 | .0791-.0792 (2.009-2.012) |

**5)** If size mark cannot be obtained, add size mark number on cylinder block and size mark number on crankshaft. The total is size mark number of main bearing to be used. For example, if size mark on cylinder block is "2" and size mark on crankshaft is "1", use main bearing with size mark "3".
**6)** Bearing thickness varies with size mark. See MAIN BEARING SPECIFICATIONS table. Ensure main bearing caps are installed in original location, with arrow pointing toward timing belt end of engine. Coat threads and seat area of main bearing cap bolt with engine oil.
**7)** Tighten main bearing cap bolts in sequence to specification. *See Fig. 30.* See appropriate TORQUE SPECIFICATIONS table at end of article. Ensure crankshaft end play is within specification. See CRANKSHAFT, MAIN & CONNECTING ROD BEARINGS table under ENGINE SPECIFICATIONS at end of article.

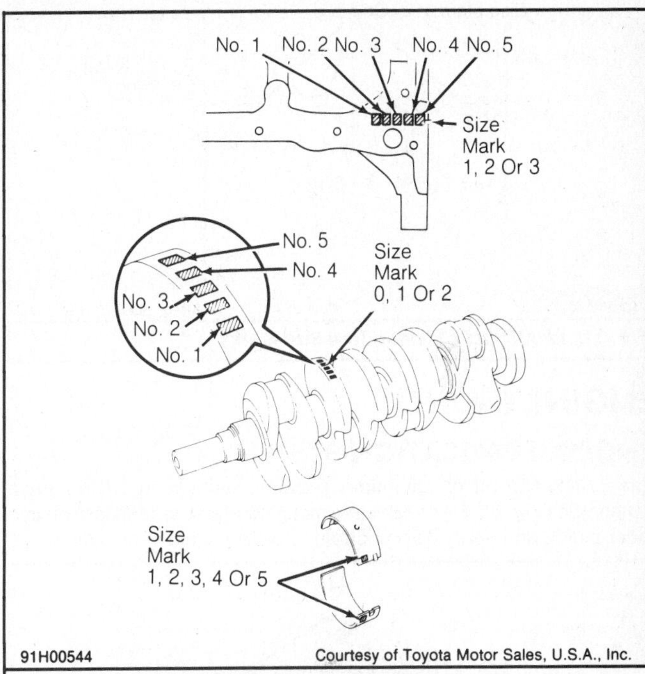

***Fig. 29: Identifying Main Bearing Size Marks***

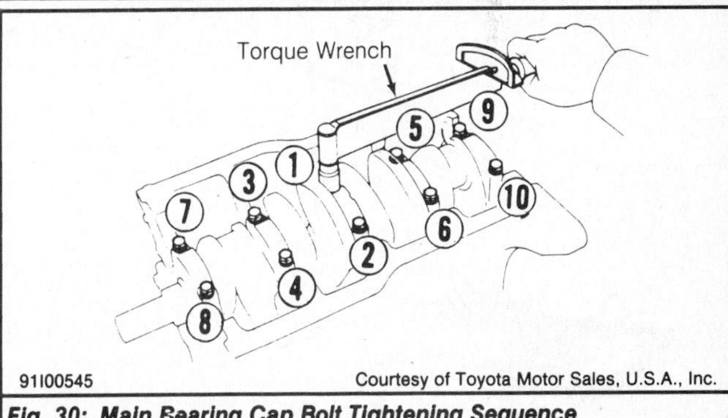

***Fig. 30: Main Bearing Cap Bolt Tightening Sequence***

**Thrust Bearing –** Install thrust bearing on No. 3 main bearing with grooves facing toward crankshaft. Thrust bearing must be replaced if crankshaft end play is not within specification. See CRANKSHAFT, MAIN & CONNECTING ROD BEARINGS table under ENGINE SPECIFICATIONS at end of article.
**Cylinder Block – 1)** Inspect cylinder block deck surface for warpage. Replace cylinder block if deck warpage exceeds specification. See CYLINDER BLOCK table under ENGINE SPECIFICATION at end of article.
**2)** Different cylinder bore sizes are used and can be identified by size mark stamped on cylinder block deck surface. *See Fig. 31.* Measure

# 1991 ENGINES
# 2.0L 4-Cylinder (Cont.)

cylinder bore diameter at .39" (10 mm) from top and bottom and at middle of cylinder bore. Check cylinder bore diameter, taper and out-of-round.

**3)** Ensure cylinder bore diameter is within specification. See CYLINDER BLOCK table under ENGINE SPECIFICATIONS at end of article. If cylinder bore diameter exceeds 3.3949" (86.230 mm), replace cylinder block.

**4)** Ensure main bearing bore I.D. is within specification with main bearing caps installed and bolts tightened to specification. See CYLINDER BLOCK table.

***NOTE: Main bearing bore I.D. is determined by main bearing bore size mark stamped on cylinder block. See Fig. 29.***

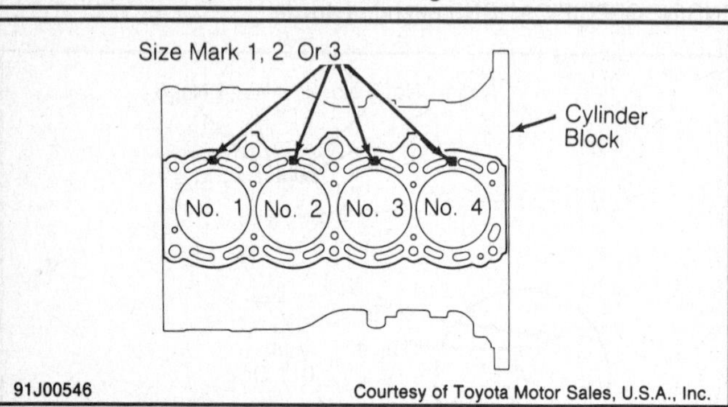


***Fig. 31: Identifying Cylinder Bore Size Marks***

## ENGINE OILING

### ENGINE LUBRICATION SYSTEM

The crankshaft-driven oil pump provides lubrication to the main gallery. *See Fig. 32.* Oil nozzles are mounted above crankshaft, on cylinder block, and spray oil on bottom of piston to aid in cooling.

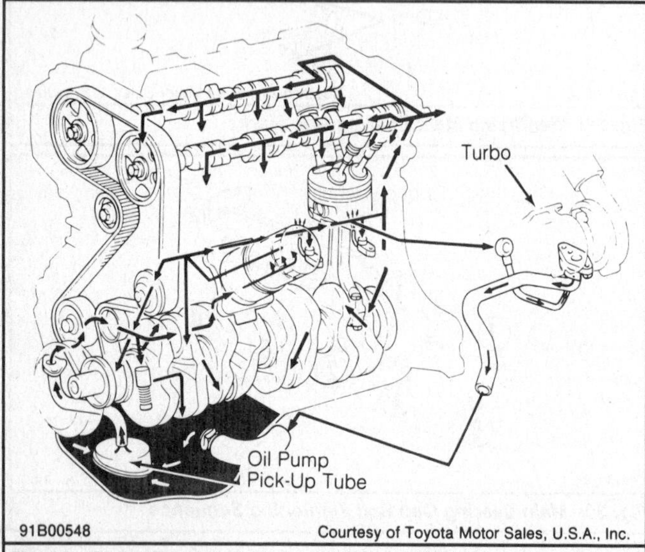


***Fig. 32: Cross-Sectional View of Engine Oil Circuit***

**Crankcase Capacity** – Crankcase capacity with oil filter is 4.1 qts. (3.9L).

**Oil Pressure** – With engine at normal operating temperature, oil pressure should be at least 4.3 psi (0.3 kg/cm²) at idle and 36-71 psi (2.5-5.0 kg/cm²) at 3000 RPM.

### OIL PUMP

**Removal & Disassembly** – Remove timing belt and crankshaft sprocket. See TIMING BELT under REMOVAL & INSTALLATION. Remove oil pan. See OIL PAN under REMOVAL & INSTALLATION. Remove retaining bolts, oil pump and gasket. Remove oil pump body cover, and disassemble oil pump components. *See Fig. 33.*

**Inspection** – **1)** Inspect components for damage. Ensure relief valve slides freely in bore. With rotors installed, use feeler gauge to measure clearance between driven rotor and oil pump housing. Replace rotor assembly if clearance exceeds specification. See OIL PUMP SPECIFICATIONS table.

**2)** Measure rotor tip clearance between tip of both rotors. Replace rotor assembly if clearance exceeds specification. See OIL PUMP SPECIFICATIONS table.

***OIL PUMP SPECIFICATIONS***

| Application | In. (mm) |
|---|---|
| Driven Rotor-To-Housing Clearance | |
| Standard | .0039-.0063 (.099-.160) |
| Wear Limit | .0079 (.201) |
| Rotor Tip Clearance | |
| Standard | .0016-.0063 (.041-.160) |
| Wear Limit | .0079 (.201) |

**Reassembly & Installation** – **1)** To reassemble, reverse disassembly procedure using new "O" ring. Ensure reference marks on rotors face toward the outside of oil pump housing (away from cylinder block surface).

**2)** Using Seal Installer (SST 09620-30010), install oil pump seal (if removed). *See Fig. 33.* Coat seal lip with grease.

**3)** Using hammer and Seal Installer (SST 09226-10010), install crankshaft front seal until seal surface is even with oil pump housing (if removed).

**4)** Install oil pump housing and retaining bolts. Ensure the 2 longest bolts are located in the outside holes nearest to oil pan flange. Tighten bolts to specification. See appropriate TORQUE SPECIFICATIONS table at end of article. To install remaining components, reverse removal procedure.

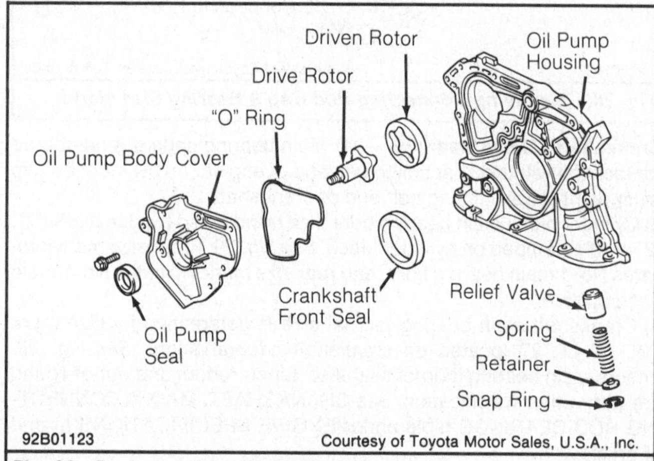


***Fig. 33: Exploded View Of Oil Pump***

### OIL COOLER

**Removal (Celica All-Trac)** – **1)** Disconnect negative battery cable. Remove alternator and oil filter. Drain cooling system. Disconnect coolant hose from oil cooler. Remove relief valve and plate washer from oil cooler housing. *See Fig. 12.*

**2)** Remove retaining nuts, oil cooler and "O" ring. Disconnect coolant hose from oil cooler bracket on cylinder block. Remove retaining bolts, oil cooler bracket and "O" rings.

***NOTE: Before installing relief valve, push on valve located in center of relief valve. Replace relief valve is valve fails to move.***

**Installation** – To install, reverse removal procedure. Coat new "O" rings with engine oil. Coat threads and below head of relief valve with engine oil. Tighten bolts/nuts to specification. See appropriate TORQUE SPECIFICATIONS table at end of article. Add engine oil, and fill cooling system.

# 1991 ENGINES
# 2.0L 4-Cylinder (Cont.)

**Removal (MR2) - 1)** Disconnect negative battery cable. Drain cooling system. Remove lower engine covers and hood right side panel. Remove No. 1 air intake connector. *See Fig. 23.*
**2)** Remove A/C compressor with hoses attached, and secure aside. Remove oil filter. Remove dipstick guide from coolant inlet. Disconnect coolant hose from oil cooler. Remove relief valve and plate washer from oil cooler housing. *See Fig. 12.*
**3)** Remove retaining nuts, oil cooler and "O" ring. Disconnect coolant hose from oil cooler bracket on cylinder block. Remove retaining bolts, oil cooler bracket and "O" rings.

***NOTE: Before installing relief valve, push on valve located in center of relief valve. Replace relief valve is valve fails to move.***

**Installation -** To install, reverse removal procedure. Coat new "O" rings with engine oil. Coat threads and below head of relief valve with engine oil. Tighten bolts/nuts to specification. See appropriate TORQUE SPECIFICATIONS table. Add engine oil. Fill and bleed cooling system. See COOLING SYSTEM BLEEDING under REMOVAL & INSTALLATION.

## OIL NOZZLES

**Removal & Installation - 1)** With crankshaft removed, remove oil nozzle retaining bolt. Remove oil nozzle.
**2)** Ensure small round relief valve ball, mounted in oil nozzle, can be pushed downward. Replace oil nozzle if relief valve ball fails to move.
**3)** To install, reverse removal procedure. Tighten retaining bolt to specification. See appropriate TORQUE SPECIFICATIONS table.

## TORQUE SPECIFICATIONS

### *TORQUE SPECIFICATIONS (CELICA ALL-TRAC)*

| Application | Ft. Lbs. (N.m) |
|---|---|
| A/C Compressor Bolt | 20 (27) |
| Axle Shaft Nut | 137 (186) |
| Ball Joint-To-Steering Knuckle Bolt | 94 (127) |
| Camshaft Bearing Cap Bolt [1] | 14 (19) |
| Camshaft Sprocket Bolt | 43 (58) |
| Catalytic Converter Brace Bolt | 43 (58) |
| Catalytic Converter-To-Turbo Bolt | 22 (30) |
| Connecting Rod Nut | 49 (66) |
| Crankshaft Pulley Bolt | 80 (109) |
| Cylinder Head Bolt [2] | |
| Step 1 | 36 (49) |
| Step 2 | Additional 90 Degrees |
| Delivery Pipe Bolt | 14 (19) |
| Drive Shaft Flange Bolt | 54 (73) |
| Dynamic Damper Bolt | 19 (26) |
| EGR Valve & Pipe Bolt | 14 (19) |
| Engine Mount Crossmember-To-Body Bolt | 38 (52) |
| Engine Mount Through Bolt | 64 (87) |
| Engine Mount-To-Crossmember Bolt | 54 (73) |
| Exhaust Manifold Nut | 38 (52) |
| Flywheel Bolt | 80 (109) |
| Intake Air Connector Bolt | 14 (19) |
| Intake Air Connector Brace Bolt | |
| 10-mm Bolt | [3] |
| 12-mm Bolt | 14 (19) |

[1] - Tighten bolts in sequence. *See Fig. 22.*
[2] - Tighten bolts in sequence. *See Fig. 13.*
[3] - Tighten bolt to 69 INCH lbs. (7 N.m)
[4] - Tighten bolts in sequence. *See Fig. 30.*
[5] - Tighten bolts in sequence. *See Fig. 25.*

### *TORQUE SPECIFICATIONS (CELICA ALL-TRAC - Cont.)*

| Application | Ft. Lbs. (N.m) |
|---|---|
| Intake Manifold Bolt/Nut | 14 (19) |
| Intake Manifold Brace Bolt | 19 (26) |
| Knock Sensor | 33 (45) |
| Main Bearing Cap Bolt [4] | 43 (58) |
| No. 1 Idler Pulley Bolt | 38 (52) |
| No. 2 Idler Pulley Bolt | 32 (43) |
| Oil Cooler Relief Valve | 58 (79) |
| Oil Pipe-To-Turbo Nut | 13 (18) |
| Oil Pump Sprocket Nut | 26 (35) |
| Outlet Elbow-To-Turbo Nut | 47 (64) |
| Oxygen Sensor | 33 (45) |
| Spark Plug | 13 (18) |
| Stiffener Support Brace Bolt | 27 (37) |
| Strut Tower-To-Firewall Brace | |
| Bolt | 15 (20) |
| Nut | 47 (64) |
| Suspension Crossmember Bolt | 112 (152) |
| Throttle Body Bolt | 14 (19) |
| Tie Rod Nut | 36 (49) |
| Timing Belt Side Engine Mount Bracket-To-Cylinder Block Bolt | 38 (52) |
| Timing Belt Side Engine Mount | |
| Nut | 38 (52) |
| Through Bolt | 64 (87) |
| Timing Belt Tensioner Bolt | 15 (20) |
| Turbine Outlet Elbow-To-Turbo Nut | 47 (64) |
| Turbo Brace Bolt | |
| Cylinder Block Side | 43 (58) |
| Turbo Side | 51 (69) |
| Turbo Return Oil Pipe-To-Cylinder Block Union Bolt | 38 (52) |
| Turbo-To-Exhaust Manifold Nut | 47 (64) |
| Wheel Lug Nut | 76 (103) |
| | **INCH Lbs. (N.m)** |
| Coolant By-Pass Pipe-To-Water Pump Nut | 69 (7) |
| No. 3 Timing Belt Cover Bolt | 78 (8) |
| Oil Cooler Bracket-To-Cylinder Block Bolt | 69 (7) |
| Oil Nozzle Bolt | 82 (9) |
| Oil Pan Bolt/Nut | 48 (5) |
| Oil Pump Body Cover Bolt | 78 (8) |
| Oil Pump Pick-Up Tube Bolt/Nut | 48 (5) |
| Oil Pump-To-Cylinder Block Bolt | 69 (7) |
| Rear Plate-To-Cylinder Block Bolt | 82 (9) |
| Rear Seal Housing Bolt | 82 (9) |
| Valve Cover Bolt | 21 (2) |
| Water Pump Bolt [5] | 69 (7) |
| Water Pump Cover Bolt | 82 (9) |

[1] - Tighten bolts in sequence. *See Fig. 22.*
[2] - Tighten bolts in sequence. *See Fig. 13.*
[3] - Tighten bolt to 69 INCH lbs. (7 N.m)
[4] - Tighten bolts in sequence. *See Fig. 30.*
[5] - Tighten bolts in sequence. *See Fig. 25.*

# 1991 ENGINES
# 2.0L 4-Cylinder (Cont.)

### TORQUE SPECIFICATIONS (MR2)

| Application | Ft. Lbs. (N.m) |
|---|---|
| A/C Compressor Bolt | 20 (27) |
| Air By-Pass Valve Bolt | 14 (19) |
| Air Cleaner Case Bracket Bolt | 26 (35) |
| Axle Shaft Nut | 217 (294) |
| Ball Joint Stud-To-Lower Control Arm Nut | 67 (91) |
| Bearing Bracket Support Bracket Bolt/Nut | 56 (76) |
| Bearing Bracket-To-Cylinder Block Bolt | 47 (64) |
| Bearing Retaining Bolt | 24 (33) |
| Brake Caliper Bolt | 43 (58) |
| Camshaft Bearing Cap Bolt [1] | 14 (19) |
| Camshaft Sprocket Bolt | 43 (58) |
| Catalytic Converter Brace Bolt | 43 (58) |
| Catalytic Converter-To-Turbo Bolt | 22 (30) |
| Connecting Rod Nut | 49 (66) |
| Crankshaft Pulley Bolt | 80 (109) |
| Cylinder Head Bolt [2] | |
| Step 1 | 36 (49) |
| Step 2 | Additional 90 Degrees |
| Delivery Pipe Bolt | 14 (19) |
| Dynamic Damper Bolt | 19 (26) |
| EGR Valve & Pipe Bolt | |
| Cylinder Head Side | 19 (26) |
| Intake Manifold Side | 14 (19) |
| Engine Mounts & Brackets | |
| Front Mount Bracket Bolt | 57 (77) |
| Front Mount-To-Body Bolt | 54 (73) |
| Left Mount Support Bracket Bolt | |
| Engine Side | 54 (73) |
| Transaxle Side | 18 (24) |
| Left Mount-To-Bracket Bolt | [3] |
| Mount Through Bolt | 58 (79) |
| Rear Mount-To-Body Bolt | 47 (64) |
| Right Mount Support Bracket Bolt/Nut | 54 (73) |
| Right Mount-To-Bracket Nut | 38 (52) |
| Exhaust Manifold Nut | 38 (52) |
| Flywheel Bolt | 80 (109) |
| Intake Air Connector Bolt | 14 (19) |
| Intake Air Connector Brace Bolt | |
| 10-mm Bolt | [4] |
| 12-mm Bolt | 14 (19) |
| Intake Manifold Bolt/Nut | 14 (19) |
| Intake Manifold Brace Bolt | 19 (26) |
| Knock Sensor | 33 (45) |
| Lower Control Arm-To-Body Bolt/Nut | 98 (133) |
| Main Bearing Cap Bolt [5] | 43 (58) |
| No. 1 Idler Pulley Bolt | 38 (52) |
| No. 2 Idler Pulley Bolt | 32 (43) |
| No. 4 Air Tube Brace Bolt | 14 (19) |
| Oil Cooler Relief Valve | 58 (79) |
| Oil Pipe-To-Turbo Nut | 13 (18) |
| Oil Pump Sprocket Nut | 26 (35) |

[1] – Tighten bolts in sequence. *See Fig. 22.*
[2] – Tighten bolts in sequence. *See Fig. 13.*
[3] – Tighten bolts to specification. *See Fig. 11.*
[4] – Tighten bolt to 69 INCH lbs. (7 N.m)
[5] – Tighten bolts in sequence. *See Fig. 30.*
[6] – Tighten bolts in sequence. *See Fig. 25.*

### TORQUE SPECIFICATIONS (MR2 – Cont.)

| Application | Ft. Lbs. (N.m) |
|---|---|
| Outlet Elbow-To-Turbo Nut | 47 (64) |
| Oxygen Sensor | 33 (45) |
| Rear Suspension Crossmember Bolt | 83 (113) |
| Spark Plug | 13 (18) |
| Stabilizer Link-To-Strut Nut | 36 (49) |
| Stiffener Support Brace Bolt | 27 (37) |
| Strut Rod-To-Lower Control Arm Nut | 87 (118) |
| Strut Tower-To-Firewall Brace | |
| Bolt | 54 (73) |
| Nut | 47 (64) |
| Suspension Crossmember Bolt | 112 (152) |
| Throttle Body Bolt | 14 (19) |
| Tie Rod-To-Hub Assembly Carrier Bolt | 76 (103) |
| Timing Belt Tensioner Bolt | 15 (20) |
| Turbine Outlet Elbow-To-Turbo Nut | 47 (64) |
| Turbo Brace Bolt | |
| Cylinder Block Side | 43 (58) |
| Turbo Side | 51 (69) |
| Turbo Return Oil Pipe-To-Cylinder | |
| Block Union Bolt | 38 (52) |
| Turbo-To-Exhaust Manifold Nut | 47 (64) |
| Wheel Lug Nut | 76 (103) |
| | **INCH Lbs. (N.m)** |
| Anti-Lock Brake Sensor Bolt | 69 (7) |
| Coolant By-Pass Pipe-To-Water Pump Nut | 69 (7) |
| Clutch Release Cylinder Bolt | 108 (12) |
| No. 3 Timing Belt Cover Bolt | 78 (8) |
| Oil Cooler Bracket-To-Cylinder Block Bolt | 69 (7) |
| Oil Nozzle Bolt | 82 (9) |
| Oil Pan Bolt/Nut | 48 (5) |
| Oil Pump Body Cover Bolt | 78 (8) |
| Oil Pump Pick-Up Tube Bolt/Nut | 48 (5) |
| Oil Pump-To-Cylinder Block Bolt | 69 (7) |
| Rear Plate-To-Cylinder Block Bolt | 82 (9) |
| Rear Seal Housing Bolt | 82 (9) |
| Valve Cover Bolt | 21 (2) |
| Water Pump Bolt [6] | 69 (7) |
| Water Pump Cover Bolt | 82 (9) |

[1] – Tighten bolts in sequence. *See Fig. 22.*
[2] – Tighten bolts in sequence. *See Fig. 13.*
[3] – Tighten bolts to specification. *See Fig. 11.*
[4] – Tighten bolt to 69 INCH lbs. (7 N.m)
[5] – Tighten bolts in sequence. *See Fig. 30.*
[6] – Tighten bolts in sequence. *See Fig. 25.*

## ENGINE SPECIFICATIONS

### GENERAL SPECIFICATIONS

| Application | Specification |
|---|---|
| Displacement | 122 Cu. In. (2.0L) |
| Bore | 3.39" (86.1 mm) |
| Stroke | 3.39" (86.1 mm) |
| Compression Ratio | 8.8:1 |
| Fuel System | PFI |
| Horsepower @ RPM | 200 @ 6000 |
| Torque Ft. Lbs. @ RPM | 200 @ 3200 |

# 1991 ENGINES
# 2.0L 4-Cylinder (Cont.)

## CRANKSHAFT, MAIN & CONNECTING ROD BEARINGS

| Application | In. (mm) |
|---|---|
| Crankshaft | |
| End Play | |
| Standard | .0008-.0087 (.020-.221) |
| Wear Limit | .0118 (.300) |
| Maximum Runout | .0024 (.061) |
| Main Bearings | |
| Journal Diameter [1] | |
| Size Mark "0" | 2.1653-2.1655 (54.998-55.003) |
| Size Mark "1" | 2.1651-2.1653 (54.993-54.998) |
| Size Mark "2" | 2.1649-2.1651 (54.988-54.993) |
| Journal Out-Of-Round | .0008 (.020) |
| Journal Taper | .0008 (.020) |
| Oil Clearance | |
| Standard Crankshaft Journal | |
| No. 3 Journal | |
| Standard | .0010-.0017 (.025-.043) |
| Wear Limit | .0031 (.079) |
| All Other Journals | |
| Standard | .0006-.0013 (.015-.034) |
| Wear Limit | .0031 (.079) |
| .010" (.25 mm) Undersize Crankshaft Journal | |
| No. 3 Journal | |
| Standard | .0008-.0024 (.020-.061) |
| Wear Limit | .0031 (.079) |
| All Other Journals | |
| Standard | .0011-.0027 (.028-.069) |
| Wear Limit | .0031 (.079) |
| Connecting Rod Bearings | |
| Journal Diameter | 1.8892-1.8898 (47.985-48.001) |
| Journal Out-Of-Round | .0008 (.020) |
| Journal Taper | .0008 (.020) |
| Oil Clearance | |
| Standard Crankshaft Journal | |
| Standard | .0009-.0022 (.023-.056) |
| Wear Limit | .0031 (.079) |
| .010" (.25 mm) Undersize Crankshaft Journal | |
| Standard | .0009-.0027 (.023-.069) |
| Wear Limit | .0031 (.079) |

[1] – Main journal diameter is determined by size mark on crankshaft. *See Fig. 29.*

## CONNECTING RODS

| Application | In. (mm) |
|---|---|
| Bore Diameter | |
| Pin Bushing | .8663-.8668 (22.004-22.017) |
| Maximum Bend | .0020 Per 3.94 (.051 Per 100.1) |
| Maximum Twist | .0059 Per 3.94 (.150 Per 100.1) |
| Side Play | |
| Standard | .0063-.0123 (.160-.312) |
| Wear Limit | .0138 (.350) |

## PISTONS, PINS & RINGS

| Application | In. (mm) |
|---|---|
| Pistons | |
| Clearance | |
| Standard | .0028-.0035 (.071-.089) |
| Wear Limit | .0043 (.109) |
| Diameter [1] | |
| Size Mark "1" | 3.3827-3.3831 (85.921-85.931) |
| Size Mark "2" | 3.3831-3.3835 (85.931-85.941) |
| Size Mark "3" | 3.3835-3.3839 (85.941-85.951) |
| Pins | |
| Diameter | .8660-.8665 (21.996-22.009) |
| Piston Fit | [2] |
| Rod Fit | |
| Standard | .0002-.0004 (.005-.010) |
| Wear Limit | .0020 (.051) |
| Rings | |
| No. 1 | |
| End Gap | |
| Standard | .0130-.0217 (.330-.551) |
| Wear Limit | .0335 (.851) |
| Side Clearance | .0016-.0031 (.041-.079) |
| No. 2 | |
| End Gap | |
| Standard | .0177-.0264 (.450-.079) |
| Wear Limit | .0382 (.970) |
| Side Clearance | .0012-.0028 (.030-.071) |
| No. 3 (Oil) | |
| End Gap | |
| Standard | .0079-.0236 (.201-.599) |
| Wear Limit | .0354 (.899) |

[1] – Piston diameter is determined by size mark stamped on top of piston. *See Fig. 26.*

[2] – With piston heated to 140°F (60°C), it should be possible to press piston pin into piston using thumb pressure.

## CYLINDER BLOCK

| Application | In. (mm) |
|---|---|
| Cylinder Bore | |
| Standard Diameter [1] | |
| Size Mark "1" | 3.3858-3.3862 (86.000-86.010) |
| Size Mark "2" | 3.3862-3.3866 (86.010-86.020) |
| Size Mark "3" | 3.3866-3.3870 (86.020-86.030) |
| Maximum Deck Warpage | .002 (.05) |
| Main Bearing Bore I.D. [2] | |
| Size Mark "1" | 2.3236-2.3239 (59.019-59.027) |
| Size Mark "2" | 2.3239-2.3241 (59.027-59.032) |
| Size Mark "3" | 2.3241-2.3243 (59.032-59.037) |

[1] – Cylinder bore diameter is determined by size mark on cylinder block deck surface. *See Fig. 31.*

[2] – Main bearing bore I.D. is determined by size mark on cylinder block. *See Fig. 29.*

# 1991 ENGINES
# 2.0L 4-Cylinder (Cont.)

## VALVES & VALVE SPRINGS

| Application | Specification |
|---|---|
| Intake Valves | |
| Face Angle | 44.5° |
| Minimum Margin | .020" (.51 mm) |
| Minimum Refinish Length | 4.1260" (104.80 mm) |
| Stem Diameter | .2346-.2352" (5.959-5.974 mm) |
| Exhaust Valves | |
| Face Angle | 44.5° |
| Minimum Margin | .020" (.51 mm) |
| Minimum Refinish Length | 3.8917" (98.849 mm) |
| Stem Diameter | .2344-.2350" (5.954-5.969 mm) |
| Valve Springs | |
| Free Length | 1.749" (44.42 mm) |
| Out-Of-Square | .079" (2.00 mm) |
| | **Lbs. @ In. (kg @ mm)** |
| Pressure | |
| Valve Closed | 45-53 @ 1.354 (20-24 @ 34.39) |

## CYLINDER HEAD

| Application | Specification |
|---|---|
| Maximum Warpage | |
| Cylinder Block Surface | .008" (.20 mm) |
| Intake Manifold Surface | .008" (.20 mm) |
| Exhaust Manifold Surface | .012" (.30 mm) |
| Valve Seats | |
| Intake Valve | |
| Seat Angle | 45° |
| Seat Width | .039-055" (.99-1.40 mm) |
| Exhaust Valve | |
| Seat Angle | 45° |
| Seat Width | .039-055" (.99-1.40 mm) |
| Valve Guides | |
| Intake Valve | |
| Valve Guide Cylinder Head | |
| Bore I.D. | .4326-.4333" (10.988-11.006 mm) |
| Valve Guide I.D. | .2362-.2369" (5.999-6.017 mm) |
| Valve Stem-To-Guide Oil Clearance | |
| Standard | .0010-.0023" (.025-.059 mm) |
| Wear Limit | .0031" (.079 mm) |
| Exhaust Valve | |
| Valve Guide Cylinder Head | |
| Bore I.D. | .4326-.4333" (10.988-11.006 mm) |
| Valve Guide I.D. | .2362-.2369" (5.999-6.017 mm) |
| Valve Stem-To-Guide Oil Clearance | |
| Standard | .0012-.0026" (.030-.066 mm) |
| Wear Limit | .0039" (.099 mm) |

## CAMSHAFT

| Application | In. (mm) |
|---|---|
| End Play | |
| Standard | .0047-.0094 (.119-.239) |
| Wear Limit | .0118 (.300) |
| Journal Diameter | 1.0614-1.0620 (26.960-26.975) |
| Journal Runout | .0024 (.061) |
| Lobe Height | |
| Standard | 1.6146-1.6185 (41.010-41.110) |
| Wear Limit | 1.5709 (39.991) |
| Oil Clearance | |
| Standard | .0010-.0024 (.025-.061) |
| Wear Limit | .0031 (.079) |

## VALVE LIFTERS

| Application | In. (mm) |
|---|---|
| Bore Diameter | 1.1024-1.1032 (28.001-28.021) |
| Lifter Diameter | 1.1014-1.1018 (27.976-27.986) |
| Oil Clearance | |
| Standard | .0006-.0018 (.015-.046) |
| Wear Limit | .0028 (.071) |

# 1991 ENGINES
# 2.0L & 2.2L 4-Cylinder

## Camry (2.0L), Celica (2.2L), MR2 (2.2L)

***NOTE: For Celica All-Trac and MR2 (2.0L) repair procedures, see 2.0L 4-CYLINDER article in ENGINES.***

***NOTE: For repair procedures not covered in this article, see ENGINE OVERHAUL PROCEDURES article in GENERAL INFORMATION.***

***CAUTION: Before performing service procedures on vehicle, negative battery cable should be disconnected. Wait at least 20 seconds after disconnecting negative battery cable before proceeding to avoid accidental air bag deployment on Celica and MR2.***

## ENGINE IDENTIFICATION

Engine serial number is stamped on flywheel end of cylinder block, just below cylinder head surface.

***ENGINE IDENTIFICATION CODE***

| Engine | Code |
|---|---|
| 2.0L (Camry) | 3S-FE |
| 2.2L (Celica & MR2) | 5S-FE |

## ADJUSTMENTS

### VALVE CLEARANCE ADJUSTMENT

***NOTE: Adjust valve clearance with engine cold.***

**1)** Remove valve cover and gasket. Rotate crankshaft so No. 1 cylinder is at TDC of compression stroke. Ensure timing mark on crankshaft pulley aligns with "0" mark on timing belt cover. Ensure valve lifters on No. 1 cylinder are loose and No. 4 cylinder are tight.

**2)** With No. 1 cylinder at TDC of compression stroke, check clearance on specified valves. See VALVE CLEARANCE ADJUSTMENT SEQUENCE table. Using feeler gauge, measure and record clearance between valve lifter and camshaft.

***VALVE CLEARANCE ADJUSTMENT SEQUENCE***

| Cylinder No. On TDC | Adjust Intake Valves | Adjust Exhaust Valves |
|---|---|---|
| 1 | 1 & 2 | 1 & 3 |
| 4 | 3 & 4 | 2 & 4 |

**3)** To check remaining valves, rotate crankshaft 360 degrees (one revolution) until No. 4 cylinder is at TDC of compression stroke. Measure and record valve clearance on specified valves. See VALVE CLEARANCE ADJUSTMENT SEQUENCE table.

**4)** Clearance should be as specified. See VALVE CLEARANCE SPECIFICATIONS table. If valves require adjustment, rotate camshaft so lobe on valve to be adjusted is facing upward, away from valve lifter.

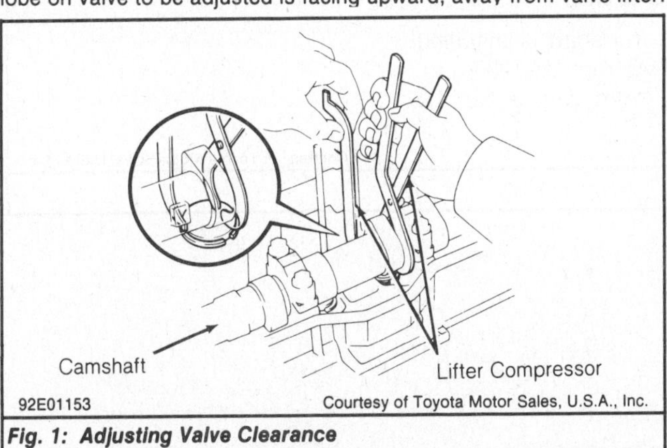


***Fig. 1: Adjusting Valve Clearance***

***VALVE CLEARANCE SPECIFICATIONS***

| Application | In. (mm) |
|---|---|
| Exhaust | .011-.015 (.28-.38) |
| Intake | .007-.011 (.19-.28) |

**5)** Rotate valve lifter so notch on valve lifter is toward the spark plug. Valve Clearance Adjuster (SST 09248-55010) is used to remove adjusting shim. Using SST (A) of valve clearance adjuster, push downward on valve lifter. Place SST (B) between camshaft and valve lifter. Remove SST (A). *See Fig. 1.*

**6)** Using small screwdriver and magnet, remove adjusting shim. Measure thickness of adjusting shim removed. Determine correct thickness of adjusting shim to be used. *See Figs. 4 and 5.*

**7)** Install adjusting shim and recheck valve clearance. Before installing valve cover and gasket, apply sealant at front and rear areas of cylinder head. *See Fig. 2.* Install valve cover and gasket.

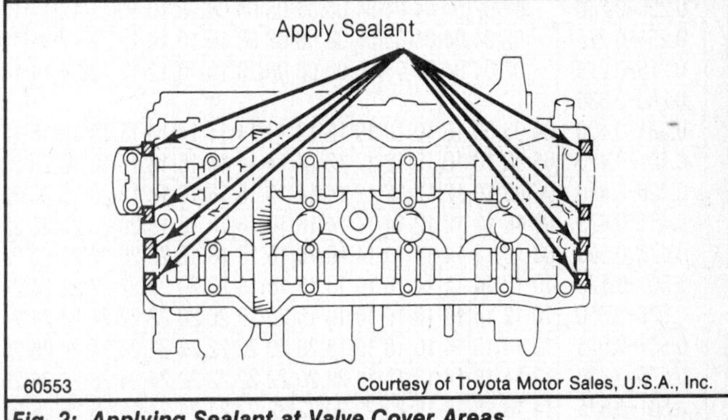


***Fig. 2: Applying Sealant at Valve Cover Areas***

**8)** When installing valve cover grommets, install grommets in original location with markings in designated area. *See Fig. 3.* Install valve cover nuts and tighten to specification. See TORQUE SPECIFICATIONS table at end of this article.

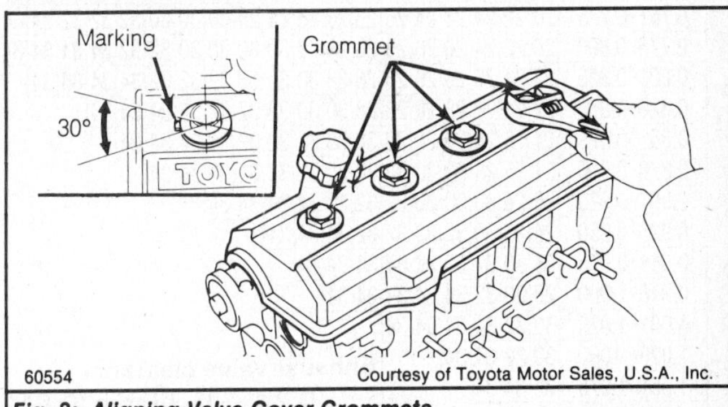


***Fig. 3: Aligning Valve Cover Grommets***

# 1991 ENGINES
# 2.0L & 2.2L 4-Cylinder (Cont.)

EXHAUST VALVES

| Measured clearance (mm) | Installed shim thickness (mm) | | | | | | | | | | | | | | | | | | | | | | | | | | | | | | | | | | | | | | | | |
|---|---|---|---|---|---|---|---|---|---|---|---|---|---|---|---|---|---|---|---|---|---|---|---|---|---|---|---|---|---|---|---|---|---|---|---|---|---|---|---|---|---|
| | 2.500 | 2.550 | 2.600 | 2.620 | 2.640 | 2.650 | 2.660 | 2.680 | 2.700 | 2.720 | 2.740 | 2.750 | 2.760 | 2.780 | 2.800 | 2.820 | 2.840 | 2.850 | 2.860 | 2.880 | 2.900 | 2.920 | 2.940 | 2.950 | 2.960 | 2.980 | 3.000 | 3.020 | 3.040 | 3.050 | 3.060 | 3.080 | 3.100 | 3.120 | 3.140 | 3.150 | 3.160 | 3.180 | 3.200 | 3.250 | 3.300 |
| 0.000-0.025 | | | | | | | | | | | | | 02 | 02 | 02 | 02 | 02 | 04 | 04 | 04 | 06 | 06 | 06 | 08 | 08 | 08 | 10 | 10 | 10 | 12 | 12 | 12 | 14 | 14 | 14 | 16 | 16 | 16 | 18 | 20 | 22 |
| 0.026-0.050 | | | | | | | | | | | 02 | 02 | 02 | 02 | 02 | 04 | 04 | 04 | 04 | 06 | 06 | 08 | 08 | 08 | 08 | 10 | 10 | 12 | 12 | 12 | 12 | 14 | 14 | 16 | 16 | 16 | 16 | 18 | 18 | 20 | 22 |
| 0.051-0.075 | | | | | | | | | | 02 | 02 | 02 | 02 | 02 | 04 | 04 | 04 | 06 | 06 | 06 | 08 | 08 | 08 | 10 | 10 | 10 | 12 | 12 | 12 | 14 | 14 | 14 | 16 | 16 | 16 | 18 | 18 | 18 | 20 | 22 | 24 |
| 0.076-0.100 | | | | | | | | 02 | 02 | 02 | 02 | 02 | 02 | 04 | 04 | 06 | 06 | 06 | 06 | 08 | 08 | 10 | 10 | 10 | 10 | 12 | 12 | 14 | 14 | 14 | 14 | 16 | 16 | 18 | 18 | 18 | 18 | 20 | 20 | 22 | 24 |
| 0.101-0.125 | | | | | | | 02 | 02 | 02 | 02 | 02 | 04 | 04 | 04 | 06 | 06 | 06 | 08 | 08 | 08 | 10 | 10 | 10 | 12 | 12 | 12 | 14 | 14 | 14 | 16 | 16 | 16 | 18 | 18 | 18 | 20 | 20 | 20 | 22 | 24 | 26 |
| 0.126-0.150 | | | | | 02 | 02 | 02 | 02 | 02 | 04 | 04 | 04 | 04 | 06 | 06 | 08 | 08 | 08 | 08 | 10 | 10 | 12 | 12 | 12 | 12 | 14 | 14 | 16 | 16 | 16 | 16 | 18 | 18 | 20 | 20 | 20 | 20 | 22 | 22 | 24 | 26 |
| 0.150-0.175 | | | | 02 | 02 | 02 | 02 | 02 | 04 | 04 | 04 | 06 | 06 | 06 | 08 | 08 | 08 | 10 | 10 | 10 | 12 | 12 | 12 | 14 | 14 | 14 | 16 | 16 | 16 | 18 | 18 | 18 | 20 | 20 | 20 | 22 | 22 | 22 | 24 | 26 | 28 |
| 0.176-0.200 | | | 02 | 02 | 02 | 02 | 02 | 04 | 04 | 06 | 06 | 06 | 06 | 08 | 08 | 10 | 10 | 10 | 10 | 12 | 12 | 14 | 14 | 14 | 14 | 16 | 16 | 18 | 18 | 18 | 18 | 20 | 20 | 22 | 22 | 22 | 22 | 24 | 24 | 26 | 28 |
| 0.201-0.225 | | | 02 | 02 | 02 | 04 | 04 | 04 | 06 | 06 | 06 | 08 | 08 | 08 | 10 | 10 | 10 | 12 | 12 | 12 | 14 | 14 | 14 | 16 | 16 | 16 | 18 | 18 | 18 | 20 | 20 | 20 | 22 | 22 | 22 | 24 | 24 | 24 | 26 | 28 | 30 |
| 0.226-0.250 | | 02 | 02 | 04 | 04 | 04 | 04 | 06 | 06 | 08 | 08 | 08 | 08 | 10 | 10 | 12 | 12 | 12 | 12 | 14 | 14 | 16 | 16 | 16 | 16 | 18 | 18 | 20 | 20 | 20 | 20 | 22 | 22 | 24 | 24 | 24 | 24 | 26 | 26 | 28 | 30 |
| 0.251-0.275 | | 02 | 04 | 04 | 04 | 06 | 06 | 08 | 08 | 08 | 08 | 10 | 10 | 10 | 12 | 12 | 12 | 14 | 14 | 14 | 16 | 16 | 16 | 18 | 18 | 18 | 20 | 20 | 20 | 22 | 22 | 22 | 24 | 24 | 24 | 26 | 26 | 26 | 28 | 30 | 32 |
| 0.275-0.279 | | 02 | 04 | 04 | 06 | 06 | 06 | 08 | 08 | 08 | 10 | 10 | 10 | 12 | 12 | 12 | 14 | 14 | 14 | 16 | 16 | 16 | 18 | 18 | 18 | 20 | 20 | 20 | 22 | 22 | 22 | 24 | 24 | 24 | 26 | 26 | 26 | 28 | 28 | 30 | 32 |
| 0.280-0.380 | | | | | | | | | | | | | | | | | | | | | | | | | | | | | | | | | | | | | | | | | |
| 0.381-0.400 | 04 | 06 | 08 | 10 | 10 | 10 | 10 | 12 | 12 | 14 | 14 | 14 | 14 | 16 | 16 | 18 | 18 | 18 | 18 | 20 | 20 | 22 | 22 | 22 | 22 | 24 | 24 | 26 | 26 | 26 | 26 | 28 | 28 | 30 | 30 | 30 | 30 | 32 | 32 | 34 | |
| 0.401-0.425 | 06 | 08 | 10 | 10 | 10 | 12 | 12 | 12 | 14 | 14 | 14 | 16 | 16 | 16 | 18 | 18 | 18 | 20 | 20 | 20 | 22 | 22 | 22 | 24 | 24 | 24 | 26 | 26 | 26 | 28 | 28 | 28 | 30 | 30 | 30 | 32 | 32 | 32 | 34 | 34 | |
| 0.426-0.450 | 06 | 08 | 10 | 12 | 12 | 12 | 12 | 14 | 14 | 16 | 16 | 16 | 16 | 18 | 18 | 20 | 20 | 20 | 20 | 22 | 22 | 24 | 24 | 24 | 24 | 26 | 26 | 28 | 28 | 28 | 28 | 30 | 30 | 32 | 32 | 32 | 32 | 34 | 34 | | |
| 0.451-0.475 | 08 | 10 | 12 | 12 | 12 | 14 | 14 | 14 | 16 | 16 | 16 | 18 | 18 | 18 | 20 | 20 | 20 | 22 | 22 | 22 | 24 | 24 | 24 | 26 | 26 | 26 | 28 | 28 | 28 | 30 | 30 | 30 | 32 | 32 | 32 | 34 | 34 | 34 | 34 | | |
| 0.476-0.500 | 08 | 10 | 12 | 14 | 14 | 14 | 14 | 16 | 16 | 18 | 18 | 18 | 18 | 20 | 20 | 22 | 22 | 22 | 22 | 24 | 24 | 26 | 26 | 26 | 26 | 28 | 28 | 30 | 30 | 30 | 30 | 32 | 32 | 34 | 34 | 34 | 34 | | | | |
| 0.501-0.525 | 10 | 12 | 14 | 14 | 14 | 16 | 16 | 16 | 18 | 18 | 18 | 20 | 20 | 20 | 22 | 22 | 22 | 24 | 24 | 24 | 26 | 26 | 26 | 28 | 28 | 28 | 30 | 30 | 30 | 32 | 32 | 32 | 34 | 34 | 34 | 34 | | | | | |
| 0.526-0.550 | 10 | 12 | 14 | 16 | 16 | 16 | 16 | 18 | 18 | 20 | 20 | 20 | 20 | 22 | 22 | 24 | 24 | 24 | 24 | 26 | 26 | 28 | 28 | 28 | 28 | 30 | 30 | 32 | 32 | 32 | 32 | 34 | 34 | 34 | | | | | | | |
| 0.551-0.575 | 12 | 14 | 16 | 16 | 16 | 18 | 18 | 18 | 20 | 20 | 20 | 22 | 22 | 22 | 24 | 24 | 24 | 26 | 26 | 26 | 28 | 28 | 28 | 30 | 30 | 30 | 32 | 32 | 32 | 34 | 34 | 34 | 34 | | | | | | | | |
| 0.576-0.600 | 12 | 14 | 16 | 18 | 18 | 18 | 18 | 20 | 20 | 22 | 22 | 22 | 22 | 24 | 24 | 26 | 26 | 26 | 26 | 28 | 28 | 30 | 30 | 30 | 30 | 32 | 32 | 34 | 34 | 34 | 34 | 34 | | | | | | | | | |
| 0.601-0.625 | 14 | 16 | 18 | 18 | 18 | 20 | 20 | 20 | 22 | 22 | 22 | 24 | 24 | 24 | 26 | 26 | 26 | 28 | 28 | 28 | 30 | 30 | 30 | 32 | 32 | 32 | 34 | 34 | 34 | 34 | | | | | | | | | | | |
| 0.626-0.650 | 14 | 16 | 18 | 20 | 20 | 20 | 20 | 22 | 22 | 24 | 24 | 24 | 24 | 26 | 26 | 28 | 28 | 28 | 28 | 30 | 30 | 32 | 32 | 32 | 32 | 34 | 34 | 34 | | | | | | | | | | | | | |
| 0.651-0.675 | 16 | 18 | 20 | 20 | 20 | 22 | 22 | 22 | 24 | 24 | 24 | 26 | 26 | 26 | 28 | 28 | 28 | 30 | 30 | 30 | 32 | 32 | 32 | 34 | 34 | 34 | 34 | | | | | | | | | | | | | | |
| 0.676-0.700 | 16 | 18 | 20 | 22 | 22 | 22 | 22 | 24 | 24 | 26 | 26 | 26 | 26 | 28 | 28 | 30 | 30 | 30 | 30 | 32 | 32 | 34 | 34 | 34 | 34 | 34 | | | | | | | | | | | | | | | |
| 0.701-0.725 | 18 | 20 | 22 | 22 | 22 | 24 | 24 | 24 | 26 | 26 | 26 | 28 | 28 | 28 | 30 | 30 | 30 | 32 | 32 | 32 | 34 | 34 | 34 | 34 | | | | | | | | | | | | | | | | | |
| 0.726-0.750 | 18 | 20 | 22 | 24 | 24 | 24 | 24 | 26 | 26 | 28 | 28 | 28 | 28 | 30 | 30 | 32 | 32 | 32 | 32 | 34 | 34 | 34 | | | | | | | | | | | | | | | | | | | |
| 0.751-0.775 | 20 | 22 | 24 | 24 | 24 | 26 | 26 | 26 | 28 | 28 | 28 | 30 | 30 | 30 | 32 | 32 | 32 | 34 | 34 | 34 | 34 | | | | | | | | | | | | | | | | | | | | |
| 0.776-0.800 | 20 | 22 | 24 | 26 | 26 | 26 | 26 | 28 | 28 | 30 | 30 | 30 | 30 | 32 | 32 | 34 | 34 | 34 | 34 | 34 | | | | | | | | | | | | | | | | | | | | | |
| 0.801-0.825 | 22 | 24 | 26 | 26 | 26 | 28 | 28 | 28 | 30 | 30 | 30 | 32 | 32 | 32 | 34 | 34 | 34 | 34 | | | | | | | | | | | | | | | | | | | | | | | |
| 0.826-0.850 | 22 | 24 | 26 | 28 | 28 | 28 | 28 | 30 | 30 | 32 | 32 | 32 | 32 | 34 | 34 | 34 | | | | | | | | | | | | | | | | | | | | | | | | | |
| 0.851-0.875 | 24 | 26 | 28 | 28 | 28 | 30 | 30 | 30 | 32 | 32 | 32 | 34 | 34 | 34 | 34 | | | | | | | | | | | | | | | | | | | | | | | | | | |
| 0.876-0.900 | 24 | 26 | 28 | 30 | 30 | 30 | 30 | 32 | 32 | 34 | 34 | 34 | 34 | 34 | | | | | | | | | | | | | | | | | | | | | | | | | | | |
| 0.901-0.925 | 26 | 28 | 30 | 30 | 30 | 32 | 32 | 32 | 34 | 34 | 34 | 34 | | | | | | | | | | | | | | | | | | | | | | | | | | | | | |
| 0.926-0.950 | 26 | 28 | 30 | 32 | 32 | 32 | 32 | 34 | 34 | 34 | | | | | | | | | | | | | | | | | | | | | | | | | | | | | | | |
| 0.951-0.975 | 28 | 30 | 32 | 32 | 32 | 34 | 34 | 34 | 34 | | | | | | | | | | | | | | | | | | | | | | | | | | | | | | | | |
| 0.976-1.000 | 28 | 30 | 32 | 34 | 34 | 34 | 34 | 34 | | | | | | | | | | | | | | | | | | | | | | | | | | | | | | | | | |
| 1.001-1.025 | 30 | 32 | 34 | 34 | 34 | 34 | | | | | | | | | | | | | | | | | | | | | | | | | | | | | | | | | | | |
| 1.026-1.050 | 30 | 32 | 34 | 34 | | | | | | | | | | | | | | | | | | | | | | | | | | | | | | | | | | | | | |
| 1.051-1.075 | 32 | 34 | 34 | | | | | | | | | | | | | | | | | | | | | | | | | | | | | | | | | | | | | | |
| 1.076-1.100 | 32 | 34 | | | | | | | | | | | | | | | | | | | | | | | | | | | | | | | | | | | | | | | |
| 1.101-1.125 | 34 | 34 | | | | | | | | | | | | | | | | | | | | | | | | | | | | | | | | | | | | | | | |
| 1.126-1.180 | 34 | | | | | | | | | | | | | | | | | | | | | | | | | | | | | | | | | | | | | | | | |

New shim thickness mm (in.)

| Shim No. | Thickness | Shim No. | Thickness |
|---|---|---|---|
| 02 | 2.50 (0.0984) | 20 | 2.95 (0.1161) |
| 04 | 2.55 (0.1004) | 22 | 3.00 (0.1181) |
| 06 | 2.60 (0.1024) | 24 | 3.05 (0.1201) |
| 08 | 2.65 (0.1043) | 26 | 3.10 (0.1220) |
| 10 | 2.70 (0.1063) | 28 | 3.15 (0.1240) |
| 12 | 2.75 (0.1083) | 30 | 3.20 (0.1260) |
| 14 | 2.80 (0.1102) | 32 | 3.25 (0.1280) |
| 16 | 2.85 (0.1122) | 34 | 3.30 (0.1299) |
| 18 | 2.90 (0.1142) | | |

**Exhaust valve clearance:**
**0.28 — 0.38 mm (0.011 — 0.015 in.)**

EXAMPLE: The 2.800 mm (0.1102 in.) shim is installed and the measured clearance is 0.450 mm (0.0177 in.). Replace the 2.800 mm (0.1102 in.) shim with a No. 18 shim.

91E00517

Courtesy of Toyota Motor Sales, U.S.A., Inc.

***Fig. 4: Selecting Exhaust Valve Adjusting Shim***

# 1991 ENGINES
# 2.0L & 2.2L 4-Cylinder (Cont.)

INTAKE VALVES

| Measured clearance (mm) | Installed shim thickness (mm) | | | | | | | | | | | | | | | | | | | | | | | | | | | | | | | | | | | | | | | | |
|---|---|---|---|---|---|---|---|---|---|---|---|---|---|---|---|---|---|---|---|---|---|---|---|---|---|---|---|---|---|---|---|---|---|---|---|---|---|---|---|---|---|
| | 2.500 | 2.550 | 2.600 | 2.620 | 2.640 | 2.650 | 2.660 | 2.680 | 2.700 | 2.720 | 2.740 | 2.750 | 2.760 | 2.780 | 2.800 | 2.820 | 2.840 | 2.850 | 2.860 | 2.880 | 2.900 | 2.920 | 2.940 | 2.950 | 2.960 | 2.980 | 3.000 | 3.020 | 3.040 | 3.050 | 3.060 | 3.080 | 3.100 | 3.120 | 3.140 | 3.150 | 3.160 | 3.180 | 3.200 | 3.250 | 3.300 |
| 0.000-0.025 | | | | | | | | 02 | 02 | 02 | 02 | 02 | 04 | 04 | 04 | 06 | 06 | 06 | 08 | 08 | 08 | 10 | 10 | 10 | 12 | 12 | 12 | 14 | 14 | 14 | 16 | 16 | 16 | 18 | 18 | 18 | 20 | 20 | 20 | 22 | 24 |
| 0.026-0.050 | | | | | 02 | 02 | 02 | 02 | 02 | 02 | 04 | 04 | 04 | 06 | 06 | 06 | 08 | 08 | 08 | 10 | 10 | 10 | 12 | 12 | 12 | 14 | 14 | 14 | 16 | 16 | 16 | 18 | 18 | 18 | 20 | 20 | 20 | 22 | 22 | 24 | 26 |
| 0.051-0.075 | | | | 02 | 02 | 02 | 02 | 02 | 02 | 04 | 04 | 04 | 06 | 06 | 06 | 08 | 08 | 08 | 10 | 10 | 10 | 12 | 12 | 12 | 14 | 14 | 14 | 16 | 16 | 16 | 18 | 18 | 18 | 20 | 20 | 20 | 22 | 22 | 22 | 24 | 26 |
| 0.076-0.100 | | | 02 | 02 | 02 | 02 | 02 | 04 | 04 | 04 | 06 | 06 | 06 | 08 | 08 | 08 | 10 | 10 | 10 | 12 | 12 | 12 | 14 | 14 | 14 | 16 | 16 | 16 | 18 | 18 | 18 | 20 | 20 | 20 | 22 | 22 | 22 | 24 | 24 | 26 | 28 |
| 0.101-0.125 | | | 02 | 02 | 02 | 02 | 04 | 04 | 04 | 06 | 06 | 06 | 08 | 08 | 08 | 10 | 10 | 10 | 12 | 12 | 12 | 14 | 14 | 14 | 16 | 16 | 16 | 18 | 18 | 18 | 20 | 20 | 20 | 22 | 22 | 22 | 24 | 24 | 24 | 26 | 28 |
| 0.126-0.150 | | 02 | 02 | 02 | 04 | 04 | 04 | 06 | 06 | 06 | 08 | 08 | 08 | 10 | 10 | 10 | 12 | 12 | 12 | 14 | 14 | 14 | 16 | 16 | 16 | 18 | 18 | 18 | 20 | 20 | 20 | 22 | 22 | 22 | 24 | 24 | 24 | 26 | 26 | 28 | 30 |
| 0.151-0.175 | | 02 | 02 | 04 | 04 | 04 | 06 | 06 | 06 | 08 | 08 | 08 | 10 | 10 | 10 | 12 | 12 | 12 | 14 | 14 | 14 | 16 | 16 | 16 | 18 | 18 | 18 | 20 | 20 | 20 | 22 | 22 | 22 | 24 | 24 | 24 | 26 | 26 | 26 | 28 | 30 |
| 0.176-0.189 | | 02 | 04 | 04 | 06 | 06 | 06 | 06 | 08 | 08 | 10 | 10 | 10 | 10 | 12 | 12 | 14 | 14 | 14 | 14 | 16 | 16 | 18 | 18 | 18 | 18 | 20 | 20 | 22 | 22 | 22 | 22 | 24 | 24 | 26 | 26 | 26 | 26 | 28 | 30 | 32 |
| 0.190-0.290 | | | | | | | | | | | | | | | | | | | | | | | | | | | | | | | | | | | | | | | | | |
| 0.291-0.300 | 04 | 06 | 08 | 10 | 10 | 10 | 10 | 12 | 12 | 14 | 14 | 14 | 14 | 16 | 16 | 18 | 18 | 18 | 18 | 20 | 20 | 22 | 22 | 22 | 22 | 24 | 24 | 26 | 26 | 26 | 26 | 28 | 28 | 30 | 30 | 30 | 30 | 32 | 32 | 34 | |
| 0.301-0.325 | 04 | 06 | 08 | 10 | 10 | 10 | 12 | 12 | 12 | 14 | 14 | 14 | 16 | 16 | 16 | 18 | 18 | 18 | 20 | 20 | 20 | 22 | 22 | 22 | 24 | 24 | 24 | 26 | 26 | 26 | 28 | 28 | 28 | 30 | 30 | 30 | 32 | 32 | 32 | 34 | |
| 0.326-0.350 | 06 | 08 | 10 | 10 | 12 | 12 | 12 | 14 | 14 | 14 | 16 | 16 | 16 | 18 | 18 | 18 | 20 | 20 | 20 | 22 | 22 | 22 | 24 | 24 | 24 | 26 | 26 | 26 | 28 | 28 | 28 | 30 | 30 | 30 | 32 | 32 | 32 | 34 | 34 | | |
| 0.351-0.375 | 06 | 08 | 10 | 12 | 12 | 12 | 14 | 14 | 14 | 16 | 16 | 16 | 18 | 18 | 18 | 20 | 20 | 20 | 22 | 22 | 22 | 24 | 24 | 24 | 26 | 26 | 26 | 28 | 28 | 28 | 30 | 30 | 30 | 32 | 32 | 32 | 34 | 34 | 34 | | |
| 0.376-0.400 | 08 | 10 | 12 | 12 | 14 | 14 | 14 | 16 | 16 | 16 | 18 | 18 | 18 | 20 | 20 | 20 | 22 | 22 | 22 | 24 | 24 | 24 | 26 | 26 | 26 | 28 | 28 | 28 | 30 | 30 | 30 | 32 | 32 | 32 | 34 | 34 | 34 | 34 | | | |
| 0.401-0.425 | 08 | 10 | 12 | 14 | 14 | 14 | 16 | 16 | 16 | 18 | 18 | 18 | 20 | 20 | 20 | 22 | 22 | 22 | 24 | 24 | 24 | 26 | 26 | 26 | 28 | 28 | 28 | 30 | 30 | 30 | 32 | 32 | 32 | 34 | 34 | 34 | 34 | | | | |
| 0.426-0.450 | 10 | 12 | 14 | 14 | 16 | 16 | 16 | 18 | 18 | 18 | 20 | 20 | 20 | 22 | 22 | 22 | 24 | 24 | 24 | 26 | 26 | 26 | 28 | 28 | 28 | 30 | 30 | 30 | 32 | 32 | 32 | 34 | 34 | 34 | 34 | | | | | | |
| 0.451-0.475 | 10 | 12 | 14 | 16 | 16 | 16 | 18 | 18 | 18 | 20 | 20 | 20 | 22 | 22 | 22 | 24 | 24 | 24 | 26 | 26 | 26 | 28 | 28 | 28 | 30 | 30 | 30 | 32 | 32 | 32 | 34 | 34 | 34 | | | | | | | | |
| 0.476-0.500 | 12 | 14 | 16 | 16 | 18 | 18 | 18 | 20 | 20 | 20 | 22 | 22 | 22 | 24 | 24 | 24 | 26 | 26 | 26 | 28 | 28 | 28 | 30 | 30 | 30 | 32 | 32 | 32 | 34 | 34 | 34 | 34 | | | | | | | | | |
| 0.501-0.525 | 12 | 14 | 16 | 18 | 18 | 18 | 20 | 20 | 20 | 22 | 22 | 22 | 24 | 24 | 24 | 26 | 26 | 26 | 28 | 28 | 28 | 30 | 30 | 30 | 32 | 32 | 32 | 34 | 34 | 34 | 34 | | | | | | | | | | |
| 0.526-0.550 | 14 | 16 | 18 | 18 | 20 | 20 | 20 | 22 | 22 | 22 | 24 | 24 | 24 | 26 | 26 | 26 | 28 | 28 | 28 | 30 | 30 | 30 | 32 | 32 | 32 | 34 | 34 | 34 | 34 | | | | | | | | | | | | |
| 0.551-0.575 | 14 | 16 | 18 | 20 | 20 | 20 | 22 | 22 | 22 | 24 | 24 | 24 | 26 | 26 | 26 | 28 | 28 | 28 | 30 | 30 | 30 | 32 | 32 | 32 | 34 | 34 | 34 | | | | | | | | | | | | | | |
| 0.576-0.600 | 16 | 18 | 20 | 20 | 22 | 22 | 22 | 24 | 24 | 24 | 26 | 26 | 26 | 28 | 28 | 28 | 30 | 30 | 30 | 32 | 32 | 32 | 34 | 34 | 34 | 34 | | | | | | | | | | | | | | | |
| 0.601-0.625 | 16 | 18 | 20 | 22 | 22 | 22 | 24 | 24 | 24 | 26 | 26 | 26 | 28 | 28 | 28 | 30 | 30 | 30 | 32 | 32 | 32 | 34 | 34 | 34 | 34 | | | | | | | | | | | | | | | | |
| 0.626-0.650 | 18 | 20 | 22 | 22 | 24 | 24 | 24 | 26 | 26 | 26 | 28 | 28 | 28 | 30 | 30 | 30 | 32 | 32 | 32 | 34 | 34 | 34 | 34 | | | | | | | | | | | | | | | | | | |
| 0.651-0.675 | 18 | 20 | 22 | 24 | 24 | 24 | 26 | 26 | 26 | 28 | 28 | 28 | 30 | 30 | 30 | 32 | 32 | 32 | 34 | 34 | 34 | | | | | | | | | | | | | | | | | | | | |
| 0.676-0.700 | 20 | 22 | 24 | 24 | 26 | 26 | 26 | 28 | 28 | 28 | 30 | 30 | 30 | 32 | 32 | 32 | 34 | 34 | 34 | 34 | | | | | | | | | | | | | | | | | | | | | |
| 0.701-0.725 | 20 | 22 | 24 | 26 | 26 | 26 | 28 | 28 | 28 | 30 | 30 | 30 | 32 | 32 | 32 | 34 | 34 | 34 | 34 | | | | | | | | | | | | | | | | | | | | | | |
| 0.726-0.750 | 22 | 24 | 26 | 26 | 28 | 28 | 28 | 30 | 30 | 30 | 32 | 32 | 32 | 34 | 34 | 34 | 34 | | | | | | | | | | | | | | | | | | | | | | | | |
| 0.751-0.775 | 22 | 24 | 26 | 28 | 28 | 28 | 30 | 30 | 30 | 32 | 32 | 32 | 34 | 34 | 34 | | | | | | | | | | | | | | | | | | | | | | | | | | |
| 0.776-0.800 | 24 | 26 | 28 | 28 | 30 | 30 | 30 | 32 | 32 | 32 | 34 | 34 | 34 | 34 | | | | | | | | | | | | | | | | | | | | | | | | | | | |
| 0.801-0.825 | 24 | 26 | 28 | 30 | 30 | 30 | 32 | 32 | 32 | 34 | 34 | 34 | 34 | | | | | | | | | | | | | | | | | | | | | | | | | | | | |
| 0.826-0.850 | 26 | 28 | 30 | 30 | 32 | 32 | 32 | 34 | 34 | 34 | 34 | | | | | | | | | | | | | | | | | | | | | | | | | | | | | | |
| 0.851-0.875 | 26 | 28 | 30 | 32 | 32 | 32 | 34 | 34 | 34 | | | | | | | | | | | | | | | | | | | | | | | | | | | | | | | | |
| 0.876-0.900 | 28 | 30 | 32 | 32 | 34 | 34 | 34 | 34 | | | | | | | | | | | | | | | | | | | | | | | | | | | | | | | | | |
| 0.901-0.925 | 28 | 30 | 32 | 34 | 34 | 34 | 34 | | | | | | | | | | | | | | | | | | | | | | | | | | | | | | | | | | |
| 0.926-0.950 | 30 | 32 | 34 | 34 | 34 | | | | | | | | | | | | | | | | | | | | | | | | | | | | | | | | | | | | |
| 0.951-0.975 | 30 | 32 | 34 | | | | | | | | | | | | | | | | | | | | | | | | | | | | | | | | | | | | | | |
| 0.976-1.000 | 32 | 34 | | | | | | | | | | | | | | | | | | | | | | | | | | | | | | | | | | | | | | | |
| 1.001-1.025 | 34 | 34 | | | | | | | | | | | | | | | | | | | | | | | | | | | | | | | | | | | | | | | |
| 1.026-1.090 | 34 | | | | | | | | | | | | | | | | | | | | | | | | | | | | | | | | | | | | | | | | |

New shim thickness mm (in.)

| Shim No. | Thickness | Shim No. | Thickness |
|---|---|---|---|
| 02 | 2.50 (0.0984) | 20 | 2.95 (0.1161) |
| 04 | 2.55 (0.1004) | 22 | 3.00 (0.1181) |
| 06 | 2.60 (0.1024) | 24 | 3.05 (0.1201) |
| 08 | 2.65 (0.1043) | 26 | 3.10 (0.1220) |
| 10 | 2.70 (0.1063) | 28 | 3.15 (0.1240) |
| 12 | 2.75 (0.1083) | 30 | 3.20 (0.1260) |
| 14 | 2.80 (0.1102) | 32 | 3.25 (0.1280) |
| 16 | 2.85 (0.1122) | 34 | 3.30 (0.1299) |
| 18 | 2.90 (0.1142) | | |

**Intake valve clearance (Cold):**
**0.19 — 0.29 mm (0.007 — 0.011 in.)**

EXAMPLE: The 2.800 mm (0.1102 in.) shim is installed and the measured clearance is 0.450 mm (0.0177 in.). Replace the 2.800 mm (0.1102 in.) shim with a No. 22 shim.

91F00518

Courtesy of Toyota Motor Sales, U.S.A., Inc.

***Fig. 5: Selecting Intake Valve Adjusting Shim***

## REMOVAL & INSTALLATION

***NOTE: For reassembly reference, label all electrical connectors vacuum hoses, and fuel lines before removal. Also place mating marks on engine hood and other major assemblies before removal.***

### FUEL PRESSURE RELEASE

With ignition off, disconnect negative battery cable. Place container under fuel line. Cover fuel line connection with shop towel. Slowly loosen fuel line connection, allowing fuel pressure to be released. Once fuel pressure is released, fuel system components can be removed.

### COOLING SYSTEM BLEEDING

**Camry & Celica** – No special cooling system bleeding procedure is required.

**MR2 – 1)** Remove spare tire, front luggage compartment trim and upper radiator support seal. Connect air bleed hoses to heater and radiator air drain plugs. Support opposite end of hoses to hood or hood support. *See Fig. 6.* Ensure hoses are not pinched shut.

**2)** Place heater control lever to the warmest position. Open heater and radiator air drain plugs at least 3 turns.

**3)** Slowly add coolant through coolant filler. *See Fig. 6.* Air will bleed from hoses on heater and radiator air drain plugs. Ensure coolant level in air bleed hoses is same level as coolant filler. *See Fig. 6.*

# 1991 ENGINES
# 2.0L & 2.2L 4-Cylinder (Cont.)

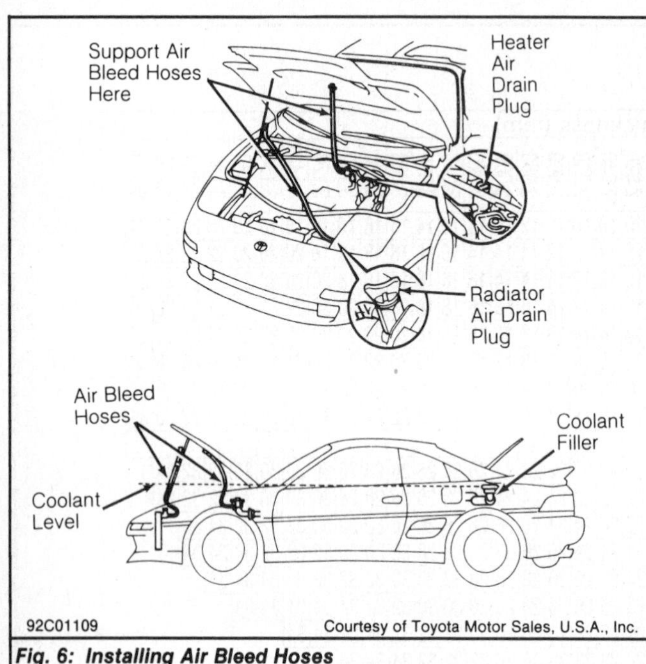


*Fig. 6: Installing Air Bleed Hoses*

4) If coolant level in air bleed hoses is lower than level in coolant filler, air still exists in cooling system. Check for pinched or restriction in air bleed hoses and repeat step 3). When proper coolant level is obtained in air bleed hoses, close air drain plugs. Remove air bleed hoses.

## ENGINE

***CAUTION: Before performing service procedures on vehicle, disconnect negative battery cable. To avoid accidental air bag deployment on Celica and MR2, wait at least 20 seconds after disconnecting negative battery cable before proceeding.***

***NOTE: Remove engine and transaxle as an assembly.***

**Removal (Camry) – 1)** Release fuel pressure. See FUEL PRESSURE RELEASE under REMOVAL & INSTALLATION.

**2)** Remove battery. Drain cooling system and engine oil. Remove hood. Disconnect electrical connections and remove ignitor and bracket. Remove radiator, cooling fans and coolant reservoir tank. Remove cruise control actuator (if equipped). Remove air cleaner assembly, air intake duct and airflow meter.

**3)** Remove A/C compressor (if equipped) and power steering pump with hoses attached and secure aside. Disconnect necessary control cables, coolant and vacuum hoses, fuel lines and electrical connections.

**4)** Remove glove box. Disconnect Electronic Control Unit (ECU) connectors and necessary wiring and pull engine wiring out through the firewall. Remove power steering reservoir.

**5)** Raise and support vehicle. On M/T models, remove clutch release cylinder with hose attached and secure aside. On A/T models, disconnect oil cooler lines at transaxle.

**6)** On all models, disconnect control cables, speedometer cable and electrical connections at transaxle. Remove crossmember, bolted to both lower suspension arm shafts.

**7)** On 4WD models, place reference marks on front and rear drive shaft flanges at center bearing. Remove flange bolts. Separate front drive shaft from rear drive shaft. Remove front drive shaft from transfer case. Install Plug (SST 09325-20010) in transfer case to prevent oil leakage. Remove seal deflector from rear of transfer case.

**8)** On all models, disconnect exhaust pipe at catalytic converter and center pipe. Remove exhaust pipe. Remove front tires and wheels.

**9)** Remove cotter pin and retainer from end of axle shaft. Apply service brake and remove axle shaft nut. Remove lower engine covers and fenderwell aprons (if equipped) for axle shaft removal. Drain transaxle fluid. Remove nut and separate tie rod from steering knuckle.

**10)** Remove ball joint-to-steering knuckle bolts. Cover axle shaft boots with shop towel to prevent damage to axle shaft boot. Using plastic hammer, tap on axle shaft until it is free of hub assembly. Separate axle shaft from hub assembly.

**11)** On 2WD models, remove right axle shaft center bearing bracket-to-cylinder block bolts. Place wooden block against transaxle case. Pry on wooden block and axle shaft until axle shaft disengages from transaxle. Remove axle shafts.

**12)** On 4WD models, to remove left axle shaft, pry between transaxle case and axle shaft until axle shaft disengages from transaxle. To remove right axle shaft, use brass drift and hammer to drive axle shaft from transaxle. *See Fig. 7.*

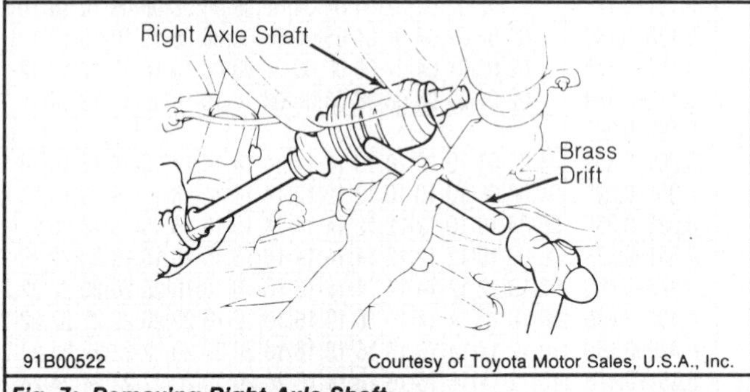


*Fig. 7: Removing Right Axle Shaft*

**13)** On all models, support engine with hoist. Remove engine mount crossmember located below engine.

**14)** Disconnect engine and transaxle mounts. Note direction of mount installation for reassembly reference. Mounts must be installed in original direction. Lift engine and transaxle from vehicle.

**Installation – 1)** To install, reverse removal procedure. Before installing axle shafts, coat transaxle seals with engine oil. Ensure opening of axle shaft snap ring is facing downward before installing axle shaft.

**2)** On 4WD models, ensure reference mark is aligned on drive shaft flanges.

**3)** On all models, tighten fasteners to specification. See TORQUE SPECIFICATIONS table at end of article. Adjust all control cables and fluid levels.

***NOTE: Remove engine and transaxle as an assembly.***

**Removal (Celica) – 1)** Release fuel pressure. See FUEL PRESSURE RELEASE under REMOVAL & INSTALLATION. Drain cooling system and engine oil. Remove hood and battery.

**2)** Remove air cleaner assembly and air intake duct. Remove engine relay box from battery. Remove relay box lower cover and disconnect fusible link and 2 electrical connectors. Remove A/C relay box from bracket, located near right front corner of engine compartment.

**3)** Remove cruise control actuator and bracket (if equipped). Remove cover and disconnect hoses at anti-lock brake actuator at right front corner of engine compartment (if equipped). Remove anti-lock brake actuator.

**4)** Remove radiator, cooling fan and coolant reservoir tank. Remove strut tower-to-firewall braces. Remove ignition coil and charcoal canister. Remove power steering pump and A/C compressor (if equipped) with hoses attached and secure aside.

**5)** Disconnect necessary control cables, coolant hoses, fuel lines, vacuum hoses and electrical connections. Disconnect Electronic Control Unit (ECU) and other connectors necessary to pull engine wiring harness out through the firewall. *See Fig. 8.*

**6)** Raise and support vehicle. On M/T models, remove starter and clutch release cylinder. On A/T models, disconnect transaxle control cables and oil cooler lines at transaxle. On all models, disconnect speedometer cable and electrical connections at transaxle.

**7)** Remove suspension crossmember, bolted to both lower suspension arm shafts. Disconnect exhaust pipe at catalytic converter and center pipe. Remove exhaust pipe. Remove front wheels. Remove cotter pin and lock nut cap from end of axle shaft. Apply service brake and remove axle shaft nut.

# 1991 ENGINES
# 2.0L & 2.2L 4-Cylinder (Cont.)

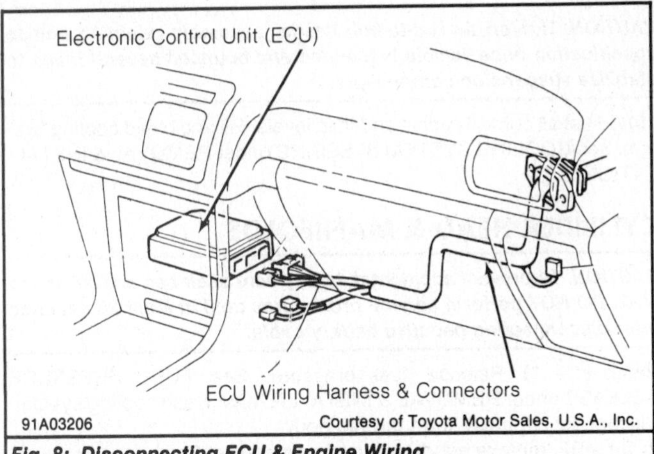


***Fig. 8: Disconnecting ECU & Engine Wiring***

**8)** Remove lower engine cover. Drain transaxle fluid. Remove brake caliper. Place reference mark on brake rotor and hub assembly for reassembly reference. Remove brake rotor.
**9)** Remove nut and separate tie rod from steering knuckle. Remove ball joint-to-lower control arm bolt and nuts. Using Hub Puller (09950-20017), press axle shaft from of hub assembly.
**10)** Cover axle shaft boot with shop towel. Using pry bar, remove left axle shaft assembly. *See Fig. 9.*

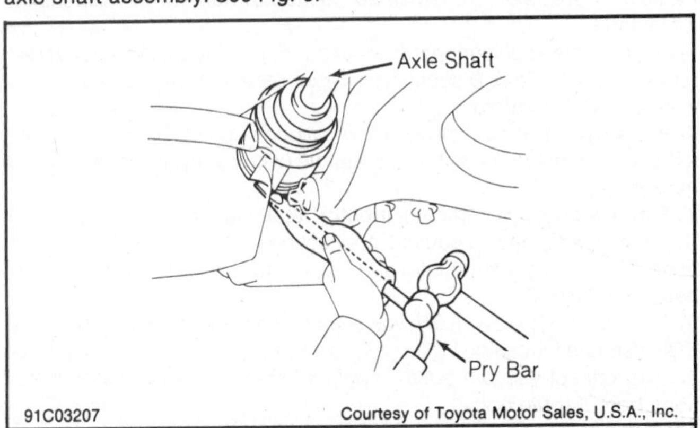


***Fig. 9: Removing Left Axle Shaft***

**11)** Remove right axle shaft center bearing bracket-to-cylinder block support bolts. Remove right axle assembly. Support engine with hoist.
**12)** Remove engine mount crossmember located below engine. Disconnect engine and transaxle mounts. Note direction of mount installation for reassembly reference. Lift engine and transaxle from vehicle.
**Installation – 1)** To install, reverse removal procedure. Before installing axle shafts, coat transaxle seals with engine oil. Ensure opening of axle shaft snap ring is facing downward before installing axle shaft. Install right axle shaft so pin on center bearing aligns with cylinder block support.
**2)** Ensure reference mark on brake rotor and hub assembly are aligned. Tighten fasteners to specification. See TORQUE SPECIFICATIONS table at end of article. Adjust all control cables and fluid levels.

***NOTE: Remove engine and transaxle as an assembly.***

**Removal (MR2) – 1)** Release fuel pressure. See FUEL PRESSURE RELEASE under REMOVAL & INSTALLATION. Drain cooling system, engine oil and transaxle oil.
**2)** Remove hood, hood side panels and lower engine covers. Remove strut tower-to-firewall braces. Remove air cleaner cap, airflow meter and air cleaner case.
**3)** Remove cruise control actuator and linkage. Disconnect necessary control cables, coolant hoses, fuel lines, vacuum hoses and electrical connections.
**4)** Remove check connector (located near vacuum sensor) and vacuum sensor from the body. *See Fig. 10.* Remove A/C vacuum switching valve assembly, located near the throttle body and mounted on side of the vehicle body.

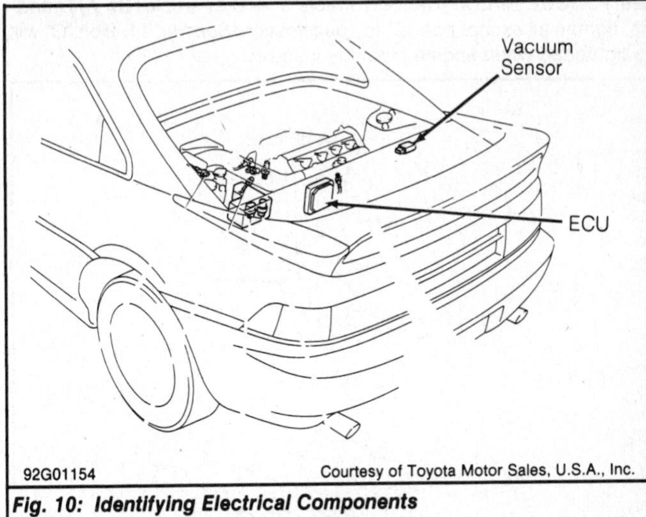


***Fig. 10: Identifying Electrical Components***

**5)** Remove radiator cap and coolant filler. *See Fig. 6.* Remove charcoal canister. Remove retaining bolts from relay box, located near strut tower. Disconnect luggage compartment cable near relay box. Remove upper and lower covers from relay box.
**6)** Disconnect positive cable and electrical connections from relay box. Remove ignition coil and ignitor. Disconnect electrical connectors from Electronic Control Unit (ECU), located near the luggage compartment. *See Fig. 10.*
**7)** Disconnect electrical connectors from starter relay and engine wiring, located near ECU. *See Fig. 10.* Pull engine wiring out through opening in luggage compartment.
**8)** Disconnect necessary control cables, coolant hoses, fuel lines, vacuum hoses and electrical connections. Raise and support vehicle. Disconnect control cables at transaxle.
**9)** Disconnect exhaust pipe located below engine. Remove support brace and remove exhaust pipe. Remove drive belt and idler pulley bracket.
**10)** Remove A/C compressor with hoses attached and secure aside. Disconnect speedometer cable and electrical connections at transaxle. On A/T models, disconnect oil cooler hoses at transaxle.
**11)** On all models, remove cotter pin and lock nut cap from end of axle shaft. Apply service brake and remove axle shaft nut. Remove brake caliper. Place reference mark on brake rotor and hub assembly for reassembly reference. Remove brake rotor.
**12)** Remove retaining nut and disconnect stabilizer link from strut assembly. Remove retaining bolt and remove anti-lock brake sensor from hub carrier assembly.
**13)** Remove ball joint-to-lower control arm bolts. Separate lower control arms from ball joint at hub carrier assembly. Remove retaining nut and separate tie rod from hub carrier assembly.
**14)** Cover axle shaft boot with shop towel. Using puller attached to hub assembly, press axle shaft from hub assembly. Using pry bar, remove left axle shaft assembly. *See Fig. 9.* To remove right axle shaft, use hammer and brass drift to drive axle shaft from transaxle. *See Fig. 7.*
**15)** Support engine with hoist. Remove through bolt and retaining bolts from front (exhaust manifold side) and rear (intake manifold side) engine mounts. Remove transaxle control cable bracket (A/T) or clutch cylinder with hose attached (M/T).
**16)** Remove air cleaner case support bracket. Remove remaining engine mount support brackets and through bolts. Lower engine and transaxle through bottom of engine compartment.
**Installation – 1)** Install right (timing belt side) engine mount to the body with through bolt loosely installed. Secure right (timing belt side)

# 1991 ENGINES
# 2.0L & 2.2L 4-Cylinder (Cont.)

engine mount insulator to mounting bracket with nuts loosely installed.

**2)** Install the left (flywheel side) engine mount bracket on transaxle. On M/T models, tighten left engine mount bracket bolts to specification. See TORQUE SPECIFICATIONS table at end of article. On A/T models, tighten all except bolt "C" to specification. *See Fig. 11.* Bolt "C" will be tightened when engine mount is installed.

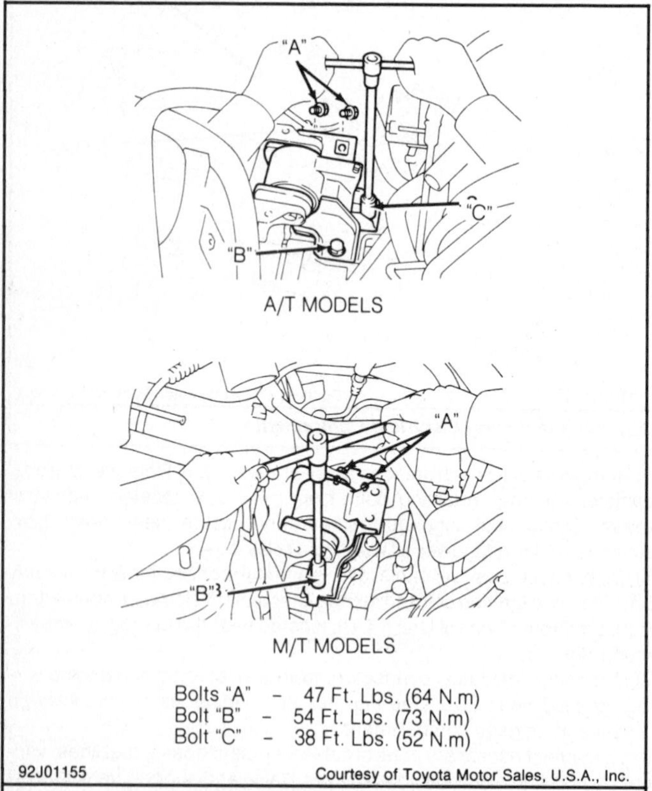


***Fig. 11: Installing Left Engine Mount Bolts***

**3)** On all models, install left (flywheel side) engine mount to the body with through bolt loosely installed. Install left (flywheel side) engine mount insulator-to-mounting bracket and tighten bolts to specification. *See Fig. 11.*

**4)** Tighten left (flywheel side) engine mount through bolt to specification. See TORQUE SPECIFICATIONS table at end of article. Tighten right (flywheel side) engine mount nuts and through bolt to specification. Install support bracket on top of right (timing belt side) engine mount. Tighten bolts and nuts to specification.

**5)** Install air cleaner case bracket and left (flywheel side) engine mount support bracket. Tighten bolts to specification. See TORQUE SPECIFICATIONS table at end of article.

**6)** Install transaxle control cable bracket (A/T) or clutch cylinder (M/T). Tighten bolts to specification. See TORQUE SPECIFICATIONS table at end of article.

**7)** Install front (exhaust manifold side) engine mount-to-body bolts. Tighten bolts to specification. Loosely install front (exhaust manifold side) engine mount through bolt. Install rear (intake manifold side) engine mount-to-body bolts and through bolt. Tighten bolts to specification. Tighten front (exhaust manifold side) engine mount through bolt to specification.

**8)** Coat lip of axle shaft oil seals with grease. Position opening of snap ring on end of axle shaft facing downward. Install axle shaft by lightly tapping axle shaft into the transaxle. Ensure axle shaft fully engages transaxle.

**9)** Ensure axle shaft end play is .08-.12" (2.0-3.0 mm). To install remaining components, reverse removal procedure. Ensure reference marks on brake rotor and hub assembly are aligned. Tighten fasteners to specification. See TORQUE SPECIFICATIONS table at end of article.

***CAUTION: Tighten tie rod-to-hub carrier assembly retaining bolt to specification once vehicle is lowered and bounced several times to stabilize suspension components.***

**10)** Adjust all control cables and fluid levels. Fill and bleed cooling system. See COOLING SYSTEM BLEEDING under REMOVAL & INSTALLATION.

## CYLINDER HEAD & MANIFOLDS

***CAUTION: To prevent accidental deployment of air bag on Celica and MR2, DO NOT perform service procedures until at least 20 seconds after disconnecting negative battery cable.***

**Removal - 1)** Release fuel pressure. See FUEL PRESSURE RELEASE under REMOVAL & INSTALLATION. Drain cooling system. Disconnect air intake from throttle body.

**2)** On MR2, remove hood and hood side panels. Remove strut tower-to-firewall braces.

**3)** On all models, remove air cleaner cap. Disconnect control cables, air intake tubing, electrical connections, coolant hoses and vacuum hoses at throttle body and intake manifold.

**4)** Remove cruise control actuator, oil pressure switch and engine hangers. *See Fig. 12.* Raise and support vehicle. Remove lower engine covers.

**5)** On Camry and Celica, remove alternator and alternator bracket. Remove suspension crossmember, bolted to both lower suspension arm shafts.

**6)** On all models, disconnect front exhaust pipe at catalytic converter on exhaust manifold. Disconnect oxygen sensor. Remove heat shield from exhaust manifold.

**7)** Remove catalytic converter-to-cylinder block brace. Remove exhaust manifold nuts, exhaust manifold (with catalytic converter) and gasket.

**8)** Remove distributor cap, distributor retaining bolts, distributor and "O" ring. Disconnect electrical connections, radiator hose, vacuum hoses. Remove coolant outlet and coolant by-pass pipe from cylinder head. *See Fig. 12.*

**9)** Remove EGR pipe, EGR valve and vacuum modulator. Remove EGR Vacuum Switching Valve (VSV) and air pipe (if equipped). *See Fig. 12.* Disconnect vacuum hoses, coolant hoses and electrical connections from throttle body.

**10)** Remove throttle body retaining bolts. Note bolt location and length for reassembly reference. Remove throttle body. Remove cold start injector pipe. *See Fig. 12.* Remove intake manifold-to-cylinder block brace.

**11)** Remove retaining bolts/nuts, intake manifold and gasket. Disconnect hoses from pressure regulator and delivery pipe and injector wiring. Remove delivery pipe retaining bolts.

**12)** Remove delivery pipe, injector assemblies, spacers and insulators from cylinder head. DO NOT allow injector assemblies to fall from delivery pipe. Remove spark plugs.

**13)** Remove timing belt, idler pulley, spring and camshaft sprocket. See TIMING BELT under REMOVAL & INSTALLATION. Remove No. 3 timing belt cover. *See Fig. 12.*

***NOTE: Manufacturer recommends removing No. 2 timing belt cover (upper cover), timing belt and camshaft sprockets while laying timing belt on No. 1 timing belt (lower cover). Ensure timing belt does not come off crankshaft sprocket or timing belt must be removed and reinstalled.***

**14)** Remove camshafts. See CAMSHAFT under REMOVAL & INSTALLATION. Remove cylinder head bolts in sequence using several steps. *See Fig. 13.* Remove cylinder head and gasket.

***CAUTION: Proper cylinder head bolt removal sequence must be used to prevent cylinder head warpage. See Fig. 13.***

# 1991 ENGINES
# 2.0L & 2.2L 4-Cylinder (Cont.)

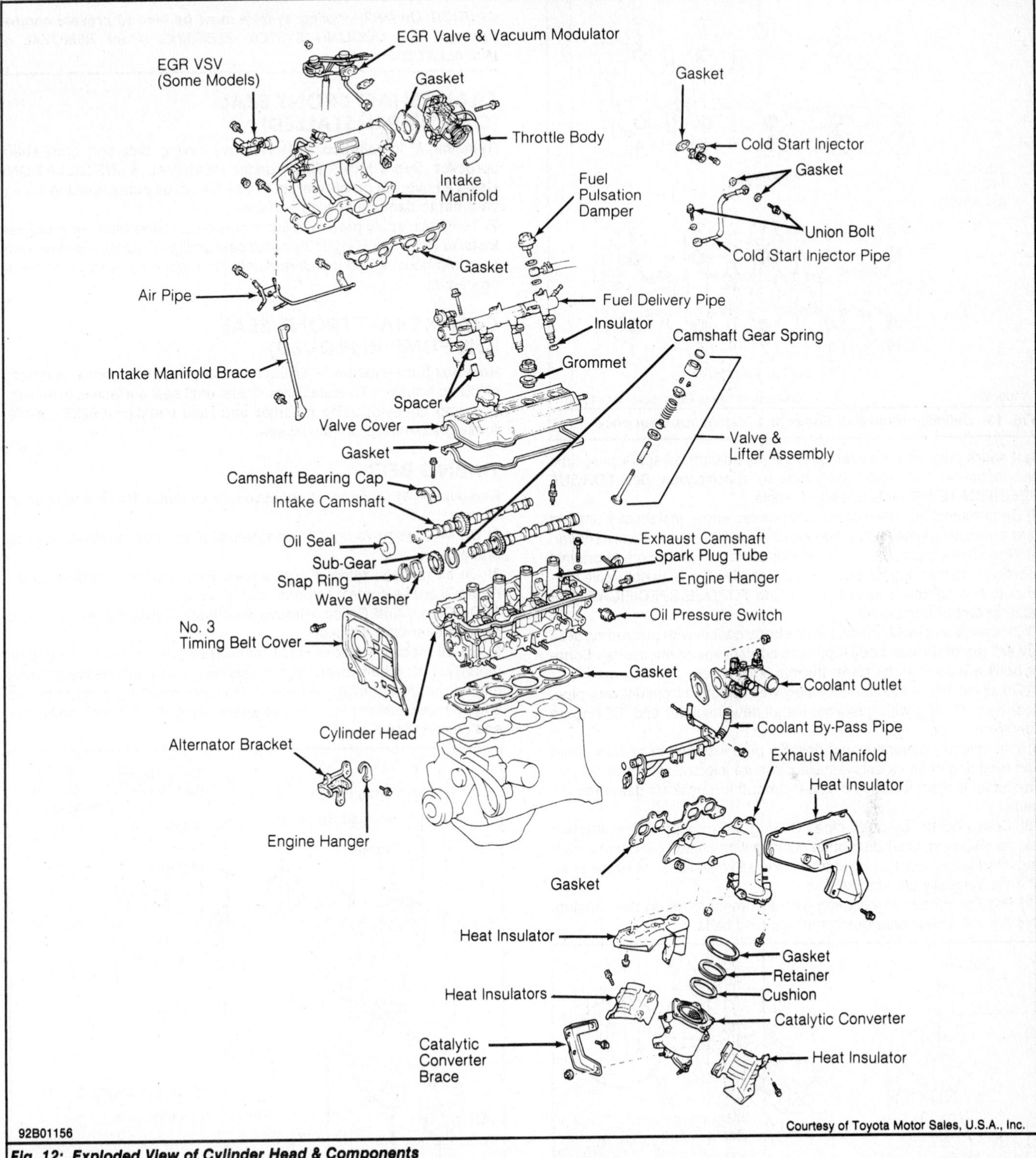


*Fig. 12: Exploded View of Cylinder Head & Components*

**Inspection** – **1)** Inspect cylinder head for warpage at cylinder block and manifold areas. Replace cylinder head if warpage exceeds specification. See CYLINDER HEAD table under ENGINE SPECIFICATIONS at end of article.

**2)** Inspect cylinder block deck surface warpage. Replace cylinder block if deck warpage exceeds specification. See CYLINDER BLOCK table under ENGINE SPECIFICATIONS at end of article.

**3)** Inspect intake and exhaust manifold surfaces for warpage. Replace manifold if warpage exceeds .012" (.30 mm).

**4)** Inspect camshaft and components. See CAMSHAFT under REMOVAL & INSTALLATION.

**Installation** – **1)** To install, reverse removal procedure. Apply engine oil on cylinder head bolt threads and cylinder head bolt-to-cylinder head contact surfaces.

**2)** Install and tighten cylinder head bolts to specification in sequence. *See Fig. 13.* See TORQUE SPECIFICATIONS table at end of article.

**3)** If camshaft or cylinder head components are serviced, adjust valve clearance. See VALVE CLEARANCE ADJUSTMENT under ADJUSTMENTS.

# 1991 ENGINES
# 2.0L & 2.2L 4-Cylinder (Cont.)

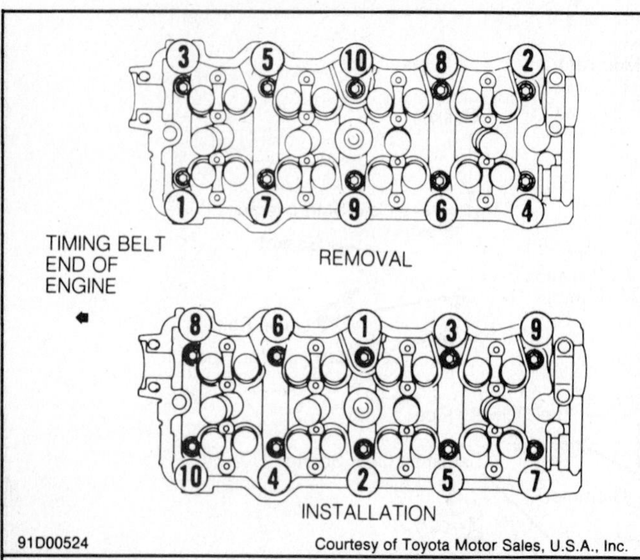


*Fig. 13: Cylinder Head Bolt Removal & Installation Sequence*

**4)** If spark plug tube was removed, apply sealant on spark plug tube and install. Tighten spark plug tube to specification. See TORQUE SPECIFICATIONS table at end of article.
**5)** Before installing valve cover and gasket, apply sealant at front and rear areas of cylinder head. *See Fig. 2.* Install gasket and valve cover.
**6)** When installing valve cover grommets, install grommets in original location with markings in designated area. *See Fig. 3.* Install valve cover nuts and tighten to specification. See TORQUE SPECIFICATIONS table at end of this article.
**7)** On Celica and MR2, install throttle body gasket with protruding area toward top of throttle body (opposite coolant line connections). Longer bolts are used in the lower throttle body holes.
**8)** On all models, if injector assembly was removed from delivery pipe, coat new "O" ring with gasoline. Install new insulator and "O" ring on injector.
**9)** With injector assembly and delivery pipe installed in cylinder head and retaining bolts loosely installed, ensure injector assembly rotates smoothly. If injector does not rotate smoothly, check for damaged "O" rings.
**10)** Coat coolant by-pass pipe "O" ring with soapy water solution before installing. Coat distributor "O" ring with engine oil. When installing distributor, rotate crankshaft clockwise so slot area of intake camshaft is vertically positioned.
**11)** Position cutout on coupling with alignment mark on the housing. *See Fig. 14.* Install distributor and retaining bolts.

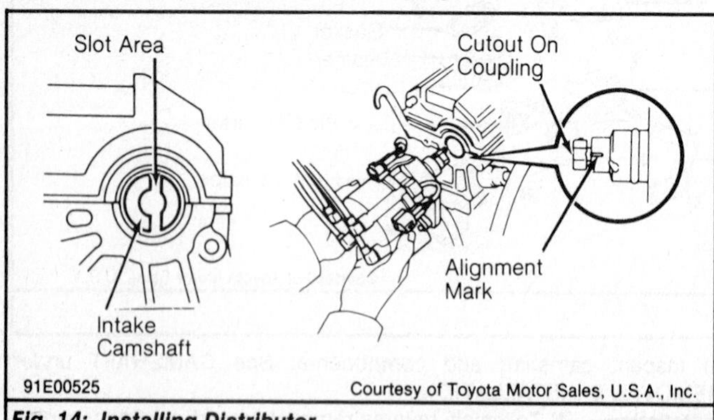


*Fig. 14: Installing Distributor*

**12)** Use new gasket when installing catalytic converter. To install remaining components, reverse removal procedure. Tighten all fasteners to specification. See TORQUE SPECIFICATIONS table at end of article. Adjust control cables. Fill cooling system.

*CAUTION: On MR2, cooling system must be bled to prevent engine damage. See COOLING SYSTEM BLEEDING under REMOVAL & INSTALLATION.*

## CRANKSHAFT FRONT SEAL (OIL PUMP INSTALLED)

**Removal & Installation – 1)** Remove timing belt and crankshaft sprocket. See TIMING BELT under REMOVAL & INSTALLATION. Using a knife, cut off oil seal lip. Pry seal from oil pump housing, using care not to damage sealing surfaces.
**2)** To install, apply grease to lip of new seal. Using hammer and Seal Installer (SST 09226-10010), install seal until seal surface is even with oil pump housing. To install remaining components, reverse removal procedure.

## CRANKSHAFT FRONT SEAL (OIL PUMP REMOVED)

**Removal & Installation –** Using hammer and drift, remove seal from oil pump housing. To install, install seal until seal surface is even with oil pump housing, using hammer and Seal Installer (09226-10010). Apply grease to lip of new oil seal.

## TIMING BELT

**Removal – 1)** Disconnect negative battery cable. Raise and support vehicle.
**2)** On MR2, remove right hood side panel and strut tower-to-firewall braces.
**3)** On all models, remove right wheel. Remove lower engine cover. Remove cruise control actuator and bracket.
**4)** On Camry and Celica, remove alternator. It may be necessary to remove alternator bracket.
**5)** On all models, remove drive belts. Remove top brace on engine mount at timing belt cover. Slightly raise engine to remove weight from engine mount at timing belt cover. Remove retaining bolts/nuts and engine mount assembly. Remove spark plugs, No. 2 timing belt cover and gasket. *See Fig. 15.*

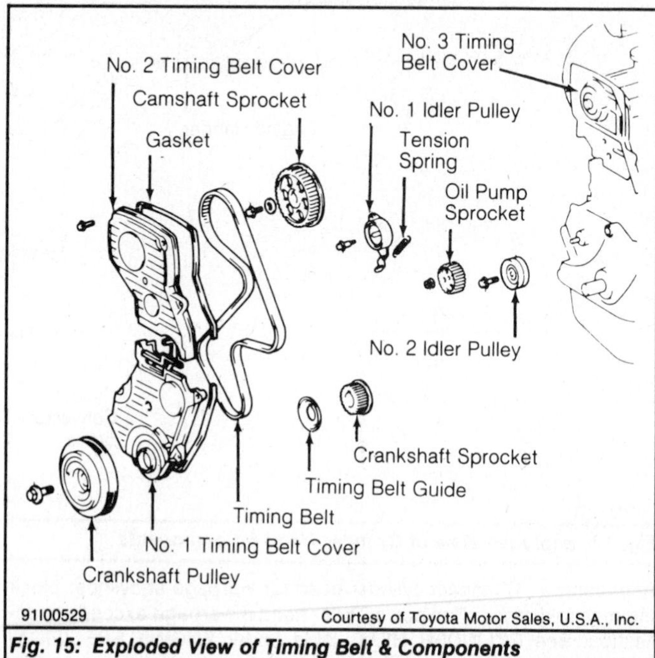


*Fig. 15: Exploded View of Timing Belt & Components*

**6)** Rotate crankshaft so No. 1 cylinder is at TDC of compression stroke and timing mark on crankshaft pulley aligns with "0" mark on No. 1 timing belt cover. Ensure hole in camshaft sprocket is aligned with alignment mark on camshaft bearing cap. *See Fig. 16.*

# 1991 ENGINES
# 2.0L & 2.2L 4-Cylinder (Cont.)

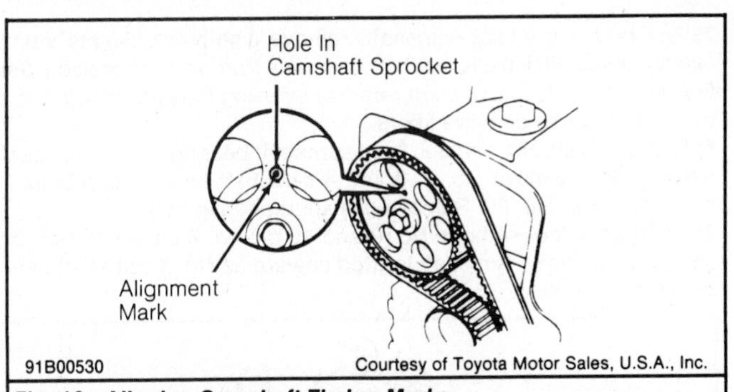


*Fig. 16: Aligning Camshaft Timing Marks*

***CAUTION: If timing belt is to be reused, mark direction of timing belt rotation and location on camshaft sprocket for reassembly reference. Also place reference mark on timing belt at upper edge of No. 1 timing belt cover.***

**7)** Loosen No. 1 idler pulley retaining bolt. Move No. 1 idler pulley outward as far as possible and temporarily retighten retaining bolt. *See Fig. 16.* Remove timing belt from camshaft sprocket.

**8)** Using Pulley Holder (SST 09213-54015), hold crankshaft pulley and remove pulley retaining bolt.

**9)** If timing belt is to be reused, ensure reference mark placed on timing belt aligns with upper edge of No. 1 timing belt cover when timing mark on crankshaft pulley is aligned with "0" mark on No. 1 timing belt cover.

**10)** Using puller, remove crankshaft pulley. DO NOT allow crankshaft to rotate. Remove No. 1 timing belt cover and gasket. If timing belt is to be reused, mark direction of belt rotation and place reference marks on timing belt and crankshaft sprocket for reassembly reference.

**11)** Note direction of timing belt guide installation. *See Fig. 15.* Remove timing belt guide and timing belt. Remove idler pulleys if necessary.

**12)** If removing camshaft sprocket, use Sprocket Holder (SST 09278-54012) to hold camshaft sprocket. Remove retaining bolt, washer and camshaft sprocket.

**13)** If removing crankshaft sprocket, place shop towels against oil pump housing. Using 2 screwdrivers, pry sprocket from crankshaft.

**14)** If removing oil pump sprocket, use Sprocket Holder (SST 09616-30011) to hold oil pump sprocket. Remove retaining nut. Remove oil pump sprocket.

**Inspection – 1)** Inspect timing belt for damaged teeth, cracking or oil contamination. Ensure idler pulleys rotate freely. Replace components if damaged.

**2)** Ensure free length of tension spring is 1.811" (45.99 mm) and installed tension is 10.5-11.6 lbs. (4.8-5.3 kg) at 1.988" (50.50 mm). Replace tension spring if not within specification.

**Installation – 1)** When installing oil pump sprocket, align cutouts of oil pump sprocket and shaft. Install nut and tighten to specification. See TORQUE SPECIFICATIONS table at end of article.

**2)** When installing crankshaft sprocket, align crankshaft sprocket with key in crankshaft.

**3)** When installing camshaft sprocket, align camshaft knock pin with groove in camshaft sprocket. Install washer and tighten bolt to specification. See TORQUE SPECIFICATIONS table at end of article.

**4)** Install No. 2 idler pulley and tighten bolt to specification. Ensure idler pulley is clean and rotates smoothly. Install No. 1 idler pulley and tension spring. Pry idler pulley away from timing belt area as far as possible and tighten retaining bolt.

**5)** Install timing belt on crankshaft, oil pump and water pump sprockets and No. 2 idler pulley.

***CAUTION: If timing belt is reused, ensure reference marks are aligned on crankshaft sprocket and timing belt is installed in original direction of rotation.***

**6)** Install timing belt guide with cupped side away from crankshaft sprocket. Install No. 1 timing belt cover and gasket. Align crankshaft key with key groove of crankshaft pulley and install. Tighten retaining bolt to specification. See TORQUE SPECIFICATIONS table at end of this article.

**7)** Rotate crankshaft pulley so timing mark on crankshaft pulley aligns with "0" mark on No. 1 timing belt cover. Rotate camshaft and align hole in camshaft sprocket with alignment mark on camshaft bearing cap. *See Fig. 16.*

**8)** Install timing belt on camshaft sprocket. If timing belt is reused, ensure reference marks are aligned on camshaft sprocket and upper edge of No. 1 timing belt cover. Ensure tension exists on timing belt between crankshaft, camshaft and water pump sprockets.

**9)** Loosen No. 1 idler pulley retaining bolt 1/2 turn. Rotate crankshaft pulley clockwise 2 full revolutions from TDC to TDC.

***CAUTION: DO NOT rotate crankshaft counterclockwise.***

**10)** Ensure timing mark on crankshaft pulley aligns with "0" mark on No. 1 timing belt cover and hole in camshaft sprocket aligns with alignment mark on camshaft bearing cap. *See Fig. 16.* If marks are not aligned, remove timing belt and reinstall.

**11)** Tighten No. 1 idler pulley retaining bolt to specification. See TORQUE SPECIFICATIONS table at end of article. Install and tighten spark plugs to specification. See TORQUE SPECIFICATIONS table at end of article.

**12)** Install No. 2 timing belt cover and gasket. To install remaining components, reverse removal procedure. Tighten fasteners to specification. See TORQUE SPECIFICATIONS table at end of article.

## CAMSHAFT

**Removal – 1)** Remove timing belt and camshaft sprocket. See TIMING BELT under REMOVAL & INSTALLATION. Remove No. 3 timing belt cover. *See Fig. 12.* Remove valve cover and gasket. Install valve cover grommets in original location to prevent oil leakage.

**2)** For servicing exhaust camshaft, rotate intake camshaft so knock pin is at 10-45 degrees from vertical position. *See Fig. 17.* This aids in camshaft removal by using lobes on No. 2 and 4 cylinders to push on valve lifters.

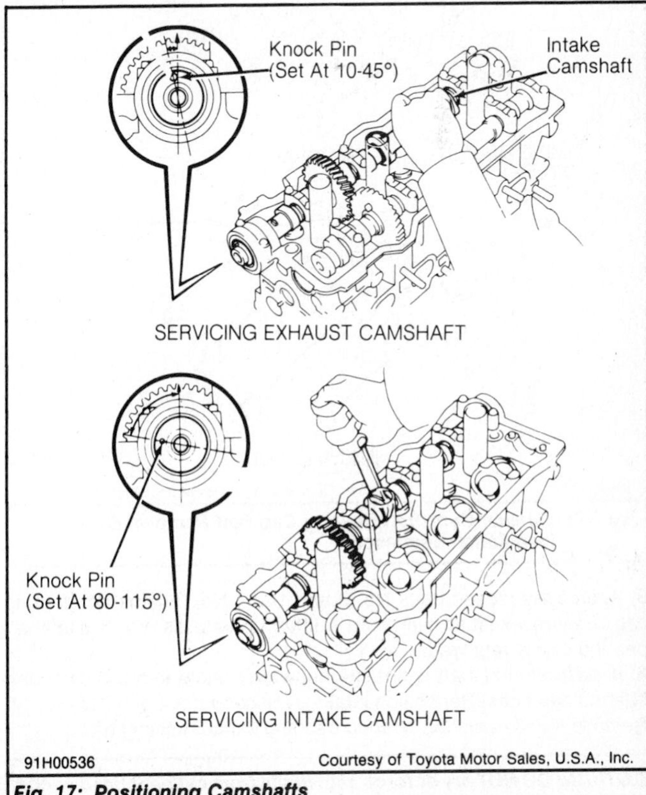


*Fig. 17: Positioning Camshafts*

# 1991 ENGINES
# 2.0L & 2.2L 4-Cylinder (Cont.)

**3)** Secure exhaust camshaft sub-gear to main gear with a 6 x 1.0 x 18 mm service bolt. *See Fig. 18.* Before removing camshaft bearing cap bolts, ensure torsional spring force of sub-gear has been held by service bolt.

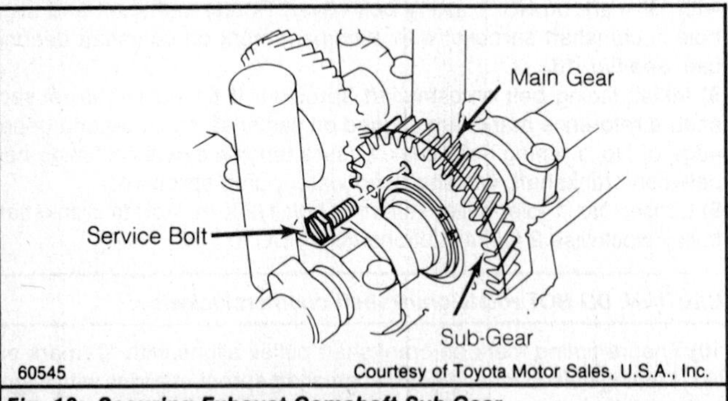


***Fig. 18: Securing Exhaust Camshaft Sub-Gear***

***NOTE: Camshaft bearing caps are numbered for location. Front bearing cap (intake camshaft) and rear bearing cap (exhaust camshaft) are not numbered for location. All others are numbered with No. 1 toward timing belt end of cylinder head.***

**4)** On exhaust camshaft, remove bolts No. 1 and 2 and rear camshaft bearing cap. *See Fig. 19.* Remove No. 1, 2 and 4 camshaft bearing cap bolts in sequence. *See Fig. 19.* Remove camshaft bearing caps.

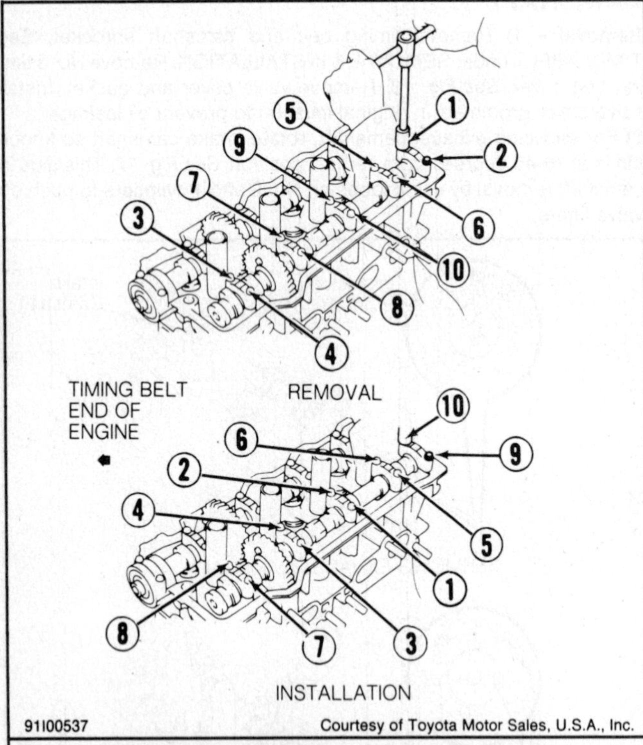


***Fig. 19: Exhaust Camshaft Bearing Cap Bolt Removal & Installation Sequence***

**5)** Alternately loosen bolts No. 9 and 10 on No. 3 camshaft bearing cap. Ensure exhaust camshaft is lifted upward as No. 3 camshaft bearing cap is removed.

**6)** If exhaust camshaft is not lifted upward, retighten No. 3 camshaft bearing cap bolts. Reposition intake camshaft knock pin. *See Fig. 17.* Remove No. 3 camshaft bearing cap and exhaust camshaft.

***CAUTION: DO NOT pry or force camshafts from cylinder head or component damage will result.***

**7)** For servicing intake camshaft, remove distributor. Rotate intake camshaft so knock pin is at 80-115 degrees from vertical position. *See Fig. 17.* This aids in camshaft removal by using lobes on No. 1 and 3 cylinders to push on valve lifters.

**8)** Remove bolts No. 1 and 2, front camshaft bearing cap and oil seal. *See Fig. 20.* Remove No. 1, 3 and 4 camshaft bearing cap bolts in sequence. *See Fig. 20.* Remove camshaft bearing caps.

**9)** Alternately loosen bolts No. 9 and 10 on No. 3 camshaft bearing cap. Ensure intake camshaft is lifted upward as No. 3 camshaft bearing cap is removed.

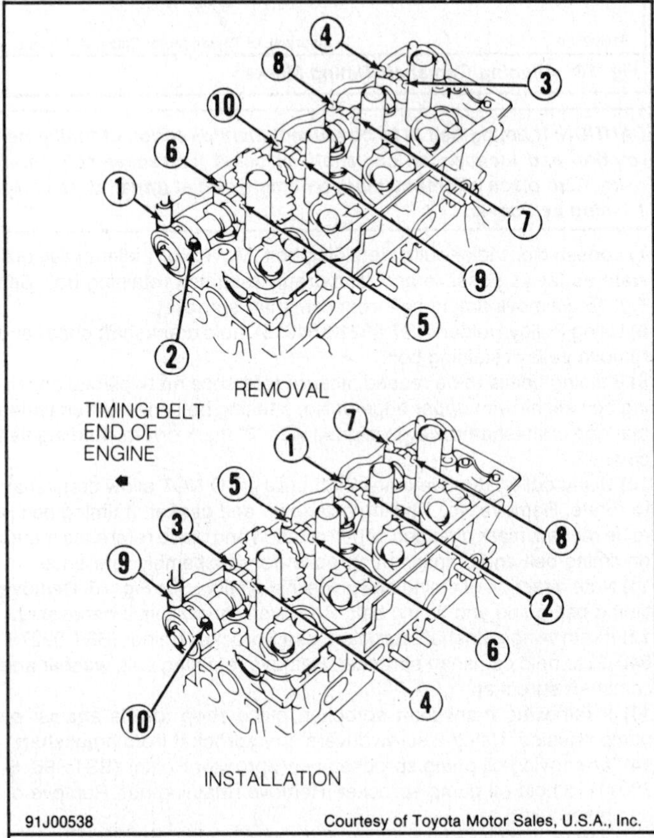


***Fig. 20: Intake Camshaft Bearing Cap Bolt Removal & Installation Sequence***

**10)** If intake camshaft is not lifted upward, retighten No. 3 camshaft bearing cap bolts. Reposition intake camshaft knock pin. *See Fig. 17.* Remove No. 2 camshaft bearing cap and intake camshaft.

***CAUTION: DO NOT pry or force camshafts from cylinder head or component damage will result.***

**11)** If sub-gear is to be removed from exhaust camshaft, install service bolts in camshaft. *See Fig. 21.* Using screwdriver, rotate sub-gear clockwise and remove service bolt "B".

**12)** Remove snap ring, wave washer, sub-gear and camshaft gear spring. *See Fig. 21.*

**Inspection – 1)** Inspect components for damage. Check camshaft journal diameter, lobe height and runout. Replace camshaft if not within specification. See CAMSHAFT table under ENGINE SPECIFICATIONS at end of article.

**2)** Install camshaft in cylinder head. Tighten camshaft bearing cap bolts to specification in sequence. *See Figs. 19 and 20.* See TORQUE SPECIFICATIONS table at end of article.

**3)** Using Plastigage, check camshaft oil clearance. Check camshaft end play. Replace camshaft and/or cylinder head if oil clearance or end play is not within specification. See CAMSHAFT table under ENGINE SPECIFICATIONS at end of article.

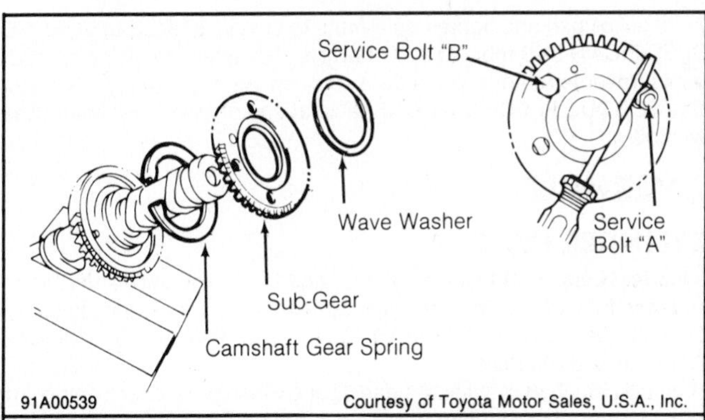


*Fig. 21: Disassembling Exhaust Camshaft Gears*

**4)** Using dial indicator, measure gear backlash with camshafts installed. Replace camshaft if gear backlash exceeds specification. See CAMSHAFT table under ENGINE SPECIFICATIONS at end of article.

**5)** Using caliper, measure width between ends of camshaft gear spring. Replace camshaft gear spring if distance exceeds .886-.902" (22.50-22.91 mm).

**Installation - 1)** Install camshaft gear spring, sub-gear, wave washer and snap ring on exhaust camshaft. Install service bolt "A" in camshaft sub-gear. *See Fig. 21.* Rotate sub-gear clockwise and align holes of camshaft main gear and sub-gear. Install service bolt "B".

**2)** Coat thrust surfaces of camshaft with grease. To install intake camshaft, rotate camshaft so knock pin is at approximately 80-115 degrees from vertical position and install in cylinder head. *See Fig. 17.*

**3)** Apply a 1/8" bead of sealant on outer edge-to-cylinder head surfaces of front camshaft bearing cap. Install remaining bearing caps in original location with arrow pointing toward timing belt end of engine.

***CAUTION: Ensure camshaft bearing caps are installed in numerical sequence with arrow pointing toward timing belt end of engine. Intake camshaft bearing caps contain an "I" stamped on the cap.***

**4)** Apply engine oil to threads and area below head of camshaft bearing cap bolt. Install and tighten camshaft bearing cap bolts to specification in sequence using several steps. *See Fig. 20.* See TORQUE SPECIFICATIONS table at end of article.

**5)** Coat new oil seal with grease. Using Seal Installer (SST 09223-46011), install oil seal. To install exhaust camshaft, rotate intake camshaft so knock pin is at approximately 10-45 degrees from vertical position. *See Fig. 17.*

**6)** Install exhaust camshaft so timing marks are engaged with intake camshaft. DO NOT use assembly reference marks. *See Fig. 22.* Install bearing caps in original location with arrow pointing toward timing belt end of engine.

***CAUTION: Ensure camshaft bearing caps are installed in numerical sequence with arrow pointing toward timing belt end of engine. Exhaust camshaft bearing caps contain an "E" stamped on the cap.***

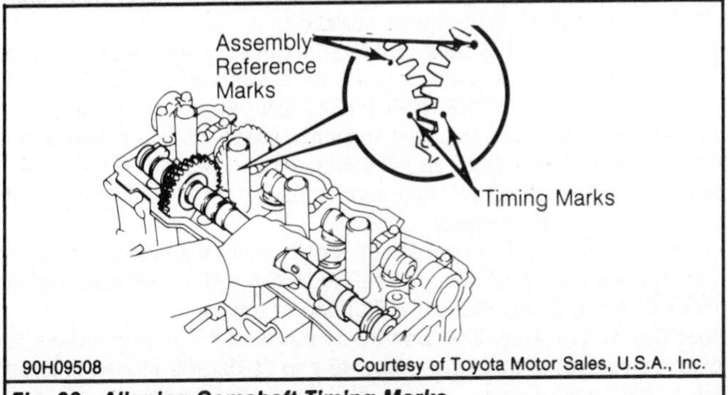


*Fig. 22: Aligning Camshaft Timing Marks*

**7)** Apply engine oil to threads and area below head of camshaft bearing cap bolt. Install and tighten camshaft bearing cap bolts to specification in sequence using several steps. *See Fig. 19.* See TORQUE SPECIFICATIONS table at end of article.

**8)** Remove service bolt from camshaft gear. *See Fig. 18.* To install remaining components, reverse removal procedure.

***CAUTION: If cylinder head or camshaft are serviced or replaced, valve clearance must be checked. See VALVE CLEARANCE ADJUSTMENT under ADJUSTMENTS.***

**9)** Apply sealant on semi-circular plugs and install in the end of cylinder head, located on exhaust camshaft side of cylinder head. Before installing valve cover and gasket, apply sealant at front and rear areas of cylinder head. *See Fig. 2.* Install valve cover and gasket.

**10)** When installing valve cover grommets, install grommets in original location with markings in designated area. *See Fig. 3.* When installing distributor, rotate crankshaft clockwise so slot area of intake camshaft is vertically positioned.

**11)** Position cutout on coupling with alignment mark on the housing. *See Fig. 14.* Install distributor and retaining bolts. To install remaining components, reverse removal procedure. Tighten all fasteners to specification. See TORQUE SPECIFICATIONS table at end of article.

## REAR CRANKSHAFT OIL SEAL

**Removal -** Remove transaxle, clutch assembly (if equipped) and flywheel/drive plate. Using a knife, cut off oil seal lip. Pry oil seal from rear seal housing, using care not to damage sealing surfaces.

**Installation - 1)** Ensure all sealing surfaces are clean. Apply grease to seal lip of new oil seal. Using Seal Installer (SST 09223-63010), install oil seal in rear seal housing until oil seal is even with rear seal housing surface.

**2)** Install flywheel/drive plate. Apply Loctite to flywheel/drive plate bolts. Install and tighten bolts to specification in a crisscross pattern. See TORQUE SPECIFICATIONS table at end of article. To install remaining components, reverse removal procedure.

## WATER PUMP

**Removal (Camry & Celica) - 1)** Disconnect negative battery cable. Drain cooling system. Remove timing belt and idler pulleys. See TIMING BELT under REMOVAL & INSTALLATION.

**2)** It may be necessary to remove alternator belt adjusting bar. Disconnect radiator hose at water pump. Remove coolant by-pass pipe-to-water pump cover retaining nuts. *See Fig. 12.*

**3)** Remove water pump bolts in sequence. *See Fig. 23.* Remove water pump, water pump cover and "O" rings. Remove retaining bolts and separate water pump and gasket from water pump cover. *See Fig. 24.*

**Installation - 1)** To install, reverse removal procedure using new gaskets and "O" rings. Apply soapy water solution to coolant by-pass pipe "O" ring before installing water pump. DO NOT tighten coolant by-pass pipe-to-water pump cover retaining nuts until water pump bolts are tightened.

**2)** Tighten water pump bolts to specification in sequence. *See Fig. 23.* See TORQUE SPECIFICATIONS table at end of article. To install remaining components, reverse removal procedure. Fill cooling system.

**Removal (MR2) - 1)** Drain cooling system. Remove timing belt and No. 2 idler pulley. See TIMING BELT under REMOVAL & INSTALLATION. Disconnect radiator hose at water pump. Remove A/C compressor idler pulley.

**2)** Remove coolant by-pass pipe-to-water pump cover retaining nuts. *See Fig. 24.* Remove water pump bolts in sequence. *See Fig. 23.* Remove water pump, water pump cover and "O" rings. Remove retaining bolts and separate water pump and gasket from water pump cover. *See Fig. 24.*

**Installation - 1)** To install, reverse removal procedure using new gaskets and "O" rings. Apply soapy water solution to coolant by-pass pipe "O" ring before installing water pump. DO NOT tighten coolant by-pass pipe-to-water pump cover retaining nuts until water pump bolts are tightened to specification.

# 1991 ENGINES
# 2.0L & 2.2L 4-Cylinder (Cont.)

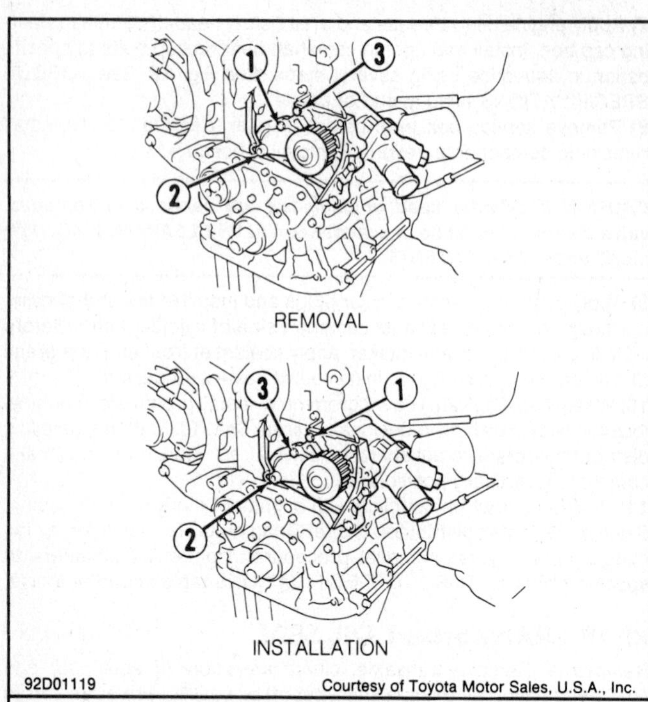


92D01119 Courtesy of Toyota Motor Sales, U.S.A., Inc.

***Fig. 23: Water Pump Bolt Removal & Installation Sequence***

91F03218 Courtesy of Toyota Motor Sales, U.S.A., Inc.

***Fig. 24: Exploded View of Water Pump Assembly***

**2)** Tighten water pump bolts to specification in sequence. *See Fig. 23.* See TORQUE SPECIFICATIONS table at end of article. To install remaining components, reverse removal procedure. Fill and bleed cooling system. See COOLING SYSTEM BLEEDING under REMOVAL & INSTALLATION.

## OIL PAN

**Removal - 1)** Disconnect negative battery cable. Raise and support vehicle. Remove lower engine covers. Drain engine oil.

**2)** On Camry and Celica, remove suspension crossmember, bolted to both lower suspension arm shafts. Remove engine mount crossmember located below engine.

**3)** On all models, remove exhaust pipe located below the engine. Remove stiffener brace at rear of oil pan. Remove dipstick. Remove retaining bolts/nuts and oil pan.

**Installation - 1)** To install, ensure sealing surfaces are clean. Apply bead of sealant at center of oil pan sealing surface between bolt/nut holes and on inside of the bolt/nut holes.

**2)** Install oil pan and tighten bolts/nuts to specification. See TORQUE SPECIFICATIONS table at end of article. To install remaining components, reverse removal procedure. Tighten fasteners to specification. See TORQUE SPECIFICATIONS table at end of article. Fill crankcase with oil.

## OVERHAUL

### CYLINDER HEAD

**Cylinder Head - 1)** Inspect cylinder head warpage at cylinder block and manifold areas. Replace cylinder head if warpage exceeds specification. See CYLINDER HEAD table under ENGINE SPECIFICATIONS at end of article.

**2)** Install camshaft in cylinder head. Using Plastigage, check camshaft oil clearance with camshaft bearing cap bolts tightened in sequence to specification. *See Figs. 19 and 20.* See TORQUE SPECIFICATIONS table at end of article. Replace camshaft and/or cylinder head if oil clearance is not within specification. See CAMSHAFT table under ENGINE SPECIFICATIONS at end of article.

**3)** Ensure valve lifter bore diameter is within specification. See VALVE LIFTERS table under ENGINE SPECIFICATIONS at end of article.

**Valve Springs -** Ensure valve spring free length, pressure and out-of-square are within specification. See VALVES & VALVE SPRINGS table under ENGINE SPECIFICATIONS at end of article.

**Valve Stem Oil Seals -** Lubricate valve stem oil seal with engine oil. Intake valve stem oil seals are Brown and exhaust valve stem oil seals are Black. Install valve stem oil seal using Oil Seal Installer (SST 09201-41020).

**Valve Guides - 1)** Check valve stem-to-valve guide clearance. Ensure valve stem diameter is within specification. Replace valve guide if clearance exceeds specification. See CYLINDER HEAD table under ENGINE SPECIFICATIONS at end of article.

**2)** Before replacing valve guide on 2.2L (Celica and MR2), wrap tape around old valve stem. Tape must be approximately .31" (7.9 mm) from end of valve stem. From top of cylinder head, install old valve in valve guide with tape area resting on valve guide. Hit old valve with hammer to break off old valve guide. Remove snap ring.

**3)** On all models when replacing valve guide, heat cylinder head to 176-212°F (80-100°C). Using hammer and Valve Guide Remover/Installer (SST 09201-70010), drive valve guide from top of cylinder head.

**4)** Measure I.D. of cylinder head valve guide bore. If bore I.D. is .4331-.4341" (11.000-11.026 mm), standard valve guide will be used. If bore I.D. is .4350-.4361" (11.049-11.077 mm), oversize valve guide will be used.

**5)** If bore I.D. exceeds .4341" (11.026 mm), valve guide bore must be machined to .4350-.4361" (11.049-11.077 mm) for oversize valve guide. If bore I.D. exceeds .4361" (11.077 mm), replace cylinder head.

**6)** To install valve guide, heat cylinder head to 176-212°F (80-100°C). Using hammer and valve guide remover/installer, drive valve guide into cylinder head from top of cylinder head.

**7)** On 2.0L (Camry), install valve guide until installed height is .323-.339" (8.20-8.61 mm). Valve guide installed height is measured from top of valve guide to cylinder head surface.

**8)** On 2.2L (Celica and MR2), drive valve guide in cylinder head until snap ring contacts cylinder head surface.

**9)** On all models, using .236" (6.00 mm) reamer, ream valve guide to obtain specified valve stem-to-guide oil clearance. See CYLINDER HEAD table under ENGINE SPECIFICATIONS at end of article.

**Valve Seat -** Ensure valve seat angle and seat width are within specification. See CYLINDER HEAD table under ENGINE SPECIFICATIONS at end of article. Valve seat replacement information is not available from manufacturer.

**Valves -** Ensure minimum refinish length, stem diameter, and valve margin are within specification. See VALVES & VALVE SPRINGS table under ENGINE SPECIFICATIONS at end of article.

**Seat Correction Angles -** Use 30-degree and 45 degree stones to lower valve seat contact area. Use 45 and 75 degree stones to raise valve seat contact area.

## VALVE TRAIN

**Valve Lifters** – Ensure valve lifter diameter, bore diameter and oil clearance is within specification. See VALVE LIFTERS table under ENGINE SPECIFICATIONS at end of article.

## CYLINDER BLOCK ASSEMBLY

**Piston & Rod Assembly (2.0L Camry)** – **1)** Ensure piston does not move on back and forth on piston pin. If movement exists, replace piston and pin as an assembly.

**2)** To disassemble, using press, press piston pin from piston and connecting rod. To reassemble, install piston with front mark on top of piston aligned with front mark (straight edge) on connecting rod. *See Fig. 25.* Press pin in connecting rod and piston.

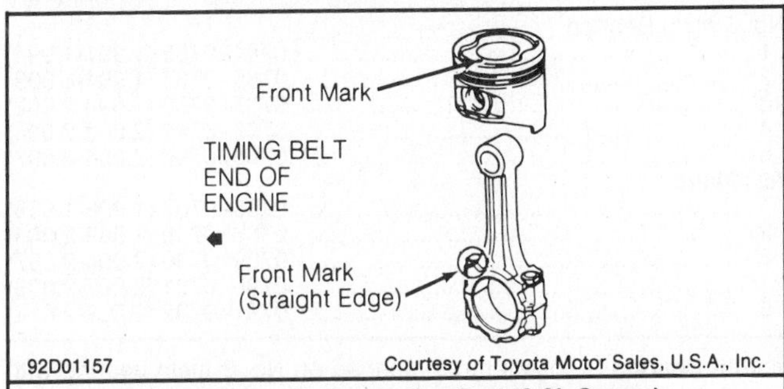


***Fig. 25: Aligning Piston & Connecting Rod (2.0L Camry)***

**Piston & Rod Assembly (2.2L Celica & MR2)** – **1)** When removing piston from connecting rod, remove snap ring from piston. Heat piston to 176-194°F (80-90°C) in water. Remove piston pin. Separate piston from connecting rod.

**2)** Ensure piston pin diameter is within specification. See PISTONS, PINS & RINGS table under ENGINE SPECIFICATIONS at end of article. Ensure connecting rod piston pin bushing bore diameter is within specification. See CONNECTING RODS table under ENGINE SPECIFICATIONS at end of article.

**3)** Bushing can be replaced in connecting rod if bore diameter is not within specification. Bushing must be honed to obtain correct piston pin clearance. See PISTONS, PINS & RINGS table under ENGINE SPECIFICATIONS at end of article.

**4)** To reassemble, install piston with front mark on top of piston aligned with protrusion on connecting rod. *See Fig. 26.*

**5)** Install new snap ring in piston. Heat piston to 176-194°F (80-90°C) in water. Install piston pin and remaining snap ring.

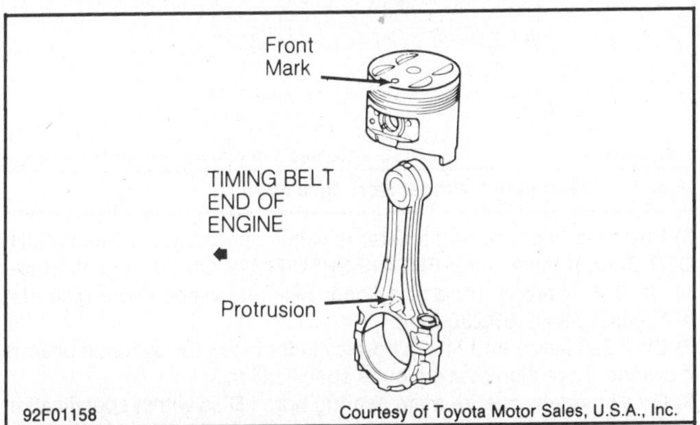


***Fig. 26: Aligning Piston & Connecting Rod (2.2L Celica & MR2)***

**Fitting Pistons** – **1)** Determine if piston-to-cylinder clearance is within specification.

**2)** On 2.0L (Camry), measure piston skirt diameter at 1.00" (25.4 mm) from top of piston at 90-degree angle to piston pin.

**3)** On 2.2L (Celica and MR2), measure piston skirt diameter at .925" (23.50 mm) from top of piston at 90-degree angle to piston pin.

**4)** On all models, different piston sizes are used. Piston size can be identified by size mark (1, 2 or 3) stamped on top of piston. *See Fig. 27.*

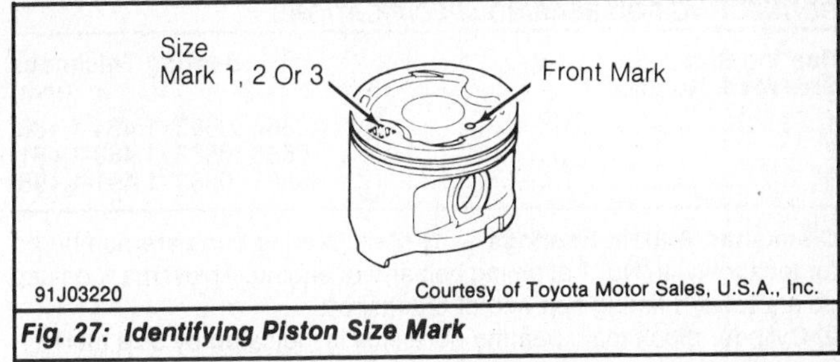


***Fig. 27: Identifying Piston Size Mark***

**5)** Ensure piston diameter is within specification. See PISTONS, PINS & RINGS table under ENGINE SPECIFICATIONS at end of article.

**6)** Measure cylinder bore diameter at .39" (10 mm) from top, bottom and middle of cylinder bore. Different cylinder bores are used and can be identified by No. 1, 2 or 3 size mark stamped on cylinder block deck surface. *See Fig. 31.*

**7)** Cylinder bore diameter must be within specification. See CYLINDER BLOCK table under ENGINE SPECIFICATIONS at end of article. Determine piston clearance.

**8)** On 2.0L (Camry), replace piston or cylinder block if clearance is not within specification. See PISTONS, PINS & RINGS table under ENGINE SPECIFICATIONS at end of article.

**9)** On 2.2L (Celica and MR2), bore cylinder block for oversize pistons if clearance is not within specification. See PISTONS, PINS & RINGS table under ENGINE SPECIFICATIONS at end of article.

**Piston Rings** – Ensure piston ring end gap and side clearance are within specification. See PISTONS, PINS & RINGS table under ENGINE SPECIFICATIONS at end of article. Position piston ring gaps in proper areas with identification mark on ring toward top of piston. *See Fig. 28.*

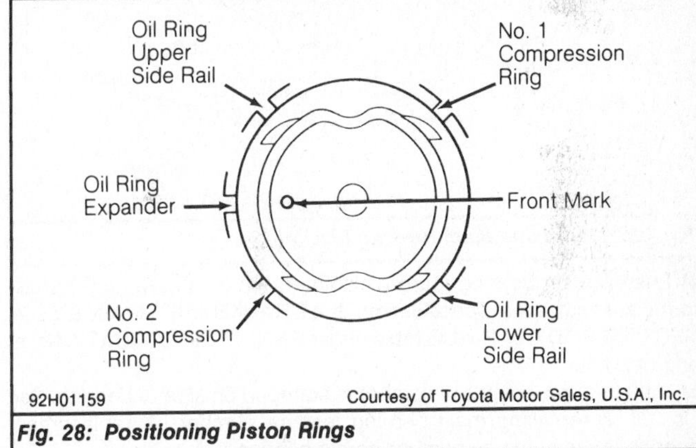


***Fig. 28: Positioning Piston Rings***

**Rod Bearings** – **1)** Note direction of connecting rod and cap installation. Connecting rod must be installed so it is properly aligned with front mark on the piston. *See Figs. 25 and 26.*

**2)** Connecting rod cap and rod bearing are marked with a No. 1, 2 or 3 size mark. Size mark is located on edge of rod bearing and on outer edge of connecting rod cap.

**3)** Size marks must be the same on connecting rod cap and rod bearing. If size mark cannot be read, measure rod bearing thickness to determine size. See CONNECTING ROD BEARING SPECIFICATIONS table.

***NOTE: If replacing rod bearing, replace with one having the same number.***

**4)** Coat nut and threads with engine oil before tightening to specification. Ensure bearing oil clearance and connecting rod side play are within specification. See CRANKSHAFT, MAIN & CONNECTING ROD BEARINGS and CONNECTING RODS tables under ENGINE SPECIFICATIONS at end of article.

# 1991 ENGINES
# 2.0L & 2.2L 4-Cylinder (Cont.)

***CONNECTING ROD BEARING SPECIFICATIONS***

| Bearing Size Size Mark Number | Bearing Thickness In. (mm) |
|---|---|
| 1 | .0584-.0586 (1.484-1.488) |
| 2 | .0586-.0587 (1.488-1.491) |
| 3 | .0587-.0589 (1.491-1.496) |

**Crankshaft & Main Bearings – 1)** Main bearing caps are numbered for location with No. 1 at timing belt end of engine. Arrow mark on cap points toward timing belt end of crankshaft.

**2)** Cylinder block main bearing bore size is indicated by size mark (1, 2 or 3) stamped on cylinder block. *See Fig. 29.* Front size mark indicates No. 1 main bearing bore and rear size mark indicates No. 5 main bearing bore.

**3)** Crankshaft main bearing journal size is determined by size mark (0, 1 or 2), located on crankshaft counterweight. *See Fig. 29.*

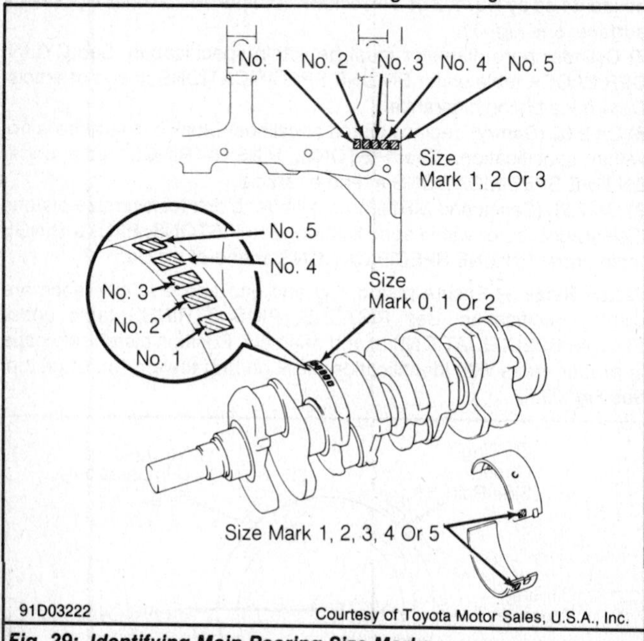


***Fig. 29: Identifying Main Bearing Size Marks***

**4)** Ensure main bearing journal diameter, taper, runout, and out-of-round are with within specification. See CRANKSHAFT, MAIN & CONNECTING ROD BEARINGS table under ENGINE SPECIFICATIONS at end of article.

**5)** Main bearing size mark number is stamped on side of bearing. *See Fig. 29.* If replacing main bearing, ensure number on replacement bearing is the same as number on old bearing.

**6)** If size mark cannot be obtained, add size marks on cylinder block and crankshaft. The total is the size mark of main bearing to be used. For example, if size mark on cylinder block is 2 and size mark on crankshaft is 1, use main bearing with size mark 3.

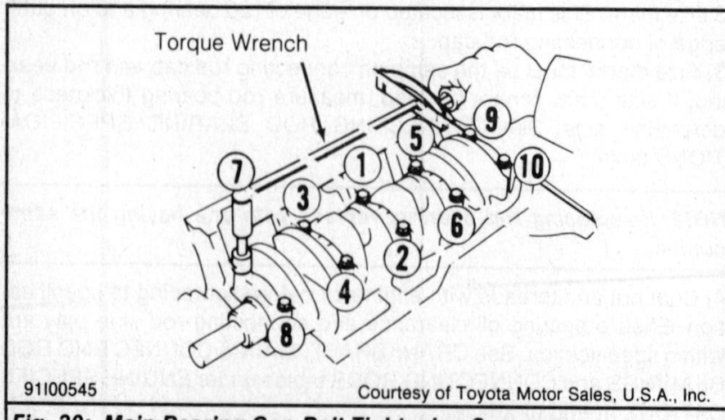


***Fig. 30: Main Bearing Cap Bolt Tightening Sequence***

**7)** Bearing thickness varies with size mark. See MAIN BEARING SPECIFICATIONS table. Ensure main bearing caps are installed in original location with arrow pointing toward timing belt end of engine. Coat main bearing cap bolt threads and seat area of the bolt with engine oil.

**8)** Tighten main bearing cap bolts to specification in sequence. *See Fig. 30.* See TORQUE SPECIFICATIONS table at end of article.

**9)** Ensure crankshaft end play is within specification. See CRANKSHAFT, MAIN & CONNECTING ROD BEARINGS table under ENGINE SPECIFICATIONS at end of article.

***MAIN BEARING SPECIFICATIONS***

| Bearing Size Mark Number | Bearing Thickness In. (mm) |
|---|---|
| No. 3 Main Bearing | |
| 1 | .0784-.0785 (1.991-1.994) |
| 2 | .0785-.0787 (1.994-1.999) |
| 3 | .0787-.0788 (1.999-2.002) |
| 4 | .0788-.0789 (2.002-2.004) |
| 5 | .0789-.0790 (2.004-2.007) |
| All Others | |
| 1 | .0786-.0787 (1.996-1.999) |
| 2 | .0787-.0789 (1.999-2.004) |
| 3 | .0789-.0790 (2.004-2.007) |
| 4 | .0790-.0791 (2.007-2.009) |
| 5 | .0791-.0792 (2.009-2.012) |

**Thrust Bearing –** Install thrust bearing on No. 3 main bearing with grooves facing toward the crankshaft. Thrust bearing must be replaced if crankshaft end play is not within specification. See CRANKSHAFT, MAIN & CONNECTING ROD BEARINGS table under ENGINE SPECIFICATIONS at end of article.

**Cylinder Block – 1)** Inspect cylinder block deck surface warpage. Replace cylinder block if deck warpage exceeds specification. See CYLINDER BLOCK table under ENGINE SPECIFICATIONS at end of article.

**2)** Different cylinder bore sizes are used and can be identified by size mark stamped on cylinder block deck surface. *See Fig. 31.* Measure cylinder bore diameter at .39" (10 mm) from top, bottom and middle of cylinder bore.

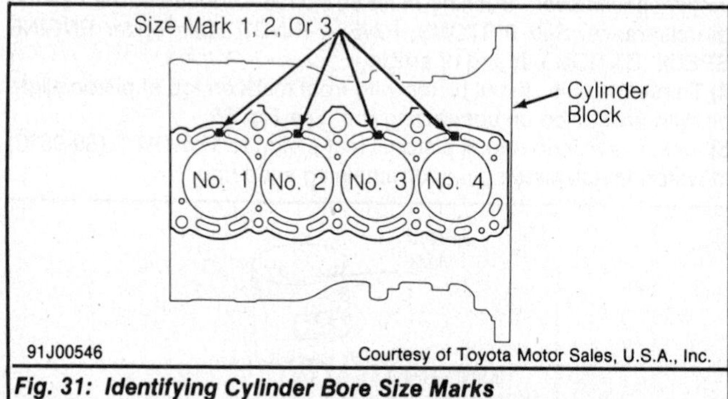


***Fig. 31: Identifying Cylinder Bore Size Marks***

**3)** Ensure cylinder bore diameter is within specification. See CYLINDER BLOCK table under ENGINE SPECIFICATIONS at end of article.

**4)** On 2.0L (Camry), replace cylinder block if cylinder bore diameter exceeds 3.3949" (86.230 mm).

**5)** On 2.2L (Celica and MR2), bore cylinder block for oversize pistons if cylinder bore diameter exceeds specification.

**6)** On all models, ensure main bearing bore I.D. is within specification with main bearing caps installed and bolts tightened to specification. See CYLINDER BLOCK table under ENGINE SPECIFICATIONS at end of article.

***NOTE: Main bearing bore I.D. will depend on main bearing bore size mark stamped on cylinder block. See Fig. 29. Main bearing bore size mark may be a 1, 2 or 3.***

# 1991 ENGINES
# 2.0L & 2.2L 4-Cylinder (Cont.)

## ENGINE OILING

### ENGINE LUBRICATION SYSTEM

The crankshaft-driven oil pump provides lubrication to the main gallery. *See Fig. 32.* On 2.2L (Celica and MR2) an oil cooler assembly may be installed at the oil filter assembly.

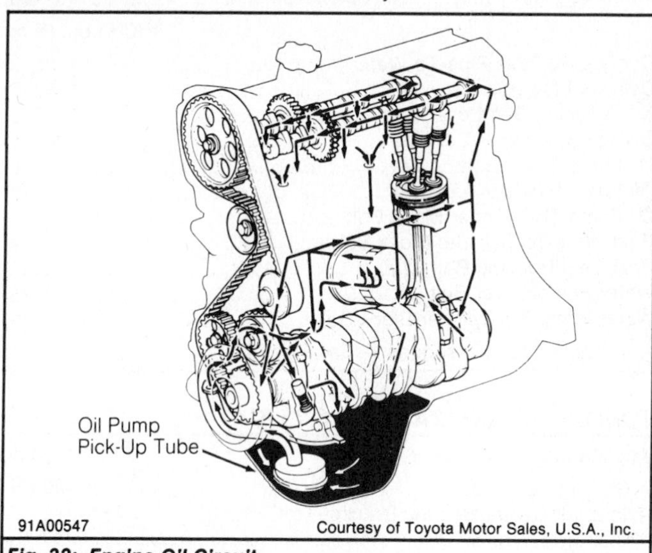


***Fig. 32: Engine Oil Circuit***

**Crankcase Capacity** – See CRANKCASE CAPACITIES table.

***CRANKCASE CAPACITIES***

| Application | Qts. (L) |
|---|---|
| Camry | 4.3 (4.1) |
| Celica & MR2 | |
| With Oil Cooler | 4.5 (4.3) |
| Without Oil Cooler | 4.2 (3.9) |

**Oil Pressure** – With engine at normal operating temperature, oil pressure should be at least 4.3 psi (0.3 kg/cm²) at idle and 36-71 psi (2.5-5.0 kg/cm²) at 3000 RPM.

### OIL PUMP

**Removal & Disassembly** – Remove timing belt and crankshaft sprocket. See TIMING BELT under REMOVAL & INSTALLATION. Remove oil pan. See OIL PAN under REMOVAL & INSTALLATION. Remove retaining bolts, oil pump and gasket. Remove oil pump body cover and oil pump components. *See Fig. 33.*

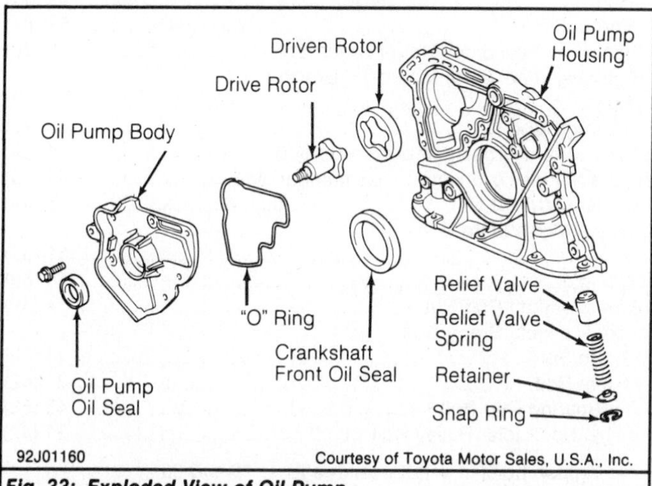


***Fig. 33: Exploded View of Oil Pump***

**Inspection** – **1)** Inspect components for damage. Ensure relief valve slides freely in bore. With rotors installed, using feeler gauge, measure clearance between driven rotor and oil pump housing. Replace rotor assembly if clearance exceeds specification. See OIL PUMP SPECIFICATIONS table.

**2)** Measure rotor tip clearance between tip of both rotors. Replace rotor assembly if clearance exceeds specification. See OIL PUMP SPECIFICATIONS table.

***OIL PUMP SPECIFICATIONS***

| Application | In. (mm) |
|---|---|
| Driven Rotor-To-Housing Clearance | |
| Standard | .0039-.0063 (.099-.160) |
| Wear Limit | .0079 (.201) |
| Rotor Tip Clearance | |
| Standard | .0016-.0063 (.041-.160) |
| Wear Limit | .0079 (.201) |

**Reassembly & Installation** – **1)** To reassemble, reverse disassembly procedure using new "O" ring.

**2)** On 2.2L (Celica and MR2), ensure reference marks on rotors are facing toward outside (away from cylinder block surface) of oil pump housing.

**3)** On all models, using Seal Installer (SST 09620-30010), install oil pump oil seal until oil seal is even with oil pump body (if removed). *See Fig. 33.* Coat oil seal lip with grease.

**4)** Using hammer and Seal Installer (SST 09226-10010), install crankshaft front seal until seal surface is even with oil pump housing (if removed).

**5)** Install oil pump housing and retaining bolts. Ensure 2 longest bolts are located in outside holes nearest oil pan flange. Tighten bolts to specification. See TORQUE SPECIFICATIONS table at end of article. To install remaining components, reverse removal procedure.

### OIL COOLER

***NOTE: Oil cooler is located between cylinder block and oil filter.***

**Removal (2.2L Celica & MR2)** – **1)** Disconnect negative battery cable. Drain cooling system. Remove lower engine cover. It may be necessary to remove alternator. Remove front exhaust pipe. Remove exhaust manifold and catalytic converter.

**2)** Remove oil filter. Disconnect coolant hoses from oil cooler. Remove relief valve and plate washer from center of oil cooler housing. Remove oil cooler-to-cylinder block retaining nuts, oil cooler and "O" ring.

***NOTE: Before installing relief valve, push on valve (located in center of relief valve). Replace relief valve is valve fails to move.***

**Installation** – To install, reverse removal procedure. Coat new "O" rings with engine oil. Coat threads and below head of relief valve with engine oil. Tighten bolts/nuts to specification. See TORQUE SPECIFICATIONS table at end of article. Add engine oil and fill cooling system.

***CAUTION: On MR2, cooling system must be bled to prevent engine damage. See COOLING SYSTEM BLEEDING under REMOVAL & INSTALLATION.***

# 1991 ENGINES
# 2.0L & 2.2L 4-Cylinder (Cont.)

## TORQUE SPECIFICATIONS

### TORQUE SPECIFICATIONS (CAMRY)

| Application | Ft. Lbs. (N.m) |
|---|---|
| A/C Compressor Bolt | 20 (27) |
| Axle Shaft Center Bearing Bracket-To-Cylinder Block Bolt | 47 (64) |
| Axle Shaft Nut | 137 (186) |
| Ball Joint-To-Steering Knuckle Bolt | 83 (113) |
| Camshaft Bearing Cap Bolt [1] | 14 (19) |
| Camshaft Sprocket Bolt | 40 (54) |
| Catalytic Converter-To-Exhaust Manifold Bolt | 22 (30) |
| Cold Start Injector Pipe Union Bolt | 13 (18) |
| Connecting Rod Nut | 36 (49) |
| Coolant Outlet Bolt | 11 (15) |
| Crankshaft Pulley Bolt | 80 (109) |
| Cylinder Head Bolt [2] | |
| Step 1 | 36 (49) |
| Step 2 | Additional 90 Degrees |
| Drive Shaft Flange Bolt | 54 (73) |
| Engine Hanger Bolt | 31 (42) |
| Engine Mounts & Brackets | |
| Front & Rear Mount Through Bolt | 64 (87) |
| Left (Timing Belt Side) Mount Bolt/Nut | |
| 2WD | |
| Bolt | 47 (64) |
| Nut-To-Body | 65 (88) |
| Nut-To-Bracket | 38 (52) |
| 4WD | |
| Nut | 38 (52) |
| Through Bolt | 64 (87) |
| Left (Timing Belt Side) Mount Brace Bolt | 54 (73) |
| Right (Flywheel Side) Mount Brace Bolt | 15 (20) |
| Right (Flywheel Side) Mount | |
| Through Bolt | 64 (87) |
| Transaxle Bracket Bolt | 38 (52) |
| Engine Mount Crossmember-To-Body Bolt | 29 (39) |
| Engine Mount-To-Engine Mount Crossmember | |
| Bolt | 54 (73) |
| Nut | 35 (47) |
| Exhaust Manifold Nut | 36 (49) |
| Flywheel/Drive Plate Bolt | |
| A/T | 61 (83) |
| M/T | 65 (88) |
| Intake Manifold Bolt/Nut | 14 (19) |
| Intake Manifold Brace Bolt | |
| 12-mm Bolt | 14 (19) |
| 14-mm Bolt | 31 (42) |
| Main Bearing Cap Bolt [3] | 43 (58) |
| No. 1 & No. 2 Idler Pulley Bolt | 31 (42) |
| Oil Pump Sprocket Nut | 21 (29) |
| Spark Plug | 13 (18) |
| Spark Plug Tube | 29 (39) |
| Stiffener Bracket Bolt | 27 (37) |
| Suspension Crossmember-To-Engine Mount Crossmember Bolt | 29 (39) |
| Suspension Crossmember-To-Lower Suspension Arm Shafts | |
| Bolt | [4] |
| Nut | [5] |
| Throttle Body Bolt | 14 (19) |

[1] – Tighten bolts in sequence. *See Figs. 19 and 20.*
[2] – Tighten bolts in sequence. *See Fig. 13.*
[3] – Tighten bolts in sequence. *See Fig. 30.*
[4] – Tighten bolts with No. 10 stamped on bolt head to 153 ft. lbs. (207 N.m) and bolts with No. 11 to 112 ft. lbs. (152 N.m).
[5] – Tighten nuts with height of .51" (13.0 mm) to 153 ft. lbs. (207 N.m) and nuts with height of .68" (17.2 mm) to 112 ft. lbs. (152 N.m).

### TORQUE SPECIFICATIONS (CAMRY Cont.)

| Application | Ft. Lbs. (N.m) |
|---|---|
| Tie Rod Nut | 36 (49) |
| Valve Cover Nut | 17 (23) |
| Wheel Lug Nut | 76 (103) |
| | INCH Lbs. (N.m) |
| Coolant By-Pass Pipe-To-Water Pump Nut | 82 (9) |
| Delivery Pipe Bolt | 108 (12) |
| No. 3 Timing Belt Cover Bolt | 69 (8) |
| Oil Pan Bolt/Nut | 48 (5) |
| Oil Pump Cover Bolt | 78 (8) |
| Oil Pump Pick-Up Tube Nut | 48 (5) |
| Oil Pump-To-Cylinder Block Bolt | 82 (9) |
| Rear Plate-To-Cylinder Block Bolt | 82 (9) |
| Rear Seal Housing Bolt | 82 (9) |
| Water Pump Cover Bolt | 78 (8) |
| Water Pump-To-Cylinder Block Bolt [6] | 82 (9) |

[6] – Tighten bolts in sequence. *See Fig. 23.*

### TORQUE SPECIFICATIONS (CELICA)

| Application | Ft. Lbs. (N.m) |
|---|---|
| A/C Compressor Bolt | 20 (27) |
| Axle Shaft Center Bearing Bracket-To-Cylinder Block Bolt | 47 (64) |
| Axle Shaft Nut | 137 (186) |
| Ball Joint-To-Lower Control Arm Bolt/Nut | 94 (127) |
| Camshaft Bearing Cap Bolt [1] | 14 (19) |
| Camshaft Sprocket Bolt | 40 (54) |
| Catalytic Converter Brace Nut | 31 (42) |
| Catalytic Converter-To-Exhaust Manifold Bolt | 22 (30) |
| Cold Start Injector Pipe Union Bolt | 13 (18) |
| Connecting Rod Nut | |
| Step 1 | 18 (24) |
| Step 2 | Additional 90 Degrees |
| Coolant Outlet Bolt | 11 (15) |
| Crankshaft Pulley Bolt | 80 (109) |
| Cylinder Head Bolt [2] | |
| Step 1 | 36 (49) |
| Step 2 | Additional 90 Degrees |
| Engine Hanger Bolt | 18 (24) |
| Engine Mounts & Brackets | |
| Front & Rear Mount Through Bolt | 64 (87) |
| Left (Timing Belt Side) Mount Brace Bolt | 54 (73) |
| Left (Timing Belt Side) Mount-To-Bracket | |
| Bolt | 47 (64) |
| Through Bolt | 64 (87) |
| Right (Flywheel Side) Mount Brace Bolt | 15 (20) |
| Right (Flywheel Side) Mount-To-Bracket | |
| Nut | 38 (52) |
| Through Bolt | 64 (87) |
| Engine Mount Crossmember-To-Body Bolt | 38 (52) |
| Engine Mount-To-Engine Crossmember Bolt | 54 (73) |
| Exhaust Manifold Nut | 36 (49) |
| Flywheel/Drive Plate Bolt | |
| A/T | 61 (83) |
| M/T | 65 (88) |
| Intake Manifold Bolt/Nut | 14 (19) |
| Intake Manifold Brace Bolt | |
| 12-mm Bolt | 14 (19) |
| 14-mm Bolt | 31 (42) |
| Main Bearing Cap Bolt [3] | 43 (58) |
| No. 1 & No. 2 Idler Pulley Bolt | 31 (42) |

[1] – Tighten bolts in sequence. *See Figs. 19 and 20.*
[2] – Tighten bolts in sequence. *See Fig. 13.*
[3] – Tighten bolts in sequence. *See Fig. 30.*

# 1991 ENGINES
# 2.0L & 2.2L 4-Cylinder (Cont.)

## TORQUE SPECIFICATIONS (CELICA Cont.)

| Application | Ft. Lbs. (N.m) |
|---|---|
| Oil Cooler-To-Cylinder Block Relief Valve | 33 (45) |
| Oil Pump Sprocket Nut | 21 (29) |
| Spark Plug | 13 (18) |
| Spark Plug Tube | 29 (39) |
| Stiffener Bracket Bolt | 27 (37) |
| Strut Tower-To-Firewall Brace Bolt/Nut | |
| Bolt | 15 (20) |
| Nut | 47 (64) |
| Suspension Crossmember Bolt | 112 (152) |
| Throttle Body Bolt | 14 (19) |
| Tie Rod Nut | 36 (49) |
| Valve Cover Nut | 17 (23) |
| Wheel Lug Nut | 76 (103) |
| | **INCH Lbs. (N.m)** |
| Coolant By-Pass Pipe-To-Water Pump Nut | 82 (9) |
| Delivery Pipe Bolt | 108 (12) |
| No. 3 Timing Belt Cover Bolt | 69 (8) |
| Oil Cooler-To-Cylinder Block Nut | 69 (8) |
| Oil Pan Bolt/Nut | 48 (5) |
| Oil Pump Cover Bolt | 78 (8) |
| Oil Pump Pick-Up Tube Nut | 48 (5) |
| Oil Pump-To-Cylinder Block Bolt | 82 (9) |
| Rear Plate-To-Cylinder Block Bolt | 82 (9) |
| Rear Seal Housing Bolt | 82 (9) |
| Water Pump Cover Bolt | 82 (9) |
| Water Pump-To-Cylinder Block Bolt [4] | 82 (9) |

[4] – Tighten bolts in sequence. *See Fig. 23.*

## TORQUE SPECIFICATIONS (MR2)

| Application | Ft. Lbs. (N.m) |
|---|---|
| A/C Compressor Bolt | 20 (27) |
| Axle Shaft Nut | 152 (206) |
| Ball Joint-To-Lower Control Arm Bolt | 83 (113) |
| Camshaft Bearing Cap Bolt [1] | 14 (19) |
| Camshaft Sprocket Bolt | 40 (54) |
| Catalytic Converter Brace Nut | 31 (42) |
| Catalytic Converter-To-Exhaust Manifold Bolt | 22 (30) |
| Cold Start Injector Pipe Union Bolt | 13 (18) |
| Connecting Rod Nut | |
| Step 1 | 18 (24) |
| Step 2 | Additional 90 Degrees |
| Coolant Outlet Bolt | 11 (15) |
| Crankshaft Pulley Bolt | 80 (109) |
| Cylinder Head Bolt [2] | |
| Step 1 | 36 (49) |
| Step 2 | Additional 90 Degrees |
| Engine Hanger Bolt | 18 (24) |
| Engine Mounts & Brackets | |
| Engine Mount Bracket-To-Transaxle Case Bolt | 38 (52) |
| Front (Exhaust Manifold Side) Mount Bolt | |
| Body Side | 54 (73) |
| Through Bolt | 58 (79) |
| Left (Flywheel Side) Mount Support Bracket Bolt | |
| A/T | 26 (35) |
| M/T | |
| Mount Side | 54 (73) |
| Transaxle Side | 18 (24) |
| Left (Flywheel Side) Mount Through Bolt | 58 (79) |
| Left (Flywheel Side) Mount-To-Mounting Bracket | [3] |

[1] – Tighten bolts in sequence. *See Figs. 19 and 20.*
[2] – Tighten bolts in sequence. *See Fig. 13.*
[3] – Tighten bolts to specification. *See Fig. 11.*

## TORQUE SPECIFICATIONS (MR2 Cont.)

| Application | Ft. Lbs. (N.m) |
|---|---|
| Right (Timing Belt Side) Mount | |
| Nut | 38 (52) |
| Through Bolt | 58 (79) |
| Rear (Intake Manifold Side) Mount Bolt | |
| Body Side | 47 (64) |
| Through Bolt | 58 (79) |
| Right (Timing Belt Side) Mount Support | |
| Bracket Bolt/Nut | 54 (73) |
| Exhaust Manifold Nut | 36 (49) |
| Flywheel/Drive Plate Bolt | |
| A/T | 61 (83) |
| M/T | 65 (88) |
| Intake Manifold Bolt/Nut | 14 (19) |
| Intake Manifold Brace Bolt | |
| 12-mm Bolt | 14 (19) |
| 14-mm Bolt | 31 (42) |
| Main Bearing Cap Bolt [4] | 43 (58) |
| No. 1 & No. 2 Idler Pulley Bolt | 31 (42) |
| Oil Cooler-To-Cylinder Block Relief Valve | 33 (45) |
| Oil Pump Sprocket Nut | 21 (29) |
| Spark Plug | 13 (18) |
| Spark Plug Tube | 29 (39) |
| Stabilizer Link Nut | 36 (49) |
| Stiffener Bracket Bolt | 27 (37) |
| Strut Tower-To-Firewall Brace Bolt/Nut | |
| Bolt | 54 (73) |
| Nut | 47 (64) |
| Throttle Body Bolt | 14 (19) |
| Tie Rod-To-Hub Carrier Assembly Bolt | 76 (103) |
| Transaxle Control Cable Bracket Bolt | 57 (77) |
| Valve Cover Nut | 17 (23) |
| Wheel Lug Nut | 76 (103) |
| | **INCH Lbs. (N.m)** |
| Anti-Lock Brake Sensor Bolt | 69 (8) |
| Clutch Master Cylinder Bolt | 108 (12) |
| Coolant By-Pass Pipe-To-Water Pump Nut | 82 (9) |
| Delivery Pipe Bolt | 108 (12) |
| No. 3 Timing Belt Cover Bolt | 69 (8) |
| Oil Cooler-To-Cylinder Block Nut | 69 (8) |
| Oil Pan Bolt/Nut | 48 (5) |
| Oil Pump Cover Bolt | 78 (8) |
| Oil Pump Pick-Up Tube Nut | 48 (5) |
| Oil Pump-To-Cylinder Block Bolt | 82 (9) |
| Rear Plate-To-Cylinder Block Bolt | 82 (9) |
| Rear Seal Housing Bolt | 82 (9) |
| Water Pump Cover Bolt | 82 (9) |
| Water Pump-To-Cylinder Block Bolt [5] | 82 (9) |

[4] – Tighten bolts in sequence. *See Fig. 30.*
[5] – Tighten bolts in sequence. *See Fig. 23.*

# 1991 ENGINES
# 2.0L & 2.2L 4-Cylinder (Cont.)

## ENGINE SPECIFICATIONS

### GENERAL SPECIFICATIONS

| Application | Specification |
|---|---|
| 2.0L | |
| Displacement | 122 Cu. In. (2.0L) |
| Bore | 3.39" (86.1 mm) |
| Stroke | 3.39" (86.1 mm) |
| Compression Ratio | 9.3:1 |
| Fuel System | PFI |
| Horsepower @ RPM | 115 @ 5200 |
| Torque Ft. Lbs. @ RPM | 124 @ 4400 |
| 2.2L | |
| Displacement | 134 Cu. In. (2.2L) |
| Bore | 3.43" (87.1 mm) |
| Stroke | 3.58" (90.9 mm) |
| Compression Ratio | 9.5:1 |
| Fuel System | PFI |
| Horsepower @ RPM | 130 @ 5400 |
| Torque Ft. Lbs. @ RPM | 140 @ 4400 |

### CRANKSHAFT, MAIN & CONNECTING ROD BEARINGS

| Application | In. (mm) |
|---|---|
| 2.0L | |
| Crankshaft End Play | |
| Standard | .0008-.0087 (.020-.221) |
| Wear Limit | .0118 (.300) |
| Maximum Runout | .0024 (.061) |
| Main Bearings | |
| Journal Diameter [1] | |
| Size Mark 0 | 2.1653-2.1655 (54.998-55.003) |
| Size Mark 1 | 2.1651-2.1653 (54.993-54.998) |
| Size Mark 2 | 2.1649-2.1651 (54.988-54.993) |
| Journal Out-Of-Round | .0008 (.020) |
| Journal Taper | .0008 (.020) |
| Oil Clearance | |
| Standard Crankshaft | |
| No. 3 Journal | |
| Standard | .0010-.0017 (.025-.043) |
| Wear Limit | .0031 (.079) |
| All Other Journals | |
| Standard | .0006-.0013 (.015-.033) |
| Wear Limit | .0031 (.079) |
| .010" (.25 mm) Undersize Crankshaft | |
| No. 3 Journal | |
| Standard | .0011-.0026 (.028-.066) |
| Wear Limit | .0031 (.079) |
| All Other Journals | |
| Standard | .0007-.0023 (.018-.058) |
| Wear Limit | .0031 (.079) |
| Connecting Rod Bearings | |
| Journal Diameter | 1.8892-1.8898 (47.986-48.001) |
| Journal Out-Of-Round | .0008 (.020) |
| Journal Taper | .0008 (.020) |
| Oil Clearance | |
| Standard Crankshaft | |
| Standard | .0009-.0022 (.022-.056) |
| Wear Limit | .0031 (.079) |
| .010" (.25 mm) Undersize Crankshaft | |
| Standard | .0009-.0027 (.022-.069) |
| Wear Limit | .0031 (.079) |

[1] – Main bearing journal diameter is determined by size mark stamped on crankshaft counterweight. *See Fig. 29.*

### CRANKSHAFT, MAIN & CONNECTING ROD BEARINGS (Cont.)

| Application | In. (mm) |
|---|---|
| 2.2L | |
| Crankshaft End Play | |
| Standard | .0008-.0087 (.020-.221) |
| Wear Limit | .0118 (.300) |
| Maximum Runout | .0024 (.061) |
| Main Bearings | |
| Journal Diameter [1] | |
| Size Mark 0 | 2.1653-2.1655 (54.998-55.003) |
| Size Mark 1 | 2.1651-2.1653 (54.993-54.998) |
| Size Mark 2 | 2.1649-2.1651 (54.988-54.993) |
| Journal Out-Of-Round | .0008 (.020) |
| Journal Taper | .0008 (.020) |
| Oil Clearance | |
| Standard Crankshaft | |
| No. 3 Journal | |
| Standard | .0010-.0017 (.025-.043) |
| Wear Limit | .0031 (.079) |
| All Other Journals | |
| Standard | .0006-.0013 (.015-.033) |
| Wear Limit | .0031 (.079) |
| .010" (.25 mm) Undersize Crankshaft | |
| No. 3 Journal | |
| Standard | .0011-.0026 (.028-.066) |
| Wear Limit | .0031 (.079) |
| All Other Journals | |
| Standard | .0007-.0023 (.018-.058) |
| Wear Limit | .0031 (.079) |
| Connecting Rod Bearings | |
| Journal Diameter | 2.0466-2.0472 (51.984-51.999) |
| Journal Out-Of-Round | .0008 (.020) |
| Journal Taper | .0008 (.020) |
| Oil Clearance | |
| Standard Crankshaft | |
| Standard | .0009-.0022 (.022-.056) |
| Wear Limit | .0031 (.079) |
| .010" (.25 mm) Undersize Crankshaft | |
| Standard | .0009-.0027 (.022-.069) |
| Wear Limit | .0031 (.079) |

[1] – Main bearing journal diameter is determined by size mark stamped on crankshaft counterweight. *See Fig. 29.*

### CYLINDER BLOCK

| Application | In. (mm) |
|---|---|
| 2.0L | |
| Cylinder Bore [1] | |
| Size Mark 1 | 3.3858-3.3862 (85.999-86.009) |
| Size Mark 2 | 3.3862-3.3866 (86.009-86.020) |
| Size Mark 3 | 3.3866-3.3870 (86.020-86.030) |
| Maximum Deck Warpage | .002 (.05) |
| Main Bearing Bore I.D. [2] | |
| Size Mark 1 | 2.3326-2.3239 (59.019-59.027) |
| Size Mark 2 | 2.3239-2.3241 (59.027-59.032) |
| Size Mark 3 | 2.3241-2.3243 (59.032-59.037) |
| 2.2L | |
| Cylinder Bore [1] | |
| Size Mark 1 | 3.4252-3.4256 (87.000-87.010) |
| Size Mark 2 | 3.4256-3.4260 (87.010-87.020) |
| Size Mark 3 | 3.4260-3.4264 (87.020-87.031) |
| Maximum Deck Warpage | .002 (.05) |
| Main Bearing Bore I.D. [2] | |
| Size Mark 1 | 2.3326-2.3239 (59.019-59.027) |
| Size Mark 2 | 2.3239-2.3241 (59.027-59.032) |
| Size Mark 3 | 2.3241-2.3243 (59.032-59.037) |

[1] – Cylinder bore diameter is determined by size mark on cylinder block deck surface. *See Fig. 31.*

[2] – Main bearing bore I.D. is determined by size mark on cylinder block. *See Fig. 29.*

# 1991 ENGINES
# 2.0L & 2.2L 4-Cylinder (Cont.)

## PISTONS, PINS & RINGS

| Application | In. (mm) |
|---|---|
| 2.0L | |
| Pistons | |
| Clearance | |
| Standard | .0018-.0026 (.046-.066) |
| Wear Limit | .0033 (.084) |
| Diameter [1] | |
| Size Mark 1 | 3.3836-3.3840 (85.943-85.953) |
| Size Mark 2 | 3.3840-3.3844 (85.953-85.964) |
| Size Mark 3 | 3.3844-3.3848 (85.964-85.974) |
| Rings | |
| No. 1 | |
| End Gap | |
| Standard | .0106-.0197 (.269-.500) |
| Wear Limit | .0433 (1.099) |
| Side Clearance | .0012-.0028 (.030-.071) |
| No. 2 | |
| End Gap | |
| Standard | .0106-.0201 (.269-.511) |
| Wear Limit | .0437 (1.110) |
| Side Clearance | .0012-.0028 (.030-.071) |
| No. 3 (Oil) | |
| End Gap | |
| Standard | .0079-.0217 (.201-.551) |
| Wear Limit | .0453 (1.151) |
| Side Clearance | .0012-.0028 (.030-.071) |
| 2.2L | |
| Pistons | |
| Clearance | |
| Standard | .0031-.0039 (.079-.099) |
| Wear Limit | .0047 (.119) |
| Diameter [1] | |
| Size Mark 1 | 3.4217-3.4221 (86.911-86.921) |
| Size Mark 2 | 3.4221-3.4225 (86.921-86.931) |
| Size Mark 3 | 3.4225-3.4229 (86.931-86.942) |
| Pins | |
| Diameter | .8660-.8665 (21.996-22.010) |
| Piston Fit | [2] |
| Rod Fit | |
| Standard | .0002-.0004 (.005-.010) |
| Wear Limit | .0020 (.051) |
| Rings | |
| No. 1 | |
| End Gap | |
| Standard | .0106-.0197 (.269-.500) |
| Wear Limit | .0433 (1.099) |
| Side Clearance | .0012-.0028 (.030-.071) |
| No. 2 | |
| End Gap | |
| Standard | .0138-.0236 (.350-.599) |
| Wear Limit | .0472 (1.199) |
| Side Clearance | .0012-.0028 (.030-.071) |
| No. 3 (Oil) | |
| End Gap | |
| Standard | .0079-.0217 (.201-.551) |
| Wear Limit | .0453 (1.15) |
| Side Clearance | .0012-.0028 (.030-.071) |

[1] - Piston diameter is determined by size mark stamped on top of piston. *See Fig. 27.*

[2] - Piston pin should slide through piston using thumb pressure with piston at 140°F (60°C).

## CYLINDER HEAD

| Application | Specification |
|---|---|
| 2.0L | |
| Maximum Warpage | |
| Cylinder Block Surface | .002" (.05 mm) |
| Intake & Exhaust Manifold Surface | .003" (.08 mm) |
| Valve Seats | |
| Intake Valve | |
| Seat Angle | 45° |
| Seat Width | .039-.055" (.99-1.40 mm) |
| Exhaust Valve | |
| Seat Angle | 45° |
| Seat Width | .039-.055" (.99-1.40 mm) |
| Valve Guides | |
| Intake Valve | |
| Valve Guide Cylinder Head | |
| Bore I.D. | .4331-.4341" (11.000-11.026 mm) |
| Valve Guide I.D. | .2366-.2374" (6.010-6.030 mm) |
| Valve Guide Installed Height | .323-.339 (8.20-8.61) |
| Valve Stem-To-Guide Oil Clearance | |
| Standard | .0010-.0024" (.025-.061 mm) |
| Wear Limit | .0031" (.079 mm) |
| Exhaust Valve | |
| Valve Guide Cylinder Head | |
| Bore I.D. | .4331-.4314" (11.000-11.026 mm) |
| Valve Guide I.D. | .2366-.2374" (6.010-6.030 mm) |
| Valve Guide Installed Height | .323-.339 (8.20-8.61) |
| Valve Stem-To-Guide Oil Clearance | |
| Standard | .0012-.0026" (.030-.066 mm) |
| Wear Limit | .0039" (.099 mm) |
| 2.0L | |
| Maximum Warpage | |
| Cylinder Block Surface | .002" (.05 mm) |
| Intake & Exhaust Manifold Surface | .003" (.08 mm) |
| Valve Seats | |
| Intake Valve | |
| Seat Angle | 45° |
| Seat Width | .039-.055" (.99-1.40 mm) |
| Exhaust Valve | |
| Seat Angle | 45° |
| Seat Width | .039-.055" (.99-1.40 mm) |
| Valve Guides | |
| Intake Valve | |
| Valve Guide Cylinder Head | |
| Bore I.D. | .4331-.4341" (11.000-11.026 mm) |
| Valve Guide I.D. | .2366-.2374" (6.010-6.030 mm) |
| Valve Stem-To-Guide Oil Clearance | |
| Standard | .0010-.0024" (.025-.061 mm) |
| Wear Limit | .0031" (.079 mm) |
| Exhaust Valve | |
| Valve Guide Cylinder Head | |
| Bore I.D. | .4331-.4314" (11.000-11.026 mm) |
| Valve Guide I.D. | .2366-.2374" (6.010-6.030 mm) |
| Valve Stem-To-Guide Oil Clearance | |
| Standard | .0012-.0026" (.030-.066 mm) |
| Wear Limit | .0039" (.099 mm) |

# 1991 ENGINES
# 2.0L & 2.4L 4-Cylinder (Cont.)

## CAMSHAFT

| Application | In. (mm) |
|---|---|
| 2.0L | |
| End Play | |
| Intake Camshaft | |
| Standard | .0018-.0039 (.046-.099) |
| Wear Limit | .0047 (.119) |
| Exhaust Camshaft | |
| Standard | .0012-.0033 (.030-.084) |
| Wear Limit | .0039 (.099) |
| Gear Backlash | |
| Standard | .0008-.0079 (.020-.201) |
| Wear Limit | .0118 (.300) |
| Journal Diameter | 1.0614-1.0620 (26.960-26.975) |
| Journal Runout | .0016 (.041) |
| Lobe Height | |
| Intake Camshaft | |
| Standard | 1.3744-1.3783 (34.910-35.009) |
| Wear Limit | 1.3701 (34.801) |
| Exhaust Camshaft | |
| Standard | 1.4000-1.4039 (35.560-35.659) |
| Wear Limit | 1.3957 (35.451) |
| Oil Clearance | |
| Standard | .0010-.0024 (.025-.061) |
| Wear Limit | .0039 (.099) |
| 2.2L | |
| End Play | |
| Intake Camshaft | |
| Standard | .0018-.0039 (.046-.099) |
| Wear Limit | .0047 (.119) |
| Exhaust Camshaft | |
| Standard | .0012-.0033 (.030-.084) |
| Wear Limit | .0039 (.099) |
| Gear Backlash | |
| Standard | .0008-.0079 (.020-.201) |
| Wear Limit | .0118 (.300) |
| Journal Diameter | 1.0614-1.0620 (26.960-26.975) |
| Journal Runout | .0016 (.041) |
| Lobe Height | |
| Intake Camshaft | |
| Standard | 1.3902-1.3941 (35.311-35.410) |
| Wear Limit | 1.3858 (35.199) |
| Exhaust Camshaft | |
| Standard | 1.4000-1.4039 (35.560-35.660) |
| Wear Limit | 1.3957 (35.451) |
| Oil Clearance | |
| Standard | .0010-.0024 (.025-.061) |
| Wear Limit | .0039 (.099) |

## CONNECTING RODS

| Application | In. (mm) |
|---|---|
| 2.0L | |
| Maximum Bend | .002 Per 3.94 (.05 Per 100.1) |
| Maximum Twist | .006 Per 3.94 (.15 Per 100.1) |
| Side Play | |
| Standard | .0063-.0123 (.160-.312) |
| Wear Limit | .0138 (.350) |
| 2.2L | |
| Bore Diameter | |
| Pin Bore | .8663-.8668 (22.004-22.017) |
| Maximum Bend | .002 Per 3.94 (.05 Per 100.1) |
| Maximum Twist | .006 Per 3.94 (.15 Per 100.1) |
| Side Play | |
| Standard | .0063-.0123 (.160-.312) |
| Wear Limit | .0138 (.350) |

## VALVES & VALVE SPRINGS

| Application | Specification |
|---|---|
| Intake Valves | |
| Face Angle | 44.5° |
| Minimum Margin | .020" (.51 mm) |
| Minimum Refinish Length | 3.941" (100.10 mm) |
| Stem Diameter | .2350-.2356" (5.969-5.984 mm) |
| Exhaust Valves | |
| Face Angle | 44.5° |
| Minimum Margin | .020" (.51 mm) |
| Minimum Refinish Length | 3.937" (99.99 mm) |
| Stem Diameter | .2348-.2354" (5.964-5.979 mm) |
| Valve Springs | |
| Free Length | 1.772" (45.01 mm) |
| Out-Of-Square | .078" (1.98 mm) |
| | **Lbs. @ In. (kg @ mm)** |
| Pressure | |
| Valve Closed | 37-43 @ 1.366 (16.7-19.5 @ 34.70) |

## VALVE LIFTERS

| Application | In. (mm) |
|---|---|
| 2.0L & 2.2L | |
| Bore Diameter | 1.1024-1.1032 (28.001-28.021) |
| Lifter Diameter | 1.1014-1.1018 (27.976-27.986) |
| Oil Clearance | |
| Standard | .0005-.0018 (.013-.046) |
| Wear Limit | .0028 (.071) |

# 1991 ENGINES
# 2.4L 4-Cylinder – Pickup & 4Runner

***NOTE: For repair procedures not covered in this article, see ENGINE OVERHAUL PROCEDURES article in GENERAL INFORMATION.***

## ENGINE IDENTIFICATION

Engine may be identified by Vehicle Identification Number (VIN) stamped on a metal pad, located near lower left corner of windshield. The forth character of VIN identifies engine model. See ENGINE IDENTIFICATION CODES table.

Engine identification number, located on cylinder block below cylinder head, may be needed when ordering replacement parts. *See Fig. 1.*

***ENGINE IDENTIFICATION CODES***

| Application | VIN | Engine Code |
|---|---|---|
| 2.4L PFI | R | 22R-E |

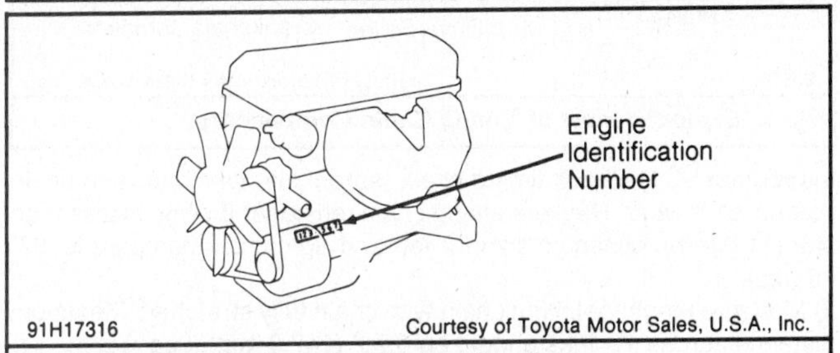


***Fig. 1: Locating Engine Identification Number***

## ADJUSTMENTS

### VALVE CLEARANCE ADJUSTMENT

**1)** Check and adjust valve clearance with engine at normal operating temperature. Remove valve cover. Rotate crankshaft pulley and align pulley groove with "0" mark on timing belt cover to set No. 1 cylinder at TDC of compression stroke.

**2)** Ensure rocker arms on cylinder No. 1 are loose, and rocker arms on cylinder No. 4 are tight. This indicates TDC compression for cylinder No. 1. If rocker arms are not as described, rotate crankshaft 360 degrees and realign timing marks.

**3)** Check intake valve clearance on cylinders No. 1 and No. 2, and exhaust valve clearance on cylinders No. 1 and No. 3. Adjust clearance to specification if necessary. See VALVE CLEARANCE SPECIFICATIONS table.

**4)** Rotate crankshaft 360 degrees and realign timing marks. Adjust intake valve clearance on cylinders No. 3 and No. 4, and exhaust valve clearance on cylinders No. 2 and No. 4.

***VALVE CLEARANCE SPECIFICATIONS***

| Valve [1] | In. (mm) |
|---|---|
| Exhaust | .012 (.30) |
| Intake | .008 (.20) |

[1] – Adjust valves with engine at normal operating temperature.

## REMOVAL & INSTALLATION

***NOTE: For installation reference, label all electrical connectors, vacuum hoses and fuel lines before removal. Also place mating marks on engine hood and other major assemblies before removal.***

### FUEL PRESSURE RELEASE

***WARNING: High fuel pressure may be present in fuel lines and component parts. Relieve fuel pressure before opening fuel system. DO NOT allow fuel to flow onto engine or electrical parts.***

Disconnect negative battery cable. Place container under fitting to be loosened. Use a rag to cover fuel line and component. Slowly loosen fitting, allowing pressurized fuel to flow into container. After fuel system has depressurized, disconnect and plug fitting.

### ENGINE

***NOTE: Engine and transaxle should be removed as an assembly.***

**Removal – 1)** Remove hood. Remove battery. Remove engine undercover (splash) shields. Drain coolant from radiator and cylinder block. Drain engine oil. Remove air cleaner case and intake air connector.

**2)** Remove radiator. Remove all accessory drive belts. Remove fan clutch along with fan. Remove fan pulley. Disconnect all necessary electrical wiring from engine. Disconnect and mark all vacuum hoses for installation reference. Disconnect all coolant hoses. Release fuel pressure. See FUEL PRESSURE RELEASE. Disconnect fuel lines.

**3)** Disconnect accelerator cable. Disconnect throttle cable and cruise control cable (if equipped). Disconnect ground straps from right side and rear side of engine. Remove drive shaft. Disconnect speedometer cable.

**4)** On models with power steering, remove power steering pump, and wire aside. DO NOT disconnect power steering hoses. Disconnect ground strap from power steering pump bracket.

**5)** On models with A/C, remove A/C compressor, and wire it aside. DO NOT disconnect A/C compressor hoses. On M/T models, remove shift lever(s) from inside vehicle. On 2WD A/T models, disconnect manual shift linkage from neutral start switch. On 4WD A/T models, disconnect transfer case shift linkage.

**6)** On all 4WD models, remove transfer case undercover (splash) shields. Remove stabilizer bar. Remove front drive shaft. Remove frame crossmember. On all models, disconnect oxygen sensor connector.

**7)** Disconnect exhaust pipe from exhaust manifold. Remove exhaust pipe clamp. Remove exhaust pipe from catalytic converter. On 2WD models, remove engine rear mount and bracket. On M/T models, remove clutch release (slave) cylinder with bracket.

**8)** On 4WD models, remove front floor heat insulator and brake tube heat insulator. Remove side frame crossmember. On all models, attach engine hoist chain to engine lift brackets. Remove engine mount nuts and bolts. Lift engine out of vehicle slowly and carefully. Ensure engine is clear of all wiring and hoses.

**Installation –** To install, reverse removal procedure. Check all fluid levels and linkage adjustments before starting engine. Tighten all nuts and bolts to specification. See TORQUE SPECIFICATIONS table at end of article.

### CYLINDER HEAD & MANIFOLDS

***NOTE: See Fig. 16 for exploded view of cylinder head and cylinder block components***

**Removal – 1)** Disconnect negative battery cable. Drain coolant from radiator and cylinder block. Remove intake air connector. Disconnect exhaust pipe from exhaust manifold.

**2)** Remove oil dipstick. Remove distributor and spark plugs. Disconnect all necessary electrical wiring from cylinder head. Disconnect and label all electrical wiring and vacuum hoses from cylinder head. Disconnect all coolant hoses from cylinder head.

**3)** Disconnect accelerator cable. Disconnect throttle cable (if equipped). Disconnect ground strap from rear of engine. Remove EGR vacuum modulator. Remove air intake chamber along with throttle body. *See Fig. 16.*

**4)** Release fuel pressure. See FUEL PRESSURE RELEASE. Disconnect fuel lines. Remove power steering pump and bracket (if equipped). Remove valve cover. Set No. 1 piston to TDC on compression stroke. Paint mating marks on camshaft sprocket and timing chain. Remove rubber half-circle seal and cam sprocket retaining bolt.

**5)** Pull distributor drive gear and cam thrust plate off sprocket. Remove sprocket from camshaft. Allow sprocket and chain to rest in cylinder head. Remove chain cover bolt in front of camshaft sprocket.

**6)** Loosen cylinder head bolts in 3 stages, in reverse order of tightening sequence. *See Fig. 2.* Remove rocker arm assembly. If necessary, pry equally at front and rear of rocker arm assembly to remove.

**7)** Lift cylinder head from dowels on cylinder block. Set cylinder head on wood blocks on work bench. If cylinder head is hard to remove, carefully pry with flat bar between cylinder head and block projection.

# 1991 ENGINES
# 2.4L 4-Cylinder – Pickup & 4Runner (Cont.)

**8)** Remove air injection manifold and reed valve from cylinder head. Remove heater inlet tube. Remove air pipe. Remove intake manifold as an assembly with fuel delivery pipe, injectors and heater water inlet pipe.

**9)** Remove EGR valve. Remove 3 bolts and exhaust manifold outer heat insulator. Remove 8 nuts, exhaust manifold and inner exhaust manifold heat insulator.

**Installation – 1)** Apply liquid sealant at 2 front corners of engine block. Position head gasket over locating dowels. Place head in position, and rotate camshaft so dowel pin is facing up. Install rocker arm assembly over locating dowels.

**2)** Tighten cylinder head bolts in 3 stages in proper sequence. *See Fig. 2.* To complete installation, reverse removal procedure. Tighten all nuts and bolts to specification. See TORQUE SPECIFICATIONS table at end of article. Ensure valve and ignition timing are properly set. Adjust valves. See VALVE CLEARANCE ADJUSTMENT under ADJUSTMENTS.

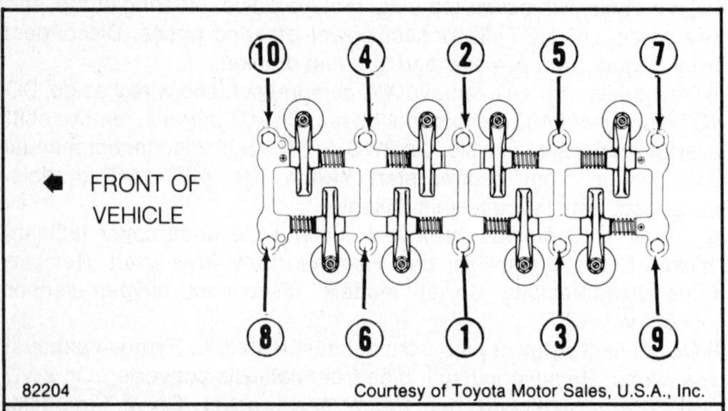


***Fig. 2: Cylinder Head/Rocker Arm Bolt Tightening Sequence***

## FRONT COVER OIL SEAL

**Removal & Installation – 1)** If oil pump is removed from cylinder block, pry out old oil seal. Using Seal Installer (09223-50010), install oil seal until oil seal surface is flush with timing chain cover. Apply multipurpose grease to oil seal lip.

**2)** If oil pump is installed to cylinder block, cut off old oil seal lip. Pry out oil seal. Use care not to damage crankshaft surface. Apply multipurpose grease to new oil seal lip. Using Seal Installer (09223-50010), install oil seal until oil seal surface is flush with timing chain cover edge.

## TIMING CHAIN

**Removal – 1)** Remove cylinder head. See CYLINDER HEAD & MANIFOLDS under REMOVAL & INSTALLATION. Remove radiator. On 4WD models, drain differential gear oil. Disconnect drive axles from side gear flanges. Index mark propeller shaft and companion flange. Disconnect propeller shaft.

**2)** Disconnect vacuum hoses and electrical connector (if equipped). Support differential assembly with jack. Remove differential assembly mounting bolts and nuts. Lower differential assembly from vehicle.

**3)** On 2WD models, place a jack under transmission, and raise engine about 1" (25.4 mm). On all models, remove 16 bolts and 2 nuts attaching oil pan. Using Oil Pan Seal Cutter (09032-00100), remove oil pan. DO NOT damage oil pan flange.

**4)** Remove power steering belt (if equipped). Remove A/C belt, compressor and bracket (if equipped), and lay them aside. Remove fan clutch along with fan. Remove water pump pulley. Set No. 1 cylinder to TDC of compression stroke. Remove crankshaft pulley. *See Fig. 3.*

**5)** Remove coolant by-pass pipe. Remove 2 bolts, and disconnect heater outlet pipe. Remove fan belt adjusting bracket.

**6)** Remove timing chain cover assembly. Remove chain from damper. Remove cam sprocket and chain. Using gear puller, remove oil pump drive spline and chain sprocket.

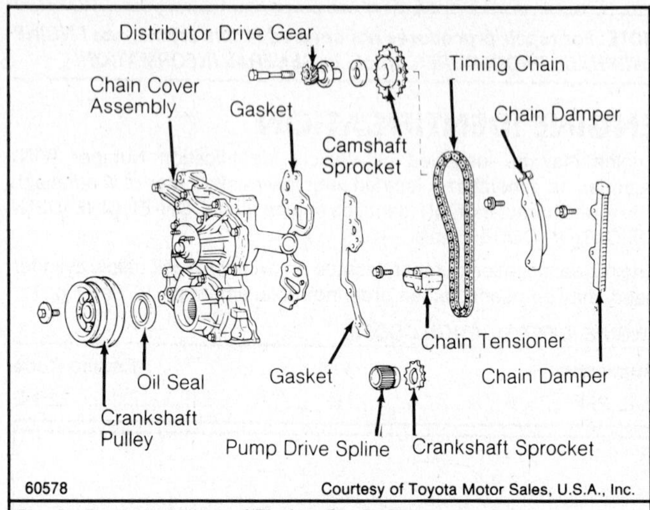


***Fig. 3: Exploded View of Timing Chain Components***

**Inspection – 1)** Check timing chain, sprockets, tensioner and chain dampers for wear. Replace timing chain tensioner if width is less than .43" (11.0 mm). Minimum size for left and right chain dampers is .02" (.5 mm).

**2)** Measure length of timing chain with chain fully stretched. Maximum distance across 17 links should be 5.79" (147.0 mm). *See Fig. 4.*

**3)** Wrap timing chain completely around camshaft sprocket. Using a Vernier caliper held parallel to sprocket, measure outer sides of chain rollers. Using same method, measure diameter of crankshaft sprocket and chain.

**4)** Minimum diameter for crankshaft sprocket and chain is 2.34" (59.4 mm). Minimum diameter for camshaft sprocket and chain is 4.48" (113.8 mm). If either measurement is less than minimum, replace timing chain and both sprockets.

**Installation – 1)** Ensure No. 1 cylinder is at TDC (crankshaft Woodruff key is in 12 o'clock position). Position sprocket on

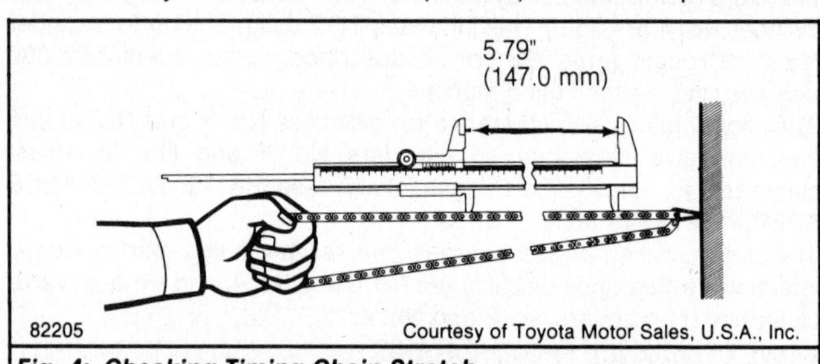


***Fig. 4: Checking Timing Chain Stretch***

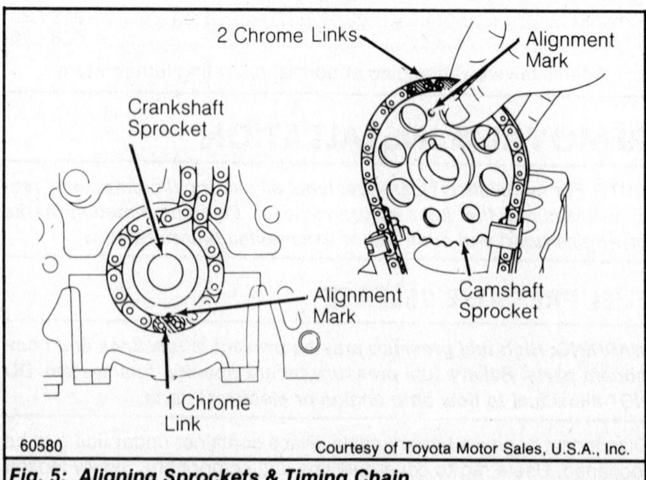


***Fig. 5: Aligning Sprockets & Timing Chain***

# 1991 ENGINES
# 2.4L 4-Cylinder – Pickup & 4Runner (Cont.)

crankshaft. Place timing chain on sprocket with single bright link aligned with timing mark on sprocket.

**2)** Install timing chain on camshaft sprocket so timing mark on sprocket is located between 2 chrome links. *See Fig. 5.* Ensure chain is positioned in dampers. Turn camshaft sprocket counterclockwise to remove slack from timing chain. Slide oil pump drive spline over crankshaft key.

**3)** Install cover assembly with new gasket over dowels and pump spline. To complete installation, reverse removal procedure. Tighten all nuts and bolts to specification. See TORQUE SPECIFICATIONS table at end of article.

## CAMSHAFT

**Removal – 1)** Measure camshaft end play before removing camshaft. End play should be within specification. See CAMSHAFT table under ENGINE SPECIFICATIONS at end of article. If end play is greater than maximum, replace cylinder head.

**2)** Remove cylinder head. See CYLINDER HEAD & MANIFOLDS under REMOVAL & INSTALLATION. Remove rocker arm assembly. Remove camshaft bearing caps. If necessary, pry equally at front and rear of rocker arm assembly to remove.

**Inspection – 1)** Check camshaft journal oil clearance using Plastigage method. If clearance exceeds specification, replace cylinder head and/or camshaft. Maximum clearance is .004" (.10 mm).

**2)** Maximum camshaft runout at center journal is .008" (.20 mm). Replace camshaft if runout is beyond limit. Replace camshaft if lobe height is less than 1.663" (42.25 mm) for intake or 1.665" (42.30 mm) for exhaust.

**Installation – 1)** To install camshaft, reverse removal procedure. Install camshaft bearing caps in numerical order with arrows pointing toward front of engine.

**2)** Tighten all nuts and bolts to specification. See TORQUE SPECIFICATIONS table at end of article. Ensure valve and ignition timing is properly set. Adjust valves. See VALVE CLEARANCE ADJUSTMENT under ADJUSTMENTS.

## REAR CRANKSHAFT OIL SEAL

**Removal & Installation –** Rear main bearing oil seal may be replaced with engine in vehicle. Remove transmission. Pry out old seal from retainer. Apply grease to lip of new oil seal. Using Seal Driver (09223-41020), drive oil seal in place until oil seal surface is flush with rear oil seal retainer edge.

## WATER PUMP

**Removal & Installation – 1)** Drain cooling system. Remove power steering pump and A/C compressor belts (if equipped). Remove fan clutch together with fan. Remove fan pulley.

**2)** Remove 6 bolts and 3 nuts attaching water pump. Remove water pump. To install water pump, reverse removal procedure. Use new gasket on clean mating surfaces.

## OIL PAN

**Removal –** Drain engine oil. Remove engine undercover (splash) shields. On 2WD models, place a jack under transmission, and raise engine about 1" (25.4 mm). On all models, remove 16 bolts and 2 nuts attaching oil pan. Using Oil Pan Seal Cutter (09032-00100), remove oil pan. DO NOT damage oil pan flange.

**Installation –** Thoroughly clean pan rail mating surface. Apply a .20" (5.0 mm) bead of Seal Packing (08826-00080) to oil pan flange. Place gasket on pan. Apply sealant to 4 corners of cylinder block, where front cover and rear seal retainer meet cylinder block. Install oil pan. To complete installation, reverse removal procedure.

# OVERHAUL

***NOTE: See Fig. 16 for exploded view of cylinder head and cylinder block components***

## CYLINDER HEAD

**Cylinder Head – 1)** Check for cracks, damage and coolant leakage. Remove scale, sealing compound and carbon deposits. Clean oil passages, and blow compressed air through passages to ensure they are not clogged.

**2)** Check EGR passage for clogging. Inspect cylinder head for warpage at deck surface. Replace cylinder if warpage exceeds specification. See CYLINDER HEAD table under ENGINE SPECIFICATIONS at end of article.

**Valve Springs –** Inspect valve spring free length, tension and installed height. Using a square, check out-of-square of each spring. Replace valve spring if measurements are not within specification. See VALVES & VALVE SPRINGS table under ENGINE SPECIFICATIONS at end of article.

**Valve Stem Oil Seals – 1)** Using a spring compressor, remove valve keepers. Remove spring retainer and springs. Remove valve stem oil seal from end of valve guide.

**2)** Carefully slide new oil seal over valve stem without damaging seal as it passes over keeper grooves. Force seal over end of valve guide. To complete oil seal installation, reverse removal procedure.

**Valve Guides –** With valves removed, measure I.D. of valve guide and O.D. of valve stem. Subtract valve stem O.D. from valve guide I.D. to obtain clearance. Replace valve and/or guide if clearance is not within specification. See CYLINDER HEAD table under ENGINE SPECIFICATIONS at end of article.

**Valve Guide Replacement – 1)** Break valve guide off at snap ring. Gradually heat cylinder head to 194°F (90°C). Using Valve Guide Remover/Installer (09201-60011), remove valve guide(s).

**2)** To install valve guide(s), allow cylinder head to cool down. Measure valve guide bore of cylinder head. If bore exceeds .5125" (13.018 mm), machine bore to .5138-.5145" (13.050-13.068 mm) for oversize valve guide. If bore is less than .5125" (13.018 mm), use standard size guide.

**3)** Heat cylinder head to 194°F (90°C). Using remover/installer, install valve guide(s) until snap ring contacts cylinder head. Ream valve guide to obtain proper clearance for valve being installed.

**Valve Seats –** No service procedure is given by manufacturer. Valve seats must be ground if valve guides are replaced.

**Valves –** Inspect each valve for wear, damage and distortion of head and stem. If stem end is pitted or worn, resurface as necessary. This correction must be limited to a minimum. Resurface valve face. If valve margin has decreased to less than the service limit, replace valve. See VALVES & VALVE SPRINGS table under ENGINE SPECIFICATIONS at end of article.

## VALVE TRAIN

***NOTE: Label all rocker arm components for reassembly reference.***

**Rocker Arm Shaft Assembly – 1)** If rocker arms appear loose, disassemble rocker arm assembly, and measure rocker arm-to-shaft clearance. Clearance should be .0004-.0020" (.010-.050 mm), with a maximum limit of .0031" (.08 mm).

**2)** If clearance exceeds maximum limit, replace rocker arms and/or shafts. Reassemble in reverse order of disassembly. Note that rocker arms are identical. *See Fig. 6.*

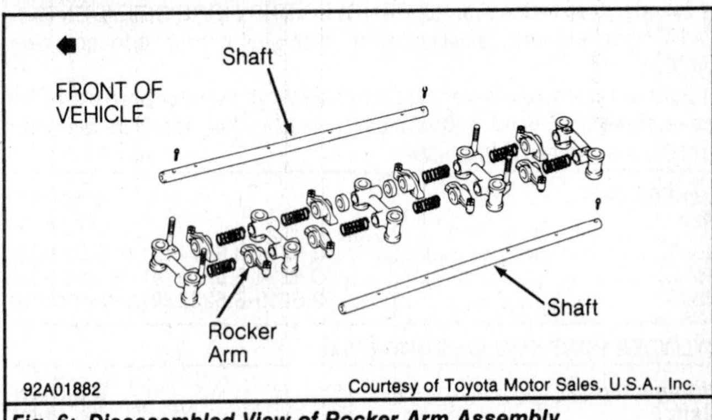


***Fig. 6: Disassembled View of Rocker Arm Assembly***

# 1991 ENGINES
# 2.4L 4-Cylinder – Pickup & 4Runner (Cont.)

## CYLINDER BLOCK ASSEMBLY

**Piston & Rod Assembly** – Ensure rod and rod cap are with matching cylinder number. Ensure piston and rod are installed in cylinder from which they were removed. Check piston and rod. Replace piston and rod if measurements are not as specified in CONNECTING RODS table and PISTONS, PINS & RINGS table under ENGINE SPECIFICATIONS at end of article.

**Piston Pins** – **1)** Remove piston pin snap ring. Heat piston in hot water to 140°F (60°C). Using hammer and driver, push piston pin out of piston and connecting rod.

**2)** Measure clearance between rod bushing and piston pin. Replace rod bushing if clearance is greater than .0006" (.015 mm).

**3)** At 176°F (80°C), it should be possible to push pin into piston with thumb pressure. If pin can be installed at lower temperature, replace pin and piston.

**4)** Inspect connecting rod for misalignment. Maximum rod bend limit is .002" (.05 mm) per 3.94" (100.0 mm). Maximum rod twist limit is .0059" (.150 mm) per 3.94" (100.0 mm). If rod is bent or twisted beyond maximum limit, replace rod.

***NOTE: Piston and pin are a matched set. Use new snap rings when reassembling.***

**5)** Heat piston to 176°F (80°C), and position piston and connecting rod so manufacturer's mark on rod and indent on piston crown face same direction. *See Fig. 7.* Push pin into piston and rod assembly. Install snap rings.

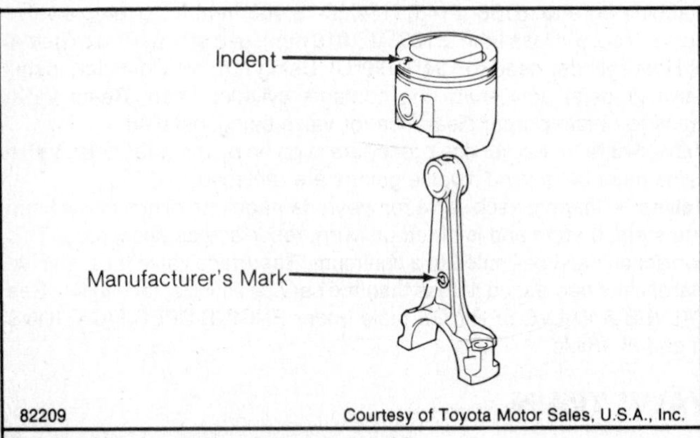


***Fig. 7: Aligning Piston & Rod Assembly***

**Fitting Pistons & Rings** – **1)** Remove carbon from top of piston. Clean piston and ring grooves. Measure piston clearance. Determine piston size by identification mark on top of piston. *See Fig. 8.* See PISTON SIZE IDENTIFICATION table. Measure piston diameter at right angles to piston pin center line. Measure 1.30" (33.0 mm) from piston head.

**2)** Determine cylinder bore size by identification mark on deck surface of cylinder block. *See Fig. 10.* See CYLINDER BORE SIZE IDENTIFICATION table. Measure cylinder bore diameter in thrust direction. *See Fig. 9.*

**3)** Subtract piston diameter measurement from cylinder bore diameter measurement. Ensure piston clearance is within specification. See PISTONS, PINS & RINGS table under ENGINE SPECIFICATIONS at end of article. If piston clearance exceeds maximum specification, replace all pistons and/or rebore all cylinders.

***PISTON SIZE IDENTIFICATION***

| Identification Mark | Diameter In. (mm) |
|---|---|
| No. 1 | 3.6211-3.6214 (91.975-91.985) |
| No. 2 | 3.6214-3.6219 (91.985-91.995) |
| No. 3 | 3.6219-3.6222 (91.995-92.005) |

***CYLINDER BORE SIZE IDENTIFICATION***

| Identification Mark | Diameter In. (mm) |
|---|---|
| No. 1 | 3.6220-3.6224 (92.000-92.010) |
| No. 2 | 3.6224-3.6228 (92.010-92.020) |
| No. 3 | 3.6228-3.6232 (92.020-92.030) |

**4)** Check end gap of ring in cylinder to which it will be installed. If end gap is greater than specification, try new set of rings. See PISTONS, PINS & RINGS table. If end gap is still greater than specification, rebore cylinder and use oversize piston rings. Properly position rings on piston before installing piston. *See Fig. 11.*

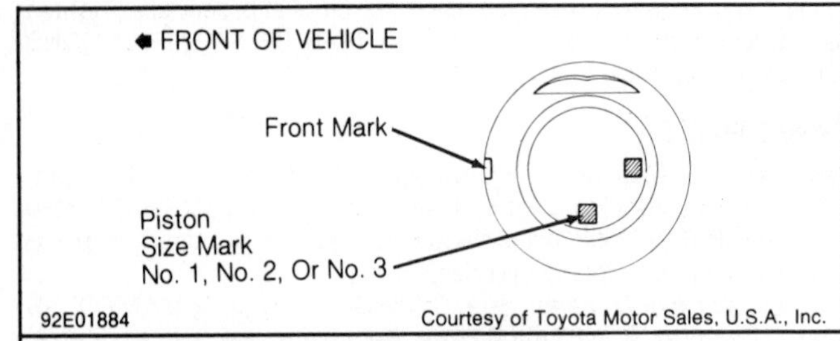


***Fig. 8: Locating Piston Identification Marks***

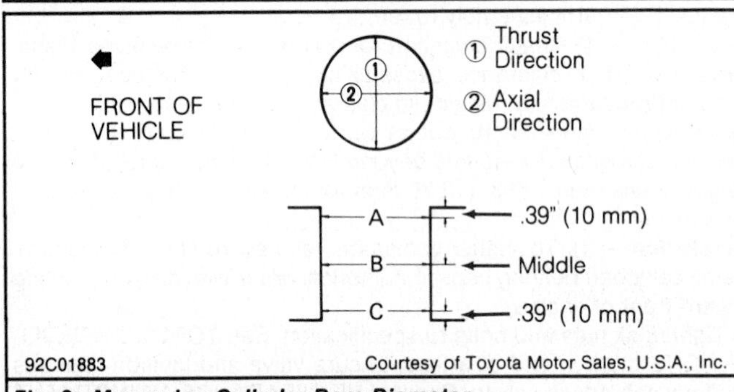


***Fig. 9: Measuring Cylinder Bore Diameter***

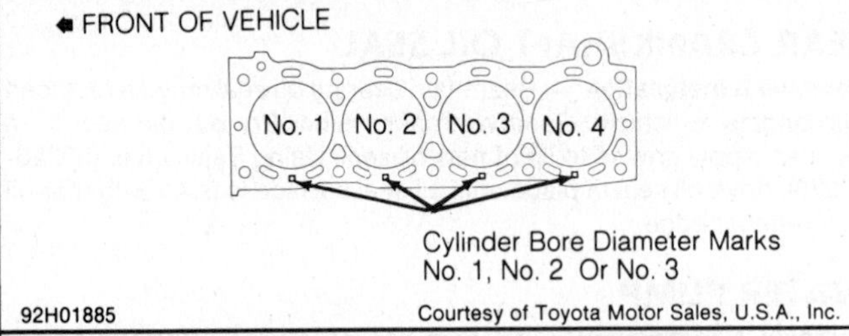


***Fig. 10: Locating Cylinder Bore Identification Marks***

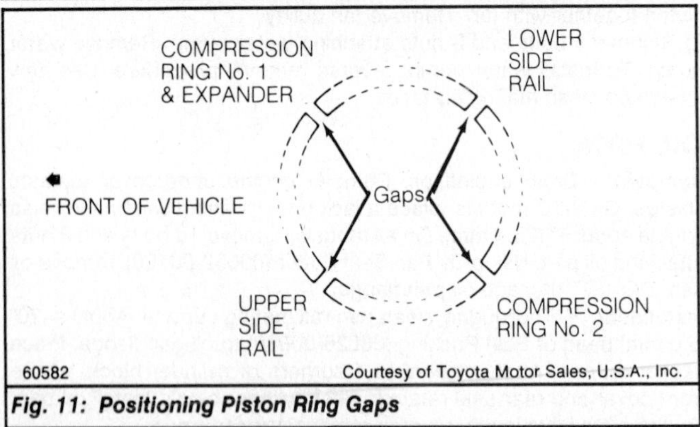


***Fig. 11: Positioning Piston Ring Gaps***

***NOTE: There are 3 standard connecting rod bearing sizes. Connecting rod cap and bearing are marked with a letter "A", "B" or "C". See Fig. 12. If replacing rod bearing, ensure letter on replacement rod bearing is the same as letter on connecting rod cap.***

**Rod Bearings** – Check crankshaft journal condition. Check rod bearing clearance. If clearance is not within specification, machine or

# 1991 ENGINES
# 2.4L 4-Cylinder – Pickup & 4Runner (Cont.)

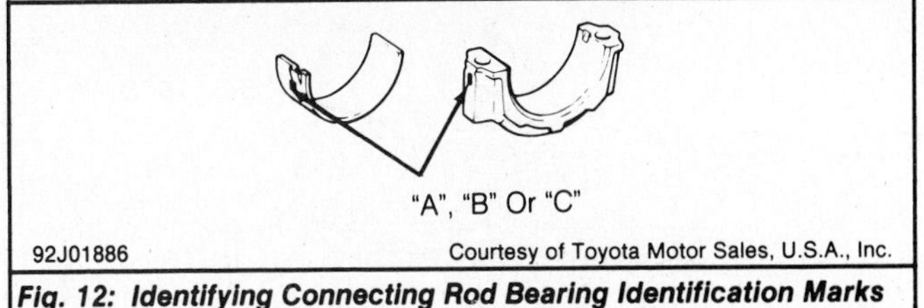


*Fig. 12: Identifying Connecting Rod Bearing Identification Marks*

***NOTE: There are 3 sizes of standard main bearings. Cylinder block and main bearing are marked with a number "3", "4" or "5". See Fig. 13. If replacing bearing, ensure number on replacement bearing is the same as number on cylinder block.***

replace as necessary. See CRANKSHAFT, MAIN & CONNECTING ROD BEARINGS table under ENGINE SPECIFICATIONS at end of article.

**Crankshaft & Main Bearings** – **1)** Remove main bearing caps evenly in 3 stages, in reverse order of tightening sequence. *See Fig. 14.* Check bearing clearance.

**2)** If bearing clearance is not within specification, machine or replace as necessary. See CRANKSHAFT, MAIN & CONNECTING ROD BEARINGS table under ENGINE SPECIFICATIONS at end of article.

**3)** Replacement main bearings must have same identification number as old main bearings. Install thrust washers on center bearing cap with oil grooves facing outward. Install bearing caps in numerical order with arrows facing forward.

**4)** Tighten main bearings to specification in sequence. *See Fig. 14*. See TORQUE SPECIFICATIONS table at end of article.

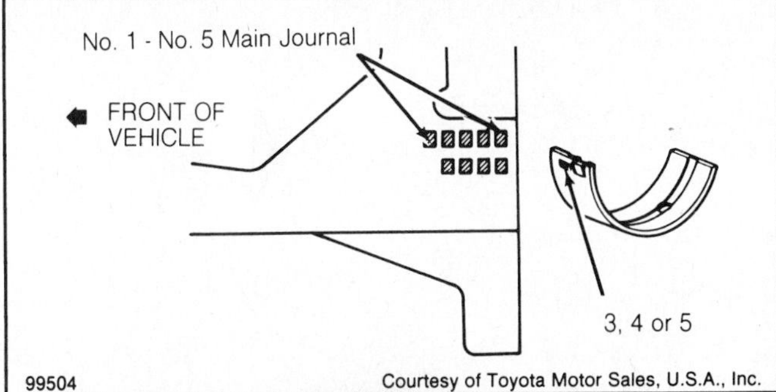


*Fig. 13: Identifying Main Bearing Identification Marks*

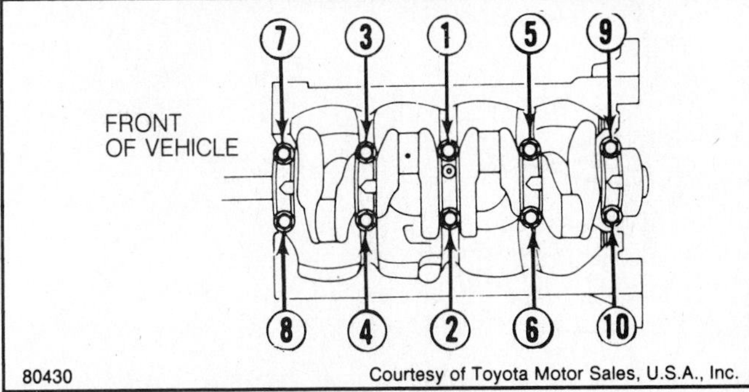


*Fig. 14: Main Bearing Tightening Sequence*

**Thrust Bearing** – Using dial indicator, measure thrust clearance. See CRANKSHAFT, MAIN & CONNECTING ROD BEARINGS table under ENGINE SPECIFICATIONS at end of article. If clearance exceeds specification, replace thrust bearings as a set. See THRUST WASHER SPECIFICATIONS table. If clearance is less than specification, remove and reinstall thrust bearing. Recheck thrust clearance.

**Cylinder Block** – **1)** Check cylinder head surface of engine block for warpage using straightedge and feeler gauge. Cylinder block warpage must be within specification. See CYLINDER BLOCK table under ENGINE SPECIFICATIONS at end of article.

***THRUST WASHER SPECIFICATIONS***

| Size | In. (mm) |
|---|---|
| Standard | .1059-.1079 (2.690-2.740) |
| .125 Oversize | .1084-.1104 (2.753-2.803) |
| .250 Oversize | .1108-.1128 (2.815-2.865) |

**2)** Different cylinder bore sizes are used and can be identified by size marks on deck surface of cylinder block. *See Fig. 10*. Measure cylinder bore diameter at positions "A", "B" and "C" in thrust and axial directions. *See Fig. 9*. If diameter is greater than maximum specification, rebore cylinders or replace cylinder block. See CYLINDER BLOCK table under ENGINE SPECIFICATIONS at end of article.

## ENGINE OILING

### ENGINE LUBRICATION SYSTEM

Oiling system is force fed using a gear-type oil pump, driven from front of crankshaft. Oil from oil pan is pumped through a full-flow oil filter to the oil galleys in cylinder block. Oil is fed to crankshaft bearings, timing chain assembly, camshaft and rocker arm assembly. *See Fig. 15* for cross-sectional view of engine oil circuit.

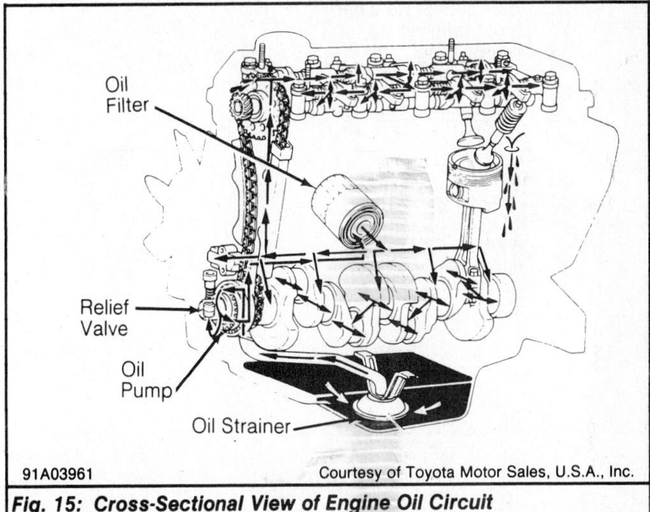


*Fig. 15: Cross-Sectional View of Engine Oil Circuit*

**Crankcase Capacity** – Engine oil capacity is 4.5 qts. (4.3L) with oil filter change. Oil capacity without oil filter change is 4.0 qts. (3.8L).

**Oil Pressure** – Oil pressure is 4.3 psi (.3 kg/cm²) at idle speed and 36-71 psi (2.5-5.0 kg/cm²) at 3000 RPM.

## OIL PUMP

***NOTE: Manufacturer recommends cleaning oil pan and strainer when servicing oil pump.***

**Removal** – **1)** Remove engine undercover (splash) shields. On 2WD models, place a jack under transmission, and raise engine about 1" (25.4 mm). On all models, remove 16 bolts and 2 nuts attaching oil pan.

**2)** Using Oil Pan Seal Cutter (09032-00100), remove oil pan. Remove oil strainer. Remove drive belts and crankshaft pulley. On models with A/C, remove A/C compressor and bracket. Wire A/C compressor aside. DO NOT disconnect A/C hoses.

**3)** On all models, loosen oil pump relief valve plug. *See Fig. 17.* Remove 5 bolts and oil pump assembly. Remove oil pump drive spline from crankshaft and "O" ring from engine block. Remove relief valve plug, spring and piston from pump body. Remove driven and drive gear from pump body.

**Installation** – Reassemble pump, and lubricate seal lip. Install new "O" ring in block, and apply sealant to upper bolt "A". *See Fig. 17*. Install and tighten pump. To complete installation, reverse removal procedure. Tighten oil pump bolts to specification. See TORQUE SPECIFICATIONS table at end of article.

# 1991 ENGINES
## 2.4L 4-Cylinder – Pickup & 4Runner (Cont.)

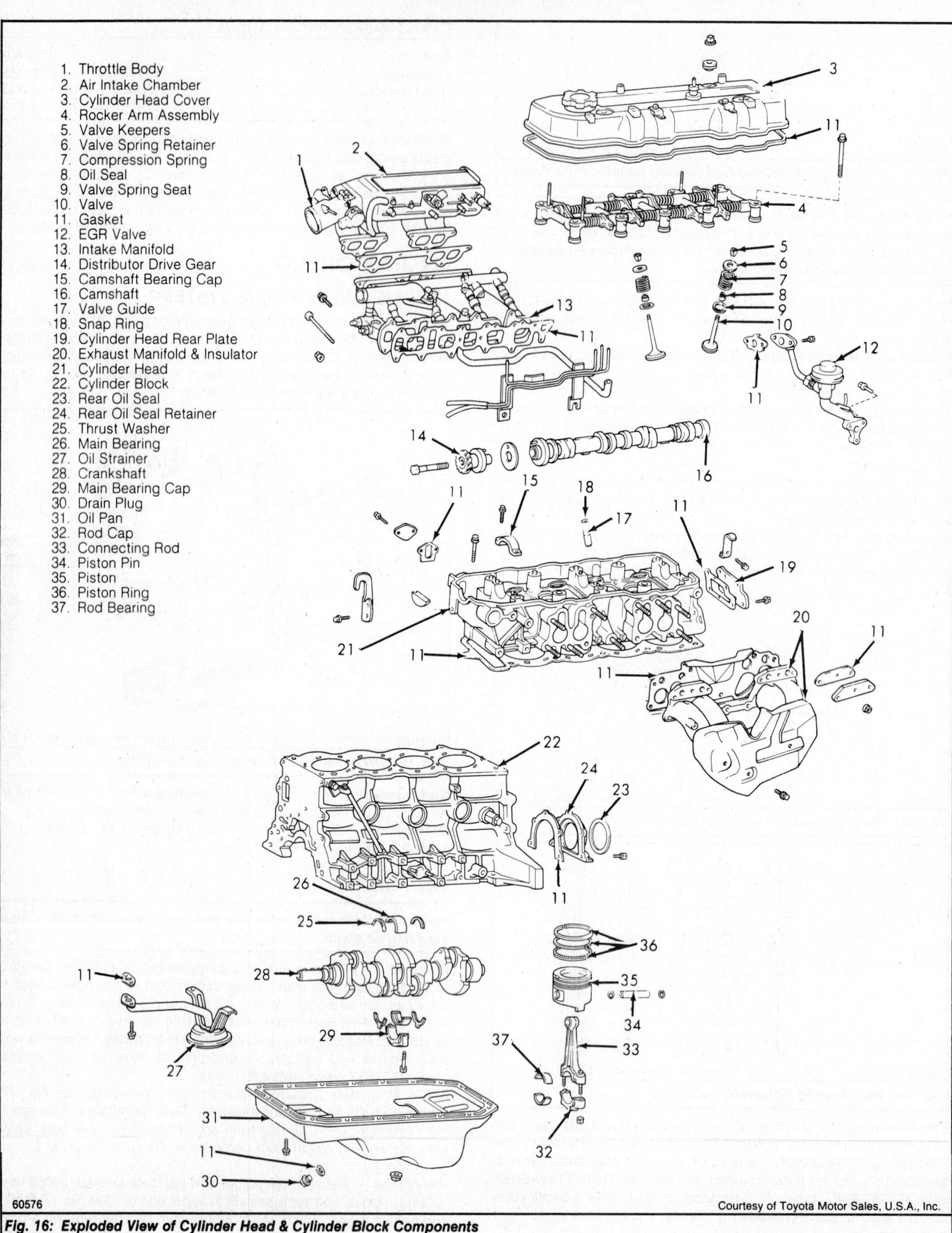


*Fig. 16: Exploded View of Cylinder Head & Cylinder Block Components*

### OIL PUMP SPECIFICATIONS

| Application | In. (mm) |
|---|---|
| Driven Gear-To-Body Clearance | |
| Standard | .0035-.0059 (.090-.150) |
| Maximum | .008 (.20) |
| Gear Side Clearance | |
| Standard | .0012-.0035 (.030-.090) |
| Maximum | .006 (.15) |
| Tip-To-Crescent Clearance | |
| Standard | |
| Drive Gear | [3] .0087-.0098 (.220-.250) |
| Driven Gear | [3] .0059-.0083 (.150-.210) |
| Maximum | .012 (.30) |

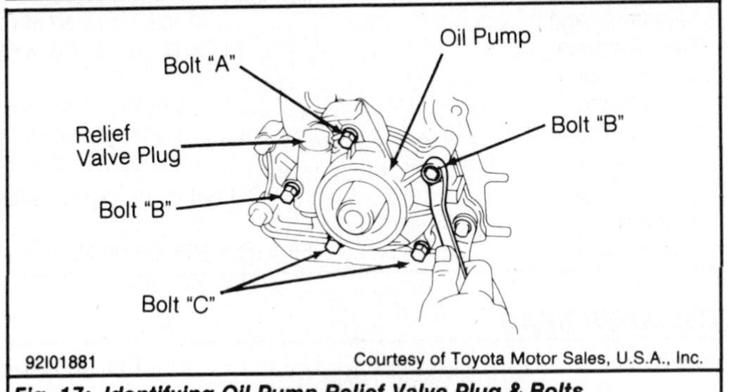


*Fig. 17: Identifying Oil Pump Relief Valve Plug & Bolts*

## TORQUE SPECIFICATIONS

### TORQUE SPECIFICATIONS

| Application | Ft. Lbs. (N.m) |
|---|---|
| Camshaft Bearing Bolts | 15 (20) |
| Camshaft Sprocket Bolt | 58 (78) |
| Chain Damper Bolts | 16 (22) |
| Chain Tensioner Bolts | 14 (19) |
| Connecting Rod Cap Bolts | 51 (69) |
| Crankshaft Pulley Bolt | 116 (157) |
| Cylinder Head/Rocker Arm Bolts [1] | 58 (78) |
| EGR Valve Bolt & Nut | 10 (13) |
| Exhaust Manifold Bolts | 32 (44) |
| Flywheel Bolts | |
| A/T | 61 (83) |
| M/T | 80 (108) |
| Intake Manifold Bolts | 14 (19) |
| Main Bearing Cap Bolts [2] | 76 (103) |
| Oil Cooler Relief Valve | 51 (69) |
| Oil Pan Drain Plug | 18 (25) |
| Oil Pump [3] | |
| Bolt "A" | 18 (25) |
| Bolt "B" | 14 (19) |
| Bolt "C" | 10 (13) |
| Oil Pump Relief Valve Plug | 27 (37) |
| Rear Oil Seal Retainer Bolts | 13 (18) |
| Timing Chain Damper Bolt | 16 (22) |
| Timing Chain Tensioner Bolt | 14 (19) |
| Timing Cover Bolts | |
| 8 mm | 9 (12) |
| 10 mm | 29 (39) |
| Rocker Arm Adjusting Screw | 18 (25) |
| | **INCH Lbs. (N.m.)** |
| Oil Pan Bolts | 108 (12) |
| Oil Pump Strainer Bolts | 108 (12) |
| Valve Cover Bolts | 52 (5.9) |

[1] – Tighten in sequence. *See Fig. 2.*
[2] – Tighten in sequence. *See Fig. 14.*
[3] – *See Fig. 17* for bolt location.

## ENGINE SPECIFICATIONS

### GENERAL SPECIFICATIONS

| Application | Specification |
|---|---|
| Displacement | 144.4 Cu. In. (2.4L) |
| Bore | 3.62" (92.0 mm) |
| Stroke | 3.50" (89.0 mm) |
| Compression Ratio | 9.3:1 |
| Fuel System | PFI |
| Horsepower @ RPM | 116 @ 4800 |
| Torque Ft. Lbs. @ RPM | 140 @ 2800 |

### CRANKSHAFT, MAIN & CONNECTING ROD BEARINGS

| Application | In. (mm) |
|---|---|
| Crankshaft | |
| End Play | .0008-.0087 (.020-.220) |
| Runout | .004 (.10) |
| Main Bearings | |
| Journal Diameter | 2.3616-2.3622 (59.984-60.000) |
| Journal Out-Of-Round | .0004 (.100) |
| Journal Taper | .0004 (.100) |
| Oil Clearance | .0010-.0022 (.025-.055) |
| Bearing Center Wall Thickness [1] | |
| Identification Mark "3" | .0783-.0784 (1.988-1.992) |
| Identification Mark "4" | .0784-.0786 (1.992-1.996) |
| Identification Mark "5" | .0786-.0787 (1.996-2.000) |
| Connecting Rod Bearings | |
| Journal Diameter | 2.0861-2.0866 (52.988-53.000) |
| Journal Out-Of-Round | .0004 (.100) |
| Journal Taper | .0004 (.100) |
| Oil Clearance | .0010-.0022 (.025-.055) |
| Bearing Center Wall Thickness [2] | |
| Identification Mark "A" | .0584-.0586 (1.484-1.488) |
| Identification Mark "B" | .0586-.0587 (1.488-1.492) |
| Identification Mark "C" | .0587-.0589 (1.492-1.496) |

[1] – Three standard main bearing sizes are used. Cylinder block is marked with a number "3", "4" or "5". *See Fig. 13.*
[2] – Three standard rod bearing sizes are used. Connecting rod caps are marked with letter "A", "B" or "C". *See Fig. 12.*

### CONNECTING RODS

| Application | In. (mm) |
|---|---|
| Bore Diameter | |
| Crankpin Bore [1] | |
| Standard Bore "A" | 2.2047-2.2050 (56.000-56.006) |
| Standard Bore "B" | 2.2050-2.2052 (56.006-56.012) |
| Standard Bore "C" | 2.2052-2.2054 (56.012-56.018) |
| Maximum Bend | .0020 (.050) |
| Maximum Twist | .0059 (.150) |
| Side Play | .0063-.0102 (.160-.260) |

[1] – Three standard crankpin sizes are used. Connecting rod caps are marked with letter "A", "B" or "C". *See Fig. 12.*

# 1991 ENGINES
# 2.4L 4-Cylinder – Pickup & 4Runner (Cont.)

## PISTONS, PINS & RINGS

| Application | In. (mm) |
|---|---|
| Pistons | |
| Clearance | .0006-.0014 (.015-.035) |
| Standard Diameter [1] | |
| Identification Mark No. 1 | 3.6211-3.6214 (91.975-91.985) |
| Identification Mark No. 2 | 3.6214-3.6219 (91.985-91.995) |
| Identification Mark No. 3 | 3.6219-3.6222 (91.995-92.005) |
| Pins | |
| Piston Fit | Thumb Pressure @ 176°F (80°C) |
| Rod Fit | Thumb Pressure @ 176°F (80°C) |
| Oil Clearance | .0002-.0004 (.005-.011) |
| Rings | |
| No. 1 | |
| End Gap | .0098-.0185 (.250-.470) |
| Side Clearance | .0012-.0028 (.030-.070) |
| No. 2 | |
| End Gap | .0236-.0323 (.600-.820) |
| Side Clearance | .0012-.0028 (.030-.070) |
| No. 3 (Oil) | |
| End Gap | .0079-.0224 (.200-.570) |
| Side Clearance | .0012-.0028 (.030-.070) |

[1] – Three piston sizes are used. Pistons are marked with No. 1, No. 2 or No. 3. *See Fig. 8.*

## CYLINDER BLOCK

| Application | In. (mm) |
|---|---|
| Cylinder Bore [1] | |
| Standard Diameter | |
| Identification Mark No. 1 | 3.6220-3.6224 (92.000-92.010) |
| Identification Mark No. 2 | 3.6224-3.6228 (92.010-92.020) |
| Identification Mark No. 3 | 3.6228-3.6232 (92.020-92.030) |
| Maximum Taper | .0008 (.020) |
| Maximum Out-Of-Round | .0008 (.020) |
| Main Journal Bore [2] | |
| Identification Mark "3" | 2.5198-2.5201 (64.004-64.010) |
| Identification Mark "4" | 2.5201-2.5203 (64.010-64.016) |
| Identification Mark "5" | 2.5203-2.5205 (64.016-64.022) |
| Maximum Deck Warpage | .002 (.05) |

[1] – Three cylinder bore sizes are used. Cylinders are marked with No. 1, No. 2 or No. 3. *See Fig. 10.*

[2] – Three standard main journal sizes are used. Cylinder block is marked with number "3", "4" or "5". *See Fig. 13.*

## VALVES & VALVE SPRINGS

| Application | Specification |
|---|---|
| Intake Valves | |
| Face Angle | 44.5° |
| Minimum Margin | .039" (1.00 mm) |
| Minimum Length | 4.449" (113.00 mm) |
| Standard Length | 4.468" (113.50 mm) |
| Stem Diameter | .3138-.3144" (7.970-7.985 mm) |
| Exhaust Valves | |
| Face Angle | 44.5° |
| Minimum Margin | .039" (1.00 mm) |
| Minimum Length | 4.406" (111.90 mm) |
| Standard Length | 4.425" (112.40 mm) |
| Stem Diameter | .3136-.3142" (7.965-7.980 mm) |
| Valve Springs | |
| Free Length | 1.909" (48.50 mm) |
| Installed Height | 1.594" (40.50 mm) |
| Out-Of-Square | .063" (1.60 mm) |
| | Lbs. @ In. (kg @ mm) |
| Pressure | |
| Valve Closed | 66.1 @ 1.595 (30.00 @ 40.50) |

## CYLINDER HEAD

| Application | Specification |
|---|---|
| Maximum Warpage | .0059" (.150 mm) |
| Valve Seats | |
| Intake Valve | |
| Seat Angle | 45° |
| Seat Width | .047-.063" (1.20-1.60 mm) |
| Exhaust Valve | |
| Seat Angle | 45° |
| Seat Width | .047-.063" (1.20-1.60 mm) |
| Valve Guides | |
| Intake Valve | |
| Bore I.D. | .5118-.5125" (13.000-13.018 mm) |
| Valve Guide I.D. | .3154-.3161" (8.010-8.030 mm) |
| Valve Stem-To-Guide | |
| Oil Clearance | .0010-.0024" (.025-.060 mm) |
| Exhaust Valve | |
| Bore I.D. | .5118-.5125" (13.000-13.018 mm) |
| Valve Guide I.D. | .3154-.3161" (8.010-8.030 mm) |
| Valve Stem-To-Guide | |
| Oil Clearance | .0012-.0026" (.030-.065 mm) |

## CAMSHAFT

| Application | In. (mm) |
|---|---|
| End Play | .0031-.0071 (.080-.180) |
| Journal Diameter | 1.2984-1.2992 (32.980-33.000) |
| Journal Runout | .008 (.20) |
| Lobe Height | |
| Intake | 1.6783-1.6891 (42.630-42.720) |
| Exhaust | 1.6807-1.6842 (42.690-42.780) |
| Oil Clearance | .0004-.0020 (.010-.050) |

# 1991 ENGINES
# 2.4L 4-Cylinder – Previa

***NOTE: For repair procedures not covered in this article, see ENGINE OVERHAUL PROCEDURES article in GENERAL INFORMATION.***

## ENGINE IDENTIFICATION

Engine serial number is stamped on cylinder block, below intake manifold. *See Fig. 1.*

***ENGINE IDENTIFICATION CODE***

| Engine | Code |
|---|---|
| 2.4L 4-Cylinder | 2TZ-FE |

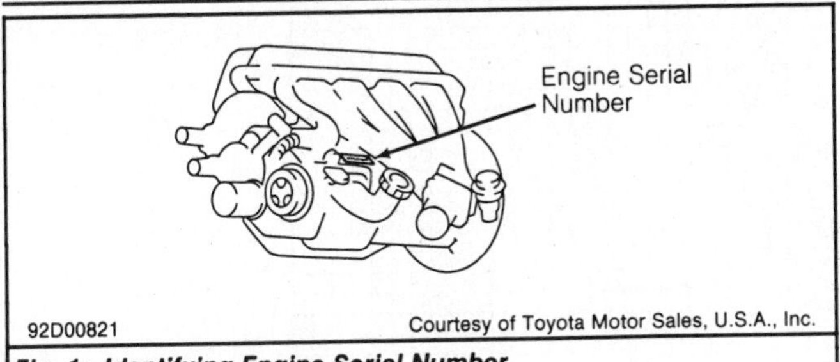


92D00821 Courtesy of Toyota Motor Sales, U.S.A., Inc.

***Fig. 1: Identifying Engine Serial Number***

## ADJUSTMENTS

### VALVE CLEARANCE ADJUSTMENT

***NOTE: Adjust valve clearance with engine cold.***

**1)** Right service cover, located below right seat must be removed to gain access to valve covers. Remove scuff plate. Disconnect right seat belt from floor panel. Remove right seat, right seat support leg, and jack holder.

**2)** Remove retaining bolts and right service cover. Remove retaining bolts, No. 2 valve cover and gasket. *See Fig. 10.* Remove PCV hose. Disconnect spark plug wires from spark plugs.

**3)** Remove retaining bolts, No. 1 valve cover and gasket. *See Fig. 10.* Install a 12-mm bolt in end of accessory drive shaft, near cooling fan and tighten nut. *See Fig. 2.* Bolt is used to rotate the engine.

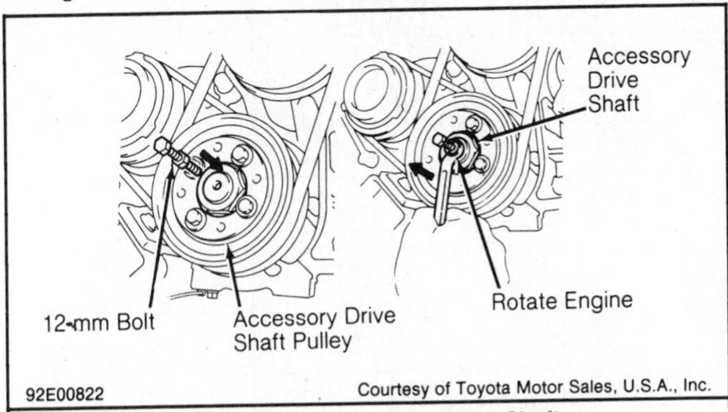


92E00822 Courtesy of Toyota Motor Sales, U.S.A., Inc.

***Fig. 2: Rotating Engine with Accessory Drive Shaft***

**4)** Rotate engine so No. 1 cylinder is at TDC on compression stroke. Ensure timing mark on crankshaft pulley aligns with "O" mark on the front cover.

**5)** If valves on No. 1 cylinder are tight, rotate crankshaft one revolution and realign timing marks. Ensure valves on No. 1 cylinder are loose and valves on No. 4 cylinder are tight.

**6)** With No. 1 cylinder at TDC, check clearance on specified valves. See VALVE CLEARANCE ADJUSTMENT SEQUENCE table. Using feeler gauge, measure and record clearance between valve lifter and camshaft.

***VALVE CLEARANCE ADJUSTMENT SEQUENCE***

| Cylinder No. On TDC | Adjust Intake Valves | Adjust Exhaust Valves |
|---|---|---|
| 1 | 1 & 2 | 1 & 3 |
| 4 | 3 & 4 | 2 & 4 |

**7)** To check remaining valves, rotate crankshaft 360 degrees (one full revolution) until No. 4 piston is at TDC of compression stroke. Measure valve clearance on specified valves. See VALVE CLEARANCE ADJUSTMENT SEQUENCE table.

**8)** Clearance should be within specification. See VALVE CLEARANCE SPECIFICATIONS table. If valves require adjustment, rotate camshaft so lobe on valve to be adjusted is facing upward, away from valve lifter.

***VALVE CLEARANCE SPECIFICATIONS*** [1]

| Application | In. (mm) |
|---|---|
| Exhaust | .010-.014 (.25-.36) |
| Intake | .006-.010 (.15-.25) |

[1] – Adjust valve clearance with engine cold.

**9)** Rotate valve lifter so notch on valve lifter is positioned upward. Valve Clearance Adjuster (SST 09248-55010) is used to remove adjusting shim. Using SST (A) of valve clearance adjuster, push downward on valve lifter. Place SST (B) between camshaft and valve lifter. Remove SST (A). *See Fig. 3.*

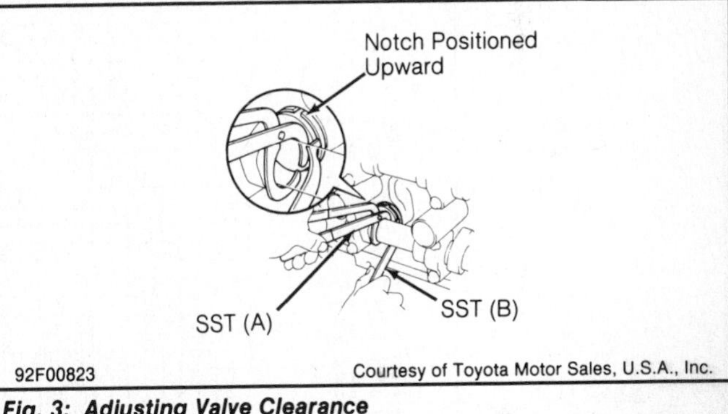


92F00823 Courtesy of Toyota Motor Sales, U.S.A., Inc.

***Fig. 3: Adjusting Valve Clearance***

**10)** Using small screwdriver and magnet, remove adjusting shim. Measure thickness of adjusting shim removed. Determine correct thickness of adjusting shim to be used. *See Figs. 4-7.* Install adjusting shim and recheck valve clearance. Remove bolt used to rotate engine from accessory drive shaft.

***CAUTION: Ensure bolt is removed from accessory drive shaft or cooling fan will be damaged.***

**11)** If spark plug tube gasket in No. 1 valve cover requires replacement, tap spark plug tube gasket from No. 1 valve cover. Note direction of spark plug tube gasket installation.

**12)** Using Handle (SST 09552-10010) and Spark Plug Tube Gasket Installer (SST 09560-10010), install spark plug tube gasket in No. 1 valve cover.

***CAUTION: Ensure spark plug tube gasket is installed evenly in No. 1 valve cover.***

**13)** Apply sealant on cylinder head at both edges of half-circular seals at front of cylinder head and on exhaust camshaft rear camshaft bearing cap-to-cylinder head surface.

**14)** Install No. 1 valve cover and gasket. Tighten retaining bolts to specification in sequence. *See Fig. 8.* See TORQUE SPECIFICATIONS table at end of article. To install remaining components, reverse removal procedure.

# 1991 ENGINES
# 2.4L 4-Cylinder – Previa (Cont.)

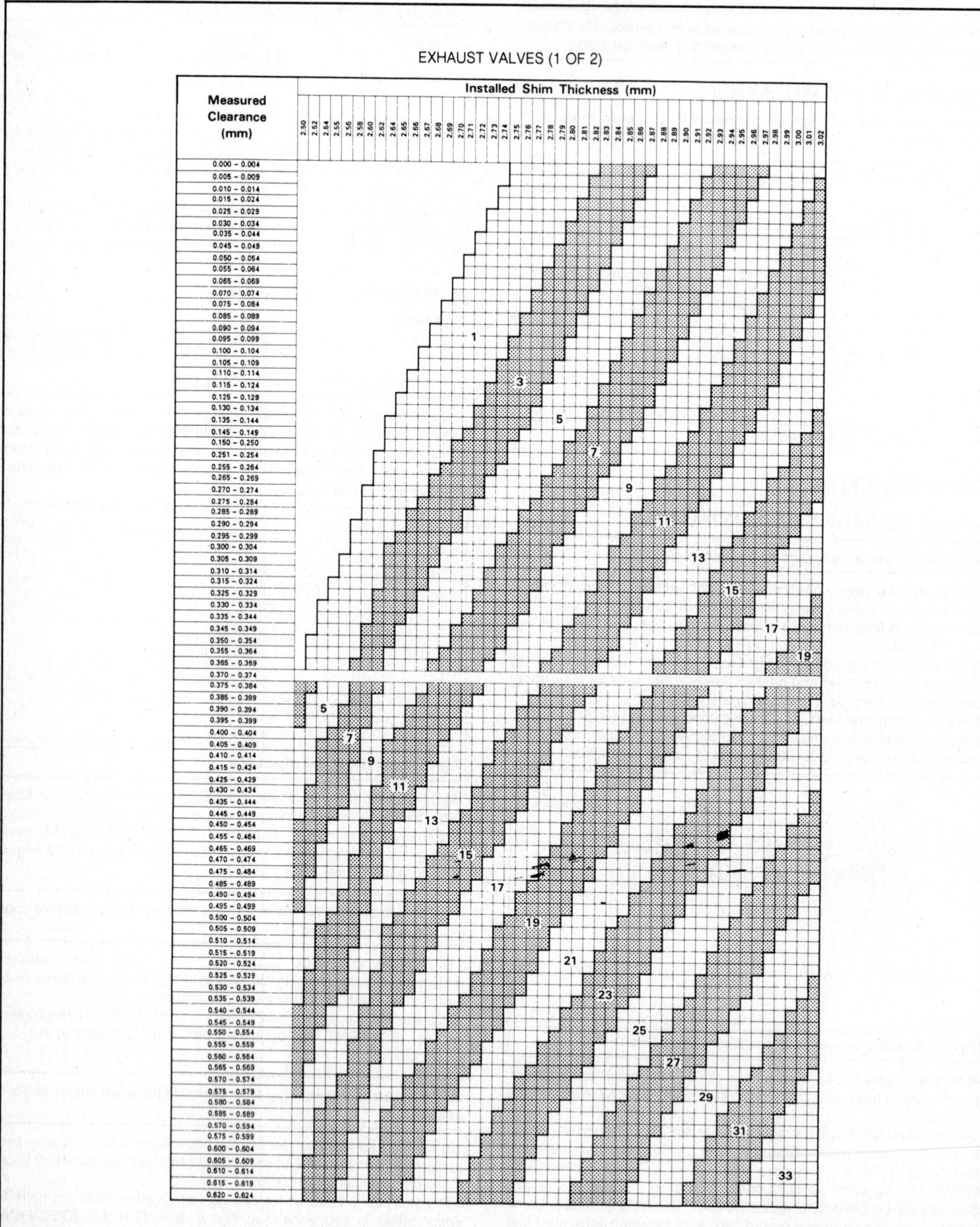


91F17892

Courtesy of Toyota Motor Sales, U.S.A., Inc.

*Fig. 4: Exhaust Valve Adjusting Shim Selection Chart (1 of 2)*

# 1991 ENGINES
## 2.4L 4-Cylinder – Previa (Cont.)

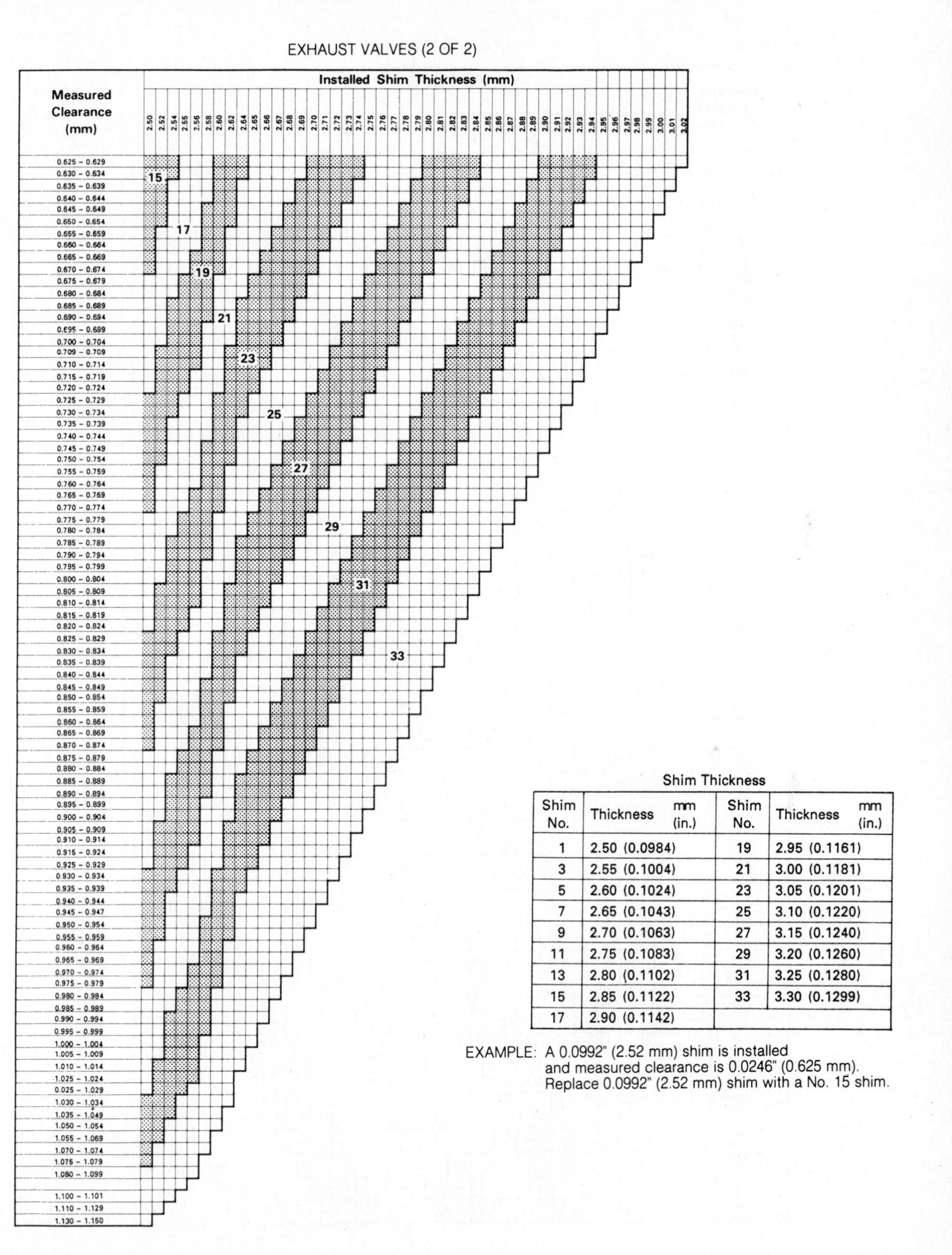


Shim Thickness

| Shim No. | Thickness mm (in.) | Shim No. | Thickness mm (in.) |
|---|---|---|---|
| 1 | 2.50 (0.0984) | 19 | 2.95 (0.1161) |
| 3 | 2.55 (0.1004) | 21 | 3.00 (0.1181) |
| 5 | 2.60 (0.1024) | 23 | 3.05 (0.1201) |
| 7 | 2.65 (0.1043) | 25 | 3.10 (0.1220) |
| 9 | 2.70 (0.1063) | 27 | 3.15 (0.1240) |
| 11 | 2.75 (0.1083) | 29 | 3.20 (0.1260) |
| 13 | 2.80 (0.1102) | 31 | 3.25 (0.1280) |
| 15 | 2.85 (0.1122) | 33 | 3.30 (0.1299) |
| 17 | 2.90 (0.1142) | | |

EXAMPLE: A 0.0992" (2.52 mm) shim is installed and measured clearance is 0.0246" (0.625 mm). Replace 0.0992" (2.52 mm) shim with a No. 15 shim.

91G17893 91H17894

Courtesy of Toyota Motor Sales, U.S.A., Inc.

***Fig. 5: Exhaust Valve Adjusting Shim Selection Chart (2 of 2)***

# 1991 ENGINES
# 2.4L 4-Cylinder – Previa (Cont.)

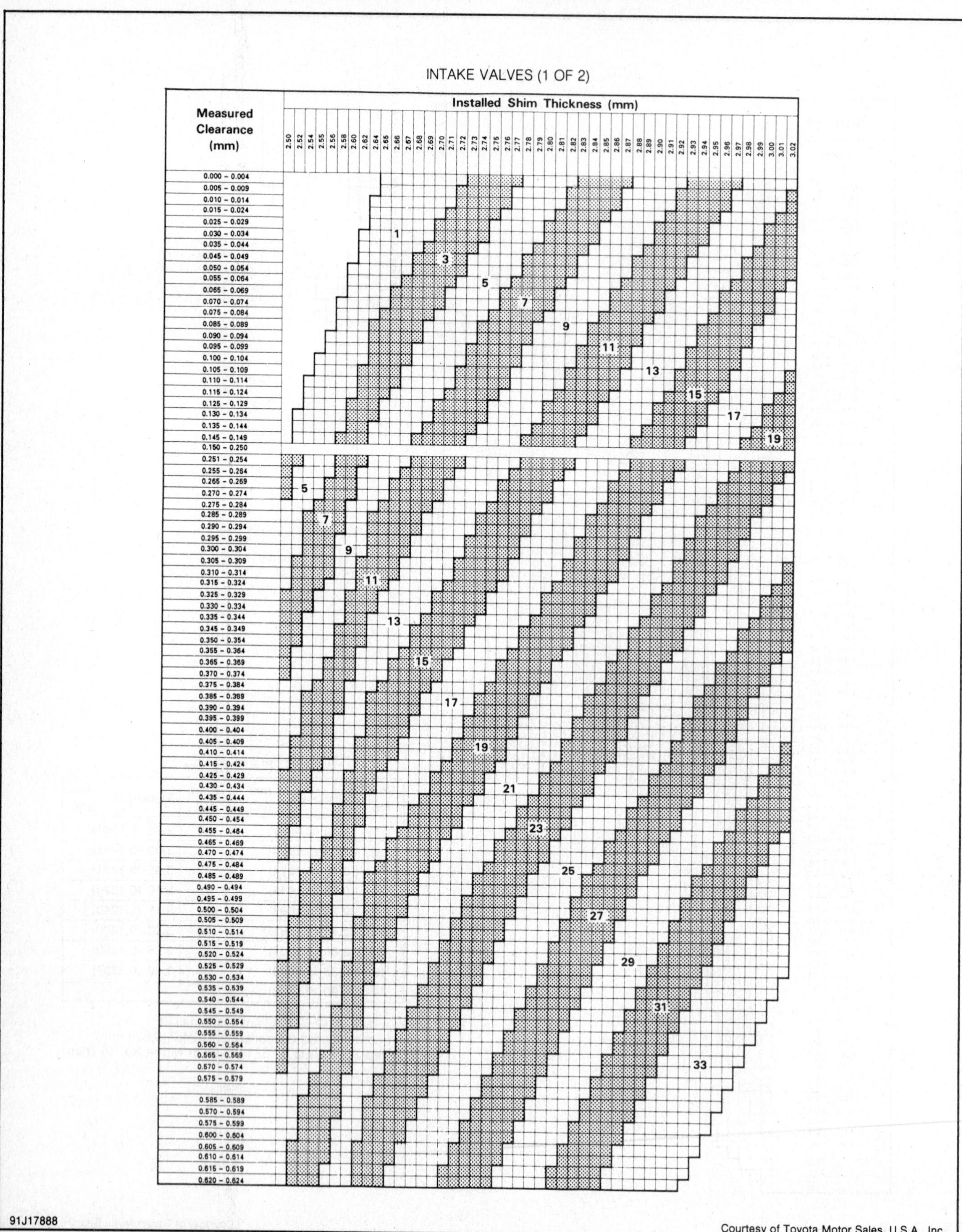


Courtesy of Toyota Motor Sales, U.S.A., Inc.

***Fig. 6: Intake Valve Adjusting Shim Selection Chart (1 of 2)***

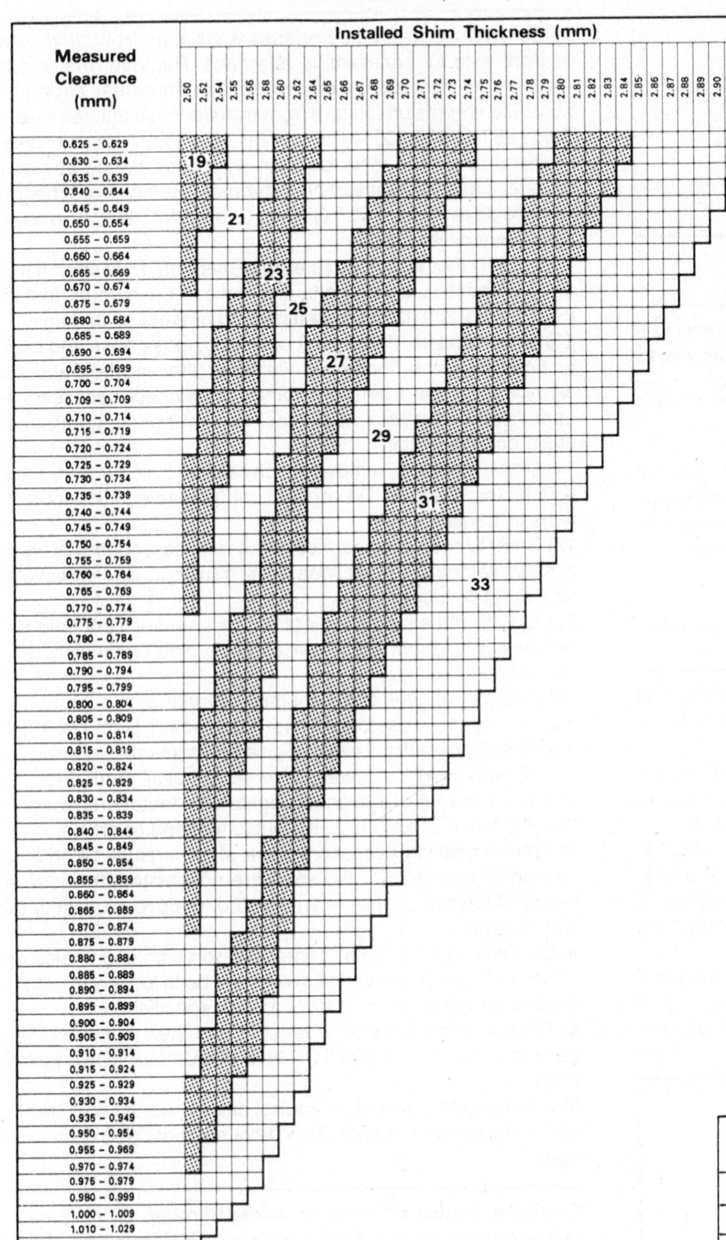


EXAMPLE: A 0.0992" (2.52 mm) shim is installed and measured clearance is 0.0246" (0.625 mm). Replace 0.0992" (2.52 mm) shim with a No. 19 shim.

Shim Thickness

| Shim No. | Thickness mm (in.) | Shim No. | Thickness mm (in.) |
|---|---|---|---|
| 1 | 2.50 (0.0984) | 19 | 2.95 (0.1161) |
| 3 | 2.55 (0.1004) | 21 | 3.00 (0.1181) |
| 5 | 2.60 (0.1024) | 23 | 3.05 (0.1201) |
| 7 | 2.65 (0.1043) | 25 | 3.10 (0.1220) |
| 9 | 2.70 (0.1063) | 27 | 3.15 (0.1240) |
| 11 | 2.75 (0.1083) | 29 | 3.20 (0.1260) |
| 13 | 2.80 (0.1102) | 31 | 3.25 (0.1280) |
| 15 | 2.85 (0.1122) | 33 | 3.30 (0.1299) |
| 17 | 2.90 (0.1142) | | |

91A17889 91D17890

Courtesy of Toyota Motor Sales, U.S.A., Inc.

*Fig. 7: Intake Valve Adjusting Shim Selection Chart (2 of 2)*

# 1991 ENGINES
# 2.4L 4-Cylinder – Previa (Cont.)

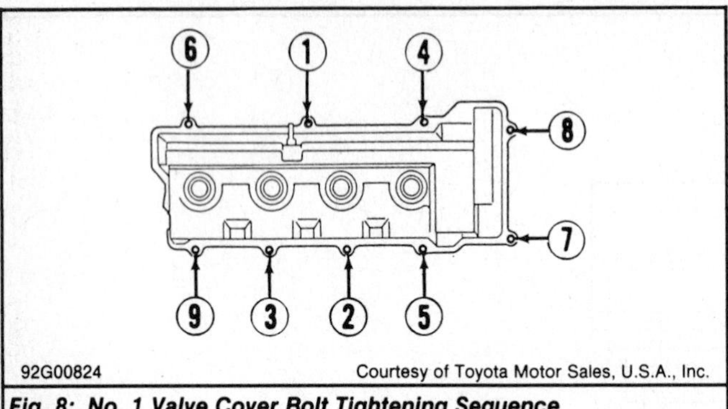


*Fig. 8: No. 1 Valve Cover Bolt Tightening Sequence*

## REMOVAL & INSTALLATION

***NOTE: For reassembly reference, label all electrical connectors, vacuum hoses and fuel lines before removal. Also place mating marks on engine hood and other major assemblies before removal.***

### FUEL PRESSURE RELEASE

With ignition off, disconnect negative battery cable. Place suitable container under fuel line. Cover fuel line connection with shop towel. Slowly loosen fuel line connection and release fuel pressure. Once pressure is released, fuel system components can be removed.

### ENGINE

***NOTE: Remove engine and transmission as an assembly.***

**Removal – 1)** Disconnect negative battery cable. Release fuel pressure. See FUEL PRESSURE RELEASE under REMOVAL & INSTALLATION.

**2)** Raise and support vehicle. Drain cooling system and engine oil. Remove lower engine covers. Place reference mark on accessory drive shaft flange at crankshaft pulley for reassembly reference.

**3)** Remove alternator and A/C compressor drive belts. Remove accessory drive shaft pulley. *See Fig. 2.* Install a 12-mm bolt in end of accessory drive shaft, near cooling fan and tighten nut. *See Fig. 2.* Using 12 mm bolt, rotate engine for access to accessory drive shaft flange-to-crankshaft pulley retaining bolts.

**4)** Remove the 3 accessory drive flange-to-crankshaft pulley retaining bolts "A" and washers. DO NOT remove retaining bolts "B". *See Fig. 9.* Remove the 3 accessory drive shaft front flange retaining bolts. *See Fig. 9.*

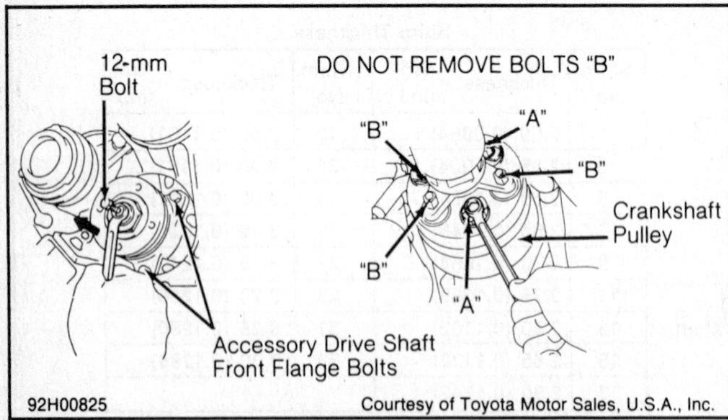


*Fig. 9: Identifying Accessory Drive Shaft Front Flange Bolts*

**5)** Rotate accessory drive shaft and front housing clockwise approximately 60 degrees and slide accessory drive shaft forward and disconnect from crankshaft pulley.

**6)** Disconnect radiator and heater hoses from the engine. Disconnect automatic engine oil feeder system return pipe. Disconnect control cable at throttle body.

***CAUTION: Accessory drive shaft front flange bolts must be removed for shaft removal. DO NOT allow drive shaft to hang with front flange bolts installed. Accessory drive shaft must be stored in a horizontal position to prevent damage to flexible couplings, located at each end of the drive shaft.***

**7)** On 4WD models, place reference mark on front drive shaft flange at front axle for reassembly reference. Remove retaining bolts and washers at front axle. Remove drive shaft center support retaining bolts. Disengage drive shaft from transfer case and remove. Install Oil Plug (SST 09325-20010) in transfer case to prevent oil leakage.

**8)** Place reference mark on rear drive shaft flange at rear axle and transfer case for reassembly reference. Remove retaining bolts and remove drive shaft. Install Oil Plug (SST 09325-20010) in transfer case to prevent oil leakage.

**9)** On 2WD models, place reference mark on drive shaft flange at rear axle. Remove retaining bolts and remove drive shaft. Install Oil Plug (SST 09325-20010) in transmission to prevent oil leakage.

**10)** On all models, disconnect coolant by-pass hose and brake booster hose from the floor pipe. Remove retaining bolt and disconnect wires and hoses from floor panel. Disconnect necessary air intake hoses, vacuum hoses, fuel lines, coolant hoses, control cables and electrical connections.

**11)** On M/T models, remove clutch release cylinder from transmission with hoses attached. Disconnect control cable and electrical connections at transmission.

**12)** On A/T models, disconnect oil cooler lines, control cables and necessary electrical connections from transmission. Remove transmission dipstick tube.

**13)** On all models, disconnect oxygen sensor connectors. Remove retaining bolts/nuts and front exhaust pipe containing the catalytic converter.

**14)** Support engine and transmission with jack assembly. Remove engine mount crossmember-to-body bolts. Remove transmission mount-to-body bolts. Lower engine and transmission from vehicle.

**Installation – 1)** To install, reverse removal procedure. Ensure all reference marks are aligned. Tighten all fasteners to specification. See TORQUE SPECIFICATIONS table at end of article.

**2)** When installing accessory drive shaft, ensure flexible couplings, located at each end of the shaft are not twisted or squeezed out of shape. If flexible couplings are twisted, remove accessory drive shaft and reinstall.

**3)** On 4WD models, install center support with drain holes on outside of center support facing downward and bolts loosely installed. Tighten drive shaft flange bolts at front axle to specification.

**4)** Ensure center support is straight and then tighten center support bolts to specification. See TORQUE SPECIFICATIONS table at end of article.

**5)** On all models, adjust all control cables. Adjust fluid levels. Ensure bolt is removed from accessory drive shaft or cooling fan will be damaged.

***CAUTION: Engine oil must be added through oil filler cap, located below driver's seat. If engine oil is added through automatic engine oil feeder system reservoir under the hood, oil will not feed into the engine.***

## CYLINDER HEAD & MANIFOLDS

***NOTE: Manufacturer recommends engine removal for servicing cylinder head. Intake and exhaust manifold procedure given is with cylinder head removed.***

**Removal – 1)** Remove engine. See ENGINE under REMOVAL & INSTALLATION. Disconnect electrical connections and remove engine wire. *See Fig. 10.* Remove retaining bolts, No. 2 valve cover and gasket.

# 1991 ENGINES
# 2.4L 4-Cylinder – Previa (Cont.)

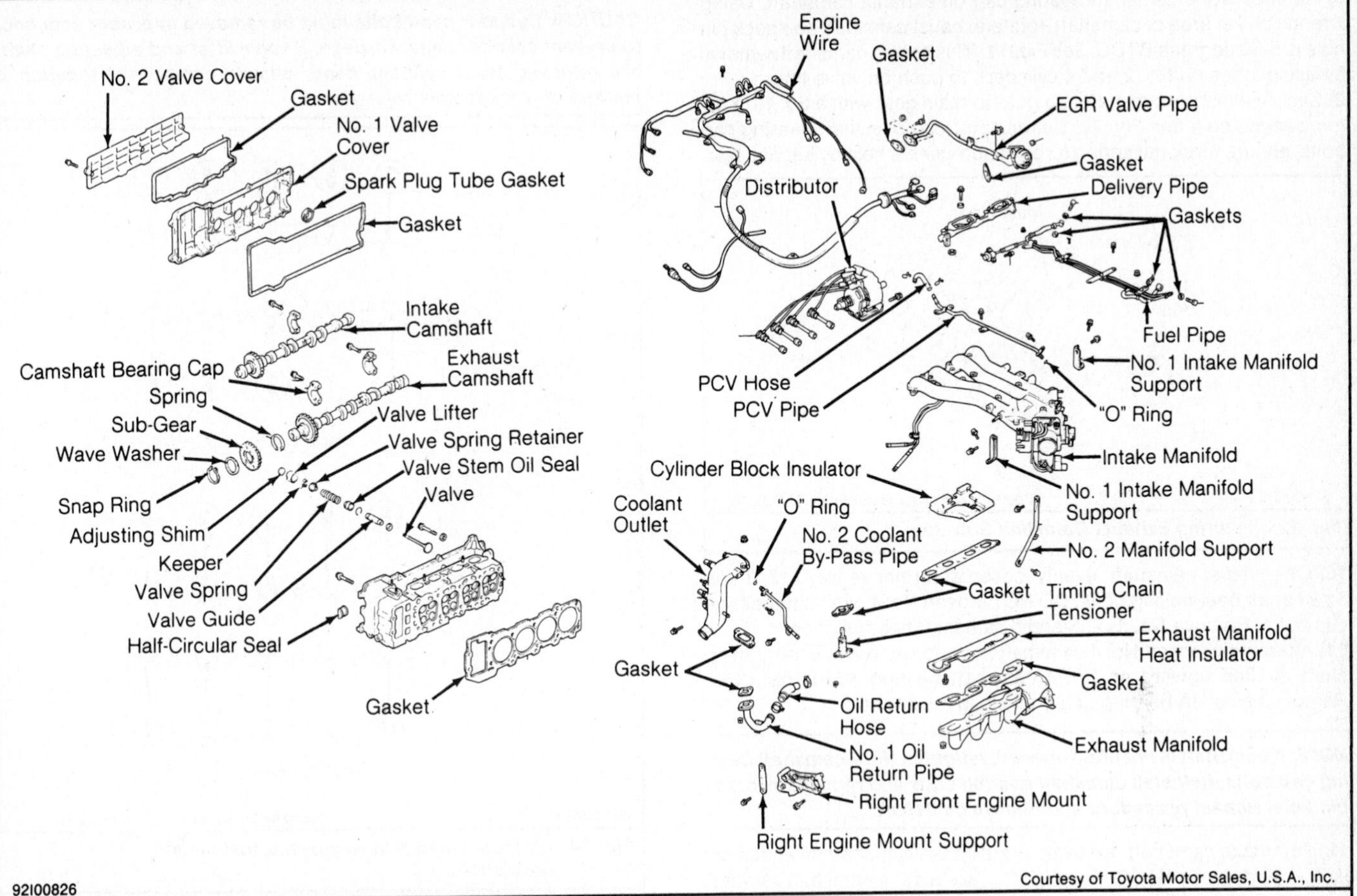

No. 2 Valve Cover
Gasket
No. 1 Valve Cover
Spark Plug Tube Gasket
Gasket
Intake Camshaft
Camshaft Bearing Cap
Exhaust Camshaft
Spring
Sub-Gear
Wave Washer
Valve Lifter
Valve Spring Retainer
Valve Stem Oil Seal
Valve
Snap Ring
Adjusting Shim
Keeper
Valve Spring
Valve Guide
Half-Circular Seal
Gasket
Engine Wire
Gasket
EGR Valve Pipe
Gasket
Distributor
Delivery Pipe
Gaskets
Fuel Pipe
No. 1 Intake Manifold Support
PCV Hose
PCV Pipe
"O" Ring
Intake Manifold
Cylinder Block Insulator
No. 1 Intake Manifold Support
Coolant Outlet
"O" Ring
No. 2 Coolant By-Pass Pipe
No. 2 Manifold Support
Gasket
Timing Chain Tensioner
Exhaust Manifold Heat Insulator
Gasket
Gasket
Oil Return Hose
No. 1 Oil Return Pipe
Exhaust Manifold
Right Front Engine Mount
Right Engine Mount Support

92I00826
Courtesy of Toyota Motor Sales, U.S.A., Inc.

**Fig. 10: Exploded View of Cylinder Head & Components**

**2)** Remove distributor. Disconnect hoses and remove EGR valve pipe. Remove union bolts and gaskets from delivery pipe and cold start injector. Remove pressure regulator from delivery pipe.

**3)** Remove retaining bolts and fuel pipe. *See Fig. 10.* Remove coolant outlet with No. 2 coolant by-pass pipe. Remove PCV hose. Remove retaining bolts, spacers, delivery pipe and insulators.

**4)** Disconnect coolant hose at water pump. Remove coolant pipe retaining bolt at front cover. Remove retaining bolts, No. 1 intake manifold supports and No. 2 manifold support. *See Fig. 10.*

**5)** Remove retaining bolts/nuts, intake manifold and gasket. Remove cylinder block insulator. Remove retaining nuts, exhaust manifold and gasket. Remove right engine mount support. *See Fig. 10.* Remove right front engine mount.

**6)** Remove exhaust manifold heat insulator and No. 1 oil return pipe. Remove No. 1 valve cover and gasket. Place reference mark on camshaft sprocket and No. 1 timing chain.

***CAUTION: DO NOT rotate engine or allow No. 1 timing chain to disengage from crankshaft sprocket.***

***NOTE: Camshaft bearing caps are numbered for location except rear bearing cap on exhaust camshaft. The No. 1 bearing cap is at timing chain end of cylinder head. Intake camshaft bearing caps are stamped with an "I" and exhaust are stamped with an "E". Arrow on bearing cap points toward timing chain end of engine.***

***CAUTION: Camshafts must be properly positioned to lift camshaft straight from cylinder head to prevent damage to cylinder head and camshaft. DO NOT pry or force camshafts from cylinder head or component damage will result.***

**7)** Hold camshaft and remove camshaft sprocket bolt. Remove retaining nuts, timing chain tensioner and gasket. Remove camshaft sprocket with No. 1 timing chain, allowing camshaft sprocket and timing chain to rest on slipper and damper. *See Fig. 22.*

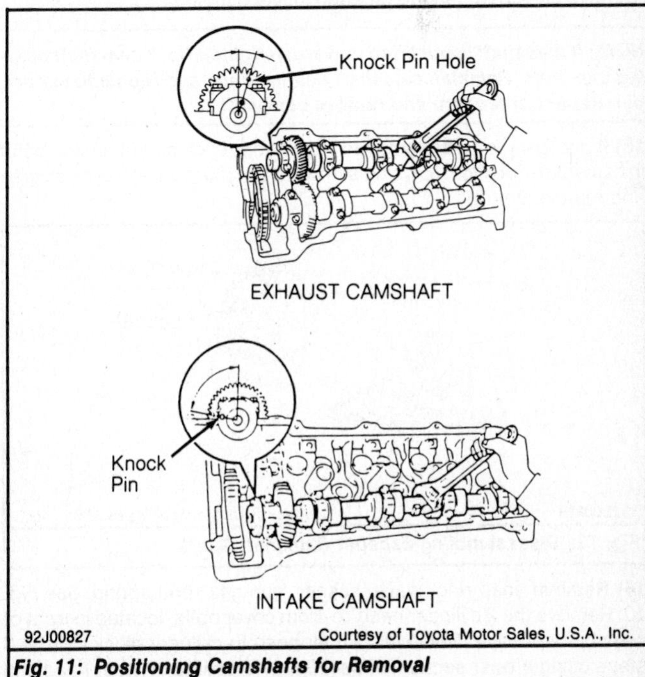


**Fig. 11: Positioning Camshafts for Removal**

# 1991 ENGINES
# 2.4L 4-Cylinder – Previa (Cont.)

**8)** Remove No. 6 camshaft bearing cap on exhaust camshaft. Using wrench on flat area of camshaft, rotate exhaust camshaft so knock pin hole is 5-30 degrees BTDC. *See Fig. 11.* This aids in camshaft removal by using lobes on No. 2 and 4 cylinders to push on valve lifters.
**9)** Secure exhaust camshaft sub-gear to main gear with a 6 x 1.0 x 18 mm service bolt. *See Fig. 12.* Before removing camshaft bearing cap bolts, ensure torsional spring force of sub-gear is held by service bolt.

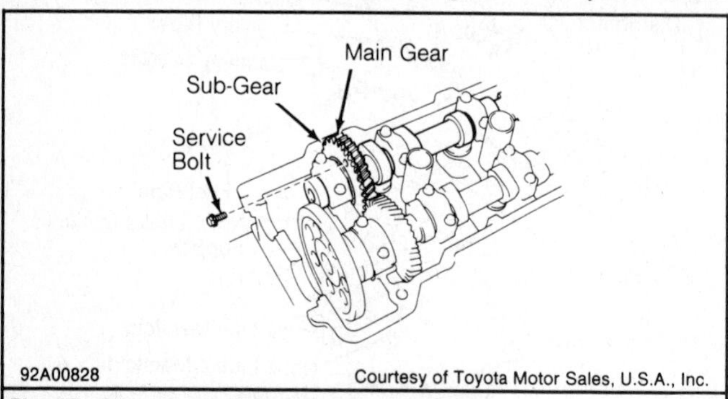


***Fig. 12: Securing Exhaust Camshaft Sub-Gear***

**10)** On exhaust camshaft, evenly loosen and remove No. 1, 2, 3 and 5 camshaft bearing cap bolts. DO NOT loosen No. 4 camshaft bearing cap bolts. Remove No. 1, 2, 3 and 5 camshaft bearing caps.
**11)** Alternately loosen No. 4 camshaft bearing cap bolts. Ensure camshaft is lifted upward as No. 4 camshaft bearing cap is removed. Remove camshaft bearing cap and exhaust camshaft.

***NOTE: If camshaft is not lifted upward, retighten No. 4 camshaft bearing cap bolts. Reinstall camshaft bearing caps and reposition knock pin hole. Repeat procedure and remove camshaft.***

**12)** For intake camshaft removal, rotate intake camshaft so knock pin is 75-100 degrees BTDC. *See Fig. 11.* This aids in camshaft removal by using lobes on No. 1 and 3 cylinders to push on valve lifters.
**13)** Evenly loosen and remove No. 1, 2, 4 and 5 camshaft bearing cap bolts. DO NOT loosen No. 3 camshaft bearing cap bolts. Remove No. 1, 2, 4 and 5 camshaft bearing caps.
**14)** Alternately loosen No. 3 camshaft bearing cap bolts. Ensure camshaft is lifted upward as No. 3 camshaft bearing cap is removed. Remove camshaft bearing cap and intake camshaft.

***NOTE: If camshaft is not lifted upward, retighten No. 3 camshaft bearing cap bolts. Reinstall camshaft bearing caps and reposition knock pin. Repeat procedure and remove camshaft.***

**15)** If sub-gear is to be removed from exhaust camshaft, install bolts in camshaft. *See Fig. 13.* Using screwdriver, rotate sub-gear clockwise and remove bolt "B".

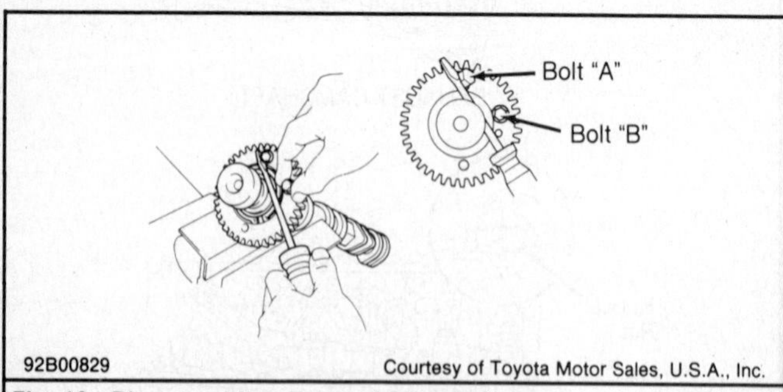


***Fig. 13: Disassembling Exhaust Camshaft Gears***

**16)** Remove snap ring, wave washer, sub-gear and spring. *See Fig. 10.* Remove the 2 cylinder head-to-front cover bolts, located in front of camshaft sprocket. Remove cylinder head-to-cylinder block bolts in 3 steps using proper sequence. *See Fig. 14.* Remove cylinder head and gasket.

***CAUTION: Cylinder head bolts must be removed in proper sequence to prevent cylinder head warpage. If valve lifter and adjusting shims are removed from cylinder head, ensure component location is marked for reassembly reference.***

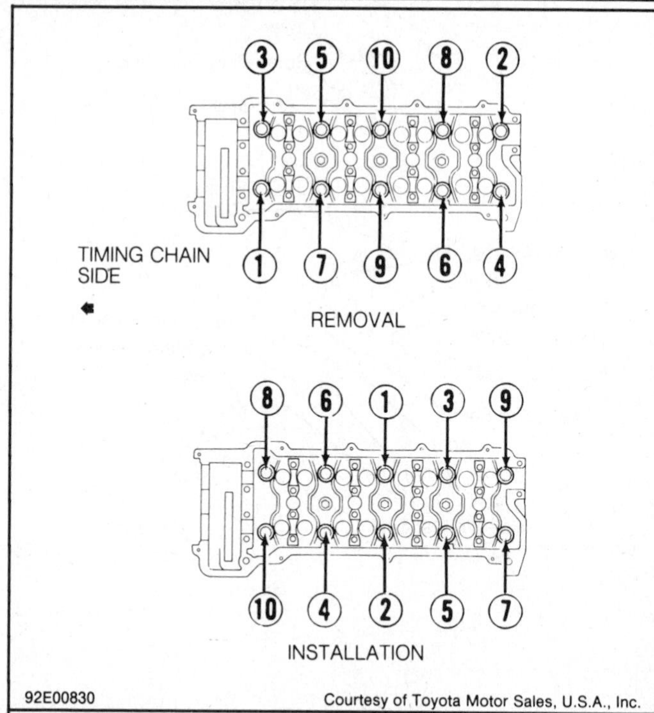


***Fig. 14: Cylinder Head Bolt Removal & Installation Sequence***

**Inspection – 1)** Inspect cylinder head warpage at cylinder block and manifold areas. Replace cylinder head if warpage exceeds specification. See CYLINDER HEAD table under ENGINE SPECIFICATIONS at end of article.
**2)** Check camshaft journal diameter, lobe height and runout. Replace camshaft if not within specification. See CAMSHAFT table under ENGINE SPECIFICATIONS at end of article.
**3)** Install camshaft in cylinder head. Using Plastigage, check camshaft oil clearance with camshaft bearing cap bolts tightened to specification. See TORQUE SPECIFICATIONS table at end of article. Replace camshaft and/or cylinder head if oil clearance is not within specification. See CAMSHAFT table under ENGINE SPECIFICATIONS at end of article.
**4)** Check camshaft end play with camshaft bearing cap bolts tightened to specification. Replace camshaft and/or cylinder head if end play is not within specification. See CAMSHAFT table under ENGINE SPECIFICATIONS at end of article.
**5)** Using dial indicator, measure gear backlash with camshafts installed. Replace camshaft if gear backlash exceeds specification. See CAMSHAFT table under ENGINE SPECIFICATIONS at end of article.
**6)** Using caliper, measure width between ends of sub-gear retaining spring. Replace spring if distance exceeds .886-.902" (22.50-22.91 mm).
**7)** Inspect intake and exhaust manifolds for warpage at cylinder head surface. Replace manifold if warpage exceeds .016" (.41 mm).
**8)** Ensure timing chain tensioner plunger moves freely when pawl is pushed downward. Perform STEP 1. *See Fig. 15.* Release pawl and ensure plunger locks and will not move. Perform STEP 2. *See Fig. 15.* Replace timing chain tensioner if defective.
**Installation – 1)** Apply sealant where front cover contacts cylinder block. *See Fig. 16.* DO NOT apply excessive sealant or sealant may block the oil hole.

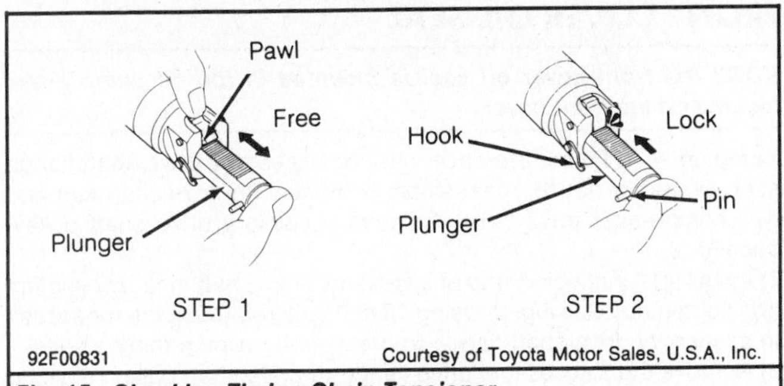


*Fig. 15: Checking Timing Chain Tensioner*

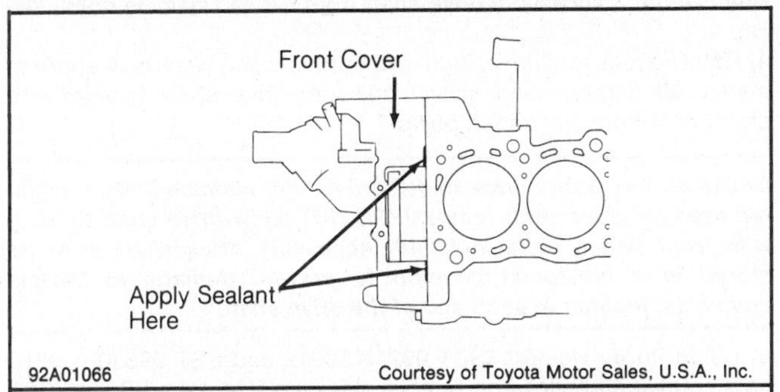


*Fig. 16: Applying Sealant at Front Cover & Cylinder Block*

**2)** Install gasket and cylinder head. Coat cylinder head bolt threads and seat area below head of bolt with oil and install. Tighten cylinder head-to-cylinder block bolts to specification in sequence. *See Fig. 14.* See TORQUE SPECIFICATIONS table at end of article.

**3)** Install cylinder head-to-front cover bolts and tighten to specification. See TORQUE SPECIFICATIONS table at end of article.

**4)** Install spring, sub-gear, wave washer and snap ring on exhaust camshaft. Install bolt "A" in camshaft sub-gear. *See Fig. 13.* Rotate sub-gear clockwise and align holes of camshaft main gear and sub-gear. Install bolt "B".

**5)** Coat thrust surfaces of camshafts with grease. To install intake camshaft, rotate camshaft so knock pin is 75-100 degrees BTDC and install in cylinder head. Perform STEP 1. *See Fig. 17.* The No. 1 and 3 cylinder camshaft lobes should contact the valve lifter.

**6)** Install camshaft bearing caps in original location with arrow pointing toward timing chain side of engine.

***CAUTION: Ensure intake camshaft bearing caps are stamped with the letter "I" and installed in numerical sequence, with arrow pointing toward timing belt end of engine.***

**7)** Apply engine oil to threads and area below head of camshaft bearing cap bolts and install. Tighten bolts to specification using proper sequence. *See Fig. 18.* See TORQUE SPECIFICATIONS table at end of article.

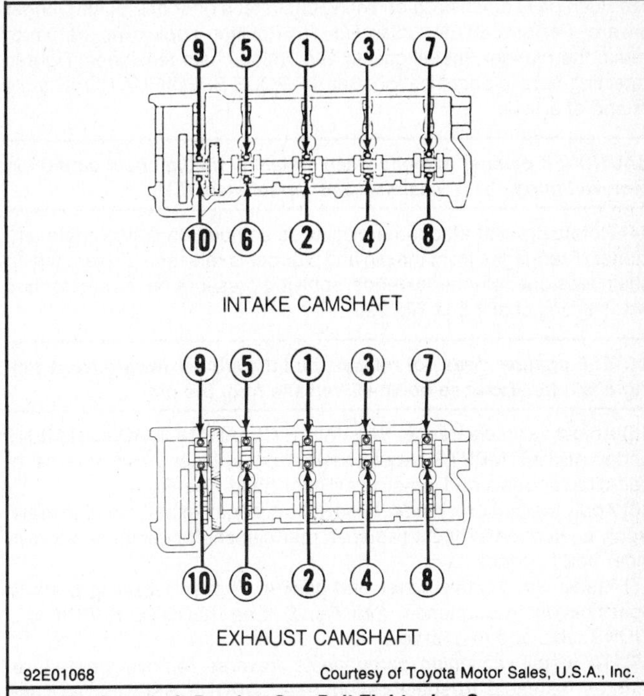


*Fig. 18: Camshaft Bearing Cap Bolt Tightening Sequence*

**8)** To install exhaust camshaft, rotate intake camshaft so knock pin is 5-30 degrees BTDC. Perform STEP 2. *See Fig. 17.* Install exhaust camshaft so installation marks are engaged with intake camshaft. Perform STEP 3. *See Fig. 17.* Ensure No. 2 and 4 cylinder camshaft lobes are contacting the valve lifter.

***CAUTION: Ensure exhaust camshaft bearing caps are stamped with the letter "E" and installed in numerical sequence, with arrow pointing toward timing belt end of engine.***

**9)** Install all camshaft bearing caps except No. 6. Ensure camshaft bearing caps are installed in original location with arrow pointing toward timing chain side of engine.

**10)** Apply engine oil to threads and area below head of camshaft bearing cap bolts and install. Tighten bolts to specification in steps using proper sequence. *See Fig. 18.* See TORQUE SPECIFICATIONS table at end of article.

**11)** Remove bolts from camshaft gear. Apply sealant on No. 6 camshaft bearing cap-to-cylinder head contact surface and install. Install camshaft bearing cap bolts and tighten to specification. See TORQUE SPECIFICATIONS table at end of article.

**12)** Ensure reference mark on camshaft sprocket and No. 1 timing chain are aligned. Install camshaft sprocket on camshaft. Install retaining bolt and tighten to specification. See TORQUE SPECIFICATIONS table at end of article.

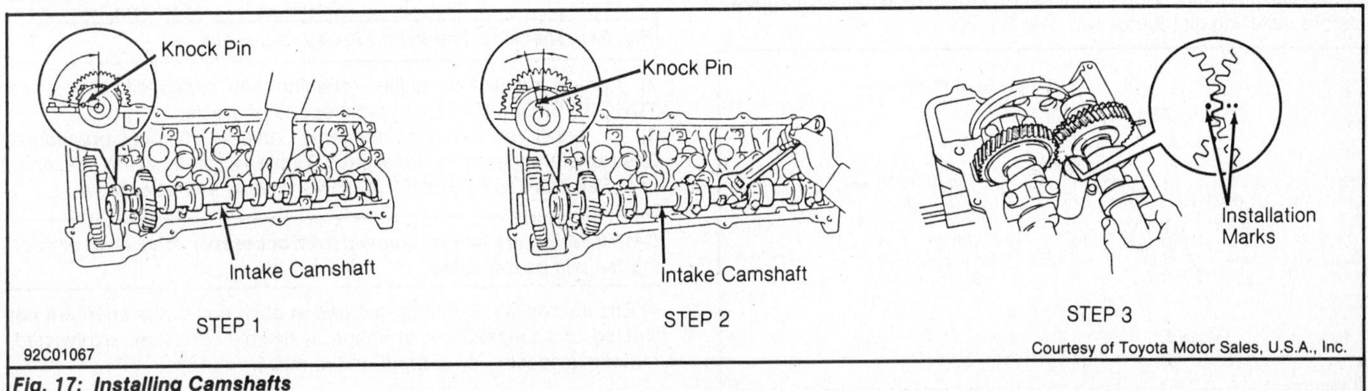


*Fig. 17: Installing Camshafts*

# 1991 ENGINES
# 2.4L 4-Cylinder – Previa (Cont.)

**13)** Push pawl downward on timing chain tensioner and push plunger inward. Perform STEP 1. *See Fig. 15.* Position hook over the pin to retain the plunger. Install gasket and timing chain tensioner. Tighten retaining nuts to specification. See TORQUE SPECIFICATIONS table at end of article.

***CAUTION: If plunger extends when installing timing chain tensioner, remove timing chain tensioner and repeat step 13).***

**14)** Rotate crankshaft counterclockwise so hook on timing chain tensioner disengages from the pin and plunger is released. Ensure timing chain tensioner plunger extends, applying pressure on the slipper and No. 1 timing chain. *See Fig. 22.*

***NOTE: If plunger does not release, pull the slipper toward No. 1 timing chain tensioner so hook will release from the pin.***

**15)** Adjust valve clearance. See VALVE CLEARANCE ADJUSTMENT under ADJUSTMENTS. Apply sealant on cylinder head surface of half-circular seals and install in cylinder head. *See Fig. 10.*
**16)** Apply sealant on cylinder head at both edges of half-circular seals. Apply sealant on exhaust camshaft rear camshaft bearing cap-to-cylinder head surface.
**17)** Install No. 1 valve cover and gasket. Tighten retaining bolts to specification in sequence. *See Fig. 8.* See TORQUE SPECIFICATIONS table at end of article.
**18)** To install remaining components, reverse removal procedure. Tighten fasteners to specification. See TORQUE SPECIFICATIONS table at end of article. Coolant outlet bolts must be tighten according to location. *See Fig. 19.*

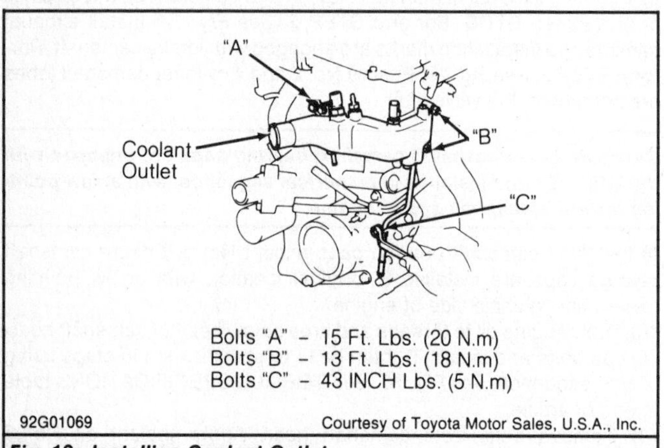


***Fig. 19: Installing Coolant Outlet***

**19)** Before installing distributor, rotate engine so No. 1 cylinder is at TDC on compression stroke. Ensure timing mark on crankshaft pulley aligns with "0" mark on front cover.
**20)** Install new "O" ring on distributor and coat with engine oil. Align cutout portion of coupling with groove on distributor housing. *See Fig. 20.* Install distributor. Apply Seal Packing (08826-00080) to distributor before installing distributor cap. *See Fig. 20.*

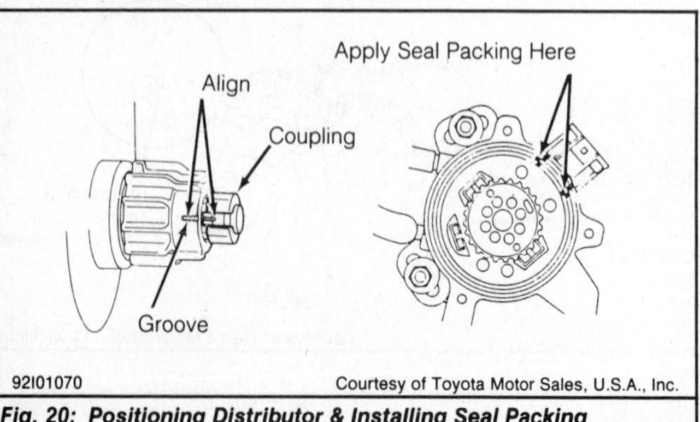


***Fig. 20: Positioning Distributor & Installing Seal Packing***

## FRONT COVER OIL SEAL

***NOTE: The front cover oil seal is mounted in the oil pump cover located on the front cover.***

**Removal – 1)** Place reference mark on accessory drive shaft flange at crankshaft pulley for reassembly reference. Remove alternator and A/C compressor drive belts. Remove accessory drive shaft pulley. *See Fig. 2.*
**2)** Install a 12-mm bolt in end of accessory drive shaft, near cooling fan and tighten nut. *See Fig. 2.* Using 12-mm bolt, rotate engine for access to accessory drive shaft flange-to-crankshaft pulley retaining bolts.
**3)** Remove the 3 accessory drive flange-to-crankshaft pulley retaining bolts "A" and washers. DO NOT remove retaining bolts "B". *See Fig. 9.* Remove the 3 accessory drive shaft front flange retaining bolts. *See Fig. 9.*
**4)** Rotate accessory drive shaft and front housing clockwise approximately 60 degrees and slide accessory drive shaft forward and disconnect from crankshaft pulley.

***CAUTION: Accessory drive shaft front flange retaining bolts must be removed for drive shaft removal. DO NOT allow drive shaft to hang with front flange bolts installed. Accessory drive shaft must be stored in a horizontal position to prevent damage to flexible couplings, located at each end of the drive shaft.***

**5)** Using Pulley Holders (SST 09213-58012 and SST 09330-00021), hold crankshaft pulley and remove retaining bolt. Using Puller (SST 09950-20017), remove crankshaft pulley.
**6)** Using knife, cut seal lip from front cover oil seal. Pry oil seal from oil pump cover on the front cover. Use care not to damage front cover and crankshaft surfaces.
**Installation – 1)** Coat oil seal lip with grease. Using Oil Seal Installer (SST 09309-36010), install oil seal in oil pump cover on the front cover. Install crankshaft pulley.

***CAUTION: Flat areas on crankshaft pulley must engage with oil pump and keyway must align with key in the crankshaft. Ensure a gap of .118-.157" (3.00-4.00 mm) exists between end of crankshaft and crankshaft pulley. See Fig. 21.***

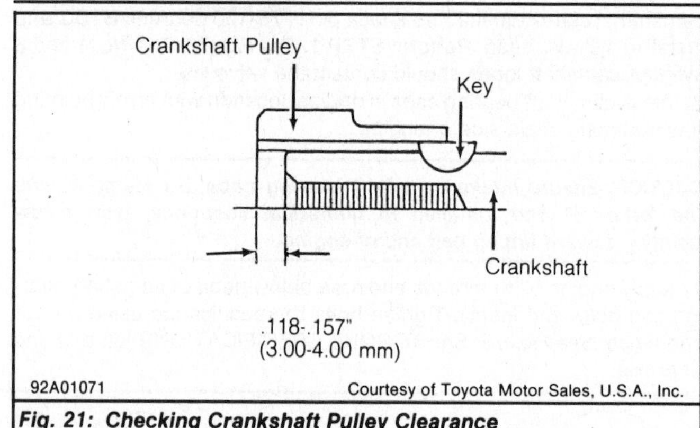


***Fig. 21: Checking Crankshaft Pulley Clearance***

**2)** Tighten crankshaft pulley retaining bolt to specification. See TORQUE SPECIFICATIONS table at end of article.
**3)** To install remaining components, reverse removal procedure. Ensure reference marks are aligned. Tighten all fasteners to specification. See TORQUE SPECIFICATIONS table at end of article.

***CAUTION: Ensure bolt is removed from accessory drive shaft or cooling fan will be damaged.***

**4)** Ensure flexible couplings, located at each end of the shaft are not twisted or squeezed out of shape. If flexible couplings are twisted, remove accessory drive shaft and reinstall.

## TIMING CHAIN

***NOTE: Manufacturer recommends cylinder head removal when servicing timing chain, as cylinder head gasket fits on top of front cover.***

**Removal – 1)** Remove cylinder head. See CYLINDER HEAD & MANIFOLDS under REMOVAL & INSTALLATION. Using Pulley Holders (SST 09213-58012 and SST 09330-00021), hold crankshaft pulley and remove retaining bolt. Using Puller (SST 09950-20017), remove crankshaft pulley.

**2)** Remove support bracket, left front engine mount, oil pressure switch and dipstick. *See Fig. 22.* Remove ventilation case and dipstick tube.

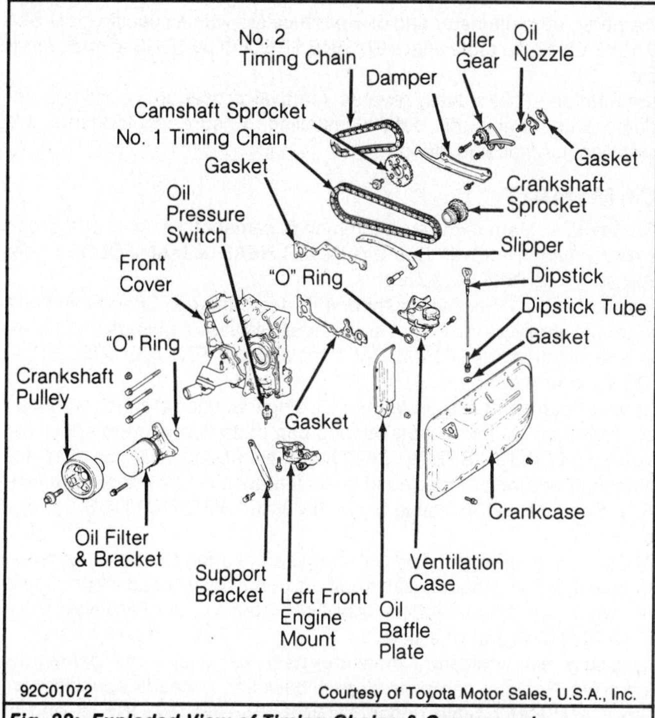


***Fig. 22: Exploded View of Timing Chains & Components***

**3)** Remove retaining bolts/nuts, crankcase and oil baffle plate. *See Fig. 22.* Remove oil filter bracket and "O" ring from front cover. Remove the 3 cylinder block-to-front cover retaining bolts. These bolts go from the front of cylinder block into the rear of front cover.

**4)** Remove retaining bolts/nuts, front cover and gasket. Remove No. 1 timing chain, slipper, damper, oil nozzle and gasket. *See Fig. 22.* Loosen 2 retaining bolts on No. 2 timing chain guide, located on left side of No. 2 timing. *See Fig. 24.* Push outward on No. 2 timing chain near timing chain guide and tighten lower retaining. This positions timing chain guide for timing chain removal.

**5)** Remove idler gear retaining bolts. Remove No. 2 timing chain and idler gear. Remove crankshaft sprockets (if necessary).

**Inspection – 1)** Inspect component for damage. Ensure idler gear rotates smoothly. Using micrometer, check amount of wear on slipper and damper. Replace slipper or damper if wear exceeds .039" (.99 mm).

**2)** Using caliper, measure length of timing chains between 16 links on No. 1 timing chain or 18 links on No. 2 timing chain. Perform STEP 1. *See Fig. 23.*

**3)** Replace timing chain if length exceeds specification. See TIMING CHAIN & SPROCKET SPECIFICATIONS table.

**4)** Wrap timing chain around each sprocket. Using caliper, measure Outside Diameter (O.D.) of timing chain. Perform STEP 2. *See Fig. 23.* Replace timing chain and sprockets or idler gear if O.D. measurement is less than specification. See TIMING CHAIN & SPROCKET SPECIFICATIONS table.

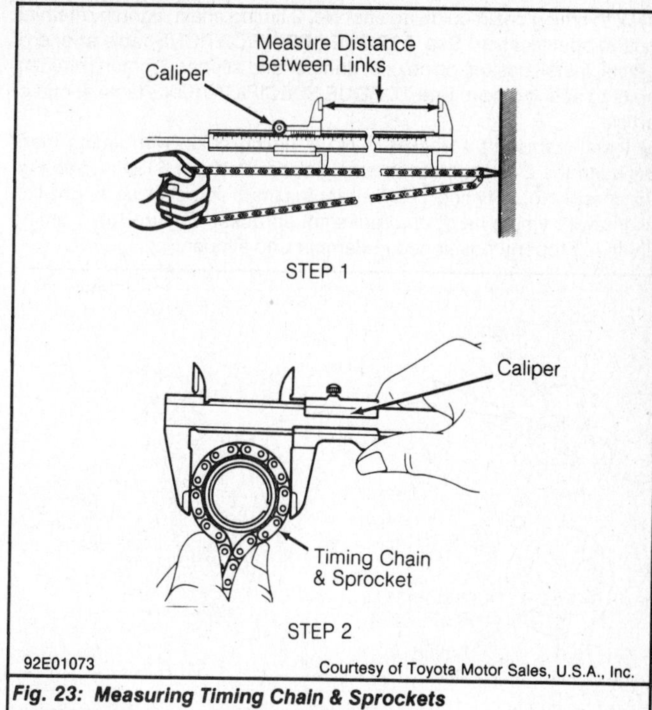


***Fig. 23: Measuring Timing Chain & Sprockets***

***TIMING CHAIN & SPROCKET SPECIFICATIONS***

| Application | In. (mm) |
|---|---|
| Sprocket & Timing Chain O.D | |
| No. 1 Timing Chain | |
| Camshaft Sprocket | 4.480 (113.79 mm) |
| Crankshaft Sprocket | 2.339 (59.41 mm) |
| No. 2 Timing Chain | |
| Crankshaft Sprocket | 2.752 (69.90 mm) |
| Idler Gear | 2.244 (57.00 mm) |
| Timing Chain Length | |
| No. 1 Timing Chain | 5.772 (146.60 mm) |
| No. 2 Timing Chain | 5.531 (140.49 mm) |

**Installation – 1)** Rotate crankshaft so key is at 12 o'clock position. Install crankshaft sprockets (if removed). It may be necessary to use Sprocket Installer (SST 09608-35014) and hammer to drive sprocket onto crankshaft.

**2)** Install No. 2 timing chain on idler gear. Install No. 2 timing chain and idler gear. Ensure timing chain properly engages crankshaft sprocket. Install and tighten idler gear retaining bolts to specification. See TORQUE SPECIFICATIONS table at end of article.

**3)** Loosen bolt on No. 2 timing chain guide, allowing timing guide to apply pressure on No. 2 timing chain. Press on No. 2 timing chain near timing guide and release. Ensure spring in timing guide maintains pressure on timing chain. *See Fig. 24.*

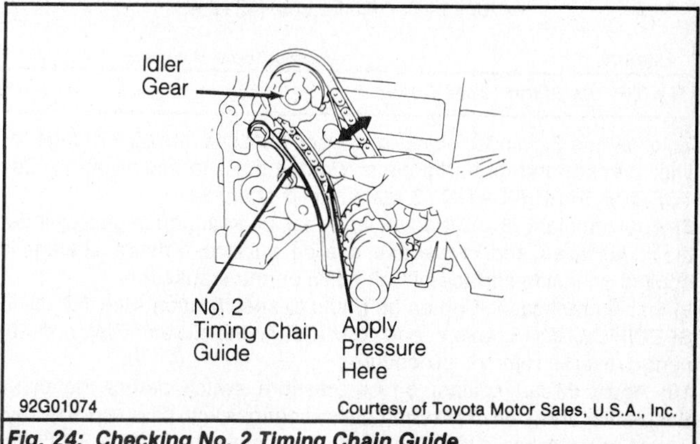


***Fig. 24: Checking No. 2 Timing Chain Guide***

# 1991 ENGINES
# 2.4L 4-Cylinder – Previa (Cont.)

**4)** With timing chain guide against No. 2 timing chain, tighten retaining bolt to specification. See TORQUE SPECIFICATIONS table at end of article. Install gasket, oil nozzle, damper and slipper. Tighten retaining bolts to specification. See TORQUE SPECIFICATIONS table at end of article.

**5)** Install camshaft sprocket in No. 1 timing chain with timing mark between the 2 bright links on timing chain. Perform STEP 1. *See Fig. 25.* Install No. 1 timing chain on crankshaft sprocket so bright link aligns with timing mark on crankshaft sprocket. Ensure No. 1 timing chain is properly positioned in damper and slipper.

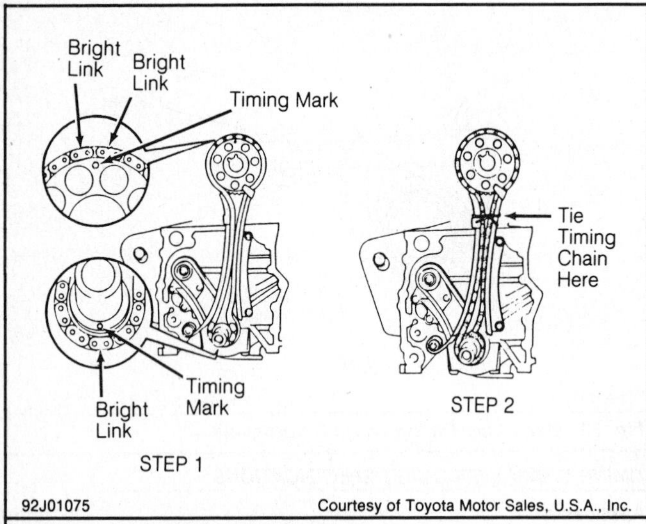


*Fig. 25: Installing No. 1 Timing Chain*

**6)** Rotate camshaft sprocket to remove slack in timing chain. Securely tie timing chain to hold components in position. Perform STEP 2. *See Fig. 25.* Install gasket and front cover. Tighten front cover-to-cylinder block bolts to specification. *See Fig. 26.*

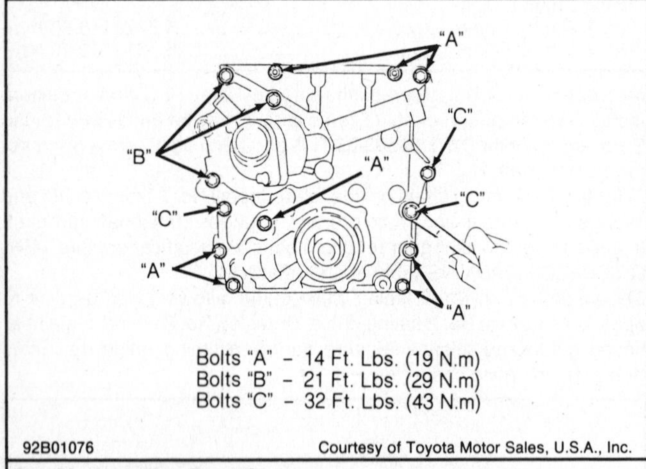


*Fig. 26: Installing Front Cover*

**7)** Install the 3 cylinder block-to-front cover bolts. Install "O" rings, oil filter bracket and oil baffle plate. Tighten bolts to specification. See TORQUE SPECIFICATIONS table at end of article.

**8)** Apply sealant at front cover and rear oil seal housing-to-cylinder block surfaces and crankcase sealing surface. Ensure sealant is applied on inside surface of bolt holes on the crankcase.

**9)** Install crankcase. Tighten bolt/nuts to specification. See TORQUE SPECIFICATIONS table at end of article. To install remaining components, reverse removal procedure.

**10)** Apply thread sealant on oil pressure switch before installing. Ensure flat areas on crankshaft pulley engages with oil pump and keyway aligns with key in the crankshaft. Ensure a gap of .118-.157" (3.00-4.00 mm) exists between end of crankshaft and crankshaft pulley. *See Fig. 21.*

**11)** Tighten all bolts/nuts to specification. See TORQUE SPECIFICATIONS table at end of article.

## VALVE LIFTER

**Removal** – Camshaft must be removed for lash adjuster removal. Manufacturer recommends camshaft removal along with cylinder head removal. See CYLINDER HEAD & MANIFOLDS under REMOVAL & INSTALLATION. With camshaft removed, remove valve lifter and adjusting shims.

***CAUTION: Mark component location for reassembly reference. Components must be installed in original location.***

**Inspection** – Inspect components for damage. Ensure lash adjuster diameter, bore diameter and oil clearance are within specification. See VALVE LIFTERS table under ENGINE SPECIFICATIONS at end of article.

**Installation** – To install, reverse removal procedure. Coat components with engine oil before installing. Ensure components are installed in original location.

## CAMSHAFT

**Removal** – Manufacturer recommends camshaft removal along with cylinder head removal. See CYLINDER HEAD & MANIFOLDS under REMOVAL & INSTALLATION.

**Inspection – 1)** Inspect components for damage. Check camshaft journal diameter, lobe height and runout. Replace camshaft if not within specification. See CAMSHAFT table under ENGINE SPECIFICATIONS at end of article.

**2)** Install camshaft in cylinder head. Using Plastigage, check camshaft oil clearance with camshaft bearing cap bolts tightened to specification See TORQUE SPECIFICATIONS table at end of article. Replace camshaft and/or cylinder head if oil clearance is not within specification. See CAMSHAFT table under ENGINE SPECIFICATIONS at end of article.

**3)** Check camshaft end play with camshaft bearing cap bolts tightened to specification. Replace camshaft and/or cylinder head if end play is not within specification. See CAMSHAFT table under ENGINE SPECIFICATIONS at end of article.

**4)** Using dial indicator, measure gear backlash with camshafts installed. Replace camshaft if gear backlash exceeds specification. See CAMSHAFT table under ENGINE SPECIFICATIONS at end of article.

**Installation** – Coat camshaft with engine oil before installing. Install camshaft using installation procedure listed under cylinder head and manifolds. See CYLINDER HEAD & MANIFOLDS under REMOVAL & INSTALLATION.

## REAR CRANKSHAFT OIL SEAL

***NOTE: A one-piece rear crankshaft oil seal is mounted in oil seal retainer on rear of cylinder block.***

**Removal & Installation – 1)** Remove transmission, clutch assembly (if equipped) and flywheel/drive plate. Using knife, cut seal lip from rear crankshaft oil seal. Pry oil seal from oil seal retainer. Use care not to damage oil seal retainer and crankshaft surfaces.

**2)** To install, coat seal lip with grease. Using Oil Seal Installer (SST 09223-56010), install oil seal in oil seal retainer. To install remaining components, reverse removal procedure. Tighten flywheel/drive plate bolts to specification. See TORQUE SPECIFICATIONS table at end of article.

## WATER PUMP

**Removal – 1)** Drain cooling system. Disconnect heater hose and radiator outlet hose. Remove retaining bolts, oil filter and bracket with "O" ring from front cover. *See Fig. 22.*

**2)** Disconnect coolant hose at water pump. Remove retaining bolts, water pump assembly and "O" ring from front cover. Remove retaining bolts and separate water pump and gasket from coolant inlet housing. *See Fig. 27.*

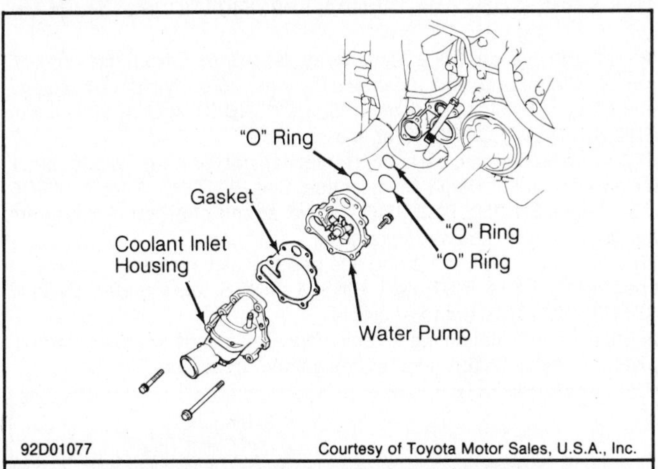


***Fig. 27: Exploded View of Water Pump & Components***

**Installation - 1)** Install water pump on coolant inlet housing using new gasket. Tighten retaining bolts to specification. See TORQUE SPECIFICATIONS table at end of article.

**2)** Install new "O" rings on front cover. Install water pump and tighten retaining bolts to specification. *See Fig. 28.* To install remaining components, reverse removal procedure. Tighten bolts to specification. See TORQUE SPECIFICATIONS table at end of article. Fill cooling system.

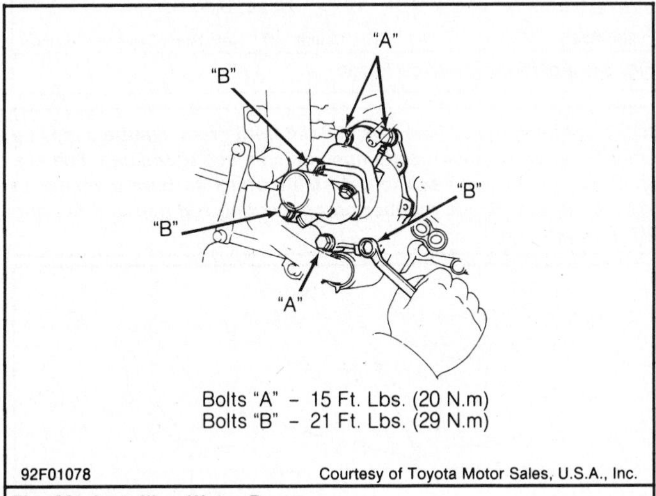


***Fig. 28: Installing Water Pump***

## OIL PAN

**Removal & Installation - 1)** Drain engine oil. Remove retaining bolts, oil level sensor and gasket from oil pan. Remove oil pan retaining bolts/nuts and oil pan. It may be necessary to use Seal Cutter (SST 09032-00100) to cut seal between oil pan and cylinder block.

**2)** To install, ensure sealing surfaces are clean. Apply bead of sealant at center of oil pan sealing surface between bolt/nut holes and on inside of the bolt/nut holes.

**3)** Install oil pan. Install and tighten bolts/nuts to specification. See TORQUE SPECIFICATIONS table at end of article. Install oil level sensor using new gasket. Tighten bolts to specification. Fill crankcase with oil.

***CAUTION: Engine oil must be added through oil filler cap, located below driver's seat. If engine oil is added through automatic engine oil feeder system reservoir under the hood, the oil will not feed into the engine.***

## OVERHAUL

### CYLINDER HEAD

**Cylinder Head - 1)** Inspect cylinder head warpage at cylinder block and manifold areas. Replace cylinder head if warpage exceeds specification. See CYLINDER HEAD table under ENGINE SPECIFICATIONS at end of article.

**2)** Install camshaft in cylinder head. Using Plastigage, check camshaft oil clearance with camshaft bearing cap bolts tightened to specification See TORQUE SPECIFICATIONS table at end of article. Replace camshaft and/or cylinder head if oil clearance is not within specification. See CAMSHAFT table under ENGINE SPECIFICATIONS at end of article.

**3)** Ensure valve lifter bore diameter is within specification. See VALVE LIFTERS table under ENGINE SPECIFICATIONS at end of article.

**4)** When using new cylinder head, spark plug tubes must be installed. Apply Sealant (08833-00070) to spark plug tube hole in cylinder head. Using press, install spark plug tube so protrusion from top of spark plug tube to cylinder head surface is 1.69-1.73" (42.9-43.9 mm). *See Fig. 29.*

***CAUTION: Measure protrusion several times while installing spark plug tube to prevent pressing spark plug tube to far into the cylinder head.***

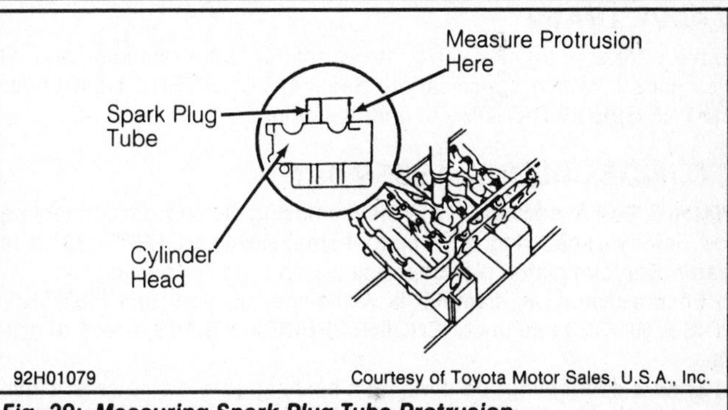


***Fig. 29: Measuring Spark Plug Tube Protrusion***

**Valve Springs -** Ensure valve spring free length, pressure and out-of-square are within specification. See VALVES & VALVE SPRINGS table under ENGINE SPECIFICATIONS at end of article.

**Valve Stem Oil Seals -** Lubricate valve stem oil seal with engine oil. Install valve stem oil seals using Oil Seal Installer (SST 09201-41020). Exhaust valve stem oil seals are Black and intake valve stem oil seals are Brown.

**Valve Guides - 1)** Check valve stem-to-valve guide clearance. See CYLINDER HEAD table under ENGINE SPECIFICATIONS at end of article. Ensure valve stem diameter is within specification. Valve guide can be replaced if clearance exceeds specification.

**2)** To replace valve guide, install old valve in top of valve guide approximately .31" (7.9 mm). Using hammer, tap on old valve and break off the top of the valve guide. *See Fig. 30.*

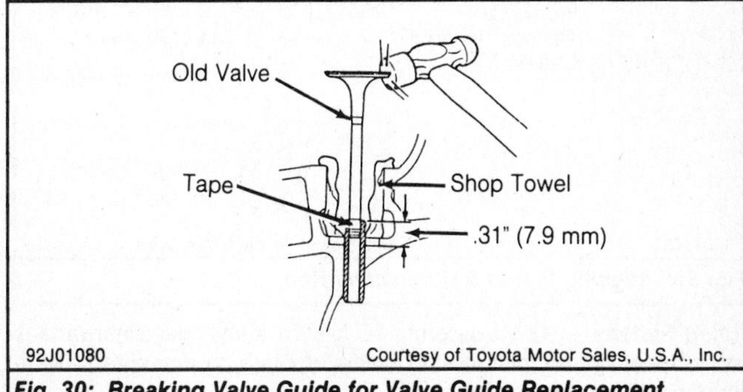


***Fig. 30: Breaking Valve Guide for Valve Guide Replacement***

# 1991 ENGINES
# 2.4L 4-Cylinder – Previa (Cont.)

**3)** Heat cylinder head to 194°F (90°C). Using hammer and Valve Guide Remover/Installer (SST 09201-70010), drive valve guide from camshaft side of cylinder head.

**4)** Using calipers, measure cylinder head valve guide bore Inside Diameter (I.D.) If cylinder head valve guide bore is .4331-.4341" (11.000-11.026 mm), a standard valve guide can be used.

**5)** If cylinder head valve guide bore is greater than .4341" (11.026 mm), machine bore to .4350-.4361" (11.049-11.077 mm) for oversize valve guide installation.

**6)** Using hammer and valve guide remover/installer, drive new valve guide in cylinder head from camshaft side of cylinder head until snap ring contacts cylinder head. Using .236" (6.00 mm) reamer, ream valve guide to obtain specified valve stem-to-guide oil clearance. See CYLINDER HEAD table under ENGINE SPECIFICATIONS at end of article.

**Valve Seat** – Ensure valve seat angle and seat width are within specification. See CYLINDER HEAD table under ENGINE SPECIFICATIONS at end of article. Valve seat replacement information not available from manufacturer.

**Valves** – Ensure minimum refinish length, stem diameter, and valve margin are within specification. See VALVES & VALVE SPRINGS table under ENGINE SPECIFICATIONS at end of article.

**Seat Correction Angles** – Use 30-degree and 45-degree stones to lower valve seat contact area. Use 45-degree and 60-degree stones to raise valve seat contact area.

## VALVE TRAIN

**Valve Lifters** – Ensure valve lifter diameter, bore diameter and oil clearance is within specification. See VALVE LIFTERS table under ENGINE SPECIFICATIONS at end of article.

## CYLINDER BLOCK ASSEMBLY

**Piston & Rod Assembly** – **1)** When removing piston from connecting rod, remove snap ring from piston. Heat piston to 176°F (80°C) in water. Remove piston pin. Separate piston from connecting rod.

**2)** Ensure piston pin diameter is within specification. See PISTONS, PINS & RINGS table under ENGINE SPECIFICATIONS at end of article.

**3)** Ensure connecting rod piston pin bushing bore diameter is within specification. See CONNECTING RODS table under ENGINE SPECIFICATIONS at end of article. Bushing can be replaced in connecting rod if bore diameter is not within specification. Bushing must be honed to obtain correct piston pin clearance.

***NOTE: With piston at 176°F (80°C), piston pin should be able to be pressed into piston using thumb pressure.***

**4)** To reassemble, install piston with front mark on top of piston and connecting rod aligned. *See Fig. 31.*

**5)** Install new snap ring in piston. Heat piston to 176°F (80°C) in water. Install piston pin and remaining snap ring.

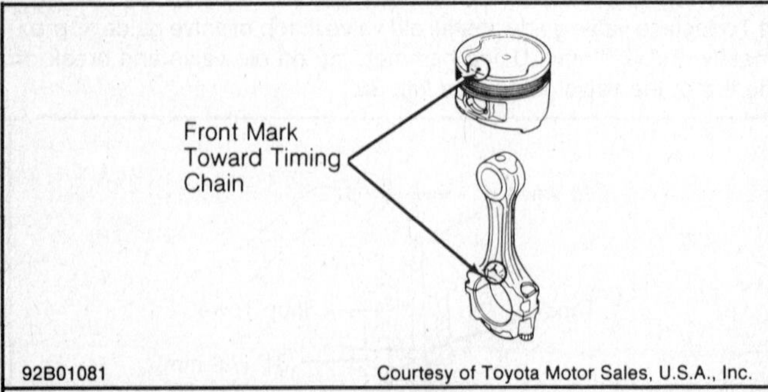


***Fig. 31: Aligning Piston & Connecting Rod***

**Fitting Pistons** – **1)** To determine if piston-to-cylinder clearance is within specification, piston skirt diameter must be measured at 90-degree angle to piston pin.

**2)** Measure piston diameter at 2.106" (53.49 mm) from bottom of piston skirt. Piston diameter must be within specification. See PISTONS, PINS & RINGS table under ENGINE SPECIFICATIONS at end of article.

**3)** Measure cylinder bore diameter at .39" (9.9 mm) from top and bottom of cylinder bore and at center of cylinder bore. Cylinder bore diameter must be within specification. See CYLINDER BLOCK table under ENGINE SPECIFICATIONS at end of article.

**4)** Determine piston clearance. Replace piston or bore cylinder block if clearance is not within specification. See PISTONS, PINS & RINGS table under ENGINE SPECIFICATIONS at end of article. Pistons are available in .020" (.50 mm) oversize.

**Piston Rings** – **1)** Ensure ring end gap and side clearance are within specification. See PISTONS, PINS & RINGS table under ENGINE SPECIFICATIONS at end of article.

**2)** Ensure identification marks on compression rings are toward top of piston. Position piston rings at designated areas. *See Fig. 32.*

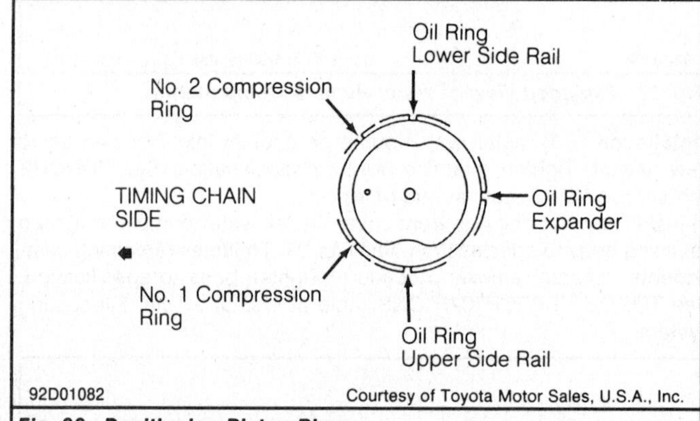


***Fig. 32: Positioning Piston Rings***

***NOTE: Connecting rod bearings of 3 different grade numbers may be used. The grade number is stamped on connecting rod cap. See Fig. 33. Grade number is used to determine crankpin bore diameter of connecting rod. Grade number on connecting rod cap and bearing MUST match.***

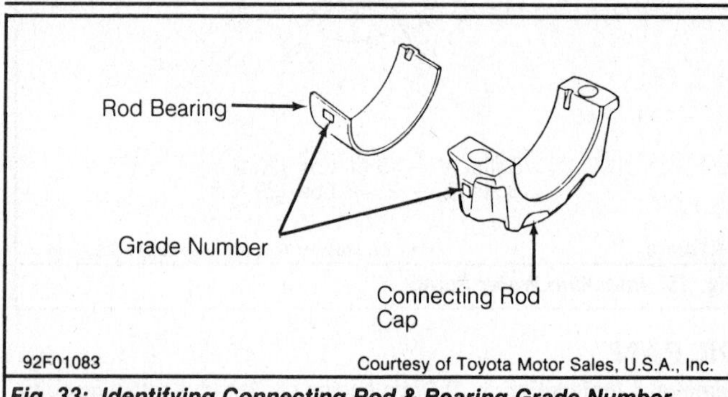


***Fig. 33: Identifying Connecting Rod & Bearing Grade Number***

**Rod Bearings** – **1)** Mark direction of connecting rod cap and cylinder number before disassembly. Connecting rod must be installed with front mark toward timing chain. *See Fig. 31.* Coat connecting rod bolt threads and seat area of the nut with oil before tightening to specification.

**2)** Ensure bearing oil clearance and connecting rod side play are within specification. See CRANKSHAFT, MAIN & CONNECTING ROD BEARINGS and CONNECTING RODS table under ENGINE SPECIFICATIONS at end of article.

***CAUTION: If connecting rod bearing is replaced, ensure grade number on connecting rod cap and connecting rod bearing are the same. See Fig. 33. Connecting rod bearing thickness varies with the grade number. See CONNECTING ROD BEARING SPECIFICATIONS table.***

**CONNECTING ROD BEARING SPECIFICATIONS**

| Bearing Grade Number | Bearing Thickness In. (mm) |
|---|---|
| 1 | .0583-.0585 (1.481-1.485) |
| 2 | .0585-.0586 (1.485-1.488) |
| 3 | .0587-.0588 (1.490-1.493) |

**Crankshaft & Main Bearings – 1)** Main bearing cap bolts must be loosened evenly in 3 steps using proper sequence. *See Fig. 34.* Remove main bearing caps.

***CAUTION: Note direction of main bearing cap installation. Main bearing caps are numbered for location on top of bearing cap with No. 1 at timing chain end. Arrow on main bearing cap should point toward timing chain end.***

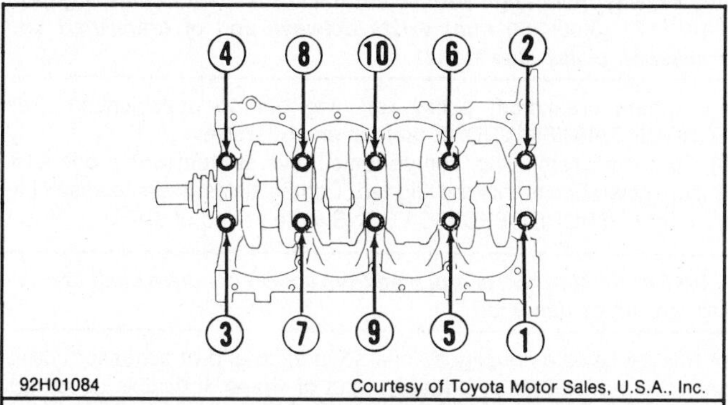


*Fig. 34: Main Bearing Bolt Removal Sequence*

**2)** Ensure main bearing journal diameter, taper, runout, and out-of-round are with within specification. See CRANKSHAFT, MAIN & CONNECTING ROD BEARINGS table under ENGINE SPECIFICATIONS at end of article.

***CAUTION: If main bearing is replaced, ensure grade number on cylinder block and main bearing are the same. See Fig. 35. Main bearing thickness varies with the grade number. See MAIN BEARING SPECIFICATIONS table.***

**MAIN BEARING SPECIFICATIONS**

| Bearing Grade Number | Bearing Thickness In. (mm) |
|---|---|
| 1 | .0782-.0783 (1.986-1.989) |
| 2 | .0784-.0785 (1.991-1.994) |
| 3 | .0785-.0787 (1.994-1.998) |

***CAUTION: Different width main bearings are used. Ensure main bearings are installed with wide main bearings on No. 1 and No. 5 main bearing journals and narrow main bearings on all other journals.***

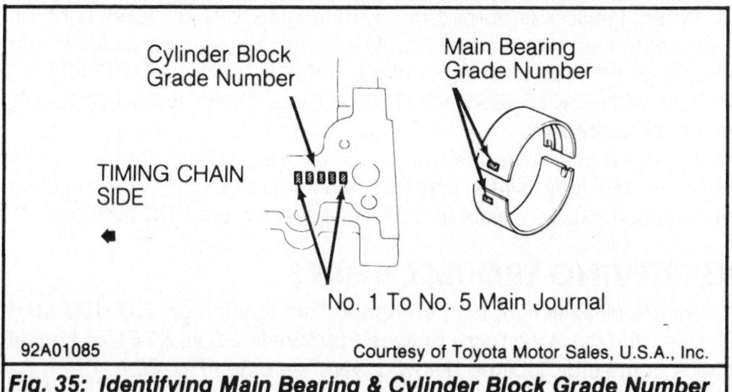


*Fig. 35: Identifying Main Bearing & Cylinder Block Grade Number*

**3)** Ensure main bearing caps are installed with No. 1 at timing chain end and arrow on main bearing cap pointing toward timing chain end. Ensure thrust bearing is installed with grooves facing toward the crankshaft.

**4)** Coat main bearing cap bolt threads and seat area of bolt with engine oil. Alternately tighten main bearing cap bolts to specification using several passes. See TORQUE SPECIFICATIONS table at end of article.

**5)** Ensure crankshaft end play is within specification. See CRANKSHAFT, MAIN & CONNECTING ROD BEARINGS table under ENGINE SPECIFICATIONS at end of article. Replace thrust bearing if crankshaft end play is not within specification.

**Thrust Bearing –** Install thrust bearing on No. 3 main bearing with grooves facing toward the crankshaft. Thrust bearing must be replaced if crankshaft end play is not within specification. See CRANKSHAFT, MAIN & CONNECTING ROD BEARINGS table under ENGINE SPECIFICATIONS at end of article.

**Cylinder Block – 1)** Inspect cylinder block deck surface warpage. Replace cylinder block if deck warpage exceeds specification. See CYLINDER BLOCK table under ENGINE SPECIFICATION at end of article.

**2)** Check cylinder bore wear, taper and out-of-round. Cylinder bore diameter is measured at .39" (9.9 mm) from top and bottom of cylinder bore and at center of cylinder bore. Bore cylinder block if not within specification. See CYLINDER BLOCK table under ENGINE SPECIFICATIONS at end of article. Pistons are available in .020" (.50 mm) oversize.

**3)** Ensure main bearing bore Inside Diameter (I.D.) is within specification with main bearing caps installed and bolts tightened to specification. See CYLINDER BLOCK table under ENGINE SPECIFICATIONS at end of article.

***NOTE: Main bearing bore I.D. will depend on main bearing bore grade number stamped on cylinder block. See Fig. 35. Main bearing bore grade number may be a 1, 2 or 3.***

# ENGINE OILING

## ENGINE LUBRICATION SYSTEM

The crankshaft driven oil pump provides pressurized lubrication for engine lubrication. *See Fig. 36.* Vehicle is equipped with a automatic engine oil feeder system which supplies additional engine oil if crankcase oil level becomes low. For additional information see AUTOMATIC ENGINE OIL FEEDER SYSTEM.

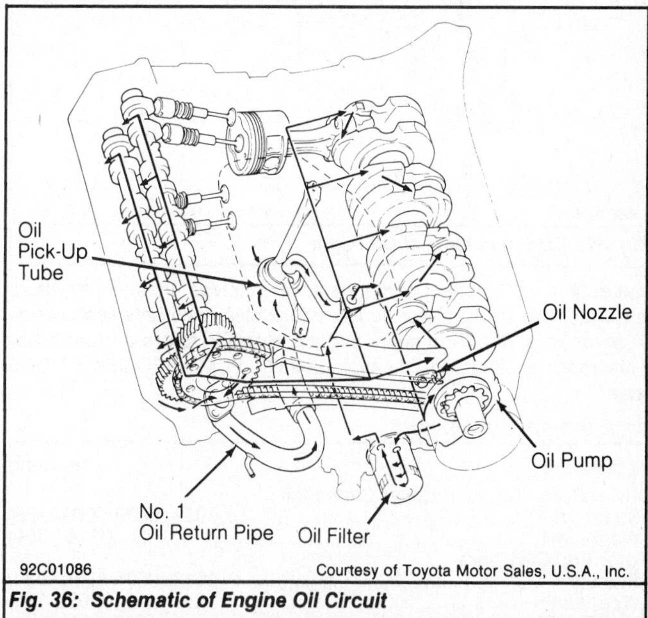


*Fig. 36: Schematic of Engine Oil Circuit*

**Crankcase Capacity –** Crankcase capacity with oil filter is 6.1 qts. (5.8L).

**Oil Pressure –** With engine at normal operating temperature, oil pressure should be at least 4.3 psi (.3 kg/cm²) at idle or at least 36 psi (2.5 kg/cm²) at 3000 RPM.

# 1991 ENGINES
# 2.4L 4-Cylinder – Previa (Cont.)

## OIL PUMP

**Removal & Disassembly – 1)** Place reference mark on accessory drive shaft flange at crankshaft pulley for reassembly reference. Remove alternator and A/C compressor drive belts. Remove accessory drive shaft pulley. *See Fig. 2.*

**2)** Install a 12 mm bolt in end of accessory drive shaft, near cooling fan and tighten nut. *See Fig. 2.* Using 12 mm bolt, rotate engine for access to accessory drive shaft flange-to-crankshaft pulley retaining bolts.

**3)** Remove the 3 accessory drive flange-to-crankshaft pulley retaining bolts "A" and washers. DO NOT remove retaining bolts "B". *See Fig. 9.* Remove the 3 accessory drive shaft front flange retaining bolts. *See Fig. 9.*

**4)** Rotate accessory drive shaft and front housing clockwise approximately 60 degrees and slide accessory drive shaft forward and disconnect from crankshaft pulley.

***CAUTION: Accessory drive shaft front flange bolts must be removed for drive shaft removal. DO NOT allow drive shaft to hang with front flange bolts installed. Accessory drive shaft must be stored in a horizontal position to prevent damage to flexible couplings, located at each end of the drive shaft.***

**5)** Using Pulley Holders (SST 09213-58012 and SST 09330-00021), hold crankshaft pulley and remove retaining bolt. Using Puller (SST 09950-20017), remove crankshaft pulley.

**6)** Remove retaining screws and oil pump cover. *See Fig. 37.* Mark component location for reassembly reference. Components must be installed in original location. Disassemble oil pump components.

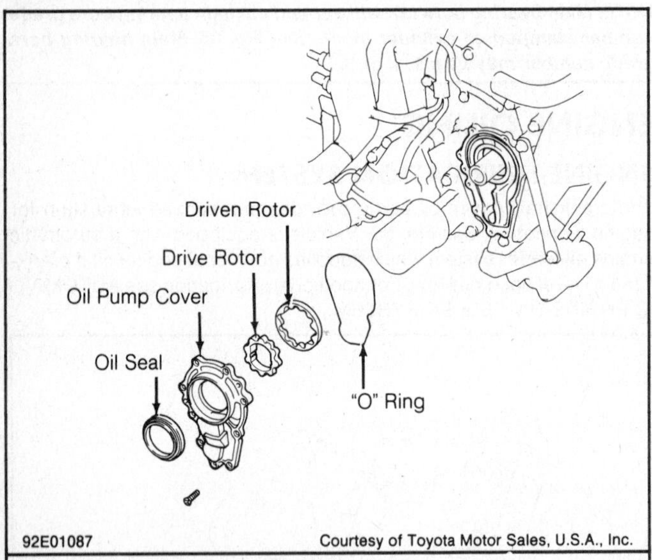


***Fig. 37: Exploded View of Oil Pump***

**Inspection – 1)** Inspect components for damage. Install both rotors in front cover. Using feeler gauge, check clearance between outside of driven rotor and front cover surface. Replace rotors or front cover if clearance exceeds specification. See OIL PUMP SPECIFICATIONS table.

***OIL PUMP SPECIFICATIONS***

| Application | In. (mm) |
|---|---|
| Driven Rotor-To-Front Cover Clearance | |
| Standard | .0039-.0069 (.099-.175) |
| Wear Limit | .0118 (.300) |
| Rotor End Clearance | |
| Standard | .0012-.0035 (.030-.089) |
| Wear Limit | .0059 (.150) |
| Rotor Tip Clearance | |
| Standard | .0043-.0094 (.109-.239) |
| Wear Limit | .0138 (.351) |

**2)** Measure rotor tip clearance between the tips of both rotors. Replace rotors if clearance exceeds specification.

**3)** Place straightedge across front cover above the rotors. Measure rotor end clearance between straightedge and surface of both rotors. Replace rotors or front cover if clearance exceeds specification. See OIL PUMP SPECIFICATIONS table.

**Reassembly & Installation – 1)** Coat all components with engine oil. To reassemble, reverse disassembly procedure. Ensure components are installed in original location.

**2)** Install oil pump cover using new "O" ring. Tighten retaining screws to specification. See TORQUE SPECIFICATIONS table at end of article.

**3)** Coat oil seal lip with grease. Using Oil Seal Installer (SST 09309-36010), install oil seal in oil pump cover (if removed). Install crankshaft pulley.

***CAUTION: Flat areas on crankshaft pulley must engage with oil pump and keyway must align with key in the crankshaft. Ensure a gap of .118-.157" (3.00-4.00 mm) exists between end of crankshaft and crankshaft pulley. See Fig. 21.***

**4)** Tighten crankshaft pulley retaining bolt to specification. See TORQUE SPECIFICATIONS table at end of article.

**5)** To install remaining components, reverse removal procedure. Ensure reference marks are aligned. Tighten all fasteners to specification. See TORQUE SPECIFICATIONS table at end of article.

***CAUTION: Ensure bolt is removed from accessory drive shaft or cooling fan will be damaged.***

**6)** Ensure flexible couplings, located at each end of accessory drive shaft are not twisted or squeezed out of shape. If flexible couplings are twisted, remove accessory drive shaft and reinstall.

## AUTOMATIC ENGINE OIL FEEDER SYSTEM

### SYSTEM OPERATION

During engine cranking, Electronic Control Unit (ECU) monitors the signal received from oil level sensor in the oil pan. If ECU determines engine oil level is low, it activates electric motor on automatic engine oil feeder system reservoir tank under the hood. Oil is pumped into oil pan until correct level is obtained.

When ignition is turned on with engine off, oil level light on instrument cluster will come on. When engine is started, oil level light should go off. If oil level decreases below specified level, oil level light will come on. If oil level light flashes, a system malfunction exists. When system malfunction exists, a trouble code will be set in the ECU memory.

The ECU contains a self-diagnostic system used to determine system trouble area by obtaining trouble codes. The ECU is located below the driver's seat.

### OIL LEVEL LIGHT

**1)** When ignition is turned on with engine off, oil level light on instrument cluster will come on. When engine is started, oil level light should go off. If oil level light did not come on, perform DIAGNOSTIC CIRCUIT CHECK or TEST NO. 1, OIL LEVEL LIGHT & ECU CIRCUIT. *See Figs. 42 and 43.*

**2)** If oil level decreases below specified level, oil level light will come on. If oil level light blinks, a system malfunction exists. When system malfunction exists, a trouble code will be set in the ECU memory.

### RETRIEVING TROUBLE CODES

**1)** Ensure oil level light is operational. Turn ignition on. DO NOT start engine. Install jumper wire between terminals E1 and TE1 of engine check connector, located below drivers seat. *See Fig. 38.*

**2)** If system is operating normally, oil level light will flash for 1/2 second every 4 1/2 seconds. If trouble code exists, oil level light will flash the trouble code. *See Fig. 39.*

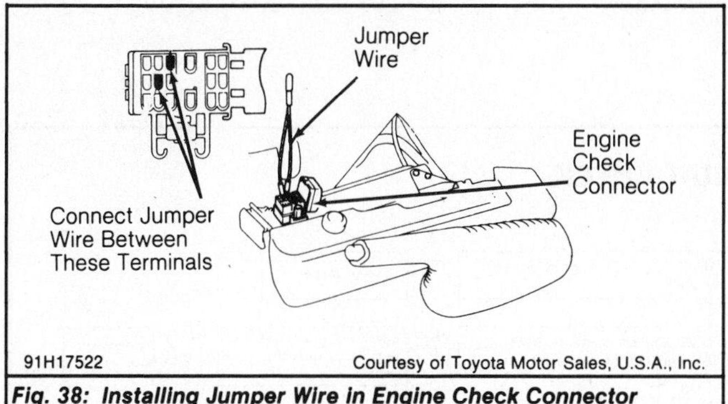


***Fig. 38: Installing Jumper Wire In Engine Check Connector***

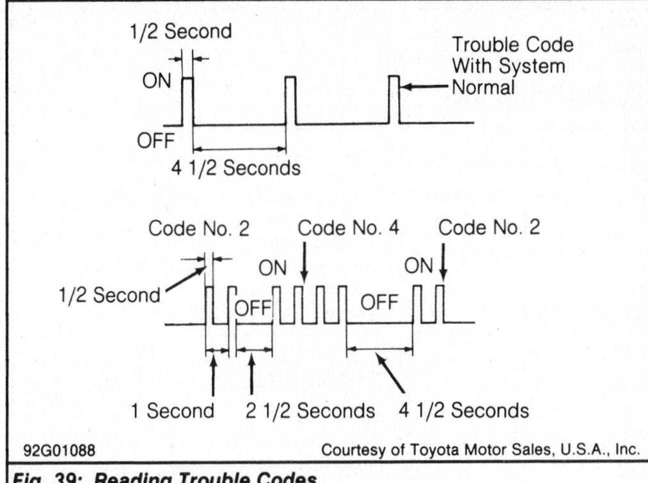


***Fig. 39: Reading Trouble Codes***

**3)** If more than one trouble code exists, there will be a 2 1/2 second pause between trouble codes. The smallest trouble code will be displayed first and continue with the larger trouble code.

**4)** Once all trouble codes are displayed, a 4 1/2 second pause will exist and then trouble codes will be displayed again. Trouble codes will be displayed as long as jumper wire is installed in engine check connector.

**5)** Once trouble code is obtained, determine probable cause. See TROUBLE CODE IDENTIFICATION table. Proceed to proper trouble code chart. *See Figs. 44 and 45.*

***CAUTION: Trouble code must be cleared from ECU memory after performing repairs. If trouble code is not cleared, trouble code will be retained in ECU memory and will be displayed with future trouble codes.***

***TROUBLE CODE IDENTIFICATION***

| Code No. | System Affected | Probable Cause |
|---|---|---|
| 2 | Oil Level Sensor OLS Circuit | Sensor, Circuit, ECU |
| 3 | Oil Level Sensor OMS Circuit | Sensor, Circuit, ECU |
| 4 | Electric Motor Circuit | Motor, Relay Circuit, ECU |

## CLEARING TROUBLE CODES

Ensure ignition is off. Remove 15-amp EFI fuse from fuse/relay block for at least 30 seconds. Fuse/relay block is located at center of instrument panel, near bottom of windshield. *See Fig. 40.* Fuse may need to be removed longer depending on ambient temperature. Reinstall fuse and road test to ensure trouble code does not reset.

***NOTE: Trouble code may also be cleared by disconnecting negative battery cable, but memory for radio, clock etc. will also be canceled.***

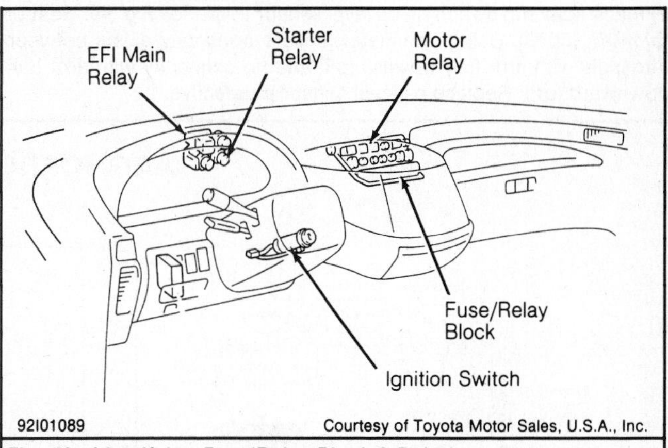


***Fig. 40: Identifying Fuse/Relay Block & Relays***

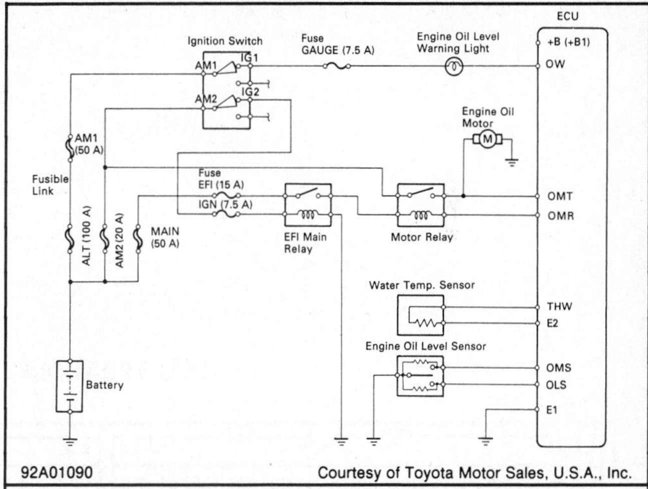


***Fig. 41: Automatic Engine Oil Feeder System Wiring Diagram***

## ECU PIN VOLTAGES

Note ECU terminal identification. *See Fig. 42.* Voltage can be checked at designated ECU pins. If voltage is not correct, proper test must be used to determine system failure. *See Fig. 46.*

***CAUTION: Perform all voltage measurements with ECU harness connector installed. Use high-impedance digital voltmeter (10,000 ohm minimum). Verify battery voltage is greater than 11 volts.***

## COMPONENT TESTING

***NOTE: Motor relay may also be referred to as engine oil level relay.***

**EFI Main Relay Or Motor Relay – 1)** Ensure ignition is off. Remove relay. *See Fig. 40.* Using ohmmeter, check continuity between specified terminals. *See Fig. 47.*

**2)** Connect battery voltage to terminals No. 1 and 3. Ensure continuity exists between terminals No. 2 and 4. Replace relay if defective.

**Oil Feeder System Electric Motor – 1)** Disconnect electrical connection from electric motor. Using ohmmeter, measure resistance between both terminals on electric motor. Replace electric motor if resistance exceeds 100 ohms.

**2)** With no battery voltage applied, ensure oil does not flow from pipe "B". *See Fig. 48.* Apply battery voltage and ensure oil flows from pipe "B". Replace electric motor if defective.

**3)** Disconnect battery voltage. Connect hand-held vacuum pump to pipe "B". Apply vacuum reading of 5.9 in. Hg on pipe "B". Replace electric motor if vacuum reading cannot be maintained.

**Oil Level Sensor – 1)** With oil level sensor removed from oil pan, connect ohmmeter to sensor terminals. Move oil level sensor arm fully upward and then downward. Continuity should exist in both positions.

# 1991 ENGINES
# 2.4L 4-Cylinder – Previa (Cont.)

**2)** Place float and switch on oil level sensor in oil. *See Fig. 49.* Heat oil to 140°F (60°C). Using ohmmeter, ensure continuity exists between terminals with arm fully upward (on) and no continuity with arm fully downward (off). Replace oil level sensor if defective.

## DIAGNOSTIC CIRCUIT CHECK

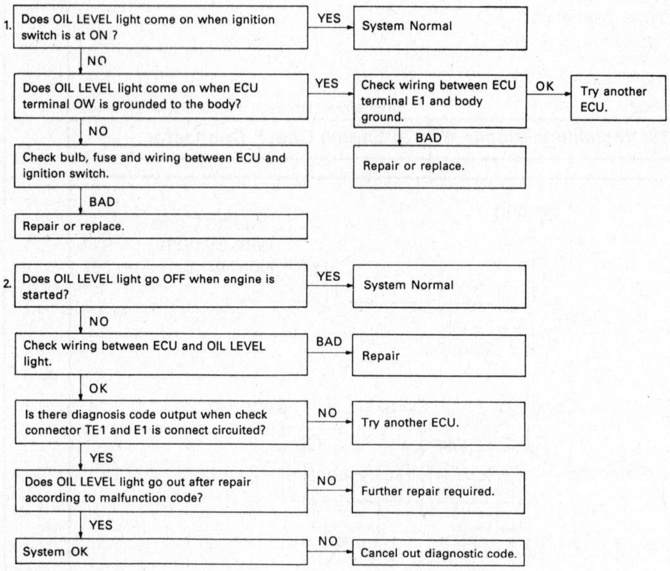

ECU
BATT
Fuse
EFI (15A)
EFI Main Relay
Ignition Switch
+B
AM2
IG2
IGN (7.5A)
+B1
GAUGE (7.5A)
AM1
IG1
"OIL LEVEL"
Warning Light
OW
Fusible Link
MAIN (50A)
AM2 (20A)
AM1 (50A)
ALT (100A)
E1
T
Battery
Check Connector

1.
Does OIL LEVEL light come on when ignition switch is at ON ?
YES
System Normal
NO
Does OIL LEVEL light come on when ECU terminal OW is grounded to the body?
YES
Check wiring between ECU terminal E1 and body ground.
OK
Try another ECU.
BAD
Repair or replace.
NO
Check bulb, fuse and wiring between ECU and ignition switch.
BAD
Repair or replace.
2.
Does OIL LEVEL light go OFF when engine is started?
YES
System Normal
NO
Check wiring between ECU and OIL LEVEL light.
BAD
Repair
OK
Is there diagnosis code output when check connector TE1 and E1 is connect circuited?
NO
Try another ECU.
YES
Does OIL LEVEL light go out after repair according to malfunction code?
NO
Further repair required.
YES
System OK
NO
Cancel out diagnostic code.

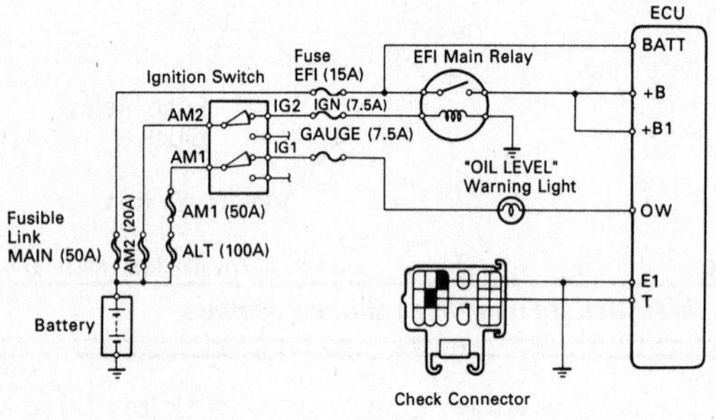

## ECU TERMINAL IDENTIFICATION

| | | | | | | | | | | | | |
|---|---|---|---|---|---|---|---|---|---|---|---|---|
| E01 | No.10 | STJ | HT | IGT | OMR | OMT | ISC1 | G2 | NE | IGF | / | SL |
| E02 | No.20 | E1 | EPU | / | / | / | ISC2 | G1 | G⊖ | / | S1 | S2 |

| | | | | | | | |
|---|---|---|---|---|---|---|---|
| VF | / | OX1 | OX2 | THW | THA | VS | VC |
| T | / | KNK | | IDL | VTA | THG | E2 |

| | | | | | | | | | | |
|---|---|---|---|---|---|---|---|---|---|---|
| STA | A/C | SP1 | SP2 | O/G | ACT | W | OW | / | / | BATT |
| NSW | OD1 | OD2 | STP | OMS | OLS | N | 2 | L | +B1 | +B |

92C01091 92E01092 91A18093

Courtesy of Toyota Motor Sales, U.S.A., Inc.

*Fig. 42: Performing Diagnostic Circuit Check & Identifying ECU Terminals*

## TEST NO. 1
## OIL LEVEL LIGHT & ECU CIRCUIT

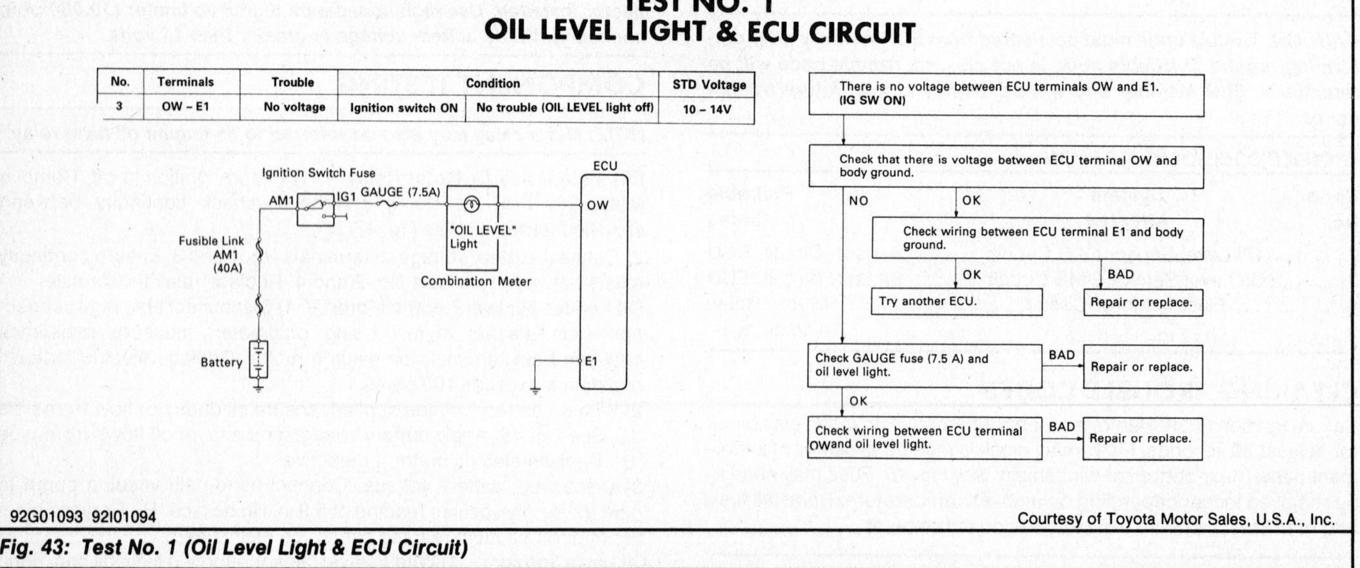

| No. | Terminals | Trouble | Condition | | STD Voltage |
|---|---|---|---|---|---|
| 3 | OW – E1 | No voltage | Ignition switch ON | No trouble (OIL LEVEL light off) | 10 – 14V |

Ignition Switch Fuse
ECU
AM1
IG1
GAUGE (7.5A)
OW
"OIL LEVEL"
Light
Fusible Link
AM1
(40A)
Combination Meter
Battery
E1

There is no voltage between ECU terminals OW and E1.
(IG SW ON)
Check that there is voltage between ECU terminal OW and body ground.
NO
OK
Check wiring between ECU terminal E1 and body ground.
OK
BAD
Try another ECU.
Repair or replace.
Check GAUGE fuse (7.5 A) and oil level light.
BAD
Repair or replace.
OK
Check wiring between ECU terminal OW and oil level light.
BAD
Repair or replace.

92G01093 92I01094

Courtesy of Toyota Motor Sales, U.S.A., Inc.

*Fig. 43: Test No. 1 (Oil Level Light & ECU Circuit)*

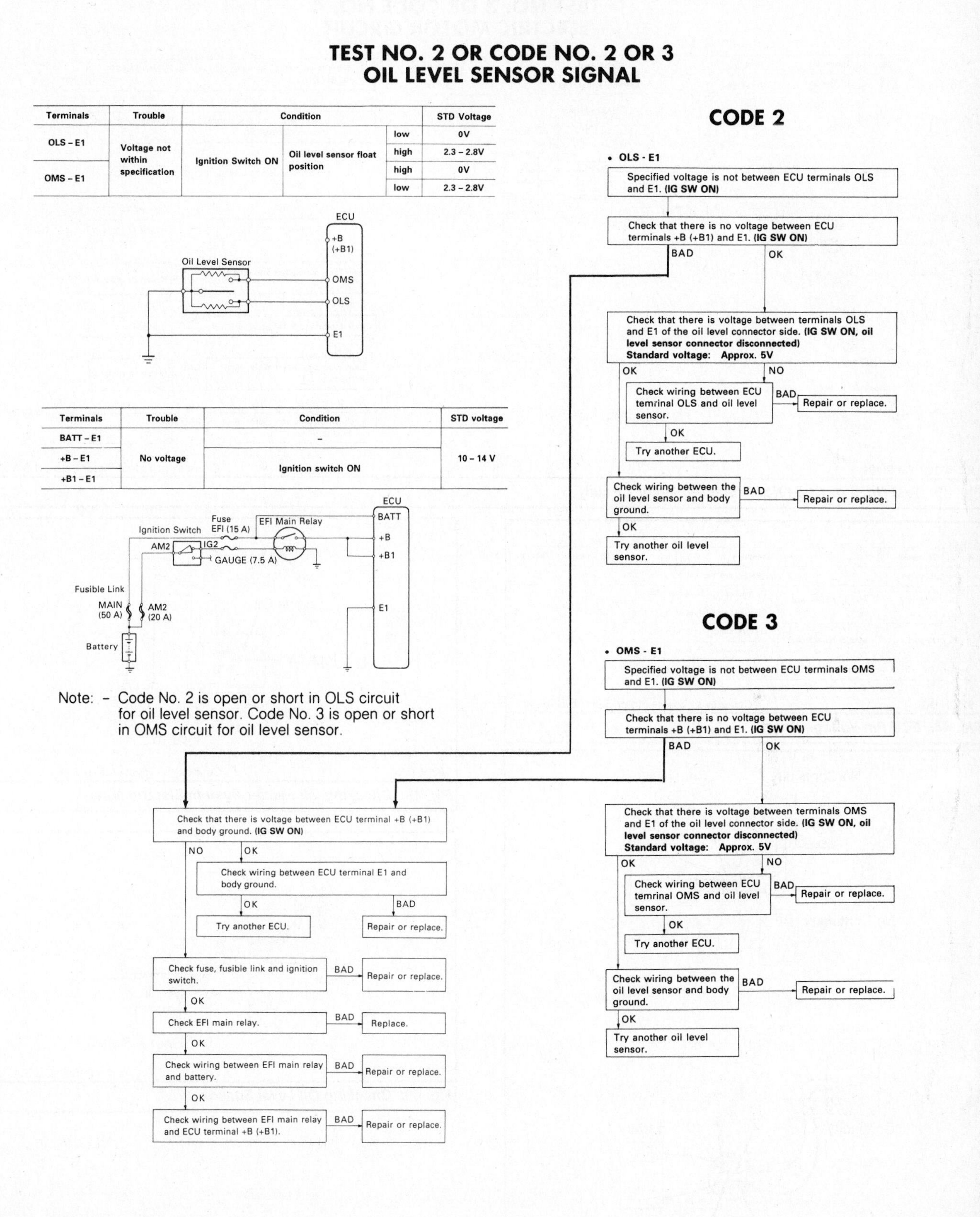

| Terminals | Trouble | Condition | | | STD Voltage |
|---|---|---|---|---|---|
| OLS – E1 | Voltage not within specification | Ignition Switch ON | Oil level sensor float position | low | 0V |
| | | | | high | 2.3 – 2.8V |
| OMS – E1 | | | | high | 0V |
| | | | | low | 2.3 – 2.8V |

| Terminals | Trouble | Condition | STD voltage |
|---|---|---|---|
| BATT – E1 | No voltage | – | 10 – 14 V |
| +B – E1 | | Ignition switch ON | |
| +B1 – E1 | | | |

TEST NO. 2 OR CODE NO. 2 OR 3
OIL LEVEL SENSOR SIGNAL
ECU
+B (+B1)
Oil Level Sensor
OMS
OLS
E1
ECU
BATT
Fuse
EFI (15 A)
EFI Main Relay
Ignition Switch
AM2
IG2
GAUGE (7.5 A)
+B
+B1
Fusible Link
MAIN (50 A)
AM2 (20 A)
Battery
E1
Note: - Code No. 2 is open or short in OLS circuit for oil level sensor. Code No. 3 is open or short in OMS circuit for oil level sensor.
CODE 2
• OLS - E1
Specified voltage is not between ECU terminals OLS and E1. (IG SW ON)
Check that there is no voltage between ECU terminals +B (+B1) and E1. (IG SW ON)
BAD
OK
Check that there is voltage between terminals OLS and E1 of the oil level connector side. (IG SW ON, oil level sensor connector disconnected)
Standard voltage: Approx. 5V
OK
NO
Check wiring between ECU temrinal OLS and oil level sensor.
BAD
Repair or replace.
OK
Try another ECU.
Check wiring between the oil level sensor and body ground.
BAD
Repair or replace.
OK
Try another oil level sensor.
CODE 3
• OMS - E1
Specified voltage is not between ECU terminals OMS and E1. (IG SW ON)
Check that there is no voltage between ECU terminals +B (+B1) and E1. (IG SW ON)
BAD
OK
Check that there is voltage between terminals OMS and E1 of the oil level connector side. (IG SW ON, oil level sensor connector disconnected)
Standard voltage: Approx. 5V
OK
NO
Check wiring between ECU temrinal OMS and oil level sensor.
BAD
Repair or replace.
OK
Try another ECU.
Check wiring between the oil level sensor and body ground.
BAD
Repair or replace.
OK
Try another oil level sensor.
Check that there is voltage between ECU terminal +B (+B1) and body ground. (IG SW ON)
NO
OK
Check wiring between ECU terminal E1 and body ground.
OK
BAD
Try another ECU.
Repair or replace.
Check fuse, fusible link and ignition switch.
BAD
Repair or replace.
OK
Check EFI main relay.
BAD
Replace.
OK
Check wiring between EFI main relay and battery.
BAD
Repair or replace.
OK
Check wiring between EFI main relay and ECU terminal +B (+B1).
BAD
Repair or replace.
92B01095 92D01096 92F01097 92H01098 92J01099
Courtesy of Toyota Motor Sales, U.S.A., Inc.

*Fig. 44: Test No. 2 or Code No. 2 or 3 (Oil Level Sensor Signal)*

# 1991 ENGINES
# 2.4L 4-Cylinder – Previa (Cont.)

## TEST NO. 3 OR CODE NO. 4
## ELECTRIC MOTOR CIRCUIT

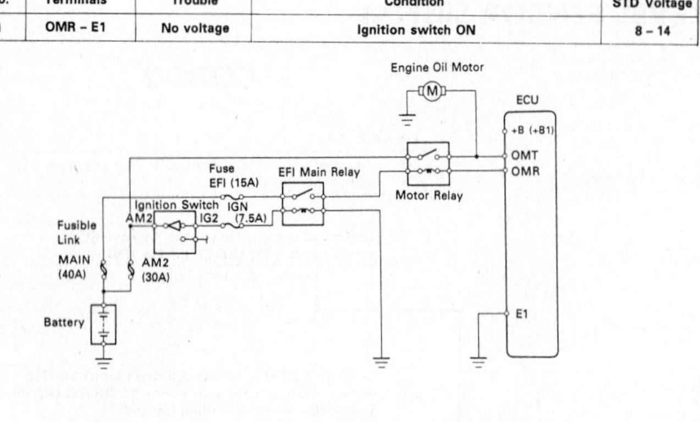

| No. | Terminals | Trouble | Condition | STD Voltage |
|---|---|---|---|---|
| 1 | OMR – E1 | No voltage | Ignition switch ON | 8 – 14 |



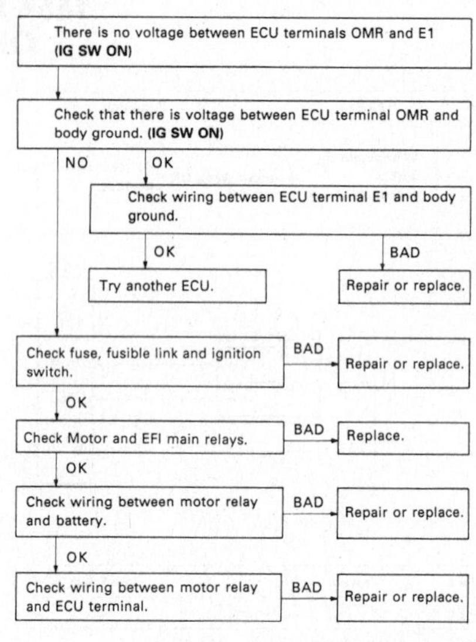



92D01100 92F01101

Courtesy of Toyota Motor Sales, U.S.A., Inc.

*Fig. 45: Test No. 3 or Code No. 4 (Electric Motor Circuit)*

| No. | Terminals | Condition | | STD voltage | Test No. |
|---|---|---|---|---|---|
| 1 | OMR – E1 | Ignition swtich ON | | 8 – 14 | 3 |
| 2 | OLS – E1 | Ignition switch ON | Oil level sensor float low position | 0 | 2 |
| | | | Oil level sensor float high position | 2.3 – 2.8 | |
| | OMS – E1 | Ignition switch ON | Oil level sensor float high position | 0 | 2 |
| | | | Oil level sensor float low position | 2.3 – 2.8 | |
| 3 | OW – E1 | Ignition switch ON | No trouble (OIL LEVEL light off) | 10 – 14 | 1 |

92H01102

Courtesy of Toyota Motor Sales, U.S.A., Inc.

*Fig. 46: ECU Pin Voltage Chart*

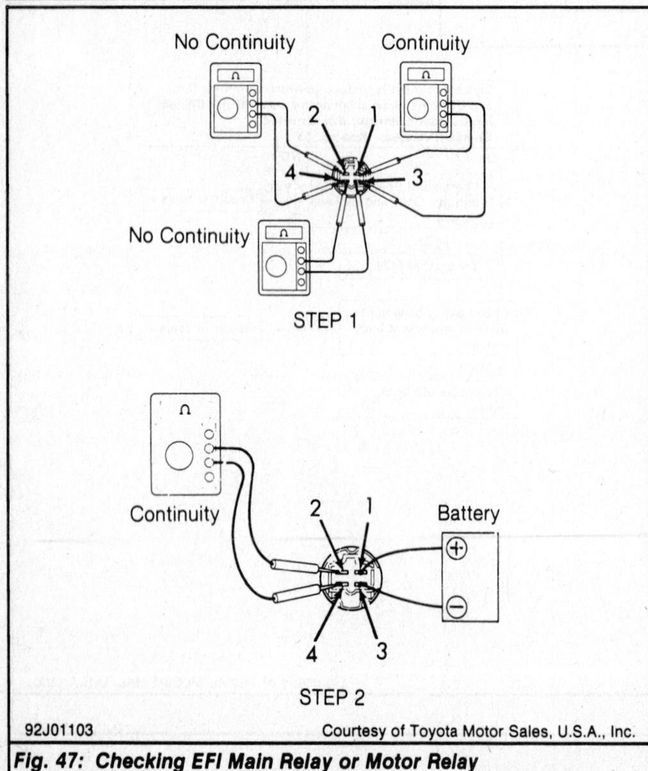



92J01103

Courtesy of Toyota Motor Sales, U.S.A., Inc.

*Fig. 47: Checking EFI Main Relay or Motor Relay*

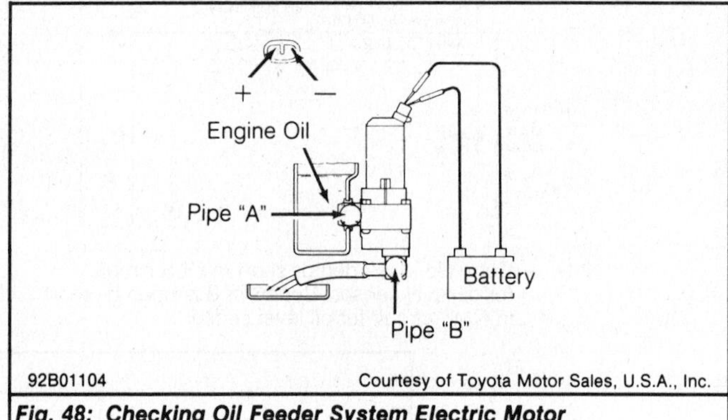



92B01104

Courtesy of Toyota Motor Sales, U.S.A., Inc.

*Fig. 48: Checking Oil Feeder System Electric Motor*

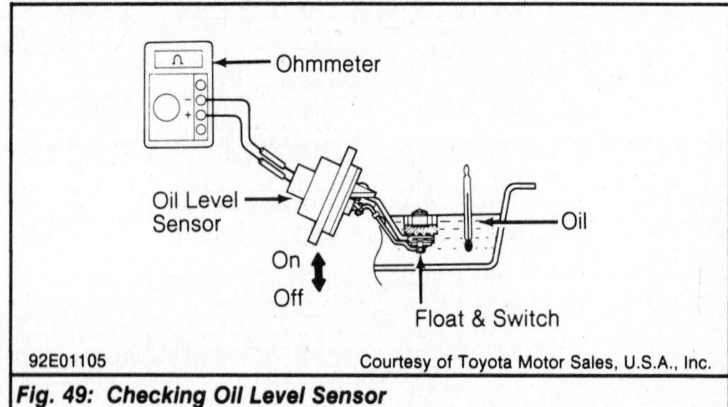



92E01105

Courtesy of Toyota Motor Sales, U.S.A., Inc.

*Fig. 49: Checking Oil Level Sensor*

# 1991 ENGINES
# 2.4L 4-Cylinder – Previa (Cont.)

## TORQUE SPECIFICATIONS

### TORQUE SPECIFICATIONS

| Application | Ft. Lbs. (N.m) |
|---|---|
| Accessory Drive Shaft Flange-To-Crankshaft Pulley Bolt | 25 (34) |
| Accessory Drive Shaft Front Flange Bolt | 38 (52) |
| Accessory Drive Shaft Pulley Bolt | 21 (29) |
| Camshaft Bearing Cap Bolt [1] | 12 (16) |
| Camshaft Sprocket Bolt | 54 (73) |
| Connecting Rod Nut | |
| Step 1 | 22 (30) |
| Step 2 | Additional 90 Degrees |
| Coolant Outlet Bolt | [2] |
| Crankshaft Pulley Bolt | 192 (260) |
| Cylinder Block-To-Front Cover Bolt | 13 (18) |
| Cylinder Head-To-Cylinder Block Bolt [3] | |
| Step 1 | 29 (39) |
| Step 2 | Additional 90 Degrees |
| Step 3 | Additional 90 Degrees |
| Cylinder Head-To-Front Cover Bolt | 15 (20) |
| Damper Bolt | 13 (18) |
| Delivery Pipe Bolt | 14 (19) |
| Dipstick Guide-To-Cylinder Block Bolt | 13 (18) |
| Dipstick Tube-To-Crankcase | 22 (30) |
| Distributor Retaining Bolt | 14 (19) |
| Drive Shaft Center Support Bolt | 27 (37) |
| Drive Shaft Flange-To-Front Axle Bolt | 31 (42) |
| Drive Shaft Flange-To-Rear Axle Bolt | 54 (73) |
| Drive Shaft Flange-To-Transfer Case Bolt | 54 (73) |
| EGR Valve Bolt | 13 (18) |
| EGR Valve Pipe-To-Intake Manifold Bolt | 13 (18) |
| Engine Mount Crossmember-To-Body Bolt | 27 (37) |
| Engine Wire Bolt | 13 (18) |
| Exhaust Manifold Heat Insulator Bolt | 13 (18) |
| Exhaust Manifold Nut | 36 (49) |
| Flywheel/Drive Plate Bolt | |
| A/T | 54 (73) |
| M/T | 65 (88) |
| Front Cover Bolt | [4] |
| Front Exhaust Pipe-To-Rear | |
| Exhaust Pipe Bolt | 32 (43) |
| Nut | 46 (62) |
| Fuel Pipe Union Bolt | |
| At Cold Start Injector | 14 (19) |
| At Delivery Pipe | 22 (30) |
| Idler Gear Bolt | 14 (19) |
| Intake Manifold Bolt/Nut | 15 (20) |
| Left Engine Mount Support Bracket Bolt | 27 (37) |
| Left Front Engine Mount Bolt | 30 (41) |
| Main Bearing Cap Bolt | |
| Step 1 | 29 (39) |
| Step 2 | Additional 90 Degrees |
| No. 1 Intake Manifold Support Bolt | |
| At Cylinder Block | 27 (37) |
| At Intake Manifold | 13 (18) |
| No. 1 Oil Return Pipe Bolt | 15 (20) |
| No. 2 Manifold Support Bolt | 27 (37) |
| No. 2 Timing Chain Guide Bolt | 14 (19) |
| Oil Filter Bracket Bolt | 14 (19) |
| Oil Nozzle Bolt | 13 (18) |
| Oil Pick-Up Tube Bolt/Nut | 13 (18) |
| Oil Pressure Switch | 11 (15) |

[1] – Tighten bolts to specification in sequence. *See Fig. 18.*
[2] – Tighten bolts to specification. *See Fig. 19.*
[3] – Tighten bolts to specification in sequence. *See Fig. 14.*
[4] – Tighten bolts to specification. *See Fig. 26.*
[5] – Tighten bolts to specification. *See Fig. 28.*

### TORQUE SPECIFICATIONS (Cont.)

| Application | Ft. Lbs. (N.m) |
|---|---|
| Rear Oil Seal Retainer Bolt | 10 (14) |
| Right Front Engine Mount-To-Cylinder Block Bolt | 30 (41) |
| Slipper Bolt | 20 (27) |
| Spark Plug | 14 (19) |
| Throttle Body Bolt | 13 (18) |
| Timing Chain Tensioner Nut | 15 (20) |
| Torque Converter-To-Drive Plate Bolt | 30 (41) |
| Transmission Mount-To-Body Bolt | 22 (30) |
| Water Pump Bolt | [5] |
| Water Pump-To-Coolant Inlet Housing Bolt | 14 (19) |
| | **INCH Lbs. (N.m)** |
| Clutch Master Cylinder Bolt | 108 (12) |
| Crankcase Bolt/Nut | 108 (12) |
| Fuel Pipe Retaining Bolt | 48 (5) |
| No. 2 Cylinder Head Cover Bolt | 48 (5) |
| Oil Baffle Plate Nut | 43 (4) |
| Oil Level Sensor Bolt | 108 (12) |
| Oil Pan Bolt/Nut | 48 (5) |
| Oil Pump Cover Screw | 96 (11) |
| Pressure Regulator Bolt | 48 (5) |
| Ventilation Case-To-Crankcase Bolt | 69 (8) |

## ENGINE SPECIFICATIONS

### GENERAL SPECIFICATIONS

| Application | Specification |
|---|---|
| 2.4L | |
| Displacement | 146 Cu. In. (2.4L) |
| Bore | 3.74" (95.0 mm) |
| Stroke | 3.39" (86.1 mm) |
| Compression Ratio | 9.3:1 |
| Fuel System | PFI |
| Horsepower @ RPM | 138 @ 5000 |
| Torque Ft. Lbs. @ RPM | 154 @ 4000 |

### CRANKSHAFT, MAIN & CONNECTING ROD BEARINGS

| Application | In. (mm) |
|---|---|
| 2.4L | |
| Crankshaft | |
| End Play | |
| Standard | .0008-.0087 (.020-.221) |
| Wear Limit | .012 (.30) |
| Runout | .0012 (.030) |
| Main Bearings | |
| Journal Diameter | 2.3617-2.3622 (59.987-60.000) |
| Journal Out-Of-Round & Taper | .0002 (.005) |
| Oil Clearance | |
| Standard | .0008-.0019 (.020-.048) |
| Wear Limit | .004 (.10) |
| Connecting Rod Bearings | |
| Journal Diameter | 2.0861-2.0866 (52.987-53.000) |
| Journal Out-Of-Round & Taper | .0002 (.005) |
| Oil Clearance | |
| Standard | .0012-.0023 (.030-.058) |
| Wear Limit | .004 (.10) |

### VALVE LIFTERS

| Application | In. (mm) |
|---|---|
| 2.4L | |
| Bore Diameter | 1.2205-1.2211 (31.001-31.016) |
| Lifter Diameter | 1.2191-1.2195 (30.965-30.975) |
| Oil Clearance | |
| Standard | .0009-.0020 (.023-.051) |
| Wear Limit | .0028 (.071) |

# 1991 ENGINES
# 2.4L 4-Cylinder – Previa (Cont.)

## CONNECTING RODS

| Application | In. (mm) |
|---|---|
| 2.4L | |
| Bore Diameter | |
| Pin Bushing Bore | .9452-.9455 (24.008-24.016) |
| Crankpin Bore [1] | |
| Grade Number 1 | .2.2047-2.2050 (55.999-56.007) |
| Grade Number 2 | .2.2051-2.2053 (56.009-56.015) |
| Grade Number 3 | .2.2054-2.2057 (56.017-56.025) |
| Maximum Bend | .002 Per 3.94 (.05 Per 100.1) |
| Maximum Twist | .0059 Per 3.94 (.150 Per 100.1) |
| Side Play | |
| Standard | .0063-.0123 (.160-.312) |
| Wear Limit | .014 (.36) |

[1] – Crankpin bore diameter is determined by grade number stamped on connecting rod cap. *See Fig. 33.*

## PISTONS, PINS & RINGS

| Application | In. (mm) |
|---|---|
| 2.4L | |
| Pistons | |
| Clearance | .0012-.0020 (.030-.050) |
| Diameter | 3.7382-3.7386 (95.451-95.461) |
| Pins | |
| Diameter | .9449-.9452 (24.000-24.008) |
| Piston Fit | [1] |
| Rod Fit | .0002-0004 (.005-.010) |
| Rings | |
| No. 1 | |
| End Gap | |
| Standard | .0118-.0169 (.300-.429) |
| Wear Limit | .0406 (1.031) |
| Side Clearance | |
| Standard | .0008-.0028 (.020-.071) |
| Wear Limit | .008 (.20) |
| No. 2 | |
| End Gap | |
| Standard | .0177-.0236 (.450-.599) |
| Wear Limit | .0472 (1.199) |
| Side Clearance | |
| Standard | .0012-.0028 (.030-.071) |
| Wear Limit | .008 (.20) |
| No. 3 (Oil) | |
| End Gap | |
| Standard | .0051-.0150 (.130-.381) |
| Wear Limit | .0386 (.980) |

[1] – Piston pin should slide in piston using thumb pressure with piston heated to 176°F (80°C).

## CYLINDER BLOCK

| Application | In. (mm) |
|---|---|
| 2.4L | |
| Cylinder Bore | |
| Standard Diameter | 3.7398-3.7402 (94.991-95.001) |
| Maximum Taper | .0004 (.010) |
| Maximum Out-Of-Round | .0008 (.020) |
| Main Journal I.D. [1] | |
| Grade Number 1 | 2.5197-2.5200 (64.000-64.008) |
| Grade Number 2 | 2.5200-2.5203 (64.008-64.016) |
| Grade Number 3 | 2.5203-2.5206 (64.016-64.023) |
| Maximum Deck Warpage | .0020 (.051) |

[1] – Cylinder block main journal I.D. is determined by grade number stamped on cylinder. *See Fig. 35.*

## VALVES & VALVE SPRINGS

| Application | Specification |
|---|---|
| 2.4L | |
| Intake Valves | |
| Face Angle | 44.5° |
| Minimum Margin | .020" (.51 mm) |
| Minimum Refinish Length | 4.0531" (102.949 mm) |
| Stem Diameter | .2350-.2356" (5.969-5.984 mm) |
| Exhaust Valves | |
| Face Angle | 44.5° |
| Minimum Margin | .020" (.51 mm) |
| Minimum Refinish Length | 4.0590" (103.099 mm) |
| Stem Diameter | .2348-.2354" (5.964-5.979 mm) |
| Valve Springs | |
| Free Length | 1.6425" (41.720 mm) |
| Installed Height | 1.406" (35.71 mm) |
| Out-Of-Square | .079" (2.01 mm) |
| | **Lbs. @ In. (kg @ mm)** |
| Pressure | |
| Valve Closed | 57-63 @ 1.406 (26-29 @ 35.71) |

## CYLINDER HEAD

| Application | Specification |
|---|---|
| 2.4L | |
| Cylinder Head | |
| Maximum Warpage | |
| Cylinder Block Surface | .0059" (.150 mm) |
| Manifold Surface | .0079" (.201 mm) |
| Valve Seats | |
| Intake | |
| Seat Angle | 45° |
| Seat Width | .039-.055" (.99-1.40 mm) |
| Exhaust | |
| Seat Angle | 45° |
| Seat Width | .039-.055" (.99-1.40 mm) |
| Valve Guides | |
| Intake Valve | |
| Valve Guide Cylinder Head | |
| Bore I.D. | .4331-.4341" (11.000-11.026 mm) |
| Valve Guide I.D. | .2366-.2374" (6.010-6.030 mm) |
| Valve Stem-To-Guide Oil Clearance | |
| Standard | .0010-.0024" (.025-.061 mm) |
| Wear Limit | .0031" (.079 mm) |
| Exhaust Valve | |
| Valve Guide Cylinder Head | |
| Bore I.D. | .4331-.4341" (11.000-11.026 mm) |
| Valve Guide I.D. | .2366-.2374" (6.010-6.030 mm) |
| Valve Stem-To-Guide Oil Clearance | |
| Standard | .0012-.0026" (.030-.066 mm) |
| Wear Limit | .0039" (.099 mm) |

## CAMSHAFT

| Application | In. (mm) |
|---|---|
| 2.4L | |
| End Play | |
| Standard | .0016-.0037 (.041-.094) |
| Wear Limit | .0047 (.119) |
| Journal Diameter | 1.0614-1.0620 (26.959-26.975) |
| Journal Runout | .0024 (.061) |
| Lobe Height | |
| Intake | 1.7839-1.7878 (45.311-45.410) |
| Exhaust | 1.7740-1.7779 (45.060-45.159) |
| Oil Clearance | |
| Standard | .0010-.0024 (.025-.061) |
| Wear Limit | .0031 (.079) |
| Gear Backlash | |
| Standard | .0008-.0079 (.020-.201) |
| Wear Limit | .0118 (.300) |

## Camry

***NOTE: For repair procedures not covered in this article, see ENGINE OVERHAUL PROCEDURES article in GENERAL INFORMATION.***

# ENGINE IDENTIFICATION

Engine serial number is stamped in front of dipstick, on cylinder block.

***ENGINE IDENTIFICATION CODES***

| Engine | Code |
|---|---|
| 2.5L V6 | 2VZ-FE |

# ADJUSTMENTS

## VALVE CLEARANCE ADJUSTMENT

***NOTE: Adjust valve clearance with engine cold.***

**1)** Remove valve covers. Rotate crankshaft so No. 1 cylinder is at TDC of compression stroke. Ensure timing mark on crankshaft pulley aligns with "0" mark on timing belt cover. Ensure intake lifters on No. 1 cylinder are loose, and exhaust lifters on No. 1 cylinder are tight. If conditions are not as described, rotate crankshaft one complete revolution.

**2)** Using feeler gauge, measure and record clearance between valve lifter and camshaft on intake valves of No. 1 and No. 6 cylinders and exhaust valves on No. 2 and No. 3 cylinders.

***NOTE: No. 1, 3 and 5 cylinders are on firewall side of engine, with No. 1 at timing belt end of engine. No. 2, 4 and 6 cylinders are on radiator side, with No. 2 at timing belt end of engine.***

**3)** Rotate crankshaft 2/3 turn (240 degrees). Measure and record clearance between valve lifter and camshaft on intake valves of No. 2 and No. 3 cylinders and exhaust valves on No. 4 and No. 5 cylinders.

**4)** Rotate crankshaft another 2/3 turn (240 degrees). Measure and record clearance between valve lifter and camshaft on intake valves of No. 4 and No. 5 cylinders and exhaust valves on No. 1 and No. 6 cylinders.

**5)** Ensure clearance is within specification. See VALVE CLEARANCE SPECIFICATIONS table.

***VALVE CLEARANCE SPECIFICATIONS*** [1]

| Application | In. (mm) |
|---|---|
| Intake Valves | .005-.009 (.13-.23) |
| Exhaust Valves | .011-.015 (.28-.38) |

1 – Adjust valves with engine cold.

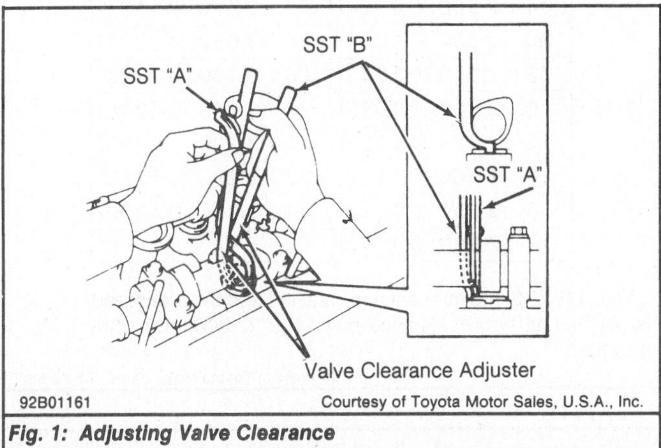


***Fig. 1: Adjusting Valve Clearance***

**6)** If valves require adjustment, rotate camshaft so lobe on valve to be adjusted is facing upward, away from valve lifter. Valve Clearance Adjuster (SST 09248-55010) is used to remove adjusting shim. Position notch on adjusting shim toward spark plug.

**7)** Using SST "A" of valve clearance adjuster, push downward on valve lifter. Place SST "B" between camshaft and valve lifter, and remove SST "A". *See Fig. 1.*

**8)** Using small screwdriver and magnet, remove adjusting shim. Measure and record thickness of shim removed. Use measured clearance and shim thickness values to select proper replacement shim from shim selection charts. *See Figs. 4 and 5.*

**9)** Install replacement adjusting shim, and recheck valve clearance. Before installing valve cover and gasket, apply sealant at front and rear areas of cylinder head. *See Fig. 2.*

**10)** Install gasket and valve cover. Tighten nuts to specification. See TORQUE SPECIFICATIONS table at end article.

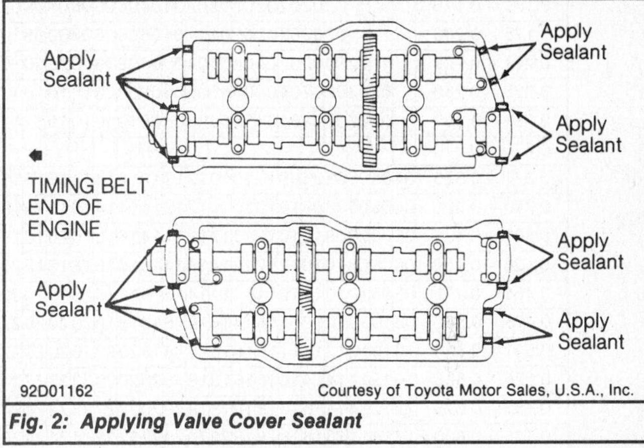


***Fig. 2: Applying Valve Cover Sealant***

# REMOVAL & INSTALLATION

***NOTE: For installation reference, label all electrical connectors, vacuum hoses and fuel lines before removal. Also place mating marks on engine hood and other major assemblies before removal.***

## FUEL PRESSURE RELEASE

With ignition off, disconnect negative battery cable. Place suitable container under fuel line. Cover fuel line connection with shop towel. Slowly loosen fuel line connection to release fuel pressure. Once fuel pressure is released, fuel system components can be removed.

## COOLING SYSTEM BLEEDING

**1)** Loosen union bolt on coolant outlet approximately 5 revolutions. *See Fig. 3.* Slowly fill cooling system. Allow air to bleed from union bolt.

**2)** Once coolant flows from union bolt, tighten union bolt to 13 ft. lbs. (18 N.m). Finish filling cooling system.

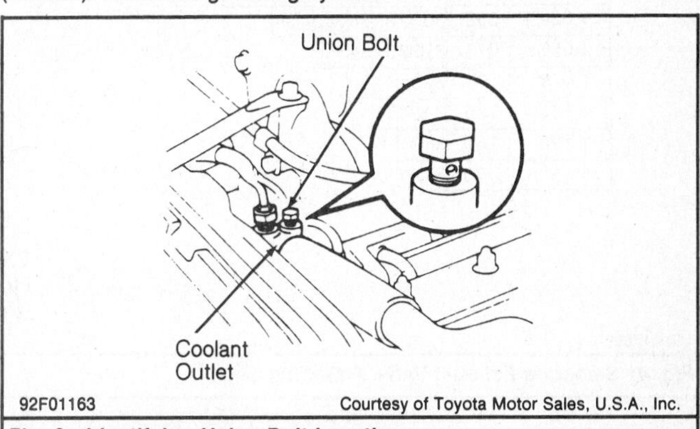


***Fig. 3: Identifying Union Bolt Location***

# 1991 ENGINES
# 2.5L V6 (Cont.)

EXHAUST VALVES

| Measured clearance (mm) | Installed shim thickness (mm) | | | | | | | | | | | | | | | | | | | | | | | | | | | | | | | | | | | | | | | | | | | | |
|---|---|---|---|---|---|---|---|---|---|---|---|---|---|---|---|---|---|---|---|---|---|---|---|---|---|---|---|---|---|---|---|---|---|---|---|---|---|---|---|---|---|---|---|---|---|
| | 2.500 | 2.525 | 2.550 | 2.575 | 2.600 | 2.620 | 2.640 | 2.650 | 2.660 | 2.680 | 2.700 | 2.720 | 2.740 | 2.750 | 2.760 | 2.780 | 2.800 | 2.820 | 2.840 | 2.850 | 2.860 | 2.880 | 2.900 | 2.920 | 2.940 | 2.950 | 2.960 | 2.980 | 3.000 | 3.020 | 3.040 | 3.050 | 3.060 | 3.080 | 3.100 | 3.120 | 3.140 | 3.150 | 3.160 | 3.180 | 3.200 | 3.225 | 3.250 | 3.275 | 3.300 |
| 0.000 - 0.025 | | | | | | | | | | | | | | 02 | 02 | 02 | 02 | 02 | 04 | 04 | 04 | 04 | 06 | 06 | 08 | 08 | 08 | 08 | 10 | 10 | 12 | 12 | 12 | 12 | 14 | 14 | 16 | 16 | 16 | 16 | 18 | 18 | 20 | 20 | 22 |
| 0.026 - 0.050 | | | | | | | | | | | | 02 | 02 | 02 | 02 | 02 | 02 | 04 | 04 | 04 | 06 | 06 | 06 | 08 | 08 | 08 | 10 | 10 | 10 | 12 | 12 | 12 | 14 | 14 | 14 | 16 | 16 | 16 | 18 | 18 | 18 | 20 | 20 | 22 | 22 |
| 0.051 - 0.075 | | | | | | | | | | | 02 | 02 | 02 | 02 | 02 | 02 | 04 | 04 | 06 | 06 | 06 | 06 | 08 | 08 | 10 | 10 | 10 | 10 | 12 | 12 | 14 | 14 | 14 | 14 | 16 | 16 | 18 | 18 | 18 | 18 | 20 | 20 | 22 | 22 | 24 |
| 0.076 - 0.100 | | | | | | | | | | 02 | 02 | 02 | 02 | 02 | 04 | 04 | 04 | 06 | 06 | 06 | 08 | 08 | 08 | 10 | 10 | 10 | 12 | 12 | 12 | 14 | 14 | 14 | 16 | 16 | 16 | 18 | 18 | 18 | 20 | 20 | 20 | 22 | 22 | 24 | 24 |
| 0.101 - 0.125 | | | | | | | | 02 | 02 | 02 | 02 | 02 | 04 | 04 | 04 | 04 | 06 | 06 | 08 | 08 | 08 | 08 | 10 | 10 | 12 | 12 | 12 | 12 | 14 | 14 | 16 | 16 | 16 | 16 | 18 | 18 | 20 | 20 | 20 | 20 | 22 | 22 | 24 | 24 | 26 |
| 0.126 - 0.150 | | | | | | 02 | 02 | 02 | 02 | 02 | 02 | 04 | 04 | 04 | 06 | 06 | 06 | 08 | 08 | 08 | 10 | 10 | 10 | 12 | 12 | 12 | 14 | 14 | 14 | 16 | 16 | 16 | 18 | 18 | 18 | 20 | 20 | 20 | 22 | 22 | 22 | 24 | 24 | 26 | 26 |
| 0.151 - 0.175 | | | | | 02 | 02 | 02 | 02 | 02 | 02 | 04 | 04 | 06 | 06 | 06 | 06 | 08 | 08 | 10 | 10 | 10 | 10 | 12 | 12 | 14 | 14 | 14 | 14 | 16 | 16 | 18 | 18 | 18 | 18 | 20 | 20 | 22 | 22 | 22 | 22 | 24 | 24 | 26 | 26 | 28 |
| 0.176 - 0.200 | | | | 02 | 02 | 02 | 02 | 02 | 04 | 04 | 04 | 06 | 06 | 06 | 08 | 08 | 08 | 10 | 10 | 10 | 12 | 12 | 12 | 14 | 14 | 14 | 16 | 16 | 16 | 18 | 18 | 18 | 20 | 20 | 20 | 22 | 22 | 22 | 24 | 24 | 24 | 26 | 26 | 28 | 28 |
| 0.201 - 0.225 | | | 02 | 02 | 02 | 02 | 04 | 04 | 04 | 04 | 06 | 06 | 08 | 08 | 08 | 08 | 10 | 10 | 12 | 12 | 12 | 12 | 14 | 14 | 16 | 16 | 16 | 16 | 18 | 18 | 20 | 20 | 20 | 20 | 22 | 22 | 24 | 24 | 24 | 24 | 26 | 26 | 28 | 28 | 30 |
| 0.226 - 0.250 | | 02 | 02 | 02 | 02 | 04 | 04 | 04 | 06 | 06 | 06 | 08 | 08 | 08 | 10 | 10 | 10 | 12 | 12 | 12 | 14 | 14 | 14 | 16 | 16 | 16 | 18 | 18 | 18 | 20 | 20 | 20 | 22 | 22 | 22 | 24 | 24 | 24 | 26 | 26 | 26 | 28 | 28 | 30 | 30 |
| 0.251 - 0.269 | | 02 | 02 | 02 | 04 | 04 | 06 | 06 | 06 | 06 | 08 | 08 | 10 | 10 | 10 | 10 | 12 | 12 | 14 | 14 | 14 | 14 | 16 | 16 | 18 | 18 | 18 | 18 | 20 | 20 | 22 | 22 | 22 | 22 | 24 | 24 | 26 | 26 | 26 | 26 | 28 | 28 | 30 | 30 | 32 |
| 0.270 - 0.370 | | | | | | | | | | | | | | | | | | | | | | | | | | | | | | | | | | | | | | | | | | | | | |
| 0.371 - 0.375 | 04 | 06 | 06 | 08 | 08 | 08 | 10 | 10 | 10 | 12 | 12 | 12 | 14 | 14 | 14 | 16 | 16 | 16 | 18 | 18 | 18 | 20 | 20 | 20 | 22 | 22 | 22 | 24 | 24 | 24 | 26 | 26 | 26 | 28 | 28 | 28 | 30 | 30 | 30 | 32 | 32 | 34 | 34 | 34 | |
| 0.376 - 0.400 | 04 | 06 | 06 | 08 | 08 | 10 | 10 | 10 | 12 | 12 | 12 | 14 | 14 | 14 | 16 | 16 | 16 | 18 | 18 | 18 | 20 | 20 | 20 | 22 | 22 | 22 | 24 | 24 | 24 | 26 | 26 | 26 | 28 | 28 | 28 | 30 | 30 | 30 | 32 | 32 | 32 | 34 | 34 | 34 | |
| 0.401 - 0.425 | 06 | 06 | 08 | 08 | 10 | 10 | 12 | 12 | 12 | 12 | 14 | 14 | 16 | 16 | 16 | 16 | 18 | 18 | 20 | 20 | 20 | 20 | 22 | 22 | 24 | 24 | 24 | 24 | 26 | 26 | 28 | 28 | 28 | 28 | 30 | 30 | 32 | 32 | 32 | 32 | 34 | 34 | 34 | | |
| 0.426 - 0.450 | 06 | 08 | 08 | 10 | 10 | 12 | 12 | 12 | 14 | 14 | 14 | 16 | 16 | 16 | 18 | 18 | 18 | 20 | 20 | 20 | 22 | 22 | 22 | 24 | 24 | 24 | 26 | 26 | 26 | 28 | 28 | 28 | 30 | 30 | 30 | 32 | 32 | 32 | 34 | 34 | 34 | 34 | | | |
| 0.451 - 0.475 | 08 | 08 | 10 | 10 | 12 | 12 | 14 | 14 | 14 | 14 | 16 | 16 | 18 | 18 | 18 | 18 | 20 | 20 | 22 | 22 | 22 | 22 | 24 | 24 | 26 | 26 | 26 | 26 | 28 | 28 | 30 | 30 | 30 | 30 | 32 | 32 | 34 | 34 | 34 | 34 | 34 | | | | |
| 0.476 - 0.500 | 08 | 10 | 10 | 12 | 12 | 14 | 14 | 14 | 16 | 16 | 16 | 18 | 18 | 18 | 20 | 20 | 20 | 22 | 22 | 22 | 24 | 24 | 24 | 26 | 26 | 26 | 28 | 28 | 28 | 30 | 30 | 30 | 32 | 32 | 32 | 34 | 34 | 34 | 34 | 34 | | | | | |
| 0.501 - 0.525 | 10 | 10 | 12 | 12 | 14 | 14 | 16 | 16 | 16 | 16 | 18 | 18 | 20 | 20 | 20 | 20 | 22 | 22 | 24 | 24 | 24 | 24 | 26 | 26 | 28 | 28 | 28 | 28 | 30 | 30 | 32 | 32 | 32 | 32 | 34 | 34 | 34 | 34 | 34 | | | | | | |
| 0.526 - 0.550 | 10 | 12 | 12 | 14 | 14 | 16 | 16 | 16 | 18 | 18 | 18 | 20 | 20 | 20 | 22 | 22 | 22 | 24 | 24 | 24 | 26 | 26 | 26 | 28 | 28 | 28 | 30 | 30 | 30 | 32 | 32 | 32 | 34 | 34 | 34 | 34 | 34 | | | | | | | | |
| 0.551 - 0.575 | 12 | 12 | 14 | 14 | 16 | 16 | 18 | 18 | 18 | 18 | 20 | 20 | 22 | 22 | 22 | 22 | 24 | 24 | 26 | 26 | 26 | 26 | 28 | 28 | 30 | 30 | 30 | 30 | 32 | 32 | 34 | 34 | 34 | 34 | 34 | | | | | | | | | | |
| 0.576 - 0.600 | 12 | 14 | 14 | 16 | 16 | 18 | 18 | 18 | 20 | 20 | 20 | 22 | 22 | 22 | 24 | 24 | 24 | 26 | 26 | 26 | 28 | 28 | 28 | 30 | 30 | 30 | 32 | 32 | 32 | 34 | 34 | 34 | 34 | 34 | | | | | | | | | | | |
| 0.601 - 0.625 | 14 | 14 | 16 | 16 | 18 | 18 | 20 | 20 | 20 | 20 | 22 | 22 | 24 | 24 | 24 | 24 | 26 | 26 | 28 | 28 | 28 | 28 | 30 | 30 | 32 | 32 | 32 | 32 | 34 | 34 | 34 | 34 | 34 | | | | | | | | | | | | |
| 0.626 - 0.650 | 14 | 16 | 16 | 18 | 18 | 20 | 20 | 20 | 22 | 22 | 22 | 24 | 24 | 24 | 26 | 26 | 26 | 28 | 28 | 28 | 30 | 30 | 30 | 32 | 32 | 32 | 34 | 34 | 34 | 34 | 34 | | | | | | | | | | | | | | |
| 0.651 - 0.675 | 16 | 16 | 18 | 18 | 20 | 20 | 22 | 22 | 22 | 22 | 24 | 24 | 26 | 26 | 26 | 26 | 28 | 28 | 30 | 30 | 30 | 30 | 32 | 32 | 34 | 34 | 34 | 34 | 34 | | | | | | | | | | | | | | | | |
| 0.676 - 0.700 | 16 | 18 | 18 | 20 | 20 | 22 | 22 | 22 | 24 | 24 | 24 | 26 | 26 | 26 | 28 | 28 | 28 | 30 | 30 | 30 | 32 | 32 | 32 | 34 | 34 | 34 | 34 | 34 | | | | | | | | | | | | | | | | | |
| 0.701 - 0.725 | 18 | 18 | 20 | 20 | 22 | 22 | 24 | 24 | 24 | 24 | 26 | 26 | 28 | 28 | 28 | 28 | 30 | 30 | 32 | 32 | 32 | 32 | 34 | 34 | 34 | 34 | 34 | | | | | | | | | | | | | | | | | | |
| 0.726 - 0.750 | 18 | 20 | 20 | 22 | 22 | 24 | 24 | 24 | 26 | 26 | 26 | 28 | 28 | 28 | 30 | 30 | 30 | 32 | 32 | 32 | 34 | 34 | 34 | 34 | 34 | | | | | | | | | | | | | | | | | | | | |
| 0.751 - 0.775 | 20 | 20 | 22 | 22 | 24 | 24 | 26 | 26 | 26 | 28 | 28 | 30 | 30 | 30 | 30 | 32 | 32 | 34 | 34 | 34 | 34 | 34 | 34 | | | | | | | | | | | | | | | | | | | | | | |
| 0.776 - 0.800 | 20 | 22 | 22 | 24 | 24 | 26 | 26 | 26 | 28 | 28 | 28 | 30 | 30 | 30 | 32 | 32 | 32 | 34 | 34 | 34 | 34 | 34 | | | | | | | | | | | | | | | | | | | | | | | |
| 0.801 - 0.825 | 22 | 22 | 24 | 24 | 26 | 26 | 28 | 28 | 28 | 28 | 30 | 30 | 32 | 32 | 32 | 32 | 34 | 34 | 34 | 34 | 34 | | | | | | | | | | | | | | | | | | | | | | | | |
| 0.826 - 0.850 | 22 | 24 | 24 | 26 | 26 | 28 | 28 | 28 | 30 | 30 | 30 | 32 | 32 | 32 | 34 | 34 | 34 | 34 | 34 | | | | | | | | | | | | | | | | | | | | | | | | | | |
| 0.851 - 0.875 | 24 | 24 | 26 | 26 | 28 | 28 | 30 | 30 | 30 | 30 | 32 | 32 | 34 | 34 | 34 | 34 | 34 | | | | | | | | | | | | | | | | | | | | | | | | | | | | |
| 0.876 - 0.900 | 24 | 26 | 26 | 28 | 28 | 30 | 30 | 30 | 32 | 32 | 32 | 34 | 34 | 34 | 34 | 34 | | | | | | | | | | | | | | | | | | | | | | | | | | | | | |
| 0.901 - 0.925 | 26 | 26 | 28 | 28 | 30 | 30 | 32 | 32 | 32 | 32 | 34 | 34 | 34 | 34 | 34 | | | | | | | | | | | | | | | | | | | | | | | | | | | | | | |
| 0.926 - 0.950 | 26 | 28 | 28 | 30 | 30 | 32 | 32 | 32 | 34 | 34 | 34 | 34 | 34 | | | | | | | | | | | | | | | | | | | | | | | | | | | | | | | | |
| 0.951 - 0.975 | 28 | 28 | 30 | 30 | 32 | 32 | 34 | 34 | 34 | 34 | 34 | | | | | | | | | | | | | | | | | | | | | | | | | | | | | | | | | | |
| 0.976 - 1.000 | 28 | 30 | 30 | 32 | 32 | 34 | 34 | 34 | 34 | 34 | | | | | | | | | | | | | | | | | | | | | | | | | | | | | | | | | | | |
| 1.001 - 1.025 | 30 | 30 | 32 | 32 | 34 | 34 | 34 | 34 | 34 | | | | | | | | | | | | | | | | | | | | | | | | | | | | | | | | | | | | |
| 1.026 - 1.050 | 30 | 32 | 32 | 34 | 34 | 34 | 34 | | | | | | | | | | | | | | | | | | | | | | | | | | | | | | | | | | | | | | |
| 1.051 - 1.075 | 32 | 32 | 34 | 34 | 34 | | | | | | | | | | | | | | | | | | | | | | | | | | | | | | | | | | | | | | | | |
| 1.076 - 1.100 | 32 | 34 | 34 | 34 | | | | | | | | | | | | | | | | | | | | | | | | | | | | | | | | | | | | | | | | | |
| 1.101 - 1.125 | 34 | 34 | 34 | | | | | | | | | | | | | | | | | | | | | | | | | | | | | | | | | | | | | | | | | | |
| 1.126 - 1.150 | 34 | 34 | | | | | | | | | | | | | | | | | | | | | | | | | | | | | | | | | | | | | | | | | | | |
| 1.151 - 1.170 | 34 | | | | | | | | | | | | | | | | | | | | | | | | | | | | | | | | | | | | | | | | | | | | |

New shim thickness mm (in.)

| Shim No. | Thickness | Shim No. | Thickness |
|---|---|---|---|
| 02 | 2.500 (0.0984) | 20 | 2.950 (0.1161) |
| 04 | 2.550 (0.1004) | 22 | 3.000 (0.1181) |
| 06 | 2.600 (0.1024) | 24 | 3.050 (0.1201) |
| 08 | 2.650 (0.1043) | 26 | 3.100 (0.1220) |
| 10 | 2.700 (0.1063) | 28 | 3.150 (0.1240) |
| 12 | 2.750 (0.1083) | 30 | 3.200 (0.1260) |
| 14 | 2.800 (0.1102) | 32 | 3.250 (0.1280) |
| 16 | 2.850 (0.1122) | 34 | 3.300 (0.1299) |
| 18 | 2.900 (0.1142) | | |

EXAMPLE: The .1102" (2.800 mm) shim is installed and the measured clearance is .0177" (.450 mm). Replace the .1102" (2.800 mm) shim with a No. 18 shim.

91C17899

Courtesy of Toyota Motor Sales, U.S.A., Inc.

***Fig. 4: Selecting Exhaust Valve Adjusting Shim***

# 1991 ENGINES
# 2.5L V6 (Cont.)

INTAKE VALVES

| Measured clearance (mm) | Installed shim thickness (mm) | | | | | | | | | | | | | | | | | | | | | | | | | | | | | | | | | | | | | | | | | | | | |
|---|---|---|---|---|---|---|---|---|---|---|---|---|---|---|---|---|---|---|---|---|---|---|---|---|---|---|---|---|---|---|---|---|---|---|---|---|---|---|---|---|---|---|---|---|---|
| | 2.500 | 2.525 | 2.550 | 2.575 | 2.600 | 2.620 | 2.640 | 2.650 | 2.660 | 2.680 | 2.700 | 2.720 | 2.740 | 2.750 | 2.760 | 2.780 | 2.800 | 2.820 | 2.840 | 2.850 | 2.860 | 2.880 | 2.900 | 2.920 | 2.940 | 2.950 | 2.960 | 2.980 | 3.000 | 3.020 | 3.040 | 3.050 | 3.060 | 3.080 | 3.100 | 3.120 | 3.140 | 3.150 | 3.160 | 3.180 | 3.200 | 3.225 | 3.250 | 3.275 | 3.300 |
| 0.000 - 0.025 | | | | | | 02 | 02 | 02 | 02 | 02 | 04 | 04 | 04 | 06 | 06 | 06 | 08 | 08 | 08 | 10 | 10 | 10 | 12 | 12 | 12 | 14 | 14 | 14 | 16 | 16 | 16 | 18 | 18 | 18 | 20 | 20 | 20 | 22 | 22 | 22 | 24 | 24 | 26 | 26 | 28 |
| 0.026 - 0.050 | | | | | 02 | 02 | 02 | 02 | 02 | 04 | 04 | 06 | 06 | 06 | 06 | 08 | 08 | 10 | 10 | 10 | 10 | 12 | 12 | 14 | 14 | 14 | 14 | 16 | 16 | 18 | 18 | 18 | 18 | 20 | 20 | 22 | 22 | 22 | 22 | 24 | 24 | 26 | 26 | 28 | 28 |
| 0.051 - 0.075 | | | | 02 | 02 | 02 | 02 | 04 | 04 | 04 | 06 | 06 | 06 | 08 | 08 | 08 | 10 | 10 | 10 | 12 | 12 | 12 | 14 | 14 | 14 | 16 | 16 | 16 | 18 | 18 | 18 | 20 | 20 | 20 | 22 | 22 | 22 | 24 | 24 | 24 | 26 | 26 | 28 | 28 | 30 |
| 0.076 - 0.100 | | | 02 | 02 | 02 | 04 | 04 | 04 | 04 | 06 | 06 | 08 | 08 | 08 | 08 | 10 | 10 | 12 | 12 | 12 | 12 | 14 | 14 | 16 | 16 | 16 | 16 | 18 | 18 | 20 | 20 | 20 | 20 | 22 | 22 | 24 | 24 | 24 | 24 | 26 | 26 | 28 | 28 | 30 | 30 |
| 0.101 - 0.125 | | 02 | 02 | 02 | 04 | 04 | 04 | 06 | 06 | 06 | 08 | 08 | 08 | 10 | 10 | 10 | 12 | 12 | 12 | 14 | 14 | 14 | 16 | 16 | 16 | 18 | 18 | 18 | 20 | 20 | 20 | 22 | 22 | 22 | 24 | 24 | 24 | 26 | 26 | 26 | 28 | 28 | 30 | 30 | 32 |
| 0.126 - 0.129 | | 02 | 02 | 04 | 04 | 04 | 06 | 06 | 06 | 08 | 08 | 08 | 10 | 10 | 10 | 12 | 12 | 12 | 14 | 14 | 14 | 16 | 16 | 16 | 18 | 18 | 18 | 20 | 20 | 20 | 22 | 22 | 22 | 24 | 24 | 24 | 26 | 26 | 26 | 28 | 28 | 28 | 30 | 30 | 32 |
| 0.130 - 0.230 | | | | | | | | | | | | | | | | | | | | | | | | | | | | | | | | | | | | | | | | | | | | | |
| 0.231 - 0.250 | 04 | 06 | 06 | 08 | 08 | 10 | 10 | 10 | 10 | 12 | 12 | 14 | 14 | 14 | 14 | 16 | 16 | 18 | 18 | 18 | 18 | 20 | 20 | 22 | 22 | 22 | 22 | 24 | 24 | 26 | 26 | 26 | 26 | 28 | 28 | 30 | 30 | 30 | 30 | 32 | 32 | 34 | 34 | 34 | |
| 0.251 - 0.275 | 06 | 06 | 08 | 08 | 10 | 10 | 10 | 12 | 12 | 12 | 14 | 14 | 14 | 16 | 16 | 16 | 18 | 18 | 18 | 20 | 20 | 20 | 22 | 22 | 22 | 24 | 24 | 24 | 26 | 26 | 26 | 28 | 28 | 28 | 30 | 30 | 30 | 32 | 32 | 32 | 34 | 34 | 34 | 34 | |
| 0.276 - 0.300 | 06 | 08 | 08 | 10 | 10 | 12 | 12 | 12 | 12 | 14 | 14 | 16 | 16 | 16 | 16 | 18 | 18 | 20 | 20 | 20 | 20 | 22 | 22 | 24 | 24 | 24 | 24 | 26 | 26 | 28 | 28 | 28 | 28 | 30 | 30 | 32 | 32 | 32 | 32 | 34 | 34 | 34 | 34 | | |
| 0.301 - 0.325 | 08 | 08 | 10 | 10 | 12 | 12 | 12 | 14 | 14 | 14 | 16 | 16 | 16 | 18 | 18 | 18 | 20 | 20 | 20 | 22 | 22 | 22 | 24 | 24 | 24 | 26 | 26 | 26 | 28 | 28 | 28 | 30 | 30 | 30 | 32 | 32 | 32 | 34 | 34 | 34 | 34 | 34 | | | |
| 0.326 - 0.350 | 08 | 10 | 10 | 12 | 12 | 14 | 14 | 14 | 14 | 16 | 16 | 18 | 18 | 18 | 18 | 20 | 20 | 22 | 22 | 22 | 22 | 24 | 24 | 26 | 26 | 26 | 26 | 28 | 28 | 30 | 30 | 30 | 30 | 32 | 32 | 34 | 34 | 34 | 34 | 34 | 34 | | | | |
| 0.351 - 0.375 | 10 | 10 | 12 | 12 | 14 | 14 | 14 | 16 | 16 | 16 | 18 | 18 | 18 | 20 | 20 | 20 | 22 | 22 | 22 | 24 | 24 | 24 | 26 | 26 | 26 | 28 | 28 | 28 | 30 | 30 | 30 | 32 | 32 | 32 | 34 | 34 | 34 | 34 | 34 | | | | | | |
| 0.376 - 0.400 | 10 | 12 | 12 | 14 | 14 | 16 | 16 | 16 | 16 | 18 | 18 | 20 | 20 | 20 | 20 | 22 | 22 | 24 | 24 | 24 | 24 | 26 | 26 | 28 | 28 | 28 | 28 | 30 | 30 | 32 | 32 | 32 | 32 | 34 | 34 | 34 | 34 | 34 | | | | | | | |
| 0.401 - 0.425 | 12 | 12 | 14 | 14 | 16 | 16 | 16 | 18 | 18 | 18 | 20 | 20 | 20 | 22 | 22 | 22 | 24 | 24 | 24 | 26 | 26 | 26 | 28 | 28 | 28 | 30 | 30 | 30 | 32 | 32 | 32 | 34 | 34 | 34 | 34 | 34 | | | | | | | | | |
| 0.426 - 0.450 | 12 | 14 | 14 | 16 | 16 | 18 | 18 | 18 | 18 | 20 | 20 | 22 | 22 | 22 | 22 | 24 | 24 | 26 | 26 | 26 | 26 | 28 | 28 | 30 | 30 | 30 | 30 | 32 | 32 | 34 | 34 | 34 | 34 | 34 | 34 | | | | | | | | | | |
| 0.451 - 0.475 | 14 | 14 | 16 | 16 | 18 | 18 | 18 | 20 | 20 | 20 | 22 | 22 | 22 | 24 | 24 | 24 | 26 | 26 | 26 | 28 | 28 | 28 | 30 | 30 | 30 | 32 | 32 | 32 | 34 | 34 | 34 | 34 | 34 | | | | | | | | | | | | |
| 0.476 - 0.500 | 14 | 16 | 16 | 18 | 18 | 20 | 20 | 20 | 20 | 22 | 22 | 24 | 24 | 24 | 24 | 26 | 26 | 28 | 28 | 28 | 28 | 30 | 30 | 32 | 32 | 32 | 32 | 34 | 34 | 34 | 34 | 34 | | | | | | | | | | | | | |
| 0.501 - 0.525 | 16 | 16 | 18 | 18 | 20 | 20 | 20 | 22 | 22 | 22 | 24 | 24 | 24 | 26 | 26 | 26 | 28 | 28 | 28 | 30 | 30 | 30 | 32 | 32 | 32 | 34 | 34 | 34 | 34 | 34 | | | | | | | | | | | | | | | |
| 0.526 - 0.550 | 16 | 18 | 18 | 20 | 20 | 22 | 22 | 22 | 22 | 24 | 24 | 26 | 26 | 26 | 26 | 28 | 28 | 30 | 30 | 30 | 30 | 32 | 32 | 34 | 34 | 34 | 34 | 34 | 34 | | | | | | | | | | | | | | | | |
| 0.551 - 0.575 | 18 | 18 | 20 | 20 | 22 | 22 | 22 | 24 | 24 | 24 | 26 | 26 | 26 | 28 | 28 | 28 | 30 | 30 | 30 | 32 | 32 | 32 | 34 | 34 | 34 | 34 | 34 | | | | | | | | | | | | | | | | | | |
| 0.576 - 0.600 | 18 | 20 | 20 | 22 | 22 | 24 | 24 | 24 | 24 | 26 | 26 | 28 | 28 | 28 | 28 | 30 | 30 | 32 | 32 | 32 | 32 | 34 | 34 | 34 | 34 | 34 | | | | | | | | | | | | | | | | | | | |
| 0.601 - 0.625 | 20 | 20 | 22 | 22 | 24 | 24 | 24 | 26 | 26 | 26 | 28 | 28 | 28 | 30 | 30 | 30 | 32 | 32 | 32 | 34 | 34 | 34 | 34 | 34 | | | | | | | | | | | | | | | | | | | | | |
| 0.626 - 0.650 | 20 | 22 | 22 | 24 | 24 | 26 | 26 | 26 | 26 | 28 | 28 | 30 | 30 | 30 | 30 | 32 | 32 | 34 | 34 | 34 | 34 | 34 | 34 | | | | | | | | | | | | | | | | | | | | | | |
| 0.651 - 0.675 | 22 | 22 | 24 | 24 | 26 | 26 | 26 | 28 | 28 | 28 | 30 | 30 | 30 | 32 | 32 | 32 | 34 | 34 | 34 | 34 | 34 | | | | | | | | | | | | | | | | | | | | | | | | |
| 0,676 - 0.700 | 22 | 24 | 24 | 26 | 26 | 28 | 28 | 28 | 28 | 30 | 30 | 32 | 32 | 32 | 32 | 34 | 34 | 34 | 34 | 34 | | | | | | | | | | | | | | | | | | | | | | | | | |
| 0.701 - 0.725 | 24 | 24 | 26 | 26 | 28 | 28 | 28 | 30 | 30 | 30 | 32 | 32 | 32 | 34 | 34 | 34 | 34 | 34 | | | | | | | | | | | | | | | | | | | | | | | | | | | |
| 0.726 - 0.750 | 24 | 26 | 26 | 28 | 28 | 30 | 30 | 30 | 30 | 32 | 32 | 34 | 34 | 34 | 34 | 34 | | | | | | | | | | | | | | | | | | | | | | | | | | | | | |
| 0.751 - 0.775 | 26 | 26 | 28 | 28 | 30 | 30 | 30 | 32 | 32 | 32 | 34 | 34 | 34 | 34 | 34 | | | | | | | | | | | | | | | | | | | | | | | | | | | | | | |
| 0.776 - 0.800 | 26 | 28 | 28 | 30 | 30 | 32 | 32 | 32 | 32 | 34 | 34 | 34 | 34 | 34 | | | | | | | | | | | | | | | | | | | | | | | | | | | | | | | |
| 0.801 - 0.825 | 28 | 28 | 30 | 30 | 32 | 32 | 32 | 34 | 34 | 34 | 34 | 34 | | | | | | | | | | | | | | | | | | | | | | | | | | | | | | | | | |
| 0.826 - 0.850 | 28 | 30 | 30 | 32 | 32 | 32 | 34 | 34 | 34 | 34 | 34 | | | | | | | | | | | | | | | | | | | | | | | | | | | | | | | | | | |
| 0.851 - 0.875 | 30 | 30 | 32 | 32 | 34 | 34 | 34 | 34 | 34 | | | | | | | | | | | | | | | | | | | | | | | | | | | | | | | | | | | | |
| 0.876 - 0.900 | 30 | 32 | 32 | 34 | 34 | 34 | 34 | 34 | | | | | | | | | | | | | | | | | | | | | | | | | | | | | | | | | | | | | |
| 0.901 - 0.925 | 32 | 32 | 34 | 34 | 34 | 34 | | | | | | | | | | | | | | | | | | | | | | | | | | | | | | | | | | | | | | | |
| 0.926 - 0.950 | 32 | 34 | 34 | 34 | 34 | | | | | | | | | | | | | | | | | | | | | | | | | | | | | | | | | | | | | | | | |
| 0.951 - 0.975 | 34 | 34 | 34 | 34 | | | | | | | | | | | | | | | | | | | | | | | | | | | | | | | | | | | | | | | | | |
| 0.976 - 1.000 | 34 | 34 | 34 | | | | | | | | | | | | | | | | | | | | | | | | | | | | | | | | | | | | | | | | | | |
| 1.001 - 1.025 | 34 | 34 | | | | | | | | | | | | | | | | | | | | | | | | | | | | | | | | | | | | | | | | | | | |
| 1.026 - 1.030 | 34 | | | | | | | | | | | | | | | | | | | | | | | | | | | | | | | | | | | | | | | | | | | | |

New shim thickness mm (in.)

| Shim No. | Thickness | Shim No. | Thickness |
|---|---|---|---|
| 02 | 2.500 (0.0984) | 20 | 2.950 (0.1161) |
| 04 | 2.550 (0.1004) | 22 | 3.000 (0.1181) |
| 06 | 2.600 (0.1024) | 24 | 3.050 (0.1201) |
| 08 | 2.650 (0.1043) | 26 | 3.100 (0.1220) |
| 10 | 2.700 (0.1063) | 28 | 3.150 (0.1240) |
| 12 | 2.750 (0.1083) | 30 | 3.200 (0.1260) |
| 14 | 2.800 (0.1102) | 32 | 3.250 (0.1280) |
| 16 | 2.850 (0.1122) | 34 | 3.300 (0.1299) |
| 18 | 2.900 (0.1142) | | |

EXAMPLE: The .1102" (2.800 mm) shim is installed and the measured clearance is .0177" (.450 mm). Replace the .1102" (2.800 mm) shim with a No. 18 shim.

91B17898

Courtesy of Toyota Motor Sales, U.S.A., Inc.

***Fig. 5: Selecting Intake Valve Adjusting Shim***

# 1991 ENGINES
# 2.5L V6 (Cont.)

## ENGINE

***NOTE: Remove engine and transaxle as an assembly.***

**Removal - 1)** Release fuel pressure. See FUEL PRESSURE RELEASE under REMOVAL & INSTALLATION. Drain cooling system and engine oil. Remove hood, battery, ignition coil, ignitor and bracket assembly. Remove radiator, radiator reservoir tank, alternator and alternator adjusting bar.

**2)** Disconnect necessary control cables, fuel lines, vacuum hoses, coolant hoses and electrical connections. Remove cruise control actuator assembly and vacuum pump. Remove air cleaner case assembly.

**3)** Remove glove box. Disconnect necessary electrical connections so engine wiring can be pulled out through firewall.

**4)** Remove A/C compressor, power steering pump and power steering fluid reservoir with lines attached, and secure them aside. Raise and support vehicle. Remove lower engine covers and starter.

**5)** On M/T models, remove clutch release cylinder with hoses attached, and secure them aside. On A/T models, disconnect oil cooler hoses at transaxle.

**6)** On all models, disconnect control cables, speedometer cable and electrical connections at transaxle. Remove suspension crossmember bolted to both lower suspension arm shafts. Remove front exhaust pipe.

**7)** Remove front wheels. Remove cotter pin, retainer, axle shaft nut and washer. Remove nut, and separate tie rod from steering knuckle.

**8)** Remove ball joint-to-steering knuckle bolts. Cover axle shaft boot with shop towel. Using soft-faced hammer, tap axle shaft from hub assembly.

**9)** For right axle shaft, remove axle shaft bearing retaining bolt on axle shaft support bracket. Remove bearing retaining snap ring from axle shaft support bracket. Using soft-faced hammer, tap axle shaft and center shaft from transaxle. For left axle shaft, tap axle shaft from transaxle.

***NOTE: Left axle shaft may also be removed by separating axle shaft at axle shaft flange near transaxle. If axle shaft is separated here, ensure to mark flanges for reassembly reference. Also, if axle shaft is separated, flange must be repacked with grease before reconnecting axle shaft flanges.***

**10)** Support engine with hoist. Remove engine crossmember located below engine. Remove engine and transaxle mounts. Remove engine and transaxle.

**Installation - 1)** To install, reverse removal procedure. Before installing axle shafts, ensure opening of snap ring on end of axle shaft is facing downward.

**2)** Ensure reference marks are aligned on drive shaft flanges. Tighten fasteners to specification. See TORQUE SPECIFICATIONS table at end of article. Adjust all control cables and fluid levels. Fill and bleed cooling system. See COOLING SYSTEM BLEEDING under REMOVAL & INSTALLATION.

## CYLINDER HEAD & MANIFOLDS

**Removal - 1)** Release fuel pressure. See FUEL PRESSURE RELEASE under REMOVAL & INSTALLATION. Drain cooling system. Remove lower engine covers. Disconnect necessary electrical connections, control cables and hoses from throttle body and intake manifold.

**2)** Remove cruise control actuator and vacuum pump. Remove air cleaner cap, airflow meter and air cleaner hose assembly. Raise and support vehicle. Remove right lower engine cover. Remove suspension crossmember bolted to both lower suspension arm shafts.

**3)** Remove front exhaust pipe and alternator. Disconnect electrical connector from Idle Speed Control (ISC) valve. Remove retaining bolts, ISC valve and gasket. Remove retaining bolts, throttle body and gasket. Remove EGR valve pipe, EGR valve, vacuum modulator and vacuum pipe. *See Fig. 6.*

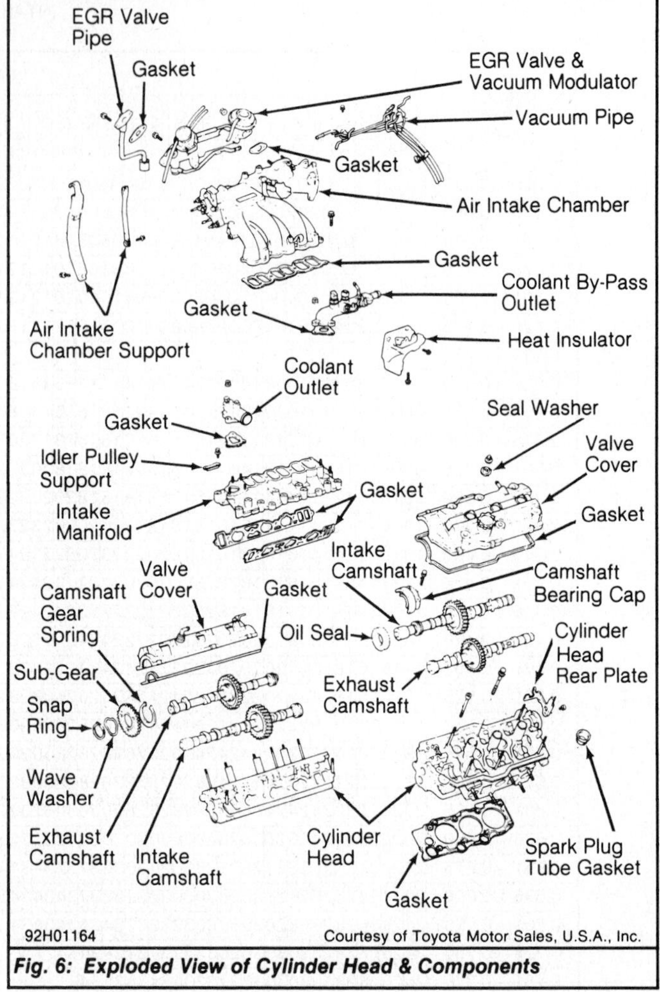

***Fig. 6: Exploded View of Cylinder Head & Components***

**4)** Disconnect spark plug wires, and remove distributor. Remove exhaust crossover pipe. Disconnect electrical connector at cold start injector. Remove union bolt, and disconnect cold start injector tube. Remove retaining bolts, cold start injector and gasket.

**5)** Remove retaining bolts/nuts, air intake chamber supports, air intake chamber and gaskets. *See Fig. 6.* Disconnect electrical connectors at fuel injectors.

**6)** Disconnect fuel lines. Remove union bolts from No. 2 fuel line, located between ends of fuel delivery pipes for fuel injectors. Remove retaining bolts, delivery pipe and fuel injectors.

***CAUTION: DO NOT allow fuel injectors to fall from delivery pipe when removing from intake manifold.***

**7)** Remove retaining nuts, coolant outlet and gasket. Remove coolant by-pass outlet, cylinder head rear plate and idler pulley support. *See Fig. 6.*

**8)** Remove retaining bolts/nuts, intake manifold and gaskets. Disconnect electrical connector on oxygen sensor, located in exhaust manifold. Remove heat insulator from exhaust manifolds.

**9)** Remove retaining nuts, exhaust manifolds and gaskets. Remove heat insulator located between exhaust manifold and cylinder head.

**10)** Remove spark plugs. Remove timing belt and camshaft sprockets. See TIMING BELT under REMOVAL & INSTALLATION. Remove No. 3 timing belt cover. *See Fig. 9.*

**11)** Remove camshafts. See CAMSHAFTS under REMOVAL & INSTALLATION. Using 8-mm hexagon wrench, remove recessed cylinder head bolts. *See Fig. 7.* Loosen cylinder head bolts in sequence in several steps. *See Fig. 7.* Remove remaining cylinder head bolts, cylinder head and gasket.

***CAUTION: Remove cylinder head bolts in proper sequence to prevent cylinder head warpage.***

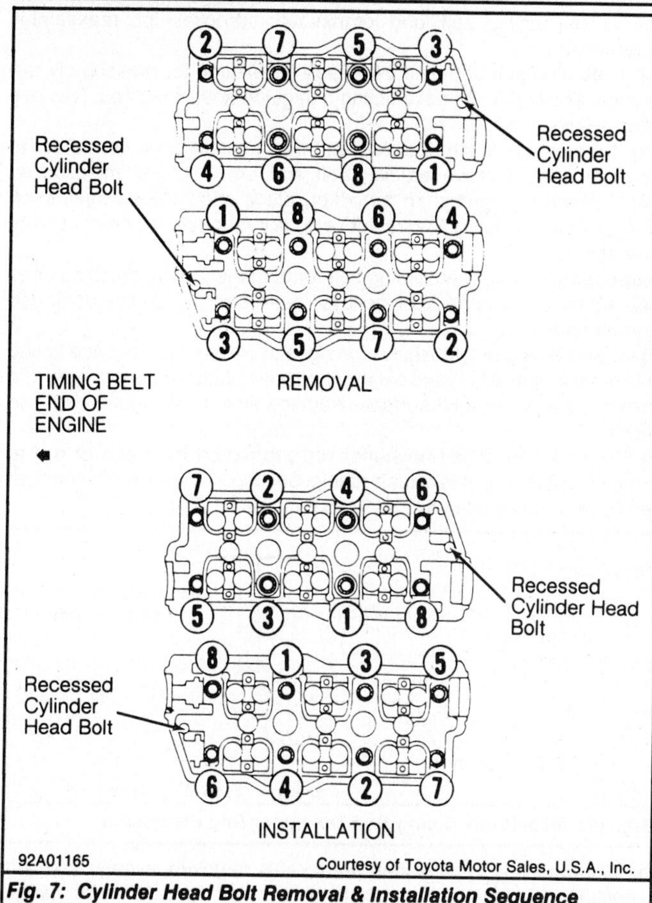


*Fig. 7: Cylinder Head Bolt Removal & Installation Sequence*

**Inspection - 1)** Inspect cylinder head for warpage at cylinder block area. Replace cylinder head if warpage exceeds specification. See CYLINDER HEAD table under ENGINE SPECIFICATIONS at end of article.

**2)** Inspect cylinder block deck surface for warpage. Replace cylinder block if deck warpage exceeds specification. See CYLINDER BLOCK table under ENGINE SPECIFICATIONS at end of article.

**3)** Inspect camshaft and components. See CAMSHAFT under REMOVAL & INSTALLATION.

**Installation - 1)** To install, reverse removal procedure. Apply engine oil on cylinder head bolt threads and cylinder head bolt-to-cylinder head contact surfaces.

***CAUTION: Ensure all holes in cylinder head gaskets align with cylinder block.***

**2)** Install and tighten cylinder head bolts to specification in sequence. *See Fig. 7.* See TORQUE SPECIFICATIONS table at end of article.

**3)** Install recessed cylinder head bolts, and tighten to specification. See TORQUE SPECIFICATIONS table at end of article. If camshaft or cylinder head components are serviced, adjust valve clearance. See VALVE CLEARANCE ADJUSTMENT under ADJUSTMENTS.

**4)** Before installing valve cover and gasket, apply sealant at front and rear areas of cylinder head. *See Fig. 2.* Install gasket and valve cover. Tighten nuts to specification. See TORQUE SPECIFICATIONS table at end article.

**5)** If fuel injector was removed from delivery pipe, coat new "O" ring with gasoline. Install new "O" ring on fuel injector.

**6)** Coat distributor "O" ring with engine oil. When installing distributor, rotate crankshaft clockwise so No. 1 cylinder is at TDC on compression stroke.

**7)** Ensure timing mark on crankshaft pulley aligns with "0" mark on timing belt cover. Ensure slot area of intake camshaft on right cylinder head is positioned properly. *See Fig. 8.*

**8)** Position cutout area on coupling with alignment mark on distributor housing. *See Fig. 8.* Install distributor and retaining bolts.

**9)** To install remaining components, reverse removal procedure. Tighten all fasteners to specification. See TORQUE SPECIFICATIONS table at end of article. Adjust control cables. Fill and bleed cooling system. See COOLING SYSTEM BLEEDING under REMOVAL & INSTALLATION.

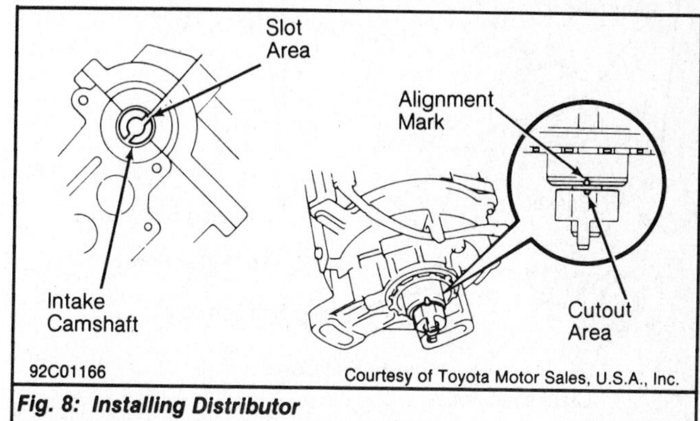


*Fig. 8: Installing Distributor*

## CRANKSHAFT FRONT SEAL (OIL PUMP INSTALLED)

**Removal & Installation - 1)** Remove timing belt and crankshaft sprocket. See TIMING BELT under REMOVAL & INSTALLATION. Using a knife, cut off oil seal lip. Pry seal from oil pump body. Be careful not to damage sealing surfaces.

**2)** To install, apply grease to lip of new seal. Using hammer and Seal Installer (SST 09309-37010), install seal until seal surface is even with oil pump body. To install remaining components, reverse removal procedure.

## CRANKSHAFT FRONT SEAL (OIL PUMP REMOVED)

**Removal & Installation -** Using hammer and drift, remove seal from oil pump body. To install, use hammer and Seal Installer (09309-37010). Install seal until seal surface is even with oil pump body. Apply grease to lip of new oil seal.

## TIMING BELT

**Removal - 1)** Disconnect negative battery cable. Remove cruise control actuator and vacuum pump. Remove power steering reservoir with hoses attached, and secure them aside.

**2)** Raise and support vehicle. Remove right front wheel. Remove right lower engine cover. Remove all drive belts.

**3)** Remove top braces on right engine mount at timing belt cover. Slightly raise engine to remove weight from right engine mount. Remove retaining bolts/nuts and right engine mount assembly.

**4)** Remove spark plugs. Remove retaining bolts, No. 2 timing belt cover, gasket and right engine mount bracket. *See Fig. 9.* Note bolt length and location of No. 2 timing belt cover bolts for reassembly reference.

***CAUTION: If timing belt is to be reused, mark direction of timing belt rotation and location on camshaft sprockets for reassembly reference. Also place reference mark on timing belt at upper edge of No. 1 timing belt cover.***

**5)** Rotate crankshaft clockwise so No. 1 cylinder is at TDC of compression stroke. Ensure timing mark on crankshaft pulley aligns with "0" mark on No. 1 timing belt cover.

**6)** Ensure timing marks on camshaft sprockets are aligned with timing marks on No. 3 timing belt cover. *See Fig. 10.* Remove retaining bolts and timing belt tensioner.

# 1991 ENGINES
# 2.5L V6 (Cont.)

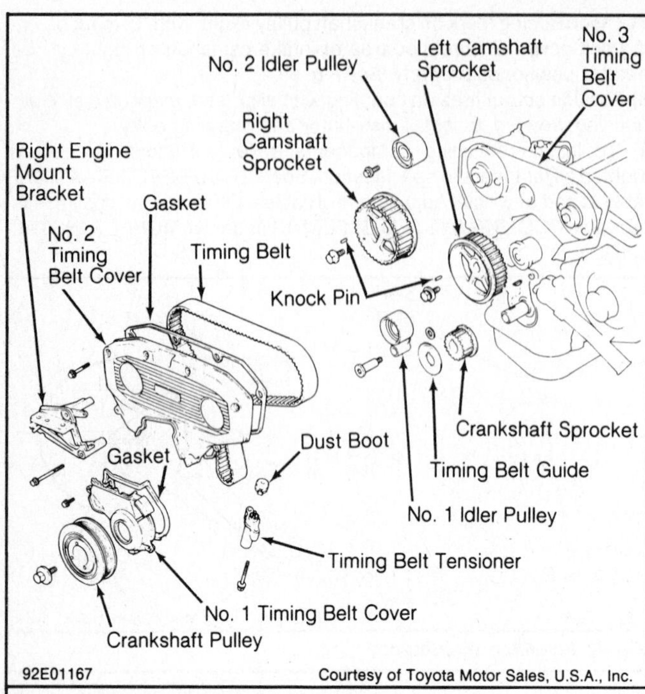


*Fig. 9: Exploded View of Timing Belt & Components*

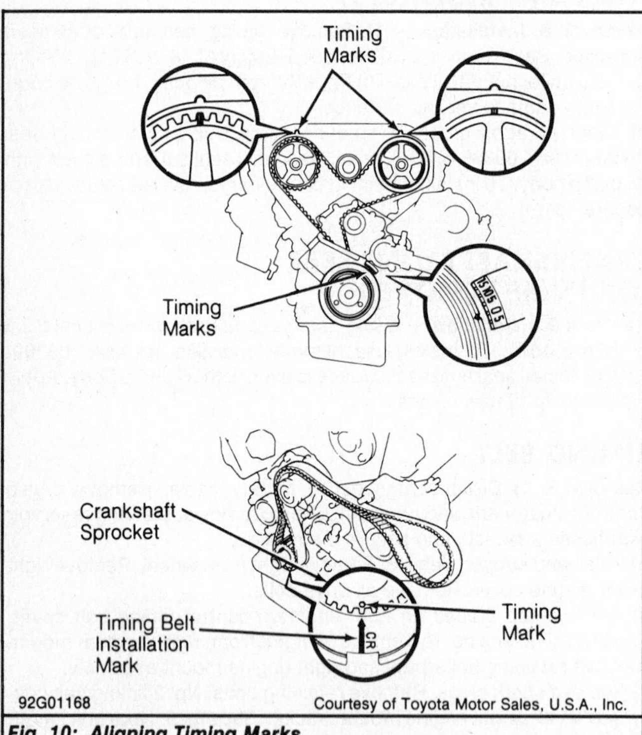


*Fig. 10: Aligning Timing Marks*

**7)** Install Camshaft Sprocket Holder (SST 09278-54012) in holes on front of right camshaft sprocket. Slightly rotate right camshaft sprocket clockwise to release tension on timing belt between camshaft sprockets. Remove timing belt from camshaft sprockets.
**8)** Using Pulley Holder (SST 09213-54014) and Handle (SST 09330-00021), hold crankshaft pulley, and remove retaining bolt.
**9)** If timing belt is to be reused, ensure reference mark placed on timing belt aligns with upper edge of No. 1 timing belt cover when timing mark on crankshaft pulley is aligned with "0" mark on No. 1 timing belt cover.
**10)** Using puller, remove crankshaft pulley. DO NOT allow crankshaft to rotate. Remove No. 1 timing belt cover and gasket. If timing belt is to be reused, mark direction of belt rotation, and place reference marks on timing belt and crankshaft sprocket for reassembly reference.
**11)** Note direction of timing belt guide installation for reassembly reference. *See Fig. 9.* Remove timing belt guide and timing belt. Remove idler pulleys (if necessary).
**12)** If removing camshaft sprocket, use camshaft sprocket holder to hold sprocket. Remove retaining bolt, and remove camshaft sprocket.
**13)** If removing crankshaft sprocket, place shop towels against oil pump housing. Using 2 screwdrivers, pry crankshaft sprocket from crankshaft.

**Inspection - 1)** Inspect timing belt for damaged teeth, cracking or oil contamination. Ensure idler pulleys rotate freely. Replace damaged components.
**2)** Inspect timing belt tensioner for signs of oil leakage. Replace timing belt tensioner if oil leakage exists. Hold timing belt tensioner body, and press rod against solid surface. Replace timing belt tensioner if rod moves.
**3)** Measure timing belt tensioner rod protrusion from end of rod to edge of timing belt tensioner housing. *See Fig. 11.* Replace timing belt tensioner if distance is not .413-.453" (10.49-11.51 mm).

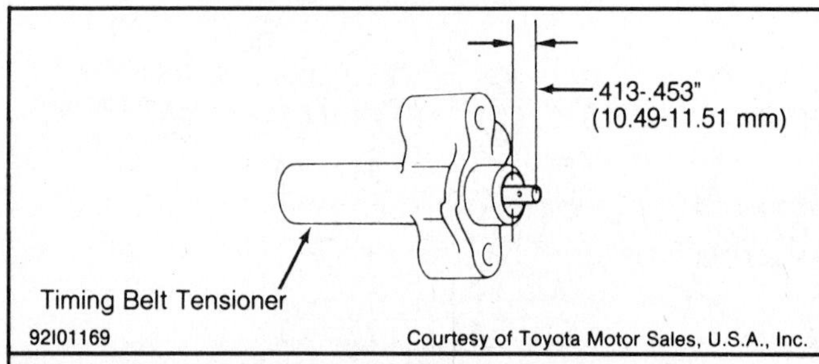


*Fig. 11: Measuring Timing Belt Tensioner Rod Protrusion*

**Installation - 1)** If crankshaft sprocket is removed, align crankshaft sprocket with key in crankshaft, and install sprocket with flange toward cylinder block.
**2)** Install No. 1 idler pulley (if removed). Apply Loctite 242 on threads of No. 1 idler pulley retaining bolt. Install and tighten retaining bolt to specification. See TORQUE SPECIFICATIONS table at end of article. Ensure idler pulley is clean, and pulley rotates smoothly.
**3)** Install timing belt on crankshaft sprocket with installation mark on timing belt aligned with timing mark on crankshaft sprocket. *See Fig. 10.*

***CAUTION: If reusing timing belt, ensure timing mark on crankshaft sprocket is aligned with reference mark placed on timing belt, and timing belt is installed in original direction of rotation.***

**4)** Install timing belt guide with cupped side away from crankshaft sprocket. Install No. 1 timing belt cover and gasket. Align crankshaft key with key groove of crankshaft pulley and install crankshaft pulley. Tighten retaining bolt to specification.
**5)** Install No. 2 idler pulley. Tighten retaining bolt to specification. Ensure idler pulley rotates smoothly. Install left camshaft sprocket with flange side facing away from cylinder head. *See Fig. 9.*
**6)** Align knock pin hole in camshaft sprocket with hole in camshaft, and install knock pin. Install and tighten camshaft sprocket retaining bolt to specification. See TORQUE SPECIFICATIONS table at end of article.
**7)** Rotate crankshaft pulley so timing mark on crankshaft pulley aligns with "0" mark on No. 1 timing belt cover. Rotate left camshaft so timing mark on camshaft sprocket aligns with timing mark on No. 3 timing belt cover. *See Fig. 10.*
**8)** Rotate right camshaft so knock pin hole in camshaft aligns with timing mark on No. 3 timing belt cover. *See Fig. 10.*

**9)** If reusing timing belt, ensure reference mark placed on timing belt aligns with upper edge of No. 1 timing belt cover when timing mark on crankshaft pulley is aligned with "0" mark on No. 1 timing belt cover.

**10)** Using camshaft sprocket holder, slightly rotate left camshaft sprocket clockwise, and install timing belt on camshaft sprocket. Ensure reference mark on timing belt aligns with timing mark on camshaft sprocket.

**11)** Using camshaft sprocket holder, slightly rotate left camshaft sprocket, and align timing mark on camshaft sprocket with timing mark on No. 3 timing belt cover. Ensure tension exists on timing belt between crankshaft sprocket and left camshaft sprocket.

**12)** Align reference mark on timing belt with timing mark on right camshaft sprocket. Install right camshaft sprocket on camshaft with flange side toward cylinder head. Ensure timing mark on right camshaft sprocket aligns with timing mark on No. 3 timing belt cover. *See Fig. 10.*

**13)** Using camshaft sprocket holder, slightly rotate right camshaft sprocket so knock pin hole in camshaft sprocket aligns with knock pin hole in camshaft.

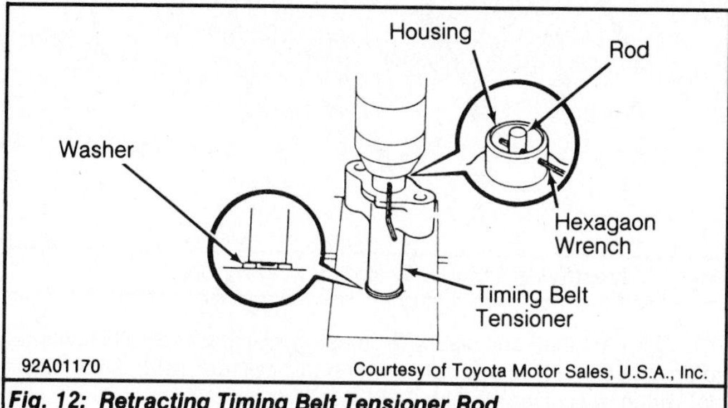


***Fig. 12: Retracting Timing Belt Tensioner Rod***

**14)** Install knock pin in right camshaft. Install right camshaft sprocket retaining bolt, and tighten it to specification. See TORQUE SPECIFICATIONS table at end of article.

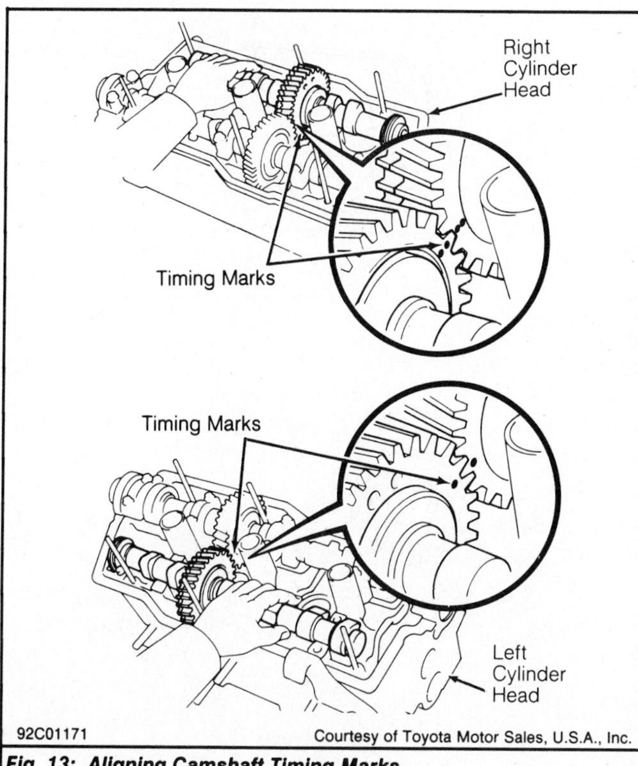


***Fig. 13: Aligning Camshaft Timing Marks***

**15)** Place washer on bottom side of timing belt tensioner. Using press, apply pressure on rod of timing belt tension until rod is retracted, and holes in rod and housing are aligned. *See Fig.12.*

**16)** Install hexagon wrench through holes in housing and rod to hold rod in retracted position. *See Fig. 12.* Release press, and install dust boot on timing belt tensioner. Install timing belt tensioner. Tighten retaining bolts to specification. See TORQUE SPECIFICATIONS table at end of article.

**17)** Remove hexagon wrench from timing belt tensioner. Rotate crankshaft clockwise 2 full revolutions from TDC to TDC. Ensure timing marks on camshaft sprockets align with those on No. 3 timing belt cover. *See Fig. 10.*

***CAUTION: Crankshaft must always be rotated clockwise. DO NOT rotate crankshaft counterclockwise.***

**18)** To install remaining components, reverse removal procedure. Tighten all fasteners to specification. See TORQUE SPECIFICATIONS table at end of article.

## CAMSHAFT

**Removal – 1)** Remove timing belt and camshaft sprockets. See TIMING BELT under REMOVAL & INSTALLATION. Remove No. 3 timing belt cover. *See Fig. 9.* When removing intake camshaft, remove distributor.

**2)** Remove retaining nuts, seal washers, valve cover and gasket. Remove spark plug tube gaskets. *See Fig. 6.* Align timing marks of camshaft gears by rotating exhaust camshaft using hex area of camshaft. *See Fig. 13.*

***NOTE: Camshaft bearing caps are numbered for location. Number is stamped on top of camshaft bearing cap. Top of camshaft bearing cap is also stamped with either an "I" for intake or an "E" for exhaust. See Figs. 15 and 17.***

**3)** Install service bolt "B" to retain exhaust camshaft sub-gear to main gear. *See Fig. 14.* Note location of camshaft bearing caps. *See Figs. 15 and 17.*

**4)** Remove exhaust camshaft bearing cap bolts in sequence in several steps. *See Fig. 16.* Remove exhaust camshaft. Remove intake camshaft bearing cap bolts in sequence in several steps. *See Fig. 18.* Remove intake camshaft and oil seal.

**5)** If disassembling exhaust camshaft, mount hexagonal area of camshaft in soft-faced vise. Install service bolt "A" in sub-gear. *See Fig. 19.* Using screwdriver, rotate sub-gear clockwise, and remove service bolt "B". Remove snap ring, wave washer, sub-gear and camshaft gear spring. *See Fig. 6.*

***CAUTION: Remove camshaft bearing caps in proper sequence to prevent damage to cylinder head and camshaft thrust surfaces.***

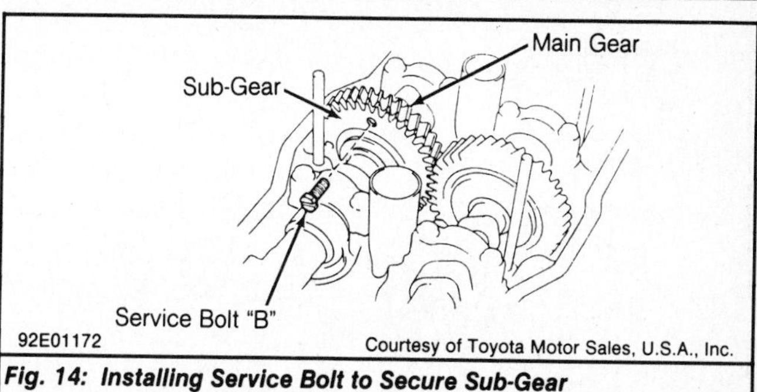


***Fig. 14: Installing Service Bolt to Secure Sub-Gear***

**Inspection – 1)** Inspect components for damage. Check camshaft journal diameter, lobe height and runout. Replace camshaft if measurements are not within specification. See CAMSHAFT table under ENGINE SPECIFICATIONS at end of article.

# 1991 ENGINES
# 2.5L V6 (Cont.)

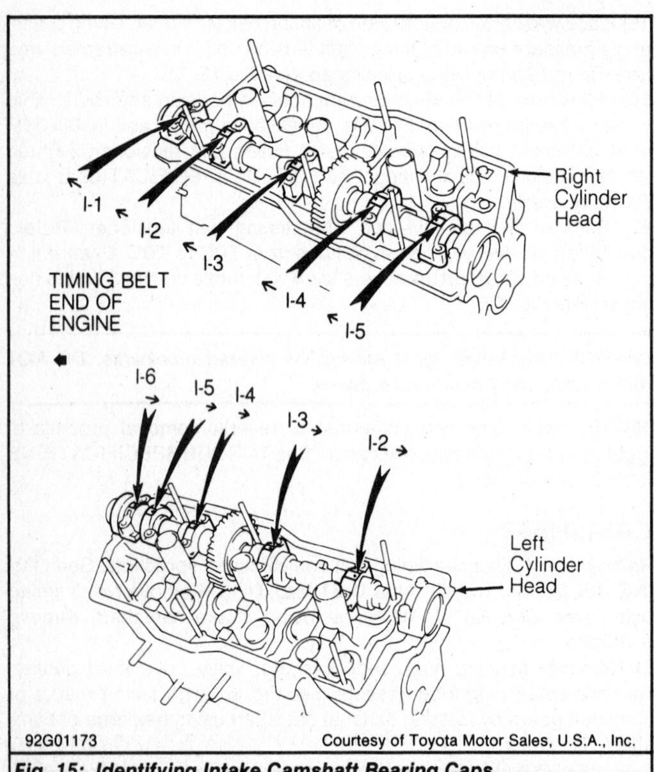


*Fig. 15: Identifying Intake Camshaft Bearing Caps*

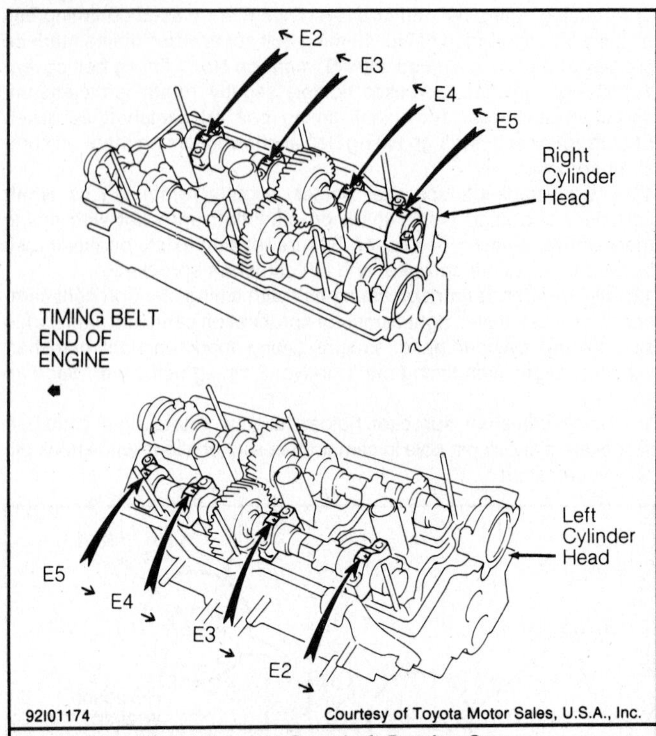


*Fig. 17: Identifying Exhaust Camshaft Bearing Caps*

**2)** Install camshaft in cylinder head. Using Plastigage, check camshaft oil clearance. Tighten camshaft bearing cap bolts to specification in sequence when checking oil clearance. *See Figs. 16 and 18.* See TORQUE SPECIFICATIONS table at end of article.

**3)** Replace camshaft and/or cylinder head if oil clearance is not within specification. See CAMSHAFT table under ENGINE SPECIFICATIONS.

**4)** Check camshaft end play with camshaft bearing cap bolts tightened to specification. Replace camshaft and/or cylinder head if end play is not within specification. See CAMSHAFT table.

**5)** Install both camshafts without sub-gear installed on exhaust camshaft. Tighten camshaft bearing cap bolts to specification. Check gear backlash between camshaft gears.

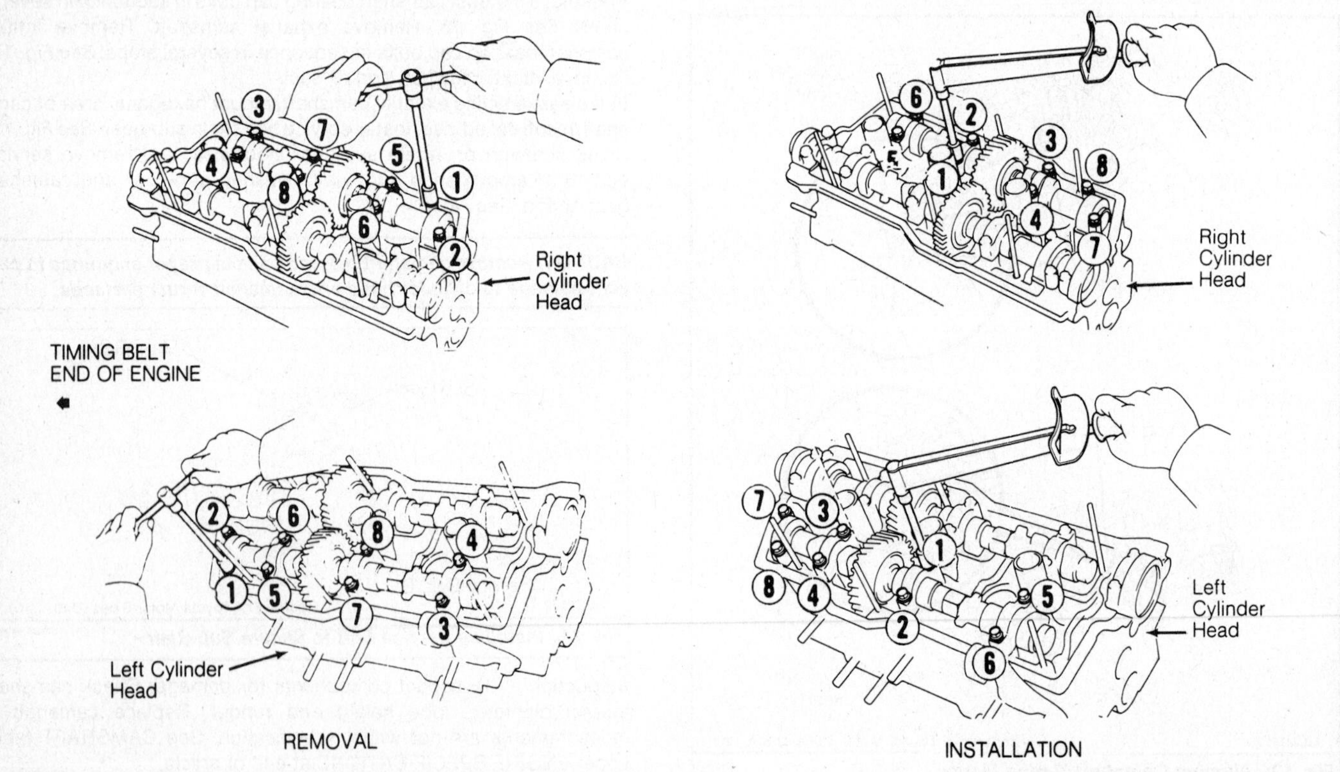

Right Cylinder Head
TIMING BELT END OF ENGINE
Left Cylinder Head
REMOVAL
INSTALLATION
92B01175
Courtesy of Toyota Motor Sales, U.S.A., Inc.

*Fig. 16: Exhaust Camshaft Bearing Cap Bolt Removal & Installation Sequence*

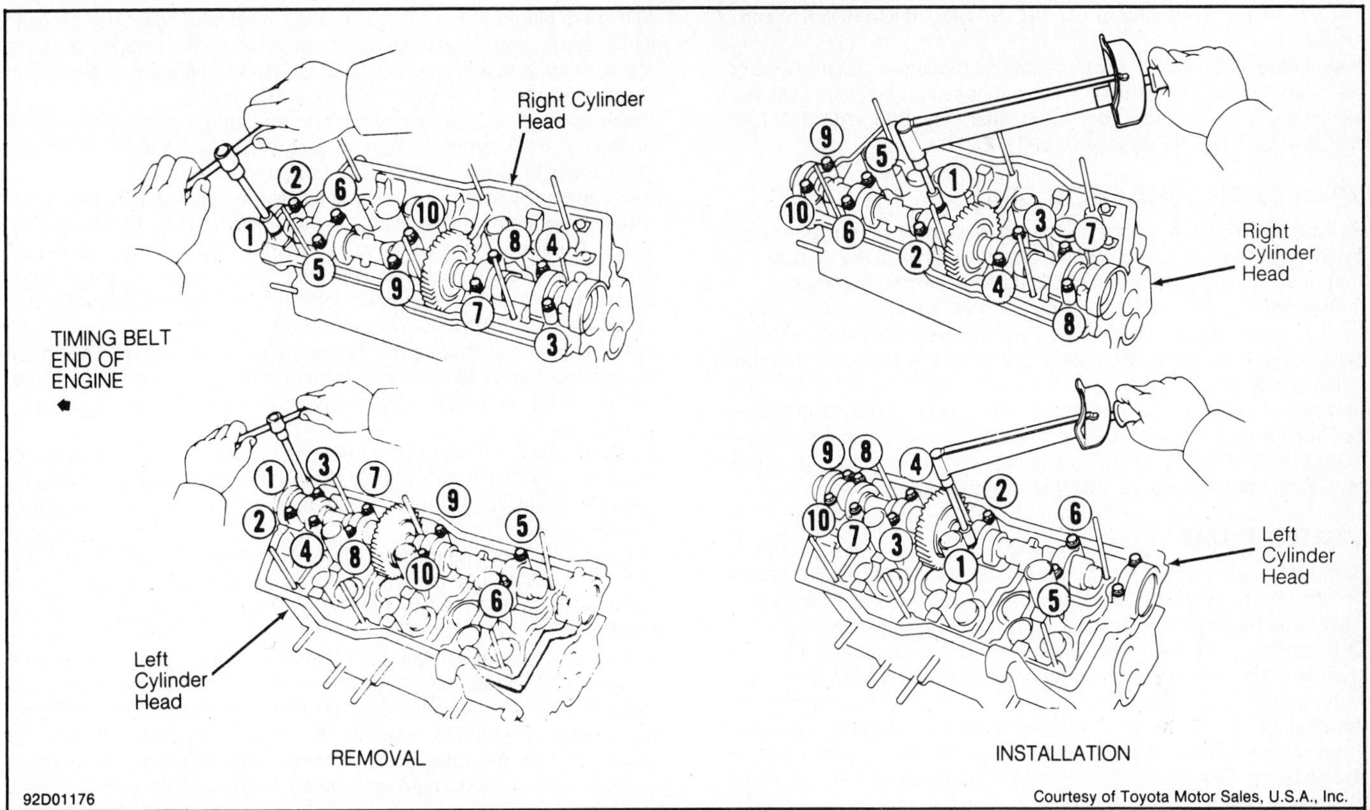

92D01176 Courtesy of Toyota Motor Sales, U.S.A., Inc.

*Fig. 18: Intake Camshaft Bearing Cap Bolt Removal & Installation Sequence*

6) Replace camshaft if gear backlash exceeds specification. See CAMSHAFT table. Measure distance between ends of camshaft gear spring. Replace camshaft gear spring if distance is not .712-.470" (18.1-18.9 mm).

**Installation – 1)** If exhaust camshaft was disassembled, reassemble camshaft by installing camshaft gear spring, sub-gear, wave washer and snap ring. Install service bolt "A". *See Fig. 19.* Using screwdriver, rotate sub-gear clockwise, and install service bolt "B". Remove service bolt "A".

**2)** Apply grease to thrust surfaces of camshafts. Install intake camshaft in cylinder head with timing mark properly aligned. *See Fig. 13.* Apply sealant on No. 1 camshaft bearing cap-to-cylinder head surface.

**3)** Install intake camshaft bearing caps in proper location. *See Fig. 15.* Ensure arrows on camshaft bearing caps point in proper direction.

**4)** Coat bottom of heads and threads of camshaft bearing cap bolts with oil. Install and tighten bolts in sequence to specification in several steps. *See Fig. 18.*

**5)** Install exhaust camshaft in cylinder head with timing mark properly aligned. *See Fig. 13.* Install exhaust camshaft bearing caps in proper location. *See Fig. 17.* Ensure arrows on camshaft bearing caps point in proper direction.

**6)** Coat bottom of heads and threads of camshaft bearing cap bolts with oil. Install and tighten bolts in sequence to specification in several steps. *See Fig. 16.*

**7)** Coat lip of intake camshaft oil seal with grease. Using Oil Seal Installer (SST 09223-46011), install oil seal in cylinder head.

***CAUTION: Ensure service bolt "B" is remove from sub-gear on exhaust camshafts.***

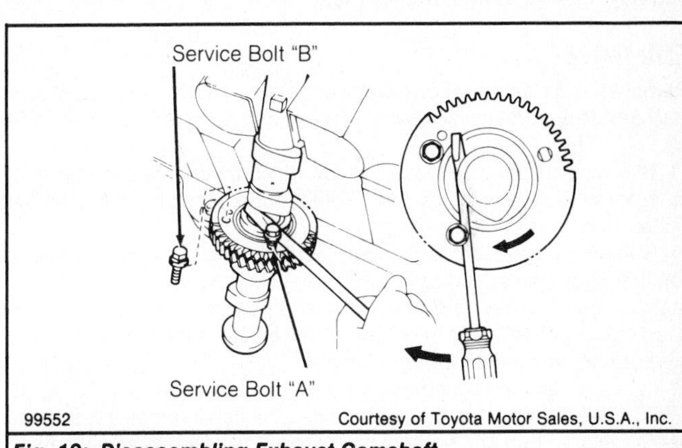


99552 Courtesy of Toyota Motor Sales, U.S.A., Inc.

*Fig. 19: Disassembling Exhaust Camshaft*

**8)** Check and adjust valve clearance. See VALVE CLEARANCE ADJUSTMENT under ADJUSTMENTS. To install remaining components, reverse removal procedure.

**9)** Before installing valve cover and gasket, apply sealant at front and rear areas of cylinder head. *See Fig. 2.* Tighten bolts/nuts to specification. See TORQUE SPECIFICATIONS table at end article.

## VALVE LIFTER

**Removal –** Remove camshaft. See CAMSHAFT under REMOVAL & INSTALLATION. Note location of adjusting shims and valve lifter for installation reference. Remove adjusting shim and valve lifter from cylinder head.

**Inspection –** Inspect components for damage. Measure lifter diameter and bore diameter. Ensure oil clearance is within specification. Replace components if measurements are not within specification.

# 1991 ENGINES
# 2.5L V6 (Cont.)

See VALVE LIFTERS table under ENGINE SPECIFICATIONS at end of article.

**Installation** – To install, reverse removal procedure. Ensure components are installed in original location. If camshaft, adjusting shims or valve lifter are replaced, check valve clearance. See VALVE CLEARANCE ADJUSTMENT under ADJUSTMENTS.

## REAR CRANKSHAFT OIL SEAL

**Removal** – Remove transaxle, clutch assembly (if equipped) and flywheel/drive plate. Using a knife, cut off oil seal lip. Pry oil seal from rear seal housing. Be careful not to damage sealing surfaces.

**Installation** – **1)** Ensure all sealing surfaces are clean. Apply grease to seal lip of new oil seal. Using Seal Installer (SST 09223-56010), install oil seal in rear seal housing until oil seal is even with rear seal housing surface.

**2)** Apply Loctite to flywheel/drive plate bolts. Install and tighten flywheel/drive plate bolts to specification in a crisscross pattern. See TORQUE SPECIFICATIONS table at end of article. To install remaining components, reverse removal procedure.

## WATER PUMP

**Removal** – **1)** Disconnect negative battery cable. Drain cooling system. Remove timing belt. See TIMING BELT under REMOVAL & INSTALLATION.

**2)** Disconnect necessary coolant hoses. Remove coolant inlet pipe and thermostat housing from water pump. Remove retaining bolts and water pump.

**Installation** – **1)** To install, reverse removal procedure. Apply sealant in groove on back of water pump before installing. Tighten bolts to specification. See TORQUE SPECIFICATIONS table at end of article.

**2)** Apply soapy water solution on inlet pipe "O" ring before installing. Fill and bleed cooling system. See COOLING SYSTEM BLEEDING under REMOVAL & INSTALLATION.

## OIL PAN

**Removal** – **1)** Disconnect negative battery cable. Remove hood. Raise and support vehicle. Remove lower engine covers. Drain engine oil.

**2)** Remove exhaust pipe located below oil pan. Remove stiffener support brace near rear of oil pan. Remove suspension crossmember bolted to both lower suspension arm shafts.

**3)** Remove engine crossmember located below engine. Remove retaining bolts/nuts, and remove oil pan.

**Installation** – **1)** To install, ensure sealing surfaces are clean. Apply bead of sealant on inside of bolt/nut holes and at center of oil pan sealing surface between bolt/nut holes.

**2)** Install oil pan, and tighten bolts/nuts to specification. See TORQUE SPECIFICATIONS table at end of article. To install remaining components, reverse removal procedure. Tighten fasteners to specification. See TORQUE SPECIFICATIONS table at end of article. Fill crankcase with oil.

# OVERHAUL

## CYLINDER HEAD

**Cylinder Head** – **1)** Inspect cylinder head warpage at cylinder block area. Replace cylinder head if warpage exceeds specification. See CYLINDER HEAD table under ENGINE SPECIFICATIONS at end of article.

**2)** Install camshaft in cylinder head. Using Plastigage, check camshaft oil clearance with camshaft bearing cap bolts tightened in sequence to specification. *See Figs. 16 and 18.* See TORQUE SPECIFICATIONS table at end of article. Replace camshaft and/or cylinder head if oil clearance is not within specification. See CAMSHAFT table under ENGINE SPECIFICATIONS at end of article.

**3)** Ensure valve lifter bore diameter is within specification. See VALVE LIFTERS table under ENGINE SPECIFICATIONS at end of article.

**4)** If spark plug tubes are to be installed in cylinder head, use press to install spark plug tube. Install spark plug tube until distance between top surface of spark plug tube and camshaft bearing cap surface of cylinder head is 1.791-1.807" (45.49-45.90 mm).

**Valve Springs** – Ensure valve spring free length, pressure and out-of-square are within specification. See VALVES & VALVE SPRINGS table under ENGINE SPECIFICATIONS at end of article.

**Valve Stem Oil Seals** – Lubricate valve stem oil seal with engine oil. Install valve stem oil seal using Oil Seal Installer (SST 09201-41020).

**Valve Guides** – **1)** Check valve stem-to-valve guide clearance. Ensure valve stem diameter is within specification. Replace valve guide if clearance exceeds specification. See CYLINDER HEAD table under ENGINE SPECIFICATIONS at end of article.

**2)** To replace valve guide, wrap tape around old valve stem. Tape must be approximately .39" (9.9 mm) from end of valve stem. From top of cylinder head, install old valve in valve guide with tape area resting on valve guide.

**3)** Hit old valve with hammer to break off old valve guide. Heat cylinder head to 176-212°F (80-100°C). Using hammer and Valve Guide Remover/Installer (SST 09201-70010), drive valve guide from top of cylinder head.

**4)** Measure I.D. of cylinder head valve guide bore. If bore I.D. is .4331-.4341" (11.001-11.026 mm), standard valve guide will be used. If bore I.D. is .4350-.4361" (11.049-11.077 mm), oversize valve guide will be used.

**5)** If bore I.D. exceeds .4341" (11.026 mm), valve guide bore must be machined to .4350-.4361" (11.049-11.077 mm) for oversize valve guide. If bore I.D. exceeds .4361" (11.077 mm), replace cylinder head.

**6)** To install valve guide, heat cylinder head to 176-212°F (80-100°C). Using hammer and valve guide remover/installer, drive valve guide in from top of cylinder head until snap ring contacts cylinder head surface.

**7)** Using .236" (6.00 mm) reamer, ream valve guide to obtain specified valve stem-to-guide oil clearance. See CYLINDER HEAD table under ENGINE SPECIFICATIONS at end of article.

**Valve Seat** – Ensure valve seat angle and seat width are within specification. See CYLINDER HEAD table under ENGINE SPECIFICATIONS at end of article. Valve seat replacement information is not available from manufacturer.

**Valves** – Ensure minimum refinish length, stem diameter and valve margin are within specification. See VALVES & VALVE SPRINGS table under ENGINE SPECIFICATIONS at end of article.

**Seat Correction Angles** – Use 30-degree and 45-degree stones to lower valve seat contact area. Use 60-degree and 75-degree stones to raise valve seat contact area.

## VALVE TRAIN

**Valve Lifters** – Ensure valve lifter diameter, bore diameter and oil clearance are within specification. See VALVE LIFTERS table under ENGINE SPECIFICATIONS at end of article.

## CYLINDER BLOCK ASSEMBLY

**Piston & Rod Assembly** – Piston must be installed on connecting rod with front mark on top of piston aligned with front mark on connecting rod. *See Fig. 20.* Piston must be installed in cylinder block with front mark toward timing belt end of engine.

**Fitting Pistons** – **1)** To determine if piston-to-cylinder clearance is within specification, measure piston skirt diameter at .955" (24.25 mm) from top of piston, at 90-degree angle to piston pin.

**2)** Different piston sizes are used. Piston diameter is determined by size mark ("1", "2" or "3") stamped on top of piston. *See Fig. 20.*

**3)** Ensure piston diameter is within specification. See PISTONS, PINS & RINGS table under ENGINE SPECIFICATIONS at end of article.

**4)** Measure cylinder bore diameter at .39" (10 mm) from top and bottom cylinder bore, and at middle of cylinder bore. Different cylinder bore sizes are used. Cylinder bore diameter can be identified by size mark ("1", "2" or "3") stamped on cylinder block deck surface. *See Fig. 25.*

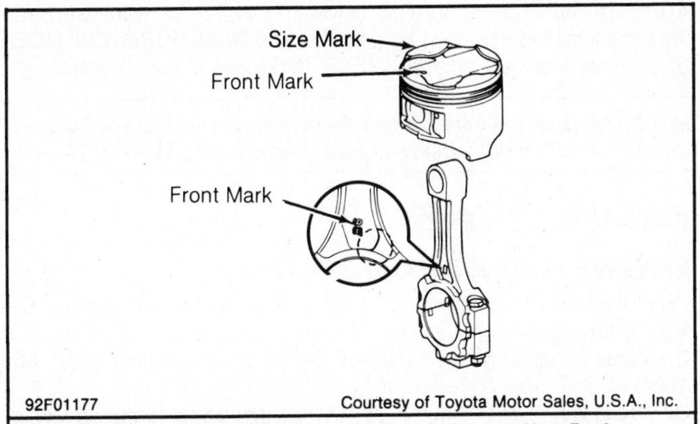


**Fig. 20: Aligning Front Marks on Piston & Connecting Rod**

**5)** Ensure cylinder bore diameter is within specification. See CYLINDER BLOCK table under ENGINE SPECIFICATIONS at end of article. Determine piston clearance. Replace piston, or bore cylinder block if clearance is not within specification. See PISTONS, PINS & RINGS table under ENGINE SPECIFICATIONS at end of article.

**Piston Rings** - Ensure piston ring end gap and side clearance are within specification. See PISTONS, PINS & RINGS table under ENGINE SPECIFICATIONS at end of article. Position piston ring gaps in proper areas, with identification mark on ring toward top of piston. *See Fig. 21.*

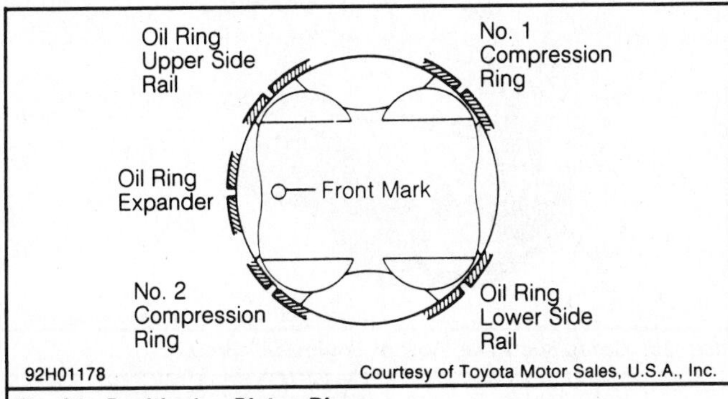


**Fig. 21: Positioning Piston Rings**

**Rod Bearings - 1)** Note direction of connecting rod and cap installation. Connecting rod must be installed so front mark at center of connecting rod is toward timing belt end of engine. *See Fig. 20.*

**2)** Connecting rod cap and rod bearing are stamped with size mark "1", "2" or "3". *See Fig. 22.* Size marks on connecting rod cap and rod bearing must be the same. If size mark cannot be read, measure rod bearing thickness to determine bearing size. See CONNECTING ROD BEARING SPECIFICATIONS table.

***NOTE: If replacing rod bearing, ensure number on replacement bearing is the same number on old bearing.***

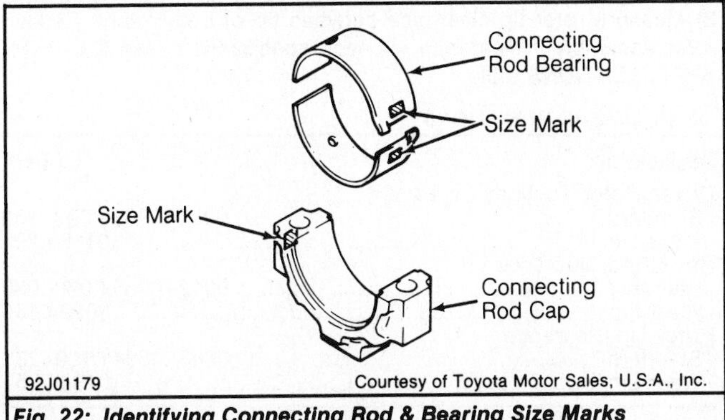


**Fig. 22: Identifying Connecting Rod & Bearing Size Marks**

**3)** Coat nut and threads with engine oil before tightening to specification. Ensure bearing oil clearance and connecting rod side play are within specification. See CRANKSHAFT, MAIN & CONNECTING ROD BEARINGS and CONNECTING RODS tables under ENGINE SPECIFICATIONS at end of article.

***CONNECTING ROD BEARING SPECIFICATIONS***

| Size Mark | Bearing Thickness In. (mm) |
|---|---|
| "1" | .0584-.0586 (1.484-1.488) |
| "2" | .0586-.0587 (1.488-1.491) |
| "3" | .0587-.0589 (1.491-1.496) |

**Crankshaft & Main Bearings - 1)** Remove main bearing cap in sequence. *See Fig. 23.* Cylinder block main bearing bore diameter is determined by size mark ("1", "2" or "3") stamped on cylinder block. *See Fig. 24.* Front size mark indicates No. 1 main bearing bore, and rear size mark indicates No. 4 main bearing bore.

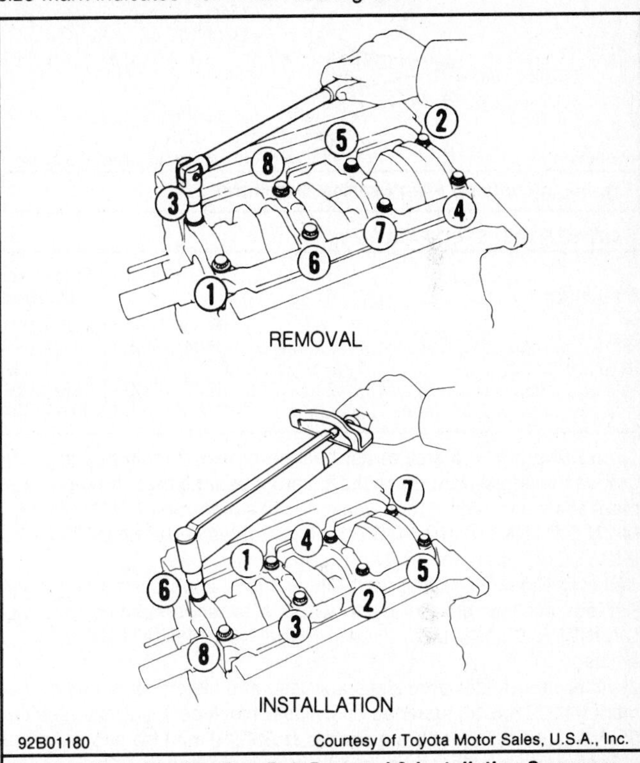


**Fig. 23: Main Bearing Cap Bolt Removal & Installation Sequence**

**2)** Main bearing journal diameter is determined by size mark ("0", "1" or "2") located on crankshaft counterweight. *See Fig. 24.* Ensure main bearing journal diameter, taper and out-of-round are with within specification. See CRANKSHAFT, MAIN & CONNECTING ROD BEARINGS table under ENGINE SPECIFICATIONS at end of article.

**3)** Main bearing size mark ("1", "2", "3", "4" or "5") is located on side of main bearing. *See Fig. 24.* If replacing main bearing, ensure number on replacement bearing is the same as number on old bearing.

**4)** If bearing size mark cannot be obtained, add size marks on cylinder block and crankshaft to determine size mark of main bearing to be used. For example, if size mark on cylinder block is "2" and size mark on crankshaft is "1", use main bearing with size mark "3".

**5)** Bearing thickness is determined by size mark. See MAIN BEARING SPECIFICATIONS table. Coat main bearing cap bolt threads and seat area of bolt with engine oil.

**6)** Tighten main bearing cap bolts to specification in sequence. *See Fig. 23.* See TORQUE SPECIFICATIONS table at end of article. Ensure crankshaft end play is within specification. See CRANKSHAFT, MAIN & CONNECTING ROD BEARINGS table under ENGINE SPECIFICATIONS at end of article.

# 1991 ENGINES
# 2.5L V6 (Cont.)

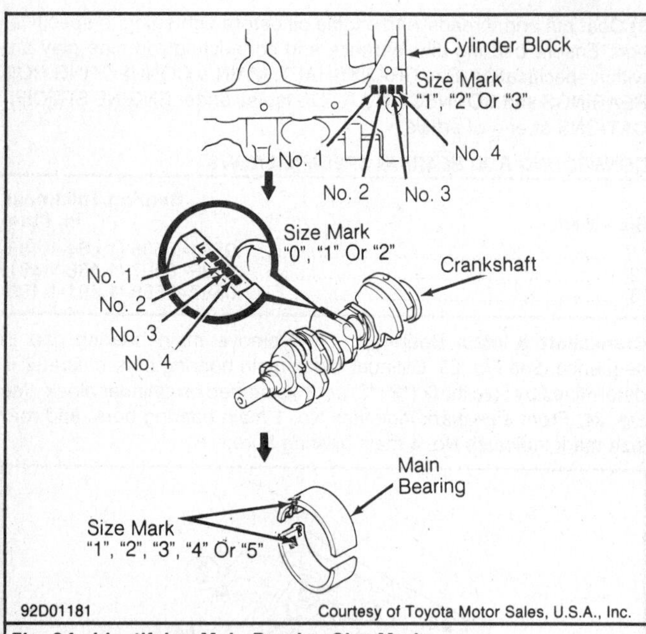


*Fig. 24: Identifying Main Bearing Size Marks*

***MAIN BEARING SPECIFICATIONS***

| Size Mark | Bearing Thickness In. (mm) |
|---|---|
| "1" | .0783-.0784 (1.989-1.991) |
| "2" | .0784-.0785 (1.991-1.994) |
| "3" | .0785-.0787 (1.994-1.999) |
| "4" | .0787-.0788 (1.999-2.001) |
| "5" | .0788-.0789 (2.001-2.004) |

**Thrust Bearing** - Install thrust bearing on No. 2 main bearing, with grooves facing toward crankshaft. Thrust bearing must be replaced if crankshaft end play is not within specification. See CRANKSHAFT, MAIN & CONNECTING ROD BEARINGS table under ENGINE SPECIFICATIONS at end of article.

**Cylinder Block** - **1)** Inspect cylinder block deck surface warpage. Replace cylinder block if deck warpage exceeds specification. See CYLINDER BLOCK table under ENGINE SPECIFICATION at end of article.

**2)** Different cylinder bore sizes are used and can be identified by size mark ("1", "2" or "3") stamped on cylinder block deck surface. *See Fig. 25.* Measure cylinder bore diameter at .39" (10 mm) from top and bottom of cylinder bore, and at middle of cylinder bore.

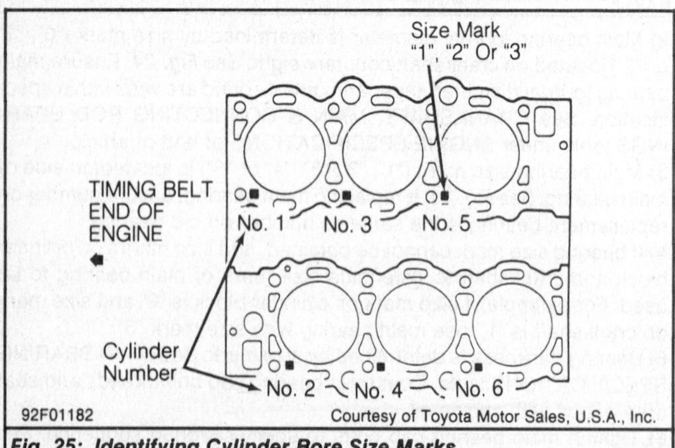


*Fig. 25: Identifying Cylinder Bore Size Marks*

**3)** Ensure cylinder bore diameter is within specification. See CYLINDER BLOCK table under ENGINE SPECIFICATIONS at end of article. Bore cylinder block if cylinder bore diameter exceeds specification.

**4)** Ensure main bearing bore I.D. is within specification with main bearing caps installed and bolts tightened to specification. See CYLINDER BLOCK table under ENGINE SPECIFICATIONS at end of article.

***NOTE: Main bearing bore I.D. is determined by main bearing bore size mark ("1", "2" or "3") stamped on cylinder block. See Fig. 24.***

## ENGINE OILING

### ENGINE LUBRICATION SYSTEM

Crankshaft-driven oil pump provides lubrication to main gallery. *See Fig. 26* for cross-sectional view of engine oil circuit.

**Crankcase Capacity** - Crankcase capacity with oil filter is 4.1 qts. (3.9L).

**Oil Pressure** - With engine at normal operating temperature, oil pressure should be at least 4.3 psi (0.3 kg/cm²) at idle and 43-78 psi (3.0-5.5 kg/cm²) at 3000 RPM.

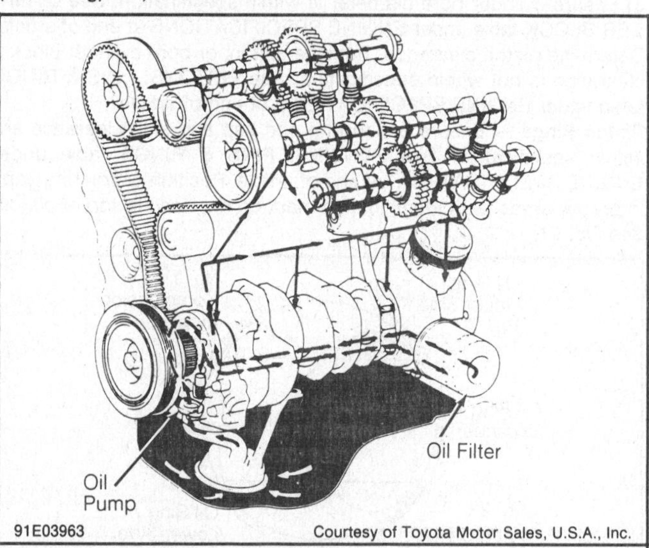


*Fig. 26: Cross-Sectional View of Engine Oil Circuit*

### OIL PUMP

**Removal & Disassembly** - **1)** Remove timing belt and crankshaft sprocket. See TIMING BELT under REMOVAL & INSTALLATION. Remove oil pan. See OIL PAN under REMOVAL & INSTALLATION.

**2)** Remove oil pump pick-up tube. Remove retaining bolts, oil pump and "O" ring. Note bolt length and location for reassembly reference. Remove oil pump body cover and oil pump components. *See Fig. 27* for exploded view of oil pump.

**Inspection** - **1)** Inspect components for damage. Ensure relief valve slides freely in bore. With rotors installed, using feeler gauge, measure clearance between driven rotor and oil pump body. Replace rotor assembly if clearance exceeds specification. See OIL PUMP SPECIFICATIONS table.

**2)** Measure rotor tip clearance between tip of both rotors. Replace rotor assembly if clearance exceeds specification. See OIL PUMP SPECIFICATIONS table.

***OIL PUMP SPECIFICATIONS***

| Application | In. (mm) |
|---|---|
| Driven Rotor-To-Body Clearance | |
| Standard | .0039-.0063 (.099-.160) |
| Wear Limit | .0118 (.299) |
| Rotor End Clearance | |
| Standard | .0012-.0035 (.030-.089) |
| Wear Limit | .0059 (.150) |
| Rotor Tip Clearance | |
| Standard | .0043-.0094 (.109-.239) |
| Wear Limit | .0138 (.351) |

# 1991 ENGINES
# 2.5L V6 (Cont.)

**3)** Place straightedge across oil pump body, above both rotors. Measure rotor end clearance between straightedge and rotor surface. Replace rotor assembly or oil pump body if clearance exceeds specification. See OIL PUMP SPECIFICATIONS table.

**Reassembly & Installation – 1)** To reassemble, reverse disassembly procedure using new "O" ring. Ensure reference marks on rotors face toward outside of oil pump body (toward cylinder block surface). Install oil pump body cover.

**2)** Using Seal Installer (SST 09309-37010), install crankshaft front seal (if removed) until seal surface is even with oil pump body. *See Fig. 27.* Coat seal lip with grease.

**3)** To install, apply sealant on rear of oil pump. Install "O" ring and oil pump assembly. Ensure splined teeth on rotor of oil pump engages with splines on crankshaft.

**4)** Install and tighten retaining bolts to specification. See TORQUE SPECIFICATIONS table at end of article. To install remaining components, reverse removal procedure.

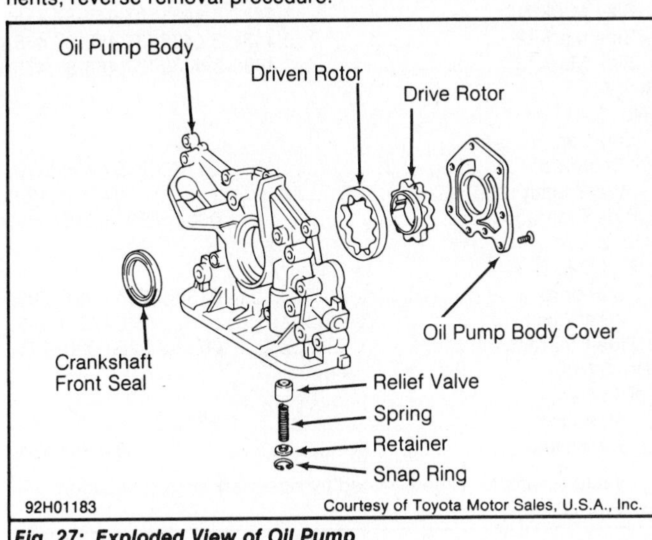


*Fig. 27: Exploded View of Oil Pump*

## TORQUE SPECIFICATIONS

### *TORQUE SPECIFICATIONS*

| Application | Ft. Lbs. (N.m) |
|---|---|
| A/C Compressor Bolt | 18 (24) |
| Air Intake Chamber Bolt | 32 (43) |
| Air Intake Chamber Support Bolt | 27 (37) |
| Axle Shaft Flange Bolt | 47 (64) |
| Axle Shaft Nut | 137 (186) |
| Axle Shaft Support Bracket-To-Cylinder Block Bolt | 47 (64) |
| Ball Joint-To-Steering Knuckle Bolt | 83 (113) |
| Camshaft Bearing Cap Bolt [1] | 12 (16) |
| Camshaft Sprocket Bolt | 80 (109) |
| Cold Start Injector Union Bolt | 14 (19) |
| Connecting Rod Nut | |
| Step 1 | 18 (24) |
| Step 2 | Additional 90 Degrees |
| Coolant By-Pass Outlet Nut | 14 (19) |
| Crankshaft Pulley Bolt | 181 (245) |

[1] – Tighten bolts to specification in sequence. *See Figs. 16 and 18.*
[2] – Tighten bolts to specification in sequence. *See Fig. 7.*
[3] – Tighten bolts to specification in sequence. *See Fig. 23.*
[4] – Tighten bolts with No. 10 stamped on bolt head to 153 ft. lbs. (207 N.m) and bolts with No. 11 to 112 ft. lbs. (152 N.m).
[5] – Tighten nuts with height of .51" (13.0 mm) to 153 ft. lbs. (207 N.m) and nuts with height of .68" (17.2 mm) to 112 ft. lbs. (152 N.m).

### *TORQUE SPECIFICATIONS (Cont.)*

| Application | Ft. Lbs. (N.m) |
|---|---|
| Cylinder Head Bolt [2] | |
| 12-Point Bolt | |
| Step 1 | 25 (34) |
| Step 2 | Additional 90 Degrees |
| Step 3 | Additional 90 Degrees |
| Recessed Hexagon Bolt | 13 (18) |
| EGR Valve Bolt/Nut | 13 (18) |
| EGR Valve Pipe | |
| Bolt | 13 (18) |
| Nut | 58 (79) |
| Engine Crossmember-To-Body Bolt | 29 (39) |
| Engine Mount Through Bolt | 64 (87) |
| Engine Mount-To-Engine Crossmember Bolt | 54 (73) |
| Exhaust Crossover Pipe | |
| Bolt | 25 (34) |
| Nut | 29 (39) |
| Exhaust Manifold Nut | 29 (39) |
| Flywheel/Drive Plate Bolt | 61 (83) |
| Front (Exhaust Manifold Side) Engine Mount Bracket Bolt | 57 (77) |
| Idler Pulley Bolt | |
| No. 1 Idler Pulley | 25 (34) |
| No. 2 Idler Pulley | 29 (39) |
| Idler Pulley Support Bolt | 13 (18) |
| Intake Manifold Bolt/Nut | 13 (18) |
| Left (Transaxle Side) Engine Mount Support Bracket Bolt | |
| A/T | |
| 12-mm Nut | 15 (20) |
| 14-mm Nut | 38 (52) |
| M/T | |
| Bolt | 14 (19) |
| Nut | 38 (52) |
| Left (Transaxle Side) Engine Mount Through Bolt | 64 (87) |
| Main Bearing Cap Bolt [3] | |
| Step 1 | 45 (61) |
| Step 2 | Additional 90 Degrees |
| Mount Bracket-To-Transaxle Bolt | 38 (52) |
| No. 2 Fuel Line Union Bolt | 24 (33) |
| Oil Pump-To-Cylinder Block Bolt | |
| 12-mm Bolt | 14 (19) |
| 14-mm Bolt | 30 (41) |
| Rear (Intake Manifold Side) Engine Mount Bracket Bolt | 57 (77) |
| Right (Timing Belt Side) Engine Mount | |
| Bolt | 47 (64) |
| Nut | |
| Bracket Side | 38 (52) |
| Body Side | 65 (88) |
| Spark Plug | 13 (18) |
| Stiffener Support Brace Bolt | 27 (37) |
| Suspension Crossmember-To-Lower Suspension Arm Shafts | |
| Bolt | [4] |
| Nut | [5] |
| Thermostat Housing Bolt | 14 (19) |
| Tie Rod Nut | 36 (49) |
| Timing Belt Tensioner Bolt | 20 (27) |
| Water Pump Bolt | 14 (19) |
| Wheel Lug Nut | 76 (103) |

[1] – Tighten bolts to specification in sequence. *See Figs. 16 and 18.*
[2] – Tighten bolts to specification in sequence. *See Fig. 7.*
[3] – Tighten bolts to specification in sequence. *See Fig. 23.*
[4] – Tighten bolts with No. 10 stamped on bolt head to 153 ft. lbs. (207 N.m) and bolts with No. 11 to 112 ft. lbs. (152 N.m).
[5] – Tighten nuts with height of .51" (13.0 mm) to 153 ft. lbs. (207 N.m) and nuts with height of .68" (17.2 mm) to 112 ft. lbs. (152 N.m).

# 1991 ENGINES
# 2.5L V6 (Cont.)

### TORQUE SPECIFICATIONS (Cont.)

| Application | INCH Lbs. (N.m) |
|---|---|
| Cold Start Injector Bolt | 48 (5) |
| Coolant Outlet Bolt | 73 (9) |
| Delivery Pipe Bolt | 108 (12) |
| No. 3 Timing Belt Cover Bolt | 65 (7) |
| Oil Pan Bolt/Nut | 52 (6) |
| Pick-Up Tube Bolt/Nut | 65 (7) |
| Rear Oil Seal Housing Bolt | 69 (8) |
| Rear Plate-To-Cylinder Block Bolt | 65 (7) |
| Throttle Body Bolt | 108 (12) |
| Valve Cover Nut | 52 (6) |

## ENGINE SPECIFICATIONS

### GENERAL SPECIFICATIONS

| Application | Specification |
|---|---|
| Displacement | 152.6 Cu. In. (2.5L) |
| Bore | 3.44" (87.3 mm) |
| Stroke | 2.74" (69.6 mm) |
| Compression Ratio | 9.0:1 |
| Fuel System | PFI |
| Horsepower @ RPM | 156 @ 5600 |
| Torque Ft. Lbs. @ RPM | 160 @ 4400 |

### CRANKSHAFT, MAIN & CONNECTING ROD BEARINGS

| Application | In. (mm) |
|---|---|
| Crankshaft | |
| End Play | |
| Standard | .0008-.0087 (.020-.220) |
| Wear Limit | .0118 (.299) |
| Runout | .0024 (.061) |
| Main Bearings | |
| Journal Diameter [1] | |
| Size Mark "0" | 2.5195-2.5197 (63.995-64.000) |
| Size Mark "1" | 2.5193-2.5195 (63.990-63.995) |
| Size Mark "2" | 2.5191-2.5193 (63.985-63.990) |
| Journal Out-Of-Round | .0008 (.020) |
| Journal Taper | .0008 (.020) |
| Oil Clearance | |
| Standard | .0011-.0022 (.028-.056) |
| Wear Limit | .0031 (.079) |
| Connecting Rod Bearings | |
| Journal Diameter | 1.8892-1.8898 (47.986-48.001) |
| Journal Out-Of-Round | .0008 (.020) |
| Journal Taper | .0008 (.020) |
| Oil Clearance | |
| Standard Crankshaft | |
| Standard | .0011-.0026 (.028-.066) |
| Wear Limit | .0031 (.079) |
| .010" (.25 mm) Undersize Crankshaft | |
| Standard | .0011-.0031 (.028-.079) |
| Wear Limit | .0031 (.079) |

[1] – Main bearing journal diameter is determined by size mark on the crankshaft. *See Fig. 24.*

### CONNECTING RODS

| Application | In. (mm) |
|---|---|
| Maximum Bend | .002 Per 3.94 (.05 Per 100.1) |
| Maximum Twist | .0059 Per 3.94 (.150 Per 100.1) |
| Side Play | |
| Standard | .0059-.0130 (.150-.330) |
| Wear Limit | .015 (.38) |

### PISTONS, PINS & RINGS

| Application | In. (mm) |
|---|---|
| Pistons | |
| Clearance | |
| Standard | .0018-.0026 (.046-.066) |
| Wear Limit | .0033 (.084) |
| Diameter [1] | |
| Size Mark "1" | 3.4427-3.4431 (87.445-87.455) |
| Size Mark "2" | 3.4431-3.4435 (87.455-87.465) |
| Size Mark "3" | 3.4435-3.4439 (87.465-87.475) |
| Rings | |
| No. 1 | |
| End Gap | |
| Standard | .0118-.0205 (.300-.520) |
| Wear Limit | .0441 (1.120) |
| Side Clearance | .0004-.0031 (.010-.079) |
| No. 2 | |
| End Gap | |
| Standard | .0138-.0236 (.351-.599) |
| Wear Limit | .0472 (1.199) |
| Side Clearance | .0012-.0028 (.030-.071) |
| No. 3 (Oil) | |
| End Gap | |
| Standard | .0079-.0217 (.201-.551) |
| Wear Limit | .0453 (1.151) |

[1] – Piston diameter is determined by size mark on top of piston. *See Fig. 20.*

### CYLINDER BLOCK

| Application | In. (mm) |
|---|---|
| Cylinder Bore | |
| Standard Diameter [1] | |
| Size Mark "1" | 3.4449-3.4453 (87.500-87.511) |
| Size Mark "2" | 3.4453-3.4457 (87.511-87.521) |
| Size Mark "3" | 3.4457-3.4461 (87.521-87.531) |
| Main Bearing Bore I.D. [2] | |
| Size Mark "1" | 2.6776-2.6778 (68.011-68.016) |
| Size Mark "2" | 2.6778-2.6780 (68.016-68.021) |
| Size Mark "3" | 2.6780-2.6783 (68.021-68.029) |
| Maximum Deck Warpage | .002 (.05) |

[1] – Cylinder bore diameter is determined by size mark on cylinder block deck surface. *See Fig. 25.*

[2] – Main bearing bore diameter is determined by size mark on cylinder block oil pan flange. *See Fig. 24.*

# 1991 ENGINES
# 2.5L V6 (Cont.)

## VALVES & VALVE SPRINGS

| Application | Specification |
|---|---|
| Intake Valves | |
| Face Angle | 45° |
| Minimum Margin | .020" (.51 mm) |
| Minimum Refinish Length | 3.764" (95.61 mm) |
| Stem Diameter | .2350-.2356" (5.969-5.984 mm) |
| Exhaust Valves | |
| Face Angle | 45° |
| Minimum Margin | .020" (.51 mm) |
| Minimum Refinish Length | 3.768" (95.71 mm) |
| Stem Diameter | .2348-.2354" (5.964-5.979 mm) |
| Valve Springs | |
| Free Length | 1.677" (42.60 mm) |
| Installed Height | 1.331" (33.81 mm) |
| Out-Of-Square | .079" (2.00 mm) |
| | **Lbs. @ In. (kg @ mm)** |
| Pressure | |
| Valve Closed | 41.0-47.2 @ 1.331 (18.6-21.4 @ 33.81) |

## CYLINDER HEAD

| Application | Specification |
|---|---|
| Maximum Warpage | .0039" (.099 mm) |
| Valve Seats | |
| Intake Valve | |
| Seat Angle | 45° |
| Seat Width | .039-.055" (.99-1.40 mm) |
| Exhaust Valve | |
| Seat Angle | 45° |
| Seat Width | .039-.055" (.99-1.40 mm) |
| Valve Guides | |
| Intake Valve | |
| Valve Guide Cylinder Head | |
| Bore I.D. | .4331-.4341" (11.001-11.026 mm) |
| Valve Guide I.D. | .2366-.2374" (6.010-6.030 mm) |
| Valve Stem-To-Guide Oil Clearance | |
| Standard | .0010-.0024" (.025-.061 mm) |
| Wear Limit | .0031" (.079 mm) |
| Exhaust Valve | |
| Valve Guide Cylinder Head | |
| Bore I.D. | .4331-.4341" (11.001-11.026 mm) |
| Valve Guide I.D. | .2366-.2374" (6.010-6.030 mm) |
| Valve Stem-To-Guide Oil Clearance | |
| Standard | .0012-.0026" (.030-.066 mm) |
| Wear Limit | .0039" (.099 mm) |

## CAMSHAFT

| Application | In. (mm) |
|---|---|
| End Play | |
| Standard | .0012-.0031 (.030-.079) |
| Wear Limit | .0047 (.119) |
| Journal Diameter | 1.0610-1.0616 (26.949-26.965) |
| Journal Runout | .0024 (.061) |
| Lobe Height | |
| Intake | |
| Standard | 1.5555-1.5594 (39.510-39.609) |
| Wear Limit | 1.5496 (39.360) |
| Exhaust | |
| Standard | 1.5339-1.5378 (38.961-38.060) |
| Wear Limit | 1.5279 (38.809) |
| Oil Clearance | |
| Standard | .0014-.0028 (.036-.071) |
| Wear Limit | .0039 (.099) |
| Gear Backlash | |
| Standard | .0008-.0079 (.020-.201) |
| Wear Limit | .0118 (.299) |

## VALVE LIFTERS

| Application | In. (mm) |
|---|---|
| Bore Diameter | 1.1024-1.1032 (28.001-28.021) |
| Lifter Diameter | 1.1014-1.1018 (27.976-27.986) |
| Oil Clearance | |
| Standard | .0006-.0018 (.015-.046) |
| Limit | .0028 (.071) |

# 1991 ENGINES
# 3.0L V6

## Pickup, 4Runner

***NOTE: For repair procedures not covered in this article, see ENGINE OVERHAUL PROCEDURES article in GENERAL INFORMATION.***

## ENGINE IDENTIFICATION

Engine may be identified by Vehicle Identification Number (VIN) stamped on a metal pad, located near lower left corner of windshield. The fourth character of VIN identifies engine model. See ENGINE IDENTIFICATION CODES table.

Engine identification number, located on left front corner of cylinder block, near oil filter, may be required when ordering replacement parts.

***ENGINE IDENTIFICATION CODES***

| Application | VIN Code | Engine Code |
|---|---|---|
| 3.0L V6 | V | 3VZ-E |

## ADJUSTMENTS

### VALVE CLEARANCE ADJUSTMENT

***NOTE: Adjust valve clearance with engine cold.***

**1)** Disconnect throttle position sensor connector. Release fuel pressure. See FUEL PRESSURE RELEASE under REMOVAL & INSTALLATION. Disconnect vacuum and fuel lines at fuel pressure regulator. Disconnect PCV hose at union.
**2)** Drain cooling system. Remove coolant hoses from intake manifold and coolant by-pass pipe. Remove cold start injector tube. Disconnect EGR temperature sensor connector (Calif. only) and vacuum hoses at air pipe and vacuum modulator.
**3)** Remove EGR valve assembly. Disconnect hose from reed valve. Remove air intake chamber retaining bolts. Remove air intake chamber. *See Fig. 10*.
**4)** Label and unplug electrical connectors. Remove engine wiring harness across front of engine. Remove valve covers and spark plugs. Rotate crankshaft pulley, and align pulley groove with "0" mark on timing belt cover to set cylinder No. 1 at TDC of compression stroke.
**5)** Ensure cylinder No. 1 valve lifters are loose and cylinder No. 4 valve lifters are tight. If valve lifters are not as described, rotate crankshaft 360 degrees, and realign timing marks.
**6)** Measure and record clearance of exhaust valve on cylinder No. 2 and intake valve on cylinder No. 6. *See Fig. 1*. Rotate crankshaft pulley 120 degrees (1/3 of a revolution). Measure and record clearance of intake valve on cylinder No. 1 and exhaust valve on cylinder No. 3.

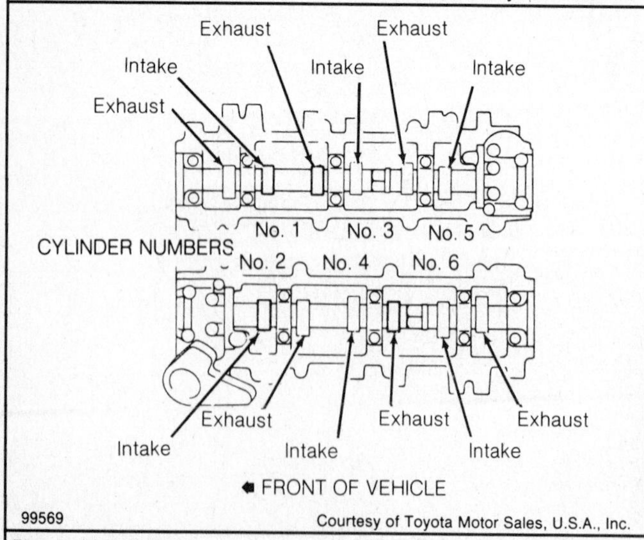


***Fig. 1: Identifying Locations of Intake & Exhaust Valves***

**7)** Rotate crankshaft pulley 120 degrees (1/3 of a revolution). Measure and record clearance of intake valve on cylinder No. 2 and exhaust valve on cylinder No. 4.
**8)** Rotate crankshaft pulley 120 degrees (1/3 of a revolution). Measure and record clearance of intake valve on cylinder No. 3 and exhaust valve on cylinder No. 5. Rotate crankshaft pulley 120 degrees (1/3 of a revolution). Measure and record clearance of intake valve on cylinder No. 4 and exhaust valve on cylinder No. 6.
**9)** Rotate crankshaft pulley 120 degrees (1/3 of a revolution). Measure and record clearance of intake valve on cylinder No. 5 and exhaust valve on cylinder No. 1.
**10)** Ensure clearance is within specification. See VALVE CLEARANCE SPECIFICATIONS table. If clearance adjustment is required, rotate crankshaft pulley so camshaft lobe on valve to be adjusted faces up.

***VALVE CLEARANCE SPECIFICATIONS***

| Application [1] | In. (mm) |
|---|---|
| Exhaust Valve | .009-.013 (.22-.32) |
| Intake Valve | .007-.011 (.18-.28) |

[1] – Adjust valve clearance with engine cold.

**11)** Position adjusting shim notch area in direction in which shim will be removed. Use Valve Clearance Adjuster (09248-55010) and SST (A) to press valve lifter down. *See Fig. 2*. Install SST (B) between camshaft and valve lifter. Remove SST (A). Using a small screwdriver and magnet, remove adjusting shim.

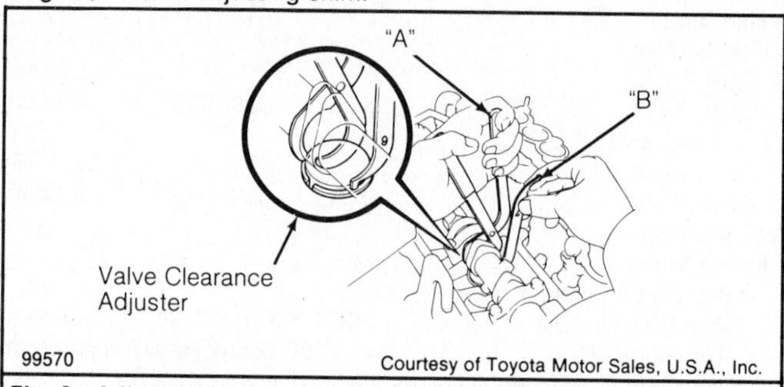


***Fig. 2: Adjusting Valve Clearance***

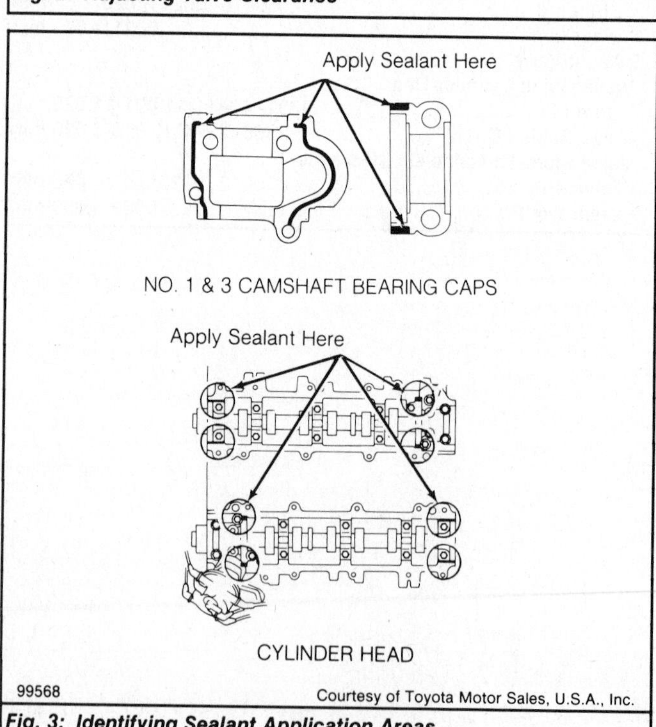


***Fig. 3: Identifying Sealant Application Areas***

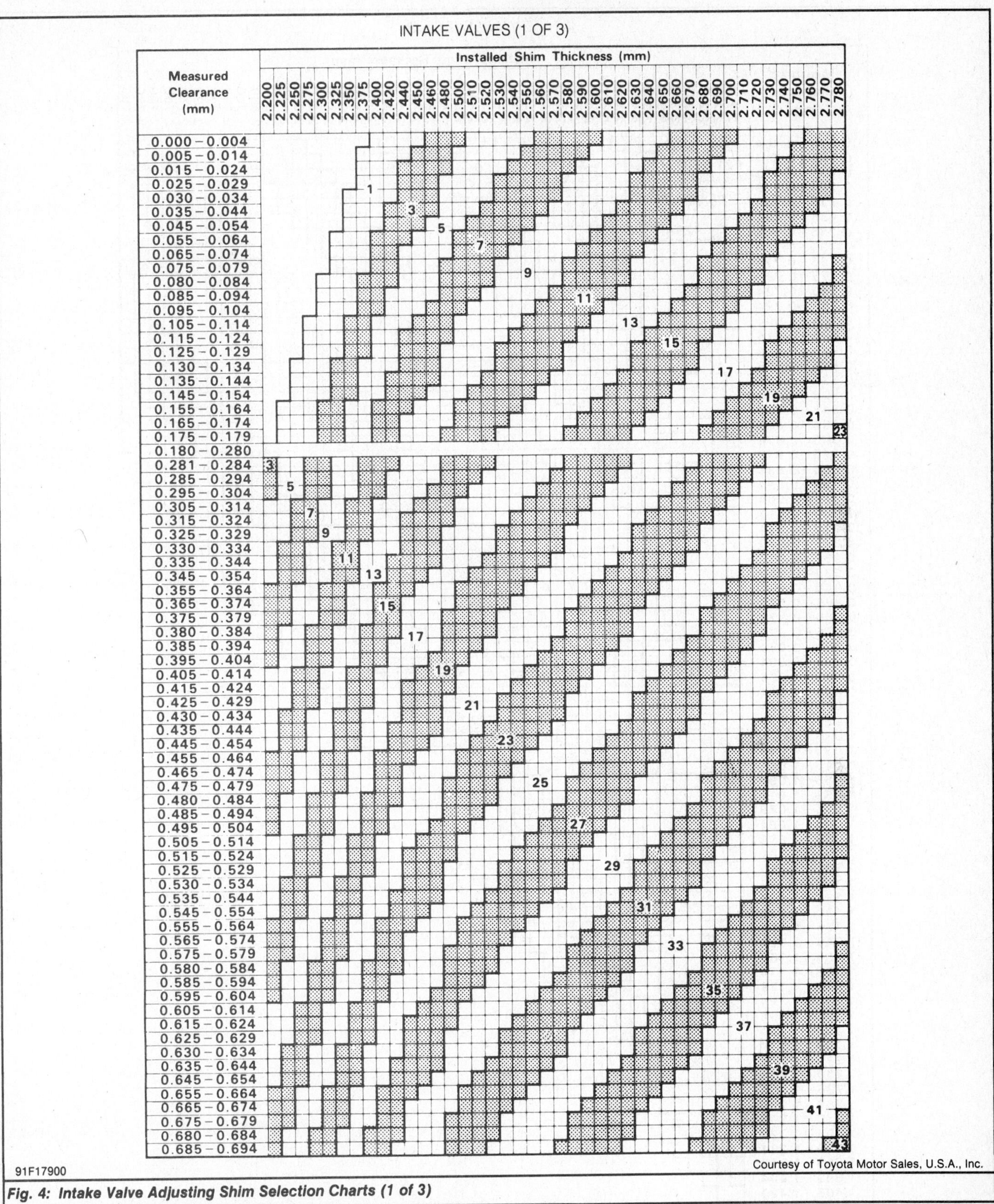


***Fig. 4: Intake Valve Adjusting Shim Selection Charts (1 of 3)***

**12)** Using micrometer, measure thickness of shim removed. Determine correct thickness of replacement shim to be used. *See Figs. 4-9*. Install proper shim. Using SST (A), press valve lifter down, and remove SST (B). Recheck valve clearance.

**13)** Install gasket on valve cover. Apply sealant to indicated areas on cylinder head. *See Fig. 3*. Install valve cover. Install air intake chamber with new gaskets.

**14)** Install EGR valve and gaskets, and tighten designated bolts to specification. *See Fig. 14*. To install remaining components, reverse removal procedure. Tighten all nuts and bolts to specification. See TORQUE SPECIFICATIONS table at end of article.

# 1991 ENGINES
# 3.0L V6 (Cont.)

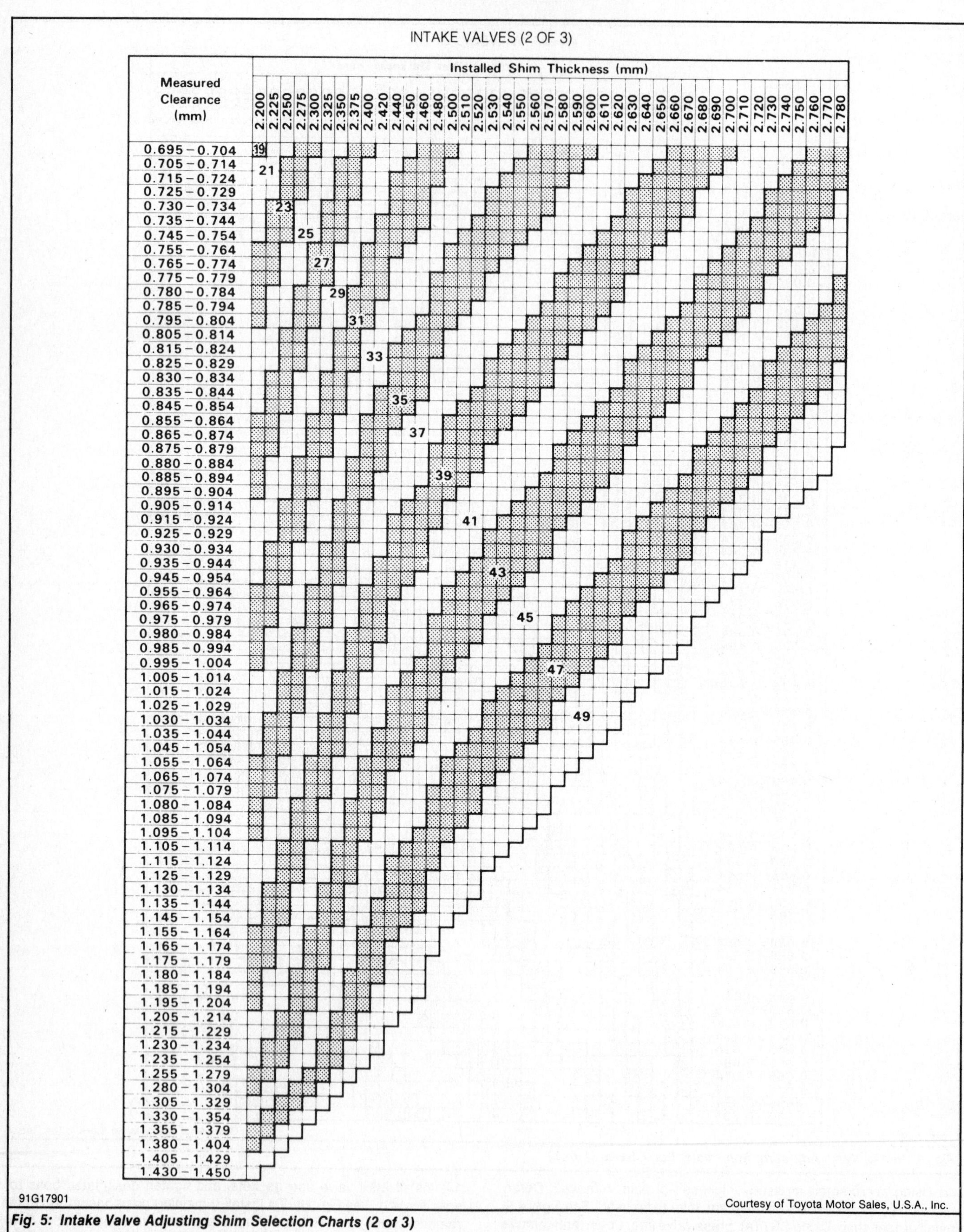


*Fig. 5: Intake Valve Adjusting Shim Selection Charts (2 of 3)*

# 1991 ENGINES
# 3.0L V6 (Cont.)

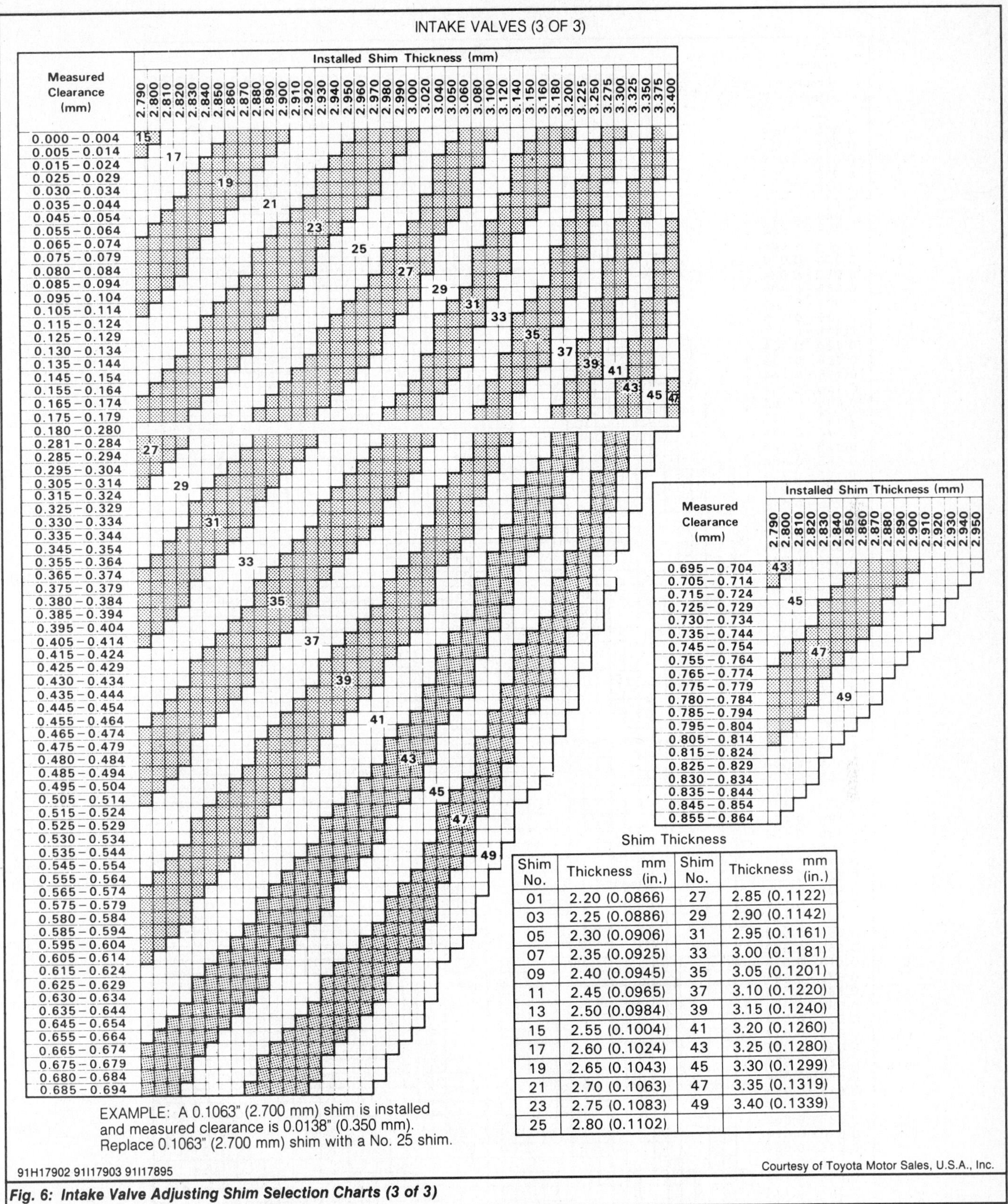


Shim Thickness

| Shim No. | Thickness mm (in.) | Shim No. | Thickness mm (in.) |
|---|---|---|---|
| 01 | 2.20 (0.0866) | 27 | 2.85 (0.1122) |
| 03 | 2.25 (0.0886) | 29 | 2.90 (0.1142) |
| 05 | 2.30 (0.0906) | 31 | 2.95 (0.1161) |
| 07 | 2.35 (0.0925) | 33 | 3.00 (0.1181) |
| 09 | 2.40 (0.0945) | 35 | 3.05 (0.1201) |
| 11 | 2.45 (0.0965) | 37 | 3.10 (0.1220) |
| 13 | 2.50 (0.0984) | 39 | 3.15 (0.1240) |
| 15 | 2.55 (0.1004) | 41 | 3.20 (0.1260) |
| 17 | 2.60 (0.1024) | 43 | 3.25 (0.1280) |
| 19 | 2.65 (0.1043) | 45 | 3.30 (0.1299) |
| 21 | 2.70 (0.1063) | 47 | 3.35 (0.1319) |
| 23 | 2.75 (0.1083) | 49 | 3.40 (0.1339) |
| 25 | 2.80 (0.1102) | | |

EXAMPLE: A 0.1063" (2.700 mm) shim is installed and measured clearance is 0.0138" (0.350 mm). Replace 0.1063" (2.700 mm) shim with a No. 25 shim.

91H17902 91I17903 91I17895

Courtesy of Toyota Motor Sales, U.S.A., Inc.

***Fig. 6: Intake Valve Adjusting Shim Selection Charts (3 of 3)***

# 1991 ENGINES
# 3.0L V6 (Cont.)

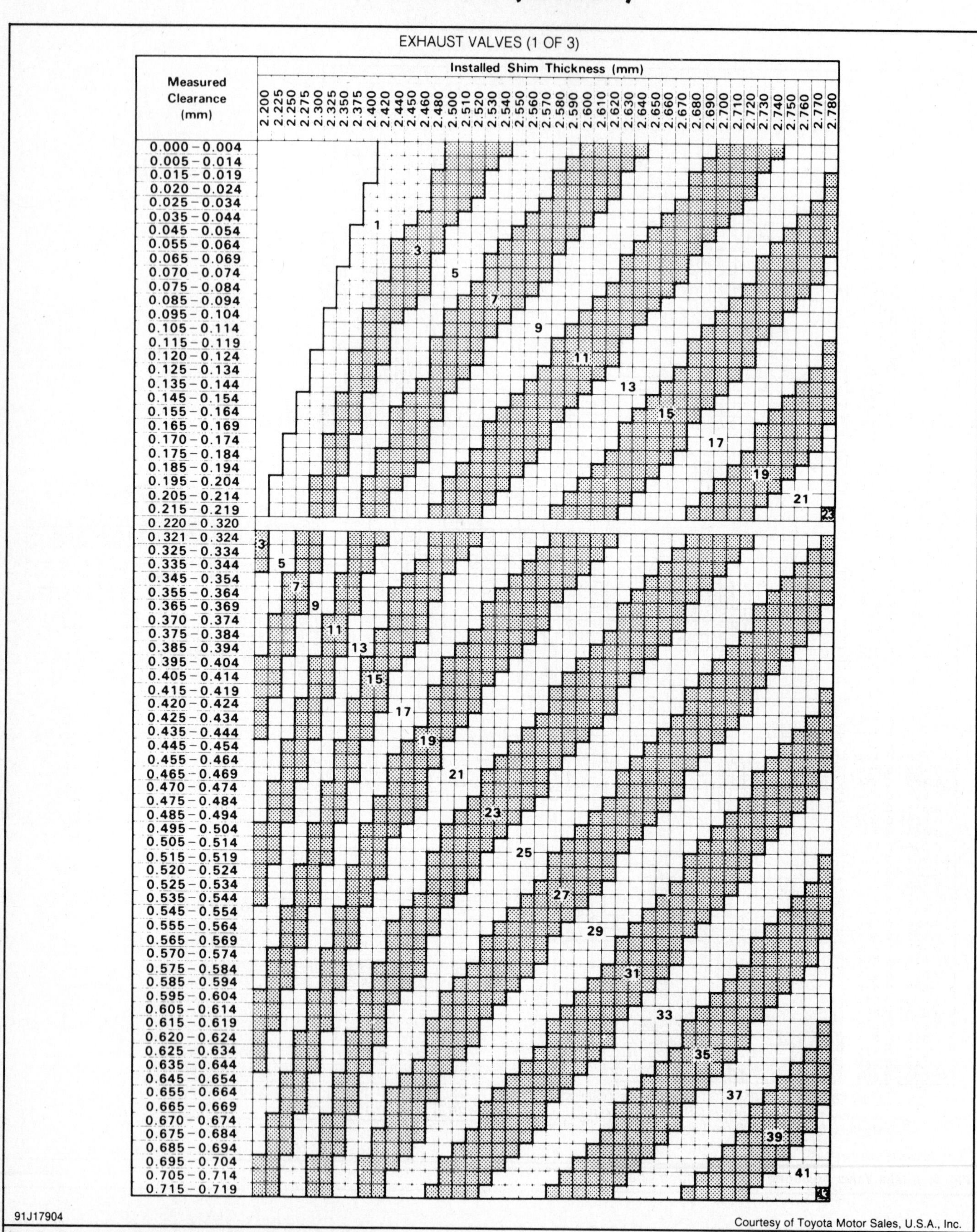


*Fig. 7: Exhaust Valve Adjusting Shim Selection Charts (1 of 3)*

# 1991 ENGINES
# 3.0L V6 (Cont.)

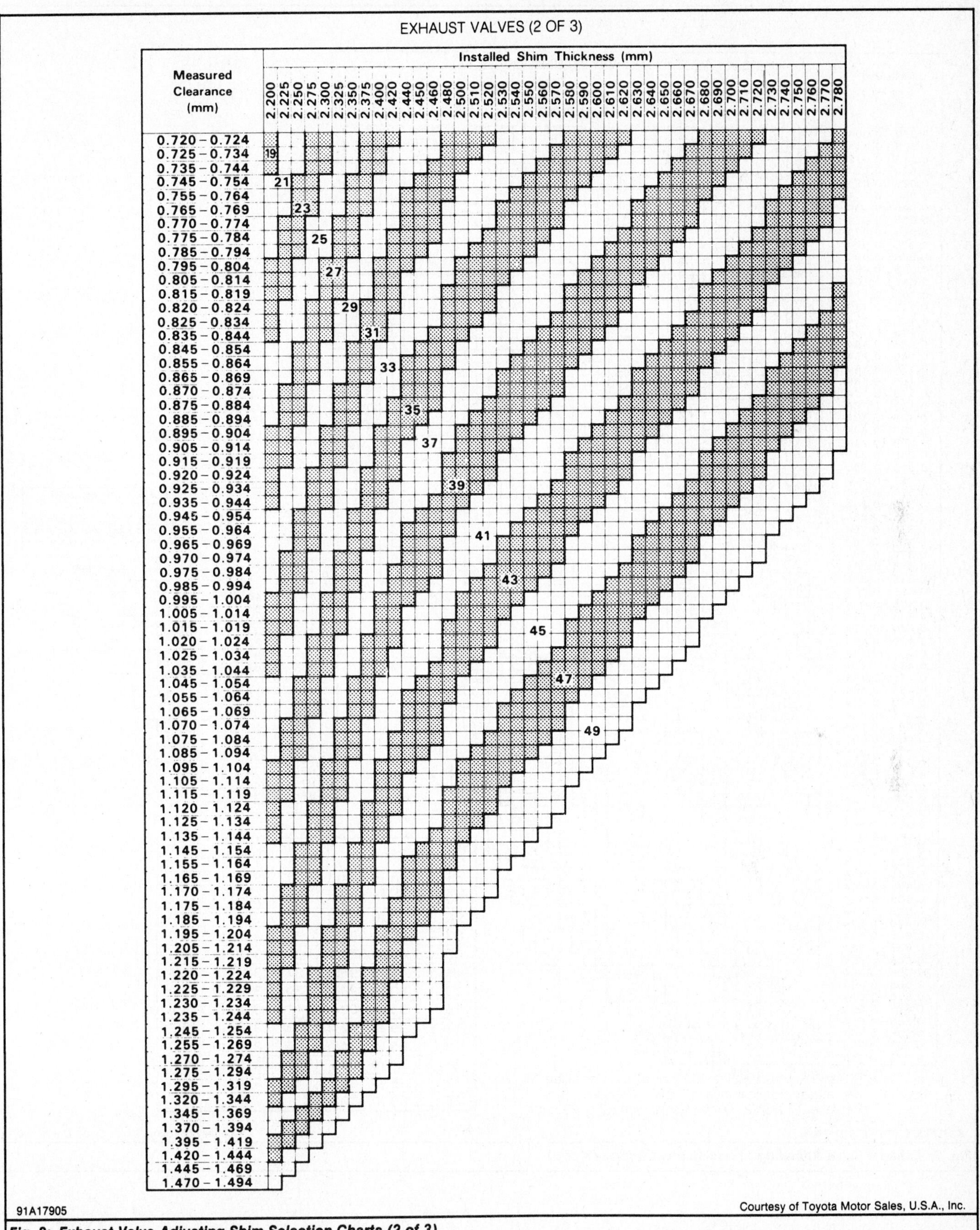


*Fig. 8: Exhaust Valve Adjusting Shim Selection Charts (2 of 3)*

# 1991 ENGINES
# 3.0L V6 (Cont.)

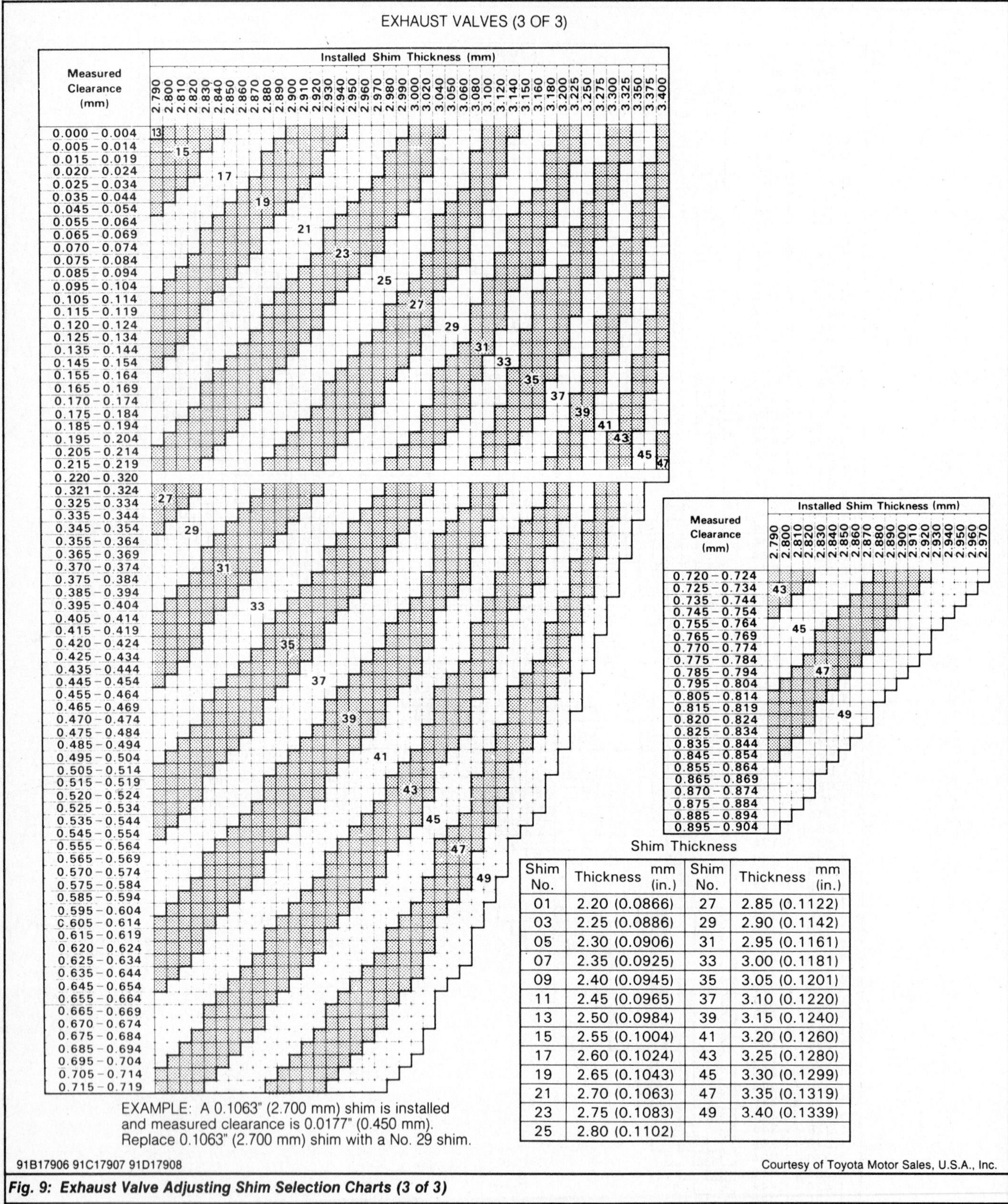


Shim Thickness

| Shim No. | Thickness mm (in.) | Shim No. | Thickness mm (in.) |
|---|---|---|---|
| 01 | 2.20 (0.0866) | 27 | 2.85 (0.1122) |
| 03 | 2.25 (0.0886) | 29 | 2.90 (0.1142) |
| 05 | 2.30 (0.0906) | 31 | 2.95 (0.1161) |
| 07 | 2.35 (0.0925) | 33 | 3.00 (0.1181) |
| 09 | 2.40 (0.0945) | 35 | 3.05 (0.1201) |
| 11 | 2.45 (0.0965) | 37 | 3.10 (0.1220) |
| 13 | 2.50 (0.0984) | 39 | 3.15 (0.1240) |
| 15 | 2.55 (0.1004) | 41 | 3.20 (0.1260) |
| 17 | 2.60 (0.1024) | 43 | 3.25 (0.1280) |
| 19 | 2.65 (0.1043) | 45 | 3.30 (0.1299) |
| 21 | 2.70 (0.1063) | 47 | 3.35 (0.1319) |
| 23 | 2.75 (0.1083) | 49 | 3.40 (0.1339) |
| 25 | 2.80 (0.1102) | | |

EXAMPLE: A 0.1063" (2.700 mm) shim is installed and measured clearance is 0.0177" (0.450 mm). Replace 0.1063" (2.700 mm) shim with a No. 29 shim.

91B17906 91C17907 91D17908

Courtesy of Toyota Motor Sales, U.S.A., Inc.

***Fig. 9: Exhaust Valve Adjusting Shim Selection Charts (3 of 3)***

## REMOVAL & INSTALLATION

***NOTE: For installation reference, label all electrical connectors, vacuum hoses and fuel lines before removal. Also place mating marks on engine hood and other major assemblies before removal.***

## FUEL PRESSURE RELEASE

***WARNING: High fuel pressure may be present in fuel lines and component parts. Relieve fuel pressure before opening fuel system. DO NOT allow fuel to flow onto engine or electrical parts.***

Disconnect negative battery cable. Place container under the fitting that will be loosened. Use a rag to cover fuel line and component. Slowly loosen fitting, allowing pressurized fuel to flow into container. After fuel system has been depressurized, disconnect and plug fitting.

## ENGINE

***NOTE: Engine and transmission should be removed as an assembly.***

**Removal - 1)** Disconnect negative battery cable. Drain cooling system. Remove radiator. Remove air cleaner assembly. Remove all drive belts and fan pulley. Mark all electrical connectors and vacuum hoses for installation reference, and then disconnect them.

**2)** Release fuel pressure. See FUEL PRESSURE RELEASE. Disconnect fuel inlet and return hoses. Disconnect accelerator cable. Disconnect throttle and cruise control cables (if equipped). Remove power steering pump and A/C compressor with hoses connected (if equipped).

**3)** On M/T models, remove shift levers. Disconnect clutch release cylinder hose. On all models, place alignment marks on drive shafts and companion flange. Remove drive shafts. Disconnect heater hoses. On A/T models, disconnect shift linkage.

**4)** On all models, disconnect speedometer cable. Remove front crossmember. On 4WD models, remove transfer case shift linkage, and remove stabilizer bar. Remove front floor heat insulator and brakeline heat insulator. On all models, disconnect oxygen sensor connector.

**5)** Remove exhaust pipe from exhaust manifold and catalytic converter. Support transmission with a jack. Remove transmission mount bolts and rear crossmember. Support engine with hoist. Remove engine mount bolts. Lift engine and transmission out of vehicle.

**Installation -** To install, reverse removal procedure. Tighten all nuts and bolts to specification. See TORQUE SPECIFICATIONS table at end of article. Refill fluid levels. Check for leaks.

## CYLINDER HEAD & MANIFOLDS

**Removal - 1)** Disconnect negative battery cable. Remove air cleaner. Drain cooling system, and remove radiator. Remove all drive belts. Remove power steering pump with hoses connected (if equipped).

**2)** Remove fan, fan clutch and fan pulley. Mark all electrical connectors on engine wiring harness for installation reference, and then disconnect them. Label vacuum hoses, and disconnect them from intake manifold and cylinder head.

**3)** Release fuel system pressure. See FUEL PRESSURE RELEASE. Disconnect fuel inlet and return hoses. Disconnect accelerator cable. Disconnect throttle and cruise control cables (if equipped).

**4)** Disconnect clutch release (slave) cylinder hose (if equipped). Disconnect heater hoses. Disconnect oxygen sensor connector. Remove front exhaust pipe from exhaust manifold and catalytic converter.

**5)** Remove timing belt. See TIMING BELT under REMOVAL & INSTALLATION. Mark distributor and spark plug wires for installation reference, and remove them. Disconnect coolant hoses from air intake chamber.

**6)** Remove cold start injector connector and cold start injector tube from air intake chamber. Remove EGR valve assembly. Remove reed valve hoses. Remove air intake chamber.

**7)** Remove engine wiring harness from front of engine. Remove No. 2 and 3 fuel pipes. *See Fig. 10.* Remove No. 4 timing belt cover, No. 2 idler pulley and No. 3 timing belt cover. *See Figs. 11 and 12.* Remove oil dipstick guide bolt from left side of cylinder head.

**8)** Remove fuel delivery pipes, injectors and delivery pipe spacers. Remove coolant by-pass outlet. *See Fig. 10.* Remove intake manifold bolts/nuts, and remove intake manifold. Remove exhaust crossover pipe between exhaust manifolds.

***CAUTION: Cylinder head bolts must be loosened in proper sequence to prevent cylinder head warping or cracking.***

**9)** Remove reed valve and air injection manifold on right cylinder head. Remove alternator. Remove valve cover and camshaft housing rear cover. *See Fig. 10.* Using proper sequence, loosen cylinder head bolts in 3 steps. *See Fig. 13.* Remove cylinder head. Remove exhaust manifold.

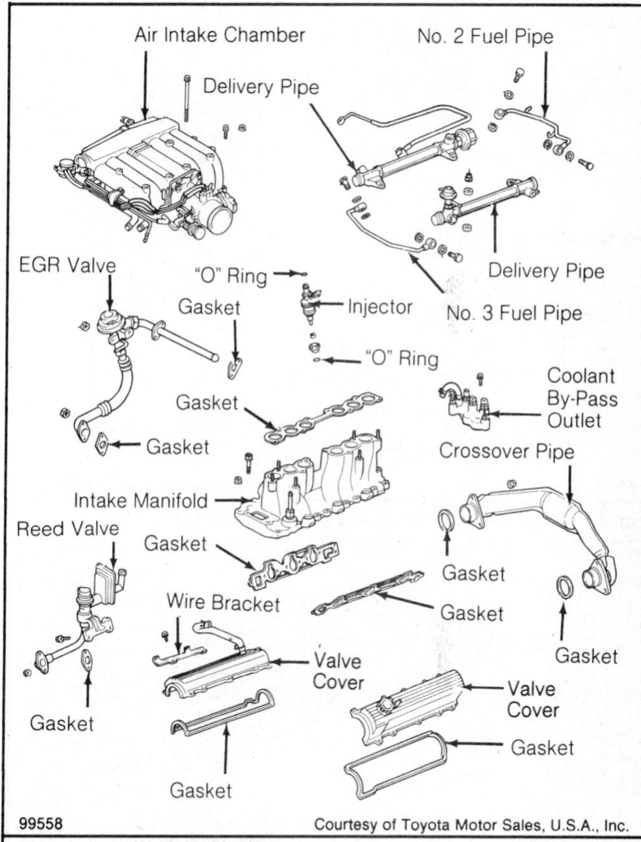


***Fig. 10: Exploded View of Intake Manifold & Components***

**Inspection - 1)** Measure cylinder head warpage. Replace cylinder head if warpage exceeds specification. See CYLINDER HEAD table under ENGINE SPECIFICATIONS at end of article.

**2)** Check intake and exhaust manifolds and air intake chamber warpage. If warpage exceeds specification, replace appropriate component(s). See WARPAGE SPECIFICATIONS table.

***WARPAGE SPECIFICATIONS***

| Application | Warpage In. (mm) |
|---|---|
| Air Intake Chamber | .0039 (.100) |
| Exhaust Manifold | .0276 (.701) |
| Intake Manifold | .0039 (.100) |

**Installation - 1)** Ensure mating surfaces are clean and dry. Ensure No. 1 piston is at TDC and camshafts are timed correctly. *See Fig. 16.* Install cylinder head gasket. Coat cylinder head bolt threads with oil. Using several steps, tighten cylinder head bolts, except bolt "A", in sequence to 32 ft. lbs. (44 N.m). *See Fig. 13.*

# 1991 ENGINES
# 3.0L V6 (Cont.)

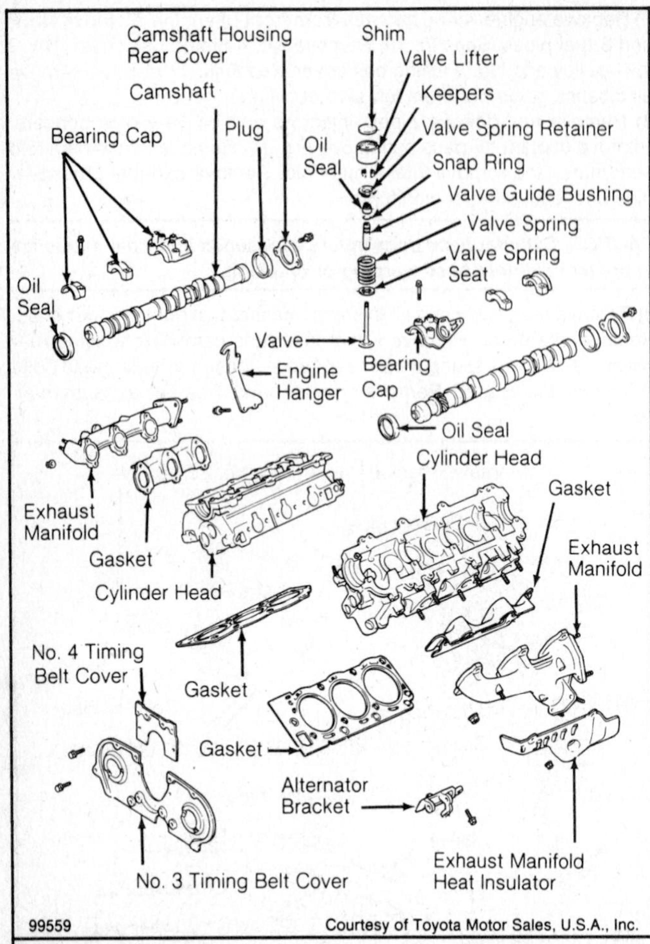


*Fig. 11: Exploded View of Cylinder Head & Components*

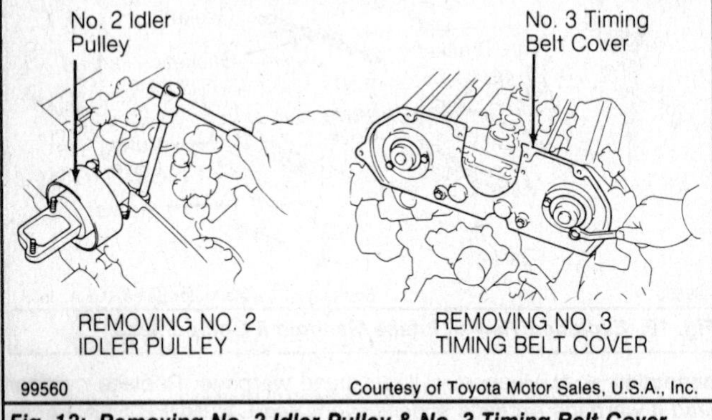


*Fig. 12: Removing No. 2 Idler Pulley & No. 3 Timing Belt Cover*

2) Place a mark on top of cylinder head bolts, toward the front. Tighten bolts 90 degrees, in sequence. Ensure mark on cylinder head bolt is pointing to the side. Tighten bolts an additional 90 degrees, in sequence. Ensure mark on cylinder head bolt faces rearward. Install bolt "A", and tighten it to 27 ft. lbs. (37 N.m).

3) Install alternator, air suction reed valve, oil dipstick guide and exhaust crossover pipe. Connect knock sensor wire. Install intake manifold and coolant by-pass outlet.

4) Install new "O" rings on injectors. Coat "O" rings with gasoline before installing injectors in delivery pipes. Ensure injectors rotate smoothly in delivery pipe and intake manifold after installation.

5) Apply sealant to sealing surface of No. 2 idler pulley and No. 4 timing belt cover. Apply sealant to coolant outlet before installation. Install front and rear fuel pipes. Install timing belt. See TIMING BELT under REMOVAL & INSTALLATION. When installing valve cover, apply sealant to indicated areas on cylinder head. *See Fig. 3.*

6) Install air intake chamber. Install EGR valve and gaskets, and tighten designated bolts to specification. *See Fig. 14.* Install new "O" ring on distributor.

7) Align protrusion area on distributor driven gear with groove of distributor housing. Install distributor while aligning housing groove with groove of No. 4 camshaft bearing cap.

8) To install remaining components, reverse removal procedure. Tighten bolts to specification. See TORQUE SPECIFICATIONS table at end of article. Fill cooling system, and check for leaks.

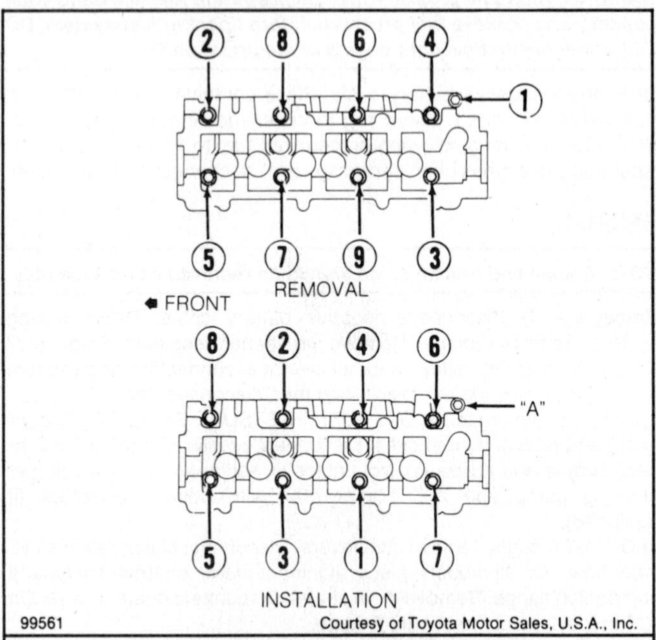


*Fig. 13: Cylinder Head Bolt Removal & Tightening Sequence*

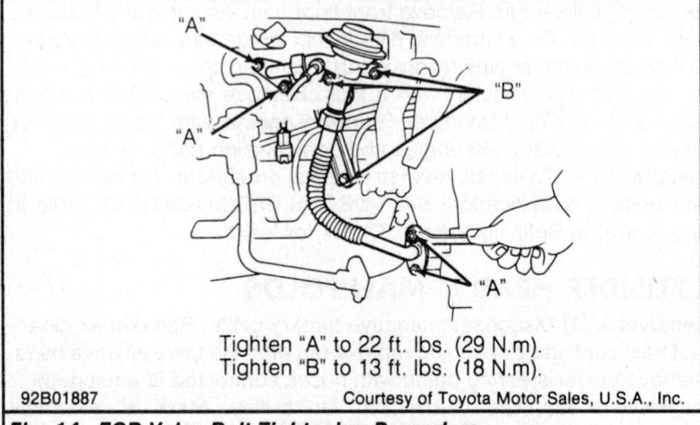


*Fig. 14: EGR Valve Bolt Tightening Procedure*

## FRONT COVER OIL SEAL

**Removal & Installation (Oil Pump Installed) – 1)** Remove timing belt and crankshaft timing pulley. See TIMING BELT. Using a knife, cut off oil seal lip. Pry seal from oil pump housing. Use care not to damage crankshaft sealing surfaces.

2) To install new oil seal, apply grease to oil seal lip. Using Seal Installer (09309-37010), install oil seal until oil seal is even with oil pump body. To install remaining components, reverse removal procedure.

**Removal & Installation (Oil Pump Removed) –** Using hammer and drift, remove oil seal from oil pump housing. Apply grease to new oil seal lip. Using Seal Installer (09309-37010), install oil seal until oil seal is even with oil pump housing surface.

## TIMING BELT

**Removal – 1)** Drain cooling system. Remove radiator. Remove all accessory drive belts. Remove power steering pump belt pulley (if equipped). Remove power steering pump with hoses connected (if equipped). Remove spark plugs. Disconnect hoses from air pipe.

**2)** Remove fan, belt guide and fan pulley. Remove spark plug wire clamps. Remove No. 2 timing belt cover bolts and cover. *See Fig. 15.* Rotate engine until No. 1 cylinder is at TDC, and groove on crankshaft pulley aligns with "0" mark on No. 1 timing belt cover.

**3)** Ensure camshaft and No. 3 timing belt cover marks are aligned. *See Fig. 16.* If marks are not aligned, rotate crankshaft 360 degrees and recheck alignment.

**4)** Remove power steering belt pulley. Using Pulley Holder (09213-58011) and Flange Holder (09330-00021), hold crankshaft pulley, and remove crankshaft pulley retaining bolt. Using puller, remove crankshaft pulley.

**5)** Remove fan pulley bracket. Remove No. 1 timing belt cover and gaskets. If timing belt is to be reused, place arrow on belt to indicate belt rotation direction, and place alignment marks on all timing pulleys and timing belt.

***NOTE: If timing belt is to be reused, place arrow on belt to indicate direction of belt rotation, and scribe alignment marks on all pulleys and timing belt.***

**6)** Remove timing belt guide and tension spring. *See Fig. 15.* Loosen No. 1 idler pulley retaining bolt. Move pulley to the left as far as possible, and temporarily tighten bolt. Remove timing belt.

**7)** If camshaft timing pulleys require removal, use Holder (09278-54012) to hold pulley while removing pulley retaining bolt.

***CAUTION: DO NOT use timing belt tension to hold timing belt pulley during retaining bolt removal and installation.***

**8)** Remove camshaft timing belt pulley and pin. To remove crankshaft timing belt pulley, pry pulley off of crankshaft using 2 screwdrivers.

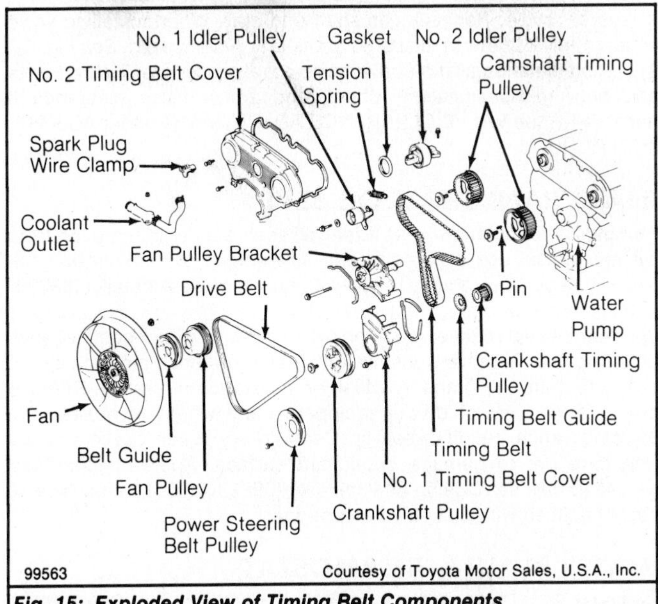


***Fig. 15: Exploded View of Timing Belt Components***

**Inspection – 1)** Inspect timing belt for wear on rounded edges of drive teeth. Inspect belt for signs of oil contamination. Replace timing belt if damaged or contaminated.

**2)** Inspect idler pulleys and fan pulley bracket for smooth rotation. For No. 2 idler pulley replacement, see NO. 2 IDLER PULLEY. Inspect idler pulley tension spring for damage and free length. Tension spring free length should be 2.216" (56.28 mm). Replace damaged components.

**Installation – 1)** Install Woodruff key in crankshaft (if removed). Using Crankshaft Pulley Installer (09214-60010), install crankshaft timing pulley. Align groove of crankshaft timing pulley with cavity of oil pump.

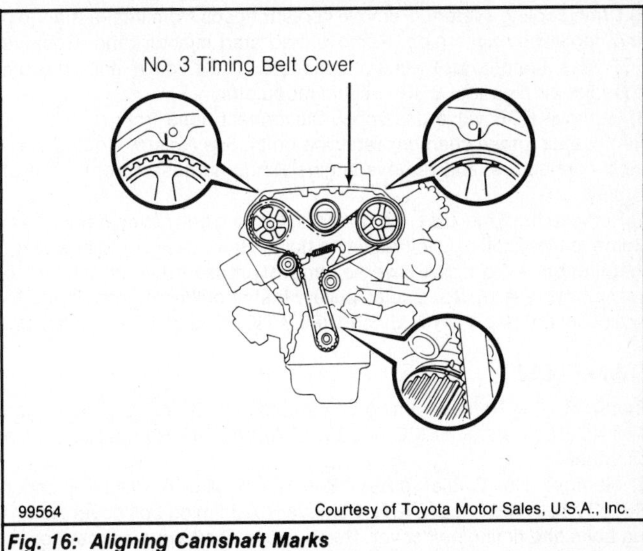


***Fig. 16: Aligning Camshaft Marks***

**2)** Install No. 1 idler pulley as far to the left as possible, and temporarily tighten bolt. Align camshaft pin holes with reference marks on No. 3 timing belt cover. *See Fig. 17.*

**3)** Install camshaft timing pulleys and retaining bolts. DO NOT install pins at this time. Ensure head of retaining bolt does not contact pulley. Align pulley reference mark with mark on No. 3 timing belt cover. *See Fig. 16.*

**4)** Install timing belt. If installing used belt, ensure belt is installed in proper direction of rotation, and reference marks on belt align with all pulleys.

**5)** Loosen No. 1 idler pulley bolt, pry pulley toward the right as far as possible, and temporarily tighten bolt. Install tension spring. Loosen No. 1 idler pulley bolt until pulley moves with spring force tension.

**6)** Temporarily install crankshaft pulley bolt, and rotate crankshaft clockwise 2 full revolutions. Ensure all pulley timing marks are properly aligned. *See Fig. 16.* Tighten No. 1 idler pulley bolt to 27 ft. lbs. (37 N.m).

**7)** Remove camshaft timing pulley retaining bolts. Align camshaft pin holes with hole of pulley. Install pin and retaining bolt. Using Pulley Holder (09278-54012), hold pulley, and tighten bolt to specification. See TORQUE SPECIFICATIONS table at end of article. DO NOT use timing belt to hold pulley while tightening.

**8)** Remove crankshaft pulley bolt. Install timing belt guide with cupped side toward front of engine. To install remaining components, reverse removal procedure. Tighten bolts to specification. Apply sealant to coolant outlet before installation.

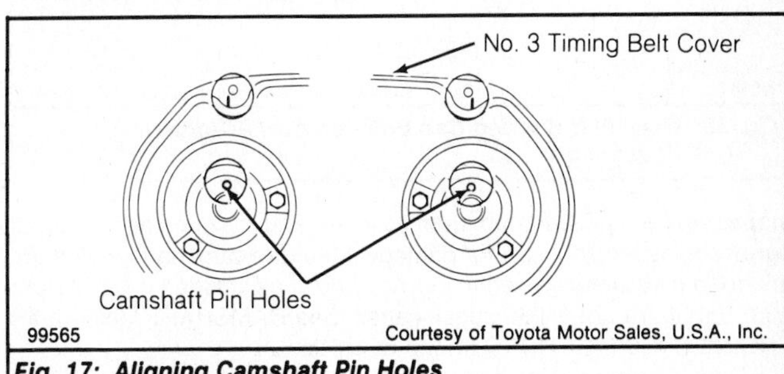


***Fig. 17: Aligning Camshaft Pin Holes***

## NO. 2 IDLER PULLEY

**Removal – 1)** Disconnect throttle position sensor connector. Release fuel pressure. See FUEL PRESSURE RELEASE. Disconnect vacuum and fuel lines at pressure regulator. Disconnect PCV hose at union.

# 1991 ENGINES
# 3.0L V6 (Cont.)

2) Drain cooling system. Remove coolant hoses from intake manifold and coolant by-pass pipe. Remove cold start injector tube. Remove EGR gas temperature sensor connector (Calif. only) and vacuum hoses at air pipe and EGR vacuum modulator.
3) Remove EGR valve assembly. Disconnect hose from reed valve. Remove air intake chamber retaining bolts. *See Fig. 10.* Unplug electrical connectors, and remove engine wiring harness across front of engine.
4) Remove front fuel pipe. Remove No. 4 timing belt cover. *See Fig. 11.* Remove No. 2 idler pulley retaining bolts. Remove No. 2 idler pulley.
**Installation** – To install, reverse removal procedure. Apply sealant to sealing surface of No. 2 idler pulley. Install pulley. Tighten bolts to specification. See TORQUE SPECIFICATIONS table at end of article.

## CAMSHAFT

**Removal** – 1) Remove timing belt and camshaft timing pulleys. See TIMING BELT under REMOVAL & INSTALLATION. Remove air intake chamber.
2) Remove No. 2 idler pulley. See NO. 2 IDLER PULLEY under REMOVAL & INSTALLATION. Remove No. 3 timing belt cover retaining bolts and timing belt cover. Remove camshaft housing rear cover.
3) Remove all other hoses, electrical connectors, vacuum lines and components necessary to access valve covers. Remove valve covers. Loosen camshaft bearing cap bolts in sequence, in 3 steps. *See Fig. 18.*
4) Note camshaft bearing cap arrow direction for reassembly reference. *See Fig. 19.* Remove bearing caps and camshaft. Remove valve lifters and shims from cylinder head. Mark component location for installation reference.

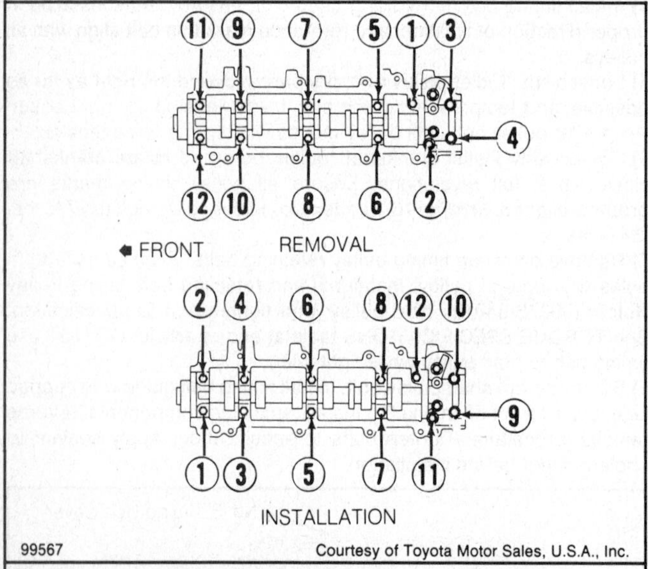


***Fig. 18: Camshaft Bearing Cap Bolt Removal & Tightening Sequence***

**Inspection** – 1) Clean camshaft journals and cylinder head journal surfaces. Inspect journals for damage. Measure camshaft lobe height and runout at center camshaft journal. Replace camshaft if lobe height and runout are not within specification. See CAMSHAFT table under ENGINE SPECIFICATIONS at end of article.
2) Using Plastigage method, check camshaft oil clearance. Install camshaft and bearing caps. Ensure bearing caps are installed with arrows on caps pointing toward front (right side) and rear (left side). *See Fig. 19.*
3) Tighten bearing caps in sequence to 12 ft. lbs. (16 N.m) in 3 steps. *See Fig. 18.* Remove bearing caps, and check clearance. Replace cylinder head or camshaft if clearance is not within specification. See CAMSHAFT table. With camshaft installed, check camshaft end play. Replace camshaft or cylinder head if end play exceeds specification.
4) Determine oil clearance between cylinder head and valve lifter. Replace components if clearance is not within specification. See VALVE LIFTERS table under ENGINE SPECIFICATIONS at end of article.

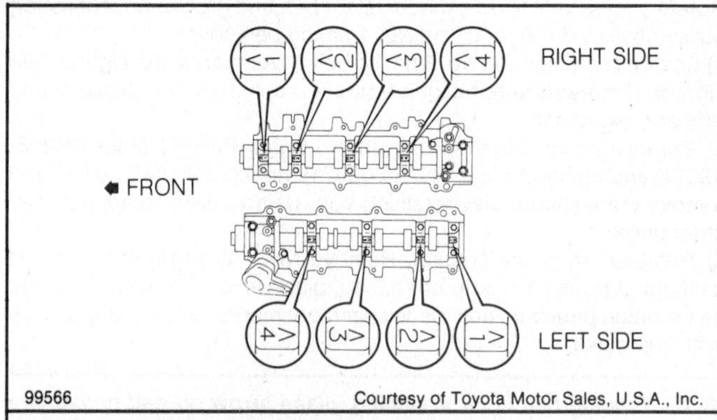


***Fig. 19: Identifying Camshaft Bearing Cap Installation Directions***

**Installation** – 1) Coat oil seal lip and bearing journals with oil. Install camshaft on cylinder head. Install oil seal on front of camshaft. Install camshaft housing plug. Apply sealant to No. 1 and No. 3 bearing caps. *See Fig. 3.*
2) Install bearing caps. Ensure arrows on caps point toward front on right side and rear on left side. *See Fig. 19.* Install bearing cap bolts. Slightly tighten bolts in small increments using proper sequence to secure components during oil seal installation. *See Fig. 18.*
3) Using Seal Installer (09214-60010), drive in camshaft oil seals. Using proper sequence, tighten bearing cap bolts to specification in small increments. *See Fig. 18.* See TORQUE SPECIFICATIONS table at end of article. Recheck camshaft end play. When installing valve cover, apply sealant to indicated areas on cylinder head. *See Fig. 3.*
4) To complete installation, reverse removal procedure. Tighten bolts and nuts to specification. Check and adjust valve clearance if necessary. See VALVE CLEARANCE ADJUSTMENT under ADJUSTMENTS.

## REAR CRANKSHAFT OIL SEAL

**Removal & Installation** – 1) If rear oil seal retainer is removed from cylinder block, use a hammer and screwdriver to remove oil seal. Apply multipurpose grease to new oil seal. Using Seal Installer (09223-41020), install oil seal.
2) If rear oil seal retainer is still on cylinder block, disconnect negative battery cable. Remove transmission. Place reference mark on clutch pressure plate (M/T) and flywheel for installation reference. Remove pressure plate, clutch disc (if equipped) and flywheel/drive plate.
3) Using a knife, cut off oil seal lip. Carefully pry oil seal out of retainer. Use care not to damage crankshaft surface. Apply multipurpose grease to new seal. Using Seal Installer (09223-41020), install new oil seal until flush with oil seal retainer edge.

## WATER PUMP & THERMOSTAT

**Removal** – 1) Drain cooling system. Remove timing belt. See TIMING BELT. Remove No. 1 idler pulley. *See Fig. 15.* Remove radiator hose at thermostat housing.
2) Remove coolant inlet, gasket and thermostat. Remove water pump bolts and water pump.
**Installation** – 1) Ensure water pump bearing rotates smoothly. Apply sealant to water pump sealing area. Install water pump. Install bolts and tighten them to specification. See TORQUE SPECIFICATIONS table at end of article.
2) Install thermostat with valve facing upward. Install coolant inlet and gasket. Tighten bolts to specification. Install remaining components.

***NOTE: For more information on cooling systems, see SPECIFICATIONS & ELECTRIC COOLING FANS article in ENGINE COOLING.***

# 1991 ENGINES
# 3.0L V6 (Cont.)

## OIL PAN

**Removal - 1)** On 4WD models, front differential must be removed. See appropriate article in DRIVE AXLES. On all models, drain engine oil. Remove oil pan retaining bolts.

***CAUTION: DO NOT damage baffle plate flange during removal.***

**2)** Using Seal Cutter (09032-00100) and brass drift, separate oil pan from cylinder block. If oil pan baffle plate requires removal, remove oil strainer. Using seal cutter and brass drift, separate baffle plate from cylinder block.

**Installation - 1)** Apply sealant to sealing surface of baffle plate. Install baffle plate, oil strainer and gasket. Tighten bolts to specification. Apply one continuous bead of Sealant (08826-00080) to oil pan mating surface.

**2)** Apply sealant to inner surface around bolt hole area. Tighten oil pan bolts to specification. See TORQUE SPECIFICATIONS table at end of article. To complete installation, reverse removal procedure. Fill engine with oil. Start engine, and check for leaks.

# OVERHAUL

## CYLINDER HEAD

**Cylinder Head - 1)** Remove and disassemble cylinder head. See CYLINDER HEAD & MANIFOLDS under REMOVAL & INSTALLATION. Remove camshaft bearing caps in sequence. *See Fig. 18.* Keep disassembled parts in removal order for reassembly. Mark parts for reassembly reference.

***CAUTION: DO NOT clean cylinder head in hot tank.***

**2)** Inspect cylinder head for cracks. Thoroughly clean cylinder head gasket mating surfaces. Check cylinder head for warpage. If warpage exceeds specification, resurface or replace as necessary. See CYLINDER HEAD table under ENGINE SPECIFICATIONS at end of article.

**Valve Springs -** Measure free length of valve springs. Check spring tension at specified height. Check valve spring out-of-square. Replace springs if measurements are not within specification. See VALVES & VALVE SPRINGS table under ENGINE SPECIFICATIONS at end of article.

**Valve Guides - 1)** To obtain valve stem-to-valve guide oil clearance, subtract measured valve stem diameter from measured valve guide I.D. Replace valve guide and valve if oil clearance is not within specification. See CYLINDER HEAD table under ENGINE SPECIFICATIONS at end of article. To replace valve guide, go to step **2)**.

***NOTE: Valve guide bore of cylinder head can be reamed to accommodate .002" (.05 mm) oversize replacement valve guide.***

**2)** Insert an old valve wrapped with tape into valve guide. *See Fig. 20.* Tap valve firmly with hammer to break guide off flush with cylinder head surface. Be careful not to damage lifter bore. Remove snap ring.

**3)** Using water or oil bath, gradually heat cylinder head to about 194°F (90°C). Using Valve Guide Remover/Installer (09201-70010), drive guide out from camshaft side. Using telescopic hole gauge, measure inside diameter (I.D.) of cylinder head valve guide bore.

**4)** Valve guide bore I.D. should be .5118-.5129" (13.000-13.027 mm). If valve guide bore I.D. exceeds .5129" (13.027 mm), ream valve guide bore to .5138-.5148" (13.050-13.076 mm) for .002" (.05 mm) O/S guide.

**5)** To install new valve guide, heat cylinder head as explained previously in step **3)**. Using valve guide remover/installer, drive in new valve guide from camshaft side until snap ring contacts cylinder head. Using a sharp .31" (8.0 mm) reamer, ream valve guide until standard valve stem-to-guide oil clearance is obtained. See CYLINDER HEAD table under ENGINE SPECIFICATIONS at end of article.

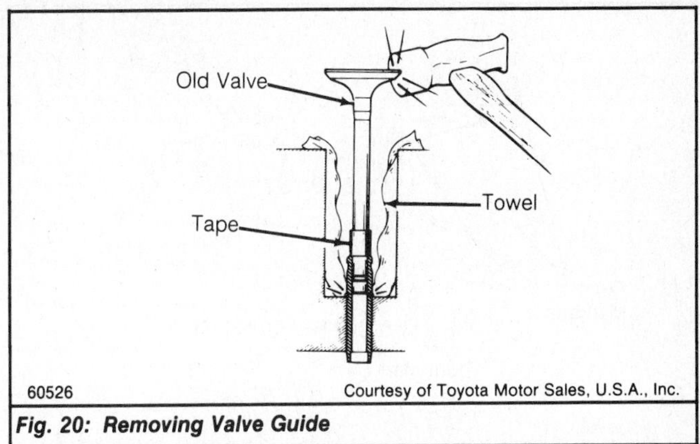


*Fig. 20: Removing Valve Guide*

***NOTE: Always reface valve seat after replacing valve guide.***

**Valve Seat - 1)** Before refacing valve seats, inspect valves and valve guides. If measurements are not within specification, replace components as necessary. See VALVES & VALVE SPRINGS and CYLINDER HEAD tables under ENGINE SPECIFICATIONS at end of article.

**2)** Inspect valve seat for evidence of pitting at valve contact surface. Reface seat as necessary. Valve seat replacement procedure is not available from manufacturer.

**Valves -** Measure valve stem diameter, valve margin and overall length. Replace valves if measurements are not within specification. See VALVES & VALVE SPRINGS table under ENGINE SPECIFICATIONS at end of article.

**Seat Correction Angles - 1)** Replace valve guides, if necessary, before refacing valve seats. After refacing, if valve seat is too high on face of valve, use 30-degree and 45-degree stones/cutters to correct seat.

**2)** If valve seat is too low, use 60-degree and 30-degree stones/cutters to correct seat. Ensure valve seat margin is within specification. See CYLINDER HEAD table under ENGINE SPECIFICATIONS at end of article.

## CYLINDER BLOCK ASSEMBLY

**Piston & Rod Assembly - 1)** Before removing bearing caps, mark caps and rods with punch for reassembly reference. Measure connecting rod side play clearance with dial indicator. If clearance exceeds .015" (.38 mm), replace connecting rod and/or crankshaft.

**2)** Using a connecting rod aligner, check rod for bends or twists. Maximum bend limit is .0020" (.050 mm) per 3.94" (100.0 mm) length or less. Maximum twist limit is .0059" (.150 mm) per 3.94" (100.0 mm) length or less.

**3)** Install piston on connecting rod so that front mark on connecting rod aligns with FRONT mark on top of piston. *See Fig. 21.*

**Fitting Pistons - 1)** Measure cylinder bore and piston skirt diameter. Piston skirt diameter should be measured at 90-degree angle to piston pin. Measure at approximately .921" (23.39 mm) from piston head. Ensure clearance between piston and cylinder bore is within specification. See PISTONS, PINS & RINGS table under ENGINE SPECIFICATIONS at end of article.

**2)** There are 3 standard piston sizes. Pistons may be identified by size mark ("1", "2" or "3") located on top of piston. *See Fig. 21.* When installing new piston into cylinder block that has not been bored for oversize, ensure size mark on new piston matches cylinder bore size mark stamped on left side of cylinder block, near each cylinder bore. *See Fig. 22.*

**Piston Rings -** Ensure ring end gap and side clearance are within specification. See PISTONS, PINS & RINGS table under ENGINE SPECIFICATIONS at end of article. Ensure identification marks on rings are toward top of piston. Position piston rings at designated areas. *See Fig. 23.*

# 1991 ENGINES
# 3.0L V6 (Cont.)

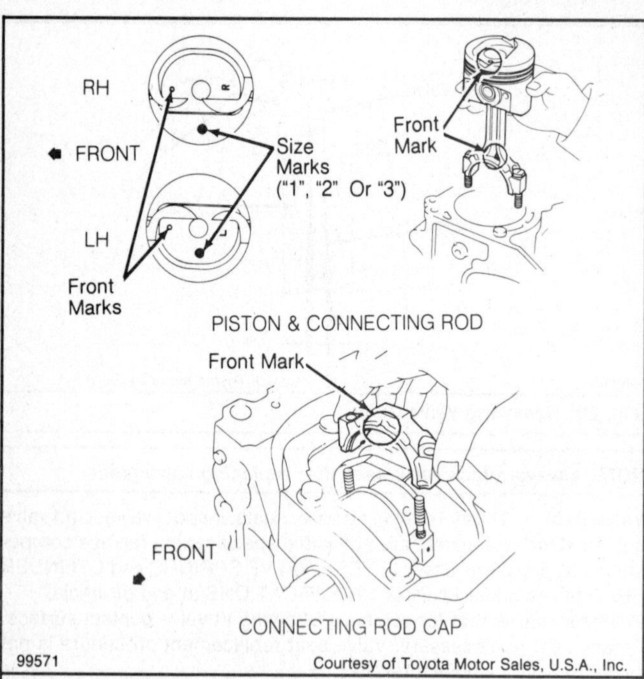


***Fig. 21: Identifying Piston & Connecting Rod Marks***

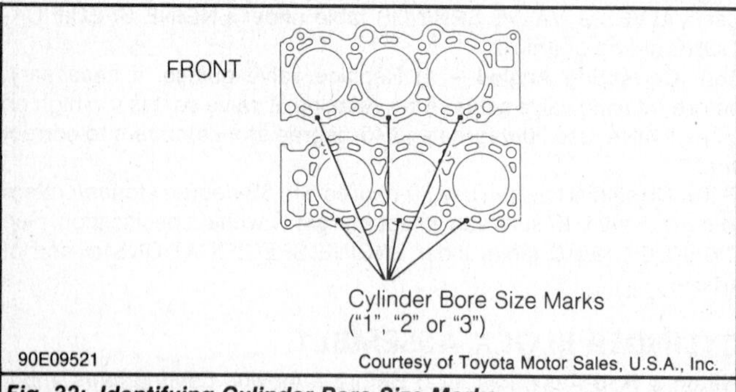


***Fig. 22: Identifying Cylinder Bore Size Marks***

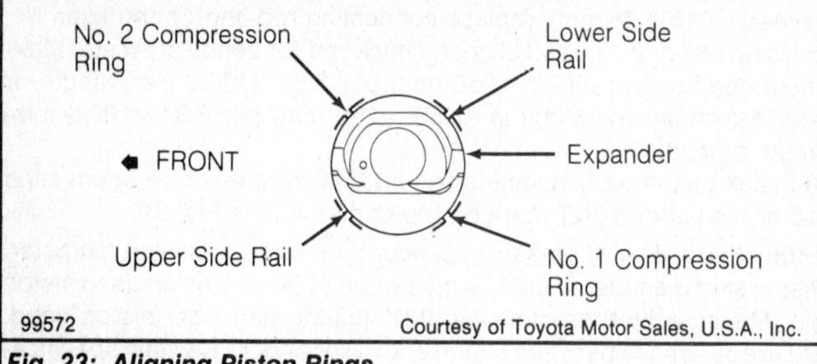


***Fig. 23: Aligning Piston Rings***

**Rod Bearings – 1)** Mark bearing cap and connecting rod for location. Remove connecting rod cap and bearing. Note size mark ("1", "2" or "3") stamped on connecting rod cap and bearing. *See Fig. 25.* If replacing standard size bearing, ensure number on replacement bearing is same as number on connecting rod cap and old bearing.

**2)** Different bearing sizes are used. Bearing size (thickness) is determined by size mark ("1", "2" or "3") stamped on connecting rod cap and bearing. See CONNECTING ROD BEARING SPECIFICATIONS table.

**3)** Install replacement bearing. Install connecting rod cap with front mark toward front of engine. *See Fig. 21.* Using Plastigage method, check bearing clearance. See CONNECTING RODS table under ENGINE SPECIFICATIONS at end of article.

**4)** Tighten connecting rod nuts in 2 steps. Tighten rod nuts to 18 ft. lbs. (24 N.m). Place reference point on top of each connecting rod nut, and tighten each nut 90 degrees.

**5)** If connecting rod nut cannot be tightened to specification, or nut binds on connecting rod stud threads, replace connecting rod nuts and/or bolts. Check connecting rod side clearance. See CONNECTING RODS table under ENGINE SPECIFICATIONS.

***NOTE: Install rod bearings with oil hole in the connecting rod.***

***CONNECTING ROD BEARING SPECIFICATIONS***

| Size Mark [1] | Thickness In. (mm) |
|---|---|
| "1" | .0584-.0586 (1.484-1.488) |
| "2" | .0586-.0587 (1.489-1.492) |
| "3" | .0588-.0589 (1.493-1.496) |

[1] – Bearing number is stamped on bearing and connecting rod cap. *See Fig. 25.*

**Crankshaft & Main Bearings – 1)** Mark connecting rod and main bearing caps for reassembly reference. Remove connecting rod caps and bearings. Note direction of arrow on main bearing cap.

**2)** Loosen main bearing cap bolts in 3 steps using proper sequence. *See Fig. 24.* Remove main bearing caps. Keep all bearing inserts in original location. Remove crankshaft. Remove main bearings from cylinder block. Mark bearings for location.

***CAUTION: Use size mark on crankshaft to determine journal diameter. See Fig. 25.***

**3)** Inspect crankshaft for cracks. Check crankshaft for runout at center journal. If runout is greater than .0024" (.060 mm), replace crankshaft. Measure crankshaft journals out-of-round and taper. If either measurement exceeds .0008" (.020 mm), regrind and/or replace crankshaft.

**4)** Cylinder block main journal bore diameter is determined by size mark ("1", "2" or "3") stamped on oil pan rail of cylinder block. *See Fig. 25.* Main bearing journal diameter is determined by size mark ("0", "1" or "2") stamped on crankshaft counterweight. Size marks are placed in order with corresponding cylinders. *See Fig. 25.*

**5)** Ensure main bearing journal diameter is within specification. See CRANKSHAFT, MAIN & CONNECTING ROD BEARINGS table under ENGINE SPECIFICATIONS at end of article. Install bearing with oil hole in the engine block.

**6)** Main bearings are available in .010" (.25 mm) and .020" (.50 mm) undersize. Install thrust washers on No. 2 main bearing cap, with oil grooves facing away from cap. Install main bearing cap with arrow pointing toward front of engine.

**7)** Tighten main bearing cap bolts to specification in sequence. *See Fig. 24.* See TORQUE SPECIFICATIONS at end of article. Ensure crankshaft rotates smoothly. Check crankshaft end play. See CRANKSHAFT, MAIN & CONNECTING ROD BEARINGS table under ENGINE SPECIFICATIONS.

***NOTE: Install main bearing with oil hole in cylinder block.***

**Thrust Bearing –** Check crankshaft end play. See CRANKSHAFT, MAIN & CONNECTING ROD BEARINGS table under ENGINE SPECIFICATIONS at end of article. If end play exceeds maximum limit, replace thrust washers as a set and/or replace crankshaft. Thrust washers are installed on No. 2 main bearing journal.

**Cylinder Block – 1)** Inspect cylinder block for cracks. Measure warpage, taper and out-of-round. Replace or repair cylinder block if measurements are not within specification. See CYLINDER BLOCK table under ENGINE SPECIFICATIONS at end of article.

**2)** Measure cylinder bore. There are 3 standard cylinder bore sizes. Cylinder bore size (diameter) is determined by size mark ("1", "2" or "3") stamped on left side of block, near each cylinder bore. *See Fig. 22.*.

***NOTE: If boring cylinder block, allow less than .0008" (.020 mm) in cylinder bore for final honing.***

**3)** If cylinder bore is okay, hone cylinder to obtain a 60-degree cross-hatch pattern. After honing, wash cylinder bore with hot soapy water. Air-dry cylinder bore, and apply engine oil to prevent rusting.

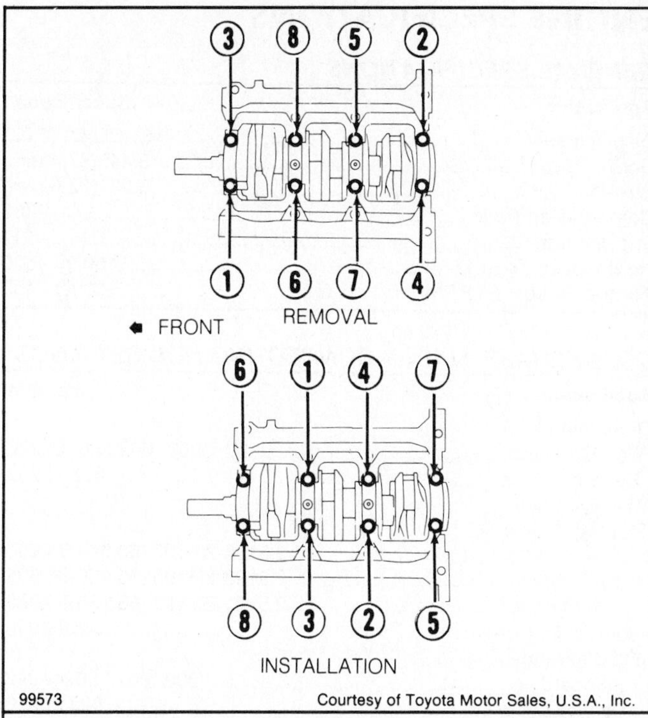


*Fig. 24: Main Bearing Cap Bolt Removal & Tightening Sequence*

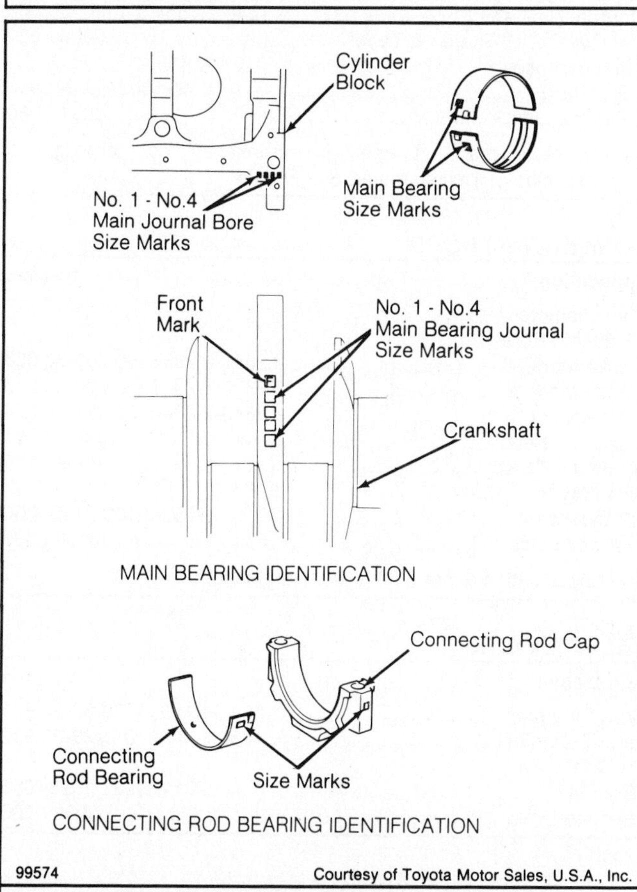


*Fig. 25: Locating Cylinder Block, Main Bearing, Crankshaft, Connecting Rod Cap & Rod Bearing Size marks*

# ENGINE OILING

## ENGINE LUBRICATION SYSTEM

Oil pressure is provided by a rotor-type pump, which is driven by the crankshaft. Pressure relief valve is located in the oil pump body. *See Fig. 26* for cross-sectional view of engine oil circuit.

**Crankcase Capacity** – On 4WD models, crankcase oil capacity is 4.8 qts. (4.5L) with filter replacement. On 2WD models, crankcase capacity is 4.5 qts. (4.3L) with filter replacement.

**Normal Oil Pressure** – With engine at normal operating temperature, oil pressure should exceed 4 psi (.3 kg/cm²) at idle and should be 36-75 psi (2.5-5.3 kg/cm²) at 3000 RPM.

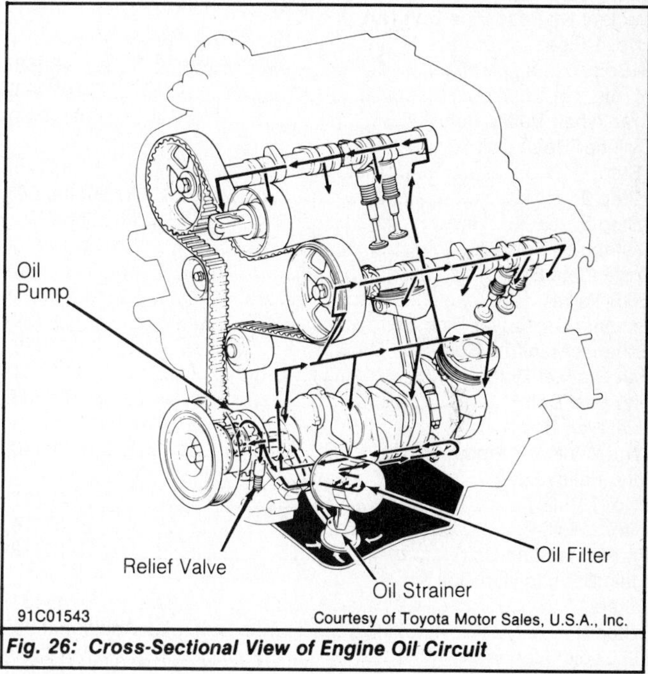


*Fig. 26: Cross-Sectional View of Engine Oil Circuit*

## OIL PUMP

**Removal** – Remove engine undercover (splash) shields. Remove oil pan and baffle. Remove timing belt and crankshaft timing pulley. See TIMING BELT under REMOVAL & INSTALLATION. Remove oil pump bolts. Remove oil pump and "O" ring from cylinder block.

**Inspection** – **1)** Disassemble pump. Install rotors in pump body. Check rotor tip clearance and clearance between driven rotor and pump body. Place straightedge across pump body to check rotor side clearance.

**2)** Check clearance between straightedge and both rotors. Replace rotor set or pump assembly if any clearance measurement is not within specification. See OIL PUMP SPECIFICATIONS table.

**Installation** – **1)** If oil seal was removed, coat new seal with grease, and install seal using Seal Installer (09309-37010). Reassemble pump. Install new "O" ring on front of cylinder block.

**2)** Apply Sealant (08826-00080) to rear of oil pump. Install oil pump on cylinder block. Ensure splined teeth of oil pump aligns with teeth of crankshaft. To complete installation, reverse removal procedure. Install bolts, and tighten them to specification.

***OIL PUMP SPECIFICATIONS***

| Application | In. (mm) |
|---|---|
| Driven Rotor-To-Pump Body | |
| Standard | .0039-.0051 (.100-.130) |
| Service Limit | .0118 (.300) |
| Rotor Side Clearance | |
| Standard | .0012-.0035 (.030-.090) |
| Service Limit | .0059 (.150) |
| Rotor Tip Clearance | |
| Standard | .0043-.0094 (.110-.240) |
| Service Limit | .0138 (.350) |

# 1991 ENGINES
# 3.0L V6 (Cont.)

## TORQUE SPECIFICATIONS

### TORQUE SPECIFICATIONS

| Application | Ft. Lbs. (N.m) |
|---|---|
| Air Intake Chamber Bolt | 13 (18) |
| Camshaft Bearing Cap Bolt | 12 (16) |
| Camshaft Timing Pulley Bolt | 80 (109) |
| Cold Start Injector Tube Bolt | 13 (18) |
| Connecting Rod Nut | |
| Step 1 | 18 (24) |
| Step 2 | Additional 90° |
| Coolant By-Pass Outlet Bolt | 13 (18) |
| Coolant By-Pass Pipe Bolt/Nut | |
| No. 1 Pipe | |
| Bolt | 43 (58) |
| Nut | 61 (83) |
| Crankshaft Pulley Bolt | 181 (245) |
| Cylinder Head Bolt [1] | |
| Step 1 | 33 (45) |
| Step 2 | Additional 90° |
| Step 3 | Additional 90° |
| Distributor Bolt | 13 (18) |
| Drive Plate Bolt [2] | 61 (83) |
| EGR Valve | [3] |
| Exhaust Crossover Pipe Bolt | 29 (39) |
| Exhaust Manifold Bolt | 29 (39) |
| Fan Bracket Bolt | 30 (41) |
| Flywheel Bolt [2] | 65 (88) |
| Fuel Pipe Bolt | |
| No. 2 & No. 3 Pipes | 22 (30) |
| Idler Pulley Bolt | |
| No. 1 Pulley | 27 (37) |
| No. 2 Pulley | 13 (18) |
| Intake Manifold Bolt | 13 (18) |
| Main Bearing Cap Bolt [4] | |
| Step 1 | 45 (61) |
| Step 2 | Additional 90° |
| Oil Cooler Center Bolt | 43 (58) |
| Oil Filter Union | 18 (24) |
| Oil Pan | 18 (24) |
| Oil Pump Bolt | 14 (19) |
| Power Steering Pump Pulley Nut | 32 (43) |
| Rear Crossmember-To-Frame Bolt | 70 (95) |
| Rear Mount-To-Crossmember Bolt | 13 (18) |
| Reed Valve-To-Cylinder Head Bolt | 27 (37) |
| Reed Valve-To-Exhaust Manifold Bolt | 22 (30) |
| Tension Spring Bracket Bolt | 13 (18) |
| Thermostat Housing Bolt | 14 (19) |
| Water Pump Bolt | |
| Long Bolt | 13 (18) |
| Short Bolt | 14 (19) |
| | **INCH Lbs. (N.m)** |
| Delivery Pipe Bolt | 108 (12) |
| Fan Pulley Nut | 48 (5) |
| Oil Strainer Bolt | 61 (7) |
| Rear Oil Seal Retainer Bolt | 69 (8) |
| Rear Plate Bolt | 61 (7) |
| Timing Belt Cover Bolt | |
| No. 1 & No. 2 Covers | 48 (5) |
| No. 3 & No. 4 Covers | 74 (8) |

[1] – Tighten all bolts to specification, except bolt "A". Then install bolt "A" and tighten to 27 ft. lbs. (37 N.m). *See Fig. 13.*

[2] – Tighten in a crisscross pattern.

[3] – *See Fig. 14.*

[4] – Tighten in sequence. *See Fig. 24.*

## ENGINE SPECIFICATIONS

### GENERAL SPECIFICATIONS

| Application | Specification |
|---|---|
| Displacement | 181 Cu. In. (3.0L) |
| Bore | 3.44" (87.4 mm) |
| Stroke | 3.23" (82.0 mm) |
| Compression Ratio | 9.0:1 |
| Fuel System | PFI |
| Horsepower @ RPM | 150 @ 4800 |
| Torque Ft. Lbs. @ RPM | 180 @ 3400 |

### CRANKSHAFT, MAIN & CONNECTING ROD BEARINGS

| Application | In. (mm) |
|---|---|
| Crankshaft | |
| End Play | .0008-.0090 (.020-.220) |
| Runout | .0024 (.060) |
| Main Bearings [1] | |
| Journal Diameter | |
| Size Mark "0" | 2.5195-2.5197 (63.996-64.000) |
| Size Mark "1" | 2.5193-2.5195 (63.990-63.995) |
| Size Mark "2" | 2.5191-2.5192 (63.985-63.989) |
| Journal Out-Of-Round & Taper | .0008 (.020) |
| Oil Clearance | |
| Standard | .0009-.0017 (.024-.042) |
| Service Limit | .0031 (.080) |
| Connecting Rod Bearings | |
| Journal Diameter | 2.1648-2.1654 (54.987-55.000) |
| Journal Out-Of-Round & Taper | .0008 (.020) |
| Oil Clearance | |
| Standard | .0009-.0021 (.024-.053) |
| Service Limit | .0031 (.080) |

[1] – Use size mark stamped on crankshaft counterweight to determine journal diameter. *See Fig. 25.*

### CONNECTING RODS

| Application | In. (mm) |
|---|---|
| Bore Diameter | |
| Crankpin Bore | |
| Size Mark "1" | 2.2835-2.2838 (58.000-58.008) |
| Size Mark "2" | 2.2838-2.2841 (58.009-58.016) |
| Size Mark "3" | 2.2843-2.2844 (58.017-58.024) |
| Maximum Bend [1] | .0020 (.051) |
| Maximum Twist [1] | .0059 (.150) |
| Side Play | |
| Standard | .0059-.0130 (.150-.330) |
| Service Limit | .0150 (.380) |

[1] – Specification is per 3.94" (100.0 mm) length.

### VALVE LIFTERS

| Application | In. (mm) |
|---|---|
| Bore Diameter | 1.4945-1.4951 (37.960-37.975) |
| Lifter Diameter | 1.4930-1.4934 (37.922-37.932) |
| Oil Clearance | |
| Standard | .0011-.0021 (.028-.053) |
| Service Limit | .0039 (.100) |

# 1991 ENGINES
# 3.0L V6 (Cont.)

## PISTONS, PINS & RINGS

| Application | In. (mm) |
|---|---|
| Pistons | |
| Clearance | .0031-.0039 (.080-.100) |
| Diameter [1] | |
| Size Mark "1" | 3.4413-3.4417 (87.410-87.420) |
| Size Mark "2" | 3.4418-3.4421 (87.421-87.430) |
| Size Mark "3" | 3.4422-3.4425 (87.431-87.440) |
| Rings | |
| No. 1 | |
| End Gap | |
| Standard | .0091-.0130 (.231-.330) |
| Service Limit | .0327 (.831) |
| Side Clearance | .0012-.0028 (.030-.071) |
| No. 2 | |
| End Gap | |
| Standard | .0150-.0189 (.381-.480) |
| Service Limit | .0366 (.930) |
| Side Clearance | .0012-.0028 (.030-.071) |
| No. 3 (Oil) | |
| End Gap | |
| Standard | .0059-.0157 (.150-.400) |
| Service Limit | .0354 (.900) |

[1] - Piston diameter is determined size mark on top of piston. *See Fig. 21.*

## CYLINDER BLOCK

| Application | In. (mm) |
|---|---|
| Cylinder Bore | |
| Standard Diameter [1] | |
| Size Mark "1" | 3.4449-3.4453 (87.500-87.510) |
| Size Mark "2" | 3.4453-3.4457 (87.511-87.520) |
| Size Mark "3" | 3.4457-3.4461 (87.521-87.530) |
| Main Journal Bore Diameter [2] | |
| Size Mark "1" | 2.6776-2.6778 (68.010-68.016) |
| Size Mark "2" | 2.6778-2.6780 (68.017-68.022) |
| Size Mark "3" | 2.6781-2.6783 (68.023-68.028) |
| Maximum Taper | .0008 (.020) |
| Maximum Out-Of-Round | .0008 (.020) |
| Maximum Deck Warpage | .002 (.05) |

[1] - Cylinder bore diameter is determined by size mark stamped on left side of block, near each cylinder bore. *See Fig. 22.*

[2] - Main journal bore diameter is determined by size mark located on cylinder block oil pan rail. *See Fig. 25.*

## VALVES & VALVE SPRINGS

| Application | Specification |
|---|---|
| Face Angle | 44.5° |
| Head Diameter | [1] |
| Minimum Margin | .051" (1.30 mm) |
| Minimum Refinish Length | 4.094" (104.00 mm) |
| Stem Diameter | |
| Intake Valve | .3138-.3144" (7.970-7.985 mm) |
| Exhaust Valve | .3136-.3142" (7.965-7.980 mm) |
| Valve Springs | |
| Free Length | 1.8508" (47.010 mm) |
| Installed Height | 1.575" (40.00 mm) |
| Out-Of-Square | .0484" (1.230 mm) |
| | **Lbs. @ In. (kg @ mm)** |
| Pressure | |
| Intake & Exhaust | 57 @ 1.58 (26 @ 40.0) |

[1] - Information is not available from manufacturer.

## CYLINDER HEAD

| Application | Specification |
|---|---|
| Cylinder Head | |
| Maximum Warpage | .0039" (.100 mm) |
| Valve Seats | |
| Seat Angle | 45° |
| Seat Width | .047-.063" (1.20-1.60 mm) |
| Valve Guide | |
| Bore I.D. | |
| Standard | .5118-.5129" (13.000-13.027 mm) |
| Oversize | .5138-.5148" (13.050-13.077 mm) |
| Valve Guide I.D. | .3154-.3161" (8.010-8.030 mm) |
| Valve Guide O.D | |
| Standard | .5134-.5138" (13.040-13.051 mm) |
| Over Size | .5154-.5158" (13.090-13.101 mm) |
| Valve Stem-To-Guide | |
| Oil Clearance | |
| Intake Valve | |
| Standard | .0010-.0024" (.025-.060 mm) |
| Service Limit | .0031" (.079 mm) |
| Exhaust Valve | |
| Standard | .0012-.0026" (.030-.065 mm) |
| Service Limit | .0039" (.100 mm) |

## CAMSHAFT

| Application | In. (mm) |
|---|---|
| End Play | |
| Standard | .0031-.0075 (.080-.190) |
| Service Limit [1] | .0098 (.250) |
| Journal Diameter | 1.3370-1.3376 (33.959-33.975) |
| Journal Runout | .0024 (.060) |
| Lobe Height | 1.8830-1.8870 (47.828-47.930) |
| Oil Clearance | |
| Standard | .0010-.0026 (.025-.066) |
| Service Limit | .0039 (.100) |

[1] - If measurement exceeds service limit, replace camshaft and/or cylinder head.

# 1991 ENGINES
# 3.0L & 3.0L Turbo 6-Cylinder

## Cressida, Supra

***NOTE: For repair procedures not covered in this article, see ENGINE OVERHAUL PROCEDURES article in GENERAL INFORMATION.***

## ENGINE IDENTIFICATION

Engine may be identified by using Vehicle Identification Number (VIN) stamped on a metal pad, located near lower left corner of windshield. The fourth character identifies the engine model.

Engine identification number, located on right front of cylinder block below cylinder head, may be required when ordering replacement parts (if needed).

***ENGINE IDENTIFICATION CODES***

| Application | VIN Code | Engine Code |
|---|---|---|
| Cressida & Supra Non-Turbo | M | 7M-GE |
| Supra Turbo | M | 7M-GTE |

## ADJUSTMENTS

### VALVE CLEARANCE ADJUSTMENT

**1)** With engine cold, remove valve covers. Place No. 1 cylinder on TDC of compression stroke. Ensure lifters on No. 1 cylinder are loose and lifters on No. 6 cylinder are tight. If not, turn crankshaft clockwise one complete revolution.
**2)** Using feeler gauge, measure and record clearance of intake valves on No. 1 and No. 4 cylinders and exhaust valves on No. 1 and No. 5 cylinders. Rotate crankshaft 2/3 turn (240 degrees). Measure and record clearance of intake valves on No. 3 and No. 5 cylinders and exhaust valves on No. 3 and No. 6 cylinders.
**3)** Rotate crankshaft another 2/3 turn (240 degrees). Measure and record clearance of intake valves on No. 2 and No. 6 cylinders and exhaust valves on No. 2 and No. 4 cylinders. If clearance is not within specification, change adjusting shim to adjust valve clearance. See VALVE CLEARANCE SPECIFICATIONS (COLD) table.

***VALVE CLEARANCE SPECIFICATIONS (COLD)***

| Valve | In. (mm) |
|---|---|
| Intake | .006-.010 (.15-.25) |
| Exhaust | .008-.012 (.20-.30) |

**4)** To remove adjusting shim, depress valve lifter with Lifter Depressor (09248-55010 A and B). Before depressing lifter, position notch on depressor toward spark plug. Use small screwdriver to remove shim from top of lifter.
**5)** Measure thickness of shim removed with a micrometer. If valve clearance is greater than specified, use thicker shim. If valve clearance is less than specified, use thinner shim. Adjusting shims are available in .002" (.05 mm) increments ranging from .0984" (2.500 mm) to .1299" (3.299 mm). Install new shims using lifter depressor.

## REMOVAL & INSTALLATION

***NOTE: For reassembly reference, label all electrical connectors, vacuum hoses and fuel lines before removal. Also place mating marks on engine hood and other major assemblies before removal.***

### FUEL PRESSURE RELEASE

With ignition off, disconnect negative battery cable. Place suitable container under fuel line at fuel filter. Cover fuel line connection with shop towel. Slowly loosen fuel line connection, allowing fuel pressure to be released.

### ENGINE

**Removal – 1)** Remove hood. Disconnect battery cables. Remove battery and battery tray. Drain cooling system. Disconnect air hoses from airflow meter and power steering unit. Remove 3 attaching bolts from air cleaner case. Remove air cleaner with hoses attached.
**2)** Disconnect A/C condenser fan motor connector. Disconnect radiator and coolant reservoir hoses. On automatic transmission models, disconnect and plug transmission cooler lines. On all models, remove radiator supports and radiator.
**3)** Remove accessory drive belts. Remove radiator fan and water pump pulley. Disconnect brake booster, heater valve, cruise control and charcoal canister hoses. Disconnect engine ground straps (one on left front fender apron and one at rear of engine). Label and disconnect all electrical connections between engine and chassis.
**4)** Disconnect cruise control and accelerator cables. On automatic transmission models, disconnect throttle cable. On all models, disconnect heater hoses. Remove A/C compressor and power steering pump and lay aside. DO NOT disconnect hoses from A/C compressor and power steering pump.
**5)** On manual transmission models, remove shift lever from inside vehicle. On all models, disconnect ground strap from fuel hose clamp. Release fuel pressure. See FUEL PRESSURE RELEASE under REMOVAL & INSTALLATION. Disconnect fuel lines.
**6)** Raise and support vehicle. Remove lower engine cover. Drain engine oil. Remove exhaust pipe. Remove drive shaft and insert Transmission Oil Plug (09325-40010) for automatic transmission or (09325-20010) for manual transmission to prevent oil leakage. Remove front suspension crossmember. Disconnect speedometer cable.
**7)** Remove manual shift linkage (automatic transmission). Remove clutch slave cylinder (manual transmission). Lower vehicle. Using a jack, support transmission with wooden block between jack and transmission oil pan.
**8)** Remove rear engine support member from body with ground strap attached. Attach lifting chain to engine hangers. Remove engine mounting nuts and washers. Ensure all electrical wiring and hoses are disconnected. Carefully lift engine with transmission assembly from engine compartment.
**Installation – 1)** With engine connected to transmission, carefully lower engine/transmission assembly into engine compartment. On models with manual transmission, install clutch slave cylinder and bleed hydraulic system, if necessary.
**2)** Ensure proper placement of all electrical harnesses and vacuum lines. Adjust drive belt tension. Refill fluids before starting engine. To complete installation, reverse removal procedure. Tighten nuts and bolts to specification. See TORQUE SPECIFICATIONS table at end of article. Install hood, start engine and check for leaks.

## INTAKE MANIFOLD

***NOTE: Manufacturer recommends removing intake manifold after removing cylinder head from engine. See CYLINDER HEAD under REMOVAL & INSTALLATION.***

**Removal – 1)** With cylinder head resting on wooden blocks, remove No. 2 timing belt cover. *See Fig. 1.* Remove alternator bracket, heater inlet hose and heater union.

**2)** Remove 3 fuel supply rail retaining bolts. Remove fuel supply rail with injectors attached. Remove fuel injector insulators and collars from cylinder head. Remove EGR valve, vacuum switching valve, intake manifold and gasket.
**Inspection –** Check intake manifold and intake chamber for surface warpage. Maximum warpage limit is .004" (.10 mm). Replace manifold if warpage exceeds maximum limit.
**Installation –** Thoroughly clean all gasket surfaces and install NEW gaskets. Install intake manifold. Gradually tighten bolts to specification, working from center outward. See TORQUE SPECIFICATIONS table at end of article. To complete installation, reverse removal procedure.

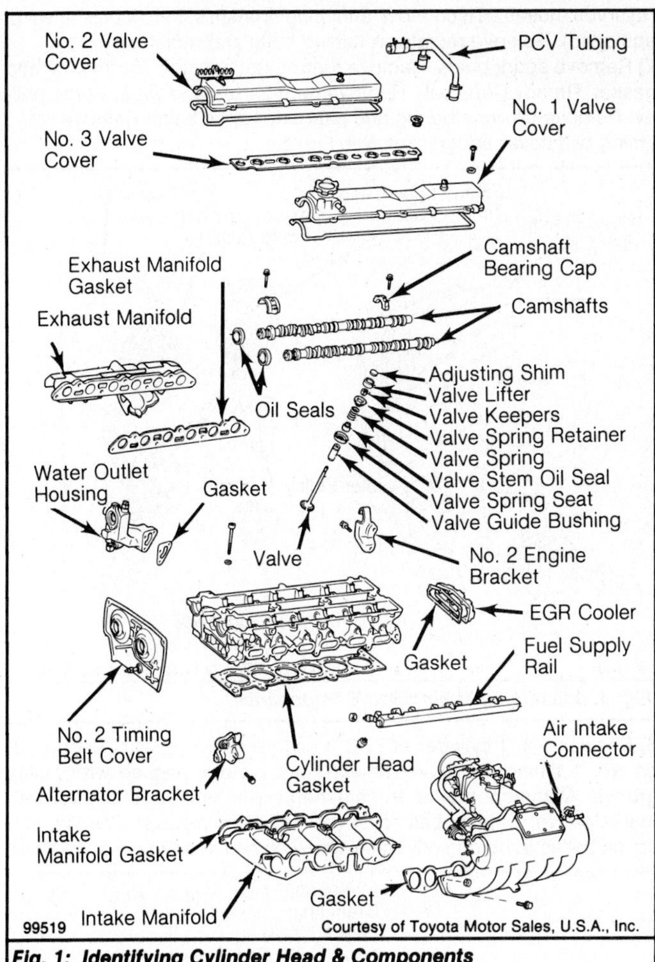


***Fig. 1: Identifying Cylinder Head & Components***

## EXHAUST MANIFOLD

**Removal - 1)** Disconnect negative battery cable. Release fuel pressure. See FUEL PRESSURE RELEASE under REMOVAL & INSTALLATION. Drain cooling system. Disconnect exhaust pipe from exhaust manifold. Disconnect cruise control cable, accelerator cable and throttle cable (automatic transmission). Disconnect ground strap at rear of engine.

**2)** Remove air cleaner hose with intake air connector tube (nearest fender panel). Disconnect cruise control vacuum hose and charcoal canister hose. Remove heater and radiator inlet hoses. Disconnect PCV hose. Remove alternator belt, alternator and adjusting bracket.

**3)** Remove PCV tubing. Disconnect electrical connectors from cold start injector, throttle position sensor and Idle Speed Control (ISC) valve. Disconnect bimetallic vacuum switching valve and EGR hoses from throttle body. Disconnect vacuum tube hose from air intake chamber. Disconnect fuel pressure regulator hose. Disconnect vacuum switching valve hoses. Disconnect diaphragm hose.

**4)** Disconnect coolant by-pass hoses from ISC valve and from throttle body. Remove EGR tube mounting bolts. Remove manifold support mounting bolt. Remove throttle body bracket. Remove air intake connector bracket mounting bolts.

**5)** Remove cold start injector tube. Remove EGR vacuum modulator from mounting bracket. Disconnect wiring harness from routing clamps on air intake chamber. Remove retaining nuts/bolts from air intake chamber.

**6)** Remove vacuum transmitting pipes and air intake chamber with connector and gasket as an assembly. Identify and disconnect all necessary wiring. Separate wiring from routing clamps.

**7)** Remove pulsation damper and No. 1 fuel supply line. Disconnect fuel hose from No. 2 fuel supply line. Remove mounting bolt, union bolt, No. 2 fuel supply line and gaskets. Mark and remove spark plug cables and distributor. Remove oil dipstick. Remove exhaust manifold and gasket.

**Inspection -** Check exhaust manifold for surface warpage. Maximum warpage limit is .0295" (.749 mm) or .0197" (.50 mm) on turbo model. Replace manifold if warpage exceeds maximum limit.

**Installation -** Thoroughly clean all gasket surfaces and install NEW gasket. Install exhaust manifold and tighten nuts to specification. See TORQUE SPECIFICATIONS table at end of article. To complete installation, reverse removal procedure.

## CYLINDER HEAD

**Removal - 1)** Remove timing belt. See TIMING BELT under REMOVAL & INSTALLATION. Remove turbocharger (if equipped). Remove exhaust manifold as previously outlined.

**2)** Remove union bolts and coolant by-pass hose with gaskets at coolant outlet housing. Disconnect coolant by-pass hose from coolant by-pass tube. Remove bolt, nuts, coolant outlet housing and gasket.

**3)** Remove accelerator link. Remove No. 1 and No. 2 valve covers. Using Clamp Adapter (09923-00010), remove heater hose clamp and No. 3 valve cover (cover between camshafts). Remove spark plugs.

**4)** Using 10 mm Hex Adapter (09043-38100), loosen cylinder head bolts in 3 stages in reverse order of tightening sequence. *See Fig. 2.*

***NOTE: Cylinder head bolts must be removed in correct order to prevent warpage or cracking of cylinder head.***

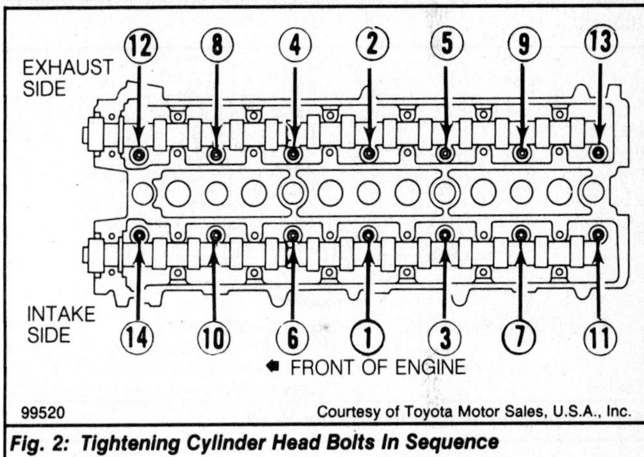


***Fig. 2: Tightening Cylinder Head Bolts In Sequence***

**5)** Lift cylinder head off dowels on engine block. While lifting head, separate coolant by-pass hose from union. Place head on wooden blocks on work bench.

***NOTE: Cylinder head can be pried from engine block with pry bar inserted between head and block projections only. DO NOT damage head or block surfaces during prying operation.***

**Inspection -** Check cylinder head for cracks, flaws or damage. Inspect cylinder head and block mating surfaces for warpage. Cylinder head warpage limit is .004" (.10 mm). If beyond limit, replace cylinder head. Maximum warpage for cylinder block is .002" (.05 mm). If warpage exceeds maximum, replace cylinder block.

**Installation - 1)** Clean all surfaces. Apply sealant to front of cylinder block. *See Fig. 3.* Install NEW head gasket. Ensure gasket is properly installed. Carefully lower cylinder head into position over dowels. Connect coolant by-pass hose to union.

**2)** Apply light coat of oil to threads and underside of cylinder head bolts. Using 10 mm Hex Adapter (09043-38100), tighten cylinder head bolts in 3 stages in tightening sequence. *See Fig. 2* and TORQUE SPECIFICATIONS table at end of article. Install timing belt. See TIMING BELT under REMOVAL & INSTALLATION. Install spark plugs.

# 1991 ENGINES
# 3.0L & 3.0L Turbo 6-Cylinder (Cont.)

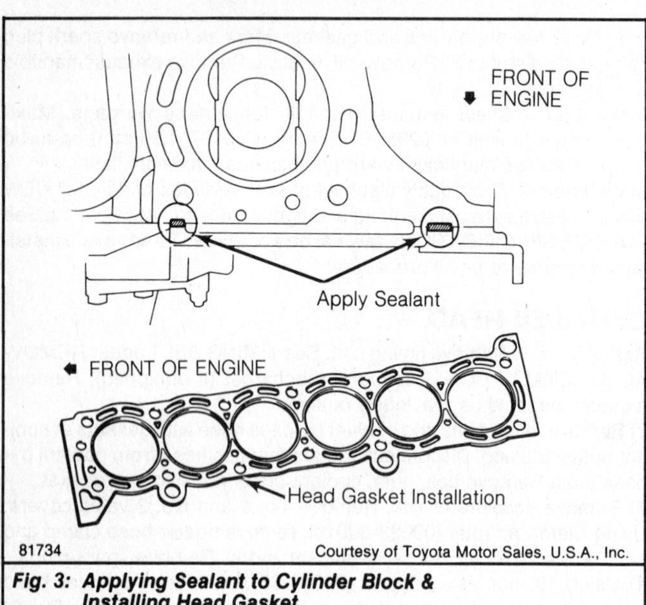


***Fig. 3: Applying Sealant to Cylinder Block & Installing Head Gasket***

**3)** Using Clamp Adapter (09923-00010), install heater hose clamp and No. 3 valve cover (cover between camshafts). Apply sealant to cylinder head as shown. *See Fig. 4*. Install valve covers. Install accelerator link.

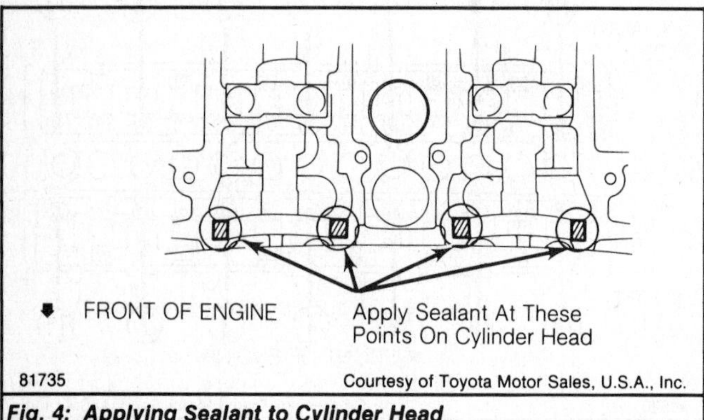


***Fig. 4: Applying Sealant to Cylinder Head***

**4)** Install NEW coolant outlet housing gasket. Install coolant outlet housing. Connect coolant by-pass hose. Install NEW gaskets, union and union bolt to coolant outlet housing. To complete installation, reverse removal procedure. Tighten nuts and bolts to specification. See TORQUE SPECIFICATIONS table at end of article.

## FRONT CRANKSHAFT OIL SEAL

**Removal & Installation (With Timing Case Installed)** – Remove timing belt. See TIMING BELT under REMOVAL & INSTALLATION. Using Seal Puller (09308-55010) remove seal from timing case. Apply multipurpose grease to NEW seal. Using Seal Installer and Driver (09214-60010 and 09506-35010), install oil seal. To complete installation, reverse removal procedure.

**Removal & Installation (With Timing Case Removed)** – Using a screwdriver and a hammer, remove oil seal from timing case. Apply multipurpose grease to NEW seal. Using Seal Installer and Driver (09214-60010 and 09506-35010), drive in oil seal.

## TIMING BELT

***NOTE: Timing belt should be replaced at 60,000 mile intervals.***

**Removal – 1)** Disconnect negative battery cable. Drain cooling system. Remove fan shroud. Disconnect radiator and coolant reservoir hoses. Disconnect and plug transmission cooler lines (if equipped). Remove radiator retaining bolts and radiator.

**2)** Remove spark plugs. Remove thermostat housing, thermostat and gasket. Remove A/C belt. Remove radiator fan and water pump pulley. Remove power steering and alternator drive belts. Remove No. 3 timing belt cover and gasket. *See Fig. 5*.

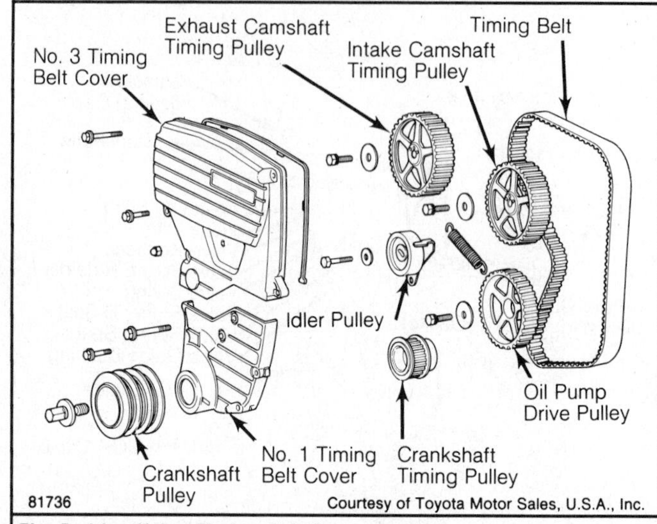


***Fig. 5: Identifying Timing Belt Components***

**3)** Position No. 1 cylinder at TDC on compression stroke. Ensure "0" on No. 1 timing belt cover timing mark plate is aligned with pulley groove. Alignment marks on camshaft pulleys must be aligned with marks on No. 2 timing belt cover (cover behind pulleys). *See Fig. 6*. If timing belt is to be reused, place arrow on belt in direction of rotation.

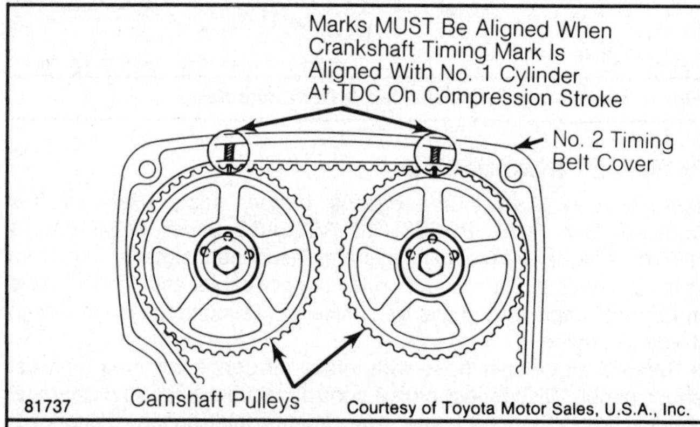


***Fig. 6: Aligning Camshaft Pulley Timing Marks***

**4)** Loosen idler pulley bolt. Pry the idler pulley as far left as it will go and tighten pulley bolt. Relieve timing belt tension and remove belt from camshaft and idler pulleys. Support belt in such a way that alignment marks on camshaft pulleys and crankshaft pulley are not disturbed.

**5)** Using Camshaft Pulley Holder (09278-54012), hold pulley and remove bolt. Remove camshaft pulleys and dowel pins (center pin only on each pulley). Using Crankshaft Pulley Adapter and Bar (09213-70010 and 09330-00021), hold pulley and remove bolt. Using Crankshaft Pulley Puller (09213-31021), remove crankshaft pulley.

***NOTE: DO NOT use belt tension to hold camshaft pulley while removing bolt.***

**6)** Remove air tube from power steering unit. Remove A/C compressor without disconnecting hoses. Remove A/C idler pulley bracket, compressor bracket and No. 1 timing belt cover. Remove timing belt. Remove idler pulley and spring.

**7)** Using Crankshaft Timing Pulley Puller (09213-60017) and socket, remove crankshaft timing pulley. Using Oil Pump Drive Pulley Holder (09278-54012), remove oil pump drive pulley.

**Inspection – 1)** Check belt teeth for cracks or damage. If tooth damage is found, ensure camshafts are not locked. If wear or cracks on flat belt race are found, check for nicks on one side of idler pulley lock.

**2)** If wear or damage to only one side of belt is found, check belt guide and alignment of each pulley. If noticeable wear is found on belt teeth, check timing cover gasket for damage and proper installation.

**3)** Ensure there is no foreign material on pulley teeth. Check timing belt idler pulley for smooth rotation. Replace if roughness or noise is found. Check free length of idler pulley tension spring. If free length is not 2.72" (69 mm), replace spring.

**Installation – 1)** Install oil pump drive pulley. Using oil pump drive pulley holder, install and tighten pulley bolt to specification. Using Crankshaft Timing Pulley Installer (09214-60010), drive pulley onto crankshaft. Install idler pulley and spring. Pry the idler pulley as far left as it will go and tighten pulley bolt. Keep idler pulley clean.

**2)** Install timing belt on crankshaft, oil pump drive and idler pulleys. If reusing old belt, install belt with arrow pointing in direction of rotation. Install No. 1 timing belt cover, A/C compressor bracket and idler pulley bracket. Install A/C compressor. Install air tube on power steering unit.

**3)** Align Woodruff key and install crankshaft pulley. Using crankshaft pulley adapter and bar, hold pulley and tighten bolt to specification. Turn crankshaft pulley to align "0" on No. 1 timing belt cover timing mark plate with crankshaft pulley groove.

**4)** Align marks on camshaft pulleys with marks on No. 2 timing belt cover and install pulleys. *See Fig. 6*. Install dowel pin in middle hole of each pulley. Install bolt. Using camshaft pulley holder, hold pulley and tighten bolt to specification. Ensure camshaft pulley marks are still aligned.

**5)** Install timing belt. Loosen idler pulley bolt and allow tensioner to re position. Tighten idler pulley bolt to specification. Rotate crankshaft pulley 2 revolutions clockwise (TDC to TDC). Ensure camshaft timing marks are aligned with marks on timing cover No. 2.

**6)** If timing marks do not align, remove timing belt. Align camshaft timing marks and install timing belt. Ensure timing belt deflection (stretch) is within specification.

**7)** To check timing belt deflection, remove slack in timing belt by rotating both intake and exhaust camshaft pulleys inward. Measure timing belt deflection at center of timing belt between intake and exhaust cams. If measurement is not within specification, readjust belt tension. See TIMING BELT DEFLECTION SPECIFICATIONS table.

**8)** To complete installation, reverse removal procedure. Tighten nuts and bolts to specification. See TORQUE SPECIFICATIONS table at end of article.

***TIMING BELT DEFECTION SPECIFICATIONS***

| Application | In. (mm) |
|---|---|
| Used Belt | .20-.28 (.5-.7) |
| New Belt | .16-.24 (.4-.6) |

## CAMSHAFT

**Removal – 1)** Remove timing belt and camshaft pulleys. See TIMING BELT under REMOVAL & INSTALLATION. Remove air intake chamber. Remove all other hoses, vacuum lines and components as necessary to access cylinder head covers.

**2)** Remove No. 1 and No. 2 cylinder head covers. Remove No. 2 engine bracket. Remove heater pipe union, gaskets and pipe. Remove EGR cooler. Loosen bearing cap bolts in 3 steps in reverse order of tightening sequence. *See Fig. 9*.

**3)** Remove bearing caps, oil seal and camshaft. Keep bearing caps in order for reassembly reference. DO NOT disturb shim placement on cam followers.

***NOTE: Camshaft rides directly on cylinder head bearing surfaces and caps. There are no replaceable camshaft bearings in head.***

**Inspection – 1)** Clean camshaft. Measure runout. Mount dial indicator so tip is touching center journal. If runout exceeds limit, replace camshaft. Measure camshaft lobe height. If lobe height is less than minimum limit, replace camshaft. See CAMSHAFT table under ENGINE SPECIFICATIONS at end of article.

**2)** Using a micrometer, measure camshaft journal diameter. If journal diameter is less than specified, replace camshaft. Clean camshaft bearing caps. Using Plastigage method, install camshaft in cylinder head to measure camshaft oil clearance.

**3)** Install bearing caps with arrow stamped in cap facing front of head in numerical sequence. Tighten bearing cap bolts in 3 stages in tightening sequence. *See Fig. 9* and TORQUE SPECIFICATIONS table at end of article. Remove bearing caps. Measure Plastigage at widest point. If maximum oil clearance is exceeded, replace cylinder head and/or camshaft.

**4)** Clean camshaft and install bearing caps. Using a dial indicator, measure camshaft end play. If end play is not within specification, replace cylinder head and/or camshaft. See CAMSHAFT table under ENGINE SPECIFICATIONS at end of article.

**Installation – 1)** Ensure No. 1 cylinder is at TDC on compression stroke. Coat lip of NEW oil seal with engine oil and install seal on camshaft. Coat all bearing journals with engine oil.

**2)** Ensure camshafts are positioned correctly and install camshafts on cylinder head. *See Fig. 7.* Exhaust camshaft has distributor drive gear (non-turbo) or cam position sensor (turbo) drive gear.

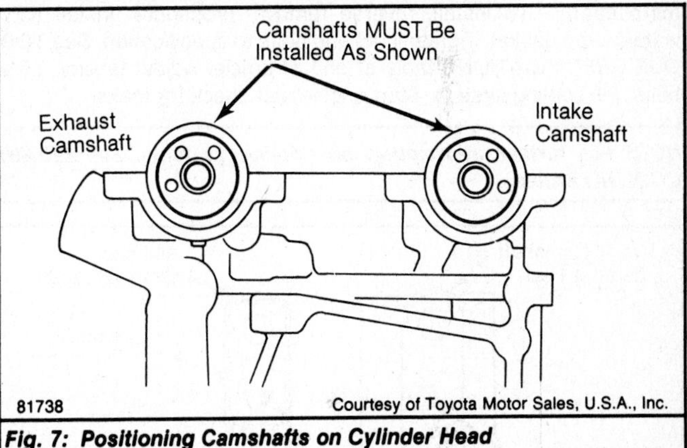


***Fig. 7: Positioning Camshafts on Cylinder Head***

**3)** Apply a bead of sealant .08-.12" (2.0-3.0 mm) thick on each side of camshaft at No. 1 bearing cap locations. After applying sealant, install No. 1 bearing caps. No. 1 bearing caps are identified by "I" for intake side and "E" for exhaust side. *See Fig. 8*.

**4)** Install remaining bearing caps in correct order with arrows pointing toward front of cylinder head. Loosely tighten all bearing caps in tightening sequence. *See Fig. 9* (Step 1). Using Camshaft Oil Seal Installer (09223-50010), drive in NEW camshaft oil seals.

**5)** Tighten No. 3 and No. 7 bearing caps to specification in 3 stages in sequence. *See Fig. 9* (Step 2). Tighten all remaining bearing caps to specification in 3 stages in sequence. *See Fig. 9* (Step 3). Recheck camshaft end play.

**6)** To complete installation, reverse removal procedure. Install EGR cooler. Install heater pipe union, gaskets and pipe. Install engine bracket. Tighten nuts and bolts to specification. See TORQUE SPECIFICATIONS table at end of article.

## CAMSHAFT OIL SEALS

**Removal & Installation –** Camshafts must be removed to replace camshaft oil seals. For removal and installation of oil seals, see CAMSHAFT under REMOVAL & INSTALLATION.

## REAR MAIN BEARING OIL SEAL

**Removal & Installation – 1)** If rear oil seal retainer is removed from block, use a hammer and screwdriver to remove oil seal. Apply multipurpose grease to NEW seal. Using Seal Installer (09223-41020), install oil seal.

**2)** If rear oil seal retainer is still on cylinder block, disconnect negative battery cable. Remove transmission. Place reference mark on clutch pressure plate (M/T) and flywheel for reassembly reference. Remove pressure plate, clutch disc and flywheel/drive plate.

**3)** Cut off lip of oil seal with knife at 8 o'clock position. Cover crankshaft with shop towel and pry seal out of retainer. Ensure crankshaft is free of burrs. Apply multipurpose grease to NEW seal. Using Seal Installer (09223-41020), drive in oil seal.

**4)** To complete installation, reverse removal procedure. Tighten nuts and bolts to specification. See TORQUE SPECIFICATIONS table at end of article.

## WATER PUMP

**Removal – 1)** Drain coolant from block and radiator. Remove A/C belt. Loosen water pump pulley nuts. Remove alternator drive belt. Remove radiator fan and water pump pulley.

**2)** Remove air tube from power steering pump. Remove water pump retaining bolts, water pump and gasket. Clean all gasket material from water pump and block.

**Inspection –** Check water pump body and timing belt case for cracks and damaged gasket surfaces. Repair and/or replace as necessary. Replace water pump if bearing operation is rough or noisy. Replace fan fluid coupling if damaged or if silicone leakage is present.

**Installation –** To install, reverse removal procedure. Install NEW water pump gasket. Tighten nuts and bolts to specification. See TORQUE SPECIFICATIONS table at end of article. Adjust tension of all belts. Fill cooling system. Start engine and check for leaks.

***NOTE: For further information on cooling systems, see ENGINE COOLING article.***

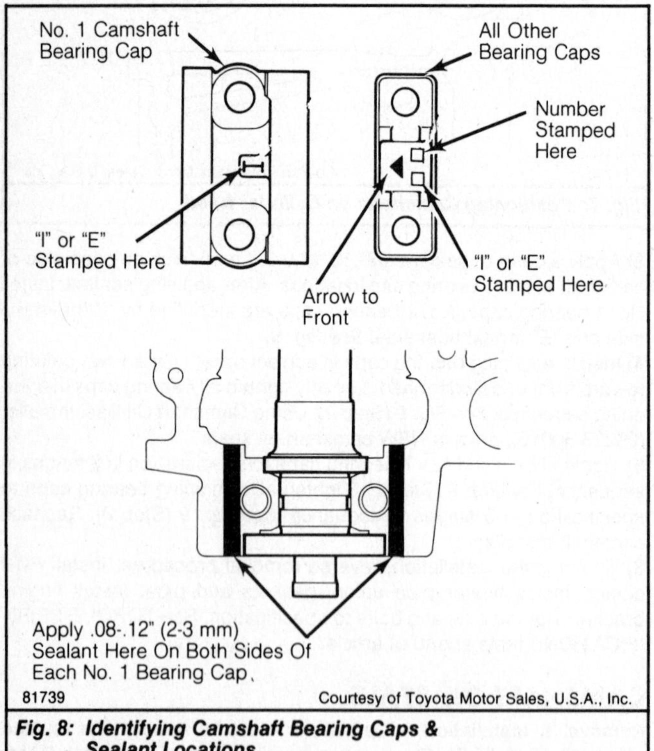


***Fig. 8: Identifying Camshaft Bearing Caps & Sealant Locations***

## OIL PAN

**Removal – 1)** Raise and support vehicle. Remove lower engine cover. Drain engine oil. Remove front wheels. On models with automatic transmission, disconnect and plug transmission oil cooler lines. On all models, remove front crossmember. Remove front exhaust pipe bracket and stiffener plates.

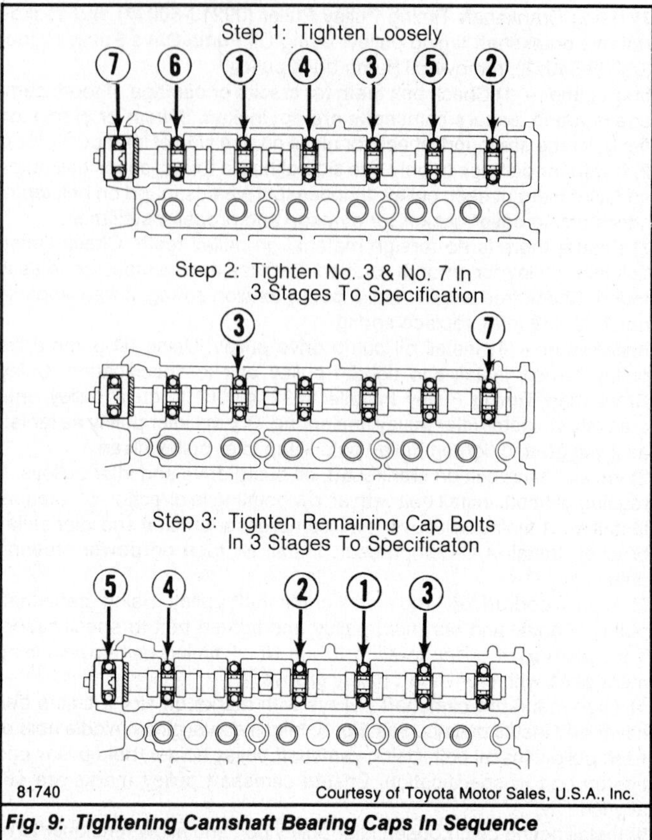


***Fig. 9: Tightening Camshaft Bearing Caps In Sequence***

**2)** Remove brake hose brackets and clips. Loosen intermediate steering shaft pinch bolt. Disconnect intermediate steering shaft. Disconnect stabilizer bar links from lower control arms.

**3)** Lower vehicle. Attach engine lifting chain to engine hangers. Support engine and remove engine mounting nuts and washers. Remove electronic suspension actuators from strut assemblies.

**4)** Remove top strut mounting bolts. Support front suspension member with floor jack. Remove nuts/bolts securing assembly to body. Lower suspension member and support on jack stands. Remove oil pan nuts/bolts and remove oil pan.

**Installation – 1)** To install, reverse removal procedure. Apply one continuous bead of gasket Sealant (08826-00080) to mating surface of oil pan. Sealant should be applied to inner surface around bolt hole area.

**2)** Tighten oil pan nuts/bolts to specification. See TORQUE SPECIFICATIONS table at end of article. Fill engine with oil. Start engine and check for leaks. Check front wheel alignment. See SPECIFICATIONS & PROCEDURES article in WHEEL ALIGNMENT.

# OVERHAUL

## CYLINDER HEAD

**Cylinder Head – 1)** Remove cylinder head and disassemble. See CYLINDER HEAD under REMOVAL & INSTALLATION. Remove camshaft bearing caps in reverse order of tightening sequence. *See Fig. 9.* Keep disassembled parts in order and mark parts for reassembly reference.

**2)** Thoroughly clean cylinder head gasket mating surfaces. Check cylinder head for warpage. If not within specification, resurface or replace as necessary. See CYLINDER HEAD table under ENGINE SPECIFICATIONS at end of article.

**Valve Springs – 1)** Remove camshafts as previously outlined. Remove valve lifters and shims. Keep lifters and shims in order for

reassembly reference. Using Valve Spring Compressor (09202-70010), remove valve springs. Keep all components in order for reassembly reference. Remove valve stem oil seals.
**2)** Using steel square, measure squareness of valve springs. Replace spring if squareness limit is exceeded. Measure free length of valve springs. If free length is not within specification replace valve spring.
**3)** Using spring tester, check tension of each valve spring at specified installed height. If valve spring tension is not within specification replace spring. See VALVE & VALVE SPRINGS table under ENGINE SPECIFICATIONS at end of article.
**Valve Stem Oil Seals -** Use Valve Stem Oil Seal Installer (09201-41020) to install NEW oil seal on valve guide.
**Valve Guides - 1)** To measure valve stem-to-valve guide clearance, subtract the valve stem diameter measurement from valve guide inside diameter measurement.
**2)** Replace valve guide and valve if oil clearance is not within specification. See CYLINDER HEAD table under ENGINE SPECIFICATIONS at end of article. To replace valve guide, go to step **3)**.

***NOTE: Replacement valve guides are available in .002" (.05 mm) oversize.***

**3)** Insert an old valve wrapped with tape into valve guide. Tap valve with hammer firmly enough to break guide off flush with cylinder head surface. Be careful not damage lifter bore. Remove snap ring.
**4)** Using water or oil bath, gradually heat cylinder head to about 194°F (90°C). Using Valve Guide Remover/Installer (09201-70010), drive guide out from camshaft side. Using telescopic hole gauge, measure inside diameter of valve guide bore.
**5)** If valve guide bore is .4331-.4341" (11.001-11.026 mm), install standard valve guide. If valve guide bore is greater than .4341" (11.026 mm), rebore guide bore to .4350-.4361" (11.049-11.077 mm).
**6)** To install NEW valve guide, reheat cylinder head as explained in step **4)**. Using valve guide remover/installer, drive in valve guide from camshaft side until snap ring contacts cylinder head. Using a sharp .24" (6.1 mm) reamer, ream valve guide until standard valve stem-to-guide clearance is obtained.

***NOTE: Always reface valve seat after replacing valve guide.***

**Valve Seat - 1)** Before refacing valve seats, check valve and valve guide for wear. If not within specification, replace components as necessary. See CYLINDER HEAD table under ENGINE SPECIFICATIONS at end of article.
**2)** Inspect valve seat for any evidence of pitting at valve contact surface. Reface seat if worn excessively. Valve seat replacement is not available from manufacturer.
**Valves - 1)** Mark valves for installation reference. Disassemble cylinder head. Measure valve stem diameter. Replace valves if not within specification. See VALVES & VALVE SPRINGS table under ENGINE SPECIFICATIONS at end of article.
**2)** Measure valve margin. Replace valves if valve margin is not within specification. Measure valve margin after grinding valves.
**Valve Seat Correction Angles - 1)** If valve guides need to be replaced, perform replacement before refacing valve seats. After refacing, if valve seating is too high on face of valve, use a 30-degree and 45-degree stone/cutter to correct seat.
**2)** If valve seating is too low, use a 60-degree and 30-degree stone/cutter to correct seat. Ensure valve seat margin is within specification. See CYLINDER HEAD table under ENGINE SPECIFICATIONS at end of article.

## CYLINDER BLOCK ASSEMBLY

**Piston & Rod Assembly - 1)** Before removing bearing caps, mark caps and rods with punch for reassembly reference. Measure connecting rod side play clearance with dial indicator. If clearance exceeds .012" (.3 mm), replace connecting rod and/or crankshaft.
**2)** Using a connecting rod aligner, check rod for bends or twists. If maximum bend limit or maximum twist limit exceeds specification, replace connecting rod. See CONNECTING RODS table under ENGINE SPECIFICATIONS at end of article.
**3)** Piston must be installed on connecting rod so that front mark on connecting rod aligns with front mark on top of piston. *See Fig. 10.*

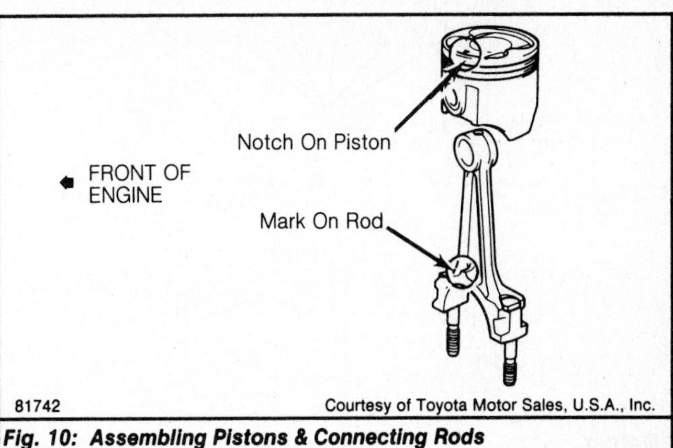

***Fig. 10: Assembling Pistons & Connecting Rods***

**Piston Pin - 1)** Check fit between piston and pin by moving piston back and forth on piston pin. If any movement is felt, replace piston and pin.
**2)** To separate piston from connecting rod, remove snap rings from piston with needle-nose pliers. Heat piston and rod assembly to 140°F (60°C). Drive pin out of piston with plastic-faced hammer and driver.

***NOTE: Piston and pin are a matched set. Keep piston, pin, rings and connecting rod together for each cylinder.***

**3)** Measure clearance between connecting rod bushing and piston pin. Standard clearance is .0002-.0004" (.005-.010 mm). If maximum clearance of .0008" (.020 mm) is exceeded, replace connecting rod bushing. To replace bushing, use press and Connecting Rod Bushing Remover/Installer (09222-30010) to press out bushing.
**4)** Use press and bushing remover/installer to install bushing. Ensure oil holes in bushing and connecting rod are aligned. Hone new bushing to ensure standard clearance between piston pin and bushing.
**5)** Coat pin with oil. Install NEW snap ring on one side of piston. Install pin into piston and rod. Ensure notch on piston and mark on connecting rod are aligned. *See Fig. 10*. Install other NEW snap ring.
**Fitting Pistons - 1)** Five different standard pistons sizes and cylinder bore diameters are used. Pistons are marked "0", "1", "2", "3" or "4" on top of piston near front mark. See PISTON, PINS & RINGS table under ENGINE SPECIFICATIONS at end of article.
**2)** Cylinder bore diameters are marked "0", "1", "2", "3", "4". Identification mark is located on left side of block near each cylinder bore and on oil pan gasket surface between cylinders No. 4 and 5. *See Fig. 11* and CYLINDER BLOCK table under ENGINE SPECIFICATIONS at end of article.
**3)** To determine if piston-to-cylinder clearance is within specification, measure piston skirt diameter at right angles to piston pin center line, .87" (22.1 mm) from top of piston. Replace piston or rebore cylinder block if clearance is not within specification. See PISTONS, PINS & RINGS table under ENGINE SPECIFICATIONS at end of article
**4)** To determine amount of cylinder rebore, add piston clearance of .0031-.0039" (.08-.10 mm) or .0028-.0035" (.07-.09 mm) on turbo model, to measured piston diameter. From this figure, subtract maximum honing amount of .0008" (.020 mm).
**5)** After honing cylinder to final fit, measure piston-to-cylinder clearance. Clearance should be .0031-.0039" (.08-.10 mm) or .0028-.0035" (.07-.09 mm) on turbo model.
**6)** If reusing pistons, clean ring grooves with groove cleaner or broken ring. Using solvent and soft brush (not wire brush), thoroughly clean piston. Check for scratches, wear or damage.

***NOTE: Pistons are available only in .50 mm oversize.***

# 1991 ENGINES
# 3.0L & 3.0L Turbo 6-Cylinder (Cont.)

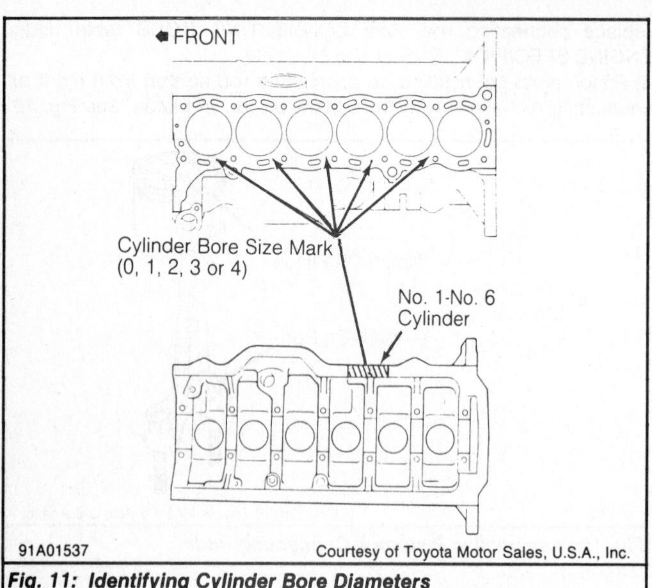


*Fig. 11: Identifying Cylinder Bore Diameters*

**Piston Rings** – Ensure ring end gap and side clearance are within specification. See PISTONS, PINS & RINGS table under ENGINE SPECIFICATIONS at end of article. Ensure identification marks on rings are toward top of piston. Position piston rings at designated areas. *See Fig. 12.*

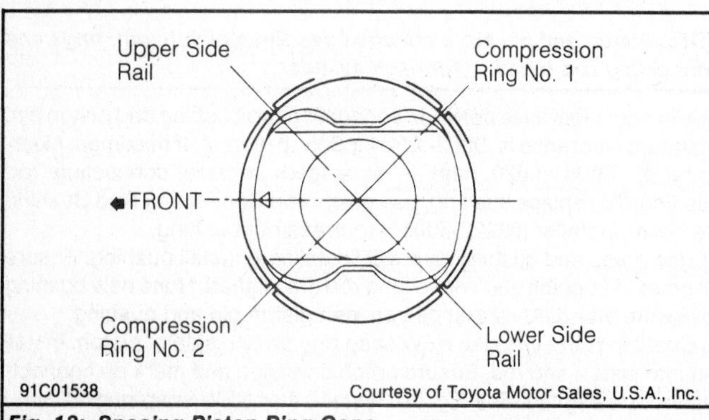


*Fig. 12: Spacing Piston Ring Gaps*

**Rod Bearings** – **1)** Note connecting rod and cap direction before disassembly. Ensure bearing oil clearance and side play are within specification. If clearance exceeds maximum limit, replace bearings and/or grind crankshaft journals. See CRANKSHAFT, MAIN & CONNECTING ROD BEARINGS table under ENGINE SPECIFICATIONS at end of article.

***NOTE: Five different standard connecting rod bearings are available. Each bearing is identified by a "1", "2", "3", "4" or "5" mark. Always replace bearings with those having the same number.***

**2)** Crankshaft rod bearing journal diameter is determined by a size mark on crankshaft counterweight. *See Fig. 13.* Ensure rod bearing journal diameter is within specification. See CRANKSHAFT, MAIN & CONNECTING ROD BEARINGS table under ENGINE SPECIFICATIONS at end of article.

**3)** Connecting rod bearing size is determined by size mark on side of bearing. If rod bearing size mark is unreadable, add number on crankshaft counterweight and number on connecting rod cap to determine size mark number of rod bearing to be used. *See Fig. 13.*

**4)** See ROD BEARING SPECIFICATIONS table. Rod bearings are available in .010" (.25 mm) undersize. Tighten connecting rod bearing cap nuts to specification. See TORQUE SPECIFICATIONS table at end of article.

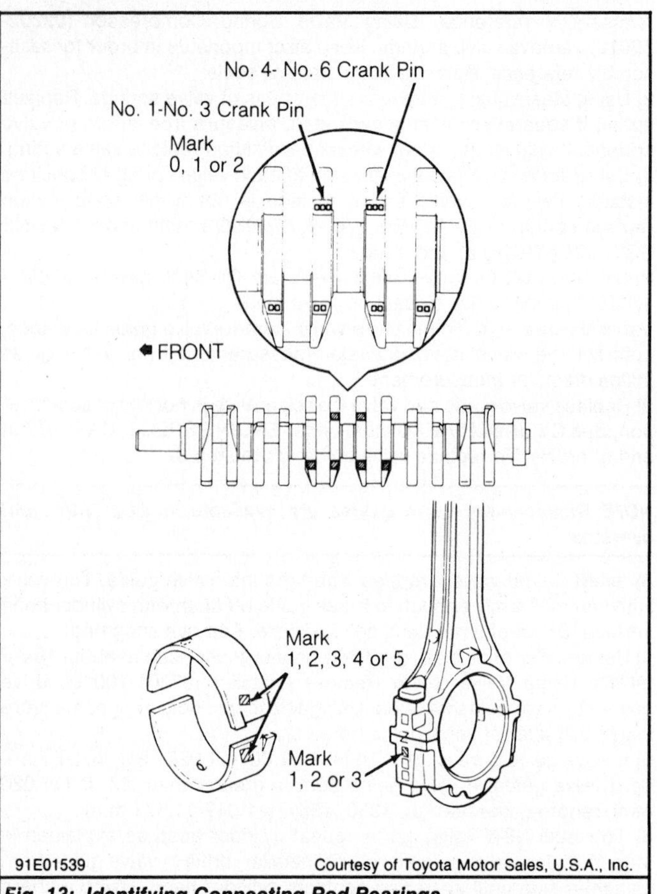


*Fig. 13: Identifying Connecting Rod Bearings*

***NOTE: Install rod bearings with oil hole in connecting rod.***

***ROD BEARING SPECIFICATIONS***

| Bearing Size Mark | Bearing Thickness In. (mm) |
|---|---|
| 1 | .0587-.0589 (1.490-1.495) |
| 2 | .0589-.0591 (1.496-1.500) |
| 3 | .0591-.0593 (1.501-1.505) |
| 4 | .0593-.0594 (1.506-1.510) |
| 5 | .0595-.0596 (1.511-1.515) |
| O/S | .0639-.0643 (1.622-1.632) |

**Crankshaft & Main Bearings** – **1)** Ensure main bearing caps are numbered for location. Loosen main bearing cap bolts in 3 steps and in reverse order of tightening sequence. *See Fig. 15.*

**2)** Cylinder block main bearing journal bore size is indicated by a number, located on cylinder block oil pan rail *See Fig. 14.* Ensure cylinder block main bearing journal bore is within specification. See CYLINDER BLOCK table under ENGINE SPECIFICATIONS at end of article.

**3)** Crankshaft main bearing journal size is also indicated by a number, located on crankshaft counterweight. *See Fig. 14.* Ensure main bearing journal is within specification. See CRANKSHAFT, MAIN & CONNECTING ROD BEARINGS table under ENGINE SPECIFICATIONS at end of article.

**4)** If main bearing number is unreadable, add number on crankshaft counterweight and number on cylinder block rail to determine proper size main bearing to be used. See corresponding number in CRANKSHAFT MAIN BEARING SELECTION table.

# 1991 ENGINES
# 3.0L & 3.0L Turbo 6-Cylinder (Cont.)

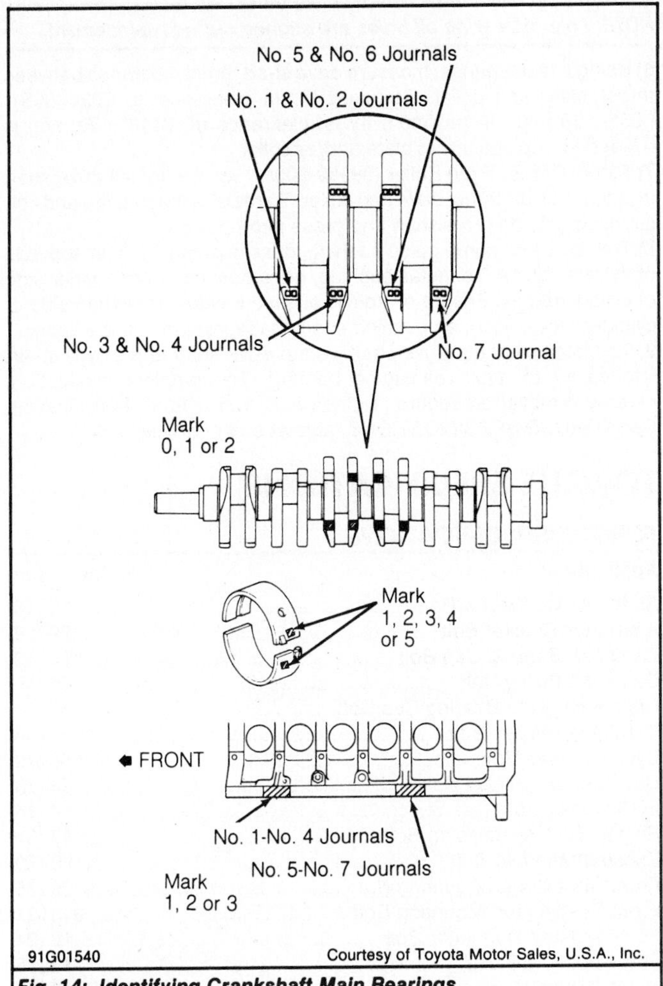


*Fig. 14: Identifying Crankshaft Main Bearings*

***CRANKSHAFT MAIN BEARING SELECTION***

| Bearing Number | Bearing Thickness In. (mm) |
|---|---|
| 1 | .0783-.0784 (1.988-1.991) |
| 2 | .0784-.0785 (1.992-1.994) |
| 3 | .0785-.0786 (1.994-1.996) |
| 4 | .0787-.0788 (1.998-2.000) |
| 5 | .0788-.0789 (2.000-2.003) |
| O/S | .0086-.0840 (2.123-2.133) |

***NOTE: Install main bearings with oil hole in cylinder block.***

5) Install bearing. Main bearings are available in .010" (.25 mm) undersize. Tighten main bearing caps to specification in sequence. *See Fig. 15* and TORQUE SPECIFICATIONS table at end of article. Ensure crankshaft rotates smoothly.

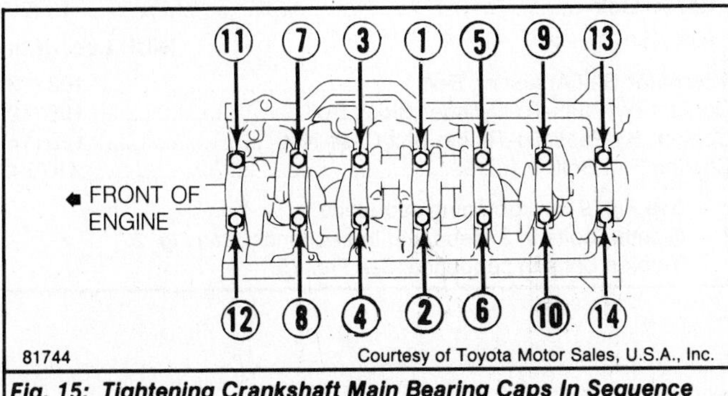


*Fig. 15: Tightening Crankshaft Main Bearing Caps In Sequence*

**Thrust Bearing** – Check crankshaft end play. See CRANKSHAFT, MAIN & CONNECTING ROD BEARINGS table under ENGINE SPECIFICATIONS at end of article. If end play exceeds maximum limit, replace thrust washers as a set and/or replace crankshaft. Thrust washers are installed on No. 4 main bearing journal.

***NOTE: Thrust washers are available in standard thickness of .1152-.1171" (2.926-2.974 mm) and oversize of .1176-.1196" (2.988-3.038 mm).***

**Cylinder Block** – **1)** Using a feeler gauge and straightedge, inspect cylinder block deck surface for warpage. Maximum warpage is .002" (.05 mm). If warpage is greater than maximum, replace cylinder block.
**2)** Measure cylinder bore out-of-round and taper. See CYLINDER BLOCK table under ENGINE SPECIFICATIONS at end of article. If either out-of-round or taper exceeds service limit, rebore all cylinders for oversize pistons.
**3)** There are 5 different standard cylinder diameters, marked "0", "1", "2", "3", "4" located on left side of block near each cylinder bore and on oil pan gasket surface between cylinders No. 4 and 5. *See Fig. 11* and CYLINDER BLOCK table under ENGINE SPECIFICATIONS at end of article.
**4)** If cylinder bore is okay, hone cylinder to obtain a 60-degree cross-hatch pattern. After honing, wash cylinder bore with hot soapy water. Air dry cylinder bore and apply engine oil to prevent rusting.

## ENGINE OILING

### ENGINE LUBRICATING SYSTEM

System is force-fed with full-flow filtering unit. Pressure is delivered by a gear-driven oil pump. Oil travels from filter through cylinder block passages to lubricate internal components. *See Fig. 16.*

**Crankcase Capacity** – Total oil capacity (dry) on non-turbo engines is 5.2 qts. (4.9L). Drain and refill capacity is 4.7 qts. (4.4L) with filter. On turbo engines, total oil capacity (dry) is 5.7 qts. (5.4L). Drain and refill capacity is 5.0 qts. (4.7L) with filter.
**Oil Pressure** – Normal oil pressure at idle should be a minimum of 4.3 psi (.3 kg/cm²). At 3000 RPM, oil pressure should be 36-71 psi (2.5-5.0 kg/cm²).
**Oil Pressure Relief Valve** – The oil pressure relief valve is a nonadjustable type located in the oil pump and opens between 63-71 psi (4.4-5.0 kg/cm²).

### OIL PUMP

**Removal & Disassembly** – **1)** Remove oil pan. See OIL PAN under REMOVAL & INSTALLATION. Unbolt and remove oil pump assembly. Remove oil pick-up and discharge tubes.
**2)** Unscrew relief valve plug. Carefully remove plug, spring and relief valve. Remove 5 bolts from pump cover. Remove cover and driven gear. Remove snap ring, shaft gear, Woodruff key and drive shaft.
**Inspection** – Check relief valve for scoring or wear. If damaged, replace valve or pump assembly. Measure clearances between driven gear and pump body, drive gear and driven gear and check gear-to-body clearance.
**Reassembly & Installation** – **1)** Reassemble pump in reverse order of disassembly. Replace all "O" rings. After reassembly, check pump operation. Immerse inlet tube in clean engine oil and turn drive shaft counterclockwise.
**2)** Oil should flow from discharge hole. Cover hole with thumb and turn drive shaft counterclockwise. Shaft should be difficult to turn. Install oil pump. Apply one continuous bead of gasket sealant (08826-00080) to mating surface of oil pan.
**3)** Sealant should be applied to inner surface around bolt hole area. Tighten oil pan to specification. To complete installation, reverse removal procedure. Fill engine with oil. Start engine and check for leaks. Check front wheel alignment. See SPECIFICATIONS & PROCEDURES article in WHEEL ALIGNMENT.

# 1991 ENGINES
# 3.0L & 3.0L Turbo 6-Cylinder (Cont.)

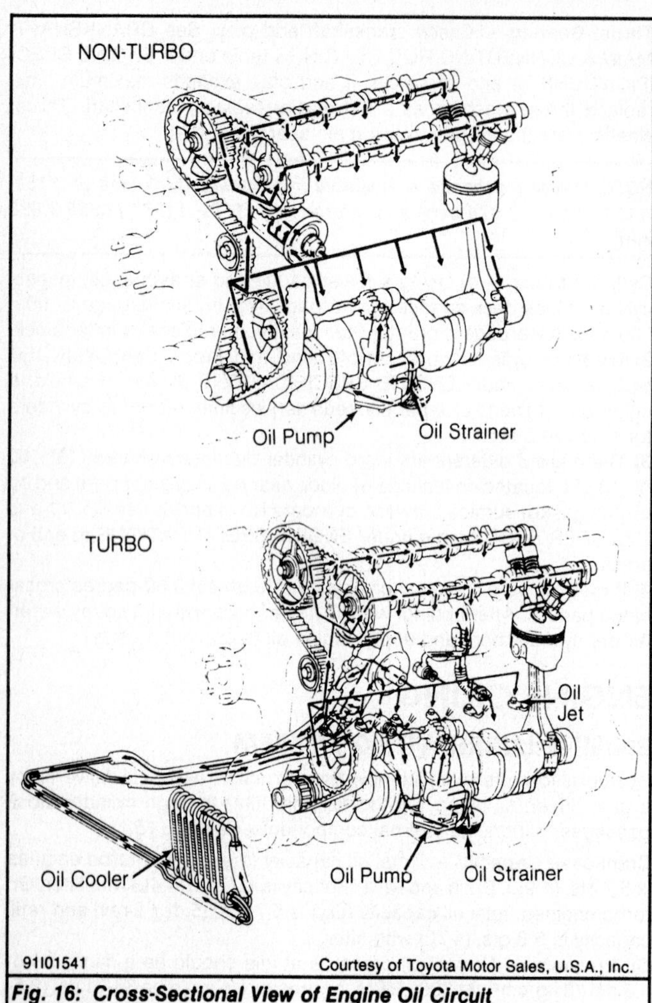


*Fig. 16: Cross-Sectional View of Engine Oil Circuit*

### *OIL PUMP SPECIFICATIONS*

| Application | In. (mm) |
|---|---|
| Driven Gear-To-Body | |
| Standard Clearance | .0041-.0069 (.104-.175) |
| Maximum Clearance | .008 (.20) |
| Drive Gear-To-Driven Gear | |
| Standard Backlash | .020-.024 (.51-.61) |
| Maximum Backlash | .035 (.89) |
| Gear-To-Body | |
| Standard Clearance | .0012-.0035 (.030-.089) |
| Maximum Clearance | .0059 (.150) |

**Oil Pump Drive Shaft, Bearings & Bushings – 1)** Remove oil pump drive pulley. See TIMING BELT under REMOVAL & INSTALLATION. Remove oil pan. See OIL PAN under REMOVAL & INSTALLATION. Remove retaining bolt and oil pump drive shaft. Remove oil pump.

**2)** Using a micrometer, measure and record oil pump drive shaft journal diameter. Standard journal diameter is 1.6126-1.6132" (40.960-40.975 mm) for front journal and 1.2976-1.2982" (32.959-32.974 mm) for rear journal.

**3)** Using a telescopic bore gauge, measure and record front and rear drive shaft bearing bore diameters. To obtain clearance, subtract journal diameter readings from bore diameter readings.

**4)** Standard clearance is .0010-.0026" (.025-.066 mm). If maximum clearance of .0031" (.078 mm) is exceeded, replace bearings and/or drive shaft.

**5)** Using Bearing Remover/Replacer Set (09215-00100), replace bearings. Replace No. 1 bearing using No. 2 bearing as a guide. Replace No. 2 bearing using No. 1 bearing as a guide.

***NOTE: Ensure bearing oil holes are aligned during replacement.***

**6)** Using a feeler gauge, measure drive shaft thrust clearance between thrust plate and collar. Standard thrust clearance is .0024-.0051" (.061-.130 mm). If maximum thrust clearance of .0118" (.30 mm) is exceeded, replace thrust plate and/or collar.

**7)** Mount Thrust Plate Puller (09950-20017) in vise. Install drive shaft in puller. Pull off thrust plate and collar. To replace thrust plate and collar, assemble on drive shaft and press into position.

**8)** To replace oil pump guide bushing, drive bushing out from top side of cylinder block. To install bushing, drive bushing in from inner side of cylinder block. Ensure oil hole is aligned toward crankshaft side of cylinder block. Mark on bushing should face front of cylinder block.

**9)** To install oil pump drive shaft, rotate drive shaft and slowly insert into cavity to avoid damaging bearing. To complete installation, reverse removal procedure. Tighten nuts and bolts to specification. See TORQUE SPECIFICATIONS table at end of article.

## TORQUE SPECIFICATIONS

### *TORQUE SPECIFICATIONS*

| Application | Ft. Lbs. (N.m) |
|---|---|
| Air Intake Connector Bolt | 13 (18) |
| Alternator Bracket Bolt | 29 (39) |
| Camshaft Bearing Cap Bolt | [1] 14 (19) |
| Camshaft Pulley Bolt | 36 (49) |
| Connecting Rod Bearing Cap Bolt | 47 (64) |
| Crankshaft Pulley Bolt | 195 (264) |
| Cylinder Head Bolt | [2] 58 (79) |
| Drive Plate/Flywheel Bolt | 54 (73) |
| EGR Cooler Bolt | 10 (14) |
| Engine-To-Transmission Bolt | 47 (64) |
| Exhaust Manifold Bolt | 29 (39) |
| Front Strut Upper Mounting Nut | 26 (35) |
| Front Suspension Mounting Bolt | 94 (127) |
| Fuel Pressure Regulator Bolt | 18 (24) |
| Fuel Supply Rail Bolt | 13 (18) |
| Heater Union Bolt | 43 (58) |
| Intake Manifold Bolt | 13 (18) |
| Intermediate Steering Shaft Bolt | 26 (35) |
| Main Bearing Cap Bolt | [3] 75 (102) |
| No. 2 Engine Bracket Bolt | 29 (39) |
| Oil Pump Drive Pulley Bolt | 16 (22) |
| Oil Pump Mounting Bolt | 16 (22) |
| Oil Pump Outlet Tube Union | 25 (34) |
| Oil Pump Relief Valve Plug | 27 (37) |
| Oil Pump Union Nut | 25 (34) |
| Propeller Shaft Center Support Bolt | 36 (49) |
| Propeller Shaft-To-Differential Bolt | 54 (73) |
| Spark Plug | 13 (18) |
| Stabilizer Bar-To-Lower Arm Nut | 47 (64) |
| Timing Belt Idler Pulley Bolt | 36 (49) |
| Water Pump Bolt | |
| 10-mm Bolt | 13 (18) |
| 12-mm Bolt | 15 (20) |
| | **INCH Lbs. (N.m)** |
| Alternator Belt Adjusting Bolt | 108 (12) |
| Coolant By-Pass-To-Cylinder Block Bolt | 108 (12) |
| Coolant By-Pass-To-Timing Belt Case Nut | 120 (14) |
| Cooling Fan Bolt | 48 (5.4) |

[1] – *See Fig. 9* for tightening sequence.
[2] – Tighten bolts in 3 steps and in sequence. *See Fig. 2.*
[3] – Tighten bolts in sequence. *See Fig. 15.*

# 1991 ENGINES
# 3.0L & 3.0L Turbo 6-Cylinder (Cont.)

### TORQUE SPECIFICATIONS (Cont.)

| Application | INCH Lbs. (N.m) |
|---|---|
| Fuel Return Line Support Bolt | 108 (12) |
| Oil Pan Bolt & Nut | 108 (12) |
| Oil Pump Cover Bolt | 65 (7) |
| Oil Pump Drive Shaft Retaining Nut | 108 (12) |
| Oil Pump Strainer Bolt | 69 (8) |
| Rear Main Oil Seal Retainer Bolt | 108 (12) |
| Valve Cover Bolt | 22 (2.5) |

[1] – *See Fig. 9* for tightening sequence.
[2] – Tighten bolts in 3 steps and in sequence. *See Fig. 2.*
[3] – Tighten bolts in sequence. *See Fig. 15.*

## ENGINE SPECIFICATIONS

### GENERAL SPECIFICATIONS

| Application | Specification |
|---|---|
| Displacement | 180.2 Cu. In. (3.0L) |
| Bore | 3.27" (83 mm) |
| Stroke | 3.58" (91 mm) |
| Compression Ratio | |
| Non-Turbo | 9.2:1 |
| Turbo | 8.4:1 |
| Fuel System | PFI |
| Horsepower @ RPM | |
| Non-Turbo | 200 @ 6000 |
| Turbo | 232 @ 6000 |
| Torque Ft. Lbs. @ RPM | |
| Non-Turbo | 188 @ 3600 |
| Turbo | 254 @ 3200 |

### CRANKSHAFT, MAIN & CONNECTING ROD BEARINGS

| Application | In. (mm) |
|---|---|
| Crankshaft | |
| End Play | .002-.010 (.05-.25) |
| Runout | .0024 (.060) |
| Main Bearings [1] | |
| Journal Diameter | |
| Mark 0 | 2.3625-2.3627 (60.007-60.012) |
| Mark 1 | 2.3622-2.3624 (60.001-60.006) |
| Mark 2 | 2.3620-2.3622 (59.994-60.000) |
| Journal Out-Of-Round | .0008 (.020) |
| Journal Taper | .0008 (.020) |
| Oil Clearance | |
| Standard | .0012-.0019 (.030-.048) |
| Service Limit | .0028 (.071) |
| Connecting Rod Bearings | |
| Journal Diameter | |
| Mark 0 | 2.0470-2.0472 (51.993-52.000) |
| Mark 1 | 2.0466-2.0489 (51.985-51.992) |
| Mark 2 | 2.0463-2.0466 (51.976-51.984) |
| Journal Out-Of-Round | .0008 (.020) |
| Journal Taper | .0008 (.020) |
| Oil Clearance | |
| Standard | .0008-.0021 (.020-.053) |
| Service Limit | .0031 (.080) |

[1] – Use number stamped on crankshaft counterweight to determine journal diameter. *See Fig. 14.*

### PISTONS, PINS & RINGS

| Application | In. (mm) |
|---|---|
| Pistons | |
| Clearance | |
| Non-Turbo | |
| Standard | .0031-.0039 (.079-.099) |
| Service Limit | .0051 (.130) |
| Turbo | |
| Standard | .0028-.0035 (.071-.089) |
| Service Limit | .0051 (.130) |
| Diameter [1] | |
| Non-Turbo | |
| Mark No. 0 | 3.2638-3.2642 (82.900-82.910) |
| Mark No. 1 | 3.2642-3.2646 (82.911-82.920) |
| Mark No. 2 | 3.2646-3.2650 (82.921-82.930) |
| Mark No. 3 | 3.2650-3.2653 (82.931-82.940) |
| Mark No. 4 | 3.2654-3.2657 (82.941-82.950) |
| Turbo | |
| Mark No. 0 | 3.2642-3.2646 (82.910-82.920) |
| Mark No. 1 | 3.2646-3.2650 (82.921-82.930) |
| Mark No. 2 | 3.2650-3.2653 (82.931-82.940) |
| Mark No. 3 | 3.2654-3.2657 (82.941-82.950) |
| Mark No. 4 | 3.2658-3.2661 (82.951-82.960) |
| Pins | |
| Diameter | .8660-.8665 (21.996-22.009) |
| Piston Fit | [2] |
| Rod Fit | [3] |
| Rings | |
| No. 1 | |
| End Gap | |
| Non-Turbo | |
| Standard | .009-.015 (.23-.38) |
| Service Limit | .027 (.68) |
| Turbo | |
| Standard | .011-.017 (.29-.44) |
| Service Limit | .029 (.74) |
| Side Clearance | .0012-.0028 (.030-.071) |
| No. 2 | |
| End Gap | |
| Standard | .010-.021 (.25-.53) |
| Service Limit | .045 (1.13) |
| Side Clearance | .0008-.0024 (.020-.061) |
| No. 3 (Oil) | |
| End Gap | |
| Non-Turbo | |
| Standard | .004-.016 (.10-.40) |
| Service Limit | .039 (1.00) |
| Turbo | |
| Standard | .004-.017 (.10-.44) |
| Service Limit | .041 (1.04) |

[1] – Piston diameter is determined by piston identification mark on top of piston. *See Fig. 10.*
[2] – Indicates interference fit. Piston pin is installed using thumb pressure at 140°F (60°C). If pin can be replaced at lower temperature, replace piston.
[3] – Piston pin is installed using thumb pressure at room temperature.

### VALVE LIFTERS

| Application | In. (mm) |
|---|---|
| Bore Diameter | 1.1024-1.1032 (28.000-28.021) |
| Lifter Diameter | 1.1014-1.1018 (27.975-27.985) |
| Oil Clearance | |
| Standard | .0006-.0018 (.015-.046) |
| Service Limit | .0039 (.10) |

# 1991 ENGINES
# 3.0L & 3.0L Turbo 6-Cylinder (Cont.)

## CYLINDER BLOCK

| Application | In. (mm) |
|---|---|
| Cylinder Bore | |
| Standard Diameter [1] | |
| Mark 0 | 3.2673-3.2677 (82.990-83.000) |
| Mark 1 | 3.2677-3.2681 (83.001-83.010) |
| Mark 2 | 3.2681-3.2685 (83.011-83.020) |
| Mark 3 | 3.2685-3.2689 (83.021-83.030) |
| Mark 4 | 3.2689-3.2693 (83.031-83.040) |
| Main Journal Inner Diameter [2] | |
| Mark 1 | 2.5206-2.5209 (64.024-64.030) |
| Mark 2 | 2.5209-2.5211 (64.031-64.036) |
| Mark 3 | 2.5211-2.5213 (64.037-64.042) |
| Maximum Taper | .0008 (.020) |
| Maximum Out-Of-Round | .0008 (.020) |
| Maximum Deck Warpage | .002 (.05) |

[1] – Cylinder bore diameter is determined by mark stamped on top of engine block and on oil pan rail. *See Fig. 11.*

[2] – Cylinder block main bearing journal bore size is indicated by a number, located on cylinder block oil pan rail *See Fig. 14.*

## VALVES & VALVE SPRINGS

| Application | Specification |
|---|---|
| Intake & Exhaust Valves | |
| Face Angle | 44.5° |
| Head Diameter | N/A |
| Minimum Margin | .020" (.51 mm) |
| Minimum Refinish Length | 3.848" (97.75 mm) |
| Stem Diameter | |
| Intake Valve | .2350-.2356" (5.970-5.985 mm) |
| Exhaust Valve | .2348-.2354" (5.965-5.980 mm) |
| Valve Springs | |
| Free Length | 1.6394" (41.64 mm) |
| Out-Of-Square | .059" (1.50 mm) |
| | **Lbs. @ In. (kg @ mm)** |
| Pressure | |
| Intake & Exhaust | 35 @ 1.38 (16 @ 35) |

## CYLINDER HEAD

| Application | Specification |
|---|---|
| Maximum Warpage | .004" (.10 mm) |
| Valve Seats | |
| Seat Angle | 45° |
| Seat Width | .039-.055" (1.0-1.4 mm) |
| Valve Guides | |
| Valve Guide Cylinder Head Bore I.D. | |
| Standard | .4331-.4341" (11.000-11.027 mm) |
| Oversize | .4350-.4361" (11.050-11.077 mm) |
| Valve Guide I.D. | .2366-.2374" (6.010-6.030 mm) |
| Valve Guide O.D. | |
| Standard | .4344-.4348" (11.033-11.044 mm) |
| Over Size | .4363-.4368" (11.083-11.094 mm) |
| Valve Stem-To-Guide Oil Clearance | |
| Intake Valve | |
| Standard | .0010-.0024" (.025-.060 mm) |
| Service Limit | .0031" (.079 mm) |
| Exhaust Valve | |
| Standard | .0012-.0026" (.030-.065 mm) |
| Service Limit | .0039" (.099 mm) |

## CAMSHAFT

| Application | In. (mm) |
|---|---|
| End Play | |
| Standard | .003-.008 (.08-.19) |
| Service Limit [1] | .012 (.30) |
| Journal Diameter | |
| No. 1 Journal | 1.0610-1.0616 (26.949-26.965) |
| All Others | 1.0586-1.0620 (26.888-26.975) |
| Journal Runout | .0012 (.030) |
| Lobe Height | |
| Non-Turbo | |
| Intake | 1.502 (38.16) |
| Exhaust | 1.510 (38.35) |
| Turbo | 1.510 (38.35) |
| Oil Clearance | |
| Standard | |
| No. 1 Journal | .0014-.0028 (.035-.072) |
| All Others | .0010-.0037 (.025-.093) |
| Service Limit | .0051 (.13) |

[1] – If clearance is greater than maximum, replace camshaft and/or cylinder head

## CONNECTING RODS

| Application | In. (mm) |
|---|---|
| Bore Diameter | |
| Pin Bore | .8660-.8665 (21.996-22.009) |
| Crankpin Bore | |
| Mark 0 | 2.1659-2.1663 (55.015-55.025) |
| Mark 1 | 2.1664-2.1667 (55.026-55.035) |
| Mark 2 | 2.1668-2.1671 (55.036-55.045) |
| Maximum Bend [1] | .0020 (.051) |
| Maximum Twist [1] | .0059 (.150) |
| Side Play | |
| Standard | .0063-.0117 (.160-.296) |
| Service Limit | .012 (.30) |

[1] – Per 3.94" (100 mm) length.

# 1991 ENGINES
# 4.0L 6-Cylinder

## Land Cruiser

***NOTE: For repair procedures not covered in this article, see ENGINE OVERHAUL PROCEDURES article in GENERAL INFORMATION.***

## ENGINE IDENTIFICATION

Engine serial number is stamped on right side of cylinder block, near distributor.

***ENGINE IDENTIFICATION CODE***

| Engine | Code |
|---|---|
| 4.0L 6-Cylinder | 3F-E |

## ADJUSTMENTS

### VALVE CLEARANCE ADJUSTMENT

***NOTE: Adjust valve clearance with engine at normal operating temperature.***

**1)** Remove valve cover and gasket. Rotate crankshaft so No. 1 cylinder is at TDC of compression stroke. Ensure timing mark on flywheel aligns with mark on flywheel housing, located above the starter.
**2)** Ensure rocker arms on No. 1 cylinder are loose and No. 6 cylinder are tight. Adjust clearance on intake valves of cylinders No. 1, 2 and 4 to .008" (.20 mm) and exhaust valves of cylinders No. 1, 3 and 5 to .014" (.35 mm). Rotate crankshaft 360 degrees and realign timing mark.
**3)** Adjust remaining valves to specified clearance. Install valve cover and gasket. Tighten nuts to specification. See TORQUE SPECIFICATIONS table at end of article.

## REMOVAL & INSTALLATION

***NOTE: For reassembly reference, label all electrical connectors, vacuum hoses and fuel lines before removal. Also place mating marks on engine hood and other major assemblies before removal.***

### FUEL PRESSURE RELEASE

With ignition off, disconnect negative battery cable. Place suitable container under fuel line. Cover fuel line connection with shop towel. Slowly loosen fuel line connection, allowing fuel pressure to be released. Once pressure is released, fuel system components can be removed.

### ENGINE

***NOTE: Remove engine and transmission as an assembly.***

**Removal - 1)** Release fuel pressure. See FUEL PRESSURE RELEASE under REMOVAL & INSTALLATION.
**2)** Drain engine oil and cooling system. Remove battery, battery tray and hood. Remove air cleaner assembly, air intake duct and airflow meter. Remove coolant recovery tank, fan shroud, cooling fan and radiator.
**3)** Disconnect necessary control cables, coolant hoses, fuel lines, vacuum hoses and electrical connections. Remove glove box. Disconnect Electronic Control Unit (ECU) electrical connectors and necessary wiring. Pull engine wiring out through the firewall.
**4)** Remove A/C compressor (if equipped) and power steering pump with hoses attached and secure aside. Raise and support vehicle. Remove lower transfer case covers. Place reference marks on front and rear drive shaft flanges. Remove flange bolts and drive shafts.
**5)** Disconnect speedometer cable, necessary electrical connections, shift linkages and hoses from transmission and transfer case. Disconnect exhaust pipe at exhaust manifold. Support transmission with floor jack. Remove crossmember located below transmission.
**6)** Support engine with hoist. Remove engine mount nuts. Remove engine and transmission assembly.

**Installation -** To install, reverse removal procedure. Ensure reference marks are aligned on drive shaft flanges. Tighten fasteners to specification. See TORQUE SPECIFICATIONS table at end of article. Adjust all control cables and fluid levels.

### INTAKE & EXHAUST MANIFOLDS

**Removal - 1)** Release fuel pressure. See FUEL PRESSURE RELEASE under REMOVAL & INSTALLATION. Drain cooling system. Disconnect air intake duct from throttle body.
**2)** Remove air cleaner assembly. Disconnect necessary control cables, hoses, electrical connections and vacuum hoses. It may be necessary to remove upper intake manifold.
**3)** If removing upper intake manifold, disconnect EGR pipe and cold start injector pipe. Remove support braces. Remove retaining bolts and upper intake manifold.
**4)** It may be necessary to remove fuel rail and injectors. If removing fuel rail, disconnect fuel lines and electrical connections. Remove retaining nuts, washers, spacers, insulators and fuel rail with injectors. DO NOT allow injectors to fall during fuel rail removal.
**5)** Disconnect exhaust pipe from exhaust manifold. Remove retaining bolts/nuts, manifolds and gasket.

**Inspection - 1)** Inspect lower intake and exhaust manifold surfaces for warpage. Replace manifold if warpage exceeds .020" (.50 mm).
**2)** Inspect upper intake manifold surface for warpage. Replace manifold if warpage exceeds .008" (.20 mm).

**Installation - 1)** To install, reverse removal procedure. Lower intake and exhaust manifold gaskets must be installed with FRONT mark on the gasket toward front engine. Tighten bolts/nuts to specification. See TORQUE SPECIFICATIONS table at end of article.
**2)** If injector was removed from fuel rail, coat new "O" ring with gasoline and install on injector. Install new grommet on injector.

***NOTE: Once fuel rail and injector assembly are installed, injector assembly should rotate smoothly. If injector does not rotate smoothly, check for damaged "O" ring.***

**3)** To install remaining components, reverse removal procedure. Tighten all fasteners to specification. See TORQUE SPECIFICATIONS table at end of article. Adjust control cables. Fill cooling system.

### CYLINDER HEAD

**Removal - 1)** Remove intake and exhaust manifolds. See INTAKE & EXHAUST MANIFOLDS under REMOVAL & INSTALLATION.
**2)** Remove A/C compressor (if equipped) and power steering pump with hoses attached and secure aside. Disconnect necessary electrical connections and hoses. Remove air pump.
**3)** Remove rocker arm shaft and push rods. See ROCKER ARM & PUSH ROD under REMOVAL & INSTALLATION. Loosen cylinder head bolts using 3 steps in reverse order of tightening sequence. *See Fig. 1.* Remove cylinder head and gasket.

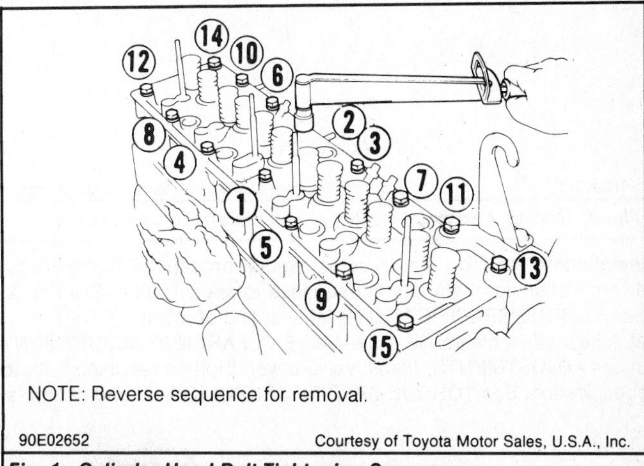


***Fig. 1: Cylinder Head Bolt Tightening Sequence***

# 1991 ENGINES
# 4.0L 6-Cylinder (Cont.)

**Inspection** - Inspect cylinder head warpage at cylinder block and manifold surfaces. Replace cylinder head if warpage exceeds specification. See CYLINDER HEAD table under ENGINE SPECIFICATIONS at end of article.

**Installation** - **1)** Install gasket and cylinder head. Coat cylinder head bolt threads and seat area below head of bolt with oil and install. Tighten cylinder head bolts to specification in sequence using several steps. *See Fig. 1.* See TORQUE SPECIFICATIONS table at end of article.

**2)** To install remaining components, reverse removal procedure. Adjust valve clearance. See VALVE CLEARANCE ADJUSTMENT under ADJUSTMENTS.

## FRONT COVER OIL SEAL

**Removal** - **1)** Remove drive belts and power steering pulley. Using Pulley Holders (SST 09213-58011 and SST 09330-00021), hold crankshaft pulley and remove retaining bolt.

**2)** Using puller, remove crankshaft pulley. Using Seal Remover (SST 09308-10010), remove oil seal from front cover.

**Installation** - **1)** Coat lip of new oil seal with grease. Using hammer and Seal Installer (SST 09238-47012), install oil seal in front cover.

**2)** Using Pulley Installer (SST 09214-60010), install and tighten crankshaft pulley retaining bolt to specification. See TORQUE SPECIFICATIONS table at end of article. To install remaining components, reverse removal procedure.

## ROCKER ARM & PUSH ROD

**Removal** - Remove valve cover and gasket. Remove rocker arm retaining bolts/nuts in sequence. *See Fig. 2.* Remove rocker arm and push rods. Mark component location for reassembly reference.

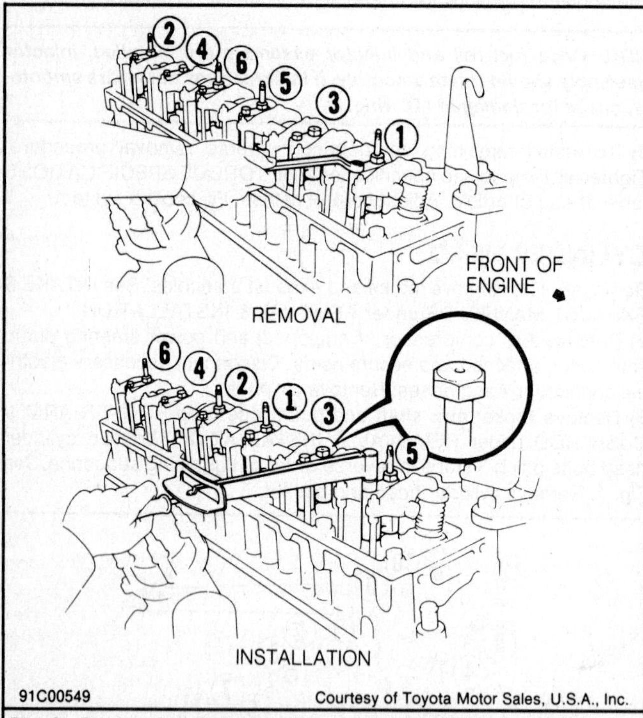

Courtesy of Toyota Motor Sales, U.S.A., Inc.

*Fig. 2: Rocker Arm Bolt/Nut Removal & Installation Sequence*

**Installation** - **1)** To install, reverse removal procedure. Tighten rocker arm retaining bolts/nuts in sequence to specification. *See Fig. 2.* See TORQUE SPECIFICATIONS table at end of article.

**2)** Adjust valve clearance. See VALVE CLEARANCE ADJUSTMENT under ADJUSTMENTS. Install valve cover. Tighten retaining nuts to specification. See TORQUE SPECIFICATIONS table at end of article.

## VALVE LIFTER

**Removal** - **1)** Remove rocker arms and push rods. See ROCKER ARM & PUSH ROD under REMOVAL & INSTALLATION. Remove push rod side cover from right side of cylinder block.

**2)** Remove valve lifter. Mark valve lifter location for reassembly reference. Components must be installed in original location.

**Inspection** - Inspect components for damage. Measure valve lifter diameter and bore diameter. Determine oil clearance. Replace valve lifter and or cylinder block if clearance exceeds specification. See VALVE LIFTERS table under ENGINE SPECIFICATIONS at end of article.

**Installation** - To install, reverse removal procedure. Ensure components are installed in original location. Tighten bolts/nuts to specification. See TORQUE SPECIFICATIONS table at end of article. Adjust valve clearance. See VALVE CLEARANCE ADJUSTMENT under ADJUSTMENTS. Install valve cover.

## CAMSHAFT & TIMING GEARS

**Removal** - **1)** Drain cooling system. Remove air cleaner assembly, air intake duct and airflow meter. Remove radiator, cooling fan and water pump pulley.

**2)** Remove A/C compressor (if equipped) and power steering pump with hoses attached and secure aside.

**3)** Remove A/C compressor and power steering pump brackets. Remove distributor. Remove valve lifter. See VALVE LIFTER under REMOVAL & INSTALLATION.

**4)** Remove drive belts and power steering pulley. Using Pulley Holders (SST 09213-58011 and SST 09330-00021), hold crankshaft pulley and remove retaining bolt. Using puller, remove crankshaft pulley.

**5)** Remove oil cooler pipe with hose. Remove retaining bolts, front cover and gasket. Note bolt length and location for reassembly reference.

**6)** Before removing camshaft, measure timing gear backlash using dial indicator. Timing gears must be replaced if backlash is not within specification. See CAMSHAFT table under ENGINE SPECIFICATIONS at end of article.

**7)** Remove camshaft thrust plate retaining bolts and camshaft. If removing timing gear from crankshaft, remove key from crankshaft. Using Puller (SST 09213-60017), remove crankshaft timing gear.

**8)** If removing timing gear from camshaft, using feeler gauge, check clearance between timing gear and thrust plate. Replace thrust plate or camshaft if clearance exceeds .013" (.33 mm).

**9)** Remove snap ring from camshaft. Note direction of snap ring installation for reassembly reference. Support timing gear in press. Press camshaft from timing gear.

**Inspection** - **1)** Inspect components for damage. Check camshaft journal diameter, lobe height and runout. Replace camshaft if not within specification. See CAMSHAFT table under ENGINE SPECIFICATIONS at end of article.

**2)** Check camshaft bearing bore I.D. and camshaft-to-bearing oil clearance. Replace components if not within specification. See CAMSHAFT table under ENGINE SPECIFICATIONS at end of article.

**3)** If timing gear is installed on camshaft, using feeler gauge, measure clearance between timing gear and thrust plate. Replace thrust plate or camshaft if clearance exceeds .013" (.33 mm).

**Installation** - **1)** If installing camshaft timing gear, install thrust plate on camshaft. Using press, press timing gear on camshaft with timing mark away from camshaft. Install snap ring with raised area on sides of snap ring away from timing gear.

**2)** If installing crankshaft timing gear, place timing gear on crankshaft with timing mark facing outward. Using hammer and Timing Gear Installer (SST 09214-60010), install timing gear on crankshaft.

**3)** Rotate crankshaft so keyway is at 12 o'clock position with No. 6 cylinder at TDC. Install camshaft so timing marks are aligned. *See Fig. 3.*

**4)** Install camshaft thrust plate retaining bolts. Tighten bolts to specification. See TORQUE SPECIFICATIONS table at end of article.

**5)** Ensure camshaft end play and gear backlash are as specified. See CAMSHAFT table under ENGINE SPECIFICATIONS at end of article. Ensure oil nozzle spray hole is toward timing gears. *See Fig. 4.*

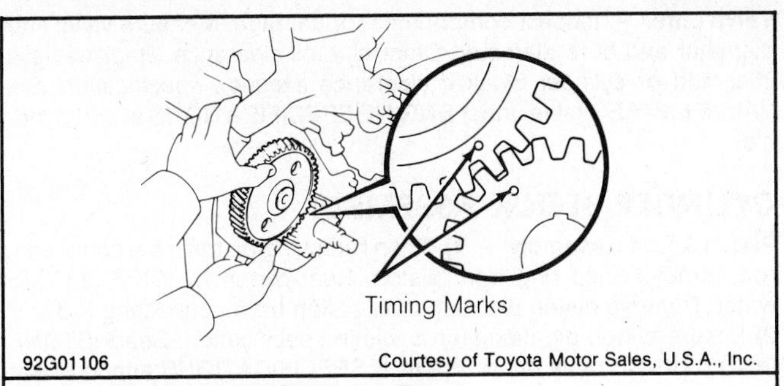


*Fig. 3: Aligning Timing Marks on Gears*

***CAUTION: Ensure oil nozzle threads are staked against cylinder block.***

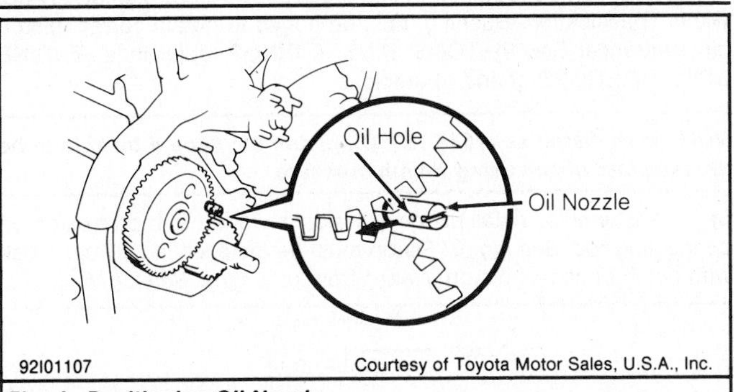


*Fig. 4: Positioning Oil Nozzle*

**6)** Install front cover and gasket with bolts finger tight. Apply Loctite 242 to the lower 2 bolts (long bolts) for front cover. Coat lip of front cover oil seal with grease. Using Pulley Installer (SST 09214-60010), install crankshaft pulley.
**7)** Tighten front cover bolts to specification. See TORQUE SPECIFICATIONS table at end of article. To install remaining components, reverse removal procedure. Ensure valve lifters are installed in original location.
**8)** Tighten all fasteners to specification. See TORQUE SPECIFICATIONS table at end of article. Fill cooling system. Adjust valve clearance. See VALVE CLEARANCE ADJUSTMENT under ADJUSTMENTS. Install valve cover.

## CAMSHAFT BEARING

***NOTE: Camshaft bearings are available for .010" (.25 mm) and .020" (.50 mm) undersize camshafts. Camshaft bearing bore I.D. should be within specification. See CAMSHAFT table under ENGINE SPECIFICATIONS at end of article.***

**Removal** – Drive out camshaft rear expansion plug from cylinder block. Using Camshaft Bearing Remover/Installer (09215-00100), remove camshaft bearings. Note diameter and location of each camshaft bearing.
**Installation** – **1)** Using camshaft bearing remover/installer, install camshaft bearing. Camshaft bearing O.D. varies with the largest at the No 1 (front) and smallest at No. 4 (rear).
**2)** Ensure camshaft bearing oil holes align with those of cylinder block. Ream camshaft bearings to finished diameter. See CAMSHAFT table under ENGINE SPECIFICATIONS at end of article. Coat rear expansion plug with sealer and install in cylinder block.

## REAR CRANKSHAFT OIL SEAL

**Removal & Installation** – **1)** Remove transmission and flywheel. Cut seal lip from oil seal. Pry oil seal from housing, using care not to damage sealing surfaces.
**2)** To install, coat oil seal lip with grease. Using Seal Installer (SST 09223-60010), install oil seal so oil seal surface is even with cylinder block surface.
**3)** Apply thread sealant to flywheel bolts and install. Tighten bolts in a crisscross pattern in several steps to specification. See TORQUE SPECIFICATIONS table at end of article. To install remaining components, reverse removal procedure.

***CAUTION: Ensure thread sealant is applied on flywheel bolts.***

## WATER PUMP

**Removal & Installation** – **1)** Drain cooling system. Remove drive belts. Disconnect necessary coolant hoses. Remove fan shroud, cooling fan and water pump pulley. Remove alternator. Remove retaining bolts/nuts, brackets, water pump and gasket.
**2)** To install, reverse removal procedure. Tighten bolts/nuts to specification. See TORQUE SPECIFICATIONS table at end of article. Adjust drive belts and fill cooling system.

## OIL PAN

**Removal & Installation** – **1)** Raise and support vehicle. Drain engine oil. Remove retaining bolts, oil pan and gasket.
**2)** To install, reverse removal procedure. Apply sealant at front and rear main bearing caps-to-cylinder block surfaces before installing gasket.
**3)** Install gasket and oil pan. Tighten bolts to specification. See TORQUE SPECIFICATIONS table at end of article. Fill engine with oil.

# OVERHAUL

## CYLINDER HEAD

**Cylinder Head** – Inspect cylinder head warpage at cylinder block and manifold surfaces. Replace cylinder head if warpage exceeds specification. See CYLINDER HEAD table under ENGINE SPECIFICATIONS at end of article.
**Valve Springs** – Ensure valve spring free length, out-of-square and pressure are within specification. See VALVES & VALVE SPRINGS table under ENGINE SPECIFICATIONS at end of article.

***CAUTION: Ensure valve spring is installed with painted area toward cylinder head surface. Intake valve spring retainers or keepers use 3 internal ridges and exhaust valves use only one internal ridge, as these valves use a valve rotator.***

**Valve Stem Oil Seals** – Coat oil seal with engine oil and install using Oil Seal Installer (SST 09201-31010).
**Valve Guides** – **1)** Check valve stem-to-valve guide clearance and valve guide inside diameter (I.D.). Ensure valve stem diameter is within specification. Replace valve guide if clearance or I.D. exceeds specification. See CYLINDER HEAD table under ENGINE SPECIFICATIONS at end of article.
**2)** To replace valve guide, use hammer and Valve Guide Remover/Installer (SST 09201-60011). Drive out valve guide from top of cylinder head.
**3)** Measure I.D. of cylinder head valve guide bore. Bore I.D. should be .5512-.5519" (14.000-14.018 mm). If bore I.D. is greater than .5519" (14.018 mm), machine bore to .5531-.5539" (14.050-14.068 mm) for an oversize valve guide. If bore I.D. is greater than .5539" (14.068 mm), replace cylinder head.
**4)** To install valve guide, use hammer and valve guide remover/installer. Install valve guide from top of cylinder head so valve guide installed height is within specification. See CYLINDER HEAD table under ENGINE SPECIFICATIONS at end of article.

***CAUTION: Intake valve guide length is 2.13" (54.1 mm) and exhaust valve guide is 2.32" (58.9 mm). Valve guide installed height is measured from top of valve guide to cylinder head surface, near valve guide.***

**5)** Ream valve guide to obtain specified valve stem-to-guide oil clearance. See CYLINDER HEAD table under ENGINE SPECIFICATIONS at end of article.

# 1991 ENGINES
# 4.0L 6-Cylinder (Cont.)

**Valve Seat** - Ensure valve seat angle and seat width are within specification. See CYLINDER HEAD table under ENGINE SPECIFICATIONS at end of article. Valve seat replacement information not available from manufacturer.

**Valves** - Ensure valve stem diameter, minimum refinish length and margin are within specification. See VALVES & VALVE SPRINGS table under ENGINE SPECIFICATIONS at end of article.

**Seat Correction Angles** - On intake valves, use 25-degree and 45-degree stones to lower valve seat contact area on the valve or 70-degree and 45-degree stones to raise valve seat contact area. On exhaust valves, no information is provided on lowering valve seat contact area. Use 65 and 45 degree stones to raise valve seat contact area on the valve.

## VALVE TRAIN

**Rocker Arm Shaft Assembly** - **1)** Mark component location for reassembly reference. Disassemble rocker arm shaft. *See Fig. 5.*

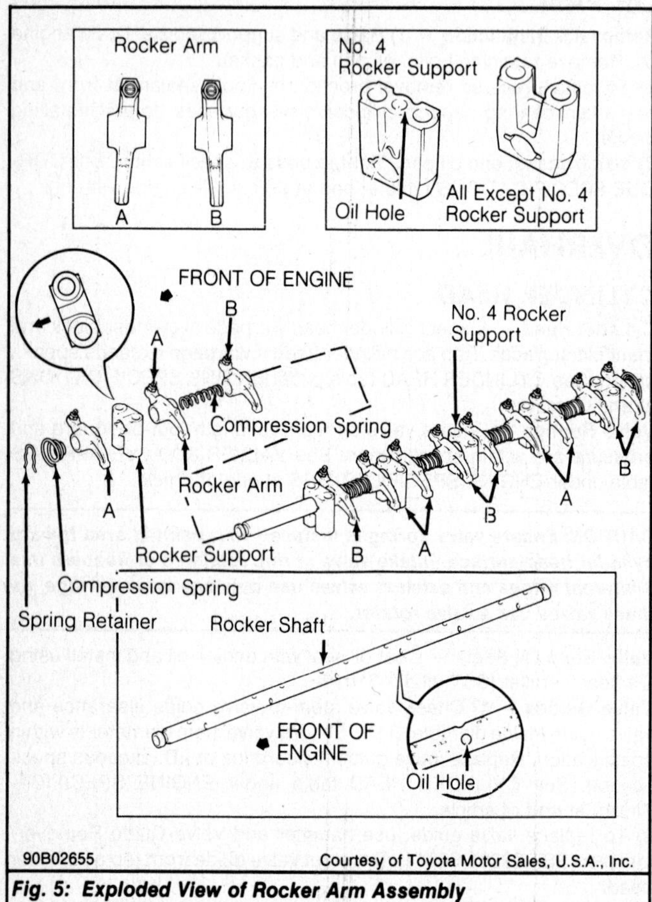


*Fig. 5: Exploded View of Rocker Arm Assembly*

**2)** Inspect components for damage. Measure rocker shaft outside diameter (O.D.) in rocker arm operating area. Measure rocker arm inside diameter (I.D.). Determine oil clearance. Replace components if not within specification. See ROCKER ARM SPECIFICATIONS table.

***ROCKER ARM SPECIFICATIONS***

| Application | In. (mm) |
|---|---|
| Rocker Arm I.D. | .7281-.7289 (18.494-18.514) |
| Rocker Arm Oil Clearance | |
| Standard | .0004-.0020 (.010-.051) |
| Wear Limit | .0031 (.079) |
| Rocker Arm Shaft O.D. | .7269-.7278 (18.463-18.486) |

**3)** Reassemble rocker arm assembly. Components must be installed in original location. Ensure oil hole in rocker shaft aligns with oil hole in No. 4 rocker support. *See Fig. 5.*

**Valve Lifter** - Inspect components for damage. Measure valve lifter diameter and bore diameter. Determine oil clearance. Replace valve lifter and or cylinder block if clearance exceeds specification. See VALVE LIFTERS table under ENGINE SPECIFICATIONS at end of article.

## CYLINDER BLOCK ASSEMBLY

**Piston & Rod Assembly** - **1)** When removing piston from connecting rod, remove snap ring from piston. Heat piston to 176°F (80°C) in water. Remove piston pin. Separate piston from connecting rod.

**2)** Ensure piston pin diameter is within specification. See PISTONS, PINS & RINGS table under ENGINE SPECIFICATIONS at end of article.

**3)** Ensure connecting rod piston pin bushing bore diameter is within specification. See CONNECTING RODS table under ENGINE SPECIFICATIONS at end of article.

**4)** Bushing can be replaced in connecting rod if bore diameter is not within specification. Bushing must be honed to obtain correct piston pin clearance. See PISTONS, PINS, & RINGS table under ENGINE SPECIFICATIONS at end of article.

***NOTE: With piston at 176°F (80°C), piston pin should be able to be pressed into piston using thumb pressure.***

**5)** To reassemble, install piston with notch aligned with protrusion on connecting rod. *See Fig. 6.* Piston must be installed in cylinder block with notch on top of piston toward front of engine. *See Fig. 6.*

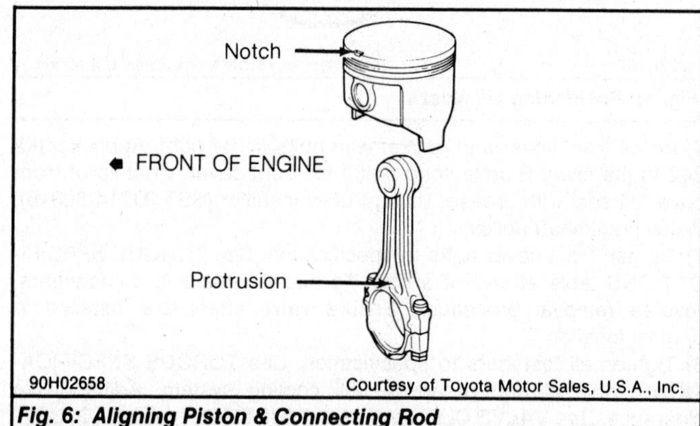


*Fig. 6: Aligning Piston & Connecting Rod*

**Fitting Pistons** - **1)** To determine if piston-to-cylinder clearance is within specification, measure piston skirt diameter .630" (16.00 mm) from bottom of piston skirt at 90-degree angle to piston pin.

**2)** Different piston sizes are used. Piston size can be identified by size mark stamped on top of piston. *See Fig. 7.*

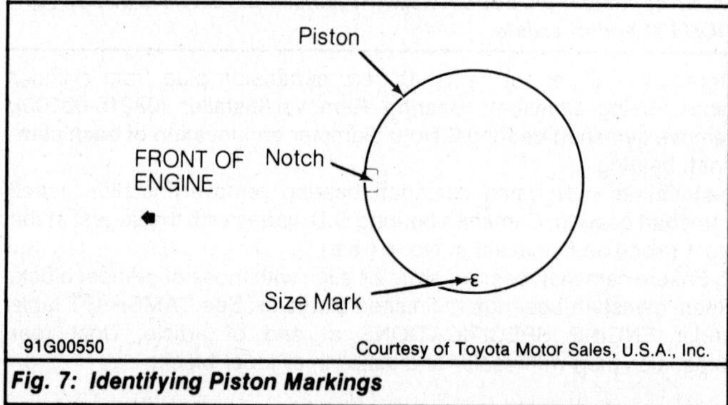


*Fig. 7: Identifying Piston Markings*

**3)** Ensure piston diameter is within specification. See PISTONS, PINS & RINGS table under ENGINE SPECIFICATIONS at end of article.

**4)** Different standard cylinder bore sizes are used and can be identified by size marks (1, 2 or 3) on deck surface of cylinder block. *See Fig. 13.* Measure cylinder bore diameter .39" (9.9 mm) from top and bottom and at middle of cylinder bore.

# 1991 ENGINES
# 4.0L 6-Cylinder (Cont.)

**5)** Ensure cylinder bore diameter is within specification. See CYLINDER BLOCK table under ENGINE SPECIFICATIONS at end of article. Check piston-to-cylinder bore clearance. Clearance should be within specification. See PISTONS, PIN & RINGS table under ENGINE SPECIFICATIONS at end of article.
**6)** If diameter of cylinder bore or piston clearance exceeds specification, cylinder block can be bored for oversize pistons.
**Piston Rings** – Ensure ring end gap and side clearance are within specification. See PISTONS, PINS & RINGS table under ENGINE SPECIFICATIONS at end of article. Position piston ring gaps in proper areas with identification mark on piston ring toward top of piston. *See Fig. 8.*

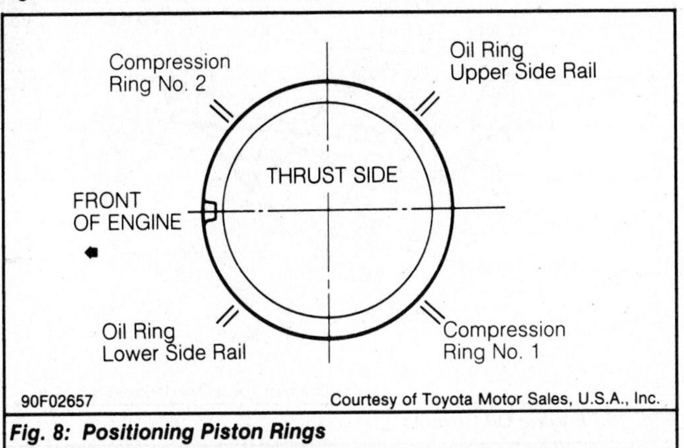

***Fig. 8: Positioning Piston Rings***

**Rod Bearings** – **1)** Note direction of connecting rod and cap installation. Connecting rod must be installed so protrusion at center of connecting rod is toward front of engine. *See Fig. 6.*
**2)** Connecting rod bearing cap and rod bearing are marked with an "A", "B" or "C code to indicate the size. *See Fig. 9.* Ensure codes are the same on connecting rod cap and rod bearing.

***NOTE: If replacing rod bearings, replace rod bearing with one having the same code.***

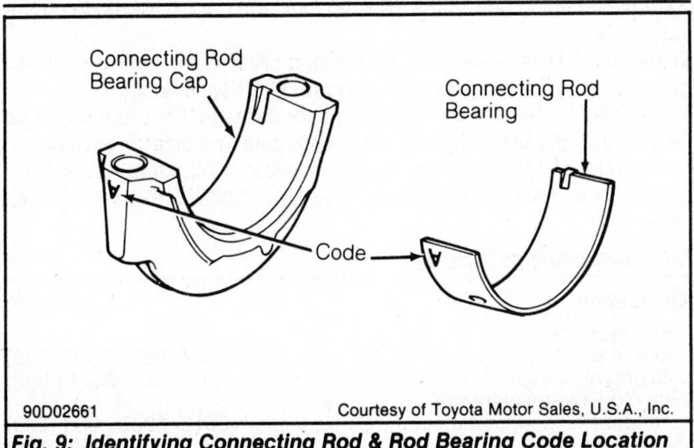

***Fig. 9: Identifying Connecting Rod & Rod Bearing Code Location***

**3)** If bearing code cannot be read, measure bearing thickness to determine bearing code. See CONNECTING ROD BEARING SPECIFICATIONS table.
**4)** Ensure bearing oil clearance and connecting rod side play are within specification. See CRANKSHAFT, MAIN & CONNECTING ROD BEARINGS and CONNECTING RODS table under ENGINE SPECIFICATIONS at end of article.

***CONNECTING ROD BEARING SPECIFICATIONS***

| Bearing Code | Bearing Thickness In. (mm) |
|---|---|
| Code "A" | .0584-.0586 (1.483-1.488) |
| Code "B" | .0586-.0587 (1.488-1.491) |
| Code "C" | .0587-.0589 (1.491-1.496) |

**Crankshaft & Main Bearings** – **1)** Ensure main bearing caps are numbered for location with No. 1 at front of engine. Arrow mark on main bearing cap points toward front of crankshaft. Remove main bearing cap bolts in sequence. *See Fig. 12.*
**2)** Cylinder block main bearing bore size is indicated by cylinder block code (6, 7 or 8) stamped on cylinder block. *See Fig. 10.* Front code indicates No. 1 main bearing bore and rear code indicates No. 4 main bearing bore. Ensure main bearing bore inside diameter (I.D.) is within specification. See CYLINDER BLOCK table under ENGINE SPECIFICATIONS at end of article.

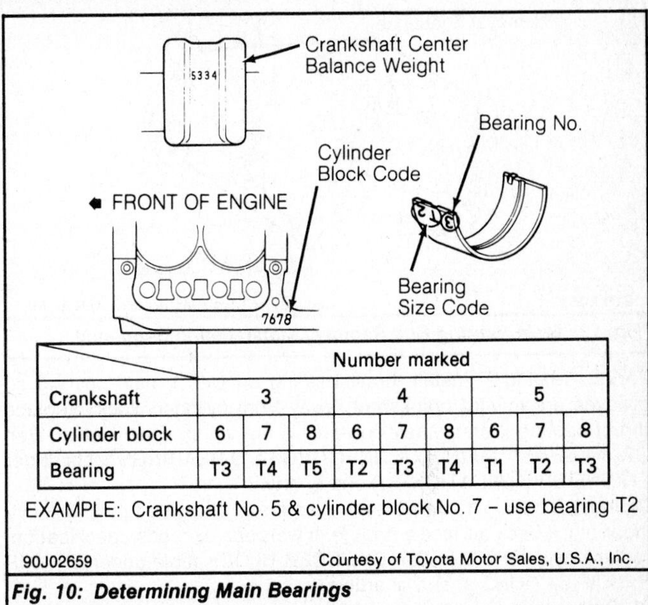


| | Number marked | | | | | | | | |
|---|---|---|---|---|---|---|---|---|---|
| Crankshaft | 3 | | | 4 | | | 5 | | |
| Cylinder block | 6 | 7 | 8 | 6 | 7 | 8 | 6 | 7 | 8 |
| Bearing | T3 | T4 | T5 | T2 | T3 | T4 | T1 | T2 | T3 |

EXAMPLE: Crankshaft No. 5 & cylinder block No. 7 – use bearing T2

90J02659 Courtesy of Toyota Motor Sales, U.S.A., Inc.

***Fig. 10: Determining Main Bearings***

**3)** Crankshaft main bearing journal size is determined by size mark (3, 4 or 5), located on crankshaft center balance weight. *See Fig. 10.* Main bearings are marked with a bearing size code on side of bearing shell. *See Fig. 10.*

***NOTE: If replacing main bearings, replace with one having the same bearing size code.***

**4)** If bearing size code cannot be obtained, use cylinder block code and main bearing journal size mark to determine main bearing to be used. *See Fig. 10.*
**5)** Main bearing thickness varies with size code. See MAIN BEARING SPECIFICATIONS table. The No. 1 and No. 4 main bearing thickness should be measured at designated area. *See Fig. 11.*

***MAIN BEARING SPECIFICATIONS***

| Main Bearing Size Code | Bearing Thickness In. (mm) |
|---|---|
| T1 | .0981-.0983 (2.492-2.497) |
| T2 | .0983-.0985 (2.497-2.502) |
| T3 | .0985-.0986 (2.502-2.504) |
| T4 | .0986-.0988 (2.504-2.510) |
| T5 | .0988-.0989 (2.510-2.512) |

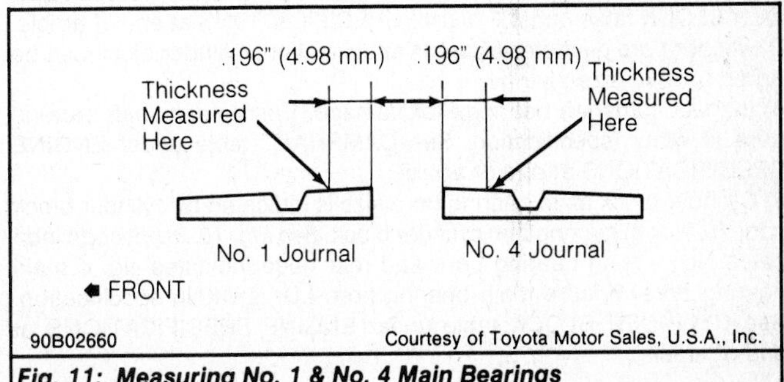

***Fig. 11: Measuring No. 1 & No. 4 Main Bearings***

# 1991 ENGINES
# 4.0L 6-Cylinder (Cont.)

**6)** When installing main bearing caps, ensure arrow on cap points toward front of crankshaft. Coat main bearing bolt threads with engine oil.

**7)** Install and tighten bolts in sequence to specification. *See Fig. 12.* See TORQUE SPECIFICATIONS table at end of article. Ensure crankshaft end play and oil clearance are within specification. See CRANKSHAFT, MAIN & CONNECTING ROD BEARINGS table under ENGINE SPECIFICATIONS at end of article.

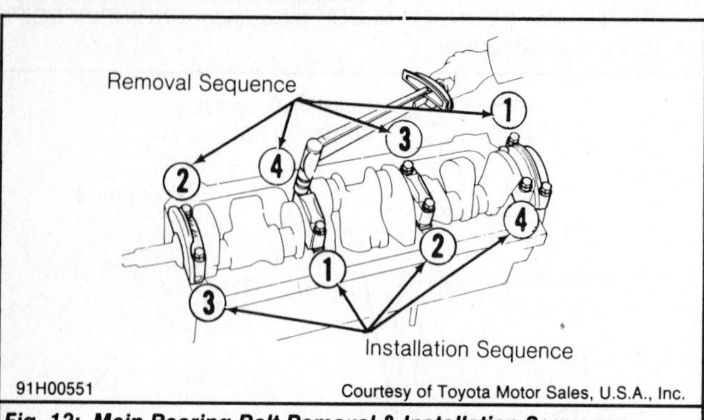


***Fig. 12: Main Bearing Bolt Removal & Installation Sequence***

**Thrust Bearing** – Install thrust bearing on No. 3 main bearing so grooves are toward crankshaft, away from cylinder block. Replace thrust bearing if crankshaft end play is not within specification. See CRANKSHAFT, MAIN & CONNECTING ROD BEARINGS table under ENGINE SPECIFICATIONS at end of article.

**Cylinder Block** – **1)** Using feeler gauge and straightedge, check cylinder block deck surface warpage. If warpage exceeds specification, replace cylinder block. See CYLINDER BLOCK table under ENGINE SPECIFICATIONS at end of article.

**2)** Different standard cylinder bore sizes are used and can be identified by size marks (1, 2 or 3) on deck surface of cylinder block. *See Fig. 13.* Measure cylinder bore diameter .39" (9.9 mm) from top and bottom and at middle of cylinder bore.

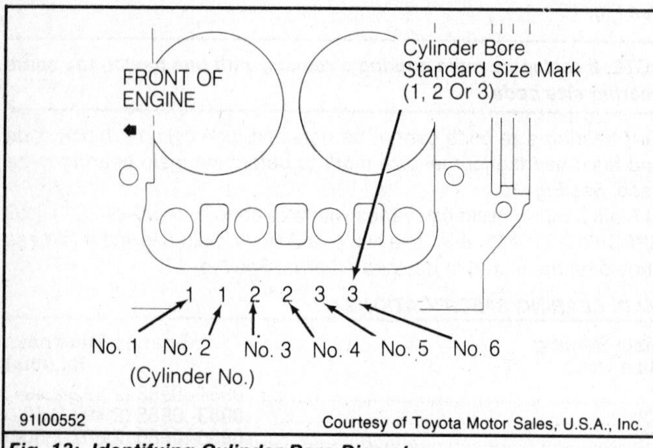


***Fig. 13: Identifying Cylinder Bore Diameter***

**3)** Ensure cylinder bore diameter is within specification. See CYLINDER BLOCK table under ENGINE SPECIFICATIONS at end of article. If cylinder bore diameter exceeds specification, cylinder block can be bored for oversize pistons.

**4)** Inspect camshaft bearings for damage. Ensure camshaft bearing bore is within specification. See CAMSHAFT table under ENGINE SPECIFICATIONS at end of article.

**5)** Cylinder block main bearing bore size is indicated by cylinder block code (6, 7 or 8) stamped on cylinder block. *See Fig. 10.* Front code indicates No. 1 main bearing bore and rear code indicates No. 4 main bearing bore. Ensure main bearing bore I.D. is within specification. See CYLINDER BLOCK table under ENGINE SPECIFICATIONS at end of article.

## ENGINE OILING

### ENGINE LUBRICATION SYSTEM

The distributor-driven oil pump provides lubrication to the main gallery. *See Fig. 14.*

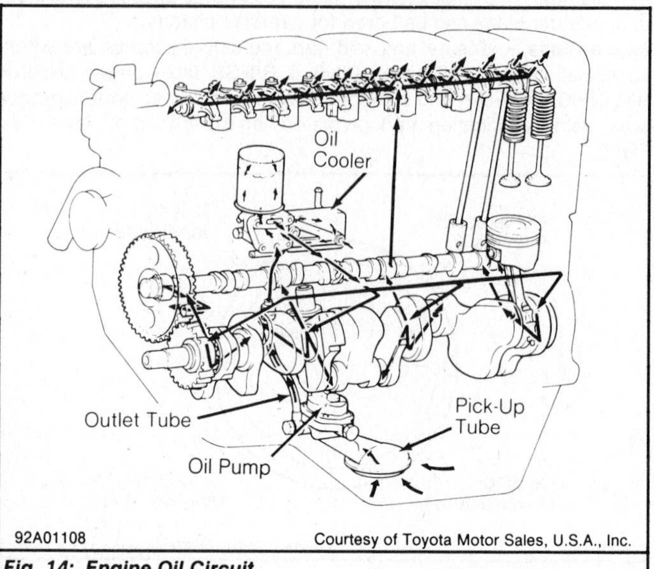


***Fig. 14: Engine Oil Circuit***

**Crankcase Capacity** – Crankcase capacity with oil filter change is 8.2 qts. (7.8L).

**Oil Pressure** – With engine at normal operating temperature, oil pressure should be 4.3 psi (0.3 kg/cm²) at idle and 36-71 psi (2.5-5.0 kg/cm²) at 3000 RPM.

## OIL PUMP

**Removal & Disassembly** – **1)** Remove oil pan. See OIL PAN under REMOVAL & INSTALLATION. Remove outlet tube from oil pump. Remove retaining bolts/nuts, pick-up tube and gasket. Remove retaining bolt and oil pump.

**2)** Remove relief valve plug, spring and relief valve. Remove driven gear. Remove driven gear and oil pump shaft assembly.

**Inspection** – **1)** Inspect components for damage. Ensure relief valve slides freely in bore. Using feeler gauge, measure clearance between both gears and the housing. Replace gears or oil pump assembly if clearance exceeds specification. See OIL PUMP SPECIFICATIONS table.

***OIL PUMP SPECIFICATIONS***

| Application | In. (mm) |
|---|---|
| Gear Backlash | |
| Standard | .0197-.0236 (.500-.599) |
| Maximum | .0374 (.950) |
| Gear-To-Cover Clearance | |
| Standard | .0012-.0035 (.030-.089) |
| Maximum | .0059 (.150) |
| Gear-To-Housing Clearance | |
| Standard | .0037-.0069 (.094-.175) |
| Maximum | .0079 (.201) |

**2)** With all gears in oil pump housing, place straightedge across cover surface of the housing. Measure gear-to-cover clearance between gears and straightedge. Replace gears or oil pump assembly if clearance exceeds specification. See OIL PUMP SPECIFICATIONS table.

**3)** Using dial indicator, check gear backlash while holding one gear and slightly rotating the other gear. Replace gears if gear backlash exceeds specification. See OIL PUMP SPECIFICATIONS table.

**Reassembly & Installation** – **1)** To reassemble, reverse disassembly procedure. Check pump operation by submerging inlet hole in clean engine oil.

2) Rotate shaft clockwise with a screwdriver and check for oil flow from discharge hole. Cover discharge hole with thumb and turn shaft. Turning resistance should be felt.

***CAUTION: When tightening pick-up tube retaining nuts, push pick-up tube downward so no gap exists between pick-up tube and cylinder block.***

3) To install, reverse removal procedure. Ensure oil pump shaft engages with distributor drive shaft. To install remaining components, reverse removal procedure. Tighten bolts/nuts to specification. See TORQUE SPECIFICATIONS table at end of article.

## OIL COOLER

**Removal & Installation** – **1)** Drain cooling system. Remove air cleaner intake hose, oil filter and oil pressure sender. Disconnect hoses from oil cooler.

**2)** Remove oil cooler-to-oil filter bracket bolts, oil cooler and "O" rings. To install, reverse removal procedure. Tighten retaining bolts to specification. See TORQUE SPECIFICATIONS table.

## TORQUE SPECIFICATIONS

### *TORQUE SPECIFICATIONS*

| Application | Ft. Lbs. (N.m) |
|---|---|
| A/C Compressor Bolt | 18 (24) |
| Air Injection Manifold Nut | 15 (20) |
| Connecting Rod Nut | 43 (58) |
| Crossmember Retaining Bolt | 29 (39) |
| Crossmember Retaining Nut | 43 (58) |
| Crankshaft Pulley Bolt | 253 (343) |
| Cylinder Head Bolt [1] | 90 (122) |
| Drive Shaft Flange Bolt | 65 (88) |
| EGR Pipe Nut | 47 (64) |
| Flywheel Bolt | 64 (87) |
| Front Cover Bolt | |
| Large Bolt | 18 (24) |
| Small Bolt | [2] |
| Front Plate-To-Cylinder Block | |
| Bolt | 22 (30) |
| Torx Screw | 18 (24) |
| Intake/Exhaust Manifold Bolt/Nut | |
| Large Bolt | 51 (69) |
| Nut | 41 (56) |
| Small Bolt | 37 (51) |
| Main Bearing Cap Bolt [3] | |
| 17mm Bolt | 85 (115) |
| 19mm Bolt | 99 (134) |
| Oil Cooler Bolt | 47 (64) |
| Oil Pump Relief Valve Plug | 27 (37) |
| Oil Pump-To-Cylinder Block Bolt | 13 (18) |
| Outlet Pipe Bolt | 33 (45) |
| Pick-Up Tube-To-Cylinder Block Bolt | 13 (18) |
| Pick-Up Tube-To-Oil Pump Nut | 10 (14) |
| Power Steering Pulley-To-Crankshaft Pulley Bolt | 13 (18) |
| Rocker Arm Bolt/Nut [4] | |
| Large Bolt & Nut | 25 (34) |
| Small Bolt | 17 (23) |
| Spark Plug | 13 (18) |
| Upper Intake Manifold-To-Lower Manifold Bolt/Nut | 18 (24) |
| Water Pump Bolt/Nut | 27 (37) |

1 – Tighten bolts to specification in sequence. *See Fig. 1.*
2 – Tighten bolts to 43 INCH lbs. (5 N.m).
3 – Tighten bolts to specification in sequence. *See Fig. 12.*
4 – Tighten bolts to specification in sequence. *See Fig. 2.*

### *TORQUE SPECIFICATIONS (Cont.)*

| Application | INCH Lbs. (N.m) |
|---|---|
| Camshaft Thrust Plate Bolt | 108 (12) |
| Fuel Rail Nut | 108 (12) |
| Oil Pan Bolt | 69 (8) |
| Oil Pump Cover Bolt | 84 (9) |
| Push Rod Side Cover Bolt/Nut | 35 (4) |
| Throttle Body Bolt | 108 (12) |
| Upper Intake Manifold Brace Bolt | 108 (12) |
| Valve Cover Nut | 78 (9) |

## ENGINE SPECIFICATIONS

### *GENERAL SPECIFICATIONS*

| Application | Specification |
|---|---|
| 4.0L | |
| Displacement | 244 Cu. In. (4.0L) |
| Bore | 3.70" (94.0 mm) |
| Stroke | 3.74" (95.0 mm) |
| Compression Ratio | 8.1:1 |
| Fuel System | PFI |
| Horsepower @ RPM | 155 @ 4000 |
| Torque Ft. Lbs. @ RPM | 220 @ 3000 |

### *PISTONS, PINS & RINGS*

| Application | In. (mm) |
|---|---|
| 4.0L | |
| Pistons | |
| Clearance | .0011-.0019 (.028-.048) |
| Diameter [1] | |
| Size Mark 1 | 3.6993-3.6997 (93.962-93.972) |
| Size Mark 2 | 3.6997-3.7001 (93.972-93.983) |
| Size Mark 3 | 3.7001-3.7005 (93.983-93.993) |
| Pins | |
| Diameter | .8663-.8669 (22.004-22.019) |
| Piston Fit | [2] |
| Rod Fit | .0002-.0004 (.005-.010) |
| Rings | |
| No. 1 | |
| End Gap | |
| Standard | .0079-.0165 (.201-.419) |
| Wear Limit | .040 (1.02) |
| Side Clearance | .0012-.0028 (.030-.071) |
| No. 2 | |
| End Gap | |
| Standard | .0197-.0283 (.500-.719) |
| Wear Limit | .052 (1.32) |
| Side Clearance | .0020-.0035 (.051-.089) |
| No. 3 (Oil) | |
| End Gap | |
| Standard | .0079-.0323 (.201-.820) |
| Wear Limit | .056 (1.42) |

1 – Piston diameter is determined by size mark stamped on top of piston. *See Fig. 7.*
2 – Piston pin should slide in piston using thumb pressure with piston heated to 176°F (80°C).

# 1991 ENGINES
# 4.0L 6-Cylinder (Cont.)

## CRANKSHAFT, MAIN & CONNECTING ROD BEARINGS

| Application | In. (mm) |
|---|---|
| 4.0L | |
| Crankshaft | |
| End Play | |
| Standard | .0006-.0080 (.015-.203) |
| Wear Limit | .0118 (.300) |
| Maximum Runout | .0048 (.121) |
| Main Bearings | |
| Journal Diameter [1] | |
| Size Mark 3 | |
| No. 1 Journal | 2.6367-2.6370 (66.972-66.980) |
| No. 2 Journal | 2.6957-2.6961 (68.471-68.481) |
| No. 3 Journal | 2.7548-2.7551 (69.972-69.980) |
| No. 4 Journal | 2.8139-2.8142 (71.473-71.481) |
| Size Mark 4 | |
| No. 1 Journal | 2.6370-2.6373 (66.980-66.987) |
| No. 2 Journal | 2.6961-2.6964 (68.481-68.489) |
| No. 3 Journal | 2.7551-2.7554 (69.980-69.987) |
| No. 4 Journal | 2.8141-2.8145 (71.480-71.488) |
| Size Mark 5 | |
| No. 1 Journal | 2.6373-2.6376 (66.987-66.995) |
| No. 2 Journal | 2.6964-2.6967 (68.489-68.496) |
| No. 3 Journal | 2.7554-2.7557 (69.987-69.995) |
| No. 4 Journal | 2.8145-2.8148 (71.488-71.496) |
| Journal Out-Of-Round & Taper | .0008 (.020) |
| Oil Clearance | |
| **Standard Crankshaft** | |
| Standard | .0006-.0022 (.015-.056) |
| Wear Limit | .0039 (.099) |
| **.010" (.25 mm) & .020" (.50 mm) Undersize Crankshaft** | |
| Standard | .0008-.0026 (.020-.066) |
| Wear Limit | .0039 (.099) |
| Connecting Rod Bearings | |
| Journal Diameter | 2.0861-2.0866 (52.987-52.999) |
| Journal Out-Of-Round & Taper | .0008 (.020) |
| Oil Clearance | |
| **Standard Crankshaft** | |
| Standard | .0008-.0020 (.020-.051) |
| Wear Limit | .0039 (.099) |
| **.010" (.25 mm) & .020" (.50 mm) Undersize Crankshaft** | |
| Standard | .0007-.0025 (.018-.064) |
| Wear Limit | .0039 (.099) |

[1] – Journal diameter is determined by size mark on crankshaft center balance weight. *See Fig. 10.*

## CONNECTING RODS

| Application | In. (mm) |
|---|---|
| 4.0L | |
| Bore Diameter | |
| Bushing Pin Bore | .8666-.8672 (22.012-22.027) |
| Maximum Bend | .002 Per 3.94 (.05 Per 100.1) |
| Maximum Twist | .0059 Per 3.94 (.150 Per 100.1) |
| Side Play | |
| Standard | .0063-.0118 (.160-.300) |
| Wear Limit | .0157 (.399) |

## CYLINDER BLOCK

| Application | In. (mm) |
|---|---|
| 4.0L | |
| Cylinder Bore | |
| Standard Diameter [1] | |
| Size Mark 1 | 3.7008-3.7012 (94.000-94.010) |
| Size Mark 2 | 3.7012-3.7016 (94.010-94.021) |
| Size Mark 3 | 3.7016-3.7020 (94.021-94.031) |
| Maximum Deck Warpage | .0059 (.150) |
| Main Bearing Bore I.D. [2] | |
| Code Number 6 | |
| No. 1 Journal | 2.8350-2.8353 (72.009-72.017) |
| No. 2 Journal | 2.8941-2.8944 (73.510-73.518) |
| No. 3 Journal | 2.9531-2.9535 (75.009-75.019) |
| No. 4 Journal | 3.0122-3.0125 (76.510-76.518) |
| Code Number 7 | |
| No. 1 Journal | 2.8353-2.8357 (72.017-72.027) |
| No. 2 Journal | 2.8944-2.8947 (73.518-73.525) |
| No. 3 Journal | 2.9535-2.9538 (75.019-75.027) |
| No. 4 Journal | 3.0125-3.0128 (76.518-76.525) |
| Code Number 8 | |
| No. 1 Journal | 2.8357-2.8360 (72.027-72.034) |
| No. 2 Journal | 2.8947-2.8950 (73.525-73.533) |
| No. 3 Journal | 2.9538-2.9541 (75.026-75.034) |
| No. 4 Journal | 3.0128-3.0131 (76.525-76.533) |

[1] – Diameter is determined by size mark on cylinder block deck surface. *See Fig. 13.*

[2] – Main bearing bore diameter is determined by cylinder block code. *See Fig. 10.*

## VALVES & VALVE SPRINGS

| Application | Specification |
|---|---|
| 4.0L | |
| Intake Valves | |
| Face Angle | 44.5° |
| Minimum Margin | .039" (.99 mm) |
| Minimum Refinish Length | 4.894" (124.31 mm) |
| Stem Diameter | .3138-.3144" (7.970-7.985 mm) |
| Exhaust Valves | |
| Face Angle | 44.5° |
| Minimum Margin | .047" (1.19 mm) |
| Minimum Refinish Length | 5.020" (127.51 mm) |
| Stem Diameter | .3134-.3140" (7.960-7.976 mm) |
| Valve Springs | |
| Free Length | |
| Standard | 2.028" (51.51 mm) |
| Wear Limit | 1.969" (50.012 mm) |
| Out-Of-Square | .071" (1.80 mm) |
| | Lbs. @ In. (kg @ mm) |
| Pressure | |
| Valve Closed | |
| Standard | 71 @ 1.693 (32 @ 43.00) |
| Wear Limit | 59.5 @ 1.693 (26.9 @ 43.00) |

# 1991 ENGINES
# 4.0L 6-Cylinder (Cont.)

## CYLINDER HEAD

| Application | Specification |
|---|---|
| 4.0L | |
| Maximum Warpage | |
| Cylinder Block Surface | .0059" (.150 mm) |
| Manifold Surface | .0039" (.099 mm) |
| Valve Seats | |
| Intake Valve | |
| Seat Angle | 45° |
| Seat Width | .043-067" (1.09-1.70 mm) |
| Exhaust Valve | |
| Seat Angle | 45° |
| Seat Width | .055-079" (1.40-2.01 mm) |
| Valve Guides | |
| Intake Valve | |
| Valve Guide Cylinder Head Bore I.D. | .5512-.5519" (14.000-14.018 mm) |
| Valve Guide I.D. | .3154-.3161" (8.011-8.030 mm) |
| Valve Guide Installed Height | .681-.697" (17.30-17.70 mm) |
| Valve Stem-To-Guide Oil Clearance | |
| Standard | .0010-.0024" (.025-.061 mm) |
| Wear Limit | .0039" (.099 mm) |
| Exhaust Valve | |
| Valve Guide Cylinder Head Bore I.D. | .5512-.5519" (14.000-14.018 mm) |
| Valve Guide I.D. | .3154-.3161" (8.011-8.030 mm) |
| Valve Guide Installed Height | .681-.697" (17.30-17.70 mm) |
| Valve Stem-To-Guide Oil Clearance | |
| Standard | .0014-.0028" (.036-.071 mm) |
| Wear Limit | .0047" (.119 mm) |

## VALVE LIFTERS

| Application | In. (mm) |
|---|---|
| 4.0L | |
| Bore Diameter | .8432-.8442 (21.417-21.443) |
| Lifter Diameter | .8420-.8427 (21.387-21.405) |
| Oil Clearance | |
| Standard | .0005-.0022 (.013-.056) |
| Wear Limit | .0039 (.099) |

## CAMSHAFT

| Application | In. (mm) |
|---|---|
| 4.0L | |
| Bearing Bore I.D. | |
| **Standard Camshaft** | |
| No. 1 Bearing | 1.8898-1.8909 (48.001-48.029) |
| No. 2 Bearing | 1.8307-1.8319 (46.500-46.530) |
| No. 3 Bearing | 1.7717-1.7728 (45.000-45.029) |
| No. 4 Bearing | 1.7126-1.7138 (43.500-43.531) |
| **.010" (.25 mm) Undersize Camshaft** | |
| No. 1 Bearing | 1.8799-1.8829 (47.749-47.826) |
| No. 2 Bearing | 1.8209-1.8238 (46.251-46.325) |
| No. 3 Bearing | 1.7618-1.7646 (44.750-44.821) |
| No. 4 Bearing | 1.7028-1.7055 (43.251-43.320) |
| **.020" (.50 mm) Undersize Camshaft** | |
| No. 1 Bearing | 1.8701-1.8730 (47.501-47.574) |
| No. 2 Bearing | 1.8110-1.8140 (46.000-46.076) |
| No. 3 Bearing | 1.7520-1.7547 (44.501-44.570) |
| No. 4 Bearing | 1.6929-1.6957 (43.000-43.071) |
| End Play | |
| Standard | .0079-.0114 (.201-.290) |
| Wear Limit | .0130 (.330) |
| Gear Backlash | |
| Standard | .0039-.0072 (.099-.183) |
| Wear Limit | .0098 (.249) |
| Journal Diameter | |
| **Standard Camshaft** | |
| No. 1 Journal | 1.8880-1.8887 (47.955-47.973) |
| No. 2 Journal | 1.8289-1.8297 (46.454-46.474) |
| No. 3 Journal | 1.7699-1.7707 (44.955-44.976) |
| No. 4 Journal | 1.7108-1.7116 (43.454-43.475) |
| **.010" (.25 mm) Undersize Camshaft** | |
| No. 1 Journal | 1.8785-1.8789 (47.714-47.724) |
| No. 2 Journal | 1.8195-1.8199 (46.215-46.225) |
| No. 3 Journal | 1.7604-1.7608 (44.714-44.724) |
| No. 4 Journal | 1.7014-1.7018 (43.216-43.226) |
| **.020" (.50 mm) Undersize Camshaft** | |
| No. 1 Journal | 1.8687-1.8691 (47.465-47.475) |
| No. 2 Journal | 1.8096-1.8100 (45.964-45.975) |
| No. 3 Journal | 1.7506-1.7510 (44.465-44.475) |
| No. 4 Journal | 1.6915-1.6919 (42.964-42.974) |
| Journal Runout | .0118 (.300) |
| Lobe Height | |
| Intake | |
| Standard | 1.5102-1.5142 (38.359-38.461) |
| Wear Limit | 1.496 (37.998) |
| Exhaust | |
| Standard | 1.5059-1.5098 (38.250-38.349) |
| Wear Limit | 1.492 (37.897) |
| Oil Clearance | |
| **Standard Camshaft** | |
| Standard | .0010-.0030 (.025-.076) |
| Wear Limit | .0039 (.099) |
| **.010" (.25 mm) & .020" (.50 mm) Undersize Camshaft** | |
| Journals No. 1 & No. 2 | |
| Standard | .0010-.0043 (.025-.109) |
| Wear Limit | .0059 (.150) |
| Journals No. 3 & No. 4 | |
| Standard | .0010-.0041 (.025-.104) |
| Wear Limit | .0059 (.150) |

# 1991 ENGINE COOLING
# Specifications & Electric Cooling Fans

**Camry, Celica, Corolla, Cressida, Land Cruiser, MR2, Pickup, Previa, Supra, Tercel, 4Runner**

## SPECIFICATIONS

### BELT ADJUSTMENT

*ENGINE BELT ADJUSTMENT (4-CYLINDER)* [1]

| Application | New Belt | Used Belt |
|---|---|---|
| Camry | | |
| Alternator | | |
| Without A/C | 125 (57) | 95 (43) |
| With A/C | 175 (79) | 130 (59) |
| P/S | 125 (57) | 80 (36) |
| Celica | | |
| 3S-GTE Engine | | |
| Alternator | | |
| With A/C | 175 (79) | 115 (52) |
| Without A/C | 150 (68) | 130 (59) |
| P/S | 125 (57) | 80 (36) |
| 4A-FE Engine | | |
| Alternator | 160 (73) | 130 (59) |
| A/C Compressor | 160 (73) | 100 (45) |
| P/S | 125 (57) | 80 (36) |
| 5S-FE Engine | | |
| Alternator | | |
| With A/C | 175 (79) | 130 (59) |
| Without A/C | 125 (57) | 95 (43) |
| P/S | 125 (57) | 80 (36) |
| Corolla | | |
| 4A-FE | | |
| A/C | 160 (73) | 100 (45) |
| Alternator | 160 (73) | 130 (59) |
| P/S | 100 (45) | 55 (25) |
| 4A-GE | | |
| A/C & P/S | 165 (75) | 90 (41) |
| Alternator | 175 (79) | 115 (52) |
| MR2 | | |
| Alternator | 120 (54) | 104 (47) |
| A/C | 160 (73) | 100 (45) |
| Pickup & 4Runner | 125 (57) | 80 (36) |
| Previa | | |
| Alternator & P/S | 170 (77) | 125 (57) |
| A/C | 140 (64) | 120 (54) |
| Tercel | | |
| A/C Only | 165 (75) | 110 (50) |
| All Others | 160 (73) | 100 (45) |

1 – Tension in lbs. (kg) using Burroughs tension gauge.

*ENGINE BELT ADJUSTMENT (6-CYLINDER & V6)* [1]

| Application | New Belt | Used Belt |
|---|---|---|
| Camry V6 | | |
| Alternator | 175 (79) | 115 (52) |
| P/S | 125 (57) | 80 (36) |
| Cressida | | |
| Alternator | 175 (79) | 115 (52) |
| A/C | 160 (73) | 105 (48) |
| P/S | 160 (73) | 100 (45) |
| Land Cruiser | | |
| A/C | 125 (57) | 80 (36) |
| Alternator & P/S | 145 (66) | 100 (45) |
| Pickup & 4Runner V6 | | |
| Alternator | 160 (73) | 100 (45) |
| A/C & P/S | 125 (57) | 80 (36) |
| Supra | | |
| Alternator | 175 (79) | 115 (52) |
| A/C & P/S | 160 (73) | 105 (48) |

1 – Tension in lbs. (kg) using Burroughs tension gauge.

## COOLING SYSTEM SPECIFICATIONS

*ENGINE COOLING SYSTEM SPECIFICATIONS (4-CYLINDER)*

| Application | Specification |
|---|---|
| Coolant Replacement Interval | |
| First Service | 45,000 Miles or 36 Months |
| Subsequent Servicing | 30,000 Miles or 24 Months |
| Coolant Capacity | |
| Camry | |
| 2WD | 6.8 Qts. (6.4L) |
| 4WD | 7.2 Qts. (6.8L) |
| Celica | |
| 3S-GTE | 6.9 Qts. (6.5L) |
| 4A-FE | |
| A/T | 5.9 Qts. (5.6L) |
| M/T | 5.5 Qts. (5.2L) |
| 5S-FE | |
| A/T | 6.4 Qts. (6.1L) |
| M/T | 6.6 Qts. (6.2L) |
| Corolla | |
| 4A-FE | [2] 6.5 Qts. (6.2L) |
| 4A-GE | 6.3 Qts. (6.0L) |
| MR2 | |
| 3S-GTE | 14.4 Qts. (13.6L) |
| 5S-FE | 13.7 Qts. (13.0L) |
| Pickup & 4Runner | |
| 4WD A/T | 9.6 Qts. (9.1L) |
| All Others | 8.9 Qts. (8.4L) |
| Previa | 12.3 Qts. (11.6L) |
| Tercel | |
| A/T | 5.7 Qts. (5.4L) |
| M/T | 5.2 Qts. (4.9L) |
| Pressure Cap Standard Opening Pressure | 10.7-14.9 psi |
| Thermostat Opens [1] | |
| Camry (4-Cyl.), Celica, Corolla, MR2, Previa & Tercel | 176-183°F (80-84°C) |
| Pickup & 4Runner (4-Cyl.) | 187-194°F (86-90°C) |

1 – If thermostat is equipped with a "jiggle valve" on its flange, install "jiggle valve" properly. On Camry, Celica, MR2, Previa and Tercel, align "jiggle valve" with protrusion on thermostat housing. On Corolla, align "jiggle valve" with stud bolt or above water inlet housing.

2 – Some models have a coolant capacity of 5.9 Qts. (5.6L).

*ENGINE COOLING SYSTEM SPECIFICATIONS (6-CYLINDER & V6)*

| Application | Specification |
|---|---|
| Coolant Replacement Interval | |
| First Service | 45,000 Miles or 36 Months |
| Subsequent Servicing | 30,000 Miles or 24 Months |
| Coolant Capacity | |
| Camry V6 | 10.0 Qts. (9.5L) |
| Cressida | 8.8 Qts. (8.3L) |
| Land Cruiser | |
| Without Rear Heater | 18.5 Qts. (17.5L) |
| With Rear Heater | 20.6 Qts. (19.5L) |
| Pickup & 4Runner V6 | |
| A/T | 10.9 Qts. (10.3L) |
| M/T | 11.1 Qts. (10.5L) |
| Supra | 8.6 Qts. (8.1L) |
| Pressure Cap Standard Opening Pressure | 10.7-14.9 psi |
| Thermostat Opens [1] | |
| Camry V6, Pickup & 4Runner | 176-183°F (80-84°C) |
| Cressida, Land Cruiser & Supra | 187-194°F (86-90°C) |

1 – If thermostat is equipped with a "jiggle valve" on its flange, ensure "jiggle valve" is installed at 12 o'clock (straight-up) position. This applies to engines where thermostat flange is vertical when installed.

## ELECTRIC COOLING FAN

***NOTE: On models with A/C, electric radiator cooling fans are also controlled by A/C system. See Mitchell's AIR CONDITIONING & HEATING, IMPORT SERVICE & REPAIR manual for additional information.***

### COOLING FAN QUICK TEST

**Engine Compartment Fan (MR2 Turbo) – 1)** Ensure engine compartment temperature is below 113°F (45.5°C). Turn ignition on. Fan motor should not run. If fan operates, check cooling fan relays, engine compartment temperature switch and wiring.

# 1991 ENGINE COOLING
# Specifications & Electric Cooling Fans (Cont.)

**2)** With ignition on, unplug engine compartment temperature switch. Fan motor should operate. If fan does not operate, check ignition main relay, cooling fan relays, cooling fan ECU, fan motor, fuse and wiring.
**3)** Reconnect engine compartment temperature switch. Start engine and raise engine compartment temperature above 144.5°F (62.5°C). Fan motor should operate. If fan does not operate, replace engine compartment temperature switch.

**Radiator Cooling Fan (Camry 4-Cyl., Celica, Corolla, MR2 & Tercel) – 1)** Ensure engine coolant temperature is below STEP 1 temperature. See COOLING FAN QUICK TEST TEMPERATURE SPECIFICATIONS table. Turn ignition on. Fan motor should not run. If it does, check cooling fan relays, coolant temperature switch and wiring.
**2)** With ignition on, unplug coolant temperature switch. Fan motor should operate. If fan does not operate, check cooling fan relays, fan motor, engine main relay, fuse and wiring.
**3)** Reconnect coolant temperature switch. Start engine and raise coolant temperature above STEP 2 temperature. See RADIATOR COOLING FAN QUICK TEST TEMPERATURE SPECIFICATIONS table. Fan motor should operate. If fan does not operate, replace coolant temperature switch.

***RADIATOR COOLING FAN QUICK TEST TEMPERATURE SPECIFICATIONS***

| Application | Step 1 Temperature °F (°C) | Step 2 Temperature °F (°C) |
|---|---|---|
| Camry (4-Cyl.), Celica | | |
| & Corolla | 181 (83) | 199 (93) |
| MR2 | | |
| With A/C | 185 (85) | 194 (90) |
| Without A/C | 181 (83) | 199 (93) |
| Tercel | 181 (89) | 201 (94) |

**Radiator Cooling Fan (Camry V6) – 1)** Ensure engine coolant temperature is below 185°F (85°C). Turn ignition on. Fan motor should not run. If it does, check cooling fan relay, coolant temperature sensor and wiring.
**2)** With ignition on, unplug coolant temperature sensor. Fan motor should operate. If fan does not operate, check cooling fan relay, fan motor, engine main relay, fuse, coolant temperature sensor and wiring.
**3)** Reconnect coolant temperature sensor connector. Start engine and raise coolant temperature to 185-194°F (85-90°C). Fan motor should operate at low speed. If fan does not operate at low speed, replace coolant temperature sensor.
**4)** With engine on continue to raise coolant temperature above 194°F (90°C). Fan motor should operate at high speed. If fan does not operate at high speed, replace coolant temperature sensor.

## COMPONENT TESTING

**A/C Amplifier Circuit (MR2) –** Disconnect wiring harness from A/C amplifier. A/C amplifier is located behind glove box. Check for continuity between harness connector terminals and ground under conditions specified. See A/C AMPLIFIER CIRCUIT TEST (MR2) table. *See Fig. 1.*

***A/C AMPLIFIER CIRCUIT TEST (MR2)***

| Wiring Harness Terminal Check | Condition | Specification |
|---|---|---|
| No. 3 - Ground | Always | Continuity |
| No. 4 - Ground | Ignition On | Battery Voltage |
| No. 9 - No. 15 | 185°F (85°C) [1] | 1350 Ohms |
| | 194°F (90°C) [1] | 1190 Ohms |
| | 203°F (95°C) [1] | 1050 Ohms |
| No. 10 - Ground | Ignition On | Battery Voltage |
| No. 13 - Ground | Always | Continuity |

[1] – Coolant temperature.

**Cooling Fan ECU Circuit (Camry V6 & MR2 Turbo) – 1)** Disconnect wiring harness from cooling fan ECU. On Camry V6, radiator cooling fan ECU is located under right side of dash, behind glove box. On MR2 Turbo, engine compartment cooling fan ECU is located on rear wall of engine compartment.
**2)** Check for continuity between wiring harness terminals and ground under conditions specified. See COOLING FAN ECU CIRCUIT TEST (CAMRY V6 & MR2 TURBO) table. *See Fig. 2 or 3.*

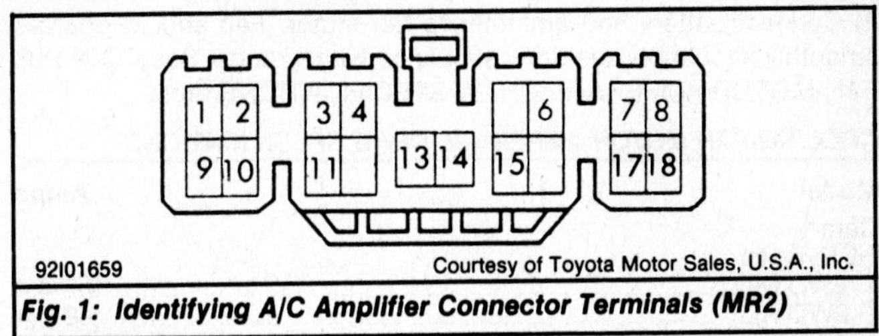

***Fig. 1: Identifying A/C Amplifier Connector Terminals (MR2)***

***NOTE: Cooling fan ECU controls radiator cooling fan on Camry V6 and engine compartment cooling fan on MR2 turbo.***

***COOLING FAN ECU CIRCUIT TEST (CAMRY V6 & MR2 TURBO)***

| Wiring Harness Terminal Check | Condition | Specification |
|---|---|---|
| Camry V6 | | |
| No. 2-Ground | Always | Continuity |
| No. 3-Ground | Ignition On | Battery Voltage |
| No. 4-Ground | Ignition On | Battery Voltage |
| No. 5-No. 7 | 176°F (80°C) [1] | 1530 Ohms |
| | 194°F (90°C) [1] | 1180 Ohms |
| | 203°F (95°C) [1] | 1030 Ohms |
| No. 6-Ground | Always | Continuity |
| MR2 Turbo | | |
| No. 1 - Ground | Always | Continuity |
| No. 2 - Ground | Ignition On | Battery Voltage |
| No. 3 - Ground | Ignition On | Battery Voltage |
| No. 5 - No. 6 | 68°F (20°C) [2] | 2450 Ohms |
| | 136°F (58°C) [2] | 630 Ohms |
| | 176°F (80°C) [2] | 320 Ohms |
| No. 7 - Ground | Ignition On | Battery Voltage |
| No. 9 - Ground | Ignition On | Battery Voltage |

[1] – Coolant temperature.
[2] – Engine compartment temperature.

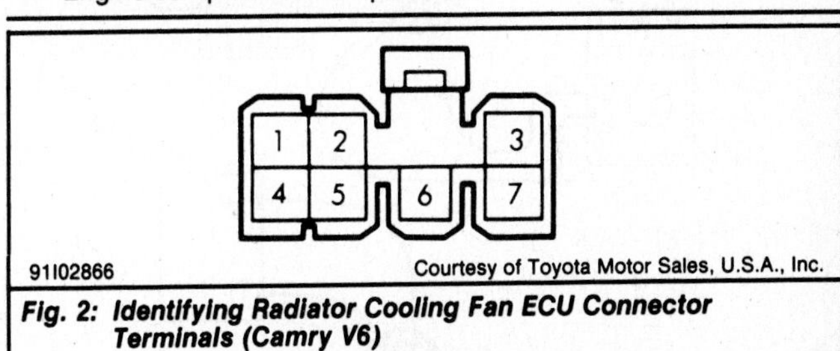

***Fig. 2: Identifying Radiator Cooling Fan ECU Connector Terminals (Camry V6)***

***Fig. 3: Identifying Engine Compartment Cooling Fan ECU Connector Terminals (MR2 Turbo)***

**Cooling Fan Motor (Camry, Celica, Corolla, Land Cruiser, MR2 & Tercel) – 1)** On Land Cruiser, remove shroud from fan motor. On all models, disconnect wiring harness from fan motor.

# 1991 ENGINE COOLING
# Specifications & Electric Cooling Fans (Cont.)

2) Connect battery and ammeter to fan motor. Fan should operate smoothly and amperage draw should be within range. See COOLING FAN MOTOR AMPERAGE DRAW SPECIFICATIONS table.

***COOLING FAN MOTOR AMPERAGE DRAW SPECIFICATIONS***

| Model | Amps |
|---|---|
| Camry | |
| 4-Cylinder | |
| 2WD M/T | 3.2-4.4 |
| 2WD A/T | 5.8-7.4 |
| 4WD | 8.8-10.8 |
| V6 | |
| Cooling Fan No. 1 (Driver's Side) | 12.1-15.1 |
| Cooling Fan No. 2 | 6.0-7.4 |
| Celica | |
| 3S-GTE Engine | 8.8-10.8 |
| 4A-FE & 5S-FE Engines | 5.8-7.4 |
| Corolla | |
| Coupe | 8.8-10.8 |
| All Others | 5.8-7.4 |
| Land Cruiser | 2.8-3.8 |
| MR2 | |
| Radiator Cooling Fans | |
| A/T | 8.8-10.8 |
| M/T | 5.8-7.4 |
| Engine Compartment Cooling Fan | 3.1-4.3 |
| Tercel | |
| A/T | 8.8-10.8 |
| M/T | 6.0-7.4 |

**Cooling Fan Relay(s) (Camry, Celica, Corolla, Land Cruiser, MR2 & Tercel) – 1)** Disconnect wiring harness from cooling fan relay. On Land Cruiser, cooling fan relay is located behind driver's side kick panel. On all other models, cooling fan relay is located in engine compartment relay/fuse box.

**2)** Check continuity between relay terminals as shown. *See Figs. 4-8.* Replace relay if continuity is not as specified.

***NOTE: MR2 fan main relay may be tested using engine main relay test procedure. See Fig. 10.***

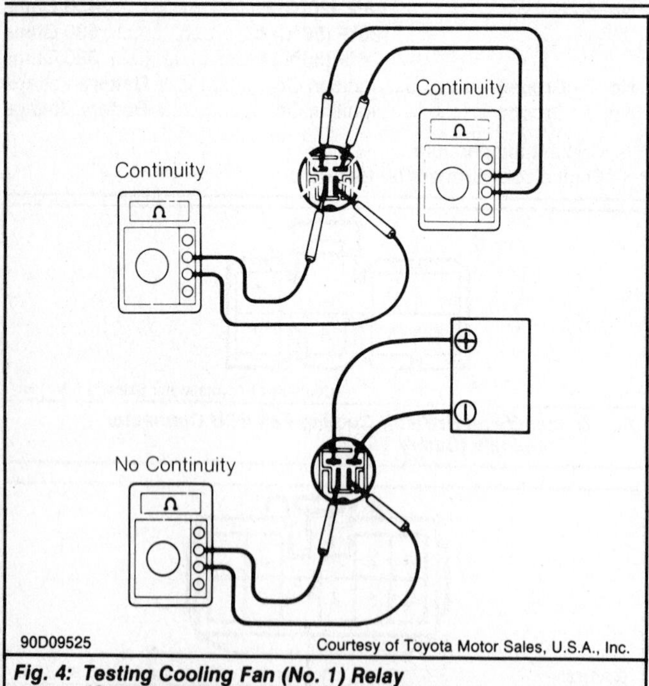


***Fig. 4: Testing Cooling Fan (No. 1) Relay (Camry, Celica, Corolla, MR2 & Tercel)***

**Cooling Fan Relay Circuit (Land Cruiser)** – Disconnect wiring harness from cooling fan relay. Cooling fan relay is located behind passenger's side kick panel. Check for continuity between terminals and ground under conditions specified. See COOLING FAN RELAY CIRCUIT TEST (LAND CRUISER) table. *See Fig. 9.*

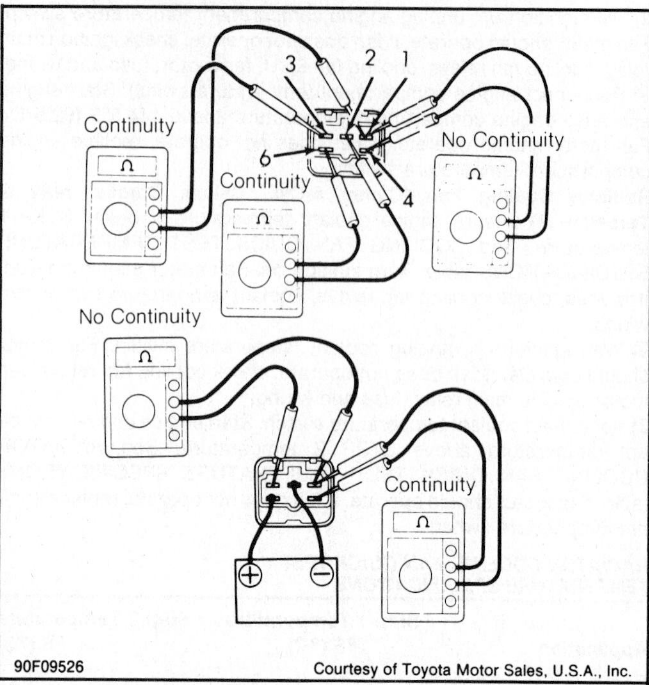


***Fig. 5: Testing Cooling Fan (No. 2) Relay (Camry V6 With A/C)***

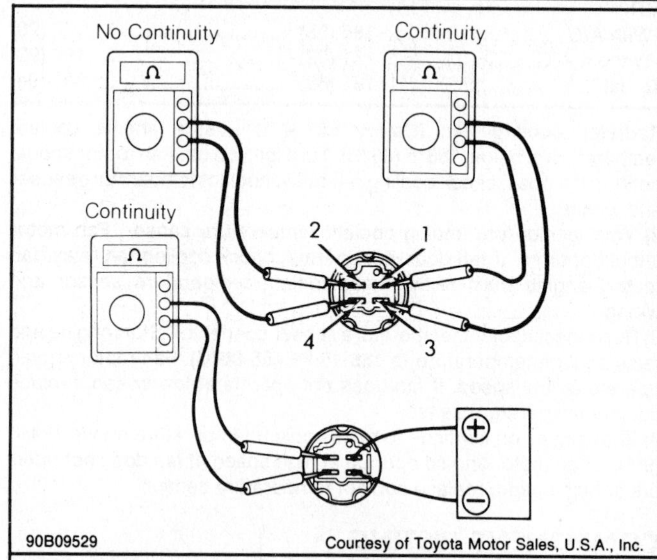


***Fig. 6: Testing Cooling Fan (No. 3) Relay (Camry V6 With A/C & Land Cruiser No. 1)***

***COOLING FAN RELAY CIRCUIT TEST (LAND CRUISER)***

| Wiring Harness Terminal Check | Condition | Specification |
|---|---|---|
| No. 1 - Ground | Always | Battery Voltage |
| No. 2 - Ground | Always | Continuity |
| No. 3 - Ground | Ignition On | Battery Voltage |
| No. 5 - Ground | Always | Continuity |
| No. 6 - Ground | Fan Inoperative | Battery Voltage |

**Coolant Temperature Sensor (Camry V6 & MR2) – 1)** Remove sensor from vehicle. Coolant temperature sensor is located in upper radiator hose coolant inlet on engine.

**2)** Using ohmmeter, measure resistance between sensor terminals while heating sensor in coolant. See COOLANT TEMPERATURE SENSOR RESISTANCE (CAMRY V6 & MR2) table.

# 1991 ENGINE COOLING
# Specifications & Electric Cooling Fans (Cont.)

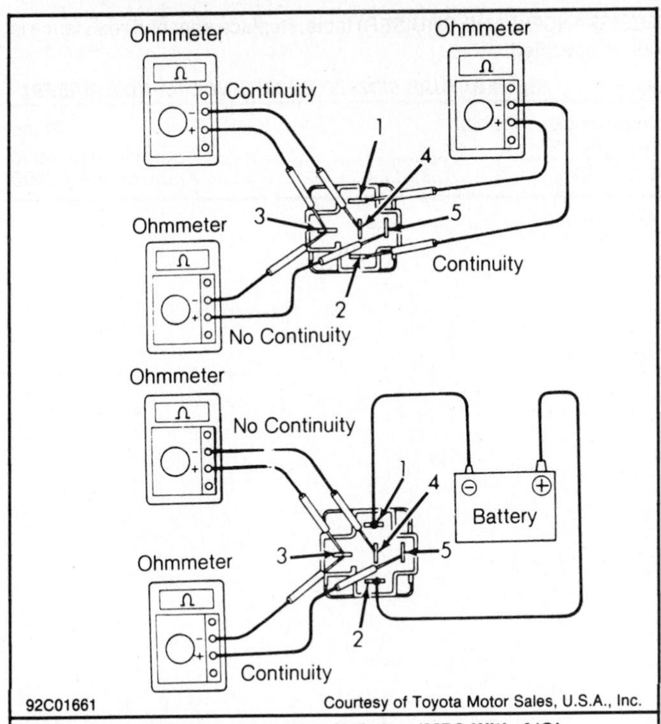


Courtesy of Toyota Motor Sales, U.S.A., Inc.

*Fig. 7: Testing Cooling Fan (No. 2) Relay (MR2 With A/C)*

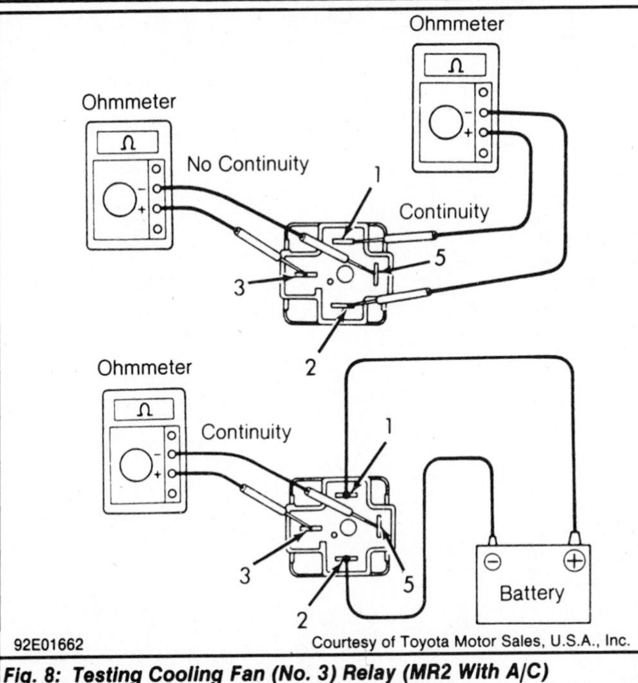


Courtesy of Toyota Motor Sales, U.S.A., Inc.

*Fig. 8: Testing Cooling Fan (No. 3) Relay (MR2 With A/C)*

### COOLANT TEMPERATURE SENSOR RESISTANCE (CAMRY V6 & MR2)

| Temperature °F (°C) | Ohms |
|---|---|
| Camry V6 | |
| 176 (80) | 1530 |
| 194 (90) | 1180 |
| 203 (95) | 1030 |
| MR2 | |
| 185 (85) | 1350 |
| 194 (90) | 1190 |
| 203 (95) | 1050 |

**Coolant Temperature Switch (Camry 4-Cylinder, Celica, Corolla & Tercel) – 1)** Remove switch from vehicle. Coolant temperature switch is located in upper radiator hose coolant inlet on engine. Most switches have a single terminal. Some switches have 2 terminals.

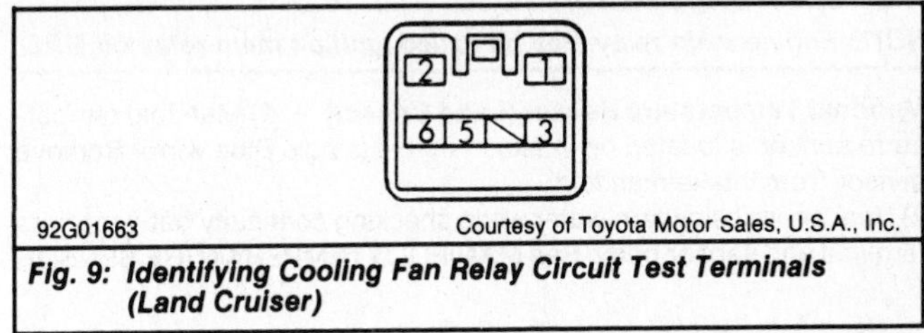


Courtesy of Toyota Motor Sales, U.S.A., Inc.

*Fig. 9: Identifying Cooling Fan Relay Circuit Test Terminals (Land Cruiser)*

**2)** Place switch in container of coolant and heat container. Using ohmmeter, ensure continuity is correct between wire connector and switch body or between both terminals. See COOLANT TEMPERATURE SWITCH CONTINUITY SPECIFICATIONS table.

### COOLANT TEMPERATURE SWITCH CONTINUITY SPECIFICATIONS [1]

| Model | No Continuity °F (°C) | Continuity °F (°C) |
|---|---|---|
| Camry (4-Cyl.), Celica & Corolla | Above 199 (93) | Below 181 (83) |
| Tercel | Above 201 (94) | Below 181 (89) |

[1] – As measured between wire connector and switch body or between switch terminals.

**Engine Compartment Temperature Sensor (MR2 Turbo) –** Remove sensor from forward section of engine compartment. Using ohmmeter, measure resistance between sensor terminals while heating sensor in water. See ENGINE COMPARTMENT TEMPERATURE SENSOR RESISTANCE (MR2 TURBO) table.

### ENGINE COMPARTMENT TEMPERATURE SENSOR RESISTANCE (MR2 TURBO)

| Temperature °F (°C) | Ohms |
|---|---|
| 68 (20) | 2450 |
| 136 (58) | 630 |
| 176 (80) | 320 |

**Engine Main Relay (Camry, Celica, Corolla, MR2 & Tercel) –** Engine main relay supplies power to cooling fan relay. Disconnect wiring harness from engine main relay. Relay is located in engine compartment relay/fuse box. Check continuity between relay terminals as shown. *See Fig. 10.*

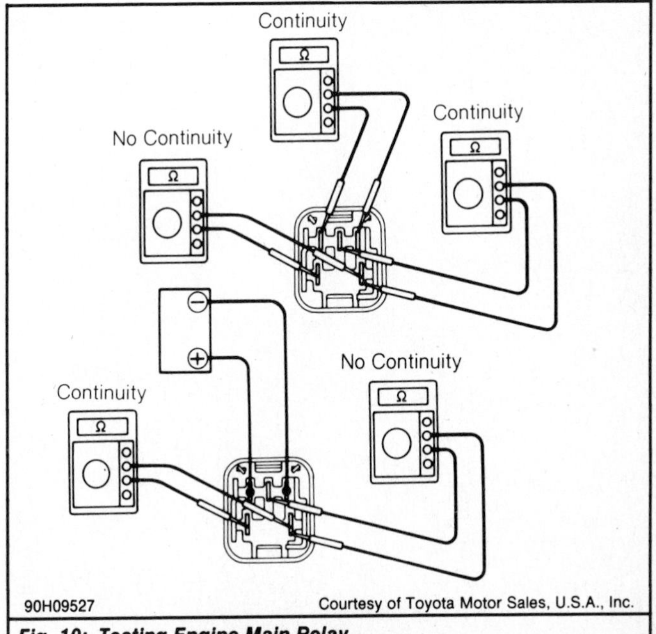


Courtesy of Toyota Motor Sales, U.S.A., Inc.

*Fig. 10: Testing Engine Main Relay (Camry, Celica, Corolla, MR2 & Tercel)*

# 1991 ENGINE COOLING
# Specifications & Electric Cooling Fans (Cont.)

***NOTE: Engine main relay may be called ignition main relay on MR2.***

**Manifold Temperature Sensor (Land Cruiser) – 1)** Manifold temperature sensor is located on intake manifold (single Blue wire). Remove sensor from intake manifold.

**2)** Heat sensor slowly in water while checking continuity between wire terminal and sensor body. See MANIFOLD TEMPERATURE SENSOR RESISTANCE (LAND CRUISER) table. Replace sensor if resistance is not as specified.

***MANIFOLD TEMPERATURE SENSOR RESISTANCE (LAND CRUISER)***

| Temperature °F (°C) | Ohms |
|---|---|
| 194 (90) | Approximately 4000 |
| 230 (110) | Approximately 2000 |

## Camry, Celica, Corolla, Tercel

# DESCRIPTION

Clutch is a single, dry disc type using a hydraulically-operated master cylinder and clutch housing mounted release cylinder. Clutch release cylinder is not adjustable. Clearance is automatically compensated for by internal design of cylinder.

# ADJUSTMENTS

## CLUTCH PEDAL HEIGHT

Pedal height is measured from highest point of pedal pad to area of floor contacted when pedal is fully depressed. Loosen pedal stop bolt at top of pedal assembly to adjust pedal height from floor. *See Fig. 1.* See CLUTCH PEDAL HEIGHT SPECIFICATIONS table.

**CLUTCH PEDAL HEIGHT SPECIFICATIONS**

| Application | In. (mm) |
|---|---|
| Camry | 7.13-7.52 (181.1-191.0) |
| Celica | 6.41-6.80 (162.8-172.7) |
| Corolla | 5.71-6.10 (145.0-154.9) |
| Tercel | |
| 4-Speed | 5.69-6.08 (144.5-154.4) |
| 5-Speed | 5.51-5.91 (140.0-150.1) |

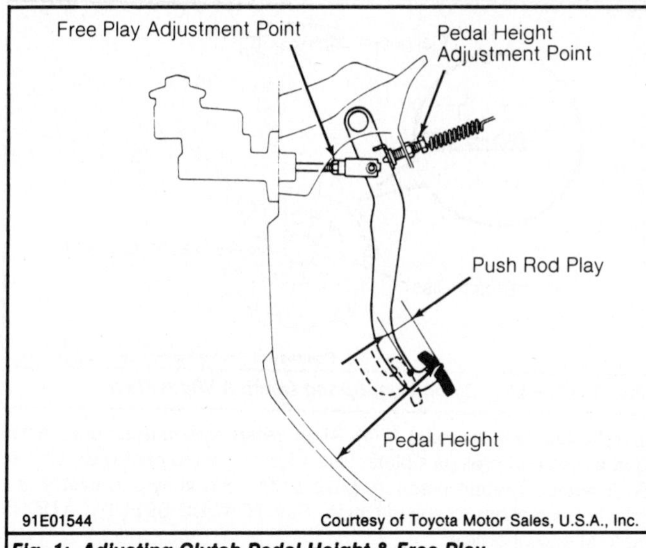


**Fig. 1: Adjusting Clutch Pedal Height & Free Play**

## CLUTCH PEDAL FREE PLAY

**1)** Push in on clutch pedal until beginning of clutch resistance is felt. Clutch pedal free play should be .20-.59" (5.0-15.0 mm). *See Fig. 2.*

**2)** To adjust free play, loosen lock nut on master cylinder push rod and turn push rod to obtain correct pedal free play. *See Fig. 1.* Tighten lock nut, and recheck pedal height.

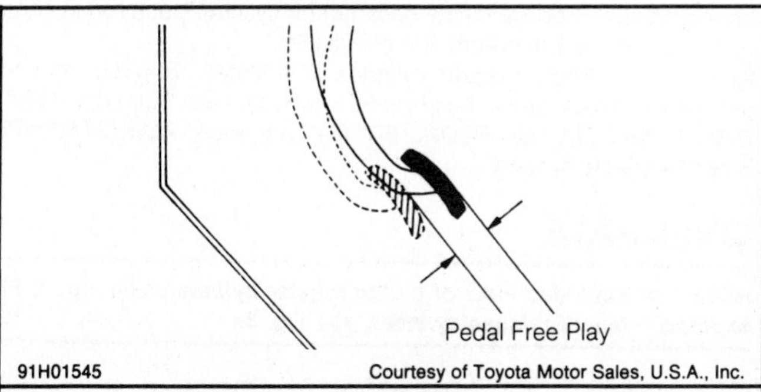


**Fig. 2: Measuring Clutch Pedal Free Play**

## CLUTCH START SYSTEM

**Switch Adjustment – 1)** Ensure engine does not start when clutch pedal is released. Ensure engine starts when clutch pedal is fully depressed. On Corolla, ensure clearance "A" is greater than 0.04" (1.0 mm) when clutch is fully depressed. *See Fig. 3.*

**2)** For all models, if system is not operating correctly, check clutch start switch. With switch in ON (pushed) position, continuity should exist. With switch in OFF (free) position, continuity should not exist. See CLUTCH SWITCH PLUNGER CONTINUITY SPECIFICATIONS table. *See Fig. 4.* Replace or adjust switch as necessary.

**CLUTCH SWITCH PLUNGER CONTINUITY SPECIFICATIONS** [1]

| Application | In. (mm) |
|---|---|
| Camry, Celica & Tercel | .176-.216 (4.5-5.5) |
| Corolla | .374-.414 (9.5-10.5) |

[1] – Distance from threaded end of switch where continuity changes. *See Fig. 4.*

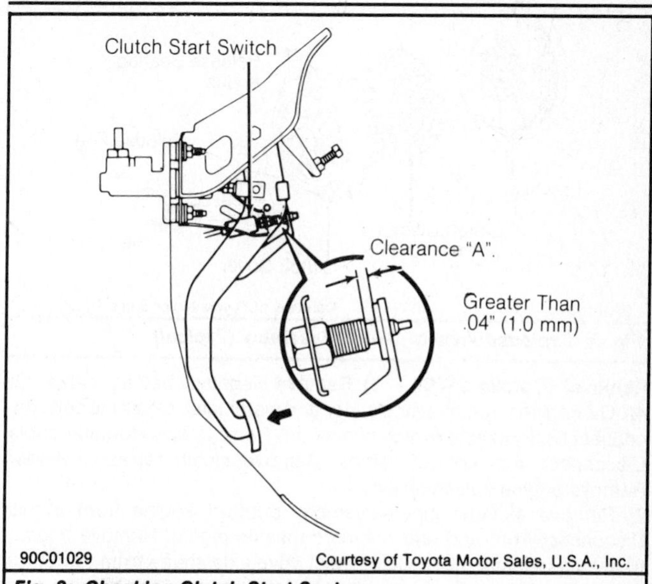


**Fig. 3: Checking Clutch Start System (Corolla Shown; Camry, Celica & Tercel Are Similar)**

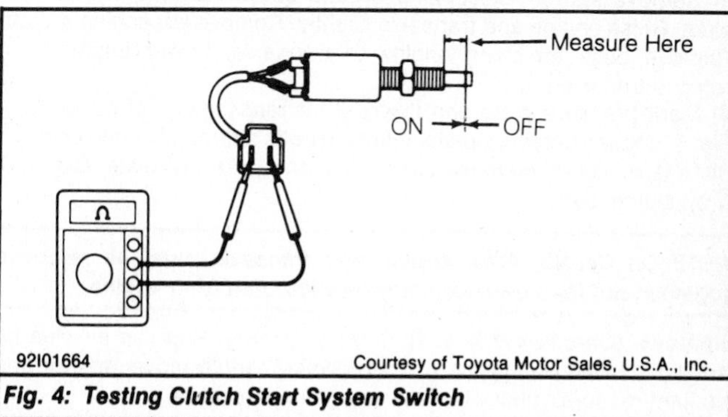


**Fig. 4: Testing Clutch Start System Switch**

# REMOVAL & INSTALLATION

## CLUTCH ASSEMBLY

**Removal (Camry, Celica & Tercel) – 1)** Remove negative battery cable. Remove air cleaner. Remove clutch release cylinder, bracket and starter. Disconnect back-up light switch connector and shift control cables.

**2)** Remove upper transaxle mounting bolts. Raise and support vehicle. Remove engine splash shield(s). Drain transaxle fluid. Disconnect speedometer cable. Remove suspension lower crossmember and engine mounting centermember (if equipped).

# 1991 CLUTCHES
# FWD (Cont.)

3) Disconnect drive axle shafts from transaxle. See FWD AXLE SHAFTS article in DRIVE AXLES. On Camry, remove intermediate shaft and stabilizer bar. Disconnect left steering knuckle from lower arm, and remove left drive shaft.
4) On all vehicles, raise engine and transaxle slightly using a jack. Disconnect necessary engine mountings. Remove bolts attaching engine to transaxle. Lower engine, and remove transaxle.

***NOTE: On Celica 4WD, when removing transaxle from engine, pull transaxle straight away from engine and rotate end of transaxle rearward until transaxle can be removed.***

5) Mark pressure plate and flywheel for reassembly reference. *See Fig. 5.* Loosen pressure plate attaching bolts alternately until pressure plate is released. Remove clutch disc and pressure plate. DO NOT drop clutch disc.

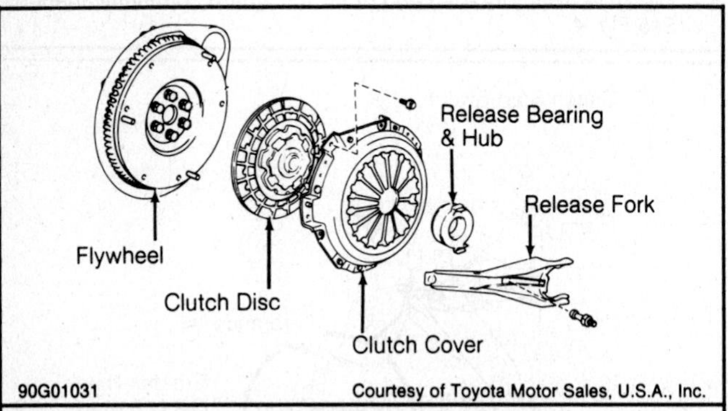


***Fig. 5: Exploded View of Clutch Assembly (Typical)***

**Removal (Corolla 2WD) – 1)** Remove negative battery cable. On 4A-GE engines, remove air cleaner and water inlet. On all models, disconnect back-up light switch connector. Remove speedometer cable. Disconnect shift control cables. Remove clutch release cylinder. Remove engine splash shield.
**2)** Remove exhaust pipe assembly. Support engine from above. Disconnect front and rear engine/transaxle mount. Remove engine/transaxle crossmember. Disconnect drive axle shafts from transaxle. Disconnect left steering knuckle from lower control arm. Remove left drive shaft. See FWD AXLE SHAFTS article in DRIVE AXLES.
**3)** Remove starter. Disconnect ground strap. Remove engine rear plate. Raise engine and transaxle slightly. Remove left engine mount. Remove bolts attaching engine to transaxle. Lower engine, and remove transaxle.
**4)** Mark pressure plate and flywheel for reassembly reference. *See Fig. 5.* Loosen pressure plate attaching bolts alternately until pressure plate is released. Remove clutch disc and pressure plate. DO NOT drop clutch disc.

***NOTE: On Corolla 4WD, engine and transaxle must be removed together and then transaxle may be separated from engine.***

**Removal (Corolla 4WD) – 1)** Remove battery. Remove air cleaner and windshield washer tank. Drain coolant, and remove radiator and coolant reservoir tank. Remove engine undercovers.
**2)** Remove power steering pump drive belt and power steering pump. Raise and support vehicle. Disconnect tie rod ends from steering knuckles. Remove left and right drive shafts. See FWD AXLE SHAFTS article in DRIVE AXLES. Remove propeller shaft.
**3)** Remove front exhaust pipe. Disconnect steering knuckles from lower arms. Disconnect all electrical wiring and vacuum hoses from engine and transaxle. Disconnect fuel lines from engine. Remove throttle cable. Disconnect speedometer cable and shift control cables. Drain transaxle fluid.
**4)** Remove clutch release cylinder and starter. Support engine/transaxle assembly using jack. Disconnect engine/transaxle mounts. Remove engine/transaxle crossmember (if equipped). Slowly lower engine/transaxle assembly. Remove power steering pump bracket and transfer stiffener plates.
**5)** Remove transfer case vacuum actuator. Remove bolts attaching engine to transaxle. Pull transaxle straight out of engine 2-3" (51-76 mm). Rotate transfer output shaft down and remove transaxle.
**6)** Mark pressure plate and flywheel for reassembly reference. *See Fig. 5.* Loosen pressure plate attaching bolts alternately until pressure plate is released. Remove clutch disc and pressure plate. DO NOT drop clutch disc.

**Inspection (All Models) – 1)** Check wear on facings of clutch disc by measuring depth of each rivet head. Minimum depth at any rivet is .012" (.30 mm). Maximum runout of clutch disc facing is .031" (.79 mm). Replace clutch disc if it is not within specifications.
**2)** Check diaphragm spring and pressure plate for wear and damage. If assembly is excessively worn or damaged, replace pressure plate. Check pilot bearing rotation. If bearing rotates roughly, replace bearing. Check release bearing for rough rotation. Replace bearing and hub as necessary.
**3)** Inspect flywheel runout. Maximum runout is .004" (.10 mm). If runout is excessive, replace flywheel. Clean flywheel and pressure plate of all oil, grease and metal deposits. Inspect for damage, cracks and warpage. Slight surface scoring can be removed using sandpaper. Replace or repair as necessary.
**4)** Using calipers, inspect diaphragm spring for depth and width of wear. *See Fig. 6.* Maximum depth is .024" (.060 mm); maximum width is .197" (5.0 mm).

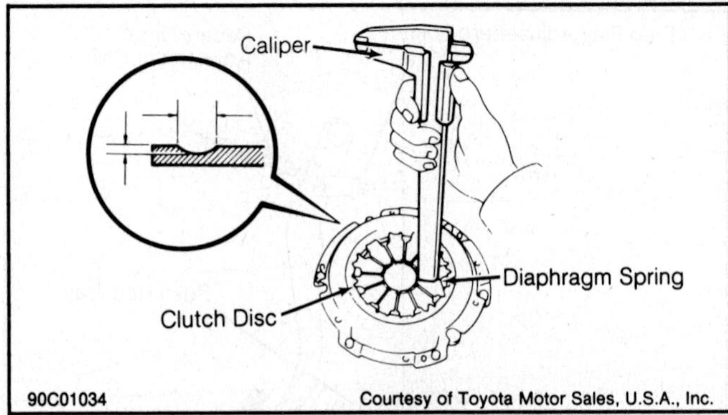


***Fig. 6: Checking Diaphragm Spring Depth & Width Wear***

**Installation (All Models) – 1)** Align reference marks, and install clutch disc and pressure plate. Use aligning tool to center clutch disc on flywheel. Tighten pressure plate bolts alternately and evenly in a crisscross pattern to specification. See TORQUE SPECIFICATIONS table at end of article.
**2)** Apply molybdenum disulfide grease to release fork contact surfaces, release bearing and hub, and clutch disc splines. Reverse removal procedure to complete installation.

## CLUTCH MASTER CYLINDER

**Removal & Installation – 1)** On Camry, remove lower instrument finish panel, and disconnect air duct from panel. On Celica Turbo, remove front suspension brace. On Corolla (4A-GE), remove brake booster. On all models, disconnect master cylinder push rod at clutch pedal. Disconnect hydraulic line at cylinder.
**2)** Remove clutch master cylinder. To install, reverse removal procedure. Adjust pedal height and free play. See CLUTCH PEDAL HEIGHT and CLUTCH PEDAL FREE PLAY under ADJUSTMENTS. Bleed hydraulic system.

# OVERHAUL

***NOTE: For exploded view of clutch master cylinder, see Fig. 7. For exploded view of release cylinder, see Fig. 8.***

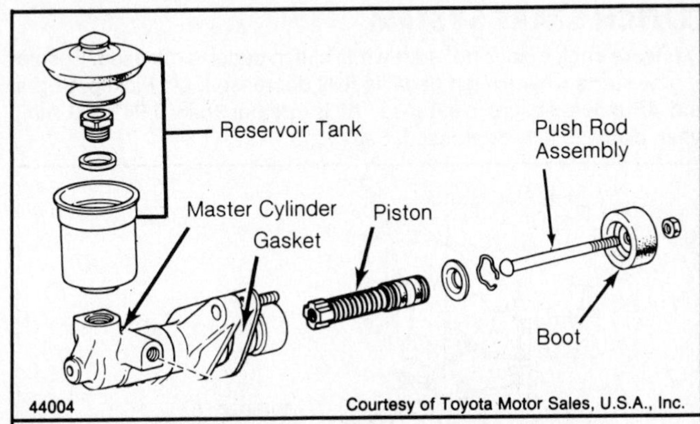


**Fig. 7: Exploded View of Clutch Master Cylinder (Typical)**

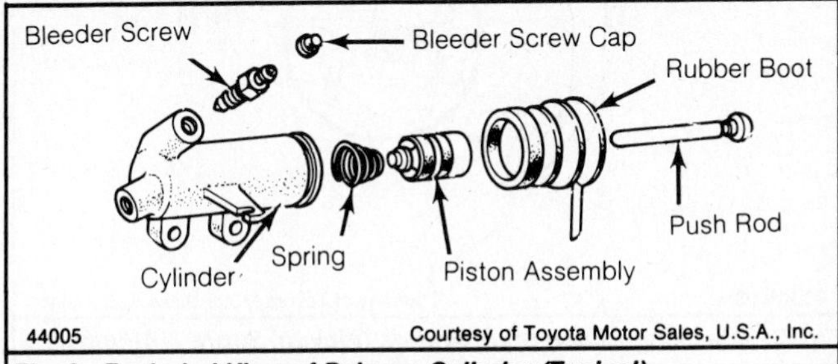


**Fig. 8: Exploded View of Release Cylinder (Typical)**

# TORQUE SPECIFICATIONS

***TORQUE SPECIFICATIONS***

| Application | Ft. Lbs. (N.m) |
|---|---|
| Flywheel Bolts | |
| Camry | |
| 4-Cylinder | 65 (88) |
| V6 | 61 (83) |
| Celica | |
| 4A-FE | 58 (79) |
| 3S-GTE | 80 (108) |
| 5S-FE | 72 (98) |
| Corolla | |
| 4A-FE | 58 (79) |
| 4A-GE | 54 (73) |
| Tercel | 65 (88) |
| Pressure Plate Bolts | 14 (19) |
| Transaxle-To-Engine Bolts | |
| 10-mm Bolts | 34 (46) |
| 12-mm Bolts | 47 (64) |

# 1991 CLUTCHES
# RWD

## MR2, Pickup, Previa, Supra, 4Runner

## DESCRIPTION

Clutch is a single, dry disc type using a hydraulically operated master cylinder and clutch housing mounted release cylinder. Clutch release cylinder is nonadjustable. Clearance is automatically compensated by internal design of cylinder. Previa also has an accumulator.

## ADJUSTMENTS

### CLUTCH PEDAL HEIGHT

**Adjustment** – Pedal height is measured from highest point of pedal pad to area of floor contacted when pedal is fully depressed. Loosen pedal stop bolt at top of pedal assembly to adjust pedal height from floor. *See Fig. 1.* See CLUTCH PEDAL HEIGHT SPECIFICATIONS table.

***CLUTCH PEDAL HEIGHT SPECIFICATIONS***

| Application | In. (mm) |
|---|---|
| MR2 | 7.20-7.60 (182.9-193.0) |
| Pickup & 4Runner | |
| 2WD | 6.08 (154.4) |
| 4WD | 5.96 (151.4) |
| Previa | 6.46 (164.1) |
| Supra | 6.18-6.57 (157.0-166.8) |

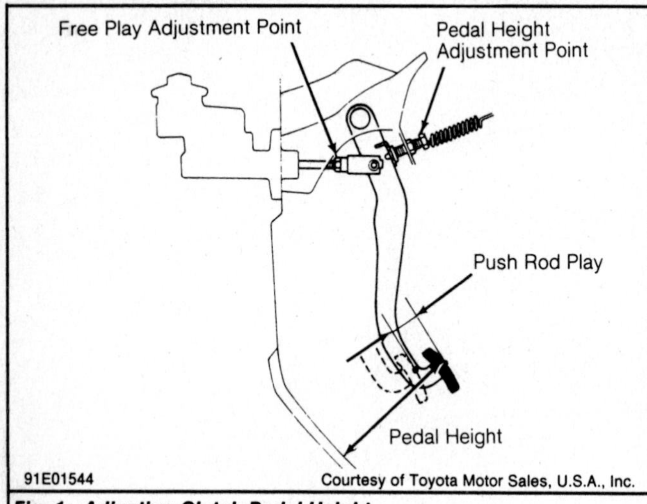


***Fig. 1: Adjusting Clutch Pedal Height***

### CLUTCH PEDAL FREE PLAY

**Adjustment** – **1)** Push in on clutch pedal until the beginning of clutch resistance is felt. *See Fig. 2.* Clutch pedal free play should be .20-.59" (5.0-15.0 mm).

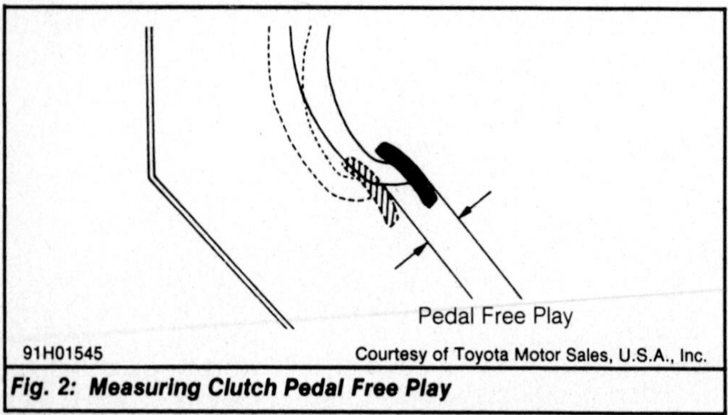


***Fig. 2: Measuring Clutch Pedal Free Play***

**2)** To adjust, loosen lock nut on master cylinder push rod and turn push rod to obtain correct pedal free play. *See Fig. 1.* Tighten lock nut and recheck pedal height.

### CLUTCH START SYSTEM

**1)** Ensure engine does not start when clutch pedal is released. Ensure engine starts when clutch pedal is fully depressed. On Pickup, Supra and 4Runner, ensure clearance "A" is greater than 0.04" (1.0 mm) when clutch is fully depressed. *See Fig. 3.*

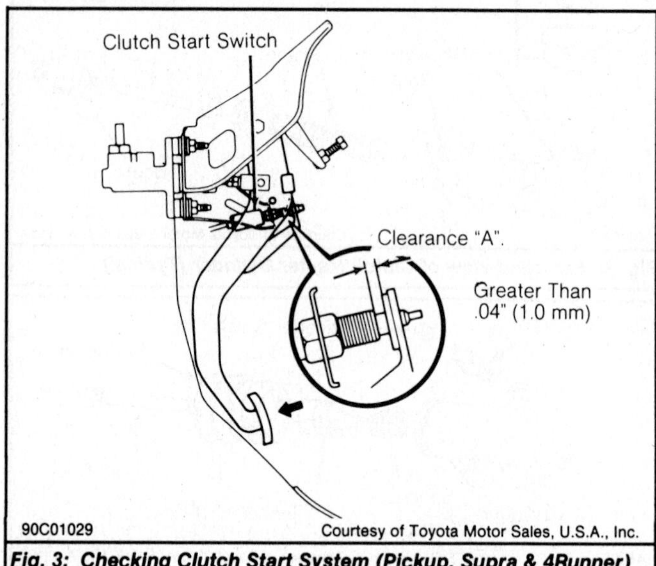


***Fig. 3: Checking Clutch Start System (Pickup, Supra & 4Runner)***

**2)** For all models, if system is not operating correctly, check clutch start switch. See CLUTCH START SWITCH under TESTING.

## TESTING

### CLUTCH START CANCEL SWITCH

**Continuity Inspection (Pickup & 4Runner)** – **1)** Remove clutch start cancel switch from dash. Using an ohmmeter, ensure there is no continuity between switch connector terminals No. 1 (negative lead) and No. 2 (positive lead). *See Fig. 4.* Replace switch if continuity is present.

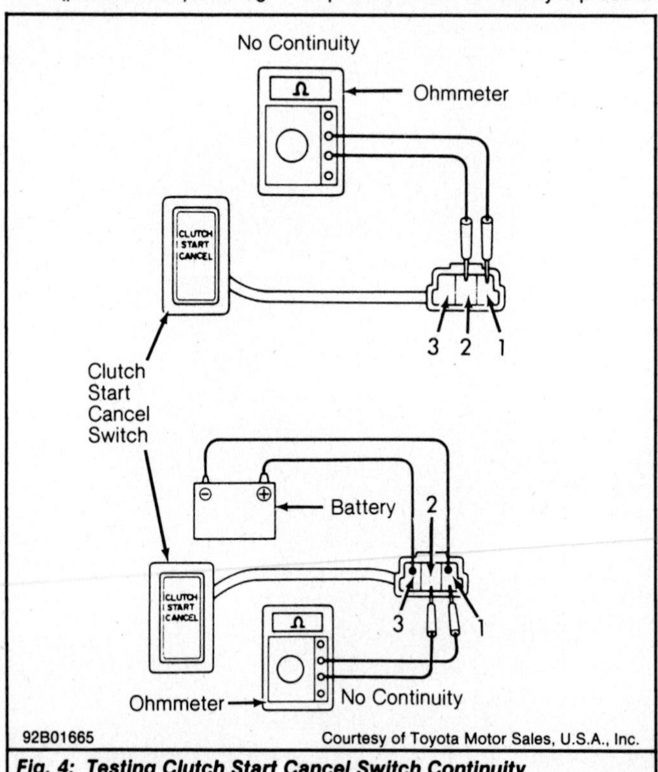


***Fig. 4: Testing Clutch Start Cancel Switch Continuity (Pickup & 4Runner)***

**2)** Check for continuity between switch connector terminals No. 1 and No. 3 and between terminals No. 2 and No. 3. *See Fig. 4*. If continuity is not present, go to next step. If continuity is present, replace switch.
**3)** Connect battery voltage to switch connector terminals No. 3 (positive) and No. 1 (negative). *See Fig. 4*. Using an ohmmeter, ensure that no continuity is present between switch connector terminals No. 1 and No. 2. Replace switch if continuity is present.
**4)** With battery still connected and ohmmeter still connected between terminals No. 1 and No. 2, press switch button. *See Fig. 4*. Continuity should be present. Replace switch if continuity is not present when switch button is pressed.
**5)** Disconnect battery positive lead. Continuity should no longer be present between terminals No. 1 and No. 2. Replace switch if continuity is still present.

## CLUTCH START SWITCH

**Continuity Testing** – With switch in the ON (pushed) position, continuity should exist. With switch in the OFF (free) position, continuity should not exist. See CLUTCH START SWITCH CONTINUITY SPECIFICATIONS table. *See Fig. 5*. Replace or adjust switch as necessary.

***CLUTCH START SWITCH CONTINUITY SPECIFICATIONS*** [1]

| Application | In. (mm) |
|---|---|
| MR2 & Previa | .176-.216 (4.5-5.5) |
| Pickup, Supra & 4Runner | .374-.414 (9.5-10.5) |

[1] – Distance of plunger tip from threaded end of switch where continuity changes. *See Fig. 5*.

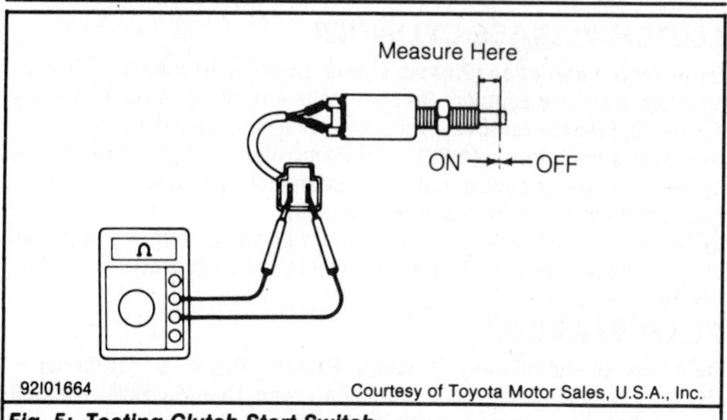


***Fig. 5: Testing Clutch Start Switch***

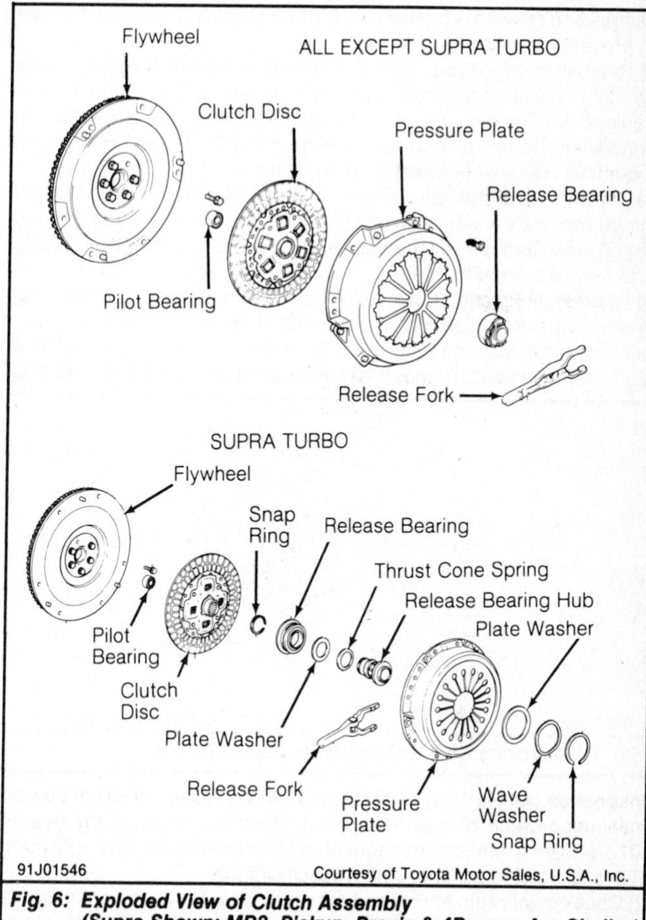


***Fig. 6: Exploded View of Clutch Assembly (Supra Shown; MR2, Pickup, Previa & 4Runner Are Similar)***

# REMOVAL & INSTALLATION

## CLUTCH ASSEMBLY

**Removal (MR2)** – **1)** Disconnect negative battery cable. Remove air cleaner assembly. Disconnect control cables, speedometer cable and ground cable. Remove left side engine mounting stay. Remove starter. Remove clutch release cylinder with hydraulic line connected.
**2)** Raise and support vehicle. Remove engine under covers and front exhaust pipe. Disconnect stabilizer bar from strut. Disconnect tie rod ends and lower arms from knuckles.
**3)** Remove drive axle shafts from transaxle. See RWD AXLE SHAFTS article in DRIVE AXLES. Raise transaxle slightly with jack. Disconnect front and rear engine mounting brackets. Remove transaxle mounting bolts. Pull transaxle from engine.
**4)** Reference mark pressure plate and flywheel for reassembly. *See Fig. 6*. Alternately loosen pressure plate attaching bolts until pressure plate is released. Remove clutch disc and pressure plate.
**Removal (Pickup & 4Runner)** – **1)** Disconnect battery cable. Remove fan shroud bolts. On 4WD V6, remove heater hose clamp. On all models, remove transmission shift lever and transfer case shift lever (if equipped). Raise and support vehicle.
**2)** Drain transmission and transfer case fluid (if equipped). Remove propeller shaft dust cover (if equipped). Disconnect propeller shaft. Disconnect speedometer cable, back-up light switch connector and transfer indicator switch connector (if equipped).
**3)** Remove exhaust pipe, clamp and bracket (if equipped). Remove clutch release cylinder from transmission but do not disconnect hydraulic line. On 4WD V6, remove front differential set bolts and support differential. On all models, remove stabilizer bracket bolts.
**4)** On 2WD 4-cylinder, remove frame auxiliary crossmember. On all models, raise transmission slightly with a jack. Remove crossmember (V6) or engine rear mounting and bracket (4-cylinder). Place a small piece of wood on front crossmember. Lower transmission slightly.
**5)** Remove starter, exhaust pipe bracket and stiffener plate. Remove remaining transmission bolts. Slowly pull transmission (and transfer case, if equipped) rearward. On some 2WD V6 models, transmission may need to be rotated clockwise 45 degrees before removing.
**6)** Reference mark pressure plate and flywheel for reassembly. *See Fig. 6*. Alternately loosen pressure plate attaching bolts until pressure plate is released. Remove clutch disc and pressure plate.
**Removal (Previa)** – **1)** Disconnect negative battery cable. Raise and support vehicle. Reference mark propeller shaft flanges and remove propeller shaft(s). Insert plug into extension housing to prevent oil spillage.
**2)** Remove starter and front propeller shaft bracket (if equipped). Remove clutch release cylinder with hydraulic line connected. Remove exhaust pipe and bracket. Disconnect control cables and speed sensor connection. Remove control cable bracket and stiffener plate.
**3)** Raise transmission slightly with jack. Remove rear engine mounting bolts. Raise rear of engine slightly with jack. Remove remaining transmission mounting bolts. Pull transmission rearward and remove.
**4)** Reference mark pressure plate and flywheel for reassembly. *See Fig. 6*. Alternately loosen pressure plate attaching bolts until pressure plate is released. Remove clutch disc and pressure plate.
**Removal (Supra)** – **1)** Disconnect negative battery cable. Remove center cluster finish panel. Remove shift lever. Raise and support vehicle. Drain transmission fluid. Reference mark propeller shaft

# 1991 CLUTCHES RWD (Cont.)

flanges and remove propeller shaft. Insert plug into extension housing to prevent oil spillage.

**2)** Remove front exhaust pipe. Disconnect speedometer cable, back-up light switch connector and rear speed sensor connector (if equipped). Remove clutch release cylinder with hydraulic line connected. Raise transmission slightly with jack. Remove rear engine mounting. Remove flywheel housing cover.

**3)** On non-turbo models, remove transmission mounting bolts and slowly remove transmission. On turbo models, remove 2 clutch housing covers. Remove clutch release fork. Reference mark clutch cover and flywheel. *See Fig. 6.*

**4)** Alternately loosen clutch cover bolts while rotating flywheel from crankshaft pulley. *See Fig. 7.* After clutch cover bolts are removed, push clutch cover and disc toward transmission. Remove transmission mounting bolts. Remove transmission with clutch cover and disc.

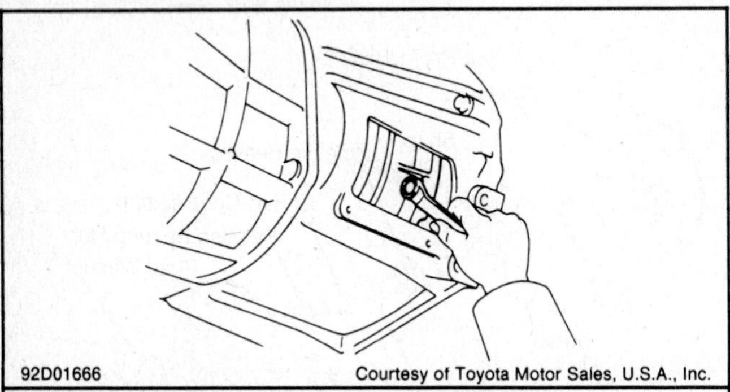

92D01666 Courtesy of Toyota Motor Sales, U.S.A., Inc.

***Fig. 7: Removing Clutch Cover Bolts (Supra Turbo)***

**Inspection (All Models) - 1)** Check wear on facings of clutch disc by measuring depth of each rivet head. Minimum depth at any rivet is .012" (.30 mm). Maximum runout of clutch disc facing is .031" (.79 mm). Replace clutch disc if not within specifications.

**2)** Check diaphragm spring and pressure plate for wear or damage. If the assembly is excessively worn or damaged, replace pressure plate. Check pilot bearing rotation. If bearing rotates roughly, replace bearing. Check release bearing for smooth rotation. Replace bearing and hub as necessary.

**3)** Inspect flywheel runout. Maximum runout is .008" (.20 mm) for Supra and .004" (.10 mm) for all others. If runout is excessive, replace flywheel. Clean flywheel and pressure plate of all oil, grease, and metal deposits. Inspect for damage, cracks or warpage. Slight surface scoring can be removed with sandpaper. Replace or repair as necessary.

**4)** Using calipers, inspect diaphragm spring for depth and width of wear. Maximum depth is .024" (.060 mm). Maximum width is .197" (5.0 mm). *See Fig. 8.*

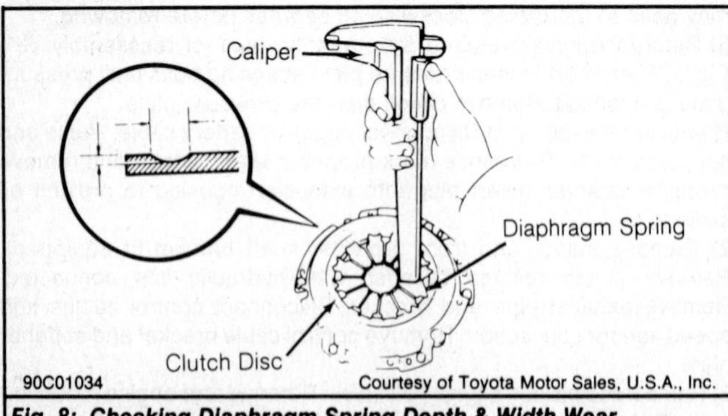


90C01034 Courtesy of Toyota Motor Sales, U.S.A., Inc.

***Fig. 8: Checking Diaphragm Spring Depth & Width Wear***

**Installation (MR2, Pickup, Previa, Supra Non-Turbo & 4Runner) - 1)** Align reference marks and install clutch disc and pressure plate. Use aligning tool to center clutch disc on flywheel. Tighten pressure plate bolts alternately and evenly in a crisscross pattern to specification. See TORQUE SPECIFICATIONS table at end of article.

**2)** Apply molybdenum disulfide grease to release fork contact surfaces, release bearing and hub, and clutch disc splines. Reverse removal procedure to complete installation.

**Installation (Supra Turbo) - 1)** Apply molybdenum disulfide grease to release fork contact surfaces, release bearing and hub, and clutch disc splines. Install clutch cover and clutch disc on transmission input shaft.

**2)** Install transmission to engine and tighten transmission-to-engine bolts. See TORQUE SPECIFICATIONS table at end of article. Align reference marks and install clutch cover bolts through access holes. *See Fig. 7.*

**3)** Tighten clutch cover bolts alternately and evenly in a crisscross pattern to specification. See TORQUE SPECIFICATIONS table at end of article. Reverse removal procedure to complete installation.

## CLUTCH MASTER CYLINDER

**Removal & Installation - 1)** On MR2, remove retractor control relay from engine compartment. On Previa, remove lower instrument finish panel and steering column cover. On Supra, remove lower instrument finish panel and disconnect air duct from panel.

**2)** On all models, disconnect master cylinder push rod at clutch pedal. On Previa, disconnect reservoir hose at cylinder. On all models, disconnect hydraulic line at cylinder.

**3)** Remove clutch master cylinder. To install, reverse removal procedure. Adjust pedal height and free play. See CLUTCH PEDAL HEIGHT and CLUTCH PEDAL FREE PLAY under ADJUSTMENTS in this article. Bleed hydraulic system.

## CLUTCH RELEASE CYLINDER

**Removal & Installation (Pickup, Previa, Supra & 4Runner) -** Disconnect hydraulic line at union. Remove bolts and clutch release cylinder. To install, reverse removal procedure. Bleed hydraulic system.

**Removal & Installation (MR2) - 1)** Remove engine under cover. Disconnect transaxle control cables. Disconnect hydraulic line at union. Support engine and transaxle with a jack.

**2)** Remove front engine mounting bracket bolts. Remove bolts and clutch release cylinder. To install, reverse removal procedure. Bleed hydraulic system.

## PILOT BEARING

**Removal & Installation (Pickup, Previa, Supra & 4Runner) -** Remove pilot bearing from crankshaft with Bearing Puller (09303-3011). Coat new bearing with multipurpose grease and drive into crankshaft with Bearing Driver (09304-30012).

# OVERHAUL

***NOTE: For exploded view of clutch master cylinder, see Fig. 9 or 10. For exploded view of clutch release cylinder, see Fig. 11.***

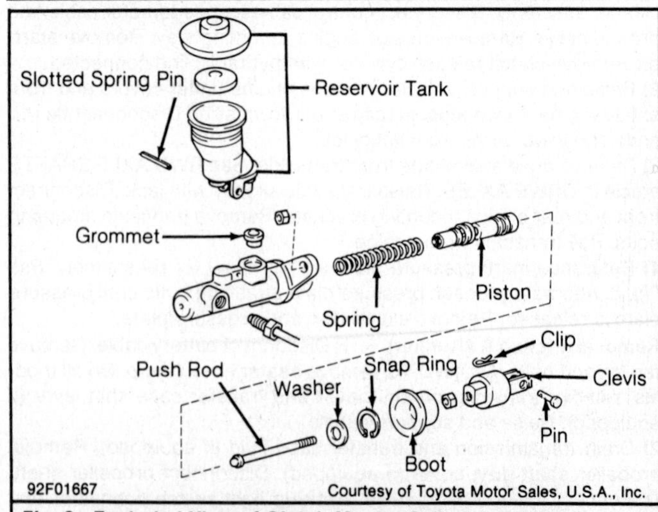


92F01667 Courtesy of Toyota Motor Sales, U.S.A., Inc.

***Fig. 9: Exploded View of Clutch Master Cylinder (Pickup & 4Runner Shown; MR2, Previa & Supra Are Similar)***

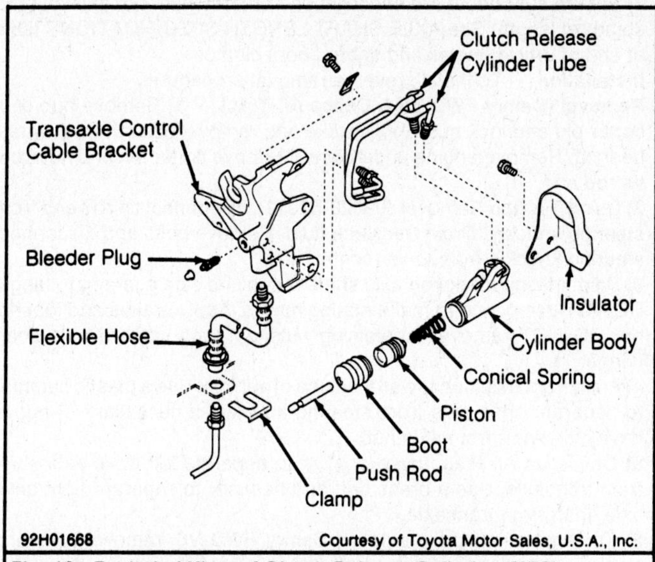


***Fig. 10: Exploded View of Clutch Release Cylinder (MR2)***

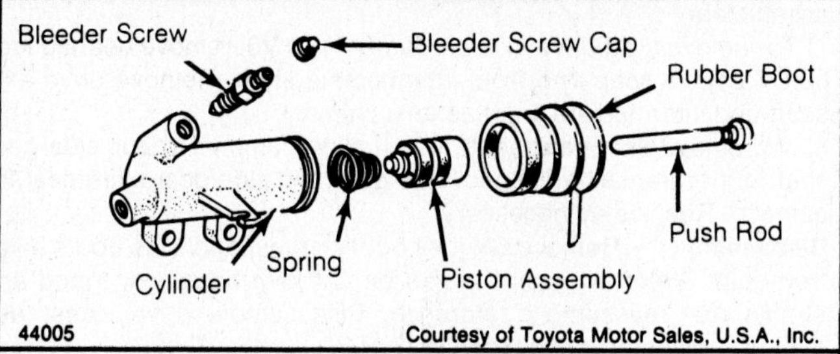


***Fig. 11: Exploded View of Clutch Release Cylinder (Supra Shown; Pickup, Previa & 4Runner Are Similar)***

## TORQUE SPECIFICATIONS

***TORQUE SPECIFICATIONS***

| Application | Ft. Lbs. (N.m) |
|---|---|
| Clutch Cover Bolts (Supra) | 14 (19) |
| Flywheel Bolts | |
| MR2 | 72 (98) |
| Pickup & 4Runner | |
| 22R-E | 80 (109) |
| 3VZ-E | 65 (88) |
| Previa | 65 (88) |
| Supra | 54 (73) |
| Pressure Plate Bolts | 14 (19) |
| Propeller Shaft Flange Bolts | |
| Previa Front Shaft (4WD) | 31 (42) |
| All Others | 54-56 (73-76) |
| Starter Mounting Bolts | 29 (39) |
| Transmission-To-Engine Bolts | |
| MR2 | 47 (64) |
| Pickup, Previa & 4Runner | |
| Upper | 53 (72) |
| Lower | 27 (37) |
| Supra | 29 (39) |

# 1991 DRIVE AXLES
# FWD Axle Shafts

## Camry, Celica, Corolla, Tercel

## DESCRIPTION

Axle shafts transfer power from transaxle to driving wheels. All axle shafts consist of a shaft and flexible Constant Velocity (CV) joint at each end. Inner CV joint is splined or bolted to transaxle. Outer CV joint is splined to hub assembly and secured by axle shaft nut.

The inner CV joint is a plunging tripod joint. The plunging action allows for axle shaft length change as suspension moves up and down.

The inner and outer CV joints are enclosed by a CV joint boot. The boot maintains lubrication in the joint and prevents contamination of CV lubricant. Boots must be replaced when signs of leakage or cracks are present. The inner CV joint can be repaired without replacing assembly. The outer CV joint must be replaced as an assembly.

## REMOVAL, DISASSEMBLY, REASSEMBLY & INSTALLATION

***NOTE: Manufacturer recommends removing right drive axle and intermediate shaft as an assembly***

**Removal (Camry FWD 4-Cylinder) - 1)** Remove hub cap, cotter pin and lock nut. Apply brake and remove lock nut from wheel bearing. Remove engine splash shields. Drain transaxle fluid. Remove cotter pin and nut from tie rod end.

**2)** Using Tie Rod Remover (09628-62011), disconnect tie rod end from steering knuckle. Remove bolts and disconnect steering knuckle from lower control arm.

**3)** Using a plastic hammer, drive axle shaft out of bearing hub. Using a pry bar, pry drive axle from transaxle and remove axle. Inspect drive axle seal and replace as necessary.

**Disassembly -** Remove CV joint boot clamps and slide boots away from joint. Paint alignment marks on CV joint housings, tripod and shaft(s) for reassembly reference. Disassemble drive axles; use exploded views for guide. *See Fig. 3.*

**Reassembly - 1)** To reassemble drive axles, reverse disassembly procedure. Ensure dust covers are 3.39-3.43" (86-87 mm) from end of shaft (splined end). *See Fig. 1.* On GKN drive axles, clearance between dust cover and bearing should be .04-.08" (1-2 mm).

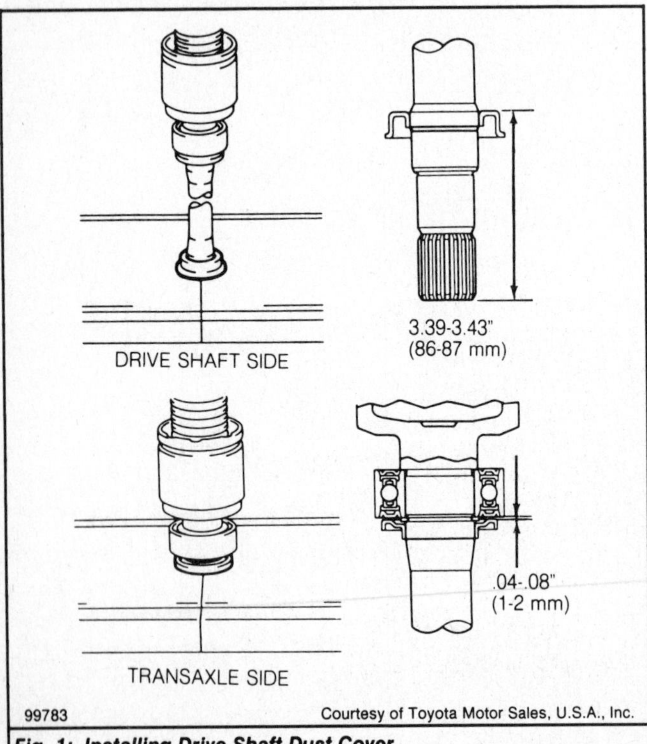


***Fig. 1: Installing Drive Shaft Dust Cover***

**2)** Ensure dust boots are not collapsed or stretched. Set axle shaft to standard length. See AXLE SHAFT LENGTH SPECIFICATIONS table at end of article. Install and tighten boot clamps.

**Installation -** To install, reverse removal procedure.

**Removal (Camry FWD V6 & Celica All-Trac) - 1)** Remove hub cap, cotter pin and lock nut. Apply brake and remove lock nut from wheel bearing. Remove engine undercover. Remove cotter pin and nut from tie rod end.

**2)** Using Tie Rod Remover (09628-62011), disconnect tie rod end from steering knuckle. Drain transaxle fluid. Remove bolts and disconnect steering knuckle from lower control arm.

**3)** Paint mating marks on axle shaft flange and side gear shaft flange. DO NOT use punch to make mating marks. Apply brakes and loosen, but DO NOT remove, 6 retaining nuts on each inboard axle shaft flange.

**4)** Push front axle hub toward outside of vehicle. Use a plastic hammer to separate drive axle from steering knuckle, if necessary. Remove drive axle shaft from axle hub.

**5)** On Celica All-Trac, use a pry bar to separate left drive axle shaft from transaxle. Use a brass drift and hammer to separate right drive axle shaft from transaxle.

**6)** To remove left drive axle on Camry FWD V6, remove bolts and washers from inboard axle shaft flange. Carefully remove drive axle shaft. DO NOT compress inboard CV joint boot or CV joint will be disassembled.

**7)** To remove right drive axle on Camry FWD V6, remove bearing lock bolt. Remove snap ring from intermediate shaft. Remove drive axle shaft and intermediate shaft as an assembly.

**8)** To remove side gear shaft, use a slide hammer to pull side gear shaft out of transaxle. Inspect side gear and side gear shaft seal for damage. Replace as necessary.

**Disassembly -** Remove CV joint boot clamps, and slide boots away from joint. Paint alignment marks on CV joint housings, tripod and shaft(s) for reassembly reference. Disassemble drive axles; use exploded view for guide. *See Fig. 2 or 3.*

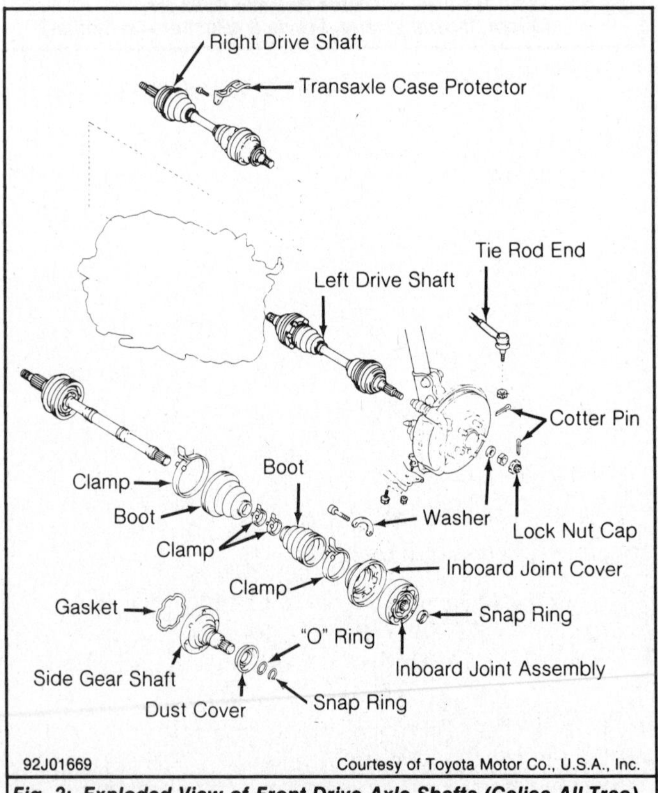


***Fig. 2: Exploded View of Front Drive Axle Shafts (Celica All-Trac)***

# 1991 DRIVE AXLES
# FWD Axle Shafts (Cont.)

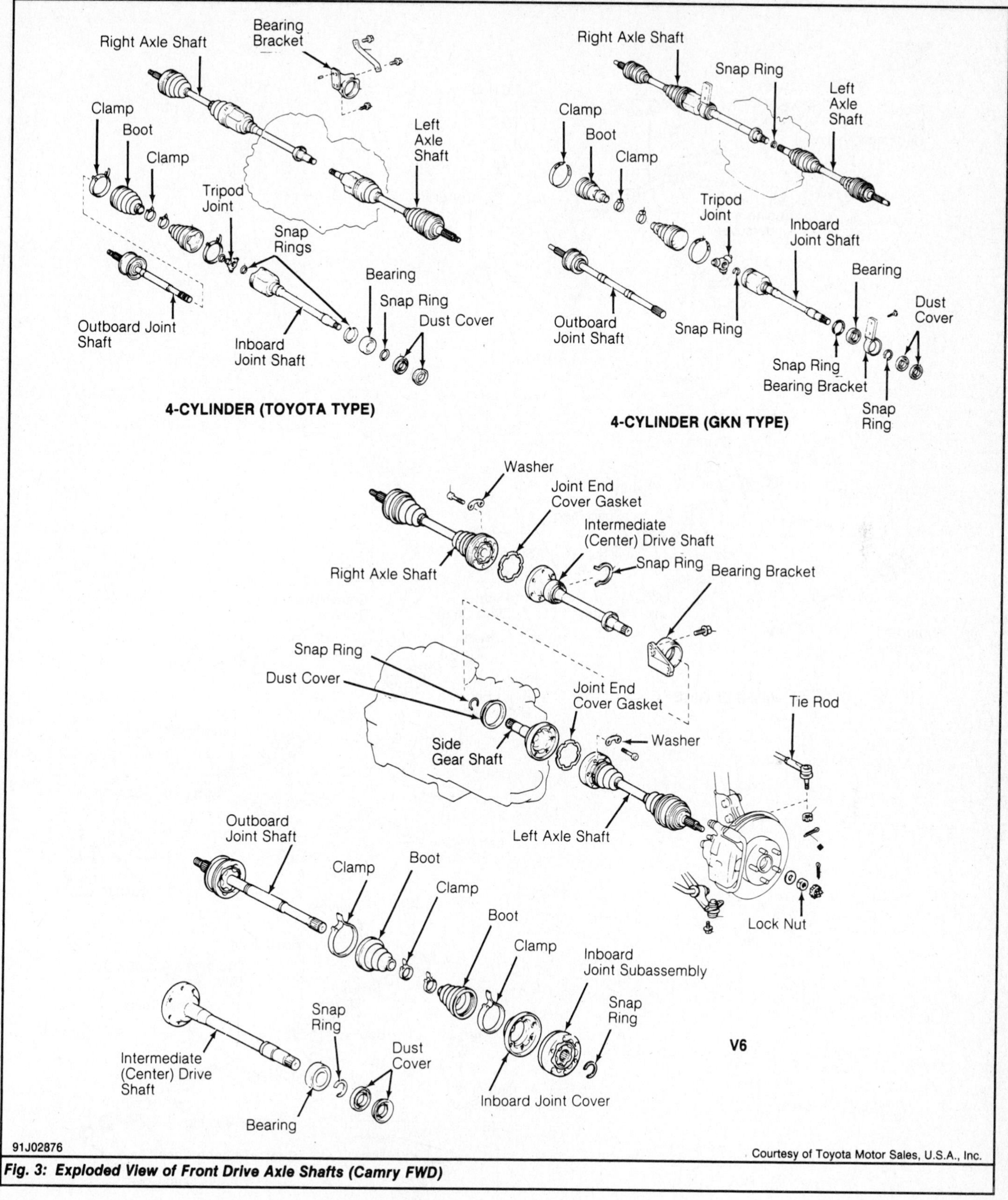




*Fig. 3: Exploded View of Front Drive Axle Shafts (Camry FWD)*

# 1991 DRIVE AXLES
# FWD Axle Shafts (Cont.)

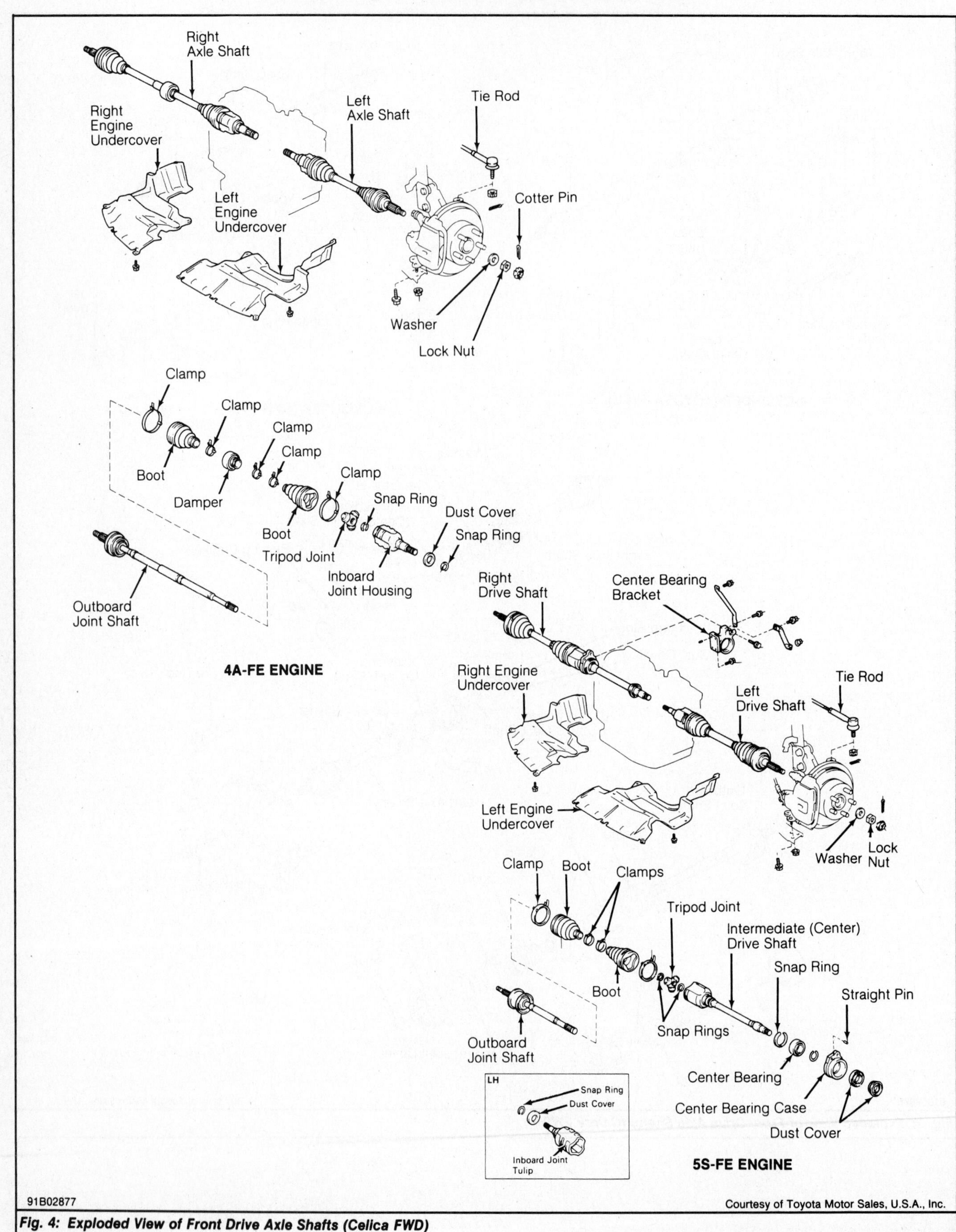


*Fig. 4: Exploded View of Front Drive Axle Shafts (Celica FWD)*

# 1991 DRIVE AXLES
# FWD Axle Shafts (Cont.)

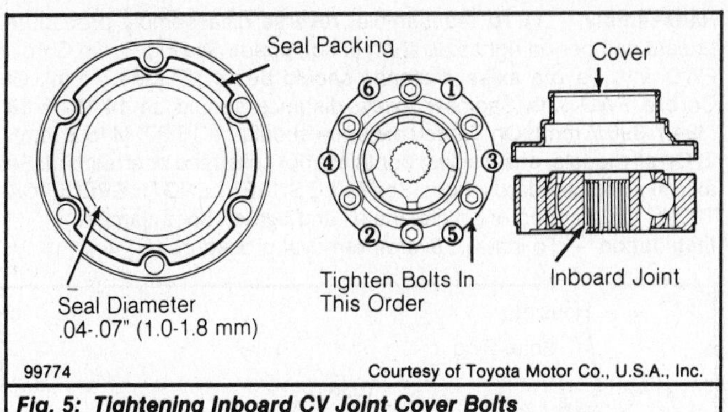


***Fig. 5: Tightening Inboard CV Joint Cover Bolts (Camry FWD V6 & Celica All-Trac)***

**Reassembly** – **1)** To reassemble drive axles, reverse disassembly procedure. Tighten inboard CV joint cover bolts as shown. *See Fig. 5.* On Camry FWD V6, ensure dust covers are 3.39-3.43" (86-87 mm) from end of shaft (splined end). *See Fig. 1.* Ensure clearance between dust cover and bearing is .04-.08" (1-2 mm).

**2)** On all models, ensure dust boots are not collapsed or stretched. Set axle shaft to standard length. See AXLE SHAFT LENGTH SPECIFICATIONS table at end of article. *See Fig. 10.* Install and tighten boot clamps.

**Installation** – To install, reverse removal procedure. On Camry FWD V6, use NEW intermediate axle shaft bearing lock bolt.

**Removal (Celica FWD)** – **1)** Remove cotter pin and lock nut cap. Apply brakes and remove axle shaft/bearing lock nut. Remove lower engine undercover (if equipped).

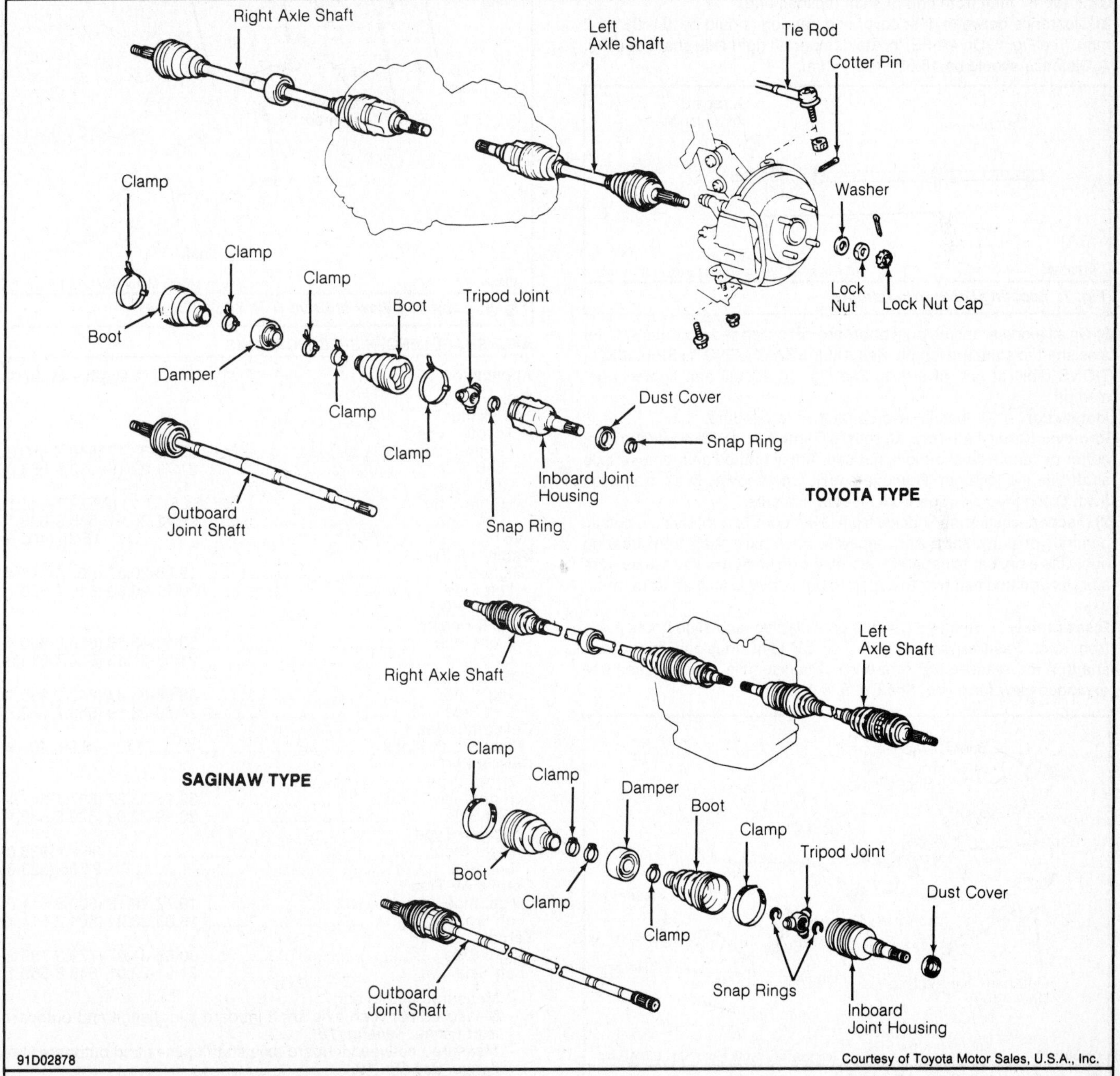

91D02878

Courtesy of Toyota Motor Sales, U.S.A., Inc.

***Fig. 6: Exploded View of Front Drive Axle Shafts (Corolla FWD)***

# 1991 DRIVE AXLES
# FWD Axle Shafts (Cont.)

**2)** Drain transaxle fluid. Remove brake caliper with hydraulic line attached, and wire aside. Mark front brake disc-to-axle hub position for reassembly reference. Remove brake disc.

**3)** Remove nut and disconnect tie rod end from steering knuckle. Disconnect lower control arm from steering knuckle. Using universal puller, separate drive axle shaft from steering knuckle. Using a pry bar, remove left drive axle from transaxle case.

**4)** On 5S-FE engine, remove 2 bolts from center bearing bracket; remove right drive axle and intermediate shaft as an assembly. On 4A-FE engine, using a hammer and brass punch, remove right drive axle from transaxle case.

**Disassembly** – Remove CV joint boot clamps, and slide boots away from joint. Paint alignment marks on CV joint housings, tripod and shaft(s) for reassembly reference. Disassemble drive axles; use exploded view for guide. *See Fig. 4.*

**Reassembly** – **1)** To reassemble, reverse disassembly procedure. On 5S-FE engine, right drive shaft dust cover must be located 3.39-3.43" (86-87 mm) from end of shaft (splined end).

**2)** Clearance between dust cover and bearing should be .04-.08" (1-2 mm). *See Fig. 1.* On 4A-FE, locate damper on right axle shaft. *See Fig. 7.* Distance should be 16.68" (423.7 mm).

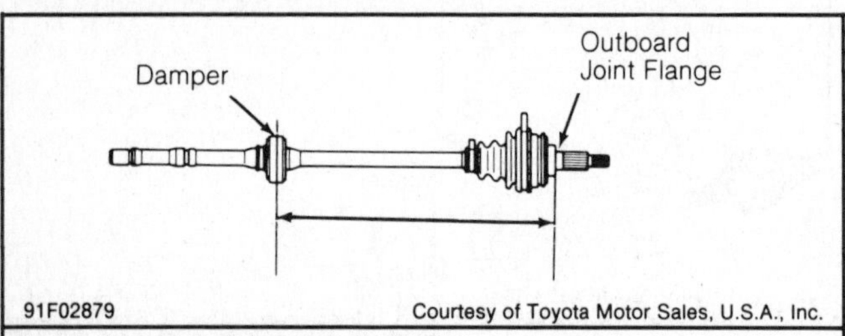


***Fig. 7: Locating Drive Axle Damper***

**3)** On all models, ensure dust boots are not collapsed or stretched. Set axle shaft to standard length. See AXLE SHAFT LENGTH SPECIFICATIONS table at end of article. *See Fig. 10.* Install and tighten boot clamps.

**Installation** – To install, reverse removal procedure.

**Removal (Camry All-Trac, Corolla & Tercel)** – **1)** Remove hub cap, cotter pin and axle shaft lock nut cap. Apply brakes and remove axle shaft/bearing lock nut. Remove engine undercover. Drain transaxle fluid. Disconnect tie rods from steering knuckle.

**2)** Disconnect steering knuckle from lower control arm. Using a plastic hammer or universal puller, separate drive axle shaft from bearing hub. Use a pry bar to separate left drive axle shaft from transaxle. Use a brass drift and hammer to separate right drive axle shaft from transaxle.

**Disassembly** – Remove CV joint boot clamps, and slide boots away from joint. Paint alignment marks on CV joint housings, tripod and shaft(s) for reassembly reference. Disassemble drive axles; use exploded view for guide. *See Fig. 6, 8 or 9.*

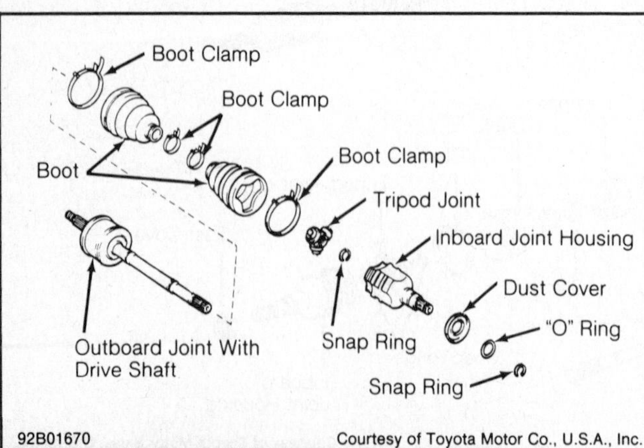


***Fig. 8: Exploded View of Front Drive Axle Shafts (Camry All-Trac & Corolla All-Trac)***

**Reassembly** – **1)** To reassemble, reverse disassembly procedure. Locate damper on right axle shaft (if equipped). *See Fig. 7.* On Corolla FWD with Toyota axles, distance should be 14.15" (384.7 mm). On Corolla FWD with Saginaw axles, distance should be 14.15-15.38" (384.7-390.7 mm). On Tercel, distance should be 16.37" (415.8 mm).

**2)** On all models, ensure dust boots are not collapsed or stretched. Set axle shaft to standard length. See AXLE SHAFT LENGTH SPECIFICATIONS table at end of article. Install and tighten boot clamps.

**Installation** – To install, reverse removal procedure.

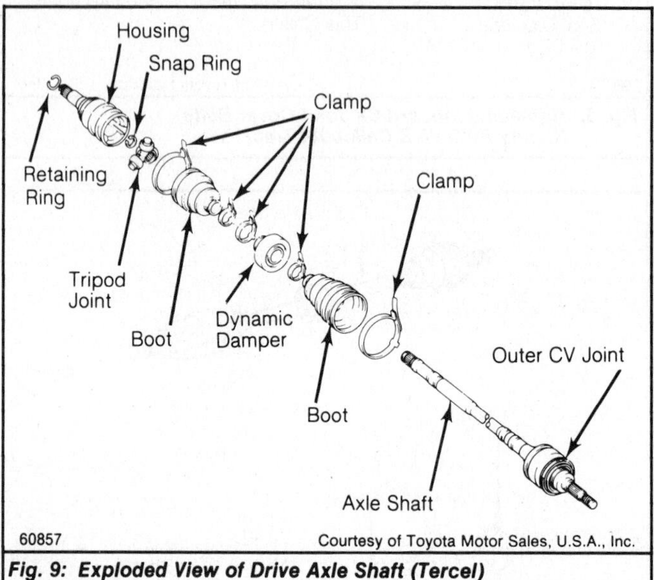


***Fig. 9: Exploded View of Drive Axle Shaft (Tercel)***

***AXLE SHAFT LENGTH SPECIFICATIONS***

| Application | Length – In. (mm) |
|---|---|
| **Camry FWD** | |
| 4-Cylinder [1] | |
| Toyota Type | |
| Right Side | 33.08-33.47 (840.2-850.2) |
| Left Side | 21.79-22.19 (553.5-563.6) |
| GKN Type | |
| Right Side | 36.65-37.13 (930.9.7-943.1) |
| Left Side | 25.43-25.91 (645.9-658.1) |
| V6 [2] | 15.98 (405.8) |
| **Camry All-Trac** [3] | |
| Right Side | 19.98-20.37 (507.5-517.4) |
| Left Side | 20.11-20.50 (510.7-520.7) |
| **Celica FWD** [3] | |
| 4A-FE Engine | |
| Right Side | 33.50-33.89 (850.9-860.8) |
| Left Side | 21.05-21.45 (534.7-544.8) |
| 5S-FE Engine | |
| Right Side | 33.08-33.47 (840.2-850.1) |
| Left Side | 21.80-22.19 (553.7-563.7) |
| **Celica All-Trac** [4] | |
| Right & Left Sides | 15.96 (405.4) |
| **Corolla FWD** | |
| Toyota Type [3] | |
| Right Side | 32.98-33.37 (837.7-847.6) |
| Left Side | 20.59-20.99 (522.9-533.1) |
| Saginaw Type [1] | |
| Right Side | 36.93 (938.0) |
| Left Side | 24.55 (623.6) |
| **Corolla All-Trac** [3] | |
| Right Side | 19.72-20.12 (500.9-511.0) |
| Left Side | 19.85-20.24 (504.2-514.1) |
| **Tercel** [3] | |
| Right Side | 30.68-31.07 (779.3-789.2) |
| Left Side | 21.61-22.01 (548.8-559.1) |

[1] – Measured end to end.
[2] – Measured between axle shaft inboard joint flange and outboard joint flange. *See Fig. 10.*
[3] – Measured between inboard axle shaft splines and outboard joint flange. *See Fig. 10.*
[4] – Measured between axle shaft inboard joint flange and outboard end of splines.

# 1991 DRIVE AXLES
# FWD Axle Shafts (Cont.)

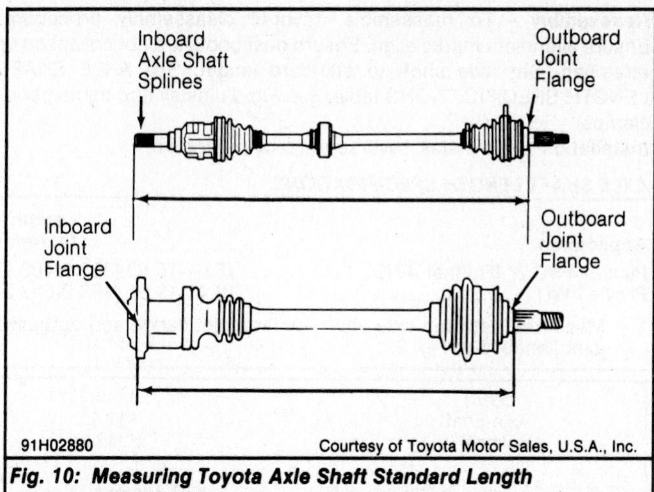


*Fig. 10: Measuring Toyota Axle Shaft Standard Length*

## TORQUE SPECIFICATIONS

*TORQUE SPECIFICATIONS (CAMRY)*

| Application | Ft. Lbs. (N.m) |
|---|---|
| Axle Shaft/Bearing Lock Nut | 137 (187) |
| Axle Shaft Inboard Joint Flange Bolts (V6) | 48 (65) |
| Bearing Bracket Bolts (4-Cylinder) | |
| Toyota Type | 47 (64) |
| GKN Type | 24 (32) |
| Lower Ball Joint-To-Steering Knuckle Bolts/Nuts | 83 (113) |
| Tie Rod Nuts | 36 (49) |

*TORQUE SPECIFICATIONS (CELICA)*

| Application | Ft. Lbs. (N.m) |
|---|---|
| Axle Shaft/Bearing Lock Nut | 137 (187) |
| Bearing Bracket Bolts (5S-FE Engine) | 47 (64) |
| Brake Caliper Bolts | |
| 13" Wheel | 18 (24) |
| 14" & 15" Wheels | 29 (39) |
| Lower Arm-To-Steering Knuckle Bolts/Nuts | 94 (127) |
| Tie Rod Nuts | 36 (49) |

*TORQUE SPECIFICATIONS (COROLLA)*

| Application | Ft. Lbs. (N.m) |
|---|---|
| Axle Shaft/Bearing Lock Nut | 137 (187) |
| Lower Arm-To-Steering Knuckle Bolts/Nuts | 105 (142) |
| Tie Rod Nuts | 36 (49) |

*TORQUE SPECIFICATIONS (TERCEL)*

| Application | Ft. Lbs. (N.m) |
|---|---|
| Axle Shaft Hub Nut | 137 (187) |
| Brake Caliper Bolts | 65 (88) |
| Lower Arm-To-Steering Knuckle Bolts/Nuts | 59 (80) |
| Tie Rod Nuts | 36 (49) |

# 1991 DRIVE AXLES
# 4WD Front Axle Shafts

## Pickup 4WD, Previa 4WD, 4Runner 4WD

***NOTE: This article covers 4WD vehicles with independent front suspension. For Land Cruiser front axle, see DIFFERENTIALS & AXLE SHAFTS - SEPARATE CARRIER article in DRIVE AXLES.***

## DESCRIPTION

Axle shafts transfer power from transaxle to driving wheels. All axle shafts consist of a shaft and flexible Constant Velocity (CV) joint at each end. Inner CV joint is bolted to transaxle. Outer CV joint is splined to hub assembly and secured by axle shaft nut.

The inner CV joint is a plunging tripod joint. The plunging action allows for axle shaft length change as suspension moves up and down.

The inner and outer CV joints are enclosed by a CV joint boot. The boot maintains lubrication in the joint and prevents contamination of CV lubricant. Boots must be replaced if leaking or cracked. The inner CV joint can be repaired without replacing assembly. The outer CV joint must be replaced as an assembly.

## TROUBLE SHOOTING

***NOTE: See TROUBLE SHOOTING article in GENERAL INFORMATION.***

## REMOVAL, DISASSEMBLY, REASSEMBLY & INSTALLATION

**Removal (Pickup 4WD & 4Runner 4WD) - 1)** Place free-wheeling hub cover in FREE position. Remove center hub body bolt and washer. Remove hub body mounting nuts and washers.

**2)** Remove cone washers by tapping on bolt heads using brass drift and hammer. Remove hub body. Apply brakes and loosen 6 inboard CV joint flange-to-front differential nuts. Remove snap ring and spacer from outboard end of axle shaft.

**3)** On 4Runner 4WD, disconnect stabilizer bar from lower arm. Support front differential using jack. Remove differential mounting bolt and nut. Raise differential slightly using jack. Raise lower arm using a second jack.

**4)** On all models, remove nuts, and slide axle shaft toward steering knuckle until it is free of differential. *See Fig. 1.* Pull axle shaft down and away, out of steering knuckle.

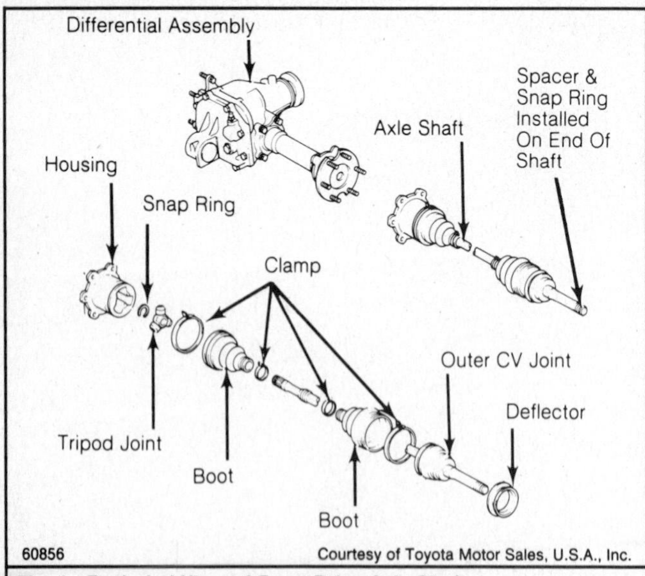


***Fig. 1: Exploded View of Front Drive Axle Shaft (Pickup 4WD & 4Runner 4WD)***

**Disassembly -** Remove CV joint boot clamps, and slide boots from joint. Paint alignment marks on CV joint housings, tripod and shaft(s) for reassembly reference. Disassemble drive axles. *See Fig. 1.*

**Reassembly -** To reassemble, reverse disassembly procedure. Ensure alignment marks align. Ensure dust boots are not collapsed or stretched. Set axle shaft to standard length. See AXLE SHAFT LENGTH SPECIFICATIONS table. *See Fig. 2.* Install and tighten boot clamps.

**Installation -** To install, reverse removal procedure.

***AXLE SHAFT LENGTH SPECIFICATIONS***

| Application | Length [1] In. (mm) |
|---|---|
| Pickup 4WD & 4Runner 4WD | 15.51-15.90 (393.9-403.9) |
| Previa 4WD | 19.41-19.81 (493.0-503.2) |

[1] - Measured between axle shaft inboard joint flange and outboard joint flange. *See Fig. 2.*

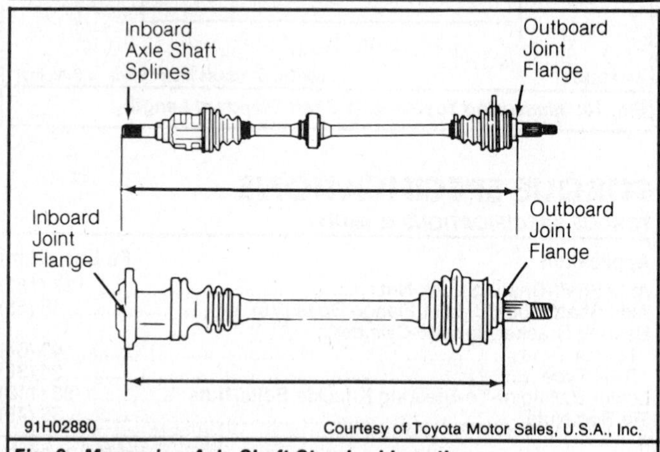


***Fig. 2: Measuring Axle Shaft Standard Length***

**Removal (Previa 4WD) - 1)** Remove front wheel. Remove hub cap, cotter pin and lock nut. Apply brake and remove wheel bearing lock nut. Remove cotter pin and nut from tie rod end. Using Tie Rod Remover (09628-62011), disconnect tie rod end from steering knuckle.

**2)** Paint mating marks on axle shaft flange and side gear shaft flange. DO NOT use punch to make mating marks. Apply brakes and remove

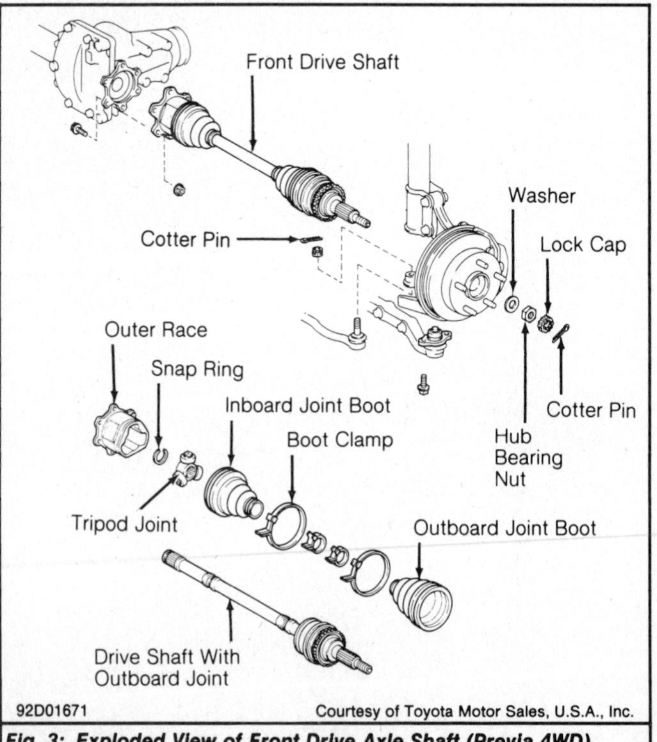


***Fig. 3: Exploded View of Front Drive Axle Shaft (Previa 4WD)***

# 1991 DRIVE AXLES
# 4WD Front Axle Shafts (Cont.)

retaining nuts on each inboard axle shaft flange. Remove bolts, and disconnect steering knuckle from lower control arm. Separate steering knuckle from drive shaft.

***CAUTION: DO NOT damage oil seal, drive shaft boots or ABS speed sensor rotor (if equipped) during axle shaft removal or installation.***

**Disassembly** – Remove CV joint boot clamps, and slide boots from joint. Paint alignment marks on CV joint housings, tripod and shaft(s) for reassembly reference. Disassemble drive axles. *See Fig. 3.*

**Reassembly** – To reassemble, reverse disassembly procedure. Ensure alignment marks align. Ensure dust boots are not collapsed or stretched. Set axle shaft to standard length. See AXLE SHAFT LENGTH SPECIFICATIONS table. *See Fig. 2.* Install and tighten boot clamps.

**Installation** – To install, reverse removal procedure.

## TORQUE SPECIFICATIONS

***TORQUE SPECIFICATIONS (PICKUP 4WD & 4RUNNER 4WD)***

| Application | Ft. Lbs. (N.m) |
|---|---|
| Axle Shaft-To-Differential Drive Flange Nuts | 61 (83) |
| Differential Mounting Bolt (4Runner 4WD) | 109 (148) |
| Freewheel Hub Body Center Bolt | 13 (18) |
| Freewheel Hub Body-To-Axle Hub Nuts | 23 (31) |
| Stabilizer Bar-To-Lower Arm Nut (4Runner 4WD) | 19 (26) |
| | **INCH Lbs. (N.m)** |
| Freewheel Hub Cover-To-Hub Body Bolts | 84 (10) |

***TORQUE SPECIFICATIONS (PREVIA 4WD)***

| Application | Ft. Lbs. (N.m) |
|---|---|
| Axle Shaft Hub Nut | 137 (187) |
| Axle Shaft-To-Differential Drive Flange Nuts | 51 (69) |
| Steering Knuckle-To-Lower Arm Bolts | 94 (127) |
| Tie Rod Nuts | 36 (49) |

# 1991 DRIVE AXLES
# RWD Axle Shafts

## Camry All-Trac, Celica All-Trac, Cressida, MR2, Supra

***NOTE: Information in this article only applies to models with independent rear suspension. For other models, see appropriate DIFFERENTIALS & AXLE SHAFTS article.***

## DESCRIPTION & OPERATION

Axle shafts transfer power from differential or transaxle to driving wheels. All axle shafts consist of a shaft and flexible Constant Velocity (CV) joint at each end. Inner CV joint is bolted or splined to differential or transaxle. Outer CV joint is splined to hub assembly and secured by axle shaft nut.

Inner CV joint is a plunging tripod joint. The plunging action allows for axle shaft length change as suspension moves up and down.

Inner and outer CV joints are enclosed by a CV joint boot. Boot maintains lubrication in the joint and prevents contamination of CV lubricant. Boots must be replaced when signs of leakage or cracks are present. Inner CV joint can be repaired without replacing assembly. Outer CV joint must be replaced as an assembly.

## TROUBLE SHOOTING

***NOTE: See TROUBLE SHOOTING article in GENERAL INFORMATION.***

## REMOVAL, DISASSEMBLY, REASSEMBLY & INSTALLATION

### REAR AXLE SHAFT

**Removal (Camry All-Trac & Celica All-Trac) - 1)** Raise and support vehicle. Remove rear wheels. From center of disc brake hub, remove cotter pin and lock nut. On Celica All-Trac, disconnect left side strut rod from lower suspension arm. *See Fig. 1.*

**2)** On all models, place match marks on inboard axle shaft flange and differential flange. Remove nuts (4) securing drive axle shaft to differential flange. Disconnect axle from differential. Slide axle shaft out of wheel hub and remove from vehicle.

**Inspection -** Ensure no play exists in inboard and outboard joints. Inboard joint must slide smoothly in the thrust direction and be free from excessive play in the radial direction. Check for torn or damaged boots.

**Disassembly - 1)** Remove inboard joint boot clamps and slide boot off of inboard joint tulip. *See Fig. 1.* Paint match marks on inboard joint tulip and axle shaft. Remove inboard tulip from axle shaft.

**2)** Remove snap ring from tripod spider. Paint matching marks on tripod spider and axle shaft. Drive tripod spider from axle using hammer and brass drift.

**3)** Remove inboard boot. Remove outboard boot clamps and slide boot from joint.

***NOTE: Toyota does not recommend overhaul of outboard CV joint assembly.***

**Reassembly - 1)** Wrap axle shaft splines with vinyl tape. Temporarily install new boots and clamps. Inboard and outboard boots are not the same design. *See Fig. 2.*

**2)** Aligning matching marks made at disassembly, install tripod spider onto axle shaft. Install snap ring.

**3)** Pack inboard joint tulip with CV joint grease supplied in overhaul kit. Slide tulip over onto axle shaft. Install inboard boot, but do not tighten clamps yet.

**4)** Pack outboard joint with CV joint grease supplied in overhaul kit. Slide boot over joint; do not tighten clamps. Ensure boots are not stretched or compressed with shaft at standard length. *See Fig. 3.* Tighten boot clamps.

**Installation -** To install rear drive axle shaft, reverse removal procedure. Tighten fasteners to specification. See TORQUE SPECIFICATIONS table at end of article.

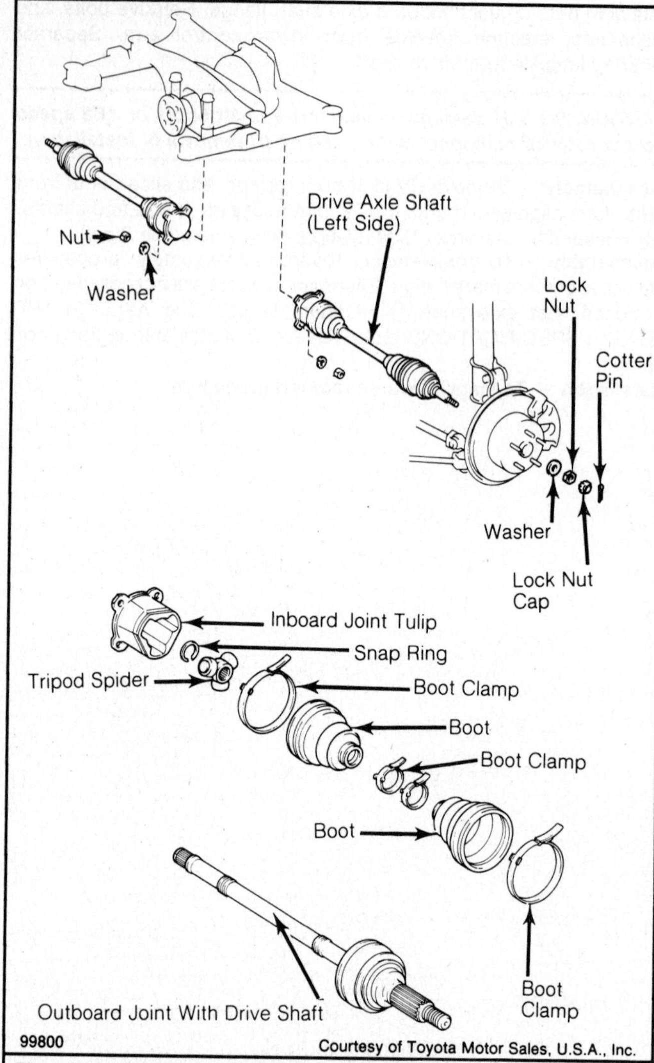


***Fig. 1: Identifying Rear Axle Shaft Components (Camry All-Trac & Celica All-Trac)***

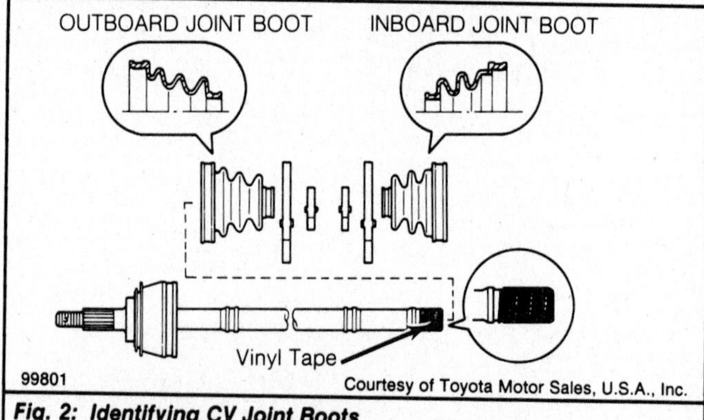


***Fig. 2: Identifying CV Joint Boots (Camry All-Trac, Celica All-Trac & Cressida)***

**Removal (Cressida & Supra) - 1)** Raise and support vehicle. Remove rear wheels. On Cressida left rear, support tail pipe and remove rubber hangers. On all models, use a jack to raise the lower suspension arm until arm is horizontal.

**2)** Paint matching marks on inboard drive axle flange and side gear flange. Remove 6 flange retaining nuts. *See Fig. 4.* On outboard end of drive axle shaft, remove cotter pin, lock nut cap and hub nut. Tap axle shaft out of hub carrier, and remove drive axle shaft from vehicle.

# 1991 DRIVE AXLES
# RWD Axle Shafts (Cont.)

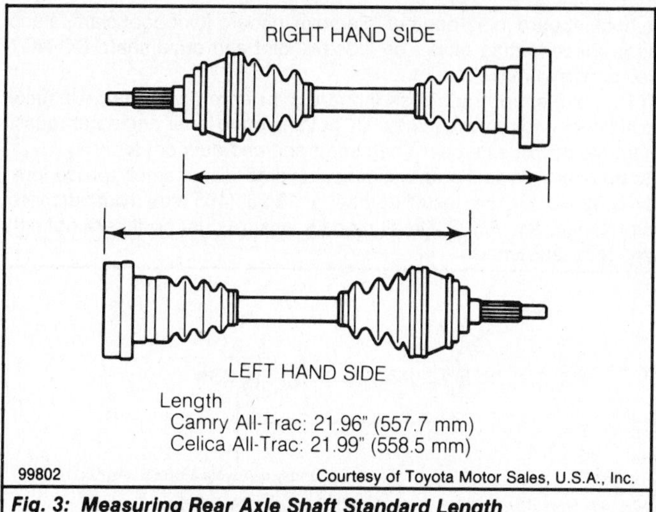


***Fig. 3: Measuring Rear Axle Shaft Standard Length (Camry All-Trac & Celica All-Trac)***

**Disassembly - 1)** Check for play in CV joints. Ensure CV joints slide smoothly in thrust direction. Remove inboard joint boot clamps and slide boot back. Using paint, mark inboard joint tulip and tripod. DO NOT use a punch to mark parts.

**2)** Remove inboard joint tulip. Remove snap ring. Using scribe, place matching marks on axle shaft and tripod joint. Using brass bar and hammer, drive tripod joint off of axle shaft. Remove inboard boot. Remove outboard joint boot clamps. Remove dust deflector.

***NOTE: Toyota does not recommend overhaul of outboard CV joint assembly.***

**Reassembly - 1)** Install dust deflector. Wrap shaft splines with tape. Temporarily install outboard and inboard joint boots. On Cressida, inboard and outboard boots are not the same design. *See Fig. 2.*

**2)** On all models, align marks made during disassembly and install tripod joint on shaft with beveled side of tripod splines facing toward outboard joint. Install snap ring on tripod joint side of axle shaft. Apply CV joint grease to outboard joint and boot. Install outboard boot, but do not tighten clamps.

**3)** Pack inboard joint tulip with grease. Aligning marks made during disassembly, place inboard tulip onto tripod spider. Install boot, but do not tighten clamps.

**4)** On Supra, set axle shaft to standard length of 21.724-21.842" (551.80-554.80 mm). Measure length from differential side of inboard flange to shoulder of outboard joint that seats against the hub bearing. On all models, boots should not be compressed or expanded. Tighten boot clamps. *See Fig. 3.*

**Installation -** Grease splines of outboard joint. With lower suspension arm horizontal, install axle splines into hub carrier. Continue installation in reverse of removal procedure. Tighten hub nut and axle flange nuts to specification. See TORQUE SPECIFICATIONS table at end of article.

**Removal (MR2) - 1)** Raise and support vehicle. Remove rear wheels and engine under cover. Drain transaxle fluid. Remove cotter pin and lock nut cap. *See Fig. 5 or 6.* Apply parking brake and remove bearing lock nut.

**2)** On MR2 Turbo, paint mating marks on axle shaft flange and side gear shaft flange. *See Fig. 6.* DO NOT use punch to make mating marks. Loosen, but do not remove, 6 bolts connecting axle shaft flange to differential side gear shaft flange.

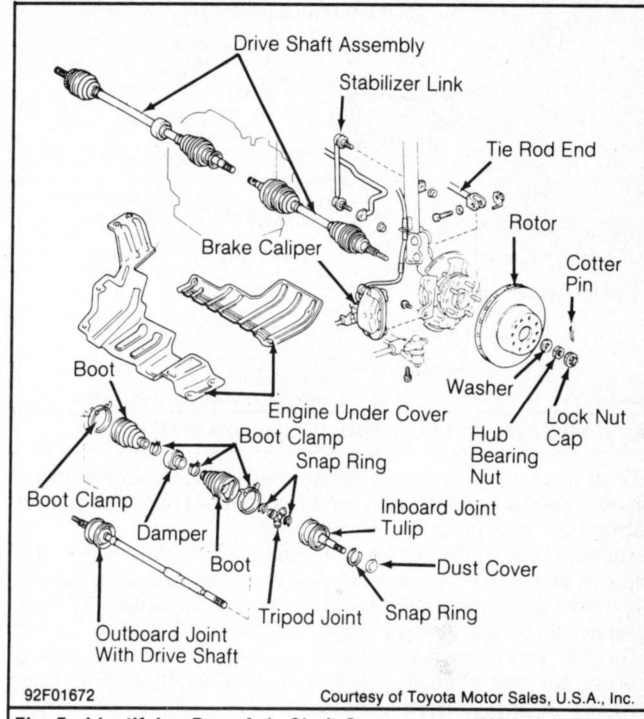


***Fig. 5: Identifying Rear Axle Shaft Components (MR2 Non-Turbo)***

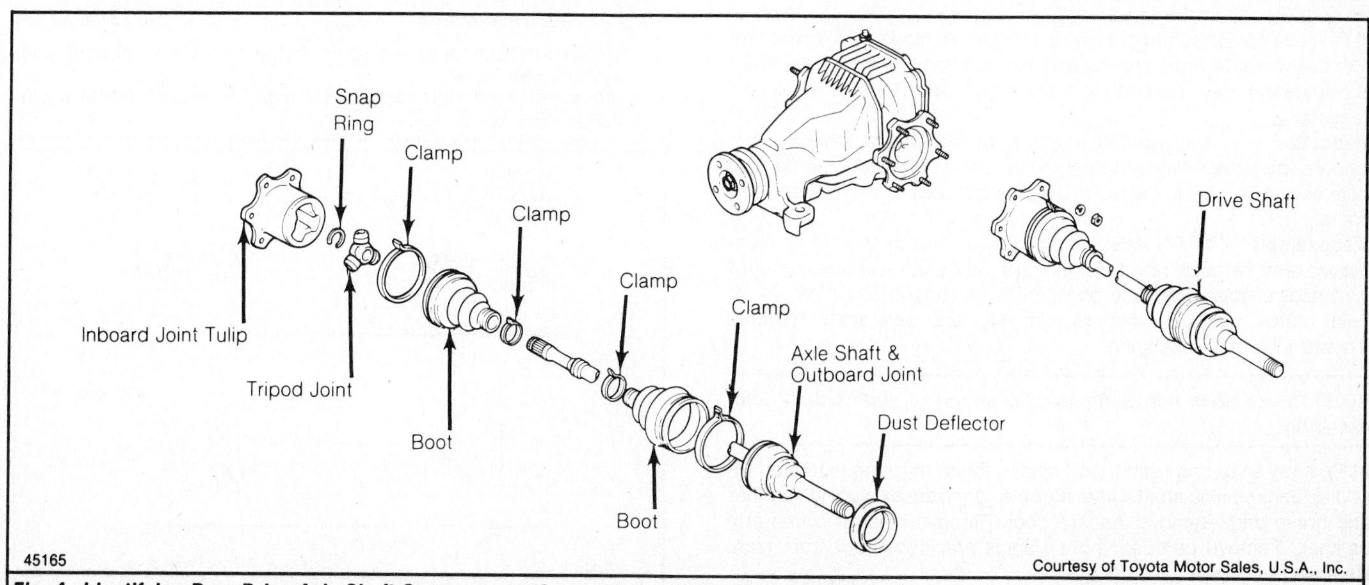


***Fig. 4: Identifying Rear Drive Axle Shaft Components (Supra Shown; Cressida Is Similar)***

# 1991 DRIVE AXLES
# RWD Axle Shafts (Cont.)

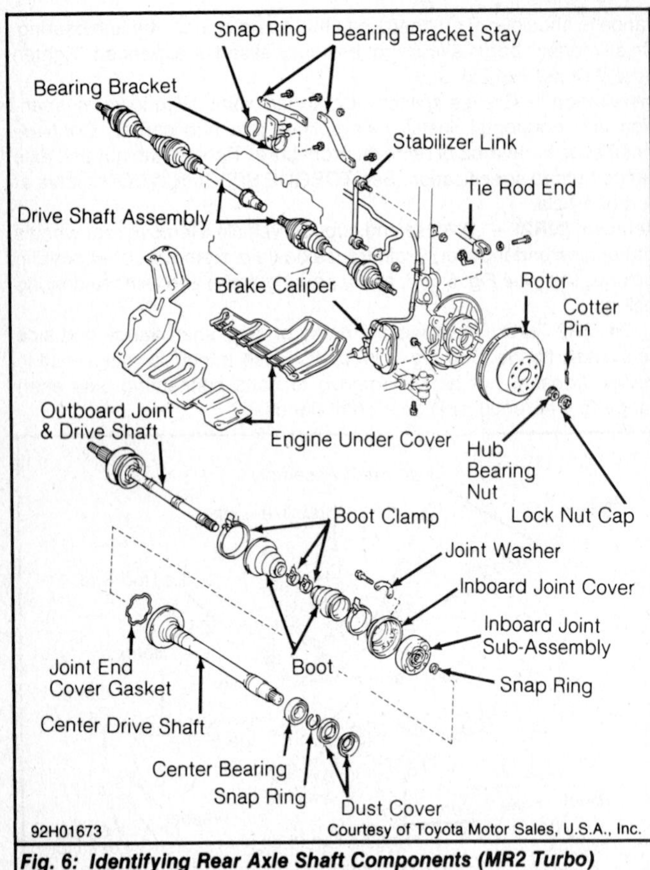


*Fig. 6: Identifying Rear Axle Shaft Components (MR2 Turbo)*

**3)** On all models, remove brake caliper from axle carrier and suspend with wire leaving hydraulic line connected. Remove rotor. Disconnect stabilizer bar link from strut. *See Fig. 5 or 6*.

**4)** Remove rear speed sensor (if equipped). Disconnect lower arm from rear axle carrier. Disconnect tie rod ends from axle carrier. Using a universal puller, separate drive shaft from axle carrier. DO NOT damage boot or speed sensor rotor.

**5)** On MR2 Non-Turbo, pry left side drive shaft from transaxle. Using a brass bar and hammer, separate right side drive shaft from transaxle. Replace oil seals if necessary.

**6)** On MR2 Turbo, use a brass bar and hammer to separate left side drive shaft from transaxle. On right axle shaft, use a hammer and screwdriver to remove snap ring from bearing bracket.

**7)** Remove center bolt from bearing bracket. Remove right drive shaft with intermediate shaft. Use a brass bar and hammer to remove shaft (if necessary). Remove bearing bracket and stay. Replace oil seals if necessary.

**Inspection** – Ensure no play exists in inboard and outboard joints. Inboard joint must slide smoothly in the thrust direction and be free from excessive play in the radial direction. Check for torn or damaged boots.

**Disassembly** – **1)** For MR2 Turbo, go to step **3)**. For MR2 Non-Turbo, remove snap ring from inboard joint shaft. Remove inboard joint boot clamps and slide boot toward outboard joint. *See Fig. 5*. Paint match marks on inboard joint tulip and axle shaft. Remove inboard tulip from axle shaft.

***NOTE: Toyota does not recommend overhaul of outboard CV joint assembly.***

**2)** Remove snap ring from tripod spider. Paint matching marks on tripod spider and axle shaft. Drive tripod spider from axle using hammer and brass drift. Remove inboard boot. Remove damper clamp and damper. Remove outboard boot clamps and slide boot from joint. Remove dust cover.

**3)** For MR2 Turbo, remove bolts and disconnect side gear shaft from drive axle shaft. *See Fig. 6*. Reinstall nuts, bolts and washers by hand to hold inboard joint together. Remove inboard joint boot clamps and boot. Place mating marks on inboard joint and drive shaft. DO NOT use punch to make marks.

**4)** Remove snap ring. Press inboard joint from drive shaft. Unstake joint cover and remove joint while holding on to inner and outer races. Remove boots, side gear shaft snap ring and dust cover.

**Reassembly** – **1)** To reassemble, reverse disassembly procedure. On MR2 Non-Turbo, install damper at 18.23" (463 mm) from outboard joint flange. *See Fig. 7*. On all models, ensure dust boots are not collapsed or stretched.

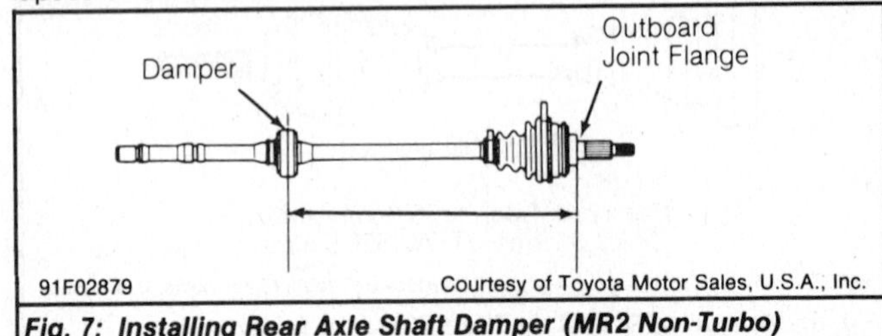


*Fig. 7: Installing Rear Axle Shaft Damper (MR2 Non-Turbo)*

**2)** On MR2 Turbo, tighten inboard joint cover bolts in proper sequence. *See Fig. 8*.

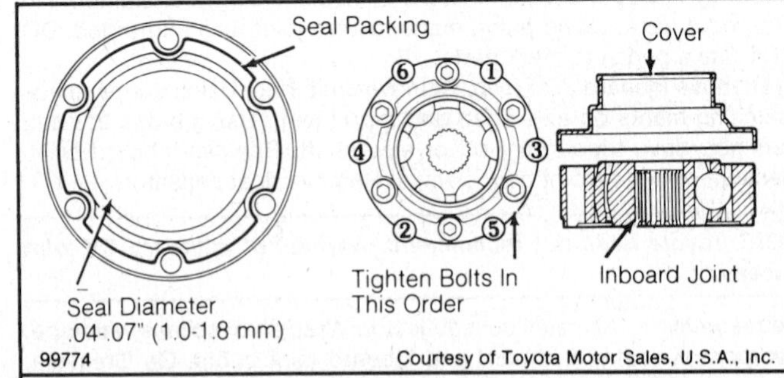


*Fig. 8: Tightening Inboard Joint Cover Bolts (MR2 Turbo)*

**3)** On all models, set axle shaft to standard length. See AXLE SHAFT LENGTH SPECIFICATIONS table. *See Fig. 9*. Install and tighten boot clamps. Install snap ring (if equipped).

***AXLE SHAFT LENGTH SPECIFICATIONS (MR2)***

| Application | In. (mm) |
|---|---|
| Non-Turbo | |
| Right Drive Shaft | [1] 32.54-32.93 (826.5-836.4) |
| Left Drive Shaft | [1] 21.08-21.47 (535.4-545.3) |
| Turbo | |
| Right & Left Drive Shafts | [2] 15.15-15.54 (384.8-394.7) |

[1] – Measured from outboard joint flange to end of inboard joint splines. *See Fig. 9*.

[2] – Measured from outboard joint flange to end of inboard joint flange. *See Fig. 9*.

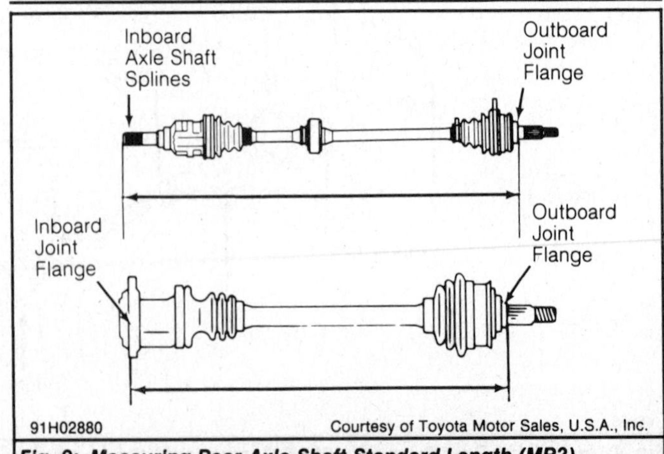


*Fig. 9: Measuring Rear Axle Shaft Standard Length (MR2)*

**Installation - 1)** To install, reverse removal procedure. DO NOT damage speed sensor rotor or joint boots. On MR2 Non-Turbo, after installing drive shaft to transaxle, ensure axial play is .08-.12" (2.0-3.0 mm). Ensure drive shaft cannot be pulled out by hand.
**2)** On all models, tighten all fasteners to specification. See TORQUE SPECIFICATIONS table at end of article. DO NOT fully tighten tie rod ends or hub bearing lock nut until vehicle wheels are resting on ground.

## REAR AXLE HUB & CARRIER

**Removal (Camry All-Trac & Celica All-Trac) - 1)** Raise and support vehicle. Remove rear wheel. Disconnect parking brake cable. Remove disc brake caliper without disconnecting hydraulic line. Place matching marks on rotor and axle hub and remove rotor. *See Fig. 10.*

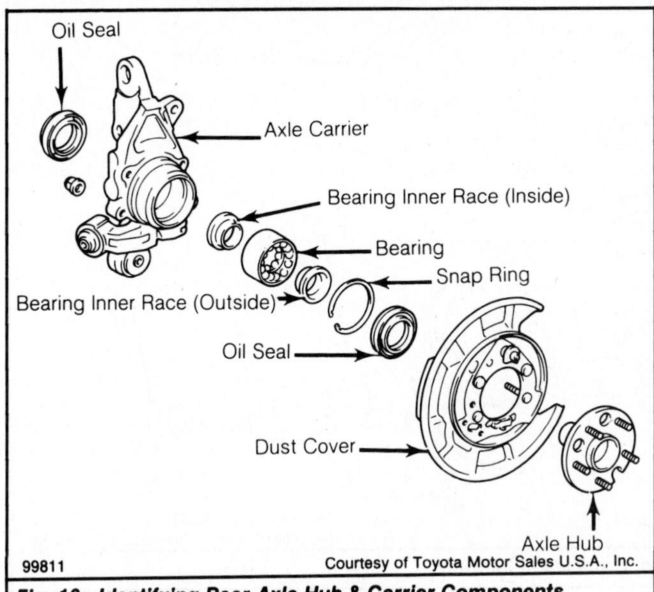


***Fig. 10: Identifying Rear Axle Hub & Carrier Components (Camry All-Trac & Celica All-Trac)***

**2)** Check hub bearing end play and axle hub runout. *See Fig. 11.* If bearing end play is greater than .002" (.05 mm), replace bearing. If hub runout is greater than .0028" (.07 mm), replace hub. Remove parking brake assembly and cable. Remove cotter pin, lock nut cap and drive axle shaft hub nut. Remove rear speed sensor (if equipped).

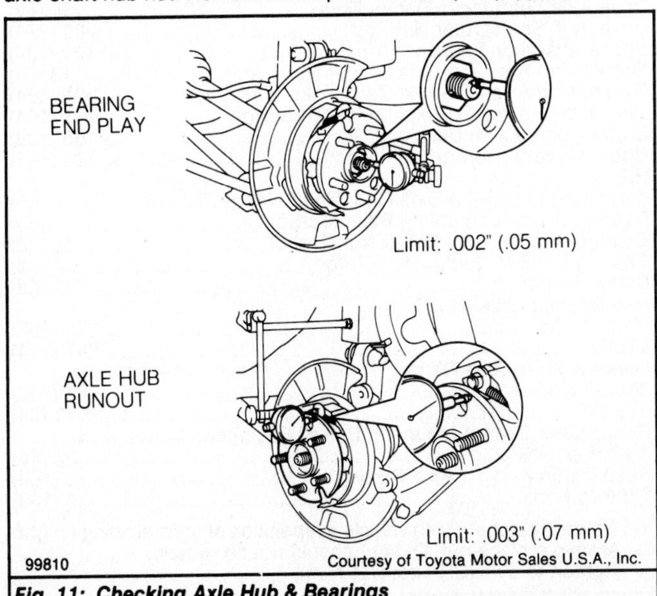


***Fig. 11: Checking Axle Hub & Bearings***

**3)** After noting the camber setting on adjusting cam, remove the 2 bolts securing the axle carrier to the shock strut. Disconnect strut rod and suspension arms from the axle carrier.
**4)** Tap drive axle shaft from center of axle hub, and remove axle carrier from vehicle.
**Disassembly & Reassembly - 1)** Press axle hub from carrier. Press bearing inner race off of axle hub. Remove the dust cover from the carrier.
**2)** Remove retaining snap ring from carrier. Remove outer oil seal from axle carrier. Press bearing from axle carrier. To reassemble axle carrier, reverse disassembly procedure.
**Installation - 1)** To install axle carrier, reverse removal procedure. Tighten the 2 axle carrier-to-strut nuts to 188 ft. lbs. (255 N.m).
**2)** After attaching suspension strut rod and lower suspension arm, do not final tighten bolts and nuts until suspension is at normal riding height. Check rear wheel alignment.
**Removal (Cressida & Supra) - 1)** Raise vehicle. Remove rear wheel. Remove caliper and support out of way, without disconnecting brake line. Release parking brake fully and remove rotor. *See Fig. 12.*
**2)** Check bearing end play and axle hub runout. *See Fig. 11.* If bearing end play or axle hub runout exceeds .002" (.05 mm), replace bearing or hub. Remove drive axle shaft from vehicle.
**3)** Remove parking brake assembly. Disconnect lower suspension arms, shock absorber and strut rod from axle carrier. Remove upper arm from body and remove axle carrier assembly from vehicle.
**Disassembly - 1)** Remove backing plate from axle carrier. Using Pullers (09950-00020 and 09950-20017), separate upper arm from axle carrier.
**2)** Remove deflector. *See Fig. 12.* Remove inner oil seal. Press axle hub from axle carrier. Remove inner bearing race from axle hub. Remove oil outer seal. Remove snap ring and press bearing outer race from axle carrier.
**Reassembly & Installation - 1)** To reassemble axle carrier, reverse disassembly procedure. Coat the bearings, races and interior of hub with multipurpose grease.
**2)** Reverse removal procedure to complete installation. Use NEW nut on upper control arm ball joint. Do not final tighten strut rod, No. 2 suspension arm and upper control arm nuts until suspension is at normal riding height.
**Removal (MR2) - 1)** Raise and support rear of vehicle. Remove rear wheels. Remove disc brake caliper without disconnecting hydraulic line. Place matching marks on rotor and axle hub and remove disc brake rotor.
**2)** Check hub bearing end play and axle hub runout. *See Fig. 11.* If bearing end play is greater than .002" (.05 mm), replace bearing. Remove cotter pin and lock nut cap. Apply parking brake and remove drive axle shaft hub nut.
**3)** Disconnect stabilizer link. Remove rear speed sensor (if equipped). Disconnect lower arm and suspension arm from axle carrier. Remove steering knuckle-to-strut bolts and remove axle carrier with axle shaft.

***NOTE: Cover drive shaft boots to protect from damage. DO NOT damage speed sensor rotor (if equipped).***

**Disassembly & Reassembly -** Secure axle carrier in a vise. Remove dust deflector and snap ring. *See Fig. 13.* Remove disc brake dust cover bolts. Using puller, remove axle shaft. Remove disc brake dust cover. Press outboard inner race and axle bearing from carrier. To reassemble, reverse disassembly procedure.
**Installation -** To install, reverse removal procedure. Tighten all fasteners to specification. See TORQUE SPECIFICATIONS table at end of article.

# 1991 DRIVE AXLES
# RWD Axle Shafts (Cont.)

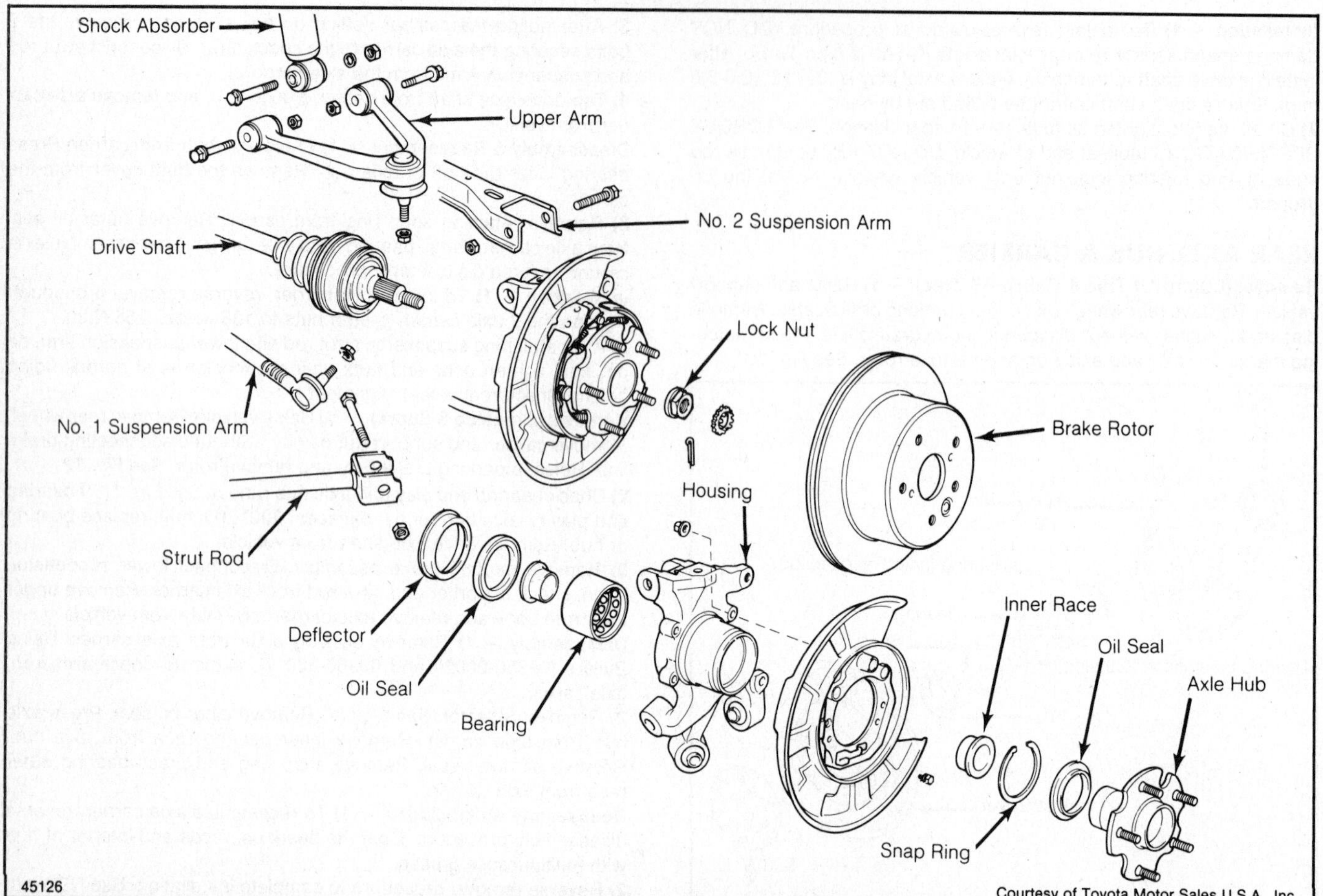

45126 Courtesy of Toyota Motor Sales U.S.A., Inc.

***Fig. 12: Identifying Rear Axle Carrier Assembly Components (Supra Shown; Cressida Is Similar)***

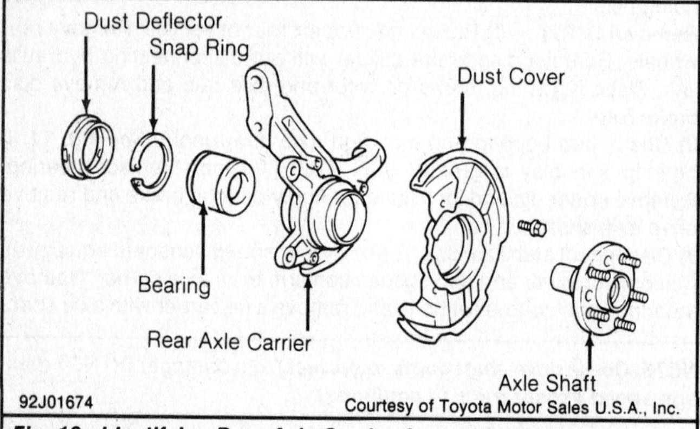


***Fig. 13: Identifying Rear Axle Carrier Assembly Components (MR2)***

## TORQUE SPECIFICATIONS

***TORQUE SPECIFICATIONS***

| Application | Ft. Lbs. (N.m) |
|---|---|
| **Camry All-Trac & Celica All-Trac** | |
| Axle Carrier-To-Strut Nuts | 188 (255) |
| Disc Brake Caliper | |
| Camry | 29 (39) |
| Celica | |
| 13" Wheel | 18 (24) |
| 14" & 15" Wheels | 29 (39) |
| Drive Axle Shaft Hub Nut | 137 (186) |
| Inboard Axle Shaft Flange Nuts | 51 (69) |
| Strut Rod-To-Lower Suspension Arm Bolt (Celica) | 83 (113) |

***TORQUE SPECIFICATIONS (Cont.)***

| Application | Ft. Lbs. (N.m) |
|---|---|
| **Cressida & Supra** | |
| Adjusting Cam Nuts (Cressida) | 134 (182) |
| Backing Plate Bolt | 19 (26) |
| Backing Plate Nut | 43 (58) |
| Disc Brake Caliper | 34 (47) |
| Drive Axle Shaft Inner Flange Nuts | 51 (69) |
| Drive Axle Shaft Outer Hub Nut | 203 (275) |
| Shock Absorber-To-Upper Arm | 101 (137) |
| Suspension Arms-To-Axle Carrier No. 1 Arm | 43 (59) |
| Suspension Arms-To-Axle Carrier No. 2 Arm [1] | 121 (164) |
| Suspension Arms-To-Axle Carrier Strut Rod [1] | 121 (164) |
| Upper Control Arm Ball Joint Nut [2] | 80 (108) |
| Upper Control Arm-to-Body Nuts [1] | 121 (164) |
| **MR2** | |
| Axle Shaft Flange-To-Side Gear Shaft Flange (Turbo) | 48 (65) |
| Bearing Bracket Mounting Bolts (Turbo) | 47 (64) |
| Bearing Bracket Stay Bolt & Nut (Turbo) | 56 (76) |
| Bearing Bracket Center Bolt (Turbo) | 24 (33) |
| Brake Caliper | 43 (58) |
| Hub Bearing Lock Nut | |
| Non-Turbo | 152 (206) |
| Turbo | 217 (294) |
| Lower Arm-To-Axle Carrier | |
| Non-Turbo | 83 (113) |
| Turbo | 73 (99) |
| Rear Speed Sensor Mounting Bolt (If Equipped) | [3] |
| Stabilizer Link | 36 (49) |
| Suspension Arm-To-Axle Carrier | 76 (103) |
| Tie Rod Ends | 76 (103) |

[1] – Tighten fasteners with vehicle suspension at normal riding height.
[2] – Always replace nut. Old nut should not be reused.
[3] – Tighten to 69 INCH Lbs. (7.4 N.m).

# 1991 DRIVE AXLES
# Differentials & Axle Shafts – Integral Housing

**Camry All-Trac, Celica All-Trac, Cressida, Pickup 4WD, Previa 4WD, Supra, 4Runner 4WD**

## DESCRIPTION

Drive axle assembly is a hypoid type with integral carrier housing. Drive pinion preload is adjusted using collapsible spacer. Side bearing preload is adjusted using shims.

Limited Slip Differential (LSD) is available on Cressida and Supra. On Pickup 4WD and 4Runner 4WD, front differential may be Automatic Disconnecting Differential (ADD).

***INTEGRAL HOUSING DIFFERENTIAL APPLICATION***

| Application | Location |
|---|---|
| Camry All-Trac, Celica All-Trac, Cressida & Supra | Rear |
| Pickup 4WD, Previa 4WD & 4Runner 4WD | Front |

## AXLE RATIO & IDENTIFICATION

Integral carrier-type drive axle is identified on inspection cover, on rear of carrier housing. Axle ratio is determined by dividing number of ring gear teeth by number of pinion gear teeth.

***AXLE RATIO SPECIFICATIONS***

| Application | Ratio |
|---|---|
| Camry All-Trac & Celica All-Trac | 2.928 |
| Cressida | 3.909 |
| Pickup 4WD & 4Runner 4WD | |
| A/T | |
| 4-Cylinder | 4.556 |
| V6 | 4.100 |
| M/T | [1] 4.100 |
| Previa 4WD | 4.300 |
| Supra | |
| Non-Turbo | 4.300 |
| Turbo | 3.727 |

[1] – 4.556 with V6 and optional 31 x 10.5" tires.

## LUBRICATION

### FLUID TYPE & CAPACITY

All models should use SAE 90 (API GL-5) for temperatures above 0°F (-18°C) and SAE 80W-90 (API GL-5) for temperatures below 0°F (-18°C). Limited Slip Differential (LSD) should use only LSD approved oil. See FLUID CAPACITY SPECIFICATIONS table.

***FLUID CAPACITY SPECIFICATIONS***

| Application | Pts. (L) |
|---|---|
| Camry All-Trac & Celica All-Trac | 2.4 (1.1) |
| Cressida & Supra | 2.8 (1.3) |
| Pickup 4WD & 4Runner 4WD | |
| With ADD | 4.0 (1.9) |
| Without ADD | 3.4 (1.6) |
| Previa 4WD | 2.2 (1.0) |

## TROUBLE SHOOTING

***NOTE: See TROUBLE SHOOTING article in GENERAL INFORMATION.***

## REMOVAL & INSTALLATION

***NOTE: During removal and installation procedures, refer to Fig. 2, 3, 4, 5 or 6.***

### ADD ACTUATOR

**Removal (Pickup 4WD & 4Runner 4WD With Automatic Disconnecting Differential)** – Remove Automatic Disconnecting Differential (ADD) actuator from left side gear shaft tube. Remove left side gear shaft and tube. See SIDE GEAR SHAFTS & OIL SEALS under REMOVAL & INSTALLATION. Remove snap ring and clutch hub from side gear shaft.

**Inspection – 1)** Using feeler gauge, measure clearance between side of sleeve fork and clutch sleeve. If clearance is greater than .014" (.36 mm), replace fork and/or sleeve.

**2)** Apply vacuum of 19.69 in. Hg to actuator port "A". Ensure sleeve fork moves toward actuator. *See Fig. 1.* Apply vacuum of 19.69 in. Hg to port "B". Ensure sleeve fork moves from actuator. *See Fig. 1.* Replace actuator if vacuum leaks or sleeve fork does not function properly.

**Installation** – To install, reverse removal procedure. Use new "O" ring. Tighten fasteners to specification. See TORQUE SPECIFICATIONS table at end of article.

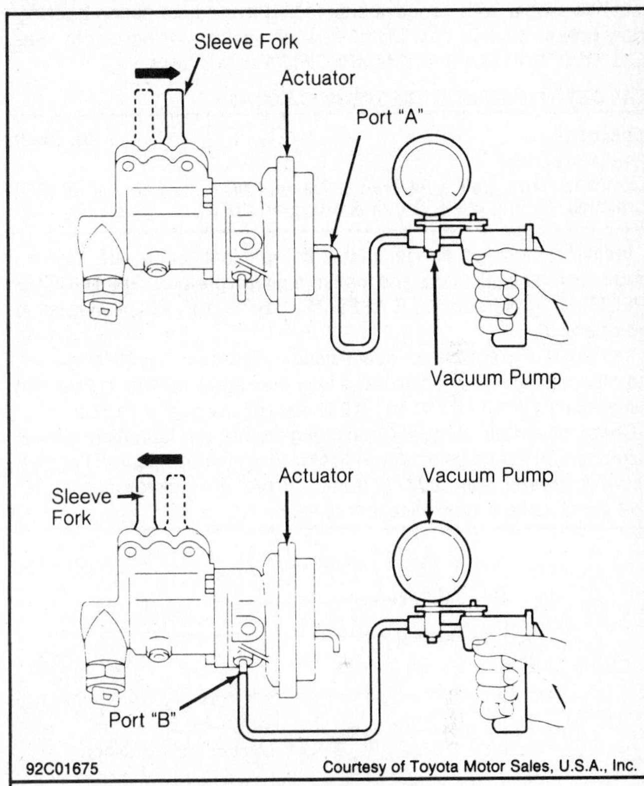


***Fig. 1: Testing ADD Actuator Operation (Pickup 4WD & 4Runner 4WD with ADD)***

## AXLE SHAFTS & BEARINGS

***NOTE: For Camry All-Trac, Celica All-Trac, Cressida and Supra rear axle shaft removal and installation procedure, see RWD AXLE SHAFTS article in DRIVE AXLES. For Pickup 4WD, Previa 4WD and 4Runner 4WD front axle shaft removal and installation procedure, see 4WD FRONT AXLE SHAFTS article in DRIVE AXLES.***

### DIFFERENTIAL ASSEMBLY

**Removal – 1)** Drain gear oil. On Camry All-Trac and Celica All-Trac, remove rear crossmember. On all models, disconnect drive axles from side gear flanges. Mark drive shaft and companion flange for installation reference. Disconnect drive shaft.

**2)** Disconnect vacuum hoses and electrical connector (if equipped). On Cressida, remove stabilizer links and bar. On all models, support differential assembly using jack. Remove differential assembly mounting bolts and nuts. Lower differential assembly from vehicle.

**Installation** – To install, reverse removal procedure. Ensure reference marks on drive shaft and companion flange align. Tighten all fasteners to specification. See TORQUE SPECIFICATIONS table at end of article.

# 1991 DRIVE AXLES
## Differentials & Axle Shafts – Integral Housing (Cont.)

### PINION FLANGE & OIL SEAL

**Removal** – **1)** Drain gear oil. On Camry All-Trac and Celica All-Trac, remove rear crossmember. On all models, mark drive shaft and drive pinion companion flange for installation reference. Remove drive shaft. Reverse staked portion of companion flange nut. Remove flange nut.

**2)** Remove companion flange. Remove oil seal from housing. Remove oil slinger. Using a puller, remove front bearing from housing. Remove and discard collapsible spacer.

***NOTE: Replace collapsible spacer whenever companion flange nut is loosened or removed.***

**Installation** – **1)** Install new collapsible spacer and front bearing. Install oil slinger with concave side facing front drive pinion bearing. Apply grease to seal lips. Install new oil seal to correct depth. See SEAL DEPTH INSTALLATION SPECIFICATIONS table.

***SEAL DEPTH INSTALLATION SPECIFICATIONS***

| Application | In. (mm) |
|---|---|
| Drive Pinion Seal | |
| Camry All-Trac, Celica All-Trac & Previa 4WD | .08 (2.0) |
| Cressida, Pickup 4WD, Supra & 4Runner 4WD | .06 (1.5) |

**2)** Install companion flange. Install companion flange nut. Tighten flange nut to specification, and measure pinion preload. See TORQUE SPECIFICATIONS and AXLE ASSEMBLY SPECIFICATIONS tables at end of article.

**3)** If preload is greater than specification, replace collapsible spacer, and repeat procedure. If preload is less than specification, tighten nut in increments of 108 INCH lbs. (12 N.m) until preload is correct.

**4)** Check pinion nut torque. Check longitudinal and latitudinal runout of companion flange using dial indicator. Replace companion flange if runout is greater than .004" (.10 mm). Stake drive pinion nut. Install drive shaft. Ensure reference marks align.

### SIDE GEAR SHAFTS & OIL SEALS

**Removal (Camry All-Trac, Celica All-Trac & Previa 4WD)** – **1)** Drain gear oil. Remove drive axle shaft. See RWD AXLE SHAFTS or 4WD FRONT AXLE SHAFTS article in DRIVE AXLES. Remove differential cover.

**2)** Remove side gear shaft snap ring. Remove side gear shaft. On Previa 4WD, remove side gear shaft tube. On all models, remove oil seal.

**Installation** – Install and grease oil seal. Install side gear shaft and tube (if equipped) to differential. Install new snap ring on side gear shaft. Ensure side gear shaft cannot be pulled out by hand.

**Removal (Cressida & Supra)** – Drain gear oil. Remove drive axle shaft. See RWD AXLE SHAFTS article in DRIVE AXLES. Using puller, remove side gear shaft. Remove snap ring from end of shaft. Remove oil seal.

**Installation** – Install and grease oil seal. Install new snap ring on side gear shaft. Install side gear shaft to differential. Ensure side gear shaft cannot be pulled out by hand.

**Removal (Pickup 4WD & 4Runner 4WD With Automatic Disconnecting Differential)** – **1)** Drain gear oil. Remove drive axle shaft. See 4WD FRONT AXLE SHAFTS article in DRIVE AXLES. Remove vacuum actuator and differential carrier cover. Remove left side gear shaft tube Torx bolts.

**2)** Tighten bolts to specification. See TORQUE SPECIFICATIONS table at end of article. Ensure side gear shaft cannot be pulled out by hand.

**Removal (Pickup 4WD & 4Runner 4WD Without Automatic Disconnecting Differential)** – Drain gear oil. Remove drive axle shaft. See 4WD FRONT AXLE SHAFTS article in DRIVE AXLES. Using puller, remove side gear shaft. Remove snap ring from end of shaft. Remove left side differential tube. Remove oil seal.

**Installation** – Install and grease oil seal. Install differential tube. Install new snap ring on side gear shaft. Install side gear shaft to differential. Ensure side gear shaft cannot be pulled out by hand.

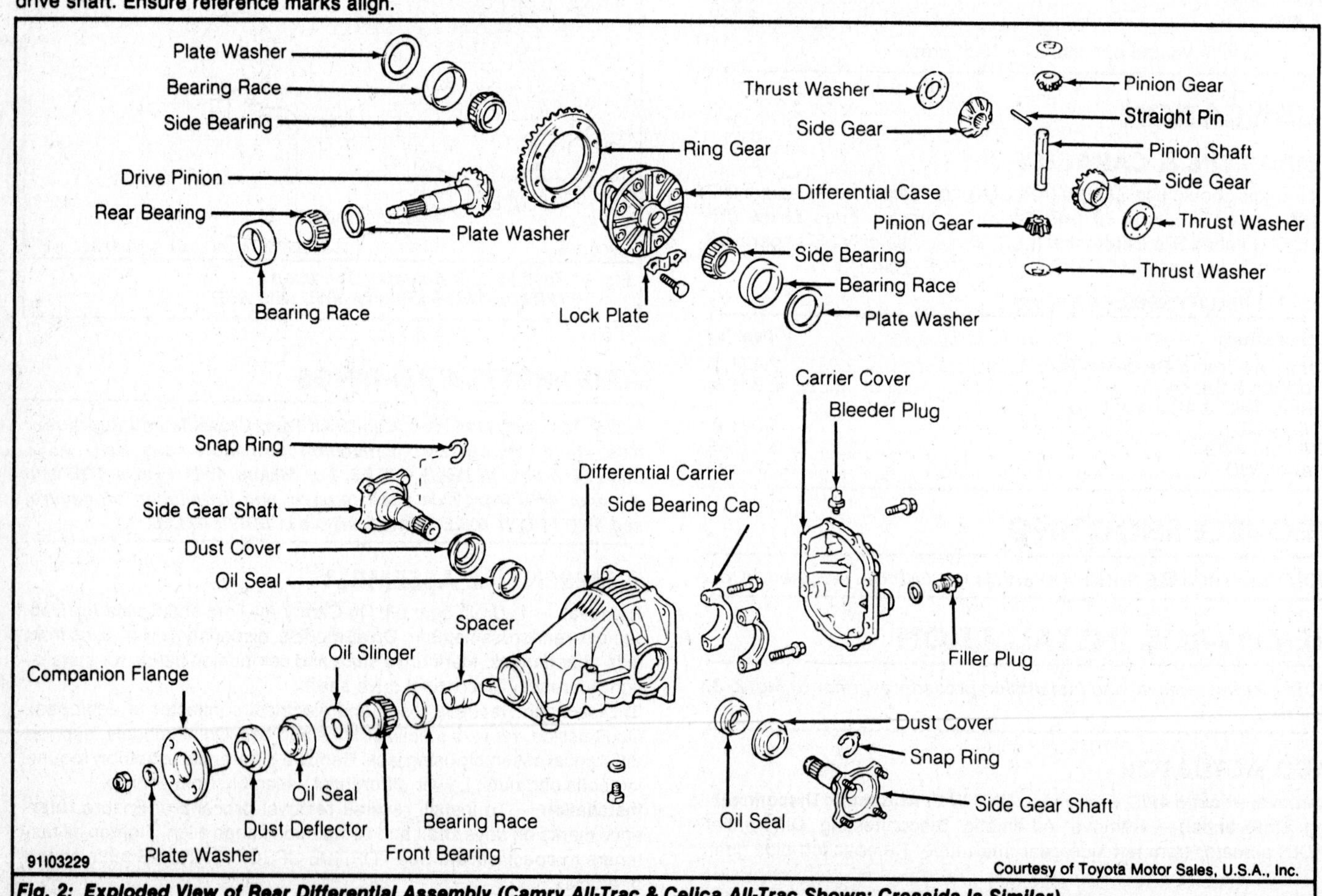


***Fig. 2: Exploded View of Rear Differential Assembly (Camry All-Trac & Celica All-Trac Shown; Cressida Is Similar)***

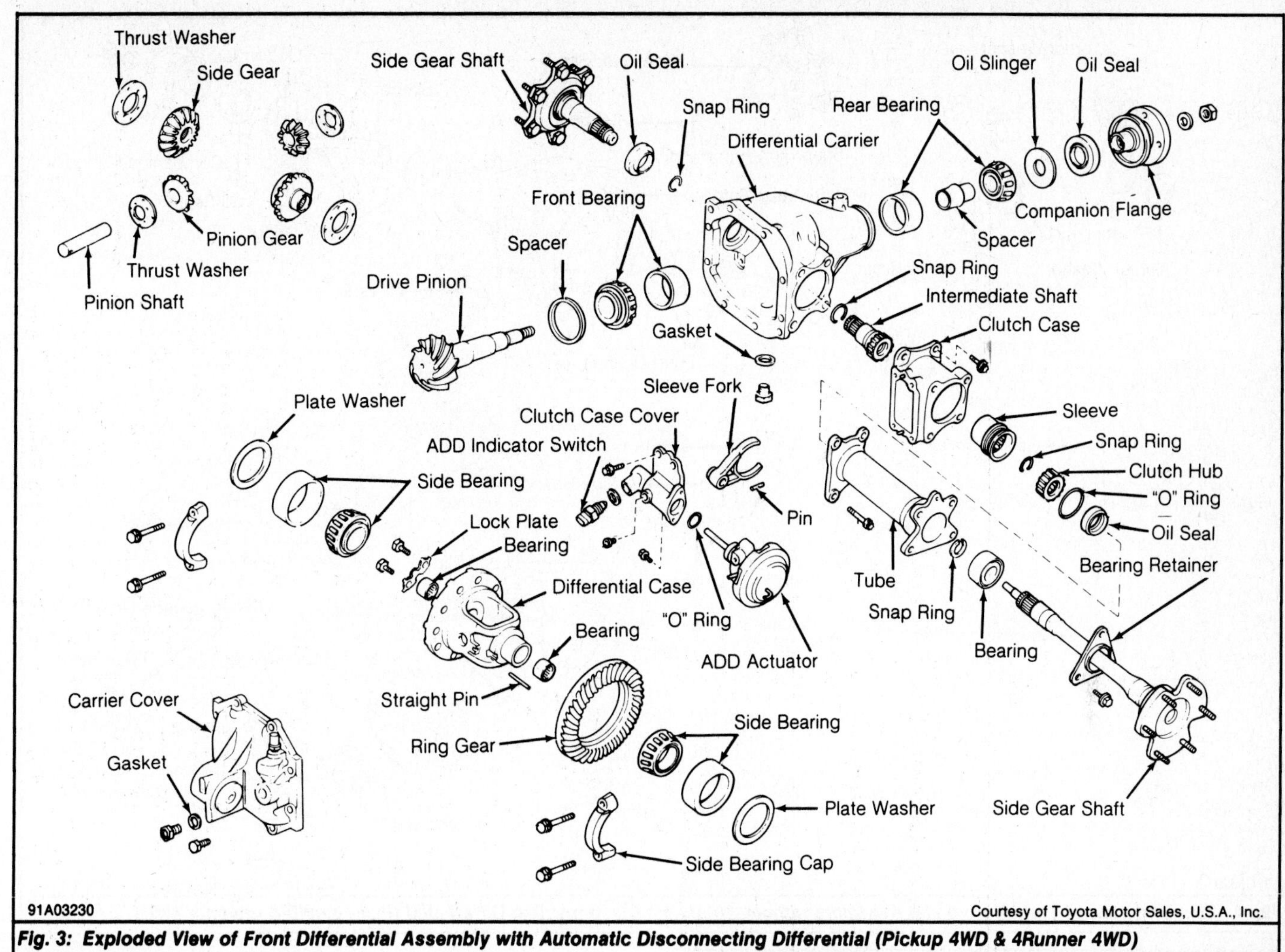


***Fig. 3: Exploded View of Front Differential Assembly with Automatic Disconnecting Differential (Pickup 4WD & 4Runner 4WD)***

# OVERHAUL

## DIFFERENTIAL ASSEMBLY

***NOTE: Refer to Fig. 2, 3, 4, 5 or 6 during overhaul procedures.***

**Disassembly – 1)** Remove differential carrier cover. Check pinion companion flange lateral and radial runout. If runout exceeds .004" (.10 mm), replace companion flange.

**2)** Using INCH-pound torque wrench, measure drive pinion starting preload and total preload. See AXLE ASSEMBLY SPECIFICATIONS table at end of article.

**3)** Check ring gear runout and backlash. See AXLE ASSEMBLY SPECIFICATIONS table. Check gear tooth contact pattern. See GEAR TOOTH CONTACT PATTERNS article in GENERAL INFORMATION.

**4)** On 2-pinion conventional differentials, check side gear backlash. See AXLE ASSEMBLY SPECIFICATIONS table. On all models, remove side gear shafts, oil seals and differential tube (if equipped). See SIDE GEAR SHAFTS & OIL SEALS under REMOVAL & INSTALLATION.

**5)** Remove drive pinion flange and oil seal. See PINION FLANGE & OIL SEAL under REMOVAL & INSTALLATION. Paint mating marks on bearing caps, and remove caps. Remove 2 side bearing preload adjusting plate washers. Measure washers, and record thicknesses.

**6)** Remove differential case and ring gear. Remove differential case side bearing outer races. Index mark bearings, gears and thrust washers. Remove drive pinion shaft from differential carrier. Press rear bearing from pinion shaft.

**7)** Drive front and rear drive pinion bearing outer races from carrier. Inspect bearings, outer races and pinion shaft for wear and damage. Discard collapsible spacer. Ring gear and drive pinion must be replaced as a set.

**8)** Remove side bearings from differential case using puller. Keep side bearings together with correct outer races, and mark for reassembly. Place alignment marks on ring gear and differential case.

**9)** Remove ring gear bolts and locking tabs. Tap ring gear using plastic hammer to remove. Disassemble differential case. See DIFFERENTIAL CASE under OVERHAUL.

**Reassembly – 1)** Clean contact surfaces of differential case. Heat ring gear to 212°F (100°C) in oil bath. DO NOT heat ring gear warmer than 230°F (110°). Clean ring gear contact surface with solvent.

**2)** Install ring gear on differential case while it is still hot. Align index marks on ring gear and case. Coat ring gear bolts with hypoid oil, and install with lock plates.

**3)** Tighten ring gear bolts gradually in diagonal sequence to specification. See TORQUE SPECIFICATIONS table at end of article. Stake lock plates with one tab flush against flat of bolt head. Tab resting on point should be staked on tightening side of point.

**4)** Press side bearings onto differential case. Install case, with side bearings, into carrier. Install plate washers until no play exists in bearing. Temporarily install bearing caps.

**5)** Check ring gear runout using dial indicator against back of gear (opposite teeth). See AXLE ASSEMBLY SPECIFICATIONS table at end of article. If runout exceeds specification, rotate ring gear on case, and remeasure. If runout cannot be brought within specified range, case or ring gear must be replaced.

**6)** Install front and rear bearing outer races into carrier. Press rear drive pinion bearing, with depth shim under bearing, onto drive pinion. Install drive pinion into carrier. Install front bearing.

# 1991 DRIVE AXLES
## Differentials & Axle Shafts – Integral Housing (Cont.)

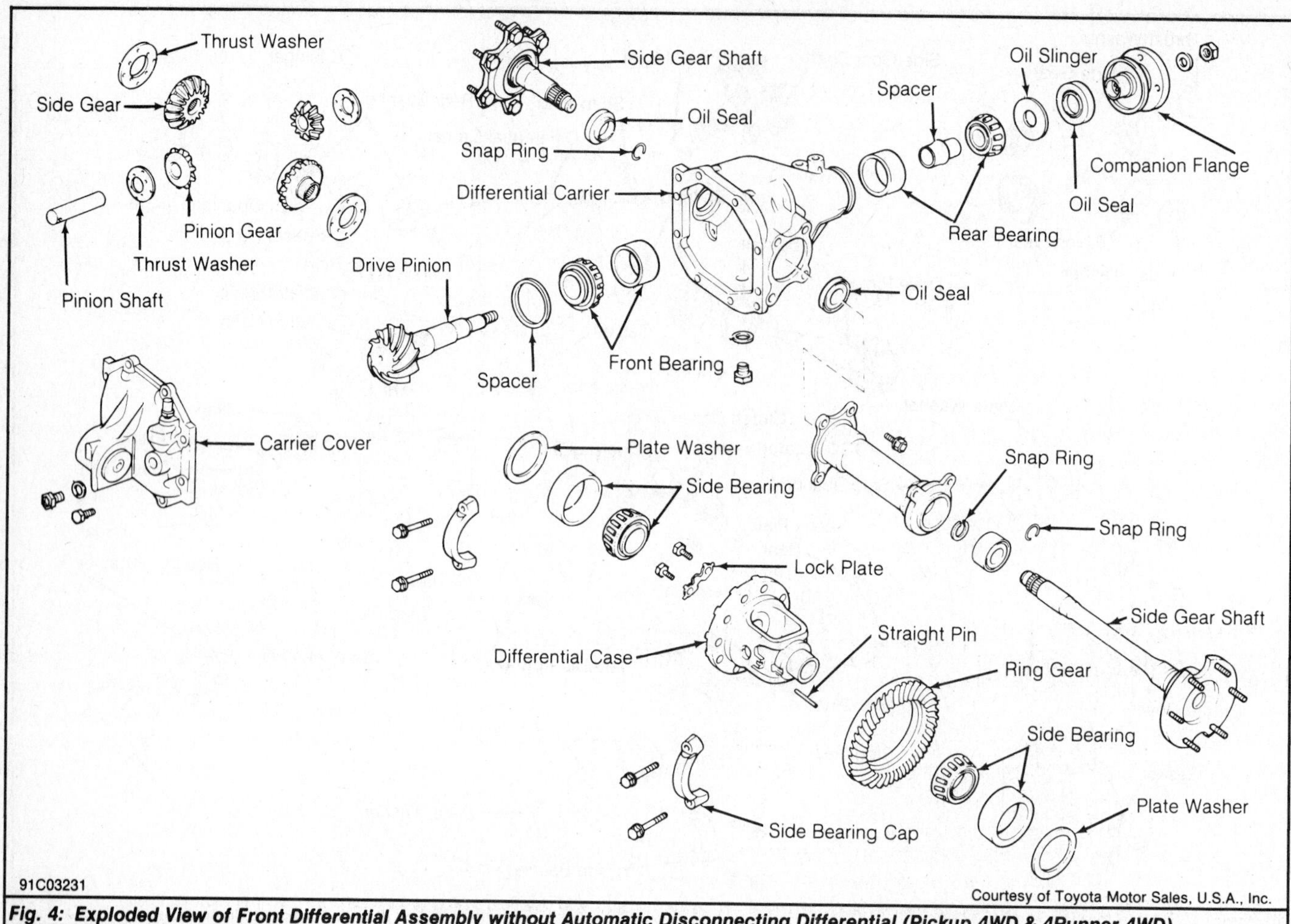


*Fig. 4: Exploded View of Front Differential Assembly without Automatic Disconnecting Differential (Pickup 4WD & 4Runner 4WD)*

***NOTE: Drive pinion preload is set in 2 stages. Initial adjustment is made without collapsible spacer, oil slinger or oil seal installed. Final adjustment is made with differential case installed and ring and pinion backlash set.***

**7)** Install companion flange, and lightly grease threads of flange nut. Install flange nut, and adjust drive pinion preload by slowly tightening nut. Measure preload using torque wrench. See AXLE ASSEMBLY SPECIFICATIONS table.

***CAUTION: Since spacer is not yet installed, tighten pinion nut slowly until desired preload is obtained. DO NOT exceed torque specification. See TORQUE SPECIFICATIONS table.***

**8)** Place bearing outer races on respective bearings, and install differential case into carrier. Install plate washer only on side opposite ring gear teeth. Tap ring gear using plastic hammer to seat washer and bearing.

**9)** Install dial indicator with plunger on tooth surface of ring gear. Apply downward pressure on side bearing boss. Measure ring gear-to-drive pinion reference backlash. See RING GEAR INITIAL BACKLASH SPECIFICATIONS table.

***RING GEAR INITIAL BACKLASH SPECIFICATIONS***

| Application | In. (mm) |
|---|---|
| Camry All-Trac & Celica All-Trac | .005-.007 (.13-.18) |
| Cressida & Supra | .004 (.10) |
| Pickup 4WD, Previa 4WD & 4Runner 4WD | .005 (.13) |

**10)** Using initial backlash as reference, select ring gear (back side) plate washer. Select ring gear side (tooth side) plate washer just thick enough to eliminate clearance between outer race and case. Remove plate washers and differential case from carrier.

**11)** Install plate washer into lower part of carrier. Place other plate washer on differential case with outer race. Install case assembly into carrier housing. Seat washer and bearing by tapping ring gear using plastic hammer. Measure ring gear backlash using dial indicator.

**12)** See AXLE ASSEMBLY SPECIFICATIONS table. Adjust backlash by increasing or decreasing washers on both sides by equal amounts. Ensure no clearance exists between plate washer and case. Ensure ring gear backlash exists at all times.

**13)** After adjustment, remove ring gear (tooth side) plate washer, and measure thickness. Install washer .002-.004" (.05-.10 mm) thicker than washer removed.

***NOTE: Select washer which can be pressed in 2/3 of way by finger pressure. Backlash will change approximately .0008" (.020 mm) for every .0012" (.030 mm) change in washer thickness.***

**14)** Using a plastic hammer, tap washer in place. Recheck ring gear backlash. See AXLE ASSEMBLY SPECIFICATIONS table. Adjust as necessary. Align index marks on caps and carrier. Install cap bolts, and tighten to specification. See TORQUE SPECIFICATIONS table.

**15)** Measure total drive pinion preload. Ensure total preload equals drive pinion preload plus assembled preload. See AXLE ASSEMBLY SPECIFICATIONS table. Coat 3 or 4 teeth at 3 different positions on ring gear with red lead.

**16)** Hold companion flange firmly and rotate ring gear in both directions. Inspect gear tooth contact pattern. Adjust as necessary by changing shims on drive pinion. See GEAR TOOTH CONTACT PATTERNS article in GENERAL INFORMATION.

# 1991 DRIVE AXLES
## Differentials & Axle Shafts – Integral Housing (Cont.)

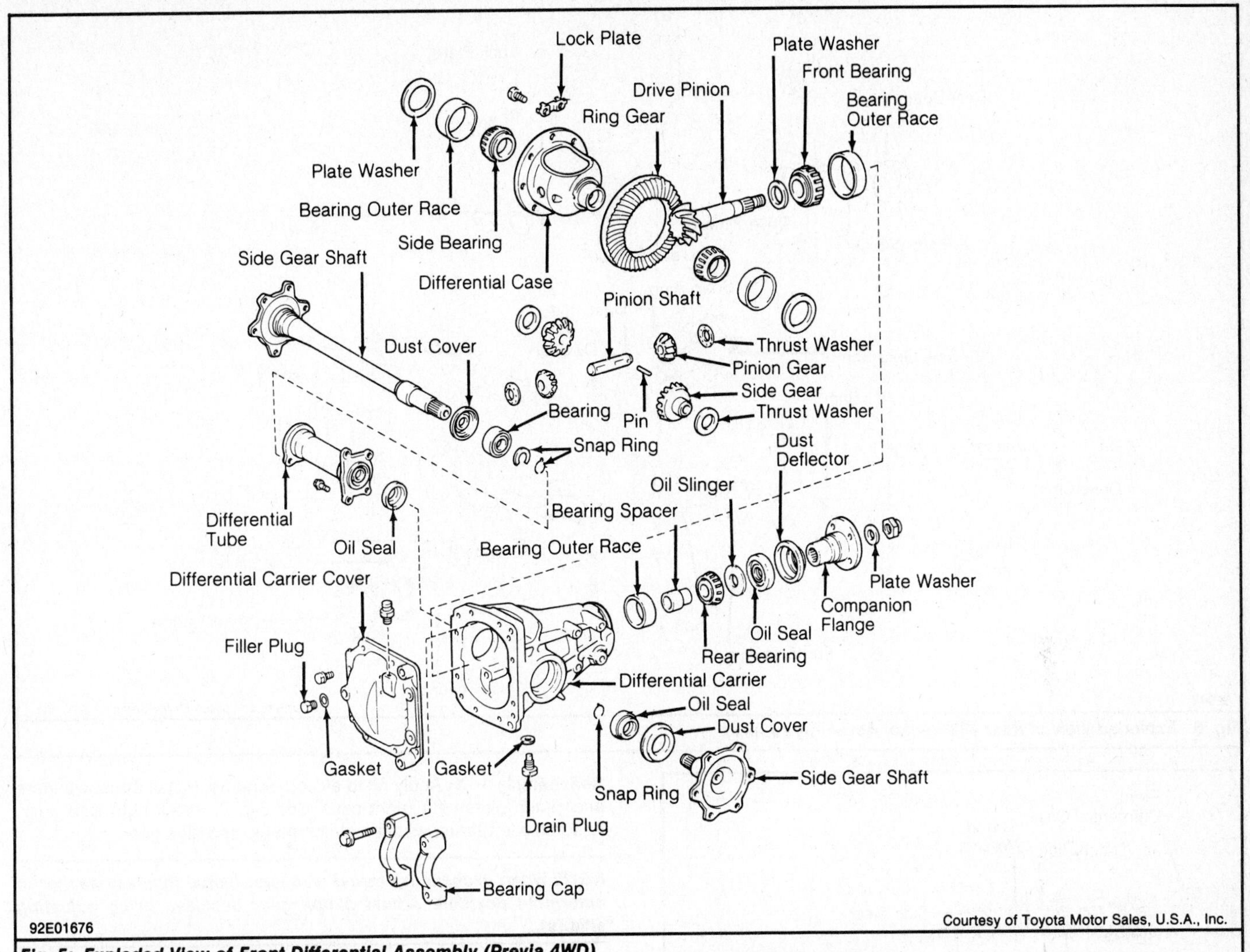


***Fig. 5: Exploded View of Front Differential Assembly (Previa 4WD)***

**17)** Remove companion flange and front bearing. See PINION FLANGE & OIL SEAL under REMOVAL & INSTALLATION. Install new bearing collapsible spacer, front bearing, oil slinger and oil seal. Install companion flange, and tighten pinion nut to minimum specification. See TORQUE SPECIFICATIONS table.

**18)** Check total differential preload. Total preload range equals measured drive pinion preload plus assembled preload. See AXLE ASSEMBLY SPECIFICATIONS table.

**19)** If preload is greater than specification, replace collapsible spacer, and repeat procedure. If preload is less than specification, tighten pinion companion flange nut in increments of 108 INCH lbs. (13 N.m).

***NOTE: If maximum pinion flange nut torque is reached before minimum preload is attained, replace collapsible spacer, and repeat procedure. See TORQUE SPECIFICATIONS table.***

**20)** Ensure companion flange longitudinal and latitudinal runout do not exceed .004" (.10 mm). Stake drive pinion flange nut. Install side gear shafts and oil seals. See SIDE GEAR SHAFTS & OIL SEALS under REMOVAL & INSTALLATION.

**21)** Apply sealant to differential cover, and install cover. Tighten bolts to specification. See TORQUE SPECIFICATIONS table.

### DIFFERENTIAL CASE

**Disassembly (Conventional Differential) – 1)** On 2-pinion differentials, use hammer and punch to drive out pinion shaft-to-case lock pin. On 4-pinion differentials, mark case halves for reassembly reference, and remove bolts retaining case halves.

**2)** On all differentials, remove pinion shaft, pinion gears, side gears and thrust washers. Thoroughly clean and inspect all parts for wear and damage. Repair or replace parts as necessary.

**Reassembly – 1)** Install side gears and thrust washers in case. *See Fig. 2, 3, 4, 5 or 6*. Thrust washers should be same size for both sides. Install pinion gears with thrust washers. Tap pinion shaft into place. Hold pinion gear toward case. Check side gear backlash.

**2)** Change thickness of thrust washers until side gear backlash is .002-.008" (.05-.20 mm). On 2-pinion differentials, install lock pin through case and hole in pinion shaft. Stake pin to differential case.

**3)** On 4-pinion differentials, align marks, and install case halves. Alternately tighten bolts to specification. See TORQUE SPECIFICATIONS table at end of article.

**Disassembly (Limited Slip Differential) –** Mark case halves for reassembly reference. Remove bolts, and separate case halves. Remove side gears, thrust washers, spring and clutch plates, and mark for reassembly reference. *See Fig. 7*. Replace damaged or worn parts.

# 1991 DRIVE AXLES
## Differentials & Axle Shafts – Integral Housing (Cont.)

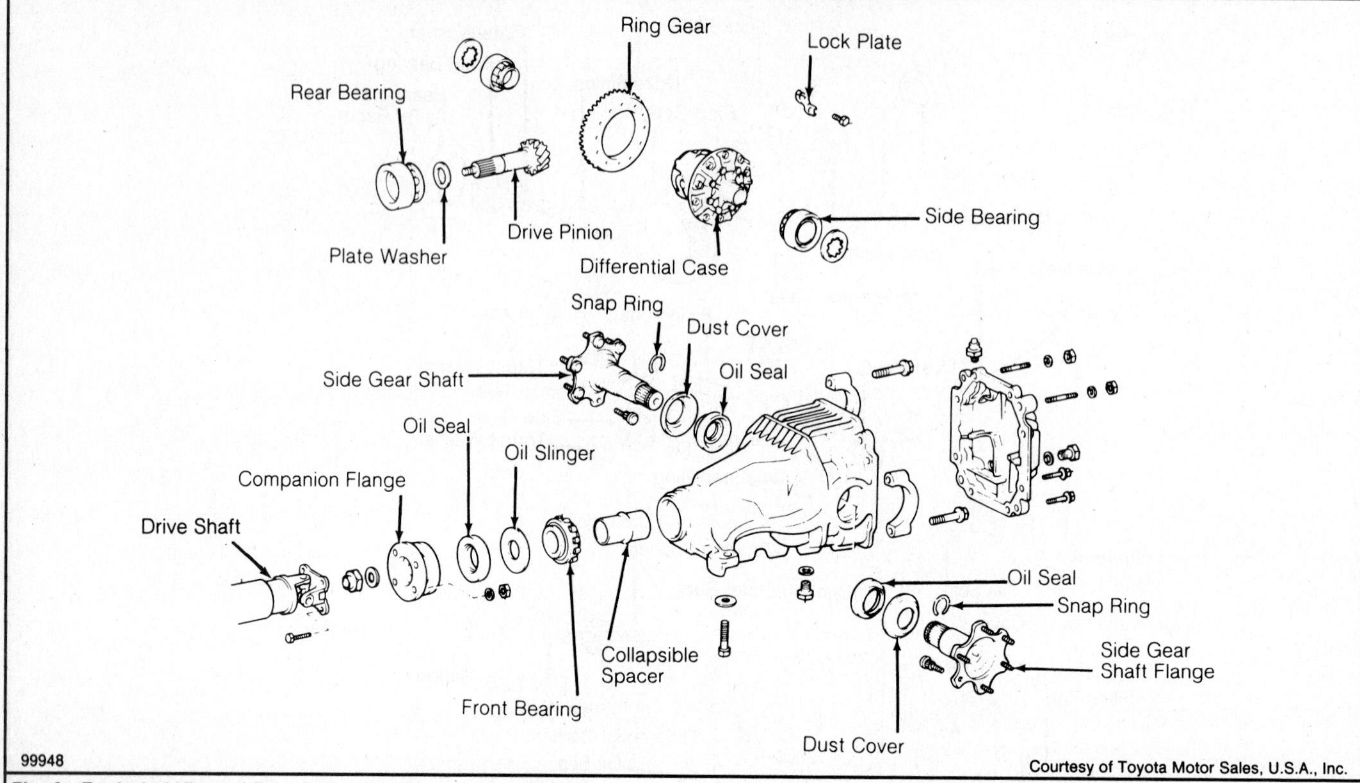

99948 Courtesy of Toyota Motor Sales, U.S.A., Inc.

***Fig. 6: Exploded View of Rear Differential Assembly (Supra)***

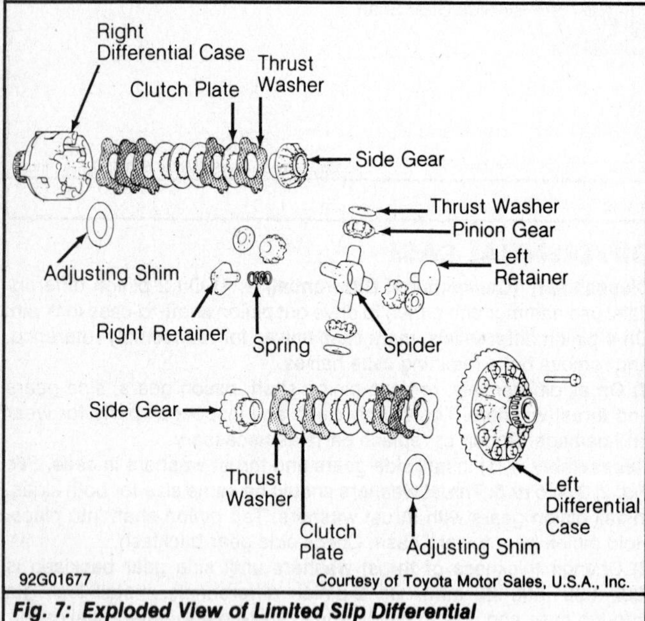


***Fig. 7: Exploded View of Limited Slip Differential (Cressida & Supra)***

**Reassembly** – **1)** Apply oil to all components. Install thrust washers and clutch plates into right case. *See Fig. 7.* Install right side gear. Assemble left thrust washer, clutch plates and side gear.

***NOTE: When exchanging thrust washers, install thinnest washer in outermost position. Adjust pinion gear backlash using adjusting shim(s).***

**2)** Install pinion gears, washers and right retainer to spider. Ensure retainer holes align with knock pins in spider. Install spider assembly into differential case.

**3)** Measure side gear-to-pinion gear backlash. If backlash is not .002-.008" (.05-.20 mm), replace shim. See LSD SIDE GEAR BACKLASH SHIM ADJUSTMENT SPECIFICATIONS table.

***LSD SIDE GEAR BACKLASH SHIM ADJUSTMENT SPECIFICATIONS***

| Shim Indication | Thickness – In. (mm) |
|---|---|
| A | .006 (.15) |
| B | .008 (.20) |
| C | .010 (.25) |
| D | .012 (.30) |
| E | .014 (.35) |

**4)** Check backlash of all pinion gears. Check left case gears using same procedure. Install spring, and assemble case halves. Ensure reference marks align.

**5)** Apply oil to bolts of case halves. Tighten bolts alternately and evenly to specification. See TORQUE SPECIFICATIONS table at end of article.

# 1991 DRIVE AXLES
# Differentials & Axle Shafts – Integral Housing (Cont.)

## AXLE ASSEMBLY SPECIFICATIONS

*AXLE ASSEMBLY SPECIFICATIONS*

| Application | In. (mm) |
|---|---|
| Pinion Flange Runout | |
| Latitudinal | .004 (.10) |
| Longitudinal | .004 (.10) |
| Ring Gear Backlash | .005-.007 (.13-.18) |
| Ring Gear Runout | |
| Cressida & Supra | .004 (.10) |
| Except Cressida & Supra | .003 (.07) |
| Side Gear Backlash | .002-.008 (.05-.20) |
| Side Gear Flange Runout (Supra) | .008 (.20) |
| Side Gear Shaft Runout (Supra) | .008 (.20) |
| | INCH Lbs. (N.m) |
| Assembled Preload [1] | |
| Camry All-Trac, Celica All-Trac & Previa 4WD | 2.6-4.3 (.29-.49) |
| Cressida, Pickup 4WD, Supra & 4Runner 4WD | 3.5-5.2 (.40-.59) |
| Drive Pinion Preload | |
| Camry All-Trac, Celica All-Trac, Previa 4WD & Supra | |
| New Bearings | 8.7-13.9 (1.0-1.6) |
| Used Bearings | 4.3-6.9 (.5-.8) |
| Cressida | 4.3-6.9 (.5-.8) |
| Pickup 4WD & 4Runner 4WD | |
| New Bearings | 10.4-16.5 (1.2-1.9) |
| Used Bearings | 5.2-8.7 (.6-1.0) |
| Side Gear Bearing Preload | .9-3.5 (.1-.4) |

[1] – Add this amount to drive pinion preload to obtain total preload.

## TORQUE SPECIFICATIONS

*TORQUE SPECIFICATIONS*

| Application | Ft. Lbs. (N.m) |
|---|---|
| ADD Actuator Bolts | 15 (20) |
| Clutch Case Bolts (With ADD) | 58 (78) |
| Drain Plug | 36 (49) |
| Differential Mounting Bolt & Nut | |
| Camry All-Trac & Celica All-Trac | |
| Front | 70 (95) |
| Rear | 108 (146) |
| Cressida | |
| Forward Case Mount | 71 (96) |
| Rear Cover Mount Bolt | 90 (122) |
| Pickup 4WD & 4Runner 4WD | |
| Forward Crossmember Mount | 108 (146) |
| Side Mounts | 148 (201) |
| Previa 4WD | 54 (73) |
| Supra | |
| Forward Case Mount | 123 (167) |
| Rear Cover Stud Nuts | 67 (91) |
| Differential Tube Bolts | 65 (88) |
| Drive Shaft Flange Bolts | |
| Except Previa 4WD | 54 (73) |
| Previa 4WD | 27 (37) |
| Filler Plug | 29 (39) |
| Pinion Flange Nut | |
| Cressida & Supra | [1] 134-250 (182-339) |
| Camry All-Trac, Celica All-Trac & Previa 4WD | [1] 80-174 (108-236) |
| Pickup 4WD & 4Runner 4WD | [1] 89-165 (121-224) |
| Rear Cover Bolt | 34 (46) |
| Rear Crossmember Bolt (Camry All-Trac & Celica All-Trac) | 53 (72) |
| Ring Gear Bolts | 71 (96) |
| Side Bearing Cap Bolts | 58 (78) |
| Side Gear Flange-To-Drive Axle Nut | |
| Except Pickup 4WD & 4Runner 4WD | 51 (69) |
| Pickup 4WD & 4Runner 4WD | 61 (83) |
| Side Gear Shaft Tube Bolts | |
| Except Pickup 4WD & 4Runner 4WD With ADD | 65 (88) |
| Pickup 4WD & 4Runner 4WD With ADD | 58 (78) |

[1] – Minimum and maximum torque for adjustment of drive pinion preload. See DIFFERENTIAL ASSEMBLY under OVERHAUL.

# 1991 DRIVE AXLES
# Differentials & Axle Shafts – Separate Carrier

## Corolla All-Trac, Land Cruiser, Pickup, Previa, 4Runner

**NOTE: For models with independent suspension, see RWD AXLE SHAFTS, FWD AXLE SHAFTS or 4WD FRONT AXLE SHAFTS article for axle shaft overhaul.**

## DESCRIPTION

The axle assembly is a hypoid-gear type with separate carrier housing. One-piece differential cases use 2 pinion gears. Two-piece differential cases use 4 pinion gears. Drive pinion preload is adjusted using a collapsible spacer. Side bearing preload is adjusted using adjustable nuts. On Land Cruiser, rear axle shafts are held in place by a shaft lock clip.

## AXLE RATIO & IDENTIFICATION

Toyota uses one basic type of separate carrier axle assembly. Any differences in removal, installation or overhaul procedures between vehicle models will be noted where they occur. Axle ratio is determined by dividing the number of ring gear teeth by the number of pinion gear teeth.

**AXLE RATIO SPECIFICATIONS**

| Application | Ratio |
|---|---|
| Corolla All-Trac | 2.929:1 |
| Land Cruiser | |
| Front | [1] |
| Rear | 4.100:1 |
| Pickup | |
| 2WD | |
| 4-Cylinder | |
| Automatic Transmission | 3.727:1 |
| Manual Transmission | 3.583:1 |
| V6 | |
| Automatic Transmission | 3.417:1 |
| Manual Transmission | |
| 1-Ton Models | 3.900:1 |
| Cab Chassis Model | 4.100:1 |
| All Others | 3.417:1 |
| 4WD | |
| 4-Cylinder | |
| Automatic Transmission | 4.556:1 |
| Manual Transmission | 4.100:1 |
| V6 | |
| Automatic Transmission | 4.100:1 |
| Manual Transmission | [2] 4.100:1 |
| Previa | 4.300:1 |
| 4Runner | |
| 4-Cylinder | |
| Automatic Transmission | 4.556:1 |
| Manual Transmission | 4.100:1 |
| V6 | |
| 2WD | 3.900:1 |
| 4WD | [2] 4.100:1 |

[1] – Information is not available from manufacturer.
[2] – 4.556 with optional 31" aluminum wheels.

## LUBRICATION

### FLUID TYPE & CAPACITY

All models should use SAE 90 (API GL-5) for temperatures greater than 0°F (-18°C) and SAE 80W-90 (API GL-5) for temperatures less than 0°F (-18°C). See FLUID CAPACITY SPECIFICATIONS table.

**FLUID CAPACITY SPECIFICATIONS**

| Application | Pts. (L) |
|---|---|
| Corolla All-Trac | 2.4 (1.1) |
| Land Cruiser | |
| Front | 5.4 (2.6) |
| Rear | 6.0 (2.8) |
| Pickup & 4Runner | |
| 2WD | |
| 7.5" Ring Gear | 2.8 (1.4) |
| 8.0" Ring Gear | 3.8 (1.8) |
| 4WD | 4.6 (2.2) |
| Previa | 3.2 (1.5) |

## TROUBLE SHOOTING

**NOTE: See TROUBLE SHOOTING article in GENERAL INFORMATION.**

## REMOVAL & INSTALLATION

### FRONT AXLE SHAFT & BEARING

**Removal (Land Cruiser) – 1)** Raise and support vehicle. Disconnect brake line, and remove brake caliper. Set hub control handle to FREE position. Remove control handle cover bolts and cover. *See Fig. 1.*

**2)** Remove snap ring. Remove free wheel hub body mounting nuts. Using a brass punch and hammer, tap bolt heads, and remove cone washers.

**3)** Remove free wheel hub body. Bend back tabs on spindle nut lock plate. Remove lock nut. Remove lock plate and adjusting nut. Remove axle hub with brake disc attached. Remove thrust washer and outer bearing. Remove axle hub with disc. Remove oil seal and inner wheel bearing.

**4)** Drive outer bearing races from hub. Remove dust shield retaining bolts. Remove dust seal, gasket and shield. Remove spindle assembly by tapping with a brass drift. Remove gasket. Position one flat of Constant Velocity (CV) joint pointing upward. Remove axle shaft assembly.

**NOTE: DO NOT disconnect steering knuckle. Front end alignment and knuckle bearing preload settings will be affected and will require readjustment.**

**Installation – 1)** Install axle shaft with one flat of CV joint pointing upward. Pack steering knuckle cavity with grease to about 3/4 of knuckle volume. Install spindle on knuckle with new gasket.

**2)** Install dust cover, new gasket and dust seal on spindle. Tighten 8 spindle mounting bolts. Pack front hub bearings, and coat inside of hub with multipurpose grease. Install inner bearing and oil seal. Lightly coat lips of seal with grease.

**3)** Install axle hub on spindle. Install outer bearing and thrust washer. Tighten adjusting nut to 43 ft. lbs. (58 N.m). Rotate hub several times in each direction. Loosen adjusting nut until finger tight. Retighten adjusting nut to 48 INCH lbs. (5.4 N.m).

**4)** Check axle hub preload starting torque with spring scale. If preload is 6.2-12.6 lbs. (2.8-5.7 kg), install lock washer and lock nut. Tighten lock nut to 47 ft. lbs. (64 N.m), and bend one tab of lock washer in and one tab out to secure. If preload is not within specification, adjust preload by adjusting wheel bearing adjusting nut.

**5)** Install locking hub. Install cone washers and nuts. Tighten nuts evenly. Install a bolt in end of axle shaft and then pull axle shaft out of hub far enough to install snap ring. Install snap ring.

**6)** Apply grease to inner hub splines. Ensure hub control handle is in FREE position. Install new gasket and hub cover. Install dust cap. To complete installation, reverse removal procedure. Bleed brakes.

### REAR AXLE SHAFT & BEARING

**Removal (Corolla All-Trac) – 1)** Raise and support vehicle. Remove wheel. Disconnect and plug brake line at wheel cylinder. Remove brake drum. *See Fig. 2.*

**2)** Remove backing plate. Using puller, remove axle shaft. DO NOT damage oil seal. Remove end gasket. Grind down bearing retainer and remove using chisel. Press bearing from shaft.

**Installation – 1)** Press outer retainer and new bearing onto axle shaft. Heat inner retainer to 302°F (150°C) in an oil bath. Clean retainer and axle shaft of oil and grease. While still hot, press inner retainer onto axle shaft.

**2)** Replace oil seal (if necessary). Install new seal to a depth of .22" (5.6 mm). To complete installation, reverse removal procedure. Tighten axle flange bolts to specification. See appropriate TORQUE SPECIFICATIONS table at end of article.

**CAUTION: On Land Cruiser, remove rear differential inspection cover BEFORE attempting to remove axle shaft.**

# Differentials & Axle Shafts – Separate Carrier (Cont.)

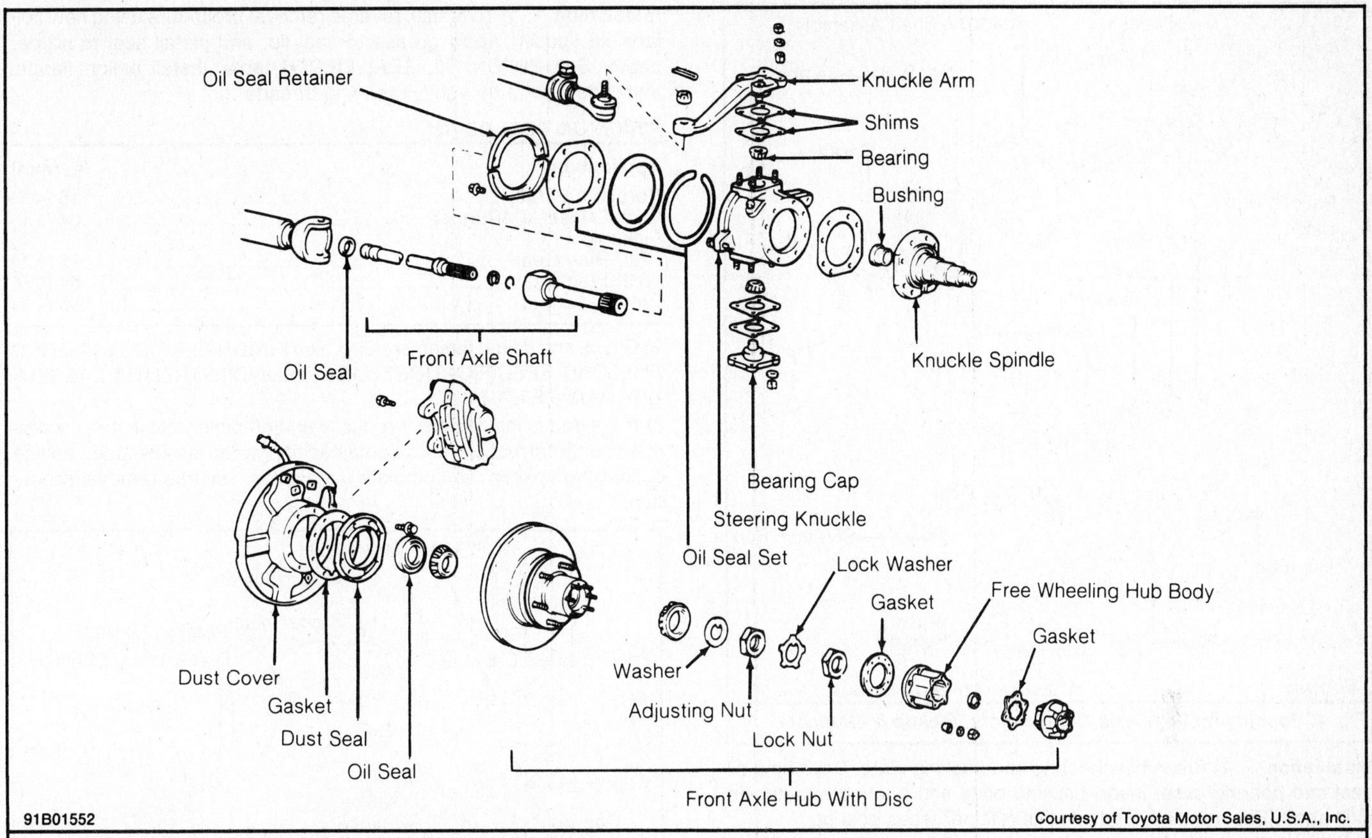

91B01552 Courtesy of Toyota Motor Sales, U.S.A., Inc.

*Fig. 1: Identifying Front Axle Shaft Components (Land Cruiser)*

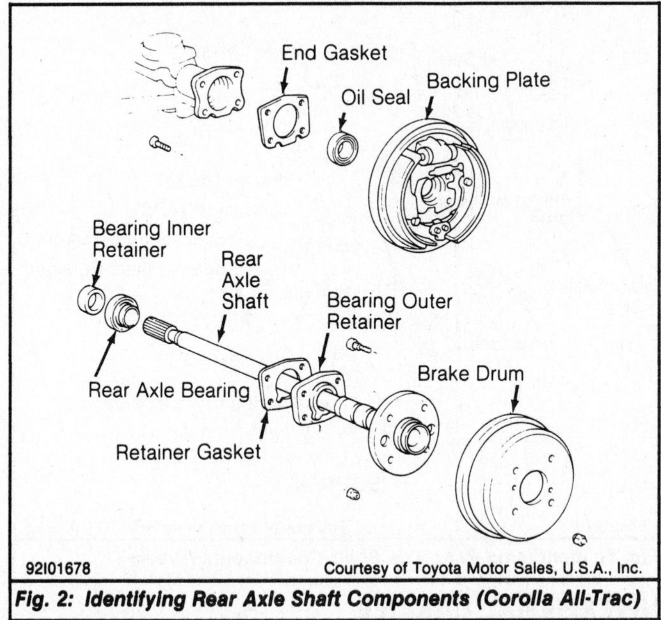


*Fig. 2: Identifying Rear Axle Shaft Components (Corolla All-Trac)*

**Removal (Land Cruiser) – 1)** Raise and support vehicle. Remove wheel and brake drum. Drain differential housing. Remove proportioning valve shackle bracket and brake cable clamp. Remove differential cover and gasket. *See Fig. 3.*

**2)** Remove differential pinion shaft lock pin. Remove pinion shaft and spacer. Push axle shaft inward. Remove axle lock circlip. Remove axle shaft. Using bearing puller, remove axle bearing and oil seal together.

**Installation – 1)** Apply multipurpose grease to new bearing. Drive bearing and new oil seal into housing. Coat lip of seal with grease. Install rear axle shaft.

**2)** To complete installation, reverse removal procedure. Check axle shaft end thrust clearance. Select pinion shaft spacer that gives maximum clearance of .020" (.50 mm) between axle shaft and spacer.

**Removal (Pickup & 4Runner) – 1)** Raise and support vehicle. Disconnect parking brake cable. *See Fig. 4*. Disconnect and plug brake line at wheel cylinder. Remove brake drum.

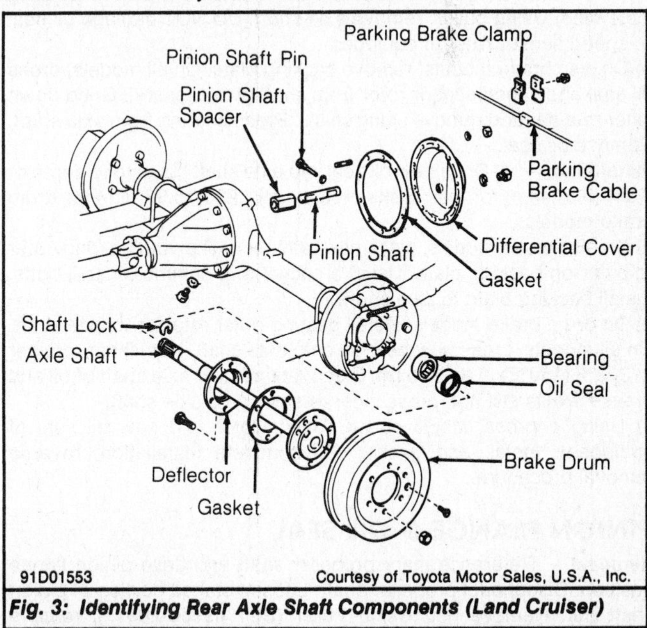


*Fig. 3: Identifying Rear Axle Shaft Components (Land Cruiser)*

**2)** Remove backing plate and axle shaft. Remove "O" ring. Remove axle shaft snap ring. Press out axle shaft from backing plate. Remove bearing retainer from axle shaft. Remove outer oil seal. Press old bearing from backing plate.

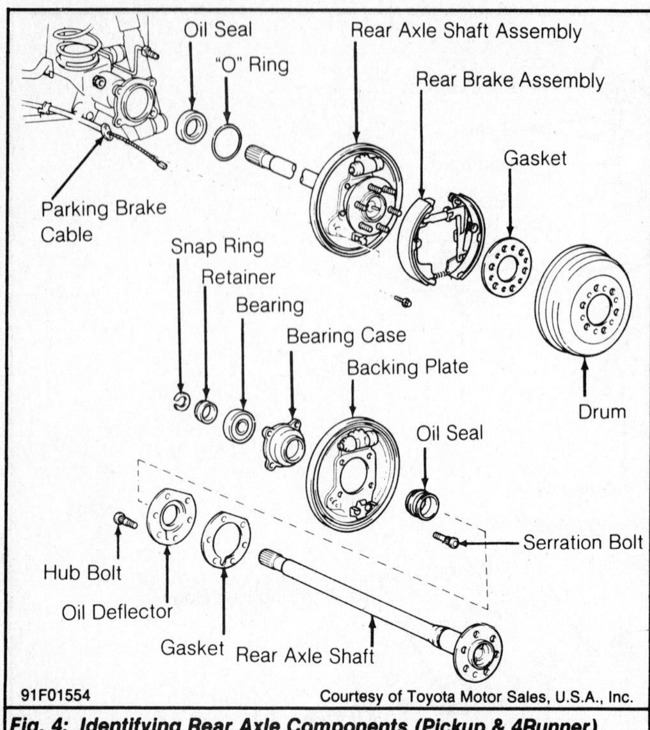


*Fig. 4: Identifying Rear Axle Components (Pickup & 4Runner)*

**Installation – 1)** Press new bearing into backing plate. Drive new oil seal into bearing case. Insert backing plate and bearing retainer on axle shaft. Ensure unbeveled edge of retainer faces bearing.

**2)** Press rear axle shaft into backing plate. Install snap ring. Install new "O" ring. Install rear axle shaft in housing. To complete installation, reverse removal procedure.

**Removal (Previa) – 1)** Raise and support vehicle. Remove rear wheel and speed sensor (if equipped). Disconnect and plug brake line at wheel cylinder. On drum brake models, remove drum and shoes. On disc brake models, remove cylinder and rotor. *See Fig. 5.*

**2)** On all models, disconnect parking brake cable. Remove backing plate nuts. Using puller, remove axle shaft. DO NOT damage oil seal or speed sensor rotor (if equipped).

**3)** On disc brake models, remove backing plate. On all models, press oil seal and speed sensor rotor from shaft (if necessary). Grind down inner retainer and remove using chisel. Press bearing from axle shaft. Remove oil seal.

**Installation – 1)** Drive new oil seal into axle shaft housing to depth of .138" (3.51 mm) for disc brake models and .236" (5.99 mm) for drum brake models.

**2)** On disc brake models, place new retainer gasket and bearing outer retainer on backing plate. Using a socket and hammer, install bolts. Install backing plate to axle shaft.

**3)** On drum brake models, install bearing outer retainer to axle shaft. On all models, press new bearing onto axle shaft. Heat inner retainer to 302°F (150°C) in an oil bath. Clean retainer and axle shaft of oil and grease. While still hot, press inner retainer onto axle shaft.

**4)** Using a press, install speed sensor rotor and new oil seal (if equipped). Install end gasket. To complete installation, reverse removal procedure.

## PINION FLANGE & OIL SEAL

**Removal –** Reference mark propeller shaft and drive pinion flange position. Disconnect propeller shaft. Loosen staked portion of pinion shaft nut. Remove nut. Using Puller (SST 09950-20017), remove pinion flange. Remove oil seal. Remove oil slinger. Remove front bearing. Remove and discard collapsible spacer.

***NOTE: Install new collapsible spacer whenever pinion companion flange nut is loosened or removed.***

**Installation – 1)** To install, reverse removal procedure using new collapsible spacer. Apply grease to seal lip, and install seal to proper depth. See PINION OIL SEAL DEPTH table. Install pinion flange. Install new nut after lightly greasing threads.

***PINION OIL SEAL DEPTH***

| Application | In. (mm) |
|---|---|
| Corolla All-Trac | .16 (4.1) |
| Land Cruiser & 4Runner | .04 (1.0) |
| Pickup | |
| 7.5" Ring Gear | .06 (1.5) |
| 8.0" Ring Gear | .04 (1.0) |
| Previa | .06 (1.5) |

**2)** Check and adjust pinion preload. See PINION BEARING STARTING PRELOAD SPECIFICATIONS table under DIFFERENTIAL ASSEMBLY under OVERHAUL.

**3)** If preload is insufficient, gradually tighten pinion nut in small increments until correct preload is obtained. If preload is exceeded, replace collapsible spacer. To complete installation, reverse removal procedure.

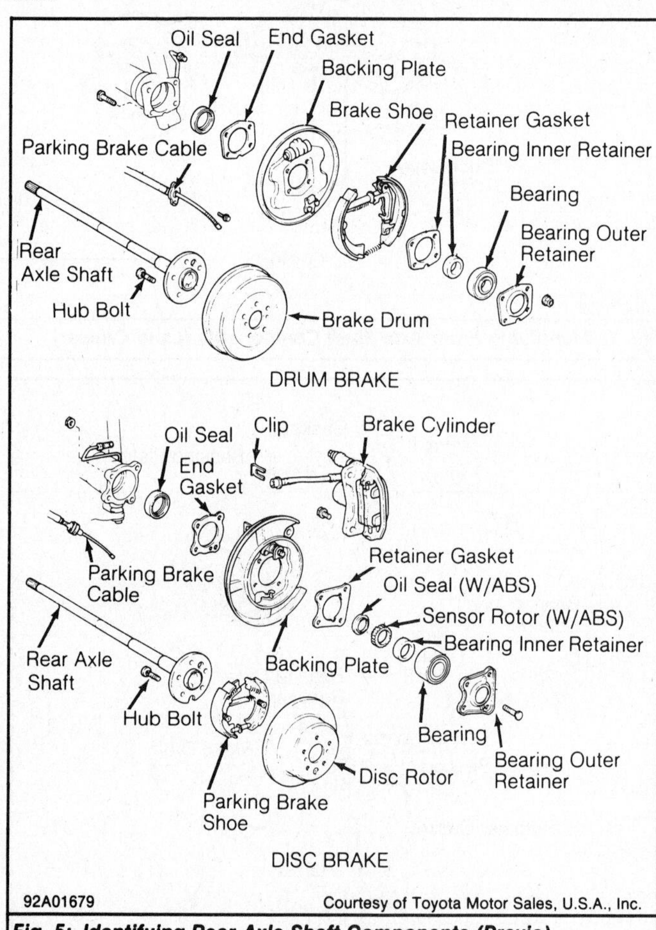


*Fig. 5: Identifying Rear Axle Shaft Components (Previa)*

## DIFFERENTIAL CARRIER

**Removal & Installation – 1)** Remove wheels. Index propeller shaft to pinion flange. Remove propeller shaft. Remove speed sensor and bracket (if equipped). Remove axle shafts. See FRONT AXLE SHAFT & BEARING or REAR AXLE SHAFT & BEARING under REMOVAL & INSTALLATION.

**2)** On Land Cruiser's rear axle, reinstall pinion shaft and lock pin. On all models, remove differential carrier retaining bolts and carrier. To install, reverse removal procedure. Coat both sides of carrier-to-housing gasket with sealant before installation. Add differential fluid, and bleed brakes.

# 1991 DRIVE AXLES
# Differentials & Axle Shafts – Separate Carrier (Cont.)

## OVERHAUL

### FRONT AXLE SHAFT & SPINDLE

**Disassembly (Land Cruiser) – 1)** Mount spindle in vise. Remove bushing with puller. Using a press, install new bushing into spindle. Inspect axle shaft for wear or damage. Carefully inspect Constant Velocity (CV) joint for rust, dirt or excessive looseness. If CV joint needs to be replaced, go to next step.

**2)** Mount inner axle shaft in a vise with CV joint pointing upward. Place a brass drift against CV joint inner race, and drive CV joint off inner shaft. DO NOT drop CV joint. Remove snap rings from inner axle shaft. Tilt cage and inner race outward from housing.

**3)** Remove 6 ball bearings individually. Turn cage and inner race 90 degrees from outer CV joint race. Align 2 larger openings of cage with protrusions of outer CV joint race. Remove inner race and cage. Turn inner race perpendicular to large cage openings, and pull race out. *See Figs. 6 and 8.*

Constant Velocity
(CV) Joint
Large
Opening
Small
Opening
CV Joint
Cage
44186
Courtesy of Toyota Motor Sales, U.S.A., Inc.

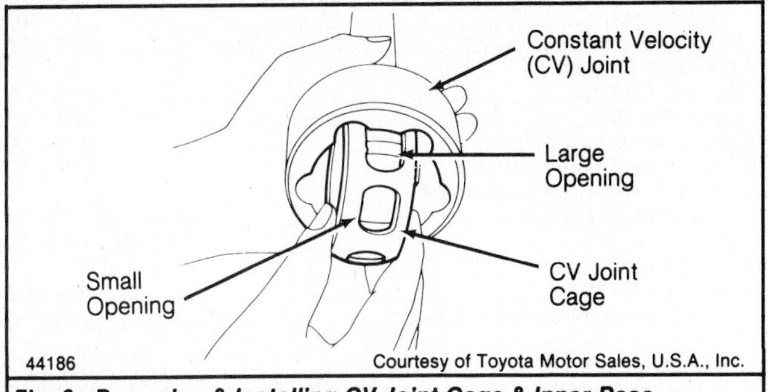

***Fig. 6: Removing & Installing CV Joint Cage & Inner Race***

CV Joint
Cage
Small
Opening
Large
Opening
CV Joint
Inner Race
Flat End
Narrow
Side
Wide
Side
Protrusion
End
44187
Courtesy of Toyota Motor Sales, U.S.A., Inc.

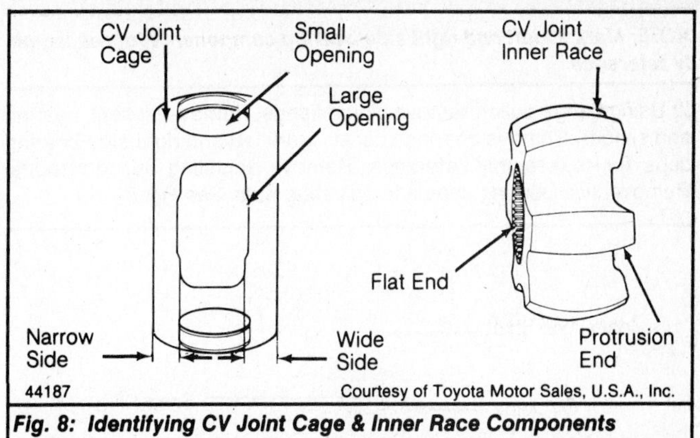

***Fig. 8: Identifying CV Joint Cage & Inner Race Components***

**Reassembly – 1)** Coat inner race, cage and balls with wheel bearing grease. Reverse disassembly procedure. Ensure protruding end of inner race is covered by wide portion of cage during reassembly.

**2)** When installing inner race and cage into outer race, wide side of cage must face outward. Fit 6 balls into cage. After reassembly, pack stub axle end with lithium-base grease. Install new snap rings on axle shaft. *See Fig. 9.* Insert inner axle shaft into CV joint inner race, keeping inner snap ring compressed.

### DIFFERENTIAL ASSEMBLY

**Disassembly – 1)** Before disassembling differential, check tooth contact pattern, ring gear runout (measure at back of gear, in 4 places), ring gear-to-drive pinion backlash and total drive preload. Record readings. Loosen staked portion of pinion shaft/companion flange nut. Remove nut.

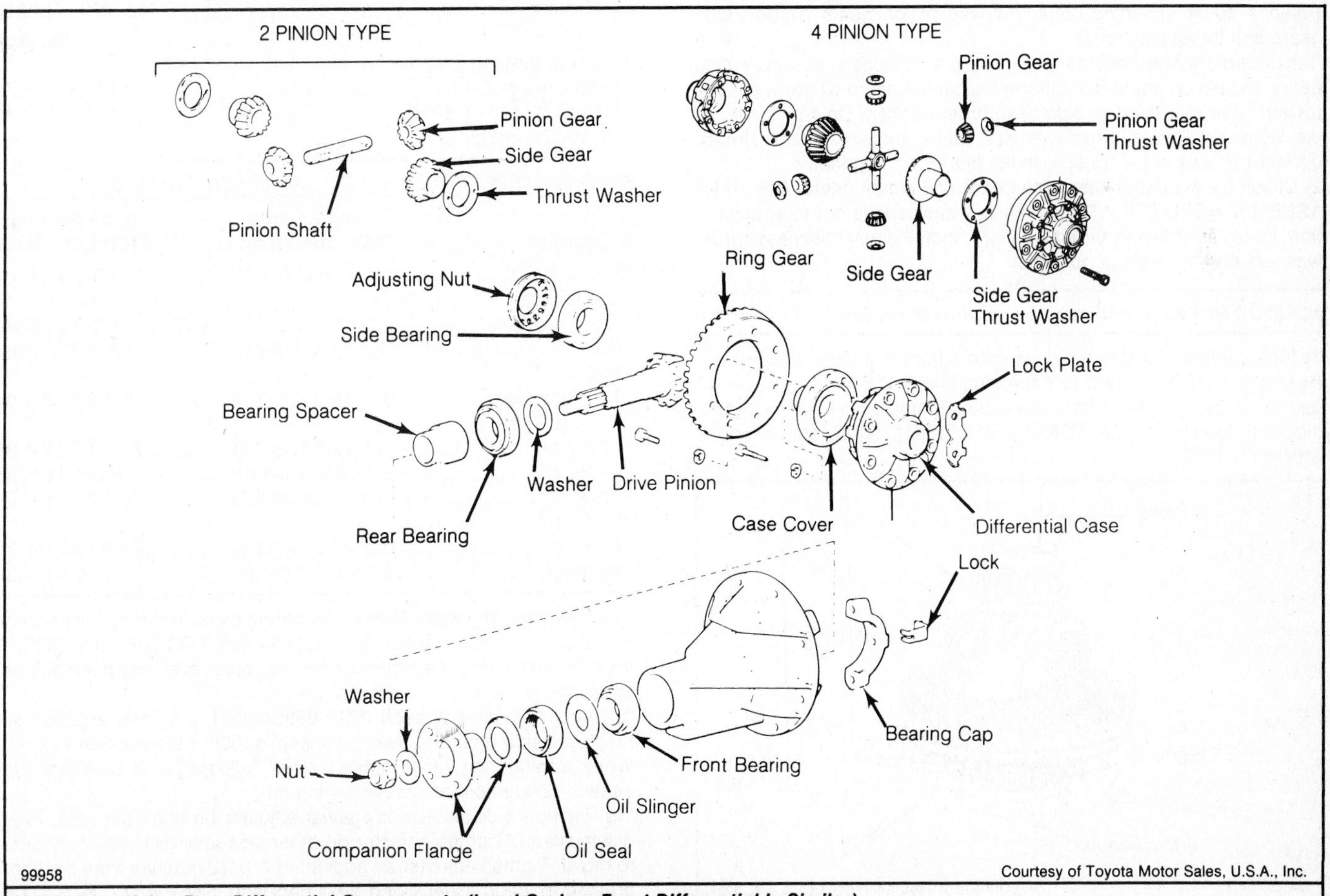

2 PINION TYPE
4 PINION TYPE
Pinion Gear
Side Gear
Thrust Washer
Pinion Shaft
Pinion Gear
Pinion Gear
Thrust Washer
Ring Gear
Side Gear
Side Gear
Thrust Washer
Adjusting Nut
Side Bearing
Lock Plate
Bearing Spacer
Washer
Drive Pinion
Rear Bearing
Case Cover
Differential Case
Lock
Washer
Nut
Bearing Cap
Front Bearing
Oil Slinger
Companion Flange
Oil Seal
99958
Courtesy of Toyota Motor Sales, U.S.A., Inc.

***Fig. 7: Identifying Rear Differential Components (Land Cruiser Front Differential Is Similar)***

# 1991 DRIVE AXLES
## Differentials & Axle Shafts – Separate Carrier (Cont.)

***NOTE: Mark all left and right side bearing components for reassembly reference.***

**2)** Using flange puller, remove pinion flange. Remove oil seal, bearing and slinger. Remove bearing spacer. Mark left and right side bearing caps for reassembly reference. Remove adjusting nut lock bolts. Remove side bearing caps and adjusting nuts. *See Fig. 7.*

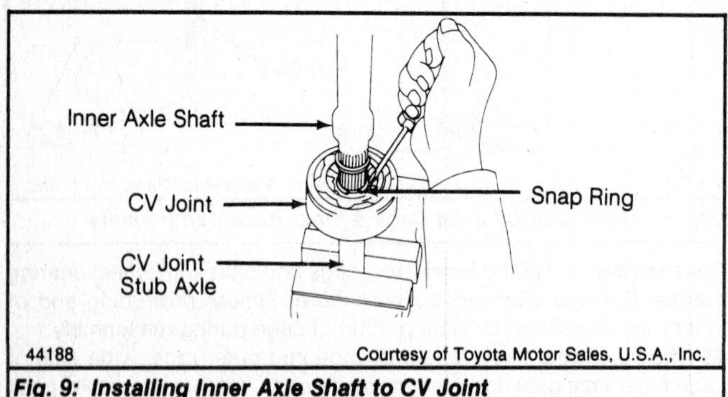


***Fig. 9: Installing Inner Axle Shaft to CV Joint***

**3)** Remove differential case assembly with side bearings. Remove drive pinion, and mount it in holder. Using puller, remove rear pinion bearing. Press out front and rear pinion bearing outer races. Remove side bearings from differential case.

**4)** Index ring gear to case. Remove ring gear bolt lock plates and bolts. Remove ring gear. Tap ring gear from case using a soft-faced hammer (if necessary). On 2-pinion differentials, remove pinion gear shaft retaining pin. Drive out pinion shaft. Remove pinion gears, side gears and thrust washers.

**5)** On 4-pinion differentials, index differential case cover to case. Remove cover attaching bolts. Remove pinion gears, spider, side gears and thrust washer(s).

**Reassembly & Adjustments – 1)** On 2-pinion models, assemble side gears and pinion gears into differential case. Ensure oil groove faces toward gear (if present on side gear thrust washer). On 4-pinion models, install side gears, thrust washers, spider and pinion gears. Install differential case cover. Ensure index marks are aligned.

**2)** Check backlash between side gears and pinion gears. See AXLE ASSEMBLY SPECIFICATIONS table. If backlash is not to specification, install selective fit thrust washers. Install equal thickness thrust washers on each side (if possible).

***NOTE: DO NOT allow ring gear temperature to exceed 230°F (110°C).***

**3)** Press differential side bearings onto differential case. *See Fig. 10.* Heat ring gear in oil bath to approximately 212°F (100°C). Wipe off gear, and press it onto differential case. Tighten bolts evenly to specification. See appropriate TORQUE SPECIFICATIONS table at end of article.

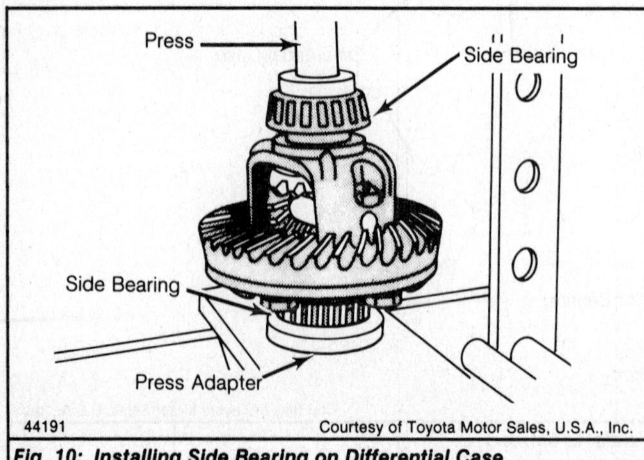


***Fig. 10: Installing Side Bearing on Differential Case***

**4)** Bend lock tabs over. Install differential case assembly into differential carrier. Tighten adjusting nut until no play exists in bearings. Measure ring gear runout. See AXLE ASSEMBLY SPECIFICATIONS table.

**5)** If runout exceeds specification, shift ring gear on differential case, and measure runout again. If runout still exceeds specification, replace ring gear.

**6)** Install drive pinion with rear bearing and front bearing into differential carrier. Install pinion flange and nut with threads lightly greased. DO NOT install oil seal, slinger or collapsible spacer at this time.

**7)** Using a torque wrench, measure pinion bearing staring preload, and tighten companion flange nut until starting preload is to specification. See PINION BEARING STARTING PRELOAD SPECIFICATIONS table. Install differential in case.

***AXLE ASSEMBLY SPECIFICATIONS***

| Application | In. (mm) |
|---|---|
| Axle Shaft Flange Runout | |
| Corolla All-Trac | .004 (.10) |
| Land Cruiser | N/A |
| Pickup, Previa & 4Runner | .008 (.20) |
| Axle Shaft Runout | |
| Corolla All-Trac | .059 (1.5) |
| Land Cruiser | .031 (.80) |
| Pickup, Previa & 4Runner | .079 (2.0) |
| Drive Pinion Flange Runout | .004 (.10) |
| Drive Pinion-To-Ring Gear Backlash | |
| Land Cruiser (Rear) | .006-.008 (.15-.20) |
| All Others | .005-.007 (.13-.18) |
| Ring Gear Runout [1] | |
| Corolla All-Trac | .003 (.07) |
| Land Cruiser, Previa & 4Runner | .004 (.10) |
| Pickup | |
| 7.5" Ring Gear | .003 (.07) |
| 8.0" Ring Gear | .004 (.10) |
| Side Gear-To-Pinion Gear Backlash | |
| Land Cruiser (Rear) | .0008-.0078 (.020-.200) |
| All Others | .002-.008 (.05-.20) |
| | **Lbs. (kg)** |
| Axle Hub Preload Starting Torque | |
| Land Cruiser (Front) | 6.2-12.6 (2.8-5.7) |
| Pickup W/ Dual Wheels | .2-3.3 (.1-1.5) |

[1] – Maximum runout.

***PINION BEARING STARTING PRELOAD SPECIFICATIONS***

| Application | New Bearings INCH Lbs. (N.m) | Used Bearings INCH Lbs. (N.m) |
|---|---|---|
| Corolla All-Trac | 8.7-13.9 (1.0-1.6) | 4.3-6.9 (.5-.8) |
| Land Cruiser | | |
| Front | 8.7-13.9 (1.0-1.6) | 4.3-6.9 (.5-.8) |
| Rear | 11.3-17.4 (1.3-2.0) | 6.1-8.7 (.7-1.0) |
| Pickup | | |
| 7.5" Ring Gear | 10.4-16.5 (1.2-1.9) | 5.2-8.7 (.6-1.0) |
| 8" Ring Gear | | |
| 2 Pinion | 16.5-22.6 (1.9-2.5) | 7.8-11.3 (.9-1.3) |
| 4 Pinion | 8.7-13.9 (1.0-1.6) | 4.3-6.9 (.5-.8) |
| Previa | 10.4-16.5 (1.2-1.9) | 5.2-8.7 (.6-1.0) |
| 4Runner | | |
| 2 Pinion | 16.5-22.6 (1.9-2.5) | 7.8-11.3 (.9-1.3) |
| 4 Pinion | 8.7-13.9 (1.0-1.6) | 4.3-6.9 (.5-.8) |

**8)** Install adjusting nuts. Align side bearing caps. Tighten side bearing cap bolts to specification. See appropriate TORQUE SPECIFICATIONS table at end of article. Loosen cap bolts, and then hand tighten them.

**9)** Using Adjusting Wrench (SST 09504-00011), tighten adjuster on ring gear side until ring gear backlash is .008" (.2 mm). *See Fig. 11.* While turning ring gear, tighten other adjuster until bearings are settled. Loosen pinion side adjusting nut.

**10)** Position a dial indicator against adjuster on ring gear side. Zero dial indicator. Tighten adjuster on other side until dial indicator starts to move. Tighten adjuster an additional 1-1 1/2 notches from the zero preload position. Check ring gear backlash. *See Fig. 11.* See AXLE ASSEMBLY SPECIFICATIONS table.

# 1991 DRIVE AXLES
# Differentials & Axle Shafts – Separate Carrier (Cont.)

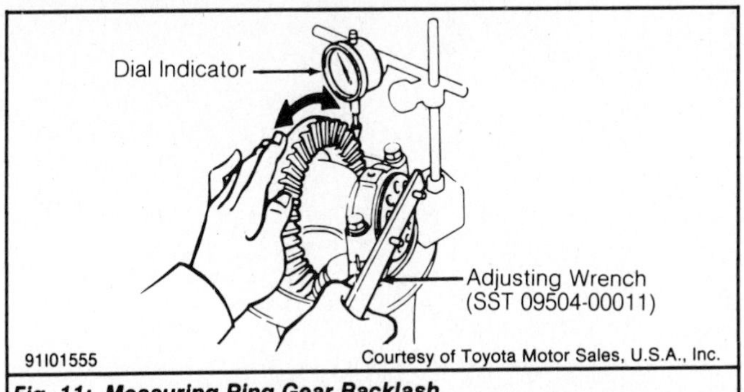


*Fig. 11: Measuring Ring Gear Backlash*

**11)** If backlash is not as specified, loosen one adjuster while tightening other adjuster an equal amount until backlash is to specification. Tighten bearing cap bolts to specification. See appropriate TORQUE SPECIFICATIONS table at end of article. Recheck ring gear backlash and pinion preload.

**12)** Check tooth contact pattern. See GEAR TOOTH CONTACT PATTERNS article in GENERAL INFORMATION. If gear tooth contact patterns are not correct, install correct washer behind rear pinion bearing. See PINION FLANGE & OIL SEAL under REMOVAL & INSTALLATION.

**13)** If gear tooth contact patterns are correct, remove companion flange and front bearing. Install new collapsible spacer, front bearing, new oil seal and slinger. See PINION FLANGE & OIL SEAL under REMOVAL & INSTALLATION.

**14)** Tighten pinion flange nut to minimum specification. See appropriate TORQUE SPECIFICATIONS table at end of article. Check total starting preload. See PINION BEARING STARTING PRELOAD SPECIFICATIONS and TOTAL PRELOAD SPECIFICATIONS tables.

***TOTAL PRELOAD SPECIFICATIONS*** [1]

| Application | INCH Lbs. (N.m) |
|---|---|
| Corolla All-Trac | 2.6-4.3 (.3-.5) |
| All Other Models | 3.5-5.2 (.4-.6) |

[1] – Add this amount to drive pinion preload.

**15)** If preload is less than specification, adjust preload by tightening flange nut in increments of 108 INCH lbs. (13 N.m) up to maximum torque. If preload exceeds specification or flange nut is tightened to maximum torque before preload reaches specification, replace collapsible spacer, and repeat procedure.

**16)** Check pinion flange runout and end play with a dial indicator. If end play or runout exceeds .004" (.10 mm), bearings must be checked. Stake drive pinion nut. Install adjuster locks.

## TORQUE SPECIFICATIONS

***TORQUE SPECIFICATIONS (COROLLA ALL-TRAC)***

| Application | Ft. Lbs. (N.m) |
|---|---|
| Axle Retainer Flange Bolts | 48 (65) |
| Brake Line | 11 (15) |
| Differential | |
| Adjusting Nut Locks | 10 (14) |
| Carrier-To-Axle Housing | 23 (31) |
| Drain & Fill Plug | 36 (49) |
| Pinion Flange Nut | [1] 80-174 (109-236) |
| Ring Gear-To-Case Bolts | 71 (96) |
| Side Bearing Cap Bolts | 58 (79) |
| Propeller Shaft Bolts | 27 (37) |

[1] – Minimum and maximum torque. See REASSEMBLY & ADJUSTMENTS procedure under DIFFERENTIAL ASSEMBLY under OVERHAUL.

***TORQUE SPECIFICATIONS (LAND CRUISER)***

| Application | Ft. Lbs. (N.m) |
|---|---|
| Brake Caliper Mounting Bolts | 90 (122) |
| Brake Line | 11 (15) |
| Differential | |
| Adjusting Lock Nuts | 10 (14) |
| Bearing Cap Bolt | 58 (79) |
| Bearing Cap Nut Lock Bolt | 10 (14) |
| Differential Carrier-To-Housing Nuts | |
| Front | 18 (24) |
| Rear | 34 (46) |
| Drain & Fill Plug | 36 (49) |
| Pinion Flange Nut | |
| Front | [1] 145-253 (197-343) |
| Rear | [1] 181-326 (245-442) |
| Pinion Shaft Pin (Rear) | 20 (27) |
| Ring Gear-To-Differential Case Nuts | |
| Front | 71 (96) |
| Rear | 81 (110) |
| Dust Cover Mounting Bolts | 34 (46) |
| Front Wheel Bearing Adjusting Nut | |
| Step 1 | 43 (58) |
| Step 2 | Loosen Nut |
| Step 3 | [2] |
| Front Wheel Bearing Lock Nut | 47 (64) |
| Hub Body Nuts (6) | 23 (31) |
| Propeller Shaft Bolts | |
| Front | 54 (73) |
| Rear | 65 (88) |
| Proportioning Valve Shackle Bracket Bolt | 14 (19) |
| Tie Rod End Nut | 67 (91) |

[1] – Minimum and maximum torque. See REASSEMBLY & ADJUSTMENTS procedure under DIFFERENTIAL ASSEMBLY under OVERHAUL.

[2] – Tighten to 48 INCH lbs. (5.4 N.m).

***TORQUE SPECIFICATIONS (PICKUP)***

| Application | Ft. Lbs. (N.m) |
|---|---|
| Axle Retainer Flange Bolts | 21 (29) |
| Backing Plate Mounting Bolts | 51 (69) |
| Bearing Retainer Bolt | 51 (69) |
| Differential | |
| Adjusting Lock Nuts | 10 (14) |
| Case Cover Bolts (4 Pinion) | 35 (47) |
| Carrier-To-Axle Housing | |
| Single Wheel | 18 (24) |
| Dual Wheel | 23 (31) |
| Drain Plug | 36 (49) |
| Drive Pinion Flange Nut | |
| 7.5" Ring Gear | [1] 80-174 (109-236) |
| 8" Ring Gear | [1] 145-253 (197-343) |
| Ring Gear-To-Case Bolts | 71 (96) |
| Side Bearing Cap Bolts | 58 (79) |
| Propeller Shaft Bolts | |
| V6 (Manual Transmission) | 56 (76) |
| All Others | 54 (73) |
| Speed Sensor Mounting Bolt | 14 (19) |

[1] – Minimum and maximum torque. See REASSEMBLY & ADJUSTMENTS procedure under DIFFERENTIAL ASSEMBLY under OVERHAUL.

***TORQUE SPECIFICATIONS (PREVIA)***

| Application | Ft. Lbs. (N.m) |
|---|---|
| Backing Plate Mounting Bolts | 53 (72) |
| Brake Caliper Mounting Bolts | 65 (88) |
| Brake Line | 11 (15) |
| Differential | |
| Adjusting Nut Locks | 10 (14) |
| Carrier-To-Axle Housing | 23 (31) |
| Drain & Fill Plug | 36 (49) |
| Pinion Flange Nut | [1] 80-174 (109-236) |
| Ring Gear-To-Case Bolts | 71 (96) |
| Side Bearing Cap Bolts | 58 (79) |
| Propeller Shaft Bolts | 54 (73) |
| Speed Sensor Mounting Bolt | [2] |

[1] – Minimum and maximum torque. See REASSEMBLY & ADJUSTMENTS procedure under DIFFERENTIAL ASSEMBLY under OVERHAUL.

[2] – Tighten to 70 INCH lbs. (7.9 N.m).

# 1991 DRIVE AXLES
## Differentials & Axle Shafts – Separate Carrier (Cont.)

***TORQUE SPECIFICATIONS (4RUNNER)***

| Application | Ft. Lbs. (N.m) |
|---|---|
| Axle Retainer Flange Bolts | 25 (34) |
| Backing Plate Mounting Bolts | 51 (69) |
| Brake Line | 11 (15) |
| Differential | |
| Adjusting Nut Locks | 10 (14) |
| Case Cover Bolts (4 Pinion) | 35 (47) |
| Carrier-To-Axle Housing | 18 (24) |
| Drain & Fill Plug | 36 (49) |
| Pinion Flange Nut | [1] 145-253 (197-343) |
| Ring Gear-To-Case Bolts | 71 (96) |
| Side Bearing Cap Bolts | 58 (79) |
| Propeller Shaft Bolts | 54 (73) |
| Speed Sensor Mounting Bolt | 14 (19) |

[1] – Minimum and maximum torque. See REASSEMBLY & ADJUSTMENTS procedure under DIFFERENTIAL ASSEMBLY under OVERHAUL.

# 1991 DRIVE AXLES
# Locking Hubs

## Pickup, 4Runner

## DESCRIPTION

4WD vehicles are equipped with front locking hubs. When locking hubs are set in locked position, front wheels are engaged with and driven by front axle shafts. Setting locking hubs in unlocked position, disengages front wheels from front axle shafts and wheels spin freely.

Locking hub wheel-to-drive axle engagement is accomplished through gear and spring mechanisms within free wheeling hub. *See Fig. 1*. In locked position, a hub clutch engages inner hub, which is permanently connected to axle shaft by inner splines. Hub clutch is permanently connected by outer splines to hub body. Hub cover and handle are marked LOCK and FREE for position designation.

## REMOVAL & INSTALLATION

**Removal - 1)** Set control hub to FREE position. Remove cover bolts and cover. Remove center bolt with washer.

**2)** Remove freewheeling hub nuts and washers. Using a brass drift and hammer, tap on end of each stud and remove cone washers. Remove freewheeling hub body and gasket.

**Installation - 1)** Place a new gasket in position on front axle hub. Install freewheeling hub body with 6 cone washers and nuts. Tighten nuts to specification. See TORQUE SPECIFICATIONS table at end of article.

**2)** Install center bolt and washer and tighten to specification. See TORQUE SPECIFICATIONS table at end of article. Apply grease to inner hub splines. Set control handle and clutch to FREE position. Place a new gasket in position on cover.

**3)** Install cover to body with follower pawl tabs aligned with non-toothed portions of body. *See Fig. 2*. Tighten freewheeling hub cover bolts to specification. See TORQUE SPECIFICATIONS table at end of article.

## OVERHAUL

**Disassembly** - While compressing spring, remove pawl tab from handle cam and remove clutch. Using snap ring pliers, remove snap ring. *See Fig. 3*. Remove control handle. Remove steel ball and spring from control handle.

**Inspection** - Inspect cover, handle and seal. Install handle in cover and check that handle moves smoothly and freely. Check that clutch moves smoothly in body.

**Reassembly - 1)** Apply grease to all parts with sliding surfaces. Install seal, spring and steel ball to handle. Insert handle in cover and install snap ring with snap ring pliers.

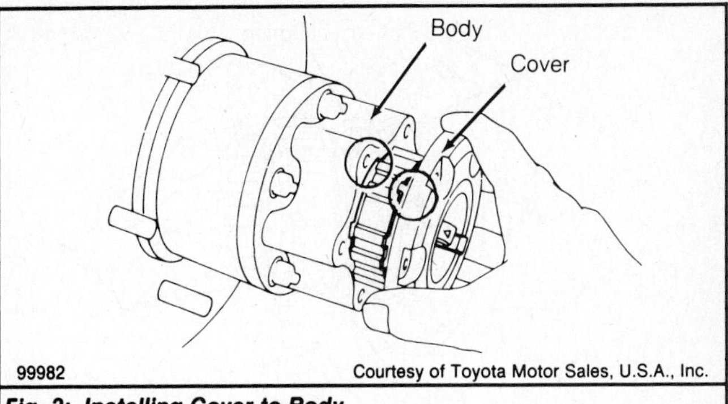


***Fig. 2: Installing Cover to Body***

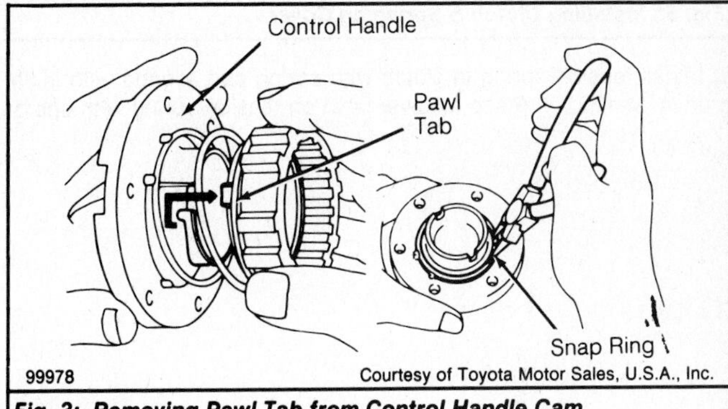


***Fig. 3: Removing Pawl Tab from Control Handle Cam***

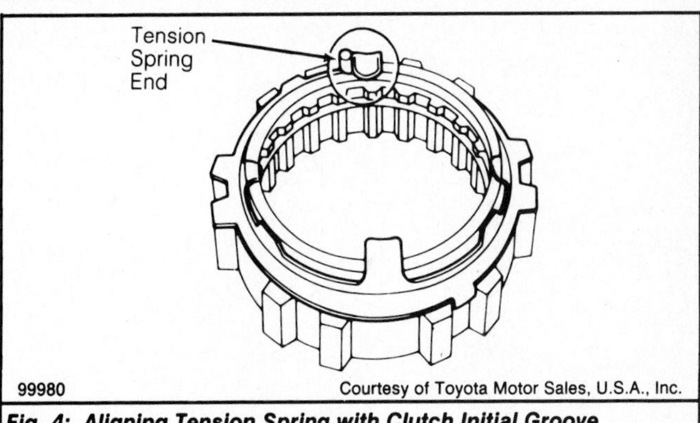


***Fig. 4: Aligning Tension Spring with Clutch Initial Groove***

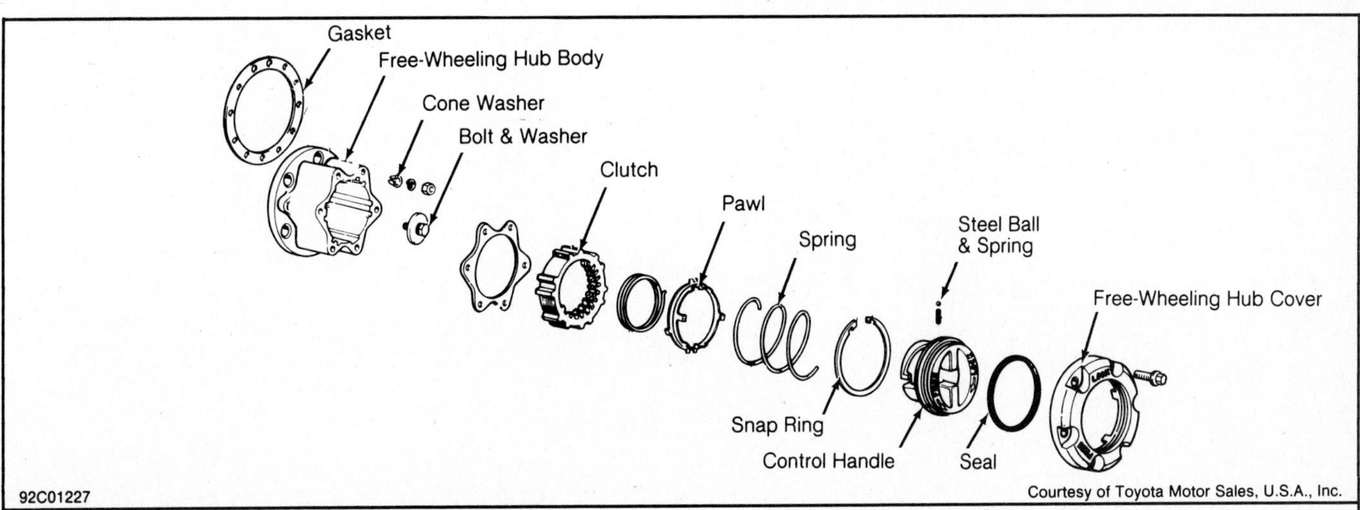


***Fig. 1: Identifying Locking Hub Assembly Components***

# 1991 DRIVE AXLES
## Locking Hubs (Cont.)

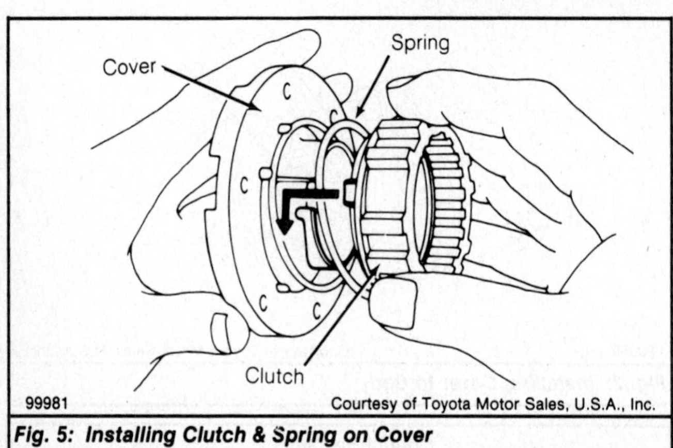


*Fig. 5: Installing Clutch & Spring on Cover*

**2)** Install tension spring in clutch with spring end aligned with initial groove. *See Fig. 4*. Place follower pawl on tension spring with one of the large tabs against bent spring end. Place top ring of spring on small tabs.

**3)** Place spring between freewheeling hub cover and clutch with large spring end toward cover. Compress spring and install clutch with pawl tab fit to handle cam. *See Fig. 5*.

**4)** Temporarily install hub cover to hub body and check freewheeling hub operation. Set control handle and clutch to FREE position. Remove hub cover from hub body. Install new gasket. See INSTALLATION under REMOVAL & INSTALLATION.

## TORQUE SPECIFICATIONS

***TORQUE SPECIFICATIONS***

| Application | Ft. Lbs. (N.m) |
|---|---|
| Center Bolt | 13 (18) |
| Hub Body Nut | 23 (31) |
| | **INCH Lbs. (N.m)** |
| Hub Cover Bolt | 84 (9) |

# 1991 BRAKES
# Disc & Drum – FWD Cars

## Camry, Celica, Corolla, Tercel

***WARNING:** For warnings and procedures regarding vehicles equipped with Anti-Lock Brake Systems (ABS), see appropriate ANTI-LOCK article.*

## DESCRIPTION & OPERATION

The hydraulic brake system uses a tandem master cylinder with a vacuum power assist servo. All models are equipped with front disc and rear drum brakes standard. Rear disc brakes are available on Camry, Celica and Corolla.

A proportioning valve is used to regulate brake pressure between front and rear brakes. Proportioning valve on Camry is load-sensing. Rear brakes on all models are self-adjusting.

Parking brake lever mechanically activates rear brakes. On models with rear drum brakes, a cable applies rear shoes. On Corolla models with rear disc brakes, parking brake applies rear pads. On Camry and Celica with rear disc brakes, parking brake is a duo servo mechanical drum brake design built into bell of rear rotor assemblies.

## BLEEDING BRAKE SYSTEM

### BLEEDING PROCEDURES

***CAUTION:** Use only clean brake fluid. Ensure no dirt or other foreign matter contaminates brake fluid. DO NOT mix different brands of brake fluid as they may not be compatible. DO NOT spill brake fluid on car as it may damage paint. If brake fluid contacts paint, immediately wash with water.*

Ensure master cylinder reservoir is full. Begin bleeding procedure on longest hydraulic line first and then go to next longest line until all lines have been bled. Road test vehicle and check brake performance. Check reservoir fluid level.

## ADJUSTMENTS

### BRAKE PEDAL HEIGHT

**1)** Brake pedal height is measured from face of pedal pad to asphalt sheet under carpet. To adjust clearance, loosen stoplight switch and lock nut on brake push rod. *See Fig. 1.*

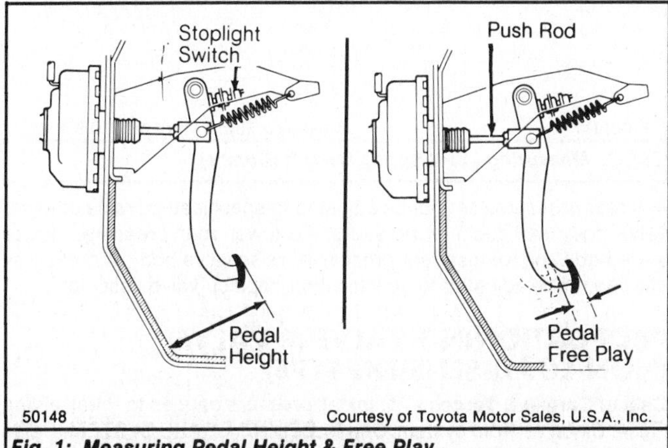


***Fig. 1: Measuring Pedal Height & Free Play***

**2)** Adjust pedal height by turning push rod. See BRAKE PEDAL HEIGHT SPECIFICATIONS table for correct specification. After setting pedal height, tighten lock nut on push rod. See appropriate TORQUE SPECIFICATIONS table at end of article.

**3)** Adjust stoplight switch and tighten switch lock nut. See STOPLIGHT SWITCH under ADJUSTMENTS.

***BRAKE PEDAL HEIGHT SPECIFICATIONS***

| Application | In. (mm) |
|---|---|
| Camry | 7.0-7.4 (178-187) |
| Celica | 6.6-7.0 (168-178) |
| Corolla | 5.5-5.9 (139-149) |
| Tercel | |
| 4-Speed M/T | 5.6-6.0 (142-152) |
| All Others | 5.5-5.9 (139-149) |

### BRAKE PEDAL FREE PLAY

**1)** Brake pedal free play is distance brake pedal travels before feeling resistance with engine stopped. To check pedal free play, depress brake pedal several times to exhaust vacuum from servo. Depress pedal and measure travel until initial resistance is felt.

**2)** Brake pedal free play should be .12-.24" (3.0-6.0 mm). If free play is not within specification, adjust by turning push rod. *See Fig. 1.* Check brake pedal height. See BRAKE PEDAL HEIGHT under ADJUSTMENTS.

### BRAKE PEDAL RESERVE DISTANCE

**1)** Pedal reserve distance is measured from face of pedal pad to asphalt sheet under carpet with brakes applied. Measure reserve distance with engine running and weight of 110 lbs. (50 kg) applied against pedal.

**2)** See BRAKE PEDAL RESERVE DISTANCE table for minimum reserve distance. If measured reserve distance is less than minimum distance specified in table, inspect brake system.

***BRAKE PEDAL RESERVE DISTANCE***

| Application | In. (mm) |
|---|---|
| Camry | 3.35 (85) |
| Celica | |
| With ABS | 3.54 (90) |
| Without ABS | 3.35 (85) |
| Corolla | |
| 2WD Rear Disc | 2.36 (60) |
| 2WD Rear Drum | 2.17 (55) |
| 4WD | 2.56 (65) |
| Tercel | 1.97 (50) |

## LOAD-SENSING PROPORTIONING VALVE (LSPV)

***NOTE:** See LOAD-SENSING PROPORTIONING VALVE (LSPV) under TESTING.*

## PARKING BRAKE

***NOTE:** Service brake must be correctly adjusted before adjusting parking brake. See REAR DRUM BRAKE SHOES under ADJUSTMENTS.*

Pull on parking brake lever with weight of 44 lbs. (20 kg) to check parking brake adjustment. Count number of notches (clicks) until parking brake is fully applied. Compare actual count to specification in PARKING BRAKE LEVER STROKE SPECIFICATIONS table. Adjust parking brake if travel is not within specification.

***PARKING BRAKE LEVER STROKE SPECIFICATIONS***

| Application | Notches |
|---|---|
| Camry | 5-8 |
| Celica & Tercel | 4-7 |
| Corolla | |
| Rear Disc | 5-8 |
| Rear Drum | 4-7 |

**Adjustment (Camry, Celica, Corolla With Rear Drum & Tercel) –** Remove center console or parking brake lever boot to uncover base of lever. Loosen lock nut. Turn adjusting nut on cable until lever travel is correct. Tighten lock nut. Install console or boot.

# 1991 BRAKES
# Disc & Drum – FWD Cars (Cont.)

**Adjustment (Corolla With Rear Disc) – 1)** Disc brake caliper is activated by emergency brake lever. System is self adjusting. Ensure cable lever on caliper moves freely and is against stop pin when emergency brake is off.
**2)** Pull up and release parking lever a few times. Depress brake pedal. Pull up brake lever. If an excessive number of clicks is required to activate brake, adjust cable nut until lever travel is correct.

## POWER BRAKE UNIT PUSH ROD

**Clearance Adjustment –** Check and adjust clearance between power brake unit push rod and master cylinder piston if either unit is replaced or overhauled. Set clearance to zero. *See Fig. 2*. If clearance is not to specification, adjust male portion of push rod with open end wrench while holding female portion of rod with pliers.

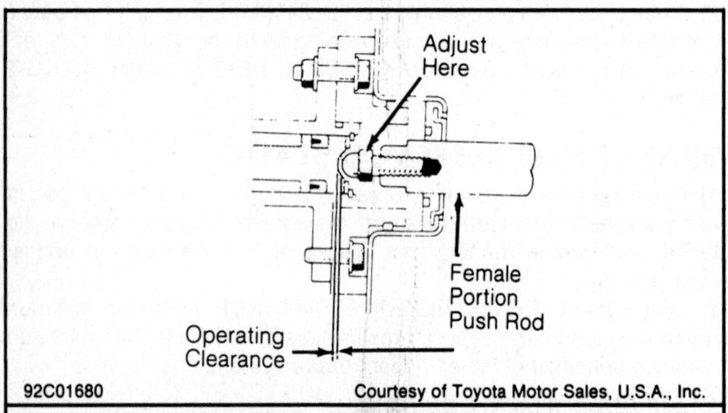


***Fig. 2: Measuring Clearance Between Master Cylinder Piston & Power Brake Unit Push Rod***

## REAR DRUM BRAKE SHOES

***NOTE: All rear drum brakes have a self-adjuster which is activated when brake pedal is applied as vehicle travels in reverse.***

Raise and support rear of vehicle. Release parking brake. Remove adjustment hole plug from backing plate. Turn adjusting nut until brake shoes lock wheel. Back adjuster off until wheel turns freely or drags slightly. Measured clearance between linings and braking surface of drum should be .024" (.60 mm).

## STOPLIGHT SWITCH

Stoplight switch is located above brake pedal. *See Fig. 1*. To adjust, remove panel and air duct (if necessary). Ensure brake pedal height is correct. See BRAKE PEDAL HEIGHT under ADJUSTMENTS. Loosen lock nuts and turn stoplight switch until it touches pedal stop. Tighten lock nut. Check brake light operation.

# TESTING

## POWER BRAKE UNIT

**Functional Test – 1)** Start engine. Turn ignition off. Depress brake pedal several times. Depress pedal firmly and hold pressure for 15 seconds. If pedal sinks, master cylinder, brake line or caliper piston is faulty.
**2)** Start engine with pedal depressed. If pedal sinks slightly, vacuum unit is working properly. If pedal height does not vary, booster or check valve is faulty. Replace as necessary.
**Leak Test – 1)** Depress brake pedal with engine running. Turn ignition off. If pedal height does not vary while depressed for 30 seconds, vacuum booster is okay. If pedal height changes, check for air leaks.
**2)** With engine stopped, depress brake pedal several times using normal pressure. Pedal should be low when first depressed. On consecutive applications, pedal height should gradually rise. If pedal height does not increase, check for air leaks.

## LOAD-SENSING PROPORTIONING VALVE (LSPV)

**Camry – 1)** Measure and record unladen rear axle load. Set total rear axle load to unladen load plus 220 lbs. (100 kg) for testing purposes. Attach Pressure Gauge Set (09709-29017) to front caliper and rear wheel cylinder or caliper.
**2)** Bleed system. See BLEEDING BRAKE SYSTEM. Depress brake pedal until front pressure reading is as specified. See LSPV PRESSURE SPECIFICATIONS (CAMRY) table. Wait 2 seconds and record rear pressure reading.

***NOTE: DO NOT depress brake pedal more than once or release pedal while setting pressure on front gauge.***

***LSPV PRESSURE SPECIFICATIONS (CAMRY)***

| Application | Front Pressure psi ($kg/cm^2$) | Rear Pressure psi ($kg/cm^2$) |
|---|---|---|
| With ABS | | |
| Test 1 | 1422 (100) | 937-1122 (65.9-78.9) |
| Test 2 | 1707 (120) | 1043-1277 (73.3-86.3) |
| Without ABS | | |
| 4-Cylinder | | |
| Test 1 | 1138 (80) | 583-768 (41.0-54.0) |
| Test 2 | 1422 (100) | 688-873 (48.4-61.4) |
| V6 | | |
| Test 1 | 1422 (100) | 906-1091 (63.7-76.7) |
| Test 2 | 1707 (120) | 1011-1196 (71.1-84.1) |

**3)** If rear pressure is not to specification, adjust spring length. To increase rear pressure, lengthen spring (dimension "A"). *See Fig. 3*. To decrease rear pressure, shorten spring length. Tighten lock nuts.

***NOTE: A .04" (1.0 mm) change in spring length changes fluid pressure approximately 14.2 psi (1.0 $kg/cm^2$).***

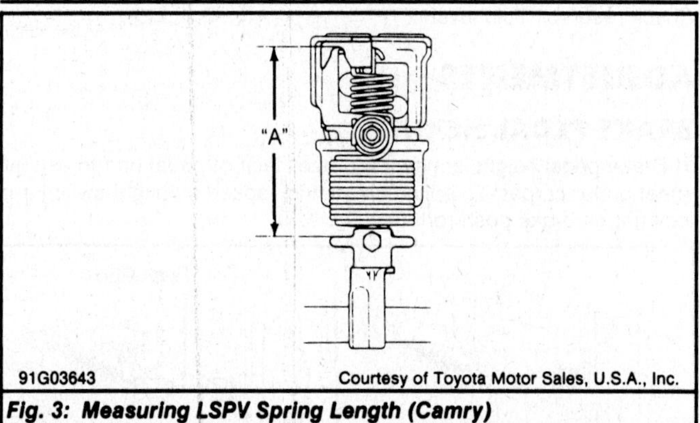


***Fig. 3: Measuring LSPV Spring Length (Camry)***

**4)** If rear pressures cannot be adjusted to specification, raise or lower valve body and recheck pressure. To lower rear pressures, lower valve body and to raise rear pressures, raise valve body. If pressures still cannot be adjusted to specification, replace valve assembly.

## PROPORTIONING VALVE (P VALVE) (NON-LOAD-SENSING TYPE)

**Celica, Corolla & Tercel – 1)** Install pressure gauges to P Valve. *See Fig. 4*. Bleed air from system. See BLEEDING BRAKE SYSTEM. Raise master cylinder (front wheel) pressure and read rear wheel pressure gauges. Check system at specified pressures.
**2)** Rear pressure increase should be less than front pressure. If rear wheel cylinder pressure is not to specification, replace valve. See PROPORTIONING VALVE PRESSURE SPECIFICATIONS table.

# 1991 BRAKES
# Disc & Drum – FWD Cars (Cont.)

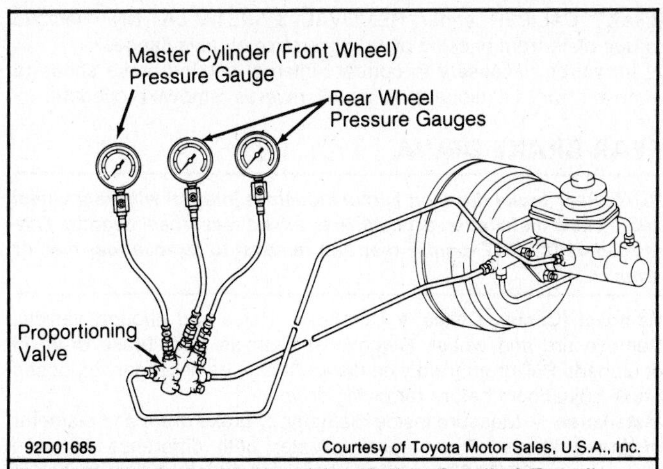


***Fig. 4: Testing Proportioning Valve (Celica, Corolla & Tercel)***

***PROPORTIONING VALVE PRESSURE SPECIFICATIONS***

| Application | Front Pressure psi (kg/cm²) | Rear Pressure psi (kg/cm²) |
|---|---|---|
| **Celica** | | |
| 3S-GTE | 569 (40) | 569 (40) |
| | 1280 (90) | 832 (58.5) |
| 4A-FE | 427 (30) | 427 (30) |
| | 1138 (80) | 690 (49) |
| 5S-FE | | |
| Rear Disc Brakes | 284 (20) | 284 (20) |
| | 1138 (80) | 600 (42) |
| Rear Drum Brakes | 427 (30) | 427 (30) |
| | 1138 (80) | 605 (42.5) |
| **Corolla** | | |
| 4A-FE Engine | 498 (35) | 498 (35) |
| | 1138 (80) | 735 (51.7) |
| 4A-GE Engine | 284 (20) | 284 (20) |
| | 1138 (80) | 600 (42.2) |
| **Tercel** | | |
| 4-Speed M/T | 356 (25) | 356 (25) |
| | 1138 (80) | 644 (43.5) |
| All Others | 356 (25) | 356 (25) |
| | 1138 (80) | 552 (38.8) |

## REMOVAL & INSTALLATION

***NOTE: Location and number of anti-rattle springs, anti-squeal shims, pad support and guide plates varies between models. Note component locations during removal process for reassembly reference.***

### FRONT DISC BRAKE PADS

***NOTE: Pushing piston into caliper bore will force fluid back into master cylinder reservoir. Remove reservoir cap when compressing piston.***

**Removal – 1)** Remove small amount of fluid from master cylinder. Raise vehicle and support securely. Remove wheels and hold rotor in place with lug nuts. Remove caliper guide bolts. *See Fig. 5.*

**2)** Leave hose connected and hang caliper from suspension. Remove anti-squeal springs (if equipped), brake pads, anti-squeal shims, pad wear indicator plates and pad support plates.

***NOTE: Some models have one or more sets of anti-squeal shims. If one set of shims is vented, place it between pad and outer anti-squeal shim.***

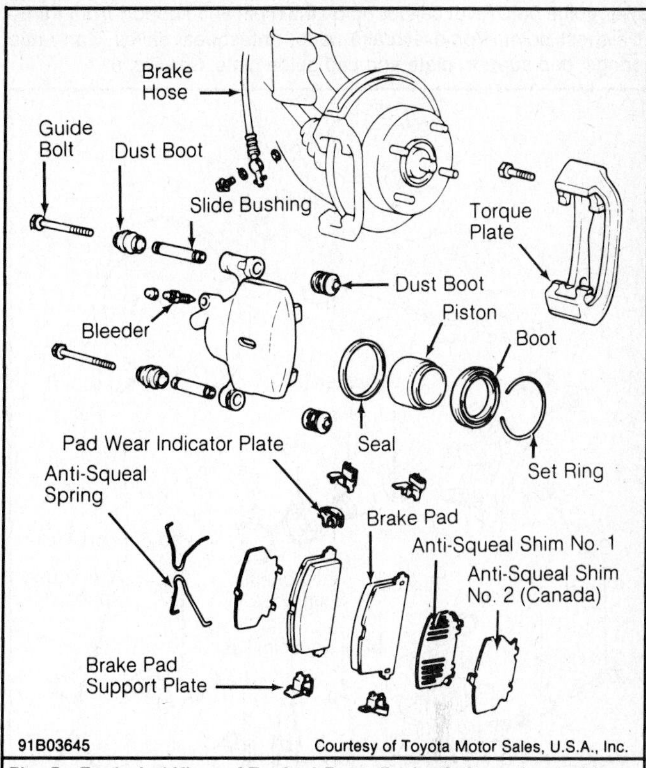


***Fig. 5: Exploded View of Typical Front Brake Caliper Assembly***

**Installation – 1)** Install new pad support plates on torque plate. Put new pad wear indicators on pads. Arrow on wear indicators must point in direction rotor turns. Put new anti-squeal shims on pads.

**2)** Cover both sides of No. 1 anti-squeal shim with disc brake grease. Install pads on support plates. Press piston into caliper with "C" clamp or wooden hammer handle. Install caliper carefully so that piston dust boot DOES NOT wedge against brake pads.

**3)** Check reservoir fluid level. Tighten bolts to specification. See appropriate TORQUE SPECIFICATIONS table at end of article.

### FRONT BRAKE CALIPER

**Removal & Installation – 1)** Raise vehicle and remove wheels. Disconnect hydraulic line and spring clip. Plug line to prevent fluid spillage. Remove caliper mounting bolts or slide pins as necessary.

**2)** On models with fixed main pin, pivot caliper up to clear edge of rotor. Slide caliper off main pin. On all other models, remove caliper from knuckle or torque plate.

**3)** To install, reverse removal procedure. On units with fixed main pin, boot end must be installed in groove of main pin. See appropriate TORQUE SPECIFICATIONS table at end of article.

### FRONT BRAKE ROTOR

**Removal & Installation – 1)** Remove caliper assembly with hose connected. See FRONT BRAKE CALIPER under REMOVAL & INSTALLATION. Support caliper from frame with wire.

**2)** Remove torque plate from knuckle. Slide rotor off hub assembly. To install, reverse removal procedure. Tighten all bolts to specification. See appropriate TORQUE SPECIFICATIONS table at end of article.

### REAR DISC BRAKE PADS

***NOTE: Pushing piston into caliper bore will force fluid back into master cylinder reservoir. Remove reservoir cap when compressing piston.***

**Removal & Installation (Camry, Celica & Corolla) –** Raise vehicle and remove wheels. Install 2 lug nuts to hold rotor in place. Remove lower guide bolt. Pivot caliper up on main pin and support from frame at highest point. Remove brake pads, anti-squeal shims, anti-rattle springs, pad support plate and pad guide plate. *See Fig. 6.*

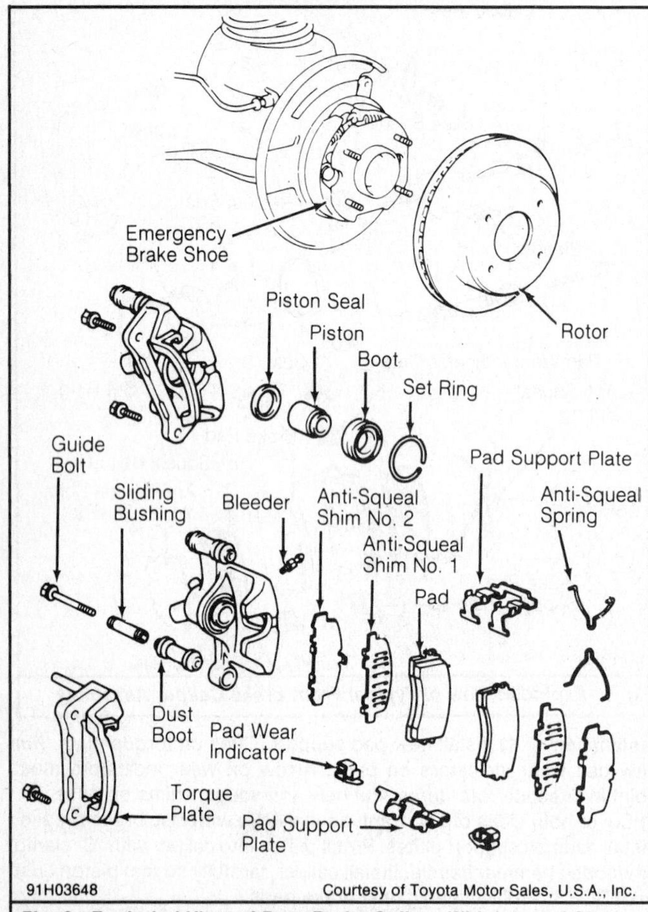


***Fig. 6: Exploded View of Rear Brake Caliper With Internal Shoe Parking Brake (Camry & Celica)***

**Installation – 1)** Install pad support plate, anti-rattle springs and pad guide plates on torque plate. Place new anti-squeal shims onto pads. Install pads in torque plate. Wear indicator should be on top edge of outer pad.

**3)** On Camry and Celica, compress piston with "C" clamp or hammer handle. On Corolla, use Piston Spanner (09719-00020) to turn piston clockwise until it locks. Align pad projection with piston stopper.

**4)** On all models, swing caliper down, ensuring boot does not wedge against pad. Install guide bolt and tighten to specification. See appropriate TORQUE SPECIFICATIONS table at end of article.

**5)** Install wheels. Ensure reservoir fluid level is correct. On Corolla, set automatic parking brake adjuster by pumping brake pedal several times.

## REAR BRAKE CALIPER

**Removal & Installation (Camry, Celica & Corolla) –** Remove pads. See REAR DISC BRAKE PADS under REMOVAL & INSTALLATION. Disconnect brake hose and mounting bolts. Disconnect parking brake cable if attached to caliper. Remove caliper.

**Installation –** To install, reverse removal procedure. On fixed pin type caliper, ensure that boot end is installed in groove of pin. On Corolla, align pad projection with piston stopper groove.

## REAR BRAKE ROTOR

**Removal & Installation (Camry, Celica & Corolla) – 1)** Remove caliper and suspend from underbody with hose connected. See REAR BRAKE CALIPER under REMOVAL & INSTALLATION. Remove torque plate from backing plate. Slide rotor off axle flange.

**2)** It may be necessary to contract internal parking brake shoes to remove rotor (if equipped). To install, reverse removal procedure.

## REAR BRAKE DRUM

***NOTE: Rear brake drum on Tercel models is integral with rear wheel hub. Follow installation procedure to adjust rear wheel bearing. Other models DO NOT require rear hub removal to remove rear disc or drum.***

**Removal (Camry, Celica & Corolla) –** Raise and support vehicle. Remove tire and wheel. Remove set screws from brake drum (if equipped). Pull drum from axle flange. It may be necessary to loosen brake adjustment before removing drum.

**Installation –** Measure inside diameter of brake drum and diameter of brake shoes. Turn brake adjuster until difference between diameters is .024" (.60 mm). Install brake drum and adjust brakes (if required).

**Removal (Tercel) –** Raise and support vehicle. Remove tire and wheel. Remove grease cap, cotter pin, lock nut and bearing nut. Remove brake hub together with outer bearing and thrust washer. It may be necessary to contract brake shoes before removing drum.

**Installation – 1)** Pack wheel bearings with MP grease. Tighten wheel bearings to 22 ft. lbs. (30 N.m) while turning drum. Loosen nut until it can be turned by hand. Using a spring scale, measure rotational preload.

**2)** Slowly tighten bearing nut until rotational preload is 0-2.6 lbs. (0-11.8 N). Install lock cap and cotter pin. If pin will not go into hole in spindle, loosen nut to obtain alignment. Reverse removal procedure to complete installation.

## REAR DRUM BRAKE SHOES

**Removal (Camry, Celica & Corolla) – 1)** Remove wheel and brake drum. See REAR BRAKE DRUM under REMOVAL & INSTALLATION. Remove tension spring, hold-down pins and clips, brake shoes, adjusting lever, anchor spring and adjuster strut. *See Fig. 7.*

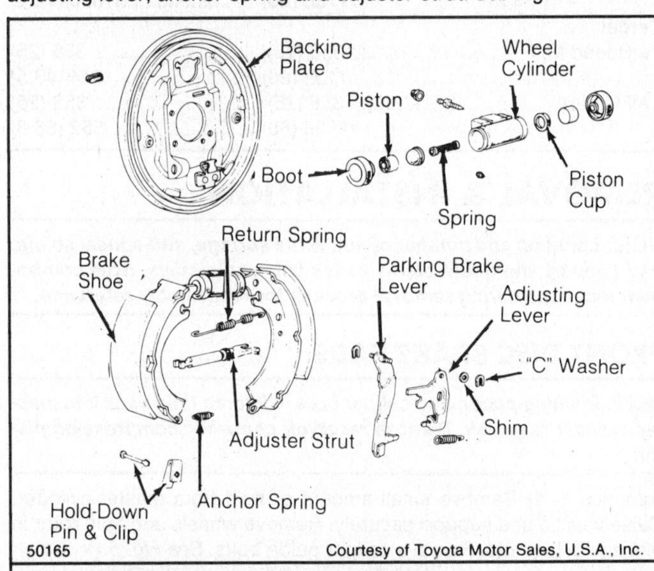


***Fig. 7: Exploded View of Rear Drum Brakes (Camry Shown; Celica & Corolla are Similar)***

**2)** Disconnect parking brake cable from adjusting lever. Remove "C" washer, adjusting lever and parking brake lever from rear shoe.

**Installation – 1)** Install adjusting lever and parking brake lever to rear shoe with new "C" washer. Measure clearance between adjusting lever and shoe. Remove "C" washer and install shim(s) to provide clearance of 0-.0138" (0-.35 mm).

2) Install and stake "C" washer. To complete installation, reverse removal procedure. Adjuster assemblies are not interchangeable. Left-hand thread is for right wheel and right-hand thread is for left wheel. Install drum and adjust brakes.

**Removal (Tercel) – 1)** Remove wheel and brake drum. See REAR BRAKE DRUM under REMOVAL & INSTALLATION. Disconnect return spring. *See Fig. 8.* Remove hold-down springs and pins.

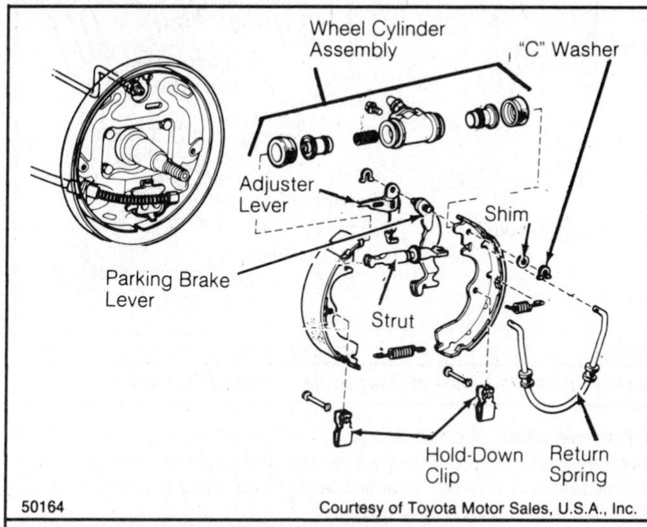


*Fig. 8: Exploded View of Rear Drum Brakes (Tercel)*

2) Disconnect front shoe from parking brake strut and disconnect lower spring. Remove front shoe. Disconnect parking brake lever return spring. Remove rear shoe from backing plate.

3) Disconnect parking brake cable from lever. Remove "C" washer, adjuster lever and parking brake lever from rear shoe. Remove "C" washer retaining parking brake lever on adjuster lever and separate levers.

**Installation** – Install parking brake lever onto adjusting lever with new "C" washer. Ensure lever moves. To complete installation, reverse removal procedure.

## REAR WHEEL CYLINDER

**Removal & Installation** – With brake drum and shoes removed, disconnect hydraulic line from wheel cylinder. Remove mounting bolts and remove wheel cylinder. To install, reverse removal procedure. Adjust brakes and bleed system. See BLEEDING BRAKE SYSTEM.

## REAR PARKING BRAKE (INTERNAL SHOE)

**Removal (Camry & Celica With Rear Disc Brake) – 1)** Remove rotor. See REAR BRAKE ROTOR under REMOVAL & INSTALLATION. Remove shoe return springs and shoe strut with spring.

2) Pull out on front shoe and remove adjusting screw set. Remove hold down spring, front shoe and tension spring. Remove rear shoe and disconnect parking brake cable from lever. *See Fig. 9.*

**Inspection** – Clearance between parking brake shoe and lever must be .014" (.35 mm) or less. If not, replace shim under parking brake lever. Shims are available in sizes from .008" (.20 mm) to .035" (.90 mm) in .004" (.10 mm) increments. Use new "C" washer when installing lever.

**Installation** – To install, reverse removal procedure. Apply non-melting grease to sliding surfaces of shoes and adjusting screw threads. Align groove of rear axle shaft flange with service hole on disc and install disc.

## REAR PARKING BRAKE (CALIPER)

**Removal & Installation (Corolla With Rear Disc Brake)** – See REAR BRAKE CALIPER under REMOVAL & INSTALLATION.

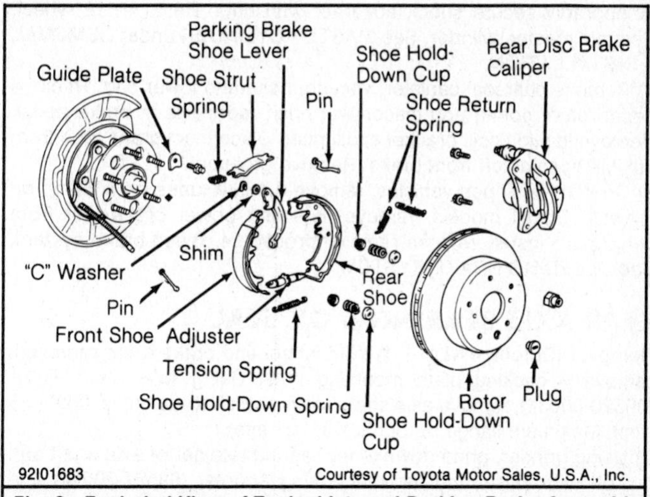


*Fig. 9: Exploded View of Typical Internal Parking Brake Assembly (Camry & Celica With Rear Disc Brake)*

## LOAD-SENSING PROPORTIONING VALVE (LSPV)

**Removal & Installation (Camry)** – Disconnect brake lines from LSPV. Loosen adjuster. Disconnect spring. *See Fig. 10.* Remove LSPV. To install, reverse removal procedure. Tighten mounting bolts to specification. See appropriate TORQUE SPECIFICATIONS table at end of article.

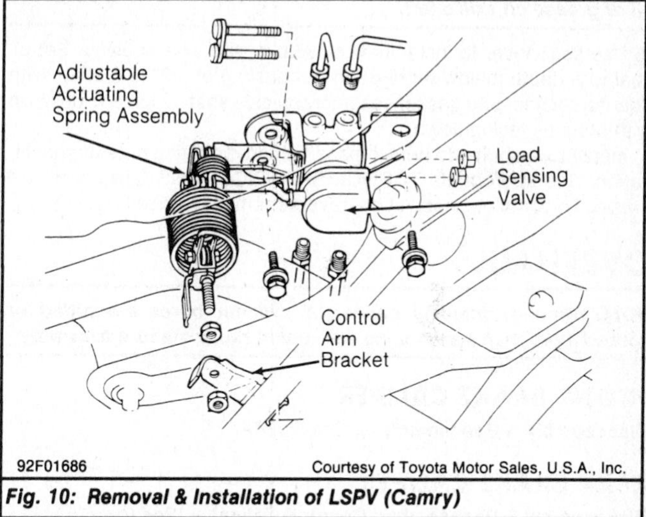


*Fig. 10: Removal & Installation of LSPV (Camry)*

## MASTER CYLINDER

**Removal** – Unplug sensor lead (if equipped). Remove brake fluid from reservoir. Disconnect and plug hydraulic lines. Remove master cylinder-to-power brake unit nuts. Remove master cylinder.

**Installation** – Check and adjust clearance between power brake unit push rod and master cylinder piston if either unit is replaced or overhauled. See POWER BRAKE UNIT PUSH ROD under ADJUSTMENTS. To complete installation, reverse removal procedure. Bleed brake system. See BLEEDING BRAKE SYSTEM.

## POWER BRAKE UNIT

**Removal & Installation (Camry, Corolla & Tercel)** – Remove master cylinder assembly from vehicle. See MASTER CYLINDER under REMOVAL & INSTALLATION. Disconnect vacuum hose from booster. Disconnect push rod clevis at brake pedal. Remove power brake unit from vehicle. To install, reverse removal procedure.

**Removal & Installation (Celica) – 1)** Remove wiper arms. Remove outside lower windshield molding. Remove upper suspension brace.

# 1991 BRAKES
# Disc & Drum – FWD Cars (Cont.)

Temporarily secure shock absorber with nuts. Remove left wheel. Remove master cylinder. See MASTER CYLINDER under REMOVAL & INSTALLATION.

**2)** Remove charcoal canister, vacuum hose and lower pad. Remove pedal return spring and disconnect push rod clevis at brake pedal. Remove ignition coil, bracket and igniter. Disconnect brake tube from flexible hose at left front brake. Remove grommet.

**3)** On ABS-equipped vehicles, remove 3 brake tubes from clamp on firewall. On all models, remove nuts and power brake unit from vehicle. To install, reverse removal procedure. Bleed brake system. See BLEEDING BRAKE SYSTEM.

## REAR AXLE BEARING & OIL SEAL

**Removal (Corolla 4WD) – 1)** With wheel and brake drum removed, remove 4 backing plate mounting nuts. Using Axle Shaft Puller (09520-00031), remove axle shaft. Maximum shaft runout is .059" (1.5 mm). Maximum flange runout is .004" (.1 mm).

**2)** Using grinder, grind down inner bearing retainer of axle shaft and cut off with chisel and hammer. Using Adapter (09527-30010) and press, remove bearing from axle shaft. Use seal puller to remove oil seal from housing. Clean all parts.

**Installation – 1)** Position outer bearing retainer and new bearing on axle shaft. Using press and Adapter (09515-21010), press bearing onto axle shaft.

**2)** Heat new inner bearing retainer to 302°F (150°C) in oil bath. While still hot, face non-beveled side toward bearing and press onto axle shaft, using Adapter (09515-21010).

***NOTE: When installing hot inner bearing retainer, ensure there is no oil or grease on axle shaft.***

**3)** Use seal driver to install new oil seal in rear axle housing. Set oil seal to a depth (below outer edge of housing) of .22" (5.6 mm). With bearing retainer and gasket assembly on axle shaft, align and position with notches facing down.

**4)** Install axle shaft into housing and tighten mounting nuts to specification. See appropriate TORQUE SPECIFICATIONS table at end of article. To complete installation, reverse removal procedure.

# OVERHAUL

***NOTE: When overhauling caliper, if cylinder bores are pitted or scored more than light honing will repair, replace entire assembly.***

## FRONT BRAKE CALIPER

**Disassembly & Reassembly** – *See Fig. 5.*

## REAR BRAKE CALIPER

**Disassembly & Reassembly (Camry & Celica)** – *See Fig. 6.*

**Disassembly (Corolla) – 1)** Remove sliding bushing and dust boot. Use screwdriver to remove retaining set ring and dust boot. Using Piston Spanner (09719-14020), turn piston counterclockwise to remove. Remove piston seal from bore of cylinder. *See Fig. 11.*

**2)** Using Spring Compressor (09756-00010) over adjusting bolt, gently tighten spring with 14-mm socket. Remove snap ring from bore of caliper. Remove spring compressor.

***CAUTION: Always use Spring Compressor (09756-00010) when removing snap ring to prevent accidental spring disengagement. DO NOT overtighten spring compressor as spring retainer could be damaged.***

**3)** Pull spring retainer, spring, spring plate and stopper out with adjusting bolt connected. DO NOT use excessive force to pry out adjusting bolt. Ensure "O" ring on adjusting bolt is not damaged. Disassemble adjusting bolt by removing retainer, spring, spring plate and stopper. Remove "O" ring from bolt.

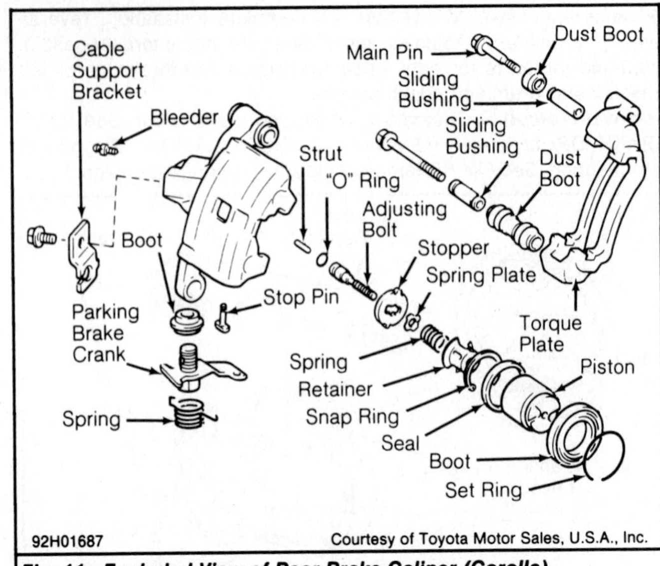


***Fig. 11: Exploded View of Rear Brake Caliper (Corolla)***

**4)** Remove cable support bracket. Disconnect spring from parking brake lever. Remove parking brake lever from caliper. Turn lever so it will not catch on stop pin. If lever boot is to be replaced, remove it. DO NOT disassemble lever any further.

**Reassembly – 1)** Apply lithium soap base glycol grease on main pin, sliding bushing, strut pin, adjusting bolt, piston and all rubber parts. Install stopper pin. Pin should be .098" (2.5 mm) from caliper to underside of head.

**2)** Install cable support bracket. Install lever boot and lever, ensuring boot aligns with groove in lever seal. Install spring and ensure lever touches stopper pin.

**3)** Ensure clearance between cable support bracket and upper side of lever is .236" (.60 mm). Use cable support bracket mount bolt to adjust clearance.

**4)** Install strut. Ensure needle rollers DO NOT catch on caliper hole. Install new "O" ring on adjusting bolt. Assemble adjuster bolt with stopper, plate, spring and spring retainer.

**5)** Use spring compressor to tighten component parts of adjusting bolt assembly. Ensure inscribed surface of stopper faces UP and notches of spring case align with notches on stopper.

**6)** Install adjusting bolt assembly. Install snap ring with opening toward bleeder side of caliper. Remove threaded compressor. Move parking brake lever by hand. Ensure adjusting bolt moves smoothly. Install piston seal in cylinder bore.

**7)** Using piston spanner, slowly turn piston clockwise into caliper until it bottoms. Align piston stopper groove with protrusion on caliper. Place dust boot and retaining ring into caliper. Install sliding bushing and boot. Ensure seal does not fold under piston.

# 1991 BRAKES
# Disc & Drum – FWD Cars (Cont.)

## MASTER CYLINDER

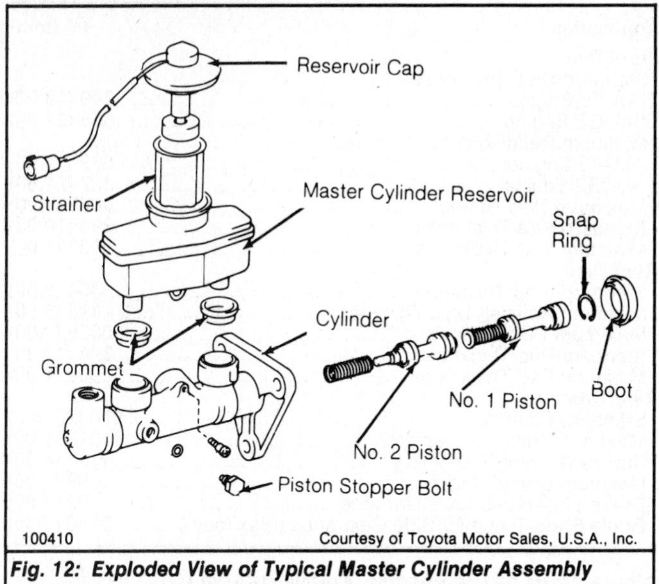


*Fig. 12: Exploded View of Typical Master Cylinder Assembly*

## TORQUE SPECIFICATIONS

*TORQUE SPECIFICATIONS (CAMRY)*

| Application | Ft. Lbs. (N.m) |
|---|---|
| Axle Carrier Upper Bolt | 166 (225) |
| Brake Booster Clevis Lock Nut | 19 (26) |
| Brake Hose Union Bolt | 22 (30) |
| Brake Line Fittings | 11 (15) |
| Caliper Guide Bolts | |
| Front | 29 (39) |
| Rear | 14 (20) |
| Caliper Support Bracket (Torque Plate) Bolts | |
| Front | 79 (107) |
| Rear | 34 (46) |
| LSPV Adjusting Lock Nuts | 19 (26) |
| LSPV Mounting Bolts | 19 (26) |
| Wheel Lug Nuts | 76 (103) |
| | **INCH Lbs. (N.m)** |
| Bleeder Screws | 72 (8) |
| Master Cylinder Mounting Nuts | 108 (13) |
| Parking Brake Adjustment Lock Nut | 48 (5.4) |
| Rear Brake Cylinder-To-Backing Plate | 89 (10) |

*TORQUE SPECIFICATIONS (CELICA)*

| Application | Ft. Lbs. (N.m) |
|---|---|
| Axle Carrier Upper Bolt | 166 (225) |
| Brake Booster Clevis Lock Nut | 19 (26) |
| Brake Line Fittings | 11 (15) |
| Caliper Guide Bolts | |
| Front | |
| 13" Wheel | 18 (24) |
| 14" & 15" Wheel | 29 (39) |
| Rear | 14 (19) |
| Caliper Support Bracket (Torque Plate) Bolts | |
| Front | 79 (107) |
| Rear | 34 (46) |
| Union Bolt | 22 (30) |
| Upper Suspension Brace | |
| Bolt | 15 (20) |
| Nut | 27 (37) |
| Wheel Lug Nuts | 76 (103) |
| | **INCH Lbs. (N.m)** |
| Bleeder Screw | 72 (8) |
| Master Cylinder Mounting Nuts | 108 (13) |
| Parking Brake Adjustment Lock Nut | 48 (5.4) |

*TORQUE SPECIFICATIONS (COROLLA)*

| Application | Ft. Lbs. (N.m) |
|---|---|
| Brake Booster Clevis Lock Nut | 19 (26) |
| Brake Line Fittings | 11 (15) |
| Caliper Guide Bolts | |
| Front | 18 (25) |
| Rear | 14 (19) |
| Caliper Support Bracket (Torque Plate) Bolts | |
| Front | 65 (88) |
| Rear | 34 (46) |
| Hub-to-Carrier Bolts | 59 (80) |
| Rear Caliper Cable Support Bracket Bolts | 34 (46) |
| Union Bolt | 22 (30) |
| Wheel Lug Nuts | 76 (103) |
| | **INCH Lbs. (N.m)** |
| Bleeder Screw | 72 (8) |
| Brake Booster Mounting Nuts | 108 (13) |
| Master Cylinder Mount Bolts | 108 (13) |
| Parking Brake Adjustment Lock Nut | 48 (5.4) |

*TORQUE SPECIFICATIONS (TERCEL)*

| Application | Ft. Lbs. (N.m) |
|---|---|
| Backing Plate-to-Rear Axle | 51 (70) |
| Brake Booster Clevis Lock Nut | 19 (26) |
| Brake Line Fittings | 11 (15) |
| Brake Line Union Bolt | 22 (30) |
| Caliper Guide Bolts | 18 (25) |
| Caliper Support Bracket (Torque Plate) Bolts | 65 (88) |
| Wheel Lug Nuts | 76 (103) |
| | **INCH Lbs. (N.m)** |
| Bleeder Screws | 72 (8) |
| Master Cylinder Mounting Nuts | 108 (13) |
| Parking Brake Adjusting Nuts | 48 (5.4) |

## DISC & DRUM BRAKE SPECIFICATIONS

*DISC & DRUM BRAKE SPECIFICATIONS (CAMRY)*

| Application | In. (mm) |
|---|---|
| **Front Disc** | |
| Standard Disc Thickness | .984 (25.00) |
| Minimum Refinish Disc Thickness | .945 (24.00) |
| Maximum Disc Runout | .0028 (.070) |
| Standard Pad Thickness | .394 (10.00) |
| Minimum Pad Thickness | .039 (1.00) |
| **Rear Disc** | |
| Standard Disc Thickness | .394 (10.00) |
| Minimum Refinish Disc Thickness | .354 (9.00) |
| Maximum Disc Runout | .0059 (.150) |
| Standard Pad Thickness | .394 (10.00) |
| Minimum Pad Thickness | .039 (1.00) |
| **Rear Emergency Brake Drum (Integral With Rear Disc)** | |
| Standard Diameter | 6.69 (170.0) |
| Maximum Refinish Diameter | 6.73 (171.0) |
| Standard Lining Thickness | .079 (2.00) |
| Minimum Lining Thickness | .039 (1.00) |
| Brake Shoe-To-Lever Side Clearance (Maximum) | .0138 (.350) |
| **Rear Brake Drum** | |
| Standard Diameter | 9.000 (228.60) |
| Maximum Refinish Diameter | 9.079 (230.61) |
| Standard Lining Thickness | .197 (5.00) |
| Minimum Lining Thickness | .039 (1.00) |
| Brake Shoe-To-Drum Clearance | .024 (.60) |
| Brake Shoe-To-Lever Side Clearance (Maximum) | .0138 (.350) |

# 1991 BRAKES
# Disc & Drum – FWD Cars (Cont.)

**DISC & DRUM BRAKE SPECIFICATIONS (CELICA)**

| Application | In. (mm) |
|---|---|
| **Front Disc** | |
| Standard Disc Thickness | .866 (22.00) |
| Minimum Refinish Disc Thickness | .787 (20.00) |
| Maximum Disc Runout | .0028 (.070) |
| Standard Pad Thickness | .39 (10.0) |
| Minimum Pad Thickness | .039 (1.00) |
| **Rear Disc** | |
| Standard Disc Thickness | .394 (10.00) |
| Minimum Refinish Disc Thickness | .354 (9.00) |
| Maximum Disc Runout | .0059 (.150) |
| Standard Pad Thickness | .394 (10.00) |
| Minimum Pad Thickness | .039 (1.00) |
| **Rear Emergency Brake Drum (Integral With Rear Disc)** | |
| Standard Diameter | 6.69 (170.0) |
| Maximum Refinish Diameter | 6.73 (171.0) |
| Standard Lining Thickness | .079 (2.00) |
| Minimum Lining Thickness | .039 (1.00) |
| Brake Shoe-To-Lever Side Clearance (Maximum) | .0138 (.350) |
| **Rear Brake Drum** | |
| Standard Diameter | 7.874 (200.00) |
| Maximum Refinish Diameter | 7.913 (201.00) |
| Standard Lining Thickness | .157 (4.00) |
| Minimum Lining Thickness | .039 (1.00) |
| Brake Shoe-To-Drum Clearance | .024 (.60) |
| Brake Shoe-To-Lever Side Clearance (Maximum) | .0138 (.350) |

**DISC & DRUM BRAKE SPECIFICATIONS (COROLLA)**

| Application | In. (mm) |
|---|---|
| **Front Disc** | |
| Standard Disc Thickness | |
| 4A-FE Engine | .709 (18.00) |
| 4A-GE Engine | .866 (22.00) |
| Minimum Refinish Disc Thickness | |
| 4A-FE Engine | .669 (17.00) |
| 4A-GE Engine | .827 (21.00) |
| Maximum Disc Runout | .0035 (.090) |
| Standard Pad Thickness | .394 (10.00) |
| Minimum Pad Thickness | .039 (1.00) |
| **Rear Disc** | |
| Standard Disc Thickness | .354 (9.00) |
| Minimum Refinish Disc Thickness | .315 (8.00) |
| Maximum Disc Runout | .0039 (.100) |
| Standard Pad Thickness | .394 (10.00) |
| Minimum Pad Thickness | .039 (1.00) |
| **Rear Drum** | |
| Standard Diameter | 7.874 (200.00) |
| Maximum Refinish Diameter | 7.913 (201.00) |
| Standard Lining Thickness | .157 (4.00) |
| Minimum Lining Thickness | .039 (1.00) |
| Brake Shoe-To-Drum Clearance | .024 (.60) |
| Brake Shoe-To-Lever Side Clearance (Maximum) | .0138 (.350) |

**DISC & DRUM BRAKE SPECIFICATIONS (TERCEL)**

| Application | In. (mm) |
|---|---|
| **Front Disc** | |
| Standard Disc Thickness | .709 (18.00) |
| Minimum Refinish Disc Thickness | .669 (17.00) |
| Maximum Disc Runout | .0035 (.090) |
| Standard Pad Thickness | .394 (10.00) |
| Minimum Pad Thickness | .039 (1.00) |
| **Rear Brake Drum** | |
| Standard Diameter | 7.087 (180.00) |
| Maximum Refinish Diameter | 7.126 (181.00) |
| Standard Lining Thickness | .157 (4.00) |
| Minimum Lining Thickness | .039 (1.00) |
| Brake Shoe-To-Drum Clearance | .024 (.60) |

# 1991 BRAKES
# Disc & Drum – RWD Cars

## Cressida, MR2, Supra

***WARNING: For warnings and procedures regarding vehicles equipped with Anti-Lock Brake System (ABS), see appropriate ANTI-LOCK article in BRAKES.***

## DESCRIPTION & OPERATION

The hydraulic brake system uses a tandem master cylinder with a vacuum power assist servo. All models are equipped with 4-wheel disc brakes.

A load-sensing proportioning valve is used on Cressida and MR2 to regulate brake pressure between front and rear brakes. Rear brakes on all models are self-adjusting.

Parking brake lever mechanically activates rear brakes. On Cressida and Supra models, parking brake is a duo servo mechanical drum brake design built into bell of rear rotor assemblies. On MR2 models, parking brake applies rear pads.

## BLEEDING BRAKE SYSTEM

### BLEEDING PROCEDURES

***CAUTION: Use only clean brake fluid. Ensure no dirt or other foreign matter contaminates brake fluid. DO NOT mix different brands of brake fluid as they may not be compatible. DO NOT spill brake fluid on car as it may damage paint. If brake fluid contacts paint, immediately wash with water.***

Ensure master cylinder reservoir is full. Begin bleeding procedure on longest hydraulic line, and then go to next longest line until all lines have been bled. Road test vehicle, and check brake performance. Check reservoir fluid level.

## ADJUSTMENTS

### BRAKE PEDAL HEIGHT

**1)** Brake pedal height is measured from face of pedal pad to asphalt sheet under carpet. *See Fig. 1.* To adjust clearance, loosen lock nut on brake pedal push rod.

**2)** Adjust pedal height by turning push rod. See BRAKE PEDAL HEIGHT & FREE PLAY SPECIFICATIONS table for specification.

***BRAKE PEDAL HEIGHT & FREE PLAY SPECIFICATIONS***

| Application | Free Play In. (mm) | Pedal Height In. (mm) |
|---|---|---|
| Cressida | .12-.24 (3.0-6.0) | 6.2-6.6 (157-167) |
| MR2 | .12-.20 (3.0-5.0) | 7.0-7.4 (178-188) |
| Supra | .12-.24 (3.0-6.0) | 6.0-6.4 (152-162) |

**3)** After setting pedal height, tighten lock nut on push rod. See appropriate TORQUE SPECIFICATIONS table at end of article. Adjust stoplight switch, and tighten switch lock nut. See STOPLIGHT SWITCH under ADJUSTMENTS.

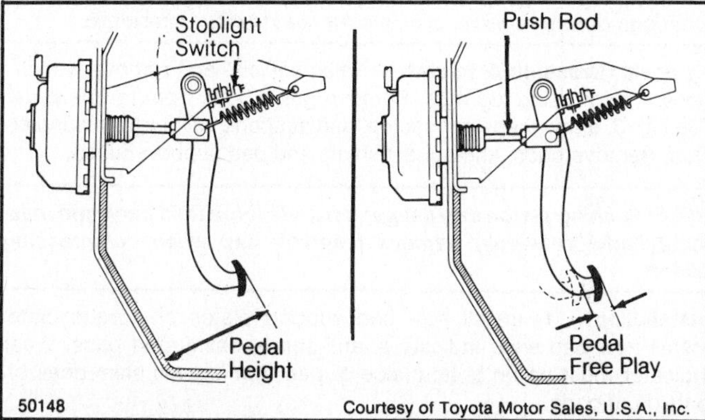


***Fig. 1: Measuring Pedal Height & Free Play***

### BRAKE PEDAL FREE PLAY

**1)** Brake pedal free play is distance brake pedal travels with engine stopped before resistance is felt. *See Fig. 1.* To check pedal free play, depress brake pedal several times to exhaust vacuum from power brake unit.

**2)** Depress pedal, and measure travel until initial resistance is felt. See BRAKE PEDAL HEIGHT & FREE PLAY SPECIFICATIONS table. If free play is not as specified, adjust by turning push rod. Check brake pedal height. See BRAKE PEDAL HEIGHT under ADJUSTMENTS.

### BRAKE PEDAL RESERVE DISTANCE

**1)** Pedal reserve distance is measured from face of pedal pad to asphalt sheet under carpet with brakes applied. Measure reserve distance with engine running and weight of 110 lbs. (50 kg) applied against pedal.

**2)** If measured reserve distance is less than specification, inspect brake system. See BRAKE PEDAL MINIMUM RESERVE DISTANCE SPECIFICATIONS table.

***BRAKE PEDAL MINIMUM RESERVE DISTANCE SPECIFICATIONS***

| Application | In. (mm) |
|---|---|
| Cressida | 3.03 (77) |
| MR2 | 4.61 (117) |
| Supra | 3.15 (80) |

### PARKING/EMERGENCY BRAKE

**Inspection** – Pull on parking brake lever with weight of 44 lbs. (20 kg) to check parking brake adjustment. Count number of notches (clicks) until parking brake is fully applied. Adjust parking brake if lever stroke travel is not 5-8 notches.

**Adjustment (Cressida)** – Loosen lock nuts on turnbuckle (under vehicle, in right cable) and pull rod (at equalizer). Tighten cables first at turnbuckle and then at pull rod. Tighten lock nuts.

**Adjustment (MR2)** – **1)** Disc brake caliper is activated by emergency brake lever. System is normally self-adjusting. Ensure cable lever on caliper moves freely and is against stop pin when emergency brake is off.

**2)** Pull up and release parking lever a few times. Depress brake pedal several times. Pull up brake lever. If an excessive number of clicks is required to activate brake, remove fuel tank undercover and adjust cable at equalizer link until lever travel is correct. Ensure lock nuts are tightened with equalizer link in horizontal position.

**Adjustment (Supra)** – Remove center console or parking brake lever boot to uncover base of lever. Loosen lock nut. Turn adjusting nut on cable until lever travel is correct. Tighten lock nut. Install console or boot.

### PARKING BRAKE SHOES

**Cressida & Supra** – Raise and support rear of vehicle. Remove rear wheel. Release parking brake. Remove adjustment hole plug from rear rotor. Turn adjusting nut until parking brake shoes lock rotor. Back off adjuster 8 notches. Install hole plug.

### POWER BRAKE UNIT PUSH ROD

**1)** Check and adjust clearance between power brake unit push rod and master cylinder piston if either unit is replaced or overhauled. *See Fig. 2.*

**2)** If clearance is not zero, adjust male portion of push rod using open end wrench while holding female portion of rod using pliers.

### STOPLIGHT SWITCH

**1)** Remove lower instrument panel and air duct (if necessary). Loosen lock nuts. Turn switch until clearance between switch and pedal stop is as specified. *See Fig. 1.* See STOPLIGHT SWITCH CLEARANCE SPECIFICATIONS table.

**2)** Check brake pedal height. See BRAKE PEDAL HEIGHT under ADJUSTMENTS. Check brakelight operation.

# 1991 BRAKES
# Disc & Drum – RWD Cars (Cont.)

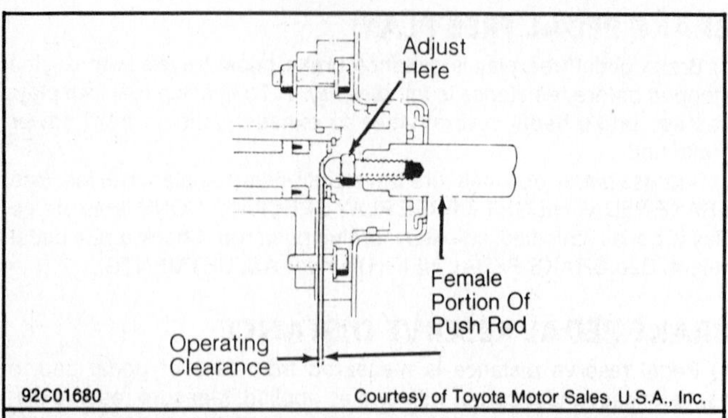

Courtesy of Toyota Motor Sales, U.S.A., Inc.

***Fig. 2: Measuring Clearance Between Master Cylinder Piston & Power Brake Unit Push Rod***

## TESTING

### POWER BRAKE UNIT

**Functional Test – 1)** Start engine. Turn ignition off. Depress brake pedal several times. Depress pedal firmly and hold pressure for 15 seconds. If pedal sinks, master cylinder, brake line or caliper piston is faulty.

**2)** Start engine with pedal depressed. If pedal sinks slightly, vacuum unit is working properly. If pedal height does not vary, booster or check valve is faulty. Replace as necessary.

**Leak Test – 1)** Depress brake pedal with engine running. Turn ignition off. If pedal height does not vary while depressed for 30 seconds, vacuum booster is okay. If pedal height changes, check for air leaks.

**2)** With engine stopped, depress brake pedal several times using normal pressure. Pedal should be low when first depressed. On consecutive applications, pedal height should gradually increase. If pedal height does not increase, check for air leaks.

### PROPORTIONING & BY-PASS VALVE

**Cressida & MR2 – 1)** Install SST (09709-29017) gauge set on front and rear calipers. Bleed air from system. See BLEEDING BRAKE SYSTEM. Raise master cylinder (front) pressure and read gauge at front wheel. See PROPORTIONING & BY-PASS VALVE PRESSURE SPECIFICATIONS table.

**2)** Check system at specified pressures. Rear pressure increase should be less than front pressure increase. If rear wheel cylinder pressure is not within specification, replace valve assembly.

## REMOVAL & INSTALLATION

### FRONT DISC BRAKE PADS

***NOTE: Location and number of anti-rattle springs, anti-squeal shims, pad support and guide plates varies with models. Note component locations during removal process for reassembly reference.***

**Removal – 1)** Loosen master cylinder reservoir cap. Raise and support vehicle. Remove wheels, and install wheel nuts to temporarily retain discs. On Supra, remove brake hose bracket. On all models, remove brake caliper from torque plate, and hang aside leaving hydraulic line connected.

**2)** Remove anti-squeak springs, shims and pads. Remove anti-squeak shims and pad support plates. Check disc thickness and runout. Measure brake pads, and replace as necessary. See appropriate DISC BRAKE SPECIFICATIONS or DISC & DRUM BRAKE SPECIFICATIONS table at end of article.

***NOTE: Some models have one or more sets of anti-squeal shims. If one set of shims is vented, place it between pad and outer anti-squeal shim.***

***STOPLIGHT SWITCH CLEARANCE SPECIFICATIONS***

| Application | In. (mm) |
|---|---|
| Cressida | .02-.09 (.5-2.3) |
| MR2 & Supra | 0 (0) |

***PROPORTIONING & BY-PASS VALVE PRESSURE SPECIFICATIONS***

| Application | Front Pressure psi (kg/cm²) | Rear Pressure psi (kg/cm²) |
|---|---|---|
| Cressida | 569 (40) | 569 (40) |
| | 1138 (80) | 779 (54.8) |
| MR2 | | |
| Non-Turbo | 427 (30) | 427 (30) |
| | 1138 (80) | 853 (60) |
| Turbo | 853 (60) | 853 (60) |
| | 1422 (100) | 1195 (84) |

**Installation – 1)** Install new pad support plates, pad guides and anti-rattle springs on torque plate. Push piston(s) into caliper bore. Wear indicator must be on top side of pad on Cressida and MR2 and bottom side of pad on Supra.

***NOTE: Pushing piston into caliper bore will force fluid back into master cylinder reservoir. Remove reservoir cap when compressing piston.***

**2)** Reverse removal procedure to complete installation. DO NOT let piston dust boot wedge against edge of pads. Check reservoir fluid level, and tighten cap.

### FRONT BRAKE CALIPER

**Removal –** Raise vehicle, and remove wheels. Disconnect hydraulic line and spring clip. Plug line to prevent fluid spillage. Remove caliper mounting bolts or slide pins as necessary. Remove caliper from torque plate.

**Installation –** Compress piston(s) using hammer handle and wooden plate (if necessary). Reverse removal procedure to complete installation. Tighten bolts to specification. See appropriate TORQUE SPECIFICATIONS table at end of article.

### FRONT BRAKE ROTOR

**Removal & Installation – 1)** Remove caliper assembly with hose connected. See FRONT BRAKE CALIPER under REMOVAL & INSTALLATION. Support caliper from frame using wire. Remove torque plate from knuckle.

**2)** Mark rotor and hub for installation reference. Slide rotor off hub assembly. To install, reverse removal procedure. Tighten all bolts to specification. See appropriate TORQUE SPECIFICATIONS table at end of article.

### REAR DISC BRAKE PADS

***NOTE: Location and number of anti-rattle springs, anti-squeal shims, pad support and guide plates varies with models. Note component locations during removal process for reassembly reference.***

**Removal (Cressida & Supra) –** Raise vehicle, and remove wheels. Secure rotor using lug nuts. Remove guide bolts from torque plate. *See Fig. 3.* Leave hose connected, and suspend caliper from suspension. Remove pads, anti-squeal shims and pad support plates.

***NOTE: Pushing piston into caliper bore will force fluid back into master cylinder reservoir. Remove reservoir cap when compressing piston.***

**Installation – 1)** Install new pad support plates on torque plate. Install new pad wear indicators, anti-squeal shims and pads. Wear indicator must be on bottom side of pad. Anti-squeal shim goes on outside of pads.

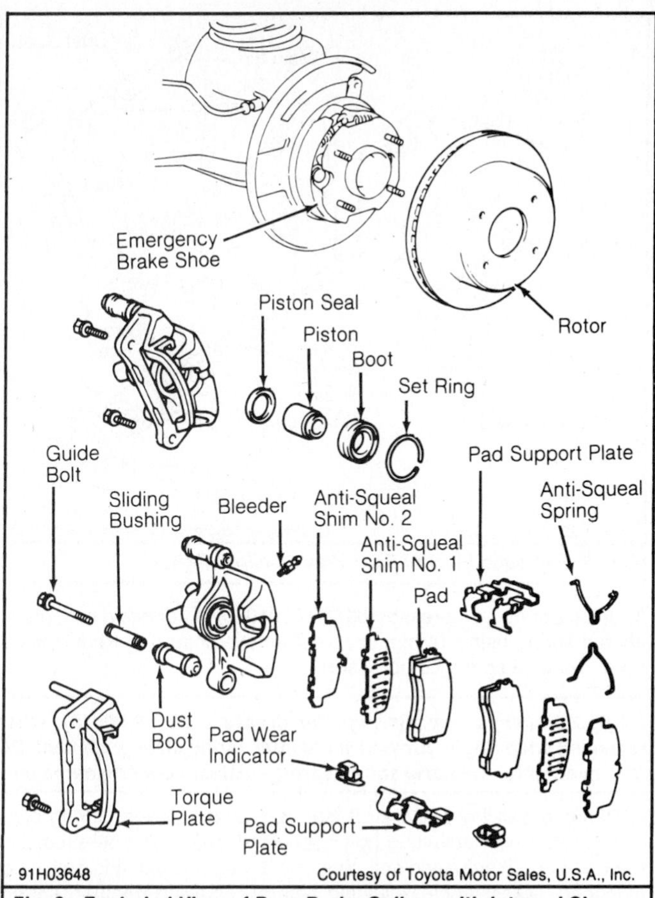


*Fig. 3: Exploded View of Rear Brake Caliper with Internal Shoe Parking Brake (Cressida & Supra)*

**2)** Push piston into bore using "C" clamp or wooden hammer handle. Put new anti-squeal shim on piston. Slide caliper onto torque plate carefully to avoid damaging boot on edge of pad.

**Removal (MR2)** – Raise vehicle, and remove wheels. Secure rotor using 2 lug nuts. Remove lower guide bolt. Pivot caliper up on main pin and support from frame at highest point. Remove brake pads, anti-squeal shims, anti-rattle springs and pad guide plates.

**Installation** – **1)** Install anti-rattle springs and pad guide plates on torque plate. Place new anti-squeal shims onto pads. Install pads in torque plate. Wear indicator should be on top edge of outer pad.

**2)** Using Piston Spanner (09719-00020), turn piston clockwise until it turns freely. Align pad projection with piston stopper. Swing caliper down, ensuring boot does not wedge against pad.

**3)** Install lower guide bolt. See TORQUE SPECIFICATIONS (MR2) table at end of article. Install wheels. Ensure fluid level is correct. Set automatic parking brake adjuster by pumping brake pedal several times.

## REAR BRAKE CALIPER

**Removal & Installation** – Remove pads. See REAR DISC BRAKE PADS under REMOVAL & INSTALLATION. Disconnect brake hose from caliper. Disconnect parking brake cable if attached to caliper. To install, reverse removal procedure.

## REAR BRAKE ROTOR

**Removal & Installation** – **1)** Remove caliper, and suspend from underbody with hose connected. See REAR BRAKE CALIPER under REMOVAL & INSTALLATION. Remove torque plate from backing plate.

**2)** Mark rotor and axle shaft flange for installation reference. Slide rotor off axle flange. On Cressida and Supra, contract parking brake shoe adjuster (if necessary) to remove rotor. To install, reverse removal procedure.

## MASTER CYLINDER

**Removal** – Unplug sensor lead (if equipped). Drain brake fluid from reservoir. Disconnect and plug hydraulic lines. Remove master cylinder-to-power brake unit nuts. Remove master cylinder.

**Installation** – Check and adjust power brake unit push rod. See POWER BRAKE UNIT PUSH ROD under ADJUSTMENTS. To complete installation, reverse removal procedure and bleed brake system. See BLEEDING BRAKE SYSTEM.

## POWER BRAKE UNIT

**Removal & Installation (Cressida)** – **1)** Remove master cylinder. See MASTER CYLINDER under REMOVAL & INSTALLATION. Disconnect vacuum hose from booster. Disconnect clevis at brake pedal.

**2)** Remove alternator, PCV pipe and hose. Remove Idle Speed Control (ISC) valve. Disconnect water by-pass hose from throttle body. Remove EGR pipe bolts. Remove cold start injector tube and gaskets. Clean up any spilled fuel. Remove manifold stay.

**3)** Remove air intake chamber bolts, and move chamber forward. Remove power brake unit. To install, check and adjust push rod. See POWER BRAKE UNIT PUSH ROD under ADJUSTMENTS. Reverse removal procedure to complete installation.

**Removal & Installation (MR2 & Supra)** – **1)** Remove master cylinder. See MASTER CYLINDER under REMOVAL & INSTALLATION. Disconnect vacuum hose from booster. Disconnect push rod clevis at brake pedal.

**2)** Remove power brake unit from vehicle. To install, reverse removal procedure. Check and adjust push rod. See POWER BRAKE UNIT PUSH ROD under ADJUSTMENTS.

## REAR PARKING BRAKE (CALIPER)

**Removal & Installation (MR2)** – See REAR BRAKE CALIPER under REMOVAL & INSTALLATION.

## REAR PARKING BRAKE (INTERNAL SHOE)

**Removal (Cressida & Supra)** – **1)** Remove rotor. See REAR BRAKE ROTOR under REMOVAL & INSTALLATION. Remove shoe return springs and shoe strut with spring. *See Fig. 4*. Pull out on front shoe and remove adjusting screw.

**2)** Remove hold-down spring, front shoe and tension spring. Remove rear shoe, and disconnect parking brake cable from lever.

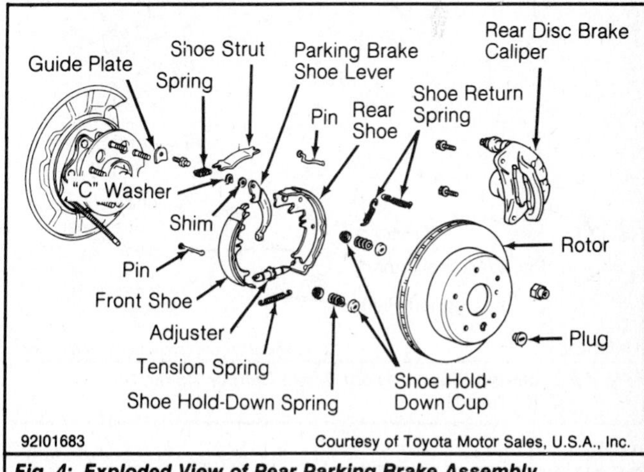


*Fig. 4: Exploded View of Rear Parking Brake Assembly (Cressida & Supra)*

**Inspection** – Clearance between parking brake shoe and lever must be .0138" (.350 mm) or less. If clearance is more than .0138" (.350 mm), replace shim under parking brake lever. Shims are available from .012-.035" (.30-.90 mm) in .012" (.30 mm) increments. Use new "C" washer when installing lever.

**Installation** – To install, reverse removal procedure. Apply non-melting grease to sliding surfaces of shoes and adjusting screw threads. Align groove of rear axle shaft flange with service hole on rotor, and install rotor. Adjust parking brake shoe clearance. See PARKING BRAKE SHOES under ADJUSTMENTS.

## OVERHAUL

### FRONT BRAKE CALIPER

***NOTE:* For exploded view of front brake caliper assembly, see Fig. 5 or 6.**

***NOTE:* When overhauling caliper, replace entire assembly if cylinder bores are pitted or scored more than light honing will repair.**

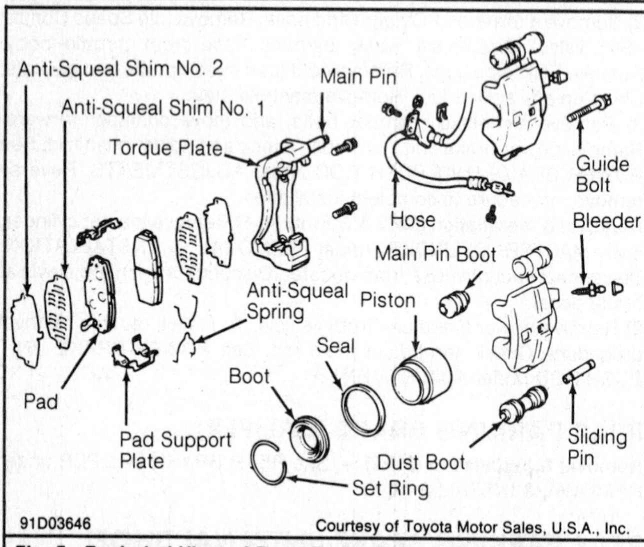


***Fig. 5:* Exploded View of Front Brake Caliper Assembly (Supra Shown; Cressida & MR2 Non-Turbo Are Similar)**

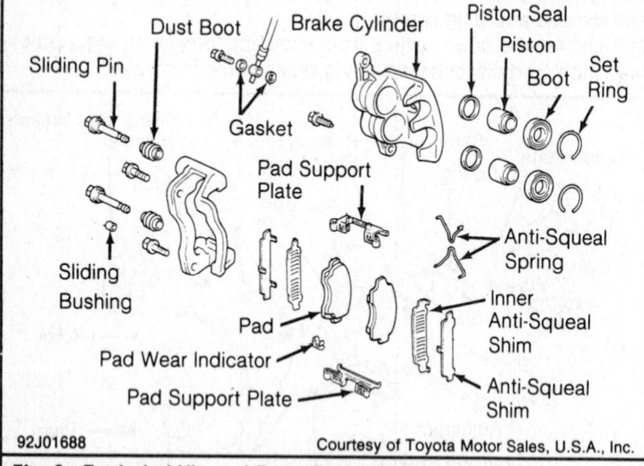


***Fig. 6:* Exploded View of Front Brake Caliper Assembly (MR2 Turbo)**

### REAR BRAKE CALIPER

**Disassembly & Reassembly (Cressida & Supra)** – *See Fig. 3.*

**Disassembly (MR2)** – **1)** Remove sliding bushing and dust boot. *See Fig. 7.* Remove main pin boots. Use screwdriver to remove cylinder boot retaining set ring and dust boot. Remove piston from bore by turning it counterclockwise using Piston Spanner (09719-14020). Remove piston seal from cylinder bore.

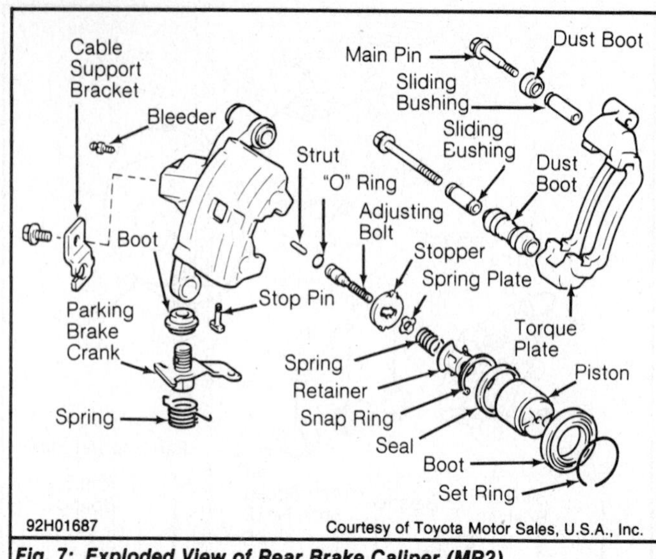


***Fig. 7:* Exploded View of Rear Brake Caliper (MR2)**

**2)** Using Spring Compressor (09756-00010) over adjusting bolt, gently tighten spring using 14-mm socket. Remove snap ring from cylinder bore. Remove spring compressor.

***CAUTION:* Always use Spring Compressor (09756-00010) when removing snap ring to prevent accidental spring disengagement. DO NOT overtighten compressor as spring retainer could be damaged.**

**3)** Remove parking brake strut, spring retainer, spring, spring plate and stopper with adjusting bolt connected. DO NOT use excessive force to pry out adjusting bolt. Ensure "O" ring on adjusting bolt is not damaged. Disassemble adjusting bolt by removing retainer, spring, spring plate and stopper. Remove "O" ring from bolt.

**4)** Remove cable support bracket. Disconnect spring from parking brake lever. Remove parking brake lever from caliper. Turn lever so it will not catch on stop pin. If lever boot is to be replaced, remove it. DO NOT disassemble lever any further.

**Reassembly** – **1)** Apply lithium soap base glycol grease on main pin, sliding bushing, strut pin, adjusting bolt, piston and all rubber parts. Install stopper pin. Pin should be .098" (2.5 mm) from caliper to underside of head.

**2)** Install cable support bracket. Install lever boot and lever, ensuring boot aligns with groove in lever seal. Install spring, and ensure lever touches stopper pin.

**3)** Ensure clearance exists between cable support bracket and upper side of lever. Use cable support bracket mount bolt to adjust clearance.

**4)** Install strut. Ensure needle rollers do not catch on caliper hole. Install new "O" ring on adjusting bolt. Assemble adjuster bolt with stopper, plate, spring and spring retainer.

**5)** Use spring compressor to tighten component parts of adjusting bolt assembly. Ensure inscribed surface of stopper faces up and notches of spring case align with notches on stopper.

**6)** Install adjusting bolt assembly. Install snap ring with opening toward bleeder side of caliper. Remove threaded compressor. Move parking brake lever by hand. Ensure adjusting bolt moves smoothly. Install piston seal in cylinder bore.

**7)** Using piston spanner, slowly turn piston clockwise into caliper until it bottoms. Align piston stopper groove with protrusion on caliper. Place dust boot and retaining ring into caliper. Install sliding bushing and boot. Ensure seal does not fold under piston.

### MASTER CYLINDER

***NOTE:* For exploded view of master cylinder assembly, see Fig. 8.**

# 1991 BRAKES
# Disc & Drum – RWD Cars (Cont.)

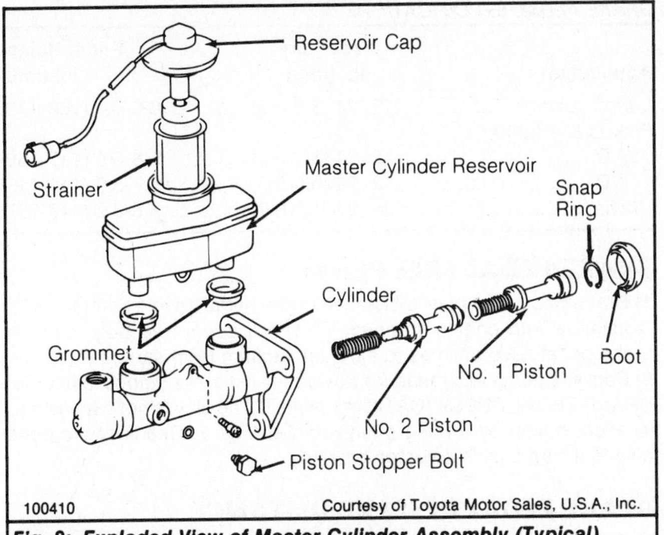


*Fig. 8: Exploded View of Master Cylinder Assembly (Typical)*

## TORQUE SPECIFICATIONS

*TORQUE SPECIFICATIONS (CRESSIDA)*

| Application | Ft. Lbs. (N.m) |
|---|---|
| Air Intake Chamber Mounting Bolts | 13 (18) |
| Brake Hose-To-Caliper Fitting | 17 (23) |
| Brake Line Fittings | 11 (15) |
| Brake Pedal Clevis Rod Lock Nut | 19 (26) |
| Caliper Guide Bolts | |
| Front | 65 (88) |
| Rear | 18 (24) |
| Caliper Support Bracket (Torque Plate) Bolts | |
| Front | 67 (91) |
| Rear | 34 (46) |
| EGR Pipe Mounting Bolts | 13 (18) |
| Reservoir Mounting Bolt (Without ABS) | 18 (24) |
| Wheel Lug Nuts | 76 (103) |
| | **INCH Lbs. (N.m)** |
| Bleeder Screw | 72 (8) |
| Master Cylinder Mounting Nuts | 108 (13) |
| Power Brake Unit Mounting Nuts | 108 (13) |

*TORQUE SPECIFICATIONS (MR2)*

| Application | Ft. Lbs. (N.m) |
|---|---|
| Brake Hose-To-Caliper Fitting | 22 (30) |
| Brake Line Fittings | 11 (15) |
| Brake Pedal Clevis Rod Lock Nut | 19 (26) |
| Cable Support Bracket Bolt | 34 (46) |
| Caliper Guide Bolts | |
| Front (Non-Turbo) | 18 (24) |
| Front (Turbo) | 25 (34) |
| Rear | 14 (19) |
| Caliper Support Bracket (Torque Plate) Bolts | |
| Front | 65 (88) |
| Rear | 43 (58) |
| Parking Brake Equalizer Lock Nuts | 12 (16) |
| Wheel Lug Nuts | 76 (103) |
| | **INCH Lbs. (N.m)** |
| Bleeder Screw | 72 (8) |
| Master Cylinder Mounting Nuts | 108 (13) |
| Proportioning Valve/Power Brake Unit Mounting Nuts | 108 (13) |

*TORQUE SPECIFICATIONS (SUPRA)*

| Application | Ft. Lbs. (N.m) |
|---|---|
| Brake Hose Support Bracket Bolts | 14 (19) |
| Brake Hose-To-Caliper Fitting | |
| Front | 22 (30) |
| Rear | 17 (23) |
| Brake Line Fittings | 11 (15) |
| Brake Pedal Clevis Rod Lock Nut | 19 (26) |

*TORQUE SPECIFICATIONS (SUPRA – Cont.)*

| Application | Ft. Lbs. (N.m) |
|---|---|
| Caliper Guide Bolts | |
| Front | 27 (37) |
| Rear | 14 (19) |
| Caliper Support Bracket (Torque Plate) Bolts | |
| Front | 77 (104) |
| Rear | 34 (46) |
| Parking Brake Guide Plate Bolt | 13 (18) |
| Wheel Lug Nuts | 76 (103) |
| | **INCH Lbs. (N.m)** |
| Bleeder Screw | 72 (8) |
| Master Cylinder Mounting Nuts | 108 (13) |
| Parking Brake Lever Adjustment Lock Nut | 48 (5.4) |
| Power Brake Unit Mounting Nuts | 108 (13) |

## DISC & DRUM BRAKE SPECIFICATIONS

*DISC & DRUM BRAKE SPECIFICATIONS (CRESSIDA)*

| Application | In. (mm) |
|---|---|
| Front Disc | |
| Standard Disc Thickness | .866 (22.00) |
| Minimum Refinish Disc Thickness | .827 (21.00) |
| Maximum Disc Runout | .0028 (.070) |
| Standard Lining Thickness | .394 (10.00) |
| Minimum Pad Thickness | .039 (1.00) |
| Rear Disc | |
| Standard Disc Thickness | .709 (18.00) |
| Minimum Refinish Disc Thickness | .669 (17.00) |
| Maximum Disc Runout | .0051 (.130) |
| Standard Lining Thickness | .354 (9.00) |
| Minimum Pad Thickness | .039 (1.00) |
| Rear Parking Brake Drum | |
| Standard Diameter | 6.93 (176.0) |
| Maximum Refinish Diameter | 6.97 (177.0) |
| Standard Lining Thickness | .079 (2.00) |
| Minimum Lining Thickness | .039 (1.00) |
| Brake Shoe-To-Lever Side Clearance (Maximum) | .0138 (.350) |

*DISC BRAKE SPECIFICATIONS (MR2)*

| Application | In. (mm) |
|---|---|
| Front Disc | |
| Standard Disc Thickness | .984 (25.00) |
| Minimum Refinish Disc Thickness | .945 (24.00) |
| Maximum Disc Runout | .0028 (.070) |
| Standard Lining Thickness | .394 (10.00) |
| Minimum Pad Thickness | .039 (1.00) |
| Rear Disc | |
| Standard Disc Thickness | .630 (16.00) |
| Minimum Refinish Disc Thickness | .591 (15.00) |
| Maximum Disc Runout | .0039 (.100) |
| Standard Lining Thickness | .394 (10.00) |
| Minimum Pad Thickness | .039 (1.00) |

*DISC & DRUM BRAKE SPECIFICATIONS (SUPRA)*

| Application | In. (mm) |
|---|---|
| Front Disc | |
| Standard Disc Thickness | .866 (22.00) |
| Minimum Refinish Disc Thickness | .827 (21.00) |
| Maximum Disc Runout | .0051 (.130) |
| Standard Lining Thickness | .394 (10.00) |
| Minimum Pad Thickness | .039 (1.00) |
| Rear Disc | |
| Standard Disc Thickness | .709 (18.00) |
| Minimum Refinish Disc Thickness | .669 (17.00) |
| Maximum Disc Runout | .0051 (.130) |
| Standard Lining Thickness | .394 (10.00) |
| Minimum Pad Thickness | .039 (1.00) |
| Rear Parking Brake Drum | |
| Standard Diameter | 7.48 (190.0) |
| Maximum Refinish Diameter | 7.52 (191.0) |
| Standard Lining Thickness | .098 (2.50) |
| Minimum Lining Thickness | .039 (1.00) |
| Brake Shoe-To-Lever Side Clearance (Maximum) | .0138 (.350) |

# 1991 BRAKES
# Disc & Drum – Light Trucks & Vans

## Land Cruiser, Pickup, Previa, 4Runner

***WARNING:*** *For warnings and procedures regarding vehicles equipped with Anti-Lock Brake Systems (ABS), see appropriate ANTI-LOCK article.*

***NOTE:*** *Pickup in this article includes Cab and Chassis (C & C) with Single Rear Wheels (SRW) and Dual Rear Wheels (DRW).*

## DESCRIPTION & OPERATION

Hydraulic brake system uses a tandem master cylinder with a vacuum power assist servo. All models are equipped with front disc brakes and rear drum brakes standard. Rear disc brakes are optional on Previa models.

A load-sensing proportioning valve is used to regulate brake pressure between front and rear brakes. Rear brakes on all models are self-adjusting.

Parking brake lever mechanically activates rear brakes. On models with rear drum brakes, a cable applies rear shoes. On Previa with rear disc brakes, parking brake is internal with rear disc rotor assembly.

## BLEEDING BRAKE SYSTEM

### BLEEDING PROCEDURES

***CAUTION:*** *Use only clean brake fluid. Ensure no dirt or other foreign matter contaminates brake fluid. DO NOT mix different brands of brake fluid as they may not be compatible. DO NOT spill brake fluid on car as it may damage paint. If brake fluid contacts paint, immediately wash with water.*

Ensure master cylinder reservoir is full. Begin bleeding procedure on longest hydraulic line first and then go to next longest line until all lines have been bled. Road test vehicle and check brake performance. Check reservoir fluid level.

## ADJUSTMENTS

### BRAKE PEDAL HEIGHT

**1)** Brake pedal height is measured from face of pedal pad to asphalt sheet under carpet. To adjust clearance, loosen stoplight switch and lock nut on brake push rod. *See Fig. 1.*

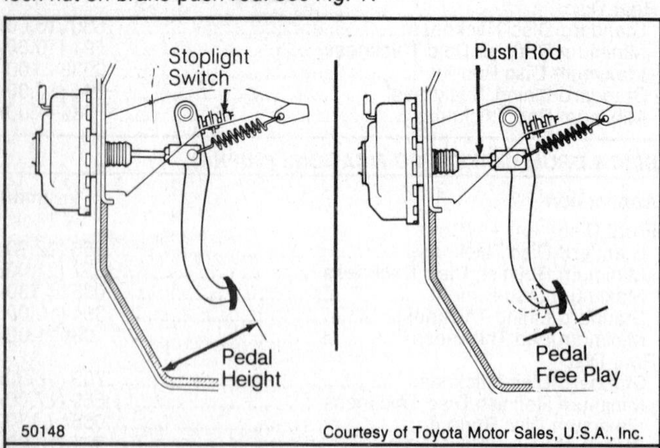


***Fig. 1: Measuring Brake Pedal Height & Free Play***

**2)** Adjust pedal height by turning push rod. See BRAKE PEDAL SPECIFICATIONS table for correct specification. After setting pedal height, tighten lock nut on push rod. Adjust stoplight switch and tighten switch lock nut.

***BRAKE PEDAL SPECIFICATIONS***

| Application | Free Play In. (mm) | Pedal Height In. (mm) |
|---|---|---|
| Land Cruiser | .12-.24 (3.0-6.0) | 6.3-6.7 (160-170) |
| Pickup & 4Runner | | |
| 2WD | .12-.24 (3.0-6.0) | 5.8-6.0 (147-153) |
| 4WD | .12-.24 (3.0-6.0) | 5.7-5.9 (145-150) |
| Previa | .04-.24 (1.0-6.0) | 5.8-6.2 (147-157) |

## BRAKE PEDAL FREE PLAY

**1)** Brake pedal free play is distance brake pedal travels before feeling resistance with engine stopped. To check pedal free play, depress brake pedal several times to exhaust vacuum from servo.

**2)** Depress pedal and measure travel until initial resistance is felt. See BRAKE PEDAL SPECIFICATIONS table. If free play is not within specification, adjust by turning push rod. *See Fig. 1.* Check brake pedal height, if free play is adjusted properly.

## BRAKE PEDAL RESERVE DISTANCE

**1)** Pedal reserve distance is measured from face of pedal pad to asphalt sheet under carpet with brakes applied. Measure reserve distance with engine running and weight of 110 lbs. (50 kg) applied against pedal.

**2)** See BRAKE PEDAL MINIMUM RESERVE DISTANCE SPECIFICATIONS table for minimum reserve distance. If measured reserve distance is less than specification, inspect brake system.

***BRAKE PEDAL MINIMUM RESERVE DISTANCE SPECIFICATIONS***

| Application | In. (mm) |
|---|---|
| Land Cruiser | 2.32 (58) |
| Pickup & 4Runner | |
| 2WD | |
| 22R-E Engine | 2.76 (70) |
| 3VZ-E Engine | |
| 1/2-Ton | 2.56 (65) |
| 1-Ton | 2.95 (75) |
| C & C | |
| DRW | 2.17 (55) |
| SRW | 2.95 (75) |
| 4WD | 2.56 (65) |
| Previa | 2.95 (75) |

## LOAD-SENSING PROPORTIONING & BY-PASS VALVE (LSP & BV or LSPV)

***NOTE:*** *See LOAD-SENSING PROPORTIONING & BY-PASS VALVE (LSP & BV or LSPV) under TESTING.*

## PARKING BRAKE

***NOTE:*** *Rear service brakes must be correctly adjusted before adjusting parking brake. See REAR BRAKE DRUM under REMOVAL & INSTALLATION.*

**Lever Stroke Adjustment – 1)** Pull on parking brake lever with weight of 44 lbs. (20 kg) to check parking brake adjustment. Count number of notches (clicks) until parking brake is fully applied. See PARKING BRAKE LEVER STROKE SPECIFICATIONS table. Adjust parking brake if travel is not within specification.

***PARKING BRAKE LEVER STROKE SPECIFICATIONS***

| Application | Notches |
|---|---|
| Land Cruiser | 7-9 |
| Pickup | |
| 1-Ton & 4WD | 11-17 |
| 2WD | 12-18 |
| Previa | 4-5 |
| 4Runner | 13-19 |

**2)** On Land Cruiser, remove center console or parking brake lever boot to uncover base of lever. Loosen adjusting cap. Turn adjusting

# 1991 BRAKES
# Disc & Drum – Light Trucks & Vans (Cont.)

nut on cable until lever travel is correct. Tighten adjusting cap. Install console or boot.

**3)** On Pickup, Previa and 4Runner, release parking brake. From beneath vehicle, loosen lock nut on equalizer bar pull rod. Turn adjuster nut until lever travel is correct. Tighten lock nut.

## PARKING BRAKE SHOES

**Previa With Rear Disc Brakes –** Raise and support rear of vehicle. Release parking brake. Remove adjustment hole plug from backing plate. Turn adjuster until parking brake shoes lock wheel. Back adjuster off 8 notches. Install hole plug.

## POWER BRAKE UNIT PUSH ROD

**Clearance Adjustment – 1)** Check and adjust clearance between power brake unit push rod and master cylinder piston if either unit is replaced or overhauled. Set clearance to zero. *See Fig. 2*.

**2)** If clearance is not to specification, adjust male portion of push rod with open end wrench while holding female portion of rod with pliers.

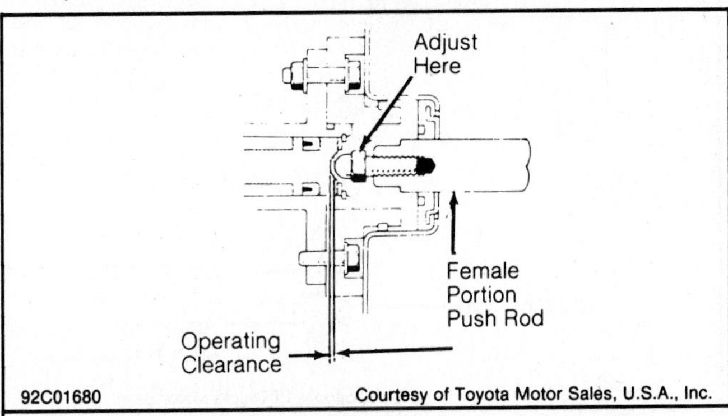


***Fig. 2: Measuring Clearance Between Master Cylinder Piston & Power Brake Unit Push Rod***

## REAR DRUM BRAKE SHOES

***NOTE: All rear drum service brakes have a self-adjuster which is activated when brake pedal is applied as vehicle travels in reverse.***

To set initial lining-to-drum clearance, raise and support rear of vehicle. Release parking brake. Remove adjustment hole plug from backing plate. Turn adjusting nut until brake shoes lock wheel. Back adjuster off until wheel turns freely. Measured clearance between linings and braking surface of drum should be .024" (.60 mm).

## STOPLIGHT SWITCH

Remove lower instrument panel and air duct (if necessary). Loosen lock nuts. Turn switch until clearance between switch and pedal stop is as specified. *See Fig. 1*. See STOPLIGHT SWITCH CLEARANCE SPECIFICATIONS table. Check brake pedal height and brake light operation.

***STOPLIGHT SWITCH CLEARANCE SPECIFICATIONS***

| Application | In. (mm) |
|---|---|
| Land Cruiser & 4Runner | 0 (0) |
| Pickup & Previa | .02-.09 (.5-2.3) |

# TESTING

## POWER BRAKE UNIT

**Functional Test – 1)** Start engine. Turn ignition off. Depress brake pedal several times. Depress pedal firmly and hold pressure for 15 seconds. If pedal sinks, master cylinder, brake line or caliper piston is faulty.

**2)** Start engine with pedal depressed. If pedal sinks slightly, vacuum unit is working properly. If pedal height does not vary, booster or check valve is faulty. Replace as necessary.

**Leak Test – 1)** Depress brake pedal with engine running. Turn ignition off. If pedal height does not vary while depressed for 30 seconds, vacuum booster is okay. If pedal height changes, check for air leaks.

**2)** With engine stopped, depress brake pedal several times using normal pressure. Pedal should be low when first depressed. On consecutive applications, pedal height should gradually rise. If pedal height does not increase, check for air leaks.

## LOAD-SENSING PROPORTIONING & BY-PASS VALVE (LSP & BV or LSPV)

**Land Cruiser, Pickup & 4Runner – 1)** For testing purposes, rear axle is loaded to a specified weight. Set total rear axle weight to specified amount. See LSPV REAR AXLE TEST WEIGHT table.

***LSPV REAR AXLE TEST WEIGHT***

| Application | Lbs. (kg) |
|---|---|
| Land Cruiser | 2535 (1150) |
| Pickup | |
| 2WD | |
| 1/2-Ton | 1764 (800) |
| 1-Ton & C & C SRW [1] | 1984 (900) |
| C & C DRW [1] | 2535 (1150) |
| 4WD | 1764 (800) |
| Previa | 2028 (920) |
| 4Runner | 2310 (1048) |

[1] – On Pickup C & C models, if unladen weight exceeds specification, set rear axle load to 3699 lbs. (1678 kg) with SRW and 4400 lbs. (1996 kg) with DRW.

**2)** Attach Pressure Gauge Set (09709-29017) to front caliper and rear wheel cylinder. Bleed air from system. See BLEEDING BRAKE SYSTEM. Depress brake pedal until front pressure is as specified. See LSPV PRESSURE SPECIFICATIONS table. Wait 2 seconds and record rear pressure reading.

***NOTE: DO NOT depress brake pedal more than once or release pedal while setting pressure on front gauge.***

***LSPV PRESSURE SPECIFICATIONS***

| Application | Front Pressure psi (kg/cm²) | Rear Pressure psi (kg/cm²) |
|---|---|---|
| Land Cruiser | 1138 (80) | 555-725 (39-51) |
| Pickup | | |
| 2WD | | |
| 1/2-Ton | 1138 (80) | 555-697 (39-49) |
| 1-Ton | 1138 (80) | 569-711 (40-50) |
| C & C | | |
| DRW [1] | 1138 (80) | 612-754 (43-53) |
| DRW [2] | 1707 (120) | 1124-1294 (79-91) |
| SRW [1] | 1138 (80) | 569-711 (40-50) |
| SRW [2] | 1707 (120) | 1323-1493 (93-105) |
| 4WD | | |
| Regular Cab | 1138 (80) | 498-640 (35-45) |
| Extra Cab | 1138 (80) | 555-697 (39-49) |
| Previa | | |
| Rear Disc Brake | 1707 (120) | 1508-1749 (106-123) |
| Rear Drum Brake | 1422 (100) | 868-925 (61-65) |
| 4Runner | 1138 (80) | 615-757 (43.2-53.2) |

[1] – Total rear axle weight set to 1984 lbs. (900 kg) on SRW and to 2535 lbs. (1150 kg) on DRW.

[2] – Total rear axle weight set to 4400 lbs. (1996 kg) on SRW and to 3699 lbs. (1678 kg) on DRW.

**3)** Adjust rear pressure by changing length of No. 2 shackle (if necessary). *See Fig. 3*. To increase rear pressure reading, increase distance "A". To decrease rear pressure reading, decrease distance "A".

**4)** Repeat pressure tests after adjusting shackle length. If rear pressures fail specification after adjustment, reposition valve body.

# 1991 BRAKES
# Disc & Drum – Light Trucks & Vans (Cont.)

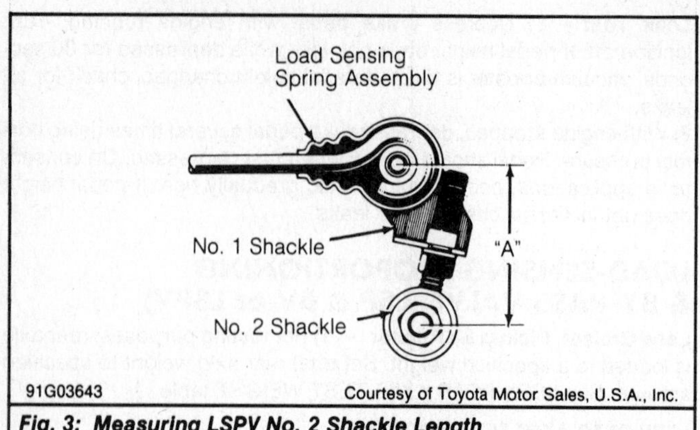


**Fig. 3: Measuring LSPV No. 2 Shackle Length (Land Cruiser, Pickup & 4Runner)**

Raise valve body if rear pressures are too high, lower valve body if rear pressures are too low.

**5)** Ensure No. 2 shackle length is within adjustment range. If shackle is removed or replaced, adjust No. 2 shackle to standard length. See NO. 2 SHACKLE LENGTH SPECIFICATIONS table.

***NO. 2 SHACKLE LENGTH SPECIFICATIONS***

| Application | Standard Length In. (mm) | Adjustment Range In. (mm) |
|---|---|---|
| Land Cruiser | 3.54 (90) | 3.31-3.78 (84-96) |
| Pickup | | |
| 2WD | 3.07 (78) | 2.83-3.31 (72-84) |
| 4WD | 4.72 (120) | 4.49-4.96 (114-126) |
| 4Runner | 3.07 (78) | 2.68-3.46 (68-88) |

**6)** If pressures cannot be adjusted to specification, check valve housing. Position valve body in uppermost position. Apply brakes and record rear brake pressures. See VALVE BODY ADJUSTMENT PRESSURE SPECIFICATIONS (LAND CRUISER, PICKUP & 4RUNNER) table. If measured value does not meet specification, replace valve assembly.

***VALVE BODY ADJUSTMENT PRESSURE SPECIFICATIONS (LAND CRUISER, PICKUP & 4RUNNER)***

| Application | Front Pressure psi (kg/cm²) | Rear Pressure psi (kg/cm²) |
|---|---|---|
| Land Cruiser & 4Runner | | |
| 1st Reading | 142 (10) | 142 (10) |
| 2nd Reading | 356 (25) | 168-225 (11.8-15.8) |
| 3rd Reading | 853 (60) | 270-370 (19-26) |
| Pickup | | |
| 2WD (SRW) | | |
| 1st Reading | 71 (5) | 71 (5) |
| 2nd Reading | 356 (25) | 128-185 (9-13) |
| 3rd Reading | 853 (60) | 256-356 (18-25) |
| 2WD (DRW) | | |
| 1st Reading | 71 (5) | 71 (5) |
| 2nd Reading | 356 (25) | 148-205 (10.4-14.4) |
| 3rd Reading | 853 (60) | 311-411 (21.9-28.9) |
| 4WD (Regular Cab) | | |
| 1st Reading | 142 (10) | 142 (10) |
| 2nd Reading | 356 (25) | 156-213 (11-15) |
| 3rd Reading | 853 (60) | 235-334 (16.5-23.5) |
| 4WD (Extra Cab) | | |
| 1st Reading | 142 (10) | 142 (10) |
| 2nd Reading | 356 (25) | 168-225 (11.8-15.8) |
| 3rd Reading | 853 (60) | 270-370 (19-26) |

**Previa – 1)** For testing purposes, rear axle is loaded to a specified weight. Set total rear axle weight to specified amount. See LSPV REAR AXLE TEST WEIGHT table.

**2)** Install Pressure Gauge Set (09709-29017) gauge set on front and rear calipers. Bleed air from system. See BLEEDING BRAKE SYSTEM. Depress brake pedal until front pressure is as specified. See LSPV PRESSURE SPECIFICATIONS table. Wait 2 seconds and record rear pressure reading.

**3)** Adjust rear pressure by changing length of spring shaft. *See Fig. 4*. To increase rear pressure reading, increase distance "A". To decrease rear pressure reading, decrease distance "A". If valve cannot be adjusted to specification, replace valve assembly.

***NOTE: On Previa, turn adjustment nut one complete turn (360 degrees) for pressure change of 51.2 psi (3.6 kg/cm²) on rear disc brakes or 28.4 psi (2.0 kg/cm²) for rear drum brakes.***

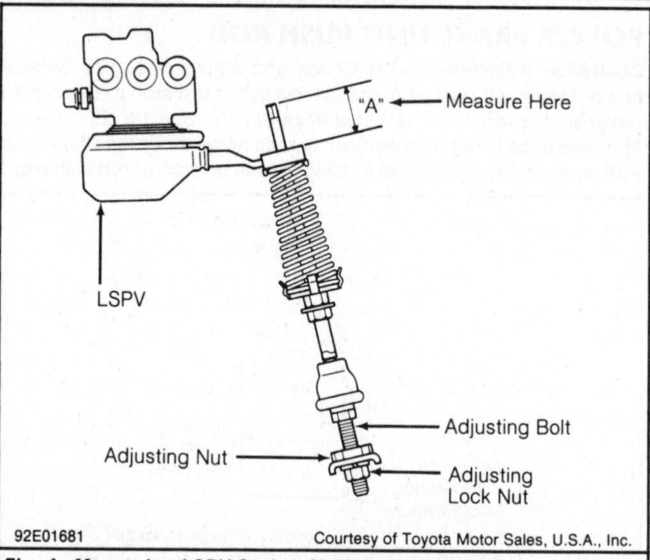


**Fig. 4: Measuring LSPV Spring Shaft Length (Previa)**

## REMOVAL & INSTALLATION

***NOTE: Location and number of anti-rattle springs, anti-squeal shims, pad support and guide plates varies between models. Note component locations during removal process for reassembly reference.***

### FRONT DISC BRAKE PADS

***NOTE: Pushing piston into caliper bore will force fluid back into master cylinder reservoir. Remove reservoir cap when compressing piston.***

**Removal (Land Cruiser, Pickup 4WD & 4Runner 4WD)** – Loosen master cylinder reservoir cap. Raise vehicle and remove wheels. Remove clip, 2 pins and anti-rattle spring. Remove pads and shims. *See Fig. 5.*

***NOTE: Always change pads on one wheel at a time. Opposite piston may be pressed out by brake pressure.***

**Installation** – Seat pistons using a hammer handle or equivalent. Slide new pads and anti-rattle shims into caliper. Install retaining pins and anti-rattle spring. Install clip into retaining pin holes. Check reservoir fluid level.

**Removal & Installation (Pickup 2WD & Previa) – 1)** Raise and support vehicle. Remove front wheel. On Previa, install 2 lug nuts to hold rotor in place. On all models, remove lower guide pin. Rotate caliper upward and suspend with wire.

**2)** Remove springs, pads, shims and support plates. *See Fig. 6 or 7.* To install, reverse removal procedure. Tighten lower guide pin to specification. See appropriate TORQUE SPECIFICATIONS table at end of article. Check reservoir fluid level.

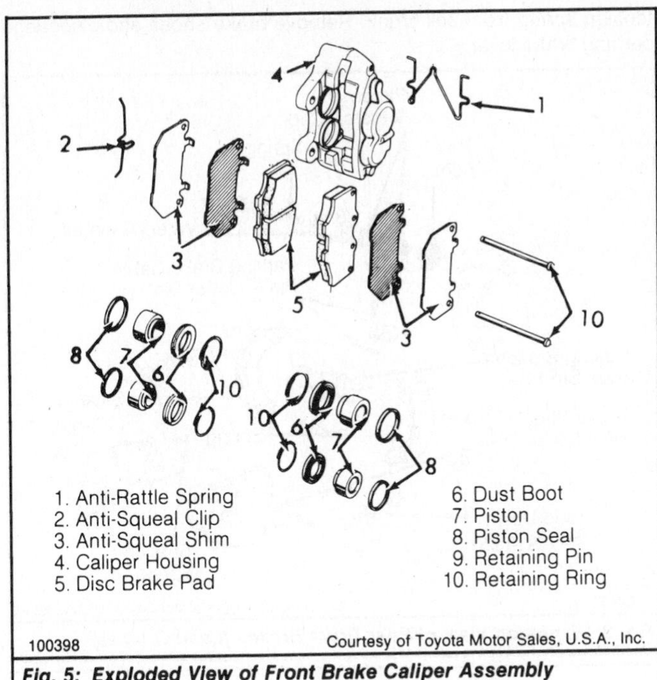


*Fig. 5: Exploded View of Front Brake Caliper Assembly (Land Cruiser, Pickup 4WD & 4Runner 4WD)*

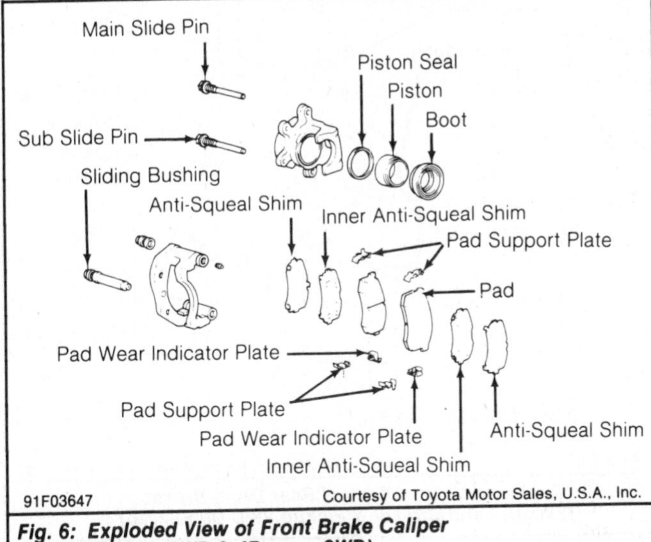


*Fig. 6: Exploded View of Front Brake Caliper (Pickup 2WD & 4Runner 2WD)*

## FRONT BRAKE CALIPER

**Removal & Installation – 1)** Raise vehicle and remove wheels. Disconnect hydraulic line and spring clip. Plug line to prevent fluid spillage. Remove caliper mounting bolts or slide pins as necessary.

**2)** On models with fixed main pin, pivot caliper up to clear edge of rotor. Slide caliper off main pin. On all other models, remove caliper from knuckle or torque plate.

**3)** To install, reverse removal procedure. On units with fixed main pin, boot end must be installed in groove of main pin.

## FRONT BRAKE ROTOR

**Removal (Land Cruiser, Pickup 4WD & 4Runner 4WD) – 1)** Raise vehicle and remove wheels. Disconnect brake line from caliper (if necessary). Remove caliper.

**2)** On models with free wheeling hub, set control handle to FREE position. On all models, remove hub cover, bolt/washer and hub body. Use tapered punch to open slits of conical washers. Remove axle shaft snap ring (if equipped).

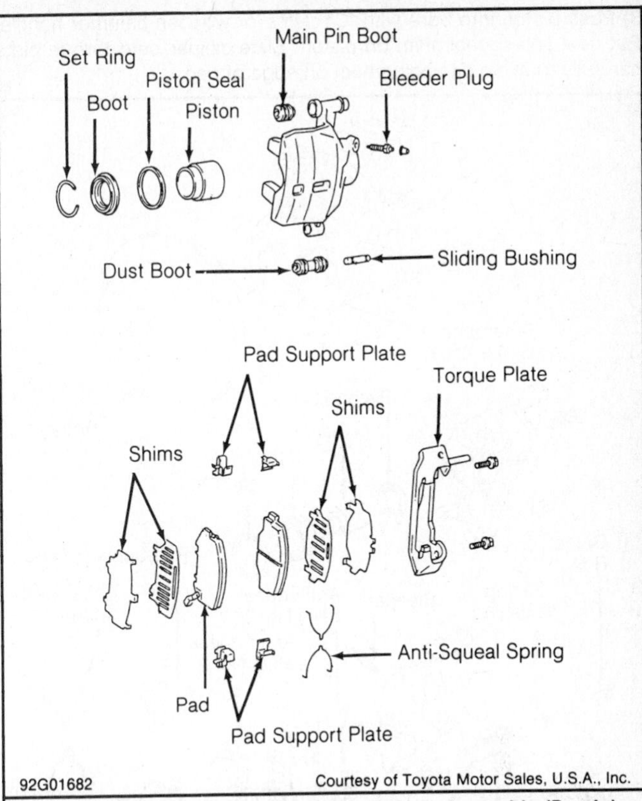


*Fig. 7: Exploded View of Front Brake Caliper Assembly (Previa)*

**3)** Straighten tabs of outer lock washer. Using Spindle Socket (09607-60020), remove lock nut, lock washer and adjusting nut. Remove thrust washer and outer bearing. Remove axle hub and rotor. Remove grease seal and inner bearing. Press hub bolts out of axle hub. Remove retaining bolts and separate rotor from hub.

**Installation** – To install, reverse removal procedure. Adjust wheel bearings. See appropriate SUSPENSION article. Tighten all bolts to specification. See appropriate TORQUE SPECIFICATIONS table at end of this article.

**Removal & Installation (Pickup 2WD & 4Runner 2WD) – 1)** Remove caliper. Remove grease cap, cotter pin, washer and castellated nut. Remove thrust washer and outer wheel bearing. Remove rotor and hub assembly.

**2)** Place alignment marks on rotor and hub for reassembly reference. Remove retaining bolts and separate hub from rotor.

**3)** To complete installation, reverse removal procedures. Adjust wheel bearings. See appropriate SUSPENSION article. Tighten all bolts to specification. See appropriate TORQUE SPECIFICATIONS table at end of this article.

**Removal & Installation (Previa)** – Remove caliper assembly with hose connected. Support caliper from frame with wire. Remove torque plate from knuckle. Slide rotor off hub assembly. To install, reverse removal procedure. Tighten all bolts to specification. See appropriate TORQUE SPECIFICATIONS table at end of article.

## REAR DISC BRAKE PADS

***NOTE: Pushing piston into caliper bore will force fluid back into master cylinder reservoir. Remove reservoir cap when compressing piston.***

**Removal & Installation (Previa) – 1)** Raise and support vehicle. Remove wheels. Secure rotor with lug nuts. Remove guide bolts from torque plate. Leave hose connected and suspend caliper from suspension. Remove pads, anti-squeal shims and pad support plates. *See Fig. 8.*

**2)** Install new pad support plates on torque plate. Install new pad wear indicators, anti-squeal shims and pads. Position wear indicators on lower edge of pad. Anti-squeal shim goes on outside of pads.

# 1991 BRAKES
# Disc & Drum – Light Trucks & Vans (Cont.)

3) Push piston into bore with "C" clamp or wooden hammer handle. Put new anti-squeal shim on piston. Slide caliper onto torque plate carefully to avoid damaging boot on edge of pad.

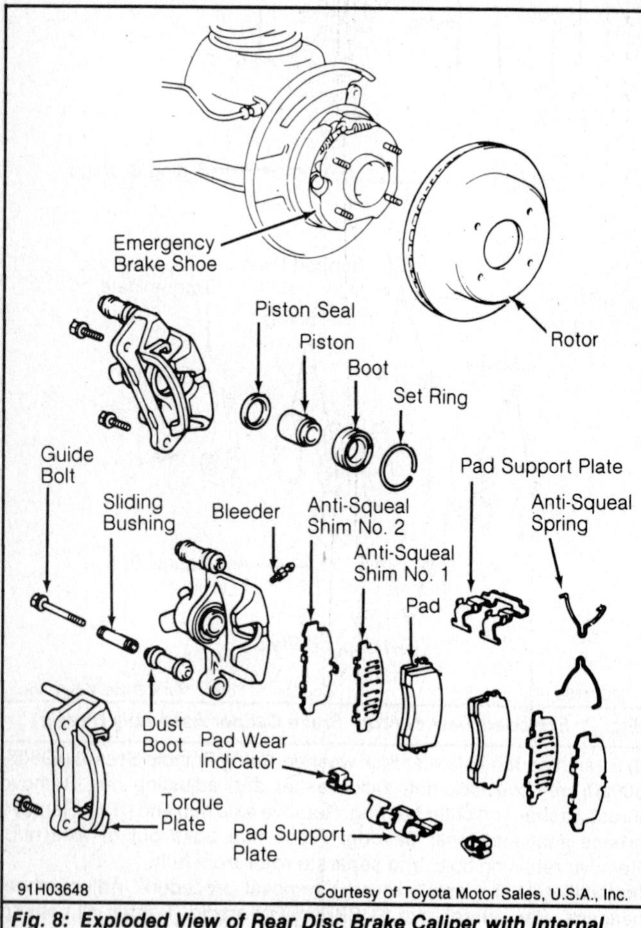


***Fig. 8: Exploded View of Rear Disc Brake Caliper with Internal Shoe Parking Brake (Previa)***

## REAR BRAKE CALIPER

**Removal & Installation (Previa)** – Disconnect brake hose and mounting bolts. Remove caliper from knuckle or torque plate. To install, reverse removal procedure. Bleed hydraulic system. See BLEEDING BRAKE SYSTEM.

## REAR BRAKE ROTOR

**Removal & Installation (Previa)** – Remove caliper and suspend from underbody with hose connected. See REAR BRAKE CALIPER under REMOVAL & INSTALLATION. Remove torque plate from backing plate. Slide rotor off axle flange. To install, reverse removal procedure.

## REAR BRAKE DRUM

**Removal** – Raise and support vehicle. Remove tire and wheel. Remove set screws from brake drum (if equipped). Pull drum from axle flange. It may be necessary to loosen brake shoe adjuster before removing drum.

**Installation** – Measure inside diameter of brake drum and diameter of brake shoes. Turn brake adjuster until difference between diameters is .02" (.6 mm). Install brake drum and adjust brakes, if required.

## REAR DRUM BRAKE SHOES

**Removal (All Except Pickup 2WD Duo-Servo)** – Remove brake drum, tension spring and hold-down springs. *See Fig. 9 or 10*. Remove tension spring from bell crank. Remove brake shoes and disengage parking brake lever.

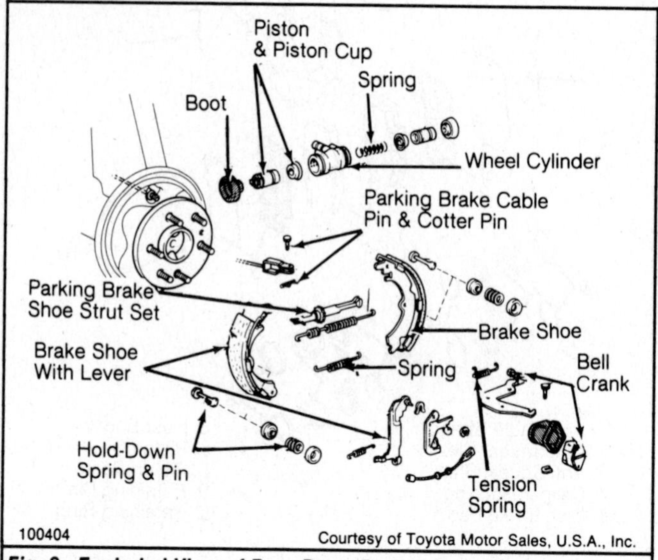


***Fig. 9: Exploded View of Rear Drum Brakes (Land Cruiser)***

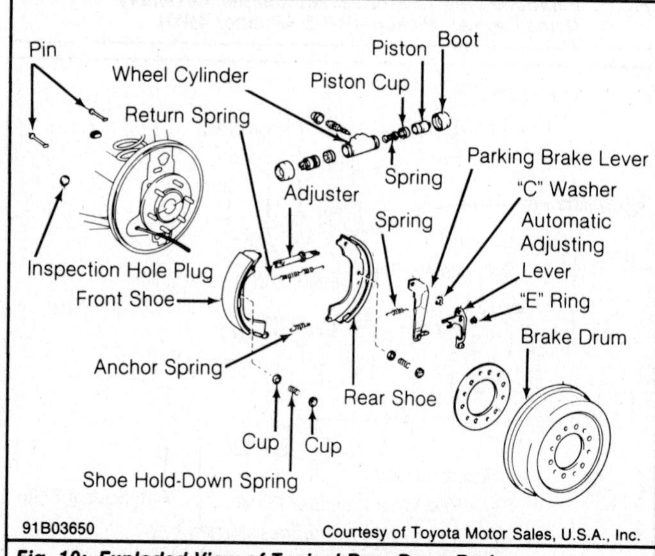


***Fig. 10: Exploded View of Typical Rear Drum Brakes (Except Land Cruiser & Pickup 2WD Duo-Servo)***

**Installation** – Position brake shoes over wheel cylinders with front return spring hooked on inner side of shoe. Install hold-down springs. To complete installation, reverse removal procedures. Adjust brake shoes.

**Removal (Pickup 2WD Duo-Servo)** – **1)** With brake drum removed, disconnect upper tension springs. *See Fig. 11*. Remove adjusting cable, cable guide, adjusting lever and guide plate. Remove adjuster lever tension springs and strut. Remove hold-down springs and pins.

**2)** Pull brake shoes from backing plate. Separate adjuster mechanism and tension spring. Disconnect parking brake cable from lever. Secure rear shoe and remove "C" washer retaining parking lever to shoe. Remove parking brake lever.

**Installation** – Install parking brake on lever and secure with new "C" washer. Ensure lever moves. To complete installation, reverse removal procedures. Install brake drum. Adjust brake shoes.

## REAR WHEEL CYLINDER

**Removal & Installation** – With brake drum and shoes removed, disconnect hydraulic line from wheel cylinder. Remove mounting bolts

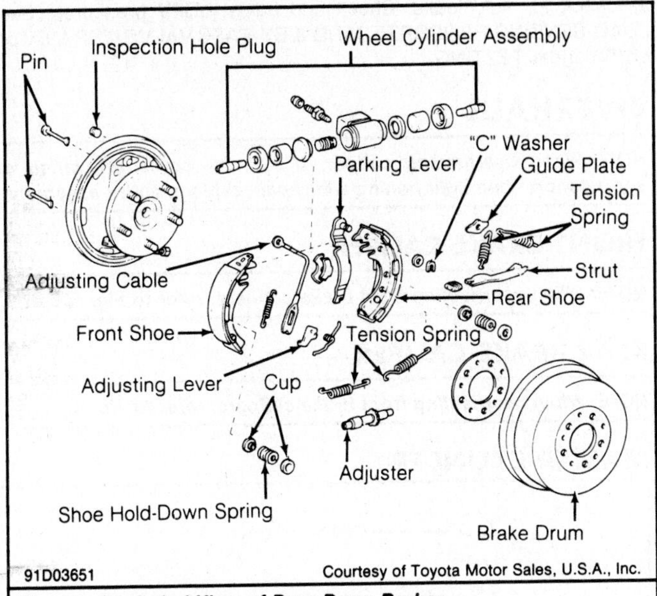


***Fig. 11: Exploded View of Rear Drum Brakes (Pickup 2WD Duo-Servo)***

and remove wheel cylinder. To install, reverse removal procedure. Adjust brakes and bleed system. See BLEEDING BRAKE SYSTEM.

## REAR AXLE BEARING & OIL SEAL

**Removal (Land Cruiser) – 1)** Drain axle housing and remove inspection cover. Remove differential pinion shaft lock pin. Remove pinion shaft and spacer.

**2)** Push axle shaft to center of vehicle and remove axle lock circlip. Remove axle shaft. Use seal remover to remove oil seal. Using Bearing Remover (09514-35011), remove rear axle bearing.

**Installation –** Using Bearing Installer (09608-20011), drive new bearing and oil seal into rear housing. To complete installation, reverse removal procedure.

**Removal (Pickup & 4Runner) – 1)** Remove wheel and brake drum. Disconnect line at wheel cylinder. Disconnect parking brake cable. Remove backing plate mounting nuts. Pull out axle shaft and backing plate together. Remove snap ring from axle shaft.

**2)** Attach Pressing Tube (09521-25011) to rear of backing plate. Press axle shaft from backing plate. Using slide hammer with inside puller, remove outer oil seal. Support backing plate around bearing. Using press with bearing driver, press bearing out of bearing case.

**3)** If bearing case is worn or damaged, put nuts on serration bolts and drive bolts out with hammer. Using slide hammer with inside puller, remove inner oil seal from axle shaft. Clean all parts before reinstallation.

**Installation – 1)** Place backing plate on new bearing case. Using 2 sockets as adapters, press serration bolts into place. Flat side of bearing case and 2 long serration bolts should be on upper side of backing plate. Using press, bearing driver and support for backing plate, press new bearing into case.

**2)** Using seal driver, install new oil seal into bearing case. Install backing plate and bearing retainer onto axle shaft. Using press and adapter for backing plate and bearing case, press axle shaft into backing plate and bearing case.

**3)** Install snap ring to axle shaft. Use seal driver to install seal in housing. Coat oil seal lips with grease before final installation. Install rear axle shaft in housing. Replace backing plate nuts and tighten to 51 ft. lbs. (69 N.m).

**4)** Connect brake line to wheel cylinder. Install drum and wheel. Fill differential with gear oil. Connect parking brake cable to equalizer and install clip and clamp bolt to frame. Bleed brake system. See BLEEDING BRAKE SYSTEM.

**Removal (Previa) – 1)** Raise and support vehicle. Remove rear wheel and speed sensor (if equipped). Disconnect and plug brake line at wheel cylinder. On drum brake models, remove drum and shoes. On disc brake models, remove cylinder and rotor.

**2)** On all models, disconnect parking brake cable. Remove backing plate nuts. Using puller, remove axle shaft. DO NOT damage oil seal or speed sensor rotor (if equipped).

**3)** On disc brake models, remove backing plate. On all models, press oil seal and speed sensor rotor from shaft (if necessary). Grind down inner retainer and remove with chisel. Press bearing from axle shaft. Remove oil seal.

**Installation – 1)** Drive new oil seal into axle shaft housing to depth of .138" (3.51 mm) for disc brake models and .236" (5.99 mm) for drum brake models.

**2)** On disc brake models, place new retainer gasket and bearing outer retainer on backing plate. Using a socket and hammer, install bolts. Install backing plate to axle shaft.

**3)** On drum brake models, install bearing outer retainer to axle shaft. On all models, press new bearing onto axle shaft. Heat inner retainer to 302°F (150°C) in an oil bath. Clean retainer and axle shaft of oil and grease. While still hot, press inner retainer onto axle shaft.

**4)** Using a press, install speed sensor rotor and new oil seal (if equipped). Install end gasket. To complete installation, reverse removal procedure. Bleed brake system. See BLEEDING BRAKE SYSTEM.

## MASTER CYLINDER

**Removal –** Unplug sensor lead. Drain brake fluid from reservoir. Disconnect and plug hydraulic lines. Remove master cylinder-to-power brake unit nuts. Remove master cylinder.

**Installation –** If master cylinder has been overhauled or replaced, check and adjust power brake unit push rod. See POWER BRAKE UNIT PUSH ROD under ADJUSTMENTS. To install, reverse removal procedure. Bleed brake system. See BLEEDING BRAKE SYSTEM.

## POWER BRAKE UNIT

**Removal & Installation –** Remove master cylinder assembly from vehicle. See MASTER CYLINDER under REMOVAL & INSTALLATION. Disconnect push rod clevis at brake pedal. Remove power brake unit from vehicle. To install, reverse removal procedure.

## PARKING BRAKE SHOES (INTERNAL)

**Removal (Previa With Rear Disc Brakes) – 1)** Remove rotor. See REAR DISC BRAKE ROTOR under REMOVAL & INSTALLATION. Remove shoe return springs and shoe strut with spring.

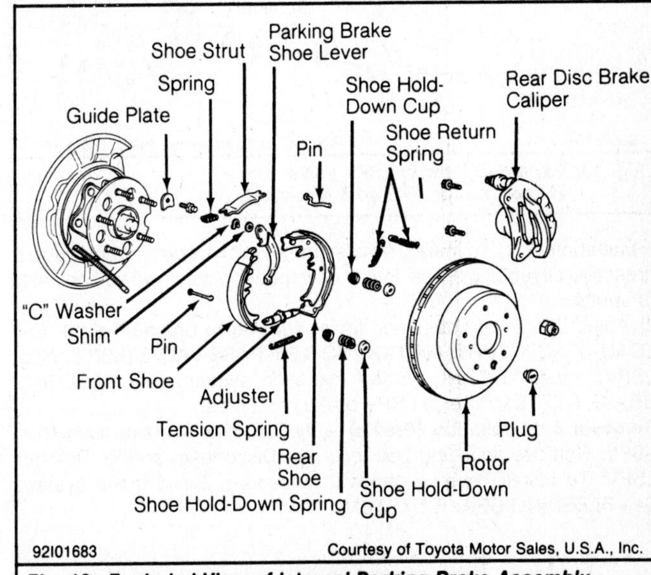


***Fig. 12: Exploded View of Internal Parking Brake Assembly (Previa with Rear Disc Brakes)***

# 1991 BRAKES
# Disc & Drum – Light Trucks & Vans (Cont.)

**2)** Pull out on front shoe and remove adjusting screw set. Remove hold down spring, front shoe and tension spring. Remove rear shoe and disconnect parking brake cable from lever. *See Fig. 12.*

**Inspection** – Clearance between parking brake shoe and lever must be .014" (.35 mm) or less. If not, replace shim under parking brake lever. Shims are available in sizes from .008" (.20 mm) to .035" (.90 mm) in .004" (.10 mm) increments. Use new "C" washer when installing lever.

**Installation** – Reverse removal procedure to complete installation. Apply non-melting grease to sliding surfaces of shoes and adjusting screw threads. Align groove of rear axle shaft flange with service hole on rotor. Install rotor.

## LOAD-SENSING PROPORTIONING & BY-PASS VALVE (LSP & BV or LSPV)

**Removal (Land Cruiser, Pickup & 4Runner)** – Raise and support vehicle. Disconnect No. 2 shackle from bracket. *See Fig. 13.* Disconnect and plug hydraulic lines from LSPV. Remove clip from brake hose. Remove mounting bolts from valve bracket and remove LSPV assembly. Separate valve body from bracket.

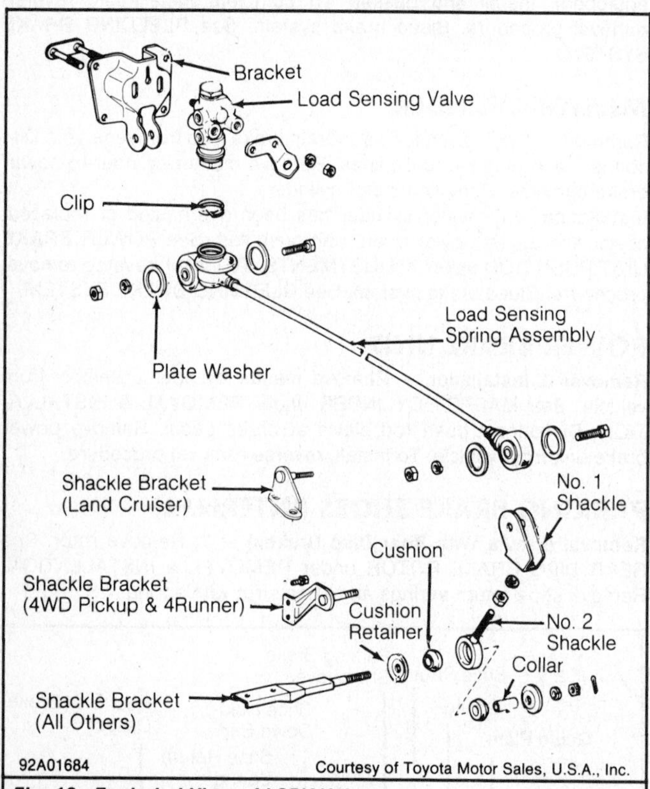


***Fig. 13: Exploded View of LSPV Valve (Land Cruiser, Pickup & 4Runner)***

**Installation** – **1)** To install, reverse removal procedure. Apply rubber grease to all rubbing areas. Install new rubber plate on valve body side of spring.

**2)** Adjust length of upper and lower shackle to original height. See LOAD-SENSING PROPORTIONING & BY-PASS VALVE (LSP & BV or LSPV) under TESTING. Bleed hydraulic system. See BLEEDING BRAKE SYSTEM. Check LSPV brake pressures.

**Removal & Installation (Previa)** – **1)** Disconnect brake lines from LSPV. Remove adjusting bolt lock nut. Disconnect spring. Remove LSPV. To install, reverse removal procedure. Bleed brake system. See BLEEDING BRAKE SYSTEM.

**2)** Check for fluid leaks. Check and adjust LSPV pressures. See LOAD-SENSING PROPORTIONING & BY-PASS VALVE (LSP & BV or LSPV) under TESTING.

# OVERHAUL

***NOTE: When overhauling caliper, if cylinder bores are pitted or scored more than light honing will repair, replace entire assembly.***

## FRONT BRAKE CALIPER

***NOTE: When overhauling front brake calipers, refer to Fig. 5, 6 or 7.***

## REAR BRAKE CALIPER

***NOTE: When overhauling front brake calipers, refer to Fig. 8.***

## MASTER CYLINDER

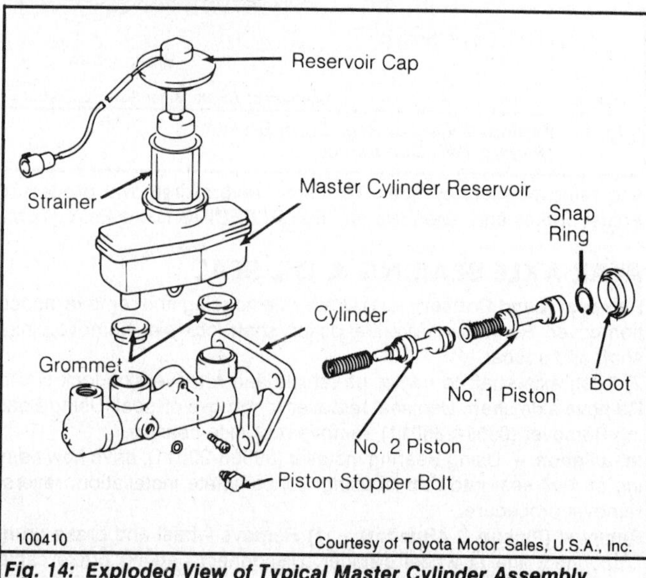


***Fig. 14: Exploded View of Typical Master Cylinder Assembly***

## LOAD-SENSING PROPORTIONING & BY-PASS VALVE (LSP & BV or LSPV)

***NOTE: When overhauling front brake calipers for Land Cruiser, Pickup and 4Runner, refer to Fig. 13. If LSPV is faulty on Previa, replace entire assembly.***

# TORQUE SPECIFICATIONS

***TORQUE SPECIFICATIONS (LAND CRUISER)***

| Application | Ft. Lbs. (N.m) |
|---|---|
| Caliper Mounting Bolts | 90 (123) |
| LSPV No. 1 Shackle Lock Nut | 18 (25) |
| LSPV No. 2 Shackle Bracket-to-Axle Bolts | 14 (19) |
| LSPV Mounting Bolts | 13 (18) |
| Master Cylinder Outlet Pipe Fitting | 11 (15) |
| Master Cylinder Outlet Reducer Fitting | 33 (44) |
| Parking Brake Adjusting Nuts | 12 (16) |
| Reservoir Mounting Bolt | 18 (25) |
| Wheel Lug Nuts | 116 (157) |
| | **INCH Lbs. (N.m)** |
| Brake Bleeder Fitting | 72 (8) |
| Master Cylinder Mounting Nuts | 108 (13) |

# 1991 BRAKES
# Disc & Drum – Light Trucks & Vans (Cont.)

*TORQUE SPECIFICATIONS (PICKUP & 4RUNNER)*

| Application | Ft. Lbs. (N.m) |
|---|---|
| Cable Support Bracket Bolts | 34 (46) |
| Caliper Torque Plate-to-Knuckle Bolts | |
| PD60 & 66 (2WD) | 80 (108) |
| Caliper Mounting Bolts/Slide Pins | |
| FS17 & 18 (2WD) | 65 (88) |
| PD60 & 66 (2WD) | 24 (39) |
| S12 + 12 (4WD) | 90 (123) |
| Hub-to-Rotor Bolts | 47 (64) |
| LSPV Mounting Bolts | 11 (15) |
| Master Cylinder Outlet Fittings | 11 (15) |
| Parking Brake Adjusting Lock Nuts | 12 (16) |
| Rear Brake Cylinder-to-Backing Plate Bolt | 10 (14) |
| Wheel Lug Nuts | |
| Pickup 2WD | |
| SRW | 101 (137) |
| DRW | 170 (230) |
| Pickup 4WD & 4Runner | 76 (103) |
| | **INCH Lbs. (N.m)** |
| Brake Bleeder Fitting | 72 (8) |
| LSPV Adjusting Screws/Nuts | 115 (13) |
| Master Cylinder-to-Booster Nuts | 115 (13) |

*TORQUE SPECIFICATIONS (PREVIA)*

| Application | Ft. Lbs. (N.m) |
|---|---|
| Backing Plate Mounting Nuts | 53 (72) |
| Brake Line Fittings | 11 (15) |
| Caliper Torque Plate Bolts | |
| Front | 77 (104) |
| Rear | 65 (88) |
| Caliper Slide Pins | |
| Front | 27 (37) |
| Rear | 18 (24) |
| LSPV Mounting Bolts | 14 (19) |
| LSPV Adjustment Lock Nut | 10 (14) |
| Union Bolt | 22 (30) |
| Wheel Lug Nuts | 76 (103) |
| | **INCH Lbs. (N.m)** |
| Brake Bleeder Screw | 96 (11) |
| Master Cylinder Mounting Nuts | 108 (13) |
| Reservoir Mounting Screw | 15 (1.7) |

# 1991 BRAKES
# Anti-Lock – Camry

## DESCRIPTION

The Anti-Lock Brake System (ABS) consists of hydraulic unit, brake actuator, four 3-position actuator solenoids, pump motor, deceleration sensor (All-Trac), ABS computer, and 4 speed sensors. *See Fig. 1.*

An ABS indicator light is located on the instrument panel in the combination meter. Indicator light comes on for 3 seconds as a bulb test when ignition is turned on. A primary check is performed after each engine start and initial vehicle speed exceeds 4 MPH. An actuator noise is heard as vehicle speed exceeds 4 MPH, this is normal. If brake pedal is depressed before vehicle exceeds 4 MPH, the primary check will not occur until brake pedal is released.

***NOTE: For more information on brake system, see DISC & DRUM – FWD CARS article.***

## OPERATION

Under normal driving conditions, ABS functions as a standard brake system. With detection of wheel lock-up, short pedal pulsations occurring in rapid succession will be felt in brake pedal. Pedal pulsation will continue until there is no longer a need for ABS function or until vehicle is stopped. Maintaining a constant force on the brake pedal provides shortest stopping distance.

***CAUTION: See ANTI-LOCK BRAKE SAFETY PRECAUTIONS article in GENERAL INFORMATION.***

## BLEEDING BRAKE SYSTEM

***CAUTION: Brake fluid will damage painted surfaces. If brake fluid gets on a painted surface, wipe off immediately and clean with alcohol. Use only DOT 3 brake fluid from a sealed container. Do not mix brake fluid with any other type.***

Brake bleeding procedure is same procedure used to bleed non-ABS systems. If master cylinder was rebuilt or reservoir ran empty, bleed master cylinder first. Bleed remaining wheels starting with wheel having longest hydraulic line working to shortest hydraulic line.

## ADJUSTMENTS

### MASTER CYLINDER PUSH ROD

**1)** Install Adjusting Gauge (09737-00010) on master cylinder with master cylinder gasket in place. Lower adjusting gauge pin until pin slightly touches master cylinder piston. Perform STEP 1. *See Fig. 2.* Turn adjusting gauge upside down and install on power brake unit.

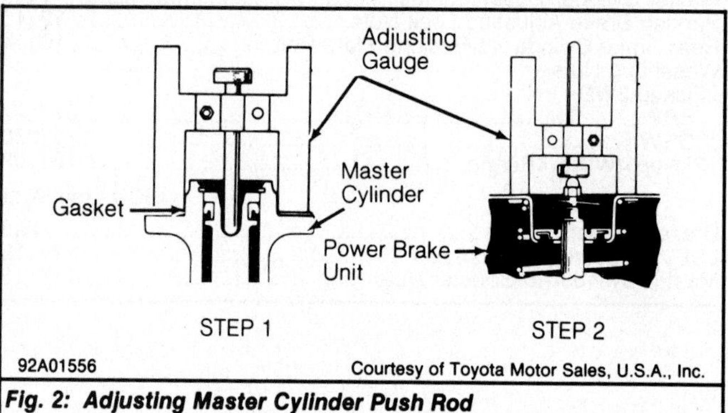


***Fig. 2: Adjusting Master Cylinder Push Rod***

**2)** Measure clearance between power brake unit push rod and adjusting gauge pin head. Perform STEP 2. *See Fig. 2.* Measured clearance should be zero. If clearance is not zero, adjust power brake unit push rod length until push rod lightly touches adjusting gauge pin head.

### BRAKE PEDAL HEIGHT

**1)** Remove instrument lower finish panel and air duct (if necessary). Brake pedal height is measured from face of brake pedal pad to asphalt sheet under carpet. *See Fig. 3*

**2)** Brake pedal height should be 7.0-7.4" (178-188 mm). To adjust brake pedal height, loosen stoplight switch and lock nut on brake pedal push rod. Adjust pedal height by turning push rod.

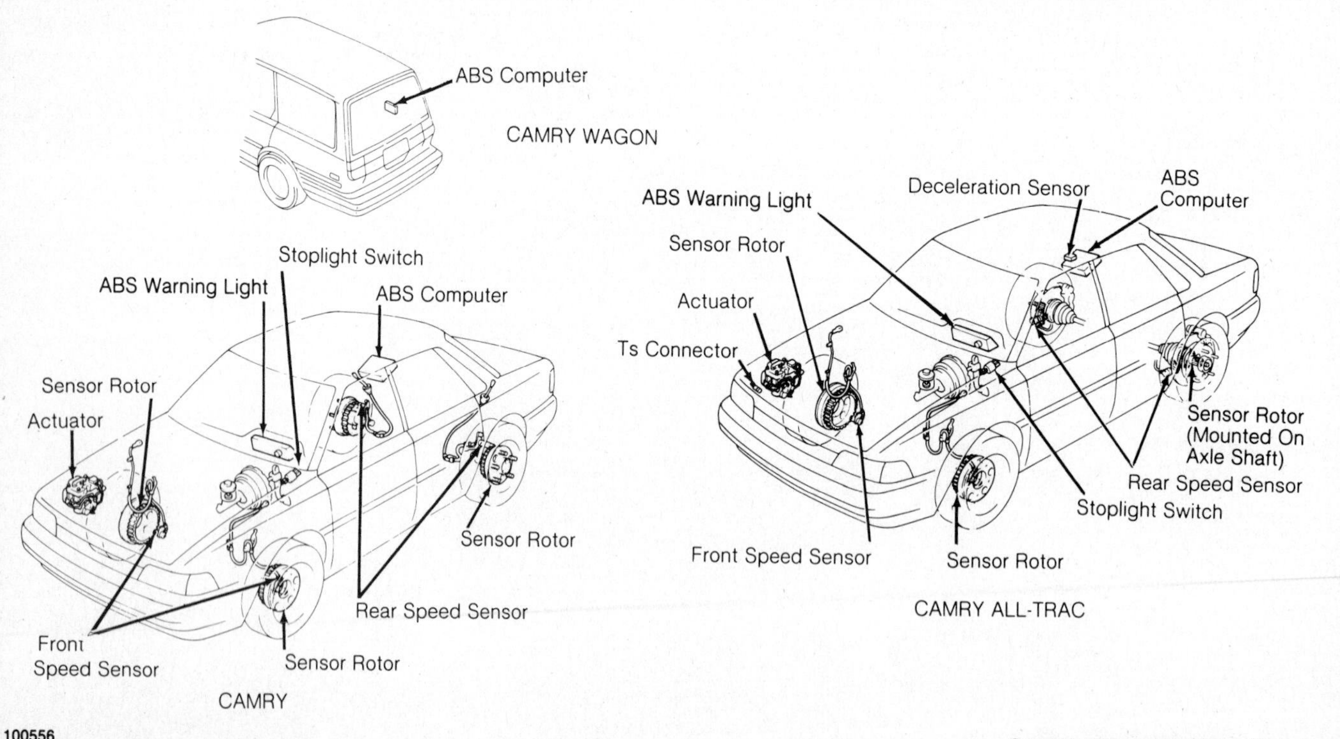

100556

Courtesy of Toyota Motor Sales, U.S.A., Inc.

***Fig. 1: Locating ABS Components***

# 1991 BRAKES
# Anti-Lock – Camry (Cont.)

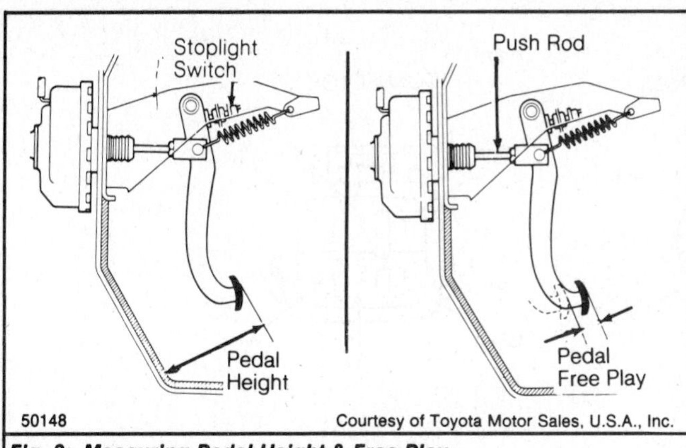


***Fig. 3: Measuring Pedal Height & Free Play***

**3)** After adjusting brake pedal height, tighten push rod lock nut. Adjust stoplight switch. See STOPLIGHT SWITCH. Check and adjust brake pedal free play. See BRAKE PEDAL FREE PLAY.

## BRAKE PEDAL FREE PLAY

**1)** Brake pedal free play is distance brake pedal travels before feeling resistance with engine stopped. To check brake pedal free play, depress brake pedal several times to exhaust vacuum from power brake unit. Depress brake pedal and measure travel until initial resistance is felt.

**2)** Brake pedal free play should be .12-.24" (3.0-6.0 mm). If free play is not within specification, adjust by turning push rod. *See Fig. 3*. After adjusting brake pedal free play, check brake pedal height. Install air duct and instrument lower finish panel (if previously removed).

## STOPLIGHT SWITCH

**1)** Stoplight switch is located above brake pedal. *See Fig. 3*. To adjust stoplight switch, remove instrument lower finish panel and air duct (if necessary).

**2)** Loosen stoplight switch lock nuts and turn stoplight switch until it touches brake pedal stop. Tighten lock nut. Check brake light operation.

## BRAKE PEDAL DEPRESSED HEIGHT

Brake pedal depressed height is measured from face of brake pedal pad to asphalt sheet under carpet with brakes applied. Measure brake pedal depressed height with engine running and weight of 110 lbs. (50 kg) applied against brake pedal. Minimum brake pedal depressed height should be 3.35" (85.0 mm). If measured distance is less than minimum height, inspect brake system.

## REAR DRUM BRAKE SHOES

***NOTE: Rear drum brakes have a self-adjuster which activates when brake pedal is applied as vehicle travels in reverse.***

Raise and support vehicle. Remove brake drum. Measure brake drum inside diameter and diameter of brake shoes. Clearance between diameters should be .024" (6.00 mm). Adjust self-adjuster length to adjust clearance.

## REAR DISC PARKING BRAKE SHOES

Raise and support vehicle. Remove wheels. Temporarily install hub nuts to hold disc brake rotor in place. Remove hole plug to gain access to adjuster. Turn adjuster and expand shoes until disc brake rotor locks. Return adjuster 8 notches. Install hole plug.

## PARKING BRAKE CABLE

***NOTE: Service brake on rear drum brakes and parking brake shoe clearance on rear disc brakes must be adjusted before adjusting parking brake cable.***

Parking brake lever stroke should be 5-8 notches (clicks) with a pull force of 44 lbs. (20 kg). To adjust, remove console box. Loosen cable lock nut and turn adjusting nut until parking brake lever travel is correct. Tighten lock nut. Install console box.

# TROUBLE SHOOTING

## SYMPTOM DIAGNOSTICS

**ABS Light Illuminates – 1)** Turn ignition on. Disconnect actuator check connector. *See Fig. 4*. If ABS light blinks codes or illuminates constantly, see DIAGNOSTIC CODES under DIAGNOSIS & TESTING. If ABS light does not illuminate, go to next step.

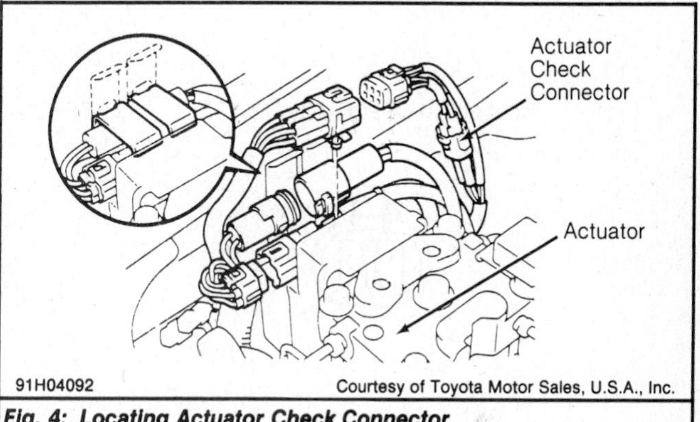


***Fig. 4: Locating Actuator Check Connector***

**2)** Ensure ABS computer connector is properly connected and connector terminals are not damaged. Repair connector as necessary. Turn ignition on. Using a voltmeter, check for 10-16 volts between ABS computer connector terminal No. 19 (Black/Red wire) and ground. *See Fig. 5*. If 10-16 volts is not present, repair faulty Black/Red wire. If 10-16 volts is present, go to next step.

**3)** Turn ignition off. Disconnect ABS computer connector. Turn ignition on. If ABS light illuminates, repair short circuit between actuator check connector terminal "W" and ABS computer connector terminal No. 2 (Red/Yellow wire). *See Fig. 5*. If ABS light does not illuminate, replace faulty ABS computer.

**ABS Light Does Not Illuminate For 3 Seconds After Ignition Is Turned On – 1)** Turn ignition on. Disconnect actuator check connector. Using a jumper wire, ground check connector terminal "W" on harness side. *See Fig. 5*. If ABS light does not illuminate, replace faulty ABS light bulb or repair open circuit between ABS light and actuator check connector terminal "W". If ABS light illuminates, go to next step.

**2)** Turn ignition off. Disconnect ABS computer connector and brake actuator connectors. Using a jumper wire, ground ABS computer connector terminal No. 2 on wire harness side. Turn ignition on. ABS light should illuminate. If ABS light does not illuminate, repair open circuit in wiring harness between ABS computer terminal No. 2 and ABS light. If ABS light illuminates, go to next step.

**3)** Turn ignition off. Disconnect brake actuator connectors. Using an ohmmeter, ensure continuity is present between brake actuator connector "A" terminal No. 2 and brake actuator connector "C" terminal No. 6. *See Fig. 5*. Reverse ohmmeter leads. Check for continuity between actuator connectors again.

**4)** If continuity is present both ways between brake actuator connectors, repair short circuit in actuator diode. If continuity is present only one way between brake actuator connectors, replace faulty ABS computer.

**5)** Connect ABS computer connector. When brake actuator connectors are disconnected, turn ignition on. ABS light should illuminate. If ABS light illuminates, this ensures ABS computer connector terminal No. 2 is okay.

**ABS Light Illuminates Intermittently – 1)** Ensure actuator check connector is not disconnected. Check for an open circuit between ABS computer terminal No. 16 and brake actuator connector "C" terminal No. 3. *See Fig. 5*.

# 1991 BRAKES
## Anti-Lock – Camry (Cont.)

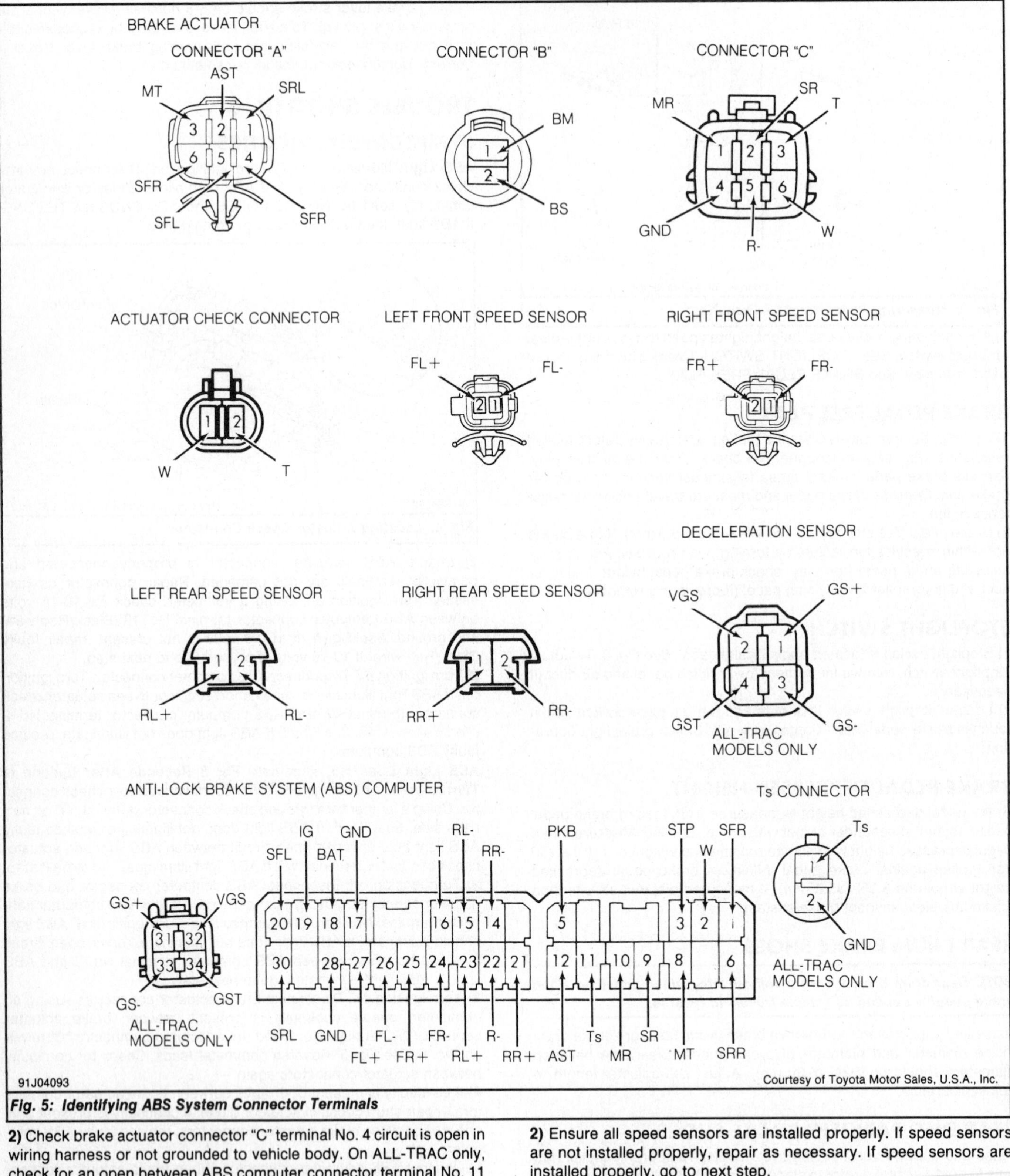



***Fig. 5: Identifying ABS System Connector Terminals***

**2)** Check brake actuator connector "C" terminal No. 4 circuit is open in wiring harness or not grounded to vehicle body. On ALL-TRAC only, check for an open between ABS computer connector terminal No. 11 and Ts connector terminal No. 1 (Ts). *See Fig. 5.*

**Brakes Pull, Braking Inefficient, ABS Operates With Ordinary Braking, ABS Operates Just Before Stopping With Ordinary Braking, & Brake Pedal Pulsates Abnormally With ABS Functioning – 1)** Turn ignition on. Disconnect actuator check connector. *See Fig. 4.* ABS light should blink a normal code. If ABS light does not blink a normal code, refer to DIAGNOSTIC CODES. If ABS light blinks a normal code, go to next step.

**2)** Ensure all speed sensors are installed properly. If speed sensors are not installed properly, repair as necessary. If speed sensors are installed properly, go to next step.

**3)** Turn ignition off. Disconnect ABS computer connectors. Ensure continuity is present between each speed sensor connector (wire harness side) of ABS computer connector. Check continuity between FL+ and FL- (left front speed sensor), FR+ and FR- (right front speed sensor), RL+ and RL- (left rear speed sensor), and RR+ and RR- (right rear speed sensor). *See Fig. 5.*

**4)** If continuity readings change when wiring harness is twisted and moved, repair faulty wiring harness between speed sensor and ABS

# 1991 BRAKES
# Anti-Lock – Camry (Cont.)

computer connector. If continuity readings do not change, go to next step.

**5)** Ensure all foreign and metal chips are cleaned from speed sensor tip. Enter speed sensor diagnostics. See SPEED SENSOR DIAGNOSTICS under DIAGNOSIS & TESTING. If speed sensor signal change is okay, go to next step if vehicle is an ALL-TRAC. If vehicle is not an ALL-TRAC, go to step **7)**. If speed sensor signal level is not okay, inspect sensor and sensor rotor. Replace as necessary. If sensor and sensor rotor are okay and vehicle is an ALL-TRAC, go to next step. If vehicle is not an ALL-TRAC, go to step **7)**.

**6)** Enter deceleration sensor diagnostics. See DECELERATION SENSOR DIAGNOSTICS (ALL-TRAC) under DIAGNOSIS & TESTING. If deceleration sensor does not operate okay, ensure deceleration sensor is installed properly. If deceleration sensor is installed properly, replace faulty sensor. If deceleration sensor operation is okay, go to next step.

**7)** Check actuator operation. See ACTUATOR CHECK under DIAGNOSIS & TESTING. If actuator operates okay, replace faulty ABS computer. See ABS COMPUTER under REMOVAL & INSTALLATION. If actuator does not operate okay, replace faulty actuator.

**ABS System Works Inefficiently – 1)** Turn ignition on. Disconnect actuator check connector. *See Fig. 4.* ABS light should blink a normal code. If ABS light does not blink a normal code, refer to DIAGNOSTIC CODES under DIAGNOSIS & TESTING. If ABS light blinks a normal code, go to next step.

**2)** Ensure battery voltage is present between ABS computer terminal No. 3 and ground when brake pedal is depressed. If battery voltage is not present when brake pedal is depressed, repair open circuit in stoplight switch or wiring harness. Check actuator operation. See ACTUATOR CHECK under DIAGNOSIS & TESTING.

## DIAGNOSIS & TESTING

***NOTE: DO NOT start engine when accessing diagnostic codes.***

### ACCESSING TROUBLE CODES

**ABS Light Diagnostics – 1)** Ensure battery voltage is 12 volts. Turn ignition switch to ON position. ABS light should illuminate, then go out after 3 seconds. If warning light does not illuminate, check fuse, bulb, and wiring harness.

**2)** With ignition on, disconnect actuator check connector. *See Fig. 4.* If a malfunction is detected, 4 seconds will elapse and ABS light will begin to flash a 2-digit code. First number of blinks will equal first digit in a code. After a 1.5-second pause, second number of blinks will equal second digit in a code.

**3)** If 2 or more codes are stored, there will be a 4-second pause between each code. If ABS system is functioning properly, ABS light will blink once every .5 second. For code interpretation, see DIAGNOSTIC CODES.

**4)** After replacing or repairing malfunctioning components, clear diagnostic codes. If a battery cable was disconnected during repairs, all codes will be erased. If battery cable was not disconnected during repairs, see CLEARING CODES.

### DIAGNOSTIC CODES

Check suspect components in order given. See COMPONENT TESTING. Checks will consist mainly of a visual inspection and continuity checks.

**Code 11** – Open solenoid relay circuit. Check actuator wiring harness, solenoid relay, solenoid relay wiring harness and solenoid relay connector.

**Code 12** – Short in solenoid relay circuit. Check actuator wiring harness, solenoid relay, solenoid relay wiring harness and solenoid relay connector.

**Code 13** – Open pump motor relay circuit. Check actuator wiring harness, pump motor wiring harness, pump motor relay circuit and pump motor connector.

**Code 14** – Short in pump motor relay circuit. Check actuator wiring harness, pump motor wiring harness, pump motor relay circuit and pump motor connector.

**Code 21** – Open or short circuit in 3-position solenoid for right front wheel. Check 3-position actuator solenoid, wiring harness and connector.

**Code 22** – Open or short circuit in 3-position solenoid for left front wheel. Check 3-position actuator solenoid, wiring harness and connector.

**Code 23** – Open or short circuit in 3-position solenoid for right rear wheel. Check 3-position actuator solenoid, wiring harness and connector.

**Code 24** – Open or short circuit in 3-position solenoid for left rear wheel. Check 3-position actuator solenoid, wiring harness and connector.

**Code 31** – Malfunction of right front wheel speed sensor signal. Check speed sensor, sensor rotor, wiring harness and connector.

**Code 32** – Malfunction of left front wheel speed sensor signal. Check speed sensor, sensor rotor, wiring harness and connector.

**Code 33** – Malfunction of right rear wheel speed sensor signal. Check speed sensor, sensor rotor, wiring harness and connector.

**Code 34** – Malfunction of left rear wheel speed sensor signal. Check speed sensor, sensor rotor, wiring harness and connector.

**Code 35** – Open in left front or right rear wheel speed sensor circuit. Check speed sensor, sensor rotor, wiring harness and connector.

**Code 36** – Open in right front or left rear wheel speed sensor circuit. Check speed sensor, sensor rotor, wiring harness and connector.

**Code 37** – Wrong rear axle hubs on both sides. Check rear sensor rotors.

**Code 41** – Battery voltage is 9.5 volts or less. Check battery and voltage regulator.

**Code 42** – Battery voltage is 16.2 volts or more. Check battery and voltage regulator.

**Code 43** – Deceleration sensor malfunction. Check deceleration sensor, deceleration sensor installation, wiring harness and connector.

**Code 44** – Open or short circuit in deceleration sensor. Check deceleration sensor, deceleration sensor installation, wiring harness and connector.

**Code 51** – Actuator pump motor is locked or pump motor circuit open. Check pump motor, pump motor relay, vehicle battery, actuator wiring harness, connectors, actuator pump motor circuit and actuator ground bolt.

**Always On** – Malfunction of ABS computer. Ensure ABS computer connector is properly connected and terminals are not damaged. If connector is okay, replace ABS computer. See ABS COMPUTER under REMOVAL & INSTALLATION.

### CLEARING CODES

Turn ignition on. Disconnect actuator check connector. *See Fig. 4.* With vehicle stopped, depress brake pedal 8 or more times within 3 seconds. Codes are now erased. Ensure ABS light shows a normal code. Connect actuator check connector.

### ACTUATOR CHECK

***NOTE: Actuator Checker (09990-00150) and Sheet "A" (09990-00163) are needed to perform ACTUATOR CHECK.***

**1)** Turn ignition off. Disconnect actuator electrical connectors. *See Fig. 4.* Connect Actuator Checker (09990-00150) to actuator. Connect actuator checker positive and negative power cables to vehicle battery.

**2)** Place Sheet "A" (09990-00163) on actuator checker. Start engine and let idle. Turn actuator checker SELECTOR switch to FRONT RH position. *See Fig. 6.* Press and hold MOTOR switch for a few seconds. Press and hold brake pedal.

***NOTE: DO NOT press POWER switch for more than 10 seconds.***

**3)** Press POWER switch. When POWER switch is pressed, brake pedal should not go down. Release POWER SWITCH. Brake pedal should lower. Press and hold MOTOR switch for a few seconds. Brake pedal should return. Release MOTOR switch. Release brake pedal.

# 1991 BRAKES
# Anti-Lock – Camry (Cont.)

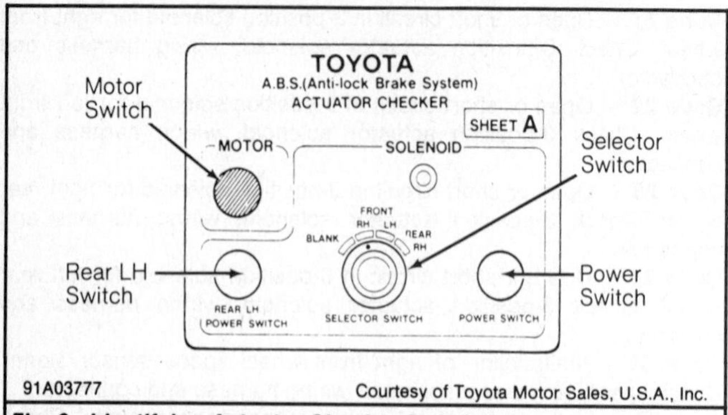


*Fig. 6: Identifying Actuator Checker Switches*

**4)** Press and hold MOTOR switch for a few seconds. Release MOTOR switch. Press brake pedal and hold for approximately 15 seconds. As brake pedal is being held, press MOTOR switch for a few seconds. Ensure brake pedal does not pulsate.
**5)** Repeat steps **2)** through **4)** for FRONT LH, REAR RH, and REAR LH by turning SELECTOR switch on actuator checker. When checking REAR LH position, press REAR LH switch, instead of POWER SWITCH. After checking remaining wheels, press and hold MOTOR switch for a few seconds. Remove actuator checker. Connect actuator wiring harness to actuator. Clear diagnostic codes. See CLEARING CODES.

## SPEED SENSOR DIAGNOSTICS

***NOTE: While diagnosing speed sensors, brake system functions as a conventional system.***

**1)** Ensure battery voltage is approximately 12 volts. Turn ignition on. Ensure ABS light illuminates, then goes out after approximately 3 seconds. If ABS light does not illuminate, check fuse, bulb and wiring harness. If vehicle is a FWD model, go to next step. If vehicle is an ALL-TRAC model, go to step **3)**.
**2)** Turn ignition off. Disconnect actuator check connector. *See Fig. 4.* Engage parking brake. Start engine. Press brake pedal 4-6 times within 2 seconds. ABS light will illuminate 4 times a second. Go to step **4)**.
**3)** Turn ignition off. Using a jumper wire, connect terminals of Trouble Shooting (Ts) connector. *See Fig. 7.* Engage parking brake. Start engine. DO NOT depress brake pedal. ABS light will illuminate 4 times a second. Go to next step.

***NOTE: While ABS light is off, DO NOT accelerate, decelerate, brake, shift, move steering or drive on rough road surfaces as these conditions will affect test.***

**4)** Drive vehicle straight ahead at 2.5-3.7 MPH. Ensure ABS light illuminates after a one second pause. If ABS light illuminates without blinking when vehicle is NOT within specified speed, stop vehicle and record diagnostic codes. Turn ignition off. Repair as necessary. See SPEED SENSOR DIAGNOSTIC CODES.
**5)** If ABS light illuminates while vehicle speed is within specified range, check is completed. If vehicle speed exceeds 3.7 MPH, ABS light will blink again. If ABS light blinks when vehicle speed exceeds 3.7 MPH, speed sensors are okay.
**6)** Drive vehicle straight ahead at 28-34 MPH. Ensure ABS light illuminates after a one second pause. If ABS light illuminates without blinking when vehicle is NOT within specified speed, stop vehicle and record diagnostic codes. Turn ignition off. Repair as necessary. See SPEED SENSOR DIAGNOSTIC CODES.
**7)** If ABS light illuminates while vehicle speed is within specified range, check is completed. If vehicle speed exceeds 34 MPH, ABS light will blink again. If ABS light blinks when vehicle speed exceeds 34 MPH, sensor rotors are okay.
**8)** On FWD models, leave ignition on. Connect actuator check connector. Clear diagnostic codes. See CLEARING CODES. On ALL-TRAC models, turn ignition off. Remove jumper wire from Ts connector. Install rubber cap on Ts connector. Connect actuator check connector. Clear diagnostic codes. See CLEARING CODES.

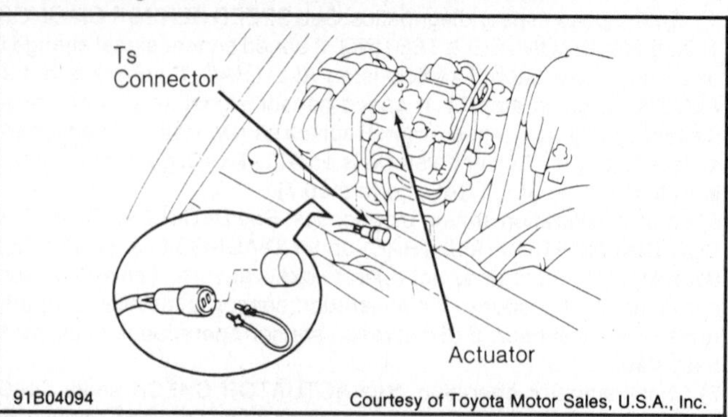


*Fig. 7: Locating All-Trac Trouble Shooting (Ts) Connector*

## SPEED SENSOR DIAGNOSTIC CODES

**Code 71** – Low voltage of right front speed sensor signal. Check right front speed sensor and sensor installation.
**Code 72** – Low voltage of left front speed sensor signal. Check left front speed sensor and sensor installation.
**Code 73** – Low voltage of right rear speed sensor signal. Check right rear speed sensor and sensor installation.
**Code 74** – Low voltage of left rear speed sensor signal. Check left rear speed sensor and sensor installation.
**Code 75** – Abnormal signal from right front speed sensor. Check right front sensor rotor.
**Code 76** – Abnormal signal from left front speed sensor. Check right front sensor rotor.
**Code 77** – Abnormal signal from right rear speed sensor. Check right rear sensor rotor.
**Code 78** – Abnormal signal from left rear speed sensor. Check left rear sensor rotor.
**Light Illuminates 4 Times A Second** – All speed sensors and sensor rotors are normal.

## DECELERATION SENSOR DIAGNOSTICS (ALL-TRAC)

***NOTE: While diagnosing deceleration sensor, brake system functions as a conventional system.***

**1)** Ensure battery voltage is 12 volts. Turn ignition on. ABS light should illuminate, then go out after 3 seconds. If ABS light does not illuminate, check fuse, bulb, and wiring harness.
**2)** Remove rubber cap from Trouble Shooting (Ts) connector. Connect a jumper wire between Ts connector terminals. *See Fig. 7.* Engage parking brake, depress brake pedal and start engine.
**3)** Ensure ABS light blinks about once every second. If ABS light does not blink, inspect parking brake switch, stoplight switch, Ts connector, deceleration sensor installation and ABS computer. If ABS light blinks, go to next step.
**4)** To inspect sensor detection point, raise rear of vehicle 32-35" (813-889 mm). When measuring height, measure from bottom of rear bumper to ground. Ensure ABS light is off. As vehicle is lowered, ABS light will start blinking. Completely lower rear of vehicle. On models with a spoiler, raise front of vehicle 24-27" (610-686 mm). On models with spoiler, raise front of vehicle 26-28" (660-711 mm). When measuring height, measure from lower body or spoiler edge to ground.
**5)** Ensure ABS light is off. As vehicle is lowered, ABS light will start blinking. If ABS light illuminates steadily, inspect deceleration sensor installation. If deceleration sensor installation is okay, replace deceleration sensor.
**6)** To inspect sensor operation, drive vehicle straight about 6.2 MPH or more. Lightly depress brake pedal. ABS light should blink once every second with no change in pattern.

# 1991 BRAKES
# Anti-Lock – Camry (Cont.)

**7)** Drive vehicle straight about 12.4 MPH or more. Using a little force, depress brake pedal. ABS light should stay on while braking. Drive vehicle about 12.4 MPH or more. Strongly depress brake pedal. ABS light should blink approximately 7 times per second.

**8)** If ABS light does not respond correctly, check deceleration sensor installation. If deceleration sensor installation is okay, replace deceleration sensor. Turn engine off. Remove jumper wire from Ts connector. Install rubber cap on Ts connector.

## COMPONENT TESTING

**Front Speed Sensors – 1)** Remove front wheel speed sensor from vehicle. See FRONT WHEEL SPEED SENSORS under REMOVAL & INSTALLATION. Using a DVOM, measure resistance between speed sensor terminals. Resistance should be 850-1300 ohms.

**2)** Ensure continuity is not present between each sensor terminal and sensor body. If resistance and continuity readings are as specified, speed sensor is okay. If resistance and continuity readings are not as specified, replace speed sensor.

**Rear Speed Sensors – 1)** Remove rear wheel speed sensor from vehicle. See REAR WHEEL SPEED SENSORS under REMOVAL & INSTALLATION. Using a DVOM, measure resistance between speed sensor terminals.

**2)** Resistance should be 850-1500 ohms. Ensure continuity is not present between each sensor terminal and sensor body. If resistance and continuity readings are as specified, speed sensor is okay. If resistance and continuity readings are not as specified, replace speed sensor.

**Pump Motor Relay Continuity – 1)** Remove pump motor relay from actuator. *See Fig. 8*. See SOLENOID & PUMP MOTOR RELAYS under REMOVAL & INSTALLATION.

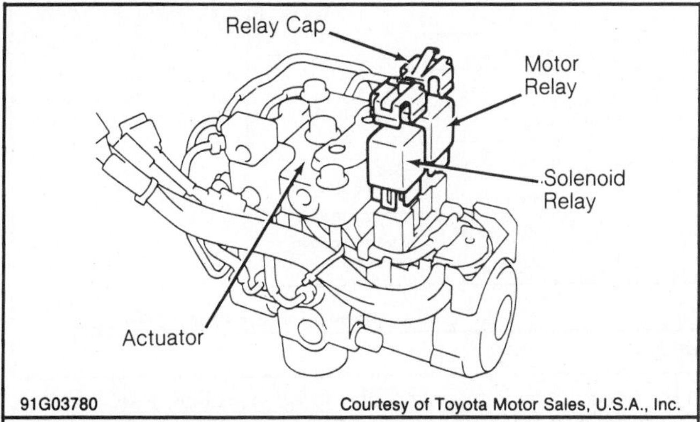


***Fig. 8: Identifying ABS Relays***

**2)** Using a DVOM, check for continuity between relay terminals No. 1 and No. 2. *See Fig. 9*. Continuity should be present. Ensure continuity is not present between relay terminals No. 3 and No. 4. Ensure continuity is not present between relay terminals No. 1 and No. 4. If continuity readings are not as specified, replace pump motor relay. If continuity readings are as specified, pump motor relay is okay.

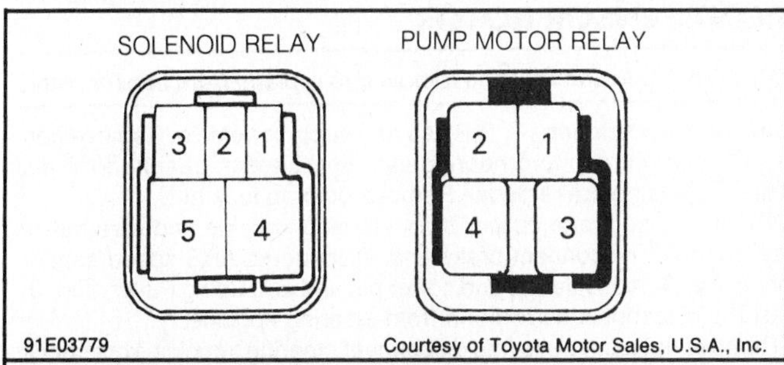


***Fig. 9: Identifying ABS Relay Terminals***

**Pump Motor Relay Operation – 1)** Remove pump motor relay from actuator. *See Fig. 8*. See SOLENOID & PUMP MOTOR RELAYS under REMOVAL & INSTALLATION. Using a 12-volt battery, connect jumper wires from positive battery terminal to relay terminal No. 1. and from negative battery terminal to relay terminal No. 2. *See Fig. 9*.

**2)** Ensure continuity is present between relay terminals No. 3 and No. 4. Ensure continuity is not present between relay terminals No. 1 and No. 4. If continuity is not as specified, replace pump motor relay. If continuity readings are as specified, pump motor relay is okay.

**Solenoid Relay Continuity – 1)** Remove solenoid relay from actuator. *See Fig. 8*. See SOLENOID & PUMP MOTOR RELAYS under REMOVAL & INSTALLATION. Using a DVOM, check for continuity between relay terminals No. 1 and No. 3. *See Fig. 9*. Continuity should be present.

**2)** Ensure continuity is present between relay terminals No. 2 and No. 4. Ensure continuity is not present between relay terminals No. 4 and No. 5. If continuity readings are not as specified, replace solenoid relay. If continuity readings are as specified, solenoid relay is okay.

**Solenoid Relay Operation – 1)** Remove solenoid relay from actuator. *See Fig. 8*. See SOLENOID & PUMP RELAYS under REMOVAL & INSTALLATION. Connect a jumper wire between battery positive terminal and relay terminal No. 3. Connect a second jumper wire between ground and relay terminal No. 1. *See Fig. 9*.

**2)** Check for continuity between relay terminals No. 4 and No. 5. Ensure continuity is not present between relay terminals No. 2 and No. 4. If continuity is not as specified, replace solenoid relay. If continuity readings are as specified, solenoid relay is okay.

**Sensor Rotors –** Remove sensor rotor. See FRONT SENSOR ROTOR or REAR SENSOR ROTOR under REMOVAL & INSTALLATION. Visually inspect sensor rotor serrations for scratches, cracks, missing teeth and warping. If sensor rotor is damaged, replace sensor rotor. If sensor rotor is okay, install sensor rotor.

**ABS Computer Wiring Harness – 1)** Remove ABS computer. See ABS COMPUTER under REMOVAL & INSTALLATION. With ABS computer connectors connected, backprobe ABS computer connector terminals. Measure voltage at each terminal and ground as specified in table. *See Fig. 10*. If circuit(s) do not test as specified, check and repair or replace trouble part shown in table.

**2)** Disconnect ABS computer connectors. Check voltage and resistance on wire harness side of ABS computer connector terminals as specified in table. *See Fig. 11*. If circuit(s) do not test as specified, check and repair or replace troubled part shown in table.

## REMOVAL & INSTALLATION

***WARNING: Hydraulic system may be under high pressure. Use caution when opening hydraulic system.***

### ACTUATOR

***NOTE: If actuator is being replaced, remove proportioning valve and 3-way union connection from actuator.***

**Removal & Installation – 1)** Turn ignition off. Remove actuator cover. Disconnect 3 actuator electrical connectors. Remove cover bracket and stud bolt. Disconnect 6 brake lines attaching to actuator.

**2)** Remove 3 nuts, washers and wave washers. Remove actuator from actuator bracket. To install, reverse removal procedure. Bleed brake system. See BLEEDING BRAKE SYSTEM.

### ABS COMPUTER

**Removal & Installation – 1)** Ensure ignition is off. Disconnect negative battery cable. Access ABS computer in right side of luggage compartment. Remove 5 screws attaching ABS computer to vehicle.

**2)** Disconnect wiring harness from ABS computer bracket clamp. Disconnect ABS computer connector. Remove ABS computer from vehicle. To install, reverse removal procedure.

### FRONT WHEEL SPEED SENSORS

**Removal & Installation – 1)** Loosen front wheel lug nuts. Raise and support front of vehicle. Remove front wheel. Remove wheel speed sensor mounting bolt.

# 1991 BRAKES
# Anti-Lock – Camry (Cont.)

ANTI-LOCK BRAKE SYSTEM (ABS) COMPUTER CONNECTOR

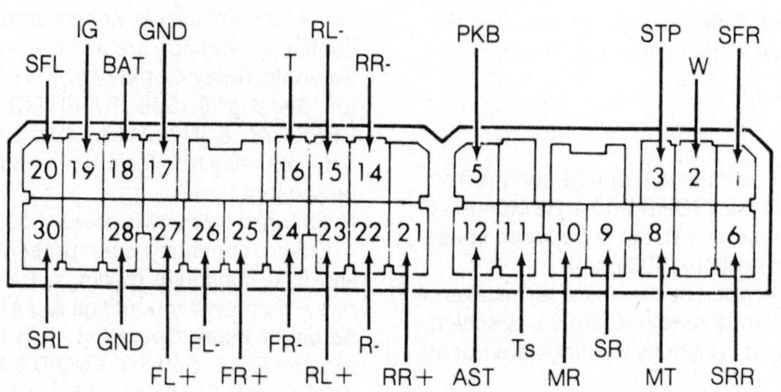


| Tester Connection | Condition | Voltage | Trouble Part |
|---|---|---|---|
| SFL – Body ground | Ignition switch on | Battery voltage | Actuator, control relays |
| | Ignition switch on and "ABS" warning light goes on | About 0 V | |
| SFR – Body ground | Ignition switch on | Battery voltage | |
| | Ignition switch on and "ABS" warning light goes on | About 0 V | |
| SRL – Body ground | Ignition switch on | Battery voltage | |
| | Ignition switch on and "ABS" warning light goes on | About 0 V | |
| SRR – Body ground | Ignition switch on | Battery voltage | |
| | Ignition switch on and "ABS" warning light goes on | About 0 V | |
| AST – Body ground | Ignition switch on | Battery voltage | |
| | Ignition switch on and "ABS" warning light goes on | About 0 V | |
| W – Body ground | Ignition switch on | Battery voltage | "ABS" warning light bulb |
| | Ignition switch on and "ABS" warning light goes on | About 0 V | |
| T – Body ground | Check connector disconnected | Battery voltage | Check connector, computer |
| | Check connector connected | About 0 V | |

92C01557



***Fig. 10: Testing Specifications Table for ABS Computer Wiring Harness (1 of 2)***

**2)** Disconnect wheel speed sensor connector. Remove wheel speed sensor from vehicle. To install, reverse removal procedure. Tighten wheel speed sensor mounting bolt to specification. See TORQUE SPECIFICATIONS table at end of article.

## REAR WHEEL SPEED SENSORS

**Removal & Installation (FWD) – 1)** Remove rear seat cushion. Disconnect wheel speed sensor connector. Pull sensor wire from wiring harness. Remove 2 sensor wiring harness-to-body and suspension arm clamp bolts.

**2)** Remove rear brake assembly. Suspend rear brake assembly so brake hose is not stretched. DO NOT disconnect brake line. Remove disc brake rotor. Remove axle carrier upper mounting bolt. Remove 4 axle hub mounting bolts. Remove rear axle hub. Remove backing plate with parking brake assembly and "O" ring.

**3)** Remove wheel speed sensor mounting bolt from backing plate. Remove wheel speed sensor. To install, reverse removal procedure. Install a new "O" ring onto axle carrier. Tighten wheel speed sensor and brake components to specification. See TORQUE SPECIFICATIONS table at end of article.

**Removal & Installation (ALL-TRAC) – 1)** Loosen rear wheel lug nuts. Raise and support front of vehicle. Remove rear wheel. Remove wheel speed sensor mounting bolt.

**2)** Disconnect wheel speed sensor connector. Remove wheel speed sensor from vehicle. To install, reverse removal procedure. Tighten wheel speed sensor mounting bolt to specification. See TORQUE SPECIFICATIONS table at end of article.

## SOLENOID & PUMP MOTOR RELAYS

**Removal & Installation –** Remove connector from wire harness clamp. Remove screw and wire harness clamp. Remove relay case. Remove relay cap from relays. Remove relays from actuator. *See Fig. 8.* To install, reverse removal procedure.

## FRONT SENSOR ROTOR

***NOTE: Front axle hub must be removed to replace front sensor rotor.***

**Removal & Installation – 1)** Raise and support vehicle. Remove cotter pin, lock nut cap and bearing lock nut. Loosen bearing lock nut while depressing brake pedal. Remove bearing lock nut.

**2)** Remove disc brake caliper from steering knuckle and wire out of way. DO NOT disconnect brake line. Disconnect ABS speed sensor connector. Remove tie rod end cotter pin and nut. Using Puller (09610-550120), disconnect tie rod end from steering knuckle.

**3)** Remove nuts and bolts and disconnect steering knuckle from shock absorber. Remove cotter pin and nut attaching steering knuckle to lower suspension arm. Using Puller (09610-55012), disconnect steering knuckle from lower suspension arm.

# 1991 BRAKES
# Anti-Lock – Camry (Cont.)

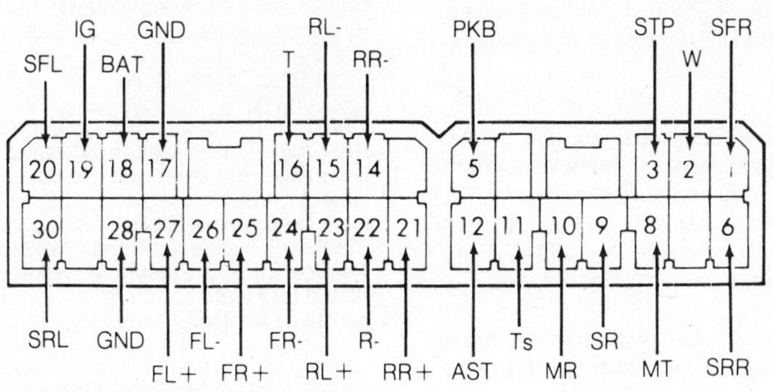


| Tester Connection | Check Item | Condition | Voltage or Resistance Value | Trouble Part |
|---|---|---|---|---|
| SFR – AST | Resistance | Ignition switch off | About 6 Ω | Actuator |
| STP – Body ground | Voltage | Ignition switch off and brake pedal depressed | Battery voltage | Stop light switch, stop light |
| | Continuity | Ignition switch off and brake pedal returned | Continuity | |
| PKB – Body ground | Voltage | Ignition switch on and PKB lever pulled | About 0 V | Parking brake switch, level warning switch |
| | | Engine running and PKB lever returned | Battery voltage | |
| SRR – AST | Resistance | Ignition switch off | About 6 Ω | Actuator |
| MT – Body ground | Continuity | Ignition switch off | Continuity | |
| SR – R ⊖ | Resistance | Ignition switch off | 65 – 100 Ω | |
| MR – R ⊖ | Resistance | Ignition switch off | 50 – 80 Ω | |
| Ts – Body ground (For 4WD) | Continuity | – | No continuity | Ts connector, wiring harness |
| | | Ts connector shorted | Continuity | |
| AST – Body ground | Resistance | Ignition switch off | About 5 Ω | Wiring harness |
| RR ⊖ – Body ground | Continuity | Ignition switch off | No continuity | Rear RH speed sensor |
| RL ⊖ – Body ground | Continuity | Ignition switch off | No continuity | Rear LH speed sensor |
| T – Body ground | Continuity | Ignition switch off | Continuity | Check connector, wiring harness |
| GND – Body ground | Continuity | Ignition switch off | Continuity | Wiring harness |
| BAT – Body ground | Voltage | – | Battery voltage | FOG fuse |
| IG – Body ground | Voltage | Ignition switch on | Battery voltage | ECU-IG fuse |
| SFL – AST | Resistance | Ignition switch off | About 6 Ω | Actuator |
| RR ⊕ – RR ⊖ | Resistance | – | 0.85 – 1.50 kΩ | Rear RH speed sensor |
| R ⊖ – Body ground | Continuity | Ignition switch off | No continuity | Wiring harness |
| RL ⊕ – RL ⊖ | Resistance | – | 0.85 – 1.50 kΩ | Rear LH speed sensor |
| FR ⊖ – Body ground | Continuity | – | No continuity | Front RH speed sensor |
| FR ⊕ – FR ⊖ | Resistance | – | 0.85 – 1.30 kΩ | |
| FL ⊖ – Body ground | Continuity | – | No continuity | Front LH speed sensor |
| FL ⊕ – FL ⊖ | Resistance | – | 0.85 – 1.30 kΩ | |
| SRL – AST | Resistance | Ignition switch off | About 6 Ω | Actuator |

92E01558

Courtesy of Toyota Motor Sales, U.S.A., Inc.

***Fig. 11: Testing Specifications Table for ABS Computer Wiring Harness (2 of 2)***

# 1991 BRAKES
# Anti-Lock – Camry (Cont.)

**4)** Using a plastic hammer, tap drive shaft inward and remove steering knuckle. Attach steering knuckle in a vise. Using Puller (09950-20017), remove axle hub. Remove hub bearing inner race.
**5)** Using a Torx wrench, remove bolts attaching front sensor rotor to axle hub. Remove sensor rotor.
**6)** To install, reverse removal procedure. Tighten all nuts and bolts to specification. See TORQUE SPECIFICATIONS table at end of article.

## REAR SENSOR ROTOR

**Removal & Installation – 1)** Remove seat cushion. Disconnect sensor connector. Pull out sensor wire harness. Remove 2 clamp bolts holding sensor wire harness to body and suspension arm.
**2)** Raise and support vehicle. Remove upper axle carrier mounting bolt. Remove disc brake assembly and wire out of way. DO NOT disconnect brake line. Remove disc brake rotor. Remove 4 axle hub mounting bolts.
**3)** Remove axle hub. Remove backing plate with parking brake assembly and "O" ring. Remove 4 speed sensor mounting bolts. Remove speed sensor.
**4)** To install, reverse removal procedure. Tighten all nuts and bolts to specification. See TORQUE SPECIFICATIONS table at end of article.

## OVERHAUL

DO NOT attempt to overhaul or disassemble actuator assembly. If actuator is defective, replace entire assembly.

## TORQUE SPECIFICATIONS

*TORQUE SPECIFICATIONS*

| Application | Ft. Lbs. (N.m) |
|---|---|
| Ball Joint-To-Lower Arm | 90 (122) |
| Ball Joint-To-Steering Knuckle Nut | 83 (112) |
| Brake Line Nuts | 11 (15) |
| Front Axle Nut | 137 (186) |
| Front Disc Caliper Bolts | |
| ALL-TRAC | 79 (107) |
| FWD | 69 (93) |
| Rear Axle Carrier Upper Mounting Bolt | 152 (206) |
| Rear Axle Hub Bolts | 59 (80) |
| Rear Axle Nut | 90 (122) |
| Rear Disc Caliper Bolts | 34 (46) |
| Steering Knuckle-To-Shock Absorber Bolt | 224 (304) |
| Tie Rod End-To Steering Knuckle Nut | 36 (49) |
| Wheel Lug Nuts | 76 (103) |
| 3-Way Union Bolt | 12 (16) |
| | **INCH Lbs. (N.m)** |
| ABS Computer Mounting Screws | 28 (3) |
| Actuator Mounting Nuts | 48 (5) |
| Deceleration Sensor Mounting Bolts | 28 (3) |
| Proportioning Valve Bolts | 78 (9) |
| Wheel Speed Sensor Mounting Bolt | 69 (8) |

## WIRING DIAGRAM

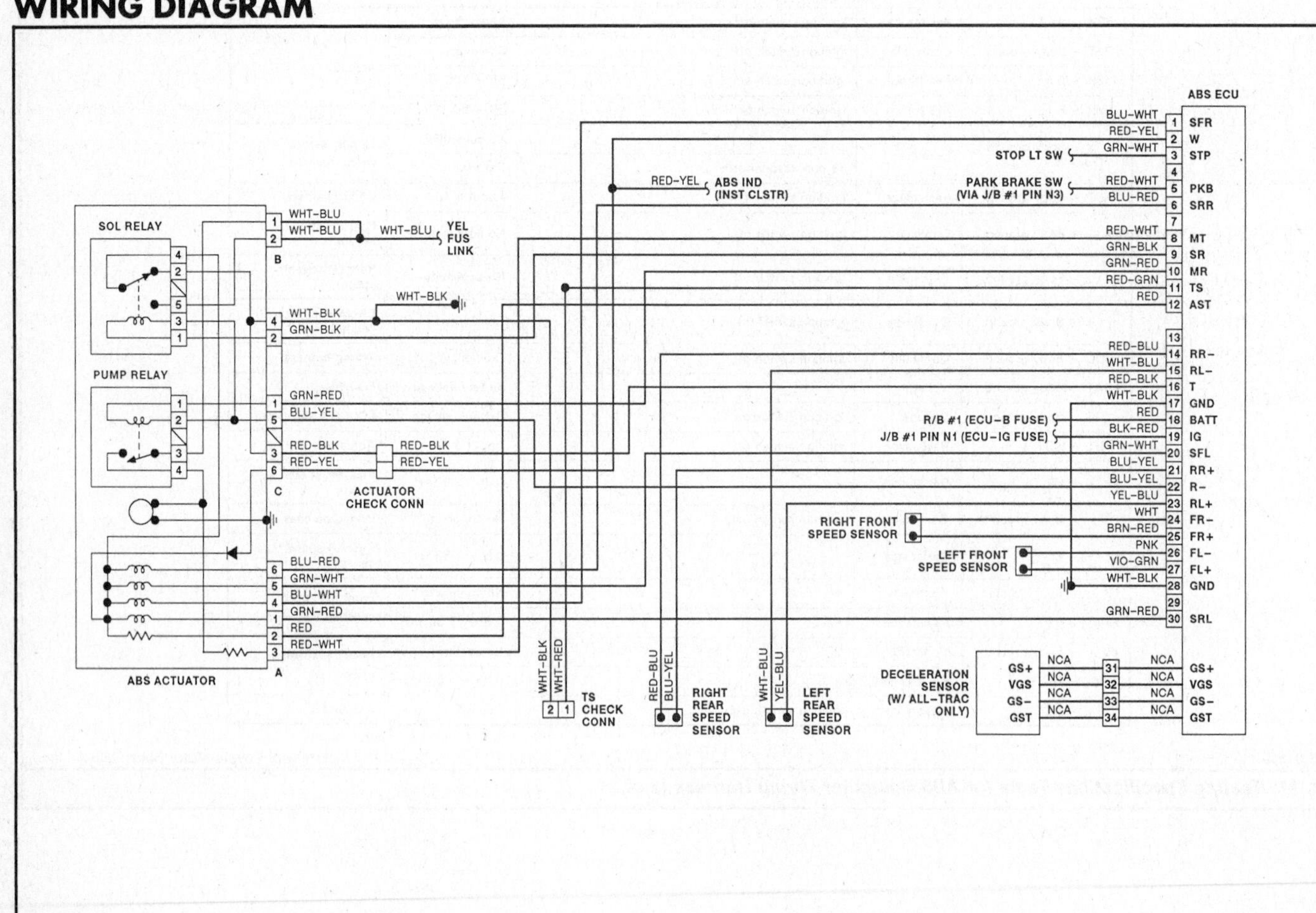


*Fig. 12: Anti-Lock Brake System (ABS) Wiring Diagram*

# 1991 BRAKES
# Anti-Lock – Celica

## DESCRIPTION

The Anti-Lock Brake System (ABS) consists of hydraulic unit, ABS control relay, brake actuator, four 3-position actuator solenoids, pump motor, deceleration sensor (All-Trac), ABS computer and 4 speed sensors. *See Fig. 1.*

An ABS indicator light is located on the instrument panel in the combination meter. ABS indicator light comes on for 3 seconds as a bulb test when ignition is turned on. A primary check is performed after each engine start and initial vehicle speed exceeds 4 MPH. An actuator noise is heard as vehicle speed exceeds 4 MPH, this is normal. If brake pedal is depressed before vehicle exceeds 4 MPH, primary check will not occur until brake pedal is released.

***NOTE: For more information on brake system, see DISC & DRUM – FWD CARS article.***

## OPERATION

Under normal driving conditions, the ABS functions as a standard brake system. With detection of wheel lock-up, short pedal pulsations occurring in rapid succession will be felt in brake pedal. Pedal pulsation will continue until there is no longer a need for ABS function or until vehicle is stopped. Maintaining a constant force on brake pedal provides shortest stopping distance.

***CAUTION: See ANTI-LOCK BRAKE SAFETY PRECAUTIONS article in GENERAL INFORMATION.***

## BLEEDING BRAKE SYSTEM

***CAUTION: Brake fluid will damage painted surfaces. If brake fluid gets on a painted surface, wipe off immediately and clean with alcohol. Use only DOT 3 brake fluid from a sealed container. Do not mix brake fluid with any other type.***

Brake bleeding procedure is same procedure used to bleed non-ABS systems. If master cylinder was rebuilt or reservoir ran empty, bleed master cylinder first. Bleed remaining wheels starting with wheel having longest hydraulic line working to shortest hydraulic line.

## ADJUSTMENTS

### MASTER CYLINDER PUSH ROD

**1)** Install Adjusting Gauge (09737-00010) on master cylinder with master cylinder gasket in place. Lower adjusting gauge pin until pin slightly touches master cylinder piston. Perform STEP 1. *See Fig. 2.* Turn adjusting gauge upside down and install on power brake unit.

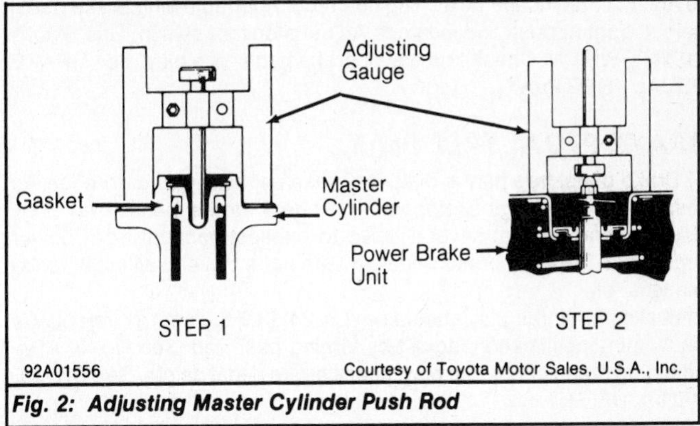


***Fig. 2: Adjusting Master Cylinder Push Rod***

**2)** Measure clearance between power brake unit push rod and adjusting gauge pin head. Perform STEP 2. *See Fig. 2.* Measured clearance should be zero. If clearance is not zero, adjust power brake unit push rod length until push rod lightly touches adjusting gauge pin head.

### BRAKE PEDAL HEIGHT

**1)** Brake pedal height is measured from face of brake pedal pad to rib of floor panel. *See Fig. 3.* On A/T models, brake pedal height should be 6.61-7.01" (167.9-178.0 mm). On M/T models, brake pedal height should be 6.64-7.03" (168.6-178.5 mm). To adjust brake pedal height, loosen stoplight switch and lock nut on brake pedal push rod.

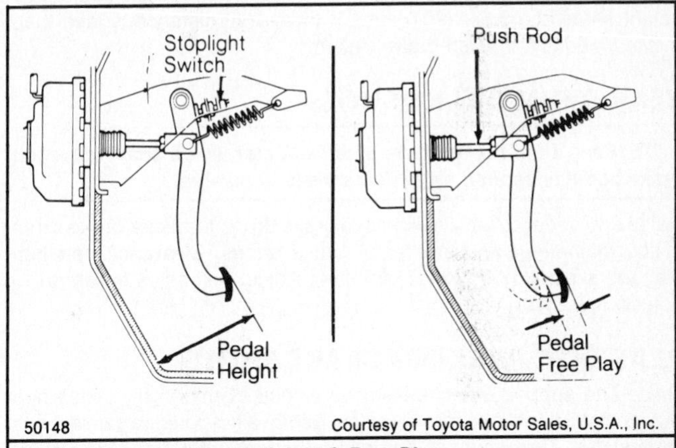


***Fig. 3: Measuring Pedal Height & Free Play***

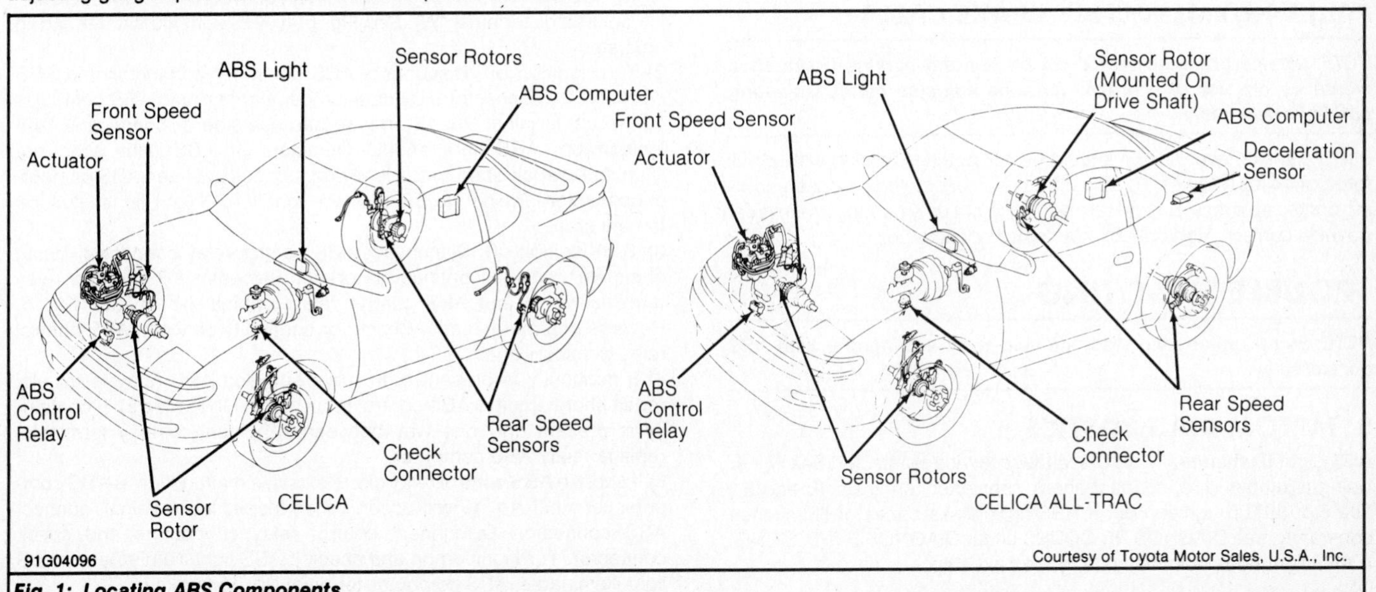


***Fig. 1: Locating ABS Components***

# 1991 BRAKES
# Anti-Lock – Celica (Cont.)

**2)** Adjust pedal height by turning push rod. After adjusting brake pedal height, tighten push rod lock nut. Adjust stoplight switch. See STOPLIGHT SWITCH. Check and adjust brake pedal free play. See BRAKE PEDAL FREE PLAY.

## BRAKE PEDAL FREE PLAY

**1)** Brake pedal free play is distance brake pedal travels before feeling resistance with engine stopped. To check brake pedal free play, depress brake pedal several times to exhaust vacuum from power brake unit. Depress brake pedal and measure travel until initial resistance is felt.

**2)** Brake pedal free play should be .12-.24" (3.0-6.0 mm). If free play is not within specification, adjust by turning push rod. *See Fig. 3.* After adjusting brake pedal free play, check brake pedal height. See BRAKE PEDAL HEIGHT.

## STOPLIGHT SWITCH

Stoplight switch is located above brake pedal. *See Fig. 3.* To adjust stoplight switch, loosen stoplight switch lock nuts and turn stoplight switch until it touches brake pedal stop. Tighten lock nut. Check stoplight operation.

## BRAKE PEDAL DEPRESSED HEIGHT

Brake pedal depressed height is measured from face of brake pedal pad to asphalt sheet under carpet with brakes applied. Measure brake pedal depressed height with engine running and weight of 110 lbs. (50 kg) applied against brake pedal. Minimum brake pedal depressed height should be 3.54" (90.0 mm). If measured distance is less than minimum height, inspect brake system.

## REAR DRUM BRAKE SHOES

***NOTE: Rear drum brakes have a self-adjuster which activates when brake pedal is applied as vehicle travels in reverse.***

Raise and support vehicle. Remove brake drum. Measure brake drum inside diameter and diameter of brake shoes. Clearance between diameters should be .024" (6.00 mm). Adjust self-adjuster length to adjust clearance.

## REAR DISC PARKING BRAKE SHOES

Raise and support vehicle. Remove wheels. Temporarily install hub nuts to hold disc brake rotor in place. Remove hole plug to gain access to adjuster. Turn adjuster and expand shoes until disc brake rotor locks. Return adjuster 8 notches. Install hole plug.

## PARKING/EMERGENCY BRAKE CABLE

***NOTE: Service brake on rear drum brakes and parking brake shoe clearance on rear disc brakes must be adjusted before adjusting parking brake cable.***

Parking brake lever stroke should be 4-7 notches (clicks) with a pull force of 44 lbs. (20 kg). To adjust, remove console box. Loosen parking brake cable lock nut and turn adjusting nut until parking brake lever travel is correct. Tighten lock nut. Install console box.

# TROUBLE SHOOTING

***NOTE: Pump motor relay and solenoid relay are integral with ABS control relay.***

## SYMPTOM DIAGNOSTICS

**ABS Light Illuminates – 1)** Disconnect service connector. *See Fig. 4.* Using a jumper wire, connect check connector terminals Tc and $E_1$. *See Fig. 5.* Turn ignition on. If ABS light blinks codes or illuminates constantly, see DIAGNOSTIC CODES under DIAGNOSIS & TESTING. If ABS light does not illuminate, go to next step.

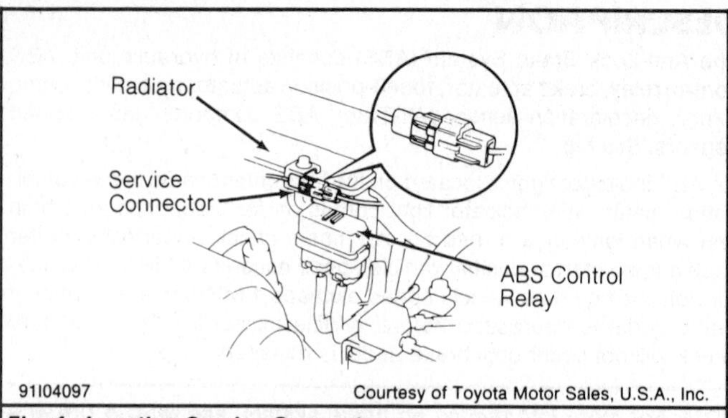


*Fig. 4: Locating Service Connector*

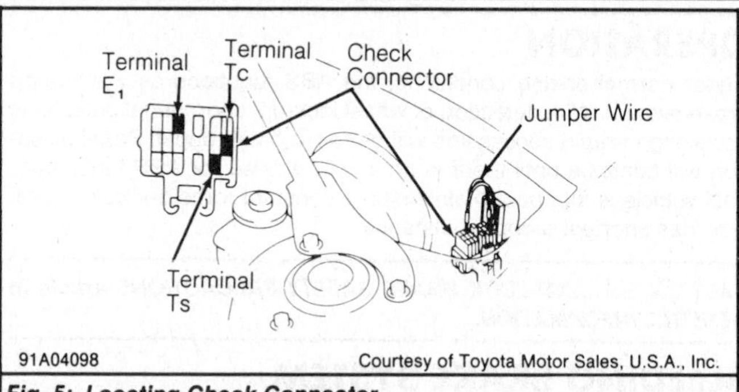


*Fig. 5: Locating Check Connector*

**2)** Ensure ABS computer connector is properly connected and connector terminals are not damaged. Repair connector as necessary. Turn ignition on. Using a voltmeter, check for 10-16 volts between ABS computer connector terminal No. 1 (Black/Red wire) and ground. *See Fig. 6.* If 10-16 volts is not present, repair faulty Black/Red wire. If 10-16 volts is present, go to next step.

**3)** Turn ignition off. Disconnect ABS computer connector. Disconnect service connector if not previously disconnected. Turn ignition on. If ABS light illuminates, repair short circuit between ABS control relay terminal "W" (Green wire) and ABS computer connector terminal No. 15 (Gray wire) *See Fig. 6.* If ABS light does not illuminate, replace faulty ABS computer.

**ABS Light Does Not Illuminate For 3 Seconds After Ignition Is Turned On – 1)** Disconnect service connector. *See Fig. 4.* Using a jumper wire, ground service connector terminal "W" on harness (female) side. Turn ignition on. If ABS does not illuminate, replace faulty ABS light bulb or repair open circuit between ABS light and service connector terminal "W". *See Fig. 6.* If ABS light illuminates, go to next step.

**2)** Turn ignition off. Disconnect ABS computer connector and ABS control relay connectors. Using a jumper wire, ground ABS computer connector terminal No. 15 on wire harness side of connector. Turn ignition on. ABS light should illuminate. If ABS light does not illuminate, repair open circuit in wiring harness between ABS computer connector terminal No. 15 and ABS light. If ABS light illuminates, go to next step.

**3)** Turn ignition off. Disconnect ABS control relay connector. Using ohmmeter, ensure continuity is present between ABS control relay terminal No. 4 and ABS control relay terminal No. 5. *See Fig. 6.* Reverse ohmmeter leads. Check for continuity between ABS control relay terminals again.

**4)** If continuity is present both ways between ABS relay terminals, repair short circuit in ABS control relay diode. Go to step **5)**. If continuity is present only one way between ABS control relay terminals, replace faulty ABS computer.

**5)** If short in ABS control relay diode exists, a malfunction at ABS computer terminal No. 15 will occur. When inspecting terminal, connect ABS connector. Disconnect control relay connectors and check connector. Turn ignition on and check if ABS light illuminates. If ABS light illuminates, ABS computer terminal No. 15 is okay.

# 1991 BRAKES
# Anti-Lock – Celica (Cont.)

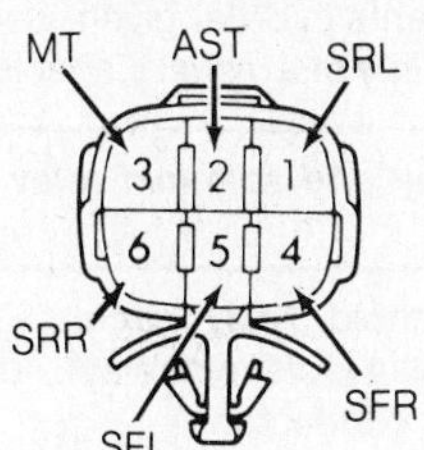


BRAKE ACTUATOR
CONNECTOR "B"

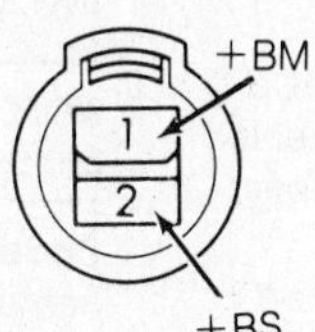


LEFT REAR SPEED SENSOR

LEFT FRONT SPEED SENSOR

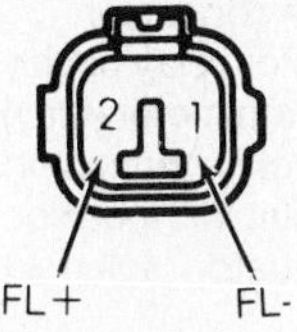


RIGHT FRONT SPEED SENSOR

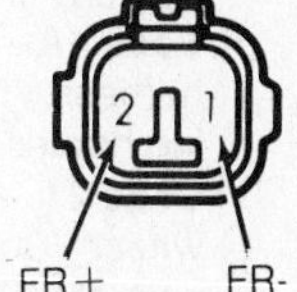


RIGHT REAR SPEED SENSOR

ABS CONTROL RELAY

BM +BM TC +BS SR

Solenoid Relay

Pump Motor Relay

8 7 3 2 1

10 9 6 5 4

MR R- GND BS W

SERVICE CONNECTOR

1

W

DECELERATION SENSOR

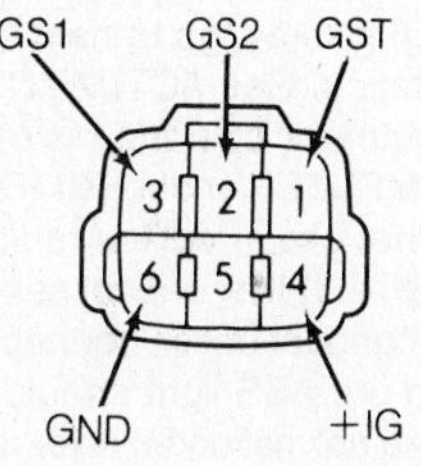


ABS COMPUTER

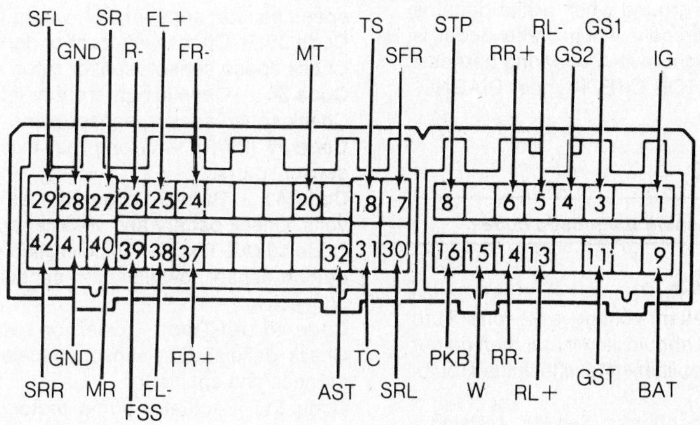


91C04099

Courtesy of Toyota Motor Sales, U.S.A., Inc.

*Fig. 6: Identifying ABS System Connector Terminals*

# 1991 BRAKES
# Anti-Lock – Celica (Cont.)

**ABS Light Illuminates Intermittently** – Check for a short in wiring harness between check connector terminals Tc and $E_1$ or Ts and $E_1$. *See Fig. 5*.

**Brakes Pull, Braking Inefficient, ABS Operates With Ordinary Braking, ABS Operates Just Before Stopping With Ordinary Braking, & Brake Pedal Pulsates Abnormally With ABS Functioning – 1)** Disconnect service connector. *See Fig. 4*. Using a jumper wire, connect check connector terminals Tc and $E_1$. *See Fig. 5*. Turn ignition on. ABS light should blink a normal code. If ABS light does not blink a normal code, refer to DIAGNOSTIC CODES under DIAGNOSIS & TESTING. If ABS light blinks a normal code, go to next step.

**2)** Enter speed sensor diagnostics. See SPEED SENSOR DIAGNOSTICS under DIAGNOSIS & TESTING. If speed sensor signal level is okay, go to next step. If speed sensor signal level is not okay, inspect sensor and sensor rotor. Replace as necessary.

**3)** Ensure all speed sensors are installed properly. If speed sensors are not installed properly, repair as necessary. If speed sensors are installed properly, ensure all foreign and metal chips are cleaned from speed sensor tip. Go to next step.

**4)** Turn ignition off. Disconnect ABS computer connector. Ensure continuity is present between each speed sensor connector (wire harness side) of ABS computer connector. Check continuity between FL+ and FL- (left front speed sensor), FR+ and FR- (right front speed sensor), RL+ and RL- (left rear speed sensor), and RR+ and RR- (right rear speed sensor).

**5)** If continuity readings change when wiring harness is twisted or moved, repair faulty wiring harness between speed sensor and ABS computer connector. If vehicle is an All-Trac and continuity readings do not change, go to step **6)**. If vehicle is not an All-Trac, go to step **7)**.

**6)** Enter deceleration sensor diagnostics. See DECELERATION SENSOR DIAGNOSTICS (ALL-TRAC) under DIAGNOSIS & TESTING. If deceleration sensor operation is not okay, ensure sensor is installed properly. If sensor is installed properly, replace faulty sensor. If deceleration sensor operation is okay, go to next step.

**7)** Check actuator operation. See ACTUATOR CHECK under DIAGNOSIS & TESTING. If actuator operation is okay, replace faulty ABS computer. See ABS COMPUTER under REMOVAL & INSTALLATION. If actuator operation is not okay, replace faulty actuator.

**ABS Works Inefficiently – 1)** Disconnect service connector. *See Fig. 4*. Using a jumper wire, connect check connector terminals Tc and $E_1$. *See Fig. 5*. Turn ignition on. ABS light should blink a normal code. If ABS light does not blink a normal code, refer to DIAGNOSTIC CODES under DIAGNOSIS & TESTING. If ABS light blinks a normal code, go to next step.

**2)** Ensure battery voltage exists between ABS computer connector terminal No. 8 (Green/White wire) and ground when brake pedal is depressed. If battery voltage is not present when brake pedal is depressed, repair open circuit in stoplight switch or wiring harness. Check actuator operation. See ACTUATOR CHECK under DIAGNOSIS & TESTING.

## DIAGNOSIS & TESTING

***NOTE: DO NOT start engine when accessing diagnostic codes.***

### ACCESSING TROUBLE CODES

**ABS Light Diagnostics – 1)** Ensure battery voltage is 12 volts. Turn ignition switch to ON position. ABS light should illuminate, then go out after 3 seconds. If warning light does not illuminate, check fuse, bulb, and wiring harness.

**2)** With ignition on, disconnect service connector. *See Fig. 4*. Using a jumper wire, connect check connector terminals Tc and $E_1$. *See Fig. 5*. If a malfunction is detected, 4 seconds will elapse and ABS light will begin to flash a 2-digit code. First number of blinks will equal first digit in a code. After a 1.5-second pause, second number of blinks will equal second digit in a code.

**3)** If 2 or more codes are stored, there will be a 4.5-second pause between each code. If ABS system is functioning properly, ABS light will blink once every .5 second. For code interpretation, see DIAGNOSTIC CODES.

**4)** After replacing or repairing malfunctioning components, clear diagnostic codes. If a battery cable was disconnected during repairs, all codes will be erased. If battery cable was not disconnected during repairs, see CLEARING CODES.

### DIAGNOSTIC CODES

Check suspect components in order given. See COMPONENT TESTING. Checks consist mainly of a visual inspection and continuity tests.

***NOTE: Pump motor relay and solenoid relay are integral with ABS control relay.***

**Code 11** – Open solenoid relay circuit. Check actuator wiring harness, ABS control relay (solenoid relay), solenoid relay wiring harness and solenoid relay connector.

**Code 12** – Short in solenoid relay circuit. Check actuator wiring harness, ABS control relay (solenoid relay), solenoid relay wiring harness and solenoid relay connector.

**Code 13** – Open pump motor relay circuit. Check actuator wiring harness, ABS control relay (pump motor relay), pump motor relay wiring harness and pump motor relay connector.

**Code 14** – Short in pump motor relay circuit. Check actuator wiring harness, ABS control relay (pump motor relay), pump motor relay wiring harness and pump motor relay connector.

**Code 21** – Open or short circuit in 3-position solenoid for right front wheel. Check 3-position actuator solenoid, wiring harness and connector.

**Code 22** – Open or short circuit in 3-position solenoid for left front wheel. Check 3-position actuator solenoid, wiring harness and connector.

**Code 23** – Open or short circuit in 3-position solenoid for right rear wheel. Check 3-position actuator solenoid, wiring harness and connector.

**Code 24** – Open or short circuit in 3-position solenoid for left rear wheel. Check 3-position actuator solenoid, wiring harness and connector.

**Code 31** – Malfunction of right front wheel speed sensor signal. Check speed sensor, sensor rotor, wiring harness and connector.

**Code 32** – Malfunction of left front wheel speed sensor signal. Check speed sensor, sensor rotor, wiring harness and connector.

**Code 33** – Malfunction of right rear wheel speed sensor signal. Check speed sensor, sensor rotor, wiring harness and connector.

**Code 34** – Malfunction of left rear wheel speed sensor signal. Check speed sensor, sensor rotor, wiring harness and connector.

**Code 35** – Open in left front or right rear wheel speed sensor circuit. Check speed sensor, sensor rotor, wiring harness and connector.

**Code 36** – Open in right front or left rear wheel speed sensor circuit. Check speed sensor, sensor rotor, wiring harness and connector.

**Code 37 (FWD)** – Wrong rear axle hubs on both sides. Check rear sensor rotors.

**Code 41** – Battery voltage is less than 9.5 volts or more than 16.2 volts. Check battery and voltage regulator.

**Code 43 (All-Trac)** – Deceleration sensor malfunction. Check deceleration sensor, deceleration sensor installation, wiring harness and connector.

**Code 44 (All-Trac)** – Open or short circuit in deceleration sensor. Check deceleration sensor, deceleration sensor installation, wiring harness and connector.

**Code 51** – Actuator pump motor is locked or pump motor circuit open. Check pump motor, ABS control relay (pump motor relay), vehicle battery, actuator wiring harness, connectors, actuator pump motor circuit and actuator ground bolt.

**Always On** – Malfunction of ABS computer. Ensure ABS computer connector is properly connected and terminals are not damaged. If connector is okay, replace ABS computer. See ABS COMPUTER under REMOVAL & INSTALLATION.

# 1991 BRAKES
# Anti-Lock – Celica (Cont.)

## CLEARING CODES

Turn ignition on. Using a jumper wire, connect check connector terminals Tc and $E_1$. *See Fig. 5*. With vehicle stopped, depress brake pedal 8 or more times within 3 seconds. Codes are now erased. Turn ignition on. Ensure ABS light goes out after 3 seconds. Ensure ABS light shows a normal code. See ABS LIGHT DIAGNOSTICS under ACCESSING TROUBLE CODES.

## ACTUATOR CHECK

***NOTE: Actuator Checker (09990-00150) and Sheet "A" (09990-00163) are needed to perform ACTUATOR CHECK.***

**1)** Turn ignition off. Disconnect actuator electrical connectors. Disconnect ABS control relay connectors. Connect Actuator Checker (09990-00150) to actuator and ABS control relay. Connect actuator checker positive and negative power cables to vehicle battery.
**2)** Place Sheet "A" (09990-00163) on actuator checker. Start engine. Turn actuator checker SELECTOR switch to FRONT RH position. *See Fig. 7*. Press and hold MOTOR switch for a few seconds. Press and hold brake pedal.

***NOTE: DO NOT press POWER switch for more than 10 seconds.***

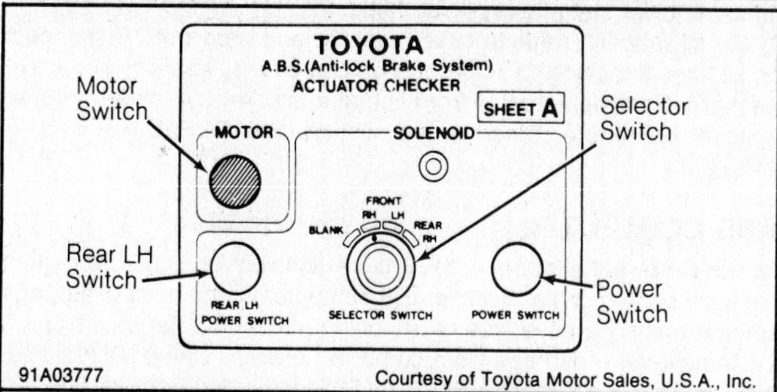


***Fig. 7: Identifying Actuator Checker Switches***

**3)** Press POWER switch. When POWER switch is pressed, brake pedal should not go down. Release POWER SWITCH. Brake pedal should lower. Press and hold MOTOR switch for a few seconds. Brake pedal should return. Release MOTOR switch. Release brake pedal.
**4)** Press and hold MOTOR switch for a few seconds. Release MOTOR switch. Press brake pedal and hold for approximately 15 seconds. As brake pedal is being held, press MOTOR switch for a few seconds. Ensure brake pedal does not pulsate.
**5)** Repeat steps **2)** through **4)** for FRONT LH, REAR RH, and REAR LH by turning SELECTOR switch on actuator checker. When checking REAR LH position, press REAR LH switch, instead of POWER SWITCH. After checking remaining wheels, press and hold MOTOR switch for a few seconds.
**6)** Remove actuator checker. Connect actuator wiring harness to actuator. Connect ABS control relay wiring harness to relay. Clear diagnostic codes. See CLEARING CODES.

## SPEED SENSOR DIAGNOSTICS

***NOTE: During diagnosis, DO NOT turn ignition off, pull parking brake lever and press brake pedal more than 16 times or diagnostic codes will be erased. While diagnosing speed sensors, brake system functions as a conventional system.***

**1)** Ensure battery voltage is approximately 12 volts. Turn ignition on. Ensure ABS light illuminates, then goes out after approximately 3 seconds. If ABS does not illuminate, check fuse, bulb and wiring harness.
**2)** Turn ignition off. Using a jumper wire, connect check connector terminals Tc, and $E_1$ to Ts. *See Fig. 5*. Engage parking brake. Start engine. DO NOT press brake pedal. ABS light will illuminate 4 times a second. Go to next step.

***NOTE: While ABS light is off, DO NOT accelerate, decelerate, brake, shift, move steering or drive on rough road surfaces as these conditions will affect test.***

**3)** Drive vehicle straight ahead at 2.5-3.7 MPH. Ensure ABS light illuminates after a one second pause. If ABS light illuminates without blinking when vehicle is NOT within specified speed, stop vehicle and record diagnostic codes. Turn ignition off. Repair as necessary. See SPEED SENSOR DIAGNOSTIC CODES.
**4)** If ABS light illuminates while vehicle speed is within specified range, check is completed. If vehicle speed exceeds 3.7 MPH, ABS light will blink again. If ABS light blinks when vehicle speed exceeds 3.7 MPH, speed sensors are okay.
**5)** Drive vehicle straight ahead at 28-34 MPH. Ensure ABS light illuminates after a one second pause. If ABS light illuminates without blinking when vehicle is NOT within specified speed, stop vehicle and record diagnostic codes. Turn ignition off. Repair as necessary. See SPEED SENSOR DIAGNOSTIC CODES.
**6)** If ABS light illuminates while vehicle speed is within specified range, check is completed. If vehicle speed exceeds 34 MPH, ABS light will blink again. If ABS light blinks when vehicle speed exceeds 34 MPH, sensor rotors are okay.
**7)** Turn ignition off. Remove jumper wire from check connector. Clear diagnostic codes. See CLEARING CODES.

## SPEED SENSOR DIAGNOSTIC CODES

**Code 71** – Low voltage of right front speed sensor signal. Check right front speed sensor and sensor installation.
**Code 72** – Low voltage of left front speed sensor signal. Check left front speed sensor and sensor installation.
**Code 73** – Low voltage of right rear speed sensor signal. Check right rear speed sensor and sensor installation.
**Code 74** – Low voltage of left rear speed sensor signal. Check left rear speed sensor and sensor installation.
**Code 75** – Abnormal signal from right front speed sensor. Check right front sensor rotor.
**Code 76** – Abnormal signal from left front speed sensor. Check right front sensor rotor.
**Code 77** – Abnormal signal from right rear speed sensor. Check right rear sensor rotor.
**Code 78** – Abnormal signal from left rear speed sensor. Check left rear sensor rotor.
**Light Illuminates 4 Times A Second** – All speed sensors and sensor rotors are normal.

## DECELERATION SENSOR DIAGNOSTICS (ALL-TRAC)

***NOTE: While diagnosing deceleration sensor, brake system functions as a conventional system.***

**1)** Ensure battery voltage is 12 volts. Turn ignition on. ABS light should illuminate, then go out after 3 seconds. If ABS light does not illuminate, check fuse, bulb, and wiring harness.
**2)** Turn ignition off. Using a jumper wire, connect check connector terminals $E_1$ and Ts. *See Fig. 5*. Engage parking brake, depress brake pedal and start engine.
**3)** Ensure ABS light blinks about once every second. If ABS light does not blink, inspect parking brake switch, stoplight switch, check connector Ts terminal, deceleration sensor installation and ABS computer. If ABS blinks, go to next step.
**4)** To inspect sensor detection point, raise rear of vehicle 26-28" (660-710 mm). When measuring height, measure from bottom of rear bumper to ground. Ensure ABS light is off. As vehicle is lowered, ABS light will start blinking. Completely lower rear of vehicle. Raise front of vehicle 21-24" (533-610 mm). Measure distance from lower body or spoiler edge of vehicle to ground.
**5)** Ensure ABS light is off. As vehicle is lowered, ABS light will start blinking. If ABS light illuminates steadily, inspect deceleration sensor installation. If sensor installation is okay, replace deceleration sensor.

# 1991 BRAKES
# Anti-Lock – Celica (Cont.)

**6)** To inspect sensor operation, drive vehicle straight about 6.2 MPH or more. Lightly depress brake pedal. ABS light should blink once every second with no change in pattern.
**7)** Drive vehicle straight about 12.4 MPH or more. Using a little force, depress brake pedal. ABS light should stay on while braking. Drive vehicle about 12.4 MPH or more. Strongly depress brake pedal. ABS light should blink approximately 7 times per second.
**8)** If ABS light does not respond correctly, check deceleration sensor installation. If sensor installation is okay, replace deceleration sensor. Turn engine off. Remove jumper wire from check connector terminals $E_1$ and Ts.

## COMPONENT TESTING

**Front Speed Sensors – 1)** Remove front wheel speed sensor from vehicle. See FRONT WHEEL SPEED SENSORS under REMOVAL & INSTALLATION. Using a DVOM, measure resistance between speed sensor terminals. Resistance should be 800-1300 ohms.
**2)** Ensure continuity is not present between each sensor terminal and sensor body. If resistance and continuity readings are as specified, speed sensor is okay. If resistance and continuity readings are not as specified, replace speed sensor.
**Rear Speed Sensors – 1)** Remove rear seat cushion. Disconnect wheel speed sensor connector. Using a DVOM, measure resistance between speed sensor terminals. On FWD models, resistance should be 1100-1700 ohms. On All-Trac models, resistance should be 800-1500 ohms.
**2)** Ensure continuity is not present between each sensor terminal and sensor body. If resistance and continuity readings are as specified, speed sensor is okay. If resistance and continuity readings are not as specified, replace speed sensor.

***NOTE: Pump motor relay and solenoid relay are integral with ABS control relay.***

**ABS Control Relay – 1)** Remove ABS control relay. *See Fig. 1*. Using ohmmeter, check that continuity exists between ABS control relay terminals No. 4 and 3. *See Fig. 6*. Reverse ohmmeter leads. Check that continuity does not exist between terminals No. 3 and 4. If ABS control relay tests as specified, go to next step. If ABS control relay does not test as specified, replace ABS control relay.
**2)** Check that continuity exists between ABS control relay terminals No. 3 and 5, and between terminals No. 3 and 6. If continuity exists, go to next step. If continuity does not exist, replace ABS control relay.
**3)** Check that continuity exists between ABS control relay terminals No. 4 and 5, and between terminals No. 4 and 6. Reverse ohmmeter leads. Check that continuity does not exist between terminals No. 5 and 4, and terminals No. 6 and 4. If ABS control relay tests as specified, go to next step. If ABS control relay does not test as specified, replace ABS control relay.
**4)** Check that continuity exists between ABS control relay terminals No. 5 and 6. If continuity exists, go to next step. If continuity does not exist, replace ABS control relay.
**5)** Using a 12-volt battery, apply battery positive terminal to ABS control relay terminal No. 10. Apply battery negative terminal to ABS control relay terminal No. 9. Ensure continuity is present between relay terminals No. 7 and 8.
**6)** If continuity is not as specified, replace ABS control relay. If continuity readings are as specified, apply battery positive terminal to relay terminal No. 1. Apply battery negative terminal to relay terminal No. 9.
**7)** Ensure continuity exists between relay terminals No. 2 and 5. If continuity does not exist, replace ABS control relay. If continuity exists, go to next step.
**8)** Using a 12-volt battery, apply battery positive terminal to ABS control relay terminal No. 1. Apply battery negative terminal to ABS control relay terminal No. 9. Ensure continuity exists between relay terminals No. 3 and 5. If continuity exists, ABS control relay is okay. If continuity does not exist, replace ABS control relay.
**Sensor Rotors –** Visually inspect sensor rotor serrations for scratches, cracks, missing teeth and warping. Replace sensor rotor if damaged.

**ABS Computer Wiring Harness – 1)** Remove ABS computer. See ABS COMPUTER under REMOVAL & INSTALLATION. With ABS computer connectors connected, backprobe ABS computer connector terminals. Measure voltage and resistance at each terminal as specified in table. *See Fig. 8*. If circuit(s) do not test as specified, check and repair or replace trouble part shown in table.
**2)** Disconnect ABS computer connectors. Check resistance on wire harness side of ABS computer connector terminals as specified in table. *See Fig. 9*. If circuit(s) do not test as specified, check and repair or replace troubled part shown in table.

## REMOVAL & INSTALLATION

***WARNING: Hydraulic system may be under high pressure. Use caution when opening hydraulic system.***

## ACTUATOR

***NOTE: If actuator is being replaced, remove proportioning valve and 3-way union connection from actuator.***

**Removal & Installation – 1)** Turn ignition off. Remove actuator cover. Disconnect actuator electrical connectors. On All-Trac models, remove power steering reservoir tank.
**2)** On all models, remove cover bracket and stud bolt. Disconnect brake lines attaching to actuator. Remove 3 nuts, washers and wave washers. Remove actuator from actuator bracket. To install, reverse removal procedure. Bleed brake system. See BLEEDING BRAKE SYSTEM.

## ABS COMPUTER

**Removal & Installation – 1)** Ensure ignition is off. Disconnect negative battery cable. Access ABS computer in right side of luggage compartment. Remove screws attaching ABS computer to vehicle.
**2)** Remove wire harness from computer bracket clamp. Disconnect ABS computer connector. Remove ABS computer from vehicle. To install, reverse removal procedure.

## FRONT WHEEL SPEED SENSORS

**Removal & Installation – 1)** Loosen front wheel lug nuts. Raise and support front of vehicle. Remove front wheel. Remove wheel speed sensor mounting bolt.
**2)** Disconnect wheel speed sensor connector. Remove wheel speed sensor from vehicle. To install, reverse removal procedure. Tighten wheel speed sensor mounting bolt to specification. See TORQUE SPECIFICATIONS table at end of article.

## REAR WHEEL SPEED SENSORS

**Removal & Installation (FWD) – 1)** Remove rear seat cushion. Disconnect wheel speed sensor connector. Pull sensor wire from wiring harness. Remove sensor wiring harness-to-body and suspension arm clamp bolts.
**2)** Remove rear brake assembly. Suspend rear brake assembly so brake hose is not stretched. Remove rear rotor disc. Remove axle carrier upper mounting bolt. Remove 4 axle hub mounting bolts. Remove rear axle hub. Remove backing plate with parking brake assembly and "O" ring.
**3)** Remove wheel speed sensor mounting bolt. Remove wheel speed sensor. To install, reverse removal procedure. Install a new "O" ring onto axle carrier. Tighten wheel speed sensor and brake components to specification. See TORQUE SPECIFICATIONS table at end of article.
**Removal & Installation (All-Trac) – 1)** Loosen rear wheel lug nuts. Raise and support rear of vehicle. Remove rear wheel. Remove wheel speed sensor mounting bolt.
**2)** Disconnect wheel speed sensor connector. Remove wheel speed sensor from vehicle. To install, reverse removal procedure. Tighten wheel speed sensor mounting bolt to specification. See TORQUE SPECIFICATIONS table at end of article.

# 1991 BRAKES
# Anti-Lock – Celica (Cont.)

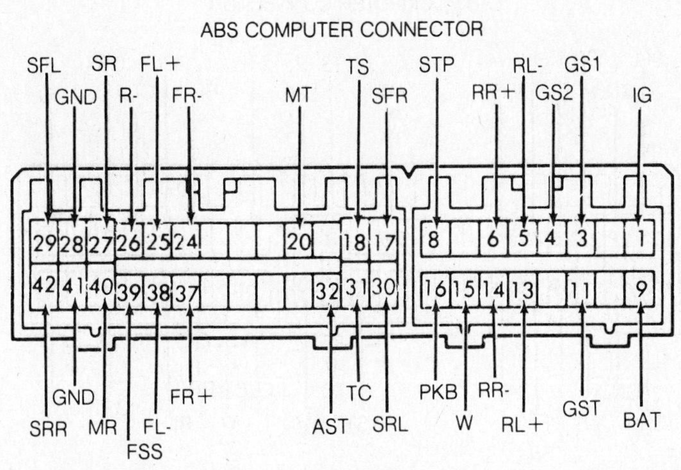


| Tester Connection | Check Item | Condition | Specified Value | Trouble Part |
|---|---|---|---|---|
| IG | Voltage | IG switch on | Battery voltage | ECU-IG Fuse |
| GS1 (4WD) | Voltage | IG switch on | 4 ~ 6 V | Deceleration Sensor |
| GS2 (4WD) | Voltage | IG switch on | 4 ~ 6 V | |
| RL– | Continuity | IG switch off | Continuity | ABS ECU |
| STP | Voltage | IG switch off and brake pedal depressed | Battery voltage | Stop light switch Stop light |
| | Continuity | IG switch off and brake pedal returned | Continuity | |
| BAT | Voltage | IG switch off | Battery voltage | DOME Fuse |
| RR– | Continuity | IG switch off | Continuity | ABS ECU |
| W | Voltage | IG switch on and "ABS" warning light goes on | About 0V | ABS ECU "ABS" warning light |
| | | IG switch on and "ABS" warning light goes off | Battery voltage | |
| PKB | Voltage | IG switch on and PKB lever pulled | About 0V | Parking brake switch Level warning switch |
| | | IG switch on and PKB lever returned | Battery voltage | |
| SFR | Voltage | IG switch on and "ABS" warning light goes on | About 0V | Actuator |
| | | IG switch on and "ABS" warning light goes off | Battery voltage | |
| TS | Voltage | IG switch on and check connector Ts-$E_1$ not connected | Battery voltage | ABS ECU |
| | | IG switch on and check connector Ts-$E_1$ connected | About 0V | |
| D/G | Voltage | IG switch on and check connector Ts-$E_1$ not connected | About 0V | |
| FR– | Continuity | IG switch off | Continuity | |
| R– | Continuity | IG switch off | Continuity | ABS ECU |
| SR | Voltage | IG switch on and "ABS" warning light goes on | About 0V | |
| | | IG switch on and "ABS" warning light goes off | Battery voltage | |
| GND | Continuity | IG switch off | Continuity | Wiring harness |
| SFL | Voltage | IG switch on and "ABS" warning light goes on | About 0V | Actuator |
| | | IG switch on and "ABS" warning light goes off | Battery voltage | |

| Tester Connection | Check Item | Condition | Specified Value | Trouble Part |
|---|---|---|---|---|
| SRL | Voltage | IG switch on and "ABS" warning light goes on | About 0V | Actuator |
| | | IG switch on and "ABS" warning light goes off | Battery voltage | |
| TC | Voltage | IG switch on and check connector Tc-$E_1$ not connected | Battery voltage | ABS ECU |
| | | IG switch on and check connector Tc-$E_1$ connected | About 0V | |
| AST | Voltage | IG switch on and "ABS" warning light goes on | About 0V | Actuator |
| | | IG switch on and "ABS" warning light goes off | Battery voltage | |
| FL– | Continuity | IG switch off | Continuity | ABS ECU |
| FSS | Continuity | IG switch off | Continuity | |
| SRR | Voltage | IG switch on and "ABS" warning light goes on | About 0V | Actuator |
| | | IG switch on and "ABS" warning light goes off | Battery voltage | |

92A01820



***Fig. 8: Testing Specifications Table for ABS Computer Wiring Harness (1 of 2)***

# 1991 BRAKES
# Anti-Lock – Celica (Cont.)

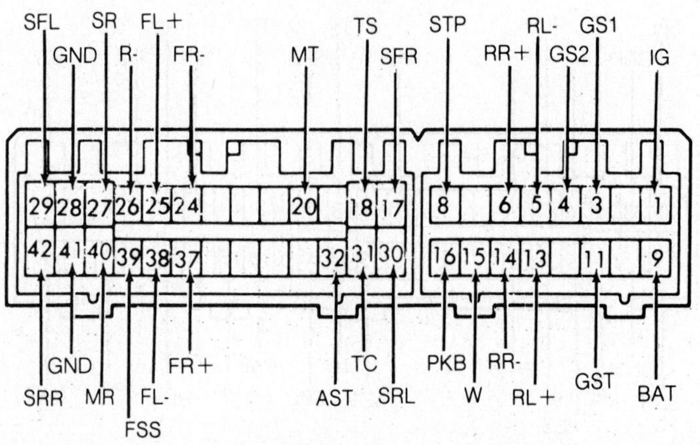


| Tester Connection | Check Item | Specified Value | Trouble Part | Tester Connection | Check Item | Specified Value | Trouble Part |
|---|---|---|---|---|---|---|---|
| RR+ ↔ RR– | Resistance | 1.1 ~ 1.7 kΩ<br>★ 0.8 ~ 1.5 kΩ | Rear RH speed sensor | SFL ↔ AST | Resistance | About 6 Ω | Actuator |
| RL+ ↔ RL– | Resistance | 1.1 ~ 1.7 kΩ<br>★ 0.8 ~ 1.5 kΩ | Rear LH speed sensor | SRL ↔ AST | Resistance | About 6 Ω | Actuator |
| SFR ↔ AST | Resistance | About 6 Ω | Actuator | AST ↔ Body ground | Resistance | About 5 Ω | Actuator |
| MT ↔ Body ground | Continuity | Continuity | Actuator | FR+ ↔ FR– | Resistance | 0.8 ~ 1.3 Ω | Front RH speed sensor |
| FL+ ↔ FL– | Resistance | 0.8 ~ 1.3 kΩ | Front LH speed sensor | MR ↔ R– | Resistance | 50 ~ 80 Ω | Control relay |
| SR ↔ R– | Resistance | 60 ~ 100 Ω | Control relay | SRR ↔ AST | Resistance | About 6 Ω | Actuator |

92C01821

Courtesy of Toyota Motor Sales, U.S.A., Inc.

*Fig. 9: Testing Specifications Table for ABS Computer Wiring Harness (2 of 2)*

## ABS CONTROL RELAY

**Removal & Installation** – Remove connector from wire harness clamp. Remove bolt mounting relay to vehicle. Remove relay from vehicle. *See Fig. 1.* To install, reverse removal procedure.

## FRONT SENSOR ROTOR

Information is not available from manufacturer.

## REAR SENSOR ROTOR

Information is not available from manufacturer.

## OVERHAUL

DO NOT attempt to overhaul or disassemble actuator assembly. If actuator is defective, replace entire assembly.

## TORQUE SPECIFICATIONS

***TORQUE SPECIFICATIONS***

| Application | Ft. Lbs. (N.m) |
|---|---|
| Brake Line Nuts | 11 (15) |
| Front Axle Nut | 137 (186) |
| Front Disc Caliper Bolts | 79 (107) |
| Power Steering Reservoir Tank Mounting Bolts | 14 (19) |
| Rear Axle Hub Bolts | 59 (80) |
| Rear Axle Nut | 90 (122) |
| Rear Disc Caliper Bolts | 34 (46) |
| Wheel Lug Nuts | 76 (103) |
| 3-Way Union Bolt | 12 (16) |
| | **INCH Lbs. (N.m)** |
| ABS Computer Mounting Screws | 28 (3) |
| Actuator Mounting Nuts | 48 (5) |
| Deceleration Sensor Mounting Bolts | 28 (3) |
| Proportioning Valve Bolts | 78 (9) |
| Wheel Speed Sensor Mounting Bolt | 69 (8) |

## WIRING DIAGRAM

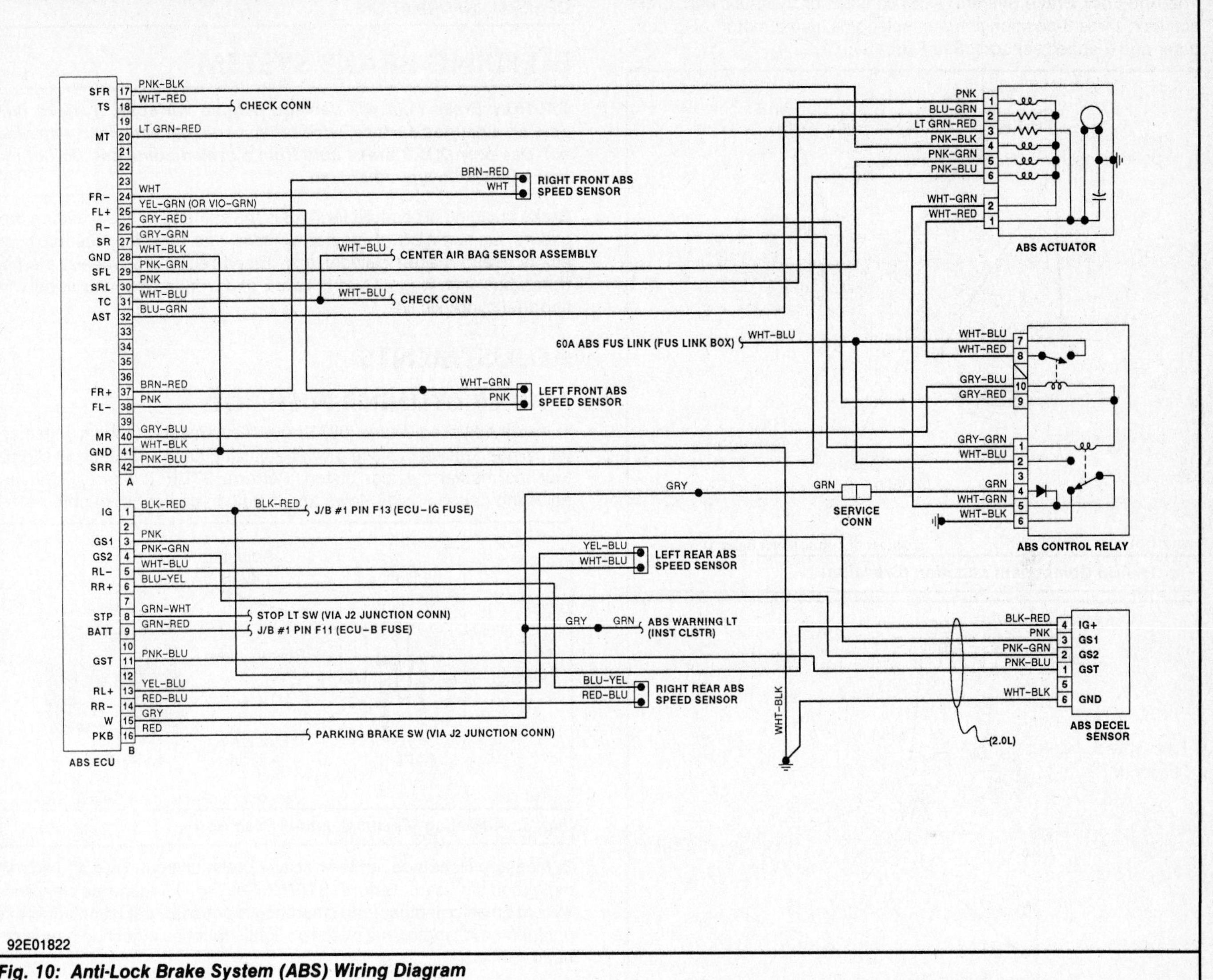


*Fig. 10: Anti-Lock Brake System (ABS) Wiring Diagram*

# 1991 BRAKES
# Anti-Lock – Cressida & Supra

## DESCRIPTION

The Anti-Lock Brake System (ABS) consists of hydraulic unit, brake actuator, three 3-position actuator solenoids, pump motor, ABS computer and 3 speed sensors. *See Figs. 1 and 2.*

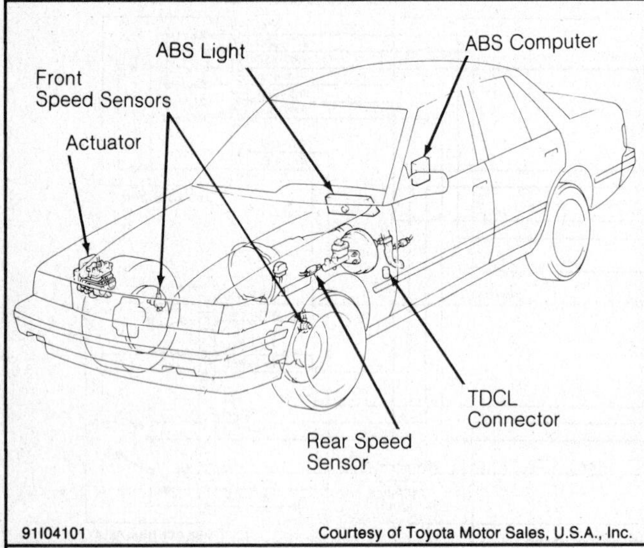


***Fig. 1: ABS Component Location (Cressida)***

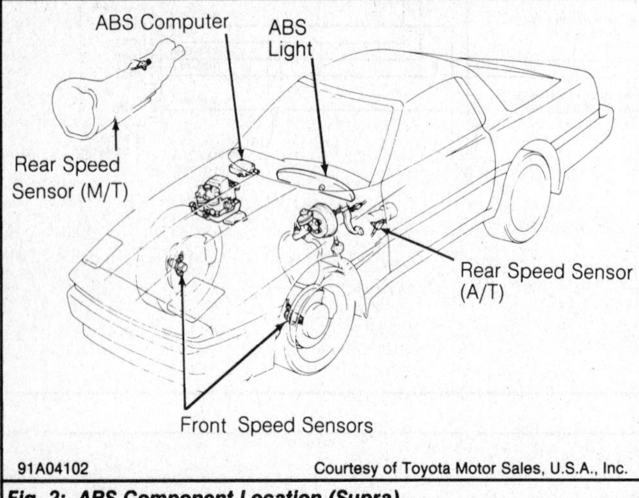


***Fig. 2: ABS Component Location (Supra)***

An ABS indicator light is located on the instrument panel, in the combination meter. Indicator light comes on for 3 seconds as a bulb test when ignition is turned on. A primary check is performed after each engine start and after initial vehicle speed exceeds 4 MPH. An actuator noise will be heard as vehicle speed exceeds 4 MPH. If brake pedal is depressed before vehicle exceeds 4 MPH, primary check will not occur until brake pedal is released.

***NOTE: For more information on brake system, see DISC & DRUM – RWD CARS article.***

## OPERATION

Under normal driving conditions, ABS functions as a standard brake system. Upon detection of wheel lock-up, short pedal pulsations, occurring in rapid succession, will be felt in brake pedal. Pedal pulsations will continue until there is no longer a need for ABS function or until vehicle is stopped. Applying constant force on pedal results in shortest stopping distance.

***CAUTION: See ANTI-LOCK BRAKE SAFETY PRECAUTIONS article in GENERAL INFORMATION.***

## BLEEDING BRAKE SYSTEM

***CAUTION: Brake fluid will damage painted surfaces. If brake fluid gets on a painted surface, wipe off immediately and clean with alcohol. Use only DOT 3 brake fluid from a sealed container. Do not mix brake fluid with any other type.***

Brake bleeding procedure for ABS is the same as brake bleeding procedure for non-ABS. If master cylinder was rebuilt or reservoir ran empty, bleed master cylinder first. Bleed remaining wheels, starting from wheel with longest hydraulic line and working down to wheel with shortest hydraulic line.

## ADJUSTMENTS

### MASTER CYLINDER PUSH ROD

**1)** Install Adjusting Gauge (09737-00010) on master cylinder with master cylinder gasket in place. Lower adjusting gauge pin until pin slightly touches master cylinder piston. Perform STEP 1. *See Fig. 3.* Turn adjusting gauge upside down and install on power brake unit.

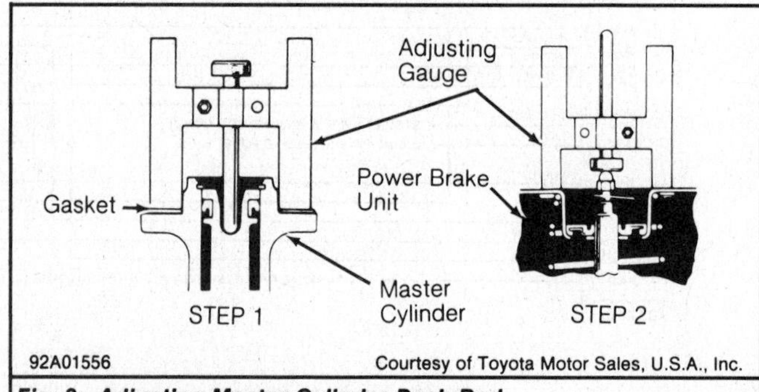


***Fig. 3: Adjusting Master Cylinder Push Rod***

**2)** Measure clearance between power brake unit push rod and adjusting gauge pin head. Perform STEP 2. *See Fig. 3.* Measured clearance should be zero. If measured clearance is not zero, adjust power brake unit push rod length until push rod lightly touches adjusting gauge pin head.

### BRAKE PEDAL HEIGHT

**1)** Brake pedal height is measured from face of brake pedal pad to asphalt sheet under carpet. *See Fig. 4.* On Cressida, brake pedal height should be 6.18-6.57" (157.0-167.0 mm). On Supra, brake pedal height should be 5.96-6.36" (151.4-161.5 mm).

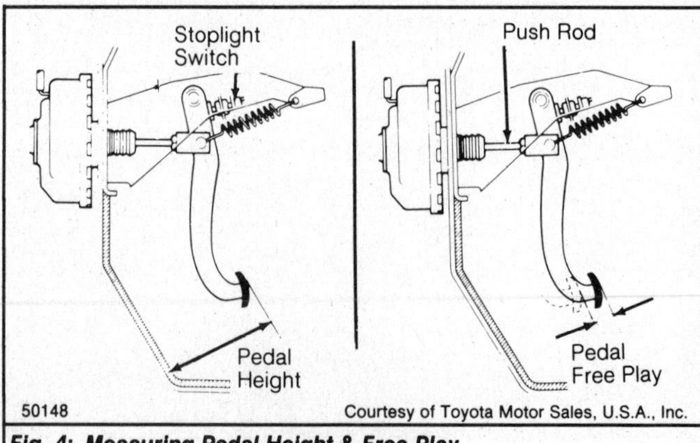


***Fig. 4: Measuring Pedal Height & Free Play***

# 1991 BRAKES
# Anti-Lock – Cressida & Supra (Cont.)

**2)** To adjust brake pedal height, remove instrument lower finish panel and air duct (if necessary). Disconnect stoplight switch connector. Loosen stoplight switch lock nut. Remove stoplight switch.
**3)** Adjust pedal height by turning push rod. After adjusting brake pedal height, tighten push rod lock nut. Install and adjust stoplight switch. See STOPLIGHT SWITCH under ADJUSTMENTS. Check and adjust brake pedal free play. See BRAKE PEDAL FREE PLAY.

## BRAKE PEDAL FREE PLAY

**1)** Brake pedal free play is distance brake pedal travels before feeling resistance with engine stopped. To check brake pedal free play, depress brake pedal several times to exhaust vacuum from power brake unit. Depress brake pedal and measure travel until initial resistance is felt.
**2)** Brake pedal free play should be .12-.24" (3.0-6.0 mm). If free play is not within specification, adjust by turning push rod. *See Fig. 4*. After adjusting brake pedal free play, check brake pedal height. See BRAKE PEDAL HEIGHT.

## STOPLIGHT SWITCH

**Cressida – 1)** Stoplight switch is located above brake pedal. *See Fig. 4*. To adjust stoplight switch, loosen stoplight switch lock nuts and turn stoplight switch until it touches brake pedal stop.
**2)** Turn switch counterclockwise one turn. Check clearance "A" between stoplight switch and brake pedal. *See Fig. 5*. Clearance "A" should be .02-.09" (.5-2.3 mm). Tighten stoplight switch lock nut. Check stoplight operation.

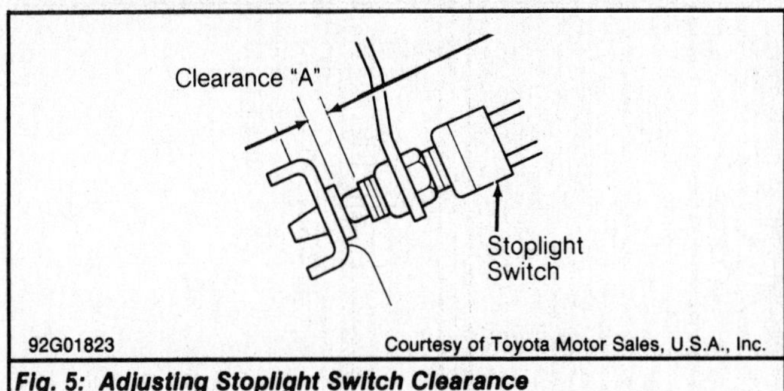


***Fig. 5: Adjusting Stoplight Switch Clearance***

**Supra –** Stoplight switch is located above brake pedal. *See Fig. 4*. To adjust stoplight switch, loosen stoplight switch lock nuts and turn stoplight switch until it touches brake pedal stop. Tighten lock nut. Check stoplight operation.

## BRAKE PEDAL DEPRESSED HEIGHT

**1)** Brake pedal depressed height is measured from face of brake pedal pad to asphalt sheet under carpet with brakes applied. Measure brake pedal depressed height with engine running and weight of 110 lbs. (50 kg) applied against brake pedal.
**2)** On Cressida, minimum brake pedal depressed height should be 3.03" (77.0 mm). On Supra, minimum brake pedal depressed height should be 3.15" (80.0 mm). On all models, if measured distance is less than minimum height, inspect brake system.

## REAR DISC PARKING BRAKE SHOES

Raise and support vehicle. Remove wheels. Temporarily install hub nuts to hold disc brake rotor in place. Remove hole plug to gain access to parking brake shoe adjuster. Turn adjuster to expand shoes until disc brake rotor locks. Return adjuster 8 notches. Install hole plug.

## PARKING BRAKE CABLE

***NOTE: Parking brake shoe clearance on rear disc brakes must be adjusted before adjusting parking brake cable.***

**Cressida –** Parking brake lever stroke should be 5-8 notches (clicks) with a pull force of 44 lbs. (20 kg). To adjust, loosen lock nut and adjust the adjuster or pull rod until parking brake lever stroke is correct. *See Fig. 6*.

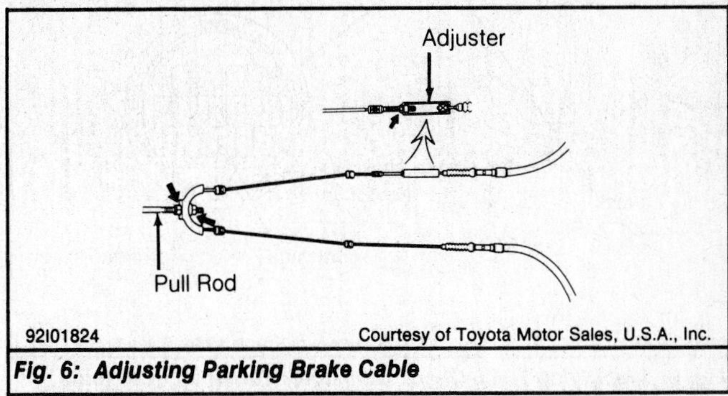


***Fig. 6: Adjusting Parking Brake Cable***

**Supra –** Parking brake lever stroke should be 5-8 notches (clicks) with a pull force of 44 lbs. (20 kg). To adjust, remove console box. Loosen parking brake cable lock nut and turn adjusting nut until parking brake lever travel is correct. Tighten lock nut. Install console box.

# TROUBLE SHOOTING

## SYMPTOM DIAGNOSTICS

**ABS Light Illuminates – 1)** Disconnect actuator check connector. *See Fig. 7 or 8*. On Cressida, using a jumper wire, connect Toyota Diagnostic Communication Link (TDCL) check connector terminals Tc and $E_1$. *See Fig. 9*. On all models, turn ignition on. If ABS light blinks codes or illuminates constantly, see DIAGNOSTIC CODES under DIAGNOSIS & TESTING. If ABS light does not illuminate, go to next step.

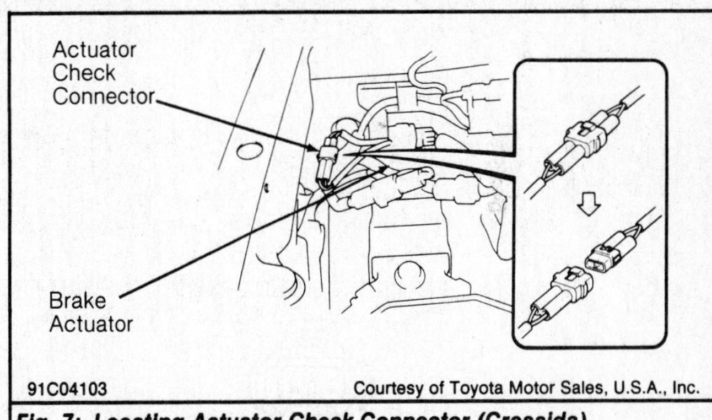


***Fig. 7: Locating Actuator Check Connector (Cressida)***

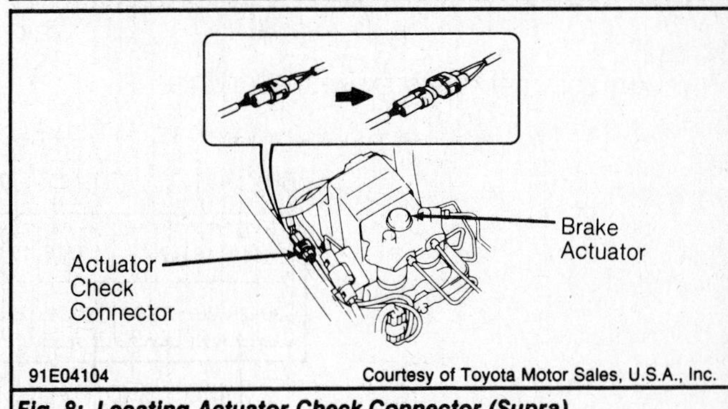


***Fig. 8: Locating Actuator Check Connector (Supra)***

# 1991 BRAKES
## Anti-Lock – Cressida & Supra (Cont.)

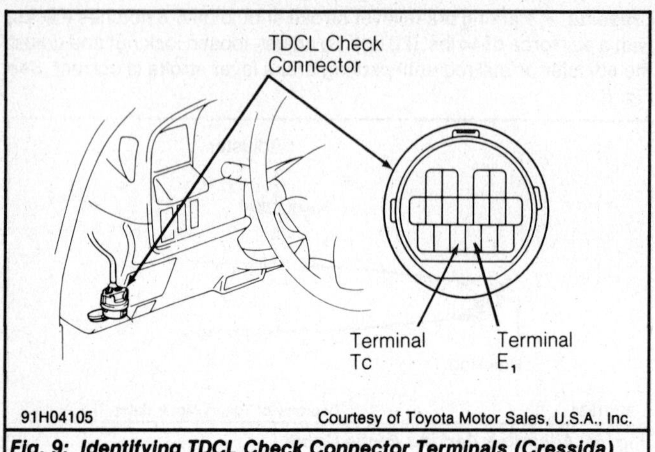


***Fig. 9: Identifying TDCL Check Connector Terminals (Cressida)***

**2)** Ensure front axle hub is serrated. If front axle hub is not serrated, replace faulty front axle hub. If front axle hub is serrated, ensure ABS computer connector is properly connected and connector terminals are not damaged. Repair connector as necessary.

**3)** Turn ignition on. Using a voltmeter, check for 10-16 volts between ABS computer connector terminal No. 19 (Pink wire on Cressida, Black/Red wire on Supra) and ground. *See Fig. 10 or 11*. If 10-16 volts is not present, repair faulty circuit. If 10-16 volts is present, go to next step.

**4)** Turn ignition off. Disconnect ABS computer connector and brake actuator connectors. Turn ignition on. If ABS light illuminates, repair short circuit between terminal No. 6 of actuator connector "A" and terminal No. 17 of ABS computer connector. *See Fig. 10 or 11*. If ABS light does not illuminate, replace faulty ABS computer.

**ABS Light Does Not Illuminate For 3 Seconds After Ignition Is Turned On – 1)** Disconnect actuator check connector. *See Fig. 7 or 8*. Using a jumper wire, ground check connector terminal "W" on harness side. *See Fig. 10 or 11*. Turn ignition on. If ABS light does not illuminate, replace faulty ABS light bulb or repair open circuit between ABS light and actuator check connector terminal "W". If ABS light illuminates, go to next step.

**2)** Turn ignition off. Disconnect ABS computer connector and actuator connectors. Using a jumper wire, ground ABS computer connector terminal No. 17 *See Fig. 10 or 11*. Turn ignition on. ABS light should illuminate. If ABS light does not illuminate, repair open circuit in wiring harness between ABS computer terminal No. 17 and ABS light. If ABS light illuminates, go to next step.

**3)** Turn ignition off. Ensure actuator connectors are disconnected. Using ohmmeter, ensure continuity is present between terminal No. 6 of actuator connector "A" and terminal No. 2 of actuator connector "B". *See Fig. 10 or 11*. Reverse ohmmeter leads between terminals and recheck continuity.

**4)** If continuity between actuator connectors is present in both directions, repair short circuit in actuator diode. If continuity between actuator connectors is only present in one direction, replace faulty ABS computer.

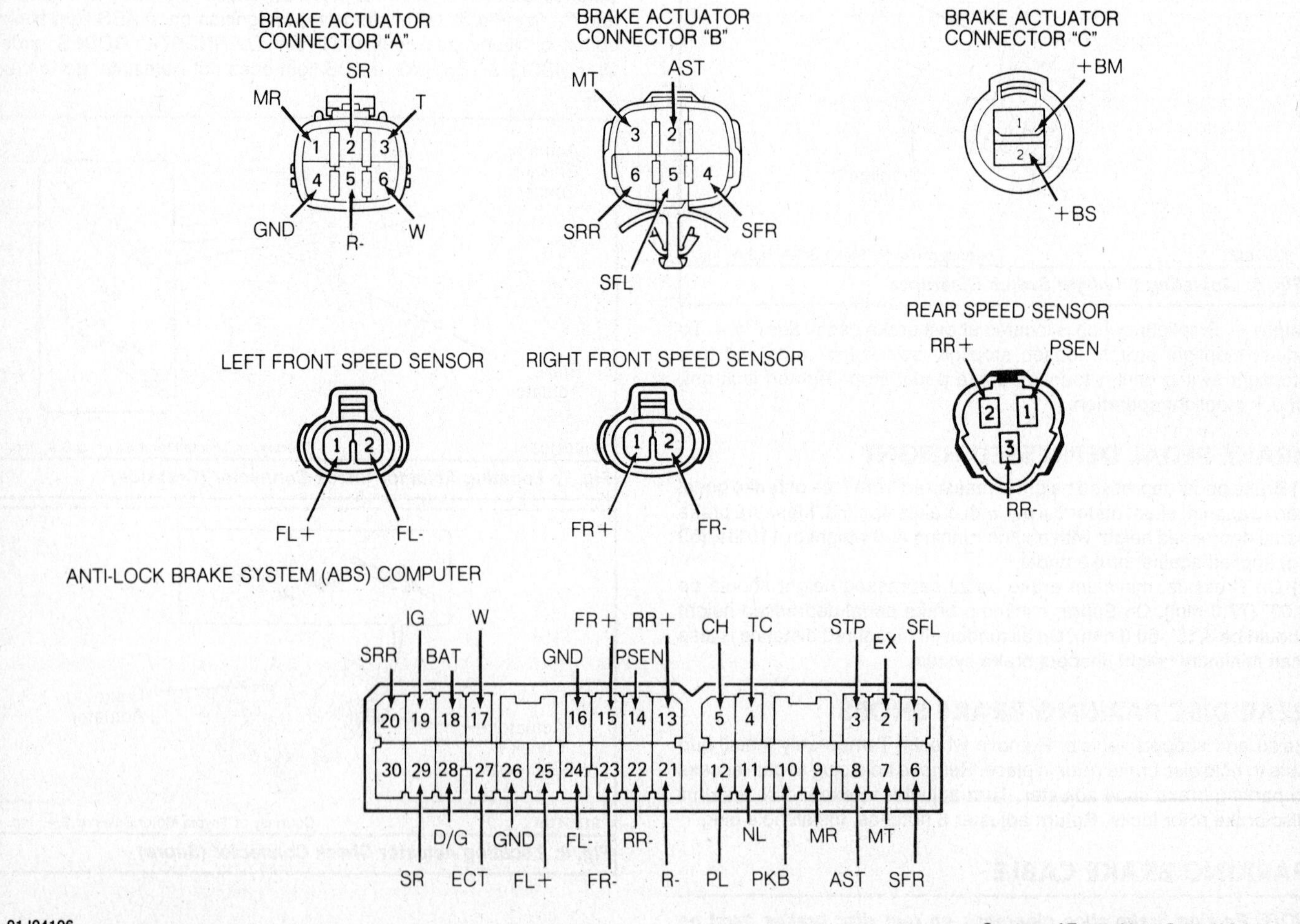

91J04106

Courtesy of Toyota Motor Sales, U.S.A., Inc.

***Fig. 10: Identifying ABS System Connector Terminals (Cressida)***

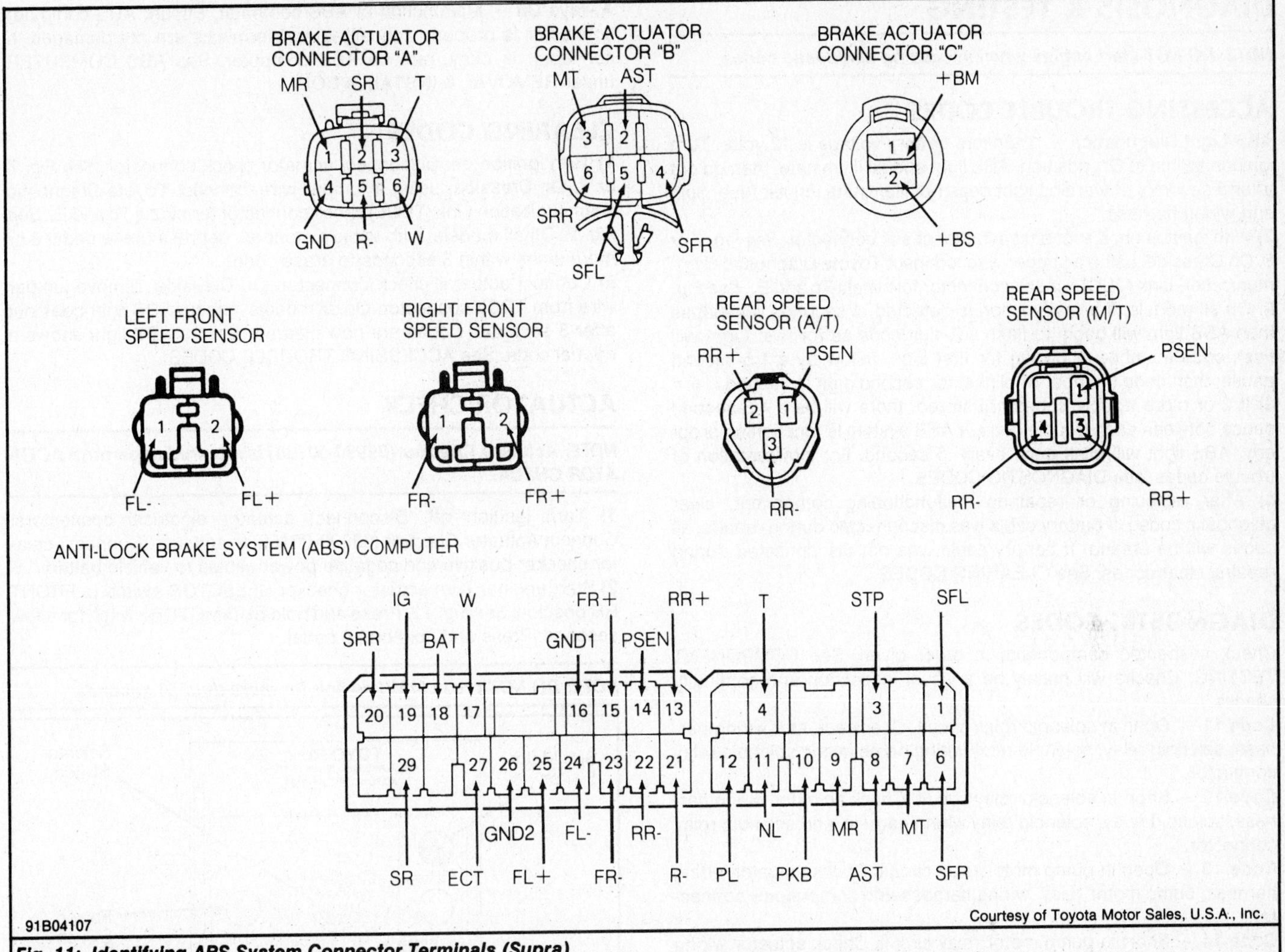


***Fig. 11: Identifying ABS System Connector Terminals (Supra)***

**5)** Connect ABS computer connector. Ensure actuator connectors are disconnected. Turn ignition on. ABS light should illuminate. If ABS light illuminates, ABS computer connector terminal No. 17 is okay.

**ABS Light Illuminates Intermittently – 1)** On Cressida, check for short circuit between TDCL check connector terminals Tc and $E_1$. *See Fig. 9.*

**2)** On Supra, ensure actuator check connector is not disconnected. *See Fig. 8.* Check for open circuit between terminal No. 4 of ABS computer and terminal No. 3 of actuator connector "A". *See Fig. 11.* Check for open circuit in wiring harness of actuator connector "A" terminal No. 4, or check for actuator not grounded to vehicle body.

**Brakes Pull, Braking Inefficient, ABS Operates With Ordinary Braking, ABS Operates Just Before Stopping With Ordinary Braking & Brake Pedal Pulsates Abnormally With ABS Functioning – 1)** Disconnect actuator check connector. *See Fig. 7 or 8.* On Cressida, using a jumper wire, connect Toyota Diagnostic Communication Link (TDCL) check connector terminals Tc and $E_1$. *See Fig. 9.* On all models, turn ignition on. ABS light should blink a normal code. If ABS light does not blink a normal code, refer to DIAGNOSTIC CODES under DIAGNOSIS & TESTING. If ABS light blinks a normal code, go to next step.

**2)** Ensure all speed sensors are properly installed. If speed sensors are not properly installed, repair as necessary. Turn ignition off. Disconnect ABS computer connector. Ensure continuity is present between each speed sensor connector (wire harness side) of ABS computer connector.

**3)** Check continuity between FL+ and FL– (left front speed sensor), FR+ and FR– (right front speed sensor), RL+ and RL– (left rear speed sensor), and RR+ and RR– (right rear speed sensor).

**4)** If continuity readings change when wiring harness is twisted or moved, repair faulty circuit between speed sensor and ABS computer connector. If continuity readings do not change, go to next step.

**5)** Ensure all foreign and metal chips are cleaned from speed sensor tip. On Cressida, enter speed sensor diagnostics. See SPEED SENSOR DIAGNOSTICS (CRESSIDA) under DIAGNOSIS & TESTING. If speed sensor signal level is okay, go to next step. If speed sensor signal level is not okay, inspect sensor and sensor rotor. Replace as necessary. On Supra, inspect front and rear sensor rotor serrations. See SENSOR ROTORS under COMPONENT TESTING.

**6)** On all models, check actuator operation. See ACTUATOR CHECK under DIAGNOSIS & TESTING. On Cressida, if actuator operation is okay, replace faulty ABS computer. See ABS COMPUTER under REMOVAL & INSTALLATION. On Supra, if actuator operation is okay, replace faulty speed sensor for a faulty inner magnet. On all models, if actuator operation is not okay, replace faulty actuator.

**ABS Works Inefficiently – 1)** Disconnect actuator check connector. *See Fig. 7 or 8.* On Cressida, using a jumper wire, connect Toyota Diagnostic Communication Link (TDCL) check connector terminals Tc and $E_1$. *See Fig. 9.* On all models, turn ignition on. ABS light should blink a normal code. If ABS light does not blink a normal code, refer to DIAGNOSTIC CODES under DIAGNOSIS & TESTING. If ABS light blinks a normal code, go to next step.

**2)** Ensure battery voltage is present between ABS computer terminal No. 3 and ground when brake pedal is depressed. If battery voltage is not present when brake pedal is depressed, repair open circuit in stoplight switch or wiring harness. Check actuator operation. See ACTUATOR CHECK under DIAGNOSIS & TESTING.

# 1991 BRAKES
# Anti-Lock – Cressida & Supra (Cont.)

## DIAGNOSIS & TESTING

*NOTE: DO NOT start engine when accessing diagnostic codes.*

### ACCESSING TROUBLE CODES

**ABS Light Diagnostics** – **1)** Ensure battery voltage is 12 volts. Turn ignition switch to ON position. ABS light should illuminate, then go out after 3 seconds. If warning light does not illuminate, check fuse, bulb and wiring harness.

**2)** With ignition on, disconnect actuator check connector. *See Fig. 7 or 8*. On Cressida, using a jumper wire, connect Toyota Diagnostic Communication Link (TDCL) check connector terminals Tc and $E_1$. *See Fig. 9*. On all models, if a malfunction is detected, 4 seconds will elapse then ABS light will begin to flash a 2-digit code as follows. Light will flash code (number of blinks) for first digit, follow by a 1.5-second pause, then code (number of blinks) for second digit is flashed.

**3)** If 2 or more trouble codes are stored, there will be a 4.5-second pause between each trouble code. If ABS system is functioning properly, ABS light will blink once every .5 second. For interpretation of trouble codes, see DIAGNOSTIC CODES.

**4)** After replacing or repairing malfunctioning component, clear diagnostic codes. If battery cable was disconnected during repairs, all codes will be erased. If battery cable was not disconnected during repairs, clear codes. See CLEARING CODES.

### DIAGNOSTIC CODES

Check suspected components in order given. See COMPONENT TESTING. Checks will mainly be a visual inspection and continuity checks.

**Code 11** – Open in solenoid relay circuit. Check actuator wiring harness, solenoid relay, solenoid relay wiring harness and solenoid relay connector.

**Code 12** – Short in solenoid relay circuit. Check actuator wiring harness, solenoid relay, solenoid relay wiring harness and solenoid relay connector.

**Code 13** – Open in pump motor relay circuit. Check actuator wiring harness, pump motor relay, wiring harness and pump motor connector.

**Code 14** – Short in pump motor relay circuit. Check actuator wiring harness, pump motor relay, wiring harness, and pump motor connector.

**Code 21** – Open or short circuit in 3-position solenoid for right front wheel. Check 3-position actuator solenoid, wiring harness and connector.

**Code 22** – Open or short circuit in 3-position solenoid for left front wheel. Check 3-position actuator solenoid, wiring harness and connector.

**Code 23** – Open or short circuit in 3-position solenoid for rear wheels. Check 3-position actuator solenoid, wiring harness and connector.

**Code 31** – Malfunction of right front wheel speed sensor signal. Check speed sensor, sensor rotor, wiring harness and connector.

**Code 32** – Malfunction of left front wheel speed sensor signal. Check speed sensor, sensor rotor, wiring harness and connector.

**Code 33** – Malfunction of rear wheels speed sensor signal. Check speed sensor, sensor rotor, wiring harness and connector.

**Code 34 (Supra)** – Open in front wheel speed sensor circuit. Check speed sensor, sensor rotor, wiring harness and connector.

**Code 35 (Cressida)** – Open in front wheel speed sensor circuit. Check speed sensor, sensor rotor, wiring harness and connector.

**Code 37 (Cressida)** – Wrong front axle hubs on both sides. Check front sensor rotors.

**Code 41** – Battery voltage is 9.5 volts or less. Check battery and voltage regulator.

**Code 42** – Battery voltage is 17.2 volts or more. Check battery and voltage regulator.

**Code 51** – Actuator pump motor is locked or pump motor circuit open. Check pump motor, pump motor relay, vehicle battery, actuator wiring harness, connectors, actuator pump motor circuit and actuator ground bolt.

**Always On** – Malfunction of ABS computer. Ensure ABS computer connector is properly connected and terminals are not damaged. If connector is okay, replace ABS computer. See ABS COMPUTER under REMOVAL & INSTALLATION.

### CLEARING CODES

**1)** Turn ignition on. Disconnect actuator check connector. *See Fig. 7 or 8*. On Cressida, using a jumper wire, connect Toyota Diagnostic Communication Link (TDCL) check connector terminals Tc and $E_1$. *See Fig. 9*. On all models, with vehicle stopped, depress brake pedal 8 or more times within 3 seconds to erase codes.

**2)** Connect actuator check connector. On Cressida, remove jumper wire from TDCL connector. On all models, ensure ABS light goes out after 3 seconds. Codes are now cleared. Ensure ABS light shows a normal code. See ACCESSING TROUBLE CODES.

### ACTUATOR CHECK

***NOTE: Actuator Checker (09990-00150) is required to perform ACTUATOR CHECK.***

**1)** Turn ignition off. Disconnect actuator electrical connectors. Connect Actuator Checker (09990-00150) to actuator. Connect actuator checker positive and negative power cables to vehicle battery.

**2)** Start engine. Turn actuator checker SELECTOR switch to FRONT RH position. *See Fig. 12*. Press and hold SUB MOTOR switch for a few seconds. Press and hold brake pedal.

***NOTE: DO NOT press MAIN switch for more than 10 seconds.***

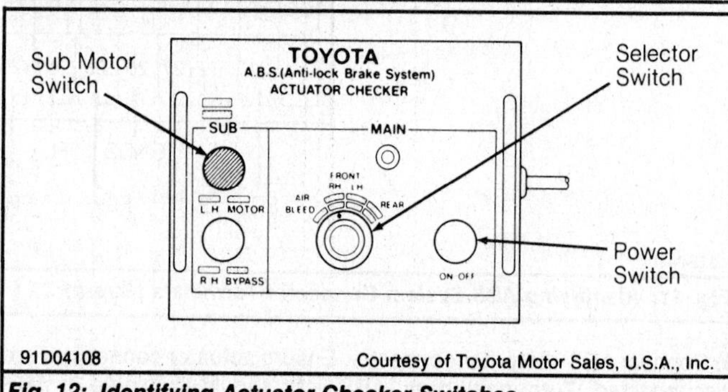


***Fig. 12: Identifying Actuator Checker Switches***

**3)** Press MAIN switch. When MAIN switch is pressed, brake pedal should not go down. Release MAIN switch. Brake pedal should lower (move down). Press and hold SUB MOTOR switch for a few seconds. Brake pedal should return. Release SUB MOTOR switch. Release brake pedal.

**4)** Press and hold SUB MOTOR switch for a few seconds. Release SUB MOTOR switch. Depress brake pedal and hold for approximately 15 seconds. While depressing brake pedal, press SUB MOTOR switch for a few seconds. Ensure brake pedal does not pulsate.

**5)** Repeat steps **2)** through **4)** for FRONT LH and REAR by turning SELECTOR switch on actuator checker. After checking remaining wheels, press and hold SUB MOTOR switch for a few seconds. Remove actuator checker. Connect actuator wiring harness to actuator. Clear diagnostic codes. See CLEARING CODES.

### SPEED SENSOR DIAGNOSTICS (CRESSIDA)

***NOTE: While diagnosing speed sensors, brake system functions as a conventional system.***

**1)** Ensure battery voltage is approximately 12 volts. Turn ignition on. Ensure ABS light illuminates then goes out after about 3 seconds. If ABS light does not illuminate, check fuse, bulb and wiring harness.

# 1991 BRAKES
# Anti-Lock – Cressida & Supra (Cont.)

**2)** Turn ignition off. Using a jumper wire, connect Toyota Diagnostic Communication Link (TDCL) check connector terminals Tc and $E_1$. *See Fig. 9.* Engage parking brake. Start engine. Press brake pedal 4-6 times within 2 seconds. ABS light should illuminate 4 times per second. Go to next step.

***NOTE: While ABS light is off, DO NOT accelerate, decelerate, brake, shift, move steering or drive on rough road surfaces, as these conditions will affect test.***

**3)** Drive vehicle straight ahead at 2.5-3.7 MPH. Ensure ABS light illuminates after a one-second pause. If ABS light illuminates without blinking when vehicle speed is NOT in the specified range, stop vehicle and record diagnostic codes. Turn ignition off. Repair as necessary. See SPEED SENSOR DIAGNOSTIC CODES (CRESSIDA).

**4)** If ABS light illuminates when vehicle speed is in the specified range, check is completed. If vehicle speed exceeds 3.7 MPH, ABS light will blink. If ABS light blinks when vehicle speed exceeds 3.7 MPH, speed sensors are okay.

**5)** Drive vehicle straight ahead at 28-34 MPH. Ensure ABS light illuminates after a one-second pause. If ABS light illuminates without blinking when vehicle speed is NOT in the specified speed, stop vehicle and record diagnostic codes. Turn ignition off. Repair as necessary. See SPEED SENSOR DIAGNOSTIC CODES (CRESSIDA).

**6)** If ABS light illuminates when vehicle speed is in the specified range, check is completed. If vehicle speed exceeds 34 MPH, ABS light will blink. If ABS light blinks when vehicle speed exceeds 34 MPH, sensor rotors are okay.

**7)** Turn ignition off. Remove jumper wire from TDCL check connector. Clear diagnostic codes. See CLEARING CODES.

## SPEED SENSOR DIAGNOSTIC CODES (CRESSIDA)

Code 71 – Low voltage in right front speed sensor signal. Check right front speed sensor and sensor installation.

**Code 72** – low voltage in left front speed sensor signal. Check left front speed sensor and sensor installation.

**Code 73** – Low voltage in rear speed sensor signal. Check rear speed sensor and sensor installation.

**Code 75** – Abnormal signal from right front speed sensor. Check right front sensor rotor.

**Code 76** – – Abnormal signal from left front speed sensor. Check left front sensor rotor.

**Code 77** – Abnormal signal from rear speed sensor. Check rear sensor rotor.

**Light Illuminates 4 Times Per Second** – All speed sensors and sensor rotors are normal.

## COMPONENT TESTING

**Front Speed Sensor – 1)** Remove front wheel speed sensor from vehicle. See FRONT WHEEL SPEED SENSORS under REMOVAL & INSTALLATION. Using a DVOM, measure resistance between speed sensor terminals. On Cressida, resistance should be 1200-1600 ohms. On Supra, resistance should be 800-1300 ohms.

**2)** On all models, ensure continuity is NOT present between each sensor terminal and sensor body. If resistance and continuity readings are NOT as specified, replace speed sensor.

**Rear Speed Sensor – 1)** Disconnect rear wheel speed sensor connector. Check for continuity between sensor terminal and sensor body. If continuity is present, replace rear speed sensor. If continuity is not present, remove rear wheel speed sensor from vehicle. See REAR WHEEL SPEED SENSOR under REMOVAL & INSTALLATION.

**2)** Connect positive voltmeter lead to rear sensor terminal RR+. Connect negative voltmeter lead to rear sensor terminal RR–. *See Fig. 13.* Connect positive battery terminal to rear sensor terminal PSEN. Connect negative battery terminal to rear sensor terminal RR–. Connect a 2000-10,000 ohm resistor between rear speed sensor terminal RR+ and battery positive terminal.

***CAUTION: Cover shaft of screwdriver with a rag to prevent chipping sensor tip.***

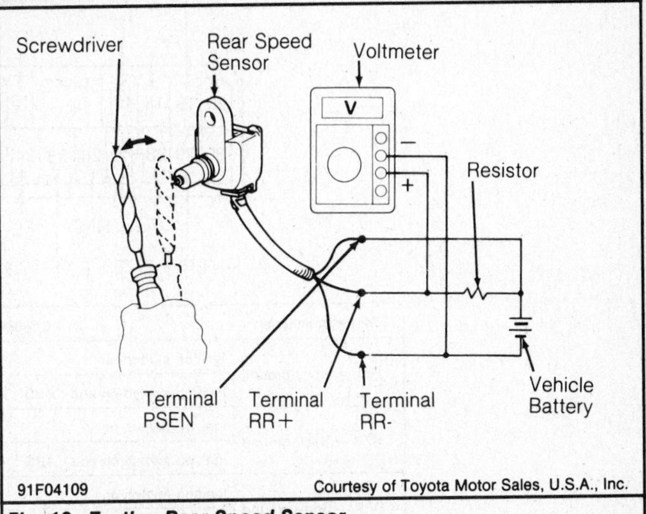


***Fig. 13: Testing Rear Speed Sensor***

**3)** Cover shaft of screwdriver with a rag. Wave screwdriver past tip of speed sensor. As screwdriver is waved in front of sensor tip, voltage should alternate between less than 2 volts and more than 2 volts (up to 12 volts maximum).

**4)** If voltage changes but stays above 2 volts, replace rear speed sensor. If voltage remains less than 2 volts or if voltage is more than 12 volts, replace rear speed sensor.

**Pump Motor Relay Continuity – 1)** Remove pump motor relay from actuator. *See Fig. 14.* See SOLENOID & PUMP MOTOR RELAYS under REMOVAL & INSTALLATION. Using a DVOM, check continuity between pump motor relay terminals No. 1 and 2. *See Fig. 15.* Ensure continuity is present.

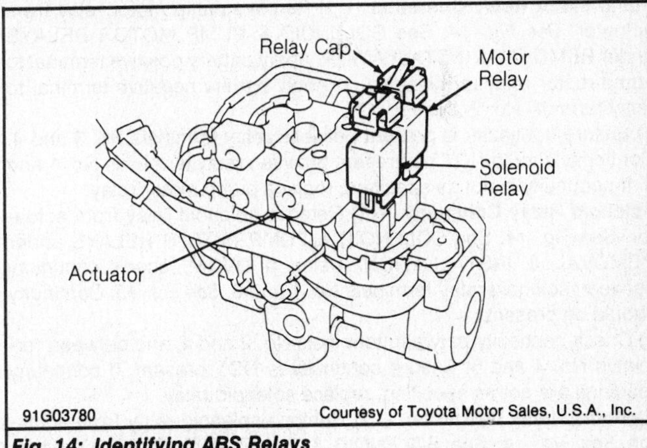


***Fig. 14: Identifying ABS Relays***

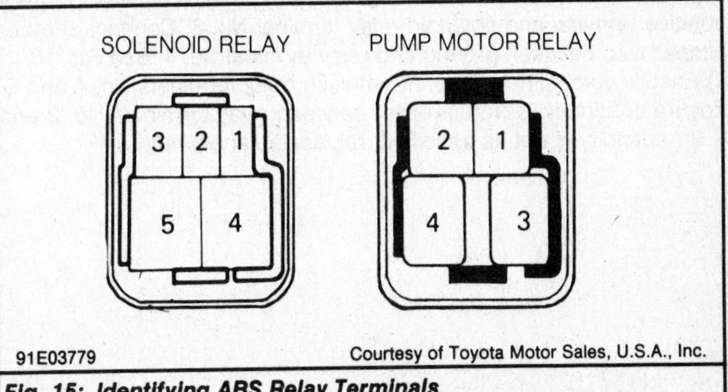


***Fig. 15: Identifying ABS Relay Terminals***

# 1991 BRAKES
# Anti-Lock – Cressida & Supra (Cont.)

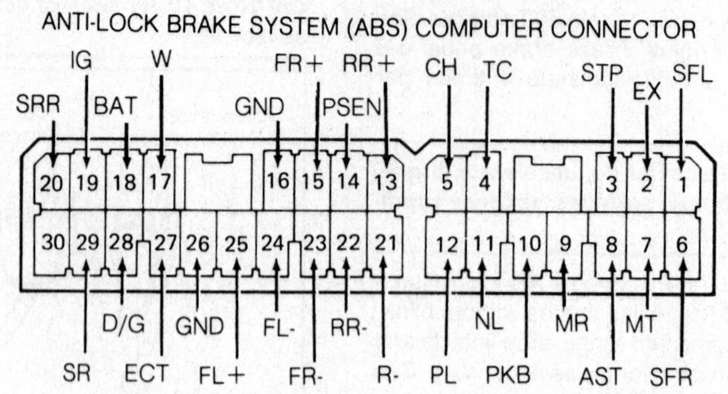


| Tester Connection | Condition | Voltage | Trouble Part |
|---|---|---|---|
| SFL – Body ground | Ignition switch on | Battery voltage | Actuator, control relays |
| | Ignition switch on and "ABS" warning light goes on | About 0 V | |
| SFR – Body ground | Ignition switch on | Battery voltage | |
| | Ignition switch on and "ABS" warning light goes on | About 0 V | |
| SRR – Body ground | Ignition switch on | Battery voltage | |
| | Ignition switch on and "ABS" warning light goes on | About 0 V | |
| AST – Body ground | Ignition switch on | Battery voltage | |
| | Ignition switch on and "ABS" warning light goes on | About 0 V | |
| W – Body ground | Ignition switch on | Battery voltage | "ABS" warning light bulb |
| | Ignition switch on and "ABS" warning light goes on | About 0 V | |

92B01825

Courtesy of Toyota Motor Sales, U.S.A., Inc.

***Fig. 16: Testing Specifications Table for ABS Computer Wiring Harness (Cressida – 1 of 2)***

**2)** Check continuity between terminals No. 3 and 4, and between terminals No. 1 and 4. Ensure continuity is NOT present. If continuity readings are not as specified, replace pump motor relay.

**Pump Motor Relay Operation – 1)** Remove pump motor relay from actuator. *See Fig. 14*. See SOLENOID & PUMP MOTOR RELAYS under REMOVAL & INSTALLATION. Apply battery positive terminal to pump motor relay terminal No. 1. Apply battery negative terminal to relay terminal No. 2. *See Fig. 11*.

**2)** Ensure continuity is present between relay terminals No. 3 and 4. Continuity should NOT be present between relay terminals No. 1 and 4. If continuity is not as specified, replace pump motor relay.

**Solenoid Relay Continuity – 1)** Remove solenoid relay from actuator. *See Fig. 14*. See SOLENOID & PUMP MOTOR RELAYS under REMOVAL & INSTALLATION. Using a DVOM, check continuity between solenoid relay terminals No. 1 and 3. *See Fig. 15*. Continuity should be present.

**2)** Check continuity between terminals No. 2 and 4, and between terminals No. 4 and 5. Ensure continuity is NOT present. If continuity readings are not as specified, replace solenoid relay.

**Solenoid Relay Operation – 1)** Remove solenoid relay from actuator. *See Fig. 14*. See SOLENOID & PUMP MOTOR RELAY under REMOVAL & INSTALLATION. Connect jumper wire between battery positive terminal and solenoid relay terminal No. 3. Connect another jumper wire between ground and relay terminal No. 1. *See Fig. 15*.

**2)** Ensure continuity is present between relay terminals No. 4 and 5. Ensure continuity is NOT present between relay terminals No. 2 and 4. If continuity is not as specified, replace solenoid relay.

**Sensor Rotors (Front)** – Remove front wheel assembly. Visually inspect sensor rotor serrations for scratches, cracks, missing teeth and warping. If sensor rotor is damaged, replace front axle hub. On Supra, measure rotor serrations at .08" (2 mm) from serration edge. Maximum fluctuation allowed, measured at top of 3 consecutive serrations, is .004" (.1 mm). If runout is more than maximum allowed, replace front axle hub.

**Sensor Rotors (Rear)** – Remove transmission extension housing to access rear sensor rotor. See SENSOR ROTOR under REMOVAL & INSTALLATION. On Supra with M/T, rear sensor rotor is the reverse gear inside transmission. On all models, visually inspect sensor rotor serrations for scratches, cracks, missing teeth and warping. If sensor rotor is damaged, replace sensor rotor.

**ABS Computer Wiring Harness (Cressida) – 1)** Remove ABS computer cover. Remove ABS computer. See ABS COMPUTER under REMOVAL & INSTALLATION. With ABS computer connector connected, backprobe ABS computer connector terminals. Measure voltage at each terminal as specified in table. *See Fig. 16*. If circuit(s) do not test as specified, check and repair or replace trouble part shown in table.

**2)** Disconnect ABS computer connectors. Check resistance and voltage on wire harness side of ABS computer connector terminals as specified in table. *See Fig. 17*. If circuit(s) do not test as specified, check and repair or replace troubled part shown in table.

**ABS Computer Wiring Harness (Supra)** – Remove ABS computer. See ABS COMPUTER under REMOVAL & INSTALLATION. With ABS computer connector connected, backprobe connector terminals. Check voltage or resistance at ABS computer harness connector terminals referring to tables. *See Figs. 18 and 19*.

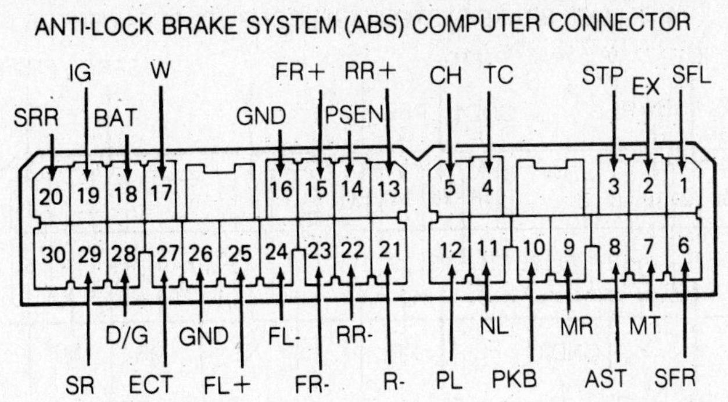


| Tester Connection | Check Item | Condition | Voltage or Resistance Value | Trouble Part |
|---|---|---|---|---|
| SFR – AST | Resistance | Ignition switch off | About 6 Ω | Actuator |
| STP – Body ground | Voltage | Ignition switch off and brake pedal depressed | Battery voltage | Stop light switch, stop light |
| | Continuity | Ignition switch off and brake pedal returned | Continuity | |
| PKB – Body ground | Voltage | Ignition switch on and PKB lever pulled | About 0 V | Parking brake switch, level warning switch |
| | | Ignition switch on and PKB lever returned | Battery voltage | |
| SRR – AST | Resistance | Ignition switch off | About 6 Ω | Actuator |
| MT – Body ground | Continuity | Ignition switch off | Continuity | |
| SR – R ⊖ | Resistance | Ignition switch off | 65 – 100 Ω | |
| MR – R ⊖ | Resistance | Ignition switch off | 50 – 80 Ω | |
| AST – Body ground | Resistance | Ignition switch off | About 5 Ω | Wiring harness |
| RR ⊖ – Body ground | Continuity | Ignition switch off | No continuity | Rear speed sensor |
| Tc – Body ground | Continuity | Ignition switch off | No continuity | Check TDCL connector wiring harness |
| GND – Body ground | Continuity | Ignition switch off | Continuity | Wiring harness |
| BAT – Body ground | Voltage | | Battery voltage | FOG fuse |
| IG – Body ground | Voltage | Ignition switch on | Battery voltage | ECU-IG fuse |
| SFL – AST | Resistance | Ignition switch off | About 6 Ω | Actuator |
| R ⊖ – Body ground | Continuity | Ignition switch off | No continuity | Wiring harness |
| FR ⊖ – Body ground | Continuity | | No continuity | Front RH speed sensor |
| FR ⊕ – FR ⊖ | Resistance | | 1.2 – 1.6 kΩ | |
| FL ⊖ – Body ground | Continuity | | No continuity | Front LH speed sensor |
| FL ⊕ – FL ⊖ | Resistance | Ignition switch off | 1.2 – 1.6 kΩ | |

92D01826

Courtesy of Toyota Motor Sales, U.S.A., Inc.

*Fig. 17: Testing Specifications Table for ABS Computer Wiring Harness (Cressida – 2 of 2)*

# 1991 BRAKES
# Anti-Lock – Cressida & Supra (Cont.)

ANTI-LOCK BRAKE SYSTEM (ABS) COMPUTER CONNECTOR

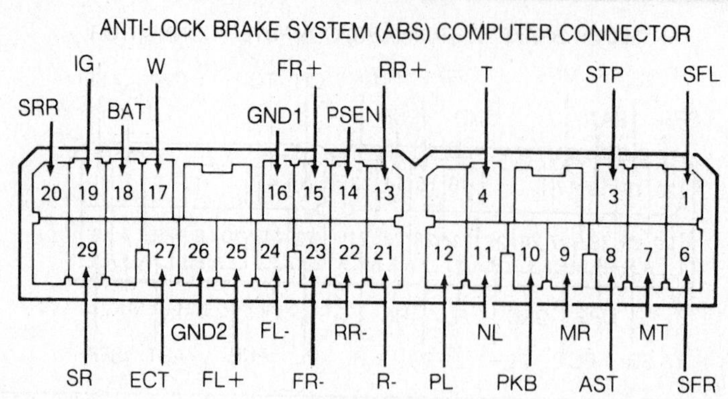


| Tester Connection | Condition | Voltage |
|---|---|---|
| SFL – Body ground | Ignition switch on | Battery voltage |
| | Ignition switch on and "ABS" warning light goes on | About 0 V |
| SFR – Body ground | Ignition switch on | Battery voltage |
| | Ignition switch on and "ABS" warning light goes on | About 0 V |
| AST – Body ground | Ignition switch on | Battery voltage |
| | Ignition switch on and "ABS" warning light goes on | About 0 V |
| PESN – Body ground | Ignition switch on | Battery voltage |
| W – Body ground | Ignition switch on | Battery voltage |
| | Ignition switch on and "ABS" warning light goes on | About 0 V |
| SRR – Body ground | Ignition switch on | Battery voltage |
| | Ignition switch on and "ABS" warning light goes on | About 0 V |

92F01827

Courtesy of Toyota Motor Sales, U.S.A., Inc.

*Fig. 18: Testing Specifications Table for ABS Computer Wiring Harness (Supra – 1 of 2)*

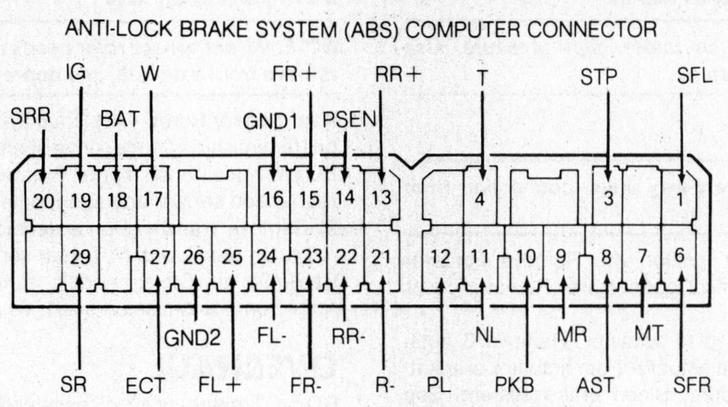


| Tester Connection | Check Item | Condition | Voltage or Resistance Value |
|---|---|---|---|
| SFL – AST | Resistance | Ignition switch off | About 1 Ω |
| STP – Body ground | Voltage | Ignition switch off and brake pedal depressed | Battery voltage |
| | Continuity | Ignition switch off and brake pedal returned | Continuity |
| T – Body ground | Continuity | Ignition switch off | Continuity |
| SFR – AST | Resistance | Ignition switch off | About 1 Ω |
| MT – Body ground | Continuity | Ignition switch off | Continuity |
| AST – Body ground | Continuity | Ignition switch off | Continuity |
| MR – R ⊖ | Resistance | Ignition switch off | 50 – 80 Ω |
| PKB – Body ground | Voltage | Ignition switch on and PKB lever pulled | About 0 V |
| | | Engine running and PKB lever returned | Battery voltage |
| NL – Body ground | Voltage | Ignition switch on and shift into "N" range | Battery voltage |
| PL – Body ground | Voltage | Ignition switch on and shift into "P" range | Battery voltage |
| FR ⊕ – FR ⊖ | Resistance | Ignition switch off | 0.8 – 1.3 kΩ |
| GND1 – Body ground | Continuity | Ignition switch off | Continuity |
| BAT – Body ground | Voltage | – | Battery voltage |
| IG – Body ground | Voltage | Ignition switch on | Battery voltage |
| SRR – AST | Resistance | Ignition switch off | About 1 Ω |
| R ⊖ – Body ground | Continuity | Ignition switch off | No continuity |
| RR ⊖ – Body ground | Continuity | Ignition switch off | No continuity |
| FR ⊖ – Body ground | Continuity | Ignition switch off | No continuity |
| FL ⊖ – Body ground | Continuity | Ignition switch off | No continuity |
| FL ⊕ – FL ⊖ | Resistance | Ignition switch off | 0.8 – 1.3 kΩ |
| GND2 – Body ground | Continuity | Ignition switch off | Continuity |
| ECT – Body ground | Voltage | Ignition switch on and shift into "N" or "P" range | About 5 V |
| SR – R ⊖ | Resistance | Ignition switch off | 65 – 100 Ω |

92H01828

Courtesy of Toyota Motor Sales, U.S.A., Inc.

*Fig. 19: Testing Specifications Table for ABS Computer Wiring Harness (Supra – 2 of 2)*

# 1991 BRAKES
# Anti-Lock – Cressida & Supra (Cont.)

## REMOVAL & INSTALLATION

***WARNING:** Hydraulic system may be under high pressure. Use caution when opening hydraulic system.*

## ACTUATOR

***NOTE:** If replacing actuator, remove 2-way union connection from actuator.*

**Removal & Installation – 1)** Turn ignition off. Remove actuator cover. Disconnect 3 actuator electrical connectors. Remove cover bracket and stud bolt.
**2)** Disconnect 5 brake lines attached to actuator. Remove 3 nuts, washers and wave washers. Remove actuator from actuator bracket. To install, reverse removal procedure. Bleed brake system. See BLEEDING BRAKE SYSTEM.

## ABS COMPUTER

**Removal & Installation – 1)** Ensure ignition is off. Disconnect negative battery cable. On Cressida, access ABS computer in right side of luggage compartment. On Supra, access ABS computer in right side of dashboard, above glove box.
**2)** On all models, remove ABS computer-to-vehicle screws. Remove wire harness from computer bracket clamp. Disconnect ABS computer connector. Remove ABS computer from vehicle. To install, reverse removal procedure.

## FRONT WHEEL SPEED SENSORS

**Removal & Installation – 1)** Loosen front wheel lug nuts. Raise and support front of vehicle. Remove front wheel. Remove wheel speed sensor mounting bolt.
**2)** Disconnect wheel speed sensor connector. Remove wheel speed sensor from vehicle. To install, reverse removal procedure. Tighten wheel speed sensor mounting bolt to specification. See TORQUE SPECIFICATIONS table at end of article.

## REAR WHEEL SPEED SENSOR

**Removal & Installation – 1)** Raise and support vehicle. Disconnect rear wheel speed sensor connector. Remove wheel speed sensor mounting bolt from transmission.
**2)** Remove wheel speed sensor. Install a new "O" ring onto speed sensor. To install, reverse removal procedure. Tighten wheel speed sensor mounting bolt to specification. See TORQUE SPECIFICATIONS table at end of article.

## SOLENOID & PUMP MOTOR RELAYS

**Removal & Installation –** Remove connector from wire harness clamp. Remove screw and wire harness clamp. Remove relay case. Remove relay cap from relays. Remove relays from actuator. *See Fig. 14.* To install, reverse removal procedure.

## SENSOR ROTOR

***NOTE:** If front sensor rotor needs replacing, install a new axle hub. To remove front axle hub, see appropriate SUSPENSION article.*

**Rear Sensor Rotor – 1)** Drain transmission fluid. Paint mating marks on transmission flange, drive shaft flange and center support bearing. DO NOT use punch marks. Remove drive shaft from vehicle. Remove rear speed sensor and speedometer cable from transmission.
**2)** Remove transmission extension housing to access rear sensor rotor. On Supra with M/T, rear sensor rotor is the reverse gear inside transmission. On all models, remove sensor rotor key and sensor rotor from transmission shaft. To install, reverse removal procedure.

## OVERHAUL

DO NOT overhaul or disassemble actuator assembly. If actuator is defective, replace entire assembly.

## TORQUE SPECIFICATIONS

***TORQUE SPECIFICATIONS***

| Application | Ft. Lbs. (N.m) |
|---|---|
| Brake Line Nuts | 11 (15) |
| Center Support Bearing Bolts | |
| Cressida | 27 (37) |
| Supra | 36 (49) |
| Drive Shaft Bolts | 54 (73) |
| Front Axle Nut | |
| Cressida | 108 (146) |
| Supra | 147 (199) |
| Front Disc Caliper Bolts | |
| Cressida | 67 (91) |
| Supra | 77 (104) |
| Front Wheel Speed Sensor Bolt | |
| Supra | 14 (19) |
| Rear Axle Nut | 203 (275) |
| Rear Disc Caliper Bolts | 34 (46) |
| Rear Speed Sensor Bolt | |
| A/T | 12 (16) |
| M/T | 21 (28) |
| Wheel Lug Nuts | 76 (103) |
| 2-Way Union Bolt | 12 (16) |
| | **INCH Lbs. (N.m)** |
| ABS Computer Mounting Screws | 28 (3) |
| Actuator Mounting Nuts | 48 (5) |
| Front Wheel Speed Sensor Bolt | |
| Cressida | 108 (12) |

# 1991 BRAKES
# Anti-Lock – Cressida & Supra (Cont.)

## WIRING DIAGRAMS

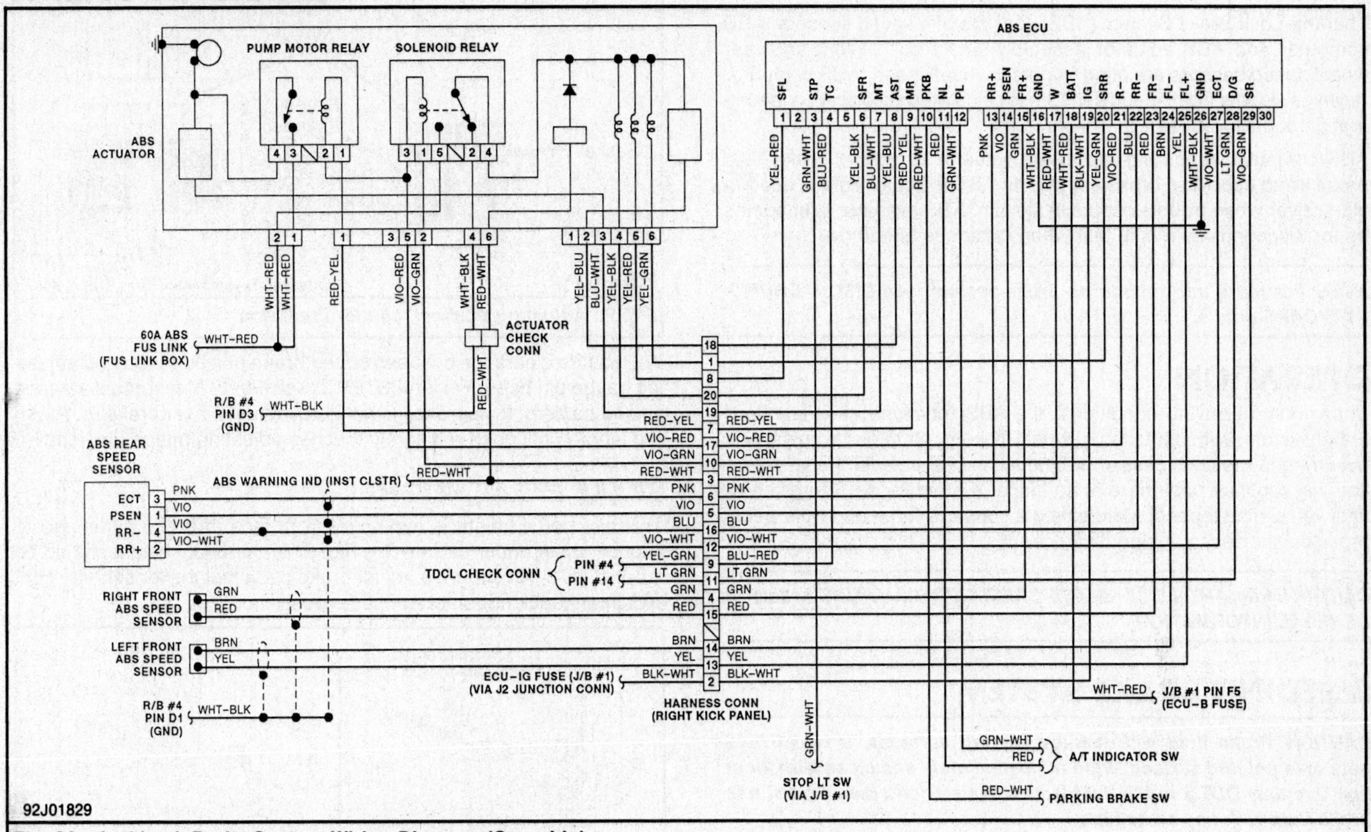

92J01829

*Fig. 20: Anti-Lock Brake System Wiring Diagram (Cressida)*

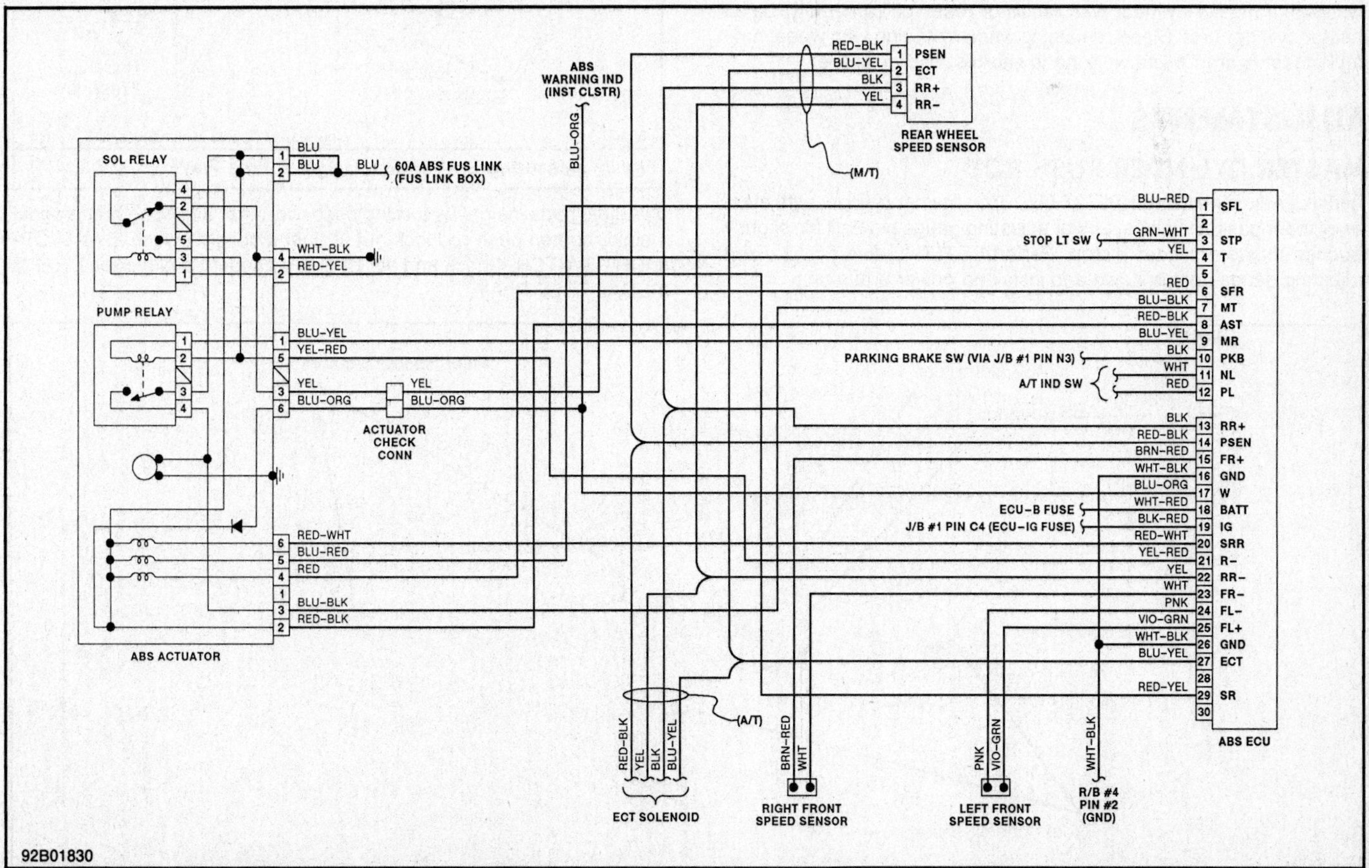

92B01830

*Fig. 21: Anti-Lock Brake System Wiring Diagram (Supra)*

# 1991 BRAKES
# Anti-Lock – MR2

## DESCRIPTION

The Anti-Lock Brake System (ABS) consists of 4 speed sensors, ABS computer and ABS actuator assembly. *See Fig. 1.* Front and rear wheel speed sensors are used to detect wheel speed. ABS computer receives signals from speed sensors to calculates acceleration, deceleration and slip values.

ABS computer sends signals to the actuator to control brake fluid pressure to each disc brake caliper. An ABS indicator light is used to alert driver when trouble occurs in system. ABS indicator light comes on for 3 seconds as a bulb test when ignition is turned on.

***NOTE: For more information on brake system, see DISC & DRUM – RWD CARS article.***

## OPERATION

Under normal driving conditions, the ABS functions as a standard brake system. With detection of wheel lock-up, short pedal pulsations occurring in rapid succession will be felt in brake pedal. Pedal pulsation will continue until there is no longer a need for ABS function or until vehicle is stopped. Maintaining a constant force on brake pedal provides shortest stopping distance.

***CAUTION: See ANTI-LOCK BRAKE SAFETY PRECAUTIONS article in GENERAL INFORMATION.***

## BLEEDING BRAKE SYSTEM

***CAUTION: Brake fluid will damage painted surfaces. If brake fluid gets on a painted surface, wipe off immediately and clean with alcohol. Use only DOT 3 brake fluid from a sealed container. Do not mix brake fluid with any other type.***

Brake bleeding procedure is same procedure used to bleed non-ABS systems. If master cylinder was rebuilt or reservoir ran empty, bleed master cylinder first. Bleed remaining wheels starting with wheel having longest hydraulic line working to shortest hydraulic line.

## ADJUSTMENTS

### MASTER CYLINDER PUSH ROD

**1)** Install Adjusting Gauge (09737-00010) on master cylinder with master cylinder gasket in place. Lower adjusting gauge pin until pin slightly touches master cylinder piston. Perform STEP 1. *See Fig. 2.* Turn adjusting gauge upside down and install on power brake unit.

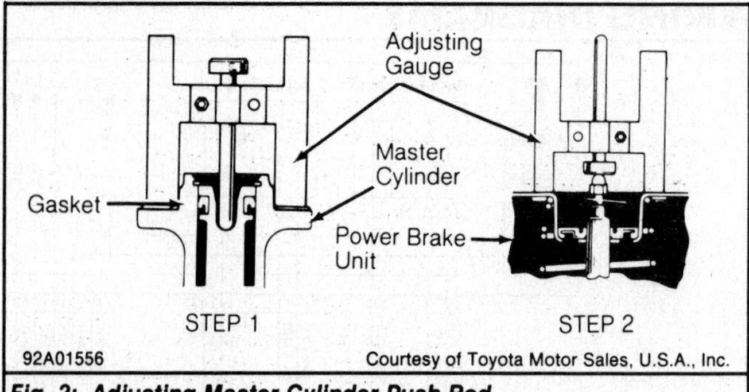


***Fig. 2: Adjusting Master Cylinder Push Rod***

**2)** Measure clearance between power brake unit push rod and adjusting gauge pin head. Perform STEP 2. *See Fig. 2.* Measured clearance should be zero. If clearance is not zero, adjust power brake unit push rod length until push rod lightly touches adjusting gauge pin head.

### BRAKE PEDAL HEIGHT

**1)** Brake pedal height is measured from face of brake pedal pad to asphalt sheet under carpet. *See Fig. 3.* Brake pedal height should be 7.0-7.4" (178-187 mm). To adjust brake pedal height, loosen stoplight switch and lock nut on brake pedal push rod.

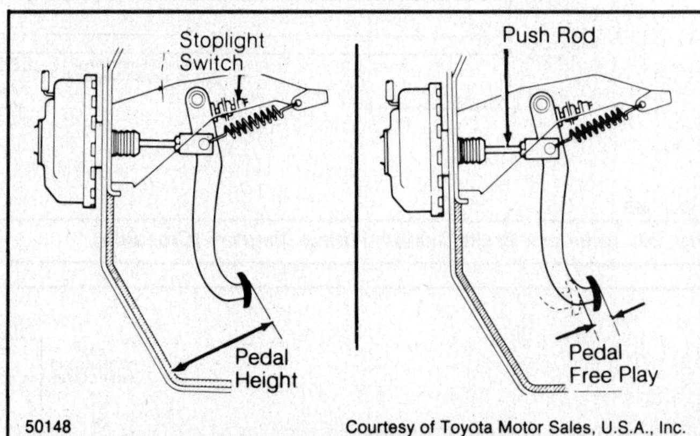


***Fig. 3: Measuring Brake Pedal Height & Free Play***

**2)** Adjust pedal height by turning push rod. After adjusting brake pedal height, tighten push rod lock nut. Adjust stoplight switch. See STOPLIGHT SWITCH. Check and adjust brake pedal free play. See BRAKE PEDAL FREE PLAY.

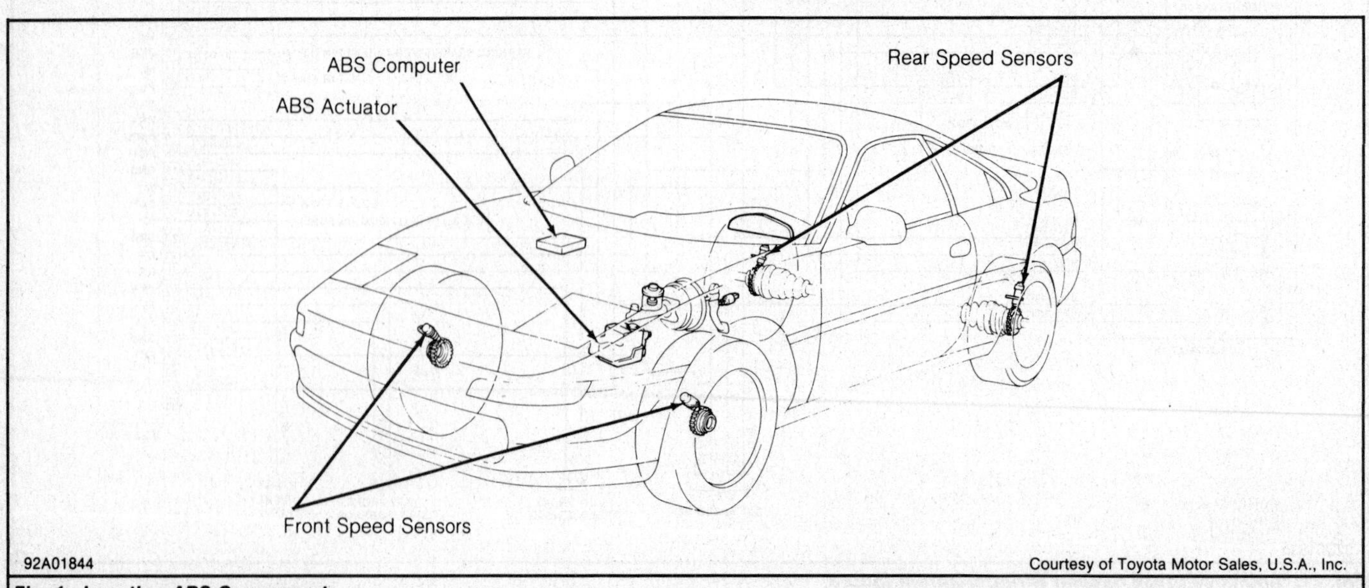


***Fig. 1: Locating ABS Components***

## BRAKE PEDAL FREE PLAY

**1)** Brake pedal free play is distance brake pedal travels before feeling resistance with engine stopped. To check brake pedal free play, depress brake pedal several times to exhaust vacuum from power brake unit.
**2)** On single booster power brake unit, depress brake pedal and measure travel until initial resistance is felt. On tandem booster power brake unit, depress brake pedal and measure travel until beginning of second resistance is felt. First resistance is due to play between clevis and pin, .04-.12" (1-3 mm).
**3)** On all models, brake pedal free play should be .12-.20" (3.0-5.0 mm). If free play is not within specification, adjust by turning push rod. *See Fig. 3*. After adjusting brake pedal free play, check brake pedal height. See BRAKE PEDAL HEIGHT.

## STOPLIGHT SWITCH

Stoplight switch is located above brake pedal. *See Fig. 3*. To adjust stoplight switch, loosen stoplight switch lock nuts and turn stoplight switch until it touches brake pedal stop. Tighten lock nut. Check stoplight operation.

## BRAKE PEDAL DEPRESSED HEIGHT

Brake pedal depressed height is measured from face of brake pedal pad to asphalt sheet under carpet with brakes applied. Measure brake pedal depressed height with engine running and weight of 110 lbs. (50 kg) applied against brake pedal. Minimum brake pedal depressed height should be 4.6" (117 mm). If measured distance is less than specified, inspect brake system.

## PARKING BRAKE CABLE

**1)** Parking brake lever stroke should be 5-8 notches (clicks) with a pull force of 44 lbs. (20 kg). To adjust, pull parking brake lever all the way up and down 2 or 3 times. Release parking brake lever.
**2)** Depress brake pedal several times. Remove fuel tank protector. Loosen parking brake cable by turning adjusting nuts on equalizer. Perform STEP 1. *See Fig. 4*. Check that parking brake crank touches stopper pin. Perform STEP 2. *See Fig. 4*.

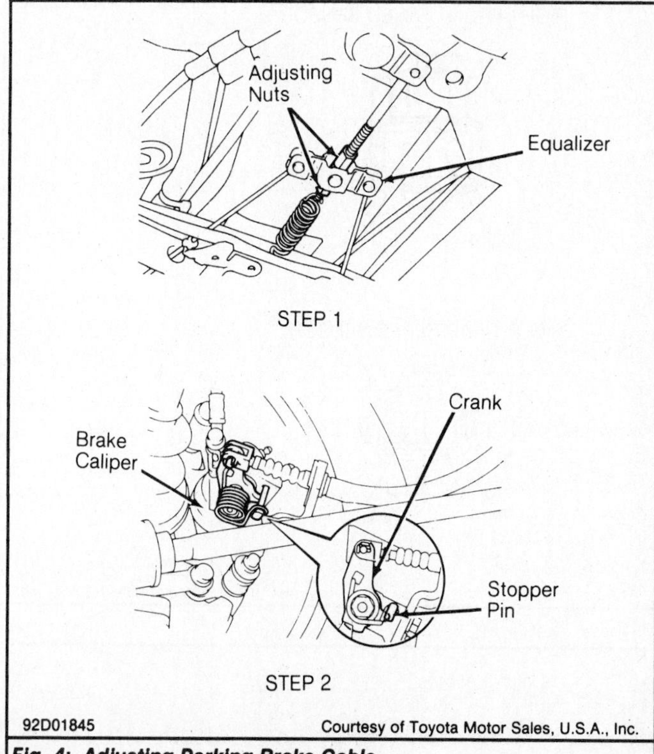


***Fig. 4: Adjusting Parking Brake Cable***

**3)** Tighten parking brake cable by turning adjusting nuts on equalizer until crank just begins to move. Tighten adjusting nuts so equalizer is horizontal to ground. Install fuel tank protector.

## TROUBLE SHOOTING

### SYMPTOM DIAGNOSTICS

**ABS Light Illuminates – 1)** Disconnect service connector. *See Fig. 5*. Using jumper wire, connect check connector terminals Tc and $E_1$. *See Fig. 6*. Turn ignition on. If ABS light blinks codes or illuminates constantly, see DIAGNOSTIC CODES under DIAGNOSIS & TESTING. If ABS light does not illuminate, go to next step.

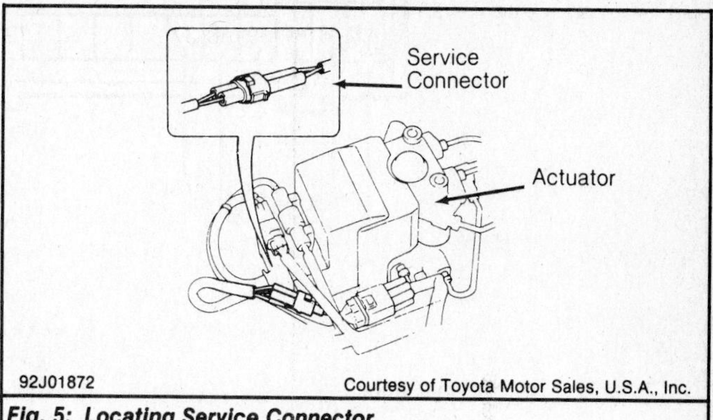


***Fig. 5: Locating Service Connector***

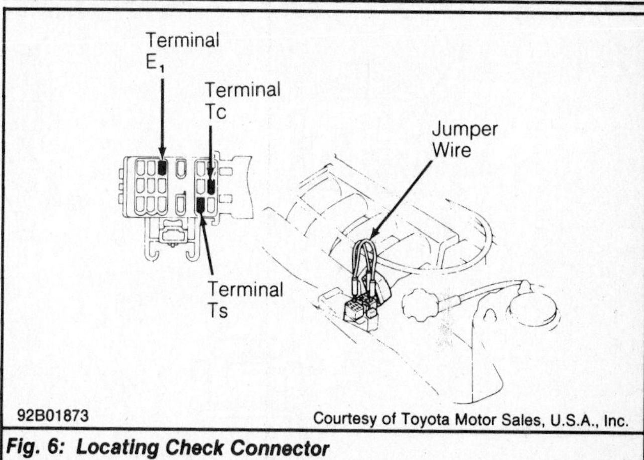


***Fig. 6: Locating Check Connector***

**2)** Ensure ABS computer connector is properly connected and connector terminals are not damaged. Repair connector as necessary. Turn ignition on. Using voltmeter, check for 10-16 volts between ABS computer connector terminal No. 1 (Black/Yellow wire) and ground on wire harness side. *See Fig. 7*. If 10-16 volts is not present, repair faulty Black/Yellow wire. If 10-16 volts is present, go to next step.
**3)** Turn ignition off. Disconnect ABS computer connector. Disconnect service connector if not previously disconnected. Turn ignition on. If ABS light illuminates, repair short circuit between ABS computer connector terminal No. 15 and actuator connector "A" terminal No. 6. *See Fig. 7*. If ABS light does not illuminate, replace faulty ABS computer.

**ABS Light Does Not Illuminate For 3 Seconds After Ignition Is Turned On – 1)** Disconnect service connector. *See Fig. 5*. Using a jumper wire, ground service connector on harness (female) side. Turn ignition on. If ABS light does not illuminate, replace faulty ABS light bulb or repair open circuit between ABS light and service connector. If ABS light illuminates, go to next step.
**2)** Turn ignition off. Disconnect ABS computer connector and actuator connectors. Using a jumper wire, ground ABS computer connector terminal No. 15 on wire harness side of connector. *See Fig. 7*. Turn ignition on. ABS light should illuminate. If ABS light does not

# 1991 BRAKES
## Anti-Lock – MR2 (Cont.)

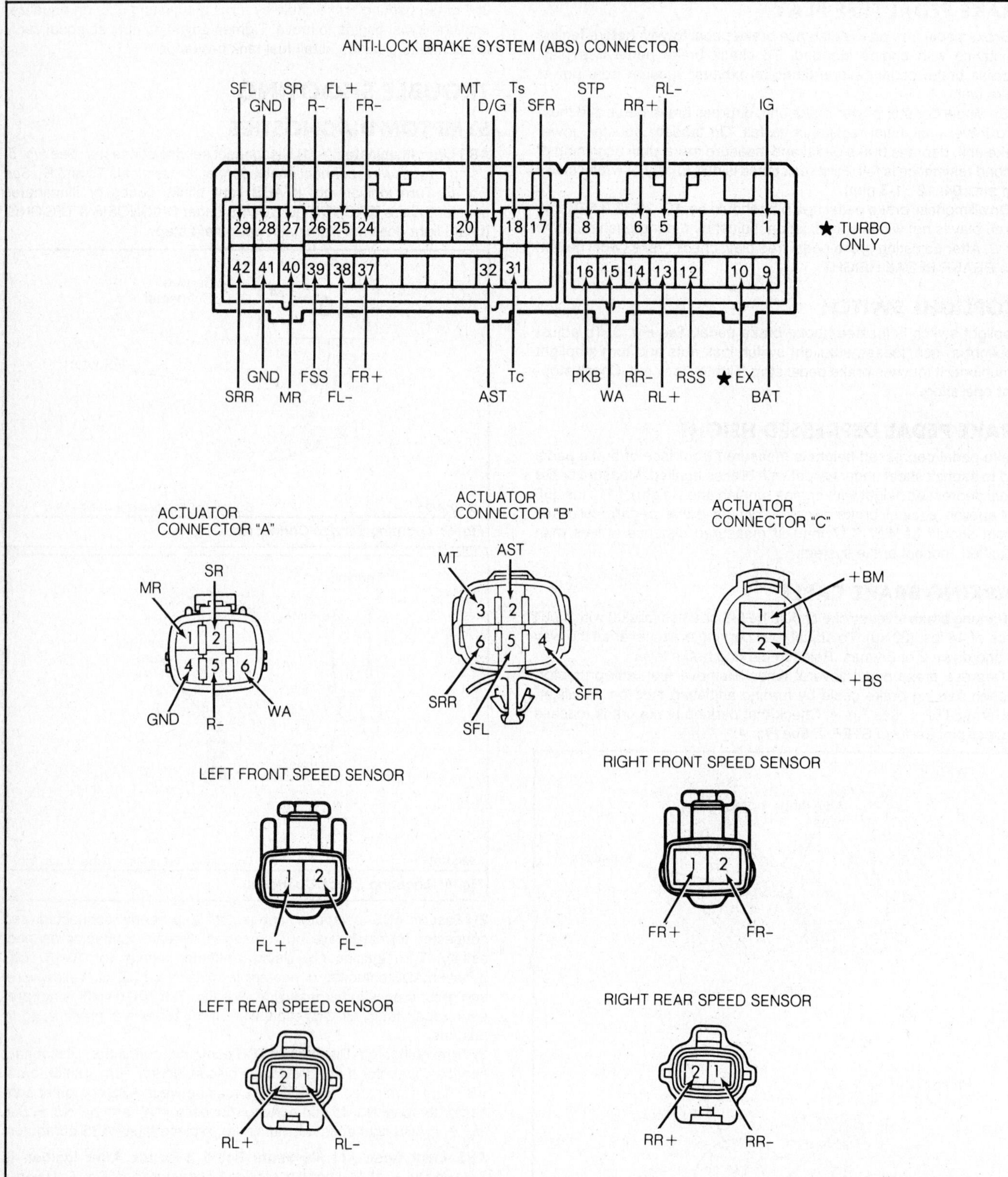


Courtesy of Toyota Motor Sales, U.S.A., Inc.

***Fig. 7: Identifying ABS Connector Terminals***

illuminate, repair open circuit in wiring harness between ABS computer connector terminal No. 15 and ABS light. If ABS light illuminates, go to next step.
**3)** Turn ignition off. Disconnect actuator connectors. Using ohmmeter, ensure continuity is present between actuator connector "A" terminal No. 6 and actuator connector "B" terminal No. 2 on actuator side. *See Fig. 7*. Reverse ohmmeter leads and check again.
**4)** If continuity is present both ways between actuator terminals, repair short circuit in actuator diode. Go to step next step. If continuity is present only one way between actuator terminals, replace faulty ABS computer.
**5)** If short in actuator diode exists, a malfunction at ABS computer terminal No. 15 will occur. When inspecting terminal, connect ABS computer connector. Disconnect actuator connectors. Turn ignition on and check if ABS light illuminates. If ABS light illuminates, ABS computer connector terminal No. 15 is okay.
**ABS Light Illuminates Intermittently –** Check for a short in wiring harness between check connector terminals Tc and $E_1$ or Ts and $E_1$. *See Fig. 6*.
**Brakes Pull, Braking Inefficient, ABS Operates With Ordinary Braking, ABS Operates Just Before Stopping With Ordinary Braking, & Brake Pedal Pulsates Abnormally With ABS Functioning – 1)** Disconnect service connector. *See Fig. 5*. Using a jumper wire, connect check connector terminals Tc and $E_1$. *See Fig. 6*. Turn ignition on. ABS light should blink a normal code. If ABS light does not blink a normal code, refer to DIAGNOSTIC CODES under DIAGNOSIS & TESTING.
**2)** Enter speed sensor diagnostics. See SPEED SENSOR DIAGNOSTICS under DIAGNOSIS & TESTING. If speed sensor signal level is okay, go to next step. If speed sensor signal level is not okay, inspect sensor and sensor rotor. Replace as necessary.
**3)** Ensure all speed sensors are installed properly. If speed sensors are not installed properly, repair as necessary. If speed sensors are installed properly, ensure all foreign and metal chips are cleaned from speed sensor tip. Go to next step.
**4)** Turn ignition off. Disconnect ABS computer connector. Ensure continuity is present between each speed sensor connector (wire harness side) of ABS computer connector. Check continuity between FL+ and FL- (left front speed sensor), FR+ and FR- (right front speed sensor), RL+ and RL- (left rear speed sensor), and RR+ and RR- (right rear speed sensor).
**5)** If continuity readings change when wiring harness is twisted or moved, repair faulty wiring harness between speed sensor and ABS computer connector. Check actuator operation. See ACTUATOR CHECK under DIAGNOSIS & TESTING. If actuator operation is okay, replace faulty ABS computer. ABS computer is located under right side of dash. *See Fig. 1*. If actuator operation is not okay, replace faulty actuator.
**ABS Works Inefficiently – 1)** Disconnect service connector. *See Fig. 5*. Using jumper wire, connect check connector terminals Tc and $E_1$. *See Fig. 6*. Turn ignition on. ABS light should blink a normal code. If ABS light does not blink a normal code, refer to DIAGNOSTIC CODES under DIAGNOSIS & TESTING. If ABS light blinks a normal code, go to next step.
**2)** Ensure battery voltage exists between ABS computer connector terminal No. 8 (Green/White wire) and ground when brake pedal is depressed. If battery voltage is not present when brake pedal is depressed, repair open circuit in stoplight switch or wiring harness. Check actuator operation. See ACTUATOR CHECK under DIAGNOSIS & TESTING.

## DIAGNOSIS & TESTING

***NOTE: DO NOT start engine when accessing trouble codes.***

### ACCESSING TROUBLE CODES

**ABS Light Diagnostics – 1)** Ensure battery voltage is 12 volts. Turn ignition switch to ON position. ABS light should illuminate, then go out after 3 seconds. If ABS light does not illuminate, check fuse, bulb, and wiring harness.
**2)** With ignition on, disconnect service connector. *See Fig. 5*. Using jumper wire, connect check connector terminals Tc and $E_1$. *See Fig. 6*. If a malfunction is detected, 4 seconds will elapse and ABS light will begin to flash a 2-digit code. First number of blinks will equal first digit in a code. After a 1.5-second pause, second number of blinks will equal second digit in a code.
**3)** If 2 or more codes are stored, there will be a 4.5-second pause between each code. If ABS system is functioning properly, ABS light will blink once every .5 second. For code interpretation, see DIAGNOSTIC CODES.
**4)** After replacing or repairing malfunctioning components, clear diagnostic codes. If a battery cable was disconnected during repairs, all codes will be erased. If battery cable was not disconnected during repairs, see CLEARING CODES.

### DIAGNOSTIC CODES

Check suspect components in order given. See COMPONENT TESTING. Checks consist mainly of a visual inspection and continuity tests.
**Code 11 –** Open solenoid relay circuit. Check actuator wiring harness, ABS solenoid relay, solenoid relay wiring harness and solenoid relay connector.
**Code 12 –** Short in solenoid relay circuit. Check actuator wiring harness, ABS solenoid relay, solenoid relay wiring harness and solenoid relay connector.
**Code 13 –** Open pump motor relay circuit. Check actuator wiring harness, ABS pump motor relay, pump motor relay wiring harness and pump motor relay connector.
**Code 14 –** Short in pump motor relay circuit. Check actuator wiring harness, ABS pump motor relay, pump motor relay wiring harness and pump motor relay connector.
**Code 21 –** Open or short circuit in 3-position solenoid for right front wheel. Check 3-position actuator solenoid, wiring harness and connector.
**Code 22 –** Open or short circuit in 3-position solenoid for left front wheel. Check 3-position actuator solenoid, wiring harness and connector.
**Code 23 –** Open or short circuit in 3-position solenoid for rear wheels. Check 3-position actuator solenoid, wiring harness and connector.
**Code 31 –** Malfunction of right front wheel speed sensor signal. Check speed sensor, sensor rotor, wiring harness and connector.
**Code 32 –** Malfunction of left front wheel speed sensor signal. Check speed sensor, sensor rotor, wiring harness and connector.
**Code 33 –** Malfunction of right rear wheel speed sensor signal. Check speed sensor, sensor rotor, wiring harness and connector.
**Code 34 –** Malfunction of left rear wheel speed sensor signal. Check speed sensor, sensor rotor, wiring harness and connector.
**Code 35 –** Open in left front or right rear wheel speed sensor circuit. Check speed sensor, sensor rotor, wiring harness and connector.
**Code 36 –** Open in right front or left rear wheel speed sensor circuit. Check speed sensor, sensor rotor, wiring harness and connector.
**Code 41 –** Abnormally high or low battery voltage. Battery voltage is 17 volts or more, or 9.5 volts or less. Check battery and voltage regulator.
**Code 51 –** Actuator pump motor is locked or pump motor circuit open. Check pump motor, pump motor relay, vehicle battery, actuator wiring harness, connectors, actuator pump motor circuit and actuator ground bolt.
**Always On –** Malfunction of ABS computer. Ensure ABS computer connector is properly connected and terminals are not damaged. If connector is okay, replace ABS computer. ABS computer is located under right side of dash.

### CLEARING CODES

Turn ignition on. Disconnect service connector. *See Fig. 5*. Using jumper wire, connect check connector terminals Tc and $E_1$. *See Fig. 6*. With vehicle stopped, depress brake pedal 8 or more times within 3 seconds. Codes are now erased. Turn ignition on. Ensure ABS light goes out after 3 seconds. Ensure ABS light shows a normal code. See ABS LIGHT DIAGNOSTICS under ACCESSING TROUBLE CODES.

# 1991 BRAKES
# Anti-Lock - MR2 (Cont.)

## ACTUATOR CHECK

***NOTE:** Actuator Checker (09990-00150) is needed to perform ACTUATOR CHECK.*

**1)** Turn ignition off. Disconnect actuator electrical connectors. Connect Actuator Checker (09990-00150) to actuator and body side wire harness through sub-wire harness. Connect actuator checker positive and negative power cables to vehicle battery.
**2)** Start engine and let idle. Turn actuator checker selector switch to FRONT RH position. *See Fig. 8.* Press and hold SUB MOTOR switch for a few seconds. Press and hold brake pedal.

***NOTE:** DO NOT press MAIN switch for more than 10 seconds.*

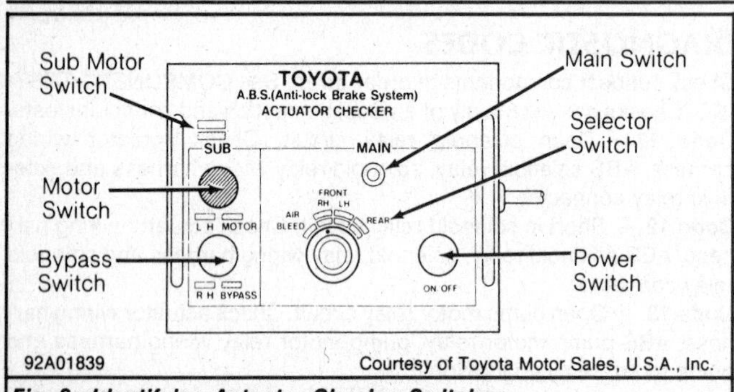

***Fig. 8:** Identifying Actuator Checker Switches*

**3)** Press MAIN switch. When MAIN switch is pressed, brake pedal should not go down. Release MAIN SWITCH. Brake pedal should lower. Press and hold SUB MOTOR switch for a few seconds. Brake pedal should return. Release brake pedal.
**4)** Press and hold SUB MOTOR switch for a few seconds. Press brake pedal and hold for approximately 15 seconds. As brake pedal is being held, press SUB MOTOR switch for a few seconds. Ensure brake pedal does not pulsate.
**5)** Repeat steps **2)** through **4)** for FRONT LH, REAR RH, and REAR LH by turning selector switch on actuator checker. After checking remaining wheels, press and hold MOTOR switch for a few seconds.
**6)** Disconnect actuator checker and sub-wire harness from actuator. Connect actuator connectors. Clear diagnostic codes. See CLEARING CODES.

## SPEED SENSOR DIAGNOSTICS

***NOTE:** During diagnosis, DO NOT turn ignition off, pull parking brake lever and press brake pedal more than 16 times or diagnostic codes will be erased. While diagnosing speed sensors, brake system functions as a conventional system.*

**1)** Ensure battery voltage is approximately 12 volts. Turn ignition on. Ensure ABS light illuminates, then goes out after approximately 3 seconds. If ABS light does not illuminate, check fuse, bulb and wiring harness. Check that ABS light turns off.
**2)** Turn ignition off. Using a jumper wire, connect check connector terminals Tc and Ts to $E_1$. *See Fig. 6.* Engage parking brake. Start engine. DO NOT press brake pedal. ABS light will illuminate 4 times a second. Go to next step.

***NOTE:** While ABS light is off, DO NOT accelerate, decelerate, brake, shift, move steering or drive on rough road surfaces as these conditions will affect test.*

**3)** Drive vehicle straight ahead at 2.5-3.7 MPH. Ensure ABS light illuminates after a one second pause. If ABS light illuminates without blinking when vehicle is NOT within specified speed, stop vehicle and record diagnostic codes. Turn ignition off. Repair as necessary. See SPEED SENSOR DIAGNOSTIC CODES.
**4)** If ABS light illuminates while vehicle speed is within specified range, check is completed. If vehicle speed exceeds 3.7 MPH, ABS light will blink again. If ABS light blinks when vehicle speed exceeds 3.7 MPH, speed sensors are okay.
**5)** Drive vehicle straight ahead at 28-34 MPH. Ensure ABS light illuminates after a one second pause. If ABS light illuminates without blinking when vehicle is NOT within specified speed, stop vehicle and record diagnostic codes. Turn ignition off. Repair as necessary. See SPEED SENSOR DIAGNOSTIC CODES.
**6)** If ABS light illuminates while vehicle speed is within specified range, check is completed. If vehicle speed exceeds 34 MPH, ABS light will blink again. If ABS light blinks when vehicle speed exceeds 34 MPH, sensor rotors are okay.
**7)** Turn ignition off. Remove jumper wire from check connector. Clear diagnostic codes. See CLEARING CODES.

## SPEED SENSOR DIAGNOSTIC CODES

**Code 71** - Low voltage of right front speed sensor signal. Check right front speed sensor and sensor installation.
**Code 72** - Low voltage of left front speed sensor signal. Check left front speed sensor and sensor installation.
**Code 73** - Low voltage of right rear speed sensor signal. Check right rear speed sensor and sensor installation.
**Code 74** - Low voltage of left rear speed sensor signal. Check left rear speed sensor and sensor installation.
**Code 75** - Abnormal signal from right front speed sensor. Check right front sensor rotor.
**Code 76** - Abnormal signal from left front speed sensor. Check right front sensor rotor.
**Code 77** - Abnormal signal from right rear speed sensor. Check right rear sensor rotor.
**Code 78** - Abnormal signal from left rear speed sensor. Check left rear sensor rotor.
**Light Illuminates 4 Times A Second** - All speed sensors and sensor rotors are normal.

## COMPONENT TESTING

**Front & Rear Speed Sensors** - **1)** Remove speed sensor from vehicle. See SPEED SENSORS under REMOVAL & INSTALLATION. Using a DVOM, measure resistance between speed sensor terminals. Resistance should be 900-1500 ohms.
**2)** Ensure continuity is not present between each sensor terminal and sensor body. If resistance and continuity readings are as specified, speed sensor is okay. If resistance and continuity readings are not as specified, replace speed sensor.
**Pump Motor Relay Continuity** - **1)** Remove pump motor relay, located on top of actuator. Using a DVOM, check continuity between pump motor relay terminals No. 1 and No. 2. *See Fig. 9.* Ensure continuity is present.

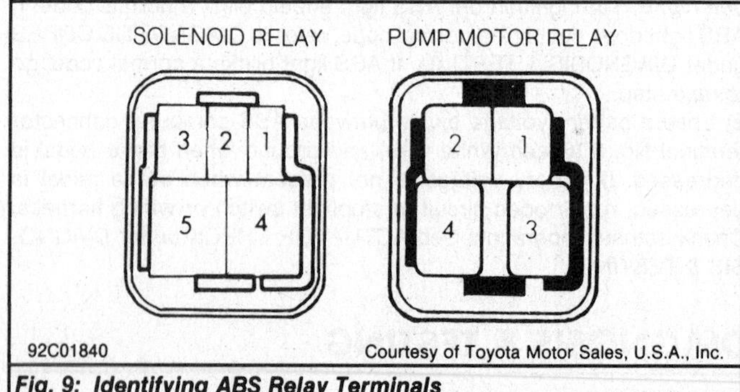

***Fig. 9:** Identifying ABS Relay Terminals*

**2)** Check continuity between terminals No. 3 and No. 4, and between terminals No. 1 and No. 4. Ensure continuity is NOT present. If continuity readings are not as specified, replace pump motor relay.

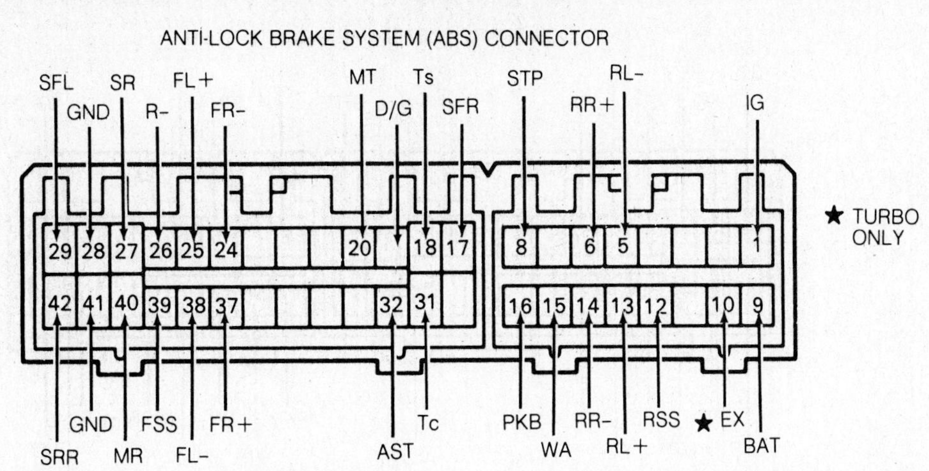


| Tester Connection | Check Item | Condition | Specified Value | Trouble Part |
|---|---|---|---|---|
| IG | Voltage | IG switch on | Battery voltage | ECU-IG Fuse |
| RL– | Continuity | IG switch off | Continuity | ABS ECU |
| STP | Voltage | IG switch off and brake pedal depressed | Battery voltage | Stop light switch<br>Stop light |
| | Continuity | IG switch off and brake pedal returned | Continuity | |
| BAT | Voltage | IG switch off | Battery voltage | ECU +B Fuse |
| EX | Voltage | IG switch on | Battery voltage | ABS ECU. EFI ECU |
| RSS | Continuity | IG switch off | Continuity | ABS ECU |
| RR– | Continuity | IG switch off | Continuity | ABS ECU |
| WA | Voltage | IG switch on and "ABS" warning light goes on | About 0V | ABS ECU<br>"ABS" warning light |
| | | IG switch on and "ABS" warning light goes off | Battery voltage | |
| PKB | Voltage | IG switch on and PKB lever pulled | About 0V | Parking brake switch<br>Level warning switch |
| | | Engine running on and PKB lever returned | Battery voltage | |
| SFR | Voltage | IG switch on and "ABS"warning light goes on | About 0V | Actuator |
| | | IG switch on and "ABS" warning light goes off | Battery voltage | |
| TS | Voltage | IG switch on and check connector Ts-$E_1$ not connected | Battery voltage | ABS ECU |
| | | IG switch on and check connector Ts-$E_1$ connector | About 0V | |
| FR– | Continuity | IG switch off | Continuity | |
| R– | Continuity | IG switch off | Continuity | ABS ECU |
| SR | Voltage | IG switch on and "ABS" warning light goes on | About 0V | |
| | | IG switch on and "ABS" warning light goes off | Battery voltage | |
| GND | Continuity | IG switch off | Continuity | Wiring harness |
| SFL | Voltage | IG switch on and "ABS" warning light goes on | About 0V | Actuator |
| | | IG switch on and "ABS" warning light goes off | Battery voltage | |
| TC | Voltage | IG switch on and check connector Tc-$E_1$ not connected | Battery voltage | ABS ECU |
| | | IG switch on and check connector Tc-$E_1$ connected | About 0V | |
| AST | Voltage | IG switch on and "ABS" warning light goes on | About 0V | Actuator |
| | | IG switch on and "ABS" warning light goes off | Battery voltage | |
| FL– | Continuity | IG switch off | Continuity | ABS ECU |
| FSS | Continuity | IG switch off | Continuity | |
| SRR | Voltage | IG switch on and "ABS" warning light goes on | About 0V | Actuator |
| | | IG switch on and "ABS" warning light goes off | Battery voltage | |

92G01875



***Fig. 10: Testing Specifications Table for ABS Computer Wiring Harness (1 of 2)***

# 1991 BRAKES
# Anti-Lock – MR2 (Cont.)

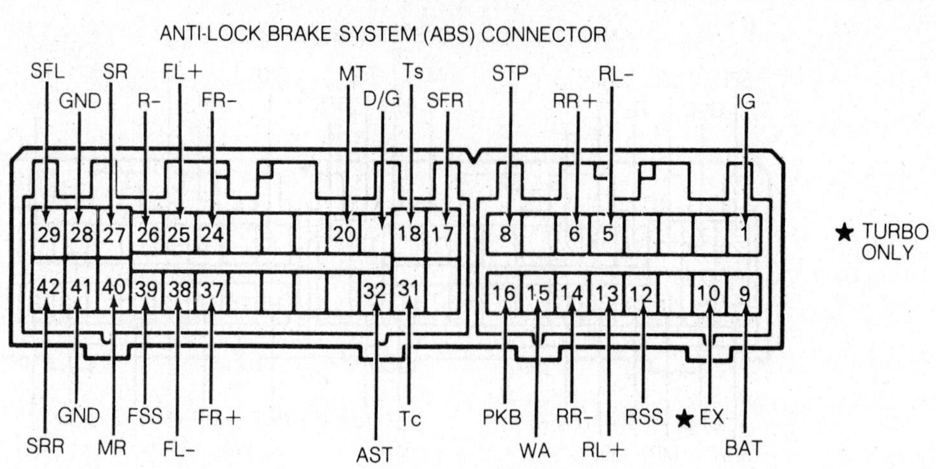


| Tester Connection | Check Item | Specified Value | Trouble Part | Tester Connection | Check Item | Specified Value | Trouble Part |
|---|---|---|---|---|---|---|---|
| RR+ ↔ RR- | Resistance | 0.9 ~ 1.5 kΩ | Rear RH speed sensor | SFL ↔ AST | Resistance | About 6 Ω | Actuator |
| RL+ ↔ RL- | Resistance | 0.9 ~ 1.5 kΩ | Rear LH speed sensor | AST ↔ Body ground | Resistance | About 5 Ω | Actuator |
| SFR ↔ AST | Resistance | About 6 Ω | Actuator | FR+ ↔ FR- | Resistance | 0.8 ~ 1.5 Ω | Front RH speed sensor |
| MT ↔ Body ground | Resistance | About 5 Ω | Actuator | MR ↔ R- | Resistance | 50 ~ 80 Ω | Control relay |
| FL+ ↔ FL- | Resistance | 0.8 ~ 1.5 kΩ | Front LH speed sensor | SRR ↔ AST | Resistance | About 6 Ω | Actuator |
| SR ↔ R- | Resistance | 60 ~ 100 Ω | Control relay | | | | |

92I01876

Courtesy of Toyota Motor Sales, U.S.A., Inc.

***Fig. 11: Testing Specifications Table for ABS Computer Wiring Harness (2 of 2)***

**Pump Motor Relay Operation – 1)** Remove pump motor relay, located on top of actuator. Apply battery positive terminal to pump motor relay terminal No. 1. Apply battery negative terminal to pump motor relay terminal No. 2. *See Fig. 9.*

**2)** Ensure continuity is present between relay terminals No. 3 and No. 4. Continuity should NOT be present between relay terminals No. 1 and No. 4. If continuity is not as specified, replace pump motor relay.

**Solenoid Relay Continuity – 1)** Remove solenoid relay, located on top of actuator. Using a DVOM, check continuity between solenoid relay terminals No. 1 and No. 3. *See Fig. 9.* Continuity should be present.

**2)** Check continuity between terminals No. 2 and No. 4. Continuity should be present. Check continuity between terminals No. 4 and No. 5. Continuity should NOT be present. If continuity readings are not as specified, replace solenoid relay.

**Solenoid Relay Operation – 1)** Remove solenoid relay, located on top of actuator. Connect jumper wire between battery positive terminal and solenoid relay terminal No. 3. Connect another jumper wire between ground and relay terminal No. 1. *See Fig. 9.*

**2)** Ensure continuity is present between relay terminals No. 4 and No. 5. Ensure continuity is NOT present between relay terminals No. 2 and No. 4. If continuity is not as specified, replace solenoid relay.

**Sensor Rotors –** Visually inspect sensor rotor serrations for scratches, cracks, missing teeth and warping. Replace sensor rotor if damaged.

**ABS Computer Wiring Harness – 1)** Remove ABS computer. ABS computer is located under right side of dash. With ABS computer connector connected, backprobe ABS computer connector terminals. Measure voltage and resistance at each terminal as specified in table. *See Fig. 10.* If circuit(s) do not test as specified, check and repair or replace trouble part shown in table.

**2)** Disconnect ABS computer connector. Check resistance on wire harness side of ABS computer connector terminals as specified in table. *See Fig. 11.* If circuit(s) do not test as specified, check and repair or replace troubled part shown in table.

## REMOVAL & INSTALLATION

***WARNING: Hydraulic system may be under high pressure. Use caution when opening hydraulic system.***

### ACTUATOR

**Removal & Installation – 1)** Disconnect actuator electrical connectors. Disconnect brake lines connected to actuator. Remove actuator mounting bolts. Remove actuator with bracket.

**2)** Remove actuator from actuator bracket. To install, reverse removal procedure. Bleed brake system. See BLEEDING BRAKE SYSTEM. Check for fluid leaks.

### ABS COMPUTER

ABS computer is located under right side of dash. *See Fig. 1.* Removal and installation procedure is not available from manufacturer

### SPEED SENSORS

**Removal & Installation – 1)** Loosen wheel lug nuts. Raise and support vehicle. Remove wheel. Remove wheel speed sensor mounting bolt. Disconnect wheel speed sensor connector.

**2)** Remove wheel speed sensor from vehicle. To install, reverse removal procedure. Tighten wheel speed sensor mounting bolt to specification. See TORQUE SPECIFICATIONS table at end of article.

# 1991 BRAKES
# Anti-Lock – MR2 (Cont.)

## FRONT SENSOR ROTOR

***NOTE: Front axle hub must be removed to service sensor rotor.***

**Removal & Installation – 1)** Loosen front wheel lug nuts. Raise and support front of vehicle. Remove front wheel. Remove wheel speed sensor mounting bolt.
**2)** Disconnect wheel speed sensor connector. Remove wheel speed sensor from vehicle. Remove disc brake rotor and wire out of way. DO NOT disconnect brake line. Remove disc brake rotor.
**3)** Loosen 2 nuts on lower side of shock absorber. DO NOT remove bolts. Loosen 2 bolts of lower ball joint. DO NOT remove bolts. Disconnect tie rod end from steering knuckle. Remove 2 bolts on lower ball joint and disconnect steering knuckle.
**4)** Remove 2 nuts and bolts on lower side of shock absorber. Remove steering knuckle with axle hub. Mount axle hub in vise. Remove grease cap. Chisel staked part of axle shaft hub lock nut. Remove axle shaft hub lock nut. Remove speed sensor rotor.
**5)** To install, reverse removal procedure. Install new axle shaft hub lock nut. Tighten axle shaft hub lock nut to specification and stake nut. Tighten all nuts and bolts to specification. See TORQUE SPECIFICATIONS table at end of article.

## REAR SENSOR ROTOR

***NOTE: Rear speed sensor rotor is an integral part of axle shaft.***

**Removal – 1)** Raise and support vehicle. Remove rear wheels and engine under cover. Drain transaxle fluid. Remove cotter pin and lock nut cap. Apply parking brake and remove bearing lock nut.
**2)** On MR2 Turbo, paint mating marks on axle shaft flange and side gear shaft flange. DO NOT use punch to make mating marks. Loosen, but do not remove, 6 bolts connecting axle shaft flange to differential side gear shaft flange.
**3)** On all models, remove brake caliper from axle carrier and suspend with wire leaving hydraulic line connected. Remove rotor. Disconnect stabilizer bar link from strut.
**4)** Remove rear speed sensor. Disconnect lower arm from rear axle carrier. Disconnect tie rod ends from axle carrier. Using a universal puller, separate axle shaft from axle carrier. DO NOT damage boot or speed sensor rotor.
**5)** On MR2 Non-Turbo, pry left side axle shaft from transaxle. Using a brass bar and hammer, separate right side axle shaft from transaxle. Replace oil seals if necessary.
**6)** On MR2 Turbo, use a brass bar and hammer to separate left side axle shaft from transaxle. On right axle shaft, use a hammer and screwdriver to remove snap ring from bearing bracket.
**7)** Remove center bolt from bearing bracket. Remove right axle shaft with intermediate shaft. Use a brass bar and hammer to remove shaft (if necessary). Remove bearing bracket and stay. Replace oil seals if necessary.
**Installation – 1)** To install, reverse removal procedure. DO NOT damage speed sensor rotor or joint boots. On MR2 Non-Turbo, after installing axle shaft to transaxle, ensure axial play is .08-.12" (2.0-3.0 mm). Ensure axle shaft cannot be pulled out by hand.
**2)** On all models, tighten all fasteners to specification. See TORQUE SPECIFICATIONS table at end of article. DO NOT fully tighten tie rod ends or hub bearing lock nut until vehicle wheels are resting on ground.

## OVERHAUL

DO NOT attempt to overhaul or disassemble actuator assembly. If actuator is defective, replace entire assembly.

## TORQUE SPECIFICATIONS

***TORQUE SPECIFICATIONS***

| Application | Ft. Lbs. (N.m) |
|---|---|
| Brake Caliper | 43 (58) |
| Front Axle Hub Lock Nut | 90 (122) |
| Front Tie Rod-To-Steering Knuckle Nut | 36 (49) |
| Rear Axle Shaft Flange-To-Side Gear Shaft Flange (Turbo) | 48 (65) |
| Rear Bearing Bracket Center Bolt (Turbo) | 24 (33) |
| Rear Bearing Bracket Mounting Bolts (Turbo) | 47 (64) |
| Rear Bearing Bracket Stay Bolt & Nut (Turbo) | 56 (76) |
| Rear Hub Bearing Lock Nut | |
| Non-Turbo | 152 (206) |
| Turbo | 217 (294) |
| Rear Lower Arm-To-Axle Carrier | |
| Non-Turbo | 83 (112) |
| Turbo | 73 (99) |
| Rear Stabilizer Link | 36 (49) |
| Rear Suspension Arm-To-Axle Carrier | 76 (103) |
| Rear Tie Rod Ends | 76 (103) |
| Steering Knuckle-To-Ball Joint Nut | 59 (80) |
| Steering Knuckle-To-Shock Absorber Bolts | 188 (255) |
| | **INCH Lbs. (N.m)** |
| Actuator Mounting Bolts | 168 (19) |
| Speed Sensor Mounting Bolt | 69 (8) |

# 1991 BRAKES
# Anti-Lock – MR2 (Cont.)

## WIRING DIAGRAM

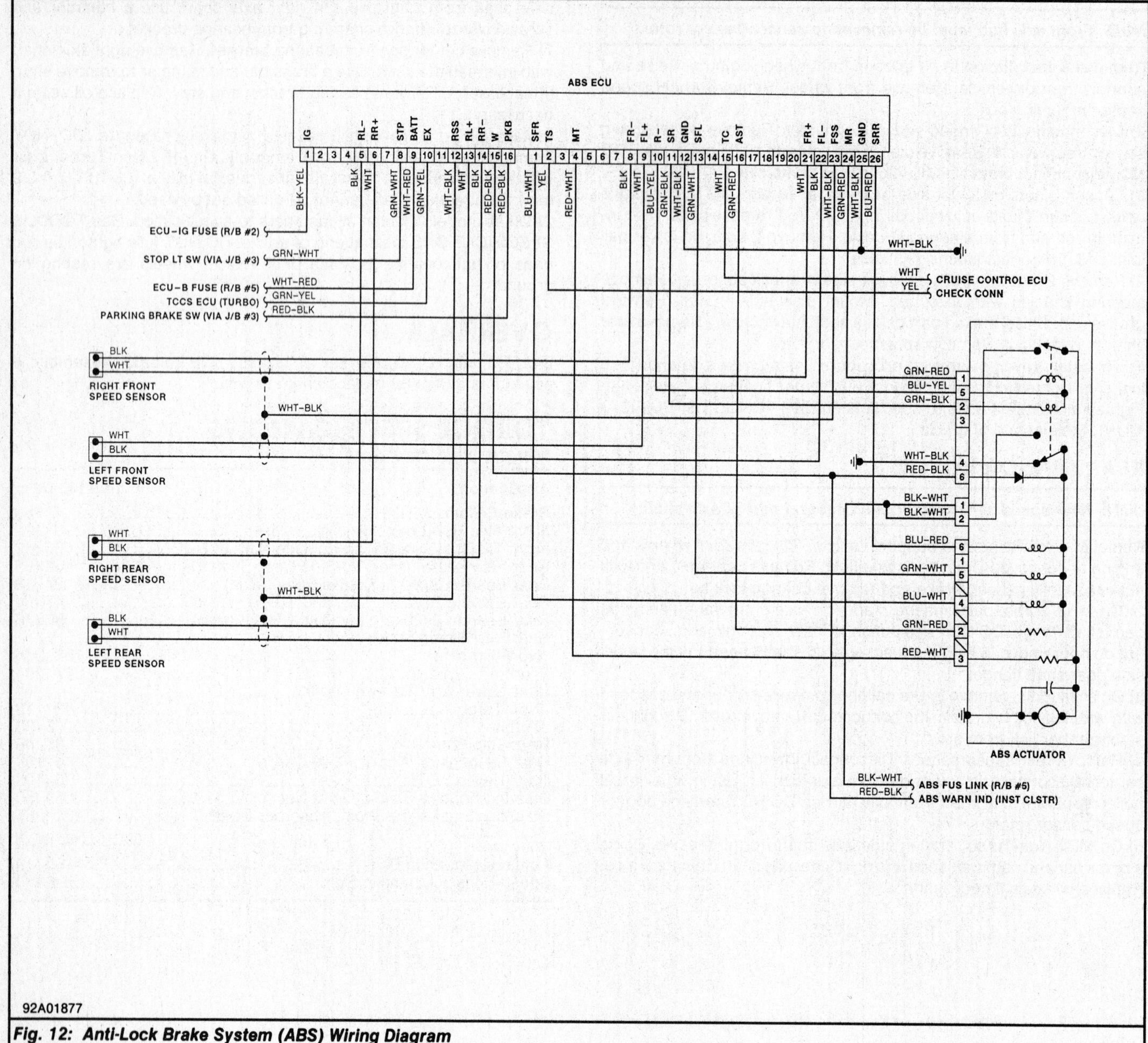


*Fig. 12: Anti-Lock Brake System (ABS) Wiring Diagram*

# 1991 BRAKES
# Anti-Lock – Pickup & 4Runner

## DESCRIPTION

Rear Anti-Lock Brake System (ABS) consists of power steering pump, brake actuator, ABS relay, deceleration sensor, actuator solenoid, ABS computer and speed sensor. *See Figs. 1 and 2.*

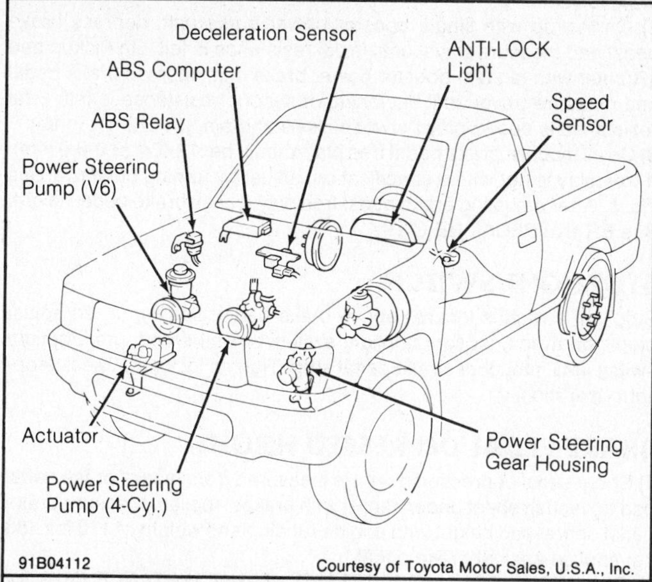


***Fig. 1: Locating ABS Components (Pickup)***

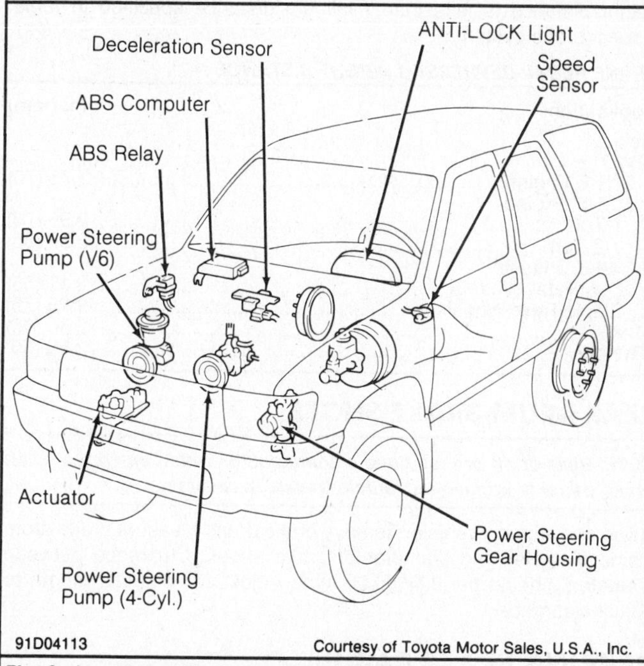


***Fig. 2: Locating ABS Components (4Runner)***

REAR ANTI-LOCK indicator light is located in the combination meter on instrument panel. Indicator light comes on for 2 seconds as a bulb test when ignition is turned on. A primary check is performed after each engine start and after initial vehicle speed exceeds 4 MPH.

An actuator noise will be heard as vehicle speed exceeds 4 MPH. If brake pedal is depressed before vehicle exceeds 4 MPH, primary check will not occur until brake pedal is released.

***NOTE: For more information on brake system, see DISC & DRUM – LIGHT TRUCKS & VANS article.***

## OPERATION

Under normal driving conditions, ABS functions as a standard brake system. Upon detection of wheel lock-up, short pedal pulsations, occurring in rapid succession, will be felt in brake pedal. Pedal pulsation will continue until there is no longer a need for anti-lock function or until vehicle is stopped. Applying constant force on pedal results in shortest stopping distance.

***CAUTION: See ANTI-LOCK BRAKE SAFETY PRECAUTIONS article in GENERAL INFORMATION.***

## BLEEDING BRAKE SYSTEM

***CAUTION: Brake fluid will damage painted surfaces. If brake fluid gets on a painted surface, wipe off immediately and clean with alcohol. Use only DOT 3 brake fluid from a sealed container. Do not mix brake fluid with any other type.***

Normally, brake bleeding procedure for ABS is the same as brake bleeding procedure for non-ABS. If master cylinder was rebuilt or reservoir ran empty, bleed master cylinder first. Bleed remaining wheels, starting from wheel with longest hydraulic line and working down to wheel with shortest hydraulic line.

If a power steering hose is disconnected or actuator is removed, the following brake bleeding procedure using Actuator Checker (09990-00150) is required.

**1)** Fill fluid in power steering reservoir. Start engine. With engine speed less than 1000 RPM, turn steering wheel from side to side against lock 2-3 times.

**2)** Turn engine off. Connect a clear hose to bleeder plug located on top of steering gear. *See Fig. 3.* Start engine. Turn steering wheel from side to side against lock 2-3 times.

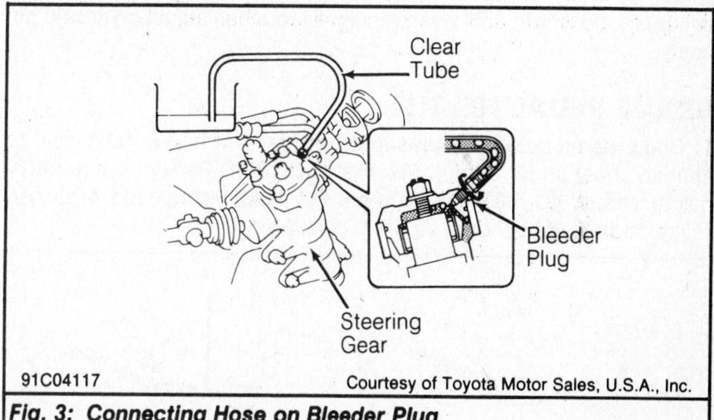


***Fig. 3: Connecting Hose on Bleeder Plug***

**3)** Place wheels in straight-ahead position. Loosen bleeder plug. Tighten bleeder plug when bubbles no longer exist in clear hose. Ensure power steering fluid level does not rise and foaming of fluid does not exist.

**4)** If fluid level rises or foaming occurs, repeat procedure until air is no longer present. Tighten bleeder plug to 69 INCH lbs. (8 N.m). Bleed brake system with engine running, then bleed system again with engine off. When bleeding brake system, start with longest line first. Tighten bleeder screw to 96 INCH lbs. (11 N.m).

**5)** Bleed power steering system again. Turn ignition off. Disconnect actuator electrical connector. Disconnect ABS relay. Connect Actuator Checker (09990-0150) to actuator and ABS relay. Connect actuator checker positive and negative cables to battery.

***CAUTION: Master cylinder may be damaged if these cautions are not followed. DO NOT press POWER switch for more than 10 seconds. DO NOT press POWER switch without depressing brake pedal. DO NOT release brake pedal while pressing POWER switch.***

# 1991 BRAKES
# Anti-Lock – Pickup & 4Runner (Cont.)

6) Start engine. Turn actuator checker SELECTOR switch to AIR BLEED position. *See Fig. 9.* Strongly press and hold brake pedal. Press POWER switch for 3 seconds and then release. Repeat this procedure 5 times.
7) Ensure POWER switch is released, then release brake pedal. Check brake and power steering fluid. Fill as necessary. Remove actuator checker from vehicle.

## ADJUSTMENTS

### MASTER CYLINDER PUSH ROD

1) Install Adjusting Gauge (09737-00010) on master cylinder with master cylinder gasket in place. Lower adjusting gauge pin until pin slightly touches master cylinder piston. Perform STEP 1. *See Fig. 4.* Turn adjusting gauge upside down and install on power brake unit.

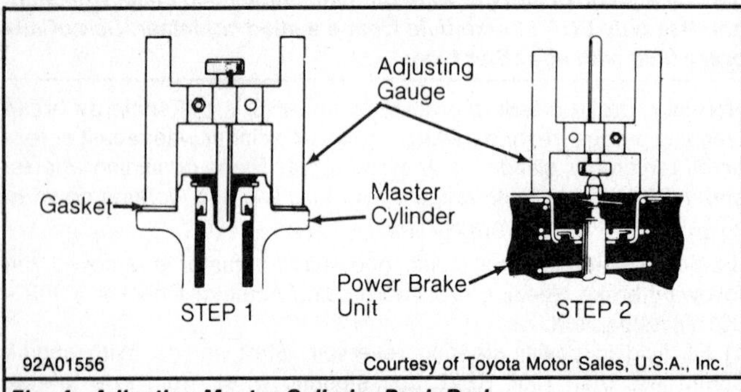


***Fig. 4: Adjusting Master Cylinder Push Rod***

2) Measure clearance between power brake unit push rod and adjusting gauge pin head. Perform STEP 2. *See Fig. 4.* Measured clearance should be zero. If measured clearance is not zero, adjust power brake unit push rod length until push rod lightly touches adjusting gauge pin head.

### BRAKE PEDAL HEIGHT

1) Brake pedal height is measured from face of brake pedal pad to asphalt sheet under carpet. *See Fig. 5.* On 2WD Pickup, brake pedal height should be 5.83" (148.0 mm). On 4WD Pickup and 4Runner, brake pedal height should be 5.71" (145.0 mm).

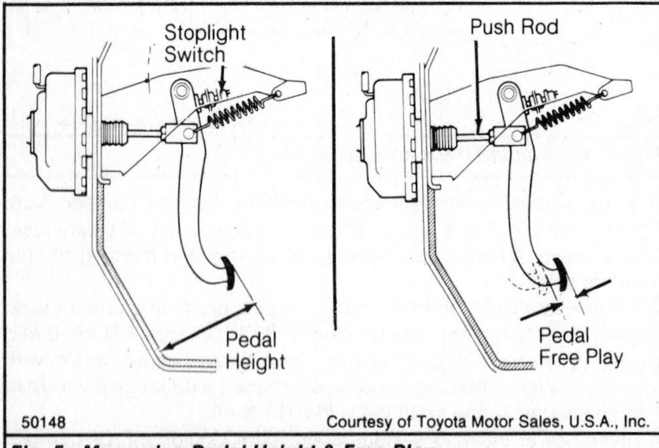


***Fig. 5: Measuring Pedal Height & Free Play***

2) To adjust brake pedal height, disconnect stoplight switch connector. Loosen stoplight switch lock nut. Remove stoplight switch.
3) Adjust pedal height by turning push rod. After adjusting brake pedal height, tighten push rod lock nut. Install and adjust stoplight switch. See STOPLIGHT SWITCH. Check and adjust brake pedal free play. See BRAKE PEDAL FREE PLAY.

### BRAKE PEDAL FREE PLAY

1) Brake pedal free play is distance brake pedal travels before feeling resistance with engine stopped. To check brake pedal free play, depress brake pedal several times to exhaust vacuum from power brake unit.
2) On Pickup with single booster power brake unit, depress brake pedal and measure travel until initial resistance is felt. On Pickup and 4Runner with tandem booster power brake unit, depress brake pedal and measure travel until beginning of second resistance is felt. First resistance is due to play between clevis and pin, .04-.12" (1-3 mm).
3) On all models, brake pedal free play should be .12-.24" (3.0-6.0 mm). If free play is not within specification, adjust by turning push rod. *See Fig. 5.* After adjusting brake pedal free play, check brake pedal height. See BRAKE PEDAL HEIGHT.

### STOPLIGHT SWITCH

Stoplight switch is located above brake pedal. *See Fig. 5.* To adjust stoplight switch, loosen stoplight switch lock nuts and turn stoplight switch until it touches brake pedal stop. Tighten lock nut. Check stoplight operation.

### BRAKE PEDAL DEPRESSED HEIGHT

1) Brake pedal depressed height is measured from face of brake pedal pad to asphalt sheet under carpet with brakes applied. Measure brake pedal depressed height with engine running and weight of 110 lbs. (50 kg) applied against brake pedal.
2) See BRAKE PEDAL DEPRESSED HEIGHT DISTANCE table for minimum depressed height. If measured brake pedal depressed height distance is less than minimum distance specified in table, inspect brake system.

***BRAKE PEDAL DEPRESSED HEIGHT DISTANCE***

| Application | In. (mm) |
|---|---|
| Pickup | |
| 2WD | |
| 22R-E Engine | 2.76 (70) |
| 3VZ-E Engine | |
| 1 Ton | 2.95 (75) |
| 1/2 Ton | 2.56 (65) |
| Cab & Chassis | |
| Dual Rear Wheels | 2.17 (55) |
| Single Rear Wheels | 2.95 (75) |
| 4WD | 2.56 (65) |
| 4Runner | 2.56 (65) |

### REAR DRUM BRAKE SHOES

***NOTE: Rear drum brakes have a self-adjuster which activates when brake pedal is applied as vehicle travels in reverse.***

Raise and support vehicle. Remove brake drum. Measure brake drum inside diameter and diameter of brake shoes. Clearance between diameters should be .024" (6.00 mm). Adjust self-adjuster length to adjust clearance.

### PARKING BRAKE CABLE

***NOTE: Service brake must be correctly adjusted before adjusting parking brake.***

1) Pull on parking brake lever with weight of 44 lbs. (20 kg) to check parking brake adjustment. Count number of notches (clicks) until parking brake is fully applied. Compare actual count to specification in PARKING BRAKE ADJUSTMENT table. Adjust parking brake if travel is not within specification.
2) To adjust, release parking brake. From beneath vehicle, loosen lock nut on equalizer bar pull rod. Turn adjuster nut until lever travel is correct. Tighten lock nut.

**PARKING BRAKE ADJUSTMENT**

| Application | Notches |
|---|---|
| Pickup | |
| 2WD | 12-18 |
| 1 Ton & 4WD | 11-17 |
| 4Runner | 13-19 |

## TROUBLE SHOOTING

### SYMPTOM DIAGNOSTICS

**Rear Anti-Lock Light Illuminates – 1)** Disconnect service connector. *See Fig. 6*. Using a jumper wire, connect check connector terminals Tc and $E_1$. *See Fig. 7*. Turn ignition on. If REAR ANTI-LOCK light blinks codes or illuminates constantly, see DIAGNOSTIC CODES under DIAGNOSIS & TESTING. If REAR ANTI-LOCK light does not illuminate, go to next step.

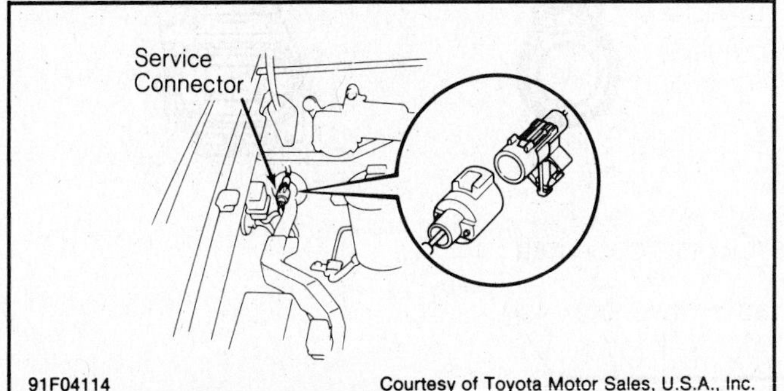


***Fig. 6: Service Connector Location***

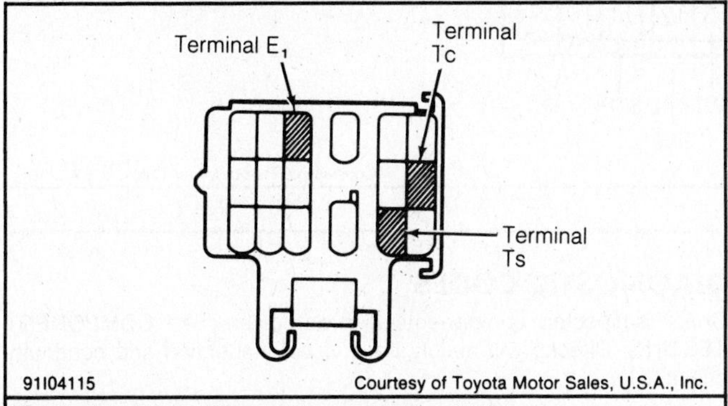


***Fig. 7: Identifying Check Connector Terminals***

**2)** Turn ignition off. Ensure ABS computer connector is properly connected and connector terminals are not damaged. Repair connector as necessary. Turn ignition on. Using a voltmeter, ensure 10-14 volts exists between ABS computer connector terminal No. 8 (Black wire) and ground. *See Fig. 8*. If 10-14 volts does not exist, repair faulty circuit.

**3)** Turn ignition off. Disconnect ABS computer connector. Disconnect ABS relay connector. Turn ignition on. If REAR ANTI-LOCK light illuminates, repair short circuit between ABS relay connector terminal No. 4 and ABS computer connector terminal No. 10 (Black/Red wire). *See Fig. 8*. If REAR ANTI-LOCK light does not illuminate, replace faulty ABS computer.

**Rear Anti-Lock Light Does Not Illuminate For 2 Seconds After Ignition Is Turned On – 1)** Disconnect service connector. *See Fig. 6*. Using a jumper wire, ground service connector terminal on harness side. Turn ignition on. If REAR ANTI-LOCK light does not illuminate, replace faulty REAR ANTI-LOCK light bulb or repair open circuit between REAR ANTI-LOCK light and service connector terminal. *See Fig. 8*. If REAR ANTI-LOCK light illuminates, go to next step.

**2)** Turn ignition off. Disconnect ABS computer connector. Disconnect ABS relay connector. Using a jumper wire, ground ABS computer connector terminal No. 10 (Black/Red wire) on wire harness side. *See Fig. 8*. Turn ignition on. REAR ANTI-LOCK light should illuminate. If REAR ANTI-LOCK light does not illuminate, repair open circuit in wiring harness between ABS computer terminal No. 10 and REAR ANTI-LOCK light. If REAR ANTI-LOCK light illuminates, go to next step.

**3)** Turn ignition off. Disconnect ABS relay connector. Using ohmmeter, ensure continuity is present between ABS relay terminal No. 4 and ABS relay terminal No. 2. *See Fig. 8*. Reverse ohmmeter leads between terminals and recheck continuity.

**4)** If continuity between ABS relay connector terminals is present both ways, repair short circuit in ABS relay diode. If continuity between terminals is only present in one direction, replace faulty ABS computer.

**5)** Connect ABS computer connectors. Ensure ABS relay connector is disconnected. Turn ignition on. REAR ANTI-LOCK light should illuminate. If REAR ANTI-LOCK light illuminates, ABS computer connector terminal No. 10 is okay.

**Rear Anti-Lock Light Illuminates Intermittently – 1)** Check for short circuit between check connector terminal Ts and ABS computer connector terminal No. 14 (Red/Yellow and Black/Red wires). *See Figs. 7 and 8*.

**2)** Check for short circuit between check connector terminal Tc and ABS computer connector terminal No. 6 (Blue/Black and Yellow/Black wires).

**Braking Inefficient, ABS Operates With Ordinary Braking, ABS Operates Just Before Stopping With Ordinary Braking & Brake Pedal Pulsates Abnormally With ABS Functioning – 1)** Disconnect service connector. *See Fig. 6*. Using a jumper wire, connect check connector terminals Tc and $E_1$. *See Fig. 7*. Turn ignition on. REAR ANTI-LOCK light should blink a normal code. If REAR ANTI-LOCK light does not blink a normal code, see DIAGNOSTIC CODES under DIAGNOSIS & TESTING. If REAR ANTI-LOCK light blinks a normal code, go to next step.

**2)** Enter deceleration sensor diagnostics. See DECELERATION SENSOR DIAGNOSTICS under DIAGNOSIS & TESTING. If deceleration sensor does not function properly, check installation of sensor. If deceleration sensor is properly installed, replace faulty deceleration sensor. If deceleration sensor operation is okay, go to next step.

**3)** Enter speed sensor diagnostics. See SPEED SENSOR DIAGNOSTICS under DIAGNOSIS & TESTING. If speed sensor signal level is okay, go to next step. If speed sensor signal level is not okay, check speed sensor. See SPEED SENSOR under COMPONENT TESTING. Replace as necessary.

**4)** Ensure speed sensors is installed properly. If speed sensor is not installed properly, repair as necessary. Ensure all foreign and metal chips are cleaned from speed sensor tip.

**5)** Turn ignition off. Disconnect ABS computer connector. Ensure continuity is present between each speed sensor terminal and ABS computer connector terminal. Twist and move wiring harness. If continuity readings change, repair faulty wiring harness between speed sensor and ABS computer connector. If continuity readings do not change, go to next step.

**6)** Check actuator operation. See ACTUATOR CHECK under DIAGNOSIS & TESTING. If actuator operation is not okay, replace faulty actuator. If actuator operation is okay, inspect differential ring gear serrations. See DIFFERENTIAL RING GEAR under COMPONENT TESTING. Replace as necessary. If differential ring gear is okay, replace ABS computer.

**Anti-Lock Works Inefficiently – 1)** Disconnect service connector. *See Fig. 6*. Using a jumper wire, connect check connector terminals Tc and $E_1$. *See Fig. 7*. Turn ignition on. REAR ANTI-LOCK light should blink a normal code. If REAR ANTI-LOCK light does not blink a normal code, see DIAGNOSTIC CODES under DIAGNOSIS & TESTING. If REAR ANTI-LOCK light blinks a normal code, go to next step.

**2)** Ensure battery voltage is present between ABS computer terminal No. 11 (Green/White wire) and ground when brake pedal is depressed. *See Fig. 8*. If battery voltage is not present when brake pedal is depressed, repair open circuit in stoplight switch or wiring harness. Check actuator operation. See ACTUATOR CHECK under DIAGNOSIS & TESTING.

# 1991 BRAKES
# Anti-Lock – Pickup & 4Runner (Cont.)

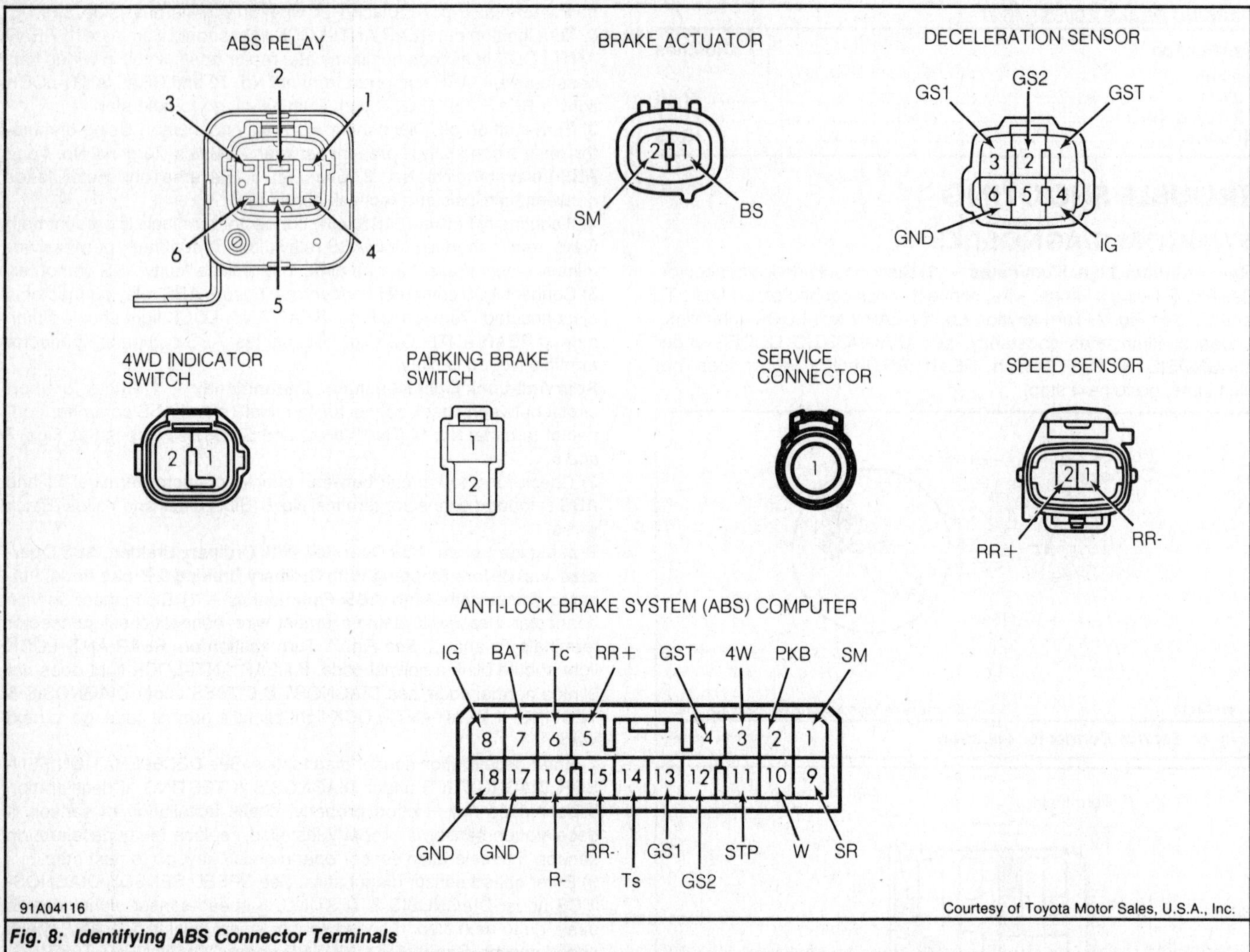


***Fig. 8: Identifying ABS Connector Terminals***

## DIAGNOSIS & TESTING

***NOTE: DO NOT start engine when accessing trouble codes.***

### ACCESSING TROUBLE CODES

**Rear Anti-Lock Light Diagnostics** – **1)** Ensure battery voltage is 12 volts. Turn ignition switch to ON position. REAR ANTI-LOCK light should illuminate then go out after 2 seconds. If REAR ANTI-LOCK light does not illuminate, check fuse, bulb and wiring harness.

**2)** With ignition on, disconnect service connector. *See Fig. 6.* Using a jumper wire, connect check connector terminals Tc and $E_1$. *See Fig. 7.* If a malfunction is detected, 4 seconds will elapse and REAR ANTI-LOCK light will begin to flash a 2-digit code as follows. Light will flash code for first digit (number of blinks), follow by a 1.5-second pause, then code for second digit (number of blinks) is flashed.

**3)** If 2 or more trouble codes are stored, there will be a 4-second pause between each code. If ABS system is functioning properly, REAR ANTI-LOCK light will blink once every .5 second. For code interpretation, see DIAGNOSTIC CODES.

**4)** After replacing or repairing malfunctioning components, clear diagnostic codes. If battery cable was disconnected during repairs, all codes will be erased. If battery cable was not disconnected during repairs, see CLEARING CODES.

## DIAGNOSTIC CODES

Check suspected components in order given. See COMPONENT TESTING. Checks will mainly be a visual inspection and continuity checks.

***NOTE: To prevent false ABS Codes 11 and 25, a production change was made to power transistor circuit inside ABS computer. Contact local Toyota dealer to check if production change affects your vehicle. Before replacing ABS computer, always inspect actuator solenoid and ABS relay circuits for an open or short.***

**Code 11** – Open in ABS relay circuit. Check actuator solenoid, ABS relay, wiring harness, actuator solenoid connector and ABS relay connector.

**Code 12** – Short in ABS relay circuit. Check actuator solenoid, ABS relay, wiring harness, actuator solenoid connector and ABS relay connector.

**Code 25** – Short in solenoid circuit. Check actuator solenoid, ABS relay, wiring harness, actuator solenoid connector and ABS relay connector.

**Code 33** – Open or short in speed sensor circuit. Check speed sensor, sensor wiring harness and connector.

**Code 41** – Battery voltage is 9.5 volts or less. Check vehicle battery.

**Code 42** – Battery voltage is 17 volts or more. Check vehicle battery.

**Code 43** – Mechanical malfunction of deceleration sensor. Check deceleration sensor, wiring harness, sensor connector and sensor circuit.

**Code 44** – Electrical malfunction of deceleration sensor circuit. Check deceleration sensor, wiring harness, sensor connector and sensor circuit.

**Always On** – Malfunction of ABS computer. Ensure ABS computer connector is properly connected and terminals are not damaged. If connector is okay, replace ABS computer. See ABS COMPUTER under REMOVAL & INSTALLATION.

## CLEARING CODES

**1)** Turn ignition on. Disconnect service connector. *See Fig. 6.* Using a jumper wire, connect check connector terminals Tc and $E_1$. *See Fig. 7.* With vehicle stopped, depress brake pedal 8 or more times within 3 seconds to erase codes.

**2)** REAR ANTI-LOCK light should show a normal code. Connect service connector. Remove jumper wire from check connector. Ensure REAR ANTI-LOCK light goes out after 2 seconds. Codes are now cleared. Ensure REAR ANTI-LOCK light shows a normal code. See ACCESSING TROUBLE CODES.

## ACTUATOR CHECK

***NOTE: Actuator Checker (09990-00150) is required to perform ACTUATOR CHECK.***

**1)** Turn ignition off. Disconnect actuator electrical connector. Disconnect ABS relay. *See Fig. 1 or 2.* Connect Actuator Checker (09990-00150) to actuator and ABS relay. Connect actuator checker positive and negative power cables to vehicle battery.

***NOTE: DO NOT press POWER switch for more than 10 seconds.***

**2)** Start engine. Turn actuator checker SELECTOR switch to REAR position. *See Fig. 9.* Strongly press and hold brake pedal. Press POWER switch (DO NOT press more than 10 seconds). When POWER switch is pressed, brake pedal should not go down. Release POWER switch. Brake pedal should lower. If brake pedal does not respond as specified, replace brake actuator.

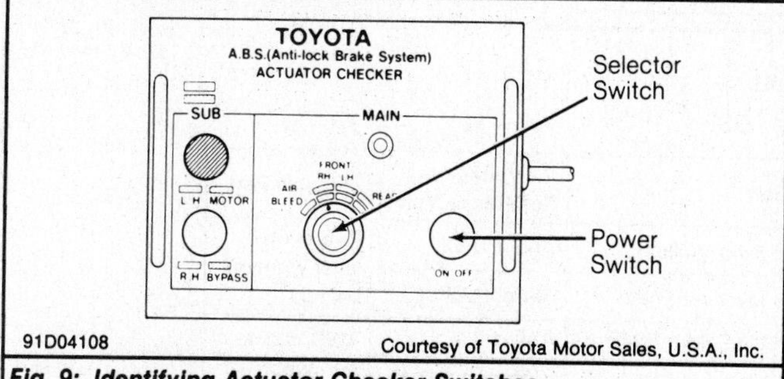


Courtesy of Toyota Motor Sales, U.S.A., Inc.

***Fig. 9: Identifying Actuator Checker Switches***

## SPEED SENSOR DIAGNOSTICS

***NOTE: While diagnosing speed sensor, brake system functions as a conventional system. Ensure vehicle is not in 4WD mode.***

**1)** Ensure battery voltage is approximately 12 volts. Turn ignition on. Ensure REAR ANTI-LOCK light illuminates, then goes out after about 2 seconds. If REAR ANTI-LOCK light does not illuminate, check fuse, bulb and wiring harness.

**2)** Turn ignition off. Using a jumper wire, connect check connector terminals Tc and $E_1$. *See Fig. 7.* Engage parking brake. Start engine. DO NOT press brake pedal. REAR ANTI-LOCK light should illuminate 4 times per second. If REAR ANTI-LOCK light does not illuminate, check parking brake switch, check connector, speed sensor installation and ABS computer connection.

**3)** On 4WD models, if vehicle is in 4WD mode, diagnostic code 88 will appear. Ensure vehicle is not in 4WD mode, then re-enter SPEED SENSOR DIAGNOSTICS. On all models, if REAR ANTI-LOCK light starts flashing diagnostic code, refer to DIAGNOSTIC CODES. Repair as necessary.

***NOTE: While REAR ANTI-LOCK light is off, DO NOT accelerate, decelerate, brake, shift, move steering or drive on rough road surfaces, as these conditions will affect test.***

**4)** Release parking brake. Drive vehicle straight ahead at 2.5-3.7 MPH. REAR ANTI-LOCK light should go out when vehicle speed is in the specified range. If REAR ANTI-LOCK light goes out when vehicle speed is in the specified range, and blinks when vehicle speed is not in the specified range, speed sensor low speed check is completed.

**5)** Drive vehicle straight ahead at 24-31 MPH. Ensure REAR ANTI-LOCK light illuminates after a one-second pause. If REAR ANTI-LOCK light illuminates without blinking when vehicle is NOT within specified speed, stop vehicle and record diagnostic codes. Turn ignition off. Repair as necessary. See SPEED SENSOR DIAGNOSTIC CODES.

**6)** If REAR ANTI-LOCK light illuminates while vehicle speed is in the specified range, check is completed. If vehicle speed exceeds 34 MPH, REAR ANTI-LOCK light will blink. If REAR ANTI-LOCK light blinks when vehicle speed exceeds 34 MPH, differential ring gear is okay.

**7)** Turn ignition off. Remove jumper wire from check connector. Clear diagnostic codes. See CLEARING CODES.

## SPEED SENSOR DIAGNOSTIC CODES

**Code 77** – Abnormal signal from speed sensor. Check differential ring gear.

**Code 88** – Mismatched ABS computer. Replace ABS computer.

**Light Illuminates 4 Times Per Second** – Speed sensor and differential ring gear are normal.

## DECELERATION SENSOR DIAGNOSTICS

***NOTE: While diagnosing deceleration sensor, brake system functions as a conventional system.***

**1)** Ensure battery voltage is 12 volts. Turn ignition on. REAR ANTI-LOCK light should illuminate then go out after 2 seconds. If REAR ANTI-LOCK light does not illuminate, check fuse, bulb and wiring harness.

**2)** Using a jumper wire, connect check connector terminals Tc and Ts to $E_1$. *See Fig. 7.* Engage parking brake. Depress brake pedal and start engine.

***NOTE: If brake pedal is not depressed when engine is started, vehicle will enter speed sensor diagnostics.***

**3)** Ensure REAR ANTI-LOCK light blinks about once every second. If REAR ANTI-LOCK light does not blink, inspect parking brake switch, check connector, deceleration sensor installation and ABS computer. If REAR ANTI-LOCK light flashes diagnostic code(s), see DIAGNOSTIC CODES. Repair as necessary.

**4)** Release parking brake. Drive vehicle at about 12.4 MPH or greater. Strongly depress brake pedal. REAR ANTI-LOCK light should blink about 7 times per second.

**5)** If REAR ANTI-LOCK light does not respond as specified, check deceleration sensor installation. If deceleration sensor installation is okay, replace deceleration sensor. Turn engine off. Remove jumper wire from check connector terminals.

## COMPONENT TESTING

**Speed Sensor** – Disconnect speed sensor connector. *See Fig. 1 or 2.* Using a DVOM, measure resistance between speed sensor terminals. Resistance should be 580-700 ohms. Ensure continuity is not present between each sensor terminal and sensor body. If resistance and continuity readings are not as specified, replace speed sensor.

# 1991 BRAKES
# Anti-Lock – Pickup & 4Runner (Cont.)

ANTI-LOCK BRAKE SYSTEM (ABS) COMPUTER CONNECTOR

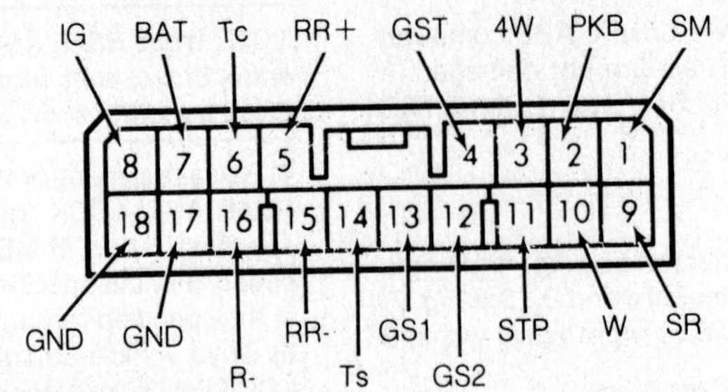


| Tester Connection | Condition | Voltage | Trouble Part |
|---|---|---|---|
| SM – Body ground | Ignition switch ON | Battery voltage | Solenoid relay, Actuator |
| | Ignition switch ON and "REAR ANTILOCK" warning light goes on | About 0 V | |
| SR – Body ground | Ignition switch ON | Battery voltage | |
| | Ignition switch ON and "REAR ANTILOCK" warning light goes on | About 0 V | |
| W – Body ground | Ignition switch ON | Battery voltage | Warning light bulb |
| | Ignition switch ON and "REAR ANTILOCK" warning light goes on | About 0 V | |

Courtesy of Toyota Motor Sales, U.S.A., Inc.

92D01831

**Fig. 10: Testing Specifications Table for ABS Computer Wiring Harness (1 of 2)**

ANTI-LOCK BRAKE SYSTEM (ABS) COMPUTER CONNECTOR

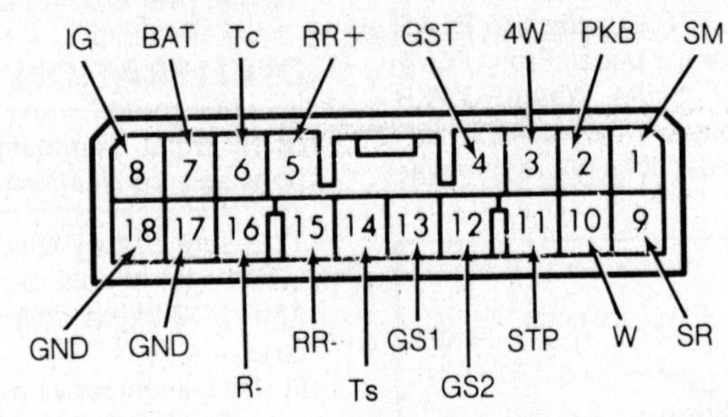


| Tester Connection | Check Item | Condition | Voltage or Resistance Value | Trouble Part |
|---|---|---|---|---|
| PKB – Body ground | Voltage | Ignition SW on and PKB lever pulled | About 0 V | PKB switch, level warning switch |
| | | Ignition SW on and PKB lever returned | Battery voltage | |
| [1] 4W – Body ground | Voltage | Ignition SW on and 4WD indicator SW on | About 0 V | 4WD indicator switch |
| | | Ignition SW on and 4WD indicator SW off | Battery voltage | |
| [2] 4W – Body ground | Continuity | – | Continuity | Wire harness |
| RR+ – RR– | Resistance | – | 580 – 700 Ω | Speed sensor |
| BAT – Body ground | Voltage | – | Battery voltage | Wire harness |
| IG – Body ground | Voltage | Ignition SW on | Battery voltage | ECU-IG fuse, wire harness |
| | | Ignition SW off | About 0 V | |
| SR – R– | Resistance | – | 80 Ω | Solenoid relay |
| STP – Body ground | Voltage | Ignition SW off and brake pedal depressed | Battery voltage | Stop light switch, stop light |
| | Continuity | Ignition SW off and brake pedal returned | Continuity | |
| GND – Body ground | Continuity | – | Continuity | Wire harness |

[1] – For 4WD models only.
[2] – For 2WD models only.

Courtesy of Toyota Motor Sales, U.S.A., Inc.

92F01832

**Fig. 11: Testing Specifications Table for ABS Computer Wiring Harness (2 of 2)**

**ABS Relay – 1)** Disconnect ABS relay connector. *See Fig. 1 or 2.* Using a DVOM, check continuity between ABS relay terminals No. 1 and No. 6. *See Fig. 8.* Continuity should be present.

**2)** Ensure continuity is present between relay terminals No. 3 and No. 5. Connect DVOM positive lead to relay terminal No. 4. Connect DVOM negative lead to relay terminal No. 5. Ensure continuity is present. Reverse DVOM connections between relay terminals No. 4 and No. 5. Continuity should NOT be present.

**3)** Apply battery voltage between relay terminals No. 1 and No. 6. Check continuity between relay terminals No. 2 and No. 5. Ensure continuity is present.

**4)** Connect DVOM positive lead to relay terminal No. 4 and negative lead to terminal No. 5. Continuity should be present. Reverse DVOM connections between relay terminals No. 4 and No. 5. Continuity should NOT be present. If continuity readings are not as specified, replace ABS relay.

**Differential Ring Gear –** Remove differential carrier. See DIFFERENTIAL RING GEAR under REMOVAL & INSTALLATION. Visually inspect differential ring gear serrations for scratches, cracks, missing teeth and warping. If differential ring gear is damaged, replace ring gear. If differential ring gear is okay, install differential carrier.

**ABS Computer Wiring Harness – 1)** Remove ABS computer. See ABS COMPUTER under REMOVAL & INSTALLATION. With ABS computer connector connected, backprobe ABS computer connector terminals. Measure voltage at each terminal and body ground as specified in table. *See Fig. 10.* If circuit(s) do not test as specified, check and repair or replace trouble part shown in table.

**2)** Disconnect ABS computer connectors. Check resistance and voltage on wire harness side of ABS computer connector terminals as specified in table. *See Fig. 11.* If circuit(s) do not test as specified, check and repair or replace troubled part shown in table.

## REMOVAL & INSTALLATION

***WARNING: Hydraulic system may be under high pressure, use caution when opening hydraulic system.***

### ACTUATOR

**Removal & Installation – 1)** Turn ignition off. Remove vehicle battery. Remove battery tray. Disconnect actuator electrical connector. Disconnect brake lines attached to actuator. Turn steering wheel clockwise to right stop. Disconnect power steering hydraulic lines from actuator.

**2)** Remove 3 bolts. Remove actuator from actuator bracket. To install, reverse removal procedure. Bleed brake and power steering system. See BLEEDING BRAKE SYSTEM.

### ABS COMPUTER

**Removal & Installation –** Ensure ignition is off. Disconnect negative battery cable. Remove glove box assembly. Access ABS computer in right side of dashboard, above glove box. Remove ABS computer-to-vehicle screws. Disconnect ABS computer connector. Remove ABS computer from vehicle. To install, reverse removal procedure.

### SPEED SENSOR

**Removal & Installation –** Disconnect rear wheel speed sensor connector. Remove wheel speed sensor mounting bolt from differential. Remove wheel speed sensor. To install, reverse removal procedure. Tighten wheel speed sensor mounting bolt to specification. See TORQUE SPECIFICATIONS table at end of article.

### ABS RELAY

**Removal & Installation –** Remove relay-to-vehicle bolt. Disconnect connector from relay. Remove relay from vehicle. To install, reverse removal procedure.

### DECELERATION SENSOR

**Removal & Installation –** Remove instrument lower center cover below dashboard. Remove 2 sensor-to-vehicle bolts. Disconnect connector from sensor. Remove sensor from vehicle. *See Fig. 12.* To install, reverse removal procedure.

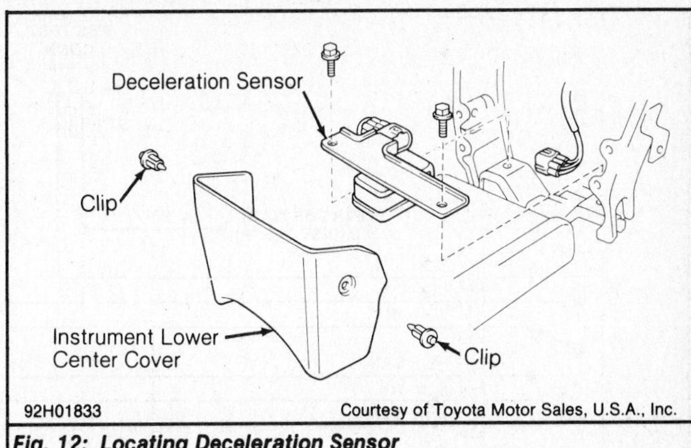


***Fig. 12: Locating Deceleration Sensor***

### DIFFERENTIAL RING GEAR

**Removal & Installation – 1)** Remove speed sensor from differential. See SPEED SENSOR. On single rear wheel models, remove wheel assembly. Disconnect parking brake and brake hose from brake assembly. Remove 4 rear brake assembly-to-axle housing bolts. Remove rear brake assembly with axle.

**2)** On dual rear wheel models, remove outboard wheel assembly. Remove 6 nuts and washers. Install 2 service bolts into axle shaft end. Tighten service bolts one turn. Tap on end of axle shaft. Remove 6 cone washers. Tighten service bolts to separate axle shaft. Remove axle shaft from axle housing. Remove 2 service bolts from axle shaft.

**3)** On all models, paint mating marks on differential flange and drive shaft flange. DO NOT use punch marks. Remove drive shaft bolts. Wire drive shaft aside. Drain differential oil. Remove 10 differential bolts. Remove differential carrier from axle housing. To install, reverse removal procedure. Fill differential to bottom of fill hole with oil.

## OVERHAUL

DO NOT overhaul or disassemble actuator assembly. If actuator is defective, replace entire assembly.

## TORQUE SPECIFICATIONS

***TORQUE SPECIFICATIONS***

| Application | Ft. Lbs. (N.m) |
|---|---|
| Axle Shaft-To-Hub Nuts | |
| Dual Rear Wheel | 25 (34) |
| Brake Line Nuts | 11 (15) |
| Drive Shaft Bolts | 54 (73) |
| Power Steering Hose-To-Actuator Bolt | 34 (46) |
| Rear Brake Assembly-To-Axle Housing Nuts | |
| Single Rear Wheel | 51 (69) |
| Speed Sensor Bolt | 14 (19) |
| Wheel Lug Nuts | 76 (103) |
| | **INCH Lbs. (N.m)** |
| ABS Computer Mounting Screws | 28 (3) |
| Actuator Mounting Bolts | 108 (12) |
| Deceleration Sensor Bolts | 48 (5) |

# 1991 BRAKES
# Anti-Lock – Pickup & 4Runner (Cont.)

## WIRING DIAGRAM

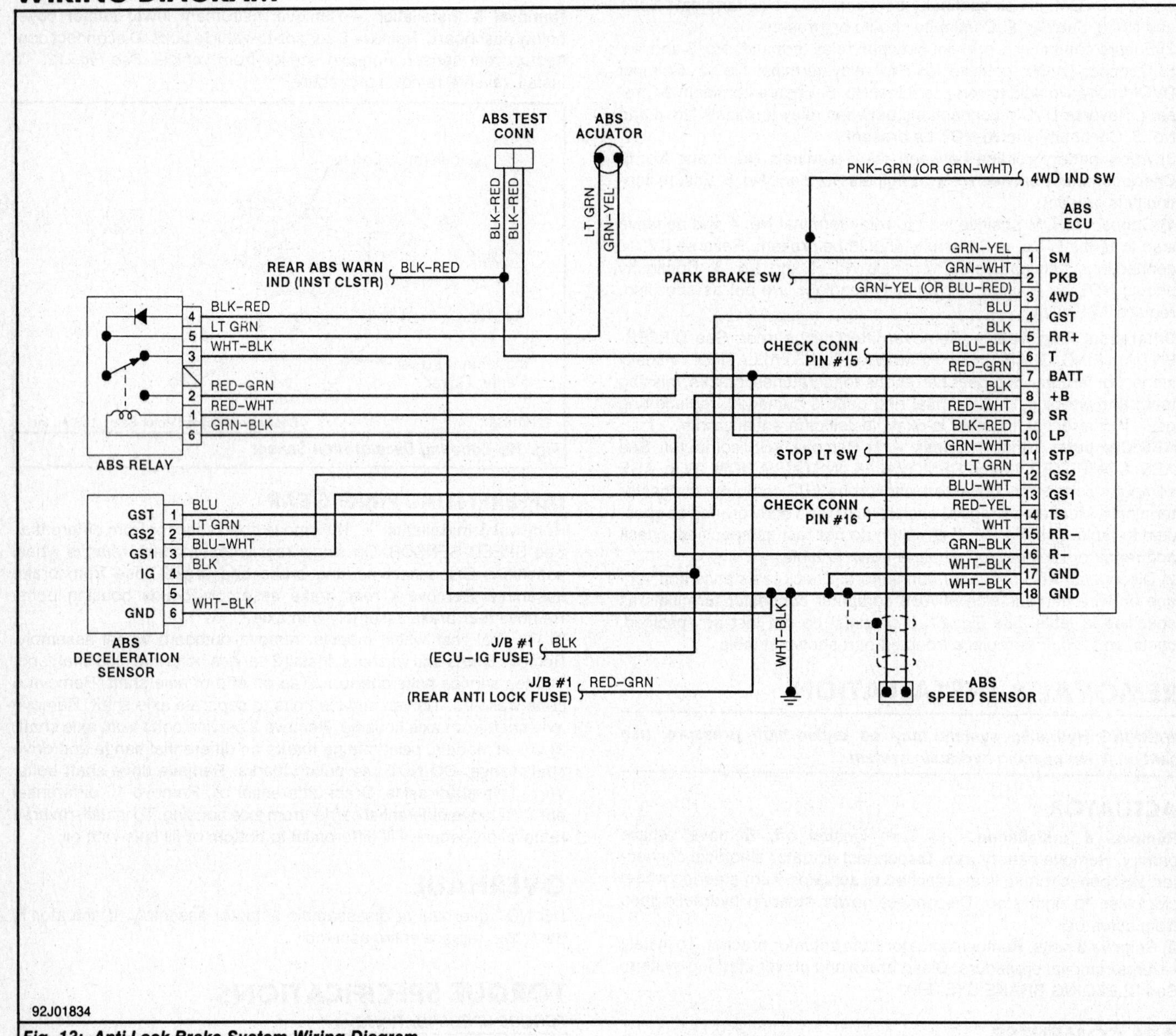


**Fig. 13: Anti-Lock Brake System Wiring Diagram**

# 1991 BRAKES
# Anti-Lock – Previa

## DESCRIPTION

The Anti-Lock Brake System (ABS) consists of deceleration sensor (4WD), ABS actuator, ABS computer and 4 speed sensors. *See Fig. 1*. An ABS indicator light is located on the instrument panel, in the combination meter. ABS indicator light comes on for 3 seconds as a bulb test when ignition is turned on.

***NOTE: For more information on brake system, see appropriate DISC & DRUM article.***

## OPERATION

Under normal driving conditions, the ABS functions as a standard brake system. Upon detection of wheel lock-up, short pedal pulsations occurring in rapid succession will be felt in brake pedal. Pedal pulsation will continue until there is no longer a need for ABS function or until vehicle is stopped. Maintaining a constant force on brake pedal provides shortest stopping distance.

***CAUTION: See ANTI-LOCK BRAKE SAFETY PRECAUTIONS article in GENERAL INFORMATION.***

## BLEEDING BRAKE SYSTEM

***CAUTION: Brake fluid will damage painted surfaces. If brake fluid contacts painted surface, wipe off immediately, and clean with alcohol. Use only DOT 3 brake fluid from a sealed container. DO NOT mix brake fluid with any other type.***

ABS bleeding procedure is the same as standard brake bleeding procedure. If master cylinder is rebuilt or reservoir is empty, bleed master cylinder first. Bleed remaining wheels starting on wheel with longest hydraulic line, and work toward wheel with shortest hydraulic line.

## ADJUSTMENTS

### MASTER CYLINDER PUSH ROD

**1)** Install Adjusting Gauge (09737-00010) on master cylinder with master cylinder gasket in place. Lower adjusting gauge pin until pin slightly touches master cylinder piston. Perform STEP 1 in illustration. *See Fig. 2*. Turn adjusting gauge upside down, and install gauge on power brake unit.

**2)** Measure clearance between power brake unit push rod and adjusting gauge pin head. Perform STEP 2 in illustration. *See Fig. 2*. Measured clearance should be zero. If clearance is not zero, adjust power brake unit push rod length until push rod lightly touches adjusting gauge pin head.

### BRAKE PEDAL HEIGHT

**1)** Brake pedal height is measured from face of brake pedal pad to asphalt sheet under carpet. *See Fig. 3*. Brake pedal height should be 5.83-6.22" (148.0-158.0 mm). To adjust brake pedal height, loosen stoplight switch and lock nut on brake pedal push rod.

**2)** Adjust pedal height by turning push rod. After adjusting brake pedal height, tighten push rod lock nut. Adjust stoplight switch. See STOPLIGHT SWITCH. Check brake pedal free play. See BRAKE PEDAL FREE PLAY.

### BRAKE PEDAL FREE PLAY

**1)** Brake pedal free play is distance brake pedal travels before feeling resistance with engine stopped. To check brake pedal free play, depress brake pedal several times to exhaust vacuum from power brake unit. Depress brake pedal until initial resistance is felt. Measure pedal free play. *See Fig. 3*.

**2)** Brake pedal free play should be .04-.24" (1.0-6.0 mm). If free play is not within specification, adjust by turning push rod. After adjusting brake pedal free play, check brake pedal height. See BRAKE PEDAL HEIGHT.

### STOPLIGHT SWITCH

**1)** Stoplight switch is located above brake pedal. *See Fig. 3*. To adjust stoplight switch, loosen stoplight switch lock nuts, and turn stoplight switch until it touches brake pedal stop.

**2)** Turn stoplight switch counterclockwise until clearance between stoplight switch and brake pedal is .02-.09" (.5-2.3 mm). Tighten stoplight switch lock nut. Check stoplight operation.

### BRAKE PEDAL DEPRESSED HEIGHT

Brake pedal depressed height is measured from face of brake pedal pad to asphalt sheet under carpet with brakes applied. Measure brake pedal depressed height with engine running and weight of 110 lbs. (50 kg) applied against brake pedal. Minimum brake pedal depressed height should be 2.95" (75.0 mm). If measured distance is less than specified, inspect brake system.

### REAR DRUM BRAKE SHOES

***NOTE: Rear drum brakes have a self-adjuster, which activates when brake pedal is applied with vehicle traveling in reverse.***

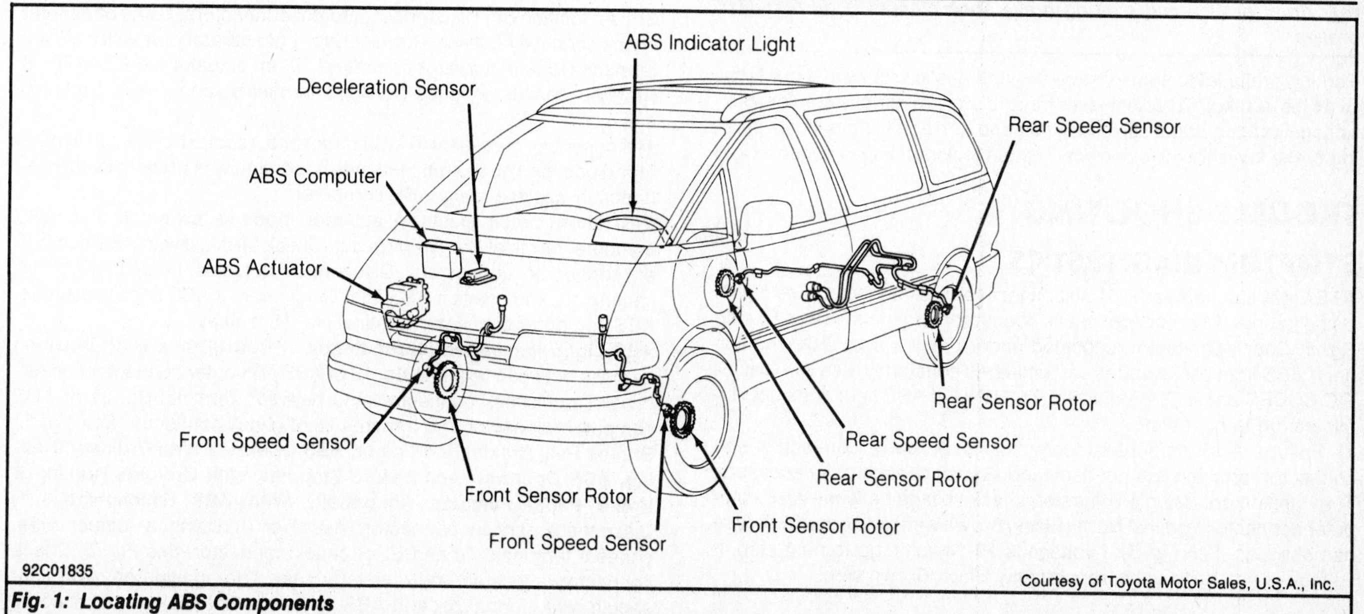


*Fig. 1: Locating ABS Components*

# 1991 BRAKES
# Anti-Lock – Previa (Cont.)

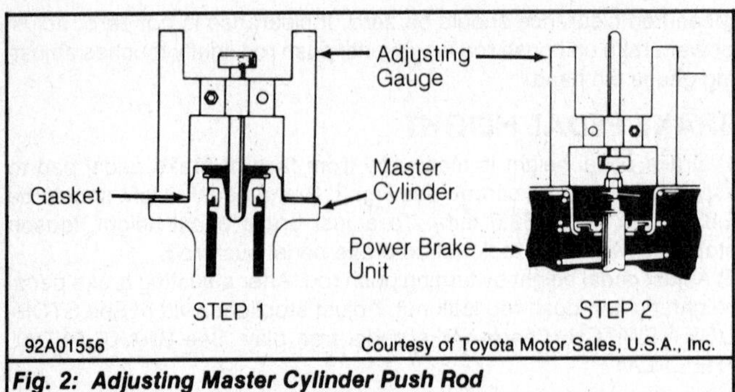


***Fig. 2: Adjusting Master Cylinder Push Rod***

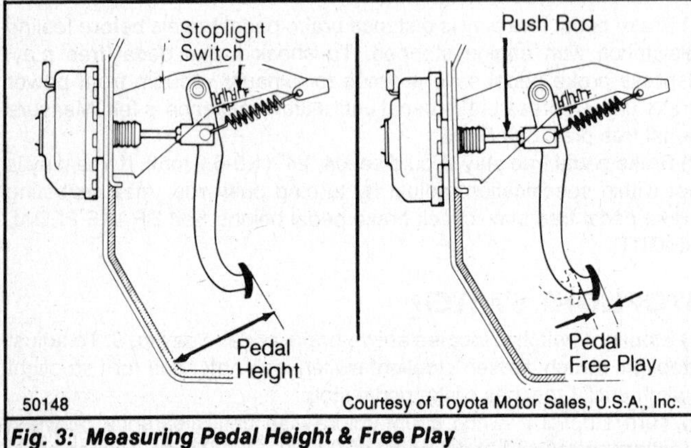


***Fig. 3: Measuring Pedal Height & Free Play***

Raise and support vehicle. Remove wheels and brake drums. Measure brake drum inside diameter and diameter of brake shoes. Clearance between diameters should be .024" (6.00 mm). To adjust clearance, adjust self-adjuster length.

## REAR DISC PARKING BRAKE SHOES

Raise and support vehicle. Remove wheels. Temporarily install hub nuts to hold disc brake rotors in place. Remove hole plug to gain access to adjuster. Turn adjuster and expand shoes until disc brake rotor locks. Return adjuster 8 notches. Install hole plug.

## PARKING/EMERGENCY BRAKE CABLE

***NOTE: Before adjusting parking brake cable, adjust service brake on rear drum brakes and parking brake shoe clearance on rear disc brakes.***

Parking brake lever should travel 4-5 notches (clicks) with a pull force of 44 lbs. (20 kg). To adjust lever travel distance, remove console box. Loosen parking brake cable lock nut, and turn adjusting nut until parking brake lever travel is correct. Tighten lock nut. Install console box.

# TROUBLE SHOOTING

## SYMPTOM DIAGNOSTICS

**ABS Light Illuminates – 1)** Disconnect service connector. *See Fig. 4*. Using jumper wire, connect check connector terminals Tc and $E_1$. *See Fig. 5*. Check connector is located under driver's seat. Turn ignition on. If ABS light blinks codes or illuminates constantly, see DIAGNOSTIC CODES under DIAGNOSIS & TESTING. If ABS light does not illuminate, go to next step.

**2)** Ensure ABS computer connector is properly connected and connector terminals are not damaged. Repair connector if necessary. Turn ignition on. Using a voltmeter, check voltage between ABS computer connector terminal No. 1 (Black/Brown wire) and ground on wire harness side. *See Fig. 6*. If voltage is 10-14 volts, go to next step. If voltage is not 10-14 volts, repair faulty Black/Brown wire.

**3)** Turn ignition off. Disconnect ABS computer connector. Disconnect service connector if not previously disconnected. Turn ignition on. If ABS light illuminates, repair short circuit between ABS computer connector terminal No. 15 and service connector terminal No. 1. *See Fig. 6*. If ABS light does not illuminate, replace faulty ABS computer.

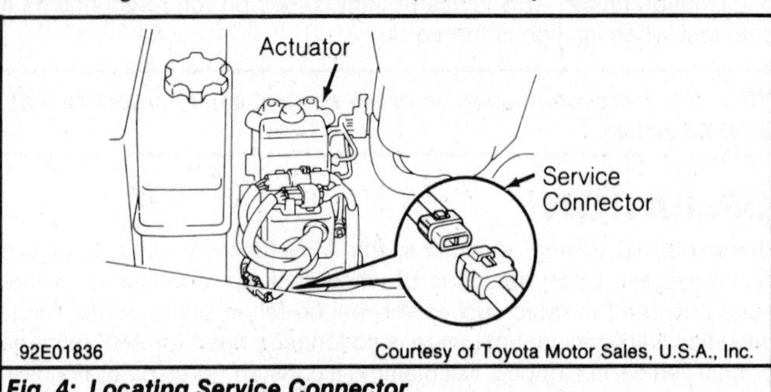


***Fig. 4: Locating Service Connector***

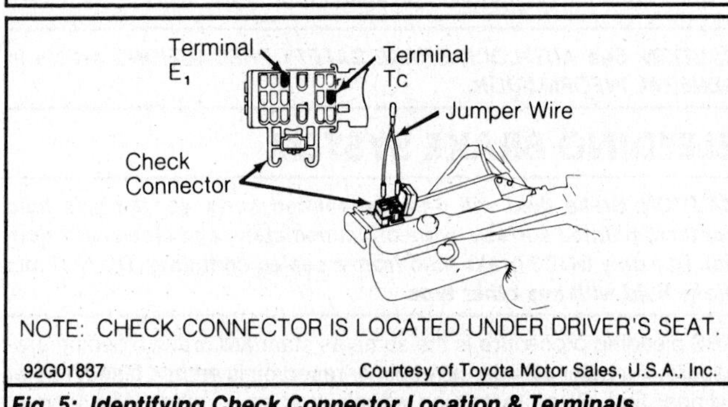


***Fig. 5: Identifying Check Connector Location & Terminals***

**ABS Light Does Not Illuminate For 3 Seconds After Ignition Is Turned On – 1)** Disconnect service connector. *See Fig. 4*. Using a jumper wire, ground service connector terminal No. 1 on harness (female) side. *See Fig. 6*. Turn ignition on. If ABS light does not illuminate, replace faulty ABS light bulb, or repair open circuit between ABS light and service connector terminal No. 1. If ABS light illuminates, go to next step.

**2)** Turn ignition off. Disconnect ABS computer connector and service connector. Using a jumper wire, ground ABS computer connector terminal No. 15 on wire harness side of connector. Turn ignition on. ABS light should illuminate. If ABS light does not illuminate, repair open circuit in wiring harness between ABS computer connector terminal No. 15 and ABS light. If ABS light illuminates, go to next step.

**3)** Turn ignition off. Disconnect actuator connectors. Using ohmmeter, check continuity between terminal No. 1 of actuator connector "A" and terminal No. 2 of actuator connector "C" on actuator side. *See Fig. 6*. Reverse ohmmeter leads between terminals, and check continuity again.

**4)** If continuity is present in both directions, repair short circuit in actuator diode, and go to step next step. If continuity is present in only one direction, replace faulty ABS computer.

**5)** If short circuit exists in actuator diode, a malfunction at ABS computer terminal No. 15 will occur. Check terminal with ABS computer connector connected. Disconnect actuator connectors. Turn ignition on, and check if ABS light illuminates. If ABS light illuminates, ABS computer connector terminal No. 15 is okay.

**ABS Light Illuminates Intermittently –** Check for a short in wiring harness between terminal No. 18 of ABS computer connector and terminal Ts of check connector, and between terminal No. 31 of ABS computer connector and terminal Tc of check connector. *See Fig. 6*.

**Brakes Pull, Braking Inefficient, ABS Operates With Ordinary Braking, ABS Operates Just Before Stopping With Ordinary Braking & Brake Pedal Pulsates Abnormally With ABS Functioning – 1)** Disconnect service connector. *See Fig. 4*. Using a jumper wire, connect terminals Tc and $E_1$ of check connector. *See Fig. 5*. Check connector is located under driver's seat. Turn ignition on. ABS light should blink normal code. If ABS light does not blink a normal code, refer to DIAGNOSTIC CODES under DIAGNOSIS & TESTING. On 4WD models, if ABS light blinks normal code, go to next step. On all other models, if ABS light blinks a normal code, go to step **3)**.

**2)** On 4WD models, enter deceleration sensor diagnostics. See DECELERATION SENSOR DIAGNOSTICS (4WD) under DIAGNOSIS & TESTING. If deceleration sensor does not operate properly, ensure deceleration sensor is installed correctly. If deceleration sensor is installed correctly, replace faulty sensor. If deceleration sensor operates properly, go to next step.

**3)** Enter speed sensor diagnostics. See SPEED SENSOR DIAGNOSTICS under DIAGNOSIS & TESTING. If speed sensor signal level is okay, go to next step. If speed sensor signal level is not okay, inspect sensor and sensor rotor. Replace if necessary.

**4)** Ensure all speed sensors are installed properly. If speed sensors are not installed properly, repair as necessary. If speed sensors are installed properly, ensure all foreign and metal chips are cleaned from speed sensor tip. Go to next step.

**5)** Turn ignition off. Disconnect ABS computer connector. Ensure continuity is present between each speed sensor connector (wire harness side) of ABS computer connector. Check continuity between FL+ and FL- (left front speed sensor), FR+ and FR- (right front speed sensor), RL+ and RL- (left rear speed sensor), and RR+ and RR- (right rear speed sensor). *See Fig. 6*.

**6)** If continuity readings change when wiring harness is twisted or moved, repair faulty wiring harness between speed sensor and ABS computer connector. Check actuator operation. See ACTUATOR CHECK under DIAGNOSIS & TESTING. If actuator operation is okay, replace faulty ABS computer. See ABS COMPUTER under REMOVAL & INSTALLATION. If actuator operation is not okay, replace faulty actuator.

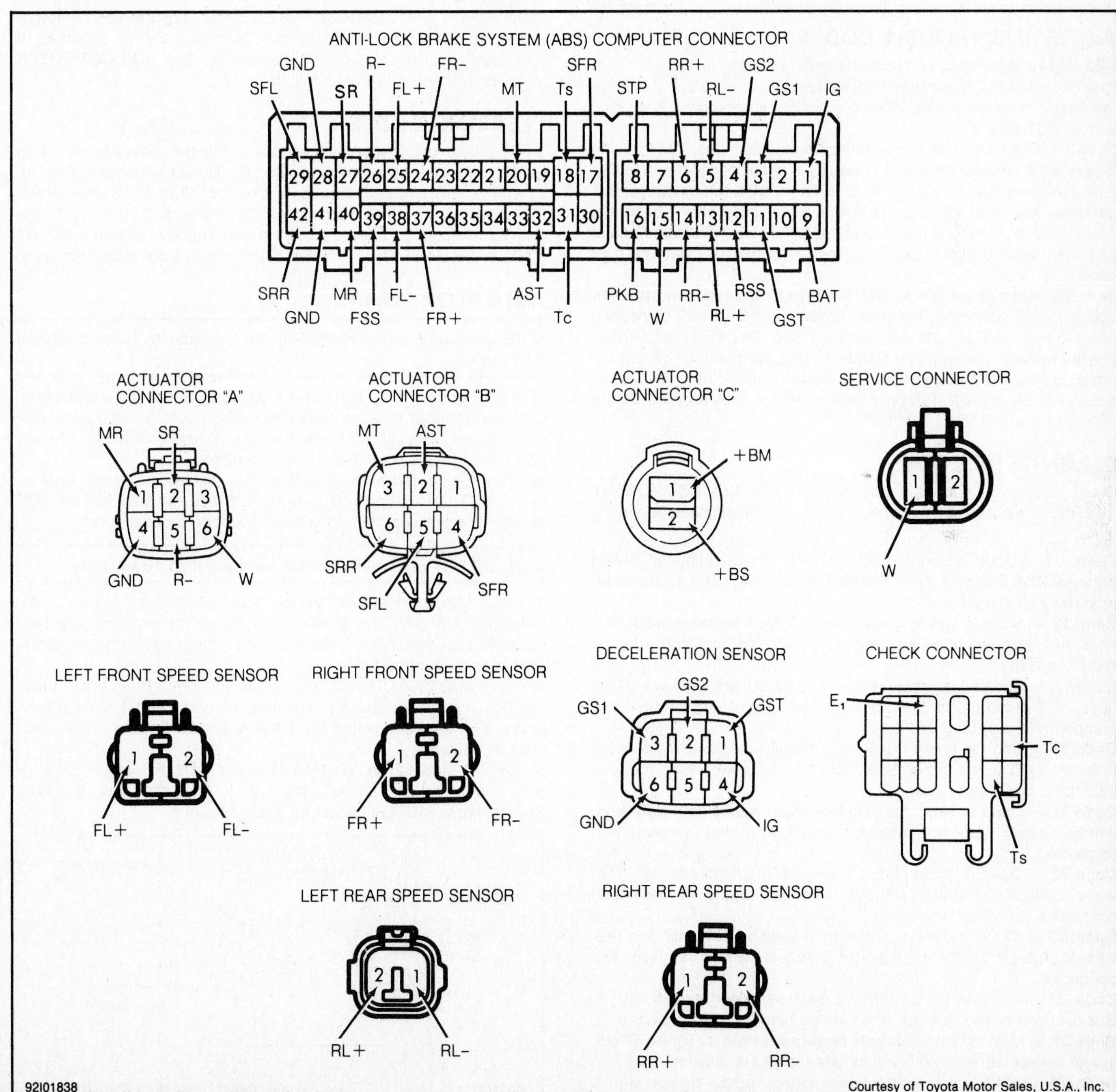


*Fig. 6: Identifying ABS Connector Terminals*

# 1991 BRAKES
# Anti-Lock – Previa (Cont.)

**ABS Works Inefficiently** – **1)** Disconnect service connector. *See Fig. 4.* Using jumper wire, connect terminals Tc and $E_1$ of check connector. *See Fig. 5.* Check connector is located under driver's seat. Turn ignition on. ABS light should blink a normal code. If ABS light does not blink a normal code, refer to DIAGNOSTIC CODES under DIAGNOSIS & TESTING. If ABS light blinks a normal code, go to next step.
**2)** Ensure battery voltage exists between ABS computer connector terminal No. 8 (Green/White wire) and ground when brake pedal is depressed. If battery voltage is not present when brake pedal is depressed, repair open circuit in stoplight switch or wiring harness. Check actuator operation. See ACTUATOR CHECK under DIAGNOSIS & TESTING.

## DIAGNOSIS & TESTING

***NOTE: DO NOT start engine when accessing diagnostic codes.***

### ACCESSING TROUBLE CODES

**ABS Light Diagnostics** – **1)** Ensure battery voltage is 12 volts. Turn ignition switch to ON position. ABS light should illuminate and then go out after 3 seconds. If ABS light does not illuminate, check fuse, bulb and wiring harness.
**2)** With ignition on, disconnect service connector. *See Fig. 4.* Using jumper wire, connect terminals Tc and $E_1$ of check connector. *See Fig. 5.* Check connector is located under driver's seat. If a malfunction is detected, ABS light will begin to flash a 2-digit code after 4 seconds. ANTI-LOCK light will flash first digit, followed by a 1.5-second pause and then second digit. Count number of flashes to identify 2-digit code.
**3)** If 2 or more codes are stored, a 4.5-second pause will separate codes. If ABS system is functioning properly, ABS light will blink once every .5 second. For code interpretation, see DIAGNOSTIC CODES.
**4)** After replacing or repairing malfunctioning components, clear diagnostic codes. If a battery cable was disconnected during repairs, all codes will be erased. If battery cable was not disconnected during repairs, see CLEARING CODES.

### DIAGNOSTIC CODES

Check suspected components in order given. See COMPONENT TESTING. Checks consist mainly of a visual inspection and continuity tests.

**Code 11** – Open solenoid relay circuit. Check actuator wiring harness, ABS solenoid relay, solenoid relay wiring harness and solenoid relay connector.
**Code 12** – Short in solenoid relay circuit. Check actuator wiring harness, ABS solenoid relay, solenoid relay wiring harness and solenoid relay connector.
**Code 13** – Open pump motor relay circuit. Check actuator wiring harness, ABS pump motor relay, pump motor relay wiring harness and pump motor relay connector.
**Code 14** – Short in pump motor relay circuit. Check actuator wiring harness, ABS pump motor relay, pump motor relay wiring harness and pump motor relay connector.
**Code 21** – Open or short circuit in 3-position solenoid for right front wheel. Check 3-position actuator solenoid, wiring harness and connector.
**Code 22** – Open or short circuit in 3-position solenoid for left front wheel. Check 3-position actuator solenoid, wiring harness and connector.
**Code 23** – Open or short circuit in 3-position solenoid for rear wheels. Check 3-position actuator solenoid, wiring harness and connector.
**Code 31** – Malfunction of right front wheel speed sensor signal. Check speed sensor, sensor rotor, wiring harness and connector.
**Code 32** – Malfunction of left front wheel speed sensor signal. Check speed sensor, sensor rotor, wiring harness and connector.
**Code 33** – Malfunction of right rear wheel speed sensor signal. Check speed sensor, sensor rotor, wiring harness and connector.
**Code 34** – Malfunction of left rear wheel speed sensor signal. Check speed sensor, sensor rotor, wiring harness and connector.
**Code 35** – Open in left front or right rear wheel speed sensor circuit. Check speed sensor, sensor rotor, wiring harness and connector.
**Code 36** – Open in right front or left rear wheel speed sensor circuit. Check speed sensor, sensor rotor, wiring harness and connector.
**Code 41** – Abnormally high or low battery voltage. Check battery and voltage regulator.
**Code 43 (4WD)** – Deceleration sensor malfunction. Check deceleration sensor, deceleration sensor installation, wiring harness and connector.
**Code 44 (4WD)** – Open or short circuit in deceleration sensor. Check deceleration sensor, deceleration sensor installation, wiring harness and connector.
**Code 51** – Actuator pump motor is locked or pump motor circuit open. Check pump motor, pump motor relay, vehicle battery, actuator wiring harness, connectors, actuator pump motor circuit and actuator ground bolt.
**Always On** – Malfunction of ABS computer. Ensure ABS computer connector is properly connected and terminals are not damaged. If connector is okay, replace ABS computer. See ABS COMPUTER under REMOVAL & INSTALLATION.

### CLEARING CODES

Turn ignition on. Disconnect service connector. *See Fig. 4.* Using jumper wire, connect terminals Tc and $E_1$ of check connector. *See Fig. 5.* With vehicle stopped, depress brake pedal 8 or more times within 3 seconds. Ensure ABS warning light flashes on and off every .5 second (normal code). Codes are now cleared. Remove jumper wire from TDCL connector. Ensure ABS warning light goes out after 3 seconds.

### ACTUATOR CHECK

***NOTE: Actuator Checker (09990-00150) is needed to perform ACTUATOR CHECK.***

**1)** Turn ignition off. Disconnect actuator electrical connectors. Connect Actuator Checker (09990-00150) to actuator and body side wire harness through sub-wire harness. Connect actuator checker positive and negative cables to vehicle battery.
**2)** Start engine and allow it to idle. Turn actuator checker selector switch to FRONT RH position. *See Fig. 7.* Press and hold SUB MOTOR switch for a few seconds. Press and hold brake pedal down.

***NOTE: DO NOT press MAIN switch for more than 10 seconds.***

**3)** Press MAIN switch, and ensure brake pedal does not go down. Release MAIN SWITCH. Brake pedal should lower. Press and hold SUB MOTOR switch for a few seconds. Brake pedal should return. Release brake pedal.
**4)** Press SUB MOTOR switch for a few seconds. Press brake pedal and hold it down for about 15 seconds. As brake pedal is being held, press SUB MOTOR switch for a few seconds. Ensure brake pedal does not pulsate.
**5)** Repeat steps **2)-4)** for FRONT LH, REAR RH and REAR LH positions of selector switch. *See Fig. 7.* After checking remaining wheels, press MOTOR switch for a few seconds.

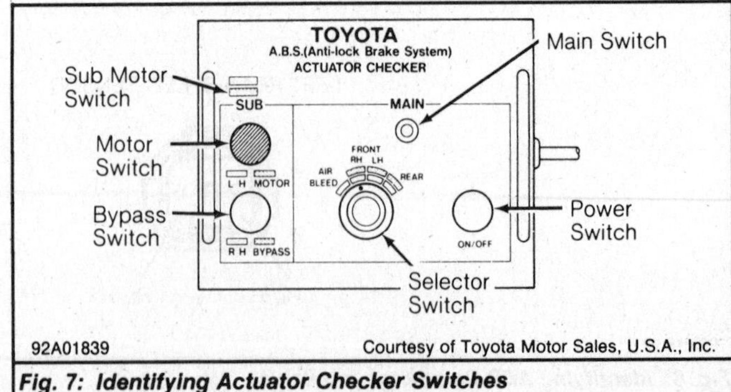


***Fig. 7: Identifying Actuator Checker Switches***

# 1991 BRAKES
# Anti-Lock – Previa (Cont.)

**6)** Disconnect actuator checker and sub-wire harness from actuator. Connect actuator connectors. Clear diagnostic codes. See CLEARING CODES under DIAGNOSIS & TESTING.

## SPEED SENSOR DIAGNOSTICS

***NOTE: During diagnosis, DO NOT turn ignition off, pull parking brake lever and press brake pedal more than 16 times or diagnostic codes will be erased. Brake system functions as a conventional system during speed sensors diagnosis.***

**1)** Ensure battery voltage is approximately 12 volts. Turn ignition on. Ensure ABS light illuminates and then goes out after approximately 3 seconds. If ABS light does not illuminate, check fuse, bulb and wiring harness. Ensure ABS light goes out.
**2)** Turn ignition off. Using a jumper wire, connect check connector terminals Tc and Ts to $E_1$. *See Fig. 6.* Engage parking brake. Start engine. DO NOT press brake pedal. ABS light will illuminate 4 times a second. Go to next step.

***NOTE: While ABS light is off, DO NOT accelerate, decelerate, brake, shift, move steering or drive on rough road surfaces as these conditions affect test.***

**3)** Drive vehicle straight ahead at 2.5-3.7 MPH. Ensure ABS light illuminates after a one-second pause. If ABS light illuminates without blinking when vehicle is not in specified speed range, stop vehicle and record diagnostic codes. Turn ignition off. Repair as necessary. See SPEED SENSOR DIAGNOSTIC CODES.
**4)** If ABS light illuminates while vehicle speed is in specified range, check is completed. If vehicle speed exceeds 3.7 MPH, ABS light will blink again. If ABS light blinks when vehicle speed exceeds 3.7 MPH, speed sensors are okay.
**5)** Drive vehicle straight ahead at 28-34 MPH. Ensure ABS light illuminates after a one-second pause. If ABS light illuminates without blinking when vehicle is not in specified speed range, stop vehicle and record diagnostic codes. Turn ignition off. Repair as necessary. See SPEED SENSOR DIAGNOSTIC CODES.
**6)** If ABS light illuminates while vehicle speed is in specified range, check is completed. If vehicle speed exceeds 34 MPH, ABS light will blink again. If ABS light blinks when vehicle speed exceeds 34 MPH, sensor rotors are okay.
**7)** Turn ignition off. Remove jumper wire from check connector. Clear diagnostic codes. See CLEARING CODES.

## SPEED SENSOR DIAGNOSTIC CODES

**Code 71** – Right front speed sensor signal voltage is low. Check right front speed sensor and sensor installation.
**Code 72** – Left front speed sensor signal voltage is low. Check left front speed sensor and sensor installation.
**Code 73** – Right rear speed sensor signal voltage is low. Check right rear speed sensor and sensor installation.
**Code 74** – Left rear speed sensor signal voltage is low. Check left rear speed sensor and sensor installation.
**Code 75** – Abnormal signal from right front speed sensor. Check right front sensor rotor.
**Code 76** – Abnormal signal from left front speed sensor. Check left front sensor rotor.
**Code 77** – Abnormal signal from right rear speed sensor. Check right rear sensor rotor.
**Code 78** – Abnormal signal from left rear speed sensor. Check left rear sensor rotor.
**Light Illuminates 4 Times A Second** – All speed sensors and sensor rotors are normal.

## DECELERATION SENSOR DIAGNOSTICS (4WD)

***NOTE: Brake system functions as a conventional system during deceleration sensor diagnosis.***

**1)** Ensure battery voltage is 12 volts. Turn ignition on. ABS light should illuminate and then go out after 3 seconds. If ABS light does not illuminate, check fuse, bulb and wiring harness.
**2)** Turn ignition off. Using a jumper wire, connect terminals $E_1$ and Ts of check connector. *See Fig. 5.* Check connector is located under driver's seat. Engage parking brake. Depress brake pedal, and start engine.
**3)** Ensure ABS light blinks about once every second. If ABS light does not blink, inspect parking brake switch, stoplight switch, terminal Ts of check connector, deceleration sensor installation and ABS computer. If ABS light blinks, go to next step.
**4)** To inspect sensor detection point, slowly raise rear of vehicle 29". Measure height from center of rear bumper to ground. Ensure ABS light is off.
**5)** If ABS warning light illuminates, inspect deceleration sensor installation. Repair as required. If deceleration sensor installation is okay, replace sensor. Slowly lower rear of vehicle. Slowly raise front of vehicle 23". Measure distance from lower body to ground.
**6)** Ensure ABS light is off. If ABS light illuminates, inspect deceleration sensor installation. Repair as required. If deceleration sensor installation is okay, replace sensor. Slowly lower vehicle.
**7)** To inspect sensor operation, drive vehicle straight at about 12.4 MPH or more. Lightly depress brake pedal. ABS light should blink once every second with no change in pattern.
**8)** Drive vehicle straight at about 12.4 MPH or more. Using a little force, depress brake pedal. ABS light should stay on during braking. Drive vehicle at about 12.4 MPH or more, and strongly depress brake pedal. ABS light should blink approximately 7 times per second.
**9)** If ABS light does not function as described, check deceleration sensor installation. If sensor installation is okay, replace deceleration sensor. Turn engine off. Remove jumper wire from terminals $E_1$ and Ts of check connector.

## COMPONENT TESTING

**Front Speed Sensors – 1)** Remove front speed sensor from vehicle. See SPEED SENSORS under REMOVAL & INSTALLATION. Using a DVOM, measure resistance between speed sensor terminals. Resistance should be 920-1220 ohms.
**2)** Ensure continuity is not present between each sensor terminal and sensor body. If resistance and continuity readings are as specified, speed sensor is okay. If resistance and continuity readings are not as specified, replace speed sensor.
**Rear Speed Sensors – 1)** Remove rear speed sensor. See SPEED SENSORS under REMOVAL & INSTALLATION. Using a DVOM, measure resistance between speed sensor terminals. Resistance should be 1050-1450 ohms.
**2)** Ensure continuity is not present between each sensor terminal and sensor body. If resistance and continuity readings are as specified, speed sensor is okay. If resistance and continuity readings are not as specified, replace speed sensor.

**Pump Motor Relay Continuity – 1)** Remove pump motor relay located on top of actuator. Using a DVOM, check continuity between pump motor relay terminals No. 1 and 2. *See Fig. 8.* Ensure continuity is present.
**2)** Check continuity between terminals No. 3 and 4, and between terminals No. 1 and 4. Ensure continuity is not present. If continuity readings are not as specified, replace pump motor relay.

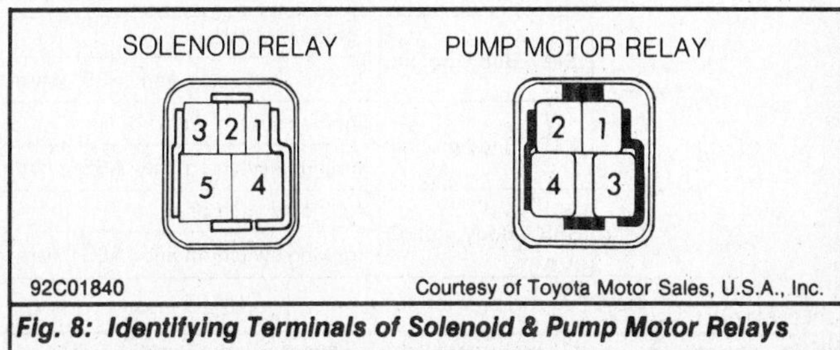


***Fig. 8: Identifying Terminals of Solenoid & Pump Motor Relays***

# 1991 BRAKES
# Anti-Lock – Previa (Cont.)

**Pump Motor Relay Operation – 1)** Remove pump motor relay located on top of actuator. Connect battery positive terminal to pump motor relay terminal No. 1. Connect battery negative terminal to pump motor relay terminal No. 2. *See Fig. 8.*
**2)** Ensure continuity is present between relay terminals No. 3 and 4. Continuity should not be present between relay terminals No. 1 and 4. If continuity is not as specified, replace pump motor relay.
**Solenoid Relay Continuity – 1)** Remove solenoid relay located on top of actuator. Using a DVOM, check continuity between solenoid relay terminals No. 1 and 3. *See Fig. 8.* Continuity should be present.
**2)** Check continuity between terminals No. 2 and 4. Continuity should be present. Check continuity between terminals No. 4 and 5. Continuity should not be present. If continuity readings are not as specified, replace solenoid relay.
**Solenoid Relay Operation – 1)** Remove solenoid relay located on top of actuator. Connect jumper wire between battery positive terminal and solenoid relay terminal No. 3. Connect another jumper wire between ground and relay terminal No. 1. *See Fig. 8.*
**2)** Ensure continuity is present between relay terminals No. 4 and 5. Ensure continuity is not present between relay terminals No. 2 and 4. If continuity is not as specified, replace solenoid relay.
**Sensor Rotors –** Visually inspect sensor rotor serrations for scratches, cracks, missing teeth and warping. Replace sensor rotor if necessary.
**ABS Computer Wiring Harness – 1)** Remove ABS computer. See ABS COMPUTER under REMOVAL & INSTALLATION. With ABS computer connector connected, backprobe ABS computer connector terminals. Measure voltage as specified in chart. *See Fig. 9.* If circuit(s) do not test as specified, check and repair or replace trouble part shown in chart.
**2)** Disconnect ABS computer connector. Check resistance and voltage as specified in chart, on wire harness side of ABS computer connector. *See Fig. 10.* If circuit(s) do not test as specified, check and repair or replace troubled part shown in chart.

## REMOVAL & INSTALLATION

***WARNING: Hydraulic system may be under high pressure. Use caution when opening hydraulic system.***

### ACTUATOR

**Removal & Installation – 1)** Disconnect actuator electrical connectors. Disconnect brake lines connected to actuator. Remove 3 bolts, and remove actuator with bracket attached.
**2)** Remove actuator from actuator bracket. To install, reverse removal procedure. Bleed brake system. See BLEEDING BRAKE SYSTEM. Check for fluid leaks.

### ABS COMPUTER

**Removal & Installation – 1)** ABS computer is located on right front side of vehicle. *See Fig. 1.* Ensure ignition is off. Disconnect negative battery cable. On models with CD player, remove 2 screws, and remove amplifier.
**2)** On all models, disconnect electrical connector in front of ABS computer. Remove ABS computer lower mounting nut. Remove 2 upper mounting bolts. Pull out ABS computer. Disconnect ABS computer connector.
**3)** To install, reverse removal procedure. Tighten ABS computer mounting nut and bolts to specification. See TORQUE SPECIFICATIONS table at end of article.

### SPEED SENSORS

**Removal & Installation – 1)** Loosen wheel lug nuts. Raise and support vehicle. Remove wheel. Remove wheel speed sensor mounting bolt. Disconnect wheel speed sensor connector.
**2)** Remove wheel speed sensor from vehicle. To install, reverse removal procedure. Tighten wheel speed sensor mounting bolt to specification. See TORQUE SPECIFICATIONS table at end of article.

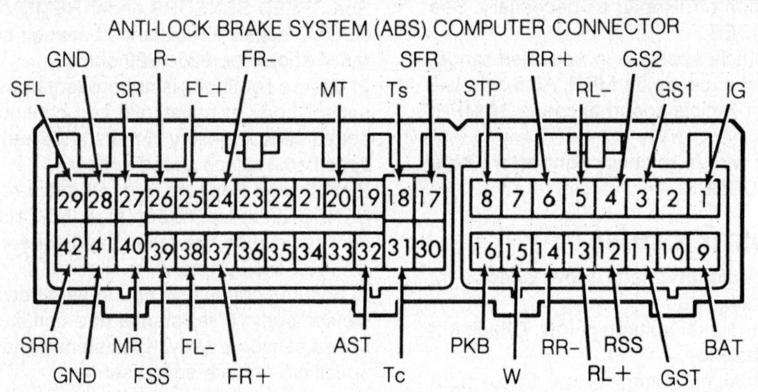


| Tester Connection | Condition | Voltage | Trouble Part |
|---|---|---|---|
| W – Body ground | Ignition switch on | Battery voltage | "ABS" warning light bulb |
| | Ignition switch on and "ABS" warning light goes on | About 0 V | |
| SFR – Body ground | Ignition switch on | Battery voltage | Actuator control relays or wire harness |
| | Ignition switch on and "ABS" warning light goes on | About 0 V | |
| SFL – Body ground | Ignition switch on | Battery voltage | |
| | Ignition switch on and "ABS" warning light goes on | About 0 V | |
| AST – Body ground | Ignition switch on | Battery voltage | |
| | Ignition switch on and "ABS" warning light goes on | About 0 V | |
| SRR – Body ground | Ignition switch on | Battery voltage | |
| | Ignition switch on and "ABS" warning light goes on | About 0 V | |

92E01841

Courtesy of Toyota Motor Sales, U.S.A., Inc.

***Fig. 9: Testing Specifications Chart for ABS Computer Wiring Harness (1 of 2)***

# 1991 BRAKES
# Anti-Lock – Previa (Cont.)

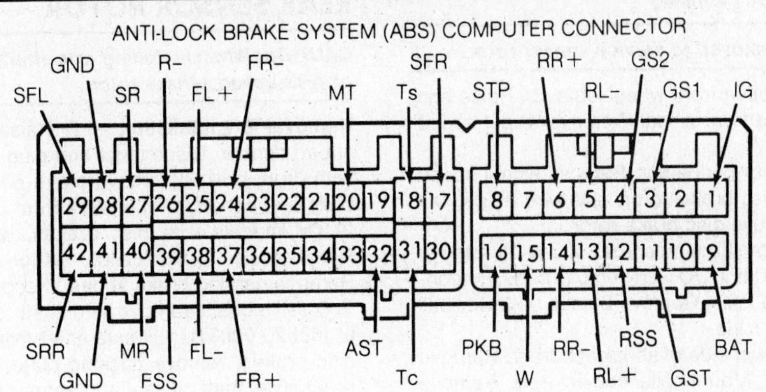


| Tester connection | Check item | Condition | Voltage or resistance value | Trouble part |
|---|---|---|---|---|
| IG – Body ground | Voltage | Ignition SW on | Battery voltage | ECU-IG fuse, wire harness |
| | | Ignition SW off | About 0 V | |
| RL– – Body ground | Continuity | — | No continuity | Rear LH speed sensor or wire harness |
| RL– – RL+ | Resistance | — | 1.05–1.45 kΩ | |
| RL+ – Body ground | Continuity | — | No continuity | |
| RR+ – Body ground | Continuity | — | No continuity | Rear RH speed sensor or wire harness |
| RR+ – RR– | Resistance | — | 1.05–1.45 kΩ | |
| RR– – Body ground | Continuity | — | No continuity | |
| STP – Body ground | Voltage | Ignition SW off and brake pedal depressed | Battery voltage | Stop light switch or stop light |
| | Continuity | Ignition SW off and brake pedal returned | Continuity | |
| BAT – Body ground | Voltage | — | Battery voltage | Wire harness |
| RSS – * | Continuity | — | Continuity | Sealed wire |

* TERMINALS NO. 1 AND NO. 6 OF INTERMEDIATE CONNECTOR ON FUEL TANK.

| Tester connection | Check item | Condition | Voltage or resistance value | Trouble part |
|---|---|---|---|---|
| PKB – Body ground | Voltage | Ignition SW on and PKB lever pulled | About 0 V | PKB switch, level warning switch |
| | | Ignition SW on and PKB lever returned | Battery voltage | |
| SFR – AST | Resistance | Ignition SW off | About 6 Ω | Actuator |
| TS – Body ground | Continuity | — | No continuity | Check connector or wire harness |
| | | Check connector terminals Ts and $E_1$ are connected | Continuity | |
| MT – Body ground | Continuity | — | Continuity | Actuator |
| FR– – Body ground | Continuity | — | No continuity | Front RH speed sensor or wire harness |
| FR– – FR+ | Resistance | — | 0.92–1.22 kΩ | |
| FR+ – Body ground | Continuity | — | No continuity | |
| FL+ – Body ground | Continuity | — | No continuity | Front LH speed sensor or wire harness |
| FL+ – FL– | Resistance | — | 0.92–1.22 kΩ | |
| FL– – Body ground | Continuity | — | No continuity | |
| R– – Body ground | Continuity | — | No continuity | Wire harness |
| R– – MR | Continuity | — | Continuity | Motor relay |
| R– – SR | Continuity | — | Continuity | Solenoid relay |
| GND – Body ground | Continuity | — | Continuity | Wire harness |
| SFL – AST | Resistance | Ignition SW off | About 6 Ω | Actuator |
| TC – Body ground | Continuity | — | No continuity | Check connector or wire harness |
| | | Terminal Tc of check connector shorted | Continuity | |
| AST – Body ground | Resistance | — | About 5 Ω | Actuator |
| SRR – AST | Resistance | Ignition SW off | About 6 Ω | |

92G01842

Courtesy of Toyota Motor Sales, U.S.A., Inc.

***Fig. 10: Testing Specifications Chart for ABS Computer Wiring Harness (2 of 2)***

# 1991 BRAKES
# Anti-Lock – Previa (Cont.)

## FRONT SENSOR ROTOR (2WD)

***NOTE: Front axle hub must be removed to service sensor rotor.***

**Removal & Installation – 1)** Loosen front wheel lug nuts. Raise and support front of vehicle. Remove front wheel. Remove wheel speed sensor mounting bolt.

**2)** Disconnect wheel speed sensor connector. Remove wheel speed sensor from vehicle. Remove disc brake rotor, and wire aside. DO NOT disconnect brake line. Remove disc brake rotor.

**3)** Loosen 2 nuts on lower side of shock absorber. DO NOT remove bolts. Loosen 2 bolts of lower ball joint. DO NOT remove bolts. Disconnect tie rod end from steering knuckle. Remove 2 bolts on lower ball joint, and disconnect steering knuckle.

**4)** Remove 2 nuts and bolts on lower side of shock absorber. Remove steering knuckle with axle hub. Mount axle hub in vise. Remove grease cap. Remove caulking from around axle shaft hub lock nut. Remove axle shaft hub lock nut. Remove speed sensor rotor.

**5)** To install, reverse removal procedure. Install new axle shaft hub lock nut. Tighten axle shaft hub lock nut to specification, and caulk nut. Tighten all nuts and bolts to specification. See TORQUE SPECIFICATIONS table at end of article.

## FRONT SENSOR ROTOR (4WD)

***CAUTION: When removing or installing axle shaft, use care not to damage oil seal, drive shaft boots or ABS speed sensor rotor.***

**Removal & Installation – 1)** Remove front wheel. Remove hub cap, cotter pin and lock nut. Apply brake, and remove wheel bearing lock nut. Remove cotter pin and nut from tie rod end. Using Tie Rod Remover (09628-62011), disconnect tie rod end from steering knuckle.

**2)** Paint mating marks on axle shaft flange and side gear shaft flange. DO NOT use punch to make mating marks. Apply brakes, and remove retaining nuts on each inboard axle shaft flange. Remove bolts, and disconnect steering knuckle from lower ball joint.

**3)** While pulling steering knuckle outward, remove axle shaft from hub. To install, reverse removal procedure. Tighten all nuts and bolts to specification. See TORQUE SPECIFICATIONS table at end of article.

## REAR SENSOR ROTOR

***CAUTION: When installing axle shaft, use care not to damage oil seal or ABS speed sensor rotor.***

**Removal & Installation – 1)** Raise and support vehicle. Remove speed sensor. Disconnect and plug brake hydraulic line. On models with drum brakes, remove brake drum and brake shoes. Remove 2 bolts and parking brake cable from backing plate.

**2)** On models with disc brakes, disconnect brake line from clip. Remove disc brake caliper assembly. Remove disc brake rotor. Remove parking brake shoes. Disconnect parking brake cable.

**3)** On all models, remove axle shaft-to-backing plate bolts. Using Puller (09520-00031), pull axle shaft from axle housing. On models with disc brakes, remove backing plate from axle shaft. On all models, press axle shaft oil seal and sensor rotor from axle shaft.

**4)** To install, reverse removal procedure. Bleed brakes. Tighten all nuts and bolts to specification. See TORQUE SPECIFICATIONS table at end of article.

# OVERHAUL

DO NOT overhaul or disassemble actuator assembly. If actuator is defective, replace entire assembly.

# TORQUE SPECIFICATIONS

***TORQUE SPECIFICATIONS***

| Application | Ft. Lbs. (N.m) |
|---|---|
| Actuator Mounting Bolts | 14 (19) |
| Front Axle Shaft Hub Nut | 137 (186) |
| Front Axle Shaft-To-Differential Drive Flange Nuts | 51 (69) |
| Disc Brake Caliper Mounting Bolts | 65 (88) |
| Lower Shock Absorber Nuts | 231 (313) |
| Rear Axle Shaft-To-Backing Plate Nuts | 53 (72) |
| Steering Knuckle-To-Lower Ball Joint Bolts | 94 (127) |
| Tie Rod Nuts | 36 (49) |
| Wheel Lug Nuts | 76 (103) |
| | **INCH Lbs. (N.m)** |
| Actuator-To-Bracket Nuts | 48 (5) |
| Deceleration Sensor Mounting Bolts | 108 (13) |
| ABS Computer Lower Mounting Nut | 108 (13) |
| ABS Computer Upper Mounting Bolts | 48 (5) |
| Speed Sensor Bolts | 69 (8) |

## WIRING DIAGRAM

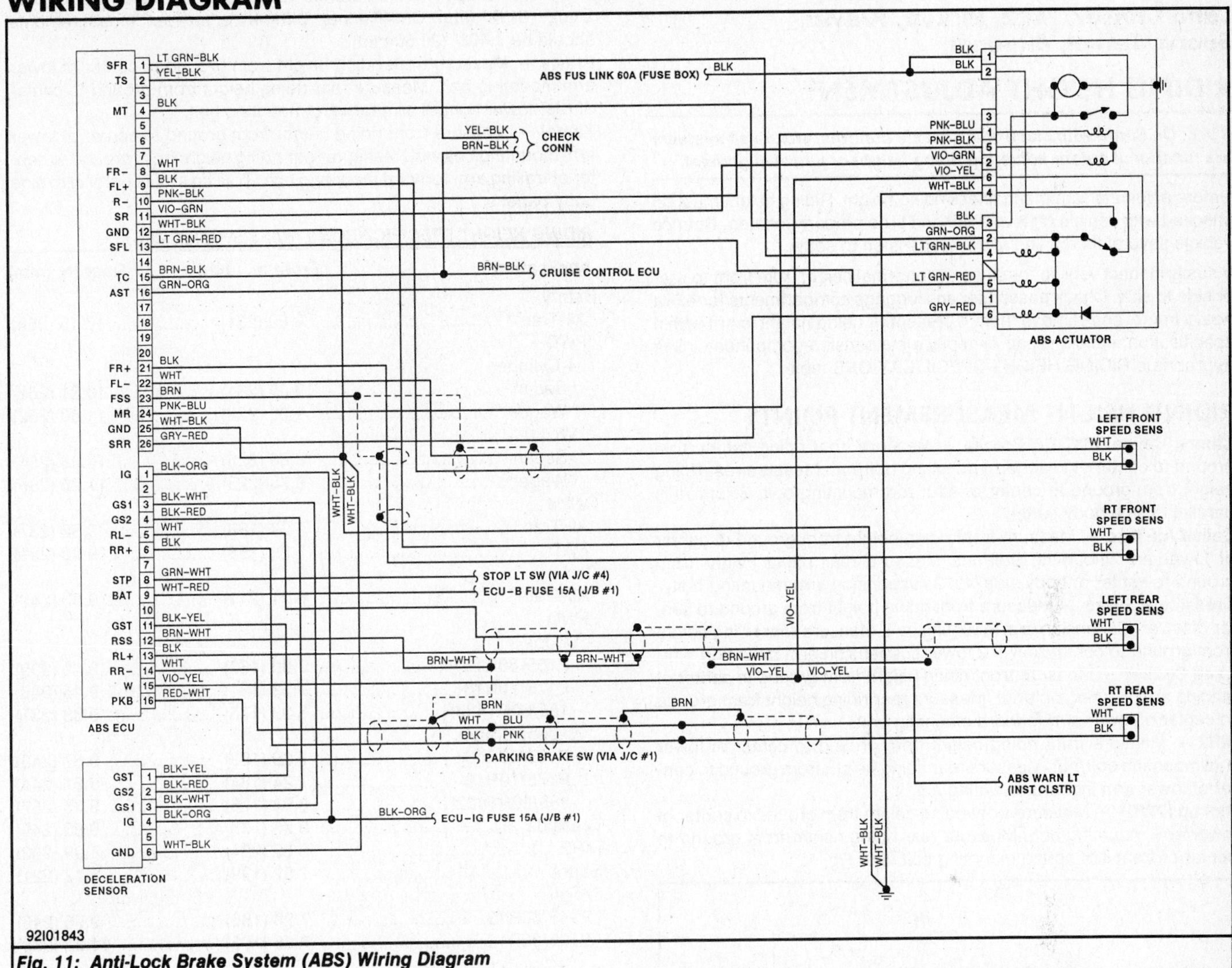


*Fig. 11: Anti-Lock Brake System (ABS) Wiring Diagram*

# 1991 WHEEL ALIGNMENT Specifications & Procedures

## Camry, Celica, Corolla, Cressida, Land Cruiser, MR2, Pickup, Previa, Supra, Tercel, 4Runner

## RIDING HEIGHT ADJUSTMENT

***NOTE: On Supra with electronic chassis controls, ensure all systems are functional before adjusting riding height or wheel alignment.***

Before adjusting alignment, check riding height. Riding height must be checked with vehicle on level floor and tires properly inflated. Bounce vehicle several times, and allow suspension to settle.

Visually inspect vehicle for signs of abnormal height from front to rear or side to side. Check passenger and luggage compartments for extra heavy items, and remove them if present. If riding height is not within specification, check, repair or replace suspension components. See appropriate RIDING HEIGHT SPECIFICATIONS table.

## RIDING HEIGHT MEASUREMENT POINTS

**Camry, Celica (FWD) & Corolla –** Measure front riding height from ground to center of lower arm mounting bolt/nut. Measure rear riding height from ground to center of strut rod mounting bolt. Strut rod is parallel to side body panel.

**Celica All-Trac –** Measure front riding height from ground to center of lower arm mounting bolt/nut. Measure rear riding height from ground to center of body side No. 2 suspension arm mounting bolt.

**Cressida & Supra –** Measure front riding height from ground to center of lower suspension arm mounting bolt. Measure rear riding height from ground to center of No. 2 lower suspension arm mounting bolt.

**Land Cruiser –** Measure front riding height from ground to center of leading arm bushing bolt/nut. Measure rear riding height from ground to center of lower arm forward mounting bolt.

**MR2 –** Measure front riding height from ground to center of lower arm mounting bolt/nut. Measure rear riding height from ground to center of lower arm inboard mounting nut.

**Pickup (2WD) –** Measure front riding height from ground to center of lower arm mounting bolt. Measure rear riding height from ground to center of front leaf spring mounting bolt. *See Fig. 1.*

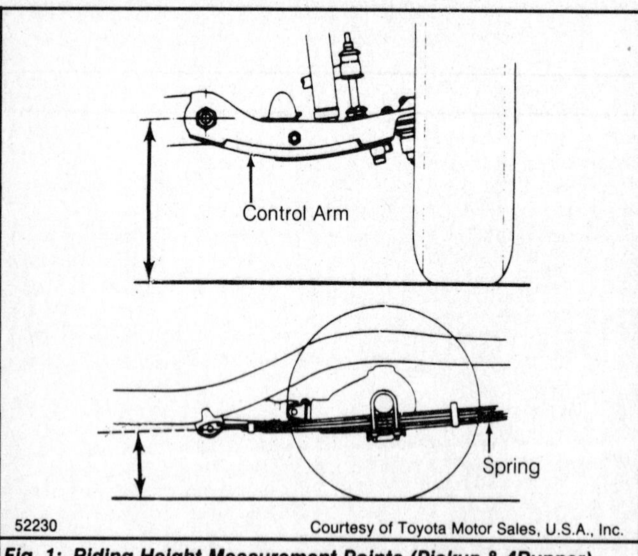


***Fig. 1: Riding Height Measurement Points (Pickup & 4Runner)***

**Pickup (4WD) & 4Runner – 1)** Measure front riding height from ground to center of lower arm mounting bolt. Measure rear riding height from ground to center of front leaf spring. *See Fig. 1*. To check for standard height differential, go to next step.

**2)** Measure front riding height differential by comparing height at center tip of spindle to height at center of lower arm adjustment cam bolt. Difference between measurements should be 2.303" (58.50 mm).

**3)** Measure rear riding height differential by comparing height at center of front leaf spring mounting bolt to height at centerline of rear axle shaft. On Pickup (4WD), difference between measurements should be 2.402" (61.00 mm). On 4Runner, difference between measurements should be 1.403" (26.50 mm).

**Previa –** Measure front riding height from ground to center of lower arm mounting bolt. Measure rear riding height from ground to center of rear lower control arm forward mounting bolt.

**Tercel –** Measure front riding height from ground to center of lower arm mounting bolt/nut. Measure rear riding height from ground to center of trailing arm forward mounting bolt. Trailing arm is parallel to side body panel.

***RIDING HEIGHT SPECIFICATIONS (PASSENGER CARS)***

| Application [1] | Front In. (mm) | Rear In. (mm) |
|---|---|---|
| Camry | | |
| All-Trac | 9.09 (231) | 10.16 (258) |
| FWD | | |
| 4-Cylinder | | |
| Sedan | 9.09 (231) | 10.31 (262) |
| Wagon | 9.02 (229) | 11.50 (292) |
| V6 | | |
| Sedan | 8.86 (225) | 10.08 (256) |
| Wagon | 8.78 (223) | 11.26 (286) |
| Celica | | |
| All-Trac | 7.39 (188) | 9.32 (237) |
| FWD | 7.28 (185) | 9.90 (251) |
| Corolla | | |
| All-Trac | 8.31 (211) | 9.53 (242) |
| FWD | | |
| Coupe | | |
| P155/80R13 | 7.09 (180) | 9.41 (239) |
| P175/70R13 | 7.13 (181) | 9.45 (240) |
| 185/60R1482H | 6.93 (176) | 9.33 (237) |
| Except Coupe | | |
| P155/80R13 | 7.20 (183) | 9.57 (243) |
| P175/70R13 | 7.24 (184) | 9.61 (244) |
| 185/60R1482H | 6.93 (176) | 9.33 (237) |
| Cressida | 9.25 (235) | 9.80 (249) |
| MR2 | 8.82 (224) | 7.99 (203) |
| Supra | 7.82 (199) | 8.72 (221) |
| Tercel | | |
| P145/80R13 | 7.28 (185) | 9.76 (248) |
| P155/80R13 | 7.56 (192) | 11.22 (285) |

[1] – Riding height will vary depending on tire size used. Recommended tire size are available for some models.

***RIDING HEIGHT SPECIFICATIONS (LAND CRUISER)***

| Application [1] | Front In. (mm) | Rear In. (mm) |
|---|---|---|
| P235/75R15 Tire | 13.19 (335) | 13.19 (335) |
| 31. x 10.50R15 LT Tire | 14.19 (360) | 14.19 (360) |

[1] – Riding height will vary depending on tire size used.

***RIDING HEIGHT SPECIFICATIONS (PICKUP 2WD)***

| Application [1] | Front In. (mm) | Rear In. (mm) |
|---|---|---|
| 4-Cylinder | | |
| Standard | | |
| Reg. Cab, Short Chassis | 10.23 (260) | 10.55 (268) |
| DLX (Deluxe) | | |
| Regular Cab | | |
| Short Chassis | 10.12 (257) | 10.35 (263) |
| Long Chassis | | |
| 5-Speed M/T | 10.35 (263) | 10.28 (261) |
| 4-Speed A/T | 10.31 (262) | 10.28 (261) |
| Xtra Cab, Xtra Long Chassis | 10.94 (278) | 10.39 (264) |
| V6 | | |
| Standard C x C DRW [2] | | |
| Long Chassis | | |
| 5-Speed M/T | 10.20 (259) | 9.21 (234) |
| 4-Speed A/T | 10.24 (260) | 9.25 (235) |
| Super Long Chassis | 10.20 (259) | 9.13 (232) |

# 1991 WHEEL ALIGNMENT
# Specifications & Procedures (Cont.)

*RIDING HEIGHT SPECIFICATIONS (PICKUP 2WD - Cont.)*

| Application [1] | Front In. (mm) | Rear In. (mm) |
|---|---|---|
| DLX (Deluxe) | | |
| Reg. Cab, Long Chassis | | |
| 5-Speed M/T | 10.24 (260) | 11.18 (284) |
| 4-Speed A/T | 10.16 (258) | 11.14 (283) |
| Xtra Cab, Xtra Long Chassis | | |
| 5-Speed M/T | 10.91 (277) | 10.47 (266) |
| 4-Speed A/T | 10.91 (277) | 10.43 (265) |
| SR5 | | |
| Xtra Cab, Xtra Long Chassis | | |
| P205/75R14 | 10.75 (273) | 10.31 (262) |
| P215/65R15 | 10.79 (274) | 10.31 (262) |

[1] - Riding height will vary depending on tire size used. Recommended tire size are available for some models.

[2] - C & C DRW is Cab and Chassis with Dual Rear Wheels.

*RIDING HEIGHT SPECIFICATIONS (PICKUP 4WD)*

| Application [1] | Front In. (mm) | Rear In. (mm) |
|---|---|---|
| 4-Cylinder | | |
| DLX (Deluxe) Reg. Cab | | |
| Standard Chassis | | |
| A/T | 11.08 (281) | 16.73 (425) |
| M/T | 11.09 (282) | 16.81 (427) |
| Long Chassis | | |
| M/T Type "W" | 11.26 (286) | 16.83 (427) |
| M/T Type "G" | 11.24 (285) | 16.83 (427) |
| DLX Xtra Cab | | |
| Xtra Long Chassis | | |
| A/T | 11.47 (291) | 16.54 (420) |
| M/T Type "W" | 11.50 (292) | 16.66 (423) |
| M/T Type "G" | 11.47 (291) | 16.66 (423) |
| V6 | | |
| DLX Reg. Cab | | |
| Standard Chassis | | |
| P225/75R15 | 11.00 (279) | 16.63 (422) |
| 31 X 10.5R15LT | 12.24 (311) | 17.88 (454) |
| Long Chassis | | |
| P225/75R15 | 11.17 (284) | 16.63 (422) |
| 31 X 10.5R15LT | 12.41 (315) | 17.88 (454) |
| DLX Xtra Cab | | |
| Xtra Long Chassis (A/T) | | |
| P225/75R15 | 11.39 (289) | 16.43 (417) |
| 31 X 10.5R15LT | 12.64 (321) | 17.68 (449) |
| Xtra Long Chassis (M/T) | | |
| P225/75R15 | 11.41 (290) | 16.45 (418) |
| 31 X 10.5R15LT | 12.65 (321) | 17.73 (450) |
| SR5 Xtra Cab | | |
| Xtra Long Chassis (A/T) | | |
| P225/75R15 | 11.13 (282) | 16.30 (414) |
| 31 X 10.5R15LT | 12.37 (314) | 17.54 (446) |
| Xtra Long Chassis (M/T) | | |
| P225/75R15 | 11.15 (283) | 16.36 (416) |
| 31 X 10.5R15LT | 12.39 (314) | 17.61 (447) |

[1] - Riding height will vary depending on tire size used. Recommended tire size are available for some models.

*RIDING HEIGHT SPECIFICATIONS (PREVIA)*

| Application [1] | Front In. (mm) | Rear In. (mm) |
|---|---|---|
| 2WD | | |
| P205/75R14 | 9.53 (242) | 11.06 (281) |
| P215/65R15 | 9.45 (240) | 10.98 (279) |
| 4WD | | |
| P205/75R14 | 9.92 (252) | 11.46 (291) |
| P215/65R15 | 9.84 (250) | 11.38 (289) |

[1] - Riding height will vary depending on tire size used.

*RIDING HEIGHT SPECIFICATIONS (4RUNNER)*

| Application [1] | Front In. (mm) | Rear In. (mm) |
|---|---|---|
| 2WD | | |
| SR5 4-Door A/T | | |
| 4-Cylinder | 11.17 (284) | 13.04 (331) |
| V6 | 11.14 (283) | 12.94 (329) |
| 4WD | | |
| SR5 4-Cylinder | | |
| 2-Door | | |
| A/T | 11.15 (283) | 12.83 (326) |
| M/T | 11.18 (284) | 12.87 (327) |
| 4-Door | | |
| A/T | 11.15 (283) | 12.78 (325) |
| M/T | 11.17 (284) | 12.81 (325) |
| SR5 V6 | | |
| 2-Door | | |
| A/T | | |
| P225/75R15 | 10.98 (279) | 12.96 (329) |
| 31 X 10.5R15LT | 12.19 (310) | 14.15 (359) |
| M/T | | |
| P225/75R15 | 11.00 (280) | 13.01 (330) |
| 31 X 10.5R15LT | 12.21 (310) | 14.19 (360) |
| 4-Door | | |
| A/T | | |
| P225/75R15 | 10.95 (278) | 13.12 (333) |
| 31 X 10.5R15LT | 12.16 (309) | 14.29 (363) |
| M/T | | |
| P225/75R15 | 10.98 (279) | 13.14 (334) |
| 31 X 10.5R15LT | 12.19 (310) | 14.03 (356) |

[1] - Riding height will vary depending on tire size used. Recommended tire size are available for some models.

## JACKING & HOISTING

### FLOOR JACK

**Camry, Celica & Corolla** - To raise vehicle, place floor jack under center of front longitudinal engine crossmember. For rear of FWD models, place floor jack under rear suspension crossmember. For rear of All-Trac models, place floor jack under rear differential support member.

**Cressida & Supra** - To raise vehicle, place floor jack under front suspension crossmember and under rear differential carrier.

**Land Cruiser** - Place floor jack under front/rear differential to raise vehicle.

**MR2** - To raise vehicle, place floor jack under front undercover support and under rear suspension crossmember.

**Pickup, Previa & 4Runner** - To raise vehicle, place floor jack under front suspension crossmember and under rear axle housing/differential.

**Tercel** - To raise vehicle, place floor jack under front crossmember and under center of rear axle beam.

### EMERGENCY JACKING

**Camry, Celica, Corolla, Cressida, MR2, Supra & Tercel** - Place emergency jack on reinforced support points of side body panel (between front and rear wheels). Safety stands may also be placed at these points. *See Fig. 2.*

**Land Cruiser** - To raise vehicle, place emergency jack under front/rear axle.

**Pickup & 4Runner** - Place emergency jack under front suspension crossmember and under rear axle housing/differential.

**Previa** - To raise vehicle, place emergency jack under frame support points between front and rear wheels.

### HOIST

**Camry, Celica, Corolla, Cressida, MR2, Supra & Tercel** - Place lift blocks on reinforced support points of side body panel (between front

# 1991 WHEEL ALIGNMENT
# Specifications & Procedures (Cont.)

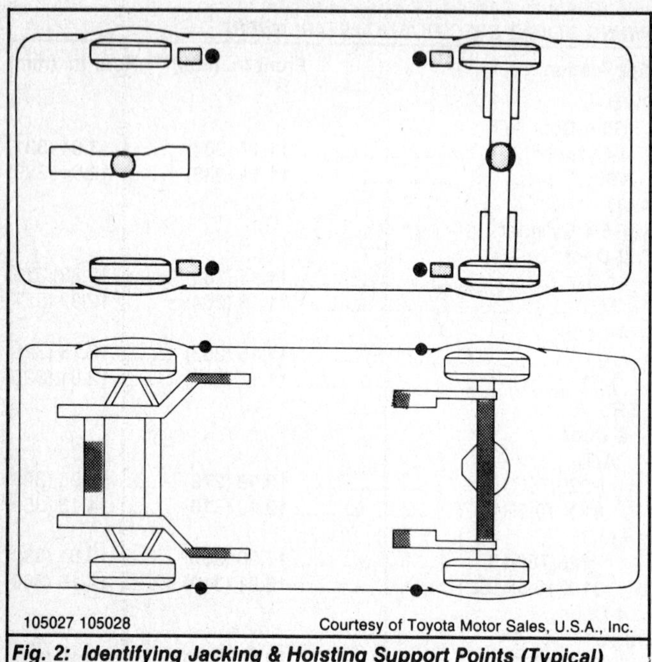
105027 105028 Courtesy of Toyota Motor Sales, U.S.A., Inc.

*Fig. 2: Identifying Jacking & Hoisting Support Points (Typical)*

and rear wheels). Safety stands may also be placed at these points. *See Fig. 2.*

**Land Cruiser** – Place lift blocks under front/rear axle to raise vehicle.

**Pickup & 4Runner** – On 2WD models, place lift blocks under frame side rail and under rear axle housing to raise vehicle. On 4WD models, place lift blocks under front suspension crossmember and under rear axle housing to raise vehicle.

**Previa** – Place lift blocks under frame side rail supports.

## WHEEL ALIGNMENT PROCEDURES

### TURNING ANGLE

On Land Cruiser, Pickup, Previa and 4Runner, remove steering knuckle stopper bolts. On all models, turn steering wheel fully to the right and then left, and observe turning radius on both wheels. If turning radius is incorrect, inspect and replace any damaged or worn front suspension components. See appropriate WHEEL ALIGNMENT SPECIFICATIONS table at end of article.

### CAMBER ADJUSTMENT

**Front Suspension (Camry, Celica, Corolla, Cressida, Land Cruiser, MR2, Previa & Tercel) – 1)** Check tires for wear and improper inflation. Check front wheel bearings for looseness. Check wheel runout. Wheel runout should not exceed .039" (1 mm).

**2)** Check front suspension components for looseness. Ensure front shock absorbers work properly. Check vehicle riding height. See RIDING HEIGHT ADJUSTMENT.

**3)** Check camber of both front wheels. See appropriate WHEEL ALIGNMENT SPECIFICATIONS table at end of article. If camber is not within specification, inspect and replace any damaged or worn front suspension components. Camber is NOT adjustable.

**Front Suspension (Pickup & 4Runner) – 1)** Check tires for wear and improper inflation. Check front wheel bearings for looseness. Check wheel runout. Wheel runout should not exceed .047" (1.2 mm).

**2)** Check front suspension components for looseness. Ensure front shock absorbers work properly. Check vehicle riding height. See RIDING HEIGHT ADJUSTMENT.

**3)** Check camber of both front wheels. See appropriate WHEEL ALIGNMENT SPECIFICATIONS table at end of article. If camber is not within specification, add or remove shims on upper control arms on 2WD models. On 4WD models, loosen and turn adjustment cams. *See Fig. 3.*

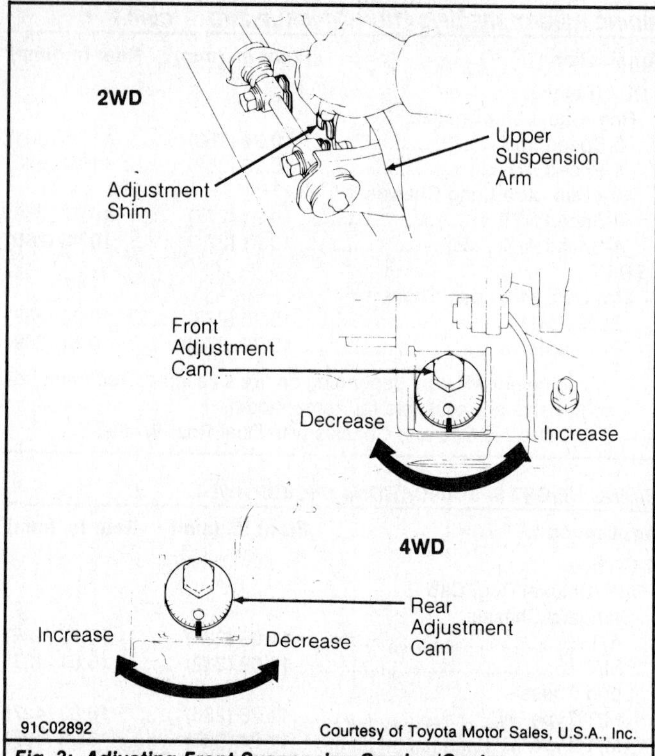

91C02892 Courtesy of Toyota Motor Sales, U.S.A., Inc.

*Fig. 3: Adjusting Front Suspension Camber/Caster (Pickup & 4Runner)*

**Front Suspension (Supra) – 1)** Check tires for wear and improper inflation. Check front wheel bearings for looseness. Check wheel runout. Wheel runout should not exceed .047" (1.2 mm).

**2)** Check front suspension components for looseness. Ensure front shock absorbers work properly. Check vehicle riding height. See RIDING HEIGHT ADJUSTMENT.

**3)** Check camber of both front wheels. See appropriate WHEEL ALIGNMENT SPECIFICATIONS table at end of article. If camber is not within specification, loosen and turn adjustment cams. *See Fig. 4.*

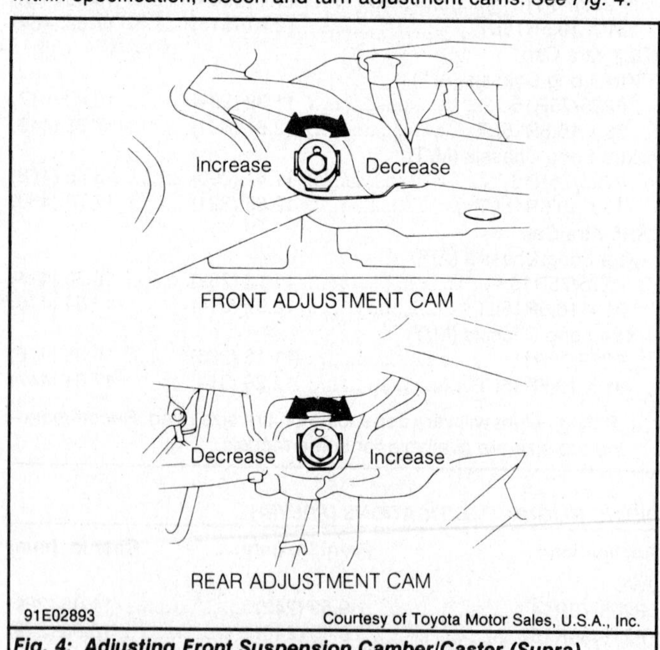

91E02893 Courtesy of Toyota Motor Sales, U.S.A., Inc.

*Fig. 4: Adjusting Front Suspension Camber/Caster (Supra)*

**Rear Suspension (Camry, Celica, Corolla FWD & MR2)** – Check tires for wear and improper inflation. Check camber of both rear wheels. See appropriate WHEEL ALIGNMENT SPECIFICATIONS

# 1991 WHEEL ALIGNMENT
# Specifications & Procedures (Cont.)

table at end of article. If camber is not within specification, inspect and replace any damaged or worn rear suspension components. Camber is NOT adjustable.

**Rear Suspension (Cressida & Supra)** – Check tires for wear and improper inflation. Ensure left and right lengths of No. 1 and No. 2 lower suspension arms are equal. *See Fig. 5*. Check camber of both rear wheels. See appropriate WHEEL ALIGNMENT SPECIFICATIONS table at end of article. If camber is not within specification, adjust camber by turning adjustment cams. *See Fig. 5*.

## STEERING AXIS/KING PIN INCLINATION

**Except Supra** – Ensure riding height and camber are correctly set. See appropriate WHEEL ALIGNMENT SPECIFICATIONS table at end of article. If adjustment is necessary, see appropriate adjustment procedure in this article. Check steering axis inclination of both front wheels. If steering axis inclination is not within specification, inspect and replace any damaged or worn front suspension components. See appropriate WHEEL ALIGNMENT SPECIFICATIONS table. Steering axis/king pin inclination is NOT adjustable.

**Supra** – Ensure riding height, camber and caster are correctly set. See appropriate WHEEL ALIGNMENT SPECIFICATIONS table at end of article. If adjustment is necessary, see appropriate adjustment procedure in this article. Check steering axis inclination of both front wheels. If steering axis inclination is not within specification, inspect wheel bearing for looseness, or replace steering knuckle. See appropriate WHEEL ALIGNMENT SPECIFICATIONS table.

## CASTER ADJUSTMENT

**Front Suspension (Camry & Cressida)** – **1)** Ensure riding height, camber and steering axis inclination are correctly set. See appropriate WHEEL ALIGNMENT SPECIFICATIONS table at end of article. If adjustment is necessary, see appropriate adjustment procedure in this article.

**2)** Check caster of both front wheels. If caster is not within specification, add or remove spacers on stabilizer bar (strut rod on Cressida). DO NOT use more than 2 spacers to adjust caster.

**Front Suspension (Celica, Corolla, Land Cruiser, Previa & Tercel)** – **1)** Ensure riding height, camber and steering axis inclination are correctly set. See appropriate WHEEL ALIGNMENT SPECIFICATIONS table at end of article. If adjustment is necessary, see appropriate adjustment procedure in this article.

**2)** Check caster of both front wheels. If caster is not within specification, inspect and replace any damaged or worn front suspension components. Caster is NOT adjustable.

**Front Suspension (MR2)** – **1)** Ensure riding height, camber and steering axis inclination are correctly set. See appropriate WHEEL ALIGNMENT SPECIFICATIONS table at end of article. If adjustment is necessary, see appropriate adjustment procedure in this article.

**2)** Check caster of both front wheels. If caster is not within specification, loosen strut bar front nut, and adjust camber adjusting nut. *See Fig. 6*. Tighten strut bar front nut after adjustment.

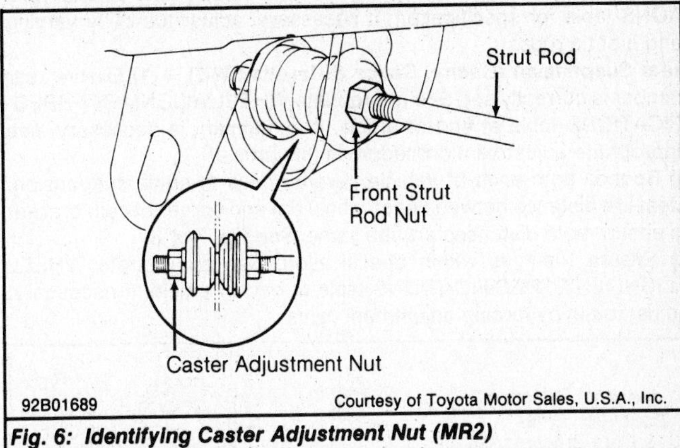


*Fig. 6: Identifying Caster Adjustment Nut (MR2)*

**Front Suspension (Pickup & 4Runner)** – **1)** Ensure riding height, camber and steering axis inclination are correctly set. See appropriate WHEEL ALIGNMENT SPECIFICATIONS table at end of article. If adjustment is necessary, see appropriate adjustment procedure in this article.

**2)** Check caster of both front wheels. If caster is not within specification, add or remove shims on upper control arms on 2WD models. DO NOT use more than 2 shims to adjust caster. On 4WD models, loosen and turn adjustment cams. *See Fig. 3*.

**Front Suspension (Supra)** – **1)** Ensure riding height, camber and steering axis inclination are correctly set. See appropriate WHEEL ALIGNMENT SPECIFICATIONS table at end of article. If adjustment is necessary, see appropriate adjustment procedure in this article.

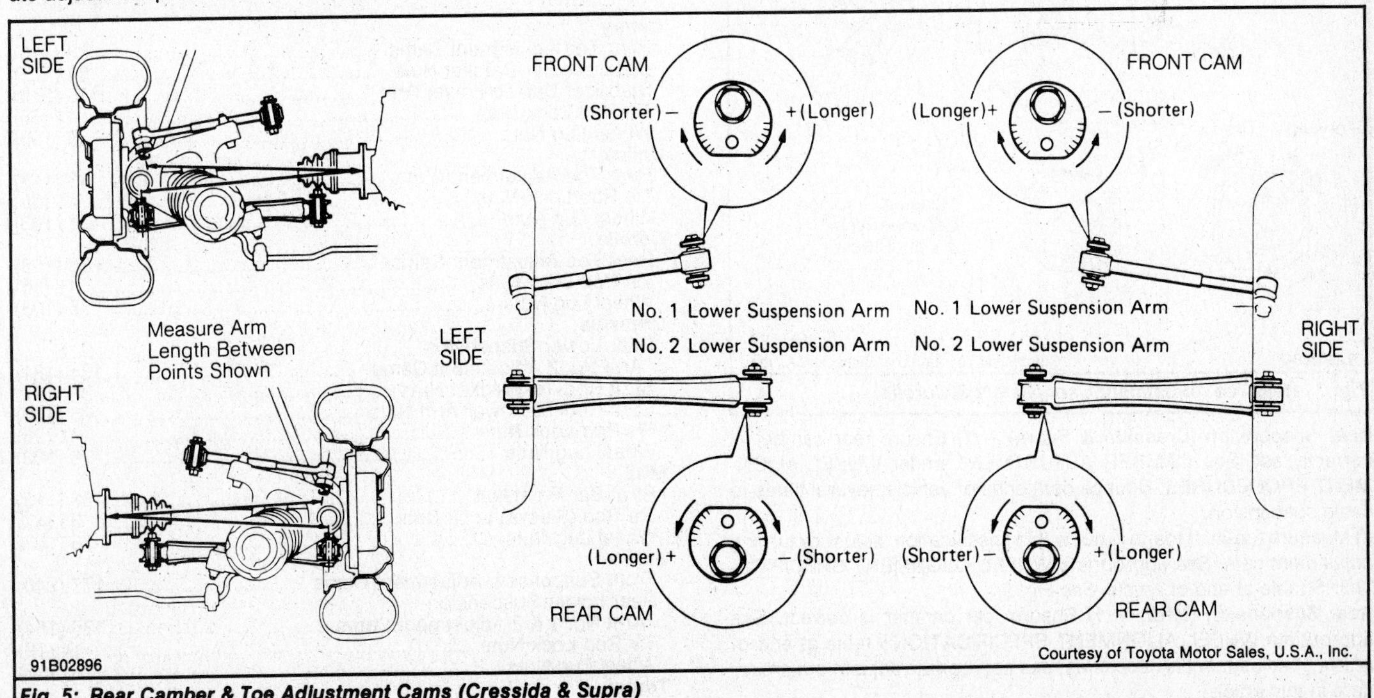


*Fig. 5: Rear Camber & Toe Adjustment Cams (Cressida & Supra)*

# 1991 WHEEL ALIGNMENT
# Specifications & Procedures (Cont.)

**2)** Check caster of both front wheels. If caster is not within specification, loosen and turn adjustment cams. *See Fig. 4*.

## TOE-IN ADJUSTMENT

**Front Suspension (All Models) – 1)** Ensure riding height, camber, steering axis inclination and caster are correctly set. See appropriate WHEEL ALIGNMENT SPECIFICATIONS table at end of article. Ensure steering wheel is in straight-ahead position. Bounce both ends of vehicle several times to settle suspension.
**2)** Measure toe-in. See appropriate WHEEL ALIGNMENT SPECIFICATIONS table for specification. If necessary, adjust toe-in by varying length of tie rods.

**Rear Suspension (Camry, Celica & Corolla FWD) – 1)** Ensure rear camber is correctly set. See appropriate WHEEL ALIGNMENT SPECIFICATIONS table at end of article. If adjustment is necessary, see appropriate adjustment procedure in this article.
**2)** Bounce both ends of vehicle several times to settle suspension. Measure distance between each wheel rim and corner of cam bracket to ensure both distances are the same. *See Fig. 7 or 8*.
**3)** Ensure toe-in is within specification. See appropriate WHEEL ALIGNMENT SPECIFICATIONS table at end of article. If necessary, adjust toe-in by turning adjustment cams.

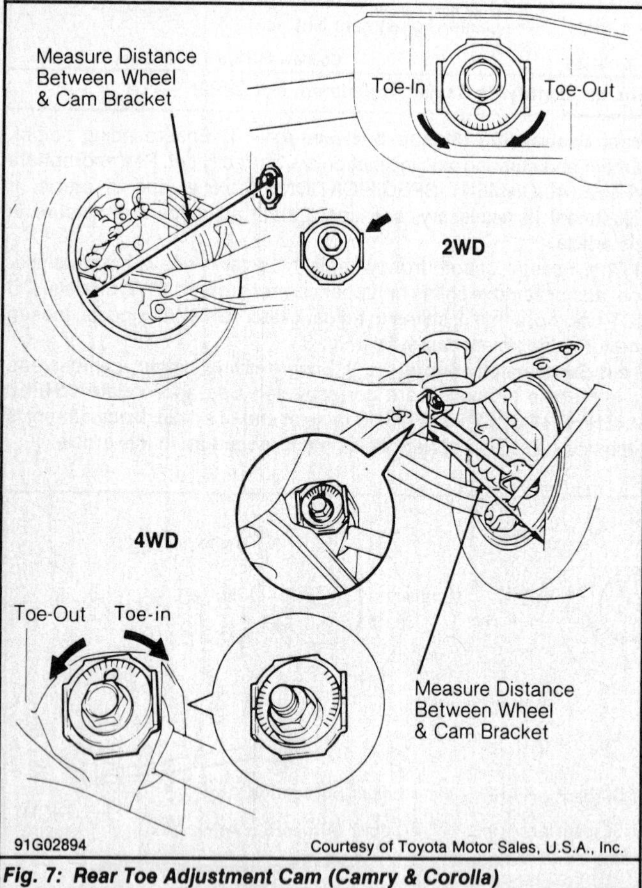


*Fig. 7: Rear Toe Adjustment Cam (Camry & Corolla)*

**Rear Suspension (Cressida & Supra) – 1)** Ensure rear camber is correctly set. See CAMBER ADJUSTMENT under WHEEL ALIGNMENT PROCEDURES. Bounce both ends of vehicle several times to settle suspension.
**2)** Measure toe-in. If toe-in is not within specification, adjust by turning adjustment cam. See appropriate WHEEL ALIGNMENT SPECIFICATIONS table at end of article. *See Fig. 5*.

**Rear Suspension (MR2) – 1)** Ensure rear camber is correct. See appropriate WHEEL ALIGNMENT SPECIFICATIONS table at end of article. If adjustment is necessary, see appropriate adjustment procedure in this article.
**2)** Bounce both ends of vehicle several times to settle suspension. Measure rear wheel toe-in. See appropriate WHEEL ALIGNMENT SPECIFICATIONS table at end of article. If necessary, adjust rear toe-in by rotating rear tie rod sleeves.

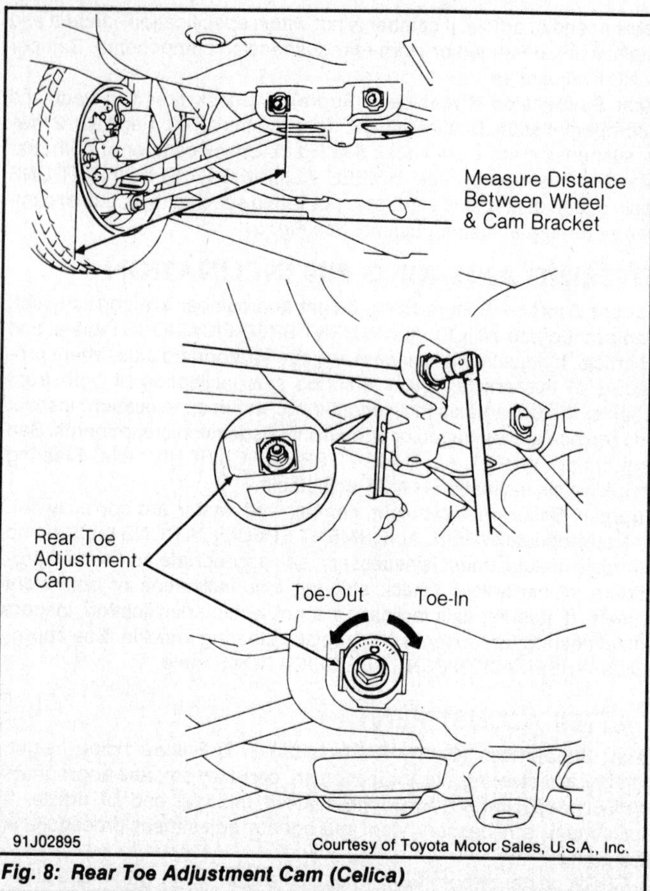


*Fig. 8: Rear Toe Adjustment Cam (Celica)*

## TORQUE SPECIFICATIONS

*TORQUE SPECIFICATIONS (PASSENGER CARS)*

| Application | Ft. Lbs. (N.m) |
|---|---|
| **Camry** | |
| Rear Toe Adjustment Cams | 83 (113) |
| Stabilizer Bar Bracket Nuts | 94 (127) |
| Stabilizer Bar-To-Lower Arm | 156 (212) |
| Tie Rod Lock Nuts | 41 (56) |
| Wheel Lug Nuts | 76 (103) |
| **Celica** | |
| Rear Toe Adjustment Cams | 83 (113) |
| Tie Rod Lock Nuts | 41 (56) |
| Wheel Lug Nuts | 76 (103) |
| **Corolla** | |
| Rear Toe Adjustment Cams | 80 (108) |
| Tie Rod Lock Nuts | 41 (56) |
| Wheel Lug Nuts | 76 (103) |
| **Cressida** | |
| Rear Lower Suspension Arm No. 2 Adjustment Cams | 134 (181) |
| Strut Rod-To-Bracket Nuts | 94 (127) |
| Strut Rod-To-Lower Arm Nuts | 76 (103) |
| Tie Rod Lock Nuts | 41 (56) |
| Wheel Lug Nuts | 76 (103) |
| **MR2** | |
| Strut Bar Front Nut | 83 (113) |
| Tie Rod (Sleeve) Lock Nuts | 35 (47) |
| Wheel Lug Nuts | 76 (103) |
| **Supra** | |
| Front Suspension Adjustment Cams | 177 (240) |
| Rear Lower Suspension Arm No. 1 & 2 Adjustment Cams | 136 (184) |
| Tie Rod Lock Nuts | 14 (19) |
| Wheel Lug Nuts | 76 (103) |
| **Tercel** | |
| Tie Rod Lock Nuts | 35 (57) |
| Wheel Lug Nuts | 76 (103) |

# 1991 WHEEL ALIGNMENT Specifications & Procedures (Cont.)

*TORQUE SPECIFICATIONS (LIGHT TRUCKS)*

| Application | Ft. Lbs. (N.m) |
|---|---|
| **Land Cruiser** | |
| Steering Knuckle Stopper Bolts | 33 (44) |
| Tie Rod Lock Nuts | 27 (37) |
| Wheel Lug Nuts | 116 (157) |
| **Pickup (2WD)** | |
| Steering Knuckle Stopper Bolts | 25 (34) |
| Tie Rod Lock Nuts | 19 (25) |
| Upper Control Arm Bolts | 71 (96) |
| Wheel Lug Nuts | |
| Dual Rear Wheel | 170 (230) |
| Single Rear Wheel | 101 (137) |
| **Pickup (4WD) & 4Runner** | |
| Front Suspension Adjustment Cams | 145 (196) |
| Steering Knuckle Stopper Bolts | 35 (47) |
| Tie Rod Lock Nuts | 19 (25) |
| Wheel Lug Nuts | 76 (103) |
| **Previa** | |
| Steering Knuckle Stopper Bolts | 24 (33) |
| Tie Rod Lock Nuts | 67 (91) |
| Wheel Lug Nuts | 76 (103) |

## WHEEL ALIGNMENT SPECIFICATIONS

*WHEEL ALIGNMENT SPECIFICATIONS (CAMRY)*

| Application | Preferred | Range |
|---|---|---|
| Camber [1] | | |
| Front | | |
| Sedan FWD | 9/16 | -3/16 To 1 5/16 |
| Wagon FWD | 1/2 | -1/4 To 1 1/4 |
| Rear | | |
| Sedan FWD | -9/16 | -1 1/16 To -1/16 |
| Wagon FWD | -1/16 | -9/16 To 7/16 |
| All-Trac | -1/2 | -1 To 0 |
| Caster [1] | | |
| Sedan | 1 11/16 | 1 3/16 To 2 3/16 |
| Wagon | 1 | 1/2 To 1 1/2 |
| Steering Axis | | |
| Inclination [1] | | |
| Sedan | 12 3/4 | 12 To 13 1/2 |
| Wagon | 12 27/32 | 12 3/32 To 13 19/32 |
| Toe-In [2] | | |
| Front | 1/32 (1) | 0 To 3/32 (0 To 2) |
| Rear | 5/32 (4) | 1/8 To 3/16 (3 To 5) |
| Toe-In [1] | | |
| Front | 1/16 | 0 To 3/16 |
| Rear | 5/16 | 1/4 To 3/8 |
| Toe-Out On Turns [1] | | |
| 4-Cylinder | | |
| Inner | 37 1/2 | .... |
| Outer | 30 3/4 | .... |
| V6 | | |
| Inner | 35 3/4 | .... |
| Outer | 29 3/4 | .... |

[1] – Measurement in degrees.
[2] – Measurement in inches (mm).

*WHEEL ALIGNMENT SPECIFICATIONS (CELICA)*

| Application | Preferred | Range |
|---|---|---|
| Camber [1] | | |
| Front | -5/32 | -29/32 To 19/32 |
| Rear | -3/4 | -1 1/4 To -1/4 |
| Caster [1] | | |
| Except All-Trac | 29/32 | 5/32 To 1 21/32 |
| All-Trac | 27/32 | 3/32 To 1 19/32 |
| Steering Axis | | |
| Inclination [1] | 14 5/32 | 13 13/32 To 14 29/32 |
| Toe-In [2] | | |
| Front | 0 (0) | -3/32 To 3/32 (-2 To 2) |
| Rear | 3/16 (5) | 3/32 To 9/32 (3 To 7) |
| Toe-In [1] | | |
| Front | 0 | -3/16 To 3/16 |
| Rear | 3/8 | 3/16 To 9/16 |
| Toe-Out On Turns [1] | | |
| Inner | 33 1/2 | .... |
| Outer | 29 1/2 | .... |

[1] – Measurement in degrees.
[2] – Measurement in inches (mm).

*WHEEL ALIGNMENT SPECIFICATIONS (COROLLA)*

| Application | Preferred | Range |
|---|---|---|
| Camber [1] | | |
| Except All-Trac | | |
| Front | -3/16 | -7/8 To 1/2 |
| Rear | -11/16 | -1 3/8 To 0 |
| All-Trac | 3/16 | -5/16 To 11/16 |
| Caster [1] | | |
| Except All-Trac | 1 7/16 | 3/4 To 2 1/8 |
| All-Trac | 1 1/4 | 3/4 To 1 3/4 |
| Steering Axis | | |
| Inclination [1] | | |
| 2WD (4A-FE) | 12 21/32 | 11 29/32 To 13 13/32 |
| 2WD (4A-GE) | 12 27/32 | 12 3/32 To 13 19/32 |
| 4WD | 12 3/32 | 11 19/32 To 12 19/32 |
| Toe-In [2] | | |
| Front | 1/32 (1) | 0 To 1/16 (0 To 2) |
| Rear | 5/32 (4) | 1/8 To 3/16 (3 To 5) |
| Toe-In [1] | | |
| Front | 1/16 | 0 To 1/8 |
| Rear | 5/16 | 1/4 To 3/8 |
| Toe-Out On Turns [1] | | |
| Except All-Trac | | |
| Inner | 37 | .... |
| Outer | 32 1/2 | .... |
| All-Trac | | |
| Inner | 38 | .... |
| Outer | 32 | .... |

[1] – Measurement in degrees.
[2] – Measurement in inches (mm).

# 1991 WHEEL ALIGNMENT
# Specifications & Procedures (Cont.)

### *WHEEL ALIGNMENT SPECIFICATIONS (CRESSIDA)*

| Application | Preferred | Range |
|---|---|---|
| Camber [1] | | |
| Front | 1/2 | -1/4 To 1 1/4 |
| Rear | 0 | -3/4 To 3/4 |
| Caster [1] | 7 5/16 | 6 13/16 To 7 13/16 |
| Steering Axis | | |
| Inclination [1] | 13 5/32 | 12 13/32 To 13 29/32 |
| Toe-In [2] | | |
| Front | 1/16 (2) | 1/32 To 3/32 (1 To 3) |
| Rear | 1/16 (2) | 0 To 5/32 (0 To 4) |
| Toe-In [1] | | |
| Front | 1/8 | 1/16 To 3/16 |
| Rear | 1/8 | 0 To 5/16 |
| Toe-Out On Turns [1] | | |
| Inner | 41 7/16 | ..... |
| Outer | 34 1/4 | ..... |

[1] – Measurement in degrees.
[2] – Measurement in inches (mm).

### *WHEEL ALIGNMENT SPECIFICATIONS (LAND CRUISER)*

| Application | Preferred | Range |
|---|---|---|
| Camber [1] (Front) | 1 | 1/4 To 1 1/4 |
| Caster [1] | | |
| P235/75R | 3 | 2 To 4 |
| 31 x 10.50R LT | 1 21/32 | 21/32 To 2 21/32 |
| Steering Axis | | |
| Inclination [1] | 13 1/2 | 12 3/4 To 14 1/4 |
| Toe-In [2] | 1/32 (1) | -1/32 To 1/8 (-1 To 3) |
| Toe-In [1] | 1/16 | -1/16 To 7/32 |
| Toe-Out On Turns [1] | | |
| Inner | 35 | ..... |
| Outer | 30 | ..... |

[1] – Measurement in degrees.
[2] – Measurement in inches (mm).

### *WHEEL ALIGNMENT SPECIFICATIONS (MR2)*

| Application | Preferred | Range |
|---|---|---|
| Camber [1] | | |
| Front | -15/16 | -1 7/16 To -7/16 |
| Rear | -1 11/32 | -1 27/32 To -27/32 |
| Caster [1] | 2 3/4 | 2 3/4 To 3 1/4 |
| Steering Axis | | |
| Inclination [1] | 13 1/2 | 13 To 14 |
| Toe-In [2] | | |
| Front | 1/32 (1) | 0 To 3/32 (0 To 2) |
| Rear | 3/16 (5) | 5/32 To 1/4 (4 To 6) |
| Toe-In [1] | | |
| Front | 1/16 | 0 To 3/16 |
| Rear | 3/8 | 5/16 To 1/2 |
| Toe-Out On Turns [1] | | |
| Inner | 37 1/2 | ..... |
| Outer | 32 | ..... |

[1] – Measurement in degrees.
[2] – Measurement in inches (mm).

### *WHEEL ALIGNMENT SPECIFICATIONS (PICKUP 2WD)*

| Application | Preferred | Range |
|---|---|---|
| **4-Cylinder** | | |
| STD, Reg. Cab | | |
| Short Chassis | | |
| Camber [1] | 1/2 | -1/4 To 1 1/4 |
| Caster [1] | 21/32 | 0 To 1 1/2 |
| Steering Axis | | |
| Inclination [1] | 10 | 9 1/4 To 10 3/4 |
| Toe-In [2] | 1/16 (1.5) | -1/32 To 1/8 (-1 To 3) |
| Toe-Out On Turns [1] | | |
| Inner | 34 | 32-35 |
| Outer | 30 | ..... |
| DLX, Reg. Cab | | |
| Short Chassis | | |
| Camber [1] | 1/2 | -1/4 To 1 1/4 |
| Caster [1] | 23/32 | 0 To 1 1/2 |
| Steering Axis | | |
| Inclination [1] | 10 | 9 1/4 To 10 3/4 |
| Toe-In [2] | 1/16 (1.5) | -1/32 To 1/8 (-1 To 3) |
| Toe-Out On Turns [1] | | |
| Inner | 34 | 32-35 |
| Outer | 30 | ..... |
| Long Chassis | | |
| Camber [1] | 1/2 | -1/4 To 1 1/4 |
| Caster [1] | 1 | 1/4 To 1 3/4 |
| Steering Axis | | |
| Inclination [1] | 10 | 9 1/4 To 10 3/4 |
| Toe-In [2] | 3/32 (2) | 0 To 5/32 (0 To 4) |
| Toe-Out On Turns [1] | | |
| Inner | 34 | 32-35 |
| Outer | 30 | ..... |
| DLX, Xtra Cab | | |
| Xtra Long Chassis | | |
| Camber [1] | 3/8 | -3/8 To 1 1/8 |
| Caster [1] | 1 1/4 | 1/2 To 2 |
| Steering Axis | | |
| Inclination [1] | 10 | 9 1/4 To 10 3/4 |
| Toe-In [2] | 1/8 (3) | 1/16 To 3/16 (1 To 5) |
| Toe-Out On Turns [1] | | |
| Inner | 34 | 32-35 |
| Outer | 30 | ..... |
| **V6** | | |
| Standard | C & C DRW [3] | |
| Camber [1] | 1/2 | -1/4 To 1 1/4 |
| Caster [1] | 1 3/4 | 1 To 2 1/2 |
| Steering Axis | | |
| Inclination [1] | 10 | 9 1/4 To 10 3/4 |
| Toe-In [2] | 7/32 (5.5) | 1/8 To 5/16 (1 To 8) |
| Toe-Out On Turns [1] | | |
| Inner | 34 | 32-35 |
| Outer | 30 | ..... |
| DLX, Reg. Cab | | |
| Long Chassis (A/T) | | |
| Camber [1] | 1/2 | -1/4 To 1 1/4 |
| Caster [1] | 9/16 | -3/16 To 1 5/16 |
| Steering Axis | | |
| Inclination [1] | 10 | 9 1/4 To 10 3/4 |
| Toe-In [2] | 3/16 (5) | 1/8 To 9/32 (3 To 7) |
| Toe-Out On Turns [1] | | |
| Inner | 34 | 32-35 |
| Outer | 30 | ..... |
| Long Chassis (M/T) | | |
| Camber [1] | 1/2 | -1/4 To 1 1/4 |
| Caster [1] | 9/16 | -3/16 To 1 5/16 |
| Steering Axis | | |
| Inclination [1] | 10 | 9 1/4 To 10 3/4 |
| Toe-In [2] | 7/32 (5.5) | 1/8 To 5/16 (3 To 8) |

# 1991 WHEEL ALIGNMENT Specifications & Procedures (Cont.)

### WHEEL ALIGNMENT SPECIFICATIONS (PICKUP 2WD - Cont.)

| Application | Preferred | Range |
|---|---|---|
| Toe-Out On Turns [1] | | |
| Inner | 34 | 32-35 |
| Outer | 30 | .... |
| DLX, Xtra Cab | | |
| Xtra Long Chassis | | |
| Camber [1] | 3/8 | -3/8 To 1 1/8 |
| Caster [1] | 1 1/4 | 1/2 To 2 |
| Steering Axis | | |
| Inclination [1] | 10 | 9 1/4 To 10 3/4 |
| Toe-In [2] | 1/8 (3) | 1/16 To 3/16 (1 To 5) |
| Toe-Out On Turns [1] | | |
| Inner | 34 | 32-35 |
| Outer | 30 | .... |
| SR5, Xtra Cab | | |
| Xtra Long Chassis | | |
| Camber [1] | 13/32 | -11/32 To 1 5/32 |
| Caster [1] | 1 7/32 | 15/32 To 2 |
| Steering Axis | | |
| Inclination [1] | 10 | 9 1/4 To 10 3/4 |
| Toe-In [2] | 1/8 (3) | 1/16 To 3/16 (1 To 5) |
| Toe-Out On Turns [1] | | |
| Inner | 34 | 32-35 |
| Outer | 30 | .... |

[1] - Measurement in degrees.
[2] - Measurement in inches (mm).
[3] - C & C DRW is Cab and Chassis with Dual Rear Wheels.

### WHEEL ALIGNMENT SPECIFICATIONS (PICKUP 4WD)

| Application | Preferred | Range |
|---|---|---|
| **4-Cylinder** | | |
| All Long Chassis | | |
| Camber [1] | 11/16 | -1/16 To 1 7/16 |
| Caster [1] | 1 11/16 | 15/16 To 2 7/16 |
| Steering Axis | | |
| Inclination [1] | 11 7/8 | 11 1/8 To 12 5/8 |
| Toe-In [2] | 3/32 (2) | 0 To 5/32 (0 To 4) |
| Toe-Out On Turns [1] | | |
| Inner | 32 | 30-33 |
| Outer | 31 | .... |
| DLX, Reg. Cab | | |
| Standard Chassis | | |
| Camber [1] | 23/32 | -1/32 To 1 15/32 |
| Caster [1] | | |
| A/T | 1 29/32 | 15/16 To 2 7/16 |
| M/T | 1 5/8 | 7/8 To 2 3/8 |
| Steering Axis | | |
| Inclination [1] | 11 7/8 | 11 1/8 To 12 5/8 |
| Toe-In [2] | 3/32 (2) | 0 To 5/32 (0 To 4) |
| Toe-Out On Turns [1] | | |
| Inner | 32 | 30-33 |
| Outer | 31 | .... |
| DLX, Xtra Cab | | |
| Xtra Long Chassis | | |
| Camber [1] | 21/32 | -3/32 To 1 13/32 |
| Caster [1] | | |
| A/T | 1 7/8 | 1 1/8 To 2 5/8 |
| M/T | 1 13/16 | 1 1/16 To 2 9/16 |
| Steering Axis | | |
| Inclination [1] | 11 29/32 | 11 5/32 To 12 21/32 |
| Toe-In [2] | 3/32 (2.5) | 0 To 3/16 (0 To 5) |
| Toe-Out On Turns [1] | | |
| Inner | 32 | 30-33 |
| Outer | 31 | .... |

### WHEEL ALIGNMENT SPECIFICATIONS (PICKUP 4WD - Cont.)

| Application | Preferred | Range |
|---|---|---|
| **V6** | | |
| All Reg. Cab | | |
| Short Chassis | | |
| Camber [1] | 23/32 | -1/32 To 1 15/32 |
| Caster [1] | 1 11/16 | 15/16 To 2 7/16 |
| Steering Axis | | |
| Inclination [1] | 11 7/8 | 11 1/8 To 12 5/8 |
| Toe-In [2] | 3/32 (2) | 0 To 5/32 (0 To 4) |
| Toe-Out On Turns [1] | | |
| Inner | 32 | 30-33 |
| Outer | 31 | .... |
| Long Chassis | | |
| Camber [1] | 11/16 | -1/16 To 1 7/16 |
| Caster [1] | 1 3/4 | 1 To 2 1/2 |
| Steering Axis | | |
| Inclination [1] | 11 7/8 | 11 1/8 To 12 5/8 |
| Toe-In [2] | 3/32 (2) | 0 To 5/32 (0 To 4) |
| Toe-Out On Turns [1] | | |
| Inner | 32 | 30-33 |
| Outer | 31 | .... |
| DLX, Xtra Cab | | |
| Xtra Long Chassis | | |
| Camber [1] | 21/32 | -3/32 To 1 13/32 |
| Caster [1] | 1 7/8 | 1 1/8 To 2 5/8 |
| Steering Axis | | |
| Inclination [1] | 11 29/32 | 11 5/32 To 12 21/32 |
| Toe-In [2] | 3/32 (2.5) | 0 To 3/16 (0 To 5) |
| Toe-Out On Turns [1] | | |
| Inner | 32 | 30-33 |
| Outer | 31 | .... |
| SR5, Xtra Cab | | |
| Xtra Long Chassis | | |
| Camber [1] | 11/16 | -1/16 To 1 7/16 |
| Caster [1] | | |
| M/T | 1 29/32 | 1 5/32 To 2 21/32 |
| A/T | 1 15/16 | 1 3/16 To 2 11/16 |
| Steering Axis | | |
| Inclination [1] | 11 7/8 | 11 1/8 To 12 5/8 |
| Toe-In [2] | 3/32 (2.5) | 0 To 5/32 (0 To 4) |
| Toe-Out On Turns [1] | | |
| Inner | 32 | 30-33 |
| Outer | 31 | .... |

[1] - Measurement in degrees.
[2] - Measurement in inches (mm).

### WHEEL ALIGNMENT SPECIFICATIONS (PREVIA)

| Application | Preferred | Range |
|---|---|---|
| **2WD** | | |
| Camber [1] | 0 | -3/4 To 3/4 |
| Caster [1] | 5 1/2 | 4 3/4 To 6 1/4 |
| Steering Axis | | |
| Inclination [1] | 10 19/32 | 9 27/32 To 11 11/32 |
| Toe-In [2] | 3/32 (2) | 1/32 To 1/8 (1 To 3) |
| Toe-In [1] | 3/16 | 1/16 To 1/4 |
| Toe-Out On Turns [1] | | |
| Inner | 36 | .... |
| Outer | 33 | .... |
| **4WD** | | |
| Camber [1] | 1/4 | -1/2 To 1 |
| Caster [1] | 5 5/16 | 4 9/16 To 6 1/16 |
| Steering Axis | | |
| Inclination [1] | 10 11/32 | 9 19/32 To 11 3/32 |
| Toe-In [2] | 1/8 (3) | 3/32 To 5/32 (2 To 4) |
| Toe-Out On Turns [1] | | |
| Inner | 36 | .... |
| Outer | 33 1/2 | .... |

[1] - Measurement in degrees. [2] - Measurement in inches (mm).

# 1991 WHEEL ALIGNMENT
# Specifications & Procedures (Cont.)

### WHEEL ALIGNMENT SPECIFICATIONS (SUPRA)

| Application | Preferred | Range |
|---|---|---|
| Camber [1] | | |
| Front | -3/16 | -11/16 To 5/16 |
| Rear | -3/4 | -1 1/4 To -1/4 |
| Caster [1] | 7 11/16 | 7 3/16 To 8 3/16 |
| Steering Axis | | |
| Inclination [1] | 10 29/32 | 10 5/32 To 11 21/32 |
| Toe-In [2] | | |
| Front | 0 (0) | -1/32 To 1/32 (-1 To 1) |
| Rear | 5/32 (4) | 1/8 To 3/16 (3 To 5) |
| Toe-In [1] | | |
| Front | 0 | -1/16 To 1/16 |
| Rear | 5/16 | 1/4 To 3/8 |
| Toe-Out On Turns [1] | | |
| Inner | 34 1/2 | .... |
| Outer | 31 3/4 | .... |

[1] – Measurement in degrees.
[2] – Measurement in inches (mm).

### WHEEL ALIGNMENT SPECIFICATIONS (TERCEL)

| Application | Preferred | Range |
|---|---|---|
| Camber [1] | | |
| Front | -1/4 | -1 To 1/2 |
| Rear | -1/2 | -1 1/4 To 1/4 |
| Caster [1] | 1 1/4 | 1/2 To 2 |
| Steering Axis | | |
| Inclination [1] | 12 | 11 1/4 To 12 3/4 |
| Toe-In [2] | | |
| Front | 1/32 (1) | -1/32 To 1/8 (-1 To 3) |
| Rear | 1/8 (3) | 0 To 1/4 (0 To 6) |
| Toe-In [1] | | |
| Front | 3/32 | -3/32 To 5/16 |
| Rear | 1/4 | 0 To 1/2 |
| Toe-Out On Turns [1] | | |
| Inner | 36 5/32 | .... |
| Outer | 32 1/4 | .... |

[1] – Measurement in degrees.
[2] – Measurement in inches (mm).

### WHEEL ALIGNMENT SPECIFICATIONS (4RUNNER)

| Application | Preferred | Range |
|---|---|---|
| **2WD** | | |
| SR5 4-Door A/T | | |
| Camber [1] | 23/32 | -1/32 To 1 15/32 |
| Caster [1] | | |
| 4-Cylinder | 1 29/32 | 1 5/32 To 2 5/8 |
| V6 | 1 15/16 | 1 3/16 To 2 11/16 |
| Steering Axis | | |
| Inclination [1] | 11 7/8 | 11 1/8 To 12 5/8 |
| Toe-In [2] | 3/32 (2) | 0 To 5/32 (0 To 4) |
| Toe-Out On Turns [1] | | |
| Inner | 32 | 30-33 |
| Outer | 31 | .... |

### WHEEL ALIGNMENT SPECIFICATIONS (4RUNNER – Cont.)

| Application | Preferred | Range |
|---|---|---|
| **4WD** | | |
| SR5 4-Cylinder | | |
| Camber [1] | 23/32 | -1/32 To 1 15/32 |
| Caster [1] | | |
| 2-Door | 1 31/32 | 1 7/32 To 2 23/32 |
| 4-Door | 2 | 1 9/32 To 2 25/32 |
| Steering Axis | | |
| Inclination [1] | 11 7/8 | 11 1/8 To 12 5/8 |
| Toe-In [2] | 3/32 (2) | 0 To 5/32 (0 To 4) |
| Toe-Out On Turns [1] | | |
| Inner | 32 | 30-33 |
| Outer | 31 | .... |
| SR5 V6 | | |
| 2-Door (A/T) | | |
| Camber [1] | 23/32 | -1/32 To 1 15/32 |
| Caster [1] | | |
| P225/75R15 | 1 27/32 | 1 3/32 To 2 19/32 |
| 31 x 10.5R15 | 1 7/8 | 1 1/8 To 2 5/8 |
| Steering Axis | | |
| Inclination [1] | 11 7/8 | 11 1/8 To 12 5/8 |
| Toe-In [2] | 3/32 (2) | 0 To 5/32 (0 To 4) |
| Toe-Out On Turns [1] | | |
| Inner | 32 | 30-33 |
| Outer | 31 | .... |
| 2-Door (M/T) | | |
| Camber [1] | 23/32 | -1/32 To 1 15/32 |
| Caster [1] | | |
| P225/75R15 | 1 13/16 | 1 1/16 To 2 9/16 |
| 31 x 10.5R15 | 1 27/32 | 1 3/32 To 2 19/32 |
| Steering Axis | | |
| Inclination [1] | 11 7/8 | 11 1/8 To 12 5/8 |
| Toe-In [2] | 3/32 (2) | 0 To 5/32 (0 To 4) |
| Toe-Out On Turns [1] | | |
| Inner | 32 | 30-33 |
| Outer | 31 | .... |
| 4-Door (A/T) | | |
| Camber [1] | 23/32 | -1/32 To 1 15/32 |
| Caster [1] | | |
| P225/75R15 | 1 21/32 | 29/32 To 2 13/32 |
| 31 x 10.5R15 | 1 23/32 | 31/32 To 2 15/32 |
| Steering Axis | | |
| Inclination [1] | 11 7/8 | 11 1/8 To 12 5/8 |
| Toe-In [2] | 3/32 (2) | 0 To 5/32 (0 To 4) |
| Toe-Out On Turns [1] | | |
| Inner | 32 | 30-33 |
| Outer | 31 | .... |
| 4-Door (M/T) | | |
| Camber [1] | 23/32 | -1/32 To 1 15/32 |
| Caster [1] | | |
| P225/75R15 | 1 11/16 | 15/16 To 2 7/16 |
| 31 x 10.5R15 | 1 23/32 | 31/32 To 2 15/32 |
| Steering Axis | | |
| Inclination [1] | 11 7/8 | 11 1/8 To 12 5/8 |
| Toe-In [2] | 3/32 (2) | 0 To 5/32 (0 To 4) |
| Toe-Out On Turns [1] | | |
| Inner | 32 | 30-33 |
| Outer | 31 | .... |

[1] – Measurement in degrees.
[2] – Measurement in inches (mm).

# 1991 SUSPENSION
# Front – Camry, Celica, Corolla & Tercel

## DESCRIPTION

Vehicles are equipped with front wheel drive and independent MacPherson strut front suspension. Suspension consists of vertically mounted strut assemblies, control arms and stabilizer bar.

Struts are mounted between inner fender and steering knuckle. Tie rod ends connect rack and pinion steering to steering knuckle. Ball joint connects steering knuckle to lower control arm which attaches to frame crossmember. On Camry, Celica and Corolla, stabilizer bar attaches to lower control arms and 2 points on crossmember.

## ADJUSTMENTS & INSPECTION

### WHEEL ALIGNMENT SPECIFICATIONS & PROCEDURES

***NOTE:** See SPECIFICATIONS & PROCEDURES article in WHEEL ALIGNMENT.*

### WHEEL BEARING

Wheel bearings are not adjustable. Whenever bearings are removed, replace with new bearings, races and oil seals.

### BALL JOINT CHECKING

**1)** Raise vehicle, and place a wooden block with a height of 7.09-7.87" (180.0-200.0 mm) under either front tire. Lower floor jack until about half vehicle load is on front struts. Place safety stands under vehicle.
**2)** Place front wheels in straight-ahead position, and block them. Use a rod to move control arm up and down. Check for vertical ball joint play. If ball joint is damaged or any vertical play is found, replace ball joint. See LOWER CONTROL ARM & BALL JOINT under REMOVAL & INSTALLATION.

## REMOVAL & INSTALLATION

### WHEEL BEARING

***NOTE:** During following removal and installation procedure, refer to Fig. 1, 2, 3 or 4.*

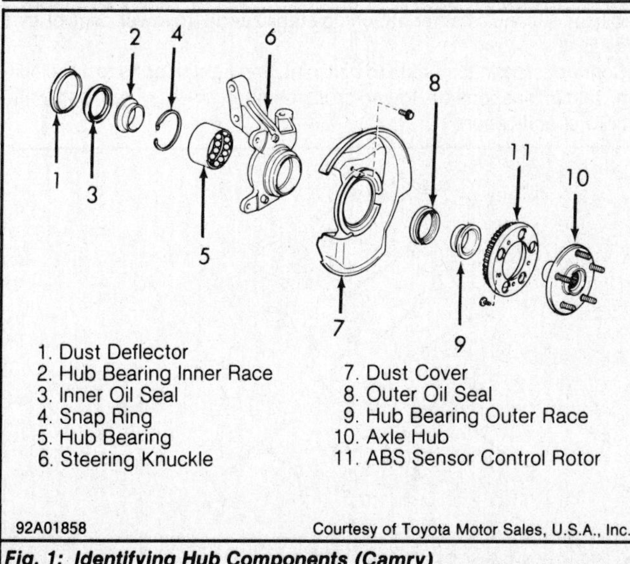

1. Dust Deflector
2. Hub Bearing Inner Race
3. Inner Oil Seal
4. Snap Ring
5. Hub Bearing
6. Steering Knuckle
7. Dust Cover
8. Outer Oil Seal
9. Hub Bearing Outer Race
10. Axle Hub
11. ABS Sensor Control Rotor

92A01858 Courtesy of Toyota Motor Sales, U.S.A., Inc.

*Fig. 1: Identifying Hub Components (Camry)*

**Removal – 1)** Remove cotter pin, bearing lock nut cap and bearing lock nut (apply brakes when removing lock nut). Remove brake caliper. DO NOT disconnect brake line. Secure caliper aside.
**2)** Remove disc brake rotor. On ABS-equipped models, remove speed sensor. Remove cotter pin and castle nut from tie rod end.

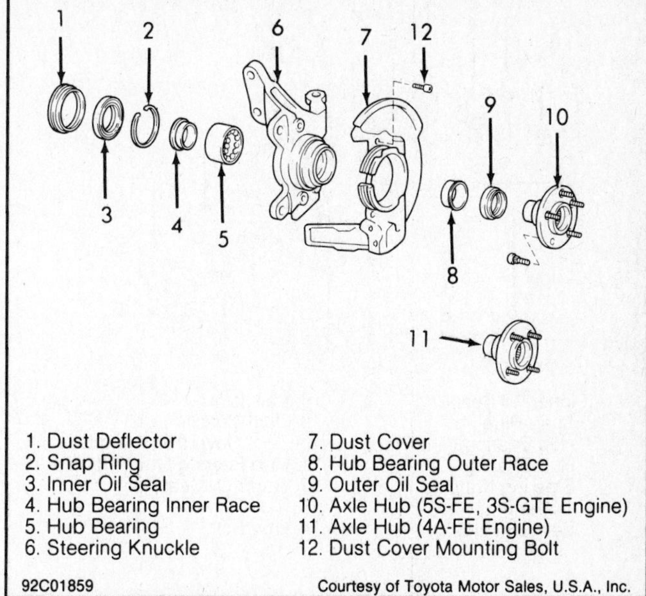

1. Dust Deflector
2. Snap Ring
3. Inner Oil Seal
4. Hub Bearing Inner Race
5. Hub Bearing
6. Steering Knuckle
7. Dust Cover
8. Hub Bearing Outer Race
9. Outer Oil Seal
10. Axle Hub (5S-FE, 3S-GTE Engine)
11. Axle Hub (4A-FE Engine)
12. Dust Cover Mounting Bolt

92C01859 Courtesy of Toyota Motor Sales, U.S.A., Inc.

*Fig. 2: Identifying Hub Components (Celica)*

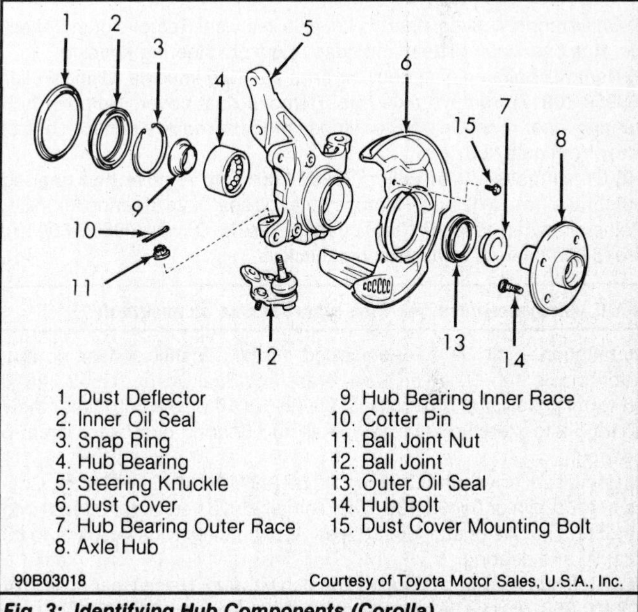

1. Dust Deflector
2. Inner Oil Seal
3. Snap Ring
4. Hub Bearing
5. Steering Knuckle
6. Dust Cover
7. Hub Bearing Outer Race
8. Axle Hub
9. Hub Bearing Inner Race
10. Cotter Pin
11. Ball Joint Nut
12. Ball Joint
13. Outer Oil Seal
14. Hub Bolt
15. Dust Cover Mounting Bolt

90B03018 Courtesy of Toyota Motor Sales, U.S.A., Inc.

*Fig. 3: Identifying Hub Components (Corolla)*

**3)** Using Puller (09610-55012 on Camry, 09628-62011 on Celica and Tercel or 09611-22012 on Corolla), pull tie rod end from steering knuckle.
**4)** Mark lower strut bracket and camber adjusting cam for installation reference. Remove bolts and nuts, and separate steering knuckle from strut.
**5)** On Camry, remove ball joint cotter pin and nut. Disconnect steering knuckle from lower control arm ball joint using Puller (09616-55012). Using a plastic hammer, tap drive shaft from splines. Remove steering knuckle.
**6)** On Celica, remove nuts and bolts attaching steering knuckle to lower control arm. Using Puller (09950-20017), disconnect steering knuckle from drive shaft. Remove steering knuckle.
**7)** On Corolla and Tercel, remove nuts and bolts attaching steering knuckle to lower control arm. Using a plastic hammer, tap drive shaft from splines, and remove steering knuckle.

# 1991 SUSPENSION
# Front – Camry, Celica, Corolla & Tercel (Cont.)

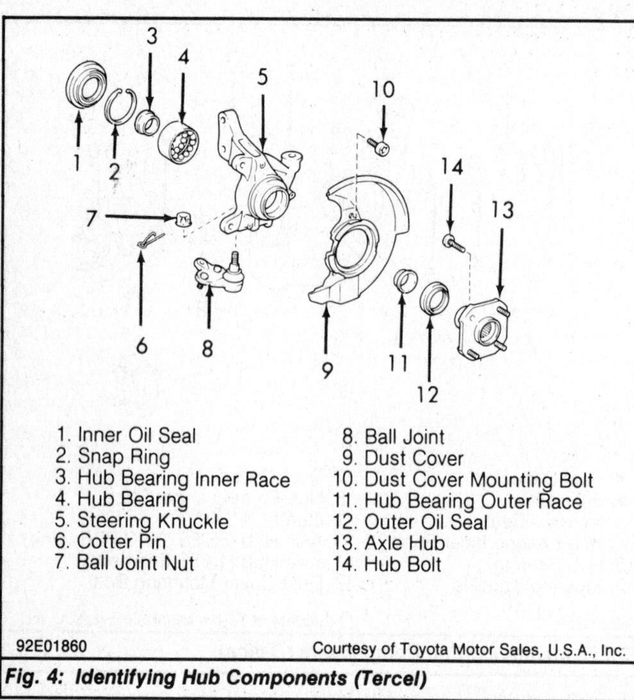

1. Inner Oil Seal
2. Snap Ring
3. Hub Bearing Inner Race
4. Hub Bearing
5. Steering Knuckle
6. Cotter Pin
7. Ball Joint Nut
8. Ball Joint
9. Dust Cover
10. Dust Cover Mounting Bolt
11. Hub Bearing Outer Race
12. Outer Oil Seal
13. Axle Hub
14. Hub Bolt

92E01860 Courtesy of Toyota Motor Sales, U.S.A., Inc.

*Fig. 4: Identifying Hub Components (Tercel)*

**8)** On all models, place steering knuckle in a vise. Remove dust deflector. Remove inner oil seal and snap ring from steering knuckle.

**9)** Remove bolts holding dust cover to steering knuckle. Using Puller (09950-20017), remove axle hub. Remove dust cover. Remove hub bearing inner race. On ABS-equipped models, remove sensor control rotor from axle hub.

**10)** On all models, use Puller (09950-20017) to remove hub bearing outer race from axle hub. Remove outer oil seal from steering knuckle. Reinstall outer race on hub bearing. Using Driver (09605-60010), press hub bearing from steering knuckle.

***NOTE: Always replace bearings and races as an assembly.***

**Installation – 1)** On ABS-equipped models, install sensor control rotor to axle hub. Using an arbor press and Seal Driver (09608-32010 on Camry, Celica and Corolla or 09608-10010 on Tercel), press new bearing into steering knuckle. Install hub bearing outer race on hub bearing.

**2)** Using seal driver and Bushing Driver (09710-14012 on Camry, Celica and Corolla or 09608-10010 on Tercel), drive new outer oil seal into steering knuckle. Install dust cover. Apply multipurpose grease to oil seal lip and bearing.

**3)** Install hub bearing inside race on hub bearing. Using Bearing Driver (09310-35010 on Camry, Celica and Corolla or 09608-10010 on Tercel), press hub into steering knuckle. Install snap ring into steering knuckle on Camry, Celica, and Corolla. Install lower ball joint on Tercel.

**4)** Using seal driver and Bushing Driver (09710-14012 on Camry, Celica and Corolla or 09608-10010 on Tercel), install new inner oil seal flush with end surface of steering knuckle. On Camry, Celica and Corolla, install new dust deflector into steering knuckle using Seal Driver (09608-35014 on Camry and Celica or 09218-46010 on Corolla).

**5)** On all models, reverse removal procedure to complete installation. Tighten all nuts and bolts to specification. See TORQUE SPECIFICATIONS table at end of article. Check front end alignment. See SPECIFICATIONS & PROCEDURES article in WHEEL ALIGNMENT.

## LOWER CONTROL ARM & BALL JOINT

**Removal (Camry) – 1)** Raise and support vehicle. Remove wheels. Disconnect lower ball joint from steering knuckle. Remove stabilizer nut holding stabilizer bar to lower control arm. Remove lower control arm shaft nut attaching lower control arm shaft to lower control arm. *See Fig. 5.*

**2)** Remove suspension crossmember. Remove lower control arm shaft mounting nut and bolt. Remove lower control arm and lower control arm shaft as an assembly.

**3)** Install lower control arm in a vise. Remove ball joint cotter pin and nut. Using ball joint Remover (09628-62011), remove ball joint from lower control arm.

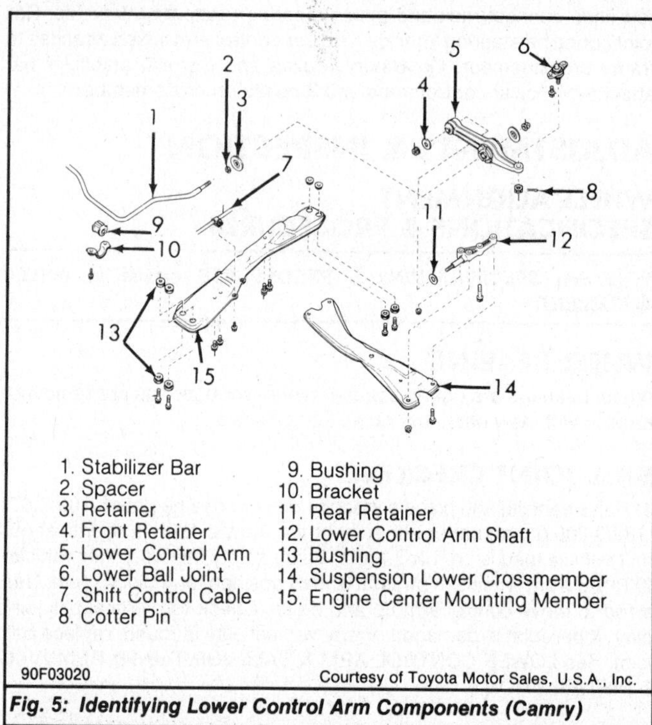

1. Stabilizer Bar
2. Spacer
3. Retainer
4. Front Retainer
5. Lower Control Arm
6. Lower Ball Joint
7. Shift Control Cable
8. Cotter Pin
9. Bushing
10. Bracket
11. Rear Retainer
12. Lower Control Arm Shaft
13. Bushing
14. Suspension Lower Crossmember
15. Engine Center Mounting Member

90F03020 Courtesy of Toyota Motor Sales, U.S.A., Inc.

*Fig. 5: Identifying Lower Control Arm Components (Camry)*

**Installation – 1)** Install ball joint to lower control arm, and tighten nut to specification. See TORQUE SPECIFICATIONS table at end of article. Install new cotter pin.

**2)** Install lower control arm shaft to lower control arm. Install, but DO NOT tighten, lower control arm nut and rear retainer attaching lower control arm to lower control arm shaft. Install, but DO NOT tighten, stabilizer nut and retainer attaching stabilizer bar to lower control arm. *See Fig. 5.*

**3)** Connect steering knuckle to ball joint, and tighten bolts to specification. Install suspension lower crossmember, and tighten bolts and nuts to specification.

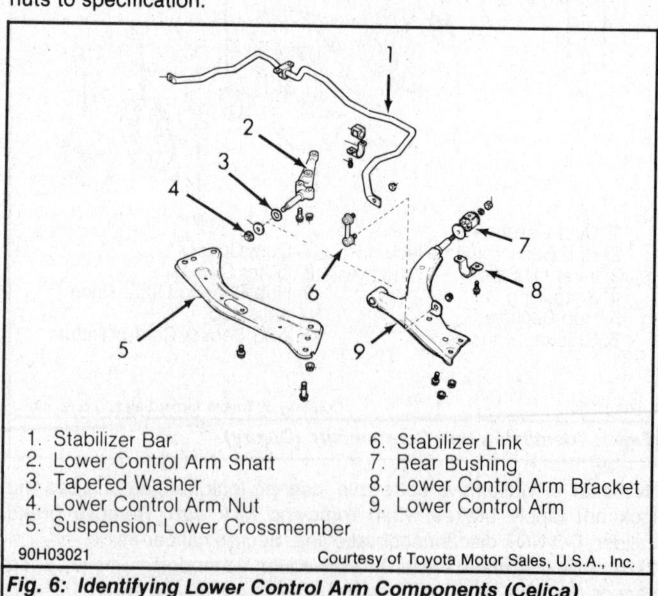

1. Stabilizer Bar
2. Lower Control Arm Shaft
3. Tapered Washer
4. Lower Control Arm Nut
5. Suspension Lower Crossmember
6. Stabilizer Link
7. Rear Bushing
8. Lower Control Arm Bracket
9. Lower Control Arm

90H03021 Courtesy of Toyota Motor Sales, U.S.A., Inc.

*Fig. 6: Identifying Lower Control Arm Components (Celica)*

**4)** Install wheels, and lower vehicle. Bounce vehicle up and down to stabilize suspension. Tighten lower control arm nut attaching lower control arm to lower control arm shaft and stabilizer bar to lower control arm to specification.
**5)** Ensure all bolts and nuts are tightened to specification. See TORQUE SPECIFICATIONS table. Check front end alignment. See SPECIFICATIONS & PROCEDURES article in WHEEL ALIGNMENT.
**Removal (Celica) – 1)** Disconnect lower control arm from steering knuckle. Disconnect stabilizer link from lower control arm. *See Fig. 6*. Remove lower control arm front setting nut and washer.

***NOTE: On A/T models, remove left lower control arm with lower control arm shaft as an assembly. Remove suspension lower crossmember before removing lower control arm and shaft assembly.***

**2)** On M/T models, remove left lower control arm and lower arm damper plate. Remove lower control arm rear bracket bolts. Remove right lower control arm. Remove suspension lower crossmember and lower control arm shaft if necessary.
**3)** On A/T models, remove suspension lower crossmember. Remove lower arm damper plate bolts and damper plate. Remove lower control arm with lower control arm shaft as an assembly.
**4)** On all models, remove ball joint cotter pin and nut to remove ball joint from steering knuckle. Using Remover (09628-62011), remove ball joint from steering knuckle.
**Installation – 1)** Install ball joint to steering knuckle, and tighten to specification. See TORQUE SPECIFICATIONS table at end of article. Install new cotter pin. To complete installation, reverse removal procedure.
**2)** Install left lower control arm. Ensure tapered side of lower control arm faces body side.

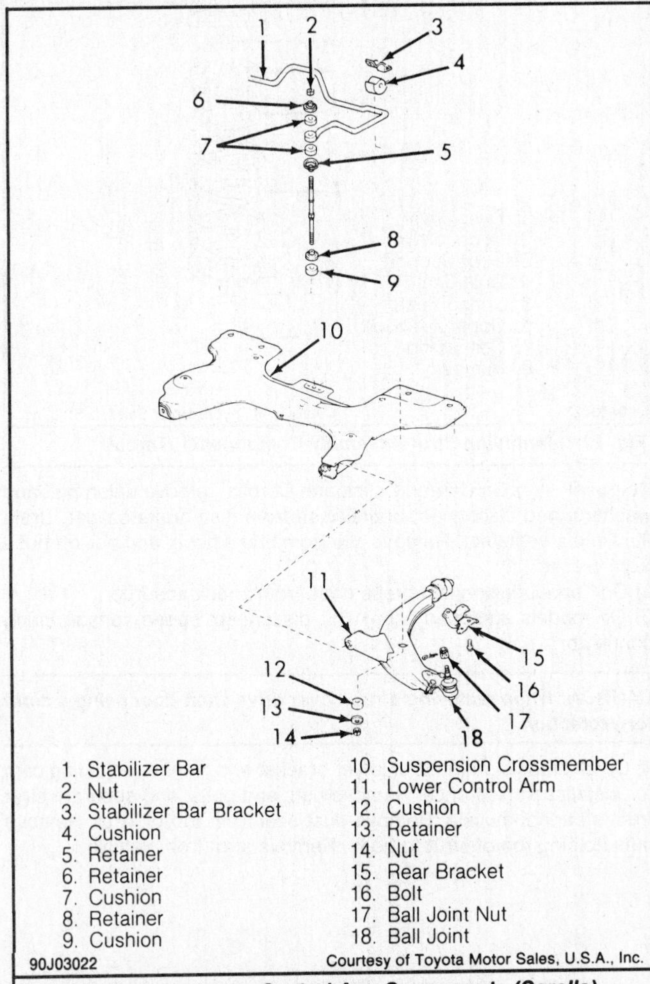


***Fig. 7: Identifying Lower Control Arm Components (Corolla)***

**3)** Install, but DO NOT tighten, nut attaching lower control arm to lower control arm shaft and lower control arm bracket bolts. Install lower arm damper plate. Connect lower control arm to steering knuckle. Connect stabilizer link to control arm.
**4)** Install wheels, and lower vehicle. Bounce vehicle up and down to stabilize suspension. See TORQUE SPECIFICATIONS table.
**5)** Ensure all bolts are tightened to specification. See TORQUE SPECIFICATIONS table. Check front end alignment. See SPECIFICATIONS & PROCEDURES article in WHEEL ALIGNMENT.
**Removal (Corolla) – 1)** On M/T models, disconnect lower control arm from steering knuckle. Disconnect stabilizer bar from lower control arm. *See Fig. 7*.
**2)** Loosen lower control arm front bolt. Remove lower control arm and stabilizer bracket. Remove lower control arm front bolt. Remove lower control arm.
**3)** On A/T models, disconnect right and left lower control arms from steering knuckles. Disconnect stabilizer bar from lower arms. Remove right and left lower control arm brackets.
**4)** Move stabilizer bar toward rear, and remove stabilizer bar bracket. Remove suspension crossmember with lower arms as an assembly. Remove lower control arms from suspension crossmember.
**5)** On all models, remove ball joint cotter pin and nut. Using Remover (09950-20017), remove ball joint from steering knuckle.
**Installation – 1)** Install ball joint to steering knuckle, and tighten to specification. Install new cotter pin. To complete installation, reverse removal procedure.
**2)** Temporarily install, but DO NOT tighten, lower control arm to suspension crossmember bolt, stabilizer bar bracket and rear bracket. *See Fig. 7*.
**3)** Install wheels, and lower vehicle. Bounce vehicle up and down to stabilize suspension. Tighten lower control arm-to-suspension crossmember bolt, stabilizer bar bracket and rear bracket to specification.
**4)** Ensure all bolts are tightened to specification. See TORQUE SPECIFICATIONS table at end of article. Check front end alignment. See SPECIFICATIONS & PROCEDURES article in WHEEL ALIGNMENT.
**Removal & Installation (Tercel) – 1)** Raise and support vehicle. Remove wheels. Disconnect lower control arm from lower ball joint. *See Fig. 8*. Remove front and rear lower control arm bracket. Remove lower control arm assembly.

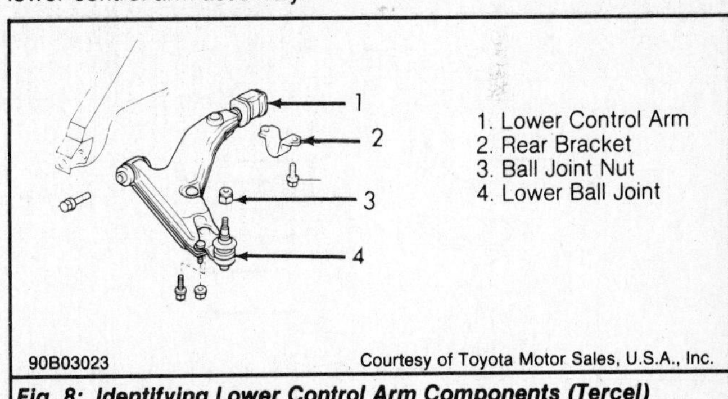


***Fig. 8: Identifying Lower Control Arm Components (Tercel)***

**2)** To remove ball joint from steering knuckle, remove ball joint cotter pin and nut. Using Remover (09628-62011), remove ball joint from steering knuckle.
**3)** Install ball joint to steering knuckle, and tighten to specification. See TORQUE SPECIFICATIONS table at end of article. Install new cotter pin. Install lower control arm to frame. Temporarily install, but DO NOT tighten, front and rear lower control arm bracket bolts.
**4)** Connect lower control arm-to-lower ball joint, and tighten to specification. Install wheels, and lower vehicle. Bounce vehicle up and down to stabilize suspension.
**5)** Tighten front and rear lower control arm bracket bolts to specification. Ensure all bolts are tightened to specification. See TORQUE SPECIFICATIONS table. Check front end alignment. See SPECIFICATIONS & PROCEDURES article in WHEEL ALIGNMENT.

# 1991 SUSPENSION
# Front – Camry, Celica, Corolla & Tercel (Cont.)

## CONTROL ARM BUSHING

**Removal & Installation (Celica & Corolla)** – Install lower control arm in a vise. Remove nut, washer and bushing from control arm. Install new bushing, washer and nut. Install washer with tapered side facing lower control arm. Tighten nut to specification. See TORQUE SPECIFICATIONS table at end of article.

## STRUT ASSEMBLY

***NOTE: During following removal, disassembly, inspection and installation procedures, refer to Fig. 9, 10, 11 or 12.***

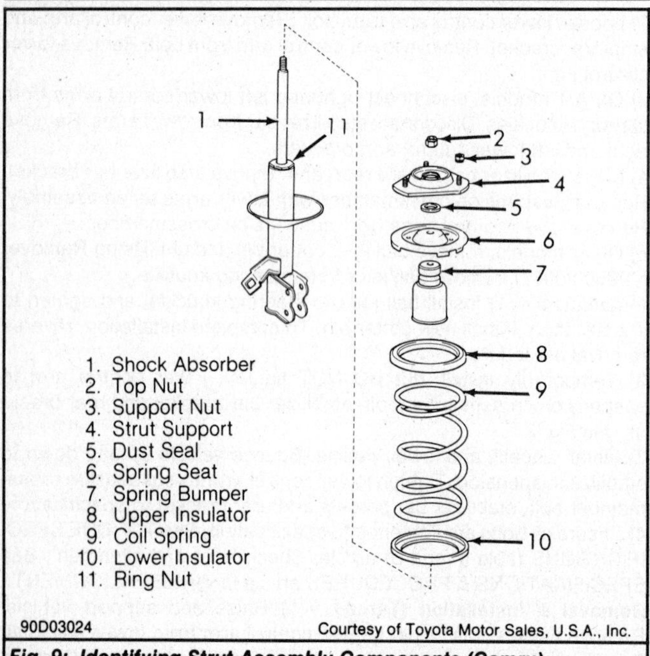


***Fig. 9: Identifying Strut Assembly Components (Camry)***

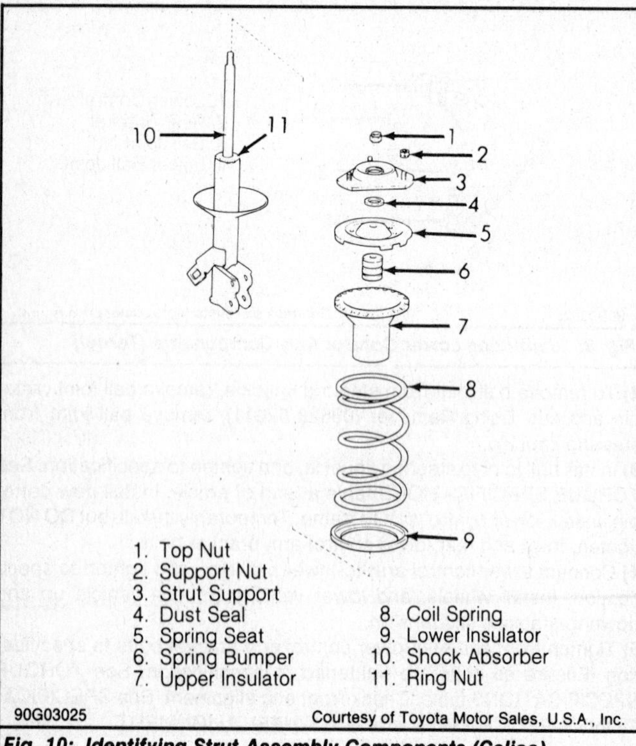


***Fig. 10: Identifying Strut Assembly Components (Celica)***

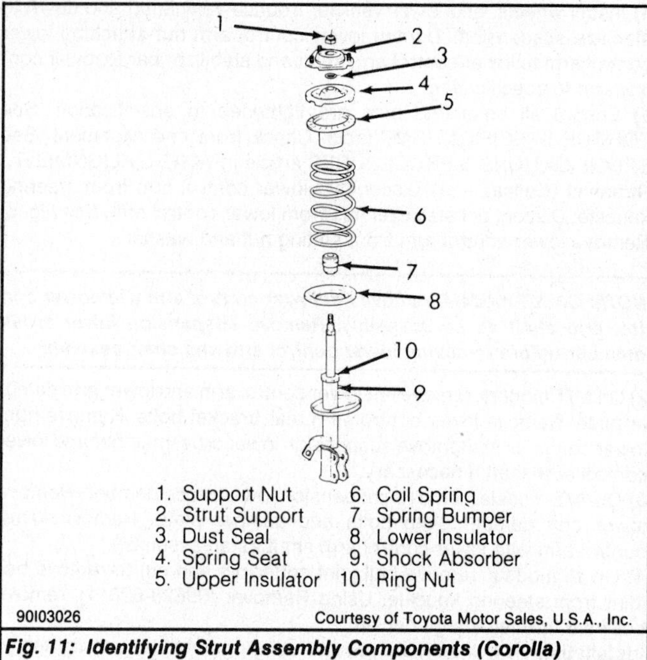


***Fig. 11: Identifying Strut Assembly Components (Corolla)***

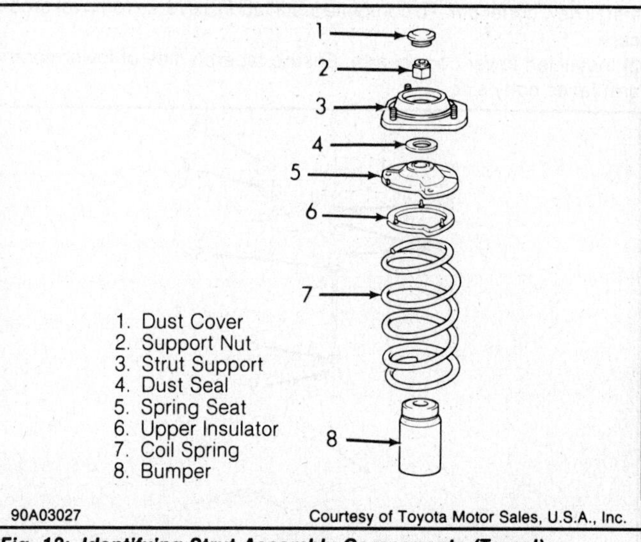


***Fig. 12: Identifying Strut Assembly Components (Tercel)***

**Removal** – **1)** On Camry, Celica and Corolla, remove union bolt and washers, and disconnect brake hose from disc brake caliper. Drain fluid into a container. Remove clip from brake hose, and pull off hose from bracket.

**2)** On Tercel, disconnect brake hose from shock absorber.

**3)** On models equipped with ABS, disconnect speed sensor wiring connector.

***CAUTION: When removing strut, cover drive shaft boot using a cloth for protection.***

**4)** On all models, mark strut lower bracket and camber adjusting cam for installation reference. Remove nuts and bolts, and separate strut from steering knuckle. Remove dust seal from top of strut. Remove nuts holding top of strut to body. Remove strut from vehicle.

# 1991 SUSPENSION
# Front – Camry, Celica, Corolla & Tercel (Cont.)

**Disassembly – 1)** Install a bolt and 2 nuts to strut lower bracket to prevent distortion of strut shell when clamped. Clamp bottom of strut in a vise.

**2)** Using Compressor (09727-30020), compress coil spring. Hold spring seat using Lever (09729-22031) and remove strut rod top nut. Remove components.

**Inspection –** Compress and extend shock rod, and ensure no abnormal resistance or noise exists. Push shock absorber piston rod in fully and release. Ensure piston rod returns at a constant speed throughout travel. If shock is defective, replace as an assembly.

***CAUTION: To prevent personal injury, discharge gas in shock absorber. On Camry, Celica and Corolla, use Shock Absorber Wrench (09720-00012) to loosen ring nut 2 or 3 turns before discarding. On Tercel, drill holes in cylinder.***

**Reassembly & Installation – 1)** To install, reverse removal procedure. On Camry, Celica and Corolla, ensure "OUT" mark on spring seat faces toward outside of vehicle. Tighten support nut to specification. See TORQUE SPECIFICATIONS table at end of article. On Tercel, install support nut, but DO NOT tighten.

**2)** On all models, install strut to body. Tighten nuts to specification. Install strut to steering knuckle, and tighten bolts. On Tercel, tighten support nut to specification.

**3)** On all models, install dust seal after packing bearing in suspension support with grease. Bleed brakes. On Camry, Celica and Corolla, ensure flexible brake hose pin aligns with caliper hole.

**4)** On Tercel, connect brake hose to shock absorber. On all models, check front end alignment. See SPECIFICATIONS & PROCEDURES article in WHEEL ALIGNMENT.

## STABILIZER BAR

**Removal (Camry) – 1)** Remove suspension lower crossmember. Remove stabilizer nuts and retainer. Remove stabilizer bar bracket.

**2)** Remove shift control cable clamp bolt from engine center mounting member. Remove engine center mounting member. *See Fig. 5.* Remove stabilizer bar.

**Removal (Celica) – 1)** Disconnect stabilizer link from lower arm and stabilizer bar. *See Fig. 6.* Disconnect exhaust pipe from manifold. Disconnect exhaust pipe from tail pipe hanger ring. Remove both brackets from body.

**2)** Remove stabilizer bar. Inspect stabilizer link ball joint arms. If movement of arms is not free in all directions, replace stabilizer link.

**Removal (Corolla) –** Disconnect bar from lower arms. *See Fig. 7.* Remove brackets from body. Remove stabilizer bar. Inspect stabilizer link ball joint arms. If movement of arms is not free in all directions, replace stabilizer link.

**Installation (Camry, Celica and Corolla) –** To install, reverse removal procedure. Check wheel alignment. See SPECIFICATIONS & PROCEDURES article in WHEEL ALIGNMENT.

## TORQUE SPECIFICATIONS

***TORQUE SPECIFICATIONS***

| Application | Ft. Lbs. (N.m) |
|---|---|
| **Camry** | |
| Axle Nut | 137 (186) |
| Ball Joint-To-Knuckle Bolts | 83 (113) |
| Ball Joint-To-Lower Control Arm Nut | 91 (123) |
| Brake Caliper Bolts | 86 (117) |
| Control Arm-To-Body Bolt | 156 (212) |
| Control Arm-To-Steering Knuckle Bolt/Nut | 156 (212) |
| Engine Mounting Member Bolts | |
| Inside | 32 (43) |
| Outside | 29 (39) |
| Stabilizer Bar Bracket Bolts | 94 (127) |
| Stabilizer-To-Lower Control Arm Nut | 156 (212) |
| Steering Knuckle-To-Strut Bolts/Nuts | 224 (304) |
| Strut Assembly-To-Body Nuts | 47 (64) |
| Strut Assembly Top Support Nut | 34 (47) |
| Tie Rod End-To-Steering Knuckle | 36 (49) |
| Wheel Lug Nuts | 76 (103) |
| **Celica** | |
| Axle Nut | 137 (186) |
| Axle Shaft Flange Bolts | |
| 2WD | 27 (36) |
| 4WD | 48 (65) |
| Ball Joint-To-Lower Arm Nut | 94 (127) |
| Ball Joint-To-Steering Knuckle Nut | 93 (126) |
| Brake Caliper-To-Knuckle Bolt | 79 (109) |
| Brake Hose-To-Caliper Bolt | 22 (30) |
| Control Arm Bracket-To-Body Bolt | 72 (98) |
| Control Arm Bushing Nut | 76 (103) |
| Crossmember Bolts (4) | 112 (152) |
| Crossmember Nuts (2) | 112 (152) |
| Drive Shaft Flange Bolts | 54 (74) |
| Exhaust Pipe-To-Manifold Bolt | 46 (62) |
| Exhaust Pipe Hanger Bolts | 14 (19) |
| Lower Arm Nut | 156 (212) |
| Lower Arm Shaft-To-Body Bolt | 112 (152) |
| Stabilizer Bracket-To-Body Bolt | 13 (18) |
| Stabilizer Lower Arm & Bar Bolt | 26 (35) |
| Steering Knuckle-To-Strut Bolt | 224 (301) |
| Strut Assembly-To-Body Nuts | 59 (80) |
| Strut Assembly Top Support Nut | 34 (47) |
| Tie Rod-To-Knuckle Nut | 36 (49) |
| Wheel Lug Nuts | 76 (103) |
| **Corolla** | |
| Axle Nut | 137 (186) |
| Ball Joint-To-Lower Control Arm | 105 (142) |
| Ball Joint-To-Steering Knuckle | 76 (103) |
| Brake Caliper Bolts | 65 (88) |
| Control Arm Bushing Nut (Rear) | 101 (137) |
| Control Arm Rear Bracket-To-Body Bolts | 94 (127) |
| Control Arm-To-Body Bolt (Front) | 173 (235) |
| Stabilizer Bar Bracket Bolts | |
| Large Bolt | 37 (50) |
| Small Bolt/Nut | 14 (19) |
| Stabilizer Bar Link Nut | 13 (18) |
| Steering Knuckle-To-Strut | 203 (275) |
| Strut Support-To-Body Nuts | 29 (39) |
| Strut Support Top Nut | 34 (47) |
| Tie Rod End-To-Steering Knuckle Nut | 36 (49) |
| Wheel Lug Nuts | 76 (103) |
| **Tercel** | |
| Axle Nut | 137 (186) |
| Ball Joint-To-Lower Control Arm Nut | 59 (80) |
| Ball Joint-To-Steering Knuckle Bolt | 72 (98) |
| Brake Caliper Bolts | 65 (88) |
| Control Arm-To-Body Bolt | |
| Front | 105 (142) |
| Rear | 94 (127) |
| Steering Knuckle-To-Strut Bolts/Nuts | 166 (226) |
| Strut Support-To-Body Nuts | 29 (39) |
| Strut Support Top Nut | 34 (47) |
| Tie Rod End-To-Steering Knuckle Nut | 36 (49) |
| Wheel Lug Nuts | 76 (103) |

# 1991 SUSPENSION
# Front – Cressida & Supra

## DESCRIPTION

The independent MacPherson strut-type front suspension consists of vertically mounted strut assemblies, control arms, strut rods and stabilizer bar. On Cressida, strut assembly is mounted to inner fender at top and to steering knuckle arm at bottom. Steering knuckle arm is mounted to ball joint, which is part of lower control arm. On Supra, strut assembly attaches to lower control arm and is not part of steering.

## ADJUSTMENTS & INSPECTION

### WHEEL ALIGNMENT SPECIFICATIONS & PROCEDURES

***NOTE: See SPECIFICATIONS & PROCEDURES article in WHEEL ALIGNMENT.***

### WHEEL BEARING

Wheel bearings are not adjustable. Bearings are pressed into housing and must be replaced if removed. Use a dial indicator to check bearing axial play. Service limit is .002" (.050 mm).

### BALL JOINT CHECKING

**1)** Jack front of vehicle and place a wooden block with a height of 7.09-7.87" (180.0-200.0 mm) under one front tire. Lower jack until there is about half a load on coil spring.

**2)** Place stands under vehicle for safety. Ensure wheels are in a straight forward position. Move lower control arm up and down. Check ball joint vertical play. Replace ball joint if vertical play exceeds .098" (2.50 mm) for Cressida or .012" (.30 mm) for Supra.

**3)** On Supra, check upper ball joint vertical play. Remove front wheels. Move upper control arm up and down. Replace upper ball joint if any vertical play is present.

**4)** Check turning torque of upper and lower ball on Supra or lower ball joint on Cressida, with ball joint removed from vehicle. Flip joint stud back and forth 5 times.

**5)** Install ball joint stud nut. Using an INCH lb. torque wrench, check turning torque. Turn nut one turn each 2-4 seconds and take torque reading on fifth turn.

**6)** On Supra, upper ball joint turning torque should be 8.7-30.0 INCH lbs. (1.0-3.4 N.m). Lower ball joint turning torque should be 0-4.3 INCH lbs. (0-.5 N.m) for Supra or 22-39 INCH lbs. (2.5-4.4 N.m) for Cressida. Replace ball joint if not within specification.

## REMOVAL & INSTALLATION

### WHEEL BEARING

***CAUTION: When removing axle hub on models with ABS, DO NOT apply excessive force to hub. DO NOT let hub fall. ALWAYS set hub down with ABS sensor rotor facing upward.***

**Removal & Installation (Cressida) – 1)** Raise and support vehicle. Remove disc brake caliper and wire out of way. Match mark rotor and axle hub for installation reference. Remove rotor. *See Fig. 1.*

**2)** Remove grease cap. Using hammer and chisel, loosen staked part of hub nut. Remove hub nut. Remove axle hub from steering knuckle.

**3)** Using Puller (09308-00010), remove grease seal. Using snap ring pliers, remove snap ring. Temporarily install hub bearing outside race in hub bearing. Using a press, remove hub bearing.

**4)** To install, reverse removal procedure. Tighten nuts and bolts to specification. See TORQUE SPECIFICATIONS table at end of this article.

**Removal (Supra) – 1)** Raise vehicle and support with safety stands. Remove wheel assembly. Remove brake ABS speed sensor and brake hose bracket. Remove disc brake caliper bolts and support caliper out of way.

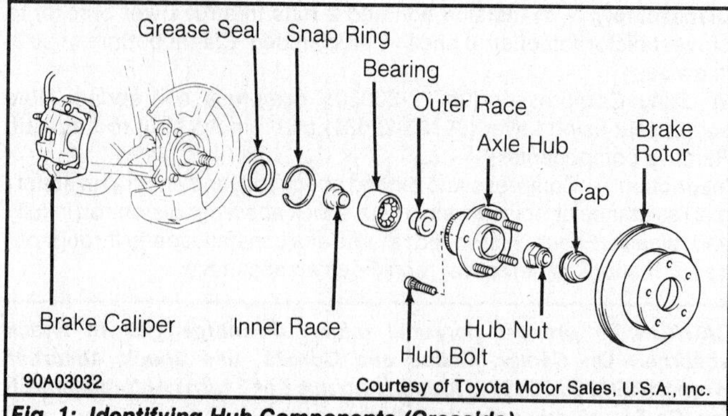


***Fig. 1: Identifying Hub Components (Cressida)***

**2)** Match mark brake disc and wheel hub for installation reference. Remove brake rotor. Remove tie rod end nut and press out rod end using Ball Joint Puller (09628-10011). Remove upper ball joint nut and press from steering knuckle, using Ball Joint Puller (09628-62011). Remove lower ball joint nut. Using same tool, press ball joint from steering knuckle. Remove steering knuckle from vehicle. *See Fig. 2.*

***NOTE: Use care when handling wheel hub. Serrations on hub trigger ABS brake system.***

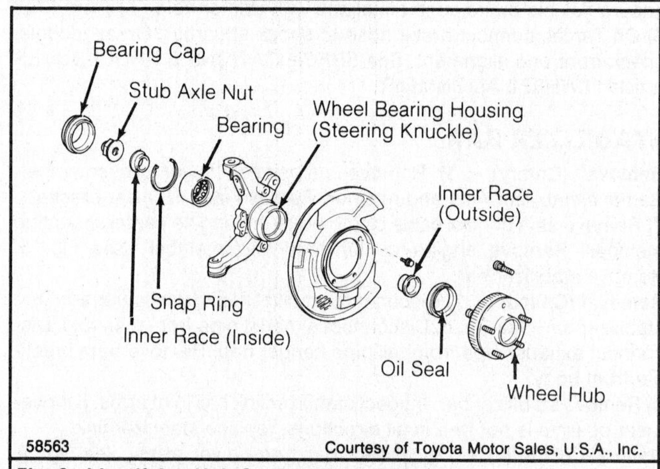


***Fig. 2: Identifying Hub Components (Supra)***

**3)** Remove hub bearing cap. Using a chisel and hammer, loosen staked part of stub axle self-locking nut and remove nut. Using a 2 jaw gear puller, remove wheel hub from bearing. Using same puller, remove inner bearing race from wheel hub.

**4)** Remove dust cover bolts and dust cover. Using a screwdriver pry out outer seal. Remove bearing snap ring. Temporarily install inner race. Using Bearing Replacer (09608-06100), press bearing out of housing.

**Installation – 1)** Press new bearing in steering knuckle with Bearing Installer (09608-06120). Install snap ring. Install bearing inner race. Using Seal Installer (09608-06020), drive in new seal. Install dust cover.

**2)** Use Press Adapter (09636-20010) to press wheel hub into steering knuckle. Install new stub axle self-locking nut and tighten to 147 ft. lbs. (199 N.m). Stake lock nut. Install hub bearing cap.

**3)** To complete installation, reverse removal procedure. Upper and lower ball joints are to be initially tightened to 14 ft. lbs. (20 N.m) using conventional nuts. Remove conventional nuts and install new self-locking nuts and tighten to specification. Tighten all bolts and nuts to specification. See TORQUE SPECIFICATIONS table at end of this article. Check wheel alignment. See SPECIFICATIONS & PROCEDURES article in WHEEL ALIGNMENT.

## CONTROL ARM & BALL JOINT

**Removal (Cressida) – 1)** Raise and support vehicle. Remove wheels. Remove bolts and disconnect strut from lower control arm. Remove cotter pin and nut holding steering knuckle arm to tie rod. *See Fig. 3.*

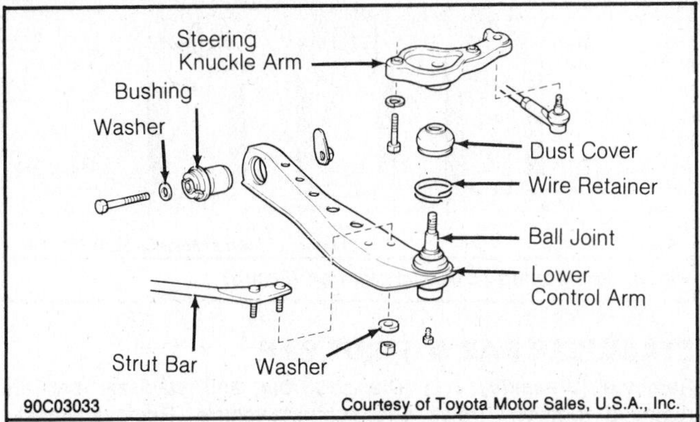


***Fig. 3: Exploded View of Lower Control Arm Assembly (Cressida)***

**2)** Using Tie Rod Puller (09610-20011), disconnect tie rod from steering knuckle arm. Remove nuts and disconnect strut bar from lower control arm. Remove bolt and lower control arm with steering knuckle arm.

**Disassembly – 1)** Use a screwdriver to remove ball joint dust cover set ring and dust cover.

***NOTE: Ball joint is not serviceable separately. If worn or damaged, ball joint and lower control arm must be replaced as a unit.***

**2)** Using Bushing Remover (09726-12022), remove bushing from lower control arm.

**Reassembly – 1)** Use Bushing Remover (09726-12022) to press new bushing into control arm. Apply ball joint grease to new dust cover. Install dust cover with grease escape valve facing rear of vehicle.

**2)** Wind wire dust cover retainer twice around dust cover and bend wire knot down facing rear of ball joint. Remove plug and install grease fitting. Fill ball joint with grease. Remove fitting and install plug.

**Installation –** To install, reverse removal procedure. Do not tighten lower control arm bolt to crossmember until vehicle has been lowered and bounced to settle suspension. Tighten all bolts and nuts to specification. See TORQUE SPECIFICATIONS table at end of this article. Check wheel alignment. See SPECIFICATIONS & PROCEDURES article in WHEEL ALIGNMENT.

**Removal (Supra) – 1)** Raise and support vehicle allowing suspension to hang free. Remove wheel assembly.

**2)** To remove upper control arm, Remove upper ball joint nut and press out using Ball Joint Puller (09628-62011). Remove upper control arm mounting bolt and nut. Remove control arm. *See Fig. 4.*

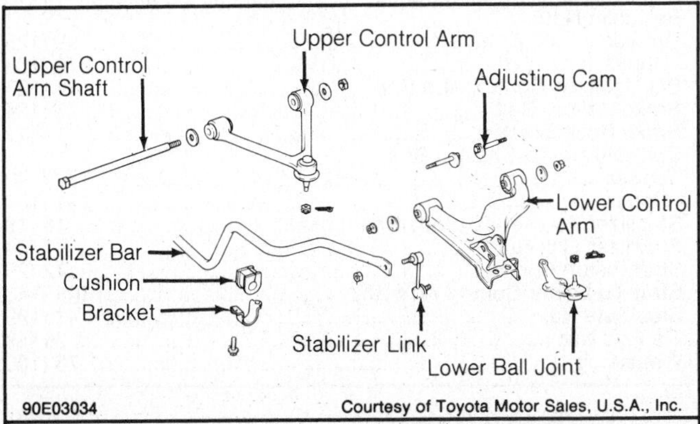


***Fig. 4: Identifying Front Suspension Components (Supra)***

**3)** To remove lower control arm, disconnect stabilizer bar link from control arm. Remove lower ball joint nut and press out of housing using same tool as upper ball joint. Remove lower strut mounting bolt at control arm.

**4)** Match mark lower control arm adjusting cams. Remove nuts and adjusting cams. Remove control arm. If ball joint is to be replaced, remove attaching bolts and remove ball joint from control arm.

**Installation – 1)** To install, reverse removal procedure. Tighten upper and lower control arm bolts with vehicle on ground after bouncing vehicle to settle suspension.

**2)** Upper and lower ball joints are to be initially tightened to 14 ft. lbs. (20 N.m) using conventional nuts. Remove conventional nuts and install new self-locking nuts and tighten to specification. Tighten all bolts and nuts to specification. See TORQUE SPECIFICATIONS table at end of this article. Check wheel alignment. See SPECIFICATIONS & PROCEDURES article in WHEEL ALIGNMENT.

## STRUT ASSEMBLY

**Removal (Cressida) – 1)** Raise and support vehicle. Remove wheels. Remove 2 clips, "E" ring and disconnect brake tube. Disconnect stabilizer bar link from strut. Place match marks on disc rotor and axle hub for installation reference. Remove brake caliper. Remove disc rotor.

**2)** On models with ABS, disconnect harness from speed sensor and remove sensor. On all models, remove axle hub. See WHEEL BEARING under REMOVAL & INSTALLATION.

**3)** Remove dust cover. Disconnect lower control arm from strut. Remove 3 upper strut-to-body nuts. Remove coil spring and strut assembly.

**Disassembly – 1)** Using Strut Holder (09720-00012), mount strut in a vise. Using Spring Compressor (09727-00045), compress coil spring. Hold spring upper seat and remove strut piston rod nut.

**2)** Remove suspension support, dust seal, spring upper seat, insulator, coil spring, and bumper. *See Fig. 5.*

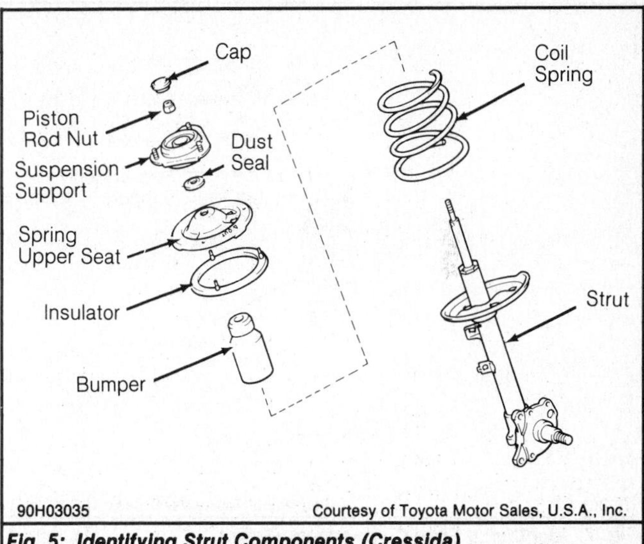


***Fig. 5: Identifying Strut Components (Cressida)***

**Inspection – 1)** Inspect strut for leaks or damage. Compress piston rod. Piston stroke should feel even, and there should be no abnormal resistance or noise. Release piston rod, and check that it returns at a constant speed.

**2)** If shock absorber is defective, use Shock Absorber Wrench (09720-00011) and loosen ring nut 2 or 3 turns and allow gas to release completely. Remove ring nut and pull out shock absorber.

**Reassembly –** To assemble, reverse disassembly procedure. Set piston rod position in proper direction. *See Fig. 6.* Align spring upper seat with piston rod. Position spring upper seat "OUT" mark toward outside of vehicle. Pack suspension support bearing with multipurpose grease.

# 1991 SUSPENSION
# Front – Cressida & Supra (Cont.)

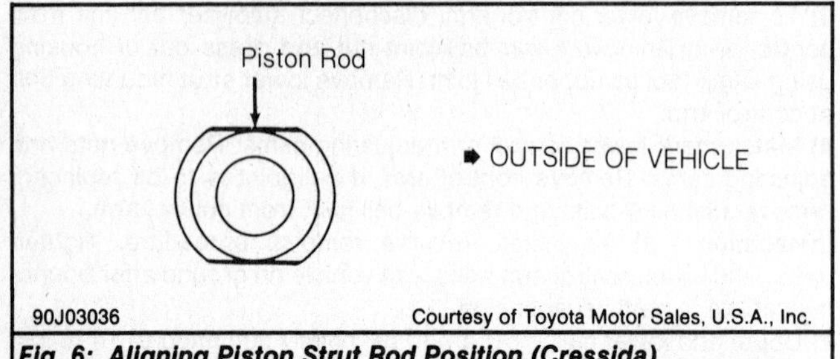


*Fig. 6: Aligning Piston Strut Rod Position (Cressida)*

**Installation** – To complete installation, reverse removal procedure. Tighten all bolts and nuts to specification. See TORQUE SPECIFICATIONS table at end of this article. Check wheel alignment. See SPECIFICATIONS & PROCEDURES article in WHEEL ALIGNMENT.

**Removal (Supra)** – **1)** Raise vehicle and support allowing suspension to hang free. Remove wheel assembly.

***NOTE: On models equipped with Toyota Electronic Modulated Suspension (TEMS), refer to ELECTRONIC article in SUSPENSION before attempting to remove strut assembly.***

**2)** Loosen but do not remove strut piston rod lock nut until nut can be turned by hand. Disconnect upper control arm from body. Remove upper strut retaining nuts. Remove lower strut mount bolt and remove strut.

**Disassembly** – **1)** Mount strut assembly in a vise. Use Spring Compressor (09727-22032) to compress coil spring. Remove piston rod lock nut.

**2)** Remove suspension support, dust seal, spring seat, coil spring, and bumper. On models with TEMS, remove actuator bracket, suspension support, spring seat, piston rod dust cover, coil spring, and bumper. *See Fig. 7.*

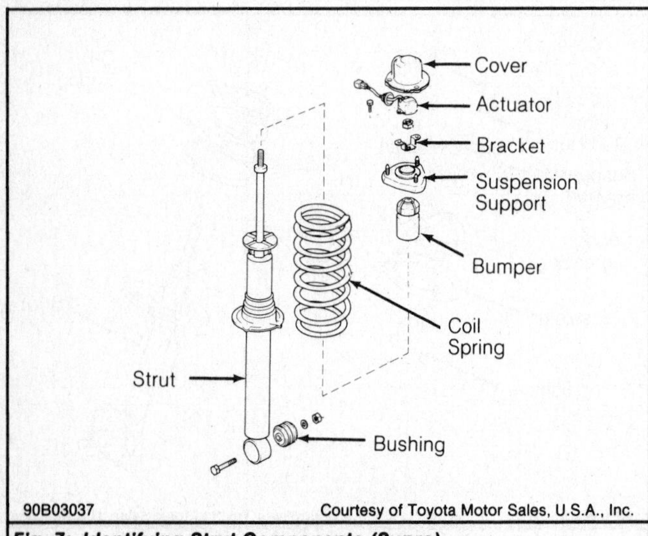


*Fig. 7: Identifying Strut Components (Supra)*

**Inspection** – **1)** Inspect strut for leakage or damage. Compress piston rod. Piston stroke should feel even, and there should be no abnormal resistance or noise. Release piston rod, and check that it returns at a constant speed. Replace if defective.

**2)** On models with TEMS, check that control rod in piston rod can be turned easily with needle nose pliers. With control rod positioned as shown, check that there is a difference in damping at each position. *See Fig. 8.*

**Reassembly & Installation** – To reassemble and install, reverse disassembly and removal procedures. Tighten upper control arm bolts and lower strut mounting bolt with vehicle on ground after bouncing to settle suspension. Tighten all bolts and nuts to specification. See TORQUE SPECIFICATIONS table at end of this article.

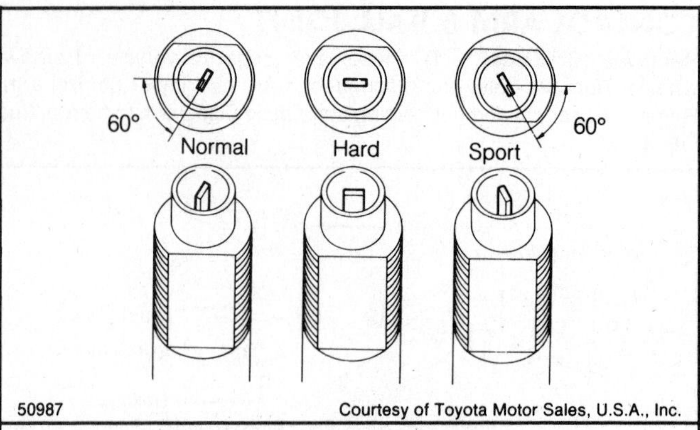


*Fig. 8: Positioning TEMS Control Rod (Supra)*

## STABILIZER BAR & STRUT BAR

**Removal (Cressida)** – **1)** The strut bar and stabilizer bar are removed together. Raise and support vehicle. Remove wheels. Remove engine under cover (splash) shield. Disconnect stabilizer bar from lower control arm.

**2)** Remove right and left stabilizer bushings. Disconnect strut bar from lower control arm. Remove strut bar with strut bar bracket. Remove nut, front retainer, strut bar, rear retainer, and spacer.

**Installation** – **1)** To install, reverse removal procedure. Install but do not tighten strut bar nut. Install wheels and lower vehicle.

**2)** Bounce vehicle up and down to stabilize vehicle. Tighten strut bar nut to specification. Ensure all nuts and bolts are tighten to specification. See TORQUE SPECIFICATIONS table.

## TORQUE SPECIFICATIONS

***TORQUE SPECIFICATIONS***

| Application | Ft. Lbs. (N.m) |
|---|---|
| **Cressida** | |
| Ball Joint Nut | 67 (91) |
| Brake Caliper Bolts | 67 (91) |
| Hub Nut | 108 (147) |
| Knuckle Arm-To-Strut Bolts | 80 (108) |
| Lower Control Arm-To-Chassis Bolt | 121 (164) |
| Lower Control Arm-To-Strut | 80 (108) |
| Shock Absorber Ring Nut | 34 (46) |
| Stabilizer Bar-To-Chassis Bracket Bolt | 22 (29) |
| Stabilizer Bar-To-Control Arm Nut | 13 (18) |
| Stabilizer Bar-To-Link | 70 (95) |
| Strut Bar-To-Chassis Nut | 94 (127) |
| Strut Bar-To-Control Arm Nut | 76 (103) |
| Strut Piston Rod Nut | 35 (48) |
| Strut Top Plate-To-Body Nut | 32 (43) |
| Tie Rod Nut | 43 (59) |
| Wheel Lug Nut | 76 (103) |
| **Supra** | |
| Anti-Lock Brake Speed Sensor | 14 (19) |
| Ball Joint Nut | |
| Lower | 92 (125) |
| Upper | 76 (103) |
| Ball Joint-To-Control Arm Bolt | 94 (127) |
| Brake Caliper Bolt | 77 (104) |
| Brake Hose Bracket | 14 (19) |
| Control Arm-To-Chassis Bolt | |
| Lower | 177 (240) |
| Upper | 121 (164) |
| Stabilizer Bracket-To-Body Bolt | 13 (18) |
| Stabilizer Link Nut | 47 (64) |
| Strut Piston Rod Nut | 22 (29) |
| Strut-To-Lower Control Arm Bolt | 106 (143) |
| Stub Axle Nut | 147 (199) |
| Tie Rod Nut | 36 (49) |
| Wheel Lug Nut | 76 (103) |

# 1991 SUSPENSION
# Front – MR2

## DESCRIPTION

Front suspension is MacPherson strut type. Lower end of strut is connected to steering knuckle. Steering knuckle is bolted to a ball joint, which is connected to lower control arm. Stabilizer bar link is connected to strut. Strut rod is connected to lower control arm and frame. *See Fig. 1.*

## ADJUSTMENTS & INSPECTION

### WHEEL ALIGNMENT SPECIFICATIONS & PROCEDURES

***NOTE: See SPECIFICATIONS & PROCEDURES article in WHEEL ALIGNMENT.***

### WHEEL BEARING

Remove brake caliper. Place match marks on rotor and hub for reassembly reference. Remove rotor. Check bearing axial play using a dial indicator. Replace wheel bearing if axial play is greater than .002" (.05 mm).

### BALL JOINT CHECKING

**1)** Raise and support front of vehicle. Place wooden block under one front tire. Lower vehicle until there is about 1/2 load on front coil spring. Support vehicle with jack stands. Ensure wheels are pointed straight-ahead and block wheels with wheel chocks.

**2)** Move lower arm up and down. Ensure there is no vertical play in ball joint. Remove ball joint from vehicle. See BALL JOINT under REMOVAL & INSTALLATION. Push ball joint stud from side-to-side 5 times. Install nut on ball joint stud.

**3)** Measure rotating torque while rotating ball joint stud one revolution every 2-4 seconds. Take torque reading on fifth turn. Rotating torque should be 7-22 INCH lbs. (.8-2.5 N.m).

## REMOVAL & INSTALLATION

### BALL JOINT

**Removal & Installation** – Raise and support vehicle. Remove cotter pin and castle nut from ball joint stud. Using puller, separate ball joint from lower control arm. Unbolt ball joint from steering knuckle. To install, reverse removal procedure. Tighten bolts and nuts to specification. See TORQUE SPECIFICATIONS table at end of article.

### HUB & KNUCKLE ASSEMBLY

**Removal** – **1)** Remove brake caliper. Place match marks on rotor and hub for reassembly reference. Remove rotor. Check bearing axial play using a dial indicator. Replace wheel bearing if axial play is greater than .002" (.05 mm).

**2)** On models with ABS, remove speed sensor. On all models, remove strut-to-knuckle mounting nuts, but do not remove bolts. Loosen lower ball joint mounting bolts.

**3)** Remove cotter pin and nut from tie rod end. Using puller, separate tie rod end from knuckle. Remove ball joint bolts. Remove strut-to-knuckle mounting bolts and remove knuckle and hub assembly. *See Figs. 2 and 3.*

**Disassembly** – **1)** Clamp knuckle in a soft-jawed vise. Remove hub bearing cap. Clamp hub in a soft-jawed vise on wheel studs. DO NOT overtighten. Unstake and remove hub nut. On models equipped with ABS, remove speed sensor rotor. Ensure sensor rotor serrations are not damaged during removal.

**2)** On models without ABS, remove bearing inner spacer. On all models, remove snap ring retaining hub bearing. Remove outer bearing inner race from hub using Puller (09950-20017). Position inner race on bearing and drive hub bearing from knuckle.

**Reassembly** – **1)** Install hub bearing using bearing driver. Install snap ring. Apply sealer to dust cover and install dust cover on knuckle. Install 4 Torx retaining bolts and tighten to specification.

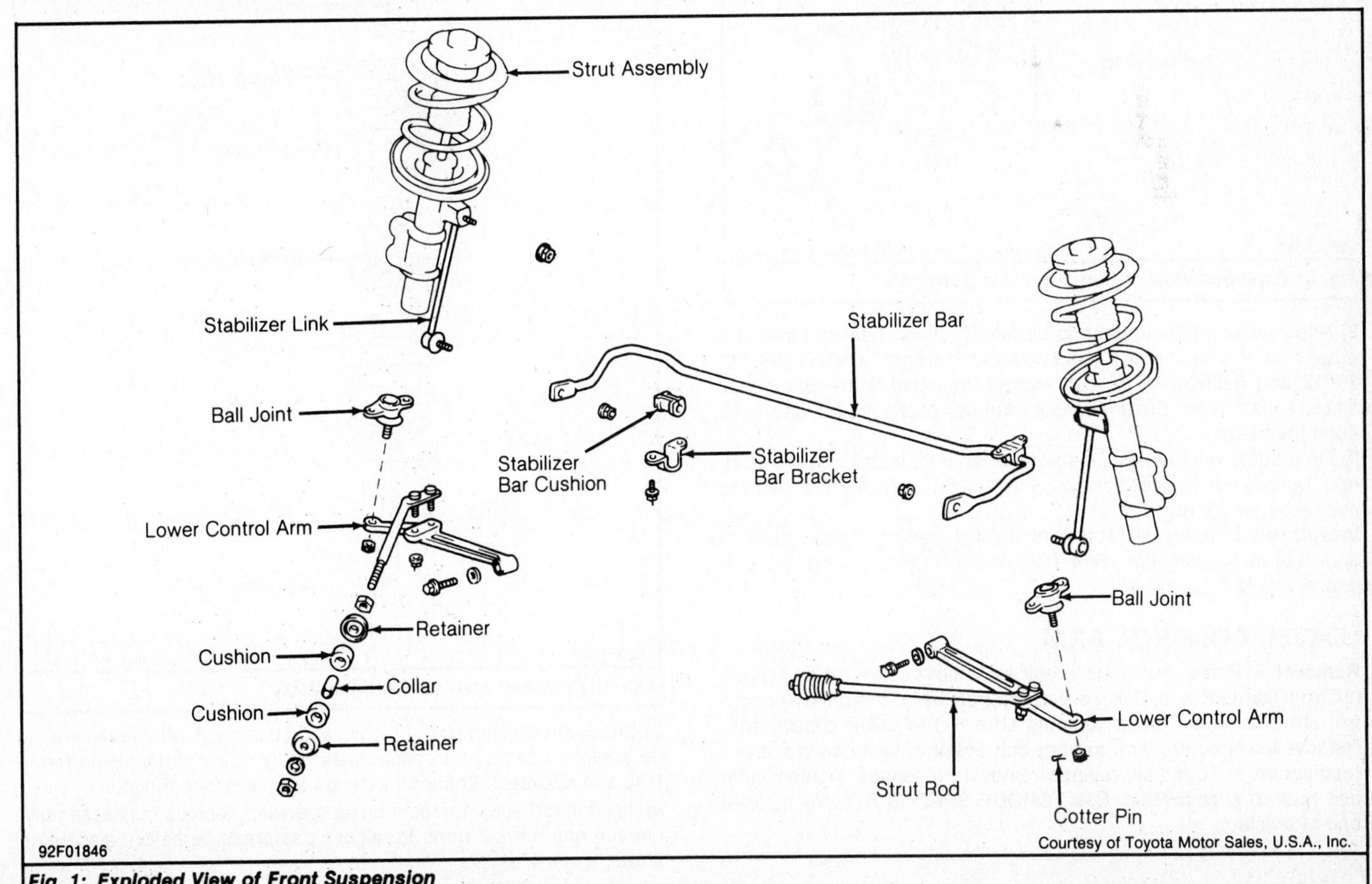


***Fig. 1: Exploded View of Front Suspension***

# 1991 SUSPENSION
# Front – MR2 (Cont.)

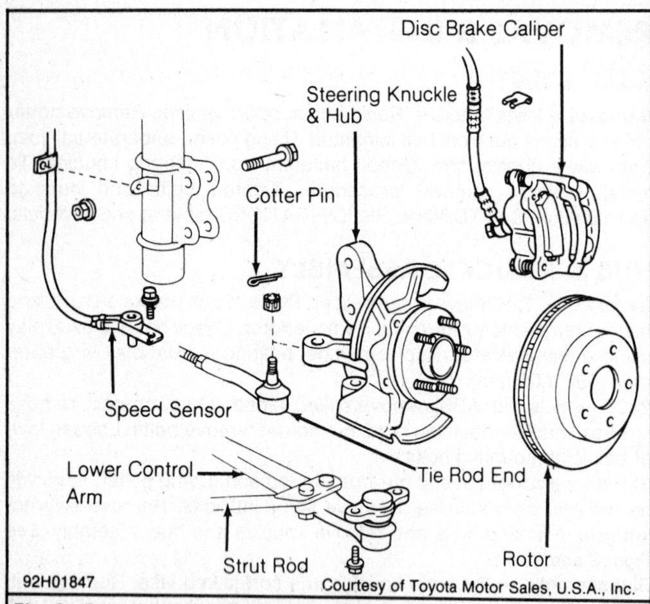


*Fig. 2: Removing Hub & Knuckle Assembly*

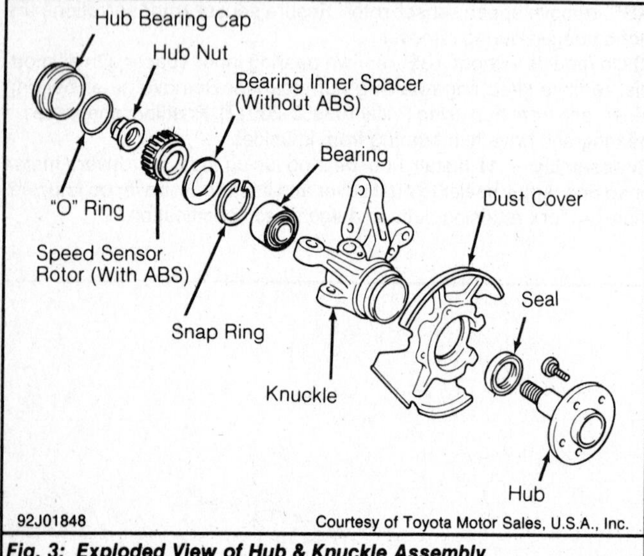


*Fig. 3: Exploded View of Hub & Knuckle Assembly*

**2)** Apply multipurpose grease to oil seal lip. Install bearing inner and outer race into hub. Press hub into knuckle using Installers (09608-30012 and 09608-040420). On models equipped with ABS, install speed sensor rotor. Ensure sensor rotor serrations are not damaged during removal.

**3)** On models without ABS, install inner spacer. Install axle hub lock nut. Tighten nut to specification. Stake lock nut. Install hub bearing cap with new "O" ring.

**Installation** – To install, reverse removal procedure. Tighten all bolts and nuts to specification. See TORQUE SPECIFICATIONS table at end of article.

## LOWER CONTROL ARM

**Removal** – Raise and support vehicle. Remove cotter pin and castle nut from ball joint stud. Using puller, separate ball joint from lower control arm. Remove 2 bolts securing strut rod to lower control arm. Remove lower control arm-to-body bolt. Remove lower control arm.

**Installation** – To install, reverse removal procedure. Tighten bolts and nuts to specification. See TORQUE SPECIFICATIONS table at end of article.

## LOWER CONTROL ARM BUSHINGS

***NOTE: Information on lower control arm bushing replacement is not available from manufacturer.***

## STABILIZER BAR & LINKS

**Removal** – Remove nut and disconnect stabilizer link from stabilizer bar. Use a 5-mm Allen wrench to hold stud if necessary. Remove stabilizer bar brackets from frame. Remove brackets and cushions from stabilizer bar. Remove stabilizer links from strut assemblies. Use a 5-mm Allen wrench to hold stud if necessary.

**Inspection** – Inspect stabilizer link ball joints. Rotate ball joint stud in all directions. Replace stabilizer link if stud does not rotate smoothly, without binding.

**Installation** – Install stabilizer bar bushings on painted marks on bar. To complete installation, reverse removal procedure. Tighten bolts and nuts to specification. See TORQUE SPECIFICATIONS table at end of article.

## STRUT ASSEMBLY

**Removal** – **1)** Remove brake hose from caliper. Remove clip retaining hose to strut. Remove brake hose from strut. On models with ABS, remove speed sensor wiring harness bracket bolt. On all models, disconnect stabilizer link from strut assembly. Use a 5-mm Allen wrench to hold stud if necessary.

**2)** Disconnect strut from steering knuckle. Remove upper strut mounting nuts and remove strut.

**Disassembly & Inspection** – **1)** Install bolt with 2 nuts on lower strut mounting brackets. Mount strut in a vise. Compress coil spring and remove nut from top of strut. Hold upper spring seat to keep it from rotating if necessary. Remove suspension support, dust seal, spring seat, spring, insulators and bumper. *See Fig. 4*.

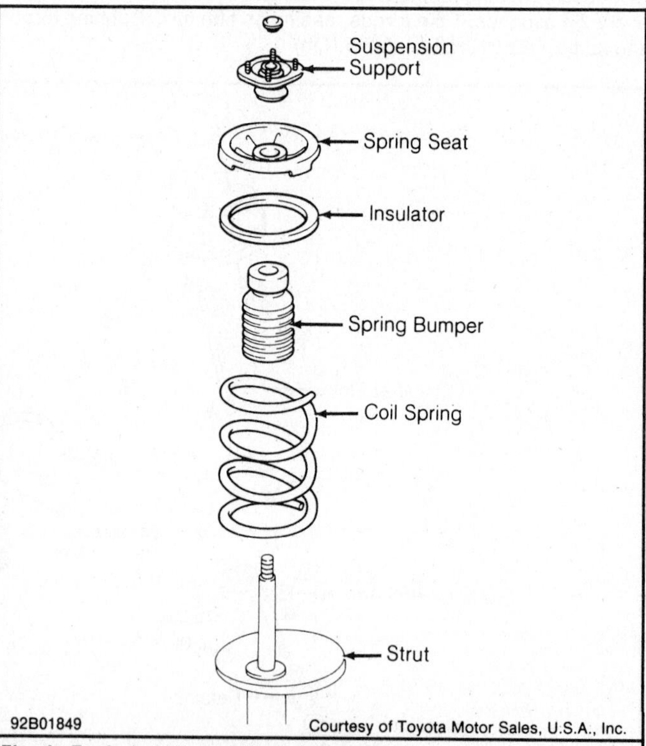


*Fig. 4: Exploded View of Strut Assembly*

**2)** Check strut piston by pushing in and pulling out. Movement should be smooth with no abnormal resistance or noise. Push piston rod in fully and release it. Ensure it extends at a constant speed.

**3)** If piston rod does not respond as specified, replace strut assembly. Loosen ring nut 2-3 turns to release gas pressure before discarding strut.

# 1991 SUSPENSION
# Front - MR2 (Cont.)

**Reassembly** - To reassemble, reverse disassembly procedure. Position spring seat with OUT mark on seat toward outside of vehicle. Tighten nut to specification while holding spring seat from turning.

**Installation** - To install, reverse removal procedure. Ensure notch in suspension support is installed toward rear of vehicle. Tighten all nuts and bolts to specification. Bleed brake system. See DISC & DRUM - RWD CARS article in BRAKES. Check wheel alignment. See SPECIFICATIONS & PROCEDURES article in WHEEL ALIGNMENT.

## STRUT ROD

**Removal** - Measure strut rod length "L" before removal. *See Fig. 5.* Remove nut, front retainer and cushion. Remove strut rod-to-lower control arm mounting bolts. Remove strut rod. Remove collar, cushion and retainer from strut rod.

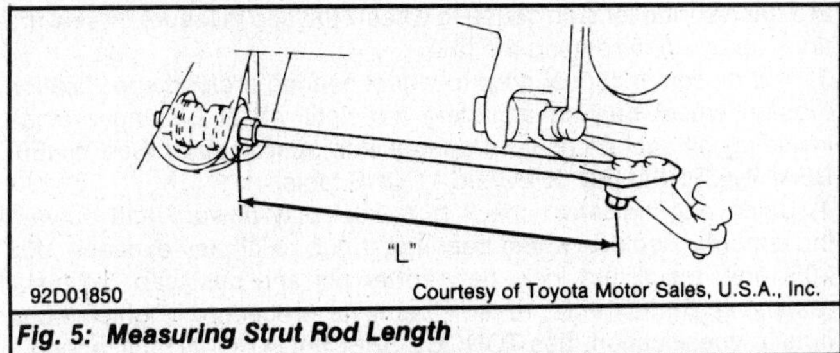


***Fig. 5: Measuring Strut Rod Length***

**Installation** - To install, reverse removal procedure. *See Fig. 6.* Ensure front and rear cushions are installed in correct location. Bounce vehicle up and down to stabilize suspension. Tighten strut rod front nut to specification.

## WHEEL BEARING

***NOTE: For wheel bearing removal and installation procedures, see HUB & KNUCKLE ASSEMBLY under REMOVAL & INSTALLATION.***

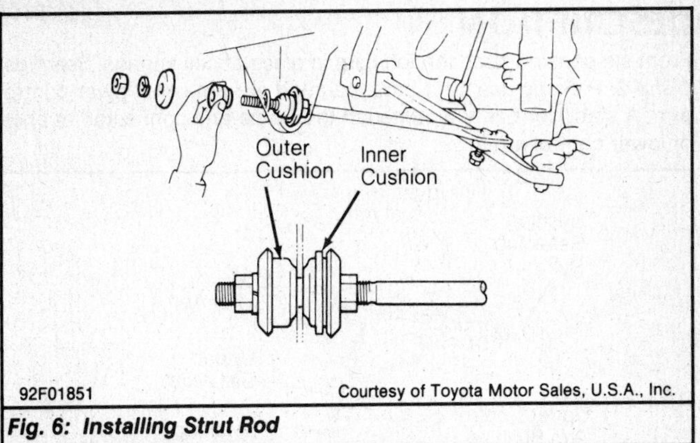


***Fig. 6: Installing Strut Rod***

## TORQUE SPECIFICATIONS

***TORQUE SPECIFICATIONS***

| Application | Ft. Lbs. (N.m) |
|---|---|
| Axle Shaft Nut | 91 (123) |
| Ball Joint Stud Nut | 58 (78) |
| Ball Joint-To-Steering Knuckle Bolts | 59 (80) |
| Brake Caliper-To-Steering Knuckle Bolt | 43 (59) |
| Brake Line-To-Caliper Union Bolt | 22 (30) |
| Lower Control Arm Bolt | 87 (118) |
| Stabilizer Bar Bracket Bolts | 14 (19) |
| Stabilizer Link Nuts | 47 (64) |
| Steering Knuckle-To-Strut Bolts | 188 (255) |
| Strut Rod Nut | 83 (113) |
| Strut Rod-To-Lower Control Arm Nut | 83 (113) |
| Tie Rod End-To-Steering Knuckle Nut | 36 (49) |
| Upper Strut Mounting Nuts | 29 (39) |
| | **INCH Lbs. (N.m)** |
| Disc Brake Dust Shield | 74 (8.3) |
| Speed Sensor Bolt | 69 (7.8) |

# 1991 SUSPENSION
# Front – 2WD Pickup & 4Runner

## DESCRIPTION

Front suspension uses torsion bars in place of coil springs. *See Figs. 1 and 2.* Pickups use strut bars mounted at frame and lower control arm. A stabilizer bar is mounted to the frame and connected at ends of lower control arms.

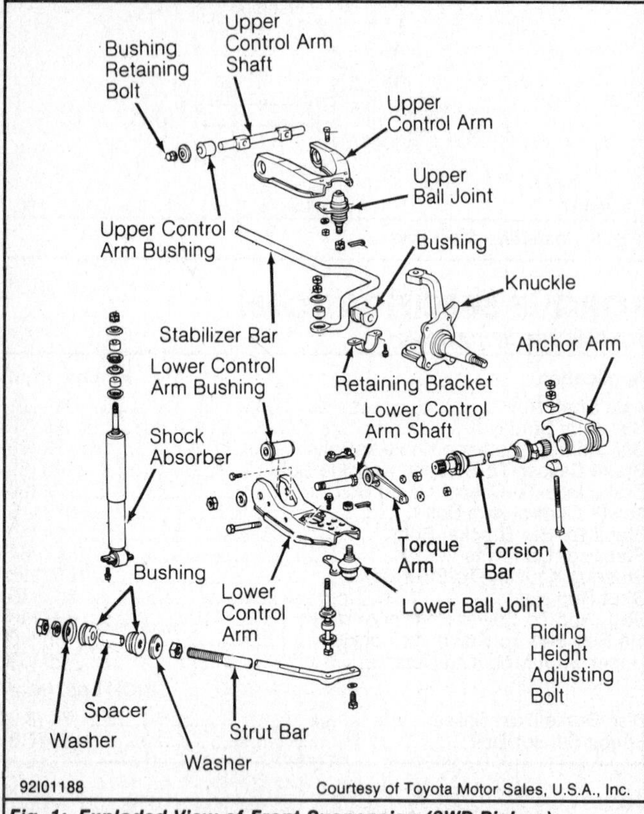


*Fig. 1: Exploded View of Front Suspension (2WD Pickup)*

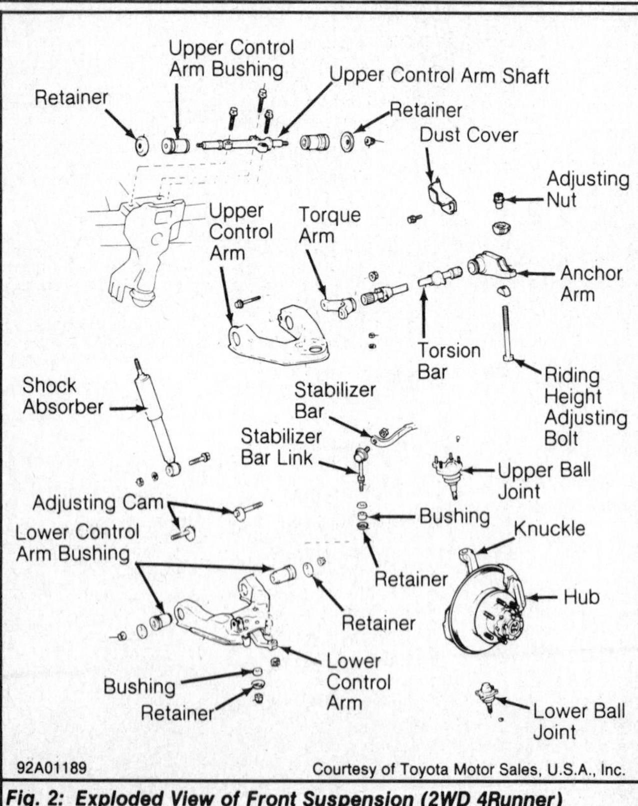


*Fig. 2: Exploded View of Front Suspension (2WD 4Runner)*

## ADJUSTMENTS & INSPECTION

### WHEEL ALIGNMENT SPECIFICATIONS & PROCEDURES

***NOTE: See SPECIFICATIONS & PROCEDURES article in WHEEL ALIGNMENT.***

### WHEEL BEARING

**Pickup – 1)** Raise and support vehicle. Remove front wheel. Remove brake caliper and secure aside. Remove dust cap, cotter pin and nut lock. Tighten wheel bearing adjusting nut to 25 ft. lbs. (34 N.m). Rotate hub several times to seat wheel bearings. Loosen wheel bearing adjusting nut until hub can be turned easily by hand.

**2)** Attach spring tension gauge to wheel stud and measure oil seal frictional drag when rotating the hub.

**3)** Add oil seal frictional drag to wheel bearing preload specification. Tighten wheel bearing adjusting nut until wheel bearing preload, including oil seal frictional drag is within specification. See WHEEL BEARING PRELOAD SPECIFICATIONS table.

**4)** Using dial indicator, check hub axial play (inward and outward movement). Replace wheel bearings if hub axial play exceeds .002" (.05 mm). Install nut lock, new cotter pin and dust cap. To install remaining components, reverse removal procedure. Tighten bolts/nuts to specification. See TORQUE SPECIFICATIONS table at end of article.

**4Runner – 1)** Raise and support vehicle. Remove front wheel. Remove brake caliper and secure aside. Remove hub grease cap.

**2)** Using screwdriver, release tab on lock washer. Remove wheel bearing lock nut and lock washer. Loosen wheel bearing adjusting nut several turns. Tighten wheel bearing adjusting nut to 44 ft. lbs. (59 N.m). Rotate hub several times. Loosen wheel bearing adjusting nut and retighten to 18 ft. lbs. (25 N.m).

**3)** Attach spring tension gauge to wheel stud. Measure wheel bearing preload required to rotate the hub. Adjust wheel bearing adjusting nut until wheel bearing preload is within specification. See WHEEL BEARING PRELOAD SPECIFICATIONS table.

**4)** Install new lock washer. Install wheel bearing lock nut. Tighten wheel bearing lock nut to specification. See TORQUE SPECIFICATIONS table at end of article.

**5)** Ensure no play exists in wheel bearing. Recheck wheel bearing preload. If not within specification, readjust wheel bearing.

**6)** Once wheel bearing preload is correct, bend one tab on lock washer inward and one tab outward. Install gasket and grease cap. Tighten retaining bolts to specification. See TORQUE SPECIFICATIONS table at end of article.

**7)** Install front wheel. To install remaining components, reverse removal procedure. Tighten bolts/nuts to specification. See TORQUE SPECIFICATIONS table at end of article.

***WHEEL BEARING PRELOAD SPECIFICATIONS***

| Application | Lbs. (kg) |
|---|---|
| Pickup | |
| Dual Rear Wheels | [1] 0.9-2.2 (0.4-1.0) |
| Single Rear Wheels | [1] 1.3-4.0 (0.6-1.8) |
| 4Runner | 6.4-12.6 (2.9-5.7) |

[1] – Add oil seal frictional drag to this specification.

### RIDING HEIGHT

***NOTE: Before measuring riding height, bounce vehicle several times to stabilize the suspension.***

**Pickup – 1)** Front suspension riding height is measured from the ground surface to center of front lower control arm chassis pivot bolt. Rear suspension riding height is measured from the ground surface and center of front leaf spring-to-frame bracket bolt.

**2)** Ensure all suspension components are okay before adjusting riding height. Adjust riding height by rotating riding height adjusting bolt. *See Fig. 1.* Rotate riding height adjusting bolt until riding height is within specification. See RIDING HEIGHT SPECIFICATIONS (PICKUP) table.

# 1991 SUSPENSION
# Front - 2WD Pickup & 4Runner (Cont.)

*RIDING HEIGHT SPECIFICATIONS (PICKUP)*

| Application [1] | Front In. (mm) | Rear In. (mm) |
|---|---|---|
| **4-Cylinder** | | |
| Standard | | |
| Regular Cab, Short Chassis | 10.23 (260) | 10.55 (268) |
| Deluxe (DLX) | | |
| Regular Cab | | |
| Short Chassis | 10.12 (257) | 10.35 (263) |
| Long Chassis | | |
| 5-Speed M/T | 10.35 (263) | 10.28 (261) |
| 4-Speed A/T | 10.31 (262) | 10.28 (261) |
| Xtra Cab, Xtra Long Chassis | 10.94 (278) | 10.39 (264) |
| **V6** | | |
| Standard Cab & Chassis [2] | | |
| Long Chassis | | |
| 5-Speed M/T | 10.20 (259) | 9.21 (234) |
| 4-Speed A/T | 10.24 (260) | 9.25 (235) |
| Super Long Chassis | 10.20 (259) | 9.13 (232) |
| DLX | | |
| Regular Cab, Long Chassis | | |
| 5-Speed M/T | 10.24 (260) | 11.18 (284) |
| 4-Speed A/T | 10.16 (258) | 11.14 (283) |
| Xtra Cab, Xtra Long Chassis | | |
| 5-Speed M/T | 10.91 (277) | 10.47 (266) |
| 4-Speed A/T | 10.91 (277) | 10.43 (265) |
| SR5 | | |
| Xtra Cab, Xtra Long Chassis | | |
| P205/75R14 | 10.75 (273) | 10.31 (262) |
| P215/65R15 | 10.79 (274) | 10.31 (262) |

[1] - Riding height will vary depending on tire size used. Riding height is based on original tire size for vehicle application.

[2] - This is cab and chassis equipped with dual rear wheels.

**4Runner - 1)** Front suspension riding height is measured from the ground surface to center of front adjusting cam at lower control arm. Rear suspension riding height is measured from the ground surface and center of front lower control arm-to-frame bracket bolt.

**2)** Ensure all suspension components are okay before adjusting riding height. Adjust riding height by rotating riding height adjusting bolt. *See Fig. 2.* Rotate riding height adjusting bolt until riding height is within specification. See RIDING HEIGHT SPECIFICATIONS (4RUNNER) table.

*RIDING HEIGHT SPECIFICATIONS (4RUNNER)*

| Application [1] | Front In. (mm) | Rear In. (mm) |
|---|---|---|
| SR5 4-Door A/T | | |
| 4-Cylinder | 11.17 (284) | 13.04 (331) |
| V6 | 11.14 (283) | 12.94 (329) |

[1] - Riding height will vary depending on tire size used. Riding height is based on original tire size for vehicle application.

## BALL JOINT CHECKING

**1)** To check lower ball joint, raise and support vehicle. Ensure wheels are positioned straight-ahead. Apply service brakes. Place a sturdy lever against wheel and under lower control arm.

**2)** Move lower control arm upward and downward, noting vertical movement in lower ball joint. Replace lower ball joint if vertical movement exceeds .091" (2.30 mm).

**3)** To check upper ball joint, use sturdy lever to move wheel upward and downward, noting vertical movement in upper ball joint. Replace upper ball joint if vertical movement exceeds .091" (2.30 mm) on Pickup or if any movement exists on 4Runner.

**4)** Ball joint rotating torque can be checked with ball joint disconnected from knuckle. With ball joint disconnected from knuckle, move ball joint stud back and forth 5 times. Install nut on ball joint stud.

**5)** Using INCH lb. torque wrench, rotate ball joint stud continuously one revolution per 2-4 seconds and note rotating torque. Replace ball joint if rotating torque exceeds specification. See BALL JOINT ROTATING TORQUE SPECIFICATIONS table.

*BALL JOINT ROTATING TORQUE SPECIFICATIONS*

| Application | INCH Lbs. (N.m) |
|---|---|
| Pickup | |
| Lower Ball Joint | 22-43 (2.5-4.9) |
| Upper Ball Joint | 17-35 (1.9-3.9) |
| 4Runner | |
| Lower Ball Joint | 26-52 (2.9-5.9) |
| Upper Ball Joint | [1] |

[1] - Turning torque specification is not available from manufacturer.

## REMOVAL & INSTALLATION

### HUB & KNUCKLE

**Removal (Pickup) - 1)** Raise and support vehicle. Remove front wheel. Remove brake caliper and secure aside. Remove dust cap, cotter pin, nut lock and wheel bearing adjusting nut. Remove hub and outer wheel bearing. Remove retaining bolts and rotor dust cover from knuckle.

**2)** Remove bolts and disconnect steering arm from knuckle. Support lower control arm with floor jack. Remove ball joint-to-knuckle retaining nuts. Using Ball Joint Separator (SST 09628-62011), separate ball joints from knuckle. Remove knuckle.

**Installation -** To install, reverse removal procedure. Tighten bolts/nuts to specification. See TORQUE SPECIFICATIONS table at end of article. Install hub and adjust wheel bearings. See WHEEL BEARING under ADJUSTMENTS & INSPECTION.

**Removal (4Runner) - 1)** Raise and support vehicle. Remove front wheel. Remove brake caliper and secure aside. Remove hub grease cap.

**2)** Using screwdriver, release tab on lock washer. Remove wheel bearing lock nut, lock washer and wheel bearing adjusting nut. Remove hub and outer wheel bearing. Remove retaining bolts and rotor dust cover from knuckle.

**3)** Remove bolts and disconnect steering arm from knuckle. Disconnect shock absorber from lower control arm. Disconnect stabilizer bar link from lower control arm. *See Fig. 2.* Support lower control arm with floor jack.

**4)** Remove upper ball joint-to-knuckle retaining nut. Using Ball Joint Separator (SST 09628-62011), separate upper ball joint from knuckle. Remove lower ball joint-to-lower control arm bolts. Lower floor jack and remove knuckle.

**Installation - 1)** To install, reverse removal procedure. Clean steering arm-to-knuckle bolt threads and apply thread sealant on threads before installing.

**2)** Tighten bolts/nuts to specification. See TORQUE SPECIFICATIONS table at end of article. Install hub and adjust wheel bearings. See WHEEL BEARING under ADJUSTMENTS & INSPECTION.

### LOWER CONTROL ARM & BALL JOINT

**Removal (Pickup) - 1)** Remove torsion bar. See TORSION BAR under REMOVAL & INSTALLATION. Remove cotter pin and nut from tie rod. Separate tie rod from knuckle.

**2)** Remove shock absorber. Disconnect stabilizer rod at lower control arm. Stabilizer rod is installed between stabilizer bar and lower control arm. Remove strut bar-to-lower control arm bolts.

**3)** Remove lower ball joint-to-lower control arm bolts. Remove lower control arm shaft and lower control arm. *See Fig. 1.*

**Installation - 1)** Install torque arm on lower control arm. *See Fig. 1.* Install lower control arm and lower control arm shaft. DO NOT tighten nut on lower control arm shaft at this time. With lower control arm shaft installed, remove torque arm.

**2)** To install remaining components, reverse removal procedure using new nut on stabilizer rod. Tighten bolts/nuts to specification. See TORQUE SPECIFICATIONS table at end of article. Check wheel alignment. See SPECIFICATIONS & PROCEDURES article in WHEEL ALIGNMENT.

# 1991 SUSPENSION
# Front – 2WD Pickup & 4Runner (Cont.)

***CAUTION: Lower vehicle and bounce vehicle several times to stabilize suspension before tightening lower control arm shaft nut to specification.***

**Removal (4Runner) – 1)** Raise and support vehicle. Remove front wheel. Remove shock absorber. Disconnect stabilizer link at lower control arm. *See Fig. 2.* Remove lower ball joint-to-lower control arm nut.
**2)** Separate lower ball joint from lower control arm. Mark position of both adjusting cams for reassembly reference. *See Fig. 2.* Remove adjusting cams and lower control arm.
**Installation – 1)** Install lower control arm and adjusting cams. DO NOT tighten adjusting cam nuts at this time.
**2)** To install remaining components, reverse removal procedure. Tighten bolts/nuts to specification. See TORQUE SPECIFICATIONS table at end of article.
**3)** Lower vehicle and bounce vehicle several times to stabilize suspension. Align reference marks on alignment cams and tighten retaining nuts to specification. See TORQUE SPECIFICATIONS table at end of article. Check wheel alignment. See SPECIFICATIONS & PROCEDURES article in WHEEL ALIGNMENT.

## LOWER CONTROL ARM BUSHINGS

**Removal & Installation (Pickup) – 1)** Remove lower control arm. See LOWER CONTROL ARM & BALL JOINT under REMOVAL & INSTALLATION. Cut rubber edge of lower control arm bushing off so it is even with surface of bushing housing.
**2)** Using Lower Control Arm Bushing Remover/Installer (SST 09726-35010), remove lower control arm bushing from lower control arm.
**3)** To install, coat rubber area of new lower control arm bushing with soapy water. Using bushing remover/installer, install lower control arm bushing in lower control arm. Install lower control arm.
**Removal & Installation (4Runner) – 1)** Remove lower control arm. See LOWER CONTROL ARM & BALL JOINT under REMOVAL & INSTALLATION. Using vise, Base (SST 09726-02060) and Bushing Remover/Installer (SST 09726-02050) from Bushing Remover/Installer Kit (SST 09726-35010), remove bushing from lower control arm.
**2)** To install, use vise, Replacer (SST 09726-02040) and base to install lower control arm bushing. Install lower control arm.

## STABILIZER BAR

**Removal & Installation (Pickup) – 1)** Remove torsion bar. See TORSION BAR under REMOVAL & INSTALLATION. Remove stabilizer rod, located between stabilizer bar and lower control arm. Remove retaining brackets, bushings and stabilizer bar. *See Fig. 1.*
**2)** To install, reverse removal procedure using new nuts on stabilizer bar rod. DO NOT tighten retaining bracket bolts to specification until stabilizer rod is installed and tightened. Tighten bolts/nuts to specification. See TORQUE SPECIFICATIONS table at end of article.
**Removal & Installation (4Runner) – 1)** Remove stabilizer bar link. *See Fig. 2.* Remove retaining brackets at the frame, bushings and stabilizer bar. Ensure stud on stabilizer bar link rotates smoothly in all directions. Replace stabilizer bar link if defective.
**2)** To install, reverse removal procedure using new nuts on stabilizer bar link. DO NOT tighten retaining bracket bolts to specification until stabilizer bar link is installed and tightened. Tighten bolts/nuts to specification. See TORQUE SPECIFICATIONS table at end of article.

## STRUT BAR

***NOTE: Strut bar is used on Pickup only.***

**Removal & Installation (Pickup) – 1)** Place reference marks on threaded portion of strut bar and adjusting nut for installation reference. Remove nut from front of strut bar. Remove strut bar-to-lower control arm bolts. Remove strut bar, washers, bushings and spacer. *See Fig. 1.*
**2)** To install, reverse removal procedure. Ensure reference marks are aligned. DO NOT tighten front nut until vehicle is lowered and bounced several times to stabilize suspension. Tighten bolts/nuts to specification. See TORQUE SPECIFICATIONS table at end of this article. Check wheel alignment. See SPECIFICATIONS & PROCEDURES article in WHEEL ALIGNMENT.

## TORSION BAR

***NOTE: Left and right torsion bars are not interchangeable. Torsion bars are marked "L" (left) or "R" (right) on rear end of torsion bar.***

**Removal (Pickup) – 1)** Raise and support vehicle. Remove front wheel. Place reference mark on anchor arm, torsion bar and torque arm for reassembly reference. *See Fig. 1.*
**2)** Remove lock nut from nut on riding height adjusting bolt. Measure distance from end of adjusting bolt to top surface of the nut. Record distance for reassembly reference. Remove torsion bar dust cover.
**3)** Loosen riding height adjusting bolt nut until all tension is removed from torsion bar. Remove retaining bolts, torque arm, torsion bar and anchor arm.
**Installation – 1)** Lightly apply grease on torsion bar splines. Align splines and reference marks and install anchor arm and torque arm on torsion bar.
**2)** Install torque arm and torsion bar on lower control arm. Tighten bolts to specification. See TORQUE SPECIFICATIONS table at end of article. Install riding height adjusting bolt.
**3)** Install nut on riding height adjusting bolt and tighten to original dimension. Install front wheel and lower vehicle. Adjusting riding height. See RIDING HEIGHT under ADJUSTMENTS & INSPECTION. Install and tighten lock nut on riding height adjusting bolt.
**Removal (4Runner) – 1)** Raise and support vehicle. Remove front wheel. Place reference mark on anchor arm, torsion bar and torque arm for reassembly reference. *See Fig. 2.*
**2)** Measure distance from end of riding height adjusting bolt to top surface of the nut. *See Fig. 2.* Record distance for reassembly for reference on setting riding height. Remove torsion bar dust cover.
**3)** Loosen riding height adjusting bolt nut until all tension is removed from torsion bar. Remove torsion bar and anchor arm.
**Installation – 1)** Lightly apply grease on torsion bar splines. Align reference marks and install anchor arm on torsion bar.

***NOTE: Torque arm, anchor arm and torque bar contain a toothless spline which must be aligned.***

**2)** Install torsion bar on lower control arm. Ensure reference mark is aligned on reference mark on torque arm.

***NOTE: If torque arm was removed from lower control arm, torque arm must be installed with protrusion facing upward. See Fig. 4.***

**3)** Install riding height adjusting bolt. Install nut on riding height adjusting bolt and tighten to original dimension. Install front wheel and lower vehicle. Adjusting riding height. See RIDING HEIGHT under ADJUSTMENTS & INSPECTION.

## UPPER CONTROL ARM

**Removal (Pickup) – 1)** Raise and support vehicle. Remove front wheel. Support lower control arm with floor jack. Remove upper ball joint-to-upper control arm bolts.
**2)** Remove retaining bolts from upper control arm shaft. Mark location of wheel alignment shims for reassembly reference. Remove upper control arm.
**Installation –** To install, reverse removal procedure. Tighten bolts/nuts to specification. See TORQUE SPECIFICATIONS table at end of article. Check wheel alignment

***NOTE: On Pickup models, if upper control arm bushings were replaced, bushing retaining bolts at ends of upper control arm shaft must be tightened to specification once vehicle is lowered and bounced several times to stabilize suspension.***

**Removal (4Runner) – 1)** Raise and support vehicle. Remove torsion bar. See TORSION BAR under REMOVAL & INSTALLATION. Support lower control arm with floor jack. Remove upper ball joint-to-upper control arm bolts.

**2)** Remove shock absorber-to-frame retaining nut, washer and bushings. Disconnect shock absorber from the frame. Disconnect intermediate shaft from steering gear. Remove upper control arm shaft retaining bolts and upper control arm shaft.

**Installation** – To install, reverse removal procedure. Tighten bolts/nuts to specification. See TORQUE SPECIFICATIONS table at end of article. Check wheel alignment. See SPECIFICATIONS & PROCEDURES article in WHEEL ALIGNMENT.

## UPPER CONTROL ARM BUSHINGS

**Removal (Pickup)** – **1)** Remove upper control arm. See UPPER CONTROL ARM under REMOVAL & INSTALLATION. Remove bushing retaining bolt from end of upper control arm shaft. *See Fig. 1.*

**2)** Using press, Upper Control Arm Bushing Remover (SST 09710-03030) and Base (SST 09710-03040) from Bushing Remover/Installer Kit (SST 09710-30020), remove bushings from upper control arm.

**Installation** – **1)** Install upper control arm shaft in upper control arm. Using press, Upper Control Arm Bushing Installer (SST 09710-03050) and Base (SST 09710-03060) from bushing remover/installer kit, install upper control arm bushings.

**2)** Install bushing retaining bolts. DO NOT tighten bolts at this time. Install lower control arm. Check wheel alignment. See SPECIFICATIONS & PROCEDURES article in WHEEL ALIGNMENT.

***CAUTION: Bushing retaining bolts must be tightened to specification once vehicle is lowered and bounced several times to stabilize suspension.***

**Removal (4Runner)** – **1)** Remove upper control arm. See UPPER CONTROL ARM under REMOVAL & INSTALLATION. Remove retaining bolts and torque arm from upper control arm. *See Fig. 2.*

**2)** Remove staked area from bushing retaining nut at each end of upper control arm shaft. Remove bushing retaining nut and retainer from upper control arm shaft.

**3)** Using press, Upper Control Arm Bushing Remover (SST 09710-05050) and Adapter (SST 09710-05040) from Bushing Remover/Installer Kit (SST 09710-26010), remove front bushing from upper control arm.

**4)** Using press, Upper Control Arm Bushing Remover (SST 09710-05030), Handle (SST 09710-05020) and Base (SST 09710-05080) from bushing remover/installer kit, rear bushing from upper control arm.

**Installation** – **1)** Using press, Upper Control Arm Bushing Installer (SST 09710-05060) and Base (SST 09710-05080) from bushing remover/installer kit, install rear upper control arm bushing.

***CAUTION: DO NOT apply oil or grease on upper control arm bushings.***

**2)** Install upper control arm shaft in upper control arm. Using press, upper control arm bushing installer and base, install front upper control arm bushing.

**3)** Install retainers and new bushing retaining nuts on upper control arm shaft. DO NOT reuse nuts. Position upper control arm shaft so upper control arm surface is level with the shaft. *See Fig. 3.*

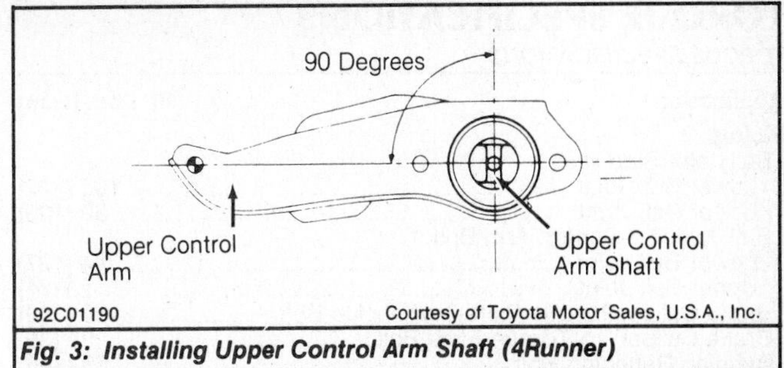


***Fig. 3: Installing Upper Control Arm Shaft (4Runner)***

**4)** Tighten bushing retaining nuts to specification. See TORQUE SPECIFICATIONS table at end of article. Stake bushing retaining nut against upper control arm shaft. Install torque arm on upper control arm with protrusion facing upward. *See Fig. 4.* Tighten bolts to specification.

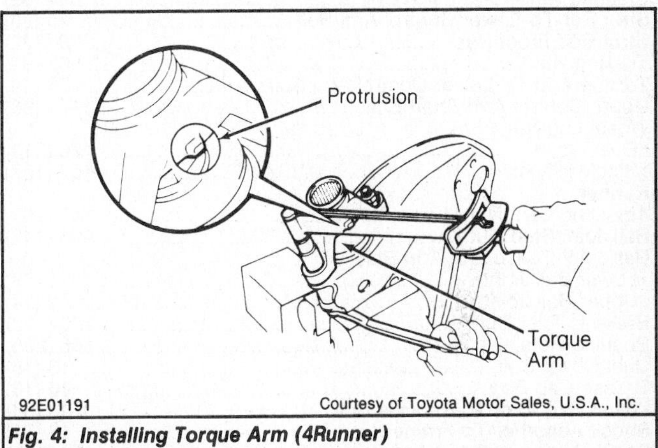


***Fig. 4: Installing Torque Arm (4Runner)***

## WHEEL BEARING

**Removal (Pickup)** – **1)** Raise and support vehicle. Remove front wheel. Remove brake caliper and secure aside. Remove dust cap, cotter pin, nut lock, wheel bearing adjusting nut, washer and hub.

**2)** Remove grease seal and inner wheel bearing. Remove wheel bearing races from hub (if necessary).

**Installation** – **1)** Clean and pack wheel bearings and center of hub with grease. Install inner wheel bearing in hub. Using Handle (SST 09608-04020) and Seal Installer (SST 09608-04100), install grease seal in hub.

**2)** Install hub, outer wheel bearing, washer and wheel bearing adjusting nut. Adjust wheel bearing preload. See WHEEL BEARING under ADJUSTMENTS & INSPECTION.

**Removal (4Runner)** – **1)** Raise and support vehicle. Remove front wheel. Remove brake caliper and secure aside. Remove hub grease cap.

**2)** Using screwdriver, release tab on lock washer. Remove wheel bearing lock nut, lock washer, wheel bearing adjusting nut, washer and hub. Remove grease seal and inner wheel bearing. Remove wheel bearing races from hub (if necessary).

**Installation** – **1)** Clean and pack wheel bearings and center of hub with grease. Install inner wheel bearing in hub. Using Handle (SST 09608-09608) and Seal Installer (SST 09608-06150), install grease seal in hub.

**2)** Install hub, outer wheel bearing, washer and wheel bearing adjusting nut. Adjust wheel bearing preload. See WHEEL BEARING under ADJUSTMENTS & INSPECTION.

# 1991 SUSPENSION
# Front – 2WD Pickup & 4Runner (Cont.)

## TORQUE SPECIFICATIONS

*TORQUE SPECIFICATIONS*

| Application | Ft. Lbs. (N.m) |
|---|---|
| **Pickup** | |
| Ball Joint Stud Nut | |
| Lower Ball Joint | 105 (142) |
| Upper Ball Joint | 80 (109) |
| Ball Joint-To-Control Arm Bolt | |
| Lower Ball Joint | 94 (127) |
| Upper Ball Joint | 23 (31) |
| Brake Caliper Torque Plate-To-Knuckle Bolt | 80 (109) |
| Brake Caliper-To-Torque Plate Bolt | 29 (39) |
| Bushing Retaining Bolt | 93 (126) |
| Lower Control Arm Shaft Nut | 166 (226) |
| Riding Height Adjusting Bolt Lock Nut | 61 (83) |
| Shock Absorber-To-Lower Control Arm Bolt | 13 (18) |
| Shock Absorber Upper Shaft Nut | 18 (24) |
| Stabilizer Bar Retaining Bracket Bolt | 22 (30) |
| Stabilizer Rod-To-Lower Control Arm Nut | 10 (14) |
| Steering Arm-To-Knuckle Bolt | 80 (109) |
| Strut Bar-To-Lower Control Arm Bolt | 70 (95) |
| Strut Rod Front Nut | 90 (122) |
| Tie Rod Nut | 67 (91) |
| Torque Arm-To-Lower Control Arm Bolt | 36 (49) |
| Upper Control Arm Shaft Bolt | 71 (96) |
| Wheel Lug Nut | |
| Dual Wheel | 170 (213) |
| Single Wheel | 101 (137) |
| **4Runner** | |
| Adjusting Cam Nut | 145 (197) |
| Ball Joint Stud Nut | 105 (142) |
| Ball Joint-To-Control Arm Bolt | |
| Lower Ball Joint | 43 (58) |
| Upper Ball Joint | 25 (34) |
| Brake Caliper Bolt | 90 (122) |
| Bushing Retaining Nut | 166 (226) |
| Dust Cover Bolt | 13 (18) |
| Grease Cap Bolt | 10 (13) |
| Lower Ball Joint-To-Knuckle Bolt | 43 (58) |
| Shock Absorber-To-Frame Nut | 18 (24) |
| Shock Absorber-To-Lower Control Arm Bolt | 101 (137) |
| Stabilizer Bar Link-To-Lower Control Arm Bolt | 19 (26) |
| Stabilizer Bar Link-To-Stabilizer Bar Nut | 70 (95) |
| Stabilizer Bar Retaining Bracket Bolt | 22 (30) |
| Steering Arm-To-Knuckle Bolt | 135 (183) |
| Torque Arm-To-Upper Control Arm Bolt | 64 (87) |
| Upper Control Arm Shaft Retaining Bolt | 131 (178) |
| Wheel Bearing Lock Nut | 35 (47) |
| Wheel Lug Nut | 76 (103) |

# 1991 SUSPENSION
# Front – 4WD Pickup & 4Runner

## DESCRIPTION

An independent front suspension, with torsion bars mounted on upper control arm, is used on 4WD Pickup and 4Runner. *See Figs. 1 and 2*. Wheel is supported by a steering knuckle mounted between the upper and lower control arms. Torsion bars are mounted between the upper control arms and vehicle frame. Vehicle roll is controlled by a stabilizer bar attached to each front lower control arm and frame. Shock absorbers are mounted between the lower control arm and frame.

## ADJUSTMENTS & INSPECTION

### WHEEL ALIGNMENT SPECIFICATIONS & PROCEDURES

***NOTE: See SPECIFICATIONS & PROCEDURES article in WHEEL ALIGNMENT.***

### RIDING HEIGHT

Ride height will vary by vehicle model and by tire size used on vehicle. Standard vehicle height is the measurement used on 4WD vehicles when suspension is being aligned. Set vehicle to this specification for alignment procedures. See STANDARD VEHICLE HEIGHT SPECIFICATIONS table. Loaded and non-loaded vehicle ride heights are adjusted for individual vehicles. See SPECIFICATIONS & PROCEDURES article in WHEEL ALIGNMENT.

***STANDARD VEHICLE HEIGHT SPECIFICATIONS***

| Application | In. (mm) |
|---|---|
| Pickup | |
| Front | 2.30 (58.5) |
| Rear | 2.40 (61.0) |
| 4Runner | |
| Front | 2.30 (58.5) |
| Rear | 1.04 (26.5) |

**Standard Vehicle Height** – On front suspension, height measurement is difference between height at center of steering knuckle spindle and height at center of front side of adjusting cam bolt. On rear suspension, height measurement is difference between height of center of rear lower control arm front bushing and height of center of rear axle shaft. *See Fig. 3*.

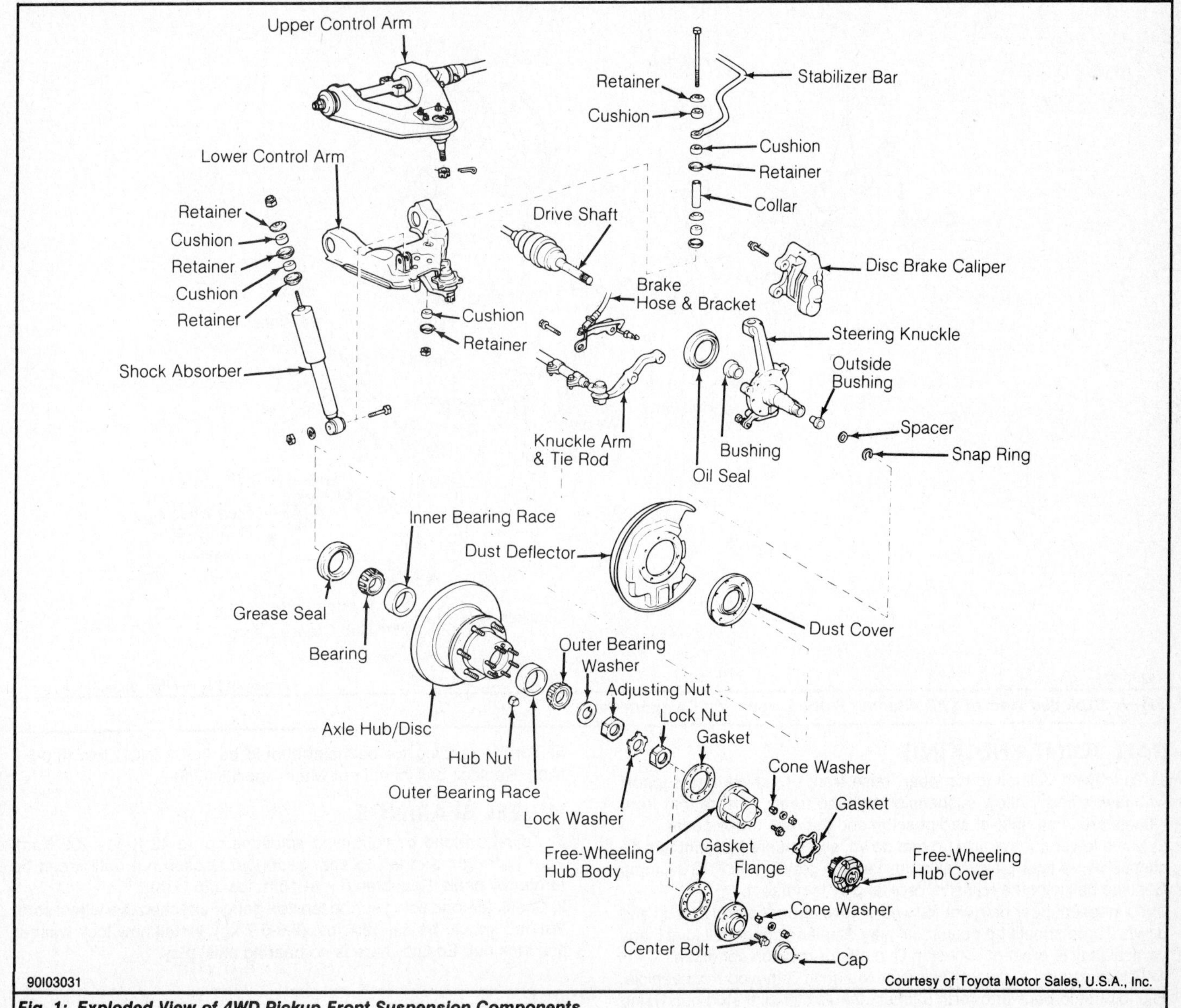


***Fig. 1: Exploded View of 4WD Pickup Front Suspension Components***

# 1991 SUSPENSION
# Front – 4WD Pickup & 4Runner (Cont.)

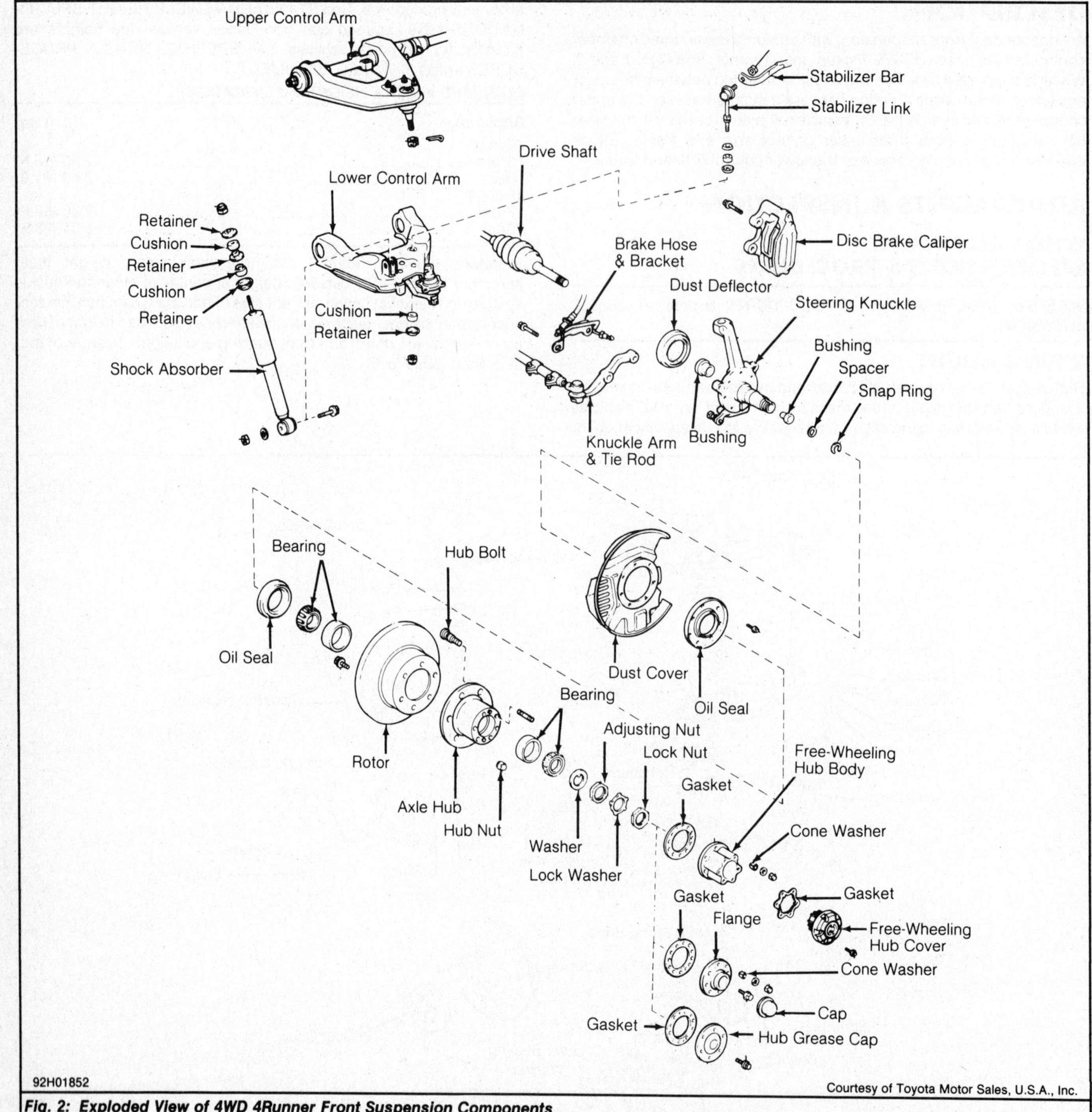


*Fig. 2: Exploded View of 4WD 4Runner Front Suspension Components*

## BALL JOINT CHECKING

**1)** To inspect ball joints for wear, raise front of vehicle and support with jack stands. Allow suspension to hang freely. Ensure that front wheels are in straight-ahead position and depress brake pedal.

**2)** Move lower control arm up and down, and ensure ball joint has no excessive vertical play. Maximum vertical play is .091" (2.30 mm). Replace ball joint if excessive vertical play is present.

**3)** To inspect upper ball joint for wear, move upper control arm up and down. There should be no vertical play. Replace upper ball joint if any vertical play is present. Check ball joints for rotation condition.

**4)** Check turning torque of ball joint with joint removed from vehicle. Flip joint stud back and forth 5 times. Install ball joint stud nut. Using an INCH lb. torque wrench, check turning torque. Turn nut one turn each 2-4 seconds and take torque reading on the fifth turn.

**5)** Torque reading for ball joint should be 26-52 INCH lbs. (3.0-5.9 N.m). Replace ball joint if not within specification.

## WHEEL BEARINGS

**1)** Adjust preload by tightening adjusting nut to 43 ft. lbs. (59 N.m). Turn hub right and left to seat bearings. Loosen nut until it can be turned by hand. Retighten nut to 18 ft. lbs. (25 N.m).

**2)** Check preload using spring tension gauge attached to a wheel stud. Preload should be 6.4-12.6 lbs. (2.9-5.7 kg). Install new lock washer and lock nut. Ensure there is no bearing axial play.

# 1991 SUSPENSION
# Front – 4WD Pickup & 4Runner (Cont.)

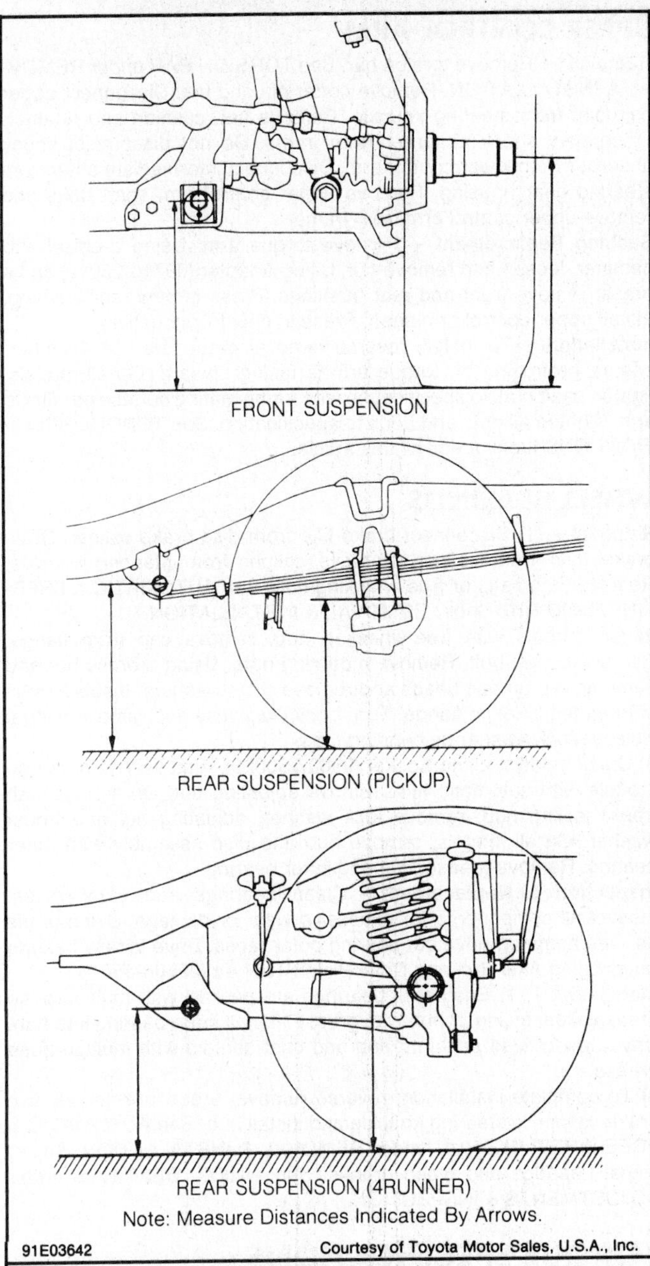


***Fig. 3: Measuring Standard Vehicle Height***

## REMOVAL & INSTALLATION

### AUTOMATIC & FREE-WHEELING HUB

**Removal** – **1)** On models with free-wheeling hubs, turn hub selector to "FREE" position. On all models, remove hub cover mounting bolts and cover. Remove center bolt and washer.

**2)** Remove mounting nuts and washers. Using brass bar and hammer, tap on bolt heads and remove cone washer. Remove hub body.

**Installation (Automatic Hubs)** – **1)** Install new gasket to axle hub. Apply multipurpose grease to hub body splines. Align spring ends of brake assembly with knock pin.

**2)** Check that outer cam stopper is secure in inner cam groove. Position inner cam protrusion so it is centered between outer cam protrusions and aligned with hub body knock pin hole.

**3)** Install automatic locking hub body to axle hub/disc so that inner cam protrusion is set between ends of brake spring. Install hub body to drive shaft spline.

**4)** Ensure hub body fits perfectly on axle hub. Install washers and nuts and tighten to specification. Install center bolt and washer. Tighten center bolt to specification. Install hub cover and tighten mounting bolts to specification. See TORQUE SPECIFICATIONS table at end of article.

**Installation (Free-Wheeling Hubs)** – **1)** Install new gasket on front axle hub. Install free-wheeling hub body with washers and nuts and tighten to specification.

**2)** Install center bolt and washer and tighten to specification. Apply multipurpose grease to inner hub splines. Set control handle and clutch to "FREE" position. Install free-wheeling hub cover with new gasket.

**3)** Install hub cover to body with follower pawl tabs aligned with non-toothed portions of body. Tighten cover mounting bolts to specification. See TORQUE SPECIFICATIONS table at end of article.

### BALL JOINTS

**Removal & Installation** – **1)** Remove steering knuckle. See STEERING KNUCKLE under REMOVAL & INSTALLATION. Remove cotter pin and nut. Remove lower ball joint from lower control arm. Remove upper ball joint from upper control arm.

**2)** To install, reverse removal procedure. Ensure all nuts and bolts are tightened to specification. See TORQUE SPECIFICATIONS table at end of this article.

### LOWER CONTROL ARM

**Removal** – Remove shock absorber, and disconnect stabilizer bar from lower control arm. Remove bolts, and disconnect lower control arm from lower ball joint. Mark front and rear adjusting cams for installation reference. Remove nuts and adjusting cams. Remove lower control arm.

**Bushing Replacement** – Using press and Adapter (09726-27011), press out bushings from lower control arms. Press in new bushings using Adapter (09726-27011). DO NOT apply grease or oil to bushings.

**Installation** – To install, reverse removal procedure. Ensure reference marks are aligned, and tighten all nuts and bolts to specification. See TORQUE SPECIFICATIONS table at end of article. Ensure adjusting cam nuts are tightened with vehicle on ground. Check front wheel alignment. See SPECIFICATIONS & PROCEDURES article in WHEEL ALIGNMENT.

### SHOCK ABSORBER

**Removal & Installation** – **1)** Raise and support vehicle. Remove wheel assembly. Remove nuts retaining shock absorber to bracket. Remove washers and cushions from shaft of shock absorber.

**2)** Remove nuts and bolts securing shock absorber to lower control arm. Compress shock absorber and remove from vehicle. To install, reverse removal procedure.

### STABILIZER BAR

**Removal** – Disconnect stabilizer link from stabilizer bar. Remove stabilizer link from lower control arm. Remove stabilizer bar brackets and stabilizer bar from vehicle.

**Inspection (4Runner)** – Rotate stabilizer link ball joint stud in all directions. If movement is not smooth and even, replace stabilizer bar link.

**Installation** – To install, reverse removal procedure. Tighten mounting nuts to specification.

### STEERING KNUCKLE

**Removal** – **1)** Remove disc brake caliper and front axle hub. Remove dust cover and grease seal. Disconnect knuckle arm from steering knuckle. Install bolt in drive shaft.

**2)** Using feeler gauge, measure front drive axle thrust clearance between steering knuckle outside bushing and spacer. See DRIVE AXLE THRUST CLEARANCE table. If measurement is within specification, go to step **4)**.

**3)** If measurement is more than maximum clearance, clearance can be altered by replacing spacers. Spacers are available in 2 sizes; .0709" (1.800 mm) and .0886" (2.250 mm). If spacers will not bring clearance within specification, replace steering knuckle outside and/or inside bushings.

# 1991 SUSPENSION
# Front – 4WD Pickup & 4Runner (Cont.)

*DRIVE AXLE THRUST CLEARANCE*

| Clearance | In. (mm) |
|---|---|
| Standard | .00295-.0272 (.075-.690) |
| Maximum | .039 (1.0) |

**4)** Disconnect front shock absorber from lower control arm. Disconnect stabilizer bar from lower control arm. Remove snap ring and spacer. Remove cotter pin and nut from upper ball joint. Using Ball Joint Puller (09308-00010), disconnect steering knuckle from upper ball joint.
**5)** Remove bolts from lower ball joint. Disconnect steering knuckle from lower ball joint. Push lower control arm down and remove steering knuckle. Using dye penetrant, check steering knuckle for cracks or excessive wear. Pry out dust deflector.
**6)** Using Puller (09308-00010), pull out steering knuckle outside bushing. Using brass bar and hammer, drive out steering knuckle inside bushing.
**Installation – 1)** Install inside and outside bushings using Bushing Replacer Set (09550-10012, 09252-10010 and 09555-10010).

***NOTE: When installing bushing, ensure that flat portion of bushing is aligned with spindle groove.***

**2)** Apply Molybdenum Disulfide Lithium (MDL) base grease to steering knuckle bushings. To complete installation, reverse removal procedure. Apply sealant to knuckle arm-to-steering knuckle bolts. Tighten all nuts and bolts to specification. See TORQUE SPECIFICATIONS table at end of article.
**3)** Install new cotter pin. If steering knuckle bushings are replaced, recheck drive axle thrust clearance.

## TORSION BAR

**Removal** – Remove dust boot protectors (if equipped). Remove boots and place match marks on torsion bar, anchor arm and torque arm for installation reference. Loosen adjusting nut. Remove anchor arm and torsion bar. Measure distance of protruding bolt from bolt end to top of adjusting nut. Use this measurement for reference when adjusting vehicle height.

***NOTE: On rear end of torsion bars, there are left and right indication marks. Ensure they are not interchanged when installing.***

**Installation (Used Torsion Bar)** – Apply light coat of MDL base grease to spline of torsion bar. Align match marks and install torsion bar to torque arm. Align match marks and install anchor arm to torsion bar. Tighten adjusting nut so that bolt protrusion is equal to original measurement. Tighten lock nut to specification and assemble boots.
**Installation (New Torsion Bar) – 1)** Remove wheel and install 2 boots to torsion bar. Apply light coat MDL base grease to spline of torsion bar.
**2)** Temporarily install anchor arm to small end of torsion bar. Place match marks on torsion bar and anchor arm for installation reference.

***NOTE: One spline on torsion bar is larger than others. Install torsion bar into anchor arm. Slowly turn anchor arm until large end of spline enters matching point in anchor arm.***

**3)** Align match marks on bottom of torsion bar and anchor arm. Remove anchor arm from torsion bar. Install torsion bar to torque arm.
**4)** Align match marks and install anchor arm to torsion bar. Tighten adjusting nut until bolt protrusion length is 3.43" (87.1 mm). Temporarily install lock nut. Install wheel and remove stands. Bounce vehicle to settle suspension.
**5)** Adjust chassis ground clearance by turning adjusting nut. Front chassis clearance is measured from ground to center of lower control arm front mounting bolt. For ground clearance specification, see SPECIFICATIONS & PROCEDURES article in WHEEL ALIGNMENT. After adjusting clearance, tighten torsion bar lock nut to specification.

## UPPER CONTROL ARM

**Removal** – Remove torsion bar. See TORSION BAR under REMOVAL & INSTALLATION. Remove cotter pin and nut. Disconnect upper ball joint from steering knuckle. Remove nut, cushion and retainer. Disconnect shock absorber from frame. Do not disconnect shock absorber from lower control arm. Disconnect intermediate shaft from steering gear housing. Remove upper control arm shaft bolts and remove upper control arm from frame.
**Bushing Replacement** – Remove torque arm. Using a chisel and hammer, loosen and remove nut. Using Adapter (09710-26010) and a press, remove front and rear bushings. Press in new rear bushing. Install upper control arm shaft. Press in new front bushing.
**Installation** – To install, reverse removal procedure. On 4Runner, ensure protrusion on torque arm is facing upward. On all models, tighten shaft nuts to specification with frame mating surface parallel to arm. Tighten all nuts and bolts to specification. See TORQUE SPECIFICATIONS table at end of this article.

## WHEEL BEARINGS

**Removal – 1)** Disconnect brake line from disc brake caliper. Drain brake fluid from caliper. Remove caliper from steering knuckle. Remove automatic or free-wheeling hub. See AUTOMATIC & FREE-WHEELING HUB under REMOVAL & INSTALLATION.
**2)** On models with free-wheeling hub, remove cap from flange. Remove center bolt. Remove mounting nuts. Using a brass bar and hammer, tap on bolt heads and remove cone washers. Install 2 bolts in threaded holes in flange. Turn bolts clockwise and remove flange. Release lock washer by bending tabs.
**3)** On all models, using Socket (09607-60020), remove lock nut or on models with automatic hub, remove adjusting nut. On models with free-wheeling hub, remove lock washer, adjusting nut and thrust washer. On all models, remove hub and disc assembly with outer bearing. Remove grease seal and inner bearing.
**Inspection & Replacement** – Clean bearings and outer races. Inspect all components for excessive wear or damage. Using brass bar and hammer, drive out bearing outer races. Drive in new bearing races using Axle Hub and Drive Pinion Tool Kit (09608-35014).
**Installation – 1)** Ensure all bearings are packed with multipurpose grease. Coat inside of hub with grease. Install inner bearing into hub. Drive new grease seal into hub and coat seal lip with multipurpose grease.
**2)** To complete installation, reverse removal procedure. Install disc brake caliper to steering knuckle and install hub. See AUTOMATIC & FREE-WHEELING HUB under REMOVAL & INSTALLATION. Adjust wheel bearings and bleed brakes. See WHEEL BEARINGS under ADJUSTMENTS & INSPECTION.

## TORQUE SPECIFICATIONS

*TORQUE SPECIFICATIONS*

| Application | Ft. Lbs. (N.m) |
|---|---|
| Automatic Hub Adjustment Preload Nut | 43 (59) |
| Automatic Hub Cone Nut | 23 (31) |
| Brake Line Nut | 11 (15) |
| Disc Brake Caliper | 90 (123) |
| Dust Cover | 13 (18) |
| Free-Wheeling Hub Adjustment Preload Nut | 35 (47) |
| Hub Bolt | 13 (18) |
| Lower Ball Joint-To-Lower Control Arm Nut | 105 (142) |
| Lower Ball Joint-To-Steering Knuckle Bolt | 43 (58) |
| Lower Control Arm Shaft Nut | 145 (196) |
| Shock Absorber-To-Frame Nut | 18 (25) |
| Shock Absorber-To-Lower Control Arm Nut & Bolt | 101 (137) |
| Stabilizer Bar-To-Lower Suspension Arm Nut | 19 (25) |
| Steering Knuckle-To-Knuckle Arm | 135 (183) |
| Tie Rod End-To-Steering Knuckle | 67 (91) |
| Torque Arm-To-Upper Arm Nut | 64 (87) |
| Upper Ball Joint-To-Steering Knuckle Nut | 105 (142) |
| Upper Ball Joint-To-Upper Control Arm Nut | 18 (25) |
| Upper Control Arm Shaft Nut | 166 (226) |
| Upper Control Arm-To-Frame Nut | 131 (178) |
| | **INCH Lbs. (N.m)** |
| Hub Cover Mounting Bolt | 84 (10) |

# 1991 SUSPENSION
# Front – Previa

## DESCRIPTION

The strut-type suspension uses the lower control arm as a pivot support. Suspension consists of strut assembly, lower control arm, knuckle assembly and stabilizer bar.

## ADJUSTMENTS & INSPECTION

### WHEEL ALIGNMENT SPECIFICATIONS & PROCEDURES

***NOTE:* *See SPECIFICATIONS & PROCEDURES article in WHEEL ALIGNMENT.***

### WHEEL BEARING & HUB

**1)** Raise and support vehicle. Remove front wheel. Remove brake caliper and secure aside. Remove brake rotor. Mount dial indicator on dust shield with indicator stem near center of hub.
**2)** Move hub inward and zero dial indicator. Pull hub outward and note dial indicator reading. Wheel bearing must be replace if reading exceeds .002" (.05 mm).
**3)** Reposition dial indicator with indicator stem on outer edge of hub, near outer edge of wheel stud. Rotate hub and note dial indictor reading. If dial indicator indicates more than .002" (.05 mm) deviation in hub surface, hub must be replace.
**4)** Reinstall components and tighten bolts to specification. See TORQUE SPECIFICATIONS table at end of article.

### BALL JOINT CHECKING

**1)** Check for vertical play at the ball joint. Ball joint must be replace if vertical movement exists.
**2)** With ball joint disconnected from knuckle, move ball joint stud back and forth 5 times. Install nut on ball joint stud.
**3)** Using INCH lb. torque wrench, rotate ball joint stud continuously one revolution per 2-4 seconds and note rotating torque. Replace ball joint if rotating torque is not 13-35 INCH lbs. (1.5-3.9 N.m).

## REMOVAL & INSTALLATION

### HUB & KNUCKLE ASSEMBLY

**Removal – 1)** Raise and support vehicle. Remove front wheel. On models with Anti-Lock Brakes (ABS), remove retaining bolt and ABS speed sensor from knuckle.
**2)** On all models, remove brake caliper and secure aside. Remove brake rotor. On 4WD models, remove cotter pin and lock cap from axle shaft nut. Apply brakes and remove axle shaft nut and washer.
**3)** On all models, loosen knuckle-to-strut and ball joint-to-knuckle bolts. DO NOT remove bolts at this time. Remove cotter pin and nut from tie rod. Separate tie rod from knuckle.
**4)** Remove ball joint-to-knuckle bolts. Separate knuckle from ball joint. Remove knuckle-to-strut bolts. Remove hub and knuckle assembly.

***CAUTION: Use care not to damage ABS speed sensor rotor or axle shaft boot (if equipped) when removing hub and knuckle assembly.***

**Installation – 1)** To install, reverse removal procedure. DO NOT tighten knuckle-to-strut or ball joint-to-knuckle bolts to specification until all bolts are installed.
**2)** Tighten all fasteners to specification. See TORQUE SPECIFICATIONS table at end of article. Check wheel alignment. See SPECIFICATIONS & PROCEDURES article in WHEEL ALIGNMENT.

### LOWER CONTROL ARM & BALL JOINT

***NOTE: Ball joint can be removed by separating ball joint from knuckle and lower control arm. Lower control does not require removal for ball joint replacement.***

**Removal – 1)** Raise and support vehicle. Remove front wheel. Remove lower cover. *See Fig. 1.* Remove ball joint-to-knuckle bolts. Separate knuckle from ball joint.

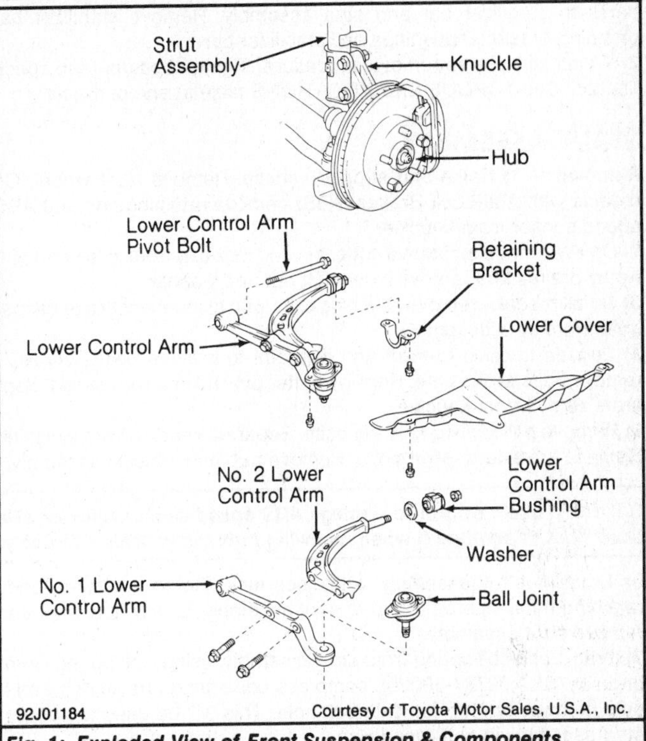


***Fig. 1: Exploded View of Front Suspension & Components***

**2)** Remove bolts and retaining bracket. *See Fig. 1.* Remove lower control arm pivot bolt. Remove lower control arm and ball joint.
**3)** Remove retaining bolts and separate No. 1 lower control arm from No. 2 lower control arm (if necessary). To remove ball joint from lower control arm, remove retaining nut. Using Puller (SST 09268-62011), separate ball joint from lower control arm.
**Installation – 1)** Install No. 1 lower control arm on No. 2 lower control arm (if disassembled). Tighten bolts to specification. See TORQUE SPECIFICATIONS table at end of article.
**2)** Install ball joint on lower control arm. Tighten nut to specification. See TORQUE SPECIFICATIONS table at end of article.
**3)** Install lower control arm with pivot bolt and retaining bracket bolts loosely installed. DO NOT tighten bolts at this time. Tighten ball joint-to-knuckle bolts to specification. See TORQUE SPECIFICATIONS table at end of article.
**4)** Install wheel and lower vehicle. Bounce vehicle several times to stabilize suspension. Raise and support vehicle under the body. Support lower control arm with floor jack.
**5)** Tighten lower control arm pivot bolt and retaining bracket bolts to specification. See TORQUE SPECIFICATIONS table at end of article. Install lower cover. Check wheel alignment. See SPECIFICATIONS & PROCEDURES article in WHEEL ALIGNMENT.

### LOWER CONTROL ARM BUSHING

**Removal & Installation – 1)** Remove lower control arm and ball joint. See LOWER CONTROL ARM & BALL JOINT under REMOVAL & INSTALLATION. Remove nut, lower control arm bushing and washer from lower control arm. *See Fig. 1.*
**2)** To install, reverse removal procedure. Ensure washer is installed on lower control arm with flat side against lower control arm and cupped side toward lower control arm bushing.
**3)** When tightening lower control arm retaining nut, ensure lower control arm bushing is positioned with bushing flat side level with upper surface of lower control arm. Tighten retaining nut to specification. See TORQUE SPECIFICATIONS table at end of article.

# 1991 SUSPENSION
# Front – Previa (Cont.)

## STABILIZER BAR

**Removal & Installation – 1)** Raise and support vehicle. Remove lower covers and front wheels. Remove stabilizer bar link, located between stabilizer bar and strut assembly. Remove stabilizer bar retaining brackets, bushings and stabilizer bar.

**2)** To install, reverse removal procedure. Tighten bolts/nuts to specification. See TORQUE SPECIFICATIONS table at end of article.

## STRUT ASSEMBLY

**Removal – 1)** Raise and support vehicle. Remove front wheel. On models with Anti-Lock Brakes (ABS), remove retaining bolt and ABS speed sensor from knuckle.

**2)** On 4WD models, remove cotter pin and lock cap from axle shaft nut. Apply brakes and remove axle shaft nut and washer.

**3)** On all models, remove retaining clips and disconnect brake caliper hose from strut assembly.

**4)** Loosen knuckle-to-strut and ball joint-to-knuckle bolts. DO NOT remove bolts at this time. Remove cotter pin and nut from tie rod. Separate tie rod from knuckle.

**5)** Remove ball joint-to-knuckle bolts. Separate knuckle from ball joint. Remove knuckle-to-strut bolts. Remove hub and knuckle assembly.

***CAUTION: Use care not to damage ABS speed sensor rotor or axle shaft boot (if equipped) when removing hub and knuckle assembly.***

**6)** Support strut assembly with floor jack. Remove strut-to-body retaining nuts, located at top of strut assembly. Lower floor jack and remove strut assembly.

**7)** If removing coil spring from strut assembly, using Coil Spring Compressor (SST 09727-30020), compress coil spring. Install bolt and 2 nuts in lower strut-to-knuckle bolt hole. This will be used to support strut assembly in soft-faced vise.

**8)** Using Spring Seat Holder (SST 09729-22031), hold upper spring seat and remove strut assembly shaft nut. Remove strut assembly components. *See Fig. 2.*

**9)** If strut assembly is to be disposed of, fully extend shaft. Drill hole in strut assembly housing near mounting bracket for stabilizer bar link on strut assembly housing to release gas from strut assembly.

***CAUTION: Use care when drilling hole in strut assembly, as gas strut assembly is filled with gas.***

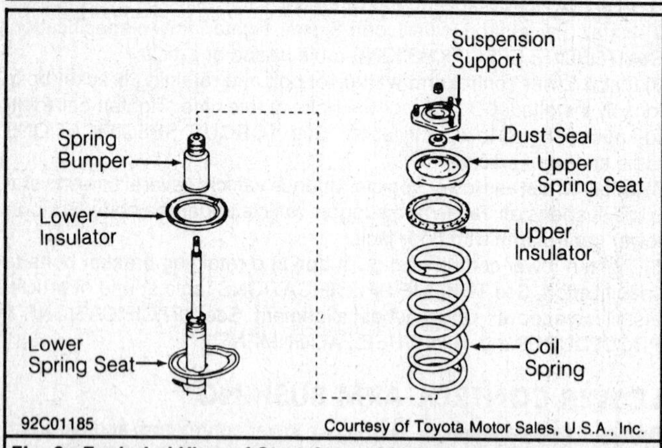


*Fig. 2: Exploded View of Strut Assembly Components*

**Installation – 1)** Install lower insulator and spring bumper on strut assembly. Using coil spring compressor, compress coil spring. Install coil spring on strut assembly. Ensure end of coil spring full seats on lower spring seat.

**2)** Install upper insulator and upper spring seat. Install dust seal and suspension support. Install new strut assembly shaft nut. DO NOT reuse nut.

**3)** Using spring seat holder, hold upper spring seat and tighten strut assembly shaft nut to specification. See TORQUE SPECIFICATIONS table at end of article.

**4)** Rotate upper spring seat so the "OUT" mark stamped on top of upper spring seat is toward outside of vehicle.

**5)** To install, reverse removal procedure. DO NOT tighten knuckle-to-strut or ball joint-to-knuckle bolts to specification until all bolts are installed.

**6)** Tighten all fasteners to specification. See TORQUE SPECIFICATIONS table at end of article. Bleed brake system. Check wheel alignment. See SPECIFICATIONS & PROCEDURES article in WHEEL ALIGNMENT.

## WHEEL BEARING

**Removal (2WD Models) – 1)** Remove grease cap. *See Fig. 3.* Using hammer and chisel, remove staked area from hub nut. Remove hub nut. Remove spacer (without ABS) or ABS speed sensor rotor (with ABS). *See Fig. 3.*

***CAUTION: Use care not to damage serrations on ABS speed sensor rotor when removing.***

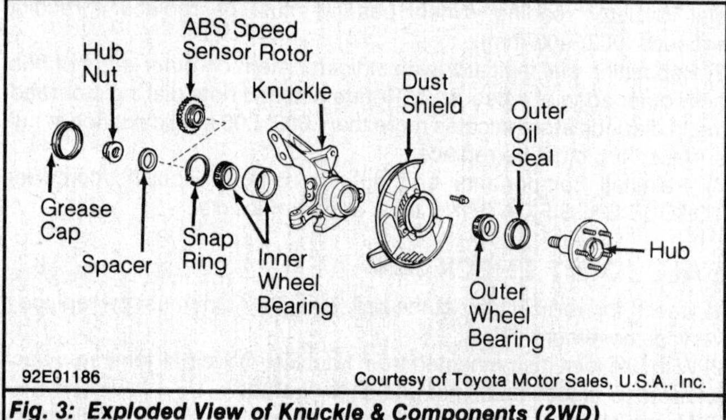


*Fig. 3: Exploded View of Knuckle & Components (2WD)*

**2)** Clamp knuckle in soft-faced vise. Using Puller (SST 09520-00031), pull hub from knuckle. Using press, and Bearing Remover (SST 09950-00020), press outer wheel bearing from hub. Remove outer oil seal from hub. Remove retaining bolts and dust shield.

**3)** Remove snap ring from rear of knuckle. Place outer wheel bearing above outer wheel bearing race on outside of knuckle. Using press and Bearing Replacing Kit (SST 09316-60010), press inner wheel bearing and wheel bearing races from knuckle.

**Installation – 1)** Using press and Bearing/Oil Seal Installer (SST 90608-10010), press new inner wheel bearing and wheel bearing races in knuckle. Install snap ring. Install outer wheel bearing in knuckle.

**2)** Using Bearing/Oil Seal Installer (SST 09608-10010), install outer oil seal in knuckle until outer oil seal is even with surface of knuckle. Install dust shield. Using press, Handle (SST 09316-00010) and bearing/oil seal installer, press hub in knuckle.

**3)** Install spacer or ABS speed sensor rotor. Install new hub nut. DO NOT reuse hub nut. Tighten hub nut to specification. See TORQUE SPECIFICATIONS table at end of article.

**4)** Stake hub nut against the hub threads. Install new grease cap. To install, remaining components, reverse removal procedure. DO NOT tighten knuckle-to-strut or ball joint-to-knuckle bolts to specification until all bolts are installed.

**5)** Tighten all fasteners to specification. See TORQUE SPECIFICATIONS table at end of article. Check wheel alignment. See SPECIFICATIONS & PROCEDURES article in WHEEL ALIGNMENT.

**Removal (4WD Models) – 1)** Clamp knuckle in soft-faced vise. Using Puller (SST 09520-00031), pull hub from knuckle. Using press, Bearing Remover/Installer (SST 09950-10012), press outer wheel bearing from hub. Remove outer oil seal from hub. Remove retaining bolts and dust shield.

**2)** Remove dust deflector. *See Fig. 4.* Using Puller (SST 09308-00010), pull inner oil seal from rear of knuckle. Remove snap ring from rear of knuckle.

# 1991 SUSPENSION
# Front – Previa (Cont.)

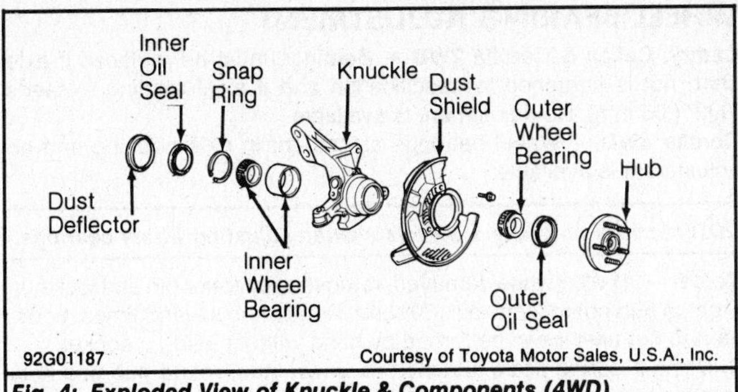


*Fig. 4: Exploded View of Knuckle & Components (4WD)*

**3)** Place outer wheel bearing above outer wheel bearing race on outside of knuckle. Using press and Bearing Replacing Kit (SST 09316-60010), press inner wheel bearing and wheel bearing races from knuckle.

**Installation – 1)** Using press and Bearing/Oil Seal Installer (SST 90608-10010), press new inner wheel bearing and wheel bearing races in knuckle. Install snap ring. Install outer wheel bearing in knuckle.

**2)** Using Bearing/Oil Seal Installer (SST 09608-10010), install outer oil seal in knuckle until outer oil seal is even with surface of knuckle. Install dust shield. Using press, Handle (SST 09316-00010) and bearing/oil seal installer, press hub in knuckle.

**3)** Using Handle (SST 09252-10010) and Oil Seal Installer (SST 09608-32010), install inner oil seal in knuckle. Using Handle (SST 09252-10010) and Dust Deflector Installer (SST 09218-56030), install dust deflector.

**4)** To install, remaining components, reverse removal procedure. DO NOT tighten knuckle-to-strut or ball joint-to-knuckle bolts to specification until all bolts are installed.

**5)** Tighten all fasteners to specification. See TORQUE SPECIFICATIONS table. Check wheel alignment. See SPECIFICATIONS & PROCEDURES article in WHEEL ALIGNMENT.

## TORQUE SPECIFICATIONS

***TORQUE SPECIFICATIONS***

| Application | Ft. Lbs. (N.m) |
|---|---|
| Axle Shaft Nut | 137 (186) |
| Ball Joint-To-Knuckle Bolt | 94 (127) |
| Ball Joint-To-Lower Control Arm Nut | 76 (103) |
| Brake Caliper Bolt | 65 (88) |
| Hub Nut | 147 (199) |
| Knuckle-To-Strut Bolt | 231 (314) |
| Lower Control Arm Bushing Retaining Nut | 141 (191) |
| Lower Control Arm Pivot Bolt | 121 (164) |
| No. 1 Lower Control Arm-To-No. 2 Lower Control Arm Bolt | 136 (184) |
| Retaining Bracket Bolt | 105 (142) |
| Stabilizer Bar Link Nut | 76 (103) |
| Stabilizer Bar Retaining Bracket Bolt | 14 (19) |
| Strut Assembly Shaft Nut | 34 (46) |
| Strut Assembly-To-Body Nut | 47 (64) |
| Tie Rod Nut | 36 (49) |
| Wheel Lug Nut | 76 (103) |
| | **INCH Lbs. (N.m)** |
| ABS Speed Sensor Bolt | 70 (8) |

# 1991 SUSPENSION
# Rear – Camry, Celica, Corolla & Tercel

## DESCRIPTION & OPERATION

On 2WD Camry, Celica and Corolla models, suspension uses MacPherson struts, fastened to rear axle carrier and wheelhousing. Wheel bearings are mounted in axle hub, bolted to rear axle carrier. *See Fig. 1.*

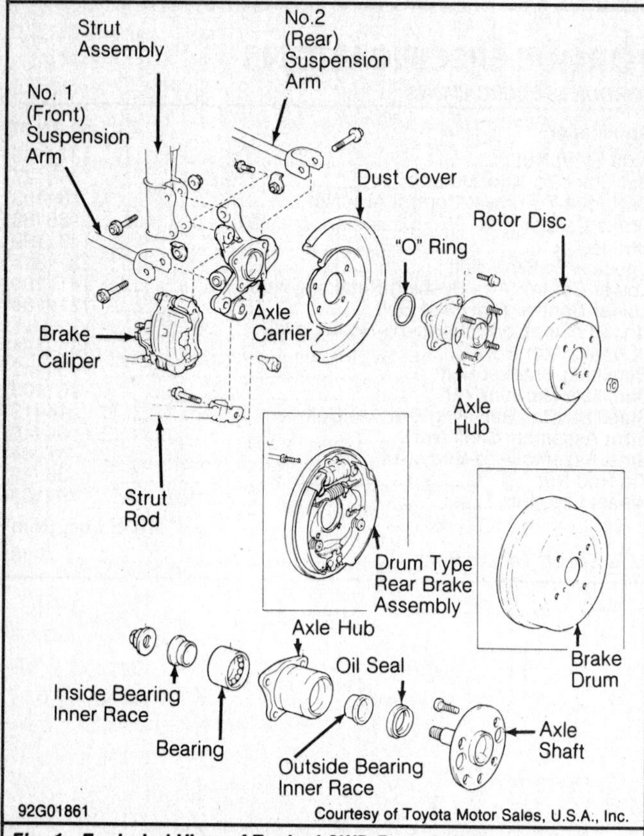


***Fig. 1: Exploded View of Typical 2WD Rear Axle Components (Camry, Celica & Corolla)***

On 4WD Camry and Celica models, suspension uses MacPherson struts, fastened to rear axle carrier and wheelhousing. Wheel bearings are mounted in axle carrier.

On 4WD Corolla models, suspension uses a solid axle with upper and lower control arms fastened to axle and the body.

Tercel models use solid axle beam with wheel bearings mounted on the axle shaft. Solid axle is supported by struts and uses a lateral control rod.

## ADJUSTMENTS & INSPECTION

### WHEEL ALIGNMENT SPECIFICATIONS & PROCEDURES

***NOTE: See SPECIFICATIONS & PROCEDURES in WHEEL ALIGNMENT article.***

### WHEEL BEARING INSPECTION

**Camry, Celica & Corolla 2WD –** Raise and support vehicle. Remove tire assembly. Place dial indicator against axle shaft. Move axle shaft in and out and note axial reading. Replace bearings if axial reading exceeds .002" (.05 mm). On Corolla, check axle hub runout using a dial indicator. Replace bearings if runout exceeds .0028" (.07 mm).

**Corolla 4WD –** Wheel bearings are mounted on axle shaft. No inspection procedure is available from manufacturer.

**Tercel –** Wheel bearing can be adjusted to obtain correct rotating torque. See WHEEL BEARING ADJUSTMENT under ADJUSTMENTS & INSPECTION.

### WHEEL BEARING ADJUSTMENT

**Camry, Celica & Corolla 2WD –** Bearings must be replaced if axle shaft nut is tightened to specification and if axial reading exceeds .002" (.05 mm). No adjustment is available.

**Corolla 4WD –** Wheel bearings are mount in axle housing and no adjustment is available.

***NOTE: Ensure no brake drag exists when adjusting wheel bearings.***

**Tercel – 1)** With wheel removed, remove cap, cotter pin and lock nut. Tighten hub nut to 22 ft. lbs. (30 N.m). Rotate hub several times. Loosen hub nut until it can be turned by hand without using a socket.

**2)** Using a spring scale attached to wheel stud, rotate hub and note rotating torque of the oil seal. Tighten axle shaft nut while rotating hub until rotating torque of oil seal and bearing is equal to oil seal rotating torque plus 0-2.6 lbs. (0-11.8 N). Install lock nut, cotter pin, cap and wheel.

## REMOVAL & INSTALLATION

### AXLE BEAM

**Removal (Tercel) – 1)** Raise and support body of vehicle. Remove tires and wheels. Remove left and right axle hubs. Remove left and right brake shoes. Disconnect parking brake cable from backing plate.

**2)** Disconnect and remove brake lines at wheel cylinders and flexible hose junction. Remove clip and separate flexible hose from bracket on axle beam.

**3)** Disconnect lateral control rod and strut from axle beam. Support axle beam. Remove axle beam-to-body bolts. Remove axle beam.

**Installation – 1)** To install, reverse removal procedure. DO NOT tighten axle beam-to-body bolts and strut assembly bolts until vehicle is at normal operating height and vehicle suspension has been bounced several times to stabilize the suspension.

**2)** Tighten all fasteners to specification. See TORQUE SPECIFICATIONS table at end of article. Fill and bleed brake system. Adjust wheel bearings. See WHEEL BEARING ADJUSTMENT under ADJUSTMENTS & INSPECTION.

### AXLE HUB, CARRIER & SHAFT

**Removal (Camry 2WD, Celica 2WD & Corolla 2WD) – 1)** Raise and support vehicle. Remove rear wheels. On models with ABS, remove rear speed sensor. On drum brake models, disconnect brake line (tube) at wheel cylinder. Plug line openings. Remove brake drum. *See Fig. 1.*

**2)** On disc brake models, remove caliper and hang aside. Remove rotor. On all applications, remove axle hub-to-axle carrier bolts, axle hub and "O" ring.

***CAUTION: Be careful not to damage ABS sensor control rotor.***

**3)** Remove nuts and bolts holding axle carrier to strut assembly and suspension arms. Note position of nuts on suspension arms and strut rods for installation reference. Remove axle carrier.

**Installation –** To install, reverse removal procedure using new "O" ring. Tighten all fasteners to specification. See TORQUE SPECIFICATIONS table at end of article. Check rear wheel alignment. Bleed brake system.

***NOTE: Tighten axle carrier-to-strut assembly and suspension arms bolts to specification with vehicle at normal operating height. Bounce vehicle several times to stabilize suspension.***

**Removal (Camry 4WD & Celica 4WD) – 1)** Raise and support vehicle. Remove wheels. Remove cotter pin and lock nut cap. With parking brake applied, remove lock nut from axle shaft.

**2)** Disconnect parking brake cable. On models with ABS, remove rear speed sensor. Remove brake caliper and secure aside. Mark axle hub-to-rotor location for reassembly reference. Remove rotor. Remove strut assembly-to-axle carrier bolts. Remove strut assembly from axle carrier. Disconnect suspension arms from axle carrier. Remove axle carrier.

***NOTE: Cover drive axle shaft boot with cloth to protect boot from damage.***

**Installation** – To install, reverse removal procedure. Tighten all fasteners to specification. See TORQUE SPECIFICATIONS table at end of article. Check rear wheel alignment. See SPECIFICATIONS & PROCEDURES article in WHEEL ALIGNMENT.

***NOTE: Tighten axle carrier-to-strut assembly and suspension arms bolts to specification with vehicle at normal operating height. Bounce vehicle several times to stabilize suspension.***

### STRUT ASSEMBLY

**Removal (Camry, Celica & Corolla 2WD)** – **1)** Raise and support vehicle. On vehicles with ABS, disconnect speed sensor wire from strut. Remove clip and brake line at strut. On disc brakes, remove brake caliper and secure aside.

**2)** Disconnect stabilizer bar link (if equipped) from strut. Support axle carrier with jack.

***NOTE: If disassembling strut assembly, loosen but DO NOT remove strut assembly shaft nut before removing strut assembly.***

**3)** Remove strut assembly-to-axle carrier bolts. Remove strut assembly-to-body retaining nuts. Remove strut assembly.

**Inspection** – While pushing strut piston rod, ensure pull throughout stroke is even and there is no abnormal resistance and noise. Push piston rod in fully and release. Ensure that piston returns at a constant speed throughout. If shock is defective, replace as an assembly.

***CAUTION: To prevent personal injury, discharge gas in shock absorber. Drill a hole .079-.118" (2-3 mm) in diameter above lower mounting bracket on cylinder.***

**Installation** – To install, reverse removal procedure. Tighten fasteners to specification. See TORQUE SPECIFICATIONS table at end of article. Bleed brake system (if necessary).

**Removal & Installation (Tercel)** – Remove rear seat cushion and seat back. Raise and support body of vehicle. Remove strut-to-axle beam bolt. Remove strut assembly-to-body nuts. Remove strut assembly. To install, reverse removal procedure. Tighten fasteners to specification. See TORQUE SPECIFICATIONS table at end of article.

### SHOCK ABSORBER

**Removal & Installation (Corolla 4WD)** – **1)** Raise and support body of vehicle. Support axle housing with jack. Remove shock absorber-to-axle housing beam bolt. Remove shock absorber-to-body nuts. Remove shock absorber.

**2)** To install, reverse removal procedure. Tighten fasteners to specification. See TORQUE SPECIFICATIONS table at end of article.

### SUSPENSION ARMS

**Removal (Camry, Celica & Corolla 2WD)** – Raise and support vehicle. On vehicles with ABS, disconnect speed sensor wire clamp from suspension arms. Remove strut rod and suspension arms from axle carrier. Remove fuel tank protector. Place match marks on cam plate, No. 2 (rear) suspension arm, and body for reassembly reference. Remove remaining suspension arm retaining bolts. Remove suspension arms.

***NOTE: Note direction of suspension arm installation for reassembly reference.***

**Installation** – **1)** To install, reverse removal procedure. Ensure components are installed in original location.

***NOTE: On Camry, right and left suspension arms are marked with an "R" (right) or "L" (left) for installation purposes. Install No. 1 (front) suspension arm with slit bushing area toward rear of vehicle and White-paint area toward outside of vehicle.***

**2)** Temporarily install all bolts, but DO NOT tighten. Install wheels and lower vehicle. Bounce vehicle to stabilize suspension.

**3)** Ensure reference marks are aligned on cam plate, No. 2 (rear) suspension arm and body. Tighten bolts to specification with vehicle resting on suspension. See TORQUE SPECIFICATIONS table at end of article. Check rear wheel alignment. See SPECIFICATIONS & PROCEDURES article in WHEEL ALIGNMENT.

### CONTROL ARMS

**Removal & Installation (Corolla 4WD)** – **1)** Raise and support vehicle. Support axle housing using jack. Remove control arm retaining bolts and control arms. *See Fig. 3.*

**2)** Temporarily install all bolts, but DO NOT tighten. Install wheels, and lower vehicle. Bounce vehicle to stabilize suspension. Tighten bolts to specification with vehicle resting on suspension. See TORQUE SPECIFICATIONS table at end of article.

### COIL SPRING

**Removal (Corolla 4WD)** – **1)** Raise and support body of vehicle. Support axle housing with jack. Remove shock absorber-to-axle housing beam bolt. Disconnect stabilizer bar and lateral control rod from axle housing.

**2)** Slightly lower axle housing. Remove coil spring and insulators. It may be necessary to disconnect brake lines to lower axle housing.

**Installation** – **1)** To install, reverse removal procedure. Ensure coil spring fully seats in the insulators.

**2)** Temporarily install lateral control rod bolts, bolts but DO NOT tighten. Install wheels and lower vehicle. Bounce vehicle to stabilize suspension. Tighten all bolts to specification with vehicle resting on suspension. See TORQUE SPECIFICATIONS table at end of article.

### STABILIZER BAR

**Removal (Camry, Celica & Corolla)** – Raise and support vehicle. Remove wheels. On Camry and Celica, use a jack and a wooden block to support fuel tank. Remove tank band bolts from body. Slightly lower fuel tank. On all models, disconnect stabilizer bar from stabilizer bar link. Remove stabilizer bar mount brackets from body. Remove stabilizer bar.

**Installation** – To install, reverse removal procedure. Tighten bolts to specification. See TORQUE SPECIFICATIONS table at end of article.

### LATERAL CONTROL ROD

**Removal & Installation (Corolla 4WD & Tercel)** – **1)** Raise and support vehicle. Disconnect lateral control rod from axle housing and body. Remove lateral control rod. *See Figs. 2 and 3.*

**2)** To install, reverse removal procedure. Temporarily install lateral control rod bolts, but DO NOT tighten. Lower vehicle. Bounce vehicle to stabilize suspension. Tighten all bolts to specification with vehicle resting on suspension. See TORQUE SPECIFICATIONS table at end of article.

### WHEEL BEARINGS

**Removal (Camry 2WD, Celica 2WD & Corolla 2WD)** – **1)** Raise and support vehicle. Remove rear wheels. Remove axle hub-to-axle carrier bolts, axle hub and "O" ring.

**2)** Using hammer and chisel, loosen staked part of axle shaft nut. Remove axle nut. Using Puller (09950-20017), remove axle shaft from axle hub. Remove inside bearing inner race. Using puller, remove outside bearing inner race from axle shaft. Remove oil seal. Press bearing from axle hub.

**Installation** – **1)** Coat outside of new bearing with grease. Press new bearing into axle hub. Install outside bearing inner race.

**2)** Coat oil seal lip with grease. Drive oil seal into axle hub. Install inside bearing inner race. Using Adapter (09636-20010), press inner races onto axle shaft. Tighten axle shaft nut to specification. See TORQUE SPECIFICATIONS table at end of article.

**3)** To install remaining components, reverse removal procedure. Tighten all bolts to specification. See TORQUE SPECIFICATIONS table at end of article.

# 1991 SUSPENSION
# Rear – Camry, Celica, Corolla & Tercel (Cont.)

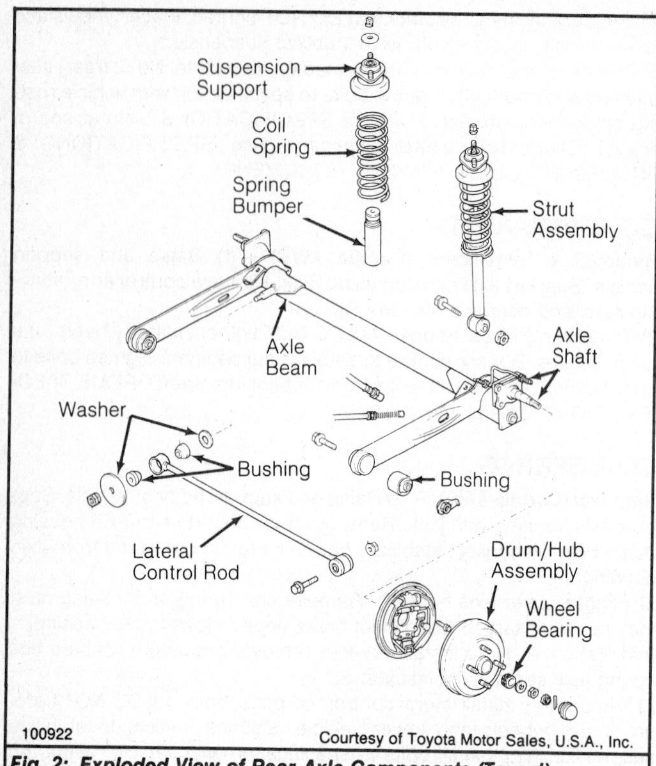


**Fig. 2: Exploded View of Rear Axle Components (Tercel)**

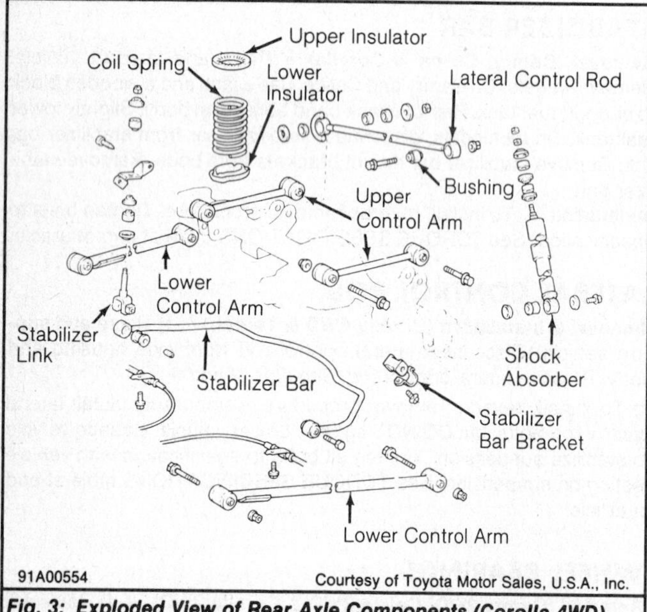


**Fig. 3: Exploded View of Rear Axle Components (Corolla 4WD)**

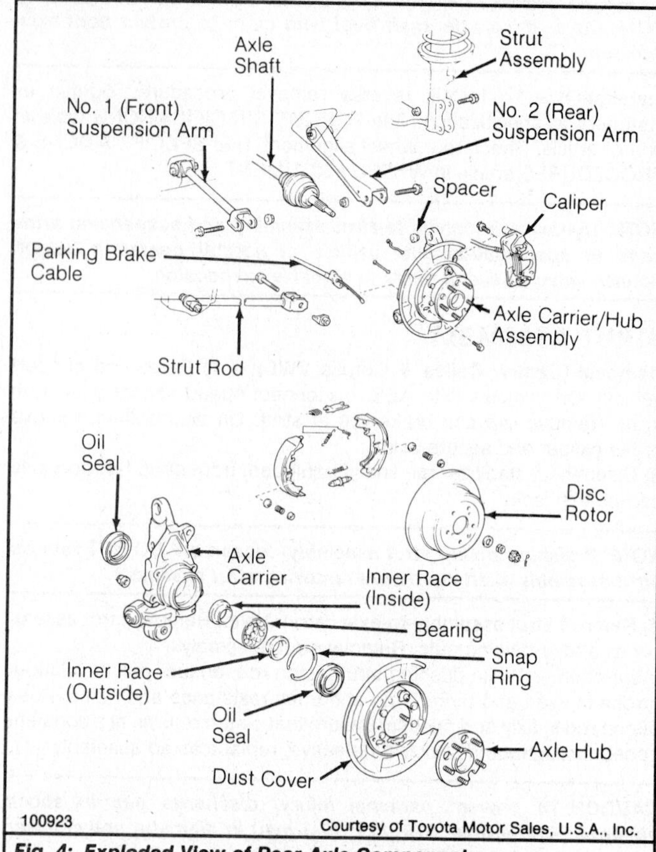


**Fig. 4: Exploded View of Rear Axle Components (Camry 4WD & Celica 4WD)**

***NOTE: Stake axle shaft nut after tightening to specification.***

**Removal (Camry 4WD & Celica 4WD) – 1)** Remove rear axle hub and carrier. See AXLE HUB, CARRIER & SHAFT under REMOVAL & INSTALLATION.

**2)** Using Puller (09950-20017), press axle hub from axle carrier. Using puller, remove outside bearing inner race from axle hub. Remove dust cover. *See Fig. 4.*

**3)** Using Puller (09308-00010), remove inner and outer oil seals from axle carrier. Remove snap ring from axle carrier. Using press and Bearing Remover (09636-20010), press bearing from axle carrier.

**Installation – 1)** Using press and Bearing Installer (09309-36010), press bearing into axle carrier. Install snap ring.

**2)** Coat inner and outer oil seals lip with grease. Using Seal Installer (09608-30012), install new outer oil seal. Install dust cover. Using bearing installer, press axle hub into axle carrier. Using seal installer, install new inner oil seal.

**3)** To install remaining components, reverse removal procedure. Tighten all bolts to specification. See TORQUE SPECIFICATIONS table at end of article.

**Removal (Corolla 4WD) – 1)** Raise and support vehicle. Remove wheel and brake drum. Remove axle shaft retaining nuts. Using Puller (09520-00031), pull axle shaft and gasket from axle housing.

**2)** Using Puller (09308-00010), pull seal from axle housing. Grind down bearing retainer on outside of wheel bearing. Using hammer and chisel, split bearing retainer and remove from axle shaft.

**3)** Support bearing in a press using Bearing Remover (09527-21011). Press axle shaft from wheel bearing.

**Installation – 1)** Using Bearing Replacer (09515-21010), press new bearing on axle shaft. Heat bearing retainer in oil to approximately 302°F (150°C). Press bearing retainer on axle shaft with beveled side away from wheel bearing.

**2)** Coat seal lip with grease. Using Seal Installer (09517-12010), install seal in axle housing. Seal must be positioned .220" (5.58 mm) below outer edge of axle housing.

**3)** Coat both sides of axle shaft gasket with sealant. Install axle shaft and gasket. Gasket must be installed with notch facing downward. Tighten axle shaft retaining nuts to specification. See TORQUE SPECIFICATIONS table at end of article.

**Removal (Tercel) –** Raise and support vehicle. Remove wheel. Remove dust cap, cotter pin, lock nut and washer. Remove brake drum/hub assembly with outer bearing. Remove outer bearing. Using Seal Remover (09308-00010), remove oil seal from drum/hub assembly. Remove inner bearing. Using a brass drift and hammer, remove bearing races.

**Installation – 1)** Using Installer (09608-30012) for inner bearing race and (09550-10012) for outer bearing race, install races. Pack bearings and center of hub with grease. Install inner bearing in drum/hub.

# 1991 SUSPENSION
# Rear – Camry, Celica, Corolla & Tercel (Cont.)

**2)** Coat oil seal lip with grease. Using Seal Installer (09550-10012), install oil seal in drum/hub. Install drum/hub and outer bearing. Adjust wheel bearings. See WHEEL BEARING ADJUSTMENT under ADJUSTMENTS & INSPECTION.

## STRUT ROD

**Removal & Installation (Camry, Celica & Corolla 2WD) – 1)** Raise and support vehicle. Remove wheels. Remove nuts and bolts holding strut rod to axle carrier and body. Remove strut rod.
**2)** To install, connect but DO NOT tighten strut rod to body and to axle carrier. Temporarily install all bolts, but DO NOT tighten. Lower vehicle. Bounce vehicle to stabilize suspension. Tighten all bolts to specification with vehicle resting on suspension. See TORQUE SPECIFICATIONS table.

## TORQUE SPECIFICATIONS

*TORQUE SPECIFICATIONS*

| Application | Ft. Lbs. (N.m) |
|---|---|
| **Camry 2WD & Celica 2WD** | |
| Axle Hub-To-Axle Carrier Bolt | 59 (80) |
| Axle Shaft Nut | 90 (122) |
| Stabilizer Bar Link Nut | |
| Camry | 47 (64) |
| Celica | 26 (35) |
| Stabilizer Bar Mount Bolt | 14 (19) |
| Strut Rod Bolt | 83 (113) |
| Strut-To-Axle Carrier Bolt | 188 (255) |
| Strut-To-Body Nut | 29 (39) |
| Suspension Arm-To-Axle Carrier Bolt | 134 (182) |
| Suspension Arm-To-Body Bolt | |
| Camry | 83 (113) |
| Celica | |
| No. 1 (Front) Arm | 83 (113) |
| No. 2 (Rear) Arm | 64 (87) |
| Suspension Arm-To-Body Nut | |
| Celica | |
| No. 2 (Rear) Arm | 166 (226) |
| Wheel Lug Nut | 76 (103) |

*TORQUE SPECIFICATIONS (Cont.)*

| Application | Ft. Lbs. (N.m) |
|---|---|
| **Camry 4WD & Celica 4WD** | |
| Axle Shaft Nut | 137 (186) |
| Strut Rod Bolt | 83 (113) |
| Strut-To-Axle Carrier Bolt | 188 (255) |
| Strut-To-Body Nut | 29 (39) |
| Suspension Arm-To-Axle Carrier Bolt | 90 (122) |
| Suspension Arm-To-Body Bolt | 83 (113) |
| Wheel Lug Nut | 76 (103) |
| **Corolla 2WD** | |
| Axle Shaft Nut | 90 (122) |
| Axle Hub-To-Axle Carrier Bolt | 59 (80) |
| No. 1 (Front) Suspension Arm | |
| Axle Carrier Bolt | 65 (88) |
| Body Mount Bolt | 65 (88) |
| No. 2 (Rear) Suspension Arm | |
| Axle Carrier Bolt | 65 (88) |
| Body Mount Bolt | 80 (109) |
| Stabilizer Bar Link Nut | 26 (35) |
| Stabilizer Bar Mount Bolt | 14 (19) |
| Strut Rod Bolt | 65 (88) |
| Strut-To-Body Nut | 29 (39) |
| Wheel Lug Nut | 76 (103) |
| **Corolla 4WD** | |
| Axle Shaft Nut | 48 (65) |
| Control Arm-To-Body Bolt | 72 (98) |
| Lateral Control Rod-To-Axle Nut | 47 (64) |
| Lateral Control Rod-To-Body Bolt | 72 (98) |
| Shock Absorber | |
| Lower Bolt | 27 (37) |
| Upper Nut | 18 (24) |
| Stabilizer Bar Mount Bolt | 27 (37) |
| Stabilizer Bar-To-Stabilizer Link Bolt | 22 (30) |
| Wheel Lug Nut | 76 (103) |
| **Tercel** | |
| Axle Beam-To-Body Bolt | 105 (142) |
| Backing Plate Bolt | 34 (47) |
| Lateral Control Rod-To-Axle Beam Nut | 43 (59) |
| Lateral Control Rod-To-Body Nut | 83 (113) |
| Strut-To-Axle Beam Bolt | 50 (68) |
| Strut-To-Body Bolt | 29 (39) |
| Wheel Lug Nut | 76 (103) |

# 1991 SUSPENSION
# Rear – Cressida

## DESCRIPTION & OPERATION

Rear suspension is fully independent type utilizing MacPherson struts. Suspension arms are mounted by bushings and pivot bolts to body and axle carrier. *See Fig. 1*. The stabilizer bar attaches to the differential support member and suspension arms.

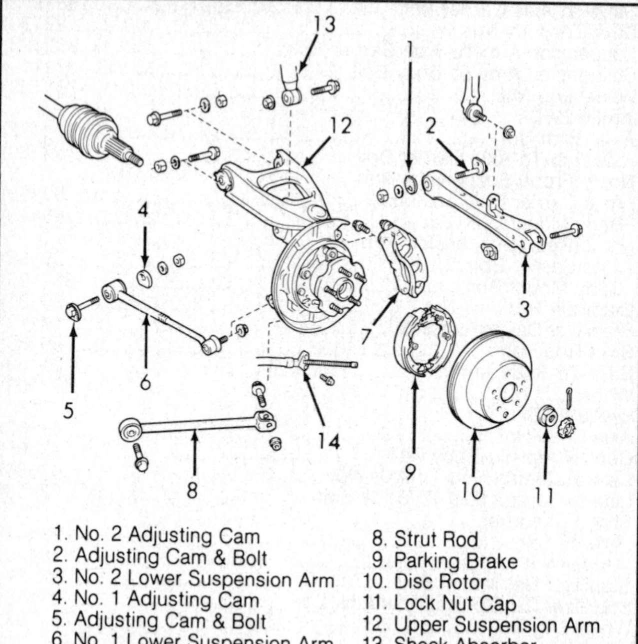


***Fig. 1: Identifying Rear Suspension Components***

## ADJUSTMENTS & INSPECTION

### WHEEL ALIGNMENT SPECIFICATIONS & PROCEDURES

***NOTE: See SPECIFICATIONS & PROCEDURES article in WHEEL ALIGNMENT.***

### WHEEL BEARING

Wheel bearings are not adjustable. Whenever bearings, races or oil seals are removed, measure axial play when reassembled. Maximum axial play is .002" (.05 mm). Replace bearing assembly if play exceeds specification.

### BALL JOINT CHECKING

**1)** Check turning torque of upper ball joint with ball joint removed from vehicle. Flip ball joint stud back and forth 5 times. Install stud nut. Using an INCH-pound torque wrench, check ball joint turning torque.
**2)** Turn ball joint stud nut one turn every 2-4 seconds, and take torque reading on fifth turn. Ball joint torque should be 9-30 INCH lbs. (1.0-3.4 N.m). Replace ball joint if not within specification. See UPPER SUSPENSION ARM under REMOVAL & INSTALLATION.

***NOTE: If ball joint is defective, ball joint and upper arm must be replaced as an assembly.***

## REMOVAL & INSTALLATION

### LOWER SUSPENSION ARM & STRUT ROD

**Removal – 1)** Raise and support vehicle. Remove wheels. Disconnect strut rod from axle carrier. Remove strut rod. Mark No. 1 lower suspension arm adjusting cam and frame for installation reference. Remove adjusting cam. *See Fig. 1*.
**2)** Remove axle carrier-to-lower suspension arm. Disconnect and remove No. 1 suspension arm using Puller (09628-10011). Disconnect stabilizer link from No. 2 lower suspension arm. Mark adjusting cam and frame for installation reference. Remove adjusting cam. Remove No. 2 lower suspension arm.
**Installation – 1)** To install, reverse removal procedure. Install, but DO NOT tighten, No. 2 lower suspension arm-to-axle carrier bolts, No. 1 and 2 adjusting cams and strut rod-to-axle carrier bolts.
**2)** Install wheels, and lower vehicle. Bounce vehicle up and down to stabilize suspension. Tighten No. 2 lower suspension arm-to-axle carrier bolts, No. 1 and 2 adjusting cams and strut rod-to-axle carrier bolts to specification.
**3)** Ensure all nuts and bolts are tightened to specification. See TORQUE SPECIFICATIONS table at end of article. Check rear wheel alignment. See SPECIFICATIONS & PROCEDURES article in WHEEL ALIGNMENT.

### SHOCK ABSORBER & COIL SPRING

**Removal – 1)** Raise and support vehicle. Remove wheels. Using a jack, support rear axle carrier. Disconnect strut rod-to-frame bolt. Remove shock absorber-to-carrier mount nut. DO NOT remove bolt yet.
**2)** Remove rear seat and package tray trim. Remove shock absorber cap. Loosen, but DO NOT remove, shock absorber rod nut. Remove suspension support nuts. Lower jack. Remove shock absorber-to-carrier mount bolt. Push rear axle carrier down and remove shock absorber.
**Disassembly –** Using spring compressor, compress coil spring. Remove shock absorber rod nut, suspension support, coil spring and bumper. *See Fig. 2*.

***NOTE: If shock absorber is being replaced, release gas before discarding shock absorber. Drill two .079-.118" (2.00-3.00 mm) holes, one .39" (10 mm) from top of shock absorber and other .79" (20 mm) from bottom of shock absorber base.***

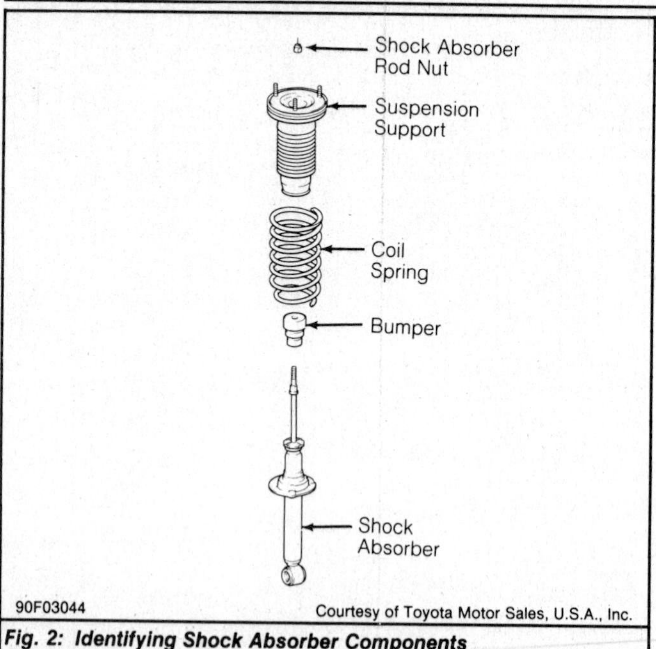


***Fig. 2: Identifying Shock Absorber Components***

**Inspection –** Check shock absorber operation. While pushing piston rod, ensure resistance throughout piston stroke is even and no abnormal resistance or noise exists. Replace shock absorber as required.
**Reassembly & Installation – 1)** Assemble strut. Align and install suspension support with piston rod. *See Fig. 3*. Install, but DO NOT tighten, shock absorber rod nut and shock absorber-to-carrier bolt. To

# 1991 SUSPENSION
# Rear – Cressida (Cont.)

complete installation, reverse removal procedure. Install wheels, and lower vehicle.

**2)** Bounce vehicle up and down to stabilize suspension. Tighten shock absorber rod nut and shock absorber-to-carrier bolt. Ensure all nuts and bolts are tightened to specification. See TORQUE SPECIFICATIONS table at end of article. Check rear wheel alignment. See SPECIFICATIONS & PROCEDURES article in WHEEL ALIGNMENT.

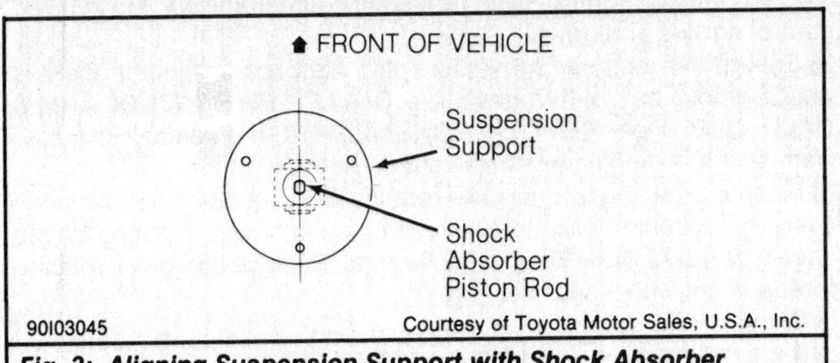


***Fig. 3: Aligning Suspension Support with Shock Absorber Piston Rod***

## STABILIZER BAR

**Removal** – Raise and support vehicle. Remove wheels. Disconnect stabilizer bar link from No. 1 lower suspension arm. Remove stabilizer bar bracket. Remove stabilizer bar from frame. Remove stabilizer bar link from stabilizer bar.

**Inspection** – Inspect stabilizer bar link. Move ball joint arm in all directions. If movement is not smooth and free, replace stabilizer bar link.

**Installation** – To install, reverse removal procedure. Tighten all nuts and bolts to specification. See TORQUE SPECIFICATIONS table at end of article. Check rear wheel alignment. See SPECIFICATIONS & PROCEDURES article in WHEEL ALIGNMENT.

## UPPER SUSPENSION ARM

**Removal – 1)** Raise and support vehicle. Remove rear wheels. Remove brake caliper, and wire aside. Remove brake disc rotor.

**2)** Remove rear drive shaft and parking brake assembly. Disconnect No. 1 (front) and 2 (rear) lower suspension arms from axle carrier. *See Fig. 1.*

**3)** Disconnect strut rod. Disconnect bottom of strut assembly. Disconnect upper suspension arm from frame, and remove axle carrier assembly with upper arm. Separate upper suspension arm from axle carrier.

**Inspection** – Check upper suspension arm ball joint turning torque. See BALL JOINT CHECKING under ADJUSTMENTS & INSPECTION.

**Installation – 1)** To install, reverse removal procedure. Install, but DO NOT tighten, upper suspension arm-to-frame, axle hub assembly-to-upper suspension arm, No. 2 lower suspension arm and strut rod bolts.

**2)** Install wheels, and lower vehicle. Bounce vehicle up and down to stabilize suspension. Tighten upper suspension arm-to-frame, axle hub assembly-to-upper suspension arm, No. 2 lower suspension arm and strut rod bolts to specification.

**3)** Ensure all nuts and bolts are tightened to specification. See TORQUE SPECIFICATIONS table at end of article. Check rear wheel alignment. See SPECIFICATIONS & PROCEDURES article in WHEEL ALIGNMENT.

## WHEEL BEARING & AXLE CARRIER

**Removal – 1)** Raise and support vehicle. Remove rear wheels. Remove brake caliper, and wire aside. Remove brake disc rotor.

**2)** Remove rear drive shaft and parking brake assembly. Disconnect No. 1 (front) and 2 (rear) lower suspension arms from axle carrier.

**3)** Disconnect strut rod. Disconnect bottom of strut assembly. Disconnect upper suspension arm from frame, and remove axle carrier assembly with upper arm. *See Fig. 4*. Separate upper suspension arm from axle carrier.

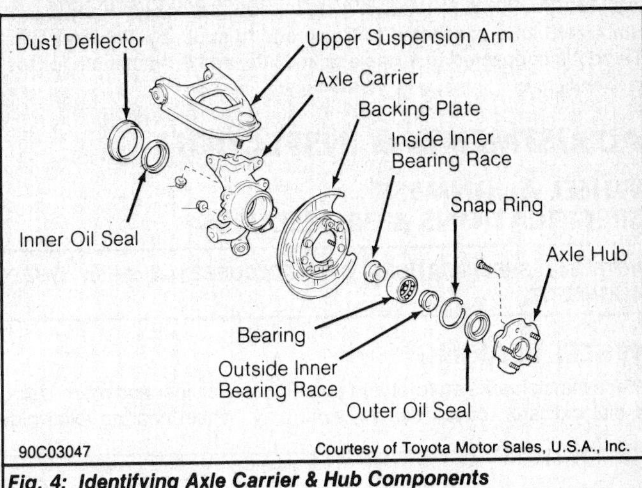


***Fig. 4: Identifying Axle Carrier & Hub Components***

**4)** Using a screwdriver, remove deflector and inner oil seal from axle carrier.

**5)** Remove axle hub using Hub Puller (09950-20017). Remove backing plate from axle carrier. Remove inner bearing race from axle hub using hub puller. Remove outer oil seal using a screwdriver, and remove snap ring.

**6)** Remove bearing from axle carrier using Driver (09608-35014).

**Installation – 1)** Pack new bearings with grease. Using Drivers (09316-60010 and 09608-32010), press new bearings into axle housing and install new snap ring.

**2)** Using Driver (09608-32010), drive in new outer oil seal. Using Driver (09223-15010), drive in new inner oil seal. Install backing plate to axle carrier. Using Driver (09608-35014), press axle carrier with bearing over hub. To complete installation, reverse removal procedure.

## TORQUE SPECIFICATIONS

***TORQUE SPECIFICATIONS***

| Application | Ft. Lbs. (N.m) |
|---|---|
| Backing Plate Bolts | 43 (58) |
| Ball Joint-To-Axle Carrier Nut | 80 (108) |
| Caliper Mount Bolts | 34 (46) |
| Hub Nut | 203 (275) |
| No. 1 Lower Suspension Arm-To-Axle Carrier Bolts | 36 (49) |
| No. 1 Lower Suspension Arm-To-Frame Bolts | 134 (181) |
| No. 2 Lower Suspension Arm-To- | |
| Axle Carrier Bolts | 119 (162) |
| Stabilizer Bar Link Bolts | 43 (58) |
| Frame Bolts | 134 (181) |
| Shock Absorber | |
| Cap Nuts | 8 (10) |
| Rod Nut | 20 (27) |
| Shock Absorber-To-Carrier Mount Nut | 101 (137) |
| Stabilizer Bar Frame Mount Bolts | 26 (35) |
| Strut Rod Bolts | 105 (142) |
| Suspension Support Nuts | 21 (28) |
| Upper Suspension Arm Bolts | 119 (162) |

# 1991 SUSPENSION
# Rear - MR2

## DESCRIPTION

Rear suspension is an independent type using MacPherson struts. Strut assembly is comprised of coil springs and gas strut cartridges. Lower end of strut is connected to upper end of knuckle. Lower end of knuckle is connected to ball joint, which is bolted to lower control arm. Lower control arm is connected to frame and to strut rod.

Stabilizer bar is connected to frame and to struts by stabilizer links. Tie rod is connected to frame and knuckle, and is adjustable for toe-in. *See Fig. 1.*

## ADJUSTMENTS & INSPECTION

### WHEEL ALIGNMENT SPECIFICATIONS & PROCEDURES

***NOTE:* See *SPECIFICATIONS & PROCEDURES* article in *WHEEL ALIGNMENT*.**

### WHEEL BEARING

Place match marks on rotor and hub. Remove caliper and rotor. Using a dial indicator, check bearing axial play. Wheel bearing axial play should be .002" (.05 mm). Replace wheel bearing if axial play is greater than .002" (.05 mm).

### BALL JOINT CHECKING

**1)** Raise and support rear of vehicle. Place 7-8" thick block of wood under one rear wheel. Lower vehicle until there is about 1/2 normal load on rear coil spring. Place jack stands under vehicle. Move lower control arm up and down.

**2)** Ensure ball joint has no vertical play. Replace ball joint if there is play. Remove ball joint from vehicle. See LOWER CONTROL ARM & BALL JOINT under REMOVAL & INSTALLATION. Push ball joint stud from side to side 5 times. Install nut on ball joint stud.

**3)** Measure rotating torque while rotating ball joint stud one revolution every 2-4 seconds. Take torque reading on fifth turn. Rotating torque should be 13-26 INCH lbs. (1.47-2.94 N.m). Replace ball joint if rotating torque is not within specification.

## REMOVAL & INSTALLATION

### HUB & KNUCKLE ASSEMBLY

**Removal - 1)** Remove cotter pin and bearing lock nut cap. Apply parking brake. Remove hub nut and washer. *See Fig. 2.* Place match

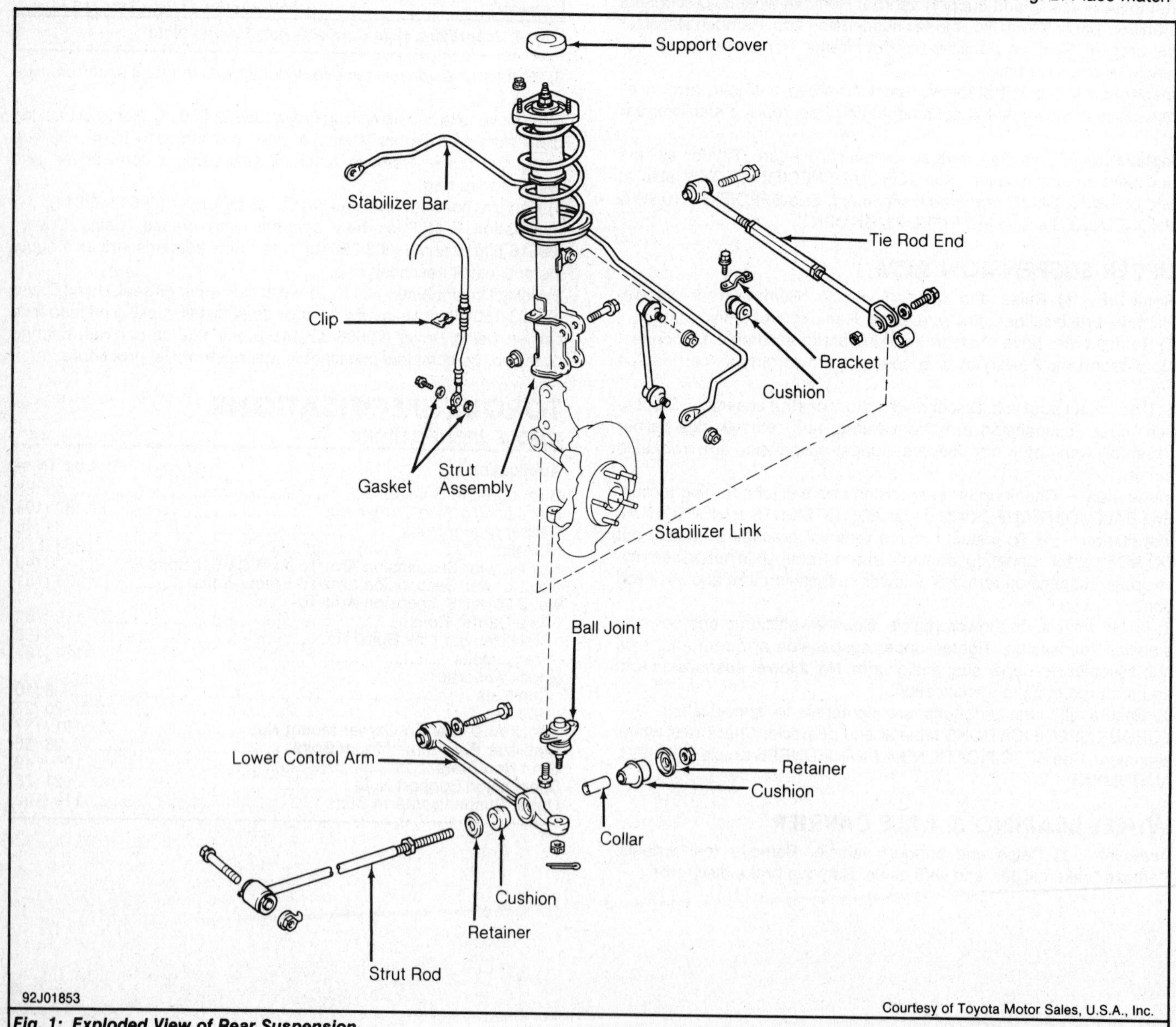


***Fig. 1:* Exploded View of Rear Suspension**

marks on rotor and hub. Remove caliper, and support it with wire. Remove rotor. Disconnect stabilizer link from strut assembly. Use a 5-mm Allen wrench to hold stud if necessary.
**2)** Remove speed sensor from knuckle (if equipped). Remove 2 bolts holding ball joint to knuckle. Disconnect tie rod from knuckle. Remove 2 bolts retaining knuckle to strut, and remove knuckle. Cover drive shaft boot to protect it from damage.

***CAUTION: Ensure speed sensor rotor on drive shaft is not damaged during removal.***

**Disassembly – 1)** Clamp knuckle in a soft-jawed vise. Remove dust deflector using a screwdriver. *See Fig. 3.* Remove snap ring from knuckle. Remove 3 bolts retaining dust shield to knuckle. Using a puller and slide hammer, remove hub. Remove dust shield.
**2)** Remove inner bearing inner race. Remove outer bearing inner race from hub using a press and bearing plate. Position inner bearing inner race on bearing in knuckle. Using a press and Adapters (09310-35010 and 09527-17101), press bearing from knuckle.
**Reassembly –** Using press and Adapter (09710-22041), install new bearing into knuckle. Install disc brake dust shield. Tighten bolts to specification. See TORQUE SPECIFICATIONS table at end of article. Press hub into knuckle. Install snap ring, being careful not to damage bearing. Install dust deflector.
**Installation –** To install, reverse removal procedure. Tighten mounting bolts to specification. See TORQUE SPECIFICATIONS table at end of article.

## LOWER CONTROL ARM & BALL JOINT

**Removal –** Remove cotter pin and castle nut from ball joint. Separate ball joint from lower control arm using a puller. Remove strut rod nut and retainer from lower control arm. Remove bolt attaching lower control arm to body, and remove lower control arm. Remove cushion, collar and retainer. Unbolt ball joint from knuckle.
**Installation –** To install, reverse removal procedure. Tighten lower control arm-to-strut rod nut and lower control arm-to-body bolt to specification with vehicle suspension at normal riding height. See TORQUE SPECIFICATIONS table at end of article.

## LOWER CONTROL ARM BUSHINGS

Bushing replacement information is not available from manufacturer.

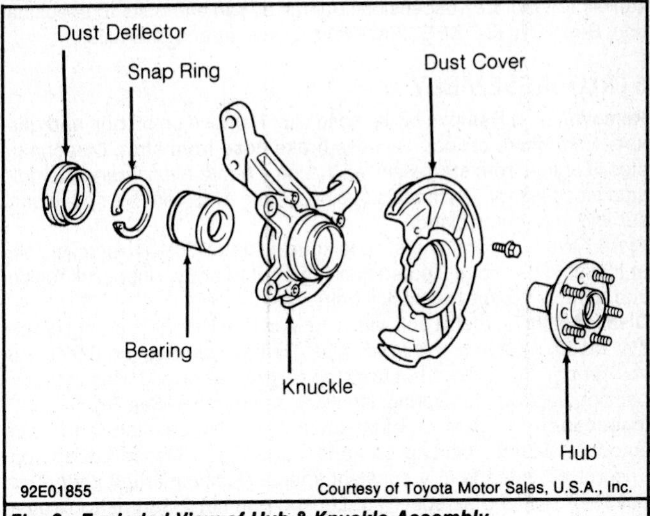


***Fig. 3: Exploded View of Hub & Knuckle Assembly***

## STABILIZER BAR & LINKS

**Removal – 1)** Remove nut, and disconnect stabilizer link from stabilizer bar. Use a 5-mm Allen wrench to hold stud if necessary. Remove speed sensor bracket (if equipped). Remove 2 bolts holding lower control arm to ball joint. Disconnect ball joint.
**2)** Disconnect tie rod end from knuckle. Disconnect exhaust pipe hanger from rear suspension. Disconnect rear engine mount from rear suspension crossmember. Support rear suspension crossmember. Remove rear suspension crossmember bolts and lower crossmember. Remove stabilizer bar brackets from crossmember.
**3)** Remove stabilizer bar. Remove brackets and cushions from stabilizer bar. Remove stabilizer links from strut assemblies. Use a 5-mm Allen wrench to hold stud if necessary.
**Inspection –** Inspect stabilizer link ball joints. Rotate ball joint stud in all directions. Replace stabilizer link if stud does not rotate smoothly, without binding.
**Installation –** Install stabilizer bar bushings so that bushings touch painted marks on bar. To complete installation, reverse removal procedure. Tighten bolts and nuts to specification. Lower vehicle. Bounce

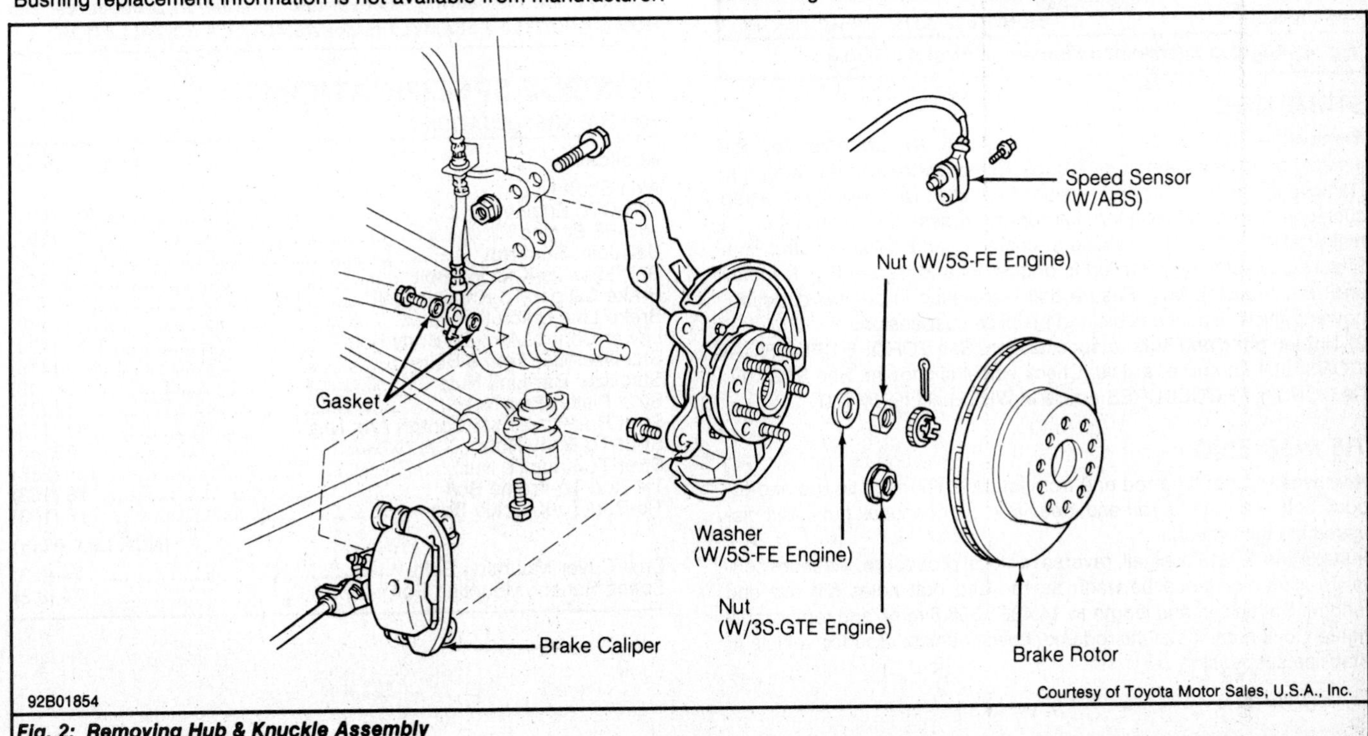


***Fig. 2: Removing Hub & Knuckle Assembly***

# 1991 SUSPENSION
# Rear – MR2 (Cont.)

vehicle to stabilize suspension. Tighten tie rod end bolts to specification. See TORQUE SPECIFICATIONS table at end of article.

## STRUT ASSEMBLY

**Removal – 1)** Remove brake hose clip. Remove union bolt and gaskets from brake caliper. Remove brake hose from strut. Disconnect stabilizer link from strut. *See Fig. 1*. Use a 5-mm Allen wrench to hold stud if necessary. On models equipped with ABS, remove speed sensor wiring harness clamp.

**2)** Remove nuts retaining strut to knuckle, but DO NOT remove bolts at this time. Remove 3 nuts attaching strut to body. Support knuckle, and remove 2 strut-to-knuckle bolts.

**Disassembly –** Install bolt with 2 nuts on lower strut mounting brackets. Clamp strut in a soft-jawed vise. Remove strut cover. Compress coil spring, and remove nut from top of strut piston rod. Remove suspension support, coil spring, insulator and bumper. *See Fig. 5*.

**Inspection –** Push in on strut piston rod. Ensure piston rod moves smoothly without binding or abnormal noise. Release piston rod. Ensure rod extends at a constant speed. Replace strut if piston rod does not respond as specified. Loosen ring nut 2-3 turns to release gas pressure before discarding strut.

**Reassembly –** To reassemble, reverse disassembly procedure. Align suspension support with strut lower mounting brackets. *See Fig. 4*. Tighten strut piston rod nut to specification. See TORQUE SPECIFICATIONS table at end of article.

**Installation –** To install, reverse removal procedure. Ensure drive axle boot is not damaged during installation. Tighten nuts and bolts to specification. See TORQUE SPECIFICATIONS table at end of article. Ensure brake hose lock pin is inserted into lock pin hole in caliper.

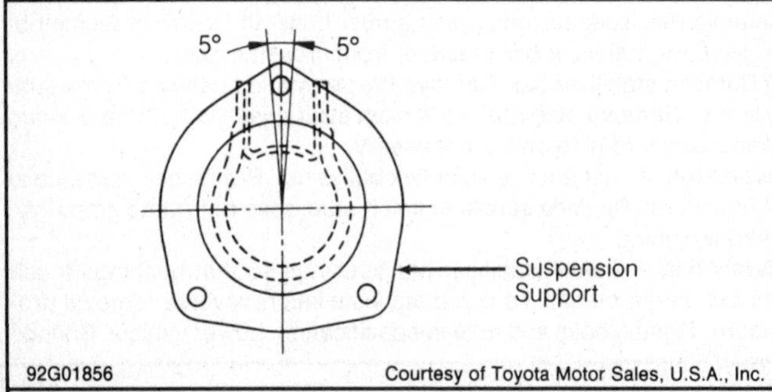


*Fig. 4: Aligning Suspension Support on Strut Assembly*

## STRUT ROD

**Removal –** Remove strut rod retaining bolt. Note direction of bolt installation for reassembly reference. Remove strut rod retaining nut. Remove cushion, collar and retainer from strut rod. *See Fig. 1*. Keep cushions, collar and retainers in order for reassembly reference.

**Installation – 1)** Install retainers, cushions and collar on strut rod. Ensure cushions are installed in original locations. *See Fig. 1*. Install strut rod retaining bolt. Ensure bolt is installed in original direction. Lower vehicle. Bounce vehicle to stabilize suspension.

**2)** Tighten bolts and nuts to specification. See TORQUE SPECIFICATIONS table at end of article. Check wheel alignment. See SPECIFICATIONS & PROCEDURES article in WHEEL ALIGNMENT.

## TIE ROD END

**Removal –** Unbolt tie rod end from knuckle. Remove tie rod end-to-body bolt. Remove tie rod end. *See Fig. 1*. Loosen lock nuts, and disassemble tie rod ends.

**Installation – 1)** To install, reverse removal procedure. Measure center-to-center distance between tie rod end bolt holes (tie rod end length). Set tie rod end length to 14.433" (366.6 mm), and temporarily tighten lock nuts. Install tie rod end. Lower vehicle. Bounce vehicle to stabilize suspension.

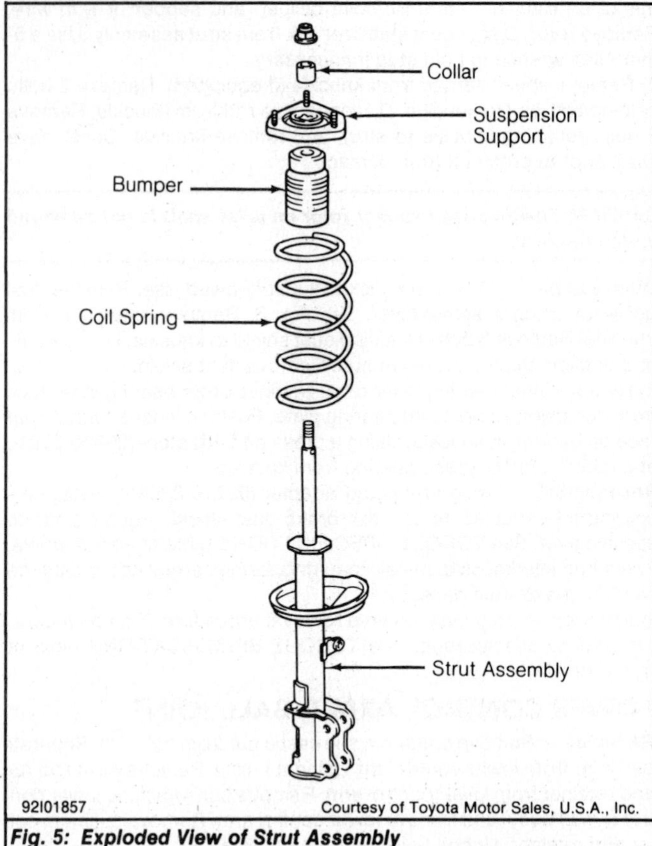


*Fig. 5: Exploded View of Strut Assembly*

**2)** Tighten tie rod end bolts to specification. See TORQUE SPECIFICATIONS table at end of article. Check wheel alignment. See SPECIFICATIONS & PROCEDURES article in WHEEL ALIGNMENT.

## WHEEL BEARING

***NOTE: For wheel bearing removal and installation procedures, see HUB & KNUCKLE ASSEMBLY under REMOVAL & INSTALLATION.***

## TORQUE SPECIFICATIONS

***TORQUE SPECIFICATIONS***

| Application | Ft. Lbs. (N.m) |
|---|---|
| Axle Shaft Nut | |
| 3S-GTE Engine | 217 (294) |
| 5S-FE Engine | 137 (186) |
| Ball Joint Stud Nut | 76 (103) |
| Ball Joint-To-Knuckle Bolt | 83 (113) |
| Brake Caliper-To-Knuckle Bolt | 43 (59) |
| Brake Line Union Bolt | 22 (30) |
| Lower Control Arm-To-Body Bolt | 83 (113) |
| Stabilizer Bar Frame Bolts | 14 (19) |
| Stabilizer Bar Link Nuts | 36 (49) |
| Strut Piston Rod Nut | 54 (73) |
| Strut Rod-To-Lower Control Arm Nut | 87 (118) |
| Strut-To-Body Nuts | 59 (80) |
| Strut-To-Knuckle Nut | 188 (255) |
| Tie Rod-To-Frame Bolt | 76 (103) |
| Tie Rod-To-Knuckle Bolt | 76 (103) |
| | **INCH Lbs. (N.m)** |
| Dust Cover Mounting Bolts | 74 (8.3) |
| Speed Sensor Mounting Bolt | 74 (8.3) |

# 1991 SUSPENSION
# Rear – Supra

## DESCRIPTION

Rear suspension is a fully independent MacPherson strut type. Suspension arms are mounted by bushings and pivot bolts to body, and are supported by the strut.

Some vehicles are equipped with Toyota Electronic Modulated Suspension (TEMS) system, allowing driver to select suspension firmness with buttons on center console. For information on this system, see ELECTRONIC article in SUSPENSION.

## ADJUSTMENTS & INSPECTION

### WHEEL ALIGNMENT SPECIFICATIONS & PROCEDURES

*NOTE: See SPECIFICATIONS & PROCEDURES article in WHEEL ALIGNMENT.*

### WHEEL BEARING

Wheel bearings are not adjustable. Measure axial play and runout at axle flange. Maximum axial play and runout is .002" (.05 mm). Replace bearing assembly if specification is exceeded.

### BALL JOINT CHECKING

**Upper & Lower Suspension Arm – 1)** Disconnect upper or lower ball joint. To check turning torque of upper or lower suspension arm ball joint, rotate ball joint back and forth 5 times.

**2)** Using an INCH-pound torque wrench, turn ball joint nut one turn every 2-4 seconds and take a torque reading on fifth turn. Turning torque should be 9-30 INCH lbs. (1.0-3.4 N.m) for upper arm ball joint or 7-30 INCH lbs. (.8-3.4 N.m) for lower arm ball joint. If turning torque is not within specification, replace suspension arm.

## REMOVAL & INSTALLATION

### LOWER SUSPENSION ARMS

**Removal – 1)** Raise and support vehicle. Remove wheels. Using a jack, raise No. 2 suspension arm until it is horizontal. Place match marks on rear drive shaft and side gear shaft flange for installation reference.

**2)** Remove nuts from drive shaft joint. Remove cotter pin and lock nut cap. Loosen bearing lock nut while depressing brake pedal. Using a plastic hammer, remove rear drive shaft.

**3)** Using Puller (09611-22012), remove nut and disconnect No. 1 lower suspension arm from axle carrier. Place match marks on adjusting cam and frame for installation reference. *See Fig. 1.* Remove cam and bolt from frame. Remove No. 1 lower suspension arm.

**4)** Remove bolt and nut, and disconnect No. 2 lower suspension arm from axle carrier. Place match marks on adjusting cam and frame for installation reference. Remove cam, bolt and No. 2 lower suspension arm.

**Inspection –** See BALL JOINT CHECKING under ADJUSTMENTS & INSPECTION.

**Bushing Replacement –** Using a press and Adapter Kit (09726-35010), press out No. 1 lower suspension arm bushings. Using a press and Adapter Kit (09710-22041), press out No. 2 lower suspension arm bushings. To install new bushings, reverse removal procedure.

**Installation – 1)** To install, reverse removal procedure. Install, but do not tighten, No. 1 and No. 2 lower suspension arm cam and bolt. Install wheels. Lower vehicle.

**2)** Bounce vehicle to stabilize suspension. Align match marks and tighten No. 1 and No. 2 lower suspension arm cam nuts to specification. Tighten all bolts and nuts to specification. See TORQUE SPECIFICATIONS table at end of article. Check rear wheel alignment. See SPECIFICATIONS & PROCEDURES article in WHEEL ALIGNMENT.

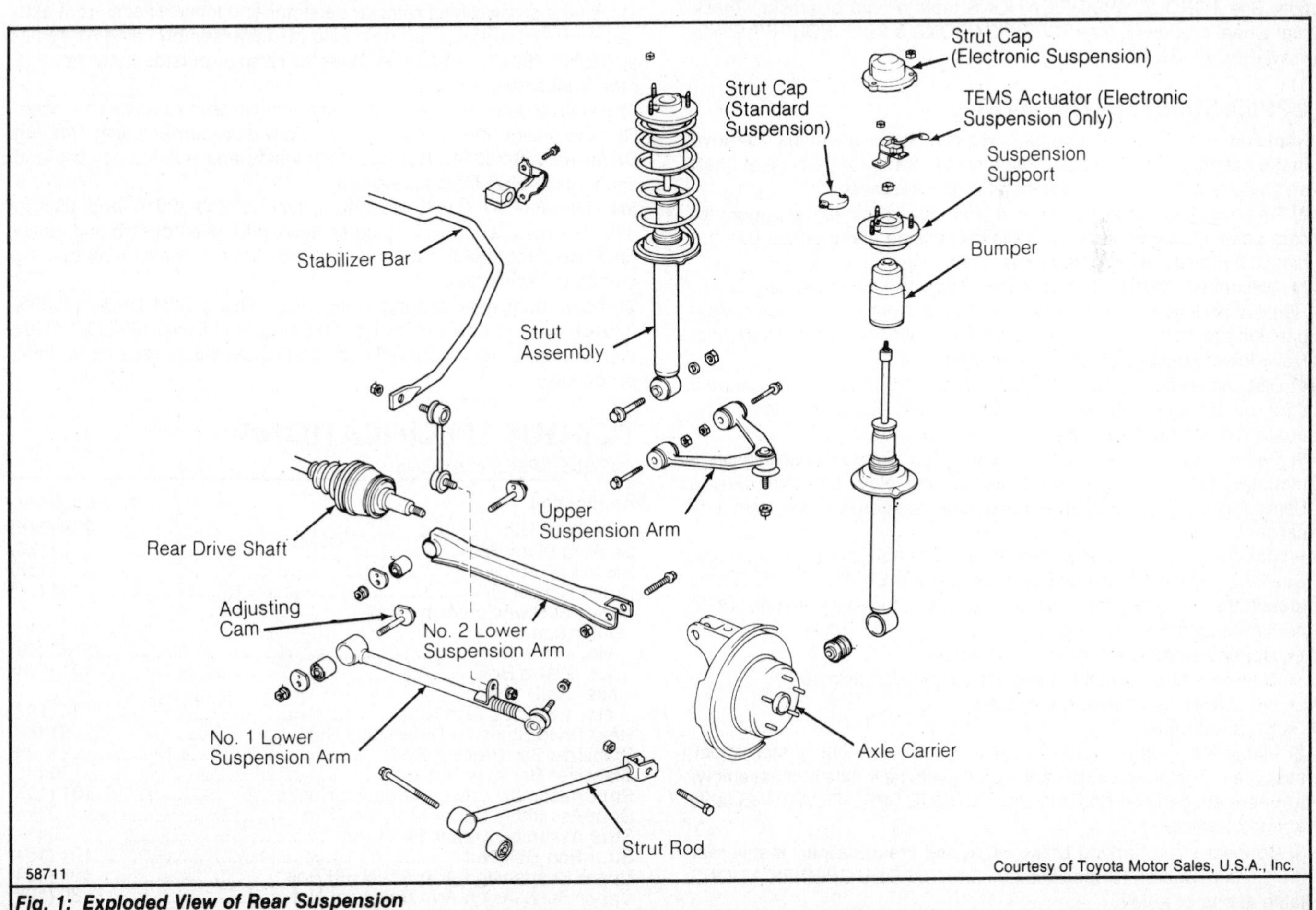


*Fig. 1: Exploded View of Rear Suspension*

# 1991 SUSPENSION
# Rear – Supra (Cont.)

## STABILIZER BAR & LINK

**Removal** – Raise and support vehicle. Remove wheels. Disconnect stabilizer bar link from No. 1 lower suspension arm. *See Fig. 1.* Remove stabilizer bar bracket. Remove stabilizer bar from frame. Remove stabilizer bar link from stabilizer bar.

**Inspection** – Move stabilizer link ball joint arm in all directions. Replace stabilizer bar link if movement is not smooth and free.

**Installation** – To install, reverse removal procedure. Tighten nuts and bolts to specification. See TORQUE SPECIFICATIONS table at end of article. Check rear wheel alignment. See SPECIFICATIONS & PROCEDURES article in WHEEL ALIGNMENT.

## STRUT ASSEMBLY

**Removal** – Remove inside rear speaker grilles and quarter trim. Raise and support vehicle. Disconnect bottom of strut assembly. Remove upper shock cap or TEMS actuator (if equipped). *See Fig. 1.* Remove upper strut assembly nuts. Remove strut assembly.

**Disassembly, Reassembly & Installation** – **1)** Secure strut assembly in vise. Using Spring Compressor (09727-30020), compress spring and remove upper strut nut. Remove suspension support, coil spring and bumper. Replace strut.

**2)** Assemble strut in reverse order. To install, reverse removal procedure. Tighten nuts and bolts to specification. See TORQUE SPECIFICATIONS table at end of article.

## STRUT ROD

**Removal & Installation** – **1)** Raise and support vehicle. Remove wheels. Remove strut rod mounting bolt and nut. *See Fig. 1.* Disconnect strut rod from axle carrier. Remove strut rod mounting bolt. Remove strut rod from frame.

**2)** To install, reverse removal procedure. Lower vehicle and bounce vehicle to stabilize suspension. Tighten all nuts and bolts to specification. See TORQUE SPECIFICATIONS table at end of article. Check rear wheel alignment. See SPECIFICATIONS & PROCEDURES article in WHEEL ALIGNMENT.

## UPPER SUSPENSION ARM

**Removal** – **1)** Raise and support vehicle. Remove wheels. Remove brake caliper and wire aside. Place match marks on rear drive shaft and side gear shaft flange for installation reference.

**2)** Remove drive shaft flange nuts. Remove cotter pin and lock nut cap. Loosen bearing lock nut while depressing brake pedal. Using a plastic hammer, remove rear drive shaft.

**3)** Disconnect parking brake cable from parking brake equalizer. Remove parking brake brackets from frame. Remove No. 1 lower suspension arm from axle carrier. Using Puller (09611-22012), disconnect No. 1 lower suspension arm from carrier. *See Fig. 1.*

**4)** Disconnect No. 2 lower suspension arm from carrier. Disconnect strut rod and shock absorber from axle carrier. Disconnect upper suspension arm from frame. Remove axle carrier assembly.

**5)** Remove upper suspension mounting nut. Remove backing plate mounting nuts and bolts. Separate backing plate and axle carrier. Using Puller (09950-00020), remove upper suspension arm from axle carrier.

**Inspection** – Check upper suspension arm ball joint turning torque. See BALL JOINT CHECKING under ADJUSTMENTS & INSPECTION.

**Installation** – **1)** To install, reverse removal procedure. Install, but do not tighten the following bolts:

- Upper suspension arm-to-frame bolts.
- New axle hub assembly-to-upper suspension arm nut.
- No. 2 lower suspension arm bolts.
- Strut rod bolts.

**2)** Install No. 1 lower suspension arm with new nut. Install shock absorber. Tighten to specification along with new axle hub assembly-to-upper suspension arm nut. See TORQUE SPECIFICATIONS table at end of article.

**3)** Connect strut, parking brake cable and brake caliper. Install rear drive shaft. Tighten to specification. See TORQUE SPECIFICATIONS table at end of article.

**4)** Install wheels and lower vehicle. Bounce vehicle to stabilize suspension. Tighten upper suspension arm to frame bolts, No. 2 lower suspension arm bolts, and strut rod bolts to specification. See TORQUE SPECIFICATIONS table at end of article.

**5)** Check rear wheel alignment. See SPECIFICATIONS & PROCEDURES article in WHEEL ALIGNMENT.

## WHEEL BEARING

**Removal** – **1)** Raise and support vehicle. Remove rear wheels. Remove brake caliper and wire out of way. Remove brake disc rotor.

**2)** Remove parking brake assembly. Disconnect No. 1 and No. 2 lower suspension arms from axle carrier. See LOWER SUSPENSION ARMS under REMOVAL & INSTALLATION.

**3)** Disconnect strut rod. Disconnect bottom of strut assembly. Disconnect upper suspension arm and remove axle carrier assembly. *See Fig. 2.* Separate upper suspension arm from axle carrier. Remove backing plate from axle carrier.

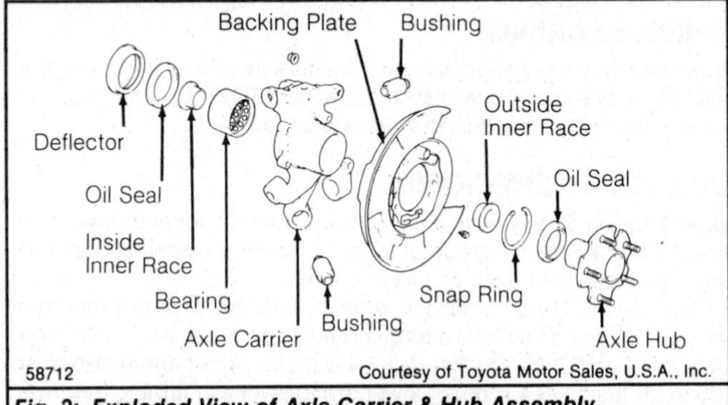


*Fig. 2: Exploded View of Axle Carrier & Hub Assembly*

**4)** Using a screwdriver, remove deflector and inner oil seal from axle carrier. Remove axle shaft from axle carrier assembly using Axle Puller (09950-20017). Use same puller to remove outside inner bearing race from axle shaft.

**5)** Remove outer oil seal with a screwdriver and remove snap ring. Remove inside inner bearing race from axle carrier using Bearing Driver (09608-35014). Remove both inside and outside bearing and cage assemblies from axle carrier.

**Installation** – **1)** Using Bearing Driver (09608-32010 and 09608-35014), press new bearings outer races into axle housing and install new snap ring. Pack new bearings with grease. Install new bearing and cage assemblies.

**2)** Install both new bearing inner races. Using Seal Driver (09608-32010), drive in new outer oil seal. Using Seal Driver (09223-15010), drive in new inner oil seal. To complete installation, reverse removal procedure.

## TORQUE SPECIFICATIONS

*TORQUE SPECIFICATIONS*

| Application | Ft. Lbs. (N.m) |
|---|---|
| Axle Shaft Nut | 203 (275) |
| Backing Plate Bolt | 19 (26) |
| Backing Plate Nut | 43 (58) |
| Brake Caliper Bolt | 34 (46) |
| Lower Suspension Arms | |
| Outer End | |
| No. 1 Arm Nut | 43 (58) |
| No. 2 Arm Bolt | 121 (164) |
| Inner End | |
| No. 1 & No. 2 Arm Nut | 136 (184) |
| Rear Drive Shaft-To-Differential Nut | 51 (69) |
| Stabilizer Bar Bracket Bolt | 21 (28) |
| Stabilizer Bar Link Nut | 26 (35) |
| Strut Assembly Lower Mounting Nut | 101 (137) |
| Strut Assembly Upper Mounting Nut | 10 (14) |
| Strut Assembly Upper Shaft Nut | 20 (27) |
| Strut Rod Bolt/Nut | 121 (164) |
| Upper Suspension Arm Attaching Bolt | 121 (164) |
| Upper Suspension Arm Ball Joint Nut | 80 (108) |

## Supra

## DESCRIPTION

Toyota Electronic-Modulated Suspension (TEMS) system electronically regulates shock absorber damping. The TEMS system has 3 modes of operation. Operational modes may be selected by a mode select switch mounted on dash or center console. *See Fig. 1*.

The TEMS computer uses information from the throttle position sensor, speed sensor, steering sensor and stoplight switch to determine the best setting for shock absorber firmness. Shock absorber firmness is accomplished by an actuator valve mounted on each shock absorber.

## OPERATION

The TEMS computer receives reference signals from various sensors and switches. The computer processes this information, and determines where to position the electrically operated shock absorber actuator valve according to mode selection.

On top of each shock absorber is an actuator valve that rotates 120 degrees to vary suspension firmness. As driving conditions vary, the TEMS indicator lights will change, informing driver of shock absorber setting. *See Fig. 2*.

## TESTING & DIAGNOSIS

***NOTE: When diagnosing TEMS computer circuit, refer to TEMS computer circuit diagnostic chart. See Fig. 8.***

### PRELIMINARY CHECK

Perform these preliminary checks before starting test procedures.

- Check cold tire inflation pressure.
- Check for proper lubrication of suspension and steering linkage.
- Check wheel alignment and vehicle height.
- Ensure battery voltage is greater than 12 volts.
- Ensure all electrical connectors are clean and secured.

### INITIAL CHECK

**1)** Check TEMS indicator lights. TEMS indicator lights "S", "M" and "F" should illuminate for 2 seconds when ignition is on. *See Fig. 2*. If lights come on, go to step **3)**. If lights do not illuminate, check for 12 volts between TEMS computer terminal B+ and GND with ignition on. *See Fig. 8*. TEMS computer is located on right side of luggage compartment. *See Fig. 1*.

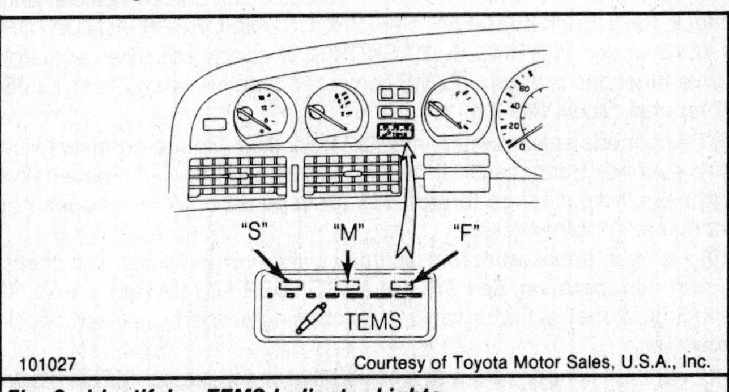


***Fig. 2: Identifying TEMS Indicator Lights***

**2)** If 12 volts is not present, check for faulty fusible link, fuse, battery cable, ignition switch or ground. If 12 volts is present, check for faulty indicator bulb, indicator bulb circuit or TEMS computer.

**3)** If TEMS indicator lights illuminate as described in step **1)**, place mode select switch to NORMAL position. TEMS indicator lights "M" and "F" should turn off, and light "S" should illuminate.

**4)** If lights do not function as described in step **3)**, check for a faulty mode select switch, mode select switch circuit or TEMS computer. If lights function as described, go to next step.

**5)** Place mode select switch in SPORT position. TEMS indicator lights "S" and "M" should illuminate. If lights do not illuminate, check for faulty mode select switch, mode select switch circuit or TEMS computer. If lights illuminate, go to next step.

**6)** Check for operational noise from each shock absorber actuator valve when mode select switch is changed from SPORT to NORMAL

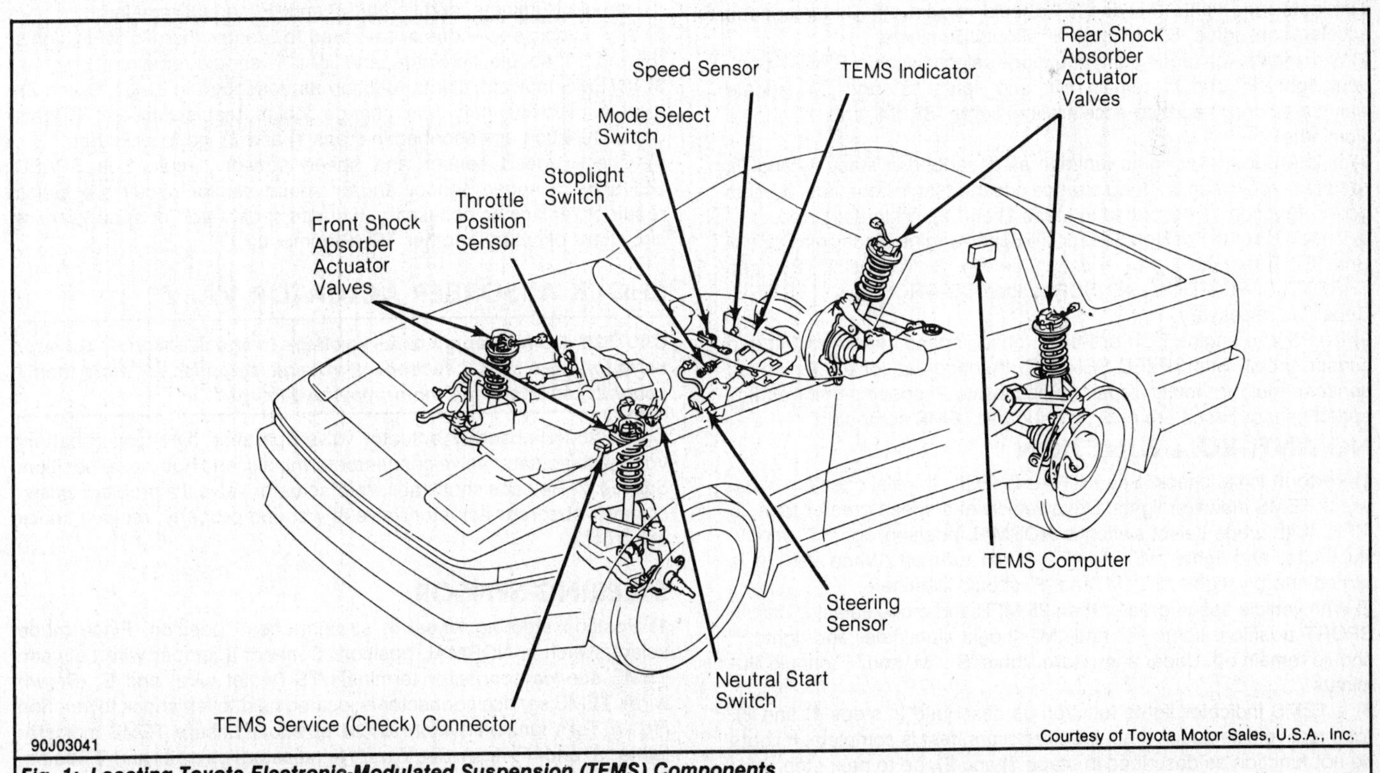


***Fig. 1: Locating Toyota Electronic-Modulated Suspension (TEMS) Components***

# 1991 SUSPENSION
# Electronic (Cont.)

to SPORT position. If noise is heard, go to step **9)**. If noise is not heard, go to next step.

**7)** Disconnect shock absorber actuator valve connector. Check for 8 or more volts to connector terminals (wiring harness side) No. 1 and 2 when mode select switch is operated. *See Fig. 7*.

**8)** If voltage to connector terminals No. 1 and 2 is 8 or more volts, shock absorber actuator valve is faulty. If voltage is not as indicated in step **7)**, remove shock absorber actuator valve from vehicle, and check for proper operation. See SHOCK ABSORBER ACTUATOR VALVE under TESTING & DIAGNOSIS. If shock absorber actuator valve functions properly, TEMS computer circuit is faulty. Test TEMS computer circuit. *See Fig. 8*.

**9)** Place mode select switch in SPORT position. Bounce vehicle twice per second. Suspension firmness should increase. If suspension firmness increases, go to step **11)**. If suspension firmness does not increase, go to next step.

**10)** Remove shock absorber actuator valve from vehicle, and check for proper operation. See SHOCK ABSORBER ACTUATOR VALVE. If shock absorber actuator valve is functioning properly, replace shock absorber.

**11)** Connect jumper wire between TEMS service connector terminals TS (Violet wire) and $E_1$ (Brown wire). TEMS service connector is located next to left shock tower. *See Fig. 1*. All TEMS indicator lights should illuminate. If lights illuminate, go to next step. If lights do not illuminate, mode select switch, mode select switch circuit or TEMS computer is faulty.

**12)** Bounce vehicle again. Suspension should become more firm. If suspension becomes more firm, initial check is complete. If suspension does not become more firm, go to next step.

**13)** Remove shock absorber actuator valve from vehicle, and check for proper operation. See SHOCK ABSORBER ACTUATOR VALVE. Replace shock absorber actuator valve if it does not function properly. If shock absorber actuator valve is functioning properly, replace shock absorber.

## NO ANTI-SQUAT FUNCTION

**1)** Perform initial check. See INITIAL CHECK. If initial check is okay, check TEMS indicator lights. *See Fig. 2*. With ignition on (engine off) and mode select switch in NORMAL position, light "S" should illuminate, and lights "M" and "F" should remain off. Under sudden acceleration, lights "S", "M" and "F" should illuminate.

**2)** With ignition on (engine off) and mode select switch in SPORT position, light "F" should remain off, and lights "S" and "M" should illuminate. Under sudden acceleration, lights "S", "M" and "F" should illuminate.

**3)** If TEMS indicator lights function as described in steps **1)** and **2)**, road test vehicle again. If no change occurs, test is complete. If lights do not function as described in steps **1)** and **2)**, go to next step.

**4)** Check Throttle Position Sensor (TPS) and engine Electronic Control Unit (ECU) circuits $L_1$, $L_2$ and $L_3$. *See Fig. 8*. To check TPS, see THROTTLE POSITION SENSOR under DIAGNOSIS & TESTING. Repair as necessary.

**5)** If TPS and engine ECU are okay, check speed sensor and speed sensor circuit. See SPEED SENSOR. If speed sensor and/or speed sensor circuit are faulty, repair as necessary. If speed sensor and/or speed sensor circuit are okay, try another TEMS computer.

## NO ANTI-ROLL FUNCTION

**1)** Perform initial check. See INITIAL CHECK. If initial check is okay, check TEMS indicator lights. Drive vehicle at a speed greater than 25 MPH. With mode select switch in NORMAL position, light "S" should illuminate, and lights "M" and "F" should turn off. When vehicle is turned sharply, lights "S", "M" and "F" should illuminate.

**2)** With vehicle speed greater than 25 MPH and mode select switch in SPORT position, lights "S" and "M" should illuminate, and light "F" should remain off. Under sharp turn, lights "S", "M" and "F" should illuminate.

**3)** If TEMS indicator lights function as described in steps **1)** and **2)**, road test vehicle again. If no change occurs, test is complete. If lights do not function as described in steps **1)** and **2)**, go to next step.

**4)** Check steering sensor and steering sensor circuit. See STEERING SENSOR. If steering sensor and/or steering sensor circuit are faulty, repair or replace as necessary. If steering sensor and/or steering sensor circuit are okay, check speed sensor and speed sensor circuit. See SPEED SENSOR. If speed sensor and/or speed sensor circuit are faulty, repair or replace as necessary. If speed sensor and circuit are okay, try another TEMS computer.

## NO ANTI-DIVE FUNCTION

**1)** Perform initial check. See INITIAL CHECK. If initial check is okay, place mode select switch in NORMAL position, and drive vehicle at a speed greater than 37 MPH. Check TEMS indicator lights. Light "S" should illuminate, and lights "M" and "F" should remain off. Depress brake pedal while vehicle is traveling at a speed greater than 37 MPH, and check indicator lights. All indicator lights should illuminate.

**2)** Place mode select switch in SPORT position, and drive vehicle at a speed greater than 37 MPH. Check indicator lights. Lights "S" and "M" should illuminate, and light "F" should remain off. Depress brake pedal while vehicle is traveling at a speed greater than 37 MPH, and check indicator lights. All indicator lights should illuminate.

**3)** If TEMS indicator lights function as described in steps **1)** and **2)**, road test vehicle again. If no change occurs, test is complete. If lights do not function as described in steps **1)** and **2)**, go to next step.

**4)** Check stoplight switch and stoplight switch circuit. If stoplight switch and/or circuit are faulty, repair or replace as necessary. If stoplight switch and/or stoplight switch circuit are okay, check speed sensor and speed sensor circuit. See SPEED SENSOR.

**5)** If speed sensor and/or speed sensor circuit are faulty, repair or replace as necessary. If speed sensor and/or speed sensor circuit are okay, try another TEMS computer.

## NO HIGH SPEED RESPONSE

***NOTE: High speed response functions only when mode select switch is in NORMAL position.***

**1)** Perform initial check. See INITIAL CHECK. If initial check is okay, check TEMS indicator lights when vehicle is accelerated gradually from less than 63 MPH to greater than 75 MPH. With vehicle speed less than 63 MPH and mode select switch in NORMAL position, light "S" should illuminate, and lights "M" and "F" should remain off.

**2)** When vehicle speed is accelerated to greater than 75 MPH, lights "S" and "M" should illuminate, and light "F" should remain off.

**3)** If TEMS indicator lights function as described in steps **1)** and **2)**, road test vehicle again. If no change occurs, test is complete. If lights do not function as described in steps **1)** and **2)**, go to next step.

**4)** Check speed sensor and speed sensor circuit. See SPEED SENSOR. If speed sensor and/or speed sensor circuit are faulty, repair or replace as necessary. If speed sensor and/or speed sensor circuit are okay, try another TEMS computer.

## SHOCK ABSORBER ACTUATOR VALVE

***CAUTION: DO NOT apply battery voltage to shock absorber actuator valve for more than 2 seconds. If voltage is applied for more than 2 seconds, solenoid and motor may be damaged.***

Check shock absorber actuator valve operation by applying battery voltage to actuator valve connector terminals, and note valve position. *See Fig. 7*. Replace shock absorber actuator valve if a problem exists. If shock absorber actuator valve is working properly, replace shock absorber.

## STEERING SENSOR

**1)** Position steering wheel in straight-ahead position. Place mode select switch in NORMAL position. Connect a jumper wire between TEMS service connector terminals TS (Violet wire) and $E_1$ (Brown wire). TEMS service connector is located next to left shock tower. *See Fig. 1*. Turn ignition switch to ON position. Ensure TEMS indicator lights "S" and "F" flash. *See Fig. 2*. If indicator lights "S" and "F" do not flash, mode select switch, service connector circuit or TEMS computer is defective.

**2)** Turn steering wheel 1/8 turn to the right from straight-ahead position. Ensure TEMS indicator light "F" flashes (right side), and light "S" (left side) goes out. Return steering wheel to straight-ahead position, and then turn steering wheel 1/8 turn to the left. Ensure TEMS indicator light "S" (left side) flashes, and light "F" (right side) goes out. System is functioning properly if lights function as indicated. If indicator lights do not function as indicated, go to next step.

**3)** Turn ignition on. Measure voltage between steering sensor connector terminals No. 1 and 2. *See Fig. 3.* Steering sensor is located in engine compartment, on top of steering column. *See Fig. 1.*

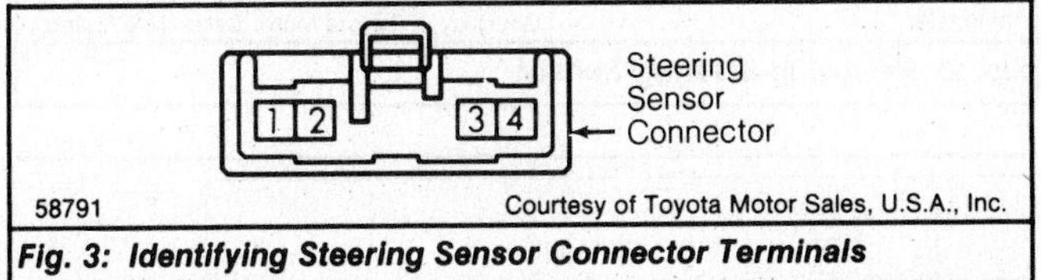


58791 Courtesy of Toyota Motor Sales, U.S.A., Inc.

***Fig. 3: Identifying Steering Sensor Connector Terminals***

**4)** Standard voltage is 3.5-4.2 volts. While slowly turning steering wheel, measure voltage between steering sensor connector terminals No. 2, 3 and 4. Standard voltage will fluctuate between 0-5 volts.

**5)** If voltage is not correct, remove steering sensor and disc. Ensure no foreign matter is in sensor groove. If necessary, clean groove with a soft cloth. Ensure sensor disc is not damaged or bent.

## MODE SELECT SWITCH

Remove mode select switch from center console box. Disconnect mode select switch connector. Using an ohmmeter, ensure continuity is present between mode select switch connector terminals No. 1 and 2 when mode select switch is in SPORT position. *See Fig. 4*. Continuity should not be present between terminals No. 1 and 2 when mode select switch is in NORMAL position.

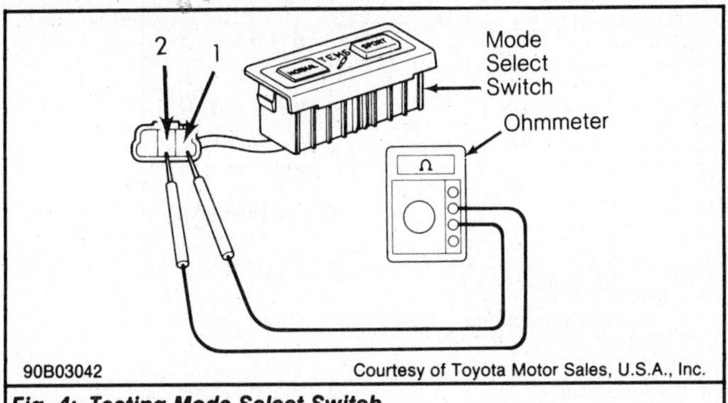


90B03042 Courtesy of Toyota Motor Sales, U.S.A., Inc.

***Fig. 4: Testing Mode Select Switch***

## SPEED SENSOR

Remove instrument cluster. Using an ohmmeter, ensure continuity between speed sensor terminals SPD + and SPD – exists 4 times per shaft revolution. *See Fig. 5.*

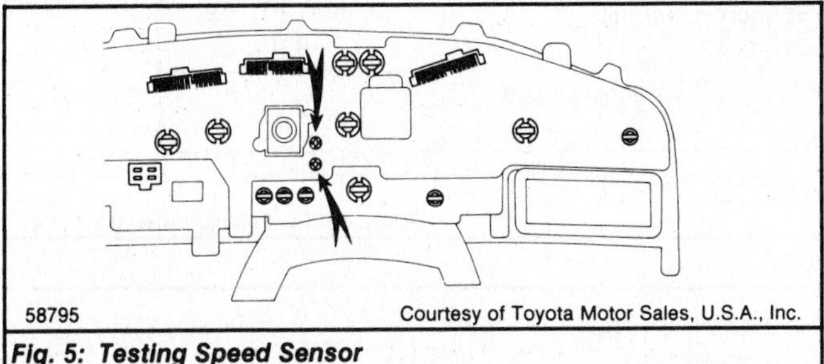

58795 Courtesy of Toyota Motor Sales, U.S.A., Inc.

***Fig. 5: Testing Speed Sensor***

## THROTTLE POSITION SENSOR

**1)** Using an ohmmeter, check resistance between throttle position sensor terminals IDL and $E_2$ with throttle valve fully closed. *See Fig. 6.* Resistance should be zero ohm. Check resistance between same terminals with throttle valve open. Ohmmeter should indicate infinity.

**2)** Check resistance between terminals VCC and $E_2$. Resistance should be 3-7 ohms. Check resistance between terminals VTA and $E_2$. With throttle valve fully closed, resistance should be .2-.8 ohm. With throttle valve open, resistance should be 3.3-10 ohms.

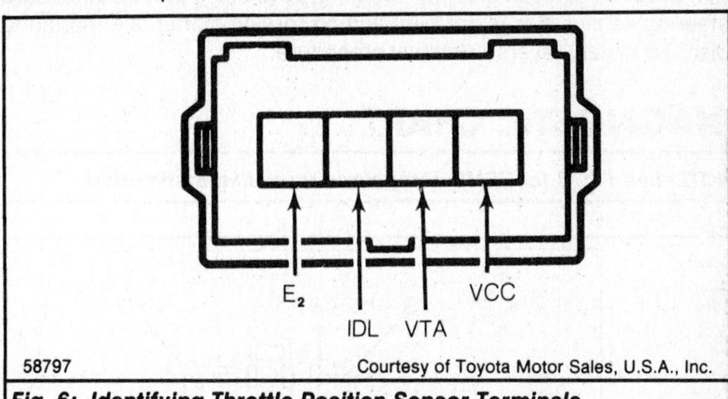


58797 Courtesy of Toyota Motor Sales, U.S.A., Inc.

***Fig. 6: Identifying Throttle Position Sensor Terminals***

# REMOVAL & INSTALLATION

## SHOCK ABSORBER ACTUATOR VALVE

**Removal – 1)** Turn ignition on. Set mode select switch to SPORT position. Using a short piece of wire, jump TEMS service connector terminals TS (Violet wire) and $E_1$ (Brown wire). TEMS service connector is located next to left shock tower. *See Fig. 1.*

**2)** Turn ignition off. Disconnect negative battery cable. Remove shock absorber actuator valve cover and connector (front only). Remove shock absorber actuator valve mounting bolts. Carefully remove shock absorber actuator valve from shock absorber.

**Installation – 1)** Ensure shock absorber actuator valve and shock absorber control rod are facing FIRM position. *See Fig. 7.*

**2)** Insert shock absorber control rod into groove of shock absorber actuator valve. Secure shock absorber actuator valve with bolts. Install shock absorber actuator valve wiring harness so it faces front of vehicle.

**3)** Install shock absorber actuator valve cover (front only). Install shock absorber actuator valve connector. Remove service wire from service connector. Check TEMS operation.

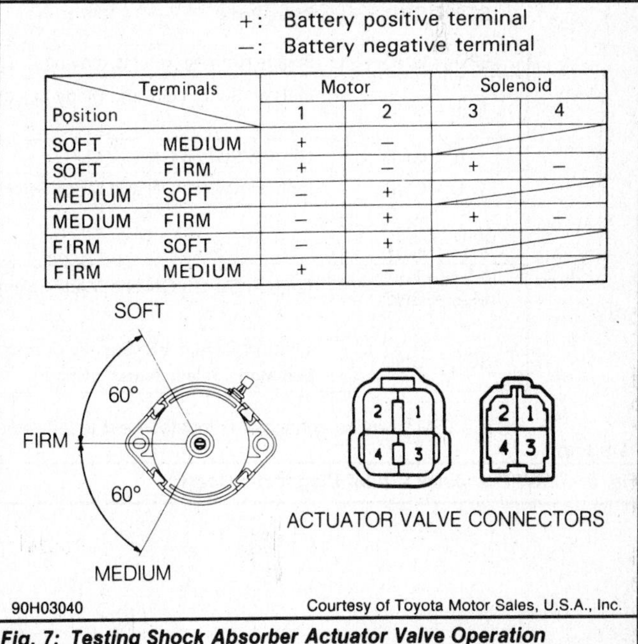

+: Battery positive terminal
–: Battery negative terminal

| Position \ Terminals | | Motor 1 | Motor 2 | Solenoid 3 | Solenoid 4 |
|---|---|---|---|---|---|
| SOFT | MEDIUM | + | – | | |
| SOFT | FIRM | + | – | + | – |
| MEDIUM | SOFT | – | + | | |
| MEDIUM | FIRM | – | + | + | – |
| FIRM | SOFT | – | + | | |
| FIRM | MEDIUM | + | – | | |



90H03040 Courtesy of Toyota Motor Sales, U.S.A., Inc.

***Fig. 7: Testing Shock Absorber Actuator Valve Operation***

# 1991 SUSPENSION
# Electronic (Cont.)

## STEERING SENSOR

**Removal & Installation – 1)** Steering sensor is located in passenger compartment, on steering column tube. Remove steering sensor mounting screws. Remove steering sensor. *See Fig. 9.* Ensure no foreign matter is in sensor groove.

**2)** If necessary, clean steering sensor groove using soft cloth. Ensure steering sensor disc is not bent and no foreign matter is adhering to disc. To install, reverse removal procedure.

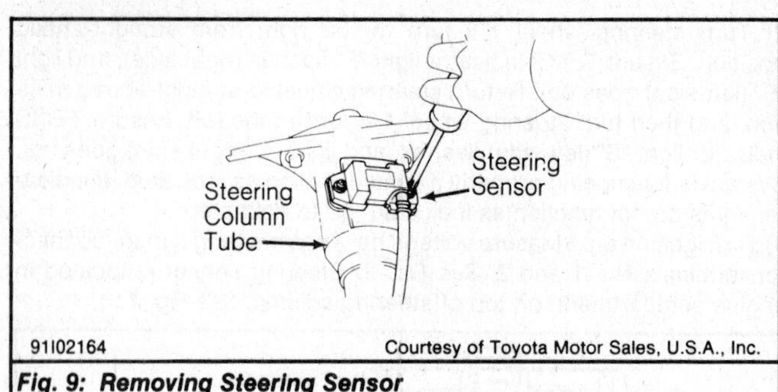


Courtesy of Toyota Motor Sales, U.S.A., Inc.

*Fig. 9: Removing Steering Sensor*

## DIAGNOSTIC CHART

***NOTE: See Fig. 8 for TEMS computer circuit diagnostic chart.***

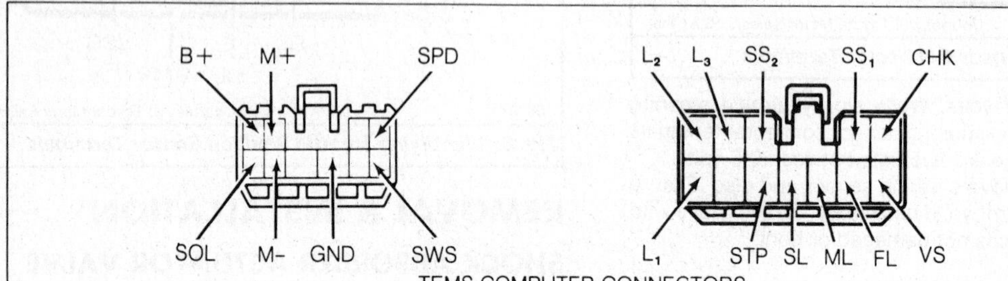


TEMS COMPUTER CONNECTORS

| Terminal | Measuring condition | | Voltage or Resistance |
|---|---|---|---|
| CHK – GND | Ignition Switch ON | Service Connector Terminals Ts – $E_1$ Open | 12 V |
| | | Service Connector Terminals Ts – $E_1$ Short | 0 V |
| $SS_1$ $SS_2$ – GND | Ignition Switch ON and turn slowly steering wheel. | | 5 → 0 → 5 → 0 V |
| $L_1$ – GND | 1. Ignition Switch ON<br>2. Depress the accelerator pedal. | | 5 → 0 V |
| $L_2$ – GND | | | 5 → 0 → 5 V |
| $L_3$ – GND | | | 5 → 0 → 5 → 0 V |
| Vs – GND | Ignition Switch ON | | 3.5 – 4.2 V |
| SL ML – GND FL | Ignition Switch ON | | 12 V (2 seconds) |
| STP – GND | Brake Pedal | Depress | 12 V |
| | | Not depress | 0 V |
| SPD – GND | Engine running, vehicle moving | | 6 V |
| M⊕ – GND | Ignition Switch ON and Mode Select Switch at Normal → Sport (Motor operating) | | Momentarily over 8 V |
| ⊕B – GND | Ignition Switch ON | | 12 V |
| SW-S – GND | Ignition Switch ON and Mode Select Switch at Sport | | Above 8 V |
| GND – Body earth | | | 0 Ω |
| M⊖ – GND | Ignition Switch ON and Mode Select Switch at Sport → Normal (Motor operating) | | Momentarily over 8 V |
| SOL – GND | Ignition Switch ON, Service Connector Terminals Ts – $E_1$ Short Circuit and Mode Select Switch at Sport | | 12 V |

NOTE: TEMS service connector is located next to left shock tower. See Fig. 1.

91B02165

Courtesy of Toyota Motor Sales, U.S.A., Inc.

*Fig. 8: TEMS Computer Circuit Diagnostic Chart*

# 1991 SUSPENSION
# Electronic (Cont.)

## WIRING DIAGRAM

See *Fig. 10*. For additional information, see appropriate chassis wiring diagram in WIRING DIAGRAMS.

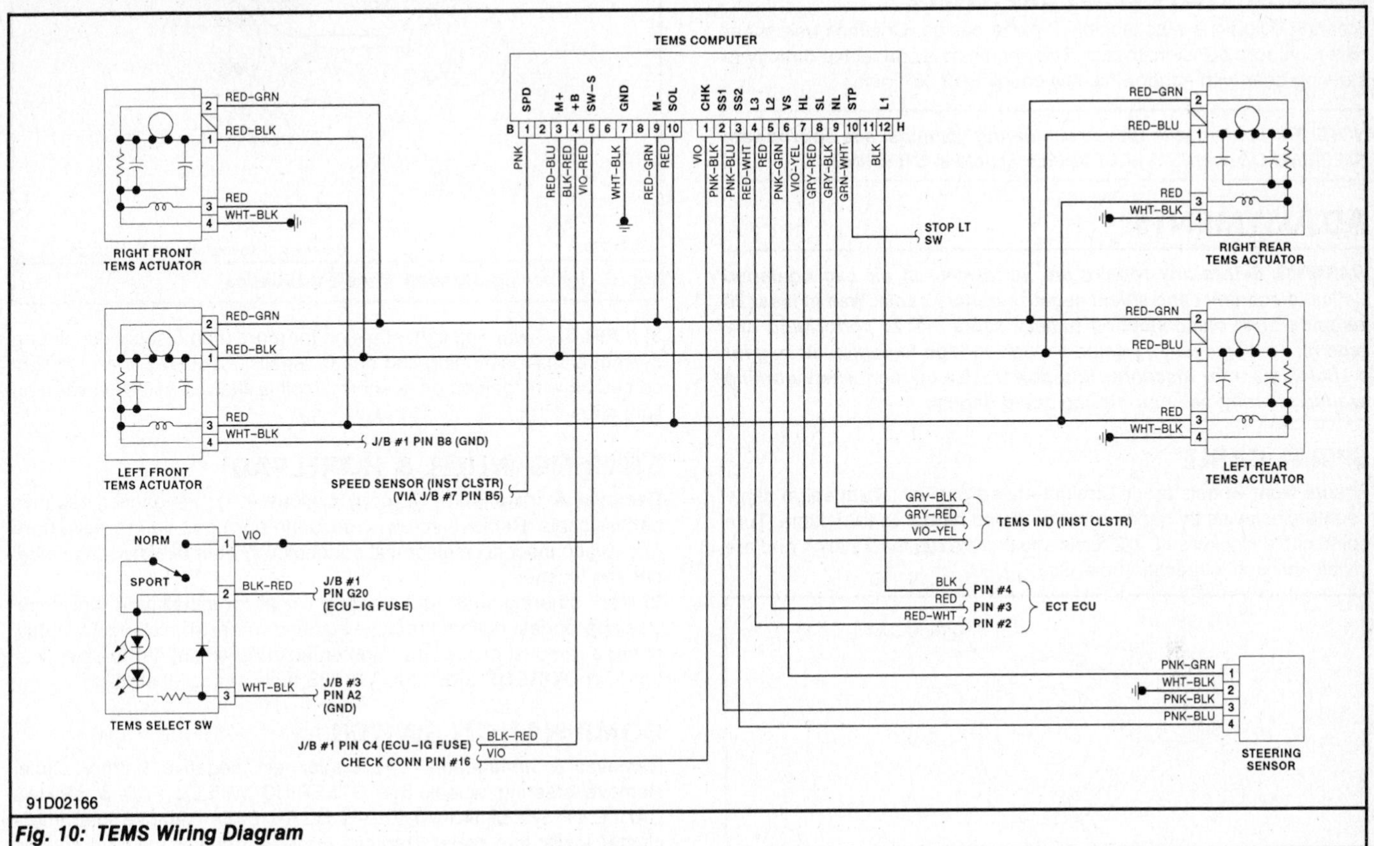


***Fig. 10: TEMS Wiring Diagram***

# 1991 STEERING
# Steering Columns – Standard

## Camry, Celica, Corolla, Pickup, Previa, Tercel, 4Runner

## DESCRIPTION & OPERATION

Steering column is a collapsible 2-piece design. Columns use shear pins to absorb collision impact. Steering shaft is connected directly to steering gear with either a flexible coupling or "U" joint.

***NOTE: For models with tilt wheel steering columns, see appropriate STEERING COLUMNS – TILT WHEEL article in STEERING.***

## ADJUSTMENTS

***WARNING: Before any repairs are performed on air bag equipped Celica, disconnect and shield negative battery cable. Wait at least 20 seconds after disconnecting battery cable before performing any repairs. Air bag system retains enough voltage to deploy air bag for a short time after disconnecting power. Use caution when working around steering column. Air bag could deploy.***

### SPIRAL CABLE

Ensure front wheels are in straight-ahead position. Turn spiral cable counterclockwise by hand until it becomes harder to turn cable. Turn spiral cable clockwise 2 1/2 turns and ensure red marks align and are visible through inspection hole. *See Fig. 1.*

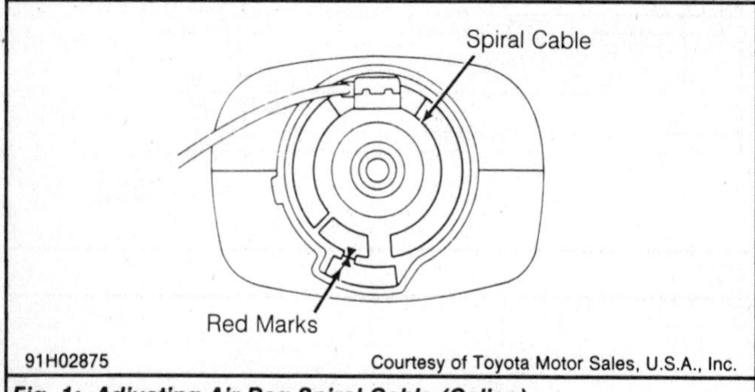


***Fig. 1: Adjusting Air Bag Spiral Cable (Celica)***

## REMOVAL & INSTALLATION

### STEERING WHEEL PAD & SPIRAL CABLE

**Removal & Installation (Celica) – 1)** Ensure front wheels are in straight-ahead position. Turn ignition switch to LOCK position. Disconnect and shield negative battery cable.

**2)** Remove screw covers, 6 screws, and lower instrument cluster trim panel(s). Loosen 4 steering wheel pad Torx screws until groove along screw circumference catches on screw case. *See Fig. 2.*

**3)** Pull steering wheel pad from steering wheel and disconnect electrical connector. Remove steering wheel pad. Place steering wheel pad on flat surface with pad cover facing up.

**4)** Mark steering wheel and steering shaft for installation reference. Remove steering wheel nut. Use appropriate puller to remove steering wheel. Remove 4 screws from upper and lower steering column covers. Remove screws attaching spiral cable to combination (headlight/turn signal/wiper) switch. Disconnect spiral cable and remove from vehicle.

**Installation – 1)** To install, reverse removal procedure. Before installing spiral cable, ensure spiral cable is properly aligned. See ADJUSTMENTS. Tighten steering wheel nut and Torx screws to specification. See TORQUE SPECIFICATIONS table at end of article.

**2)** After spiral cable and steering wheel pad are installed, ensure proper operation of air bag system by turning ignition switch to ACC or ON position. AIR BAG warning light should come on and go out after approximately 6 seconds.

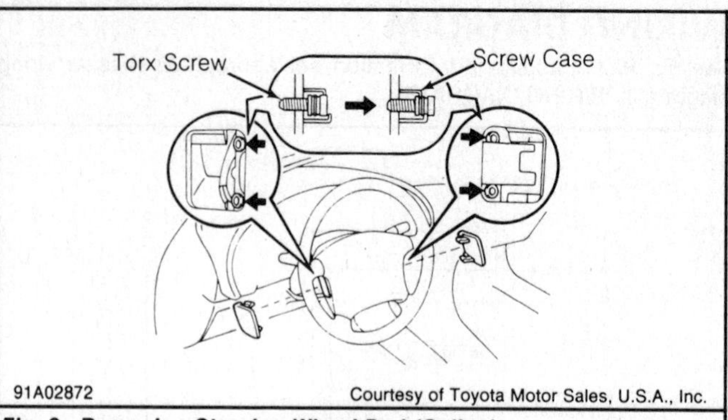


***Fig. 2: Removing Steering Wheel Pad (Celica)***

**3)** If AIR BAG warning light stays on for more than 6 seconds, air bag system is malfunctioning and needs repair. If AIR BAG warning light comes on with ignition on, a short circuit is likely in AIR BAG warning light circuit.

### STEERING WHEEL & HORN PAD

**Removal & Installation (Except Celica) – 1)** Disconnect negative battery cable. Remove screw(s) securing horn pad and remove horn pad. Disconnect horn electrical connector(s). Remove steering wheel nut and washer.

**2)** Mark steering shaft and steering wheel for installation reference. Use appropriate puller to remove steering wheel from shaft. To install, reverse removal procedure. Tighten steering wheel nut to specification. See TORQUE SPECIFICATIONS table at end of article.

### COMBINATION SWITCH

**Removal & Installation – 1)** Disconnect negative battery cable. Remove steering wheel. See STEERING WHEEL PAD & SPIRAL CABLE or STEERING WHEEL & HORN PAD. Remove instrument cluster lower trim panel. Remove upper and lower steering column covers.

**2)** Disconnect combination switch electrical connector. Remove screws securing combination switch to steering column and remove combination switch. To install, reverse removal procedure. Tighten steering wheel nut to specification. See TORQUE SPECIFICATIONS table at end of article.

### IGNITION SWITCH & LOCK CYLINDER

**Removal – 1)** Disconnect negative battery cable. Remove steering wheel. See STEERING WHEEL PAD & SPIRAL CABLE or STEERING WHEEL & HORN PAD. Remove upper and lower steering column covers. Remove combination switch (if necessary).

**2)** Disconnect ignition switch harness connectors. If shear bolt studs are accessible, use a hacksaw to cut a slot into exposed studs. Using a screwdriver, remove studs.

**3)** If shear bolt studs are recessed or hard to reach with a hacksaw, center punch studs. Using a drill bit and a screw extractor, remove studs. Remove ignition switch and lock cylinder.

**Installation – 1)** To install, reverse removal procedure. Install NEW shear bolts. Tighten shear bolts finger tight. Ensure proper operation of ignition switch and lock cylinder.

**2)** Tighten shear bolts until heads break off. Install combination switch, upper and lower steering column covers and steering wheel. Tighten steering wheel nut to specification. See TORQUE SPECIFICATIONS table at end of article.

### STEERING COLUMN

**Removal & Installation – 1)** Disconnect negative battery cable. Remove steering wheel pad. Mark steering shaft and steering wheel for installation reference. Remove steering wheel. See STEERING WHEEL PAD & SPIRAL CABLE or STEERING WHEEL & HORN PAD.

# 1991 STEERING
# Steering Columns – Standard (Cont.)

**2)** Remove instrument cluster lower trim panel. Remove air duct from under steering column (if equipped). Remove steering column upper and lower covers. Remove combination switch.

**3)** On passenger vehicles, mark "U" joint and steering shaft for installation reference. Remove bolt(s) and disconnect "U" joint from bottom of steering column shaft. Remove bolts securing steering column.

**4)** On Pickup and 4Runner, mark steering gearbox and steering column shaft for installation reference. Remove bolts securing steering column. On all models, remove steering column from vehicle. To install, reverse removal procedure. Tighten nuts and bolts to specification. See TORQUE SPECIFICATIONS table at end of article.

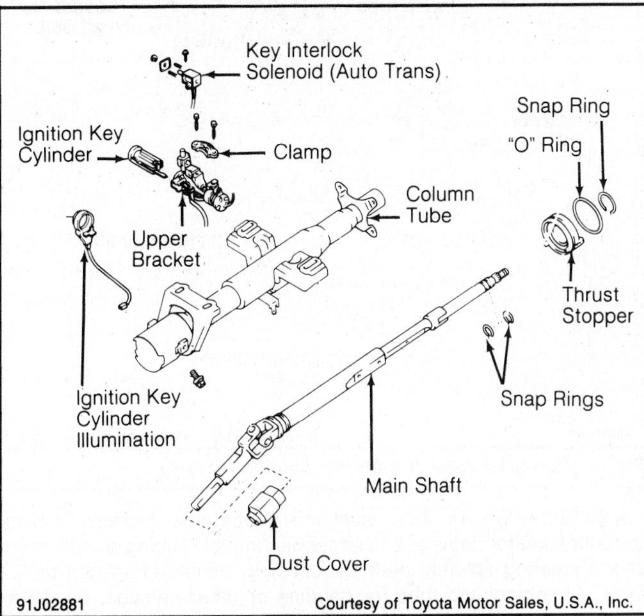


***Fig. 3: Exploded View of Steering Column (Camry)***

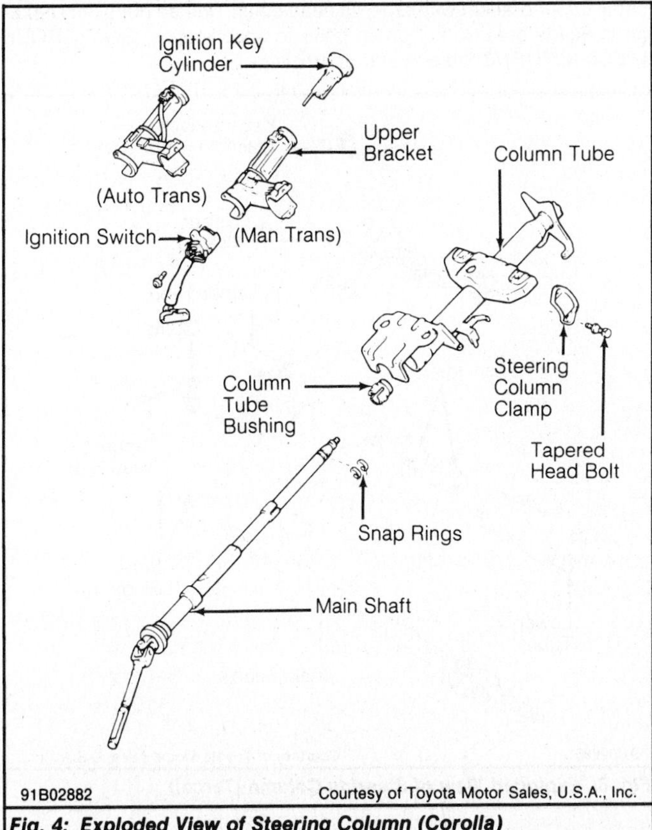


***Fig. 4: Exploded View of Steering Column (Corolla)***

## OVERHAUL

### CAMRY & COROLLA

**Disassembly** – **1)** Drill out tapered head bolts and use screw extractor to remove upper bracket bolts. Remove upper bracket from column tube.

**2)** On Camry, remove thrust stopper set bolts. Use a screwdriver to remove snap ring from thrust stopper. Remove thrust stopper. Remove snap ring from main shaft and remove steering column main shaft from column tube. *See Fig. 3.*

**3)** On Corolla, remove upper snap ring and remove steering column main shaft from column tube. Remove snap ring from main shaft. *See Fig. 4.*

**Inspection** – Ensure lock mechanism operates properly. Check upper bracket for damage and bearings for rotating smoothness. Check steering shafts for bending, damaged splines, or damaged "U" joints. Check column tube for bending or other damage. Repair or replace components as necessary.

**Reassembly** – To reassemble, reverse disassembly procedure. Apply molybdenum disulfide lithium base grease to thrust stopper. Install upper bracket with tapered head bolts. Tighten bolts until hexagonal heads break off.

### CELICA

**Disassembly** – **1)** Drill out tapered head bolts and use screw extractor to remove upper bracket bolts. Remove upper bracket from column tube. Remove upper snap ring. Remove steering column main shaft from column tube. *See Fig. 5.*

**2)** Remove lower snap ring. Remove collar from main shaft. Use a screwdriver to remove bushing. Place ignition key lock in ACC position. Push down on stop pin and pull out key cylinder.

**Inspection** – Ensure lock mechanism operates properly. Check upper bracket for damage and upper bearing for rotating smoothness.

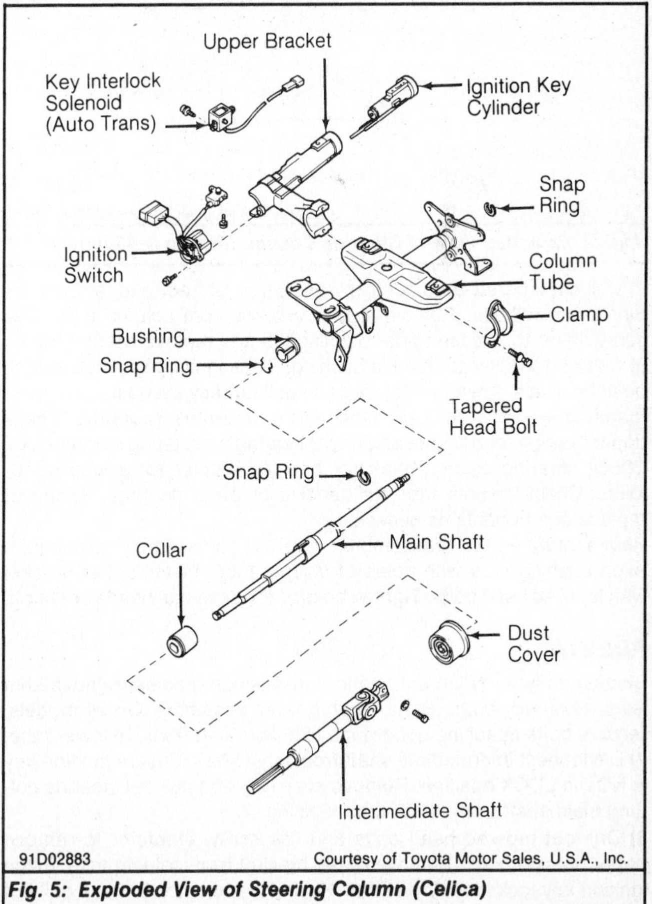


***Fig. 5: Exploded View of Steering Column (Celica)***

# 1991 STEERING
# Steering Columns – Standard (Cont.)

Check steering shafts for bending, damaged splines, or damaged "U" joints. Check column tube for bending or other damage. Repair or replace components as necessary.

**Reassembly** – To reassemble, reverse disassembly procedure. Align bushing tabs with holes of column tube. Install upper bracket with tapered head bolts. Tighten bolts until hexagonal heads break off.

## PICKUP & 4RUNNER

**Disassembly** – **1)** Disconnect intermediate shaft from steering column main shaft. Remove bolts and dust seal. Remove steering column hole cover. Remove steering column protector. Ensure ignition key is NOT in LOCK position. Remove snap ring and pull out steering column main shaft from column tube. *See Fig. 6.*

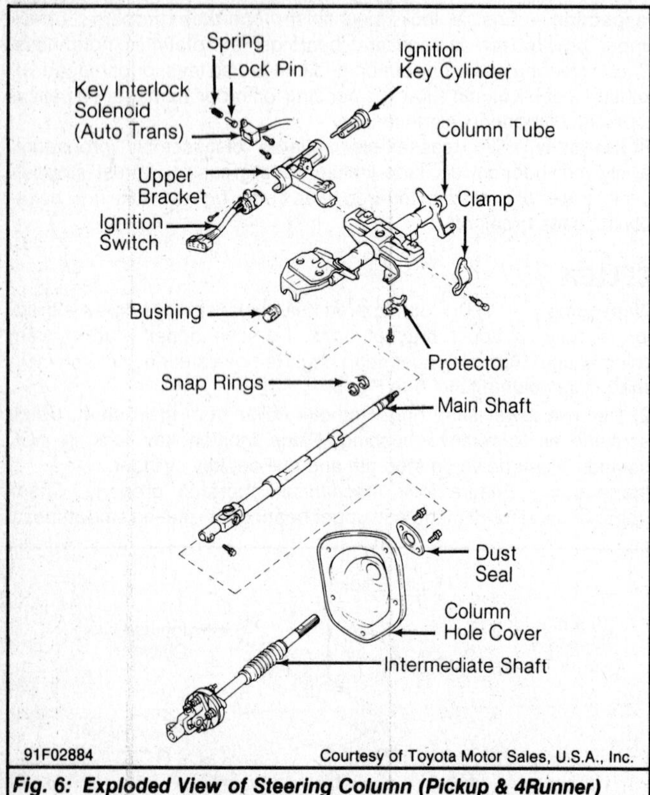


***Fig. 6: Exploded View of Steering Column (Pickup & 4Runner)***

**2)** Drill out tapered head bolts and use screw extractor to remove column bracket bolts. Remove upper bracket from column tube. Use screwdriver to release upper bushing tab and remove column tube.

**3)** Use screwdriver to remove bushing. Place ignition key lock in ACC position. Push down on stop pin and pull out key cylinder.

**Inspection** – Ensure lock mechanism operates properly. Check upper bracket for damage and upper bearing for rotating smoothness. Check steering column shaft for bending, damaged splines or "U" joints. Check column tube for bending or other damage. Repair or replace components as necessary.

**Reassembly** – To reassemble, reverse disassembly procedure. Align bushing tabs with holes of column tube. Install upper bracket with tapered head bolts. Tighten bolts until hexagonal heads break off.

## PREVIA

**Disassembly** – **1)** On automatic transmission models, remove shift lever assembly bolts. Remove shift lever assembly. On all models, remove bolts attaching upper tube to lower tube. Remove lower tube.

**2)** Disconnect intermediate shaft from main shaft. Ensure ignition key is NOT in LOCK position. Remove snap ring and pull out steering column main shaft from upper tube. *See Fig. 7.*

**3)** Drill out tapered head bolts and use screw extractor to remove upper bracket bolts. Remove upper bracket from column tube. Place ignition key lock in ACC position. Push down on stop pin and pull out key cylinder.

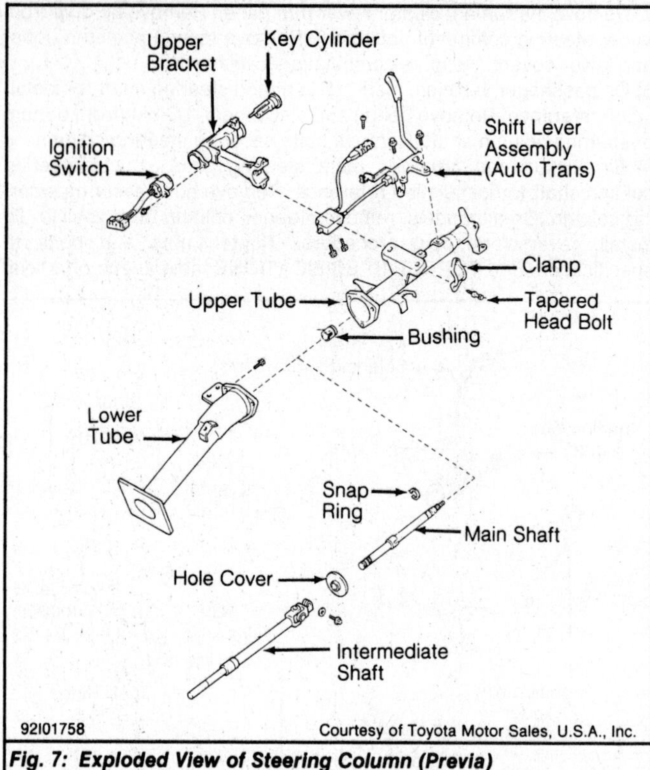


***Fig. 7: Exploded View of Steering Column (Previa)***

**Inspection** – Ensure lock mechanism operates properly. Check upper bracket for damage and upper bearing for rotating smoothness. Check steering column shaft for bending, damaged splines or "U" joints. Check column tube for bending or other damage. Repair or replace components as necessary.

**Reassembly** – To reassemble, reverse disassembly procedure. Install upper bracket with tapered head bolts. Tighten bolts until hexagonal heads break off. Tighten bolts to specification. See TORQUE SPECIFICATIONS table at end of article.

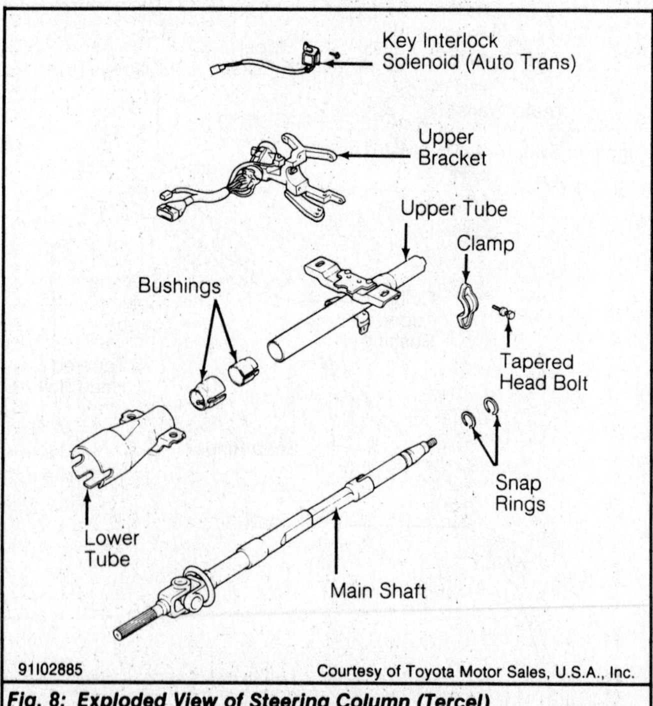


***Fig. 8: Exploded View of Steering Column (Tercel)***

# 1991 STEERING
# Steering Columns – Standard (Cont.)

## TERCEL

**Disassembly** – **1)** Drill out tapered head bolts and use screw extractor to remove column bracket bolts. Remove upper bracket from upper tube. Place ignition key lock in ACC position. Push down on stop pin and pull out key cylinder.

**2)** Remove snap ring and pull out steering column main shaft from upper tube. Use screwdriver to release upper bushing tab and remove upper tube. Use a screwdriver to remove upper and lower bushings. *See Fig. 8.*

**Inspection** – Ensure lock mechanism operates properly. Check upper bracket for damage and upper bearing for rotating smoothness. Check steering shafts for bending, damaged splines, or damaged "U" joints. Check column tube for bending or other damage. Repair or replace components as necessary.

**Reassembly** – To reassemble, reverse disassembly procedure. Apply molybdenum disulfide lithium base grease to upper bushing. Align upper and lower bushing tabs with holes of upper tube. Install upper bracket with tapered head bolts. Tighten bolts until hexagonal heads break off.

## TORQUE SPECIFICATIONS

*TORQUE SPECIFICATIONS*

| Application | Ft. Lbs. (N.m) |
|---|---|
| Intermediate Shaft-To-Main Shaft Bolt | 26 (35) |
| Lower Tube-To-Upper Tube Bolt | 14 (19) |
| Shift Lever Assembly Bolt | 14 (19) |
| Steering Column Bracket-To-Instrument Panel Bolt/Nut | 19 (26) |
| Steering Wheel Nut | 25 (34) |
| Thrust Stopper Bolt | 10 (13) |
| "U" Joint Bolt | 26 (35) |
| | **INCH Lbs. (N.m)** |
| Column Hole Cover Bolt | 62 (7) |
| Column Hole Dust Seal Bolt | 62 (7) |
| Steering Wheel Pad Torx Screw | 62 (7) |

# 1991 STEERING
# Steering Columns – Tilt Wheel – Cars

## Camry, Celica, Corolla, Cressida, MR2, Supra

## DESCRIPTION

Tilt steering wheels incorporate an upper steering shaft, attached by a "U" joint to an intermediate steering shaft. These shafts are held in place by upper and lower brackets. Brackets are pinned together so upper bracket can move up or down. Upper bracket is locked in place by pawl attached to lever. Steering columns are collapsible.

## ADJUSTMENTS

### SPIRAL CABLE

Make sure front wheels are in a straight-ahead position. Turn spiral cable COUNTERCLOCKWISE by hand until it becomes hard to turn cable. Turn spiral cable CLOCKWISE 2.5 turns and ensure Red marks align and are visible through inspection hole. *See Fig. 1.*

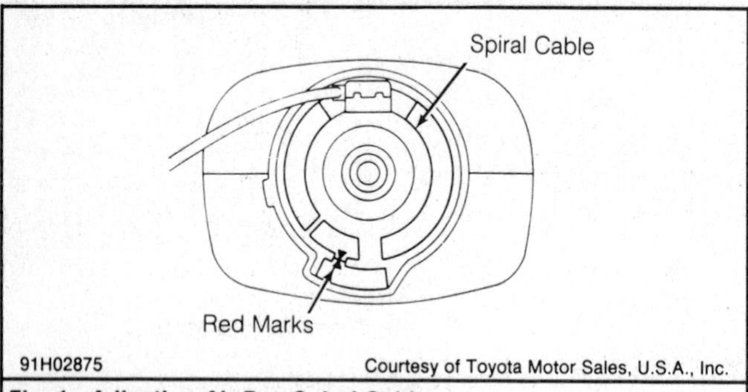


***Fig. 1: Adjusting Air Bag Spiral Cable***

## REMOVAL & INSTALLATION

***WARNING: Before working on air bag-equipped Celica, MR2 or Supra, ensure ignition switch is in LOCK position. Wait at least 20 SECONDS after disconnecting battery before proceeding with repair. Air bag system retains enough voltage to deploy air bag for a short time after disconnecting power.***

### STEERING WHEEL PAD & SPIRAL CABLE

**Removal (Celica, MR2 & Supra) – 1)** Make sure front wheels are in a straight-ahead position. Turn ignition off. Disconnect negative battery cable.

**2)** Remove engine hood release lever. Remove screw covers, 6 screws and lower instrument cluster trim panel(s). Loosen 4 steering wheel pad Torx screws until groove along screw circumference catches on screw case. *See Fig. 2.*

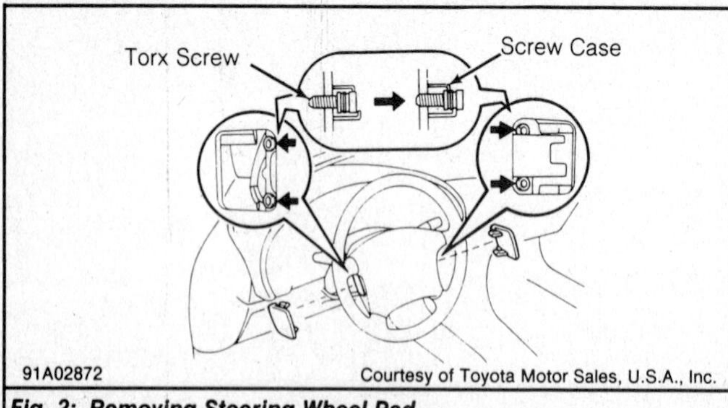


***Fig. 2: Removing Steering Wheel Pad***

**3)** Pull steering wheel pad from steering wheel and disconnect air bag. Remove steering wheel pad assembly. Place steering wheel pad assembly on a flat surface with pad cover facing upward.

**4)** Place a mark on steering wheel and main shaft for installation reference. Using steering wheel puller, remove steering wheel. Remove 4 screws from upper and lower steering column covers. Remove spiral cable-to-combination (headlight/turn signal/wiper) switch screws. Disconnect spiral cable and remove from vehicle.

**Installation – 1)** To install, reverse removal procedure. Before installing spiral cable, ensure spiral cable is properly aligned. See SPIRAL CABLE under ADJUSTMENTS.

**2)** After steering wheel pad and spiral cable are installed, ensure proper operation of air bag system by turning ignition switch to ACC or ON position. AIR BAG warning light should come on and go out after about 6 seconds.

**3)** If AIR BAG warning light stays on for more than 6 seconds, air bag system is malfunctioning and needs repair. If AIR BAG warning light comes on with ignition off, a short circuit may be present in AIR BAG warning light circuit.

### STEERING WHEEL & HORN PAD

**Removal & Installation (Camry, Corolla & Cressida) –** Remove screw securing horn pad and remove horn pad. Disconnect horn electrical connector(s). Remove lock nut and washer. Make alignment mark on steering shaft and steering wheel for installation reference. Install steering wheel puller and pull steering wheel from shaft. To install, reverse removal procedure.

### COMBINATION SWITCH

**Removal & Installation –** Remove steering wheel. See STEERING WHEEL PAD & SPIRAL CABLE or STEERING WHEEL & HORN PAD under REMOVAL & INSTALLATION. Remove instrument cluster lower trim panel. Remove upper and lower steering column covers. Disconnect combination switch electrical connector. Remove combination switch-to-steering column screws. Remove combination (headlight/turn signal/wiper) switch. To install, reverse removal procedure.

### IGNITION SWITCH

**Removal – 1)** Remove steering wheel, upper and lower steering column covers and combination (headlight/turn signal/wiper) switch (if necessary). Disconnect ignition switch harness connectors. If shear bolt studs are accessible, use a hacksaw to cut a slot into exposed studs.

**2)** Remove studs using a screwdriver. If shear bolt studs are recessed or hard to reach with a hacksaw, use a center punch on studs. Using drill bit and screw extractor, remove studs. Remove steering lock and ignition switch.

**Installation –** To install, reverse removal procedure. Install new shear bolts. Tighten shear bolts finger tight. Ensure proper operation of steering lock and ignition switch. Tighten shear bolts until heads break off. Install combination switch, upper and lower steering column covers and steering wheel (if removed).

### STEERING COLUMN

**Removal & Installation – 1)** Disconnect negative battery cable. Remove steering wheel pad. Mark steering shaft and wheel for installation reference. Remove steering wheel.

**2)** Remove instrument cluster lower trim panel. Remove air duct from under steering column (if equipped). Remove steering column upper and lower covers. Remove combination (headlight/turn signal/wiper) switch.

**3)** Mark "U" joint and shaft for installation reference. Remove bolt(s) and disconnect "U" joint from bottom of steering column shaft. Remove steering column bolts and steering column. To install, reverse removal procedure.

## OVERHAUL

### STEERING COLUMN

**Disassembly (Camry) – 1)** Remove bolt from main shaft. *See Fig. 4.* Remove 2 thrust stopper set bolts. Pull intermediate shaft from column tube. Remove 4 bolts. Remove column tube. Tilt main shaft upward. Pry tip of cord to remove spring and cord.

**2)** Push down on main shaft to compress main shaft. Using snap ring pliers, remove snap ring. Pull out main shaft. Remove spring and collar from main shaft. Remove 2 tension springs. Remove tilt lever bolt, collar and cushion. Remove 2 nuts and tilt lever retainer. Remove tilt pawl spacer and release pin. Remove stopper bolt nut and column cover support.

**3)** Using a hammer, tap out stopper bolt and cushion. Remove column upper bracket nut and set bolt. Temporarily install a nut to serration bolt end. Using a hammer, tap on nut to remove serration bolt from break-away bracket. Remove upper bracket.

**4)** Remove 2 collars, shim and tilt levers from upper bracket. Remove adjusting memory cover. Loosen upper tube tapered head bolt. Remove 2 upper tube bolts. Remove upper tube. Remove thrust stopper snap ring. Remove thrust stopper. Remove "O" ring from thrust stopper.

**Inspection** – Ensure lock mechanism operates properly. Check main shaft upper bearing for rotating smoothness. Check steering shafts for bending, damaged splines, or damaged "U" joints. Check column tube for bending or other damage. Repair or replace components as necessary.

**Reassembly – 1)** Reassemble in reverse order of disassembly procedure. Apply molybdenum disulfide lithium base grease to thrust stopper. Select appropriate tilt lever and control lever collar to eliminate free play. Collars are available in diameters of .7082-.7096" (17.989-18.024 mm).

**2)** Drive serrated bolt into support. Install tilt lever retainer. Select appropriate tilt lever retainer collar to eliminate free play. Tilt lever retainer collar is available in 2 diameters of .7080-.7087" (17.982-18.000 mm) or .7087-.7094" (18.000-18.018 mm). Select a steering support shim which fits snugly when pressed in by hand. See TILT STEERING SUPPORT SHIM THICKNESS (CAMRY) table. Ensure main shaft locks securely in all positions.

***TILT STEERING SUPPORT SHIM THICKNESS (CAMRY)***

| Mark | In. (mm) |
|---|---|
| None | .0067-.0091 (.17-.23) |
| 5 | .0177-.0217 (.45-.55) |
| 8 | .0295-.0335 (.75-.85) |
| 14 | .0531-.0571 (1.35-1.45) |
| 18 | .0689-.0728 (1.75-1.85) |

**Disassembly (Celica & MR2) – 1)** Drill out tapered-head bolts. Using a screw extractor, remove column bracket bolts. Remove upper (key cylinder) bracket. *See Fig. 5.* Remove compression spring bolt. Remove compression spring.

**2)** Remove bushings from compression spring. Remove 3 tension springs. Remove 2 tilt lever "E" rings from tilt lever lock shaft. Remove tilt lever spacer. Remove 2 nuts from tilt steering bolts. Remove 2 tilt lever retainers and 2 pawl stoppers.

**3)** Remove tilt pawl nut and washers. Pull out tilt pawl bolt. Remove tilt lever assembly installation bolt. Remove 2 tilt pawls. Remove tilt lever, tilt sub lever and tilt lever assembly from tilt lever lock shaft.

**4)** Install a nut (10 mm x 1.25 mm), washer (36-mm outer diameter), and a 2" (50 mm) bolt (10 mm x 1.25 mm) to upper column tube tilt steering bolt. Using a slide hammer, remove steering column tube tilt bolts. Remove upper column tube from lower column tube. *See Fig. 3.* Remove collar from main shaft.

**5)** Using a press, compress spring on main shaft. Remove snap ring. Remove main shaft from column tube. Remove spring, thrust collar and bearing.

**Inspection** – Ensure lock mechanism operates properly. Check upper bracket for damage and upper bearing for rotating smoothness. Check steering shafts for bending, damaged splines, or damaged "U" joints. Check column tube for bending or other damage. Repair or replace components as necessary.

**Reassembly – 1)** Reassemble in reverse order of disassembly procedure. Apply molybdenum disulfide lithium base grease to tilt lever assembly, lock bolt, main shaft, and steering bolt pivot points. Install steering column tube tilt bolts.

**2)** If upper column tube mark is "1", install hollow tipped thread bolt. If upper column tube mark is "2", install plain thread bolt. With tilt pawl and ratchet engaged, install 2 pawl stoppers. Ensure alignment marks on tilt pawl and stopper align when stopper is rotated to pawl side. If alignment marks do not align, select a different size pawl stopper. See TILT PAWL STOPPER SIZE table.

***TILT PAWL STOPPER SIZE***

| Mark Tilt Lever Side | Mark Tilt Sub Lever Side | In. (mm) |
|---|---|---|
| MR2 | | |
| 1 | A | .4980-.5020 (12.65-12.75) |
| 2 | B | .4941-.4980 (12.55-12.65) |
| 3 | C | .4902-.4941 (12.45-12.55) |
| 4 | D | .4862-.4902 (12.32-12.45) |
| 5 | E | .4823-.4862 (12.25-12.35) |
| Celica | | |
| 1 | A | .4992-.5016 (12.68-12.74) |
| 2 | B | .4965-.4988 (12.61-12.67) |
| 3 | C | .4937-.4961 (12.54-12.60) |
| 4 | D | .4909-.4933 (12.47-12.53) |
| 5 | E | .4882-.4906 (12.40-12.46) |
| 6 | F | .4854-.4878 (12.33-12.39) |
| 7 | G | .4827-.4850 (12.26-12.32) |

**Disassembly (Corolla) – 1)** Drill out tapered-head bolts. Using a screw extractor, remove column bracket bolts. Remove upper key cylinder bracket. Remove 2 tension springs. *See Fig. 6.* Remove 2 compression spring bolts and compression springs.

**2)** Remove bushings from compression springs. Remove 2 tilt lever nuts from lock bolts. Remove retainer with 2 nuts. Remove 2 tilt pawls nuts and bolts. Remove 2 pawls with collars. Remove collar from pawl. Remove 2 pawl stoppers. Remove tilt lever, tilt sub lever and lever lock bolt.

**3)** Install a nut (10 mm x 1.25 mm), washer (36-mm outer diameter), and a 2" (50 mm) bolt (10 mm x 1.25 mm) to upper column tube tilt steering bolt. Using a slide hammer, remove steering column tube tilt bolts. Remove upper column tube from lower column tube. *See Fig. 3.* Remove stopper.

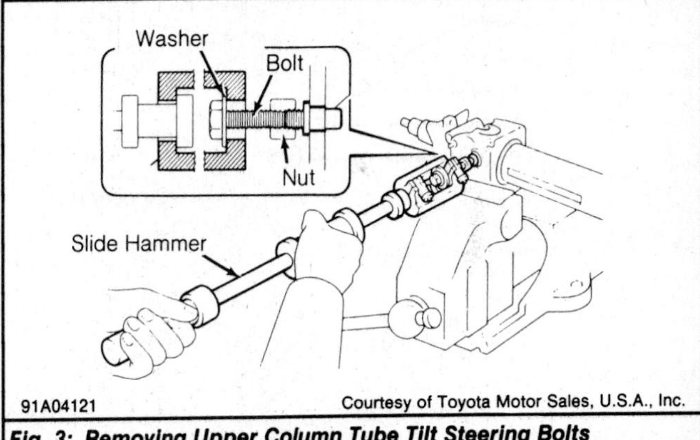


***Fig. 3: Removing Upper Column Tube Tilt Steering Bolts***

**4)** Using a press, compress spring on main shaft. Remove snap ring. Remove main shaft from upper column tube. Remove spring, thrust collar and bearing. Remove snap ring. Remove wire harness clamp. Remove 3 steering support-to-column tube bolts. Remove steering support. Remove main shaft collar snap ring from lower column tube. Remove main shaft collar.

**Inspection** – Ensure lock mechanism operates properly. Check upper bracket for damage and upper bearing for rotating smoothness. Check steering shafts for bending, damaged splines or damaged "U" joints. Check column tube for bending or other damage. Repair or replace components as necessary.

**Reassembly** – Reassemble in reverse order of disassembly procedure. Apply molybdenum disulfide lithium base grease to tilt lever assembly, lock bolt, main shaft and steering bolt pivot points. Install steering column tube tilt bolts. If upper column tube mark is "1", install plain thread bolt. If upper column tube mark is "2", install hollow tipped thread bolt. Select a tilt pawl collar which will eliminate free play. See TILT PAWL COLLAR THICKNESS table.

# 1991 STEERING
# Steering Columns – Tilt Wheel – Cars (Cont.)

*TILT PAWL COLLAR THICKNESS*

| Mark Tilt Lever Collar | Mark Sub Lever Collar | In. (mm) |
|---|---|---|
| 0 | A | .4521-.4525 (11.483-11.493) |
| 2 | 6 | .4527-.4531 (11.499-11.509) |
| 3 | 7 | .4525-.4529 (11.494-11.504) |
| 4 | 8 | .4523-.4527 (11.488-11.498) |

**Disassembly (Cressida) – 1)** Drill out tapered-head bolts. Using a screw extractor, remove steering column upper bracket bolts. Remove upper steering column bracket. Remove telescopic lever serration nut. *See Fig. 7.* Remove telescopic serration attachment. Remove telescopic lever bolt, collar, telescopic lever and washer. Remove ball and compression spring.

**2)** Install a double nut on telescopic lever lock bolt. Remove lock bolt. Remove steering column tube stopper bolt. Remove snap ring from main shaft. Remove break-away bracket from main shaft. Ensure spline shaft part of main shaft does not come loose.

**3)** Remove 2 lock wedges from break-away bracket. Remove No. 1 and No. 2 telescopic spring seats and compression spring from break-away bracket. Remove steering shaft thrust stopper from break-away bracket. Remove compression spring bolt and compression spring.

**4)** Remove 2 bushings from compression spring. Remove 3 tension springs. Remove 2 tilt lever "E" rings from tilt lever lock shaft. Remove 2 tilt lever nuts from tilt steering bolts. Remove 2 tilt lever retainers and 2 steering pawl stoppers.

**5)** Remove steering tilt pawl nut, washers and through bolt. Remove tilt lever assembly lock bolt. Remove tilt lever assembly, tilt lever lock shaft, tilt lever and sub tilt lever. Install a nut (10 mm x 1.25 mm), washer (36-mm outer diameter), and a 2" (50 mm) bolt (10 mm x 1.25 mm) to upper column tube tilt steering bolt. Using a slide hammer, remove steering column tube tilt bolts. Remove upper column tube from lower column tube. *See Fig. 3.* Remove stopper.

**6)** Using a press, compress main shaft compression spring. Remove main shaft snap ring. Remove main shaft from column tube. Remove spring, thrust collar and bearing.

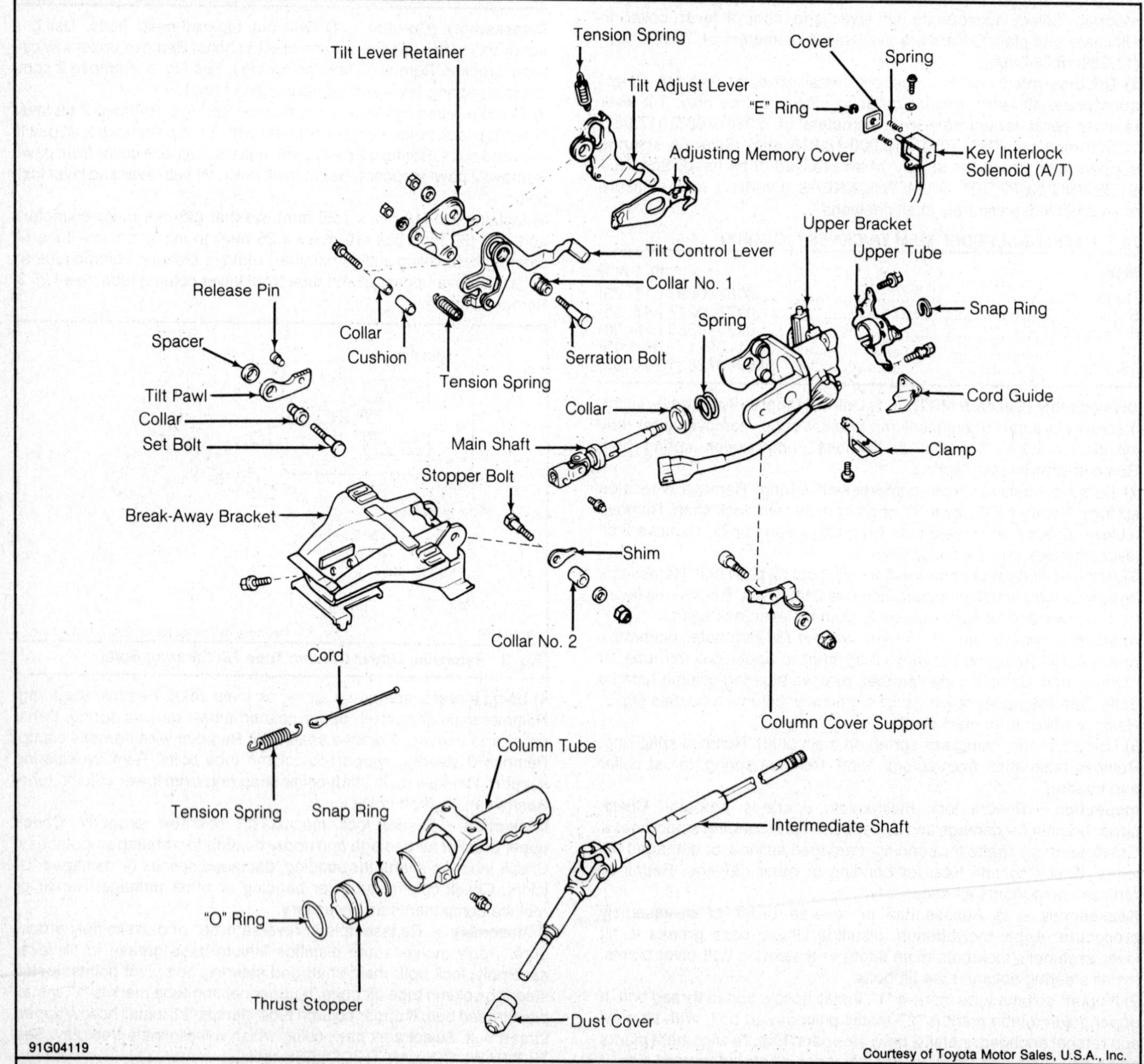


***Fig. 4: Exploded View of Steering Column (Camry)***

# 1991 STEERING
# Steering Columns – Tilt Wheel – Cars (Cont.)

**Inspection** – Ensure lock mechanism operates properly. Check upper bracket for damage and upper bearing for rotating smoothness. Check steering shafts for bending, damaged splines, or damaged "U" joints. Check column tube for bending or other damage. Repair or replace components as necessary.

**Reassembly** – Reassemble in reverse order of disassembly procedure. Apply molybdenum disulfide lithium base grease to tilt lever assembly, lock bolt, main shaft and steering bolt pivot points. Install steering column tube tilt bolts. If upper column tube mark is "1", install hollow tipped thread bolt. If upper column tube mark is "2", install plain thread bolt. Select appropriate steering pawl stopper to eliminate free play. See STEERING PAWL STOPPER SIZE table.

***STEERING PAWL STOPPER SIZE***

| Mark Tilt Lever Side | Mark Sub Lever Side | In. (mm) |
|---|---|---|
| 1 | A | .4980-.5020 (12.65-12.75) |
| 2 | B | .4941-.4980 (12.55-12.65) |
| 3 | C | .4902-.4941 (12.45-12.55) |
| 4 | D | .4862-.4902 (12.35-12.45) |
| 5 | E | .4823-.4862 (12.25-12.35) |

**Disassembly (Supra) – 1)** Remove 2 steering sensor screws. Remove steering sensor. Remove ignition key light screw. Remove

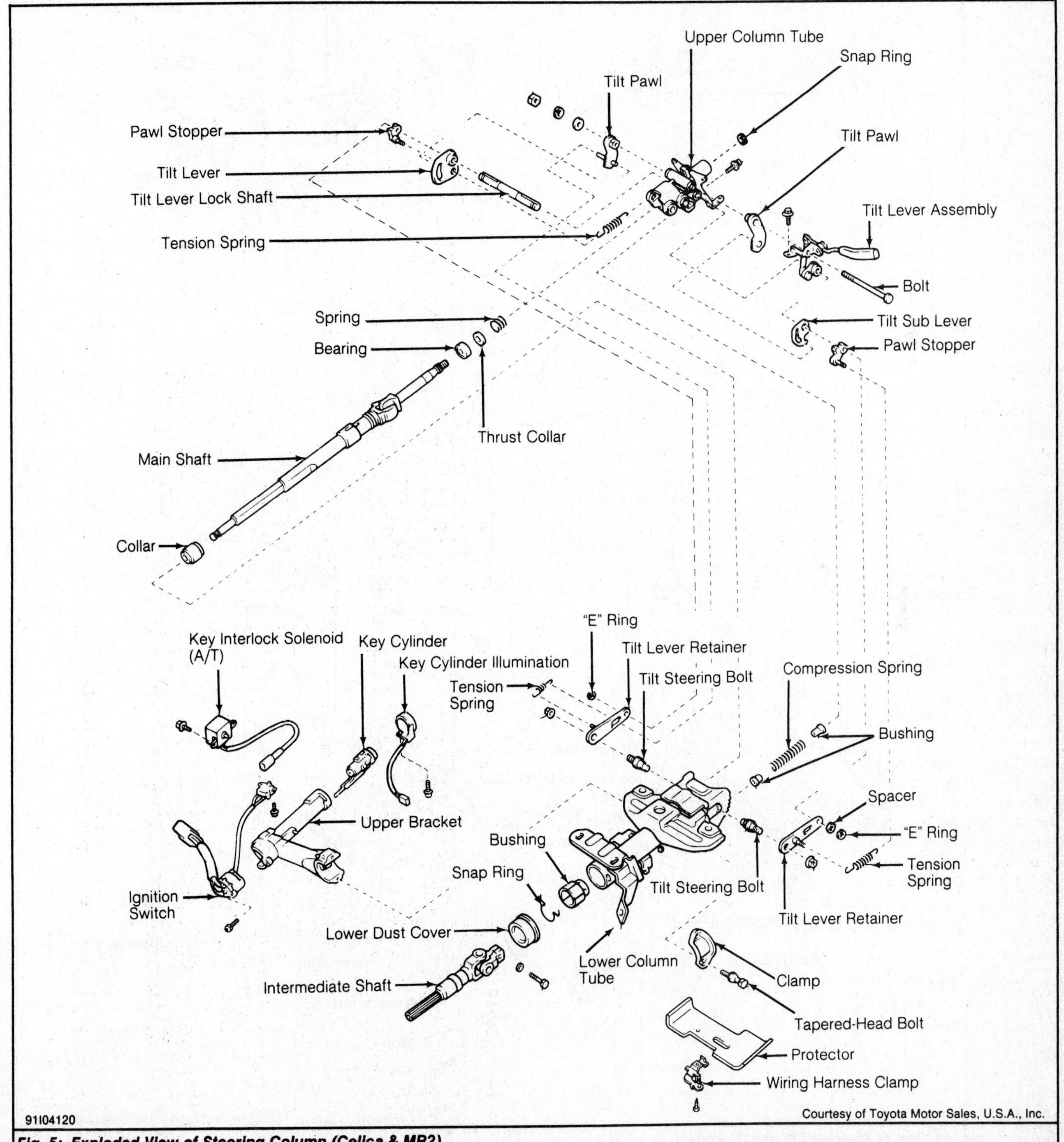


***Fig. 5: Exploded View of Steering Column (Celica & MR2)***

# 1991 STEERING
## Steering Columns – Tilt Wheel – Cars (Cont.)

ignition key light. Remove 2 column hole cover bolts. Remove "O" ring and cover plate. Remove bolt from main shaft. *See Fig. 8*.

**2)** Remove 2 bolts from retainer bracket. Pull intermediate shaft from column tube. Remove 4 break-away bracket bolts. Remove column tube. Tilt main shaft upward. Pry tip of cord to remove springs and cords.

**3)** Remove telescopic lever nut. Remove telescopic lever. Remove telescopic lever lock bolt. Remove column tube stopper. Pull out main shaft assembly. Catch 2 lock wedges as main shaft assembly is being removed. Remove tension spring.

**4)** Remove 2 tilt lever retainer bolts and nuts. Remove tilt lever retainer, collar and cushion. Remove tension spring. Remove tilt lever retainer bolt, 2 nuts and tilt lever retainer. Remove spacer and pin. Remove tilt steering adjusting nut and pin.

**5)** Remove tilt steering support stopper bolt and nut. Temporarily install a nut to serration bolt end. Using a hammer, tap on nut to

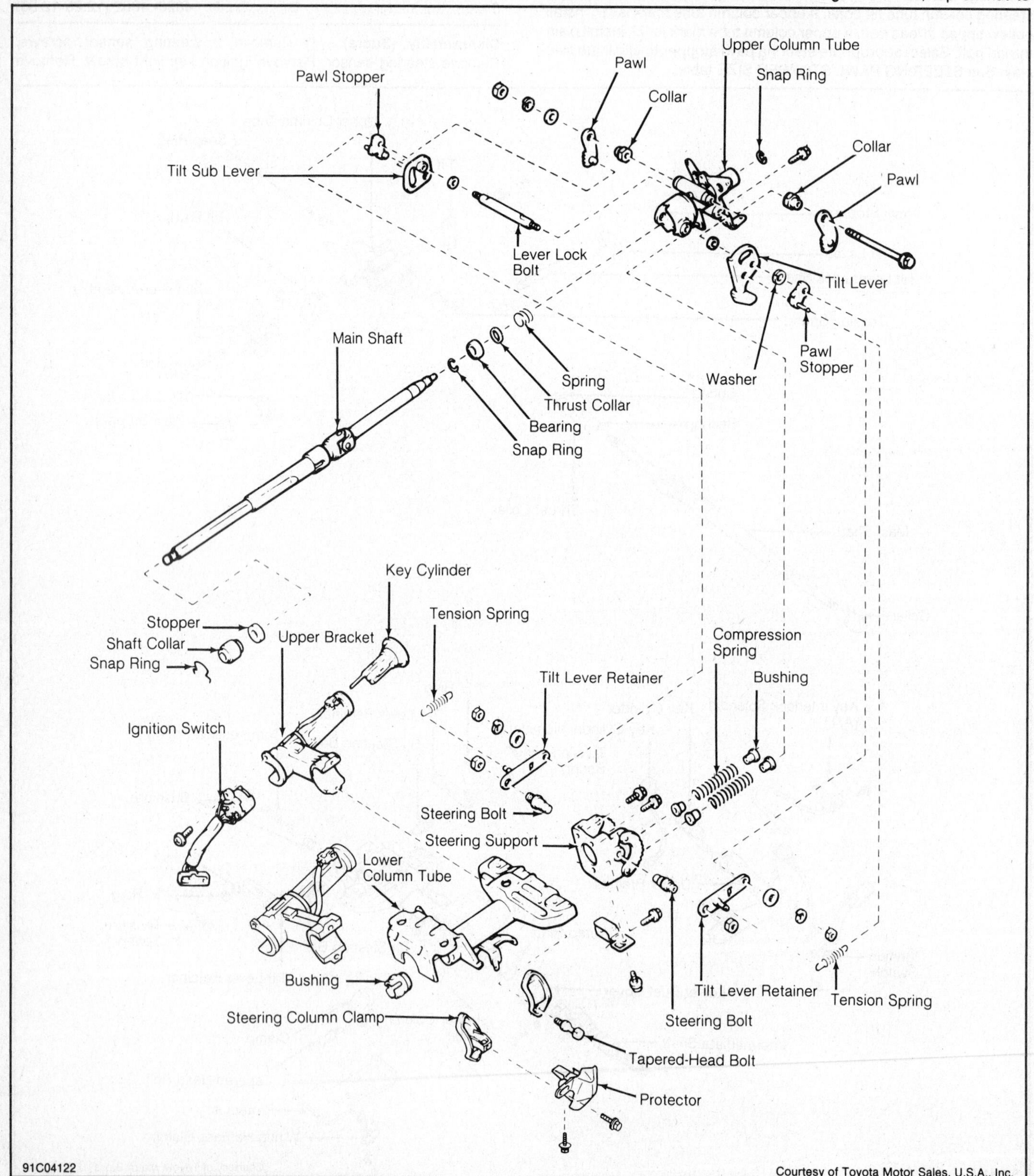


***Fig. 6: Exploded View of Steering Column (Corolla)***

# 1991 STEERING
## Steering Columns – Tilt Wheel – Cars (Cont.)

remove serration bolt from break-away bracket. Remove upper bracket. Remove 2 upper column bracket bolts.

**6)** Remove tilt steering No. 1 support collar, tilt lever, No. 1 tilt sub lever, tilt steering No. 2 support collar, No. 2 tilt sub lever and support shim. Using a chisel, remove steering shaft thrust stopper with 3 screws. Remove 2 steering pawls.

**7)** Temporarily install a nut to serration bolt end. Using a hammer, tap on nut to remove serration bolt from break-away bracket. Using a hammer and brass bar, remove sensor disc from intermediate shaft. Remove sensor disc snap ring. Remove thrust stopper snap ring. Remove thrust stopper and thrust stopper "O" ring.

**Inspection** – Ensure lock mechanism operates properly. Check main shaft upper bearing for rotating smoothness. Check steering shafts for bending, damaged splines or damaged "U" joints. Check column tube for bending or other damage. Repair or replace components as necessary.

**Reassembly – 1)** Reassemble in reverse order of disassembly procedure. Apply molybdenum disulfide lithium base grease to thrust

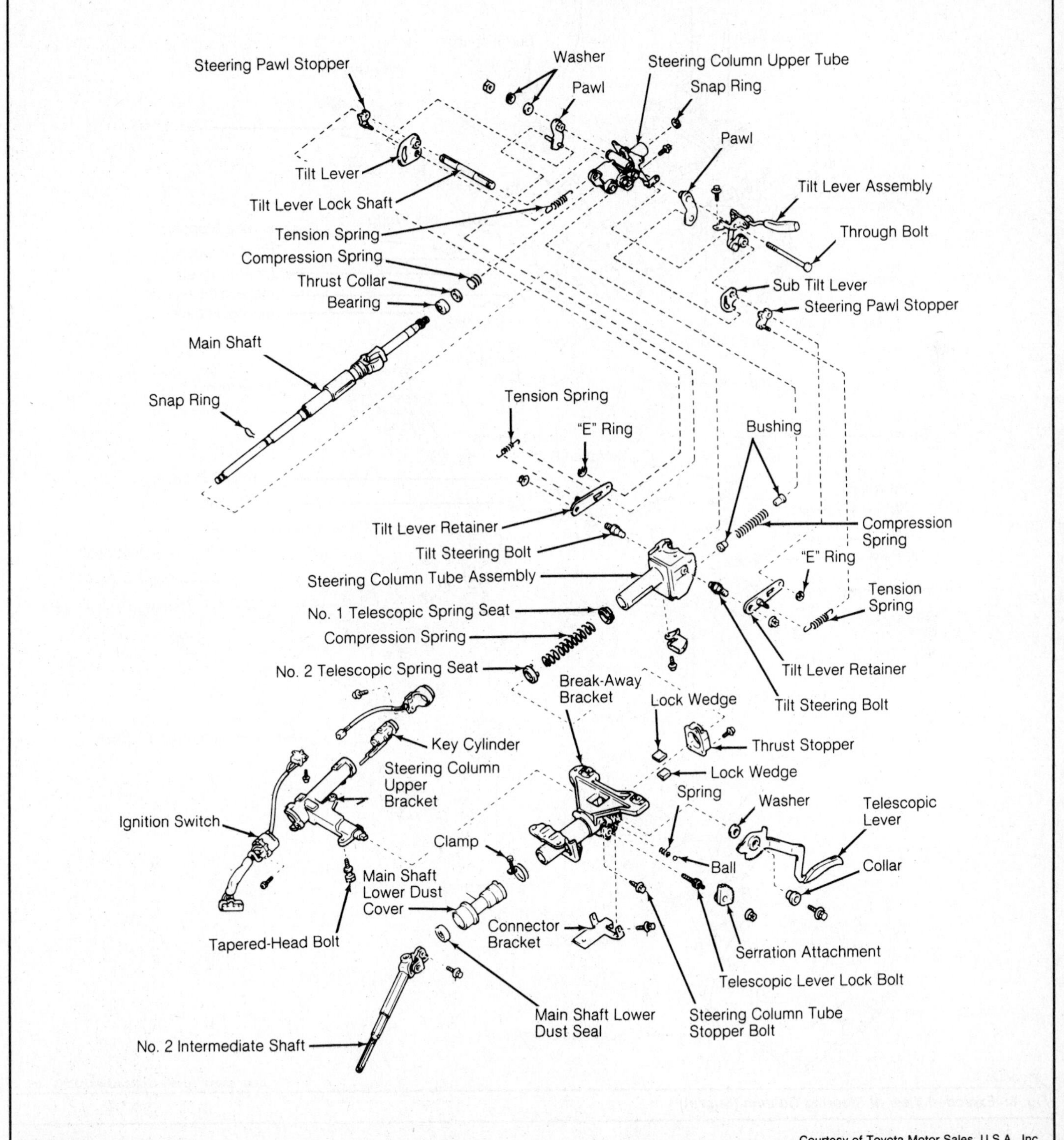


*Fig. 7: Exploded View of Steering Column (Cressida)*

# 1991 STEERING
## Steering Columns – Tilt Wheel – Cars (Cont.)

stopper. Select a No. 1 and No. 2 support collar which will eliminate free play. Collars are available in diameters of .7082-.7096" (17.989-18.024 mm).

**2)** Drive in serrated bolt into support. Install tilt lever retainer. Select a steering support shim which fits snugly when pressed in by hand. See TILT STEERING SUPPORT SHIM THICKNESS (SUPRA) table. Ensure main shaft locks securely in all positions.

***TILT STEERING SUPPORT SHIM THICKNESS (SUPRA)***

| Mark | In. (mm) |
|---|---|
| None | .0078-.0080 (.197-.203) |
| 5 | .0195-.0199 (.495-.505) |
| 8 | .0313-.0317 (.795-.805) |
| 14 | .0549-.0553 (1.395-1.405) |
| 18 | .0707-.0711 (1.795-1.805) |

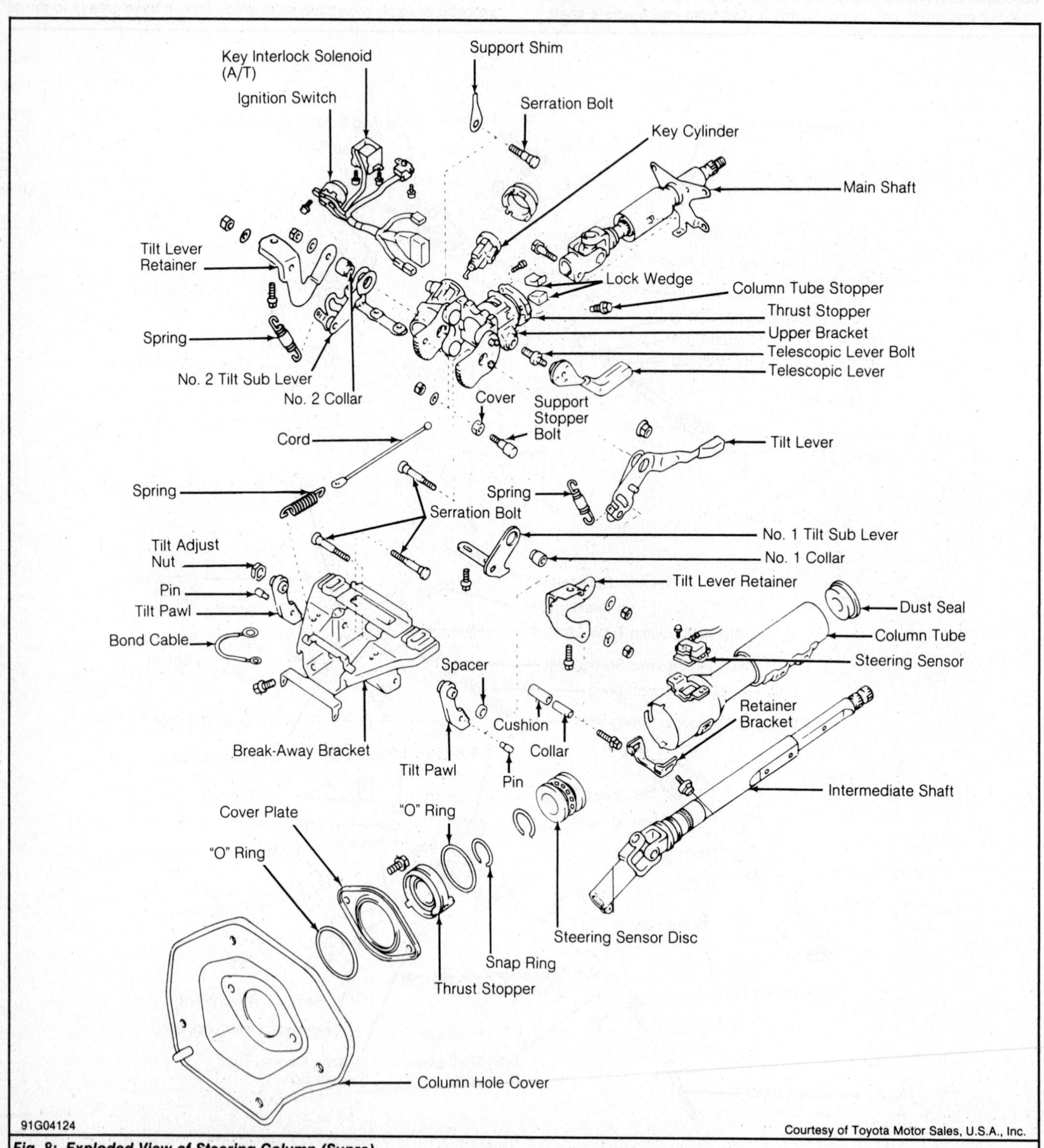


***Fig. 8: Exploded View of Steering Column (Supra)***

## TORQUE SPECIFICATIONS

### TORQUE SPECIFICATIONS (CAMRY)

| Application | Ft. Lbs. (N.m) |
|---|---|
| Column Tube Break-Away Bolt | 13 (18) |
| No. 1 & No. 2 Collar Nut | 14 (19) |
| Steering Wheel Nut | 25 (34) |
| Tilt Lever Retainer Nut | 14 (19) |
| "U" Joint Clamp Bolt | 19 (26) |
| Upper Tube Bolts | 13 (18) |
| | **INCH Lbs. (N.m)** |
| Stopper Bolt | 96 (11) |

### TORQUE SPECIFICATIONS (CELICA & MR2)

| Application | Ft. Lbs. (N.m) |
|---|---|
| Tilt Lever Retainer Nut | 11 (15) |
| Steering Wheel Nut | 25 (34) |
| Tilt Sub Lever Retainer Nut | 11 (15) |
| "U" Joint Clamp Bolt | 26 (35) |
| | **INCH Lbs. (N.m)** |
| Compression Spring Bolt | 69 (8) |
| Tilt Lever Bolt | 26 (3) |
| Tilt Sub Lever Bolt | 52 (6) |

### TORQUE SPECIFICATIONS (COROLLA)

| Application | Ft. Lbs. (N.m) |
|---|---|
| Steering Support Bolts | 14 (19) |
| Steering Wheel Nut | 25 (34) |
| | **INCH Lbs. (N.m)** |
| Compression Spring Bolt | 69 (8) |
| Tilt Lever Retainer Nut | 84 (9) |
| Tilt Pawl Nut | 69 (8) |

### TORQUE SPECIFICATIONS (CRESSIDA)

| Application | Ft. Lbs. (N.m) |
|---|---|
| Column Tube Stopper Bolt | 14 (19) |
| Steering Wheel Nut | 25 (34) |
| Telescopic Lever Bolt | 19 (26) |
| Tilt Lever Retainer Nut | 11 (15) |
| "U" Joint Clamp Bolt | 26 (35) |
| | **INCH Lbs. (N.m)** |
| Compression Spring Bolt | 69 (8) |
| Telescopic Lever Serration Bolt | 106 (12) |
| Tilt Lever Lock Bolt | 26 (3) |
| Tilt Lever Side Pawl Nut | 52 (6) |

### TORQUE SPECIFICATIONS (SUPRA)

| Application | Ft. Lbs. (N.m) |
|---|---|
| Column Tube Break-Away Bolts | 14 (19) |
| Retainer Bracket Bolts | 20 (27) |
| Serration Bolt Nuts | 14 (19) |
| Steering Wheel Nut | 25 (34) |
| Telescopic Lever Set Nut | 10 (14) |
| Tilt Lever Retainer Bolt | 14 (19) |
| "U" Joint Clamp Bolt | 24 (32) |
| | **INCH Lbs. (N.m)** |
| Column Tube Stopper Bolt | 69 (8) |
| Serration Bolts | 69 (8) |
| Steering Wheel Pad Torx Screws | 65 (7) |
| Support Stopper Bolt | 96 (11) |

# 1991 STEERING
# Steering Columns – Tilt Wheel – Light Trucks

**Land Cruiser, Pickup, 4Runner**

## DESCRIPTION & OPERATION

Tilt steering wheels incorporate an upper steering shaft, attached by a "U" joint to an intermediate steering shaft. Shafts are held in place by upper and lower brackets.

Brackets are pinned together so upper bracket can move up or down. Upper bracket is locked in place by pawl attached to lever. Steering columns are collapsible.

## REMOVAL & INSTALLATION

### STEERING WHEEL & HORN PAD

**Removal & Installation** – Disconnect battery ground cable. Remove screw securing horn pad and remove horn pad. Disconnect horn electrical connector(s). Remove lock nut and washer. Mark steering shaft and steering wheel for installation reference. Install steering wheel puller and remove steering wheel from shaft. To install, reverse removal procedure.

### COMBINATION SWITCH

**Removal & Installation** – Disconnect battery ground cable. Remove steering wheel. See STEERING WHEEL & HORN PAD in this article. Remove instrument cluster lower trim panel. Remove upper and lower steering column covers. Disconnect combination switch electrical connector. Remove combination switch securing screws and remove combination switch. To install, reverse removal procedure.

### IGNITION SWITCH & LOCK CYLINDER

**Removal** – **1)** Disconnect battery ground cable. Remove steering wheel, upper and lower steering column covers and combination switch (if necessary). Disconnect ignition switch harness connectors.
**2)** If shear bolt studs are accessible, use a hacksaw to slot exposed studs. Using a screwdriver, remove studs.
**3)** If shear bolt studs are recessed or hard to reach with hacksaw, center punch studs. Using a drill bit and a screw extractor, remove studs. Remove steering lock and ignition switch.
**Installation** – **1)** To install, reverse removal procedure. Install new shear bolts. Tighten shear bolts finger tight. Ensure proper operation of steering lock and ignition switch.

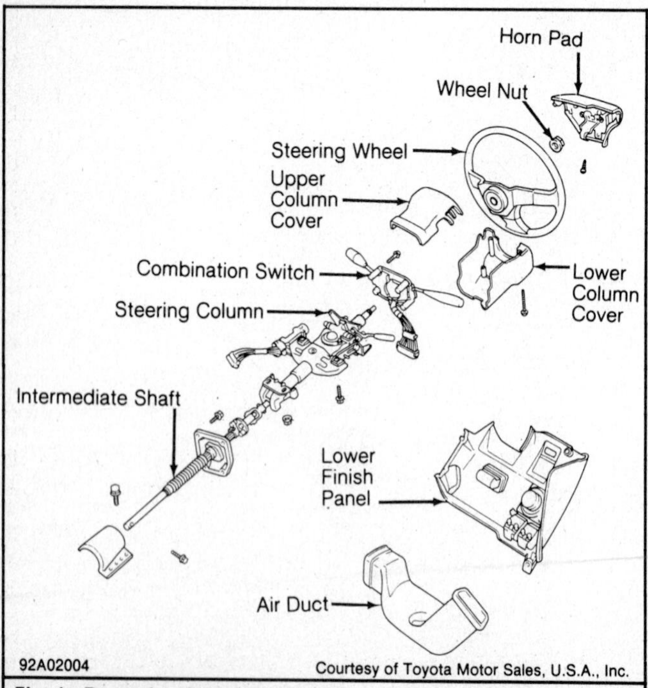


***Fig. 1: Removing Steering Column (Land Cruiser Shown; Pickup & 4Runner Are Similar)***

**2)** Tighten shear bolts until heads break off. Install combination switch, upper and lower steering column covers and steering wheel.

### STEERING COLUMN

**Removal & Installation** – **1)** Disconnect battery ground cable. Remove steering wheel. See STEERING WHEEL & HORN PAD under REMOVAL & INSTALLATION. *See Fig. 1.*
**2)** Remove instrument cluster lower trim panel. Remove air duct from under steering column (if equipped). Remove steering column upper and lower covers. Remove combination switch.
**3)** On Land Cruiser, remove lower finish panel. Mark "U" joint and shaft for installation reference. Remove bolt and disconnect "U" joint from bottom of steering column shaft. Remove bolts securing steering column.
**4)** On Pickup and 4Runner, mark steering gearbox and steering column shaft for installation reference. Remove bolts securing steering column. On all models, remove steering column from vehicle. To install, reverse removal procedure.

## OVERHAUL

### STEERING COLUMN

**Disassembly (Land Cruiser)** – **1)** Mark worm shaft and main shaft for assembly. Disconnect mainshaft from worm shaft. Mark "U" joint and shaft. Remove "U" joint bolt and "U" joint. *See Fig. 2.*

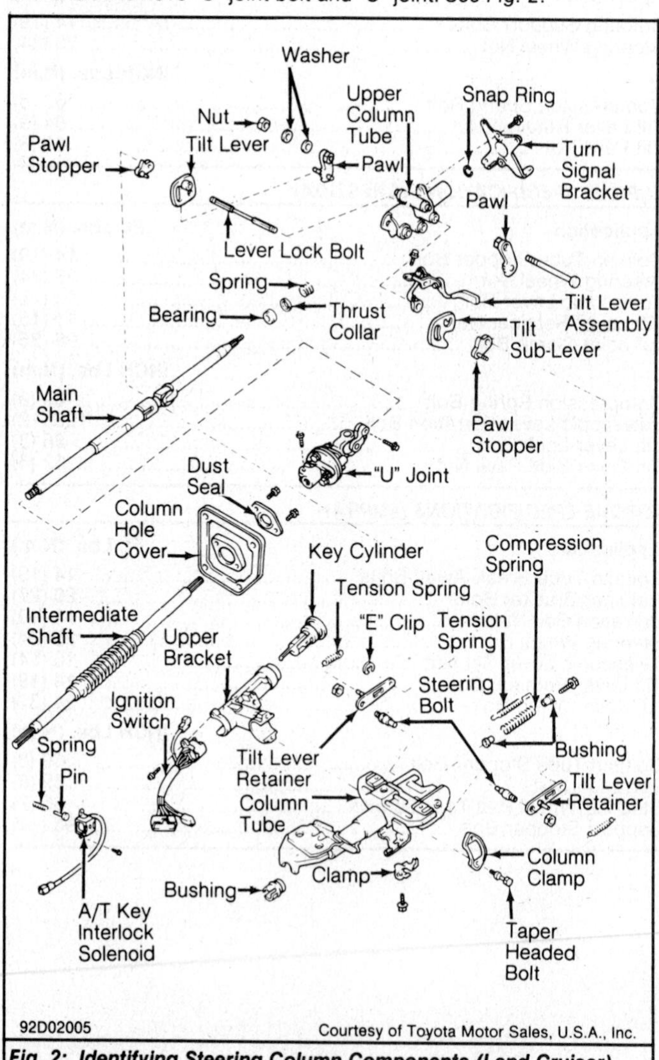


***Fig. 2: Identifying Steering Column Components (Land Cruiser)***

# 1991 STEERING
## Steering Columns – Tilt Wheel – Light Trucks (Cont.)

2) Mark flexible coupling and shaft. Remove bolt and shaft. Remove 2 bolts and dust shield. Remove column hole cover.
3) Drill tapered head column bracket bolts and use a screw extractor to remove. Remove upper steering column bracket.
4) Remove bolt and compression spring. Remove bushings from spring. Remove 3 tension springs. Remove "E" clips, retainers, and nuts. Remove 2 pawl stoppers. Remove nut, bolt, tilt pawls, and collars. Remove tilt lever, sub-lever, and lever lock bolt.
5) Install a nut (10 x 1.25 mm), washer (36 mm outer diameter), and a 2" (50 mm) bolt (10 x 1.25 mm) to upper column tube. Using slide hammer, remove steering column bolts. *See Fig. 3*. Remove upper column tube and stopper.

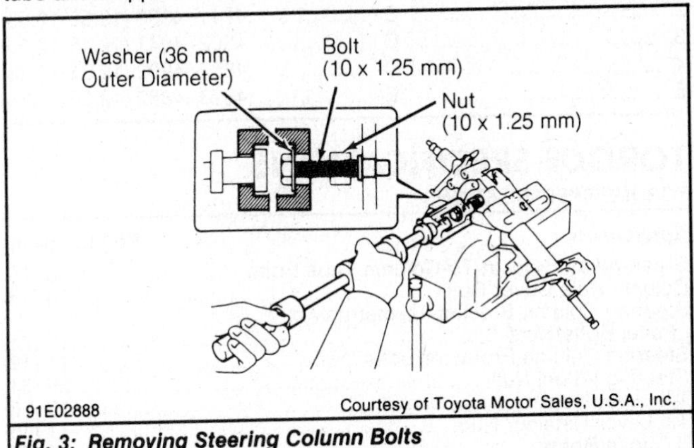


**Fig. 3: Removing Steering Column Bolts**

6) Remove turn signal bracket. Attach a universal puller to upper column tube and compress main shaft. Remove snap ring, puller, main shaft, spring, thrust collar, and bearing. Remove snap ring and main shaft collar from lower column tube.

**Inspection** – Ensure lock mechanism operates properly. Check upper bracket for damage and bearings for rotating smoothness. Check steering shafts for bending, damaged splines, or damaged "U" joints. Check column tube for bending or other damage. Repair or replace components as necessary.

**Reassembly – 1)** To reassemble, reverse disassembly procedure. Align bushing tab with hole of column tube. Apply molybdenum disulfide lithium base grease to tilt lever assembly, lock bolt, main shaft, and steering column bolt pivot points.
2) Select steering column bolt WITH center hole when upper column tube is marked "1" (select bolt WITHOUT hole when mark is "2"). *See Fig. 4*. Tap steering column bolts into place.

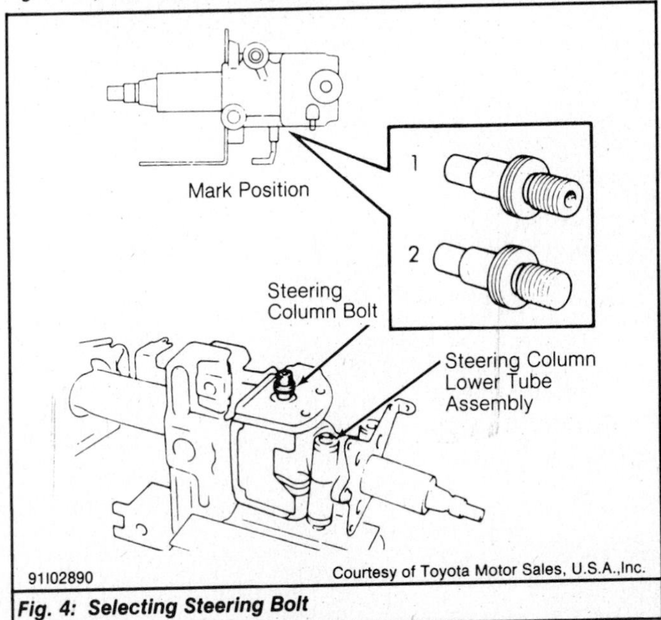


**Fig. 4: Selecting Steering Bolt**

3) Engage tilt sub-lever side pawl to center of ratchet. While turning tilt lever side collar, engage tilt lever side pawl to ratchet. *See Fig. 5*. Install and tighten tilt pawl nut.

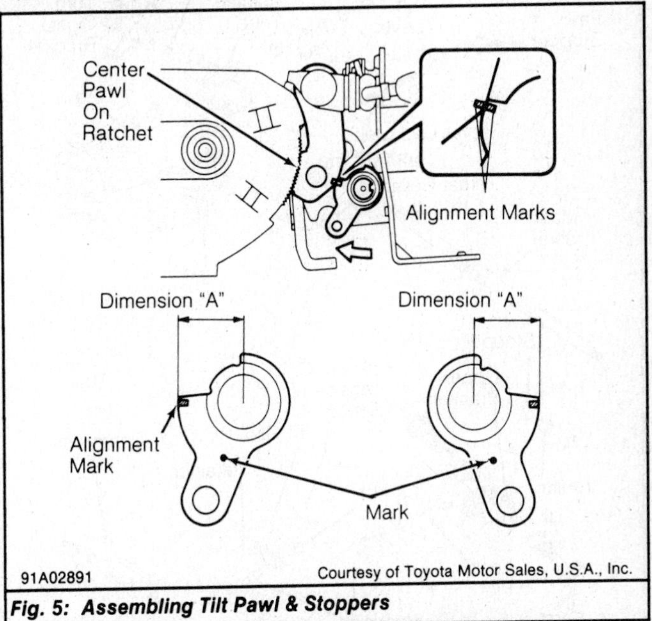


**Fig. 5: Assembling Tilt Pawl & Stoppers**

4) With tilt pawl and ratchet engaged, install 2 tilt pawl stoppers. Check that alignment marks on stopper and tilt pawl align when stopper is rotated to pawl side. *See Fig. 5*.
5) If alignment marks do not align, select replacement tilt pawl stoppers. See TILT PAWL STOPPER SELECTION table. After selecting tilt pawl stoppers, ensure that both sides of pawl and ratchet are fully engaged.
6) Tighten steering column clamp tapered head bolts until hexagonal head breaks off. Check that main shaft locks securely in uppermost and lowermost positions.

**Disassembly (Pickup & 4Runner) – 1)** Drill out tapered head bolts and use a screw extractor to remove column bracket bolts. Remove upper steering column bracket. *See Fig. 6*.
2) Remove bolt and compression spring. Remove bushings from spring. Remove 3 tension springs. Remove "E" clips, retainers, and nuts. Remove 2 pawl stoppers. Remove nut, bolt, tilt pawls, and collars. Remove tilt lever, sub-lever, and lever lock bolt.
3) Install a nut (10 x 1.25 mm), washer (36 mm outer diameter), and a 2" (50 mm) bolt (10 x 1.25 mm) to upper column tube. Use a slide hammer to remove steering column bolts. *See Fig. 3*. Remove upper column tube and stopper.
4) Remove turn signal bracket. Attach a universal puller to upper column tube and compress main shaft. Remove snap ring, puller, main shaft, spring, thrust collar, and bearing. Remove snap ring and main shaft collar from lower column tube.

**Inspection** – Check that lock mechanism operates properly. Check upper bracket for damage. Check steering shafts for bending, damaged splines, or damaged "U" joints. Check column tube for bending or other damage. Repair or replace components as necessary.

**Reassembly – 1)** To reassemble, reverse disassembly procedure. Align bushing tab with hole of column tube. Apply molybdenum disulfide lithium base grease to tilt lever assembly, lock bolt, main shaft, and steering column bolt pivot points.
2) Select steering column bolt WITH center hole when upper column tube is marked "1" (select bolt WITHOUT hole when mark is "2"). *See Fig. 4*. Tap steering column bolts into place.
3) Engage tilt sub-lever side pawl to center of ratchet. While turning tilt lever side collar, engage tilt lever side pawl to ratchet. *See Fig. 5*. Install and tighten tilt pawl nut.
4) With tilt pawl and ratchet engaged, install 2 tilt pawl stoppers. Check that alignment marks on stopper and tilt pawl align when stopper is rotated to pawl side. *See Fig. 5*.

# Steering Columns – Tilt Wheel – Light Trucks (Cont.)

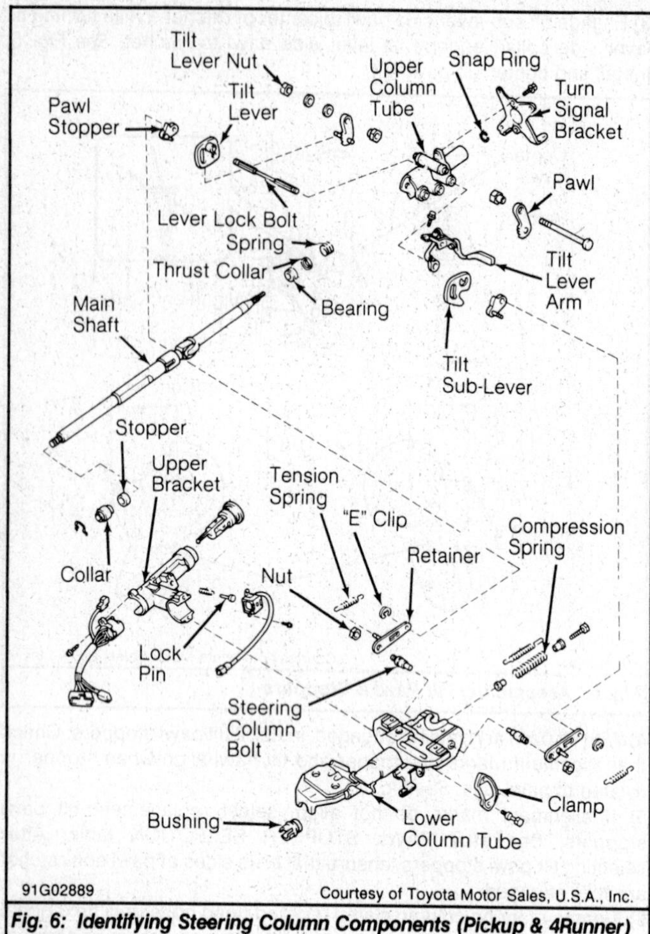


*Fig. 6: Identifying Steering Column Components (Pickup & 4Runner)*

**5)** If alignment marks do not align, select replacement tilt pawl stoppers. See TILT PAWL STOPPER SELECTION table. After selecting tilt pawl stoppers, ensure that both sides of pawl and ratchet are fully engaged.

**6)** Tighten steering column clamp tapered head bolts until hexagonal head breaks off. Check that main shaft locks securely in uppermost and lowermost positions.

***TILT PAWL STOPPER SELECTION***

| Tilt Lever Side (Mark) | Tilt Sub-Lever Side (Mark) | Dimension "A" In. (mm) |
|---|---|---|
| 1 | A | .4980-.5020 (12.65-12.75) |
| 2 | B | .4941-.4980 (12.55-12.65) |
| 3 | C | .4902-.4941 (12.45-12.55) |
| 4 | D | .4862-.4902 (12.35-12.45) |
| 5 | E | .4823-.4862 (12.25-12.35) |

## TORQUE SPECIFICATIONS

***TORQUE SPECIFICATIONS***

| Application | Ft. Lbs. (N.m) |
|---|---|
| Break-Away Bracket-To-Column Tube Bolts | 13 (18) |
| Column Hole Cover Bolts | 10 (13) |
| Steering Column Bracket-To-Instrument Panel Bolts/Nuts | 18 (25) |
| Steering Column Protector Bolts | 14 (19) |
| Steering Wheel Nut | 25 (34) |
| Tilt Lever Nuts | 13 (18) |
| Tilt Lever Retainer Nuts | 11 (15) |
| "U" Joint Bolts | 26 (35) |
| | **INCH Lbs. (N.m)** |
| Column Hole Cover Bolts | 65 (7) |
| Compression Spring Bolts | 65 (7) |
| Support Stopper Nut | 65 (7) |
| Support-To-Upper Bracket Bolts | 65 (7) |
| Tilt Lever Bolts | 17 (2) |
| Tilt Pawl Nuts | 52 (6) |
| Turn Signal Bracket Bolts | 65 (7) |

# 1991 STEERING
# Manual Rack & Pinion

## Corolla, MR2, Tercel

## DESCRIPTION

Steering assembly is a rack and pinion type. Unit consists of a toothed rack and toothed pinion. Pinion gear preload is adjustable.

## ADJUSTMENTS

Adjustments are made during the reassembly procedure. See OVERHAUL.

## REMOVAL & INSTALLATION

### STEERING GEAR

***WARNING: On MR2, to avoid possible damage to air bag restraint system spiral cable, ensure steering wheel is firmly fixed in position and NOT turned. If steering wheel turns, inspect and re-center spiral cable. See AIR BAG RESTRAINT SYSTEM article in SAFETY EQUIPMENT.***

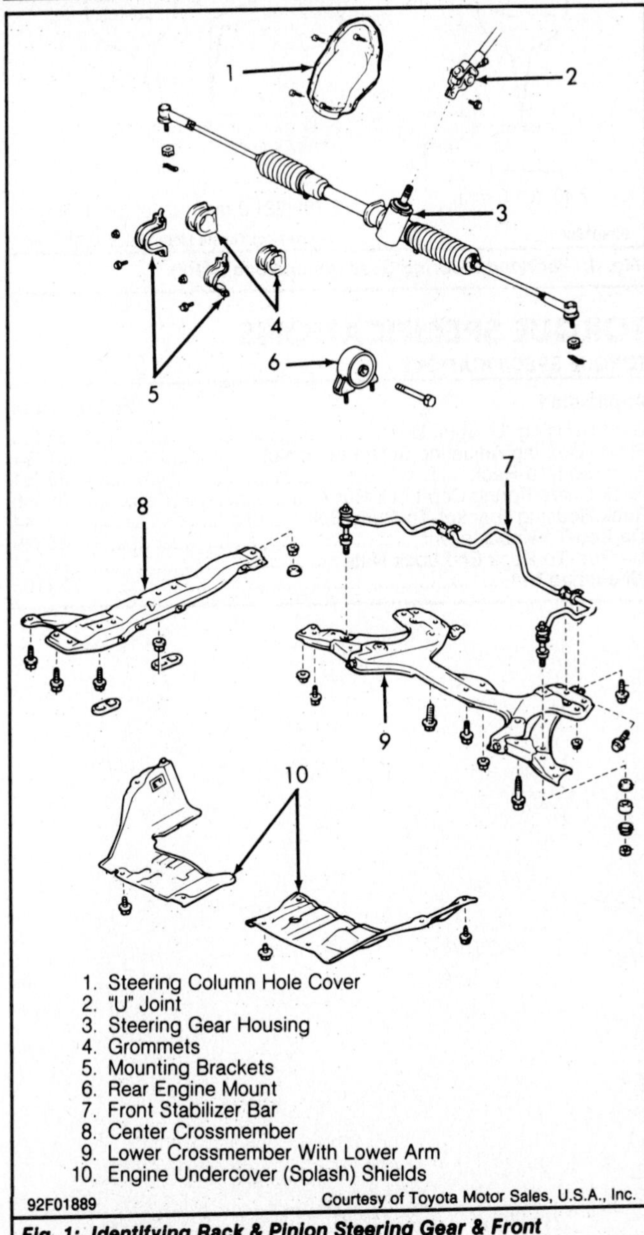


***Fig. 1: Identifying Rack & Pinion Steering Gear & Front Suspension Components (Corolla)***

**Removal – 1)** Position front wheels facing straight-ahead. On MR2, secure steering wheel from turning. On all models, raise and support vehicle. Remove front wheels. Disconnect tie rod ends at steering knuckles. Match mark steering shaft "U" joint and pinion shaft. Loosen upper "U" joint bolt.

**2)** Remove lower "U" joint bolt. Pull "U" joint upward from pinion shaft. On MR2 and Tercel, remove gear housing mounting nuts and bolts. Slide gear housing to right side and pull gear housing out through body panel opening.

**3)** On Corolla, remove gear housing mounting bracket nuts. Attach engine hoist to engine hangers to support engine. Remove lower crossmember with lower arm. *See Fig. 1.*

**4)** Remove engine undercover (splash) shields. Remove center crossmember. Remove rear engine mount. Remove gear housing mounting bracket bolts. Slide gear housing to left to remove.

**Installation –** To install, reverse removal procedure. Check toe-in. See SPECIFICATIONS & PROCEDURES article in WHEEL ALIGNMENT. On MR2, if steering wheel turns during removal and installation procedure, inspect and re-center spiral cable. See AIR BAG RESTRAINT SYSTEM article in SAFETY EQUIPMENT.

## OVERHAUL

### STEERING GEAR

**Disassembly – 1)** Place steering gear in a soft-jawed vise. Mark tie rod ends and rack ends for reassembly reference. Loosen tie rod end lock nuts.

***NOTE: Left and right tie rod ends, boots and rack ends are different. Mark them accordingly.***

**2)** Remove boot clips and clamps. Mark left and right boots accordingly. Remove rack boots. Unstake claw washer and remove rack ends using End Remover/Installer (09617-10020). *See Fig. 2.*

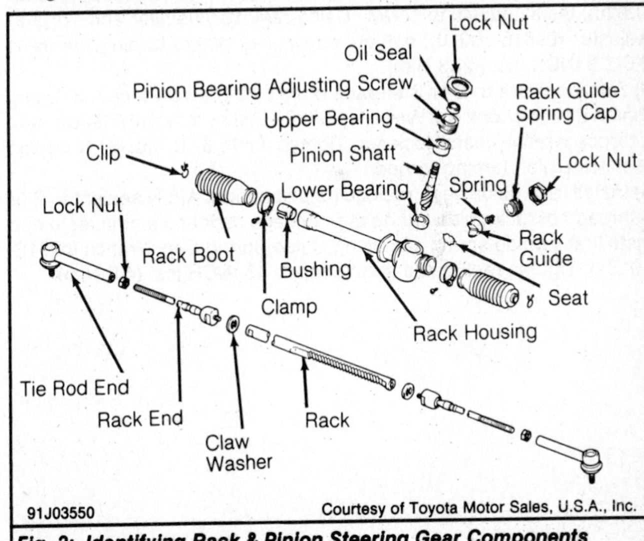


***Fig. 2: Identifying Rack & Pinion Steering Gear Components***

**3)** Using Guide Spring Cap Wrench (09612-10131), remove rack guide spring cap. Remove rack guide spring and rack guide. Using Pinion Bearing Lock Nut Wrench (09612-10093), remove pinion bearing adjusting screw lock nut. Using pinion bearing adjusting screw Remover/Installer (09616-10020), remove pinion bearing adjusting screw.

**4)** Withdraw rack from gear end of housing until notched portion of rack is aligned with pinion. Remove pinion together with upper bearing. Remove rack from pinon end of housing. DO NOT rotate rack. Remove rack bushing if necessary.

**Inspection – 1)** Check all parts for damage or deterioration. Check for play in rack ends and tie rod end ball joints. Check pinion teeth surfaces for wear or damage. If pinion upper bearing must be replaced, remove with bearing puller. Drive new bearing on (seal side down).

# 1991 STEERING
# Manual Rack & Pinion (Cont.)

**2)** If pinion lower bearing must be replaced, heat pinion housing to at least 176°F (80°C). Tap bearing out with plastic hammer. Reheat pinion housing. Drive in new bearing. Check rack for runout and excessive tooth wear. Runout must not exceed .012" (.30 mm).

**Reassembly – 1)** Pack steering gear components with Molybdenum Disulfide Lithium base grease. *See Fig. 3.* If rack bushing was removed, install new rack bushing into rack housing. Ensure new bushing holes properly align with rack housing holes. Fill rack housing about half full of grease. Insert rack from pinion housing side into rack housing.

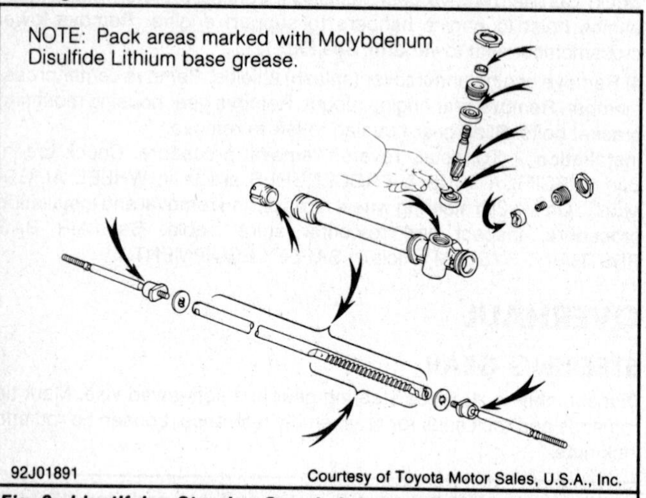


***Fig. 3: Identifying Steering Gear Lubrication Points***

**2)** Position notched portion of rack so pinion can be inserted. Ensure pinion seats properly in lower bearing. Install sealant to 2 or 3 threads of pinion bearing adjusting screw.

**3)** Using pinion bearing adjusting screw Remover/Installer (09616-10020), install adjusting screw. Using remover/installer and Torque/Adjuster (09616-10010), tighten screw until pinion turning torque is 2.0-2.9 INCH lbs. (.2-.3 N.m).

**4)** Apply sealant to 2 or 3 threads of adjusting screw lock nut. Using Pinion Bearing Lock Nut Wrench (09612-10093), remover/installer and a torque wrench, install lock nut. Tighten nut to 67 ft. lbs. (91 N.m) and recheck pinion turning torque.

**5)** Install rack guide seat, rack guide and spring. Apply sealant to 2 or 3 threads of rack guide spring cap. Engage rack and pinion teeth and install rack guide spring cap using Guide Spring Cap Wrench (09612-10131). Tighten rack guide spring cap to 43 INCH lbs. (4.9 N.m).

**6)** Recheck pinion turning torque. Turning torque should now be 5.2-10.4 INCH lbs. (.6-1.2 N.m). If turning torque is greater than specification, loosen rack guide spring cap until torque is within specification.

**7)** Apply sealant to 2 or 3 threads of spring cap lock nut. Install lock nut and tighten to 35 ft. lbs. (48 N.m). Recheck pinion turning torque. Readjust if necessary.

**8)** Install new claw washer. Align claw of washer with rack groove. Using End Remover/Installer (09617-10020), install rack ends. Tighten ends to 38 ft. lbs. (51 N.m). Using a brass bar, stake claw washer in place.

**9)** Install rack boots with seamed portion in a straight line with center of rack guide spring cap lock nut. Ensure rack boots are installed on proper ends. Install boot clamps and clips. Face open end of boot clips upward to avoid damage to boot. Screw lock nuts and tie rod ends onto rack ends.

**10)** Align marks made during disassembly. Tighten tie rod lock nuts to 35 ft. lbs. (47 N.m). On MR2, adjust steering gear dimensions before installing steering gear. *See Fig. 4.*

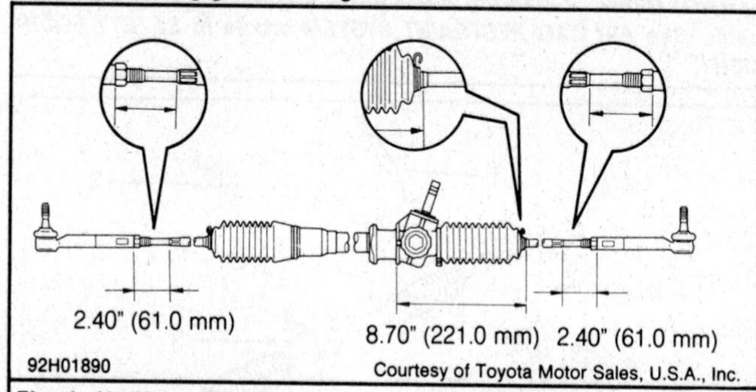


***Fig. 4: Verifying Steering Gear Dimensions (MR2)***

## TORQUE SPECIFICATIONS

***TORQUE SPECIFICATIONS***

| Application | Ft. Lbs. (N.m) |
|---|---|
| Gear Housing "U" Joint Bolts | 26 (35) |
| Pinion Bearing Adjusting Screw Lock Nut | 67 (91) |
| Rack End-To-Rack | 38 (51) |
| Rack Guide Spring Cap Lock Nut | 35 (48) |
| Rack Housing Bracket-To-Body Bolt | 32 (44) |
| Tie Rod-To-Knuckle Nut | 36 (49) |
| Tie Rod-To-Rack End Lock Nuts | 35 (47) |
| Wheel Lug Nut | 76 (103) |

# 1991 STEERING
# Power Rack & Pinion

**Camry, Celica, Corolla, Cressida, Previa, Supra, Tercel**

## DESCRIPTION & OPERATION

System consists of a rack and pinion assembly, flow control valve, hydraulic pump and hoses. An air control valve increases idle speed when the power steering pump is loaded.

## LUBRICATION

### FLUID TYPE

Use Dexron-II fluid.

### FLUID LEVEL CHECK

If fluid is at operating temperature, fluid level should be between HOT range marks on fluid reservoir or dipstick. If fluid is cold, fluid level should be between COLD range marks on fluid reservoir or dipstick.

### HYDRAULIC SYSTEM BLEEDING

**1)** Raise and support vehicle. Fill fluid to proper level in reservoir. Turn wheels fully in both directions. Recheck fluid level. Start engine, and let it idle. Turn steering from lock to lock 2 or 3 times. Lower vehicle. Run engine at 1000 RPM or less.
**2)** Turn wheel from lock to lock 2 or 3 times. Center steering wheel. If fluid level does not rise and no foaming of fluid is evident, bleeding is complete. If level rises more than .20" (5.0 mm) or foaming is evident, repeat procedure until air is released.

## ADJUSTMENTS

### POWER STEERING PUMP BELT

Using belt tension gauge, measure belt tension. See BELT TENSION SPECIFICATIONS table.

***BELT TENSION SPECIFICATIONS***

| Application | Lbs. (kg) |
|---|---|
| Camry & Celica | |
| New | 100-150 (45-68) |
| Used [1] | 60-100 (27-45) |
| Corolla | |
| 4A-FE | |
| New | 100-150 (45-68) |
| Used [1] | 60-100 (27-45) |
| 4A-GE | |
| New | 170-180 (77-82) |
| Used [1] | 95-135 (43-61) |
| Cressida & Supra | |
| New | 140-180 (63-82) |
| Used [1] | 80-120 (36-54) |
| Previa | |
| New | 160-180 (73-82) |
| Used [1] | 115-135 (52-67) |
| Tercel | |
| New | 170-180 (77-82) |
| Used [1] | 95-135 (43-61) |

[1] - Belt is used if it has been in operation longer than 5 minutes.

## TESTING

### AIR CONTROL VALVE

Start engine. Ensure A/C is off. Turn steering wheel right and left. Ensure engine RPM does not decrease more than 50 RPM. Pinch air hose shut. Turn steering wheel right and left. Ensure engine RPM decreases about 200 RPM. If system fails any of these tests, check vacuum hoses and air control valve.

### HYDRAULIC SYSTEM PRESSURE

**1)** Disconnect pressure line at line joint. Attach pressure gauge with gauge side connected to pump. Attach valve side of gauge to rack and pinion side. Bleed air from system. Check fluid level. With engine at idle and valve closed, check fluid pressure. See HYDRAULIC PRESSURE table.

***HYDRAULIC PRESSURE***

| Application | psi (kg/cm²) |
|---|---|
| Camry | |
| 2.0L | 925 (65) |
| 2.5L | 1067 (75) |
| Celica | 966 (70) |
| Corolla | 925 (65) |
| Cressida, Supra & Previa | 1067 (75) |
| Tercel | 811 (57) |

***NOTE: DO NOT keep pressure gauge valve closed longer than 10 seconds. Fluid testing temperature should be 176°F (80°C).***

**2)** Open valve fully. Note pressure with engine at idle and at 3000 RPM. Pressure difference should be less than 71 psi (5 kg/cm²). If difference is more than specified, check flow control valve.
**3)** With steering wheel at lock position and pressure valve open, recheck pressure. See HYDRAULIC PRESSURE table.

### STEERING WHEEL TURNING FORCE

**1)** On Camry, Corolla, Cressida and Tercel, center steering wheel. With engine idling, measure steering turning force at steering wheel nut using an INCH-pound torque wrench. If turning force exceeds specification, replace power steering pump. See STEERING WHEEL NUT TURNING FORCE table.

***STEERING WHEEL NUT TURNING FORCE***

| Application | INCH Lbs. (N.m) |
|---|---|
| Camry | 61 (6.9) |
| Corolla | 51 (5.8) |
| Cressida & Tercel | 69 (7.8) |

**2)** On Celica and Previa, attach spring scale to steering wheel. Steering effort should not exceed 8.8 lbs. (4 kg). If steering effort is high, repair or replace power steering pump.
**3)** On Supra, attach spring scale to steering wheel. On models without Progressive Power Steering (PPS), steering effort should not exceed 10.36 lbs. (4.7 kg). On models with PPS, steering effort should not exceed 5.95 lbs. (2.7 kg). If steering effort is high, repair or replace power steering pump.

## REMOVAL & INSTALLATION

### POWER STEERING PUMP

**Removal (Camry 2.0L & Celica FWD) – 1)** Raise and support vehicle. Remove engine undercover. Remove right front wheel. Remove lower crossmember. Remove air control valve vacuum hose.
**2)** Remove pressure and return lines. Plug and elevate lines to prevent loss of fluid. Remove pulley nut. Remove mounting bolts, belt and pump.
**Removal (Camry 2.5L & Celica All-Trac) –** Raise and support vehicle. Remove right front wheel. Disconnect pressure line at joint. Plug line opening. Disconnect right tie rod from steering knuckle. Remove pump bracket. Remove pump brace. Disconnect return line, and plug openings. Remove pump.
**Removal (Previa) –** Remove air duct and fan shroud. Remove fan, fan coupling and drive belt. Disconnect pressure and return hoses from pump. Remove pump mounting hardware and pump.
**Removal (Supra) – 1)** On turbo models, loosen air hose clips as necessary to remove hoses from airflow meter. Unplug electrical connector at airflow meter. Remove airflow meter bracket bolt and air cleaner box clips. Remove airflow meter. Remove reservoir.

# 1991 STEERING
# Power Rack & Pinion (Cont.)

**2)** On all models, loosen clamps, and remove reservoir-to-pump hoses. Disconnect hoses from air control valve on pump. Remove adjustment strut and engine undercover. Remove pressure line. Remove pulley nut, belt and pulley. Remove pump.

**Removal (Tercel)** – Remove air intake hose. Disconnect fluid line from pump. Remove bolts retaining pump bracket. Remove pump and bracket as an assembly.

**Removal (Corolla & Cressida)** – Remove oil from reservoir. Disconnect pressure and return lines at pump. Remove air control valve hoses (if equipped). Remove engine undercover. Remove drive belt and pump.

**Installation (All Models)** – To install, reverse removal procedure. Fill and bleed system. See HYDRAULIC SYSTEM BLEEDING under LUBRICATION. On FWD models, check front end alignment (if necessary). See SPECIFICATIONS & PROCEDURES article in WHEEL ALIGNMENT.

## POWER RACK & PINION

**Removal (FWD) – 1)** Raise and support vehicle. Remove wheel assemblies. Remove engine undercover. Disconnect tie rod ends from steering arms. On Tercel, remove charcoal canister, canister bracket and steering column hole cover for access to bolts.

**2)** On Camry All-Trac, disconnect speedometer cable. On all models, mark and disconnect steering coupler "U" joint. Remove pressure and return lines. Remove air control vacuum valve hose (if equipped). On Tercel, remove exhaust pipe. On Camry 2.0L, Celica and Corolla, remove engine mount bracket and center crossmembers. Disconnect exhaust pipe.

**3)** On Camry and Celica All-Trac, mark and remove drive shaft. Remove right stabilizer bar bracket. Disconnect stabilizer link from lower arm. On all models, remove steering gear mounting brackets. Remove steering gear. Use care not to tear rack boots when removing from chassis.

**Installation** – To install, reverse removal procedure. Check front end alignment.

**Removal (RWD Except Previa) – 1)** Raise and support vehicle. Remove wheel assemblies. Separate tie rod ends from steering arms. Remove engine undercover (if equipped). Mark and disconnect steering coupler "U" joint. On Supra Turbo, remove air intake hose.

**2)** On all models, remove steering damper. Disconnect solenoid wires on Cressida. Remove any line clamp bolts which may interfere with gear removal. Remove steering gear mounting brackets and steering gear. Use care not to tear rack boots when removing from chassis.

**Installation** – To install, reverse removal procedure.

**Removal (Previa) – 1)** Separate tie rod ends from steering knuckles. Mark universal joint and steering shaft. Disconnect "U" joint. Disconnect lines at steering gear. On 4WD, remove front differential assembly. See DIFFERENTIALS & AXLE SHAFTS - INTEGRAL HOUSING article in DRIVE AXLES.

**2)** On all models, remove No. 3 drive housing bracket. Remove No. 2 drive housing insulator. Remove brackets and grommets from steering gear. Move steering gear to right side. Turn steering gear pinion shaft as necessary to work steering gear through opening on left side of vehicle.

**Installation** – To install, reverse removal procedure. Check front end alignment.

# OVERHAUL

## POWER STEERING PUMP

**Disassembly (Cressida & Supra) – 1)** Remove air control valve. Remove bolts and suction port union with "O" ring. Remove pressure port union. Remove "O" rings from union and housing. Remove flow control valve and spring. *See Fig. 1.* Temporarily install bolt in flow control valve spring seat. Push bolt inward to remove snap ring. Pull bolt out. Remove spring seat.

**2)** Mark front and rear housings for reassembly reference. Remove bolts, rear housing and "O" ring. Tap rotor shaft using plastic mallet to remove rear side plate, and then remove "O" rings. Using plastic mallet, tap out rotor shaft assembly, being careful not to scratch parts. Remove long straight pin from front housing. Remove wave washer and "O" ring.

**3)** Remove cam ring gear and vane plates. Remove snap ring. Remove rotor and plate from rotor shaft, being careful not to scratch rotor. Remove "O" ring from front side plate. Remove straight pin from front side plate.

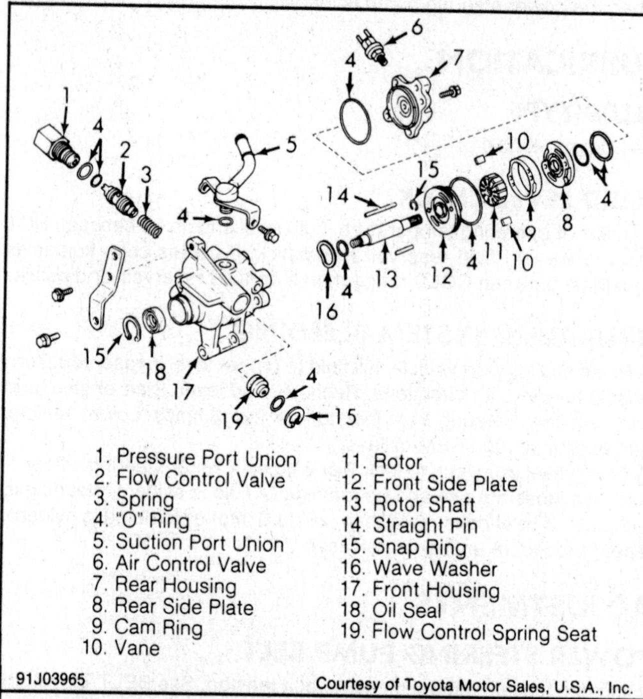


***Fig. 1: Identifying Power Steering Pump Components (Cressida & Supra Shown; Previa Is Similar)***

**Disassembly (Camry, Celica, Corolla & Tercel) – 1)** Remove drive pulley. Place power steering pump in vise. Remove reservoir tank and bracket. Remove air control valve (if equipped). *See Fig. 2 or 3.* Remove pressure feed tube, pressure port union, flow control valve and spring. Using 2 screwdrivers, remove rear housing snap ring.

**2)** Using plastic mallet, tap end of shaft to remove rear housing and wave washer. Remove vane pump shaft, cam ring and vane plates. Remove rotor and side plate. Using pin punch, drive out straight pin.

**Disassembly (Previa) – 1)** Mount pump in vise. Pull drive pulley from shaft. Remove pressure and return line fittings and "O" rings. Remove flow control valve and spring. *See Fig. 1.*

**2)** Remove rear plate and wave washer. Remove cam ring, rotor and vane plates. Pull straight pin from housing. Remove retaining clip, and then press out shaft and bearing.

**Inspection (All Models) – 1)** Check oil clearance between pump housing bushing and rotor shaft. *See Fig. 4.* If difference is greater than .0028" (.07 mm), replace complete pump assembly. Discard all "O" rings, and replace with new ones.

**2)** Check vane plates for wear and damage. See VANE PLATE SPECIFICATIONS table. Maximum clearance between vane plate and rotor groove is .0028" (.071 mm) on Cressida, and .0011" (.028 mm) on all other models. If clearance exceeds specification, replace rotor and vane plate as an assembly.

***VANE PLATE SPECIFICATIONS***

| Application | In. (mm) |
|---|---|
| Camry, Celica, Corolla, Previa & Tercel | |
| Minimum Height | .315 (8.00) |
| Minimum Thickness | .0697 (1.770) |
| Minimum Length | .5894 (14.970) |
| Cressida & Supra | |
| Minimum Height | .319 (8.10) |
| Minimum Thickness | .0707 (1.797) |
| Minimum Length | .5901 (14.988) |

# 1991 STEERING
# Power Rack & Pinion (Cont.)

1. Union Bolt
2. Pressure Feed Tube
3. Gasket
4. "O" Ring
5. Reservoir Tank
6. Flow Control Valve
7. Spring
8. Front Housing
9. Snap Ring
10. Rear Housing
11. Wave Washer
12. Rear Side Plate
13. Straight Pin
14. Cam Ring
15. Vane
16. Front Side Plate
17. Shaft
18. Rotor
19. Oil Seal
20. Air Control Valve
21. Union Seat
22. Pressure Port Union

91F03968 Courtesy of Toyota Motor Sales, U.S.A., Inc.

***Fig. 2: Identifying Power Steering Pump Components (Celica 4A-FE & Corolla)***

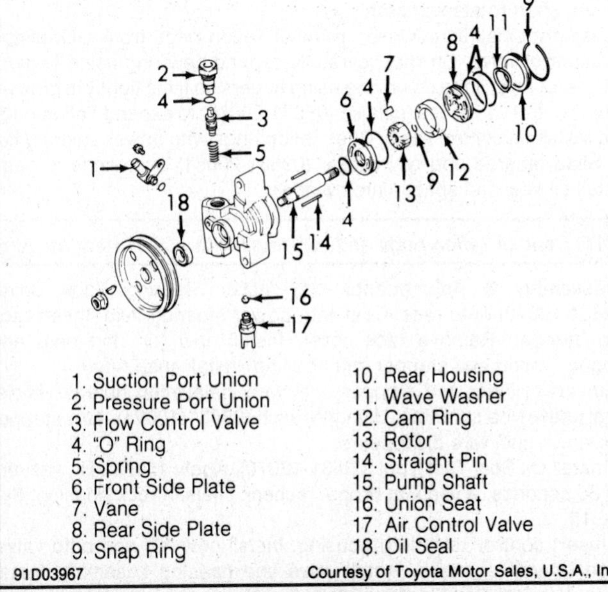

1. Suction Port Union
2. Pressure Port Union
3. Flow Control Valve
4. "O" Ring
5. Spring
6. Front Side Plate
7. Vane
8. Rear Side Plate
9. Snap Ring
10. Rear Housing
11. Wave Washer
12. Cam Ring
13. Rotor
14. Straight Pin
15. Pump Shaft
16. Union Seat
17. Air Control Valve
18. Oil Seal

91D03967 Courtesy of Toyota Motor Sales, U.S.A., Inc.

***Fig. 3: Identifying Power Steering Pump Components (Camry, Celica 5S-FE & Tercel)***

**3)** Using 57-71 psi (4.0-5.0 kg/cm²) compressed air, check flow control valve for leakage. *See Fig. 5.* Control valve spring length should be 1.42-1.49" (36-38 mm) on Camry, Celica, Corolla, Previa and Tercel, 1.85-1.97" (47-50 mm) on Cressida and 1.46-1.54" (37-39 mm) on Supra. Replace spring if length is not as specified.

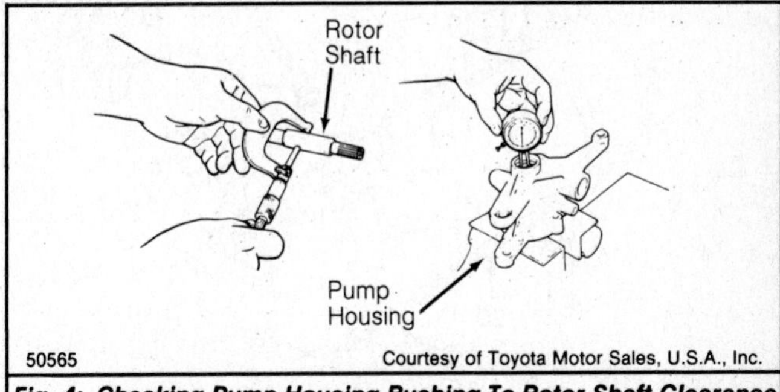


50565 Courtesy of Toyota Motor Sales, U.S.A., Inc.

***Fig. 4: Checking Pump Housing Bushing-To-Rotor Shaft Clearance***

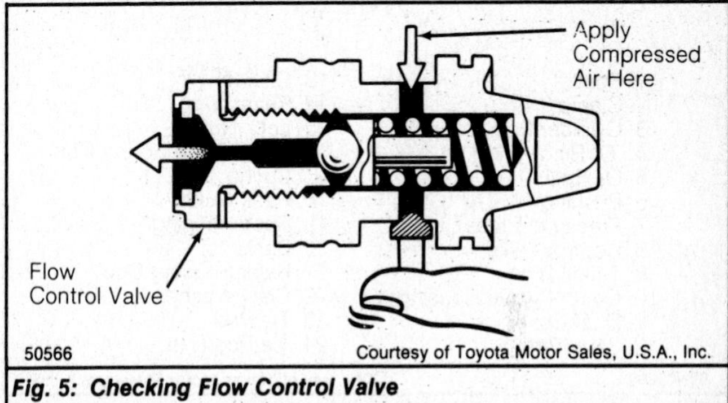


50566 Courtesy of Toyota Motor Sales, U.S.A., Inc.

***Fig. 5: Checking Flow Control Valve***

**Reassembly (All Models) – 1)** Coat all sliding surfaces with ATF. Assemble front plate and rotor assembly on pump shaft. Ensure rotor is installed properly. *See Fig. 6.* Coat shaft seal with grease. Install longer pin into housing. Align pin and hole in front plate.

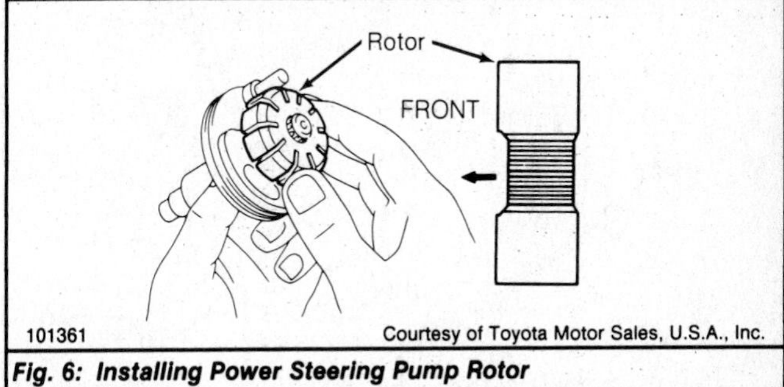


101361 Courtesy of Toyota Motor Sales, U.S.A., Inc.

***Fig. 6: Installing Power Steering Pump Rotor***

**2)** Using a plastic mallet, tap pump shaft into housing. Install cam ring with inscribed mark toward rear of pump. Install vane plates with rounded end facing rear of pump. Install rear side plate and "O" ring. Install wave washer, "O" ring and rear housing.

**3)** Using a torque wrench, measure pump shaft rotating preload. If preload exceeds 2.7 INCH lbs. (.3 N.m), disassemble pump, and check components. If preload is okay, install spring seat. Bolt hole should face outward.

**4)** Install snap ring. Install spring and flow control valve. Tighten pressure port to 34 ft. lbs. (46 N.m) on Tercel or 51 ft. lbs. (69 N.m) on all other models. Tighten return line port to 106 INCH lbs. (12 N.m). Install air control valve and pulley.

## STEERING GEAR

**Disassembly (Corolla & Tercel) – 1)** Remove left and right turn tubes. Clamp steering gear in soft-jawed vise. Loosen lock nuts on tie rod ends, and mark tie rod ends for reassembly reference. Remove tie rod ends. *See Fig. 7, 8 or 9.* Remove outer clips, inner clamps and rack boots.

# 1991 STEERING
# Power Rack & Pinion (Cont.)

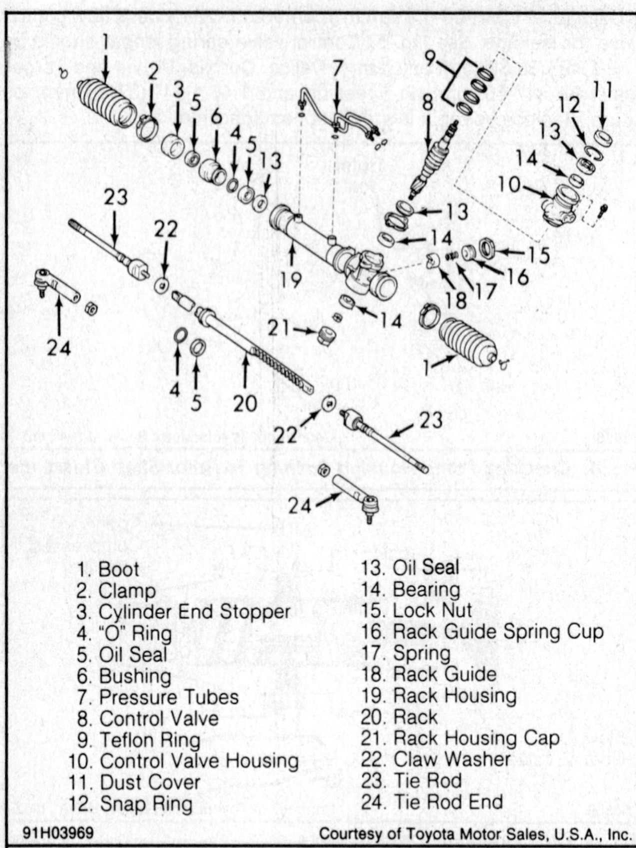

1. Boot
2. Clamp
3. Cylinder End Stopper
4. "O" Ring
5. Oil Seal
6. Bushing
7. Pressure Tubes
8. Control Valve
9. Teflon Ring
10. Control Valve Housing
11. Dust Cover
12. Snap Ring
13. Oil Seal
14. Bearing
15. Lock Nut
16. Rack Guide Spring Cup
17. Spring
18. Rack Guide
19. Rack Housing
20. Rack
21. Rack Housing Cap
22. Claw Washer
23. Tie Rod
24. Tie Rod End

91H03969 Courtesy of Toyota Motor Sales, U.S.A., Inc.

**Fig. 7: Identifying Power Rack & Pinion Steering Gear Components (Corolla – KOYO Type Rack)**

1. Cylinder End Stopper
2. Oil Seal
3. Spacer
4. "O" Rings
5. Bushing
6. Control Valve
7. Dust Cover
8. Snap Ring
9. Bearing
10. Teflon Ring
11. Rack Guide Spring Cap
12. Spring
13. Rack Guide
14. Rack Guide Seat
15. Lock Nut
16. Rack
17. Self-Locking Nut
18. Rack Housing Cap
19. Rack Housing
20. Boot
21. Tie Rod
22. Claw Washer
23. Tie Rod End

91J03970 Courtesy of Toyota Motor Sales, U.S.A., Inc.

**Fig. 8: Identifying Power Rack & Pinion Steering Gear Components (Corolla – Toyota Type Rack)**

Rack Boot
Clip
Clamp
Snap Ring
Dust Cover
Upper Bearing
Snap Ring
Oil Seal
Control Valve
Telfon Ring
Spacer
Bushing
Cylinder End Stopper
Oil Seal
Seat
Spring
Oil Seal
Rack End
Claw Washer
Spacer
Lower Bearing
Rack
Rack Guide
"O" Ring
Lock Nut
Rack Guide Spring Cap
Rack Housing Cap
Lock Nut
Telfon Ring
Tie Rod

101362 Courtesy of Toyota Motor Sales, U.S.A., Inc.

**Fig. 9: Identifying Power Rack & Pinion Steering Gear Components (Tercel)**

**2)** Unstake claw washer. Remove rack ends and claw washer. Remove rack guide spring cap lock nut. Remove spring cap. Remove rack guide spring, seat and dust boot.

**3)** Using Wrench (09612-10020), remove pinion bearing lock nut. Using Wrench (09616-10020), remove pinion bearing adjustment screw. Carefully remove pinion and bearing as an assembly. Remove rack from pinion side without rotating rack. DO NOT remove rack from tube side.

**4)** Mark control valve housing and rack. Remove control valve lock nut. Remove lower bearing and spacer. Remove snap ring. Using Puller (09613-12010), remove control valve, upper bearing and oil seal. Remove snap ring. Remove cylinder end stopper and spacer. Using a brass drift, remove rack and oil seal.

**Inspection & Repair – 1)** Place rack on "V" blocks. Using a dial indicator, measure runout at center of rack. Maximum runout is .012" (.30 mm).

**2)** Measure clearance between control valve shaft and bushing. If clearance exceeds .0059" (.150 mm), replace bushing. Remove oil seal. Press in new oil seal. Temporarily install control valve shaft. Ensure shaft rotates smoothly.

**3)** Using a small screwdriver, remove Teflon rings from rack piston and control valve. On rack, carefully expand new ring using fingers, and install ring. Snug down ring using fingers so it fits tightly in groove.

**4)** On control valve, use Installer (09631-20070) to expand Teflon rings and install on control valve. Coat Teflon rings with power steering fluid. Slide tapered end of Installer (09631-20081) over rings to seat. Install oil seal and spacer into cylinder.

***NOTE: Coat all Teflon rings and "O" rings with power steering fluid.***

**Reassembly & Adjustments – 1)** Install Steering Rack Cover (09631-10040) onto rack. Coat with power steering fluid. Insert rack into cylinder. Remove rack cover. Install new "O" ring onto end stopper. Insert end stopper into housing. Install snap ring.

**2)** Insert cylinder end stopper until wire installation hole is visible. Insert new wire into hole. Using Wrench (09631-10021), turn stopper clockwise until wire disappears.

**3)** Install Oil Seal Test Tool (09631-12070). Apply 15.8 in. Hg vacuum for 30 seconds. If vacuum drops, recheck seals in rack housing. *See Fig. 10.*

**4)** Insert control valve into housing. Install new "O" ring onto valve. Align reference marks. Install valve and housing assembly. Install upper bearing. *See Fig. 11*. Install oil seal, snap ring and dust cover.

# 1991 STEERING
# Power Rack & Pinion (Cont.)

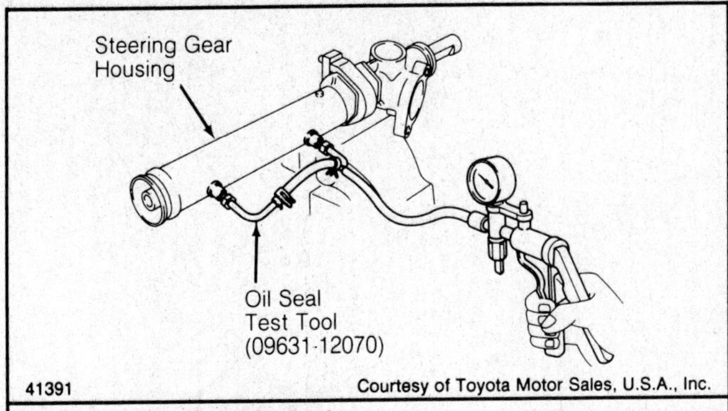


*Fig. 10: Testing Rack Oil Seal*

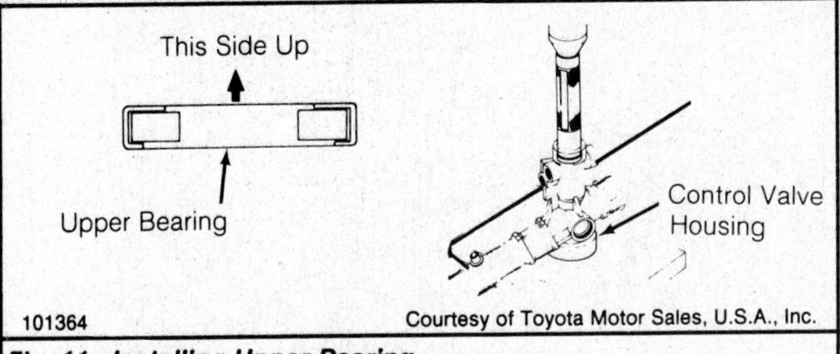


*Fig. 11: Installing Upper Bearing*

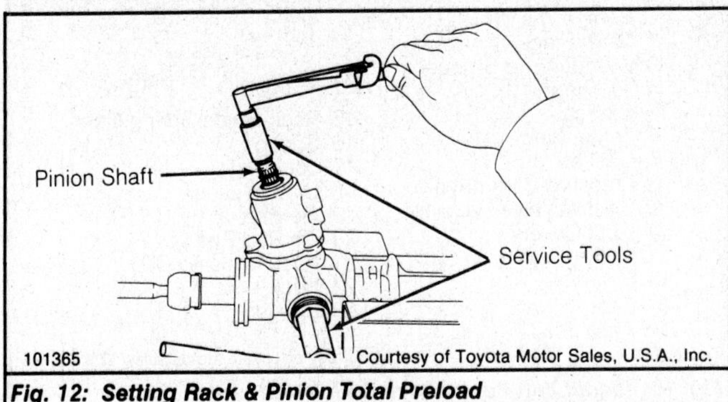


*Fig. 12: Setting Rack & Pinion Total Preload*

**5)** Using Socket (09616-00010), install new self-locking nut onto bottom of control valve. Tighten to 18 ft. lbs. (25 N.m). Apply liquid sealer to a new rack housing cap. Install cap, and tighten to 43 ft. lbs. (58 N.m). Stake housing cap in 2 places.

**6)** Install rack guide and guide spring. Apply liquid sealer to threads of rack guide spring cap. Temporarily install and tighten spring cap to 18 ft. lbs. (24 N.m). Back off spring cap 12-15 degrees. Turn control valve shaft left and right twice.

**7)** Loosen spring cap until preload is eliminated. Turn spring cap in until turning preload is 7.1-11.5 INCH lbs. (0.8-1.3 N.m). *See Fig. 12.* Apply liquid sealer to threads of lock nut, and install lock nut. Tighten lock nut to 28 ft. lbs. (38 N.m). Recheck preload. Ensure preload has not changed.

**8)** Align claw of new claw washers with rack groove. Install claw washer and rack ends. Tighten rack ends to 38 ft. lbs. (51 N.m) using Lock Nut Wrench (09628-10020). Stake claw washers.

**9)** Coat rack end dust seals with grease. Remove any grease from housing tube hole. Install boots, clamps and clips. Install outer clips with ends facing upward. Align reference marks when installing tie rod ends. Tie rod lock nuts will be tightened when wheels are aligned. Install new "O" ring seals. Install left and right turn tubes.

**Disassembly (Camry, Celica & Supra) – 1)** Using Rack Housing Stand (09612-00012), mount steering gear in vise. Remove left and right turn tubes. Mark and remove tie rod ends. Remove rack boots. *See Figs. 13, 14 or 15.*

**2)** Unstake claw washers. Mark left and right rack ends for reassembly reference. Using Wrench (09628-10020), remove rack ends and claw washers. Remove rack guide spring cap lock nut. Remove spring cap. Remove rack guide spring, guide and seat.

**3)** Remove bearing guide lock nut and guide nut. Remove dust cover. Mark control valve housing and rack. Remove control valve housing. Remove control valve and bearing. Remove "O" ring from housing. Remove spool valve spring and seat (if equipped).

**4)** Remove snap ring from end of housing. Using Bearing Replacer (09612-10061), press cylinder end stopper out until end stopper touches press plate. Pull out rack with cylinder end stopper, spacer and oil seal.

**Inspection & Repair – 1)** Placing rack on "V" blocks. Using a dial indicator, measure runout at center of rack. Maximum runout is .012" (.30 mm). Check all bearings and seals for damage. Replace control valve bearing and housing oil seal.

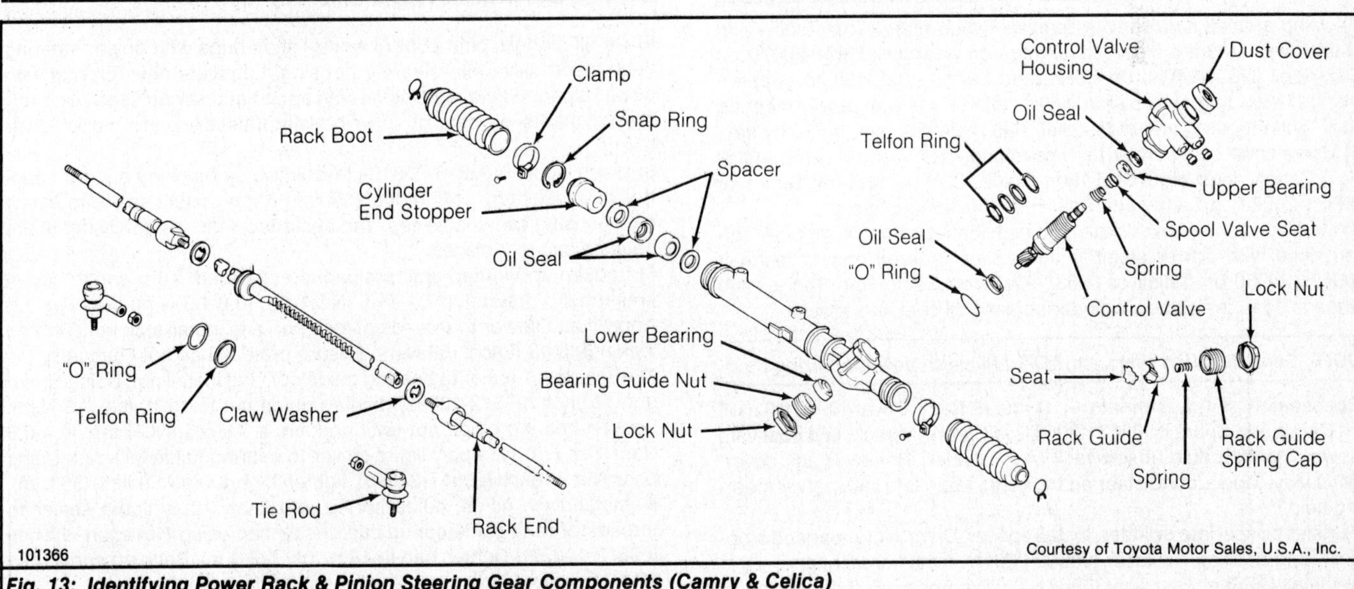


*Fig. 13: Identifying Power Rack & Pinion Steering Gear Components (Camry & Celica)*

# 1991 STEERING
## Power Rack & Pinion (Cont.)

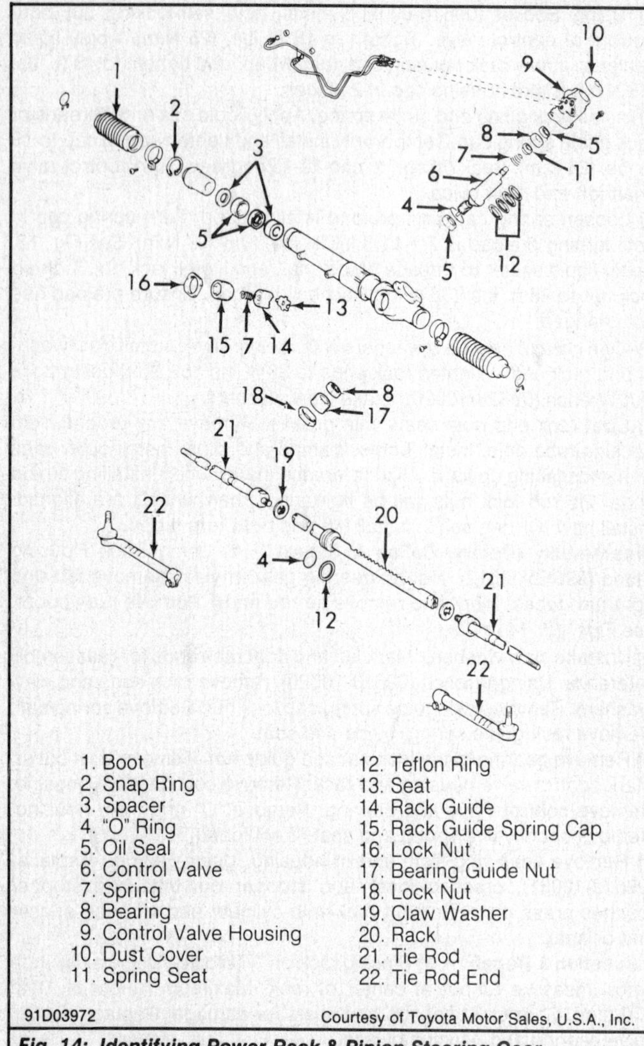


***Fig. 14: Identifying Power Rack & Pinion Steering Gear Components (Supra without PPS)***

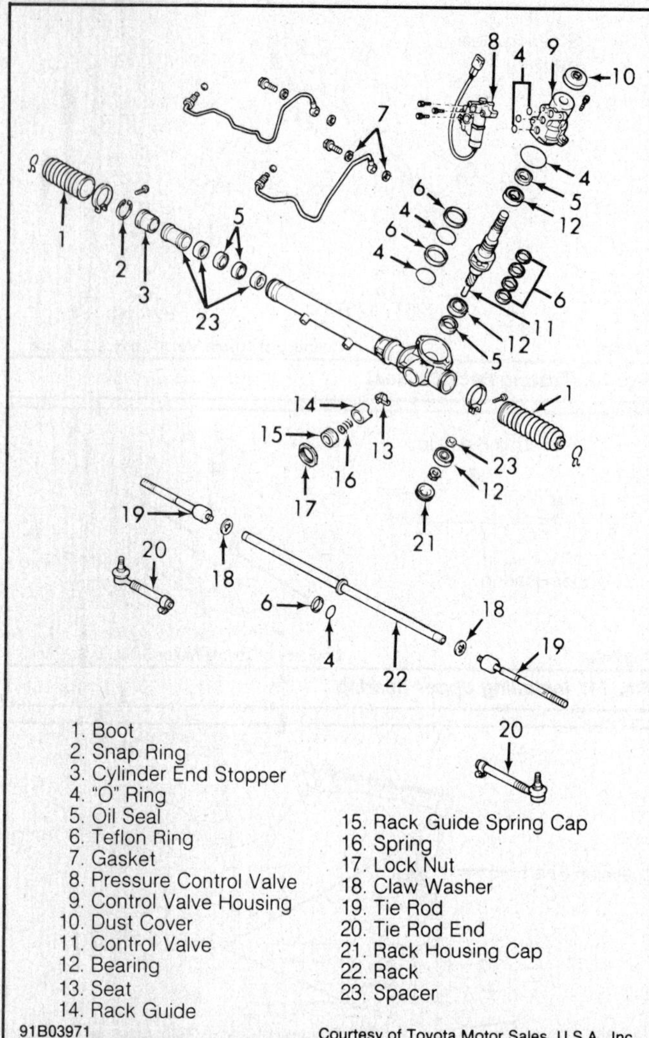


***Fig. 15: Identifying Power Rack & Pinion Steering Gear Components (Supra with PPS)***

**2)** Using a small screwdriver, remove Teflon rings. Coat Teflon ring with power steering fluid. Install rings on Adapter (09631-20070 on Camry or 09631-24020 on Celica and Supra), and expand adapter. Install Teflon ring onto piston. Coat Teflon rings with power steering fluid. Slide tapered end of Installer (09631-24030) over rings to seat.

**3)** Use a small screwdriver to remove rings from control valve. Install new Teflon rings onto Seal Ring Guide (09620-24040 on Supra or 09631-20070 on Camry and Celica), and expand guide.

**4)** Install and snug down expanded rings onto control valve. Coat Teflon rings with power steering fluid. Slide tapered end of Installer (09631-24050 on Celica or 09631-20081 on Camry and Supra) over rings to seat. Install new cylinder housing oil seal and spacer.

***NOTE: Coat all Teflon rings and "O" rings with power steering fluid.***

**Reassembly & Adjustments – 1)** Install Rack Cover (09631-32010 on Celica and Supra or 09631-20051 on Camry) to rack, and coat with power steering fluid. Insert rack into cylinder. Remove rack cover. Wind vinyl tape around steering rack end. Lubricate with power steering fluid.

**2)** Insert oil seal into cylinder. Install spacer. Drive in cylinder end stopper using Bearing Replacer (09612-22011). Install snap ring.

**3)** Install Oil Seal Test Tool (09631-12070). Apply 15.75 in. Hg for 30 seconds. If vacuum drops, recheck seals in rack housing. *See Fig. 10.*

**4)** On all models, coat control valve Teflon rings with power steering fluid. Insert valve into steering housing. Lubricate new "O" ring with power steering fluid, and install with spring and spring seat. Align reference marks on control valve housing. Install control valve lower bearing.

**5)** Using Socket (09616-00010), install new self-locking nut onto control valve. Tighten to 44 ft. lbs. (59 N.m). Apply liquid sealer to a new rack housing cap. Install cap, and tighten to 44 ft. lbs. (58 N.m). Stake housing cap in 2 places.

**6)** Loosen spring cap until preload is eliminated. Turn spring cap in until turning preload is 7.1-11.5 INCH lbs. (0.8-1.3 N.m). *See Fig. 12.* Apply liquid sealer to threads of lock nut, and install lock nut. Tighten lock nut to 43 ft. lbs. (58 N.m). Ensure preload has not changed.

**7)** Apply liquid sealer to bearing guide nut, and install nut. Using Hexagon Wrench (09612-10022), tighten guide nut to 11 ft. lbs. (15 N.m). Loosen bearing guide nut until preload is 3.9-5.6 INCH lbs. (0.4-0.6 N.m). *See Fig. 12.* Apply liquid sealer to bearing guide lock nut. Using Lock Nut Wrench (09617-24020), tighten lock nut to 41 ft. lbs. (56 N.m).

**8)** Install rack guide, guide spring and seat. Apply liquid sealer to threads of rack guide spring cap. Install cap using Hexagon Wrench (09612-10022). Tighten cap to 18 ft. lbs. (25 N.m). Back off spring cap 12-15 degrees. Turn control valve shaft left and right twice.

**9)** Loosen spring cap until preload is eliminated. Turn spring cap in until turning preload is 8.0-10.6 INCH lbs. (0.9-1.2 N.m). Apply liquid sealer to threads of lock nut, and install lock nut. Tighten lock nut to 41 ft. lbs. (56 N.m).

# 1991 STEERING
# Power Rack & Pinion (Cont.)

**10)** Align new claw washer with rack groove. Install rack end. Tighten rack end to 68 ft. lbs. (92 N.m) on Supra and 53 ft. lbs. (72 N.m) on all others. Stake claw washers.

**11)** Install steering damper (if equipped). Install new "O" ring seals. Install left and right turn tubes. Tighten tubes to 11 ft. lbs. (15 N.m). Coat rack end dust seals with grease. Remove any grease in housing tube hole. Install boots, clamps and clips. Install outer clips with ends facing up. Install tie rod ends, aligning reference marks.

**Disassembly (Cressida) – 1)** Mount steering gear in vise using Rack Housing Stand (09612-00012). Remove left and right turn tubes. Mark and remove tie rod ends. *See Fig. 16.* Remove outer clips and inner clamps. Remove boots.

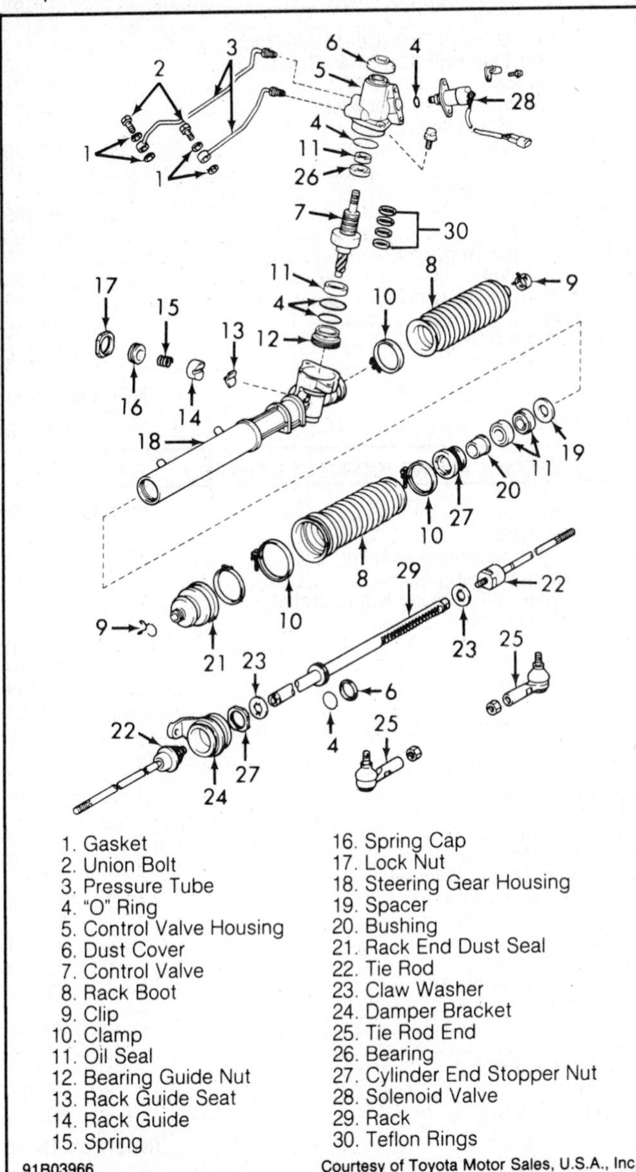


***Fig 16: Identifying Power Rack & Pinion Steering Gear Components (Cressida Shown; Previa Is Similar)***

**2)** Mark rack tie rods for reassembly reference. Using chisel and hammer, unstake claw washers. Remove tie rods using Lock Nut Wrench (09617-14010 and 09612-24014). Remove claw washers. Remove inboard rack boot and solenoid valve. Remove steering damper support. Lock nut has left-hand thread.

**3)** Remove rack guide spring cap lock nut. Remove spring cap. Remove rack guide spring, guide and seat.

**4)** Remove dust cover. Mark control valve housing and rack. Remove control valve and housing. Remove cylinder end stopper nut using Stopper Nut Wrench (09631-20090).

**5)** Using Bearing Replacer (09612-10061), press out rack and oil seal. Pull out steering rack, oil seal and rack end guide from cylinder. Remove dust cover. Using Bearing Guide Nut Wrench (09631-20060), remove bearing guide nut and "O" ring. Tap out control valve using a plastic mallet.

**Inspection & Repair – 1)** Check all parts for damage and deterioration. Place rack on "V" blocks. Using a dial indicator, measure runout at center of rack. Maximum runout is .012" (.30 mm). Check all bearings and seals for damage.

**2)** Using Oil Seal Remover (09620-24010) and Handle (09631-12020), press out oil seal and bearing. Using same tools, press in new oil seal. Using Bearing Installer (09620-24030), press in new bearing.

**3)** Drive out cylinder housing oil seal and spacer using Oil Seal Remover (09631-22040). Install new oil seal and spacer onto Seal Installer (09631-12040). Tap in using plastic mallet. Press out bearing guide nut seal using a socket wrench. Press new seal into guide nut using Seal Installer (09631-20040).

**4)** Use a small screwdriver to remove Teflon rings from rack piston. On rack, carefully expand new ring and install ring onto piston. Coat Teflon ring with power steering fluid, and snug down into groove using fingers.

**5)** Use a small screwdriver to remove rings from control valve. Install new Teflon rings onto Seal Ring Guide (09631-20070). Install rings onto control valve. Lubricate Teflon rings with power steering fluid. Slide tapered end of Installer (09631-20081) over rings to seat them.

**Reassembly & Adjustments – 1)** Install Steering Rack Cover (09631-20102) onto rack. Lubricate assembly with power steering fluid. Insert rack into cylinder. Remove rack cover. Insert end guide into cylinder. Wind vinyl tape around rack end, and lubricate with power steering fluid. Coat oil seal with power steering fluid. Press oil seal into cylinder. Remove vinyl tape. Install end stopper nut. Stake end stopper nut and cylinder end to prevent turning.

**2)** Lubricate control valve Teflon rings with power steering fluid. Insert valve into control valve housing. Lubricate new "O" ring with power steering fluid, and install ring. Install bearing guide nut. Stake nut. Install dust cover.

**3)** Install Oil Seal Test Tool (09631-22030). Apply 15.75 in. Hg for 30 seconds. If vacuum drops, recheck seals in rack housing. *See Fig. 10.* Align reference marks on control valve housing, and install housing. Tighten bolts to 13 ft. lbs. (18 N.m).

**4)** Install rack guide, guide spring and seat. Apply liquid sealer to threads of rack guide spring cap. Install cap using Hexagon Wrench (09612-10022). Tighten to 18 ft. lbs. (25 N.m). Back off spring cap 30 degrees. Turn control valve shaft left and right twice.

**5)** Loosen spring cap until preload is eliminated. Turn spring cap in until turning preload is 4.4-8.9 INCH lbs. (.5-1.0 N.m). Apply liquid sealer to threads of lock nut. Tighten lock nut to 44 ft. lbs. (60 N.m). Stake lock nut.

**6)** Install steering damper lock nut and bracket to cylinder side of housing. Align new claw washer with rack groove. Install rack tie rods. Using Lock Nut Wrench (09628-10020), tighten tie rods to 61 ft. lbs. (83 N.m). Stake claw washers. Align damper support bracket. Tighten and stake lock nut.

**7)** Install new "O" ring seals. Remove any grease in housing tube hole. Install left and right turn tubes. Coat rack end dust seals with grease. Install boots, clamps and clips. Install outer clips with ends facing up. Install tie rod ends, aligning reference marks. Tie rod lock nuts are to be tightened when wheels are aligned.

**Disassembly (Previa) – 1)** Mount steering gear in vise using Rack Housing Stand (09612-00012). Remove left and right turn tubes. Mark and remove tie rod ends. *See Fig. 16.* Remove outer clips and inner clamps. Remove boots and dust cover.

**2)** Unstake claw washers. Remove tie rods using Lock Nut Wrench (09617-14010 and 09612-24014). Remove claw washers. Remove rack guide spring cap lock nut, spring cap, rack guide and seat.

**3)** Mark control valve housing and rack housing. Remove control valve and control valve housing as an assembly. Wrap vinyl tape around shaft. Using a plastic mallet, tap out control valve together with bearing guide nut. Remove guide nut.

# 1991 STEERING
# Power Rack & Pinion (Cont.)

**4)** Remove cylinder end stopper nut using Stopper Nut Wrench (09631-20090). Remove "O" ring. Press out rack using Bearing Replacer (09612-10061). Remove oil seal.

**Inspection & Repair – 1)** Check all parts for damage and deterioration. Place rack on "V" blocks. Using a dial indicator, measure runout at center of rack. Maximum runout is .006" (.15 mm). Check all bearings and seals for damage. Replace as necessary. Replace all "O" rings. Check needle bearing for pits and damage. Replace rack housing if defective.

**2)** Using a small screwdriver, remove Teflon ring from rack. Lubricate new ring with power steering fluid. Expand ring using fingers. DO NOT expand ring more than necessary to install. Install ring onto rack, and snug down.

**3)** Remove Teflon rings from control valve in similar manner. Lubricate Teflon rings with power steering fluid. Slide rings over Installer (09631-20070). Install rings onto control valve. Snug down using fingers. Slide chamfered end of Seal Ring Setter (09631-20081) over assembly to seat seal rings.

***NOTE: Lubricate components with power steering fluid during assembly.***

**Reassembly & Adjustments – 1)** Tap in new housing oil seal. Install Steering Rack Cover (09631-20111) onto rack. Insert rack into housing. Remove steering rack cover. DO NOT move rack until control valve is installed.

**2)** Install steering rack cover onto opposite end of rack. Grease lip of oil seal, and then insert oil seal into steering rack cover. Remove steering rack cover.

**3)** Install new "O" ring onto end stopper. Tap end stopper into housing using a block of wood and hammer. Tighten end stopper using Stopper Nut Wrench (09631-20090). Stake rack housing.

**4)** Install Oil Seal Test Tool (09631-22030). Apply 15.75 in. Hg for 30 seconds. If vacuum drops, recheck seals, "O" rings and Teflon rings in rack housing. *See Fig. 10.*

**5)** Wind vinyl tape around serrations of control valve shaft. Insert control valve into housing. Install new "O" ring. Install and tighten guide nut to 18 ft. lbs. (25 N.m). Stake guide nut.

**6)** Install control valve housing "O" ring. Install control valve housing into rack housing. Ensure reference marks align. Install rack guide and rack guide spring. Apply sealant to threads of rack guide spring cap. Install rack guide spring cap.

**7)** Tighten rack guide spring cap to 18 ft. lbs. (25 N.m). Turn control valve shaft left and right twice. Loosen spring cap until preload is eliminated. Turn spring cap in until turning preload is 6.2-11.5 INCH lbs. (.7-1.3 N.m). Apply liquid sealer to threads of lock nut, and install lock nut. Tighten lock nut to 41 ft. lbs. (56 N.m). Stake lock nut.

**8)** Install boots and pressure tubes. Align reference marks when installing tie rod ends. Stake claw washers. Tie rod lock nuts are to be tightened when wheels are aligned.

## TORQUE SPECIFICATIONS

***TORQUE SPECIFICATIONS (CAMRY, CELICA & SUPRA)***

| Application | Ft. Lbs. (N.m) |
|---|---|
| Air Control Valve | 27 (37) |
| Control Valve Bearing Guide Lock Nut | 41 (56) |
| Control Valve Housing Bolts | 23 (31) |
| Control Valve Lower Bearing Self-Locking Nut | |
| Camry, Celica FWD & Supra | 18 (25) |
| Celica All-Trac | 11 (15) |
| Pressure Port | 51 (69) |
| Pulley Bolt Or Nut | 32 (43) |
| Pump Bracket Bolt | 29-33 (39-45) |
| Rack Guide Spring Cap Lock Nut | 51 (69) |
| Rear Housing Bolt | 34 (46) |
| Stabilizer Bar Bracket Bolt (Celica All-Trac) | 14 (19) |
| Stabilizer Bar Link Bolt (Celica All-Trac) | 26 (35) |
| Steering Damper | 20 (26) |
| Steering Damper Bracket Lock Nut | 61 (83) |
| Steering Gear-To-Chassis | |
| Camry & Celica | 43 (58) |
| Supra | 56 (76) |
| Steering Rack Tie Rod | |
| Camry & Celica | 61 (83) |
| Supra | 76 (103) |
| Tie Rod Clamp Bolt (Supra) | 14 (19) |
| Tie Rod Lock Nut | 41 (56) |
| Tie Rod-To-Steering Arm Nut | 36 (49) |
| Turn Tubes | 14 (19) |
| "U" Joint Pinch Bolt | 24 (32) |
| Wheel Lug Nuts | 76 (103) |
| | **INCH Lbs. (N.m)** |
| Return Port Bolt | 108 (12) |

***TORQUE SPECIFICATIONS (COROLLA & TERCEL)***

| Application | Ft. Lbs. (N.m) |
|---|---|
| Air Control Valve | 18 (25) |
| Center Engine Mounting Bracket | 29 (39) |
| Control Valve Housing Bolts | 18 (25) |
| Control Valve Self-Locking Nut (Corolla) | 18 (25) |
| Cylinder End Set Nut | 123 (167) |
| Cylinder End Stopper Nut | 87 (116) |
| Pressure Port Bolt | 34 (46) |
| Pressure Port Union | 51 (69) |
| Pulley Nut | 32 (43) |
| Pump Bracket Bolt & Nut | 29 (39) |
| Rack End Nuts | 38 (51) |
| Rack Guide Spring Cap Lock Nut | |
| Corolla | 100 (136) |
| Tercel | 28 (38) |
| Rack Housing Cap | 43 (58) |
| Rear Cover Bolt | 34 (46) |
| Rear Engine Mount Bracket | 38 (51) |
| Steering Gear-To-Chassis | 43 (58) |
| Steering Rack Tie Rod | 61 (83) |
| Tie Rod Clamp Bolt | 14 (19) |
| Tie Rod Lock Nut | 41 (56) |
| Tie Rod-To-Steering Arm | 36 (49) |
| Turn Tubes | |
| Corolla | 33 (44) |
| Tercel | 11 (15) |
| "U" Joint Pinch Bolt | |
| Corolla | 26 (35) |
| Tercel | 33 (44) |
| | **INCH Lbs. (N.m)** |
| Reservoir Bolt | 108 (12) |

# 1991 STEERING
# Power Rack & Pinion (Cont.)

*TORQUE SPECIFICATIONS (CRESSIDA)*

| Application | Ft. Lbs. (N.m) |
|---|---|
| Air Control Valve | 27 (36) |
| Control Valve Bearing Guide Nut | 18 (25) |
| Control Valve Housing Bolts | 13 (17) |
| Cylinder End Stopper Nut | 43 (58) |
| Pressure Port Union | 51 (69) |
| Pressure Port Union Bolt | 34 (46) |
| Pulley Nut | 32 (44) |
| Pump Housing Bolt | 34 (46) |
| Pump Mounting Bolt | |
| Except Through Bolt | 29 (39) |
| Through Bolt | 43 (58) |
| Rack Guide Spring Cap Lock Nut | 51 (69) |
| Steering Damper Bolt | 20 (26) |
| Steering Damper Lock Nut | 61 (83) |
| Steering Gear-To-Chassis | 56 (76) |
| Steering Rack Tie Rod | 61 (83) |
| Tie Rod Lock Nut | 41 (56) |
| Tie Rod-To-Steering Arm Nut | 43 (58) |
| Torque Shaft-To-Pinion Shaft Bolts | 26 (35) |
| Turn Tubes | 18 (25) |
| "U" Joint Pinch Bolt | 26 (35) |
| Wheel Lug Nuts | 76 (103) |
| | **INCH Lbs. (N.m)** |
| Return Port Bolt | 108 (12) |

*TORQUE SPECIFICATIONS (PREVIA)*

| Application | Ft. Lbs. (N.m) |
|---|---|
| Bearing Guide Lock Nut | 51 (69) |
| Control Valve Retaining Bolt | 13 (17) |
| Inner Tie Rod End Joint | 65 (88) |
| No. 2 Drive Housing Insulator Bolt | 18 (25) |
| No. 3 Drive Housing Bracket Bolt | 13 (17) |
| Rack Cylinder End Stopper | 58 (78) |
| Rear Pump Housing-To-Front Housing Bolt | 13 (17) |
| Steering Gear Bracket Bolt | 56 (76) |
| Tie Rod End Castle Nuts | 36 (49) |
| Tie Rod End Lock Nut | 67 (91) |
| "U" Joint Clamp Bolt | 26 (35) |

# 1991 STEERING
# Manual Recirculating Ball

### Pickup, 4Runner

## DESCRIPTION & OPERATION

Steering gear is a variable ratio, recirculating ball type. Ball bearings circulate within grooves in worm and nut. As worm shaft turns, ball nut moves up or down, turning sector shaft and pitman arm.

Linkage consists of an idler arm, center relay rod, adjustable tie rods and steering knuckles. A steering damper is attached to center relay rod. Components are connected by ball joints. Linkage assembly is connected to steering gear by a pitman arm.

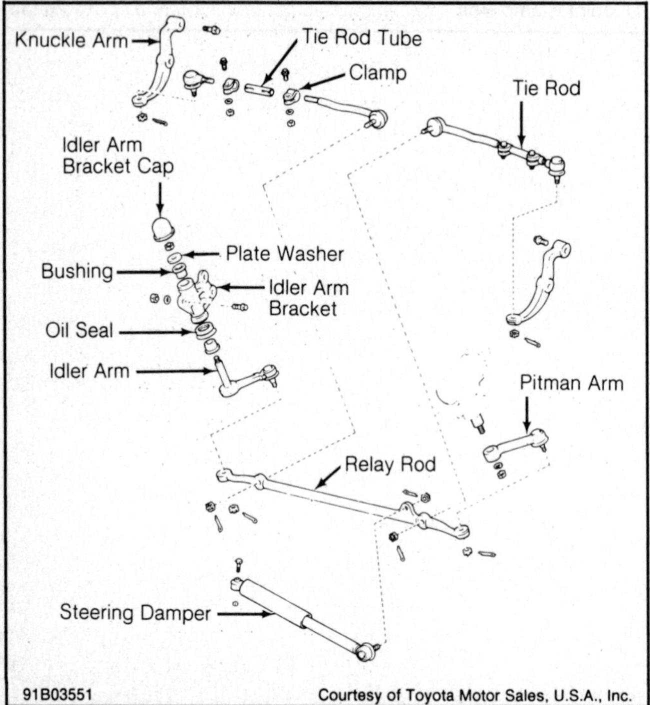


***Fig. 1: Exploded View of Steering Linkage (4Runner & Pickup 4WD Shown; Pickup 2WD Is Similar)***

## ADJUSTMENTS

Adjustments are performed during reassembly. See OVERHAUL procedure.

## REMOVAL & INSTALLATION

### STEERING GEAR

**Removal & Installation – 1)** Mark steering gear shaft at flexible coupling or "U" joint for installation reference. Remove coupling or "U" joint bolt. Mark sector shaft at pitman arm. Disconnect pitman arm from sector shaft.

**2)** Remove steering gear-to-frame retaining bolts. Separate steering gear from steering shaft while removing steering gear from vehicle. To install, reverse removal procedure. Align marks made during removal.

### STEERING LINKAGE

**Removal – 1)** Mark pitman arm at sector shaft for installation reference. Remove cotter pins and nuts from sector shaft, tie rod ends and idler arm. Using a puller, disconnect pitman arm from sector shaft and tie ends from steering arms. Disconnect idler arm from relay rod. *See Fig. 1.*

**2)** Disconnect steering damper from crossmember (if equipped). Remove steering linkage assembly from vehicle. Remove idler arm bracket nuts and bolts. Remove idler arm.

**Installation** – To install, reverse removal procedure. Align marks made during removal. Ensure tie rod lengths are to specification. Measure tie rod lengths from center to center of tie rod ball joints. Tie rod length should be 12.38" (314.5 mm).

## OVERHAUL

### STEERING GEAR

**Disassembly – 1)** Mark pitman arm at sector shaft for reassembly reference. Remove pitman arm. Remove sector shaft adjusting screw lock nut. Remove sector shaft cover and sector shaft.

**2)** DO NOT lose adjusting screw and shim. Remove worm assembly lock nut, bearing adjusting screw and oil seal. Remove worm assembly and bearings. *See Fig. 2.*

***NOTE: DO NOT remove ball nut from worm shaft. If recirculating ball assembly has damaged or worn components, replace entire assembly.***

**Inspection (2WD) – 1)** Check all components for excessive wear or damage. Measure clearance between adjusting screw (with shim installed) and sector shaft. Maximum clearance should be .002" (.05 mm).

**2)** If clearance is not within specification, replace shim. Shims are available from .0767-.0847" (1.95-2.15 mm) in .0020" (.05 mm) increments.

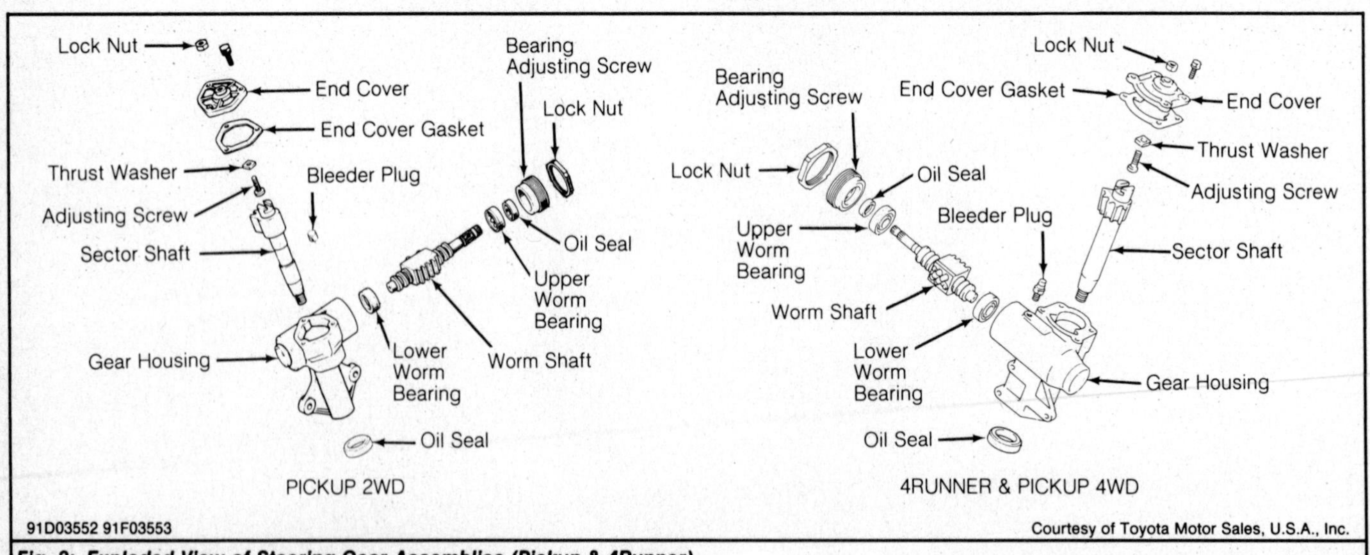


***Fig. 2: Exploded View of Steering Gear Assemblies (Pickup & 4Runner)***

# 1991 STEERING
# Manual Recirculating Ball (Cont.)

**3)** Carefully check worm gear and ball nut without letting ball nut bottom out on either end of worm gear. If ball nut bottoms out, worm assembly will be damaged.
**4)** Check worm bearings and races for pitting and smooth operation. Replace, if damaged. Replace oil seal. Replace end cover bushing and needle bearings, if necessary.
**Inspection (4WD) - 1)** Check all components for excessive wear or damage. Measure clearance between adjusting screw (with shim installed) and sector shaft. Maximum clearance should be .002" (.05 mm).
**2)** If clearance is not within specification, replace shim. Shims are available from .0767-.0807" (1.95-2.05 mm) in .0020" (.05 mm) increments. Ensure inside diameter of sector shaft end cover bushing is 1.4201" (36.07 mm).
**3)** Carefully check worm gear and ball nut without letting ball nut bottom out on either end of worm gear. If ball nut bottoms out, worm assembly will be damaged.
**Reassembly & Adjustment (2WD & 4WD) - 1)** Grease all bearings and sliding surfaces. Install bearings on worm assembly. Install worm assembly to gear housing.
**2)** Install oil seal and bearing adjusting screw. To seat bearings, tighten adjusting screw while rotating worm gear. Loosen adjusting screw. Tighten adjusting screw again.
**3)** Measure initial preload. See INITIAL WORM BEARING PRELOAD table. If preload is not within specification, loosen and tighten adjusting screw until preload is correct.

***INITIAL WORM BEARING PRELOAD***

| Application | INCH Lbs. (N.m) |
|---|---|
| 2WD | 2.6-4.3 (.29-.48) |
| 4WD | 3.0-4.3 (.34-.50) |

**4)** With initial preload to specification, hold adjusting screw in position. Install and tighten lock nut to specification. See TORQUE SPECIFICATIONS table at end of article.
**5)** Center ball nut on worm shaft. Install sector shaft so center teeth of both shafts mesh. Install shim (selected previously) to sector shaft adjusting screw. Install adjusting screw on sector shaft.
**6)** Apply liquid sealer to adjusting screw threads. Install sector shaft end cover to housing. Loosen sector shaft adjusting screw as far as possible. Install and tighten cover bolts. Center worm shaft in neutral position.
**7)** Adjust final worm bearing preload by tightening adjusting screw. *See Fig. 3.* See FINAL WORM BEARING PRELOAD table. Install lock nut. While holding adjusting screw in position, tighten lock nut to specification. See TORQUE SPECIFICATIONS table at end of article.

***FINAL WORM BEARING PRELOAD***

| Application | INCH Lbs. (N.m) |
|---|---|
| 2WD | 6.9-9.1 (.78-1.03) |
| 4WD | 6.9-9.5 (.78-1.07) |

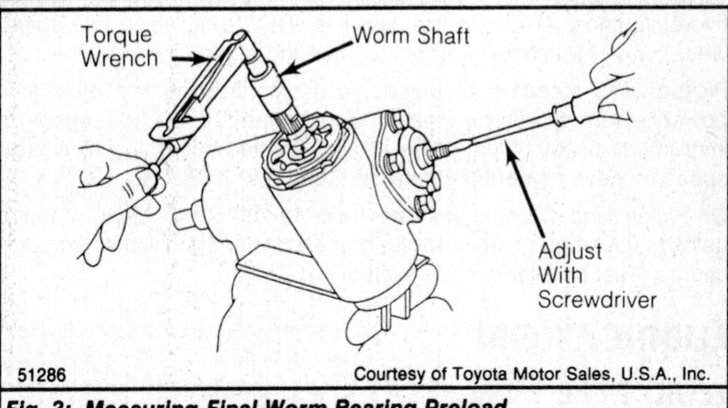


***Fig. 3: Measuring Final Worm Bearing Preload***

**8)** Align marks made during removal and install pitman arm and nut. To measure back lash, attach dial indicator so plunger touches end of pitman arm. Sector shaft should have zero backlash when measured at any point 100 degrees on either side of centered position.
**9)** Remove fill plug. Fill steering gear with fluid type API GL-4, SAE 90W gear oil. Fluid level should be below top surface of sector shaft end cover approximately 0.71"-1.10 (18-28 mm) for 2WD, and "0.55"-0.67" (14-17 mm) for 4WD.

## TORQUE SPECIFICATIONS

***TORQUE SPECIFICATIONS***

| Application | Ft. Lbs. (N.m) |
|---|---|
| Idler Arm Bracket Nut | |
| 2WD | 87 (118) |
| 4WD | 105 (142) |
| Idler Arm-To-Relay Rod Nut | 43 (59) |
| Intermediate Shaft Coupling or "U" Joint Bolt | 26 (35) |
| Pitman Arm-To-Relay Rod Nut | 67 (90) |
| Pitman Arm-To-Sector Shaft Nut | |
| 2WD | 90 (123) |
| 4WD | 130 (177) |
| Sector Shaft Adjusting Screw Lock Nut | |
| 2WD | 20 (27) |
| 4WD | 33 (44) |
| Sector Shaft End Cover Bolt | |
| 2WD | 13 (18) |
| 4WD | 72 (98) |
| Steering Gear-To-Frame Bolt | |
| 2WD | 87 (118) |
| 4WD | 105 (142) |
| Tie Rod-To-Steering Knuckle Nut | 67 (90) |
| Worm Shaft Adjusting Screw Lock Nut | 108 (147) |

# 1991 STEERING
# Power Recirculating Ball

## Land Cruiser, Pickup, 4Runner

## DESCRIPTION & OPERATION

Power steering system consists of a belt-driven pump with air control valve (if equipped), variable-assist steering gear and connecting hydraulic lines. An air control valve is used to increase idle speed when heavy loads exists on power steering pump.

Pickup uses standard or electronic power steering. On electronic power steering, vehicle speed is detected by speed sensor in instrument cluster. Fluid pressure is regulated according to vehicle speed by power steering Electronic Control Unit (ECU).

On Pickup and 4Runner with anti-lock brakes, power steering pump delivers fluid through actuator for brake system. Special bleeding procedure must be used on this system.

## LUBRICATION

### FLUID TYPE

Fluid type is Dexron II-ATF.

### FLUID LEVEL CHECK

With engine at 1000 RPM, turn wheels from side to side several times to increase fluid temperature. With engine idling, remove cap (dipstick) from power steering pump. Fluid level should be at HOT LEVEL on dipstick. Add fluid if necessary. DO NOT overfill.

### HYDRAULIC SYSTEM BLEEDING

**Land Cruiser** – **1)** Fill fluid to proper level in reservoir. Start engine. With engine speed less than 1000 RPM, turn steering wheel completely to one side and hold for 2-3 seconds.

**2)** Turn wheels completely in opposite direction for 2-3 seconds. Return steering wheel to center position. Ensure fluid level did not rise and foaming fluid does not exist. If fluid level rose or foaming exists, repeat procedure until air is gone.

**Pickup & 4Runner (With Anti-Lock Brakes)** – **1)** Fill fluid to proper level in reservoir. Start engine. With engine speed less than 1000 RPM, turn steering wheel from side to side against lock 2-3 times.

**2)** Shut off engine. Connect clear hose to bleeder plug, located on top of steering gear. *See Fig. 1.* Start engine. Turn steering wheel from side to side against lock 2-3 times.

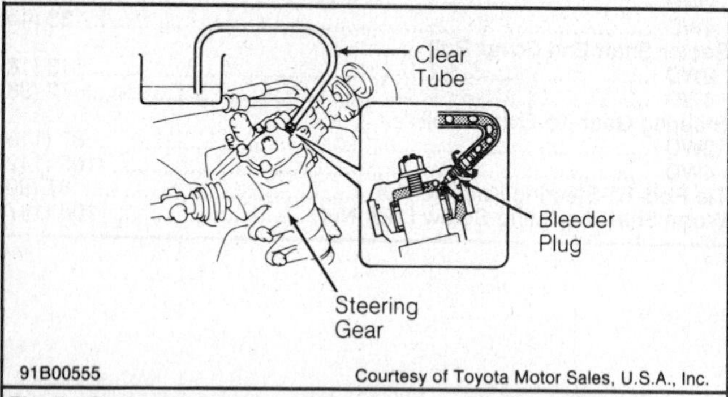


***Fig. 1: Connecting Hose on Bleeder Plug (Pickup & 4Runner)***

**3)** Place wheels in straight-ahead position. Loosen bleeder plug. Tighten bleeder plug when no bubbles exist in hose. Ensure fluid level did not rise and foaming does not exist.

**4)** If fluid level rose or foaming exists, repeat procedure until air is no longer present. Tighten bleeder plug to 69 INCH lbs. (8 N.m).

**5)** Bleed brake system with engine running and again with engine off. Start with longest line when bleeding brake system. Tighten bleeder screws to 96 INCH lbs. (11 N.m).

**6)** Power steering system must be bled again. Remove electrical connector from actuator and solenoid relay. *See Fig. 2.* Using Sub Wire Harness (09990-00205), connect Actuator Checker (09990-00150) to actuator and solenoid wiring harness connectors.

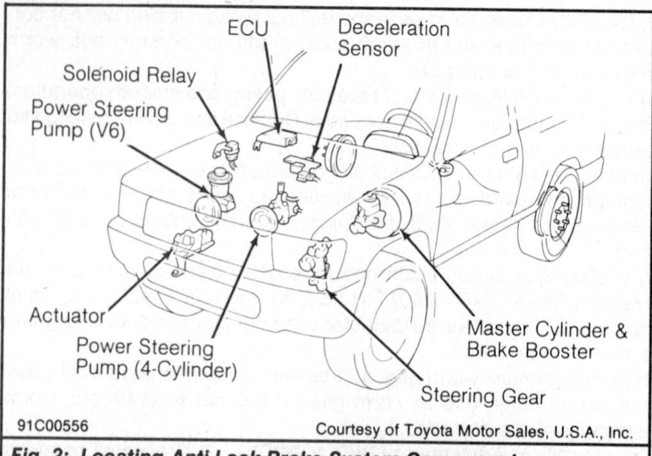


***Fig. 2: Locating Anti-Lock Brake System Components (Pickup & 4Runner)***

**7)** Connect Red lead of actuator checker to positive battery terminal and Black lead to negative battery terminal. Start engine, and allow it to idle. Turn actuator checker selector switch to AIR BLEED position. *See Fig. 3.*

**8)** Firmly depress and hold brake pedal. Turn power switch to ON position for 3 seconds and then to OFF position. Repeat power switch operation 5 times.

***CAUTION: DO NOT turn power switch to ON position before depressing brake pedal or release brake pedal before turning power switch to OFF position. DO NOT leave power switch in ON position longer than 10 seconds.***

**9)** Turn power switch to OFF position and release brake pedal. Check power steering fluid level. Add fluid if necessary. Remove actuator checker, and reconnect electrical connections.

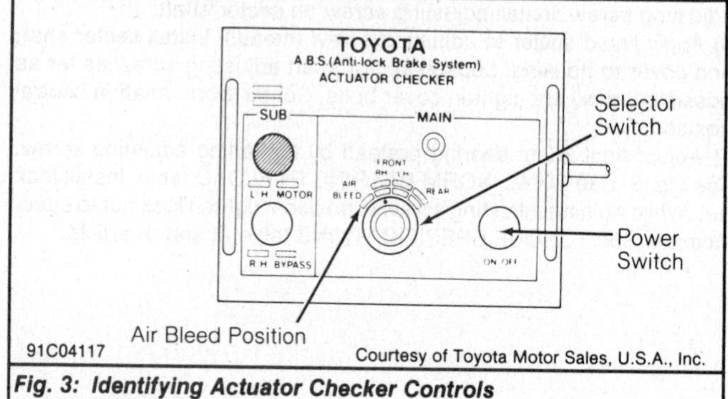


***Fig. 3: Identifying Actuator Checker Controls***

**Pickup & 4Runner (Without Anti-Lock Brakes)** – **1)** Fill fluid to proper level in reservoir. Start engine. With engine speed less than 1000 RPM, turn steering wheel from side to side against lock 2-3 times.

**2)** Shut off engine. Connect clear hose to bleeder plug, located on top of steering gear. *See Fig. 1.* Start engine. Turn steering wheel from side to side against lock 2-3 times.

**3)** Place wheels in straight-ahead position. Loosen bleeder plug. Tighten bleeder plug when no bubbles exist in hose. Ensure fluid level did not rise and no foaming of fluid exists.

**4)** If fluid level rose or foaming exists, repeat procedure until air is no longer present. Tighten bleeder plug to 69 INCH lbs. (8 N.m).

## ADJUSTMENTS

### POWER STEERING PUMP BELT

Using belt tension gauge, check belt tension. Adjust belt to obtain correct belt tension. See BELT TENSION SPECIFICATIONS table.

# 1991 STEERING
# Power Recirculating Ball (Cont.)

***BELT TENSION SPECIFICATIONS***

| Application | New Belt Lbs. (kg) [1] | Used Belt Lbs. (kg) |
|---|---|---|
| Land Cruiser | 120-170 (54-77) | 80-120 (36-54) |
| Pickup & 4Runner | 100-150 (45-68) | 60-100 (27-45) |

[1] - New belt is a belt in operation less than 5 minutes.

## TESTING

### HYDRAULIC SYSTEM PRESSURE TEST

***NOTE: Before testing, fluid temperature should be at least 176°F (80°C).***

**1)** Disconnect pressure lines from steering gear and pump. Install Pressure Gauge (09631-22020) with gauge side connected to pump and valve side of gauge connected to pressure line. *See Fig. 4.*

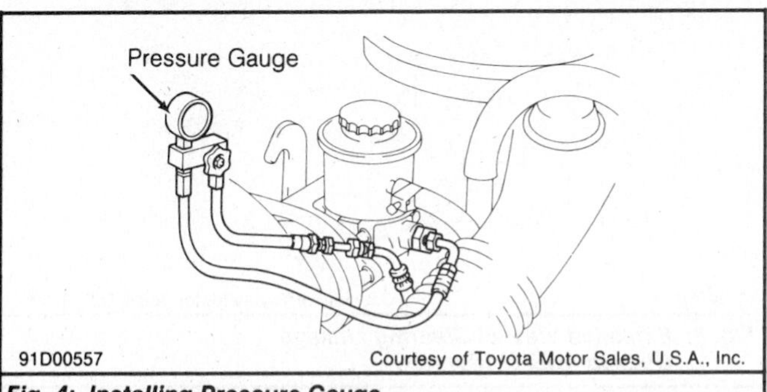


***Fig. 4: Installing Pressure Gauge***

**2)** Bleed air from system. See HYDRAULIC SYSTEM BLEEDING under LUBRICATION. Ensure fluid level is correct. Start engine, and allow it to idle. Close valve and note pressure reading. Open valve.

***CAUTION: DO NOT close valve longer than 10 seconds.***

**3)** Pressure should be at least 1067 psi (75 kg/cm²). Replace power steering pump if pressure is low.
**4)** With valve open, record pressure with engine speed at 1000 and 3000 RPM. Difference between readings should not exceed 71 psi (4.9 kg/cm²). Replace flow control valve in power steering pump if difference exceeds specification.
**5)** On all models except Pickup with electronic power steering, turn wheels against lock and note pressure reading with valve open. Pressure should be at least 1067 psi (75 kg/cm²). If pressure is low, steering gear has internal leakage and must be repaired.
**6)** On Pickup with electronic power steering, turn wheels to full lock position. Disconnect electrical connector from solenoid valve located on steering gear. *See Fig. 5.*

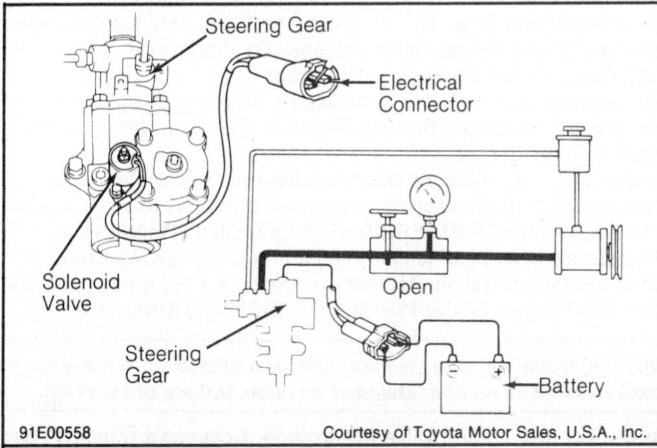


***Fig. 5: Connecting Wiring to Solenoid Valve (Pickup with Electronic Power Steering)***

**7)** With valve open and engine speed at 1000 RPM, note pressure reading. Pressure should be at least 1067 psi (75 kg/cm²). If pressure is low, steering gear has internal leakage or solenoid valve is defective.
**8)** Connect battery voltage to solenoid valve electrical connector. *See Fig. 5.* Note pressure reading. Maximum pressure should be 569 psi (40 kg/cm²).

***CAUTION: DO NOT connect voltage to solenoid valve longer than 30 seconds. Allow solenoid valve to cool between test procedures.***

**9)** If pressure is high, check resistance between solenoid terminals. Replace solenoid if resistance is not 6-11 ohms. If resistance is okay, connect battery voltage and ground to solenoid connector terminals.
**10)** Solenoid valve needle should be drawn into solenoid valve approximately .79" (20.0 mm). Replace solenoid valve if needle does not operate as specified.
**11)** Reconnect electrical connector at solenoid valve and note pressure reading. Pressure should be at least 1067 psi (75 kg/cm²). If pressure is low, check electronic power steering system. See ELECTRONIC POWER STEERING article in STEERING.

## REMOVAL & INSTALLATION

### POWER STEERING PUMP

**Removal & Installation - 1)** Drain fluid from pump. Disconnect lines, and plug openings. Remove drive belt. Remove power steering pump.
**2)** To install, reverse removal procedure. Tighten bolts to specification. See TORQUE SPECIFICATIONS table at end of article. Adjust drive belt tension. See POWER STEERING PUMP BELT under ADJUSTMENTS. Fill and bleed system. See HYDRAULIC SYSTEM BLEEDING under LUBRICATION.

### STEERING GEAR

**Removal - 1)** Disconnect fluid lines at steering gear. On electronic power steering models, disconnect solenoid valve electrical connector. On all models, place wheels in straight-ahead position. Mark joint and steering gear shaft for reassembly reference.
**2)** Remove bolt, and separate joint from steering shaft. Mark pitman arm and steering gear shaft for reassembly reference. Remove pitman arm retaining nut. Using puller, separate pitman arm from steering gear. Remove steering gear-to-frame bolts. Remove steering gear.
**Installation -** To install, reverse removal procedure. Ensure all reference marks align. Tighten bolts to specification. See TORQUE SPECIFICATIONS table at end of article. Fill and bleed system. See HYDRAULIC SYSTEM BLEEDING under LUBRICATION.

### STEERING LINKAGE

**Removal (Land Cruiser) - 1)** Raise and support vehicle. Remove wheels. Remove relay rod end-to-pitman arm nut. *See Fig. 6.* Using Puller (09628-62011), separate relay rod end from pitman arm.
**2)** Remove nut, and disconnect tie rods from steering knuckle arms. Disconnect steering damper from bracket and relay rod. Remove steering damper.
**3)** Remove nut, and separate relay rod from tie rod. Remove steering linkage. If removing pitman arm from steering gear, mark pitman arm and steering gear shaft for reassembly reference. Remove pitman arm retaining nut. Using puller, separate pitman arm from steering gear.
**Inspection -** Place nut on tie rod ends. Using INCH-pound torque wrench, check rotating torque of tie rod ends. Replace tie rod end if rotating torque is not 8.7-26.0 INCH lbs. (.9-3 N.m). Inspect relay rod end components for damage. Replace components if damaged.
**Installation - 1)** To install, reverse removal procedure. If relay rod components were disassembled, reassemble, and tighten plug. Loosen plug 1-1 1/2 turns.
**2)** Adjust relay rod ends so relay rod length is approximately 37.80" (960.12 mm) before installing. Adjust tie rod ends so tie rod length is approximately 47.51" (1206.7 mm) before installing.

# 1991 STEERING
# Power Recirculating Ball (Cont.)

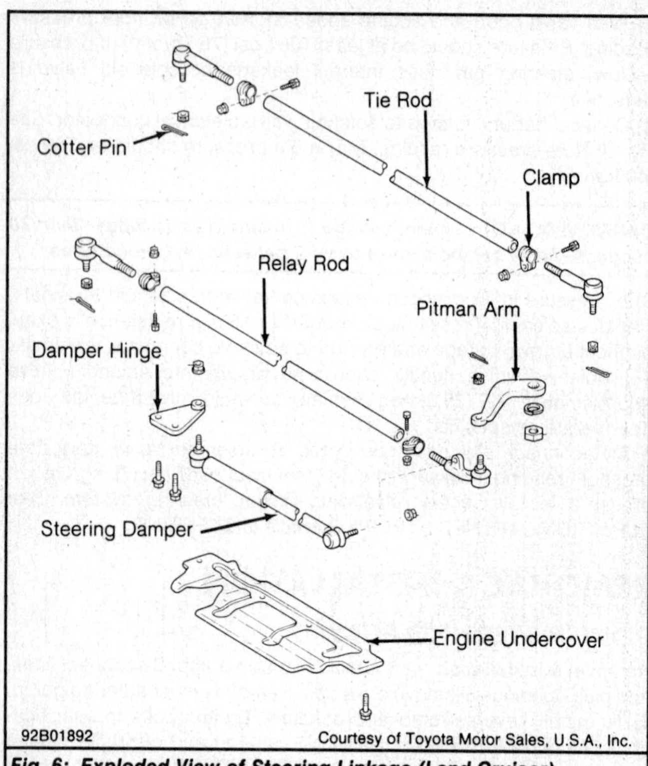


*Fig. 6: Exploded View of Steering Linkage (Land Cruiser)*

**3)** Tighten fasteners to specification. See TORQUE SPECIFICATIONS table at end of article. Lubricate all grease fittings. Adjust toe-in.

**Removal (Pickup & 4Runner) - 1)** Raise and support vehicle. Remove wheels. Mark pitman arm and steering gear shaft for reassembly reference. Remove pitman arm retaining nut. Using puller, separate pitman arm from steering gear.

**2)** Disconnect pitman arm from relay rod. *See Fig. 7 or 8.* Disconnect tie rod from relay rod and steering knuckle arm. Remove steering linkage. If removing idler arm from idler arm bracket, remove idler arm bracket cap. *See Fig. 7 or 8.* Remove nut and plate washer. Remove idler arm from idler arm bracket. Remove oil seal.

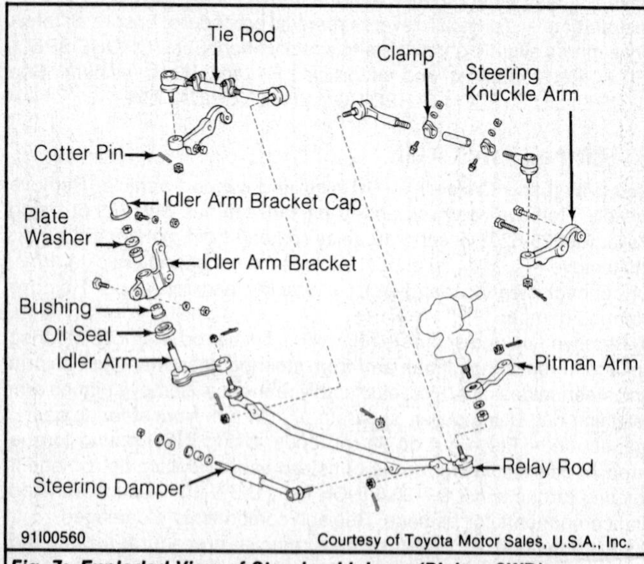


*Fig. 7: Exploded View of Steering Linkage (Pickup 2WD)*

**Installation - 1)** If idler arm was removed from idler arm bracket, install new oil seal. Coat oil seal lip with grease. Install idler arm in idler arm bracket.

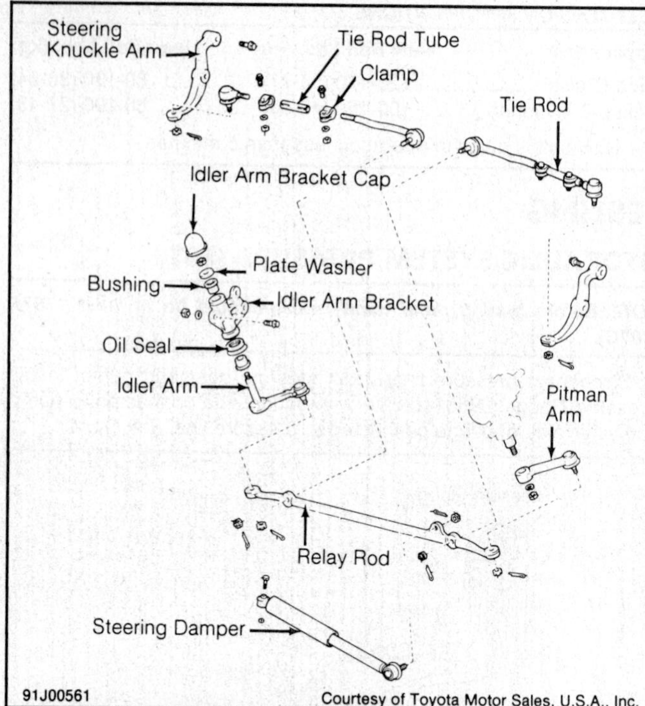


*Fig. 8: Exploded View of Steering Linkage (Pickup 4WD & 4Runner)*

**2)** Install plate washer and nut. Tighten nut to specification. See TORQUE SPECIFICATIONS table at end of article.

**3)** On Pickup 4WD and 4Runner, attach INCH-pound torque wrench to idler arm nut. Rotate idler arm and note rotating torque. Replace bushings if rotating torque is not 5-26 INCH lbs. (.6-3 N.m).

**4)** On all models, coat idler arm bracket cap sealing surface with sealant. Install idler arm bracket cap. To complete installation, reverse removal procedure. Adjust tie rod ends so tie rod length is approximately 12.38" (314.5 mm) before installing. Tighten all fasteners to specification. See TORQUE SPECIFICATIONS table. Adjust toe-in.

## OVERHAUL

### POWER STEERING PUMP

***NOTE: On Pickup and 4Runner, 2.4L and 3.0L engines use different power steering pumps.***

**Disassembly (Land Cruiser, Pickup 3.0L & 4Runner 3.0L) - 1)** Remove pulley, reservoir, "O" ring, air control valve and pressure port union. Remove flow control valve and spring. *See Fig. 9.*

**2)** Remove snap ring. Tap on pump shaft until rear housing, wave washer, "O" ring and rear plate are removed. Remove pump shaft with cam ring and vane plates from front housing.

**3)** Separate cam ring and vane plates from pump shaft. Remove straight pin from front housing. Remove snap ring, front plate and rotor from pump shaft.

**Inspection - 1)** Measure clearance between pump shaft and front housing bushing. Replace components if clearance exceeds specification. See POWER STEERING PUMP SPECIFICATIONS table.

**2)** Measure vane plate length, height and thickness. Measure vane plate-to-rotor clearance. Replace components if not within specification. See POWER STEERING PUMP SPECIFICATIONS table.

***NOTE: If replacing rotor, ensure number stamped on outer edge of rotor is same as number stamped on outer surface of cam ring.***

**3)** Inspect flow control valve for damage. Coat valve with ATF, and ensure flow control valve moves freely in housing bore. Close one hole on side of flow control valve.

# 1991 STEERING
# Power Recirculating Ball (Cont.)

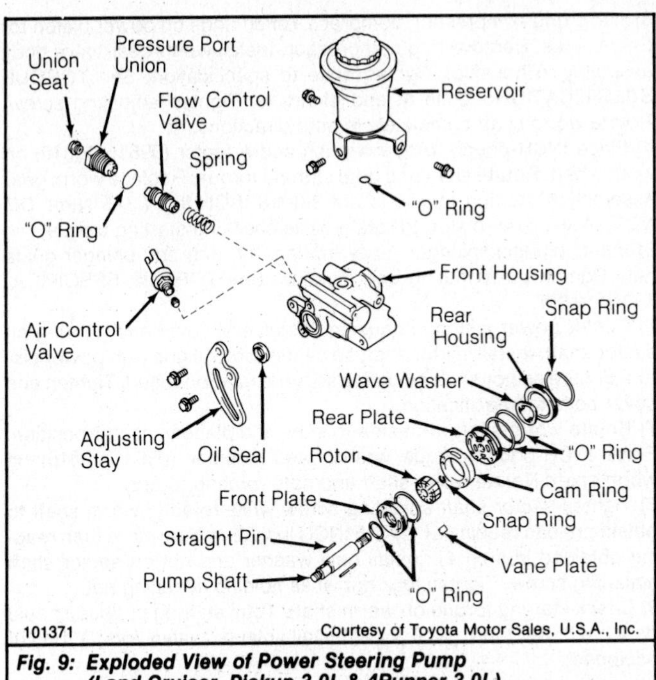


***Fig. 9: Exploded View of Power Steering Pump (Land Cruiser, Pickup 3.0L & 4Runner 3.0L)***

**4)** Apply 57-71 psi (4-5 kg/cm²) of compressed air in opposite hole on side of valve. Replace flow control valve if air escapes from hole on bottom of valve. Ensure flow control valve spring free length is within specification. See POWER STEERING PUMP SPECIFICATIONS table.

***CAUTION: If replacing flow control valve, ensure replacement valve has same letter as stamped on outer edge of original valve.***

***POWER STEERING PUMP SPECIFICATIONS***

| Application | In. (mm) |
|---|---|
| **Land Cruiser, Pickup 3.0L & 4Runner 3.0L** | |
| Flow Control Valve Spring Free Length | 1.38-1.46 (35.0-37.1) |
| Pump Shaft-To-Bushing Maximum Clearance | .0028 (.071) |
| Vane Plate Height (Minimum) | .3190 (8.103) |
| Vane Plate Length (Minimum) | .5901 (14.998) |
| Vane Plate-To-Rotor Maximum Clearance | .0011 (.028) |
| Vane Plate Thickness (Minimum) | .0707 (1.796) |
| **Pickup & 4Runner (2.4L)** | |
| Flow Control Valve Spring Free Length | 1.85-1.97 (46.9-50.0) |
| Rotor Shaft-To-Bushing Maximum Clearance | .0028 (.071) |
| Vane Plate Height (Minimum) | .3070 (7.800) |
| Vane Plate Length (Minimum) | .5894 (14.970) |
| Vane Plate-To-Cam Ring Maximum Clearance | .0024 (.061) |
| Vane Plate-To-Rotor Maximum Clearance | .0024 (.061) |
| Vane Plate Thickness (Minimum) | .0667 (1.770) |

**Reassembly - 1)** To reassemble, reverse disassembly procedure using new "O" rings. Coat oil seal lip with grease before installing. Lubricate all components with ATF.

**2)** Install rotor with inscribed mark facing from front plate. Install cam ring with inscribed mark facing from front housing. Install vane plates with rounded edge facing from rotor. Tighten bolts to specification. See TORQUE SPECIFICATIONS table at end of article.

**Disassembly (Pickup & 4Runner - 2.4L) - 1)** Remove pulley, air control valve (if equipped), union seat and suction port. *See Fig. 10.*

**2)** Mark front and rear housing for reassembly reference. Remove front housing bolts.

**3)** Tap on front housing, and remove. DO NOT allow vane plates, cam ring and rotor to come out of rear housing. *See Fig. 10.* Remove vane plates, cam ring and rotor. Remove oil seal and snap ring.

**4)** Using press, press rotor shaft from front housing. Tap on bottom of rear housing, and remove rear plate and spring. Remove "O" rings from front housing and rear plate. Remove union, flow control valve and spring. Remove snap ring, flow control valve spring seat and "O" ring.

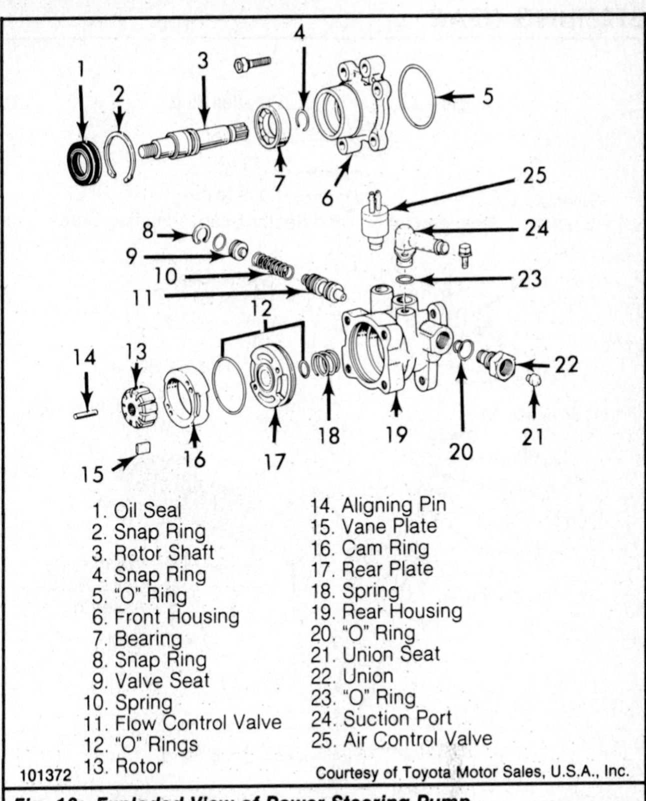


***Fig. 10: Exploded View of Power Steering Pump (Pickup & 4Runner - 2.4L)***

**Inspection - 1)** Measure clearance between rotor shaft and front housing bushing. Replace components if clearance exceeds specification. See POWER STEERING PUMP SPECIFICATIONS table.

**2)** Place rotor and vanes plate in cam ring. Measure clearance between vane plate and cam ring. Replace cam ring if clearance exceeds specification. See POWER STEERING PUMP SPECIFICATIONS table.

***NOTE: If replacing cam ring, ensure number stamped on outer edge of cam ring is same as number stamped on outer surface of rotor.***

**3)** Measure vane plate length, height and thickness. Measure vane plate-to-rotor clearance. Replace components if not within specification. See POWER STEERING PUMP SPECIFICATIONS table.

**4)** Inspect flow control valve for damage. Coat valve with ATF, and ensure flow control valve moves freely in housing bore. Close one hole on side of flow control valve.

**5)** Apply 57-71 psi (4-5 kg/cm²) of compressed air in opposite hole on side of valve. Replace flow control valve if air escapes from hole on bottom of valve. Ensure flow control valve spring free length is within specification. See POWER STEERING PUMP SPECIFICATIONS table.

***CAUTION: If replacing flow control valve, ensure replacement valve has same letter as stamped on outer edge of original valve.***

**Reassembly - 1)** To reassemble, reverse disassembly procedure using new "O" rings. Coat oil seal lip with grease before installing. Lubricate all components with ATF.

***NOTE: Install rotor with chamfered edge toward front housing.***

**2)** Install vane plates with rounded edge facing from rotor. Ensure reference marks align on front and rear housing. Tighten bolts to specification. See TORQUE SPECIFICATIONS table at end of article.

# 1991 STEERING
# Power Recirculating Ball (Cont.)

## STEERING GEAR

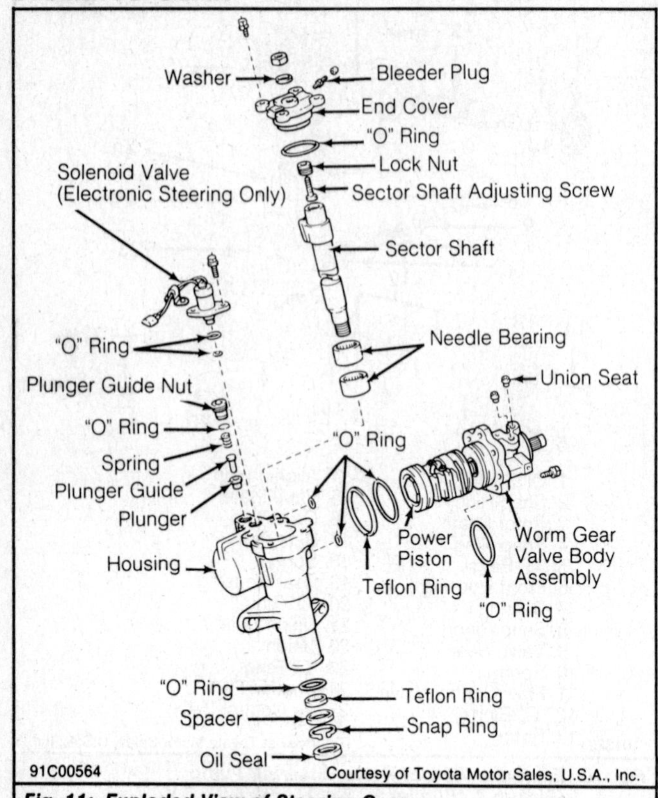


*Fig. 11: Exploded View of Steering Gear (Land Cruiser, Pickup & 4Runner)*

**Disassembly - 1)** Attach steering gear to holding fixture. Mount assembly in vise. Remove solenoid valve (if equipped). Remove pitman arm. Remove sector shaft adjusting screw lock nut and end cover retaining bolts. *See Fig. 11.*

**2)** Rotate sector shaft adjusting screw clockwise until end cover is removed. Using a mallet, tap sector shaft from housing. *See Fig. 11.*

**3)** Remove plunger guide nut, "O" ring, spring, plunger guide and plunger. Remove worm gear valve body-to-housing bolts. Hold power piston while turning worm shaft clockwise. Remove valve assembly and power piston from housing.

***CAUTION: Ensure power piston does not come off worm shaft. DO NOT disassemble valve assembly or power piston.***

**4)** If removing needle bearings, remove oil seal, snap ring, spacer and Teflon ring. *See Fig. 11.* Press needle bearings from housing using Bearing Remover/Installer (09630-00070).

**Inspection - 1)** Clamp sector shaft in soft-jawed vise. Using dial indicator, check thrust clearance of sector shaft adjusting screw. Thrust clearance should be .0012-.0020" (.030-.050 mm). If thrust clearance is not within specification, unstake lock nut.

**2)** Adjust lock nut to obtain correct thrust clearance. Restake lock nut. Inspect components for damage. Replace components as necessary.

**3)** Clamp worm gear valve body assembly in soft-jawed vise using bolt hole area of valve cap. Ensure power piston moves freely.

**4)** Using dial indicator, measure movement of power piston when pushing piston toward top of worm shaft. Replace assembly if movement exceeds .0059" (.150 mm).

**Reassembly - 1)** If needle bearings were removed, use bearing remover/installer to install upper bearing even with housing inner surface. Install outer bearing so bearing is positioned .909" (23.09 mm) from outer edge of housing.

**2)** Install "O" ring, Teflon ring, spacer and snap ring. Insert Ring Former (09631-00120) into Teflon ring to form ring to correct size. Using Seal Installer (09631-00170), install oil in housing. Coat seal with grease. Install new Teflon rings on power piston.

**3)** Using ring compressor, compress Teflon rings on power piston for 5-7 minutes. Remove ring compressor. Install worm gear valve body assembly in housing. Tighten bolts to specification. See TORQUE SPECIFICATIONS table at end of article. Tighten adjusting screw. Rotate worm shaft completely in both directions.

**4)** Place INCH-pound torque wrench and Adapter (09616-00010) on worm shaft. Rotate shaft and note starting torque. Replace worm gear assembly if starting torque is not 2.6-4.8 INCH lbs. (.3-.5 N.m). DO NOT allow power piston to rotate while checking starting torque.

**5)** Install plunger, plunger guide, spring, "O" ring and plunger guide nut. Tighten guide nut to specification. See TORQUE SPECIFICATIONS table.

**6)** Center power piston in housing. Install end cover and "O" ring on sector shaft. Install sector shaft so center tooth aligns with power piston. Ensure sector shaft adjusting screw is fully loosened. Tighten end cover bolts to specification.

**7)** Rotate worm shaft from side to side, and place in center position. Place INCH-pound torque wrench and Adapter (09631-00010) on worm shaft. Rotate worm shaft and note rotating torque.

**8)** Tighten sector shaft adjusting screw while rotating worm shaft to obtain preload reading of 1.7-3.5 INCH lbs. (.2-.4 N.m) more than reading obtained in step **4)**. Install new washer and nut on sector shaft adjusting screw. Tighten lock nut while holding adjusting nut.

**9)** Check starting torque on worm shaft. Total starting preload should be 4.3-8.3 INCH lbs. (.5-.9 N.m). Install solenoid valve and "O" ring (if equipped).

## TORQUE SPECIFICATIONS

*TORQUE SPECIFICATIONS*

| Application | Ft. Lbs. (N.m) |
|---|---|
| Air Control Valve | 27 (37) |
| End Cover Bolt | 34 (46) |
| Front Housing Bolt (Pickup & 4Runner - 2.4L) | 34 (46) |
| Guide Nut | 15 (20) |
| Idler Arm Bracket-To-Frame Bolt | |
| Pickup 2WD | 87 (118) |
| Pickup 4WD & 4Runner | 105 (142) |
| Idler Arm-To-Idler Arm Bracket Nut | 58 (79) |
| Idler Arm-To-Relay Rod Nut | 43 (58) |
| Pitman Arm Nut | 130 (176) |
| Power Steering Pump Pulley Nut | 32 (43) |
| Power Steering Pump-To-Bracket Bolt | |
| Pickup & 4Runner (2.4L) | 29 (39) |
| Pickup & 4Runner (3.0L) | |
| Long Bolt | 43 (58) |
| Short Bolt | 29 (39) |
| Pressure Line Bolt | 33 (45) |
| Pressure Port Union | 51 (69) |
| Reservoir Bolt | |
| Pickup & 4Runner (3.0L) | |
| 12-mm Bolt | [1] |
| 14-mm Bolt | 30 (41) |
| Sector Shaft Adjusting Screw Lock Nut | 34 (46) |
| Steering Damper-To-Bracket Nut | |
| Land Cruiser | 55 (74) |
| Pickup 2WD | [1] |
| Pickup 4WD & 4Runner | 19 (26) |
| Steering Damper-To-Relay Rod Nut | |
| Pickup & 4Runner | 43 (58) |
| Steering Damper-To-Tie Rod Nut (Land Cruiser) | 55 (74) |
| Steering Gear-To-Frame Bolt | |
| Pickup 2WD | 87 (118) |
| Land Cruiser, Pickup 4WD & 4Runner | 105 (142) |
| Steering Knuckle Arm-To-Frame Bolt | |
| Pickup 2WD | 80 (109) |
| Pickup 4WD & 4Runner | 135 (183) |
| Steering Shaft Joint-To-Steering Gear Bolt | 26 (35) |
| Tie Rod Clamp Bolt | 19 (26) |
| Tie Rod Nut | 67 (91) |
| Wheel Lug Nut | 76 (103) |
| Worm Gear Valve-To-Housing Bolt | 34 (46) |
| | **INCH Lbs. (N.m)** |
| Bleeder Plug | 71 (8) |
| Solenoid Valve Bolt | 80 (9) |
| Suction Port Bolt (Pickup & 4Runner - 2.4L) | 89 (10) |

[1] - Tighten bolts to 89 INCH lbs. (10 N.m).

# 1991 STEERING
# Electronic Power Steering

### Cressida, Pickup, Supra

## DESCRIPTION

The electronically controlled power steering system consists of a speed sensor (driven off speedometer), computer, a solenoid valve and other conventional power steering components.

The computer-controlled solenoid valve reduces hydraulic pressure to the rack at high speeds to increase steering effort. With vehicle at low speeds or stationary, the solenoid valve increases hydraulic pressure to the rack to reduce steering effort. *See Fig. 1.*

## TROUBLE SHOOTING

A malfunction in the electronically controlled power steering system will usually cause sensitive steering during high-speed driving and hard steering during idle or low-speed driving. However, these problems do not necessarily indicate a malfunction in the electronically controlled power steering system. Always check the following components before testing the electronically controlled power steering system.

- Tire Pressure
- Suspension & Steering Linkage Lubrication
- Front Wheel Alignment
- Steering System & Suspension Ball Joints
- Bent Steering Column
- Power Steering System Leakage
- Power Steering Pump Pressure

## ADJUSTMENTS

There are no adjustments for this system.

## TESTING

***NOTE: For wiring diagrams, see Figs. 8-10.***

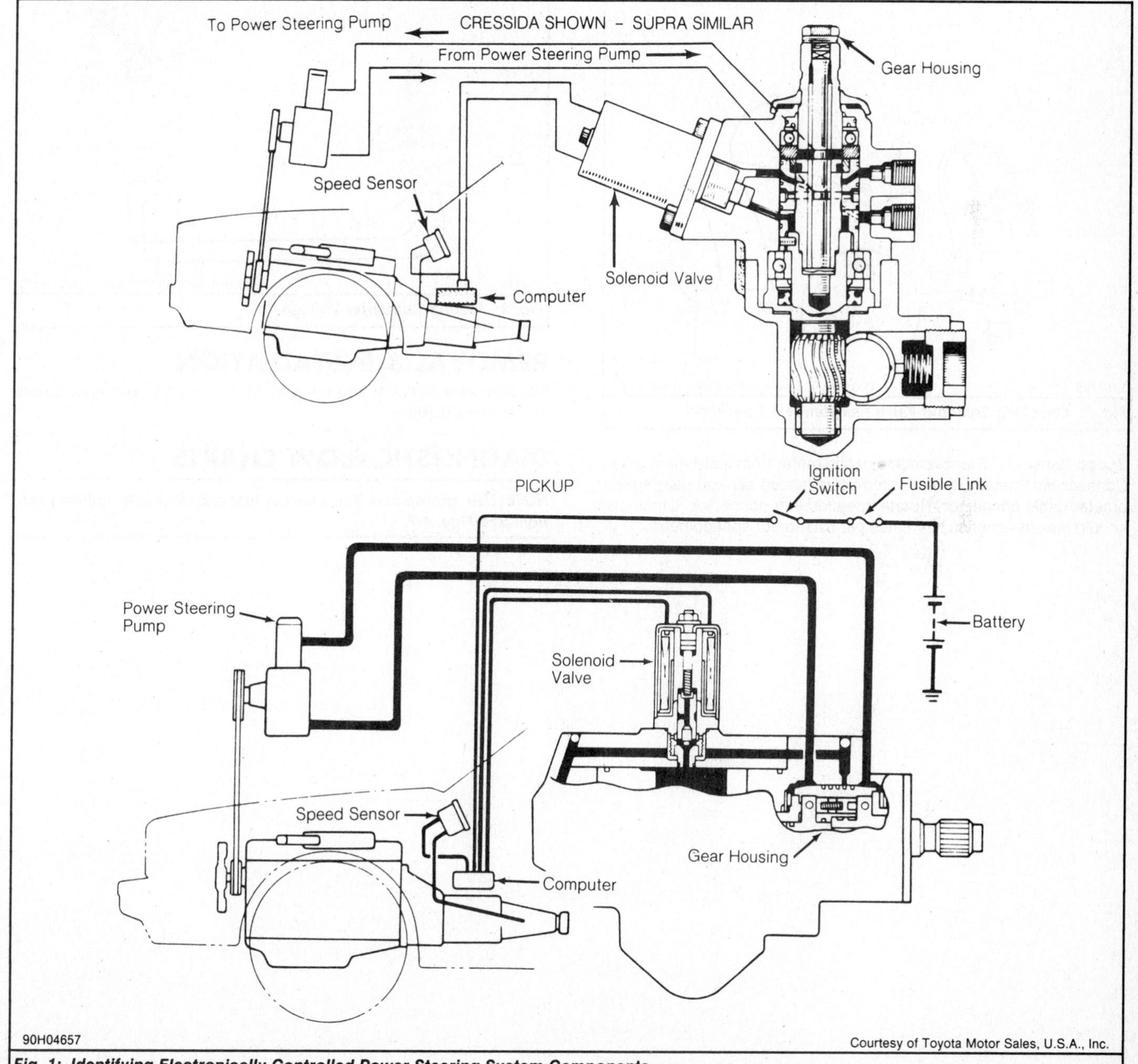


***Fig. 1: Identifying Electronically Controlled Power Steering System Components***

# 1991 STEERING
# Electronic Power Steering (Cont.)

## COMPONENT TESTING

**Solenoid Valve - 1)** Disconnect wiring connector from solenoid valve. Using an ohmmeter, measure resistance between solenoid valve terminals. Resistance should be 6.0-11.0 ohms. *See Fig. 2.* If resistance is not 6.0-11.0 ohms, replace solenoid valve.

**2)** Remove solenoid valve from steering gear housing. Using jumper wires, connect battery voltage to solenoid valve terminals. *See Fig. 2.* Ensure needle valve withdraws about .080" (2.0 mm). If needle valve does not function as described, replace solenoid valve.

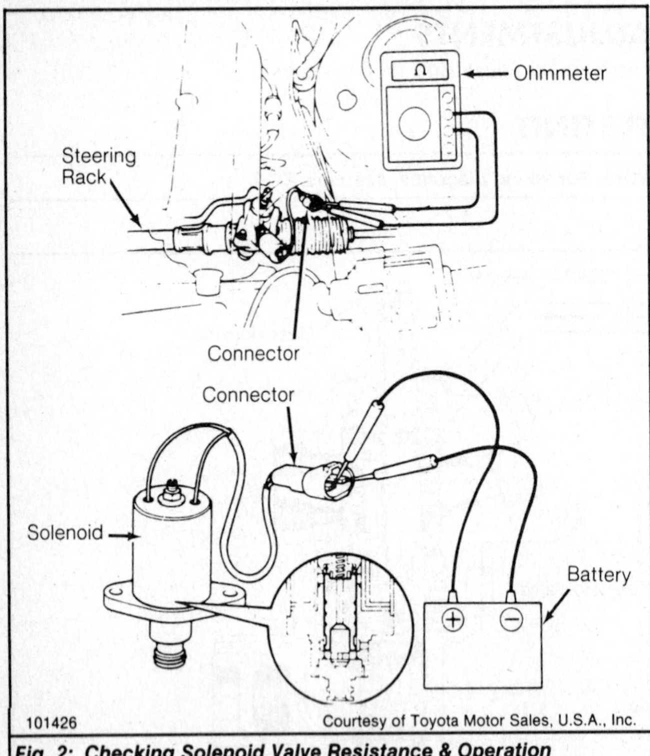

Courtesy of Toyota Motor Sales, U.S.A., Inc.

*Fig. 2: Checking Solenoid Valve Resistance & Operation*

**Speed Sensor** - Remove combination meter from instrument panel. Connect ohmmeter between 2 terminals (speed sensor) near speedometer cable connector. Rotate speedometer connector. Ohmmeter should indicate continuity 4 times per rotation of speedometer.

**Computer** - Raise vehicle, and support it on chassis stands. Remove glove box or console. DO NOT disconnect computer connector. Start engine. Using a voltmeter, check voltage between computer terminals SOL (+) and SOL (-) with engine idling. *See Fig. 3.* On Cressida and Pickup, ensure voltage is 0-.05 volt. On Supra, voltage should be .32-.44 volt. Place transmission in gear, and check computer voltage as indicated in COMPUTER VOLTAGE SPECIFICATIONS table. If voltage is not to specification, replace computer.

***COMPUTER VOLTAGE SPECIFICATIONS***

| Test Between | Vehicle Speed MPH (km/h) | Volts |
|---|---|---|
| SOL (-) & Ground | | |
| Cressida | 37 (60) | .12-.24 |
| Pickup | 37 (60) | .12-.24 |
| Supra | 31 (50) | .09-.24 |

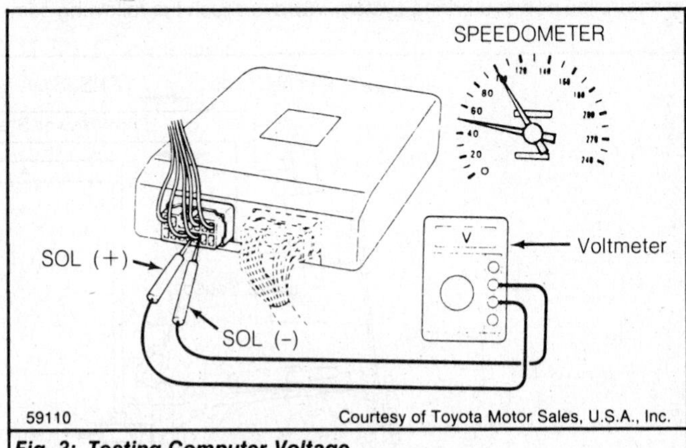

Courtesy of Toyota Motor Sales, U.S.A., Inc.

*Fig. 3: Testing Computer Voltage*

## REMOVAL & INSTALLATION

For complete removal and installation procedures, see appropriate article in STEERING.

## DIAGNOSTIC FLOW CHARTS

***NOTE: Use appropriate flow chart to test and diagnose system function. See Figs. 4-7.***

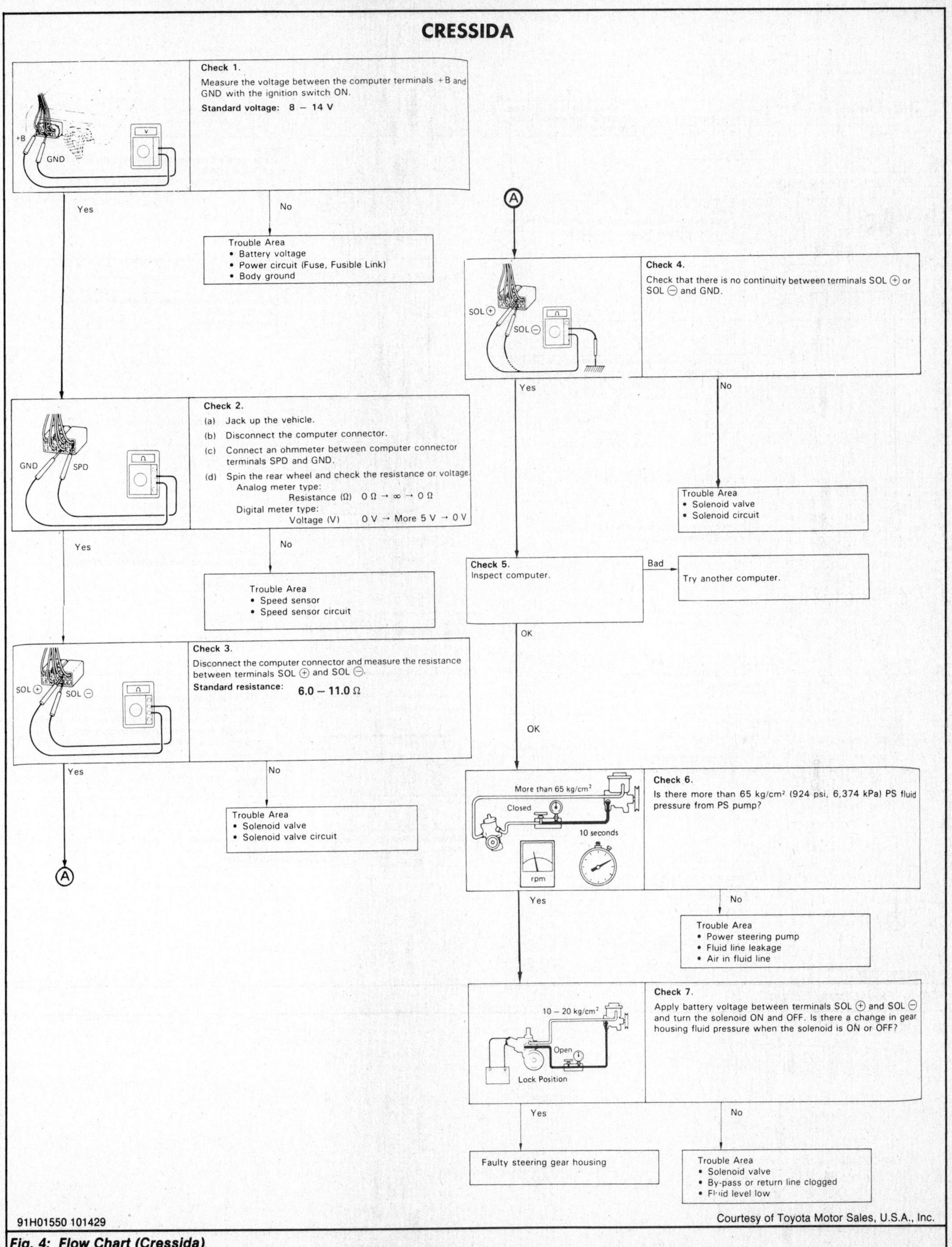

CRESSIDA
Check 1.
Measure the voltage between the computer terminals +B and GND with the ignition switch ON.
Standard voltage: 8 – 14 V
+B
GND
Yes
No
Trouble Area
• Battery voltage
• Power circuit (Fuse, Fusible Link)
• Body ground
Check 2.
(a) Jack up the vehicle.
(b) Disconnect the computer connector.
(c) Connect an ohmmeter between computer connector terminals SPD and GND.
(d) Spin the rear wheel and check the resistance or voltage.
Analog meter type:
Resistance (Ω) 0 Ω → ∞ → 0 Ω
Digital meter type:
Voltage (V) 0 V → More 5 V → 0 V
GND
SPD
Yes
No
Trouble Area
• Speed sensor
• Speed sensor circuit
Check 3.
Disconnect the computer connector and measure the resistance between terminals SOL ⊕ and SOL ⊖.
Standard resistance: 6.0 – 11.0 Ω
SOL ⊕
SOL ⊖
Yes
No
Trouble Area
• Solenoid valve
• Solenoid valve circuit
A
A
Check 4.
Check that there is no continuity between terminals SOL ⊕ or SOL ⊖ and GND.
SOL ⊕
SOL ⊖
Yes
No
Trouble Area
• Solenoid valve
• Solenoid circuit
Check 5.
Inspect computer.
Bad
Try another computer.
OK
OK
Check 6.
Is there more than 65 kg/cm² (924 psi, 6,374 kPa) PS fluid pressure from PS pump?
More than 65 kg/cm²
Closed
10 seconds
rpm
Yes
No
Trouble Area
• Power steering pump
• Fluid line leakage
• Air in fluid line
Check 7.
Apply battery voltage between terminals SOL ⊕ and SOL ⊖ and turn the solenoid ON and OFF. Is there a change in gear housing fluid pressure when the solenoid is ON or OFF?
10 – 20 kg/cm²
Open
Lock Position
Yes
No
Faulty steering gear housing
Trouble Area
• Solenoid valve
• By-pass or return line clogged
• Fluid level low
91H01550 101429
Courtesy of Toyota Motor Sales, U.S.A., Inc.


***Fig. 4: Flow Chart (Cressida)***

# 1991 STEERING
# Electronic Power Steering (Cont.)

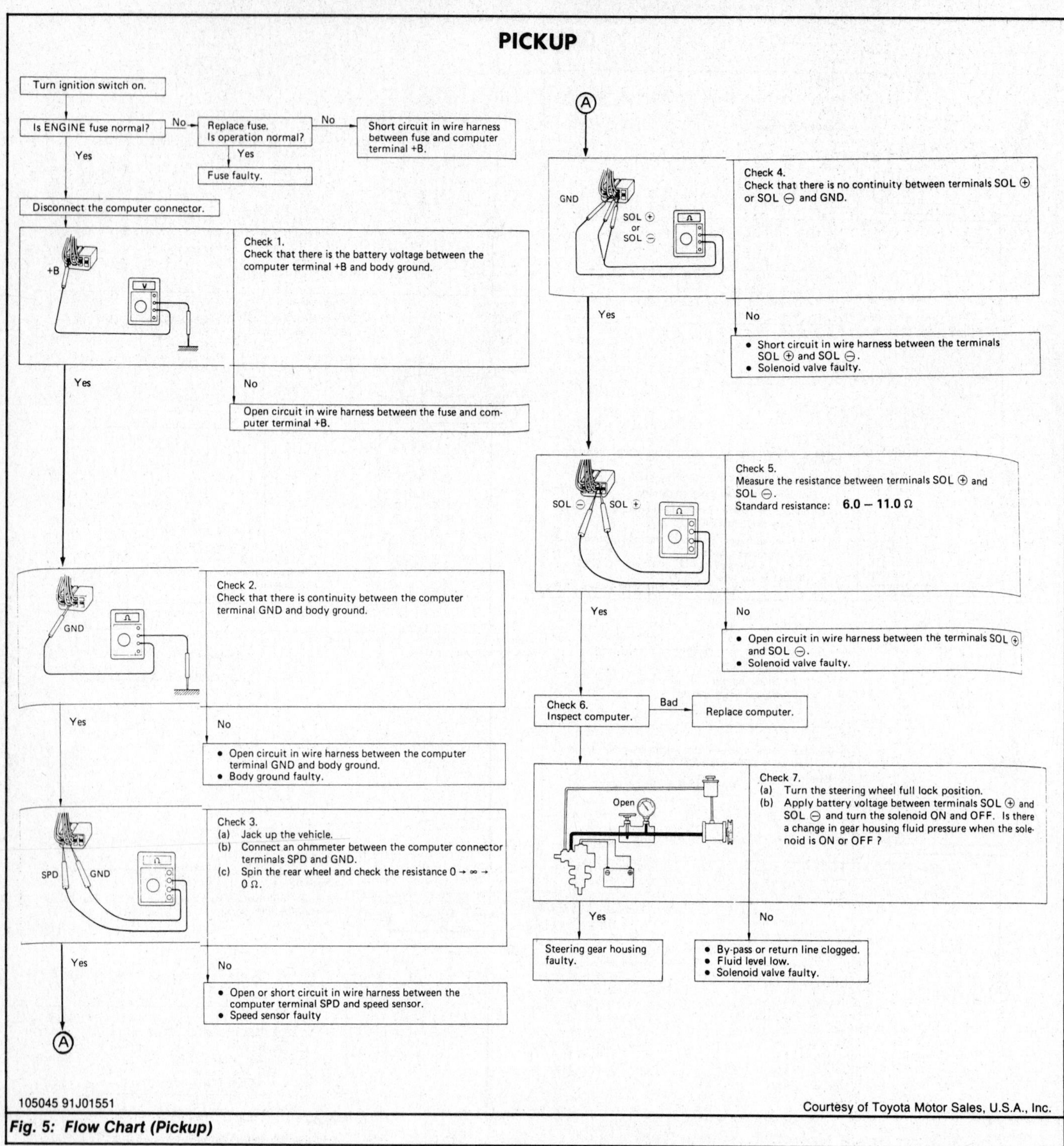

PICKUP
Turn ignition switch on.
Is ENGINE fuse normal?
No
Replace fuse.
Is operation normal?
No
Short circuit in wire harness between fuse and computer terminal +B.
Yes
Fuse faulty.
Yes
Disconnect the computer connector.
+B
Check 1.
Check that there is the battery voltage between the computer terminal +B and body ground.
Yes
No
Open circuit in wire harness between the fuse and computer terminal +B.
GND
Check 2.
Check that there is continuity between the computer terminal GND and body ground.
Yes
No
• Open circuit in wire harness between the computer terminal GND and body ground.
• Body ground faulty.
SPD
GND
Check 3.
(a) Jack up the vehicle.
(b) Connect an ohmmeter between the computer connector terminals SPD and GND.
(c) Spin the rear wheel and check the resistance 0 → ∞ → 0 Ω.
Yes
No
• Open or short circuit in wire harness between the computer terminal SPD and speed sensor.
• Speed sensor faulty
A
A
GND
SOL ⊕
or
SOL ⊖
Check 4.
Check that there is no continuity between terminals SOL ⊕ or SOL ⊖ and GND.
Yes
No
• Short circuit in wire harness between the terminals SOL ⊕ and SOL ⊖.
• Solenoid valve faulty.
SOL ⊖
SOL ⊕
Check 5.
Measure the resistance between terminals SOL ⊕ and SOL ⊖.
Standard resistance: 6.0 – 11.0 Ω
Yes
No
• Open circuit in wire harness between the terminals SOL ⊕ and SOL ⊖.
• Solenoid valve faulty.
Check 6.
Inspect computer.
Bad
Replace computer.
Open
Check 7.
(a) Turn the steering wheel full lock position.
(b) Apply battery voltage between terminals SOL ⊕ and SOL ⊖ and turn the solenoid ON and OFF. Is there a change in gear housing fluid pressure when the solenoid is ON or OFF ?
Yes
No
Steering gear housing faulty.
• By-pass or return line clogged.
• Fluid level low.
• Solenoid valve faulty.
105045 91J01551
Courtesy of Toyota Motor Sales, U.S.A., Inc.


*Fig. 5: Flow Chart (Pickup)*

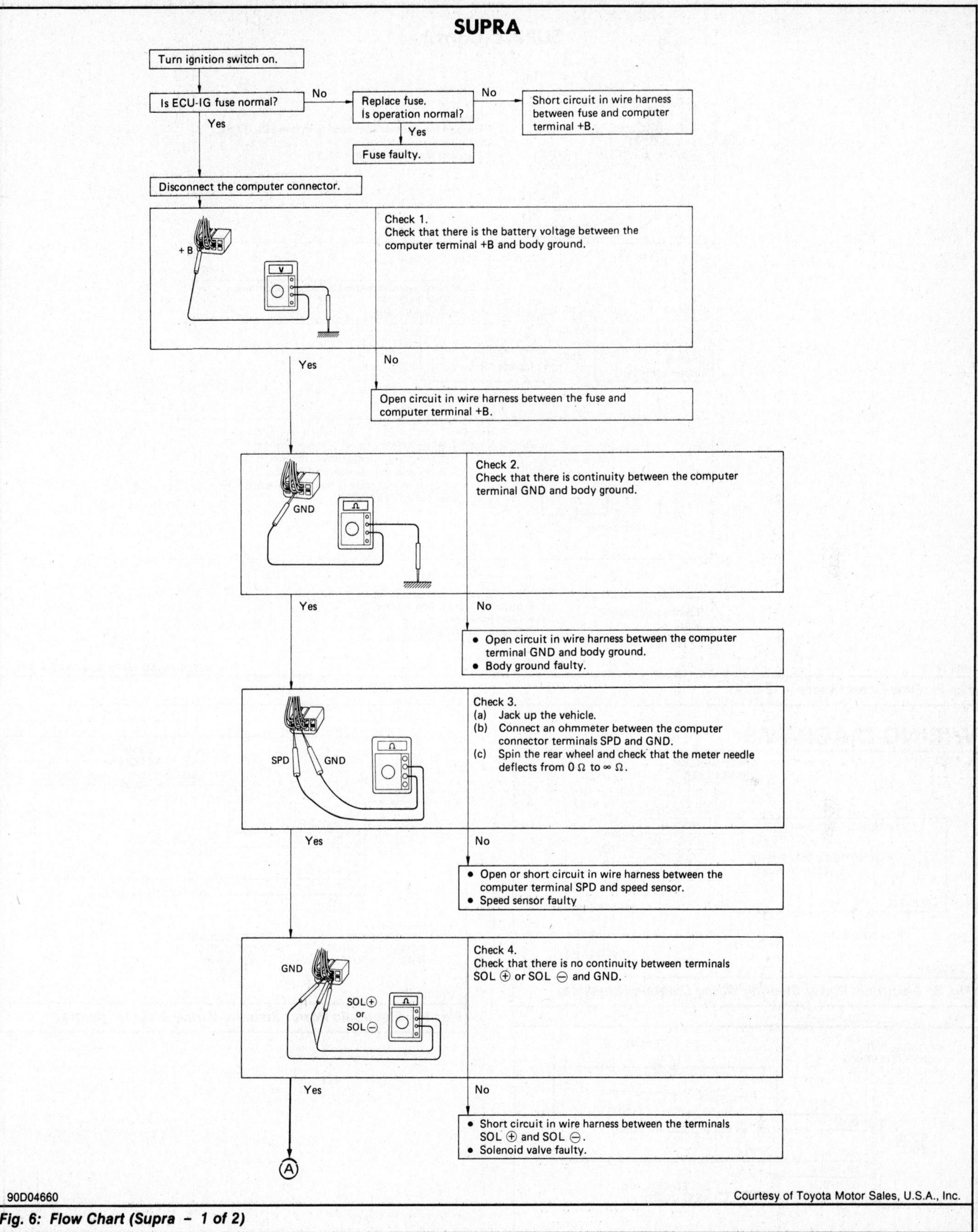
SUPRA
Turn ignition switch on.
Is ECU-IG fuse normal?
No
Replace fuse.
Is operation normal?
No
Short circuit in wire harness between fuse and computer terminal +B.
Yes
Fuse faulty.
Yes
Disconnect the computer connector.
+B
V
Check 1.
Check that there is the battery voltage between the computer terminal +B and body ground.
Yes
No
Open circuit in wire harness between the fuse and computer terminal +B.
GND
Ω
Check 2.
Check that there is continuity between the computer terminal GND and body ground.
Yes
No
• Open circuit in wire harness between the computer terminal GND and body ground.
• Body ground faulty.
SPD
GND
Ω
Check 3.
(a) Jack up the vehicle.
(b) Connect an ohmmeter between the computer connector terminals SPD and GND.
(c) Spin the rear wheel and check that the meter needle deflects from 0 Ω to ∞ Ω.
Yes
No
• Open or short circuit in wire harness between the computer terminal SPD and speed sensor.
• Speed sensor faulty
GND
SOL⊕
or
SOL⊖
Ω
Check 4.
Check that there is no continuity between terminals SOL ⊕ or SOL ⊖ and GND.
Yes
No
• Short circuit in wire harness between the terminals SOL ⊕ and SOL ⊖.
• Solenoid valve faulty.
A
90D04660
Courtesy of Toyota Motor Sales, U.S.A., Inc.

***Fig. 6: Flow Chart (Supra – 1 of 2)***

# 1991 STEERING
# Electronic Power Steering (Cont.)

## SUPRA (Cont.)

(A) Yes

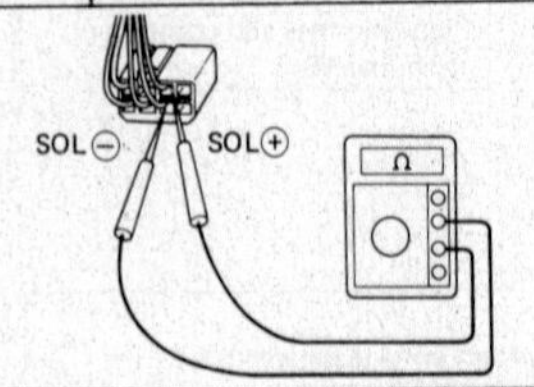

Check 5.
Measure the resistance between terminals SOL ⊕ and SOL ⊖.
Standard resistance: **6.0 – 11.0 Ω**

SOL⊖ SOL⊕ Ω

Yes / No

No:
- Open circuit in wire harness between the terminals SOL ⊕ and SOL ⊖.
- Solenoid valve faulty.

Yes:

Check 6.
Inspect computer.

Bad → Replace computer.

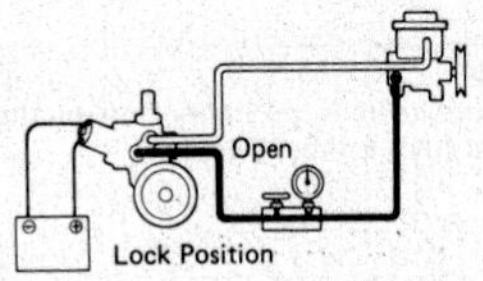

Check 7.
(a) Turn the steering wheel full lock position.
(b) Apply battery voltage between terminals SOL ⊕ and SOL ⊖ and turn the solenoid ON and OFF. Is there a change in gear housing fluid pressure when the solenoid is ON or OFF?

Open
Lock Position

Yes: Steering gear housing faulty.

No:
- By-pass or return line clogged.
- Fluid level low.
- Solenoid valve faulty.

90F04661

Courtesy of Toyota Motor Sales, U.S.A., Inc.

*Fig. 7: Flow Chart (Supra – 2 of 2)*

## WIRING DIAGRAMS

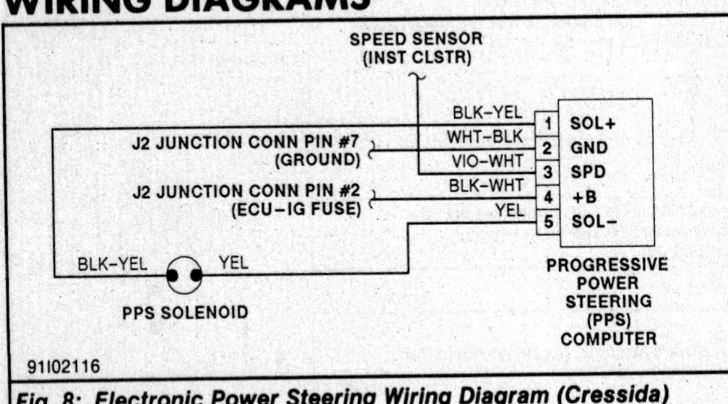

*Fig. 8: Electronic Power Steering Wiring Diagram (Cressida)*

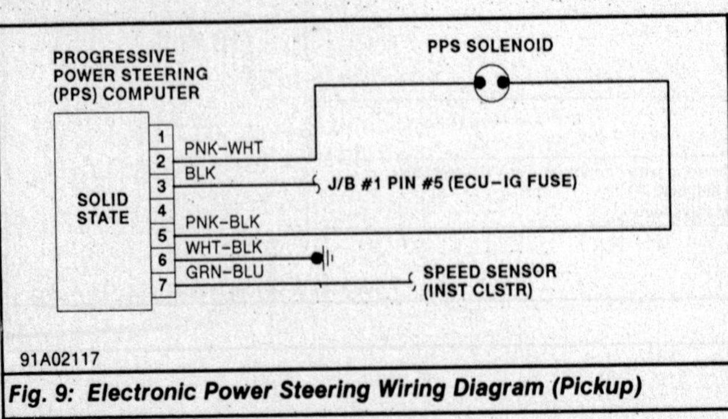

*Fig. 9: Electronic Power Steering Wiring Diagram (Pickup)*

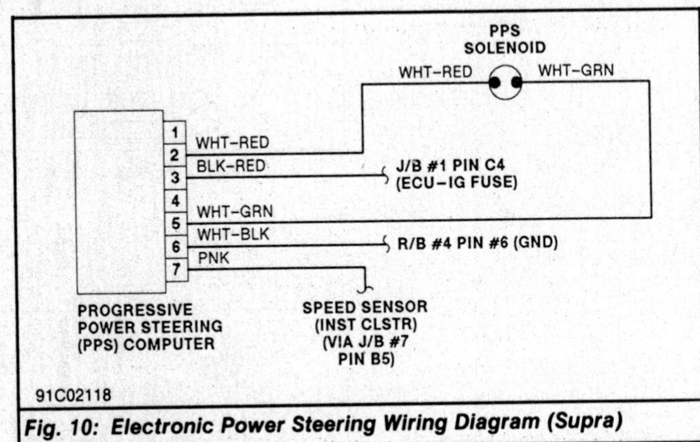

*Fig. 10: Electronic Power Steering Wiring Diagram (Supra)*

# 1991 TRANSMISSION SERVICING
# Automatic Transmission

## Camry, Celica, Corolla, Cressida, Land Cruiser, MR2, Pickup, Previa, Supra, Tercel, 4Runner

## LUBRICATION

### SERVICE INTERVALS

Inspect fluid level every 15,000 miles. Under severe operating conditions, change ATF and filter every 15,000 miles or 24 months.

### CHECKING FLUID LEVEL

**Transmission** - Check fluid with vehicle on level surface and at normal operating temperature. With engine idling, shift each gear from "P" through "L" and back to "P". Fluid level should be in "HOT" range marked on dipstick. DO NOT overfill.

***NOTE: If vehicle has been operated in heavy traffic, pulling a trailer or at high speeds in hot weather, wait 30 minutes before checking fluid level.***

**Differential** - Remove filler plug. Fluid should be level with bottom edge of filler plug hole. If fluid is level with opening, install fill plug. If fluid is low, fill until fluid is level with fill plug opening.

### RECOMMENDED FLUID

All transmissions use Dexron-II automatic transmission fluid. See TRANSMISSION REFILL CAPACITIES table.

### FLUID CAPACITY

***TRANSMISSION REFILL CAPACITIES***

| Application [1] | Refill Qts. (L) | Dry-Fill Qts. (L) |
|---|---|---|
| Camry | 1.7 (1.6) | 7.6 (7.2) |
| 2WD | 2.6 (2.5) | 8.1 (7.7) |
| All-Trac [2] | 3.5 (3.3) | 8.5 (8.0) |
| Celica | | |
| 1.6L | 3.5 (3.3) | 8.1 (7.7) |
| 2.2L | 3.5 (3.3) | 8.5 (8.0) |
| Cressida | 1.7 (1.6) | 7.6 (7.2) |
| Land Cruiser | 6.3 (6.0) | [3] 15.9 (15.0) |
| MR2 | 8.5 (8.0) | 3.5 (3.3) |
| Pickup & 4Runner | 1.7 (1.6) | 8.0 (7.6) |
| Previa | 2.5 (2.4) | 6.0 (5.7) |
| Tercel | 2.6 (2.5) | 5.7 (5.5) |
| Supra | 1.7 (1.6) | 7.6 (7.2) |

1 - All except All-Trac use Dexron-II ATF.
2 - Uses Toyota A/T Fluid.
3 - For vehicles with oil cooler, total capacity is 16.3 qts. (15.4 L).

***DIFFERENTIAL REFILL CAPACITIES***

| Application | Qts. (L) |
|---|---|
| Camry | |
| 2WD [1] | |
| 3S-FE | 1.7 (1.6) |
| 2VZ-FE | 1.1 (1.0) |
| All-Trac [2] | |
| Front | .74 (.70) |
| Rear | 1.2 (1.1) |
| Celica [2] | 1.2 (1.1) |
| Corolla [2] | 1.2 (1.1) |
| Cressida [2] | 1.4 (1.3) |
| Land Cruiser [2] | |
| Front | 3.2 (3.0) |
| Rear | 2.6 (2.5) |
| Pickup & 4Runner [2] | |
| Front | 1.7 (1.6) |
| Rear | 2.3 (2.2) |
| Previa [2] | |
| Front | 1.1 (1.05) |
| Rear | 1.6 (1.5) |
| Supra [2] | 1.4 (1.3) |

1 - Use Dexron-II ATF.
2 - Use SAE 90 with GL5 rating.

***TRANSFER CASE REFILL CAPACITIES***

| Application | Qts. (L) |
|---|---|
| Camry All-Trac [1] | .74 (.70) |
| Land Cruiser [1] | 2.2 (2.1) |
| Pickup & 4Runner [2] | .85 (.80) |
| Previa [1] | 1.4 (1.3) |

1 - Use SAE 90 with GL5 rating.
2 - Use Dexron-II ATF.

## DRAINING & REFILLING

**Transmission - 1)** Remove engine under cover if necessary. Remove drain plug and drain fluid. If replacing transmission filter, remove oil pan. Thoroughly clean transmission oil pan. Install filter and pan with new gasket.

***CAUTION: When removing transmission filter, note different size bolt lengths for reassembly reference.***

**2)** Replace pan drain plug and fill transmission with approximate amount of ATF fluid. See TRANSMISSION REFILL CAPACITIES table.
**3)** Start engine and shift through all gears. Shift into "P" and check fluid level. Add fluid as necessary. DO NOT overfill.
**Differential** - Some FWD models have separate drain plugs for transmission and differential. Both transmission and differential plugs must be removed to drain all fluid from both units. Transaxle is filled through dipstick tube, and differential is filled through a separate fill plug. *See Fig. 1.* Fill differential until fluid is level with fill hole.

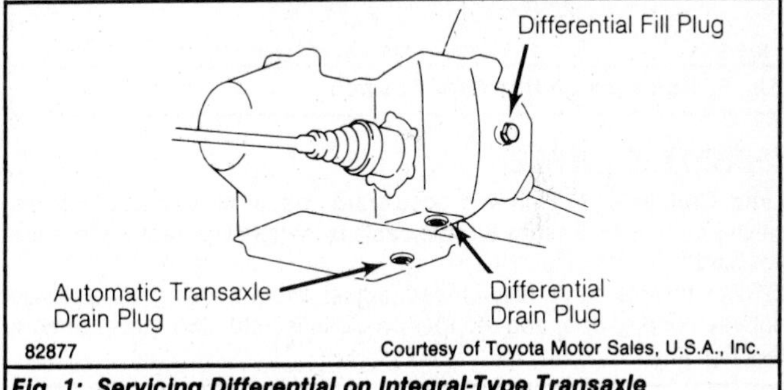


***Fig. 1: Servicing Differential on Integral-Type Transaxle***

## ADJUSTMENTS

### SHIFT CABLE

**Camry, Celica, Corolla, MR2 & Tercel - 1)** Loosen swivel nut on manual shift lever. Push manual shift lever fully toward right side of vehicle.
**2)** Return lever 2 notches to Neutral position. Ensure shift lever is in "N". While holding lever lightly toward "R" range side, tighten swivel nut to 61 INCH lbs. (6 N.m). *See Fig. 2.*

### SHIFT LINKAGE

**Pickup, Previa & 4Runner - 1)** Remove swivel nut from shift linkage. Push manual shift lever fully downward. Return lever 3 notches to Neutral position. Ensure shift lever is in "N" position. While holding lever lightly toward "R" range side, install swivel nut and tighten to 61 INCH lbs. (6 N.m).

# 1991 TRANSMISSION SERVICING
## Automatic Transmission (Cont.)

2) Start engine and ensure vehicle moves forward and reverse when shifting shift lever from "N" to "D", then to "R" positions.

**Cressida, Land Cruiser & Supra – 1)** Loosen swivel nut on shift linkage. Push manual shift lever fully toward rear of vehicle. *See Fig. 3.* Return lever 2 notches to Neutral position. Ensure shift lever is in "N" position. While holding lever lightly toward "R" range side, tighten swivel nut to 61 INCH lbs. (6 N.m).
2) Start engine and ensure vehicle moves forward and reverse when shifting shift lever from "N" to "D", then to "R" positions.

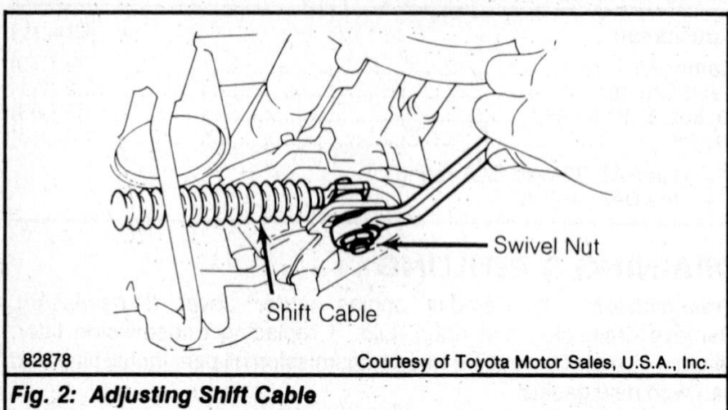


*Fig. 2: Adjusting Shift Cable*

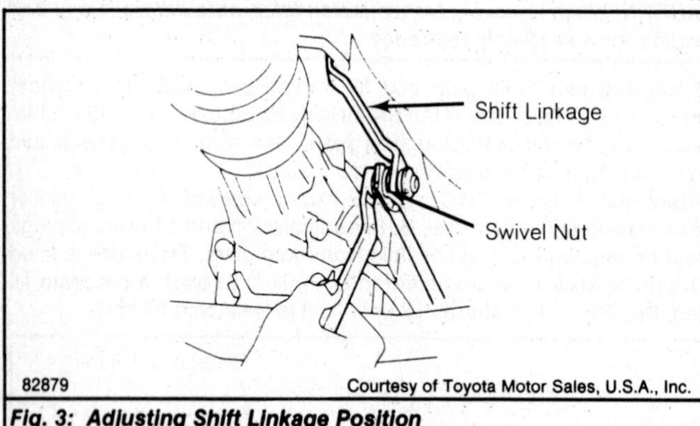


*Fig. 3: Adjusting Shift Linkage Position*

## THROTTLE CABLE

**Land Cruiser – 1)** Depress accelerator pedal and ensure throttle valve opens fully. Ensure throttle cable is installed correctly and does not bind.
2) With throttle valve fully closed, adjust cable housing so distance between end of boot and stopper on cable is .020-.059" (0.5-1.5 mm). *See Fig. 4.*

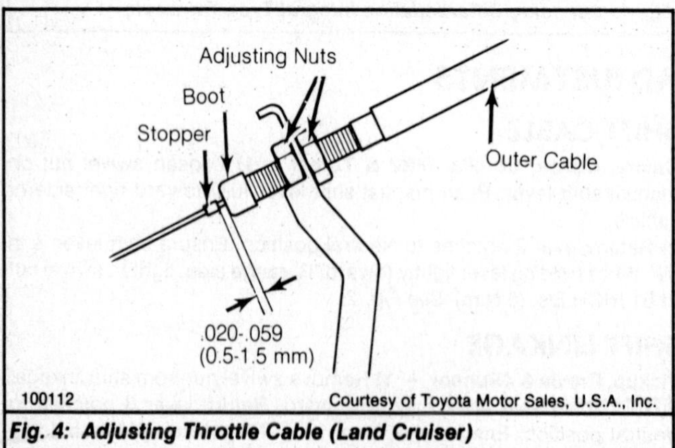


*Fig. 4: Adjusting Throttle Cable (Land Cruiser)*

**All Models Except Land Cruiser – 1)** Remove air cleaner. Check throttle cable bracket and linkage for looseness or bending. Depress accelerator to wide open throttle position.
2) Adjust cable housing so distance between rubber boot end and inner cable stopper or paint mark is .04" (1.0 mm). *See Fig. 5.* Tighten lock nut.
3) For new throttle cables, stopper or paint mark will not be in place. With new cable securely installed in transmission, pull inner cable slightly until resistance is felt. *See Fig. 6.* Stake new stopper or paint a mark as shown.

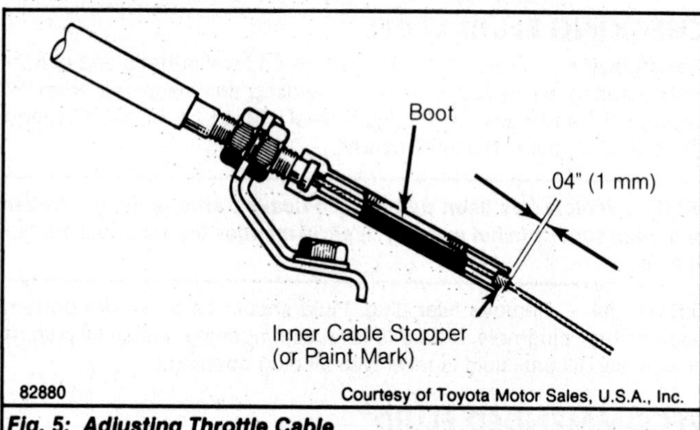


*Fig. 5: Adjusting Throttle Cable*



*Fig. 6: Marking New Throttle Cable*

## NEUTRAL SAFETY SWITCH

Loosen neutral safety switch bolts. Position shift lever in "N". Align switch shaft groove to neutral basic line. *See Fig. 7.* Tighten adjusting bolt.

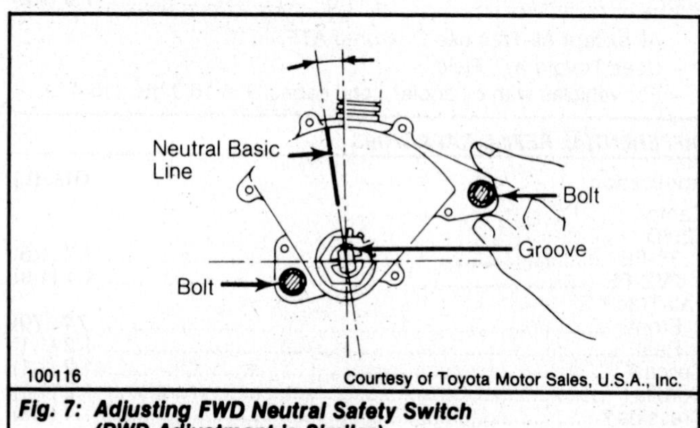


*Fig. 7: Adjusting FWD Neutral Safety Switch (RWD Adjustment Is Similar)*

# 1991 TRANSMISSION SERVICING
# Manual Transmission

## Camry, Celica, Corolla, MR2 Pickup, Previa, Supra, Tercel, 4Runner

## IDENTIFICATION

***MANUAL TRANSMISSION/TRANSAXLE APPLICATIONS***

| Model | Transmission/Transaxle |
|---|---|
| Camry | |
| FWD | 5-Speed - Model S51 & E52 |
| All-Trac | 5-Speed - Model E56F5 |
| Celica | |
| FWD | 5-Speed - Model S53 & C52 |
| All-Trac | 5-Speed - Model E150F |
| Corolla | |
| FWD | 5-Speed - Model C50 & C52 |
| All-Trac | 5-Speed - Model E55F5 & E57F5 |
| MR2 | |
| Non-Turbo | 5-Speed - Model S54 |
| Turbo | 5-Speed - Model E153 |
| Pickup & 4Runner | |
| 2WD | 4-Speed - Model W46 & G40 |
| 2WD | 5-Speed - Model W55, G57 & R150 |
| 4WD | 5-Speed - Model W56 & R150F (V6) |
| Previa | |
| 2WD | 5-Speed - Model G59 |
| 4WD | 5-Speed - Model G57 |
| Supra | 5-Speed - Model R154 & W58 |
| Tercel | 4-Speed - Model C140 & C141 |
| | 5-Speed - Model C150 |

## LUBRICATION

### SERVICE INTERVALS

Check lubricant level every 15,000 miles or 24 months. Replace fluid at 15,000 mile intervals if vehicle is operated in severe service conditions. Severe service conditions include trailer towing, repeated short trips in cold weather and operation on dusty or salt spread roads.

### CHECKING FLUID LEVEL

**Transmission/Transaxle** - Remove left engine undercover (if necessary). Check fluid level at fill plug hole. Lubricant should be level with bottom of fill hole.

**Transfer Case** - Drain and fill plugs on 4WD transfer cases are separate from main transmission/transaxle case. Lubricant should be level with bottom of fill hole.

### RECOMMENDED FLUID

All transmission/transaxles except S54 and E153 (used on MR2), use API GL-4 or GL-5, SAE 75W-90 or 80W-90 gear oil. The S54 transmission uses Dexron-II ATF. The E153 uses E50 transaxle oil.

### FLUID CAPACITY

***TRANSMISSION/TRANSAXLE REFILL CAPACITIES***

| Application | Qts. (L) |
|---|---|
| Camry (SAE 75W-90) | |
| 2WD | 2.7 (2.6) |
| All-Trac | 5.3 (5.0) |
| Celica (SAE 75W-90) | |
| 2WD | 2.7 (2.6) |
| All-Trac | 5.5 (5.2) |
| Corolla (SAE 75W-90) | |
| FWD | 2.7 (2.6) |
| All-Trac | 5.3 (5.0) |
| MR2 | |
| Non-Turbo (Dexron II) | 2.7 (2.6) |
| Turbo (E50) | 4.4 (4.2) |
| Pickup & 4Runner (SAE 75W-90 or 80W-90) | |
| 4-Cylinder | |
| 2WD | 2.5 (2.4) |
| 4WD | [1] 3.2 (3.0) |
| V6 | |
| 2WD & 4WD | 3.2 (3.0) |
| Previa | |
| 2WD | 2.7 (2.6) |
| 4WD | 2.3 (2.2) |
| Supra (SAE 75W-90 or 80W-90) | |
| Non-Turbo | 2.5 (2.4) |
| Turbo | 3.2 (3.0) |
| Tercel (SAE 75W-90 or 80W-90) | 2.5 (2.4) |

[1] - Use 4.1 qts. (3.9L) for 5-speed with 4WD.

***TRANSFER CASE REFILL CAPACITIES***

| Application | Qts. (L) |
|---|---|
| Land Cruiser | 2.2 (2.1) |
| Pickup & 4Runner (Dexron-II) | .85 (.80) |
| Previa | 1.4 (1.3) |

## ADJUSTMENTS

***NOTE: Adjustments during routine servicing and maintenance are not required.***

# 1991 TRANSMISSION SERVICING
# Transmission Removal & Installation

## Camry, Celica, Corolla, Cressida, Land Cruiser, MR2, Pickup, Previa, Supra, Tercel, 4Runner

## MANUAL

***NOTE: For manual transmission/transaxle replacement procedures, see appropriate CLUTCHES article.***

## AUTOMATIC

**Removal (Camry & Celica) - 1)** Disconnect negative battery cable. Remove airflow meter and air cleaner. Disconnect neutral safety switch connector and all external electrical connectors. Remove ground strap.

**2)** Disconnect transaxle throttle valve cable at throttle linkage and remove cable from bracket. Remove transaxle case protector and disconnect speedometer cable. Disconnect shift control cable at lever and remove from bracket.

**3)** Disconnect oil cooler hoses and remove starter motor bolts. Remove 2 upper transaxle-to-engine bolts. Remove insulator bracket set bolt for rear engine mount. Raise and support vehicle. Drain transaxle oil. Disconnect and plug oil cooler hoses.

**4)** Remove left front fender apron. Disconnect both axle shafts from transaxle. Remove lower suspension crossmember. Using pliers, remove snap ring on center axle shaft bearing bracket. Remove bearing bracket bolt and pull center axle shaft assembly out.

**5)** Disconnect control cable clamp and remove crossmember bolts supporting center mounts of engine. Remove crossmember. Remove stabilizer bar and left steering knuckle from lower control arm.

**6)** Pull steering knuckle outward and remove left axle shaft. Remove bellhousing cover and remove 6 bolts attaching torque converter to drive plate. On Camry, remove engine-to-transmission stiffener plate.

**7)** On all models, support engine with jack stand and secure transaxle jack under transaxle. Lower rear end of transaxle and remove remaining transaxle-to-engine bolts. Separate transaxle from engine and lower transaxle assembly.

**Installation - 1)** Apply multipurpose grease to center hub of torque converter. Install one guide pin in threaded mounting pad of torque converter to align torque converter. Distance from torque converter drive lug to engine mating surface of transaxle should be at least .51" (13 mm). *See Fig. 1*.

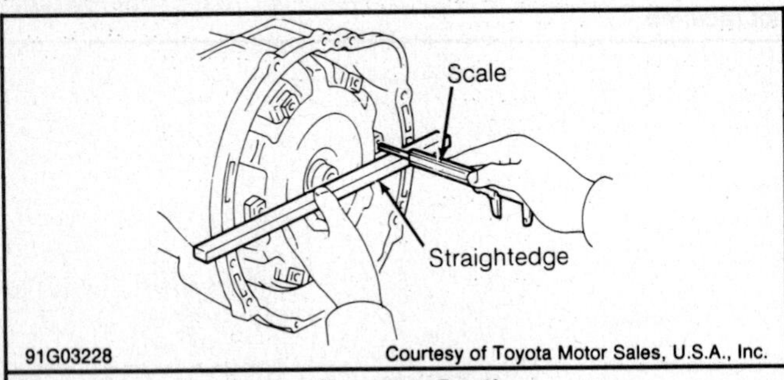


91G03228 Courtesy of Toyota Motor Sales, U.S.A., Inc.

***Fig. 1: Measuring Torque Converter Depth***

**2)** Reverse removal procedure to complete installation of transaxle. Torque converter bolts are color coded. Install Gray bolt first, then the remaining 5 bolts. Tighten torque converter bolts.

**3)** Fill transaxle to proper capacity. Check and adjust throttle cable and control cable.

**Removal (Corolla) - 1)** Disconnect negative battery cable and remove air cleaner. Disconnect neutral safety switch connector, solenoid valve connector, speed sensor connector and speedometer cable.

**2)** Disconnect transaxle throttle valve cable from throttle linkage and remove cable and bracket. Disconnect and plug oil cooler hoses. Raise and support vehicle.

**3)** Drain transaxle and remove engine undercover. Remove 2 dust covers from center crossmember and remove crossmember. On models with 4A-GE engines, remove front exhaust from manifold.

**4)** Remove left and right side axle shafts and remove starter motor. Remove bellhousing stiffener plate. Manually turn crankshaft and remove 6 torque converter bolts.

**5)** Support engine with jack stand and secure transaxle jack under transaxle. Remove engine rear mounting bolts and slightly lower transaxle assembly. Remove transaxle mounting bolts to separate transaxle from engine. Lower transaxle from vehicle.

**Installation - 1)** Apply multipurpose grease to center hub of torque converter. Install one guide pin in threaded mounting pad of torque converter to align torque converter.

**2)** Torque converter is correctly installed if torque converter drive lugs are at least .91" (23 mm) below engine mating surface. *See Fig. 1*. Reverse removal procedure to complete installation of transaxle. Torque converter bolts are color coded.

**3)** Install the White bolt and then the 5 remaining Yellow bolts. Tighten torque converter bolts. Fill transaxle to proper capacity. Check and adjust throttle cable.

**Removal (Cressida & Supra) - 1)** Disconnect negative battery cable. Disconnect transmission throttle cable from throttle linkage and remove cable housing from bracket. Disconnect cable from engine rear end. Raise and support vehicle. Drain transmission oil.

**2)** Disconnect all electrical connectors that lead to transmission (located near starter). Index mark propeller shaft flanges before removal. Disconnect shaft at differential flange and remove both sections as one assembly with center bearing support.

**3)** All models, disconnect catalytic converter from tail pipe and remove rubber hangers. Remove pipe clamp from transmission housing and remove front exhaust pipe from exhaust manifold.

**4)** Remove oil cooler pipe clamp from transmission housing, and disconnect oil cooler lines at transmission fittings. Remove oil filler tube and disconnect manual shift linkage at rear connection. Disconnect speedometer cable and remove stiffener plate(s).

**5)** Remove bellhousing cover and manually rotate crankshaft to remove 6 torque converter bolts. Secure transmission jack under transmission and raise enough to remove weight from transmission mount.

**6)** Disconnect ground strap and remove crossmember and transmission mount from vehicle. Place rag between steering gear housing and engine oil pan to prevent damage. Remove starter motor and all transmission-to-engine bolts.

**7)** Separate transmission along with torque converter from engine. Ensure that all cables and electrical harnesses are free from snagging when lowering transmission from vehicle.

**Installation - 1)** Apply multipurpose grease to center hub of torque converter. Install one guide pin in threaded mounting pad of torque converter to align torque converter.

**2)** Torque converter is correctly installed if torque converter drive lugs are at least 1.04" (26.5 mm) below engine mating surface. *See Fig. 1*. Reverse removal procedure to complete installation of transmission.

**3)** Tighten torque converter bolts. Fill transaxle to proper capacity. Check and adjust throttle cable.

**Removal (Land Cruiser) - 1)** Disconnect negative battery cable. Drain coolant at radiator drain cock and disconnect upper radiator hose. Disconnect transmission throttle cable from throttle linkage and remove cable from bracket.

**2)** Disconnect electrical connectors located near starter. Remove transfer case shift lever knob and 4 bolts to remove shift lever boot. Raise and support vehicle. Drain transmission oil and transfer case oil.

**3)** Remove transmission and transfer case undercovers. Remove clip and pin to disconnect shift rod from transfer case. Remove nut and washers to remove transfer case shift lever with control rod. Disconnect control rod from control shaft lever by removing nut on lever.

**4)** On models with mechanical winch, remove shifter knob button and spring. Using an Allen wrench, remove two set screws and shift lever knob. Remove shift lever boot. Remove nut and disconnect shift rod from Power Take-Off (PTO).

**5)** Remove bolt and remove shift lever with shift rod. Index mark propeller shaft flanges and remove both front and rear shafts. Mark and remove PTO drive shaft (if applicable). Disconnect speedometer cable and 2 vacuum hoses from transfer case. Disconnect oil cooler tubes.

# 1991 TRANSMISSION SERVICING
# Transmission Removal & Installation (Cont.)

**6)** Remove starter and transmission oil filler tube. Pry hole cover from bellhousing cover plate. Manually turn crankshaft and remove 6 torque converter bolts. Secure a transmission jack under transmission/transfer case assembly.
**7)** Remove 8 bolts and 2 nuts and remove frame crossmember. Remove flange bolts and exhaust pipe clamp to remove front pipe from tail pipe. Remove front pipe from exhaust manifold.
**8)** Support engine with a jack and wooden block. Lower rear of transmission/transfer case assembly. Remove 9 transmission mounting bolts. Ensure that throttle cable and all electrical harnesses are clear from snagging. Carefully draw assembly down and toward the rear when lowering.
**Installation - 1)** Apply multipurpose grease to center hub of torque converter. Install one guide pin in threaded mounting pad of torque converter to align torque converter.
**2)** Torque converter is correctly installed if torque converter drive lugs are at least .65" (16.5 mm) below engine mating surface. *See Fig. 1*. Reverse removal procedure to complete installation of transmission/transfer case assembly.
**3)** Tighten torque converter bolts. Fill transmission, transfer case and PTO to proper fluid capacities. Check and adjust shift control linkage for transmission and transfer case. Check and adjust PTO linkage and transfer shift control lever. Adjust throttle cable.
**Removal (MR2 & Tercel) - 1)** Disconnect negative battery cable. On MR2, remove air cleaner assembly. On all models, disconnect neutral safety switch and all other electrical connectors. Disconnect speedometer cable. Disconnect transaxle throttle cable from throttle linkage and remove cable from bracket.
**2)** Remove wiring for starter and remove starter motor. Remove upper transaxle-to-engine bolts. Raise and support vehicle. Drain transaxle oil and drain oil from differential cavity.
**3)** Disconnect oil cooler hoses from pipes and remove engine undercovers. Disconnect shift control cable at shift lever and remove cable from bracket. Remove both axle shafts.
**4)** Manually turn engine crankshaft and remove 6 torque converter bolts from access hole in bellhousing cover. Remove ground cable from left side engine mounting bracket.
**5)** Remove left side engine mount. Support engine with one jack and secure a transaxle jack under transaxle assembly. Remove 4 bolts and disconnect rear mounting bracket from body.
**6)** Remove 3 bolts and remove engine rear mounting bracket. Remove remaining transaxle-to-engine bolts. Ensure that all electrical harnesses and cables do not snag when lowering transaxle assembly with jack.
**Installation - 1)** Apply multipurpose grease to center hub of torque converter. Install one guide pin in threaded mounting pad of torque converter to aid in aligning torque converter.
**2)** Torque converter is correctly installed if torque converter drive lugs are at least .53" (13.4 mm) on Tercel and .51" (13 mm) on MR2, from edge of housing surface. *See Fig. 1*. Reverse removal procedure to complete installation of transaxle.
**3)** Tighten torque converter bolts. Fill transaxle to proper capacity. Check and adjust throttle cable.
**Removal (Pickup & 4Runner) - 1)** Disconnect and remove negative battery cable. Remove air cleaner assembly and ducting (if necessary). Disconnect transmission throttle valve cable from linkage and remove from bracket.
**2)** Remove upper starter mounting nut. On 4WD Pickup and 4Runner, disconnect 5 electrical connectors. On all models, raise and support vehicle. Drain transmission and disconnect all external electrical connectors.
**3)** Remove starter motor and support alongside of engine. Index mark and remove propeller shaft(s). Disconnect speedometer cable and manual shift linkage. Disconnect and plug transmission oil cooler lines.
**4)** On 2WD models, remove exhaust pipe support clamp, exhaust bracket and filler tube. On 4WD Pickup and 4Runner, remove clips and disconnect No. 1 and No. 2 shift linkage from cross shaft. Remove cross shaft from body. Disconnect exhaust pipe from tail pipe and remove clamp from transmission case.
**5)** Remove clamp holding oil cooler lines to transfer chain case and disconnect transfer case oil cooler lines. On all models, secure transmission jack under transmission oil pan. Raise transmission enough to remove weight from rear engine mount.
**6)** Remove rear engine mount along with bracket. Remove engine undercover to gain access to crankshaft pulley. On 4WD Pickup and 4Runner, remove crossmember and install a wood block between firewall and rear of cylinder head.
**7)** On 2WD models, insert a piece of wood between engine oil pan and top of front crossmember. All models, pry hole covers off of bellhousing cover plate. Turn crankshaft to gain access to torque converter bolts and remove 6 bolts.
**8)** Install a guide pin in one torque converter bolt hole. Remove bolts attaching support braces to front of bellhousing and engine block, and remove support braces. Remove all bellhousing-to-engine mounting bolts.
**9)** Pry on end of guide pin to begin moving torque converter and transmission from engine. Ensure that all cables and electrical harnesses are free from snagging when lowering transmission. Remove transmission from vehicle.
**Installation - 1)** Apply multipurpose grease to center hub of torque converter and pilot hole in crankshaft. Install one guide pin in threaded mounting pad of torque converter to aid in aligning torque converter.
**2)** Torque converter is correctly installed if torque converter drive lugs are at least .79" (20 mm) below engine mating surface on 2.4L models, or .71" (18 mm) on 3.0L models. *See Fig. 1*.
**3)** Reverse removal procedure to complete installation of transmission. Tighten torque converter bolts. Fill transmission and transfer case (if applicable) to proper capacity. Check and adjust throttle cable.
**Removal & Installation (Previa) - 1)** Disconnect negative battery cable. Remove ATF oil level gauge. Remove throttle cable clamp and disconnect throttle. Raise vehicle. Remove filler tube. On 4WD, remove front propeller shaft.
**2)** On both models, remove shift control cables. On 2WD, remove starter. On 4WD, remove starter and front propeller shaft bracket. On 2WD, remove stiffener plates. On both models, remove torque converter bolts.
**3)** Remove oil cooler tubes. Remove exhaust pipe bracket. On 2WD, remove propeller shaft. On 4WD, remove rear propeller shaft. Jack up transmission. Remove rear engine mount bolts.
**4)** Remove remaining transmission bolts and pull out transmission. To install, reverse removal procedure. Torque converter is properly install when 1.250" (31.75 mm) of space exists between torque converter drive lugs and front surface of bell housing.

## TORQUE SPECIFICATIONS

***TORQUE SPECIFICATIONS***

| Application | Ft. Lbs. (N.m) |
|---|---|
| **Camry, Cressida & Supra** | |
| Center Support Bearing | 27 (37) |
| Cooler Line | 25 (34) |
| Drain Plug | 36 (49) |
| Intermediate Shaft-To-Propeller Shaft | 54 (74) |
| Propeller Shaft-To-Differential | 54 (74) |
| Torque Converter-To Drive Plate | 20 (27) |
| Transaxle-To-Engine 10-mm Bolt | 34 (46) |
| Transaxle-To-Engine 12-mm Bolt | 47 (64) |
| **Celica & Tercel** | |
| Drain Plug | 25 (34) |
| Exhaust Pipe Nut | 46 (62) |
| Left Engine Mount Bracket Bolt | 32 (43) |
| Lower Control Arm-To-Knuckle Bolt | 59 (80) |
| Right Engine Mount Bracket Bolt | 47 (64) |
| Starter Bolt | 29 (39) |
| Tie Rod-To-Knuckle Nut | 36 (49) |
| Torque Converter-To-Drive Plate Bolt | 13 (18) |
| Transaxle-To-Engine Bolt | 47 (64) |

# 1991 TRANSMISSION SERVICING
## Transmission Removal & Installation (Cont.)

***TORQUE SPECIFICATIONS (Cont.)***

| Application | Ft. Lbs. (N.m) |
|---|---|
| **Land Cruiser, Pickup & 4-Runner** | |
| ATF Fluid Sensor | 25 (34) |
| Crossmember Bolt | 45 (61) |
| Crossmember Nut | 43 (59) |
| Drain Plug | 20 (27) |
| Oil Cooler Line | 25 (34) |
| Propeller Shaft-To-Differential | 65 (88) |
| Propeller Shaft-To-Transfer Case | 65 (88) |
| Rear Transmission Mount | 43 (59) |
| Torque Converter-To-Drive Plate | 21 (28) |
| Transmission-To-Engine 14-mm Bolt | 27 (37) |
| Transmission-To-Engine 17-mm Bolt | 53 (72) |
| **MR2** | |
| Drain & Filler Plugs | 36 (49) |
| Engine Mount-To-Bracket Bolt | 58 (78) |
| Exhaust Pipe Nut | 46 (62) |
| Bracket-To-Transmission Bolts | |
| Front Engine Mount | 57 (77) |
| Rear Engine Mount | 38 (52) |
| Lower Control Arm-To-Knuckle Bolt | 59 (80) |
| Starter Bolt | 29 (39) |
| Stiffener Plate Bolt | 27 (37) |
| Stabilizer-To-Strut Nut | 36 (49) |
| Tie Rod-To-Knuckle Bolt | 76 (103) |
| Torque Converter-To-Drive Plate Bolt | 20 (27) |
| Transaxle-To-Engine | 47 (64) |
| **Previa** | |
| Cooler Lines | 25 (34) |
| Exhaust Pipe Bracket Nut | |
| Exhaust Side | 32 (43) |
| Transmission Side | 37 (51) |
| Propeller Shaft Bracket | 41 (56) |
| Starter Bolt | 30 (41) |
| Stiffener Plate Bolt | 27 (37) |
| Torque Converter-To-Drive Plate Bolt | 54 (76) |
| Transmission-To-Engine Bolt | 53 (72) |

# VOLKSWAGEN

# 1991 VOLKSWAGEN CONTENTS

## GENERAL INFORMATION [1]

### ALL MODELS



[1] – For all GENERAL INFORMATION, see front of Volume 1.

## ENGINE PERFORMANCE

### INTRODUCTION



### EMISSION APPLICATIONS



### SERVICE & ADJUSTMENT SPECIFICATIONS



## ENGINE PERFORMANCE (Cont.)

### ON-VEHICLE ADJUSTMENTS — Page



### THEORY & OPERATION – CIS-E MOTRONIC



### THEORY & OPERATION – DIGIFANT



### THEORY & OPERATION – DIESEL

## ENGINE PERFORMANCE (Cont.)

### BASIC DIAGNOSTIC PROCEDURES



### TROUBLE SHOOTING – NO CODES



### SYSTEM & COMPONENT TESTING



### PIN VOLTAGE CHARTS



## ENGINE PERFORMANCE (Cont.)

### SENSOR OPERATING RANGE CHARTS



### WIRING DIAGRAMS



### VACUUM DIAGRAMS



### REMOVAL, OVERHAUL & INSTALLATION

# 1991 VOLKSWAGEN CONTENTS (Cont.)

## ELECTRICAL

### ALTERNATORS & REGULATORS - BOSCH



### ALTERNATORS & REGULATORS - SEV MOTOROLA



### STARTERS - BOSCH



## WIRING DIAGRAMS

### CHASSIS WIRING DIAGRAMS



## SAFETY EQUIPMENT

### AIR BAG RESTRAINT SYSTEM



### INSTRUMENT PANELS



### POWER MIRRORS



### STEERING COLUMN SWITCHES



### WIPER/WASHER SYSTEMS

## ENGINES

### 1.8L & 2.0L 4-CYLINDER



### 2.1L OPPOSED 4-CYLINDER



## CLUTCHES

### FWD



### RWD



## DRIVE AXLES

### FWD AXLE SHAFTS



### RWD AXLE SHAFTS



## BRAKES

### DISC & DRUM



### ANTI-LOCK



## WHEEL ALIGNMENT

### SPECIFICATIONS & PROCEDURES

# 1991 VOLKSWAGEN CONTENTS (Cont.)

## SUSPENSION

### FRONT



### REAR



## STEERING

### STEERING COLUMNS



### MANUAL RACK & PINION



### POWER RACK & PINION



## TRANSMISSION SERVICING

### AUTOMATIC TRANSMISSION



### MANUAL TRANSMISSION



### TRANSMISSION REMOVAL & INSTALLATION

# 1991 ENGINE PERFORMANCE
# Volkswagen Introduction

## 1991 MODEL COVERAGE

| MODEL | BODY CODE | ENGINE | ENGINE ID | FUEL SYSTEM | IGNITION SYSTEM |
|---|---|---|---|---|---|
| Cabriolet | 15 | 1.8L 8-Valve | 2H | AFC-Digifant II [2] | Hall Effect |
| Corrado | 50 | 1.8L 8-Valve [1] | PG | Digifant | Hall Effect |
| Fox | 30 | 1.8L 8-Valve | ABG | AFC-Digifant II [2] | Hall Effect |
| Golf GL | 1G | 1.8L 8-Valve | RV | AFC-Digifant II [2] | Hall Effect |
| GTI | 1G | 1.8L 8-Valve | PF or RV | AFC-Digifant [3] | Hall Effect |
| GTI | 1G | 2.0L 16-Valve | 9A | CIS-E Motronic | Hall Effect |
| Jetta | 1G | 1.6L Diesel | ME or 1V [4] | Mechanical Injection | |
| Jetta | 1G | 1.8L 8-Valve | RV | AFC-Digifant II [2] | Hall Effect |
| Jetta GLI | 1G | 2.0L 16-Valve | 9A | CIS-E Motronic | Hall Effect |
| Passat | 31 | 2.0L 16-Valve | 9A | CIS-E Motronic | Hall Effect |
| Vanagon | 25 | 2.1L | MV | AFC-Digifant I | Hall Effect |

[1] – Supercharged engine.
[2] – California vehicles are equipped with Digifant I.
[3] – Vehicles with 1.8L (PF) engines are equipped with Digifant II. Vehicles with 1.8L (RV) engines are equipped with Digifant I.
[4] – Vehicles with build dates through 12/90 will be equipped with 1.6L (ME) engine. Vehicles with build dates after 1/91 will be equipped with 1.6L Turbo (1V) engine.

## VIN DEFINITION

**WVWCB5152MC000001**

① ② ③ ④ ⑤ ⑥ ⑦ ⑧ ⑨ ⑩ ⑪ ⑫ ⑬ ⑭ ⑮ ⑯ ⑰

①②③ Indicates Nation of Origin.
④ Indicates Series.
⑤ Indicates Engine Type.
⑥ Indicates Restraint System.
**⑦⑧ Indicates Body Code.**
⑨ Indicates Check Digit.
**⑩ Indicates Model Year.**
⑪ Indicates Assembly Plant.
⑫⑬⑭⑮⑯⑰ Indicates Production Sequence.

90J04385

### *MODEL YEAR VIN CODE APPLICATION*

| VIN Code | Model Year |
|---|---|
| J | 1988 |
| K | 1989 |
| L | 1990 |
| M | 1991 |

## ENGINE CODE LOCATION

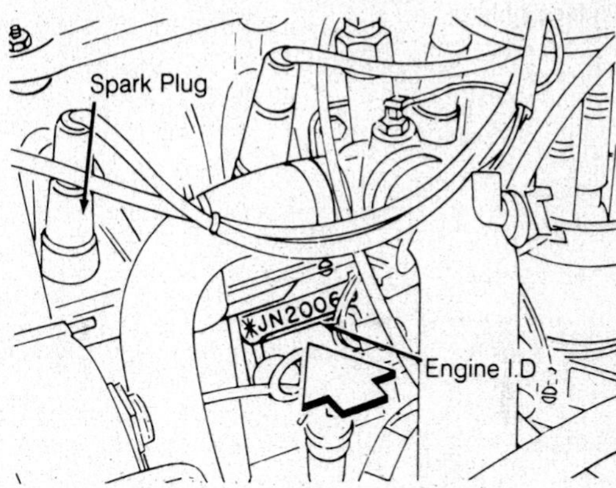


ALL MODELS EXCEPT VANAGON

121484 Courtesy of Volkswagen United States, Inc.

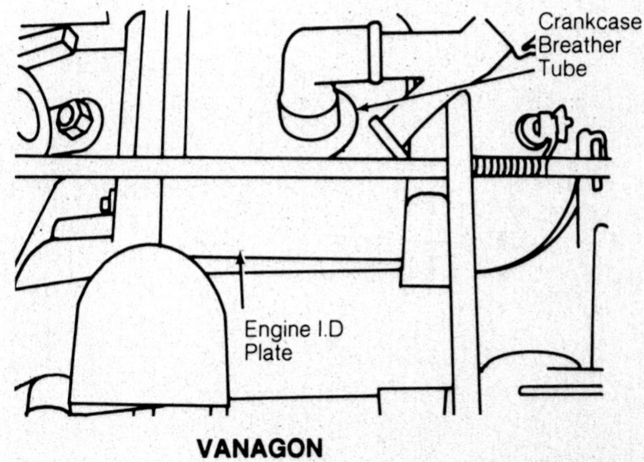


VANAGON

121485 Courtesy of Volkswagen United States, Inc.

# 1991 ENGINE PERFORMANCE
# Emission Applications

### *1991 VOLKSWAGEN EMISSION SYSTEMS*

| Model, Engine & Fuel System | Emission Control Systems & Devices | Remarks |
|---|---|---|
| Gasoline | | [1] – Calif. vehicles only. |
| Cabriolet 1.8L Digifant | **PCV, EVAP, TWC, SPK, $O_2$, CEC, CE** [1], EVAP-PV, EVAP-VC, SPK-CC, HAI [2] | [2] – Digifant II only. |
| Corrado 1.8L Digifant | **PCV, EVAP, TWC, SPK, $O_2$, CEC, CE** [1], EVAP-PV, EVAP-VC, SPK-CC | [3] – $O_2$ light. |
| Fox 1.8L Digifant | **PCV, EVAP, EGR** [1]**, TWC, SPK, $O_2$, CEC, CE** [1], EVAP-PV, EVAP-VC, EGR-VA, EGR-TVV, SPK-CC, HAI [2] | [4] – Not applicable. |
| Golf GL, GTI & Jetta 1.8L Digifant | **PCV, EVAP, TWC, SPK, $O_2$, CEC, CE** [1], EVAP-PV, EVAP-VC, SPK-CC, HAI [2] | |
| GTI & Jetta GLI 2.0L CIS-E | **PCV, EVAP, TWC, EGR** [1]**, SPK, $O_2$, CEC, CE** [1], EVAP-PV, EVAP-VC, EGR-TVV, EGR-VA, EGR-TS | |
| Passat 2.0L CIS-E | **PCV, EVAP, TWC, EGR** [1]**, SPK, $O_2$, CEC, CE** [1], EVAP-PV, EVAP-VC, EGR-VA, EGR-TVV, SPK-CC, EGR-TS | |
| Vanagon 2.1L Digifant | **PCV, EVAP, TWC, $O_2$, CEC, EMR** [1] [3]**, CE** [1], EVAP-VC, EVAP-PV, SPK-CC, PCV-HCB | |
| Diesel | | |
| Jetta 1.6L Mechanical Injection | [4] | |

**NOTE:** Major emission control systems are listed in bold type; components are listed in light type.

**CE** – CHECK ENGINE Light
**CEC** – Computerized Engine Control System
**CIS-E** – Continuous Injection System Electronic
**EGR** – Exhaust Gas Recirculation
**EGR-TS** – EGR Temperature Sensor
**EGR-TVV** – EGR Thermal Vacuum Valve
**EGR-VA** – EGR Vacuum Amplifier
**EMR** – Emission Maintenance Reminder Light
**EVAP** – Fuel Evaporative System
**EVAP-PV** – EVAP Purge Valve
**EVAP-VC** – EVAP Vacuum Canister
**HAI** – Hot Air Intake
**$O_2$** – Oxygen Sensor
**PCV** – Positive Crankcase Ventilation
**PCV-HCB** – PCV Heated Crankcase Breather
**SPK** – Spark Timing Control
**SPK-CC** – SPK Computer Controlled
**TWC** – Three-Way Catalyst

# 1991 ENGINE PERFORMANCE
# Service & Adjustment Specifications

**Cabriolet, Corrado, Fox, Golf GL, GTI, Jetta, Jetta GLI, Passat, Vanagon**

## INTRODUCTION

Use this article to quickly find specifications related to servicing and on-vehicle adjustments. This is a quick-reference article for when you are familiar with an adjustment procedure and only need a specification.

## CAPACITIES

*BATTERY SPECIFICATIONS*

| Application | Amp Hr. Rating |
|---|---|
| Cabriolet, Fox, Jetta, Jetta GLI & Passat | |
| Without A/C | 54 |
| With A/C | 63 |
| Corrado, Golf GL, GTI & Vanagon | 63 |

*FLUID CAPACITIES*

| Application | Quantity |
|---|---|
| Auto. Transaxle (Dexron-II) | [1] 3.2 Qts. (3.0L) |
| Auto. Transaxle Final Drive (SAE 90/API GL-5) | |
| Except Vanagon | [2] .8 Qts. (.76L) |
| Vanagon | 1.4 Qts. (1.3L) |
| Cooling System (Includes Heater) | |
| Cabriolet | 5.1 Qts. (4.8L) |
| Corrado | 6.0 Qts. (5.5L) |
| Fox | 6.9 Qts. (6.5L) |
| Golf GL, GTI, Jetta & Jetta GLI | 7.0 Qts. (6.6L) |
| Passat | 5.9 Qts. (5.6L) |
| Vanagon | 18.4 Qts. (17.5L) |
| Crankcase (Includes Filter) | |
| Fox | 3.7 Qts. (3.5L) |
| Vanagon | 4.8 Qts. (4.5L) |
| All Other Models | 4.3 Qts. (4.1L) |
| Man. Transaxle (SAE 80W-90/API GL-4) | |
| Fox | 1.8 Qts. (1.7L) |
| Vanagon | 3.2 Qts. (3.0L) |
| All Other Models | 2.1 Qts. (2.0L) |

[1] – Refill capacity.
[2] – Filled for service life. No oil change.

## QUICK-SERVICE

### SERVICE INTERVALS & SPECIFICATIONS

*BELT ADJUSTMENT*

| Application | [1] Deflection – In. (mm) |
|---|---|
| All Models Except Vanagon | |
| Alternator | |
| New | [2] 5/64 (2) |
| Old | 13/64 (5) |
| A/C Compressor | |
| New | 3/8 (10) |
| Old | 3/8 (10) |
| Power Steering | |
| New | 5/64 (2) |
| Old | 13/64 (5) |
| Vanagon | |
| Alternator | 3/8-9/16 (10-15) |
| A/C Compressor | 3/8 (10) |

[1] – Deflection is with 22 lbs. (10 kg) pressure applied midway on longest belt run.
[2] – 3/8" (10 mm) on models with A/C.

*REPLACEMENT INTERVALS*

| Component | Miles |
|---|---|
| Air Filter | 30,000 |
| Coolant | 30,000 |
| Fuel Filter [1] | 15,000 |
| Oil & Filter | 7500 |
| Spark Plugs | 30,000 |

[1] – Discard mini-fuel filter at 1000-mile maintenance interval. Install new copper gaskets.

## MECHANICAL CHECKS

### ENGINE COMPRESSION

*COMPRESSION SPECIFICATION*

| Application | Compression Pressure psi (kg/cm²) | Compression Ratio |
|---|---|---|
| Cabriolet | 131-174 (9.0-12.0) | 8.5:1 |
| Corrado | 116-174 (8.0-12.0) | 8.0:1 |
| Fox | 131-174 (9.0-12.0) | 9.0:1 |
| Golf GL & GTI | 131-174 (9.0-12.0) | 10.0:1 |
| Jetta | 131-174 (9.0-12.0) | 10.0:1 |
| Jetta GLI | 145-190 (10.0-13.0) | 10.0:1 |
| Passat | 116-174 (8.0-12.0) | 10.8:1 |
| Vanagon | 145-190 (10.0-13.0) | 9.0:1 |

### VALVE CLEARANCE

***NOTE:** All models are equipped with hydraulic lifters. No adjustments are required.*

***NOTE:** Right and left sides refer to engine, as viewed from flywheel.*

### VALVE ARRANGEMENT

**1.8L & 2.0L**
**Left Side** – All Intake
**Right Side** – All Exhaust
**2.1L**
**Both Banks** – E-I-I-E

## IGNITION SYSTEM

### IGNITION COIL

*IGNITION COIL RESISTANCE – Ohms @ 68°F (20°C)*

| Application | Primary | Secondary |
|---|---|---|
| Jetta GLI & Passat | .60-.70 | 6500-8500 |
| All Other Models | .52-.76 | 2400-3500 |

### HIGH TENSION WIRE RESISTANCE

*HIGH TENSION WIRE RESISTANCE*

| Application | Ohms |
|---|---|
| Vanagon | |
| Coil Wire With Connectors | 1200-2800 |
| Spark Plug Wire/Connector | 4600-7400 |
| Spark Plug Connector | 4000-6000 |
| Suppressor [1] | 600-1400 |
| Except Vanagon | |
| Coil Wire Only | [1] |
| Coil Wire With Connector | 1600-2400 |
| Spark Plug Wire/ Connector | 4000-6000 |
| Suppressor [2] | 600-1400 |

[1] – Check for continuity.
[2] – Suppressor is located between ignition wire and distributor cap.

# 1991 ENGINE PERFORMANCE
# Service & Adjustment Specifications (Cont.)

## SPARK PLUGS

### SPARK PLUG TYPE

| Application | Bosch | Champion |
|---|---|---|
| Cabriolet | W7DTC | N7BYC |
| Corrado, Fox Golf GL & Jetta 1.8L | WR7DS | N8GY |
| Jetta GLI 2.0L & Passat | F6DSR | N8GY |
| Vanagon | W7CCO | N288 |

### SPARK PLUG SPECIFICATIONS

| Application | Gap In. (mm) | Torque Ft. Lbs. (N.m) |
|---|---|---|
| All Models | .028-.032 (.70-.80) | 14 (19) |

## FIRING ORDER & TIMING MARKS

**1.8L & 2.0L** – Timing mark location is on flywheel. Timing pointer is on timing hole on transaxle bellhousing.

**2.1L** – Timing mark on crankshaft belt pulley and notch on "V" belt pulley must align with separating line of crankcase.

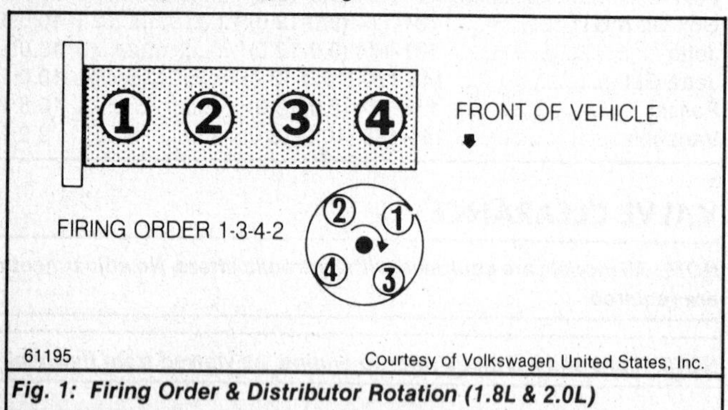


*Fig. 1: Firing Order & Distributor Rotation (1.8L & 2.0L)*

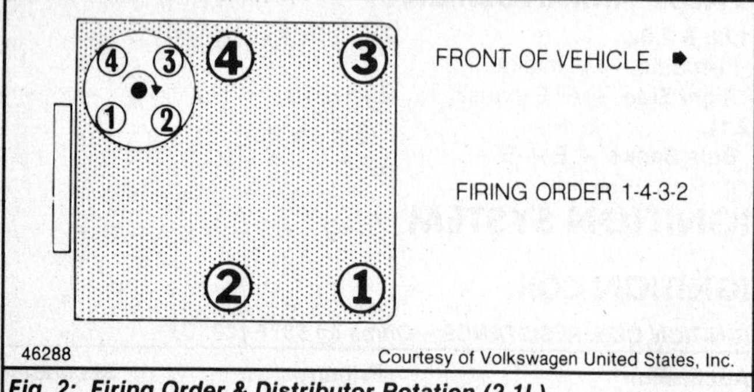


*Fig. 2: Firing Order & Distributor Rotation (2.1L)*

## IGNITION TIMING

***NOTE: Always reference under-hood label for latest specifications.***

### IGNITION TIMING (Degrees BTDC @ RPM)

| Application | Checking | Adjusting |
|---|---|---|
| 1.8L | 4-8 @ 870-930 | 5-7 @ 870-930 |
| 2.0L | 4-8 @ 770-830 | 5-7 @ 770-830 |
| 2.1L | 4-8 @ 800-900 | 5-7 @ 800-900 |

***NOTE: Off idle timing is computer controlled on models with knock sensor. For adjustment procedures, see ON-VEHICLE ADJUSTMENTS article.***

## DISTRIBUTOR SPECIFICATIONS

### DISTRIBUTOR ADVANCE

| Application | Degrees Total Advance | RPM |
|---|---|---|
| Cabriolet & Fox | 22-26 | 4500 |
| Golf GL, Jetta & Passat | 23-27 | 6000 |
| Vanagon | 21-25 | 3400 |

## FUEL SYSTEM

### FUEL PUMP

***NOTE: Fuel pump performance measures fuel pressure and volume availability, not regulated fuel pressure.***

#### FUEL PUMP PERFORMANCE (AFC-Digifant)

| Application | Pressure psi (kg/cm²) | Min. Vol. in 30 Sec. Pts. (L) |
|---|---|---|
| Cabriolet, Corrado, Golf GL, GTI & Jetta | 29-36 (2.0-2.5) | 1.0 (.5) |
| Vanagon | 33-39 (2.3-2.7) | 1.0 (.5) |

#### FUEL PUMP PERFORMANCE (CIS-E & CIS-Motronic)

| Application @ Voltage | Min. Vol. in 30 Sec. Pts. (L) |
|---|---|
| Fox | |
| 10 | .8 (.36) |
| 11 | 1.1 (.52) |
| 12 | 1.4 (.68) |
| Jetta GLI & Passat | |
| 10 | 1.0 (.46) |
| 11 | 1.3 (.62) |
| 12 | 1.6 (.75) |

#### REGULATED FUEL PRESSURE

| Application | [1] Engine Off psi (kg/cm²) | At Idle psi (kg/cm²) |
|---|---|---|
| Fox | 38.0 (2.6) | 75-82 (5.3-5.8) |
| Jetta GLI | 48.0 (3.3) | 89-95 (6.1-6.6) |
| Cabriolet, Corrado, Golf GL, GTI, Jetta & Passat | 29-36 (2.0-2.5) | 75-82 (5.2-5.6) |
| Vanagon | 29-36 (2.0-2.5) | [2] 33 (2.2) |

[1] – After checking fuel pressure at idle, turn ignition switch to OFF position.

[2] – With pressure regulator vacuum hose disconnected, pressure should be 36 psi (2.5 kg/cm²).

## INJECTOR RESISTANCE

### INJECTOR RESISTANCE SPECIFICATIONS

| Application | Ohms |
|---|---|
| Vanagon | 16.0-16.4 |
| Except Vanagon | [1] 3.7-5.0 |

[1] – Resistance measured at main electrical connector on end of fuel rail.

## IDLE SPEED & MIXTURE

***IDLE SPEED & CO LEVEL***

| Application | Idle RPM | CO Level % |
|---|---|---|
| Cabriolet | 750-850 [1] | .3-1.1 |
| Corrado | 750-850 | .3-1.1 |
| Fox | 875-925 | [2] 1.2-1.5 |
| Golf GL, Jetta & GTI | | |
| 1.8L (Digifant) | 750-850 | .3-1.1 |
| 2.0L (CIS-E) | N/A [3] | .2-1.2 |
| Passat | 700-900 [3] | .2-1.2 |
| Vanagon | 830-930 | .3-1.1 |

[1] – Disconnect Blue coolant temperature sensor connector.
[2] – Clamp crankcase breather hose near emission control valve.
[3] – Not adjustable.

# 1991 ENGINE PERFORMANCE
# On-Vehicle Adjustments

## Cabriolet, Corrado, Fox, Golf GL, GTI, Jetta, Jetta GLI, Passat, Vanagon

## ENGINE MECHANICAL

Before performing any on-vehicle adjustments to fuel or ignition systems, ensure engine mechanical condition is okay.

## ENGINE COMPRESSION

Check engine compression with engine at normal operating temperature at specified cranking speed, all spark plugs removed and throttle wide open.

*ENGINE COMPRESSION SPECIFICATIONS*

| Model | Standard psi (kg/cm²) | Minimum psi (kg/cm²) |
|---|---|---|
| Cabriolet | 131-174 (9.0-12.0) | 109 (7.5) |
| Corrado | 116-174 (8.0-12.0) | 87 (6.0) |
| Fox | 131-174 (9.0-12.0) | 102 (7.0) |
| Golf GL & GTI 1.8L | 131-174 (9.0-12.0) | 102 (7.0) |
| GTI 2.0L & Jetta GLI | 145-190 (10.0-13.0) | 109 (7.5) |
| Jetta | 131-174 (9.0-12.0) | 102 (7.0) |
| Passat | 116-174 (8.0-12.0) | 109 (7.5) |
| Vanagon | 87-131 (6.1-9.2) | 87 (6.0) |

## VALVE CLEARANCE

***NOTE: All models use hydraulic lifters. No adjustments are required.***

## IGNITION TIMING

***NOTE: Basic timing readings are only valid when engine idle speed and idle mixture are within specifications. For best results, manufacturer recommends ignition timing, idle CO and idle speed be checked and adjusted in that order.***

### IGNITION TIMING

***NOTE: Off idle timing is computer controlled on models with knock sensor(s). Only idle ignition timing can be set.***

**Except Vanagon – 1)** Warm engine to normal operating temperature (cooling fan should cycle at least once). Remove the 27 mm plastic plug from timing check hole on transaxle bellhousing.

**2)** With ignition off, connect a tachometer and timing light to vehicle. Start engine, raise speed above 2100 RPM a few times, and allow engine to idle normally. With distributor vacuum hoses connected, timing mark on flywheel should appear at pointer in hole.

***NOTE: Before checking engine timing, raise engine speed above 2100 RPM at least 4 times. This must be done each time ignition is turned off and restarted to clear ECU memory and by-pass hot-start, fast-idle function.***

**3)** If an adjustment is needed, turn ignition off and loosen distributor hold-down bolt (2.0L has 2 hold-down bolts) just enough to move distributor by hand. Start engine and allow to idle. Turn distributor until timing mark is aligned with pointer in bellhousing.

**4)** Stop engine and tighten hold down bolt to 18 ft. lbs. (24 N.m). On 2.0L tighten hold-down bolts to 87 INCH lbs. (10 N.m). Check and readjust if necessary and install plastic plug in inspection hole.

**Vanagon – 1)** Engine oil temperature must be 176° F (80° C). Connect timing light and tachometer. Start engine and allow to idle. Check ignition timing at 800-1000 RPM.

***NOTE: Before checking engine timing, raise engine speed above 2100 RPM at least 4 times. This must be done each time ignition is turned off and restarted to clear ECU memory and by-pass hot-start, fast-idle function.***

**2)** If an adjustment is needed, turn ignition off and loosen distributor hold-down bolt just enough to move distributor by hand. Remove connectors from idle stabilizer by squeezing connectors then pulling apart. Plug idle stabilizer connectors together.

**3)** Start and allow engine to idle. Turn distributor until notch on V-belt pulley matches separation in case. Set timing and RPM. Reconnect electrical connectors to idle stabilizer. Tighten distributor clamp bolt.

*IGNITION TIMING (Degrees BTDC @ RPM)*

| Application | Checking | Adjusting |
|---|---|---|
| 1.8L | 4-8 @ 870-930 | 5-7 @ 870-930 |
| 2.0L | 4-8 @ 770-830 | 5-7 @ 770-830 |
| 2.1L | 4-8 @ 800-900 | 5-7 @ 800-900 |

## COLD (FAST) IDLE

Fast idle RPM is NOT adjustable.

## IDLE SPEED & MIXTURE

***NOTE: Mixture adjustment is NOT a part of normal tune-up procedure and should NOT be performed unless mixture control unit is replaced or vehicle fails emissions testing.***

***NOTE: Ensure fuel system pressure is correct before attempting idle speed or mixture adjustment.***

### IDLE SPEED & MIXTURE ADJUSTMENT

**Fox (CIS-E), GTI 2.0L (CIS-Motronic) & Jetta GLI (CIS-Motronic) – 1)** Ignition timing and idle speed must be checked before CO is adjusted. See CHECKING & ADJUSTING under IGNITION TIMING. With ignition timing properly adjusted, check and adjust idle speed, differential pressure regulator current and idle mixture. Repeat adjustments until correct.

**2)** Warm engine to normal operating temperature. Radiator fan must come on at least once and engine oil temperature must be at least 176°F (80°C). Turn off all electrical equipment, including A/C and radiator fan. Disconnect all fuel pressure test equipment (if installed). If injection lines have been removed or replaced, run engine several times to 3000 RPM for about 2 minutes.

**3)** Ensure idle switch is properly adjusted. Check that auxiliary air regulator valve is fully closed. Pinch shut the hose leading from idle speed boost valve(s). Remove temperature sensor harness connector from temperature sensor. Pull crankcase breather hoses off valve cover and air filter, vent to atmosphere.

**4)** Remove suction hose from carbon canister. Disconnect "T" fitting from carbon canister at air intake boot. On Fox, remove connector from coolant temperature sensor and install 15,000-Ohm Resistor (VW 1490) on temperature sensor harness. *See Fig. 1.*

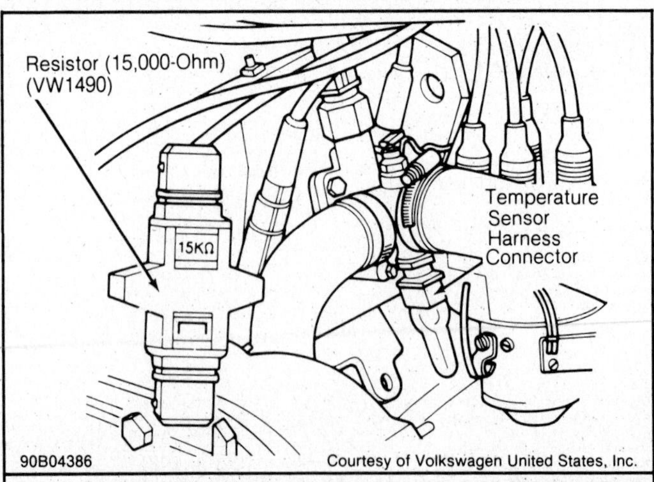


***Fig. 1: Locating Coolant Temperature Sensor & 15,000-Ohm Test Resistor (Fox)***

**5)** Turn "T" fitting 90 degrees and insert blank side with .059" (1.5 mm) restrictor into hole in intake air boot. If vehicle is not equipped with this type of connector, use Plug (026 133 382D) with .059" (1.5 mm) orifice. Adjust idle speed if not within specification. See IDLE SPEED & CO LEVEL table.

**6)** Connect fuel pressure gauge and ensure system fuel pressure is correct. See FUEL SYSTEM in BASIC DIAGNOSTIC PROCEDURES article. Connect an inductive tachometer or Tester (VW 1367) and Test Lead (VW 1473). *See Fig. 2.*

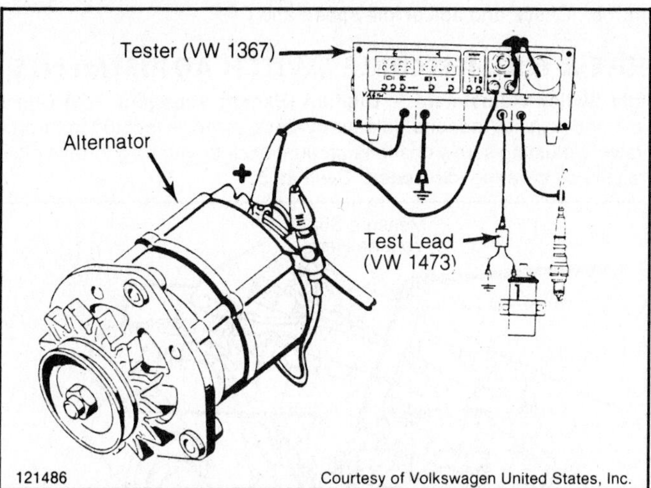


***Fig. 2: Tester (VW 1367) & Test Lead (VW 1473)***

**7)** Remove CO probe receptacle cap and connect CO meter. Ensure fit is snug to prevent exhaust leaks. Connect Digital Multimeter (US 1119) with Adapter (VW 1315 A/1) to differential pressure regulator. *See Fig. 3.*

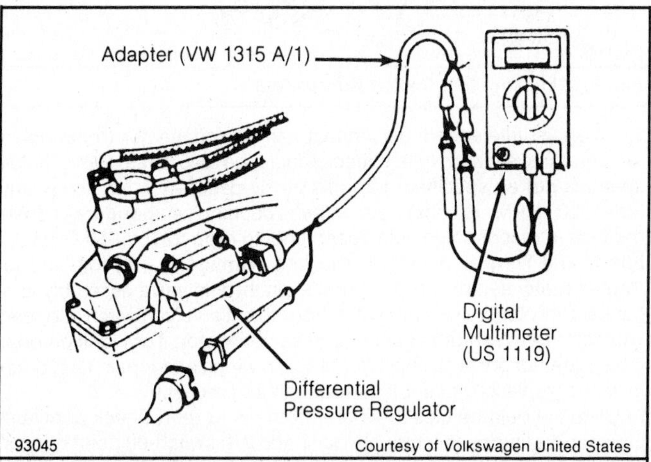


***Fig. 3: Making Digital Multimeter Hook-Up***

**8)** Connect adapter between connector and regulator. Connect multimeter to adapter and turn switch to DCA 200-mA range. Read and compare current (4-16 mA) and CO values to specifications. Turn engine off.

**9)** If CO reading is more than 1.2% at current reading of 4-16 mA, check for exhaust system leaks, ignition timing, injector inserts for leaks, and fuel distributor for uneven fuel distribution. If required, seal injector inserts with sealing compound and tighten to 15 ft. lbs. (20 N.m).

**10)** If current reading is less than 4 mA or more than 16 mA, adjustment must be made with CO adjustment screw.

**11)** Remove boot from mixture control unit. Center punch plug in CO adjusting hole and drill a 3/32" hole to a depth of 5/32" (4 mm). DO NOT drill completely through as adjustment screw will be damaged. Install a 1/8" sheet metal screw and remove plug using pliers.

**12)** Start engine and run at idle. Adjust current reading to 10 mA by turning CO adjustment screw with Wrench (P 377). Turn screw clockwise to lower reading, counterclockwise to raise reading. *See Fig. 4.*

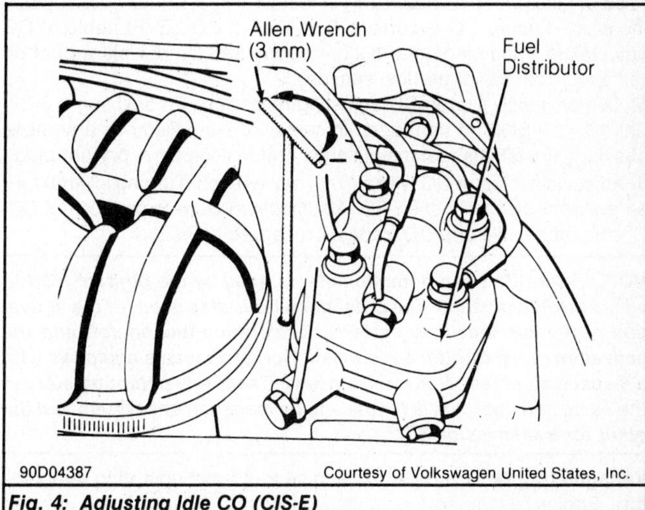


***Fig. 4: Adjusting Idle CO (CIS-E)***

**13)** Readjust idle speed if required. Turn engine off. Install new plug in mixture control unit and seat plug flush with unit. Remove all test equipment and reconnect all hoses and wiring.

**Cabriolet, Corrado, Golf GL & GTI 1.8L, Jetta & Passat (Digifant) –**

**1)** For correct system operation basic adjustments to ignition timing, CO content and idle speed must be correct. These adjustments are inter-related and must be checked/adjusted together.

**2)** Warm engine to normal operating temperature (radiator fan should have cycled at least once). Engine oil temperature must be at least 176°F (80°C). All electrical components must be off. Ensure idle speed stabilization system is okay (with ignition ON idle stabilizer valve must hum/buzz). Ensure throttle valve switch is adjusted correctly.

***NOTE: Before checking engine timing, raise engine speed above 2100 RPM at least 4 times. This must be done each time engine is turned off and restarted to clear ECU memory and by-pass hot-start, fast-idle function.***

**3)** Connect an inductive tachometer or Tester (VW 1367) to alternator, Test Lead (VW 1473) to ignition coil, and timing light lead to No. 1 spark plug wire. *See Fig. 2.* Start engine and ensure engine speed and timing are correct. If NOT, adjust to specification.

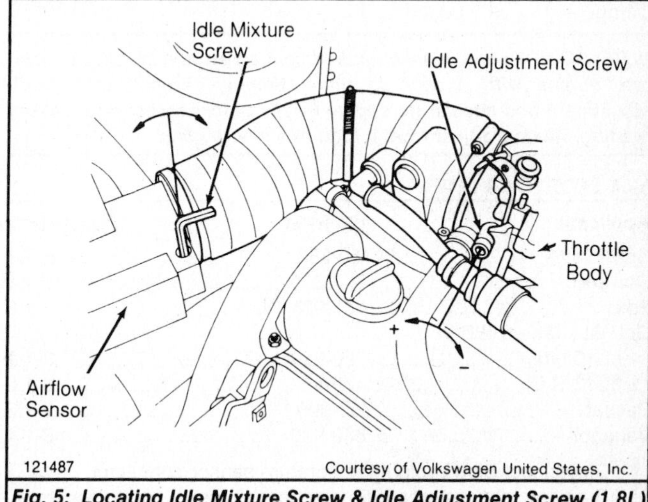


***Fig. 5: Locating Idle Mixture Screw & Idle Adjustment Screw (1.8L)***

# 1991 ENGINE PERFORMANCE
# On-Vehicle Adjustments (Cont.)

**4)** Remove Blue cap from CO tap tube rising from exhaust manifold and connect exhaust gas analyzer. Disconnect coolant sensor harness connector. Raise oil dipstick slightly to vent crankcase. Disconnect and plug crankcase ventilation hose. Start engine and raise engine speed to 2100 RPM at least 4 times. Check idle, adjust if incorrect. Ensure CO is correct. See IDLE & CO LEVEL table. If CO adjustment is needed, idle mixture screw anti-tamper plug must be removed from top of air flow sensor.
**5)** Center punch plug in CO adjusting hole. *See Fig. 5.* Using a 3/32" drill bit, drill 5/32" (4 mm) deep in center of plug. Remove any metal shavings. Install a sheet metal screw and, using pliers, pry out plug.
**6)** Adjust idle mixture CO with a 5 mm hex wrench. Turning idle mixture screw clockwise will richen CO. Adjust idle mixture to get correct CO. Check engine idle and CO, repeat procedure if needed.

***NOTE: A throttle valve potentiometer is used by the Digifant ECU to sense throttle position. The potentiometer is also used for the activation of the idle stabilizer system, deceleration fuel shutoff and the activation of full throttle enrichment. Corrado models equipped with a 4-speed automatic transmission have 2 separate potentiometers in the same housing. One is for the engine management system and the other for transmission ECU.***

**Vanagon (Digifant) – 1)** Warm engine to normal operating temperature. Engine oil temperature must be at least 176°F (80°C). Connect an inductive tachometer or Tester (VW 1367) to alternator, Test Lead (VW 1473) to ignition coil, and timing light lead to No. 1 spark plug wire. Start engine and ensure engine speed and timing are correct. If speed and timing are incorrect, adjust to specification.
**2)** Remove connectors from idle stabilizer by squeezing connectors then pulling apart. Plug idle stabilizer connectors together. Turn idle speed screw until idle speed is correct. To adjust timing, see CHECKING & ADJUSTING under IGNITION TIMING in this article.
**3)** Ensure all vehicle electrical equipment is off. Place exhaust gas analyzer in exhaust pipe. See IDLE SPEED & CO LEVEL table. If adjustment is needed, go to next step.
**4)** If adjustment is needed in step **2)**. Remove intake air sensor from engine. Center punch plug in CO adjusting hole. Using a 3/32" drill bit, drill hole 5/32" (4 mm) deep in center of plug. Remove any metal shavings. Install a sheet metal screw and, using pliers, pry out plug.
**5)** Disconnect oxygen sensor connector on left side of engine compartment (Green wire). Start engine. Set idle speed and CO reading by alternately turning mixture and idle speed adjustment screws. Reconnect oxygen sensor and idle stabilizer connectors. Let engine idle for 2 minutes.
**6)** Check CO value. If incorrect, repeat adjusting procedure. If correct turn ignition off. Drive in new adjusting hole plug flush with air intake sensor. Remove all test equipment and reconnect all hoses and wiring.

***NOTE: DO NOT push down on adjustment screw and DO NOT accelerate engine with wrench in plate. Remove wrench after each adjustment and accelerate engine briefly before measuring current reading. Always adjust from a high to a low reading.***

***IDLE SPEED & CO LEVEL***

| Application | Idle RPM | CO Level % |
|---|---|---|
| Cabriolet | 750-850 [1] | .3-1.1 |
| Corrado | 750-850 | .3-1.1 |
| Fox | 875-925 | [2] 1.2-1.5 |
| Golf GL, Jetta & GTI | | |
| 1.8L (Digifant) | 750-850 | .3-1.1 |
| 2.0L (CIS-E) | N/A [3] | .2-1.2 |
| Passat | 700-900 [3] | .2-1.2 |
| Vanagon | 830-930 | .3-1.1 |

[1] – Disconnect Blue coolant temperature sensor connector.
[2] – Clamp crankcase breather hose near emission control valve.
[3] – Not adjustable.

## IDLE & FULL THROTTLE SWITCHES

### THROTTLE STOP SCREW

***NOTE: Stop screw is set by manufacturer and should NOT be moved.***

If basic factory setting has been changed, turn throttle stop screw counterclockwise until there is a gap between stop and screw. Turn screw in until it just touches stop. Turn screw 1/2 turn (180 degrees) further. Check and adjust idle speed and CO.

### IDLE & FULL THROTTLE SWITCH ADJUSTMENTS

**Idle Switch Adjustment – Digifant (Except Vanagon) – 1)** Check idle and adjust if needed. Idle air by-pass screw is located in throttle valve. Adjusting screw changes amount of air by-passing throttle plate, raising or lowering idle speed. *See Fig. 6.*

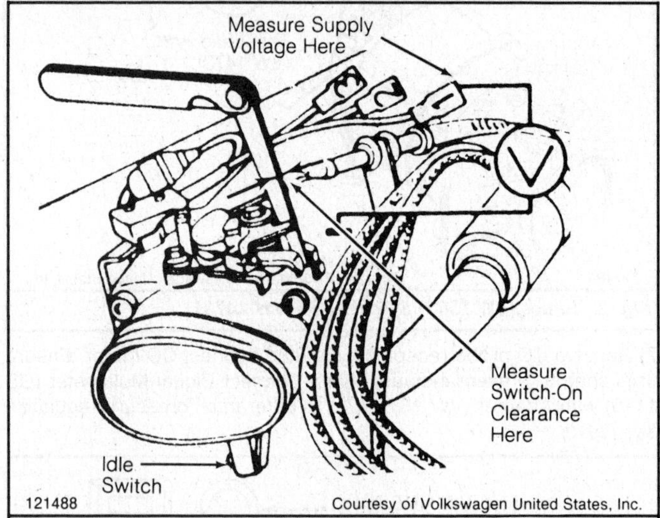


***Fig. 6: Checking Idle Switch Adjustment***

**2)** To adjust idle speed, disconnect harness connector from coolant temperature sensor. Idle speed should be 925-1025 RPM. If idle speed is not as specified, turn idle air by-pass adjusting screw until 950-1000 RPM is obtained. When coolant temperature sensor harness is reconnected, idle speed should drop to 750-850 RPM.
**Idle & Full Throttle Switch – Digifant (Vanagon) – 1)** Idle and full throttle switches are wired in parallel on throttle valve assembly. Disconnect throttle valve connector from throttle valve switch. Connect voltmeter between terminal in harness connector. Turn ignition on. If 5 volts are not present, check for break in wiring and repair. If no break in wiring, replace Digifant II control unit and recheck.
**2)** Circuit should be closed when throttle is at rest. Check continuity between test harness terminals No. 1 and 2. If switch-on point is incorrect, loosen and adjust idle switch position. Recheck clearance between throttle valve lever and stop. Ensure clearance is .002-.006 (.15-.05 mm). Throttle switch is located on underside of throttle valve housing, opposite idle stop.

***NOTE: Airflow potentiometer is factory adjusted. No adjustment should be needed, unless component is replaced.***

**Airflow Sensor Potentiometer Adjustment – CIS-E (Fox) – 1)** Disconnect airflow sensor potentiometer. Loosen 4 retaining screws and adjust airflow sensor potentiometer until voltage between center terminal and ground is 0.2-0.3 volt.
**2)** Carefully tighten mounting screws. Raise the sensor plate. Voltage should increase to approximately 7.0 volts. If increase is not as specified, readjust airflow sensor potentiometer. *See Fig. 7.*

# 1991 ENGINE PERFORMANCE
# On-Vehicle Adjustments (Cont.)

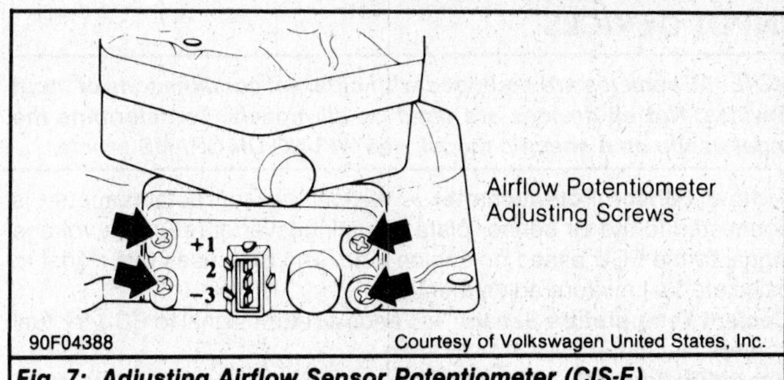


***Fig. 7: Adjusting Airflow Sensor Potentiometer (CIS-E)***

**Airflow Sensor Potentiometer Adjustment - CIS-E Motronic (GTI 2.0L & Jetta GLI) - 1)** Install Test Connector (VW 1501) between airflow sensor potentiometer connector and airflow sensor potentiometer on airflow meter. Check input voltage between terminals No. 1 and 3 with ignition on. *See Fig. 8.* Voltage should be 4.35-5.35 volts. Turn off ignition.

**2)** Connect a voltmeter between terminals No. 2 and 3. Output voltage should be within specifications, see AIRFLOW SENSOR - CIS-E MOTRONIC table. If voltage is not as specified, carefully melt sealer from potentiometer adjusting screw and adjust output voltage.

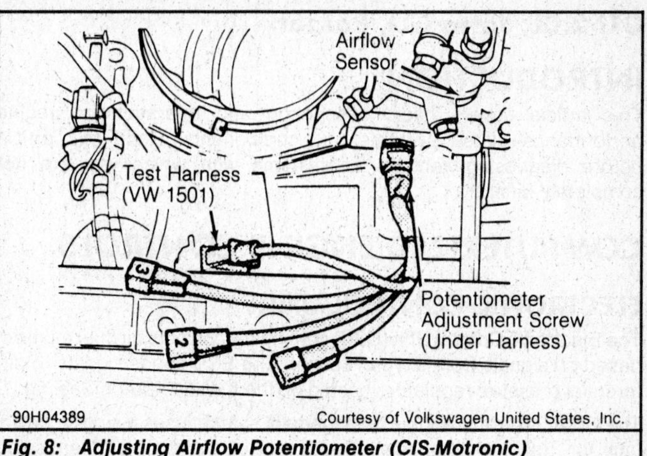


***Fig. 8: Adjusting Airflow Potentiometer (CIS-Motronic)***

***AIRFLOW SENSOR (CIS-E MOTRONIC)***

| Input Voltage | Output Voltage |
|---|---|
| 4.35 | 0.43-0.75 |
| 4.50 | 0.45-0.77 |
| 4.60 | 0.47-0.79 |
| 4.70 | 0.48-0.80 |
| 4.80 | 0.49-0.81 |
| 4.90 | 0.50-0.83 |
| 5.00 | 0.51-0.85 |
| 5.10 | 0.52-0.87 |
| 5.20 | 0.53-0.89 |
| 5.30 | 0.54-0.90 |
| 5.40 | 0.55-0.91 |

# 1991 ENGINE PERFORMANCE
# Theory & Operation – CIS-E Motronic

**GTI 2.0L, Jetta GLI, Passat**

## INTRODUCTION

This article covers basic description and operation of engine performance-related systems and components. Read this article before diagnosing vehicles or systems with which you are not completely familiar.

## COMPUTERIZED ENGINE CONTROLS

### ELECTRONIC CONTROL UNIT

The Electronic Control Unit (ECU) continually corrects air/fuel mixture based on signals from oxygen sensor. The ECU sends signals to differential pressure regulator located on the fuel distributor. *See Fig. 1*.

The CIS-E Motronic engine management system uses a single control unit for fuel injection, idle speed control, ignition, and emission controls. The oxygen sensor in the CIS-E Motronic system can adjust its range in response to changes in operating conditions.

***ECU LOCATION***

| Application | Location |
|---|---|
| Passat | Behind Firewall In Rear Center Of Engine Compartment |
| GTI 2.0L & Jetta GLI | Behind Firewall In Left Rear Of Engine Compartment. |

***NOTE: Components are grouped into 2 categories. The first category covers INPUT DEVICES, which control or produce voltage signals monitored by the control unit. The second category covers OUTPUT SIGNALS, which are components controlled by the control unit.***

### INPUT DEVICES

***NOTE: All vehicles are equipped with different combinations of input devices. Not all devices are used on all models. To determine the input usage on a specific model, see WIRING DIAGRAMS article.***

**Airflow Sensor Potentiometer** – Airflow sensor potentiometer is connected to the air sensor plate actuating lever. It returns a voltage signal to the ECU based on engine load. The ECU uses this signal to calculate fuel mixture adjustments.

**Coolant Temperature Sensor** – Feeds a return signal to ECU for fuel control.

**Heated/Exhaust Gas Oxygen Sensor** – Located in exhaust manifold, the heated/exhaust gas oxygen sensor measures amount of unburned oxygen in exhaust. If oxygen is low (rich mixture), higher voltage will be generated by sensor. If oxygen is high (lean mixture), lower voltage will be generated. Voltage signal from oxygen sensor is sent to ECU which controls fuel mixture through the differential pressure regulator. The heated portion is used to rapidly warm the oxygen sensor for more effective emission controls.

**Hall Effect Sensor** – See IGNITION SYSTEM in this article.

**Idle Switch** – With the throttle closed, the idle switch supplies the ECU inputs for the following.

- Idle Air Stabilizer
- Deceleration Fuel Shutoff
- Electronic Control Unit (ECU)

The idle switch supplies ECU with information to cut fuel during deceleration, and activate idle stabilizer to control idle speed.

### OUTPUT SIGNALS

- **Idle Air Stabilizer** – See IDLE SPEED.
- **Cold Start Valve** – See FUEL CONTROL.
- **Differential Pressure Regulator** – See FUEL CONTROL.
- **Fuel Injectors** – See FUEL CONTROL.

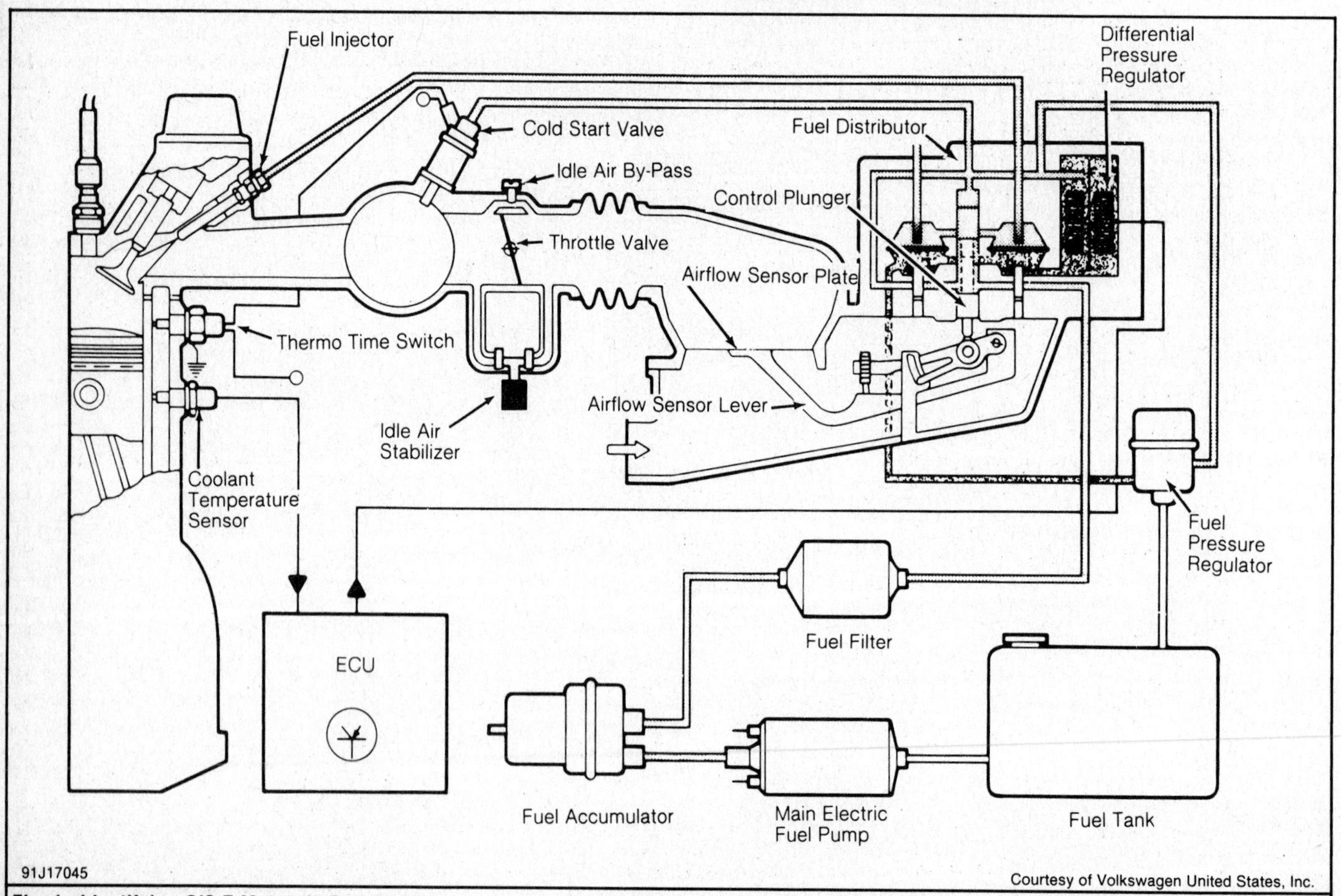


***Fig. 1: Identifying CIS-E Motronic Components***

## FUEL SYSTEM

### FUEL DELIVERY

**Fuel Pump** – Main pump is located to rear of vehicle on frame cross-member. A transfer pump is located inside fuel tank. Main fuel pump assembly, has a pressure damper at the suction end. Fuel pumps are activated during start-up and when engine is running.

The main electric fuel pump provides fuel system pressure of 88-95 psi (6.2-6.7 kg/cm²). The transfer pump pulls fuel from the tank and pushes it to the main fuel pump. Fuel pump control relay prevents continued operation of fuel pumps if engine stalls. To aid in starting, a fuel accumulator and check valves in the pump and at fuel filter maintain line pressure when engine is not running.

**Fuel Pressure Regulator** – System pressure is created by the fuel pump and controlled by fuel pressure regulator. The fuel pressure regulator returns fuel to fuel tank when system pressure exceeds need. System is self-adjusting.

**Fuel Pump Relay** – Fuel pump relay switches off fuel pumps when ignition signal is cut off.

### FUEL CONTROL

**Cold Start Valve** – Cold start valve, mounted on intake manifold, sprays fuel to enrich mixture during starting so engine will start easily. The cold start valve is powered through starter circuits and grounded through thermo time switch. It operates for 3-10 seconds when cold engine is being cranked only.

**Differential Pressure Regulator (DPR)** – The DPR, mounted on side of fuel distributor, is an electrically operated plate valve. Combined with fixed outlet orifice, the DPR governs pressure in lower chamber. Pressure change in lower chamber moves diaphragm and adjusts fuel volume flow to injectors. Actuating signal comes from ECU and ranges from 9-15 mA (after idle stabilization) with engine at an idle condition. The actuating signal will change depending upon engine operating conditions.

**Fuel Distributor** – The fuel distributor mechanically controls fuel to the injectors. Air being drawn over the sensor plate raises or lowers the fuel distributor control plunger. Differential pressure is the difference between upper (injector supply) and lower (fuel return) chambers of the fuel distributor, controlled by the differential pressure regulator. This controls the pressure differential at the fuel distributor metering ports, which determines the fuel flow to the injectors and air/fuel mixture.

**Fuel Injectors** – Fuel injectors in CIS-E system open at a preset pressure. Fuel is always present in lines between fuel distributor and injectors to ensure good starting. As pressure from fuel distributor increases (when engine is started), valves open and spray constantly. Amount of fuel injected will be determined by position of control plunger in fuel distributor and amount of voltage to differential pressure regulator.

**Thermo Time Switch** – Energizes the cold start valve to provide cold start enrichment when engine temperature is below 86°F (30°C).

### IDLE SPEED

**Idle Air Stabilizer Valve** – The electronic idle air stabilizer valve adjusts the amount of air by-passing the throttle valve to control engine idle speed under all operating conditions. The stabilizer valve receives signals from ECU based on engine RPM, idle switch and other inputs. Adjustment is not necessary with idle air by-pass adjusting screw. The idle air by-pass adjusting screw should be turned in all the way against its stop.

## IGNITION SYSTEM

### ELECTRONIC IGNITION SYSTEM

The Hall Effect sending unit in the distributor uses a shutter window wheel mounted on the distributor shaft. The shutter blades pass in and out of the air gap of the hall effect sender resulting in signal pulses. There is one shutter window for each engine cylinder.

Signals from distributor hall sender are sent to the ECU. The ECU sends a switching voltage signal to the ignition coil primary circuit to discharge secondary spark voltage.

### IGNITION TIMING CONTROL SYSTEM

**Ignition Timing Control** – The Transistorized Coil Ignition with Hall Sender (TCI-h) ignition system uses engine load, engine RPM, ignition quality (knock) and coolant temperature to control ignition timing. Two knock sensors are used to control spark knock. Using 2 knock sensors the ECU is able to determine which pair of cylinders is knocking and adjust ignition timing appropriately.

## EMISSION SYSTEMS

**Evaporative Emissions Systems** – As fuel expands in fuel tank, vapor is forced out of the fuel tank to the expansion tank. In the expansion tank liquid fuel condenses and returns to fuel tank as temperature drops. Fuel vapor then flows from expansion tank through gravity/vent valve, and into the charcoal canister.

When engine is running, solenoid valve I (closest to charcoal canister) operates as a duty solenoid. The ECU varies the on-off time of solenoid valve I according to engine operating conditions. Solenoid valve II (farthest from charcoal canister) functions as a simple on-off valve. With engine speed more than 300 RPM, solenoid valve II opens allowing charcoal canister to purge. Canister vapor is drawn from canister through solenoid valve I and solenoid valve II into intake manifold for burning.

## MISCELLANEOUS CONTROLS

***NOTE: Although not considered true engine performance-related systems, some controlled devices may affect driveability if they malfunction.***

### COOLING FAN

***NOTE: If detonation is a problem, it is possible the cooling fan is not coming on at proper temperature and should be considered as a possible cause.***

**Cooling Fan Motor** – The cooling fan is either a 1- or 2-speed motor. If vehicle is equipped with single-speed motor, the fan comes on at 198-207°F (92-97°C) and off at 183-196°F (84-91°C). If equipped with a 2-speed motor, low speed of cooling fan should come on at 198-208°F (92-98°C) on vehicles without A/C, or 183-207°F (84-97°C) on vehicles with A/C. Low speed will shut off at 183-196°F (84-91°C) on all vehicles. High speed comes on at 210-226°F (99-108°C) on vehicles without A/C, or 201-226°F (94-108°C) on vehicles with A/C. High speed will shut off at 196-220°F (91-104°C) on all vehicles.

# 1991 ENGINE PERFORMANCE
# Theory & Operation - Digifant

**Cabriolet, Corrado, Fox, Golf GL, GTI 1.8L, Jetta, Vanagon**

## INTRODUCTION

This article covers basic description and operation of engine performance-related systems and components. Read this article before diagnosing vehicles or systems with which you are not completely familiar.

## AIR INDUCTION SYSTEM

### SUPERCHARGER

**Corrado** - The supercharger works like an air pump. Driven constantly off the crankshaft by a toothed belt, the supercharger compresses air. This compressed or boosted air is cooled by an intercooler before entering intake manifold.

Excess boost air is controlled by a mechanically-operated boost control valve and idle stabilizer. The boost control valve moves in the opposite direction of the throttle valve. As throttle valve opens, the boost control closes, directing most of the boost air back to the supercharger intake. *See Fig. 1.*

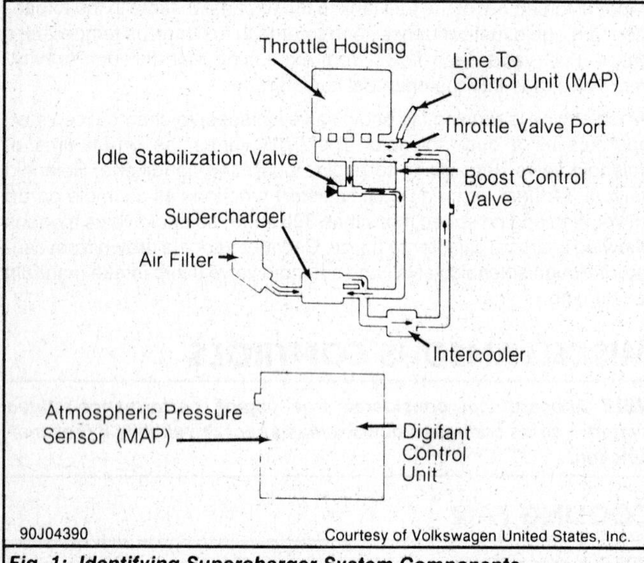


*Fig. 1: Identifying Supercharger System Components*

## COMPUTERIZED ENGINE CONTROLS

The Bosch AFC Digifant system is a computer-controlled fuel injection system. The system does not use cold start injector or thermo time switch for cold start enrichment. Different sensors and switches, along with Electronic Control Unit (ECU), regulate fuel injection and ignition timing.

### ELECTRONIC CONTROL UNIT

The ECU controls all engine operations, and limits maximum engine speed. It receives information from various input devices, and cannot be repaired.

***ECU LOCATION***

| Application | Location |
|---|---|
| Cabriolet, Golf GL, GTI 1.8L & Jetta | Behind Firewall In Left Rear Of Engine Compartment |
| Corrado | Behind Firewall In Rear Center Of Engine Compartment |
| Fox | Behind Glove Box Passenger Side |
| Vanagon | Right Side Of Engine Compartment |

### IDLE STABILIZATION CONTROL UNIT

**Vanagon** - The idle stabilization control unit is located in front of the right-hand taillight assembly. If engine idle speed differs from the value stored in the idle stabilization control unit, the idle air stabilizer valve adjusts the volume of air entering the engine at idle. The idle stabilization control unit receives information from the following.

- Coolant Temperature Sensor
- ECU Control Relay
- ECU
- Oxygen Sensor
- Power Steering Oil Pressure Switch

***NOTE: Components are grouped into 2 categories. The first category covers INPUT DEVICES, which control or produce voltage signals monitored by the control unit. The second category covers OUTPUT SIGNALS, which are components controlled by the control unit.***

### INPUT DEVICES

**Airflow Sensor (Except Corrado)** - All intake air is drawn through the airflow sensor. The airflow sensor contains a tunnel with a measuring flap and dampening flap. The measuring flap swings with intake air stream against pressure of a spiral spring and is connected to a potentiometer.

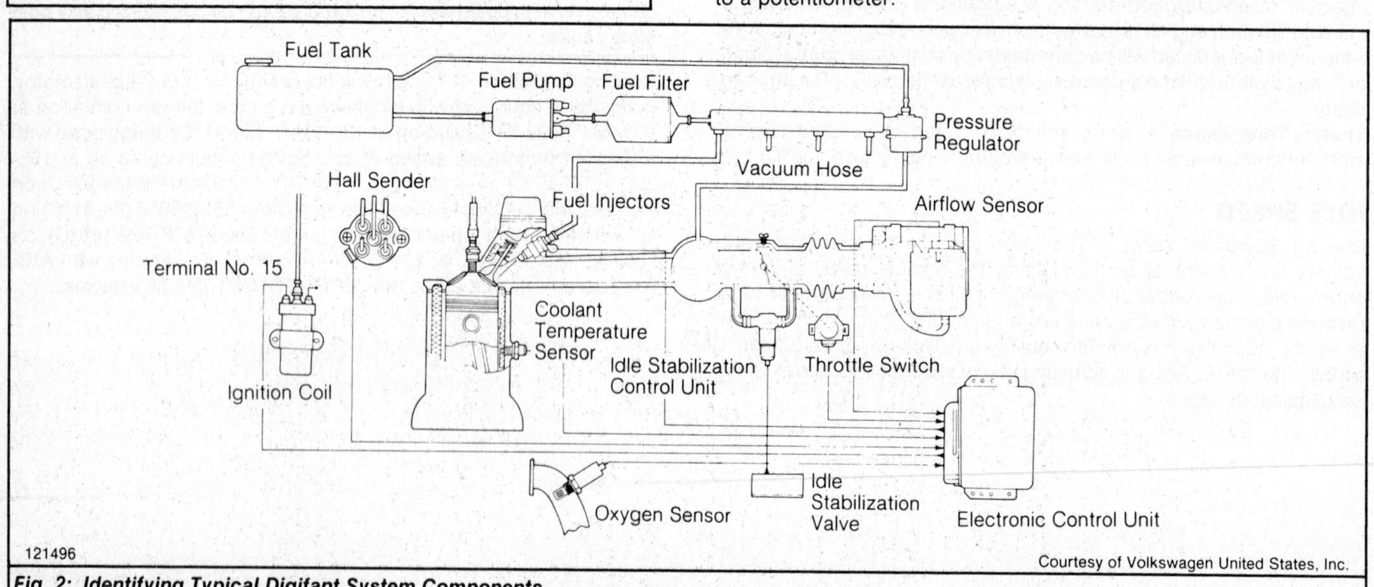


*Fig. 2: Identifying Typical Digifant System Components*

The potentiometer transmits an electrical signal determined by measuring flap position to inform ECU of engine load. At idle, the measuring flap is almost closed due to spring pressure. *See Fig. 3.*

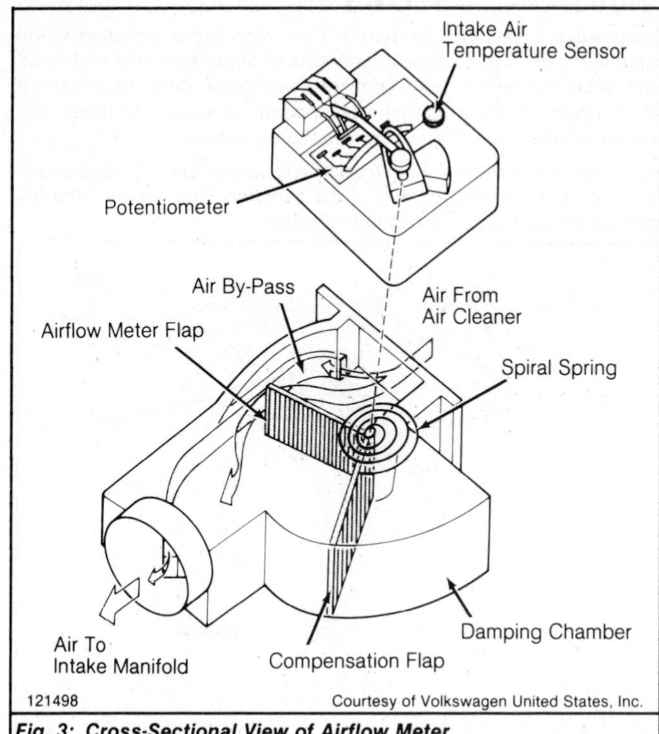


***Fig. 3: Cross-Sectional View of Airflow Meter***

The potentiometer within the airflow sensor prevents loss of engine power during engine load or sudden acceleration (along with engine speed and coolant temperature) by signaling the ECU of necessary enrichment and timing requirements.

The airflow sensor contains an intake air temperature sensor. An adjustable idle air by-pass screw influences CO levels at low engine speeds. A tamper-proof plug is installed over this screw.

**Coolant Temperature Sensor (Digifant I)** - Is a temperature sensitive variable resistor sensor (less resistance as temperature increases). This sensor returns signals to the ECU to determine amount of cold start enrichment, ignition timing and idle stabilization during warm-up. The sensor return signal has input to the ECU when the oxygen sensor, idle stabilization, and full throttle enrichment functions are activated.

**Coolant Temperature Sensor (Digifant II & Corrado)** - Is a temperature sensitive variable resistor sensor (less resistance as temperature increases). This sensor returns signals to the ECU to determine amount of cold start enrichment, enrichment during warm-up and ignition timing control.

**CO Potentiometer (Corrado)** - The CO potentiometer adjusts CO mixture. Located on the intake air duct before the throttle housing. The adjustment screw has a tamper-proof plug. An air temperature sensor located within the potentiometer housing is used to calculate air density.

**Full Throttle Switch (Digifant II)** - The full throttle switch closes approximately 10 degrees before Wide Open Throttle (WOT). The ECU uses this signal for full throttle enrichment.

**Hall Effect Sensor** - See ELECTRONIC IGNITION SYSTEM under IGNITION SYSTEM in this article.

**Idle Switch (Digifant II)** - Idle switch closes when throttle is closed. The ECU uses idle switch input for idle stabilizer valve, deceleration fuel shut-off and activation of ignition timing map for deceleration. Idle switch opens when throttle is opened approximately one degree.

**Intake Air Temperature Sensor** - Intake air temperature sensor is a thermistor-type variable resistor (resistance decreases with increase of temperature). This sensor voltage signal varies to ECU in relation to engine air temperature. Sensor is located inside the airflow meter.

**Knock Sensor** - Vibrations in engine block will cause the quartz crystal inside knock sensor to produce a small voltage. The ECU monitors this small voltage. Ignition timing is retarded 3 degrees initially when detonation begins to occur. Timing is retarded only in the cylinder which is detonating.

When detonation stops, ignition timing is advanced in .33 degree increments until a preprogrammed value is reached. If detonation continues or reoccurs in a cylinder, ignition timing can be retarded up to 15 degrees for each cylinder. The difference between any 2 cylinders is limited to 9 degrees.

**Manifold Absolute Pressure (MAP) Sensor (Corrado)** - MAP is located inside the ECU. The MAP sensor signal is used by ECU to determine engine load and manifold boost pressure. This signal along with RPM and intake air temperature is used to calculate fuel injection quantity.

**Oxygen ($O_2$) Sensor** - The $O_2$ sensor detects oxygen content in the exhaust gas and sends this information to the ECU. In operation, the ECU receives signals from the $O_2$ sensor and varies the duration during which fuel is injected. A high voltage signal indicates a rich mixture. A low voltage signal indicates a lean mixture.

The $O_2$ sensor is heated electrically for rapid warm-up and constant operating temperature. Power to the heating element is supplied whenever ignition switch is turned to ON position.

**Power Steering (P/S) Pressure Switch** - The P/S oil pressure switch signals the ECU when the power steering load is high. The ECU then sends a voltage signal to the idle stabilization valve to increase idle speed with power steering load.

**Throttle Potentiometer (Digifant I)** - Throttle potentiometer is used by ECU to sense throttle position. This signal is also used for activation of idle stabilization system and deceleration fuel shut-off.

**Throttle Potentiometer (Corrado)** - Throttle potentiometer is used by ECU to sense throttle position. This signal is also used for activation of idle stabilization system, deceleration fuel shut-off and full throttle enrichment. On vehicles equipped with a 4-speed automatic transmission, 2 throttle potentiometers are used. One throttle potentiometer is used for engine management and the other potentiometer is used for automatic transmission control.

**Throttle Valve Switch (Vanagon)** - Throttle valve switch supplies ECU with information that throttle valve is closed. If engine is above 1250 RPM with throttle closed, fuel will be shut off to the injectors. At idle speed, this switch signals control unit to regulate amount of fuel injected.

## OUTPUT SIGNALS

***NOTE: Each vehicle may be equipped with different combinations of computer controlled components. The following listed components may NOT be used on all models. For theory and operation on each output component, refer to the system indicated in brackets, to the right of each component.***

- **Idle Air Stabilizer Valve** - See IDLE SPEED.
- **Fuel Injectors** - See FUEL CONTROL.
- **Ignition Coil Control** - See IGNITION SYSTEM.

# FUEL SYSTEM

## FUEL DELIVERY

**Electric Fuel Pump** - The fuel pump provides fuel under pressure to the fuel pressure regulator. Power for operation during cranking mode is provided from starter relay via the fuel pump relay. After the engine has started, control of the fuel pump is through the ignition signal. The fuel pump is sealed unit.

**Fuel Pump Relay** - When energized by the ignition switch and grounded by the ECU. The fuel pump relay provides battery voltage to the fuel pumps, injectors, idle stabilization control unit, oxygen sensor heating element and the power steering pressure switch.

# 1991 ENGINE PERFORMANCE
# Theory & Operation – Digifant (Cont.)

**Fuel Pressure Regulator** – The fuel pressure regulator is a sealed, spring loaded diaphragm with connection for intake manifold vacuum. Fuel pressure is maintained at about 36 psi (2.5 kg/cm²) pressure.

A connection for intake manifold vacuum provides a constant pressure differential which ensures that the amount of fuel injected is solely dependent upon injector open ON time. Excess fuel is returned to fuel tank. No service of pressure regulator is required. The pressure regulator is located on or near fuel rail.

## FUEL CONTROL

Data on engine temperature, engine speed, intake air volume, throttle position, exhaust oxygen content and intake air temperature are used by ECM to determine injection pulse width.

**Fuel Injectors** – A fuel rail links the fuel pressure regulator with the fuel injectors. Each cylinder is provided with a solenoid-operated injector which sprays fuel toward backside of each inlet valve. Each injector is energized through the ignition coil and grounded through the ECU to complete the circuit

Each injector is linked to a resistor (resistor may be external or integral with injector or ECU) to reduce operating voltage to 3 volts and to protect injectors from power surges. The ECU controls length of time each injector is open. The ON time of the injector governs the amount of fuel delivered. The injector delivers 1/2 the amount of fuel required for an operating cycle each time they open (twice per cycle).

**Fuel Pump After-Run Relay (Corrado)** – The purpose of the after-run fuel pump relay system is to reduce the chance of fuel vaporizing in fuel rail. Both transfer pump and fuel pump are used to recirculate fuel. The after-run relay switches the pumps on for 2 minutes after ignition is turned off or when under hood temperature exceeds 194° F (90° C) and fuel pressure is above 17 psi (1.2 kg/cm²). The pumps operate a maximum of 8 minutes.

## IDLE SPEED

***NOTE: On Vanagon, idle stabilizer valve is controlled by a separate idle stabilizer controller. See IDLE STABILIZATION CONTROL UNIT.***

**Auxiliary Air Regulator (Fox)** – When engine is cold, air is by-passed around throttle plates to raise engine RPM. As engine warms up, an electric heating element warms a bimetallic strip inside regulator gradually closing regulator.

**Idle Stabilization System (Fox)** – The idle stabilization system uses an idle air by-pass valve and an A/C by-pass valve on vehicles equipped with A/C. The idle air by-pass valve opens to compensate for engine RPM changes at idle. The A/C by-pass valve opens when A/C is activated.

**Digital Idle Stabilization (DIS) (Fox)** – In addition to the idle stabilization, the ECU is equipped with DIS. If engine RPM changes during idle due to different engine loads, the DIS will adjust engine RPM by adjusting ignition timing to maintain a stable idle speed.

**Idle Stabilization System (Except Fox & Vanagon)** – The idle stabilization system is ECU controlled. If engine speed varies from a predetermined RPM, the idle stabilizer will adjust engine RPM accordingly.

# IGNITION SYSTEM

## ELECTRONIC IGNITION SYSTEM

The Hall Effect sending unit in the distributor uses a shutter window wheel, mounted on the distributor shaft. The shutter blades pass in and out of the air gap of the hall effect sender, resulting in signal pulses. There is one shutter window for each engine cylinder.

Signals from distributor hall sender are sent to the ECU. The ECU sends a switching voltage signal to the ignition coil primary circuit to discharge secondary spark voltage.

## IGNITION TIMING CONTROL SYSTEM

**Ignition Timing Control** – Signals from distributor hall sender are sent to the ECU, which produces a pulsating signal to the ignition coil. This computed signal from ECU to ignition coil controls ignition timing according to engine load (airflow sensor signal), engine speed (Hall Effect signal) and engine coolant temperature.

# EMISSION SYSTEMS

**Evaporative Emissions System** – Fuel vapors are collected in the expansion tank. Liquid gasoline collects in expansion tank and flows back to the fuel tank through vent lines. *See Fig. 4.* When engine is not running, fuel vapors are drawn from tops of the expansion tanks, and flow into carbon canister, where vapors are stored.

After engine is started, the control valve is opened by throttle vacuum. Fresh air is drawn into bottom of the canister. Fuel vapors from the canister are drawn into the intake manifold.

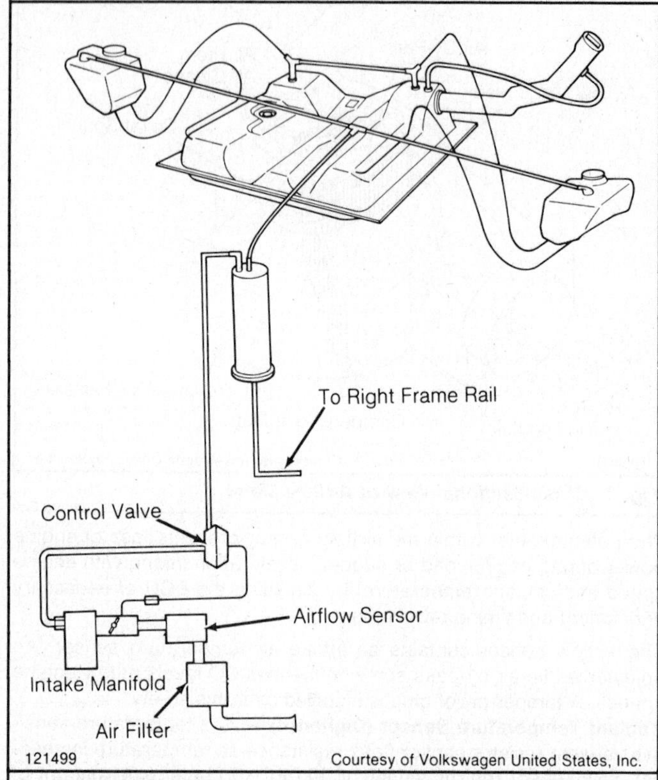


***Fig 4: Identifying Evaporative Emissions System Components***

**Thermostatic Air Cleaner** – During cold engine operation a regulator flap located inside air cleaner assembly is opened so engine can draw warmed air from around exhaust system. Vacuum from throttle valve operates regulator flap. The regulator flap is controlled by a temperature regulator valve located in upper part of air cleaner assembly. When engine becomes warm, temperature regulator valve should close causing regulator flap to close, stopping warm airflow from around exhaust.

# SELF-DIAGNOSTIC SYSTEM

## $O_2$ SENSOR WARNING LIGHT

All vehicles are equipped with an $O_2$ sensor warning light, located on the instrument panel. The light illuminates when a mileage counter reaches 60,000 miles (90,000 miles on Vanagon) indicating recommended $O_2$ sensor replacement and mileage counter reset.

## CHECK ENGINE LIGHT

**California** – California vehicles are equipped with a CHECK engine light and rocker switch on the instrument panel. The light illuminates when the ignition switch is turned to the ON position (for bulb check) and when engine management systems malfunction during normal engine operation. For additional information see appropriate SELF-DIAGNOSTICS article.

## MISCELLANEOUS CONTROLS

***NOTE: Although not considered true engine performance-related systems, some controlled devices may affect driveability if they malfunction.***

## CRANKCASE VENT LINE HEATING ELEMENT

A heating element is used in the crankcase vent line to prevent icing during cold engine operation, this element has a 5.5-mm hole in the restrictor plate. *See Fig. 5*. The circuitry to operate heating element is protected by an in-line 5-amp fuse located in the wiring connector box, in engine compartment.

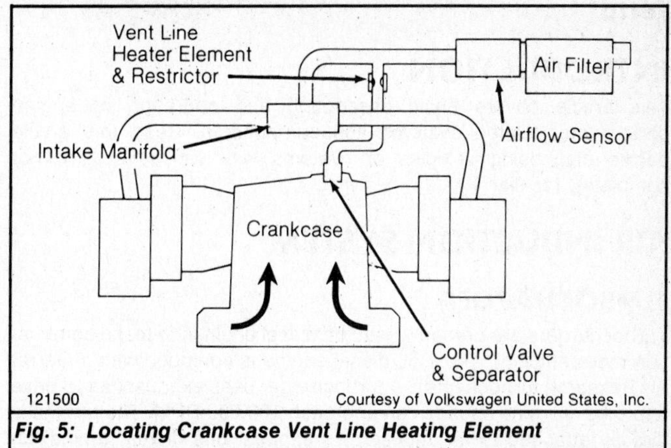


***Fig. 5: Locating Crankcase Vent Line Heating Element***

## COOLING FAN

**Cooling Fan Motor** - The cooling fan is either a 1- or 2-speed motor. If vehicle is equipped with single-speed motor, the fan comes on at 198-207°F (92-97°C) and off at 183-196°F (84-91°C). If equipped with a 2-speed motor, low speed of cooling fan should come on at 198-208°F (92-98°C) on vehicles without A/C, or 183-207°F (84-97°C) on vehicles with A/C. Low speed will shut off at 183-196°F (84-91°C) on all vehicles. High speed comes on at 210-226°F (99-108°C) on vehicles without A/C, or 201-226°F (94-108°C) on vehicles with A/C. High speed will shut off at 196-220°F (91-104°C) on all vehicles.

**After-Run Thermoswitch** - An after-run switch is used to help prevent fuel vaporization. The thermoswitch turns cooling fan on when temperatures in engine compartment exceed 230°F (110°C), and turns it off at 217°F (103°C).

# 1991 ENGINE PERFORMANCE
# Theory & Operation – Diesel

**Jetta**

## INTRODUCTION

This article covers basic description and operation of engine performance-related systems and components. Read this article before diagnosing vehicles or systems with which you are not completely familiar.

## AIR INDUCTION SYSTEM

### TURBOCHARGER

Turbochargers are primarily used on diesel engines to make combustion more efficient. The 1.6L diesel engine is equipped with a Garret Air Research turbocharger. A turbocharger uses exhaust gas to drive a turbine. Turbine speeds can approach 100,000 RPM. The turbine is directly attached to an impeller. As exhaust gas drives turbine, an impeller is driven at the same RPM. The impeller pressurizes air entering engine. By pressurizing air entering engine, this increases amount of intake air, making engine operation more efficient.

The turbocharger is lubricated with engine oil. Engine oil flows to the turbocharger bearings under pressure and is returned to engine through an oil line attached to bottom of turbocharger.

If turbocharger boost exceeds a predetermined amount, a poppet valve in the wastegate is opened. With poppet valve opened, exhaust gas by-passes turbo and flows directly into exhaust system. The wastegate limits turbocharger RPM and boost pressure. *See Fig. 1.*

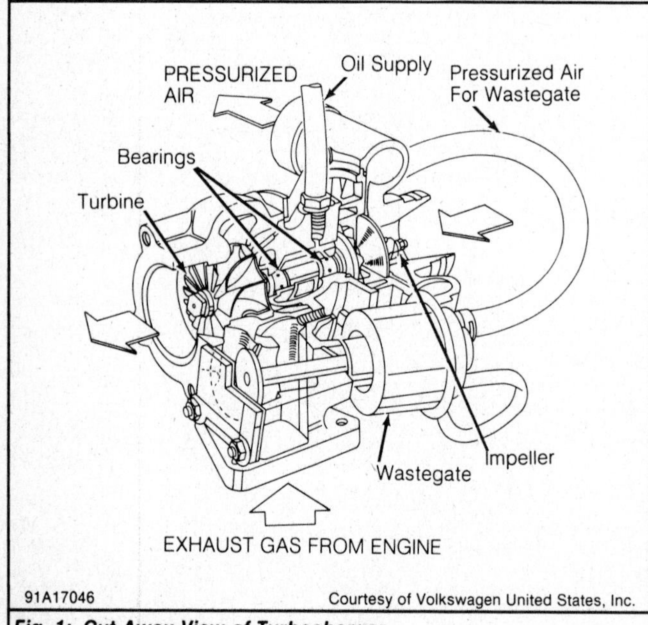


***Fig. 1: Cut-Away View of Turbocharger***

Excess turbocharger boost can cause engine damage. If wastegate malfunctions a blow-off valve will act as a safety device. The blow-off valve opens when boost pressure exceeds 11.5-12.2 psi (.81-.85 kg/cm²). Excess boost is vented to air intake pipe between air cleaner and turbocharger.

## FUEL SYSTEM

### FUEL DELIVERY

The injection pump draws fuel from fuel tank through fuel filter. It distributes, meters, pressurizes and times fuel to fuel injectors. Excess fuel from injection pump and injectors returns to fuel tank through a return line. *See Fig. 2.* Diesel fuel cools and lubricates injection pump and injectors. Circulating diesel fuel aids in warming fuel in tank and fuel lines to prevent waxing in cold weather.

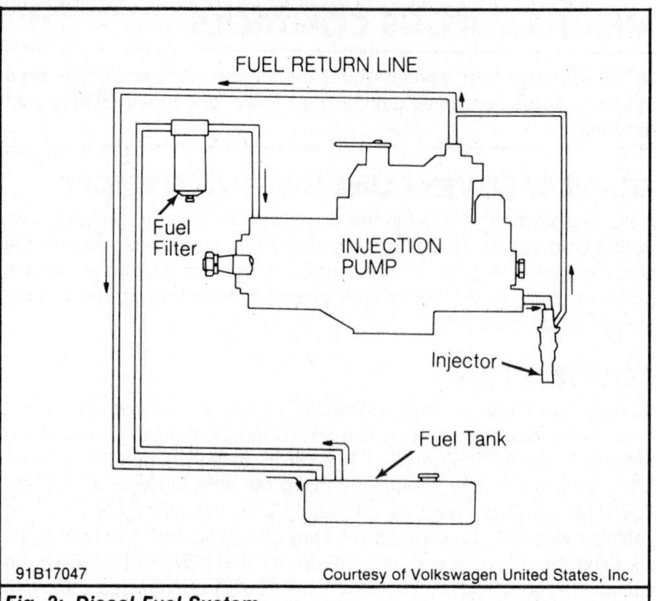


***Fig. 2: Diesel Fuel System***

### FUEL CONTROL

**Fuel Delivery Valves** – Fuel delivery valves are located on injection pump. Their main function is to ensure fuel injectors close quickly after injecting fuel. This prevents fuel dribble, which can cause pre-ignition problems and high emissions. *See Fig. 3.*

When fuel injection starts, the delivery valve opens allowing pressurized fuel from injection pump to flow to fuel injectors. As fuel injection ends, the fuel delivery valve closes, trapping fuel in the injection line. The force of a spring inside fuel delivery valve pushes valve further into its seat causing trapped fuel to expand. This sudden drop in pressure, caused by expanding fuel, allows fuel injector to snap shut.

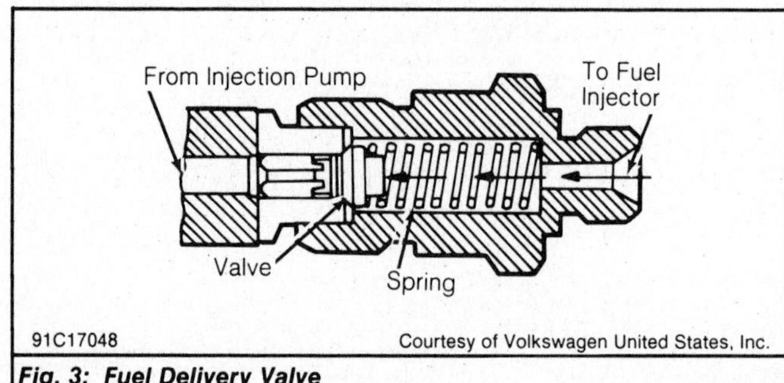


***Fig. 3: Fuel Delivery Valve***

**Fuel Injectors** – Fuel injectors are located in the swirl chambers. They are protected from combustion chamber temperatures by a heat shield. As fuel delivery valves open, fuel pressure from injection pump forces the needle up against spring pressure. Fuel injector sprays a cone-shaped spray of fuel at the precise time ignition is to occur. A small amount of fuel bleeds around injector needle to cool injector. This fuel is then circulated back to fuel tank. *See Fig. 4.*

**Fuel Shutoff Solenoid** – The fuel shutoff solenoid is located on injection pump. With ignition switch on, voltage is supplied to fuel shutoff solenoid, energizing solenoid open. When solenoid is open, fuel is allowed to flow from vane pump (inside injection pump) to fuel delivery valves.

If fuel shutoff solenoid sticks closed (or doesn't open because no voltage is reaching solenoid), vehicle will not start. If fuel shutoff solenoid sticks open, engine will continue to run even when ignition is switched off. *See Fig. 5.*

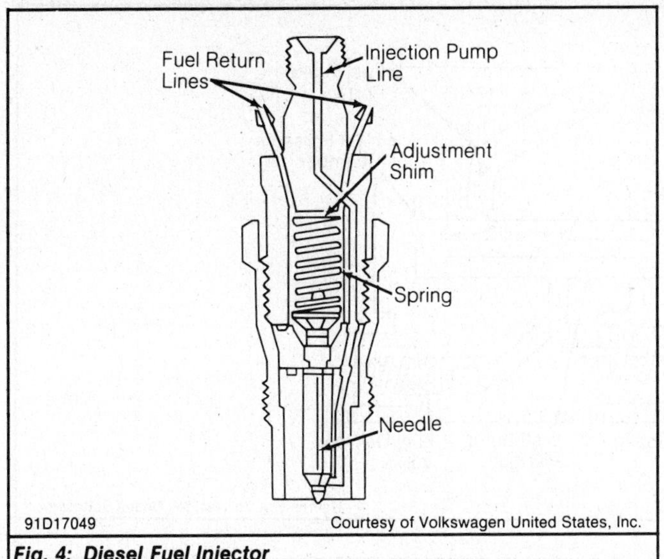


*Fig. 4: Diesel Fuel Injector*

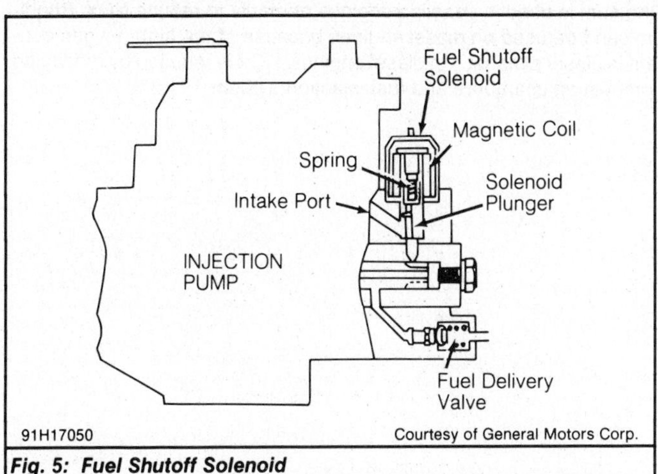


*Fig. 5: Fuel Shutoff Solenoid*

**Glow Plugs** – Glow plugs are located in swirl chamber. Battery voltage is applied to glow plugs to help with cold engine starting by preheating swirl chamber. When glow plugs are energized, glow plug temperature can reach 538°F (1000°C) or more.

**Glow Plug Relay** – The glow plug relay controls glow plug on-time. The glow plug relay performs 3 functions:

- Pre-Glow – Pre-heating time with ignition switch on.
- After-Glow – Pre-heating time with ignition switch on after glow plug light goes out (after glow lasts a few seconds).
- Cranking Glow – Pre-heating time with ignition switch on and engine in cranking mode.

**Injection Pump** – Injection pump is a single-plunger mechanical pump. It distributes fuel to fuel injectors in correct firing order, meters fuel according to engine load and speed, pressurizes fuel, and precisely times fuel delivery. *See Fig. 6*. The injection pump uses a centrifugal governor to limit engine speed to 5400 RPM.

The maintenance-free injection pump is belt driven at one half crankshaft speed. It is lubricated by the diesel fuel passing through it. Clean fuel is essential for trouble-free pump operation.

The injection pump driveshaft turns the vane pump, cam plate and distributor plunger. Springs hold cam plate and distributor plunger against 4 rollers, allowing plunger to turn and move back and forth.

When an intake port on plunger is in line with a filling port in pump body, fuel from vane pump fills the high pressure chamber. The cam plate pushes the plunger squeezing fuel into the high pressure chamber. High pressure chamber pressure can reach approximately 1800 psi (126.6 kg/cm²). *See Fig. 7*.

As plunger continues to turn, outlet ports align with injection ports in pump body. The delivery valve opens under pressure, supplying fuel to fuel injector. Ports in injection pump are arranged so injectors receive fuel in correct firing order.

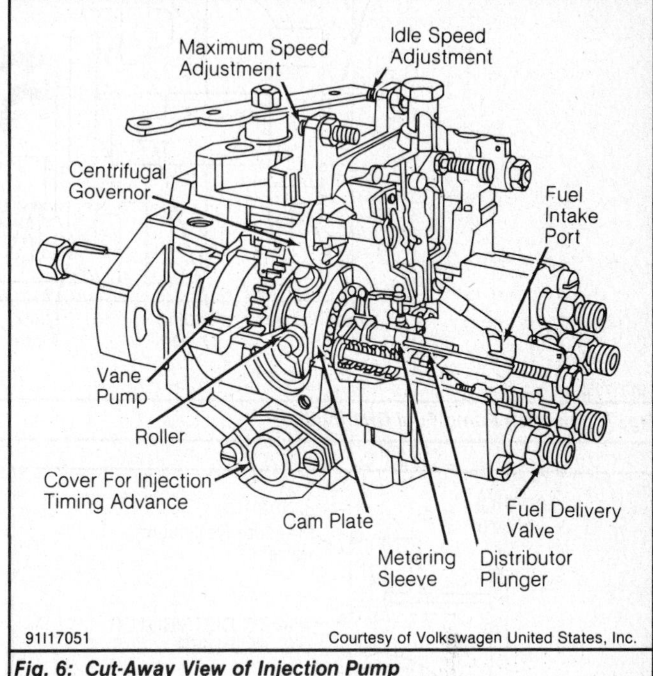


*Fig. 6: Cut-Away View of Injection Pump*

**Manual Injection Pump Shutoff** – On vehicles equipped with an automatic transmission, the injection pump will have a manual injection pump shutoff lever. Shutoff lever is located on top rear of injection pump. If fuel shutoff solenoid malfunctions, engine can be shut down by turning shutoff lever.

**Temperature Sensor** – The temperature sensor is connected to a time circuit for glow plug relay. It determines if glow plug relay gets activated and pre-heat time.

**Injection Vane Pump** – The injection vane pump is located inside injection pump. It draws fuel from fuel tank through fuel filter into injection pump. Vane pump is driven from injection pump driveshaft.

Centrifugal force holds vanes against walls of pressure chamber as rotor spins. This squeezes fuel trapped between vanes forcing it toward distributor plunger. Injection vane pump supplies a constant fuel quantity per revolution.

Fuel pressure in pressure chamber is regulated by a pressure regulating valve between 44-102 psi (3.1-7.2 kg/cm²). Fuel pressure depends upon engine load and speed conditions. *See Fig. 8*.

**Water Separator** – The water separator is located under vehicle in front of fuel tank on right side. It is connected to fuel supply line between fuel tank and fuel filter. The water separator stops and retains any water that may be present in fuel.

When water contamination reaches a predetermined level inside water separator, an internal sensor illuminates glow plug indicator on instrument panel continuously. Water can be drained from water separator by opening a drain valve on bottom of unit. Fuel filter is also equipped with a water drain valve, which should be drained at normal maintenance intervals.

## EMISSION SYSTEMS

### CATALYTIC CONVERTER

An oxidation catalyst is used to lower carbon monoxide by 90 percent and hydrocarbon compounds by 65 percent. The diesel catalyst uses platinum as a catalyst instead of rhodium, as used in gasoline engines.

# 1991 ENGINE PERFORMANCE
# Theory & Operation – Diesel (Cont.)

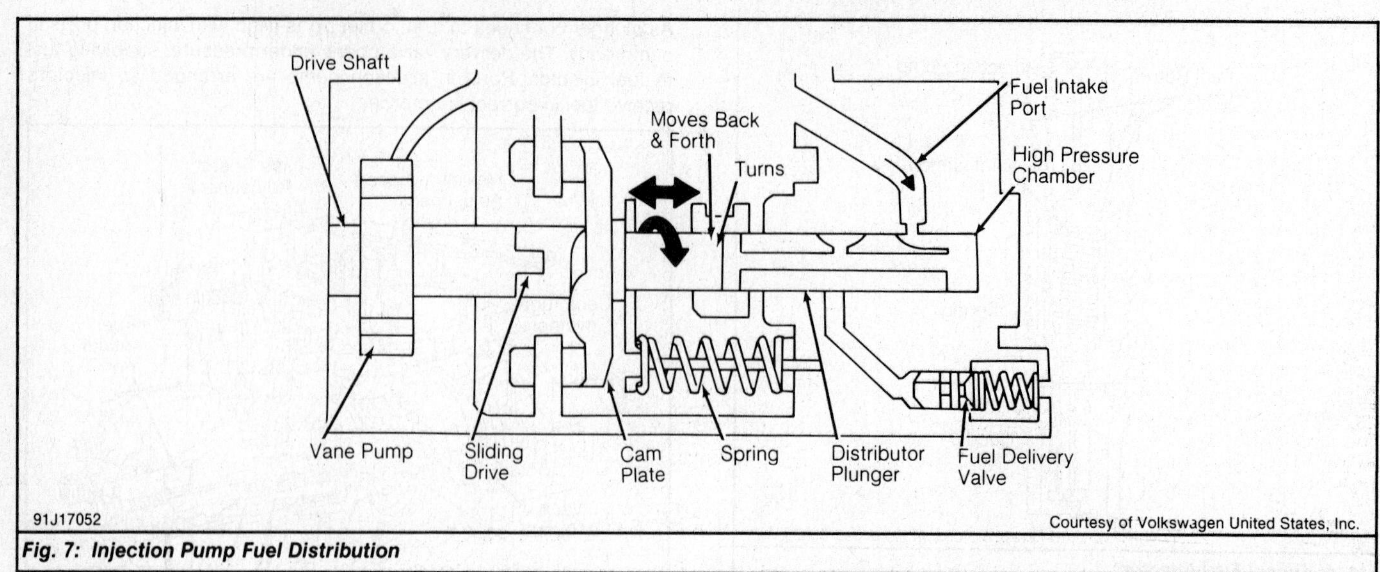


*Fig. 7: Injection Pump Fuel Distribution*

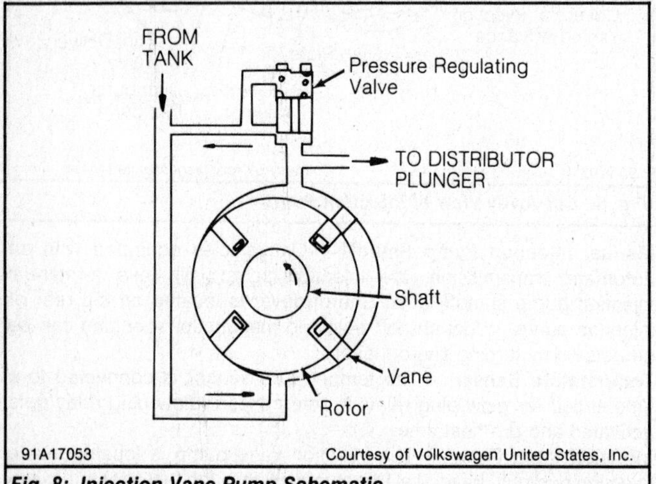


*Fig. 8: Injection Vane Pump Schematic*

Rhodium is used in gasoline engines primarily to reduce NOx. Rhodium can't be used on diesel engines because of the high oxygen content in diesel exhaust. On diesel engines, NOx is reduced by modifying combustion chambers and fuel injection system.

# 1991 ENGINE PERFORMANCE
# Basic Diagnostic Procedures

**Cabriolet, Corrado, Fox, Golf GL, GTI, Jetta, Jetta GLi, Passat, Vanagon**

## INTRODUCTION

The following diagnostic steps will help prevent overlooking a simple problem. This is also where to begin diagnosis for a no-start condition.

The first step in diagnosing any driveability problem is verifying the customer's complaint with a test drive under the conditions the problem reportedly occurred.

Before entering self-diagnostics (if equipped), perform a careful and complete visual inspection. Most engine control problems result from mechanical breakdowns, poor electrical connections, or damaged/misrouted vacuum hoses. Before condemning the computerized system, perform each test listed in this article.

***NOTE: Perform all voltage tests with a Digital Volt-Ohmmeter (DVOM) with a minimum 10-megohm input impedance, unless stated otherwise in test procedure.***

## PRELIMINARY INSPECTION & ADJUSTMENTS

### VISUAL INSPECTION

Visually inspect all electrical wiring, looking for chafed, stretched, cut or pinched wiring. Ensure electrical connectors fit tightly and are not corroded. Ensure vacuum hoses are properly routed and are not pinched or cut. See VACUUM DIAGRAMS article to verify routing and connections (if necessary). Inspect air induction system for possible vacuum leaks.

### MECHANICAL INSPECTION

**Compression** - Check engine mechanical condition with a compression gauge, vacuum gauge, or an engine analyzer. See engine analyzer manual for specific instructions.

***WARNING: DO NOT use ignition switch during compression tests on fuel injected vehicles. Use a remote starter to crank engine. Fuel injectors on many models are triggered by ignition switch during cranking mode, which can create a fire hazard or contaminate the engine's oiling system.***

***ENGINE COMPRESSION***

| Application | psi ($kg/cm^2$) |
|---|---|
| Normal Compression Pressure | |
| 1.8L | |
| Except Corrado | 131-174 (9-12) |
| Corrado | 116-174 (8-12) |
| 2.0L & 2.1L | 145-189 (10-13) |
| Minimum Compression Pressure | |
| 1.8L | |
| Except Corrado & Fox | 109 (8) |
| Corrado | 87 (6) |
| Fox | 102 (7) |
| 2.0L | 109 (8) |
| 2.1L | 116 (8) |
| Maximum Variation Between Cylinders | |
| All Models | 44 (3) |

**Exhaust System Backpressure** - The exhaust system can be checked with a vacuum or pressure gauge. Remove $O_2$ sensor or air injection check valve (if equipped). Connect a 0-5 psi pressure gauge and operate engine at 2500 RPM. If exhaust system backpressure is greater than 1 3/4 - 2 psi, exhaust system or catalytic converter is plugged.

If a vacuum gauge is used, connect vacuum gauge hose to intake manifold vacuum port and start engine. Observe vacuum gauge. Open throttle part way and hold steady. If vacuum gauge reading slowly drops after stabilizing, check exhaust system for restriction.

## FUEL SYSTEM

***FUEL SYSTEM APPLICATION***

| Application | Fuel System |
|---|---|
| 1.8L | |
| Except Corrado | AFC-Digifant |
| Corrado | Digifant |
| 2.0L | CIS-E Motronic |
| 2.1L | AFC-Digifant |

### FUEL PRESSURE

Basic diagnosis of fuel system should begin with determining fuel system pressure.

***WARNING: ALWAYS relieve fuel pressure before disconnecting any fuel injection-related component. DO NOT allow fuel to contact engine or electrical components.***

**CIS-E Motronic - 1)** Ensure ignition is off. Wrap a shop rag around fuel distributor port near cold start valve. Slowly loosen distributor port near cold start valve to release fuel pressure. Connect fuel pressure gauge between fuel distributor port and end of fuel line to cold start valve. Disconnect differential pressure regulator harness connector.

**2)** Start engine and let it run. System fuel pressure should 89-96 psi (6.3-6.7 $kg/cm^2$). If system fuel pressure is lower than specification, perform fuel volume check. If fuel volume is okay, replace fuel pressure regulator.

**3)** If fuel pressure is greater than specification, remove return hose from pressure regulator and place in a container. Repeat test. If system pressure is okay, check for restricted fuel return line. If pressure is incorrect, replace fuel pressure regulator.

**4)** Turn ignition off. After 10 minutes, residual pressure should be 48 psi (3.4 $kg/cm^2$). After 20 minutes, residual pressure should be 46 psi (3.2 $kg/cm^2$). If system fuel pressure is low, check fuel pump check valve, sensor plate free play, fuel distributor "O" rings and seats. Replace if necessary. If these components are okay, replace fuel pressure regulator.

**Digifant (Except Vanagon) - 1)** Ensure ignition is off. Wrap a shop rag around service port on fuel plenum. Slowly loosen service port on fuel plenum to release fuel pressure. Install fuel pressure gauge at service port on fuel plenum. Fuel pressure gauge must have reading range of 0-50 psi. Start engine and allow it to idle. System fuel pressure should be approximately 36 psi (2.5 $kg/cm^2$).

**2)** Disconnect vacuum hose from top of fuel pressure regulator. Fuel pressure should increase to approximately 44 psi (3 $kg/cm^2$). Turn engine off. After 10 minutes, residual pressure should be 29 psi (2 $kg/cm^2$). If system pressure is too high, replace fuel pressure regulator.

**3)** If residual pressure is too low, operate engine until system pressure builds up, then pinch off Blue fuel return line. If pressure holds, replace the fuel regulator. If fuel pressure is low, check the following for leaks.

- Fuel Lines
- Fuel Injectors
- Fuel Pump Check Valve

**Digifant (Vanagon) - 1)** Remove fuel pump relay. Start engine. Operate engine until it stalls. Crank engine to ensure all fuel pressure is relieved. Install Fuel Pressure Gauge (VW 1318) at fuel supply hose 3-way "T" connector. *See Fig. 1.* Turn ignition on. Ensure there are no fuel leaks.

**2)** Start engine. With engine idling, minimum pressure should be 29 psi (2 $kg/cm^2$). Remove vacuum hose from fuel pressure regulator. Fuel pressure should increase to 36 psi (2.5 $kg/cm^2$).

**3)** Turn engine off. After 10 minutes, residual pressure should be 29-36 psi (2-2.5 $kg/cm^2$). If fuel pressure is incorrect, check for restricted fuel lines, defective fuel pump, or weak control pressure regulator. If these items are okay, go to MAIN FUEL PUMP VOLUME CHECK.

# 1991 ENGINE PERFORMANCE
# Basic Diagnostic Procedures (Cont.)

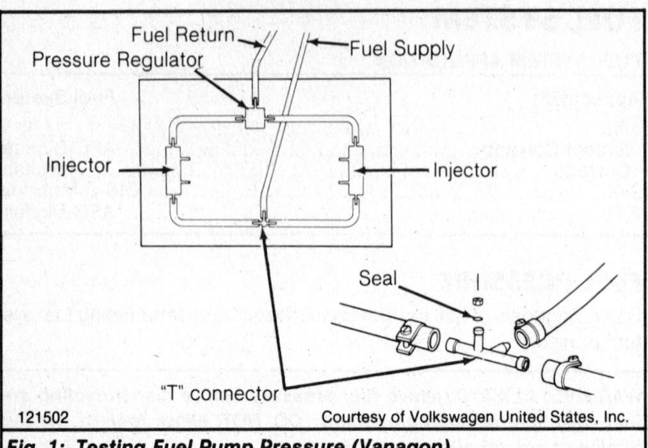


*Fig. 1: Testing Fuel Pump Pressure (Vanagon)*

## TRANSFER PUMP CHECK

**Transfer Pump Fuel Volume Check** – **1)** Turn ignition off. To check transfer pump (in tank), remove rear seat. Remove fuel sending unit access cover. Disconnect ignition coil secondary wire and jumper to ground. With transmission in Neutral, crank engine for 3-4 seconds. While starter is turning and for a few seconds afterwards, an audible sound should be heard at the pump. If sound is not heard, go to next step. If sound is heard, go to step **4)**.

**2)** Remove fuel pump relay from relay panel. On Corrado and Passat, activate fuel pumps using Remote Control (VAG1348/3A). On all other models, activate fuel pumps using Remote Control (US4480/3). On all models, if pump does not operate, remove transfer pump wire harness connector. *See Fig. 2*.

**3)** Using test light, check voltage between middle wire and outer Brown wire of fuel pump connector for Digifant fuel system, or between Brown wire and Red/Yellow wire for CIS-E fuel system. If voltage is present, replace transfer pump. If voltage is not present, repair open or short circuit in wiring.

**4)** Remove fuel pump relay jumper wire. Disconnect and plug transfer pump output hose. Attach a hose to pump outlet connector and place other end of hose in a graduated container. Activate fuel pump for 10 seconds.

**5)** Minimum fuel flow should be 10 ounces (.3 liter). If fuel flow is low, check fuel tank filter for restriction. If fuel tank filter is okay, replace transfer pump.

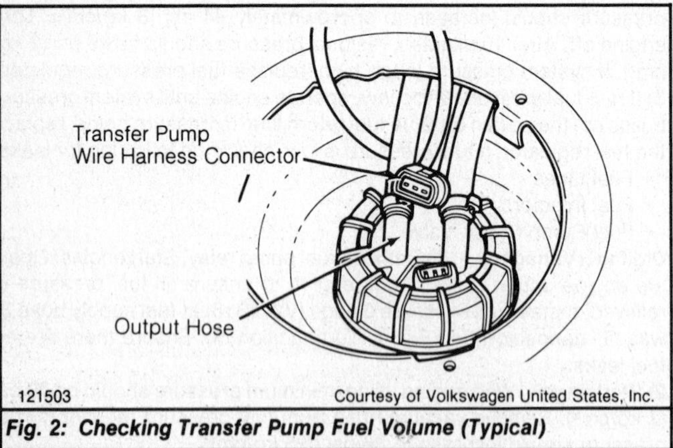


*Fig. 2: Checking Transfer Pump Fuel Volume (Typical)*

## MAIN FUEL PUMP VOLUME CHECK

***NOTE: Before testing main fuel pump, check transfer pump. See TRANSFER PUMP CHECK in this article.***

**Cabriolet, Fox, Golf & Jetta** – Remove fuel pump relay from relay panel. Activate fuel pumps using Remote Control (US4480/3). Activate fuel pumps for 30 seconds. Compare fuel volume with values in FUEL PUMP PERFORMANCE table.

**Corrado, GTI, Jetta GLI & Passat** – Remove fuel pump relay from relay panel. On Corrado and Passat, activate fuel pumps using Remote Control (VAG1348/3A). On GTI and Jetta GLI, activate fuel pumps using Remote Control (US4480/3). On all models, measure voltage being applied to fuel pump when activating with remote control. Record voltage. Fuel volume is relational to voltage applied to fuel pumps. Activate fuel pumps for 30 seconds. Compare volume with values in FUEL PUMP PERFORMANCE table.

**Vanagon** – **1)** Remove return line from pressure regulator located in engine compartment, on left side. Push a piece of hose onto open connection of pressure regulator. Insert hose into a 1-quart (1 liter) graduated container.

**2)** Remove fuel pump relay from relay panel. Activate fuel pumps using Remote Control (US4480/3). Activate fuel pumps for 30 seconds. Compare volume with values in FUEL PUMP PERFORMANCE table.

***FUEL PUMP PERFORMANCE***

| Application | Pressure psi ($kg/cm^2$) | Min. Vol. in 30 Sec. Pts. (L) |
|---|---|---|
| Cabriolet, Fox, | | |
| Golf & Jetta | 29-36 (2.0-2.5) | 1.0 (.5) |
| Vanagon | 33-39 (2.3-2.7) | 1.0 (.5) |
| Corrado & Passat | | |
| 10 Volts | N/A | 1.0 (.460) |
| 11 Volts | N/A | 1.3 (.620) |
| 12 Volts | N/A | 1.6 (.750) |
| GTI & Jetta GLI | | |
| 10 Volts | N/A | .8 (.375) |
| 11 Volts | N/A | 1.1 (.520) |
| 12 Volts | N/A | .4 (.675) |

# IGNITION CHECKS

***NOTE: Ignition checks are divided according to fuel system.***

## SPARK TEST

**1)** Using an ohmmeter, check resistance of each spark plug wire. See HIGH TENSION WIRE RESISTANCE table. Check for a strong Blue spark at coil wire and each spark plug wire by holding wire terminal 5/16" from ground while cranking engine.

***HIGH TENSION WIRE RESISTANCE***

| Application | Ohms |
|---|---|
| **1.8L** | |
| Except Fox | |
| Coil Wire Only | [2] |
| Coil Wire With Connector | 1600-2400 |
| Spark Plug Wire/ Connector | 4000-6000 |
| Suppressor [1] | 600-1400 |
| Fox | |
| Coil Wire With Connectors | 1600-2400 |
| Spark Plug Wire With Connectors | 4800-7200 |
| Spark Plug Connector | 4000-6000 |
| Suppressor | 800-1200 |
| **2.0L** | |
| Coil Wire With Connectors | 1600-2400 |
| Spark Plug Wire With Connectors | 4800-7200 |
| Spark Plug Connector | 4000-6000 |
| Suppressor [1] | 800-1200 |
| **2.1L** | |
| Coil Wire With Connectors | 1200-2800 |
| Spark Plug Wire/Connector | 4600-7400 |
| Spark Plug Connector | 4000-6000 |
| Suppressor [1] | 600-1400 |

[1] – Suppressor is located between ignition wire and distributor cap.
[2] – Check for continuity.

# 1991 ENGINE PERFORMANCE
# Basic Diagnostic Procedures (Cont.)

**2)** Disconnect and inspect all related ignition system connectors and harness. Clean or repair if necessary. If related connectors and harness are okay, remove negative battery cable. Disconnect secondary and primary leads from ignition coil.
**3)** Using ohmmeter, check primary resistance between primary terminals of coil. Check secondary resistance between coil secondary terminal and primary positive terminal. Replace coil if readings are not within specifications. See IGNITION COIL RESISTANCE table.

## IGNITION COIL

***IGNITION COIL RESISTANCE - Ohms @ 68°F (20°C)***

| Application | Primary | Secondary |
|---|---|---|
| All Models | .5-.7 | 3000-4000 |

## DISTRIBUTOR

**Hall Effect Sender - 1)** Remove coil secondary and attach to ground. Disconnect Hall Effect sender harness connector at distributor. Using a LED Test Light (US 1115), check for voltage between outer terminals of connector. *See Figs. 3 and 4*. With ignition on, light should be on. If light is on, go to step **2)**. If light is not on, check wiring for short or open circuit. If wiring is okay, replace ignition control unit.
**2)** Reconnect Hall Effect sender harness connector. Pull back Hall Effect sender boot to expose contact terminals. Apply LED Test Light (US 1115) probe to center contact and battery positive terminal. *See Fig. 3*. Observe test light while cranking engine. If test light blinks, Hall Effect sender is okay. If light does not blink, replace Hall Effect sender.

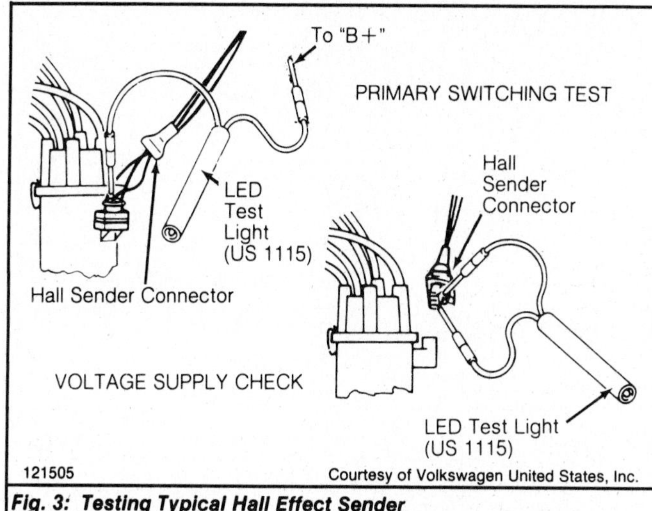


***Fig. 3: Testing Typical Hall Effect Sender***

**Voltage Supply & Ground To Hall Effect Sender - 1)** With ignition off, disconnect Hall Effect sender harness connector. Using a voltmeter, check for voltage between outer terminals No. 1 and No. 3. *See Fig. 4*. Turn ignition on. There should be a minimum of 9 volts on vehicles with CIS-E fuel system, or 10 volts on vehicles with Digifant fuel system.
**2)** If there is no voltage, check for open wire between terminal No. 3 of Hall Effect sender connector and ECU. Also check for voltage between terminal No. 1 of Hall Effect sender and ground. Repair open and recheck.

## POWER STAGE

***POWER STAGE APPLICATION***

| Application | Fuel System |
|---|---|
| 1.8L | |
| Corrado | Digifant |
| Fox | Digifant |
| Golf, Jetta & GTI | Digifant I |
| 2.0L | CIS-E |

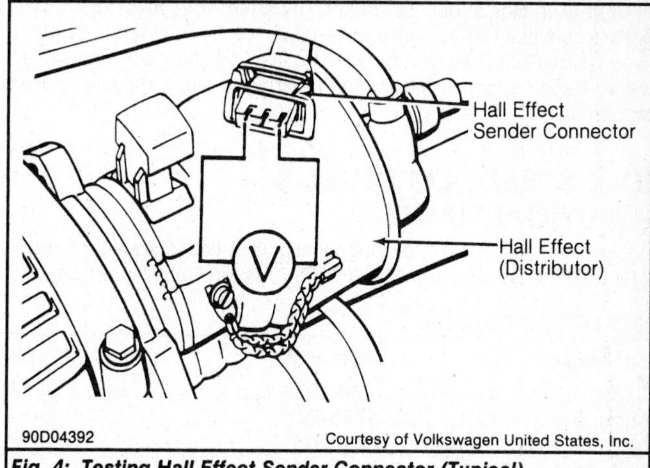


***Fig. 4: Testing Hall Effect Sender Connector (Typical)***

**Voltage Supply & Ground To Power Stage - 1)** With ignition off, disconnect coil power stage harness connector. Connect a voltmeter to terminals No. 1 and No. 3. *See Fig. 5*.
**2)** Turn ignition on. Ensure battery voltage is present. Turn ignition off. If voltage is not present, check for open wire from fuse box to terminal No. 1, or open from terminal No. 3 to ground. Repair open wire and recheck.

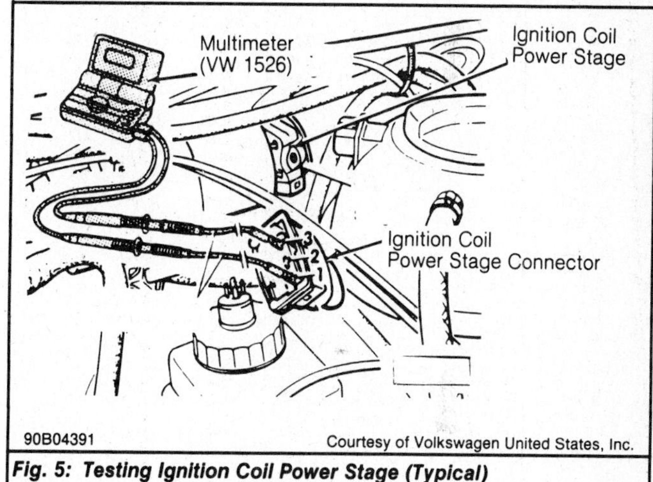


***Fig. 5: Testing Ignition Coil Power Stage (Typical)***

## HALL CONTROL UNIT

**Cabriolet, Fox, Golf, Jetta, & GTI With Digifant II - 1)** Perform spark test. See SPARK TEST under IGNITION CHECKS. If secondary spark is present, ignition control unit is okay. If secondary spark is not present, turn ignition off. Disconnect ignition control unit wire harness connector. Turn ignition on. Using a voltmeter, measure voltage between terminal No. 2 (–) and terminal No. 4 (+) of connector. *See Fig. 6*.

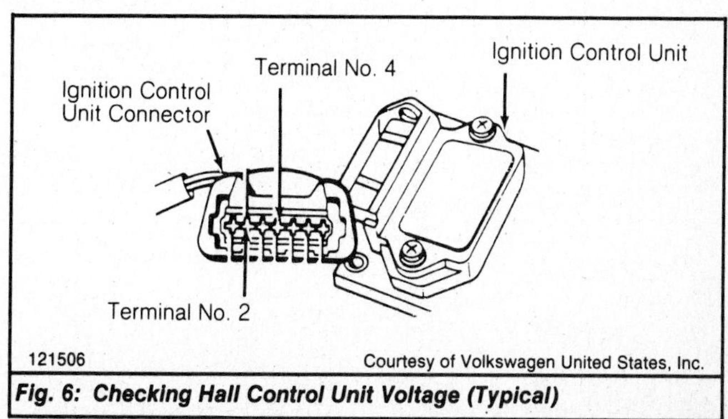


***Fig. 6: Checking Hall Control Unit Voltage (Typical)***

# 1991 ENGINE PERFORMANCE
# Basic Diagnostic Procedures (Cont.)

**2)** Battery voltage should be present. If battery voltage is not present, ensure continuity exists between terminal No. 2 and ground. Continuity must also exist between terminal No. 4 and ignition coil positive terminal. Repair wiring if necessary. If wiring is okay, replace ignition control unit.

## IDLE SPEED, CO LEVEL & IGNITION TIMING

Ensure idle speed, CO level and base ignition timing are set to specification. If necessary, see ON-VEHICLE ADJUSTMENTS article.

***IDLE SPEED & CO LEVEL***

| Application | Idle RPM | CO Level % |
|---|---|---|
| Cabriolet | 750-850 [1] | .3-1.1 |
| Corrado | 750-850 | .3-1.1 |
| Fox | 875-925 | [2] 1.2-1.5 |
| Golf, Jetta & GTI | | |
| 1.8L (Digifant) | 750-850 | .3-1.1 |
| 2.0L (CIS-E) | N/A [3] | .2-1.2 |
| Passat | 700-900 [3] | .2-1.2 |
| Vanagon | 830-930 | .3-1.1 |

[1] – Disconnect Blue coolant temperature sensor connector.
[2] – Clamp crankcase breather hose near emission control valve.
[3] – Not adjustable.

***IGNITION TIMING (Degrees BTDC @ RPM)***

| Application | Checking | Adjusting |
|---|---|---|
| Except Vanagon [1] | 4-8 @ 2000-2500 | 5-7 @ 2000-2500 |
| Vanagon [1] | 3-7 @ 2000-2500 | 4-6 @ 2000-2500 |

[1] – Disconnect coolant temperature sensor.

## SUMMARY

If no faults were found while performing BASIC DIAGNOSTIC PROCEDURES, go to TROUBLE SHOOTING – NO CODES article for diagnosis by symptom (i.e., ROUGH IDLE, NO START, etc.) or intermittent diagnostic procedures.

# 1991 ENGINE PERFORMANCE
# Trouble Shooting – No Codes

## Cabriolet, Corrado, Fox, Golf GL, GTI, Jetta, Jetta GLI, Passat, Vanagon

## INTRODUCTION

Before diagnosing symptoms or intermittent faults, perform steps in BASIC DIAGNOSTIC PROCEDURES article. Use this article to diagnose driveability problems existing when a hard fault code is not present or vehicle is not equipped with a self-diagnostic system.

***NOTE: Some driveability problems may have been corrected by manufacturer with a revised computer calibration chip or computer control unit. Check with manufacturer for latest chip or computer application.***

Symptom checks can direct the technician to malfunctioning component(s) for further diagnosis. A symptom should lead to a specific component, system test or an adjustment.

Use intermittent test procedures to locate driveability problems that DO NOT occur when the vehicle is being tested. These test procedures should also be used if a soft (intermittent) trouble code was present, but no problem was found during self-diagnostic testing.

***NOTE: For specific testing procedures, see SYSTEM & COMPONENT TESTING article. For specifications, see ON-VEHICLE ADJUSTMENTS or SERVICE & ADJUSTMENT SPECIFICATIONS article.***

## SYMPTOMS

### SYMPTOM DIAGNOSIS

Symptom checks cannot be used properly unless the problem is actually happening while the vehicle is being tested. To reduce diagnostic time, ensure steps in BASIC DIAGNOSTIC PROCEDURES article have been performed before attempting to diagnose a symptom. Symptoms available for diagnosis include the following.

- Will Not Start Or Starts Hard Cold (Cranks Okay)
- Will Not Start Or Starts Hard Hot (Cranks Okay)
- Engine Stalls Or Idles Rough
- Engine Misfires Or Hesitates
- Excessive Fast Idle
- Engine Hesitates On Acceleration
- Engine Lacks Power
- Poor Fuel Mileage
- Engine Dieseling
- Failed Emissions Test

### WILL NOT START OR STARTS HARD COLD (CRANKS OKAY)

- Check ignition fuse (if equipped).
- Check fuel pump fuse and fuel pump relay.
- Verify air intake system is unrestricted.
- Ensure fuel system pressure and volume are correct.
- Check cold start valve and thermo time switch operation.
- Ensure airflow sensor plate is in rest position. Adjust as necessary.
- Test coolant temperature sensor and wiring. Repair or replace as required.
- Check for poor ignition ground.
- Check for poor quality or contaminated fuel.
- Check condensation (water) in fuel tank causing fuel pump to freeze (cold climate).
- Check exhaust system for restriction.
- Test airflow meter. Replace if faulty.
- Ensure sufficient secondary spark is available.
- Check air induction system for cracks or restriction.
- Ensure vacuum hoses are not disconnected or damaged.
- Ensure fuel system residual pressure is correct.
- Ensure fuel injector operation is correct.
- Ensure EGR valve operation is correct and valve closes completely (if equipped).
- Check for cracks or poor connections at throttle body.
- Ensure ignition and valve timing are correct.
- Check ignition coil primary connections and wiring harness.
- Ensure ignition coil resistance is within specification.
- Check air temperature sensor operation (if equipped).
- Ensure electrical harness and connectors are not broken or loose.
- Ensure ECU or ignition control unit has correct voltage supply and is properly grounded.
- Ensure engine has sufficient compression.
- Inspect intake air components for leaking hoses, connections or cracks. Repair as required.

### WILL NOT START OR STARTS HARD HOT (CRANKS OKAY)

- Check ignition fuse (if equipped).
- Check fuel system fuse and fuel pump relay.
- Check for poor quality or contaminated fuel.
- Check condensation (water) in fuel tank causing fuel pump to freeze (cold climate).
- Check exhaust system for restriction.
- Check cold start valve and thermo time switch operation.
- Check fuel system and control system pressure. Replace pressure regulator if necessary.
- Check residual fuel pressure. Replace fuel pump check valve or fuel accumulator as necessary.
- Check oxygen sensor system operation.
- Ensure airflow sensor plate is in rest position. Adjust as necessary.
- Ensure injector spray patterns and volume are correct. Replace faulty injectors.
- Inspect fuel lines and connections for leaks.
- Check carbon canister solenoid valves (if equipped).
- Test airflow meter. Replace if faulty.
- Ensure sufficient secondary spark is available.
- Check air induction system for cracks or restriction.
- Check airflow sensor plate rest position.
- Ensure vacuum hoses are not disconnected or damaged.
- Ensure EGR valve operation is correct and valve closes completely (if equipped).
- Check for cracks or poor connections at throttle body.
- Ensure ignition and valve timing are correct.
- Check ignition coil primary connections and wiring harness.
- Ensure ignition coil resistance is within specification.
- Check air temperature sensor operation.
- Check coolant temperature sensor operation.
- Ensure electrical harness and connectors are not broken or loose.
- Ensure ECU or ignition control unit has correct voltage supply and is properly grounded.
- Ensure engine has sufficient compression.

### ENGINE STALLS OR IDLES ROUGH

- Check fuel system and control system pressure. Replace pressure regulator if necessary.
- Check cold start valve for leaking (engine warm).
- Ensure injector spray patterns and volume are correct. Replace faulty injectors.
- Test coolant temperature sensor and wiring. Repair or replace as required.
- Inspect intake air components for leaking hoses, connections or cracks. Repair as required.
- Ensure airflow sensor plate movement and rest position. Adjust as necessary.
- Test idle switch and idle air stabilizer valve.
- Perform system electrical checks.
- Check airflow meter. Replace if faulty.
- Ensure idle RPM is correct.
- Check auxiliary air by-pass regulator.
- Check fuel injector electrical connections.
- Use stethoscope to verify fuel injectors are operating.
- Ensure sufficient secondary spark is available in all cylinders.
- Verify vacuum hose routing is correct and there are no vacuum leaks.

# 1991 ENGINE PERFORMANCE
# Trouble Shooting – No Codes (Cont.)

- Check idle stabilizer operation.
- Check for EGR system malfunction (if equipped).
- Check $O_2$ sensor operation.
- Check for distortion or cracks in fuel injector(s) plastic connecting flange(s).
- Check for use of poor quality fuel containing insufficient cleaning additives. Prolonged use of poor quality fuel can cause injector clogging and carbon build-up on intake system.

## ENGINE MISFIRES OR HESITATES

**CIS-E Motronic**

- Ensure injector spray patterns and volume are correct. Replace faulty injectors.
- Check fuel system and control system pressure. Replace pressure regulator if necessary.
- Check Oxygen ($O_2$) sensor system operation.
- Check fuel lines and connections for leaks.
- Test coolant temperature sensor and wiring. Repair or replace as required.
- Check airflow meter and throttle switch. Replace if faulty.
- Ensure vacuum hoses are not disconnected or damaged.
- Ensure electrical harness connectors and wires are not broken or loose.
- Check cold start valve for leaking (engine warm).

**Digifant**

- Check airflow sensor flap and sensor resistance. Replace if faulty.
- Inspect intake air components for leaking hoses, connections or cracks. Repair as required.
- Test intake air preheating system. Replace faulty components as required.
- Check fuel system and control system pressure. Replace pressure regulator if necessary.
- Ensure vacuum hoses are not disconnected or damaged.
- Ensure electrical harness connectors and wires are not broken or loose.
- Check cold start valve for leaking (engine warm).
- Check coolant temperature sensor operation.
- Check Oxygen ($O_2$) sensor voltage output.

## EXCESSIVE FAST IDLE

- Inspect accelerator pedal and cable for worn parts or binding.
- Test idle switch (if equipped).
- Test auxiliary air regulator and replace if necessary (if equipped).
- Inspect throttle valve and adjust or replace as required.
- Check carbon canister solenoid valves (if equipped).
- Test idle boost valve system operation (if equipped). Replace faulty parts as necessary.
- Test coolant temperature sensor and wiring. Repair or replace as required.
- Check throttle cable adjustment.
- Verify vacuum hose routing is correct.
- Ensure there are no vacuum leaks.
- Check idle stabilizer operation (if equipped).
- Ensure fuel system pressure and volume are correct.
- Check auxiliary air by-pass regulator.
- Check cold start valve for leaking (engine warm).

## ENGINE HESITATES ON ACCELERATION

- Inspect intake air components for leaking hoses
- Check injector spray pattern. Check for faulty injectors.
- Check cold start valve for leaking (engine warm).
- Check airflow sensor plate movement. Replace fuel distributor as necessary.
- Check airflow sensor plate position. Adjust as necessary.
- Check fuel system and control system pressure. Replace pressure regulator if necessary.
- Test airflow sensor plate potentiometer. Adjust or replace as necessary.
- Perform system electrical checks.
- Check idle mixture CO adjustment. Adjust as necessary.

## ENGINE LACKS POWER

- Test coolant temperature sensor and wiring. Repair or replace as required.
- Check fuel system and control system pressure. Replace pressure regulator if necessary.
- Check throttle cable adjustment.
- Check throttle switch. Adjust or replace as necessary.
- Check airflow sensor screen for damage or incorrect installation (if equipped).
- Check ignition timing and knock sensor control (if equipped). Adjust as necessary.
- Check EGR system for correct operation (if equipped).
- Ensure base timing is correct and timing advance system is functional.
- Check transmission for correct downshift (auto. trans.)
- Check fuel tank filler tube for tampering of restrictor. If tampering has occurred, check catalytic converter for lead contamination and exhaust system restriction.
- Check for use of poor quality fuel containing insufficient cleaning additives. Prolonged use of poor quality fuel can cause injector clogging and carbon build-up on intake system.
- Inspect intake air element, housing, and preheating system.
- Check airflow sensor plate movement. Replace if necessary.

## POOR FUEL MILEAGE

- Ensure idle speed, base timing and timing advance are set to specifications.
- Check cold start valve for leaking (engine warm).
- Check fuel system and control system pressure. Replace pressure regulator if necessary.
- Check thermo time switch operation.
- Check airflow sensor voltage output.
- Check air induction system for leaks.
- Check fuel injector operation.
- Check coolant temperature sensor operation.
- Check Oxygen ($O_2$) sensor operation.

## ENGINE DIESELING

- Ensure ignition timing is set to specifications.
- Check for engine overheating.
- Check cold start valve for leaking (engine warm).
- Check for leaking injectors.
- Check airflow sensor plate/control plunger rest position (CIS-E Motronic). Adjust as necessary.
- Check carbon canister solenoid valve.
- Verify no leaks in exhaust system.

## FAILED EMISSIONS TEST

- Test lambda control system. Replace if faulty.
- Check air/fuel mixture. Adjust if necessary.
- Ensure air intake system is not restricted.
- Ensure engine is at normal operating temperature.
- Ensure fuel system pressure is correct.
- Check cold start valve for leaking (engine warm).
- Check thermo time switch operation.
- Verify base timing is correct.
- Check for correct PCV valve operation.
- Check crankcase for gasoline contamination.
- Check idle stabilizer operation.
- Check EGR system for correct operation (if equipped).
- Check vapor recovery system operation.
- Check operation of coolant temperature sensor.
- Check fuel tank filler tube for tampering of restrictor. If tampering has occurred, check catalytic converter for lead contamination and exhaust system restriction.
- Check for use of poor quality fuel containing insufficient cleaning additives. Prolonged use of poor quality fuel can cause injector clogging and carbon build-up on intake system.

## INTERMITTENTS

### INTERMITTENT PROBLEM DIAGNOSIS

Intermittent fault testing requires duplicating circuit or component failure to identify the problem. If necessary, monitor voltage or resistance values using a DVOM while attempting to reproduce conditions causing intermittent fault.

A status change on DVOM indicates a fault has been located. When monitoring voltage, ensure ignition switch is in ON position or engine is running. Ensure ignition switch is in OFF position or negative battery cable is disconnected when monitoring circuit resistance.

### TEST PROCEDURES

**Intermittent Simulation** – To reproduce the conditions creating an intermittent fault, use the following methods:

- Lightly vibrate component.
- Heat component.
- Wiggle or bend wiring harness.
- Spray component with water.
- Remove/apply vacuum source.

# 1991 ENGINE PERFORMANCE
# System & Component Testing

**Cabriolet, Corrado, Fox, Golf GL, GTI, Jetta, Jetta GLI, Passat, Vanagon**

## INTRODUCTION

Before testing separate components or systems, perform procedures in BASIC DIAGNOSTIC PROCEDURES article. Since many computer-controlled and monitored components set a trouble code if they malfunction, also perform procedures in SELF-DIAGNOSTICS article.

***NOTE: Testing individual components does not isolate shorts or opens. Perform all voltage tests with a Digital Volt-Ohmmeter (DVOM) with a minimum 10-megohm input impedance, unless stated otherwise in test procedure. Use ohmmeter to isolate wiring harness shorts or opens.***

## AIR INDUCTION SYSTEMS

### SUPERCHARGER

**Boost Pressure** - **1)** Before checking supercharger boost pressure, ensure engine idle speed is correct. See ON-VEHICLE ADJUSTMENTS article. Ensure engine oil temperature is 176°F (80°C). Check knock sensor operation. See KNOCK SENSOR under IGNITION SYSTEM.

**2)** Connect Pressure Gauge (VW 1397) to pressure regulator hose using "T" adapter. Open pressure gauge check valve to position "A" and start engine.

**3)** Remove harness connector from CO potentiometer and Blue connector from temperature sensor (in front flange on cylinder head). Accelerate to full throttle. Engine speed must increase periodically then drop (surge). Watch pressure gauge. Boost pressure must reach 8.7 psi (0.6 kg/cm²). If boost does not reach specification, check for leaks in air system and correct by-pass valve setting. Check supercharger.

### TURBOCHARGER

***NOTE: Faulty turbocharger is replaced as a unit. Wastegate is press-fit and not available separately.***

***WARNING: Turbocharger and related components operate at very high temperature. Always allow system to cool or use proper protective clothing to prevent severe burns.***

***CAUTION: Thoroughly clean all joints, pipe unions and connections before disconnecting or reconnecting turbocharger. Prevent dust and dirt contamination. Cover all components with dust-free paper, or seal in plastic bags. DO NOT use cloth or rags. Avoid nearby use of compressed air. DO NOT move vehicle or work in dusty conditions while turbocharger is open or removed.***

Wastegate and blow-off valve are both normally closed, opening only when boost pressure becomes too high. Not opening will allow turbocharger to create too much boost pressure, which can cause immediate and serious engine damage. Opening too soon will limit boost pressure and reduce engine power.

Before testing wastegate and blow-off valve regulating functions, inspect system for leaks and ensure control line to wastegate is not plugged, loose or leaking. To achieve valid test results, other engine performance factors, such as injection timing and valve clearance, should be within specification or adjusted correctly. Engine should be warmed to normal operating temperature for pressure tests.

Boost pressure specifications are "overpressure" values, given in relation to normal atmospheric pressure. For example, zero pressure on gauge is actually atmospheric pressure or 14.5 psi (1.02 kg/cm²) absolute pressure. A boost pressure specification of 10.2 psi (0.72 kg/cm²) as given in this test would be read as 10.2 psi (0.72 kg/cm²) on an overpressure gauge, or 24.7 psi (1.74 kg/cm²) on an absolute pressure gauge. Ensure identification of gauge type and, if necessary, convert specifications and readings to the same scale using PRESSURE CONVERSION GRAPH. *See Fig. 1.*

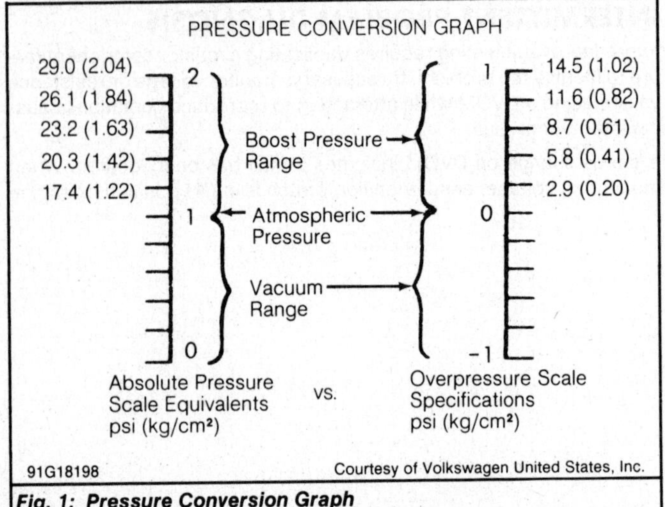


***Fig. 1: Pressure Conversion Graph***

**Testing Turbocharger Wastegate & Blow-Off Valve** - **1)** Using a "T" fitting, install a pressure gauge in air pressure line that links air intake manifold with boost enrichment device on fuel injection pump. Install a tachometer that can be seen from driver's seat. Place pressure gauge inside vehicle where it can be easily read from driver's seat. Ensure hose is not kinked or pinched. Start engine and open gauge's valve, if equipped.

**2)** Road test using brakes or steep hill to hold vehicle at 35 MPH with throttle fully open, in 2nd gear with manual transmission, or in drive range 1 with automatic transmission.

***WARNING: For safety during road test, it is advisable to have a helper read gauge or, if gauge is equipped with a valve, close valve at peak boost and record value later.***

**3)** If testing on a dynamometer, hold the engine at 4000 RPM with throttle fully open. Transmission should be in 3rd gear with a manual transmission, or in drive range 2 with an automatic transmission.

***CAUTION: To avoid unnecessary engine strain, road test or dynamometer measurement time should be limited to a maximum of 10 seconds.***

**4)** Boost pressure should be 9.3-10.4 psi (0.65-0.73 kg/cm²). If pressure indicated is greater, wastegate is faulty and turbocharger should be replaced. If maximum boost is lower, blow-off valve may be sticking open.

**5)** Disconnect blow-off valve outlet hose from intake air duct. Plug hose and secure plug with a hose clamp. Repeat test. Correct boost pressure at this point indicates that blow-off valve is faulty and should be replaced. Boost pressure still below specification indicates that turbocharger is faulty and should be replaced. SEE TURBOCHARGER BOOST PRESSURE table.

**Replacing Blow-Off Valve** - Allow engine to cool. Disconnect outlet hose from blow-off valve and loosen clamp securing valve to intake manifold. For installation, reverse removal procedure. Always use a new "O" ring.

***TURBOCHARGER BOOST PRESSURE***

| Mode | Pressure |
|---|---|
| Maximum Pressure, Regulated By Wastegate (Boost) | [1] 9.3-10.4 psi (0.65-0.73 kg/cm²) |
| Maximum Intake Manifold Pressure Allowed By Blow-Off Valve | [1] 11.2-12.6 psi (0.79-0.89 kg/cm²) |

[1] - Above atmospheric pressure.

## COMPUTERIZED ENGINE CONTROLS

***NOTE: To identify fuel system used on model being tested, see FUEL SYSTEM APPLICATION table.***

***FUEL SYSTEM APPLICATION***

| Application | Fuel System |
|---|---|
| Cabriolet 1.8L 8-Valve | [1] AFC-Digifant |
| Corrado 1.8L 8-Valve | [2] Digifant |
| Fox 1.8L 8-Valve | [1] AFC-Digifant |
| Golf GL 1.8L 8-Valve | [1] AFC-Digifant |
| GTI | |
| 1.8L 8-Valve Engine | AFC-Digifant |
| 2.0L 16-Valve Engine | CIS-E Motronic |
| Jetta | |
| 1.6L Diesel | [3] Mechanical Injection |
| 1.8L 8-Valve | [1] AFC-Digifant |
| Jetta GLI 2.0L 16-Valve | CIS-E Motronic |
| Passat 2.0L 16-Valve | CIS-E Motronic |
| Vanagon 2.1L | AFC-Digifant |

[1] California vehicles are equipped with Digifant.
[2] Supercharged engine.
[3] Vehicles with build dates through 12/90 will be equipped with 1.6L (ME) engine. Vehicles with build dates after 1/91 will be equipped with 1.6L (1V) engine.

## ELECTRONIC CONTROL UNIT (AFC-DIGIFANT)

***NOTE: Before checking ECU terminal voltages, check all terminals and connections for looseness or corrosion. Repair as needed, before continuing.***

**Ground Circuits** – Using Multimeter (US 1119), check resistance of ground connections for ECU. Remove ECU connector. Check continuity to ground on terminals No. 13 and 19. *See Fig. 4.* Resistance should be zero ohms. If resistance is not zero ohms, repair open or short in wiring.

**Power Circuits** – **1)** Turn ignition off. Disconnect ECU connector. Turn ignition on and, using a voltmeter, check for battery voltage between ECU connector terminals No. 13 (negative) and No. 14 (positive). *See Fig. 4.* If battery voltage is not present, repair wiring as required.

**2)** Check terminals No. 13 (negative) and No. 1 (positive) for battery voltage. If battery voltage is not present, check fuse No. 18 on fuse block. If fuse is okay, check wiring from ECU connector to fuse box for open.

## ELECTRONIC CONTROL UNIT (CIS-E MOTRONIC)

**Ground Circuits** – Using Multimeter (US 1119), check resistance of ground circuits for ECU. Remove ECU connector. Check continuity to ground on terminals No. 2 and No. 9. *See Fig. 4.* Resistance should be zero ohms. If resistance is not zero ohms, repair open or short in wiring.

**Power Circuits** – Turn ignition off. Disconnect ECU connector. Turn ignition on and, using a voltmeter, check for battery voltage between ECU connector terminals No. 2 (negative) and No. 1 (positive). *See Fig. 4.* If battery voltage is not present, check fuse No. 23 on fuse block. If fuse is okay, check CIS-E ECU connector to fuse box wiring for open.

## ENGINE SENSORS & SWITCHES

**Airflow Sensor (Fox, Jetta GLI, GTI 2.0L & Passat)** – **1)** Start engine to pressurize fuel system. Turn engine off and remove intake boot from top of airflow sensor. Disconnect coil secondary wire at coil, and jumper secondary wire to ground.

**2)** Check sensor play by slowly moving sensor plate through travel range with a magnet. *See Fig. 2* Resistance should be felt. Move plate back to rest position. There should be no resistance. If binding is felt, loosen sensor plate hold-down bolt and adjust plate to center of venturi.

**3)** If resistance is uneven, remove airflow sensor from housing and clean and lubricate lever assembly. If resistance is caused by control plunger, remove and clean control plunger assembly. If binding continues, replace fuel distributor.

**4)** Check position of airflow sensor plate. Airflow sensor plate edge must be within .075" (1.9 mm) below narrowest section of venturi. If not, bend sensor spring until correct specification is obtained. Ensure a small gap exists between sensor lever and control plunger.

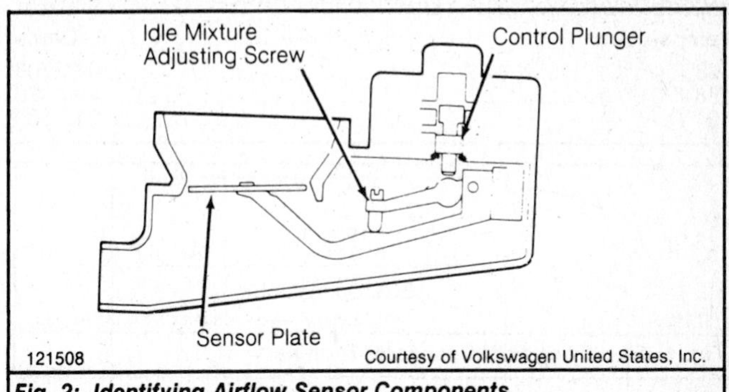


***Fig. 2: Identifying Airflow Sensor Components***

**Airflow Sensor (Golf GL & Jetta)** – **1)** Start engine to pressurize fuel system. Turn engine off and remove intake boot from top of airflow sensor. Check sensor plate by lifting plate through travel cycle with magnet or pliers.

**2)** Continuous resistance should be felt. Move plate back to rest position. There should be no resistance. If resistance is felt, replace airflow sensor. If sensor plate lever is difficult to move upward but moves freely downward, check sensor plate for correct centering.

**3)** Sensor plate should be evenly centered in housing with plate edge at narrowest section of venturi while at rest position. If sensor plate adjustment is correct, check control plunger for sticking. If control plunger is sticking, replace fuel distributor assembly.

**Airflow Sensor (Vanagon)** – **1)** Turn ignition off. Remove Electronic Control Unit (ECU) connector. Attach ohmmeter to ECU connector. *See Fig. 4.* Resistance should correspond to ECU PIN CHECK in AFC-DIGIFANT AIRFLOW SENSOR RESISTANCE table.

**2)** With ignition off, unplug connector from airflow sensor. Attach ohmmeter to airflow sensor terminal. *See Fig. 3.* Resistance should correspond to AIRFLOW SENSOR PIN CHECK in AFC-DIGIFANT AIRFLOW SENSOR RESISTANCE table.

***AFC-DIGIFANT AIRFLOW SENSOR RESISTANCE***

| Terminal | Ohms |
|---|---|
| ECU Pin Check | |
| No. 6 & No. 17 | 500-1000 |
| No. 17 & No. 21 | [1] |
| Airflow Sensor Pin Check | |
| No. 3 & No. 4 | 500-1000 |
| No. 2 & No. 3 | [1] |

[1] – Resistance should fluctuate as sensor door is moved.

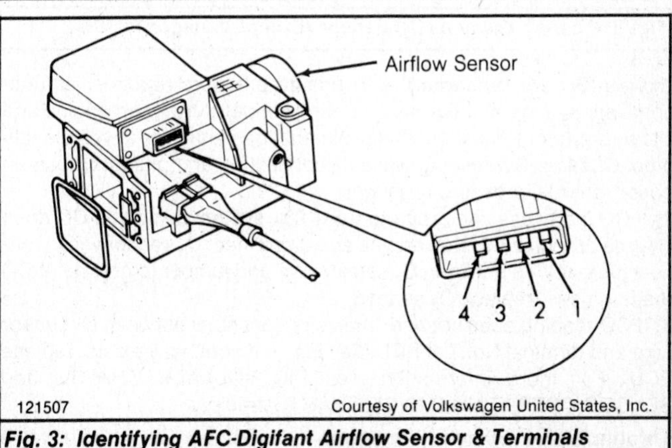


***Fig. 3: Identifying AFC-Digifant Airflow Sensor & Terminals***

**Coolant Temperature Sensor** – Turn ignition off. Use a thermometer to measure coolant temperature. Unplug connector from Electronic

# 1991 ENGINE PERFORMANCE
# System & Component Testing (Cont.)

Control Unit (ECU). Attach an ohmmeter between terminals No. 6 and No. 10 of ECU connector. *See Fig. 4*. Resistance should decrease as coolant temperature increases. See COOLANT TEMPERATURE SENSOR RESISTANCE table. Replace sensor if resistance is NOT within specification.

***COOLANT TEMPERATURE SENSOR RESISTANCE***

| Temperature | Ohms |
|---|---|
| 68°F (20°C) | 2200-2700 |
| 158°F (70°C) | 400-480 |
| 194°F (90°C) | 210-280 |

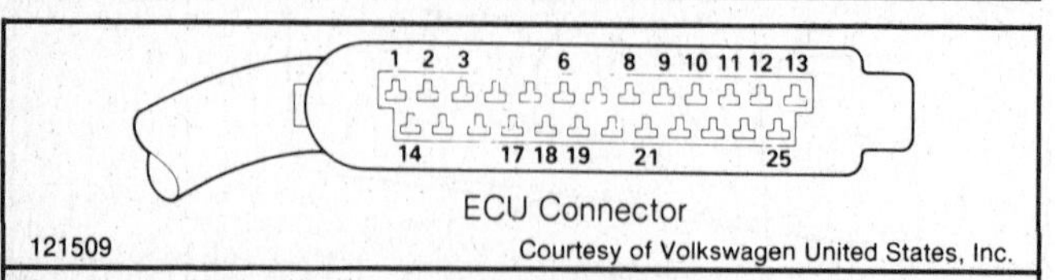


***Fig. 4: Identifying ECU Connector Terminals***

**Hall Effect Sender** – For Hall Effect sender testing, see BASIC DIAGNOSTIC PROCEDURES article.

**Oxygen Sensor (Except Vanagon) – 1)** Ensure exhaust system is not leaking. Warm engine to normal operating temperature with all accessories off. Remove differential pressure regulator connector. Connect Wiring Harness Adapter (VW 1315 A/1) in series. *See Fig. 5*.
**2)** Attach Multimeter (US 1119) to adapter and set meter on DCA 200m scale. Remove PCV hose and vent to atmosphere. Remove 90-degree "T" connector and insert port with small vent hole into intake air boot. *See Fig. 6*.
**3)** Start engine and allow to run for 2 minutes. Meter reading should start fluctuating. If reading does not fluctuate, raise engine speed to 3000 RPM. If meter reading fluctuates, oxygen sensor is okay. If reading still does not fluctuate, check control unit and wiring harness for short or open circuit.

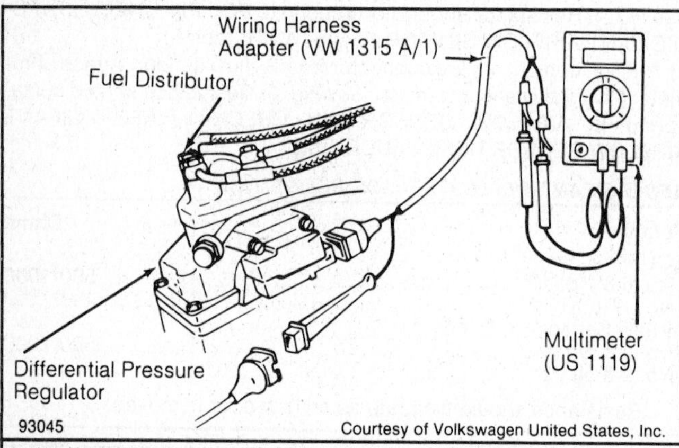


***Fig. 5: Testing Oxygen ($O_2$) Sensor (Except Vanagon)***

**Oxygen Sensor (Vanagon) – 1)** Ensure pressure regulator is functional and engine is at normal operating temperature. Start engine and allow to run for 2 minutes. Install exhaust gas analyzer at vehicle tailpipe. Observe CO reading while disconnecting and plugging vacuum hose from fuel pressure regulator.
**2)** If CO increases and drops to 0.3-1.0%, system is okay. If CO does change as indicated, stop engine and disconnect $O_2$ sensor wire. Connect jumper wire between $O_2$ sensor wire and jumper to ground. If CO reading rises, replace $O_2$ sensor.
**3)** If CO reading does not rise, check for continuity between $O_2$ sensor wire and terminal No. 2 of ECU. *See Fig. 4*. If continuity exists, replace ECU. For more information, see PIN VOLTAGE CHARTS and SENSOR OPERATING RANGE CHARTS articles.

**Throttle Valve Switch (Vanagon) – 1)** Disconnect throttle valve switch connector. With ohmmeter set on 200-ohm scale, attach probes to male terminals. Ensure throttle valve switch is completely closed. With throttle valve closed, meter reading should be zero.

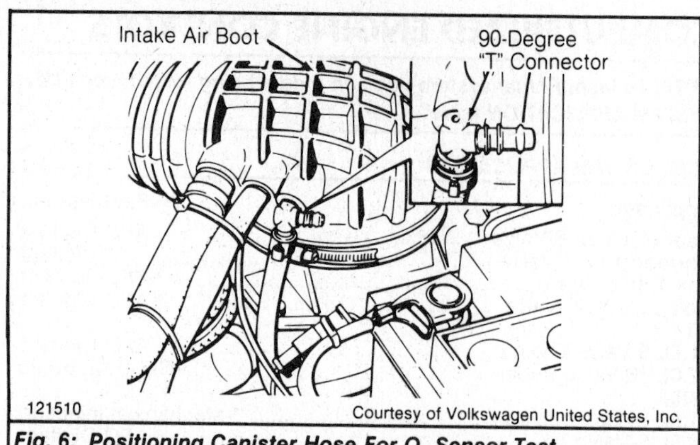


***Fig. 6: Positioning Canister Hose For $O_2$ Sensor Test***

**2)** Position throttle valve to half open position. Ohmmeter reading should be infinite. Position throttle to fully open position. Ohmmeter reading should be zero. If any reading is incorrect, perform throttle valve switch adjustment. See ON-VEHICLE ADJUSTMENTS article.
**3)** If correct specifications cannot be obtained, check throttle shaft play, accelerator cable adjustment and throttle switch actuating cam. If okay, replace throttle valve switch.

## RELAYS

**Fuel Pump Relay (Cabriolet, Golf GL, GTI, Jetta, Jetta GLI & Passat) – 1)** Ensure fuel pump fuse (No. 5) is okay. Remove fuel pump relay (No. 2) from fuse/relay panel. *See Fig. 7*. With ignition on, check for battery voltage between the following locations:

- Terminal No. 2 and ground
- Terminals No. 2 and No. 1
- Terminal No. 4 and No. 1.

If voltage is not present, repair wiring and recheck fuel pump operation.
**2)** With battery voltage present between terminal No. 1 and terminal No. 5, lightly touch middle wire of ignition distributor harness connector to ground. If voltage drops, replace fuel pump relay and check Hall Effect sender.
**3)** If voltage does not drop, check Hall Effect sender. See HALL EFFECT SENDER in BASIC DIAGNOSTIC PROCEDURES article. For fuel pump and fuse number/location, see FUEL PUMP RELAY & FUSE NUMBER table.

**Fuel Pump Relay (Corrado) – 1)** Ensure fuel pump fuse No. 18 is okay. Remove fuel pump relay No. 12 from fuse/relay panel. *See Fig. 7*. With ignition on, check for battery voltage between the following locations:

- Terminal No. 6 and ground
- Terminal No. 2 and ground
- Terminals No. 6 and No. 4.

**2)** If battery voltage is not present, check wiring and repair as needed. Check fuel pump operation. With ignition off, connect voltmeter between terminals No. 2 and No. 3. Turn ignition on. Voltage should be present for one second. If voltage is not present for one second, check wiring to ECU or replace ECU. Check fuel pump relay operation. For fuel pump and fuse number/location, see FUEL PUMP RELAY & FUSE NUMBER table.

**Fuel Pump Relay (Fox) – 1)** Ensure fuel pump fuse (No. 13) is okay. Remove fuel pump relay. Note terminals numbers molded on fuse/relay panel. With ignition on, check for battery voltage between the following locations:

- Terminal No. 46 and ground
- Terminal No. 48 and ground

*See Fig. 7*.
**2)** If voltage is not present, current is not reaching relay. Repair wiring. Check fuel pump operation. If voltage is present, check for battery voltage between the following locations:

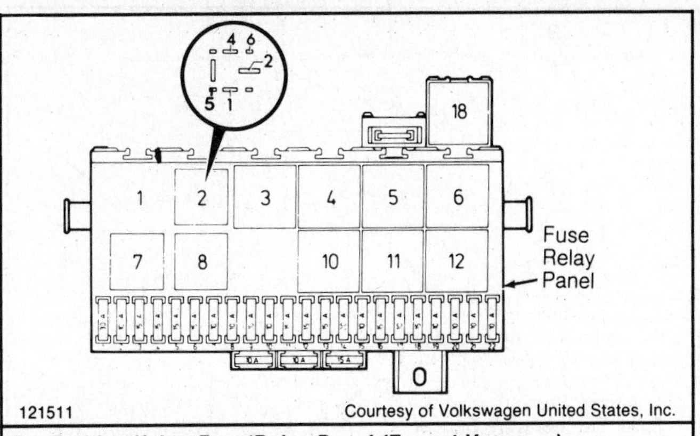


*Fig. 7: Identifying Fuse/Relay Panel (Except Vanagon)*

- Terminals No. 48 and No. 50
- Terminals No. 46 and No. 50

If voltage is not present, terminal No. 50 (ground circuit) is open. Repair wiring. Check fuel pump operation.

**3)** If voltage is present, check for battery voltage between terminals No. 50 and No. 51. If voltage is not present, ignition signal is not reaching fuel pump relay. Repair wiring. Check fuel pump operation.

**4)** If no faults can be found and fuel pump operates when relay is bypassed, replace fuel pump relay. For fuel pump relay and fuse number, see FUEL PUMP RELAY & FUSE NUMBER table.

**Fuel Pump Relay (Vanagon) - 1)** Check terminal No. 30 and terminal No. 86 of fuel pump relay for battery voltage. *See Fig. 8.* If battery voltage is not present, check circuit for short or open circuit.

**2)** If battery voltage is present, remove relay and attach ohmmeter probe to relay box terminal No. 85. Attach other probe to ground. Continuity should be present while cranking engine.

**3)** If continuity is not present, check for continuity between terminal No. 85 of fuel pump relay and terminal No. 3 of ECU connector. If continuity is present, circuit is okay but ECU is not switching to ground. Replace ECU and install fuel pump relay.

**4)** If fuel pump will not operate, turn ignition switch off, then on. Ensure battery voltage is present at fuel pump relay No. 87 for about 5 seconds after ignition is switched on. If battery voltage is not present, replace fuel pump relay. If battery voltage is present, check voltage supply and ground circuit of fuel pump. If fuel pump wiring is okay, replace fuel pump.

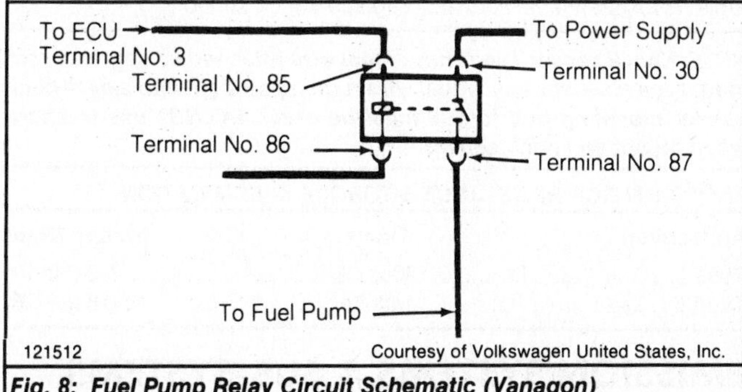


*Fig. 8: Fuel Pump Relay Circuit Schematic (Vanagon)*

***FUEL PUMP RELAY & FUSE NUMBER***

| Application | Relay No. | Fuse No. |
|---|---|---|
| Cabriolet | 2 | 5 |
| Corrado, Golf GL, GTI, Jetta, Jetta GLI & Passat | 12 | 18 |
| Fox | 10 | 13 |
| Vanagon | [1] | [2] |

[1] - Relay located in relay box left side of engine compartment, fused through AFC-Digifant ECU control relay.

[2] - Fuse and terminal number molded into plastic fuse box housing.

# FUEL SYSTEM

## FUEL DELIVERY

***NOTE: For FUEL SYSTEM PRESSURE TESTING, see BASIC DIAGNOSTIC PROCEDURES article.***

## FUEL CONTROL

***NOTE: On AFC-Digifant System, cold start valve is NOT used. Cold starts are controlled by ECU.***

**Cold Start Valve (Except Vanagon) - 1)** Engine temperature must be below 85°F (30°C). Disconnect cold start valve attaching screws and remove valve with harness connector and fuel line attached.

**2)** Remove ignition coil secondary wire and jumper to ground. Attach metal housing of cold start valve to ground. Direct cold start valve injector into a clean container. *See Fig. 9.* Have assistant turn ignition switch to START position, while observing cold start valve spray pattern.

**3)** The valve should deliver a consistent cone-shaped pattern until thermo time switch interrupts fuel flow. Ensure valve does not leak after fuel flow stops. If spray pattern is uneven or inconsistent, check for plugged or defective cold start valve. If valve does not function, proceed to THERMO TIME SWITCH.

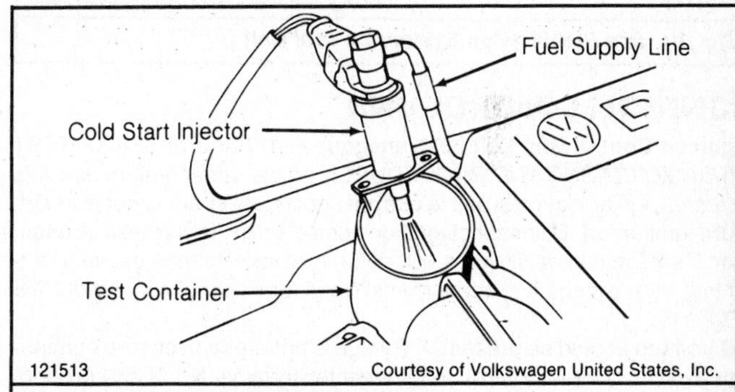


*Fig. 9: Testing Typical Cold Start Valve*

**Thermo Time Switch - 1)** Engine temperature must be below 86°F (30°C). Disconnect cold start valve wiring harness connector and attach LED test light to terminals. Have assistant hold ignition switch in START position while observing test light.

**2)** Light should stay on for 3-8 seconds depending on coolant temperature. If light does not come on, check voltage supply to cold start valve and repair as necessary. If voltage to cold start valve is okay, check ground circuit through thermo time switch. Replace thermo time switch if contact to ground cannot be made.

# IDLE CONTROL SYSTEM

**Idle Stabilization System - 1)** Attach Test Meter (VW 1315/2) and Adapter (US 1119) to idle stabilization valve. Set meter to milliampere scale. Start engine. Observe test meter while turning A/C control switch to on position. If milliampere reading increases, system is okay.

**2)** If milliampere reading does not increase, turn ignition switch off. Connect test light between terminals No. 2 and No. 5 of idle stabilization control unit connector. *See Fig. 10.* Start engine and cycle A/C switch on and off.

**3)** Test light should be on when A/C switch is in on position. If light is on, replace idle stabilization valve. If light does not go on, repair wiring between idle stabilization control unit terminal No. 2 and A/C compressor clutch.

# IGNITION SYSTEM

***NOTE: For basic ignition checks, see BASIC DIAGNOSTIC PROCEDURES article.***

# 1991 ENGINE PERFORMANCE
# System & Component Testing (Cont.)

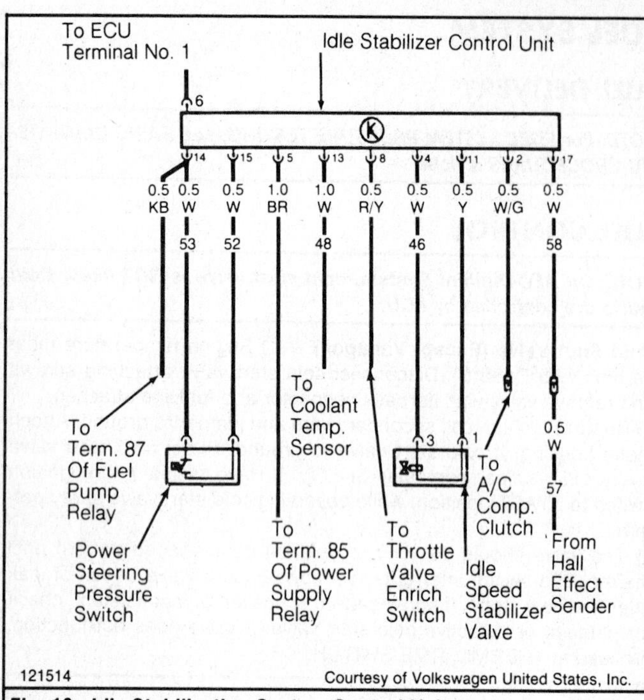


*Fig. 10: Idle Stabilization System Control Unit*

## IGNITION CONTROL UNIT

**Ignition Control Unit (Except Vanagon) – 1)** Perform SPARK TEST in BASIC DIAGNOSTIC PROCEDURES article. If secondary spark is present, ignition control unit is okay. If secondary spark is not present, turn ignition off. Disconnect ignition control unit wire harness connector. Turn ignition on. Using a voltmeter, measure voltage between terminal No. 2 (negative) and terminal No. 4 (positive) of connector. *See Fig. 11.*

**2)** Voltage should be present. If voltage is not present, ensure continuity exists between control unit connector terminal No. 2 and ground. Continuity should also exist between terminal No. 4 and ignition coil positive terminal. Repair wiring if necessary. If wiring is okay, replace ignition control unit.

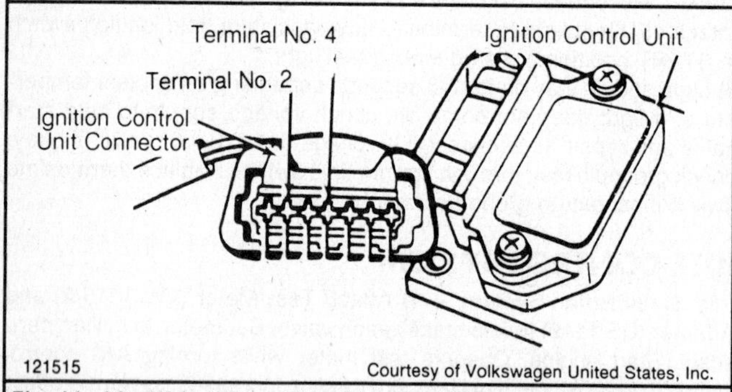


*Fig. 11: Identifying Typical Ignition Control Unit Connector*

**Ignition Control Unit (Vanagon) – 1)** Turn ignition off. Attach DVOM to ignition coil primary terminals. Disconnect Hall Effect sender wire harness connector from distributor. *See Fig. 12.* Turn ignition on.

**2)** While observing DVOM reading, attach center terminal of connector to ground for 3 seconds. Voltage reading should briefly increase to 4.5 volts. If voltage reading did not increase, check wiring for short or open circuit. If wiring is okay, replace ignition control unit.

***NOTE: Knock control is integral in AFC-Digifant ECU.***

**Knock Sensor Control Unit (Except Vanagon) – 1)** Check ignition coil and Hall Effect sender before checking knock sensor control unit. Remove knock sensor control unit harness connector. Turn ignition

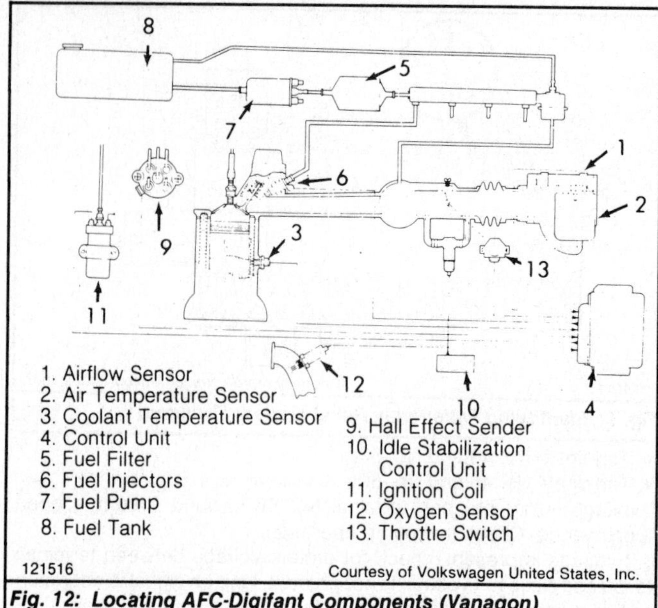


*Fig. 12: Locating AFC-Digifant Components (Vanagon)*

on. Using a voltmeter, check for battery voltage between terminals No. 3 and No. 5, and terminals No. 6 and No. 3 of knock sensor control unit. *See Fig. 13.* Open throttle valve. Voltage should drop to zero volt.

**2)** If voltage does not drop to zero volt, check voltage between terminals No. 8 and No. 3 of knock sensor control unit while fully opening throttle valve. If battery voltage is not present when throttle opens fully, replace throttle valve switch.

**3)** Remove Hall Effect sender connector and connect voltmeter to outside terminals. Turn ignition on. There should be 5 volts present. Turn ignition off. Connect voltmeter between terminals No. 1 (negative) and No. 15 (positive) of ignition coil. Turn ignition on and touch center terminal of Hall Effect sender briefly to ground. Voltage should jump momentarily to approximately 2 volts. If voltage does not jump, replace knock sensor control unit.

**Knock Sensor(s) –** Before replacing knock sensor, check knock sensor torque and resistance. Remove knock sensor connector and check resistance between terminals No. 13 and No. 14. *See Fig. 13.* See KNOCK SENSOR RESISTANCE & TORQUE SPECIFICATION table. If resistance is incorrect, replace knock sensor.

***NOTE: Knock sensor Type I has signal wire attached 90 degrees from side. Type II sensor has signal wire running straight into side. Knock sensor mounting bolt torque must be exact. DO NOT use washers when mounting knock sensor.***

***KNOCK SENSOR RESISTANCE & TORQUE SPECIFICATION***

| Application | Ohms | Ft. Lbs (N.m) |
|---|---|---|
| Type I | 300,000 | 7-9 (10-12) |
| Type II | Infinite | 15-18 (20-25) |

# EMISSION SYSTEMS & SUB-SYSTEMS

## EXHAUST GAS RECIRCULATION (EGR)

**1)** With engine idling, apply about 12 in. Hg to EGR valve with a hand-held vacuum pump. Engine should run rough or stall. If idle does not change, remove EGR valve and inspect for restricted port passage. Clean as required.

**2)** If port is clean, apply about 12 in. Hg to EGR valve with vacuum pump. If valve does not move, replace EGR valve. If valve moves, go to next step.

**3)** Install EGR valve and new gasket. Connect vacuum gauge to EGR vacuum line with a "T" fitting. Start engine and increase engine speed to about 3000 RPM. If vacuum gauge indicates vacuum, test is complete. If gauge does not indicate vacuum, vacuum source is plugged. Repair as necessary and repeat test.

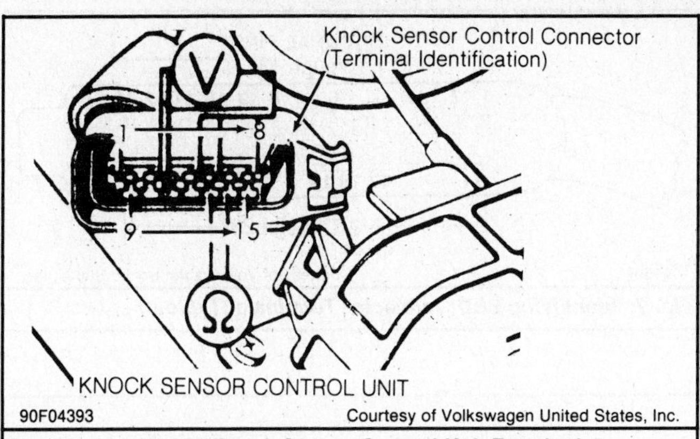


*Fig. 13: Identifying Knock Sensor Control Unit Terminals*

## FUEL EVAPORATION

**EVAP Canister By-Pass Valve (Except Vanagon) - 1)** Remove both vent hoses and vacuum hose from canister by-pass valve. *See Fig. 14.* Apply very low air pressure to vent hoses individually. There should be no airflow. If air passes through, replace by-pass valve.

**2)** Attach vacuum pump to vacuum hose and apply 5-10 in. Hg. Apply low air pressure to vent hoses individually. Valve should be open and air should flow. If air does not flow, replace by-pass valve.

**EVAP Canister By-Pass Valve (Vanagon) - 1)** Start and warm engine to normal operating temperature. Disconnect White nylon hose from rubber boot at rear of intake manifold. Attach vacuum pump and apply 5-10 in. Hg. If vacuum holds, control valve is okay.

**2)** If vacuum does not hold, disconnect Purple vacuum hose from throttle body. Attach vacuum gauge. If less than one in. Hg is present, replace control valve. If more than one in. Hg is present, adjust throttle valve stop screw and repeat test.

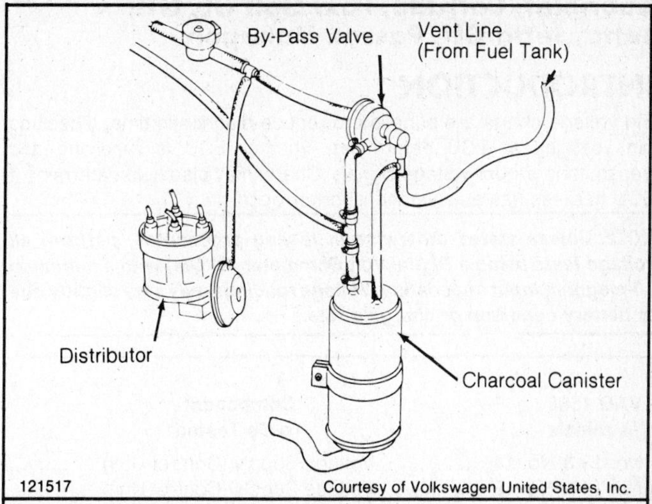


*Fig. 14: Identifying Typical Fuel Evaporation System Components*

## MISCELLANEOUS CONTROLS

***NOTE:** Although some controlled devices are not technically engine performance components, they can affect driveability if they malfunction.*

## A/C CLUTCH

See IDLE CONTROL SYSTEM.

# 1991 ENGINE PERFORMANCE
# Pin Voltage Charts

## Cabriolet, Corrado, Fox, Golf GL, GTI, Jetta, Jetta GLI, Passat, Vanagon

## INTRODUCTION

Pin voltage charts are supplied to reduce diagnostic time. Checking pin voltages at ECU determines whether ECU is receiving and transmitting proper voltage signals. Charts may also help determine if ECU harness has an electrical short or open.

***NOTE: Unless stated otherwise in testing procedures, perform all voltage tests using a Digital Volt-Ohmmeter (DVOM) with a minimum 10-megohm input impedance. Voltage readings may vary slightly due to battery condition or charging rate.***

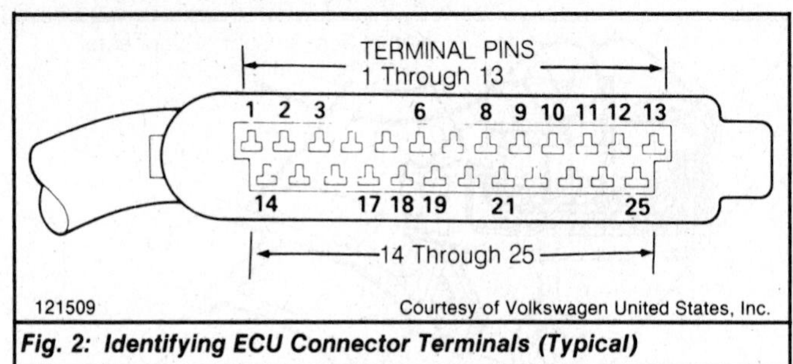


*Fig. 2: Identifying ECU Connector Terminals (Typical)*

| VAG 1598 Terminals | Component To Be Tested | Test Conditions | Specified Value Or Result |
|---|---|---|---|
| No. 13 & No. 14 | Voltage Supply (Control Unit) | Ignition On | Battery Voltage |
| No. 14 & No. 19 | Voltage Supply (Control Unit) | Ignition On | Battery Voltage |
| No. 3 & No. 13 (Jumper) | Wires To Fuel Pump Relay | Ignition On | Pumps Must Run Audibly |
| No. 1 & No. 25 (M/T) | Wires From Starter Term. 50 | Ignition Off, Operate Starter | 8 Volts Minimum |
| No. 19 & No. 25 (A/T) | Wiring to Starter Lockout Relay | Ignition On, Select "P" Then "N" | Battery Voltage |
| | | Ign. On, Select "1", "2", "3", "D" & "R" | No Voltage |
| No. 1 & No. 19 | Voltage To Control Unit | Ignition On | Battery Voltage |
| No. 19 & No. 35 | Voltage To Control Unit | Ignition On | Battery Voltage |
| No. 1 & No. 6 | Wires To Coil | Ignition On | Battery Voltage |
| No. 1 & No. 4 | Fault Indicator Light | Ignition On | Battery Voltage |
| No. 1 & No. 23 | Idle Stabilizer Valve | Ignition On | Battery Voltage |
| No. 1 & No. 24 (Jumper) | Wires To Fuel Pump Relay | Ignition On | Pumps Must Run Audibly |
| | Wiring To Injectors | | |
| No. 1 & No. 20 | Cylinder No. 1 | [1] | Battery Voltage |
| No. 1 & No. 21 | Cylinder No. 2 | [1] | Battery Voltage |
| No. 1 & No. 3 | Cylinder No. 3 | [1] | Battery Voltage |
| No. 1 & No. 2 | Cylinder No. 4 | [1] | Battery Voltage |
| No. 28 & No. 34 | Throttle Potentiometer (Power) | Ignition On | 4.5-5.0 Volts |
| No. 33 & No. 28 | Throttle Potentiometer | Connect Potentiometer, Ignition On | |
| | | Throttle Setting: | |
| | | Idle | 0.3-1.7 Volts |
| | | Full Throttle | 3-5 Volts |
| No. 28 & No. 38 | Hall Sender (Power) | Ignition On | 10 Volts Minimum |
| No. 37 & No. 38 | Hall Sender (Signal) | [2] Ignition Off, Operate Starter | LED Must Flicker |
| No. 1 & No. 6 | Ignition Signal Function | [2] Ignition Off, Operate Starter | LED Must Flicker |
| **ECU Connector Terminals** | | | |
| No. 1 & No. 2 | | Ignition On | Battery Voltage |
| No. 2 & No. 3 | | Ignition On | Battery Voltage |
| No. 2 & No. 4 | | Ignition On | Battery Voltage |
| No. 2 & No. 5 | | Ignition On | |
| | | Operate Full Throttle Switch | Battery Voltage |
| No. 2 & No. 13 | | Ignition On | |
| | | Operate Throttle Idle Switch | Battery Voltage |
| Vehicles With A/C | | | |
| No. 2 & 6 | | Ignition & A/C On | Battery Voltage |
| No. 2 & 16 | | Ignition & A/C On | Battery Voltage |
| No. 2 & 19 | | Ignition & A/C On | Battery Voltage |
| No. 2 & No. 24 | | Ignition Off, Operate Starter | 8 Volts Minimum |
| No. 2 & No. 25 | Hall Sender (Signal) | [3] Ignition Off, Operate Starter | LED Must Flicker |

1 – With ignition on and fuse No. 18 removed, jump terminals No. 1 and 24 together.

2 – With ignition off, use LED Tester (US 1115) with Adapters (VW 1594) instead of multimeter. Disconnect harness from fuel rail (main injector connector). Perform test only if engine will not start.

3 – Connect LED Tester (US 1115) instead of DVOM (US 1119).

91A18200

*Fig. 1: Checking ECU Pin Voltages (Cabriolet)*

# 1991 ENGINE PERFORMANCE
# Pin Voltage Charts (Cont.)

| VAG 1598 Terminals | Component To Be Tested | Test Conditions | Specified Value Or Result |
|---|---|---|---|
| No. 13 & No. 19 | Voltage Supply | Ignition On | Battery Voltage |
| No. 13 & No. 14 | Voltage Supply (Control Unit) | Ignition On | Battery Voltage |
| No. 14 & No. 19 | Voltage Supply (Control Unit) | Ignition On | Battery Voltage |
| No. 13 & No. 25 | Wire To Term. 1 (Coil) | Ignition On | Battery Voltage |
| No. 3 & No. 14 (Jumper) | Wires To Fuel Pump Relay | Ignition On | Pumps Must Run Audibly |
| No. 12 & No. 10 | Wires To Injectors | [1] | Battery Voltage |
| No. 13 & No. 16 | Signal From A/C | [2] | Battery Voltage |
| No. 1 & No. 14 (A/T) | Wiring to Starter Lockout Relay | Ignition On, Select "P" Then "N" | Battery Voltage |
| | | Ign. On, Select "1", "2", "3", "D" & "R" | No Voltage |
| No. 1 & No. 13 (M/T) | Wires From Starter Term. 50 | Ignition Off, Operate Starter | 8 Volts Minimum |
| No. 8 & No. 6 | Hall Sender Voltage Supply | Ignition On | 10 Volts Minimum |
| No. 6 & No. 10 | Coolant Temp. Curve | [3] | Voltage Decreases Uniformly |
| No. 6 & No. 18 | Signal From Hall Sender | Ignition Off, Operate Starter | [4] Tester Must Flicker |
| No. 1 & No. 19 | Voltage To Control Unit | Ignition On | Battery Voltage |
| No. 19 & No. 35 | Voltage To Control Unit | Ignition On | Battery Voltage |
| No. 1 & No. 6 | Wires To Coil | Ignition On | Battery Voltage |
| No. 1 & No. 4 | Fault Indicator Light | Ignition On | Battery Voltage |
| No. 1 & No. 23 | Idle Stabilizer Valve | Ignition On | Battery Voltage |
| No. 1 & No. 24 (Jumper) | Wires To Fuel Pump Relay | Ignition On | Pumps Must Run Audibly |
| | Wiring To Injectors | | |
| No. 1 & No. 20 | Cylinder No. 1 | [5] | Battery Voltage |
| No. 1 & No. 21 | Cylinder No. 2 | [5] | Battery Voltage |
| No. 1 & No. 3 | Cylinder No. 3 | [5] | Battery Voltage |
| No. 1 & No. 2 | Cylinder No. 4 | [5] | Battery Voltage |
| No. 33 & No. 34 | Throttle Potentiometer (Power) | Disconnect Potentiometer, Ignition Off | 3.5-5.0 Volts |
| No. 28 & No. 34 | Throttle Potentiometer (Power) | Ignition On | 4.5-5.0 Volts |
| No. 33 & No. 28 | Throttle Potentiometer | Connect Potentiometer, Ignition On | |
| | | Throttle Setting: | |
| | | Idle | 0.3-1.7 Volts |
| | | Full Throttle | 3-5 Volts |
| No. 28 & No. 38 | Hall Sender (Power) | Ignition On | 10 Volts Minimum |
| No. 28 & No. 37 | Hall Sender (Signal) | [6] Ignition Off, Operate Starter | LED Must Flicker |
| No. 1 & No. 6 | Ignition Signal Function | [6] Ignition Off, Operate Starter | LED Must Flicker |
| No. 18 & No. 28 | RPM Signal | [6] Ignition Off, Operate Starter | LED Must Flicker |

[1] – Turn ignition on, remove fuse No. 13 and jump terminals No. 3 and 13 together.

[2] – A/C system operation okay: Ignition and A/C switch on.

[3] – Start engine cold and allow to warm up while observing multimeter.

[4] – With ignition off, disconnect multimeter and adapters from test box. Disconnect power output stage of ignition coil. Connect LED Tester (US 1115 or VAG 1527B) to test box terminals No. 30 and 35 using Adapter Kit (VW 1594).

[5] – With ignition on and fuse No. 18 removed, jump terminals No. 1 and 24 together.

[6] – Perform test only if engine will not start. Turn ignition off. Instead of multimeter, connect LED Tester (US 1115) using Adapter Kit (VW 1594). Disconnect harness from fuel rail (main injector connector).

91B18201

*Fig. 3: Checking ECU Pin Voltages (Corrado)*

# 1991 ENGINE PERFORMANCE
## Pin Voltage Charts (Cont.)

| VAG 1598 Terminals | Component To Be Tested | Test Conditions | Specified Value Or Result |
|---|---|---|---|
| No. 1 & No. 19 | Voltage To Control Unit | Ignition On | Battery Voltage |
| No. 19 & No. 35 | Voltage To Control Unit | Ignition On | Battery Voltage |
| No. 1 & No. 6 | Wires To Coil | Ignition On | Battery Voltage |
| No. 1 & No. 4 | Fault Indicator Light | Ignition On | Battery Voltage |
| No. 1 & No. 23 | Idle Stabilizer Valve | Ignition On | Battery Voltage |
| No. 1 & No. 24 (Jumper) | Wires To Fuel Pump Relay | Ignition On | Pumps Must Run Audibly |
| | Wiring To Injectors | | |
| No. 1 & No. 20 | Cylinder No. 1 | [1] | Battery Voltage |
| No. 1 & No. 21 | Cylinder No. 2 | [1] | Battery Voltage |
| No. 1 & No. 3 | Cylinder No. 3 | [1] | Battery Voltage |
| No. 1 & No. 2 | Cylinder No. 4 | [1] | Battery Voltage |
| No. 19 & No. 25 (A/T) | Wiring To Starter Lockout Relay | Ignition On, Select "P" Then "N" | Battery Voltage |
| | | Ign. On, Select "1", "2", "3", "D" & "R" | No Voltage |
| No. 28 & No. 34 | Throttle Potentiometer (Power) | Ignition On | 4.5-5.0 Volts |
| No. 28 & No. 33 | Throttle Potentiometer | Connect Potentiometer, Ignition On | |
| | | Throttle Setting: | |
| | | Idle | 0.3-1.7 Volts |
| | | Full Throttle | 3-5 Volts |
| No. 28 & No. 38 | Hall Sender (Power) | Ignition On | 10 Volts Minimum |
| No. 37 & No. 38 | Hall Sender (Signal) | [2] Ignition Off, Operate Starter | LED Must Flicker |
| No. 1 & No. 6 | Ignition Signal Function | [2] Ignition Off, Operate Starter | LED Must Flicker |
| **ECU Connector Terminals** | | | |
| No. 1 & No. 2 | Control Unit Voltage & Ground Connection | Ignition On | Battery Voltage |
| No. 1 & No. 2 | Voltage Supply | Ignition Off, Operate Starter | 8 Volts Minimum |

[1] – With ignition on and fuse No. 18 removed, jump terminals No. 1 and 24 together.

[2] – Perform test only if engine will not start. Turn ignition off. Instead of multimeter, connect LED Tester (US 1115) using Adapter Kit (VW 1594). Disconnect harness from fuel rail (main injector connector).

91C18202

*Fig. 4: Checking ECU Pin Voltages (Fox)*

# 1991 ENGINE PERFORMANCE
# Pin Voltage Charts (Cont.)

| VAG 1598 Terminals | Component To Be Tested | Test Conditions | Specified Value Or Result |
|---|---|---|---|
| No. 13 & No. 14 | Voltage Supply (Control Unit) | Ignition On | Battery Voltage |
| No. 14 & No. 19 | Voltage Supply (Control Unit) | Ignition On | Battery Voltage |
| No. 1 & No. 24 (Jumper) | Wires To Fuel Pump Relay | Ignition On | Pumps Must Run Audibly |
| No. 1 & No. 25 (M/T) | Wires From Starter Term. 50 | Ignition Off, Operate Starter | 8 Volts Minimum |
| No. 19 & No. 34 (M/T) | Ground To Pin No. 34 | Ignition Off | Battery Voltage |
| No. 19 & No. 25 (A/T) | Wiring To Starter Lockout Relay | Ignition On, Select "P" Then "N" | Battery Voltage |
| | | Ign. On, Select "1", "2", "3", "D" & "R" | No Voltage |
| No. 34 & No. 35 (A/T) | Wiring To Starter Lockout Relay | Select "P", Operate Starter | Less Than Battery Voltage |
| No. 1 & No. 19 | Voltage To Control Unit | Ignition On | Battery Voltage |
| No. 19 & No. 35 | Voltage To Control Unit | Ignition On | Battery Voltage |
| No. 1 & No. 6 | Wires To Coil | Ignition On | Battery Voltage |
| No. 1 & No. 4 | Fault Indicator Light | Ignition On | Battery Voltage |
| No. 1 & No. 23 | Idle Stabilizer Valve | Ignition On | Battery Voltage |
| No. 1 & No. 24 (Jumper) | Wires To Fuel Pump Relay | Ignition On | Pumps Must Run Audibly |
| | Wiring To Injectors | | |
| No. 1 & No. 20 | Cylinder No. 1 | [1] | Battery Voltage |
| No. 1 & No. 21 | Cylinder No. 2 | [1] | Battery Voltage |
| No. 1 & No. 3 | Cylinder No. 3 | [1] | Battery Voltage |
| No. 1 & No. 2 | Cylinder No. 4 | [1] | Battery Voltage |
| No. 33 & No. 19 | A/C Compressor On | [2] | Click From Compr. Clutch |
| No. 28 & No. 34 | Throttle Potentiometer (Power) | Ignition On | 4.5-5.0 Volts |
| No. 33 & No. 28 | Throttle Potentiometer | Connect Potentiometer, Ignition On | |
| | | Throttle Setting: | |
| | | Idle | 0.3-1.7 Volts |
| | | Full Throttle | 3-5 Volts |
| No. 28 & No. 38 | Hall Sender (Power) | Ignition On | 10 Volts Minimum |
| No. 37 & No. 38 | Hall Sender (Signal) | [3] Ignition Off, Operate Starter | LED Must Flicker |
| No. 1 & No. 6 | Ignition Signal Function | [3] Ignition Off, Operate Starter | LED Must Flicker |
| **ECU Connector Terminals** | | | |
| No. 1 & No. 2 | Control Unit Voltage & Ground Connection | Ignition On | Battery Voltage |
| No. 1 & No. 2 | Voltage Supply | Ignition Off, Operate Starter | 8 Volts Minimum |
| No. 2 & No. 3 | Power Supply Wires | Ignition On | Battery Voltage |
| No. 2 & No. 4 | Power Supply Wires | Ignition On | Battery Voltage |
| No. 2 & No. 5 | | Ignition On | |
| | | Operate Full Throttle Switch | Battery Voltage |
| No. 2 & No. 13 | | Ignition On | |
| | | Operate Throttle Idle Switch | Battery Voltage |
| Vehicles With A/C | | | |
| No. 2 & 6 | | Ignition & A/C On | Battery Voltage |
| No. 2 & 16 | | Ignition & A/C On | Battery Voltage |
| No. 2 & 19 | | Ignition & A/C On | Battery Voltage |
| No. 2 & No. 24 | | Ignition Off, Operate Starter | 8 Volts Minimum |
| No. 2 & No. 25 | Hall Sender (Signal) | [4] Ignition Off, Operate Starter | LED Must Flicker |

[1] – With ignition on and fuse No. 18 removed, jump terminals No. 1 and 24 together.

[2] – Jump terminals together. DO NOT use multimeter.

[3] – Perform test only if engine will not start. Turn ignition off. Instead of a multimeter, connect LED Tester (US 1115) using Adapter Kit (VW 1594). Disconnect harness from fuel rail (main injector connector).

[4] – Connect LED Tester (US 1115) instead of DVOM (US 1119).

91D18203

*Fig. 5: Checking ECU Pin Voltages (Golf GL, GTI, Jetta & Jetta GLI)*

# 1991 ENGINE PERFORMANCE
# Pin Voltage Charts (Cont.)

| VAG 1598 Terminals | Component To Be Tested | Test Conditions [1] | Specified Value Or Result |
|---|---|---|---|
| No. 18 & No. 19 | Voltage Supply | Ignition Off | Battery Voltage |
| No. 14 & No. 35 | Voltage Supply | Ignition On | Battery Voltage |
| No. 17 & No. 35 | Idle Stabilizer Valve | Ignition On | Battery Voltage |
| No. 33 & No. 19 | A/C Compressor On | [2] | Audible Click From Compressor Clutch |
| No. 19 & No. 34 (M/T) | Ground To Pin No. 1 | Ignition Off | Battery Voltage |
| No. 34 & No. 35 (A/T) | Wiring To Starter Lockout Relay | Select "P", Operate Starter | 2 Volts Less Than Battery Voltage |
| No. 21 & No. 35 | Hall Sender Voltage Supply | Ignition On | 10 Volts Minimum |
| No. 2 & No. 35 | Signal From Speed Sender | [3] | [3] |
| No. 3 & No. 35 | Coolant Temp. Curve | [4] | Voltage Must Lower Uniformly |
| No. 30 & No. 35 | Signal From Hall Sender | Ignition Off, Operate Starter | [5] Tester Must Flicker |

[1] – TESTING CONDITIONS: Disconnect ECU Connector with ignition off. Remove and ground high tension lead (from coil) at distributor cap. Set multimeter to 20-volt DC scale.

[2] – Jump terminals with jumper wire. DO NOT use multimeter.

[3] – With ignition on and L/F wheel rolled very slowly, approximately every 10-degrees of rotation, voltage will switch from near zero to roughly 10 volts. This is an on-off signal; exact voltages are not critical.

[4] – Start engine cold and allow to warm up while observing multimeter.

[5] – With ignition off, disconnect multimeter and adapters from test box. Disconnect power output stage of ignition coil. Connect LED Tester (US 1115 or VAG 1527B) to test box terminals No. 30 and 35 using Adapter Kit (VW 1594).

91E18204

*Fig. 6: Checking ECU Voltage (Passat)*

| ECU Connector Terminals | Component To Be Tested | Test Conditions | Specified Value Or Result |
|---|---|---|---|
| No. 13 & No. 14 | Voltage Supply (Control Unit) | Ignition On | Battery Voltage |
| No. 14 & No. 19 | Voltage Supply (Control Unit) | Ignition On | Battery Voltage |
| No. 3 & No. 13 (Jumper) | Wires To Fuel Pump Relay | Ignition On | Pumps Must Run Audibly |
| No. 13 & No. 25 | Wire From Coil Term. 1 | Ignition On | Battery Voltage |
| No. 1 & No. 7 | AEG Hall Control Unit | Ignition On | Battery Voltage |
| No. 1 & No. 15 | FAIRCHILD Hall Control Unit | Ignition On | Battery Voltage Or Less |
| No. 1 & No. 13 | Wire From Starter Term. 50 & | Ground Center Distributor Connector Wire | 1.5 Volts Or Less |
| | From Adapter For Idle Stabilizer Control Unit Terminal 50 | Disconnect Connector From Injectors. Operate Starter Select "P" Then "N" | 8 Volts Minimum |

91F18205

*Fig. 7: Checking ECU Voltage (Vanagon)*

# 1991 ENGINE PERFORMANCE
# Sensor Operating Range Charts

## Cabriolet, Corrado, Fox, Golf GL, GTI, Jetta, Jetta GLI, Passat, Vanagon

## INTRODUCTION

Sensor operating range information can help determine if a sensor is out of calibration. An out-of-calibration sensor may not set a trouble code, but it may cause driveability problems.

***NOTE: Unless stated otherwise in test procedure, perform all voltage tests using a Digital Volt-Ohmmeter (DVOM) with a minimum 10-megohm input impedance.***

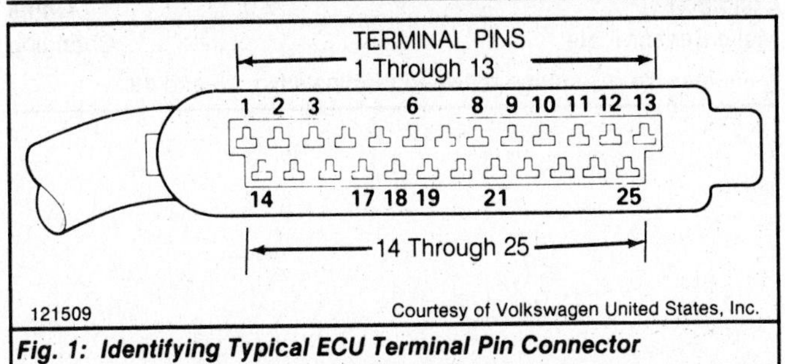


***Fig. 1: Identifying Typical ECU Terminal Pin Connector***

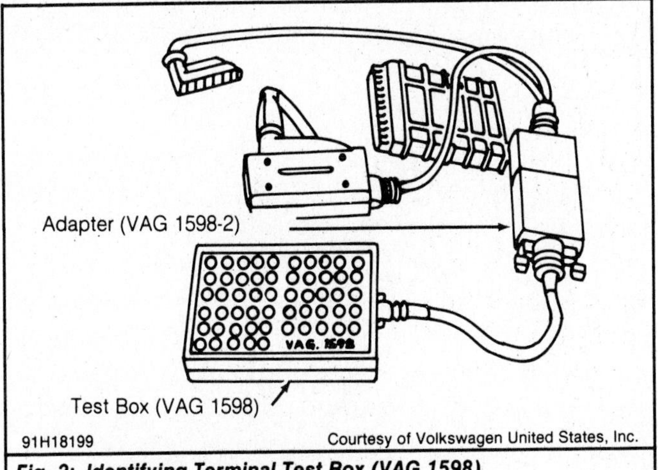


***Fig. 2: Identifying Terminal Test Box (VAG 1598) & Adapter (VAG 1598-2)***

***NOTE: Not all vehicles have all sensors listed.***

***AIRFLOW SENSOR POTENTIOMETER RESISTANCE TEST***

| Application | Conditions | Ohms |
|---|---|---|
| Cabriolet, Fox, Golf GL & Jetta | [1] Ignition On | 500-1000 |
| | [2] Move Sensor Flap | Changing |
| Corrado | [3] Ignition On | 500-1000 |
| | [4] Move Sensor Flap | Changing |
| GTI, Jetta GLI & Passat | [5] Sensor At Rest | 4500-5500 |
| | [6] Sensor At Rest | 3800-4200 |
| Vanagon | [7] Sensor At Rest | Less Than 1000 |
| | [8] Sensor At Rest | Greater Than 4000 |

[1] - Measure resistance between terminals No. 6 and 17.
[2] - Measure resistance between terminals No. 17 and 21.
[3] - Measure resistance between terminals No. 15 and 28.
[4] - Measure resistance between terminals No. 13 and 15.
[5] - Measure resistance between terminals No. 23 and 26.
[6] - Measure resistance between terminals No. 26 and 35.
[7] - Measure resistance between terminals No. 14 and 17.
[8] - Measure resistance between terminals No. 17 and 18.

***COLD START VALVE TEST***

| Application | Between Terminals | Ohms |
|---|---|---|
| 2.0L | No. 14 & 16 | 8-13 |

***COOLANT TEMPERATURE SENSOR RESISTANCE TEST***

| Application | Temperature °F (°C) | Ohms |
|---|---|---|
| Cabriolet [1], Corrado [1], Fox [2], Golf GL [1], Jetta [2], Passat [3] & Vanagon [1] | 122 (50) | 800-1000 |
| | 176 (80) | 250-350 |
| | 212 (100) | 100-200 |

[1] - Measure resistance between terminals No. 6 and 10.
[2] - Measure resistance between terminals No. 11 and 28.
[3] - Measure resistance between terminals No. 3 and 35.

***CYLINDER HEAD TEMPERATURE SENSOR RESISTANCE TEST (VANAGON) [1]***

| Temperature °F (°C) | Ohms |
|---|---|
| 68 (20) | 2,100-2,900 |
| 176 (80) | 270-390 |

[1] - Measure resistance between terminal No. 13 and ground.

***DIFFERENTIAL PRESSURE REGULATOR TEST***

| Application | Between Terminals | Ohms |
|---|---|---|
| 1.8L | No. 10 & 12 | 17.5-21.5 |
| 2.0L | No. 4 & 5 | 15-20 |

***EGR TEMPERATURE SENSOR RESISTANCE TEST (2.0L) [1]***

| Temperature °F (°C) | Ohms |
|---|---|
| 122 (50) | 500,000-600,000 |
| 257 (125) | 35,000-40,000 |
| 392 (200) | 4,500-6500 |

[1] - Measure resistance between terminals No. 9 and 35.

***INTAKE AIR TEMPERATURE SENSOR RESISTANCE TEST***

| Application | Temperature °F (°C) | Ohms |
|---|---|---|
| Cabriolet, Corrado, Fox, Golf & Jetta [1] | 32 (0) | 5000-6500 |
| | 122 (50) | 950-1000 |
| | 212 (100) | 150-250 |
| Vanagon [2] | 68 (20) | 2300-2700 |

[1] - On Cabriolet and Corrado (California), measure resistance between terminals No. 28 and 30. On all others, measure resistance between terminals No. 6 and 9.
[2] - Measure resistance between terminals No. 6 and 14.

***OIL TEMPERATURE SENSOR RESISTANCE TEST (VANAGON) [1]***

| Temperature °F (°C) | Ohms |
|---|---|
| 14 (10) | 7,000-11,600 |
| 68 (20) | 2,100-3,100 |
| 176 (80) | 270-390 |

[1] - Measure resistance between temperature sensor and ground.

# 1991 ENGINE PERFORMANCE
## Sensor Operating Range Charts (Cont.)

### OXYGEN SENSOR RESISTANCE TEST

| Application | Condition | Ohms |
|---|---|---|
| Cabriolet, Fox & Golf GL (Fed.) [1] | Disconnect & Ground Harness Wire | 0.5 |
| | Reconnect Sensor | Open Circuit |
| Cabriolet, Fox & Golf GL (Calif.) [2] | Disconnect & Ground Harness Wire | 1 |
| | Reconnect Sensor | Open Circuit |
| Corrado [3] | Disconnect Sensor | 1.5 |
| | Reconnect Sensor | Open Circuit |
| GTI, Jetta GLI & Passat (Fed.) [4] | Disconnect Sensor & Ground GRN Wire | 0 |
| | Reconnect Sensor | Open Circuit |
| GTI, Jetta GLI & Passat (Calif.) [5] | Disconnect & Ground Harness Wire | 1 |
| | Reconnect Sensor | Open Circuit |
| Vanagon [6] | Disconnect & Ground Harness Wire | 0 |
| | Reconnect Sensor | Open Circuit |

[1] - Measure resistance between terminals No. 2 and 13.
[2] - Measure resistance between terminals No. 2 and 8.
[3] - Measure resistance between terminals No. 1 and 2.
[4] - Measure resistance between terminals No. 7 and 35.
[5] - Measure resistance between terminals No. 2 and 8.
[6] - Measure resistance between terminals No. 5 and 7.

### THROTTLE POSITION SENSOR RESISTANCE TEST

| Application | Position | Ohms |
|---|---|---|
| Except Corrado [1] | Disconnect Potentiometer | 1.5 |
| Corrado [2] | Throttle Closed | 0.5 |
| | Off Full Throttle | Open Circuit |
| | Full Throttle | 0.5 |

[1] - Measure resistance between terminals No. 1 and 34.
[2] - Measure resistance between terminals No. 6 and 11.

### VACUUM SENSOR RESISTANCE TEST [1]

| Condition | Ohms |
|---|---|
| Move Sensor Plate | Changing |

[1] - Measure resistance between terminals No. 15 and 19.

# 1991 ENGINE PERFORMANCE
# Wiring Diagrams

## Cabriolet, Corrado, Fox, Golf GL, GTI, Jetta, Jetta GLI, Passat, Vanagon

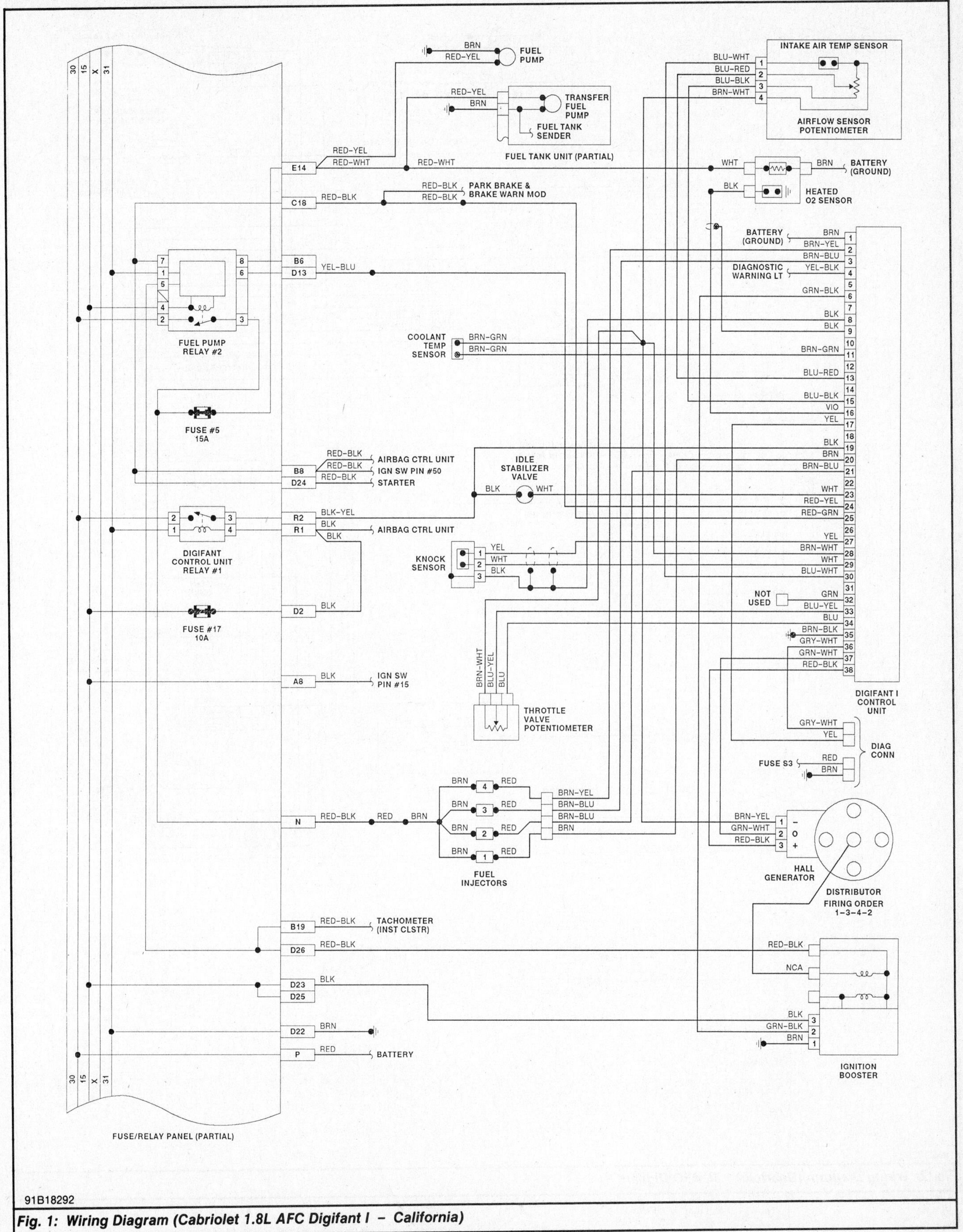


*Fig. 1: Wiring Diagram (Cabriolet 1.8L AFC Digifant I – California)*

# 1991 ENGINE PERFORMANCE
## Wiring Diagrams (Cont.)

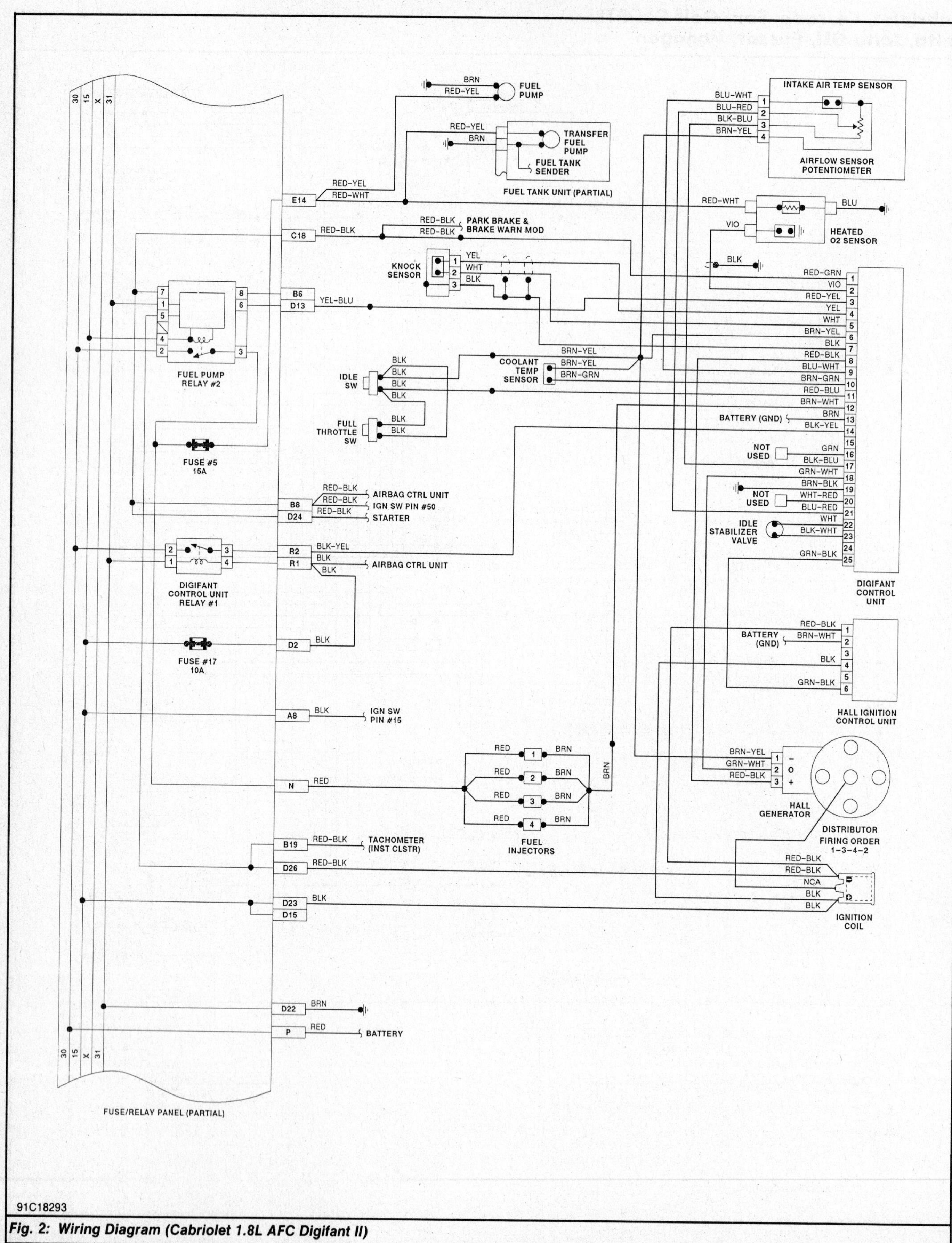


*Fig. 2: Wiring Diagram (Cabriolet 1.8L AFC Digifant II)*

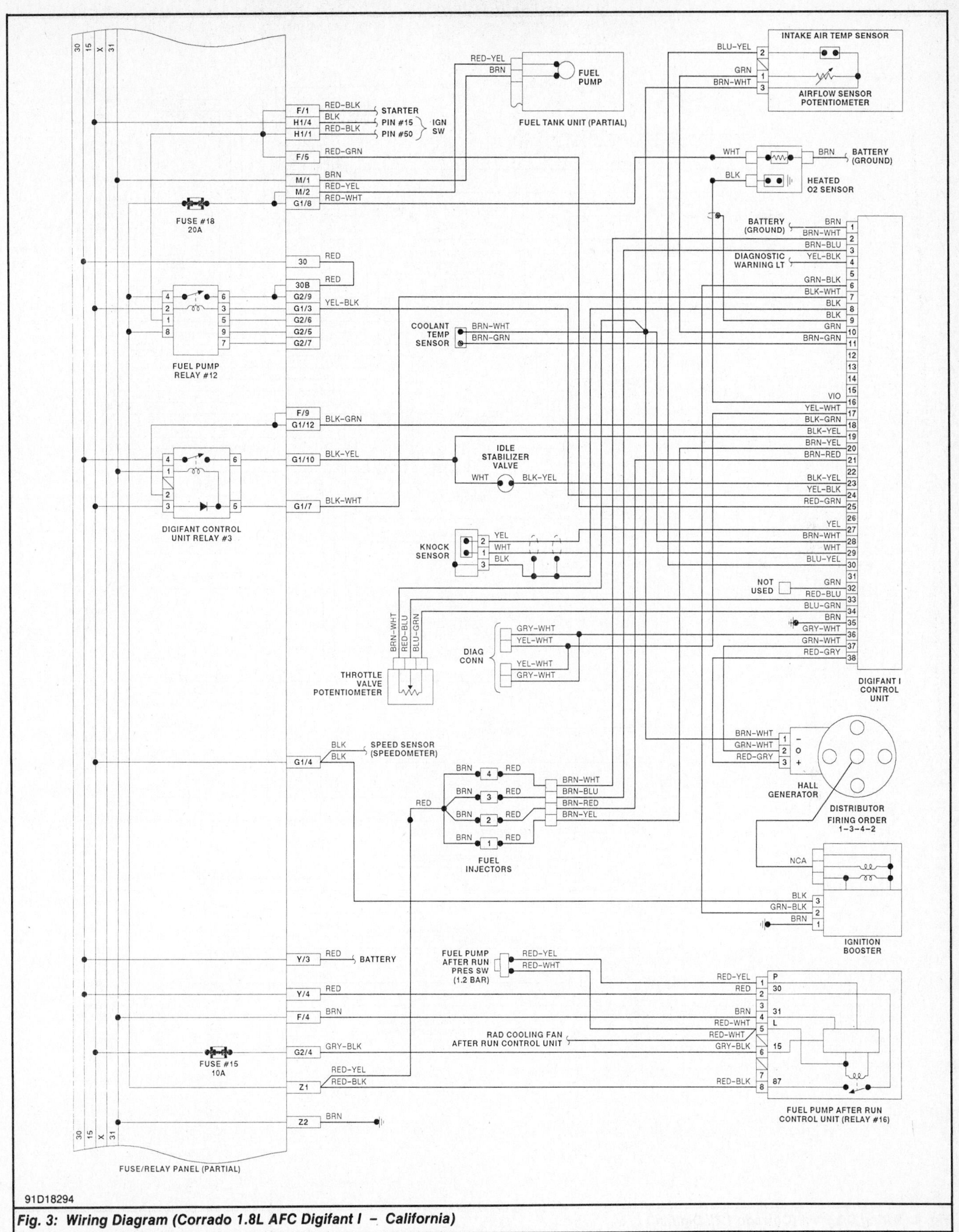


*Fig. 3: Wiring Diagram (Corrado 1.8L AFC Digifant I – California)*

# 1991 ENGINE PERFORMANCE
## Wiring Diagrams (Cont.)

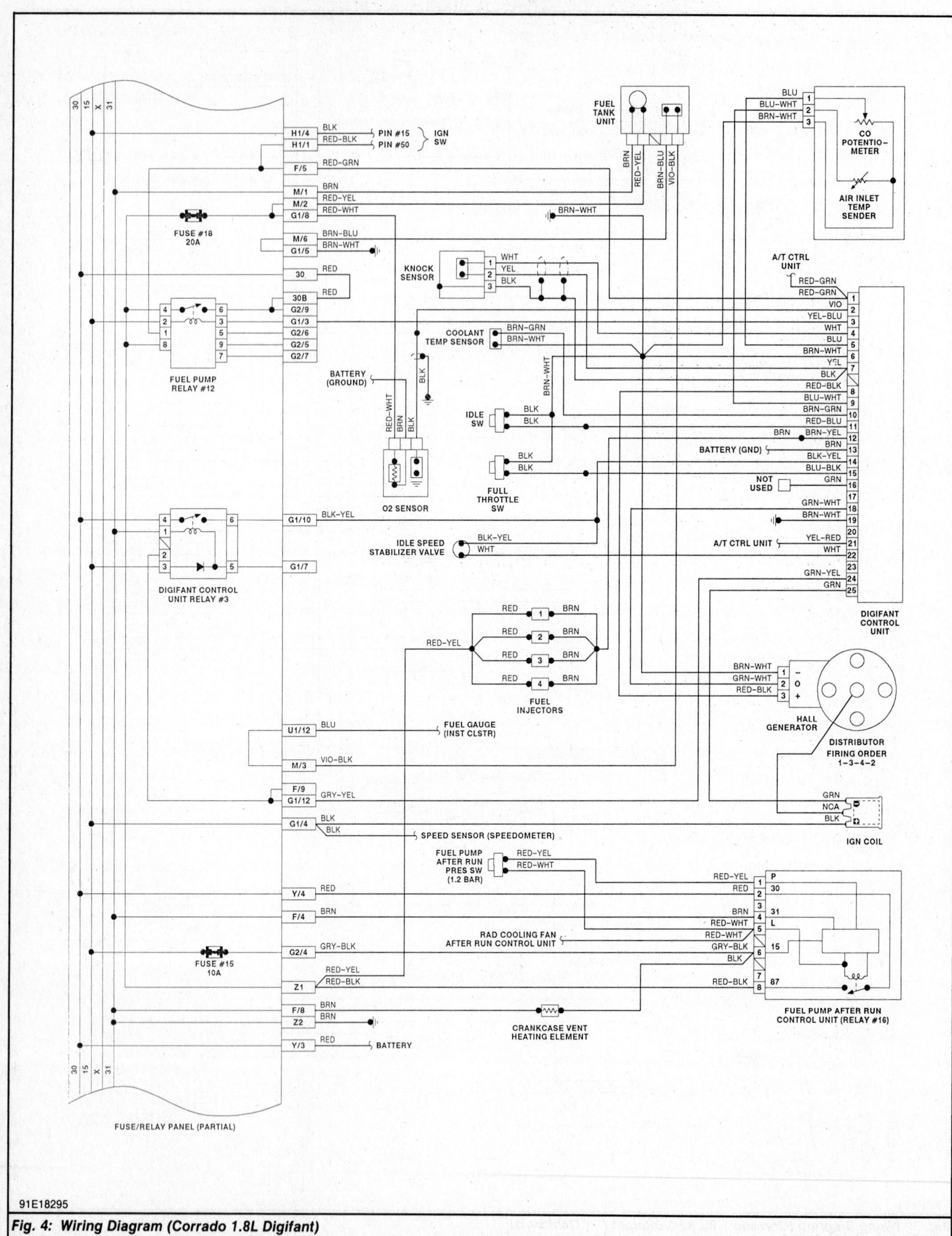


Fig. 4: Wiring Diagram (Corrado 1.8L Digifant)

# 1991 ENGINE PERFORMANCE
## Wiring Diagrams (Cont.)

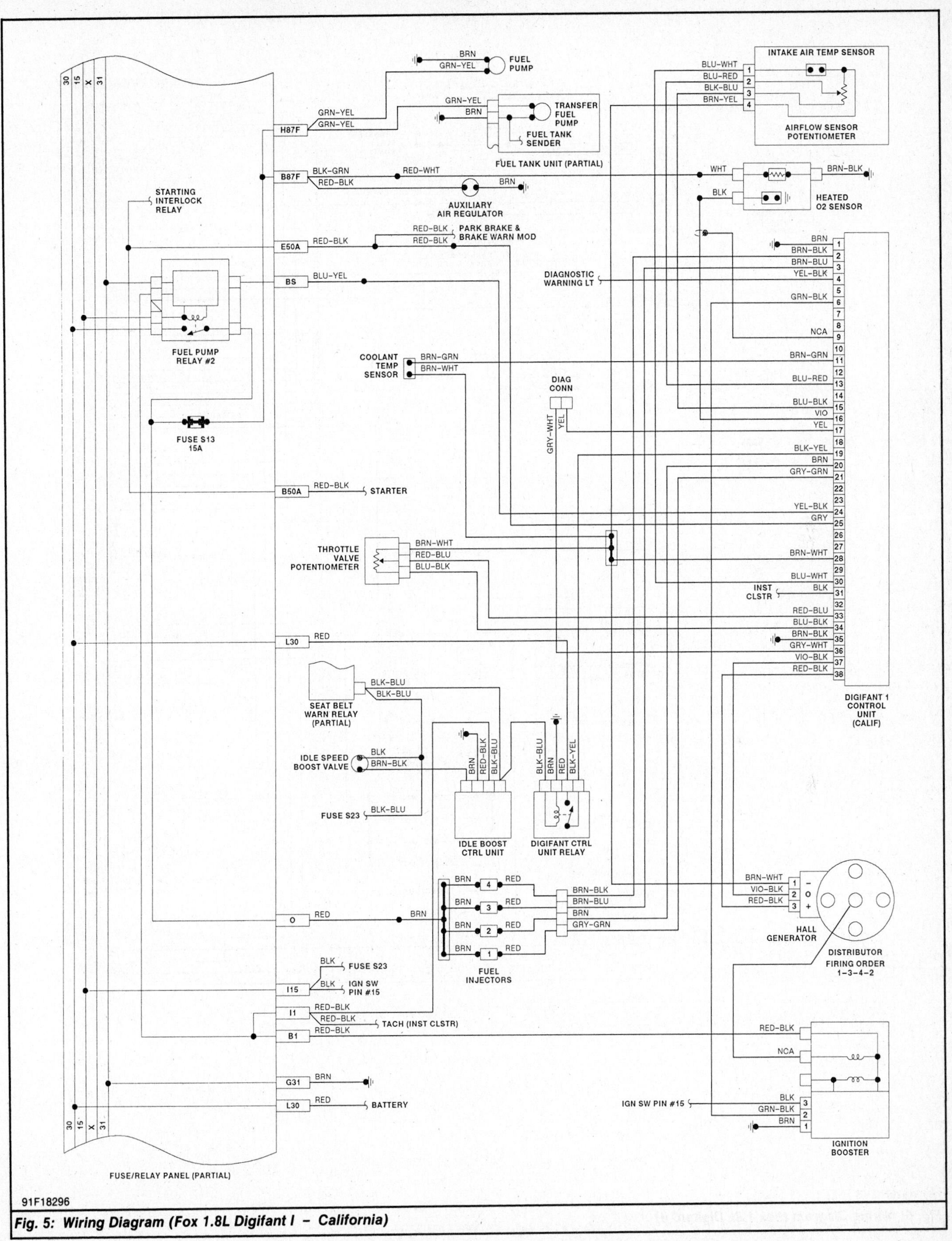


*Fig. 5: Wiring Diagram (Fox 1.8L Digifant I – California)*

# 1991 ENGINE PERFORMANCE
## Wiring Diagrams (Cont.)

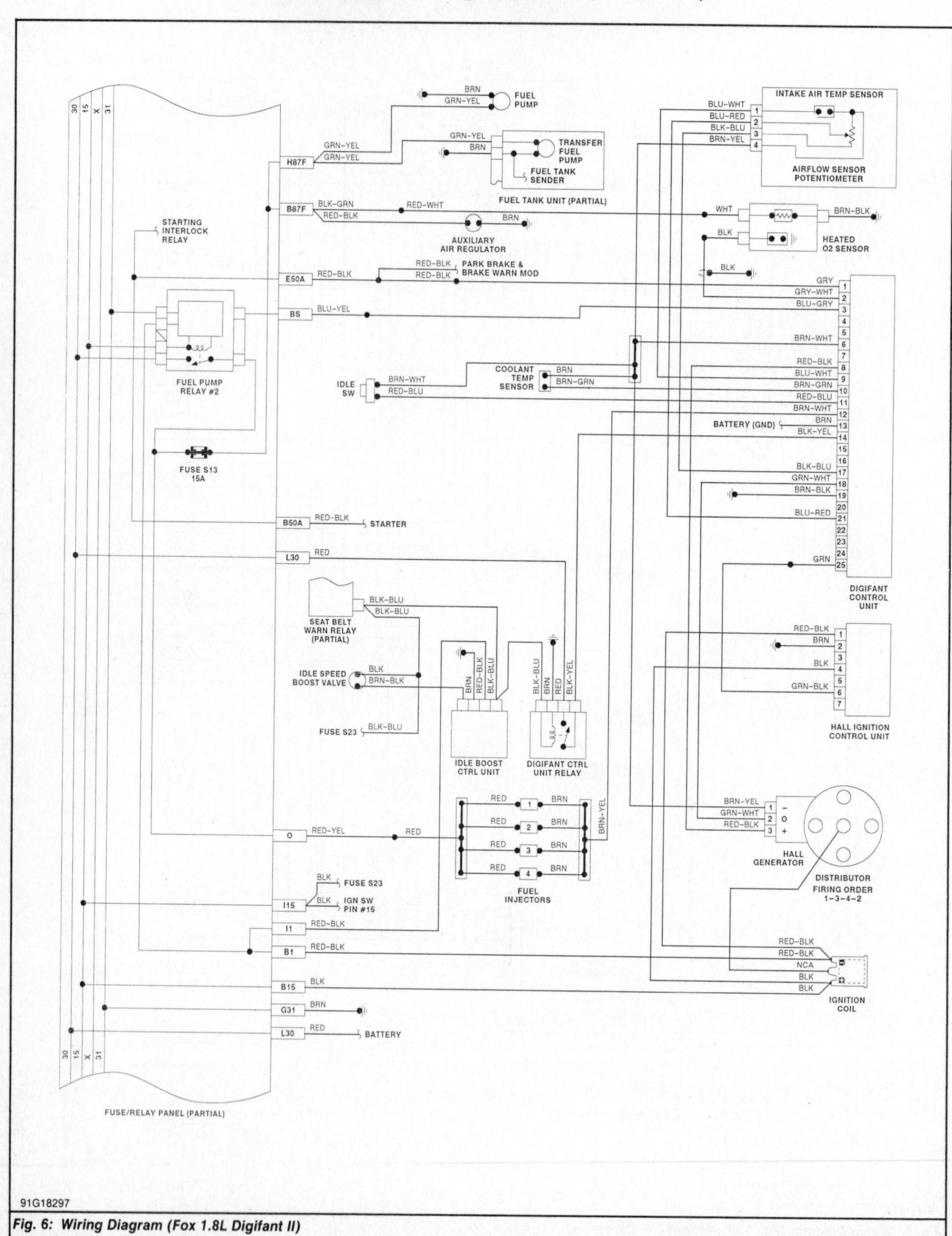


*Fig. 6: Wiring Diagram (Fox 1.8L Digifant II)*

# 1991 ENGINE PERFORMANCE
## Wiring Diagrams (Cont.)

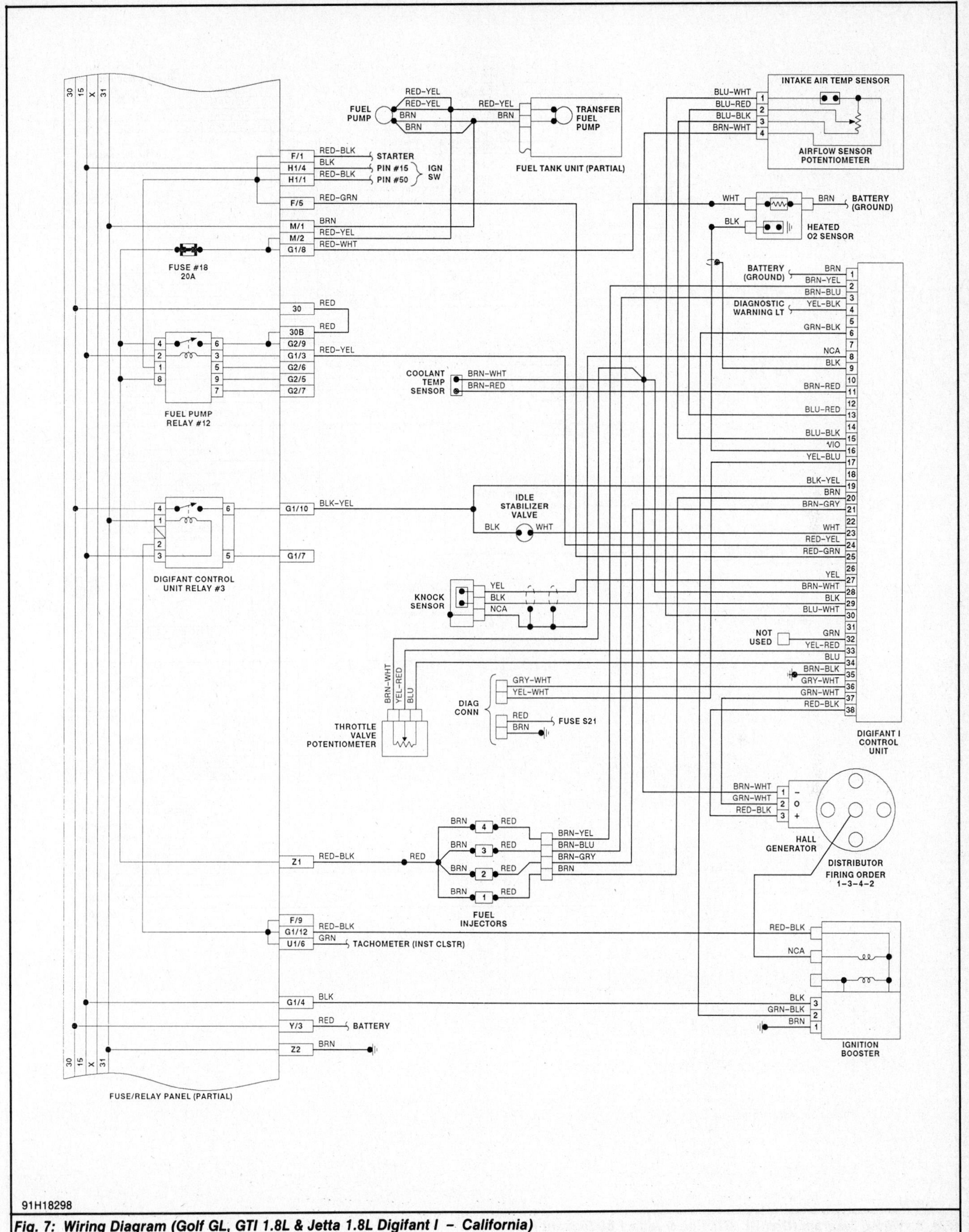


Fig. 7: Wiring Diagram (Golf GL, GTI 1.8L & Jetta 1.8L Digifant I – California)

# 1991 ENGINE PERFORMANCE
## Wiring Diagrams (Cont.)

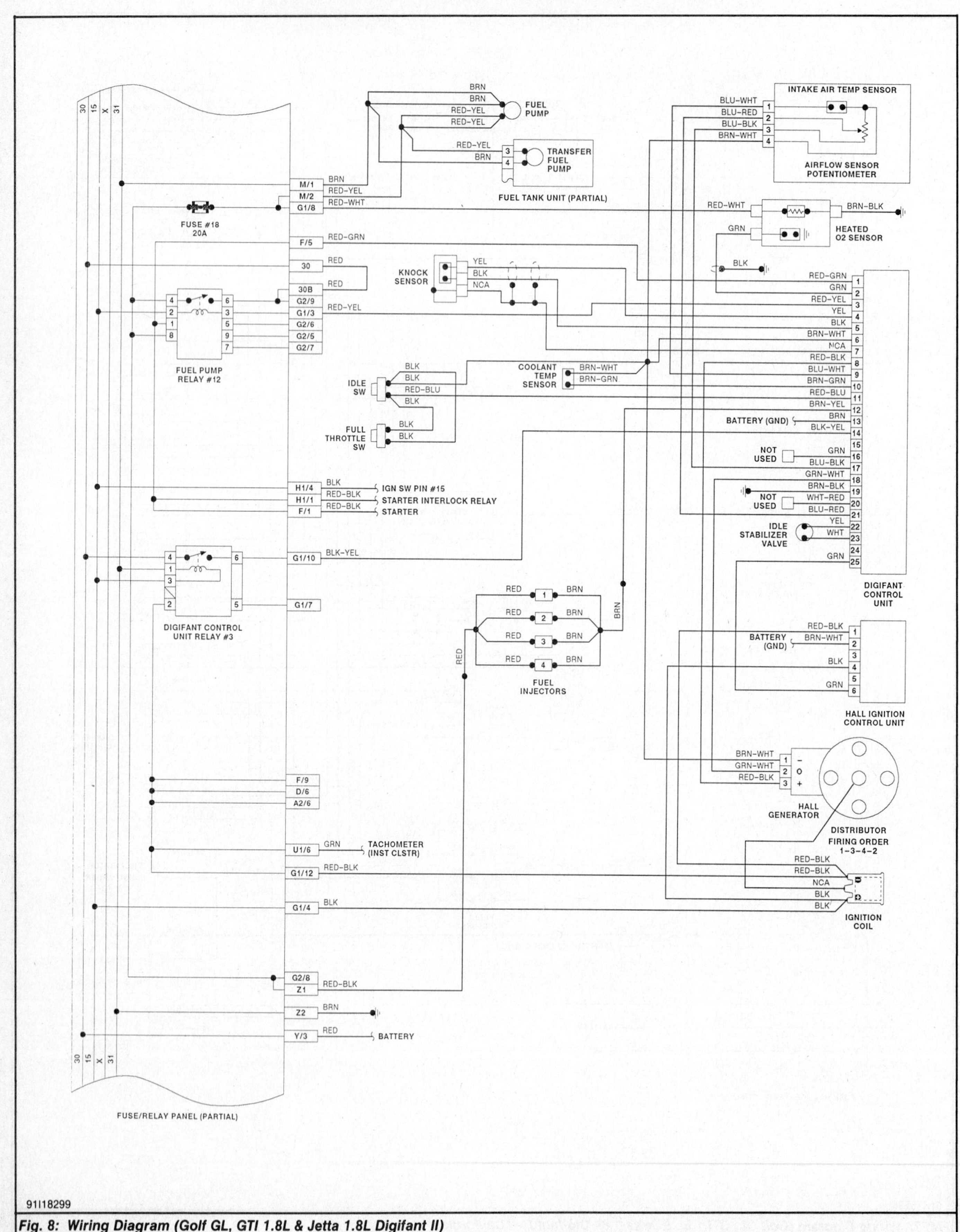


**Fig. 8: Wiring Diagram (Golf GL, GTI 1.8L & Jetta 1.8L Digifant II)**

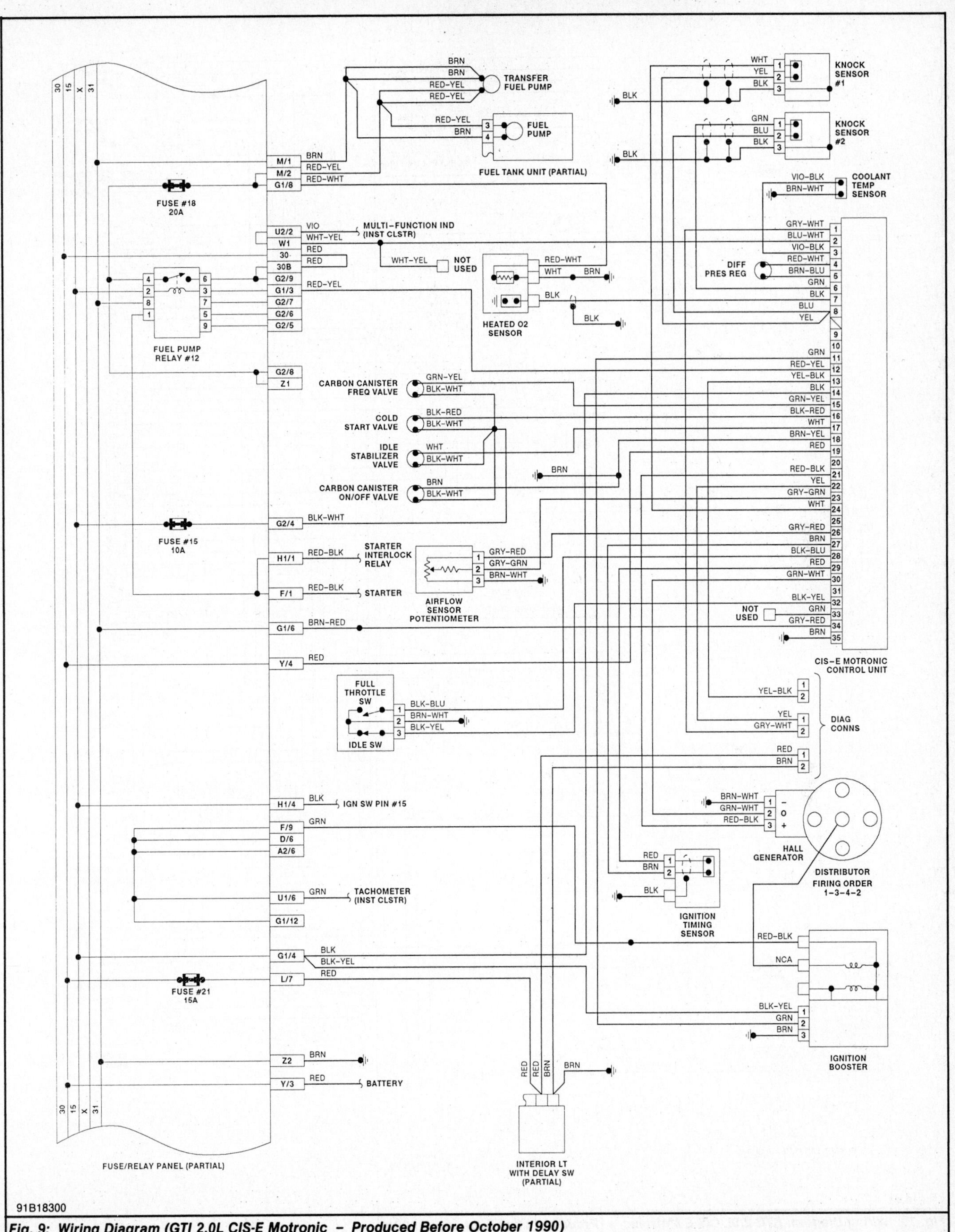


*Fig. 9: Wiring Diagram (GTI 2.0L CIS-E Motronic – Produced Before October 1990)*

# 1991 ENGINE PERFORMANCE
# Wiring Diagrams (Cont.)

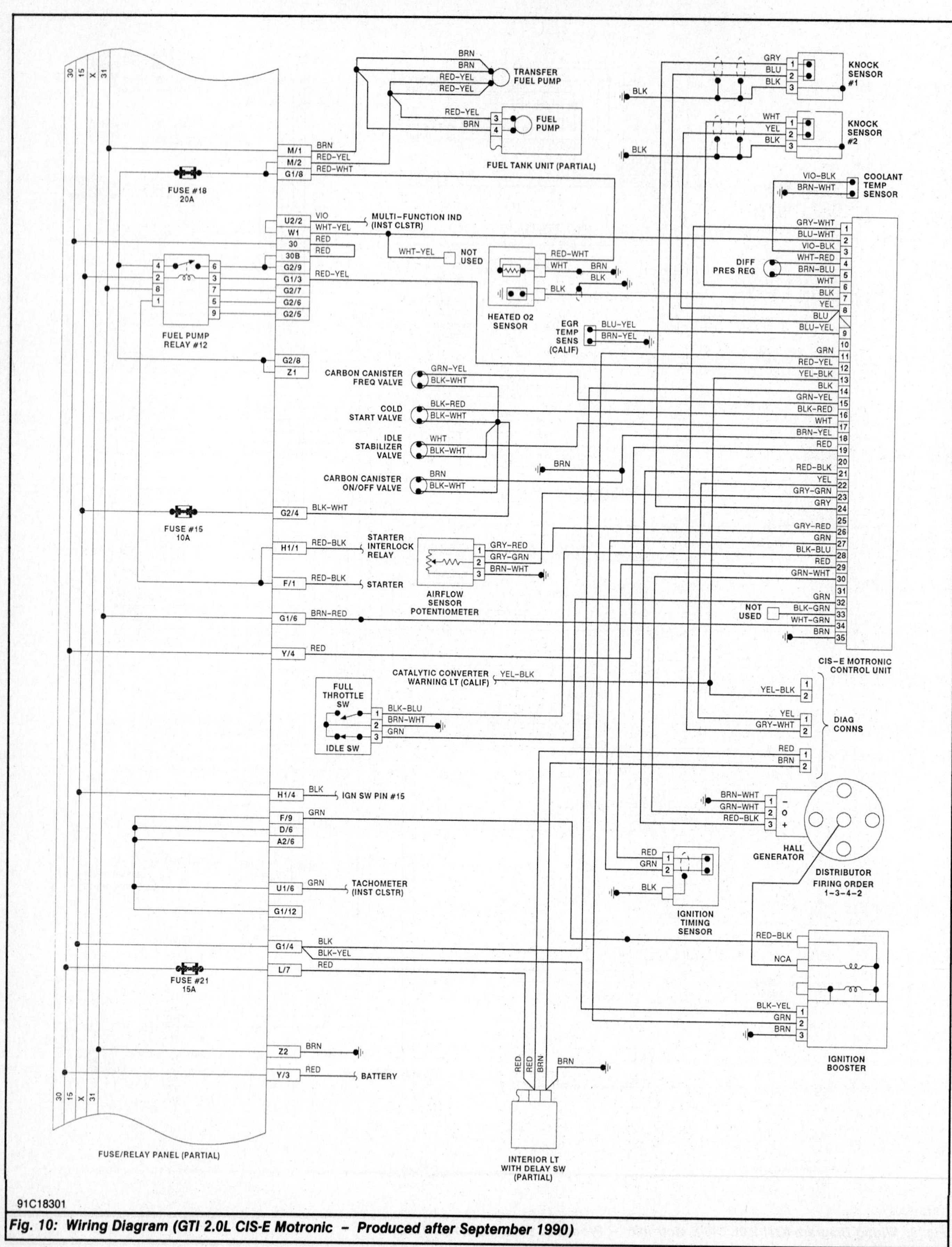


Fig. 10: Wiring Diagram (GTI 2.0L CIS-E Motronic – Produced after September 1990)

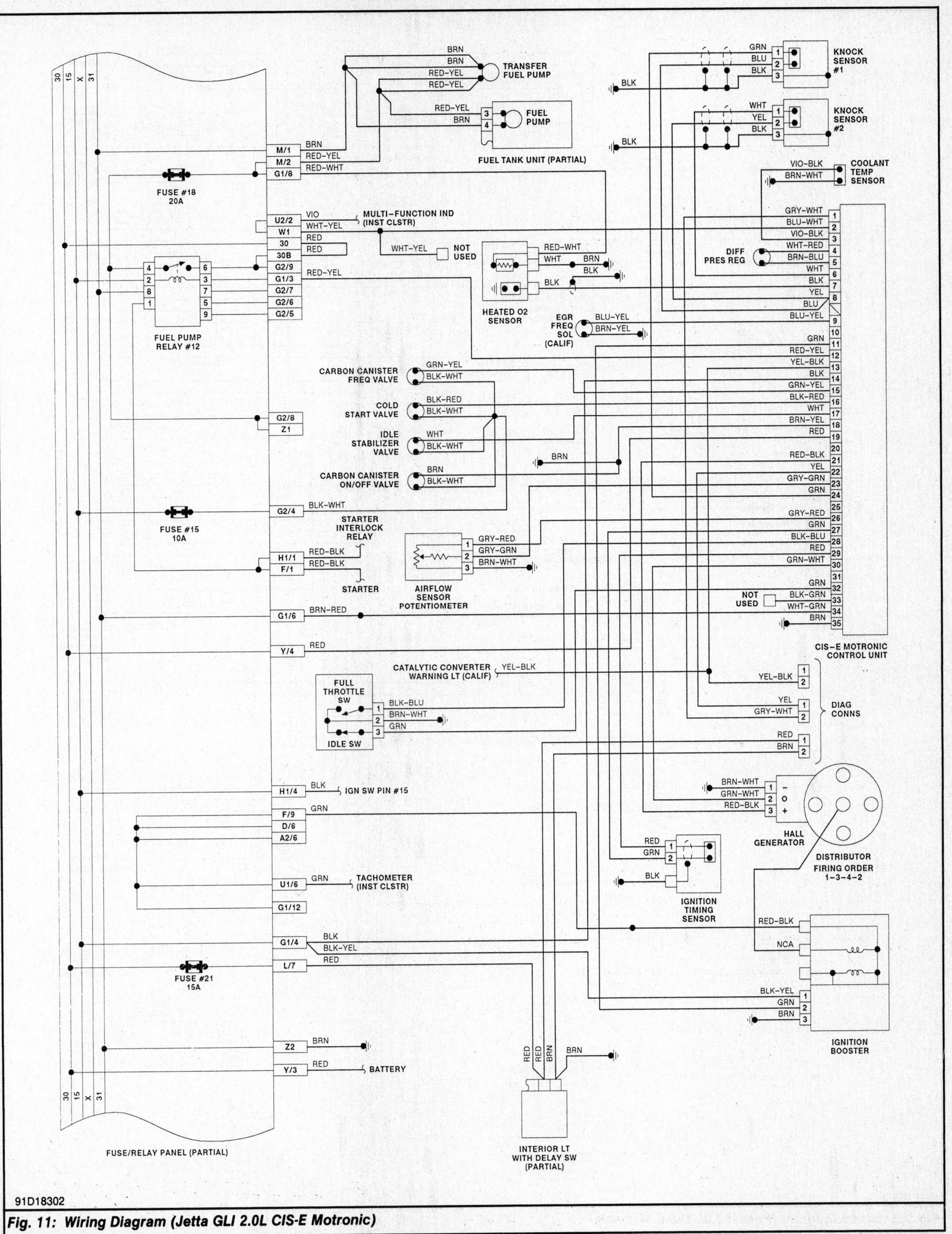


*Fig. 11: Wiring Diagram (Jetta GLI 2.0L CIS-E Motronic)*

# 1991 ENGINE PERFORMANCE
## Wiring Diagrams (Cont.)

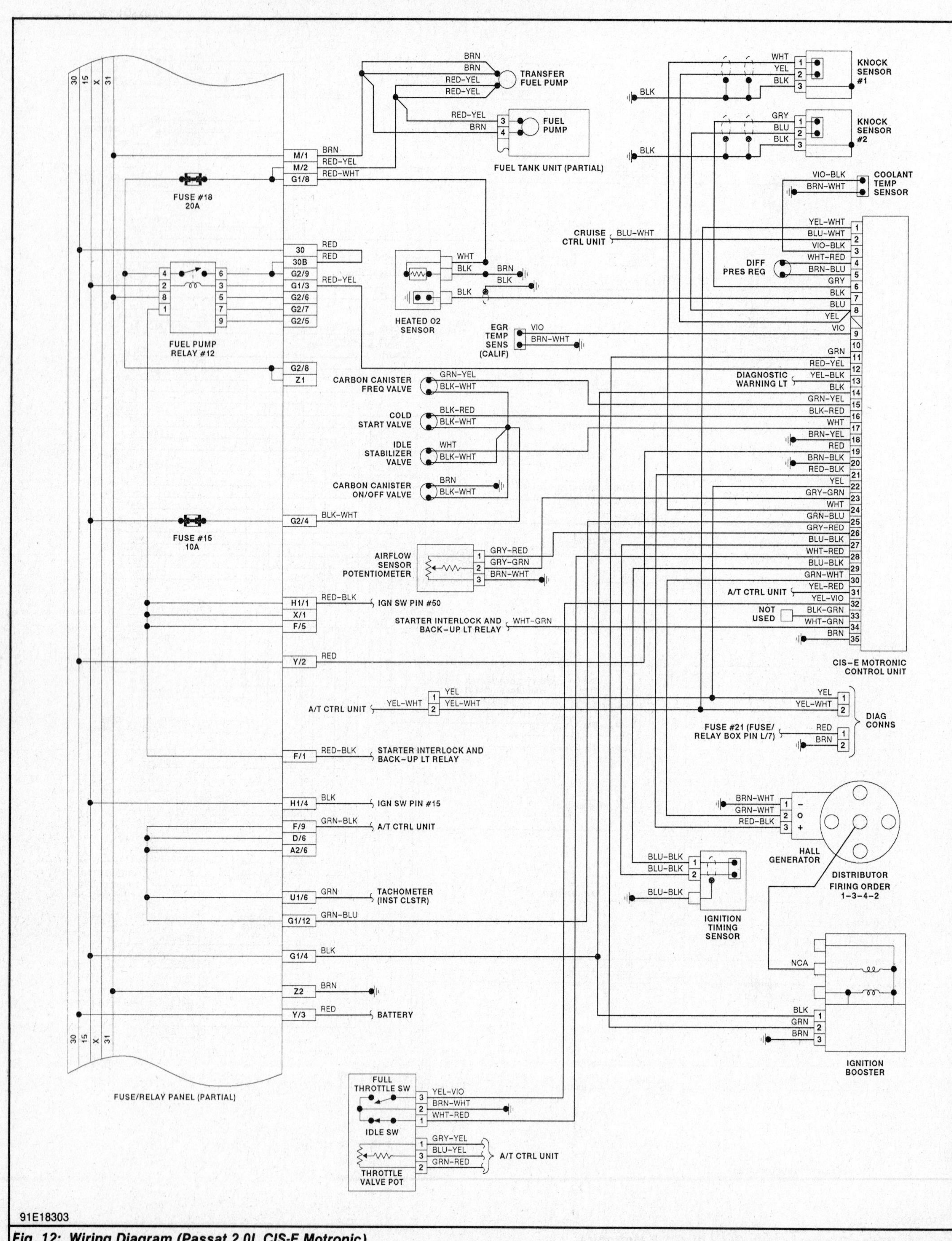


*Fig. 12: Wiring Diagram (Passat 2.0L CIS-E Motronic)*

# 1991 ENGINE PERFORMANCE
## Wiring Diagrams (Cont.)

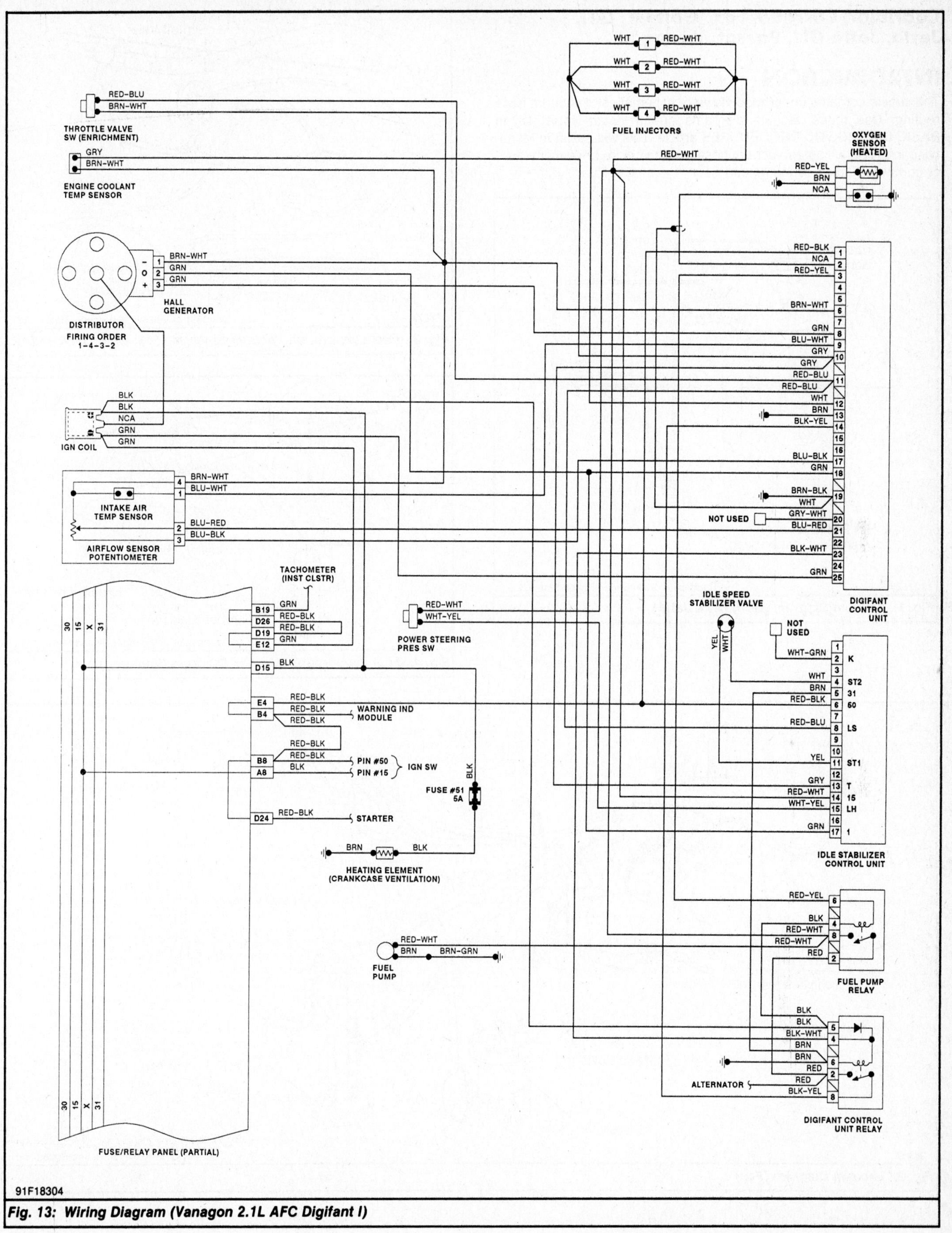


Fig. 13: Wiring Diagram (Vanagon 2.1L AFC Digifant I)

# 1991 ENGINE PERFORMANCE
# Vacuum Diagrams

## Cabriolet, Corrado, Fox, Golf GL, GTI, Jetta, Jetta GLI, Passat, Vanagon

## INTRODUCTION

This article contains underhood views or schematics of vacuum hose routing. Use these vacuum diagrams during visual inspection in BASIC DIAGNOSTIC PROCEDURES article. This will assist in identifying improperly routed vacuum hoses which cause driveability and/or computer-indicated malfunctions.

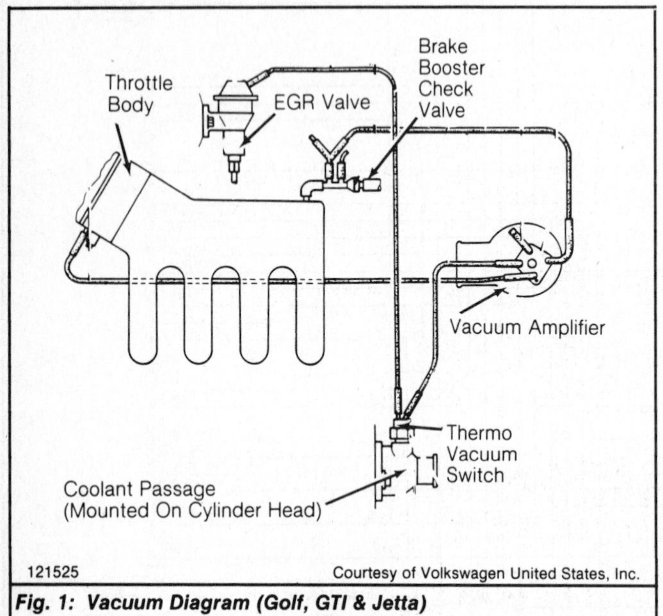


*Fig. 1: Vacuum Diagram (Golf, GTI & Jetta)*

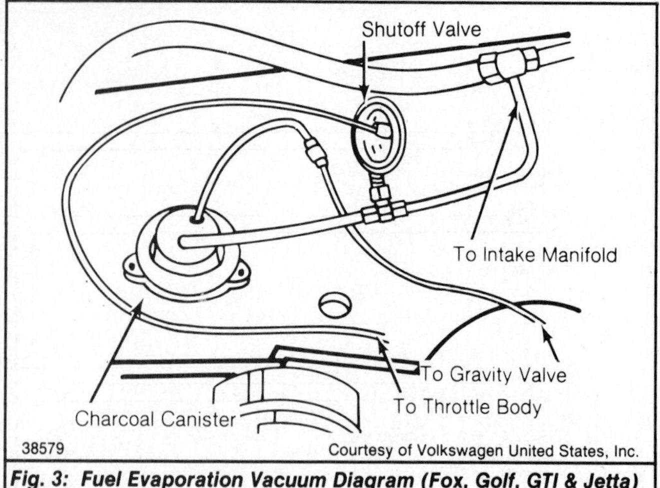


*Fig. 3: Fuel Evaporation Vacuum Diagram (Fox, Golf, GTI & Jetta)*

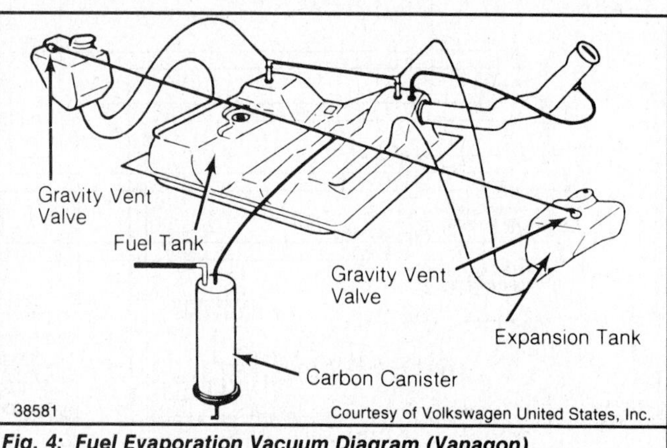


*Fig. 4: Fuel Evaporation Vacuum Diagram (Vanagon)*

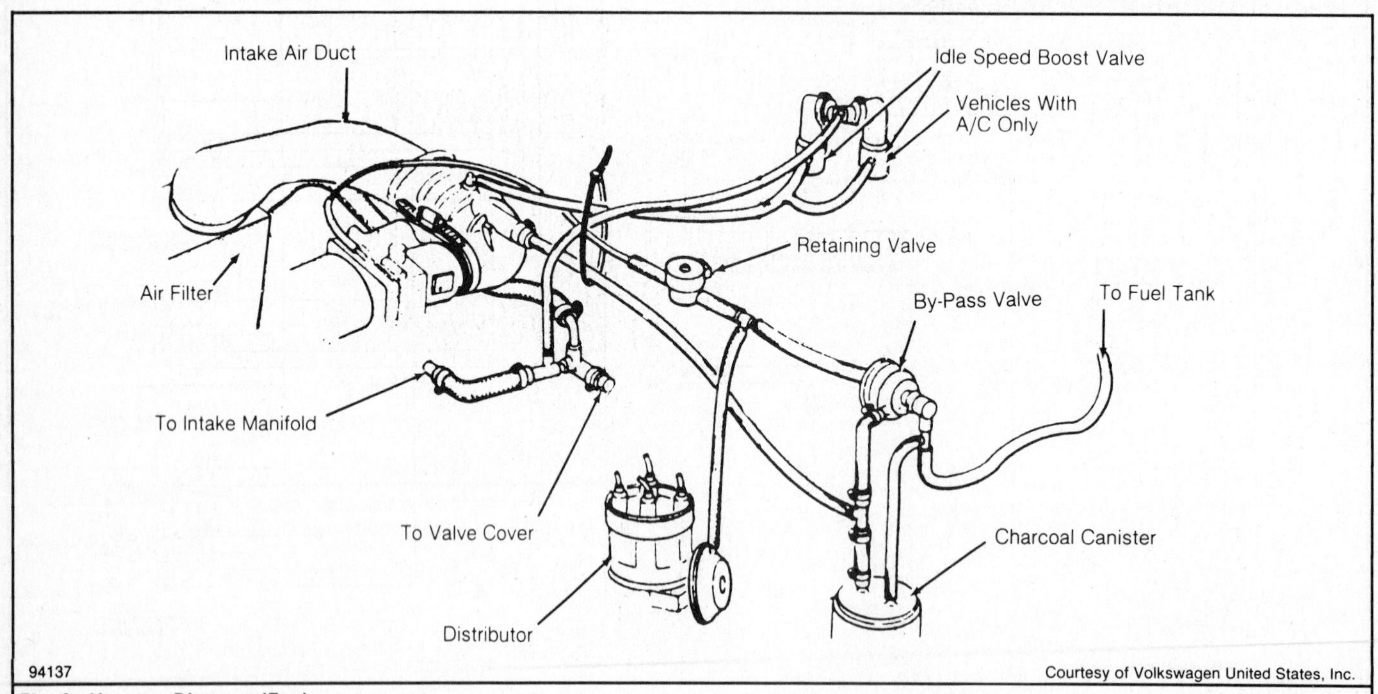


*Fig. 2: Vacuum Diagram (Fox)*

# 1991 ENGINE PERFORMANCE
# Vacuum Diagrams (Cont.)

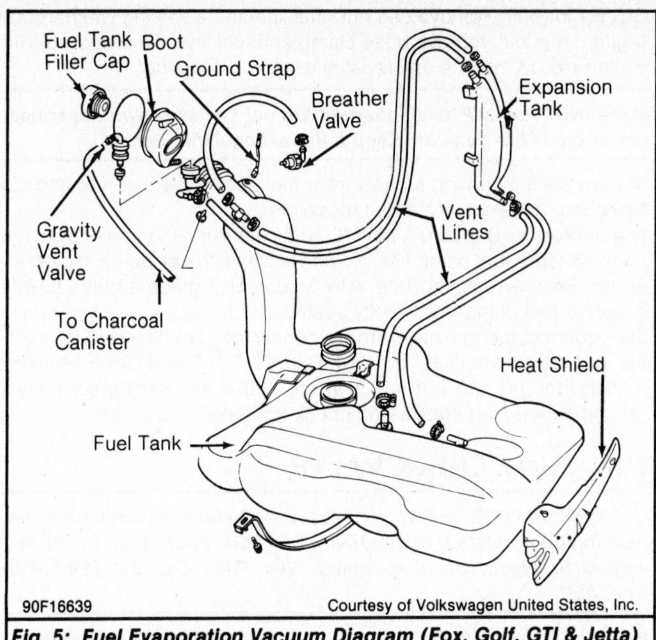


**Fig. 5: Fuel Evaporation Vacuum Diagram (Fox, Golf, GTI & Jetta)**

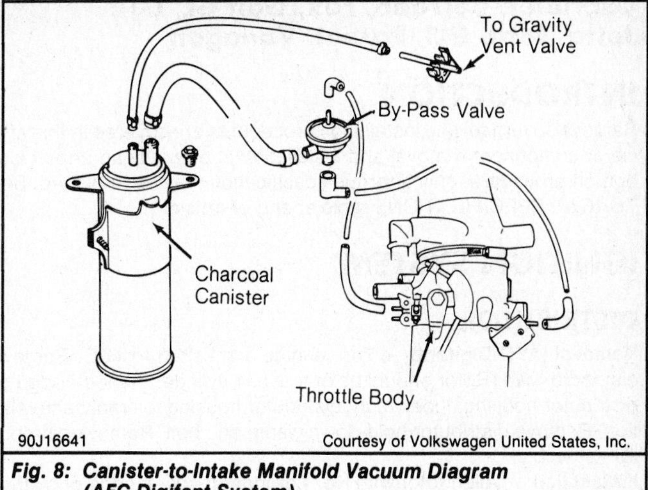


**Fig. 8: Canister-to-Intake Manifold Vacuum Diagram (AFC-Digifant System)**

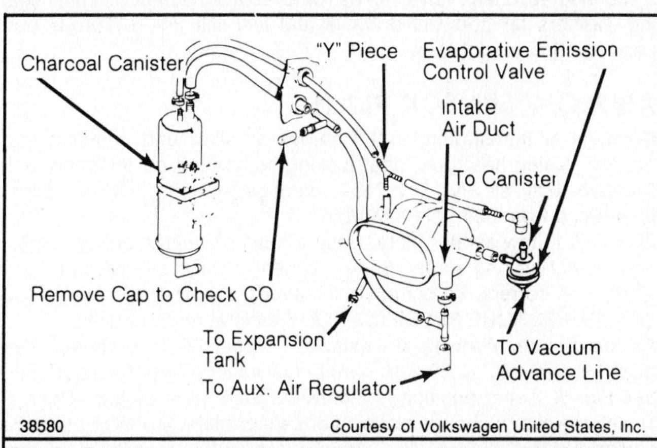


**Fig. 6: Canister-to-Intake Manifold Vacuum Diagram (Cabriolet)**

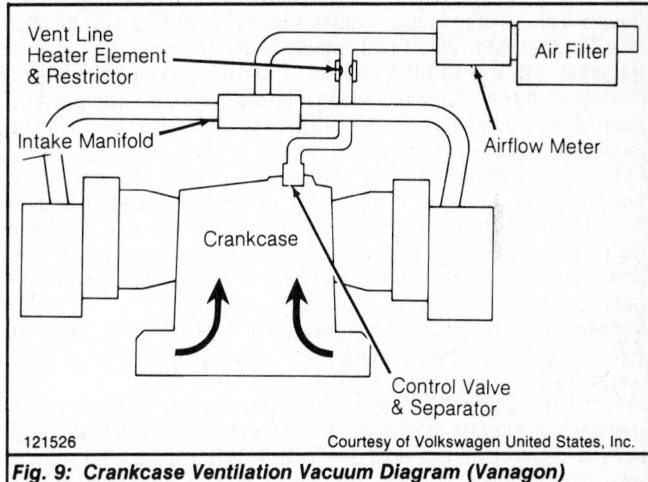


**Fig. 9: Crankcase Ventilation Vacuum Diagram (Vanagon)**

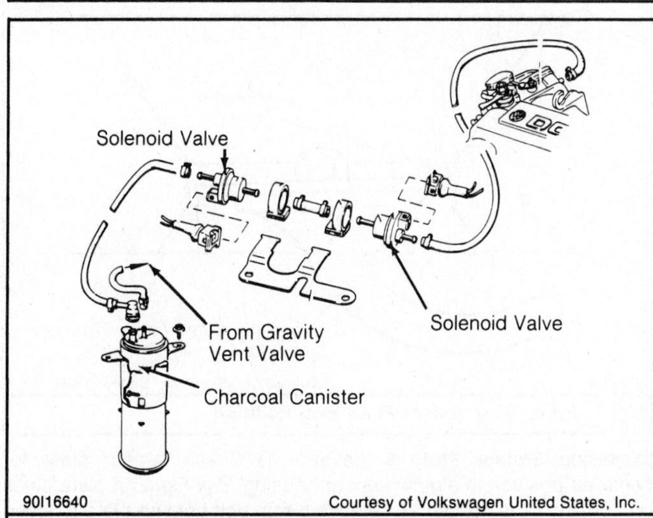

**Fig. 7: Canister-to-Intake Manifold Vacuum Diagram (CIS-E Motronic System)**

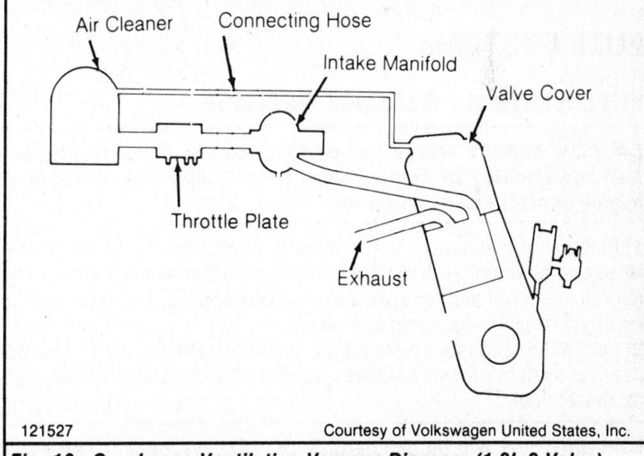


**Fig. 10: Crankcase Ventilation Vacuum Diagram (1.8L 8-Valve)**

# 1991 ENGINE PERFORMANCE
# Removal, Overhaul & Installation

## Cabriolet, Corrado, Fox, Golf GL, GTI, Jetta, Jetta GLI, Passat, Vanagon

## INTRODUCTION

Removal, overhaul and installation procedures are covered in this article. If component removal and installation is primarily an unbolt and bolt-on procedure, only a torque specification may be furnished. See TORQUE SPECIFICATIONS table at end of article.

## IGNITION SYSTEM

### DISTRIBUTOR

**Removal (AFC-Digifant)** – Turn engine crankshaft to TDC. Remove distributor cap. Rotor should point to No. 1 cylinder mark on edge of distributor housing. Index mark distributor housing to crankcase relation. Remove distributor hold-down clamp and bolt. Remove distributor assembly.
**Installation** – Align rotor with No. 1 cylinder mark on edge of distributor housing. Install distributor and align housing to index mark made on crankcase. Install distributor hold-down clamp and bolt. Install distributor cap. Check timing. Tighten hold-down bolt to specification. See TORQUE SPECIFICATIONS table at end of article.
**Removal (CIS-E & CIS-E Motronic)** – **1)** Turn engine crankshaft to TDC. Marking on vibration dampener pulley must align with drive belt guard pointer. Marking on cam shaft gear sprocket must align with cylinder head cover.
**2)** Remove distributor cap and mark position of rotor. Rotor should be pointing to No. 1 cylinder in distributor firing sequence. Mark position of distributor housing for installation reference. Remove distributor hold-down clamp and bolt. Remove distributor assembly, noting position of rotor when distributor shaft gear is disengaged from driving gear.
**Installation** – **1)** Align oil pump drive pinion lug parallel to crankshaft. Set rotor pointing toward mark made when distributor was disengaged from drive gear.
**2)** Install distributor. Rotor should now point to mark made for No. 1 cylinder in distributor firing sequence. Align mark for distributor housing and install distributor hold-down clamp and bolt. Install distributor cap. Check timing. Tighten hold-down bolt to specification. See TORQUE SPECIFICATIONS table at end of article.

## FUEL SYSTEM

### FUEL SYSTEM PRESSURE RELEASE

***CAUTION: ALWAYS relieve fuel pressure before disconnecting any fuel injection-related component. DO NOT allow fuel to contact engine or electrical components.***

**1)** Pinch shut fuel supply line to transfer pump from fuel tank. With a large container under pump and reservoir, disconnect output fuel line to drain reservoir and relieve pressure. Be prepared, with rags, to mop up any to residue escaping container.
**2)** Locate fuel pressure testing port on end of fuel rail. As an alternative fuel system pressure release, open port slowly, using clean rags to absorb fuel.

***WARNING: Fuel will be discharged! DO NOT disconnect any wires that could cause electrical sparks. DO NOT smoke or work near heaters or other fire hazards. Keep a fire extinguisher handy.***

### FUEL PUMP

**Removal** – **1)** Disconnect battery ground lead. Working under vehicle, disconnect harness connector from fuel pump. Thoroughly clean around outside of fuel line unions.
**2)** Temporarily pinch shut supply line from pump to fuel tank. With a large container under pump and reservoir, disconnect output fuel line to drain reservoir and relieve pressure. On models with CIS, CIS-E or CIS-E Motronic, remove cap nut, fuel line and 2 sealing washers. On Digifant models, remove hose clamp and fuel line. Be prepared, with clean rags, to mop up any residue escaping container.

***WARNING: Fuel will be discharged! Do not smoke or work near heaters or other fire hazards. Keep a fire extinguisher handy.***

**3)** Remove 3 mounting screws from fuel pump retaining ring and pull fuel pump assembly from fuel reservoir.
**Installation** – **1)** Moisten new "O" ring with fuel and install over fuel pump. Ensure fuel pump filter screen is clean. Install pump in fuel reservoir. Secure retaining ring with 3 screws. Tighten screws evenly, ensuring fuel pump is correctly seated.
**2)** Reconnect fuel line and harness connector. Use new sealing washers and hose clamps as required. On CIS, CIS-E and CIS-E Motronic models, torque cap nut to 15 ft. lbs. (20 N.m). Reconnect battery ground cable, start engine and check for leaks.

### FUEL PUMP CHECK VALVE

***CAUTION: ALWAYS relieve fuel pressure before disconnecting any fuel injection-related component. DO NOT allow fuel to contact engine or electrical components. See FUEL SYSTEM PRESSURE RELEASE.***

**Removal & Installation** – Clean and disconnect fuel line. With line disconnected, check valve can be removed from pump. Use new sealing washers for both check valve and fuel line union. Torque both parts to 15 ft. lb. (20 N.m).

### AIRFLOW SENSOR PLATE

**Removal & Installation** – **1)** Remove air filter and unscrew stop bracket. Using heat gun, heat locking compound on fastening bolt. Remove bolt slowly. DO NOT damage threads. Clean locking compound from bolt hole threads.
**2)** Install airflow sensor plate. Ensure 5 dimple marks are up. Lightly tighten self-locking screw. Ensure sensor plate is centered and rest position is correct. To complete installation, reverse removal procedure. See TORQUE SPECIFICATIONS table at end of article.
**Airflow Sensor Plate Rest Position** – Upper edge of sensor plate must be .070-080" (1.80-2.10 mm) below lower edge of sensor cone. *See Fig. 1.* If rest position is incorrect, raise sensor plate. Open or close wire clip to change position of sensor plate. DO NOT bend leaf spring.

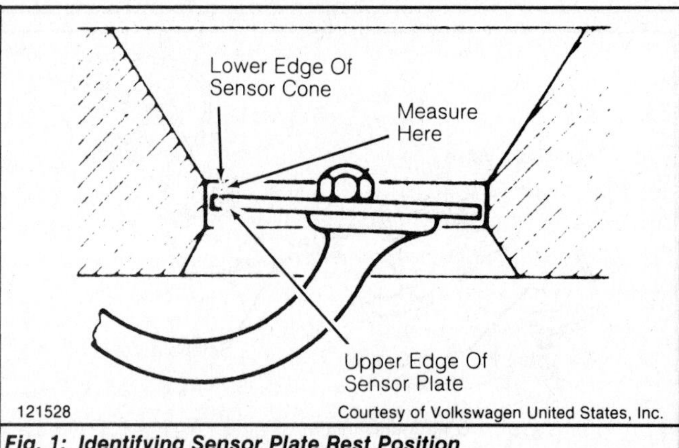


***Fig. 1: Identifying Sensor Plate Rest Position***

**Centering Sensor Plate & Lever** – **1)** Check sensor plate for centered position in airflow sensor housing. *See Fig. 2.* If plate binds on housing or is off-center, remove 6-mm bolt holding plate to lever. Coat bolt with locking compound and install finger tight.
**2)** Use Centering Gauge (US 1109) or .004" (.10 mm) feeler gauge to set plate an equal distance from sensor housing. If plate cannot be centered, remove airflow sensor housing.

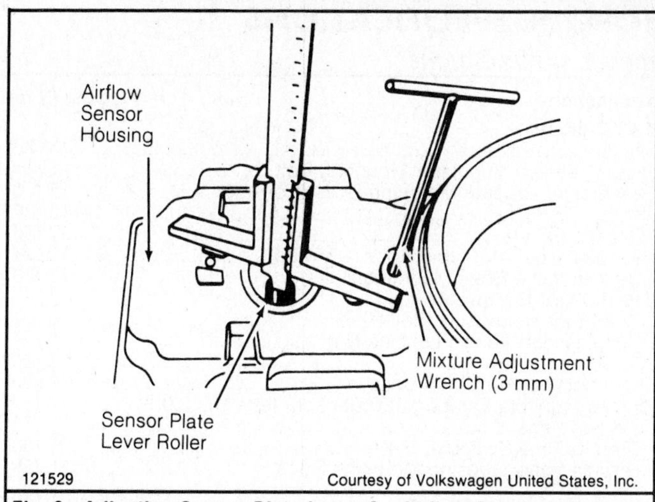


***Fig. 2: Adjusting Sensor Plate Lever On Airflow Sensor Housing***

**3)** Turn housing upside-down and remove counterweight-to-sensor lever bolt. Coat bolt with locking compound and install finger tight. Center sensor plate lever in housing and tighten bolt. Complete centering of plate.

**Checking Sensor Plate Free Play - 1)** Free play is measured between control piston and adjusting lever. To ensure Differential Pressure Regulator (DPR) current is 4-16 mA, sensor plate lever must be positioned correctly. Measure free play on side of sensor cone closest to fuel distributor. *See Fig. 3.*

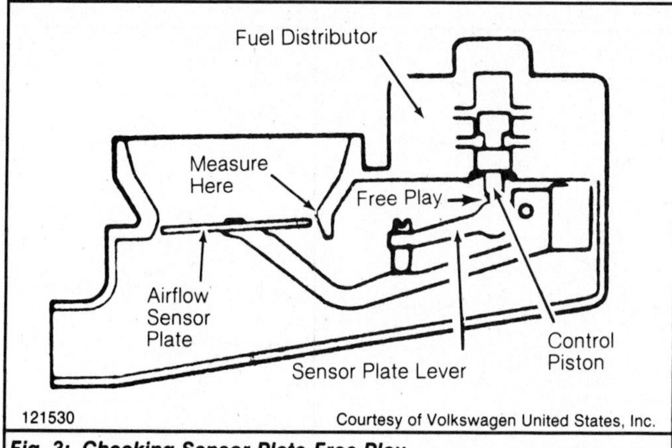


***Fig. 3: Checking Sensor Plate Free Play***

**2)** Crank starter motor for 10 seconds to develop fuel pressure. Lift sensor plate slightly until resistance is felt. Minimum clearance is any noticeable free play. Maximum clearance is .083" (2.1 mm) up to sensor cone.

**3)** If free play clearance is incorrect, remove fuel distributor. Check basic adjustment of sensor plate lever. See SENSOR PLATE LEVER ADJUSTMENT. Recheck free play clearance. If free play clearance is still incorrect, adjust sensor plate clearance with control piston stop screw.

**Sensor Plate Lever Adjustment - 1)** With fuel distributor removed from airflow sensor housing, measure distance between roller on sensor plate lever and contact points of fuel distributor on top of airflow sensor housing. *See Fig. 2.*

**2)** Use a depth gauge or vernier caliper for measuring distance. Distance should be .74-.75" (18.9-19.1 mm). If distance is out of specified range, correct it by adjusting mixture screw.

**3)** Lightly lubricate new sealing "O" ring and mount on fuel distributor. Install fuel distributor. See TORQUE SPECIFICATIONS table at end of article. Connect all fuel lines except those to fuel injectors. Check sensor plate adjusting lever and fuel distributor control piston for smooth operation. *See Fig. 3.*

**4)** Remove fuel pump relay and bridge fuel pump circuit. Use Jumper Switch (US 4480/3) in place of fuel pump relay. When pressure has built up, turn off fuel pump. Move sensor plate from rest position to end of travel.

**5)** Uniform resistance should be felt during entire movement. No resistance should be felt on quick return to rest position. Connect injector lines. Install fuel pump relay. Start engine and check for leaks.

## AIRFLOW SENSOR POTENTIOMETER

**Removal & Installation - 1)** Remove differential pressure regulator. Remove insulating compound covering mounting screws. Remove potentiometer. DO NOT touch or damage slide contact and conductor.

**2)** To install, reverse removal procedure. See TORQUE SPECIFICATIONS table at end of article. Adjust potentiometer. See ON-VEHICLE ADJUSTMENTS article.

## FUEL DISTRIBUTOR (1.8L ONLY)

***CAUTION: ALWAYS relieve fuel pressure before disconnecting any fuel injection-related component. DO NOT allow fuel to contact engine or electrical components. Wipe up any spilled fuel BEFORE continuing service.***

**Removal & Installation - 1)** Disconnect battery and remove air cleaner. Disconnect all fuel and injector lines from fuel distributor. Plug fuel supply and return lines. Use clean rags to catch any fuel spilled.

**2)** Disconnect wiring from differential pressure regulator. Remove screws holding fuel distributor to airflow sensor housing. Remove fuel distributor by turning back and forth while lifting up. To install, reverse removal procedure.

## INJECTORS

***CAUTION: ALWAYS relieve fuel pressure before disconnecting any fuel injection-related component. DO NOT allow fuel to contact engine or electrical components. Wipe up any spilled fuel BEFORE continuing service.***

**Removal (AFC-Digifant) - 1)** Disconnect negative battery cable. Disconnect main electrical connector from fuel rail. Remove idle stabilizer valve. Loosen and remove both hoses on each end of fuel rail. Remove fuel pressure regulator and mounting bracket.

**2)** Remove fuel rail mounting bolts. Pry off injector mounting clips. Disconnect injector electrical connectors. Remove fuel rail. Remove each injector from its insert.

**Installation -** To install injectors, reverse removal procedures. Use new "O" rings when installing injectors. Replace hose clamps if necessary. See TORQUE SPECIFICATIONS table at end of this article. Check for fuel leaks.

**Removal (CIS-E & CIS-E Motronic) -** Remove injectors from inserts in cylinder head with fuel lines attached. Using 12-mm or 13-mm hex wrench, remove inserts from head. Use 2 wrenches to remove injectors from fuel lines.

**Installation -** To install, reverse removal procedures. Use 2 wrenches when tightening injector lines to injectors. Use new "O" rings lightly lubricated. On models with 2-piece inserts, replace insert sealing washer (against head) and use sealing compound on upper insert threaded portion. See TORQUE SPECIFICATIONS table at end of article.

## OXYGEN ($O_2$) SENSOR

**Removal & Installation - 1)** Oxygen ($O_2$) sensor is mounted in exhaust pipe in front of catalytic converter. Disconnect permanent pigtail from sensor. Ensure sensor is free of contaminants, avoid using any cleaning solvents. Sensor may be difficult to remove when engine temperature is less than 118°F (48°C).

**2)** Always use anti-seize compound on threads before installation. Tighten sensor to specification. See TORQUE SPECIFICATIONS table at end of article.

# 1991 ENGINE PERFORMANCE
# Removal, Overhaul & Installation (Cont.)

## THROTTLE VALVE HOUSING (TVH)

**Removal & Installation – 1)** Disconnect accelerator cable from linkage. Disconnect return spring on TVH. Remove cruise control connecting rod on TVH (if equipped). Pull off vacuum hoses. Remove TVH mounting nuts.

**2)** Disconnect throttle valve switch. Remove 2 TVH to metallic front vibration mounts nuts. Disconnect fuel return hose from pressure regulator. Lift sensor housing upward and remove TVH. Remove gasket.

**3)** To install, reverse removal procedure. Ensure all surfaces are clean and mate correctly. Use new gaskets when assembling. Adjust accelerator linkage and idle speed. See TORQUE SPECIFICATIONS table.

## TORQUE SPECIFICATIONS

*TORQUE SPECIFICATIONS*

| Application | Ft. Lbs. (N.m) |
|---|---|
| **AFC-Digifant** | |
| Fuel Injector Inserts | 15 (20) |
| Fuel Pressure Regulator Mounting Bolt | 11 (15) |
| Intercooler Bracket Mounting Bolts (Corrado) | 15 (20) |
| Knock Sensor | 15 (20) |
| Oxygen Sensor | 37 (50) |
| Supercharger Mounting Bolts (Corrado) | 18 (24) |
| Throttle Valve Body Mounting Bolts | 15 (20) |
| **CIS-E & CIS-E Motronic** | |
| Distributor Hold-Down Bolt (Fox) | 18 (24) |
| Fuel Injection Valve Fuel Line Nut | 18 (24) |
| Fuel Return Line Fitting | 15 (20) |
| Fuel Supply Line Union Bolts | 15 (20) |
| Intake Manifold Temperature Sensor (Jetta GLi 2.0L) | 15 (20) |
| Oxygen Sensor | 37 (50) |
| Thermo Time Switch (CIS-E) | 22 (30) |
| Throttle Valve Housing Mounting Bolts | 15 (20) |
| | **INCH Lbs. (N.m)** |
| **AFC-Digifant** | |
| Fuel Rail Mounting Bolts | 87 (10) |
| Idle Stabilizer Valve Mounting Nuts | 87 (10) |
| Intercooler Mounting Bolts (Corrado) | 87 (10) |
| Supercharger Air Hose Mounting Bolts (Corrado) | 87 (10) |
| **CIS-E & CIS-E Motronic** | |
| Auxiliary Air Regulator Mounting Bolts | 87 (10) |
| Cold Start Valve Mounting Bolts | 87 (10) |
| Coolant Temperature Sensor | 87 (10) |
| Distributor Hold-Down Bolt (Jetta GLi) | 87 (10) |
| EGR Valve Mounting Bolts | 87 (10) |
| Fuel Distributor Mounting Bolts | 30 (3.4) |
| Fuel Line Fittings | 87 (10) |
| Test Port Plug | 87 (10) |

# 1991 ELECTRICAL
# Alternators & Regulators – Bosch

**Cabriolet, Corrado, Fox, Golf GL, GTI, Jetta, Passat, Vanagon**

***NOTE: Some Golf, GTI, Jetta, Jetta GLi and Vanagon models may use a Motorola alternator. See ALTERNATORS & REGULATORS - SEV MOTOROLA article.***

## DESCRIPTION

Bosch alternators are conventional 3-phase, self-rectifying type alternators. Bosch 65 through 75-amp alternators use 3 positive and 3 negative diodes connected to stator windings to rectify current. Bosch 90-amp alternators use 14 diodes.

All alternators use 3 exciter diodes connected to stator windings. These diodes turn off the alternator indicator light and supply power to the voltage regulator while the engine is running. Bosch regulators are transistorized and integral with alternator.

## TROUBLE SHOOTING

***NOTE: See TROUBLE SHOOTING article in GENERAL INFORMATION.***

## ADJUSTMENTS

### BELT TENSION

***BELT TENSION***

| Application | [1] Deflection - In. (mm) |
|---|---|
| New Belt | 5/64 (2) |
| Used Belt | 13/64 (5) |

[1] - Deflection is with 22 lbs. (10 kg) pressure applied midway on longest belt run.

## ON-VEHICLE TESTING

### WIRING CONTINUITY TEST

**1)** With ignition off, connect a voltmeter between alternator B+ terminal and ground. Voltmeter should indicate battery voltage. If not, check wiring between alternator and battery.

**2)** Turn ignition on and ensure alternator indicator light comes on. If light does not come on, check wiring between alternator and warning light, including indicator bulb.

### OUTPUT TEST

**1)** Ensure connections at battery, alternator, and starter (most vehicles) are clean and tight. Ensure alternator, engine and body are properly grounded. Ensure alternator drive belt is tight and in good condition.

**2)** Start engine and allow to idle. Connect ammeter following manufacturer's instructions. Connect voltmeter leads to battery terminals. Adjust carbon pile on tester until voltmeter reads 13.5 volts. Alternator output should be 28-35 amps.

**3)** Repeat process at 1000 RPM. Alternator output should be 75-85 amps. Repeat test at 2000 RPM. Alternator output should be 89 amps. If alternator output is low, remove alternator for testing and repairs.

**4)** Start engine and run at 3000 RPM. Adjust carbon pile on tester to obtain maximum alternator output. DO NOT allow voltage to drop to less than 12.6 volts.

**5)** Alternator output should equal alternator rated output, minus 16-20 amps. If reading is 16-20 amps less than alternator rating, replace regulator and retest. If output is still low, repair or replace alternator.

### REGULATOR CONTROL VOLTAGE TEST

**1)** Connect ammeter following manufacturer's instructions. Connect voltmeter leads to battery terminals. Start engine and run at 3000 RPM.

**2)** Run engine until voltage stops rising. Voltage should be 13.5-14.5 volts. If reading is incorrect, remove regulator and ensure brushes are longer than 7/32" (6 mm). Replace if necessary.

**3)** If brushes are okay and regulator fails to keep voltage within specified limits, replace regulator and retest. If voltage is still incorrect, repair or replace alternator.

## BENCH TESTING

**Diode Assembly – 1)** Place ohmmeter on X 100 scale. Connect ohmmeter leads across B+ terminal and 3 stator terminals one at a time. Reverse leads. Ohmmeter should indicate continuity in one direction only.

**2)** Connect ohmmeter leads across negative plate and 3 stator terminals one at a time. *See Fig. 1.* Reverse leads. Ohmmeter should indicate continuity in one direction only.

**3)** Connect ohmmeter leads across D+ terminal and 3 stator terminals one at a time. Reverse leads. Ohmmeter should indicate continuity in one direction only. Replace diode assembly if defective.

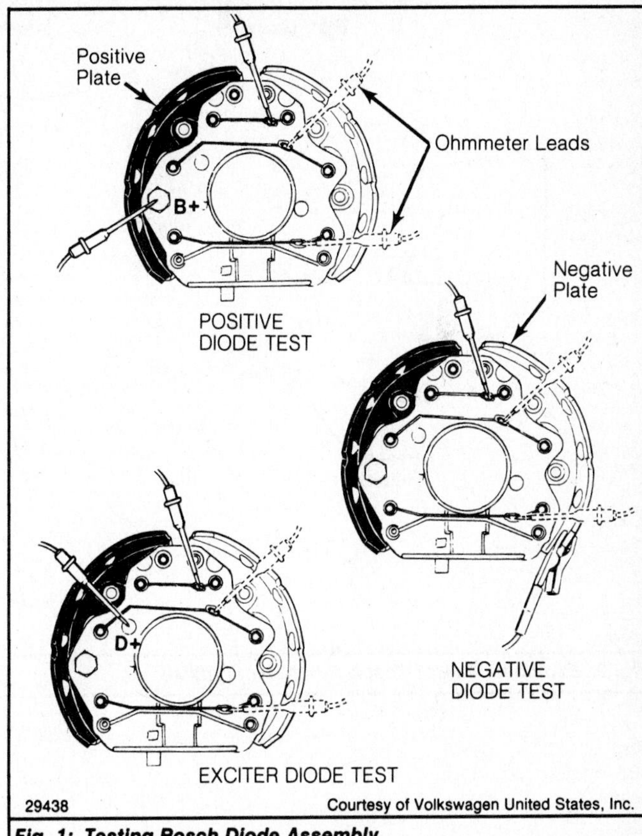


***Fig. 1: Testing Bosch Diode Assembly***

**Stator – 1)** Place ohmmeter on lowest scale. Connect ohmmeter across stator leads. Resistance should be approximately .09-.10 ohms. If resistance is incorrect, stator has open or shorted windings and must be replaced.

**2)** Place ohmmeter on X 1000 scale. Connect ohmmeter between stator core and stator lead. No continuity should exist. If continuity exists, stator is grounded and must be replaced.

**Rotor – 1)** Place ohmmeter on lowest scale. Connect ohmmeter across slip rings. Resistance should be 2.8-3.1 ohms.

**2)** If resistance is too low, rotor has short circuit and must be replaced. If resistance is infinity (no continuity), rotor has open circuit and must be replaced.

**3)** Place ohmmeter on X 1000 scale. Connect ohmmeter between either slip ring and rotor core. No continuity should exist. If continuity exists, rotor is grounded and must be replaced.

**4)** Clean slip rings using fine sandpaper. Rings which are worn or pitted should be turned on lathe. Minimum ring diameter is 1 1/16".

**5)** If slip rings are beyond repair, remove rear bearing from slip ring end of rotor. Unsolder wires from slip rings and bend up ends of rotor winding. Pull off slip rings. Ensure ends of rotor winding are not damaged.

# 1991 ELECTRICAL
# Alternators & Regulators – Bosch (Cont.)

**6)** Insert ends of rotor winding into slip ring and press new slip ring onto rotor. Slip ring end must be 9/64" from end of collar. Solder rotor winding to slip ring terminals. Turn rings on lathe and retest rotor. Maximum slip ring runout is .0012" (.03 mm).

**Bearings** – Always replace bearings. If replacement front bearing is sealed on one side only, open side must face rotor. If replacement rear bearing is sealed on one side only, open side must face away from rotor.

**Brushes** – Ensure brushes are longer than 7/32". Replace if necessary. Unsolder brushes from voltage regulator. Solder new brushes. DO NOT allow solder to run into strands of brush leads. Brushes must be free to slide in brush holder with normal spring tension of 10-14 ozs. (283-397 g).

## OVERHAUL

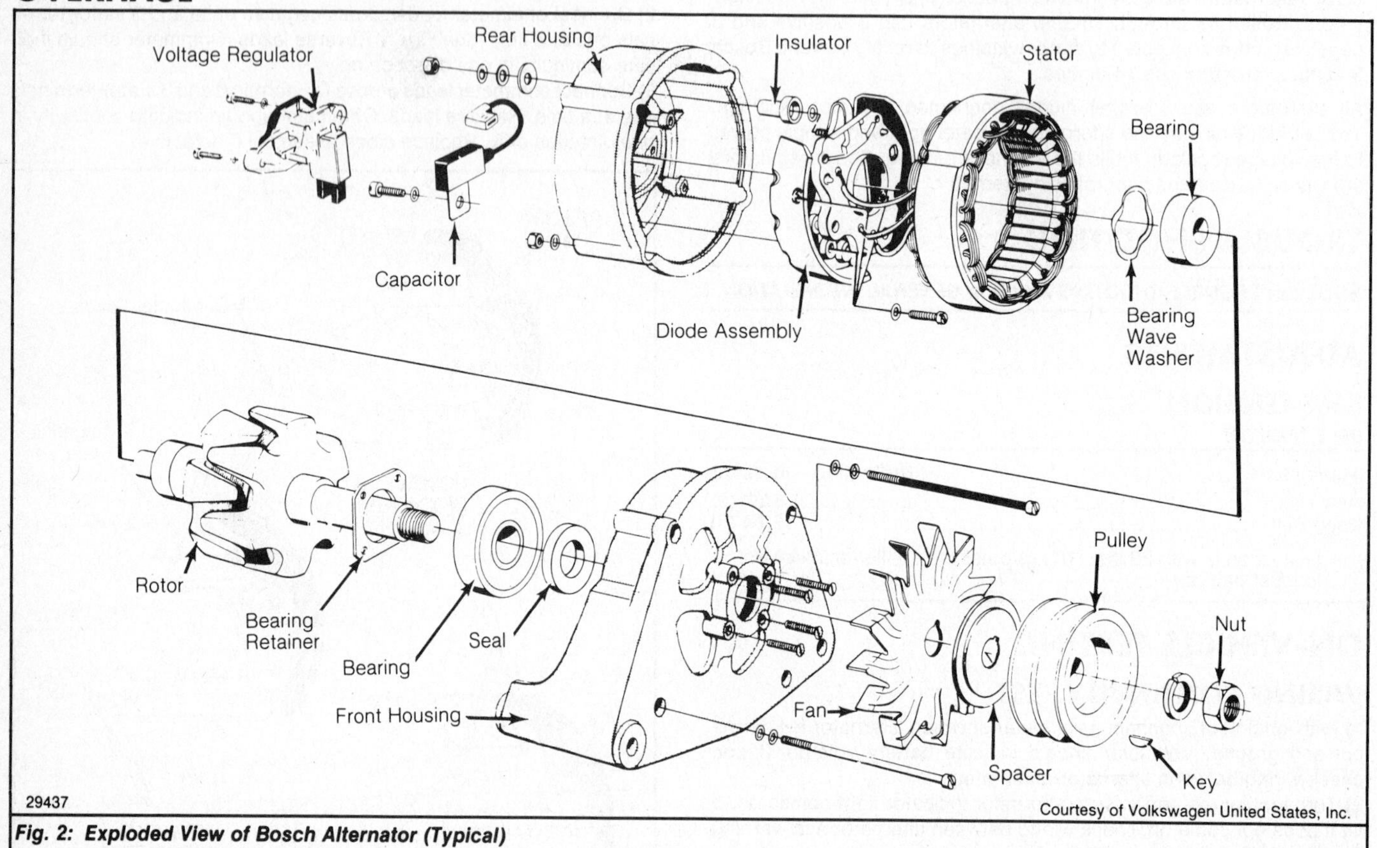


*Fig. 2: Exploded View of Bosch Alternator (Typical)*

# 1991 ELECTRICAL
# Alternators & Regulators – SEV Motorola

## Golf, GTI, Jetta, Vanagon

## DESCRIPTION

SEV Motorola alternators are conventional 3-phase, self-rectifying type alternators. Three positive and 3 negative silicon diodes are used to rectify AC current.

## TROUBLE SHOOTING

***NOTE: See TROUBLE SHOOTING article in GENERAL INFORMATION.***

## ADJUSTMENTS

### BELT TENSION

***BELT TENSION***

| Application | [1] Deflection – In. (mm) |
|---|---|
| Vanagon | 3/8-9/16 (10-15) |
| All Others | |
| New Belt | 5/64 (2) |
| Used Belt | 13/64 (5) |

[1] – Deflection is with 22 lbs. (10 kg) pressure applied midway on longest belt run.

## ON-VEHICLE TESTING

**1)** Disconnect battery cables and install cut-out switch, variable resistor, ammeter and voltmeter. *See Fig. 1.* Connect ground cable and ensure cut-out switch is in closed position.

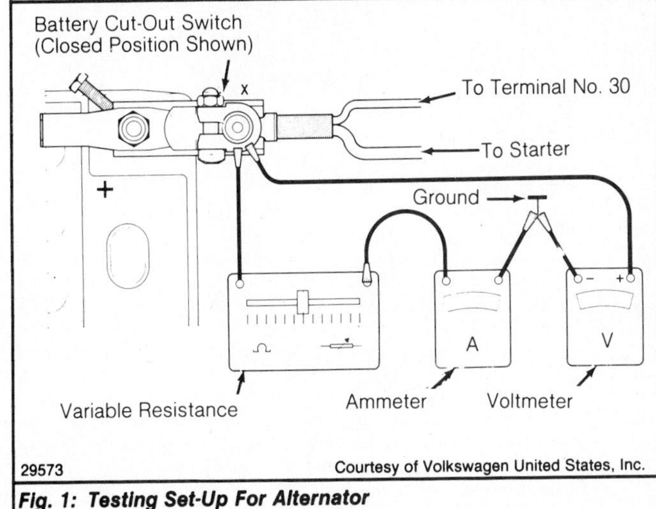


***Fig. 1: Testing Set-Up For Alternator***

**2)** Start engine and run at 3000-4000 RPM. Turn battery cut-out switch to OFF position. On 65-amp alternators, adjust variable resistor to 45 amps and on 55-amp alternators adjust variable resistor to 25 amps. System is okay if voltmeter reads 12.5-14.5 volts.

**3)** If system does not read correct voltage, substitute a known good voltage regulator and repeat test. If correct voltage is still not present, alternator is defective.

## BENCH TESTING

**Stator – 1)** With alternator disassembled, check stator for short circuits. If one or more coils are burned, stator may be shorted. *See Fig. 2.*

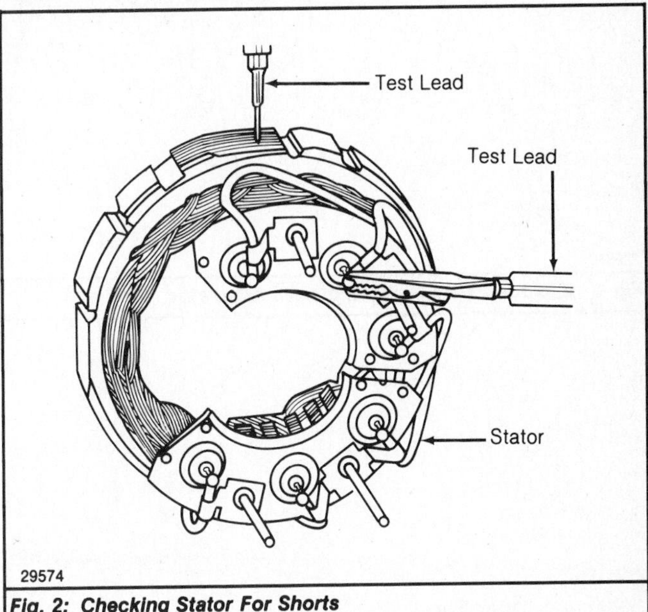


***Fig. 2: Checking Stator For Shorts***

**2)** Connect a self-powered low voltage test light between stator plates and stator terminal. If light illuminates, insulation between stator winding and stator plates is defective and stator should be replaced.

***CAUTION: Use only specified test light. DO NOT use 110 or 220-volt test light on this or any other alternator test procedure.***

**Diodes – 1)** Check diodes with a diode tester for shorts or open circuits. If any diode is defective, entire diode assembly must be replaced.

**2)** If diode tester is not available, diode leads should be quickly and carefully unsoldered and tested with an ohmmeter. Diodes should show low resistance in flow direction and high resistance in reverse direction.

**Rotor – 1)** Ensure slip rings are not dirty or burned. Check winding for breakage or damaged insulation. Measure resistance between slip rings.

**2)** Normal resistance should be about 4.5 ohms. If winding is faulty, rotor must be replaced.

**Brush Holder – 1)** Connect a self-powered low voltage test light between brushes. Test light should not illuminate. Connect test light between DF terminal and positive brush. Test light should give steady light even if brush and/or terminal cable is moved.

**2)** Connect 1 2-volt test light between brush holder frame and negative brush. Light should give steady light. If test results are not satisfactory or brush length is less than .51 (13 mm), replace brush holder. *See Fig. 3.*

# 1991 ELECTRICAL
# Alternators & Regulators – SEV Motorola (Cont.)

## OVERHAUL

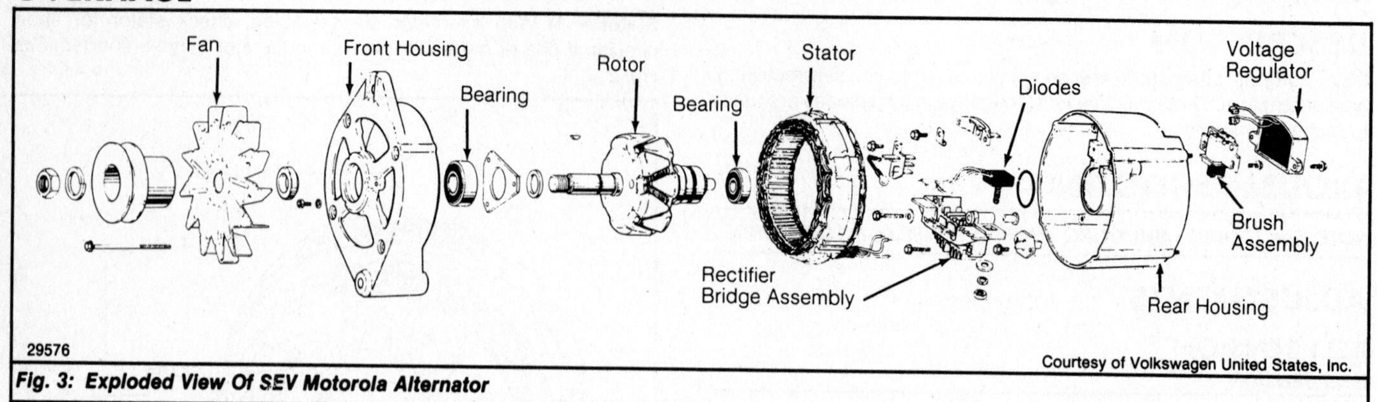


*Fig. 3: Exploded View Of SEV Motorola Alternator*

# 1991 ELECTRICAL
# Starters – Bosch

## Cabriolet, Corrado, Fox, Golf GL, GTI, Jetta, Passat, Vanagon

## DESCRIPTION

Starter is a brush type, series-wound electric motor with an overrunning clutch. Field frame is enclosed by commutator end frame and drive bushing and carries pole shoes and field coils. A splined armature shaft drive end carries drive assembly.

## TROUBLE SHOOTING

*NOTE: See TROUBLE SHOOTING article in GENERAL INFORMATION.*

## ON-VEHICLE TESTING

### STARTER DOES NOT CRANK ENGINE

**1)** Ensure battery is fully charged. Make sure electrical and ground connections are clean and tight. With ignition switch in START position, measure voltage at spade terminal of starter solenoid. Reading should be at least 8 volts (9.5 volts on Fox). If so, check engine for mechanical problems. If voltage is not as specified, go to next step.
**2)** Measure voltage at ignition switch. If reading is at least 8 volts (9.5 volts on Fox), check wiring between ignition switch and starter solenoid. If voltage is not as specified, replace ignition switch.
**3)** Measure voltage at field (starter) terminal of starter solenoid. If reading is 8 volts or more, repair or replace starter. If reading is less than 8 volts, replace starter solenoid.

*NOTE: On vehicles with automatic transmission, also check park/ neutral switch.*

### STARTER CRANKS TOO SLOWLY

Ensure engine crankcase is filled with recommended viscosity oil. Check charging system to ensure battery is fully charged. Make sure electrical and ground connections are clean and tight. If starter still turns slowly, repair or replace starter.

### VOLTAGE DROP TEST

**Starter Main Terminal** – Connect a voltmeter between starter main terminal and starter body. Disconnect ignition coil positive terminal and operate starter. Voltage reading should not be more than 1.0 volt less than battery voltage. If a larger voltage drop is indicated, circuit between battery and starter terminal may be defective.
**Main Starter Case** – Connect a voltmeter between positive battery terminal and starter motor "M" terminal. With ignition off, operate starter for 2-3 seconds. Battery voltage should be present, then drop to less than one volt. If voltage is greater than specification, high resistance may be present in circuit. Go to ACROSS SOLENOID SWITCH test.
**Across Solenoid Switch** – Connect a voltmeter between 2 starter solenoid terminal stud connections. With ignition disconnected, operate starter for 2-3 seconds and note meter reading. Initially, battery voltage should be present, then voltage should drop to less than .5 volts. If voltage is not as specified, check for damaged switch or loose or dirty connections. If high resistance is present, terminal may be loose or corroded.
**Ground Return Line** – Connect a voltmeter between battery ground terminal and starter main housing. With ignition off, operate starter for 2-3 seconds. If ground is okay, voltage reading should be less than .5 volt. If reading is .6 volt or more, high resistance is present in ground return side of circuit.

## BENCH TESTING

### STARTER SOLENOID

**1)** Remove bridge strap connecting solenoid to motor. Check windings by connecting a 12-volt battery operated test light between solenoid main terminal STA and solenoid body. If light illuminates, both windings are satisfactory.
**2)** Ensure that contacts open and close satisfactorily by connecting 12-volt battery and a high wattage test light between main solenoid terminals. Test light should not illuminate.
**3)** Close switch by energizing solenoid windings. Solenoid should be heard to operate and closing of solenoid contacts will be indicated by test light illuminating to full brilliance. On opening switch, test light should go out.

### STARTER LOAD (LOCK) TEST

With starter on test bench, lock starter drive pinion. Voltmeter should read 4.5 volts and ammeter should read 700-800 amps.

### STARTER NO-LOAD TEST

With starter on test bench, operate starter and check ammeter, voltage, and RPM. Readings should be within specification. See STARTER NO-LOAD TEST SPECIFICATIONS table.

***STARTER NO-LOAD TEST SPECIFICATIONS***

| Volts | Amps | RPM |
|---|---|---|
| 11.5 | 65-95 | 6500 |

## REMOVAL & INSTALLATION

### VANAGON

**Removal & Installation** – **1)** Disconnect battery ground strap. Before raising vehicle, remove upper starter mounting bolt. Release handbrake (to allow axle rotation) and raise vehicle on hoist.
**2)** Disconnect right rear axle from transmission and wire aside. Cover exposed CV joint with plastic bag to prevent entry of dirt or other foreign material.
**3)** Loosen clamp securing cooling hoses to chassis. Wire hoses aside. Remove bolt "A" from differential lock servo. Loosen bolt "B" and withdraw as far as possible. Lack of clearance prevents complete removal of bolt "B". *See Fig. 1.*

*NOTE: Nuts are welded to bracket. DO NOT attempt to loosen.*

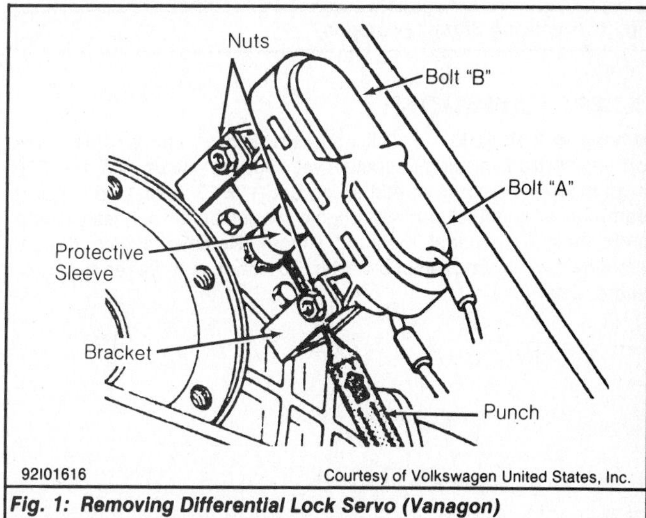


*Fig. 1: Removing Differential Lock Servo (Vanagon)*

**4)** Push back protective sleeve and drive out spring pin. With bolt "B" withdrawn as far as possible, give servo a slight upward twist and remove from bracket. *See Fig. 1.*
**5)** Remove circlip, bracket securing bolts and bracket. *See Fig. 2.*
**6)** Disconnect wires from starter solenoid. Remove lower mounting nut, push up slightly on starter and remove. *See Fig. 3.* To install, reverse removal procedure.

# 1991 ELECTRICAL
# Starters – Bosch (Cont.)

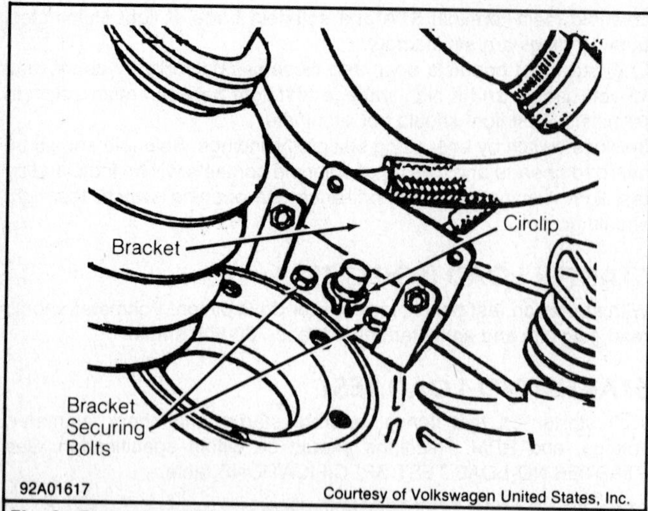


*Fig. 2: Removing Differential Lock Servo Bracket (Vanagon)*

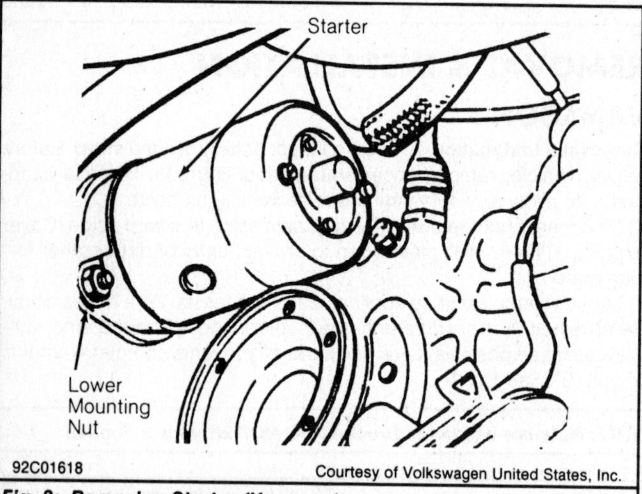


*Fig. 3: Removing Starter (Vanagon)*

## EXCEPT VANAGON

**Removal & Installation** – Disconnect negative battery cable. Support engine/transmission assembly with Support Beam (VW 10-222). On all models except Fox, add a Leg Set (VW 10-2224/1) to support beam. On all models, remove engine mount bolts, nut, and clamp screw (next to exhaust manifold flange). Remove engine mount. Disconnect wiring and remove starter. To install, reverse removal procedure. *See Fig. 4.*

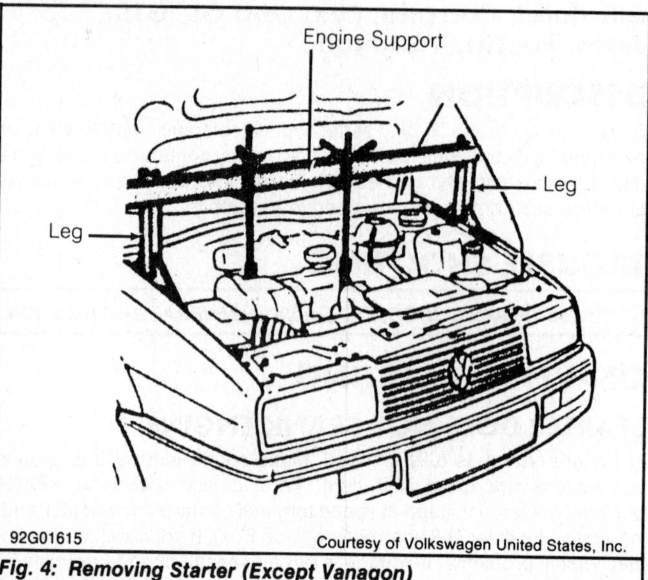


*Fig. 4: Removing Starter (Except Vanagon)*

## STARTER SPECIFICATIONS

*STARTER SPECIFICATIONS*

| Application | Specification |
|---|---|
| Armature | |
| Runout | .002" (.05mm) |
| End Play | .002" (.05mm) |
| Cold Cranking | |
| Test Voltage | 12 |
| Minimum Voltage | 9 |
| Amps | 90 |
| Minimum RPM | 1500 |
| Solenoid Hold-In Winding Voltage | 4 Volts (Min.) |
| Solenoid Pull-In Winding Voltage | 7 |
| Commutator Runout | .0004" (.01mm) |
| Cranking Voltage | 9 Volts Min. |
| Starter Current Draw | 170 Amps Max. |

## TORQUE SPECIFICATIONS

*TORQUE SPECIFICATIONS*

| Application | Ft. Lbs. (N.m) |
|---|---|
| Starter-To-Block Bolts | |
| All Except Vanagon | 32.5-44.3 (44-60) |
| Vanagon | 21 (28) |
| | INCH Lbs. (N.m) |
| Solenoid Bolts | 96 (10.8) |
| Through Bolts | 54 (6.1) |

## OVERHAUL

For overhaul, see exploded view of typical Bosch starter. *See Fig. 5.*

# 1991 ELECTRICAL
## Starters – Bosch (Cont.)

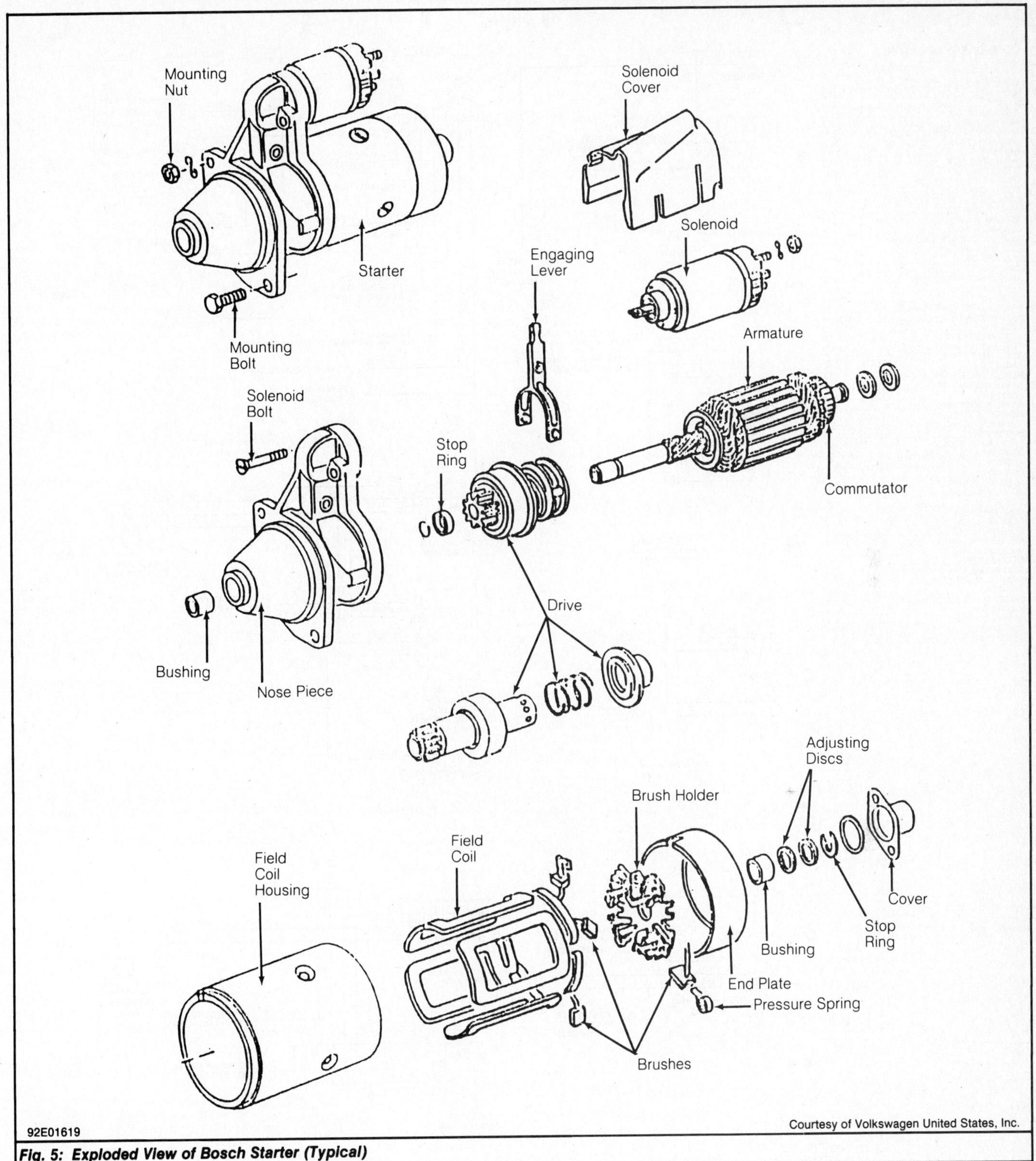


*Fig. 5: Exploded View of Bosch Starter (Typical)*

# 1991 WIRING DIAGRAMS
## Cabriolet

**COMPONENT LOCATOR:**

| | |
|---|---|
| A/C COMP CLUTCH | E 17 |
| A/C FUSE | E 17 |
| A/C SW | E 18 |
| AIRBAG SYSTEM | A–C 28–29 |
| ALTERNATOR | A 3 |
| AMPLIFIED SPEAKERS (PARTIAL) | D–E 17 |
| BACK-UP LT SW | A 21 |
| BATTERY | A 2 |
| BEAM SELECT SW | A 15 |
| BRAKE FLUID LEVEL SW | A 17 |
| CIGARETTE LIGHTER | E 16 |
| CONVERTIBLE TOP | C–D 28–30 |
| COOLANT LOW LEVEL CONTROL UNIT | A 24 |
| CRUISE CONTROL | A 8–11 |
| DEFOGGER GRID | B 19 |
| DEFOGGER SW | A 19 |
| DIGIFANT CONTROL UNIT (CALIF) | A–B 7 |
| DIGIFANT CONTROL UNIT (EX CALIF) | D–E 7 |
| DIR SW | A 16 |
| EMERGENCY FLASHER SW | A 17 |
| FAN MOTOR | E 18 |
| FRESH AIR FAN | D 18 |
| FRESH AIR FAN SW ILLUM LT | E 16 |
| FUEL INJECTORS | A 5, E 6 |
| FUEL PUMP | E 10 |
| FUSE/RELAY PANEL | C 9–23 |
| FUSE/RELAY PANEL LAYOUT | D–E 28–30 |
| GEAR SELECT SW | A 21–23 |
| HEADLT SW | A 14 |
| HEADLT SW ILLUM LT | E 17 |
| HEATED O2 SENSOR | B 4, D 4 |
| HORN SW | B 18 |
| IGNITION BOOSTER | C 4 |
| IGNITION COIL | E 4 |
| IGNITION CONTROL UNIT | E 7 |
| IGNITION SW | A 12 |
| INSTRUMENT CLUSTER | A–D 26–27 |
| INSTRUMENT GAUGES | A–B 24 |
| INTERIOR LT | B 31 |
| LEFT DOOR SW | B 31 |
| LUGGAGE COMPT LT | C 31 |
| OIL PRES GAUGE | B 24 |
| OIL PRES SWS | B 22 |
| OIL TEMP GAUGE | A 24 |
| PARK BRAKE SW | A 19 |
| POWER WINDOWS | C–E 24–26 |
| RAD COOLING FAN SYSTEM | B–C 2–3, D 2–3 |
| RADIO (PARTIAL) | E 27 |
| SEAT BELT SW | B 17 |
| SEAT BELT/BRAKE WARN IND | A 18 |
| SHIFT LOCK CONTROL UNIT | E 12 |
| STARTER | A 3 |
| STARTING INTERLOCK RELAY | C–D 8 |
| STOP LT SW | A 20 |
| VAC VENT VALVE | A 8 |
| VOLTMETER | B 24 |
| WIPER SYSTEM | E 20–22 |

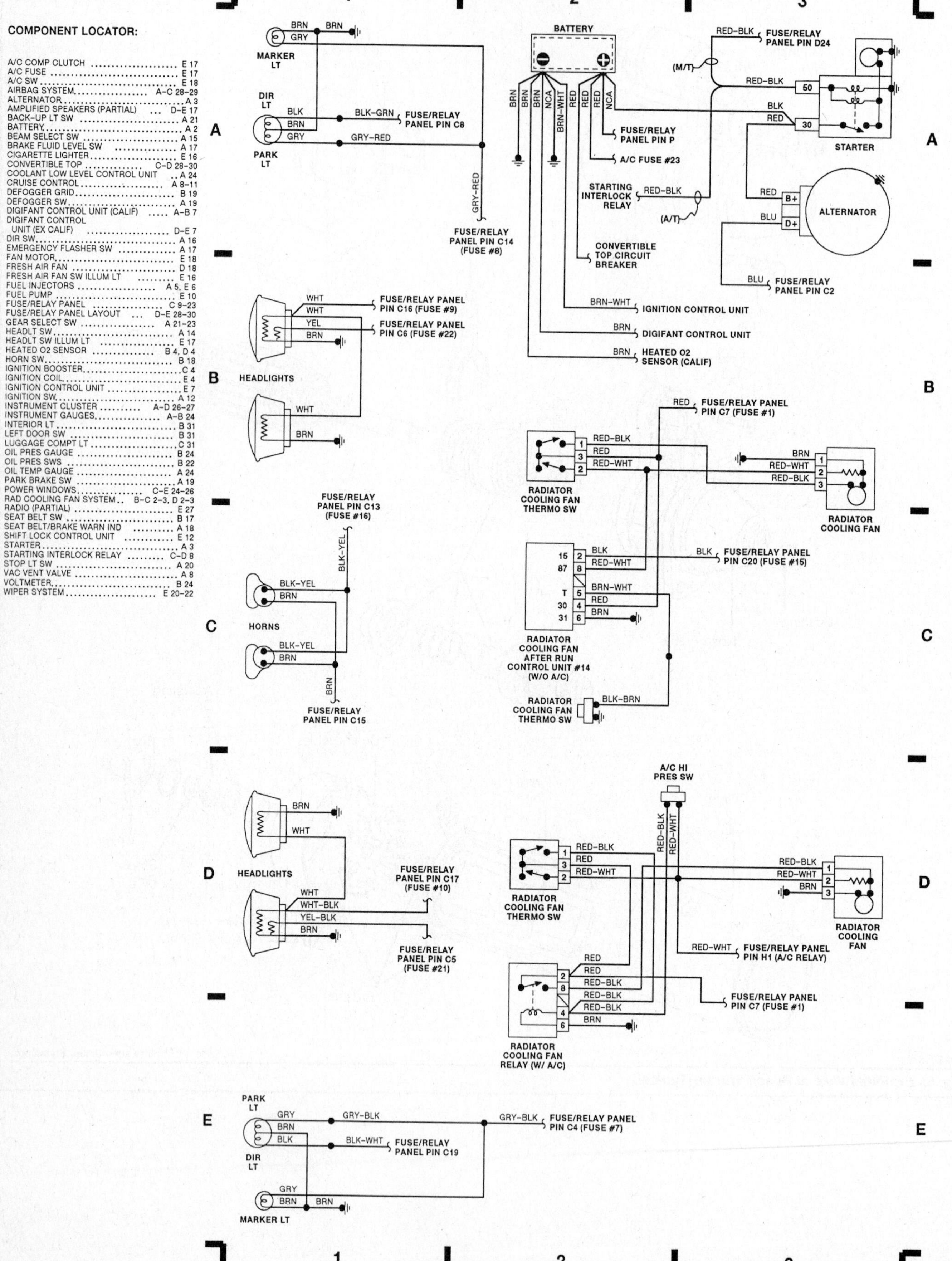

# 1991 WIRING DIAGRAMS
## Cabriolet (Cont.)

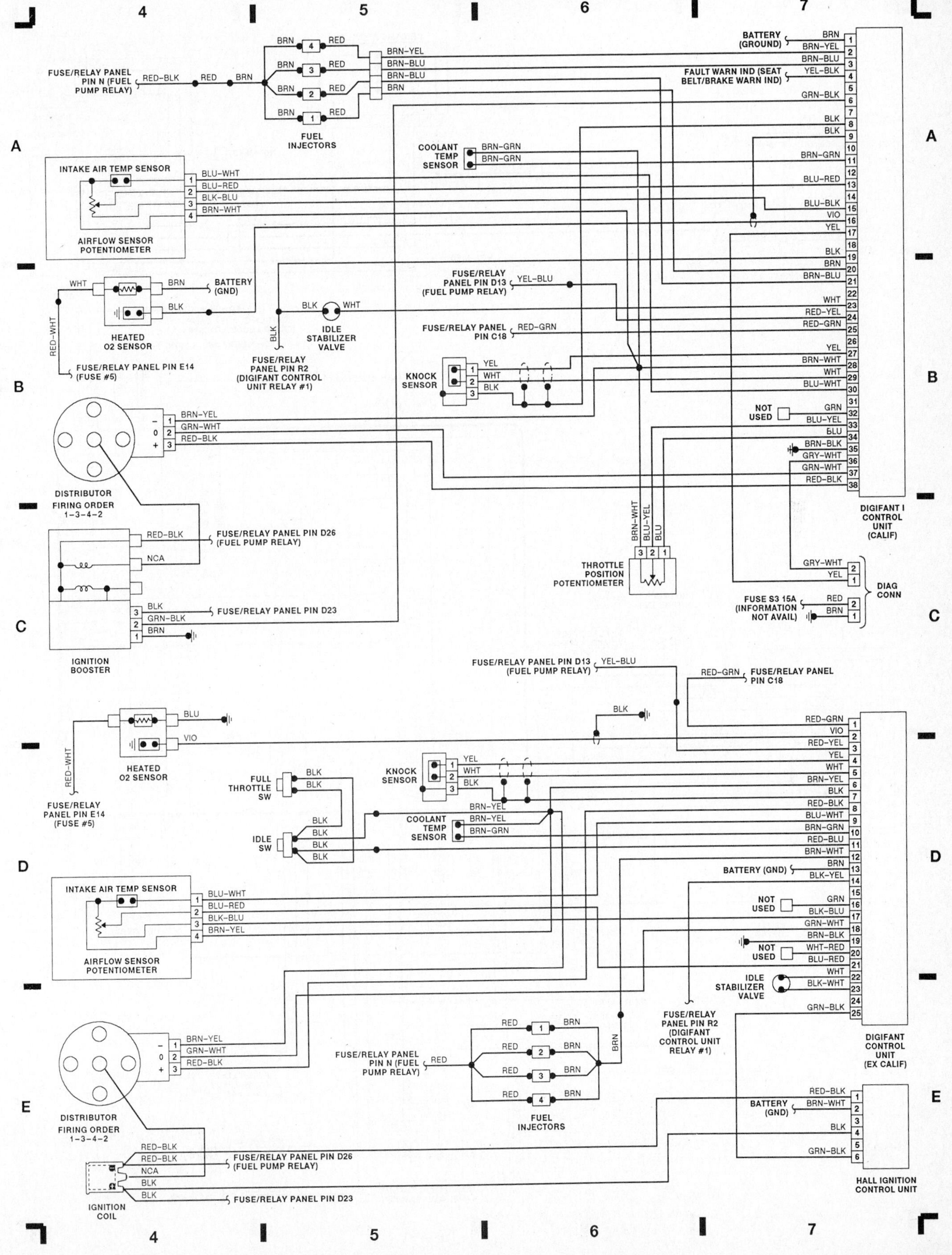

# 1991 WIRING DIAGRAMS
## Cabriolet (Cont.)

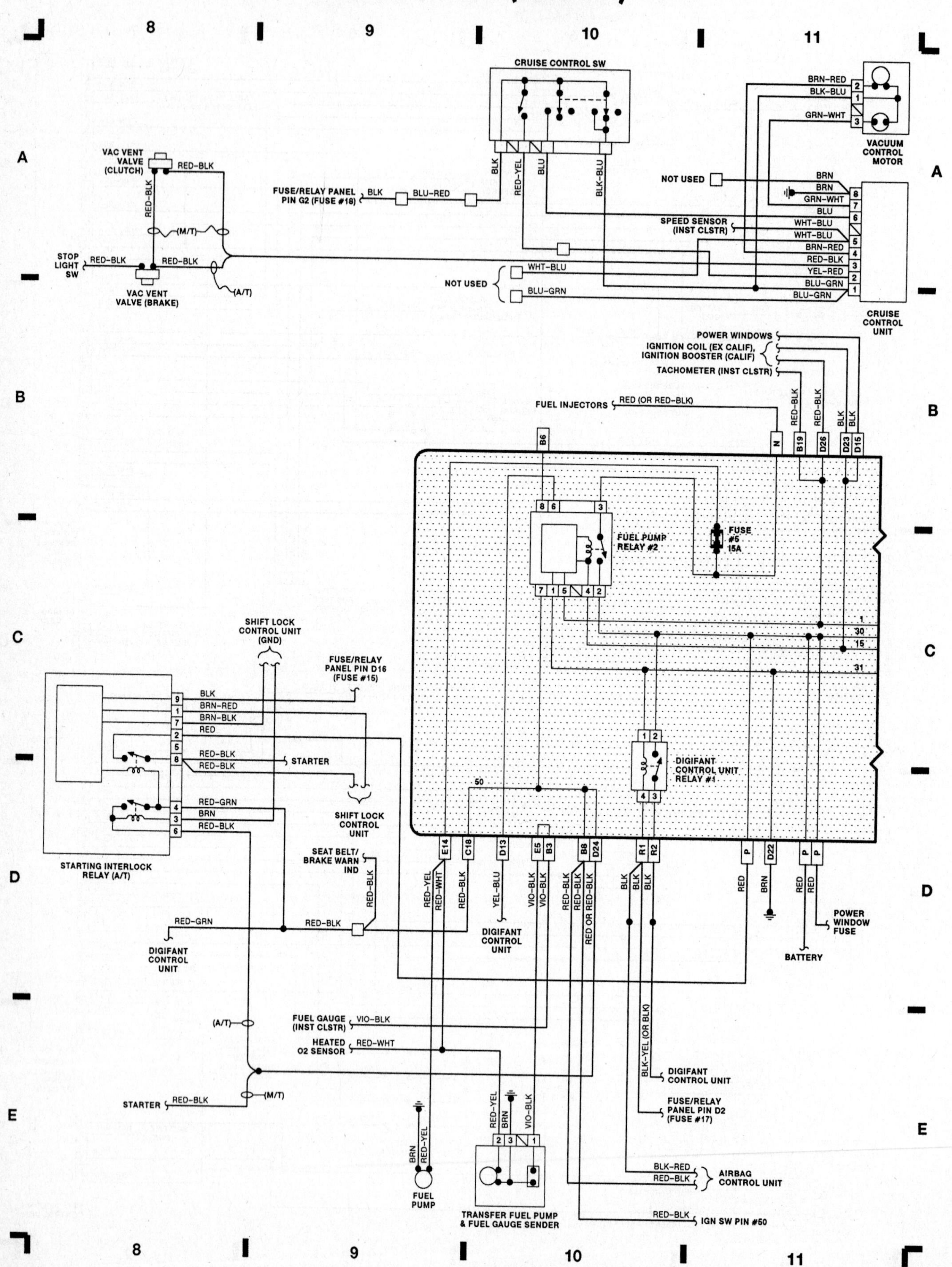

# 1991 WIRING DIAGRAMS
# Cabriolet (Cont.)

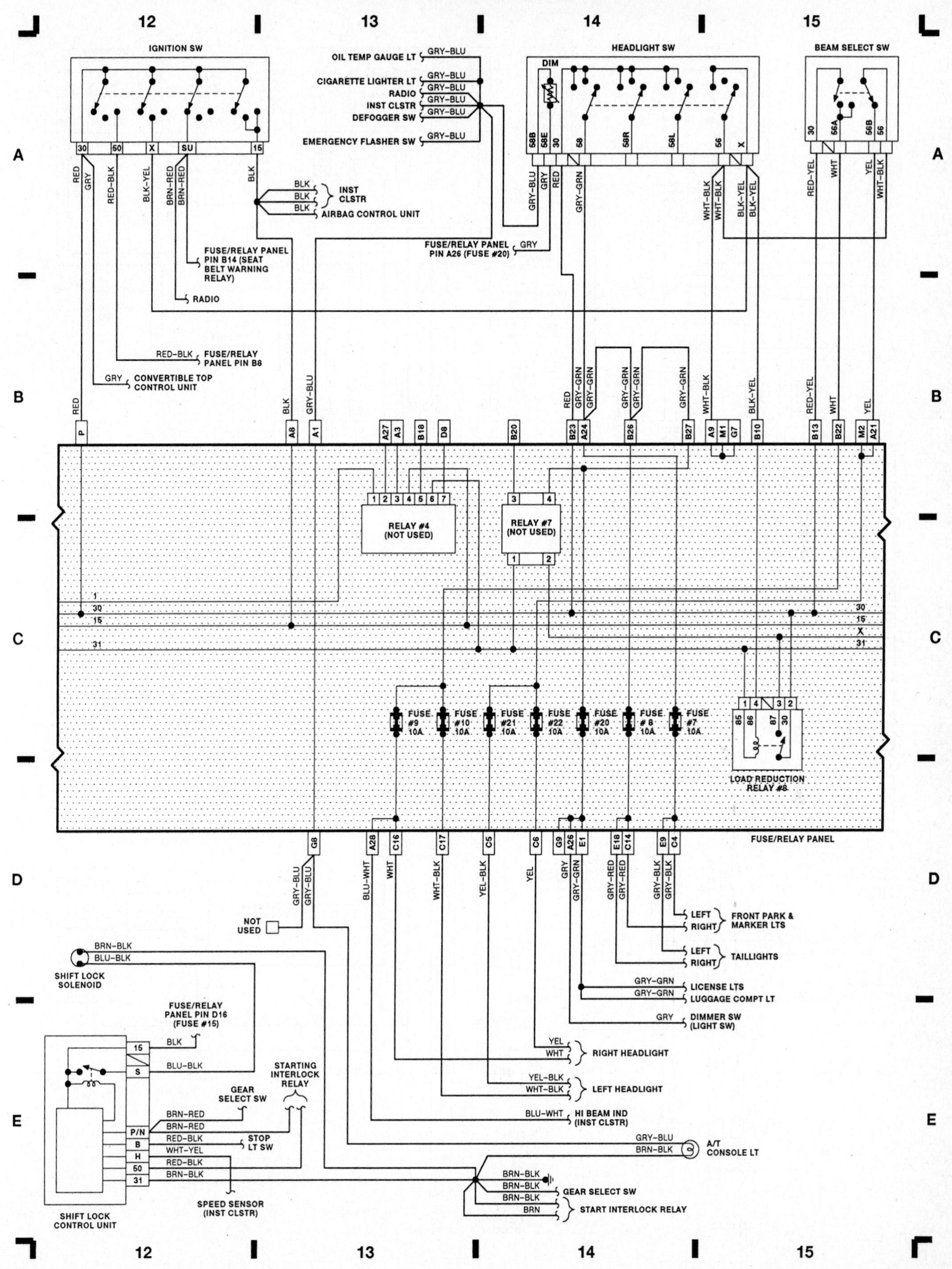

# 1991 WIRING DIAGRAMS
## Cabriolet (Cont.)

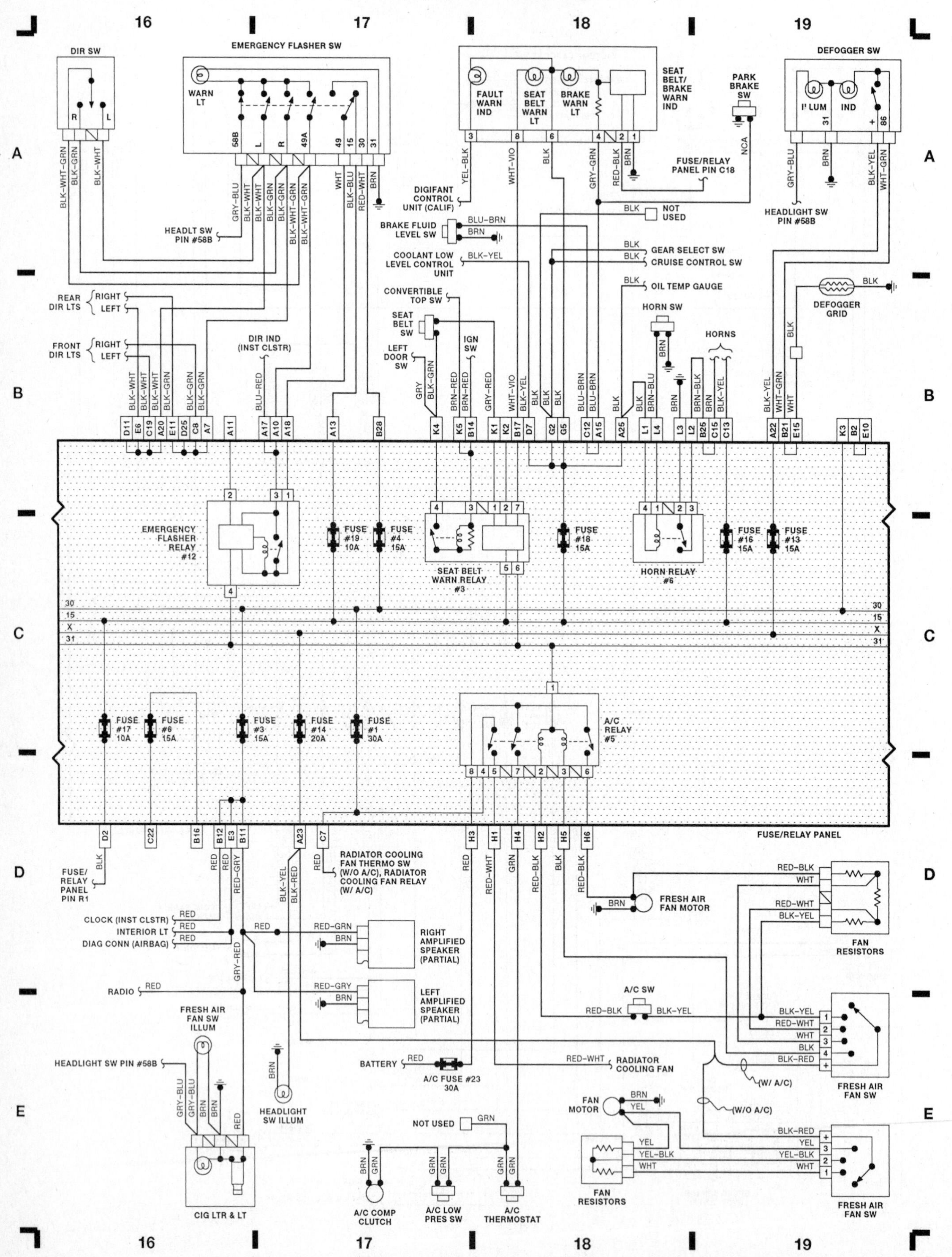

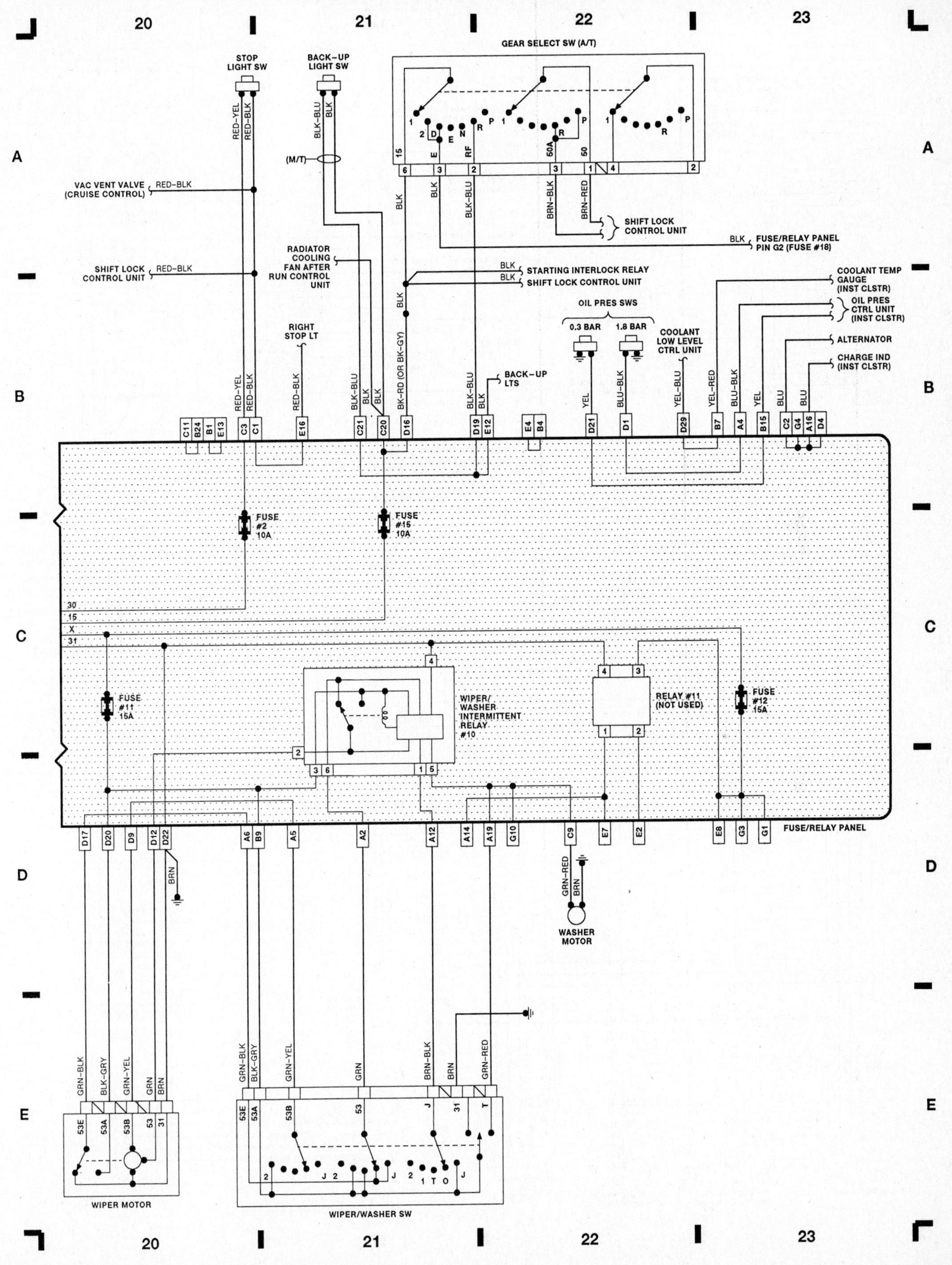
GEAR SELECT SW (A/T)
STOP LIGHT SW
BACK-UP LIGHT SW
VAC VENT VALVE (CRUISE CONTROL)
SHIFT LOCK CONTROL UNIT
RADIATOR COOLING FAN AFTER RUN CONTROL UNIT
RIGHT STOP LT
BACK-UP LTS
SHIFT LOCK CONTROL UNIT
FUSE/RELAY PANEL PIN G2 (FUSE #18)
STARTING INTERLOCK RELAY
SHIFT LOCK CONTROL UNIT
OIL PRES SWS
0.3 BAR
1.8 BAR
COOLANT LOW LEVEL CTRL UNIT
COOLANT TEMP GAUGE (INST CLSTR)
OIL PRES CTRL UNIT (INST CLSTR)
ALTERNATOR
CHARGE IND (INST CLSTR)
FUSE #2 10A
FUSE #15 10A
FUSE #11 15A
WIPER/ WASHER INTERMITTENT RELAY #10
RELAY #11 (NOT USED)
FUSE #12 15A
FUSE/RELAY PANEL
WASHER MOTOR
WIPER MOTOR
WIPER/WASHER SW

# 1991 WIRING DIAGRAMS
# Cabriolet (Cont.)

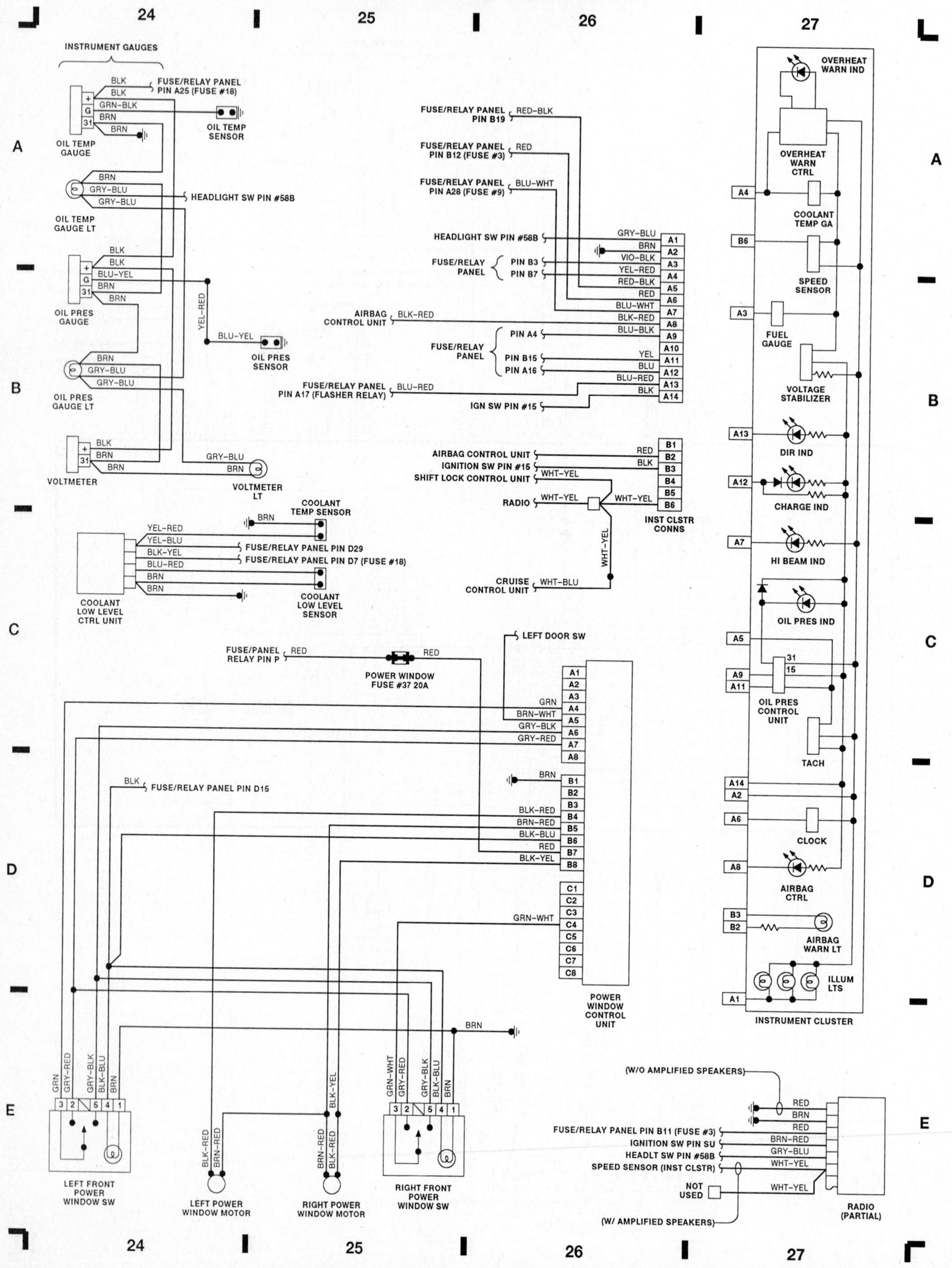

# 1991 WIRING DIAGRAMS
# Cabriolet (Cont.)

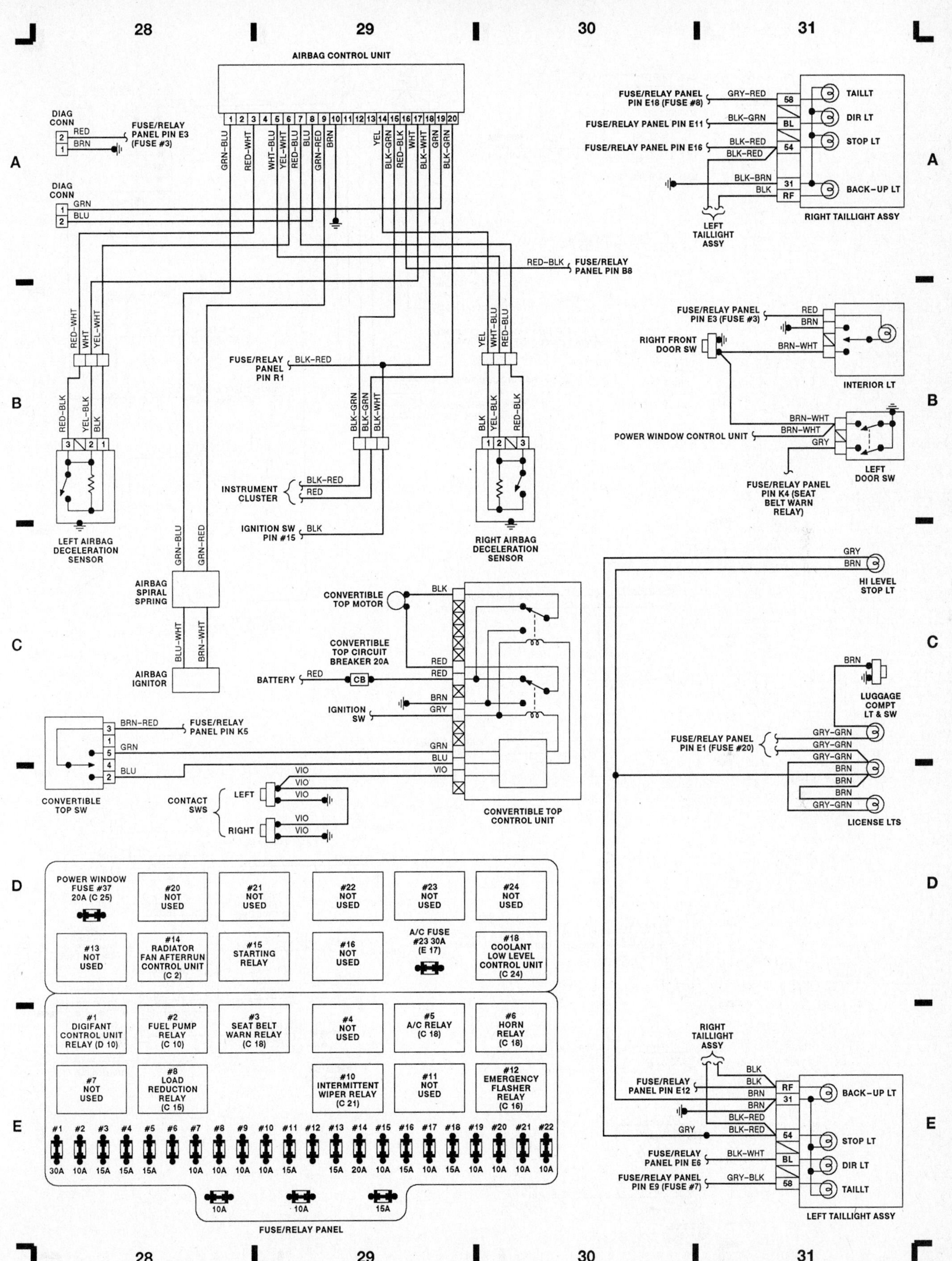

# 1991 WIRING DIAGRAMS
## Corrado

COMPONENT LOCATOR:

| | |
|---|---|
| A/C COMP CLUTCH | D 22 |
| A/T CONTROL UNIT | A–C 11 |
| ABS DIAG CONNS | D 15 |
| ABS SYSTEM | B–E 12–15 |
| ALTERNATOR | C 3 |
| ANTI–THEFT ALARM CONTROL | E 8 |
| AUTO SEAT BELTS | B–E 33–35 |
| BACK–UP LT SW | E 28 |
| BATTERY | A 2 |
| BRAKE FLUID LEVEL SW (W/ ABS) | B 15 |
| BRAKE FLUID LEVEL SW (W/O ABS) | A 31 |
| CENTRAL LOCK SYSTEM | A–B 36–39 |
| CENTRAL LOCKING SWS | A 36 |
| CIG LTR | A 24 |
| COOLANT LOW LEVEL SENDER | B 25 |
| COOLANT TEMP SENDER | A 25 |
| CRUISE CONTROL | A 12–15 |
| DEFOGGER SW | E 29 |
| DIGIFANT CONTROL UNIT (CALIF) | A–B 7 |
| DIGIFANT CONTROL UNIT (EX CALIF) | D 7 |
| DOOR SWS | B 38, E 43 |
| EMERGENCY FLASHER SW | A 20–22 |
| FOG LT SW | A 23 |
| FRESH AIR SW | E 20, E 23 |
| FRESH AIR SW ILLUM LT | D 20 |
| FUEL INJECTORS | A 5, E 5 |
| FUEL PUMP AFTER RUN CONTROL UNIT | E 19 |
| FUEL TANK SENDER | E 18 |
| FUSE #23 | D 20 |
| FUSE #51 | D 34 |
| FUSE/RELAY PANEL | C 16–31 |
| FUSE/RELAY PANEL LAYOUT | D–E 37–39 |
| GLOVE COMPT LT | D 30 |
| HEATED SEATS | C–E 40–42 |
| HYDRAULIC PUMP RELAY | D–E 15 |
| HYDRAULIC UNIT | E 13–14 |
| IGNITION BOOSTER | C 4 |
| IGNITION COIL | E 4 |
| IGNITION SW | A 16 |
| INST CLSTR | A–E 32–34 |
| INST PANEL DIMMER | A 18 |
| INTERIOR LT W/ DELAY | D 41 |
| LIGHT SW | A 18–19 |
| LUGGAGE COMPT LT SW | A 26 |
| MULTI–FUNCTION IND SW | A 27 |
| O2 SENSOR | B 4, C 6 |
| OIL PRES GAUGE | A 35 |
| OIL PRES SWS | A 25 |
| PARK BRAKE SW | A 31 |
| POWER WINDOW CB | A 38 |
| POWER WINDOWS | B–D 36–39 |
| PROGRAM SW | B 8 |
| RAD COOL FAN RELAY | D 22 |
| RADIATOR COOLING FAN | E 2, D 20 |
| RADIATOR COOLING FAN AFTER RUN CONTROL UNIT | D 3 |
| RADIO (PARTIAL) | B 41 |
| REAR SPOILER | A 40–42 |
| SEAT BELT CONTROL UNITS | C–D 35 |
| SEAT BELT SW | E 31 |
| SHOULDER BELTS | B–E 33–35 |
| SPEED SENSOR | B 26 |
| STARTER | A 3 |
| STARTER INTERLOCK/BACK–UP LT RELAY | A 8 |
| STOP LT SW | B 29 |
| SUNROOF | E 36–37 |
| THROTTLE POSITION POTENTIOMETER | C 5, D 4 |
| VACUUM VENT VALVE | A 13, A 14 |
| VOLTMETER | B 35 |
| W/SHIELD WIPER SYSTEM | D–E 24–27 |
| WARNING MODULE (ABS) | C 12 |
| WARNING MODULE (W/O ABS) | A 28 |
| WASHER NOZZLE HEATERS | E 27 |

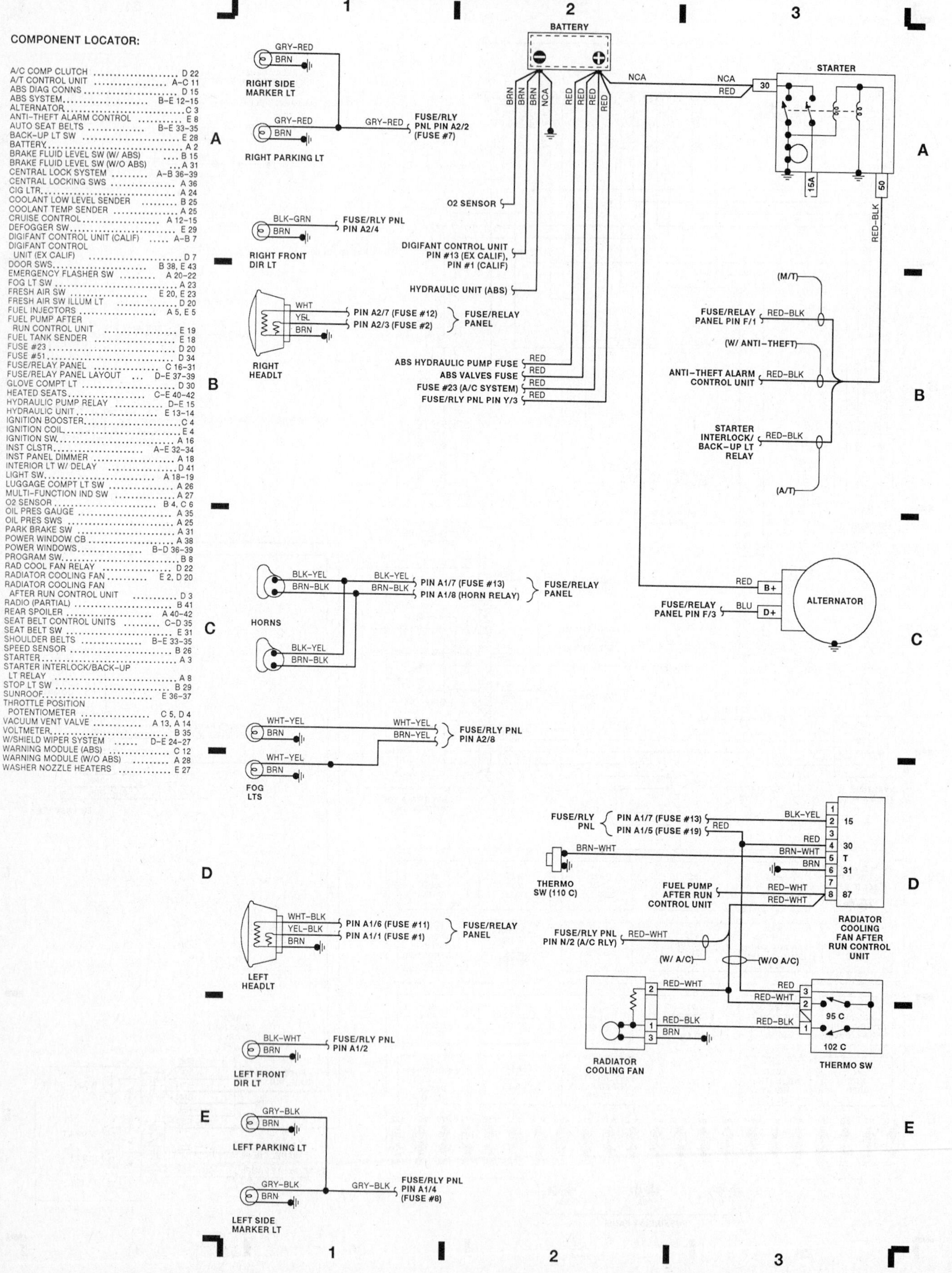

# 1991 WIRING DIAGRAMS
## Corrado (Cont.)

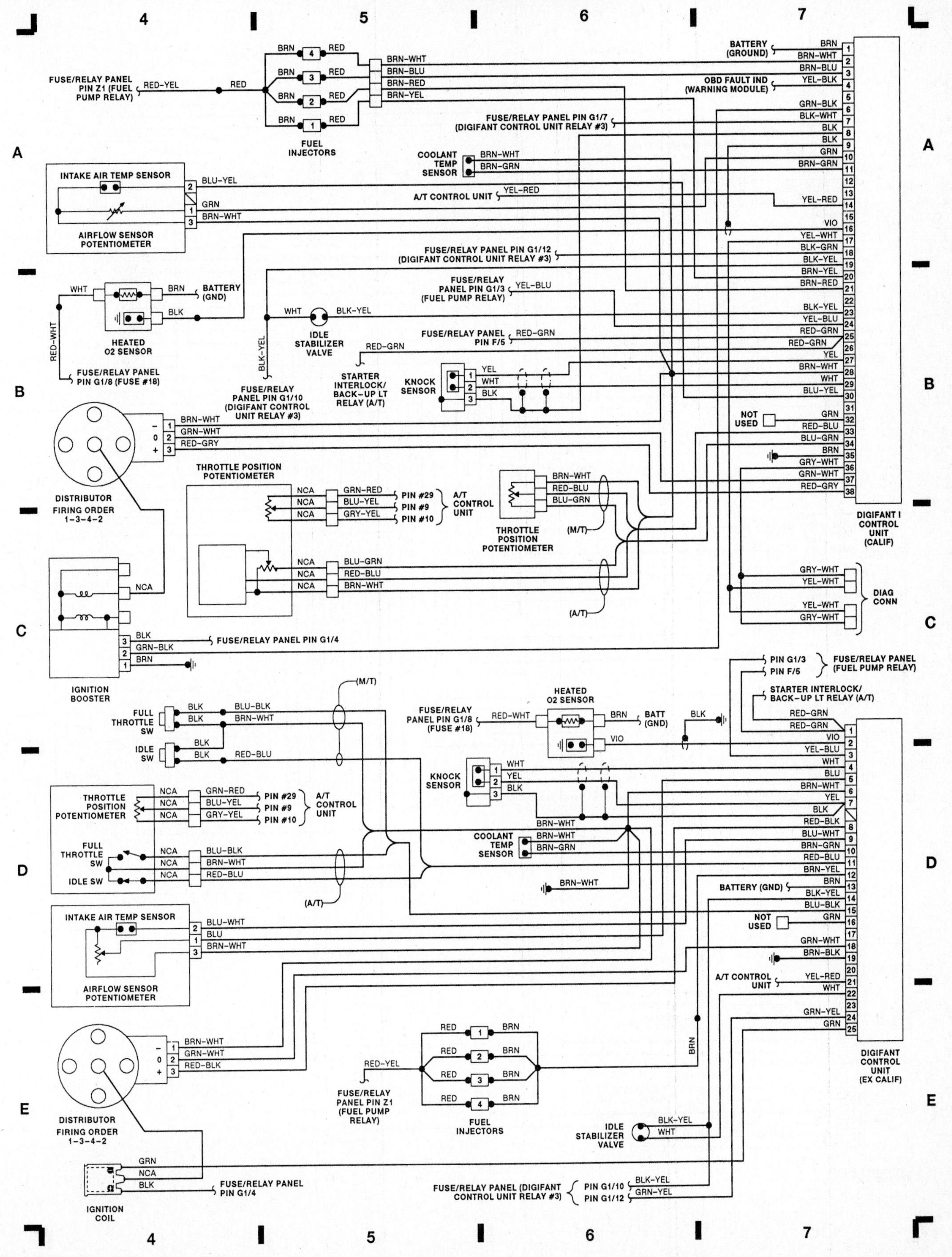

# 1991 WIRING DIAGRAMS
## Corrado (Cont.)

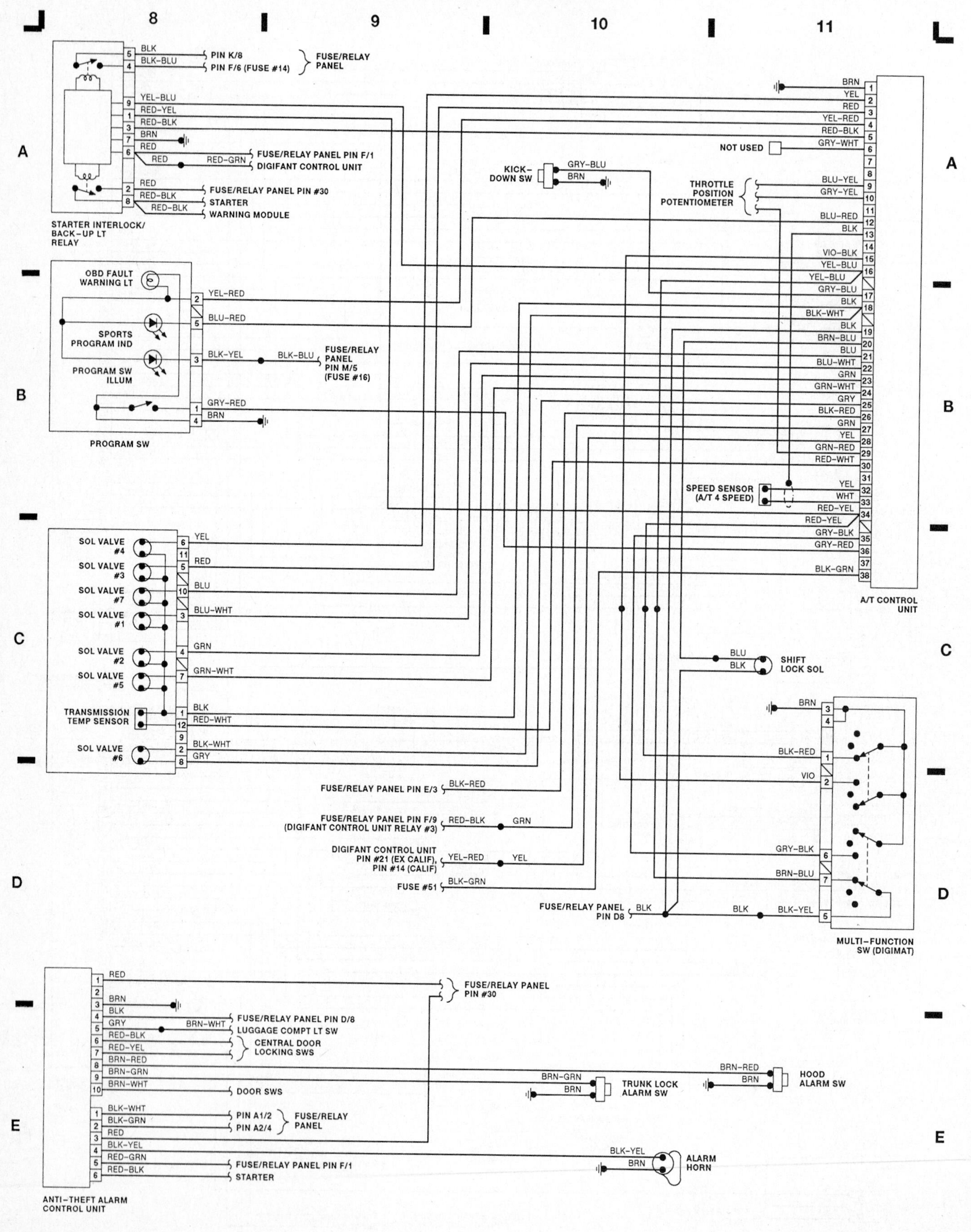

# 1991 WIRING DIAGRAMS
# Corrado (Cont.)

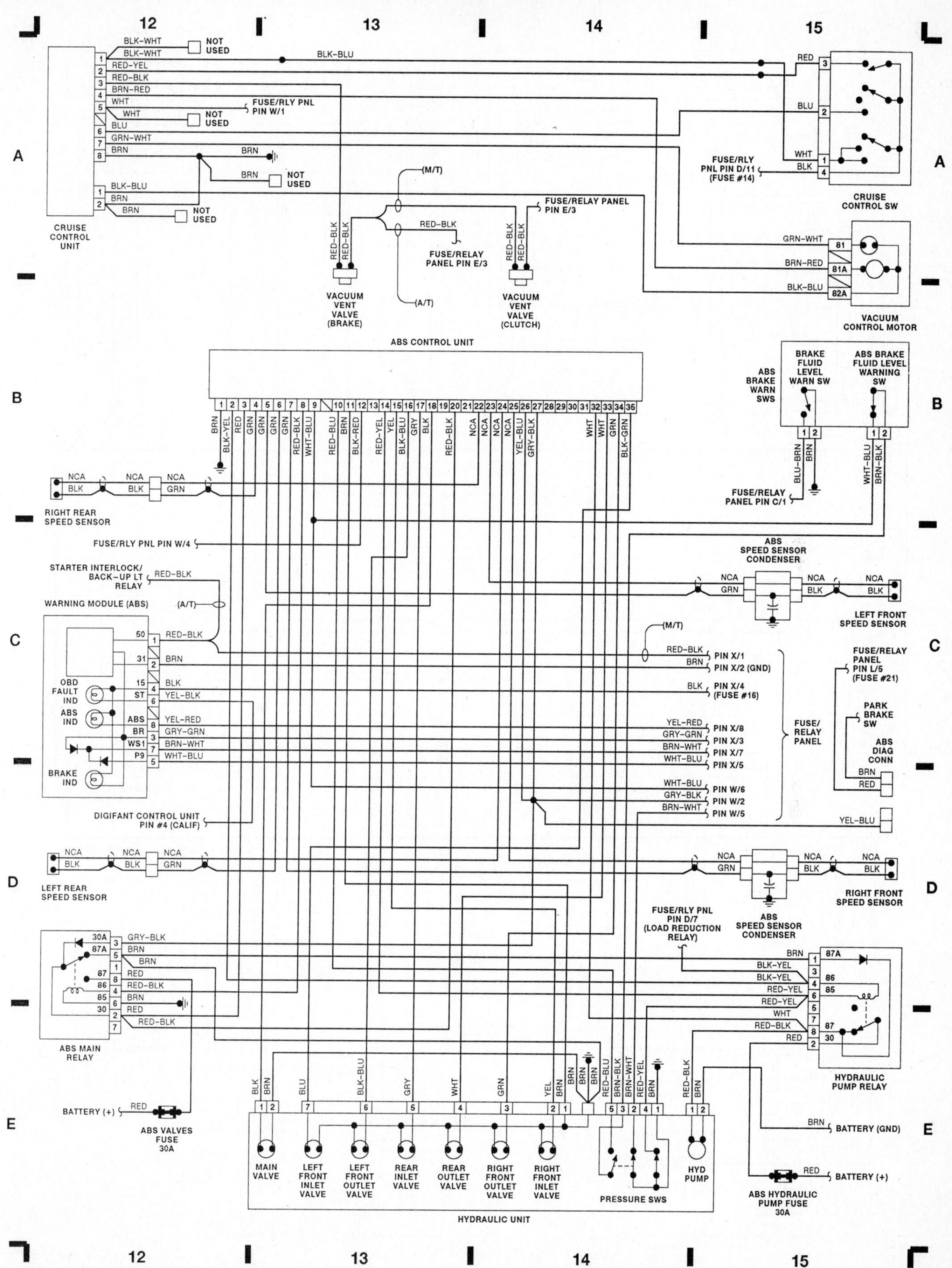

# 1991 WIRING DIAGRAMS
## Corrado (Cont.)

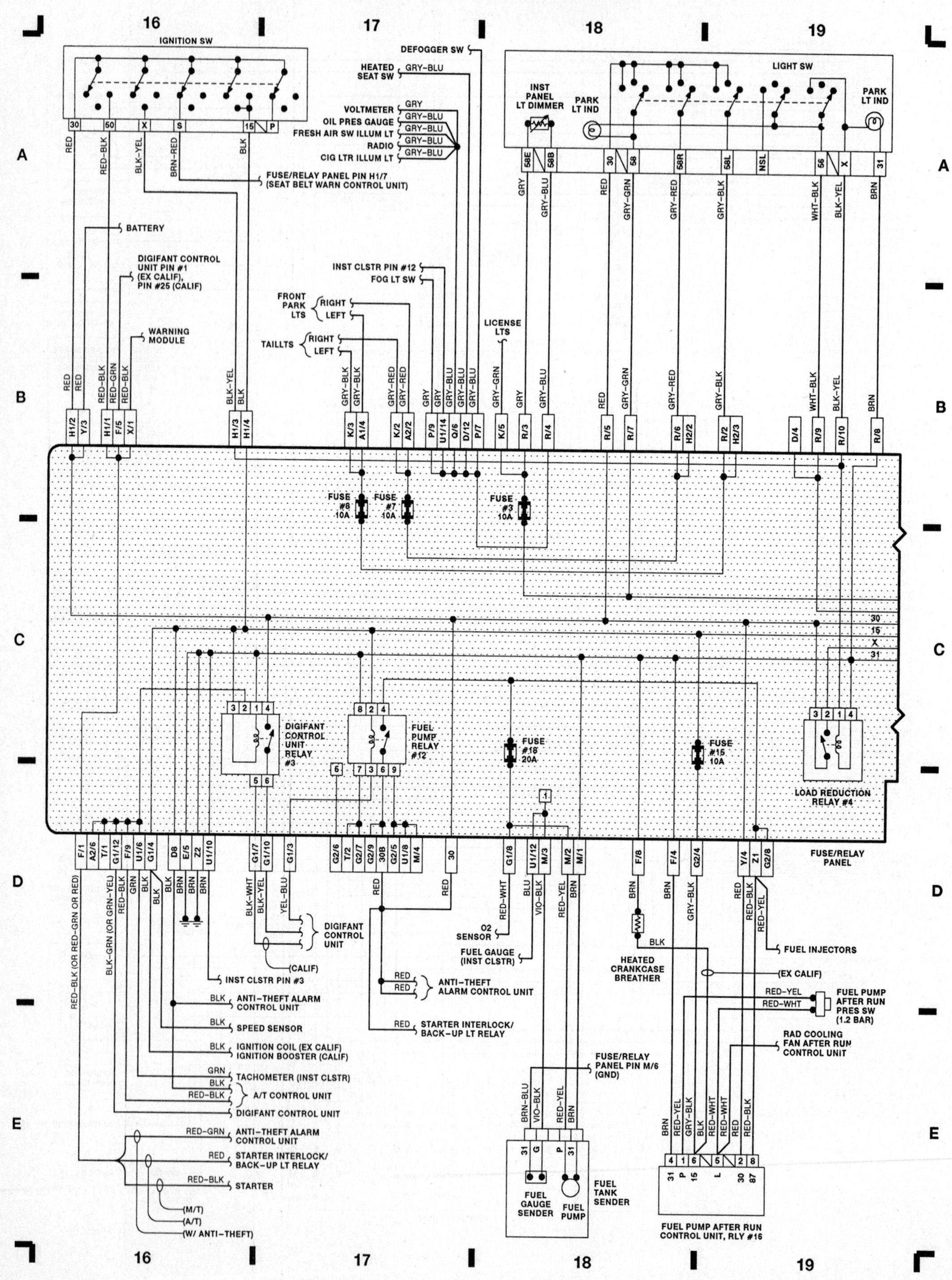

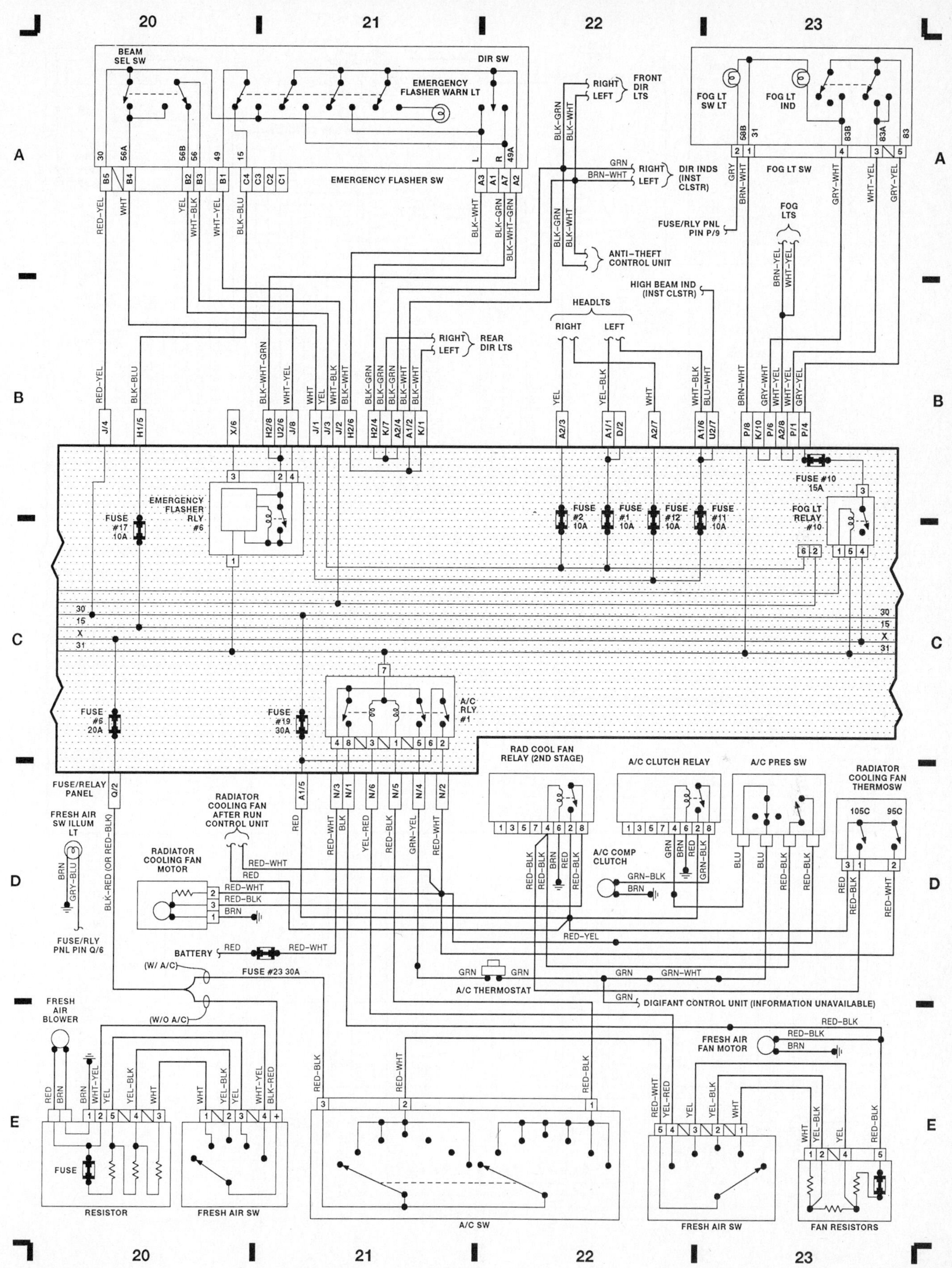

BEAM SEL SW
DIR SW
EMERGENCY FLASHER WARN LT
EMERGENCY FLASHER SW
RIGHT
LEFT
FRONT DIR LTS
DIR INDS (INST CLSTR)
FUSE/RLY PNL PIN P/9
ANTI-THEFT CONTROL UNIT
HIGH BEAM IND (INST CLSTR)
HEADLTS
REAR DIR LTS
FOG LT SW LT
FOG LT IND
FOG LT SW
FOG LTS
EMERGENCY FLASHER RLY #6
FUSE #17 10A
FUSE #2 10A
FUSE #1 10A
FUSE #12 10A
FUSE #11 10A
FUSE #10 15A
FOG LT RELAY #10
FUSE #6 20A
FUSE #19 30A
A/C RLY. #1
FUSE/RELAY PANEL
FRESH AIR SW ILLUM LT
FUSE/RLY PNL PIN Q/6
RADIATOR COOLING FAN AFTER RUN CONTROL UNIT
RADIATOR COOLING FAN MOTOR
RAD COOL FAN RELAY (2ND STAGE)
A/C CLUTCH RELAY
A/C PRES SW
RADIATOR COOLING FAN THERMOSW
105C
95C
A/C COMP CLUTCH
BATTERY
FUSE #23 30A
(W/ A/C)
(W/O A/C)
A/C THERMOSTAT
DIGIFANT CONTROL UNIT (INFORMATION UNAVAILABLE)
FRESH AIR BLOWER
FRESH AIR FAN MOTOR
FUSE
RESISTOR
FRESH AIR SW
A/C SW
FAN RESISTORS

# 1991 WIRING DIAGRAMS
## Corrado (Cont.)

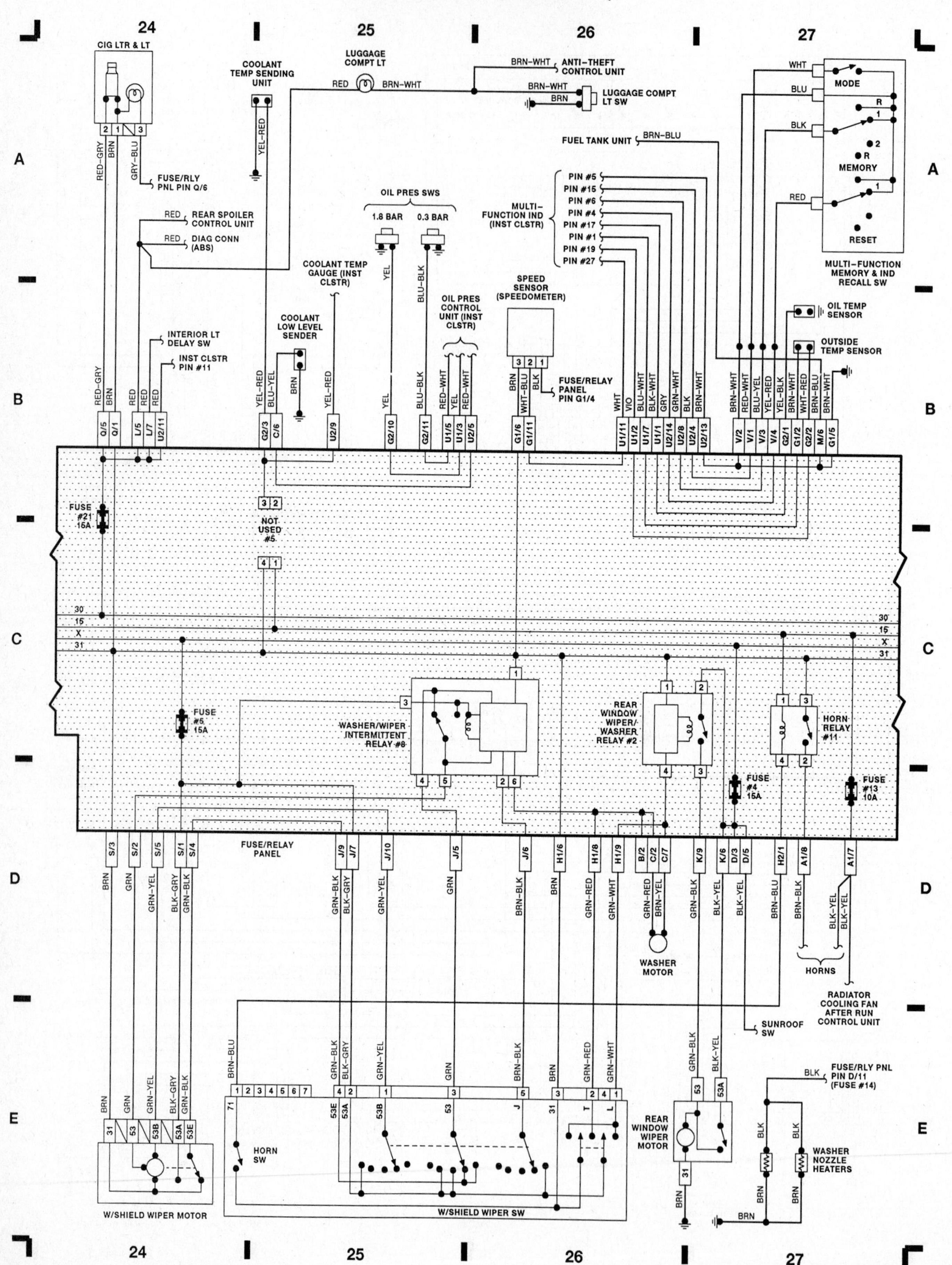

# 1991 WIRING DIAGRAMS
## Corrado (Cont.)

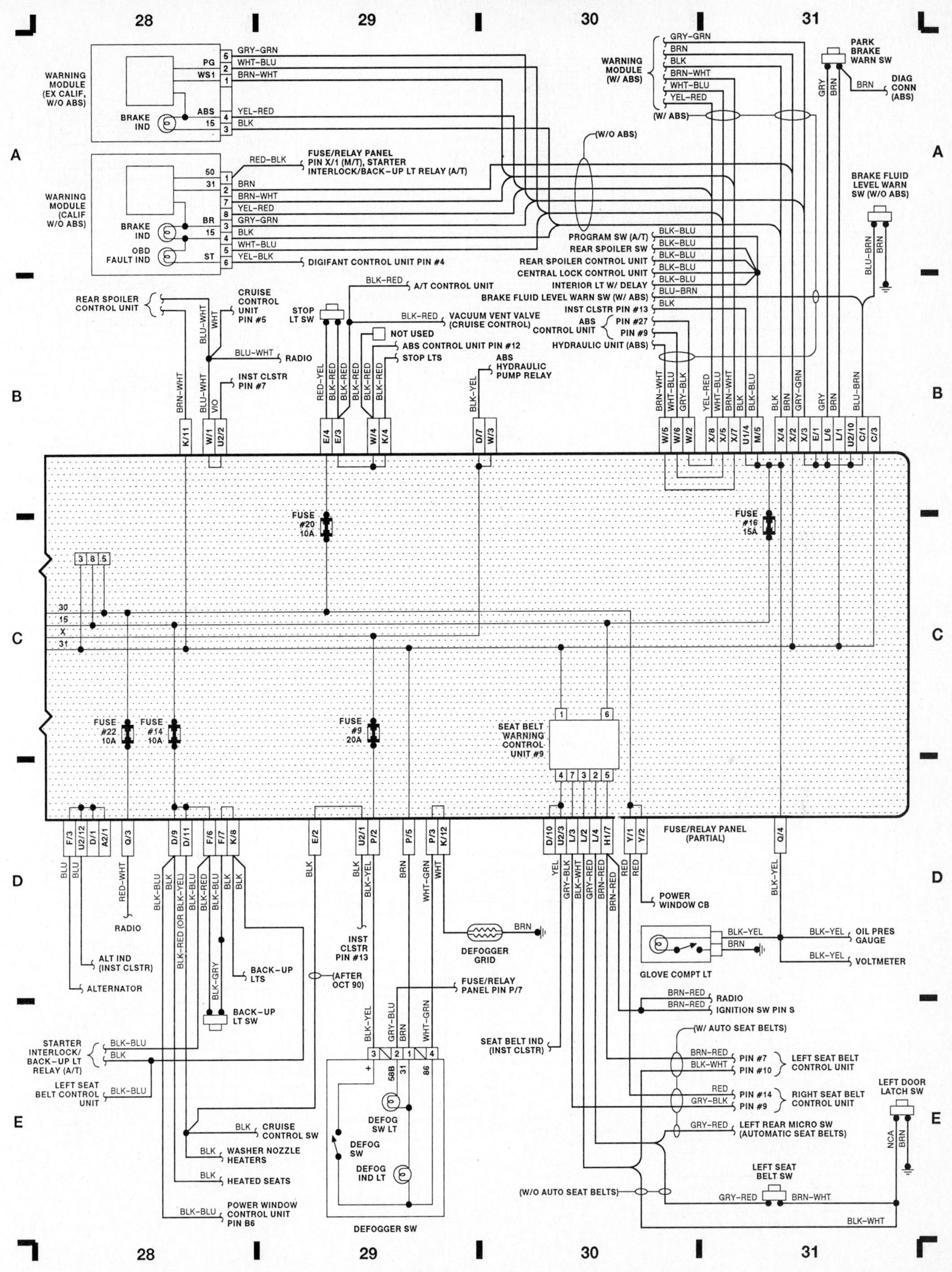

# 1991 WIRING DIAGRAMS
## Corrado (Cont.)

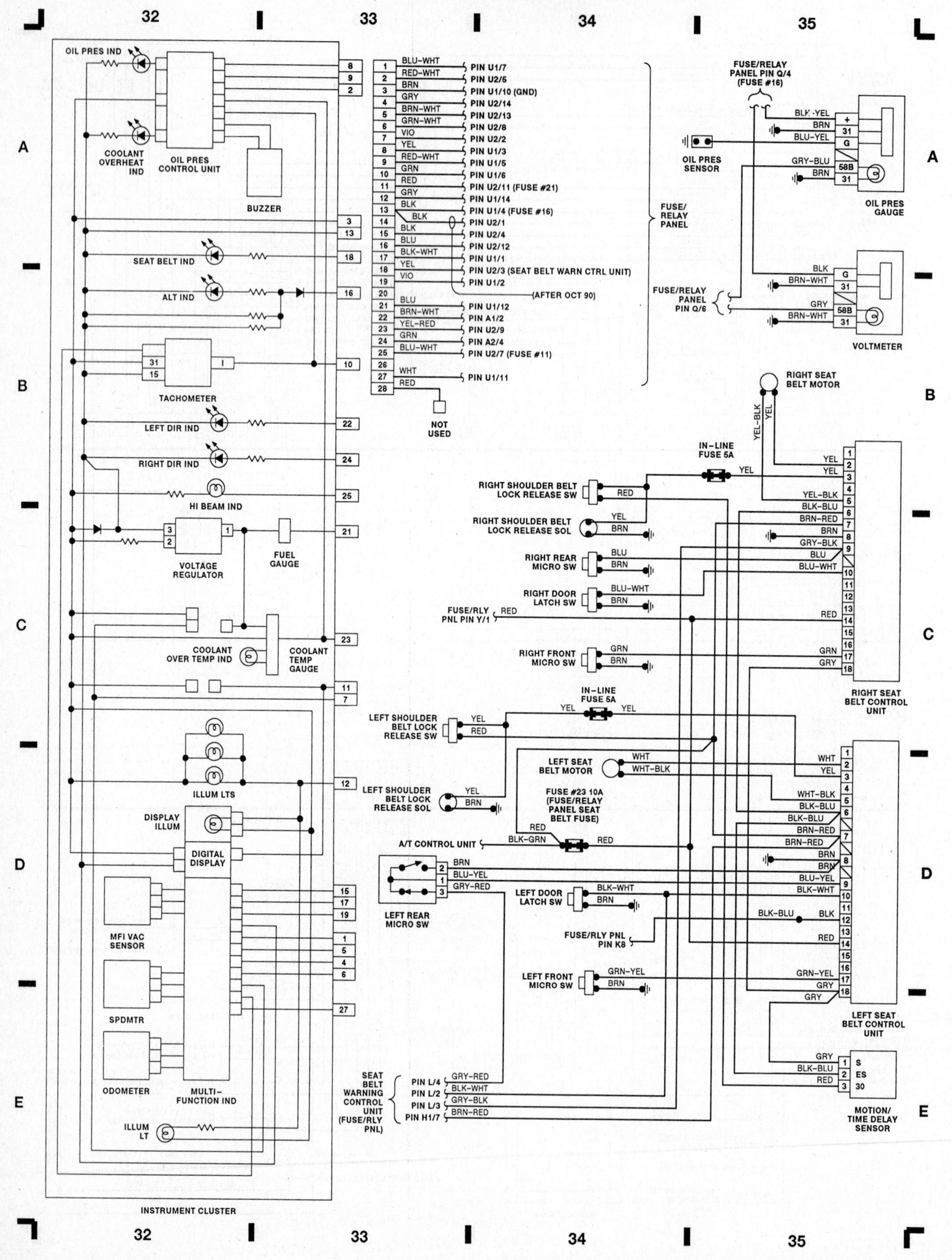

# 1991 WIRING DIAGRAMS
## Corrado (Cont.)

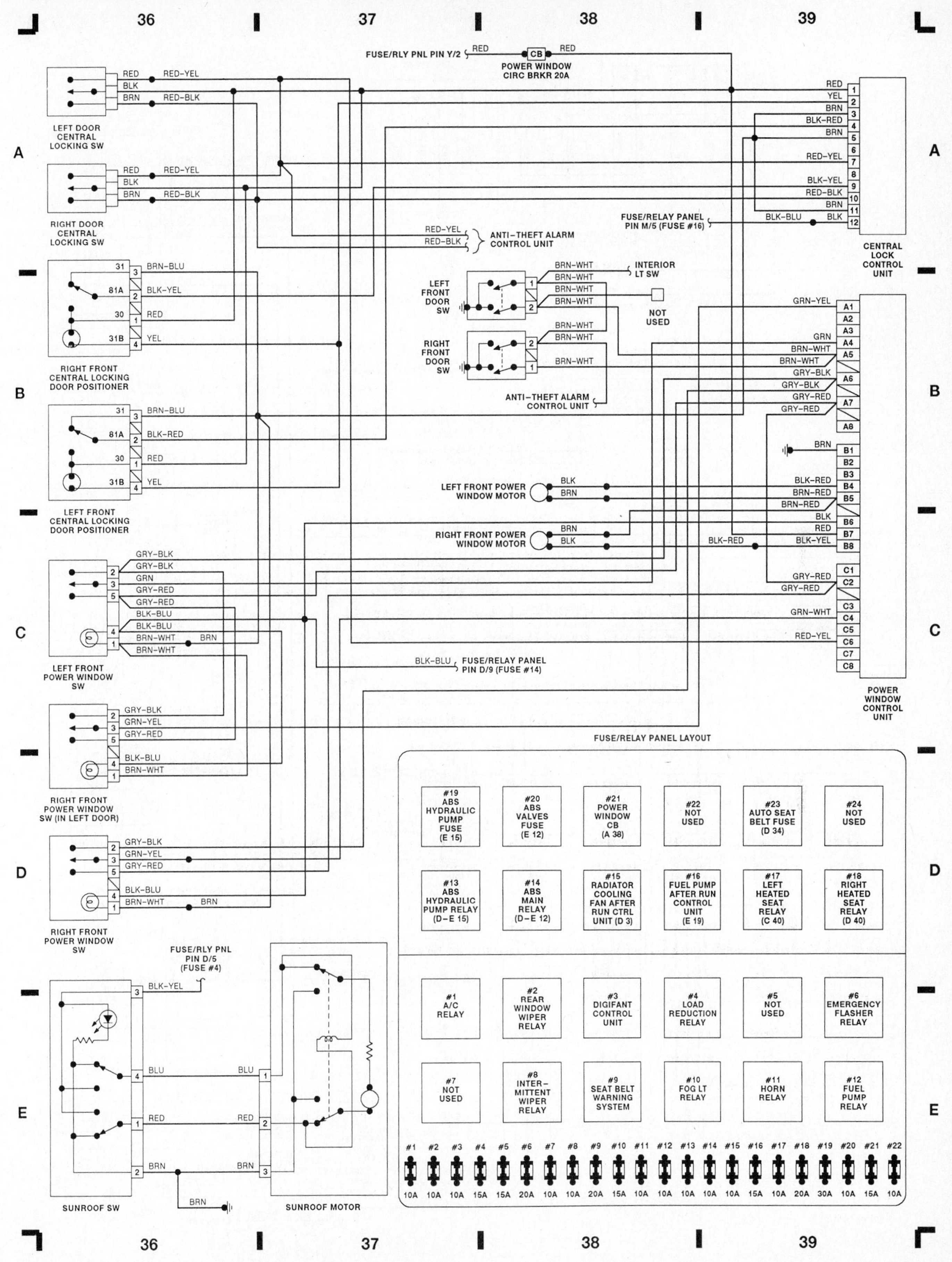

# 1991 WIRING DIAGRAMS
# Corrado (Cont.)

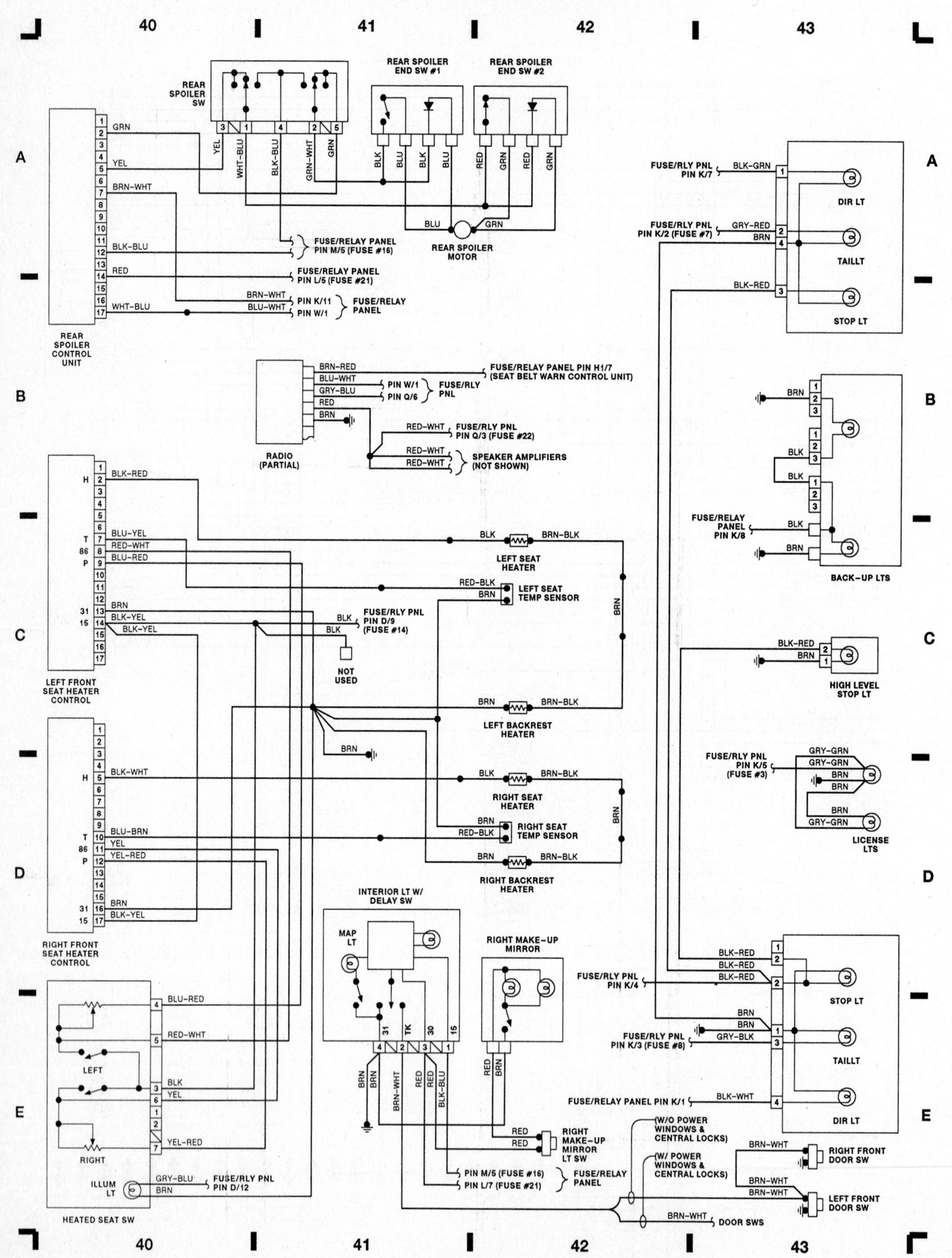

# 1991 WIRING DIAGRAMS
# Fox

**COMPONENT LOCATOR:**

| Component | Location |
|---|---|
| A/C CTRL HEAD | E 8-9 |
| A/C HI PRES SW | E 10-11 |
| A/C RELAY | C-D 10 |
| ALTERNATOR | A-B 3 |
| BACK-UP LT SW | A-B 15 |
| BATTERY | A 2 |
| BEAM SELECT/FLASHER SW | A 11 |
| BRAKE FLUID LEVEL SW | A 16 |
| CIG LTR | C 16 |
| COOLANT FAN | E 12 |
| COOLANT FAN THERMO SW | E 13 |
| COOLANT TEMP SENSOR | B 5-6 |
| COOLANT TEMP SENSOR | A 16 |
| DEFOGGER SW | C 16 |
| DIGIFANT CTRL UNIT RELAY | E 6 |
| DIGIFANT CTRL UNITS | A-C 4-7 |
| DIR SW | A 13 |
| DOOR SWS | A 14 |
| EMERGENCY FLASHER SW | A 12 |
| FLASHER RELAY | B-C 12 |
| FRESH AIR FAN SW | C-D 16 |
| FRONT WIPER MOTOR | E 3 |
| FUEL INJECTORS | E 4-7 |
| FUEL PUMP RELAY | C-D 8-9 |
| FUEL TANK UNIT | E 8 |
| HEADLIGHT SW | A 10-11 |
| HEATED O2 SENSOR | A 4 |
| HORN RELAY | C-D 12 |
| HORN SW | D-E 12 |
| IDLE BOOST CTRL UNIT | E 5-6 |
| IDLE SPEED BOOST VALVE | E 4 |
| IGNITION COILS | D 5-7 |
| IGNITION SW | A 8 |
| INSTRUMENT CLUSTER | A-D 16 |
| LOAD REDUCTION RELAY | C-D 11 |
| OIL PRES SWS | B 16 |
| PANEL DIMMER | A 13 |
| PARKING BRAKE SW | A 16 |
| RADIATOR COOLANT FAN RELAY | C-D 13 |
| READING SW | A 15 |
| REAR COMPARTMENT/TRUNK LT SW | B-C 17 |
| SEAT BELT SW | A 14 |
| SEAT BELT WARN RELAY | B-C 14 |
| STARTER | A 3 |
| STARTER INTERLOCK RELAY | B-C 8 |
| STOP LT SW | E 12 |
| WIPER/WASHER INTERMITTENT RELAY | C-D 14 |
| WIPER/WASHER SW | E 13-15 |

GRY-RED
BRN
MARKER LT
PARK LT
GRY-RED
BRN
BLK-GRN
DIR LT
FUSE/RELAY PANEL PIN E58R
EMERG FLASHER SW
BATTERY
NCA
BRN
RED
RED
BLK
FUSE/RELAY PANEL PIN L30
BLK
RED
RED-BLK
FUSE/RELAY PANEL PIN B50A
15A
30
50
STARTER
WHT
YEL
BRN
HEADLIGHT
PIN D56AR
PIN D56BR
FUSE/RELAY PANEL
RED
BLU
B+
B+
D+
ALTERNATOR
CHARGE IND (INST CLSTR)

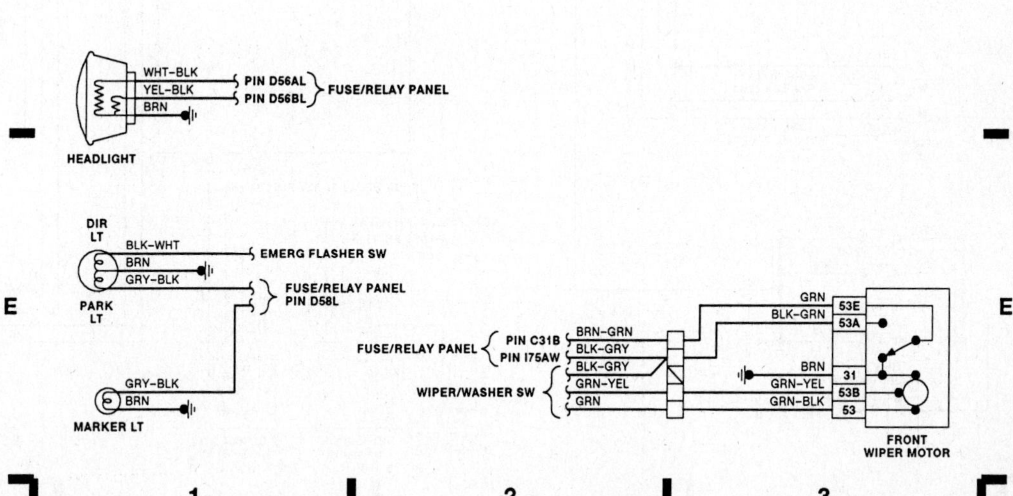

# 1991 WIRING DIAGRAMS
## Fox (Cont.)

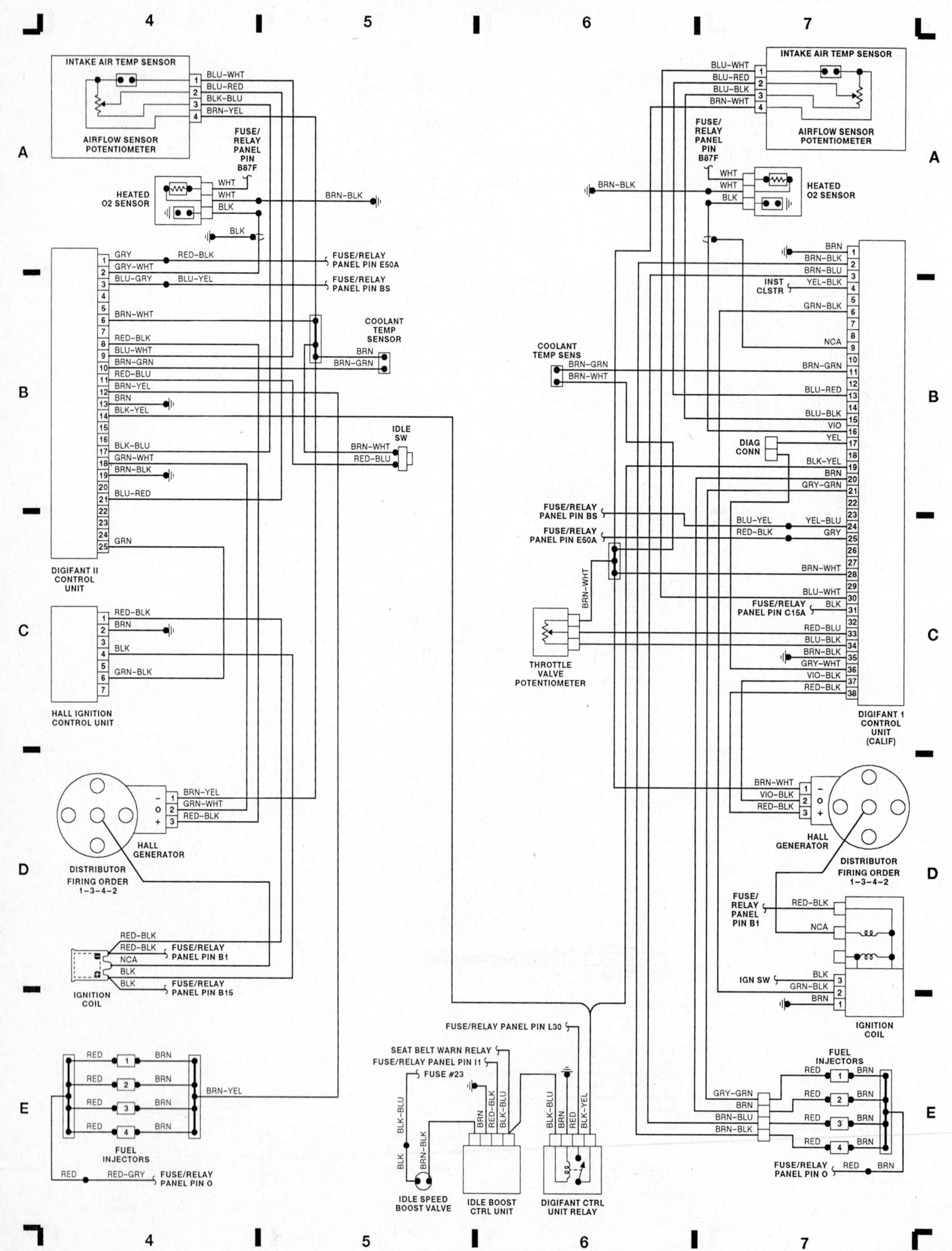

# 1991 WIRING DIAGRAMS
# Fox (Cont.)

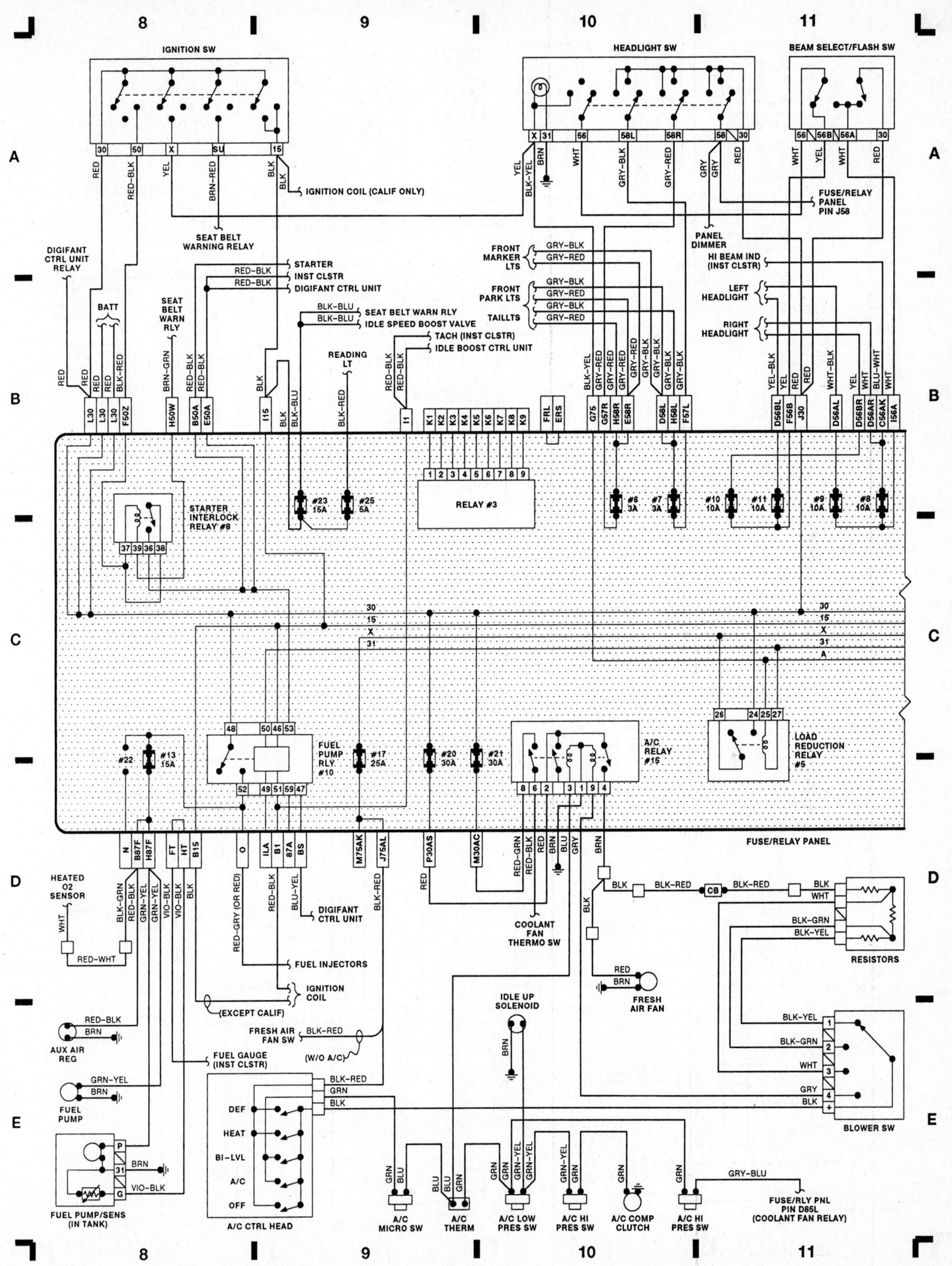

# 1991 WIRING DIAGRAMS
## Fox (Cont.)

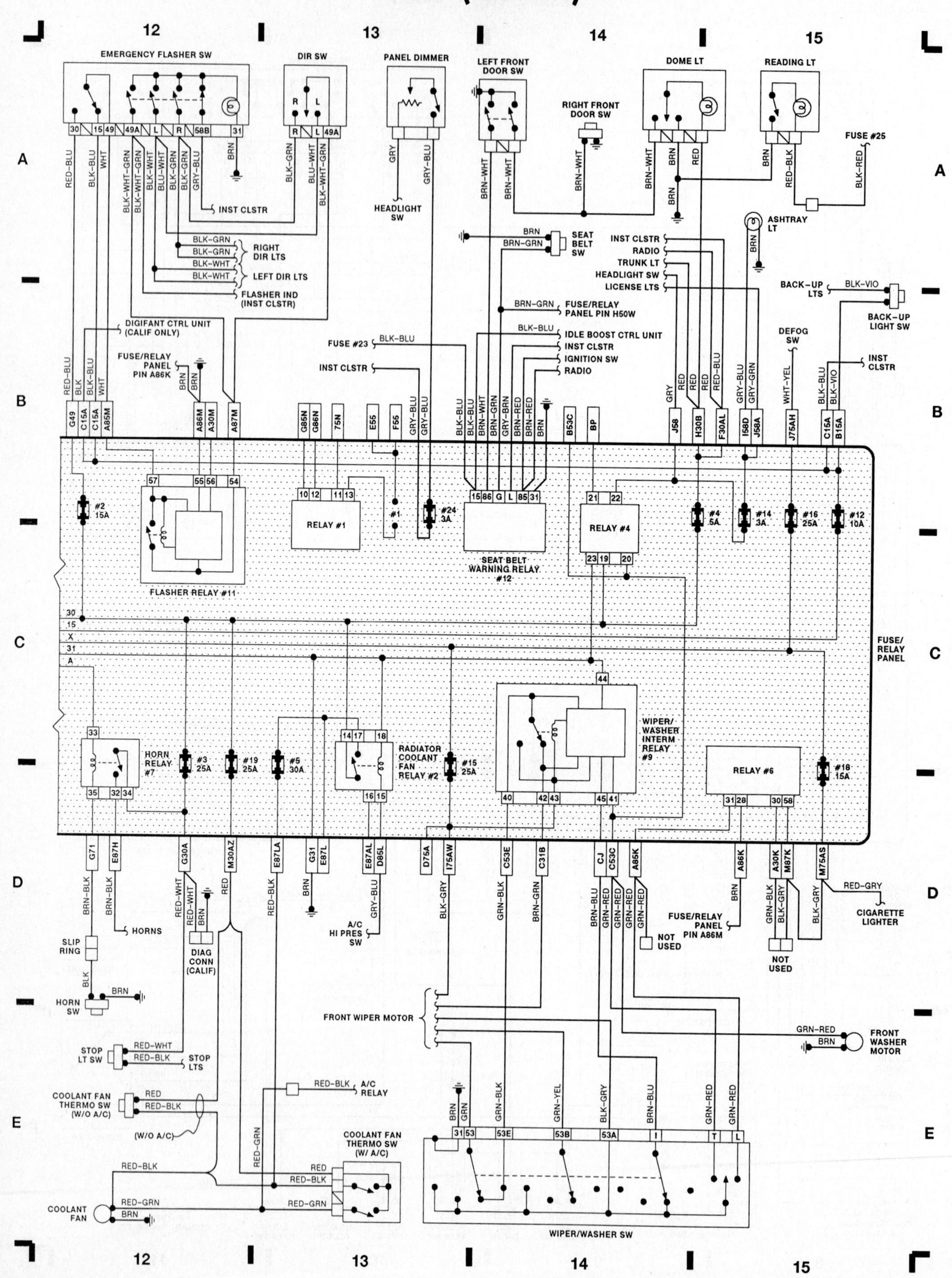

# 1991 WIRING DIAGRAMS
## Fox (Cont.)

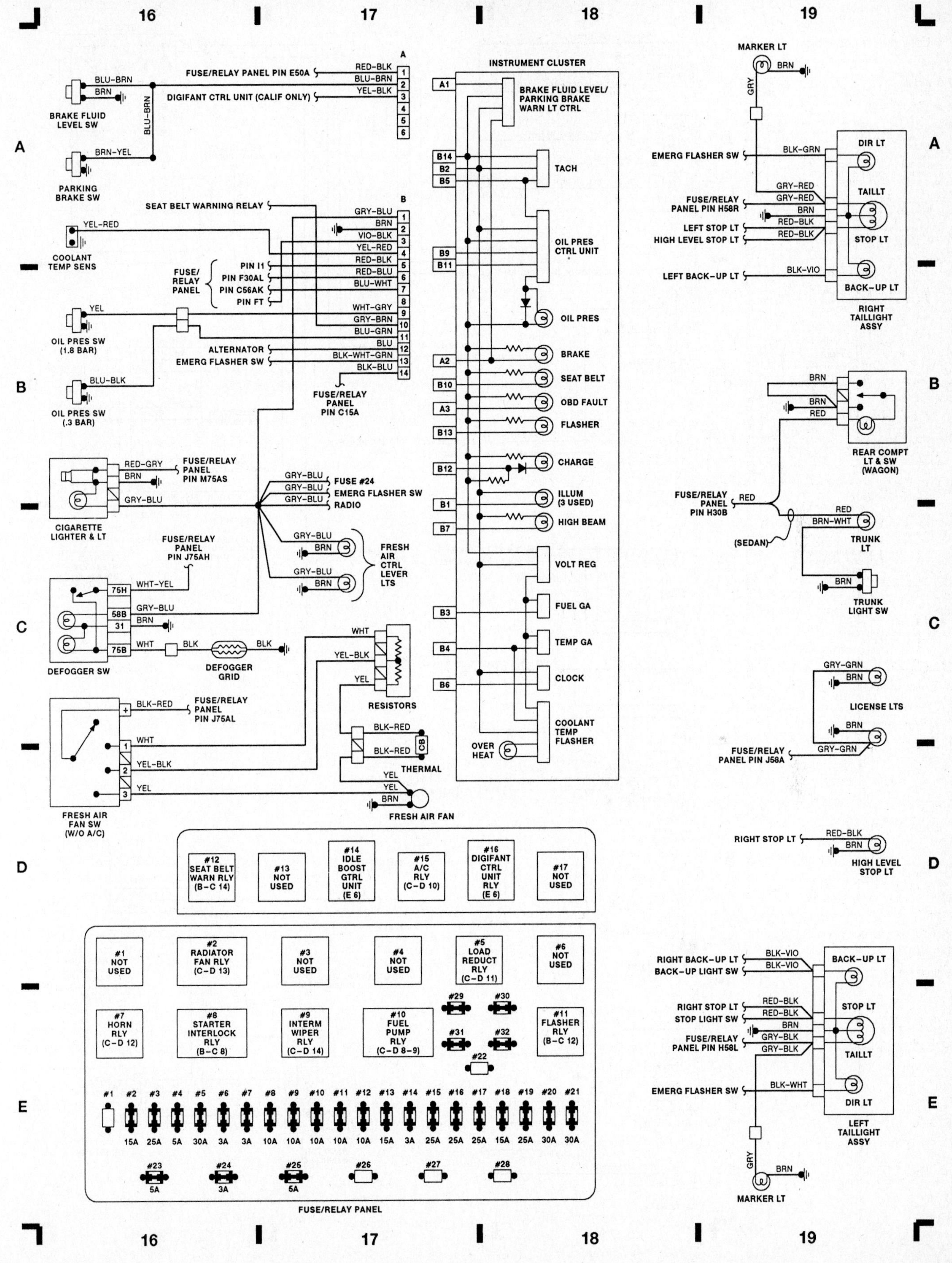

# 1991 WIRING DIAGRAMS
# Golf & GTI

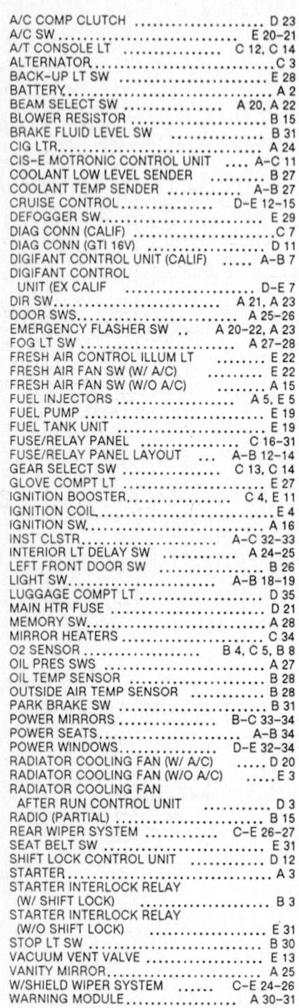

COMPONENT LOCATOR:

| | |
|---|---|
| A/C COMP CLUTCH | D 23 |
| A/C SW | E 20–21 |
| A/T CONSOLE LT | C 12, C 14 |
| ALTERNATOR | C 3 |
| BACK-UP LT SW | E 28 |
| BATTERY | A 2 |
| BEAM SELECT SW | A 20, A 22 |
| BLOWER RESISTOR | B 15 |
| BRAKE FLUID LEVEL SW | B 31 |
| CIG LTR | A 24 |
| CIS-E MOTRONIC CONTROL UNIT | A–C 11 |
| COOLANT LOW LEVEL SENDER | B 27 |
| COOLANT TEMP SENDER | A–B 27 |
| CRUISE CONTROL | D–E 12–15 |
| DEFOGGER SW | E 29 |
| DIAG CONN (CALIF) | C 7 |
| DIAG CONN (GTI 16V) | D 11 |
| DIGIFANT CONTROL UNIT (CALIF) | A–B 7 |
| DIGIFANT CONTROL UNIT (EX CALIF | D–E 7 |
| DIR SW | A 21, A 23 |
| DOOR SWS | A 25–26 |
| EMERGENCY FLASHER SW | A 20–22, A 23 |
| FOG LT SW | A 27–28 |
| FRESH AIR CONTROL ILLUM LT | E 22 |
| FRESH AIR FAN SW (W/ A/C) | E 22 |
| FRESH AIR FAN SW (W/O A/C) | A 15 |
| FUEL INJECTORS | A 5, E 5 |
| FUEL PUMP | E 19 |
| FUEL TANK UNIT | E 19 |
| FUSE/RELAY PANEL | C 16–31 |
| FUSE/RELAY PANEL LAYOUT | A–B 12–14 |
| GEAR SELECT SW | C 13, C 14 |
| GLOVE COMPT LT | E 27 |
| IGNITION BOOSTER | C 4, E 11 |
| IGNITION COIL | E 4 |
| IGNITION SW | A 16 |
| INST CLSTR | A–C 32–33 |
| INTERIOR LT DELAY SW | A 24–25 |
| LEFT FRONT DOOR SW | B 26 |
| LIGHT SW | A–B 18–19 |
| LUGGAGE COMPT LT | D 35 |
| MAIN HTR FUSE | D 21 |
| MEMORY SW | A 28 |
| MIRROR HEATERS | C 34 |
| O2 SENSOR | B 4, C 5, B 8 |
| OIL PRES SWS | A 27 |
| OIL TEMP SENSOR | B 28 |
| OUTSIDE AIR TEMP SENSOR | B 28 |
| PARK BRAKE SW | B 31 |
| POWER MIRRORS | B–C 33–34 |
| POWER SEATS | A–B 34 |
| POWER WINDOWS | D–E 32–34 |
| RADIATOR COOLING FAN (W/ A/C) | D 20 |
| RADIATOR COOLING FAN (W/O A/C) | E 3 |
| RADIATOR COOLING FAN AFTER RUN CONTROL UNIT | D 3 |
| RADIO (PARTIAL) | B 15 |
| REAR WIPER SYSTEM | C–E 26–27 |
| SEAT BELT SW | E 31 |
| SHIFT LOCK CONTROL UNIT | D 12 |
| STARTER | A 3 |
| STARTER INTERLOCK RELAY (W/ SHIFT LOCK) | B 3 |
| STARTER INTERLOCK RELAY (W/O SHIFT LOCK) | E 31 |
| STOP LT SW | B 30 |
| VACUUM VENT VALVE | E 13 |
| VANITY MIRROR | A 25 |
| W/SHIELD WIPER SYSTEM | C–E 24–26 |
| WARNING MODULE | A 30–31 |

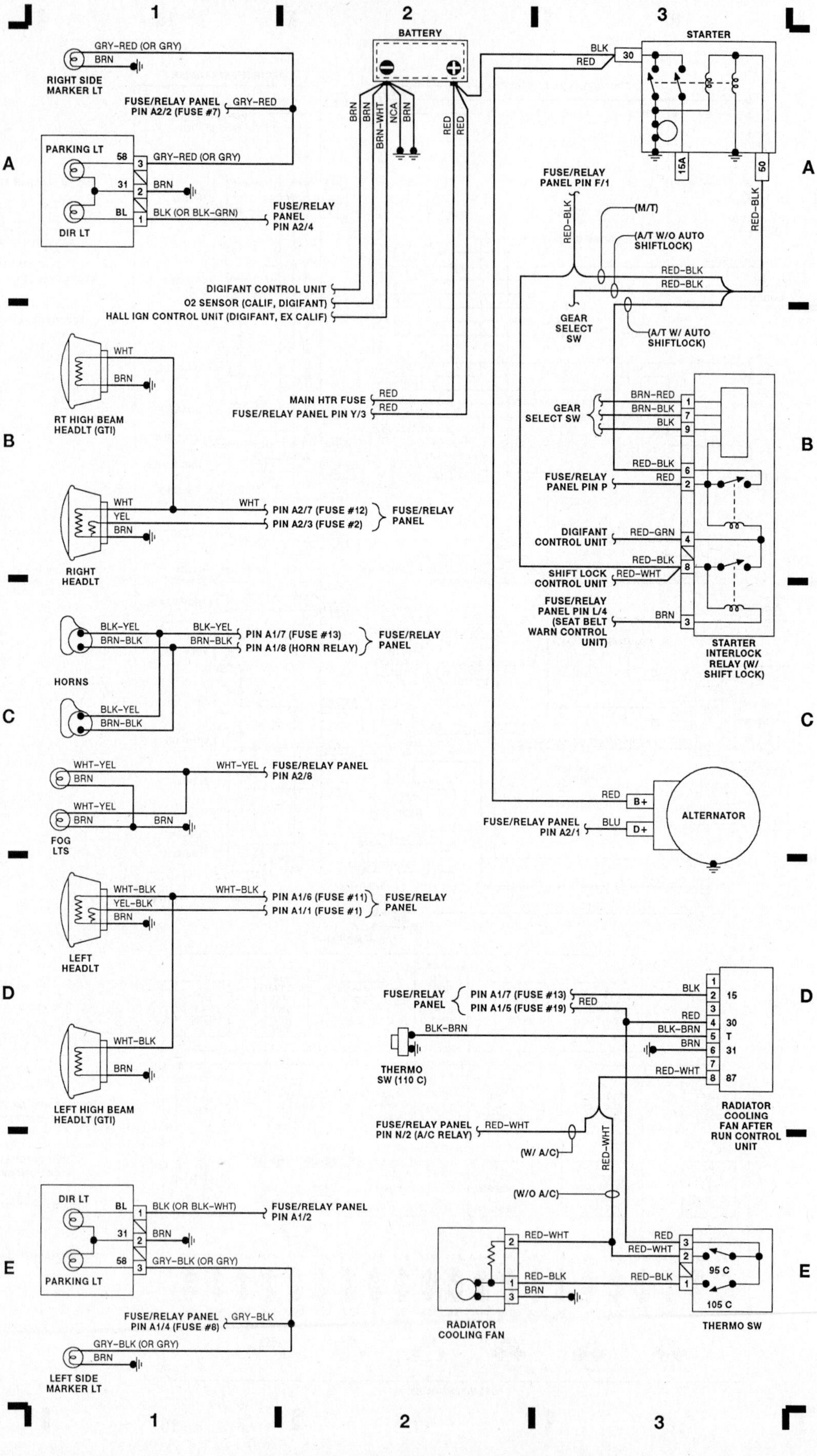

RIGHT SIDE MARKER LT
PARKING LT
DIR LT
BATTERY
STARTER
DIGIFANT CONTROL UNIT
O2 SENSOR (CALIF, DIGIFANT)
HALL IGN CONTROL UNIT (DIGIFANT, EX CALIF)
GEAR SELECT SW
RT HIGH BEAM HEADLT (GTI)
MAIN HTR FUSE
FUSE/RELAY PANEL PIN Y/3
RIGHT HEADLT
STARTER INTERLOCK RELAY (W/ SHIFT LOCK)
HORNS
FOG LTS
ALTERNATOR
LEFT HEADLT
LEFT HIGH BEAM HEADLT (GTI)
THERMO SW (110 C)
RADIATOR COOLING FAN AFTER RUN CONTROL UNIT
RADIATOR COOLING FAN
THERMO SW
LEFT SIDE MARKER LT

# 1991 WIRING DIAGRAMS
# Golf & GTI (Cont.)

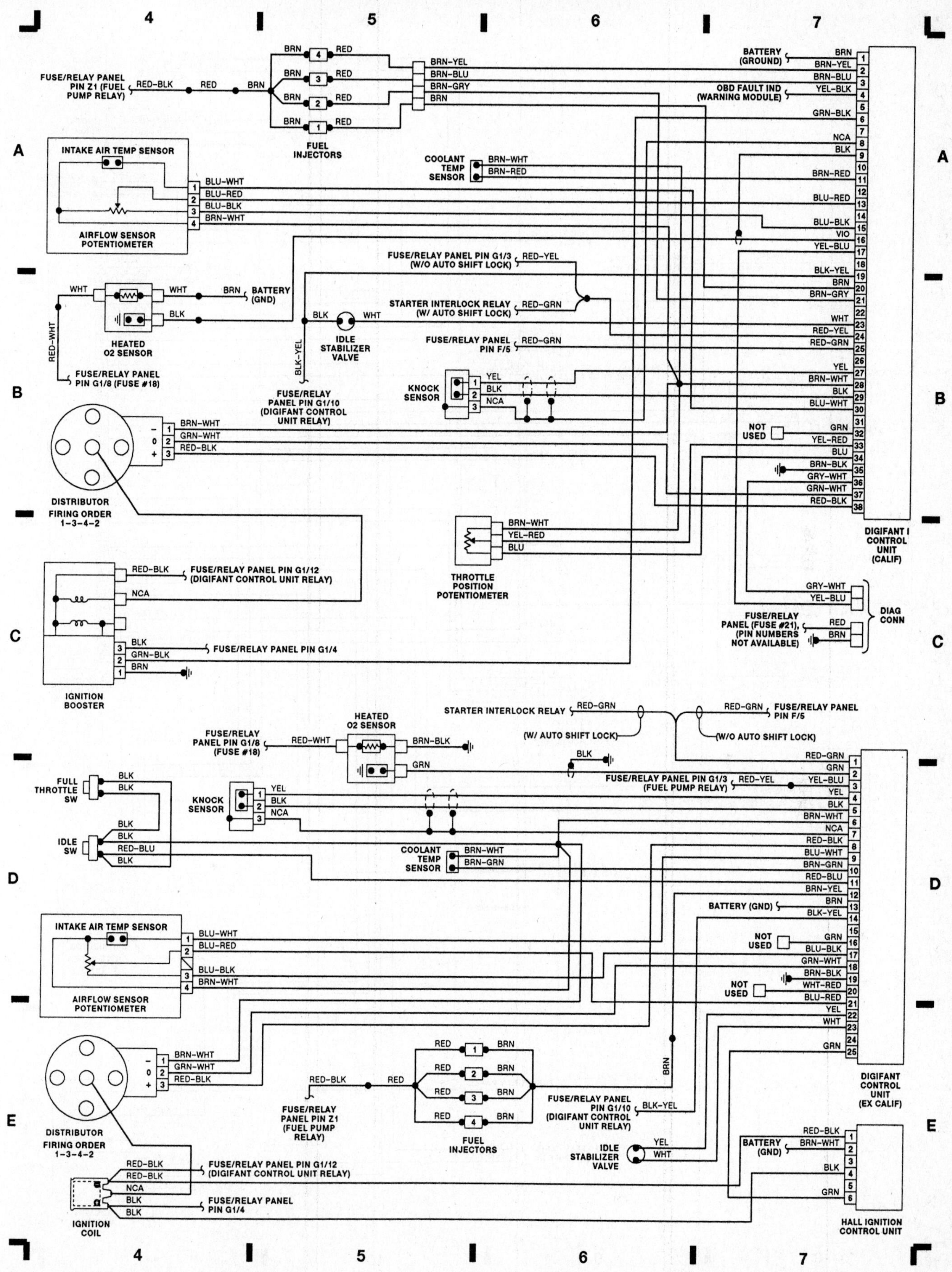

# 1991 WIRING DIAGRAMS
## Golf & GTI (Cont.)

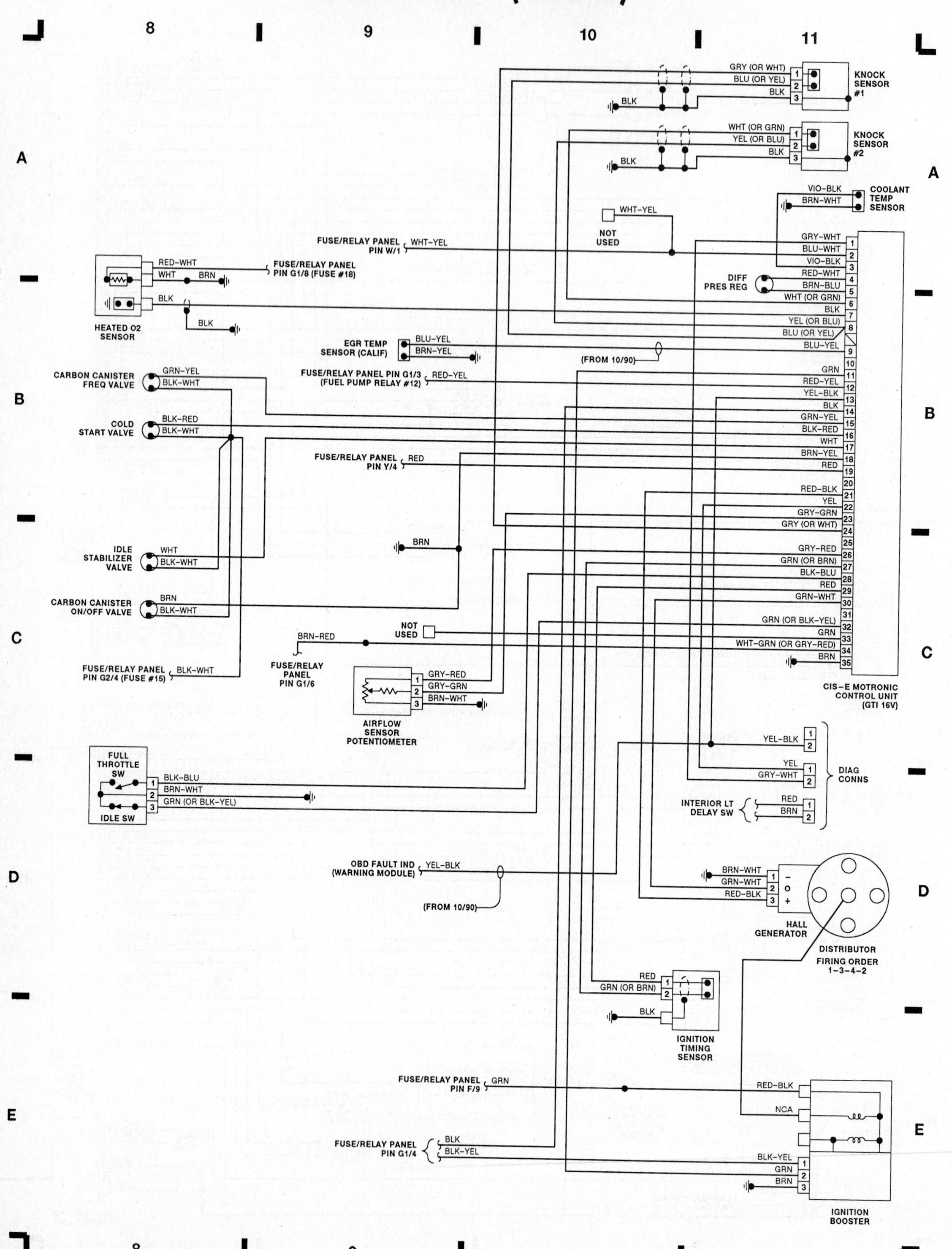

# 1991 WIRING DIAGRAMS
## Golf & GTI (Cont.)

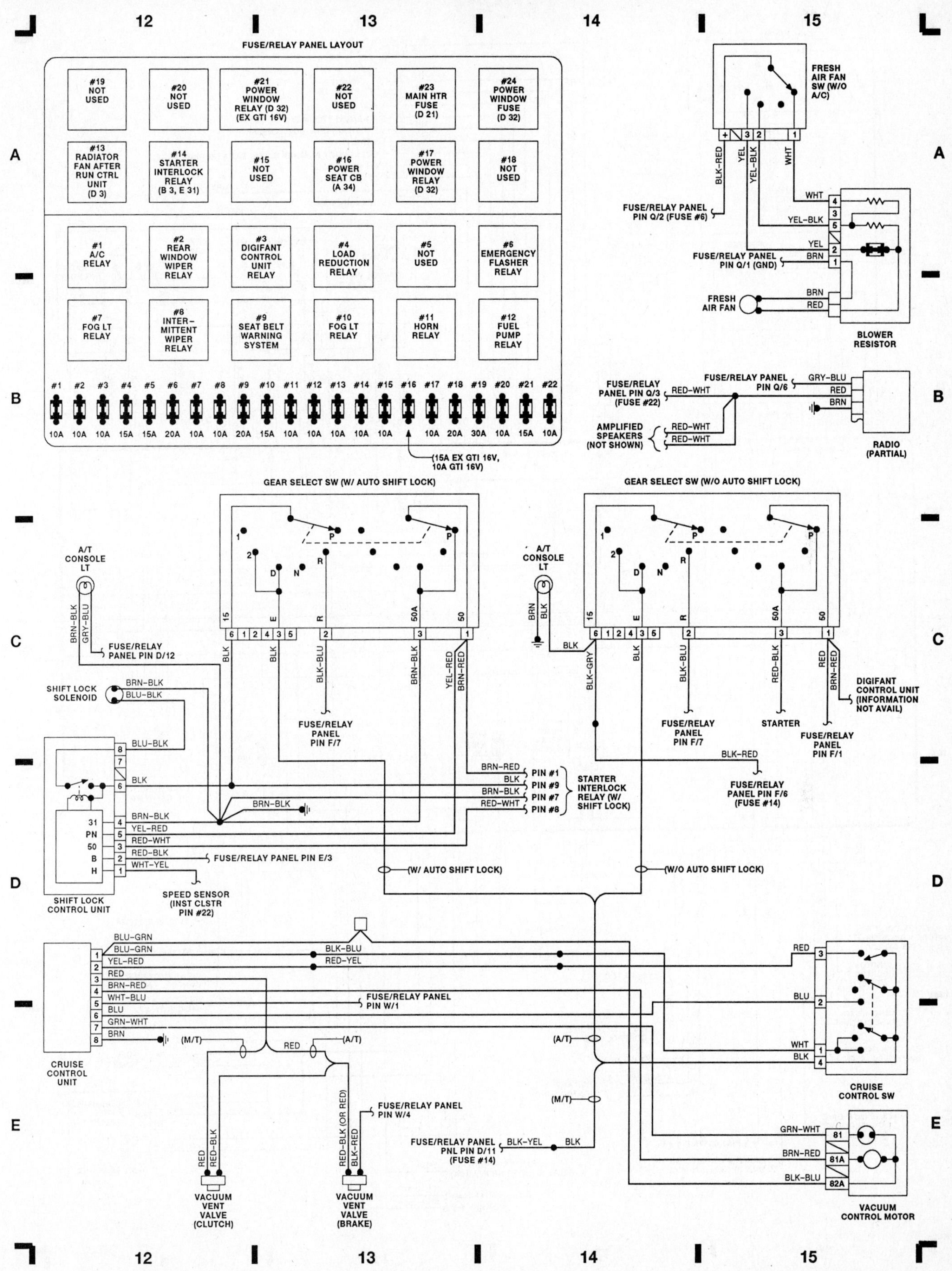

# 1991 WIRING DIAGRAMS
## Golf & GTI (Cont.)

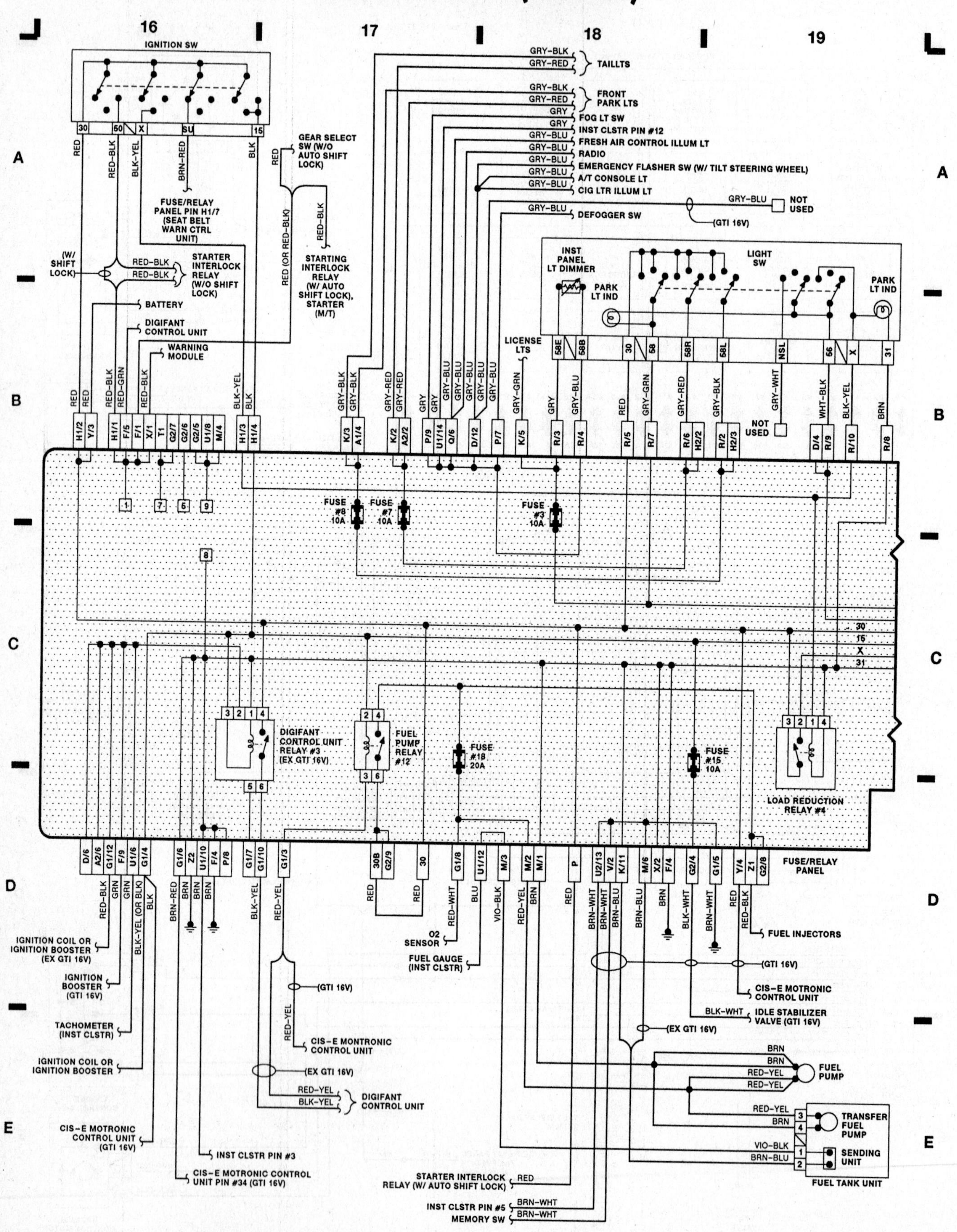

# 1991 WIRING DIAGRAMS
# Golf & GTI (Cont.)

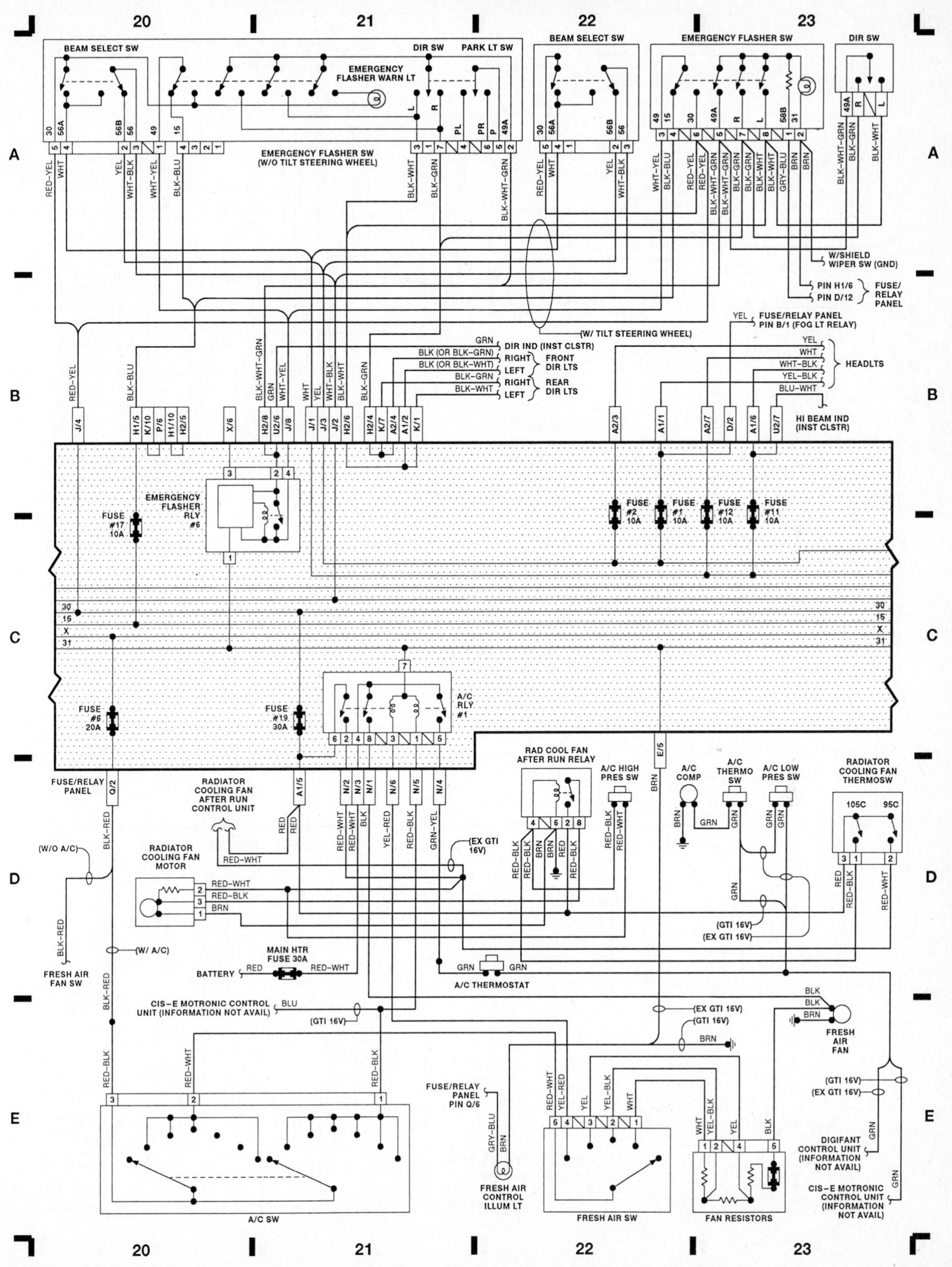

# 1991 WIRING DIAGRAMS
## Golf & GTI (Cont.)

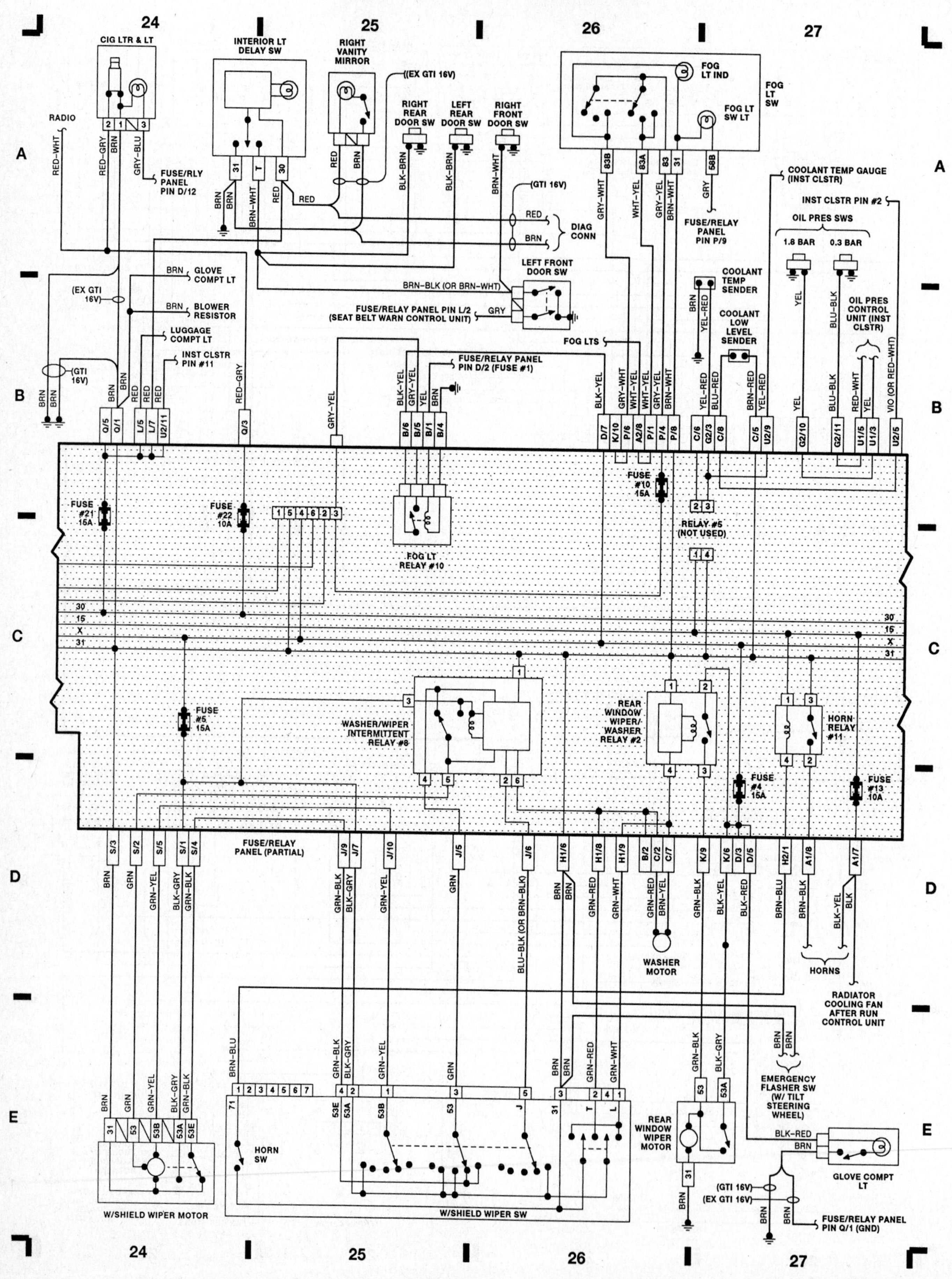

# 1991 WIRING DIAGRAMS
# Golf & GTI (Cont.)

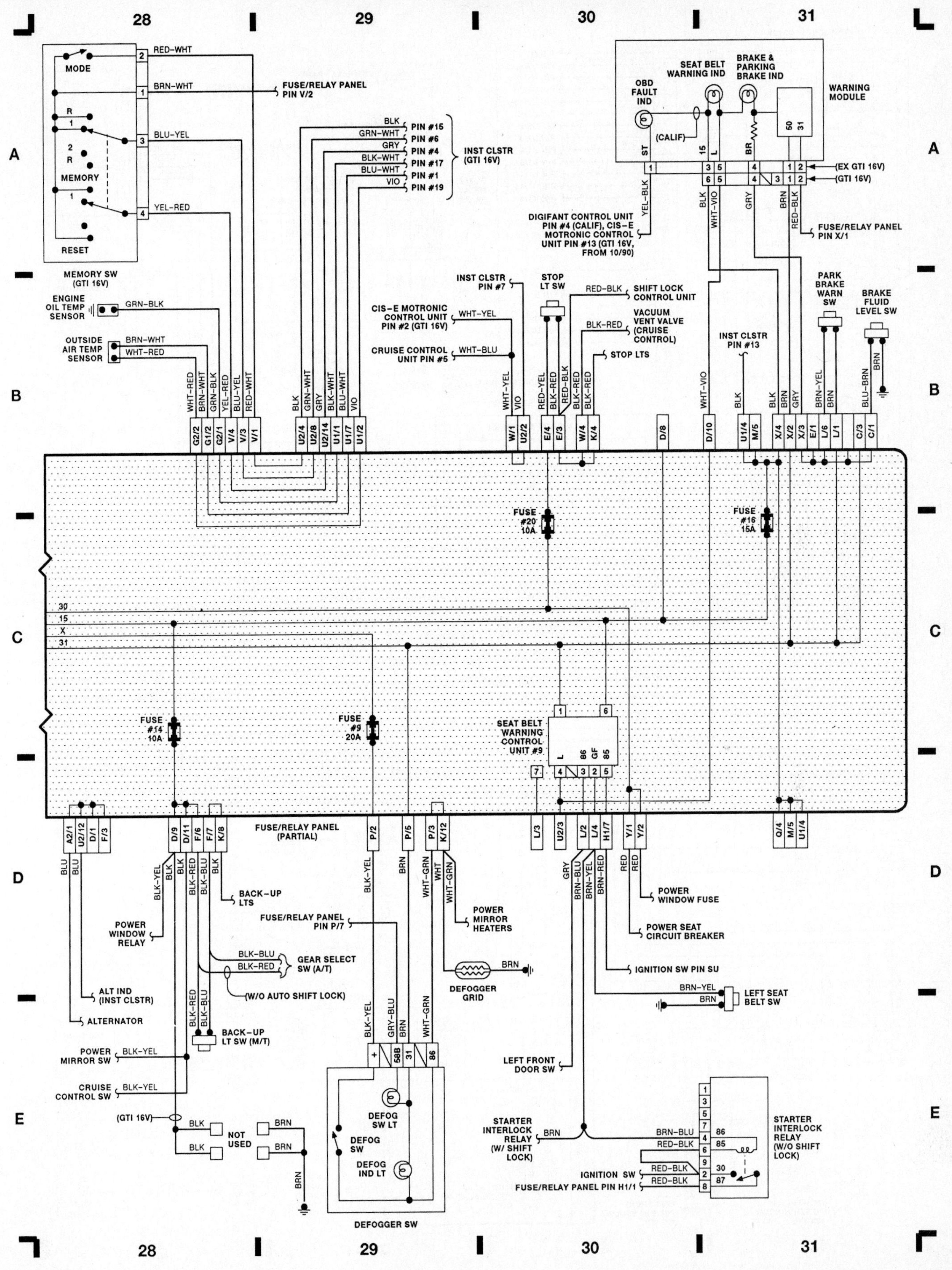

# 1991 WIRING DIAGRAMS
# Golf & GTI (Cont.)

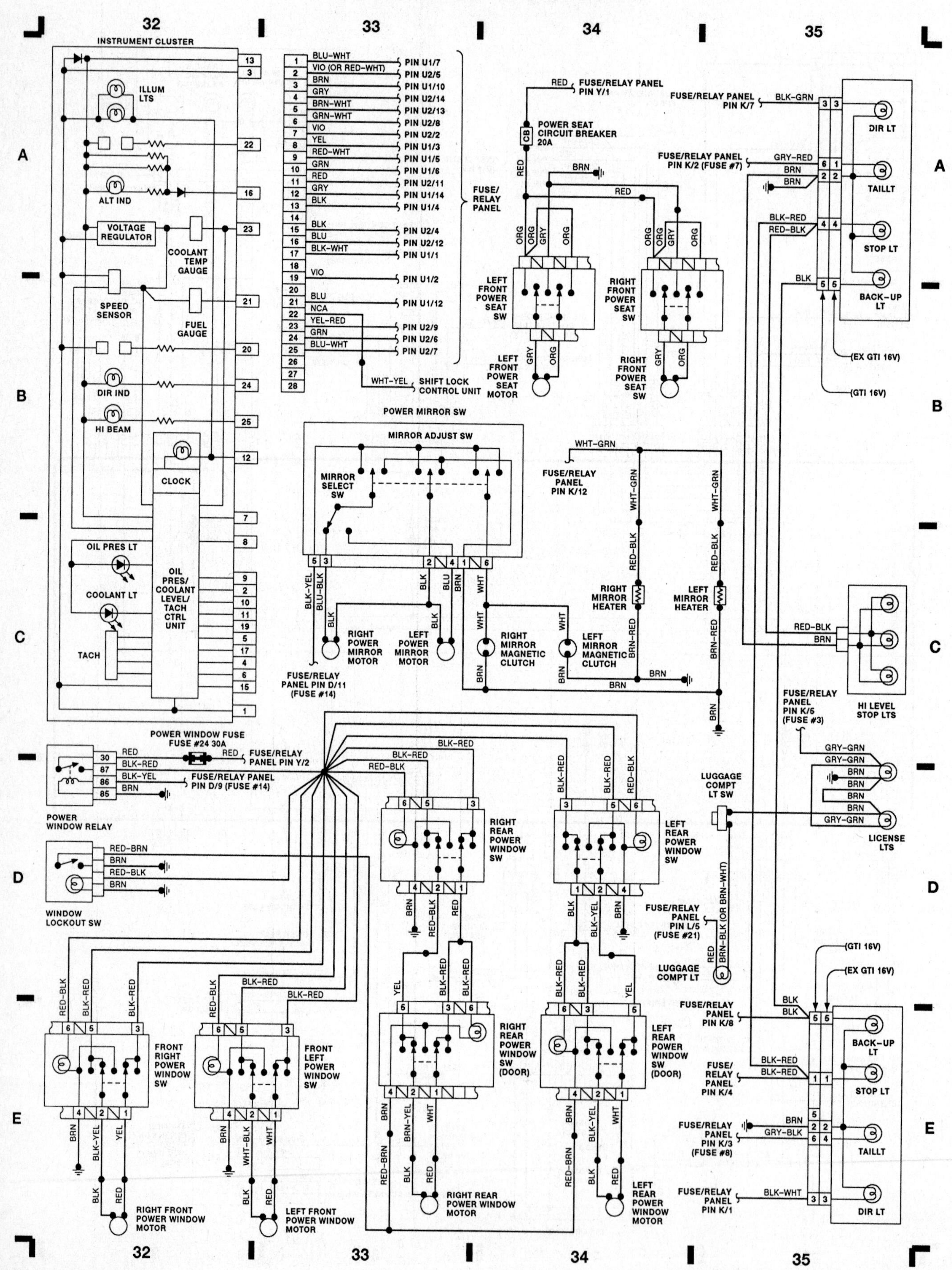

# 1991 WIRING DIAGRAMS
# Jetta & Jetta GLi

## COMPONENT LOCATOR:

| | |
|---|---|
| A/C CLUTCH RELAY (16V GLI) | D 23 |
| A/C COMP CLUTCH (16V GLI) | D 23 |
| A/C COMP CLUTCH (DIGIFANT & DIESEL) | D 23 |
| A/C COMP CLUTCH (ECO DIESEL) | E 11 |
| A/C EVAP TEMP SW (ECO DIESEL) | D 23 |
| A/C LOW PRES SW (ECO DIESEL) | E 9 |
| A/C REFRIG LOW PRES SW (16V GLI) | C 1 |
| A/C SW | E 21–22 |
| A/C TIME DELAY RELAY | B–C 1 |
| A/T CONSOLE LT | A 29 |
| ABS BRAKE WARN SWS | B 15 |
| ABS SYSTEM | B–E 12–15 |
| ABS WARNING LT | C 12 |
| ALTERNATOR | B 3 |
| ALTITUDE CORRECTION VALVE (DIESEL) | E 16 |
| BACK-UP LT SW | B 29 |
| BATTERY | A 2 |
| BEAM SELECT SW | A 20, A 22 |
| BLOWER RESISTOR | E 20, E 23 |
| CENTRAL LOCKING SW | C 33 |
| CIG LTR & LT | A 24 |
| CIS-E MOTRONIC CONTROL UNIT (16V GLI) | A–C 11 |
| COOLANT LOW LEVEL SW | B 25 |
| COOLANT TEMP SENDER | A 25 |
| CRUISE CONTROL SYSTEM | A 12–15 |
| DEFOGGER SW | E 29 |
| DIAG CONN (16V GLI) | C 11 |
| DIAG CONN (DIGIFANT, CALIF) | C 7 |
| DIGIFANT CONTROL UNIT (CALIF) | A–B 7 |
| DIGIFANT CONTROL UNIT (EX CALIF) | D 7 |
| DIR SW | A 21, A 23 |
| EMERGENCY FLASHER SW | A 20–22, A 23 |
| FRESH AIR SW ILLUM LT | D 20 |
| FUEL CUT-OFF VALVE (DIESEL) | E 16 |
| FUEL GAUGE SENDER (DIESEL) | E 18 |
| FUEL INJECTORS (DIGIFANT) | A 5, E 5–6 |
| FUEL PUMP (GAS) | E 19 |
| FUEL TANK UNIT (GAS) | E 19 |
| FUSE #23 | D 21 |
| FUSE/RELAY LAYOUT | D–E 33–35 |
| FUSE/RELAY PANEL | C 16–31 |
| GEAR SELECTOR SW | A 28–29 |
| GLOVE COMPT LT | E 26 |
| GLOW PLUGS (DIESEL) | E 17 |
| HYDRAULIC PUMP RELAY | E 15 |
| HYDRAULIC UNIT | E 13–15 |
| IDLE STAB VALVE (16V GLI) | B 8 |
| IGNITION BOOSTER (16V GLI) | D 11 |
| IGNITION BOOSTER (DIGIFANT, CALIF) | C 4 |
| IGNITION COIL (DIGIFANT, EX CALIF) | E 4 |
| IGNITION CONTROL UNIT (DIGIFANT, EX CALIF) | E 7 |
| IGNITION SW | A 16 |
| INST CLSTR | A–E 32–34 |
| INTERIOR LT DELAY SW | D–E 36–37 |
| LEFT FRONT DOOR SW | E 37–38 |
| LIGHT SW | A 18–19 |
| LUGGAGE COMPT LT SW | A 25 |
| MULTI-FUNCTION SW | A 27 |
| O2 SENSOR (DIGIFANT) | B 4, C 5 |
| OIL PRES SWS | A 25 |
| PARK BRAKE SW | E 31 |
| POWER MIRRORS | C–D 36–38 |
| POWER SEATS | B–C 35 |
| POWER WINDOWS | A–C 36–38 |
| RADIATOR COOLING SYSTEM (DIESEL) | C–E 8–11 |
| RADIATOR COOLING SYSTEM (GAS) | C–E 1–3 |
| RADIO (PARTIAL) | A 38 |
| SEAT BELT SW | E 30 |
| SHIFT LOCK CONTROL UNIT | A 31, E 30 |
| STARTER | A 3 |
| STARTING INTERLOCK RELAY | B 31 |
| STOP LT SW | D 28 |
| WARNING MODULE | B–C 33–34 |
| WATER SEPARATOR SENDER (DIESEL) | E 19 |
| WIPER SYSTEM | D–E 24–27 |

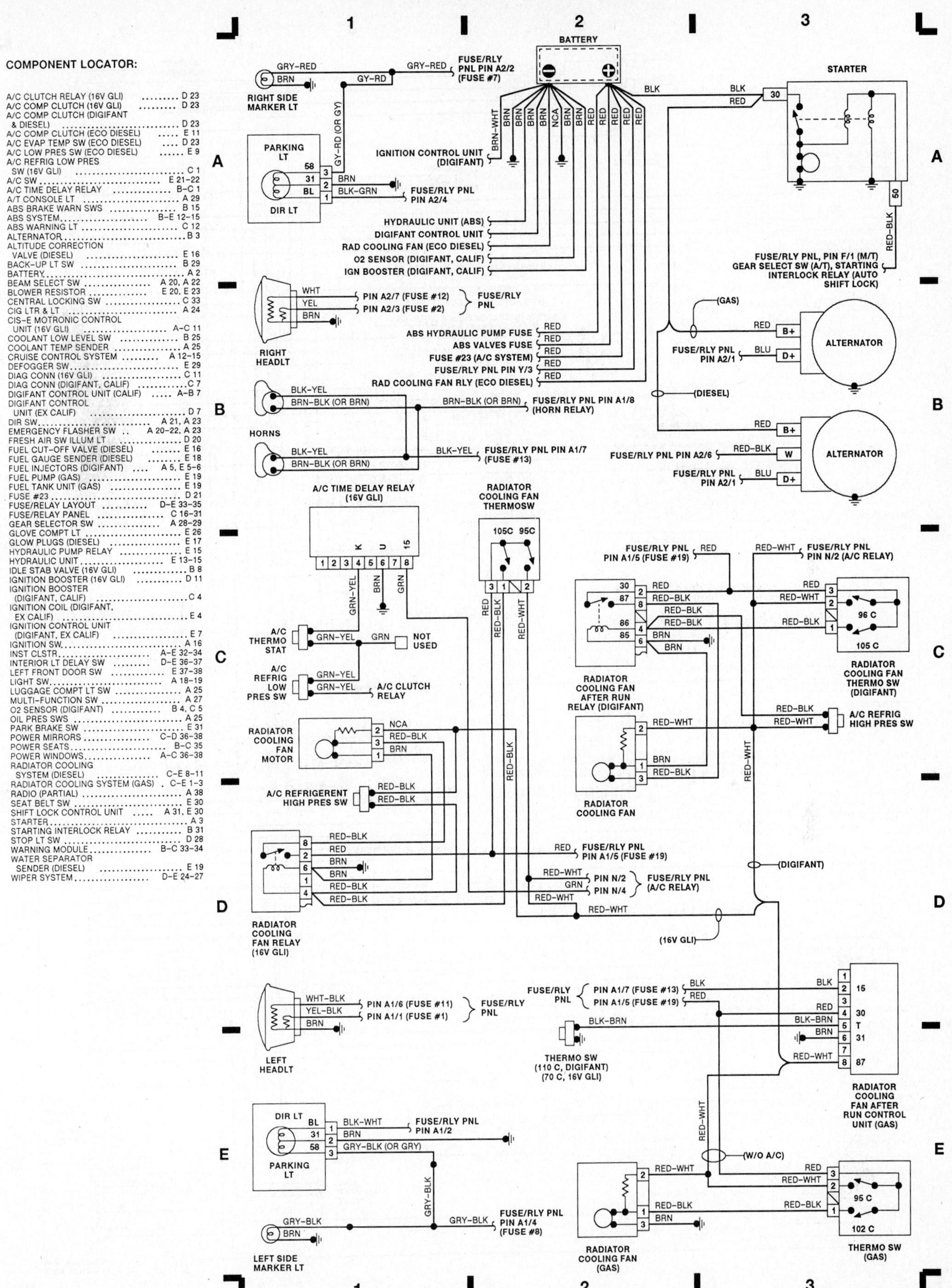

# 1991 WIRING DIAGRAMS
## Jetta & Jetta GLi (Cont.)

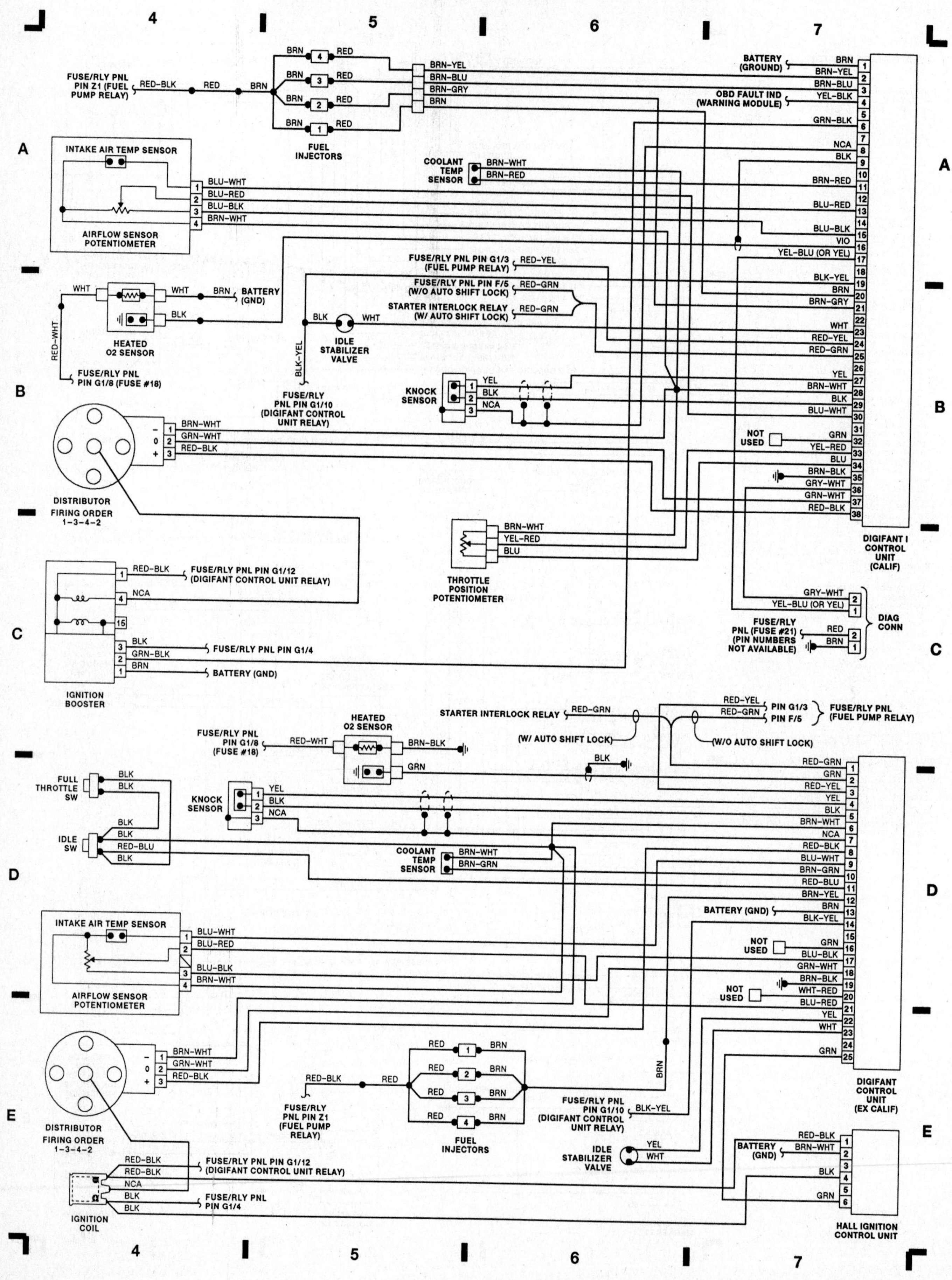

# 1991 WIRING DIAGRAMS
# Jetta & Jetta GLi (Cont.)

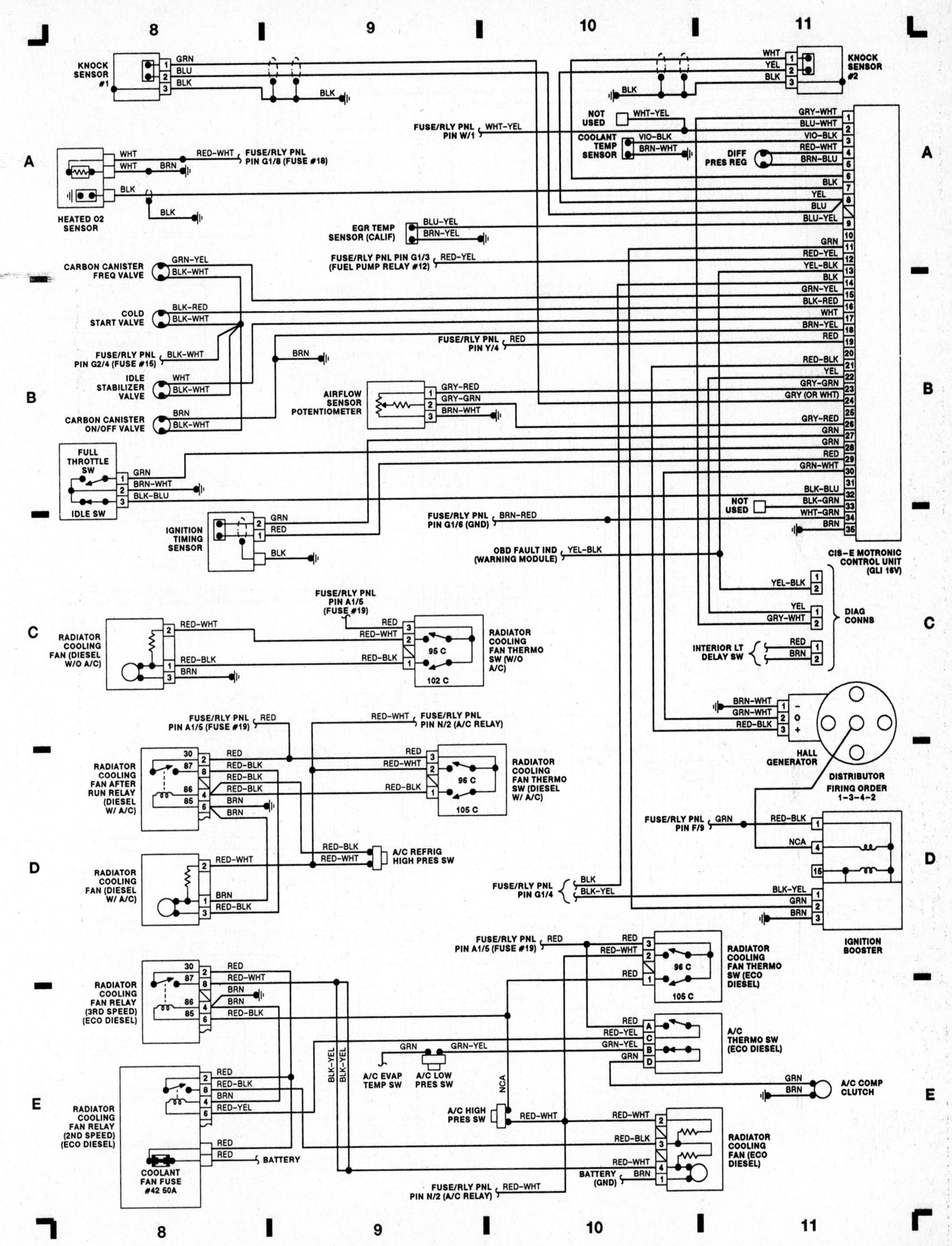

# 1991 WIRING DIAGRAMS
# Jetta & Jetta GLi (Cont.)

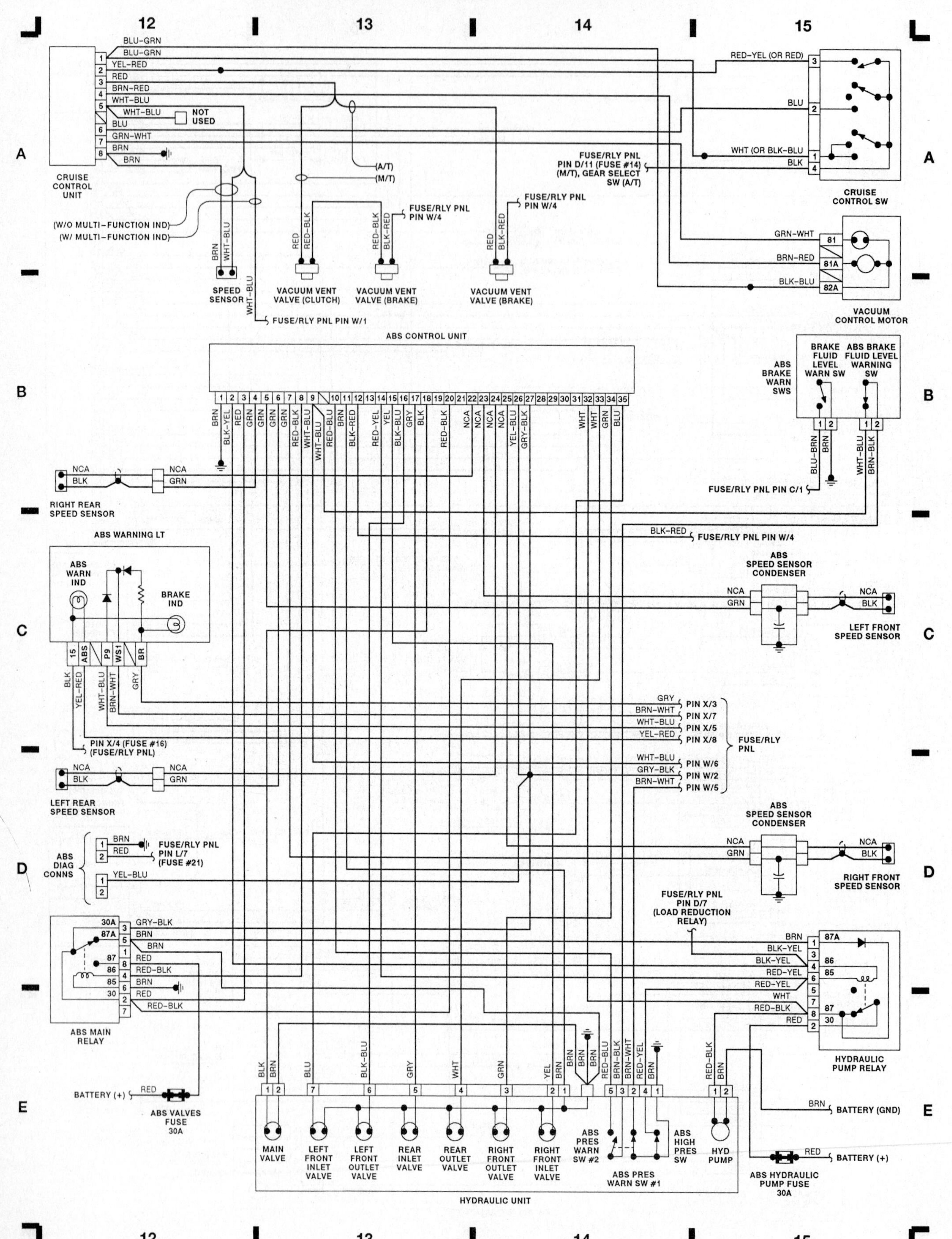

# 1991 WIRING DIAGRAMS
# Jetta & Jetta GLi (Cont.)

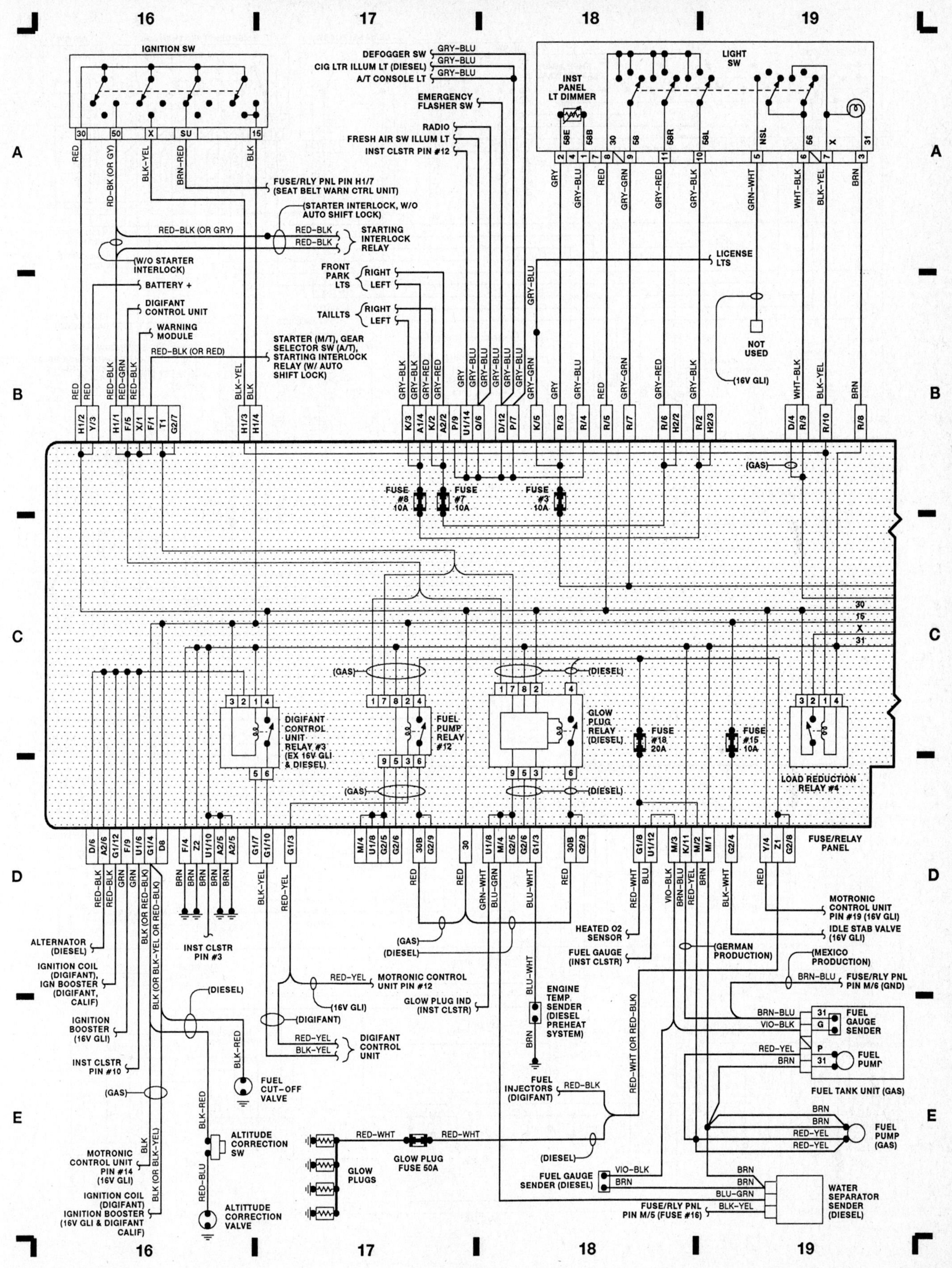

# 1991 WIRING DIAGRAMS
# Jetta & Jetta GLi (Cont.)

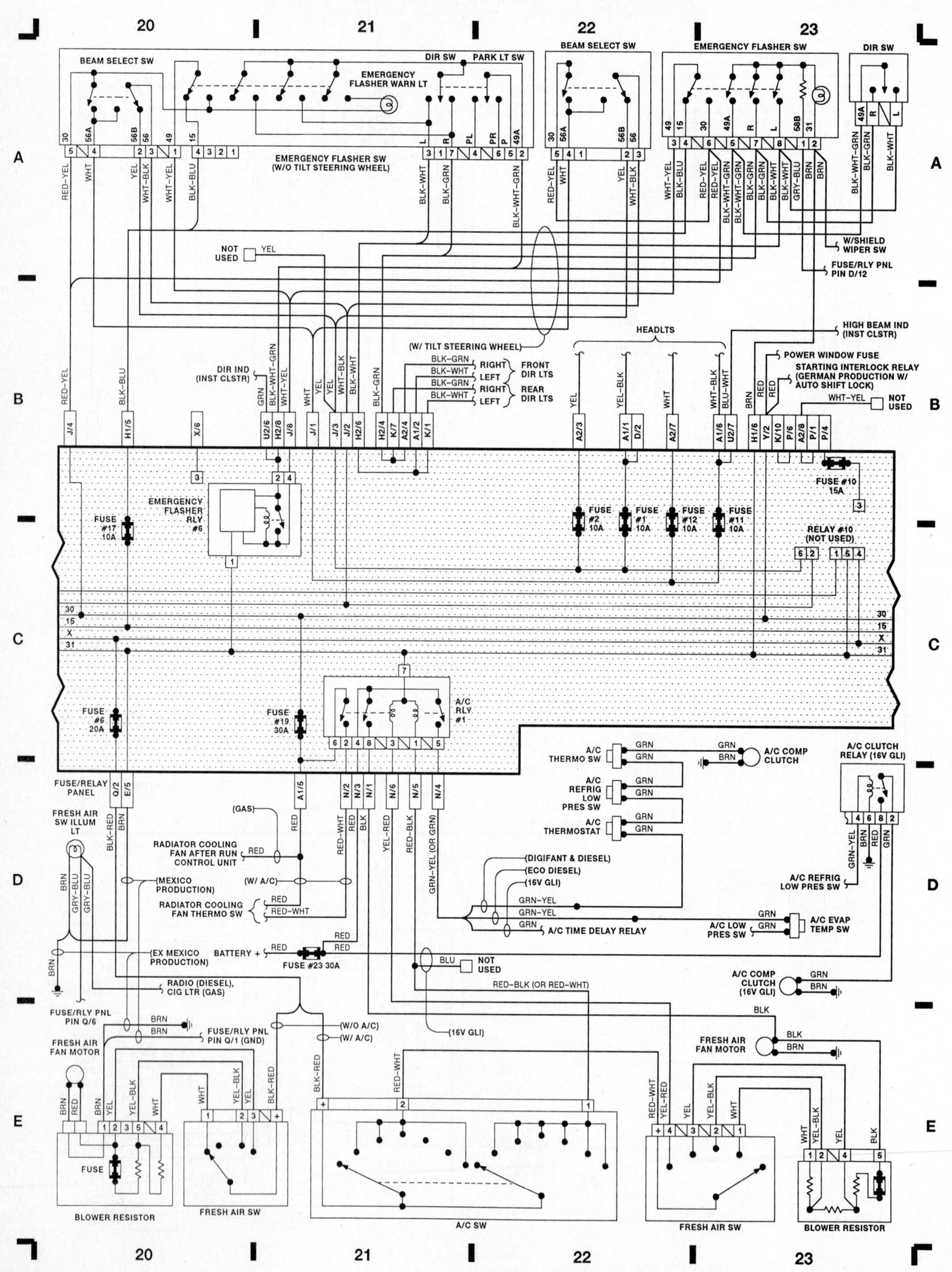

# 1991 WIRING DIAGRAMS
## Jetta & Jetta GLi (Cont.)

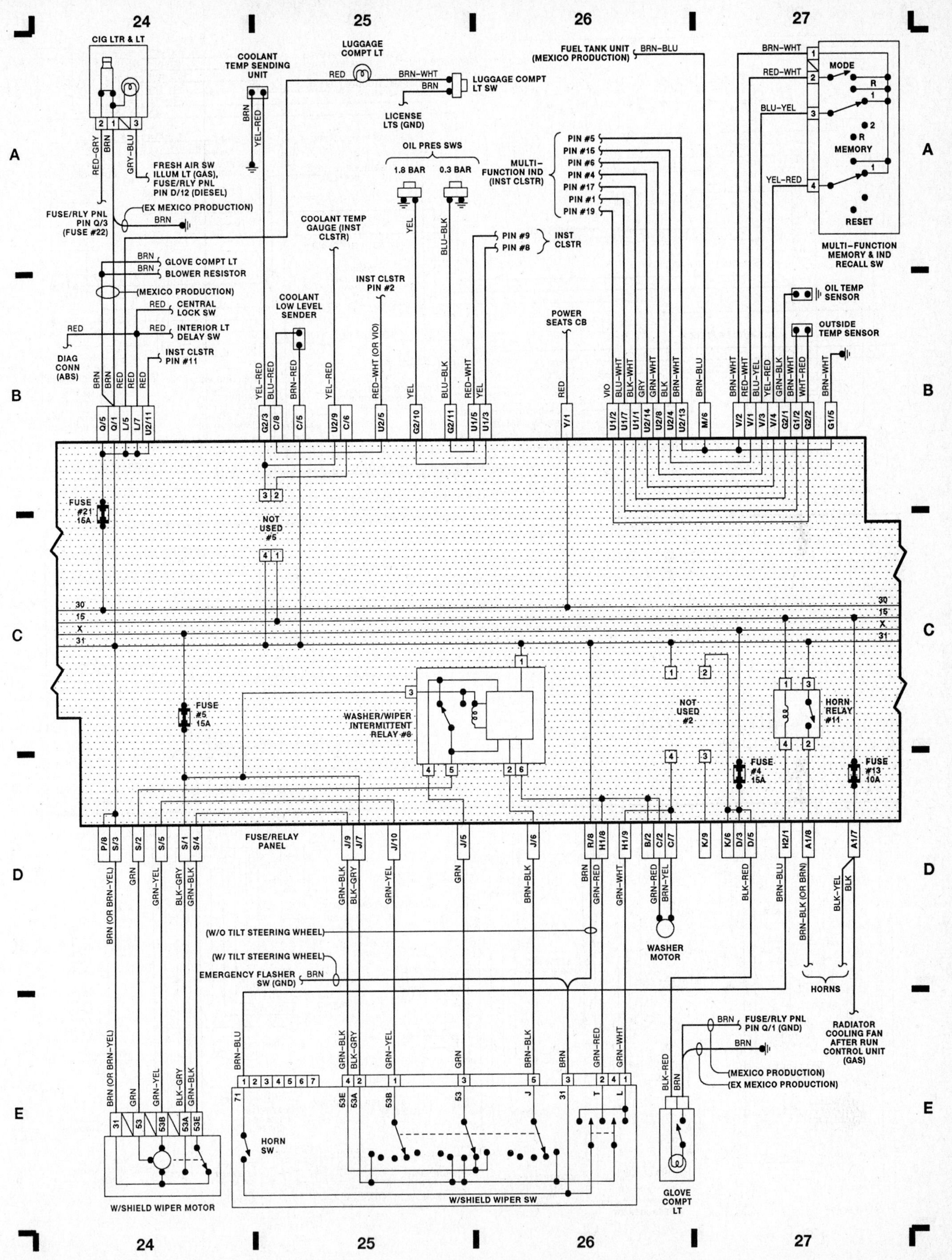

# 1991 WIRING DIAGRAMS
## Jetta & Jetta GLi (Cont.)

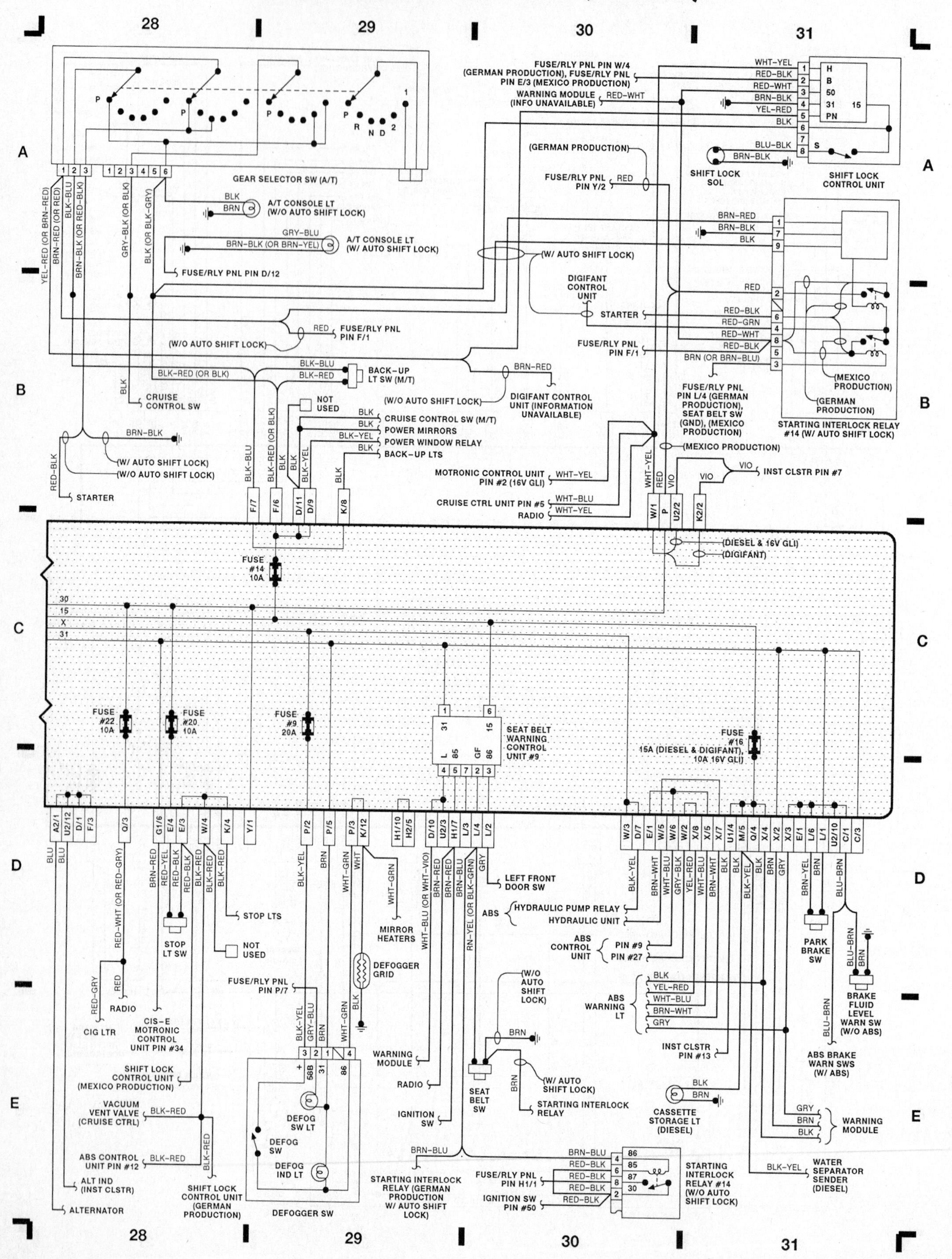

# 1991 WIRING DIAGRAMS
# Jetta & Jetta GLi (Cont.)

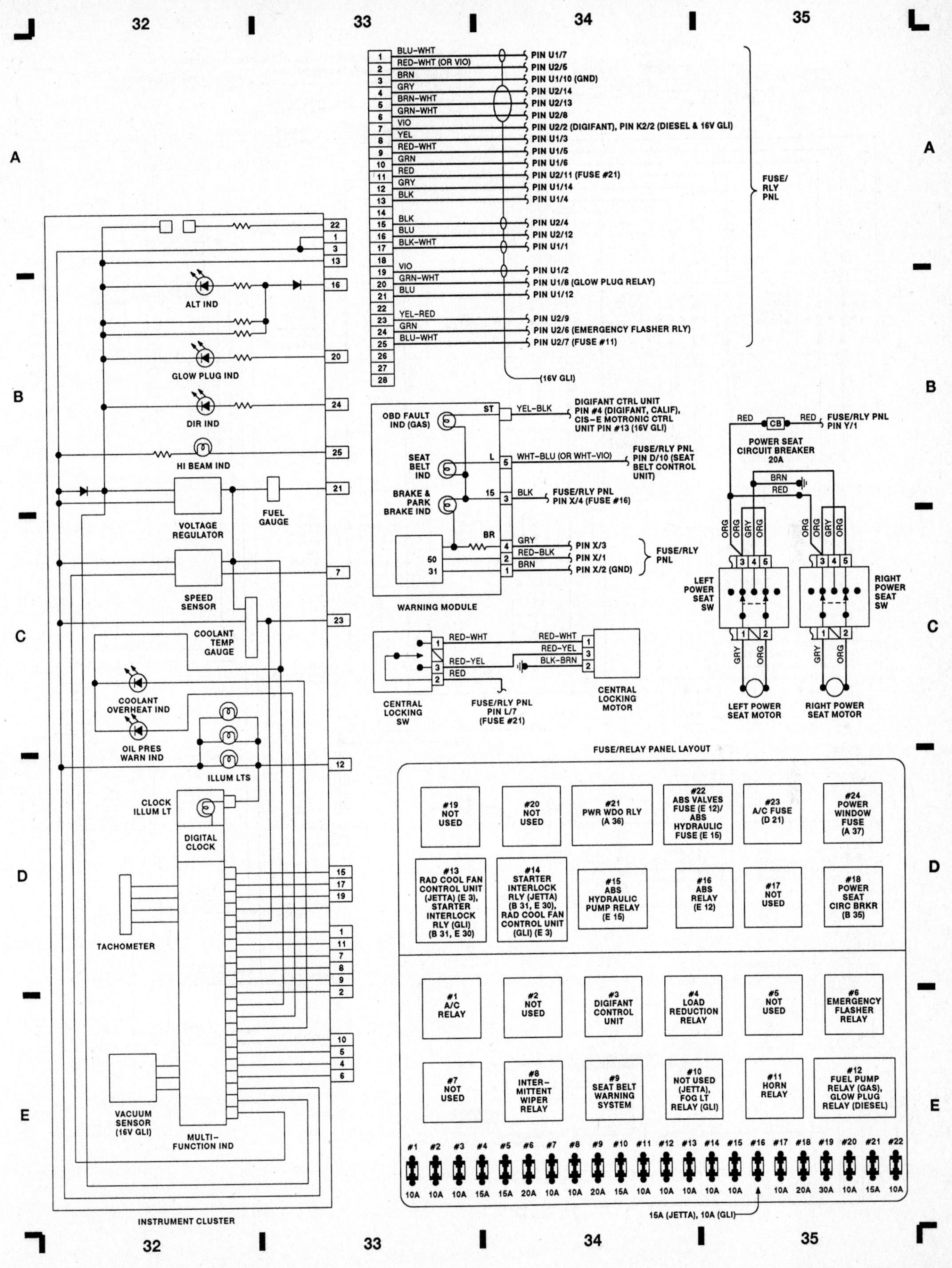

# 1991 WIRING DIAGRAMS
# Jetta & Jetta GLi (Cont.)

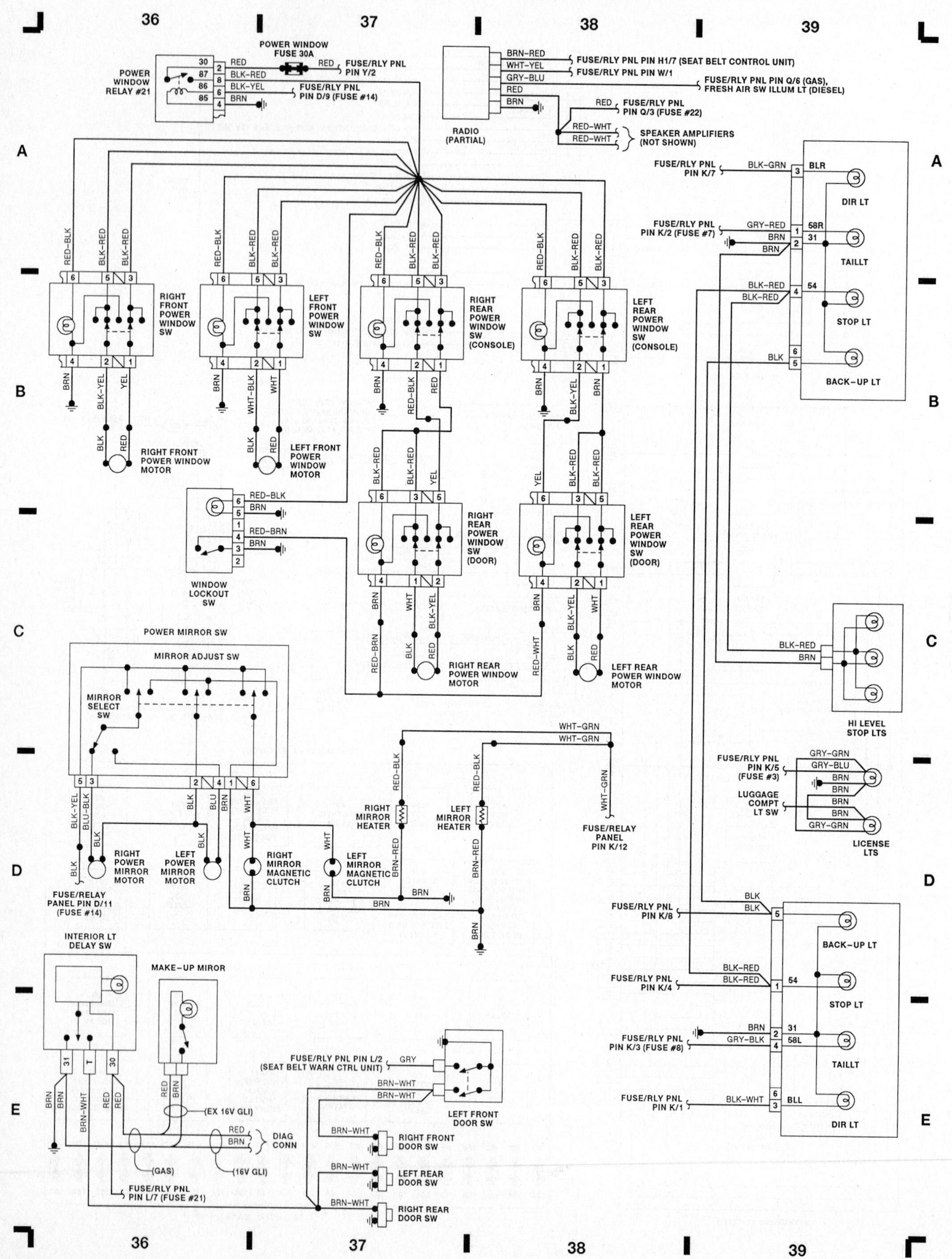

# 1991 WIRING DIAGRAMS
## Passat

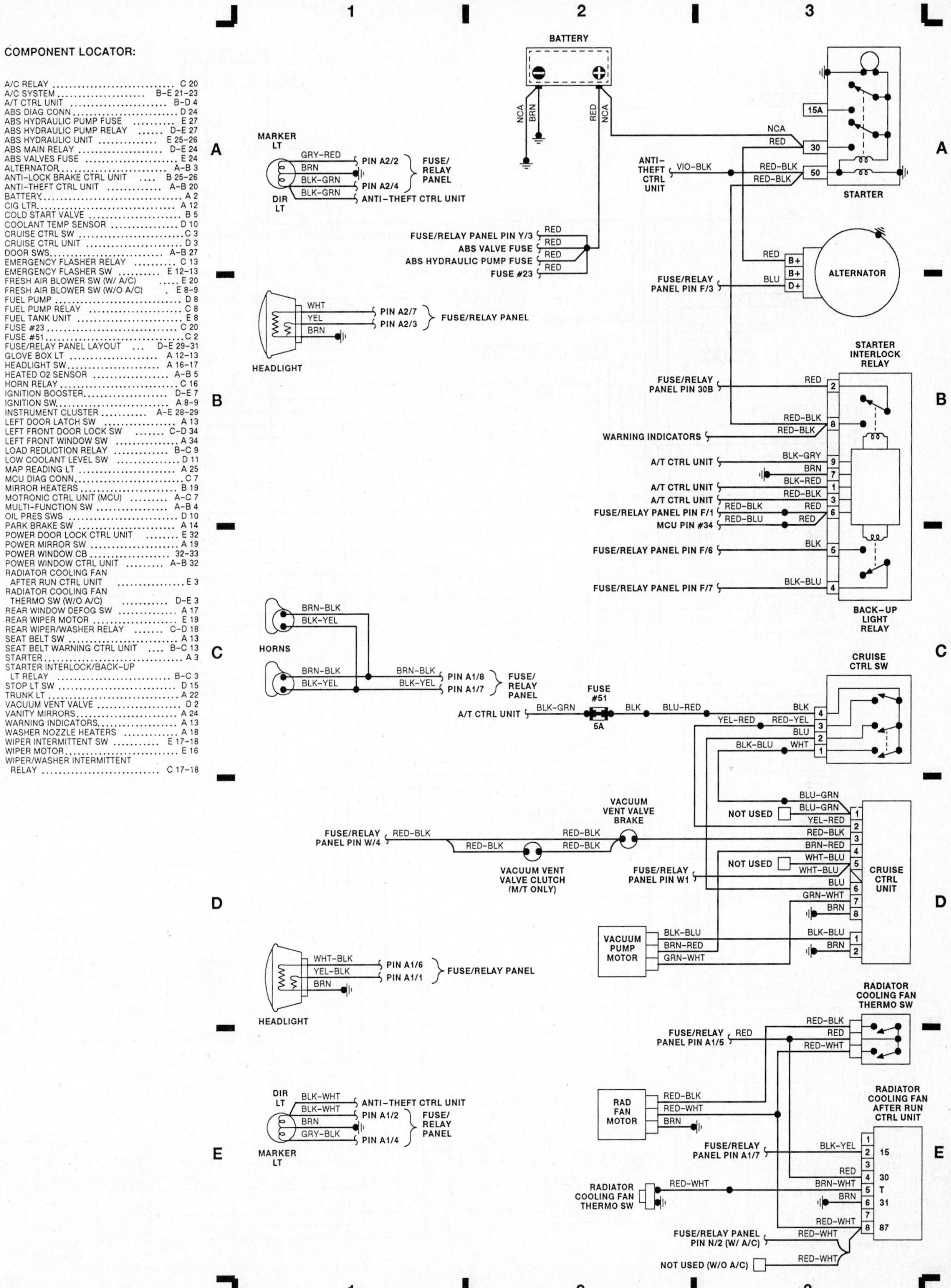

# 1991 WIRING DIAGRAMS
## Passat (Cont.)

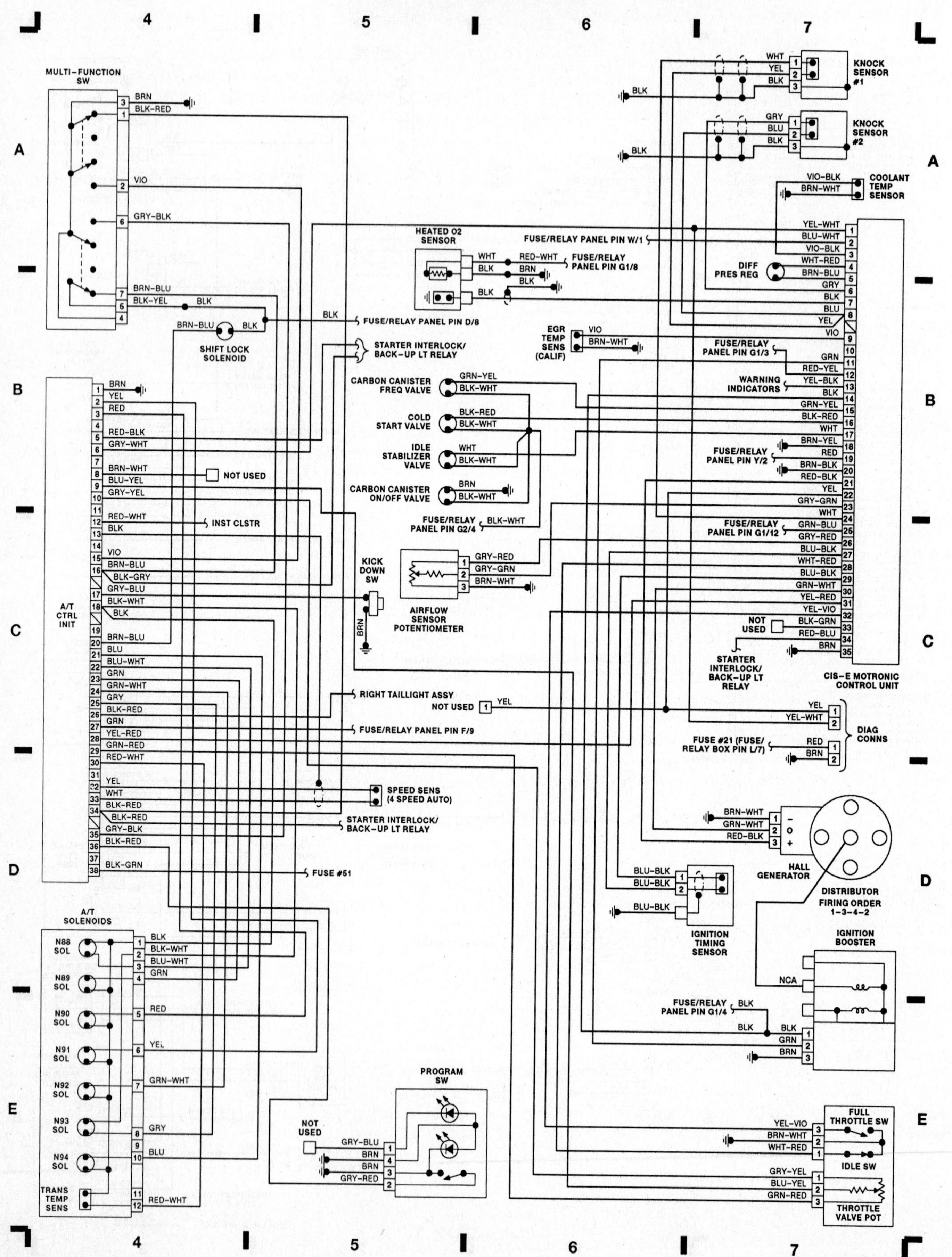

# 1991 WIRING DIAGRAMS
# Passat (Cont.)

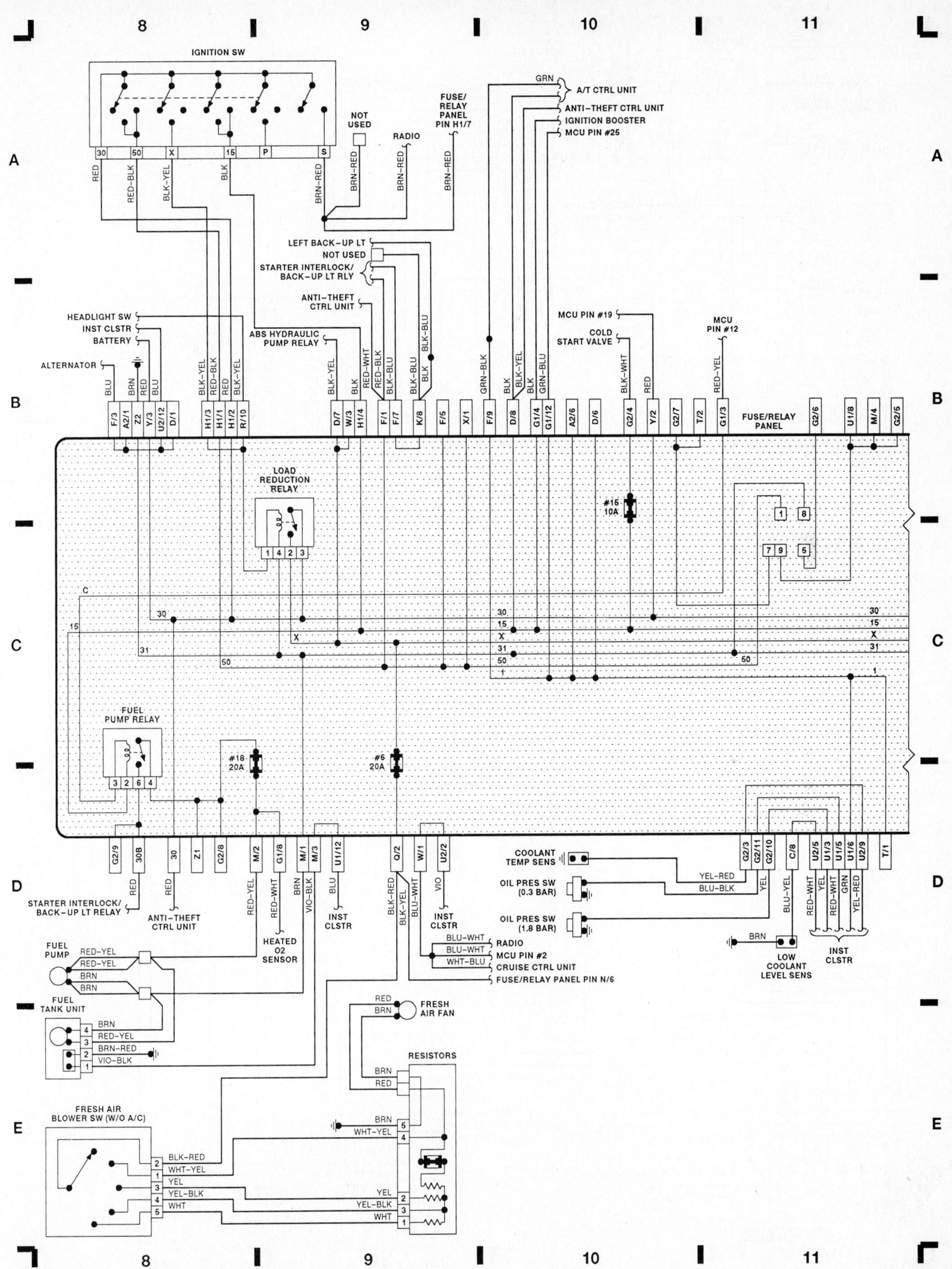

# 1991 WIRING DIAGRAMS
## Passat (Cont.)

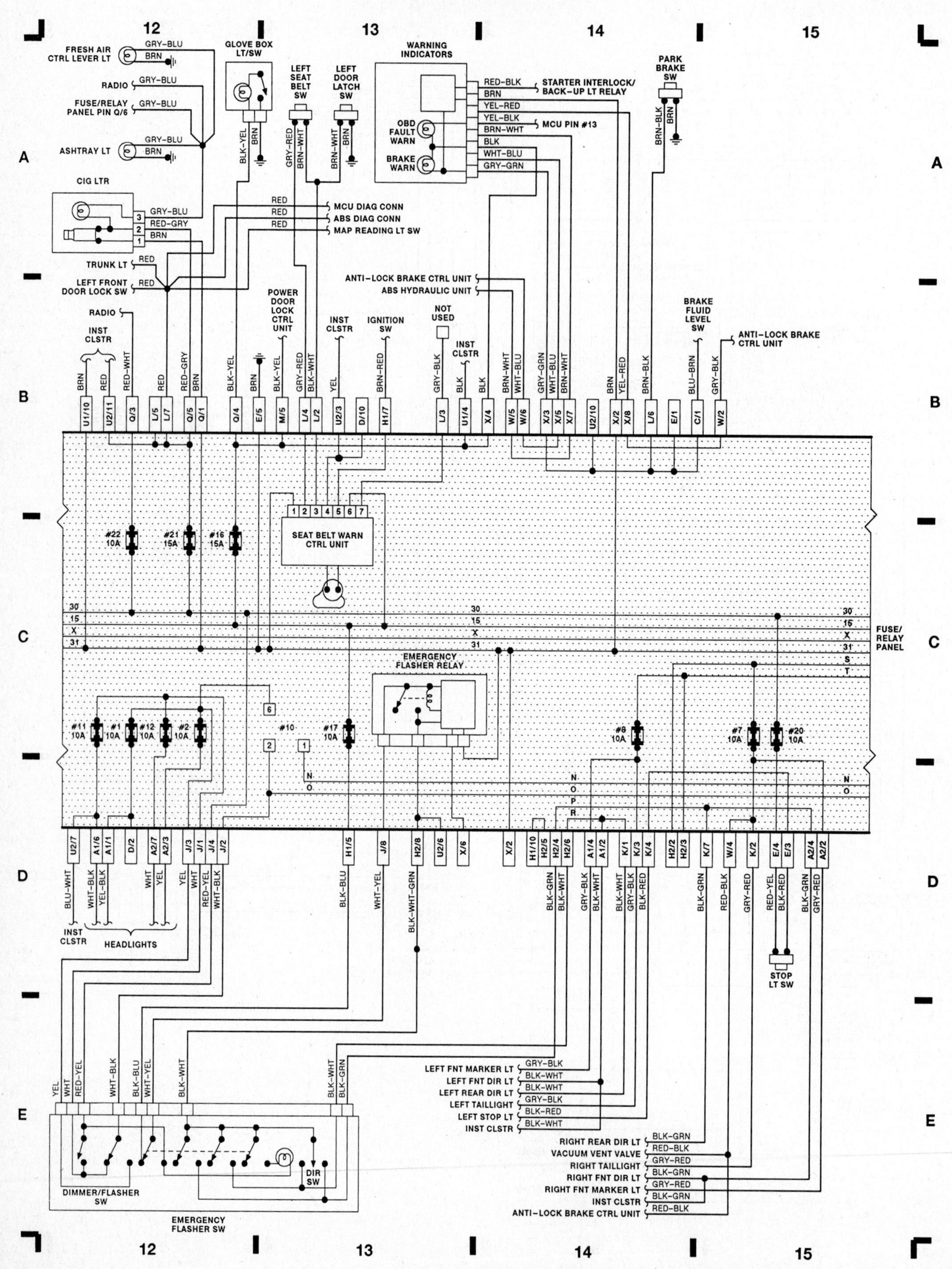

# 1991 WIRING DIAGRAMS
# Passat (Cont.)

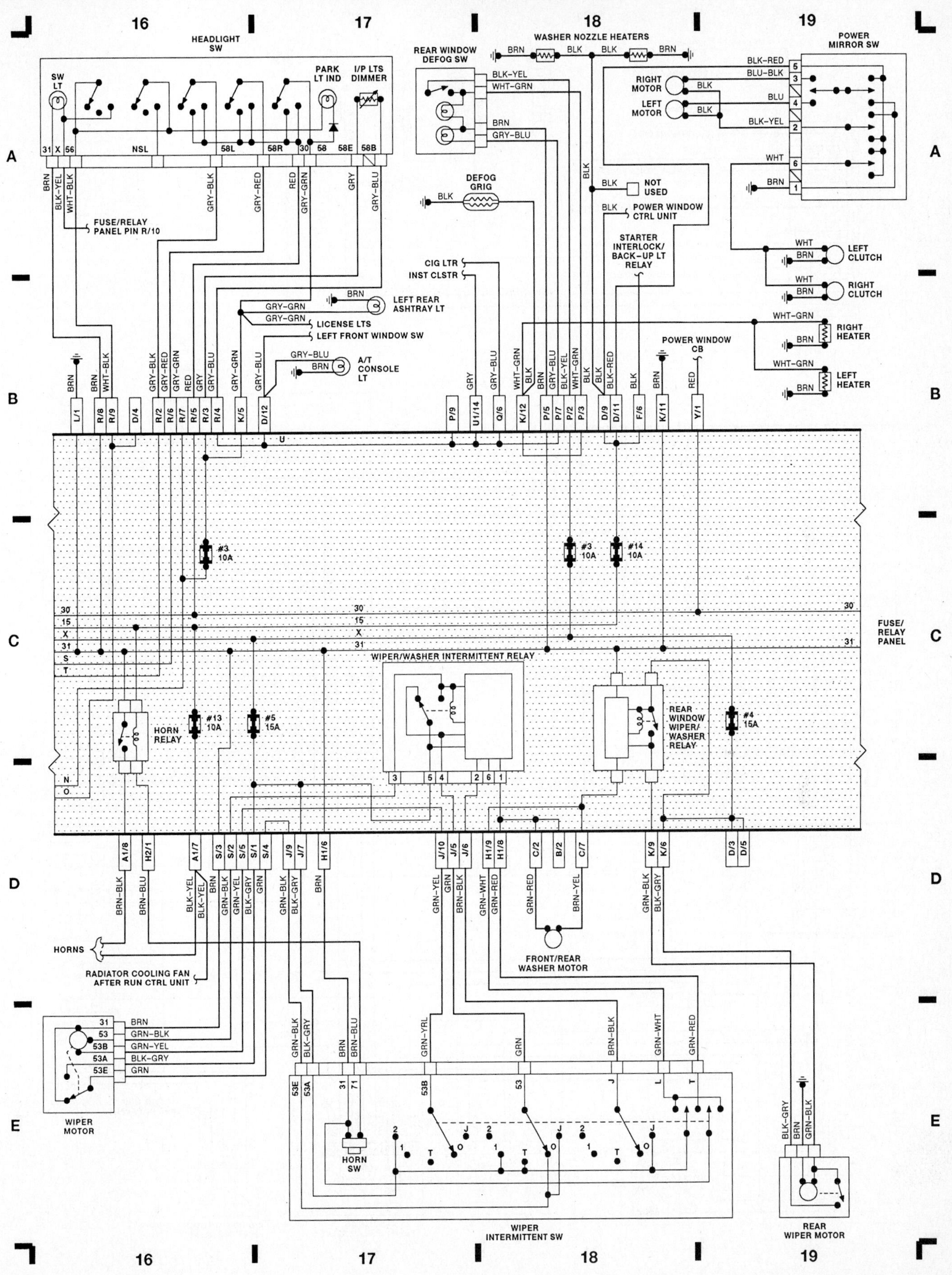

# 1991 WIRING DIAGRAMS
## Passat (Cont.)

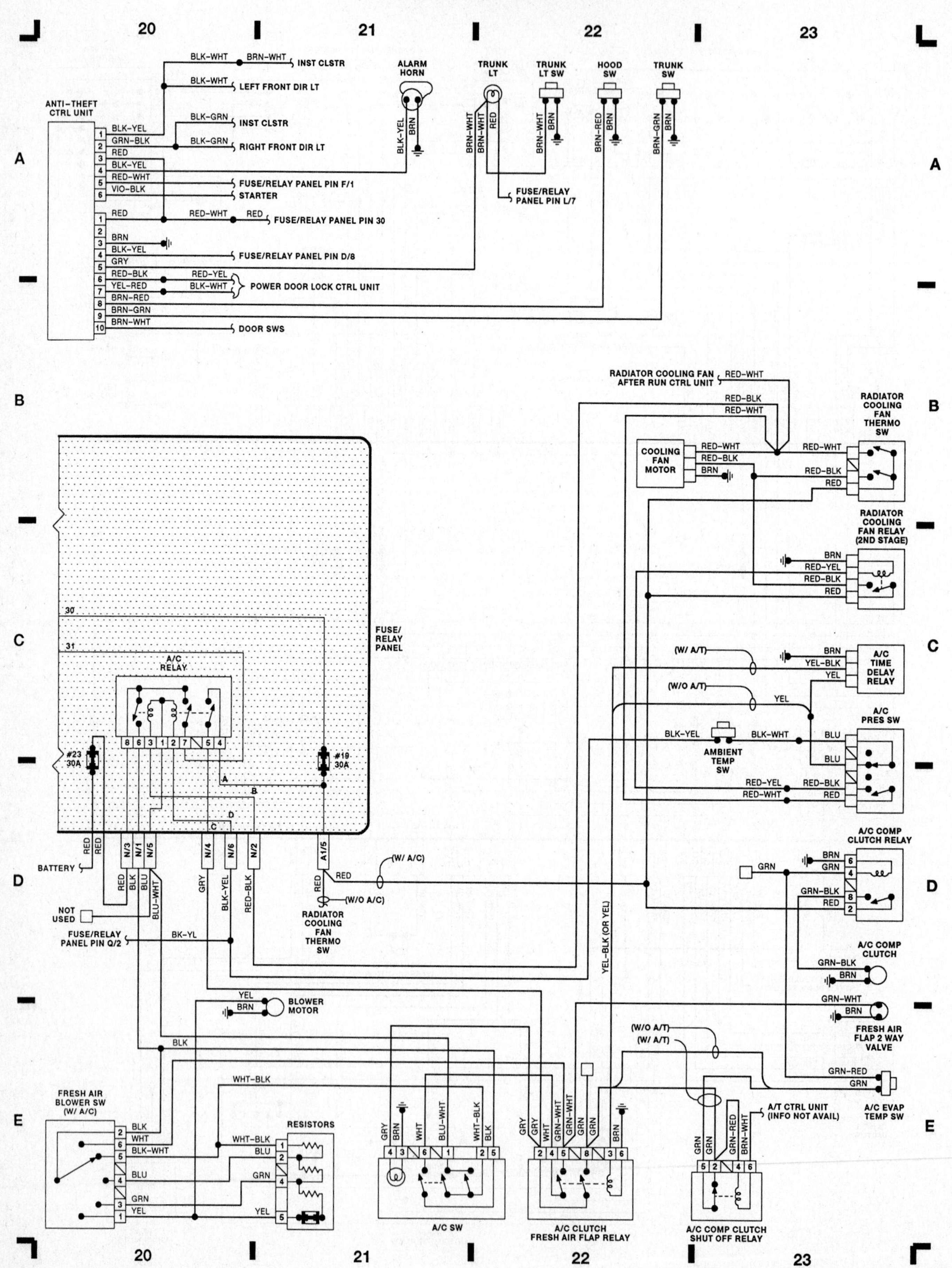

# 1991 WIRING DIAGRAMS
## Passat (Cont.)

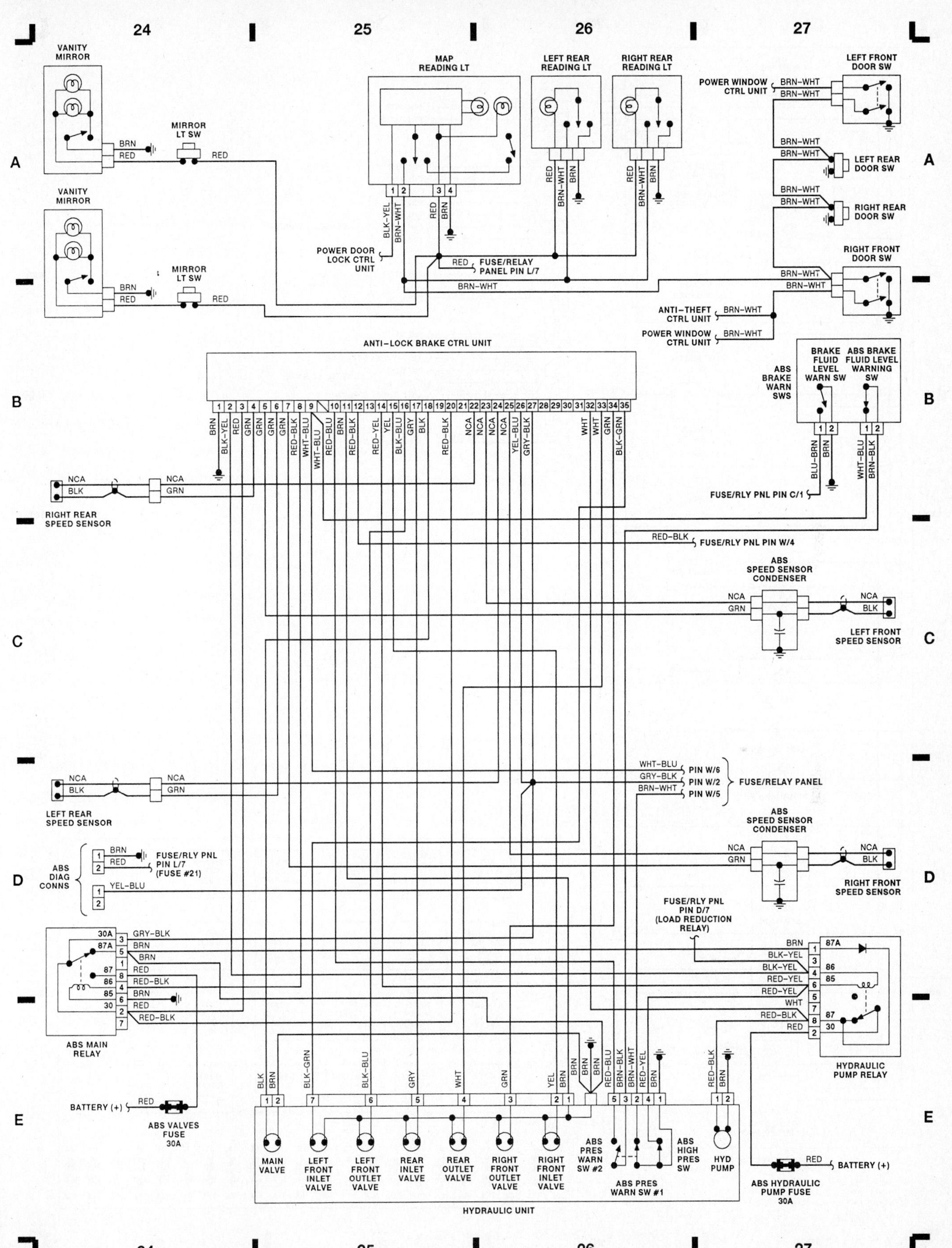

# 1991 WIRING DIAGRAMS
## Passat (Cont.)

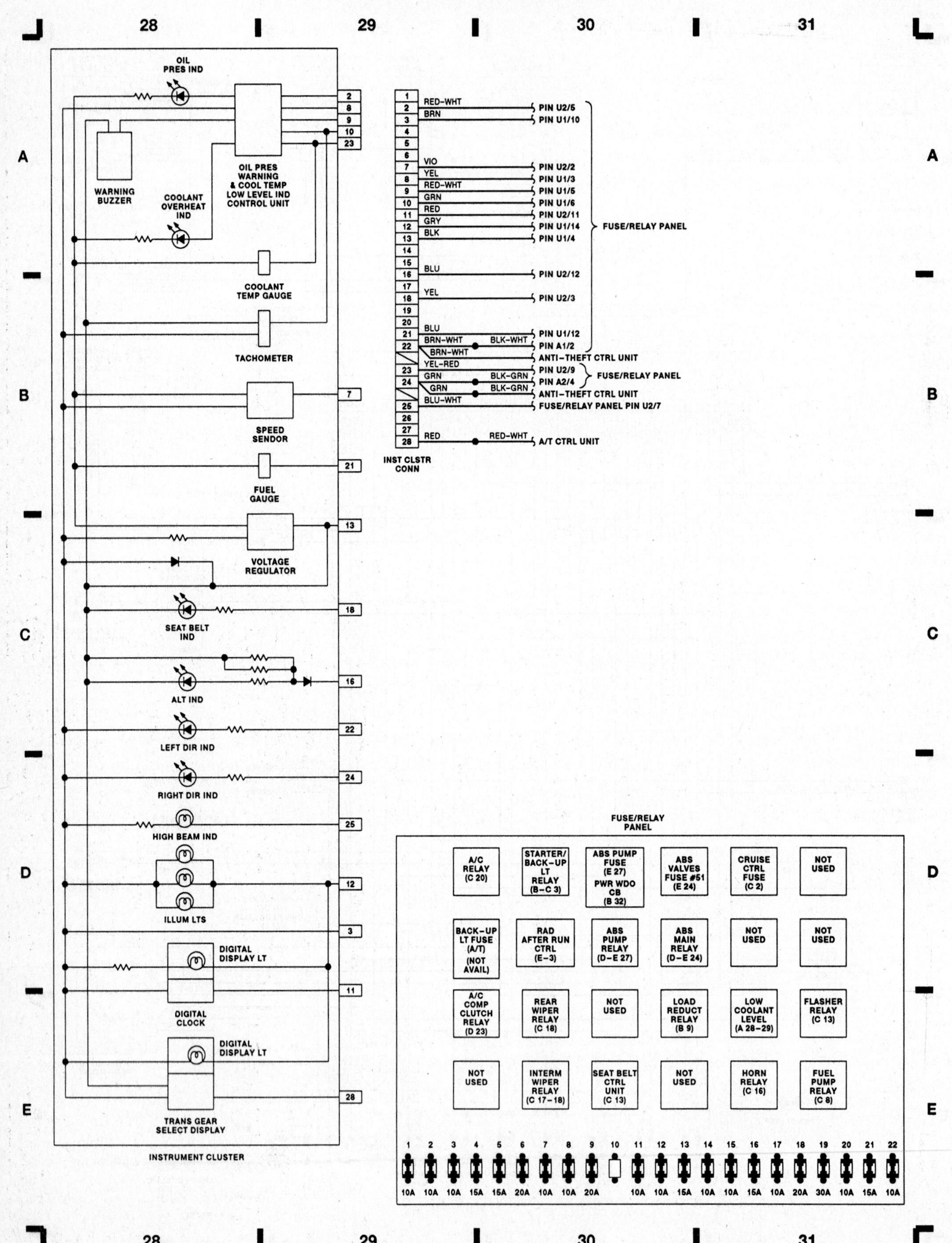

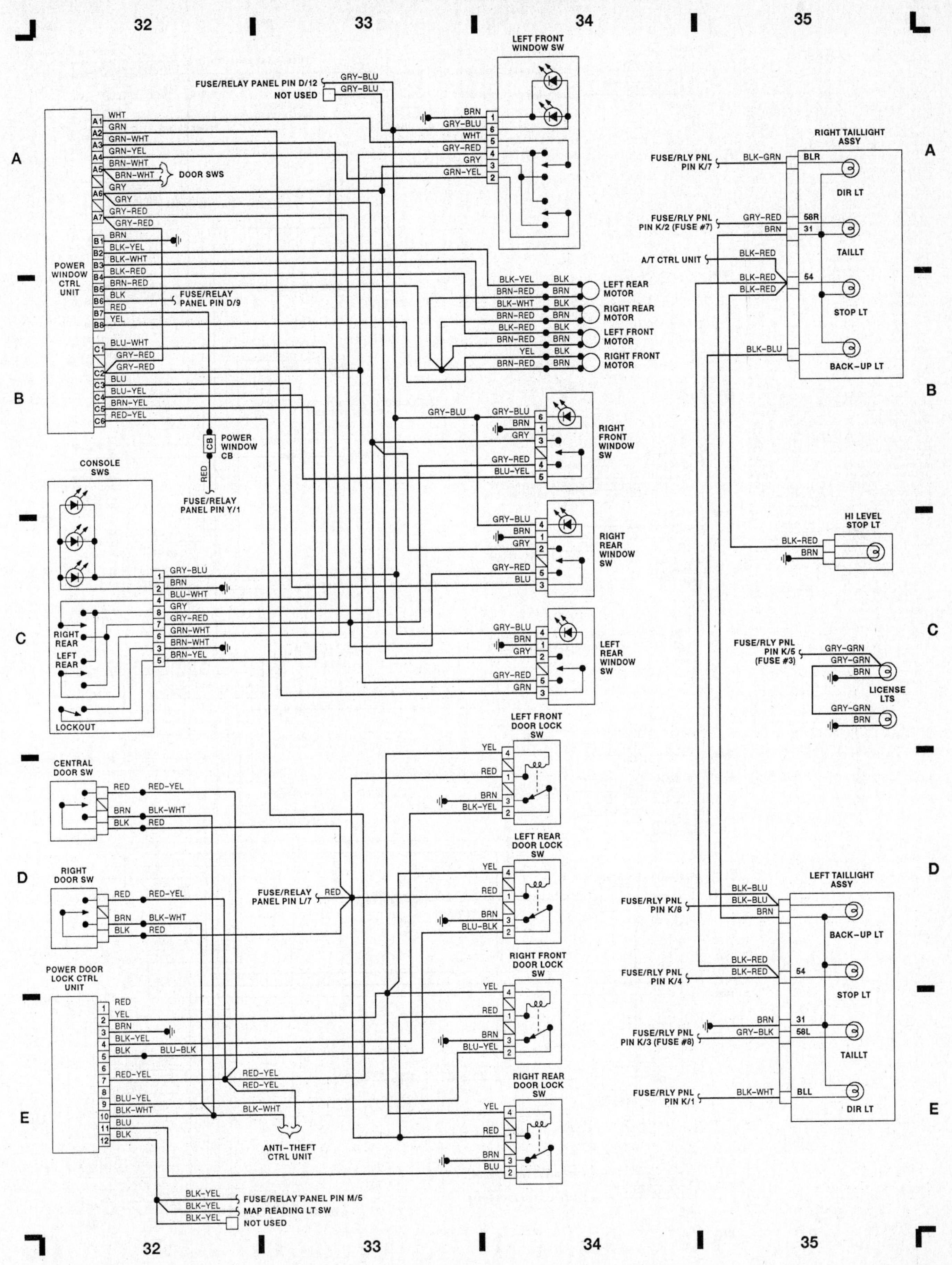

LEFT FRONT WINDOW SW
FUSE/RELAY PANEL PIN D/12
NOT USED
POWER WINDOW CTRL UNIT
DOOR SWS
FUSE/RELAY PANEL PIN D/9
LEFT REAR MOTOR
RIGHT REAR MOTOR
LEFT FRONT MOTOR
RIGHT FRONT MOTOR
POWER WINDOW CB
FUSE/RELAY PANEL PIN Y/1
RIGHT FRONT WINDOW SW
RIGHT REAR WINDOW SW
LEFT REAR WINDOW SW
CONSOLE SWS
RIGHT REAR
LEFT REAR
LOCKOUT
LEFT FRONT DOOR LOCK SW
CENTRAL DOOR SW
LEFT REAR DOOR LOCK SW
RIGHT DOOR SW
FUSE/RELAY PANEL PIN L/7
RIGHT FRONT DOOR LOCK SW
POWER DOOR LOCK CTRL UNIT
RIGHT REAR DOOR LOCK SW
ANTI-THEFT CTRL UNIT
FUSE/RELAY PANEL PIN M/5
MAP READING LT SW
NOT USED
RIGHT TAILLIGHT ASSY
FUSE/RLY PNL PIN K/7
DIR LT
FUSE/RLY PNL PIN K/2 (FUSE #7)
TAILLT
A/T CTRL UNIT
STOP LT
BACK-UP LT
HI LEVEL STOP LT
FUSE/RLY PNL PIN K/5 (FUSE #3)
LICENSE LTS
LEFT TAILLIGHT ASSY
FUSE/RLY PNL PIN K/8
BACK-UP LT
FUSE/RLY PNL PIN K/4
STOP LT
FUSE/RLY PNL PIN K/3 (FUSE #8)
TAILLT
FUSE/RLY PNL PIN K/1
DIR LT

# 1991 WIRING DIAGRAMS
## Vanagon

COMPONENT LOCATOR:

A/C HI PRES SW .......................... C 2
A/C SW .......................... E 3
A/T CONSOLE LTS .......................... A 12
A/T RELAY .......................... D 13
ALTERNATOR .......................... D–E 26–27
AUXILIARY BATTERY .......................... D 24
BACK–UP LT SW .......................... B 12
BATTERY .......................... E 24
BATTERY CUTOUT RELAY .......................... D 24
BATTERY VOLTAGE INDS .......................... C 17
BEAM SELECT SW .......................... A 7
BRAKE FLUID LEVEL WARNING SW ..... B 10
CIG LTR & LT .......................... E 7
COOLANT LOW LEVEL CTRL UNIT ... B–C 14–15
COOLANT LOW LEVEL WARNING SW . A–B 14
COOLANT TEMP SENDING UNIT ......... A 15
CRUISE CTRL SW .......................... D–E 15
DEFOGGER SW .......................... A 11
DIGIFANT CTRL UNIT .......................... A–B 26
DIGIFANT CTRL UNIT RELAY ........... C 26
DIRECTIONAL SW (DIR SW) .......................... A 8
EMERGENCY FLASHER RELAY #12 ...... C 8
EMERGENCY FLASHER SW ........... A 8–9
FRESH AIR FAN SW .......................... D 7
FRONT WIPER MOTOR .......................... E 8
FUEL GAUGE SENDING UNIT ........... D 12
FUEL INJECTORS .......................... C–D 24
FUEL PUMP .......................... D 25
FUEL PUMP RELAY .......................... D 26
FUSE #23 (A/C SYSTEM) .......................... D 2
FUSE #37 .......................... B 4
FUSE #42 (COOLING FAN) .......................... B 2
FUSE #52 .......................... A 4
FUSE/RELAY PANEL .......................... B–D 4–7
FUSE/RELAY PANEL LAYOUT ... D–E 20–23
GAS FLAME ON WARNING IND .......... D 16
GEAR SELECT SW .......................... A 12–13
HEADLIGHT SW .......................... A 6
HORN SW .......................... B 11
IDLE STABILIZER CONTROL UNIT .... B–C 26
IGNITION COIL .......................... A 24
IGNITION SW .......................... A 4
INSTRUMENT CLUSTER .......................... A–C 19
LEFT FRONT DOOR SW .......................... E 4–5
LOAD REDUCTION RELAY #8 ......... C–D 7
MAP READING LT .......................... D 19
OIL PRES SWS .......................... A–B 14
OXYGEN SENSOR .......................... C 24
P/S PRES SW .......................... C 25
PARK BRAKE WARNING SW ........... B 10
POWER DOOR LOCKS .......................... A 20–23
POWER MIRROR SYSTEM .......................... B 20–23
POWER WINDOW SYSTEM .......................... C 20–23
RADIATOR COOLING FAN (W/O A/C) .... A 2
RADIATOR COOLING FAN
RELAY 2ND STAGE #5 .......................... C 5
RADIATOR COOLING FAN RESISTORS ..... B 3
RADIATOR COOLING FAN
THERMO SW (W/O A/C) .......................... A 3
RADIO (PARTIAL) .......................... D 19
REAR WINDOW WIPER MOTOR ........... E 10
REAR WIPER/WASHER RELAY #11 ...... C 10
REFRIGERATOR 110 VOLT SOCKETS .... E 16
REFRIGERATOR 12V HEATER RELAY .. A 18–19
SEAT BELT WARNING RELAY ......... A 9–10
SEAT BELT/BRAKE WARNING INDS ..... A 10
STARTER .......................... E 24
STOP LT SW .......................... E 12
TDC SENSOR .......................... A 24
THROTTLE VALVE SW .......................... B 24
WARM AIR BLOWER SW .......................... E 11
WASHER MOTORS .......................... E 10
WATER TANK (LOW LEVEL SENS,
WATER PUMP & WATER PUMP SW .. B 16
WATER TANK LEVEL INDS .......................... C 16
WIPER/WASHER INTERMITTENT
RELAY #10 .......................... C 9
WIPER/WASHER SW .......................... E 9

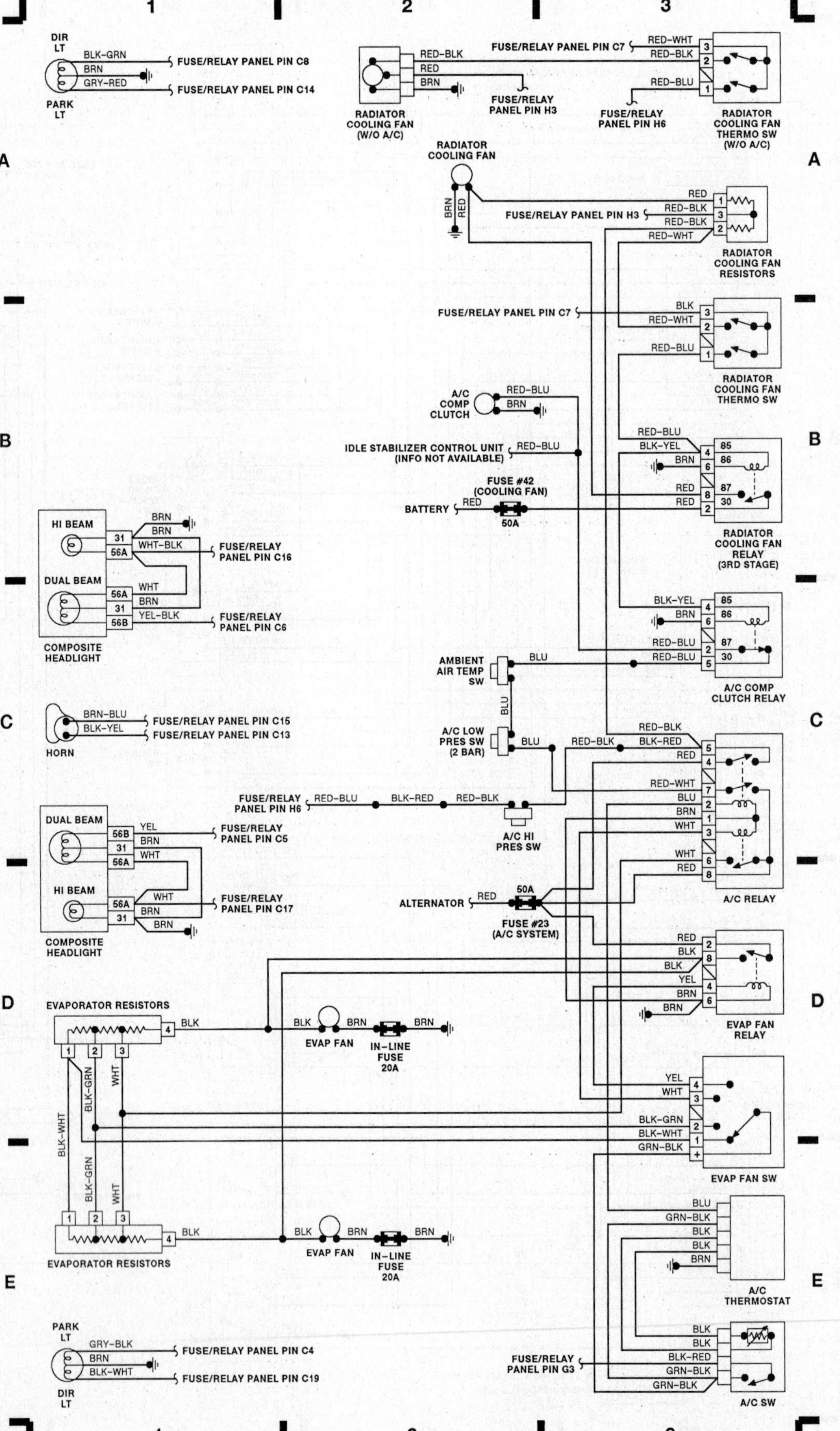

# 1991 WIRING DIAGRAMS
## Vanagon (Cont.)

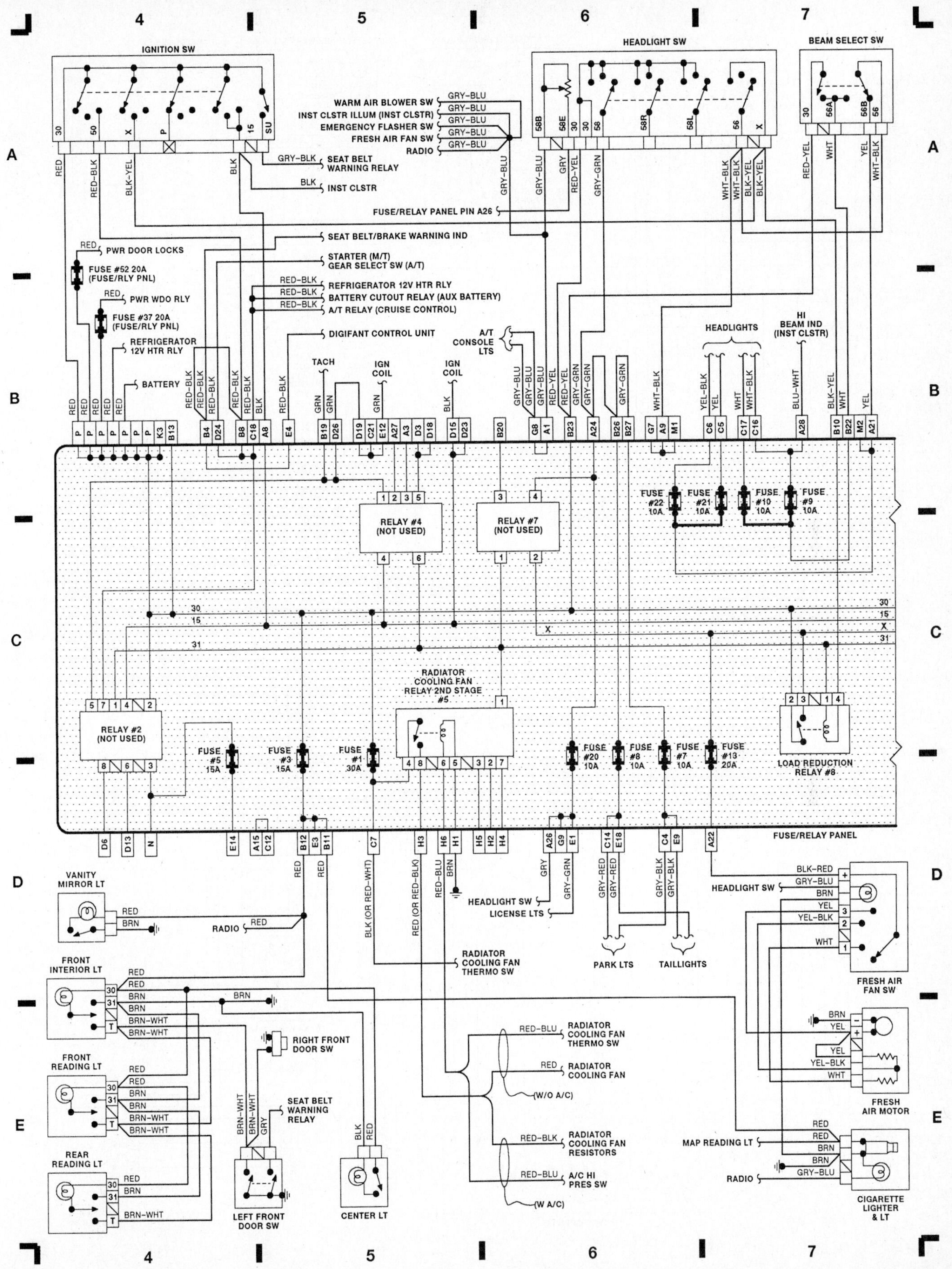

# 1991 WIRING DIAGRAMS
# Vanagon (Cont.)

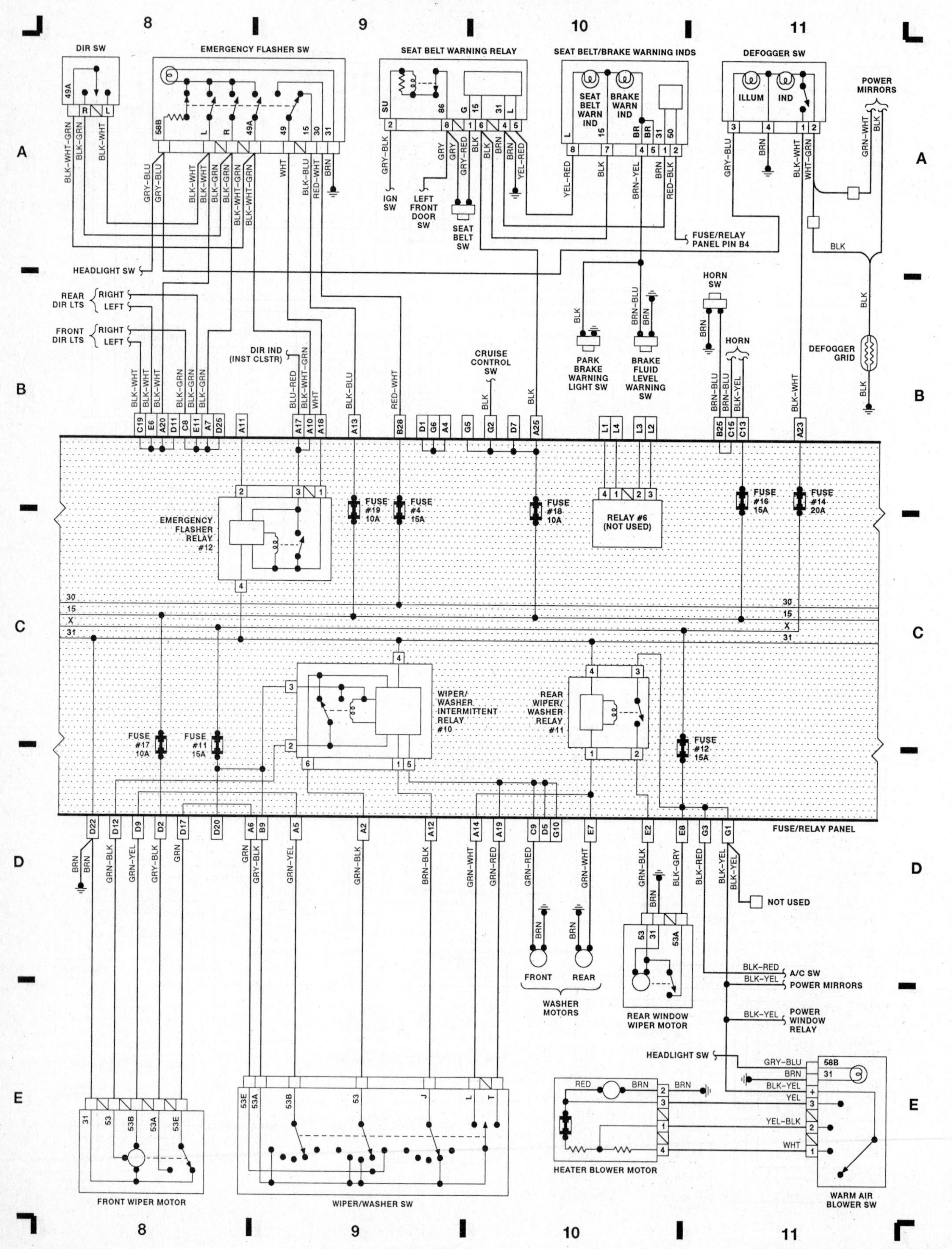

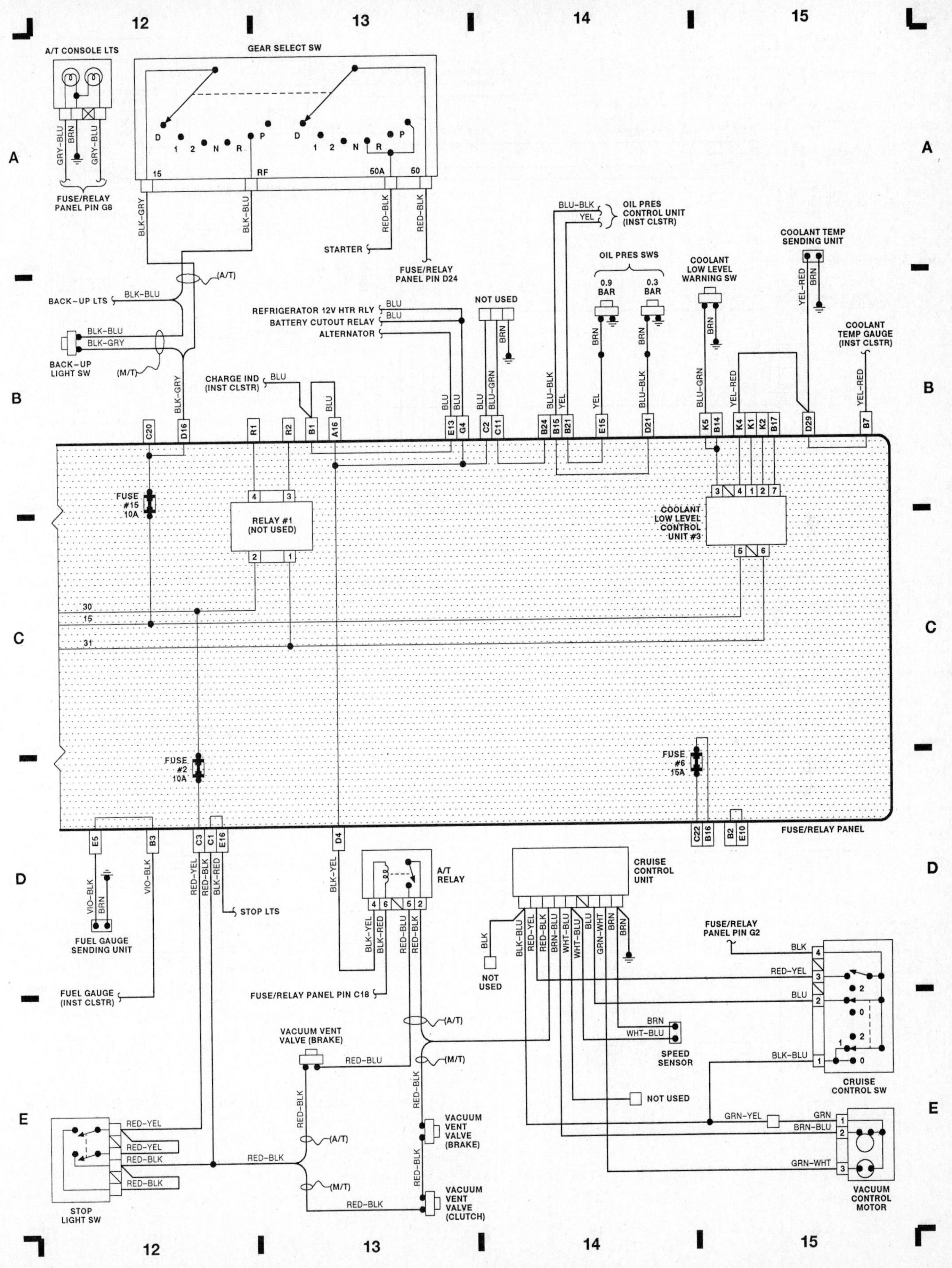

A/T CONSOLE LTS
GEAR SELECT SW
FUSE/RELAY PANEL PIN G8
STARTER
FUSE/RELAY PANEL PIN D24
BACK-UP LTS
BACK-UP LIGHT SW
REFRIGERATOR 12V HTR RLY
BATTERY CUTOUT RELAY
ALTERNATOR
CHARGE IND (INST CLSTR)
NOT USED
OIL PRES CONTROL UNIT (INST CLSTR)
OIL PRES SWS
0.9 BAR
0.3 BAR
COOLANT LOW LEVEL WARNING SW
COOLANT TEMP SENDING UNIT
COOLANT TEMP GAUGE (INST CLSTR)
FUSE #15 10A
RELAY #1 (NOT USED)
COOLANT LOW LEVEL CONTROL UNIT #3
FUSE #2 10A
FUSE #6 15A
FUSE/RELAY PANEL
FUEL GAUGE SENDING UNIT
FUEL GAUGE (INST CLSTR)
STOP LTS
A/T RELAY
FUSE/RELAY PANEL PIN C18
CRUISE CONTROL UNIT
NOT USED
FUSE/RELAY PANEL PIN G2
SPEED SENSOR
CRUISE CONTROL SW
VACUUM VENT VALVE (BRAKE)
VACUUM VENT VALVE (CLUTCH)
VACUUM CONTROL MOTOR
STOP LIGHT SW

# 1991 WIRING DIAGRAMS
## Vanagon (Cont.)

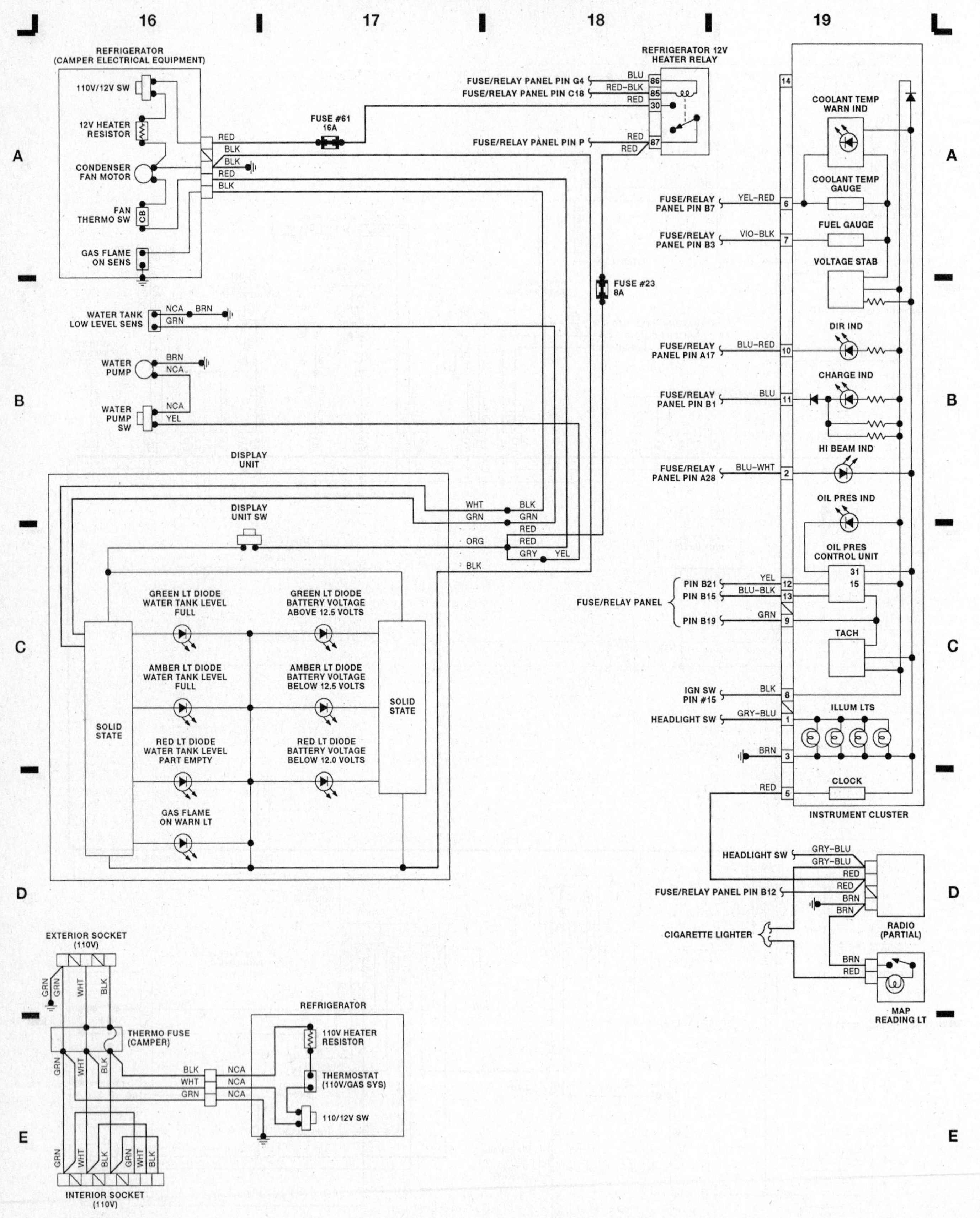

# 1991 WIRING DIAGRAMS
# Vanagon (Cont.)

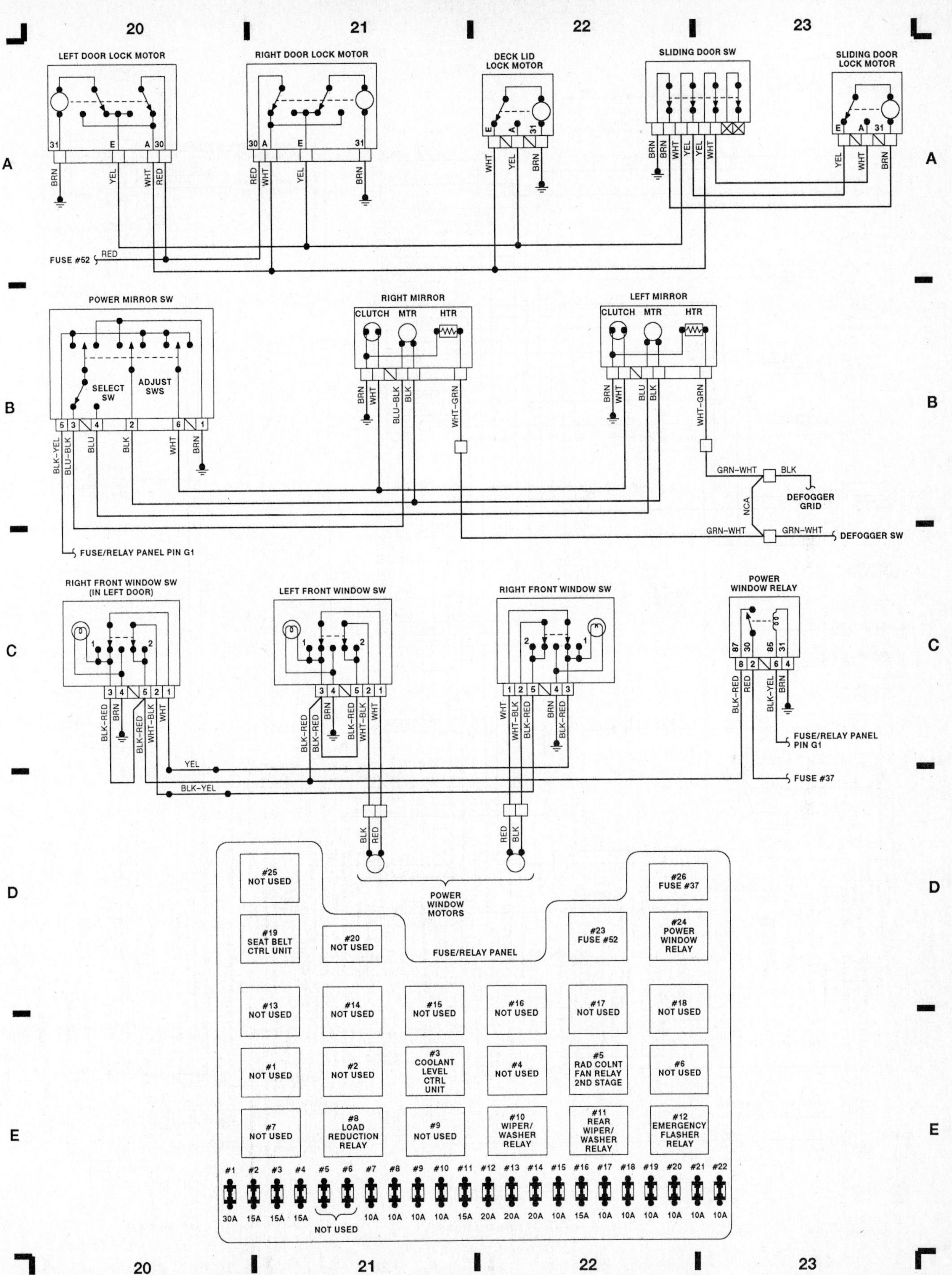

# 1991 WIRING DIAGRAMS
## Vanagon (Cont.)

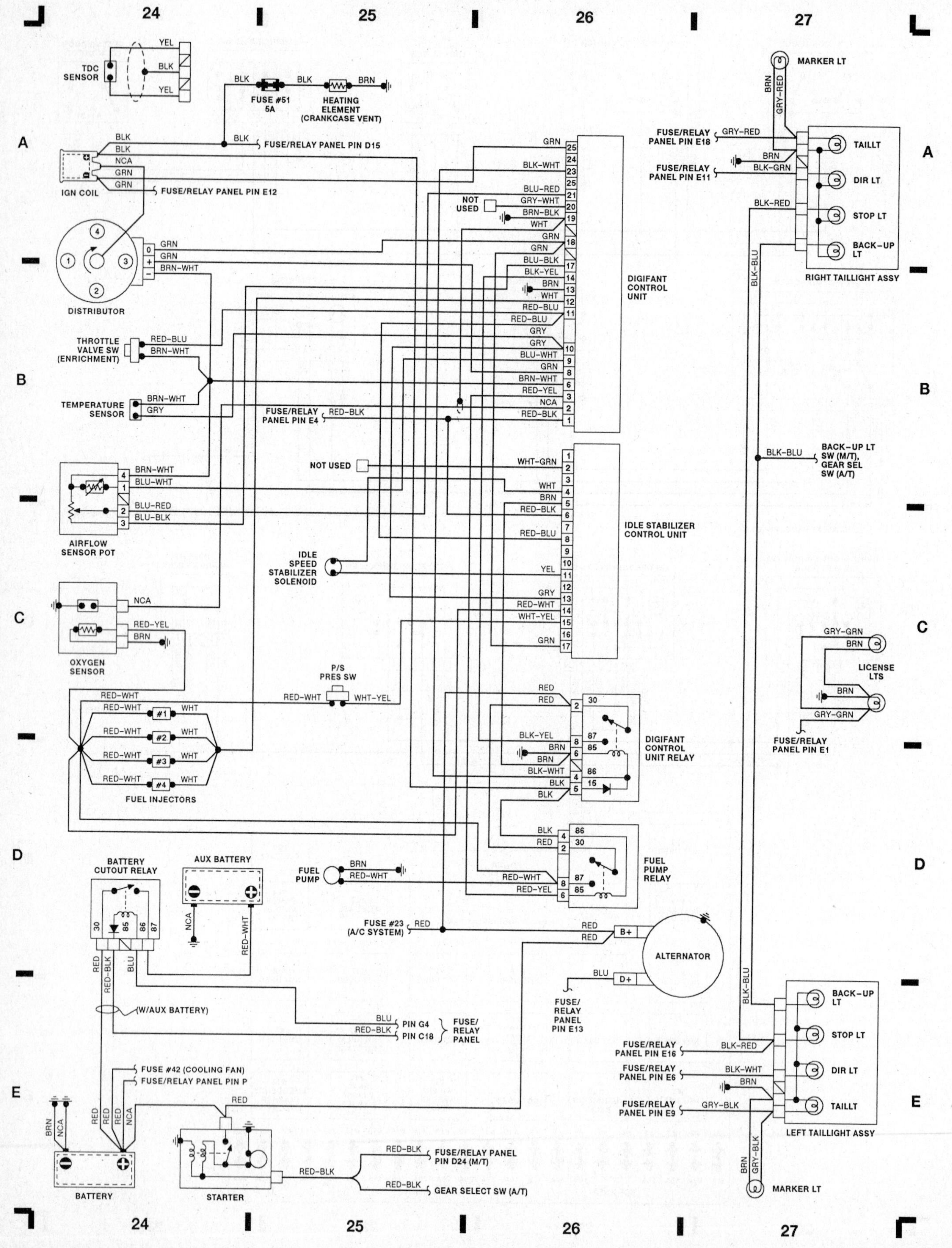

# 1991 SAFETY EQUIPMENT
# Air Bag Restraint System

## Cabriolet

***WARNING: To avoid injury from accidental air bag deployment, read and carefully follow all WARNINGS and SERVICE PRECAUTIONS.***

***NOTE: For information on air bag DIAGNOSIS & TESTING or DISPOSAL PROCEDURES, see MITCHELL'S AIR BAG SERVICE & REPAIR MANUAL, DOMESTIC & IMPORTED MODELS.***

## DESCRIPTION & OPERATION

The air bag is a supplementary restraint system designed to operate with seat belts. Air bag is folded within steering wheel and activates if vehicle is in a frontal collision at a speed greater than 9-12 MPH.

Air bag inflates within 25-30 milliseconds, acting as a cushion between driver and steering wheel. Air bag can only be inflated once, after which it must be replaced. It cannot be reused.

Main system components include front impact sensors (in fresh air plenum), air bag control unit (behind center console), air bag module (in steering wheel), diagnostic connector (in center console), air bag warning and control lights (in instrument cluster) and clockspring assembly (under steering wheel, in steering column). *See Fig. 1.*

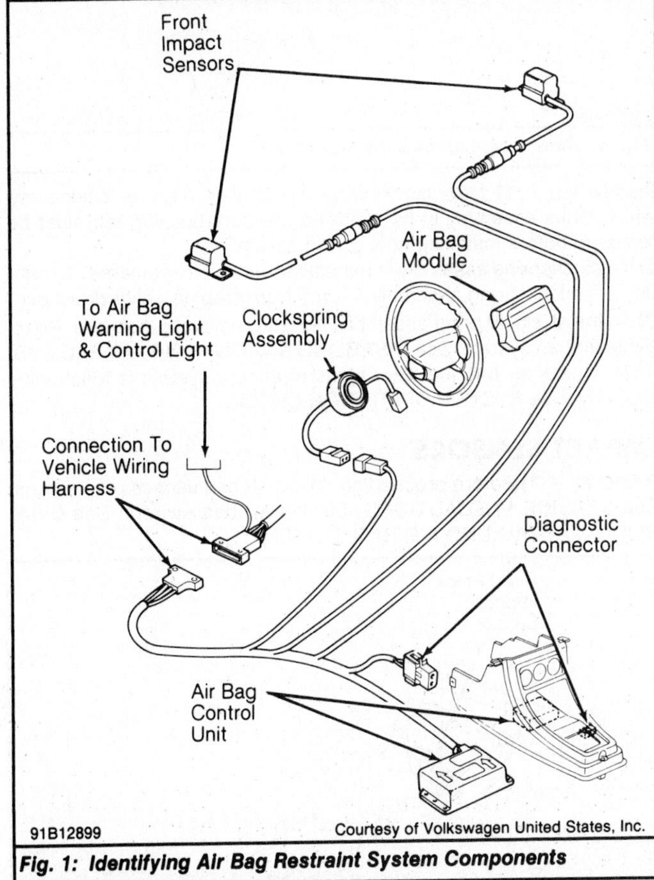


***Fig. 1: Identifying Air Bag Restraint System Components***

Air bag control unit is capable of system self-diagnosis. Air bag system components are monitored electrically, and any interferences in operation can be detected. These interferences (faults) are then stored in air bag control unit memory, which differentiates between 20 types of malfunctions. After diagnosis and servicing, fault memory can be erased.

Self-diagnosis can only be performed when Diagnostic Tester (VAG 1551) is connected to air bag control unit memory. Tester must be connected to vehicle's remote diagnostic connector, located under center console, near shift selector lever.

## SERVICING

Manufacturer recommends replacing air bag system every 10 years.

## SYSTEM OPERATION CHECK

Two lights pertaining to air bag system are located directly above air bag symbol in instrument cluster. *See Fig. 2.*

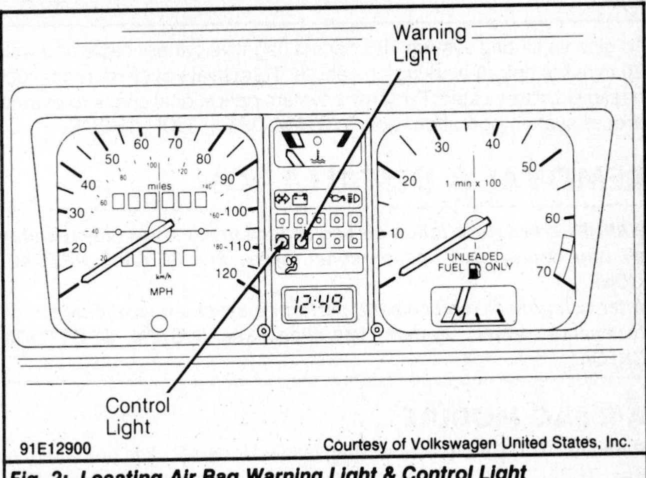


***Fig. 2: Locating Air Bag Warning Light & Control Light***

Control light is used to indicate readiness of system. This light, which illuminates when ignition switch is on or engine is started, will stay on approximately 5-8 seconds while diagnosis unit in air bag control unit performs an electronic test cycle of system.

If control light does not illuminate when ignition is on or does not go out after 5-8 seconds, a fault exists in system. If a fault occurs while ignition is on, it is stored in fault memory. Warning light will then illuminate and air bag system will be switched off. If warning light illuminates or flickers while driving, air bag system should be tested. See DIAGNOSIS & TESTING in MITCHELL'S AIR BAG SERVICE & REPAIR MANUAL, DOMESTIC & IMPORTED MODELS.

## SERVICE PRECAUTIONS

Observe these precautions when working with air bag systems:

- Disable air bag system before servicing any air bag system or steering column component. See DISABLING & ACTIVATING AIR BAG SYSTEM.
- Wait about 20 minutes after deactivating air bag system before servicing. Air bag system voltage is maintained for about 20 minutes after system is deactivated. Servicing system before 20 minutes may cause accidental air bag deployment and possible personal injury.
- Because of critical operating requirements of system, DO NOT attempt to service any air bag system component.
- Air bag parts should not be left unattended. They should be installed in vehicle immediately after obtaining them.
- Air bag components which have been dropped more than 18 inches should not be used.
- Chemical cleaners or oil and grease should not come in contact with vinyl covering on air bag module.
- Do not place stickers or covers on steering wheel.
- Always disable air bag system before performing electric welding on vehicle.
- Air bag system can only be tested with Diagnostic Tester (VAG 1551) and Multimeter (US 1119). Never use test light on air bag system.

# 1991 SAFETY EQUIPMENT
# Air Bag Restraint System (Cont.)

## DISABLING & ACTIVATING AIR BAG SYSTEM

***WARNING: Wait about 20 minutes after deactivating air bag system before servicing. Air bag system voltage is maintained for about 20 minutes after system is deactivated. Servicing system before 20 minutes may cause accidental air bag deployment and possible personal injury.***

To disable air bag system, disconnect negative battery cable and wait 20 minutes before working on vehicle. To activate system, reconnect negative battery cable. Perform a system operational check to ensure proper system operation. See SYSTEM OPERATION CHECK.

## REMOVAL & INSTALLATION

***WARNING: Failure to follow air bag service precautions may result in air bag deployment and personal injury. See SERVICE PRECAUTIONS.***

***After component replacement, perform a system operational check to ensure proper system operation. See SYSTEM OPERATION CHECK.***

### AIR BAG MODULE

**Removal - 1)** Before proceeding, follow air bag service precautions. See SERVICE PRECAUTIONS. Disable air bag system. See DISABLING & ACTIVATING AIR BAG SYSTEM.

**2)** Air bag module is located on steering wheel hub. Remove Torx head retaining screws on rear of steering wheel. *See Fig. 3.* Lift off air bag module from steering wheel, and tilt air bag module downward. Disconnect wiring connector from air bag module.

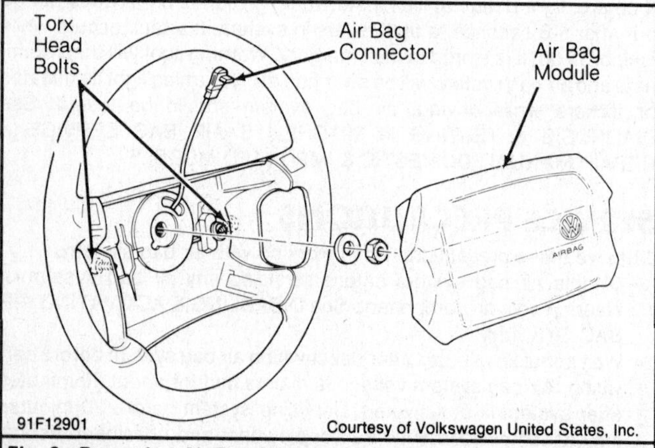


***Fig. 3: Removing Air Bag Module***

**Installation** - To install, reverse removal procedure. Tighten air bag module retaining screws to specification. See TORQUE SPECIFICATIONS table at end of article. Reactivate air bag system. See DISABLING & ACTIVATING AIR BAG SYSTEM. Check air bag indicator lights to ensure system is functioning properly. See SYSTEM OPERATION CHECK.

### STEERING WHEEL

**Removal - 1)** Follow air bag service precautions. See SERVICE PRECAUTIONS. Disable air bag system. See DISABLING & ACTIVATING AIR BAG SYSTEM.

**2)** Turn front wheels to straight-ahead position. Remove air bag module. See AIR BAG MODULE under REMOVAL & INSTALLATION. Remove steering wheel nut and spring washer. Mark steering wheel and shaft for reassembly reference. Remove steering wheel.

**Installation** - To install, reverse removal procedure. Tighten steering wheel nut to specification. See TORQUE SPECIFICATIONS table at end of article. Reactivate air bag system. See DISABLING & ACTIVATING AIR BAG SYSTEM. Check air bag indicator lights to ensure system is functioning properly. See SYSTEM OPERATION CHECK.

### CLOCKSPRING

**Removal - 1)** Before proceeding, follow air bag service precautions. See SERVICE PRECAUTIONS. Disable air bag system. See DISABLING & ACTIVATING AIR BAG SYSTEM.

**2)** Remove air bag module. See AIR BAG MODULE. Remove steering wheel. See STEERING WHEEL. Remove knee bar panel and steering column lower trim. Disconnect 2-pin wiring connector (Green/Black and Green/Red wires) at base of steering column. Remove 3 clockspring retaining screws, and remove clockspring. *See Fig. 4.*

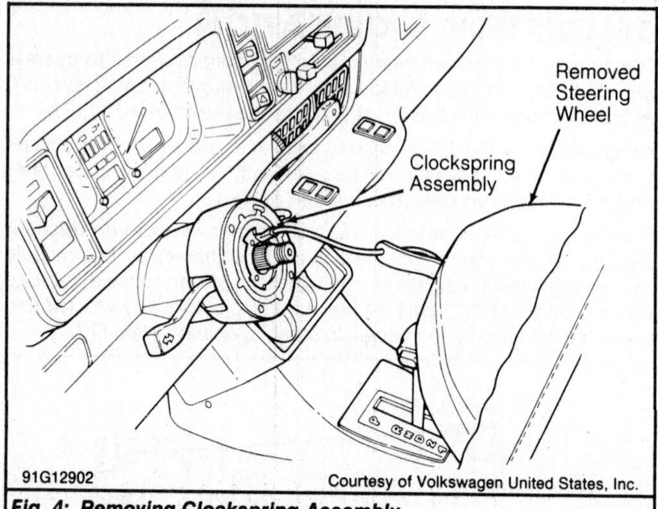


***Fig. 4: Removing Clockspring Assembly***

**Installation - 1)** New clockspring assemblies have a locking tab which locks assembly in its centered position. Locking tab must be removed before installing new spring assembly.

**2)** If a clockspring assembly is reinstalled, it must be centered. To center, turn clockspring assembly 4 turns from stop, in either direction.

**3)** To install clockspring assembly, reverse removal procedure. Reactivate air bag system. See DISABLING & ACTIVATING AIR BAG SYSTEM. Check air bag indicator lights to ensure system is functioning properly. See SYSTEM OPERATION CHECK.

### IMPACT SENSORS

**Removal - 1)** Before proceeding, follow air bag service precautions. See SERVICE PRECAUTIONS. Disable air bag system. See DISABLING & ACTIVATING AIR BAG SYSTEM.

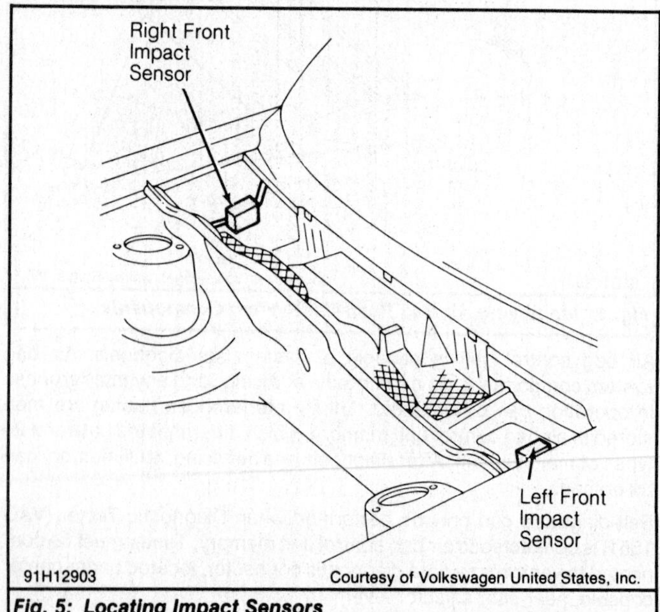


***Fig. 5: Locating Impact Sensors***

# 1991 SAFETY EQUIPMENT
# Air Bag Restraint System (Cont.)

**2)** Impact sensors are located in fresh air plenum. Remove knee bar panel. Loosen fuse/relay panel, and pull it down to access left impact sensor connector. Disconnect left and right impact sensors, located under left and right sides of instrument panel, near A-pillar. *See Fig. 5.*
**3)** Remove shear nuts from sensor mounting studs. Remove sensor while sliding wire through grommet.

**Installation - 1)** Place sensor lead through grommet in body. Ensure arrow on sensor points toward front of vehicle, and place sensor on welded mounting studs. Install new shear nuts. Hex head of shear nut rounds off when correct torque is reached. Connect impact sensor connectors. To complete installation, reverse removal procedure.
**2)** Reactivate air bag system. See DISABLING & ACTIVATING AIR BAG SYSTEM. Check air bag indicator lights to ensure system is functioning properly. See SYSTEM OPERATION CHECK.

## AIR BAG CONTROL UNIT

**Removal - 1)** Before proceeding, follow air bag service precautions. See SERVICE PRECAUTIONS. Disable air bag system. See DISABLING & ACTIVATING AIR BAG SYSTEM.
**2)** Air bag control unit is located behind center console. *See Fig. 6.* Remove lower instrument panel trim covers. Remove power window switches and ash tray. Remove center console and knee bar. Disconnect and remove air bag module. See AIR BAG MODULE.

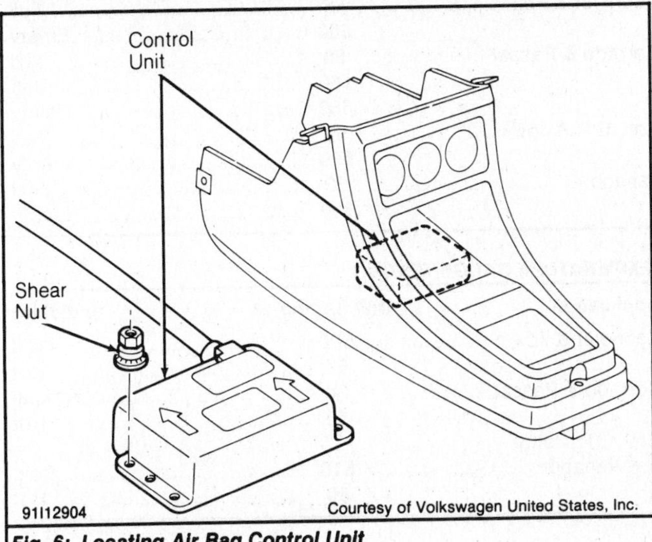


***Fig. 6: Locating Air Bag Control Unit***

**3)** Remove steering column trim. Disconnect air bag clockspring 2-pin wiring connector (Green/Black and Green/Red wires) at base of steering column. Remove shear nuts from air bag control unit.
**4)** Remove air duct and vacuum lines from A/C valve. Remove radio and fresh air controls. Remove instrument cluster trim and switches. Remove fresh air control unit.
**5)** Disconnect speedometer and wiring, and remove instrument cluster. Remove bolts securing instrument panel. Remove tie wraps and center bracket. Remove instrument panel. Disconnect air bag impact sensors. See IMPACT SENSORS. Remove air bag control unit and wiring.

**Installation - 1)** To install, reverse removal procedure. Ensure arrows on air bag control unit point toward front of vehicle. Use new shear nuts to mount air bag control unit. During tightening, hex head of shear nut rounds off when correct torque has been reached.
**2)** Reactivate air bag system. See DISABLING & ACTIVATING AIR BAG SYSTEM. Check air bag indicator lights to ensure system is functioning properly. See SYSTEM OPERATION CHECK.

# ADJUSTMENTS

## AIR BAG CLOCKSPRING

To center a clockspring assembly, turn spring assembly 4 turns from stop in either direction.

# WIRE REPAIR

Manufacturer does not recommend repair on air bag system wiring or component pigtail wiring. Air bag control unit is supplied with system's wiring harness. Wiring harness cannot be separated from air bag control unit. These 2 items must be replaced as a unit if a problem occurs in either.

# TORQUE SPECIFICATIONS

*TORQUE SPECIFICATIONS*

| Application | Ft. Lbs. (N.m) |
|---|---|
| Steering Wheel Nut | 30 (40) |
| | **INCH Lbs. (N.m)** |
| Air Bag Module-To-Steering Wheel Screws | 89 (10) |

# 1991 SAFETY EQUIPMENT
# Instrument Panels

## Cabriolet, Corrado, Fox, Golf, GTI, Jetta, Passat, Vanagon

## DESCRIPTION & OPERATION

Instrument cluster for most models includes speedometer, fuel gauge and temperature gauge. Optional instruments include clock, tachometer, voltmeter and oil temperature gauge. *See Fig. 2.*

Printed circuit provides voltage to gauges. A voltage regulator attached to printed circuit controls voltage to fuel and temperature gauges. Most warning lights are Light Emitting Diodes (LEDs). To replace diode, pull from printed circuit socket.

## TESTING

***NOTE: Volkswagen Tester (VW 1301) is required for resistance tests. Tester settings are numerical. Settings do not indicate resistance in ohms. Manufacturer does not supply resistance values in ohms.***

### VOLTAGE REGULATOR TEST

**1)** If only one gauge is inoperative, regulator is not defective. If both fuel and temperature gauges are inoperative, voltage regulator may be faulty or have a bad ground connection.

**2)** Partially remove instrument cluster. Position cluster so regulator can be reached with voltmeter probes. Leave chassis harness connected. Ensure ground connection at regulator is tight.

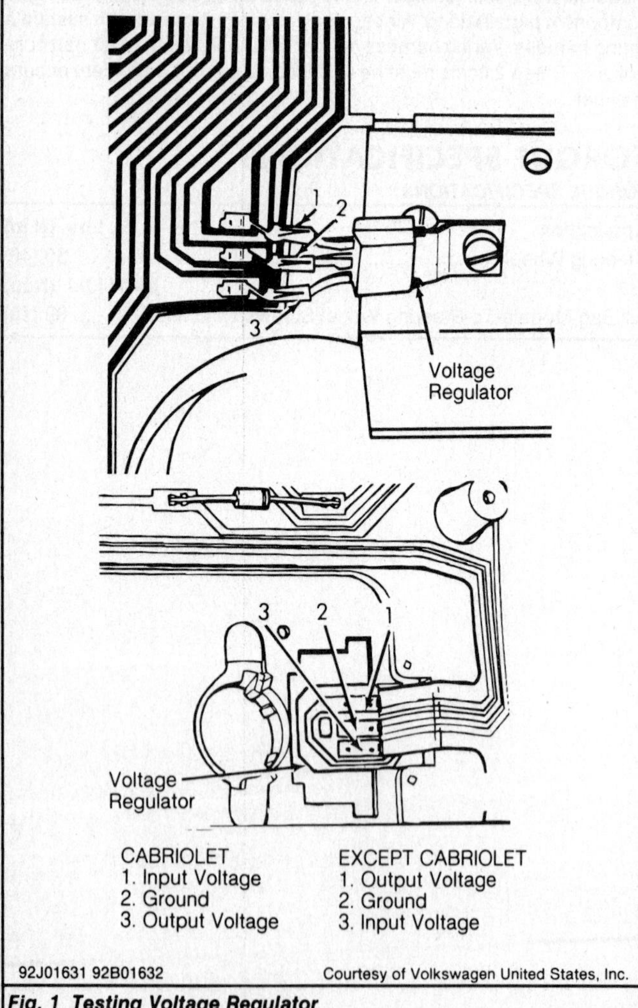


***Fig. 1 Testing Voltage Regulator***

**3)** On all except Cabriolet, turn ignition on. Connect voltmeter negative (-) lead to terminal No. 2 of regulator. Connect positive (+) lead to terminal No 1. *See Fig. 1.* Meter reading should be 9.5-10.5 volts. If reading exceeds specification, replace voltage regulator.

**4)** For Cabriolet, turn ignition on. Connect voltmeter negative (-) lead to terminal No. 2 of regulator. Connect positive lead (+) to terminal No 3. *See Fig. 1.* Meter reading should be 9.5-10.5 volts. If reading exceeds specification, replace voltage regulator.

### FUEL & TEMPERATURE GAUGE TEST

**1)** Disconnect wire from fuel tank or temperature sending unit. Connect VW Tester (VW 1301) between wire and ground. Turn ignition on and allow 2 minutes for gauge reading to stabilize. Use FUEL GAUGE TESTING or TEMPERATURE GAUGE TESTING table to compare gauge reading. Gauge should be within one pointer width of specification.

**2)** If gauge needle does not move, check continuity between sender wire and gauge. If needle moves, but does not match specifications, replace gauge. If gauge works correctly with tester, but not sending unit, replace sending unit.

***FUEL GAUGE TESTING***

| Application | Dial Setting | Indicator |
|---|---|---|
| Cabriolet & Fox | 55 | Full |
| | 560 | Empty |
| Corrado & Passat | 50 | Full |
| | 160 | Half |
| | 350 | Empty |
| Golf, GTI & Jetta | 52 | Full |
| | 550 | Empty |
| Vanagon | 50 | Full |
| | 320 | Empty |

***TEMPERATURE GAUGE TESTING***

| Application | Dial Setting | Indicator |
|---|---|---|
| Cabriolet & Fox | 500 | Cold |
| | 62 | Hot |
| Corrado & Passat | 80 | Normal |
| | 50 | Hot |
| Golf, GTI, Jetta & Vanagon | 510 | Cold |
| | 50 | Hot |

## WIPER/WASHERS

Testing information is not available from manufacturer.

## REMOVAL & INSTALLATION

### INSTRUMENT CLUSTER

***CAUTION: To disable air bag system, disconnect negative battery cable and wait 20 minutes before working on vehicle. To activate system, reconnect negative battery cable. Perform a system operational check to ensure proper system operation. See SYSTEM OPERATION CHECK in AIR BAG RESTRAINT SYSTEM article in SAFETY EQUIPMENT.***

***WARNING: Failure to follow air bag service precautions may result in air bag deployment and personal injury. See SERVICE PRECAUTIONS in AIR BAG RESTRAINT SYSTEM article in SAFETY EQUIPMENT.***

**Removal & Installation (Cabriolet) – 1)** Disconnect battery ground cable. Disable air bag. Remove steering wheel.

# 1991 SAFETY EQUIPMENT
# Instrument Panels (Cont.)

**2)** Tilt shelf downward, remove mounting screws and remove shelf. Remove instrument panel cover screws and mounting clips. Remove instrument panel cover. Remove instrument panel insert trim screws and pull off instrument panel insert trim.

**3)** Remove instrument panel insert screw and tip instrument panel insert forward. Press speedometer cable lugs together and disconnect speedometer cable from instrument panel insert.

**4)** Disconnect multi-point connector and remove instrument panel insert. To install, reverse removal procedure.

**Removal & Installation (Corrado) - 1)** Disconnect battery ground cable. Remove steering wheel only when removing complete instrument cluster housing. Remove trim screw caps and screws located on lower part of instrument cluster trim. Remove instrument cluster trim.

**2)** Remove trip odometer reset button. Remove trim cover retaining screws. Remove trim cover from instrument cluster. Remove instrument cluster housing retaining screws. Pull instrument cluster from dash panel. Disconnect multi-point connector, MFI vacuum hose (if equipped) and speedometer drive cable. Remove instrument cluster housing.

***NOTE: All components in instrument cluster, except for printed circuit, can be removed from front, without removing complete instrument cluster housing.***

**3)** Disconnect speedometer cable, remove mounting screws and pull speedometer from housing. Squeeze locating pins on other instruments and pull from housing. To install, reverse removal procedure.

**Removal & Installation (Fox) - 1)** Disconnect battery ground cable. Remove steering wheel. Carefully remove covers from vacant switch positions. Depress switch spring retainer and remove switches from instrument panel. Mark for reassembly and disconnect wire connectors from switches.

**2)** Remove 4 instrument cluster trim retaining screws. Remove instrument cluster trim panel. Remove 2 instrument cluster retaining screws. Remove speedometer cable. Disconnect cluster wire connector and remove instrument cluster. To install, reverse removal procedure.

**Removal & Installation (Golf, GTI & Jetta) - 1)** Disconnect battery ground cable. Remove steering wheel. Remove lower instrument panel retaining screws, and lower on left side. Remove remaining retaining screws, and lower instrument panel tray on right side.

**2)** Remove gearshift lever knob and boot. Remove retaining screw(s) and slide console rearward. Separate all electrical connections and lift out console.

**3)** Pull off all temperature control knobs/levers. Unclip trim plate and remove. Remove radio (or tray). Remove switches from instrument panel trim plate. Remove all retaining screws and remove instrument panel trim plate.

**4)** Remove instrument cluster retaining screws. Squeeze clips and remove speedometer cable from instrument cluster. Disconnect all vacuum hose connections and separate all electrical connectors. Remove instrument cluster. To install, reverse removal procedure.

**Removal & Installation (Passat) - 1)** Remove battery ground cable. Remove instrument cluster trim. Remove instrument cluster trim cover. For tachometer and combination gauge, carefully pull gauge from housing and connector. For mechanical speedometer, remove mounting screws and carefully pull speedometer from housing.

**2)** To install, reverse removal procedure. Carefully guide plugs on rear of instruments into connector on printed circuit board.

***CAUTION: DO NOT damage printed circuit when installing instruments.***

**Removal & Installation (Vanagon) -** Disconnect battery ground cable. Reach behind cluster hood and pull back of hood upward. Pull hazard switch forward. Pull brake warning light housing toward front of vehicle. Remove 4 mounting screws and remove cluster. To install, reverse removal procedure.

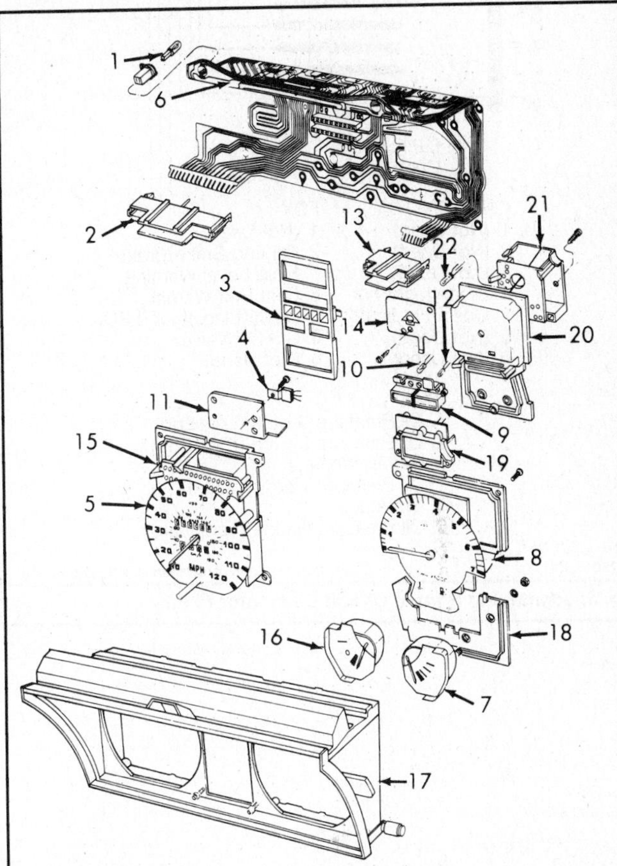


***Fig. 2: Exploded View of Instrument Cluster (Fox Shown; Other Models Are Similar)***

# 1991 SAFETY EQUIPMENT
# Instrument Panels (Cont.)

## PRINTED CIRCUIT CONNECTORS

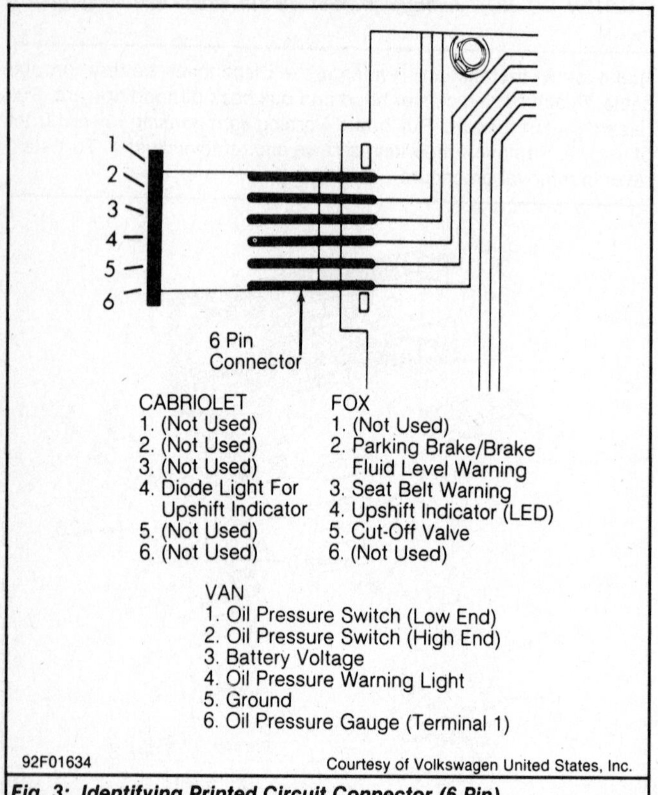


*Fig. 3: Identifying Printed Circuit Connector (6 Pin)*

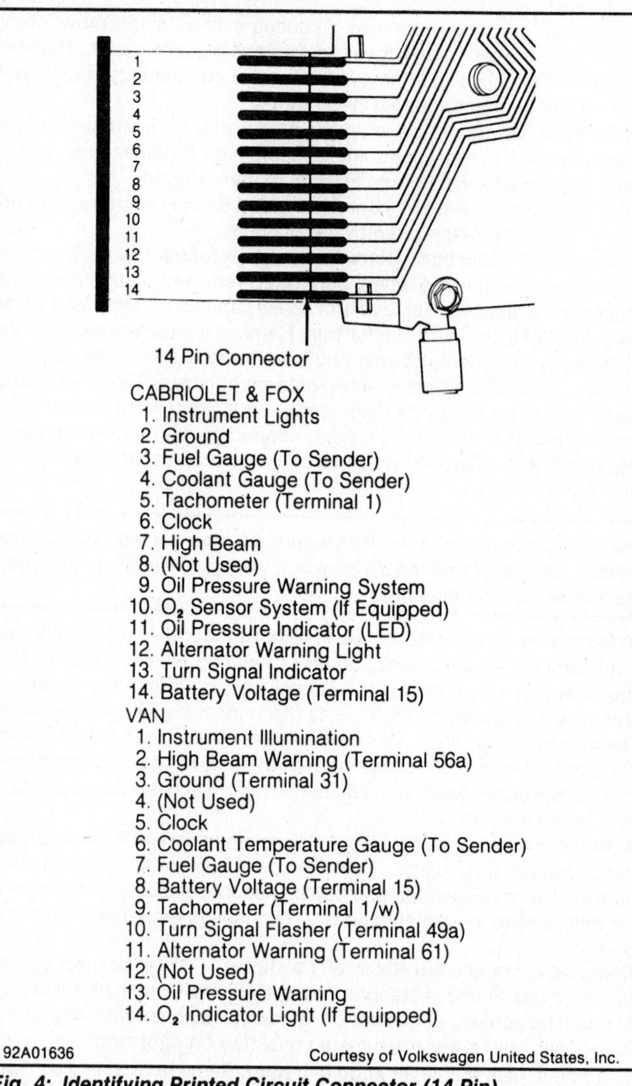


*Fig. 4: Identifying Printed Circuit Connector (14 Pin)*

# 1991 SAFETY EQUIPMENT
# Instrument Panels (Cont.)

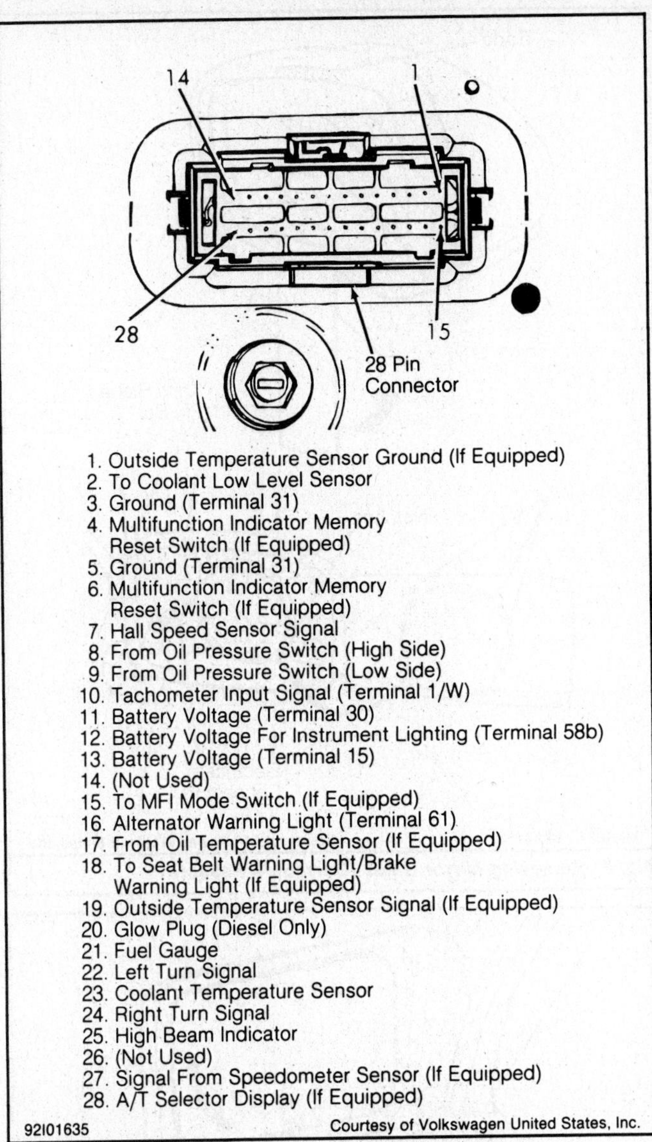


***Fig. 5: Identifying Printed Circuit Connector (28 Pin)***

## WIRING DIAGRAMS

See appropriate chassis wiring diagram in WIRING DIAGRAMS.

# 1991 SAFETY EQUIPMENT
# Power Mirrors

**Corrado, Golf, GTI, Jetta, Passat, Vanagon**

## DESCRIPTION & OPERATION

Mirrors can be adjusted electrically from inside by operating control knob on driver door panel. Adjustment control operates only when ignition is on. To adjust driver-side or passenger-side mirror, rotate control knob to "L" or "R". Control knob is a 4-way rocker switch which is pressed top (up), bottom (down), left (out) or right (in). *See Fig. 1.*

If electrical control of mirror does not operate, adjust mirror by hand by pushing lightly on edge of mirror glass. When rear defogger is on, outside mirrors are electrically heated.

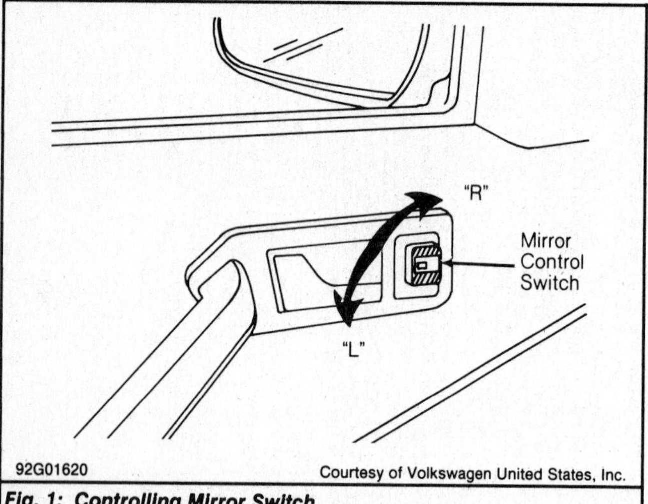


*Fig. 1: Controlling Mirror Switch*

## TROUBLE SHOOTING

**Left Or Right Power Mirror Inoperative** – Check power mirror switch, power mirror motor(s), wiring, ground connection(s) and fuse(s). Use driver manual to identify fuse(s).

## REMOVAL & INSTALLATION

### MIRROR GLASS

***CAUTION: Press only on center of glass. Always wear protective gloves while handling mirror glass in case of accidental breakage.***

**Removal & Installation (Corrado & Passat)** – Tape upper and lower edges of mirror housing. *See Fig. 2.* Remove mirror glass using knife blade Pry Bar (VW-80-200). Pry off at bottom and then top. While holding mirror, unplug electrical connector, and remove mirror glass. To install, connect electric connector. Put mirror pins in notches, and press mirror into place. *See Fig. 2.* Check mirror for proper function.

***NOTE: Mirror glass is only clipped in place.***

**Removal & Installation (Golf GL, GTI, Jetta & Jetta GLi)** – Push glass in at bottom, and turn lock ring counterclockwise using a screwdriver. *See Fig. 3.* Remove mirror glass, and disconnect electrical wires. To install, connect electrical wires. *See Fig. 3.* Ensure lock ring is rotated clockwise to stop. Insert mirror in housing, and lock mirror in place using screwdriver.

**Removal & Installation (Vanagon)** – Push mirror glass at outer edge until locking lever is accessible. *See Fig. 4.* Push locking lever counterclockwise to unlock mirror assembly. Tilt and remove mirror glass. Disconnect electric heater element. To install, reverse removal procedure. Ensure dust boot is properly seated and locking pins are engaged in lock ring. *See Fig. 4.* Check mirror for proper function.

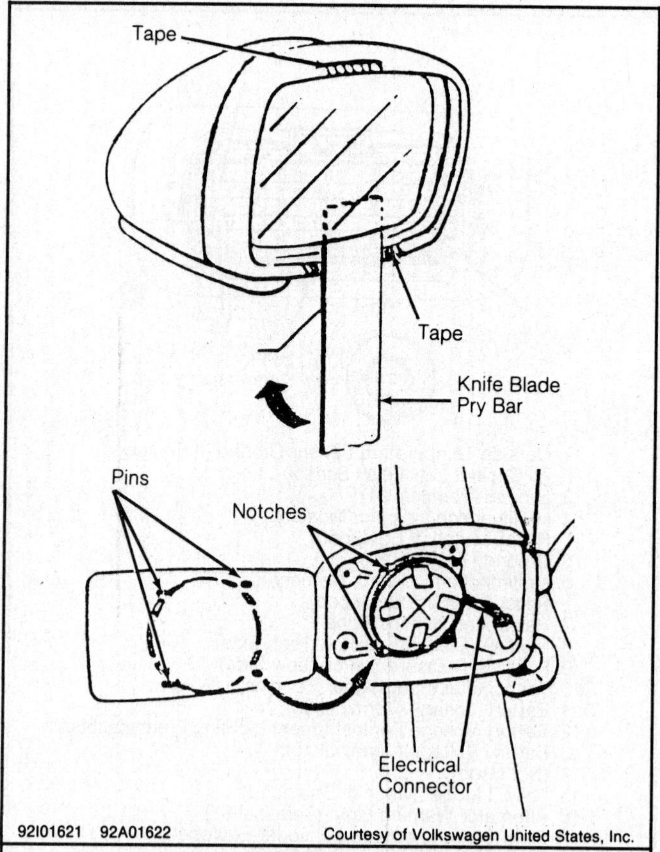


*Fig. 2: Removing Mirror Glass (Corrado & Passat)*

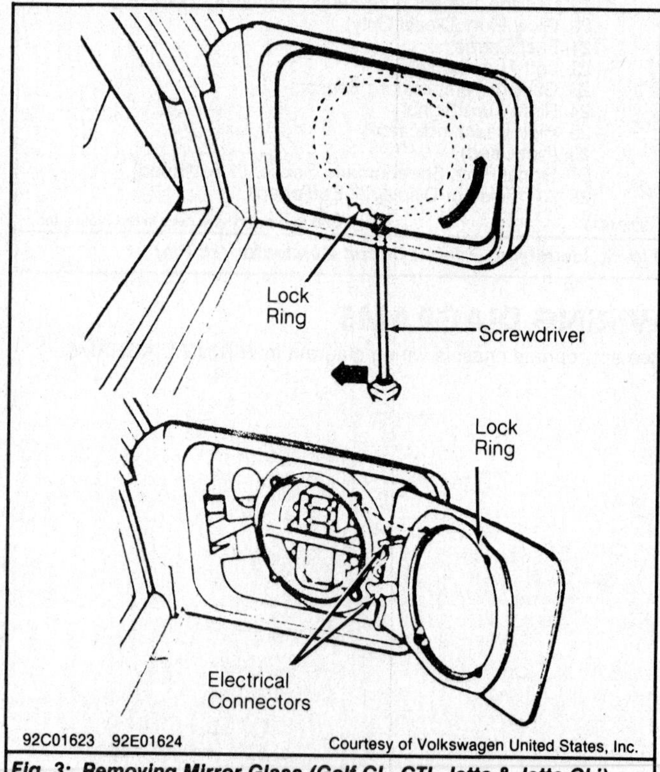


*Fig. 3: Removing Mirror Glass (Golf GL, GTI, Jetta & Jetta GLi)*

# 1991 SAFETY EQUIPMENT
# Power Mirrors (Cont.)

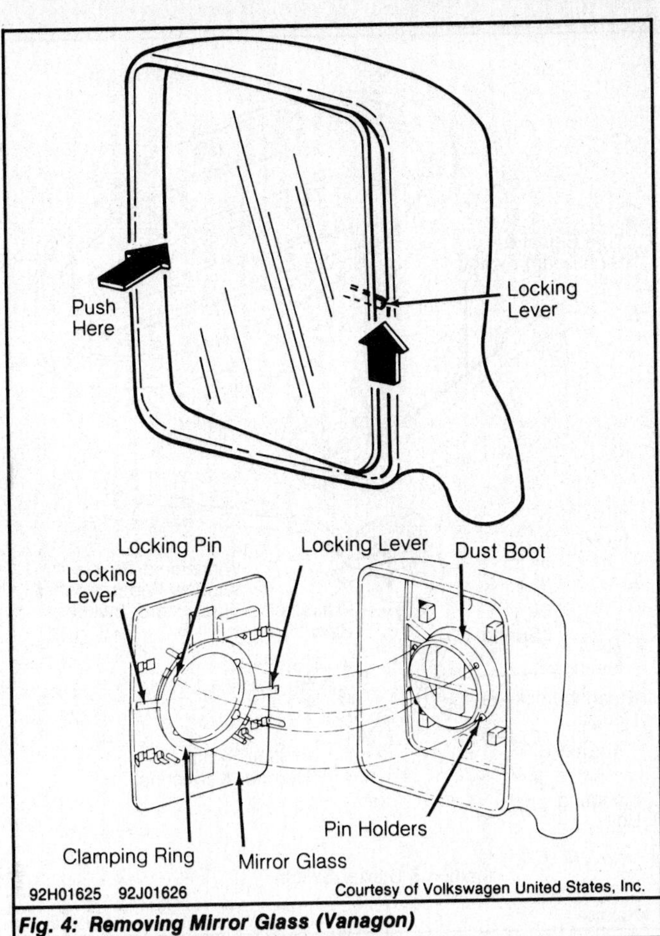


*Fig. 4: Removing Mirror Glass (Vanagon)*

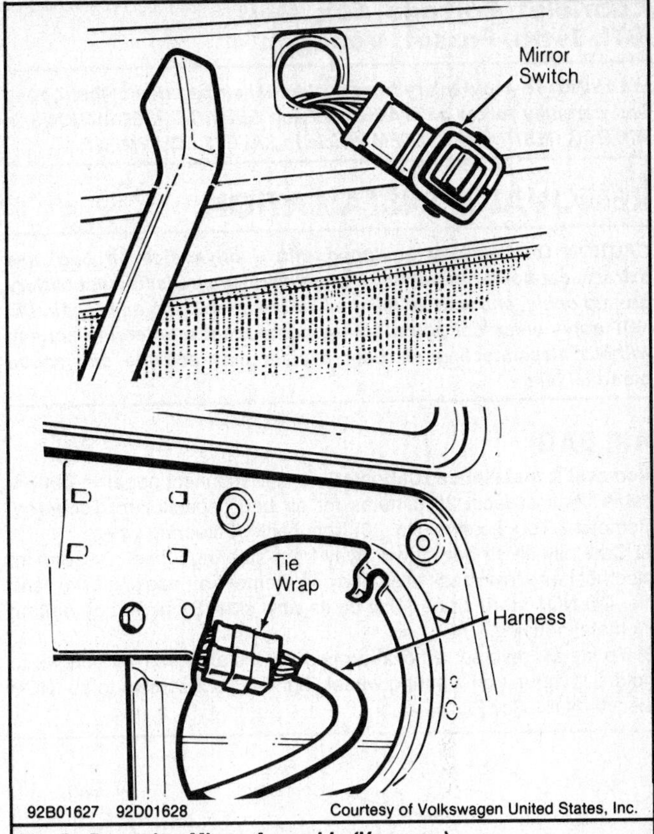


*Fig. 5: Removing Mirror Assembly (Vanagon)*

## POWER MIRROR ASSEMBLY

***CAUTION: Always wear protective gloves while handling mirror glass in case of accidental breakage. Hold glass to prevent it from falling out.***

**Removal & Installation (Corrado & Passat) – 1)** Disconnect battery ground cable. Lower window. Remove control knob and boot. Remove door trim, and loosen moisture barrier in area of rearview mirror control. Remove lock nut. Unplug electrical connector.

**2)** Pivot mirror inward, and remove mounting screw. Pivot mirror outward, and remove second mounting screw. Remove mirror with base and control. To install, reverse removal procedure.

**Removal & Installation (Golf GL, GTI, Jetta & Jetta GLi) – 1)** Disconnect battery ground cable. Remove mirror glass and electrical wires. See MIRROR GLASS under REMOVAL & INSTALLATION. Remove mirror adjustment motor securing screws and motor. Disconnect electrical wires. Carefully pry mirror adjustment switch from door panel. Unplug electrical connector.

**2)** Remove door trim panel and protective cover from door near mirror wire connectors. Disconnect terminals. To install, connect adjustment motor wires according to marked color identification. Reverse removal procedure to complete installation.

**Removal & Installation (Vanagon) – 1)** Disconnect battery ground strap. Pry out and disconnect electric mirror switch from door trim panel. *See Fig. 5.* Remove door trim panel, and carefully pull back plastic moisture barrier. Cut tie wraps securing wiring harness to door. *See Fig. 5.* Open harness far enough to expose and label individual wires. Remove labeled wires from plug connector.

**2)** Pry off plastic cap at base of mirror bracket, and remove 3 bracket securing screws. *See Fig. 6.* Remove mirror assembly with wiring harness. To install, reverse removal procedure, ensuring seal is positioned for proper fit and wire harness is secured to door frame with tie wraps. *See Fig. 6.* Check mirror for proper function.

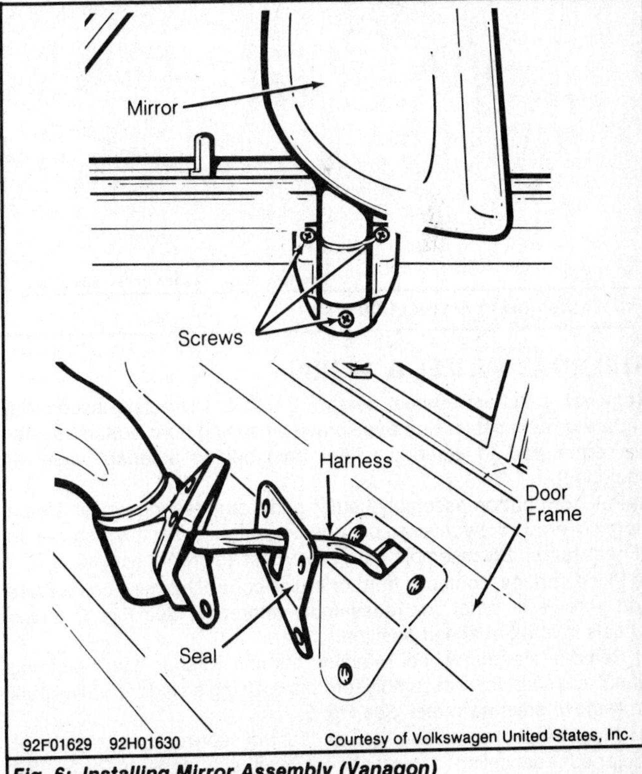


*Fig. 6: Installing Mirror Assembly (Vanagon)*

## WIRING DIAGRAMS

See appropriate chassis wiring diagram in WIRING DIAGRAMS.

# 1991 SAFETY EQUIPMENT
# Steering Column Switches

## Cabriolet, Corrado, Fox, Golf, GTI, Jetta, Passat, Vanagon

***WARNING: To avoid injury from accidental air bag deployment, read and carefully follow all WARNINGS and SERVICE PRECAUTIONS in AIR BAG RESTRAINT SYSTEM article in SAFETY EQUIPMENT.***

## REMOVAL & INSTALLATION

***CAUTION: On Cabriolet equipped with a driver-side air bag, use extreme caution while servicing steering column. Disconnect battery ground cable, and wait 20 minutes before attempting any repair. DO NOT apply electrical power to any component on steering column without disconnecting air bag. System may activate and cause personal injury.***

### AIR BAG

**Removal & Installation (Cabriolet) - 1)** Disconnect negative battery cable. Wait at least 20 minutes for air bag capacitor to discharge. Remove 2 Torx screws (No. 30) from back of steering wheel.

**2)** Carefully tilt air bag down away from steering wheel. Disconnect electrical wire from back of air bag unit. Remove air bag unit from vehicle. DO NOT store air bag unit on its vinyl side. Store air bag unit on its metal housing.

**3)** To install, reverse removal procedure. Install new Torx screws to hold air bag unit on steering wheel. Tighten Torx screws to 89 INCH lbs. (10 N.m). *See Fig. 1.*

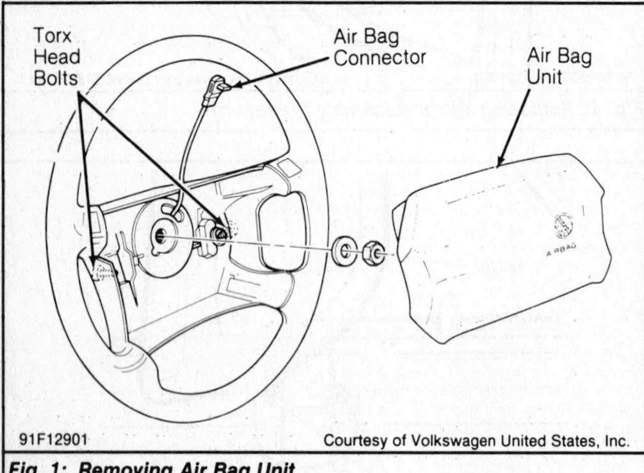


***Fig. 1: Removing Air Bag Unit***

### STEERING WHEEL & HORN

**Removal - 1)** For Cabriolet, see AIR BAG. For all models, disconnect battery ground cable. Remove screws attaching horn button assembly/center pad to steering wheel from behind steering wheel (if equipped).

**2)** Pull horn button assembly/center pad from steering wheel. Use a cloth covered screwdriver to pry off horn button assembly/center pad (if necessary). Disassemble horn button assembly (if necessary).

**3)** Place springs, contacts, horn or cruise control harness connectors and screws in order for reassembly reference. *See Fig. 2.* Place wheels in straight-ahead position.

**4)** Remove steering wheel retaining nut and washer. Mark steering wheel and shaft for reassembly reference. Using a steering wheel puller, remove steering wheel. *See Fig. 3.*

**5)** Place steering wheel, cruise control set/resume switch (if equipped), canceling cams, springs and slip rings in order for reassembly reference.

**Installation - 1)** Coat slip ring contact surfaces with a light electrical grease. Assemble horn button assembly (if disassembled). Ensure wheels are in a straight-ahead position.

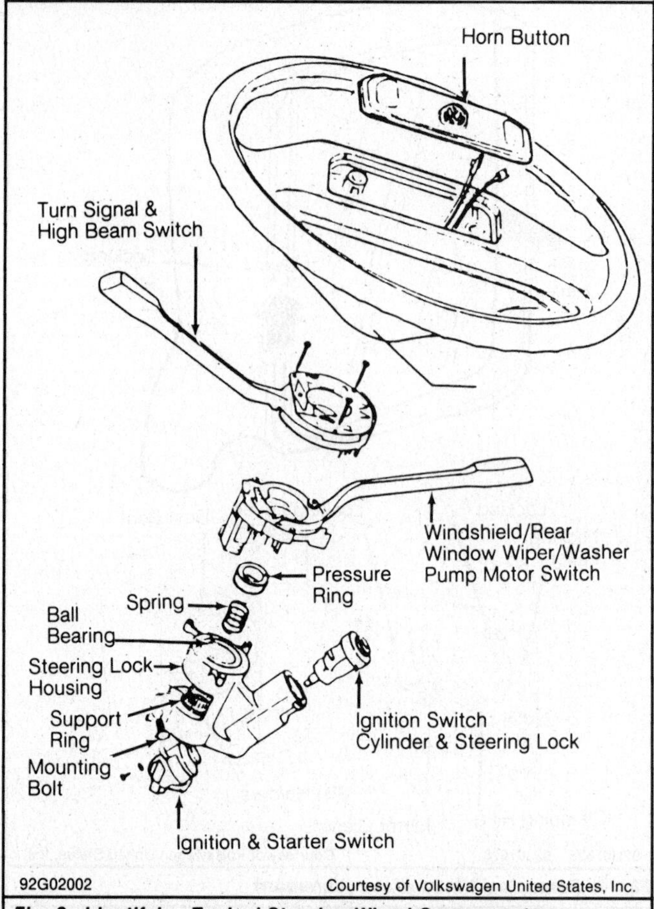


***Fig. 2: Identifying Typical Steering Wheel Components (Without Air Bag - Fox Shown; Others Are Similar)***

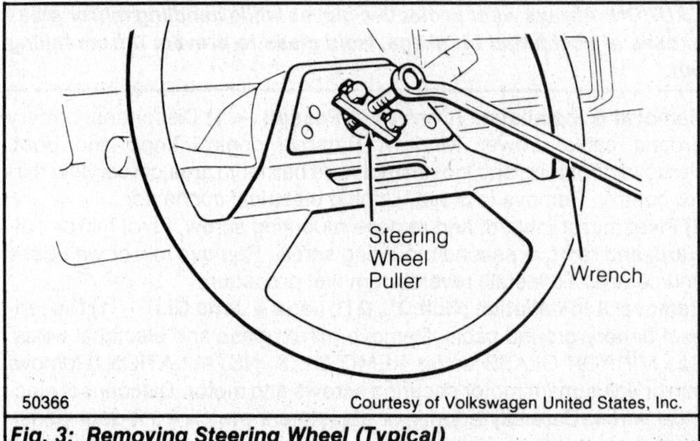


***Fig. 3: Removing Steering Wheel (Typical)***

**2)** Aligning marks made during removal, place slip ring, springs, canceling cams, steering wheel, washer and steering wheel retaining nut on shaft.

**3)** Tighten nut to 30 ft. lbs. (40 N.m). To complete installation, reverse removal procedure.

### COMBINATION SWITCH

**Removal -** Remove steering wheel. Remove upper and lower steering column covers. Disconnect combination switch harness connectors. Remove snap ring and washer from steering shaft (if equipped). Remove combination switch attaching screws. Remove combination switch.

**Installation -** To install, reverse removal procedure. Ensure all electrical connections are tight. Check canceling operation of turn signal switch.

## STEERING LOCK & IGNITION SWITCH

**Removal - 1)** Remove steering wheel, upper and lower steering column covers and combination switch. Disconnect ignition switch harness connectors.

**2)** Remove clamping washers, spring and contact ring from steering column. Remove steering lock housing mounting bolt. Remove steering lock housing from steering column.

**Installation - 1)** To install, reverse removal procedure. Slide steering lock housing onto steering column. Install contact ring, spring and clamping washers onto steering column. Ensure proper operation of steering lock and ignition switch.

***NOTE: On Corrado, pull steering column upward from steering column tube as far as possible to ensure proper column position.***

**2)** Install combination switch, upper and lower steering column covers and steering wheel. Tighten steering wheel nut to 30 ft. lbs. (40 N.m).

## LOCK CYLINDER

**Removal - 1)** Remove steering wheel. Remove combination switch and upper and lower steering wheel covers. Mark steering lock housing at intersection of "A" and "B" for hole. *See Fig. 4.* "A"=12 mm; "B"=10 mm.

**2)** Drill 3 mm hole into steering lock housing at mark until lock cylinder stop spring is visible. Hole depth will be approximately 3 mm. Compress stop spring with punch and pull lock cylinder out.

**Installation - 1)** Insert lock cylinder into steering lock housing. Insert key into lock cylinder. Push lock cylinder fully into housing while gently turning key.

**2)** Install combination switch and upper and lower steering column covers. Install steering wheel and torque steering wheel nut to 30 ft. lbs. (40 N.m).

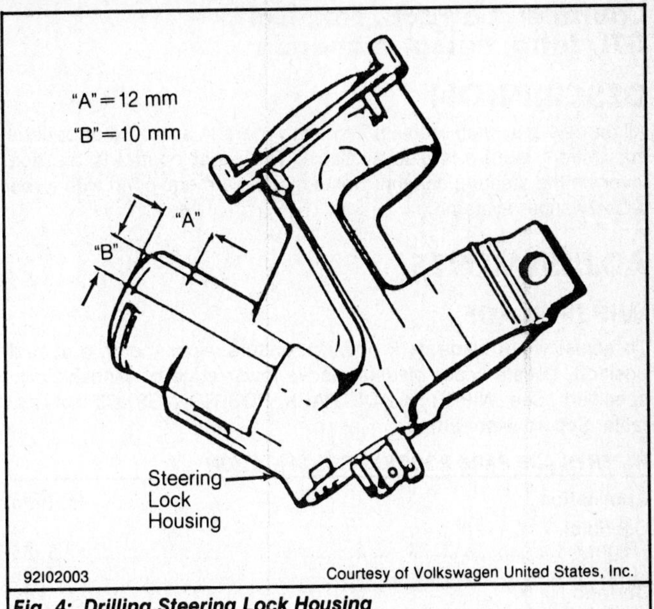


***Fig. 4: Drilling Steering Lock Housing***

# 1991 SAFETY EQUIPMENT
# Wiper/Washer Systems

## Cabriolet, Corrado, Fox, Golf, GTI, Jetta, Passat, Vanagon

## DESCRIPTION

All models are equipped with 2-speed wipers. A standard or optional intermittent feature is also available. The wiper control is the right lever on the steering column. Some models are equipped with a rear wiper/washer system.

## ADJUSTMENTS

### WIPER BLADE

To adjust wiper blade park position, ensure wiper motor is at park position. Locate wiper blade(s) above lower edge of windshield as specified. See WIPER BLADE PARK POSITION SPECIFICATION table. Secure wiper arm.

***WIPER BLADE PARK POSITION SPECIFICATION***

| Application | In. (mm) |
|---|---|
| Cabriolet | |
| Right | 2.5 (65) |
| Left | 1.4 (35) |
| Corrado | |
| Right | 1.0 (25) |
| Left | 1.8 (47) |
| Fox | |
| Front | 1.8 (47) |
| Rear | [1] 1.4 (35) |
| Golf, GTI & Jetta | |
| Front | 2.4 (60) |
| Rear | [2] |
| Passat | |
| Front | |
| Right | 2.0 (50) |
| Left | 1.4 (35) |
| Rear | .8 (20) |
| Vanagon | |
| Front | 2.8 (70) |
| Rear | 1.0 (25) |

[1] – Measured from top of blade to left edge of glass.
[2] – Specification is not available from manufacturer.

## TESTING

Testing information is not available from manufacturer.

## REMOVAL & INSTALLATION

### FRONT WIPER MOTOR

**Removal (Cabriolet & Passat)** – Open hood, and unplug wiring connector. Pry linkage off motor crank arm. Remove 4 bolts and motor. DO NOT remove motor bracket when removing motor.

**Installation** – Check crank arm alignment by running motor and allowing arm to park. Crank arm should be at 20-degree angle to motor centerline. *See Fig. 1.* To complete installation, reverse removal procedure, installing left linkage rod first.

**Removal & Installation (Corrado & Fox)** – For removal and installation of wiper motor and components, refer to illustration. *See Fig. 2.*

**Removal (Golf, GTI & Jetta)** – Remove connecting linkage from motor crank arm. Unplug wiring connector. Mark position of wiper motor crank arm. Remove wiper motor crank arm and 3 mounting bolts. Slide motor out from beneath bracket, and remove motor.

**Installation** – Check crank arm alignment by running motor and allowing arm to park. Crank arm should be in line with motor centerline and linkage ball should point from motor. *See Fig. 1.* Reverse removal procedure to complete installation.

**Removal (Vanagon)** – Remove wipers, arms and shaft nuts. Remove glove box and instrument cluster. Remove wiper linkage rods by extending fully to passenger side. Unplug wiring connector. Remove wiper bracket bolts and bracket. Remove crank arm, 3 bolts and wiper motor.

**Installation** – Connect motor wiring, run motor and allow arm to park. Align crank arm and linkage rod as shown. *See Fig. 1.* Reverse removal procedure to install.

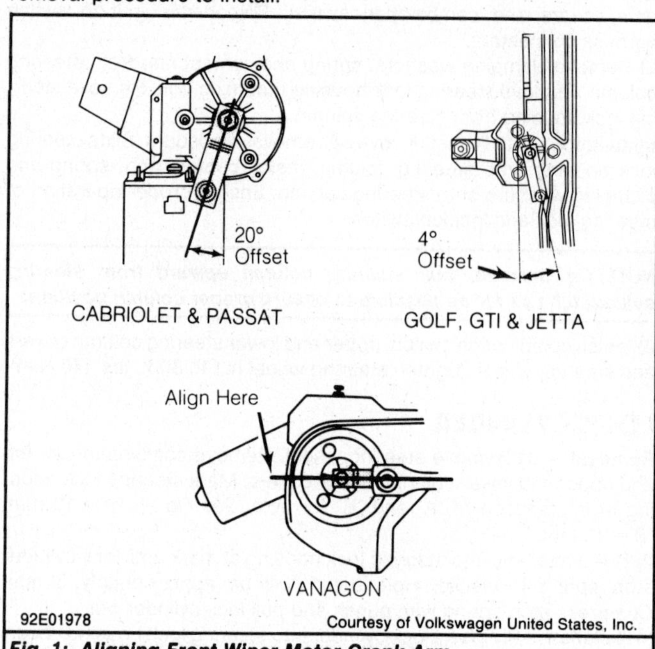


***Fig. 1: Aligning Front Wiper Motor Crank Arm***

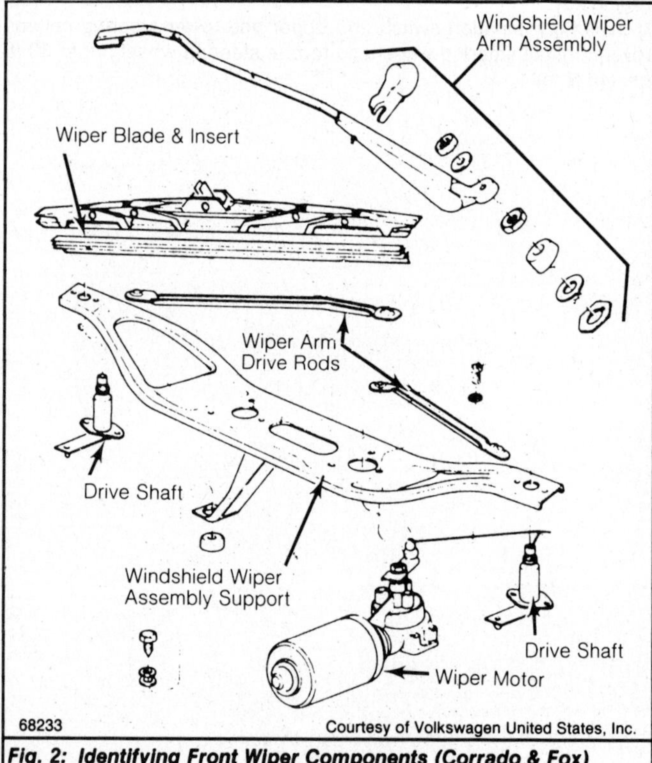


***Fig. 2: Identifying Front Wiper Components (Corrado & Fox)***

### REAR WIPER MOTOR

**Removal** – Remove inner trim panel on rear hatch. Unplug wiring connector, and pry linkage off motor crank arm. Remove motor crank arm, motor bolts and motor.

**Installation** – On Golf and GTI, check crank arm alignment by running motor and allowing arm to park. Install crank arm in correct position. *See Fig. 3.* On all models, ensure motor is in Park and install wiper blade arm. Reverse removal procedure to complete installation.

# 1991 SAFETY EQUIPMENT
# Wiper/Washer Systems (Cont.)

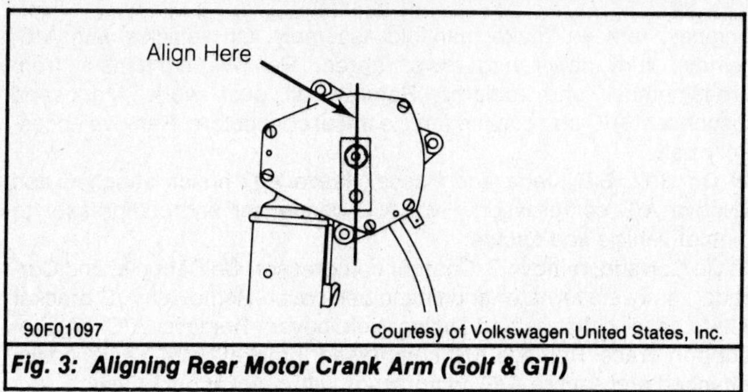


*Fig. 3: Aligning Rear Motor Crank Arm (Golf & GTI)*

## WIRING DIAGRAMS

See appropriate chassis wiring diagram in WIRING DIAGRAMS.

# 1991 ENGINES
# 1.8L & 2.0L 4-Cylinder

**Cabriolet, Corrado, Fox, Golf, GTI, Jetta, Passat**

***NOTE: For repair procedures not covered in this article, see ENGINE OVERHAUL PROCEDURES article in GENERAL INFORMATION.***

## ENGINE IDENTIFICATION

Engine identification number is stamped on a machined pad, left side of engine block, near distributor assembly (1.8L) or over crankcase ventilation area (2.0L). *See Fig. 1.* The first 2 characters (3 characters on Fox) designate engine code.

***ENGINE CODES***

| Application | Code |
|---|---|
| Cabriolet (1.8L 8-Valve) | JH |
| Corrado (1.8L 8-Valve) | PG |
| Fox (1.8L 8-Valve) | ABG |
| Golf & GTI (1.8L 8-Valve) | RV |
| Jetta (1.8L 8-Valve) | |
| Except Carat (Federal) | RV |
| Carat (Federal) | PF |
| GTI, Jetta GLi & Passat (2.0L 16-Valve) | 9A |

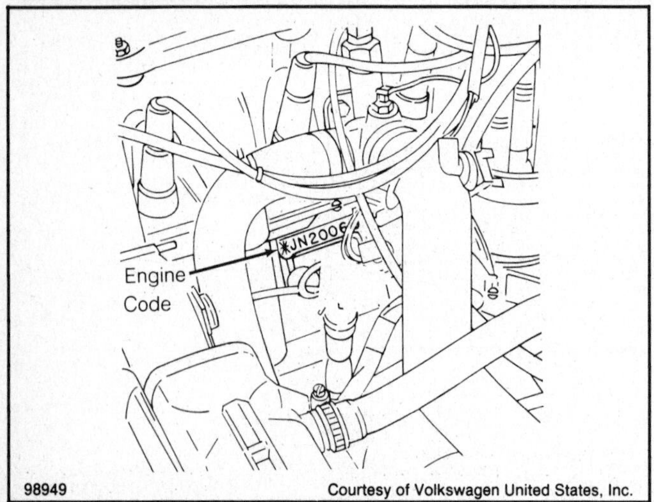


***Fig. 1: Locating Engine Identification Number***

## ADJUSTMENTS

### HYDRAULIC LIFTER (CAM FOLLOWER) TEST

To determine weak or noisy lifter, position camshaft lobe high point upward. Using a piece of wood, push cam follower down. *See Fig. 3 or 4.* If cam follower moves down more than .004" (.10 mm), replace cam follower. If cam follower moves less than .004" (.10 mm), cam follower is okay. Repeat procedure for remaining cam followers.

## REMOVAL & INSTALLATION

***NOTE: Match mark engine mounts to ensure original alignment position after installation. On vehicles with Power Steering (P/S), remove P/S unit with hoses attached and secure out of way.***

### FUEL PRESSURE RELEASE

On models with Digifant fuel injection, remove fuel pump relay (located in fuse/relay panel. Crank engine for 5 seconds. Reinstall fuel pump relay. On models with CIS-E fuel injection, apply 12 volts to cold start injector valve for 3-5 seconds.

### ENGINE

**Removal (Except Fox) – 1)** Disconnect and remove battery. Open fuel tank fill cap and radiator cap. Remove intake air duct. On 16-valve engines, remove intake manifold assembly. On vehicles with A/C, remove trim panel and lower apron. Remove condenser from crossmember and radiator. Remove all duct work. Mark and disconnect A/C and cooling fan electrical connectors. Remove accessory belts.

**2)** On Golf, GTI, Jetta and Passat, leave A/C hoses attached and remove A/C compressor. Pivot A/C condenser and compressor to side of vehicle and secure.

**3)** On Corrado, remove G-Charger compressor. On Cabriolet and Corrado, remove alternator and timing belt cover. Remove 3 A/C bracket Allen head bolts behind timing belt cover. Remove A/C bracket support brace. Remove A/C compressor bracket bolts. Leave hoses attached and secure A/C compressor with bracket out of way.

**4)** On all models, open heater controls. Remove cooling hose from thermostat housing flange and drain coolant. Remove thermostat housing flange. Mark and remove all cooling system hoses.

**5)** On Golf, GTI, Jetta and Passat, remove grille from radiator support. Disconnect electrical connectors at radiator support. Remove radiator-to-support bolts. Remove radiator support using care not damage headlights. Remove radiator, fan and shroud assembly.

**6)** On all models, remove axle shafts from transaxle. See FWD AXLE SHAFTS article. Mark and disconnect shift linkage and speedometer cable. Mark and remove electrical connectors and vacuum hoses. Disconnect throttle, cruise and kickdown cables. On Golf, Jetta GLi and Passat, leave fuel lines connected and remove cold start injector and warm-up regulator.

**7)** On all models, remove fuel injectors. Remove rear engine mount. Remove complete transaxle mount. On Cabriolet and Corrado, remove right front tire assembly. Remove right and left engine mount through bolts.

**8)** On all models, install engine sling on engine lift hooks. Carefully raise engine and transaxle out of vehicle. Separate transaxle from engine.

**Installation – 1)** To install, reverse removal procedure. Engine alignment adjustment is necessary whenever engine is removed or mounts are loosened. To adjust, loosen through bolt on engine mount "A". Loosen transmission transaxle mount "B" bolts. Loosen front engine mount and bracket. *See Fig. 2.*

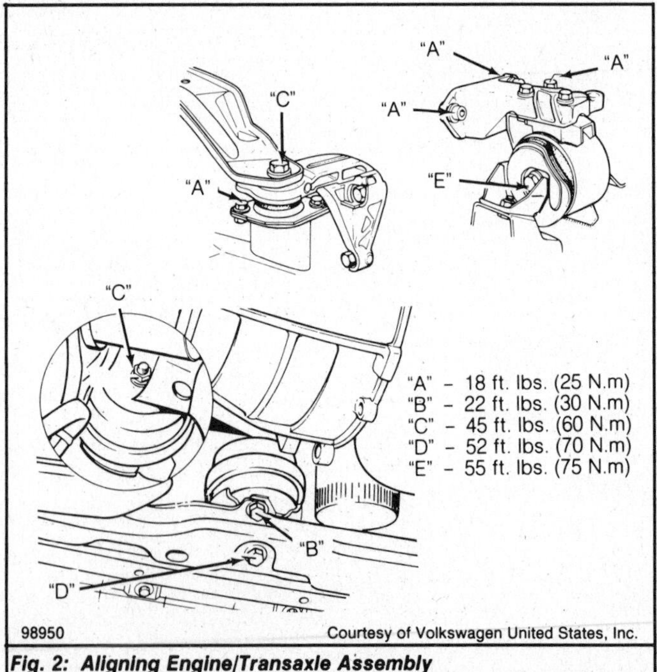


***Fig. 2: Aligning Engine/Transaxle Assembly***

**2)** Lightly rock engine and transaxle to allow position to shift as necessary. Evenly tighten mount bolts in reverse order of loosening. Fill fluids to proper level. Adjust clutch pedal (if equipped). Tighten all bolts and nuts to specification. See TORQUE SPECIFICATIONS table at end of article.

**Removal (Fox)** - **1)** Disconnect negative battery cable. Open heater valve. Drain radiator. Remove fan, shroud and radiator. Remove M/T clutch cable (if equipped).

**2)** Mark and disconnect electrical wiring and vacuum hoses. Disconnect throttle, cruise and kickdown linkage. Remove fuel injectors. Remove charcoal canister and set aside.

**3)** Remove 3 upper engine-to-transaxle bolts. Remove left and right engine mount nuts. Disconnect and remove starter. Remove 2 lower engine-to-transaxle bolts. Remove transaxle inspection cover plate. Disconnect exhaust inlet pipe support and separate inlet pipe from exhaust manifold.

**4)** Support transaxle. Attach engine sling to engine lifting hooks. Raise engine/transaxle until engine clears engine mounts. Ensure transaxle is supported. Remove remaining engine-to-transaxle bolts. Lift and separate engine from vehicle without transaxle.

**Installation** - Lubricate transaxle main shaft splines and contact area between clutch release bearing and clutch pressure plate with molybdenum disulphide grease. DO NOT lubricate guide sleeve for clutch release bearing. To complete installation, reverse removal procedure. DO NOT reuse self-locking nuts. Ensure engine mounts are installed to original location. Tighten engine mounts and subframe bolts to specification with engine running at idle. See TORQUE SPECIFICATIONS table at end of article.

## INTAKE MANIFOLD

Removal and installation procedure is not available from manufacturer. See TORQUE SPECIFICATIONS table at end of article.

## EXHAUST MANIFOLD

Removal and installation procedure is not available from manufacturer. See TORQUE SPECIFICATIONS table at end of article.

## CYLINDER HEAD

**Removal** - **1)** Removal and installation procedure is not available from manufacturer. Cylinder head may be removed with engine in vehicle. Match mark all components for installation reference. Remove timing belt. See TIMING BELT under REMOVAL & INSTALLATION. *See Fig. 3 or 4.*

**2)** Remove cylinder head bolts in reverse sequence of installation. *See Fig. 5.* Replace cylinder head bolts after loosening or removing.

**Inspection** - Thoroughly clean all gasket mating surfaces. Check cylinder head for warpage. Maximum warpage is .004" (.10 mm). Check minimum head height and replace cylinder (if necessary). The 1.8L cylinder head can be machined. DO NOT machine 2.0L (16-valve) cylinder head.

***NOTE: DO NOT reuse antifreeze after replacing cylinder block, cylinder head, head gasket, radiator and/or heater core.***

**Installation** - **1)** Ensure "OBEN" marking on cylinder head gasket faces up. Install gasket on cylinder block. Do not use any type of sealant. Carefully position cylinder head on cylinder. Install head bolts No. 9 and 10 hand tight to ensure cylinder head position. Install remaining head bolts hand tight.

**2)** Tighten cylinder head bolts (in 3 steps) in sequence to specification. *See Fig. 5.* See TORQUE SPECIFICATIONS table at end of article. No further information is available from manufacturer.

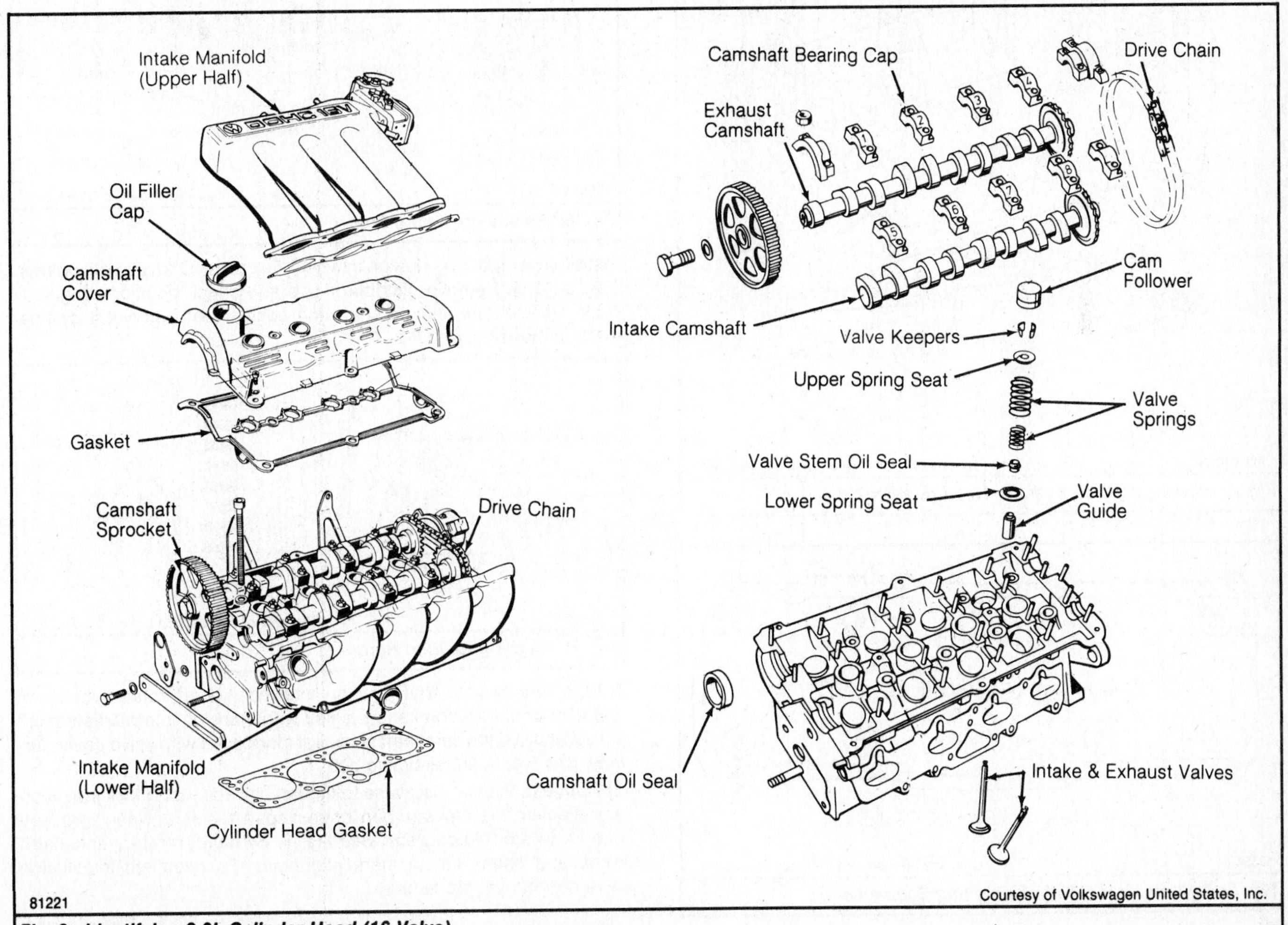


***Fig. 3: Identifying 2.0L Cylinder Head (16-Valve)***

# 1991 ENGINES
# 1.8L & 2.0L 4-Cylinder (Cont.)

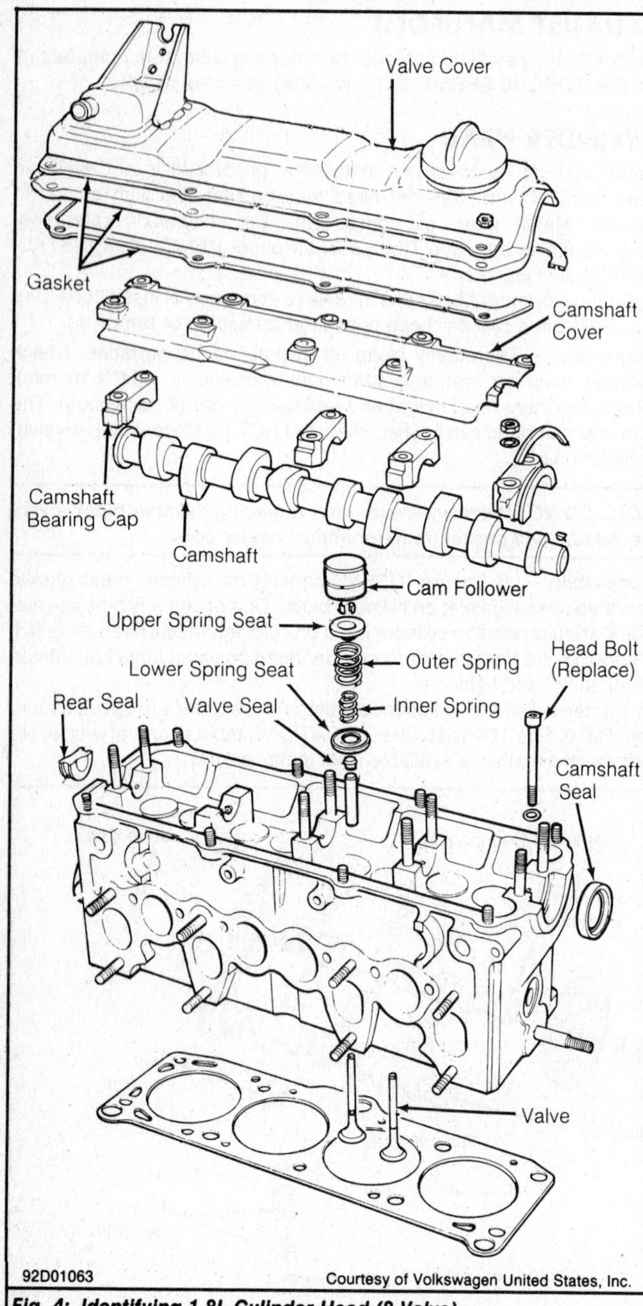


*Fig. 4: Identifying 1.8L Cylinder Head (8-Valve)*

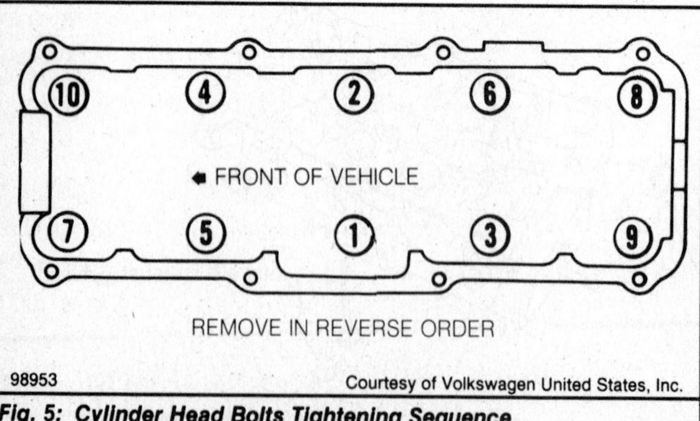


*Fig. 5: Cylinder Head Bolts Tightening Sequence*

## FRONT COVER OIL SEAL

**Removal** – Remove timing belt. See TIMING BELT under REMOVAL & INSTALLATION. Rotate inner part of Oil Seal Extractor (2085) outward 2 turns and tighten set screw. *See Fig. 11.* Lubricate threaded area of extractor and push in as far as possible. Loosen set screw and turn inner part of extractor until oil seal is removed.

**Installation** – Lubricate outer edge and lip of new seal. Place guide sleeve from Seal Installer (3083) onto crankshaft. Push oil seal over guide sleeve. Press seal completely into position. To complete installation, reverse removal procedure.

## TIMING BELT

**Removal (All Models)** – Information is not available from manufacturer. Match mark all components to ensure reassembly to original position. *See Fig. 6.* DO Not turn crankshaft without belt attached, valve damage may result.

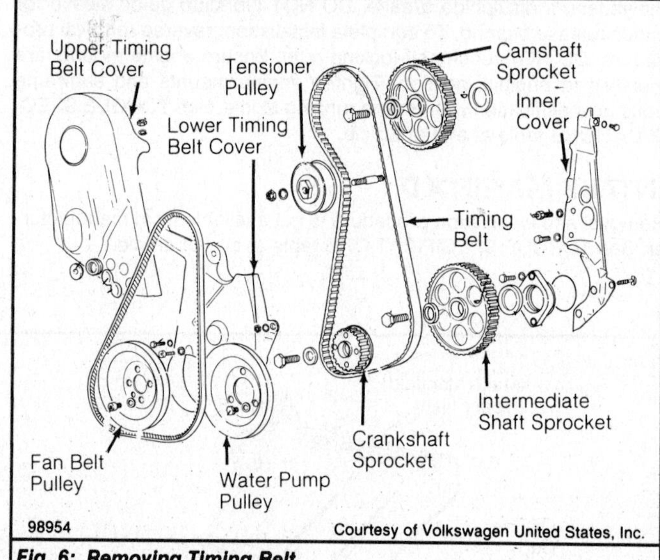


*Fig. 6: Removing Timing Belt*

**Installation (1.8L)** – **1)** Align flywheel/flex plate "O" mark with pointer. This is TDC. Remove distributor cap and check position of ignition rotor. Rotate intermediate shaft and position rotor at No. 1 cylinder mark on housing. *See Fig. 7.*

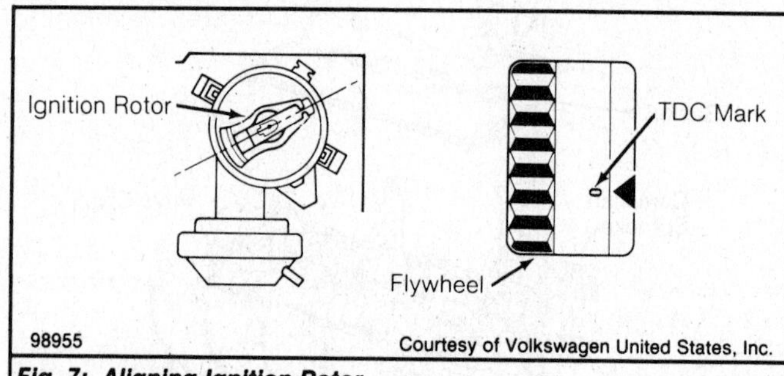


*Fig. 7: Aligning Ignition Rotor*

**2)** With intermediate shaft/ignition rotor positioned, rotate crankshaft and align mark on crankshaft pulley with mark on intermediate shaft sprocket. Position camshaft sprocket mark even with valve cover surface. *See Fig. 8.* Install timing belt.

**3)** Rotate tensioner clockwise to tighten belt and install lock nut. Proper deflection is achieved when longest span of belt between sprockets can be twisted 90 degrees. *See Fig. 9.* By hand, rotate crankshaft 2 turns and check timing mark alignment. To complete installation, reverse removal procedure.

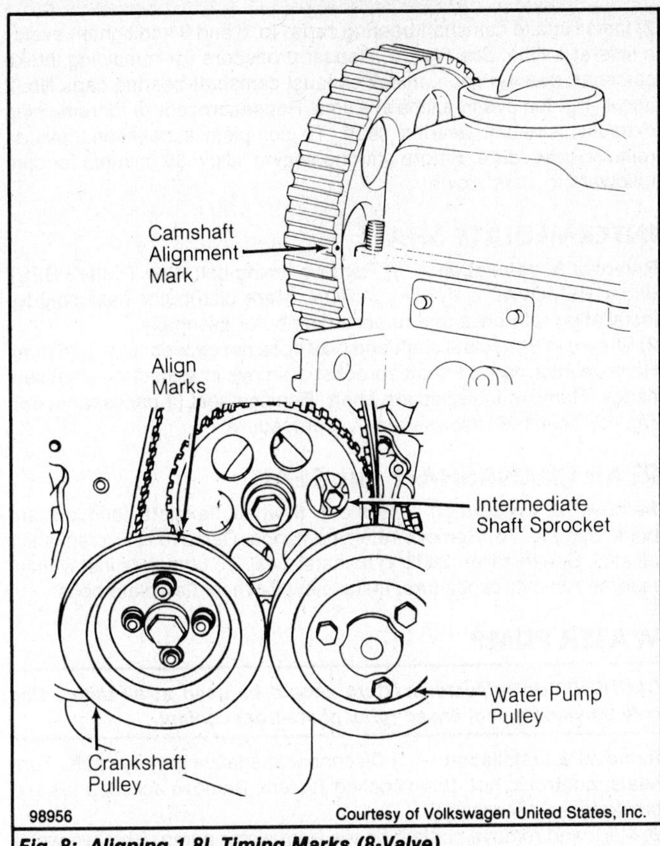

***Fig. 8: Aligning 1.8L Timing Marks (8-Valve)***

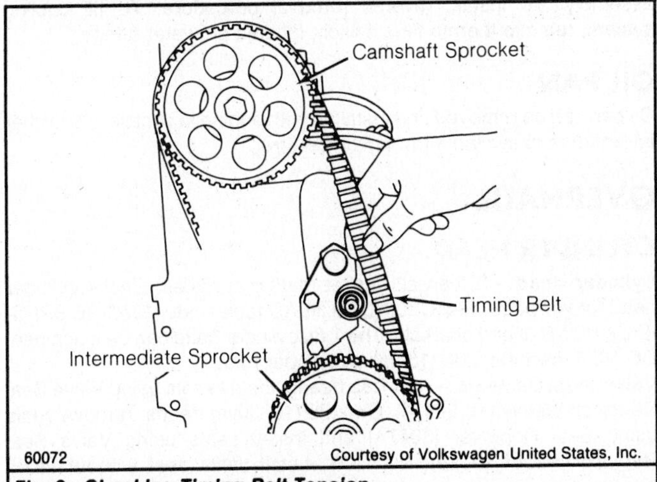


***Fig. 9: Checking Timing Belt Tension***

**Installation (2.0L)** – **1)** Install timing belt around crankshaft and intermediate shaft sprockets. Install lower timing belt cover. Install vibration damper, noting offset holes.

**2)** If valve cover is installed, mark on front of camshaft sprocket must align with mark on valve cover. If valve cover is removed, place camshaft sprocket mark even with valve cover surface. *See Fig. 10.*

**3)** Align vibration damper mark with mark on lower timing belt cover. *See Fig. 10.* Install timing belt around camshaft sprocket. Install Timing Belt Tension Scale (VW 210). To tension belt, rotate belt tensioner clockwise until tension scale reads 13-14. By hand, rotate crankshaft 2 turns and check timing mark alignment. To complete installation, reverse removal procedure.

## CAMSHAFT OIL SEAL

**Removal** – **1)** Remove upper timing belt cover. Place crankshaft at TDC with No. 1 cylinder on compression stroke. Remove timing belt

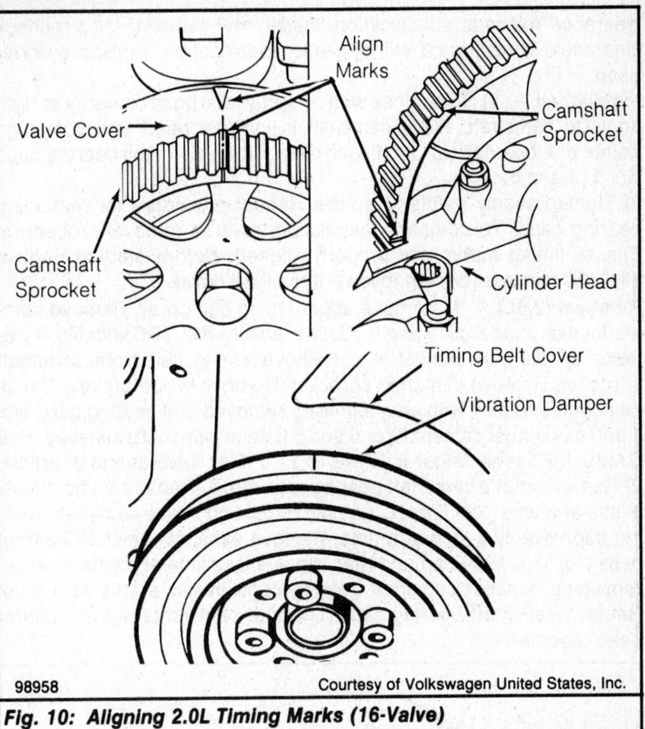


***Fig. 10: Aligning 2.0L Timing Marks (16-Valve)***

from camshaft sprocket. Remove camshaft sprocket. Remove Woodruff key. Install camshaft sprocket bolt and washer until washer is tight against camshaft.

**2)** Rotate inner part of Oil Seal Extractor (2085) outward 2 turns and tighten set screw. *See Fig. 11.* Lubricate threaded area of extractor and push in as far as possible. Loosen set screw and turn inner part of extractor until oil seal is removed.

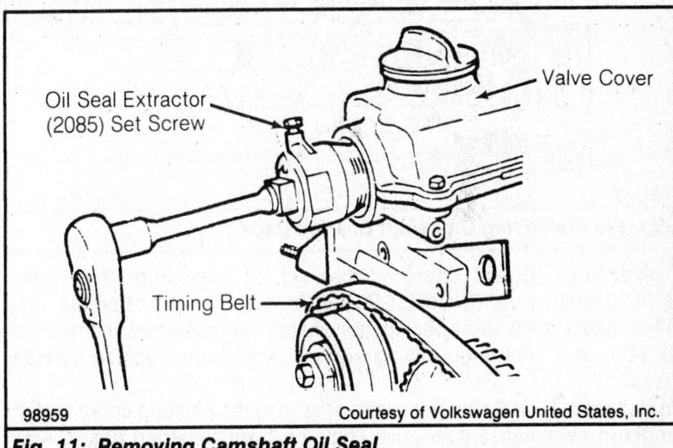


***Fig. 11: Removing Camshaft Oil Seal***

**Installation** – Coat new seal seat and lips lightly with engine oil. On 1.8L engines, using Installer (10-203), install seal until flush. On 2.0L engines, use Special Hex Head Bolt (10-203/1) to press seal into place. To complete installation, reverse removal procedure.

## CAMSHAFT

**Removal (1.8L)** – **1)** Remove upper timing belt cover. *See Fig. 6.* Remove valve cover. Place crankshaft at TDC with No. 1 cylinder on compression stroke. Remove timing belt from camshaft sprocket. Remove camshaft sprocket. Remove Woodruff key. Check camshaft end play with cam followers removed and bearing caps No. 1 and 5 installed. See CAMSHAFT table under ENGINE SPECIFICATIONS at end of article.

**2)** Remove bearing caps No. 1, 3 and 5 evenly a little at a time. Repeat for remaining caps. Remove camshaft.

**Inspection** – Check camshaft bearing oil clearance. See CAMSHAFT table under ENGINE SPECIFICATIONS at end of article. If oil

# 1991 ENGINES
# 1.8L & 2.0L 4-Cylinder (Cont.)

clearance exceeds specification, install new camshaft and recheck clearance. If clearance still exceeds specification, replace cylinder head.

**Installation** - **1)** On engines with oil spray jets, position spray at right angle to camshaft. Place camshaft in cylinder head with both high points of lobes, for No. 1 cylinder facing upward. Install bearing caps No. 1, 3 and 5.

**2)** Tighten evenly a little at a time. Repeat procedure for remaining bearing caps. To complete installation, reverse removal procedure. Ensure timing marks are properly aligned. Before starting engine, allow 30 minutes for cam followers to bleed down.

**Removal (2.0L)** - **1)** Remove upper timing belt cover. Remove camshaft cover. *See Figs. 3 and 6.* Place crankshaft at TDC with No. 1 cylinder on compression stroke. Remove timing belt from camshaft sprocket. Remove camshaft sprocket. Remove Woodruff key. Check camshaft end play with cam followers removed and bearing caps No. 1 and 4 (exhaust camshaft) or 5 and 8 (intake camshaft) installed. See CAMSHAFT table under ENGINE SPECIFICATIONS at end of article.

**2)** Remove intake camshaft bearing caps No. 5, 7 and rear cap evenly a little at a time. *See Fig. 12.* Loosen remaining intake camshaft bearing caps evenly a little at a time. Remove exhaust camshaft bearing caps No. 1, 3, front cap and rear cap evenly a little at a time. Loosen remaining exhaust camshaft bearing caps evenly a little at a time. Remove camshaft bearing caps. Lift both camshafts out of cylinder head together.

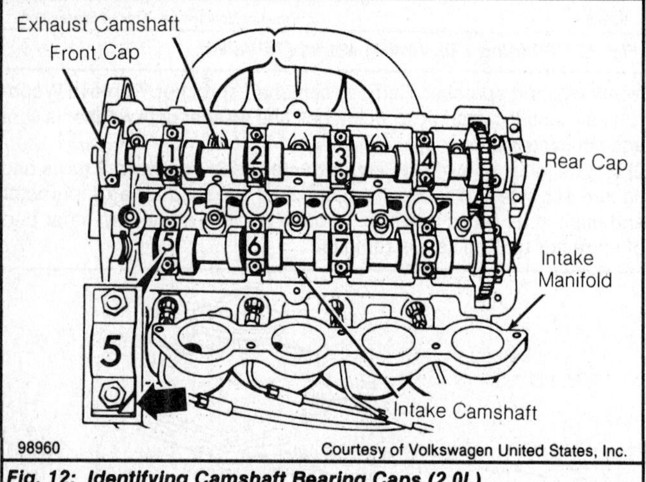


*Fig. 12: Identifying Camshaft Bearing Caps (2.0L)*

**Inspection** - Check camshaft bearing oil clearance. See CAMSHAFT table under ENGINE SPECIFICATIONS at end of article. If oil clearance is not within specification, install new camshaft and recheck clearance. If clearance still exceeds specification, replace cylinder head.

**Installation** - **1)** On engines with oil spray jets, position spray at right angle to camshaft. Place drive chain on both camshaft gears. Align matching marks on gears and place both camshafts in cylinder head. *See Fig. 13.*

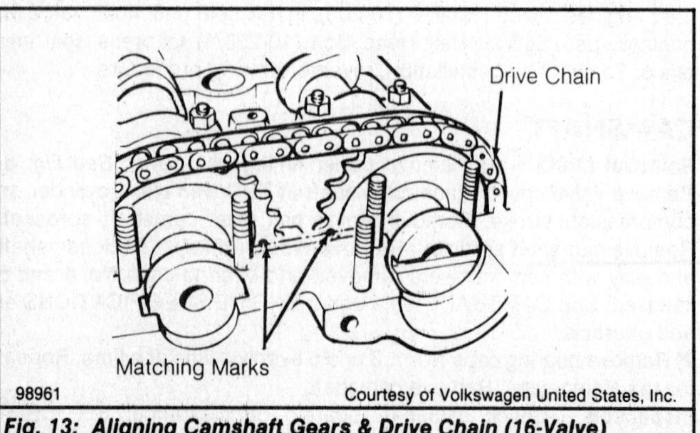


*Fig. 13: Aligning Camshaft Gears & Drive Chain (16-Valve)*

**2)** Install intake camshaft bearing caps No. 6 and 8 and tighten evenly a little at a time. *See Fig. 12.* Repeat procedure for remaining intake camshaft bearing caps. Install exhaust camshaft bearing caps No. 2 and 4. Tighten evenly a little at a time. Repeat procedure for remaining exhaust camshaft bearing caps. To complete installation, reverse removal procedure. Before starting engine, allow 30 minutes for cam followers to bleed down.

## INTERMEDIATE SHAFT

**Removal & Installation** - **1)** Remove timing belt. See TIMING BELT under REMOVAL & INSTALLATION. Mark distributor assembly for installation reference and remove distributor assembly.

**2)** Ensure intermediate shaft end play does not exceed .010" (.25 mm). Remove intermediate shaft sprocket. Remove intermediate shaft seal flange. Remove intermediate shaft. Replace seal (if necessary). *See Fig. 16.* To install, reverse removal procedure.

## REAR CRANKSHAFT OIL SEAL

**Removal & Installation** - Remove flywheel/flexplate, and discard bolts. *See Fig. 16.* Remove retaining flange. Remove rear crankshaft oil seal. Use Installer (2003/1) to install seal. To complete installation, reverse removal procedure. Install new flywheel/flex plate bolts.

## WATER PUMP

***CAUTION: Coolant/water mixture should be used at all times. Use only ethylene glycol based (phosphate-free) coolant.***

**Removal & Installation** - **1)** Disconnect negative battery cable. Turn heater control to hot. Drain cooling system. Remove accessories and brackets (as necessary).

**2)** Mark and remove coolant hoses from water pump. Remove water pump pulley. *See Fig. 8.* Remove bolts and remove water pump assembly. To install, reverse removal procedure. To fill cooling system, remove thermo time switch, located on water flange.

## OIL PAN

Oil pan can be removed and installed with engine in vehicle. No further information is available from manufacturer.

# OVERHAUL

## CYLINDER HEAD

**Cylinder Head** - Clean all gasket mating surfaces. Check cylinder head for warpage. See CYLINDER HEAD table under ENGINE SPECIFICATIONS at end of article. The 1.8L cylinder head can be machined. DO NOT machine 2.0L (16-valve) cylinder head.

**Valve Stem Oil Seals** - On 1.8L heads, install seals using Valve Seal Replacer/Sleeve (10-204/A). On 2.0L (16-valve) heads, remove seals using Seal Remover (3047A) and install seals using Valve Seal Replacer/Sleeve (3129). DO NOT install valve seal without using sleeve.

**Valve Springs** - No information is available from manufacturer.

**Valve Guides** - Check valve-to-guide clearance specification. See CYLINDER HEAD table under ENGINE SPECIFICATIONS at end of article. To replace valve guide, press guide out from combustion chamber side. Press guide in cold cylinder head as far as guide will go. DO NOT exceed one ton pressure. Ream guides to proper valve-to-guide clearance. See CYLINDER HEAD table under ENGINE SPECIFICATIONS at end of article.

**Valve Seats** - **1)** Check valve seats before any other cylinder head service. Insert the valve and hold firmly against the valve seat. Measure valve stem tip-to-cylinder head distance. *See Fig. 14.*

**2)** This measurement determines installed valve height. Subtract measured distance from minimum specification. See VALVE INSTALLED HEIGHT table.

# 1991 ENGINES
# 1.8L & 2.0L 4-Cylinder (Cont.)

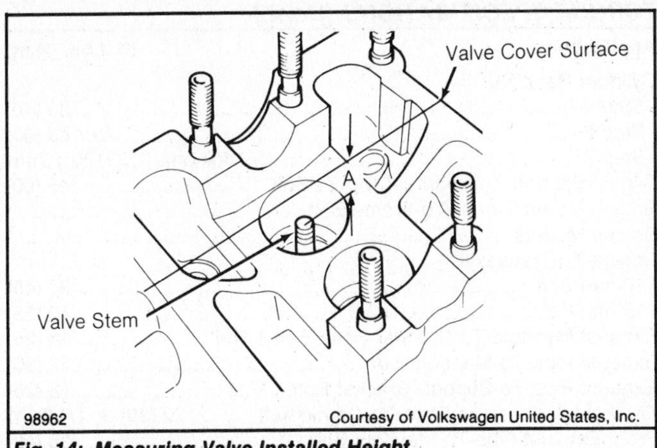


*Fig. 14: Measuring Valve Installed Height*

***VALVE INSTALLED HEIGHT***

| Application | In. (mm) |
|---|---|
| 1.8L | |
| Intake Valve | 1.330 (33.78) |
| Exhaust Valve | 1.342 (34.09) |
| 2.0L | |
| Intake Valve | [1] |
| Exhaust Valve | [1] |

[1] - DO NOT remove more than .078" (2.0 mm) of material from valve and/or valve seat.

**3)** The difference is maximum refacing allowable for valve and seat. If valve installed height is too high, replace cylinder head assembly. If valve installed height is too low or too high, cam followers will not work correctly.

**Valves** - Measure valve stem diameter and valve margin. If not within specification, replace valves. DO NOT reface exhaust valves (or intake valves on 2.0L engines) with machine. Lap valves by hand or replace as necessary. See VALVES & VALVE SPRINGS table under ENGINE SPECIFICATIONS at end of article.

## CYLINDER BLOCK ASSEMBLY

**Piston & Rod Assembly** - **1)** Make sure piston, rod and rod caps are marked with matching cylinder number prior to removal. Ensure engine front arrow is marked on top of piston. *See Fig. 15*. Pistons and rods are to be replaced in sets of 4. Rod cap bolts and nuts must be replaced after removing or loosening.

**2)** Mark piston in relation to pin. Remove circlips from ends of pin bore. Use Piston Pin Replacer/Installer (VW 207C) to remove and install piston pin. If pin is too tight, heat piston to 140°F (60°C). Ensure rod is properly positioned with piston. *See Fig. 15*.

**Fitting Pistons** - Measure clearances with cylinder block supported on work bench. Check clearance of piston-to-cylinder bore. Piston diameter is stamped on top of piston in millimeters.

***PISTON-TO-CYLINDER BORE DIMENSIONS***

| Size | Piston Diameter In. (mm) | Cylinder Bore In. (mm) |
|---|---|---|
| 1.8L | | |
| Standard | 3.188 (80.98) | 3.189 (81.01) |
| 1st Over | 3.198 (81.23) | 3.199 (81.26) |
| 2nd Over | 3.208 (81.48) | 3.209 (81.51) |
| 2.0L | | |
| Standard | 3.245 (82.43) | 3.248 (82.51) |
| 1st Over | 3.257 (82.73) | 3.258 (82.76) |
| 2nd Over | 3.267 (82.98) | 3.268 (83.01) |

**Piston Rings** - Measure ring end gap. Measure ring side clearance with piston. If not within specification, replace as necessary. See PISTONS, PINS & RINGS table under ENGINE SPECIFICATIONS at end of article. Install rings on piston with TOP mark facing upward.

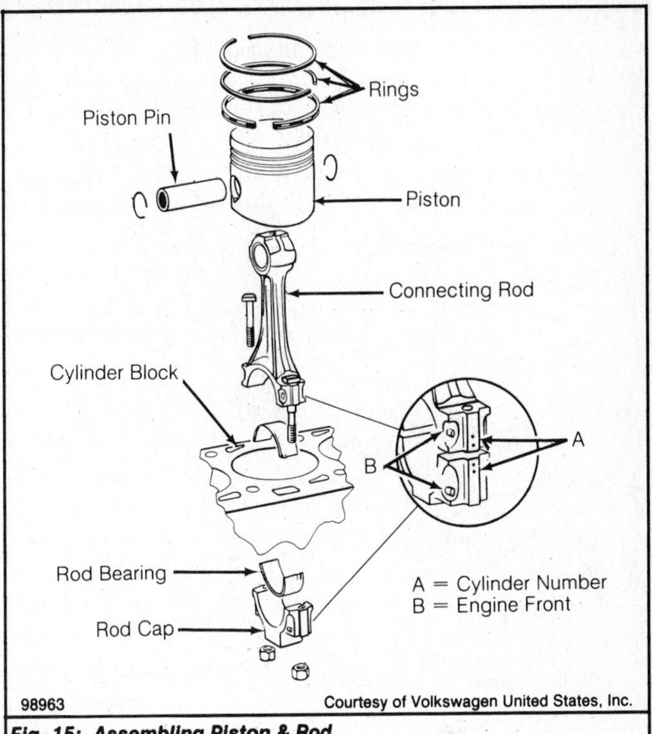


*Fig. 15: Assembling Piston & Rod*

Recessed edge on outside of center ring must face piston pin (down). Position ring ends. *See Fig. 15*.

**Rod Bearings** - Mark rod caps for reinstallation. Use Plastigage to measure bearing clearances. Measure connecting rod side play. Replace or machine as necessary. See CRANKSHAFT, MAIN & CONNECTING ROD BEARINGS table under ENGINE SPECIFICATIONS at end of article. Tighten evenly to specification in several steps. See TORQUE SPECIFICATIONS table at end of article.

**Crankshaft & Main Bearings** - Main bearing caps are marked with matching journal for installation in original position. *See Fig. 16*. Measure crankshaft end play. See THRUST BEARING.

**Thrust Bearing** - Insert feeler gauge between No. 3 main bearing and crankshaft thrust face to measure end play. *See Fig. 16*. Replace thrust bearing as necessary. See CRANKSHAFT, MAIN & CONNECTING ROD BEARINGS table under ENGINE SPECIFICATIONS at end of article.

**Cylinder Block** - Measure cylinder block while supported on work bench. Check cylinder bore for wear, out-of-round and taper. Check cylinder block for warpage. See CYLINDER BLOCK table under ENGINE SPECIFICATIONS at end of article.

# ENGINE OILING

## ENGINE LUBRICATION SYSTEM

**Crankcase Capacity** - See CRANKCASE CAPACITY table.

***CRANKCASE CAPACITY***

| Model | With Filter Replacement | Without Filter Replacement |
|---|---|---|
| Fox | 3.7 Qts. (3.5L) | 3.2 Qts. (3.0L) |
| All Others | 4.3 Qts. (4.1L) | 3.7 Qts. (3.5L) |

**Oil Pressure** - Check oil pressure with engine at warm operating temperature. Minimum oil pressure at idle is 4.3 psi (.3 kg/cm²). Minimum oil pressure at 2000 RPM is 29 psi (2.0 kg/cm²).

## OIL PUMP

**Removal & Installation** - Remove oil pan. Remove oil pump attaching bolts and remove oil pump assembly. To install, reverse removal procedure.

# 1991 ENGINES
# 1.8L & 2.0L 4-Cylinder (Cont.)

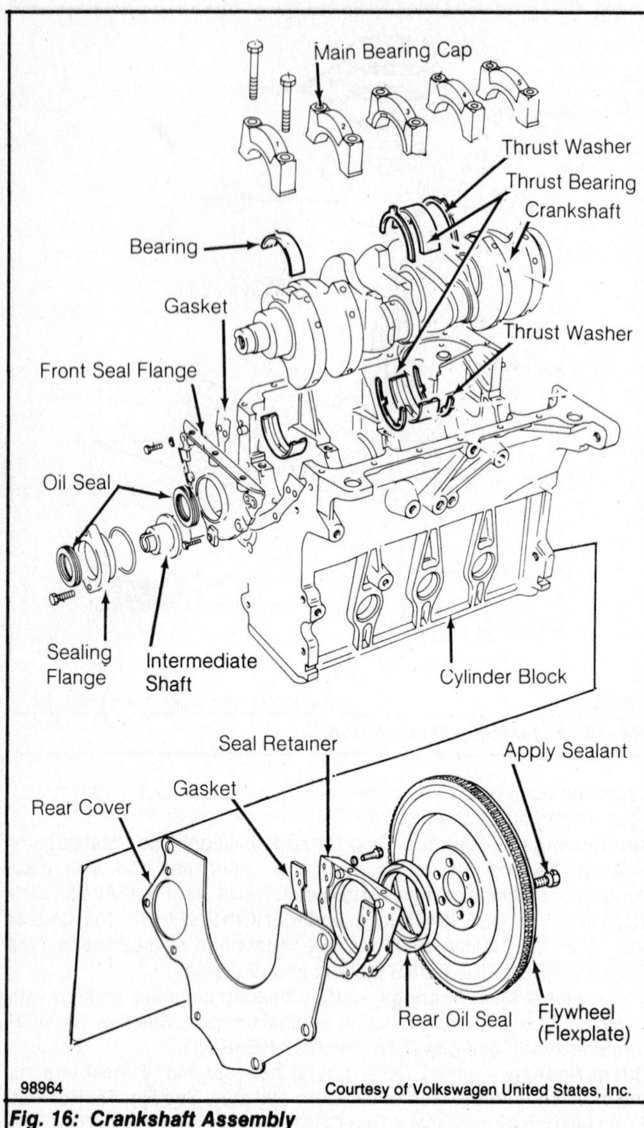


*Fig. 16: Crankshaft Assembly*

**Inspection** – Check oil pump backlash and oil pump axial play. If not within specification, replace oil pump assembly. See OIL PUMP SPECIFICATIONS table.

### OIL PUMP SPECIFICATIONS

| Application | In. (mm) |
|---|---|
| Backlash | |
| New | .002 (.05) |
| Limit | .008 (.20) |
| Axial Play Limit | .006 (.15) |

## TORQUE SPECIFICATIONS

### TORQUE SPECIFICATIONS

| Application | Ft. Lbs. (N.m) |
|---|---|
| A/C Bracket-To-Engine Bolt | 22 (30) |
| Axle Shaft-To-Transaxle Drive Flange Bolt | 33 (45) |
| Camshaft Bearing Cap Bolt | 15 (20) |
| Camshaft Drive Gear Bolt (2.0L) | |
| GTI & Jetta GLi | 60 (80) |
| Passat | 48 (65) |
| Clutch Cover Bolt | 15 (20) |
| Crankshaft Main Bearing Cap Bolt | 50 (65) |
| Crankshaft Timing Sprocket Bolt | 66 (90) + 1/2 Turn |

### TORQUE SPECIFICATIONS (Cont.)

| Application | Ft. Lbs. (N.m) |
|---|---|
| Cylinder Head Nut | |
| Step 1 | 30 (40) |
| Step 2 | 45 (60) |
| Step 3 | Additional 1/2 (180°) Turn |
| Engine Bracket-To-Hydraulic Mount Bolt | 45 (60) |
| Engine Mount Carrier-To-Frame Bolt | [1] |
| Engine Mounts | [1] |
| Engine-To-Transaxle | |
| 10-mm Bolt | 33 (45) |
| 12-mm Bolt | 40 (55) |
| Exhaust Manifold-To-Cylinder Head Bolt & Nut | 18 (25) |
| Exhaust Pipe-To-Manifold Nut | 22 (30) |
| Exhaust Pipe-To-Support Bracket Bolt | 18 (25) |
| Flywheel or Pressure Plate-To-Crankshaft | 22 (30) + 1/4 Turn |
| Front Exhaust Pipe-To-Manifold Bolt | 30 (40) |
| G-Charger Pulley Bolt | 18 (25) |
| G-Charger-To-Block | 25 (35) |
| Intake Manifold | 18 (25) |
| Intermediate Shaft Sprocket Bolt | 60 (80) |
| Knock Sensor | 15-18 (20-25) |
| Lower Pulley Bolt | 15 (20) |
| Oil Pan Bolt | 15 (20) |
| Oil Pan Drain Plug | 22 (30) |
| Oil Pump Cover Bolt | |
| Short | 7 (10) |
| Long | 15 (20) |
| Rod Bearing Cap Nut | 22 (30) + 1/4 Turn |
| Starter Mount Bolt | 18 (25) |
| Timing Belt Tensioner Nut | 33 (45) |
| Torque Converter-To-Carrier Plate Bolt | 22 (30) |
| Water Pump Pulley Bolt | 15 (20) |
| Water Pump Housing-To-Engine Bolt | 15 (20) |
| | **INCH Lbs. (N.m)** |
| Piston Oil Jet Nozzle | 84 (10) |
| Transaxle/Engine Cover Plate Bolt | 84 (10) |
| Valve Cover Retaining Nut | 84 (10) |
| Water Pump-To-Housing | 84 (10) |

[1] – *See Fig. 2.*

## ENGINE SPECIFICATIONS

### GENERAL SPECIFICATIONS

| Application | Specification |
|---|---|
| **1.8L** | |
| Displacement | 109 Cu. In. (1.8L) |
| Bore | 3.19" (81.0 mm) |
| Stroke | 3.40" (86.4 mm) |
| Compression Ratio | |
| Cabriolet | 8.5:1 |
| Corrado | 8.0:1 |
| Fox | 9.0:1 |
| Golf, GTI & Jetta | 10.0:1 |
| Fuel System | |
| Cabriolet | Digifant |
| Corrado | CIS-E |
| Fox | |
| California | Digifant I |
| Federal | Digifant II |
| Golf, GTI & Jetta | Digifant |
| Horsepower @ RPM | |
| Cabriolet | 90 @ 5500 |
| Corrado | 158 @ 5600 |
| Fox | 81 @ 5500 |
| Golf, GTI & Jetta | |
| Engine Code PF | 105 @ 5400 |
| Engine Code RV | 100 @ 5400 |

# 1991 ENGINES
# 1.8L & 2.0L 4-Cylinder (Cont.)

## GENERAL SPECIFICATIONS

| Application | Specification |
|---|---|
| **1.8L (Cont.)** | |
| Torque Ft. Lbs @ RPM | |
| Cabriolet | 102 @ 3000 |
| Corrado | 166 @ 4000 |
| Fox | 93 @ 3250 |
| Golf, GTI & Jetta | |
| Engine Code PF | 114 @ 3800 |
| Engine Code RV | 109 @ 3800 |
| **2.0L** | |
| Displacement | 121 Cu. In. (2.0L) |
| Bore | 3.25" (82.5 mm) |
| Stroke | 3.65" (92.8 mm) |
| Compression Ratio | 10.0:1 |
| Fuel System | CIS-E |
| Horsepower @ RPM | 134 @ 5800 |
| Torque Ft. Lbs @ RPM | 133 @ 4400 |

## CRANKSHAFT, MAIN & CONNECTING ROD BEARINGS

| Application | In. (mm) |
|---|---|
| Crankshaft | |
| End Play | |
| Standard | .003-.008 (.07-.17) |
| Service Limit | .010 (.25) |
| Runout | .001 (.03) |
| Main Bearings | |
| Journal Diameter | 2.124-2.125 (53.96-53.98) |
| Journal Out-Of-Round | .001 (.03) |
| Journal Taper | .001 (.03) |
| Oil Clearance | |
| Standard | .001-.003 (.03-.08) |
| Service Limit | .007 (.17) |
| Connecting Rod Bearings | |
| Journal Diameter | 1.880-1.881 (47.76-47.78) |
| Journal Out-Of-Round | .001 (.03) |
| Journal Taper | .001 (.03) |
| Oil Clearance | |
| Except Passat | .002-004 (.05-.10) |
| Passat | .0004-002 (.01-.06) |

## CYLINDER HEAD

| Application | Specification |
|---|---|
| Cylinder Head Height | |
| 1.8L (Minimum) | 5.22" (132.60 mm) |
| 2.0L (Minimum) | 4.65" (118.10 mm) |
| Maximum Warpage | .004" (1.00 mm) |
| Valve Seats | |
| Intake Valve | |
| Seat Angle | 45° |
| Seat Width | |
| 1.8L | .078" (2.00 mm) |
| 2.0L | .060-.070" (1.50-1.80 mm) |
| Exhaust Valve | |
| Seat Angle | 45° |
| Seat Width | |
| Except Fox | .070-.078" (1.80-2.00 mm) |
| Fox | .094" (2.40 mm) |
| Valve Guides | |
| Intake Valve | |
| Valve Guide Installed Height | [1] |
| Oil Clearance | [2] .039" (1.0 mm) |
| Exhaust Valve | |
| Valve Guide Installed Height | [1] |
| Valve Stem-to-Guide Oil Clearance | [2] .051" (1.3 mm) |

[1] – Valve guide shoulder flush with cylinder head.
[2] – New valve installed in cylinder head. Dial indicator used to measure valve rock in guide.

## PISTONS, PINS & RINGS

| Application | In. (mm) |
|---|---|
| Pistons | |
| Clearance | .0016 (.040) |
| Diameter | |
| 1.8L | 3.187 (80.96) |
| 2.0L | 3.245-3.247 (82.44-82.48) |
| Pins | |
| Diameter | .787 (20.00) |
| Piston Fit | Interference |
| Rod Fit | Interference |
| Rings | |
| No. 1 | |
| End Gap | |
| Standard | .012-.018 (.30-.45) |
| Service Limit | .040 (1.0) |
| Side Clearance | |
| Standard | .001-.002 (.02-.05) |
| Service Limit | .006 (.15) |
| No. 2 | |
| End Gap | |
| Standard | .012-.018 (.30-.45) |
| Service Limit | .040 (1.0) |
| Side Clearance | .001-.002 (.02-.05) |
| No. 3 (Oil) | |
| End Gap | |
| Standard | .010-.018 (.25-.45) |
| Service Limit | .040 (1.0) |
| Side Clearance | .001-.002 (.02-.05) |

## VALVES & VALVE SPRINGS

| Application | Specification |
|---|---|
| **1.8L** | |
| Intake Valves | |
| Face Angle | 45° |
| Head Diameter | 1.496" (38.00 mm) |
| Length | |
| Except Corrado | 3.58" (91.0 mm) |
| Corrado | 3.60" (91.4 mm) |
| Minimum Margin | [1] |
| Stem Diameter | .314" (7.97 mm) |
| Exhaust Valves | |
| Face Angle | 45° |
| Head Diameter | 1.300" (33.00 mm) |
| Length | |
| Cabriolet & Fox | 3.57" (90.8 mm) |
| Corrado | 3.60" (91.4) |
| Minimum Margin | [2] |
| Stem Diameter | .313" (7.95 mm) |
| **2.0L** | |
| Intake Valves | |
| Face Angle | 45° |
| Head Diameter | 1.25" (32.0 mm) |
| Length | 3.76" (95.5 mm) |
| Minimum Margin | [2] |
| Stem Diameter | .274" (6.97 mm) |
| Exhaust Valves | |
| Face Angle | 45° |
| Head Diameter | 1.10" (28.0 mm) |
| Length | 3.87" (98.2 mm) |
| Minimum Margin | [2] |
| Stem Diameter | .273" (7.95 mm) |

[1] – No information is available from manufacturer.
[2] – DO NOT machine valve; hand lap only.

# 1991 ENGINES
# 1.8L & 2.0L 4-Cylinder (Cont.)

## CYLINDER BLOCK

| Application | In. (mm) |
|---|---|
| Cylinder Bore | |
| Standard Diameter | |
| 1.8L | 3.189 (81.01) |
| 2.0L | 3.248 (82.51) |
| Maximum Taper | .0016 (.04) |
| Maximum Out-of-Round | .001 (.03) |

## CAMSHAFT

| Application | In. (mm) |
|---|---|
| End Play | .006 (.15) |
| Oil Clearance | .004 (.01) Maximum |

## CONNECTING RODS

| Application | In. (mm) |
|---|---|
| Bore Diameter | |
| Pin Bore | .787 (20.00) |
| Crankpin Bore | 1.992 (50.60) |
| Center-To-Center Length | 5.669 (144.00) |
| Side Play | |
| Except Passat | .014 (.37) |
| Passat | .002-.012 (.05-.13) |

# 1991 ENGINES
# 2.1L Opposed 4-Cylinder

### Vanagon

***NOTE:** For repair procedures not covered in this article, see ENGINE OVERHAUL PROCEDURES article in GENERAL INFORMATION.*

## ENGINE IDENTIFICATION

Engine code and number is stamped on right crankcase below breather. The first 2 characters designate engine code.

*ENGINE IDENTIFICATION CODE*

| Application | Code |
|---|---|
| 2.1L | MV |

## ADJUSTMENTS

### VALVE CLEARANCE ADJUSTMENT

***NOTE:** Engine uses adjustable hydraulic valve lifters. Lifters require adjustment only if rocker arms have been removed or adjuster setting has been changed.*

**1)** Place No. 1 cylinder at TDC on compression stroke. Distributor rotor will align with mark on distributor housing. Loosen adjuster lock nut on intake valve rocker arm of cylinder No. 1.

**2)** Turn adjusting screw clockwise until it contacts valve stem. Turn adjusting screw clockwise an additional 2 turns, and tighten lock nut. Repeat procedure for exhaust valve.

**3)** Rotate crankshaft counterclockwise 180 degrees. Adjust valve clearance of cylinder No. 4 as described in step **2)**. Use same procedure to adjust cylinders No. 3 and 2, respectively, rotating crankshaft 180 degrees between adjustment of each cylinder.

**4)** Install rocker arm cover and new gasket. Start engine and let idle until no lifter noise is heard. Replace lifters if oil level and pressure is normal and lifters are noisy.

## REMOVAL & INSTALLATION

### FUEL PRESSURE RELEASE

Remove fuel pump relay from fuse/relay panel. Crank engine 3-5 seconds. Reinstall fuel pump relay.

### BLEEDING COOLING SYSTEM

**1)** Set heater control valve to maximum heat. Open control valve for auxiliary heater (if equipped) under rear seat. Remove radiator grille and raise front of vehicle about 16". Open bleeder screw on upper right corner of radiator. *See Fig. 1.*

**2)** Open bleeder valve in engine compartment (turn counterclockwise). *See Fig. 1.* Fill expansion tank until full. Start and run engine at 2000 RPM. Keep topping tank until coolant flows from bleeder screw on radiator without any air bubbles. Add coolant until tank is full, and install cap on tank.

**3)** Turn engine off and restart after 20 seconds. Open expansion tank cap with engine running at 2000 RPM. Close bleeder screw on radiator when coolant is flowing out. Add coolant to expansion tank until full, and close tank tightly.

**4)** Close bleeder valve in engine compartment. Switch engine off. Top off refill tank to maximum mark. Pressure check cooling system with engine running until cooling fan has cycled.

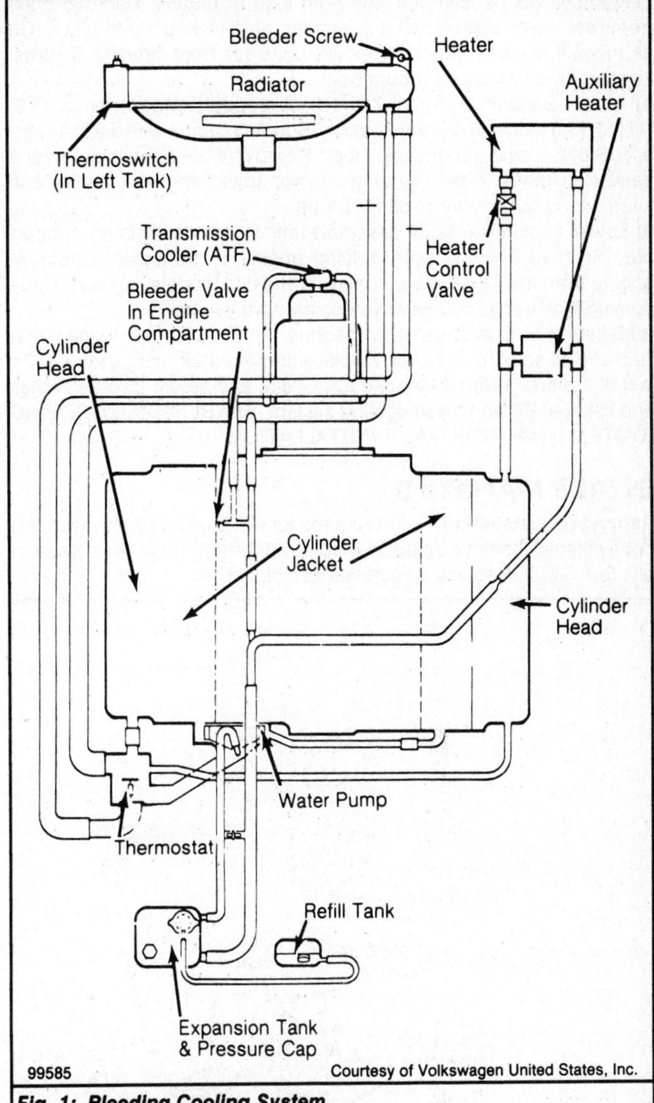


***Fig. 1: Bleeding Cooling System***

### ENGINE

***NOTE:** For reassembly reference, label all electrical connectors, vacuum hoses and fuel lines before removal. Place mating marks on major assemblies before removal.*

**Removal - 1)** Disconnect negative battery cable. Remove air cleaner with airflow sensor and air intake duct. Disconnect wires from alternator. Disconnect wiring from fuel injectors, throttle valve switch and auxiliary air regulator.

**2)** Disconnect 2 vacuum hoses from charcoal filter valve. Disconnect and plug fuel return line at pressure regulator and fuel line from fuel pump at "T" fitting. Remove throttle cable from throttle valve lever. On automatic transaxle models, remove snap ring and spring from throttle rod.

**3)** On all models, mark and disconnect coil lead and wiring plug at distributor, wiring at oxygen sensor, oil pressure switch, temperature sensor and temperature sender. Disconnect wiring to coolant level warning switch, located in expansion tank. Mark and disconnect ground leads on top left side of crankcase. *See Fig. 2.*

**4)** Clamp off both radiator hoses at thermostat housing. Clamp off both heater hoses at right rear side of engine compartment. Open expansion tank cap. Remove drain plugs at bottom of cylinder heads, and drain coolant. Disconnect coolant hoses from expansion tank at engine end. Remove expansion tank.

**5)** Disconnect brake booster vacuum line at check valve. Remove 2 upper bolts and nuts holding engine to transaxle. On models with automatic transaxle, remove 3 bolts attaching torque converter to drive plate. Access bolts through hole on top of transaxle housing. Remove rod from kickdown lever.

**6)** On all models, disconnect wiring at starter. On models with power steering, remove power steering pump with hoses attached. Secure pump in engine compartment. On models with A/C, remove compressor with hoses attached. Secure compressor in engine compartment.

# 1991 ENGINES
# 2.1L Opposed 4-Cylinder (Cont.)

**7)** Remove plates from left and right side of engine. Remove bolts from rear cover plate located at muffler, and leave plate in place. On all models, loosen transaxle mount bolts for front bracket 3 turns. Loosen lower transaxle mount bolt.
**8)** Attach Support Bar (VW 785/1B) so support pad is about 4.75" (120.0 mm) below transaxle housing. Support engine with Jack Adapter (US 612/5) and transmission jack. Remove 4 bolts retaining engine carrier at frame. While lowering engine, adjust angle of engine and keep wiring out of way of oil filler tube.
**9)** Lower engine/transaxle assembly until transaxle rests on support bar. Remove 2 lower nuts holding engine to transaxle. Separate engine from transaxle. On automatic transaxle models, secure torque converter in transaxle. Remove engine from vehicle.
**Installation** - Check release bearing and replace if necessary. Replace all self-locking nuts. Replace coolant drain plug gaskets. To install, reverse removal procedure. Check and adjust throttle cables and linkage. Fill and bleed cooling system. See BLEEDING COOLING SYSTEM under REMOVAL & INSTALLATION.

## INTAKE MANIFOLD

**Removal & Installation** - Procedures for removal and installation are not available. Remove intake manifold and throttle valve as an assembly. *See Fig. 2*. Replace all gaskets at installation.

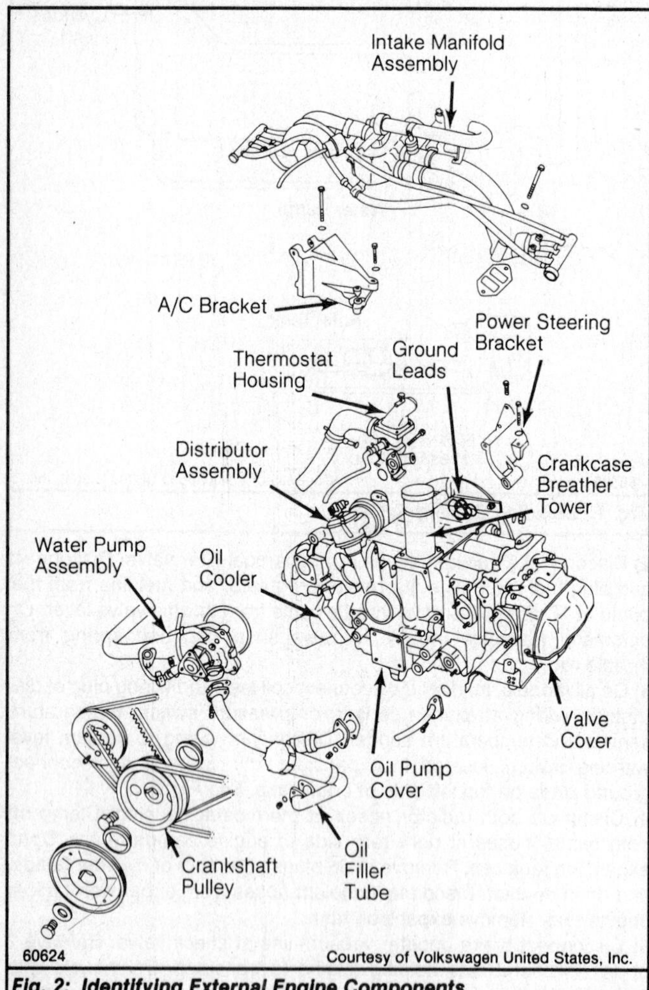


*Fig. 2: Identifying External Engine Components*

## EXHAUST MANIFOLD

**Removal & Installation** - Procedures for removal and installation are not available. *See Fig. 3*. Replace all gaskets at installation. Place metal surface of gaskets against cylinder head.

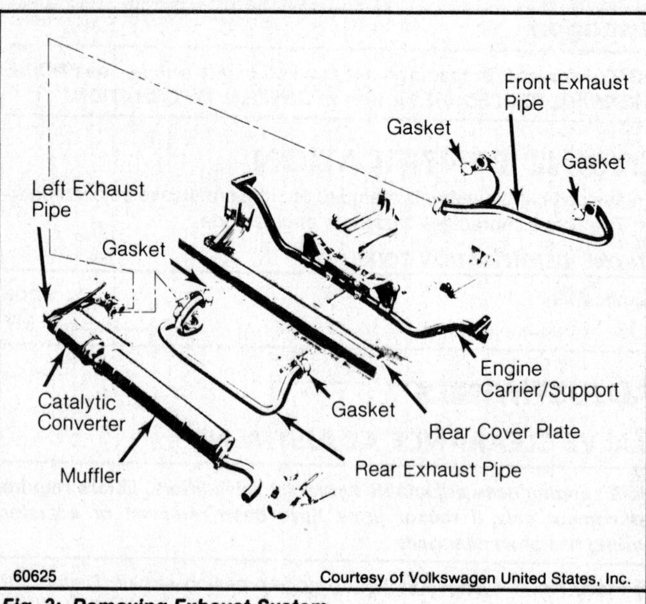


*Fig. 3: Removing Exhaust System*

## CYLINDER HEAD

***NOTE: Cylinder head may be removed with engine installed.***

**Removal** - **1)** Remove rocker arm cover. Loosen rocker arm retaining nuts so tension is relieved evenly. Remove intake manifold assembly.
**2)** Remove expansion tank cap and drain plugs under cylinder heads. Drain cooling system. Disconnect coolant hoses at cylinder head. Remove front and rear exhaust pipes from cylinder head. Remove push rods and keep in order for reassembly.
**3)** Remove 8 cap nuts holding cylinder head to block. Gradually loosen nuts in reverse order of tightening sequence. *See Fig. 4*. Remove cylinder head and gasket. Remove push rod tubes. Remove metal sealing ring and thin Green "O" ring from cylinder sleeve.

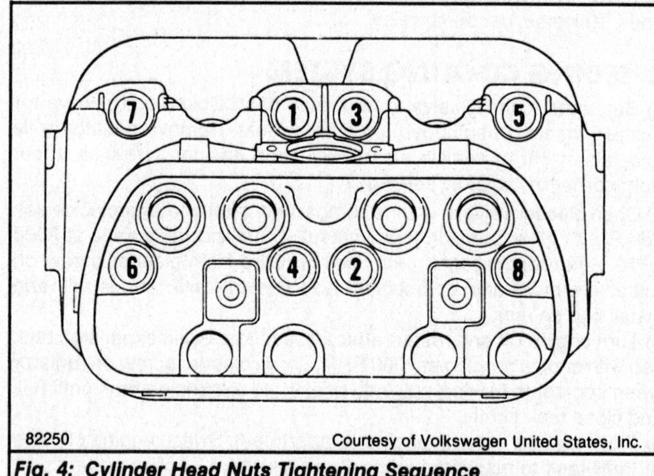


*Fig. 4: Cylinder Head Nuts Tightening Sequence*

**Installation** - **1)** Ensure push rod tube is about 7.64" (194.0 mm) long between inside edges of tube sealing "O" rings. *See Fig. 5*. Seam of tube faces upward and small end of tube faces cylinder head. Always use new sealing rings and thoroughly clean mating surfaces.

# 1991 ENGINES
# 2.1L Opposed 4-Cylinder (Cont.)

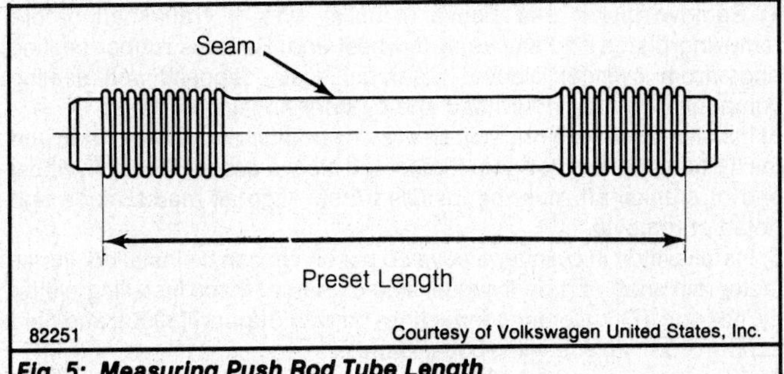


*Fig. 5: Measuring Push Rod Tube Length*

**2)** Clean cylinder head sealing surface. Install new thin Green "O" ring and metal gasket on cylinder sleeves. Apply a 1-2 mm bead of Sealing Compound (VW No. D 000 400) to center of new water jacket gasket.

***CAUTION: Using too much sealant may plug cylinder head cooling passages. Install cylinder head within 45 minutes after applying sealant.***

**3)** Coat sealing face of cap nuts with waterproof sealant. Install and snug cap nut at No. 1 stud to hold cylinder head in place. Install remaining cap nuts. Tighten cap nuts (in sequence) to 84 INCH lbs. (10 N.m). *See Fig. 4*. Make sure push rod tubes are correctly seated.
**4)** Tighten cap nuts in 2 steps (in sequence) to final torque of 37 ft. lbs. (50 N.m). Install push rods, ensuring push rods fit into cups of lifters. Install rocker assembly with slots facing upward on shaft supports. Adjust hydraulic lifters after tightening rocker arm assembly nuts. See VALVE CLEARANCE ADJUSTMENT under ADJUSTMENTS. Install rocker cover with new gasket.
**5)** Install remaining parts in reverse order of removal. Use new exhaust flange gaskets with metal surface toward head. Always use new locking nuts. Fill and bleed cooling system. See BLEEDING COOLING SYSTEM under REMOVAL & INSTALLATION.

## CRANKSHAFT FRONT SEAL

**Removal** - **1)** Loosen A/C compressor or power steering pump (if equipped). Remove drive belts from crankshaft pulley. Loosen alternator and remove drive belt.
**2)** Remove coolant expansion tank and set aside. Remove screws and bolts from exhaust heat shield. Move heat shield down and away from installed position. Rotate pulley until alignment holes are horizontal.
**3)** Insert Alignment Plate (3149) into pulley. *See Fig. 6*. Place Pad (3149) across engine mounts to hold pulley in place. Remove crankshaft pulley bolt and pulley. Pry out seal.

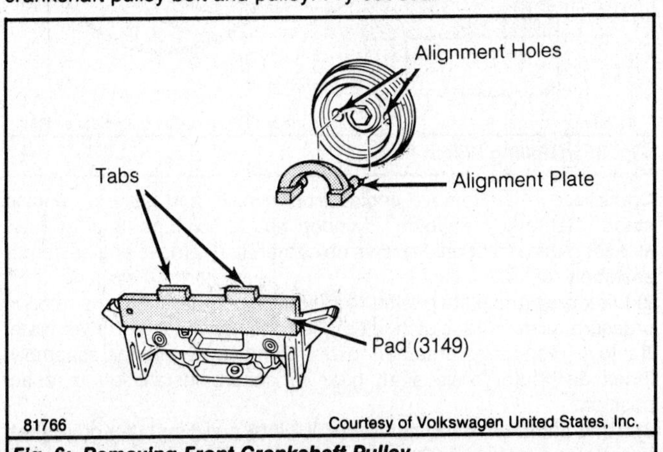


*Fig. 6: Removing Front Crankshaft Pulley*

**Installation** - Coat seal with oil. Install seal with Seal Installer (3088) and bolt without washer. Tighten bolt until stop is reached. Reverse removal procedure to install pulley.

## ROCKER ARM ASSEMBLY

***NOTE: Hydraulic valve lifters must be adjusted whenever rocker shafts have been removed and installed.***

**Removal & Installation** - Remove rocker arm cover and gasket. Gradually remove rocker arm shaft nuts. Check adjusting screw surfaces for wear or damage. Ensure threads of adjusting screws and lock nuts move freely. To install, reverse removal procedure. Adjust lifters. See VALVE CLEARANCE ADJUSTMENT under ADJUSTMENTS.

## REAR MAIN BEARING OIL SEAL

**Removal & Installation** - **1)** Remove flywheel or drive plate and pry out seal. Clean seating area for seal. Remove "O" ring from inside lip of flywheel. Check pilot bearing felt ring for damage.
**2)** Lightly oil seal and install on Seal Installer Guide (VW 191A). Attach Seal Installer Base (VW 191B) to crankshaft. Press seal and guide in until seal seats. Lightly lubricate new "O" ring and install into flywheel or drive plate. Install flywheel or drive plate.

## WATER PUMP

**Removal** - Remove expansion tank cap. Drain coolant at drain plugs on bottom of cylinder heads. Remove drive belt(s). Disconnect all hoses to water pump and thermostat housings. Remove water pump and thermostat housing as an assembly.
**Installation** - **1)** Clean all sealing surfaces and replace gaskets. Install water pump and thermostat housing assembly. Tighten bolts and nuts. See TORQUE SPECIFICATIONS table at end of article. Attach hoses and tighten clamps.
**2)** Install drive belt. Apply thumb pressure to belt, and adjust belt deflection to 3/8-9/16" (10-15 mm). Fill and bleed cooling system. See BLEEDING COOLING SYSTEM under REMOVAL & INSTALLATION.

# OVERHAUL

## CYLINDER HEAD

**Cylinder Head** - Information is not available from manufacturer.

***NOTE: Minor cracks between valve seats or between seat and spark plug thread are acceptable. Cracks may not exceed .019" (.50 mm) in width. Cracks may not extend beyond first coil of plug thread.***

**Valve Springs** - Compress spring retainer and springs. Remove keepers, and release spring compressor. Remove retainer and both inner and outer springs. Ensure springs are of equal length. To install, reverse removal procedure.
**Valve Guides** - **1)** Measure valve stem-to-guide clearance with dial indicator pointer on head of valve. Rock valve back and forth and note reading. Maximum clearance is .047" (1.20 mm). If guides are to be replaced, securely mount head in drill press with combustion chambers down.
**2)** Carefully use step drill to remove shoulder of valve guide. Avoid cutting head or valve guide boss. Using drift, tap out remaining guide toward combustion chamber side. Install new guide with drift, from side opposite combustion chamber. Ream guides to fit valve stems.

***NOTE: DO NOT machine exhaust valves. They MUST be hand lapped to seats.***

**Valves** - Check valve dimensions. Minimum length from stem tip to face is 4.823" (122.50 mm). Valve margin must not be less than specification. See CYLINDER HEAD table under ENGINE SPECIFICATIONS at end of article.

# 1991 ENGINES
# 2.1L Opposed 4-Cylinder (Cont.)

## VALVE TRAIN

**Hydraulic Valve Lifters & Rocker Arms – 1)** Remove rocker arm covers. Remove rocker arm shaft assembly. Remove push rods. Remove lower cover plate. Remove push rod tube. Remove lifters. Keep lifters in order of removal to ensure proper installation.

**2)** Looking through lifter bores, inspect camshaft lobes. Ensure lifter moves freely in bore.

**3)** Check and bleed lifters before installing. Apply firm thumb pressure to push rod socket. Push rod socket should NOT move. If socket moves, remove lock ring. Remove push rod socket, plunger, check ball, spring, check valve retainer and plunger spring.

**4)** Fill valve body bore with oil up to bleed hole. Insert plunger spring, check valve retainer, check valve spring, ball and plunger. Push downward on plunger and at the same time open ball check valve with scribe.

**5)** Place push rod socket into position. Hold a small socket on top of push rod socket, and place assembly in vise with bleeder hole facing up. Slowly tighten vise and compress lifter. Install lock ring. Recheck lifter.

***CAUTION: Failure to install lifters in original location will cause premature camshaft failure.***

**6)** Lightly oil lifter body and slide into lifter bore. Replace push rod tube sealing rings at each end. Compress push rod tube and position in cylinder block with seam facing upward. Small end of tube must be toward cylinder head.

**7)** Release push rod tube and allow it to expand into position. Ensure tube seats properly. Install push rods and ensure push rods are seated in lifter, not on lifter edge.

**8)** Install rocker arm shaft assembly. Tighten nuts evenly. Adjust hydraulic valve lifters. See VALVE CLEARANCE ADJUSTMENT under ADJUSTMENTS.

## CRANKCASE, PISTON & CYLINDER SLEEVE ASSEMBLY

**Piston & Cylinder Sleeve – 1)** With cylinder heads removed, mark pistons and cylinder sleeves with matching numbers. Note cylinder sleeve position for installation reference. Place piston at TDC.

**2)** Using slide hammer and Clamping Puller (3092), pull out sleeve until piston pin snap ring is visible through hole in cylinder housing. Remove piston pin circlip. *See Fig. 7.*

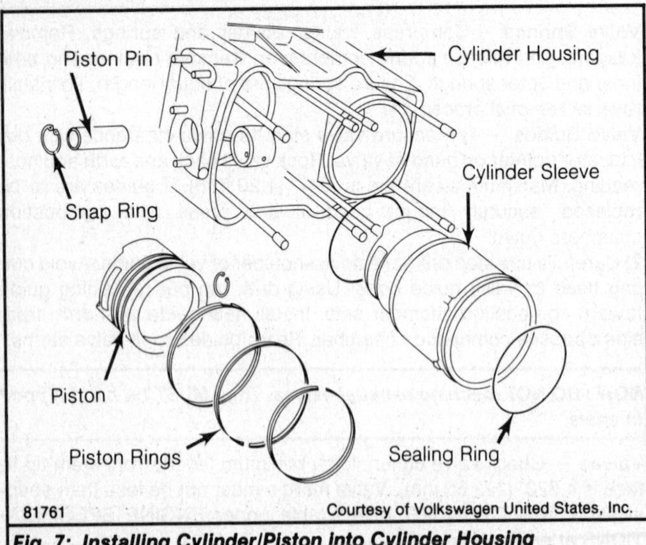


***Fig. 7: Installing Cylinder/Piston Into Cylinder Housing***

**3)** Using Piston Pin Puller/Installer (3091), remove piston pin. If piston pin cannot be pulled out, use Reamer (3159) to remove burr in piston pin bore. Remove piston and cylinder sleeve.

**4)** Remove piston and sleeve at pulley end of crankshaft before removing piston and sleeve at flywheel end. Remove rubber sealing rings from cylinder sleeve. Clean all scale deposits and sealing compound from cylinder head and cylinder housing surfaces.

**5)** Install new sealing rings on sleeve. Thick Black ring is inner ring and thin Green ring is outer ring. Piston and sleeve assemblies at flywheel end of crankshaft must be installed first. Align all marks made and noted at removal.

**6)** Install piston in cylinder sleeve so piston pin can be installed. Install piston pin snap ring on flywheel side of piston. Place installing piston cylinder on TDC. Center connecting rod with Support (3090), and hold support rod in place with rubber band.

**7)** Align connecting rod and piston. Install piston pin through access hole in cylinder housing with Piston Pin Puller/Installer (3091). Install piston pin snap ring. Ensure piston and rod move freely on pin. Push cylinder sleeve in until it seats in cylinder housing. To complete installation, reverse removal procedure.

**Fitting Pistons – 1)** Measure piston diameter at bottom of skirt, about 5/8" (15.0 mm) from edge and at 90 degrees to pin bore. Measure inside diameter of cylinder sleeve near top of sleeve. See PISTON, PINS & RINGS table under ENGINE SPECIFICATIONS at end of article.

**2)** Replace piston and/or cylinder sleeve as necessary. Arrow on piston top faces flywheel end. Size, weight and installation direction are marked on crown of piston. Weight group is indicated by "+" or "–" mark. Pistons marked "+" weigh 16.12-16.37 oz. (457-464 g). Pistons marked "–" weigh 15.80-16.08 oz. (448-456 g).

**Fitting Rings – 1)** Insert piston ring squarely into cylinder sleeve near bottom end. Using a feeler gauge, measure end clearance. See PISTON, PINS & RINGS table under ENGINE SPECIFICATIONS at end of article. If not within specification, replace as necessary.

**2)** Install rings on piston with TOP mark up. *See Fig. 8.* Using feeler gauge, measure piston ring side clearance. If clearance is not within specification, replace rings and/or pistons. See PISTON, PINS & RINGS table under ENGINE SPECIFICATIONS at end of article.

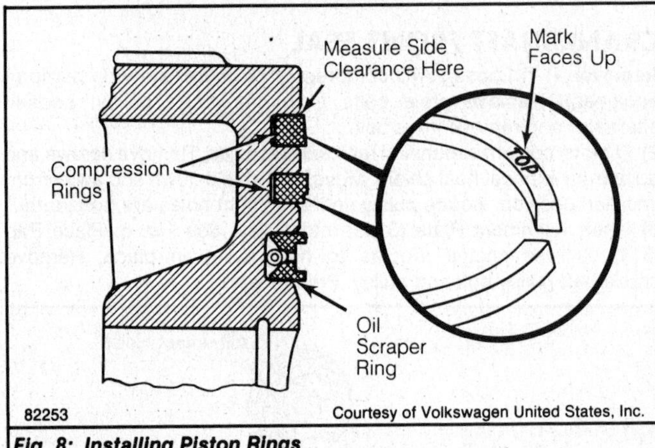


***Fig. 8: Installing Piston Rings***

**Crankcase – 1)** Remove engine from vehicle and place on engine stand. Remove manifolds, cylinder heads, pistons and cylinder sleeves. Note directional arrows on carrier, and remove engine carrier assembly.

**2)** Mark pressure plate position for installation reference, and remove pressure plate and clutch disc. Remove flywheel or drive plate. Remove crankcase breather tower. Remove distributor assembly. Index distributor drive shaft gear to ensure installation to exact position.

**3)** Using Shaft Remover/Installer (VW 228b), pull distributor drive shaft gear from crankcase. Remove 2 shims located at bottom end of distributor shaft gear and retain shims for installation. Remove water pump assembly. *See Fig. 1.* Remove thermostat housing. Remove oil filter and cooler. Pry out front and rear crankshaft seals.

# 1991 ENGINES
# 2.1L Opposed 4-Cylinder (Cont.)

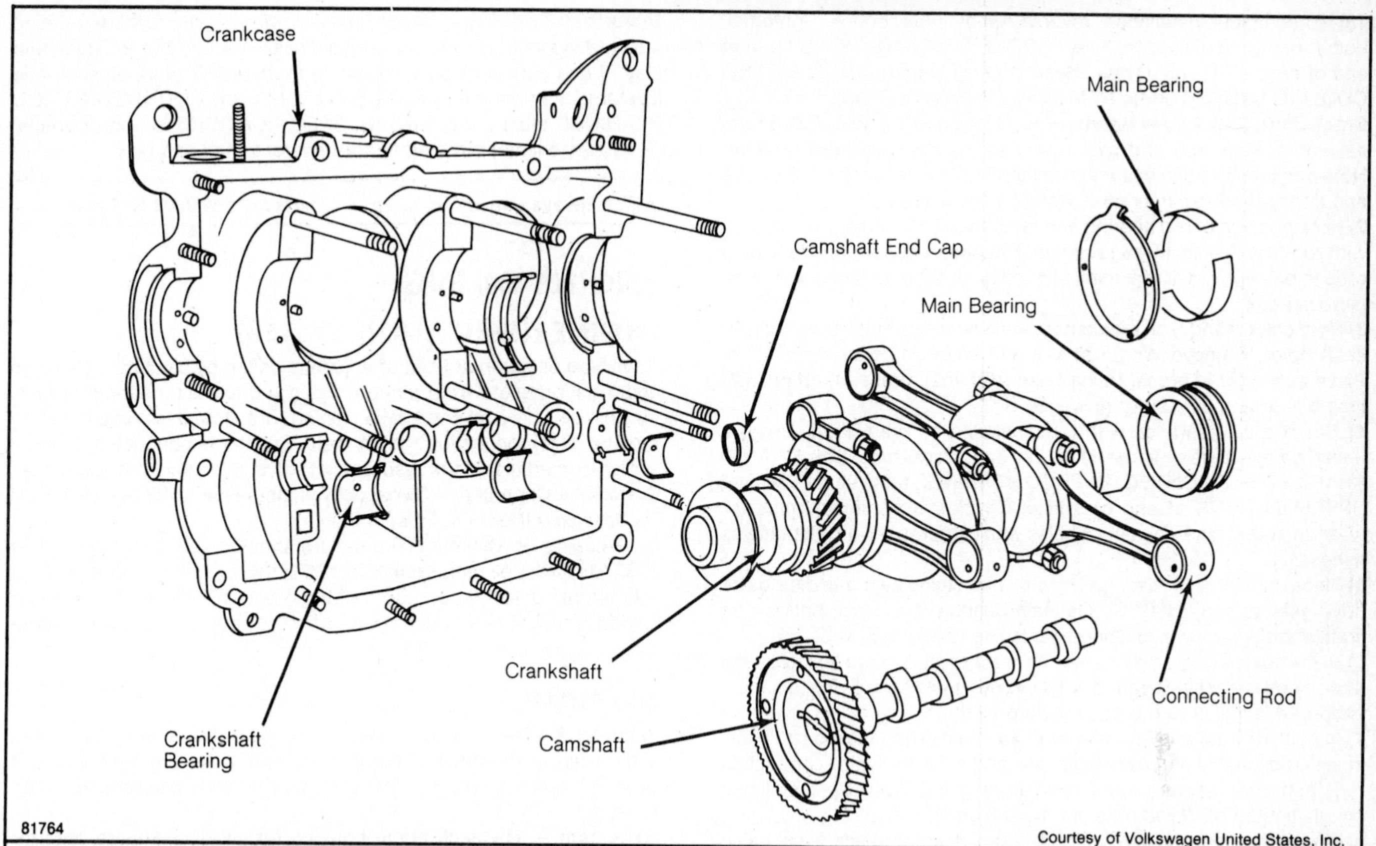

81764

Courtesy of Volkswagen United States, Inc.

***Fig. 9: Exploded View of Crankcase, Crankshaft & Camshaft Assembly***

**4)** Remove oil filler tube. Remove oil pump cover and gears. Using Puller (VW 201), remove oil pump housing and gasket. Remove lifters. Keep lifters in a marked order for installation. Remove nuts retaining crankcase halves together.

**5)** Separate crankcase halves. Use a rubber mallet if necessary. DO NOT use pry bars or levers between crankcase halves, oil leaks will occur. Lift camshaft from crankcase. Remove crankshaft and connecting rods as an assembly. *See Fig. 9.*

**6)** Remove bearings from crankcase halves. Remove main bearing locating dowels. Remove camshaft plug.

**7)** Clean all sealant from bolts, nuts and washers. Clean old sealant from crankcase. Blow out all oil galleys with compressed air. Ensure studs are tight.

***NOTE: Use only Sealant (AMV 188 000 02) on crankcase half mating surfaces.***

**8)** Ensure bearing locating dowels fit snugly in crankcase. Install main bearing and camshaft bearings in crankcases. Lubricate bearings with engine oil. Lay crankshaft and connecting rods into left half of crankcase. Properly align main bearings and locating dowels.

**9)** Install camshaft with "O" mark between marks on crankshaft gear. Check backlash of timing gears. Rotate crankshaft backward. If camshaft lifts out of bearing, install a smaller camshaft gear. Size of camshaft gear is marked on inner side of gear. Smaller size camshaft gears are available to adjust backlash. Coat edge of camshaft plug with sealant, and install plug.

**10)** Install rear thrust washer with tab on thrust washer toward main bearing and separating line of crankcase. Ensure projection on main bearing fits in notches in crankcase. Oil holes must be in left half of crankcase. *See Fig. 10.*

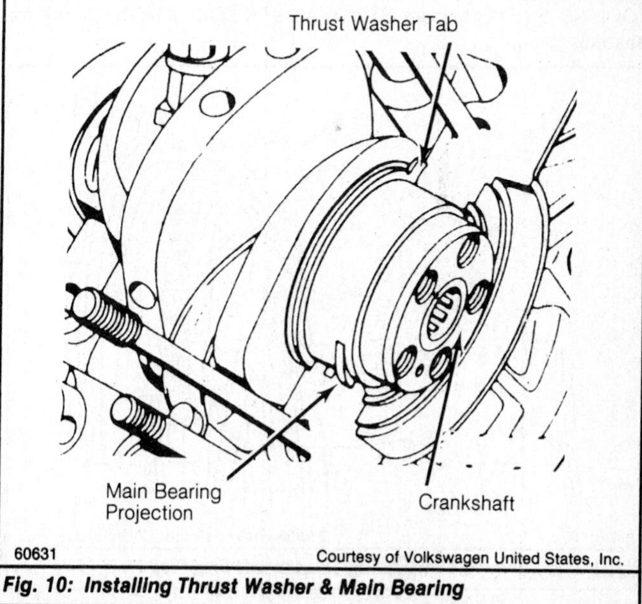


***Fig. 10: Installing Thrust Washer & Main Bearing***

**11)** Apply a thin layer of Sealant (AMV 188 000 02) to mating surfaces of both crankcase halves. Place right half of crankcase over studs, and compress crankcase halves together. Coat both sides of washers and face of cap nuts with Sealant (D3).

**12)** Tighten 8-mm nut above and behind No. 1 exhaust lifter bore first. Tighten all 10-mm nuts and then all remaining 8-mm nuts. Place No. 1 cylinder on TDC. Install distributor drive gear with Shaft Remover/ Installer (VW 228b). Ensure drive gear is in exact position as marked at removal.

# 1991 ENGINES
# 2.1L Opposed 4-Cylinder (Cont.)

**13)** To complete installation, reverse removal procedure. Tighten all bolts/nuts to specification. See TORQUE SPECIFICATIONS table at end of article. Fill fluid levels. Bleed cooling system. See BLEEDING COOLING SYSTEM under REMOVAL & INSTALLATION.

**Crankshaft, Rod & Main Bearings – 1)** Remove crankshaft and rods assembly. Mark rod and rod caps with matching cylinder number. Note position of rod to ensure installation to original position. Remove and discard rod cap nuts nuts. Remove rod and cap.

**2)** Note position of rod bearing and remove bearing. Keep rod bearing with rod from which it was removed. Repeat procedure for remaining rods to be removed. If replacing rods, they must be replaced as a complete set of 4.

**3)** Note color mark(s) on crankshaft. Main bearings must match crankshaft color. Remove Woodruff key and snap ring from crankshaft. Place assembly in press. Using Plate (VW 402), press off crankshaft timing gear and distributor drive gear.

**4)** Check side clearance with rods installed on crankshaft. Using a feeler gauge, measure between rod and crankshaft. See CRANKSHAFT, MAIN & CONNECTING ROD BEARINGS table under ENGINE SPECIFICATIONS at end of article. Check crankshaft journals for wear and damage. Blow out oil holes with compressed air. Replace as necessary.

**5)** Place crankshaft in vise. Heat crankshaft timing gear and distributor drive gear to 175°F (80° C). Oil main bearing, and place bearing on crankshaft with dowel locating hole facing crankshaft web.

**6)** Place heated gears and spacer on crankshaft. Ensure timing marks (2 dots) on crankshaft gear are facing out. Install snap ring. Oil main bearing and install with groove toward oil thrust ring.

**7)** Install oil thrust ring and Woodruff key. Install connecting rod bearings in rods and caps, with tangs engaging notches. Install connecting rods to proper cylinder, with forged mark on rod facing up. Install and snugly tighten NEW rod nuts and tighten snug.

**8)** Tap both sides of rod lightly to keep bearing shells from being pinched. Tighten rod nuts to specification. See TORQUE SPECIFICATIONS table at end of article. To complete installation, reverse removal procedure. Fill fluid levels. Bleed cooling system. See BLEEDING COOLING SYSTEM under REMOVAL & INSTALLATION. Check for leakage.

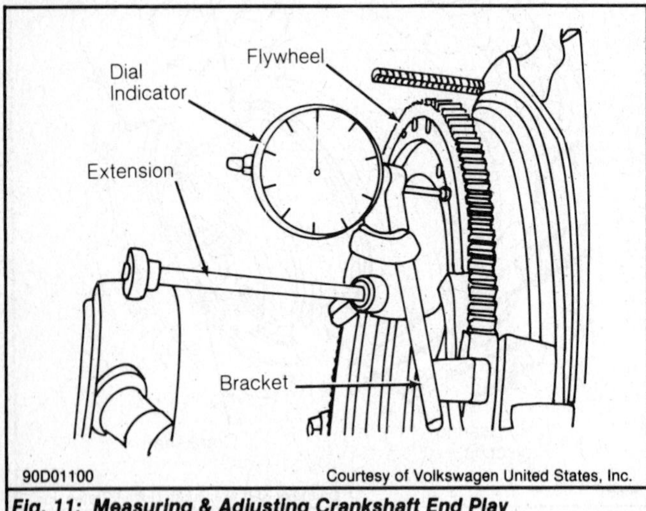


***Fig. 11: Measuring & Adjusting Crankshaft End Play***

**Crankshaft End Play –** Mount dial indicator with tip at 90 degrees to face of flywheel. *See Fig. 11*. Move flywheel in and out to check end play. If end play is incorrect, remove flywheel, "O" ring, oil seal, and adjustment shims. see CRANKSHAFT, MAIN & CONNECTING ROD BEARINGS table under ENGINE SPECIFICATIONS at end of article. Determine shim(s) required to correct crankshaft end play.

***NOTE: Always use shims to set or correct crankshaft end play.***

## ENGINE OILING

### ENGINE LUBRICATION SYSTEM

Gear-type oil pump at front of engine is driven by camshaft. Oil flows under full pressure from pump to filter and to main bearing journals through oil galleys in crankcase casting. Crankshaft is cross-drilled to provide oil to connecting rod journals. Oil filter is connected to an oil cooler. Nonadjustable pressure relief valve is located in engine case.

**Crankcase Capacity –** Oil capacity without filter is 4.2 qts. (4.0L). Oil capacity with filter is 4.7 qts. (4.5L).

**Oil Pressure –** Minimum oil pressure should be 29 psi (2 kg/cm²) at 2000 RPM with oil temperature of 176°F (80°C). Oil pressure warning light should go out at pressure of 2-6.5 psi (.15-.45 kg/cm²). Spring-loaded pressure relief valve opens when oil pressure becomes excessive.

## OIL PUMP

**Removal & Disassembly –** Remove engine. Remove exhaust and engine carrier. Remove oil pump cover with 4 sealing nuts. Remove gears from pump housing. Install Puller (VW 201) and remove pump housing.

**Inspection – 1)** Check pump housing for scoring. Ensure post for driven gear is tight in pump housing. Check lug of drive gear for excessive wear. Ensure machined surface of pump cover is smooth and flat.

**2)** Place gears in pump housing. Place straightedge across pump body and face of gears. Measure end play of gears to straightedge with feeler gauge. See OIL PUMP CLEARANCE SPECIFICATIONS table.

***OIL PUMP CLEARANCE SPECIFICATIONS***

| Application | In. (mm) |
|---|---|
| Oil Pump End Play | [1] .004 (.10) |

[1] – Maximum allowable clearance.

**Reassembly & Installation – 1)** Lightly coat THICK oil pump housing gasket with sealer. Place over studs against crankcase. Carefully tap pump housing into crankcase with soft mallet. Align studs and pump housing. Avoid tearing gasket edge.

**2)** Place drive gear in pump housing and rotate until lug fits into groove on face of camshaft. Install driven gear, rotating crankshaft slightly to align gear teeth. Install dry THIN oil pump cover gasket over studs.

**3)** Place pump cover plate on studs. Tighten new sealing nuts in diagonal pattern. Sealing ring of nut faces oil pump cover. To complete installation, reverse removal procedure.

# 1991 ENGINES
# 2.1L Opposed 4-Cylinder (Cont.)

## TORQUE SPECIFICATIONS

### TORQUE SPECIFICATIONS

| Application | Ft. Lbs. (N.m) |
|---|---|
| Connecting Rod Nuts | 33 (45) |
| Coolant Drain Plug | 37 (50) |
| Coolant Pipe-To-Cylinder Head | 15 (20) |
| Crankcase Half | |
| 8-mm Nuts | 15 (20) |
| 10-mm Nuts | 22 (30) |
| Crankshaft Pulley Bolt | 258 (350) |
| Cylinder Head-To-Crankcase Nuts [1] | |
| Step 1 | [2] |
| Step 2 | 30 (40) |
| Step 3 | 37 (50) |
| Engine-To-Transaxle Nuts | 22 (30) |
| Exhaust Flange-To-Cylinder Head Nut | 15 (20) |
| Flywheel Or Drive Plate-To-Crankshaft | 80 (110) |
| Oil Drain Plug | 20 (25) |
| Oil Pump Cover Nuts | 20 (25) |
| Pressure Plate-To-Flywheel | 15 (20) |
| Rocker Shaft-To-Cylinder Head Nuts | 20 (25) |
| Starter Mount Bolt | 18 (25) |
| Torque Converter-To-Drive Plate | 22 (30) |
| Water Pump-To-Crankcase | 15 (20) |

[1] – Tighten nuts in sequence. *See Fig. 4.*
[2] – Tighten to 84 INCH lbs (10 N.m).

## ENGINE SPECIFICATIONS

### GENERAL SPECIFICATIONS

| Application | Specification |
|---|---|
| Displacement | 128 Cu. In. (2.1L) |
| Bore | 3.701" (94.0 mm) |
| Stroke | 2.99" (76.0 mm) |
| Compression Ratio | 9.0:1 |
| Fuel System | PFI |
| Horsepower @ RPM | 95 @ 4800 |
| Torque Ft. Lbs. @ RPM | 117 @ 3200 |

### CONNECTING RODS

| Application | In. (mm) |
|---|---|
| Bore Diameter | |
| Pin Bore (Full Floating) | [1] |
| Rod Length | [1] |
| Side Play (Maximum) | .028 (.70) |

[1] – Information is not available.

### CYLINDER BLOCK

| Application | In. (mm) |
|---|---|
| Cylinder Bore | |
| Standard Diameter | 3.701-3.702 (94.00-94.03) |
| Maximum Taper | .002 (.06) |
| Maximum Out-Of-Round | .002 (.06) |

### CRANKSHAFT, MAIN & CONNECTING ROD BEARINGS

| Application | In. (mm) |
|---|---|
| Crankshaft | |
| End Play | |
| Standard | .003-.005 (.07-.13) |
| Service Limit | .006 (.15) |
| Runout | [1] |
| Main Bearings Diameter [2] | |
| Blue Dot | |
| Journal No. 1 | 2.3614-2.3618 (59.980-59.990) |
| Journals No. 2 & 3 | 2.1645-2.1649 (54.980-54.990) |
| Journal No. 4 | 1.5741-1.5748 (39.983-40.000) |
| Red Dot | |
| Journal No. 1 | 2.3610-2.3613 (59.971-59.979) |
| Journals No. 2 & 3 | 2.1642-2.1645 (54.971-54.979) |
| Journal No. 4 | 1.5741-1.5748 (39.983-40.000) |
| Journal Out-Of-Round | .001 (.03) |
| Journal Taper | .001 (.03) |
| Oil Clearance | [1] |
| Connecting Rod Bearings | |
| Journal Diameter | 2.1647-2.1651 (54.984-54.996) |
| Journal Out-Of-Round | .001 (.03) |
| Journal Taper | .001 (.03) |
| Oil Clearance | [1] |

[1] – Information is not available.
[2] – Bearing and crankcase must have same color code (Red or Blue).

### PISTONS, PINS & RINGS

| Application | In. (mm) |
|---|---|
| Pistons | |
| Diameter | 3.700 (93.98) |
| Clearance | |
| Standard | .001-.002 (.02-.05) |
| Maximum | .008 (.20) |
| Piston Pin Bore | [1] |
| Pins | |
| Pin Diameter | [1] |
| Piston Fit | Full Floating |
| Rod Fit | Full Floating |
| Rings | |
| No. 1 | |
| End Gap | |
| Standard | .012-.018 (.30-.45) |
| Service Limit | .035 (.95) |
| Side Clearance | |
| Standard | .002-.003 (.05-.08) |
| Service Limit | .005 (.12) |
| No. 2 | |
| End Gap | |
| Standard | .012-.020 (.30-.50) |
| Service Limit | .040 (1.0) |
| Side Clearance | |
| Standard | .002-.003 (.04-.07) |
| Service Limit | .004 (.10) |
| No. 3 (Oil) | |
| End Gap | |
| Standard | .010-.016 (.25-.40) |
| Service Limit | .035 (.95) |
| Side Clearance | |
| Standard | .001-.002 (.02-.05) |
| Service Limit | .004 (.10) |

[1] – Information is not available.

# 1991 ENGINES
# 2.1L Opposed 4-Cylinder (Cont.)

### CAMSHAFT

| Application | In. (mm) |
|---|---|
| End Play | .006 (.16) |
| Camshaft Runout | .0015 (.04) |
| Camshaft Backlash | .000-.002 (.00-.05) |

### VALVES & VALVE SPRINGS

| Application | Specification |
|---|---|
| Intake Valves | |
| Face Angle | 45° |
| Head Diameter | 1.575" (40.00 mm) |
| Length | 4.823" (122.50 mm) |
| Minimum Margin | .020" (.50 mm) |
| Stem Diameter | .314" (7.97 mm) |
| Exhaust Valves | |
| Face Angle | 45° |
| Head Diameter | 1.340" (34.00 mm) |
| Length | 4.823" (122.50 mm) |
| Minimum Margin | [1] |
| Stem Diameter | .3508-.3512" (8.91-8.92 mm) |

[1] - DO NOT machine; hand lap valve only.

### CYLINDER HEAD

| Application | Specification |
|---|---|
| Valve Seats | |
| Intake Valve | |
| Seat Angle | 45° |
| Seat Width | .055-.098" (1.40-2.50 mm) |
| Exhaust Valve | |
| Seat Angle | 45° |
| Seat Width | .055-.098" (1.40-2.50 mm) |
| Valve Guides | |
| Intake Valve | |
| Valve Guide I.D. | .315" (8.00 mm) |
| Valve Guide Oil Clearance | [1] .047" (1.20 mm) |
| Exhaust Valve | |
| Valve Guide I.D. | .354" (9.00 mm) |
| Valve Guide Oil Clearance | [1] .047" (1.20 mm) |
| Push Rod Tube Length [2] | 7.6" (194 mm) |

[1] - See CYLINDER HEAD under OVERHAUL.
[2] - *See Fig. 5.*

# 1991 CLUTCHES
# FWD – Except Fox

## Cabriolet, Golf, GTI, Jetta

## DESCRIPTION

The clutch is a single dry disc type, which uses a diaphragm spring-type pressure plate. The clutch is cable operated.

## ADJUSTMENTS

System is automatically adjusted and requires no manual adjustment.

## REMOVAL & INSTALLATION

### CLUTCH ASSEMBLY

***NOTE: Transaxle may be lowered out of vehicle without removing engine.***

**Removal – 1)** Disconnect negative battery cable. Attach Engine Support (10-222A) to engine. On 16-valve engines, also install Retainer (3180) to hole in intake manifold. On all engines, remove left transaxle mount. Disconnect back-up light switch wires and speedometer cable at transaxle. Disconnect clutch cable. *See Fig. 1.*

**2)** Remove upper clutch housing-to-transaxle bolts. Remove starter. Disconnect shift linkage at rod lever and relay lever. Remove front selector rod.

**3)** Remove exhaust pipe bracket. Support transaxle with floor jack. Remove rear transaxle mount. Disconnect left and right drive shafts at transaxle, and secure aside. Remove large clutch cover plate bolts (plate remains on engine). Remove small clutch cover plate bolts and clutch cover plate.

**4)** Remove right engine-to-transaxle bolt (stud/nut). Push engine as far to the right as possible. Pull transaxle away from engine while positioning engine so right drive flange clears flywheel. Lower and remove transaxle.

**5)** With transaxle removed, install Flywheel Holder (VW558) on flywheel. Remove flywheel and clutch disc. Pry retaining ring from release plate, and lift release plate from pressure plate. Remove pressure plate-to-crankshaft bolts in a diagonal pattern.

**6)** To remove clutch release bearing, pry round cover from left side of transaxle. Remove stop clip from clutch release shaft. Rotate clutch release shaft, and remove clutch release bearing.

**Installation – 1)** Install clutch release bearing. Rotate clutch release shaft into position, and replace stop clip. Install a new round cover at left side of transaxle.

**2)** Coat pressure plate bolts with Loctite 270 or 271, and reverse removal procedure. Retaining ring ends must be between 2 slots in release plate.

**3)** On 8-valve engines, center the clutch disc on flywheel. On 16-valve engines, use Clutch Aligner (3178) to center clutch disc on flywheel. On all engines, reverse removal procedure to complete installation.

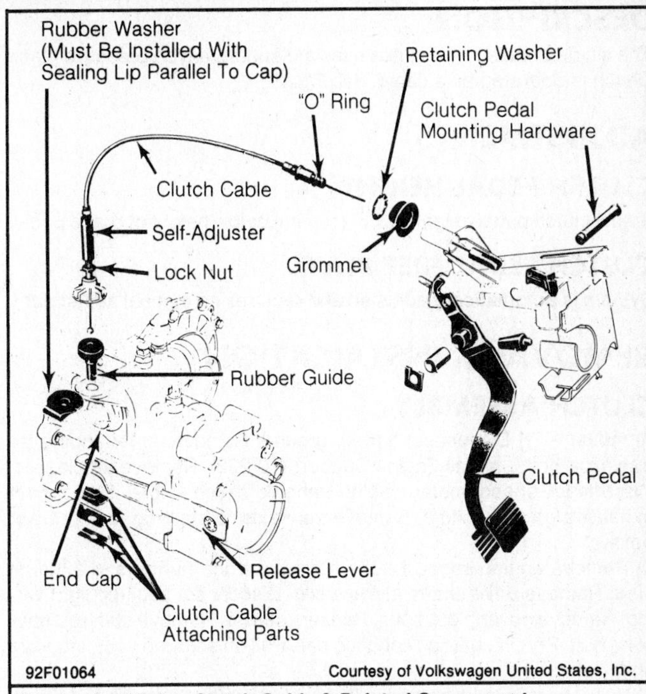


***Fig. 1: Identifying Clutch Cable & Related Components***

## TORQUE SPECIFICATIONS

***TORQUE SPECIFICATIONS***

| Application | Ft. Lbs. (N.m) |
|---|---|
| Clutch Cover Plate Bolt | 15 (20) |
| Drive Shaft-To-Transaxle Bolt | 32 (43) |
| Flywheel Bolt | 15 (20) |
| Pressure Plate Bolt | 22 (30) + 1/4 Turn |
| Starter Bolt | 44 (60) |
| Transaxle-To-Engine Bolt | 55 (75) |

# 1991 CLUTCHES
# FWD – Fox

## DESCRIPTION

The single dry disc type clutch uses a diaphragm type pressure plate. Clutch is operated by a cable. *See Fig. 2.*

## ADJUSTMENTS

### CLUTCH PEDAL HEIGHT

Adjust clutch pedal height to 3/8" (10 mm) below height of brake pedal.

### CLUTCH PEDAL FREE PLAY

System is automatically adjusted and requires no manual adjustment.

## REMOVAL & INSTALLATION

### CLUTCH ASSEMBLY

**Removal** – **1)** Disconnect battery ground. Remove upper engine-to-transaxle bolts. Install Engine Support (10-222). Remove air cleaner. Disconnect speedometer cable. Unhook clutch cable. Disconnect exhaust pipe at manifold. Remove transaxle-to-steering rack bracket bolts.

**2)** Remove engine support bolts. Remove front muffler and exhaust pipe. Remove drive shafts at transaxle. Disconnect back-up light wiring. Remove cover plate bolts. Remove starter. Remove shift rod coupling bolt. Pry off shift rod coupling ball. Pull off shift rod coupling from shift rod.

**3)** Install transaxle lift and raise transaxle slightly. Loosen bolt "A" and remove bolt "B" from rear transaxle mount. Remove rubber mount. *See Fig. 1.* Remove 3 front transaxle support bolts. Remove lower engine-to-transaxle bolts.

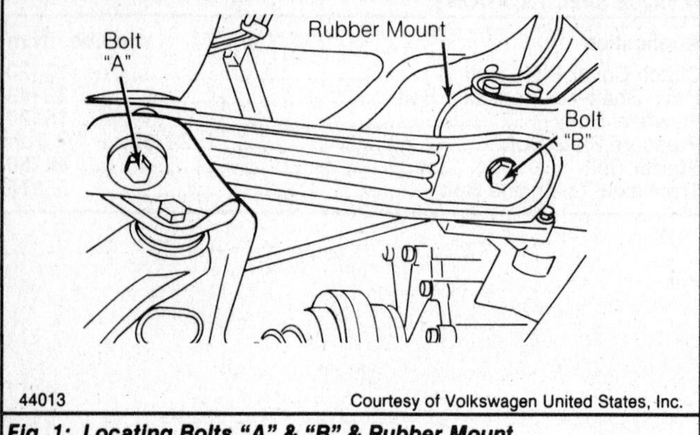


***Fig. 1: Locating Bolts "A" & "B" & Rubber Mount***

**4)** Separate transaxle from engine. Remove transaxle. Index mark pressure plate and flywheel for reassembly reference. Evenly loosen pressure plate bolts in a diagonal pattern. *See Fig. 2.* Slide pressure plate off flywheel dowels. Remove retaining clips and springs from release bearing. Remove release bearing.

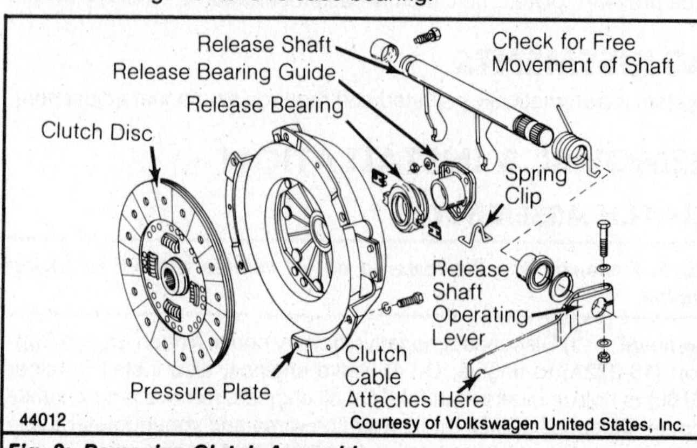


***Fig. 2: Removing Clutch Assembly***

***NOTE: Release bearing is prelubricated. DO NOT wash in solvent.***

**Installation** – **1)** Lubricate release bearing sleeve with molybdenum disulphide grease. Coat operating shaft pivot points with multipurpose grease. Position release bearing to shaft and install retaining clips and springs.

**2)** Using a clutch alignment tool match pressure plate with clutch disc. Make sure index marks are aligned. Attach and support clutch assembly.

**3)** Tighten pressure plate bolts in a crisscross pattern 2 turns at a time. Position transaxle to engine. Make sure mainshaft splines are clean and lubricated lightly with molybdenum disulphide grease. Reverse removal procedure to complete installation.

### CLUTCH CABLE

**Removal** – Loosen cable adjusting nuts and free clutch cable housing from support bracket. Separate cable from clutch operating lever (at clutch housing). Disconnect cable at pedal and force cable and housing into passenger compartment to remove.

**Installation** – To install new cable, reverse removal procedure and adjust. See CLUTCH PEDAL HEIGHT under ADJUSTMENTS.

## TORQUE SPECIFICATIONS

***TORQUE SPECIFICATIONS***

| Application | Ft. Lbs. (N.m) |
|---|---|
| Drive Shaft-To-Transaxle Bolt | 33 (45) |
| Pressure Plate-To-Flywheel Bolt | 20 (25) |
| Transaxle-To-Engine Bolt | 40 (55) |

# 1991 CLUTCHES
# RWD

### Vanagon

## DESCRIPTION

The hydraulically operated clutch is a single disc, diaphragm spring type. Master cylinder is mounted on firewall and nonadjustable clutch release cylinder is mounted on clutch housing.

## ADJUSTMENTS

System is automatically adjusted and requires no manual adjustment.

## REMOVAL & INSTALLATION

### CLUTCH ASSEMBLY

**Removal - 1)** Disconnect negative battery cable. Remove upper engine-to-transaxle bolts. Remove accelerator cable bracket. Remove left drive shaft from transaxle and support with a wire.

**2)** Remove clutch release cylinder mounting bracket. Disconnect back-up light wires. Disconnect starter wires and remove starter. Remove right drive shaft from transaxle and support with a wire.

**3)** Using VW Engine Support (VW 785/1B), support engine. Remove shift rod support and shift linkage from transaxle. Using transmission jack, support transaxle. Disconnect ground strap. Remove front transaxle mount from body.

**4)** Loosen spindle of engine support and lower front part of transaxle until room exists for transaxle removal. Remove remaining engine-to-transaxle bolts. Pull transaxle from engine guide studs and remove.

**5)** Hold flywheel. Mark position of pressure plate on flywheel for reassembly reference. Loosen pressure plate-to-flywheel bolts evenly in a diagonal pattern and remove clutch assembly.

**6)** Pry off spring clip retainers from clutch release bearing and disengage spring clips. Remove clutch release bearing. *See Fig. 1.*

**Installation - 1)** Apply molybdenum disulfide grease to clutch operating shaft, pivot points and clutch release bearing. Secure clutch release bearing with spring clips and spring clip retainers. Clean splines of transaxle input shaft and lubricate lightly with molybdenum disulfide powder. Center clutch disc against flywheel.

***NOTE: DO NOT clean clutch release bearing in solvent. Wipe clean with dry cloth.***

**2)** Install pressure plate and tighten bolts evenly in a diagonal pattern.

***NOTE: Rear mounting bolt must be installed in clutch release cylinder before attempting to install on clutch housing.***

**3)** To complete installation, reverse removal procedure. Tighten bolts to specification. See TORQUE SPECIFICATIONS table at end of article.

### CLUTCH MASTER CYLINDER

**Removal & Installation -** Disconnect master cylinder push rod at clutch pedal. Disconnect hydraulic line. Remove master cylinder from firewall. To install, reverse removal procedure and bleed hydraulic system.

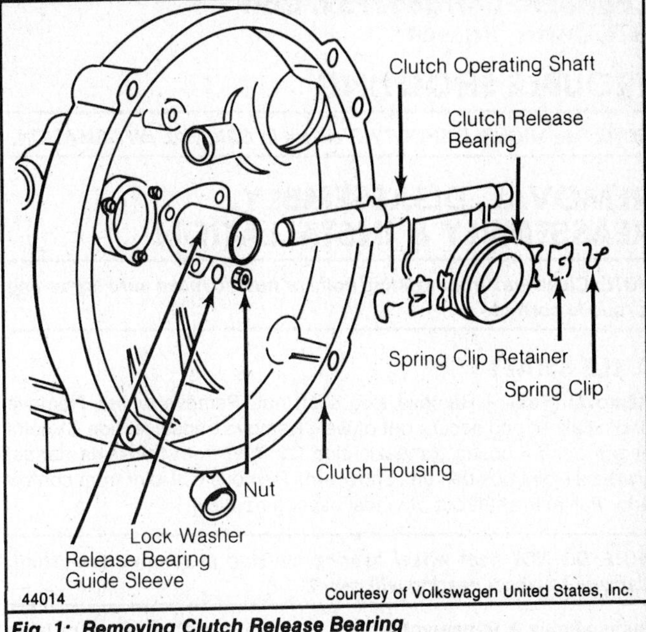


***Fig. 1: Removing Clutch Release Bearing***

### CLUTCH RELEASE CYLINDER

**Removal -** Disconnect hydraulic line from release cylinder. Remove push rod from clutch lever ball. Remove mounting bolts and remove cylinder.

**Installation -** Lightly grease clutch lever ball. Install clutch release cylinder. Attach hydraulic line and clutch lever. Bleed hydraulic system.

***NOTE: Rear mounting bolt must be installed in clutch release cylinder before attempting to install on clutch housing.***

## OVERHAUL

***NOTE: Manufacturer recommends replacement of faulty clutch master and release cylinders and does not provide overhaul procedures.***

## TORQUE SPECIFICATIONS

***TORQUE SPECIFICATIONS***

| Application | Ft. Lbs. (N.m) |
|---|---|
| Axle Shaft-To-Transaxle Bolt | 33 (45) |
| Drain Plug | 15 (20) |
| Engine-To-Transaxle Nut/Bolt | 22 (30) |
| Flywheel-To-Crankshaft Bolt | 80 (110) |
| Pressure Plate-To-Flywheel Bolt | 18 (25) |

# 1991 DRIVE AXLES
# FWD Axle Shafts

**Cabriolet, Corrado, Fox, Golf GTI, Jetta, Passat**

## TROUBLE SHOOTING

*NOTE: See TROUBLE SHOOTING article in GENERAL INFORMATION.*

## REMOVAL, DISASSEMBLY, REASSEMBLY & INSTALLATION

*NOTE: Clean wax from existing bolts or nuts to make sure tightening torque is correct.*

### AXLE SHAFT

**Removal (Fox)** – Remove axle shaft nut. Remove wheel. Remove brake caliper and secure out of way. Remove transaxle-side CV joint flange bolts. Loosen transaxle-side CV joint from transaxle flange. Mark ball joint position on control arm. Remove ball joint from control arm. Pull axle shaft out of wheel bearing housing.

*NOTE: DO NOT heat wheel bearing housing to remove axle shaft. Damage to wheel bearing will result.*

**Disassembly & Reassembly** – **1)** Remove axle shaft boot(s). Using a drift, remove protective cap from CV joint. Remove circlip from transaxle-side CV joint. Support CV joint with axle assembly on Support Stand (VW 402). Using Driver (VW 408A), press transaxle-side CV joint off axle shaft. DO NOT disassemble transaxle-side CV joint, replace complete unit.

**2)** To remove outer CV joint, use a drift and hammer to drive CV joint off axle shaft. Rotate inner race and remove balls. Inspect for galling or wear. Grease balls and reinstall. To reassemble, reverse disassembly procedure. Use new circlips and boot clamps during assembly.

**Installation** – **1)** Apply locking compound around splines, not more than 1/4" wide. Install axle shaft. Bring ball joint into same position as marked before removal. Tighten ball joint. See TORQUE SPECIFICATIONS table at end of article. Install new axle shaft nut.

**2)** Check camber, and adjust as necessary. Install wheel assembly. Allow locking compound to dry one hour before driving vehicle.

**Removal & Installation (Except Fox)** – **1)** Remove axle shaft nut. Remove wheel. Remove brake caliper, and secure aside. Remove tie rod end bolts. Remove 2 bolts attaching spindle assembly to strut assembly. Remove lower ball joint bolt or nut if necessary.

**2)** Remove spindle assembly. Loosen transaxle-side CV joint from transaxle flange. Remove axle shaft assembly. To install, reverse removal procedure. Install new axle shaft nut. See TORQUE SPECIFICATIONS table at end of article.

**Disassembly & Reassembly** – **1)** Remove axle shaft boot(s). Using a drift, remove protective cap from CV joint. Remove circlip from transaxle-side CV joint. Support CV joint with axle assembly on Support Stand (VW 402). Using Driver (VW 408A), press transaxle-side CV joint off axle shaft. DO NOT disassemble transaxle-side CV joint, replace complete unit.

**2)** To remove outer CV joint, use a drive and hammer to drive CV joint off axle shaft. Rotate inner race and remove balls. Inspect for galling or wear. Grease balls and reinstall.

**3)** To remove vibration damper, mark location on axle shaft for reassembly. On some models, drive roll pin out. On all models, remove vibration damper. To reassemble, reverse disassembly procedure. Use new circlips and boot clamps during assembly.

*AXLE SHAFT LENGTH*

| Application | In. (mm) |
|---|---|
| Corrado | |
| Left Axle | 17.20 (432.8) |
| Right Axle | 26.00 (666.5) |
| Fox | |
| Left & Right Axles | 20.12 (511.0) |
| Except Corrado & Fox | |
| Left Axle | 17.44 (442.9) |
| Right Axle | 26.66 (677.1) |

## TORQUE SPECIFICATIONS

*TORQUE SPECIFICATIONS*

| Application | Ft. Lbs. (N.m) |
|---|---|
| Cabriolet & Corrado | |
| Axle Shaft Nut | 170 (230) |
| Brake Caliper Bolt | 47 (63) |
| Lower Ball Joint Nut | 18 (25) |
| Tie Rod End Nut | 22 (30) |
| Transaxle-Side CV Joint-To-Transaxle Bolt | 33 (45) |
| Spindle Assembly-To-Strut Nut | 58 (78) |
| Fox | |
| Axle Shaft Nut | 170 (230) |
| Brake Caliper Bolt | 47 (63) |
| Lower Ball Joint Nut | 47 (63) |
| Tie Rod End Nut | 22 (30) |
| Transaxle-Side CV Joint-To-Transaxle Bolt | 33 (45) |
| Golf, GTI & Jetta | |
| Axle Shaft Nut | 170 (230) |
| Brake Caliper Bolt | 47 (63) |
| Lower Ball Joint Bolt | 36 (50) |
| Tie Rod End Nut | 26 (35) |
| Transaxle-Side CV Joint-To-Transaxle Bolt | 33 (45) |
| Spindle Assembly-To-Strut Nut | |
| Jetta with ABS | 70 (94) |
| All Others | 60 (80) |
| Passat | |
| Axle Shaft Nut | 195 (265) |
| Brake Caliper Bolt | 47 (63) |
| Lower Ball Joint Nut | 92 (125) |
| Tie Rod End Nut | 30 (40) |
| Transaxle-Side CV Joint-To-Transaxle Bolt | 33 (45) |
| Spindle Assembly-To-Strut Nut | 70 (95) |

# 1991 DRIVE AXLES
# RWD Axle Shafts

**Vanagon**

## TROUBLE SHOOTING

***NOTE: See TROUBLE SHOOTING article in GENERAL INFORMATION.***

## REMOVAL, DISASSEMBLY, REASSEMBLY & INSTALLATION

### DRIVE AXLE SHAFTS

**Removal & Installation** - **1)** Remove axle flange bolts and remove axle shafts from differential. Remove rear wheels and axle nuts. Remove brake drum. Disconnect brake line.

**2)** Remove axle shaft assembly with wheel bearing hub assembly from trailing arm. Remove axle shaft assembly from wheel bearing hub assembly. To install, reverse removal procedure.

**Disassembly & Reassembly** - Remove axle shaft boot. Remove circlip from CV joint. Remove protective cap from CV joint using a drift. Support CV joint with axle assembly on Support Stand (VW 402). Using Driver (VW 408A), press CV joint off axle shaft. To reassemble, reverse disassembly procedure. Use new circlips during assembly.

### STUB AXLE SHAFTS & BEARINGS

**Removal & Installation** - Remove wheel hub, wheel bearings and brake backing plate from wheel bearing hub assembly. Using Driver (VW 411), press stub axle from wheel bearing hub assembly. To install, reverse removal procedure.

**Disassembly** - Remove grease seals from wheel bearing hub assembly. Remove inner race from outer wheel bearing and spacer sleeve. Using a brass drift and hammer, remove outside wheel bearing. Press out inner wheel bearing.

**Reassembly** - **1)** Install inner wheel bearing, grease bearing and press until seated. Grease outer bearing and fill space between inner and outer bearings with grease.

**2)** Press outer bearing in until seated. Install spacer sleeve and inner race of outer wheel bearing. Press in flush on wheel side and against circlip on flange side. Press stub axle into wheel bearing hub assembly until seated.

## TORQUE SPECIFICATIONS

***TORQUE SPECIFICATIONS***

| Application | Ft. Lbs. (N.m) |
|---|---|
| Axle Nut | 360 (490) |
| Axle Flange Bolt | 33 (45) |
| Brake Backing Plate Bolt | |
| From Backing Plate Side | 47 (63) |
| From Wheel Bearing Hub Assembly Side | 15 (20) |
| Wheel Bearing Hub Assembly-To-Trailing Arm Bolt | 101 (136) |
| Wheel Lug Nut | 33 (45) |

# 1991 BRAKES Disc & Drum

**Cabriolet, Corrado, Fox, Golf, GTI, Jetta, Passat, Vanagon**

## DESCRIPTION

All models are equipped with front disc brakes. Rear brakes are either disc or drum. Parking brake acts on rear brakes and is cable-actuated. All models use pressure regulator between front and rear brake circuits to avoid rear wheel lock-up during hard braking.

A vacuum power-assist servo is used to ease brake pedal application. A vacuum check valve, located in vacuum supply hose, prevents vacuum leak off when engine is off.

## SERVICING

Manufacturer recommends replacing brake fluid every 2 years.

## BLEEDING BRAKE SYSTEM

***CAUTION: Ensure fluid level in master cylinder is adequate at all times during bleeding procedure. Use only DOT 4 brake fluid. DO NOT use DOT 5 silicone brake fluid.***

### BLEEDING PROCEDURES

***NOTE: Manufacturer recommends bleeding brake system using Pressure Bleeder (US 1116). If a pressure bleeder is not available, use standard bleeding procedure.***

**1)** Exhaust vacuum reserve from power unit by depressing brake pedal several times. On vehicles equipped with ABS, depress brake pedal at least 20 times to relieve system pressure.

**2)** On all vehicles, fill master cylinder with clean brake fluid. If master cylinder was replaced, bleed master cylinder before bleeding wheel calipers. Connect bleeder hose to appropriate caliper bleeder valve. See BRAKE LINE BLEEDING SEQUENCE table.

***BRAKE LINE BLEEDING SEQUENCE***

| Application [1] | Sequence |
|---|---|
| Cabriolet, Fox & Vanagon | RR, LR, RF, LF |
| Corrado | Either Front Caliper First, Either Rear Caliper First |
| Golf, GTI, Jetta & Passat | |
| Without ABS | RR, LR, RF, LF |
| With ABS | LF, RF, Either Rear Caliper First |

[1] - On all vehicles, push lever of pressure regulator in direction of rear axle when bleeding rear brakes.

**3)** Submerge other end of hose in clean glass jar partially filled with clean brake fluid. Pump brake pedal several times, then hold down. Open bleeder valve. Holding pedal down, close bleeder valve. Release brake pedal. Repeat procedure until brake fluid shows no signs of air bubbles. When bleeding rear brakes, push lever of pressure regulator in direction of rear axle.

**4)** After bleeding ABS vehicles, turn ignition on. Allow pump to run until it shuts off. If pump runs for more than 2 minutes, allow pump to cool for 10 minutes. On all vehicles, ensure master cylinder reservoir is full.

## ADJUSTMENTS

### BRAKE PRESSURE REGULATOR

***CAUTION: On all models except Vanagon, DO NOT adjust pressure regulator with brake pedal depressed.***

**Cabriolet - 1)** Raise and support vehicle. Attach Pressure Gauges (US 1016) to right front brake caliper and left rear brake cylinder. Bleed pressure gauge and hoses through valve on gauges.

**2)** Pump brake pedal several times. Press on brake pedal until reading on front gauge shows pressure given for 1st reading in BRAKE PRESSURES table. Hold brake pressure to specification. Rear gauge reading should be within specification given for 1st reading in BRAKE PRESSURES table.

**3)** Increase pressure on brake pedal until reading on front gauge shows pressure given for 2nd reading in BRAKE PRESSURES table. Hold brake pressure to specification. Rear gauge reading should be within specification given for 2nd reading in BRAKE PRESSURES table. If pressures are within specification, brake pressure regulator is functioning properly. If pressures are not within specification, replace pressure regulator. Disconnect gauges and bleed brakes.

**Corrado, Golf, GTI, Jetta & Passat - 1)** Depress brake pedal once firmly. Release brake pedal quickly, watching for regulator lever to move when pedal is released. If regulator lever does not move when pedal is released quickly, replace regulator. If regulator lever moved, go to next step.

**2)** Ensure vehicles fuel tank is full, luggage compartment is empty, and a driver is in driver's seat. Raise and support vehicle. Using Pressure Gauges (US 1016), attach one gauge to right rear brake cylinder or caliper. If vehicle is equipped with ABS, go to next step. If vehicle is not equipped with ABS, go to step **4)**.

**3)** Using Distributor (tee) (803 611 755) and an additional 8" (203 mm) of brake line, connect one gauge in front of pressure regulator. Bleed pressure gauge and hoses through valve on gauges. Lower vehicle. Bounce rear of vehicle several times. Go to step **5)**.

**4)** Attach Pressure Gauges (US 1016) to left front brake caliper. Bleed pressure gauge and hoses through valve on gauges. Lower vehicle. Bounce rear of vehicle several times.

**5)** Pump brake pedal several times. Press on brake pedal until reading on front gauge shows pressure given for 1st reading in BRAKE PRESSURES table. Hold brake pressure to specification. Rear gauge reading should be within specification given for 1st reading in BRAKE PRESSURES table.

**6)** Increase pressure on brake pedal until reading on front gauge shows pressure given for 2nd reading in BRAKE PRESSURES table. Hold brake pressure to specification. Rear gauge reading should be within specification given for 2nd reading in BRAKE PRESSURES table. If pressures are within specification, brake pressure regulator is functioning properly. If pressures are not within specification, go to next step.

**7)** If pressure is too high, decrease spring pressure on regulator. If pressure is too low, increase spring pressure on regulator. If adjusting spring pressure on regulator does not bring pressures within specification, replace pressure regulator. Disconnect gauges and bleed brakes.

**Fox - 1)** Depress brake pedal once firmly. Release brake pedal quickly, watching for regulator lever to move when pedal is released. If regulator lever does not move when pedal is released quickly, replace regulator. If regulator lever moved, go to next step.

**2)** Raise and support vehicle. Using Spring Compressors (VW 5340), compress rear suspension until measured distance between center of wheel and edge of fender lip is approximately 15" (381 mm). Compress both sides of rear suspension at the same time.

**3)** Attach Pressure Gauges (US 1016) to left front brake caliper and right rear brake cylinder. Bleed pressure gauge and hoses through valve on gauges. Pump brake pedal several times. Press on brake pedal until reading on front gauge shows pressure given for 1st reading in BRAKE PRESSURES table. Hold brake pressure to specification. Rear gauge reading should be within specification given for 1st reading in BRAKE PRESSURES table.

**4)** Increase pressure on brake pedal until reading on front gauge shows pressure given for 2nd reading in BRAKE PRESSURES table. Hold brake pressure to specification. Rear gauge reading should be within specification given for 2nd reading in BRAKE PRESSURES table. If pressures are within specification, brake pressure regulator is functioning properly. If pressures are not within specification, go to next step.

**5)** If pressure is too high, decrease spring pressure on regulator. If pressure is too low, increase spring pressure on regulator. If adjusting spring pressure on regulator does not bring pressures within specification, replace pressure regulator. Disconnect gauges and bleed brakes.

# 1991 BRAKES
# Disc & Drum (Cont.)

**Vanagon – 1)** Raise and support vehicle. Attach Pressure Gauges (US 1016) to left front brake caliper and right rear brake cylinder. Bleed pressure gauge and hoses through valve on gauges.
**2)** Pump brake pedal several times. Remove nuts holding pressure regulator. Press on brake pedal until reading on both gauges is 725 psi (51 kg/cm²).
**3)** Tilt regulator forward 30 degrees. DO NOT damage brake lines when tilting regulator. Increase pressure on brake pedal until reading on gauge connected to front caliper reads 1450 psi (102 kg/cm²).
**4)** With regulator tilted forward 30 degrees and gauge for front caliper reading 1450 psi (102 kg/cm²), reading on gauge connected to rear brake cylinder must be 798-943 psi (56-66 kg/cm²). If reading is not within specified range, replace pressure regulator. Disconnect gauges and bleed brakes. When installing pressure regulator, ensure bolt heads face in forward (driving) direction.

***BRAKE PRESSURES***

| Application | Front Gauge psi (kg/cm²) | Rear Gauge psi (kg/cm²) |
|---|---|---|
| **Cabriolet** | | |
| 1st Reading | 797 (56) | 565-623 (40-44) |
| 2nd Reading | 1450 (102) | 739-826 (52-58) |
| **Corrado** | | |
| 1st Reading | 725 (51) | 391-478 (28-34) |
| 2nd Reading | 1450 (102) | 696-783 (49-55) |
| **Fox** | | |
| Coupe & Sedan | | |
| 1st Reading | 725 (51) | 537-609 (38-43) |
| 2nd Reading | 1450 (102) | 725-958 (51-67) |
| Wagon | | |
| 1st Reading | 725 (51) | 392-479 (28-34) |
| 2nd Reading | 1450 (102) | 754-841 (53-59) |
| **Golf & Jetta** | | |
| 1st Reading | 725 (51) | [1] 450-479 (32-34) |
| 2nd Reading | 1450 (102) | [2] 812-914 (57-64) |
| **GTI & Jetta GLi** | | |
| 1st Reading | 725 (51) | [1] 450-479 (32-34) |
| 2nd Reading | 1450 (102) | [2] 754-783 (53-55) |
| **Passat** | | |
| 1st Reading | 725 (51) | 435-522 (31-37) |
| 2nd Reading | 1450 (102) | 739-826 (52-58) |
| **Vanagon** | | |
| 1st Reading | 725 (51) | ..... |
| 2nd Reading | 1450 (102) | 798-943 (56-66) |

[1] – On vehicles equipped with ABS, rear gauge 1st reading is 493-595 psi (35-42 kg/cm²).
[2] – On vehicles equipped with ABS, rear gauge 2nd reading is 812-914 psi (57-64 kg/cm²).

## MASTER CYLINDER PUSH ROD

***NOTE: Push rod is not adjustable on models not listed.***

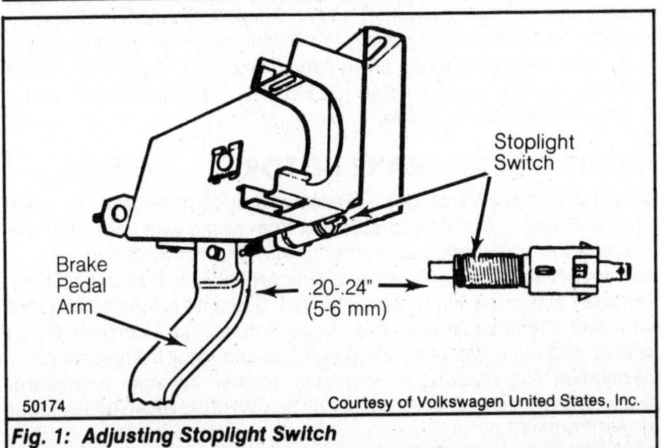


***Fig. 1: Adjusting Stoplight Switch***

**Cabriolet** – Loosen lock nut on push rod. Turn clevis until distance between booster mounting flange and center of clevis hole is 8.11" (206 mm). Tighten lock nut.

***NOTE: Adjust Vanagon push rod before installing in vehicle.***

**Vanagon** – Loosen lock nut on push rod. Turn clevis until distance between booster mounting flange and center of clevis eye is 4.40" (112 mm). Tighten lock nut.

## STOPLIGHT SWITCH

***NOTE: Stoplight switches mounted on master cylinder are nonadjustable.***

Adjustable stoplight switch is located above brake pedal. Loosen lock nut. Turn switch until distance between brake pedal arm and first thread on switch body is .20-.24" (5-6 mm). Tighten lock nut. *See Fig. 1.*

## PARKING BRAKE

**Cabriolet & Fox** – Raise and support vehicle. Apply brake pedal once firmly. On Fox, remove heat deflector plate from under vehicle to access parking brake cable adjustment. On all vehicles, pull parking brake handle up 2 notches. Loosen locking nuts, at parking brake lever. Tighten adjusting nuts until respective rear wheel is locked. Release parking brake. Ensure rear wheels rotate freely. Tighten lock nuts.

**Corrado, GTI, Jetta GLi & Passat (Rear Disc) – 1)** Raise and support vehicle. Disengage parking brake. Loosen locking nuts, at parking brake lever. Tighten adjusting nuts until levers on calipers just move off their stops. Measure gap between stop and lever. *See Fig. 2.*
**2)** Maximum clearance between parking brake lever (on caliper) and stop is .060" (1.5 mm). Apply and release parking brake. Ensure rear wheels rotate freely. Tighten lock nuts.

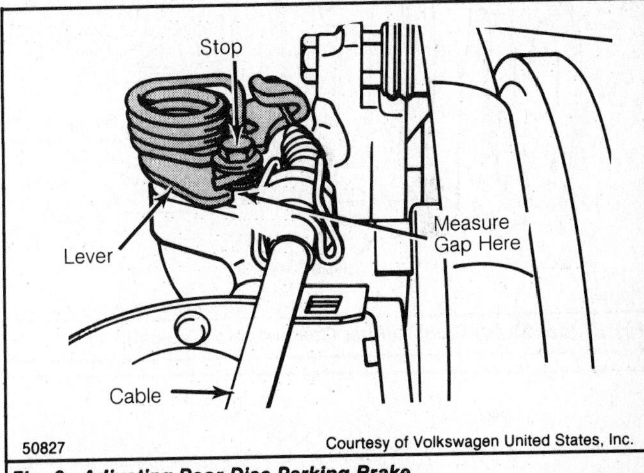


***Fig. 2: Adjusting Rear Disc Parking Brake***

**Golf, GTI & Jetta (Rear Drum)** – Raise and support vehicle. Apply brake pedal once firmly. Pull parking brake handle up 4 notches. Loosen locking nuts, at parking brake lever. Tighten adjusting nuts until respective rear wheel can just be rotated by hand. Release parking brake. Ensure rear wheels rotate freely. Tighten lock nuts.

***NOTE: On Vanagon, check rear brake adjustment before adjusting parking brake.***

**Vanagon – 1)** Raise and support vehicle. Release parking brake. Tighten self-locking adjusting nut until there is no play at brake components. Check for play by pulling on cable housings. Apply and release parking brake several times.
**2)** Check adjustment by pulling parking brake handle up 2-4 notches. Rear wheels should be too tight to turn by hand. Release parking brake. Rear wheels should rotate freely.

# 1991 BRAKES
# Disc & Drum (Cont.)

## WHEEL BEARINGS

***NOTE: FWD front wheel bearings and rear wheel bearings on Vanagon, also called hub or axle bearings, are sealed units with 1-piece outer race. Bearings are nonadjustable.***

**Rear Wheel Bearings (Except Vanagon)** – Tighten adjusting nut snugly while turning drum or rotor. Back off and retighten nut until thrust washer can just be moved with screwdriver. Install locking cap and new cotter key. Install dust cap.

**Front Wheel Bearings (Vanagon)** – Tighten adjusting nut snugly while turning rotor. Back off and retighten nut slowly until thrust washer can just be moved with screwdriver under finger pressure. After adjustment, peen flange of NEW hub nut into spindle axle shaft recess.

## REMOVAL & INSTALLATION

### FRONT DISC BRAKE PADS

**Removal (Cabriolet, Fox, Golf, GTI & Jetta)** – Raise and support vehicle. Remove front wheels. Remove retaining spring at top and bottom of caliper. Remove caliper mounting bolts. Push caliper assembly upward and swing out from bottom. Hang caliper aside with wire. Siphon small amount of brake fluid from reservoir. Remove pads and retaining springs from caliper support. Replace pads that exceed wear limit. Wear limit of pads is .28" (7.0 mm), including backing plate. *See Fig. 3, 4 or 5.*

**Installation** – **1)** Seat caliper piston fully into cylinder bore. Attach retaining springs to caliper support. Install inner pad first and then install outer pad.

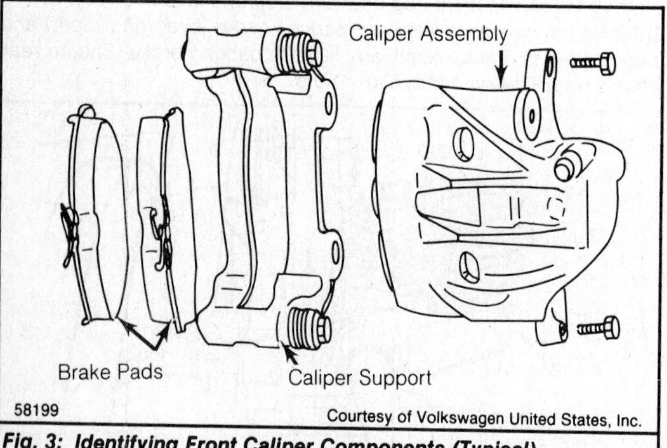


***Fig. 3: Identifying Front Caliper Components (Typical)***

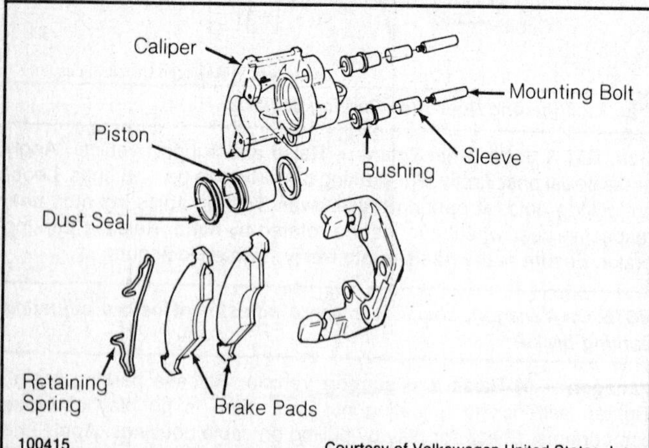


***Fig. 4: Identifying Front Disc Brake Components (Fox)***

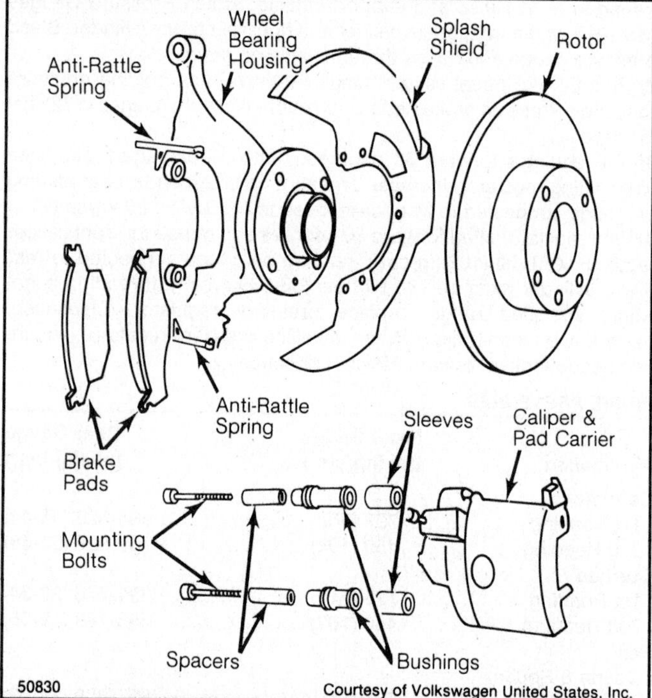


***Fig. 5: Identifying Front Disc Brake Components (Except Fox)***

**2)** Install caliper assembly into caliper support. DO NOT force caliper any further than necessary to start Allen head mounting bolts. Excessive force could distort springs, which could cause noises during braking. Depress brake pedal several times to allow pads to move into operating position. Ensure master cylinder reservoir fluid level is full.

**Removal (Corrado, Passat & Vanagon)** – Raise and support vehicle. Remove front wheels. Hold lower guide pin using an open end wrench. Remove lower caliper mounting bolt. Push caliper assembly upward and swing out from bottom. Siphon small amount of brake fluid from reservoir. Remove pads and retaining springs from caliper support. Replace pads exceeding wear limit. Wear limit of pads is .28" (7.0 mm), including backing plate. *See Fig. 3 or 5.*

**Installation** – Seat caliper piston fully into cylinder bore. Install inner pad and then outer pad. Swing caliper assembly down. Hold lower guide pin using an open end wrench. Install lower caliper mounting bolt. Depress brake pedal several times to allow pads to move into operating position. Ensure master cylinder reservoir fluid level is full.

### FRONT & REAR BRAKE CALIPER

**Removal & Installation** – Raise and support vehicle. Remove wheels. Disconnect brake line from caliper, and plug openings. Bend back locking tabs (if equipped) on mounting bolts. If removing rear brake calipers, disconnect parking brake cables. On all calipers, remove caliper mounting bolts. *See Fig. 3 or 8.* Remove caliper assembly from wheel bearing housing. To install, reverse removal procedure. Use new lock plates (if equipped) and mounting bolts. Bleed hydraulic brake system. See BLEEDING PROCEDURES under BLEEDING BRAKE SYSTEM.

### FRONT & REAR BRAKE ROTOR

**Removal (Except Vanagon)** – Raise and support vehicle. Remove wheels. Remove caliper and suspend from frame with wire. Remove countersunk screw that holds rotor to hub. Pull rotor off hub.

**Removal (Vanagon)** – Raise and support vehicle. Remove wheels. Remove caliper, leaving hose connected. Suspend caliper from frame with wire. Remove grease cap. Loosen peen nut. Remove thrust washer and outer wheel bearing. Pull hub and rotor from spindle.

**Installation (All Models)** – To install, reverse removal procedure. Adjust wheel bearings (if necessary). See WHEEL BEARINGS under ADJUSTMENTS.

# 1991 BRAKES
# Disc & Drum (Cont.)

## REAR DISC BRAKE PADS

**Removal (Corrado & Passat) -** Raise and support vehicle. Remove rear wheels. Disconnect parking brake cable from caliper. Remove caliper mounting bolts. Remove caliper and hang aside. Siphon small amount of brake fluid from reservoir. Remove pads and retaining springs from caliper support. Replace pads that exceed wear limit. Wear limit of pads is .28" (7.0 mm), including backing plate.

**Installation -** Seat caliper piston fully into cylinder bore. Install inner pad first and then install outer pad. Position caliper. Install caliper mounting bolts. Depress brake pedal several times to allow pads to move into operating position. Ensure master cylinder reservoir fluid level is full.

***CAUTION: On GTI and Jetta GLI, DO NOT depress brake pedal with engine running to reset automatic adjuster. High pressure created by booster could jam automatic adjustment piston causing premature pad wear and/or damage to automatic adjuster.***

**Removal (GTI & Jetta GLi) -** Raise and support vehicle. Remove rear wheels. Disconnect parking brake cable from caliper. Remove upper caliper mounting bolt. Swing caliper down on lower mounting bolt. Remove brake pads from carrier. Wear limit is .276" (7.0 mm), including backing plate.

**Installation -** Place brake pads in carrier. Using Allen wrench, push piston into caliper while turning it clockwise. Swing caliper into position. Install new self-locking upper mounting bolt. Reconnect parking brake cable, and check parking brake adjustment. With engine off, depress brake pedal approximately 40 times to reset automatic adjuster.

## REAR BRAKE DRUM

***CAUTION: ALWAYS loosen or tighten castellated axle nuts with wheels on ground.***

**Removal (Cabriolet, Golf, GTI & Jetta) -** Raise and support vehicle. Remove one wheel bolt. Using screwdriver inserted through wheel bolt hole, push adjusting wedge up against stop. Remove grease cap, cotter pin, nut lock and nut. Remove thrust washer and outer bearing. Remove drum with inner bearing and grease seal.

**Installation -** To install, reverse removal procedure. Adjust wheel bearings (if necessary). See WHEEL BEARINGS under ADJUSTMENTS. Apply brake pedal firmly several times to set self-adjusting mechanism.

**Removal (Fox) -** Raise and support vehicle. Remove heat deflector plate from under vehicle to access parking brake cable adjustment. Disconnect parking brake cable (at adjustment point). Remove dust cap and cotter pin. Loosen axle nut. Raise and support vehicle. Remove wheels. Pull off brake drum.

**Installation -** To install, reverse removal procedure. Adjust wheel bearings (if necessary). See WHEEL BEARINGS under ADJUSTMENTS.

**Removal (Vanagon) -** Remove dust cap and cotter pin. Loosen castellated nut. Raise and support vehicle. Remove wheels. Release parking brake at equalizer, and back off adjuster. Remove drum retaining screws. Attach a puller and remove drum. Ensure drum can rotate freely during removal.

**Installation -** To install, reverse removal procedure. Drum retaining screws must be tight. Tighten castellated axle nut to 253 ft. lbs. (345 N.m). Adjust parking brake and depress brake pedal several times to set self-adjusting mechanism.

## REAR BRAKE SHOES

**Removal (Cabriolet, Fox, Golf, GTI & Jetta) - 1)** Remove brake drum. See REAR BRAKE DRUM under REMOVAL & INSTALLATION. After removing drum, remove retainer clips, hold-down springs and anchor pins. Remove lower return spring. Disconnect parking brake cable from lever. *See Fig. 6.*

**2)** Disconnect adjusting wedge spring and upper return spring. Remove brake shoes together with push rod and tensioning spring.

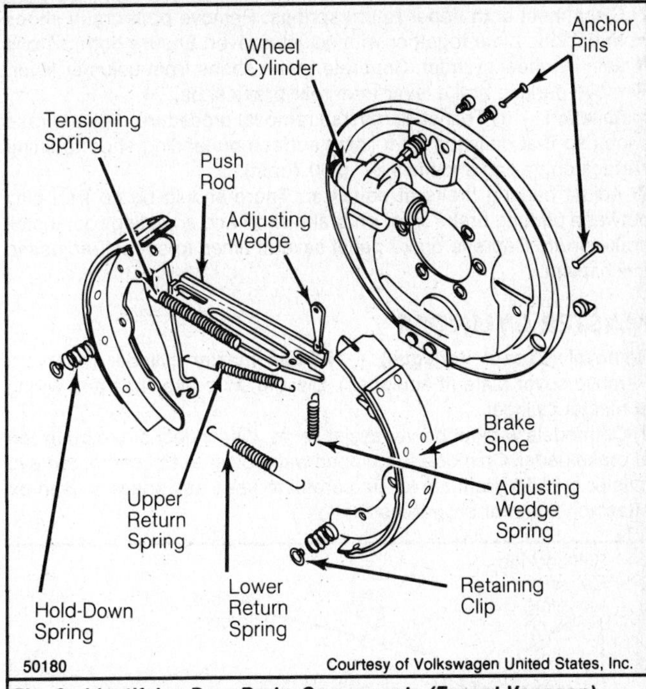


***Fig. 6: Identifying Rear Brake Components (Except Vanagon)***

Place push rod and shoes in vise. Remove tension spring. Separate shoes from push rod.

**Installation -** To install, reverse removal procedure. Ensure that lug on adjusting wedge faces backing plate. Adjust wheel bearings (if necessary). See WHEEL BEARINGS under ADJUSTMENTS. Apply brake firmly to set self-adjusting mechanism.

**Removal (Vanagon) - 1)** Remove brake drum. See REAR BRAKE DRUM under REMOVAL & INSTALLATION. After removing drum, remove retainer clips, hold-down springs and anchor pins. Disconnect parking brake cable from lever on brake shoe. Disconnect lower return and adjuster springs. Pull brake shoes out of lower support. *See Fig. 7.*

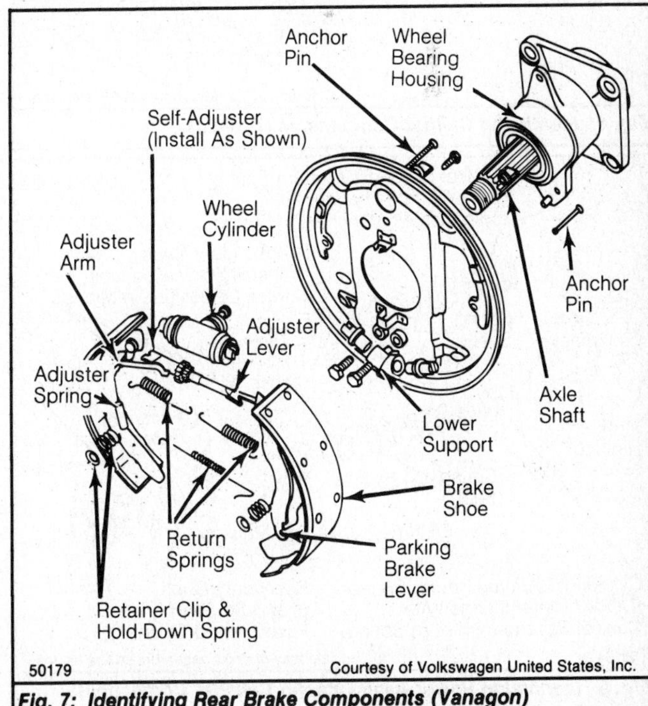


***Fig. 7: Identifying Rear Brake Components (Vanagon)***

# 1991 BRAKES
# Disc & Drum (Cont.)

**2)** Disconnect both upper return springs. Remove both brake shoes from backing plate together with adjuster lever. Ensure both pistons remain in wheel cylinder. Separate brake shoes from adjuster lever. Remove parking brake lever from rear brake shoe.

**Installation – 1)** To install, reverse removal procedure. Adjust brake shoes so that distance from lining surface on leading shoe to lining surface on trailing shoe is 9.87" (250.7 mm).

**2)** Adjust parking brake at equalizer. There should be no free play between parking brake lever on brake shoe and adjusting rod. Install brake drum. Depress brake pedal several times to set self-adjusting mechanism.

## MASTER CYLINDER

**Removal (Except Vanagon) – 1)** Drain master cylinder reservoir. Remove cover plate (if equipped). Disconnect brake lines and wiring at master cylinder.

**2)** On models without power assist servo, disconnect brake push rod at brake pedal. On models equipped with power assist servo, remove master cylinder from servo. Be careful to keep any spacers used on attaching bolts for proper installation.

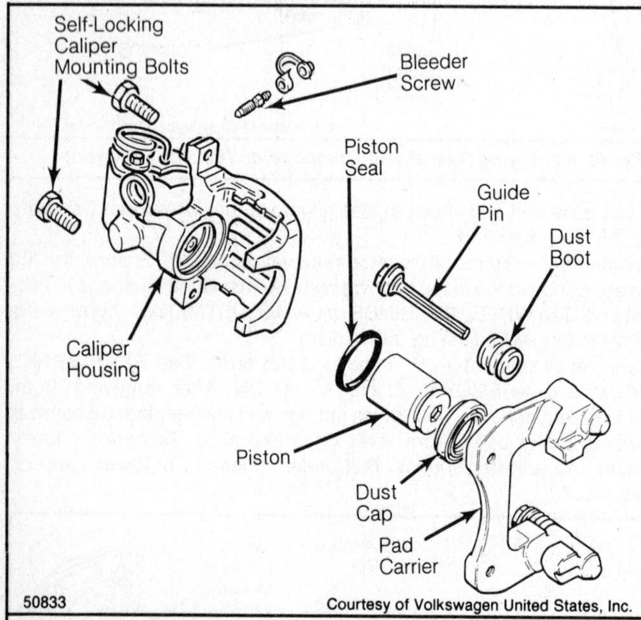


*Fig. 8: Identifying Caliper Components (Typical)*



*Fig. 9: Identifying Power Assist Master Cylinder Components*

**Installation –** To install, reverse removal procedure. Always use new "O" ring between master cylinder and power assist servo. Bleed hydraulic system.

**Removal (Vanagon) – 1)** Remove instrument panel. Drain master cylinder reservoir. Disconnect brake lines and wiring at master cylinder. Disconnect vacuum lines at power assist servo. Remove pedal and bracket assembly.

**2)** Disconnect brake push rod from brake pedal. Remove power assist servo and master cylinder assembly together from pedal bracket. Remove master cylinder from power assist servo.

**Installation –** To install, reverse removal procedure. Install new "O" ring between master cylinder and power assist servo. Adjust brake push rod length. See MASTER CYLINDER PUSH ROD under ADJUSTMENTS in this article. Bleed hydraulic system.

## VACUUM POWER ASSIST SERVO

**Removal (Except Vanagon) –** Remove master cylinder from power assist servo. Disconnect brake push rod from brake pedal. Disconnect vacuum hose from servo. Remove servo from vehicle.

**Removal (Vanagon) –** Remove instrument panel. Remove servo and master cylinder as an assembly. Separate master cylinder from servo.

**Installation (All Models) –** To install, reverse removal procedure. Before attaching brake push rod to brake pedal, check and adjust push rod length. See MASTER CYLINDER PUSH ROD under ADJUSTMENTS. Always replace damping ring, washer, filter and "O" ring (as equipped). Slots in damping washer and filter must be offset 180 degrees (if equipped). Complete installation, and bleed hydraulic system. *See Fig. 9.*

## OVERHAUL

***NOTE: Black staining from piston seal wear may show on caliper bore walls and piston. This staining is normal. DO NOT disassemble power assist servo as parts are not available.***

## TORQUE SPECIFICATIONS

***TORQUE SPECIFICATIONS***

| Application | Ft. Lbs. (N.m) |
|---|---|
| Caliper Mounting Bolts [1] | |
| Cabriolet | 29 (39) |
| Corrado, Passat & Vanagon | 26 (35) |
| Fox | 30 (41) |
| Golf, GTI & Jetta | |
| Front | 18 (25) |
| Rear | 26 (35) |
| Pad Carrier Mounting Bolt | |
| Cabriolet | 52 (70) |
| Corrado & Passat | |
| Front | 92 (125) |
| Rear | 48 (65) |
| Vanagon | 200 (271) |
| Fox, Golf, GTI & Jetta | 48 (65) |
| Rear Axle Nut | |
| Vanagon | 369 (500) |
| Rear Backing Plate-To-Flange Bolt | |
| Except Vanagon | 44 (60) |
| Vanagon | 47 (64) |
| Rear Brake Shoe Support Bolt | |
| Vanagon | 48 (65) |
| Wheel Lug Nut | |
| Except Vanagon | 81 (110) |
| Vanagon | 123 (167) |
| | **INCH Lbs. (N.m)** |
| Wheel Cylinder Bolt | |
| Except Vanagon | 80 (9) |
| Vanagon | 177 (20) |

[1] – Always replace all self-locking bolts.

# 1991 BRAKES
# Disc & Drum (Cont.)

## DISC BRAKE SPECIFICATIONS

*DISC BRAKE SPECIFICATIONS* [1]

| Application | In. (mm) |
|---|---|
| **Front** | |
| Cabriolet | |
| Original Thickness | .787 (20) |
| Wear Limit | .709 (18) |
| Corrado | |
| Disc Diameter | 11.02 (280) |
| Original Thickness | .866 (22) |
| Wear Limit | .787 (20) |
| Fox | |
| Disc Diameter | 9.41 (239) |
| Original Thickness | .472 (12) |
| Wear Limit | .394 (10) |
| Golf, GTI, Jetta & Passat | |
| Solid | |
| Original Thickness | .472 (12) |
| Wear Limit | .394 (10) |
| Vented | |
| Disc Diameter | 10.079 (256) |
| Original Thickness | .787 (20) |
| Wear Limit | .709 (18) |
| Vanagon | |
| Disc Diameter | 10.16 (258) |
| Original Thickness | .591 (15) |
| Wear Limit | .512 (13) |
| **Rear** | |
| Original Thickness | .394 (10) |
| Wear Limit | .315 (8) |

1 - Lateral runout is .002" (.05 mm)

## DRUM BRAKE SPECIFICATIONS

*DRUM BRAKE SPECIFICATIONS*

| Application | In. (mm) |
|---|---|
| **Except Vanagon** | |
| Drum Diameter | 7.087 (180) |
| Maximum Drum Refinish Diameter | 7.106 (180.5) |
| Wear Limit | 7.126 (181) |
| **Vanagon** | |
| Drum Diameter | 9.921 (252) |
| Maximum Drum Refinish Diameter | [1] 9.961 (253) |
| Wear Limit | 9.980 (253.5) |

1 - Use oversize linings after turning drum .020" (.50 mm) or more.

# 1991 BRAKES
# Anti-Lock

## Corrado, Jetta, Passat

## DESCRIPTION

All models use a Teves Anti-Lock Brake System (ABS). *See Fig. 1.* This system reduces the chance of wheel lock-up during heavy braking. The system consists of 4 wheel speed sensors, Electronic Control Unit (ECU), hydraulic modulator/pump and solenoid valves, ANTI-LOCK warning light and BRAKE warning light. There are 2 relays located at fuse/relay panel, to protect the hydraulic modulator and ECU.

***NOTE: For more information on brake system, see appropriate DISC & DRUM article.***

## OPERATION

When pressure is applied to brake pedal, the ECU monitors input signals from each wheel speed sensor. If ECU measures a rate of reduction greater than what is programmed in ECU, the ECU will output a signal to appropriate solenoid valve. Each solenoid valve allows hydraulic pressure to increase or decrease to the appropriate wheel cylinder.

If a system failure occurs, the ANTILOCK warning light, located on instrument panel, will come on. System will be deactivated, but conventional brake system will still operate. If brake fluid level drops too low, BRAKE warning light, located on instrument panel, will come on.

***CAUTION: See ANTI-LOCK BRAKE SAFETY PRECAUTIONS article in GENERAL INFORMATION.***

***CAUTION: The ABS system is under extremely high pressure. Depressurize the brake system before loosening or removing any hydraulic component.***

## DEPRESSURIZING BRAKE SYSTEM

Turn ignition off. Depress and release brake pedal 25-35 times, or until there is a noticeable increase in the effort to depress the brake pedal. Do not turn ignition on until all hydraulic lines and components are fully tighten.

## BLEEDING BRAKE SYSTEM

### FRONT BRAKES

Depressurize brake system. See DEPRESSURIZING BRAKE SYSTEM. Connect a container with hose to left front bleeder screw. Have assistant depress and release brake pedal a few times. Holding brake pedal down, open bleeder screw and allow fluid to enter container. Close bleeder screw and then release brake pedal. Continue this method until no air is present in fluid. Check master cylinder fluid level to make sure it does not go below minimum level mark. Use same procedure for right front brake.

### REAR BRAKES

***CAUTION: When bleeding rear brakes, accumulator pressure (about 3100 psi) is used to assist in procedure. Use eye protection when performing this procedure. DO NOT allow pump to run longer than 2 minutes. See ANTI-LOCK BRAKE SAFETY PRECAUTIONS article in GENERAL INFORMATION.***

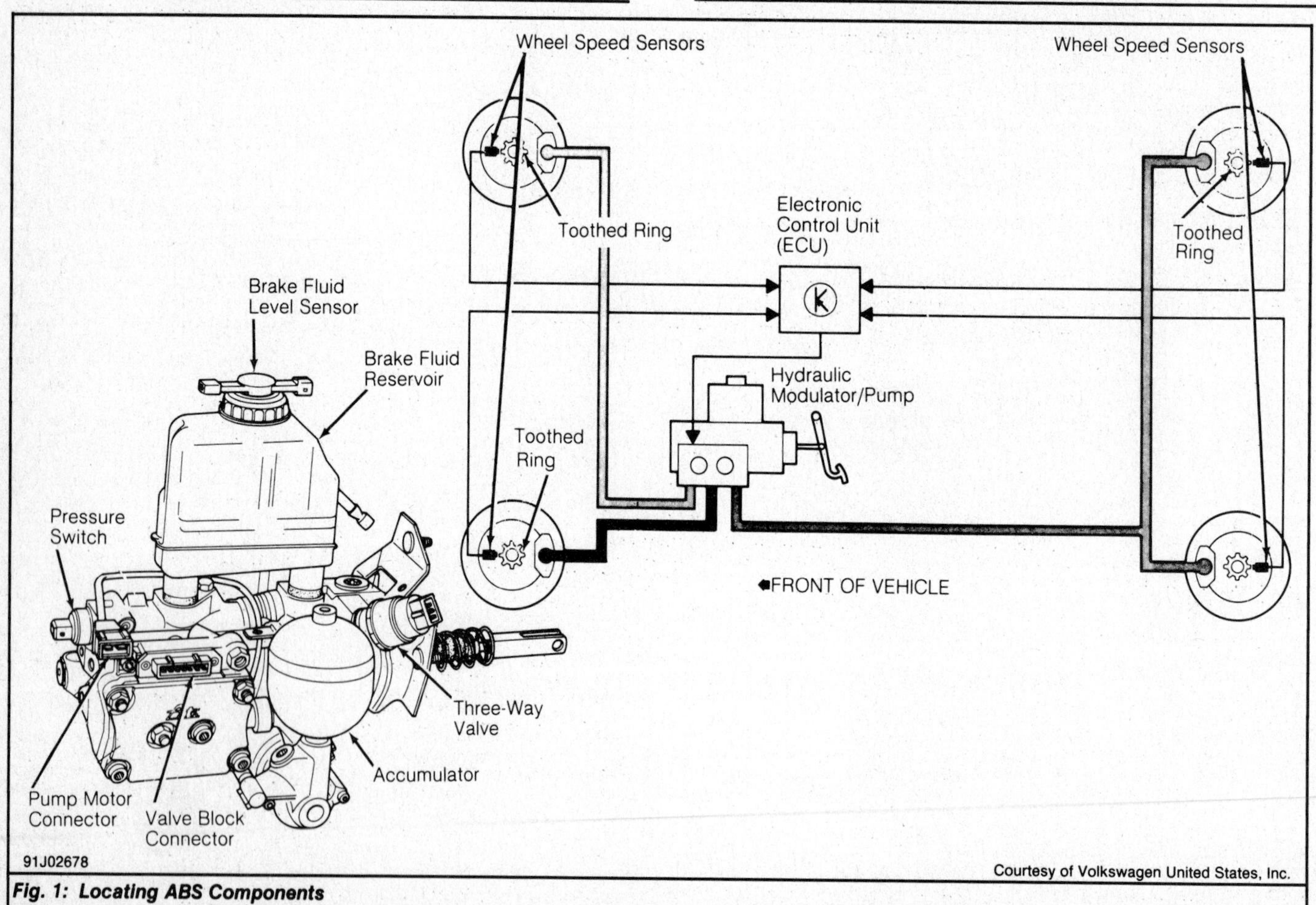


*Fig. 1: Locating ABS Components*

Attach hose and container to right rear bleeder screw. Position actuator lever on load-sensing pressure regulator toward rear of vehicle. Depress brake pedal and turn ignition on. Open bleeder screw and allow fluid to exit until no air is present in fluid. Close bleeder screw. Turn ignition off and release brake pedal. Perform same procedure for left rear brake. Ensure fluid level does not go below minimum level mark.

## ADJUSTMENTS

### PARKING BRAKE

Raise vehicle and support securely. Release parking brake lever. Apply brake pedal once. Loosen lock nuts. Tighten each adjusting nut until lever on respective caliper lifts off stop. Measure gap between stop and lever. Do not move lever off stop more than .040" (1 mm). Tighten lock nuts. Ensure wheels lock at 3 notches.

***NOTE: No other information on adjustments is available.***

## TROUBLE SHOOTING

### HYDRAULIC MODULATOR/PUMP

Depressurize brake system. See DEPRESSURIZING BRAKE SYSTEM. Turn ignition on. Hydraulic modulator/pump should operate for 60 seconds maximum, then stop. Depress brake pedal a few times, pump should operate again for a few seconds. If pump motor does not operate, check electrical system. If pump motor operates for more than 60 seconds, internal or external hydraulic leak may be indicated. Check for external leaks. If external leak is not found, further testing may be needed to check for internal leaks.

### ANTILOCK WARNING LIGHT

Start engine. ANTILOCK warning light should come on, then turn off after a few seconds. If light does not come on when engine is started, check electrical system. If light comes on and stays on, fault has been detected by the ECU and testing will be needed. See SYSTEM TESTING under DIAGNOSIS & TESTING.

## DIAGNOSIS & TESTING

### SYSTEM TESTING

***NOTE: Check battery condition, brake fluid level, electrical connections and wiring for damage. If fluid level is incorrect or battery and/or electrical connections are faulty, correct problem before proceeding. Perform each step, in sequence, to test entire system, except for ECU. If faulty ECU is suspected, replace with a known good one, and retest system. Unplug ECU connector for all test steps.***

**Power Voltage-To-ECU Test** – Turn ignition off. Unplug ECU connector. Turn ignition on. Using a voltmeter, check voltage between ECU connector terminals No. 1 and 2. *See Fig. 2.* If voltage is 10 volts or more, go to next test. If voltage is less than 10 volts, check battery, ground, ABS fuse, relay and wiring. Repair as necessary.

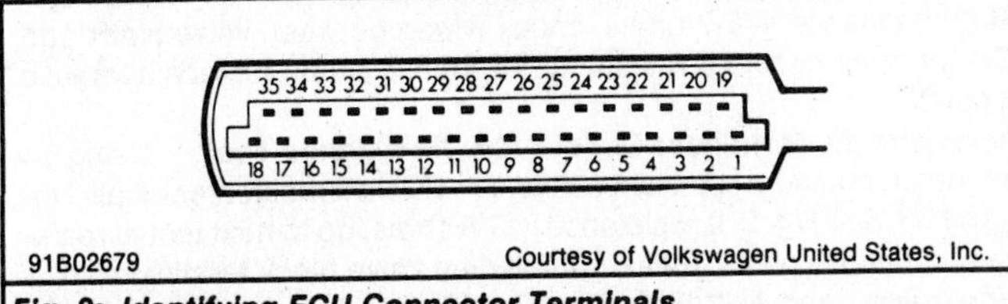


Courtesy of Volkswagen United States, Inc.

***Fig. 2: Identifying ECU Connector Terminals***

**ECU Relay Voltage Test** – Connect a jumper wire between ECU connector terminals No. 2 and 8. *See Fig. 2.* Turn ignition on. Using a voltmeter, check voltage between ECU connector terminals No. 1 and 3. If voltage is 10 volts or more, go to next test. If voltage is less than 10 volts, check ABS fuse. If fuse is faulty, replace and retest. If fuse is okay, check wiring. If wiring is faulty, repair and retest. If wiring is okay, replace relay and retest.

**Brakelight Switch** – Turn ignition on. Apply brakes. Check for 12 volts between terminals No. 12 and 1. If 12 volts are present, brakelight switch is okay. If 12 volts are not present, check fuse, brakelight switch and Black/Red wire from brakelight switch to ECU.

**Hydraulic Modulator/Pump Relay Voltage Test** – **1)** Turn ignition off. Unplug hydraulic modulator/pump connector. Depress brake pedal 25 times. Turn ignition on. Using a voltmeter, measure voltage between ECU connector terminals No. 1 and 32. *See Fig. 2.* If voltage is 10 volts or more, go to RIGHT REAR WHEEL SPEED SENSOR VOLTAGE TEST under SYSTEM TESTING.

**2)** If voltage is less than 10 volts, check hydraulic modulator/pump fuse. If fuse is okay, check wiring between ECU connector terminal No. 32 and hydraulic modulator/pump connector terminal No. 1 (large gauge Red/Black wire). *See Figs. 2, 4, 5 and 6.* If wiring is not okay, repair wiring and retest. If wiring is okay, replace relay and retest.

**Right Rear Wheel Speed Sensor Voltage Test** – Connect an AC voltmeter between ECU connector terminals No. 4 and 22. *See Fig. 2.* Rotate right rear wheel at one revolution per second. Measure voltage with wheel rotating. If voltage is 0.075 volt or more, go to next test. If voltage is less than 0.075 volt, check wheel speed sensor and/or toothed ring for damage, wear and proper installation. If damage or wear is found, replace faulty component and retest. If not properly installed, reposition and retest. If components are okay, replace wheel speed sensor and retest.

**Left Rear Wheel Speed Sensor Voltage Test** – Connect an AC voltmeter between ECU connector terminals No. 6 and 24. *See Fig. 2.* Rotate left rear wheel at one revolution per second. Measure voltage with wheel rotating. If voltage is 0.075 volt or more, go to next test. If voltage is less than 0.075 volt, check wheel speed sensor and/or toothed ring for damage, wear and proper installation. If damage or wear is found, replace faulty component and retest. If not properly installed, reposition and retest. If components are okay, replace wheel speed sensor and retest.

**Right Front Wheel Speed Sensor Voltage Test** – Connect an AC voltmeter between ECU connector terminals No. 7 and 25. *See Fig. 2.* Rotate right front wheel at one revolution per second. Measure voltage with wheel rotating. If voltage is 0.075 volt or more, go to next test. If voltage is less than 0.075 volt, check wheel speed sensor and/or toothed ring for damage, wear and proper installation. If damage or wear is found, replace faulty component and retest. If not properly installed, reposition and retest. If components are okay, replace wheel speed sensor and retest.

**Left Front Wheel Speed Sensor Voltage Test** – Connect an AC voltmeter between ECU connector terminals No. 5 and 23. *See Fig. 2.* Rotate left front wheel at one revolution per second. Measure voltage with wheel rotating. If voltage is 0.075 volt or more, go to next test. If voltage is less than 0.075 volt, check wheel speed sensor and/or toothed ring for damage, wear and proper installation. If damage or wear is found, replace faulty component and retest. If not properly installed, reposition and retest. If components are okay, replace wheel speed sensor and retest.

**ECU Relay Continuity Test** – Turn ignition off. Using an ohmmeter, check for continuity between ECU connector terminals No. 1 and 3, and between terminals No. 1 and 20. *See Fig. 2.* If there is continuity at both test points, go to next test. If there is no continuity at either or both test points, check wiring. If wiring is faulty, repair and retest. If wiring is okay, replace relay and retest.

**Solenoid Valves Ground Circuit Continuity Test** – **1)** Turn ignition off. Remove jumper wire from previous test. Using an ohmmeter, check for continuity between ECU connector terminals No. 1 and 11. *See Fig. 2.* If there is continuity, go to next step.

**2)** If there is no continuity, check for continuity between ECU connector terminal No. 1 and valve block housing, and between hydraulic modulator and valve block housing. If there is no continuity between ECU connector terminal No. 1 and valve block housing, repair wiring and retest. If there is no continuity between housings, repair as necessary.

**3)** Reconnect jumper wire between ECU connector terminals No. 1 and 11. Check for continuity between ECU connector terminal No. 11

# 1991 BRAKES
# Anti-Lock (Cont.)

and valve block connector terminal No. 1 (Brown wire). *See Figs. 2, 4, 5 and 6.* If there is no continuity, repair wiring and retest.

**Hydraulic Modulator/Pump Relay Ground Circuit Test** – Turn ignition off. Reconnect pressure switch connector. Depress brake pedal 20 times. Using an ohmmeter, check for continuity between ECU connector terminals No. 1 and 14. If continuity exists, go to next test. If continuity does not exist, check for continuity between pressure switch terminals No. 1 (Brown wire) and 4 (Red/Yellow or White wire). *See Figs. 1 and 4, 5 or 6.* If continuity does not exist, replace pressure switch, and retest. If continuity exists, check wiring between ECU terminal No. 14 and pressure switch terminal No. 4. Repair wiring, and retest.

**Low Pressure Warning Switch Test** – Turn ignition off. Ensure brake fluid level is okay and fluid level sensor switch float is in correct position (switch is in closed position). Ensure accumulator is fully charged and pump is not operating. Using an ohmmeter, check for continuity between ECU connector terminals No. 9 and 10. *See Fig. 2.* If there is continuity, switch is okay. If there is no continuity, check wiring. If wiring is okay, replace switch and retest.

**Right Rear Wheel Speed Sensor Resistance Test** – Turn ignition off. Using an ohmmeter, measure resistance between ECU connector terminals No. 4 and 22. *See Fig. 2.* If resistance is 800-1400 ohms, go to next test. If resistance is not as specified, check resistance at right rear wheel speed sensor. If resistance is correct, repair wiring and retest. If resistance is not correct, replace wheel speed sensor and retest.

**Left Rear Wheel Speed Sensor Resistance Test** – Using an ohmmeter, measure resistance between ECU connector terminals No. 6 and 24. *See Fig. 2.* If resistance is 800-1400 ohms, go to next test. If resistance is not as specified, check resistance at left rear wheel speed sensor. If resistance is correct, repair wiring and retest. If resistance is not correct, replace wheel speed sensor and retest.

**Right Front Wheel Speed Sensor Resistance Test** – Using an ohmmeter, measure resistance between ECU connector terminals No. 7 and 25. *See Fig. 2.* If resistance is 800-1400 ohms, go to next test. If resistance is not as specified, check resistance at right front wheel speed sensor. If resistance is correct, repair wiring and retest. If resistance is not correct, replace wheel speed sensor and retest.

**Left Front Wheel Speed Sensor Resistance Test** – Using an ohmmeter, measure resistance between ECU connector terminals No. 5 and 23. *See Fig. 2.* If resistance is 800-1400 ohms, go to next test. If resistance is not as specified, check resistance at left front wheel speed sensor. If resistance is correct, repair wiring and retest. If resistance is not correct, replace wheel speed sensor and retest.

**Right Rear Wheel Speed Sensor Shielding Resistance Test** – Using an ohmmeter, measure resistance between ECU connector terminals No. 4 and 1. *See Fig. 2.* If resistance is 20,000 ohms or more, go to next test. If resistance is less than 20,000 ohms, check shielding wire for damage. Replace harness if damage is found and retest.

**Left Rear Wheel Speed Sensor Shielding Resistance Test** – Using an ohmmeter, measure resistance between ECU connector terminals No. 6 and 1. *See Fig. 2.* If resistance is 20,000 ohms or more, go to next test. If resistance is less than 20,000 ohms, check shielding wire for damage. Replace harness if damage is found and retest.

**Right Front Wheel Speed Sensor Shielding Resistance Test** – Using an ohmmeter, measure resistance between ECU connector terminals No. 7 and 1. *See Fig. 2.* If resistance is 20,000 ohms or more, go to next test. If resistance is less than 20,000 ohms, check shielding wire for damage. Replace harness if damaged, and retest.

**Left Front Wheel Speed Sensor Shielding Resistance Test** – Using an ohmmeter, measure resistance between ECU connector terminals No. 5 and 1. *See Fig. 2.* If resistance is 20,000 ohms or more, go to next test. If resistance is less than 20,000 ohms, check shielding wire for damage. Replace harness if damage is found and retest.

**ECU Relay Resistance Test** – Using an ohmmeter, measure resistance between ECU connector terminals No. 1 and 8. *See Fig. 2.* If resistance is 50-100 ohms, go to next test. If resistance is not as specified, check wiring. If wiring is faulty, repair and retest. If wiring is okay, replace relay and retest. *See Fig. 3.*

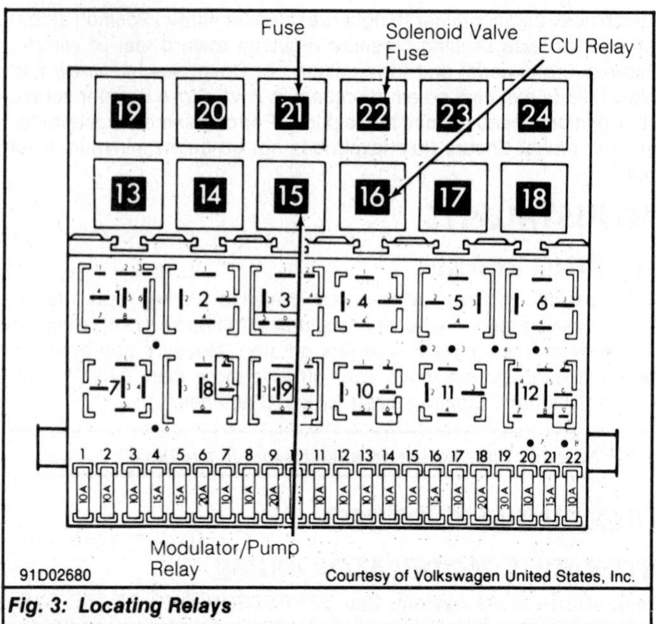


***Fig. 3: Locating Relays***

**ABS Main Valve Resistance Test** – Using an ohmmeter, measure resistance between terminals at ABS main valve terminals. *See Figs. 1, 4, 5 and 6.* If resistance is 2-5 ohms, ABS main valve is okay. If resistance is not 2-5 ohms, replace hydraulic modulator.

**ABS Main Valve Continuity Test** – Using an ohmmeter, check for continuity between ABS main valve terminal No. 1 (Black wire) and ECU connector terminal No. 18, and between ABS main valve terminal No. 2 (Brown wire) and ground. *See Figs. 1, 2, 4, 5 and 6.* There should be continuity at both test points. If there is no continuity at both test points, repair wiring and retest.

**Rear Hydraulic Modulator Inlet Valve Resistance Test** – Using an ohmmeter, measure resistance between ECU connector terminals No. 11 and 17. *See Fig. 2.* If resistance is 5-7 ohms, go to next test. If resistance is not 5-7 ohms, measure between hydraulic modulator block terminal Nos. 1 (Brown wire) and 5 (Gray wire). *See Figs. 4-6.* If resistance is 5-7 ohms, check wiring between hydraulic modulator and ECU for open circuit. If resistance is not 5-7 ohms, replace hydraulic modulator.

**Right Front Hydraulic Modulator Inlet Valve Resistance Test** – Using an ohmmeter, measure resistance between ECU connector terminals No. 11 and 15. *See Fig. 2.* If resistance is 5-7 ohms, go to next test. If resistance is not 5-7 ohms, measure between hydraulic modulator terminals No. 1 (Brown wire) and 2 (Yellow wire). *See Fig. 4, 5 or 6.* If resistance is 5-7 ohms, check wiring between hydraulic modulator and ECU for open circuit. If resistance is not 5-7 ohms, replace hydraulic modulator.

**Left Front Hydraulic Modulator Inlet Valve Resistance Test** – Using an ohmmeter, measure resistance between ECU connector terminals No. 11 and 35. *See Fig. 2.* If resistance is 5-7 ohms, go to next test. If resistance is not 5-7 ohms, measure between hydraulic modulator terminals No. 1 (Brown wire) and 7 (Blue or Black/Green wire). *See Figs. 4-6.* If resistance is 5-7 ohms, check wiring between valve block and ECU for open circuit. If resistance is not 5-7 ohms, replace hydraulic modulator.

**Rear Hydraulic Modulator Outlet Valve Resistance Test** – Using an ohmmeter, measure resistance between ECU connector terminals No. 11 and 33. *See Fig. 2.* If resistance is 3-5 ohms, go to next test. If resistance is not 3-5 ohms, measure between valve block terminals No. 1 (Brown wire) and 4 (White wire). *See Figs. 4-6.* If resistance is 3-5 ohms, check wiring between hydraulic modulator and ECU for open circuit. If resistance is not 3-5 ohms, replace hydraulic modulator.

**Right Hydraulic Modulator Block Outlet Valve Resistance Test** – Using an ohmmeter, measure resistance between ECU connector terminals No. 11 and 34. *See Fig. 2.* If resistance is 3-5 ohms, go to next test. If resistance is not 3-5 ohms, measure between hydraulic

# 1991 BRAKES
# Anti-Lock (Cont.)

modulator terminals No. 1 (Brown wire) and 3 (Green wire). *See Fig. 4, 5 or 6*. If resistance is 3-5 ohms, check wiring between hydraulic modulator and ECU for open circuit. If resistance is not 3-5 ohms, replace hydraulic modulator.

**Left Front Hydraulic Modulator Outlet Valve Resistance Test** - Using an ohmmeter, measure resistance between ECU connector terminals No. 11 and 16. *See Fig. 2*. If resistance is 3-5 ohms, go to next test. If resistance is not 3-5 ohms, measure between hydraulic modulator terminals No. 1 (Brown wire) and 6 (Black/Blue wire). *See Fig. 4, 5 or 6*. If resistance is 3-5 ohms, check wiring between hydraulic modulator and ECU for open circuit. If resistance is not 3-5 ohms, replace hydraulic modulator.

**Hydraulic Modulator/Pump Relay Resistance Test** - Turn ignition off. Unplug pressure switch connector from hydraulic modulator. Using an ohmmeter, measure resistance between ECU connector terminals No. 2 and 14. *See Fig. 2*. If resistance is 50-100 ohms, go to next test. If resistance is not 50-100 ohms, check wiring. If wiring is faulty, repair wiring and retest. If wiring is okay, replace relay and retest.

**ABS Main Valve Function Test** - Connect a jumper wire between ECU connector terminals No. 2 and 18. *See Fig. 2*. Depress brake pedal. Turn ignition on. Brake pedal should rise slightly. If brake pedal did not rise slightly, check wiring between terminals and hydraulic modulator. If wiring is okay, replace hydraulic modulator.

**Hydraulic Modulator/Pump Test** - Turn ignition off. Depress brake pedal 25 times. Turn ignition on. BRAKE and ANTILOCK lights should come on for 2-60 seconds. Pump should operate for 2-60 seconds, then turn off. If lights do not come on, check wiring and warning light bulbs, and retest. Also check bulb(s). If lights come on, then turn off, and pump operates for 60 seconds maximum, then turns off, go to next test. If pump does not operate and all other preceding tests have been performed, replace hydraulic modulator/pump.

***CAUTION: During VALVE BLOCK FUNCTION TESTS, DO NOT turn ignition on longer than 60 seconds during any test.***

**Rear Valve Block Function Test** - Connect a jumper wire ECU between ECU connector terminals No. 2, 17 and 33. *See Fig. 2*. Depress brake pedal. Rear wheels should be locked up. Turn ignition on. Rear wheels should rotate. If wheels do not rotate, replace hydraulic modulator. Turn ignition off.

**Right Front Valve Block Function Test** - Connect a jumper wire ECU between ECU connector terminals No. 2, 15 and 34. *See Fig. 2*. Depress brake pedal. Right front wheel should be locked up. Turn ignition on. Right front wheel should rotate. If wheel do not rotate, replace hydraulic modulator. Turn ignition off.

**Left Front Valve Block Function Test** - Connect a jumper wire ECU between ECU connector terminals No. 2, 16 and 35. *See Fig. 2*. Depress brake pedal. Left front wheel should be locked up. Turn ignition on. Left front wheel should rotate. If wheel do not rotate, replace hydraulic modulator. Turn ignition off.

## REMOVAL & INSTALLATION

### HYDRAULIC MODULATOR/PUMP

**Removal & Installation - 1)** Depressurize brake system. See DEPRESSURIZING BRAKE SYSTEM. Disconnect negative battery cable. Unplug all electrical connectors from hydraulic modulator/pump. Identify and disconnect all hydraulic lines from hydraulic modulator/pump. Plug all line openings.

**2)** From inside passenger compartment, remove push rod clevis pin. Remove hydraulic modulator/pump retaining nuts. Remove hydraulic modulator/pump. To install, reverse removal procedure. Tighten all fittings to specification. See TORQUE SPECIFICATIONS table at end of article. Bleed brake system. See BLEEDING BRAKE SYSTEM.

### WHEEL SPEED SENSORS

***NOTE: To protect magnetic part of sensor, always leave new wheel speed sensor in special packaging until ready for installation.***

**Removal & Installation** - Remove bolt retaining wheel speed sensor. Unplug connector. Remove wheel speed sensor. To install, apply Lubricant (G 000 650) to sensor. Install sensor and tighten retaining bolt to 84 INCH lbs. (10 N.m).

## TORQUE SPECIFICATIONS

*TORQUE SPECIFICATIONS*

| Applications | Ft. Lbs. (N.m) |
|---|---|
| Brake Lines-To-Hydraulic Modulator/Pump | 11 (15) |
| Hydraulic Modulator/Pump Retaining Nuts | 18 (25) |
| | **INCH Lbs. (N.m)** |
| Wheel Sensor Retaining Bolt | 84 (10) |

# 1991 BRAKES
# Anti-Lock (Cont.)

## WIRING DIAGRAMS

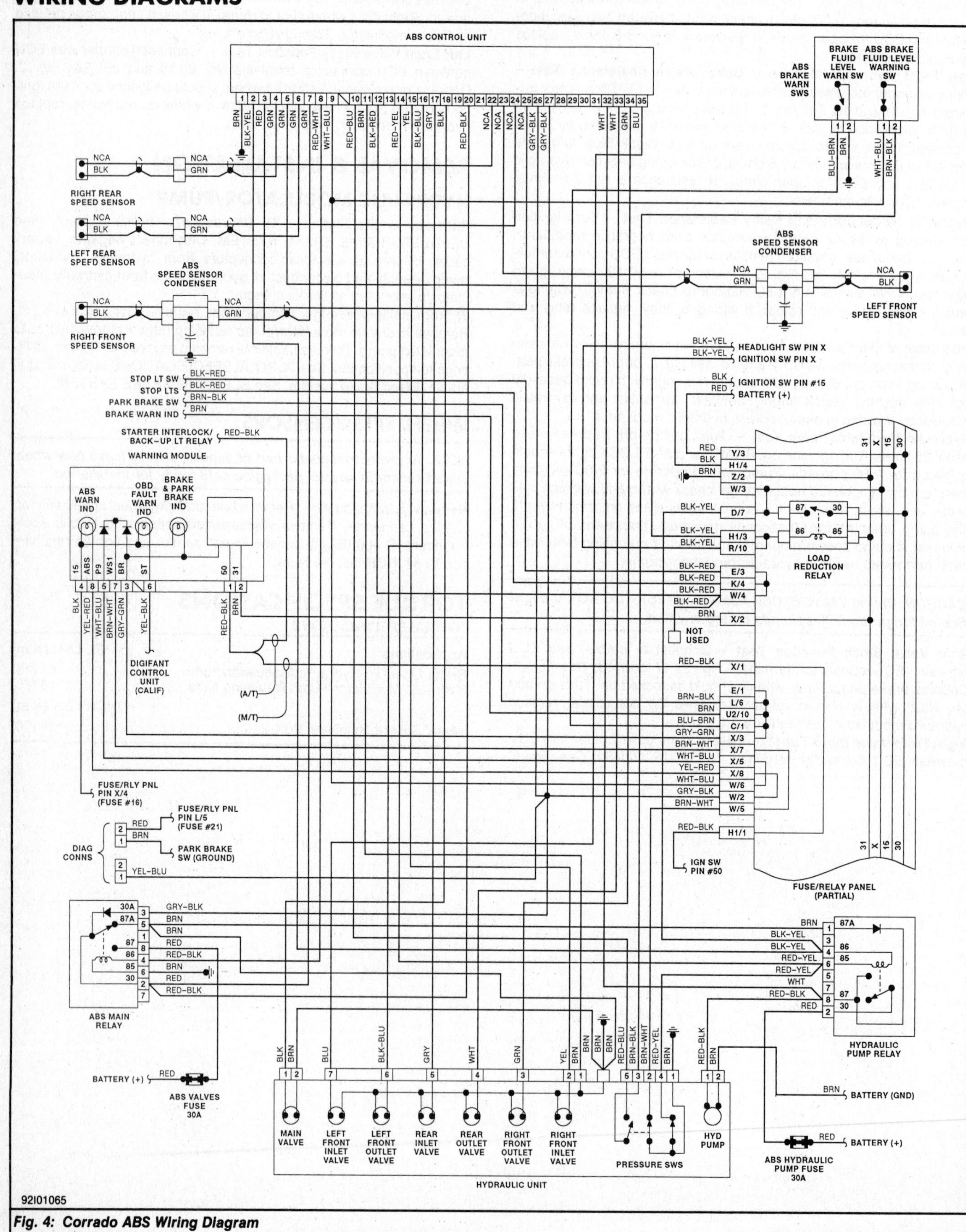


*Fig. 4: Corrado ABS Wiring Diagram*

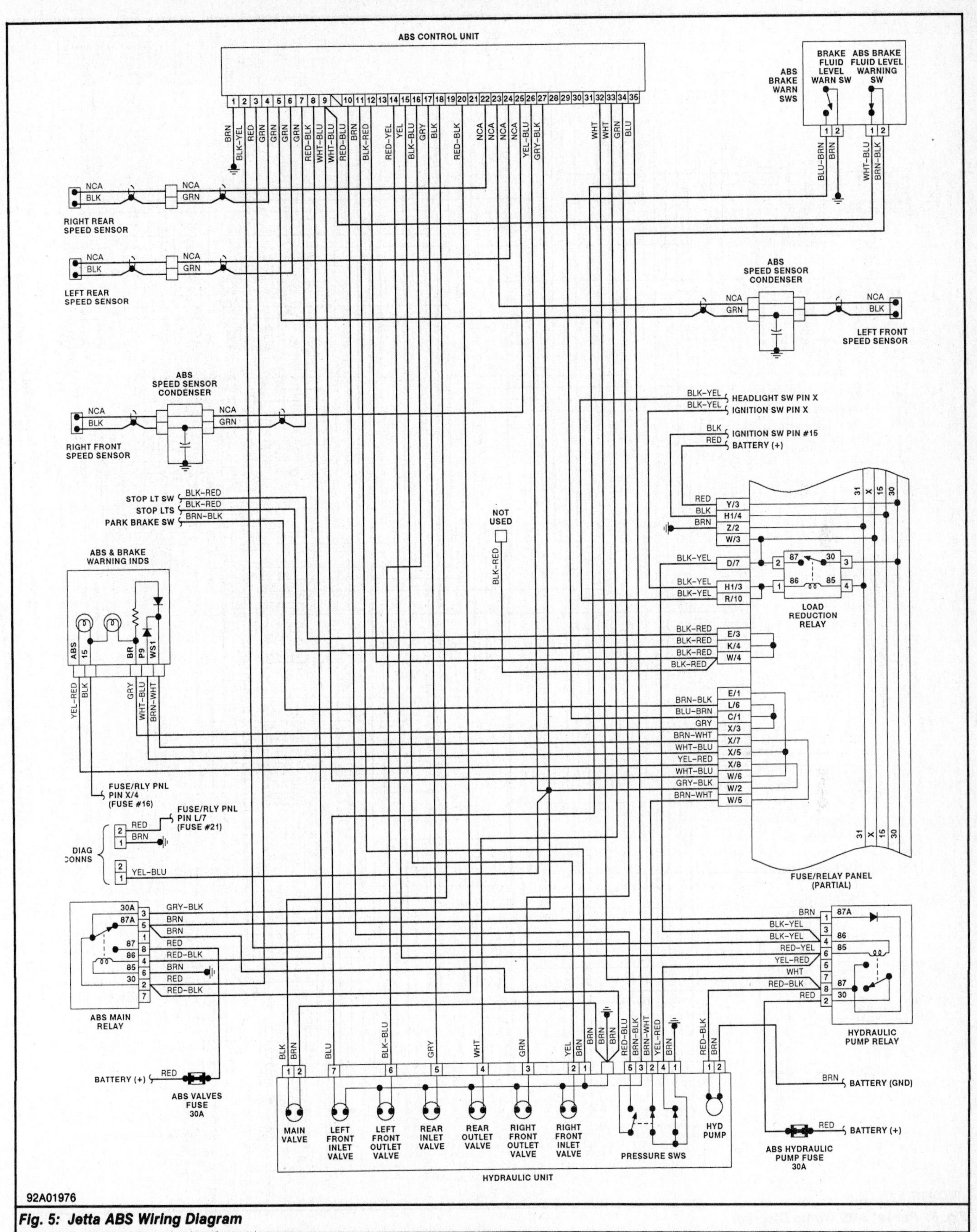


Fig. 5: Jetta ABS Wiring Diagram

# 1991 BRAKES
## Anti-Lock (Cont.)

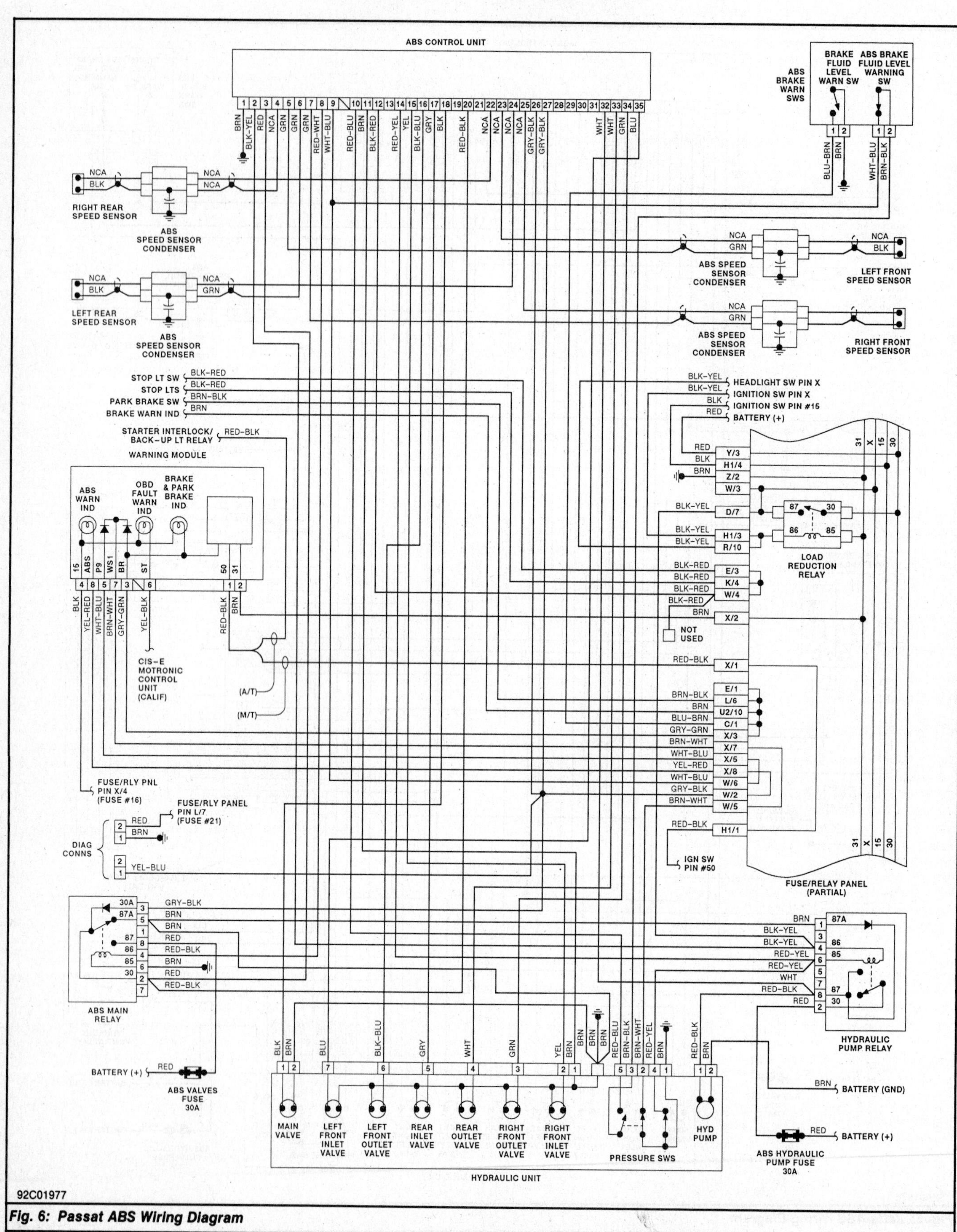


*Fig. 6: Passat ABS Wiring Diagram*

# 1991 WHEEL ALIGNMENT
# Specifications & Procedures

## Cabriolet, Corrado, Fox, Golf, GTI, Jetta, Passat, Vanagon

***NOTE: Prior to performing wheel alignment, perform preliminary visual and mechanical inspection of wheels, tires and suspension components. See PRE-ALIGNMENT INSTRUCTIONS in WHEEL ALIGNMENT THEORY & OPERATION article in GENERAL INFORMATION.***

## RIDING HEIGHT ADJUSTMENT

***NOTE: On vehicles with electronic chassis controls, all systems should be functional before attempting riding height or wheel alignment adjustment.***

Before adjusting alignment, ensure difference in riding height between left and right sides of vehicle is less than 1" (25.4 mm). Riding height must be checked with vehicle on level floor and tires properly inflated. Bounce vehicle several times and allow suspension to settle.

Visually inspect vehicle for signs of abnormal height from front to rear or side to side. Check passenger and luggage compartments for extra heavy items and remove if present. If difference in riding height between left and right sides of vehicle is NOT less than 1" (25.4 mm), check suspension components and repair or replace as necessary.

## WHEEL ALIGNMENT SPECIFICATIONS

***WHEEL ALIGNMENT SPECIFICATIONS***

| Application | Preferred | Range |
|---|---|---|
| **Cabriolet** | | |
| Camber [1] | | |
| Front | 5/16 | -3/16 To 13/16 |
| Rear | -1 1/4 | -1 13/16 To -11/16 |
| Caster [1] | 1 3/16 | 1 5/16 To 2 5/16 |
| Toe-In [2] | | |
| Front | -1/8 (-3) | -3/16 To -1/16 (-4.5 To -1.5) |
| Rear | 5/32 (4) | 1/32 To 9/32 (1 To 7) |
| Toe-In [1] | | |
| Front | -1/4 | -3/8 To -1/8 |
| Rear | 5/16 | 1/16 To 9/16 |
| Toe-Out On Turns [1] | | |
| Inner | 20 | ..... |
| Outer | 18 1/2 | ..... |
| **Corrado** | | |
| Camber [1] | | |
| Front | -21/32 | -1 To -5/16 |
| Rear | -1/2 | -1 21/32 To -1 11/32 |
| Caster [1] | 1 19/32 | 1 3/32 To 2 3/32 |
| Toe-In [2] | | |
| Front | 0 (0) | -3/32 To 3/32 (-2.5 To 2.5) |
| Rear | 5/32 (4) | 1/16 To 1/4 (1.5 To 6.5) |
| Toe-In [1] | | |
| Front | 0 | -5/32 To 5/32 |
| Rear | 11/32 | 3/16 To 1/2 |
| **Fox (Except Wagon)** | | |
| Camber [1] | | |
| Front | -1/2 | -13/16 To -3/16 |
| Rear | -1 1/2 | -2 To -1 |
| Caster [1] | 2 | 1 11/16 To 2 5/16 |
| Toe-In [2] | | |
| Front | -1/16 (-1.5) | -1/8 To 0 (-3 To 0) |
| Rear | 7/32 (5.5) | 1/8 To 9/32 (3 To 7) |
| Toe-In [1] | | |
| Front | -1/8 | -1/4 To 0 |
| Rear | 7/16 | 1/4 To 9/16 |
| **Fox Wagon** | | |
| Camber [1] | | |
| Front | -1/2 | -13/16 To 3/16 |
| Rear | -1 1/2 | -2 To 1 |

***WHEEL ALIGNMENT SPECIFICATIONS (Cont.)***

| Application | Preferred | Range |
|---|---|---|
| **Fox Wagon (Cont.)** | | |
| Caster [1] | 1 3/4 | 1 7/16 To 2 1/16 |
| Toe-In [2] | | |
| Front | -1/16 (-1.5) | -1/8 To 0 (-3 To 0) |
| Rear | 5/32 (4) | 1/16 To 1/4 (1.5 To 6.5) |
| Toe-In [1] | | |
| Front | -1/8 | -1/4 To 0 |
| Rear | 5/16 | 1/8 To 1/2 |
| **Golf & Jetta (Except GLi)** | | |
| Camber [1] | | |
| Front | -7/16 | -3/4 To -1/8 |
| Rear | -1 11/16 | -2 To -1 3/8 |
| Caster [1] | 1 1/2 | 1 To 2 |
| Toe-In [2] | | |
| Front | 0 (0) | -1/16 To 1/16 (-1.5 To 1.5) |
| Rear | 7/32 (5.5) | 1/8 To 5/16 (3 To 8) |
| Toe-In [1] | | |
| Front | 0 | -1/8 To 1/8 |
| Rear | 7/16 | 1/4 To 5/8 |
| **GTI & Jetta GLi** | | |
| Camber [1] | | |
| Front | -9/16 | -7/8 To -1/4 |
| Rear | -1 11/16 | -2 To -1 3/8 |
| Caster [1] | 1 9/16 | 1 1/16 To 2 1/16 |
| Toe-In [2] | | |
| Front | 0 (0) | -1/16 To 1/16 (-1.5 To 1.5) |
| Rear | 7/32 (5.5) | 1/8 To 5/16 (3 To 8) |
| Toe-In [1] | | |
| Front | 0 | -1/8 To 1/8 |
| Rear | 7/16 | 1/4 To 5/8 |
| **Passat** | | |
| Camber [1] | | |
| Front | -1 11/32 | -1 11/16 To -1 |
| Rear | -1 21/32 | -2 To -1 5/16 |
| Caster [1] | 1 21/32 | 1 5/32 To 2 5/32 |
| Toe-In [2] | | |
| Front | 0 (0) | -3/32 To 3/32 (-2.5 To 2.5) |
| Rear | 7/32 (5.5) | 3/32 To 11/32 (2.5 To 8.5) |
| Toe-In [1] | | |
| Front | 0 | -5/32 To 5/32 |
| Rear | 13/32 | 5/32 To 21/32 |
| **Vanagon (Except Syncro)** | | |
| Camber [1] | | |
| Front | 0 | -1/2 To 1/2 |
| Rear | -13/16 | -1 5/16 To 5/16 |
| Caster [1] | 7 1/4 | 7 To 7 1/2 |
| Toe-In [2] | | |
| Front | 5/32 (4) | 1/32 To 9/32 (1 To 7) |
| Rear | 0 (0) | -5/32 To 5/32 (-4 To 4) |
| Toe-In [1] | | |
| Front | 5/16 | 1/16 To 9/16 |
| Rear | 0 | -5/16 To 5/16 |
| **Vanagon (Syncro)** | | |
| Camber [1] | | |
| Front | 5/16 | 0 To 5/8 |
| Rear | -1/4 | -7/16 To -1/16 |
| Caster [1] | 4 5/8 | 4 3/8 To 4 7/8 |
| Toe-In [2] | | |
| Front | 0 (0) | -1/8 To 1/8 (-3 To 3) |
| Rear | 1/16 (1.5) | -1/16 To 3/16 (-1.5 To 4.5) |
| Toe-In [1] | | |
| Front | 0 | -1/4 To 1/4 |
| Rear | 1/8 | -1/8 To 3/8 |

[1] – Measurement in degrees.

[2] – Measurement in inches (mm).

# 1991 SUSPENSION
# Front – Except Fox & Vanagon

**Cabriolet, Corrado, Golf, GTI, Jetta, Passat**

## DESCRIPTION

FWD suspension system has MacPherson struts. Wheel bearing housings are supported by lower control arms and vertically mounted strut assemblies. *See Fig. 1.*

## ADJUSTMENTS & INSPECTION

### WHEEL ALIGNMENT SPECIFICATIONS & PROCEDURES

***NOTE: See SPECIFICATIONS & PROCEDURES article in WHEEL ALIGNMENT.***

### WHEEL BEARING

No adjustment is required.

### BALL JOINT CHECKING

Raise and support vehicle. Inspect ball joints for excessive play and damaged rubber boots. Maximum tolerance for ball joint play not available from manufacturer.

## REMOVAL & INSTALLATION

### HUB & KNUCKLE ASSEMBLY

Use exploded view illustration when removing or installing hub and knuckle assembly. *See Fig. 1.*

### LOWER CONTROL ARM & BALL JOINT

**Removal – 1)** Raise and support vehicle. Remove bolt retaining ball joint at wheel bearing housing. Force ball joint from of housing. Leave control arm hanging in mounts at subframe.

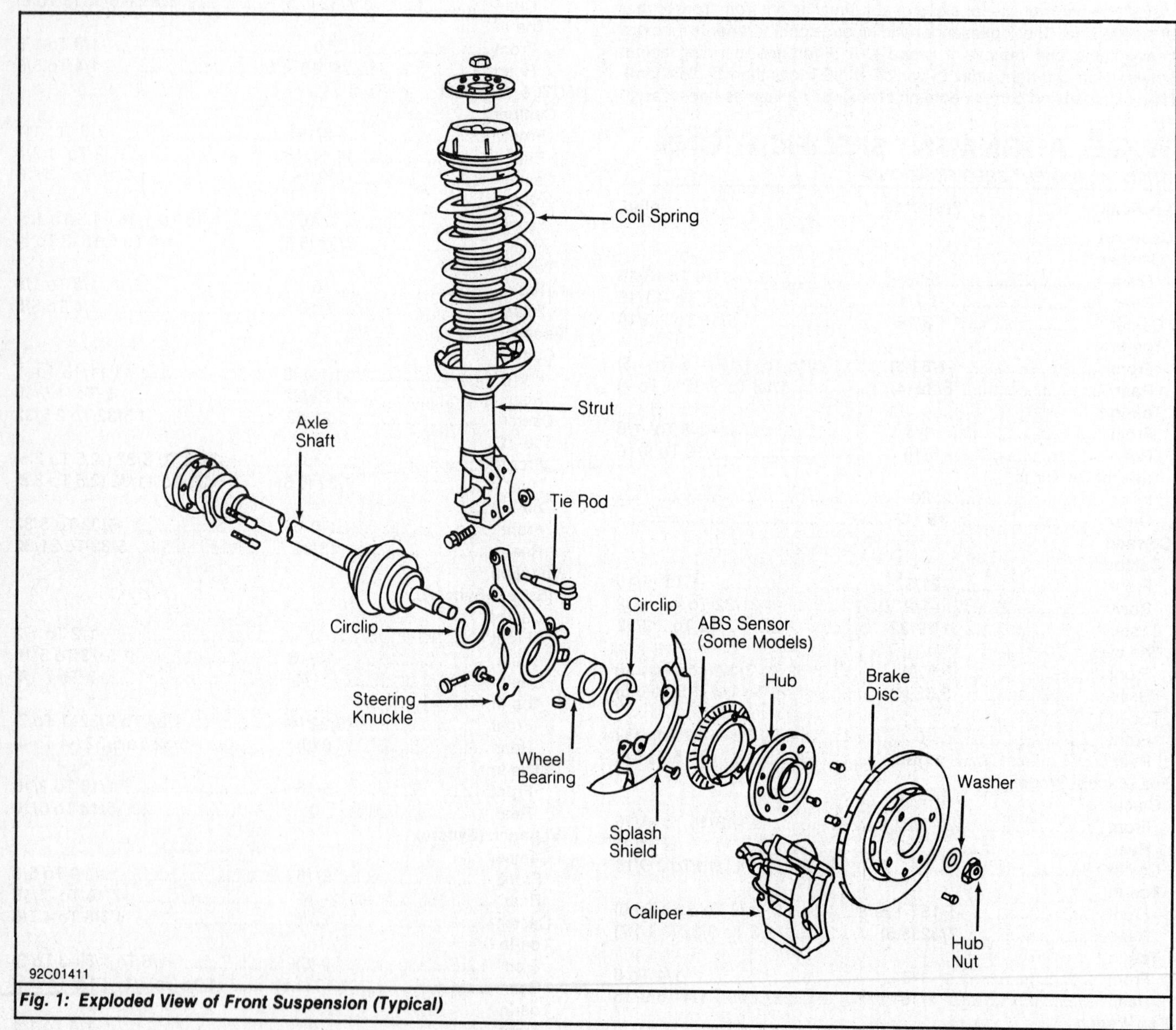


*Fig. 1: Exploded View of Front Suspension (Typical)*

# 1991 SUSPENSION
# Front – Except Fox & Vanagon (Cont.)

**2)** If control arm is not to be removed, and ball joint is riveted to control arm, drill out ball joint rivets with a 9/32" (7 mm) drill. After drilling rivets, it still may be necessary to chisel off rivet heads. Remove ball joint. *See Fig. 2.*

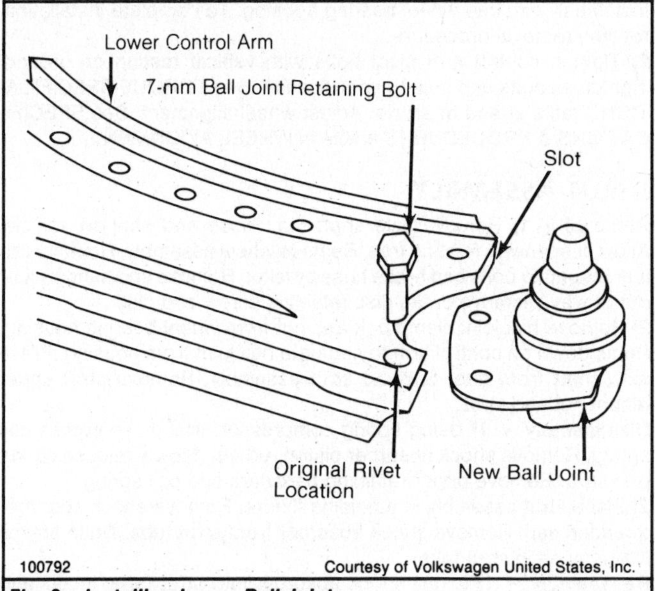


***Fig. 2: Installing Lower Ball Joint***

**3)** If control arm is to be removed, remove stabilizer bar link rod nut, washers, and bushings. Remove pivot bolt and "U" bracket housing inner pivot pin. Slide out control arm.

***NOTE: On vehicles with automatic transmission, engine may have to be lifted slightly to gain access to pivot bolts.***

**Inspection** – Check lower control arm bushings. Replace bushings if necessary. To replace bushings, press out worn bushing. Select new bushing and press into position. Make sure bushing does not twist when seating into place.

**Installation** – Slide new ball joint into slot in control arm. Install and tighten ball joint retaining bolts. Install lower control arm to subframe. Install ball joint into wheel bearing housing. To complete installation, reverse removal procedure. Tighten control arm bolts with vehicle on ground. Tighten all bolts and nuts to specification. See TORQUE SPECIFICATIONS table at end of article. Check wheel alignment. See SPECIFICATIONS & PROCEDURES article in WHEEL ALIGNMENT.

## STRUT ASSEMBLY

**Removal** – **1)** Raise and support vehicle. Remove wheel assembly. Remove and support caliper assembly out of work area. Remove bolts which retain strut to wheel bearing housing. Note that top bolt is used to adjust front wheel camber.

**2)** Support front suspension arm and related components. Pry suspension strut from wheel bearing housing. Working inside engine compartment, remove upper strut retaining nuts. Remove strut.

**Installation** – To install, reverse removal procedure. Tighten bolts and nuts to specification. See TORQUE SPECIFICATIONS table at end of article. Check wheel alignment. See SPECIFICATIONS & PROCEDURES article in WHEEL ALIGNMENT.

## FRONT SUSPENSION ASSEMBLY

**Removal** – **1)** Raise vehicle and support at center with safety stands. Disconnect brake line and plug openings. Leave flex line in place. Remove stabilizer link rod nut, bushings and washers.

**2)** Remove tie rod nut. Separate tie rod from wheel bearing housing. Remove bolts retaining inner portion of constant velocity joint to transaxle drive flange.

**3)** Remove lower control arm front pivot bolt. Remove bolts retaining "U" shaped bracket holding control arm rear pivot.

***NOTE: On vehicles with automatic transmission, engine may have to be lifted slightly to gain access to pivot bolts.***

**4)** Support suspension assembly being removed. Remove upper strut retaining nuts. Remove suspension assembly from vehicle.

**Installation** – To install, reverse removal procedure. Make sure convex side of thrust washer faces pivot bolt head. Tighten bolts and nuts to specification. Check wheel alignment. See SPECIFICATIONS & PROCEDURES article in WHEEL ALIGNMENT.

## WHEEL BEARING

***NOTE: The wheel bearing is destroyed when pressed out of housing. When either the wheel hub or bearing has been removed from housing, a new bearing must be installed.***

**Removal** – **1)** Remove axle shaft nut. Raise and support vehicle with safety stands. Allow suspension to hang free. Remove wheel assembly. Remove brake caliper attaching bolts. Remove caliper and hang out of work area. Remove brake disc retaining screw and remove disc.

**2)** Remove tie rod ball joint from wheel bearing housing. Remove nut and clamp bolt from control arm ball joint. Remove control arm ball joint from wheel bearing housing and remove housing.

**3)** Remove 2 circlips retaining bearing in hub. Using Hub Remover (VW 295a), press wheel hub from bearing housing. Using a bearing puller, remove wheel bearing inner race from hub assembly. Using Bearing Remover (VW 433), press wheel bearing from outboard end of bearing housing.

**Installation** – **1)** Press new bearing race onto hub. Using Bearing & Hub Installer (VW 472/1), press new bearing into bearing housing from outboard side. Using same adapter, press wheel hub into bearing housing. Apply a small bead of locking compound to axle splines before installing into hub.

**2)** To complete installation, reverse removal procedure. Always replace self-locking axle shaft nut. Tighten bolts and nuts to specification. See TORQUE SPECIFICATIONS table at end of article. Check wheel alignment. See SPECIFICATIONS & PROCEDURES article in WHEEL ALIGNMENT.

***NOTE: When installing hub, ensure press adapter contacts ONLY the inner bearing race.***

# TORQUE SPECIFICATIONS

***TORQUE SPECIFICATIONS***

| Application | Ft. Lbs. (N.m) |
|---|---|
| Axle Nut | 170 (230) |
| Axle Shaft-To-Transaxle Bolt | 32 (43) |
| Ball Joint Clamp Bolt | 37 (50) |
| Ball Joint-To-Control Arm Bolt | 18 (24) |
| Caliper Pin Bolt | 18 (24) |
| Control Arm Pivot Bolt | |
| Cabriolet | 50 (68) |
| All Others | 96 (130) |
| Control Arm-To-Subframe Rear Bushing Bolt | 96 (130) |
| Strut Piston Rod Nut | |
| Cabriolet | 50 (68) |
| All Others | 44 (60) |
| Suspension Strut-To-Wheel Bearing Housing Bolt | 59 (80) |
| Tie Rod Castle Nut | 26 (35) |
| Wheel Lug Bolt | 81 (110) |

# 1991 SUSPENSION
# Front – Fox

## DESCRIPTION

Vehicles are equipped with FWD and MacPherson strut independent front suspension. Wheel bearing housings and lower strut tubes are one-piece assemblies, supported by lower control arms. *See Fig. 1.*

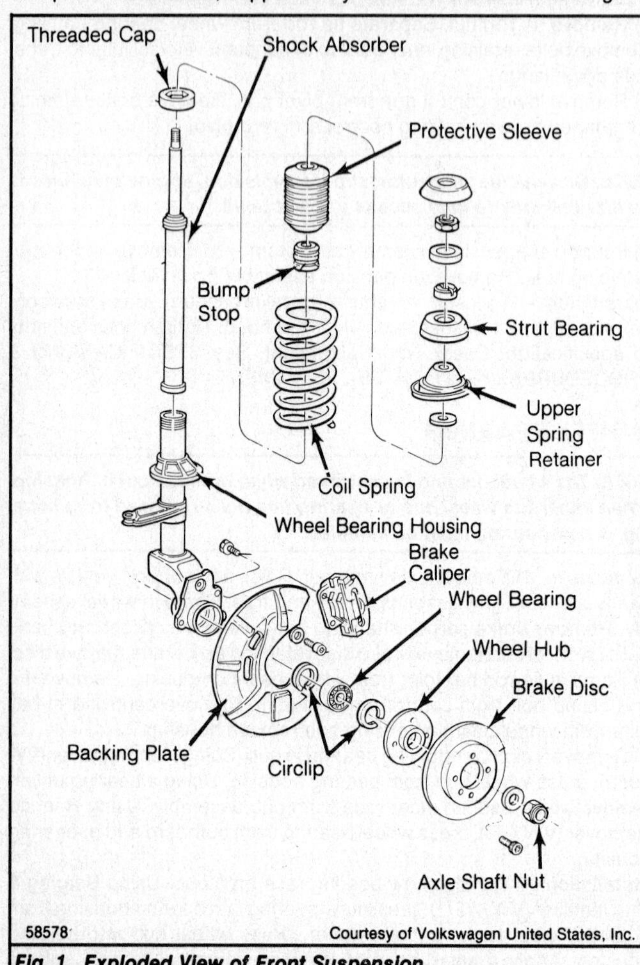


***Fig. 1. Exploded View of Front Suspension***

## ADJUSTMENTS & INSPECTION

### WHEEL ALIGNMENT SPECIFICATIONS & PROCEDURES

***NOTE: See SPECIFICATIONS & PROCEDURES article in WHEEL ALIGNMENT.***

### WHEEL BEARING

No adjustment is required.

### BALL JOINT CHECKING

Raise and support vehicle. Inspect ball joints for damaged rubber boots and play. Maximum tolerance for ball joint play is not available from manufacturer.

## REMOVAL & INSTALLATION

### LOWER CONTROL ARM & BALL JOINT

**Removal – 1)** Raise and support vehicle. Remove clamp bolt retaining ball joint to wheel bearing housing. Force ball joint from housing. Leave control arm hanging in mounts at subframe.

**2)** If control arm is not to be removed, remove ball joint clamp bolt and nut. Remove ball joint from wheel bearing housing by pressing down on lower control arm. Remove ball joint-to-control arm nuts and ball joint.

**3)** If control arm is to be removed, remove stabilizer bar link rod nut, washers, and bushings. Remove control arm pivot bolts and nuts. Remove lower control arm.

**Installation – 1)** Slide new ball joint into slot in control arm. Install and tighten ball joint retaining bolts. Install lower control arm to subframe. Install ball joint into wheel bearing housing. To complete installation, reverse removal procedure.

**2)** Tighten control arm pivot bolts with vehicle resting on ground. Tighten all bolts and nuts to specification. See TORQUE SPECIFICATIONS table at end of article. Adjust wheel alignment. See SPECIFICATIONS & PROCEDURES article in WHEEL ALIGNMENT.

### STRUT ASSEMBLY

**Removal – 1)** Remove axle shaft nut. Raise and support vehicle. Allow suspension to hang free. Remove wheel assembly. Remove caliper mounting bolts and brake hose bracket. Remove and hang caliper out of way. Remove brake disc retaining screw and disc.

**2)** Remove ball joint clamp bolt and nut from wheel bearing housing. Press down on control arm to separate ball joint from housing. Press axle shaft from hub. Support strut assembly. Remove strut upper mount nut and strut.

**Disassembly – 1)** Using spring compressor, slightly compress coil spring. Remove shock absorber piston rod nut. Slowly release spring pressure. Remove upper retaining hardware and coil spring.

**2)** Place strut assembly in a holding fixture. Remove shock absorber threaded cap. Remove shock absorber from strut tube. Drain any oil that may be in strut tube.

**Reassembly – 1)** Install shock absorber into strut tube. Install and tighten threaded cap. Install protective sleeve and bump stop over piston rod. Springs are color coded. Both coil springs must be of same type. If set cannot be matched, replace both springs.

**2)** Position coil spring into lower spring seat. Install upper spring retainer. Set entire assembly into spring compressor. Compress coil spring until all threaded portion of piston rod is exposed.

**3)** Install bearing, rubber bumper, and remaining upper retaining components. Hold piston rod while tightening piston and lock nut.

**Installation –** To install, reverse removal procedure. Tighten all bolts and nuts to specification. See TORQUE SPECIFICATIONS table at end of article. Adjust wheel alignment. See SPECIFICATIONS & PROCEDURES article in WHEEL ALIGNMENT.

### FRONT SUSPENSION ASSEMBLY

**Removal – 1)** Raise and support vehicle. Disconnect brake line, leaving flex hose in place. Plug openings. Remove stabilizer link rod nut, bushings, and washers.

**2)** Remove tie rod nut. Separate tie rod from wheel bearing housing. Remove bolts retaining inner portion of constant velocity joint to transaxle drive flange.

**3)** Remove lower control arm front pivot bolts. Support suspension assembly as it is removed. Remove upper strut retaining nuts (located in engine compartment). Remove suspension assembly from vehicle.

**Installation –** To install, reverse removal procedure. Tighten control arm pivot bolts with vehicle resting on ground. Tighten all bolts and nuts to specification. See TORQUE SPECIFICATIONS table at end of aricle. Adjust wheel alignment. See SPECIFICATIONS & PROCEDURES article in WHEEL ALIGNMENT.

### WHEEL BEARING

***NOTE: Wheel bearings are destroyed when pressed from housing. When either wheel hub or bearing has been removed from housing, new bearing must be installed.***

**Removal – 1)** Remove axle shaft nut. Raise and support vehicle. Allow suspension to hang free. Remove wheel assembly. Remove brake caliper retaining bolts and brake hose bracket. Remove caliper and hang out of way. Remove brake disc retaining screw and brake disc.

**2)** Remove tie rod ball joint from strut tube. Remove nut and clamp bolt from control arm ball joint. Remove stabilizer bracket nut from lower

# 1991 SUSPENSION
# Front – Fox (Cont.)

control arm. Remove control arm ball joint from wheel bearing housing. Press axle shaft from hub.

**3)** Support strut assembly. Remove upper strut mounting nut. Remove wheel bearing housing and strut assembly.

**4)** Using Hub Remover (VW 295a), press wheel hub from bearing housing. Using a bearing puller, remove wheel bearing inner race from hub assembly. Remove circlips retaining bearing in hub. Using Bearing Remover (VW 519), press wheel bearing from outboard end of bearing housing.

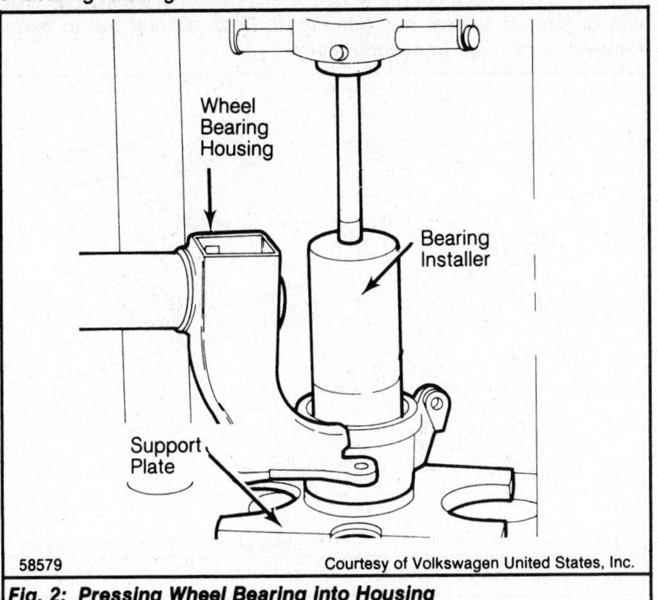


***Fig. 2: Pressing Wheel Bearing Into Housing***

**Installation – 1)** Using Bearing Installer (40-20) and Housing Support (VW 402), press new bearing into bearing housing from outboard side. *See Fig. 2.* Using same housing support and Hub Installer (VW 519), press wheel hub into bearing housing. Apply a small bead of locking compound to axle splines before installing into hub.

***NOTE: When installing hub, ensure press adapter contacts inner bearing race only.***

**2)** To complete installation, reverse removal procedure. Always replace self-locking axle shaft nut. Tighten all bolts and nuts to specification. See TORQUE SPECIFICATIONS table at end of article. Check wheel alignment. See SPECIFICATIONS & PROCEDURES article in WHEEL ALIGNMENT.

## TORQUE SPECIFICATIONS

***TORQUE SPECIFICATIONS***

| Application | Ft. Lbs. (N.m) |
|---|---|
| Axle Nut | 170 (230) |
| Axle Shaft-To-Transaxle Bolt | 32 (44) |
| Ball Joint Clamp Bolt | 48 (65) |
| Ball Joint-To-Control Arm Bolt | 48 (65) |
| Caliper Pin Bolt | 18 (24) |
| Control Arm Pivot Bolt | 44 (60) |
| Strut Upper Mount Nut | 44 (60) |
| Tie Rod Castle Nut | 22 (30) |
| Wheel Lug Bolt | 81 (110) |

# 1991 SUSPENSION
# Front – Vanagon 2WD

## DESCRIPTION

Vehicles have independent front suspension. Major components are upper and lower control arms, coil springs, and shock absorbers. A stabilizer bar is attached to the body by brackets, and to lower control arms by links. *See Fig. 1.*

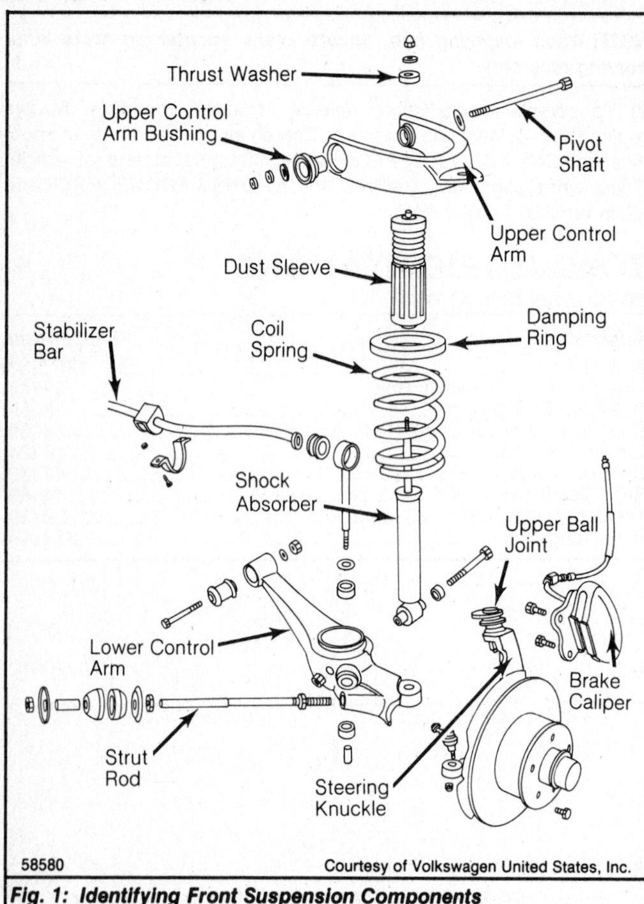


*Fig. 1: Identifying Front Suspension Components*

## ADJUSTMENTS & INSPECTION

### WHEEL ALIGNMENT SPECIFICATIONS & PROCEDURES

***NOTE: See SPECIFICATIONS & PROCEDURES article in WHEEL ALIGNMENT.***

### WHEEL BEARING

Tighten hub nut firmly while rotating brake disc by hand. Insert tip of screwdriver between thrust washer and hub. Adjustment is correct when light finger pressure against screwdriver moves thrust washer. Turn hub nut to adjust. Install and peen NEW hub nut.

### BALL JOINT CHECKING

Raise and support vehicle. Inspect ball joints for excessive play and damaged rubber boots. Maximum tolerance for ball joint play is not available from manufacturer.

## REMOVAL & INSTALLATION

### BALL JOINT

**Removal** – Remove steering knuckle. See LOWER CONTROL ARM, STEERING KNUCKLE & COIL SPRING. To remove ball joint, remove circlip or retaining bolts, then press ball joint from steering knuckle.

**Installation** – Reverse removal procedure to install ball joint. Tighten bolts and nuts to specification. See TORQUE SPECIFICATIONS table at end of article. Check wheel alignment. See SPECIFICATIONS & PROCEDURES article in WHEEL ALIGNMENT.

### LOWER CONTROL ARM, STEERING KNUCKLE & COIL SPRING

**Removal** – **1)** Raise and support vehicle. Remove wheel. Detach stabilizer link from control arm. Measure and record dimension "A" from end of threads to rear nut. *See Fig. 2.* Back off rear nut to permit removal of strut rod from control arm.

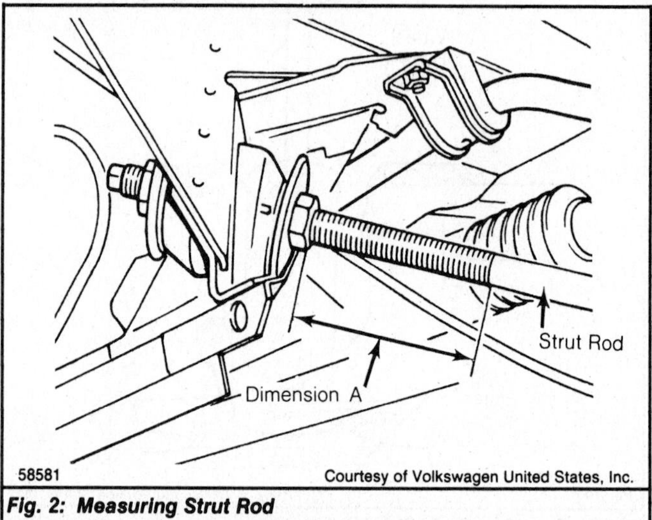


*Fig. 2: Measuring Strut Rod*

***NOTE: Length of strut rod determines caster angle. If setting at body mounting is changed, caster must be readjusted. See SPECIFICATIONS & PROCEDURES article in WHEEL ALIGNMENT.***

**2)** Remove caliper assembly and brake hose bracket. Support caliper out of work area. Separate tie rod end from steering knuckle. Using Ball Joint Remover (VW 267a), separate ball joints from steering knuckle. Remove steering knuckle.

**3)** Loosen lower shock absorber mounting bolt. Support lower control arm with floor jack. Remove lower shock absorber bolt. Lower jack slowly. Remove coil spring. Remove control arm pivot bolt and control arm.

***NOTE: Replacement steering knuckle may contact brake disc in are indicated by arrow in illustration. See Fig. 3. Grind down steering knuckle casting 5/16-3/8" (8-10 mm) to provide clearance.***

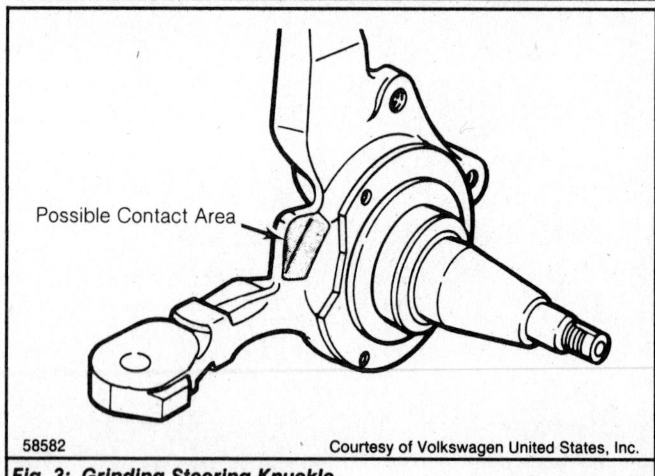


*Fig. 3: Grinding Steering Knuckle*

# 1991 SUSPENSION
# Front – Vanagon 2WD (Cont.)

**Installation – 1)** Position coil spring so straight end is at bottom. Tape damping ring to spring. Ensure spring fits into control arm depression. Reverse removal procedure to complete installation. Tighten bolts and nuts to specification. See TORQUE SPECIFICATIONS table at end of article.

**2)** Check wheel alignment. See SPECIFICATIONS & PROCEDURES article in WHEEL ALIGNMENT. Turn wheel to lock position. Ensure brake hose is 1" (25 mm) from wheel. Bend bracket as necessary to adjust.

## SHOCK ABSORBER

**Removal & Installation – 1)** Raise and support vehicle. Loosen lower shock absorber mounting bolt. Lower vehicle to floor. Remove lower mounting bolt.

**2)** Again raise and support vehicle. Avoid damaging upper ball joint when raising vehicle while shock absorber is disconnected. Remove upper shock absorber mounting hardware and shock absorber.

**3)** Reverse removal procedure to install. Tighten bolts and nuts to specification. See TORQUE SPECIFICATIONS table at end of article.

## UPPER CONTROL ARM

**Removal –** Raise and support vehicle. Remove wheel. Remove upper ball joint retaining bolts. Carefully swing steering knuckle to one side. Note position of upper control arm pivot shaft. Remove pivot shaft and control arm.

**Bushing Replacement –** Note locations of spot welds. Grind off welds. Using Adapters (VW 401, VW 412, VW 431, VW 439, and VW 459), press out bushing. Pressing in new bushing using same equipment. Spot-weld new bushing at same locations. Clean and paint welds to prevent rust.

**Installation –** Grease pivot shaft. Install pivot shaft in original position. To complete installation, reverse removal procedure. Tighten bolts and nuts to specification. See TORQUE SPECIFICATIONS table at end of article. Check wheel alignment. See SPECIFICATIONS & PROCEDURES article in WHEEL ALIGNMENT.

## STABILIZER BAR

**Removal & Installation –** Disconnect stabilizer bar from lower control arms. Remove bracket retaining bolts. Remove stabilizer bar. To install, reverse removal procedure.

## STRUT ROD

**Removal –** Measure and record dimension "A" from end of threads to rear nut. *See Fig. 2.* Note how spacers and bushings are installed. Remove retaining nuts and bolts. Remove strut rod.

**Installation –** To install, reverse removal procedure. Tighten bolts and nuts to specification. See TORQUE SPECIFICATIONS table at end of article. Check wheel alignment. See SPECIFICATIONS & PROCEDURES article in WHEEL ALIGNMENT.

## WHEEL BEARING

**Removal –** Raise and support vehicle. Remove wheel assembly. Remove caliper assembly and support it out of work area. Remove dust cap, hub nut, and thrust washer. Remove brake disc. Using a long drift, tap bearings, races, and grease seal from disc hub.

**Installation – 1)** Clean hub cavity thoroughly. Using Bearing Race Installer (VW 401, VW 407, and 30-205), press inner bearing race into bore. Using Bearing Race Installer (VW 407 and VW 447h), press outer bearing race into bore. Lubricate and install inner bearing. Using Seal Installer (VW 407 and 2051), tap grease seal into bore.

**2)** Install brake disc, outer bearing, thrust washer, and NEW hub nut. Reverse removal procedure to complete installation. Adjust wheel bearing. See WHEEL BEARING under ADJUSTMENTS & INSPECTION. Peen NEW nut.

## TORQUE SPECIFICATIONS

***TORQUE SPECIFICATIONS***

| Application | Ft. Lbs. (N.m) |
|---|---|
| Ball Joint Self-Locking Nut [1] | 80 (108) |
| Brake Caliper Bolt | 118 (160) |
| Caliper Pin Bolt | 26 (35) |
| Lower Control Arm Pivot | 66 (89) |
| Shock Absorber Mounting Bolt | |
| Lower | 110 (150) |
| Upper | 22 (30) |
| Strut Rod-To-Chassis Nut | 74 (100) |
| Strut Rod-To-Control Arm Nut | 133 (180) |
| Tie Rod-To-Steering Knuckle Nut | 22 (30) |
| Upper Ball Joint-To-Control Arm Nut | 43 (58) |
| Upper Control Arm Pivot Shaft | 54 (73) |
| Wheel Lug Bolt | 180 (133) |

[1] – Always use NEW self-locking nuts.

# 1991 SUSPENSION
# Front – Vanagon 4WD

## DESCRIPTION

Suspension consists of upper and lower control arms and ball joints connected to wheel bearing housing. Shock absorbers are part of a strut assembly. Coil springs are held between an upper mount on the frame and a spring support on the lower shock strut housing. Strut rods and stabilizer bar are used for stability. *See Fig. 1.*

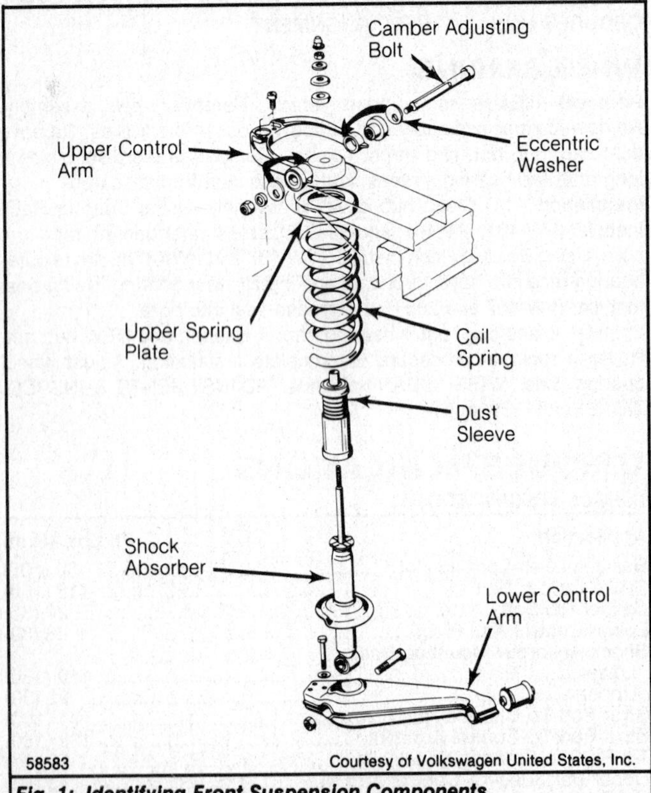


***Fig. 1: Identifying Front Suspension Components***

## ADJUSTMENTS & INSPECTION

### WHEEL ALIGNMENT SPECIFICATIONS & PROCEDURES

***NOTE: See SPECIFICATIONS & PROCEDURES article in WHEEL ALIGNMENT.***

### WHEEL BEARING

No adjustment is required.

## REMOVAL & INSTALLATION

### BALL JOINT

**Removal – 1)** Remove wheel bearing housing. See LOWER CONTROL ARM & WHEEL BEARING HOUSING.

**2)** Using Ball Joint Remover (VW 267a), separate lower ball joint bracket from ball joint. Remove ball joint circlip. Press ball joint from housing. Remove upper ball joint in same manner. Install upper ball joint with attaching bolts.

**Installation – 1)** Press in lower ball joint with flat side of shoulder facing housing. Loosely attach ball joint bracket to ball joint. Install wheel bearing housing onto vehicle.

***NOTE: Ball joint bracket must be aligned with lower control arm when installed, or ball joint rubber seal will tear.***

**2)** To complete installation, reverse removal procedure. Tighten bolts and nuts to specification. See TORQUE SPECIFICATIONS table at end of article. Check wheel alignment. See SPECIFICATIONS & PROCEDURES article in WHEEL ALIGNMENT.

### COIL SPRING & SHOCK ABSORBER

**Removal – 1)** Move front seat fully forward. Pry out rubber plug located under seat. Raise and support vehicle. Remove wheel assembly.

***WARNING: Ensure spring compressor is installed securely. Work to side of spring when removing or installing.***

**2)** Remove bolts which attach upper ball joint to control arm. Move control arm up out of way. Install spring compressor. Compress coil spring. Using Nut Holder (3017a), remove upper shock absorber mounting nut.

**3)** Push shock absorber piston rod downward. Swing shock absorber and spring outward. Remove coil spring and spring plate. Remove lower shock absorber bolt. Remove shock absorber.

**Installation – 1)** Assemble shock absorber and lower control arm. Hand-tighten nut. Install coil spring with lower spring end in spring end stop. Evenly coiled end of spring faces downward.

**2)** Tape spring plate to top of spring in at least 3 places. Swing shock absorber and spring inward. Insert "T" Handle Wrench (3141) through body access hole. Thread "T" handle onto shock. Pull shock piston rod up through hole. Remove "T" handle. Install upper mounting hardware.

**3)** Install upper ball joint to control arm. Raise lower control arm with floor jack. Remove spring compressor. Tighten nuts and bolts to specification. See TORQUE SPECIFICATIONS table at end of article. Insert plug into access hole. Install wheel assembly. Check wheel alignment. See SPECIFICATIONS & PROCEDURES article in WHEEL ALIGNMENT.

### LOWER CONTROL ARM & WHEEL BEARING HOUSING

**Removal – 1)** Remove axle nut. Raise and support vehicle. Remove wheel assembly. Remove brake line bracket from wheel bearing housing. Remove brake caliper and hang out of way.

**2)** Remove upper ball joint bolts from control arm. Remove nut from tie rod end. Press tie rod end from control arm. Remove lower ball joint bracket bolts. Separate strut rod, wheel bearing housing, and lower control arm.

**3)** Pull axle shaft from wheel hub. Remove wheel bearing housing.

***NOTE: Use press to remove axle from housing. DO NOT heat housing.***

**4)** Detach stabilizer bar bracket from control arm. Remove lower shock absorber mounting bolt. Remove lower control arm inner pivot bolt. Remove control arm.

**Bushing Replacement –** Press out old bushings using Adapters (VW 402, VW 408a, and VW 459). Press in new bushings using Adapters (VW 402, VW 411, VW 459, and 3039).

**Installation – 1)** Thoroughly clean and dry splines on axle shaft and in wheel hub. Apply locking compound around splines of axle shaft in bead approximately 1/4" wide. Allow compound to harden at least one hour before driving vehicle.

**2)** To complete installation, reverse removal procedure. Tighten nuts and bolts to specification. See TORQUE SPECIFICATIONS table at end of article. Check wheel alignment. See SPECIFICATIONS & PROCEDURES article in WHEEL ALIGNMENT.

### STABILIZER BAR

**Removal & Installation –** Disconnect stabilizer bar from strut rod. Remove bolts retaining bracket to chassis. Remove stabilizer bar. Reverse removal procedure to install.

### STRUT ROD

**Removal –** Disconnect stabilizer bar from strut rod. Remove nuts retaining strut rod, lower ball joint bracket, and lower control arm together as an assembly. Remove strut rod-to-chassis hardware. Remove strut rod.

**Installation –** To install, reverse removal procedure. Tighten nuts and bolts to specification. See TORQUE SPECIFICATIONS table at

# 1991 SUSPENSION
# Front – Vanagon 4WD (Cont.)

end of article. Check wheel alignment. See SPECIFICATIONS & PROCEDURES article in WHEEL ALIGNMENT.

## SUBFRAME

**Removal – 1)** Remove strut rods from chassis mount. Remove stabilizer mount from strut rod. Remove lower control arm inner bolt. Remove final drive support from subframe. *See Fig. 2.*

**2)** Wire final drive support to body. Remove protection bars and rubber bushings. Use Transmission Support (V.A.G 1383) to support subframe. Remove bolts which attach subframe to body. Carefully lower and remove subframe. *See Fig. 3.*

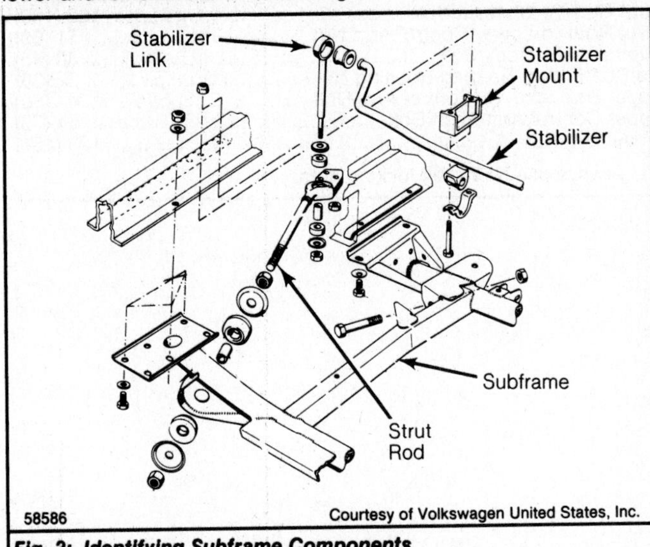


***Fig. 2: Identifying Subframe Components***

**Installation –** To install, reverse removal procedure. Tighten bolts which attach subframe to body last. Tighten nuts and bolts to specification. See TORQUE SPECIFICATIONS table at end of article. Check wheel alignment. See SPECIFICATIONS & PROCEDURES article in WHEEL ALIGNMENT.

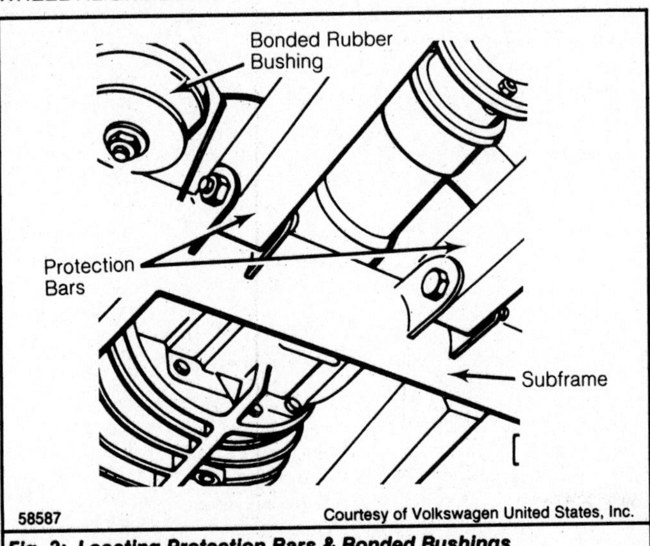


***Fig. 3: Locating Protection Bars & Bonded Bushings***

## UPPER CONTROL ARM

**Removal – 1)** Raise and support vehicle. Remove wheel assembly. Remove bolts which retain upper ball joint to upper control arm.

**2)** Carefully swing wheel bearing housing to one side. Note position of upper control arm pivot shaft. Remove pivot shaft from control arm. Remove control arm.

**Bushing Replacement –** Press bushings from upper control arm using Adapters (VW 402, VW 412, VW 439, VW 459, VW 522, and 40-105). Press in new bushing using Adapters (VW 402, VW 412, VW 454, VW 460/2, and VW 473).

**Installation –** Lubricate pivot shaft with grease. Install upper control arm to body. Position pivot shaft as noted during removal. Install ball joint. To complete installation, reverse removal procedure. Tighten bolts to specification. See TORQUE SPECIFICATIONS table at end of article. Check wheel alignment. See SPECIFICATIONS & PROCEDURES article in WHEEL ALIGNMENT.

## WHEEL BEARING

**Removal – 1)** Remove bearing housing. See LOWER CONTROL ARM & BEARING HOUSING under REMOVAL & INSTALLATION.

**2)** Mount wheel bearing housing and Housing Support (VW 401) in press. Press wheel hub from bearing using Adapters (VW 408a and 40-105). *See Fig. 4.*

***NOTE: Wheel bearing will be destroyed when wheel hub is pressed out.***

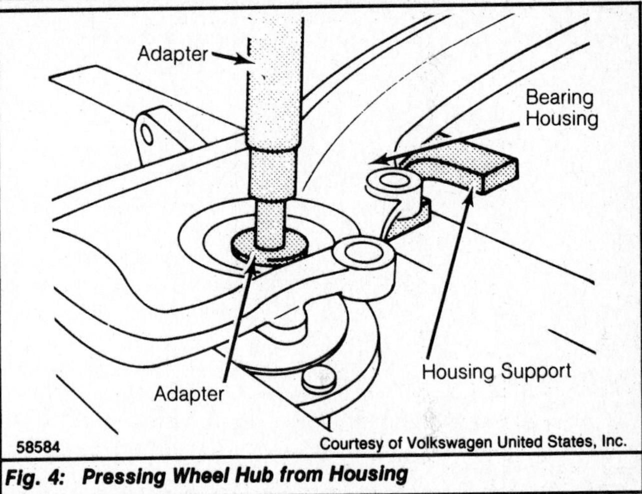


***Fig. 4: Pressing Wheel Hub from Housing***

**3)** Remove outer seal and bearing circlip. Using Housing Supports (VW 401 and 3144) and Adapters (VW 407 and 3074), press wheel bearing from housing.

**4)** Remove inner bearing race from wheel hub using Adapter (40-105) and Puller (US1015). Remove inner seal from bearing housing.

**Installation – 1)** Mount wheel bearing housing in press together with Housing Supports (VW 401 and 3144) and Adapters (VW 412 and 3124). Press wheel bearing into housing. Install seals using Installer (31430) and Support (3144).

**2)** Using Housing Supports (VW 401 and VW 415a), press wheel hub into bearing. To complete installation, reverse removal procedure. *See Fig. 5.*

# 1991 SUSPENSION
# Front – Vanagon 4WD (Cont.)

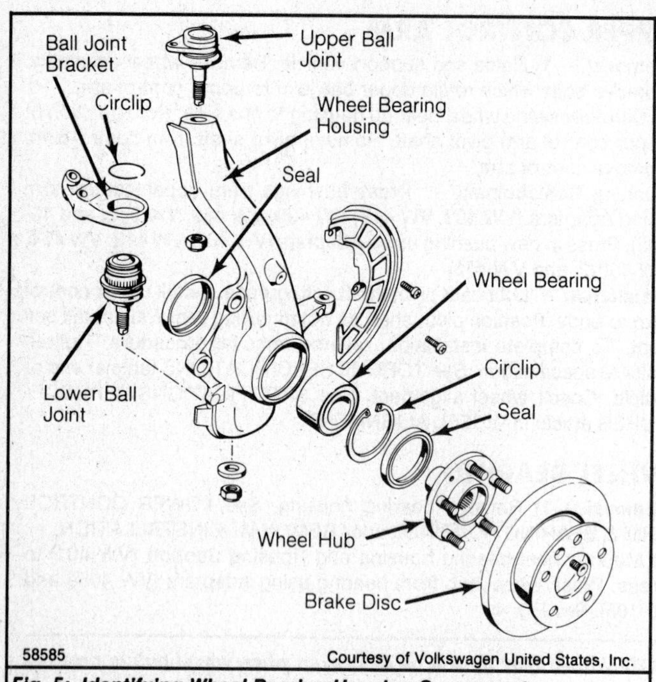


*Fig. 5: Identifying Wheel Bearing Housing Components*

## TORQUE SPECIFICATIONS

*TORQUE SPECIFICATIONS*

| Application | Ft. Lbs. (N.m) |
|---|---|
| Axle Shaft Nut | 236 (320) |
| Ball Joint Self-Locking Nut [1] | 81 (110) |
| Brake Caliper-To-Housing Bolt | 177 (240) |
| Brake Rotor-To-Hub Assembly Bolt | 14 (19) |
| Lower Control Arm Pivot Bolt | 66 (89) |
| Shock Absorber Bottom Bolt | 110 (149) |
| Shock Absorber Top Nut | 22 (30) |
| Stabilizer Link-To-Strut Rod | 22 (30) |
| Stabilizer Mount-To-Frame | 18 (24) |
| Strut Rod-To-Chassis Nut | 125 (169) |
| Strut Rod-To-Lower Control Arm Nut | 51 (69) |
| Subframe-To-Body Bolt | 33 (45) |
| Tie Rod End-to-Bearing Housing Nut | 22 (30) |
| Upper Ball Joint-To-Control Arm Bolt | 44 (60) |
| Upper Control Arm Pivot Bolt | 54 (73) |
| Wheel Lug Nut | 123 (167) |

[1] – Always use NEW self-locking nuts.

# 1991 SUSPENSION
# Rear – Except Vanagon

## Cabriolet, Corrado, Fox, Golf, GTI, Jetta, Passat

## DESCRIPTION

Rear suspension is link type with MacPherson suspension struts. Suspension uses control arms and axle beam for stabilization. Control arms and axle beam are combined as one unit. Brake drums or discs rotate on stub axles bolted to control arms. *See Fig. 1*.

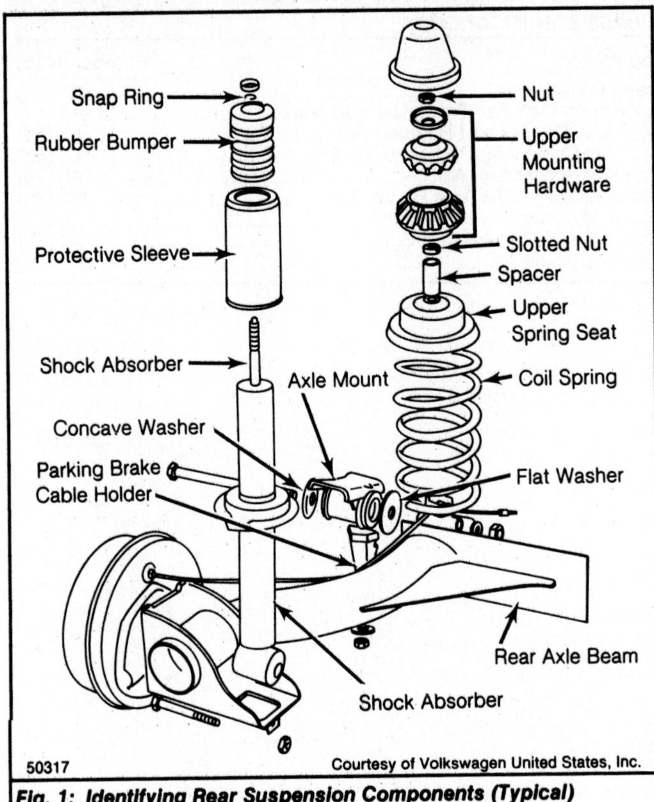


***Fig. 1: Identifying Rear Suspension Components (Typical)***

## ADJUSTMENTS & INSPECTION

### WHEEL ALIGNMENT SPECIFICATIONS & PROCEDURES

***NOTE: See SPECIFICATIONS & PROCEDURES article in WHEEL ALIGNMENT.***

### WHEEL BEARING

Tighten hub nut to 7.5 ft. lbs. (10 N.m) while rotating brake disc or drum by hand. Insert tip of screwdriver between thrust washer and hub. Adjustment is correct when light finger pressure against screwdriver moves thrust washer. Turn hub nut to adjust. Install NEW cotter pin.

## REMOVAL & INSTALLATION

### AXLE BEAM PIVOT BUSHING

**Removal** – This procedure is for replacing bushing with axle beam installed in vehicle. Raise and support vehicle. With no pressure on beam, remove nuts which retain axle beam to body. Tap out pivot bolt. Using Bushing Remover (VW 3111), press out bushing. Press new bushing into place.

**Installation** – **1)** Loosely install mounting pad onto axle beam. Install bushing to a depth of 2.42-2.44" (61.5-62.0 mm). Concave washer and bolt head must face toward outside of vehicle. Bolt head must recess into washer.

**2)** Using Mounting Bracket Aligner (VW 261 or 3021), align mount. *See Fig. 2*. With vehicle on ground, tighten pivot bolt nut to specification.

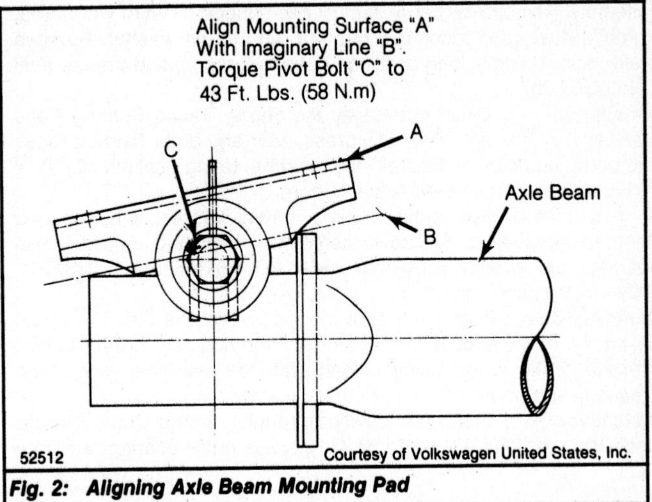


***Fig. 2: Aligning Axle Beam Mounting Pad***

### STRUT ASSEMBLY

***NOTE: DO NOT remove both suspension struts at same time, as this would overload axle beam bushings.***

**Removal** – **1)** With vehicle on floor, remove plastic cap which covers upper strut retaining nuts. Remove strut retaining nuts. Slowly raise vehicle until weight is off spring. Remove bolt which retains lower end of strut shock absorber to axle beam mount. Raise vehicle until strut can be removed. Place strut assembly in vise.

**2)** Hold piston rod. Remove strut retaining nut and related components. *See Fig. 1*. Remove slotted nut (some models). Remove spacer and coil spring. If coil spring is to be replaced, ensure paint stripe color on replacement spring matches original spring color stripe.

**Installation** – **1)** Install protective cap and tube onto shock absorber. Install rubber buffer with small end downward. Install snap ring and washer. Place spring into lower seat. Install upper retainer with spacer sleeve.

**2)** Tighten slotted nut (some models) which retains piston rod. Install upper mounting hardware. Tighten piston rod. To complete installation, reverse removal procedure. Tighten bolts and nuts to specification. See TORQUE SPECIFICATIONS table at end of article.

### SUSPENSION ASSEMBLY

***CAUTION: When removing suspension assembly, add weight to rear of vehicle to prevent tipping resulting from change in center of gravity.***

**Removal** – **1)** With vehicle on floor, disconnect upper strut mount. Raise and support vehicle. Disconnect parking brake at bracket near axle mount.

**2)** Disconnect and plug brake lines. Leave flex hose attached to suspension. Separate brake pressure regulator spring from axle beam (if equipped). Remove nuts which retain axle beam to body.

***NOTE: DO NOT install bolts and nuts fouled with undercoating. With waxy coating on threads, true tightening torque cannot be measured. Clean or replace bolts and nuts.***

**Installation** – **1)** If axle beam mounting has been removed, adjust mounting pad. *See Fig. 2*. If pad is not correctly aligned, torsional preload of mounting bushings will be incorrect.

**2)** Position rear suspension on body. Install nuts retaining axle beam to body. Raise wheel. Guide upper end of strut into body mount.

**3)** Connect parking brake cables. Connect brake lines. Lower vehicle. Tighten upper strut retaining nuts. Tighten all bolts and nuts to specification. Bleed brake system.

# 1991 SUSPENSION
# Rear – Except Vanagon (Cont.)

## WHEEL BEARING

**Removal (Disc Brakes)** – Raise and support vehicle. Remove wheel assembly. Remove caliper assembly and support it out of work area. Remove dust cap, cotter pin, hub nut, and thrust washer. Remove brake disc. Using a long drift, tap bearings, races, and grease seal from disc hub.

**Installation** – **1)** Clean hub cavity thoroughly. Using Bearing Race Installer (VW 432 and VW 411), press inner and outer bearing races into bore. Lubricate and install inner bearing. Using Seal Installer (VW 295 and 3074), tap grease seal into bore.

**2)** Install brake disc, outer bearing, thrust washer, and hub nut. Reverse removal procedure to complete installation. Adjust wheel bearing. See WHEEL BEARING under ADJUSTMENTS & INSPECTION. Install NEW cotter pin.

**Removal (Drum Brakes)** – Raise and support vehicle. Remove wheel assembly. Remove dust cap, cotter pin, hub nut, and thrust washer. Remove brake drum. Using a long drift, tap bearings, races, and grease seal from hub.

**Installation** – **1)** Clean hub cavity thoroughly. Using Outer Bearing Race Installer (VW 431 and VW 411), press outer bearing race into bore. Using Inner Bearing Race Installer (VW 432 and VW 411), press inner bearing race into bore. Lubricate and install inner bearing. Using Seal Installer (VW 295 and 3074), tap grease seal into bore.

**2)** Install brake drum, outer bearing, thrust washer, and hub nut. Reverse removal procedure to complete installation. Adjust wheel bearing. See WHEEL BEARING under ADJUSTMENTS & INSPECTION. Install NEW cotter pin.

## TORQUE SPECIFICATIONS

***TORQUE SPECIFICATIONS***

| Application | Ft. Lbs. (N.m) |
|---|---|
| Brake Caliper Bolt | 48 (65) |
| Coil Spring Retainer-To-Piston Rod Nut | 11 (15) |
| Rear Axle Beam Pivot Bushing Bolt | 43 (58) |
| Rear Axle Mounting Pad-To-Body Bolt | 63 (85) |
| Shock Absorber Slot Nut | 15 (20) |
| Shock Absorber-To-Axle Beam Nut | 52 (70) |
| Shock Absorber-To-Body Bolt | 26 (35) |
| Stub Axle-To-Control Arm Bolt | 44 (60) |
| Wheel Lug Bolt | 81 (110) |

# 1991 SUSPENSION
# Rear - Vanagon

## DESCRIPTION

Major components of rear suspension are independent trailing arms, coil springs, and shock absorbers. Trailing arms have provision for caster and toe adjustments, and mount in front to pivot brackets. Drive shafts extend through trailing arms and connect to wheel hubs. *See Fig. 1.*

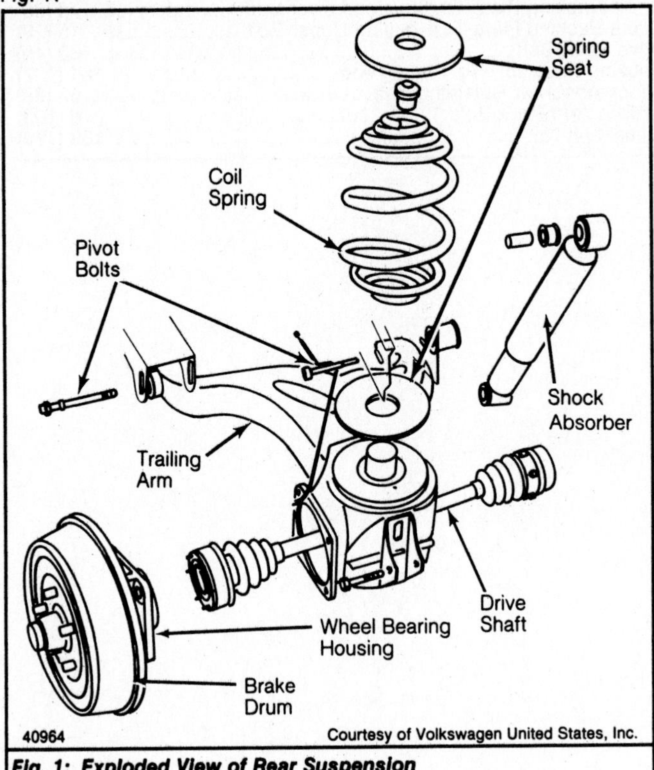


*Fig. 1: Exploded View of Rear Suspension*

## ADJUSTMENTS & INSPECTION

### WHEEL ALIGNMENT SPECIFICATIONS & PROCEDURES

*NOTE: See SPECIFICATIONS & PROCEDURES article in WHEEL ALIGNMENT.*

### WHEEL BEARING

No adjustment is required.

## REMOVAL & INSTALLATION

### COIL SPRINGS

**Removal** - Raise and support vehicle. Support trailing arm with floor jack. Remove shock absorber retaining bolts and shock absorber. Slowly lower floor jack. Remove coil spring and spring seats.

*NOTE: If only coil spring is to be removed, remove only one shock absorber mounting.*

**Installation** - To install, reverse removal procedure. End of spring must fit into spring seat depression. Depression in lower spring seat must fit into depression in trailing arm. Tighten bolts to specification. See TORQUE SPECIFICATIONS table at end of article.

### HUB & KNUCKLE ASSEMBLY

*See Fig 2.*

### TRAILING ARMS

**Removal** - **1)** Raise and support vehicle. Remove wheel assembly. Support trailing arm with floor jack. Remove nuts which retain brake drum and hub to trailing arm. Remove hex screws at axle shaft-to-transaxle joint. Remove axle shaft and brake drum assembly through opening in trailing arm.

**2)** Remove lower shock absorber retaining bolt. Slowly lower jack. Remove coil spring and spring seats. Note relative position of trailing arm and mounting brackets. Remove pivot bolts and trailing arm.

**Bushing Replacement** - **1)** Using Bushing Remover (VW 442) and Adapter (30-14), remove bushing from trailing arm. Coat washer with oil and place between nut and tool.

**2)** Lubricate bushing bore, Installer (3053), and bushing with soap solution. Pull bushing in until sleeve contacts tool. Wait about 30 seconds before removing tool. Bushing should seat itself. If necessary, press edge of bushing out.

**Installation** - **1)** To install, reverse removal procedure. Depressions in spring seats must align with ends of coil spring. Align depression in lower spring seat with depression in trailing arm.

**2)** Install trailing arm at position noted earlier. Tighten bolts to specification. See TORQUE SPECIFICATIONS table at end of article. Check wheel alignment. See SPECIFICATIONS & PROCEDURES article in WHEEL ALIGNMENT.

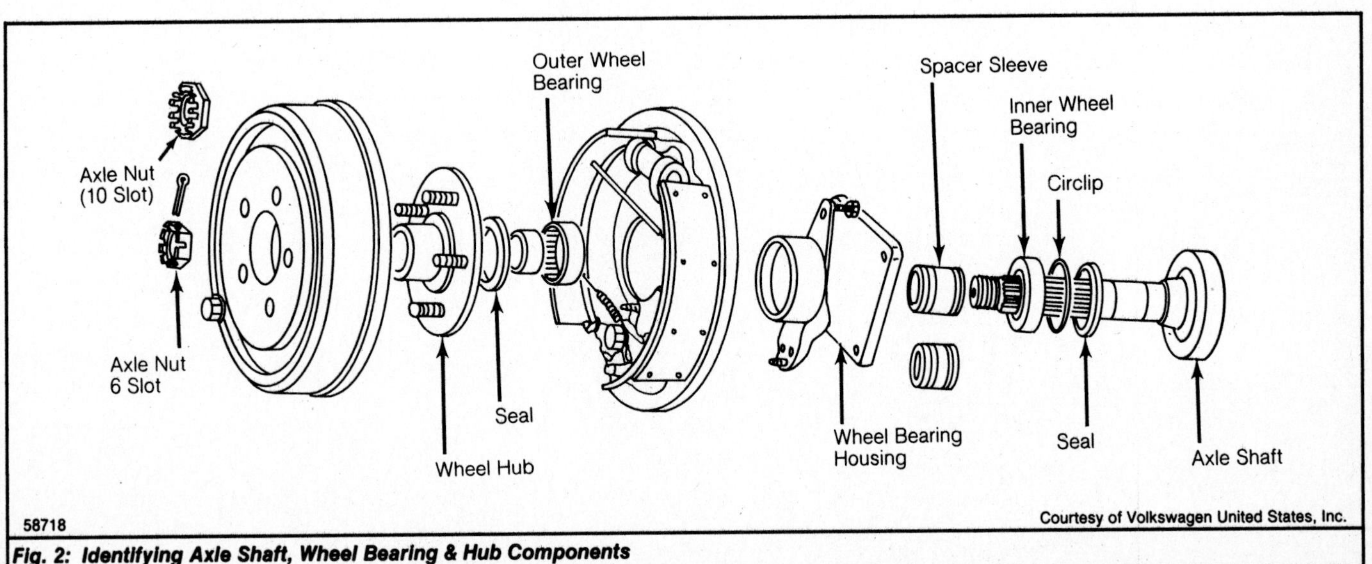


*Fig. 2: Identifying Axle Shaft, Wheel Bearing & Hub Components*

# 1991 SUSPENSION
# Rear – Vanagon (Cont.)

## WHEEL BEARING

**Removal – 1)** Remove axle nut. Raise and support vehicle. Remove wheel assembly. Remove and plug brake line. Remove brake drum and wheel hub assembly. Remove backing plate retaining bolts. Separate backing plate from housing and support it aside.

**2)** Remove bolts retaining wheel bearing housing to trailing arm. Remove hex bolts at axle shaft-to-transaxle joint. Pull hub assembly and axle through trailing arm. Remove axle shaft-to-hub bolts. Separate axle from hub. *See Fig. 2*. Using Press Adapter (VW 411), press axle from bearing housing.

**3)** Remove outer grease seal, inner grease seal, and bearing circlip. Remove inner race of outer wheel bearing. Remove spacer sleeve. Drive outer wheel bearing out with brass drift. Using Press Adapters (VW 412 and VW 244b), press inner bearing from housing.

**Installation – 1)** Using Support Plate (VW 401) and Press Adapters (VW 407 and VW 472), press inner bearing into housing until seated. Install bearing circlip. Press outer bearing into housing using same tools. Grease bearings and fill space between bearings with multi-purpose grease.

**2)** Install spacer sleeve and inner race of outer bearing. Using Seal Installer (VW 240a), install outer and inner seals. Press axle shaft into bearing housing using Press Adapters (VW 412 and 30-100). To complete installation, reverse removal procedure. Tighten all bolts and nuts to specification. See TORQUE SPECIFICATIONS table at end of article.

***NOTE: Install new spacer sleeve and axle nut on vehicles up to VIN 25ZBH119362. New nut has 10 key slots; old nut has 6 key slots.***

## TORQUE SPECIFICATIONS

***TORQUE SPECIFICATIONS***

| Application | Ft. Lbs. (N.m) |
|---|---|
| Axle Nut | |
| 10 Slot | 370 (500) |
| 6 Slot | 250 (340) |
| Brake Backing Plate-To-Housing Lower Bolt | 48 (65) |
| Brake Backing Plate-To-Housing Upper Bolt | 15 (20) |
| Drive Shaft Bolt | 33 (45) |
| Housing Assembly-To-Trailing Arm | 101 (137) |
| Shock Absorber Retaining Bolt | 65 (88) |
| Trailing Arm Pivot Bolt | 76 (103) |
| Wheel Lug Nut | 133 (180) |

# 1991 STEERING
# Steering Columns – Except Vanagon

## Cabriolet, Corrado, Fox, Golf, GTI, Jetta, Passat

## DESCRIPTION

Swing-away steering column is held by a clamp and leaf spring. On impact, the "U" joint shaft pushes steering column against the leaf spring. The spring allows the column to disengage and swing away.

***CAUTION: Applying excessive pressure or causing impact to mainshaft during service may cause the column to disengage.***

## REMOVAL & INSTALLATION

### AIR BAG

***WARNING: On Cabriolet with Supplemental Restraint System (air bag), remove air bag from vehicle before working on steering column. Follow all WARNINGS and SERVICE PRECAUTIONS to prevent injury from accidental air bag deployment. See AIR BAG RESTRAINT SYSTEM article in SAFETY EQUIPMENT.***

**Removal & Installation (Cabriolet) – 1)** Disconnect negative battery cable. Wait at least 20 minutes for air bag capacitor to discharge. Remove 2 Torx screws (No. 30) from back of steering wheel.

**2)** Carefully tilt air bag down away from steering wheel. Disconnect electrical wire from back of air bag unit. Remove air bag unit from vehicle. DO NOT store air bag unit on its vinyl side. Store air bag unit on its metal housing.

**3)** To install, reverse removal procedure. Install new Torx screws to hold air bag unit in steering wheel. Tighten Torx screws to 89 INCH lbs. (10 N.m).

### STEERING WHEEL & HORN PAD

**Removal & Installation – 1)** Disconnect negative battery cable. On Corrado and Passat, lift cover from bottom, then pull cover away from steering wheel. On Corrado and Passat, spread horn button locating lugs, then separate contact plates. On other models, pry center cover from steering wheel.

**2)** Disconnect horn wiring. Ensure steering wheel is in straight-ahead position. Mark shaft and wheel for reassembly reference. Remove retaining nut and washer. Pull steering wheel from shaft. Reverse removal procedure to install.

### TURN SIGNAL SWITCH

**Removal & Installation –** Remove steering wheel. See STEERING WHEEL & HORN PAD. Remove retaining screws. Unplug harness connector. Remove turn signal switch. To install, reverse removal procedure.

### WINDSHIELD WIPER SWITCH

**Removal & Installation –** Remove steering wheel. See STEERING WHEEL & HORN PAD. Remove turn signal switch. See TURN SIGNAL SWITCH. Remove retaining screws. Unplug harness connector. Remove windshield wiper switch. To install, reverse removal procedure.

### IGNITION SWITCH

**Removal – 1)** Remove steering wheel. See STEERING WHEEL & HORN PAD. Remove lower cover from steering column. Remove turn signal and windshield wiper switches. See TURN SIGNAL SWITCH and WINDSHIELD WIPER SWITCH. Remove lock washer, spring and horn contact ring.

**2)** Remove bolt retaining steering column tube to steering column housing. Disconnect wiring from ignition switch. Unlock steering with ignition key. Remove steering column housing, ignition lock and upper half of steering column switch cover. Remove retaining screw and ignition switch.

**Installation –** To install ignition switch, reverse removal procedure.

### STEERING COLUMN

***WARNING: On Cabriolet with Supplemental Restraint System (air bag), remove air bag from vehicle before working on steering column. See AIR BAG under REMOVAL & INSTALLATION. Failure to remove air bag may result in personal injury.***

***NOTE: Refer to illustration for exploded view of steering column components. See Fig. 1.***

**Removal (Cabriolet) – 1)** Disconnect battery ground cable. Remove steering wheel. Remove knee-bar panel. Remove steering column lower trim panel. Unplug 2 electrical connectors.

**2)** Remove spiral spring assembly retaining screws. Remove lock ring, spacer ring, spring and steering lock housing. Position Tube (VW 420) on steering column. Release lock ring tension using snap ring pliers.

**3)** Ring will slide upward with spring pressure. Remove steering column. To remove leaf spring from steering column tube, push retaining spring downward with a screwdriver. Disengage leaf spring.

**Installation –** To install, reverse removal procedure. When installing spiral spring, install 4 turns from either stop. To install leaf spring on steering column tube, insert leaf spring in bracket slot. Press lower end of leaf spring inward until it engages retaining spring.

**Removal (Except Cabriolet) – 1)** Disconnect battery ground cable. Remove steering wheel. Remove bolt and screw from switch housing recess. Tilt switch unit toward instrument panel. Pry spacer sleeve from column.

**2)** Pull up combination switch to disconnect wires. Remove combination switch. Disconnect steering shaft from "U" joint shaft. Disconnect brake pedal push rod.

**3)** Disconnect clutch cable from clutch pedal. Using a screwdriver, push down leaf spring retainer clip to disengage it from mounting slot.

**4)** Remove bolts that retain steering column under instrument panel. Drill out shear bolts. Remove column assembly from vehicle.

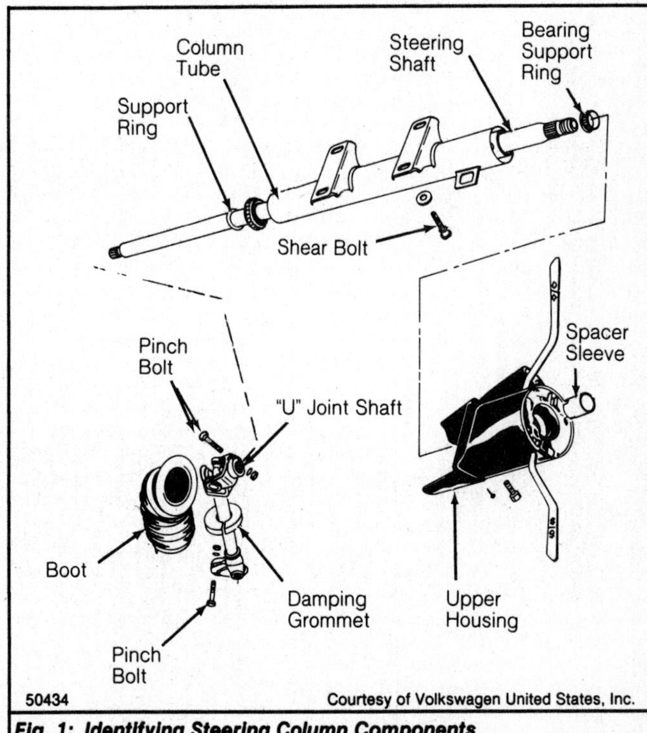


***Fig. 1: Identifying Steering Column Components***

**Installation –** To install, reverse removal procedure. Place wheels in straight-ahead position. Tighten pinch bolt. Install spacer. *See Fig. 1.* Install combination switch and steering wheel. Adjust brake pedal and clutch pedal height.

# 1991 STEERING
# Steering Columns – Except Vanagon (Cont.)

## OVERHAUL

### STEERING COLUMN

***NOTE: Refer to illustration for exploded view of steering column components. See Fig. 1.***

**Disassembly** – Press steering shaft from column. Remove bearings from steering column.

**Inspection** – Check upper bracket for damage and upper bearing for smooth rotation. Check shafts for signs of bending, damaged splines, or damaged "U" joints. Check column tube for bending or other damage. Repair or replace components as necessary.

**Reassembly** – Press in steering shaft and new bearings. DO NOT use more than 200 lbs. (90 kg) force to press shaft and bearings into column tube.

### "U" JOINT SHAFT

**Disassembly** – **1)** Remove pinch bolt that connects lower end of "U" joint shaft to steering gear pinion shaft. *See Fig. 1*. Separate manual gearshift linkage from steering box. Remove steering gear retaining nuts.

**2)** Pull box down to separate from lower "U" joint. Remove rubber boot from lower "U" joint. Remove upper "U" joint pinch bolt. Pull down joint and remove shaft with "U" joints.

**Inspection** – Inspect "U" joints for wear or excessive play. If abnormal wear or play exists, replace as necessary.

**Reassembly** – **1)** Fit "U" joint to steering shaft. Align steering shaft notch with lower "U" joint slot. Install boot and damping grommet. Fit steering box to frame while guiding pinion shaft into lower "U" joint.

**2)** Hand-tighten steering gear retaining nuts. Place wheels in straight-ahead position. Align pinion shaft and "U" joint. Tighten pinch bolt. Tighten steering gear retaining nuts. Connect gearshift linkage. Check linkage for smooth operation.

## TORQUE SPECIFICATIONS

***TORQUE SPECIFICATIONS***

| Application | Ft. Lbs. (N.m) |
|---|---|
| Pinch Bolt | 22 (30) |
| Steering Column-To-Instrument Panel | |
| Retaining Bolt | 15 (20) |
| Shear Bolt | 1 |
| Steering Gear Retaining Nut | 22 (30) |
| Steering Wheel Nut | 37 (50) |

1 – Tighten until bolt head snaps off.

# 1991 STEERING
# Steering Columns – Vanagon

## DESCRIPTION

Vanagon has an energy-absorbing 2-piece steering column, attached to the dash with brackets and to floorboard with a boot flange. Lower steering shaft connects to steering gear. *See Fig. 1.*

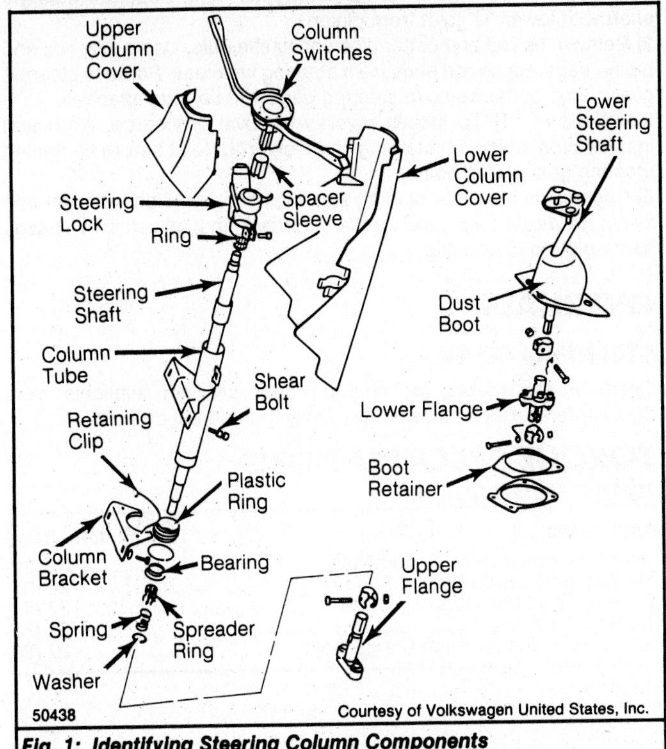


***Fig. 1: Identifying Steering Column Components***

## REMOVAL & INSTALLATION

### STEERING WHEEL & HORN PAD

**Removal & Installation – 1)** Disconnect negative battery cable. Lift center cover from steering wheel. Disconnect horn wiring.
**2)** Ensure steering wheel is in straight-ahead position. Mark shaft and wheel for reassembly reference. Remove retaining nut and washer. Pull steering wheel from shaft. Reverse removal procedure to install.

### TURN SIGNAL SWITCH

**Removal & Installation –** Remove steering wheel. See STEERING WHEEL & HORN PAD. Remove retaining screws. Unplug harness connector. Remove turn signal switch. To install, reverse removal procedure. After installation, gap between turn signal switch and steering wheel should be 1/16 – 3/16" (2 – 4 mm). *See Fig. 2.*

### WINDSHIELD WIPER SWITCH

**Removal & Installation –** Remove steering wheel. See STEERING WHEEL & HORN PAD. Remove turn signal switch. See TURN SIGNAL SWITCH. Remove retaining screws. Unplug harness connector. Remove windshield wiper switch. To install, reverse removal procedure.

### IGNITION SWITCH

**Removal - 1)** Remove steering wheel. See STEERING WHEEL & HORN PAD. Remove covers from steering column. Remove turn signal and windshield wiper switches. See TURN SIGNAL SWITCH and WINDSHIELD WIPER SWITCH. Remove lock washer, spring, and horn contact ring.
**2)** Using Ball Joint Remover ((VW 267a), hold steering column coupling. Pull steering lock housing together with spacer sleeve. Disconnect wiring from ignition switch. Remove switch.

**Installation –** Reverse removal procedure to install ignition switch. Drive spacer onto column using Tube (VW 420). Spacer upper end-to-shaft end distance must be 2" (51 mm). *See Fig. 2.*

### STEERING COLUMN

***CAUTION: Steering column incorporates shear pins, which allow column to collapse upon frontal impact. Excessive pressure or impact to shaft may cause column to collapse.***

**Removal – 1)** Remove horn pad and steering wheel. Remove column covers. Remove turn signal and windshield wiper switches. See TURN SIGNAL SWITCH and WINDSHIELD WIPER SWITCH.
**2)** Remove steering lock and spacer sleeve. See IGNITION SWITCH. Remove upper steering shaft-to-upper flange clamp bolt.
**3)** Remove lower column clamp bolts. Remove upper column retaining bolts. Remove upper steering shaft and column tube as an assembly.
**4)** Remove lower steering shaft clamp bolt. Remove dust boot retaining bolts. Remove lower steering shaft.
**Installation – 1)** To install, reverse removal procedure. Install new gasket on dust boot. Install steering shaft and column tube as an assembly.
**2)** When installing steering lock and spacer sleeve, clamp lower steering shaft to upper flange with Ball Joint Remover (VW 267a).
**3)** Ensure distance from top of spacer sleeve to top of upper steering shaft (with steering wheel and nut installed) is 2" (51 mm). Gap between turn signal switch and steering wheel should be 1/16 – 3/16" (2-4 mm). *See Fig. 2.*

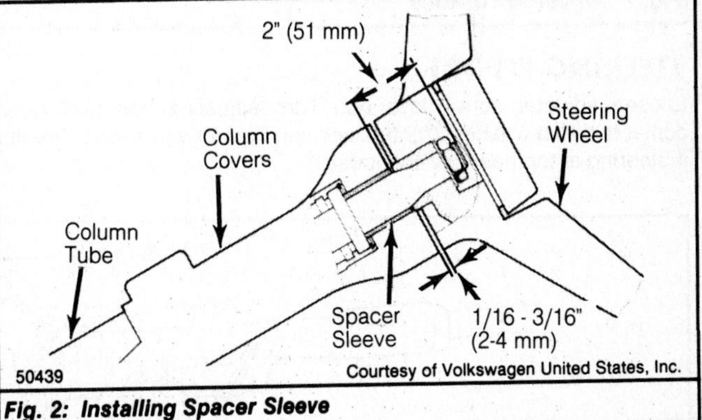


***Fig. 2: Installing Spacer Sleeve***

## OVERHAUL

### STEERING COLUMN

**Disassembly – 1)** Remove flange from lower steering shaft. Remove clamp from flange. Remove gasket and boot retainer from dust boot.
**2)** Remove washer, spring, and spreader ring from lower end of upper steering shaft. Remove bearing, plastic ring, and column bracket. *See Fig. 1.*
**3)** Remove steering lock ring from upper end of shaft. Drill out and remove shear bolt from column tube. Remove column tube from steering shaft.
**Inspection –** Check all parts for excessive wear or damage. Check steering shafts for bending, cracks, or other defects. Replace parts as necessary.
**Reassembly –** To reassemble, reverse disassembly procedure. Steering lock, spacer sleeve, and ring must be assembled before installation onto steering shaft. Tighten new shear bolt until head snaps off.

## TORQUE SPECIFICATIONS

***TORQUE SPECIFICATIONS***

| Application | Ft. Lbs. (N.m) |
|---|---|
| Clamp Bolts | 15 (20) |
| Lower Bracket Bolts | 18 (24) |
| Steering Wheel Nut | 37 (50) |

# 1991 STEERING
# Manual Rack & Pinion

## Fox, Golf

## DESCRIPTION

Steering gear is a rack and pinion type. Tie rods connect steering knuckles to ends of rack. Racks are mounted with "U" bolts and rubber bushings.

## ADJUSTMENTS

### RACK & TIE RODS

**1)** Center rack in housing so rack protrudes an equal amount from each end of rack housing. Without moving rack, adjust so that dimensions "B" and "C" are 2.77" (70.5 mm). *See Fig. 1.*

**2)** When measurements are correct, check wheel alignment. See SPECIFICATIONS & PROCEDURES article in WHEEL ALIGNMENT. Install rubber boots.

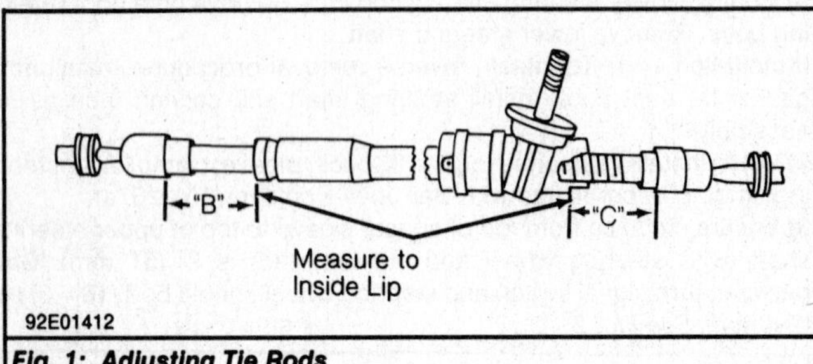


***Fig. 1: Adjusting Tie Rods***

### STEERING EFFORT

Loosen adjuster screw lock nut. Turn adjusting bolt until it just contacts thrust washer. Tighten lock nut. Test-drive vehicle. Readjust if steering is too heavy or too loose.

## REMOVAL & INSTALLATION

### STEERING GEAR

**Removal – 1)** Disconnect shift linkage bearing plate from steering gear housing. Loosen lower "U" joint pinch bolt. Separate steering shaft with lower "U" joint from pinion.

**2)** Remove tie rod end cotter pins and castle nuts. Using a tie rod end puller, separate tie rod ends from steering knuckles. Remove steering gear clamp bolts. Remove steering gear with tie rods attached.

**Installation – 1)** To install, reverse removal procedure. Align and insert pinion shaft with steering shaft lower "U" joint before tightening steering gear clamp bolts.

**2)** Connect tie rod outer ends to steering knuckles. Tighten upper and lower universal joint pinch bolts. Connect and adjust shift linkage bearing plate to housing.

## OVERHAUL

### STEERING GEAR

Overhaul procedures for steering gear are not available from manufacturer. Replace as an assembly if damaged or worn.

## TORQUE SPECIFICATIONS

***TORQUE SPECIFICATIONS***

| Application | Ft. Lbs. (N.m) |
|---|---|
| Gear Box Housing-To-Frame Nuts | 22 (30) |
| Tie Rod End Castle Nuts | 26 (35) |
| Tie Rod End Lock Nuts | 37 (50) |
| Tie Rod-To-Rack | 52 (70) |
| "U" Joint-To-Pinion Shaft Clamp Bolts | 22 (30) |

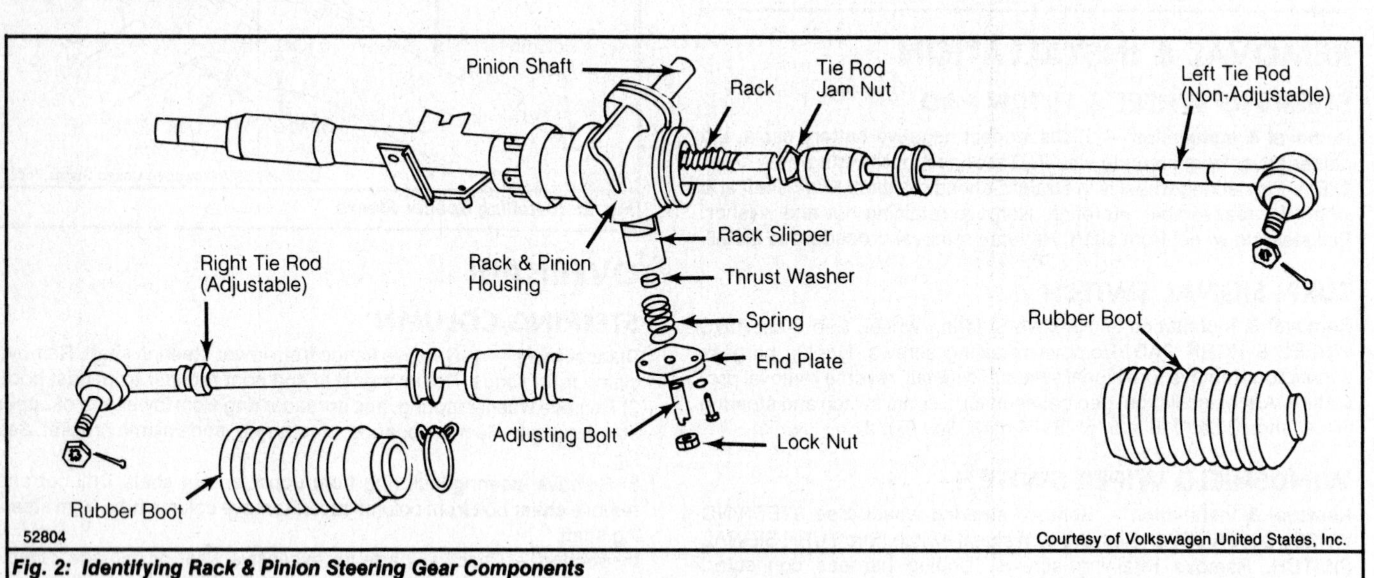


***Fig. 2: Identifying Rack & Pinion Steering Gear Components***

# 1991 STEERING
# Power Rack & Pinion

**Cabriolet, Corrado, Golf, GTI, Jetta, Passat, Vanagon**

## DESCRIPTION & OPERATION

System consists of a vane pump, rack and pinion steering gear, and an oil reservoir. Vane pump draws fluid from reservoir and supplies it to flow control valve. Control valve directs fluid to appropriate side of rack piston.

## LUBRICATION

### CAPACITY

Fluid capacity is approximately 1 qt. (.95L).

### FLUID TYPE

Recommended fluid type is Dexron-II.

### FLUID LEVEL CHECK

Remove reservoir cover. Start engine and let idle. Fluid level should be between MIN and MAX marks on reservoir.

### HYDRAULIC SYSTEM BLEEDING

**1)** Start engine and let idle. Ensure fluid is at proper level. Turn steering wheel from lock to lock several times quickly.
**2)** Continue until fluid level remains at reservoir mark. Ensure no bubbles appear in reservoir when steering wheel is turned. Shut off engine. Ensure oil level does not rise more than 3/8" (10 mm).

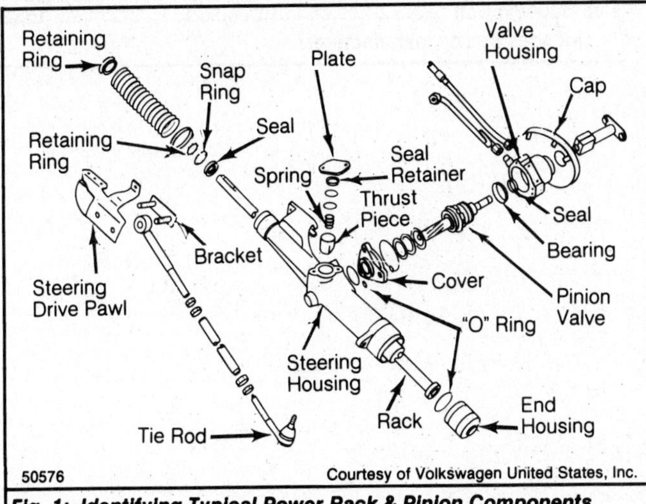


*Fig. 1: Identifying Typical Power Rack & Pinion Components*

## ADJUSTMENTS

### POWER STEERING PUMP BELT

Loosen nuts on pump mounting bracket. Turn adjuster bolt until belt deflection is 3/8" (10 mm) at center of belt. Tighten nuts to specification.

## TESTING

### HYDRAULIC SYSTEM PRESSURE TEST

**1)** Install Pressure Gauge (US1074 B) between pressure hose and pressure line at valve housing. Open pressure gauge valve. Run engine at idle. Turn steering wheel from lock to lock several times.
**2)** On Vanagon, pressure should be 1670-1750 psi (117-123 kg/cm²). On all others, pressure should be 1100-1200 psi (78-84 kg/cm²). If pressure is not within limits, see PUMP PRESSURE TEST.
**3)** If pump pressure is within specification, but system pressure is low, replace steering gear.

### PUMP PRESSURE TEST

**1)** Install Pressure Gauge (US1074 B) between pressure hose and pressure line of valve housing. Start engine and let idle. Close valve. Leave valve closed for no longer than 5 seconds. On Vanagon, pressure should be 1670-1750 psi (117-123 kg/cm²). On all others, pressure should be 1100-1200 psi (78-84 kg/cm²).
**2)** On all vehicles except Vanagon, go to step **3)**. On Vanagon, if pressure is not to specification, inspect limiting valve and housing bores and piston for obstructions. Ensure piston moves freely in housing. Install new valve if necessary.
**3)** If pump pressure is not within specification, replace pump.

### STEERING WHEEL TURNING FORCE

**Except Vanagon** – Remove steering gear. See POWER RACK & PINION under REMOVAL & INSTALLATION. Loosen lock nut. Turn adjuster bolt until pinion shaft can be turned by hand without binding. Hold adjuster bolt in position while tightening lock nut.
**Vanagon** – If steering effort is too high, check steering shaft, steering linkage, "U" joints, and ball joints for binding. If all are okay, replace steering gear.

## REMOVAL & INSTALLATION

### POWER STEERING PUMP

**Removal** – Remove alternator and pump belts. Disconnect hydraulic lines from pump. Cap lines to prevent contamination. Remove bracket bolts. Remove pump. *See Fig. 2.*

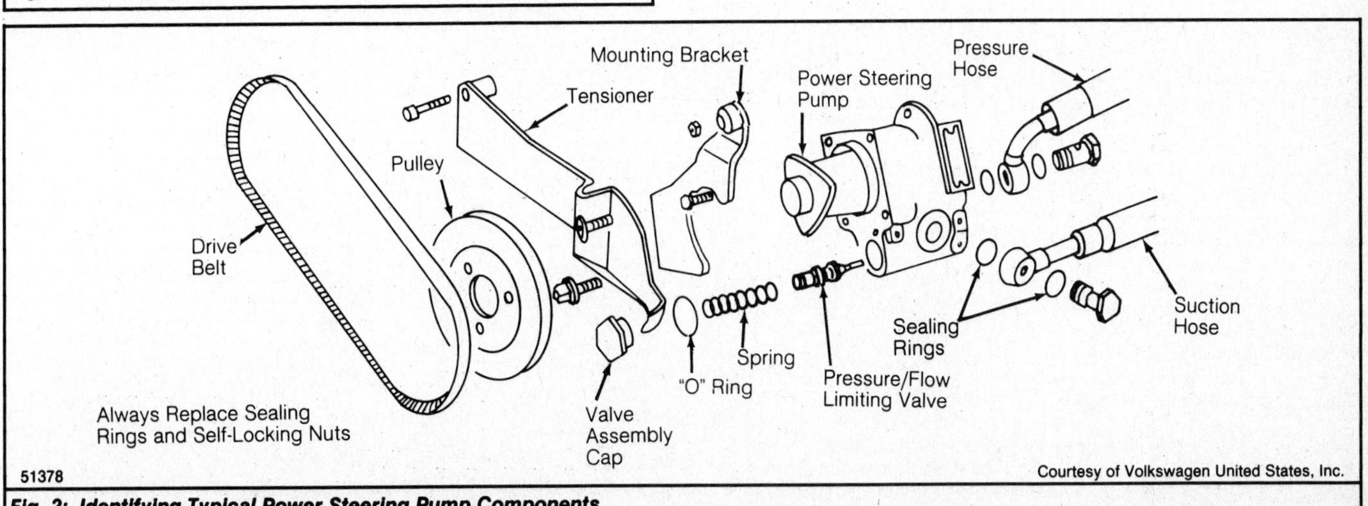


*Fig. 2: Identifying Typical Power Steering Pump Components*

# 1991 STEERING
# Power Rack & Pinion (Cont.)

**Installation** – To install, reverse removal procedure. Adjust belt tension. See POWER STEERING PUMP BELT under ADJUSTMENTS. Tighten nuts and bolts to specification. See TORQUE SPECIFICATIONS table at end of article. Fill and bleed hydraulic system. See HYDRAULIC SYSTEM BLEEDING. Start engine and check for leaks.

## POWER RACK & PINION

***NOTE:* *Refer to illustration for exploded view of power rack and pinion components. See Fig. 1.***

**Removal (Cabriolet)** – **1)** Remove pressure line from pump. Drain fluid from pump and line. Disconnect tie rod ends from steering knuckles. Remove transmission mount and bracket. Remove exhaust manifold.

**2)** Remove hydraulic lines from steering gear. Plug openings. Remove shift linkage from steering gear (if equipped). Remove ground wire. Disconnect pinion shaft at "U" joint. Remove retaining bolts and steering gear.

**Removal (Corrado)** – **1)** Disconnect return line from pump. Drain fluid from pump and line. Disconnect tie rod ends from steering knuckles.

**2)** Remove lock bolt at "U" joint. Remove steering gear retaining bolts. Disconnect hydraulic lines at steering gear. Plug openings.

**3)** Support engine and transmission. Remove subframe bolts. Remove steering gear.

**Removal (Golf, GTI & Jetta)** – **1)** Disconnect return line from pump. Drain fluid from pump and line. Disconnect tie rod ends from steering knuckles.

**2)** Remove shift linkage from steering gear (if equipped). Disconnect pinion shaft at "U" joint. Disconnect hydraulic lines from steering gear. Plug openings. Remove retaining bolts.

**3)** Support engine and transmission with Engine Support (10-222A). Remove left transmission mount bolts. Loosen right transmission mount bolts. Remove steering gear.

**Removal (Passat)** – **1)** Disconnect return line from pump. Drain fluid from pump and line. Disconnect tie rod ends from steering knuckles.

**2)** Support engine and transmission with Engine Support (10-222A and 10-222A/1). Remove steering gear boot. Remove transmission mount bolts. Lower engine/transmission sufficiently to separate steering shaft halves.

**3)** Disconnect hydraulic lines from steering gear. Plug openings. Remove retaining nuts and steering gear.

**Removal (Vanagon)** – **1)** Removal and installation information is not available from manufacturer.

**Installation (All Models)** – Reverse removal procedure to install. Tighten nuts and bolts to specification. See TORQUE SPECIFICATIONS table at end of article. Fill and bleed hydraulic system. See HYDRAULIC SYSTEM BLEEDING. Check wheel alignment. See SPECIFICATIONS & PROCEDURES article in WHEEL ALIGNMENT.

## OVERHAUL

Manufacturer recommends that power steering pump and steering gear be replaced, rather than be repaired.

## TORQUE SPECIFICATIONS

***TORQUE SPECIFICATIONS***

| Application | Ft. Lbs. (N.m) |
|---|---|
| End Housing Bolt | 37 (50) |
| Power Steering Pump Bolt | 18 (25) |
| Pressure-Flow Limiting Valve Cap | 42 (57) |
| Pressure Line Fitting | 29 (39) |
| Return Line Fitting | |
| On Pump | 29 (39) |
| On Valve Housing | 22 (30) |
| Steering Gear Adjuster Lock Nut | [1] |
| Steering Gear Retaining Bolt | 22 (30 |
| Subframe Bolt | |
| Long | 96 (130) |
| Short | 59 (80) |
| Tie Rod-to-Steering Arm | 32 (44) |
| Valve Housing Bolt | 15 (20) |

[1] – Not specified by manufacturer.

# 1991 TRANSMISSION SERVICING
# Automatic Transmission

### Cabriolet, Corrado, Golf, GTI, Jetta, Passat, Vanagon

## IDENTIFICATION

*VOLKSWAGEN AUTOMATIC TRANSMISSION APPLICATIONS*

| Model | Transmission |
|---|---|
| Cabriolet, Golf, GTI & Jetta | Model 010 Transmission |
| Corrado & Passat | Model 096 Transmission |
| Vanagon | Model 090 Transmission |

## LUBRICATION

### SERVICE INTERVALS

Check fluid level at each oil change. Change fluid every 30,000 miles under severe driving conditions. Replace ATF filter on Corrado and Passat every 30,000 miles (if equipped).

### CHECKING FLUID LEVEL

**Transmission** - Park vehicle on level surface, with transmission at normal operating temperature. Set selector lever to Park or Neutral. Apply parking brake. Allow engine to idle. Remove dipstick, wipe clean, and reinsert. Remove dipstick. Fluid level should be between marks on dipstick.

***NOTE: Normal transmission fluid color on late production vehicles is Red/Brown.***

**Final Drive (Except Corrado & Passat)** - Place vehicle on level surface. Fluid level should be up to edge of fill hole on side of case.

**Final Drive (Corrado & Passat)** - Place vehicle on level surface. Remove speedometer drive shaft. Wipe shaft clean. Reinsert and again remove shaft. Fluid level should be between MIN and MAX marks on shaft.

### RECOMMENDED FLUID

**Transmission** - Use Dexron or Dexron-II ATF.
**Final Drive** - Use G50 or SAE 75W-90.

### FLUID CAPACITY

*TRANSMISSION REFILL CAPACITIES*

| Application | Refill Qts. (L) | Dry Fill Qts. (L) |
|---|---|---|
| Corrado & Passat | 3.2 (3.0) | 5.9 (5.6) |
| Except Corrado & Passat | 3.2 (3.0) | 6.4 (6.0) |

*FINAL DRIVE REFILL CAPACITIES*

| Model | Qts. (L) |
|---|---|
| Vanagon | 1.4 (1.3) |
| Except Vanagon | .8 (.8) |

### DRAINING & REFILLING

1) Remove transmission protection plate (if necessary). Remove rear pan bolts. Loosen front pan bolts. Carefully lower pan to drain as much fluid as possible. Remove oil pan. Pour out remaining fluid. Remove filter. Clean oil pan in solvent. Dry pan with compressed air.
2) Install new filter. On all but Corrado and Passat, tighten filter retaining screws to 27 INCH lbs. (3 N.m). On Corrado and Passat, tighten filter retaining screws to 71 INCH lbs (8 N.m).
3) Install oil pan with new gasket. On all models but Corrado and Passat, tighten oil pan bolts to 15 ft. lbs. (20 N.m). On Corrado and Passat, tighten oil pan bolts to 89 INCH lbs. (10 N.m).
4) Install protection plate if it was removed. Tighten bolts to 18 ft. lbs. (25 N.m). Add 3.2 qts. (3.0L) transmission fluid. Check fluid level. Add if necessary.

## ADJUSTMENTS

### SECOND BRAKE BAND

**Cabriolet, Golf, GTI, Jetta & Vanagon** - **1)** Adjust second brake band with transmission in a horizontal position only. Loosen adjuster screw lock nut. Tighten brake band adjustment screw to 89 INCH lbs. (10 N.m). *See Fig. 1.*

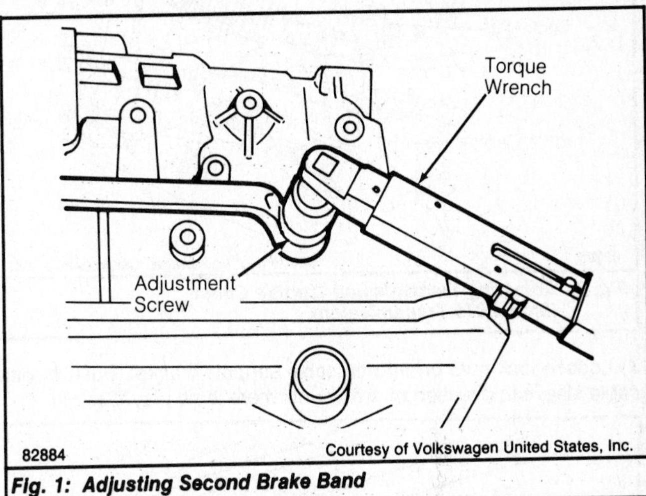


***Fig. 1: Adjusting Second Brake Band***

**2)** Loosen adjustment screw, then retighten to 44 INCH lbs. (5 N.m). Back off 2 1/2 turns. Hold adjustment screw stationary while tightening lock nut to 15 ft. lbs. (20 N.m).

### SELECTOR LEVER CABLE

**Cabriolet, Golf, GTI & Jetta** - Set transmission selector lever to Park. Loosen nut for clamping pin which retains selector cable to operating lever on transmission. Ensure selector lever and transmission operating lever are in Park. Tighten cable clamp nut to 71 INCH lbs. (8 N.m).

**Corrado & Passat** - Set transmission selector to Park. Loosen screw at gear lever shaft. Set gear lever in Park. Ensure detent engages parking lock. Tighten screw to 15 ft. lbs. (20 N.m) on Corrado, or to 18 ft. lbs. (25 N.m) on Passat.

**Vanagon** - Set transmission selector lever to Park. Loosen bolt retaining shift rod to operating lever on transmission. *See Fig. 2.* Ensure selector lever and transmission operating lever are in Park position. Push shift rod to rear. Tighten bolt.

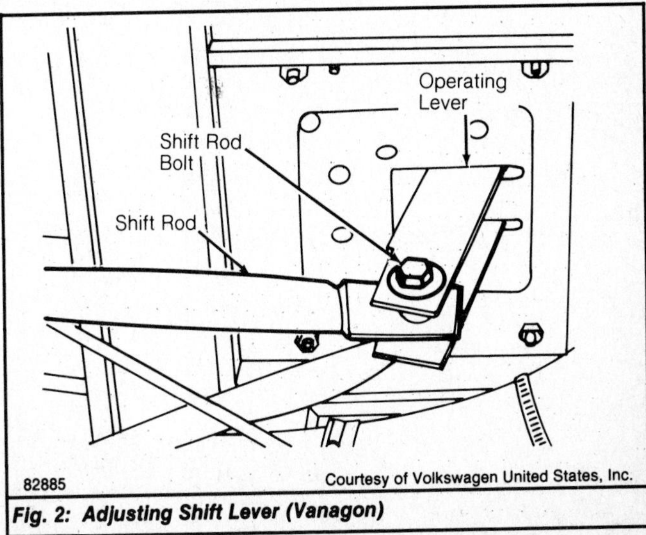


***Fig. 2: Adjusting Shift Lever (Vanagon)***

# 1991 TRANSMISSION SERVICING
# Automatic Transmission (Cont.)

## THROTTLE CABLE

***NOTE: Adjust accelerator linkage so that the operating lever on transmission is against stop when throttle valve is closed.***

**Cabriolet, Golf, GTI & Jetta - 1)** Engine must be at operating temperature and turned off. Set transmission gear selector to Park. Loosen adjustment nut and lock nut on throttle cable at transmission. Disconnect throttle cable from transmission. *See Fig. 3*.

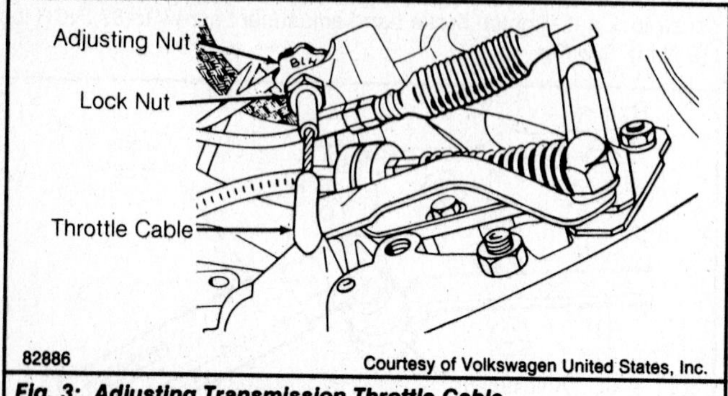


***Fig. 3: Adjusting Transmission Throttle Cable (Model 010 Transmission)***

**2)** Loosen lock nuts on throttle cable support bracket. Push throttle cable sleeve in direction of arrow until there is no play. *See Fig. 4*.

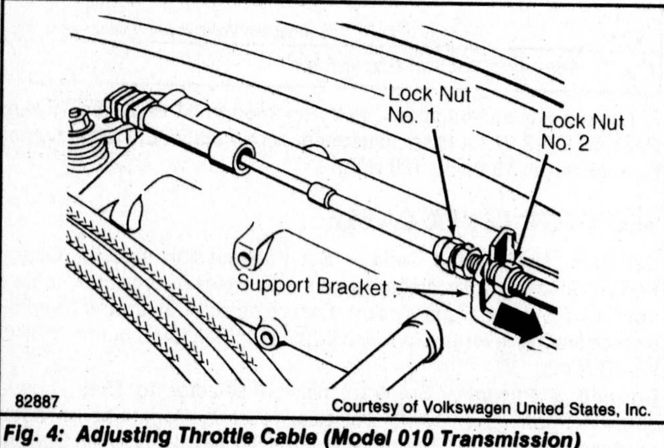


***Fig. 4: Adjusting Throttle Cable (Model 010 Transmission)***

**3)** Throttle valve must remain closed and accelerator/transmission linkage must be in closed position.
**4)** Turn lock nut No. 1 against support bracket. Tighten lock nut No. 2 to 18-89 INCH lbs. (2-10 N.m). Install accelerator cable onto transmission.

**5)** Press and hold accelerator pedal against stop. Working at transmission, push transmission operating lever against kickdown adjustment nuts.
**6)** Turn adjustment nut until all slack is removed from cable. Release accelerator pedal. Ensure transmission operating lever rests against kickdown stop. Tighten lock nut.
**Vanagon - 1)** To check adjustment, press accelerator pedal to full throttle position. Throttle lever must contact stop, but kickdown lever on transmission must NOT be in kickdown position.
**2)** Press accelerator pedal beyond full throttle position to floor. Override spring must be compressed and kickdown lever on transmission must be in kickdown position. If not, readjust.
**3)** Loosen adjustment nut. Remove override spring. *See Fig. 5*. Start engine. Adjust idle speed if necessary. Turn engine off.

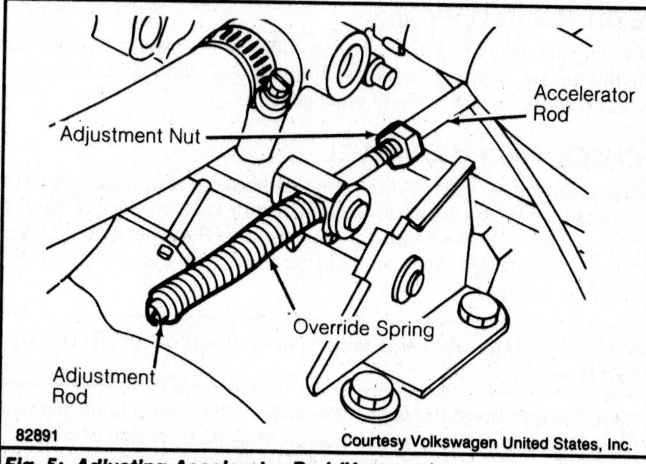


***Fig. 5: Adjusting Accelerator Rod (Vanagon)***

**4)** Move accelerator rod to closed throttle position (against stop). Using a screwdriver, turn adjustment rod until it just contacts throttle lever pivot.
**5)** Install override spring. Start engine. Check idle speed. If necessary, adjust idle speed by turning rod. Tighten lock nut on adjustment rod.
**6)** Press accelerator pedal to floor. Kickdown lever on transmission must be in kickdown position on stop.
**7)** Release accelerator pedal. Kickdown lever on transmission must return to idle position. If necessary, adjust throttle cable at clamp bolt. Clamp bolt is located at accelerator pedal end of accelerator cable.

## NEUTRAL SAFETY SWITCH

Neutral safety switch is located in shift console. Remove console cover. Adjust switch so that engine starts in Park and Neutral positions only.

# 1991 TRANSMISSION SERVICING
# Manual Transmission

## Cabriolet, Corrado, Fox, Golf, GTI, Jetta, Passat, Vanagon

## IDENTIFICATION

*MANUAL TRANSAXLE APPLICATIONS*

| Model | Transaxle |
|---|---|
| Cabriolet | 5-Speed - 020 Transaxle |
| Corrado | 5-Speed - 02A Transaxle |
| Fox | 4-Speed - 014 Transaxle |
| Golf | 5-Speed - 020 Transaxle |
| GTI | 5-Speed - 020 Transaxle |
| Jetta | 5-Speed - 020 Transaxle |
| Passat | 5-Speed - 02A Transaxle |
| Vanagon | 4-Speed - 091 Transaxle |
| Vanagon Syncro | 5-Speed - 094 Transaxle |

## LUBRICATION

### SERVICE INTERVALS

No oil changes are required.

### CHECKING FLUID LEVEL

Manufacturer states that fluid level does not have to be checked, and does not specify a procedure for doing so.

### RECOMMENDED FLUID

Use API GL-4, SAE 80W or 80W-90.

### FLUID CAPACITY

*TRANSAXLE REFILL CAPACITIES*

| Transaxle | Qts. (L) |
|---|---|
| 02A | 2.1 (2.0) |
| 014 | 1.8 (1.7) |
| 020 | 2.1 (2.0) |
| 091 | 3.2 (3.0) |
| 094 | 4.7 (4.5) |

## ADJUSTMENTS

### GEARSHIFT LINKAGE

**Cabriolet - 1)** Pull boot from housing. Loosen shift rod clamp bolt so lever moves freely on shift rod. Adjust shift finger in center of lock-out plate so that there is an equal distance on both sides of shift finger. *See Fig. 1.*

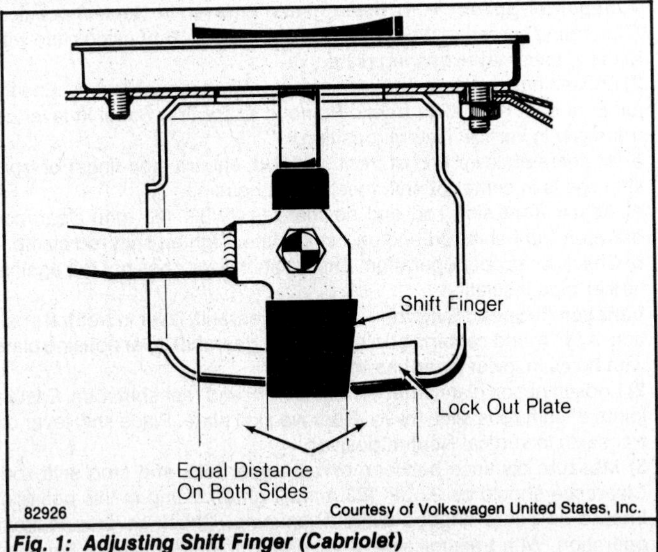


***Fig. 1: Adjusting Shift Finger (Cabriolet)***

**2)** Adjust shift rod end so distance "A" is 9/16" (14 mm). *See Fig. 2.* Tighten shift rod clamp to 14 ft. lbs (19 N.m). If shift linkage is spongy or jams after adjustment, change distance "A" to 1/2" (13 mm). If shift linkage will not stay in adjustment, install new clamp bolt and lock nut.

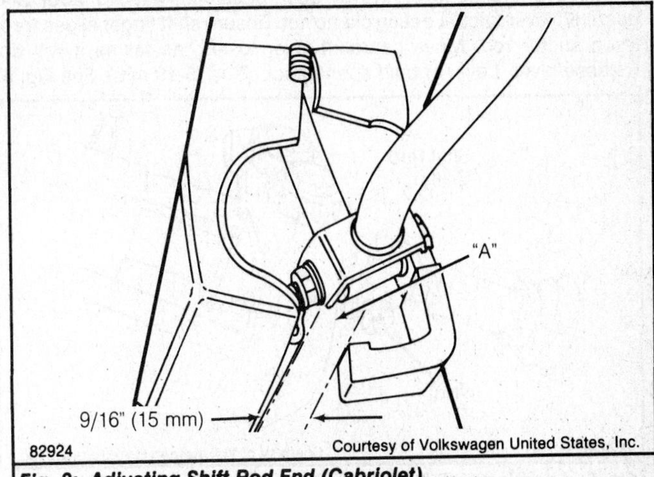


***Fig. 2: Adjusting Shift Rod End (Cabriolet)***

**Corrado & Passat - 1)** Place gearshift lever in Neutral position. Remove knob and boot. Loosen bolt "A" and nut "B" sufficiently so that operating cables move freely in centering holes. *See Fig 3.* Install Shift Linkage Gauge (3193). Loosen bolt "C". *See Fig 4.*

**2)** Pivot locating pin under bearing plate. Tighten nut "D". Place gearshift lever into left detent of slide. Move gearshift lever and slide together to left stop. Tighten slide with bolt "D". Move gearshift lever to right detent. Tighten bolt "E". Move gearshift lever to right detent. Tighten bolt "C".

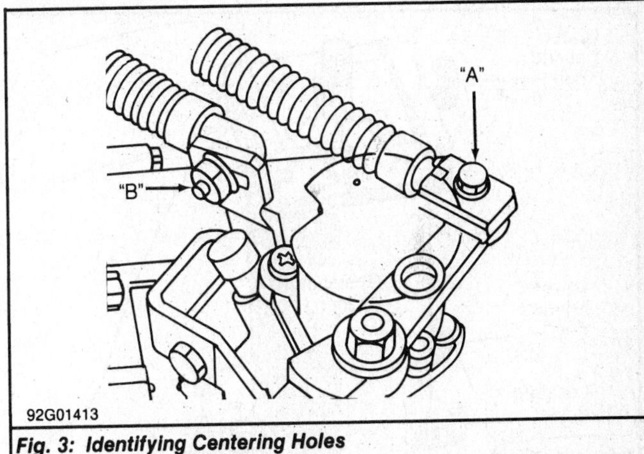


***Fig. 3: Identifying Centering Holes***

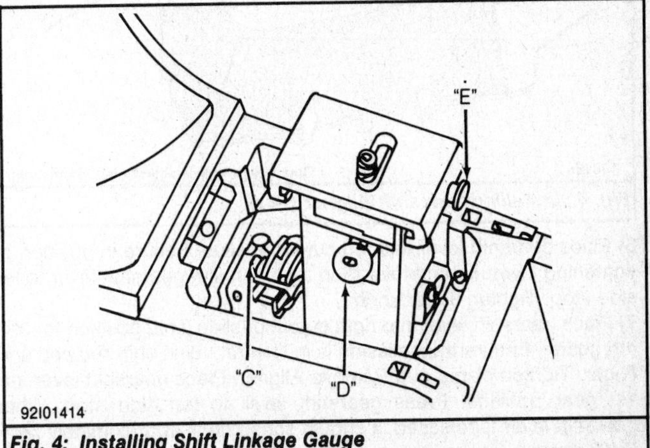


***Fig. 4: Installing Shift Linkage Gauge***

# 1991 TRANSMISSION SERVICING
## Manual Transmission (Cont.)

**Fox - 1)** Shift transaxle into 1st gear. Push gearshift lever to left stop. Release lever. If lever does not spring back .2-.4" (5-10 mm) to right, move gearshift lever housing very slightly in elongated holes. If adjustment does not correct hard shifting, go to step **2)**.

**2)** Place gearshift lever in 1st gear position. Remove boot and gearshift lever knob. Loosen clamp nut. Ensure shift finger slides freely on shifter rod. Move gearshift lever to left, as far as it will go. Release lever. Lever should spring back .2-.4" (5-10 mm). *See Fig. 5.*

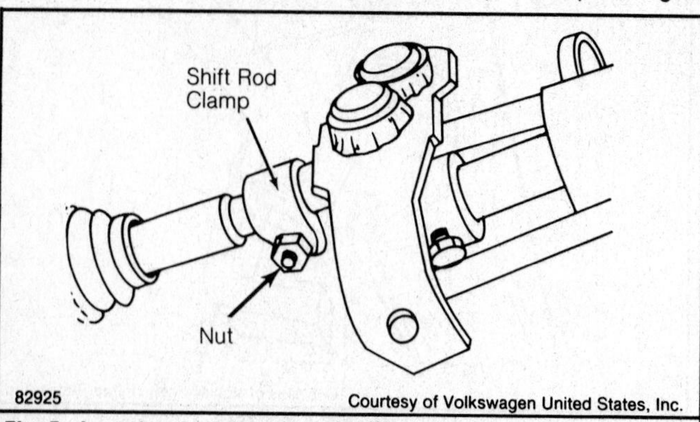


***Fig. 5: Locating Shift Rod Clamp Nut***

**3)** If lever does not spring back, move housing slightly sideways. If further adjustment is required, go to step **4)**.

**4)** Place gearshift lever in Neutral position. Place lever bearing housing in center of elongated hole. Loosen shift rod clamp nut. *See Fig. 5.* Ensure shift finger slides freely on shift rod. Remove gearshift lever knob and shift boot.

**5)** Align centering holes of gearshift lever housing and gearshift lever bearing housing. Tighten bolts. Install Gearshift Aligner (3057) with locating pin in front centering hole of vehicle. *See Fig. 6.*

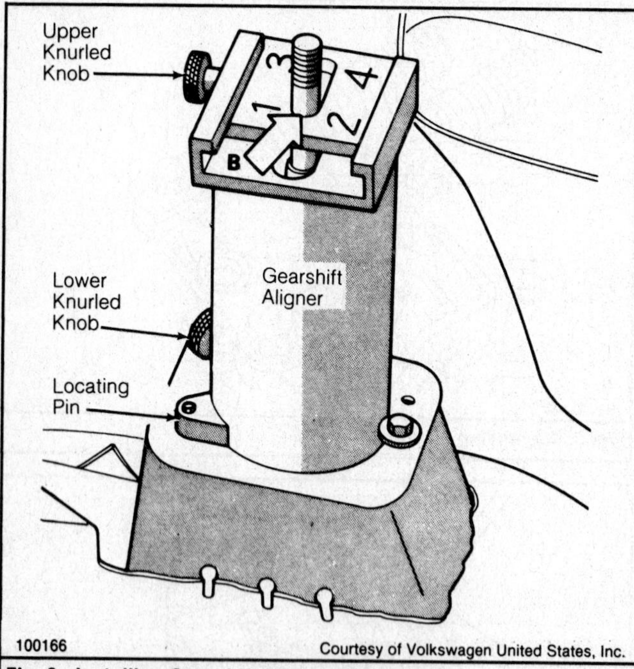


***Fig. 6: Installing Gearshift Aligner (Fox)***

**6)** Place gearshift lever into left cutout of slide. Secure in position by tightening lower knob. Move slide together with gearshift lever to left side stop. Tighten upper knob.

**7)** Place gearshift lever into right cutout of slide (shift position for 3rd/4th gears). Ensure transmission is in Neutral. Align shift rod and shift finger. Tighten clamp nut. Remove Aligner. Place gearshift lever into 1st gear position. Press gearshift lever to left side stop. When gearshift lever is released, it should spring back approximately .2-.4" (5-10 mm).

**Golf, GTI & Jetta - 1)** Place shift lever in Neutral position. Ensure transaxle is also in Neutral. Loosen lower shifter rod clamp. *See Fig. 7.* Selector lever must move freely on shifter rod.

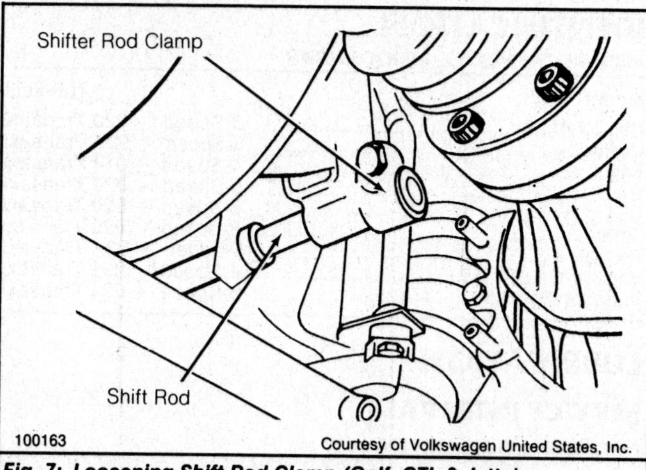


***Fig. 7: Loosening Shift Rod Clamp (Golf, GTI, & Jetta)***

**2)** Remove gearshift knob and boot. Position Adjustment Gauge (3104) over shift rod. *See Fig. 8.* With transaxle in Neutral, align shift rod with selector lever. Tighten shifter rod clamp to 19 ft. lbs. (26 N.m).

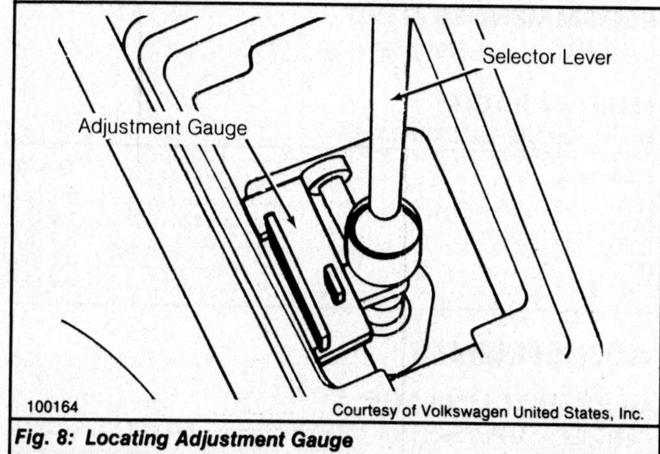


***Fig. 8: Locating Adjustment Gauge***

**3)** Move gearshift lever through all gear positions. Gears must engage smoothly and without jamming. Reinstall gearshift knob and boot.

**Vanagon (4-Speed) - 1)** Place gearshift lever in Neutral position. Align round centering holes of upper gearshift lever housing plate with holes in lower lever bearing plate.

**2)** Loosen nut on clamp that connects front and rear shift rods. Ensure joints of shift rods slide freely. Remove spare tire. Set shift lever on transaxle in vertical Neutral position.

**3)** At gearshift lever end of front shift rod, ensure stop finger of front shift rod is in center of shift mechanism housing.

**4)** Adjust front shift rod end so there is 29/32" (23 mm) clearance between front shift rod end and stop plate. Tighten shift rod clamp.

**5)** Check for proper operation. Ensure shift lever does not rub against heater pipe insulation.

**Vanagon (5-Speed Syncro) - 1)** Place gearshift lever in Neutral position. Align round centering holes of upper gearshift lever housing plate with holes in lower lever bearing plate.

**2)** Loosen nut on clamp that connects front and rear shift rods. Ensure joints of shift rods slide freely. Remove skid plate. Place shift lever on transaxle in vertical Neutral position.

**3)** Measure distance between reverse gear lock and stop shift rod. Clearance should be 29/32" (23 mm). Tighten clamp in this position. Ensure all gears engage without jamming. Check reverse lockout operation. With transmission in 1st gear, measure distance between gear shift lever and heater covering. Clearance should be 19/32" (15 mm).

# 1991 TRANSMISSION SERVICING
# Transmission Removal & Installation

**Cabriolet, Corrado, Fox, Golf GTI, Jetta, Passat, Vanagon**

## MANUAL

***NOTE: For manual transaxle replacement procedures, see appropriate article in CLUTCHES.***

## AUTOMATIC

### CABRIOLET, GOLF, GTI & JETTA

**Removal & Installation - 1)** Disconnect battery ground cable. Disconnect speedometer cable from transaxle. Raise and support vehicle. Remove left front wheel.
**2)** Support engine from above. Remove left rear transaxle mount and support. Remove upper transaxle-to-engine bolts. Remove upper bolts from front engine/transaxle mount.
**3)** Remove lower bolts on front mount and remove mount. Remove protective plate from transaxle. Remove torque converter-to-drive plate bolts.
**4)** Disconnect accelerator and selector cables from transaxle. Place mating marks on drive axle flanges and remove left and right axle shaft flange bolts.

***NOTE: If clearance is needed to remove transaxle, separate ball joint from left side steering knuckle and move axle shaft away from transaxle.***

**5)** Remove left rear engine mount. Remove starter. Remove subframe mounting bolts and allow subframe to hang free. Support transaxle with jack. Remove lower mounting bolt. Lower transaxle. To install, reverse removal procedure. Adjust accelerator and selector cables.

### CORRADO & PASSAT

**Removal & Installation - 1)** Disconnect battery ground cable. Remove air ducts to brake caliper and engine air intake. Disconnect speedometer cable from transaxle. Remove upper transaxle-to-engine bolts.
**2)** Disconnect and plug transaxle cooler lines. Support engine from above. Remove starter. Disconnect accelerator and selector cables from transaxle. Remove left transaxle mount and support.
**3)** Remove electrical wiring from transaxle. Remove lower bolts on front mount and remove mount. Place mating marks on drive axle flanges and remove left and right axle shaft flange bolts.
**4)** Disconnect right strut-to-spindle bolts. Remove right side axle. Reconnect strut. Remove protective plate from transaxle. Remove torque converter-to-drive plate bolts.
**5)** Slightly lower engine assembly. Support transaxle with jack. Remove lower transaxle-to-engine mounting bolts. Lower transaxle. To install, reverse removal procedure. Adjust accelerator and selector cables.

### VANAGON

**Removal - 1)** Disconnect battery ground cable. Remove upper engine-to-transaxle bolts. Remove dipstick and bolt for dipstick tube support bracket.
**2)** Remove 3 torque converter-to-drive bolts through hole in top of transaxle housing. Raise and support vehicle.
**3)** Disconnect both axle shafts from transaxle. Remove starter. Disconnect push rod from transaxle kickdown lever. Detach accelerator cable from transaxle. Detach selector lever cable from transaxle.
**4)** Disconnect and plug lines from transaxle cooler. Disconnect ground strap. Remove mounting bracket bolts. Support transaxle with jack.

***NOTE: Support bottom of engine when removing transaxle.***

**5)** Remove lower transaxle-to-engine bolts. Separate transaxle from engine. Lower transaxle.
**Installation -** To install, reverse removal procedure. Make sure torque converter is fully seated on one-way clutch support. Distance from engine mating surface to end of converter hub should be at least 3/8" (10 mm).

## TORQUE SPECIFICATIONS

*TORQUE SPECIFICATIONS*

| Applications | Ft. Lbs. (N.m) |
|---|---|
| Cabriolet, Golf, GTI & Jetta | |
| Axle Shaft-To-Flange Bolts | 33 (45) |
| Torque Converter-To-Drive Plate Bolts | 26 (35) |
| Transaxle-To-Engine Bolts | 55 (75) |
| Corrado & Passat | |
| Axle Shaft Nut | 195 (265) |
| Axle Shaft-To-Flange Bolts | 33 (45) |
| Strut-To-Spindle | 70 (95) |
| Torque Converter-To-Drive Plate Bolts | 45 (60) |
| Transaxle-To-Engine | |
| M10 Bolts | 45 (60) |
| M12 Bolts | 60 (80) |
| Vanagon | |
| Axle Shaft-To-Flange Bolts | 33 (45) |
| Torque Converter-To-Drive Plate Bolts | 22 (30) |
| Transaxle-To-Engine Bolts | 41 (55) |

# VOLVO

# 1991 VOLVO CONTENTS

## GENERAL INFORMATION [1]

### ALL MODELS



[1] – For all GENERAL INFORMATION, see front of Volume 1.

## ENGINE PERFORMANCE

### INTRODUCTION



### EMISSION APPLICATIONS



### SERVICE & ADJUSTMENT SPECIFICATIONS



## ENGINE PERFORMANCE (Cont.)

### ON-VEHICLE ADJUSTMENTS — Page



### THEORY & OPERATION



### BASIC DIAGNOSTIC PROCEDURES



### SELF-DIAGNOSTICS



### TROUBLE SHOOTING – NO CODES

# 1991 VOLVO CONTENTS (Cont.)

## ENGINE PERFORMANCE (Cont.)

### SYSTEM & COMPONENT TESTING



### SENSOR OPERATING RANGE CHARTS



### WIRING DIAGRAMS



### VACUUM DIAGRAMS



## ELECTRICAL

### ALTERNATORS & REGULATORS - BOSCH



### STARTERS - BOSCH & HITACHI



## WIRING DIAGRAMS

### CHASSIS WIRING DIAGRAMS



## SAFETY EQUIPMENT

### AIR BAG RESTRAINT SYSTEM



### INSTRUMENT PANELS



### STEERING COLUMN SWITCHES



### WIPER/WASHER SYSTEMS



## ENGINES

### 2.3L 4-CYLINDER

# 1991 VOLVO CONTENTS (Cont.)

## CLUTCHES



## DRIVE AXLES



## BRAKES



## WHEEL ALIGNMENT



## SUSPENSION



## STEERING

# 1991 VOLVO CONTENTS (Cont.)



## TRANSMISSION SERVICING

### AUTOMATIC TRANSMISSION



### MANUAL TRANSMISSION



### TRANSMISSION REMOVAL & INSTALLATION

# 1991 ENGINE PERFORMANCE
# Volvo Introduction

## 1991 MODEL COVERAGE

| MODEL | SERIES CODE | ENGINE | ENGINE ID | FUEL SYSTEM | IGNITION SYSTEM |
|---|---|---|---|---|---|
| 240, 240 SE | A | 2.3L SOHC [1] | 88 (B230F) | PFI | Magnetic [2,3] |
| 740 | F | 2.3L SOHC [1] | 88 (B230F) | PFI | Magnetic [2,3] |
| 740 Turbo | F | 2.3L SOHC [1] | 87 (B230FT) | PFI | Magnetic [2,3] |
| 940 GLE | J | 2.3L DOHC [4] | 89 (B234F) | PFI | Magnetic [2,3] |
| 940 Turbo | J | 2.3L SOHC [1] | 87 (B230FT) | PFI | Magnetic [2,3] |
| 940 SE Turbo | J | 2.3L SOHC [1] | 87 (B230FT) | PFI | Magnetic [2,3] |

[1] – Single Overhead Camshaft (8-Valve).
[2] – Timing is computer controlled.
[3] – Flywheel sensor type.
[4] – Double Overhead Camshaft (16-Valve).

### VIN DEFINITION

**YV1FX8850M1498000**

① ② ③ ④ ⑤ ⑥ ⑦ ⑧ ⑨ ⑩ ⑪ ⑫ ⑬ ⑭ ⑮ ⑯ ⑰

① Indicates Nation of Origin.
② Indicates Manufacturer.
③ Indicates Division.
④ **Indicates Model Series.**
⑤ Indicates Restraint System.
⑥ ⑦ **Indicates Engine Type.**
⑧ Indicates Body Type.
⑨ Indicates Check Digit.
⑩ **Indicates Model Year.**
⑪ Indicates Assembly Plant.
⑫ ⑬ ⑭ ⑮ ⑯ ⑰ Indicates Production Sequence.

91E17990

### ENGINE CODE LOCATION

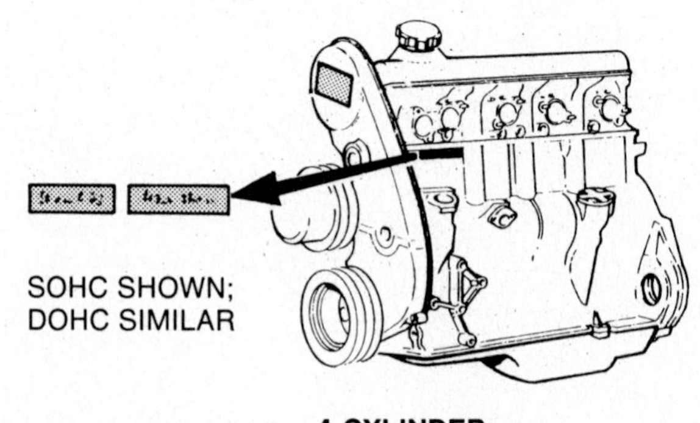


4-CYLINDER

90F17331

Courtesy of Volvo Cars of North America.

*MODEL YEAR VIN CODE APPLICATION*

| VIN Code | Model Year |
|---|---|
| K | 1989 |
| L | 1990 |
| M | 1991 |

# Emission Applications

*1991 VOLVO EMISSION SYSTEMS*

| Model, Engine & Fuel System | Emission Control Systems & Devices | Remarks |
|---|---|---|
| 240 Series 2.3L PFI<br>740 Series 2.3L PFI<br>940 Series 2.3L PFI | **PCV, TAC [1], EVAP, TWC, EGR, SPK, $O_2$, CE, CEC,** EVAP-VC, EGR-SOL [2] | [1] – 940 GLE only.<br>[2] – California only. |

**NOTE:** Major emission control systems are listed in bold type; components are listed in light type.

**CE** – CHECK ENGINE Light
**CEC** – Computerized Engine Controls
**EGR** – Exhaust Gas Recirculation
**EGR-SOL** – Exhaust Gas Recirculation Solenoid
**EVAP** – Fuel Evaporation System
**EVAP-VC** – Fuel Evaporation Vacuum Canister
**$O_2$** – Oxygen Sensor
**PCV** – Positive Crankcase Ventilation
**PFI** – Port Fuel Injection
**SPK** – Spark Control
**TAC** – Thermostatic Air Cleaner
**TWC** – Three-Way Catalyst

# 1991 ENGINE PERFORMANCE
# Service & Adjustment Specifications

**240 Series, 740 Series, 940 Series**

## INTRODUCTION

Use this article to quickly find specifications related to servicing and on-vehicle adjustments. This is a quick-reference article for when you are familiar with an adjustment procedure and only need a specification.

## CAPACITIES

*BATTERY SPECIFICATION*

| Application | Cold Cranking Amp. Rating |
|---|---|
| 240 Series, 740 Series, 940 SE & 940 Turbo | 450 |
| 940 GLE | 500 |

*FLUID CAPACITIES*

| Application | Quantity |
|---|---|
| Crankcase (Includes Filter) | |
| All Models | 4.7 Qts. (4.4L) |
| Cooling System (Includes Heater) | |
| 240 Series, 740 Series, 940 SE & 940 Turbo | 9.0 Qts. (8.5L) |
| 940 GLE | 10.0 Qts. (9.5L) |
| Man. Transmission (ATF Type F or G) | |
| M46 | |
| 740 Turbo | 2.4 Qts. (2.3L) |
| M47 | |
| 240 Series & 740 | 1.7 Qts. (1.6L) |
| Auto. Transmission (ATF Type F or G) | |
| AW-70 [1] | |
| 240 Series & 740 Series | 4.1 Qts. (3.9L) |
| AW-71 [1] | |
| 740 Turbo, 940 SE & 940 Turbo | 4.1 Qts. (3.9L) |
| AW-72L [1] | |
| 940 GLE | 4.1L Qts. (3.9L) |
| Differential (SAE 80-90W/API GL-5) | |
| 240 Series | |
| 1031 | 1.7 Qts. (1.6L) |
| 740 & 940 Series | |
| 1041 | 1.7 Qts. (1.6L) |
| 1045 | 1.5 Qts. (1.4L) |

[1] – Dry refill capacity is 7.8 qts. (7.4L).

## QUICK-SERVICE

### SERVICE INTERVALS & SPECIFICATIONS

*REPLACEMENT INTERVALS*

| Component | Miles |
|---|---|
| Air Filter | 30,000 |
| Auto. Transmission Fluid | 20,000 |
| Timing Belt | 50,000 |
| Coolant | 30,000 |
| Fuel Filter | 60,000 |
| Oil & Filter | 5000 |
| PCV (Clean) | 60,000 |
| Spark Plugs | 30,000 |

*ADJUSTMENT INTERVALS*

| Application | Miles |
|---|---|
| Valve Adjustment | |
| All Models [1] | 30,000 |

[1] – 940 GLE engine is equipped with hydraulic lifters. No adjustment is required.

*BELT ADJUSTMENT*

| Application | [1] Deflection – In. (mm) |
|---|---|
| All Belts | .2-.4 (5-10) |

[1] – Deflection is measured with moderate thumb pressure applied midway on longest belt run.

## MECHANICAL CHECKS

### ENGINE COMPRESSION

*COMPRESSION SPECIFICATIONS*

| Application | Specification |
|---|---|
| Compression Ratio | |
| 240 Series | 9.8:1 |
| 740 Series | |
| Except Turbo | 9.8:1 |
| Turbo | 8.7:1 |
| 940 GLE | 10.0:1 |
| 940 SE & 940 Turbo | 8.7:1 |
| Compression Pressure (Minimum) | |
| All Models | 128 psi (9 kg/cm²) |

### VALVE CLEARANCE

***NOTE: 940 GLE engine is equipped with hydraulic lifters. No adjustment is required.***

*VALVE CLEARANCE SPECIFICATIONS*

| Application | In. (mm) |
|---|---|
| Cold | |
| When Checking | .012-.016 (.30-.40) |
| When Setting | .014-.016 (.35-.40) |
| Warm | |
| When Checking | .014-.018 (.35-.45) |
| When Setting | .016-.018 (.40-.45) |

### VALVE ARRANGEMENT

**SOHC**

E-I-E-I-E-I-E-I (Front-to-rear).

**DOHC**

**Left Side** – All Intake.

**Right Side** – All Exhaust

## IGNITION SYSTEM

### IGNITION COIL

*IGNITION COIL RESISTANCE – Ohms @ 68°F (20°C)*

| Application | Primary | Secondary |
|---|---|---|
| All Models | 0.6-0.8 | 6900-8500 |

### SPARK PLUGS

*SPARK PLUG TYPE*

| Application | Bosch |
|---|---|
| Except 940 GLE | WR7DC |
| 940 GLE | WR6DC |

*SPARK PLUG SPECIFICATIONS*

| Application | Gap In. (mm) | Torque Ft. Lbs. (N.m) |
|---|---|---|
| All Models | .028-.032 (.70-.80) | 18 (25) |

*IGNITION TIMING (Degrees BTDC @ RPM)*

| Application | [1] Timing |
|---|---|
| Except 940 GLE | 12@725-825 |
| 940 GLE | 15@800-900 |

[1] – Ignition timing is computer controlled and is not adjustable.

# 1991 ENGINE PERFORMANCE
# Service & Adjustment Specifications (Cont.)

## FIRING ORDER

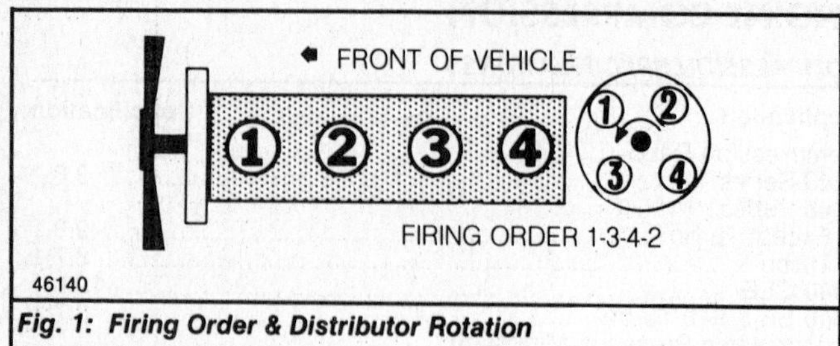


*Fig. 1: Firing Order & Distributor Rotation*

## FUEL SYSTEM

### FUEL PUMP

*FUEL PUMP PERFORMANCE* [1]

| Application | Pressure psi (kg/cm²) | Volume In 30 Sec. Pts. (L) |
|---|---|---|
| All Models | 42.0 (2.9) | 1.1 (.52) |

[1] – At 12 volts, 68°F (20°C), with engine off and fuel pump relay by-passed.

## IDLE SPEED & MIXTURE

*IDLE SPEED & CO LEVEL*

| Application | Idle RPM | [1] CO Level |
|---|---|---|
| Except 940 GLE & Turbo Models | 775 | 0.6% |
| 940 GLE | 850 | 0.6% |
| Turbo Models | 750 | 0.6% |

[1] – $O_2$ sensor disconnected. CO level is measured before catalytic converter.

## FAST IDLE

***NOTE:** All idle speeds are controlled by electronic control unit. Specifications on fast idle are not available from manufacturer.*

## THROTTLE SWITCH

See ON-VEHICLE ADJUSTMENTS article for throttle switch adjustments.

## 240 Series, 740 Series, 940 Series

# ENGINE COMPRESSION

Warm engine to normal operating temperature. Disconnect single wire from negative terminal of ignition coil. Check compression with all spark plugs removed, throttle valve wide open and at normal cranking speed (250-300 RPM).

***CAUTION: Failure to disconnect ignition coil negative terminal may cause damage to ignition system control unit(s).***

***COMPRESSION SPECIFICATIONS***

| Application | Specification |
|---|---|
| Compression Ratio | |
| 240 Series | 9.8:1 |
| 740 Series | |
| Except Turbo | 9.8:1 |
| Turbo | 8.7:1 |
| 940 GLE | 10.0:1 |
| 940 SE, 940 Turbo | 8.7:1 |
| Compression Pressure (Minimum) | |
| All Models | 128 psi (9 kg/cm²) |

# VALVE CLEARANCE

***NOTE: 940 GLE engine is equipped with hydraulic lifters. No adjustments are required.***

**1)** Remove valve cover. Turn crankshaft center bolt until camshaft is in position for firing No. 1 cylinder (TDC). Both cam lobes should point up at equally large angles. Pulley timing mark should be at zero degree mark.
**2)** Using a feeler gauge, check valve clearance of No. 1 cylinder between camshaft lobe and adjusting discs. Intake and exhaust valves have same clearance.
**3)** If clearances are incorrect, adjust by changing thickness of disc(s). Discs are available between thicknesses of .13-.18" (3.30-4.50)mm., in 002" (.05 mm) increments. Install disc with markings facing down. Use Valve Depressor (5022) and Pliers (5026) to depress and remove disc(s).
**4)** After valves for No. 1 cylinder are properly adjusted, rotate crankshaft to firing position for No. 3, No. 4 and No. 2 cylinders in sequence and repeat procedure. Install valve cover.

***VALVE CLEARANCE SPECIFICATIONS***

| Application | In. (mm) |
|---|---|
| Cold | |
| When Checking | .012-.016 (.30-.40) |
| When Setting | .014-.016 (.35-.40) |
| Warm | |
| When Checking | .014-.018 (.35-.45) |
| When Setting | .016-.018 (.40-.45) |

# IGNITION TIMING

Ignition timing is computer-controlled and is not adjustable.

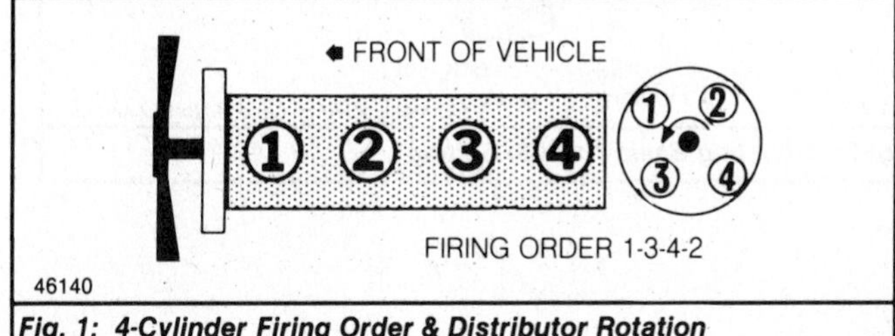


***Fig. 1: 4-Cylinder Firing Order & Distributor Rotation***

***IGNITION TIMING (Degrees BTDC @ RPM)***

| Application | [1] Timing |
|---|---|
| Except 940 GLE | 12@725-825 |
| 940 GLE | 15@800-900 |

[1] – Ignition timing is computer-controlled and is not adjustable.

# IDLE SPEED & MIXTURE

***NOTE: Cold (fast) idle is computer-controlled. Adjustment procedure is not provided by manufacturer.***

**Basic Idle Speed – 1)** Ground Red/White wire in 2-wire test lead. *See Fig. 2.* Test lead is located on right side of master cylinder. Grounding wire will set air valve wide open.

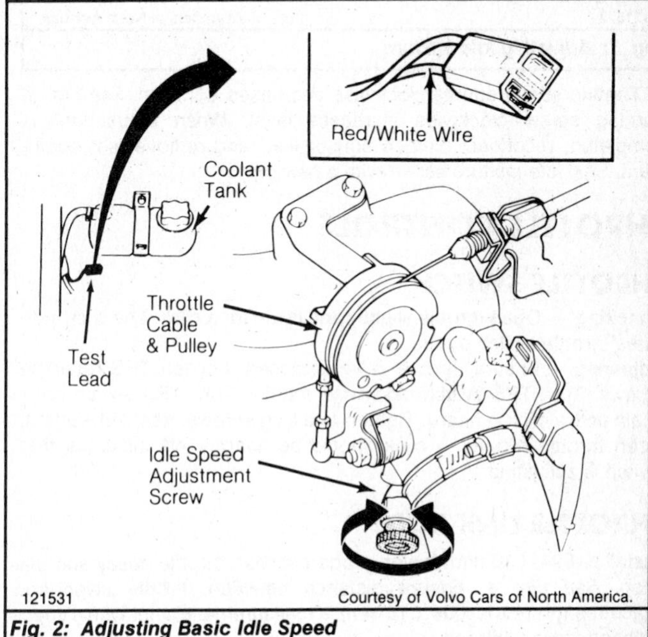


***Fig. 2: Adjusting Basic Idle Speed***

**2)** Use air bleed knob located under throttle body to set basic idle speed. See IDLE SPEED & CO LEVEL table. Disconnect ground wire from test lead. Engine speed should increase.

***IDLE SPEED & CO LEVEL***

| Application | Idle RPM | CO Level |
|---|---|---|
| Except 940 GLE & Turbo Models | 775 | [1] 0.6% |
| 940 GLE | 850 | [1] 0.6% |
| Turbo Models | 750 | [1] 0.6% |

[1] – $O_2$ sensor disconnected. CO level is measured before catalytic converter.

***NOTE: Mixture adjustment is not a normal tune-up procedure. It should not be performed unless mixture control unit is replaced or vehicle fails emissions testing.***

**Idle Mixture – 1)** Warm engine to normal operating temperature. Check idle speed and ignition timing. Disconnect oxygen sensor. Check CO level. See IDLE SPEED & CO LEVEL table.
**2)** If CO level is incorrect, turn off engine. Drill two 5/16" holes in adjustment plug. Pull out plug with snap ring pliers. Start engine and adjust CO level.

# 1991 ENGINE PERFORMANCE
# On-Vehicle Adjustments (Cont.)

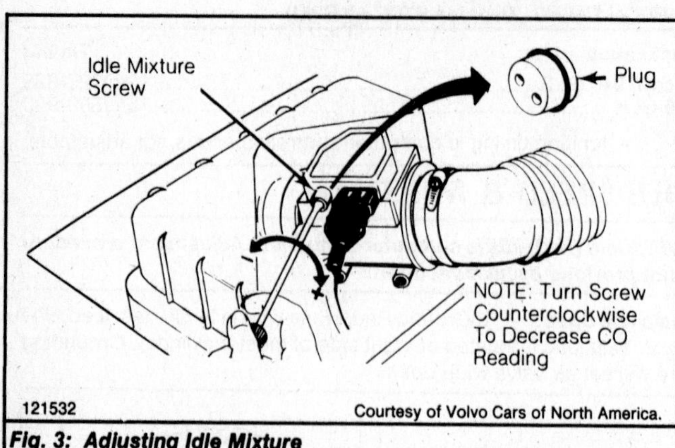


***Fig. 3: Adjusting Idle Mixture***

**3)** Turning screw counterclockwise decreases CO level. *See Fig. 3.* Turning screw clockwise increases level. When adjustment is completed, reconnect oxygen sensor lead and remove test equipment. Seal idle mixture screw with a new plug.

## THROTTLE CONTROLS

### THROTTLE SWITCH

**Checking** – Open throttle slightly and listen for a click. The click indicates throttle switch opens.

**Adjusting** – Ensure throttle valve is closed. Loosen TPS retaining screws. Turn TPS switch clockwise slightly. Turn TPS switch back again until a click is heard. Tighten retaining screws. Recheck setting. Open throttle slightly, a click should be heard. This indicates that switch is activating.

### THROTTLE LINK ROD

Install a .004" (.10 mm) feeler gauge between throttle pulley and idle stop. *See Fig. 4.* Ensure distance between throttle lever and adjustment screw is .004" (.10 mm). If measurement is not within specification, adjust link rod.

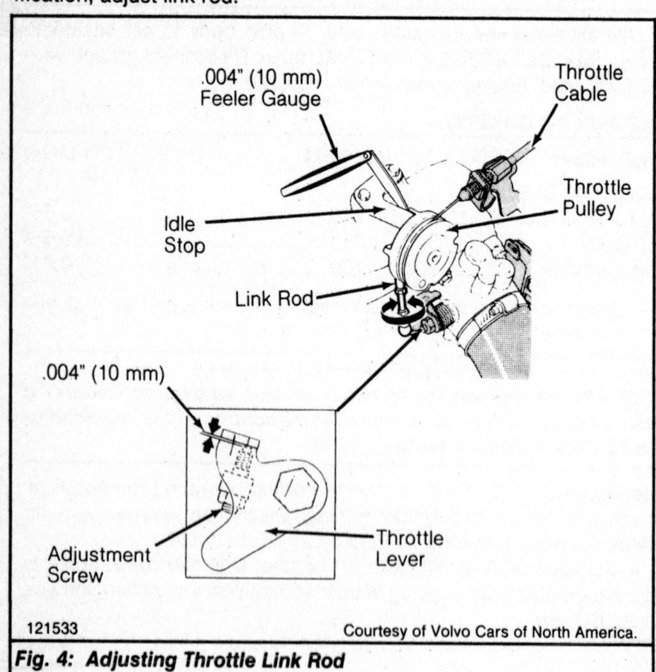


***Fig. 4: Adjusting Throttle Link Rod***

### THROTTLE CABLE

Throttle pulley should contact idle stop in the idle position. Cable should be taut but not affect position of throttle pulley. At full throttle, pulley should contact full throttle stop. Adjust throttle cable as required if out of adjustment. *See Fig. 4.*

### KICKDOWN CABLE

***NOTE: Depress accelerator pedal. DO NOT turn throttle pulley by hand or an incorrect adjustment will result.***

Fully depress accelerator pedal. At full throttle, distance between cable stop and cable casing should be 1.98-2.07" (50.4-52.6 mm). *See Fig. 5.* Adjust kickdown cable if not within specification.

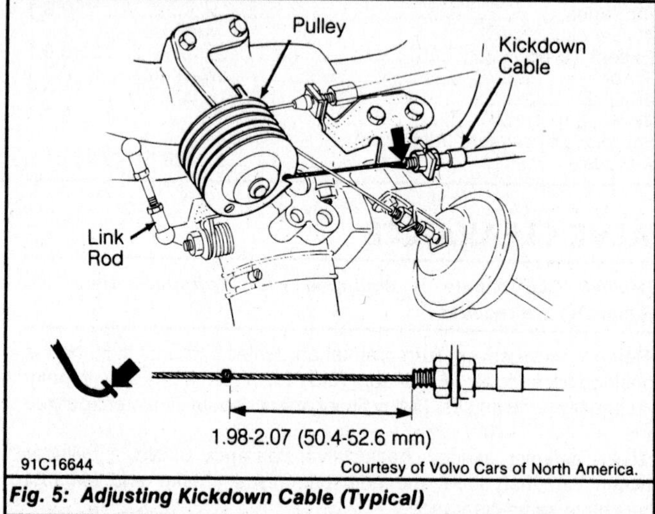


***Fig. 5: Adjusting Kickdown Cable (Typical)***

### BASIC THROTTLE SETTING

***NOTE: If basic throttle setting is adjusted, throttle position will change. Therefore, throttle switch must be adjusted whenever basic throttle setting is adjusted. See THROTTLE SWITCH under THROTTLE CONTROLS.***

Loosen basic throttle setting adjustment screw lock nut. *See Fig. 6.* Turn screw until throttle is completely closed. Tighten adjustment screw until it touches throttle lever and then turn an additional 1/4 turn (turn additional 1/2 turn on 940 GLE). On all models, tighten lock nut, making sure not to change adjustment. Recheck basic throttle setting.

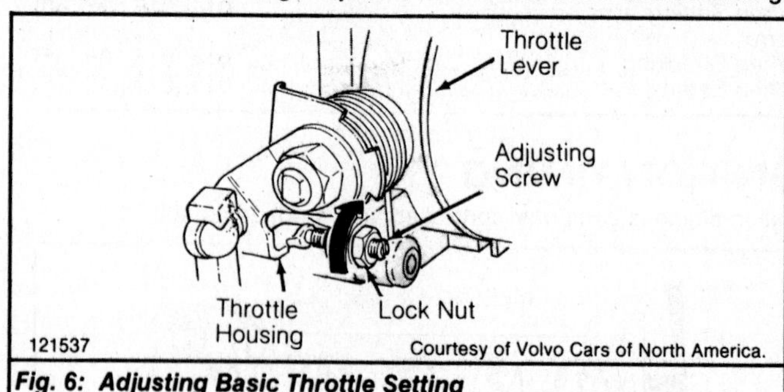


***Fig. 6: Adjusting Basic Throttle Setting***

# 1991 ENGINE PERFORMANCE
# Theory & Operation

## 240 Series, 740 Series, 940 Series

## INTRODUCTION

This article covers basic description and operation of engine performance-related systems and components. Read this article before diagnosing vehicles or systems with which you are not completely familiar.

## AIR INDUCTION SYSTEM

### TURBOCHARGERS

Turbo models use a water-cooled turbocharger, mounted directly to exhaust manifold, with a wastegate assembly attached to rear of turbine housing. Turbocharger consists of a turbine/compressor assembly, oil supply system and wastegate. Other components include impellers, impeller shaft, bearings and impeller housings.

The safety valve of system is a pressure actuated wastegate that prevents excessive intake boost pressure. The wastegate is controlled by the turbo control valve. This 3 port solenoid valve monitors boost pressure and prevents turbo lag. The control valve is activated by turbo control unit, which receives signals from throttle position sensor, fuel injection ECU and turbo pressure sensor.

If boost pressure exceeds safe limits, engine damage may result. The wastegate opens when exhaust pressure exceeds a predetermined limit and allows exhaust gases to by-pass compressor. Turbocharger operation requires a large quantity of clean oil to prevent bearing failure. Engine oil pressure provides constant lubrication to system.

At idle and light throttle, turbo engine operates like a standard engine. When more power is required, exhaust gases from exhaust manifold enter turbocharger's turbine housing and flow through turbine blades. Exhaust flow and turbine speed increase as throttle opens and RPM increases. Impeller turns with turbine and forces air into compressor housing and intake manifold. As impeller and turbine speed increases, boost pressure also increases.

## COMPUTERIZED ENGINE CONTROLS

All models use either a Bosch LH-Jetronic multi-point fuel injection system with EZ116K electronic ignition system or Regina (Bendix) multi-point fuel injection system with Rex-1 electronic ignition system. Both systems have self-diagnostic capabilities.

Both systems use an Electronic Control Unit (ECU) receiving input from engine monitoring sensors. These sensors include; coolant temperature sensor, air temperature sensor (Regina), pressure sensor (Regina), oxygen sensor, knock sensor (turbo), mass airflow meter (Bosch) and throttle switch. ECU uses these input signals to control air/fuel mixture for emission control, fuel economy and good driveability. Ignition control is provided by a separate ignition ECU. Turbo models also use a turbo ECU.

### CONTROL UNITS

All models use separate Electronic Control Units (ECUs) for fuel injection and ignition control. Turbo models also use a turbo ECU. Control units are electronically linked to provide precise control of fuel, ignition and turbo operation. Each system has self-diagnostic capabilities and use same diagnostic unit for trouble code output.

Fuel injection control unit is located behind right front kick panel. Ignition control unit is located behind left side of instrument panel, near accelerator pedal. Turbo control unit is located behind left kick panel.

***NOTE: Components are grouped into 2 categories. The first category covers INPUT DEVICES, which control or produce voltage signals monitored by control unit. The second category covers OUTPUT SIGNALS, which are components controlled by control unit.***

### INPUT DEVICES

All vehicles are equipped with different combinations of input devices. Not all devices are used on all models. To determine input usage on a specific model, see WIRING DIAGRAMS article. Available input signals include the following:

**A/C Switch** - Signals fuel injection ECU of A/C operation. This allows fuel injection ECU to control idle speed with idle valve.

**Air Temperature Sensor** - Information gathered from air temperature sensor is combined with information from pressure sensor to calculate intake air mass.

**Coolant Temperature Sensor** - Coolant temperature sensor is a negative temperature coefficient type, meaning its resistance lessens as temperature increases. Sensor unit has 2 resistors. One resistor is connected to fuel injection ECU and the other resistor is connected to the ignition ECU.

**Detonation (Knock) Sensor** - Knock sensor detects knocking and send signal to ignition ECU. ECU is able to gradually retard ignition timing to each individual cylinder. If knocking does not stop, a signal is sent to fuel injection ECU to enrich air/fuel mixture.

**Ignition Control Unit** - Ignition ECU serves as an input device for fuel injection calculation. Ignition ECU provides information on engine speed, crankshaft position, knocking, etc.

**Manifold Absolute Pressure Sensor (Regina)** - Also called a pressure sensor, measures both atmospheric and manifold absolute pressure. ECU calculates intake air mass from these inputs.

**Mass Airflow Meter** - This meter measures intake air mass. Measure sensor is a heated wire which is maintained at 250°F (120°C) hotter than intake air. Fuel injection ECU is able to calculate mass of intake air by measuring amount of current required to maintain wire temperature. When engine is turned off, any contaminants on wire is burned off by heating wire to greater than 1800°F (1000°C).

**Oxygen Sensor** - Also known as a Lambda probe, this heated oxygen sensor generates an electrical signal proportional to air/fuel mixture. Fuel injection ECU uses this information to adjust amount of injected fuel.

**Throttle Switch** - This switch signals ignition and fuel injection ECUs when throttle is fully closed or fully open.

**Turbo Control Unit** - Monitors turbo system and provides information for fuel injection control unit.

### OUTPUT SIGNALS

ECU processes information from input sensors and sends appropriate voltage control signals to control devices.

***NOTE: Vehicles are equipped with different combinations of computer-controlled components. Not all components listed below are used on every vehicle. For theory and operation of each output component, refer to system indicated after component.***

**CHECK ENGINE Light** - See CHECK ENGINE LIGHT under SELF-DIAGNOSTIC SYSTEM.

**Cold Start Valve** - See FUEL CONTROL under FUEL SYSTEM.

**EGR Control Solenoid Valve** - See EXHAUST GAS RECIRCULATION (EGR) under EMISSION SYSTEMS.

**Fuel Injectors** - See FUEL CONTROL under FUEL SYSTEM.

**Fuel Pump** - See FUEL DELIVERY under FUEL SYSTEM.

**Idle Valve** - See IDLE SPEED under FUEL SYSTEM.

**Ignition Control Unit** - See IGNITION SYSTEM.

**Oxygen Sensor Heater Control** - See OXYGEN SENSOR under EMISSION SYSTEMS.

**Power Transistor & Ignition Coil** - See ELECTRONIC IGNITION under IGNITION SYSTEM.

**Turbo Control Unit** - See TURBOCHARGERS under AIR INDUCTION SYSTEM.

## FUEL SYSTEM

### FUEL DELIVERY

**Fuel Pump** - All models are equipped with 2 fuel pumps. These are a primary low pressure pump, located in fuel tank, and a high pressure in-line pump. Both pumps are equipped with check valves to hold fuel pressure in system when ignition is off. Fuel from main pump is sent through an in-line fuel filter. Fuel is then sent to fuel pressure regulator where pressure is maintained at a constant pressure in relationship to manifold pressure. Excess fuel returns to fuel tank through a return line.

**Fuel Pressure Regulator** - Pressure regulator is a sealed unit which is divided by a diaphragm into 2 chambers (fuel and spring chambers).

# 1991 ENGINE PERFORMANCE
# Theory & Operation (Cont.)

Fuel chamber receives fuel through inlet side from injector fuel rail. Spring chamber is connected to intake manifold vacuum.

At idle, intake manifold vacuum is high. Diaphragm is pulled back by intake manifold vacuum. Any excessive fuel is returned to fuel tank. As throttle is depressed, intake manifold vacuum decreases. Regulator spring overcomes manifold vacuum, increasing fuel pressure.

### FUEL CONTROL

ECU calculates base injection pulse width by processing signals from various engine sensors. Information from crankshaft position sensor (RPM) is used to trigger timing of fuel injection. During normal driving conditions, injection duration is regulated in reference to mass air meter, engine speed, oxygen content of exhaust gases and coolant temperature. Under full throttle conditions, a richer fuel mixture is provided for increased power and to reduce combustion heat in engine and catalytic converter.

**Fuel Injectors** - Each injector incorporates a solenoid, plunger and needle valve which opens and closes an orifice. Control unit supplies current through auxiliary relay for a predetermined period, opening all injectors simultaneously to inject atomized fuel. Injection takes place twice per revolution while starter motor is running and once per revolution under normal driving conditions. Fuel is injected into intake manifold close to each inlet valve.

**Cold Start Valve** - Since fuel condenses on engine surfaces under extreme cold conditions, cold start valve compensates for this condition. Located further upstream of the engine than injectors, valve supplies fuel in more gaseous form than injectors. Operated directly by the ECU, rather than by a thermal timer, valve opens at approximately 5°F (-15°C) and stays open up to an engine speed of approximately 900 RPM. Valve remains closed at engine speeds greater than 900 RPM.

### IDLE SPEED

Engine idle speed is controlled by ECU depending upon engine operating conditions. ECU senses engine operating conditions and determines best idle speed. Idle speed is controlled by varying air passage inside idle valve.

**Idle Valve** - Idle valve uses a solenoid or motor to control by-pass air. Signal from ECU determines idle speed by controlling amount of by-pass air.

## IGNITION SYSTEM

### ELECTRONIC IGNITION

The electronic ignition ECU controls primary windings of ignition coil using signals from fuel injection ECU based on crankshaft position, engine speed and vehicle speed. Turbo models use a Hall Effect sensor, located in distributor, to determine crankshaft position and engine speed. Non-turbo models use a flywheel sensing permanent magnet generator to determine crankshaft position and engine speed.

**Power Transistor & Ignition Coil** - The ignition coil receives battery voltage through fuse panel and is grounded through power stage (power transistor). When ECU is signaled of proper crankshaft position, power stage removes ground from coil, firing plug.

### IGNITION TIMING CONTROL

**Ignition Timing Advance Control** - Ignition timing is totally controlled by ignition ECU. Ignition timing is based on preprogrammed information and modified by inputs from engine sensors.

**Detonation (Knock) Sensor** - Knock sensor is fitted to cylinder block to sense detonation inside cylinders. When detonation is detected, ignition ECU retards ignition timing in each cylinder individually until knocking stops. If knocking continues, ignition control unit signals turbo control unit to reduce boost pressure in stages.

## EMISSION SYSTEMS

### EVAPORATIVE EMISSIONS

Evaporative emissions system is designed to prevent fuel vapor from entering atmosphere. Fuel system is completely sealed and vented only through a carbon canister. System consists of pressure/vacuum relief fuel filler cap, a rollover valve, charcoal canister, purge valve and various connecting hoses.

Fuel pressure/vacuum relief filler cap allows excessive tank pressure to vent. It also allows air into fuel tank if vacuum should become excessive due to a malfunction in fuel evaporation system. Fuel tank vapor is vented by a line through rollover valve to charcoal canister.

Rollover valve is located in vent line close to fuel tank. Valve is designed to prevent fuel spillage if vehicle rolls over. Valve is open until vehicle is at a 45-degree angle or more, from horizontal.

**Canister Purge Valve** - Charcoal canister is filled with activated charcoal. Fuel vapor from tank is absorbed by charcoal when engine is not running. When engine is running faster than idle, canister purge valve opens and fuel vapor is drawn into engine and burned.

### EXHAUST GAS RECIRCULATION (EGR)

**Turbo Models** - EGR system operates by returning some exhaust gases to engine to be mixed with air/fuel mixture. This exhaust gas, which is basically inert at this stage, lowers combustion temperature. Reducing combustion temperature reduces amount of oxides of nitrogen (NOx) released into atmosphere.

**EGR Control Solenoid Valve** - When engine coolant temperature is less than 115°F (45°C), solenoid receives no current and EGR system is inactive. With engine at operating temperature, solenoid receives current from relay and opens vacuum line to EGR valve. EGR valve is opened completely by negative pressure. Even the least throttle opening opens idle switch. Time relay cuts current to solenoid, disconnecting EGR system for about 5 seconds and avoiding HC and particle build-up during acceleration from idle.

### OXYGEN SENSOR

**Oxygen Sensor Heater Control** - $O_2$ sensor operates only within a certain temperature range, approximately 545-1530°F (285-850°C). It is electrically heated to enable it to reach operating temperature quickly. When ignition is turned on, current is sent to a Positive Temperature Coefficient (PTC) resistor whose resistance increases with rising temperature. Because of this, $O_2$ sensor quickly reaches correct operating temperature, even at low exhaust gas temperatures.

### THERMOSTATIC AIR CLEANER

**940 GLE** - Thermostatic air cleaner consists of a thermostatically controlled damper and hot and cold air intake ducts. Thermostat senses air temperature and controls position of damper to vary proportions of hot and cold air entering air cleaner. This enables intake air temperature to be maintained at a constant value, regardless of outside temperature.

## SELF-DIAGNOSTIC SYSTEM

All models are equipped with self-diagnostic systems. A CHECK ENGINE light illuminates to signal driver in the event of a system malfunction. Fault codes are retrieved through the diagnostic unit, located in left rear corner of engine compartment. The diagnostic unit is equipped with an LED indicator, activation button and function select cable.

### CHECK ENGINE LIGHT

All models are equipped with a CHECK ENGINE light located on instrument panel. Light will illuminate when ignition switch is turned to ON position (bulb check) and when emission-related systems are malfunctioning during normal engine operation.

## 240 Series, 740 Series, 940 Series

# INTRODUCTION

The following diagnostic steps will help prevent overlooking a simple problem. This is also where to begin diagnosis for a no-start condition. The first step in diagnosing any driveability problem is verifying the customer's complaint with a test drive under the conditions the problem reportedly occurred.

Before entering self-diagnostics, perform a careful and complete visual inspection. Most engine control problems result from mechanical breakdowns, poor electrical connections or damaged/misrouted vacuum hoses. Before condemning the computerized system, perform each test listed in this article.

***NOTE: Perform all voltage tests with a Digital Volt-Ohmmeter (DVOM) with a minimum 10-megohm input impedance, unless stated otherwise in test procedure.***

# PRELIMINARY INSPECTION & ADJUSTMENTS

## VISUAL INSPECTION

Visually inspect all electrical wiring. Look for chafed, stretched, cut or pinched wiring. Ensure electrical connectors fit tightly and are not corroded. Ensure vacuum hoses are properly routed and not pinched or cut. See appropriate VACUUM DIAGRAMS article to verify routing and connections (if necessary). Inspect air induction system for possible vacuum leaks.

## MECHANICAL INSPECTION

**Compression** - Check engine mechanical condition with a compression gauge, vacuum gauge or an engine analyzer. See engine analyzer manual for specific instructions.

***WARNING: DO NOT use ignition switch during compression tests on fuel injected vehicles. Use a remote starter to crank engine. Fuel injectors on many models are triggered by ignition switch during cranking mode, which can create a fire hazard or contaminate the engine's oiling system.***

**Exhaust System Backpressure - 1)** The exhaust system can be checked with a vacuum or pressure gauge. Remove $O_2$ sensor or air injection check valve (if equipped).

**2)** Connect a 1-10 psi pressure gauge and run engine at 2500 RPM. If exhaust system backpressure is greater than 1 3/4 - 2 psi (.12-.14 kg/cm²), exhaust system or catalytic converter is plugged.

**3)** If a vacuum gauge is used, connect vacuum gauge hose to intake manifold vacuum port and start engine. Observe vacuum gauge. Open throttle part way and hold steadily. If vacuum gauge reading slowly drops after stabilizing, exhaust system should be checked for a restriction.

# FUEL SYSTEM

## FUEL PRESSURE

***WARNING: ALWAYS relieve fuel pressure before disconnecting any fuel injection-related component. DO NOT allow fuel to contact engine or electrical components.***

**Fuel Pump Pressure - 1)** Remove panel under right side of dash. Remove fuel injection system relay. *See Fig. 1.* Crank engine for at least 5 seconds. If engine starts, let run until it dies. Before disconnecting, cover fuel line connector with shop towel to absorb any fuel spray.

**2)** Connect a fuel pressure gauge between fuel line and injection manifold. Connect jumper wire between terminals No. 30 and 87/2 of fuel injection system relay connector. *See Fig. 2.* Fuel pressure should be 42 psi (3.0 kg/cm²).

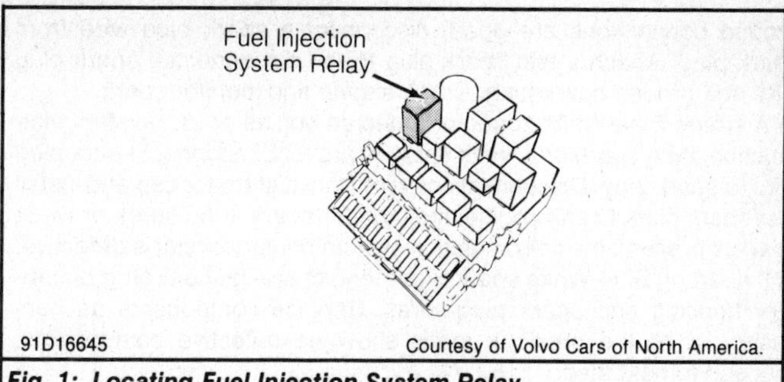


***Fig. 1: Locating Fuel Injection System Relay***

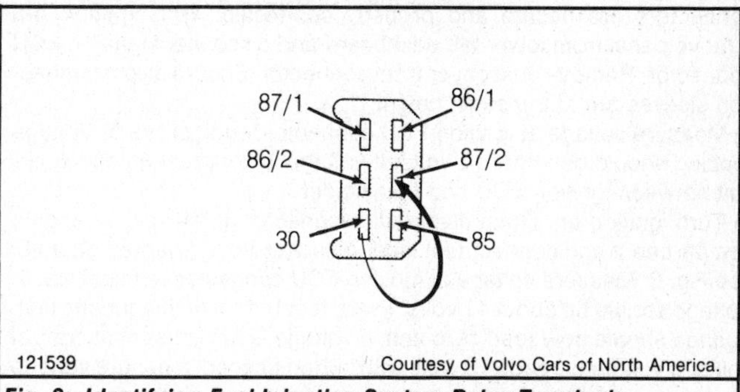


***Fig. 2: Identifying Fuel Injection System Relay Terminals***

**3)** If pressure is too low, pinch off fuel return line and recheck pressure (DO NOT allow pressure to exceed 86 psi (6.0 kg/cm²). If pressure rises quickly, pump and lines are functioning correctly. Replace pressure regulator and recheck pressure.

**4)** If pressure rises slowly, fuel filters or lines are blocked. If pressure does not rise, pump is defective.

**5)** If fuel pressure is high, disconnect fuel return line from pressure regulator and blow into line. If line is open, pressure regulator is defective and should be replaced.

**6)** Pressure may also be checked with engine off and fuel gauge connected. Attach a hand-held vacuum pump to pressure regulator. Line pressure should decrease as vacuum is applied to regulator.

**7)** With 12 volts applied, pump volume should be 1.1 qt (.52L) in 30 seconds.

**Fuel Pump Circuit - 1)** With fuel injection system relay removed, check for battery voltage at terminal No. 30. *See Fig. 2.* If battery voltage is not present, repair wiring between relay connector and battery.

**2)** Connect jumper wire between terminals No. 30 and 87/2 of fuel injection system relay connector. Fuel pump should run. If not, check wiring between pump and relay. Also check wiring between terminals No. 87/1 and 85 for continuity. Repair as necessary.

***NOTE: ECU terminal identifications are marked on unit or connector.***

***CAUTION: Ignition must be off when connecting or disconnecting ECU connector.***

**Fuel Injection System (Fuel Pump) Relay** - With ECU connector removed from ECU, ground ECU connector terminals No. 17 and No. 21. Pump relay should activate fuel pumps, and pumps should start operating. Connect voltmeter between ground and terminal 87/2 in relay. *See Fig. 2.* Battery voltage should be present. Disconnect ground leads from ECU terminals No. 17 and No. 21. Replace relay if faulty.

# IGNITION CHECKS

## BENDIX REX 1

***NOTE: ECU terminal identifications are marked on unit or connector.***

**B230F Engine (Federal) - 1)** Ensure ground connections from ignition ECU and power stage to inlet manifold ground are okay. If

# 1991 ENGINE PERFORMANCE
# Basic Diagnostic Procedures (Cont.)

ground connections are good, disconnect a spark plug wire from spark plug. Attach a test spark plug to the disconnected spark plug wire and ground spark plug. Crank engine and monitor spark.

**2)** A strong Blue-White spark indicates an engine or fuel system malfunction. If no spark or a weak spark is present, reconnect spark plug wire to spark plug. Disconnect coil wire from distributor cap and install test spark plug. Crank engine and monitor spark. If no spark or weak spark is present, the coil or ignition system primary circuit is defective.

**3)** If a strong Blue-White spark is present, check ignition rotor, distributor housing and spark plug wires. Replace components as necessary. If all the previous steps show no defective components, proceed to next step.

**4)** Turn ignition off. Reconnect disconnected components. Ensure all connectors are secure and properly connected. With ignition off, remove panel from lower left dashboard and disconnect ignition ECU connector. Remove dust cover from connector. Ensure all pin connection sleeves are at the same height.

**5)** Measure voltage at ignition ECU connector terminal No. 5. Voltage reading should be about 12 volts. If voltage is not present, check circuit between ignition ECU and fuse holder.

**6)** Turn ignition on. Open diagnostic connector at left rear of engine compartment and connect test lead to socket No. 6 (marked on unit). *See Fig. 3.* Measure voltage at ignition ECU connector terminal No. 1. Voltage should be about 12 volts. Press test button on diagnostic unit. Voltage should now read zero volt. If voltage is not present at control unit or if voltmeter reads 12 volts with button pushed, measure voltage at diagnostic unit connector.

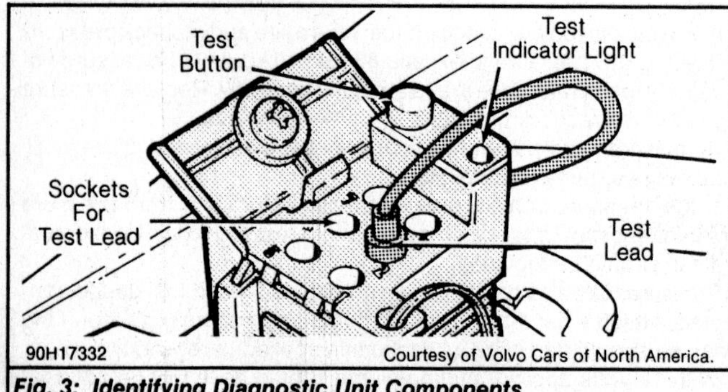


***Fig. 3: Identifying Diagnostic Unit Components***

**7)** Measure voltage at diagnostic unit connector Blue lead. Voltage should be about 12 volts. Using ohmmeter, check continuity between diagnostic unit connector Black lead and ground. Ensure continuity exists.

**8)** Turn ignition off. Check continuity between diagnostic unit test lead and pin No. 8 (under function selector button). Ohmmeter should read infinity. Press test button on diagnostic unit. Continuity should now be present.

**9)** Using ohmmeter, test for continuity of diagnostic unit LED. Connect ohmmeter leads to pin under LED and to test lead. Continuity should exist in only one direction.

**10)** Turn ignition on. Measure voltage at ignition ECU terminal No. 6 (Blue wire). Voltage should be about 12 volts. Turn ignition off. Using ohmmeter, check continuity between ignition ECU connector terminals No. 20 (Brown wire) and 14 (Black wire). Continuity should exist.

**11)** Measure resistance between ignition ECU connector terminal No. 2 (Red/Black wire) and ground. Ohmmeter reading should be as shown in COOLANT TEMPERATURE SENSOR RESISTANCE table.

***COOLANT TEMPERATURE SENSOR RESISTANCE***

| Temperature °F (°C) | Ohms |
|---|---|
| -22 (-30) | 30,000 |
| -4 (-20) | 15,000-16,000 |
| 32 (0) | 5800-6000 |
| 68 (20) | 2200-2400 |
| 104 (40) | 1000-1200 |
| 140 (60) | 600 |
| 176 (80) | 340-360 |
| 212 (100) | 180-190 |
| 248 (120) | 100-120 |

If reading is not correct, test sensor directly to determine if fault is in sensor or wiring.

**12)** Check continuity between ignition ECU connector terminal No. 7 (Orange wire) and ground. Ensure continuity exists. Depress accelerator until throttle switch opens slightly. Ohmmeter reading should increase to infinity. If reading is not correct, measure throttle switch resistance directly to determine if fault is in switch or wiring. Adjust throttle switch if necessary. See ON-VEHICLE ADJUSTMENTS article.

**13)** Remove panel under right side of dash, at right side of bulkhead. Remove glove compartment. Turn ignition off. Disconnect fuel injection ECU connector. Check for continuity between ignition ECU terminal No. 8 (Yellow wire) and fuel injection ECU terminal No. 25 (Yellow wire). If continuity is not present, check connectors and wiring. Repair as necessary. If continuity is still not present, internal fault is present in one of the ECUs. Reconnect fuel injection ECU connector and replace glove compartment and panel.

**14)** Check P/M (pulse) generator by measuring resistance between ignition ECU terminals No. 10 (Red wire) and 23 (Blue wire). Resistance should be 215-265 ohms. Ensure shield is connected to ECU terminal No. 11.

**15)** Disconnect knock sensor connector and place a jumper wire between terminals. Check continuity between ignition ECU terminals No. 12 (Black wire) and 13 (Green wire). Ohmmeter should show continuity. Ensure resistance to ground is infinity. If resistance is too high (infinity), remove jumper wire and test each wiring lead. If leads are intact, replace knock sensor.

**16)** Reconnect knock sensor connector. Reassemble and reconnect ignition ECU connector.

**17)** Disconnect connectors from ignition coil and power stage. Remove mounting screws and lift ignition coil from power stage. Measure resistance across low tension side of ignition coil. Resistance should be about .5 ohm.

**18)** Measure resistance between high tension terminal and each low tension terminal. Resistance should be about 5000 ohms. If resistance is not as specified, replace ignition coil.

**19)** Turn ignition on. Check for battery voltage at Blue wire of 3-pin power stage connector. If voltage is low or does not exist, check power supply lead connections at ignition ECU and ignition coil/power stage. Ensure voltage does not drop below 10.5 volts while engine is cranking. Turn ignition off.

**20)** Ensure ground is present at Brown/Black wire of 3-pin power stage connector and at Black wire of 2-pin power stage connector. Using a self-powered test light or buzzer, check for continuity between Orange wire of 2-pin power stage connector and ignition ECU terminal No. 16.

**21)** If no defects are found after performing all of the previous steps, or if engine still malfunctions after repairs, install a new ignition ECU. Recheck system as necessary. Reinstall ignition coil. Reassemble ignition ECU connector and reconnect to ECU. Reconnect ignition coil/power stage connectors.

## BOSCH EZ116K

***NOTE: ECU terminal identifications are marked on unit or connector.***

**B230F, B230FT & B234F Engines – 1)** Ensure ground connections from ignition ECU and power stage to inlet manifold ground are okay. If ground connections are good, disconnect a spark plug wire from spark plug. Connect a test spark plug to disconnected spark plug wire, and ground spark plug. Crank engine and monitor spark.

**2)** A strong Blue-White spark indicates an engine or fuel system malfunction. If no spark or a weak spark is present, reconnect spark plug wire to spark plug. Disconnect coil wire from distributor cap, and install test spark plug. Crank engine and monitor spark. If no spark or weak spark is present, coil or ignition system primary circuit is defective.

**3)** If a strong Blue-White spark is present, check ignition rotor, distributor housing and spark plug wires. Replace components as necessary. If previous steps show no defective components, go to next step.

4) Turn ignition off. Reconnect disconnected components. Ensure all connectors are secure and properly connected. With ignition off, remove panel from lower left dashboard and disconnect ignition ECU connector. Remove dust cover from connector. Ensure all ECU pin connection sleeves are at the same height.

5) Measure voltage at ignition ECU connector terminal No. 5. Voltage reading should be about 12 volts. If voltage is not present, check circuit between ignition ECU and fuse holder.

6) Turn ignition on. Open diagnostic connector at left rear of engine compartment and connect test lead to socket No. 6 (marked on unit). *See Fig. 3.* Measure voltage at ignition ECU connector terminal No. 1. Voltage should be about 12 volts. Press test button on diagnostic unit. Voltage should now be zero volt. If voltage is not present at control unit or if voltmeter reads 12 volts with button pushed, measure voltage at diagnostic unit connector.

7) Measure voltage at diagnostic unit connector Blue lead. Voltage should be about 12 volts. Using ohmmeter, check continuity between diagnostic connector Black lead and ground. Continuity should exist.

8) Turn ignition off. Check continuity between diagnostic test lead and pin No. 8 (under function selector button). Ohmmeter should read infinity. Press button on diagnostic unit. Ohmmeter should now show continuity.

9) Using ohmmeter, check continuity of diagnostic unit LED. Connect ohmmeter leads to test lead and to pin under LED. Continuity should exist in one direction only.

10) Turn ignition on. Measure voltage at ignition ECU terminal No. 6 (Blue wire). Voltage should be about 12 volts. Turn ignition off. Check continuity between ignition ECU connector terminals No. 20 (Brown wire) and 14 (Black wire). Continuity should be present.

11) Measure resistance between ignition ECU connector terminal No. 2 (Red/Black wire) and ground. Ohmmeter reading should be as shown in COOLANT TEMPERATURE SENSOR RESISTANCE table. If reading is not correct, test sensor directly to determine if fault is in sensor or wiring.

***COOLANT TEMPERATURE SENSOR RESISTANCE***

| Temperature °F (°C) | Ohms |
|---|---|
| -22 (-30) | 30,000 |
| -4 (-20) | 15,000-16,000 |
| 32 (0) | 5800-6000 |
| 68 (20) | 2200-2400 |
| 104 (40) | 1000-1200 |
| 140 (60) | 600 |
| 176 (80) | 340-360 |
| 212 (100) | 180-190 |
| 248 (120) | 100-120 |

12) Check continuity between ignition ECU connector terminal No. 7 (Orange wire) and ground. Ohmmeter should show continuity. Depress accelerator until throttle switch opens slightly. Ohmmeter reading should increase to infinity. If reading is not correct, measure throttle switch resistance directly to determine if fault is in switch or wiring. Adjust throttle switch if necessary. See ON-VEHICLE ADJUSTMENTS article.

13) Measure voltage at ignition ECU connector terminal No. 8 (Yellow wire). Turn ignition on. Voltmeter should read about .1 volt. If reading is not correct, check for open circuit between ignition ECU and fuel injection ECU or for fault in fuel injection ECU.

14) Turn ignition off. Measure resistance between ignition ECU connector terminals No. 10 (Red wire) and 23 (Blue wire). Resistance should be 215-265 ohms. Ensure shield is connected to ignition ECU terminal No. 11.

15) Disconnect knock sensor connector and place a jumper wire between terminals. Check continuity between ignition ECU terminals No. 12 (Black wire) and 13 (Green wire). Ohmmeter should show continuity. Ensure resistance to ground is infinity. If resistance is too high (infinity), remove jumper wire and test each wiring lead. If leads are intact, replace knock sensor.

16) Reconnect knock sensor connector. Reassemble and reconnect ignition ECU connector.

17) Remove air cleaner assembly. Ensure ignition is off and disconnect power stage connector. Power stage is located at front of left front fender panel. Remove connector dust cover. Connect multimeter negative (-) lead to ground and positive (+) lead to connector pin No. 4. Turn ignition on and note voltage reading. Voltage should be approximately 12 volts.

18) Leave multimeter attached and crank starter motor. Voltage should be at least 10.5 volts. If voltage is too low, check battery and charging system. If voltage is not present, check Blue wire from ignition ECU to ignition coil and power stage. Repair or replace as necessary.

19) Check continuity of power stage ground by connecting multimeter to power stage connector pin No. 2 and ground. Multimeter should show continuity. Check ignition coil resistance. Connect multimeter to power stage connector pins No. 1 and No. 4. Resistance should be 0.6-1.0 ohm. If resistance is less than 0.6 ohm, check wires for short circuit.

20) If wires are okay but resistance is still not 0.6-1.0 ohm, connect multimeter between ignition coil terminals No. 1 (Red/White wire) and No. 15 (Blue wire). If resistance is not 0.6-1.0 ohm, install a new ignition coil. If resistance is 0.6-1.0 ohm, check continuity of wires between ignition coil and power stage connector pins No. 1 and No. 4. Repair or replace as necessary.

21) Check shield (ground) wire between ignition ECU and power stage. Shield wire is connected to power stage connector pin No. 3 (Grey wire). Repair if necessary. Ensure power stage is receiving signal from ignition ECU. Disconnect wires from ignition coil terminal No. 1. Connect multimeter positive (+) lead to power stage connector pin No. 5 and negative (-) lead to ground.

22) Crank starter motor and monitor voltage reading. Voltage should pulsate between 0 and 2 volts. If voltage is within specifications, install a new power stage and recheck circuit. If a very low voltage is present and/or is irregular, check wiring between ignition ECU and crankshaft position sensor. Repair or replace as necessary.

23) Turn ignition off. If no defects are found after performing all of the previous steps, or if engine still malfunctions after repairs, install a new ignition ECU. Recheck system as necessary.

## IDLE SPEED & IGNITION TIMING

Ensure idle speed and ignition timing are set to specification. For idle speed adjustment procedures, see ON-VEHICLE ADJUSTMENTS article. Ignition timing is not adjustable.

***IDLE SPEED & CO LEVEL***

| Application | Idle RPM | CO Level |
|---|---|---|
| Except 940 GLE & Turbo Models | 775 | [1] 0.6% |
| 940 GLE | 850 | [1] 0.6% |
| Turbo Models | 750 | [1] 0.6% |

[1] - $O_2$ sensor disconnected. CO level is measured before catalytic converter.

***IGNITION TIMING (Degrees BTDC @ RPM)***

| Application | [1] Timing |
|---|---|
| Except 940 GLE | 12 @ 725-825 |
| 940 GLE | 15 @ 800-900 |

[1] - Ignition timing is computer-controlled and is not adjustable.

## SUMMARY

If no faults were found while performing BASIC DIAGNOSTIC PROCEDURES, proceed to SELF-DIAGNOSTICS article. If no hard codes are found in self-diagnostics, proceed to TROUBLE SHOOTING - NO CODES article for diagnosis by symptom (i.e., ROUGH IDLE, NO START, etc.) or intermittent diagnostic procedures.

# 1991 ENGINE PERFORMANCE
# Self-Diagnostics

## 240 Series, 740 Series, 940 Series

## INTRODUCTION

If no faults were found while performing BASIC DIAGNOSTIC PROCEDURES, proceed with ENTERING SELF-DIAGNOSTICS. If no fault codes or only pass codes are present, proceed to TROUBLE SHOOTING - NO CODES article for diagnosis by symptom (i.e., ROUGH IDLE, NO START, etc.).

***NOTE: All voltage tests should be performed with a Digital Volt-Ohmmeter (DVOM) with a minimum 10-megohm input impedance, unless specifically stated different in testing procedures.***

## SELF-DIAGNOSTIC SYSTEMS

***CAUTION: Self-diagnostics for fuel system, ignition system and turbocharger are covered separately in this article. Be sure you are using the proper information for the system being diagnosed.***

**Fuel Injection, Ignition & Turbo Systems** - The fuel injection, ignition and turbo systems each feature a self-diagnostic function for fault tracing. A common diagnostic unit, located in the engine compartment behind the left strut assembly, is used to retrieve codes from each control unit. The diagnostic unit is equipped with an LED indicator, activation button and function select cable. *See Fig. 1.*

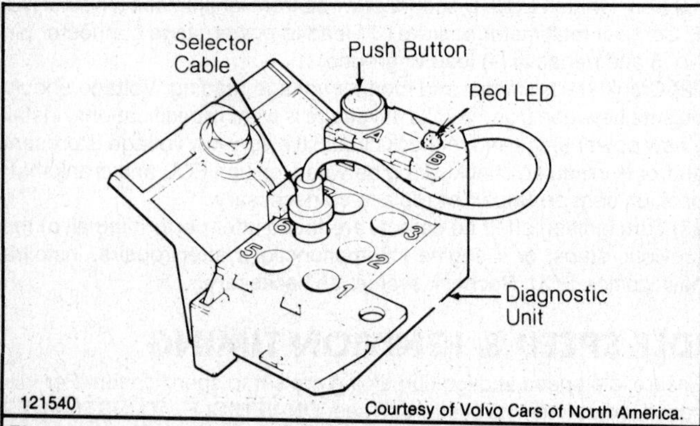


***Fig. 1: Identifying Bosch & Rex-I Diagnostic Unit***

Diagnostic unit output socket No. 2 is used for fuel injection. Socket No. 6 is used for ignition system. Socket No. 5 is used for turbo system. Once the selector cable has been inserted in the correct slot, depressing the button once, twice or 3 times selects from one of 3 control (fault tracing) functions. Faults stored in either ECU memory are read by means of a system of LED flashes.

Diagnostic system for fuel injection ECU stores 17 different fault codes. Ignition ECU stores 9 fault codes. Turbo ECU stores 8 different fault codes. All fault codes have 3 digits. Each can range from 1-to-4. Example of 3-digit code: 4-1-3. Since all codes have 3 digits, each code requires 3 series of flashes. For easier reading, a 3-second interval separates each digit of the code.

## SELF-DIAGNOSTICS - FUEL INJECTION

**Fuel Injection System Diagnostics** - The fuel injection ECU carries out continuous checks. Faults in any of the following functions are stored in system memory.

- Fuel System ECU Internal Function
- Lambda-Probe (Oxygen Sensor)
- Coolant Temperature Sensor
- Mass Airflow Meter
- Battery Voltage
- Throttle Switch
- RPM From Ignition System ECU
- Speedometer
- Knock Sensor (B234F Engine)
- Idle (Speed) Valve

## ENTERING SELF-DIAGNOSTICS

The system monitors the operation of components and switches. When the component or switch is operated according to a set procedure, the LED will display a 3-digit code. Failure to display a code indicates the control unit has failed to detect operation of the component/switch. In this case, the fault lies with the component/switch or associated connectors and wiring.

The functional check system can also test whether components/switches are correctly wired. As an example, it can be used to check whether the permanent/magnet generator (engine speed sensor) and wiring are intact if the engine fails to start.

**Control Function No. 1 (Retrieving Codes)** - This function displays any of 17 different fuel system codes stored in ECU memory during engine operation.

**Control Function No. 2 (Activating Circuit Breakers)** - This function tests fuel system circuit breakers. As it is activated, information is provided through LED in a flash code. This control function is generally used as a double-check after repairs.

**Control Function No. 3 (Testing Fuel System Components)** - This function tests fuel system components with engine stopped. It consists of a function cycle where the diagnostic system activates the components. You find out if the component is working by listening or putting a hand on it when it is activated.

## CONTROL FUNCTION NO. 1

***CAUTION: Never disconnect or connect ECU connector with ignition in ON position.***

**Retrieving Codes** - **1)** Locate the diagnostic unit and remove its cover. Connect selector cable to socket No. 2. Turn ignition to ON position. Enter control function No. 1 (retrieve codes) by pressing push button one time for at least one second and no more than 3 seconds.

***NOTE: Information on control functions No. 2 and 3 appears later in article. To enter control function No. 2, press push button 2 times for at least one second and no more than 3 seconds. To enter control function No. 3, press push button 3 times for at least one second and no more than 3 seconds.***

**2)** Watch the Red LED and count the number of flashes in the 3-flash series. The flash series are separated by a 3 second interval. *See Fig. 2.* Note all codes. Only 3 separate codes can be stored at once. If no codes are stored, the LED will flash a 1-1-1 to indicate the fuel system is operating properly.

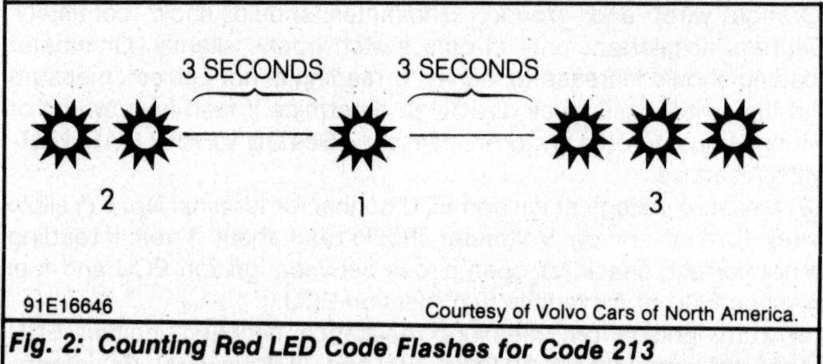


***Fig. 2: Counting Red LED Code Flashes for Code 213***

**3)** If a fault code is received, refer to FUEL INJECTION FAULT CODES table in this article. Depress push button again and check for additional codes. Depress push button a third time, if necessary. If the first code repeats, there are no other codes.

**4)** The diagnostic system memory is full when 3 codes are present. Those 3 codes must be repaired before further codes can be retrieved.

***NOTE: Not all codes listed in FUEL INJECTION FAULT CODES table are used on every vehicle.***

# 1991 ENGINE PERFORMANCE
# Self-Diagnostics (Cont.)

*FUEL INJECTION FAULT CODES*

| Code | Fault | Repair |
|---|---|---|
| 1-1-1 | No Faults | |
| 1-1-2 | ECU | Replace ECU |
| 1-1-3 | Fuel Injectors | Check Fuel Injectors<br>Check Fuel Pressure |
| 1-2-1 | Mass Airflow Signal | [1] Check Airflow Meter<br>[1] Main Relay |
| 1-2-3 | Cool. Temp. Sensor Signal | [1] Check Sensor |
| 1-3-1 | Ignition System RPM Signal | [2] |
| 1-3-2 | Battery Voltage | Check Battery<br>Check Charging System |
| 1-3-3 | Throttle Switch (Idle) | [1] Check Throttle Switch |
| 2-1-2 | $O_2$ Sensor Signal | Check Oxygen Sensor |
| 2-1-3 | Throttle Switch (Full Load) | [1] Check Throttle Switch |
| 2-2-1 | Lambda Operation | Check Intake Manifold<br>Check Fuel Pressure |
| 2-2-3 | Idle Valve Signal | [2] |
| 2-3-1 | Lambda Adjustment | Check Intake Manifold<br>Check Fuel Pressure |
| 2-3-2 | Lambda Adjustment | Check Intake Manifold<br>Check Fuel Pressure |
| 3-1-1 | Speedometer Signal | [2] |
| 3-1-2 | Knock/Fuel Enrichment Signal Missing | [2] |
| 3-2-2 | Airflow Meter Hot Wire | [1] Check Airflow Meter |

[1] – See SYSTEM & COMPONENT TESTING article.
[2] – See FAULT CODE TESTING under SELF-DIAGNOSTICS – FUEL INJECTION.

## FAULT CODE TESTING

This section will cover fault codes dealing with fuel system ECU testing. The codes will be followed by an explanation of how to test and repair the affected circuit.

**Code 1-3-1 (Ignition System RPM Signal)** – Turn ignition off. Disconnect fuel system ECU connector and remove protective sleeve. Connect a voltmeter between harness side of terminal No. 1 (Brown wire on 240 Series; Yellow/Gray wire on all others) and ground. Run starter motor. Voltage reading should be 5-7 volts. If reading is not 5-7 volts, check wiring between ignition ECU and fuel injection ECU. If wiring is okay, replace ignition ECU.

**Code 2-2-3 (Idle Valve Signal)** – Turn ignition off. Disconnect fuel system ECU connector and remove protective sleeve. Connect an ohmmeter between harness side of terminal No. 33 (Green/Red wire on 240 Series; Red/Black wire on all others) and terminal No. 9 (Orange wire on 240 Series; Blue/Yellow wire on all others). Reading should be approximately 8 ohms. If reading is not 8 ohms, check wiring and connectors. If wiring and connectors are okay, test idle valve. For idle valve testing, see SYSTEM & COMPONENT TESTING article.

**Code 3-1-1 (Speedometer Signal)** – Turn ignition off. Remove panel under instrument panel on driver's side. Disconnect 12-pin connector from speedometer. On 240 Series, connect an ohmmeter between Blue/Black wire of speedometer connector and terminal No. 34 (Blue/Black wire) of fuel system ECU. On all others, connect ohmmeter between Violet/White wire of speedometer connector and terminal No. 34 (Violet/White wire) of fuel system ECU. Resistance should be zero ohms. If resistance is present, check wiring and connectors. If problem persists, check speedometer operation and related wiring.

**Code 3-1-2 (Knock/Fuel Enrichment Signal Missing)** – Turn ignition on. Connect a voltmeter between terminal No. 28 (Brown/White wire on 240 Series; Gray/Red wire on all others) of fuel system ECU connector and ground. Reading should be approximately 0.7 volt. If voltage is not specified, check resistance between appropriate ECU connector wire and knock sensor. For knock sensor testing, see SYSTEM & COMPONENT TESTING article.

## CONTROL FUNCTION NO. 2

**Activating Circuit Breakers** – **1)** Turn ignition on. Locate diagnostic unit and remove its cover. Connect selector cable to socket No. 2. Turn throttle control at throttle body to full-load position. Depress push button twice. Each time the button is depressed, it should be held for more than 1 second and less than 3 seconds. The Red LED should flash.

**2)** Release throttle control. If flash series 3-3-3 comes up, the throttle switch works correctly in full-load position. If LED continues to flash rapidly, check throttle switch setting. See ON-VEHICLE ADJUSTMENTS article and proceed to next step.

**3)** Connect an ohmmeter between terminal No. 3 (Yellow/White wire on 240 Series; Orange wire on all others) of fuel system ECU and ground. Resistance should be infinite with throttle switch closed. Depress gas pedal slightly. Resistance should be zero ohms. If resistance is not as specified, check wiring from ECU to throttle switch.

**4)** Turn throttle control slightly and observe Red LED. If LED turns off and then flashes 3-3-2 code, the throttle switch is working properly in idle position. If LED does not flash as described, repeat step **3)**.

**5)** Start engine and check RPM signal from ignition system ECU to fuel system ECU. If LED turns off and then flashes 3-3-1 code, RPM signal is correct. If engine won't start, run the starter until the LED turns off and proceed to next step. If the LED continues to flash, check ignition system and see DIAGNOSTIC UNIT LED DOES NOT FLASH in this article.

***NOTE: Steps 6-9 are for A/C equipped vehicles and steps 10-11 are for A/T equipped vehicles.***

**6)** Check on/off function of A/C compressor. Put A/C control in ON position. If LED turns off and then flashes 1-1-4 code, A/C switch is okay. Proceed to step **8)**. If LED continues to flash, proceed to next step.

**7)** Connect an ohmmeter between terminal No. 15 (Gray/Red wire on 240 Series; Green/Yellow wire on all others) of fuel system ECU and ground. On 240 Series, resistance should be 1000 ohms with A/C off and 10 ohms with A/C on. On all others, resistance should range from infinity with A/C off and 35 ohms with A/C on. If resistance is not as specified, check wiring and connections.

**8)** Turn ignition off. The LED should flash rapidly prior to A/C compressor turning on. When the compressor turns on, the LED should turn off and then flash 1-3-4. If LED continues to flash, proceed to next step.

**9)** Connect an ohmmeter between terminal No. 15 (Green/Yellow wire) of fuel system ECU and ground. Resistance should be 35 ohms with A/C switch on. If resistance is not as specified, check wiring and connections.

**10)** This step will test idle speed compensation on A/T equipped vehicles. Depress brake pedal and place gear selector in DRIVE position and then NEUTRAL position. Observe LED while shifting. A code 1-2-4 should flash and test is complete. If LED continues to flash rapidly, proceed to next step.

**11)** Put transmission gear selector in NEUTRAL position. Connect an ohmmeter between terminal No. 30 (Blue/Yellow wire on 240 Series; Pink wire on all others) of fuel system ECU and ground. Resistance should be zero ohm in NEUTRAL position and infinity in DRIVE position. If resistance is not as specified, check wiring, connections and gear selector switch.

## CONTROL FUNCTION NO. 3

**Testing Fuel System Components** – **1)** Turn ignition on. Locate diagnostic unit and remove its cover. Connect selector cable to socket No. 2. Depress push button 3 times. Each time the button is depressed, it should be held for more than 1 second and less than 3 seconds. While LED flashes, the fuel injectors and idle valve should operate. Check by listening or feeling component when it is activated. If injectors fail to operate and LED flashes, proceed to step **2)**. If idle valve fails to operate and LED flashes, proceed to step **3)**.

# 1991 ENGINE PERFORMANCE
# Self-Diagnostics (Cont.)

**2)** To test fuel injector circuit, connect an ohmmeter between harness side of terminals No. 9 (Orange wire on 240 Series; Blue/Yellow wire on all others) and No. 18 (Green/White wire on 240 Series; Gray wire on all others) of fuel system ECU connector. Resistance should be 4 ohms.
**3)** If resistance is 5.3 ohms, one injector or wire to it is faulty. If resistance is 8.0 ohms, 2 injectors or wires to them are faulty. If resistance is 16 ohms, 3 injectors or wires to them are faulty. If resistance is incorrect, remove each injector connector. Each injector connector should have 16 ohms resistance. Repair as required.
**4)** To test idle valve circuit, connect an ohmmeter between terminals No. 33 (Green/Red wire on 240 Series; Red/Black wire on all others) and No. 9 (Orange wire on 240 Series; Blue/Yellow wire on all others) of fuel system ECU connector. Resistance should be 8 ohms. If resistance is not as specified, check wiring and connections between idle valve and ECU. If wiring is okay, check idle valve. See IDLE VALVE in SYSTEM & COMPONENT TESTING article.

## DIAGNOSTIC UNIT LED DOES NOT FLASH

**1)** If Red LED light won't flash when button is pressed or code will not flash, check grounds on intake manifold and for oxygen sensor. Check fuel pump relay and oxygen sensor heater fuses No. 4 and 6 (240 Series), 1 and 11 (740 Series) and 30 and 31 (940 Series) respectively.
**2)** If fuses are okay, go to next step. If any fuse is blown, check wiring for short. Remove glove box and right kick panel. Check ground wires at ECU. Ensure ignition is off. Remove fuel injection ECU fuses (in-line fuse near battery on 240 Series), No. 1 (740 Series) and No. 31 (940 Series).
**3)** Remove connector from ECU. Remove cover from connector. Check voltage for ECU memory by connecting voltmeter between terminal No. 4 and ground. Reading should be 12 volts. If 12 volts are not present, check wire between fuse and ECU connector.
**4)** Turn ignition on. Connect diagnostic unit select cable to socket No. 2. Connect voltmeter between terminal No. 12 and ground. Reading should be 12 volts. If 12 volts are not present, check wire between diagnostic unit and ECU. Press button on diagnostic unit, voltage reading should be zero volts. If 12 volts are present, check diagnostic unit.
**5)** Connect voltmeter between Blue wire in diagnostic unit connector and ground. Reading should be 12 volts. If 12 volts are not present, check circuit between ignition switch and diagnostic unit connector. Turn ignition off. Connect ohmmeter between Black wire in diagnostic unit connector and ground. Reading should be zero ohms.
**6)** Connect ohmmeter between selector cable end and pin under function select button. Ohmmeter should read infinite. Press function select button, reading should be zero ohms. Connect a diode tester between LED on diagnostic unit and selector cable end.
**7)** Connect Red lead of diode tester to pin under LED and Black lead to selector cable. If diode tester gives reading, LED is okay. If diode tester does not give reading, replace diagnostic unit. Turn ignition on. Connect voltmeter between terminal No. 35 on ECU connector and ground.
**8)** Reading should be about 12 volts. Voltage should also be present in start position. Turn ignition off. Separately connect ohmmeter between ECU terminals No. 5, 17, 19, 29 and ground. Reading should be zero ohms.

## CLEARING CODES

**Erasing Diagnostic System Memory – 1)** After all fault codes have been read and the faults corrected, the diagnostic system memory can be erased. Turn ignition switch to ON position. Read fault codes again. Depress push button for more than 5 seconds.
**2)** After 3 seconds, the LED should light. While the LED is lit, depress push button again for more than 5 seconds. Release button. LED should be out. Disconnect battery cable to erase codes.
**3)** To ensure memory is erased, depress push button for more than 1 second and less than 3 seconds. A flash code 1-1-1 denotes erased memory.

## SELF-DIAGNOSTICS – IGNITION SYSTEM

**Ignition System Diagnostics –** The ignition system ECU carries out continuous checks. Faults in these areas are stored in memory.

- Ignition System ECU
- Knock Sensor
- Fuel System ECU
- Coolant Temperature Sensor
- Impulse Sensor
- Throttle Switch
- EGR System
- EGR Temperature Sensor

## ENTERING SELF-DIAGNOSTICS

The system monitors the operation of certain components by operating the item(s) in question. When the component or switch is operated according to a set procedure, the LED will display a 3-digit code. Failure to display a code indicates the control unit has failed to detect operation of the component/switch. In this case, the fault lies with the component/switch, connectors and/or wiring.

The functional check system can also test whether components/switches are correctly wired. As an example, it can be used to check whether the permanent/magnet generator (engine speed sensor) and wiring are intact if the engine fails to start.
**Control Function No. 1 (Retrieving Codes) –** This function displays any codes stored in ignition system ECU memory during engine operation. The system can store 9 different ignition system faults.
**Control Function No. 2 (Testing Impulse Sensor & Throttle Switch) –** This function tests impulse sensor signal while engine is cranking and throttle switch in idle position. As each is activated, information is provided through LED in a flash code. This control function is generally used as a double-check after repairs.
**Control Function No. 3 (Testing EGR Converter – California) –** In this function, the diagnostic unit activates EGR converter. You find out if the component is working by listening or putting a hand on it when it is activated.

## CONTROL FUNCTION NO. 1

***CAUTION: Never connect or disconnect ECU connector with ignition in ON position.***

**Retrieving Codes – 1)** Locate the diagnostic unit and remove its cover. Connect selector cable to socket No. 6. Turn ignition to ON position. Enter control function No. 1 (retrieve codes) by pressing push button one time for at least one second and no more than 3 seconds.

***NOTE: Information on control functions No. 2 and 3 appears later in article. To enter control function No. 2, press push button twice for at least one second and no more than 3 seconds. To enter control function No. 3, press push button 3 times for at least one second and no more than 3 seconds.***

**2)** Watch the Red LED and count the number of flashes in the 3-flash series. The flash series are separated by a 3 second interval. *See Fig. 2.* Note all codes. Only 3 separate codes can be stored at once. If no codes are stored, the LED will flash a 1-1-1 to indicate the ignition system is operating properly.
**3)** If a fault code is received, refer to IGNITION SYSTEM FAULT CODES table in this article. Depress push button again and check for additional codes. Depress push button a third time, if necessary. If the first code repeats, there are no other codes.
**4)** The diagnostic system memory is full when 3 codes are present. Those 3 codes must be repaired before further codes can be retrieved.

***IGNITION SYSTEM FAULT CODES***

| Code | Fault | Repair |
|---|---|---|
| 1-1-1 | No Faults | |
| 1-4-2 | ECU | Replace ECU |
| 1-4-3 | Knock Sensor Signal | [1] |
| 1-4-4 | Fuel System Load Signal | [1] |
| 2-1-4 | Impulse Sensor Signal | [1] |
| 2-2-4 | Cool. Temp. Sensor | [1] |
| 2-3-4 | Throttle Switch Signal | [1] |
| 2-4-1 | EGR System | [1] |
| 4-1-3 | EGR Temperature Sensor | [1] |

[1] - See FAULT CODE TESTING under SELF-DIAGNOSTICS - IGNITION SYSTEM.

## FAULT CODE TESTING

This section will cover fault codes dealing with ignition system ECU testing. The codes will be followed by an explanation of how to test and repair the affected circuit.

***IGNITION SYSTEM ECU LOCATION***

| Application | Location |
|---|---|
| 240 Series | Behind Glove Box |
| 740/940 Series | Under Instrument Panel, Next to Gas Pedal |

**Code 1-4-3 (Knock Sensor Signal)** - Disconnect knock sensor connector and jumper terminals. Measure resistance between terminals No. 12 (Black wire) and No. 13 (Green wire). Resistance should be zero ohms. If resistance is okay, replace knock sensor. If resistance is too high, wiring is faulty.

**Code 1-4-4 (Fuel System ECU Load Signal)** - Turn ignition off. Connect a voltmeter between harness side of terminal No. 8 (Yellow/Brown wire on 240 Series; Yellow or Blue wire on all others) and ground. Turn ignition on. Reading should be approximately 0.1 volt. If reading is not 0.1 volt, check for break in wiring between electronic control units or fault in fuel system ECU.

**Code 2-1-4 (Impulse Sensor Signal)** - **1)** Turn ignition off. Connect an ohmmeter between terminals No. 10 (Blue/Yellow wire on 240 Series; Red or Blue wire on all others) and No. 23 (Yellow/Red wire on 240 Series; Red or Blue wire on all others).

**2)** Resistance should be 215-265 ohms. If engine is hot, resistance could reach 280-300 ohms. If resistance is not as specified, check wiring. If wiring is okay, check sensor. See CONTROL FUNCTION NO. 2 under SELF-DIAGNOSTICS - IGNITION SYSTEM.

**Code 2-2-4 (Coolant Temp. Signal)** - Turn ignition off. Connect an ohmmeter between terminal No. 2 and ground. *See Fig. 3* for resistance specifications.

**Code 2-3-4 (Throttle Switch Signal)** - **1)** Turn ignition off. Connect an ohmmeter between terminal No. 7 (Yellow/White wire on 240 Series; Orange wire on all others) of ignition system ECU connector. Reading should be zero ohms.

**2)** Press accelerator pedal slightly to open throttle switch. Reading should be infinite. If resistance is not as specified, check resistance at throttle switch. For throttle switch testing and adjustment, see SYSTEM & COMPONENT TESTING article.

**Code 2-4-1 (EGR System)** - Turn ignition on. Press button on diagnostic unit 3 times. Each time hold for one second. The LED should begin to flash at the same rate as EGR converter is energized. Connect ohmmeter between terminals No. 6 (Blue wire on all models) and 15 (White/Black wire on 240 Series; Red/Green wire on all others). Resistance should be 85 ohms.

**Code 4-1-3 (EGR Temperature Sensor)** - Connect ohmmeter between terminal No. 22 and ground. Reading should be 500-550 ohms at 68°F (20°C). Resistance should be approximately 1000 ohms for hot engine.

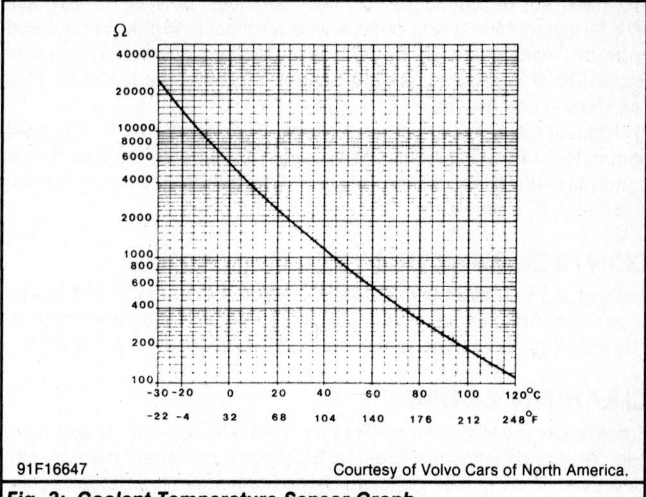


***Fig. 3: Coolant Temperature Sensor Graph***

## CONTROL FUNCTION NO. 2

**Testing Impulse Sensor & Throttle Switch** - **1)** Turn ignition on. Press diagnostic unit button twice, hold button each time for more than one second. The diagnostic unit light should flash rapidly. If light does not flash rapidly, turn ignition off. Disconnect ignition ECU connector.

***NOTE: Before removing ignition control unit connector, remove fuse No. 1 (740 Series) or fuse No. 31 (940 Series). On 240 Series, simply ensure ignition is off.***

**2)** On 240 Series, ECU is located behind panel below glove box. On 740/940 Series, ECU is located behind panel on right side of accelerator pedal. On all models, push out clip and disconnect ECU connector. Remove cover from ECU connector exposing pin identification numbers. Visually inspect all pin connector sleeves to ensure all pins are at same height.

**3)** Connect a voltmeter between ignition ECU pin No. 5 and ground. Voltmeter should read 12 volts. If voltage is not present, check wire from ignition ECU connector to in-line fuse located on left shock tower (240 Series) or check circuit between ignition ECU pin No. 5 and fuse box (all others). *See Fig. 4*.

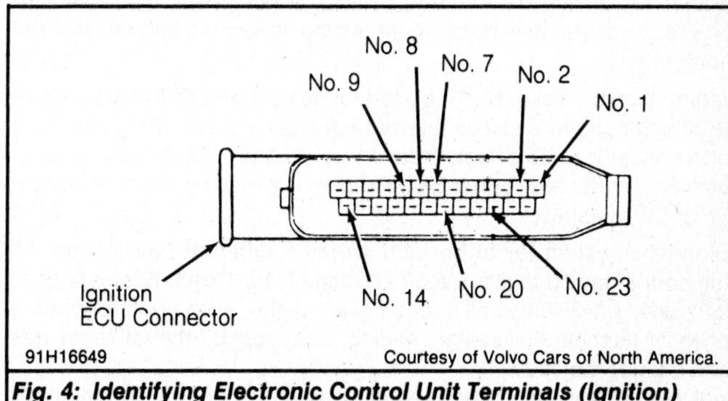


***Fig. 4: Identifying Electronic Control Unit Terminals (Ignition)***

**4)** To test diagnostic unit terminals, turn ignition on. Put diagnostic unit selector cable in socket No. 6. Connect a voltmeter between ignition control unit terminal No. 1 (White wire on 240 Series or Yellow/Red wire on 740/940 Series) and ground.

**5)** Voltage reading should be 12 volts. With button pressed, reading should be zero. If voltage is not present at ignition control unit, test for voltage at diagnostic unit socket No. 6. If 12 volts are present with button pressed, check test socket connector.

# 1991 ENGINE PERFORMANCE
# Self-Diagnostics (Cont.)

**6)** At test socket connector, connect voltmeter between Red/Black wire terminal (240 Series) or Blue wire terminal (740/940 Series) and ground. Reading should be 12 volts. Connect ohmmeter between Brown/Black wire terminal (240 Series) or Black wire terminal (740/940 Series) and ground.
**7)** Resistance should be zero ohms. Turn ignition off. Connect ohmmeter between selector cable and pin No. 8 below diagnostic unit button. Reading should be infinite. With button pressed, reading should be zero ohms.

## CONTROL FUNCTION NO. 3

**Testing EGR Converter (California)** – Press diagnostic unit button on test terminal 3 times, holding for more than one second each time. The light should flash at same rate as EGR converter is energized.

## CLEARING CODES

**Erasing Diagnostic System Memory** – **1)** After all fault codes have been read and the faults corrected, the diagnostic system memory can be erased. Turn ignition switch to ON position. Read fault codes again. Depress push button for more than 5 seconds.
**2)** After 3 seconds, the LED should light. While the LED is lit, depress push button again for more than 5 seconds. Release button. LED should be out. Disconnect battery cable to erase codes.
**3)** To ensure memory is erased, depress push button for more than 1 second and less than 3 seconds. A flash code 1-1-1 denotes erased memory.

# SELF-DIAGNOSTICS – TURBO SYSTEM

**Turbo System Diagnostics** – Turbo system carries out continuous checks. Faults in any of the following functions are stored in system memory.

- Turbo Control Valve
- Engine Knock
- A/C Blocking Relay
- Boost Pressure Sensor
- Throttle Position Sensor
- Fuel System Load Signal
- EGR Temperature Controller

## ENTERING SELF-DIAGNOSTICS

The turbo control unit has fault tracing capability. It offers 2 different control functions (No. 1 and No. 3); one for retrieving fault codes and another for testing new components. The diagnostic unit, used for code retrieval and new component testing, is located behind left front shock tower.

Diagnostic unit socket No. 5 is used for self diagnostic function. Once the selector cable has been inserted in the correct slot, depressing the button once or twice selects from one of 2 control (fault tracing) functions. Faults stored in either ECU memory are read by means of a system of LED flashes.

Diagnostic system for turbo ECU stores 8 different fault codes. All fault codes have 3 digits. Each can range from 1-to-4. Example of 3-digit code: 4-1-3. Since all codes have 3 digits, each code requires 3 series of flashes. For easier reading, a 3-second interval separates each digit of the code.
**Control Function No. 1 (Retrieving Codes)** – This function displays any of 8 different turbo system codes stored in ECU memory during engine operation.
**Control Function No. 2** – This function is not used for turbo system.
**Control Function No. 3 (Testing Turbo System Components)** – This function tests turbo system components with engine stopped. It consists of a function cycle in which diagnostic system activates components. You find out if component is working by listening or putting a hand on it when it is activated.

## CONTROL FUNCTION NO. 1

**Retrieving Codes** – **1)** Locate the diagnostic unit and remove its cover. Connect selector cable to socket No. 5. Turn ignition to ON position. Enter control function No. 1 (access codes) by pressing push button one time for at least one second and no more than 3 seconds.

***NOTE: Information on control function No. 3 appears later in article. There is no control function No. 2 for the turbo system. To enter control function No. 3, press push button 3 times for at least one second and no more than 3 seconds.***

**2)** Watch the Red LED and count the number of flashes in the 3-flash series. The flash series are separated by a 3 second interval. *See Fig. 2.* Note all codes. Only 3 separate codes can be stored at once. If no codes are stored, the LED will flash a 1-1-1 to indicate turbo system is operating properly.
**3)** If a fault code is received, refer to TURBO SYSTEM FAULT CODES table under SELF-DIAGNOSTICS – TURBO SYSTEM. Depress push button again and check for additional codes. Depress push button a third time if necessary. If first code repeats, no other codes are present.
**4)** Diagnostic system memory is full when 7 codes are present. Those 7 codes must be repaired before further codes can be retrieved.

***NOTE: Not all codes listed in FUEL INJECTION FAULT CODES table are used on every vehicle.***

***TURBO SYSTEM FAULT CODES*** [1]

| Code | Fault | Repair |
|---|---|---|
| 1-1-1 | No Faults | |
| 2-4-2 | Turbo Control Valve | Check Turbo Control Valve [2] |
| 3-1-2 | Knock Sensor Signal | Check For Knocking |
| 3-4-2 | A/C Blocking Relay | Check A/C Blocking Relay |
| 4-2-1 | Press. Sensor Signal | Check Turbo Control Valve [3] |
| 4-2-3 | Throttle Pos. Sensor | Check Sensor |
| 4-3-1 | Temp. Sensor Signal | Check Sensor |
| 4-2-4 | Load Signal | Check Load Signal |

[1] – See FAULT CODE TESTING under SELF-DIAGNOSTICS – TURBO SYSTEM.
[2] – Resistance check.
[3] – Mechanical check.

## FAULT CODE TESTING

This section will cover fault codes dealing with turbo system ECU testing. The codes will be followed by an explanation of test and repair procedure.
**Code 2-4-2 (Turbo Control Valve)** – Connect ohmmeter between turbo control unit terminals No. 1 and 23. Resistance should be 11 ohms.
**Code 3-1-2 (Knocking Detected)** – Connect voltmeter between turbo control unit terminal No. 30 and ground. Turn ignition on. Reading should be less than 1.3 volts. With engine running, voltage should be greater than 4.6 volts. When engine is knocking, voltage should be less than 1.3 volts.
**Code 3-4-2 (A/C Blocking Relay)** – **1)** Remove turbo control unit connector. Turn ignition on. Connect voltmeter between turbo control unit terminal No. 6 and ground. Reading should be 12 volts. Turn ignition off. Install control unit connector.
**2)** Start engine and turn A/C on. After A/C compressor has engaged, quickly press accelerator pedal to the floor. Compressor should disengage when throttle is fully opened. Turn ignition off.
**Code 4-2-1 (Pressure Sensor Signal)** – **1)** This is a mechanical check of turbo control valve. Disconnect hoses from valve. With control valve in rest position, blow air through fitting that connects to intake manifold. Air should come out through fitting that connects to pressure regulator.

**2)** Apply 12 volts to control valve. Blow air through fitting that connects to intake manifold. Air should come out through fitting that connects to pressure regulator and to intake side of turbo. Replace control valve as necessary.

**Code 4-2-3 (Throttle Position Sensor Signal)** - Connect ohmmeter between turbo control unit terminals No. 7 and 8. Reading should be 2500-5000 ohms in idle position and 300-500 ohms in full load position. Connect ohmmeter between turbo control unit terminals No. 7 and 24. Reading should be 3000-5000 ohms. Replace throttle position sensor a necessary.

**Code 4-3-1 (Temperature Sensor Signal)** - Connect ohmmeter between turbo control unit terminals No. 9 and 25. See TEMPERATURE SENSOR RESISTANCE table.

***TEMPERATURE SENSOR RESISTANCE***

| Temperature | Ohms |
|---|---|
| 14°F (-10°C) | 12,400 |
| 68°F (20°C) | 2800 |
| 176°F (80°C) | 280 |

**Code 4-2-4 (Load Signal)** - Check to see if code is set in ignition system control unit. See SELF DIAGNOSTICS - IGNITION SYSTEM. Connect voltmeter between turbo control unit terminal No. 14 and ground. Operate starter motor. Reading should be less than one volt. Check wiring or replace fuel injection as necessary.

## CONTROL FUNCTION NO. 3

**Testing Turbo System Components - 1)** Turn ignition on. Locate diagnostic unit and remove its cover. Connect selector cable to socket No. 5. Depress push button 3 times. Each time the button is depressed, it should be held for more than 1 second and less than 3 seconds.

**2)** While LED flashes, the cooling fan, turbo control valve and A/C blocking relay should operate. Check by listening or feeling component when it is activated. If turbo control valve does not work, go to step **3)**. If A/C blocking relay does not work go to step **4)**. If cooling fan does not operate, check both cooling fan relays. Connect voltmeter between turbo control unit terminal No. 4 and ground. Then between terminal No. 5 and ground. In both cases, reading should be 12 volts.

**3)** Connect ohmmeter between turbo control unit terminals No. 1 and 3. Resistance should be 11 ohms. Replace control valve as necessary.

**4)** Turn ignition on. Connect voltmeter between turbo control unit terminal No. 6 and ground. Reading should be 12 volts. Turn ignition off. Install turbo connector. Start engine and turn A/C on.

**5)** After compressor engages, press accelerator pedal to floor for a short time. Compressor should disengage when throttle is fully open and engage again when throttle closes slightly from fully open position. Replace A/C blocking relay as necessary. Turn ignition off.

## CLEARING CODES

**Erasing Diagnostic System Memory - 1)** After all fault codes have been read and the faults corrected, the diagnostic system memory can be erased. Turn ignition switch to ON position. Read fault codes again. Depress push button for more than 5 seconds.

**2)** After 3 seconds, the LED should light. While the LED is lit, depress push button again for more than 5 seconds. Release button. LED should be out. Disconnect battery cable to erase codes.

**3)** To ensure memory is erased, depress push button for more than 1 second and less than 3 seconds. A flash code 1-1-1 denotes erased memory.

## SUMMARY

If no hard fault codes (or only pass codes) are present, proceed to TROUBLE SHOOTING - NO CODES article for diagnosis by symptom (i.e., ROUGH IDLE, NO START, etc.) or intermittent diagnostic procedures.

# 1991 ENGINE PERFORMANCE
# Trouble Shooting – No Codes

### 240 Series, 740 Series, 940 Series

## INTRODUCTION

Before diagnosing symptoms or intermittent faults, perform steps in BASIC DIAGNOSTIC PROCEDURES and 4-cylinder SELF-DIAGNOSTICS articles. Use this article to diagnose driveability problems existing when a hard fault code is not present or if vehicle is not equipped with a self-diagnostic system.

***NOTE: Some driveability problems may have been corrected by manufacturer with a revised computer calibration chip or computer control unit. Check with manufacturer for latest chip or computer application.***

Symptom checks can direct the technician to malfunctioning component(s) for further diagnosis. A symptom should lead to a specific component, system test, or adjustment.

Use intermittent test procedures to locate driveability problems that DO NOT occur when the vehicle is being tested. These test procedures should also be used if a soft (intermittent) trouble code was present, but no problem was found during self-diagnostic testing.

***NOTE: For specific testing procedures, see SYSTEM & COMPONENT TESTING article. For specifications, see ON-VEHICLE ADJUSTMENTS or SERVICE & ADJUSTMENT SPECIFICATIONS article.***

## SYMPTOMS

### SYMPTOM DIAGNOSIS

Symptom checks cannot be used properly unless the problem is actually happening while the vehicle is being tested. To reduce diagnostic time, ensure steps in BASIC DIAGNOSTIC PROCEDURES and SELF-DIAGNOSTICS articles have been performed before attempting to diagnose a symptom. Symptoms available for diagnosis include the following:

- No Start – Cold Engine
- Starts But Stalls – Cold Engine
- Hard To Start – Cold Engine
- No Start – Warm Engine
- Erratic Idle – Warm-Up
- Backfiring
- Incorrect Idle Speed
- Hesitation – Acceleration
- Hesitation – Coasting
- Knocking
- Engine Misfire – All Conditions
- Insufficient Engine Power
- Poor Fuel Economy
- Excessive HC and NOx

### NO START – COLD ENGINE

- Ensure battery is fully charged.
- Ensure spark plugs fire strong Blue-White spark.
- Check fuel pump fuse(s).
- Check in-line fuse to control unit (if applicable).
- Ensure ignition timing and fuel pressure are correct.
- Check fuel injectors.
- Ensure timing belt is not broken (if applicable).
- Check ground connections on intake manifold for control unit and power stage.
- Ensure ignition coil resistance is correct.
- Ensure rotor, distributor and plug wires are okay.
- Check ignition control unit.
- Check coolant temperature sensor and connector.
- Check throttle switch and connector.
- Check fuel control unit.
- Check engine speed sensor or Hall Effect Sensor (turbo).
- Ensure power stage receives signal from ignition control unit.
- Check airflow sensor (if applicable).

### STARTS BUT STALLS – COLD ENGINE

- Check cold start injector.
- Check coolant temperature sensor.
- Check ignition and sensor wires for proper connection.
- Check fuel injectors.
- Check throttle switch and connector.
- Check engine speed sensor or Hall Effect Sensor (turbo).

### HARD TO START – COLD ENGINE

- Ensure spark plugs fire strong Blue-White spark.
- Check distributor.
- Ensure fuel pressure is correct.
- Check ignition timing.
- Check throttle switch and connector.

### NO START – WARM ENGINE

- Ensure fuel pressure is correct.
- Check for gasoline in oil.
- Ensure fuel injectors are not leaking.
- Check ignition and sensor wires for proper connection.
- Ensure spark plugs are not fouled.
- Check ignition and coil circuit.
- Check engine speed sensor or Hall Effect Sensor (turbo).
- Check throttle switch and connector.
- Check idle valve and ensure airflow arrow points in correct direction.

### ERRATIC IDLE – WARM-UP

- Check throttle switch and connection.
- Check coolant temperature sensor and connection.
- Check idle (air) valve.
- Check air temperature sensor and mass airflow meter.
- Check coolant temperature sensor.
- Ensure spark plugs are not fouled.
- Check ignition and sensor wires for proper connection.
- Check idle valve and ensure airflow arrow points in correct direction.
- Check distributor.
- Check ignition and coil circuit.
- Check intake system.
- Check engine speed sensor or Hall Effect Sensor (turbo).
- Check throttle switch and connector.
- Check MAP sensor (if applicable).

### BACKFIRING

- Ensure ignition timing is correct.
- Ensure timing belt has not jumped.
- Check distributor.
- Check for gasoline in oil.
- Ensure fuel injectors are not leaking.
- Ensure spark plugs fire strong Blue-White spark.
- Check ignition and coil circuit.
- Check engine speed sensor.
- Check throttle switch and connector.
- Check exhaust system.

### INCORRECT IDLE SPEED

- Check fuel injectors.
- Check intake system for leaks.
- Check coolant temperature sensor.
- Check throttle switch and connector.
- Check idle valve and ensure airflow arrow points in correct direction.
- Check distributor.

# 1991 ENGINE PERFORMANCE
# Trouble Shooting – No Codes (Cont.)

## HESITATION – ACCELERATION

- Check fuel injectors.
- Check ignition and sensor wires for proper connection.
- Check distributor cap for moisture or carbon tracking.
- Ensure spark plug wires are okay.
- Ensure spark plugs are not fouled.
- Check MAP sensor (if applicable).
- Check throttle switch and connector.
- Check ignition and coil circuit.
- Check engine speed sensor or Hall Effect Sensor (turbo).
- Check idle valve and ensure airflow arrow points in correct direction.

## HESITATION – COASTING

- Check fuel injectors.
- Check ignition and sensor wires for proper connection.
- Check throttle switch and connector.
- Check engine speed sensor or Hall Effect Sensor (turbo).
- Check for gasoline in oil.
- Check idle valve and ensure airflow arrow points in correct direction.

## KNOCKING

- Check ignition and coil circuit.
- Ensure spark plugs fire strong Blue-White spark.
- Check knock sensor.
- Check throttle switch and connector.
- Check ignition and coil circuit.
- Check engine speed sensor or Hall Effect Sensor (turbo).
- Check MAP sensor (if applicable).

## ENGINE MISFIRE – ALL CONDITIONS

- Check fuel injectors.
- Check ignition and sensor wires for proper connection.
- Check ignition and coil circuit.
- Check for gasoline in oil.
- Check intake and exhaust system.
- Check throttle switch and connector.
- Check for vacuum leaks.
- Check engine speed sensor or Hall Effect Sensor (turbo).
- Check MAP sensor (if applicable).

## INSUFFICIENT ENGINE POWER

- Check fuel injectors.
- Ensure fuel pressure is correct.
- Check airflow sensor (if applicable).
- Check for restricted exhaust.
- Check coolant temperature sensor.
- Check air temperature sensor.
- Check engine speed sensor.
- Check throttle switch and connector.
- Check ignition and coil circuit.
- Check MAP sensor (if applicable).
- Check engine speed sensor or Hall Effect Sensor (turbo).
- Check intake and exhaust system.

## POOR FUEL ECONOMY

- Check for leaky fuel injectors.
- Ensure spark plugs are not fouled.
- Check for faulty oxygen sensor.
- Check throttle switch and connector.
- Check for poor wire connections and fouled spark plugs.
- Check engine speed sensor or Hall Effect Sensor (turbo).
- Check for gasoline in oil.
- Check MAP sensor (if applicable).
- Check for malfunctioning intake system.

## EXCESSIVE HC & NOx

- Check for gasoline in oil.
- Check for leaky fuel injectors.
- Check for faulty oxygen sensor.
- Check ignition and sensor wires for proper connection.
- Check engine speed sensor.
- Check throttle switch and connector.
- Check intake system.
- Check MAP sensor (if applicable).

# INTERMITTENTS

## INTERMITTENT PROBLEM DIAGNOSIS

Intermittent fault testing requires the duplication of circuit or component failure, in order to identify the fault. These procedures may lead to the computer recording a fault code (on some systems) which may help in diagnosis.

If problem vehicle does not produce fault codes, it will be necessary to monitor voltage or resistance values using a DVOM while attempting to reproduce conditions which will create an intermittent fault. A change in status on the DVOM will indicate a fault has been located.

When using a voltmeter to pinpoint faults, monitor voltage reading with ignition on, or vehicle running. A change in status on the voltmeter while performing intermittent TEST PROCEDURES will indicate area of fault.

When using an ohmmeter to detect problems in the circuit, monitor circuit resistance (ohms) with ignition switch in the OFF position, or with battery disconnected. A change in ohmmeter reading while performing TEST PROCEDURES will indicate area of fault.

## TEST PROCEDURES

**Intermittent Simulation** – To reproduce the conditions which create an intermittent fault so that it may be identified during testing, use some of the following methods:

- Apply light vibration to components.
- Heat a component.
- Wiggle or bend wiring harnesses.
- Apply humidity to components.
- Remove or apply a vacuum supply source.

Monitor circuit/component voltage or resistance while attempting to simulate intermittent. If vehicle is running, monitor for self-diagnostic codes. Use the results of these tests to identify a faulty component or an area which should be checked closely for the problem.

# 1991 ENGINE PERFORMANCE
# System & Component Testing

## 240 Series, 740 Series, 940 Series

## INTRODUCTION

Before testing separate components or systems, perform procedures in BASIC DIAGNOSTIC PROCEDURES article. Since many computer-controlled and monitored components set a trouble code if they malfunction, also perform procedures in SELF-DIAGNOSTICS article.

***NOTE: Testing individual components does not isolate shorts or opens. Perform all voltage tests with a Digital Volt-Ohmmeter (DVOM) with a minimum 10-megohm input impedance, unless stated otherwise in test procedure. Use ohmmeter to isolate wiring harness shorts or opens.***

## AIR INDUCTION SYSTEMS

### TURBOCHARGERS
### (740, 940 & 940 SE TURBO)

**Preliminary Checks - 1)** Warm engine to normal operating temperature. Turn off engine. Turbine shaft should stop rotating shortly after engine stops. If shaft does not stop rotating shortly after engine stops, remove intake hose from compressor housing.

**2)** Verify compressor wheel rotates freely. Ensure compressor wheel does not scrape against compressor housing when wheel is pushed radially or axially.

**Check & Adjust Boost Pressure - 1)** Connect air pressure gauge in-line between fuel limiter and intake manifold hose. Use a "T" fitting and enough hose so gauge can be carried into passenger compartment.

**2)** Ensure engine is at normal operating temperature. On M/T models, drive vehicle in 3rd gear at approximately 1500 RPM. On A/T models, place selector in position "2".

***CAUTION: To prevent damage to brakes, DO NOT apply brakes longer than 5 seconds.***

**3)** Press accelerator pedal to floor. On A/T models, DO NOT engage kickdown. Increase engine speed to 3000 RPM, and apply brakes while keeping accelerator pedal down to obtain full load.

**4)** Observe boost pressure on gauge. Maximum boost pressure should be 7.0-8.0 psi (.49-.56 kg/cm²). If boost pressure is incorrect, adjust boost pressure. Go to next step.

***CAUTION: Ensure wastegate actuator rod does not turn when adjusting link rod. Damage to wastegate actuator can result.***

**5)** Remove seal and clip from wastegate actuator link rod. Turn actuator link rod to adjust boost pressure to 7.5 psi (.52 kg/cm²). *See Fig. 1.*

**6)** Turning link rod one turn will change boost pressure approximately 0.5 psi (.03 kg/cm²). Turning link rod clockwise will increase boost pressure; counterclockwise will decrease boost pressure.

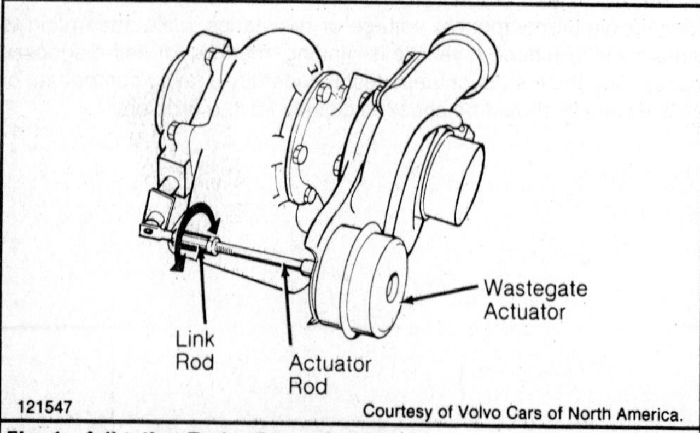


***Fig. 1: Adjusting Turbo Boost Pressure***

**Basic Adjustment Of Push Rod - 1)** Remove locking circlip from end of push rod. Connect pressure gauge (5230) and pressure tester (5496) to pressure regulator. *See Fig. 2.* Increase pressure to 7.0-7.8 psi (.49-.54 kg/cm²). Press wastegate lever against turbine housing, closing wastegate valve.

**2)** Adjust push rod length so push rod fits exactly over wastegate valve lever. Install locking circlip, and tighten push rod lock nut. Remove pressure gauge and tester.

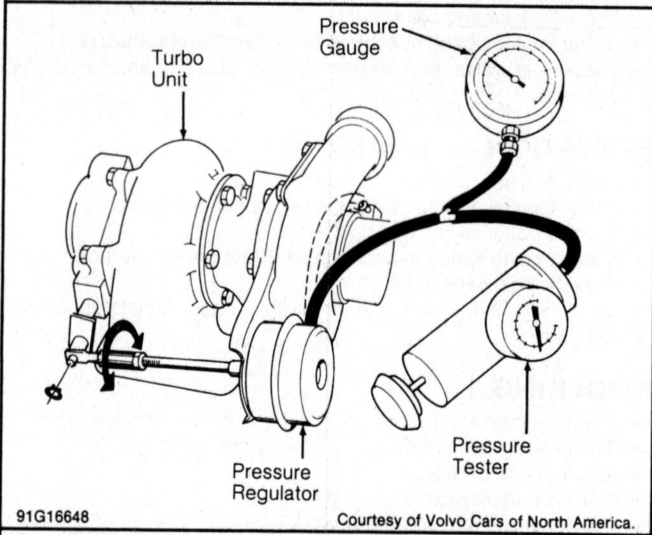


***Fig. 2: Adjusting Pressure Regulator Push Rod***

**Wastegate Valve Suction Test -** Disconnect vacuum hose from pressure regulator. Attach hand vacuum pump to fitting. Increase vacuum slightly. Look through holes in flange to see if wastegate valve opens. Wastegate valve should be fully open at 6.5 in. Hg of vacuum. Replace as necessary.

## COMPUTERIZED ENGINE CONTROLS

***CAUTION: Ensure ignition switch is in OFF position before disconnecting or connecting ignition or fuel injection Electronic Control Unit (ECU). Otherwise, damage to ECU can result.***

## ELECTRONIC CONTROL UNIT (IGNITION)

***NOTE: When measuring resistance and voltage at ECU connector, DO NOT probe into front of connector. Probe only through side of connector, just enough to make a good electrical contact. Pin identification numbers are stamped on side of ECU connector.***

***NOTE: Before removing ignition control unit connector, remove fuse No. 1 (740 Series) or fuse No. 31 (940 Series). On 240 Series, ensure ignition is off.***

**Preliminary Checks - 1)** Turn ignition off. Disconnect ignition ECU connector. On 240 Series, ECU is located behind panel below glove box. On 740 and 940 Series, ECU is located behind panel on right side of accelerator pedal.

**2)** On all models, push out clip and disconnect ECU connector. Remove cover from ECU connector exposing pin identification numbers. Visually inspect all pin connector sleeves to ensure all pins are at same height.

**Power Circuit Checks -** Connect a voltmeter between ignition ECU pin No. 5 (Red wire on 240 Series or Brown wire on 740 and 940 Series) and ground. Voltmeter should indicate 12 volts. If voltage is not present, check wire from ignition ECU connector to in-line fuse located on left shock tower (240 Series) or check circuit between ignition ECU pin No. 5 and fuse box (740 and 940 Series).

# 1991 ENGINE PERFORMANCE
# System & Component Testing (Cont.)

**Ground Circuit Checks** – Turn ignition switch to OFF position. Connect ohmmeter between ignition control unit terminals No. 20 and 14, and ground. *See Fig. 3.* Resistance should be zero ohms.

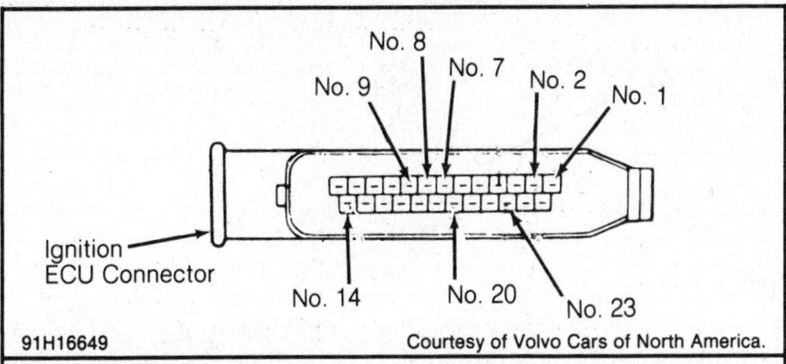


***Fig. 3: Identifying Electronic Control Unit Terminals (Ignition)***

## ELECTRONIC CONTROL UNIT (FUEL INJECTION)

***NOTE: When measuring resistance and voltage at ECU connector, DO NOT probe into front of connector. Probe only through side of connector, just enough to make a good electrical contact. Pin identification numbers are stamped on side of ECU connector.***

**Preliminary Checks** – **1)** Turn ignition switch to OFF position. Disconnect fuel injection ECU connector. Fuel injection ECU is located on right side of instrument panel, under kick panel. Push out clip and disconnect ECU connector.

**2)** Remove cover from ECU connector to expose pin identification numbers. Visually inspect all pin connector sleeves to ensure all pins are at same height.

**Power Circuit Checks** – **1)** Connect voltmeter leads between ECU connector pin No. 35 and ground.

**2)** Turn ignition switch to ON position. Voltmeter should read 12 volts. Also, crank engine and ensure battery voltage exists while engine is being cranked.

**Voltage Supply For Memory Check (Except 240 Series & Regina)** – **1)** Connect voltmeter between fuel injection ECU terminal No. 4 and ground. Reading should be 12 volts. Turn ignition on. Connect diagnostic unit select cable to socket No. 2. Connect voltmeter between fuel injection ECU terminal No. 12 and ground.

**2)** Reading should be 12 volts. Press button on diagnostic unit; voltage should drop to zero. If voltage reading is 12 volts when button is pressed, check diagnostic unit. If voltage is not present at fuel injection ECU, check for voltage at diagnostic unit output connector.

**3)** Connect voltmeter between Blue wire terminal in diagnostic unit and ground. Reading should be 12 volts. Turn ignition off. Connect ohmmeter between Black wire terminal in diagnostic unit and ground. Reading should be zero ohms. Connect ohmmeter between select cable for diagnostic unit and terminal beneath function select button.

**4)** Reading should be infinite. Press select button; resistance should be zero. Connect Red lead of a diode tester to terminal beneath LED. Connect Black lead to select cable. If diode tester gives reading, LED is okay. If diode tester does not give reading, install new diagnostic unit.

**Ground Circuit Check** – Connect ohmmeter between ground and fuel injection ECU terminals No. 5, 17, 19 and 29 (Jetronic 2.4 fuel system) or terminals No. 5, 17 and 19 (Regina fuel system). In each case, reading should be zero ohms. Wires are grounded to intake manifold.

## ENGINE SENSORS & SWITCHES

***CAUTION: Ensure ignition switch is in OFF position before disconnecting or connecting ignition or fuel injection Electronic Control Unit (ECU). Otherwise, damage to ECU may result.***

**Air Temperature Sensor** – See FUEL CONTROL under FUEL SYSTEM.

**Coolant Temperature Sensor** – **1)** Disconnect Coolant Temperature Sensor (CTS) connector. Connect ohmmeter leads between CTS terminals.

**2)** Ohmmeter should read as specified. See COOLANT TEMPERATURE SENSOR RESISTANCE table.

***COOLANT TEMPERATURE SENSOR RESISTANCE***

| Temperature °F (°C) | Ohms |
|---|---|
| 14 (-10) | 8260-10,560 |
| 68 (20) | 2280-2720 |
| 176 (80) | 290-364 |

**Oxygen ($O_2$) Sensor** – See FUEL CONTROL under FUEL SYSTEM.

**Throttle Switch** – **1)** Turn ignition switch to OFF position. Connect ohmmeter between fuel injection ECU terminal No. 2 and ground. With switch closed, reading should be zero ohms. Press accelerator pedal slightly. Resistance should increase to 2000-3000 ohms (switch opens).

**2)** Connect ohmmeter between fuel injection ECU terminal No. 3 and ground. Reading should be infinite. Press accelerator pedal to floor. Reading should be zero ohms. If a problem is found during check, perform same checks at throttle switch.

**3)** To check and adjust throttle switch, open throttle slightly and listen to switch. A click should be heard as soon as throttle is opened. If switch appears to be out of adjustment, loosen mount screws. Turn switch slightly clockwise, and then turn switch counterclockwise until switch clicks. Tighten mount screws, and check setting.

## RELAYS

**Fuel Injection Main Relay** – Connect voltmeter between fuel injection ECU terminal No. 9 and ground. Connect a jumper wire between fuel injection ECU terminal No. 21 and ground. Relay should close and voltmeter should indicate battery voltage. Replace as necessary.

**Fuel Pump Relay** – Connect jumper wire between fuel injection ECU terminal No. 21 and ground. Connect another jumper wire between fuel injection ECU terminal No. 20 and ground. Fuel pump relay should close and fuel pump should run. Replace relay as necessary.

## FUEL SYSTEM

### FUEL DELIVERY

***NOTE: For fuel system pressure testing, see BASIC DIAGNOSTIC PROCEDURES article.***

***CAUTION: DO NOT allow pressure to exceed 84 psi (5.9 kg/cm²).***

**Fuel Pressure Regulator (Non-Turbo)** – **1)** Connect a fuel pressure gauge between fuel line and fuel injection manifold. Lift out passenger compartment fuse/relay block. Remove fuel injection main relay. Connect a jumper wire between relay terminals No. 30 & 87/2. *See Fig. 4.* Fuel pump will run.

**2)** Connect a vacuum pump to pressure regulator. Apply vacuum to pressure regulator. Fuel system pressure should drop in direct proportion to amount of vacuum applied to pressure regulator. Replace regulator as necessary.

***NOTE: DO NOT increase pressure to pressure regulator more than 10 psi (.70 kg/cm²).***

**Fuel Pressure Regulator (Turbo)** – Connect a fuel pressure gauge between fuel line and fuel injection manifold. Connect pressure tester and pressure gauge to pressure regulator. Increase pressure to pressure regulator. Fuel system pressure should increase in direct proportion to pressure increase in regulator. Replace regulator as necessary.

### FUEL CONTROL

**Air Temperature Sensor (740 Regina)** – **1)** Disconnect air temperature sensor connector. Connect ohmmeter leads between air temperature sensor terminals.

**2)** Ohmmeter should read as specified. See AIR TEMPERATURE SENSOR RESISTANCE table. Replace air temperature sensor if ohmmeter reading is not as specified.

# 1991 ENGINE PERFORMANCE
# System & Component Testing (Cont.)

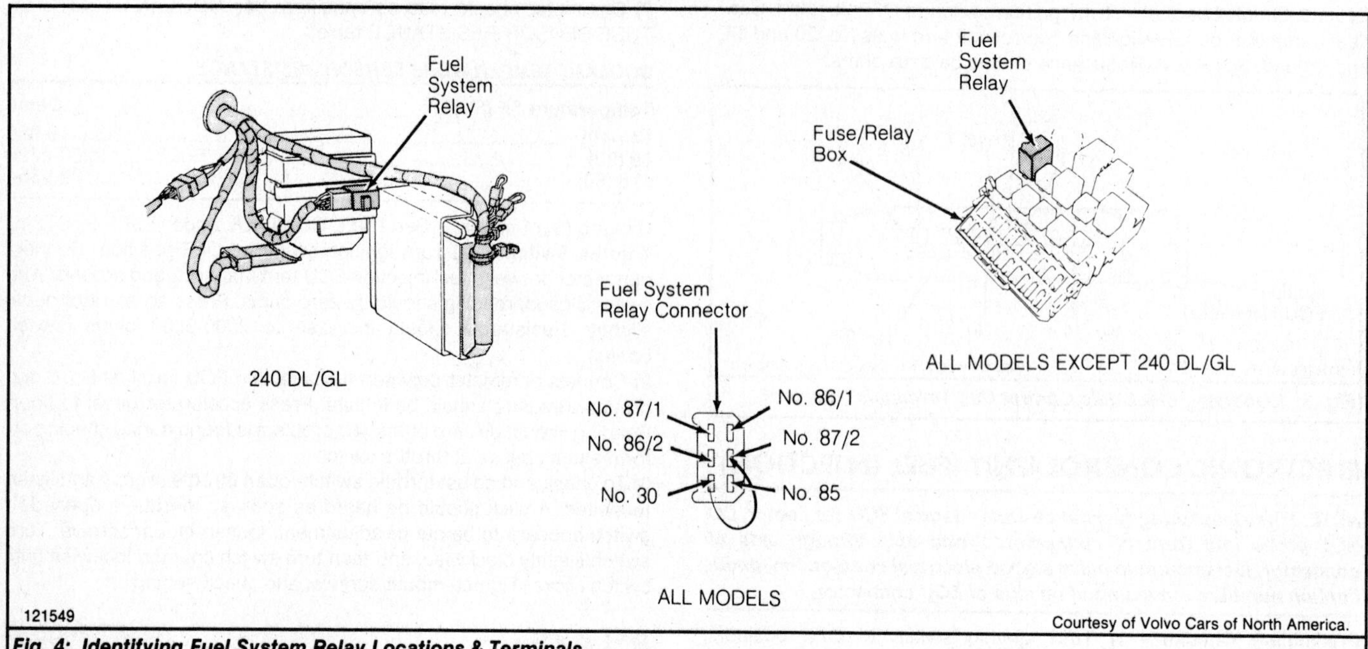


***Fig. 4: Identifying Fuel System Relay Locations & Terminals***

***AIR TEMPERATURE SENSOR RESISTANCE***

| Temperature °F (°C) | Ohms |
|---|---|
| -4 (-20) | 15,000 |
| 68 (20) | 2500 |
| 212 (100) | 160 |

**Fuel Injectors (Non-Turbo) - 1)** Remove auxiliary relay, located on left front fender panel. Jumper relay terminals No. 2 and 3. Connect ohmmeter between fuel injection ECU terminals No. 9 and 18. Resistance should be 4 ohms. If resistance is 5.3 ohms, one injector or wire is faulty.

**2)** If resistance is 8.0 ohms, 2 injectors or wires are faulty. If resistance is 16 ohms, 3 injectors or wires are faulty. To check injectors individually, disconnect injector wires and place ohmmeter across suspected injector. Resistance should be 16 ohms. Replace as necessary.

**Fuel Injectors (Turbo) - 1)** Remove auxiliary relay, located on left front fender panel. Jumper relay terminals No. 2 and 3. Connect ohmmeter between fuel injection ECU terminals No. 9 and 18. Resistance should be 2.25 ohms. If resistance is 2.9 ohms, one injector or wire is faulty.

**2)** If resistance is 4.4 ohms, 2 injectors or wires are faulty. If resistance is 8.5 ohms, 3 injectors or wires are faulty. To check injectors individually, disconnect injector wires and place ohmmeter across suspected injector. Resistance should be 2 ohms. Replace as necessary.

**Cold Start Valve - 1)** Disconnect cold start valve harness connector. Connect ohmmeter leads across cold start valve terminals.

**2)** Ohmmeter should indicate 10 ohms. If reading is not 10 ohms, replace cold start valve.

**Mass Airflow Meter - 1)** Remove rubber sleeve from airflow meter to uncover wire connector. DO NOT disconnect connector. Using a voltmeter, back probe connector terminals. Connect voltmeter leads between ground and terminal No. 5 on mass airflow connector.

**2)** Voltage reading should be 12 volts. Connect voltmeter leads between terminals No. 1 and 5 on mass airflow connector. Voltage reading should be 12 volts.

**Oxygen ($O_2$) Sensor - 1)** Warm engine to normal operating temperature. Connect exhaust gas analyzer. Disconnect $O_2$ sensor wire (at $O_2$ sensor) from ECU.

**2)** Connect a jumper wire between ECU wiring ($O_2$ sensor harness side) and ground. CO content should increase, indicating ECU and its connections are okay.

**3)** Connect a voltmeter to $O_2$ sensor. While engine is running, voltmeter should fluctuate at approximately 0.5 volts if CO constant is normal. Replace $O_2$ sensor if not within specification.

**Oxygen ($O_2$) Sensor Current Feed & Heater Resistance - 1)** Connect voltmeter between ground and terminal No. 1 of 2-wire connector located next to firewall. Voltage reading should be battery voltage. Remove ground wire from fuel injection ECU terminal No. 20.

**2)** Connect ohmmeter between oxygen sensor harness terminal No. 2 (Black wire) and ground. Connector is located next to firewall. With a cold oxygen sensor, resistance should be 2-3 ohms. With a oxygen sensor warmer than 660°F (350°C), resistance should be 7-14 ohms. Replace oxygen sensor as necessary.

## IDLE CONTROL SYSTEM

***NOTE: When measuring resistance and voltage at ECU connector, DO NOT probe into front of connector. Probe only through side of connector, just enough to make a good electrical contact. Pin identification numbers are stamped on side of ECU connector.***

**Idle Air Control Valve - 1)** Turn ignition switch to OFF position. Disconnect ECU connector. Remove cover from ECU connector to expose pin identification numbers. On 240, 740 and 940 Series with 2.4 Jetronic fuel system, connect an ohmmeter between fuel injection ECU pins No. 9 and 33.

**2)** Ohmmeter should read 8 ohms. On 740 Series with Regina fuel injection system, connect ohmmeter between fuel injection ECU pins No. 9 and 33. Ohmmeter should read 4 ohms.

## IGNITION SYSTEM

***NOTE: For basic ignition checks, see BASIC DIAGNOSTIC PROCEDURES article.***

### TIMING CONTROL SYSTEMS

**Detonation (Knock) Sensor - 1)** Disconnect knock sensor connector. Connect jumper wire across knock sensor terminals No. 1 and 2. *See Fig. 5.* Turn ignition off. Disconnect ignition ECU connector.

**2)** Remove cover from ECU connector to expose pin identification numbers. Connect ohmmeter leads between pins No. 12 and 13 of ignition ECU connector. *See Fig. 3.* Ohmmeter should indicate zero ohms.

**3)** If ohmmeter resistance is high (infinity), one or both wires may be shorted. Remove jumper wire, and take reading with ohmmeter on each wire. Replace damaged wires as required. If wires are not damaged, replace knock sensor.

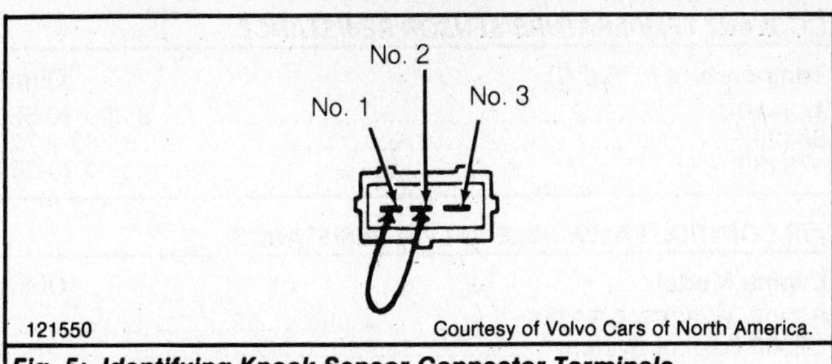


*Fig. 5: Identifying Knock Sensor Connector Terminals*

## EMISSION SYSTEMS & SUB-SYSTEMS

### EXHAUST GAS RECIRCULATION (EGR)

**1)** Ensure all connections are tight and do not leak. Ensure all vacuum hoses are connected and not kinked. Check EGR function with cold and hot engine at different engine speeds.

**2)** With engine coolant temperature below 131°F (55°C), EGR valve should be closed at all engine speeds. If EGR valve is open, replace thermostat valve.

**3)** With coolant temperature above 140°F (60°C), EGR valve should only open at partial throttle. If EGR valve remains closed, check thermostat valve by disconnecting vacuum hose from EGR valve and blowing air into it. Air should flow freely through thermostatic valve. If air does not flow freely through thermostatic valve, replace valve.

### FUEL EVAPORATION

Fuel evaporation testing procedures are not available from manufacturer. See VACUUM DIAGRAMS article for information on hose routing.

### THERMOSTATIC AIR CLEANER

**940 GLE - 1)** Check operation of air control door at various temperatures. When temperature is below 41°F (5°C), air control door should be closed, allowing only preheated air to enter air intake.

**2)** When temperature is approximately 50°F (10°C), air control door should be half-way open, allowing preheated and cold air to enter air intake.

**3)** At temperatures above 59°F (15°C), air control door should be closed, allowing only cold air to enter air intake.

# 1991 ENGINE PERFORMANCE
# Sensor Operating Range Charts

## 240 Series, 740 Series, 940 Series

## INTRODUCTION

Sensor operating range information can help determine if a sensor is out of calibration. An out-of-calibration sensor may not set a trouble code, but it may cause driveability problems.

***NOTE: Perform all voltage tests with a Digital Volt-Ohmmeter (DVOM) with a minimum 10-megohm input impedance, unless stated otherwise in test procedure.***

*AIR TEMPERATURE SENSOR RESISTANCE*

| Temperature - °F (°C) | Ohms |
|---|---|
| -4 (-20) | 15,000 |
| 32 (0) | 5800 |
| 68 (20) | 2500 |
| 176 (80) | 330 |
| 212 (100) | 160 |

*FUEL INJECTOR BALLAST RESISTOR RESISTANCE* [1]

| Application | Ohms |
|---|---|
| All Models | 5.5-6.5 |

[1] - Unit contains four resistors; one per injector. Check resistance between center terminal and 4 other terminals.

*COOLANT TEMPERATURE SENSOR RESISTANCE*

| Temperature - °F (°C) | Ohms |
|---|---|
| 14 (-10) | 8,260-10,560 |
| 68 (20) | 2,280-2,720 |
| 176 (80) | 290-364 |

*AIR CONTROL VALVE (IDLE VALVE) RESISTANCE*

| Engine Model | Ohms |
|---|---|
| B230F, B230FT & B234F | 8 |
| B230F Regina System | 4 |

*MASS AIR FLOW SENSOR RESISTANCE*

| Engine Model | Ohms |
|---|---|
| B230F & B230FT | |
| Terminals 2 & 3 [1] | 2.5-4.0 |
| B234F | |
| Terminals 2 & 3 [1] | 2.5-4.0 |
| Terminals 2 & 6 [1] | 0-1000 |

[1] - Resistance is measured between these terminals.

*OXYGEN SENSOR HEATER RESISTANCE*

| Temperature - °F (°C) | Ohms |
|---|---|
| 68 (20) | 3 |
| 660 (350) | 13 |

# 1991 ENGINE PERFORMANCE
# Wiring Diagrams

## 240 Series, 740 Series, 940 Series

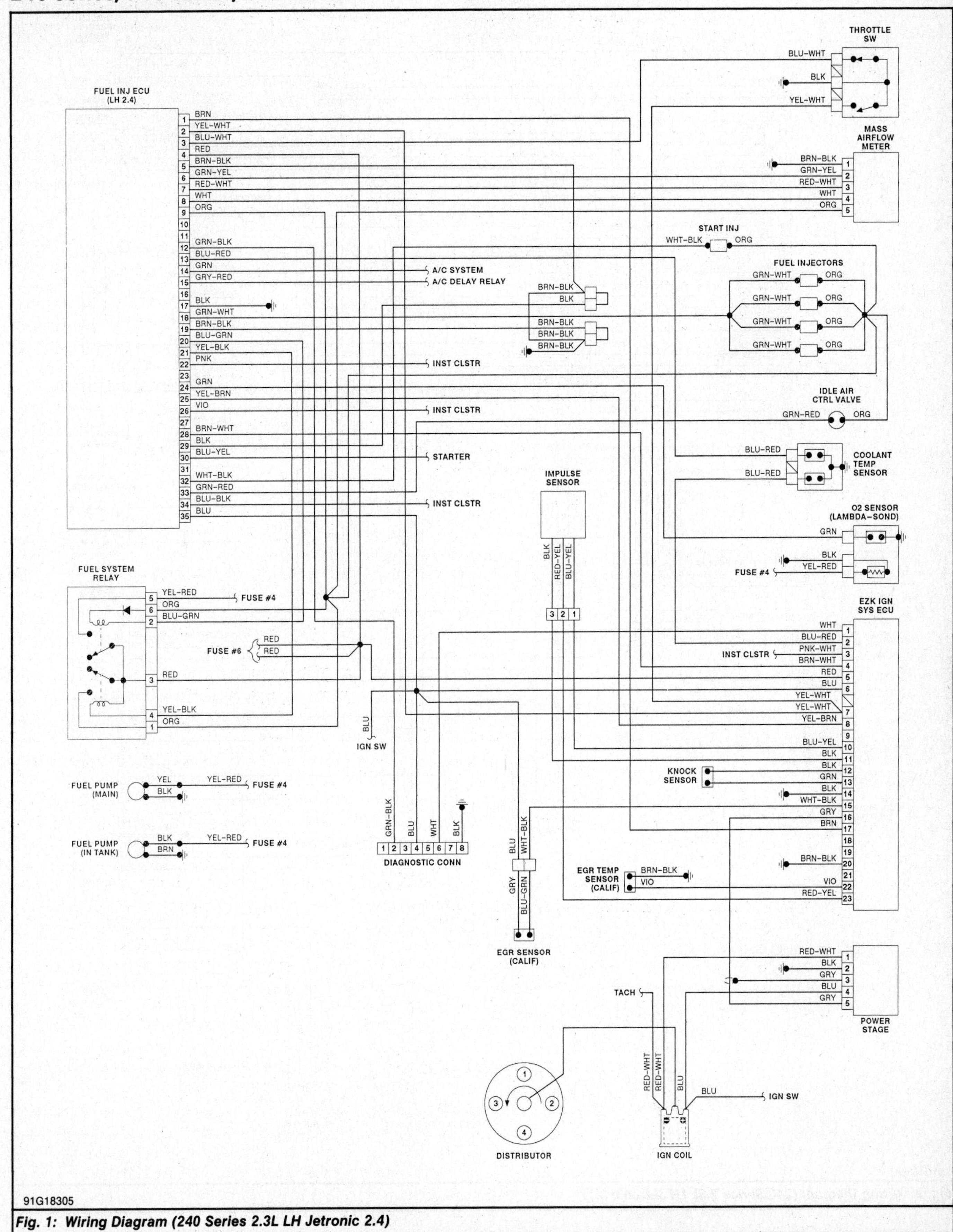

Fig. 1: Wiring Diagram (240 Series 2.3L LH Jetronic 2.4)

# 1991 ENGINE PERFORMANCE
## Wiring Diagrams (Cont.)

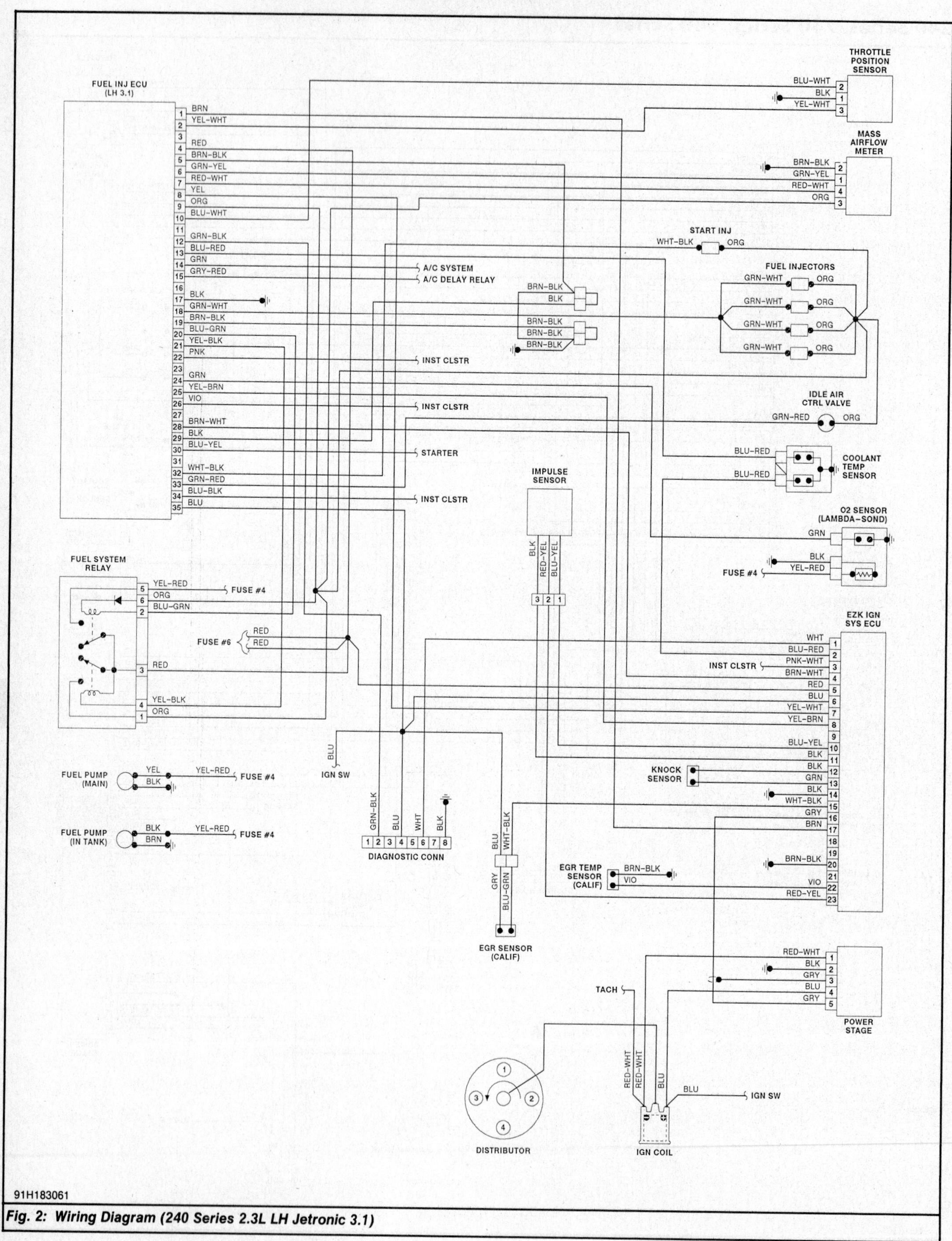


91H183061

*Fig. 2: Wiring Diagram (240 Series 2.3L LH Jetronic 3.1)*

# 1991 ENGINE PERFORMANCE
## Wiring Diagrams (Cont.)

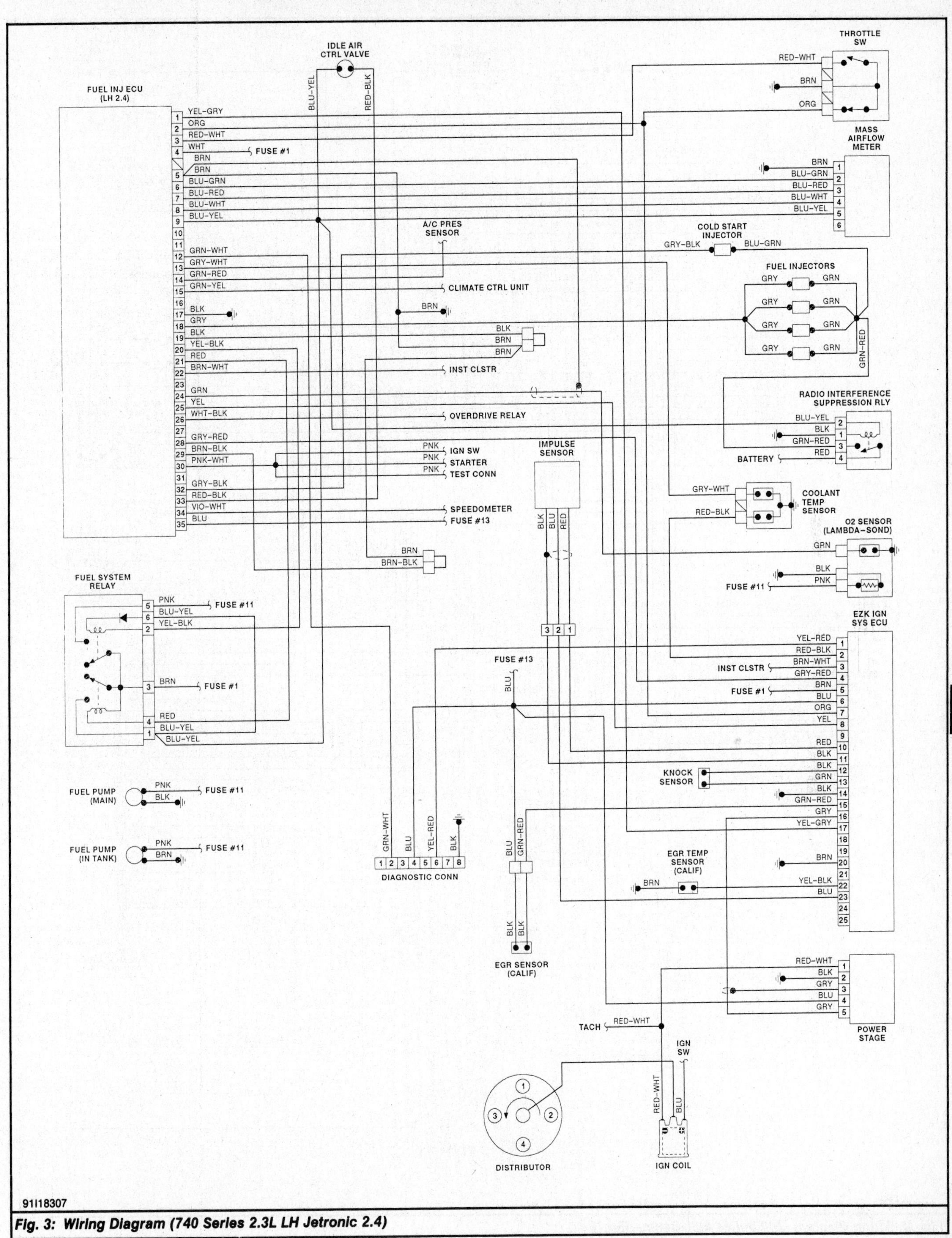


*Fig. 3: Wiring Diagram (740 Series 2.3L LH Jetronic 2.4)*

# 1991 ENGINE PERFORMANCE
## Wiring Diagrams (Cont.)

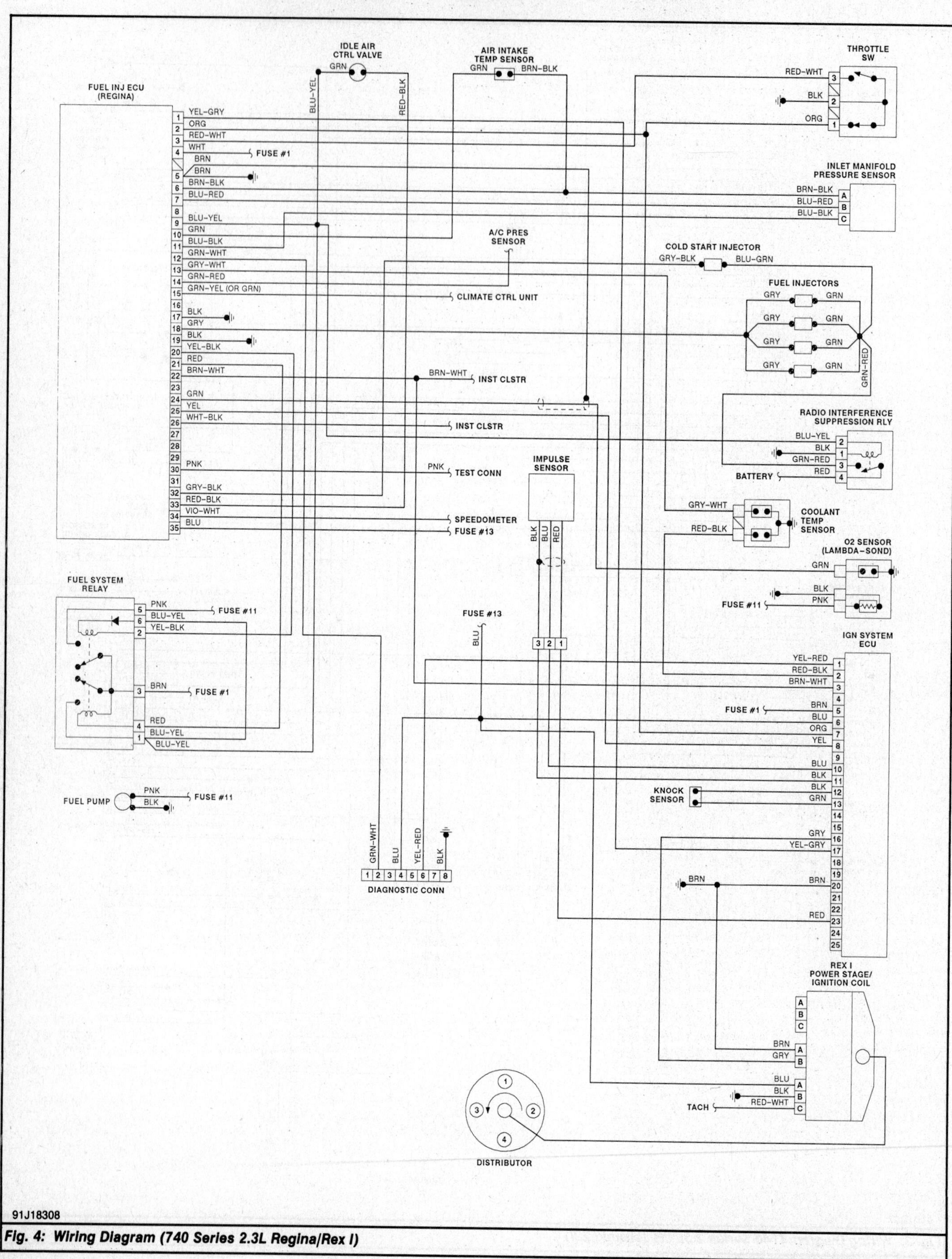


Fig. 4: Wiring Diagram (740 Series 2.3L Regina/Rex I)

# 1991 ENGINE PERFORMANCE
## Wiring Diagrams (Cont.)

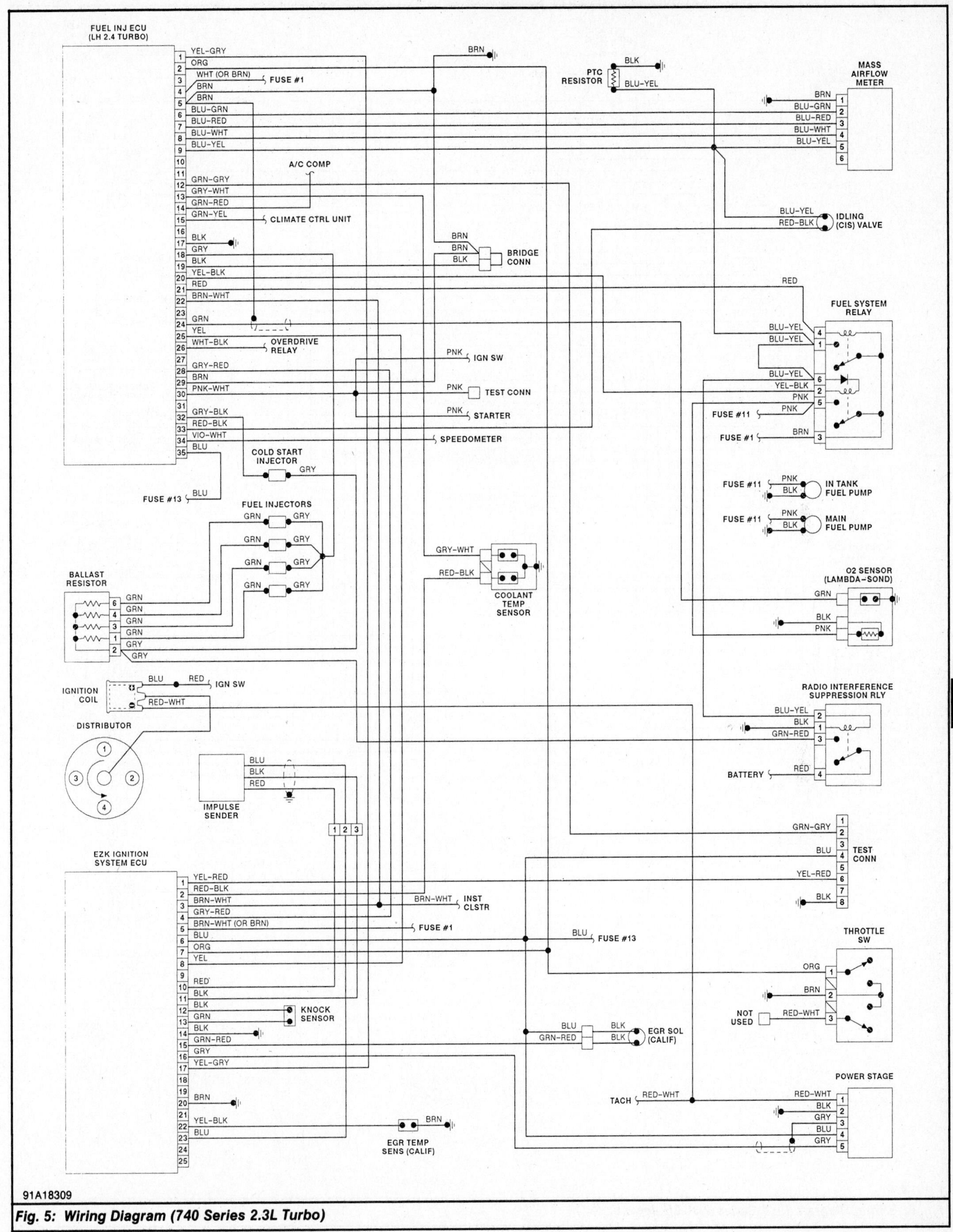

Fig. 5: Wiring Diagram (740 Series 2.3L Turbo)

# 1991 ENGINE PERFORMANCE
## Wiring Diagrams (Cont.)

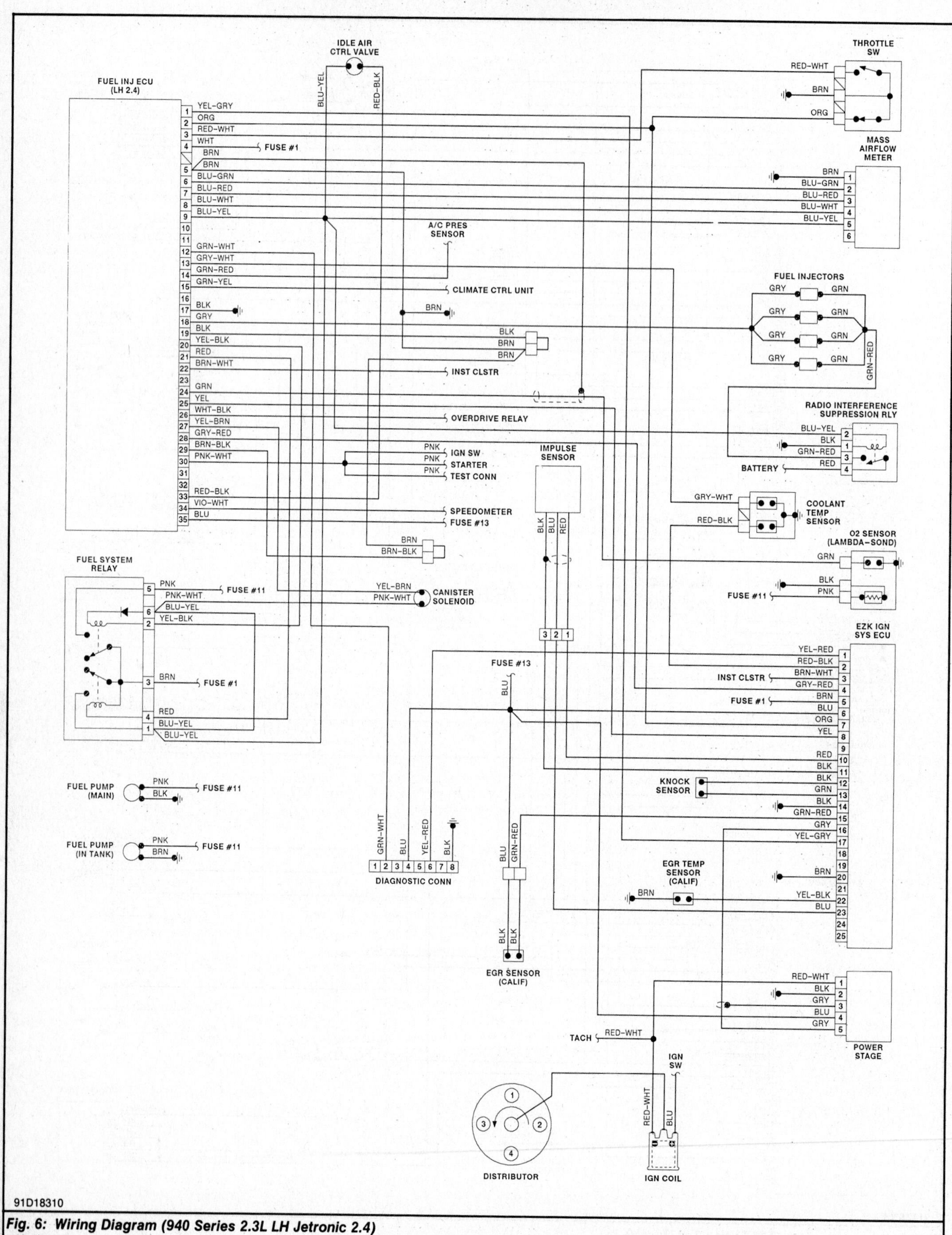


91D18310

*Fig. 6: Wiring Diagram (940 Series 2.3L LH Jetronic 2.4)*

# 1991 ENGINE PERFORMANCE
## Wiring Diagrams (Cont.)

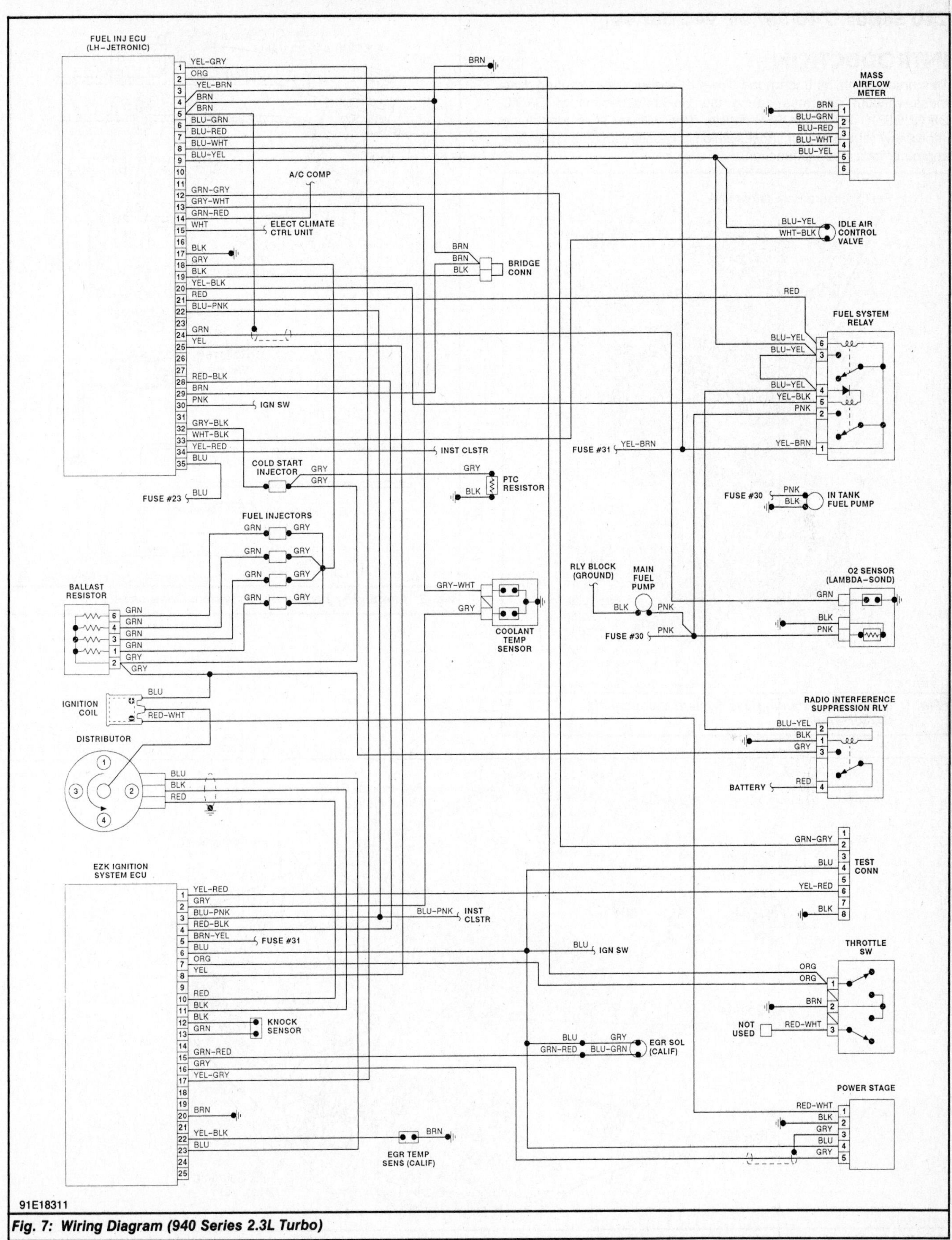

91E18311

*Fig. 7: Wiring Diagram (940 Series 2.3L Turbo)*

# 1991 ENGINE PERFORMANCE
# Vacuum Diagrams

## 240 Series, 740 Series, 940 Series

## INTRODUCTION

This article contains underhood views of vacuum hose routing. Use these vacuum diagrams during the visual inspection of BASIC DIAGNOSTIC PROCEDURES article. This will assist in identifying improperly routed vacuum hoses which may cause driveability and/or computer indicated malfunctions.

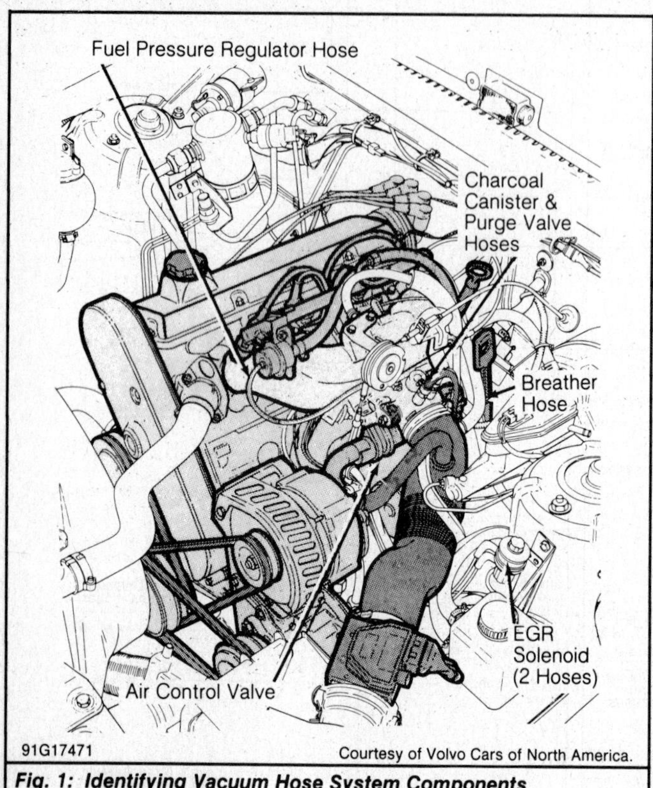


***Fig. 1: Identifying Vacuum Hose System Components (B230F Engine)***

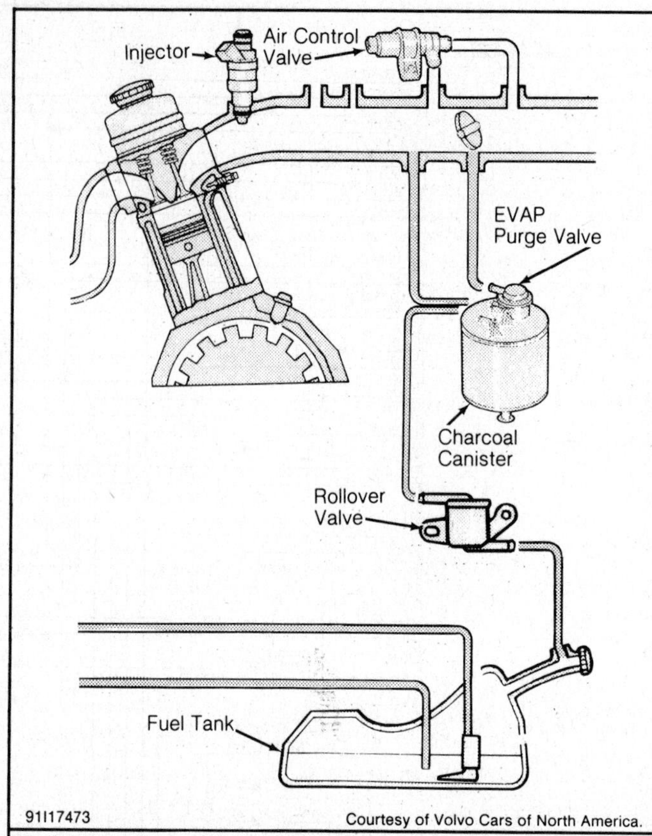


***Fig. 3: Identifying Typical EVAP System Components***



***Fig. 2: Identifying Vacuum Hose System Components (B230FT Engine)***

# 1991 ELECTRICAL
# Alternators & Regulators – Bosch

## 240, 740, 940

***NOTE:** Some Volvos may have a Toyo-Denso alternator. Information on these alternators is not available from the manufacturer.*

## DESCRIPTION

Bosch alternators are conventional 3-phase, self-rectifying type. Bosch 55-amp through 75-amp alternators have 3 positive and 3 negative diodes connected to stator windings to rectify current. Bosch 80-amp and 90-amp alternators have 14 diodes. All alternators use 3 exciter diodes connected to stator windings. These diodes turn off the alternator indicator light and supply power to voltage regulator while engine is running. Voltage regulator is transistorized.

## ADJUSTMENTS

No adjustments or maintenance is required on alternator or voltage regulator.

### BELT TENSION

*BELT ADJUSTMENT*

| Application | [1] Deflection – In. (mm) |
|---|---|
| All Belts | .2-.4 (5-10) |

[1] – Measure deflection with moderate thumb pressure midway on longest belt run.

## TROUBLE SHOOTING

***NOTE:** See TROUBLE SHOOTING article in GENERAL INFORMATION.*

## ON-VEHICLE TESTING

### WIRING CONTINUITY TEST

**1)** Connect a voltmeter between alternator B+ terminal and ground. Voltmeter should indicate battery voltage. If battery voltage is not indicated, check wiring between alternator and battery.

**2)** Turn ignition on and ensure alternator indicator light comes on. If light does not come on, check wiring between alternator and warning light, and indicator bulb.

### VOLTAGE DROP TEST – POSITIVE SIDE

**1)** Connect a voltmeter between positive battery terminal and alternator B+ terminal. Start engine and run at 2000 RPM. Turn on headlights, rear window defogger and heater blower.

**2)** If voltage drop is more than .2 volt, check circuit between alternator B+ terminal and starter for corroded or loose connections. Check circuit between starter and battery positive terminal.

### VOLTAGE DROP TEST – GROUND SIDE

**1)** Connect a voltmeter between negative battery terminal and alternator housing. Start engine and run at 2000 RPM. Turn on headlights, rear window defogger and heater blower.

**2)** If voltage drop is more than .2 volt, check battery terminals, chassis grounds and engine grounds for corroded or loose connections.

### OUTPUT TEST

**1)** Ensure connections at battery, alternator, and starter are clean and tight. Ensure alternator, engine and body are properly grounded. Ensure alternator drive belt is tight and in good condition.

**2)** Connect ammeter following manufacturer's instructions. Connect voltmeter leads to battery terminals. Run engine to 2000 RPM. Adjust carbon pile on tester until voltmeter reads 12 volts. Alternator output should be 49-55 amps. (55-amp alternator), 63-70 amps (70-amp alternator), 81-90 amps (90-amp alternator). If alternator output is low, replace alternator.

### REGULATOR CONTROL VOLTAGE TEST

**240 – 1)** Connect voltmeter to battery. Start engine and run at 2000 RPM. Run engine until voltage stops rising. Voltage should be 13.0-15.0 volts.

**2)** If reading is less than 13 volts, proceed to step **3)**. If reading is greater than 15.0 volts with integral regulator, replace regulator and retest. If reading is greater than 15 volts with external regulator, turn ignition off and disconnect harness from regulator. Connect voltmeter to battery and run engine at 2000 RPM. If reading is battery voltage, replace regulator and retest. If reading is greater than battery voltage, replace harness and retest.

**3)** Check to see if alternator warning light is on. If light is not on, check wiring between regulator and warning light. If warning light is on, perform full field test for alternators with external regulators. Pull regulator wiring harness from regulator. Connect jumper wire from D+ terminal to DF terminal.

**4)** Connect voltmeter across alternator B+ terminal and ground. Run engine to 2000 RPM. Observe voltage. If reading is greater than 15.5 volts, replace regulator and retest. If battery voltage is present, replace alternator.

**5)** If warning light is on with integral regulator, use test brush holder. With jumper wire connected to terminals D+ and DF on test brush holder, run engine to 2000 RPM. Check voltage at battery. If battery voltage is present, replace alternator. If reading is greater than 15.5 volts, replace regulator and retest.

***CAUTION:** DO NOT allow voltage to exceed 16 volts or vehicle's electrical system may be damaged.*

**740 & 940 – 1)** Connect voltmeter to battery. Run engine at 2000 RPM until voltage stops rising. Voltage should be 13.0-15.0 volts. If voltage is higher with integral regulator without temperature sensor, replace regulator. If higher with integral regulator with temperature sensor, check sensor.

**2)** Temperature sensor is located under battery. Note battery temperature and charging voltage. Check Graph A to see if temperature and voltage are within center lines of graph. *See Fig. 1.* If so, charging voltage is okay.

**3)** If voltage and temperature is not within center lines of Graph A, go to Graph B for internal temperature sensor check. *See Fig. 1.* Disconnect regulator temperature sensor. Locate temperature and voltage on Graph B. If within center lines, replace internal temperature sensor. If not within center lines, replace voltage regulator.

# 1991 ELECTRICAL
# Alternators & Regulators – Bosch (Cont.)

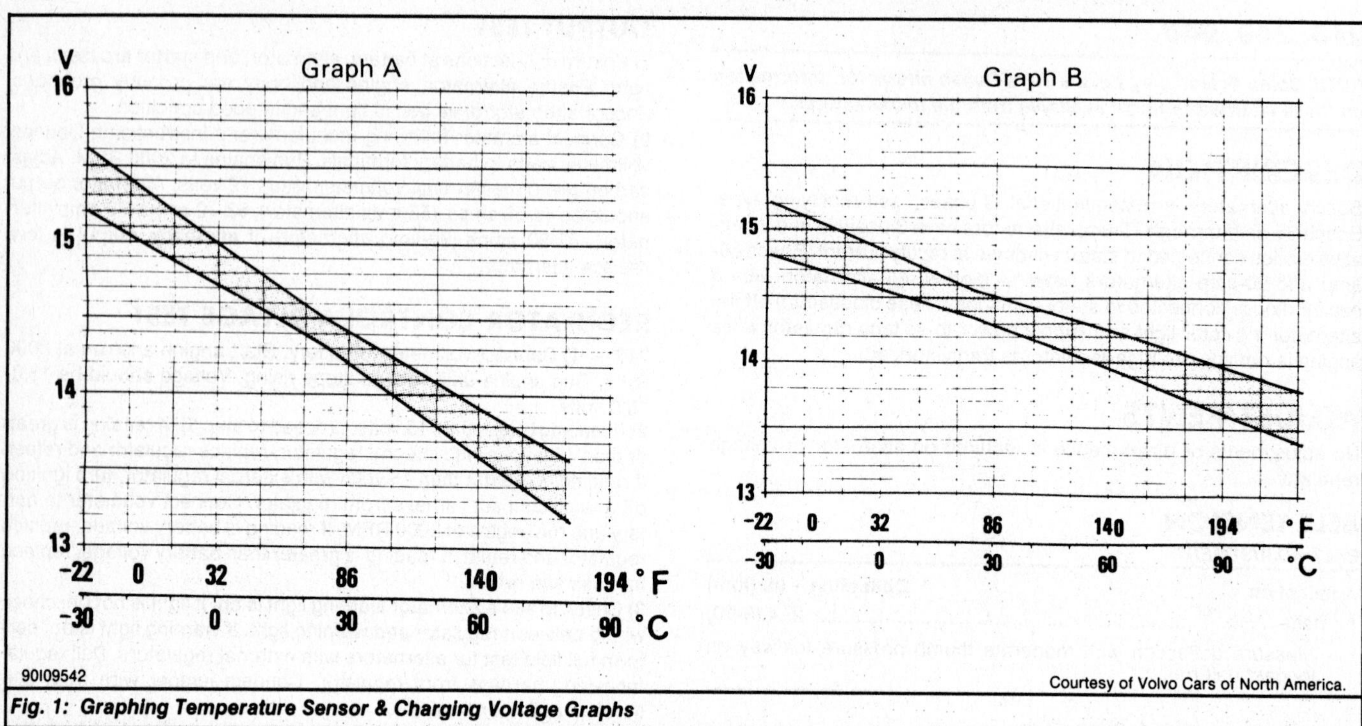


*Fig. 1: Graphing Temperature Sensor & Charging Voltage Graphs*

## OVERHAUL

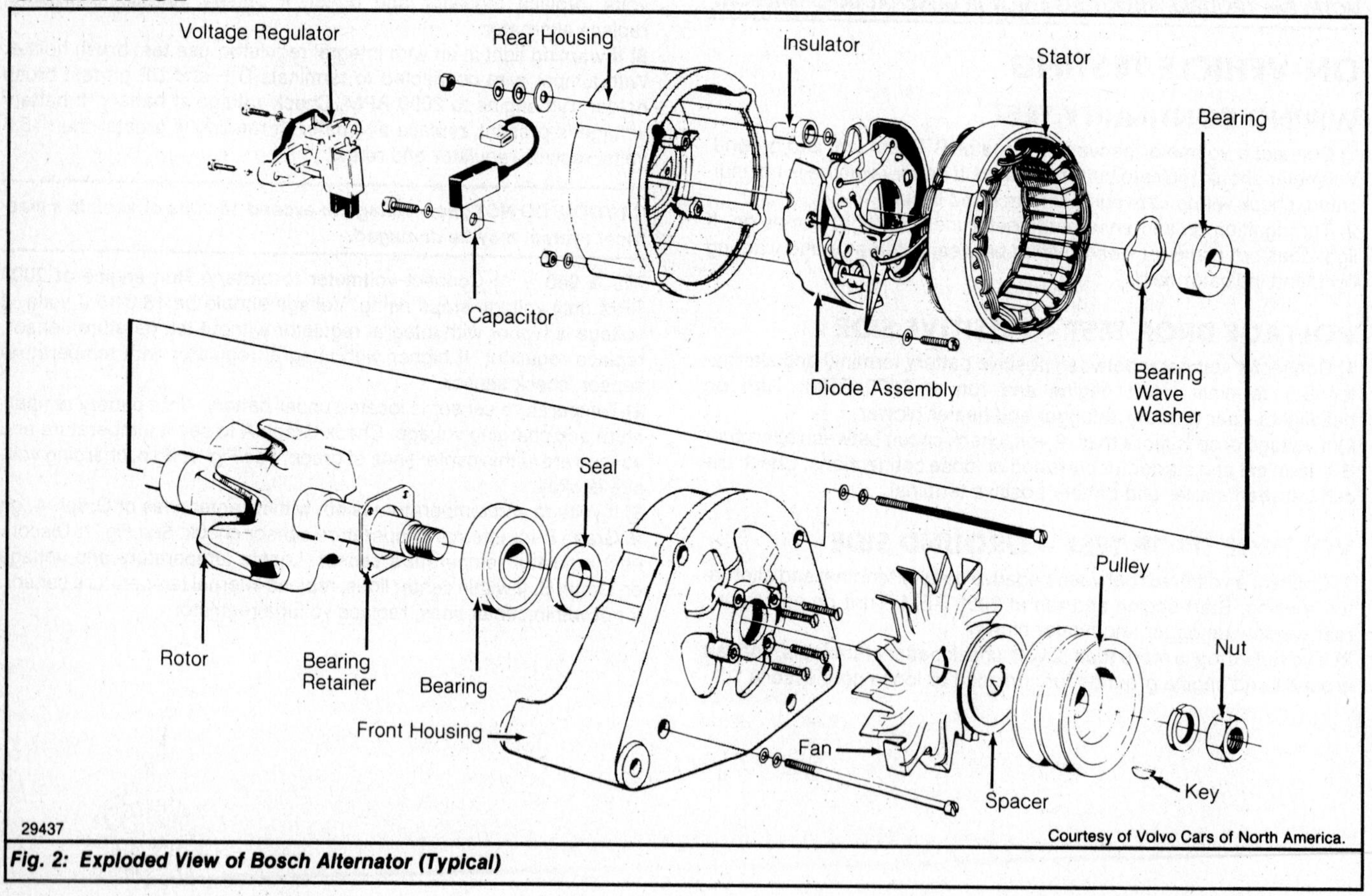

29437

Courtesy of Volvo Cars of North America.

*Fig. 2: Exploded View of Bosch Alternator (Typical)*

## WIRING DIAGRAMS

See appropriate chassis wiring diagram in WIRING DIAGRAMS.

## 240, 740, 940

## DESCRIPTION

Starter is a brush-type, series-wound electric motor with an overrunning clutch (drive assembly). Field frame is enclosed by commutator end frame and drive bushing and carries pole shoes and field coils. A spline armature shaft drive end carries drive assembly.

## TROUBLE SHOOTING

***NOTE:* See TROUBLE SHOOTING article in GENERAL INFORMATION.**

## BENCH TESTING

### STARTER LOAD (LOCK) TEST

With starter on bench, lock starter drive pinion. Voltmeter and ammeter readings should be within specification. See STARTER LOAD (LOCK) TEST SPECIFICATIONS table.

***STARTER LOAD (LOCK) TEST SPECIFICATIONS***

| Application | Volts | Amps |
|---|---|---|
| Bosch | | |
| 0 001 218 0 | 3 | 720-950 |
| 0 001 311 1 | 7.4 | [1] 480-560 |
| 0 001 362 | 4.5 | 700-880 |
| 0 001 108 | 4.5 | 625-800 |
| Hitachi | | |
| S 114-232 | 6 | 650 |
| S 13-91 | 8.8 | [2] 300 |

[1] – At 6.5 volts, ammeter reading should be 410-490 amps.
[2] – At 3 volts, ammeter reading should be 880 amps.

### STARTER NO LOAD TEST

With starter on bench, operate starter and check ammeter, voltage, and RPM. Readings should be within specification. See STARTER NO LOAD TEST SPECIFICATIONS table.

***STARTER NO LOAD TEST SPECIFICATIONS***

| Application | Volts | Amps. | RPM |
|---|---|---|---|
| Bosch | | | |
| 0 001 218 0 | 10.5 | 95 | 4200 |
| 0 001 311 1 | 11.5 | 70 | 7500 |
| 0 001 362 | 11.5 | 95 | 6500 |
| 0 001 108 | 11.5 | 75 | 2900 |
| Hitachi | | | |
| S 114-232 | 12 | 60 | 7000 |
| S 13-91 | 11 | 140 | 3900 |

### SOLENOID TEST

Connect battery negative lead to starter solenoid terminal "M". Connect battery positive lead to solenoid terminal No. 50. *See Fig. 2.* If plunger does not extend firmly, replace solenoid.

Solenoid
50
M
12V
Battery
92I01777
Courtesy of Volvo Cars of North America.

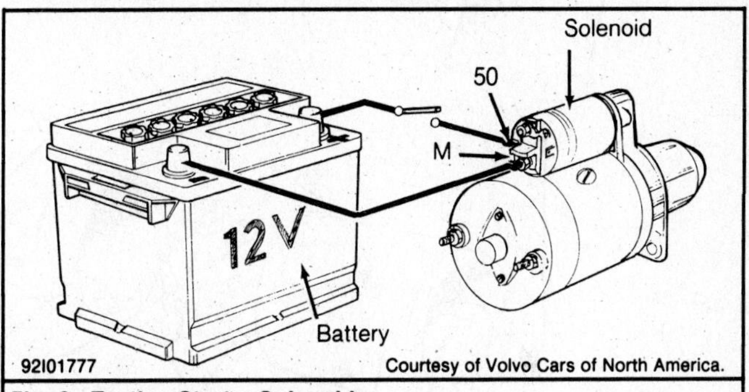

***Fig. 2: Testing Starter Solenoid***

## OVERHAUL

***NOTE:* For starter overhaul, see Figs. 1 and 3-5. View of Bosch starter (0 001 218 0) is not available from manufacturer.**

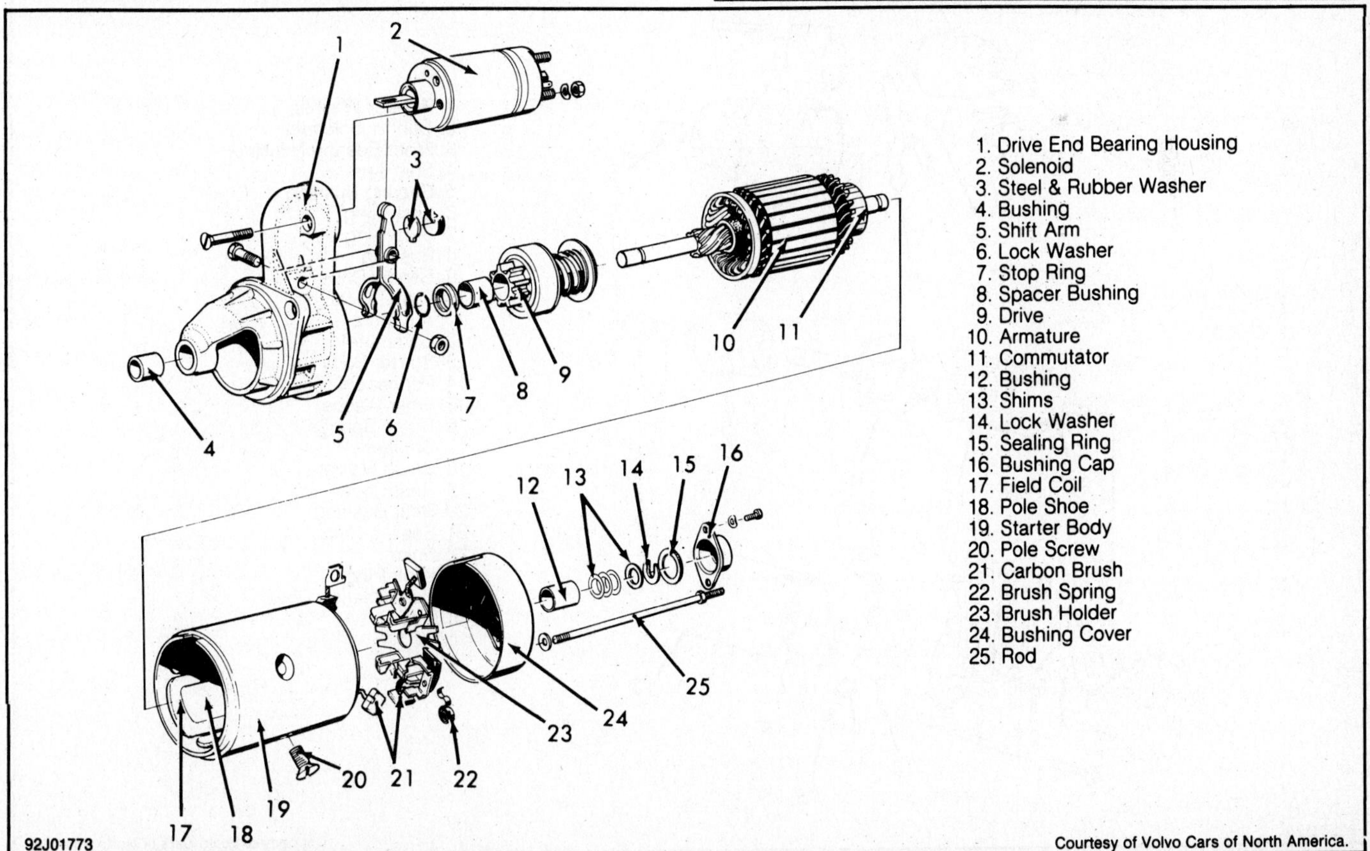

1. Drive End Bearing Housing
2. Solenoid
3. Steel & Rubber Washer
4. Bushing
5. Shift Arm
6. Lock Washer
7. Stop Ring
8. Spacer Bushing
9. Drive
10. Armature
11. Commutator
12. Bushing
13. Shims
14. Lock Washer
15. Sealing Ring
16. Bushing Cap
17. Field Coil
18. Pole Shoe
19. Starter Body
20. Pole Screw
21. Carbon Brush
22. Brush Spring
23. Brush Holder
24. Bushing Cover
25. Rod
92J01773
Courtesy of Volvo Cars of North America.

***Fig. 1: Exploded View of Bosch Starter (0 001 311)***

# 1991 ELECTRICAL
# Starters – Bosch & Hitachi (Cont.)

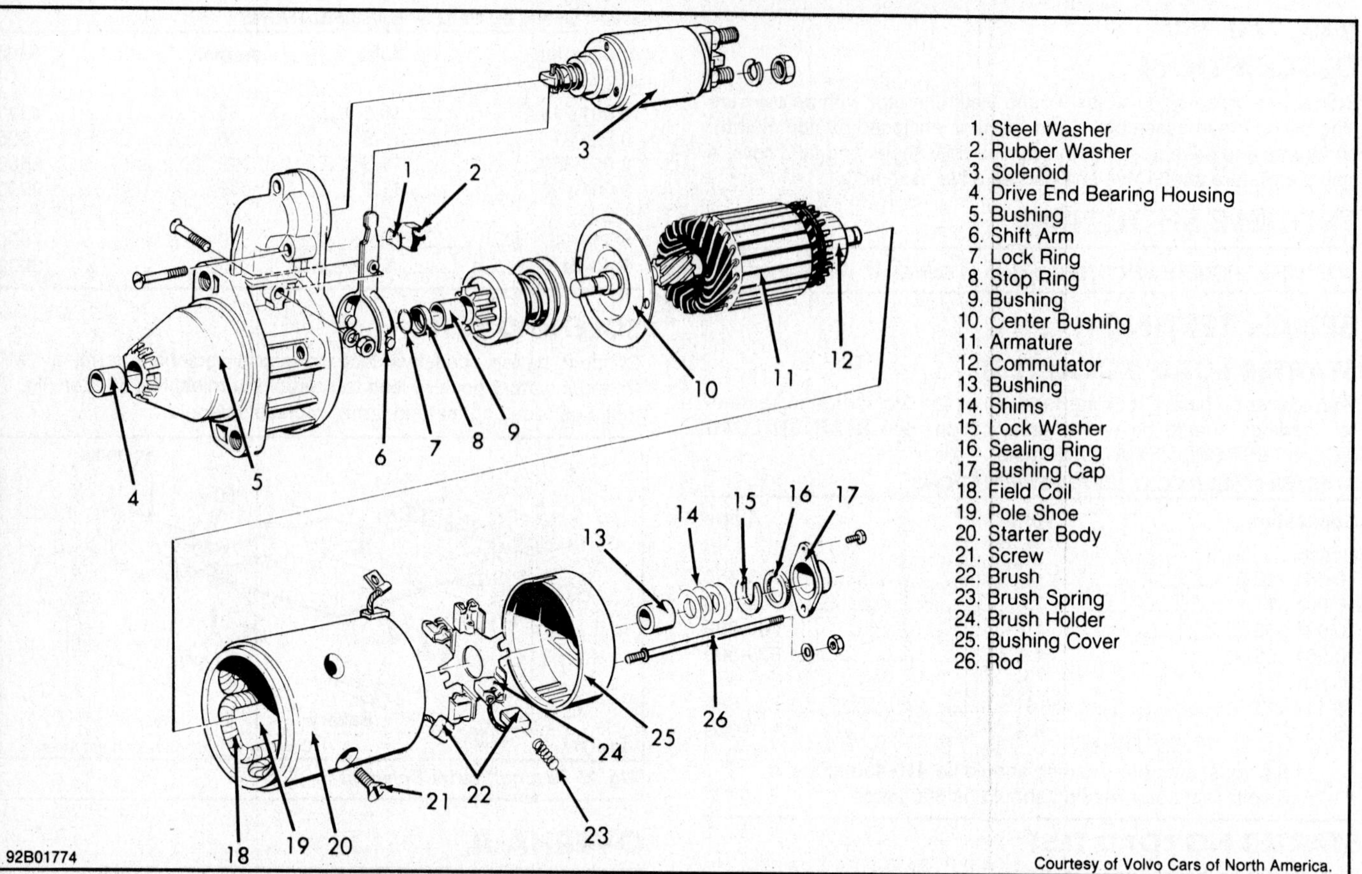

1. Steel Washer
2. Rubber Washer
3. Solenoid
4. Drive End Bearing Housing
5. Bushing
6. Shift Arm
7. Lock Ring
8. Stop Ring
9. Bushing
10. Center Bushing
11. Armature
12. Commutator
13. Bushing
14. Shims
15. Lock Washer
16. Sealing Ring
17. Bushing Cap
18. Field Coil
19. Pole Shoe
20. Starter Body
21. Screw
22. Brush
23. Brush Spring
24. Brush Holder
25. Bushing Cover
26. Rod

92B01774

Courtesy of Volvo Cars of North America.

***Fig. 3: Exploded View of Bosch Starter (0 001 362)***

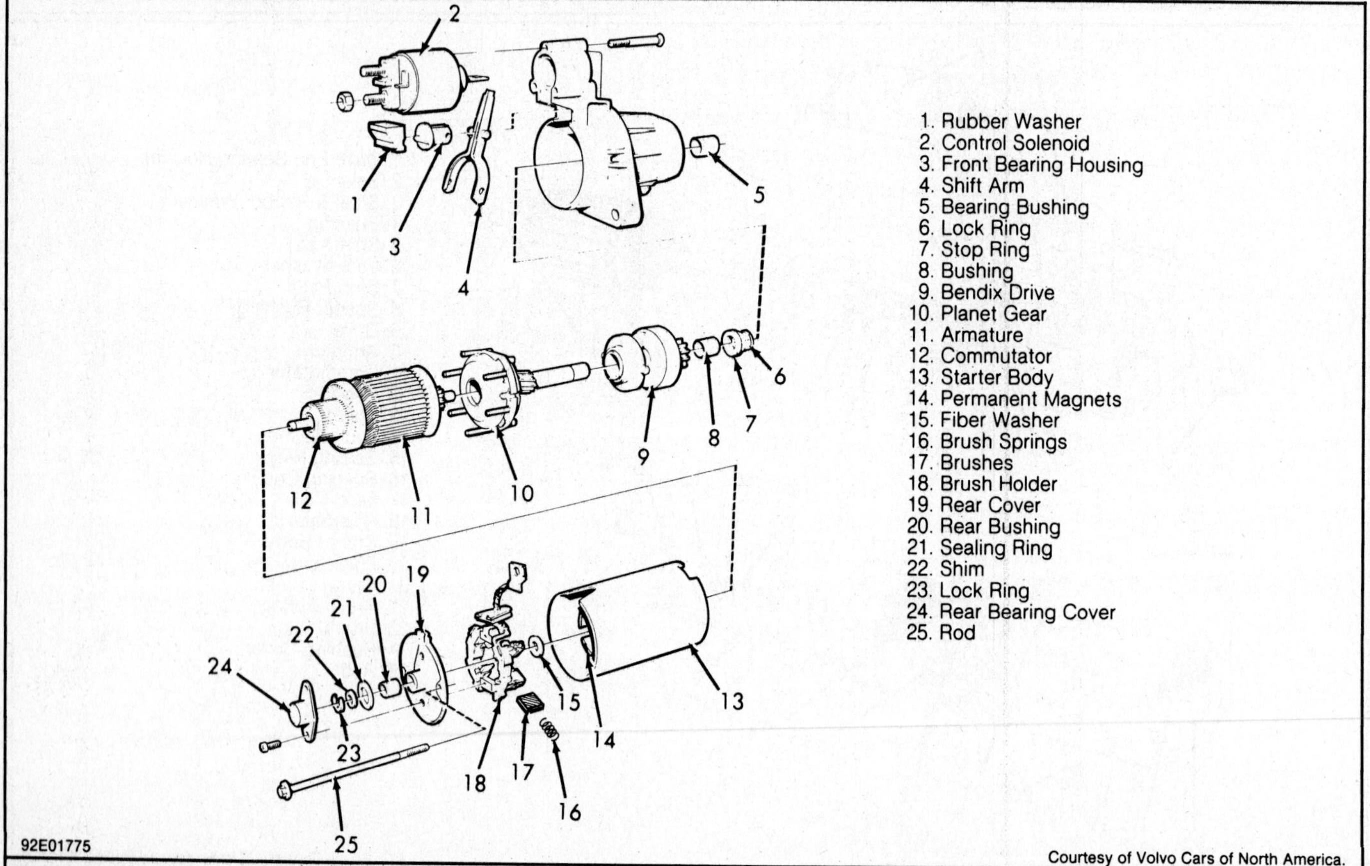

1. Rubber Washer
2. Control Solenoid
3. Front Bearing Housing
4. Shift Arm
5. Bearing Bushing
6. Lock Ring
7. Stop Ring
8. Bushing
9. Bendix Drive
10. Planet Gear
11. Armature
12. Commutator
13. Starter Body
14. Permanent Magnets
15. Fiber Washer
16. Brush Springs
17. Brushes
18. Brush Holder
19. Rear Cover
20. Rear Bushing
21. Sealing Ring
22. Shim
23. Lock Ring
24. Rear Bearing Cover
25. Rod

92E01775

Courtesy of Volvo Cars of North America.

***Fig. 4: Exploded View of Bosch Starter (0 001 108)***

# 1991 ELECTRICAL
# Starters – Bosch & Hitachi (Cont.)

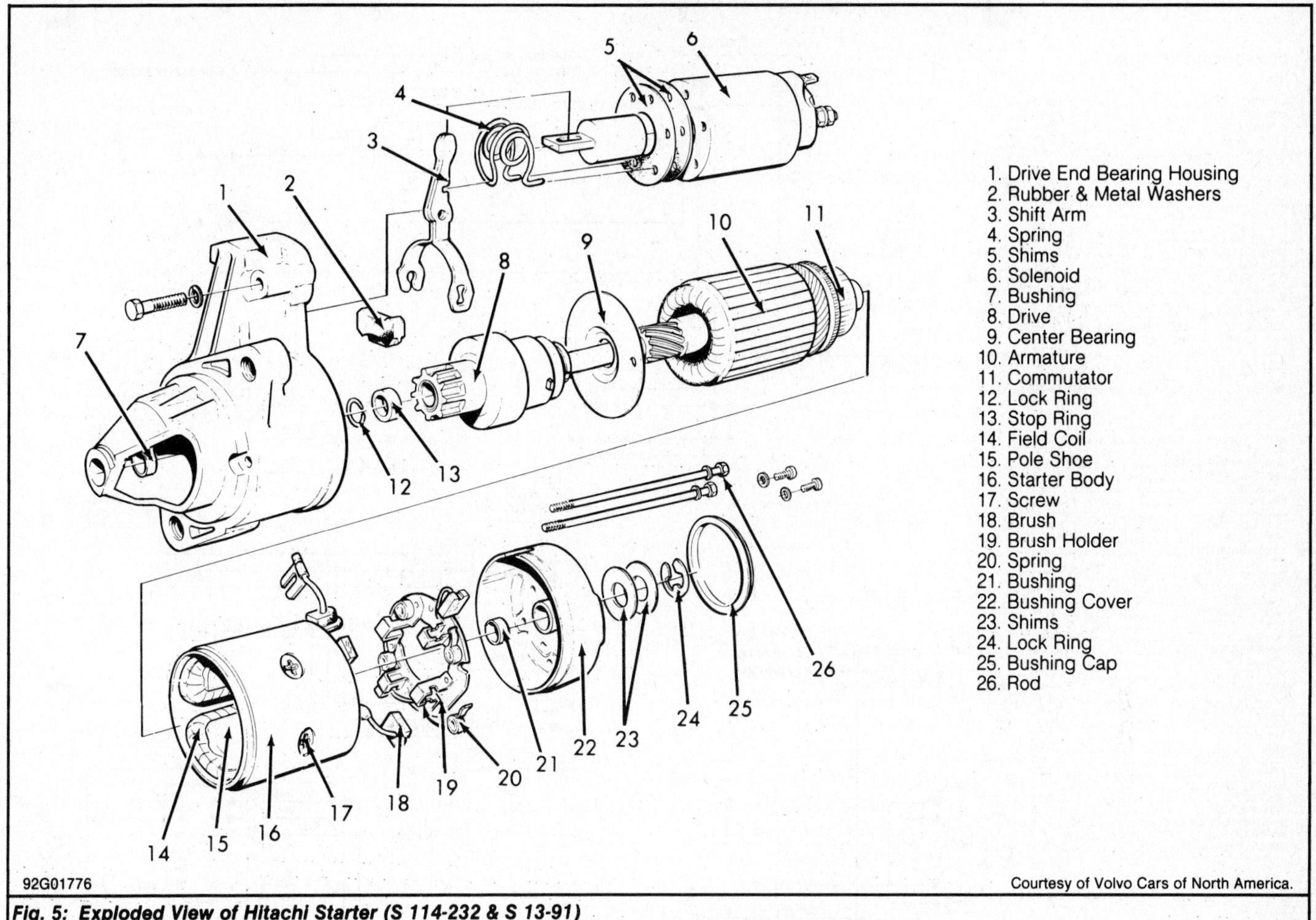


*Fig. 5: Exploded View of Hitachi Starter (S 114-232 & S 13-91)*

## STARTER SPECIFICATIONS

*STARTER SPECIFICATIONS*

| Application | Specification |
|---|---|
| Armature | |
| Core Runout | |
| Bosch (0 001 218 0) | .0019" (.050 mm) |
| Bosch (0 001 311) | .002" (.05 mm) |
| Bosch (0 001 362) | .002" (.05 mm) |
| Bosch (0 001 108) | .002" (.05 mm) |
| Hitachi (S 114-232, S 13-91) | .002" (.05 mm) |
| End Play | |
| Bosch (0 001 218 0) | .0118-.023" (.300-.60 mm) |
| Bosch (0 001 311) | .004-.012" (.10-.30 mm) |
| Bosch (0 001 362) | .004-.012" (.10-.30 mm) |
| Bosch (0 001 108) | .004-.012" (.10-.30 mm) |
| Hitachi (S 114-232, S 13-91) | .0012-.039" (.03-.10 mm) |
| Carbon Brush | |
| Min. Length | |
| Bosch (0 001 218 0) | .27" (7 mm) |
| Bosch (0 001 311) | .500" (13 mm) |
| Bosch (0 001 362) | .33" (8.5 mm) |
| Bosch (0 001 108) | .500" (13 mm) |
| Hitachi (S 114-232, S 13-91) | .44" (11 mm) |

*STARTER SPECIFICATIONS (Cont.)*

| Application | Specification |
|---|---|
| Cold Cranking | |
| Test Voltage | |
| Bosch (0 001 218 0) | 10.5 |
| Bosch (0 001 311) | 11.5 |
| Bosch (0 001 362) | 11.5 |
| Bosch (0 001 108) | 11.5 |
| Hitachi (S 114-232, S 13-91) | 12.0 |
| Commutator | |
| Diameter | |
| Bosch (0 001 218 0) | 1.30" (33.5 mm) |
| Bosch (0 001 311) | 1.30" (33.5 mm) |
| Bosch (0 001 362) | 1.60" (42.5 mm) |
| Bosch (0 001 108) | 1.60" (42.5 mm) |
| Hitachi (S 114-232, S 13-91) | 1.5" (39 mm) |
| Runout | |
| Bosch (0 001 218 0) | .0004" (.010 mm) |
| Bosch (0 001 311) | .002" (.05 mm) |
| Bosch (0 001 362) | .002" (.05 mm) |
| Bosch (0 001 108) | .002" (.05 mm) |
| Hitachi (S 114-232, S 13-91) | .002" (.05 mm) |

# 1991 WIRING DIAGRAMS
## 240 Series

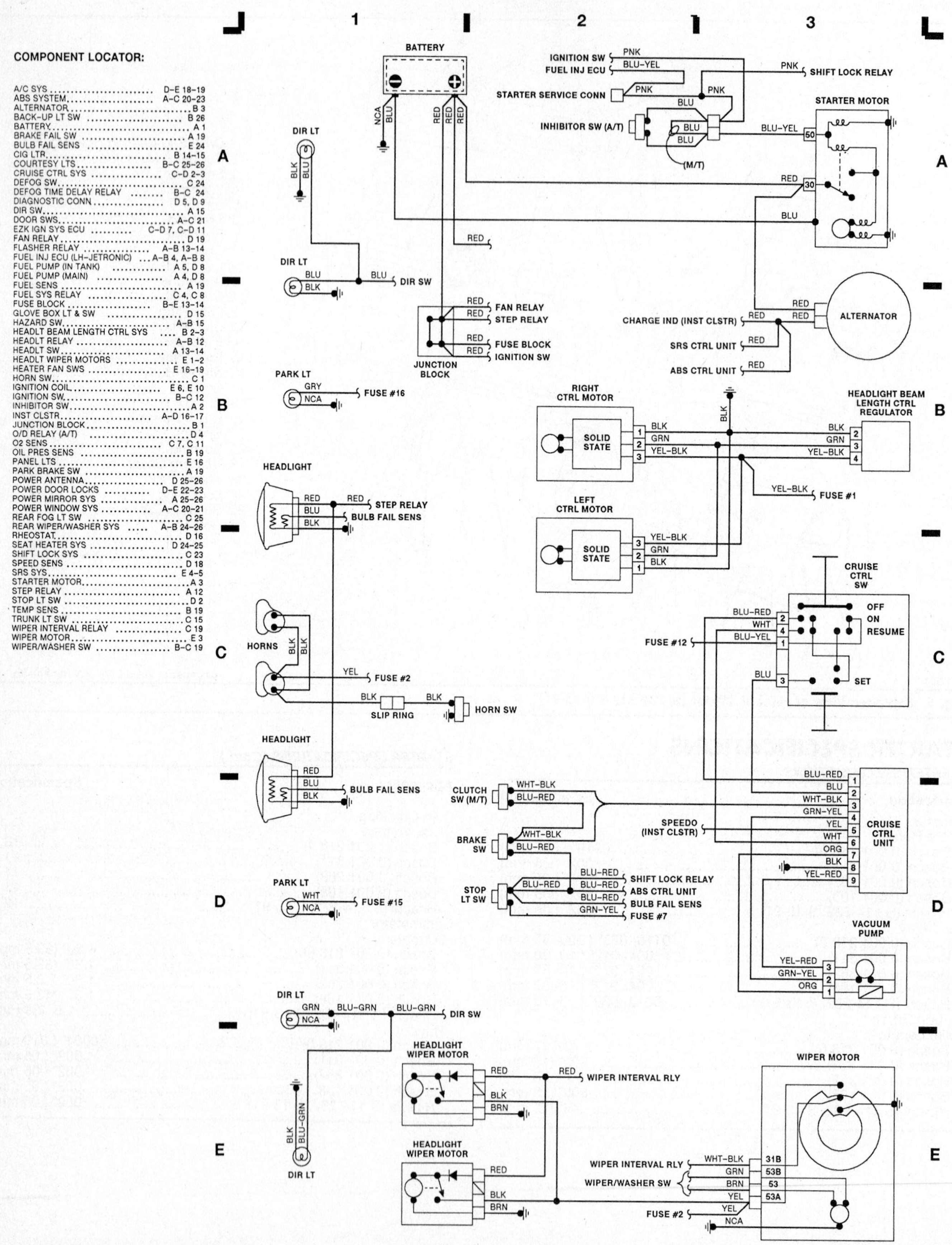


**COMPONENT LOCATOR:**

| | |
|---|---|
| A/C SYS | D–E 18–19 |
| ABS SYSTEM | A–C 20–23 |
| ALTERNATOR | B 3 |
| BACK-UP LT SW | B 26 |
| BATTERY | A 1 |
| BRAKE FAIL SW | A 19 |
| BULB FAIL SENS | E 24 |
| CIG LTR | B 14–15 |
| COURTESY LTS | B–C 25–26 |
| CRUISE CTRL SYS | C–D 2–3 |
| DEFOG SW | C 24 |
| DEFOG TIME DELAY RELAY | B–C 24 |
| DIAGNOSTIC CONN | D 5, D 9 |
| DIR SW | A 15 |
| DOOR SWS | A–C 21 |
| EZK IGN SYS ECU | C–D 7, C–D 11 |
| FAN RELAY | D 19 |
| FLASHER RELAY | A–B 13–14 |
| FUEL INJ ECU (LH-JETRONIC) | A–B 4, A–B 8 |
| FUEL PUMP (IN TANK) | A 5, D 8 |
| FUEL PUMP (MAIN) | A 4, D 8 |
| FUEL SENS | A 19 |
| FUEL SYS RELAY | C 4, C 8 |
| FUSE BLOCK | B–E 13–14 |
| GLOVE BOX LT & SW | D 15 |
| HAZARD SW | A–B 15 |
| HEADLT BEAM LENGTH CTRL SYS | B 2–3 |
| HEADLT RELAY | A–B 12 |
| HEADLT SW | A 13–14 |
| HEADLT WIPER MOTORS | E 1–2 |
| HEATER FAN SWS | E 16–19 |
| HORN SW | C 1 |
| IGNITION COIL | E 6, E 10 |
| IGNITION SW | B–C 12 |
| INHIBITOR SW | A 2 |
| INST CLSTR | A–D 16–17 |
| JUNCTION BLOCK | B 1 |
| O/D RELAY (A/T) | D 4 |
| O2 SENS | C 7, C 11 |
| OIL PRES SENS | B 19 |
| PANEL LTS | E 16 |
| PARK BRAKE SW | A 19 |
| POWER ANTENNA | D 25–26 |
| POWER DOOR LOCKS | D–E 22–23 |
| POWER MIRROR SYS | A 25–26 |
| POWER WINDOW SYS | A–C 20–21 |
| REAR FOG LT SW | C 25 |
| REAR WIPER/WASHER SYS | A–B 24–26 |
| RHEOSTAT | D 16 |
| SEAT HEATER SYS | D 24–25 |
| SHIFT LOCK SYS | C 23 |
| SPEED SENS | D 18 |
| SRS SYS | E 4–5 |
| STARTER MOTOR | A 3 |
| STEP RELAY | A 12 |
| STOP LT SW | D 2 |
| TEMP SENS | B 19 |
| TRUNK LT SW | C 15 |
| WIPER INTERVAL RELAY | C 19 |
| WIPER MOTOR | E 3 |
| WIPER/WASHER SW | B–C 19 |

# 1991 WIRING DIAGRAMS
# 240 Series (Cont.)

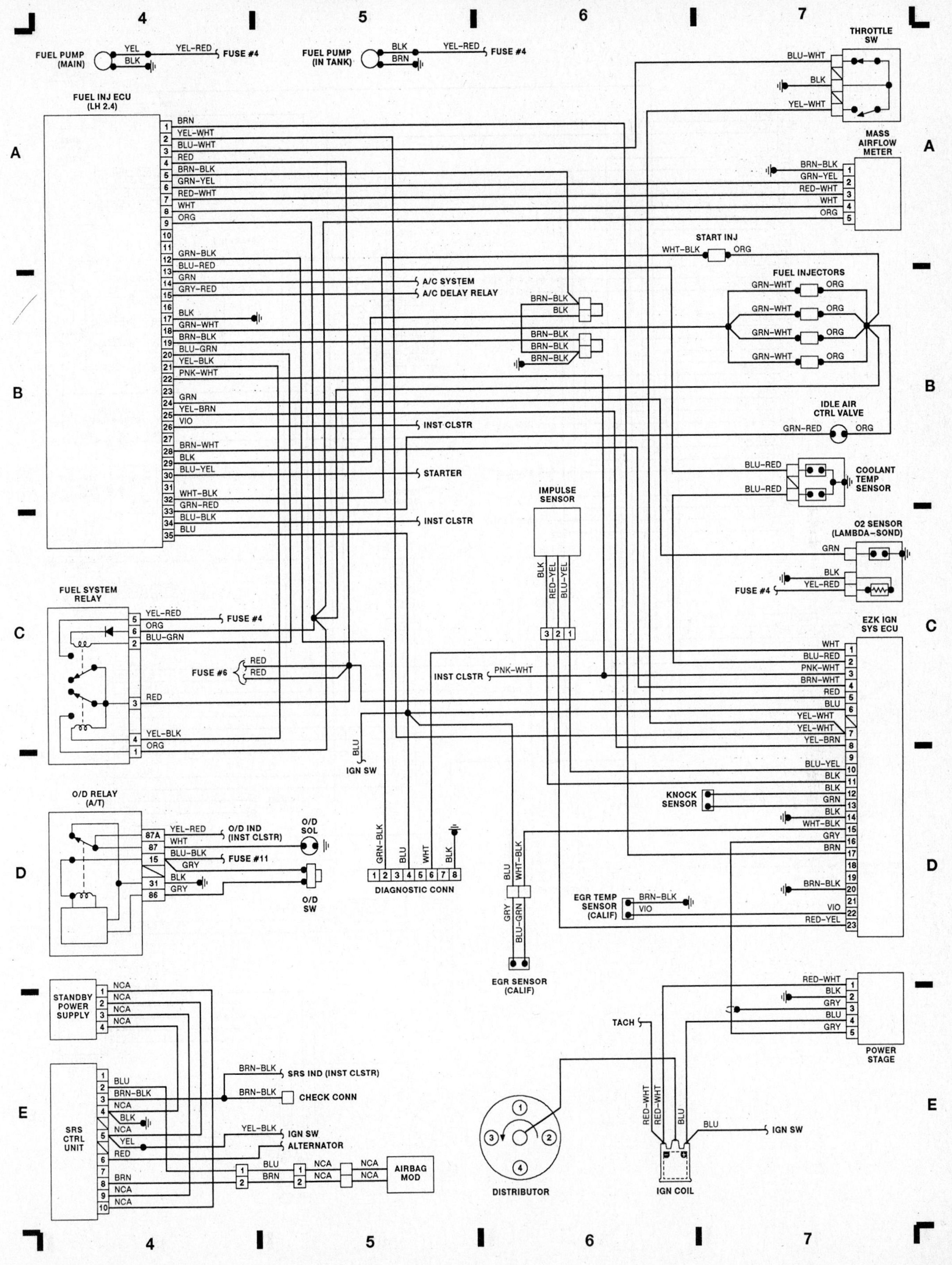

# 1991 WIRING DIAGRAMS
# 240 Series (Cont.)

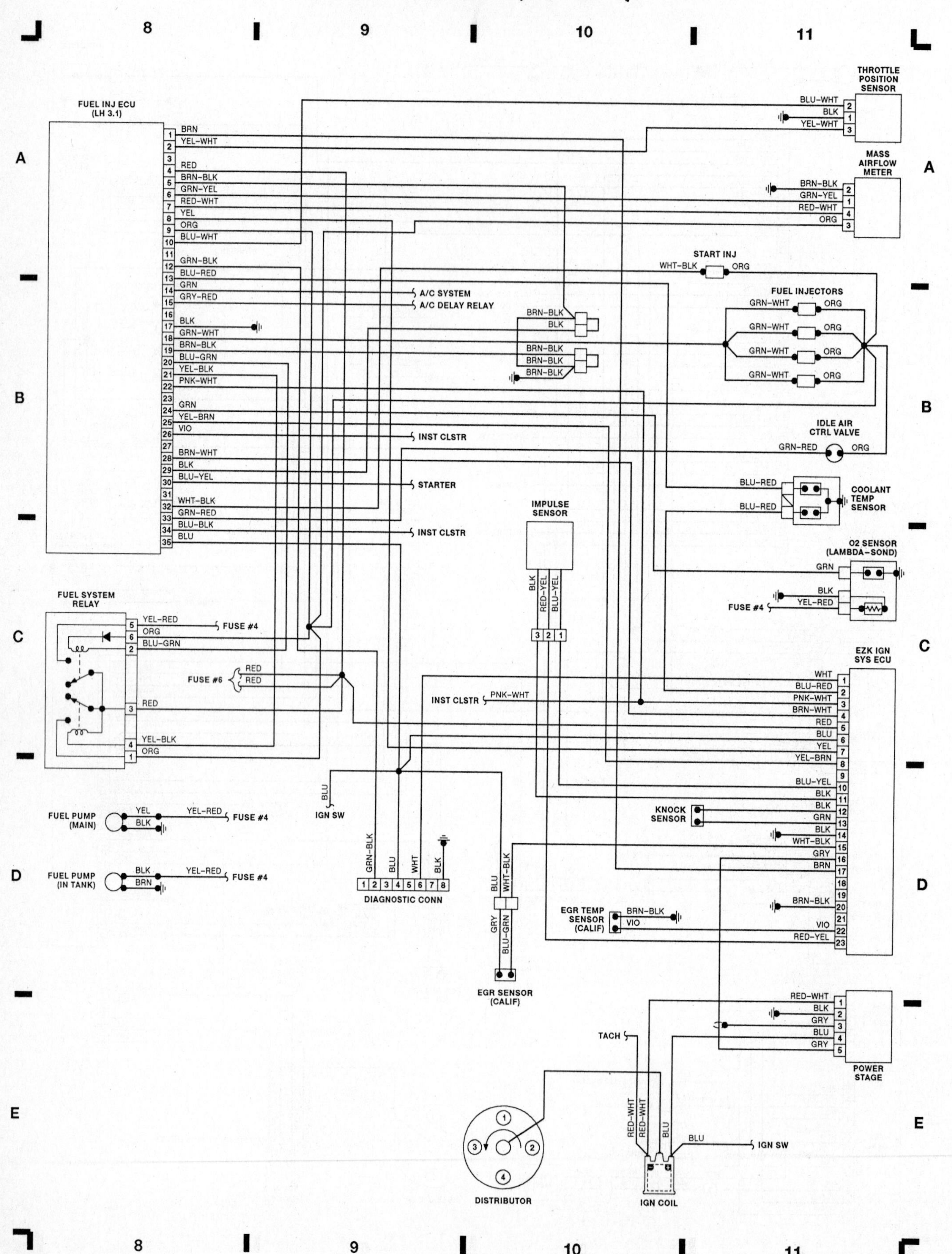

# 1991 WIRING DIAGRAMS
# 240 Series (Cont.)

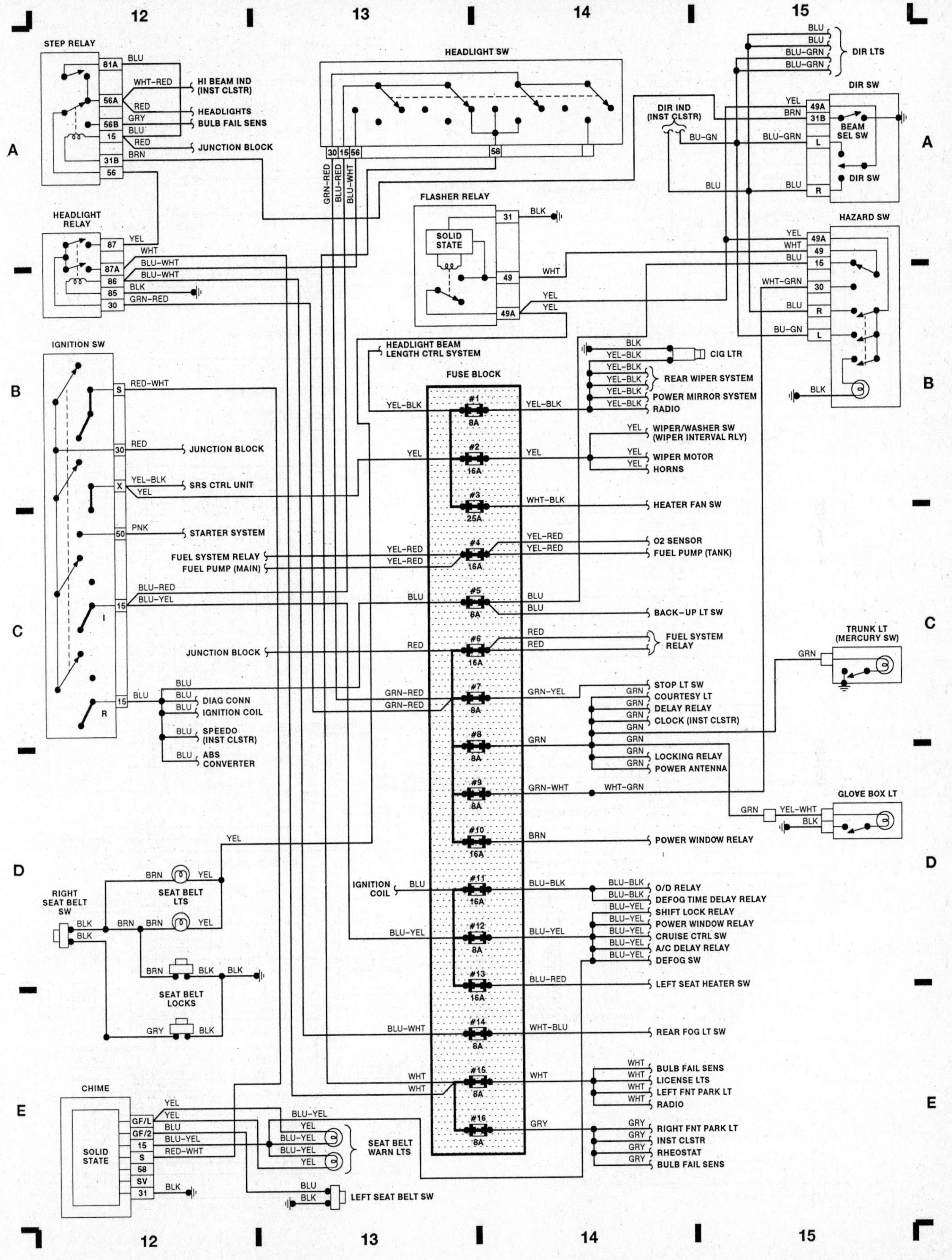

# 1991 WIRING DIAGRAMS
# 240 Series (Cont.)

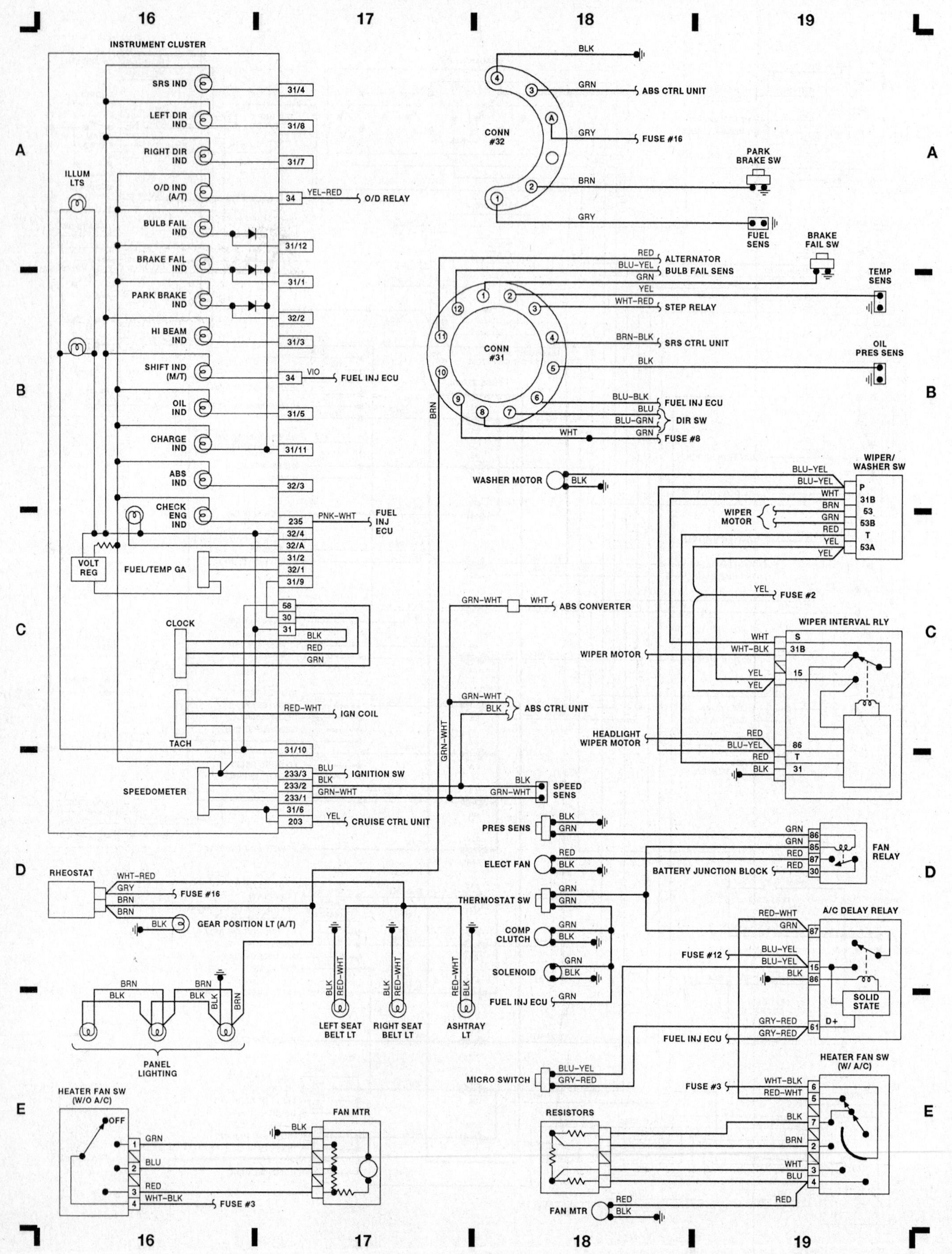

# 1991 WIRING DIAGRAMS
# 240 Series (Cont.)

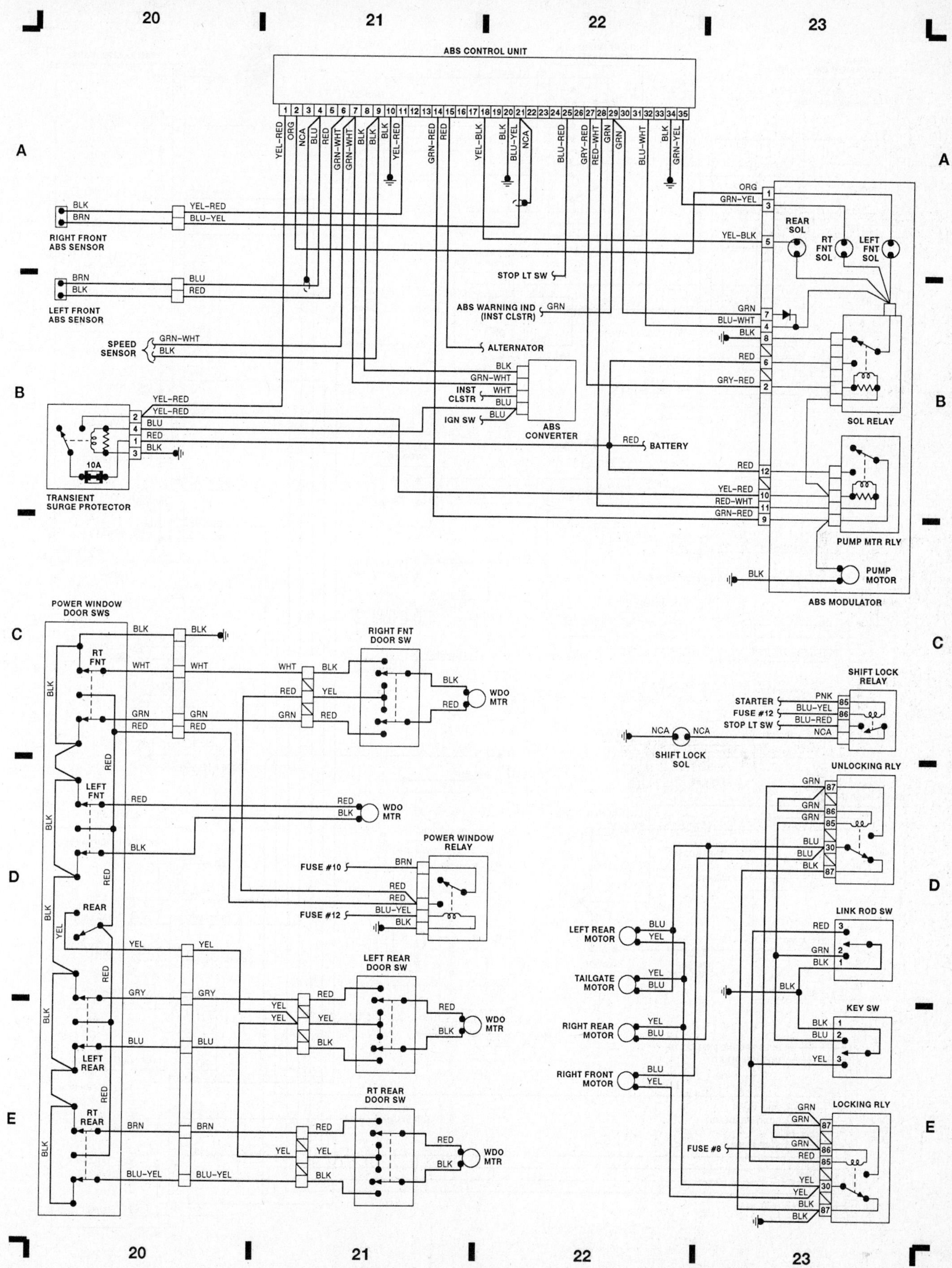

# 1991 WIRING DIAGRAMS
## 240 Series (Cont.)

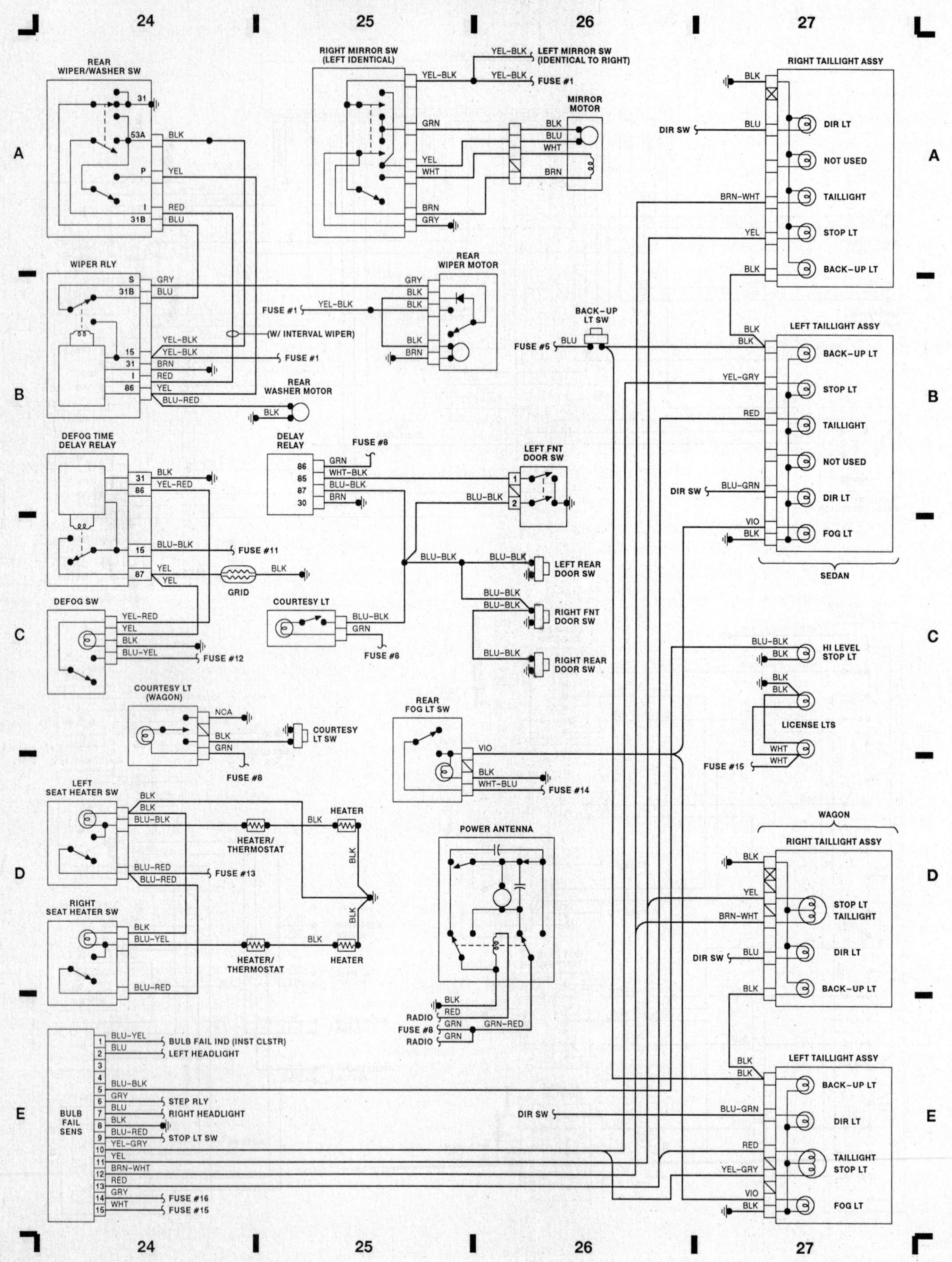

# 1991 WIRING DIAGRAMS
# 740 Series, 940GLE & 940 Turbo

COMPONENT LOCATOR:

| | |
|---|---|
| ABS CTRL UNIT | A 29-30 |
| ABS MODULATOR | A-C 31 |
| ALTERNATOR | C 3 |
| BACK-UP LT SW | C 42 |
| BATTERY | A 2 |
| BEAM LENGTH REGULATOR | A 19 |
| BULB FAILURE SENS | E 24 |
| CIG LTR | B 41 |
| COMB SW | A-C 24 |
| COOLANT FAN RELAY | A 16-18 |
| COURTESY LTS | C 24 |
| CRUISE CTRL SYS | C-D 28-30 |
| DEFOG SYS | A-B 40-41 |
| DOOR LTS | D 24 |
| ECC CTRL UNIT | C-E 23 |
| ECC POWER UNIT | E 20 |
| FLASHER RELAY | A 27 |
| FOG LT RELAY | E 28 |
| FOG LT SW | D-E 28 |
| FUEL INJ ECU (CALIF) | A-C 4 |
| FUEL INJ ECU (REGINA) | A-C 12 |
| FUEL INJ ECU (TURBO) | A-B 8 |
| FUEL PUMP (IN TANK) (CALIF) | D 4 |
| FUEL PUMP (IN TANK) (TURBO) | C 11 |
| FUEL PUMP (MAIN) (CALIF) | D 4 |
| FUEL PUMP (MAIN) (TURBO) | C 11 |
| FUEL PUMP (REGINA) | D 12 |
| FUEL SYS RELAY (CALIF) | C 4 |
| FUEL SYS RELAY (REGINA) | C 12 |
| FUEL SYS RELAY (TURBO) | B 11 |
| FUSE/RELAY BLOCK (PARTIAL) | B-D 16-19 |
| GEAR SEL LT | D 35 |
| GLOVE BOX LT | E 25 |
| HEATER CTRL SW | C 20 |
| HIGH LEVEL STOP LT | D 42 |
| HORNS & HORN SWS | C 1-2 |
| IGN COIL (CALIF) | E 6 |
| IGN COIL (REGINA) | E 15 |
| IGN COIL (TURBO) | C 8 |
| IGN SW | E 16 |
| IGN SYS ECU (CALIF) | C-D 7 |
| IGN SYS ECU (REGINA) | C-D 15 |
| IGN SYS ECU (TURBO) | D-E 8 |
| INHIBITOR SW (A/T) | B 2 |
| INST CLSTR | A-E 32-33 |
| INST PANEL LTS | E 35 |
| INTERVAL RELAY | D 27 |
| JUNCTION BLOCK | A-B 2-3 |
| LEFT FRONT DOOR SW | C 26 |
| LEFT HEADLT ADJUSTING MOTOR | C-D 1 |
| LEFT HEADLT WIPER MOTOR | E 3 |
| LIGHT RELAY | B-C 27 |
| LIGHT SW | A-B 27 |
| LOCKING RELAY | D-E 38-39 |
| MCC CTRL UNIT | B-C 23 |
| O/D RELAY (A/T) | B 20 |
| O/D RELAY (M/T) | A 20 |
| O2 SENS (CALIF) | C 7 |
| O2 SENS (REGINA) | C 15 |
| POWER ANTENNA MOTOR | E 42 |
| POWER MIRROR SYS | C-E 40-41 |
| POWER SEAT SW | B-D 38-39 |
| POWER WINDOW SYS | D-E 36-38 |
| POWER WINDOW/HEATED SEAT RELAY | C 20 |
| RADIO INTERFERENCE SUPPRESSION RELAY (CALIF) | B 7 |
| RADIO INTERFERENCE SUPPRESSION RELAY (TURBO) | D 11 |
| REAR INTERVAL RELAY | C 40 |
| REAR WIPER/WASHER SW | D-E 27 |
| RHEOSTAT & CLOCK ADJUSTER | C-D 35 |
| RIGHT HEADLT ADJUSTING MOTOR | B 1 |
| RIGHT HEADLT WIPER MOTOR | E 3 |
| SEAT BELT LOCK LTS | A-B 36 |
| SEAT BELT REMINDER | A 36 |
| SEAT HEATER SYS (DUAL) | B-C 36-37 |
| SEAT HEATER SYS (SINGLE OUTPUT) | A 38-39 |
| SHIFT LOCK SYS | E 31 |
| SRS SYS | C-D 31 |
| STARTER | B-C 3 |
| STOP LT SW | D 28 |
| SUNROOF SYS | E 40-41 |
| TRANSIENT SURGE PROTECTOR | B 28 |
| TRUNK LT | D-E 41-42 |
| WIPER MOTOR | D 3 |
| WIPER/WASHER SW | C 27 |

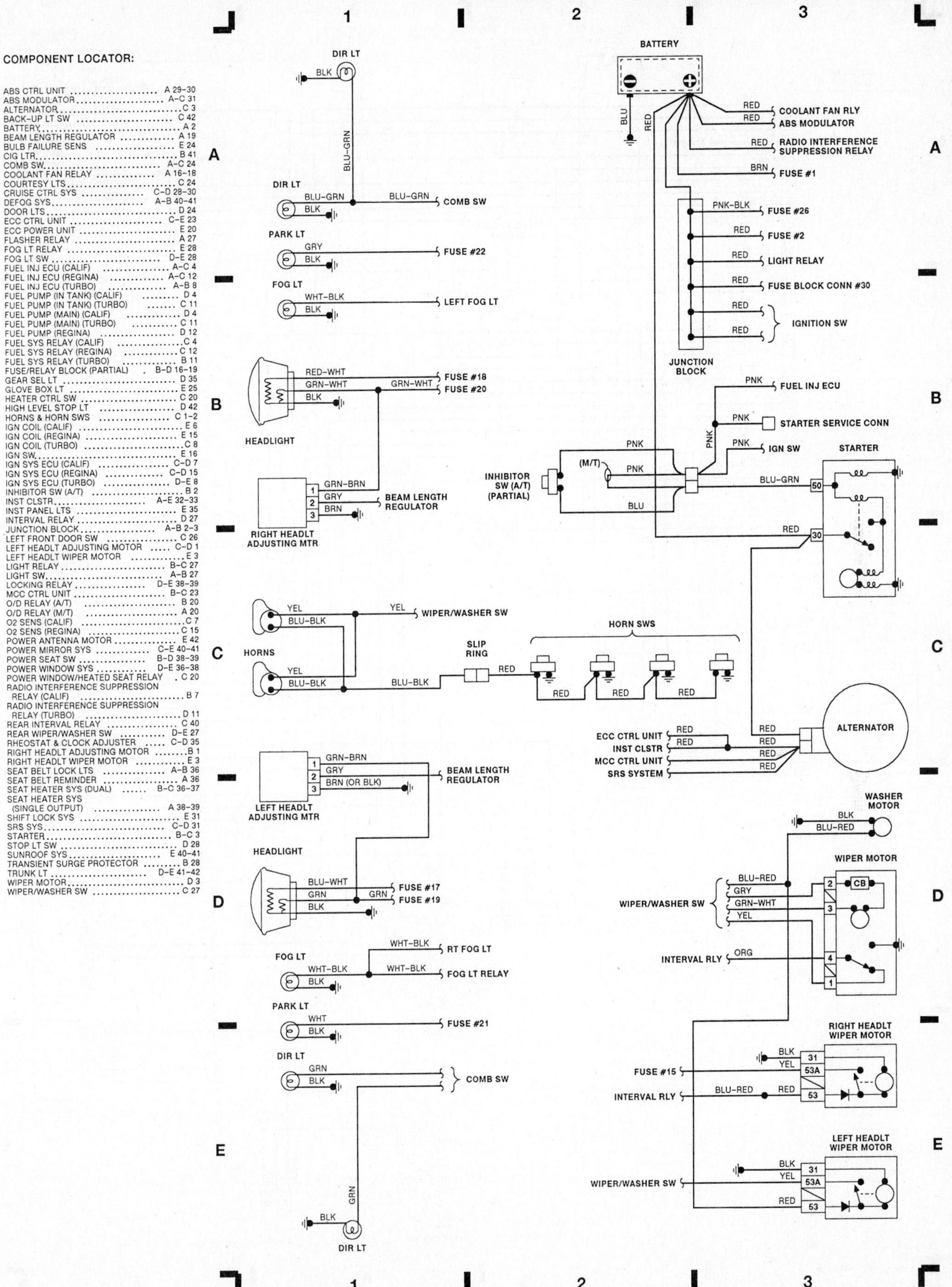

# 1991 WIRING DIAGRAMS
# 740 Series, 940GLE & 940 Turbo (Cont.)

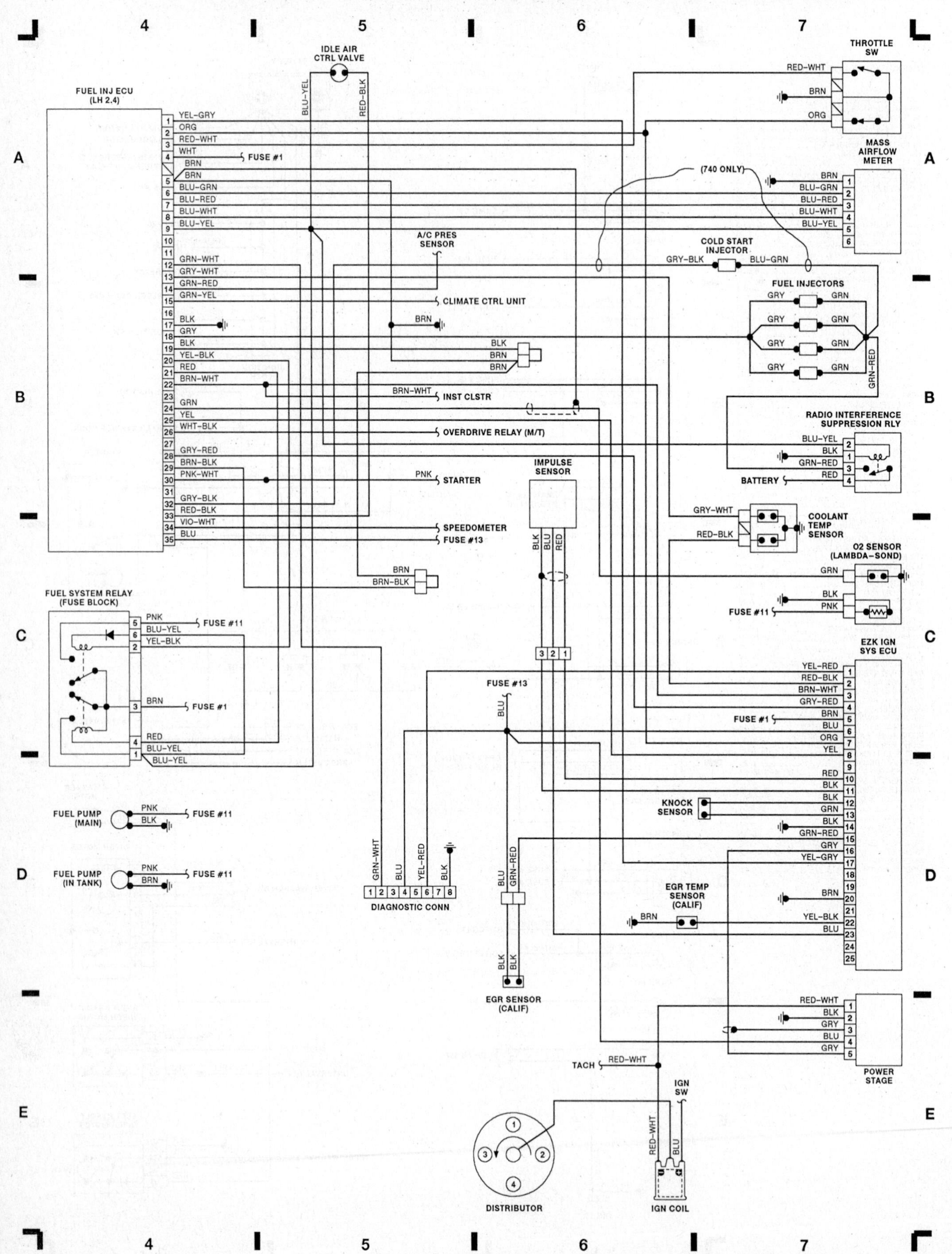

# 1991 WIRING DIAGRAMS
# 740 Series, 940GLE & 940 Turbo (Cont.)

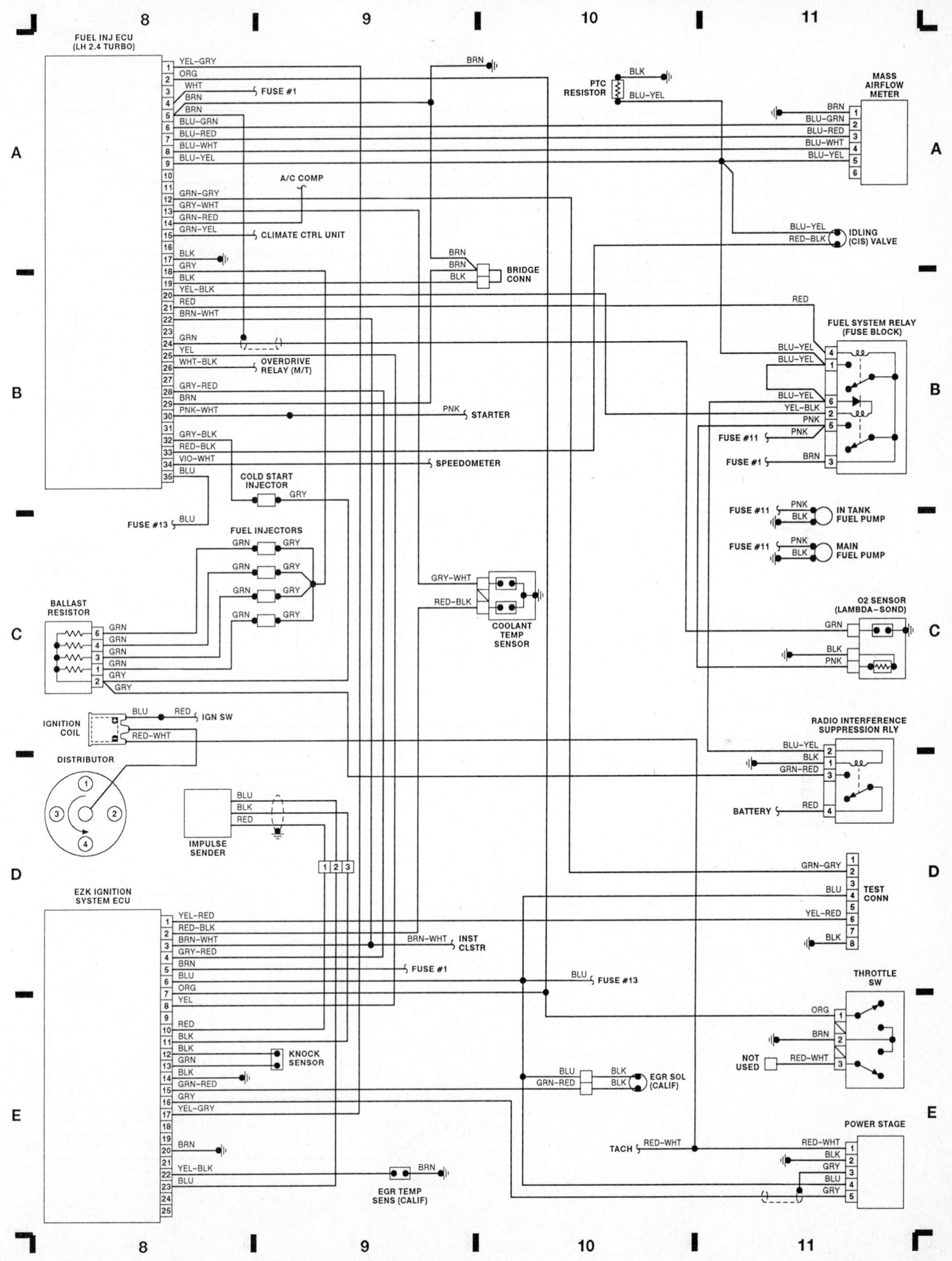

# 1991 WIRING DIAGRAMS
# 740 Series, 940GLE & 940 Turbo (Cont.)

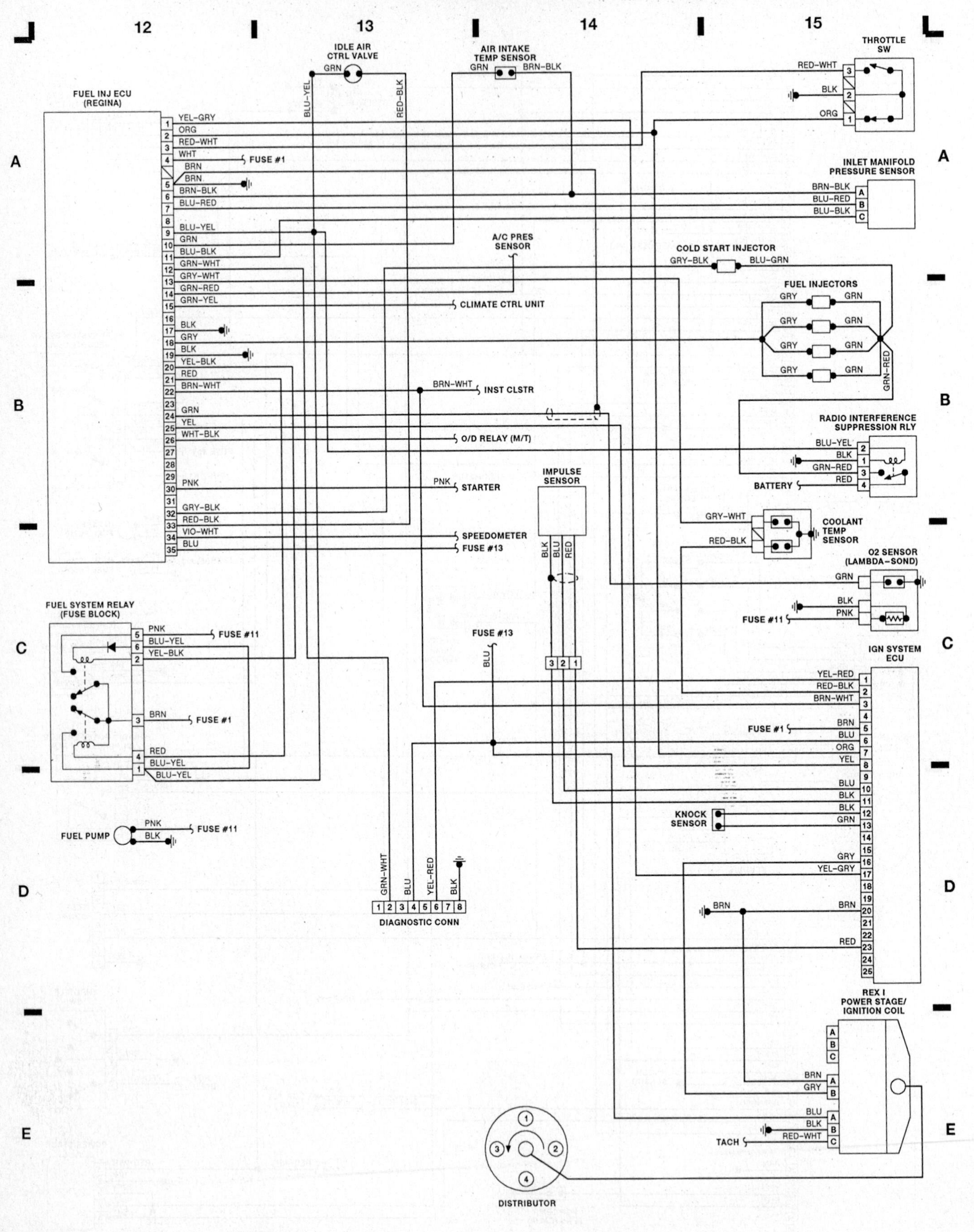

# 1991 WIRING DIAGRAMS
# 740 Series, 940GLE & 940 Turbo (Cont.)

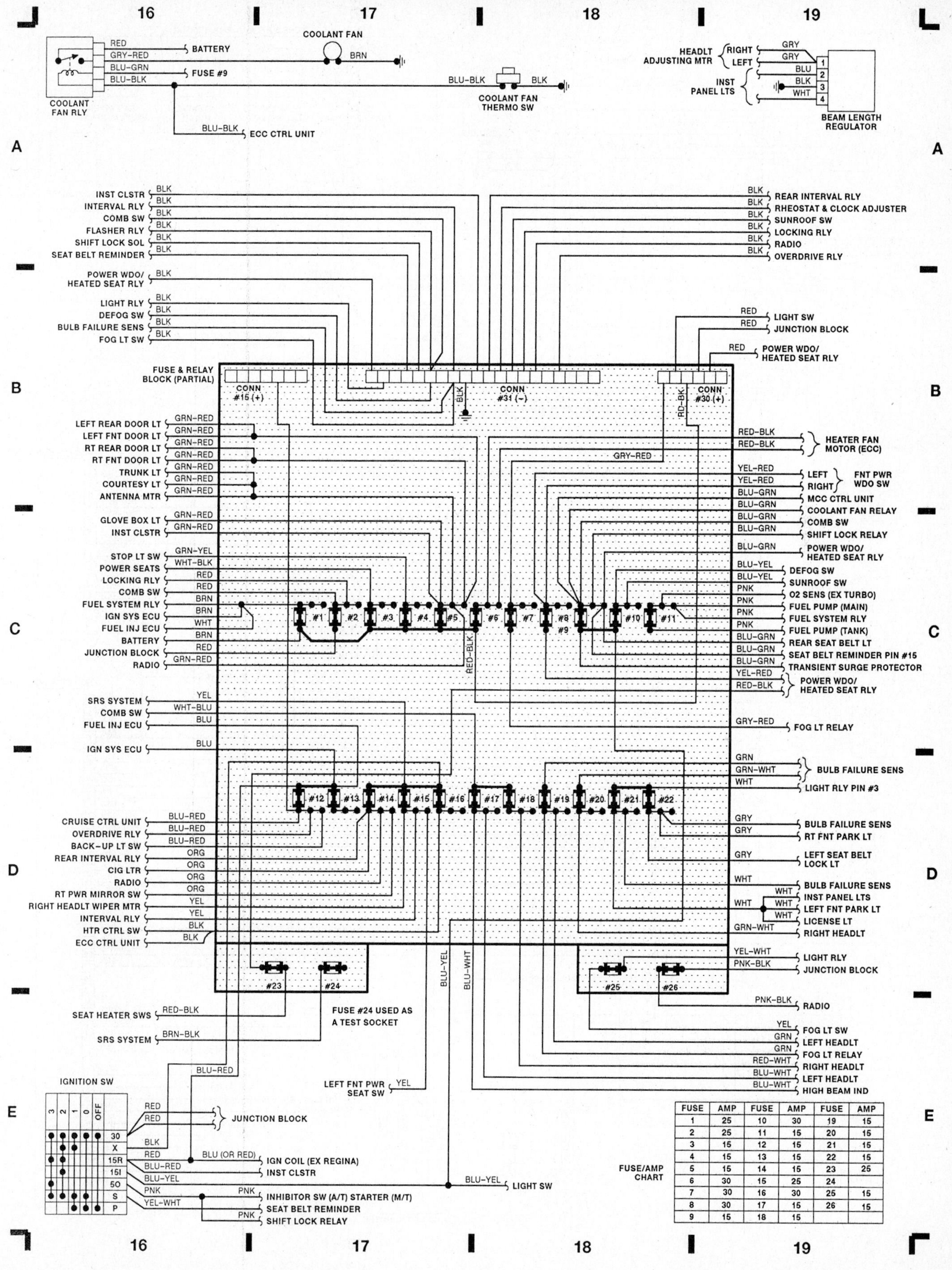


| FUSE | AMP | FUSE | AMP | FUSE | AMP |
|---|---|---|---|---|---|
| 1 | 25 | 10 | 30 | 19 | 15 |
| 2 | 25 | 11 | 15 | 20 | 15 |
| 3 | 15 | 12 | 15 | 21 | 15 |
| 4 | 15 | 13 | 15 | 22 | 15 |
| 5 | 15 | 14 | 15 | 23 | 25 |
| 6 | 30 | 15 | 25 | 24 | |
| 7 | 30 | 16 | 30 | 25 | 15 |
| 8 | 30 | 17 | 15 | 26 | 15 |
| 9 | 15 | 18 | 15 | | |

# 1991 WIRING DIAGRAMS
# 740 Series, 940GLE & 940 Turbo (Cont.)

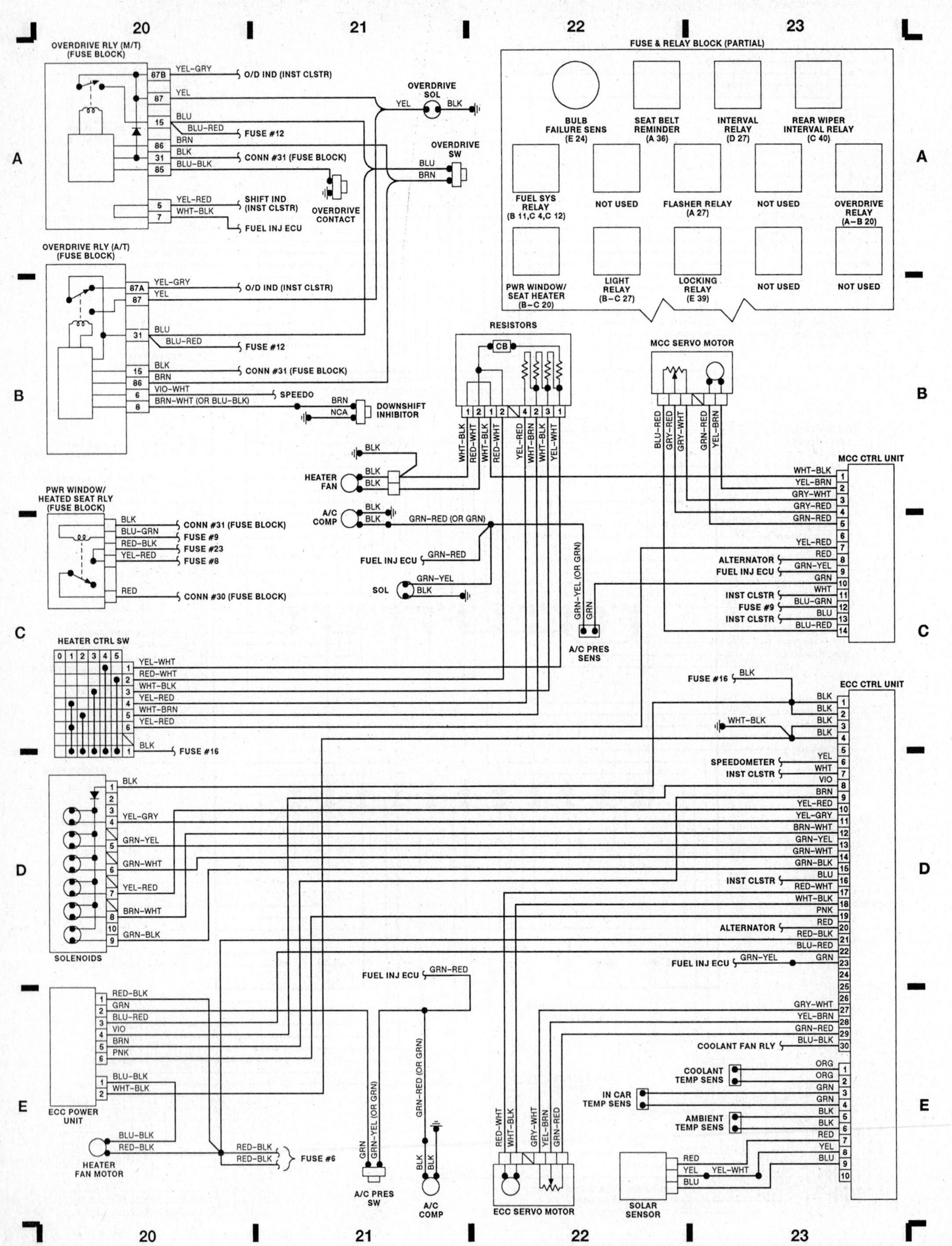

# 1991 WIRING DIAGRAMS
# 740 Series, 940GLE & 940 Turbo (Cont.)

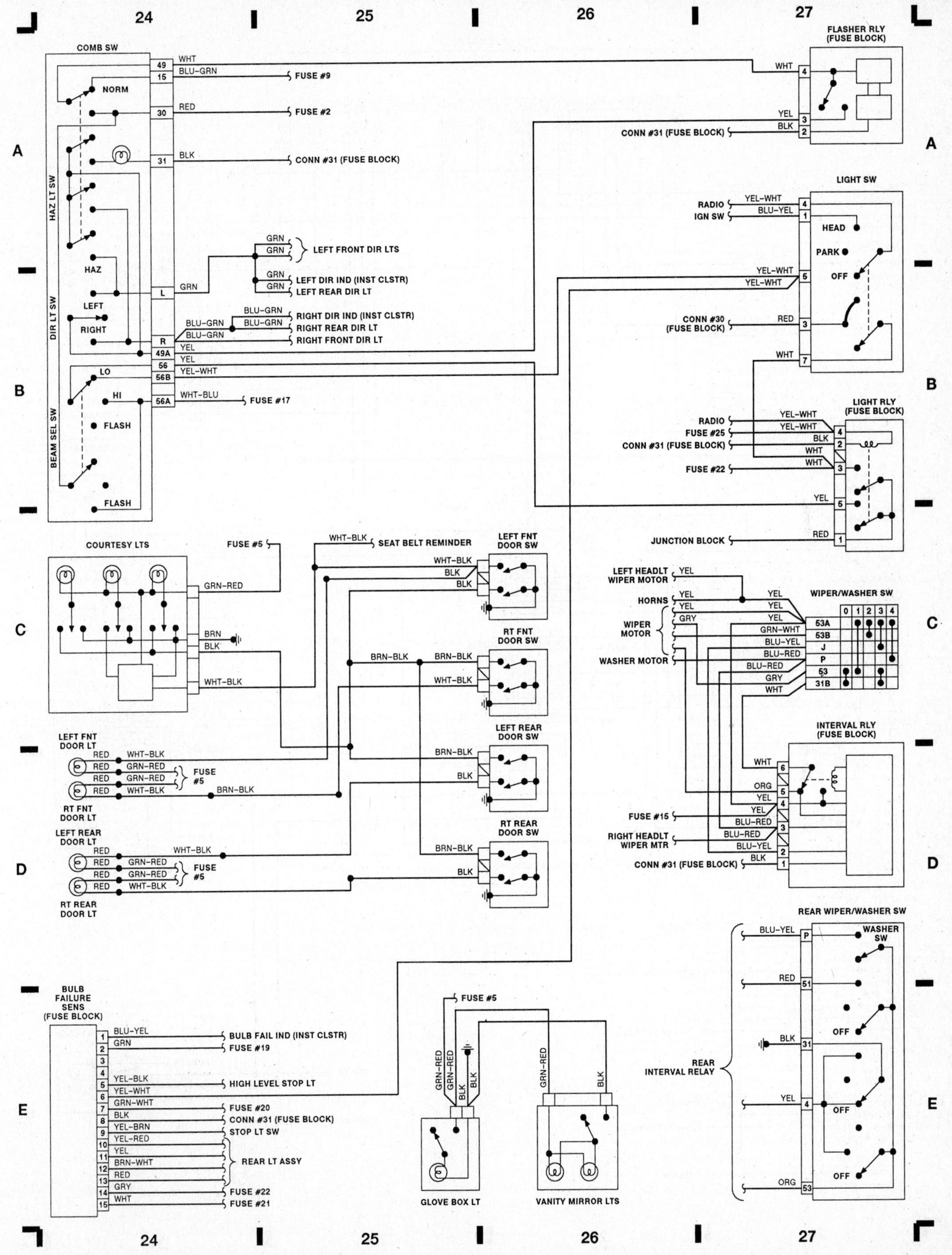

# 1991 WIRING DIAGRAMS
# 740 Series, 940GLE & 940 Turbo (Cont.)

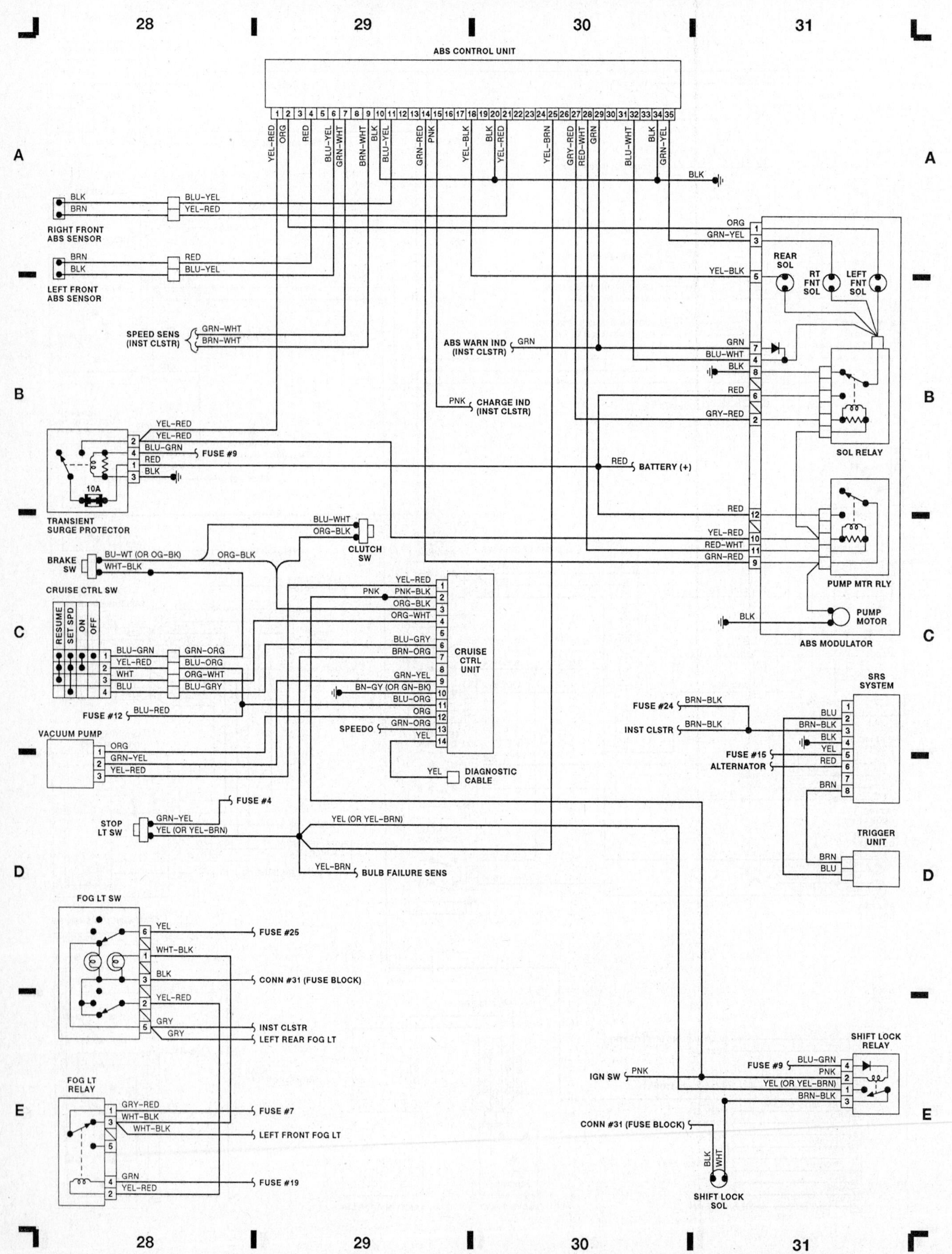

# 1991 WIRING DIAGRAMS
# 740 Series, 940GLE & 940 Turbo (Cont.)

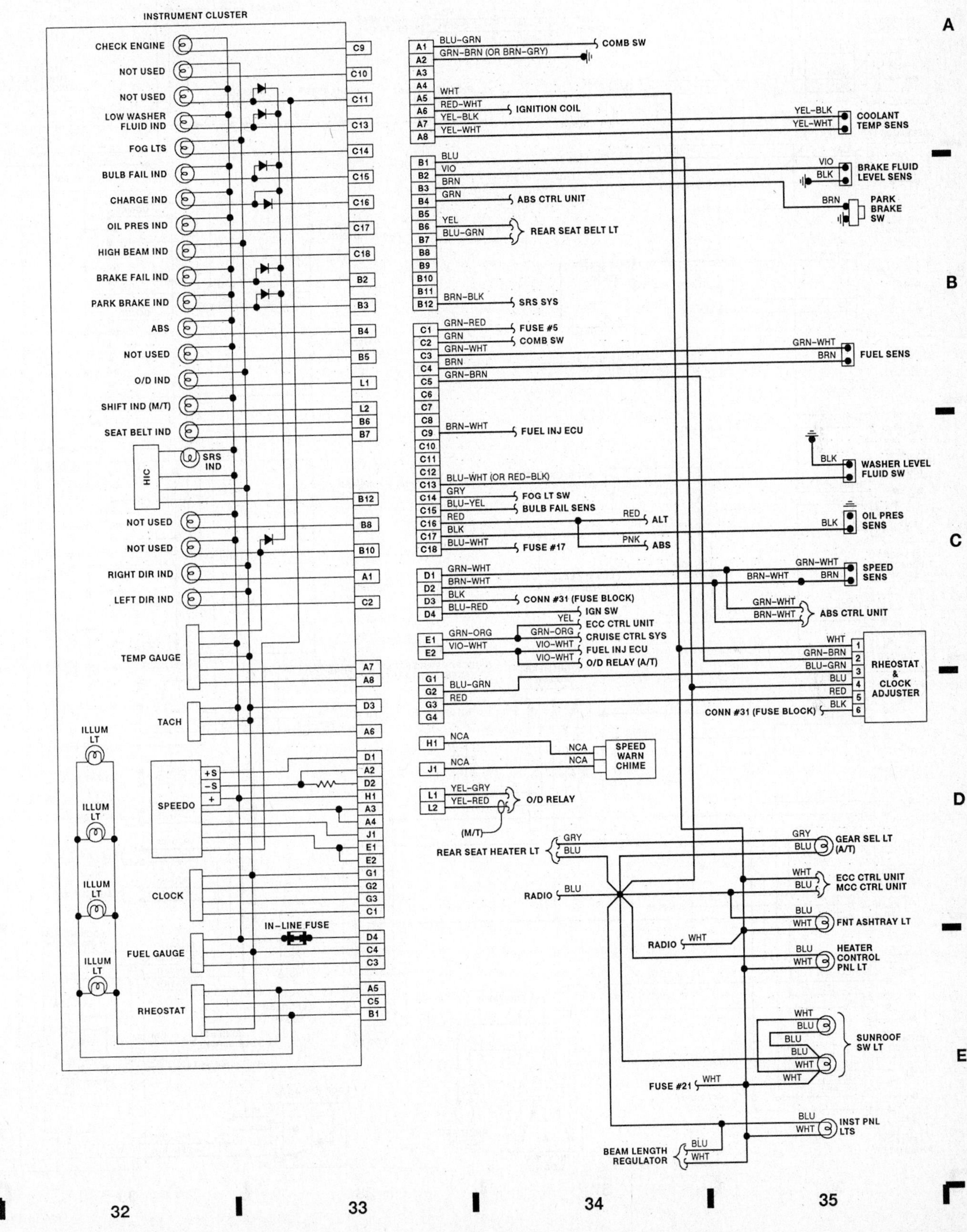

# 1991 WIRING DIAGRAMS
# 740 Series, 940GLE & 940 Turbo (Cont.)

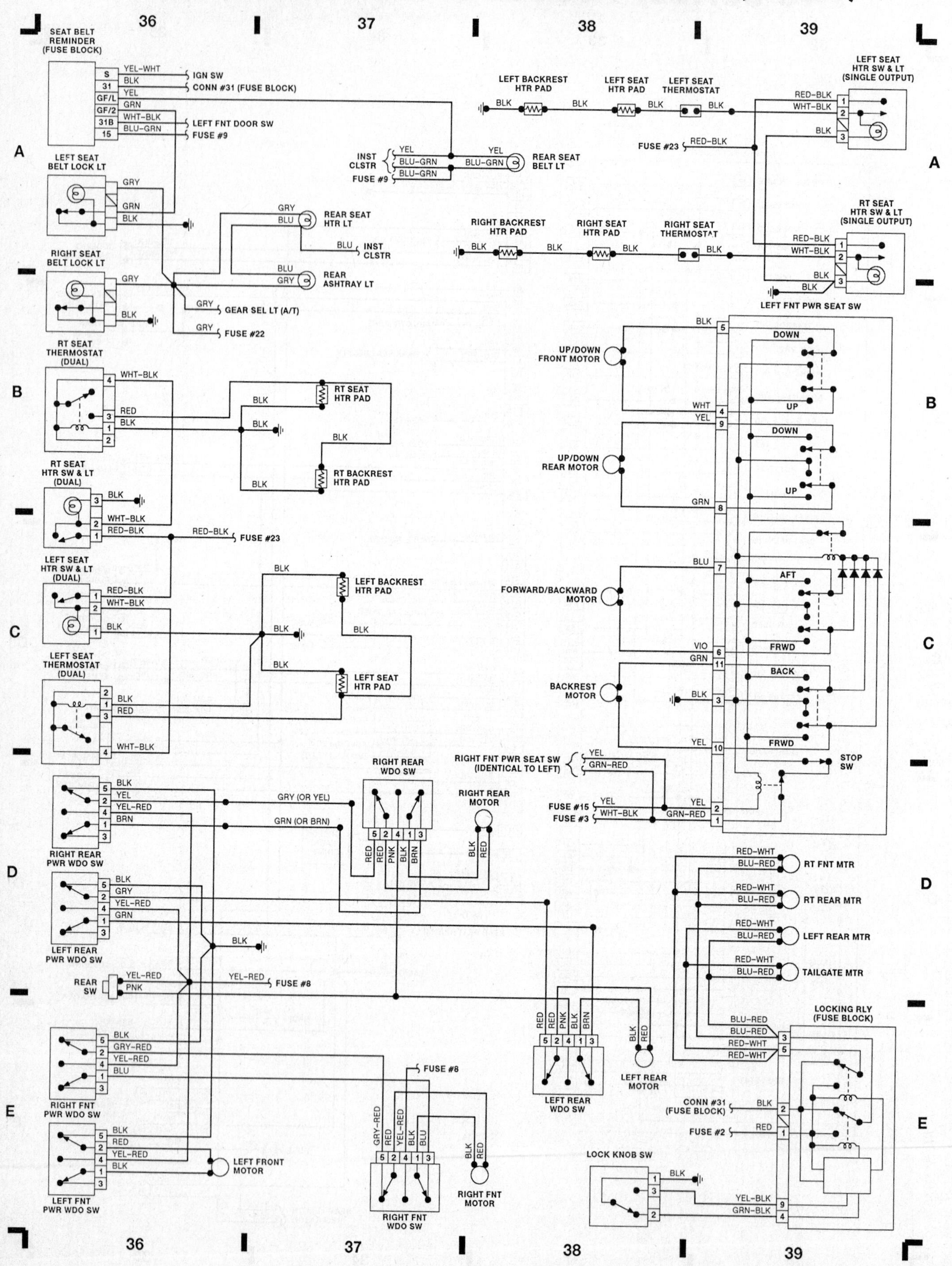

# 1991 WIRING DIAGRAMS
# 740 Series, 940GLE & 940 Turbo (Cont.)

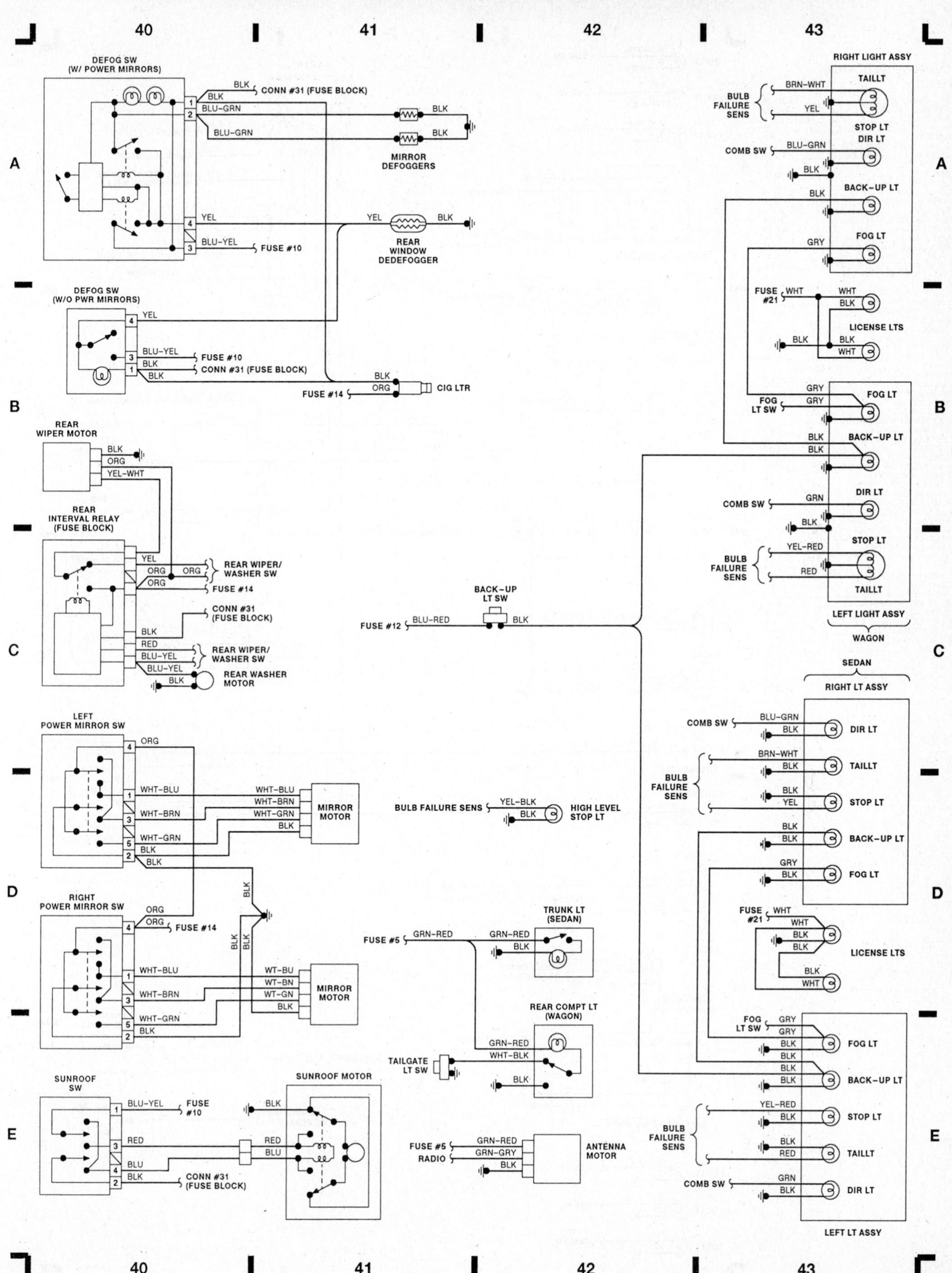

# 1991 WIRING DIAGRAMS
# 940SE

**COMPONENT LOCATOR:**

| Component | Location |
|---|---|
| ABS CTRL UNIT | A 21–22 |
| ABS MODULATOR | A–C 23 |
| ALTERNATOR | C 3 |
| BACK–UP LT SW | D 35 |
| BATTERY | A 2 |
| BEAM LENGTH REGULATOR | A 15 |
| CENTRAL LOCKING RELAY | E 31 |
| CIG LTR LT | E 8 |
| COMB SW | A–B 16 |
| COOLING FAN RELAY | C 3 |
| CRUISE CTRL SYSTEM | C 20–21 |
| DOOR WARN LTS | D–E 20 |
| ECC SYSTEM | C–E 12–15 |
| EZK IGNITION SYSTEM ECU | D–E 4 |
| FOG LT RELAY | B–C 16 |
| FOG LT SW | C 16 |
| FRONT BULB FAILURE SENS | C 31 |
| FRONT WIPER INTERVAL RELAY | D 19 |
| FRONT WIPER/WASHER MOTORS | D–E 3 |
| FRONT WIPER/WASHER SW | C 19 |
| FUEL INJ ECU (LH–JETRONIC) | A–B 4 |
| FUEL PUMP (IN TANK) | B 7 |
| FUEL PUMP (MAIN) | C 6 |
| FUEL SYSTEM RELAY | B 7 |
| FUSE BLOCK | A–E 9–10 |
| GEAR SEL SW LT | E 8 |
| GLOVE BOX LT & SW | E 16 |
| HEADLT RELAY | B 19 |
| HEADLT SW | A–B 19 |
| HORNS | C 1 |
| IGNITION COIL | C 4 |
| IGNITION SW | C 12 |
| INSTRUMENT CLUSTER | A–E 24–25 |
| INTERIOR LTS | E 25–26 |
| JUNCTION BLOCK | A 3 |
| LEFT HEADLT ADJUSTING MOTOR | D 1 |
| LEFT HEADLT WIPER | E 1 |
| LEFT SEAT HEATER SW & LT | C 28 |
| O/D RELAY | D–E 27 |
| POWER MIRROR SYSTEM | C–E 32–33 |
| POWER SEAT SW | A–C 31 |
| POWER WINDOW RELAY | D 16 |
| POWER WINDOW SYSTEM | D–E 28–30 |
| RADIO INTERFERENCE SUPPRESSION RELAY | D 7 |
| REAR ASHTRAY LT | E 8 |
| REAR BULB FAILURE SENS | B–C 32 |
| REAR WINDOW DEFOGGER SYSTEM | A–B 32–33 |
| REAR WIPER INTERVAL RELAY | E 17 |
| REAR WIPER MOTOR | E 17 |
| REAR WIPER/WASHER SW | D–E 19 |
| RELAY BOX | A–B 12–14 |
| RHEOSTAT & CLOCK ADJUSTER | C–D 27 |
| RIGHT HEADLT ADJUSTING MOTOR | B 1 |
| RIGHT HEADLT WIPER | A 1 |
| RIGHT SEAT HTR SW & LT | B 28 |
| SEAT BELT REMINDER | A 30 |
| SEAT HEATER SW LT | E 8 |
| SHIFT LOCK SYSTEM | E 26–27 |
| SPEED SENS | C 27 |
| SRS SYSTEM | C 22–23 |
| STARTER | B 3 |
| STOP LT SW | D 20 |
| TRANSIENT SURGE PROTECTOR | B 20 |
| VANITY MIRROR LTS | E 16 |

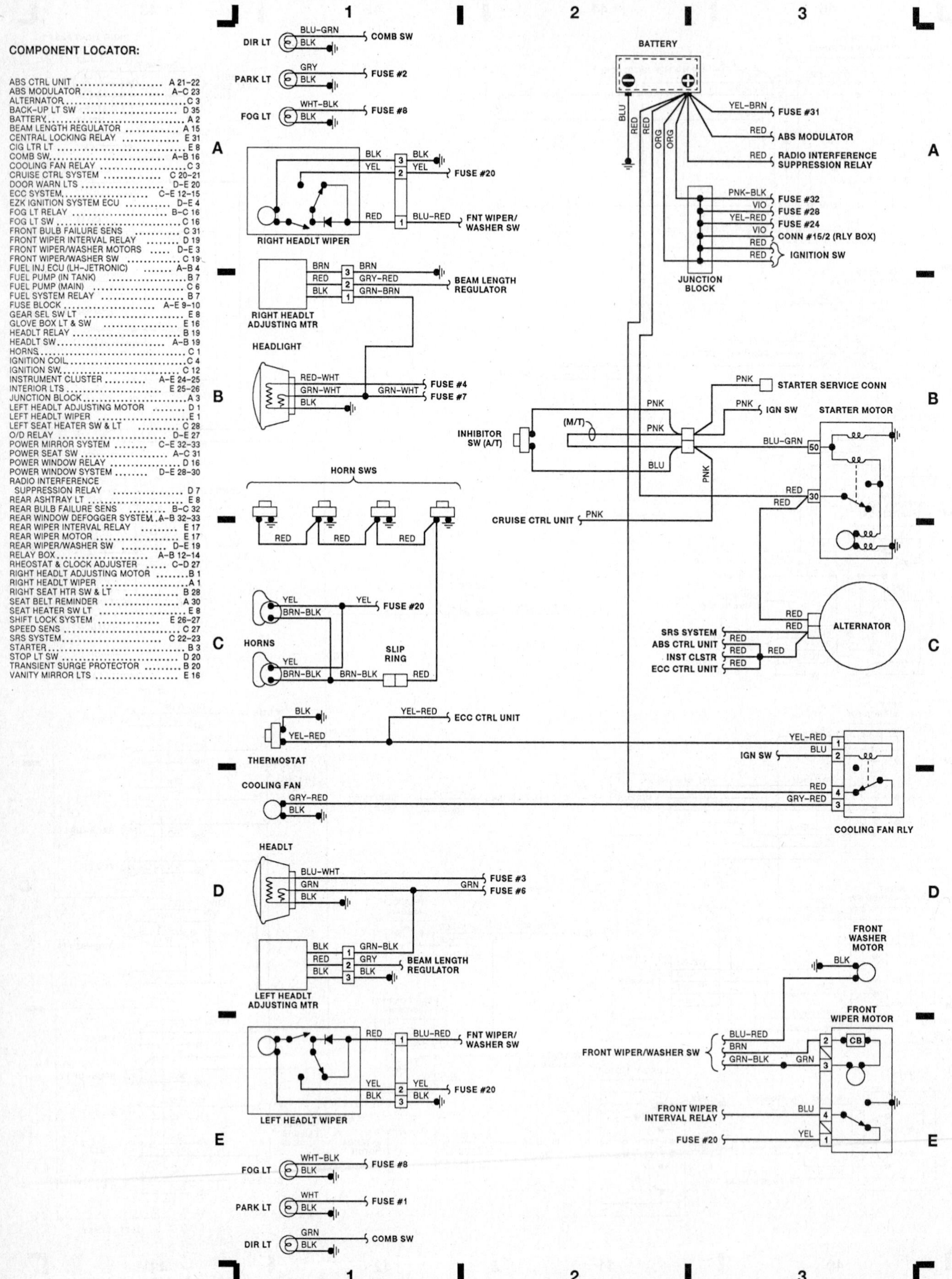

# 1991 WIRING DIAGRAMS
# 940SE (Cont.)

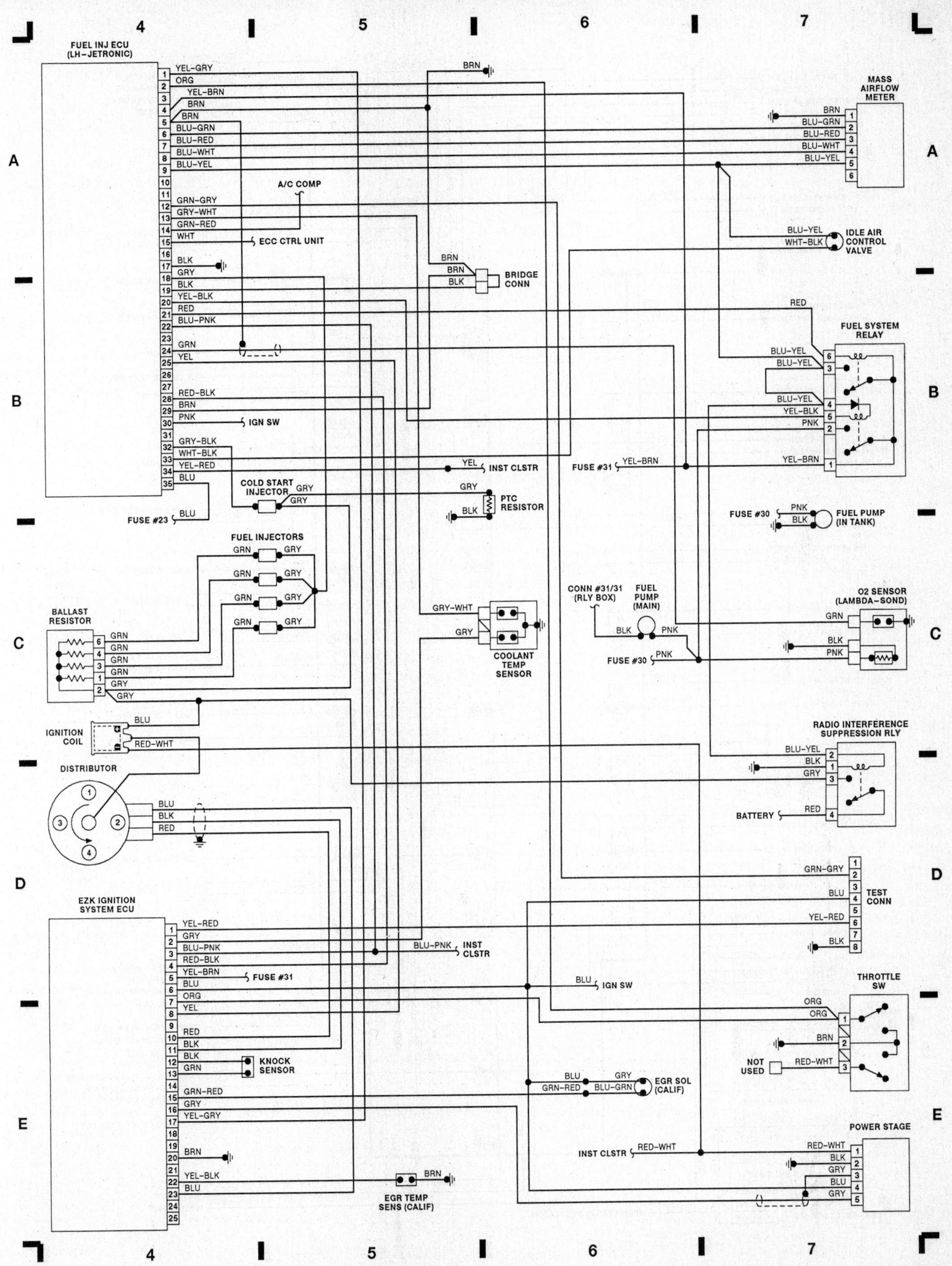

# 1991 WIRING DIAGRAMS
# 940SE (Cont.)

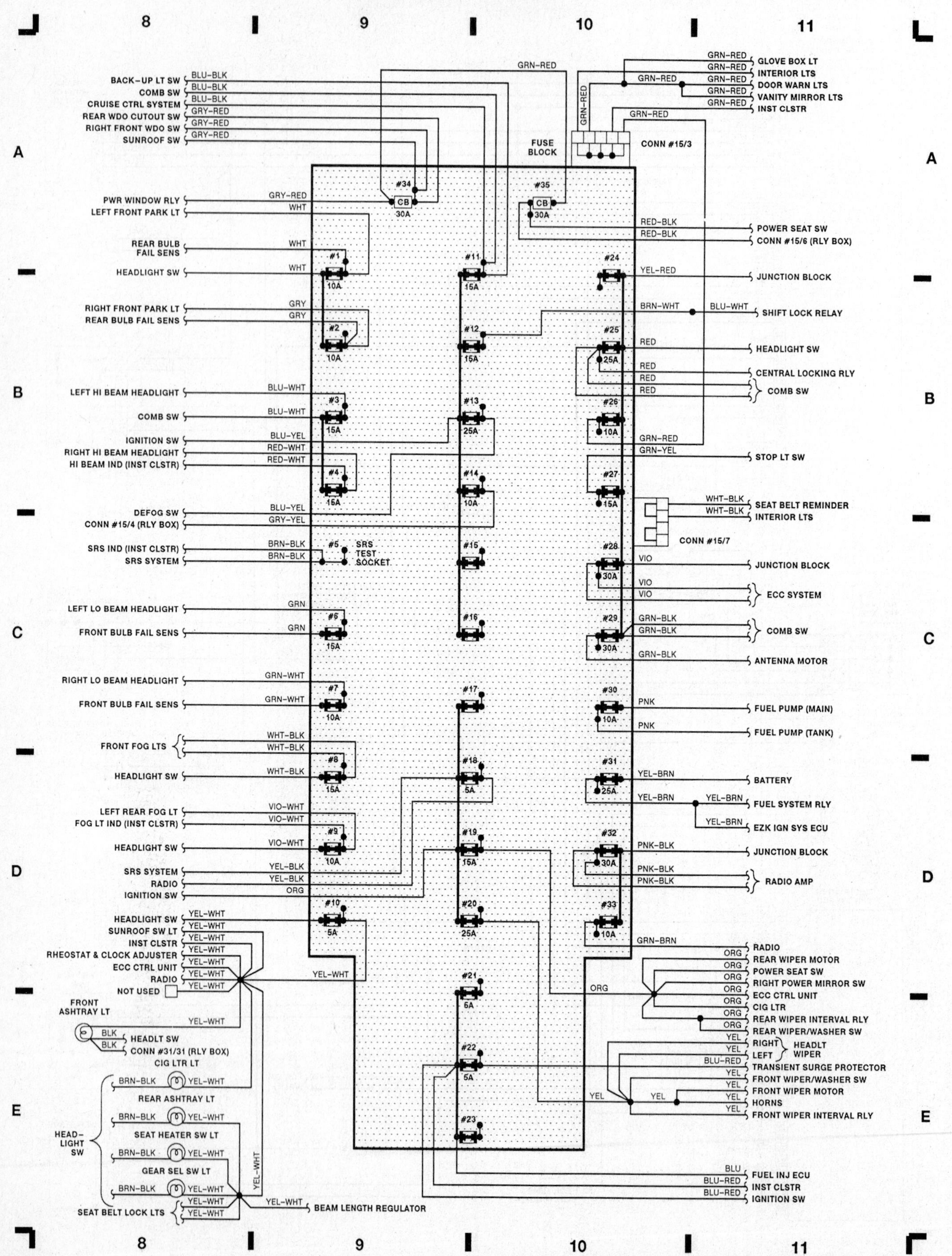

# 1991 WIRING DIAGRAMS
# 940SE (Cont.)

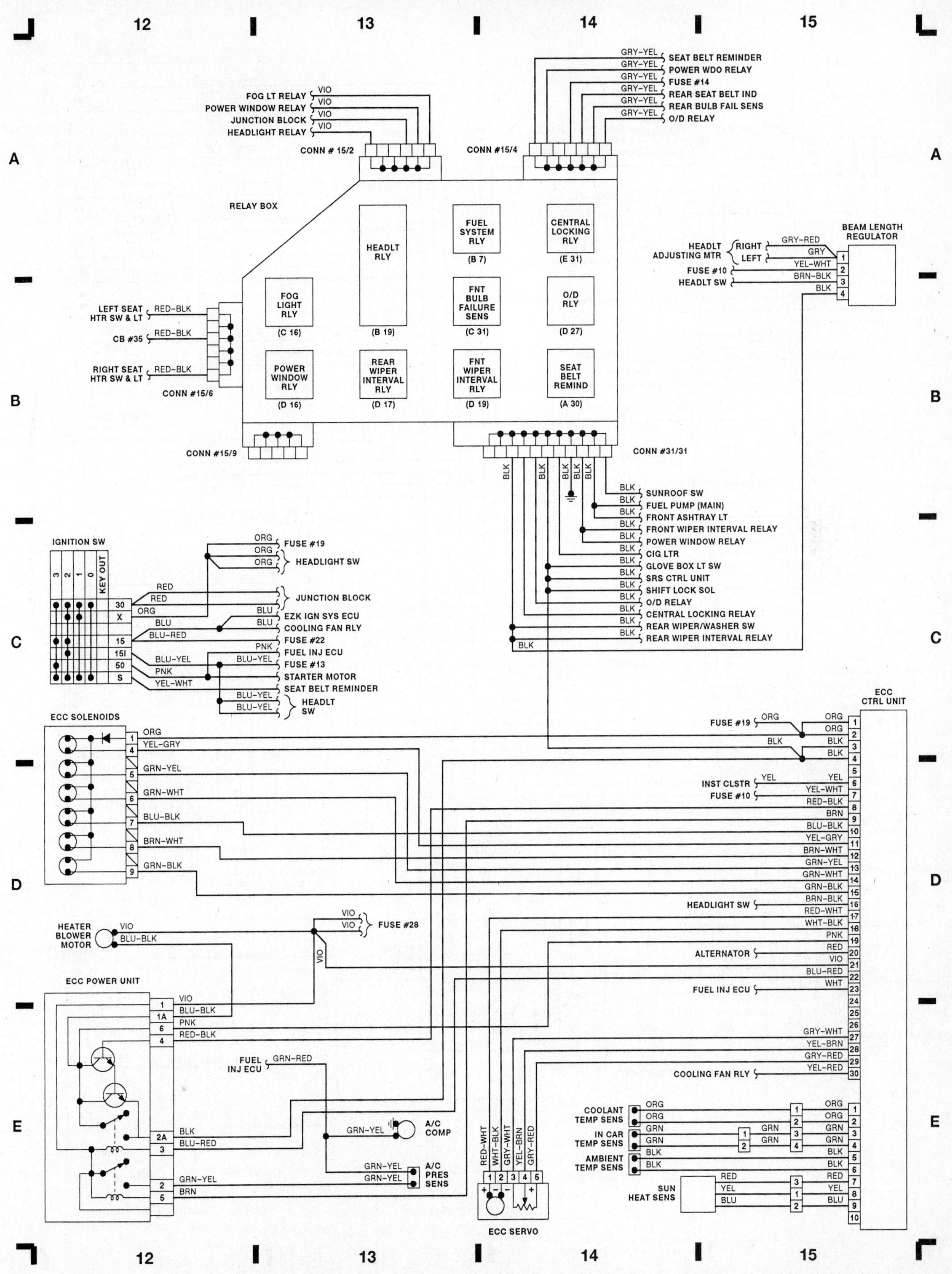

# 1991 WIRING DIAGRAMS
# 940SE (Cont.)

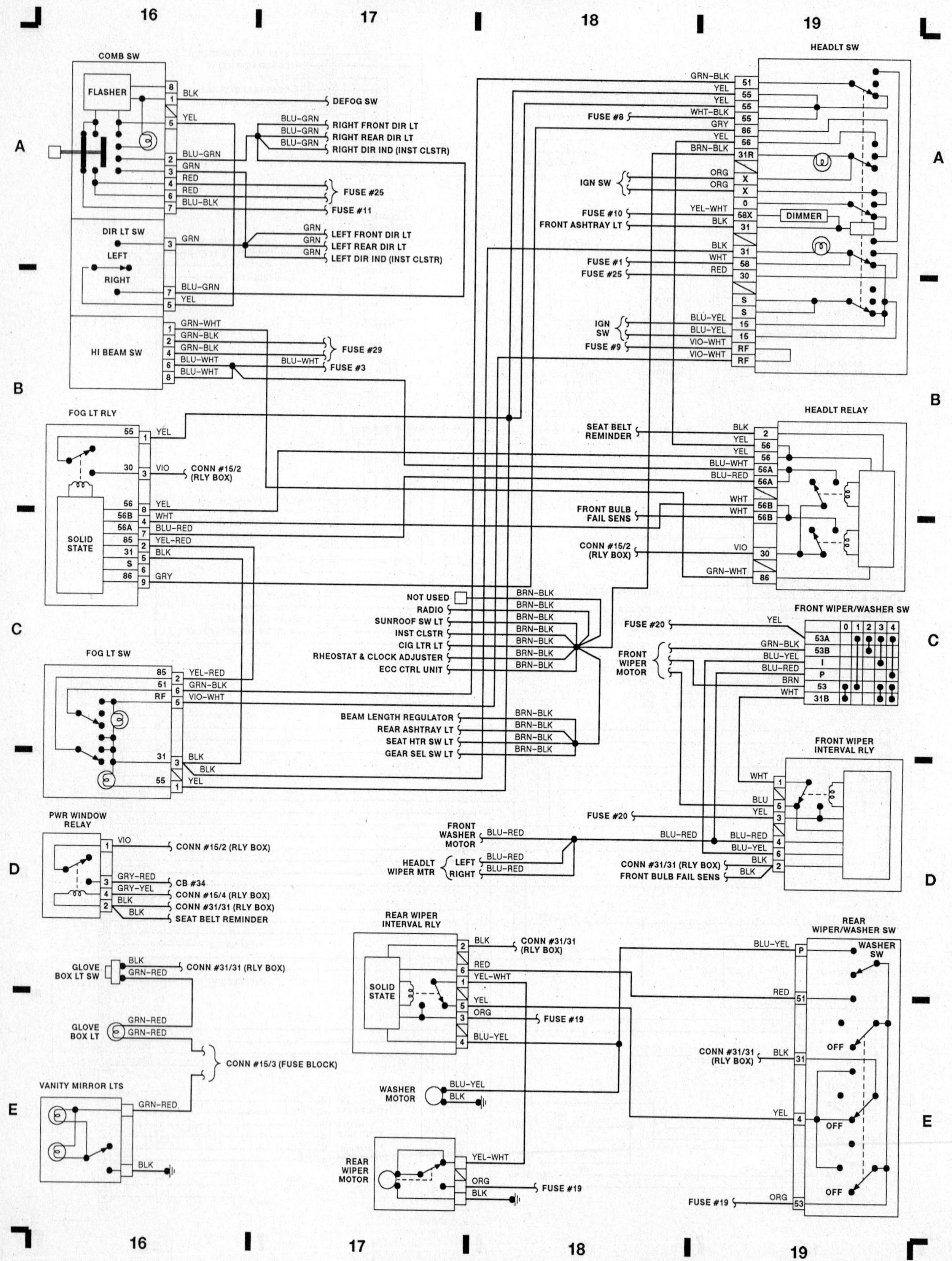

# 1991 WIRING DIAGRAMS
# 940SE (Cont.)

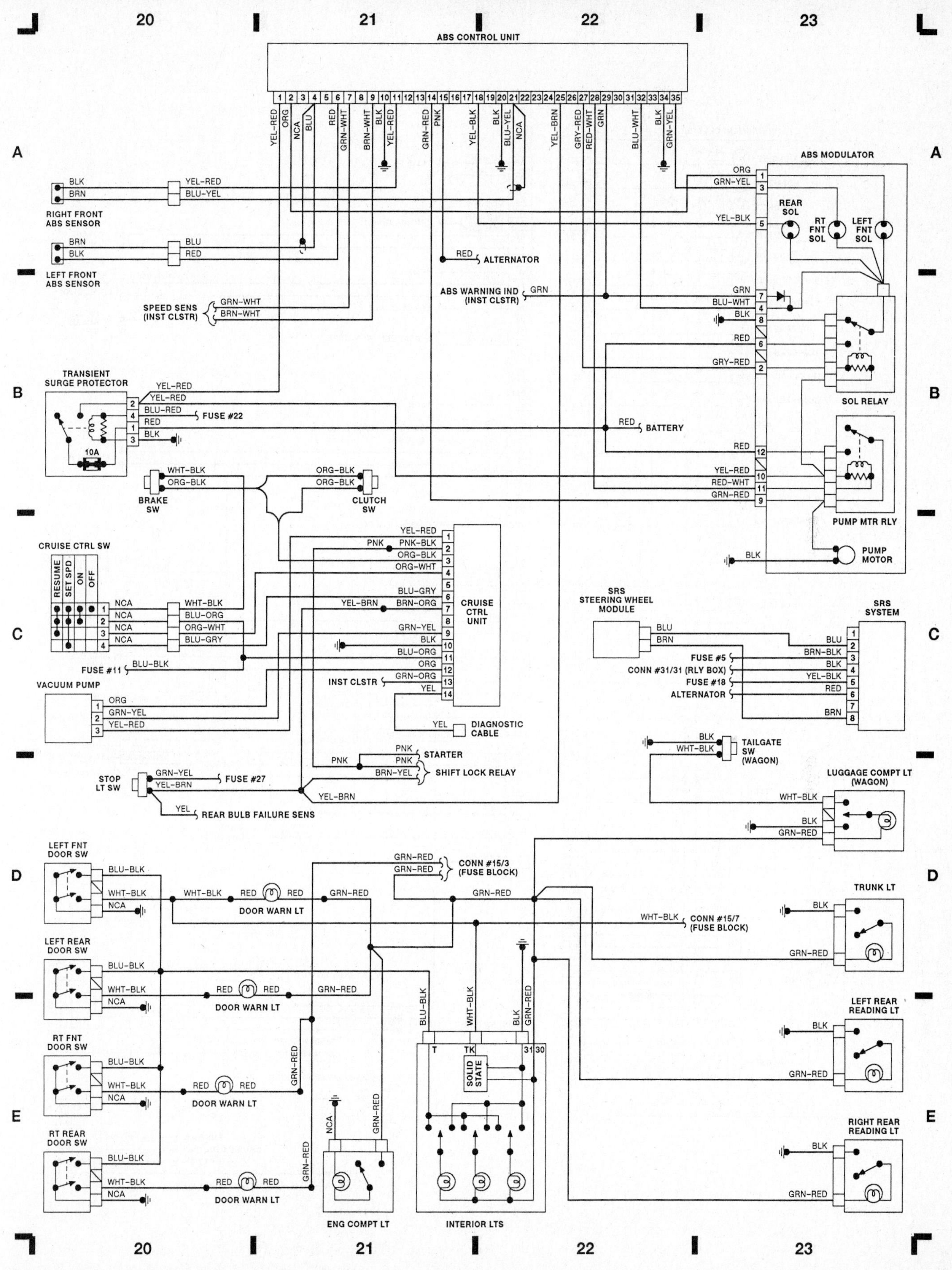

# 1991 WIRING DIAGRAMS
# 940SE (Cont.)

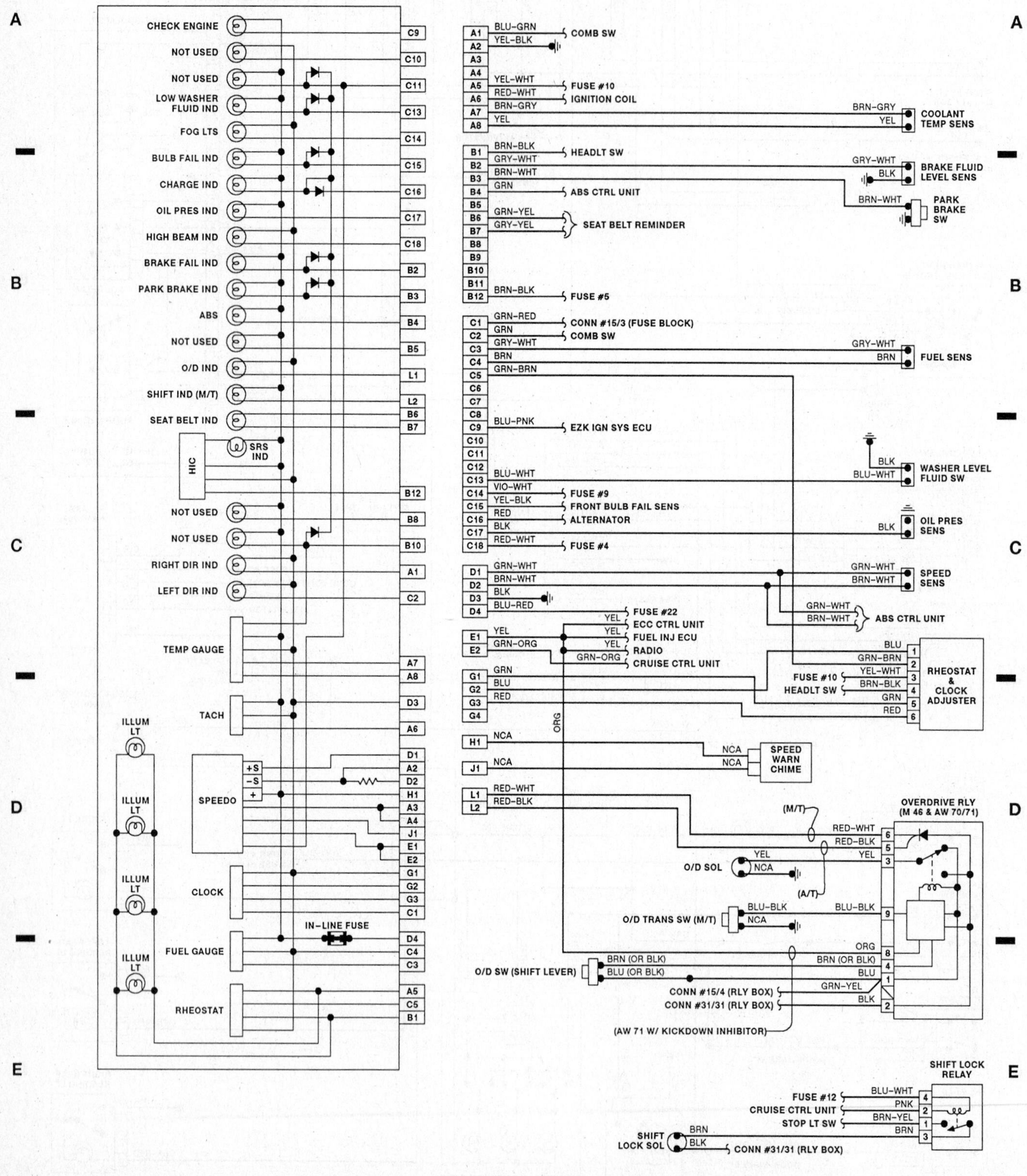

# 1991 WIRING DIAGRAMS
# 940SE (Cont.)

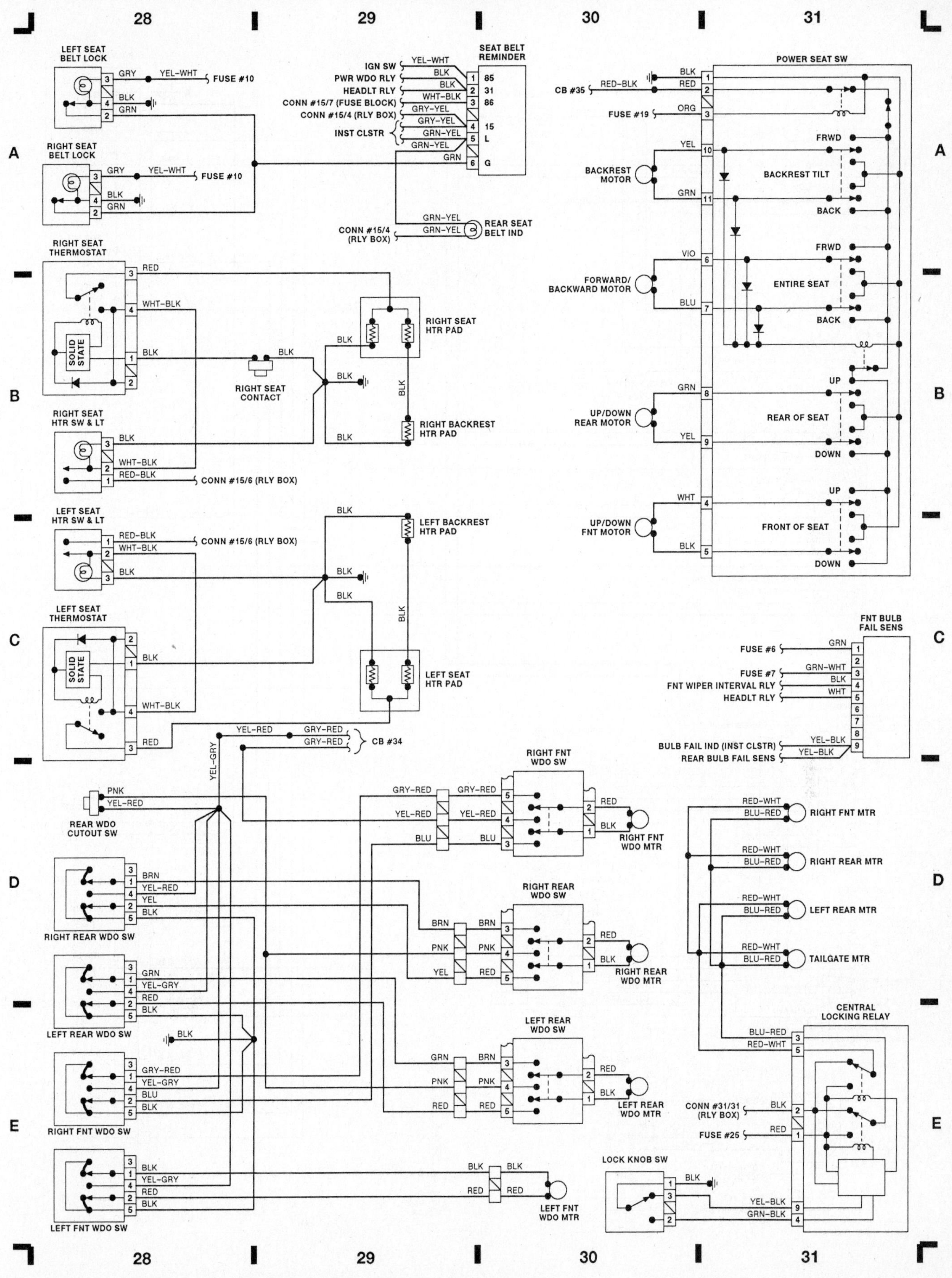

# 1991 WIRING DIAGRAMS
# 940SE (Cont.)

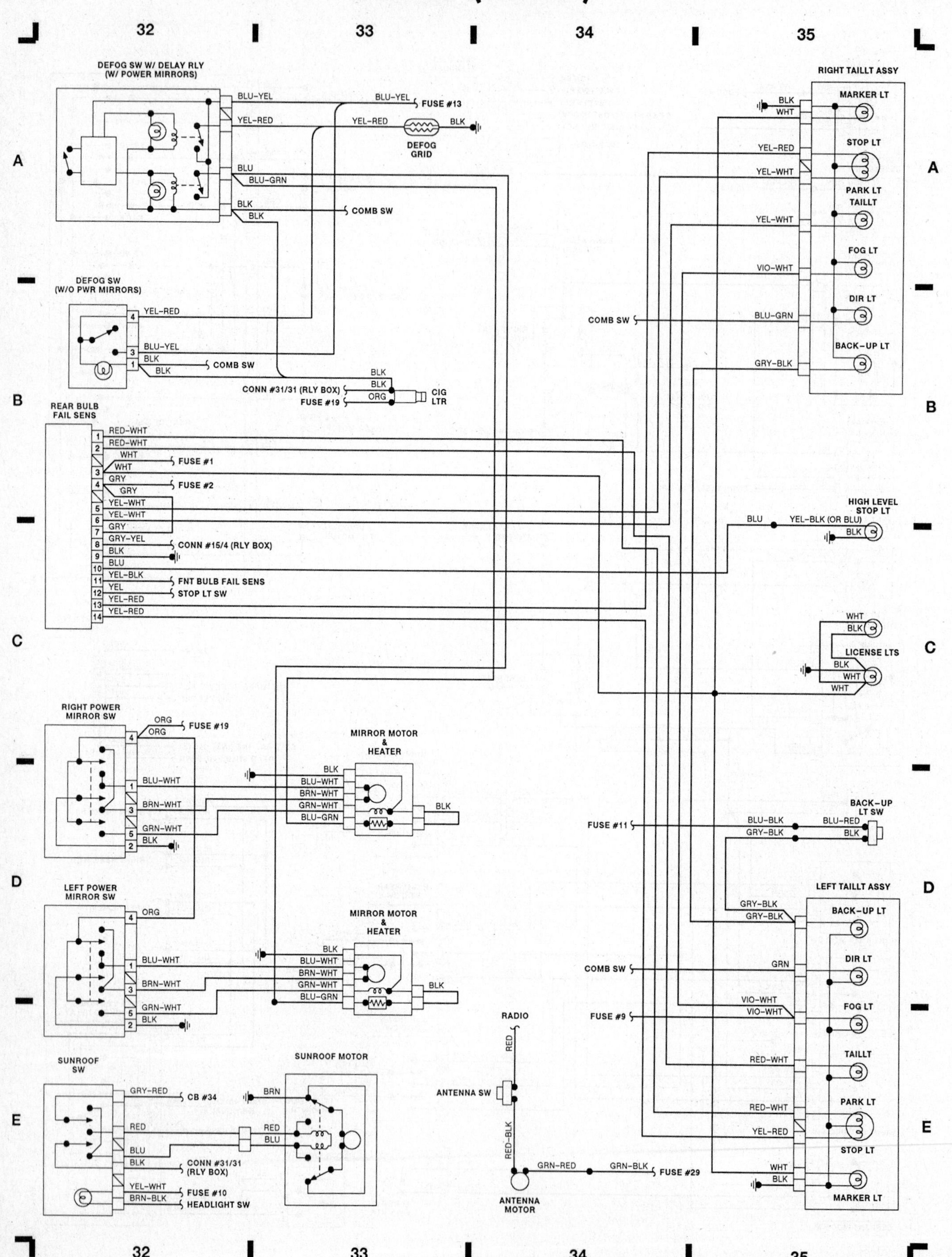

# 1991 SAFETY EQUIPMENT
# Air Bag Restraint System

## 240, 740, 940

***WARNING: To avoid injury from accidental air bag deployment, read and carefully follow all WARNINGS and SERVICE PRECAUTIONS.***

***NOTE: For information on air bag DIAGNOSIS & TESTING or DISPOSAL PROCEDURES, see MITCHELL'S AIR BAG SERVICE & REPAIR MANUAL, DOMESTIC & IMPORTED MODELS***

## DESCRIPTION & OPERATION

The main components of the Supplemental Restraint System (SRS) include an air bag/gas generator module mounted on steering wheel, contact reel (clockspring) mounted in steering column, crash sensor and standby power unit mounted under driver's seat, and SRS warning light on instrument panel.

If vehicle's deceleration recorded by crash sensor is sufficiently high, crash sensor delivers a voltage charge triggering gas generator. Gas generator then produces a quantity of non-toxic nitrogen, which fills air bag in a few hundredths of a second. Immediately after air bag inflates, gas is released through a ventilation hole on rear of air bag module, causing air bag to collapse. The entire sequence of air bag inflation and collapse takes about 0.2 seconds.

### AIR BAG MODULE

Air bag module consists of an inflatable air bag, gas generator and ignitor. Gas generator and ignitor make up the inflator unit, which is mounted to rear of air bag module. A two-pole connector with gold-plated terminals is mounted to inflator unit. If connector is disconnected for any reason, a safety shorting spring inside connector spreads open, touching both terminals and preventing accidental air bag deployment by static electricity or careless handling.

### CONTACT REEL (CLOCKSPRING)

Contact reel is a spirally-wound wire coil mounted to steering column. Contact reel unit is not a slip ring-type connection. Contact reel ensures the most reliable contact possible between gas generator and crash sensor.

### CRASH SENSOR

Crash sensor triggers air bag module inflation by measuring and recording deceleration of vehicle. Crash sensor also functions as a diagnostic monitor, which continuously monitors SRS operation and records any faults in SRS. Crash sensor incorporates an electrical sensor (to detect deceleration), a mercury switch, a microprocessor and a memory (to retain information if power supply fails).

Electrical sensor records the combination of "G" force and change in speed (deceleration). Both high "G" force and prolonged deceleration are required to activate SRS. Consequently the crash sensor cannot be activated by a hammer blow or other similar influence, which only produces a high "G" force for a short time.

The sharp deceleration produced during a collision causes the mercury switch to close, while electrical sensor simultaneously determines whether or not the impact is sufficiently serious to trigger gas generator. Operation of gas generator requires collision detection in both the mercury switch and electrical sensor.

To ensure correct operation of crash sensor, crash sensor must be properly secured to floor (securely grounded). The crash sensor is grounded by a short Black wire connected to one of crash sensor's mounting screws. SRS is monitored continuously by a microprocessor in the crash sensor, regardless of ignition switch position or engine operation.

Crash sensor will illuminate instrument panel SRS warning light until a fault is corrected and crash sensor memory is cleared. Crash sensor is powered by standby power unit if normal power source (battery voltage) is interrupted.

### ELECTRICAL SYSTEM

SRS harness connectors are Orange and Yellow. The SRS connectors between air bag module and crash sensor have gold plated terminals for maximum conductivity. These colored connectors contain a safety shorting spring. When connectors are disconnected, spring spreads open to touch both terminals, preventing accidental deployment of air bag by static electricity or careless handling.

### SRS WARNING LIGHT

When ignition is turned on, SRS warning light will illuminate. If no SRS faults are detected, SRS warning light will go out after about 10 seconds or immediately after engine is started. If SRS warning light does not go out, a fault exists in system. When SRS detects a fault, warning light will remain on until fault is corrected and memory is cleared. If warning light fails to illuminate, bulb is faulty and/or a short exists in wire to bulb.

### STANDBY POWER UNIT

Standby power unit is used to supply power to crash sensor if normal power source (battery voltage) is interrupted.

## SYSTEM OPERATION CHECK

Turn ignition switch to ON position (engine not running). If no fault codes are present, SRS warning light should go out after 10 seconds. Following conditions indicate SRS system is malfunctioning and an SRS fault code will be stored in crash sensor memory:

- SRS light does not illuminate.
- SRS light does not go out after 10 seconds.
- SRS light does not go out after engine is started.
- SRS light comes on while driving.

## SERVICE PRECAUTIONS

Observe these precautions when working with air bag systems:

- Always disable SRS before performing any air bag repairs. See DISABLING & ACTIVATING AIR BAG SYSTEM.
- Always wear safety glasses and gloves when handling a deployed air bag module. Air bag module may contain sodium hydroxide deposits, which irritates skin.
- Use caution when handling sensors. Never strike or jar sensors. All sensors and mounting bracket bolts must be tightened carefully to ensure proper sensor operation.
- Never apply power to SRS if a sensor is not securely attached to vehicle.
- To avoid accidental air bag deployment when trouble shooting SRS, DO NOT use self-powered electrical test equipment, such as battery-powered or AC-powered voltmeter, ohmmeter, etc. Wiring repairs should not be performed on any portion of SRS wiring circuit.
- Always handle air bag module with trim cover away from your body. Always place air bag module on workbench with trim cover facing up, away from loose objects.

## DISABLING & ACTIVATING AIR BAG SYSTEM

***WARNING: NEVER disconnect crash sensor connector or standby power unit to disable SRS system.***

**1)** Before proceeding, follow air bag service precautions. See SERVICE PRECAUTIONS. Before performing any repairs, disconnect and shield negative battery cable.

**2)** Locate and disconnect Orange and Yellow SRS connectors on driver's side of center console, under carpet. *See Fig. 1.* DO NOT disconnect harness connection at crash sensor or air bag will deploy.

# 1991 SAFETY EQUIPMENT
# Air Bag Restraint System (Cont.)

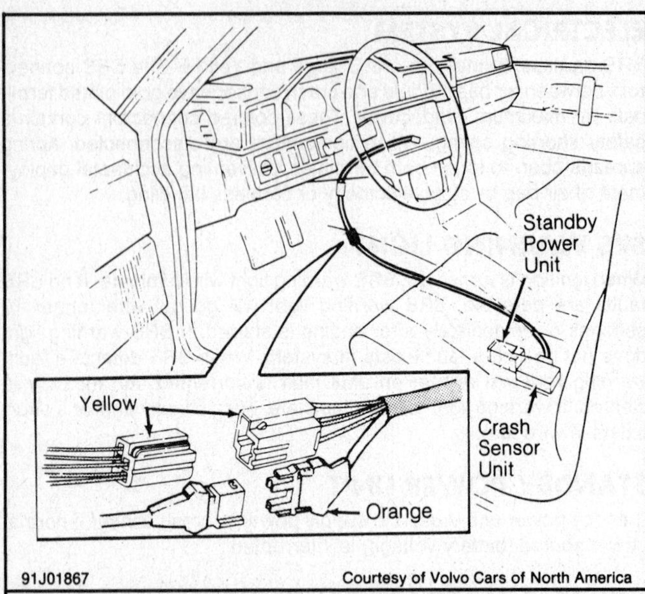


***Fig. 1: Locating SRS Disabling Connectors (740 Is Shown; Other Models Are Similar)***

**3)** After repairs, ensure all wiring and component connectors are reconnected. To activate air bag system, reconnect Orange and Yellow SRS connectors on driver's side of center console, under carpet. Reconnect negative battery cable. Check SRS warning light to ensure system is functioning properly. See SYSTEM OPERATION CHECK.

## REMOVAL & INSTALLATION

***WARNING: Failure to follow air bag service precautions may result in air bag deployment and personal injury. See SERVICE PRECAUTIONS. After component replacement, always perform a system operation check to ensure proper system operation. See SYSTEM OPERATION CHECK.***

### AIR BAG MODULE

***NOTE: If air bag deployed during a collision, contact reel and steering wheel must also be replaced.***

**Removal & Installation – 1)** Before proceeding, follow air bag service precautions. See SERVICE PRECAUTIONS. Disable SRS before removal. See DISABLING & ACTIVATING AIR BAG SYSTEM.
**2)** Turn ignition key to position No. 1 to disengage steering column lock. Remove steering column lower cover panel and knee bolster assembly. Remove 2 Torx No. 30 screws from rear of steering wheel. *See Fig. 2.*

**3)** Pull air bag module away from steering wheel just enough to disconnect wiring connector. To install, reverse removal procedure. Tighten air bag module bolts. See TORQUE SPECIFICATIONS table at end of article.
**4)** Reactivate SRS. See DISABLING & ACTIVATING AIR BAG SYSTEM. Check SRS warning light to ensure system is functioning properly. See SYSTEM OPERATION CHECK. If an air bag module fault code exists after replacing air bag module, see MITCHELL'S AIR BAG SERVICE & REPAIR MANUAL, DOMESTIC & IMPORTED MODELS.

### CRASH SENSOR & STANDBY POWER UNIT

**Removal & Installation (240) – 1)** Before proceeding, follow air bag service precautions. See SERVICE PRECAUTIONS. Before replacing crash sensor, check ground connection at Black wire terminal at crash

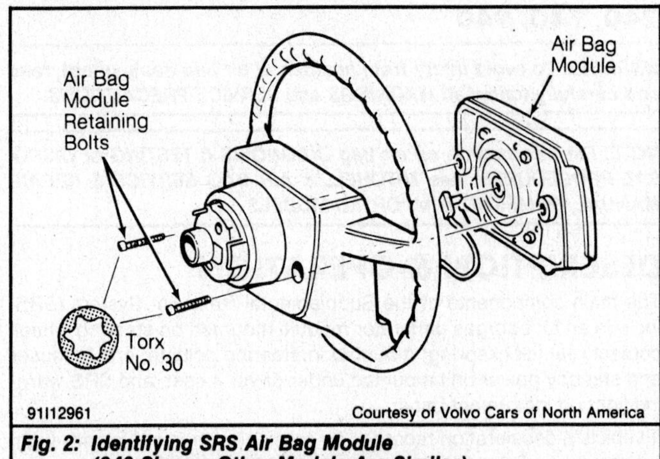


***Fig. 2: Identifying SRS Air Bag Module (240 Shown; Other Models Are Similar)***

sensor retaining screw. Crash sensor and standby power unit are located under driver's seat.

***NOTE: Before replacing crash sensor, check for poor ground connection at crash sensor. See Fig. 3. Crash sensor may still be good. Repair as required. Perform SYSTEM OPERATION CHECK to verify repair.***

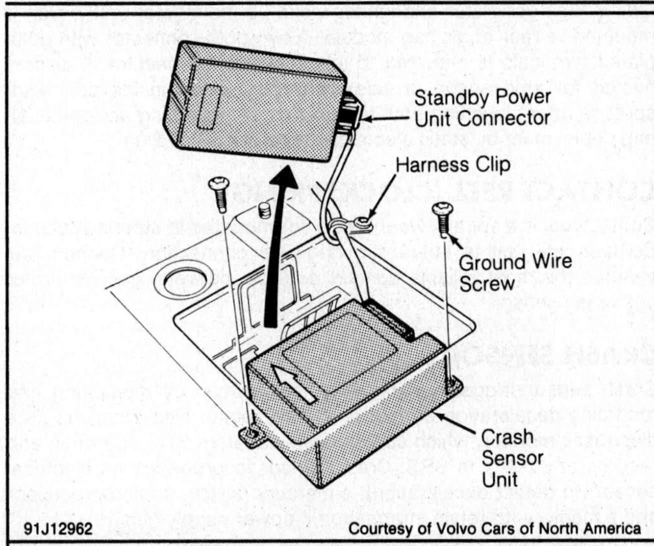


***Fig. 3: Identifying Standby Power Unit & Crash Sensor (240)***

**2)** Disable SRS before crash sensor or standby power unit removal. See DISABLING & ACTIVATING AIR BAG SYSTEM. Unbolt driver's seat guide rails from floor. Disconnect seat wiring connectors, and tilt seat rearward. Lift carpet to expose crash sensor unit.
**3)** Remove tape from standby power unit, and disconnect connector. Remove standby power unit by releasing clip. Remove crash sensor retaining screws and harness clamp. DO NOT disconnect harness connector from crash sensor. Remove crash sensor and wiring harness as an assembly.
**4)** To install, reverse removal procedure. Crash sensor connector is held in position by a fixture which is part of vehicle body. Install crash sensor carefully to avoid damage to connector or harness. Tighten all bolts to specification. See TORQUE SPECIFICATIONS table at end of article.
**5)** Reactivate SRS. See DISABLING & ACTIVATING AIR BAG SYSTEM. Check SRS warning light to ensure system is functioning properly. See SYSTEM OPERATION CHECK. If a crash sensor or standby power unit fault code exists after replacing crash sensor or

standby power unit, clear codes, and perform SYSTEM OPERATION CHECK again.

***WARNING: On 740 and 940, NEVER remove crash sensor from its bracket. Replace crash sensor and bracket as an assembly.***

**Removal & Installation (740 & 940) – 1)** Before proceeding, follow air bag service precautions. See SERVICE PRECAUTIONS. Before replacing crash sensor, check ground connection at crash sensor Black wire terminal retaining screw. If faulty ground connection exists, crash sensor may still be good. Repair as required. Perform SYSTEM OPERATION CHECK to verify repair.

**2)** Disable SRS. See DISABLING & ACTIVATING AIR BAG SYSTEM. Remove soundproofing panel under steering column. Disconnect seat belt tensioner connectors.

**3)** Crash sensor is located under driver's seat in same bracket with standby power unit. *See Fig. 4*. Unbolt driver's seat guide rails from floor. Disconnect seat wiring connectors, and tilt seat rearward. Lift carpet and remove heating duct to expose crash sensor unit. NEVER disconnect harness connector from crash sensor or separate crash sensor from bracket.

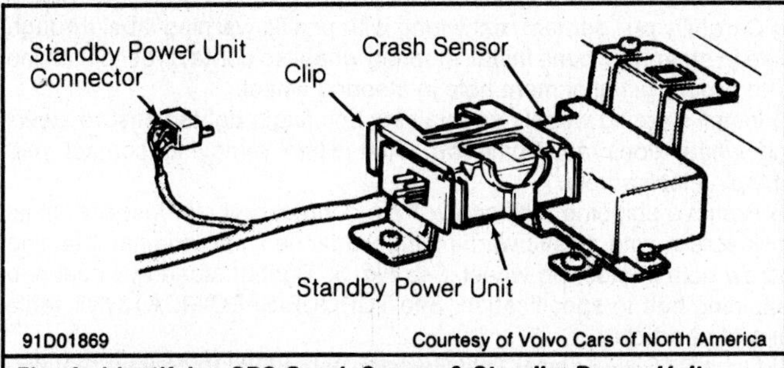


***Fig. 4: Identifying SRS Crash Sensor & Standby Power Unit (740 & 940)***

**4)** NEVER disconnect harness connector from crash sensor. Disconnect wiring harness connector from standby power unit, and remove unit from bracket by releasing clip. Remove crash sensor, harness connector and bracket as an assembly.

**5)** To install, reverse removal procedure. Install crash sensor bracket using original bolts without lock washers. Tighten all bolts to specification. See TORQUE SPECIFICATIONS table at end of article. Ensure all SRS connectors are connected.

**6)** Reactivate SRS. See DISABLING & ACTIVATING AIR BAG SYSTEM. Check SRS warning light to ensure system is functioning properly. See SYSTEM OPERATION CHECK. If a crash sensor or standby power unit fault code exists after replacing crash sensor or standby power unit, clear codes, and perform SYSTEM OPERATION CHECK again.

## STEERING WHEEL & CONTACT REEL

***NOTE: If air bag deployed during a collision, contact reel and steering wheel must be replaced.***

**Removal & Installation (740 & 940) – 1)** Before proceeding, follow air bag service precautions. See SERVICE PRECAUTIONS. Disable SRS before removal. See DISABLING & ACTIVATING AIR BAG SYSTEM.

**2)** Ensure front wheels are pointing straight ahead. Mark steering wheel to column location for reinstallation reference. Remove air bag module. See AIR BAG MODULE.

**3)** Remove steering wheel hub retaining bolt. Remove plastic warning label retaining screw from steering wheel, leaving screw attached to plastic warning label. *See Fig. 5*. Carefully pull steering wheel from column, allowing wiring and plastic warning label to pass through hole in steering wheel.

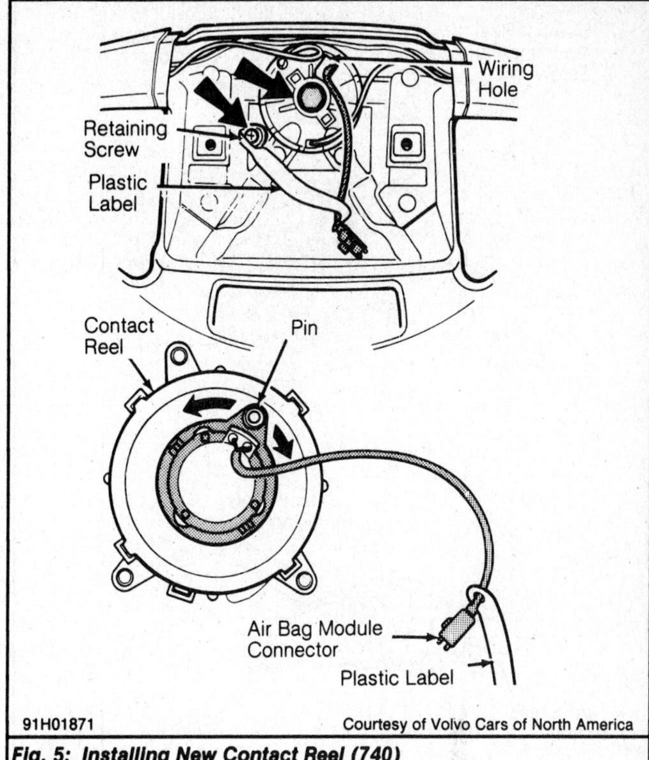


***Fig. 5: Installing New Contact Reel (740)***

**4)** Remove steering column upper and lower covers. Remove wiper and turn signal switches. *See Fig. 6*. Locate and disconnect contact reel wiring harness's Orange connector from behind instrument panel, near steering column.

**5)** Remove contact reel retaining screws. Pull contact reel off steering shaft using care to guide wiring up through steering column. To install, install new contact reel onto steering shaft, and install retaining screws. Install turn signal and wiper switches. Install column covers.

**6)** Reconnect Orange wiring connector behind instrument panel, near steering column. To properly adjust contact reel and complete installation, see CONTACT REEL CENTERING under ADJUSTMENTS.

**Removal & Installation (240) – 1)** Before proceeding, follow air bag service precautions. See SERVICE PRECAUTIONS. Disable SRS before removal. See DISABLING & ACTIVATING AIR BAG SYSTEM.

**2)** Ensure front wheels are pointing straight ahead. Mark steering wheel to column location for reassembly reference. Remove air bag module. See AIR BAG MODULE.

**3)** Remove steering wheel hub retaining bolt. Remove plastic warning label retaining screw from steering wheel, leaving screw attached to plastic warning label. Carefully pull steering wheel from column, allowing wiring and plastic warning label to pass through hole in steering wheel.

**4)** Remove steering column upper and lower covers. Remove wiper and turn signal switches. *See Fig. 6*. Locate and disconnect contact reel wiring harness's Orange connector from behind instrument panel, near steering column.

**5)** Remove both contact reel-mounting plate screws. Pull out mounting plate as far as possible to enable removal of contact reel retaining screws from behind mounting plate. Remove contact reel from mounting plate. *See Fig. 7*.

**6)** To install, install new contact reel to mounting plate. Route contact reel wiring down through steering column. Install mounting plate to column. Install turn signal and wiper switches. Install steering column covers.

**7)** Reconnect Orange wiring connector behind instrument panel, near steering column. To properly adjust contact reel and complete installation, see CONTACT REEL CENTERING under ADJUSTMENTS.

# 1991 SAFETY EQUIPMENT
# Air Bag Restraint System (Cont.)

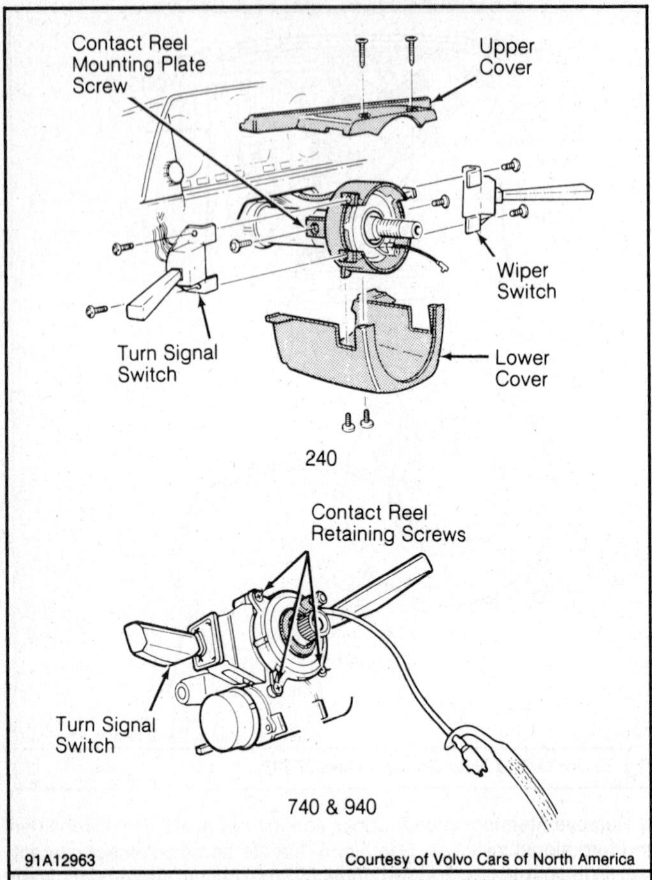


***Fig. 6: Removing Turn Signal, Wiper Switches & Contact Reel***

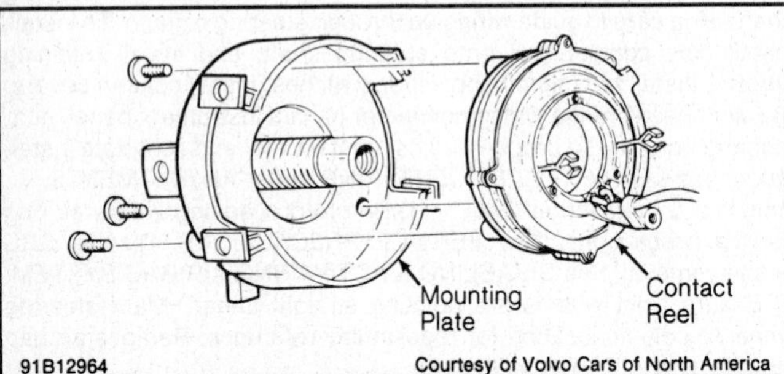


***Fig. 7: Removing Contact Reel (240)***

## ADJUSTMENTS

### CONTACT REEL CENTERING

**1)** With new contact reel installed and steering wheel still removed, remove new contact reel shipping lock screw from pin hole. *See Fig. 5 or 8.*

**2)** Turn contact reel pin to far right, then turn pin back to left about 3 turns until pin hole is at proper position. See CONTACT REEL PIN HOLE POSITION table. Lock contact reel in proper position with shipping lock screw.

***CONTACT REEL PIN HOLE POSITION***

| Model | Pin Hole Position |
|---|---|
| 240 | 6 O'Clock |
| 740 | 8 O'Clock |
| 940 | 8 O'Clock |

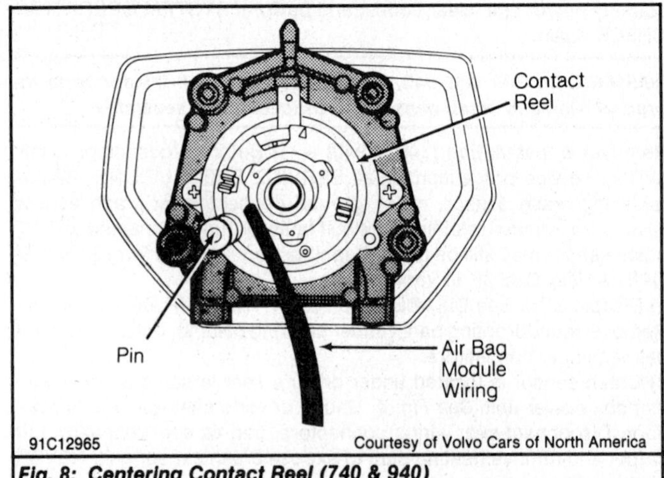


***Fig. 8: Centering Contact Reel (740 & 940)***

**3)** Carefully pull contact reel wiring with plastic warning label through hole in steering wheel. Install steering wheel so contact reel pin aligns with proper pin alignment hole in steering wheel.

**4)** Install steering wheel hub retaining bolt finger tight to ensure steering wheel does not come off shaft when removing contact reel shipping lock screw.

**5)** Remove shipping lock screw from contact reel pin. Install original lock screw, with plastic warning label attached, into original retaining screw hole in steering wheel. *See Fig. 5*. Tighten steering wheel hub retaining bolt to specification. See TORQUE SPECIFICATIONS table at end of article.

**6)** Connect SRS Special Test Resistor (998-8695) to contact reel wiring connector in place of air bag module. *See Fig. 9*. Activate SRS. See DISABLING & ACTIVATING AIR BAG SYSTEM.

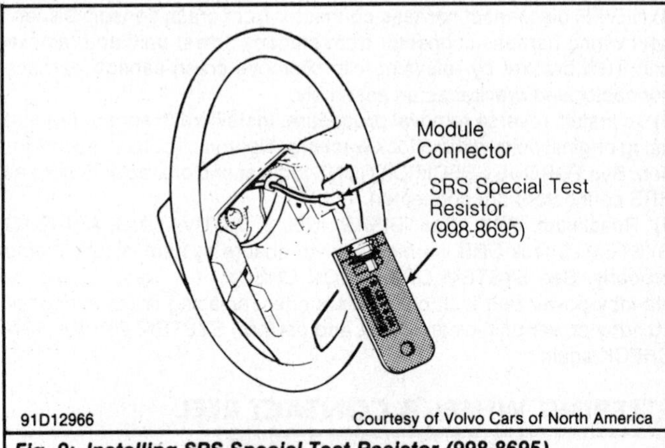


***Fig. 9: Installing SRS Special Test Resistor (998-8695) to Module Connector***

**7)** Turn ignition switch to ON position and ensure SRS warning light goes out after 10 seconds. If light does not go out, a fault code is set and memory must be cleared. See MITCHELL's AIR BAG SERVICE & REPAIR MANUAL, DOMESTIC & IMPORTED MODELS. After clearing fault codes, recheck SRS light operation. Perform SYSTEM OPERATION CHECK.

**8)** If SRS warning light goes out after about 10 seconds, turn off ignition, disconnect negative battery cable and remove Special Test Resistor (998-8695) from air bag module connector. Position air bag module to steering wheel, and install wiring connector.

# 1991 SAFETY EQUIPMENT
# Air Bag Restraint System (Cont.)

**9)** Ensure wiring connector clicks into position. Install air bag module Torx screws to rear of steering wheel, and tighten to specification. See TORQUE SPECIFICATIONS table at end of article. Install steering column undercover. Perform SYSTEM OPERATION CHECK.
**10)** After installing steering wheel, drive vehicle to check steering wheel alignment. If steering wheel is off-center, remove steering wheel assembly again.
**11)** Adjust contact reel again according to procedures. Reinstall steering wheel, and test drive vehicle to check steering wheel alignment.

## TORQUE SPECIFICATIONS

***TORQUE SPECIFICATIONS***

| Application | Ft. Lbs. (N.m) |
|---|---|
| Seat Rail-To-Floor Bolts | 35 (48) |
| Steering Wheel Bolt | |
| 240 | 44 (60) |
| 740 & 940 | 24 (33) |
| | **INCH Lbs. (N.m)** |
| Air Bag Module Bolts | 72 (8) |
| Crash Sensor Bracket Bolts | |
| 240 | 96 (11) |
| 740 & 940 | 96 (11) |
| Knee Bolster Bolts | |
| M6 Bolt | 72 (8) |
| M8 Bolt | 180 (20) |

# 1991 SAFETY EQUIPMENT
# Instrument Panels

## 240, 740, 940

***WARNING: When working around steering column and before performing repairs, disconnect and shield battery ground terminal. Disconnect YELLOW and ORANGE Supplemental Inflatable Restraint (SRS) air bag connectors located on driver's side of center console, near throttle pedal. Failure to follow precautions may result in air bag deployment and personal injury. See SERVICE PRECAUTIONS and DISABLING & ACTIVATING AIR BAG SYSTEM in AIR BAG RESTRAINT SYSTEM article.***

## DESCRIPTION & OPERATION

All models are equipped with an analog gauge instrument cluster which is either a Yazaki or VDO type. *See Fig. 1.* On 240, speedometer is centrally located with tachometer/clock on left and coolant temperature/fuel gauges on right. A warning/tell-tale light bar at bottom of cluster panel displays additional information.

On 740 and 940, speedometer is centrally located with a tachometer and clock installed on either side. Smaller gauges for coolant temperature and fuel are at opposite sides of instrument cluster. If equipped, a turbo pressure gauge is incorporated within tachometer. A warning/tell-tale light bar at bottom of cluster panel displays additional information.

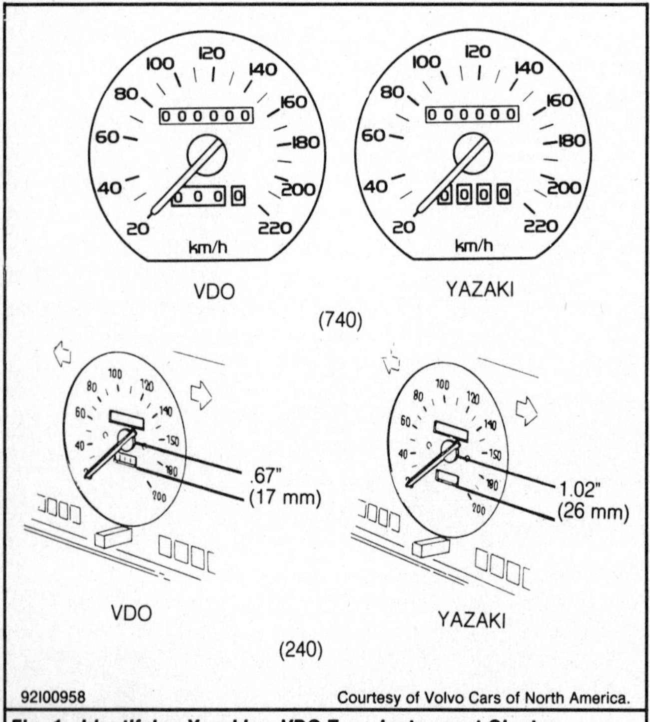


***Fig. 1: Identifying Yazaki or VDO Type Instrument Cluster***

## TESTING

***NOTE: On 240, if both fuel gauge and temperature gauge are inoperative, check voltage limiter. See VOLTAGE LIMITER. Testing information for 940 instrument panel is not available from manufacturer.***

### FUEL GAUGE TEST

**240 - 1)** Gauge can be checked with a 68-ohm Test Resistor (999-5824-1). Disconnect negative battery cable. Disconnect fuel gauge sending unit connector. Connect test resistor between ground and disconnected lead. *See Fig. 2.*

**2)** Reconnect negative battery cable and turn ignition on. If gauge is okay, needle should indicate 3/4 full and sender is defective. If reading is incorrect, gauge is defective. If gauge shows no reading, check wiring. If wiring is okay, replace gauge.

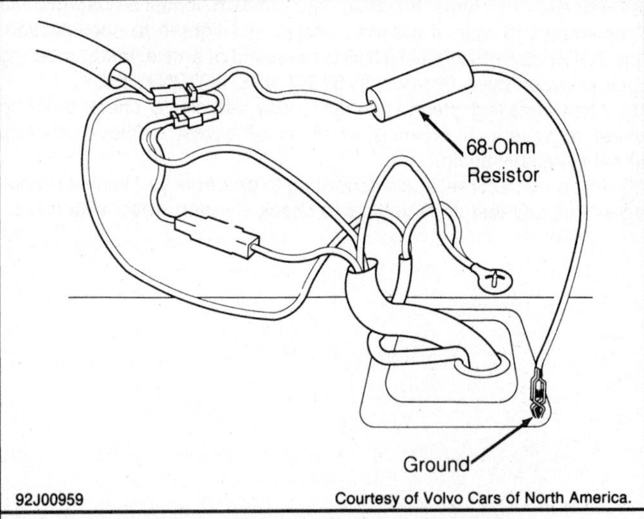


***Fig. 2: Connecting Test Resistor Between Ground & Disconnected Lead***

**740 - 1)** Ensure temperature gauge operates properly, as fuel gauge receives current from temperature gauge. If temperature gauge does not operate correctly, go to TEMPERATURE GAUGE TEST.

**2)** If temperature gauge is okay, fuel gauge can be checked with a 68-ohm Test Resistor (999-5824-1). Assemble an adapter from following components: *See Fig. 3.*

- Gray wire (954 441)
- Terminal (948 291)
- Terminal (942 201)
- Sleeve insulator (948 296)
- Cover (943511)

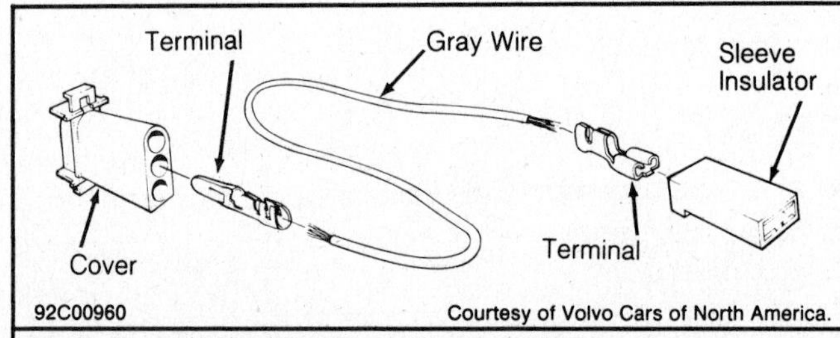


***Fig. 3: Assembling Fuel Gauge Testing Adapter***

**3)** Disconnect Gray/White wire from fuel tank sending unit. Connect test resistor between ground and disconnected wire. If gauge is okay it should indicate 1/4 full (15-gallon tank), or 1/5 full (21-gallon tank). If gauge operates as specified, sender is defective.

**4)** If needle is not on specified section, ensure gauge is set for 15-gallon or 21-gallon tank. Yazaki gauges use a screw and VDO gauges use a clip if equipped with a 15-gallon tank. *See Fig. 4.* Clip or screw should be removed for 21-gallon tank.

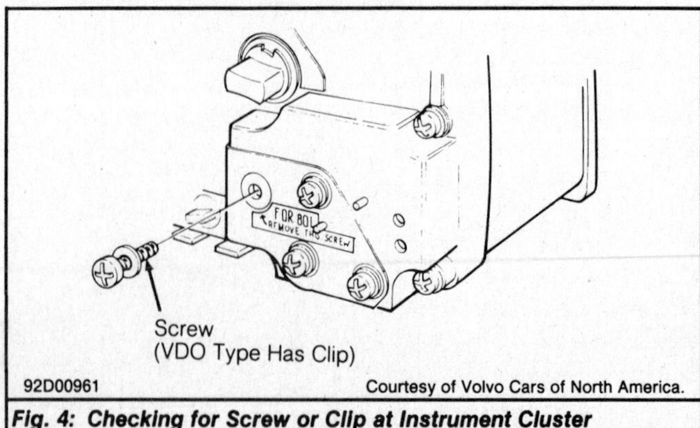


***Fig. 4: Checking for Screw or Clip at Instrument Cluster***

# 1991 SAFETY EQUIPMENT
# Instrument Panels (Cont.)

**5)** If gauge is correctly set, but still gives incorrect reading, sender is probably defective. If needle does not move at all, check continuity of wiring to gauge. If wiring is okay, gauge should be replaced.
**6)** If fuel gauge replacement is necessary, check rear side of instrument panel to see if a potentiometer has been installed. If so, gauge will require adjustment.
**7)** If not already present, Fuel Gauge Potentiometer Kit (1 398 171-7) will need to be installed in order to adjust fuel gauge. Disconnect negative battery cable. Disconnect fuel gauge sender connector and install resistor to gauge side of wiring. *See Fig. 5.*

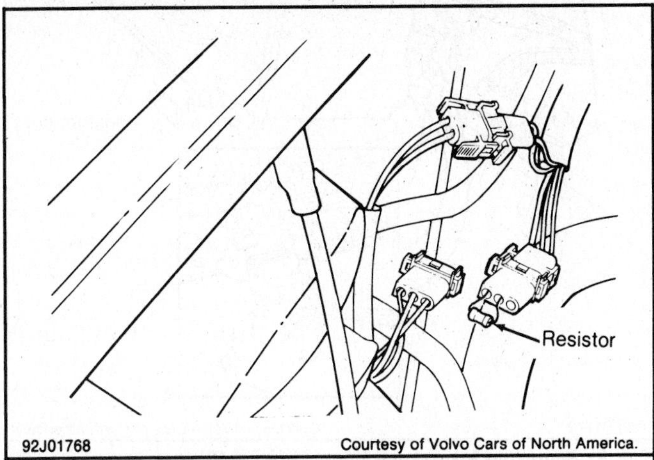


***Fig. 5: Installing Resistor In Gauge Side of Wiring***

**8)** Cut Gray/White wire next to 7-pin connector on instrument panel. Using sleeve insulators, join both sides to potentiometer. *See Fig. 6.* Reconnect negative battery cable. Turn ignition on, engine off. If needle on fuel gauge just touches Red section, go to step **10)**. If not, go to next step.

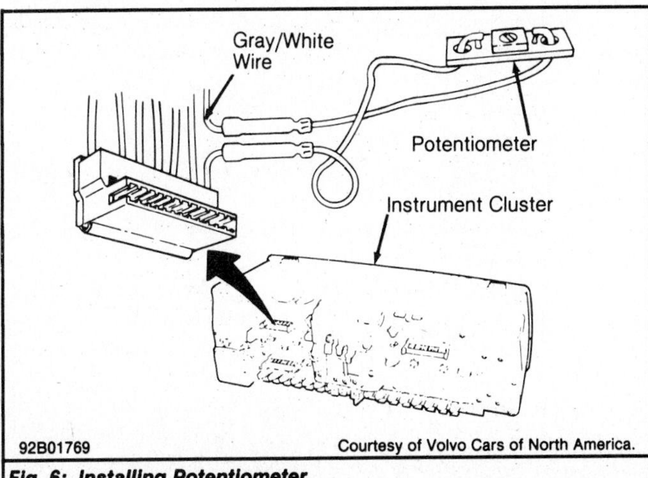


***Fig. 6: Installing Potentiometer***

**9)** Turn ignition off. Disconnect negative battery cable. Using a screwdriver, adjust potentiometer. Initial adjustment is 33 ohms. Reduce by turning screw clockwise until correct needle deflection is obtained.
**10)** Disconnect negative battery cable. Seal potentiometer with a drop of paint. Wrap electrical tape around potentiometer to prevent short circuits. Remove test resistor and reconnect wiring. Reconnect negative battery cable.

## FUEL GAUGE SENDING UNIT TEST

**240 - 1)** Drain fuel from fuel tank. Disconnect fuel tank connector. Using an ohmmeter, measure resistance between fuel level sending unit lead and ground. Resistance should be 250-350 ohms. If reading is incorrect, all fuel has not been drained or sending unit must be replaced.
**2)** Add 3 gals. (11 L) of fuel to tank. Fuel level sending unit resistance should now be 141-240 ohms. If reading is still incorrect, sending unit must be replaced.
**740 - 1)** Disconnect negative battery cable. Disconnect fuel gauge sending unit connector and measure resistance between Gray/White and Brown wires. Resistance should be 0-280 ohms (15-gallon tank), or 0-367.5 ohms (21-gallon tank). If resistance is not to specification, replace sending unit.
**2)** Add 2 1/2 gallons (9 L) of fuel to tank. Resistance should increase 5 ohms each 1/4 gallon (1 L). If resistance does not increase as specified, replace sending unit.

## TEMPERATURE GAUGE TEST

**240 - 1)** Gauge can be checked with a 68-ohm Test Resistor (999-5824-1). Disconnect negative battery cable. Disconnect coolant sender connector, located on left side of engine block, above alternator. Connect test resistor across connector terminals.
**2)** Reconnect negative battery cable and turn ignition on. If gauge is okay, needle should deflect 3/4 sweep.

***NOTE: On some instrument panels, needle will deflect 1/2 sweep.***

**3)** If gauge is correct, sender is defective. If gauge is incorrect, gauge is defective. If gauge shows no movement, check wiring. If wiring is okay, replace gauge.
**740 - 1)** Gauge can be checked with a 68-ohm Test Resistor (999-5824-1). Disconnect negative battery cable. Disconnect coolant sender wire. Connect test resistor between ground and disconnected wire. Reconnect battery cable and turn ignition on.
**2)** If gauge is okay, needle should sweep to center of Red section. If gauge is okay, sender is defective. If needle is not in Red section, gauge is defective. If needle does not move, check wiring. If wiring is okay, replace gauge.

## TEMPERATURE SENDING UNIT TEST

Drain cooling system and remove sending unit from engine head. Heat sensor in water and check sending unit resistance at temperatures listed in TEMPERATURE SENDING UNIT RESISTANCE table. If resistance is incorrect, replace sending unit.

***TEMPERATURE SENDING UNIT RESISTANCE***

| Temperature °F (°C) | Ohms |
|---|---|
| 140 (60) | 560 |
| 194 (90) | 206 |
| 212 (100) | 153 |

## VOLTAGE LIMITER

**240** - Remove voltage limiter from back of instrument cluster. *See Fig. 7.* Apply battery voltage across voltage limiter terminals. Using a voltmeter, limiter voltage should be 9.8-10.2 volts. If not, replace limiter.

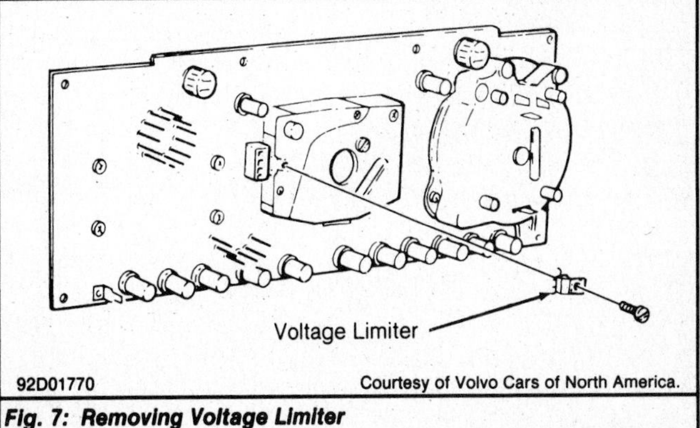


***Fig. 7: Removing Voltage Limiter***

# 1991 SAFETY EQUIPMENT
# Instrument Panels (Cont.)

## WIPER SWITCH TEST

For testing information on wipers, see WIPER/WASHER SYSTEMS article.

## REMOVAL & INSTALLATION

### INSTRUMENT CLUSTER

***NOTE: ALWAYS disconnect negative battery cable before removing ANY instrument panel components.***

**Removal & Installation (240)** – Disconnect negative battery cable. Pull off rheostat and light switch control knobs. Remove covers on each side of instrument panel. Remove instrument panel retaining screws. *See Fig. 8.* Disconnect electrical connectors and remove instrument panel. To install, reverse removal procedure.

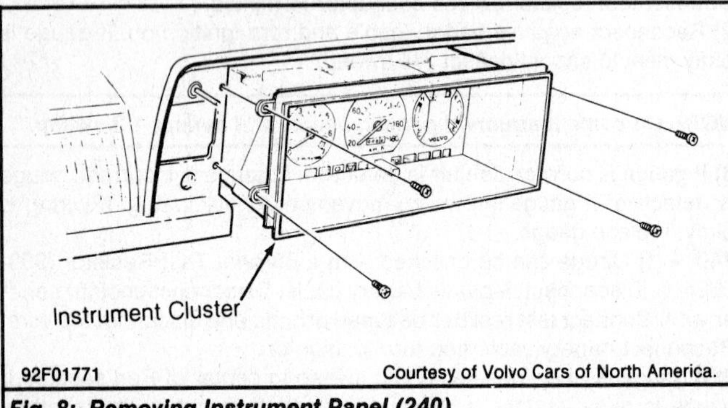


***Fig. 8: Removing Instrument Panel (240)***

**Removal & Installation (740 & 940)** – Disconnect negative battery cable. Remove 2 cover panels and screws holding instrument panel. *See Fig. 9.* Lift out instrument panel. Remove connector seal. Disconnect connectors and remove instrument panel. To install, reverse removal procedure.

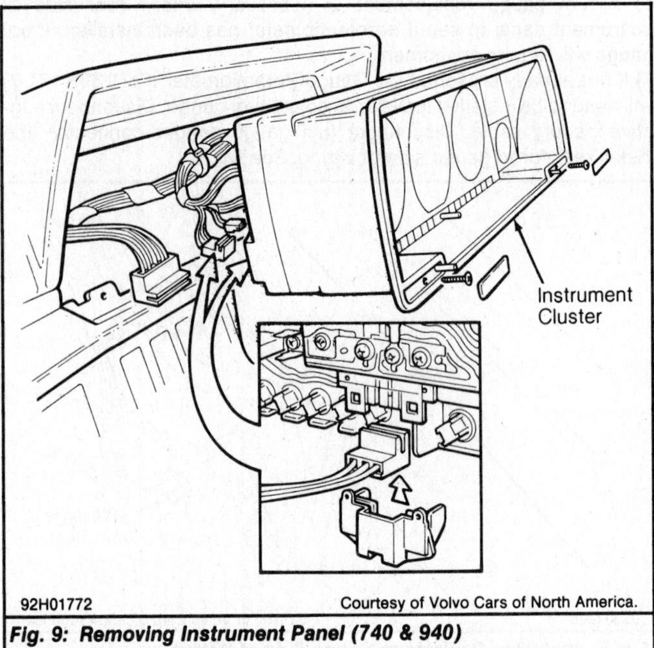


***Fig. 9: Removing Instrument Panel (740 & 940)***

## WIRING DIAGRAMS

See appropriate chassis wiring diagram in WIRING DIAGRAMS.

# 1991 SAFETY EQUIPMENT
# Steering Column Switches

## 240, 740, 940

## TESTING

***NOTE:** Testing information on steering column switches is not available from manufacturer.*

## REMOVAL & INSTALLATION

### STEERING WHEEL & HORN

***WARNING:** Before any repairs, disconnect and shield negative battery cable from ground. Disconnect Yellow and Orange Supplemental Restraint System (SRS) connectors on driver's side of center console, near accelerator pedal, to avoid accidental air bag deployment. Follow air bag service precautions. See SERVICE PRECAUTIONS in AIR BAG RESTRAINT SYSTEM article. Disable SRS before removal. See DISABLING & ACTIVATING AIR BAG SYSTEM in AIR BAG RESTRAINT SYSTEM article.*

**Removal - 1)** Ensure front wheels are pointing straight ahead. Mark steering wheel to column location for reassembly reference. Remove air bag module. *See Fig. 1.* See AIR BAG MODULE removal procedure in AIR BAG RESTRAINT SYSTEM article.

**2)** Remove steering wheel hub retaining bolt. Remove plastic warning label retaining screw from steering wheel, leaving screw attached to plastic warning label. Insert screw into hole, locking contact reel pin. Carefully pull steering wheel from column, allowing wiring and plastic warning label to pass through hole in steering wheel. *See Fig. 2.*

**Installation -** To install, reverse removal procedure. To properly adjust contact reel and complete installation, see CONTACT REEL CENTERING under ADJUSTMENTS in AIR BAG RESTRAINT SYSTEM article. Tighten steering wheel retaining bolt to specification. See TORQUE SPECIFICATIONS table.

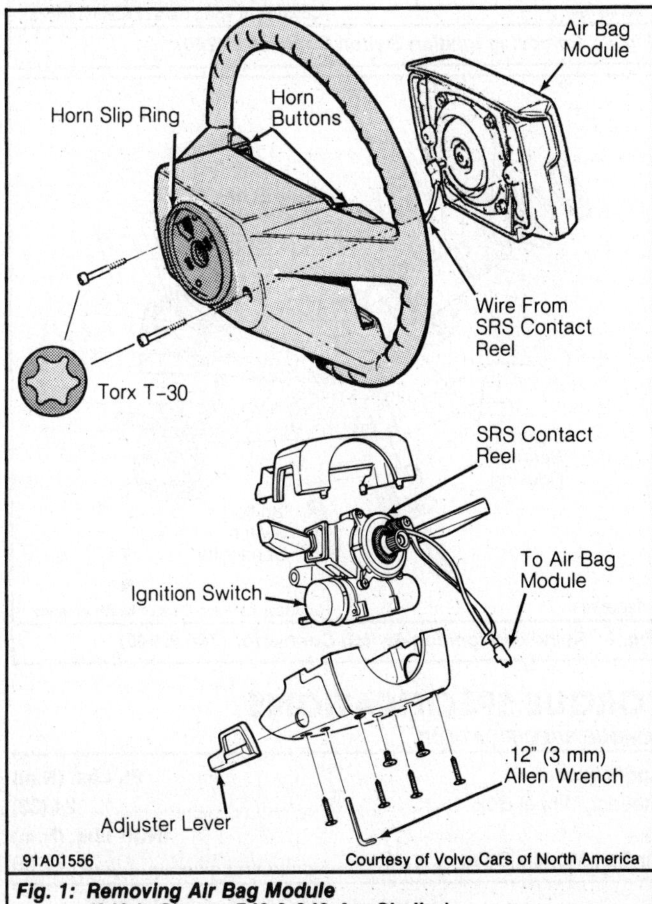


***Fig. 1:* Removing Air Bag Module (240 Is Shown; 740 & 940 Are Similar)**

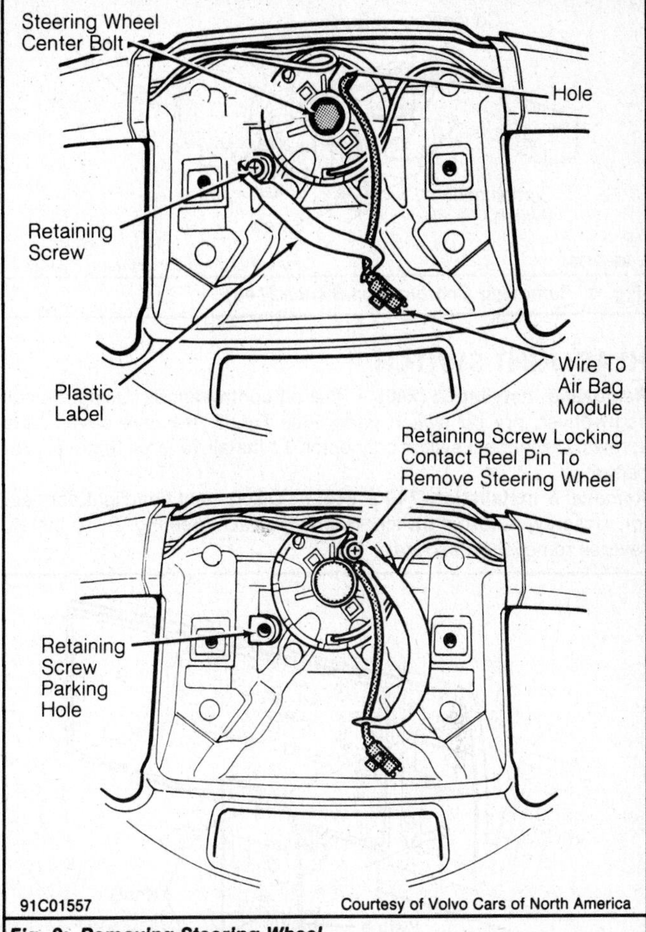


***Fig. 2:* Removing Steering Wheel**

### COMBINATION SWITCH & WIPER SWITCH

**Removal -** Remove steering wheel. See STEERING WHEEL & HORN under REMOVAL & INSTALLATION. Remove upper and lower steering column covers. *See Fig. 3.* Disconnect switch harness connectors behind instrument panel, near steering column. Remove switch attaching screws. *See Fig. 3 or 4.* Remove switch and harness.

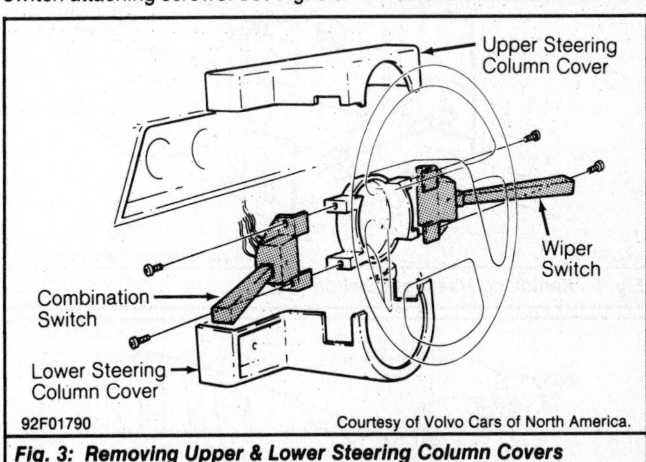


***Fig. 3:* Removing Upper & Lower Steering Column Covers (240 Is Shown; 740 & 940 Are Similar)**

**Installation -** To install, reverse removal procedure. See STEERING WHEEL & HORN under REMOVAL & INSTALLATION. Ensure all electrical connections are tight. Check turn signal switch canceling.

# 1991 SAFETY EQUIPMENT
# Steering Column Switches (Cont.)

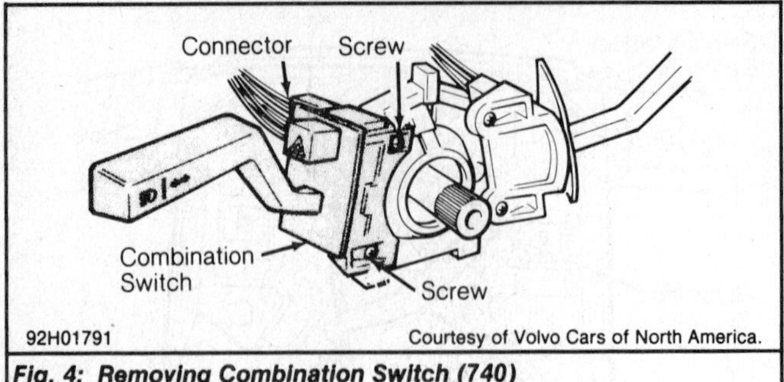


*Fig. 4: Removing Combination Switch (740)*

## HEADLIGHT SWITCH

**Removal & Installation (240)** – Pull off control knobs. Using a small screwdriver, pry off switch panel. *See Fig. 5.* Remove cover plate screws. Disconnect switch connector. To install, reverse removal procedure.

**Removal & Installation (740 & 940)** – Disconnect headlight connector. Unscrew nut from switch. Remove switch. *See Fig. 6.* To install, reverse removal procedure.

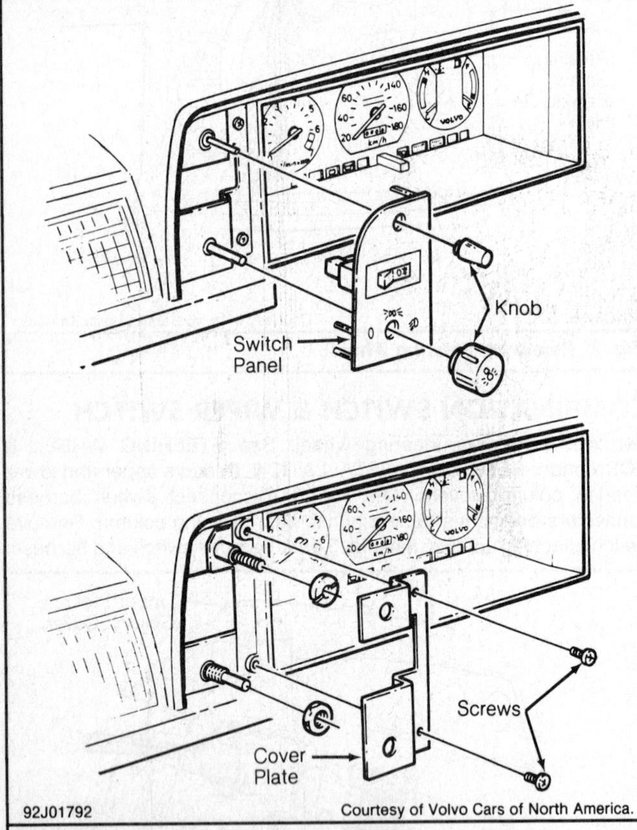


*Fig. 5: Removing Headlight Switch (240)*

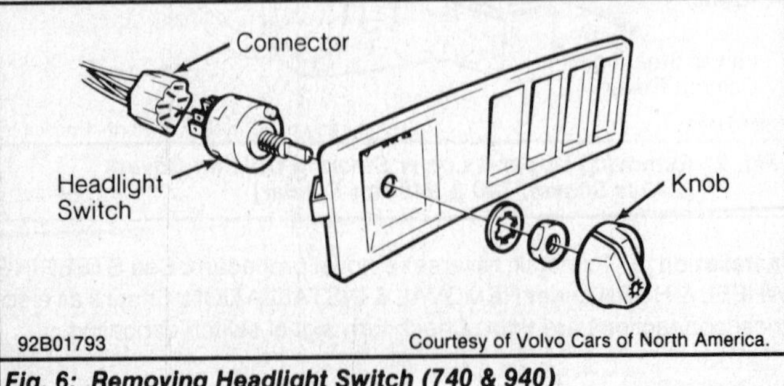


*Fig. 6: Removing Headlight Switch (740 & 940)*

## IGNITION SWITCH & LOCK CYLINDER

**Removal** – Remove sound insulation under instrument panel. Reaching up from under instrument panel, disconnect electrical connector from back of ignition lock. *See Fig. 7 or 8.* Remove upper steering column cover and ignition lock panel.

**2)** Loosen ignition lock fixing bolt, located behind upper steering column cover. Put key in ignition and turn to start position. From under instrument panel, push lock barrel back through hole and remove ignition lock.

**Installation** – Insert key in lock. Turn key and press in locking catch. Remove key. Insert lock in slot. Release barrel enough to insert key again. Tighten locking screw, and ensure key operates properly. To complete installation, reverse removal procedure.

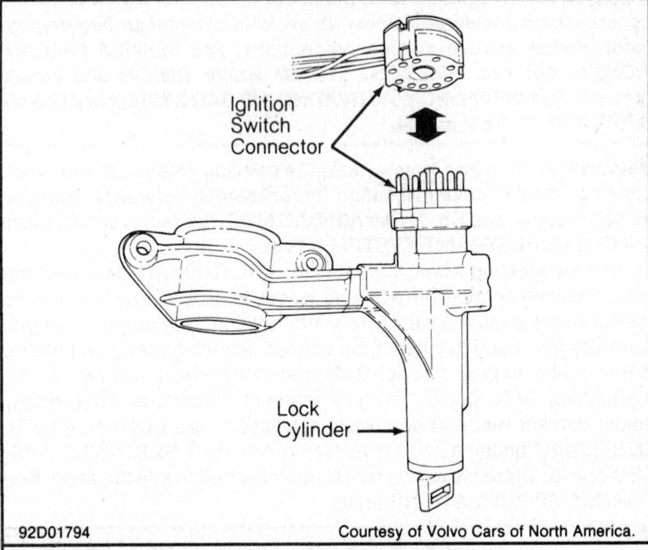


*Fig. 7: Removing Ignition Switch Connector (240)*

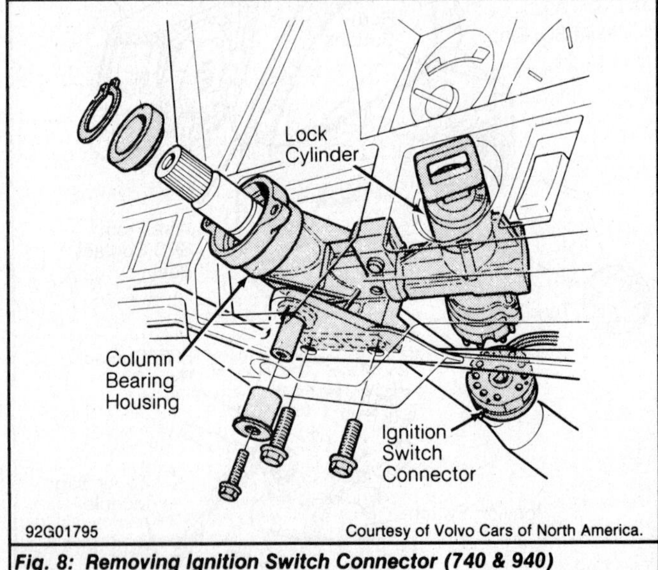


*Fig. 8: Removing Ignition Switch Connector (740 & 940)*

## TORQUE SPECIFICATIONS

*TORQUE SPECIFICATIONS*

| Application | Ft. Lbs. (N.m) |
|---|---|
| Steering Wheel Bolt | 24 (33) |
| | **INCH Lbs. (N.m)** |
| Air Bag Module Bolts | 72 (8) |

## 240, 740, 940

# DESCRIPTION & OPERATION

All models are equipped with a 2-speed front wiper motor with an adjustable intermittent feature. Wagon models are equipped with a rear wiper/washer system.

# ADJUSTMENTS

## WIPER ARM ADJUSTMENT

For wiper arm adjustment, *See Fig. 1.*

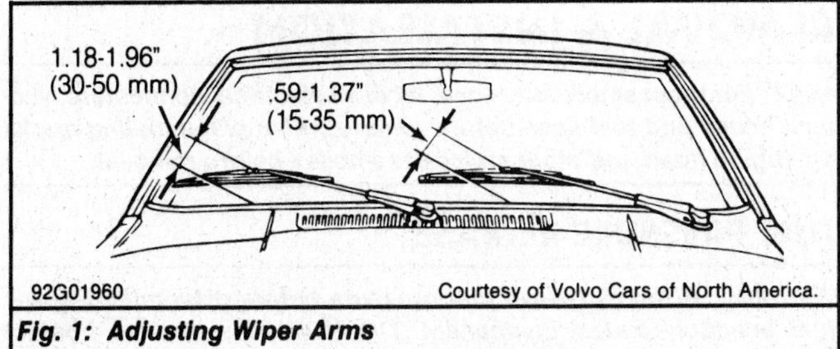


***Fig. 1: Adjusting Wiper Arms***

# REMOVAL & INSTALLATION

## FRONT WIPER MOTOR

**Removal & Installation** – For front wiper motor removal and installation, *See Fig. 2 or 3.*

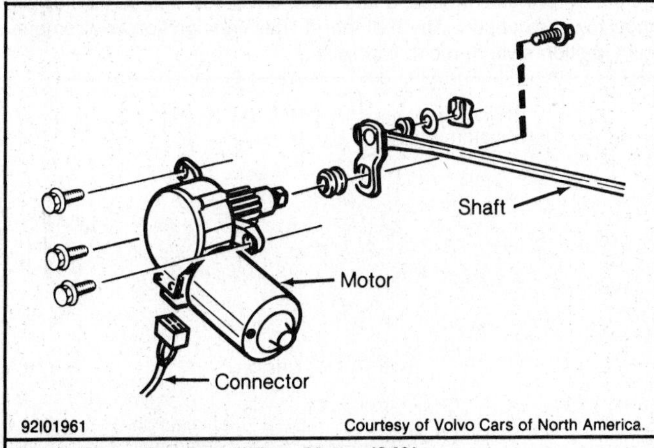


***Fig. 2: Removing Front Wiper Motor (240)***

## FRONT & REAR WIPER RELAY

**Removal & Installation (240)** – Front and rear wiper relays are located under left side of instrument panel, near kick panel.

**Removal & Installation (740 & 940)** – Front and rear wiper relays are located in relay box, in center console, behind ashtray.

## FRONT & REAR WIPER SWITCH

**Removal & Installation** – Remove steering wheel. See STEERING WHEEL under REMOVAL & INSTALLATION in appropriate AIR BAG RESTRAINT SYSTEM article. Disconnect electrical connector. Remove wiper switch retaining screws. To install, reverse removal procedure.

## FRONT & REAR WASHER MOTOR

**Removal & Installation (240)** – Washer motor is located on washer fluid reservoir, in front right corner of engine compartment. Lift pump from mounting bracket. Disconnect fluid lines and disconnect electrical connector. To install, reverse removal procedure.

**Removal & Installation (740 & 940)** – Washer motor is located on washer fluid reservoir, in front left corner of engine compartment. Disconnect electrical connector and lift motor off reservoir. Disconnect fluid lines. To install, reverse removal procedure.

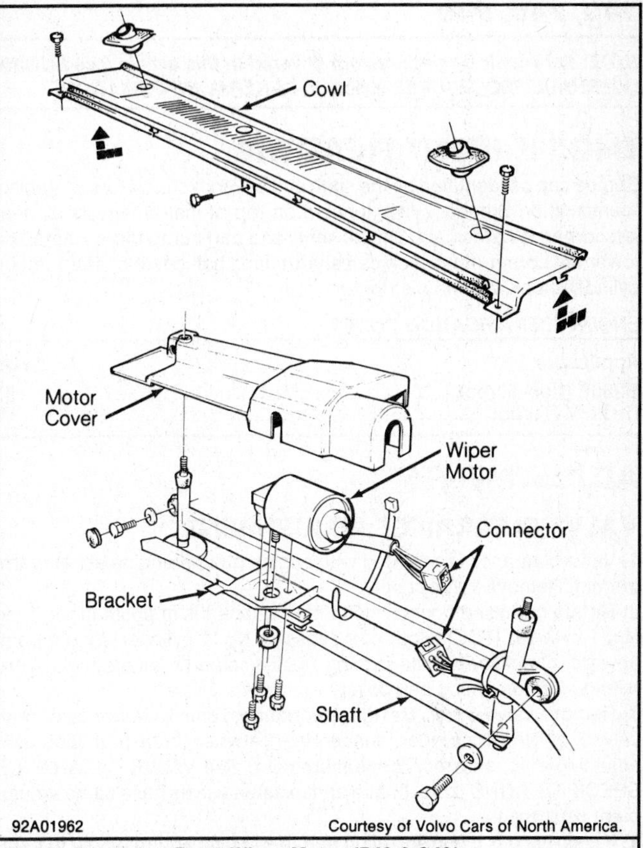


***Fig. 3: Removing Front Wiper Motor (740 & 940)***

## REAR WIPER MOTOR

**Removal & Installation** – No information is available from manufacturer. *See Fig. 4.*

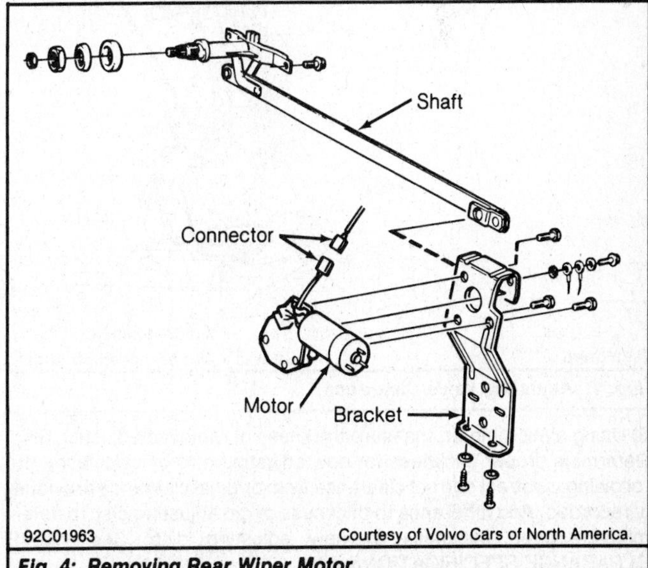


***Fig. 4: Removing Rear Wiper Motor (240 Is Shown; 740 & 940 Are Similar)***

# WIRING DIAGRAMS

See appropriate chassis wiring diagram in WIRING DIAGRAMS.

# 1991 ENGINES
# 2.3L 4-Cylinder

## 240, 740, 940

***NOTE: For repair procedures not covered in this article, see ENGINE OVERHAUL PROCEDURES article in GENERAL INFORMATION.***

## ENGINE IDENTIFICATION

Engine can be identified by the sixth and seventh characters of Vehicle Identification Number (VIN), located on top of instrument panel near left corner of windshield. Engine serial and part number are located on lower left corner of label on camshaft/timing belt cover or stamped on cylinder block, behind distributor.

***ENGINE IDENTIFICATION CODES***

| Application | Code |
|---|---|
| B230F (Non-Turbo) | 88 |
| B230FT (Turbo) | 87 |

## ADJUSTMENTS

### VALVE CLEARANCE ADJUSTMENT

**1)** Valve clearance is adjusted with engine off and engine either warm or cold. Remove valve cover.
**2)** Rotate crankshaft center bolt until camshaft is in position for firing No. 1 cylinder (TDC). Both cam lobes of No. 1 cylinder should point upward. Crankshaft pulley timing mark should be aligned with zero timing mark on timing belt cover.
**3)** Remove valve cover. Using feeler gauges, check clearance of both valves of No. 1 cylinder, measuring between camshaft lobe and adjusting disc, and record measurement. See VALVE CLEARANCE SPECIFICATIONS table. Intake and exhaust valves have same adjustment clearances.
**4)** If clearance is incorrect, align notches in disc at right angle to camshaft. Using Valve Press (5022) and Special Pliers (5026), press and remove adjusting disc. *See Fig. 1.*

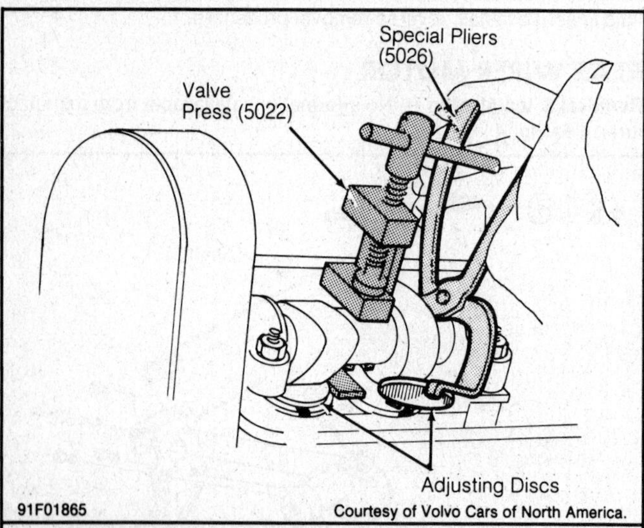


***Fig. 1: Adjusting Valve Clearance***

**5)** Using a micrometer, measure thickness of removed adjusting disc. Determine proper thickness for new adjusting disc by calculating the following: subtract correct clearance from original clearance previously recorded. Add difference to thickness of old adjusting disc to determine required thickness of new adjusting disc. See VALVE CLEARANCE SPECIFICATIONS table.
**6)** Adjusting discs are available in thicknesses ranging from .130-.177" (3.30-4.50 mm) in increments of .002" (.05 mm). Use only NEW adjusting discs.
**7)** Coat adjusting discs with oil and install with thickness markings facing down. Remove valve press. Rotate crankshaft to next firing order position and repeat procedure. Firing order is 1, 3, 4 and 2.
**8)** When all 4 cylinders have been adjusted, rotate camshaft several revolutions and recheck valve clearance on all cylinders and readjust as required. Install valve cover and gasket.

***VALVE CLEARANCE SPECIFICATIONS***

| Application | In. (mm) |
|---|---|
| Clearance When Checking | |
| Cold Engine | .012-.016 (.30-.40) |
| Hot Engine | .014-.018 (.35-.45) |
| Clearance When Adjusting | |
| Cold Engine | .014-.016 (.35-.40) |
| Hot Engine | .016-.018 (.40-.45) |

## REMOVAL & INSTALLATION

***NOTE: For reassembly reference, label all electrical connectors, vacuum hoses and fuel lines before removal. Also place mating marks on engine hood and other major assemblies before removal.***

### FUEL PRESSURE RELEASE

***WARNING: ALWAYS relieve fuel pressure before disconnecting any fuel injection-related component. DO NOT allow fuel to contact engine or electrical components.***

**Fuel Pump Pressure Release – 1)** Remove fuel injection system relay. On 240, relay is located under right side of instrument panel. On 740 and 940, relay in located behind ash tray in center console. *See Fig. 2.*
**2)** Crank engine for at least 5 seconds. If engine starts, let it run until it dies. Before disconnecting any lines, cover fuel line connector with shop towel to absorb any fuel left in line. With ignition key removed from ignition switch, reconnect relay.

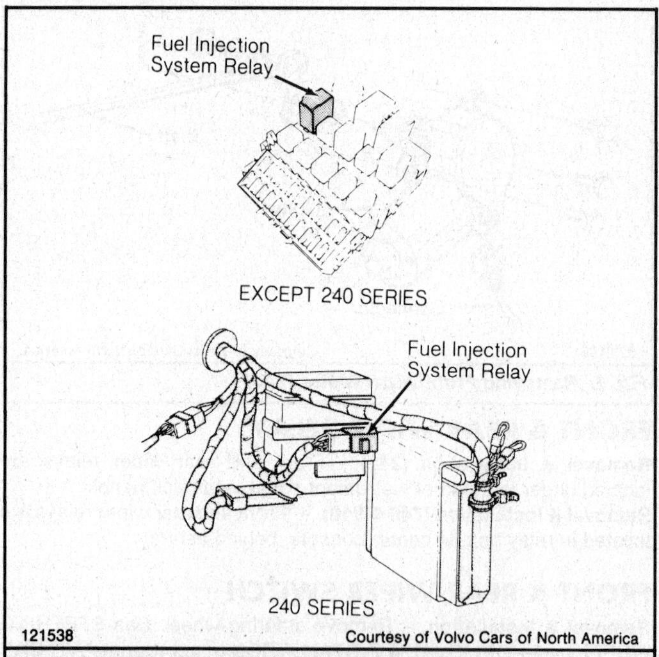


***Fig. 2: Locating Fuel Injection System Relays***

### ENGINE

**Removal – 1)** Remove hood and disconnect negative battery cable. Drain coolant and engine oil. Remove distributor cap. Disconnect coolant hoses. Remove radiator, fan shroud, air intake hoses and air cleaner assembly.
**2)** Remove power steering pump and A/C compressor with hoses attached. Disconnect vacuum hoses, electrical connections, coolant hoses and control cables at engine.

# 1991 ENGINES
# 2.3L 4-Cylinder (Cont.)

**3)** Remove fuel tank cap to relieve fuel tank pressure. See FUEL PRESSURE RELEASE. Remove fuel lines.
**4)** Raise and support vehicle. Remove splash shield located below engine. Disconnect exhaust pipe at exhaust manifold or turbo. Remove exhaust pipe support bracket.
**5)** On 240 with M/T, remove gearshift boot, gearshift lever retaining bolts and bracket. Remove gearshift lever. On 240 with A/T, disconnect control cable/linkages, noting locations.
**6)** On 740 and 940, remove rubber boot and snap ring at base of gearshift lever, pin and remove gearshift (M/T models) or disconnect control cable (A/T) models.
**7)** On all models, disconnect electrical connections and speedometer pick-up at differential. Remove propeller shaft. Support transmission and remove transmission crossmember. Remove engine mount bolts. Remove engine and transmission assembly.
**Installation – 1)** To install, reverse removal procedure. Fill fluid levels and adjust control cables.
**2)** On 240 with M/T, place gearshift in 1st gear. Adjust clearance between bracket and gearshift lever to .020-.059" (.51-1.49 mm). Recheck clearance in 2nd gear. Adjust as necessary.

## INTAKE MANIFOLD

**Removal – 1)** Disconnect negative battery cable. Remove air intake hoses at throttle body. Disconnect necessary electrical connections, control cables and vacuum hoses.
**2)** Remove fuel tank cap to relieve fuel tank pressure. See FUEL PRESSURE RELEASE. Remove fuel lines. Remove intake manifold retaining nuts and intake manifold.
**Installation –** To install, reverse removal procedure using new gaskets. If fuel rail and injectors were removed, install components using new "O" rings. Coat "O" rings with petroleum jelly before installation.

## EXHAUST MANIFOLD

***NOTE: Remove turbo before removing exhaust manifold (if necessary).***

**Removal – 1)** Disconnect negative battery cable. On turbo models, remove air delivery and intake hoses from turbo. Drain cooling system. Remove coolant lines, oil lines and vacuum hoses at turbo.
**2)** On all models, disconnect exhaust pipe. Remove manifold retaining nuts and exhaust manifold.
**Installation – 1)** To install, reverse removal procedure using new gaskets. If gaskets are marked with letters UT, marked side must face away from cylinder head.
**2)** On turbo models, if turbo was removed, apply Thread Sealant (1161078-9) to turbo retaining bolts and install using new lock plates. Tighten in a crisscross pattern.
**3)** Pour clean engine oil into turbo before installing oil supply line. When installing exhaust pipe on turbo, if studs were removed from turbo, apply Thread Sealant (1161035-9) to studs before installing into turbo housing.

## CYLINDER HEAD

***CAUTION: DO NOT rotate crankshaft or camshaft when timing belt is removed or, valves may contact the pistons.***

**Removal – 1)** Drain cooling system at radiator and cylinder block. Disconnect negative battery cable. Remove intake manifold and exhaust manifold. See INTAKE MANIFOLD and EXHAUST MANIFOLD under REMOVAL & INSTALLATION.
**2)** Remove all drive belts and water pump pulley. Remove fan, preheater hose (below fan shroud) and fan shroud. Remove timing belt cover.
**3)** Using center bolt on crankshaft, rotate crankshaft so mark on camshaft pulley aligns with timing mark on inner timing belt cover, and crankshaft pulley mark aligns with TDC mark on timing belt cover.
**4)** Loosen belt tensioner nut one turn. Pull on timing belt to compress belt tensioner spring. Tighten belt tensioner nut. Install a 3-mm drill bit through hole of belt tensioner bolt to lock tensioner spring in place.
**5)** Note location of timing belt on camshaft sprocket. Remove timing belt from camshaft sprocket.

***CAUTION: DO NOT allow timing belt to come off of crankshaft sprocket. DO NOT rotate crankshaft or camshaft when timing belt is removed, or valves may contact the pistons. See TIMING BELT under REMOVAL & INSTALLATION.***

**6)** If removing camshaft sprocket, use Holder (5034) and remove sprocket retaining bolt. Remove sprocket and spacer washer. Note direction of spacer washer installation.
**7)** Remove spark plug wires and distributor cap. Remove cylinder head bolts in proper sequence, and remove cylinder head. *See Fig. 3.*

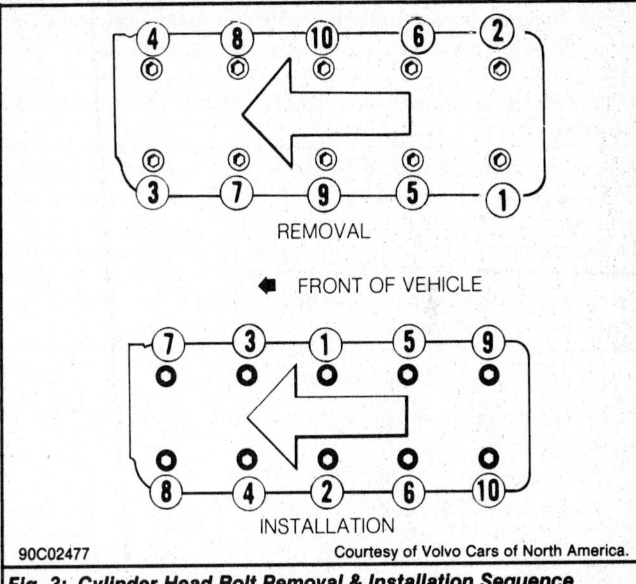


***Fig. 3: Cylinder Head Bolt Removal & Installation Sequence***

**Inspection –** Inspect cylinder head for warpage at deck surface. Resurface cylinder head if warpage exceeds specification. Cylinder head height must be within specification. See CYLINDER HEAD in ENGINE SPECIFICATIONS table.

***CAUTION: Replace cylinder head bolts if stretched or used more than 5 times. When in doubt, replace cylinder head bolts.***

**Installation – 1)** Ensure camshaft is positioned so valves are closed on No. 1 cylinder and No. 1 piston is at TDC. Install new head gasket with TOP mark upward. Ensure "O" ring for water pump sits correctly in groove. Install cylinder head.
**2)** Apply light coat of engine oil on cylinder head bolts before installation. Install and tighten bolts in sequence to specification using 3 stages. *See Fig. 3.* See TORQUE SPECIFICATIONS table at end of article.
**3)** Install remaining components. Install timing belt on camshaft sprocket in original location. Ensure all timing marks align. Adjust timing belt. See TIMING BELT under REMOVAL & INSTALLATION. To install remaining components, reverse removal procedure.

## FRONT COVER OIL SEAL (CRANKSHAFT & INTERMEDIATE SHAFT SEALS)

**Removal –** Remove timing belt. See TIMING BELT. To remove intermediate shaft seal, remove intermediate shaft sprocket and inner timing belt cover. Pry seal from front cover. To remove crankshaft seal, remove sprocket and pry seal from front cover.
**Installation –** Coat seals and seal seating areas with grease. Install seal using proper sleeve. Use Sleeve (5025) for intermediate shaft

# 1991 ENGINES
# 2.3L 4-Cylinder (Cont.)

seal or Sleeve (5283) for crankshaft seal. To install remaining components, reverse removal procedure.

## TIMING BELT

***CAUTION: Ensure timing marks align before removing timing belt. DO NOT rotate crankshaft or camshaft with timing belt removed, or valves may contact pistons.***

**Removal - 1)** Disconnect negative battery cable. Loosen adjustments and remove all drive belts and water pump pulley. Remove fan, preheater hose (below fan shroud) and fan shroud.

**2)** Using center bolt on crankshaft, rotate crankshaft so mark on camshaft pulley aligns with timing mark on inner timing belt cover, and crankshaft pulley mark aligns with TDC mark on timing belt cover.

**3)** Remove nut and washer from belt tensioner. Install Crankshaft Holder (5284) on crankshaft pulley and belt tensioner stud. Install nut on stud. Remove crankshaft center bolt, crankshaft pulley and lower timing belt cover. Ensure timing marks are aligned. *See Fig. 4.*

***NOTE: If reusing timing belt, mark direction of rotation for installation reference.***

**4)** Place mark on timing belt to indicate direction of belt rotation. Loosen belt tensioner nut one turn. Pull on timing belt to compress belt tensioner spring. Tighten belt tensioner nut.

**5)** Install a 3-mm drill bit through hole of belt tensioner bolt to lock belt tensioner spring in place. Remove timing belt from camshaft sprocket. If removing camshaft sprocket, use Holder (5034) and remove sprocket retaining bolt. Remove sprocket and spacer washer.

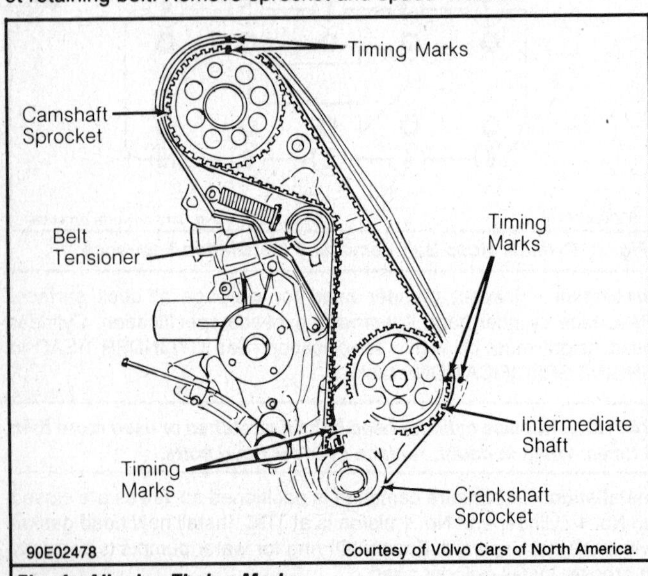


***Fig. 4: Aligning Timing Marks***

**Inspection -** Check belt teeth for cracks, damage or oil contamination. Inspect all sprockets for damage. Check belt tensioner for roughness in rotation. Replace components if damaged.

**Installation - 1)** Install belt tensioner if previously removed. Ensure all timing marks align. *See Fig. 4.*

**2)** Outer side of timing belt has 2 lines, which should fit toward crankshaft marks. Install belt over crankshaft sprocket first, then over intermediate shaft. Stretch belt on tension side and fit over camshaft sprocket. Slide back of belt onto belt tensioner.

**3)** Loosen nut on belt tensioner to permit spring tension to act against drive belt. Tighten belt tensioner nut. Ensure timing marks align. To install remaining components, reverse removal procedure.

***CAUTION: Readjust timing belt when engine reaches normal operating temperature.***

**4)** Warm engine to normal operating temperature. Remove plug from front timing belt cover. Loosen belt tensioner bolt one turn and allow belt tensioner spring to apply pressure on timing belt. This readjusts timing belt to allow for belt stretch. Tighten belt tensioner nut. Install rubber plug.

## CAMSHAFT & TAPPETS

***NOTE: Tappets may also be referred to as valve lifters. Camshaft for turbo engines are stamped with "T" and non-turbo engines are stamped with "M" at rear of camshaft.***

**Removal - 1)** Using center bolt on crankshaft, rotate crankshaft so mark on camshaft pulley aligns with timing mark on inner timing belt cover, and crankshaft pulley mark aligns with TDC mark on timing belt cover.

**2)** Loosen belt tensioner nut one turn. Pull on timing belt to compress belt tensioner spring. Tighten belt tensioner nut. Install a 3-mm drill bit through hole of belt tensioner bolt to lock tensioner spring in place.

**3)** Note location of timing belt on camshaft sprocket. Remove timing belt from camshaft sprocket.

***CAUTION: DO NOT allow timing belt to come off of crankshaft sprocket or rotate engine with timing belt removed from camshaft. It may be necessary to remove timing belt. See TIMING BELT under REMOVAL & INSTALLATION.***

**4)** Using Holder (5034), hold camshaft and remove sprocket retaining bolt. Remove sprocket and spacer washer. Note direction of spacer washer installation.

**5)** Remove valve cover and gasket. Note markings and location on camshaft bearing caps. Remove center bearing cap, and install Holder (5021) to retain camshaft in place while removing remaining bearing caps.

**6)** Remove remaining bearing caps. Remove holder, camshaft oil seal, camshaft and rubber-coated washer (at rear of camshaft).

**7)** Note location of adjusting discs for reassembly reference by recording disc thickness size marked on bottom of disc. Remove tappets, adjusting discs and valve stem rubber seals.

***CAUTION: Tappets and adjusting discs MUST be installed in original location.***

**Inspection - 1)** Inspect camshaft journal diameter, lobe lift and bearing for signs of wear. Replace camshaft if not within specification. Measure tappet diameter. Replace if not within specification. See CAMSHAFT table under ENGINE SPECIFICATIONS at end of article. Inspect tappets for scoring or wear.

**2)** Install camshaft and rear bearing cap in cylinder head. Tighten bearing cap bolts to specification. Measure camshaft end play between camshaft and thrust surface of bearing cap.

**3)** Camshaft end play should be within specification. See CAMSHAFT table. If not within specification, replace rear bearing cap.

**Installation - 1)** To install, reverse removal procedure. Lubricate all components with engine oil before installation. Install new valve stem rubber seals. Install adjusting discs and tappets in original location.

**2)** Install camshaft with dowel pin for camshaft sprocket toward top of cylinder head. Apply Sealant (1161027-6) on front and rear bearing cap-to-cylinder head sealing surfaces before installation. Once all bearing caps are installed, tighten retaining bolts to specification.

**3)** Lubricate lip of front seal and camshaft. Using Seal Installer (5025), install seal in cylinder head. To install remaining components, reverse removal procedure. Adjust valve clearance. See VALVE CLEARANCE ADJUSTMENT under ADJUSTMENTS.

## INTERMEDIATE SHAFT

**Removal - 1)** Remove timing belt. See TIMING BELT under REMOVAL & INSTALLATION. Using Holder (5034), hold intermediate shaft sprocket and remove sprocket retaining bolt. Remove intermediate shaft sprocket and crankshaft sprocket.

**2)** Remove intermediate shaft and crankshaft sprocket seals from front cover. Remove front cover-to-oil pan bolts, and remove front cover. Remove oil trap (located above oil pump drive gear), oil pump drive gear and distributor. Remove intermediate shaft.

**Inspection** – Inspect bearing journals for damage. Check bearing I.D. and intermediate shaft bearing journal O.D. Ensure oil clearance is within specification. Replace components if not within specification. See INTERMEDIATE SHAFT table under ENGINE SPECIFICATIONS at end of article.

**Installation – 1)** To install, reverse removal procedure. Lubricate intermediate shaft and oil pump drive gear with oil before installation. Ensure end play is within specification. See INTERMEDIATE SHAFT table under ENGINE SPECIFICATIONS at end of article.

**2)** Install front cover with new gasket. Install new intermediate shaft and crankshaft oil seals. Install oil trap with new "O" ring.

### REAR MAIN BEARING OIL SEAL

***NOTE: Before removing oil seal, note and record for reassembly reference if oil seal is even with seal outer housing or if seal is located .12" (3.0 mm) below outer housing lip.***

**Removal** – Remove transmission, clutch (if equipped) and flywheel or drive plate. Pry seal from housing, using care not to scratch/score crankshaft.

**Installation – 1)** Assemble Handle (1801) and Drift (5276) with all spacers. Apply oil to seal contact surface or crankshaft and oil seal lips. Install seal on drift. If crankshaft shows signs of wear, install seal beyond wear point.

**2)** Remove one spacer from drift if old seal was even with housing. Remove 2 spacers from drift if old oil seal was below seal housing .12" (3.0 mm). If no signs of wear exist, place both spacers on drift.

**3)** Install seal until drift bottoms on crankshaft. To install remaining components, reverse removal procedure.

***CAUTION: Install NEW flywheel or drive plate bolts. Apply thread sealant to new bolts before installation.***

### WATER PUMP

**Removal – 1)** Disconnect negative battery cable. On A/C-equipped models, disconnect vacuum hose from water valve. Position heater control to WARM position. Remove coolant expansion tank cap. Open drain valve on right side of engine block, and remove lower radiator hose.

**2)** Remove fan shroud, fan and preheating hose clamp (beneath fan shroud). Remove drive belts and water pump pulley. Remove upper timing belt cover. Remove coolant return pipe from water pump. Remove nuts, bolts and water pump.

**Installation** – To install, reverse removal procedure. Install water pump retaining nuts and bolts so pump does not slip but can be moved upward. Pry water pump upwards against cylinder head, while tightening nuts and bolts. Install return pipe. Check for water pump sealing before completing installation. Fill cooling system.

### OIL PAN

**Removal – 1)** Disconnect negative battery cable. Raise and support front of vehicle. Drain engine oil. Remove splash guard. Disconnect exhaust pipe at front of muffler (if necessary). Remove engine mount nuts from underside of crossmember.

**2)** Loosen steering shaft joint assembly upper bolt. Remove lower joint bolt. Slide joint assembly upward on steering shaft.

**3)** Loosen fan shroud. Remove oil dipstick. Raise engine slightly. DO NOT raise too high or distributor cap may be damaged. Remove left engine mount. Remove front axle crossmember bolts and remove crossmember.

**4)** Remove support bracket located between rear of oil pan and clutch housing (if equipped). It may be necessary to disconnect hose at power steering reservoir. Remove oil pan bolts. Turn and lower oil pan to remove.

**Installation** – To install oil pan, reverse removal procedure. Tighten all bolts to specification. See TORQUE SPECIFICATIONS table at end of article.

## OVERHAUL

### CYLINDER HEAD

**Cylinder Head** – Inspect cylinder head for warpage at manifold and cylinder block areas. Resurface or replace cylinder head if warpage exceeds specification. Ensure cylinder height is within specification. See CYLINDER HEAD table under ENGINE SPECIFICATIONS at end of article.

**Valve Springs** – Ensure valve spring free length, out-of-square and pressure is within specification. See VALVES & VALVE SPRINGS table under ENGINE SPECIFICATIONS at end of article.

**Valve Stem Oil Seals** – Seals are used only on intake valves. Use Valve Stem Oil Seal Installer (5219) to install seals. Seals should be installed with spring area toward top of valve stem.

**Valve Guides – 1)** Ensure valve stem diameter and clearance are within specification. See CYLINDER HEAD table under ENGINE SPECIFICATIONS at end of article.

**2)** If clearance exceeds specification, valve guide can be replaced with an oversized valve guide. Valve guides are identified by grooves on the guide. See OVERSIZED VALVE GUIDE SPECIFICATIONS table.

***OVERSIZED VALVE GUIDE SPECIFICATIONS***

| Number Of Grooves | Size | Reamer Part No. |
|---|---|---|
| 0 | Standard | Not Required |
| 1 | Oversize 1 | 5161 |
| 2 | Oversize 2 | 5162 |
| 3 | Oversize 3 | 5163 |

**3)** To remove valve guide, heat cylinder head to 212°F (44°C). Using Drift (5218), press valve guide from cylinder head toward combustion chamber side. Ensure valve guide does not seize during removal. If valve guide seizes, valve guide bore must be reamed to oversize.

**4)** To install, with cylinder head at room temperature, use Intake Guide Drift (5027) and Exhaust Guide Drift (5028). To obtain proper installed height, install valve guide into cylinder head until drift contacts cylinder head. Ensure replacement valve guide is same size as that removed. Once valve guide is installed, use Reamer (5224) to clean valve guide bore.

***NOTE: Force required to install valve guide should be at least 2000 lbs. (907 kg). If required force is less than specification, remove valve guide and ream to nearest oversized valve guide using proper reamer. See OVERSIZED VALVE GUIDE SPECIFICATIONS table.***

***NOTE: ALWAYS replace valve guide before replacing valve seats.***

**Valve Seat Removal – 1)** Grind 2 notches in valve seat to release valve seat tension. Grind an additional notch in valve seat.

**2)** Using chisel, split valve seat at additional notch area. From inside cylinder head, use drift to tap out valve seat.

**3)** Check valve seat recess for damage. Using micrometer, measure diameter of valve seat recess to determine if oversized valve seat is used.

**4)** Valve seats are not marked and must be measured to determine if oversized. See CYLINDER HEAD table under ENGINE SPECIFICATIONS at end of article.

***NOTE: Valve seat diameter should be .0067" (.170 mm) larger than seat bore to provide proper interference fit. If seat is not within specification, grind seat bore for oversized valve seat.***

**Valve Seat Installation** – Heat cylinder head to 212°F (100°C). Install valve seat on Valve Seat Installer (5220 for exhaust valves or 5029 for intake valves). Using carbon dioxide or similar agent, cool valve seat to -94°F (-70°C). Install valve seat within 3-4 seconds. Ensure valve seat bottoms and fits securely.

# 1991 ENGINES
# 2.3L 4-Cylinder (Cont.)

**Seat Correction Angles** - Finished seat angles are 45 degrees with intake seat face length .051-.075 (1.30-1.90 mm) and exhaust seat face length .067-.091 (70-2.30 mm).
**Valves** - Valves are stellite coated and must not be machined. They may be lapped into valve seat.

***CAUTION: Exhaust valves on turbo models are sodium filled. Use extreme care when disposing of damaged or worn sodium-filled exhaust valves.***

## CYLINDER BLOCK ASSEMBLY

**Piston & Rod Assembly** - Piston pin should slide through connecting rod and piston with light thumb pressure. Install piston on connecting rod so notch in piston aligns with identification area (number) of connecting rod. *See Fig. 5.* Install piston and rod assembly with notch on top of piston toward front of engine.

***CAUTION: DO NOT reuse connecting rod bolts if length exceeds 2.187" (55.54 mm). Apply light coat of engine oil to connecting rod bolts before installation.***

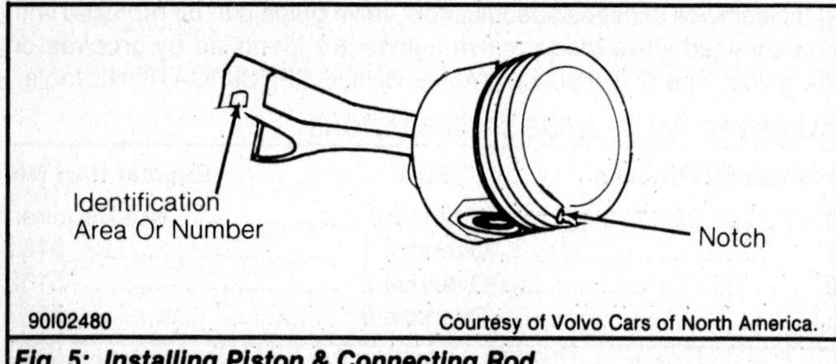


***Fig. 5: Installing Piston & Connecting Rod***

**Fitting Pistons** - **1)** Cylinder block may have different bore sizes as designated by letter marked on deck surface near cylinder bore or mark on top of piston (if used). This letter must be used to determine piston diameter.
**2)** Measure piston diameter at right angle to piston pin .28" (7 mm) from bottom of piston skirt. Replace piston if diameter is not within specification. See PISTONS, PINS & RINGS table under ENGINE SPECIFICATIONS at end of article.
**3)** Ensure piston is installed with notch toward front of engine and number on connecting rod is toward oil filter side of engine.
**Piston Rings** - Ensure ring gap and side clearance are within specification. See PISTONS, PINS & RINGS table under ENGINE SPECIFICATIONS at end of article. Ring gap is measured with piston ring at bottom of ring travel in cylinder. Install piston rings onto pistons so that ends of rings are positioned 120 degrees apart. Ensure ring gap ends DO NOT align with piston pin.
**Rod Bearings** - Connecting rod bearings are color coded. Assembly No. 1 contains Yellow color code and assembly No. 2 contains one Blue and one Red color code (Blue in connecting rod and Red in rod cap). Only Yellow color code assemblies are kept in stock for replacement. Ensure piston is installed with notch toward front of engine and number on connecting rod toward oil filter side of engine.

***NOTE: Apply light coat of engine oil on main bearing cap bolts before installation.***

**Crankshaft & Main Bearings** - Two different manufacturers supply main bearings. Ensure main bearings are supplied by same manufacturer as designated by markings on outside of bearings. Arrow on top of main bearing cap should be installed toward front of engine and in numerical sequence, according to cap number stamped near the arrow.
**Cylinder Block** - **1)** Using feeler gauge and straightedge, check cylinder block head surface warpage. If warpage exceeds specification, replace cylinder block. See CYLINDER BLOCK table under ENGINE SPECIFICATIONS at end of article.
**2)** Check diameter of cylinder bore. Different cylinder bore sizes are used and can be identified by size marks on deck surface of cylinder block.
**3)** Ensure diameter of cylinder bore is within specification. See CYLINDER BLOCK table under ENGINE SPECIFICATIONS table.

## ENGINE OILING

### ENGINE LUBRICATION SYSTEM

A gear-type, shaft-driven oil pump provides pressurized lubrication. Turbo models use an air cooled oil cooler located at the side of the radiator. An engine oil thermostat, located at oil cooler fitting, controls oil temperature.

From oil filter, oil is supplied to drilled galley in center of cylinder block and to main, connecting rod and camshaft bearings. Lubrication for camshaft bearings is used to lubricate upper valve components. Excess oil returns to sump through drain holes in block assembly and through drain hose connected to oil trap and secured to oil pump in upper block.
**Crankcase Capacity** - Oil capacity on non-turbo models with oil filter is 4.1 qts. (3.9L). On turbo models, when oil cooler is drained, oil capacity with filter is 4.7 qts. (4.5L).
**Oil Pressure** - Oil pressure is 36-85 psi (2.5-6.0 kg/cm²) at 2000 RPM with engine at normal operating temperature. Nonadjustable pressure relief valve is located in oil pump housing.

### OIL PUMP

**Removal** - Remove oil pan. See OIL PAN under REMOVAL & INSTALLATION. Remove oil pump retaining bolts and oil pump.
**Disassembly & Inspection** - Disassemble and clean all parts thoroughly. Check all parts for excessive wear. Measure clearance between teeth of pump gears. Place straightedge across pump body, above gears. Measure gear end clearance between gear and straightedge. Measure relief valve spring free length and spring pressure. Replace components if not within specification. See OIL PUMP SPECIFICATIONS table.
**Reassembly & Installation** - To reassemble, reverse disassembly procedure. Install new "O" rings on delivery pipe. To install, reverse removal procedure. Ensure oil pump properly engages in pump drive shaft.

***OIL PUMP SPECIFICATIONS***

| Application | Specification |
|---|---|
| Gear End Clearance | .0008-.0048" (.02-.12 mm) |
| Gear Teeth Clearance | .006-.014" (.15-.35 mm) |
| Relief Valve Spring | |
| Free Length | 1.54" (39.1 mm) |
| Spring Pressure | 10.0-12.0 lbs. (4.5-5.4 kg) @ 1.034" (26.26 mm) |
| | 13.6-17.2 lbs. (6.2-7.8 kg) @ .830" (21.01 mm) |

# 1991 ENGINES
# 2.3L 4-Cylinder (Cont.)

## TORQUE SPECIFICATIONS

### TORQUE SPECIFICATIONS

| Application | Ft. Lbs. (N.m) |
|---|---|
| Camshaft Bearing Cap Bolt [1] | 15 (20) |
| Camshaft Sprocket Bolt | 35 (50) |
| Connecting Rod Cap Bolt [1] [2] | |
| Step 1 | 14 (19) |
| Step 2 | Additional 90 Degrees |
| Crankshaft Pulley Bolt [1] | |
| Step 1 | 45 (60) |
| Step 2 | Additonal 60 Degrees |
| Cylinder Head Bolt [1] [3] | |
| Step 1 | 14 (19) |
| Step 2 | 43 (58) |
| Step 3 | Additional 90 Degrees |
| Exhaust Pipe-To-Turbo Bolt | 22 (30) |
| Flywheel Or Drive Plate Bolt [4] | 51 (69) |
| Intermediate Shaft Sprocket Bolt | 37 (51) |
| Main Bearing Cap Bolt [1] | 80 (110) |
| Torque Converter-To-Drive Plate Bolt | 30-37 (41-51) |

1 – Apply light coat of oil to bolts before installation.
2 – DO NOT reuse bolt if length exceeds 2.187" (55.54 mm).
3 – Tighten in sequence. *See Fig. 1.*
4 – Always use NEW bolts. Apply thread sealant to bolts before installation.

## ENGINE SPECIFICATIONS

### GENERAL SPECIFICATIONS

| Application | Specification |
|---|---|
| Displacement | 141.0 Cu In. |
| Bore | |
| Standard "C" | 3.78" (96.0 mm) |
| Stroke | 3.15" (80.0 mm) |
| Compression Ratio | |
| Non-Turbo | 9.8:1 |
| Turbo | 8.7:1 |
| Fuel System | MPI |
| HP @ RPM | |
| Non-Turbo | 114 @5400 |
| Turbo | 162 @ 4800 |
| Torque Ft. Lbs. @ RPM | |
| Non-Turbo | 136 @ 2700 |
| Turbo | 206 @ 3900 |

### CYLINDER BLOCK

| Application | In. (mm) |
|---|---|
| Cylinder Bore | |
| Diameter | |
| Standard "C" | [1] 3.7795-3.7799 (96.00-96.01) |
| Standard "D" | [1] 3.799-3.803 (96.01-96.02) |
| Standard "E" | [1] 3.7803-3.7807 (96.02-96.03) |
| Standard "G" | [1] 3.,7811-3.7815 (96.04-96.05) |
| Oversize "1" | [1] 3.7913 (96.3) |
| Oversize "2" | [1] 3.8031 (96.6) |
| Maximum Taper & Out-Of-Round | .004 (.10) |
| Minimum Deck Height | [2] |
| Maximum Deck Warpage | [2] |

1 – Cylinder bore diameter is indicated by letter or number stamped on deck surface.
2 – Information is not available from manufacturer.

### CRANKSHAFT, MAIN & CONNECTING ROD BEARINGS

| Application | In. (mm) |
|---|---|
| Crankshaft | |
| End Play | .0032-.0106 (.080-.270) |
| Runout | .0010 (.025) |
| Main Bearings | |
| Journal Diameter | |
| Standard | 2.1648-2.1694 (54.987-55.000) |
| Undersize "1" | 2.1550-2.1555 (54.737-54.750) |
| Undersize "2" | 2.1451-2.1457 (54.487-54.500) |
| Journal Out-Of-Round & Taper | .00016 (.004) |
| Oil Clearance | .0009-.0024 (.024-.061) |
| Thrust Bearing (Width) | |
| Standard | 1.258-1.260 (31.96-32.00) |
| Oversize "1" | 1.268-1.270 (32.21-32.25) |
| Oversize "2" | 1.278-1.280 (32.46-32.50) |
| Connecting Rod Bearings | |
| Journal Diameter | |
| Standard | 1.9285-1.9293 (48.984-49.005) |
| Undersize "1" | 1.9187-1.9195 (48.734-48.755) |
| Undersize "2" | 1.9088-1.9096 (48.484-48.505) |
| Journal Out-Of-Round & Taper | .00016 (.004) |
| Oil Clearance | .0009-.0026 (.023-.066) |

### CONNECTING RODS

| Application | In. (mm) |
|---|---|
| Bore Diameter | |
| Pin Bore | [1] |
| Crankpin Bore | [1] |
| Center-To-Center Length | 5.705-5.7129 (144.9-145.1) |
| Maximum Bend Or Twist | [1] |
| Side Play | .001-.018 (.03-.46) |

1 – Information is not available from manufacturer.

### PISTONS, PINS & RINGS

| Application | In. (mm) |
|---|---|
| Pistons | |
| Clearance | .0004-.0012 (.010-.030) |
| Diameter | |
| Standard ("C") | 3.7787-3.7791 (95.978-95.989) |
| Standard ("D") | 3.7791-3.7795 (95.989-95.999) |
| Standard ("E") | 3.7795-3.7799 (95.999-96.009) |
| Standard ("G") | 3.7811-3.7815 (96.039-96.050) |
| Oversize "1" | 3.7905-3.7909 (96.278-96.288) |
| Oversize "2" | 3.8024-3.8028 (96.581-96.591) |
| Pins | |
| Diameter | |
| Standard | .906 (23.00) |
| Oversize | .907 (23.05) |
| Piston fit | Thumb pressure |
| Rod Fit | Thumb pressure |
| Rings | |
| No. 1 (Top) | |
| End Gap | .012-.022 (.30-.55) |
| Side Clearance | .0024-.0036 (.060-.092) |
| No. 2 (Center) | |
| End Gap | .012-.022 (.30-.55) |
| Side Clearance | .0016-.0028 (.040-.072) |
| No. 3 (Oil) | |
| End Gap | .012-.024 (.30-.60) |
| Side Clearance | .0012-.0025 (.030-.065) |

# 1991 ENGINES
# 2.3L 4-Cylinder (Cont.)

## CYLINDER HEAD

| Application | Specification |
|---|---|
| Cylinder Head Height | 5.752" (146.1 mm) |
| Maximum Warpage | |
| Crosswise | .02" (.50 mm) |
| Lengthwise | .04" (1.00 mm) |
| Valve Seats | |
| Intake Valve | |
| Seat Angle | 45° |
| Seat Width | .051-.075" (1.27-1.91 mm) |
| Maximum Seat Runout | [1] |
| Seat Bore Diameter | [2] |
| Seat Diameter | |
| Standard | 1.8110" (45.999 mm) |
| Oversize "1" | 1.8209" (46.251 mm) |
| Oversize "2" | 1.8307" (46.499 mm) |
| Exhaust Valve | |
| Seat Angle | 45° |
| Seat Width | .066-.091" (1.68-2.31 mm) |
| Maximum Seat Runout | [1] |
| Seat Bore Diameter | [2] |
| Seat Diameter | |
| Standard | 1.4960" (37.998 mm) |
| Oversize "1" | 1.5059" (38.249 mm) |
| Oversize "2" | 1.5157" (38.498 mm) |
| Valve Guides | |
| Intake Valve | |
| Valve Guide Cylinder Head Bore I.D. | [3] |
| Valve Guide I.D. | .3150-.3158" (8.000-8.022 mm) |
| Valve Guide Installed Height | .606-.614" (15.39-15.59 mm) |
| Valve Stem-To-Guide Clearance | .0012-.0024" (.030-.060 mm) |
| Exhaust Valve | |
| Valve Guide Cylinder Head Bore I.D. | [3] |
| Valve Guide I.D. | .3150-.3158" (8.000-8.022 mm) |
| Valve Guide Installed Height | .705-.713" (17.91-18.11 mm) |
| Valve Stem-To-Guide Oil Clearance | .0024-.0035" (.060-.090 mm) |

[1] – Information not available from manufacturer.
[2] – Valve seats should have .0068" (.17 mm) interference fit to head seat bore diameter.
[3] – Valve guides are available in 3 oversizes and identified by number of outer grooves at top of guide. Installation force for guides must exceed 2000lbs. (9000 N).

## CAMSHAFT

| Application | In. (mm) |
|---|---|
| Bearing I.D. Diameter | 1.1811-1.1800 (30.000-30.021) |
| End Play | .004-.016 (.10-.40) |
| Journal Diameter | 1.1791-1.1799 (29.950-29.970) |
| Journal Runout | [1] |
| Lobe Height | [1] |
| Lobe Lift | |
| Intake | [2] .374 (9.49) |
| Exhaust | [2] .413 (10.49) |
| Oil Clearance | .0012-.0028 (.030-.071) |

[1] – Information is not available.
[2] – Lobe Lift using standard camshaft (Volvo P/N 1336779-2). Turbo model uses lobe lift of .3901" (9.908 mm) for both intake and exhaust valves.

## INTERMEDIATE SHAFT

| Application | In. (mm) |
|---|---|
| Front Bearing I.D. Diameter | 1.8512-1.8524 (47.020-47.050) |
| Front Journal O.D. Diameter | 1.8494-1.8504 (46.975-47.000) |
| Center Bearing I.D. Diameter | 1.6957-1.6969 (43.070-43.100) |
| Center Journal O.D. Diameter | 1.6939-1.6949 (43.025-43.050) |
| Rear Bearing I.D. Diameter | 1.6917-1.6929 (43.970-43.000) |
| Rear Journal O.D. Diameter | 1.6900-1.6909 (42.925-42.950) |
| Oil Clearance | .0008-.0030 (.020-.075) |

## VALVES & VALVE SPRINGS

| Application | Specification |
|---|---|
| Intake Valves [1] | |
| Face Angle | 44.5° |
| Head Diameter | 1.73" (44 mm) |
| Minimum Margin | [2] |
| Minimum Refinish Length | [2] |
| Stem Diameter | .3132-.3138" (7.955-7.970 mm) |
| Valve Tip Maximum Refinish | [2] |
| Exhaust Valves | |
| Face Angle | 44.5° |
| Head Diameter | 1.38" (35 mm) |
| Minimum Margin | [2] |
| Minimum Refinish Length | [2] |
| Stem Diameter | .3128-.3134" (7.945-7.960 mm) |
| Valve Tip Maximum Refinish | [2] |
| Valve Springs | |
| Free Length | 1.79" (45.5 mm) |
| Installed Height | |
| Valve Closed | 1.08" (27.5 mm) |
| Valve Open | 1.50" (38 mm) |
| Out-Of-Square | [2] |
| Pressure | |
| Valve Closed | 154-162 lbs. (702-782 N) |
| Valve Open | 62-70 lbs. (280-320 N) |

[1] – Valves are stellite coated and cannot be machined. Valves may ONLY be lapped to seats.
[2] – Information is not available from manufacturer.

## VALVE LIFTERS (TAPPETS)

| Application | In. (mm) |
|---|---|
| Lifter Diameter | 1.4557-1.4565 (36.975-36.995) |
| Lifter Height | 1.180-1.220 (29.97-30.99) |
| Oil Clearance | .0012-.0030 (.030-.076) |
| Adjusting Disc Diameter | 1.2984-1.2992 (32.980-33.000) |
| Adjusting Disc Thickness | In Increments of .002 (.05) |

# 1991 CLUTCHES
# RWD

## 240, 740

## DESCRIPTION

Clutch is single dry disc type, using a diaphragm spring type pressure plate. Two types of clutch systems are used: hydraulic or mechanical. *See Figs. 1 and 2.*

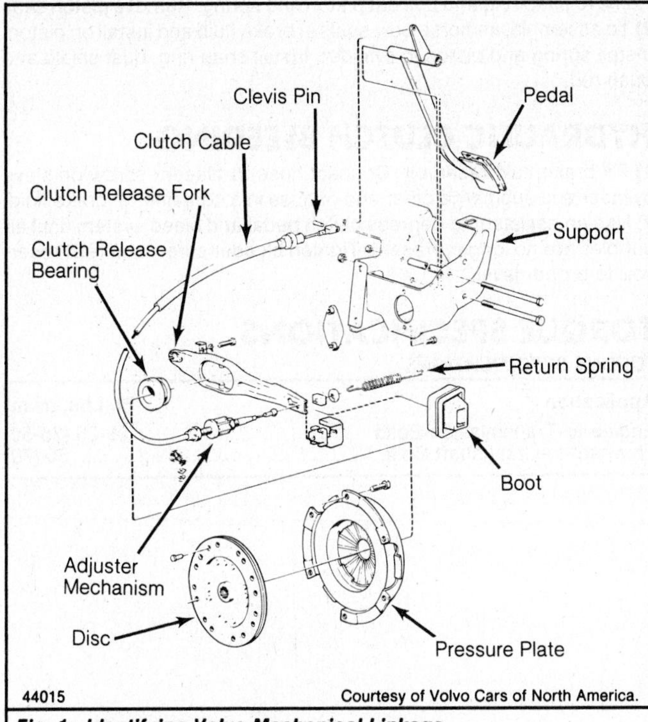


***Fig. 1: Identifying Volvo Mechanical Linkage Clutch Components***

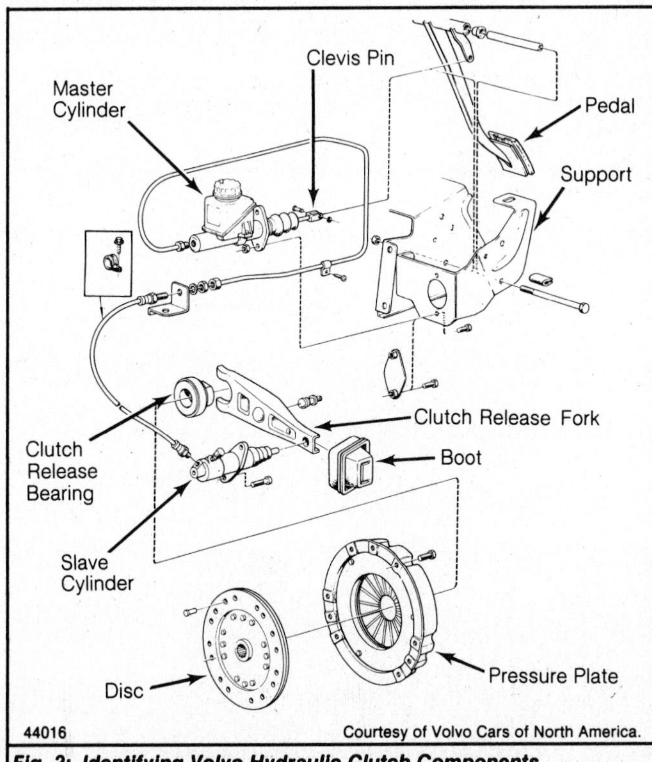


***Fig. 2: Identifying Volvo Hydraulic Clutch Components***

## ADJUSTMENTS

### CLUTCH PEDAL FREE PLAY

Rotate clutch cable at clutch housing to set free play. *See Fig. 3.* Adjustment to approximately .04-.12" (1.0-3.0 mm).

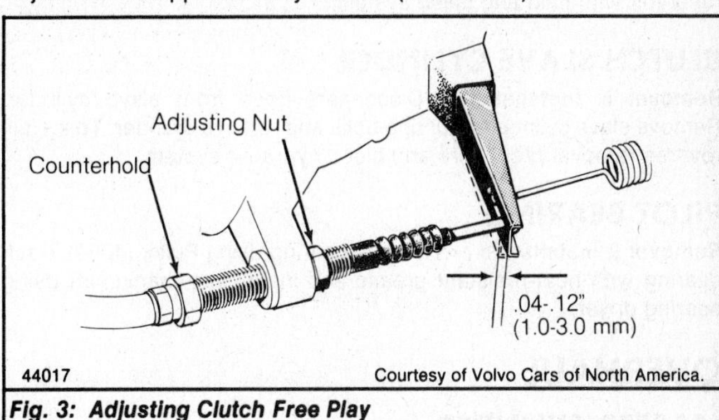


***Fig. 3: Adjusting Clutch Free Play***

## REMOVAL & INSTALLATION

### CLUTCH ASSEMBLY

**Removal - 1)** Disconnect negative battery cable and back-up light wiring harness connector. Working from under vehicle, disconnect gearshift lever from gearshift rod. Remove lock screw and pin. Avoid exerting force on transmission.

**2)** On hydraulic clutch systems, unbolt slave cylinder from housing and disconnect from release arm. On mechanical clutch systems, unhook clutch fork spring and separate cable from housing. On all models, separate shift boot from carpet.

**3)** Remove reverse gear detent plate. Remove snap ring and lift out gearshift lever. Remove front exhaust pipe bracket and position support under engine. Remove crossmember at rear of transmission. Mark drive shaft and disconnect from transmission.

**4)** Disconnect speedometer cable from transmission. Remove starter. Remove clutch housing cover plates and all bolts except 2 at bottom. Install transmission jack and remove last 2 clutch housing bolts.

**5)** Pull transmission rearward and turn to clear propeller shaft tunnel. Lower transmission from vehicle. Loosen pressure plate bolts gradually in a diagonal pattern and remove clutch assembly. Check pilot bearing and flywheel surface for any cracks or excess wear.

**Inspection - 1)** Check clutch release fork, bearing, pressure plate, disc and flywheel for damage or discoloring. Check disc for wear. Check clutch release bearing for smooth rotation.

**2)** Inspect master and slave cylinders for leakage (if equipped). Inspect clutch cable for fraying, bends or other damage (if equipped). Replace components as necessary.

**Installation -** Ensure flywheel and pressure plate are free of grease. Using clutch alignment tool, install disc with long side of hub facing back. Install pressure plate, and tighten bolts gradually in a diagonal pattern. To complete installation, reverse removal procedure.

***NOTE: Components cannot be interchanged between models.***

### CLUTCH CABLE

**Removal & Installation - 1)** Raise vehicle. On all models except Turbo, disconnect return spring and loosen cable. On all models, disconnect cable from fork, bellhousing and clamp at fuel filter.

**2)** Remove underdash panel. Remove locking pin and rubber bushing. Pull cable out of firewall. To install, reverse removal procedure. Adjust clutch free play. *See Fig. 3.*

### CLUTCH MASTER CYLINDER

**Removal & Installation - 1)** Remove panel under instrument panel. Remove pin and locking spring from clutch pedal. Disconnect hose from clutch fluid reservoir.

# 1991 CLUTCHES
# RWD (Cont.)

**2)** Open bleed nipple from cylinder housing and position container to collect fluid. Remove bolts holding cylinder and remove cylinder.
**3)** Install cylinder and attaching bolts. Install pin and locking spring making sure there is .04" (1.0 mm) clearance between push rod and piston. Adjust if necessary. Install panel under instrument panel. Fill reservoir with fluid and bleed system.

### CLUTCH SLAVE CYLINDER

**Removal & Installation** – Disconnect hose from slave cylinder. Remove slave cylinder mounting bolts and remove cylinder. To install, reverse removal procedure and bleed hydraulic system.

### PILOT BEARING

**Removal & Installation** – Remove bearing using Puller (4090). Pack bearing with heat-resistant grease and install into crankshaft using bearing driver.

## OVERHAUL

### MASTER CYLINDER

**Disassembly & Reassembly** – **1)** Remove dust shield and push rod. Remove snap ring and washer. Pull out piston and remove spring. Remove seals from piston. Clean and inspect parts that are to be reused.
**2)** To assemble, soak new piston seals in brake fluid and install on piston. Install spring and piston in cylinder. Install washer and snap ring. Install dust shield and push rod.

### SLAVE CYLINDER

**Disassembly & Reassembly** – **1)** Remove dust shield and push rod. Remove snap ring and pull out piston and spring. Remove piston seal.
**2)** To assemble, immerse new seals in brake fluid and install on piston. Install spring and piston in cylinder. Install snap ring, dust shield and push rod.

## HYDRAULIC CLUTCH BLEEDING

**1)** Fill brake fluid reservoir. Connect hose to bleeder screw on slave cylinder and submerge other end of hose in a container of brake fluid.
**2)** Use an assistant to depress clutch pedal and bleed system until air bubbles are no longer present. Tighten bleeder screw and refill reservoir to proper level.

## TORQUE SPECIFICATIONS

***TORQUE SPECIFICATIONS***

| Application | Ft. Lbs. (N.m) |
|---|---|
| Engine-to-Transmission Bolts | 25-35 (35-50) |
| Flywheel-to-Crankshaft Bolts | 50 (70) |

# 1991 DRIVE AXLES
# Differentials & Axle Shafts

## 240, 740, 940

## DESCRIPTION & OPERATION

All 240 and some 740 models use a type 1031 rear axle assembly. Axle shafts are semi-floating. *See Fig. 1*. Limited Slip Differential LSD) is available on 240 models. *See Fig. 2*. LSD cases are of 2-piece design and use 4 pinion gears mounted on a spider. Differential adjustments are made with shims.

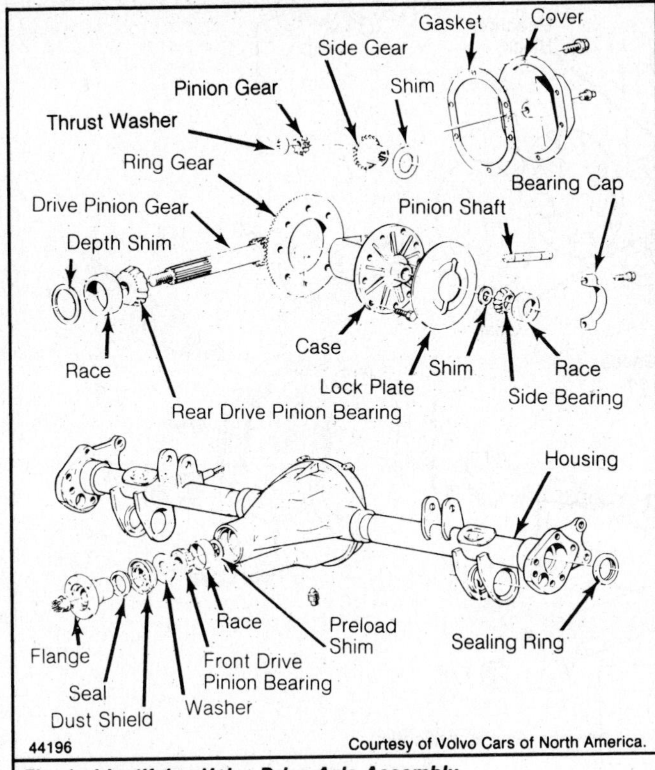


**Fig. 1: Identifying Volvo Drive Axle Assembly (Type 1031 Axle Is Shown)**

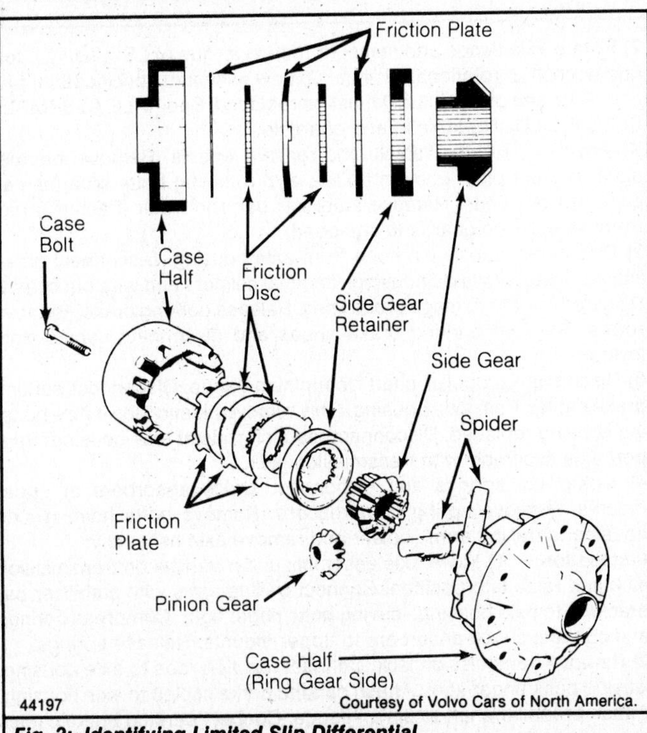


**Fig. 2: Identifying Limited Slip Differential (Type 1031 Axle Is Shown)**

Some 740 and all 940 models except 940 SE use type 1041 rear axle assembly. All 940 SE models use type 1045 multi-link axle assembly.

An automatic differential lock system is available on 1041 and 1045 axle assemblies. *See Fig. 3*. The differential locking mechanism is controlled by a centrifugal governor. After it has engaged and locked the differential automatically, the mechanism transfers the driving force to the wheel which has the most traction at the particular instant.

The device operates automatically when one of the drive wheels is spinning and the speed of the vehicle is less than 25 MPH. Under normal conditions, the unit functions as a conventional differential, even at low speeds.

## AXLE IDENTIFICATION

***AXLE IDENTIFICATION***

| Application | Axle Type |
|---|---|
| 240 | 1031 |
| 740 | 1031 or [1] 1041 |
| 940 (Except SE) | [1] 1041 |
| 940 SE | [1] 1045 |

[1] – Information on 1041 conventional axle and 1045 multi-link axle is not available from manufacturer. However, differential information on these axles equipped with automatic differential lock is available. See DIFFERENTIAL ASSEMBLY under OVERHAUL.

## AXLE RATIO

Several different ratios are used. Plate attached to left or right rear side of final drive housing gives axle ratio, part number, and serial number. Divide number of ring gear teeth by number of drive pinion gear teeth to determine axle ratio.

## LUBRICATION

### CAPACITY & FLUID TYPE

***DIFFERENTIAL CAPACITY & FLUID TYPE***

| Application | Quantity |
|---|---|
| 1031 & 1041 | 1.7 Qts. (1.6L) |
| 1045 | 1.5 Qts. (1.4L) |

## TROUBLE SHOOTING

See TROUBLE SHOOTING article in GENERAL INFORMATION.

## REMOVAL & INSTALLATION

***NOTE: Removal and installation information for 1041 and 1045 axle is not available from manufacturer. However, differential information on these axles (equipped with automatic differential lock) is available. See DIFFERENTIAL ASSEMBLY under OVERHAUL.***

### AXLE SHAFTS & BEARING

***NOTE: Although axle shaft bearing end play is not adjustable, it should be checked prior to disassembly.***

**Removal – 1)** Remove rear wheels and collision guards (if equipped). Disconnect brake line and bracket from axle housing. Remove caliper and support. Wire caliper out of way, being careful not to damage brake line. Ensure parking brake is fully released.

**2)** Remove brake rotor set screws. Take off rotors, tapping with soft mallet (if necessary). Remove parking brake shoes, unhooking retaining springs. Disconnect parking brake cables by driving out lock pin at lever.

**3)** Remove bolts for bearing retainer through holes in axle flange. Remove axle shaft using puller. Pry inner seal from housing. Press bearing and snap ring off axle shaft. Remove oil seal.

# 1991 DRIVE AXLES
# Differentials & Axle Shafts (Cont.)

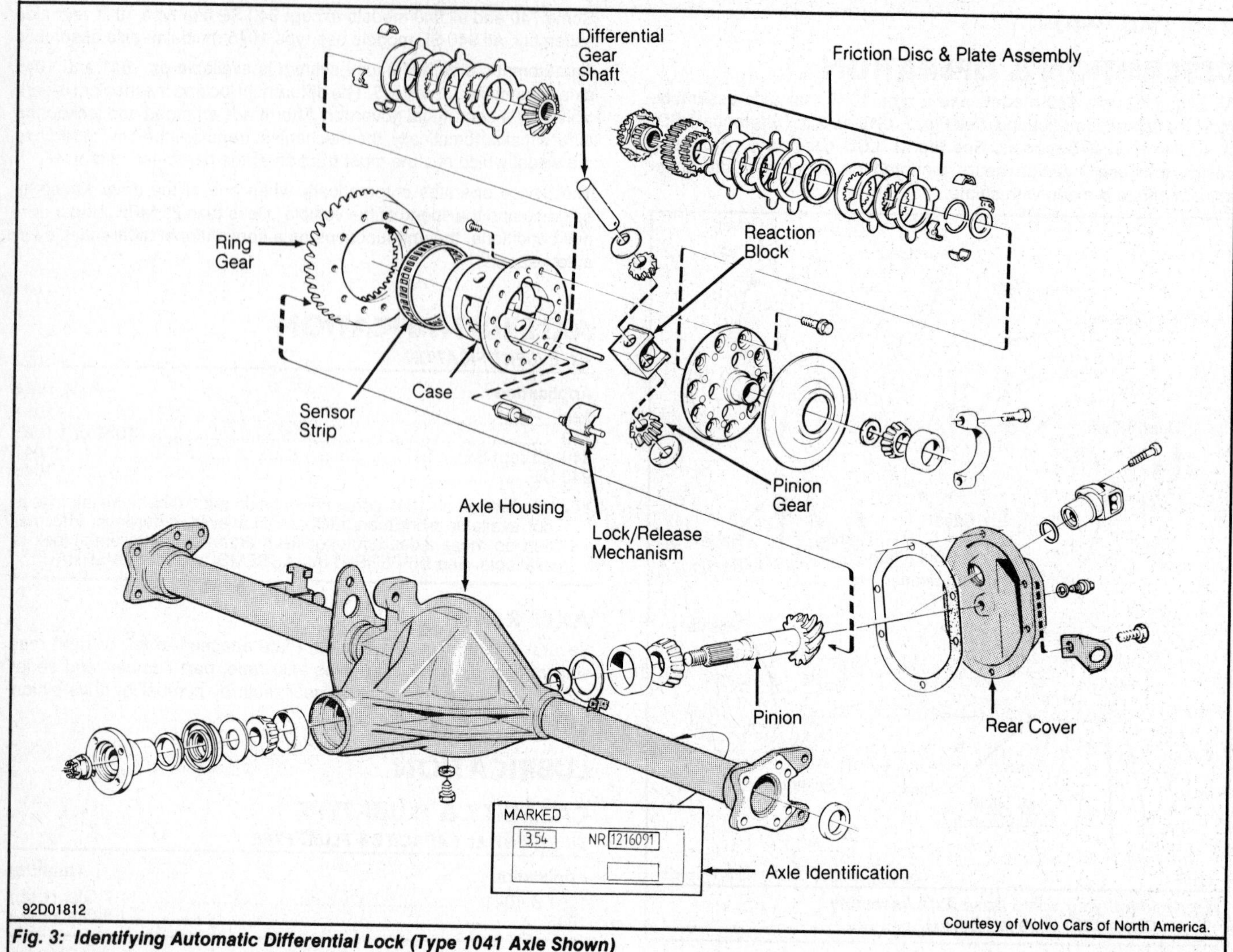


Courtesy of Volvo Cars of North America.

*Fig. 3: Identifying Automatic Differential Lock (Type 1041 Axle Shown)*

**Installation** – **1)** Pack new bearing and new seal lip groove with high temperature wheel bearing grease. Place bearing retainer and oil seal on axle shaft. Press new bearing and new snap ring onto axle shaft. Narrow side of taper fits into axle housing.

**2)** Clean axle housing and drive in new inner seal. Install axle shaft and tighten bearing retainer bolts. Install parking brake shoes and reconnect cables. Install rotors.

**3)** Check parking brake adjustment. Install brake caliper, pads, and collision guard (if equipped). Reconnect brake line and bracket to axle housing. Install wheels.

## PINION FLANGES & OIL SEAL

**Removal** – Disconnect propeller shaft at pinion flange. Remove pinion flange nut. Remove flange using puller. Remove old oil seal and dust shield.

**Installation** – Drive new seal into housing after packing seal spring and lips with grease. Unless packed, seal spring could jump out of position. Press flange onto drive pinion. Install flange washer and nut and tighten to specification. See TORQUE SPECIFICATIONS at end of article. Reconnect propeller shaft to drive pinion flange.

## AXLE ASSEMBLY

***NOTE: On models equipped with Limited Slip Differential (LSD), rotational friction of LSD must be checked with axle assembly in vehicle.***

**Checking Procedure** – **1)** Raise one rear wheel and block opposite side. Place transmission in Neutral. Release parking brake. Remove raised wheel. Attach torque wrench to axle flange.

**2)** Rotate axle flange and measure friction torque of LSD, using a torque wrench. If rotational friction is below minimum specification, friction discs and plates in LSD must be replaced. See AXLE ASSEMBLY SPECIFICATIONS table at end of article.

**Removal** – **1)** Raise vehicle and remove wheels. Remove intermediate exhaust pipe. Loosen trailing arm retaining bolts so arms can pivot at front ends. Remove stabilizer bar and track (Panhard) rod. Remove collision guards (if equipped).

**2)** Disconnect ventilation hose from axle housing. Disconnect brake line brackets from axle housing. Remove calipers and wire out of way. Be careful not to damage brake lines. Release parking brake. Remove rotors. Remove parking brake shoes and disconnect cables from levers.

**3)** Disconnect propeller shaft from pinion flange. Disconnect parking brake cables from axle housing. Only remove plastic tube if axle housing is being replaced. Disconnect reaction rods at axle housing. Support axle assembly with transmission jack.

**4)** Compress springs and disconnect shock absorbers at upper mounts. Remove spring compressors. Remove bolts holding axle housing to trailing arms. Lower and remove axle assembly.

**Installation** – **1)** Move axle assembly under vehicle on transmission jack and raise into position. Connect trailing arms with stabilizer bar brackets to axle housing, leaving bolts finger tight. Compress springs and connect shock absorbers to upper mounts. Release springs.

**2)** Remove transmission jack. Connect reaction rods to axle housing, leaving bolts finger tight. Attach parking brake cables to axle housing. Attach propeller shaft to pinion flange. Connect parking brake cables to levers and install parking brake shoes.

# 1991 DRIVE AXLES
# Differentials & Axle Shafts (Cont.)

**3)** Install rotors and check parking brake adjustment. Install calipers and attach brake line brackets to axle housing. Attach ventilation hose to axle housing. Install collision guards (if equipped). Connect Panhard rod and stabilizer bar to axle housing and trailing arms, leaving bolts finger tight.

**4)** Install wheels and tighten lug nuts. Lower and rock vehicle to settle suspension. With full weight of vehicle on suspension, tighten bolts on trailing arms, reaction rods, Panhard rod, and stabilizer bar to specifications. See TORQUE SPECIFICATIONS at end of article.

## OVERHAUL

### DIFFERENTIAL ASSEMBLY

***NOTE: Differential assembly overhaul information applies to all 1031 differentials, and 1041 and 1045 differentials with differential lock. Information for 1041 and 1045 conventional differentials is not available from manufacturer.***

**Disassembly (1031) – 1)** Support axle assembly with pinion flange down and bottom of housing toward work stand. Remove axle shafts and inner seals. Remove rear cover.

**2)** Check alignment markings on side bearing caps and carrier. Index caps to carrier for reassembly (if necessary). Remove side bearing caps. Attach Differential Housing Spreader (2394 and 2601) to carrier housing. Align pins on spreader with holes in housing and screw retainer bolts into housing.

**3)** Tighten tensioning screw until spreader fits snugly in housing. Slowly tighten tensioning screw until differential case assembly can be removed from carrier. DO NOT tighten screw more than 3 1/2 turns. Carefully pry differential assembly out of carrier.

***CAUTION: Excessive or prolonged tension by spreader can distort carrier housing.***

**4)** Remove spreader from housing. Turn axle assembly over and drain oil. Remove drive pinion flange nut. Using a puller, remove flange. Force drive pinion from carrier housing using a plastic hammer.

**5)** Drive out front drive pinion bearing, with seal and washer, from back of housing. Drive out rear drive pinion bearing race from front of housing. Press rear drive pinion bearing off drive pinion or use Puller 5216 and 5214.

**6)** For conventional differential, remove side bearings with Puller (2483), taking care not to damage shims. Mark left and right bearings, and shims for reassembly in correct position. Remove lock plate over ring gear bolts.

**7)** Index ring gear to differential case for reassembly. Loosen bolts holding ring gear to case. Tap bolts to push ring gear from case. Discard old bolts. Drive out lock pin holding differential gear shaft.

**8)** Drive out differential gear shaft. Remove differential pinion gears by rolling them out of case. Remove pinion gear shims. Lift out differential side gears with shims.

**9)** For limited slip differential, remove side bearings with Puller (2483), taking care not to damage shims. Mark left and right bearings and shims for reassembly. Index differential case halves and mark differential gear shafts for reassembly.

**10)** Remove bolts holding case halves together. Open differential case and remove side gears, side gear retainers, friction plates, friction discs, and pinion gears with spider.

**11)** Index ring gear to differential case half for reassembly. Remove and discard bolts holding ring gear to case. Remove ring gear from differential case.

**Disassembly (1041 & 1045) – 1)** On 1041 type axle, support axle in Fixture (2522) and Floor Stand (2520). Remove rear cover. Using a dial indicator, check ring gear backlash and record reading. *See Fig. 4.* Remove drive shaft pressure plates and drive shafts. Use Differential Housing Spreader (2394 and 2601) to expand rear end so differential assembly can be removed. DO NOT tighten expander screw more than 2 1/2 turns. Note position of differential bearing races for reassembly reference.

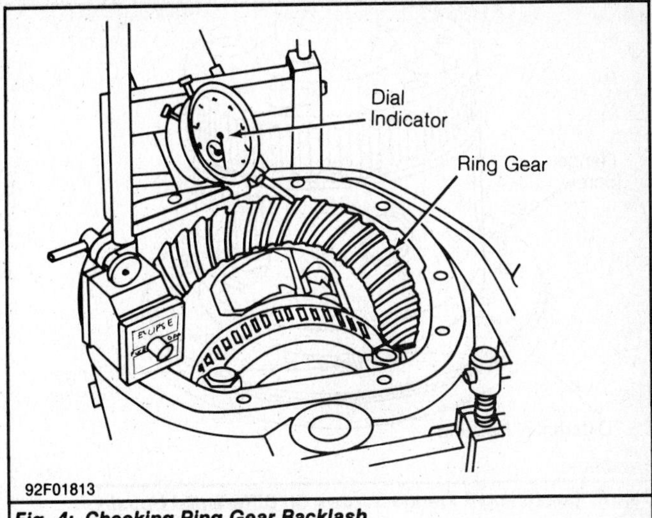


***Fig. 4: Checking Ring Gear Backlash***

**2)** On 1045 type axle, remove counterweight and side moldings for final drive lower bushings. Place final drive unit in Fixture (5370) and Floor Stand (2520). Remove rear cover. Use a large screwdriver and pry off drive shafts. Using a dial indicator, check backlash and record reading. To remove differential from final drive, remove locking washers on adjusting nuts. Using Wrench (5371), remove adjusting nuts. Note position of bearing races and adjusting nuts for reassembly reference.

**3)** On all axles, use Puller (2483) and remove differential bearings and locking plate. *See Fig. 5.* Note position of bearings for reassembly reference. On 1041 type axle, note which side spacers were installed for reassembly reference. On all axles, install differential in a vise, using Holder (5425). Remove ring gear from differential.

***NOTE: If either side of differential housing is damaged, replace differential lock.***

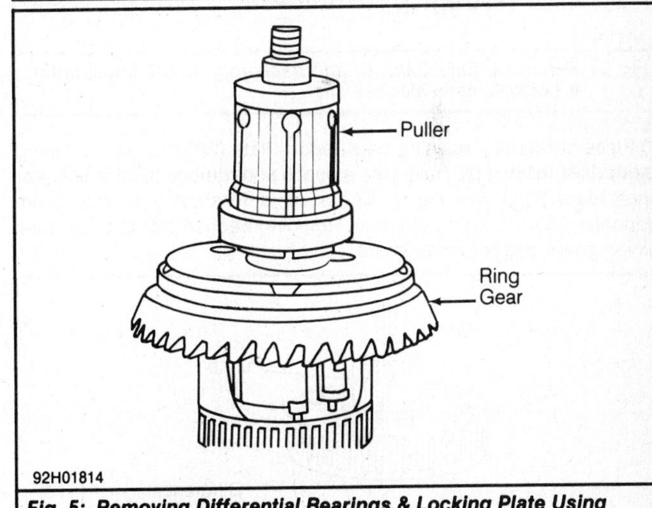


***Fig. 5: Removing Differential Bearings & Locking Plate Using Puller (2483)***

**4)** Loosen 3 flange screws on differential housing. *See Fig. 6.* Gently tap screw heads to separate differential housing from end plate. Turn housing over and remove 3 screws. Lift off housing end plate. Leave shim for side gear in housing end plate.

**5)** Lift out side gear on ring gear side with clutch assembly, guide lugs and shim (if not already removed with housing end plate). Lift out lock/release mechanism. *See Fig. 7.*

# 1991 DRIVE AXLES
# Differentials & Axle Shafts (Cont.)

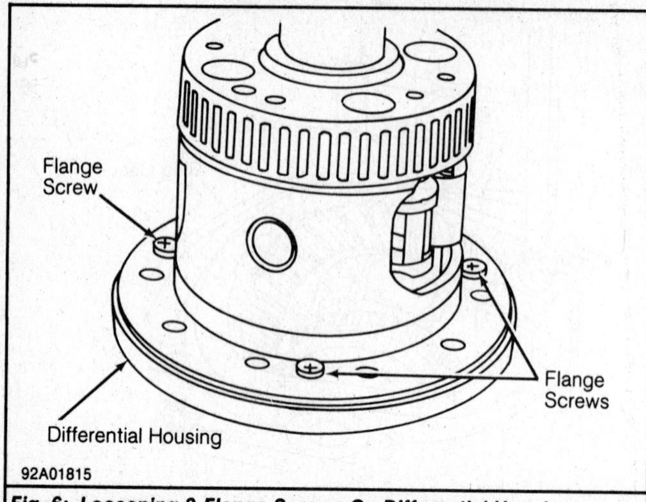


*Fig. 6: Loosening 3 Flange Screws On Differential Housing*

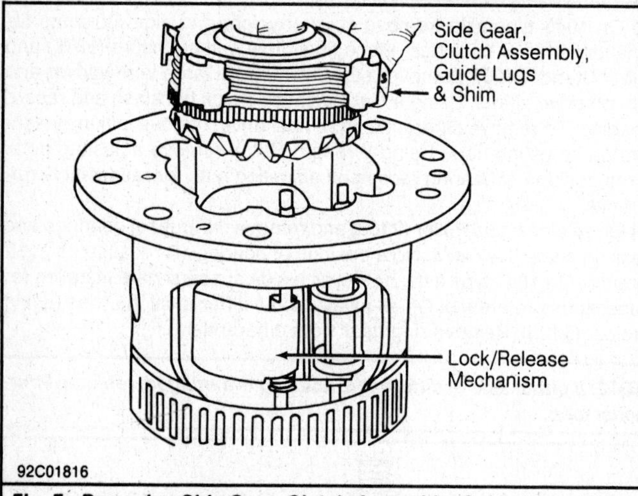


*Fig. 7: Removing Side Gear, Clutch Assembly, Guide Lugs, Shim & Lock/Release Mechanism*

**6)** Place differential housing on Support Plate (2861) so one opening is opposite locking pin hole. Use a punch and remove differential gear shaft locking pin. *See Fig. 8.* Knock out differential gear shaft from opposite side to locking pin hole. Remove reaction block, differential pinion gears and thrust washers.

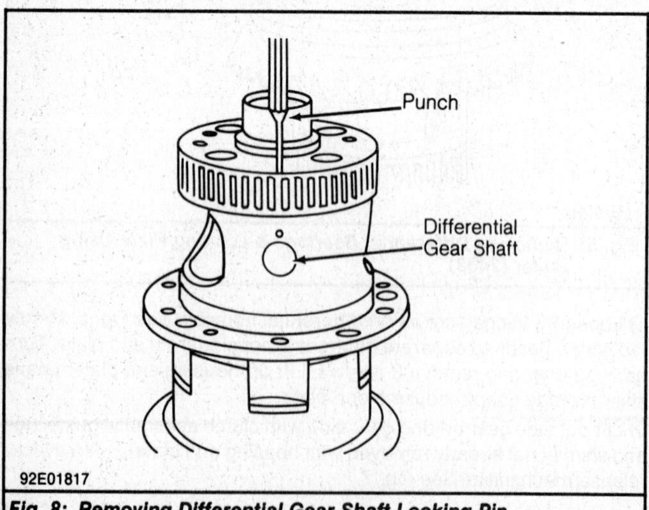


*Fig. 8: Removing Differential Gear Shaft Locking Pin*

***NOTE: Mark differential pinion gears for reassembly reference.***

**7)** Remove circlip on crown wheel side on clutch assembly. Remove clutch assembly and guide lugs. Remove cam wheel from side gear.

**Cleaning & Inspection (All Models) – 1)** Drive pinion and ring gear MUST be replaced as a set. If differential side or pinion gears show any damage, gears must be replaced as a complete set.

**2)** On models with LSD and differential lock, all friction discs should be replaced if any discs show excessive wear or heat damage.

**Reassembly & Adjustments (1031) – 1)** On conventional differential, place differential side gears together with thrust washers in differential case. Compress thrust washers so that pinion gears and thrust washers can be rolled into case as an assembly.

**2)** Drive in differential pinion shaft. Drive in shaft lock pin, using punch to stake pin in place. Line up index marks on ring gear and case. Install ring gear, ensuring that contact surfaces are clean and without any burrs. Install new ring gear bolts with locking compound. Tighten bolts in diagonal pattern.

**3)** On limited slip differentials, line up index marks on ring gear and case half. Install ring gear on case, ensuring contact surface is clean and free of burrs. Install new ring gear bolts with locking compound. Tighten bolts in diagonal pattern.

**4)** Lubricate parts in hypoid oil with limited slip additive. Install side gear and retainer, spider with pinion gears, side gear and retainer, and friction plates onto ring gear half of case. *See Fig. 2.*

**5)** Align ears on friction plates. Fit smaller half of case to ring gear half. Ensure index marks on case halves are aligned. Install case through bolts and tighten in a diagonal pattern.

**6)** To set drive pinion depth & bearing preload, clean shoulder on drive pinion with emery cloth. Install Adjusting Ring (2840) and Wrench (2841) on drive pinion. Ensure locking screw on adjusting ring is not covered by drive pinion head. *See Figs. 9 and 10.*

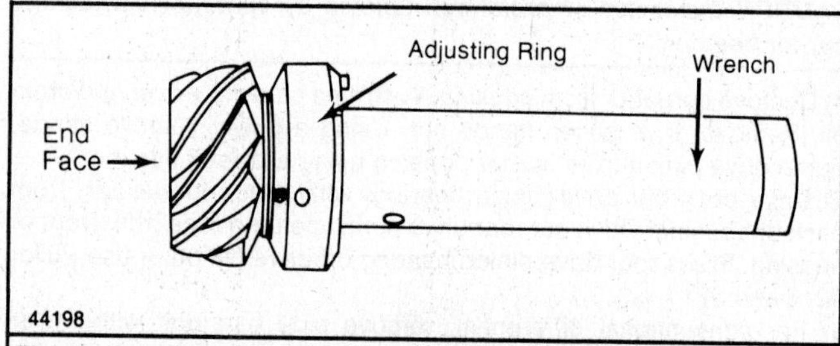


*Fig. 9: Installing Drive Pinion Adjusting Ring & Wrench*

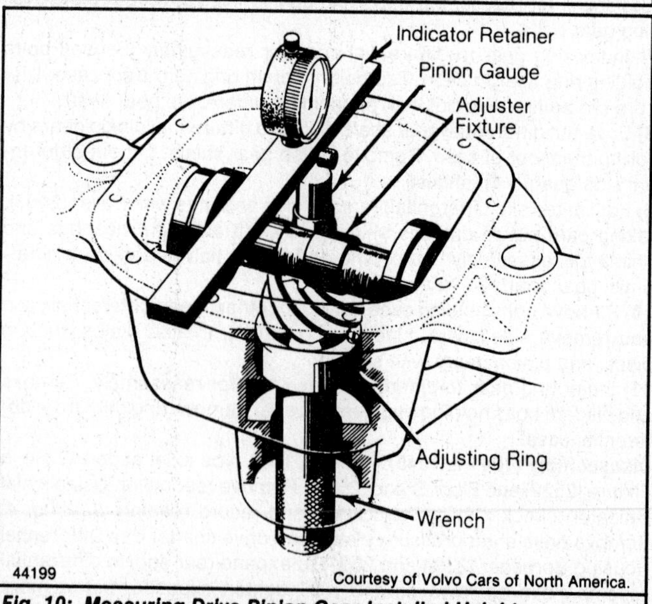


*Fig. 10: Measuring Drive Pinion Gear Installed Height*

# 1991 DRIVE AXLES
# Differentials & Axle Shafts (Cont.)

**7)** Place drive pinion in carrier so screw on adjusting ring faces large side of carrier. Ensure pin on adjusting ring fits into carrier recess. Drive pinion has a certain nominal measurement to center line of ring gear from face of drive pinion head. Due to manufacturing tolerances, deviations from this nominal measurement occur.

**8)** On rear axles made by Volvo, deviation is always positive and is indicated in hundredths of a millimeter. The plus sign is not used. Deviation from nominal measurement is recorded on drive pinion. Place Measuring Fixture (2393) in carrier, with pinion gauge on end face of pinion and adjuster fixture set in differential bearing positions.

**9)** Position dial indicator retainer so retainer sits on gasket face of axle housing with dial indicator tip touching adjuster fixture. Zero dial indicator against adjuster fixture. Move indicator over until tip touches pinion gauge. For example, if drive pinion is marked 33, the pinion gauge should lie .013" (.33 mm) under adjuster fixture. *See Fig. 11.*

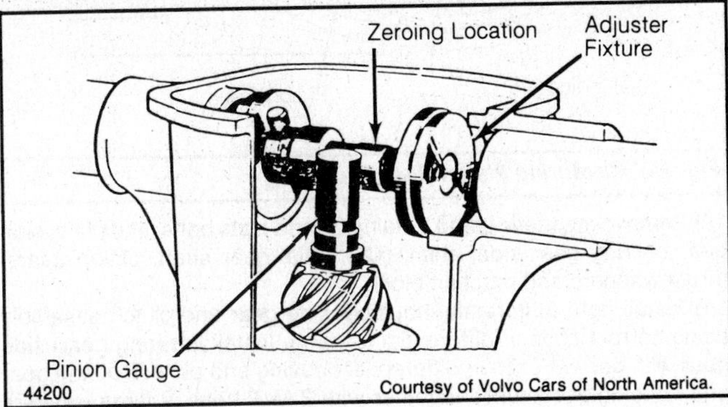


***Fig. 11: Zeroing Dial Indicator***

**10)** Adjust indicated reading by turning wrench on drive pinion until dial indicator shows correct value. Lock wrench with set screw on adjusting ring. Remove measuring fixture and drive pinion. Place complete rear pinion bearing with outer race in Measuring Fixture (2600). Assemble plate, spring, and nut with flat side of nut facing up.

**11)** Rotate plate and bearing assembly several times so that rollers settle in proper position. Place Adjusting Ring (2685 or 2840) in fixture. Place dial indicator tip against adjusting ring. Zero indicator. Move tip of indicator to outer race of bearing.

**12)** The indicator reading will now show thickness of rear drive pinion bearing shims. *See Fig. 12.* Measure shims for correct thickness with micrometer. As it is difficult to find shim of exact thickness required, shim may be .002" (.05 mm) thicker or .0008" (.020 mm) thinner than measured value. Press rear bearing onto drive pinion.

***CAUTION: When overhauling, DO NOT reinstall spacer washer under rear bearing inner race.***

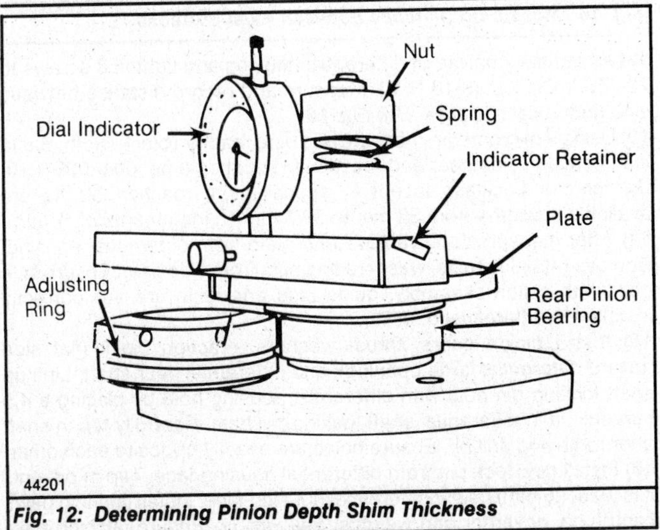


***Fig. 12: Determining Pinion Depth Shim Thickness***

**13)** Place measured shim in axle carrier housing. Press in outer races of rear and front drive pinion bearings. Insert drive pinion in housing. Install three .03" (.75 mm) thick shims and front pinion bearing. Pull pinion into housing, using Wrench (2404) and Press (1845 or 5156). Install washer and nut on pinion shaft.

**14)** Install pinion gauge, dial indicator, and dial indicator retainer. *See Fig. 13.* Pull down on drive pinion while rotating it back and forth. Zero dial indicator. Press pinion up while rotating it back and forth. Record dial indicator reading.

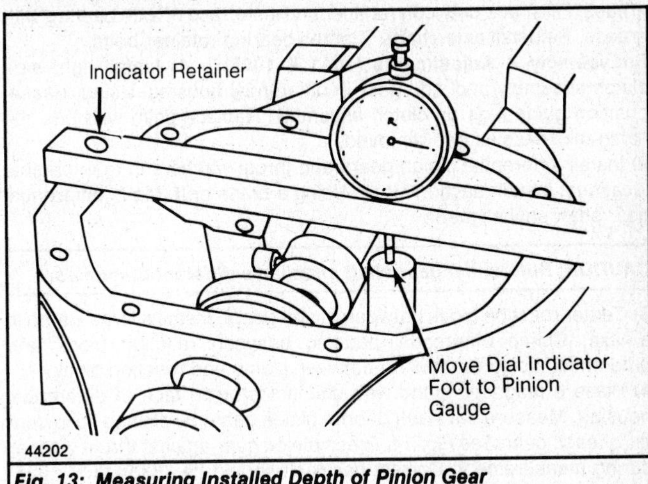


***Fig. 13: Measuring Installed Depth of Pinion Gear***

**15)** Tap drive pinion from housing. Remove shims equal to the dial indicator reading plus .0035" (.090 mm) for new bearings or .0028" (.071 mm) for used bearings. Install pinion with selected shim pack and front bearing. Press drive pinion in with Wrench (2404) and Press (1845 or 5156).

**16)** Install pinion nut with washer. Check drive pinion bearing preload with torque wrench. Adjust shim thickness to obtain specified torque (if required). Recheck pinion depth using measuring fixture as described in steps **8)** and **9)**.

**17)** To adjust backlash and side bearing preload, lubricate inside of Adjusting Ring (2595) and install them on differential carrier. Black oxidized adjusting ring should be placed on side of differential case, facing back side of ring gear. Oil bearing bores in carrier. Install differential with adjusting rings in axle housing.

**18)** Adjust rings apart until differential is held firmly without any preload. Set dial indicator tip against ring gear tooth. Adjust rings until backlash is .005-.007" (.13-.18 mm). Turn both rings in same direction. Preferred setting is .006" (.15 mm).

***NOTE: Keep bearings and shims separate so that they are installed on correct side.***

**19)** After correct backlash is obtained, lock adjusting rings in position. Remove differential with adjusting rings. Position centering plate on Measuring Fixture (2600). Place side bearing in fixture. Install plate, spring, and nut (flat side of nut faces up). Rotate plate and bearing back and forth to settle rollers.

**20)** Place adjusting ring on measuring fixture. Install Retainer (2284) with dial indicator. Zero dial indicator with tip against adjusting ring. Move tip of dial indicator to inner race of side bearing. Record measurement.

**21)** Measure shim thickness with micrometer. Total thickness of shim(s) should be measured value plus .0028" (.071 mm). Repeat measuring procedure for opposite side bearing shim pack.

**22)** Install shim pack and press side bearing opposite ring gear on first. Install lock plate for ring gear bolts. Install shim pack and press on side bearing by ring gear. Use press on both side bearings to prevent damage to side bearings.

**23)** Install Differential Housing Spreader (2394 and 2601) on carrier and expand until pins are flush against hole edges in carrier. Tighten tension screw an additional 3 1/2 turns maximum. Install differential

# 1991 DRIVE AXLES
# Differentials & Axle Shafts (Cont.)

carrier with side bearing outer races in place. Remove housing spreader. Check index marks and install side bearing caps.

**24)** Check ring gear backlash to make sure no change has occurred. Set dial indicator on back of ring gear and check runout in 4 places. Install oil slinger. Pack seal spring with grease. Drive pinion oil seal into housing. Press drive pinion flange onto drive pinion. Install pinion flange nut and washer.

**25)** Install rear cover with new gasket. If inner oil seals for axle shafts were removed, drive them into housing ends after packing lips with grease. Fill space between retainer and inner race of axle bearing with grease. Reinstall axle shafts. Tighten bearing retainer bolts.

**Reassembly & Adjustments (1041 & 1045) – 1)** Install right side clutch assembly and side gear in differential housing. Using grease, position guide lugs on clutch assembly. Replace shim with one the same thickness as one removed.

**2)** Install differential pinion gears and thrust washers in their original locations. Install reaction block. Using a brass drift, tap in differential gear shaft until aligned.

***CAUTION: Differential gear shaft ends have different diameters.***

**3)** Center reaction block between pinion gears. Install a large clamp in a vise. Clamp differential housing between reaction block and differential, using Drift (5912) between clamp and reaction block.

**4)** Place a magnetic stand with dial indicator on face of differential housing. Measure backlash of both pinion gears by placing tip in center of each gear. *See Fig. 14.* Press pinion gear against thrust washer during measurement. Correct backlash should be .0009-.005" (.025-.13 mm). If not to specification, shims are available in .25 mm, .38 mm and .64 mm sizes. After adjustment, recheck backlash.

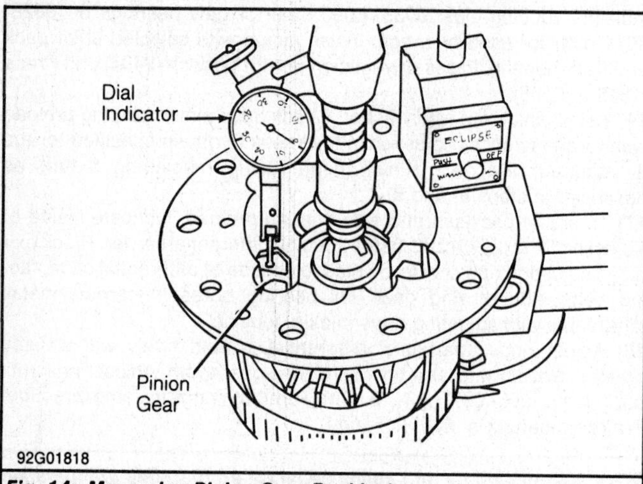


***Fig. 14: Measuring Pinion Gear Backlash***

**5)** Tap out differential gear shaft (from correct end). Remove reaction block, pinion gears and thrust washers, right gear assembly with clutch, and shim. Mark all parts for reassembly reference.

**6)** Install pinion gears on correct side. Install thrust washers and reaction block. Using a brass drift, tap in differential gear shaft until aligned.

***CAUTION: Differential gear shaft ends have different diameters.***

**7)** Using new shim with same thickness as old one, position left (ring gear side) side gear against pinion gears in differential housing. Use grease to hold in place. Install differential housing end plate and 3 flange bolts. Tighten 3 bolts to 72-156 INCH lbs. (8-10 N.m).

**8)** Reinstall differential housing in a clamp, using Drift (5912) against reaction block. Place Drift (5065) between Drift (5912) and clamp. Center reaction block and tighten clamp.

**9)** Attach Retainer (5971) in a ring gear bolt hole. Position magnetic stand on retainer. Measure pinion gear backlash. *See Fig. 15.* Correct backlash should be .0009-.016" (.25-.43 mm). If adjustment is necessary, shims are available in .56 mm, .81 mm, 1.01 mm, and 1.20 mm thicknesses. Recheck backlash after adjustment is complete.

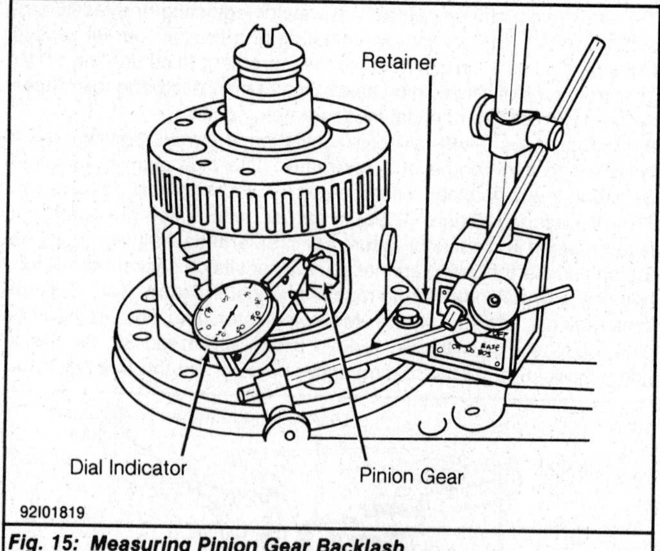


***Fig. 15: Measuring Pinion Gear Backlash***

**10)** Remove magnetic stand, retainer, 3 end plate bolts, end plate, side gear on ring gear side, shim, differential gear shaft, pinion gears, thrust washers and reaction block.

**11)** Install right (differential housing) side gear and clutch assembly using correct shim in differential housing. Install left (ring gear) side gear with correct shim in differential housing end plate. Bolt the gear and housing assemblies together with 2 M12 bolts, 2 large washers (modified to an oval shape), and nuts. *See Fig. 16.*

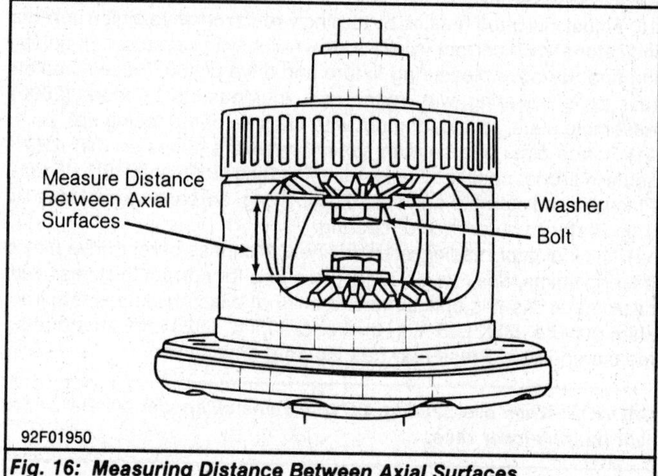


***Fig. 16: Measuring Distance Between Axial Surfaces***

**12)** Assemble 2 halves of differential housing and tighten 3 screws to 72-156 INCH lbs. (8-10 N.m). Measure and record distance between side gear axial surfaces. *See Fig. 16.*

**13)** Using a micrometer, measure and note reaction block width. Backlash between side gear and reaction block should be .004-.009" (.10-.24 mm). If backlash is not to specification, reaction blocks are available in widths from 32 mm to 32.7 mm, in increments of .1 mm.

**14)** After measurement, remove end plate from differential housing. Remove retaining bolts, washers and nuts from side gear. Ensure side gear with clutch assembly, guide lugs and shim are still correctly installed in differential housing.

**15)** Install pinion gears, thrust washers, reaction block (flat side toward differential large opening), and differential gear shaft. Line up shaft locking pin hole with differential housing hole by placing a 4.5 mm drill bit in differential shaft locking pin hole. Carefully tap in shaft after removing drill bit. Ensure holes are exactly opposite each other.

**16)** Install new lock pin from differential housing face. Tap in pin until it is .020" (.5 mm) below differential housing face. Install latching pawl, centrifugal governor and weights. *See Fig. 17.* Ensure latching pawl spring is on correct side of centrifugal governor shaft.

# 1991 DRIVE AXLES
# Differentials & Axle Shafts (Cont.)

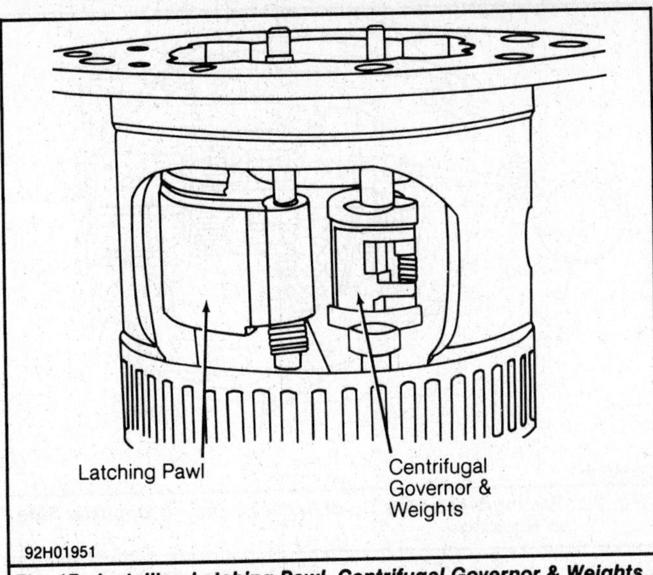


**Fig. 17: Installing Latching Pawl, Centrifugal Governor & Weights**

**17)** Install toothed cam wheel and clutch assembly on left (ring gear) side gear. Position guide lugs with grease. Place left (ring gear) side gear with clutch assembly and guide lugs into differential housing. Position shim with grease on end of side gear.
**18)** Ensure contact faces of differential housing and end plate are thoroughly clean of grease. Assemble differential housing end plate. Tighten 3 screws to 75-156 INCH lbs. (8-10 N.m).
**19)** Using cutting pliers, cut off sensor strip. *See Fig. 18*. Lubricate new strip and surface of differential housing. Carefully tap on strip until it sits level on housing. Place differential housing with new strip on Support Plate (2861) and press sensor strip onto housing until it touches support plate surface.

***CAUTION: Ensure no grease is present on facing surfaces of ring gear and differential housing.***

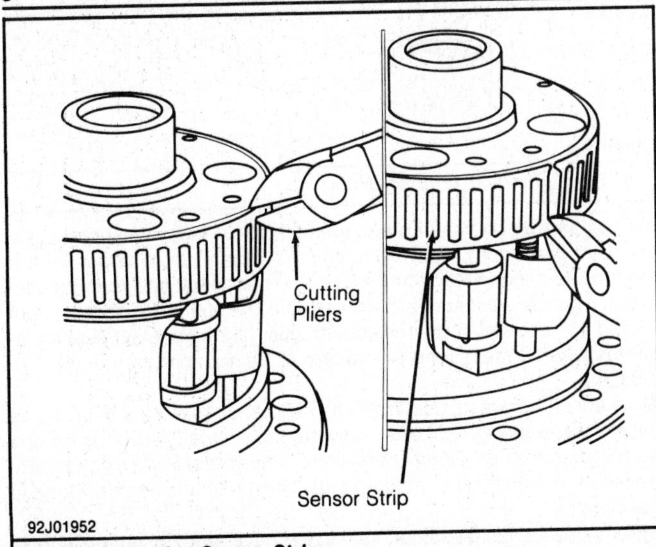


**Fig. 18: Removing Sensor Strip**

**20)** Using new bolts, install ring gear. Starting with 2 bolts in smaller holes in differential housing, tighten bolts diagonally to 26 ft. lbs. (35 N.m), then angle tighten an additional 60 degrees.
**21)** On 1041, if differential lock is replaced, new bearings installed or backlash is greater than specification, go to INSTALLATION & ADJUSTMENT (1041). If differential lock is not replaced, new bearings not installed or backlash is within specification, go to next step.
**22)** On all axles, use Drift (4112) at both ends as supports and install locking plate and differential bearings. *See Fig. 19.*

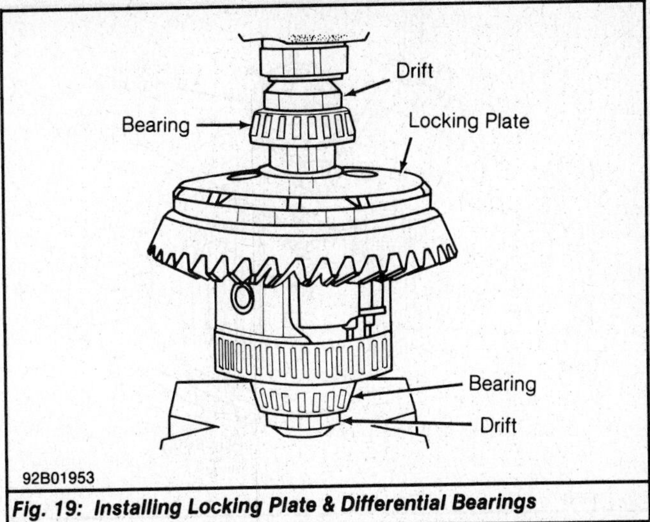


**Fig. 19: Installing Locking Plate & Differential Bearings**

**Installation & Adjustment (1041) – 1)** Lubricate Adjusting Rings (2595) and contact faces. Place rings on bearings seats, with Black ring on ring gear side. Install differential housing in rear axle housing. Expand adjusting rings until differential housing is firmly positioned but not under load. *See Fig. 20.* There should be no play between rings, differential housing and rear axle housing.

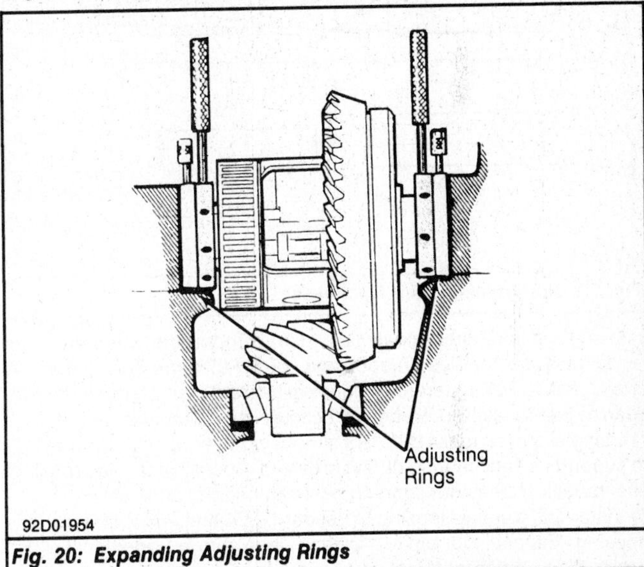


**Fig. 20: Expanding Adjusting Rings**

**2)** Position a dial indicator on rear axle housing. *See Fig. 21.* Rest measuring tip on one ring gear tooth approximately .12" (3 mm) from large end of tooth. Hold pinion and move ring gear back and forth. Acceptable backlash is .004-.006" (.10-.15 mm), but should be set as near as possible to .005" (.13 mm). Maximum variation between 3 measuring points should be no more than 0-.001" (0-.03 mm).
**3)** To adjust backlash, turn both adjusting rings in same direction. After correct backlash is obtained, lock adjusting rings in position and lift out differential housing assembly and adjusting rings.

***CAUTION: Note which side differential housing shims and bearings are to be installed, otherwise backlash will be incorrect.***

**4)** On ring gear side, place bearing with outer up in Measuring Fixture (2600) and install plate, spring and nut (flat side down). Turn plate and bearing assembly back and forth so rollers take up correct position.
**5)** Position adjusting ring on measuring fixture. Install Retainer (2284) and dial indicator. Place tip of indicator against ring and set to zero. Move tip to bearing and note reading. *See Fig. 22.*

# 1991 DRIVE AXLES
## Differentials & Axle Shafts (Cont.)

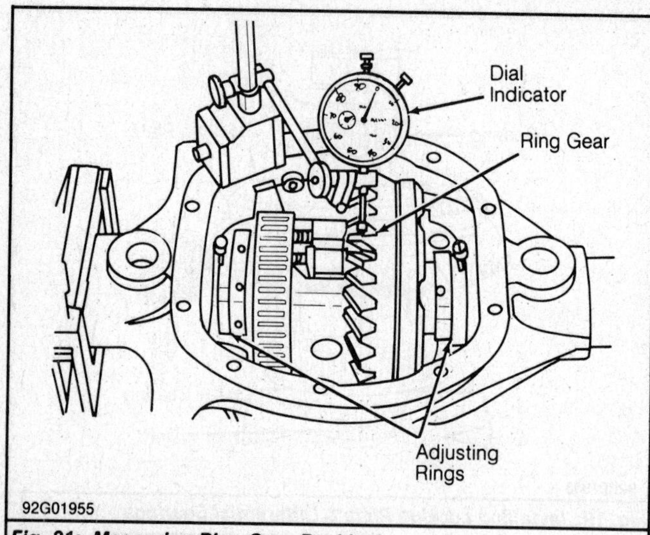


*Fig. 21: Measuring Ring Gear Backlash*

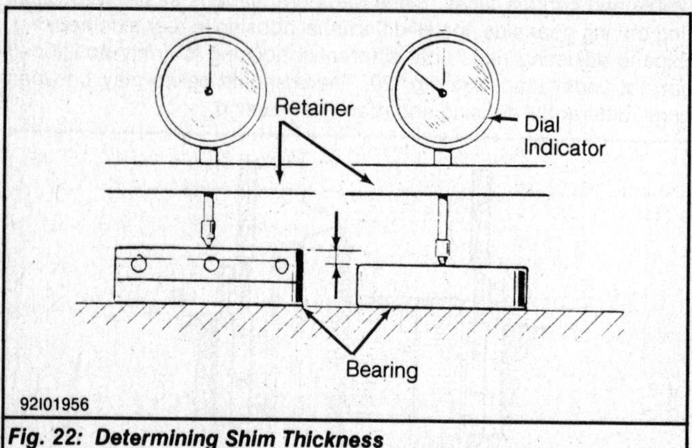


*Fig. 22: Determining Shim Thickness*

**6)** Using a micrometer, measure a shim with thickness the same as reading just taken, plus an additional .003" (.07 mm). This is done to retain preload on differential housing bearing. Put shim aside with bearing just measured. Repeat procedure for other side.

**7)** Using a press, install differential housing bearing. Use Drift (4112) to support bottom bearing during pressing procedure. While pressing, ensure lock plate is not jammed between bearing and carrier.

**8)** Install Differential Housing Spreader (2394 and 2601) on rear axle housing. Expand tool until it fastens, then turn an additional 2 1/2 turns. Place differential housing and bearing in rear axle housing. Remove expander and retainer.

**9)** Install bearing caps in original locations. Tighten bolts to 26 ft. lbs. (35 N.m), then angle tighten an additional 60 degrees.

**10)** Recheck ring gear backlash. Backlash should be .004-.006" (.10-.15 mm). Measure backlash at 3 points, .12" (3 mm) from outer edge of ring gear.

**11)** Check differential rotational torque by installing one drive shaft, Drift (2725) and a flat washer on one wheel nut, and a wheel nut with cone facing outward. Use a wrench with an extension to prevent drive pinion from turning. Turn drive shaft with a torque wrench. Rotational torque must not exceed 26 ft. lbs. (35 N.m). If not to specification, check differential bearing preload.

**12)** Install remaining drive shaft. Tighten drive shaft pressure plates to 30-42 ft. lbs. (40-56 N.m). Using new gasket, replace rear cover. Tighten rear cover bolts to 18 ft. lbs. (24 N.m).

**Installation & Adjustment (1045) – 1)** Install complete differential in rear axle housing. Install oiled adjusting nuts with new lubricated "O" rings and seals. Install Washer (5871) with one adjuster nut. Install magnetic stand with dial indicator. Place measuring tip of indicator dial on opposite side of housing. *See Fig. 23.*

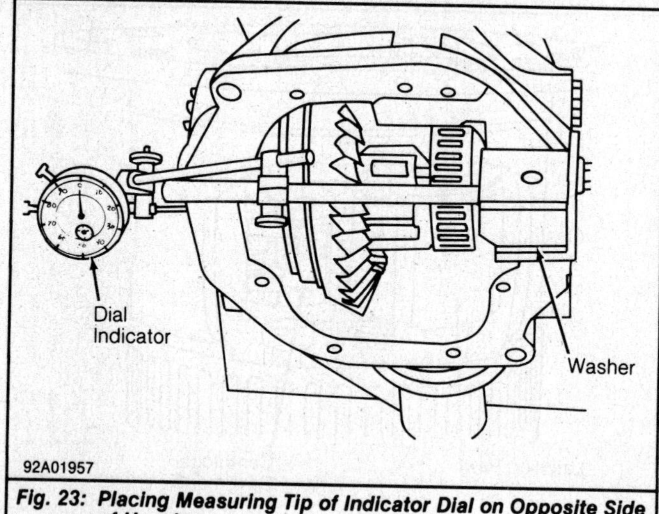


*Fig. 23: Placing Measuring Tip of Indicator Dial on Opposite Side of Housing*

**2)** Using Wrench (5371), tighten adjuster nuts on both sides. *See Fig. 24.* Turn adjuster nuts until a slight backlash can be felt on ring gear and dial indicator just begins to give a reading. Rotate differential housing several times to center roller bearings.

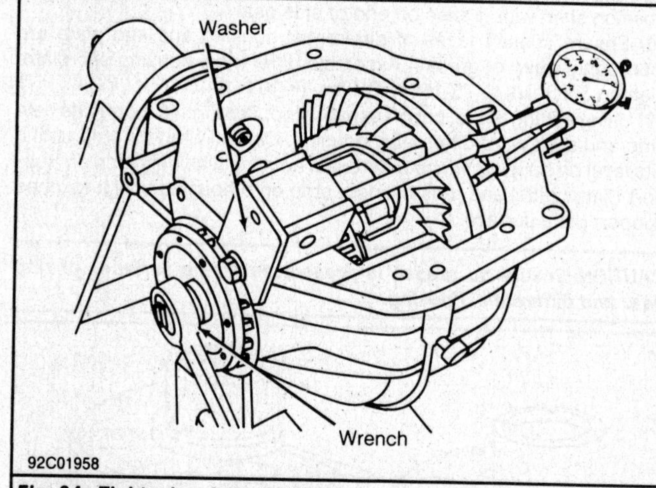


*Fig. 24: Tightening Adjuster Nuts*

**3)** Position a dial indicator on differential case. Place measuring tip on one ring gear tooth, approximately .12" (3 mm) from larger end of tooth. Hold pinion steady and move ring gear back and forth against measuring tip. Acceptable backlash is .004-.006" (.10-.15 mm), but should be set as near as possible to .005" (.13 mm). Maximum variation between 3 measuring points should be no more than 0-.001" (0-.03 mm).

**4)** To adjust backlash, use Wrench (5371) and move nuts in or out as necessary. *See Fig. 25.* After adjustment, preload the housing one notch on both sides. Rotate differential 5 turns and recheck backlash. Readjust is necessary. Adjustments can be made with preloaded bearings.

**5)** Using liquid gasket sealer, install rear cover and tighten bolts to 18 ft. lbs. (24 N.m). To complete preload, tighten adjuster nuts one more notch on both sides.

***NOTE: If old bearings were reused, tighten adjuster nuts 1/2 notch.***

**6)** Lock adjuster nuts with lock washers and tighten to 30-42 ft. lbs. (40-56 N.m). Install drive shafts. On one drive shaft and one hole for drive shaft flange, install an M10 bolt approximately .75" (20 mm) long with a flat washer. Use a wrench with an extension to prevent drive pinion from turning.

# 1991 DRIVE AXLES
# Differentials & Axle Shafts (Cont.)

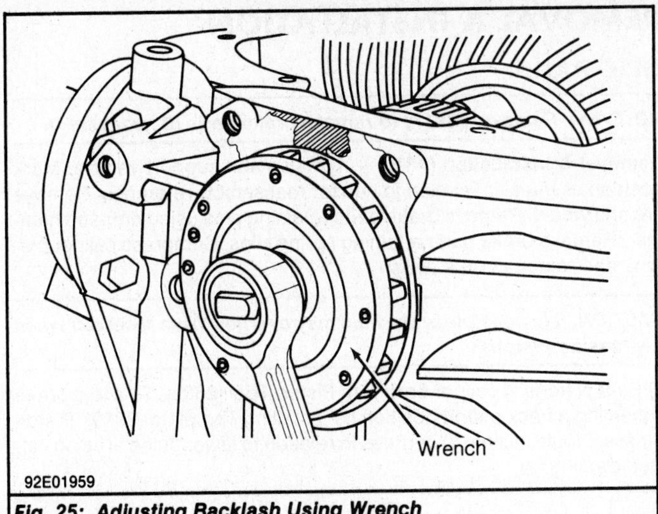


*Fig. 25: Adjusting Backlash Using Wrench*

**7)** Turn drive shaft with a torque wrench. Torque should not exceed 26 ft. lbs. (35 N.m). If not to specification, recheck differential bearing preload. Install side mountings for lower bushings. Tighten bolts to 30-75 ft. lbs. (40-56 N.m). Remove final drive from fixture and install counterweight. Tighten counterweight bolts to 15-37 ft. lbs. (20-28 N.m).

## AXLE & DIFFERENTIAL ASSEMBLY SPECIFICATIONS

*AXLE ASSEMBLY SPECIFICATIONS - 1031* [1]

| Application | In. (mm) |
|---|---|
| Axle Shaft Bearing End Play [2] | .004-.014 (.10-.36) |
| Differential Side Bearing Preload | .005-.008 (.13-.20) |
| Pinion-To-Ring Gear | |
| Backlash Preferred | .006 (.15) |
| Backlash Range | .005-.007 (.13-.18) |
| Ring Gear Runout [2] | .003 (.08) |
| Speedometer Transmitter Clearance | .019-.047 (.48-1.19) |
| | **Ft. Lbs. (N.m)** |
| Limited Slip Friction Torque | 40-110 (54-149) |
| | **INCH Lbs. (N.m)** |
| Pinion Bearing Preload Torque | |
| Oiled Used Bearings | 13-22 (1.5-2.5) |
| Oiled New Bearings | 21-30 (2.5-3.5) |

1 - Applies to 1031 rear axle and differential only.
2 - Maximum deviation allowed.

*DIFFERENTIAL ASSEMBLY SPECIFICATIONS - 1041 & 1045* [1]

| Application | In. (mm) |
|---|---|
| Ring Gear Backlash | |
| Preferred | .005" (.13 mm) |
| Range | .004-.006" (.10-.15 mm) |
| Side Gear-To-Reaction Block Backlash | .004-.009" (.10-.24 mm) |
| Pinion Gear Backlash | .0009-.005" (.025-.13) |
| | **Ft. Lbs. (N.m)** |
| Shaft Rotational Torque | 26 (35) |

1 - Applies to traction lock differential only.

## TORQUE SPECIFICATIONS

*TORQUE SPECIFICATIONS - 1031* [1]

| Application | Ft. Lbs. (N.m) |
|---|---|
| Axle Shaft Bearing Retainer Bolts | 22-36 (30-49) |
| LSD Case Through Bolts | 44-51 (60-70) |
| Pinion Flange Nut | 145-180 (197-244) |
| Rear Caliper Bolts | 42 (57) |
| Rear Cover Bolts | 14-25 (19-34) |
| Ring Gear Bolts | |
| Flanged Head | 65-80 (88-108) |
| Standard Head | 50-58 (68-79) |
| Side Bearing Cap Bolts | 35-50 (47-68) |
| Wheel Lug Nuts | 85 (115) |

1 - Applies to 1031 rear axle and differential only.

*TORQUE SPECIFICATIONS - 1041 & 1045* [1]

| Application | Ft. Lbs. (N.m) |
|---|---|
| Adjuster Nuts | 30-42 (40-56) |
| Bearing Cap Bolts | [2] 26 (35) |
| Counterweight Bolt | 15-37 (20-28) |
| Lower Bushing Side Mounting Bolt | 30-75 (40-56) |
| Rear Cover Bolts | 18 (24) |
| Ring Gear Bolts | [2] 26 (35) |
| | **INCH Lbs. (N.m)** |
| Differential Housing End Plate Flange Screws | 72-156 (8-10) |

1 - Applies to traction lock differential only.
2 - Angle tighten an additional 60 degrees.

# 1991 BRAKES
# Disc

## 240, 740

***NOTE: Information on 940 disc brakes is not available from manufacturer.***

## DESCRIPTION

All models use front and rear disc brakes. Three makes of calipers are used: ATE, Bendix (DBA) and Girling. Service brakes are hydraulically-operated by a tandem master cylinder and vacuum power brake unit. Each rear brake line has a pressure valve to prevent rear wheel lock-up. Parking brake is mechanically operated, using rear wheel disc rotor internally mounted brake shoes.

***NOTE: For information on Volvo anti-lock brake system, see ANTI-LOCK article in BRAKES.***

## BLEEDING BRAKE SYSTEM

***NOTE: Use only DOT 4 grade brake fluid.***

**1)** Raise and support vehicle. Fill master cylinder reservoir to maximum mark. Bleed brakes in sequence. See BRAKE LINE BLEEDING SEQUENCE table. After bleeding brakes, depress brake pedal with a force equal to an abrupt stop.
**2)** On 240, pedal travel should not exceed 2.4" (60 mm). On 740, pedal travel should not exceed 2.17" (55 mm). On all models, brake warning light should not illuminate. If air is still present in system, repeat procedure.

***BRAKE LINE BLEEDING SEQUENCE***

| Application | Sequence |
|---|---|
| 240 | |
| Without ABS | LF, RF, LR, RR |
| With ABS | LR, RR, LF, RF |
| 740 | |
| Without ABS | RR, LR, RF, LF |
| With ABS | LR, RR, LF, RF |

## ADJUSTMENTS

### BRAKE PEDAL HEIGHT

Brake pedal height should be equal to clutch pedal height. To adjust, loosen lock nut, remove cotter pin and turn push rod until pedal height is equal. Replace cotter pin and tighten lock nut. Pedal travel should be 6-6.5" (150-163 mm). Pedal travel can ONLY be measured during brake bleeding operation. See HYDRAULIC BRAKE BLEEDING article in GENERAL INFORMATION.

### PARKING/EMERGENCY BRAKE

**240 - 1)** Remove center console rear ashtray. Working through ashtray hole, loosen parking brake cables adjusting screw until cables are slack. Raise and support rear of vehicle. Remove rear wheels. Align hole in disc/parking brake drum with inside starwheel adjuster.
**2)** Tighten starwheel until drum can barely be rotated by hand. Back off adjuster until drum just rotates freely (no drag). Install rear wheels. Tighten parking brake cable adjusting screw until parking brake is fully applied when lever is pulled 2-8 notches. Install ashtray and lower vehicle.
**740 -** Remove cover at rear of center console. Remove adjusting screw by carefully tapping on locking sleeve spring collar with a hammer and screwdriver. Adjust cable so that parking brake is fully applied when lever is pulled 3-5 notches. Install cover.

### STOPLIGHT SWITCH

Adjust switch so brake lights come on when pedal is depressed about .30-.60" (8-14 mm).

## REMOVAL & INSTALLATION

### DISC PADS

***NOTE: Use Remover (2917) to remove brake pads (if necessary).***

**Removal & Installation (ATE) - 1)** Raise and support vehicle. Mark position of wheel in relation to hub for reassembly reference. Remove tire and wheel. Remove brake pads retaining pins using drift and hammer. Remove brake pads retaining spring clips. Compress caliper pistons and remove brake pads.

***CAUTION: It is possible brake fluid may overflow from reservoir when depressing pistons.***

**2)** Seat pistons in caliper bore with Piston Tool (2809). To avoid brake squealing, check piston position by installing Template (2919). Piston recess should incline 20 degrees in relation to lower guide area on caliper. *See Fig. 1.*

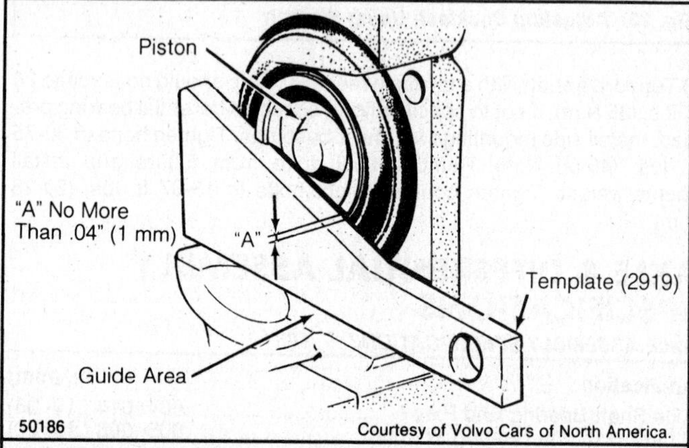


***Fig. 1: Checking ATE Rear Caliper Piston Angle To Avoid Brake Squeal***

**3)** If distance from one piston recess to the other recess at measurement "A" exceeds .04" (1 mm), adjust piston position using Adjuster (2918) to rotate piston. *See Fig. 1.*
**4)** Install intermediate plates (if equipped) or damper washers (if equipped) in original positions. Install new brake pads and ALWAYS install new brake pad tensioning spring. Install and tap one retaining guide pin into position. Install new tensioning spring. Install other retaining guide pin while holding tensioning spring in position.

***NOTE: Install the damper washers with the small contact face toward pad. DO NOT install intermediate plates in calipers equipped with damper washers.***

**Removal & Installation (Bendix & Girling) - 1)** Raise and support vehicle. Mark position of wheel in relation to hub for reassembly reference. Remove tire and wheel. Loosen caliper upper guide pin bolt and remove caliper lower guide pin bolt only from brake pad holder assembly. Swing caliper upward and remove pads. Compress caliper pistons.

***CAUTION: It is possible brake fluid may overflow from reservoir when depressing pistons.***

**2)** Inspect rubber guide pin covers and replace if defective. Install brake pads to holder and swing caliper into position. Ensure brake pad tension spring is in proper position. Tighten guide pin bolts to specification. See TORQUE SPECIFICATIONS table at end of this article.

## CALIPER ASSEMBLY

**Removal** - Raise and support vehicle. Remove wheel. Disconnect brake line connections at caliper. Cap lines to prevent entry of foreign matter. Remove caliper mounting bolts. Lift caliper from mounting bracket.

**Installation** - **1)** Position caliper assembly on mounting bracket, and install attaching bolts. After installing bolts, check clearance between disc pads and rotor on both sides of rotor.

**2)** Maximum deviation between sides should not exceed .004" (.10 mm) on front calipers or .010" (.25 mm) on rear calipers. To adjust clearance, add shims to caliper. Connect hydraulic lines and bleed hydraulic system. See BRAKE BLEEDING.

## DISC BRAKE ROTOR

**Removal & Installation (240 Front)** - With caliper assembly removed, mount a dial indicator and check rotor runout. Runout must not exceed .004" (.10 mm). Measure rotor thickness through one revolution. Thickness variance must not exceed .0008" (.020 mm). Unscrew rotor lock bolts and pull rotor from hub. To install, reverse removal procedure.

**Removal & Installation (740 Front)** - **1)** Remove caliper. Remove hub cap. Remove cotter pin and castellated nut. Remove outer wheel bearing. Remove hub and rotor assembly.

**2)** To install, reverse removal procedure. Tighten castellated nut to 42 ft. lbs. (57 N.m). Back off nut. Tighten nut to 13 INCH lbs. (1.5 N.m). Install cotter pin.

**Removal & Installation (Rear)** - Remove caliper. Remove screws retaining rotor to hub. Remove rotor. To install, reverse removal procedure.

## REAR AXLE SEAL & BEARING

***NOTE: For information on models with sealed wheel bearings, see REAR article in SUSPENSION.***

**Removal (240)** - **1)** Remove rear wheels and collision guards. Disconnect brake line and bracket from axle housing. Remove caliper and support to side with wire. Ensure parking brake is fully released. Remove brake rotor. Remove parking brake shoes, unhooking retaining springs.

**2)** Disconnect parking brake cables by driving out lock pin at lever. Remove bolts for bearing retainer through holes in axle flange. Remove axle shaft using Puller (2709). Pry inner seal from housing. Press bearing and snap ring off axle shaft. Remove oil seal.

**Installation** - **1)** Pack new bearing and new seal lip groove with high temperature wheel bearing grease. Place bearing retainer and oil seal on axle shaft. Press new bearing and new snap ring onto axle shaft. Narrow side of taper on snap ring fits into axle housing.

**2)** Install new inner seal. Install axle shaft. Tighten bearing retainer bolts. Install parking brake shoes. Reconnect cables. Install rotors. Check parking brake adjustment. Install brake caliper, pads, and collision guard (if equipped). Reconnect brake line and bracket to axle housing. Install wheels.

## PARKING BRAKE SHOES

**Removal (240)** - **1)** Remove center console rear ashtray. Loosen parking brake cable adjusting nut until cables are slack. Raise and support rear of vehicle. Remove wheels.

**2)** Remove caliper (without disconnecting hydraulic line) and support out of way. Remove rotor. Remove brake shoe return springs. Lift off shoes and adjuster. *See Fig. 2.*

**Installation** - To install, reverse removal procedure. Replace brake drum (rotor) if out-of-round exceeds .008" (.2 mm). Apply a thin coat of heat-resistant graphite grease to brake shoe sliding surfaces and to adjusting starwheel. Adjust starwheel until wheel starts to lock. Back off starwheel 4-5 notches. Ensure wheel rotates.

**Removal (740)** - Remove cover at rear of center console. Remove adjusting screw by carefully tapping on spring sleeve with a hammer and screwdriver. Unscrew adjusting screw so that cables are loose.

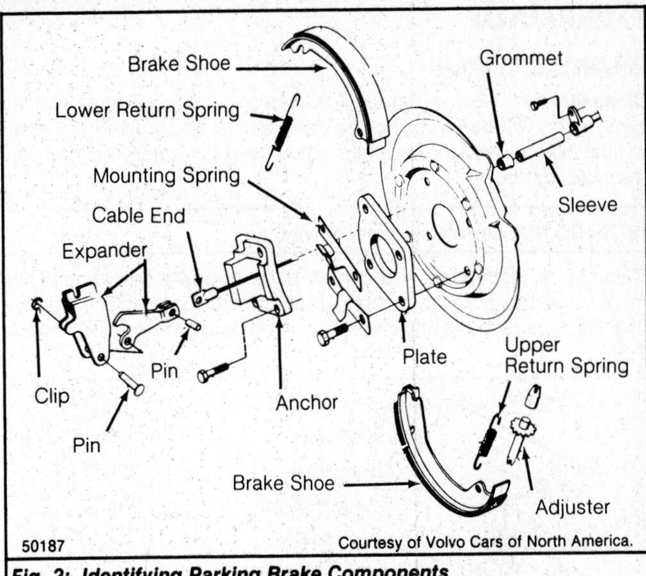


***Fig. 2: Identifying Parking Brake Components***

Raise vehicle. Remove rear wheels. Remove brake caliper and wire out of way. Remove brake rotor. Unhook rear return spring. Remove brake shoes.

**Installation** - Replace brake drum (rotor) if out-of-round exceeds .008" (.2 mm). Apply thin layer of heat resistant graphite grease on brake shoe contact surfaces. Assemble brake shoes. Install rear return spring. Using new bolts, install brake disc and caliper. Ensure that disc rotates without touching brake pads. Install wheels. Adjust parking brake cable. Lower vehicle.

## MASTER CYLINDER

**Removal & Installation** - Disconnect hydraulic lines at master cylinder. Plug openings to prevent entry of foreign matter. Remove cylinder attaching nuts. Remove cylinder assembly from vehicle. To install, reverse removal procedure. Bleed hydraulic system. See HYDRAULIC BRAKE BLEEDING article in GENERAL INFORMATION.

## POWER BRAKE UNIT

**Removal (240)** - Remove master cylinder. Disconnect vacuum hose. Remove soundproofing on left side of center console. Disconnect pressure rod from brake pedal. Remove power brake unit.

**Installation** - Apply sealing compound to contact surface on firewall. Fit other types with sealing ring. Reverse removal procedure to complete installation.

**Removal (740)** - **1)** Disconnect master cylinder and move it aside. Leave brake pipes attached to master cylinder. Disconnect vacuum hose. Using screwdriver, pry check valve from unit. Remove fuel filter and move it aside.

**2)** Disconnect vacuum pump and move it aside. Remove soundproofing on left side of center console. Disconnect push rod from brake pedal. Remove 4 nuts and power brake unit. Remove check valve seal.

**Installation** - Install seal in power brake unit. Ensure seal is correctly seated. Remove Sealing Ring (1272078-5) and install on new power brake unit. To complete installation, reverse removal procedure.

**Check Valve Replacement** - Disconnect vacuum hose from check valve. Using 2 screwdrivers, lever out check valve. Remove seal. Install new seal, ensuring that flange is properly aligned in cylinder. Coat seal with grease. Press valve carefully into place. Ensure that seal does not move out of position. Reconnect vacuum hose so that highest point is attached to valve.

# 1991 BRAKES
# Disc (Cont.)

## OVERHAUL

### BRAKE CALIPER

**Disassembly** – Remove disc pads, piston dust covers, and retaining clips. Insert wooden block into caliper housing. Apply compressed air at fluid inlet ports to force pistons out of caliper. Remove piston seals from cylinder bore.

***NOTE: DO NOT separate caliper halves.***

**Cleaning & Inspection** – Clean all parts in brake fluid or alcohol. Inspect cylinder bores for scoring, rust or corrosion. Replace if defective. Replace rubber seals and dust covers during overhaul. *See Figs. 3-6.*

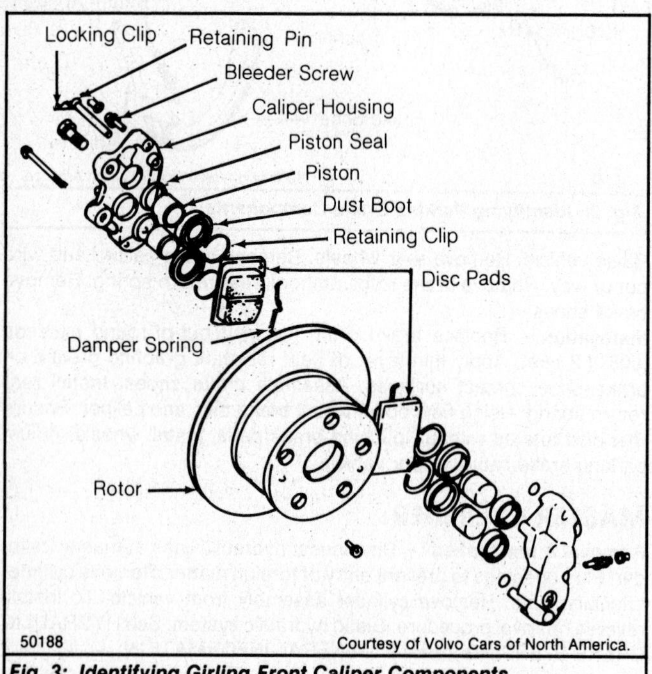


***Fig. 3: Identifying Girling Front Caliper Components***

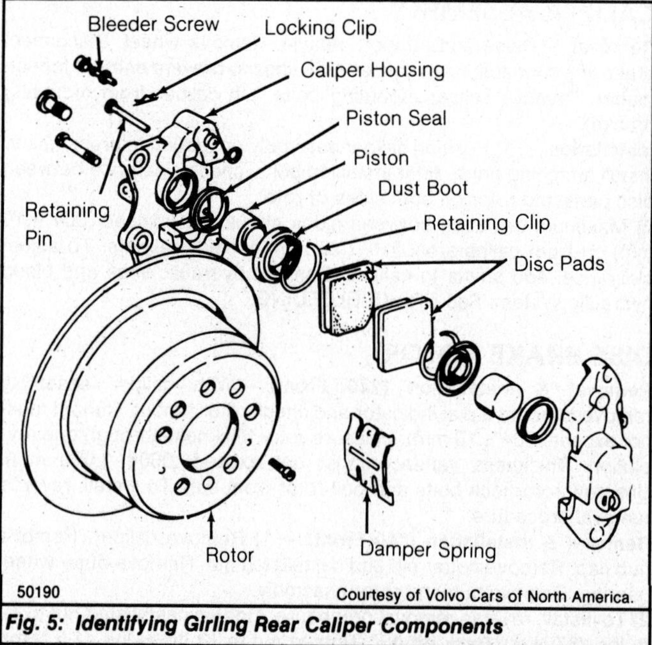


***Fig. 5: Identifying Girling Rear Caliper Components***

**Reassembly** – Coat all parts with clean brake fluid. Install new piston seals in cylinder bores. Carefully install pistons into cylinder bores. On ATE rear brake calipers, check piston position. See DISC PADS under REMOVAL & INSTALLATION. *See Fig. 1.* Install dust boots and retaining clips. Install bleeder screw and disc pads.

### MASTER CYLINDER

**Disassembly** – Remove master cylinder from vehicle. Clamp mounting flange in a vise. Remove reservoir from cylinder. Remove rubber sealing rings. Remove retainer ring from end of cylinder bore. Remove pistons from cylinder bore. *See Fig. 7.*

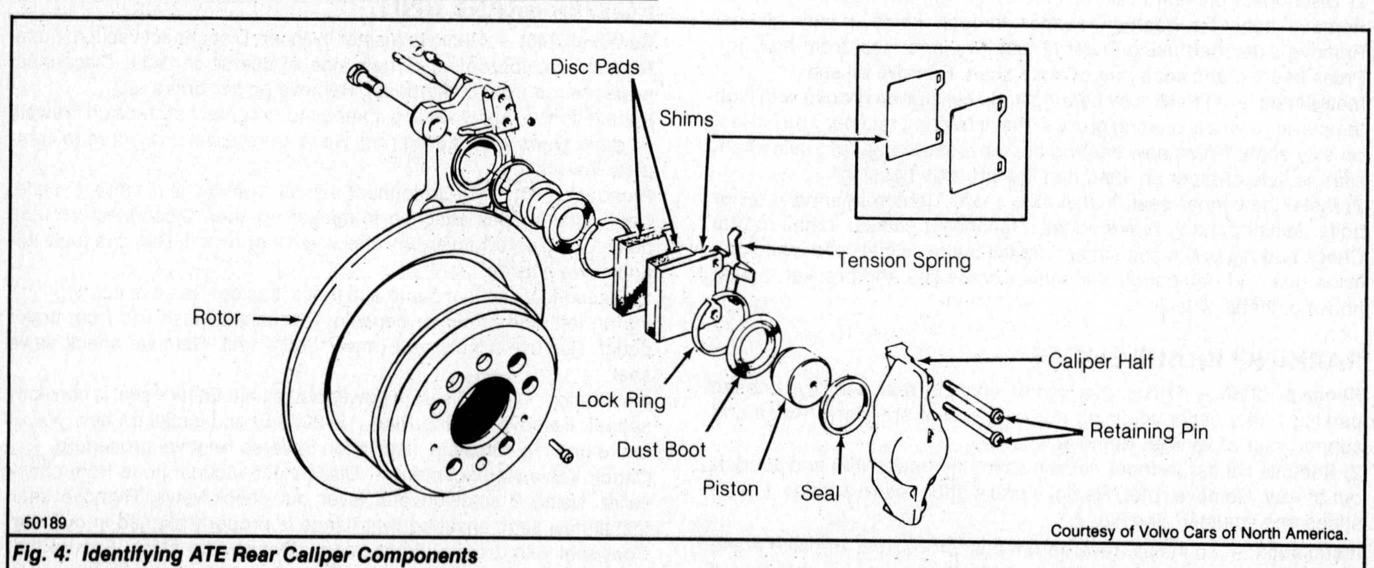


***Fig. 4: Identifying ATE Rear Caliper Components***

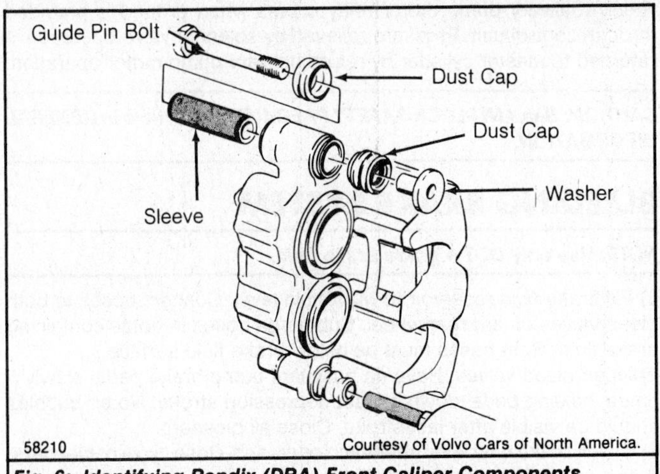


*Fig. 6: Identifying Bendix (DBA) Front Caliper Components*

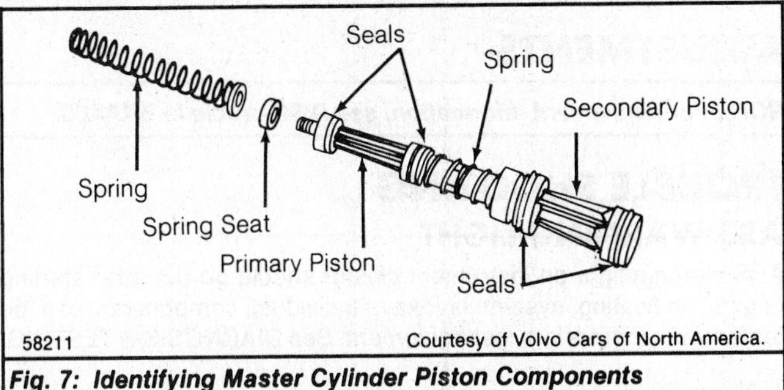


*Fig. 7: Identifying Master Cylinder Piston Components*

**Cleaning & Inspection** – Wash all parts in clean brake fluid or alcohol. Blow dry with compressed air. Inspect cylinder bore for scratches, rust or corrosion. Replace if defective. Replace both pistons with connector sleeve as an assembly.

**Reassembly – 1)** Lubricate all parts with clean brake fluid prior to reassembly. Position washer, seal, and back-up ring on secondary piston. Install spring thrust washer on piston. Install piston assembly into cylinder bore. Install washer, seal and back-up ring on primary piston.

**2)** Install spring with plate and sleeve on piston. Install piston assembly into cylinder bore. Push piston into cylinder bore. Install retaining ring. Install reservoir sealing rings, and install reservoir.

## TORQUE SPECIFICATIONS

*TORQUE SPECIFICATIONS*

| Application | Ft. Lbs. (N.m) |
|---|---|
| Caliper Guide Pin Bolts | 25 (34) |
| Front Caliper Mounting Bolts | 74 (100) |
| Master Cylinder Mounting Bolts | 22 (30) |
| Rear Caliper Mounting Bolts | 43 (58) |
| Wheel Lug Nuts | |
| 740 | 63 (86) |
| 240 | 88 (120) |
| | **INCH Lbs. (N.m)** |
| Rotor Retaining Stud | 72 (8) |

## DISC BRAKE SPECIFICATIONS

*DISC BRAKE SPECIFICATIONS*

| Application | In. (mm) |
|---|---|
| **240** | |
| Disc Diameter | |
| Front | |
| Solid | 10.33 (262) |
| Vented (ATE) | [1] |
| Vented (Girling) | [1] |
| Rear | 11.06 (281) |
| Lateral Runout (Maximum) | |
| Front & Rear | .004 (.10) |
| Original Thickness | |
| Front | |
| Solid | .563 (14.3) |
| Vented | .94 (24) |
| Rear (Solid) | .38 (9.6) |
| Minimum Refinish Thickness | [2] |
| Discard Thickness | |
| Front | |
| Solid | .52 (13.1) |
| Vented | .82 (20.8) |
| Rear | .33 (8.4) |
| Parking Brake Drum (Inside Rotor) | |
| Maximum Diameter | [1] |
| Maximum Runout | [1] |
| Master Cylinder Diameters | |
| Primary | .88 (22.3) |
| Secondary | .62 (15.75) |
| **740** | |
| Disc Diameter | |
| Front | |
| Solid | 11.02 (280) |
| Vented | |
| Type 1 | 11.30 (287) |
| Type 2 | 10.33 (262) |
| Rear | 11.06 (281) |
| Lateral Runout (Maximum) | |
| Front | .002 (.06) |
| Rear | .003 (.08) |
| Original Thickness | |
| Front | |
| Solid | .55 (14.0) |
| Vented (ATE) | .87 (22.1) |
| Vented (Girling) | 1.02 (26) |
| Rear | .38 (9.6) |
| Minimum Refinish Thickness | [2] |
| Discard Thickness | |
| Front | |
| Solid | .433 (11.0) |
| Vented | .79 (20.0) |
| Rear | .33 (8.4) |
| Parking Brake Drum (Inside Rotor) | |
| Maximum Diameter | 6.32 (160.45) |
| Maximum Runout | .006 (.15) |
| Master Cylinder Diameters | |
| Primary | .94 (23.8) |
| Secondary | .66 (16.8) |
| Rear Brake Caliper Pistons (ATE) | 1.5 (38) |

[1] – Information not available from manufacturer.
[2] – Always use minimum thickness specification stamped on rotors.

# 1991 BRAKES
# Anti-Lock

## 240, 740, 940

## DESCRIPTION

Anti-Lock Brake System (ABS) consists of speed sensors (on both front rotors and in rear axle), an Electronic Control Unit (ECU) (under right side of instrument panel on 240, left side of instrument panel on 740 and 940), and a hydraulic modulator (in engine compartment). *See Fig. 1.*

The hydraulic modulator consists of front and rear pressure control solenoids and relays, a return motor pump and relay, and ECU connector. Modulator pressure control solenoids are mounted inside hydraulic modulator and are not individually serviceable. Replace modulator assembly if solenoids are defective.

An ABS warning light in the instrument panel will remain illuminated if an ABS failure occurs. If an ABS malfunction occurs, conventional braking system takes over. The vehicle may be safely driven when ABS warning light is on.

***NOTE: For more information on brakes, see DISC article in BRAKES.***

## OPERATION

Hydraulic system consists of master cylinder, delivery lines, hydraulic modulator, electric solenoid valves, return delivery pump and brake calipers. Solenoid valves are contained within hydraulic modulator. Individual solenoid valves are used for pressure control to left and right front calipers, while rear brake line pressure is controlled by a common, regulated rear solenoid valve.

Hydraulic modulator controls hydraulic pressure to each front brake caliper or both rear calipers independent of pressure produced by brake master cylinder. However, pressure cannot exceed master cylinder pressure.

If wheel lock-up is sensed by speed sensors, ECU sends signal to hydraulic modulator. Hydraulic modulator operates electric return delivery pump to reduce hydraulic pressure at brake caliper(s). This is repeated until lock-up is eliminated.

ABS system has 2 relays (solenoid valve relay and pump motor relay), mounted on top of hydraulic modulator. Battery voltage is supplied to relays through fuse panel. ECU supplies a ground for relays when vehicle is in operation. This ECU-controlled ground supplies voltage signal from solenoid valve relay to front-control solenoid and to rear-control solenoid. Based upon speed sensor signals, ECU controls solenoid operation by supplying ground to energize individual solenoids.

Return delivery pump motor relay closes when ground is provided through control unit. Pressure relieved by solenoid valve operation is returned to master cylinder by return delivery pump motor operation.

***CAUTION: See ANTI-LOCK SAFETY PRECAUTIONS article in GENERAL INFORMATION.***

## BLEEDING BRAKE SYSTEM

***NOTE: Use only DOT 4 grade brake fluid.***

**1)** Fill brake fluid reservoir to MAX fluid level. Connect hoses to both bleed valves on left rear wheel. Submerge hoses in bottle containing brake fluid. Both hoses must be below brake fluid surface.

**2)** Open bleed valves. Have an assistant pump brake pedal slowly 5 times, holding pedal down on last depression stroke. No air bubbles should be visible after last stroke. Close all bleeders.

**3)** Check brake fluid level after each open-and-close cycle of bleeders. Bleed remaining wheels in following order: right rear, front left and front right.

## ADJUSTMENTS

***NOTE: For adjustment information, see DISC article in BRAKES.***

## TROUBLE SHOOTING

### ABS WARNING LIGHT

ABS warning light on instrument cluster should go out after starting engine, indicating system is okay. Individual components can be tested with appropriate test equipment. See DIAGNOSIS & TESTING.

## DIAGNOSIS & TESTING

### PRE-DIAGNOSIS INSPECTION

Perform a comprehensive visual inspection of system components before testing ABS system to isolate simple failures.

### ABS REPAIR PRECAUTIONS

Observe following precautions when performing repairs:

- DO NOT disconnect battery or electronic components with ignition switch in ON position.
- Disconnect ECU connector when arc welding on vehicle.
- NEVER subject ECU to temperatures greater than 180°F (82°C).
- Disconnect battery before charging with fast charger. DO NOT use fast charger to start engine.

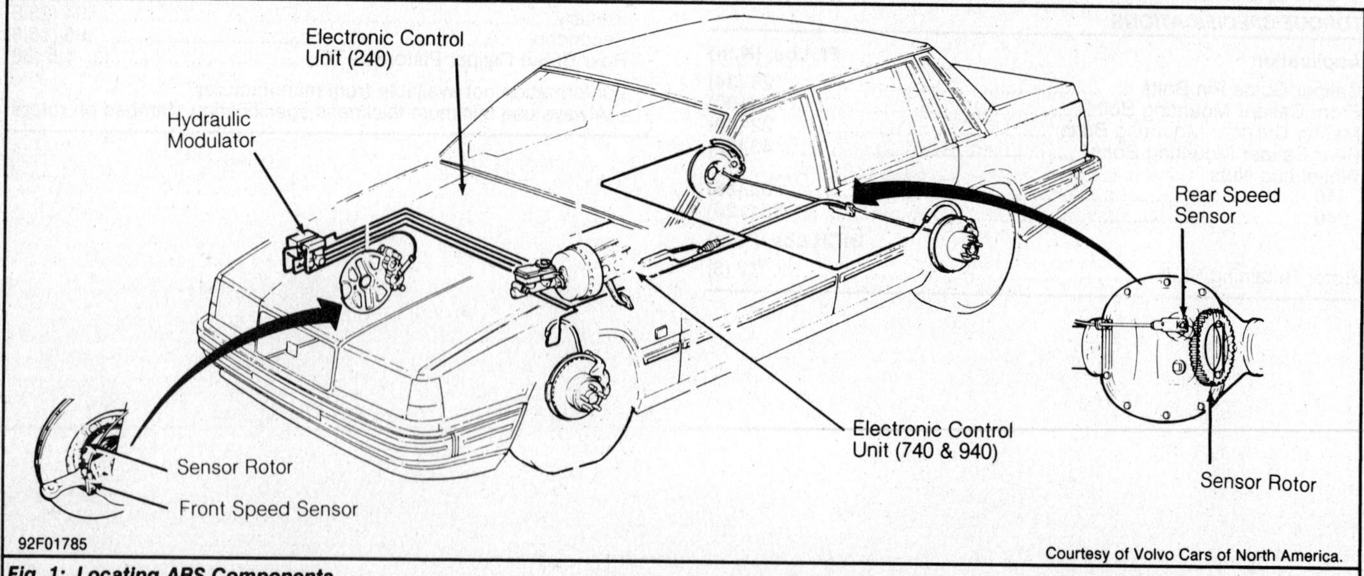


***Fig. 1: Locating ABS Components***

**NOTE: Test all ABS components and wiring before replacing ECU.**

To prepare for testing, turn ignition switch to OFF position. Remove cover from hydraulic modulator. Remove ECU connector by depressing lock spring and swinging out connector. Leave ECU connector unplugged, unless stated otherwise in testing procedure. Consult wiring diagram while performing tests. *See Fig. 6 or 7.* Check ECU connector terminals with minimum force through holes in side connector. Connector terminal numbers are molded into side of connector. To reduce diagnostic time, test components in following order.

## FUSES

Check 10-amp transient surge protector fuse. Transient surge protector is clipped to ECU. *See Fig. 1*

## ABS CIRCUIT TESTS

**Ground Circuits - 1)** Turn ignition off. Disconnect ECU connector. *See Figs. 1 and 2.* Using DVOM, check resistance between ECU connector terminals No. 10, 20, 32 and 34 and ground. Resistance should be zero in all cases.

***CAUTION: Never probe front of connectors. Check connectors only through slots in side of connector. DO NOT use more force than necessary. See Fig. 2.***

**2)** If resistance is not correct, check wiring harness between ECU and ground connections. On 240, terminals No. 10, 20 and 34 are grounded at right heater support, below carpet. On 740 and 940, these terminals are grounded on left "A" pillar. If fault is found at terminal No. 32, retest with new solenoid valve relay. *See Fig. 5.*

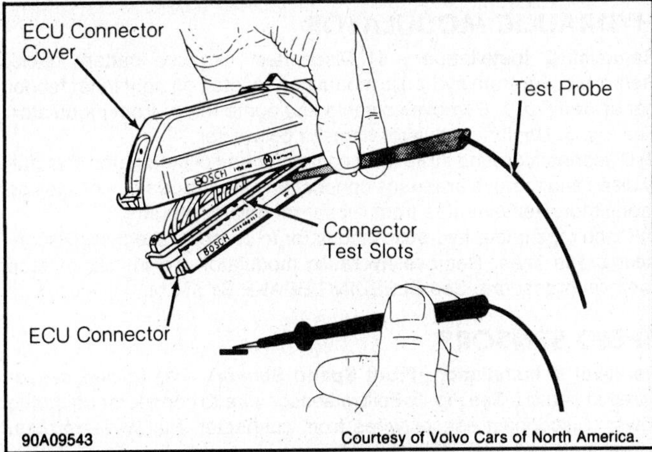


***Fig. 2: Accessing ECU Connector Test Slots***

**Transient Surge Protector - 1)** Disconnect ECU connector. *See Figs. 1 and 2.* Turn ignition on. Connect DVOM between terminal No. 1 on ECU connector and ground. DVOM should read battery voltage. If battery voltage is not present, measure voltage on transient surge protector connector. Transient surge protector is clipped to ECU.
**2)** Terminals No. 1, 2 and 4 should have battery voltage. Check for continuity between terminal No. 3 and ground. If only terminals No. 1 and 4 have voltage when terminal No. 3 is grounded, replace transient surge protector.
**Converter (240)** - Converter is located on control unit bracket. DO NOT disconnect connector. Connect voltmeter between control unit connector terminals No. 7 and 9, and ground. Voltmeter should indicate battery voltage. If no voltage is present, directly probe converter unit terminals No. 1, 2 and 4. If no terminals indicate voltage, replace converter.

**ECU Power Circuits - 1)** Turn ignition on. Disconnect ECU connector. *See Figs. 1 and 2.* Connect negative lead of DVOM to ground. Check for voltage at terminal No. 25 (while depressing brake pedal), and at terminals No. 27, 28 and 29 of ECU connector. All terminals should have battery voltage except for terminal No. 29, which should have .5-1.0 volt.
**2)** If no voltage is present at following terminals, perform appropriate repair:

- No. 25 - Check brake light switch. Replace if defective. On 240, also check connectors under instrument panel, near glove box.
- No. 27 - Replace defective solenoid valve relay.
- No. 28 - Replace defective pump motor relay.
- No. 29 - If voltage reading at terminal No. 27 is correct, voltage at terminal No. 29 should be .5-1.0 volt. If voltage at terminal No. 29 is not correct, replace solenoid relay.

**Hydraulic Modulator Power Circuits - 1)** Turn ignition off. Disconnect hydraulic modulator connector. Turn ignition on.
**2)** Connect DVOM negative lead to ground and positive lead to hydraulic modulator connector terminals No. 6, 7, 10 and 12. DVOM should indicate battery voltage. If battery voltage is not present, perform following repairs:

- No. 6 - Check wire harness and fuses.
- No. 7 - Attach connector to hydraulic modulator. ABS warning light should illuminate. If light does not illuminate, replace bulb.
- No. 10 - Check transient surge protector fuse. If fuse is okay, replace transient surge protector.
- No. 12 - On 240, check wire harness and ground wire connection behind battery. On 740 and 940, check wire harness and 80-amp fuse on top of right front wheelwell.

**3)** Turn ignition switch off. Attach connector to modulator.

## SENSORS

**Front Speed Sensors - 1)** Disconnect ECU connector. *See Figs. 1 and 2.* Using DVOM, check resistance between ECU connector terminals No. 4 and 6 (left sensor). Check resistance between ECU connector terminals No. 11 and 21 (right sensor). Resistance should vary from 900-2200 ohms as wheel is rotated.
**2)** If resistance is not within specification, check resistance at sensor connectors on suspension tower in engine compartment. If resistance is now within specification, repair wiring harness to ECU. If resistance is not within specification, replace sensor. *See Fig. 3.*
**3)** Check pulse wheels for damage. Maximum radial run-out is .006" (.15 mm)

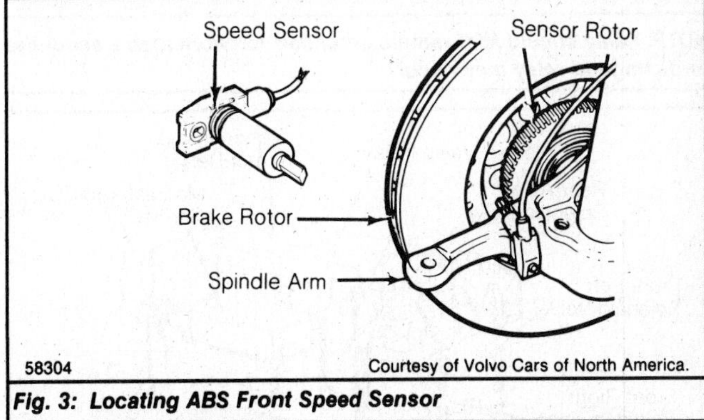


***Fig. 3: Locating ABS Front Speed Sensor***

**Rear (Axle) Speed Sensor - 1)** Disconnect ECU connector. *See Figs. 1 and 2.* Connect DVOM between ECU connector terminals No. 7 and 9. Resistance should vary from 600-1600 ohms as rear wheels are rotated.

# 1991 BRAKES
## Anti-Lock (Cont.)

**2)** If resistance is not within specification, check sensor resistance at sensor connector in rear axle casing (240), or at fuel filler pipe in trunk (740 and 940). If resistance is now within specifications, repair wiring harness to ECU. If resistance is still incorrect, replace sensor. *See Fig. 4.*
**3)** On vehicles without multi-link axle, if gap between sensor and pulse wheel is greater than .007" (.2 mm) or has damaged teeth, sensor gives incorrect signals and must be replaced.

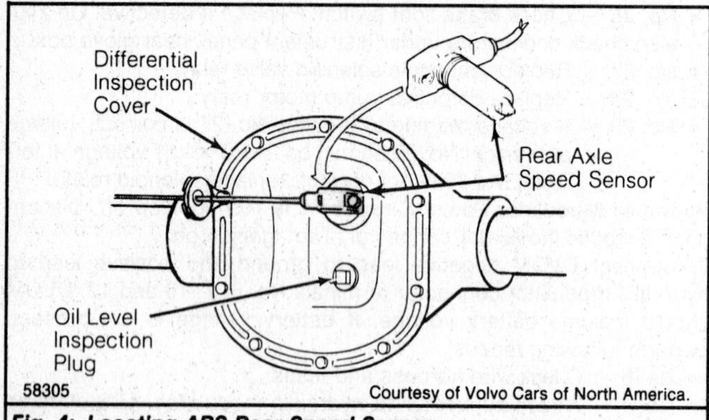


***Fig. 4: Locating ABS Rear Speed Sensor***

## SOLENOIDS

**Hydraulic Modulator – 1)** Turn ignition off. Disconnect ECU connector. *See Figs. 1 and 2.* Connect DVOM between ECU connector terminals No. 32 and 2 to check left front control solenoid. Connect DVOM between ECU connector terminals No. 18 (rear control solenoid) and No. 35 (right front control solenoid). Resistance should be .7-1.7 ohms.
**2)** If resistance is not within specification, unplug hydraulic modulator connector. Test resistance between hydraulic modulator terminal No. 4 (ground) and hydraulic modulator terminals No. 1, 3 and 5. If readings are now within specification, repair ECU wiring harness to modulator. If readings are still not within specification, replace hydraulic modulator. See HYDRAULIC MODULATOR under REMOVAL & INSTALLATION.

## RELAYS

**Pump Motor Relay – 1)** Disconnect ECU connector. *See Figs. 1 and 2.* Turn ignition on. Connect jumper wire between ECU connector terminal No. 28 and ground.

***NOTE: Relay should NOT remain grounded for more than 2 seconds, or damage to relay may occur.***

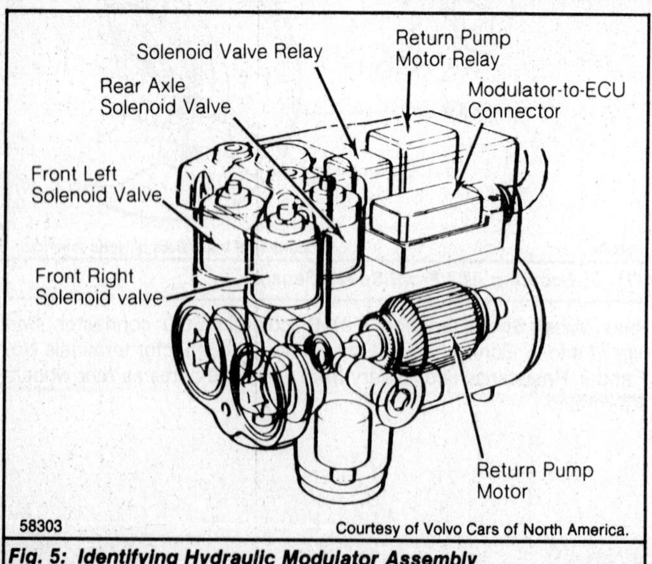


***Fig. 5: Identifying Hydraulic Modulator Assembly***

**2)** At the same time, measure voltage across connector terminal No. 14 and ground. Battery voltage should be present. If hydraulic modulator does not function, check wiring from ECU connector to modulator. If wiring is not faulty, replace and retest relay. *See Fig. 5.*

**Solenoid Valve Relay – 1)** Disconnect ECU connector. *See Figs. 1 and 2.* Turn ignition on. Connect DVOM between ground and terminal No. 32 of ECU connector. Connect jumper wire between ECU connector terminal No. 27 and ground.
**2)** Solenoid valve relay should switch on and DVOM should read battery voltage. If solenoid valve is inoperative and DVOM does not read battery voltage, check wiring harness from ECU connector and hydraulic modulator. If wiring is not faulty, replace relay and retest. *See Fig. 5.*

## ELECTRONIC CONTROL UNIT

If all other ABS components test okay, replace ECU with known good unit and check ABS operation.

# REMOVAL & INSTALLATION

## ELECTRONIC CONTROL UNIT

**Removal & Installation – 1)** Disconnect negative battery cable. On 240, remove soundproofing under right side of instrument panel. Loosen clamp and remove control unit from mounting bracket.
**2)** On 740 and 940, remove lower dash panel and knee bolster from under steering column. ECU is located behind upper left instrument panel, strapped into vertically mounted bracket. *See Fig. 1.*
**3)** On all models, release strap buckle and pull ECU down and out. Unplug connector without bending terminal pins. *See Fig. 2.* To install, reverse removal procedure.

## HYDRAULIC MODULATOR

**Removal & Installation – 1)** Disconnect negative battery cable. Remove cover from hydraulic modulator, located on right inner fender panel. *See Fig. 1.* Remove solenoid and pump relays from modulator. *See Fig. 5.* Unplug modulator harness connector.
**2)** Disconnect ground strap from connector end of modulator. Carefully clean and remove brake line connections, noting position of lines on modulator. Remove nuts from rubber modulator mounts.
**3)** Place rags under hydraulic modulator to collect brake fluid. Disconnect brake lines. Remove hydraulic modulator. To install, reverse removal procedure. See BLEEDING BRAKE SYSTEM.

## SPEED SENSORS

**Removal & Installation (Front Speed Sensor) – 1)** Locate sensor wires at sensor. *See Fig. 3.* Follow sensor wire to connector on spring tower. Disconnect sensor wires from connector. Pull wires through wheel arch and release from clamps.
**2)** Unbolt sensor from inboard side of spindle arm. Remove sensor. Before installing, coat speed sensor with small amount of Grease (1 161 037-5). To complete installation, reverse removal procedure.
**Removal (Rear Speed Sensor – Straight Axle)** – Follow sensor wires from sensor to connector. *See Fig. 4.* Cut shrink tubing from connector (if applicable). Unplug connector. Pull sensor wiring from below vehicle. Unbolt sensor from differential cover. Remove sensor.
**Installation** – To install, reverse removal procedure. Tighten bolt to 120 INCH lbs. (8 N.m).
**Removal (Rear Speed Sensor – Multi-Link Axle) – 1)** Remove spare tire. Fold back carpet to expose fuel filler pipe. Follow sensor wires from sensor. Cut shrink tubing from connector (if applicable). Disconnect connector. Press out sensor cable and rubber grommet.
**2)** Raise and support rear axle. Remove 4 bolts holding axle to body. Slightly lower rear axle. Disconnect right parking brake cable to allow access to sensor. Clean area around sensor. Remove sensor.
**Installation** – To install, reverse removal procedure. Tighten sensor screws to 120 INCH lbs. (8 N.m). Tighten rear axle-to-body bolts to 52 ft. lbs. (70 N.m), and then tighten bolts an additional 70 degrees.

# 1991 BRAKES
# Anti-Lock (Cont.)

## SENSOR ROTOR

**Removal** - Raise and support vehicle. Remove wheel assembly. Remove 2 caliper retaining bolts. Remove caliper and hang aside. Remove brake rotor. Place thumb on bearing so it does not fall out, and pull off sensor rotor.

**Installation** - **1)** Press new sensor rotor onto hub. Slide sensor rotor onto spindle. Install outer wheel bearing and nut. Torque nut to 42 ft. lbs. (57 N.m) while turning rotor. Loosen nut 1/2 turn. Ensure outer bearing inner race is not stuck. Tighten nut finger tight, then tighten nut to closest hole and insert cotter pin.

**2)** Install brake rotor. Install brake caliper using new attaching bolts. Torque caliper bolts to specification. See TORQUE SPECIFICATIONS table. To complete installation, reverse removal procedure.

## TORQUE SPECIFICATIONS

***TORQUE SPECIFICATIONS***

| Application | Ft. Lbs. (N.m) |
|---|---|
| Front Caliper Mounting Bolts | 74 (100) |
| Front Wheel Bearing Nut | 42 (57) |
| Master Cylinder Mounting Bolts | 22 (30) |
| Wheel Lug Nuts | 63 (86) |
| | **INCH Lbs. (N.m)** |
| Sensor Bolt/Screw | 120 (8 N.m) |

## WIRING DIAGRAMS

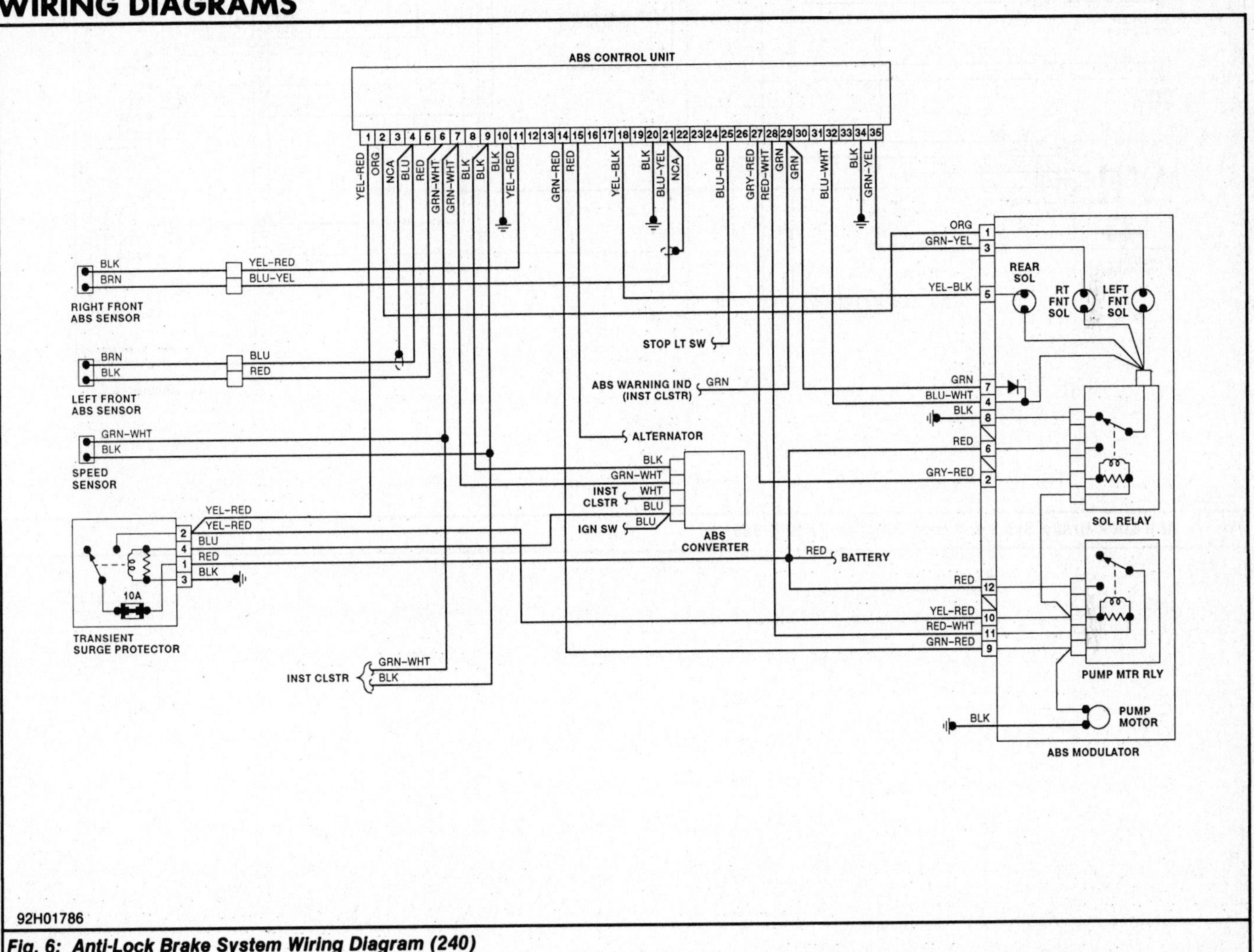


*Fig. 6: Anti-Lock Brake System Wiring Diagram (240)*

# 1991 BRAKES
## Anti-Lock (Cont.)

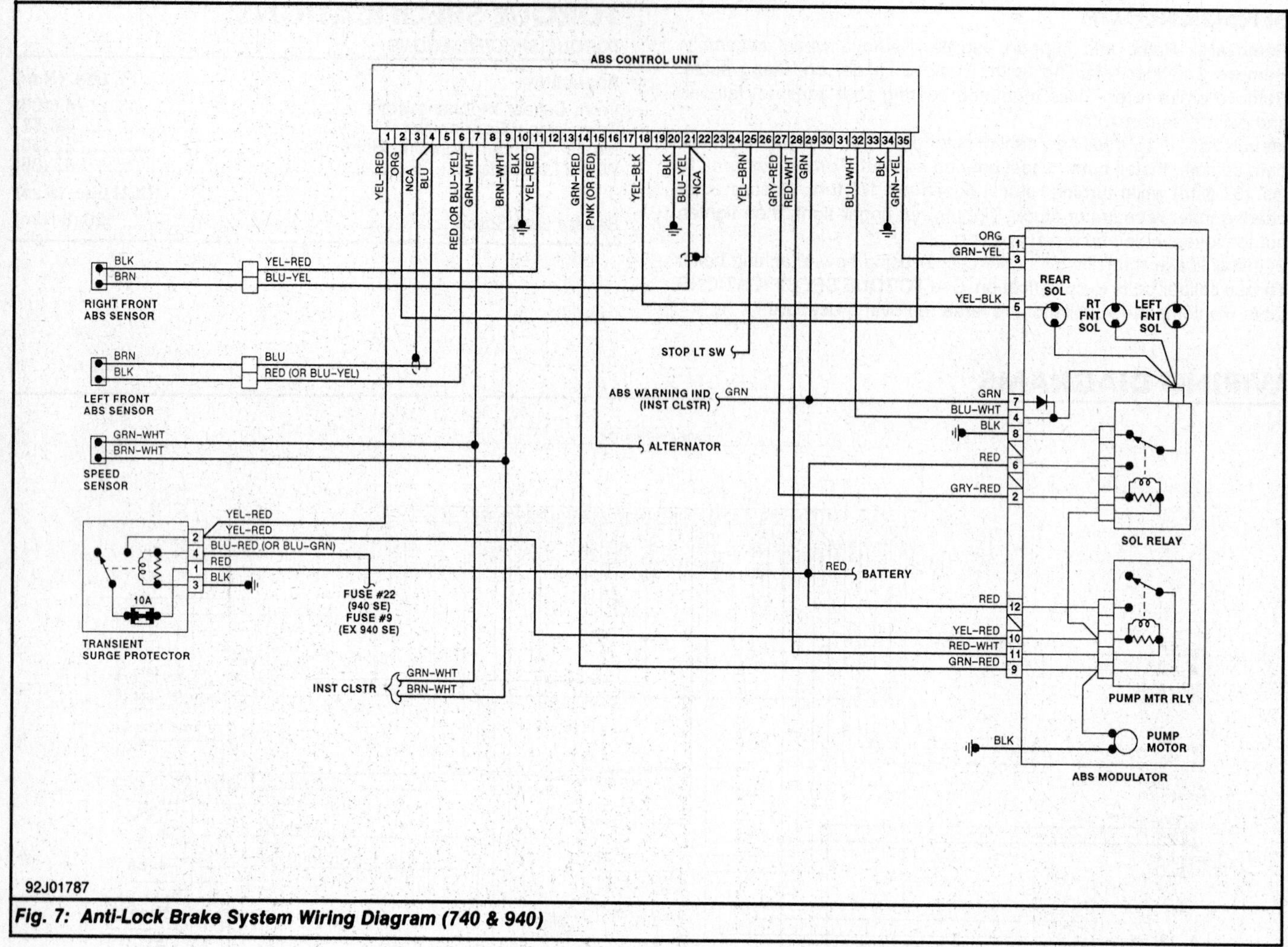


***Fig. 7: Anti-Lock Brake System Wiring Diagram (740 & 940)***

# 1991 WHEEL ALIGNMENT
# Specifications & Procedures

## 240, 740, 940

***NOTE:* Prior to performing wheel alignment, perform preliminary visual and mechanical inspection of wheels, tires and suspension components. See PRE-ALIGNMENT INSTRUCTIONS in WHEEL ALIGNMENT THEORY & OPERATION article in GENERAL INFORMATION.**

## RIDING HEIGHT ADJUSTMENT

Before adjusting alignment, check riding height. Riding height must be checked with vehicle on level floor and tires properly inflated. Bounce vehicle several times and allow suspension to settle.

Visually inspect vehicle for signs of abnormal height from front to rear or side to side. Check passenger and luggage compartments for extra heavy items and remove if present. If riding height is not within specification, check, repair or replace suspension components. Riding height between left and right side of vehicle should vary less than 1" (25.4 mm).

## JACKING & HOISTING

### FLOOR JACK OR HOIST

The following illustrations indicate areas (parts) of underbody and frame used to raise and support vehicle with either floor jack or hoist. These points are indicated by shaded areas on frame. *See Fig. 1.*

### EMERGENCY JACKING

Those points designated on body outline are designed for use with vehicle's jack and are indicated by circular dots. *See Fig. 1*. If floor jack or hoist is employed, extreme care should be exercised to avoid damaging outer body shell.

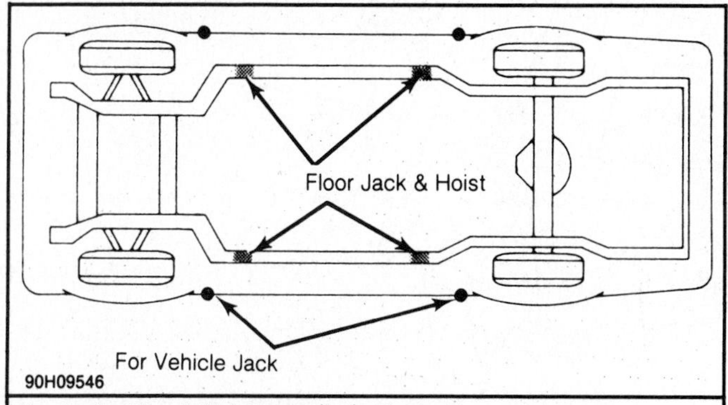


***Fig. 1: Jacking & Hoisting Points (Typical)***

## WHEEL ALIGNMENT PROCEDURES

***NOTE:* Wheel alignment adjustment procedures for 940 are not available from manufacturer.**

### CAMBER ADJUSTMENT

**240** – Remove upper spring strut mounting nuts. Using Wrench (5038), turn suspension until correct value is obtained. *See Fig. 2.* Tighten upper spring strut mounting nuts.

**740** – **1)** Camber angle can be adjusted by altering the fixing bolt hole position for the upper spring strut mount. Remove front nut in spring strut upper retaining plate. Using a soft-faced hammer, remove front press bolt.

**2)** Loosen rear bolt on retaining plate. Set Wrench (5038) on rear bolt and turn suspension assembly so hole in retaining plate passes hole in suspension tower at least .12" (3 mm). *See Fig. 2.* Mark position when hole can no longer be seen and turn wrench an additional .12" (3 mm).

**3)** Mark position of new hole with a punch. Tighten rear nut to 35 ft. lbs. (48 N.m) so strut will not move out of position.

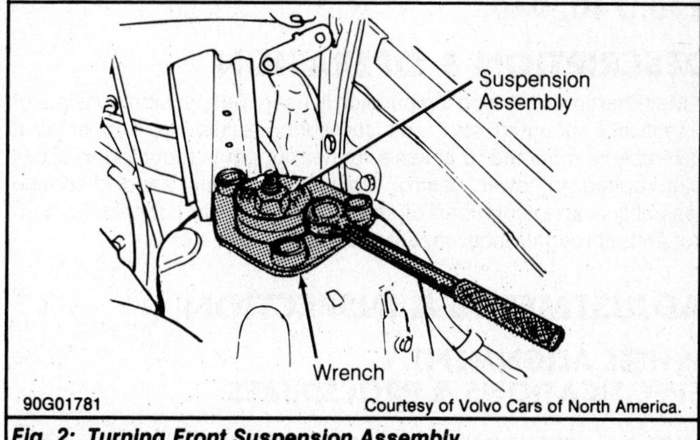


***Fig. 2: Turning Front Suspension Assembly***

**4)** Drill a new hole in retaining plate, through hole in top of suspension tower. Use care not to damage hole in suspension tower. Install and tighten front press bolt and nut. Tighten bolt in retaining plate. Remove front press bolt and replace with new bolt, nut and lock washer. Tighten bolt to 35 ft. lbs. (48 N.m).

### CASTER ADJUSTMENT

**240** – Caster angle is not adjustable. If value is incorrect, suspension components must be checked and replaced as necessary.

**740** – Caster angle can be adjusted by replacing the control arm strut. A shorter strut reduces caster angle by .8 degrees. A longer strut increases caster angle by .8 degrees.

### TOE-IN ADJUSTMENT

To adjust toe-in, lengthen or shorten tie-rod ends as necessary.

## TORQUE SPECIFICATIONS

***TORQUE SPECIFICATIONS***

| Application | Ft. Lbs. (N.m) |
|---|---|
| Upper Strut Bolt | |
| 240 | 15 (20) |
| 740 | 35 (48) |
| Wheel Lug Nuts | |
| 240 | 72-95 (98-129) |
| 740 & 940 | 63 (85) |

## WHEEL ALIGNMENT SPECIFICATIONS

***WHEEL ALIGNMENT SPECIFICATIONS***

| Application | Preferred | Range |
|---|---|---|
| **240** | | |
| Camber [1] | | |
| Front | 1/2 | 1/4 To 3/4 |
| Caster [1] | 3 1/2 | 3 To 4 |
| Toe-In [2] | | |
| Front | 1/8 (3) | 1/16 To 3/16 (1.5 To 5) |
| Toe-In [1] | | |
| Front | 1/4 | 1/8 To 3/8 |
| Toe-Out On Turns [1] | | |
| Inner | 20 3/4 | ..... |
| Outer | 20 | ..... |
| **740 & 940** | | |
| Camber [1] | | |
| Front | 3/8 | -1/8 To 7/8 |
| Caster [1] | 5 | 4 1/2 To 5 1/2 |
| Toe-In [2] | | |
| Front | 1/8 (3) | 1/16 To 3/16 (1.5 To 5) |
| Toe-In [1] | | |
| Front | 1/4 | 1/8 To 3/8 |

[1] – Measurement in degrees.

[2] – Measurement in inches (mm).

# 1991 SUSPENSION
# Front

**240, 740, 940**

## DESCRIPTION & OPERATION

A MacPherson strut-type suspension is used. Suspension consists of a vertically mounted strut and coil spring assembly. Top of strut assembly is mounted to chassis frame; bottom is mounted to a ball joint, bolted to lower control arm. The steering knuckle/spindle assembly is an integral part of strut. A stabilizer bar connects to control arms through rubber-mounted links. *See Fig. 1 or 2.*

## ADJUSTMENTS & INSPECTION

### WHEEL ALIGNMENT SPECIFICATIONS & PROCEDURES

***NOTE:* *See SPECIFICATIONS & PROCEDURES article in WHEEL ALIGNMENT.***

### WHEEL BEARING

While rotating hub, tighten hub nut to 42 ft. lbs. (57 N.m). Loosen nut 1/2 turn, and then tighten by hand. Ensure hub rotates freely without end play. If necessary, loosen nut to align cotter pin hole. Install new cotter pin. Recheck end play.

### BALL JOINT CHECKING

With vehicle resting on wheels, check ball joint axial play with large pair of pliers. Maximum axial play is .12" (3 mm). Maximum radial play is .02" (.5 mm). Check rubber bellows and replace as necessary.

## REMOVAL & INSTALLATION

### STABILIZER BAR

**Removal** - Raise and support vehicle. Disconnect stabilizer bar from stabilizer bar links. *See Fig. 1 or 2.* Remove stabilizer bar-to-frame brackets. Remove brackets, bushings and stabilizer bar from vehicle.

**Installation** - To install, reverse removal procedure. Ensure bushing joint faces forward. Tighten nuts and bolts to specification. See TORQUE SPECIFICATIONS table at end of article.

### WHEEL BEARING

**Removal** - **1)** Raise and support vehicle. Mark front wheels to avoid rebalancing. Remove front wheels. Remove Allen head caliper bolts. Remove and support caliper.

**2)** Remove grease cap, cotter pin, hub nut, outer bearing and brake disc. Remove inner seal, bearing, inner and outer races.

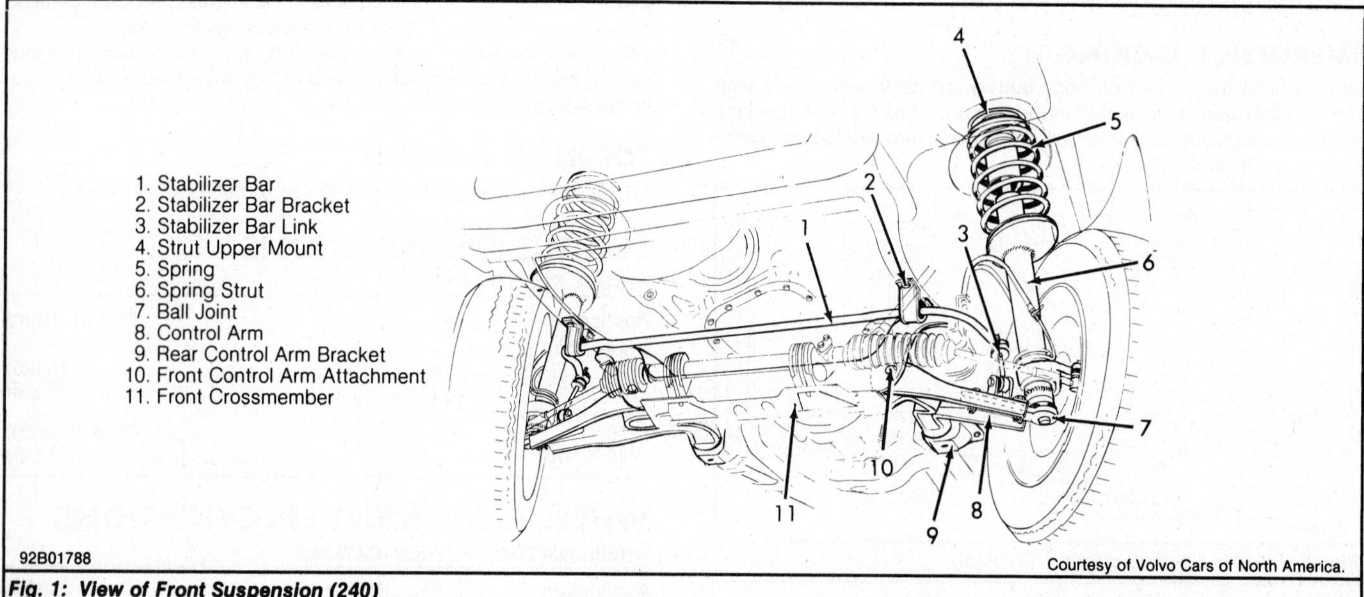


***Fig. 1: View of Front Suspension (240)***

***Fig. 2: View of Front Suspension (740 & 940)***

**Installation** – To install, reverse removal procedure. Tighten nuts and bolts to specification. See TORQUE SPECIFICATIONS table at end of article.

***NOTE: Use Puller (2722) if inner bearing is difficult to remove.***

## BALL JOINT

**Removal (240)** – **1)** Raise and support vehicle. Mark wheel-to-hub reference to avoid rebalancing front wheels. Remove front wheels. Mark nut plate at top of wheel housing and remove upper strut mount nuts.

**2)** Compress spring and remove center nut, upper spring seat and spring. Using Wrench (5173 for gas strut or 5039 for standard strut), remove strut retaining nut and strut.

**3)** Remove ball joint retaining nut, located inside strut housing. *See Fig. 3.* If necessary, use long brass drift to tap ball joint from strut housing. Remove ball joint-to-strut nuts on control arm.

**Installation** – To install, reverse removal procedure. See TORQUE SPECIFICATIONS table at end of article.

***NOTE: Left and right ball joints are different.***

**Removal (740 & 940)** – **1)** Raise and support vehicle. Mark front wheels to avoid rebalancing. Remove front wheels. Remove anti-roll link-to-control arm bolt and control arm-to-ball joint nut.

**2)** Using Puller (5259) separate control arm from ball joint stud. Remove ball joint mount bolts and ball joint.

**Installation** – To install, reverse removal procedure. See TORQUE SPECIFICATIONS table at end of this article.

***NOTE: Use NEW bolts and apply Loctite to threads.***

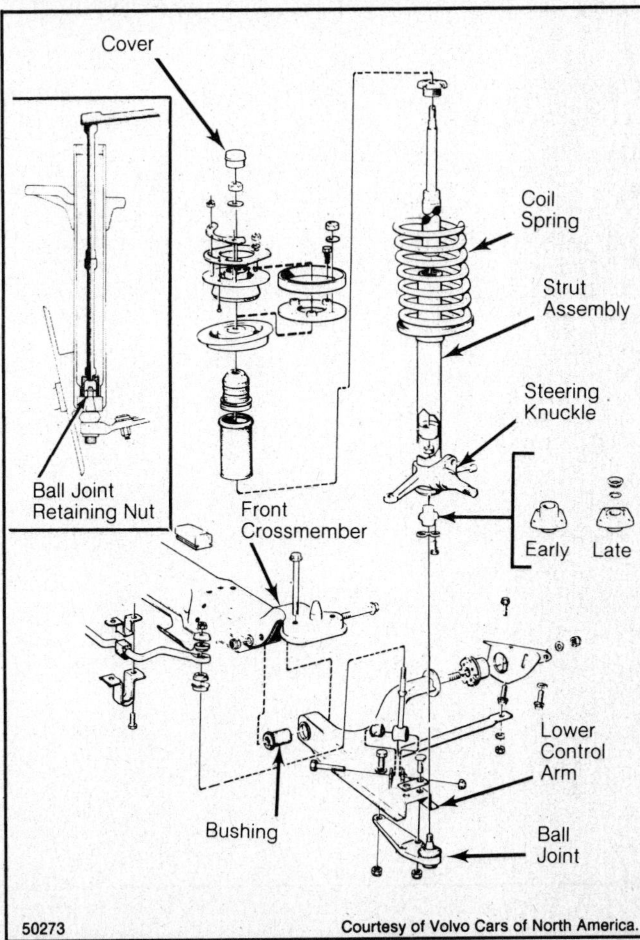


***Fig. 3: Exploded View of Front Suspension (240)***

## CONTROL ARM

**Removal (240)** – **1)** Raise and support vehicle. Mark front wheels to avoid rebalancing. Disconnect stabilizer link and ball joint from control arm. *See Fig. 3.* Disconnect rear bushing bracket from chassis.

**2)** Disconnect control arm-to-crossmember bolt and remove control arm. Separate rear bushing bracket from control arm. If control arm bushings are to be replaced, press out using Adapter Sleeve (5085) and Driver (5091).

**Installation** – To install control arm, reverse removal procedure. To install control arm bushing use adapter sleeve and driver. See TORQUE SPECIFICATIONS table at end of article.

**Removal (740 & 940)** – **1)** Raise and support vehicle. Mark front wheels to avoid rebalancing. Remove front wheels. Remove ball stud nut, anti-roll link and control arm-to-strut bolt.

**2)** Separate control arm from ball joint using Puller (5259). Remove control arm from crossmember. If bushing needs replacing use Drift (5091) and Support (5240) to remove.

**Installation** – To install control arm, reverse removal procedure. Use Drift (2904) and Support (5240) to install control arm bushing. See TORQUE SPECIFICATIONS table at end of article.

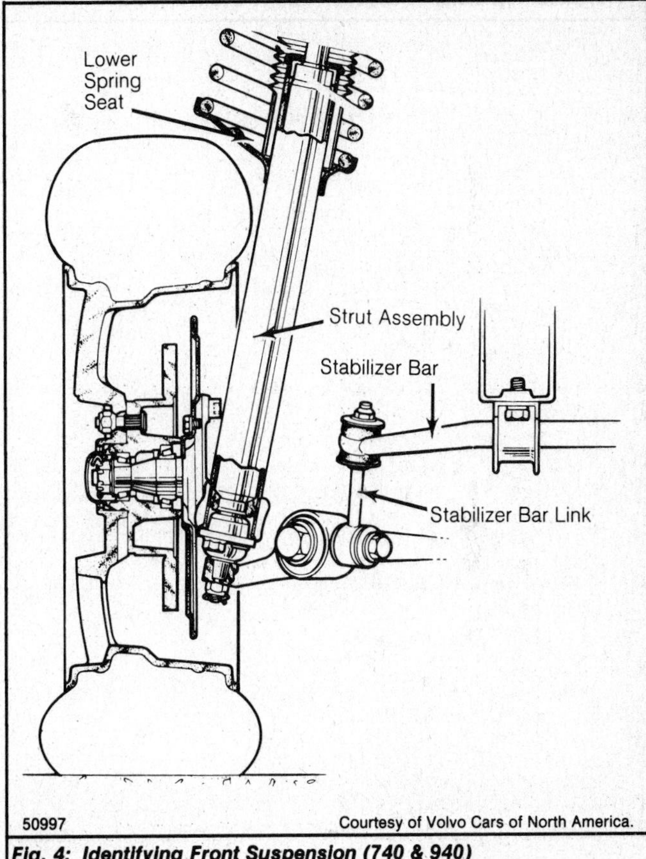


***Fig. 4: Identifying Front Suspension (740 & 940)***

## STRUT ASSEMBLY

**Removal** – **1)** Raise and support vehicle. Mark wheel-to-hub relation to avoid rebalancing wheels. Remove front wheels. Mark nut plate at top of wheel housing and remove upper strut mounting nuts.

**2)** Compress spring and remove center nut, upper spring seat and spring. Using Wrench (5039 for standard strut or 5173 for gas strut), remove strut retaining nut and strut. *See Fig. 3 or 4.*

**Installation** – To install, reverse removal procedure. See TORQUE SPECIFICATIONS table.

# 1991 SUSPENSION
## Front (Cont.)

## TORQUE SPECIFICATIONS

*TORQUE SPECIFICATIONS*

| Application | Ft. Lbs. (N.m) |
|---|---|
| **240** | |
| Ball Joint Bracket-To-Control Arm | 85 (115) |
| Ball Joint Stud Nut | 43 (58) |
| Ball Joint-To-Strut Assembly | 17 (23) |
| Control Arm Retaining Bolts | |
| Front | 40-70 (55-95) |
| Rear | 37-44 (50-60) |
| Rear Control Arm Bracket-To-Frame | 22-37 (30-50) |
| Stabilizer Bar Link Bushing Nut | [1] |
| Strut Nut (Center) | 111 (150) |
| Strut Assembly Nuts-To-Body | 15 (20) |
| Wheel Lug Nuts | 85 (115) |
| **740 & 940** | |
| Ball Joint Stud Nut | 44 (60) |
| Ball Joint-To-Strut Assembly | 22 (30) |
| Control Arm-To-Control Arm Strut | 70 (95) |
| Stabilizer Bar Link Bushing Nut | [1] |
| Strut Nut (Center) | 111 (150) |
| Wheel Lug Nuts | 63 (85) |

[1] – Tighten until distance between washers is 1.7" (42 mm).

# 1991 SUSPENSION
# Rear

## 240, 740, 940

## DESCRIPTION & OPERATION

240 rear suspension consists of coil springs mounted between trailing arms and body rubber mounts. *See Fig. 1.* Shock absorbers are mounted between trailing arms and body. A stabilizer bar is attached to control arms at both ends. Two torque rods run forward from axle brackets and are mounted to frame. A track bar is attached behind and parallel to axle housing. The bar is connected between axle housing and body bracket.

740 and 940 rear suspension consists of coil springs, self-leveling gas-filled shocks and axle with longitudinal trailing arms. *See Fig. 2.* A stabilizer bar attaches to both trailing arms. In addition, a pair of trailing arms connect the differential to a subframe.

940 SE multi-link rear suspension consists of a subframe-mounted differential. *See Fig. 3.* Independent wheel bearing housings are located near upper and lower control arms, front support arms and rear track rods. Shock absorbers and coil springs are mounted between trailing arms and body.

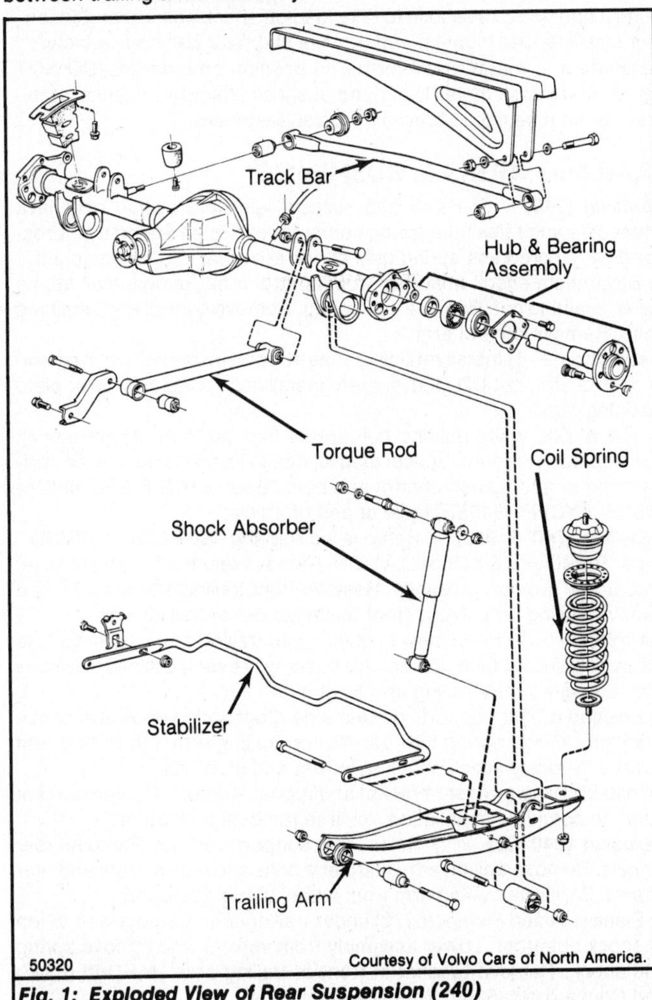

**Fig. 1: Exploded View of Rear Suspension (240)**

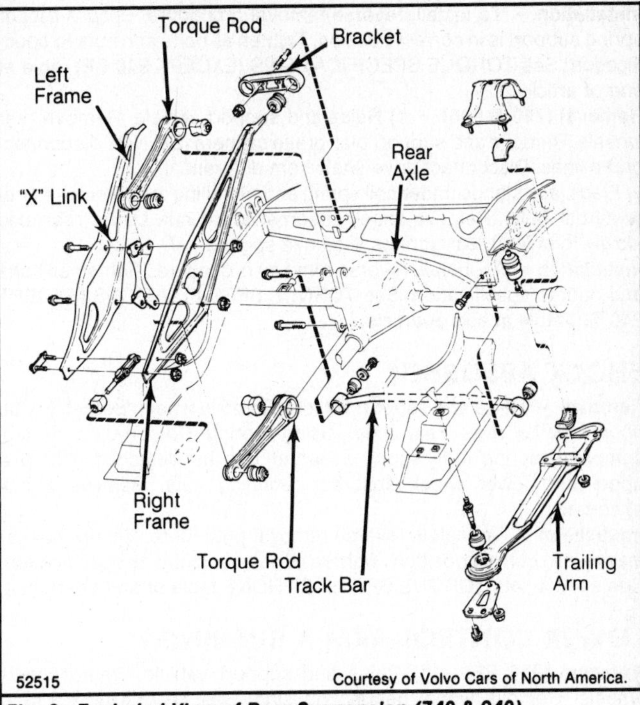

**Fig. 2: Exploded View of Rear Suspension (740 & 940)**

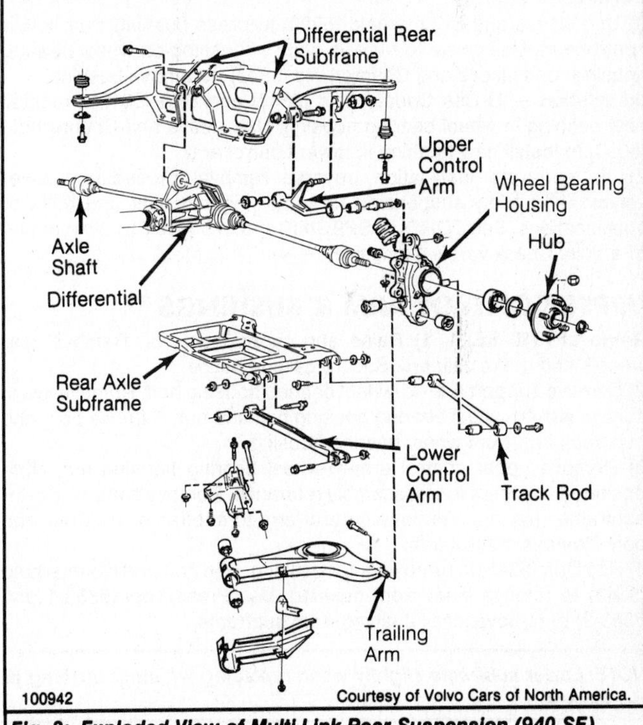

**Fig. 3: Exploded View of Multi-Link Rear Suspension (940 SE)**

## ADJUSTMENTS & INSPECTION

### WHEEL ALIGNMENT SPECIFICATIONS & PROCEDURES

***NOTE:* See *SPECIFICATIONS & PROCEDURES* article in *WHEEL ALIGNMENT.***

## REMOVAL & INSTALLATION

### COIL SPRING

**Removal (240) - 1)** Raise and support vehicle. Remove wheel assembly. Place floor jack under rear axle housing, and raise axle until spring compresses. Using Spring Compressor (5040), compress spring until shock absorber can be detached.

**2)** Disconnect lower end of shock absorber from trailing arm. *See Fig. 1.* Remove spring lower retaining nut. Lower floor jack, and remove coil spring.

# 1991 SUSPENSION
# Rear (Cont.)

**Installation** - To install, reverse removal procedure. Ensure rubber spring support is in correct position. Tighten all bolts and nuts to specification. See TORQUE SPECIFICATIONS (EXCEPT 940 SE) table at end of article.

**Removal (740 & 940)** - **1)** Raise and support vehicle. Remove rear wheels. Remove and support disc brake calipers. DO NOT disconnect brake lines. Disconnect drive shaft from differential.

**2)** Place jack stands under coil spring end of trailing arm. Remove anti-sway bar bolts. Remove shock absorber lower nut. Lower rear axle slowly to unload rear springs. Remove springs.

**Installation** - To install, reverse removal procedure. Tighten all bolts and nuts to specification. See TORQUE SPECIFICATIONS (EXCEPT 940 SE) table at end of article.

## SHOCK ABSORBER

**Removal** - Raise and support vehicle. Remove wheel assembly. Use floor jack to raise rear axle. Using Spring Compressor (5040), compress spring until shock absorber can be detached. Remove upper and lower shock absorber retaining nuts. Remove shock absorber.

**Installation** - To install, reverse removal procedure. Ensure spacer sleeve is in correct position. Tighten all bolts and nuts to specification. See appropriate TORQUE SPECIFICATIONS table at end of article.

## LOWER CONTROL ARM & BUSHINGS

**Removal (940 SE)** - **1)** Raise and support vehicle. Remove rear wheels. Remove wheel bearing housing. See TRAILING ARMS & BUSHINGS under REMOVAL & INSTALLATION. Remove lower control arm.

**2)** Use sleeve and Counterhold (5990) to press bushing from lower control arm. Use chisel to remove edge of bushing on wheel bearing housing. Use sleeve and Counterhold (5343) to remove bushing.

**Installation** - **1)** Use Counterhold (5342) and Drift (5310) to install new bushing in wheel bearing housing. Use sleeve and Counterhold (5090) to install new bushing in lower control arm.

**2)** To complete installation, reverse removal procedure. Lower vehicle, and allow suspension to settle. Tighten nuts and bolts to specifications. See TORQUE SPECIFICATIONS (940 SE) table at end of article. Check wheel alignment.

## UPPER CONTROL ARM & BUSHINGS

**Removal (940 SE)** - **1)** Raise and support vehicle. Remove rear wheels and brake calipers. Secure calipers aside.

**2)** Remove support arm-to-wheel bearing housing bolt. Remove lower control arm-to-wheel bearing housing bolt and nut. Remove bolt, and pull track arm from wheel bearing housing.

**3)** Remove upper control arm-to-wheel bearing housing nut. Note position of spacers for reassembly reference. Remove control arm-to-subframe rear nut. Remove control arm-to-subframe front nut and bolt. Remove control arm.

**4)** Use Drift (5345) to remove outer bushing. Use drift and Counterhold (5343) to remove inner front bushing. Use Press Tool (5353-1 and 5353-2) to remove inner bushing from subframe.

***NOTE: Lower subframe slightly when replacing left inner bushing (if necessary).***

**Installation** - **1)** Use Press Tool (5353-3 and 5353-4) to install new bushing in subframe. *See Fig. 4.*

**2)** Use Drift (2731) and Counterhold (2904) to install inner bushing on control arm. Use Drift (5090) and Counterhold (5087) to install new outer control arm bushing.

**3)** Reverse removal procedure to complete installation. Lower vehicle, and allow suspension to settle. Tighten nuts and bolts to specifications. See TORQUE SPECIFICATIONS (940 SE) table at end of article. Check wheel alignment.

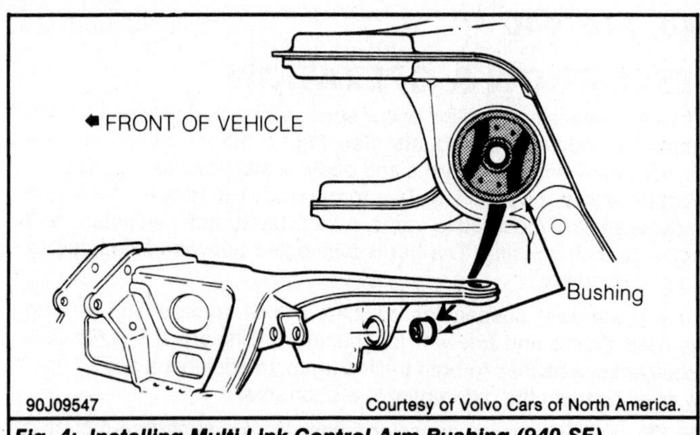


***Fig. 4: Installing Multi-Link Control Arm Bushing (940 SE)***

## STABILIZER BAR

**Removal (240)** - Raise vehicle, and support using safety stands. Using a floor jack, raise axle to take load off shock absorbers. Disconnect stabilizer bar mounts, and remove stabilizer bar from vehicle.

**Installation** - Install stabilizer bar in position on brackets (DO NOT tighten fasteners). Install lower end of shock absorber. Position stabilizer bar so it settles in bracket. Tighten fasteners.

## TRAILING ARMS & BUSHINGS

**Removal (240)** - **1)** Raise and support vehicle. Position floor jack under axle and raise until spring compresses. Using Spring Compressor (5040), compress spring until shock absorber can be detached.

**2)** Disconnect shock absorber from control arm. Remove coil spring lower retaining nut. Remove coil spring. Remove control arm retaining bolts. Remove control arm.

**Installation** - **1)** Install retaining bolts at front. Install bolts at rear end of control arm, but DO NOT tighten. Install coil spring and lower plate retaining nut.

**2)** Raise axle while guiding coil spring into position. Attach shock absorber lower mount. Spacer sleeve should lie on inside. Lower vehicle to floor, and tighten control arm bolts. See TORQUE SPECIFICATIONS (EXCEPT 940SE) table at end of article.

**Removal (740 & 940)** - Remove coil spring. See COIL SPRING under REMOVAL & INSTALLATION. Remove rear trailing arm bracket and rubber support bushings. Remove front trailing arm bracket, and remove trailing arm. Press front bushings out of trailing arm.

**Installation** - **1)** Press new bushings into trailing arms (tapered hole in bushing should face up). Ensure bushing is evenly spaced in trailing arm. Loosely install trailing arm front nuts.

**2)** Position rubber supports on rear axle. Coat spring ends with petroleum jelly. Guide spring into position on trailing arm. Lift trailing arm upward. Loosely install shock absorber and stabilizer.

**3)** Install trailing arm rear bracket and rubber support. Tighten bracket nuts. To complete installation, reverse removal procedure.

**Removal (940 SE)** - **1)** Raise and support vehicle. Remove rear wheels. Remove trailing arm guard and bolts and nuts at front and rear of arm. Separate trailing arm from wheel bearing housing.

**2)** Place jack and Fixture (5972) under trailing arm. Remove bolt at top of shock absorber. Lower assembly from vehicle, and remove spring and shock. Remove bracket at front of trailing arm. Use Drift (5347) and Counterhold (5346) to remove bushings.

**3)** Remove brake caliper, and tie it aside. Remove brake disc and handbrake cable. Remove track rod-to-wheel bearing housing bolt, and pull rod from housing. Remove hub nut. Remove upper control arm-to-wheel bearing hub nut. Retain spacers for reassembly, and remove housing.

**4)** Remove brake shield, and move it aside. Note bushing position. Use suitable sleeve and Counterhold (5343) to remove bushing.

***NOTE: Install bushing with slot at top.***

**Installation** - To install, reverse removal procedure. Lower vehicle, and allow suspension to settle. Tighten nuts and bolts to specifications. See TORQUE SPECIFICATIONS (940 SE) table at end of article.

## TORQUE RODS & TRACK BAR

**Removal (240)** - Raise and support vehicle. Disconnect track bar and torque rods from body and axle mountings. Inspect bushings and sleeves for wear and damage. Replace if necessary.

**Installation** - To install, reverse removal procedure, but DO NOT tighten nuts. Lower vehicle, and allow suspension to settle. Tighten nuts to specification.

## TORQUE RODS & BUSHINGS

**Removal (740 & 940)** - Raise and support vehicle. Remove torque rod(s). Press bushings from torque rods.

**Installation** - **1)** Coat bushing mating surfaces with petroleum jelly. Press new bushings into torque rods. Install torque rod with longer bolt in lower position.

**2)** Install rear of torque rod. Install front of torque rod. Remove front subframe mount to install front of torque rod (if necessary). Tighten front of torque rod. If removed, install and tighten front mount of subframe. Tighten rear of torque rod. See TORQUE SPECIFICATIONS (EXCEPT 940 SE) table at end of article.

## TRACK ROD BUSHINGS (MULTI-LINK REAR SUSPENSION)

**Removal & Installation (940 SE)** - Raise and support vehicle. Remove wheels and track rod. On bench, press out inner and outer track rod bushings. To install, press in new bushings. To complete assembly, reverse removal procedure. Check wheel alignment.

## SUBFRAME BUSHINGS

**Removal (740 & 940)** - **1)** Raise and support vehicle. Remove subframe front mount bolts. Pry out mount. Tap out front bracket using a hammer and drift. Remove torque rod front retaining bolts, "X" link and parking brake cable clamp.

**2)** Insert a bolt through front subframe mount hole. *See Fig. 5.* Pull subframe from rear mounting bracket using a "C" clamp. Remove rear mounting bracket from body. Use Bushing Remover (5329) to press bushings from mounting bracket.

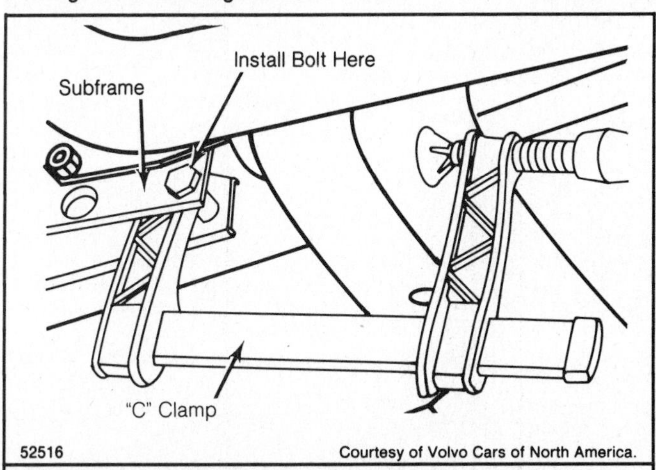


***Fig. 5: Removing Subframe from Mounting Bracket (740 & 940)***

**Installation** - **1)** Coat bushing mating surfaces with petroleum jelly. Press new bushings into torque rods. Install torque rod with longer bolt in lower position.

**2)** Attach, but DO NOT tighten, rear of torque rod. Install front of torque rod. Remove front subframe mount to install front of torque rod (if necessary).

**3)** Tighten front of torque rod. If removed, install and tighten front mount of subframe. Tighten rear of torque rod. See TORQUE SPECIFICATIONS (EXCEPT 940 SE) table at end of article.

**Removal (940 SE)** - **1)** Raise and support vehicle. Remove rear wheels and brake calipers. Tie calipers aside. Remove bolts and nuts at front and rear of trailing arm.

**2)** Remove drive shaft-to-differential coupling bolts. Place jack and Fixture (5972) under assembly. Remove 4 upper subframe-to-floor bolts. Lower assembly slightly.

**3)** Use Press Tool (5344-1 and 5344-2) to remove front bushing. Use Press Tool (5352-1 and 5352-2) to remove rear bushing.

**Installation** - Use press tool to install front bushing. Use press tool to install rear bushing. *See Fig. 6.* To complete installation, reverse removal procedure. Lower vehicle, and allow suspension to settle. Tighten nuts and bolts to specifications. See TORQUE SPECIFICATIONS (940 SE) table at end of article. Check wheel alignment.

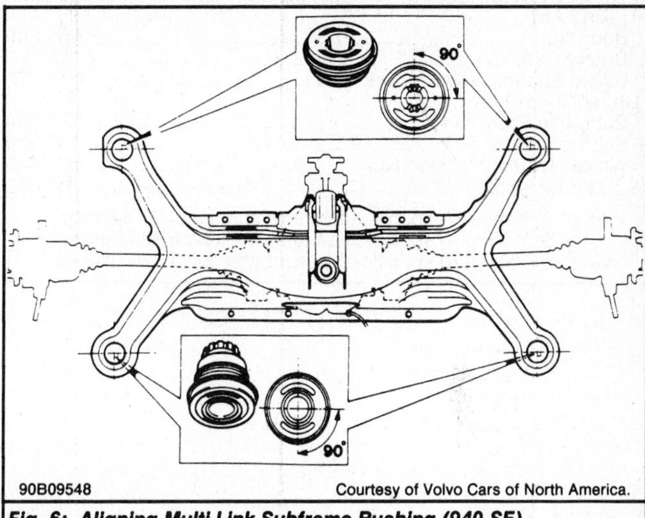


***Fig. 6: Aligning Multi-Link Subframe Bushing (940 SE)***

## TORQUE SPECIFICATIONS

***TORQUE SPECIFICATIONS (EXCEPT 940 SE)***

| Application | Ft. Lbs. (N.m) |
|---|---|
| **240** | |
| Bearing Retainer-To-Axle Housing | 22-36 (30-49) |
| Coil Spring-To-Body | 30-42 (41-57) |
| Coil Spring-To-Control Arm | 14 (19) |
| Shock Absorber Nuts | 62 (84) |
| Stabilizer Bar | |
| 10-mm Bolts | 33 (45) |
| 12-mm Bolts | 62 (84) |
| Torque Rod Bolts | 65 (85) |
| Track Bar-To-Axle | 44 (60) |
| Track Bar-To-Body | 62 (84) |
| Trailing Arm-To-Body | 85 (115) |
| Trailing Arm-To-Rear Axle | 85 (115) |
| Wheel Lug Nuts | 85 (115) |
| **740 & 940** | |
| Brake Caliper Bolts | 43 (58) |
| Rear Spring | |
| Rear Axle Bracket | 33 (45) |
| Upper Attachment | 35 (48) |
| Shock Absorber Nuts | 63 (85) |
| Stabilizer Bar | 35 (48) |
| Subframe | |
| Front Mount | 63 (85) |
| Rear Bushing Bracket | 63 (85) |
| Torque Rods | |
| Front Bolts-To-"X" Link | 103 (140) |
| Rear Bolts | 63 (85) |
| Track Rod-To-Body | 63 (85) |
| Track Rod-To-Rear Axle | 63 (85) |
| Trailing Arm | |
| Rear Axle Bracket | 33 (45) |
| Front Bracket | |
| Bolts | 35 (48) |
| Nuts | 63 (85) |
| Wheel Lug Nut | 63 (85) |

# 1991 SUSPENSION
## Rear (Cont.)

***TORQUE SPECIFICATIONS (940 SE)***

| Application | Ft. Lbs. (N.m) |
|---|---|
| **940 SE** | |
| Brake Caliper Bolts | 44 (60) |
| Hub Nut | [1] 102 (140) |
| Lower Control Arm | |
| Rear Axle Member Nut | [2] 37 (50) |
| Wheel Bearing Housing Nut | [2] 37 (50) |
| Shock Absorber Nuts | |
| Lower | 41 (56) |
| Upper | 63 (85) |
| Subframe-To-Body Bolt | [1] 51 (70) |
| Track Rod | |
| Subframe Nut | 51 (70) |
| Wheel Bearing Housing | 63 (85) |
| Trailing Arm | |
| Body Nut | [2] 51 (70) |
| Bracket Nut | [3] 125 (91) |
| Wheel Bearing Housing Bolt | [2] 44 (60) |
| Upper Control Arm | |
| Subframe Front Nut | [1] 51 (70) |
| Subframe Rear Nut | 63 (85) |
| Wheel Bearing Housing Nut | 85 (115) |
| Wheel Lug Nut | 63 (85) |

[1] – After tightening to specification, turn additional 60 degrees.
[2] – After tightening to specification, turn additional 90 degrees.
[3] – After tightening to specification, turn additional 120 degrees.

# 1991 STEERING
# Steering Columns

## 240, 740, 940

## DESCRIPTION

Steering column upper and lower sections are joined by a flange. On frontal impact, flange breaks from upper column. Upper column is carried in 2 ball bearings in jacket tube or bearing housing.

***WARNING: Before any repairs, disconnect and shield negative battery cable from ground. Disconnect Yellow and Orange Supplemental Restraint System (SRS) connectors on driver's side of center console, near accelerator pedal, to avoid accidental air bag deployment. Follow air bag service precautions. See SERVICE PRECAUTIONS in AIR BAG RESTRAINT SYSTEM article. Disable SRS before removal.***

## DISABLING & ACTIVATING AIR BAG SYSTEM

***WARNING: NEVER disconnect crash sensor connector or standby power unit to disable SRS system.***

**1)** Disconnect and shield negative battery cable. Locate and disconnect Orange and Yellow SRS connectors on driver's side of center console, under carpet. *See Fig. 1*. DO NOT disconnect harness connection at crash sensor or air bag will deploy.

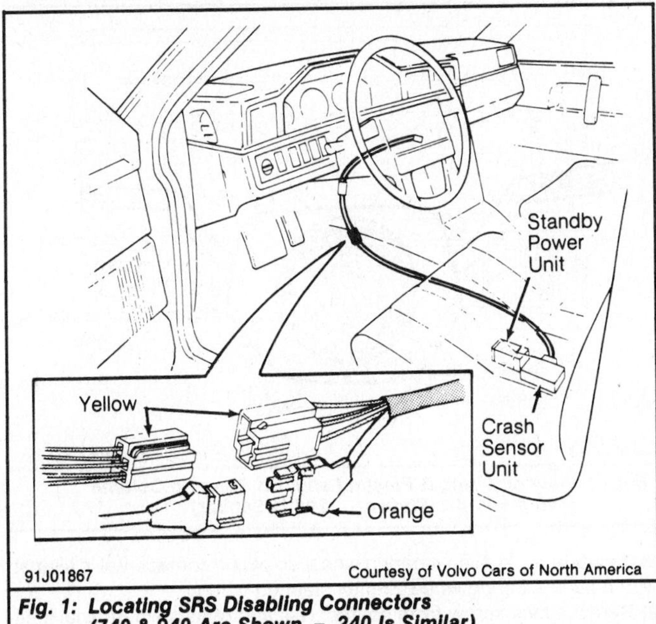


***Fig. 1: Locating SRS Disabling Connectors (740 & 940 Are Shown – 240 Is Similar)***

**2)** After repairs, ensure all wiring and component connectors are reconnected. To activate air bag system, reconnect Orange and Yellow SRS connectors on driver's side of center console, under carpet. Reconnect negative battery cable. Turn ignition switch to ON position (engine not running). If no fault codes are present, SRS warning light should go out after 10 seconds.

## ADJUSTMENTS

### CONTACT REEL CENTERING

**1)** If contact reel is new, remove new contact reel shipping pin from pin hole. *See Fig. 2*. Turn contact reel pin to far right, then turn pin back to left about 3 turns until pin hole is at proper position. See CONTACT REEL PIN HOLE POSITION table. Lock contact reel in proper position with shipping lock screw.

***CONTACT REEL PIN HOLE POSITION***

| Model | Pin Hole Position |
|---|---|
| 240 | 6 O'Clock |
| 740 | 8 O'Clock |
| 940 | 8 O'Clock |

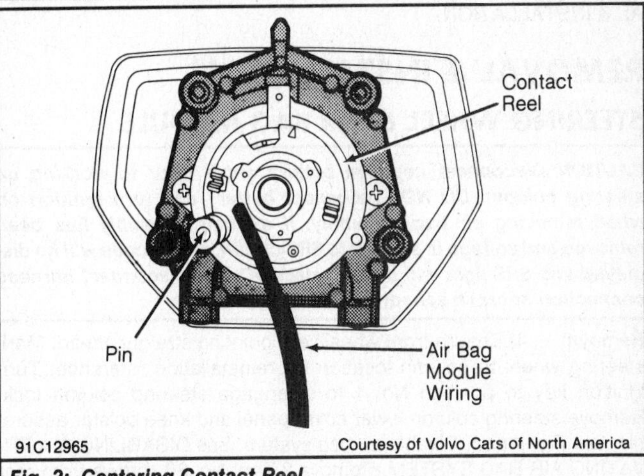


***Fig. 2: Centering Contact Reel (740 & 940 Are Shown – 240 Is Similar)***

**2)** Carefully pull contact reel wiring with plastic warning label through hole in steering wheel. Install steering wheel so contact reel pin aligns with proper pin alignment hole in steering wheel.

**3)** Install steering wheel hub retaining bolt finger tight to ensure steering wheel does not come off shaft when removing contact reel shipping lock screw.

**4)** Remove shipping lock screw from contact reel pin. Install original lock screw, with plastic warning label attached, into original retaining screw hole in steering wheel. Tighten steering wheel hub retaining bolt to specification. See TORQUE SPECIFICATIONS table at end of article.

**5)** Connect SRS Special Test Resistor (998-8695) to contact reel wiring connector in place of air bag module. *See Fig. 3*. Activate SRS. See DISABLING & ACTIVATING AIR BAG SYSTEM.

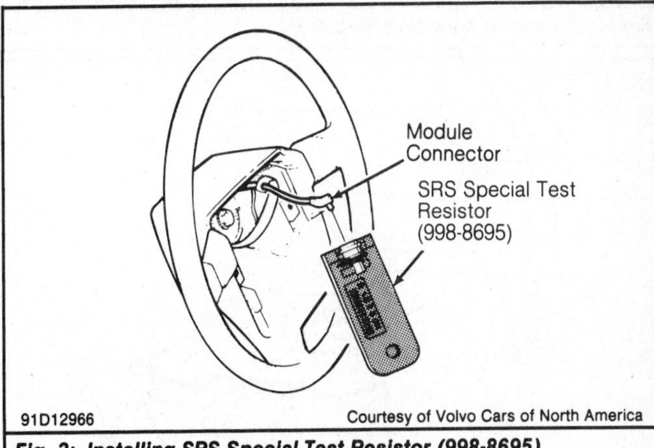


***Fig. 3: Installing SRS Special Test Resistor (998-8695) On Module Connector***

**6)** Turn ignition switch to ON position and ensure SRS warning light goes out after 10 seconds. If light does not go out, a fault code is set and memory must be cleared. See MITCHELL's AIR BAG SERVICE & REPAIR MANUAL, DOMESTIC & IMPORTED MODELS. After clearing fault codes, recheck SRS light operation. Perform SYSTEM OPERATION CHECK.

# 1991 STEERING
# Steering Columns (Cont.)

7) If SRS warning light goes out after about 10 seconds, turn off ignition, disconnect negative battery cable and remove Special Test Resistor (998-8695) from air bag module connector. Position air bag module to steering wheel, and install wiring connector. Ensure wiring connector clicks into position. Install air bag module and steering wheel. See STEERING WHEEL & AIR BAG MODULE under REMOVAL & INSTALLATION.

## REMOVAL & INSTALLATION

### STEERING WHEEL & AIR BAG MODULE

***CAUTION: Disconnect negative battery cable prior to working on steering column. DO NOT reconnect battery and turn ignition on when removing air bag assembly. If air bag assembly has been removed and voltage is applied to SRS circuit, a fault code will be displayed and SRS light will be activated. DO NOT disconnect harness connection at crash sensor or air bag will deploy.***

**Removal - 1)** Ensure front wheels are pointing straight ahead. Mark steering wheel to column location for reinstallation reference. Turn ignition key to position No. 1 to disengage steering column lock. Remove steering column lower cover panel and knee bolster assembly. *See Fig. 4 or 5.* Disable air bag system. See DISABLING & ACTIVATING AIR BAG SYSTEM. Remove 2 Torx No. 30 screws from rear of steering wheel. *See Fig. 6.*

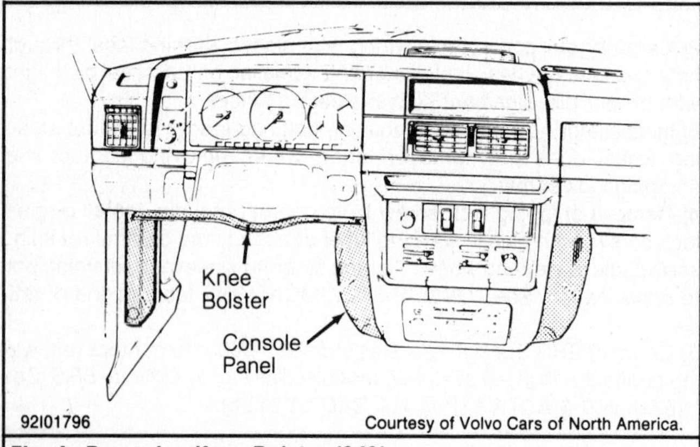


***Fig. 4: Removing Knee Bolster (240)***

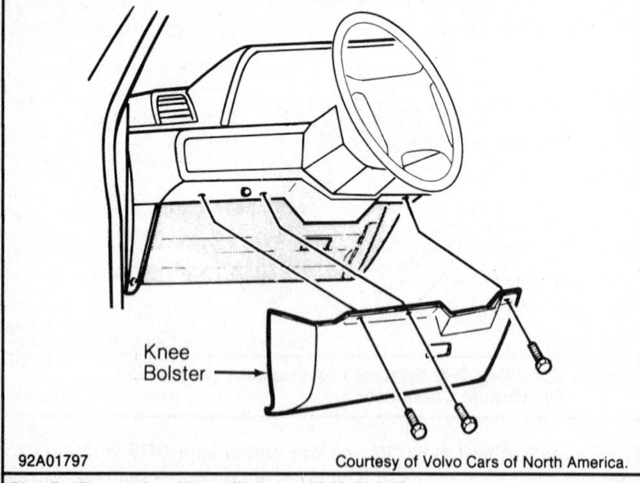


***Fig. 5: Removing Knee Bolster (740 & 940)***

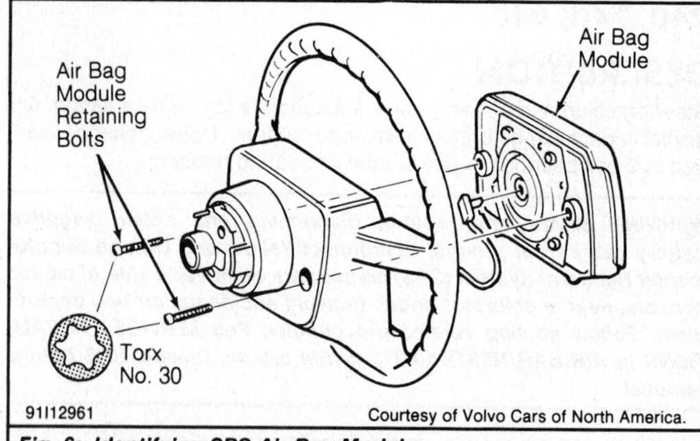


***Fig. 6: Identifying SRS Air Bag Module (240 Is Shown - Other Models Are Similar)***

2) Pull air bag module away from steering wheel and disconnect wiring connector. Remove air bag module.

3) Remove steering wheel hub retaining bolt. Remove plastic warning label retaining screw from steering wheel, leaving screw attached to plastic warning label. Carefully pull steering wheel from column, allowing wiring and plastic warning label to pass through hole in steering wheel. *See Fig. 7.*

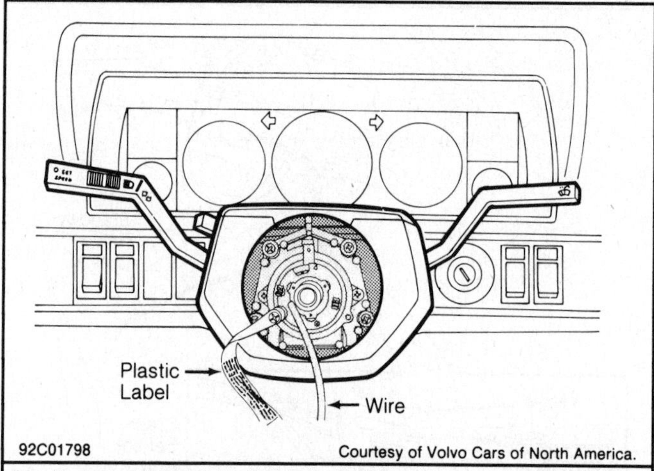


***Fig. 7: View of Wiring & Plastic Label On Steering Column (740 & 940 Are Shown - 240 Is Similar)***

**Installation - 1)** Align steering wheel so pin on contact reel is aligned with hole in steering wheel. Install steering wheel.

2) Remove lock screw from contact reel and reinstall in original location. Ensure steering wheel is centered. Install steering wheel retaining bolt.

3) Install air bag assembly. Tighten Torx bolts to specification. See TORQUE SPECIFICATIONS table at end of article. Reconnect battery.

4) Reactivate SRS. See DISABLING & ACTIVATING AIR BAG SYSTEM. Check SRS warning light to ensure system is functioning properly. If an air bag warning light stays on, see MITCHELL'S AIR BAG SERVICE & REPAIR MANUAL, DOMESTIC & IMPORTED MODELS.

### AIR BAG CONTACT REEL

1) Remove air bag module and steering wheel. See STEERING WHEEL & AIR BAG MODULE under REMOVAL & INSTALLATION. Remove steering column upper and lower covers. *See Fig. 8.* Remove wiper and turn signal switches. *See Fig. 8 or 9.* Locate and disconnect contact reel harness Orange connector from behind instrument panel, near steering column.

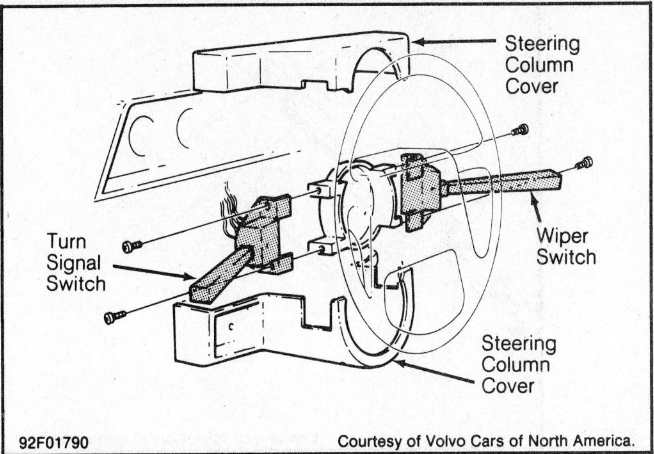


*Fig. 8: Removing Upper & Lower Steering Column Covers (240 Is Shown - Other Models Are Similar)*

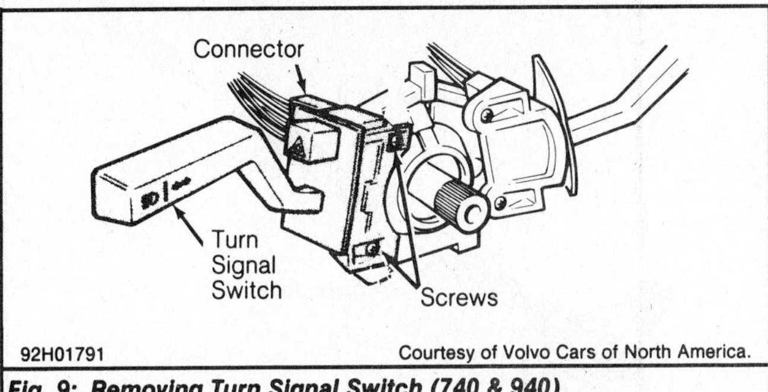


*Fig. 9: Removing Turn Signal Switch (740 & 940)*

**2)** Remove contact reel retaining screws. Pull contact reel off steering shaft using care to guide wiring up through steering column. *See Fig. 10.* To install, install new contact reel onto steering shaft, and install retaining screws. Install turn signal and wiper switches. Install column covers.

**3)** Reconnect Orange wiring connector behind instrument panel, near steering column. To properly adjust contact reel and complete installation, see CONTACT REEL CENTERING under ADJUSTMENTS.

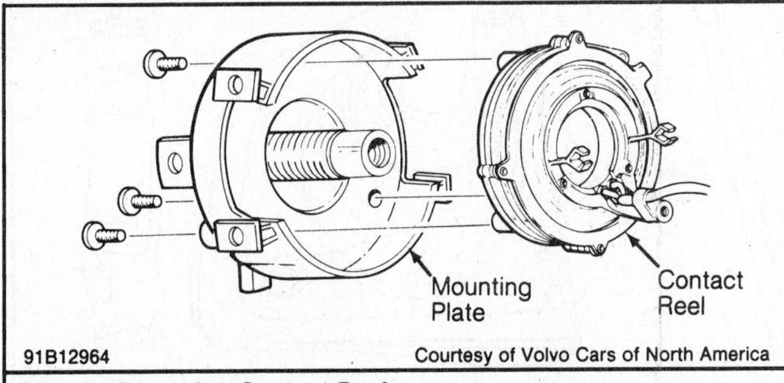


*Fig. 10: Removing Contact Reel (240 Is Shown - Other Models Are Similar)*

## COMBINATION SWITCH & WIPER SWITCH

**Removal** - Remove steering wheel. See STEERING WHEEL & AIR BAG MODULE under REMOVAL & INSTALLATION. Remove upper and lower steering column covers. *See Fig. 8.* Disconnect switch harness connectors behind instrument panel, near steering column. Remove switch attaching screws. *See Fig. 9.* Remove switch and harness.

**Installation** - To install, reverse removal procedure. See STEERING WHEEL & AIR BAG MODULE under REMOVAL & INSTALLATION. Ensure all electrical connections are tight. Check turn signal switch canceling.

## IGNITION SWITCH

**Removal** - Remove sound insulation under instrument panel. Disconnect connector from ignition lock. Remove upper steering column casing and panel of ignition lock. Loosen ignition lock fixing bolt. Put key in lock and turn to starting position. Push barrel from underneath back through hole and remove ignition lock.

**Installation** - Insert key in lock, turn, press in locking catch and remove key. Insert lock in slot. Release barrel enough to insert key again. Tighten locking screw and check function. Re-fit casing and panel by ignition lock. Reconnect connector to ignition lock. Re-fit sound insulation under instrument panel.

## STEERING COLUMN LOCK

For steering column lock removal and installation, see STEERING COLUMN under REMOVAL & INSTALLATION.

## STEERING COLUMN

**Removal (240)** - **1)** Remove air bag module. See STEERING WHEEL & AIR BAG MODULE under REMOVAL & INSTALLATION. Lock contact reel in place. See CONTACT REEL CENTERING under ADJUSTMENTS. Remove steering wheel. See STEERING WHEEL & AIR BAG MODULE under REMOVAL & INSTALLATION. Remove contact reel connectors from rear side of instrument panel. Remove contact reel. See CONTACT REEL under REMOVAL & INSTALLATION.

**2)** Working inside engine compartment, loosen upper bolts in upper and lower steering column joints. *See Fig. 11.* Pull down lower steering shaft so upper joint is free from upper steering shaft. Remove upper and lower steering column covers. *See Fig. 8.* Remove combination switch operating arms.

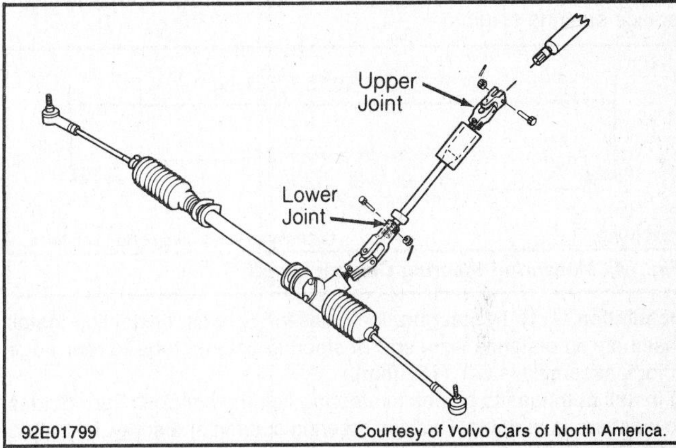


*Fig. 11: Loosening Bolts In Upper & Lower Steering Column Joint*

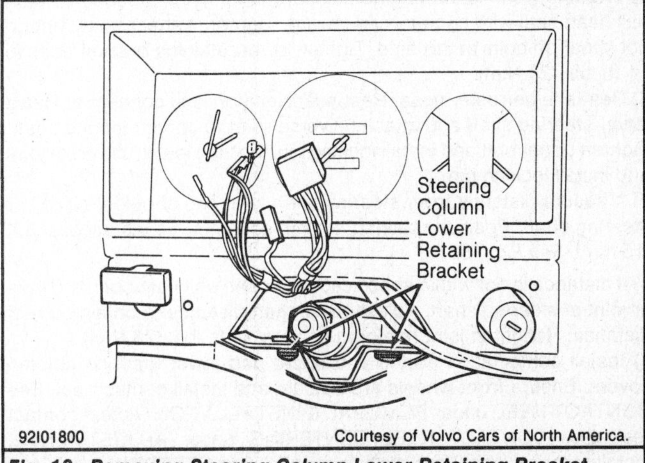


*Fig. 12: Removing Steering Column Lower Retaining Bracket*

# 1991 STEERING
## Steering Columns (Cont.)

**3)** Remove steering column lower retaining bracket. *See Fig. 12.* Remove steering column seal in bulkhead. Remove defroster hose from heater unit. Tap shearing bolts so bolts and plastic washers slide from their slots. Push steering column forward and disengage from rubber seal. Disconnect ignition switch connector. *See Fig. 13.* Lower column and lock assembly and remove from under dashboard.

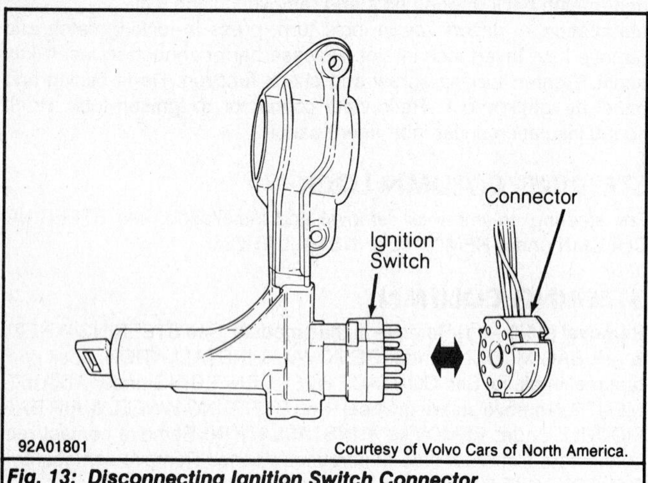


***Fig. 13: Disconnecting Ignition Switch Connector***

**4)** If steering lock assembly is to be removed, use key and unlock cylinder. Place assembly in vise and remove lock assembly retaining screws and remove lock assembly.

**Inspection** – Check steering column length. Correct length should be 27.74-27.82" (704.5-706.5 mm). *See Fig. 14.* If not to specification, replace steering column.

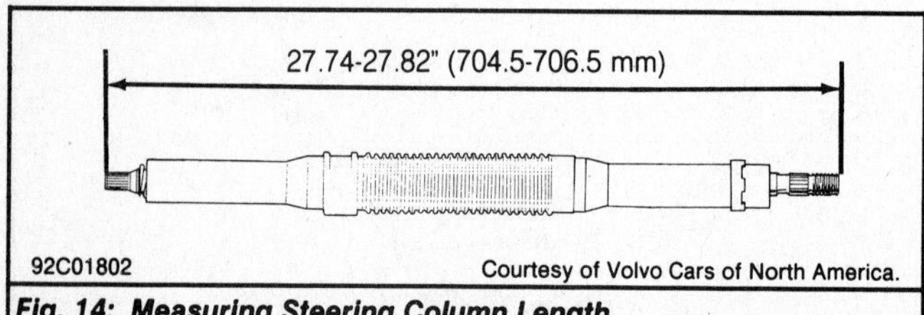


***Fig. 14: Measuring Steering Column Length***

**Installation** – **1)** If steering lock assembly was removed, install assembly so distance from end of steering column tube to rear edge of lock assembly is 6.0" (152 mm).

**2)** Install both plastic guides in steering column support. Turn guides so washers face down. Position steering column and screw in (but do not tighten) shearing bolts in column support. Install lower rubber spacer and retaining bracket. Tighten bolts by hand.

**3)** Working from inside engine compartment, install steering column bulkhead seal with cone turned inward. Tighten 4 shear bolts, but do not shear off bolts at this time. Tighten lower retaining bracket bolts to 14 ft. lbs. (20 N.m).

**4)** Reattach defroster hose. Reconnect ignition lock connector. Raise lower steering shaft and attach universal joint to upper steering shaft. Tighten upper bolt and install locking pin. Tighten lower universal joint and install locking pin.

**5)** Measure distance from steering shaft joint and shoulder on lower steering shaft. Position steering column assembly so distance is .59" (15 mm). *See Fig. 15.*

**6)** If distance is not within specification, loosen bolts at upper and lower joint at steering shaft. Adjust lower shaft distance to obtain correct distance. Retighten joint retaining bolts to 17 ft. lbs. (23 N.m).

**7)** Install combination switch and upper and lower steering column covers. Ensure front wheels are straight and install contact reel. See CONTACT REEL under REMOVAL & INSTALLATION. Adjust contact reel. See CONTACT REEL CENTERING under ADJUSTMENTS. Install steering wheel and air bag module. See STEERING WHEEL & AIR BAG MODULE under REMOVAL & INSTALLATION.

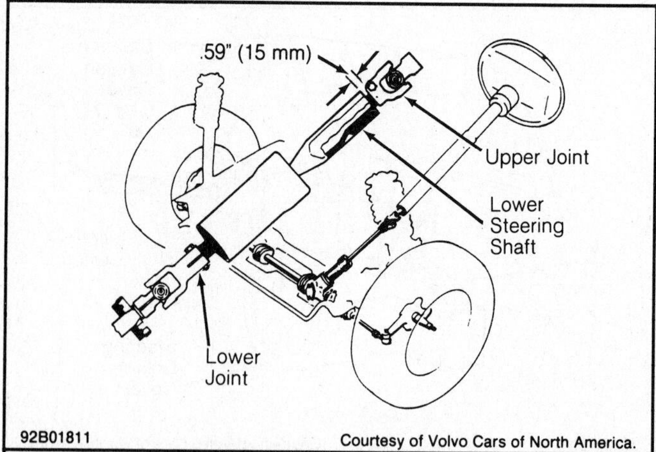


***Fig. 15: Measuring Shaft Clearance (240)***

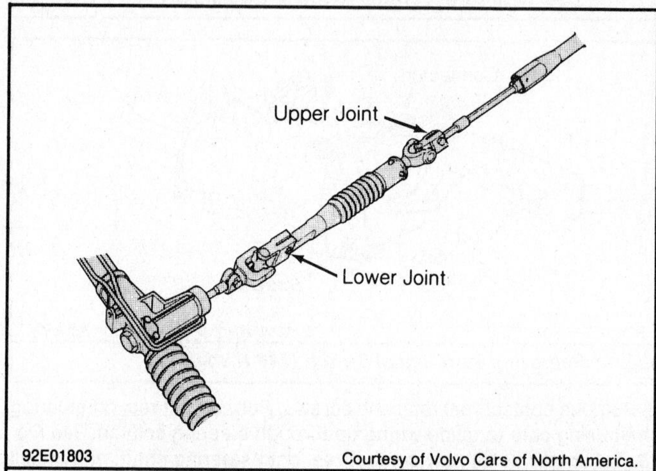


***Fig. 16: Removing Upper Steering Shaft Pin & Bolt (740 & 940)***

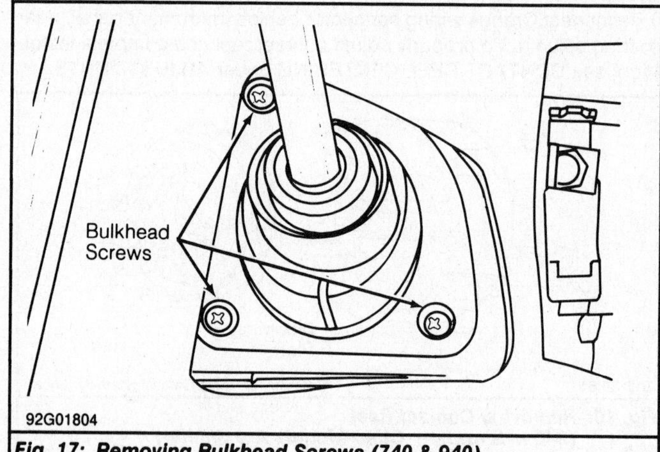


***Fig. 17: Removing Bulkhead Screws (740 & 940)***

**8)** Reactivate SRS. See DISABLING & ACTIVATING AIR BAG SYSTEM. Check SRS warning light to ensure system is functioning properly. If air bag warning light stays on, see MITCHELL'S AIR BAG SERVICE & REPAIR MANUAL, DOMESTIC & IMPORTED MODELS.

**Removal (740)** – **1)** Remove air bag module and steering wheel. See STEERING WHEEL & AIR BAG MODULE under REMOVAL & INSTALLATION. Remove upper and lower steering column covers. Remove combination switch operating arms. *See Fig. 9.*

**2)** Remove contact reel connectors from rear side of instrument panel. Remove contact reel. See CONTACT REEL under REMOVAL & INSTALLATION. Remove horn cable.

# 1991 STEERING
## Steering Columns (Cont.)

**3)** Remove knee bolster. *See Fig. 5.* Working inside engine compartment, remove locking pin and bolt on upper joint of steering shaft. *See Fig. 16.* Remove locking pin for upper bolt of lower joint and slightly loosen bolt. Move steering shaft toward steering gear and free lower steering shaft from steering column.

**4)** Remove 3 Phillips screws from lower steering column bearing plate, below steering wheel. *See Fig. 17.* Using a center punch, loosen locking bolts for bearing housing. Loosen bolt in steering pin. *See Fig. 18.*

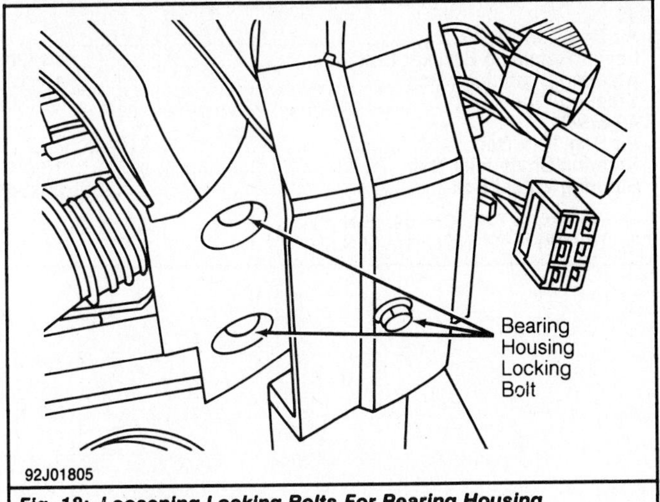


***Fig. 18: Loosening Locking Bolts For Bearing Housing (740 & 940)***

**5)** Remove locking ring and spacer ring from steering column. *See Fig. 19.* Turn ignition switch to "I" position. Push steering column back through bearing housing. Remove ignition key, locking screws for steering lock, and bolt in steering pin.

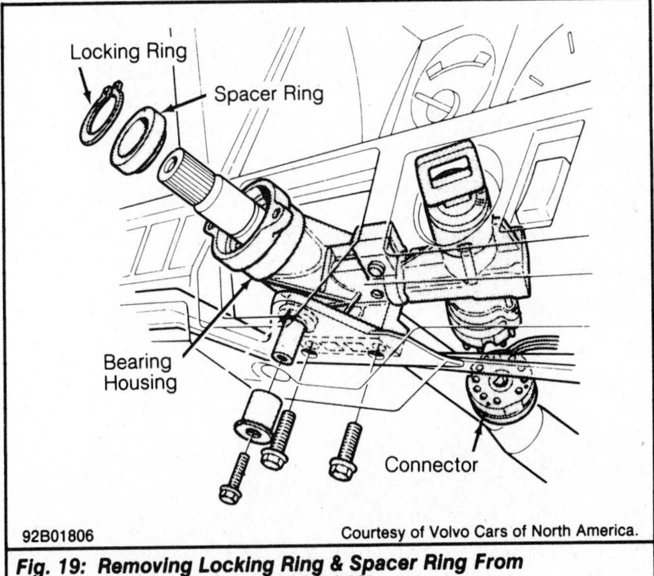


***Fig. 19: Removing Locking Ring & Spacer Ring From Steering Column (740 & 940)***

**6)** Lift up bearing housing while pressing on steering lock with one finger. Remove bearing housing and steering lock under instrument panel. Disconnect electrical connector from steering lock. Place assembly in a vise. Using center punch, loosen and remove shear bolt. *See Fig. 20.* Remove ignition switch from bearing housing.

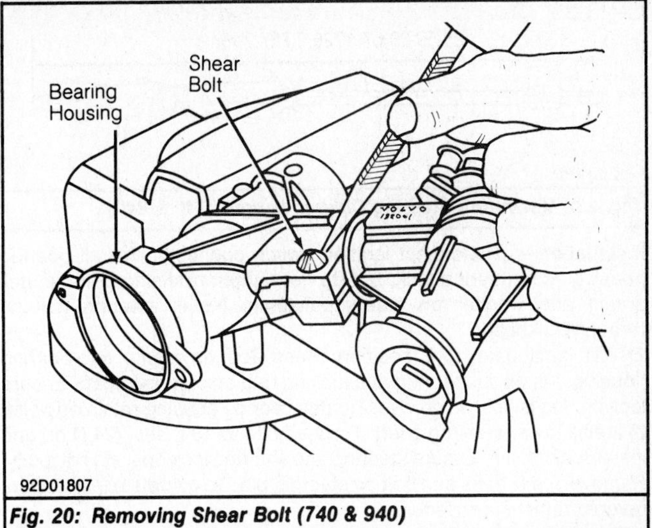


***Fig. 20: Removing Shear Bolt (740 & 940)***

**Inspection** – Check bearing housing bearings and replace as necessary. *See Fig. 21.* Check steering shaft lower bearing race position and ensure surface is not scratched. Race should be installed 1.99" (50.5 mm) from end of shaft. *See Fig. 22.* Check steering column length. Correct shaft length is 28.59-28.67" (726.2-727.2 mm). *See Fig. 23.*

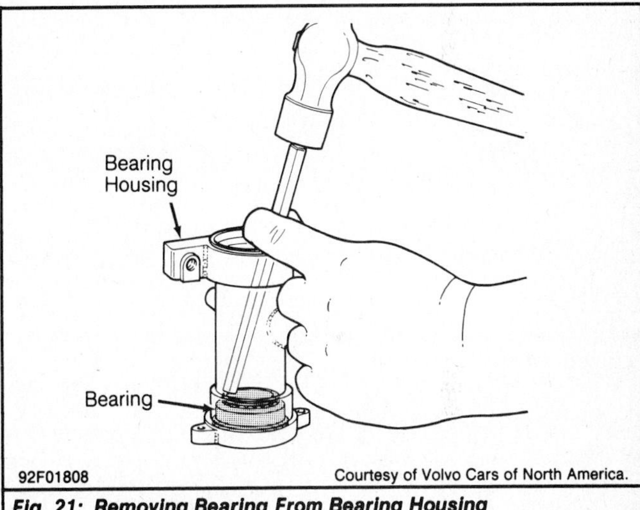


***Fig. 21: Removing Bearing From Bearing Housing (740 & 940)***

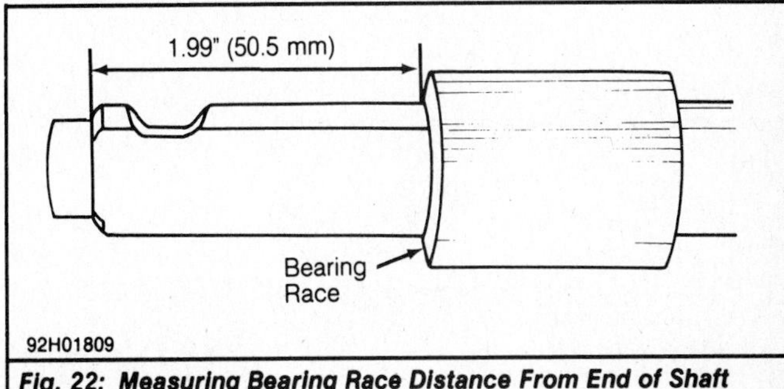


***Fig. 22: Measuring Bearing Race Distance From End of Shaft (740 & 940)***

# 1991 STEERING
# Steering Columns (Cont.)

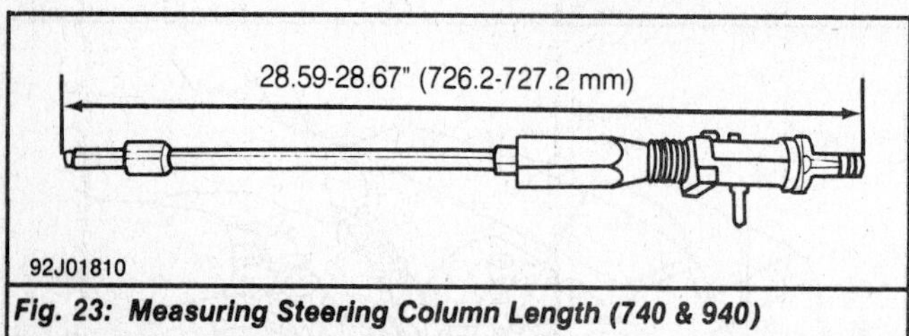


*Fig. 23: Measuring Steering Column Length (740 & 940)*

**Installation - 1)** Connect ignition switch connector. Install bearing housing with steering lock, but do not tighten retaining bolts. Install spring and washer on steering column. Install steering column through bulkhead.

**2)** Turn ignition key to "I" position. Press steering column into bearing housing. Install spacer ring and locking ring on steering shaft. Ensure locking ring is flush in groove. Tighten bearing housing retaining bolts.

**3)** Install lower steering shaft. Torque bolts to 18 ft. lbs. (24 N.m) and install locking pin. Ensure steering and steering lock operate correctly. Remove shear bolts and bolt on steering pin. To complete installation, reverse removal procedure.

**4)** Reactivate SRS. See DISABLING & ACTIVATING AIR BAG SYSTEM. Check SRS warning light to ensure system is functioning properly. If air bag warning light stays on, see MITCHELL'S AIR BAG SERVICE & REPAIR MANUAL, DOMESTIC & IMPORTED MODELS.

## TORQUE SPECIFICATIONS

***TORQUE SPECIFICATIONS***

| Application | Ft. Lbs. (N.m) |
|---|---|
| **240** | |
| Air Bag Torx Bolt | [1] |
| Lower Retaining Bracket Bolt | 14 (20) |
| Steering Shaft Joint Bolt | 17 (23) |
| Steering Wheel Nut | 22 (30) |
| **740 & 940** | |
| Air Bag Torx Bolt | [1] |
| Steering Shaft Joint Bolt | 18 (24) |
| Steering Wheel Bolt | 25 (34) |

[1] - Tighten to 72 INCH lbs. (8 N.m).
[2] - Tighten to 27 INCH lbs. (3 N.m).

# 1991 STEERING
# Power Rack & Pinion

## 240, 740, 940

***NOTE: Information on 940 power rack and pinion is not available from manufacturer.***

## DESCRIPTION

The 240 uses either a ZF gear with a non-integral housing or a cam gear type. The 740 may be equipped with either a ZF gear with an integral housing or a cam gear steering rack.

## LUBRICATION

### CAPACITY

Fluid capacity is .75 qt. (.7L) for 240 or 1 qt. (1L). for 740.

### FLUID TYPE

System uses automatic transmission fluid (ATF).

### FLUID LEVEL CHECK

Check fluid level when fluid is cold with engine off. To check and fill, remove fluid level gauge from reservoir and check fluid level. Fluid level should be between MIN and MAX marks on the gauge dipstick. Add fluid through dipstick opening as needed and recheck. DO NOT overfill.

### HYDRAULIC SYSTEM BLEEDING

**1)** Fill reservoir with fluid. Start engine and let idle. Add fluid as level drops. Turn steering wheel from lock to lock in a slow, even motion to allow pump to operate at low pressure.
**2)** Continue turning steering wheel until fluid in reservoir is free of air bubbles. Ensure fluid is at level mark. Install reservoir cap.

## ADJUSTMENTS

### POWER STEERING PUMP PRESSURE

***NOTE: Maximum power steering pump pressure is 1320-1420 psi (93.0-99.9 kg/cm²). Pump volume at 500 RPM is 5.3 qts. (5L) per minute.***

### POWER STEERING PUMP BELT

***BELT ADJUSTMENT SPECIFICATIONS***

| Application | [1] Deflection - In. (mm) |
|---|---|
| Power Steering Belt | .2-.4 (5-10) |

[1] - Deflection is measured with moderate thumb pressure applied midway on longest belt run.

## TESTING

### HYDRAULIC SYSTEM PRESSURE TEST

**1)** Connect pressure gauge between steering pump and steering gear. *See Fig. 1.* Ensure gauge can be seen from driving position. Ensure reservoir is full. Start engine.
**2)** Turn steering wheel to full left and right lock for 10 seconds maximum. On cam gear type pump, pressure should be 1102-1204 psi (77.4-84.6 kg/cm²) On ZF type pump, pressure should be 1349-1450 psi (94.8-101.9 kg/cm²).

### STEERING WHEEL TURNING FORCE

**1)** On all models, raise front wheel off ground. Connect pressure gauge between steering pump and steering gear. *See Fig. 1.* Ensure gauge can be seen from driving position. Ensure reservoir is full.
**2)** Remove air bag module from steering wheel. See STEERING WHEEL & AIR BAG MODULE removal in STEERING COLUMNS article. Place torque wrench on steering wheel nut.

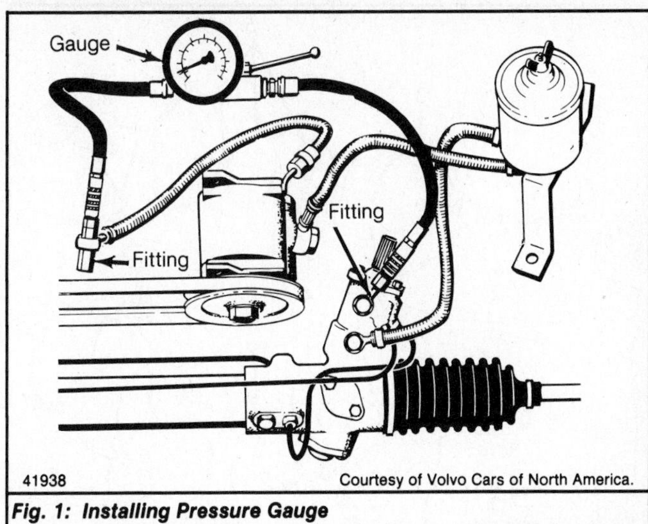

***Fig. 1: Installing Pressure Gauge***

**3)** With engine at idle, turn steering wheel slowly to the right. Read torque when pressure reaches 171 psi (12 kg/cm²) on cam gear type, 285 psi (20 kg/cm²) for ZF type.
**4)** Turn wheel to left. Torque should be 31-40 INCH lbs. (3.5-4.5 N.m) as gear approaches specified pressure. Turn steering wheel to right and read torque. Difference between both sides must not exceed 9 INCH lbs. (1 N.m) on cam gear-type. Difference must not exceed 4.4 INCH lbs. (.5 N.m) on ZF steering gear. If difference exceeds specifications, repair or replace steering gear.

***NOTE: For remaining steering gear adjustments, see OVERHAUL.***

## REMOVAL & INSTALLATION

### POWER STEERING PUMP

**Removal** - Remove pump bracket-to-pump retaining bolts. Place a drain pan below pump. Disconnect hydraulic connections at pump. Remove pump.
**Installation** - To install, reverse removal procedure. Fill and bleed system. Check for leaks.

### POWER RACK & PINION

**Removal - 1)** On 740, disconnect lower steering gear shaft by removing snap ring and lower clamp bolt. Loosen upper clamp bolt. Slide joint up on shaft. On 240, remove clamp screw and bend flange apart slightly to disconnect shaft from gear.
**2)** On all models, raise and support vehicle. Remove wheel assemblies. Remove tie rod ends from knuckles. Remove splash guard.
**3)** Disconnect hoses at steering gear. Plug hose connections. On 740, remove sway bar mounting brackets and move aside. Remove steering gear attaching bolts. Lower steering gear.
**4)** On 240, remove steering gear bolts. Pull gear down until free of steering shaft flange. Remove steering gear from left side of vehicle.
**Installation - 1)** To install, reverse removal procedure. Ensure recess on pinion shaft is aligned with lock bolt opening in flange. Install right side "U" bolt and flange, but do not tighten. Install and tighten left side bolts.
**2)** Tighten right side "U" bolt. Connect tie rods to steering gear. Ensure rods are same length. Difference should not exceed 1/16". Install lock bolt on flange. Reconnect hoses. Install splash shield and wheels.

## OVERHAUL

### POWER STEERING PUMP

***NOTE: For power steering pump overhaul, see Figs. 2-4.***

# 1991 STEERING
# Power Rack & Pinion (Cont.)

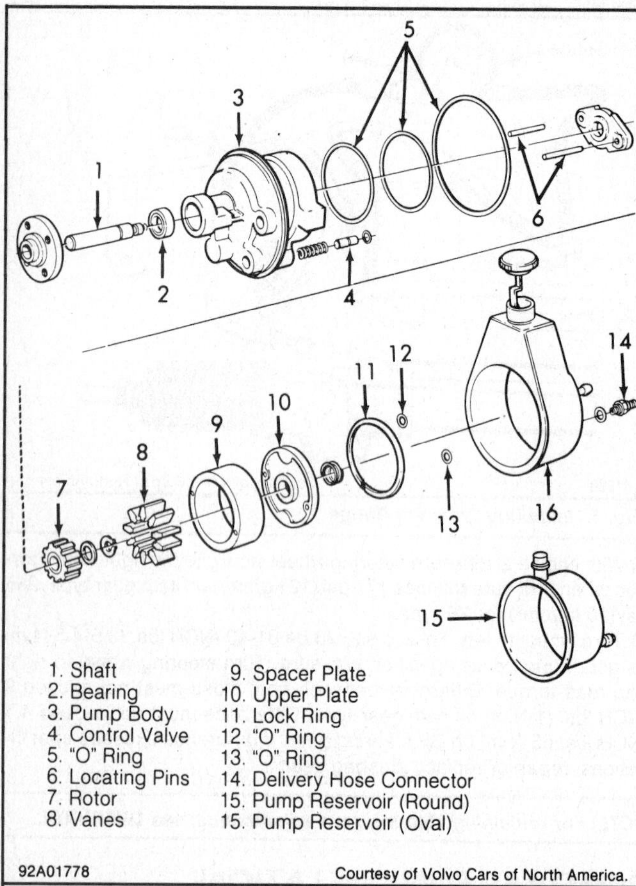


***Fig. 2: Exploded View of Saginaw "P" Power Steering Pump***

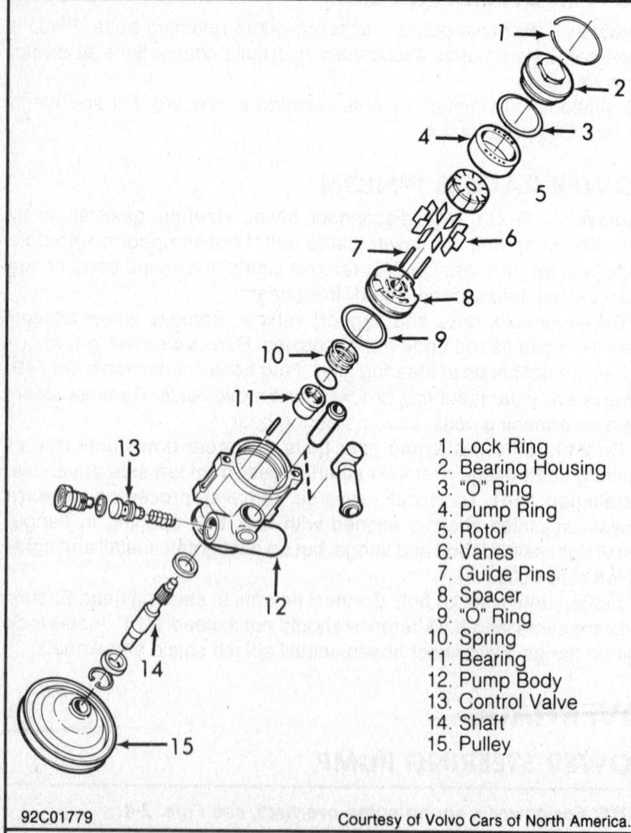


***Fig. 3: Exploded View of Saginaw TC Power Steering Pump***

1. Pump Body
2. Spring
3. Spacer Seal
4. Spacer
5. Vanes
6. Rotor
7. Pump Ring
8. "O" Ring
9. Pump Body
10. Bearing
11. Shaft
12. Pulley

92E01780 Courtesy of Volvo Cars of North America.

***Fig. 4: Exploded View of ZF Power Steering Pump***

## STEERING GEAR

**Disassembly (240 ZF Steering Gear) – 1)** Clean exterior of gear. Cut plastic clamps. Remove equalizer tube. Attach steering gear to Holding Fixture (5046). Install gear and fixture to repair stand.

**2)** Disconnect rubber boots. Unfold lock washer tab. Using a 27 mm spanner on ball joint and large adjustable wrench on rack, remove steering rods. *See Fig. 5.*

**3)** Remove pressure lines. Drain fluid. Turn rack in and out with Pinion Socket (5179) to pump out fluid. Remove preload piston by removing preload piston cover, washer, spring and piston. Remove rubber dust cover from pinion shaft.

**4)** Remove valve unit housing attaching bolts. Using Socket (5179) and Puller (4078), pull valve unit housing with pinion shaft off rack end housing.

**5)** Scratch mark center tube-to-end housing mating surfaces for reassembly reference. DO NOT use a punch to mark center tube. Using Spanner Wrench (5178), remove center tube from end housings.

***CAUTION: DO NOT clamp center tube in vise.***

**6)** Remove "O" rings from center tube. Remove lock ring (if lock collar is damaged and needs to be replaced). Pull out rack with spacer tube attached. Remove seal. If needle bearings need to be replaced, use a long punch to tap them out.

**7)** Remove spacer (inner) tube from rack. Remove lock rings, thrust washers and piston with Teflon ring and "O" ring. Fill lock ring grooves with grease. Slide off tube toward opposite end of rack teeth.

**8)** Using slide hammer and Remover (1819), remove inner spacer, seal and brass bushing. Using a screwdriver, remove "O" ring and Teflon bushing. DO NOT remove lock ring and thrust washer unless replacing those components.

**9)** Remove Teflon bushing, seal and star washer from right housing. Remove depressor and "O" ring from preload piston. Use a mallet to drive pinion from valve unit housing. Use care not to lose roller bearings.

**10)** Remove guide bushings from pinion shaft. Remove seal rings from guide bushing.

**11)** DO NOT remove small dowel pin from pinion shaft. *See Fig. 6.* Valve unit setting cannot be readjusted. Valve unit must be replaced.

**12)** Using slide hammer and Remover (1819), pull bearing cage from valve unit housing. Using a screwdriver, remove seal from valve unit housing.

**Inspection – 1)** Clean all parts and inspect for wear or damage. Replace as necessary. Check inner and outer ball joints for wear. Always use new seals during reassembly.

# 1991 STEERING
# Power Rack & Pinion (Cont.)

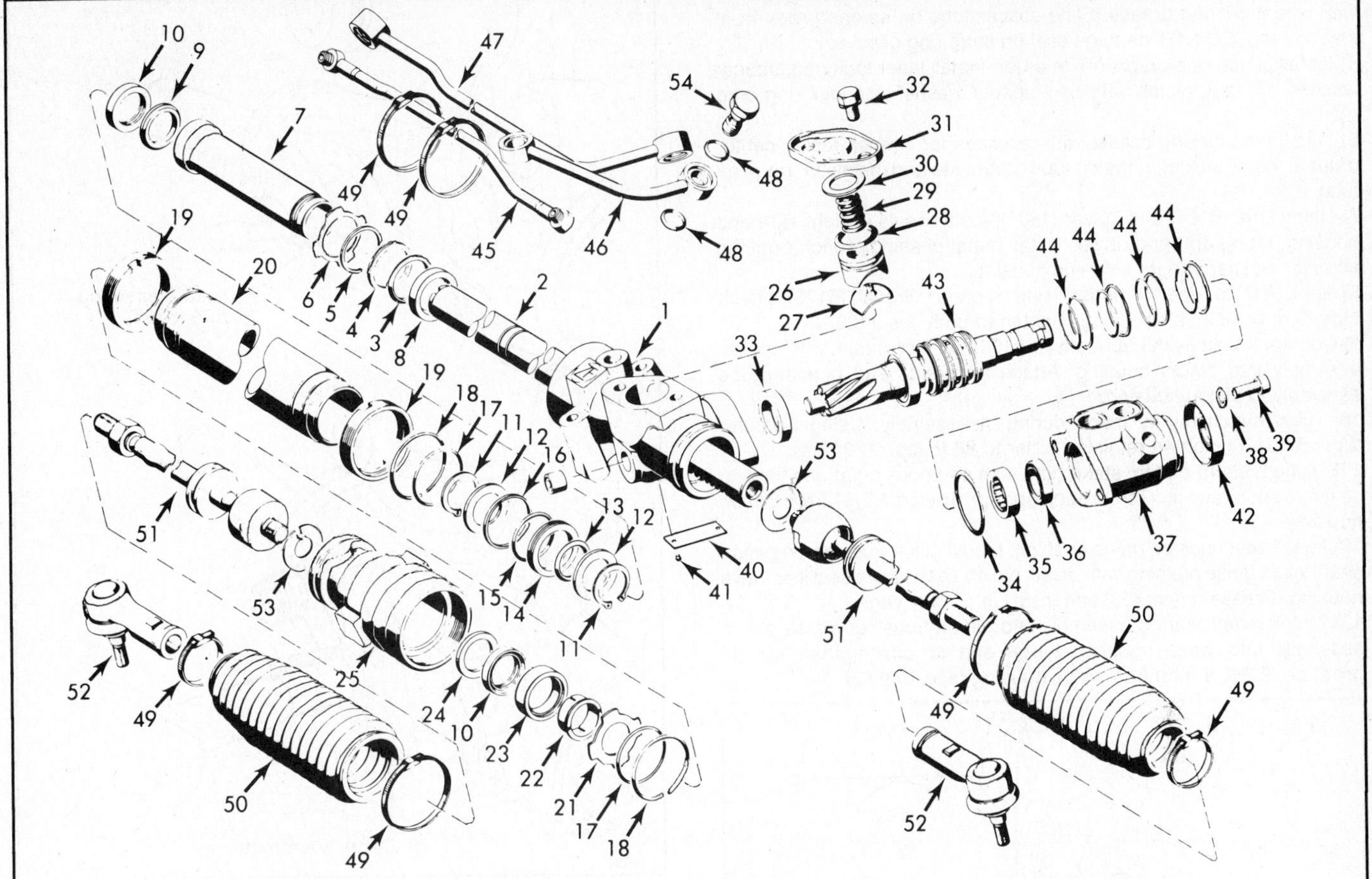

1. Needle Bearing
2. Rack
3. "O" Ring
4. Spacer Ring
5. Lock Ring
6. Thrust Washer
7. Spacer Tube
8. Supporting Ring
9. Supporting Ring
10. Seal
11. Lock Ring
12. Washer
13. "O" Ring
14. Piston
15. "O" Ring
16. Piston Ring
17. "O" Ring
18. Lock Ring
19. Nut
20. Center Tube
21. Lock Washer
22. Bearing
23. Bearing
24. Thrust Washer
25. Right End Housing
26. Preload Piston
27. Depressor
28. "O" Ring
29. Spring
30. Spacer Washer
31. Cover
32. Screw
33. Pinion Seal
34. "O" Ring
35. Bearing
36. Pinion Seal
37. Valve Housing
38. Spring Washer
39. Screw
40. Label
41. Rivet
42. Dust Seal
43. Valve Unit
44. Seal
45. Pipe (Air)
46. Pipe (Short)
47. Pipe (Long)
48. "O" Ring
49. Clamp
50. Rubber Bellows
51. Steering Rod
52. Tie Rod
53. Washer
54. Banjo Bolt

52921

Courtesy of Volvo Cars of North America.

***Fig. 5: Exploded View of ZF Steering Gear Assembly (240)***

59090

Courtesy of Volvo Cars of North America.

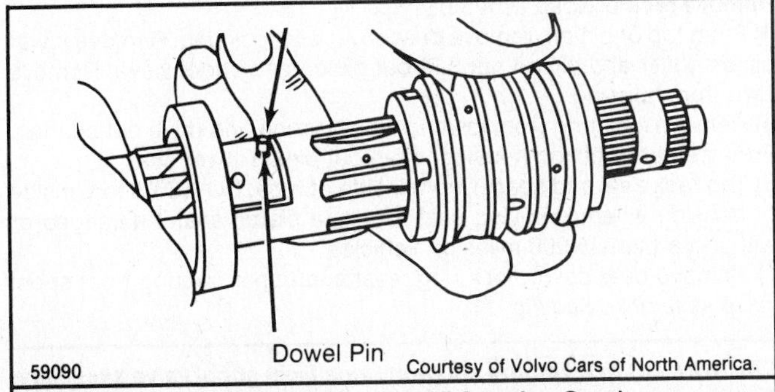

***Fig. 6: Pinion Shaft Dowel Pin (240 ZF Steering Gear)***

101381

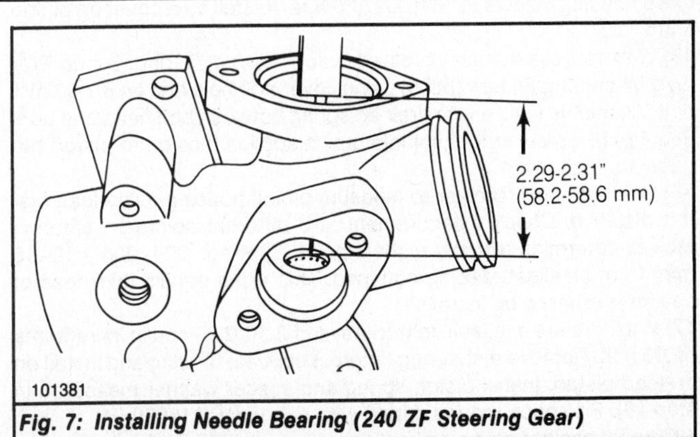

***Fig. 7: Installing Needle Bearing (240 ZF Steering Gear)***

**2)** Valve unit and guide bushing assembly must be replaced if any part of valve unit is defective.

**Reassembly – 1)** If removed, lubricate needle bearing with Lubricant (1161001-1). Install needle bearing into pinion housing, 2.29-2.31" (58.2-58.6 mm) from seal bottom. *See Fig. 7.*

**2)** Install seal and "O" ring into pinion housing. Install bronze bushing in spacer tube with chamfered side toward inside of tube.

**3)** Install seal in spacer tube with lips facing away from inside of tube. Coat seal lips with lubricant. Install spacer washer, lock ring, Teflon ring and "O" ring onto spacer tube.

# 1991 STEERING
# Power Rack & Pinion (Cont.)

**4)** Before installing spacer tube on rack, coat rack snap ring groove with wheel bearing grease. Slide spacer tube on steering rack from smooth end. DO NOT damage seal on snap ring grooves.

**5)** Install piston ring on piston. In order, install inner lock ring, spacer washer, "O" ring, piston with ring, spacer washer and lock ring onto rack.

**6)** Install tube locking collars with recesses for wrench facing center of tube. Install locking rings on tube. Lubricate and install "O" rings on tube.

**7)** Using Drift (5184) and Driver (1801), install seals in right side end housing. Using drift and driver, install metal bushing, Teflon bushing and star washer in right side end housing.

**8)** Apply ATF to tube "O" rings. Using Spanner Wrench (5178), attach tube to right side end housing. Tighten to 88 ft. lbs. (120 N.m).

**9)** Coat rack teeth with Lubricant (1161001-1). Install rack with spacer assembly into pinion housing. Attach right side end housing/tube assembly to pinion housing.

**10)** Align match marks made during disassembly. Using Spanner Wrench (5178), tighten retaining collar to 88 ft. lbs. (120 N.m).

**11)** Using a sharp punch, stake right side end housing at one locking collar wrench recess. Center rack so it protrudes 1 7/8" from pinion housing.

**12)** Install seal rings on guide bushing. Install guide bushing on pinion shaft. Align guide bushing with dowel pin on shaft. Drive seal into valve housing. Grease rollers (20) and install into roller cage.

**13)** Install roller bearing assembly into pinion housing. Install pinion assembly into valve housing. Large end of pinion shaft should protrude .20" (5.0 mm) from valve housing face. *See Fig. 8.*

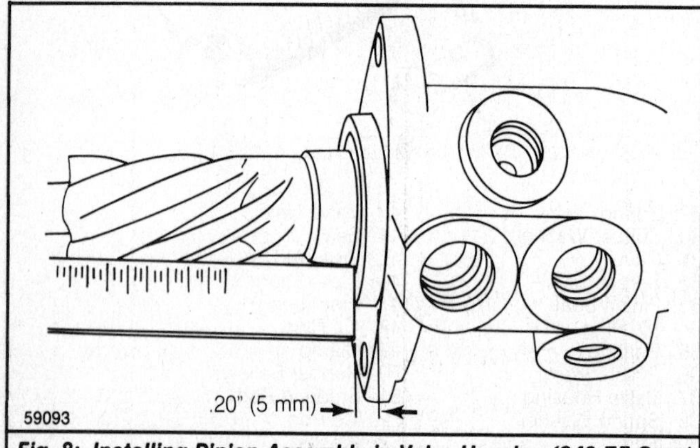


***Fig. 8: Installing Pinion Assembly in Valve Housing (240 ZF Gear)***

**14)** Install valve housing assembly to pinion housing. Flat on pinion assembly should face toward exposed rack end. DO NOT pinch "O" ring between valve and pinion housings. Install and tighten pinion-to-valve housing screws to 18 ft. lbs. (25 N.m). Install dust cover on pinion shaft.

**15)** With depressor, install preload piston without "O" ring. Set up Preload Measuring Fixture (5865) using cover bolt hole and an 8 x 45 mm bolt. Assemble fixture with preload spring between bolt head and bolt. *See Fig. 9.* Screw in tool spindle until it applies tension to piston but does not lock rack.

**16)** Use depth micrometer to measure pinion housing-to-preload piston distance. Check measurement at 3 different points on steering rack to determine piston's highest point. Subtract .004-.006" (.10-.15 mm) from smallest reading obtained. This value equals thickness of spacer washer to be installed.

**17)** Washers are available in thickness of 2.10-2.90 mm in increments of .05 mm. Remove measuring fixture. Lubricate "O" ring and install on preload piston. Install piston spring and spacer washer measured in step **16)**. Fill space around spring with Lubricant (111600-01).

**18)** Apply sealant on cover sealing surface. Install and tighten cover bolts to 16 ft. lbs. (22 N.m). Install and tighten pressure lines. Ensure "O" rings seat correctly.

**19)** Install tie rods. Bend back tie rod locking tabs. Install boots. Fill each boot with approximately 3/4 ounce of lubricant. Install boot clamps. Install equalizer tube and plastic clamps.

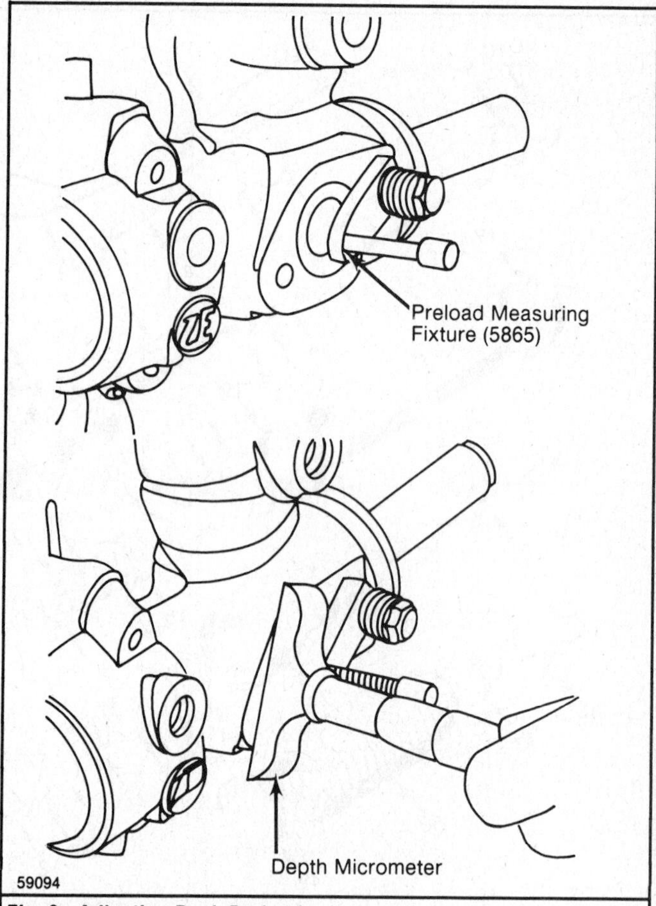


***Fig. 9: Adjusting Rack Preload***

**Disassembly & Reassembly (240 Cam Gear Type)** – Overhaul procedures are not available from manufacturer. With front end raised off ground and tie rod disconnected, turning torque of steering shaft should be 6-15 INCH lbs. (.9-1.7 N.m). *See Fig. 10* for exploded view of steering assembly.

**Disassembly (740 Cam Gear Type)** – **1)** Clean housing and remove oil pipes. Turn pinion back and forth to pump oil out of gear. Place rack in center position.

**2)** Remove clamps and boots. To prevent pinion damage, hold rack with adjustable wrench. Unscrew left steering rod completely. Loosen, but do not remove, right side steering rod. Remove right side locking wire.

**3)** Remove steering rod. Remove lock sleeve, plastic ring and bushing. Remove rack preload assembly. *See Fig. 13.*

**4)** From top of pinion, remove dust cover and lock ring. Remove lower pinion cover and pinion nut. Lift out pinion and spool valve. Remove rack from housing.

**5)** Remove lock ring from lower pinion bearing and drive out bearing. From center of pinion housing, drive out pinion lower seal.

**6)** Tap rack seal and spacer from inside of tube. DO NOT score inside of housing when removing seal. Replace piston seal if damaged or with more than 25,000 miles on vehicle.

**7)** Remove dust cover, lock ring, seal and upper bearing from spool valve assembly. *See Fig. 11.*

***CAUTION: DO NOT remove 4 Teflon rings from spool valve assembly. Replacement rings are not available. If rings are worn, replace entire steering gear.***

**Cleaning & Inspection** – Replace all seals except 4 Teflon rings on spool valve. If pinion or spool valve is damaged, replace entire steering gear. Clean and inspect rubber boots and replace if necessary.

# 1991 STEERING
# Power Rack & Pinion (Cont.)



**Reassembly - 1)** Coat all parts with ATF before assembly. Install new "O" ring and Teflon ring on rack piston. If difficult to install, heat Teflon ring in water to about 100°F (40°C).

**2)** Using Seal Drive (5277) and Handle (1801), install lower pinion seal and guide sleeve in housing. Seal ring lip must face up. If seal is not centered properly, pinion will not turn easily.

**3)** Install lower bearing and lock ring. Wrap rack teeth with tape. Install seal with lip facing piston seal. Install tapered spacer with tapered side facing seal. Install flat spacer.

**4)** Press 2 spacers together. Remove tape from rack. Lube rack teeth. Install rack in housing. As rack seats, lightly push on rack to seat seal and spacers.

**5)** To ensure seal is correctly positioned, look through pressure tube opening to ensure at least half of piston seal retainer has passed center of opening. Position rack so the end protrudes about 3/4" from end of housing next to pinion housing.

**6)** Clean end of rack with wet fine-grit sandpaper. Clean rack and wrap one turn of tape around rack edge. Lubricate rack and tape.

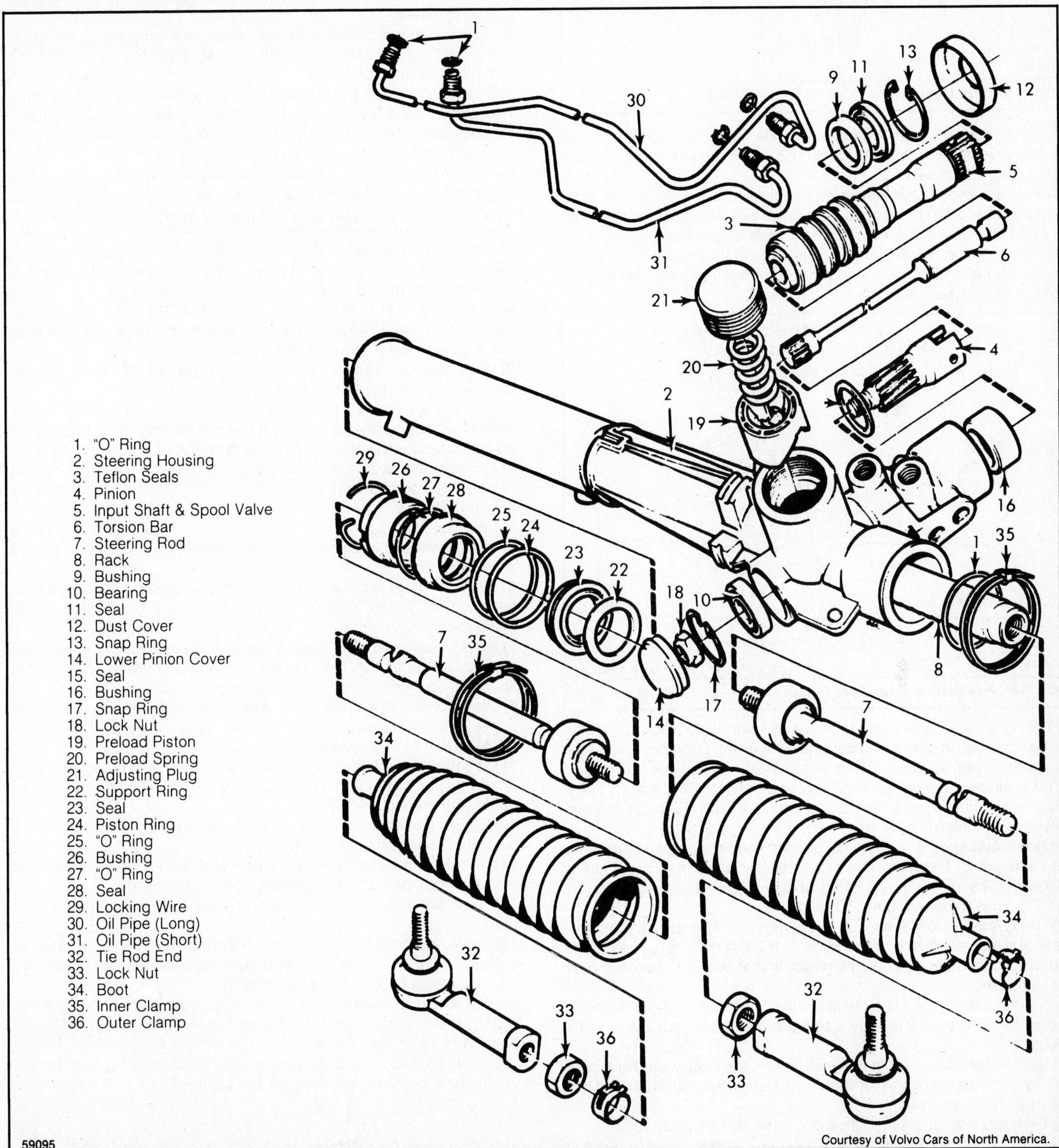


*Fig. 10: Exploded View of Cam Gear-Type Power Steering Assembly (240)*

# 1991 STEERING
# Power Rack & Pinion (Cont.)

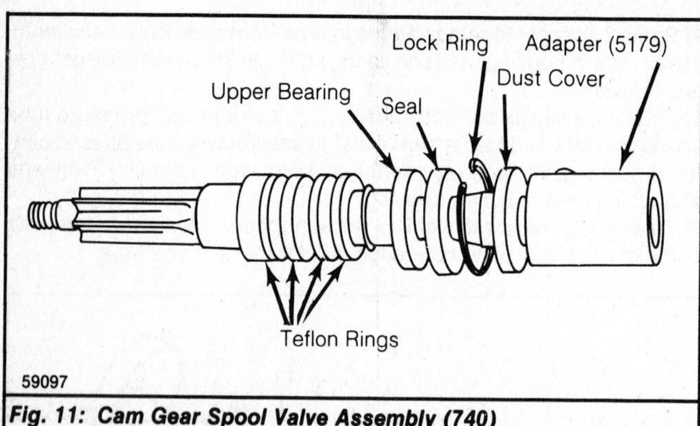


*Fig. 11: Cam Gear Spool Valve Assembly (740)*

**7)** Install plastic spacer with beveled side facing toward seal. Install lock sleeve and bushing onto rack. Use small screwdriver to lift edge of seal on end of rack.

**8)** Position end of lock sleeve so cut-out sections face end of rack. Ensure rack locking wire opening is in line with elongated hole in tube. Install locking wire. Turn bushing until wire is positioned correctly.

**9)** Center rack in housing and lubricate teeth with grease. Place pinion in housing with flat side in any one of 3 correct positions. *See Fig. 12.* End of rack should protrude 2.2" (55 mm).

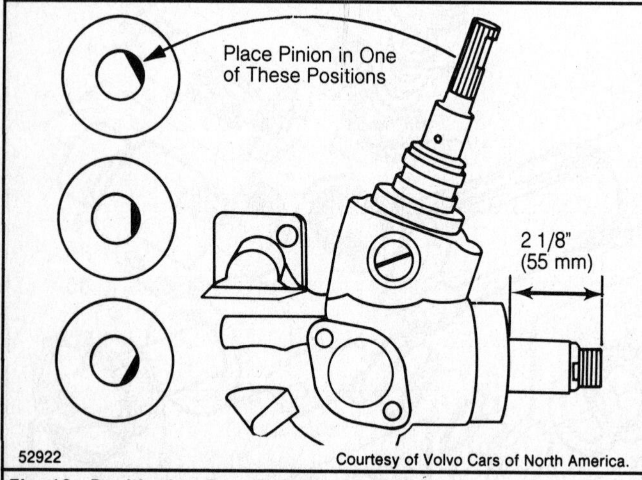


*Fig. 12: Positioning Cam Gear Pinion (740)*

**10)** Wrap pinion splines with tape. Install lower pinion lock nut. Install upper bearing on pinion with bevelled side down. Lubricate and install upper seal with lip facing down. Install snap ring and dust cover.

**11)** Install lower pinion lock nut. Tighten lock nut to 27 ft. lbs. (37 N.m). Pack lower pinion cover with Lubricant (11 61 001-1). Install preload piston assembly in housing.

**Preload Adjustment – 1)** Install preload piston spring and adjusting nut in housing. Place steering rack in center position. Tighten nut to 3.7-4.1 ft. lbs. (5.0-5.6 N.m) using Adapter (5296) and Torque Gauge (9177). Loosen adjusting nut 50-55 degrees.

**2)** Using Adapter (5179) and Torque Gauge (9177), ensure turning torque of pinion shaft is 9-18 INCH lbs. (1.0-2.0 N.m). If torque exceeds specification in any position, stop rack in that position. Readjust rack in high position.

**3)** If turning torque is still more than specification, install new steering gear. If turning torque is okay, use a punch to stake lock nut to valve housing.

**Final Reassembly – 1)** Install and tighten steering rods. Hold rack with adjustable wrench while tightening. Use narrow punch to lock ball joints to rack recesses.

**2)** Fill boots with about an ounce of grease and install on rack.

**Disassembly (740 ZF Steering Gear) – 1)** Clean exterior of steering gear. Mount steering gear in vise. Remove oil tubes. Turn steering gear back and forth to pump out oil.

**2)** Remove clamps and boots. To prevent pinion damage, hold rack with adjustable wrench. Unscrew left and right side steering rods.

**3)** Remove rack piston and preload piston assembly. *See Fig. 14.* Remove dust shield, lock ring and washer from upper part of pinion assembly. Remove lower pinion housing cover.

**4)** Secure upper pinion shaft. Remove lock nut, washer and snap ring. Withdraw pinion and spool valve assembly from housing. Remove end sleeve lock wire.

**5)** Slide rack and sleeve assembly from rack housing. Drive lower pinion bearing and seal out of pinion housing. DO NOT scratch inside of pinion housing surface.

**6)** Tap out rack seal and spacer ring from inside of steering housing. Remove "O" ring, seal, washer and bushing from rack end sleeve. Remove upper bearing housing from pinion and spool valve. Remove "O" ring and seal from upper bearing housing.

***CAUTION: Only remove 4 Teflon rings from spool valve if damaged. Replace rack piston seal only if damaged or after 25,000 miles.***

**Cleaning & Inspection –** Replace rubber boots if defective. Check all parts for wear, corrosion or damage. Replace as necessary. Replace entire steering gear if spool valve assembly is damaged.

**Reassembly – 1)** Lubricate all parts with ATF before reassembly. Install "O" ring and Teflon ring on rack piston. If difficult to install, heat Teflon ring in water to 104-122°F (40-50°C).

**2)** Install seal over rack teeth with lip facing piston. Lubricate rack piston teeth. Place spacer ring next to seal.

**3)** Install rack with seal and spacer ring into housing. When rack seats, gently push it in farther to seat seal and spacer ring. Rack is positioned correctly when rack seal is visible in center of outlet tube hole.

**4)** Position rack so end protrudes about 3/4" from pinion housing end of rack housing. DO NOT push rack farther into housing or seal may be damaged.

**5)** Install bushing, spacer washer and seal in end sleeve. Seal lips face outward from end of sleeve. Drive end sleeve in housing and secure with snap ring.

**6)** Install "O" rings and Teflon rings (if removed) on spool valve. If necessary, heat Teflon rings in water to 104-122°F (40-50°C) to ease installation.

**7)** Install bearing and "O" ring in upper bearing housing. Install seal with lip facing bearing. Install lower pinion seal in pinion housing with lip facing up. Install lower pinion bearing and lock ring.

**8)** Install pinion and spool valve assembly in pinion housing. Install upper bearing housing, spacer washer, snap ring and dust shield. Pack bottom of dust shield with grease.

**9)** On bottom of pinion and spool valve assembly, install spacer washer and tighten lock nut to 11 ft. lbs. (15 N.m). Fill pinion housing lower cover with grease and install.

**10)** Center steering rack in housing. Install preload spring WITHOUT "O" ring. Install spring in piston.

**11)** Install Counterhold (2985) on steering rack. *See Fig. 15.* Install dial indicator with stem on rack housing. Zero dial indicator.

**12)** Turn dial indicator so tip rests on face of preload piston. Note reading.

**13)** Move rack from lock to lock and note maximum indicator reading. Subtract .004" (.10 mm) from maximum indicator reading to achieve total thickness of shim to be installed.

**14)** Remove dial indicator and counterhold. Install "O" ring on preload piston. Install preload piston with spring, shim and cover. Tighten bolts to 79 INCH lbs. (9 N.m).

**15)** Install boot "O" ring and steering rods. Stake steering rods to rack to secure in position. Install boots and clamps.

# 1991 STEERING
# Power Rack & Pinion (Cont.)

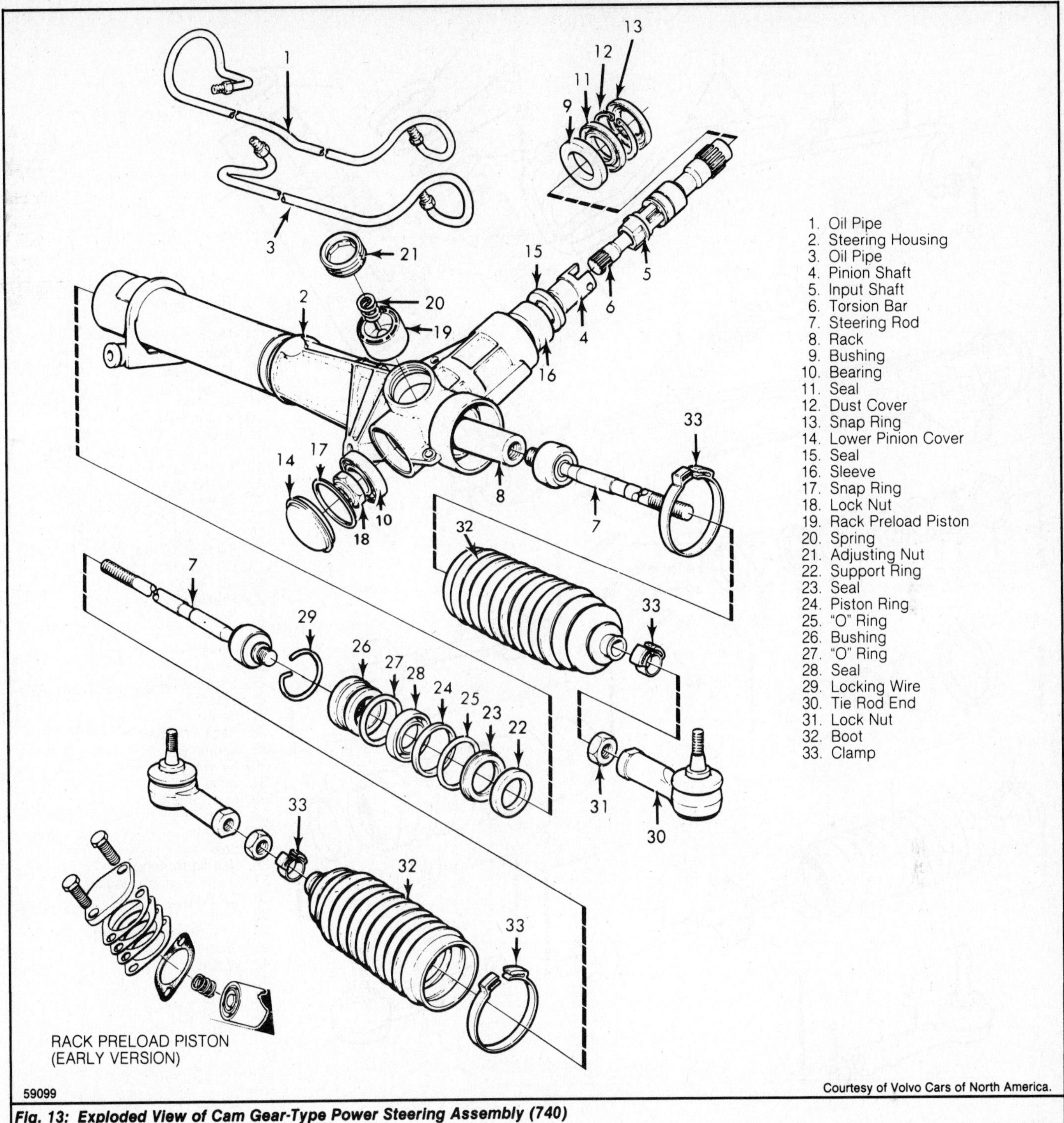


***Fig. 13: Exploded View of Cam Gear-Type Power Steering Assembly (740)***

# 1991 STEERING
## Power Rack & Pinion (Cont.)

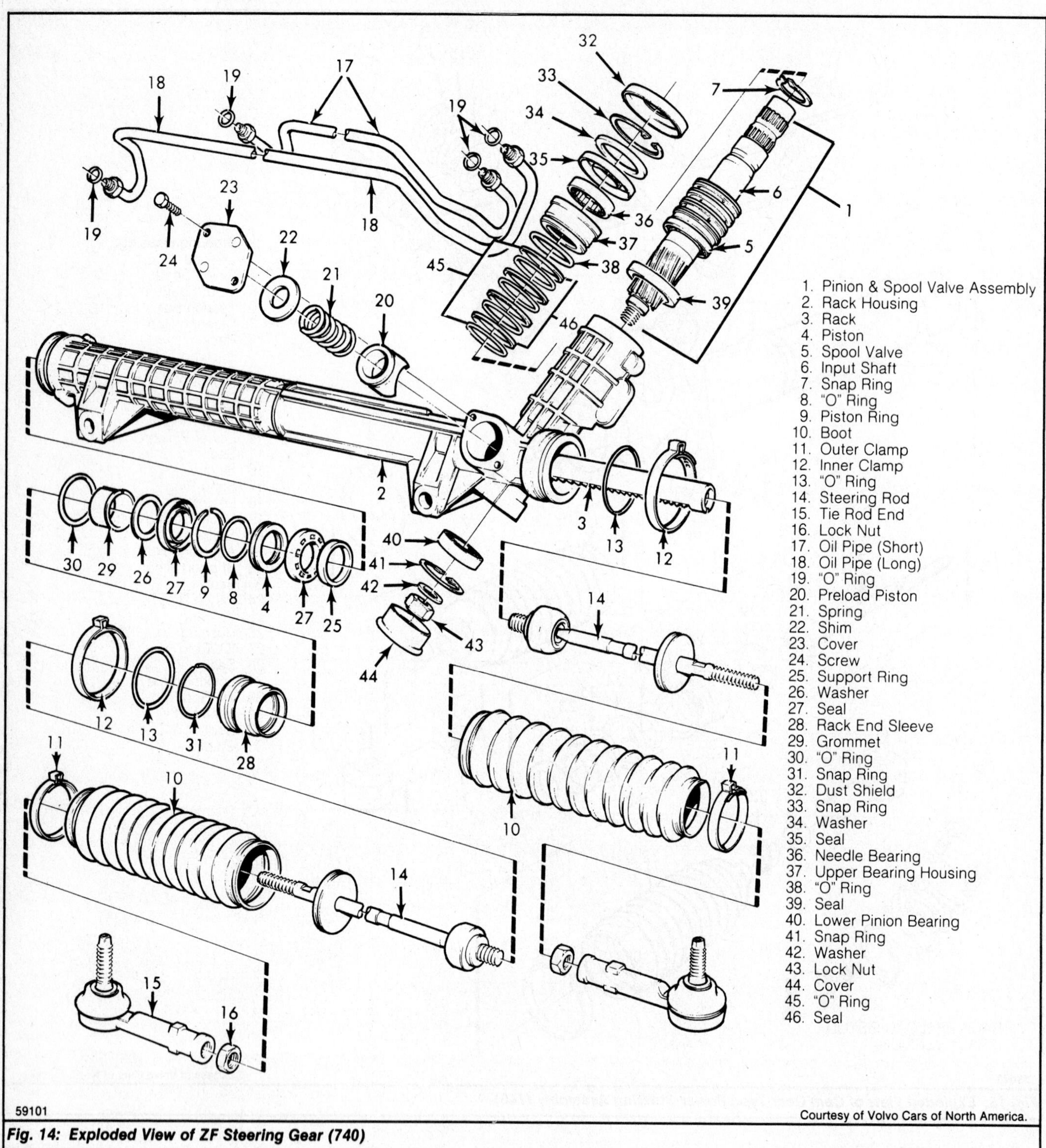


***Fig. 14: Exploded View of ZF Steering Gear (740)***

# 1991 STEERING
# Power Rack & Pinion (Cont.)

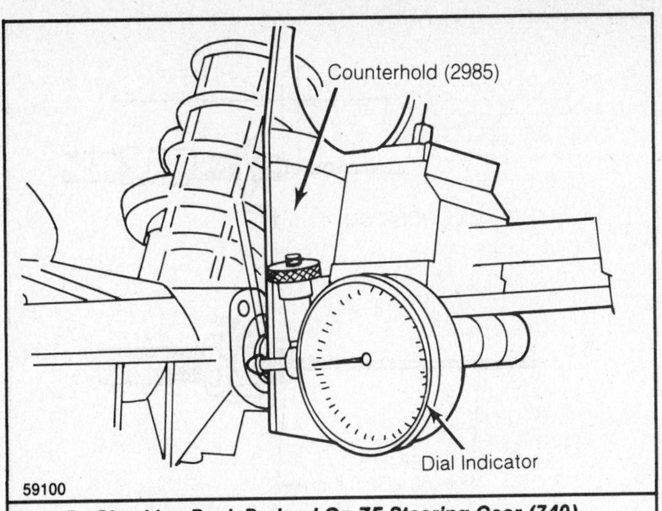


*Fig. 15: Checking Rack Preload On ZF Steering Gear (740)*

## TORQUE SPECIFICATIONS

*TORQUE SPECIFICATIONS*

| Application | Ft. Lbs. (N.m) |
|---|---|
| **240 ZF Steering Gear** | |
| Oil Line Fittings | 15 (20) |
| Preload Piston Cover | 16 (22) |
| Tube Assembly-to-Pinion Housing | 88 (120) |
| Valve Housing-to-Pinion Housing | 18 (25) |
| **740 Cam Gear** | |
| Pinion Cover Bolts | 12 (17) |
| Pinion Lower Lock Nut | 27 (37) |
| Rack Mounting Bolts | 32 (44) |
| **740 ZF Steering Gear** | |
| Rack Mounting Bolts | 32 (44) |
| | **INCH Lbs. (N.m)** |
| **740 ZF Steering Gear** | |
| Rack Preload Adjusting Cover Bolts | 79 (9) |

# 1991 TRANSMISSION SERVICING
## Automatic Transmission

**240, 740, 940**

## IDENTIFICATION

***VOLVO AUTOMATIC TRANSMISSION APPLICATIONS***

| Model | Transmission |
|---|---|
| 240 | Model AW70 |
| 740 | Model AW70L |
| 740 Turbo | Model AW71 |
| 940 | Model AW72 |
| 940 Turbo | Model AW71 |

## LUBRICATION

### SERVICE INTERVAL

Check fluid every 5000 miles. Change fluid every 20,000 miles.

### CHECKING FLUID LEVEL

**1)** Ensure vehicle is level. Apply parking brake and shift selector lever to Park. Start and idle engine. Shift selector lever through all gears, while pausing 4-5 seconds for engagement at each position.
**2)** Return selector lever to Park. Wait 2 minutes and check fluid level with engine idling. Level should be between MIN and MAX marks.

### RECOMMENDED FLUID

All transmissions use Dexron-II ATF.

### FLUID CAPACITY

***TRANSMISSION REFILL CAPACITIES***

| Application | Qts. (L) |
|---|---|
| 240 | 7.8 (7.4) |
| All Others | 7.9 (7.5) |

### DRAINING & REFILLING

**1)** Remove drain plug and drain transmission. Disconnect filler tube and remove oil pan.
**2)** Remove and clean oil strainer. Install strainer. Tighten strainer bolts to 18-25 INCH lbs. (2-3 N.m). Install oil pan with new gasket. Tighten bolts to 42 INCH lbs. (5 N.m). Tighten filler tube to 65 ft. lbs. (88 N.m).
**3)** To flush oil cooler, disconnect fluid return pipe from transmission. Place end of pipe in container. Add approximately 3.5 qts. (3.4L) of fluid in transmission.
**4)** Start engine and let idle. Turn off engine when clean oil comes out of pipe. Connect pipe and fill transmission.

## ADJUSTMENTS

### THROTTLE & KICKDOWN CABLES

Depress accelerator pedal. With pedal depressed, distance from cable sheath to clip on cable should be 1.98-2.06" (50.2-52.3 mm). *See Fig. 1.* Adjust distance on cable sheath if necessary.

### GEARSHIFT LINKAGE

**240** - Ensure gear selector linkage bushings are not worn. If worn, replace. Place transmission in Drive and move selector lever against gate. Clearance from pin to stop in "D" position should be same as clearance in "2" position. *See Fig. 2.* If clearance requires adjustment, adjust rod on gear selector.

**740 & 940** - **1)** Engine should start in Neutral or Park only. Back-up lights should only operate in Reverse. Gear selector should be vertical in Park. If gear selector is not vertical, proceed to next step.
**2)** Place gear selector in Park. Loosen lock nuts for actuator and selector rods. *See Fig. 3.* Ensure transmission lever is in Park. Rotate output shaft on transmission until it locks.
**3)** Place gear selector in a vertical position, or slightly forward, and tighten lock nut. Push reaction lever lightly rearward until a slight resistance is felt. Tighten lock nut to 42 INCH lbs. (5 N.m).

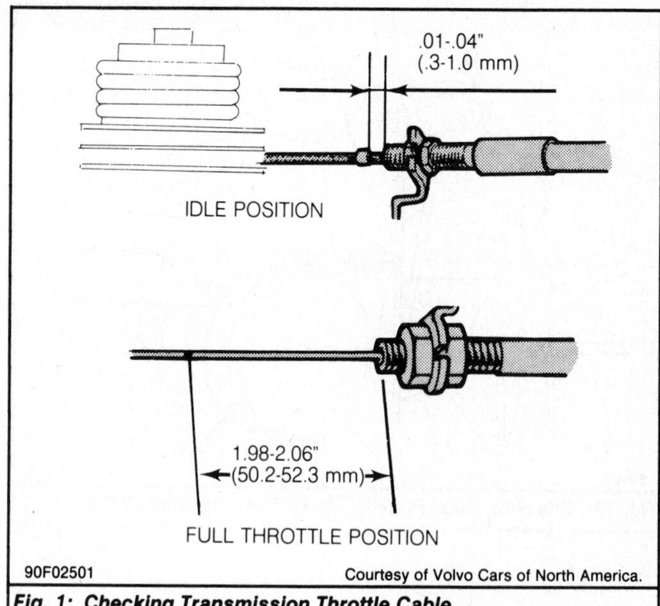


***Fig. 1: Checking Transmission Throttle Cable***

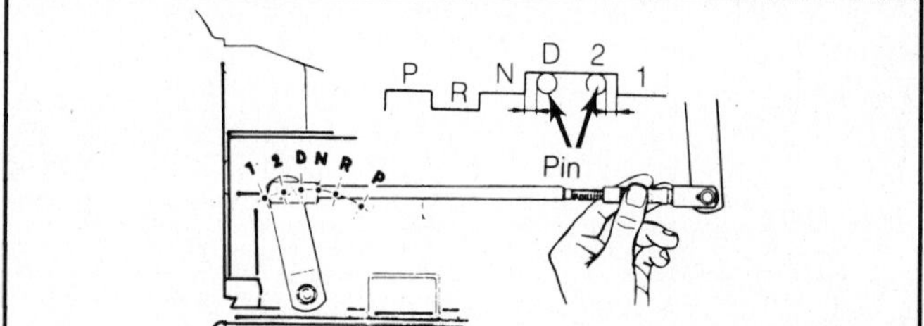


***Fig. 2: Adjusting Gear Selector (240)***

**4)** Ensure free play between pin and stop in Drive and Neutral is less than or equal to play between pin and stop in "3" and "2" positions. If free play is correct, tighten lock nut to 12-17 ft. lbs. (17-23 N.m).

***NOTE: If gear selector is stiff in "3" position, move reaction lever approximately 1/8" (3 mm) toward front and recheck operation.***

**5)** After adjustment, ensure vehicle only starts in Neutral or Park and back-up lights come on only in Reverse.

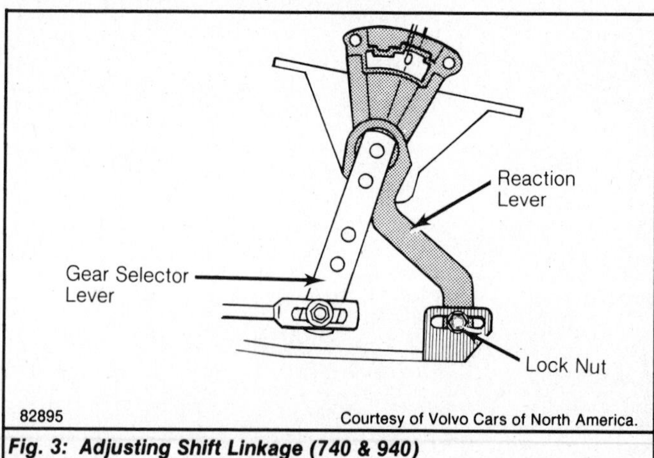


***Fig. 3: Adjusting Shift Linkage (740 & 940)***

### NEUTRAL SAFETY SWITCH

**240** - **1)** Switch is located at gear selector lever. Remove gear selector cover. Ensure "N" and "P" mark on indicator are directly oppo-

# 1991 TRANSMISSION SERVICING
## Automatic Transmission (Cont.)

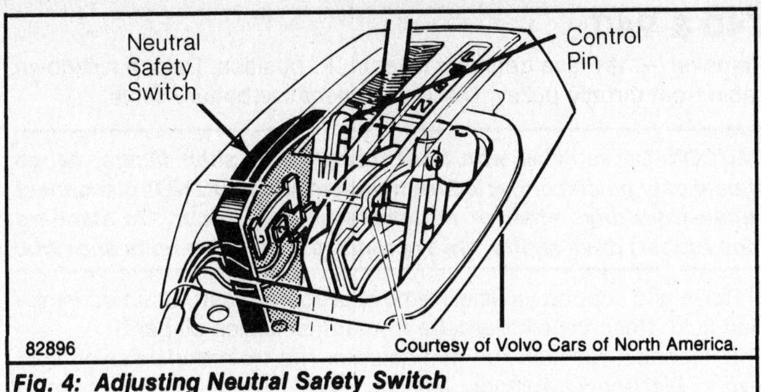


*Fig. 4: Adjusting Neutral Safety Switch*

site selector lever with transmission in Neutral and Park respectively. If not, loosen 2 retaining bolts and readjust.

**2)** Ensure engine only starts in Neutral and Park. Ensure back-up lights operate only in Reverse. Ensure control pin does not slide out of switch lever. *See Fig. 4.*

**740 & 940** – Neutral safety switch is located at bottom of selector lever. No adjustments are necessary.

# Manual Transmission

## 240, 740

## IDENTIFICATION

*VOLVO MANUAL TRANSMISSION APPLICATIONS*

| Model | Transmission |
|---|---|
| 240 | 5-Speed (M47) |
| 740 | 5-Speed (M47) |
| 740 Turbo | [1] 4-Speed (M46) |

[1] – Transmission is a 4-speed with overdrive.

## LUBRICATION

### SERVICE INTERVALS

Check fluid every 7500 miles.

### CHECKING FLUID LEVEL

**1)** Fluid should be up to bottom of fill hole. When adding oil, allow sufficient time for oil to flow into overdrive unit on M46 transmission. The M46 transmission and overdrive share fluid.

**2)** If changing fluid on M46 transmission, overdrive unit has separate oil pan and filter. *See Fig. 1.*

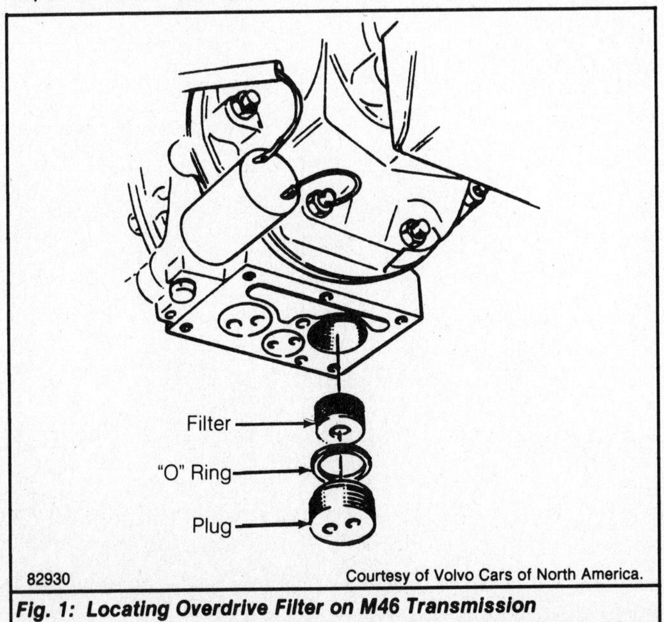


*Fig. 1: Locating Overdrive Filter on M46 Transmission*

**3)** Use Socket (2836) to remove plug. Clean strainer and magnet with solvent. Replace filter and tighten plug to 14 ft. lbs. (20 N.m). Install new gasket and tighten overdrive pan bolts to 84 INCH lbs. (10 N.m).

### RECOMMENDED FLUID

Use Type F ATF. DO NOT use Dexron-II. In climates where temperatures are consistently below 14°F (-10°C) or in high mileage vehicles, use Volvo Thermal Oil (1161243-9).

### FLUID CAPACITY

*TRANSMISSION REFILL CAPACITIES*

| Application | Qts. (L) |
|---|---|
| M46 | 2.4 (2.3) |
| M47 | 1.6 (1.55) |

## ADJUSTMENTS

### LINKAGE

No external linkage adjustment is required.

### REVERSE DETENT

Place transmission in 1st gear. Clearance between detent plate and detent screw should be .02-.06" (.5-1.5 mm). Adjust by moving detent plate. *See Fig. 2.*

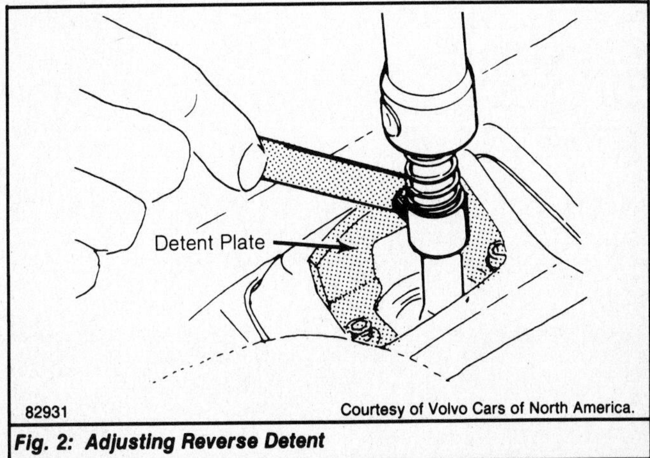


*Fig. 2: Adjusting Reverse Detent*

# 1991 TRANSMISSION SERVICING
# Transmission Removal & Installation

## 240, 740, 940

## MANUAL

***NOTE: For manual transmission replacement procedures, see CLUTCHES article.***

## AUTOMATIC

### 240

**Removal - 1)** Disconnect kickdown cable at throttle cable. Disconnect negative battery cable. Remove 2 upper transmission-to-engine bolts. Remove transmission oil dipstick tube.
**2)** Raise and support vehicle. Remove drain plug and drain transmission fluid. Disconnect shift linkage, oil filter tube, oil cooler lines and speedometer cable.

***CAUTION: On vehicles with front rubber drive shaft flange, flange should only be disconnected from transmission. DO NOT disconnect from drive shaft. Disconnecting drive shaft from flange may cause an imbalance. On standard (non-rubber) drive shafts, always replace the 4 retaining bolts and nuts.***

**3)** Remove drive shaft. Remove starter motor bolts and torque converter-to-flexplate bolts. Disconnect solenoid valve plug. Disconnect exhaust pipe bracket.
**4)** Place transmission jack under transmission. Remove rear crossmember. Remove transmission-to-engine bolts. Lower transmission.
**Installation - 1)** To install transmission, reverse removal procedures. Tighten torque converter-to-flexplate retaining bolts to 33 ft. lbs. (45 N.m). After installation, fill transmission with ATF fluid. Adjust throttle linkage and shift control linkage.
**2)** On models with rubber drive shaft flanges, retaining bolts must be tightened to 50-65 ft. lbs. (70-80 N.m). On models with standard (non-rubber) drive shafts with 4 retaining bolts, tighten 8-mm bolts to 26 ft. lbs. (35 N.m). Tighten 10-mm bolts to 37 ft. lbs. (50 N.m). Fill with ATF.

### 740 & 940

**Removal - 1)** Place gearshift lever in "P" position. Detach kickdown cable from throttle pulley. Disconnect negative battery cable.

***CAUTION: On vehicles with front rubber drive shaft flange, flange should only be disconnected from transmission. DO NOT disconnect flange from drive shaft or an imbalance may occur. On standard (non-rubber) drive shafts, always replace 4 retaining bolts and nuts.***

**2)** Raise and support vehicle. Remove propeller shaft. Drain transmission fluid. Unscrew oil filler tube from transmission oil pan.
**3)** Disconnect reaction rod and actuator rod from transmission shift levers. Disconnect solenoid lead on AW71. On all models, support transmission with jack. Remove rear transmission crossmember.
**4)** Remove starter motor bolts and cover plate. Remove torque converter-to-flexplate bolts. Disconnect oil cooler lines. Remove transmission-to-engine bolts. Slide transmission rearward and lower from vehicle.
**Installation - 1)** To install, reverse removal procedure. Tighten lower oil filler tube nut to 65 ft. lbs. (88 N.m). Tighten flexplate-to-torque converter bolts in a crisscross pattern to 32 ft. lbs. (45 N.m).
**2)** On models with rubber drive shaft flanges, retaining bolts must be tightened to 51-65 ft. lbs. (70-88 N.m). On models with standard (non-rubber) drive shafts with 4 retaining bolts, tighten 8-mm bolts to 26 ft. lbs. (35 N.m). Tighten 10-mm bolts to 37 ft. lbs. (50 N.m).
**3)** Adjust kickdown cable and gearshift linkage. Fill transmission with ATF fluid.

## TORQUE SPECIFICATIONS

***TORQUE SPECIFICATIONS***

| Application | Ft. Lbs. (N.m) |
|---|---|
| Drive Shaft Flange Retaining Bolt (Non-Rubber) | |
| 8-mm | 26 (35) |
| 10-mm | 37 (50) |
| Drive Shaft Flange Retaining Bolt (Rubber) | 52-65 (70-88) |
| Flexplate-To-Torque Converter Bolts | 33 (45) |
| Lower Oil Filler Tube Nut | 65 (88) |

# 1991 LATEST CHANGES & CORRECTIONS
# Contents

# LATEST CHANGES & CORRECTIONS 1991 & Earlier Models

## PORSCHE

### ENGINE PERFORMANCE

1 *1990 PORSCHE 911 SERIES* – Please note that information not available for use in the 1990 IMPORTED CARS, LIGHT TRUCKS & VANS SERVICE & REPAIR manual and the 1990 IMPORTED CARS, LIGHT TRUCKS & VANS ENGINE PERFORMANCE SERVICE & REPAIR supplement is now available. For 1990-91 information, please refer to the appropriate 1991 publication.

## SAAB

### ENGINE PERFORMANCE

2 *ALL 1989-90 SAAB: REVISED IGNITION COIL TESTING PROCEDURE* – Please note that ignition coil secondary resistance test procedure has been revised as follows:

**Ignition Coil Secondary Resistance** – Turn ignition switch off. Remove primary and secondary leads from ignition coil. Using ohmmeter, check secondary resistance between tower and negative terminal of coil. Replace coil if readings are not within specification. See IGNITION COIL SECONDARY RESISTANCE table.

***IGNITION COIL SECONDARY RESISTANCE – Ohms @ 68°F (20°C)***

| Application | Ohms |
|---|---|
| 900 Series | 7200-8200 |
| 9000 Series | [1] |

[1] – DIS coil specifications not available from manufacturer.

This revision applies to the following publications:
IMPORTED CARS, LIGHT TRUCKS & VANS SERVICE & REPAIR ENGINE PERFORMANCE supplement, and IMPORTED CARS, LIGHT TRUCKS & VANS SERVICE & REPAIR manual.

- 1989 – Page SAAB 1-9
- 1990 – Page SAAB 1-8

### ENGINES

3 *1990 9000 SERIES: REVISED TIMING CHAIN REMOVAL PROCEDURE* – Please note that timing chain removal procedure has been revised. For revised procedure, see the 1991 publication.

This revision applies to the following publications:
IMPORTED CARS, LIGHT TRUCKS & VANS, SERVICE & REPAIR manual and IMPORTED CARS, LIGHT TRUCKS & VANS ENGINE, CLUTCHES & DRIVE AXLE supplement.

- 1990 – Page SAAB 5-2

4 *1990 2.0L: REVISED CYLINDER HEAD SPECIFICATIONS* – Please note that cylinder head valve seat specifications have been revised as follows:

***CYLINDER HEAD***

| Application | Specification |
|---|---|
| 2.0L | |
| Valve Seat Width | .06" (1.5 mm) |

This revision applies to the following publications:
IMPORTED CARS, LIGHT TRUCKS & VANS, SERVICE & REPAIR manual and IMPORTED CARS, LIGHT TRUCKS & VANS ENGINE, CLUTCHES & DRIVE AXLE supplement.

- 1990 – Page SAAB 5-4

### CLUTCHES

5 *1990 900 SERIES: REVISED CLUTCH INSPECTION PROCEDURE* – Please note that clutch on-vehicle inspection procedure has been revised as follows:

**Inspection (On-Vehicle)** – **1)** With clutch assembly installed, remove inspection plate on top of clutch cover and look through inspection hole. Measure distance between rear edge of plastic sleeve and front edge of machined surface on slave cylinder housing.

**2)** Replace clutch disc if distance is less than .08" (2 mm). Ensure compressed thickness of disc is within limits. See CLUTCH DISC SPECIFICATIONS table. Ensure unloaded disc-to-pressure plate clearance is within specification.

This revision applies to the following publications:
IMPORTED CARS, LIGHT TRUCKS & VANS, SERVICE & REPAIR manual and IMPORTED CARS, LIGHT TRUCKS & VANS ENGINE, CLUTCHES & DRIVE AXLE supplement.

- 1990 – Page SAAB 6-2

### DRIVE AXLES

6 *1987-90 9000 SERIES: REVISED DRIVE AXLE SERVICE PROCEDURE* – Please note that drive axle disassembly & reassembly information, previously not covered is now available. For drive axle disassembly & reassembly procedure, see the 1991 publication.

This revision applies to the following publications:
IMPORTED CARS, LIGHT TRUCKS & VANS, SERVICE & REPAIR manual and IMPORTED CARS, LIGHT TRUCKS & VANS ENGINE, CLUTCHES & DRIVE AXLE supplement.

- 1987 – Page 8-21
- 1988 – Page 9-26
- 1989 – Page SAAB 7-1
- 1990 – Page SAAB 7-0

### TRANSMISSION SERVICING

7 *1990 900 SERIES: REVISED DRAINING & REFILLING PROCEDURE* – Please note that automatic transmission oil pan installation procedures have been revised. For revised procedure, see the 1991 publication.

This revision applies to the following publications:
IMPORTED CARS, LIGHT TRUCKS & VANS, SERVICE & REPAIR manual and IMPORTED CARS, LIGHT TRUCKS & VANS ENGINE, CLUTCHES & DRIVE AXLE supplement.

- 1990 – Page SAAB 12-0

8 *1990 9000 SERIES: REVISED MANUAL TRANSMISSION REMOVAL PROCEDURE* – Please note that manual transmission removal procedure has been revised. For revised procedure, see the 1991 publication.

This revision applies to the following publications:
IMPORTED CARS, LIGHT TRUCKS & VANS, SERVICE & REPAIR manual and IMPORTED CARS, LIGHT TRUCKS & VANS ENGINE, CLUTCHES & DRIVE AXLE supplement.

- 1990 – Page SAAB 12-1

## SUBARU

### ENGINE PERFORMANCE

9 *ALL 1990 SUBARU MODELS: REVISED IGNITION TIMING SPECIFICATIONS* – Please note that IGNITION TIMING SPECIFICATIONS table has been revised as follows:

***IGNITION TIMING SPECIFICATIONS (Degrees BTDC @ RPM)***

| Application | Man. Trans. | Auto. Trans. |
|---|---|---|
| 1.2L | [1] 5 @ 800 | [1] 5 @ 850 |
| 1.8L | | |
| Non-Turbo | 20 @ 700 | 20 @ 700 |
| Turbo | 20 @ 800 | 20 @ 800 |
| 2.2L | | |
| Non-Turbo | 18-22 @ 700 | 12-28 @ 700 |
| Turbo | 7-23 @ 700 | 7-23 @ 700 |
| 2.7L | 20 @ 750 | 20 @ 750 |

[1] – With test mode connector connected.

This revision applies to the following publications:
IMPORTED CARS, LIGHT TRUCKS & VANS, SERVICE & REPAIR

manual and IMPORTED CARS, LIGHT TRUCKS & VANS ENGINE PERFORMANCE supplement.

- 1990 – Page SUBARU 1-14

10 *ALL 1989-90 TURBO MODELS: REVISED TURBOCHARGER BOOST PRESSURE TEST PROCEDURE* – Please note that test procedures have been revised as follows:

## TURBOCHARGER COMPONENT TESTING

**Boost Pressure – 1)** Disconnect wastegate duty solenoid connector. Engine must be at normal operating temperature. Disconnect rubber hose from pressure switch. Using a "T" fitting, connect an air pressure gauge. Use enough hose so gauge may be brought inside passenger compartment.

**2)** Boost pressure should be checked at 2400 RPM (1.8L) or 4600 RPM (2.2L), with wide open throttle. On 1.8L engines, normal pressure is 7.2-8.3 psi (5.0-5.8 kg/cm²). On 2.2L engines, normal pressure is 6.2-7.3 psi (4.3-5.1 kg/cm²). Reconnect wastegate duty solenoid.

**3)** If boost pressure is too high, check rubber hose connecting intake manifold to wastegate valve. Replace hose if defective. If wastegate valve is not operating and remains closed, replace turbocharger. If boost pressure is too low, replace turbocharger.

This revision applies to the following publications:
IMPORTED CARS, LIGHT TRUCKS & VANS ENGINE PERFORMANCE supplement, and IMPORTED CARS, LIGHT TRUCKS & VANS SERVICE & REPAIR manual.

- 1989 – Page SUBARU 1-123
- 1990 – Page SUBARU 1-188

11 *1990 SUBARU JUSTY: REVISED PIN VOLTAGE CHART SPECIFICATIONS* – Please note that JUSTY ECU PIN SPECIFICATIONS – CARBURETED table (connector F62), has been revised as follows:

***JUSTY ECU PIN SPECIFICATIONS – CARBURETED***

| ECU Terminal No. (Wire Color) | Condition | Volts or Ohms |
|---|---|---|
| **Connector F62** | | |
| 1 (Yellow/Blue) [1] | Ign. On | 7-12V |
| 2 (Black) | Eng. On | .1-1.0V |
| 3 (White/Black) | Ign. On | .1-2V |
| 5 (Red/Yellow) | Eng. On | .1-3.0V |
| 5 (Red/Yellow) | Ign. On | 2.0-5.0V |
| 6 (Lt. Green/Black) | Eng. On | [2] 1-3V |
| 12 (Brown/Red) [1] | Ign. Off | 2-10 Ohms |
| 14 (Green/Yellow) | | |
| Release Clutch | Ign. On | 0-2V |
| Depress Clutch | Ign. On | 2-12V |
| 16 (Black) [1] | Ign. Off | 2-10 Ohms |
| 17 (Black) [1] | Ign. Off | 2-10 Ohms |
| 20 (Black/White) [1] | Ign. On | 7-12V |

[1] – ECU harness disconnected.
[2] – Fluctuates around 2 volts while driving vehicle.

This revision applies to the following publications:
IMPORTED CARS, LIGHT TRUCKS & VANS, SERVICE & REPAIR manual and IMPORTED CARS, LIGHT TRUCKS & VANS ENGINE PERFORMANCE supplement.

- 1990 – Page SUBARU 1-196

12 *1990 SUBARU LOYALE: REVISED PIN VOLTAGE CHART SPECIFICATIONS* – Please note that LOYALE ECU PIN SPECIFICATIONS table has been revised as follows:

***LOYALE ECU PIN SPECIFICATIONS – PFI***

| ECU Terminal No. (Wire Color) | Condition | Volts or Ohms |
|---|---|---|
| 2 [1] | Ign. On | 1-2V |
| 3 (Green/Blue) | Ign. On | [2] 0-10V |
| 4 (Yellow/Blue) [3] | Ign. Off | 0 Ohm in "N" |
| 6 (Blue/Black) | Ign. On | [2] 0-10V |
| 7 (Red) | Ign. On | 10-12V |
| 8 (Black) | Ign. On | [4] .1 or 4-5V |
| 9 (White/Black) [3] | Ign. Off | 100-20,000 Ohms |
| 10 (Brown/Red) [3] | Ign. Off | 0 Ohm |
| 12 [1] | Ign. On | 10-12V |
| 13 (Red/Black) | Ign. On | [2] 0-10V |
| 17 (White) | Ign. On | [5] .1 or 4-5V |
| 19 (Black/White) [3] | Ign. On | 10-12V |
| 20 (Brown/Red) [3] | Ign. Off | 0 Ohm |
| 24 (Black/White) | Ign. On | [6] 10-12V |
| 25 (Blue/White) [3] | | |
| Closed Throttle | Ign. Off | 0 Ohm |
| Open Throttle | Ign. Off | Infinity |
| 27 (White/Red) [3] | Ign. On | 10-12V |
| 29 (Yellow/Green) | Eng. On | [7] 1-3V |
| 35 (White/Red) [3] | Ign. On | 10-12V |
| 36 [1 3] | Ign. Off | 532-588 k/ohms |
| 48 [1] | Eng. On | .1-1.0V |
| 49 (White) [3] | Ign. On | 10-12V |
| 50 (White) [3] | Ign. On | 10-12V |
| 51 (White/Red) [3] | Ign. On | 10-12V |
| 52 (White/Red) [3] | Ign. On | 10-12V |
| 55 [1] | Ign. On | [2] 0-10V |
| 56 (Black) [3] | Ign. Off | 0 Ohm |
| 57 (Black) [3] | Ign. Off | 0 Ohm |
| 60 (Brown/Red) [3] | Ign. Off | 0 Ohm |
| 61 (Brown/Red) [3] | Ign. Off | 0 Ohm |
| 62 (Red) [3] | Ign. On | 10-12V |

[1] – No color available.
[2] – Fluctuates every 1.5 seconds with test connectors attached.
[3] – ECU harness disconnected.
[4] – Fluctuates 0-5 volts while cranking with starter.
[5] – Fluctuates 0-5 volts while slowly turning crankshaft hub nut with wrench.
[6] – 10-12 volts with ignition in start position.
[7] – Fluctuates around 2 volts while driving vehicle.

This revision applies to the following publications:
IMPORTED CARS, LIGHT TRUCKS & VANS, SERVICE & REPAIR manual and IMPORTED CARS, LIGHT TRUCKS & VANS ENGINE PERFORMANCE supplement.

- 1990 – Page SUBARU 1-201

13 *ALL 1990 SUBARU MODELS: REVISED THROTTLE POSITION SENSOR (TPS) SPECIFICATIONS* – Please note that THROTTLE POSITION SENSOR (TPS) RESISTANCE table has been revised as follows:

***THROTTLE POSITION SENSOR (TPS) RESISTANCE***

| Application [1] | TPS Connector [2] Terminals | Ohms |
|---|---|---|
| **Total Resistance** | | |
| Legacy | Black Wire & Red Wire | 12,000 |
| Loyale PFI | Black Wire & White Wire | 6000-18,000 |
| Loyale TBI | Black Wire & Red Wire | 3500-6500 |
| XT & XT6 | Black Wire & White Wire | 6000-18,000 |

# LATEST CHANGES & CORRECTIONS 1991 & Earlier Models (Cont.)

*THROTTLE POSITION SENSOR (TPS) RESISTANCE (Cont.)*

| Application [1] | TPS Connector [2] Terminals | Ohms |
|---|---|---|
| **Variable Resistance** | | |
| Legacy | | |
| Throttle Closed | Black Wire & White Wire | 1000 |
| Throttle Open | Black Wire & White Wire | 4300 |
| Loyale PFI | | |
| Throttle Closed | Black Wire & Red Wire | 5800-17,800 |
| Throttle Open | Black Wire & Red Wire | 1500-5100 |
| Loyale TBI | | |
| Throttle Closed | Black Wire & Green Wire | 1000 Or Less |
| Throttle Open | Black Wire & Red Wire | 2400 Or More |
| XT | | |
| Throttle Closed | Black Wire & Brown Wire | 5800-17,800 |
| Throttle Open | Black Wire & Brown Wire | 1500-5100 |
| XT6 | | |
| Throttle Closed | Black Wire & Brown Wire | 4200-15,000 |
| Throttle Open | Black Wire & Brown Wire | 100-1100 |

1 - Justy is not equipped with TPS.
2 - Disconnect TPS connector. At component side of connector, connect ohmmeter between the indicated terminals.

This revision applies to the following publications:
IMPORTED CARS, LIGHT TRUCKS & VANS, SERVICE & REPAIR manual and IMPORTED CARS, LIGHT TRUCKS & VANS ENGINE PERFORMANCE supplement.

- 1990 - Page SUBARU 1-206

## ACCESSORIES & EQUIPMENT

14 *1990 LOYALE: REVISED ILLUSTRATION* - Please note that *Fig. 3*, identifying combination switch wiring harness connector terminals, has been revised. For revised illustration, see the 1991 publication.

This revision applies to the following publications:
IMPORTED CARS, LIGHT TRUCKS & VANS, SERVICE & REPAIR manual and IMPORTED CARS, LIGHT TRUCKS & VANS ELECTRICAL SERVICE & REPAIR supplement.

- 1990 - Page SUBARU 4-7

## SUSPENSION

15 *1990 LOYALE: REVISED ILLUSTRATION* - Please note that SUSPENSION CONTROL UNIT procedures listed under TESTING, have been revised. For revised procedure, see the 1991 publication.

This revision applies to the following publications:
IMPORTED CARS, LIGHT TRUCKS & VANS, SERVICE & REPAIR manual and IMPORTED CARS, LIGHT TRUCKS & VANS CHASSIS SERVICE & REPAIR supplement.

- 1990 - Page SUBARU 10-9

## TRANSMISSION SERVICING

16 *1990 ALL MODELS: REVISED BAND ADJUSTMENT PROCEDURE* - Please note that automatic transmission band adjustment procedures have been revised as follows:

**Legacy, XT & XT6** - Band adjustment screw is located on left side of transmission housing. Hold band adjustment screw. Loosen lock nut. Tighten adjustment screw to 80 INCH lbs (9 N.m), then back off exactly 3 turns. Hold adjustment screw. Tighten lock nut to 18-21 ft. lbs. (25-28 N.m).

**Loyale** - Band adjustment screw is located on left side of transmission housing. Hold band adjustment screw. Loosen lock nut. Tighten adjustment screw to 80 INCH lbs. (9 N.m), then back off exactly 2 turns. Hold adjustment screw. Tighten lock nut to 18-21 ft. lbs. (25-28 N.m).

This revision applies to the following publications:
IMPORTED CARS, LIGHT TRUCKS & VANS, SERVICE & REPAIR manual and IMPORTED CARS, LIGHT TRUCKS & VANS ENGINE, CLUTCHES & DRIVE AXLE supplement.

- 1990 - Page SUBARU 12-0

# SUZUKI

## ENGINE PERFORMANCE

17 *1990 SUZUKI: REVISED ILLUSTRATION* - Please note that illustration given in *Fig. 6*, applies to automatic transmission vehicles only. Please disregard reference to 5th gear switch.

This revision applies to the following publications:
IMPORTED CARS, LIGHT TRUCKS & VANS, SERVICE & REPAIR manual and IMPORTED CARS, LIGHT TRUCKS & VANS ENGINE PERFORMANCE supplement.

- 1990 - Page SUZUKI 1-18

18 *1990 SUZUKI SWIFT DOHC: REVISED SELF-DIAGNOSTICS* - Please note that SWIFT (DOHC) CODE IDENTIFICATION table has been revised as follows:

*SWIFT (DOHC) CODE IDENTIFICATION*

| Code | System Affected | Probable Cause |
|---|---|---|
| 12 | System Normal | System Normal |
| 13 | Oxygen Sensor | Sensor or Circuit,ECM |
| 14 | [1] Coolant Temp. Sensor | Sensor or Circuit, ECM |
| 15 | [2] Coolant Temp. Sensor | Sensor or Circuit, ECM |
| 21 | [3] Throttle Position Sensor | Sensor or Circuit, ECM |
| 22 | [4] Throttle Position Sensor | Sensor or Circuit, ECM |
| 24 | Speed Sensor | Sensor or Circuit, ECM |
| 33 | [3] Airflow Sensor | Sensor or Circuit, ECM |
| 34 | [4] Airflow Sensor | Sensor or Circuit, ECM |
| 41 [5] | Ignition Signal Circuit | Ignition System, ECM Noise Suppressor, Wiring Circuit, ECM |
| 42 | Crank Angle Sensor | Sensor or Circuit, ECM |
| 51 [6] | EGR System | ECM, EGR Modulator, Wiring, EGR Temp. Sensor, Vacuum Switching Valve |
| 52 [6] | Fuel Injector | Fuel Injector, ECM |

1 - Low temperature is indicated.
2 - High temperature is indicated.
3 - High voltage is indicated.
4 - Low voltage is indicated.
5 - Code 41 is not stored in ECM memory. To check code when engine fails to start, crank engine, and then, with ignition still on, install fuse in diagnostic terminal of fuse block.
6 - Applicable to California models only.

This revision applies to the following publications:
IMPORTED CARS, LIGHT TRUCKS & VANS, SERVICE & REPAIR manual and IMPORTED CARS, LIGHT TRUCKS & VANS ENGINE PERFORMANCE supplement.

- 1990 - Page SUZUKI 1-26

19 *1990 SUZUKI SWIFT SOHC: REVISED MODEL APPLICATION FOR EFI MAIN RELAY TESTING* - Please note that EFI main relay test procedure is for Swift DOHC only. For Swift SOHC EFI main relay test procedure, refer to the 1991 publication.

This revision applies to the following publications:
IMPORTED CARS, LIGHT TRUCKS & VANS, SERVICE & REPAIR manual and IMPORTED CARS, LIGHT TRUCKS & VANS ENGINE PERFORMANCE supplement.

- 1990 - Page SUZUKI 1-106

20 *1990 SUZUKI SIDEKICK: REVISED MODEL APPLICATION FOR EGR TEMPERATURE SENSOR TESTING* - Please note that EGR temperature sensor test procedure, includes Sidekick.

# LATEST CHANGES & CORRECTIONS 1991 & Earlier Models (Cont.)

This revision applies to the following publications:
IMPORTED CARS, LIGHT TRUCKS & VANS, SERVICE & REPAIR manual and IMPORTED CARS, LIGHT TRUCKS & VANS ENGINE PERFORMANCE supplement.

- 1990 – Page SUZUKI 1-113

21 *ALL 1990 SUZUKI MODELS: REVISED EGR VACUUM SWITCHING VALVE (VSV) TEST PROCEDURE* – Please note that EGR VSV test procedure has been revised as follows:

**EGR VSV – 1)** Turn ignition off. Disconnect Green ECM connector and VSV connector. On Samurai and Sidekick, VSV is Blue and mounted near front right side of valve cover. On Swift DOHC, solenoid is mounted behind engine, near center of firewall. On Swift SOHC, solenoid is located between distributor and EGR modulator. Turn ignition on.

**2)** Check for battery voltage on appropriate wire terminal at VSV connector. See EGR VSV POWER TERMINAL IDENTIFICATION table. If battery voltage is present, go to next step. If battery voltage is not present, check circuit between VSV and EFI main/control relay. If circuit is okay, check EFI main relay. See EFI MAIN RELAY under RELAYS.

***EGR VSV POWER TERMINAL IDENTIFICATION***

| Application | Wire Color |
|---|---|
| Samurai & Sidekick | Blue/Black |
| Swift | White/Blue |

**3)** Turn ignition off. Check resistance between solenoid terminals. If resistance is not 33-39 ohms, replace solenoid. Disconnect upper and lower hoses from VSV. Connect short section of hose to lower horizontal port of solenoid. Blow air through hose connected to solenoid. Air should exit through filter.

**4)** If air does not exit through filter, replace solenoid. If air exits through filter, energize solenoid by applying battery voltage to appropriate wire terminal and ground the other terminal. See EGR VSV POWER TERMINAL IDENTIFICATION table.

**5)** Solenoid should click. Blow air through hose connected to solenoid. Air should now exit through other port and not through filter. If test results are not as specified, replace solenoid.

This revision applies to the following publications:
IMPORTED CARS, LIGHT TRUCKS & VANS, SERVICE & REPAIR manual and IMPORTED CARS, LIGHT TRUCKS & VANS ENGINE PERFORMANCE supplement.

- 1990 – Page SUZUKI 1-113

22 *1989-90 SUZUKI SAMURAI & SIDEKICK: REVISED ECM CONNECTOR TERMINAL LOCATION* – Please note that ECM connector terminals A1 and A12 shown in *Fig. 1* are reversed. For correct illustration, please refer to the 1991 publication.

This revision applies to the following publications:
IMPORTED CARS, LIGHT TRUCKS & VANS ENGINE PERFORMANCE supplement, and IMPORTED CARS, LIGHT TRUCKS & VANS SERVICE & REPAIR manual.

- 1989 – Page SUZUKI 1-71
- 1990 – Page SUZUKI 1-115

23 *1990 SUZUKI: REVISED ILLUSTRATION* – Please note that the abbreviations list given in *Fig. 9*, has been revised as follows:

PS – Pressure Sensor
TS – Throttle Switch
TPS – Throttle Position Sensor
Please disregard reference to Power Steering.

This revision applies to the following publications:
IMPORTED CARS, LIGHT TRUCKS & VANS, SERVICE & REPAIR manual and IMPORTED CARS, LIGHT TRUCKS & VANS ENGINE PERFORMANCE supplement.

- 1990 – Page SUZUKI 1-120

## ENGINES

24 *1990 1.3L & 1.6L: REVISED VALVE CLEARANCE SPECIFICATIONS* – Please note that valve clearance specifications have been revised as follows:

***VALVE CLEARANCE SPECIFICATIONS***

| Valve | Hot In. (mm) | Cold In. (mm) |
|---|---|---|
| Exhaust | .010-.012 (.25-.30) | .006-.008 (.15-.21) |
| Intake | .009-.011 (.23-.27) | .005-.006 (.13-.17) |

This revision applies to the following publications:
IMPORTED CARS, LIGHT TRUCKS & VANS, SERVICE & REPAIR manual and IMPORTED CARS, LIGHT TRUCKS & VANS ENGINES, CLUTCHES & DRIVE AXLES supplement.

- 1990 – Page SUZUKI 5-0

# TOYOTA

## ENGINE PERFORMANCE

25 *1990 TOYOTA PICKUP & 4RUNNER: CORRECTION OF REVERSED ILLUSTRATION* – Please note that in *Fig. 2*, the illustrations of PICKUP/4RUNNER (22-RE) and PICKUP/4RUNNER (3VZ-3) are reversed. For correct illustration, refer to the 1991 publication.

This revision applies to the following publications:
IMPORTED CARS, LIGHT TRUCKS & VANS, SERVICE & REPAIR manual and IMPORTED CARS, LIGHT TRUCKS & VANS ENGINE PERFORMANCE supplement.

- 1990 – Page TOYOTA 1-32

26 *1990 TOYOTA: REVISED SELF-DIAGNOSTICS* – Please note that trouble code clearing procedure, has been revised as follows:

## CLEARING CODES

**1)** After repairs are performed, clear ECU memory. To clear memory, turn ignition off. Remove fuse from main fuse block for about 30 seconds or more.

**2)** Fuse block is located below left side of instrument panel (Corolla), near center of instrument panel (Previa) or in engine compartment fuse/relay box (all others). See CLEARING CODES table for appropriate fuse.

**3)** Depending on ambient temperature, fuse may need to be removed for more than 30 seconds. Replace fuse and exit diagnostic mode. Codes can also be cleared by disconnecting vehicle battery. However, other memory functions, such as clock, radio, etc., will need to be reset.

***CLEARING CODES***

| Application | Fuse (Amperage) |
|---|---|
| Corolla | STOP (15) |
| Cressida | EFI (20) |
| All Others | EFI (15) |

This revision applies to the following publications:
IMPORTED CARS, LIGHT TRUCKS & VANS, SERVICE & REPAIR manual and IMPORTED CARS, LIGHT TRUCKS & VANS ENGINE PERFORMANCE supplement.

- 1990 – Page TOYOTA 1-52

27 *1990 TOYOTA CRESSIDA: REVISED SELF-DIAGNOSTICS* – Please note that step **5)** of CRESSIDA (TEST MODE), has been revised as follows:

**5)** Using a jumper wire, connect TDCL terminals TE1 and E1. Read any diagnostic codes that are stored. To read codes, see steps **4)** through **7)** of CRESSIDA (NORMAL MODE). Remove jumper wires.

This revision applies to the following publications:
IMPORTED CARS, LIGHT TRUCKS & VANS, SERVICE & REPAIR

# LATEST CHANGES & CORRECTIONS
# 1991 & Earlier Models (Cont.)

manual and IMPORTED CARS, LIGHT TRUCKS & VANS ENGINE PERFORMANCE supplement.

- 1990 – Page TOYOTA 1-52

**28** *1989-90 TOYOTA CAMRY: REVISED SELF-DIAGNOSTICS* – Please note that codes 12 and 13 test procedures for CAMRY TEST NO. 3 have been revised as follows:

Code 12 is caused by loss of NE or "G" signal from distributor to ECU for at least 2 seconds after starter signal is received at ECU. Ensure starter signal exists at ECU. See CODE 43.

Code 13 is caused by loss of NE signal from distributor to ECU when engine RPM exceeds 1000 RPM.

***NOTE: For ignition system test procedures, see BASIC DIAGNOSTIC PROCEDURE article.***

This revision applies to the following publications:
IMPORTED CARS, LIGHT TRUCKS & VANS ENGINE PERFORMANCE supplement, and IMPORTED CARS, LIGHT TRUCKS & VANS SERVICE & REPAIR manual.

- 1989 – Page TOYOTA 1-69
- 1990 – Page TOYOTA 1-59

**29** *1989-90 TOYOTA CAMRY: REVISED SELF-DIAGNOSTICS* – Please note that terminal/voltage tables for CAMRY TEST NO. 7 are reversed. For correct terminal/voltage table illustration, refer to the 1991 publication.

This revision applies to the following publications:
IMPORTED CARS, LIGHT TRUCKS & VANS ENGINE PERFORMANCE supplement, and IMPORTED CARS, LIGHT TRUCKS & VANS SERVICE & REPAIR manual.

- 1989 – Page TOYOTA 1-72
- 1990 – Page TOYOTA 1-62

**30** *1990 TOYOTA CELICA: REVISED SELF-DIAGNOSTICS* – Please note that schematics and terminal/voltage tables for CELICA TEST NO. 3, are reversed. For correct schematic and terminal/voltage table illustration, refer to the 1991 publication.

This revision applies to the following publications:
IMPORTED CARS, LIGHT TRUCKS & VANS, SERVICE & REPAIR manual and IMPORTED CARS, LIGHT TRUCKS & VANS ENGINE PERFORMANCE supplement.

- 1990 – Page TOYOTA 1-71

**31** *1990 TOYOTA TERCEL: REVISED SELF-DIAGNOSTICS* – Please note that codes 12 and 13 test procedures for TERCEL TEST NO. 3, have been revised as follows:

Code 12 is caused by loss of NE signal from distributor to ECU for at least 2 seconds after starter signal is received at ECU. Ensure starter signal exists at ECU. See CODE 43.

Code 13 is caused by loss of NE signal from distributor to ECU when engine RPM exceeds 1500 RPM.

***NOTE: For ignition system test procedures, see BASIC DIAGNOSTIC PROCEDURE article.***

This revision applies to the following publications:
IMPORTED CARS, LIGHT TRUCKS & VANS, SERVICE & REPAIR manual and IMPORTED CARS, LIGHT TRUCKS & VANS ENGINE PERFORMANCE supplement.

- 1990 – Page TOYOTA 1-150

**32** *1990 TOYOTA CELICA: REVISED ILLUSTRATION* – Please note that vacuum diagrams (2) and (3) in *Fig. 57*, are reversed. For correct illustration, refer to the 1991 publication.

This revision applies to the following publications:
IMPORTED CARS, LIGHT TRUCKS & VANS, SERVICE & REPAIR manual and IMPORTED CARS, LIGHT TRUCKS & VANS ENGINE PERFORMANCE supplement.

- 1990 – Page TOYOTA 1-211

## ELECTRICAL

**33** *1990 COROLLA (4A-FE,) LAND CRUISER, PICKUP & 4RUNNER: REVISED ILLUSTRATION* – Please note that center illustration in *Fig. 1*, is incorrectly identified as applying to Camry, Celica, Corolla (4A-GE), Cressida & Supra. The correct application is Corolla (4A-FE), Land Cruiser, Pickup & 4Runner.

This revision applies to the following publications:
IMPORTED CARS, LIGHT TRUCKS & VANS, SERVICE & REPAIR manual and IMPORTED CARS, LIGHT TRUCKS & VANS ELECTRICAL SERVICE & REPAIR supplement.

- 1990 – Page TOYOTA 2-0

## ENGINES

**34** *1990 2.0L: REVISED PISTONS & RINGS SPECIFICATIONS* – Please note that PISTONS & RING clearance specifications have been revised as follows:

***PISTONS, PINS & RINGS***

| Application | In. (mm) |
|---|---|
| Piston Clearance | |
| Camry | .0018-.0026 (.045-.066) |
| Celica | .0028-.0035 (.071-.089) |
| Rings | |
| Celica | |
| Piston No. 2 | |
| End Gap | |
| Standard | .0177-.0264 (.450-.079) |
| Wear Limit | .0382 (.970) |
| Side Clearance | .0012-.0028 (.030-.071) |

This revision applies to the following publications:
IMPORTED CARS, LIGHT TRUCKS & VANS, SERVICE & REPAIR manual and IMPORTED CARS, LIGHT TRUCKS & VANS ENGINE, CLUTCHES & DRIVE AXLE supplement.

- 1990 – Page TOYOTA 5-38

**35** *1990 2.2L: REVISED CYLINDER HEAD TORQUE SPECIFICATIONS* – Please note that cylinder head torque specifications have been revised as follows:

***TORQUE SPECIFICATIONS***

| Application | Ft. Lbs. (N.m) |
|---|---|
| Cylinder Head Bolt | |
| Step 1 | 36 (49) |
| Step 2 | Additional 90 Degrees |

This revision applies to the following publications:
IMPORTED CARS, LIGHT TRUCKS & VANS, SERVICE & REPAIR manual and IMPORTED CARS, LIGHT TRUCKS & VANS ENGINE, CLUTCHES & DRIVE AXLE supplement.

- 1990 – Page TOYOTA 5-48

**36** *1990 LAND CRUISER: REVISED ENGINE OVERHAUL PROCEDURE* – Please note that step **1)** under CRANKSHAFT & MAIN BEARINGS has been revised as follows:

**Crankshaft & Main Bearings – 1)** Ensure main bearing caps are numbered for location with No. 1 at front of engine. Arrow mark on cap points toward front of crankshaft. Remove main bearing cap bolts in sequence.

This revision applies to the following publications:
IMPORTED CARS, LIGHT TRUCKS & VANS, SERVICE & REPAIR manual and IMPORTED CARS, LIGHT TRUCKS & VANS ENGINE, CLUTCHES & DRIVE AXLE supplement.

- 1990 – Page TOYOTA 5-91

**37** *1990 LAND CRUISER: REVISED CONNECTING ROD SPECIFICATIONS* – Please note that connecting rods specifications have been revised as follows:

# LATEST CHANGES & CORRECTIONS 1991 & Earlier Models (Cont.)

***CONNECTING RODS***

| Application | In. (mm) |
|---|---|
| 4.0L | |
| Bushing Pin Bore Diameter | .8666-.8672 (22.012-22.027) |

This revision applies to the following publications:
IMPORTED CARS, LIGHT TRUCKS & VANS, SERVICE & REPAIR manual and IMPORTED CARS, LIGHT TRUCKS & VANS ENGINE, CLUTCHES & DRIVE AXLE supplement.
- 1990 - Page TOYOTA 5-93

38 *1990 LAND CRUISER: REVISED CAMSHAFT JOURNAL SPECIFICATIONS* - Please note that .020" (.50 mm) undersize camshaft No. 2 journal specifications have been revised as follows:

***CAMSHAFT***

| Application | In. (mm) |
|---|---|
| No. 2 Journal | 1.8096-1.8100 (45.964-45.975) |

This revision applies to the following publications:
IMPORTED CARS, LIGHT TRUCKS & VANS, SERVICE & REPAIR manual and IMPORTED CARS, LIGHT TRUCKS & VANS ENGINE, CLUTCHES & DRIVE AXLE supplement.
- 1990 - Page TOYOTA 5-94

39 *1990 CAMRY: REVISED COOLING FAN SPECIFICATIONS* - Please note that COOLING FAN ECU CIRCUIT TEST specifications have been revised as follows:

***CAMRY V6 COOLING FAN ECU CIRCUIT TEST***

| Wiring Harness Terminal Check | Condition | Specification |
|---|---|---|
| No. 2-Ground | Always | Continuity |
| No. 3-Ground | Ignition On | Battery Voltage |
| No. 4-Ground | Ignition On | Battery Voltage |
| No. 5-No. 7 | 176°F (80°C) [1] | 1530 Ohms |
| No. 5-No. 7 | 194°F (90°C) [1] | 1180 Ohms |
| No. 5-No. 7 | 203°F (95°C) [1] | 1030 Ohms |
| No. 6-Ground | Always | Continuity |

[1] - Coolant temperature.

This revision applies to the following publications:
IMPORTED CARS, LIGHT TRUCKS & VANS, SERVICE & REPAIR manual and IMPORTED CARS, LIGHT TRUCKS & VANS ENGINE, CLUTCHES & DRIVE AXLE supplement.
- 1990 - Page TOYOTA 5-98

## BRAKES

40 *1990 CELICA: REVISED ABS CODE CLEARING PROCEDURE* - Please note that ABS code clearing procedure has been revised as follows:
Turn ignition on. Using a jumper wire, connect check connector terminals Tc and $E_1$. *See Fig. 3.* With vehicle stopped, depress brake pedal 8 or more times within 3 seconds. Codes are now erased. Turn ignition on. Ensure ABS light goes out after 3 seconds. Ensure ABS light shows a normal code. See ABS LIGHT DIAGNOSTICS under DIAGNOSIS & TESTING.
This revision applies to the following publications:
IMPORTED CARS, LIGHT TRUCKS & VANS, SERVICE & REPAIR manual and IMPORTED CARS, LIGHT TRUCKS & VANS CHASSIS SERVICE & REPAIR supplement.
- 1990 - Page TOYOTA 8-22

41 *1990 PICKUP & 4RUNNER: REVISED ABS HYDRAULIC SYSTEM BLEEDING PROCEDURE* - Please revise the note listed under BLEEDING SYSTEM as follows:

***NOTE: If master cylinder reservoir has not been emptied, brake bleeding procedure for ABS is the same as brake bleeding procedure for non-ABS. If master cylinder has been emptied, bleed master cylinder first. Bleed remaining system, starting at wheel with longest hydraulic line and working down to wheel with shortest hydraulic line. If a power steering hose is disconnected or actuator is removed, the following brake bleeding procedure using Actuator Checker (SST 09990-00150) is required.***

This revision applies to the following publications:
IMPORTED CARS, LIGHT TRUCKS & VANS, SERVICE & REPAIR manual and IMPORTED CARS, LIGHT TRUCKS & VANS CHASSIS SERVICE & REPAIR supplement.
- 1990 - Page TOYOTA 8-38

## SUSPENSION

42 *1990 TERCEL: REVISED TORQUE SPECIFICATION* - Please revise brake caliper bolt torque specifications as follows:

***TORQUE SPECIFICATIONS***

| Application | Ft. Lbs. (N.m) |
|---|---|
| Brake Caliper Bolt | 65 (88) |

This revision applies to the following publications:
IMPORTED CARS, LIGHT TRUCKS & VANS, SERVICE & REPAIR manual and IMPORTED CARS, LIGHT TRUCKS & VANS CHASSIS SERVICE & REPAIR supplement.
- 1990 - Page TOYOTA 10-4

43 *1990 CAMRY, CELICA, COROLLA (2WD): REVISED WHEEL BEARING INSPECTION* - Please revise wheel bearing inspection as follows:
**Camry, Celica & Corolla 2WD** - Raise and support vehicle. Remove tire assembly. Place dial indicator against axle shaft. Move axle shaft in and out and note axial reading. Replace bearings if axial reading exceeds .002" (.05 mm).
This revision applies to the following publications:
IMPORTED CARS, LIGHT TRUCKS & VANS, SERVICE & REPAIR manual and IMPORTED CARS, LIGHT TRUCKS & VANS CHASSIS SERVICE & REPAIR supplement.
- 1990 - Page TOYOTA 10-16

44 *1990 TERCEL: REVISED TORQUE SPECIFICATION* - Please revise axle beam-to-body bolt torque specifications as follows:

***TORQUE SPECIFICATIONS***

| Application | Ft. Lbs. (N.m) |
|---|---|
| Axle Beam-To-Body Bolt | 105 (142) |

This revision applies to the following publications:
IMPORTED CARS, LIGHT TRUCKS & VANS, SERVICE & REPAIR manual and IMPORTED CARS, LIGHT TRUCKS & VANS CHASSIS SERVICE & REPAIR supplement.
- 1990 - Page TOYOTA 10-19

# VOLVO

## ENGINE PERFORMANCE

45 *1990 VOLVO 740 GLE: REVISED IGNITION TIMING SPECIFICATION* - Please note that the 4-CYLINDER IGNITION TIMING (DEGREES BTDC @ RPM) table has been revised as follows:

***4-CYLINDER IGNITION TIMING (Degrees BTDC @ RPM)***

| Application | [1] Timing |
|---|---|
| Except 740 GLE | 12 @ 750 |
| 740 GLE | 15 @ 850 |

[1] - Ignition timing is computer controlled and is not adjustable.

# LATEST CHANGES & CORRECTIONS 1991 & Earlier Models (Cont.)

This revision applies to the following publications:
IMPORTED CARS, LIGHT TRUCKS & VANS, SERVICE & REPAIR manual and IMPORTED CARS, LIGHT TRUCKS & VANS ENGINE PERFORMANCE supplement.

- 1990 – Page VOLVO 1-3

46 *1989-90 VOLVO: REVISED FUEL PUMP SPECIFICATION* – Please note that FUEL PUMP PERFORMANCE table has been revised as follows:

***FUEL PUMP PERFORMANCE*** [1]

| Application | Pressure psi ($kg/cm^2$) | Volume in 30 sec. Pts. (L) |
|---|---|---|
| Except 240 DL/GL & 760 GLE | 42.0 (2.9) | 1.1 (0.7) |
| 240 DL/GL | 42.6 (3.0) | 1.1 (0.7) |
| 760 GLE | 42.0 (2.9) | 1.1 (0.7) |

[1] – At 12 volts, 68°F (20°C) with engine off and fuel pump relay by-passed.

This revision applies to the following publications:
IMPORTED CARS, LIGHT TRUCKS & VANS, ENGINE PERFORMANCE supplement, and IMPORTED CARS, LIGHT TRUCKS & VANS SERVICE & REPAIR manual.

- 1989 – Page VOLVO 1-3
- 1990 – Page VOLVO 1-2

## ACCESSORIES & EQUIPMENT

47 *1990 240, 740 & 760 SERIES: REVISED AIR BAG RESTRAINT SYSTEM PROCEDURES* – Please note that air bag restraint system procedures have been revised. For revised procedures, see the 1991 publication.

This revision applies to the following publications:
IMPORTED CARS, LIGHT TRUCKS & VANS, SERVICE & REPAIR manual and IMPORTED CARS, LIGHT TRUCKS & VANS ELECTRICAL SERVICE & REPAIR supplement.

- 1990 – Page VOLVO 4-0, 4-1 & 4-2

48 *1990 240, 740 & 760 SERIES: REVISED INSTRUMENT PANEL PROCEDURES* – Please note that instrument panel procedures have been revised. For revised procedures, see the 1991 publication.

This revision applies to the following publications:
IMPORTED CARS, LIGHT TRUCKS & VANS, SERVICE & REPAIR manual and IMPORTED CARS, LIGHT TRUCKS & VANS ELECTRICAL SERVICE & REPAIR supplement.

- 1990 – Page VOLVO 4-3 & VOLVO 4-4

## ENGINE

49 *1990 2.3L: REVISED MAIN BEARING JOURNAL DIAMETER SPECIFICATIONS* –
Please note that main bearing journal diameter specifications have been revised as follows:

***CRANKSHAFT, MAIN & CONNECTING ROD BEARINGS***

| Application | In. (mm) |
|---|---|
| Crankshaft | |
| Main Bearings | |
| Journal Diameter | |
| Standard | 2.1648-2.1694 (54.987-55.000) |
| Undersize "1" | 2.1550-2.1555 (54.737-54.750) |
| Undersize "2" | 2.1451-2.1457 (54.487-54.500) |

This revision applies to the following publications:
IMPORTED CARS, LIGHT TRUCKS & VANS, SERVICE & REPAIR manual and IMPORTED CARS, LIGHT TRUCKS & VANS ENGINE, CLUTCHES & DRIVE AXLE supplement.

- 1990 – Page VOLVO 5-6

50 *1990 2.3L: REVISED PISTON RING SPECIFICATIONS* – Please note that piston ring specifications have been revised as follows:

***PISTONS, PINS & RINGS***

| Application | In. (mm) |
|---|---|
| Pistons Rings | |
| No. 1 (Top) | |
| Side Clearance | .0024-.0036 (.060-.092) |
| No. 2 (Center) | |
| Side Clearance | .0016-.0028 (.040-.072) |
| No. 3 (Oil) | |
| Side Clearance | .0012-.0025 (.030-.065) |

This revision applies to the following publications:
IMPORTED CARS, LIGHT TRUCKS & VANS, SERVICE & REPAIR manual and IMPORTED CARS, LIGHT TRUCKS & VANS ENGINE, CLUTCHES & DRIVE AXLE supplement.

- 1990 – Page VOLVO 5-6

51 *1990 2.3L: REVISED VALVE SPECIFICATIONS* – Please note that valve and valve spring specifications have been revised as follows:

***VALVES & VALVE SPRINGS***

| Application | Specification |
|---|---|
| Intake Valves [1] | |
| Stem Diameter | .3132-.3138" (7.955-7.970 mm) |
| Exhaust Valves | |
| Stem Diameter | .3128-.3134" (7.945-7.960 mm) |

[1] – Valves are stellite coated and cannot be machined. Valves may only be lapped to seats.

This revision applies to the following publications:
IMPORTED CARS, LIGHT TRUCKS & VANS, SERVICE & REPAIR manual and IMPORTED CARS, LIGHT TRUCKS & VANS ENGINE, CLUTCHES & DRIVE AXLE supplement.

- 1990 – Page VOLVO 5-7

52 *1990 2.3L: REVISED CAMSHAFT SPECIFICATIONS* – Please note that camshaft end play specifications have been revised as follows:

***CAMSHAFT***

| Application | In. (mm) |
|---|---|
| End Play | .004-.016 (.10-.40) |

This revision applies to the following publications:
IMPORTED CARS, LIGHT TRUCKS & VANS, SERVICE & REPAIR manual and IMPORTED CARS, LIGHT TRUCKS & VANS ENGINE, CLUTCHES & DRIVE AXLE supplement.

- 1990 – Page VOLVO 5-7

## BRAKES

53 *1990 740 & 760 SERIES: REVISED ABS HYDRAULIC SYSTEM BLEEDING PROCEDURE* – Please revise procedure listed under BLEEDING BRAKE SYSTEM as follows:

**1)** Fill brake fluid reservoir to MAX fluid level with DOT 4 grade brake fluid. Connect hoses to both bleed valves on left rear wheel. Submerge hoses in bottle containing brake fluid.

**2)** Both hoses must be below brake fluid surface. Open bleed valves. Have an assistant pump brake pedal slowly 5 times, holding pedal down on last depression stroke. No air bubbles should be visible from last stroke.

**3)** Close bleed valves. Check brake fluid level after each open and close cycle of bleed valves. Bleed remaining wheels in the following order: right rear, front left and front right.

This revision applies to the following publications:
IMPORTED CARS, LIGHT TRUCKS & VANS, SERVICE & REPAIR manual and IMPORTED CARS, LIGHT TRUCKS & VANS CHASSIS SERVICE & REPAIR supplement.

- 1990 – Page VOLVO 8-7

# NOTES

# NOTES

Be sure to fill out this form completely.

# COMMENTS AND SUGGESTIONS

**Please let us know if you have any comments or recommended changes to the Air Bag Service and Repair Manual. Mail this postage-paid card today. We'd like to hear from you!**

Section No. ____________ Page No. ____________ Vehicle Model & Year ____________

Comments: ________________________________

________________________________

________________________________

Name ____________ Company ____________

Address ____________ City ____________ State ________ Zip ________

Phone (   ) ____________ Date ____________ THANK YOU

ADIC 91

Be sure to fill out this form completely.

# COMMENTS AND SUGGESTIONS

**Please let us know if you have any comments or recommended changes to the Air Bag Service and Repair Manual. Mail this postage-paid card today. We'd like to hear from you!**

Section No. ____________ Page No. ____________ Vehicle Model & Year ____________

Comments: ________________________________

________________________________

________________________________

Name ____________ Company ____________

Address ____________ City ____________ State ________ Zip ________

Phone (   ) ____________ Date ____________ THANK YOU

ADIC 91

Be sure to fill out this form completely.

# COMMENTS AND SUGGESTIONS

**Please let us know if you have any comments or recommended changes to the Air Bag Service and Repair Manual. Mail this postage-paid card today. We'd like to hear from you!**

Section No. ____________ Page No. ____________ Vehicle Model & Year ____________

Comments: ________________________________

________________________________

________________________________

Name ____________ Company ____________

Address ____________ City ____________ State ________ Zip ________

Phone (   ) ____________ Date ____________ THANK YOU

ADIC 91

NO POSTAGE
NECESSARY
IF MAILED
IN THE
UNITED STATES

**BUSINESS REPLY MAIL**

FIRST CLASS PERMIT NO. 3701 SAN DIEGO, CA

POSTAGE WILL BE PAID BY ADDRESSEE

**MITCHELL INTERNATIONAL**
P.O. Box 26260
San Diego, California 92196-9984

NO POSTAGE
NECESSARY
IF MAILED
IN THE
UNITED STATES

**BUSINESS REPLY MAIL**

FIRST CLASS PERMIT NO. 3701 SAN DIEGO, CA

POSTAGE WILL BE PAID BY ADDRESSEE

**MITCHELL INTERNATIONAL**
P.O. Box 26260
San Diego, California 92196-9984

NO POSTAGE
NECESSARY
IF MAILED
IN THE
UNITED STATES

**BUSINESS REPLY MAIL**

FIRST CLASS PERMIT NO. 3701 SAN DIEGO, CA

POSTAGE WILL BE PAID BY ADDRESSEE

**MITCHELL INTERNATIONAL**
P.O. Box 26260
San Diego, California 92196-9984

# SELL MORE SERVICE!

## Designed to Help You Sell More Service, the *Mitchell® Maintenance Services Manual* Provides All the Information You Need To Service Vehicles Under Warranty.

Right now, more than 30 million vehicles are under warranty, requiring billions of dollars worth of maintenance service.

More of that business can be yours.

The *Maintenance Services Manual,* puts warranty maintenance information for all makes and models of vehicles at your fingertips. That means you can offer warranty maintenance service to all of your customers...even on vehicles you don't normally service.

And that means added sales for you.

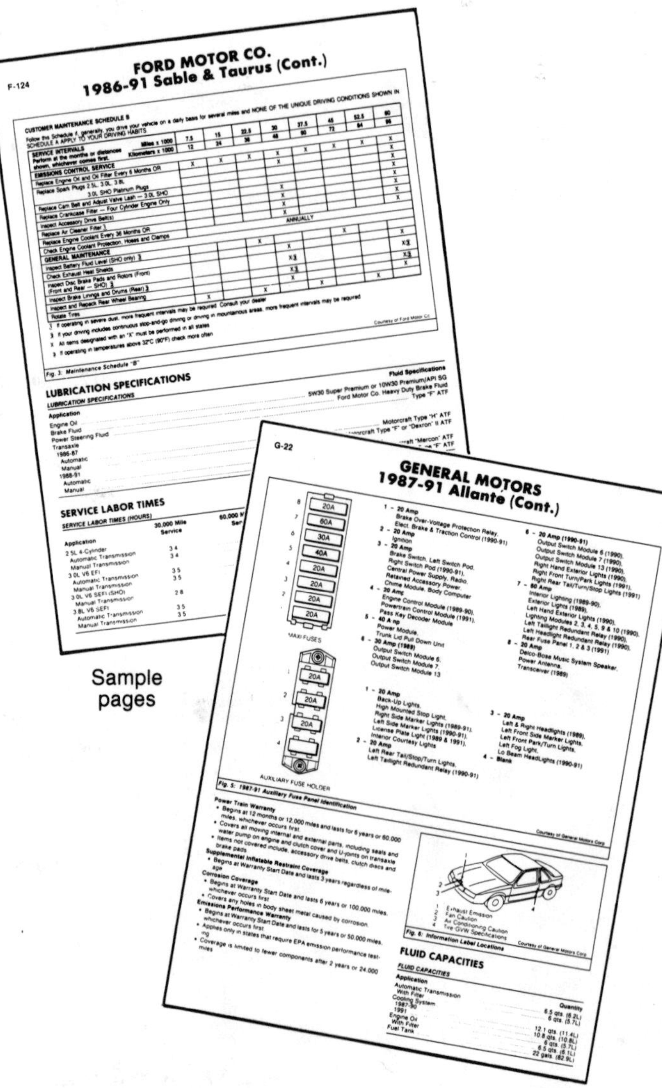
F-124 FORD MOTOR CO. 1986-91 Sable & Taurus (Cont.)

LUBRICATION SPECIFICATIONS

SERVICE LABOR TIMES

G-22 GENERAL MOTORS 1987-91 Allante (Cont.)

FLUID CAPACITIES

Sample pages

### Answers At a Glance

The *Mitchell Maintenance Services Manual* is very easy to use.

It provides the manufacturer's maintenance service schedules, so you can inform customers exactly what services are needed to keep their warranties valid.

The manual also includes:

- VIN decoding
- Fuse and flasher locations
- Wheel and tire data
- Service indicator and warning light reset procedures
- Even service labor estimating times!

The result? You get the job done properly. And profitably.

### A Vital Sales Tool

With the *Mitchell Maintenance Services Manual,* you can increase the value of some jobs, since you'll know the schedule for major vehicle maintenance operations.

And to help you sell more services, the manual includes everything from tips on customer relations to suggestions about opportunities to sell more seasonal services. And much more.

For information about updating your maintenance services coverage, call:

**1-800-648-8010**
(in the 619 area, call 578-6550)

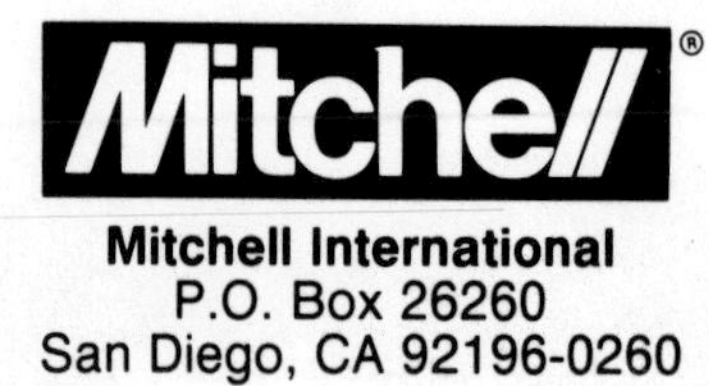


**Mitchell International**
P.O. Box 26260
San Diego, CA 92196-0260

ADIC 91